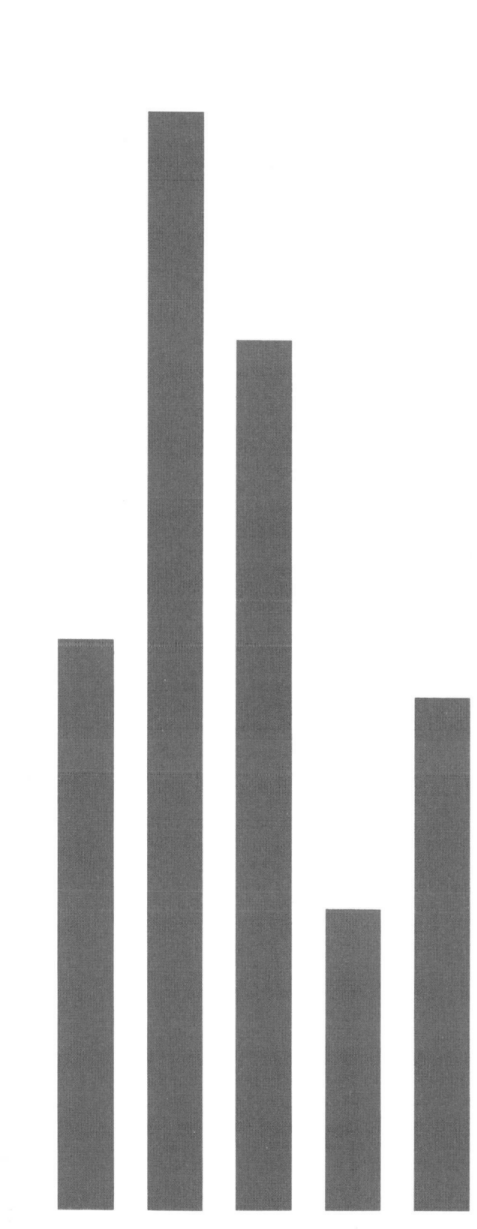

STATISTICAL REFERENCE INDEX 1993 ANNUAL

A selective guide to American statistical publications from private organizations and state government sources

Index

Congressional Information Service **CIS**

Staff

Editorial Director
Susan I. Jover

Director of Statistical Services
Darlene J. Montgomery

Managing Editor
Lynn K. Marble

Assistant Managing Editor, Collection Development
Jeanne Long

Assistant Managing Editor, Abstracts
Edie Crisostomo

Index Editor
Alistair Morrison

Abstracting and Indexing Staff
David M. Bird
David G. Johnson
Deborah Marlatt Kitchin
Michelle C. McGinnies
Mary R. Nolan

Accuracy Editor
Gale O. Holt

Acquisitions Editors
Jane Hunt
Edward Kianka

Documents Control
Sally L. MacArthur

Production Staff
Dorothy W. Rogers, *Coordinator*
Stephanie Hines, *Asst. Coordinator*

Congressional Information Service

President
Paul P. Massa

Vice President and Editorial Director
Susan I. Jover

Exec. Vice President, CIS
James F. Connolly

Vice President, Finance
Max E. Venegas

Vice President, EDP & Technology
E. Don Johnson

Senior Systems Developer
Jack Wolfire

Executive Editor
Eric Massant

Manager, Applications Programming
Andrew Ross

Manager, Systems and Operations
Mojtaba Anvari

Project Leader
Robert Starbird

Programmer/Analysts
Evette Bredel
Roger Medlin
Larry Robertson

User Support Supervisor
Pat Simons

User Support Representative
Nadine Benton

PC/LAN Specialist
Melvin Turner

Computer Operators
Marc Balthrop
Sylvia Brown
Nahid Heffernan

EDP Admin. Assistant
Paola Schrage

Finance Department
Stuart Abramowitz
Jason Balzer
Loretta Nolan
Mark Peele
David Sauer
Susan Sinicropi
Rita Skolnik-Crowley
Paula Solorzano
Gail Taylor
Nelson Toye
Emmy Wong

Director, Administrative Services
Lee Mayer

Administrative Services Coordinator
Bonnie Balzer

Mailroom Assistants
Scott Gunderson
William Sherrod

Director, Human Resources
Rebecca Warwick

Human Resources Generalist
Jonathan Markus

Receptionist
Suzanne Goldberg

Vice President, Manufacturing
William C. Smith

Plant Operations Manager
William Idol

Micropublishing Production Staff
Marjorie Abuan
Donna Barrick
Catherine Bassford
Lukman Bazarah
Sandra Bohnke
Margaret Bowles
Karla Bradburn
Deborah Briscoe
Danielle Crim
Abel David
James Day
Dorothy Faunce

Margaret Fisher
Janice Garcia
Patricia Garrison
Robert Goddard
Michelle Goostree
Matilda Gregory
Diane Harrison
Mildred Harrison
Donna Hayden
Teresa Hayden
Kimberly Hayes
Sandra Heineman
Mary Ann Hodges
Faith Holmes
Dianette Johnson
Elizabeth Kennedy
Karen Kennedy
Nancy Jane Kiger
Donna Lacey
Ida Bea Lamkin
Ethel LeBeaux
Edwin Legaspi
Robin Long
Betty Lyles
Rebecca Lyn Martin
Elaine Miles
James Mowrer
Sharon Norris
Edgar O'Bannon
Scott Owen
Marjorie Rickerson
Gloria Robinson
Elmer Rodriguez
Barbara Schumacher
Erick Shaffer
Nilza Silva
Doris Stevens
Maria Stewart
Rose Thompson
Mary Tippett
Dana Tubbs
Armando Vicente
Zina Williams
Shaun Woolcock
Gertrude Young

Director, Research
Alexander D. McRae

Research Staff
Angela Kim
Bonnie Lease
William Wears

National Sales Manager
John P. Beil

Sales Representatives
John Cox
James Drummond
Jane Edwards
Scott Eller
Christine Hansen Fitch
Paul Hennrikus
Jeffrey Strandberg

Vice President, Marketing
Richard K. Johnson

Director, Business Development
Raymond W. Crow, Jr.

Manager, International Sales
Norman Williams

Manager, Customer Service
Katie Culliton

Customer Service Representatives
Toby Holtzman
Barbara Pisano

Documents on Demand Coordinator
Sharon L. Schmedicke

Director of Communications
Jack Carey

Advertising, Publicity, and Promotion Staff
Linda Brown
Courtenay Diederich
Tom Felt
Diane Keely
Judith Silfen
Marcia Taylor
Shanon Venegas

Secretary to the President
Karen L. Grossnickle

Editorial Admin. Assistant
Melissa Krane

Finance Admin. Assistant
Susan Savage

International Book Number
For the Set: 0-88692-290-9
For Index Volume: 0-88692-291-7
For Abstract Volume: 0-88692-292-5

Congressional Information Service, Inc.
4520 East-West Highway
Bethesda, Md. 20814
(301) 654-1550

The paper used in this publication meets the minimum requirements of American National Standard for Information Sciences-Permanence of Paper for Printed Library Materials, ANSI Z39.48-1984.

©1994 by Congressional Information Service, Inc. All rights reserved.

SRI 1993 ANNUAL CONTENTS

The Statistical Reference Index 1993 Annual
is published in two volumes, the
contents of which are summarized below.

Index

Detailed Table of Contents: Index Volume v

User Guide

Introduction to SRI vii
How to Use the SRI 1993 Annual ix

Organization of SRI Indexes ix
Organization of SRI Abstracts xii
How to Acquire Source Publications xiv
Related CIS Services xiv
Acknowledgements xv

Sample Abstracts xvii
Sample Search xx
Acronyms, Selected Abbreviations, and Symbols xxii

Index by Subjects and Names 1

Index by Categories 739

Index by Issuing Sources 889

Index by Titles 925

Guide to Selected Standard Classifications 949

Abstracts

Detailed Table of Contents: Abstracts Volume v

User Guide xix

Abstracts of Statistical Publications 1

Associations 1
Business Organizations 209
Commercial Publishers 240
Independent Research Organizations 506
State Governments 564
Universities 835

NOTE: For comprehensive access to U.S. Government statistical publications, consult the American Statistics Index. ASI is published by Congressional Information Service and is available in many major libraries. Coverage begins with the early 1960s and is updated monthly.

Detailed Table of Contents: Index Volume

Index by Subjects and Names 1
(This index contains reference to subjects, to individual authors of articles and publications, and to corporate authors and data source organizations other than issuing sources.)

Index by Categories 739
(This index contains references to publications, tables, and groups of tables that contain breakdowns of statistical data by State, by industry, by age, or by some other standard category.)

Geographic Breakdowns

By Census Division	741
By City	743
By County	753
By Foreign Country or World Area	770
By Region	778
By SMSA or MSA	784
By State	787
By Urban-Rural and Metro-Nonmetro	797

Economic Breakdowns

By Commodity	801
By Government Agency	805
By Income	807
By Individual Company or Institution	810
By Industry	834
By Occupation	842

Demographic Breakdowns

By Age	846
By Disease	856
By Educational Attainment	858
By Marital Status	862
By Race	864
By Sex	874

Index by Issuing Sources 889
(This index contains a listing of all publications abstracted, arranged by issuing agency.)

Index by Titles 925
(This index contains an alphabetical listing of all publication titles abstracted.)

Guide to Selected Standard Classifications 949
(This guide outlines the major standard classification systems used by many organizations to arrange and present social and economic statistical data.)

Census Regions and Divisions	949
Outlying Areas of the U.S.	949
Federal Reserve Districts	949
Metropolitan Statistical Areas	950
Consolidated Metropolitan Statistical Areas	951
Cities with Population over 100,000	952
Consumer Price Index Cities	952
Standard Industrial Classification	953
Standard Occupational Classification	961
Standard International Trade Classification, Revision 3	964
Uniform Crime Reporting Classification of Offenses	968

INTRODUCTION TO SRI

rently published sources of statistics and focus on continuing time series data wherever possible. Priority is also given to maintaining coverage of basic social, governmental, economic, and demographic data for each of the 50 States and the District of Columbia.

This 1993 SRI Annual contains abstracts and indexing for approximately 2,010 titles, including 1,400 annual or other recurring reports (65 of which were covered in SRI for the first time during 1993), 240 monographs, 320 periodicals with regularly appearing statistical features, and over 2,000 individual statistical articles. Included are reports from all 50 States and the District of Columbia, and statistical compendia from 29 States.

During 1994, SRI will maintain current coverage of all periodicals, annuals, and other recurring reports covered since its inception in 1980, and will continue to expand that coverage with additional current titles.

Basic Objectives and Coverage

Each year, thousands of U.S. private organizations and State government agencies prepare and issue countless publications and articles, many of which contain important statistics on business, industry and finance, general economic conditions, government programs and politics, and social trends. These data are typically authoritative, timely, and well-researched, and often present results of original surveys and research. In many cases, they complement or fill important gaps in data prepared and issued by the Federal Government, and also frequently are more current than Federal data.

The *Statistical Reference Index* (SRI) service, which includes printed abstracts and indexes and a companion microfiche collection of source data, is designed to provide a reliable, centralized means of access to this large and significant body of business, financial, and social statistical data, much of which has previously been difficult to locate or obtain for research use.

Specifically, SRI has as its purpose the following functions:

- **Survey** and **review** current statistical publications issued by major U.S. associations and institutes, business organizations, commercial publishers, independent research centers, State government agencies, and universities.
- **Identify** current publications containing substantial statistical material of general research value.
- **Catalog** the publications in which the data appear, providing full bibliographic data and availability information for each publication.
- **Describe** the contents of these publications fully.
- **Index** this information in full detail for access by subject, category, issuing source, and title.
- **Micropublish** the entire content or the statistical portions of the publications covered. (During 1993, SRI obtained microfilming rights for over 90% of the publications abstracted and indexed.)

SRI data selection criteria, more fully detailed below, have been established with the objectives of covering a wide array of data publishing organizations and subject matter. Criteria also emphasize prompt coverage of cur-

Issuing Sources Covered

SRI staff have conducted comprehensive surveys of current sources of data in order to establish a well-rounded sphere of coverage for SRI. Identification and selection of issuing sources currently covered are based on:

- Review of secondary sources, including *Directory of Business and Financial Services, Business Information Sources, Guide to Special Issues and Indexes of Periodicals, Statistical Abstract of the U.S.,* and numerous other bibliographies.
- Review of the Harvard University Baker Library industry statistics file.
- Canvass of national associations with annual budgets over $1 million.
- Canvass of business-oriented periodicals ranked in order of sales in *Folio 400.*
- Canvass of 2,000 State government agencies to identify offices publishing the most comprehensive reports on State administered programs.
- Consultations with librarians who are specialists in information fields such as banking and finance, State documents, and others.
- Follow-up on references cited in current periodicals and other news media.

SRI acquisitions staff are continually reviewing additional publications and canvassing additional sources in an effort to maintain and extend SRI coverage. Within this 1993 Annual, over 1,000 issuing source organizations are represented in the following categories:

- **Trade, professional, and other nonprofit associations and institutes,** including those representing manufacturing and nonmanufacturing industries, and academic, occupational, recreational, public interest, and religious groups.
- **Business organizations,** including banks, accounting firms, stock and commodity exchanges, public opinion survey and research firms, and other private companies and corporations.
- **Commercial publishers** of business, trade association, and industry periodical and annual publications, including such major publishers as R. R. Bowker, Chilton Co., Crain Communications, Dun and Brad-

street, Forbes, Lebhar-Friedman, McGraw-Hill, and PennWell Publishing.

- **Independent research organizations,** including public policy, education, demographic, and economic research organizations.
- **State government agencies,** including those with primary responsibility in such areas as State education, employment, health and vital statistics reporting, public assistance, elections, crime and correctional institutions, the judicial system, agriculture, and regulated industries.
- **Universities and affiliated research centers,** including those focusing on demographic research, and research in the fields of business and industry, agriculture, and economic forecasting.

Criteria for Publication Selection

In selecting publications for coverage, SRI seeks to include:

- Publications presenting business, industrial, financial, and social statistics of general research value, and having national, regional, or statewide breadth of coverage. Where there is redundancy of content among groups or related series of publications, emphasis is placed upon selecting those publications presenting time series or regularly updated statistics, and those with the most comprehensive, detailed coverage.
- Publications containing statistics in subject areas or in geographic detail not well covered by Federal data, and statistics useful for comparison with Federal data.
- Publications presenting data that, while in some respects limited in scope, geographically or otherwise, are the best or most authoritative found for a given subject, or present a unique analysis or statistical base.

SRI coverage excludes:

- Ephemeral or highly localized data of very limited interest.
- Scientific or highly technical data, and instructional handbooks and manuals.
- Publications with very limited or exclusive distribution for which microfiche reproduction rights cannot be obtained, that are thus unlikely to be available to libraries in any form.
- Publications which simply republish Federal data from a single source without analysis or without additional data collected from other sources (comprehensive coverage of Federal data can be found in *American Statistics Index,* published by Congressional Information Service, Bethesda, Md.).
- Publications of municipal and county governments (coverage of this material can be found in the *Index to Current Urban Documents,* published by Greenwood Press, Westport, Conn.).

In addition, SRI excludes coverage of published current securities quotations or price data intended primarily for investment or purchasing reference purposes, as well as coverage of widely publicized and commercially

distributed monographs that are already well known and easily accessible.

Selection criteria for inclusion and exclusion are reviewed and refined on a continuing basis. We welcome comments and suggestions from SRI users that will help us in shaping future coverage policies and improving abstracting and indexing procedures.

Types of Statistics Covered

Publications covered by SRI provide users access to the following types of data:

- **National Data —** Production, costs, and earnings in major industries and business sectors; operating and market characteristics of business and commerce; rankings of products and corporations; data related to key areas of social or public interest; professional worker supply and demand; public opinion and salary surveys; demographic data; and national economic trends.
- **Statewide Data —** State statistical compendia, and 10-15 additional periodicals or annual basic reports for each of the 50 States, presenting data on such areas as vital statistics, crime, health, agriculture, business conditions and economic indicators, employment, education, taxation, State government finances, insurance, banking, public utilities, the judicial system, corrections, elections, libraries, population, and motor vehicle accidents; and State reports presenting data from the 1980 and 1990 Census of Population and Housing.
- **Data on Foreign Countries —** World economic and demographic trends; international finance, investment, and trade data; and foreign country social and economic indicators, frequently organized to permit comparison with data for the United States.
- **Local or Otherwise Narrowly Focused Data —** Detail by county and municipality is provided in most State reports selected for inclusion. In addition, selected local or narrowly focused studies or articles, from any source, may be included if the subject matter is judged to have research value beyond the limited area of coverage.

Coverage of SRI Monthly Issues, Annual Editions, and Multiple-Year Cumulations

Monthly Issues: SRI abstracts and companion indexes are issued on a monthly basis (except for the combined January/February issue). In general, SRI monthly issues cover publications acquired 8–12 weeks previously.

SRI indexes cumulate monthly within each quarter. For example, the May index contains all indexing for the April and May issues; and the June index contains all indexing for the April, May, and June issues. To search the entire SRI file for the current year, users need only consult the most recent monthly index plus any previously published quarterly indexes. For example, to search the current year file as of July, consult the July monthly index, the June index (cumulative indexing for April, May, and June), and the March index (cumulative indexing for January/February and March).

Annual Editions: SRI monthly abstracts and indexing are cumulated in an annual edition published in the spring of the following year. The annual edition replaces and fully supersedes the monthly issues.

This fourteenth SRI Annual cumulates the abstracts and indexes originally published in SRI monthly issues during 1993, generally covering publications received during Nov. 1992–Oct. 1993.

Multiple-Year Cumulations: SRI annual Index volumes are cumulated in a multiple-year index, which replaces and fully supersedes all annual indexes for the years covered, and is designed to be used in conjunction with the annual abstracts volumes as originally published for those years.

SRI's first multiple-year cumulation, published in Fall 1986, contains complete indexing for all publications covered in SRI during 1980–85. The second multiple-year cumulation, covering 1986–1989, was published in Fall 1990. The third cumulation, covering 1990–1993, will be published in Fall 1994.

HOW TO USE THE SRI 1993 ANNUAL

ORGANIZATION OF SRI INDEXES

SRI provides access to statistical data through companion volumes of indexes and abstracts. Ordinarily, research will begin with the Index volume. The Index volume contains four basic indexes to lead the user to the information he seeks from a variety of starting points.

- **Index by Subjects and Names**
- **Index by Categories**
- **Index by Issuing Sources**
- **Index by Titles**

Index by Subjects and Names

This index section contains references to specific subjects, places, personal authors (other than authors of periodical articles), and data source organizations other than issuing sources. Each index entry under a subject term contains a "notation of content," which consists of a brief description of the principal subject matter of the publication as it relates to that term, the date of data coverage or publication, major data breakdowns, and the publication periodicity. These are followed by the SRI accession number identifying the individual document as described in the abstract volume.

Notation of content entries for data of general, national, or international scope are listed first, followed by those for publications limited to individual States and local areas. The initial or key word of these notations of content is selected to provide an added level of specificity under each subject term, and serves, in a general way, to group together entries for similar data under that term.

It should be noted that the notations of content in the *State and local* section of a term (see example below), taken together constitute a unique and useful compilation of the major sources of State data on that subject. (Data in publications not focusing on a particular State, but showing breakdowns *by State*, are most easily accessible through the Index by Categories, under the heading, "By State," as detailed below.)

This index also contains *see* cross references to guide the user to the relevant term formats used in SRI; and *see also* cross references to guide the user to additional material to be found under the related or narrower terms cited.

Subject index terms are assigned for each publication abstracted to represent all subject matter and data that are covered in sufficient depth to have research value. Unusual items or items of special interest that occur in the body of a report or article, or in individual tables or groups of tables, are indexed regardless of whether they are related to the primary focus of the publication at hand.

Subject terms and cross references in the Index of Subjects and Names are based on a controlled hierarchical vocabulary. When indexing a publication to which a hierarchy of vocabulary terms might apply, SRI uses the most specific, generally applicable term or terms, and generally does not also index to broader or narrower terms that, while relevant, do not reflect so well the focus of the publication. In some cases, where the focus of the document is equally upon the more general and the more particular subject term, index references have been placed under both terms.

In general, individual cities and counties, occupations, or other commonly appearing subject breakdowns of data *within* tables are indexed in the Index by Categories and *not* also in the Index by Subjects and Names. Users are urged to review indexed category breakdowns (see section below) and to keep in mind the added depth of coverage provided. A sample search using the Subject Index is illustrated on p. xxxii.

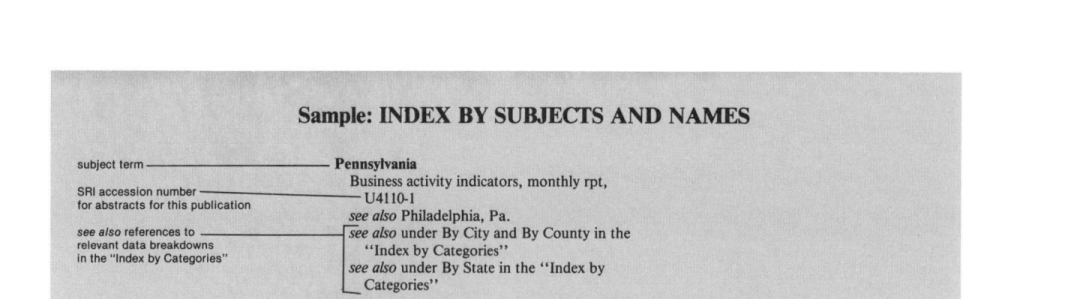

Index by Categories

This index provides special access to detailed statistical data found in tabular breakdowns and cross classifications. This index includes references to all publications that contain comparative tabular data broken down in any one or more of the following twenty standard categories:

GEOGRAPHIC BREAKDOWNS

By Census Division	By Region
By City	By SMSA or MSA
By County	By State
By Foreign Country	By Urban-Rural and
or World Area	Metro-Nonmetro

ECONOMIC BREAKDOWNS

By Commodity	By Individual
By Government Agency	Company
By Income	or Institution
By Industry	By Occupation

DEMOGRAPHIC BREAKDOWNS

By Age	By Marital Status
By Disease	By Race
By Educational	By Sex
Attainment	

For subject searches relating to any of the above breakdowns (e.g., a search for data for a specific city or county, for data on women or income, or on a particular commodity or industry), the Index by Categories is an important access tool. For all categories, this index will generally provide an added depth of coverage beyond that available through the Index by Subjects and Names.

For example, data on individual cities and counties found in detailed breakdowns in State reports will be indexed only in the Index by Categories. In addition, for searches where comparative data are desired (e.g., comparative data for different countries, different companies, different age groups or occupations), the Index by Categories is the most logical starting point.

Within each category in the index, entries are grouped according to subject matter, under one of the following 21 subject headings:

Agriculture and Food
Banking, Finance, and Insurance
Communications
Education
Energy Resources and Demand
Geography and Climate
Government and Defense
Health and Vital Statistics
Housing and Construction
Income
Industry and Commerce
Labor and Employment
Law Enforcement
Natural Resources, Environment, and Pollution
Population
Prices and Cost of Living
Public Welfare and Social Security
Recreation and Leisure
Science and Technology
Transportation and Travel
Veterans Affairs

Definitions and conventions used in assigning these headings are summarized in an introductory section preceding the Index by Categories.

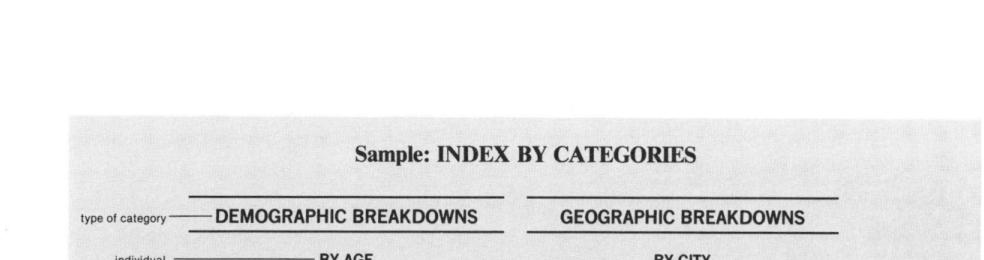

Index by Issuing Sources

This index contains references showing issuing source and publication title for all associations, business organizations, commercial publishers, independent research organizations, State agencies, and university departments or research centers whose publications have been abstracted and indexed by SRI. Periodicity and SRI microfiche status are also shown for each publication title.

Names of issuing sources generally appear in natural word order, with report titles listed below. Where issuing source names have been inverted for purposes of alphabetization by surname (e.g., Best, A.M., Co.), a cross reference from natural word order is provided. University research centers are listed first by university, and secondly by specific center or department issuing the report. In general, titles of State reports are listed under State issuing sources at the Department or highest organizational level, with cross references provided, as necessary, from names of responsible State subagencies. (See example, below.)

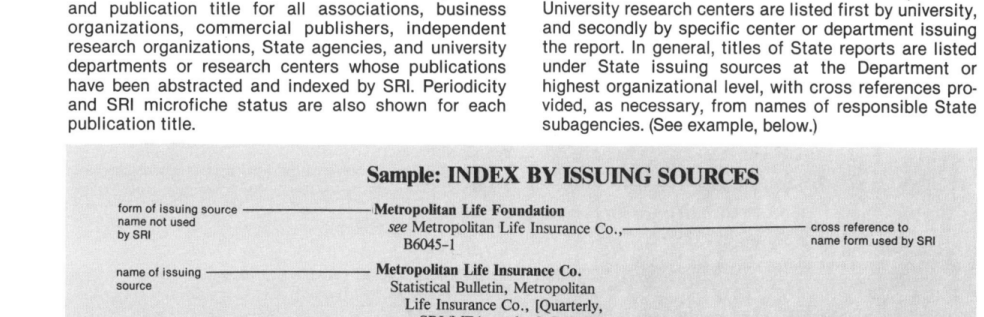

Index by Titles

This index lists titles of all publications, including individual reports within a publication series. Titles are listed alphabetically in natural word order, without initial articles (a, an, the), as they appear in the abstracts.

Titles beginning with arabic numerals appear at the end of the index (e.g., 1982 Commodity Year Book), as well as alphabetically under the first key word (e.g., Commodity Year Book, 1982).

Titles of individual articles within a given publication are not generally included in the Title Index, unless the title itself is considered to be sufficiently well known to be a useful searching tool. However, articles or publications that carry an author's name on the title page or otherwise prominently acknowledged, are listed by author in the Index by Subjects and Names.

Each title listed in the Title Index is followed by an SRI accession number, directing the user to the abstract of the publication.

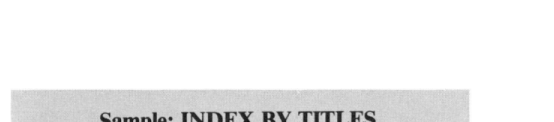

Lists of Selected Standard Classifications

Statistical data breakdowns indexed in the Index by Categories are frequently presented in accordance with several standard classification systems, and SRI abstracts generally make note of their use. To provide an easily accessible reference for the user, we have printed a number of major classification systems or lists in the "List of Selected Standard Classifications." It includes the following lists:

- Census regions and divisions; outlying areas of the U.S.; Federal Reserve Districts.
- Metropolitan Statistical Areas (MSAs); Consolidated Metropolitan Statistical Areas (CMSAs); cities with population over 100,000; and Consumer Price Index cities.
- Standard Industrial Classification (SIC), providing 1-to 4-digit codes for industry divisions through individual industries.
- Standard Occupational Classification, providing 1- to 4-digit codes for major and minor occupational groups.
- Standard International Trade Classification, a system of 3-digit codes for commodities in world trade, developed by the United Nations, used for foreign trade data, and consistent with the 7-digit codes used for U.S. import-export data.
- List of Part I (Index) and Part II (non-Index) crimes used in Uniform Crime Reporting Systems of the States.

ORGANIZATION OF SRI ABSTRACTS

SRI abstracts are based upon examination of the entire document. Abstracts differ substantially in degree of detail, depending on the type of publication and the kind of data being described. However, all abstracts are written to fulfill certain basic objectives.

These objectives are to describe a publication fully enough to allow the user to determine if it is likely to contain the specific statistical data he seeks; to tell the user how the contents of the publication are organized; to provide basic bibliographic data, availability address, price, and other ordering information; and to identify those publications for which SRI provides microfiche reproductions.

This section explains how SRI abstracts are organized in the abstract volume, the internal structure of abstracts, and the special way in which SRI handles periodicals each month.

Accession Numbers

SRI abstracts are organized by accession numbers assigned to each document abstracted and indexed. This accession number identifies not only the individual publication, but also the type of issuing source and the individual organization. It contains four basic elements, illustrated and outlined below.

- **Type of Issuing Source:** The initial letter of an accession number identifies type of issuing source, as follows:
  - A – Associations
  - B – Business organizations
  - C – Commercial publishers
  - R – Independent research centers
  - S – State agency or subagency
  - U – Universities, and affiliated research organizations.

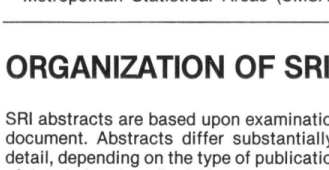

- **Individual Issuing Source:** The four digits following the initial letter, up to the hyphen, identify the individual issuing source within the issuing source type.

(Numbers have been assigned in such a way that individual sources are listed in alphabetical order within a source type.)

- **Sequential SRI Serial Number:** The digits after the hyphen form a unique serial number, sequentially assigned, basically in order of SRI acquisition, so that every publication has its own unique number which can be easily found in the abstracts volume of SRI.

- **Analytic Number:** In many cases, SRI describes publications by using a main abstract in coordination with subordinate or "analytic" abstracts. These analytic abstracts are identified by a decimal number (.1, .2, .3, etc.; or .101, .102, .103, etc.) at the end of the accession number. The analytic abstracts have the following purposes:

  (1) To describe and individually index distinct parts of a large publication, or to identify separate publications in a series. [These analytic abstracts are assigned single digit decimal numbers (A1600-1.1, A1600-1.2, etc.), followed by a heading or title.]

  (2) To describe individual issues of, or specific articles in, current issues of periodicals regularly covered by SRI. [These analytic abstracts are identified by 3-digit decimal numbers (U2735-1.101, U2735-1.102, etc.), followed by cover date of the periodical. A further explanation of periodical abstracts may be found in the section on how SRI handles periodicals, below.]

Generally, once SRI has assigned an accession number to a publication, all successive issues or updates of that publication will receive the same accession number. If the number is changed, cross-references between the old and new numbers are included in the abstracts. This will happen if, for example, the issuing agency of the publication changes.

To use SRI indexes and abstracts effectively, it is not necessary to know how SRI codes and assigns accession numbers, but familiarity with components of the accession number can speed interpretation of entries in the indexes.

Internal Organization of Abstracts

SRI abstracts provide the following information for each publication:

- Title, periodicity, publication date, collation (except for periodicals with inconsistent collation), report number (if assigned by the issuing agency), ISSN or ISBN number and Library of Congress card number (if available), and SRI microfiche coverage information.

- Overview of the publication, including principal subject and purpose, major data topics and breakdowns, geographic areas and time periods covered by data, and data sources.

- Contents summary, with page ranges, covering organization and format of the publication and the number of charts and tables presented.

- Description of statistical content. SRI abstracts present either a summary description of all tables, brief paragraphs describing groups of tables, or a complete listing of individual tables, depending on the level of detail necessary to give a clear picture of the publication's statistical content.

- Complete availability information, including issuing source address for ordering, price, and SRI microfiche coverage.

- For periodicals, cover dates of publications reviewed by SRI, and identification of cover date as either a publication date (P), or as the date of the statistical data presented (D).

Please refer to sample abstracts (p. xvii-xix) for illustrations of the above.

Special Handling of Periodicals

SRI observes a few special conventions in describing periodicals. Since most statistical periodicals retain at least some features and tables that are of constant format from issue to issue, it would be redundant to provide full abstracts for each issue. Therefore, a "base" abstract is written for each periodical, to indicate the features common to all issues and to describe tables that appear in each issue or at regular intervals.

In composing base abstracts for periodicals, we do not give specific time coverage of the data stated as a specific month or year, but describe it in a general way that will apply to all issues. Similarly, the base abstracts do not include page ranges, which may change from issue to issue.

For many periodicals, the "base" abstract suffices to describe statistical contents for all issuances during the year, since statistical contents are totally constant in format from issue to issue. However, many periodicals also contain nonrecurring feature articles and special tables, or present recurring tables at irregular intervals. These articles and tables are individually described in analytic abstracts under the heading "Statistical Features."

The "Statistical Features" analytic abstracts use 3-digit analytic numbers and are identified by the cover date of the relevant periodical issue (e.g., A1250-1.101, Nov. 7, 1988 (Vol. 66, No. 45)). For illustration of a typical "Statistical Features" abstract, see sample abstracts, p. xviii

Monthly Issues

In each SRI volume year, the base abstract of a given periodical appears in the first SRI monthly issue for which issues of the periodical are received for review. For most periodicals, the base abstract appears in SRI's combined January/February issue.

Throughout the year, a summary base abstract appears in SRI monthly issues each time an issue of a periodical is received. The summary abstract, which carries the same indexing as the full base abstract, provides a reference to the base abstract, a brief characterization of the current issue's statistical content (including any substantial changes in the regularly recurring statistics described in the base abstract), and a list of periodical issues reviewed to date. A summary base abstract appears regardless of whether a special "Statistical Features" analytic abstract is required to describe the current issue's statistical contents.

A few periodicals do not contain statistics in every issue. Each issue of these periodicals is reviewed, but an abstract is published in SRI monthly issues only when features with substantial statistical content appear.

HOW TO ACQUIRE SOURCE PUBLICATIONS

Acquiring Publications from a Library

Many of the publications abstracted in SRI are available in library collections. Ask your librarian for assistance in determining availability of specific titles.

Libraries that subscribe to the SRI Microfiche Library will have source material reproduced on microfiche as indicated in individual abstracts. (See explanation of SRI Microfiche Program, below.)

Requesting or Purchasing Publications from the Issuing Source

Information for requesting or purchasing copies of publications from the issuing source is provided in an Availability section in the SRI abstract for each publication. This information is as current and complete as possible as of SRI date of publication. See sample abstracts (p. xvii-xix) and symbols lists (p. xxii) for examples of information provided, and explanation of symbols employed.

The SRI Microfiche Program

Over 90% of the publications covered in SRI are included in the SRI Microfiche Library, available on a subscription basis and included in the collections of many major libraries. An entry in the bibliographic data section of each abstract will describe the microfiche status of that publication in one of the following ways:

- **SRI/MF/complete:** the entire publication is available in the SRI Microfiche Library. (In some series designated SRI/MF/complete, only reports with statistics are abstracted and filmed. Such exceptions are noted in the base description of the series.)
- **SRI/MF/excerpts:** only statistical portions have been filmed and are available on SRI microfiche.

Many periodicals covered in SRI are less than 50% statistical or have only one or two statistical issues per year, yet each issue averages more than 100 pages collation. Rather than inflate the size and price of SRI Microfiche Library with nonstatistical materials, only the cover, title page, table of contents, statistical content, and any accompanying narrative analysis of the statistical content will be filmed. Issues containing no statistics will not be filmed. A few large directories and calendar handbooks with limited statistical sections will also be filmed in excerpted form for similar reasons. Excerpted portions will be specified in the abstract availability information section.

- **SRI/MF/not filmed:** the publication is copyrighted, and SRI has been unable to obtain permission from the issuing agency to micropublish it.

SRI will make a continuing effort to obtain reproduction rights to provide as inclusive a microfiche library as possible.

Publications that have very limited distribution and cannot be micropublished by SRI will not be covered in SRI.

- **SRI/MF/complete, delayed; SRI/MF/excerpts, delayed:** the issuing agency has stipulated that SRI must wait to distribute the microfiche of the publication for a specified period of time as a condition of granting reproduction rights. The delay period will always be stated in the abstract availability section. Every effort will be made to keep instances of delayed shipment to a minimum.

Microfiche generally are shipped monthly and correspond to abstracts appearing in SRI monthly issues, except for selected periodicals (averaging less than 60 filmed pages) that are shipped on a quarterly basis to minimize waste space in the microfiche collection. Periodicals with quarterly microfiche shipment schedules are identified in the abstract bibliographic information following SRI/MF (e.g., SRI/MF/complete, shipped quarterly; or SRI/MF/excerpts, shipped quarterly).

SRI microfiche are sheets of film that measure 105×148 mm (approximately $4'' \times 6''$), and contain up to 98 document pages. Each has an eye-readable "title" header that identifies the accession number, issuing organization, series title (if any), and document title, for each publication filmed.

Microfiche are sequenced according to the accession numbers on the headers, which correspond to the base accession numbers in SRI abstracts (e.g., A1325–2). For separate publications in series, the accession number on the microfiche header also includes a decimal number that corresponds to the "analytic" abstract for the publication (e.g., R8750–12.7). Individual issues of periodicals are identified on microfiche headers by issue date.

Automatically updated collections of SRI current publications are available on a subscription basis. Retrospective collections, shipped in their entirety and ready for use, may also be purchased. Collections may be ordered to contain the entire range of SRI publications; or subsets may be ordered to cover only publications issued by State governments and universities or to cover only publications issued by private organizations.

RELATED CIS SERVICES

American Statistics Index and Index to International Statistics

Since 1973, Congressional Information Service has published the American Statistics Index, a comprehensive monthly abstract and index publication with annual cumulations, covering the thousands of statistical reports and publications prepared and issued by the U.S. Federal Government each year.

Beginning in January 1983, Congressional Information Service initiated publication of the Index to International Statistics, a comprehensive monthly index and abstracting service, covering the statistical publications of international intergovernmental organizations, including UN, OECD, EC, OAS, and approximately 80 other important intergovernmental organizations.

SRI abstracts and indexes are similar to ASI and IIS in many respects, and researchers generally can use SRI,

ASI, and IIS without significantly changing their search methods. However, several differences exist among the abstracts and indexes of the three services that should be noted. Major differences are:

- **Accession Number Periodicity Element**—SRI accession numbers do not indicate periodicity. IIS accession numbers include an indication of periodicity in the first letter after the hyphen, as do ASI accession numbers in the last digit before the hyphen.
- **Issuing Sources Indexing**—SRI and IIS issuing sources are indexed in a separate Index by Issuing Sources. ASI issuing agencies for publications are indexed in the ASI Index of Subjects and Names.
- **Periodicals Indexing in Monthly Issues**—SRI and IIS monthly abstracts and indexing cover all statistical contents of all periodicals received during each month. ASI monthly abstracts and indexing for periodicals cover only articles appearing in current issues, and changes from the "base" description for a periodical in the ASI Annual.
- **Periodical Currency Information in Monthly Issues**— ASI lists current issues of periodicals in a monthly "Periodicals Received and Reviewed" section. SRI and IIS incorporate this information in monthly abstracts for current periodicals.
- **Cumulation Patterns**—IIS indexes and abstracts are cumulated. ASI indexes are cumulated quarterly on the same schedule as IIS. SRI indexes are cumulated quarterly, but also cumulate throughout the quarter, so that the 2nd issue of a quarter includes indexing from the 1st issue, replacing the earlier monthly index.

All of the documents covered in ASI are included in the ASI Microfiche Library, available on a subscription basis, or through an individual Document on Demand service. The IIS Microfiche Library provides full text availability of over 95% of the publications indexed.

Statistical Masterfile

In 1989, CIS introduced a new CD-ROM product, the Statistical Masterfile, which allows users to search SRI, ASI, and IIS abstracts and indexing simultaneously. The three component databases may be purchased separately or in any combination. Both current year service and retrospective coverage are available for each index. Current service subscribers receive quarterly CD-ROM disk updates.

Other CIS Services

Since 1970, Congressional Information Service has published the CIS/Index, a monthly abstract and index publication with annual cumulations, which covers all publications of the U.S. Congress. The CIS/Microfiche Library and CIS/Documents-on-Demand services provide full-text availability of CIS/Index publications. Congressional Masterfile 2 provides CD-ROM access to CIS/Index abstracts and indexing.

Through cooperative arrangements with on-line computer services, direct on-line interactive searching of the abstracts and indexing contained in the American Statistics Index and CIS/Index databases is available to the public.

Full details on CIS publications and microform collections are available upon request from the CIS Marketing Department.

ACKNOWLEDGEMENTS

In the development of the Statistical Reference Index, we have had the help and support of so many people that it would be impossible to acknowledge them all individually.

We do wish to thank the hundreds of business organizations, publishers, associations, State government agencies, and research centers that have cooperated in providing us the information to be indexed. We appreciate the many editors, company executives, program and research directors, and State government officials and staff who have shared their expertise and often directed us to other useful sources.

Librarians and information specialists especially have offered useful advice and encouragement as we

have discussed with them various aspects of SRI over the years. Our special thanks go to the many State librarians and others who have assisted with the development of selection criteria for the publications to be covered.

The original concept of an SRI data base was developed from suggestions from Jack Leister, Head Librarian at Institute of Governmental Studies, University of California, Berkeley; and Judy Myers, Assistant to the Director, University of Houston Library. Important suggestions in expanding and developing the concept were contributed by Morris Ullman and Ruth Fine.

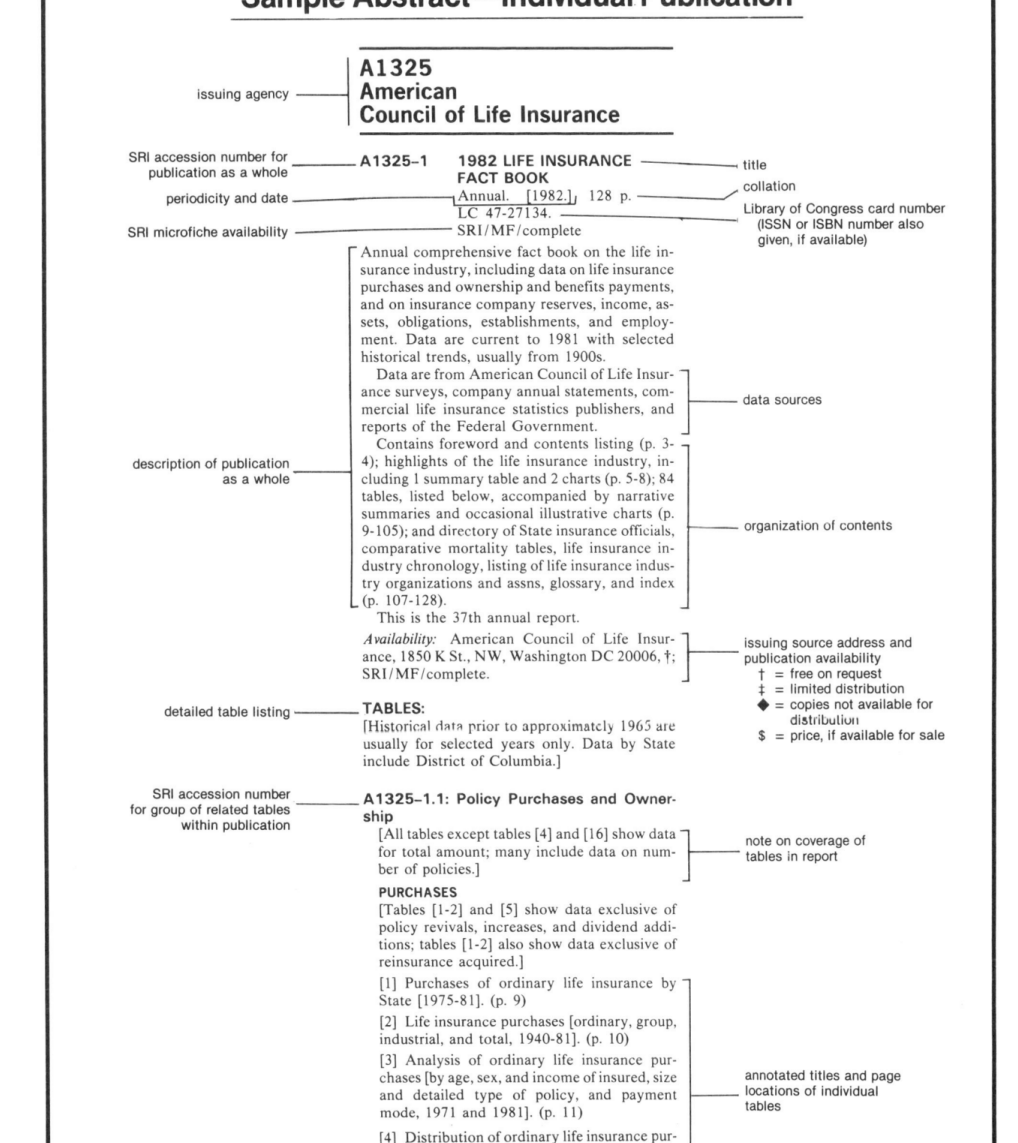

Sample Abstract—Periodical Publication

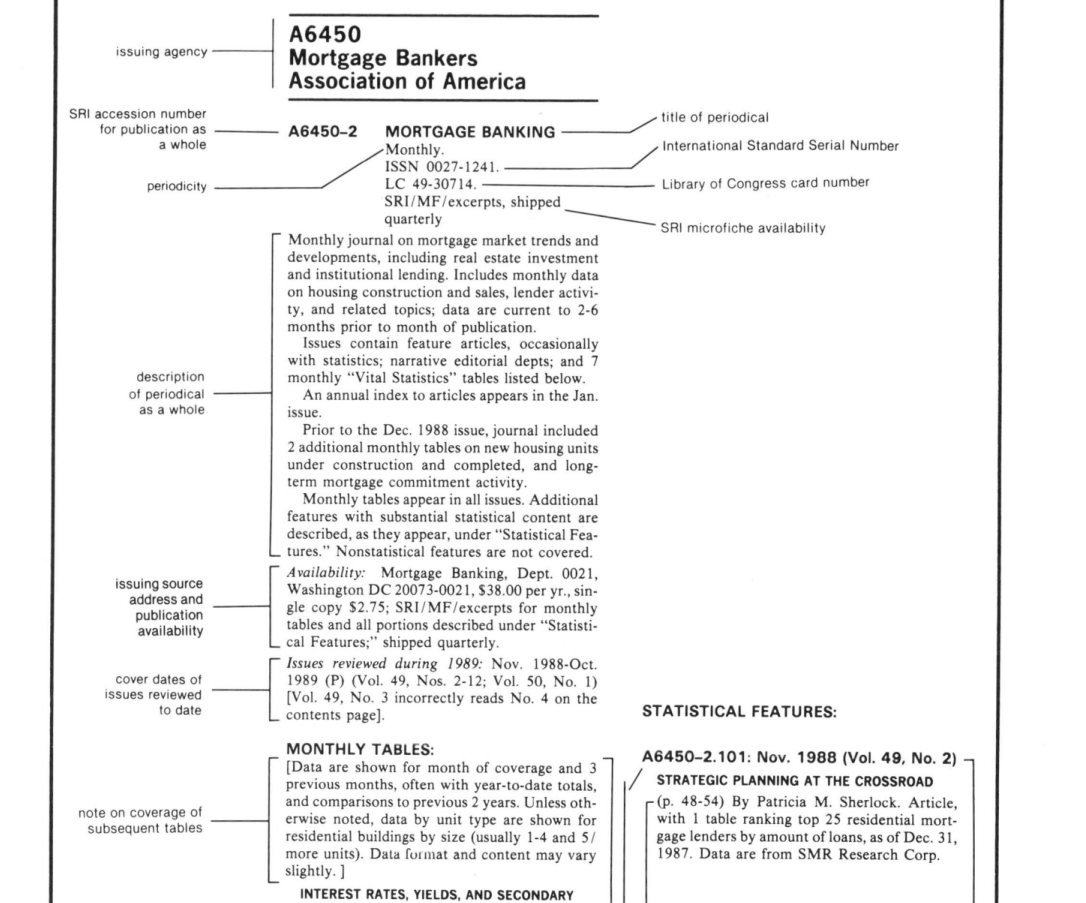

Sample Abstract—Publications in Series

U4370 Purdue University: Credit Research Center

SRI accession number for series as a whole — **U4370-1** **CREDIT RESEARCH CENTER WORKING PAPERS** — title of series

Series. For individual publication data, see below. SRI/MF/complete

description of series as a whole —

Continuing series of preliminary drafts of research study reports examining consumer and mortgage credit trends and practices, and their impact on the credit industry, consumers, and government.

Reports generally contain narrative analyses with interspersed tables and charts presenting data from government and private published sources, or from original surveys and/or survey analyses.

Recently issued report is described below.

Availability: Purdue University: Credit Research Center, Krannert Graduate School of Management, West Lafayette IN 47907, $1.50 each; SRI/MF/complete. — availability information for all reports in series

SRI accession number for individual report in series — **U4370-1.17: Second Mortgage Survey, 1981** — title of individual report

[Annual. 1982. iii+33 p. Working Paper No. 43. SRI/MF/complete.] — bibliographic data for individual report

description of report subject matter —

Annual report, by Richard L. Peterson et al., on a survey of the volume, profitability, and operating policies of the second mortgage lending market, 1980. Data are based on responses of 69 National Second Mortgage Assn members to a 1981 survey.

Includes narrative analysis, with 1 table showing survey responses, by institution type; and 10 tables generally showing low, high, average, and/or median, for the following in 1980: — contents summary

description of statistical content and page locations of tables —

a. Characteristics of second mortgage loans, including number, value, and average size of loans outstanding, extensions, and loan purchases and sales, with selected comparisons to 1979; average size of household and business extensions; ratio of new money to loan extensions; liquidation rates; and loan maturity and equity ratio requirements. Tables 2-5. (p. 6-12)

b. Operating ratios, including revenues from interest and other sources, pretax rate of return on equity and average receivables, and ratios of borrowing to receivables, and interest paid to borrowings. Table 6. (p. 14)

c. Delinquency rates by time past due; and chargeoff, foreclosure, and loss allowance ratios. Tables 7-10. (p. 16-20)

d. Comparative data, by lender type, including growth in loans and extensions, selected loan characteristics, operating ratios, delinquency rates, and foreclosures. Table 11. (p. 22)

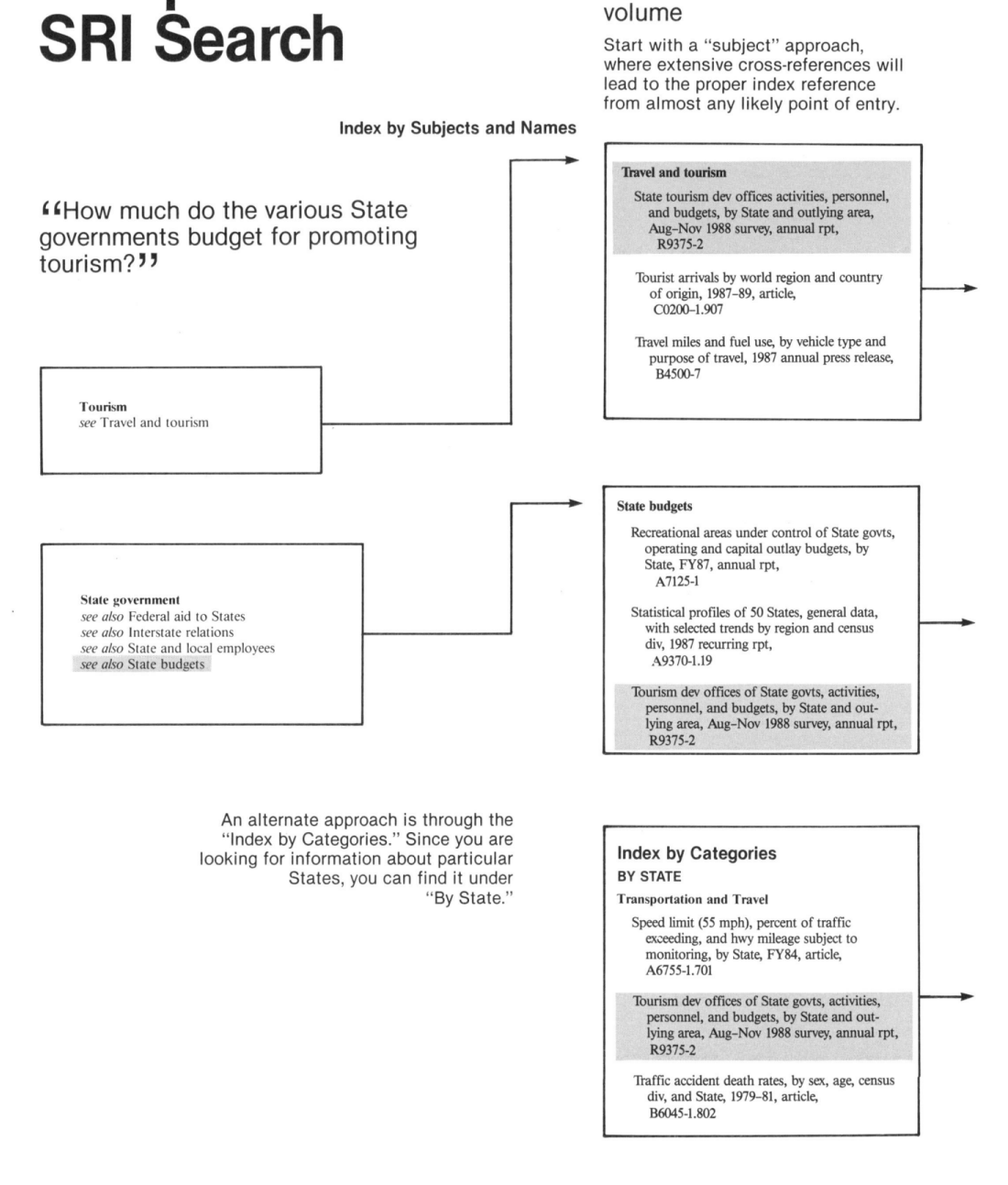

Step 2

Go from the index to the data description in the Abstracts Volume

The SRI accession number in the index will lead you to a publication entry that fully describes the document and helps you locate the tables containing the statistics you need.

Step 3

Retrieve the publication

The abstract contains the bibliographic information you need to locate the publication in a library's hardcopy collection or to obtain it from the issuing source, if copies are available.

Alternatively, if you have access to an SRI/Microfiche Library collection, the SRI accession number will lead you directly to the correct microfiche.

**R9375
U.S. Travel Data Center**

R9375-2 SURVEY OF STATE TRAVEL OFFICES, 1988-89
Annual. Dec. 1988.
1+i+94 p.
ISSN 0361-8307.
LC 74-191723.
SRI/MF/complete

Annual report, for FY89, on administration, promotional activities, budgets, and research of State travel development agencies. Data are from an Aug.-Nov. 1988 survey of agencies in each State, D.C., and selected U.S. territories.

Contains contents listing (1 p.); preface (p. i); summary and analysis, with 10 summary tables including average total and advertising budgets by census division, and trends from FY85 (p. 1-17); 17 extended tables, described below (p. 19-88); appendix, with definitions (p. 89); and index (p. 91-94).

This is the 16th annual report.

Availability: U.S. Travel Data Center, Two Lafayette Centre, 1133 21st St., NW, Washington DC 20036, $75.00; SRI/MF/complete.

TABLES:
[All data are shown for individual travel development agencies.]

- *a.* General administration: agency name, address, and telephone number; full- and part-time staff size, by job category; name and length of service of director and assistant; staff civil service status; and dept of which agency is a part. 2 tables. (p. 19-27)
- *b.* Advertising: director's name; advertising agency, years retained, and funding arrangement; whether advertising is geared toward stimulating inquiries, whether inquiries are surveyed to evaluate advertising effectiveness, and number of inquiries received in 1987. 2 tables. (p. 29-35)
- *c.* Budget: total budget and State rank, FY88-89; funding sources; State sales tax rates applicable to commercial lodging; allocations by function, with detail by advertising medium and for foreign advertising by country, FY88 and/or FY89; and travel show participation, FY89. 4 tables. (p. 37-57)
- *d.* General promotion, package tours, press/

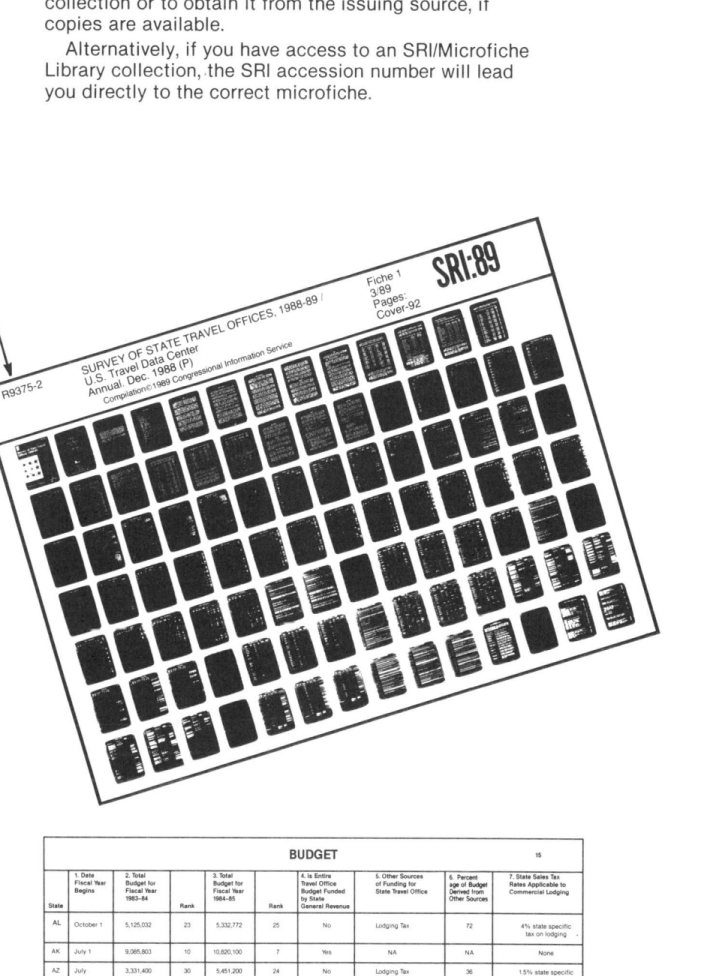

ACRONYMS, SELECTED ABBREVIATIONS, AND SYMBOLS

The following acronyms, abbreviations, and symbols may be used without further identification.

Abbreviation	Full Form
Admin	Administration
AFDC	Aid to Families with Dependent Children
AFL-CIO	American Federation of Labor-Congress of Industrial Organizations
AIDS	Acquired immune deficiency syndrome
AMEX	American Exchange
Amtrak	National Railroad Passenger Corp.
Assn	Association
Bibl	Bibliography
BLS	Bureau of Labor Statistics
Btu(h)	British thermal units
Bull.	Bulletin
Bur	Bureau
CIA	Central Intelligence Agency
CPI	Consumer Price Index
DC	District of Columbia
DEA	Drug Enforcement Administration
Dept	Department
Dev	Development
Div	Division
DOD	Department of Defense (not DON or DOA)
DOE	Department of Energy
DOT	Department of Transportation
EC	European Community
EPA	Environmental Protection Agency
FAA	Federal Aviation Administration
FBI	Federal Bureau of Investigation
FCC	Federal Communications Commission
FDA	Food and Drug Administration
FDIC	Federal Deposit Insurance Corp.
Fdn	Foundation
Fedn	Federation
FERC	Federal Energy Regulatory Commission
FHA	Federal Housing Administration
FHLBB	Federal Home Loan Bank Board
FmHA	Farmers Home Administration
FNMA	Federal National Mortgage Association
FSLIC	Federal Savings and Loan Insurance Corp.
FTC	Federal Trade Commission
FTE	Full time equivalent
FY	Fiscal Year
GDP	Gross Domestic Product
GNMA	Government National Mortgage Association
GNP	Gross National Product
Govt	Government
Govtl	Governmental
GSA	General Services Administration
GSP	Gross State Product
HHS	Department of Health and Human Services
HMO	Health Maintenance Organization
HUD	Department of Housing and Urban Development
Hwy	Highway
ICC	Interstate Commerce Commission
ILO	International Labor Organization
IMF	International Monetary Fund
Info	Information
Inst	Institute
Instn	Institution
Intl	International
IRS	Internal Revenue Service
kWh	Kilowatt hours
Metro	Metropolitan
Mgmt	Management
MSA	Metropolitan Statistical Area
NASA	National Aeronautics and Space Administration
NASDAQ	National Assn of Securities Dealers Automated Quotations
Natl	National
NATO	North Atlantic Treaty Organization
NCES	National Center for Educational Statistics
NCHS	National Center for Health Statistics
NIH	National Institutes of Health
NIMH	National Institute of Mental Health
NLRB	National Labor Relations Board
Nonmetro	Nonmetropolitan
NRC	Nuclear Regulatory Commission
NSA	National Security Agency
NSC	National Security Council
NSF	National Science Foundation
NYC	New York City
NYSE	New York Stock Exchange
OAS	Organization of American States
OASDHI	Old-Age, Survivors, Disability, and Health Insurance
OECD	Organization for Economic Cooperation and Development
OMB	Office of Management and Budget
OPEC	Organization of Petroleum Exporting Countries
OSHA	Occupational Safety and Health Administration
PAD	Petroleum Administration for Defense (abolished in 1954 but acronym is still used)
PHS	Public Health Service
P.L.	Public Law
PPI	Producer Price Index
PRC	People's Republic of China
Pub.	Publication
Qtr	Quarter
R&D	Research and Development
Res	Research
ROTC	Reserve Officers Training Corps
Rpt	Report
SALT	Strategic Arms Limitation Talks
SBA	Small Business Administration
SEC	Securities and Exchange Commission
SIC	Standard Industrial Classification
SITC	Standard International Trade Classification
SMSA	Standard Metropolitan Statistical Area
SSA	Social Security Administration
SSI	Supplemental Security Income
TSUSA	Tariff Schedules of the U.S. Annotated
TTPI	Trust Territory of the Pacific Islands
TV	Television
TVA	Tennessee Valley Authority
UK	United Kingdom
UN	United Nations
UNESCO	United Nations Educational, Scientific and Cultural Organization
UNICEF	United Nations International Children's Emergency Fund
USDA	Department of Agriculture
USITC	U.S. International Trade Commission
USMC	Marine Corps
USPS	U.S. Postal Service
USSR	Union of Soviet Socialist Republics
VA	Veterans Administration
WPI	Wholesale Price Index

Document Availability Symbols

Symbol	Meaning
†	copies are generally available free of charge from issuing source, while supplies last, inquire of issuing source
‡	copies are distributed by issuing source on a limited basis; inquire of issuing source
◆	copies are not available from issuing source; do not inquire of issuing source
SRI/MF/	notation indicating publication availability in SRI Microfiche Library; see full explanation on p. vii.

Index by Subjects and Names

Index by Subjects and Names

The Index by Subjects and Names includes references to data subjects, to individual authors of publications in which the author's name appears on the title page, and to organizations that compile or analyze data on behalf of issuing sources. (Names of issuing sources are cited separately in the Index by Issuing Sources.)

References to individual items within tabular breakdowns (e.g., data about a particular city in a table that is broken down city by city) generally are not included in the Index by Subjects and Names. For reference to these data, consult the Index by Categories.

Abandoned buildings

State and local:

- Alabama arson offenses involving uninhabited/abandoned property by type, 1992, annual rpt, S0119–1.1
- California arson offenses involving uninhabited structures by type, 1991, annual rpt, S0910–2.2
- Kansas school facilities in use and abandoned, 1990/91, annual rpt, S2945–1
- New York State arsons involving uninhabited/abandoned buildings, by location and type of property, 1991, annual rpt, S5760–3.1
- Pennsylvania arson crimes and arrests, by property type, with detail for uninhabited structures, 1992, annual rpt, S6860–1
- West Virginia arson offenses involving uninhabited buildings, by property type, 1991, annual rpt, S8610–1.2
- Wyoming arson offenses involving uninhabited/abandoned buildings, by property type, 1991, annual rpt, S8867–3.1

Abandoned property

see Vacant and abandoned property

Abbott, Langer and Associates

Engineer compensation, by work and employee characteristics, and region and metro area, 1992, annual rpt, A8460–1

Abend, Nicole

"Texas Provider Utilization and Financial Data", U8850–8.3

Abnormalities

see Birth defects

Abortion

- Black American health and vital statistics data, with comparisons to whites, 1970s-91, annual compilation, C6775–2.2
- College freshmen attitudes on legalized abortion, by sex and instn type, fall 1992, annual survey, U6215–1
- Congressional campaign finances, with detailed data for individual Members, and leading contributors by type and industry, 1990 election and trends, biennial rpt, R3828–2.2
- Developing countries family planning efforts, including abortion legal status, availability, prevalence, and cost, by country, 1988 or 1989, R8720–1.1
- Europe public opinion on political, economic, and social issues, for 9 countries and 3 Soviet Union Republics, 1991 survey, C8915–8.1
- Hospital patient discharges and length of stay, by diagnosis, type of operation, age, and region, 1991, annual rpt series, B4455–1
- Hospital patient discharges and length of stay, by diagnostic related group (DRG), payment source, age, and region, 1991, annual rpt series, B4455–3
- House of Representatives women members elected in Nov 1992, by abortion views, article, C5800–7.504
- Irish women obtaining abortions in England, characteristics and contraceptive use by marital status, 1988-90, article, A5160–1.501
- Public opinion on abortion as affected by survey question formulation, with detail for 6 States, Sept/Oct 1989 survey, article, A5160–1.504
- Public opinion on abortion as issue in 1992 presidential campaign, and preferred policy for Republican Party, 1992 Gallup Polls, C4040–1.502
- Public opinion on abortion legality, Supreme Court decision in Planned Parenthood v Casey, and related issues, June 1992 Gallup Poll and trends, C4040–1.501
- Public opinion on French abortion pill (RU-486) availability in US, Feb 1993 Gallup Poll, C4040–1.509
- Public opinion on religious preference and commitment compared to views on abortion, Mar 1993 Gallup Poll and trends, C4040–1.510
- Public opinion on social, political, and economic issues, detailed data, 1972-91 surveys, annual rpt, U6395–1
- Soviet Union former central Asian Republics population, and fertility, abortion, and contraceptive use rates, for 5 Republics, 1993 article, A5160–1.504
- State social, economic, and govtl indicators, with rankings, 1993 semiannual rpt, B8500–1.9
- Statistical profiles of 50 States and DC, general data, 1993 annual almanac, C4712–1
- Teenage abortion, birth, and pregnancy rates, by race, age group, and State, 1988, article, A5160–1.504
- World population access to affordable abortion, by country, 1992/93 biennial rpt, R9455–1.5
- Youth (male) attitudes on abortion, by respondent characteristics, 1988 survey, article, A5160–1.505
- Youth opinions about selected social issues, by religion, 1991-93 surveys, R8780–1.510

State and local:

- Arizona State constitutional amendment protecting preborn children, election results by county, 1992, biennial rpt, S0520–1
- Arkansas vital statistics, including births, deaths by cause, marriages, and divorces, by age, sex, race, and county, 1991 and trends, annual rpt, S0685–1
- Colorado vital statistics, including population, births, deaths by cause, abortion, marriage and divorce, and adoption, by demographic characteristics and location, 1990 and trends, annual rpt, S1010–1
- DC statistical profile, general data, 1992 annual rpt, S1535–3.5
- Florida abortion clinics, by district and county, 1992, annual rpt, S1746–1.2
- Georgia vital statistics, including population, births, abortions, marriages, and divorces, by demographic characteristics and location, 1991 and trends, annual rpt, S1895–1.1
- Hawaii abortions, by patient characteristics and location, 1990, annual rpt, S2065–1.2
- Idaho vital statistics, including births, deaths by cause, abortions, marriages, and divorces, by demographic characteristics and county, 1991 and trends, annual rpt, S2250–2
- Illinois criminal abortions and arrests, 1990-91, annual report, S2536–1
- Kansas vital statistics, including population, births, deaths by cause, abortions, marriages, and divorces, by demographic characteristics and location, 1991 and trends, annual rpt, S2975–1
- Louisiana vital statistics, including population, births, deaths by cause, reportable diseases, marriages, and divorces, by demographic characteristics and locality, 1989-90 and trends, annual rpt, S3295–1
- Maine vital statistics, including births, deaths by cause, abortions, and marriages and divorces, by demographic characteristics and location, 1991 and trends, annual rpt, S3460–2
- Maryland State referendum on abortion law, election results by county, 1992, biennial rpt, S3615–1
- Minnesota vital statistics, including population, births, abortions, deaths, marriages, and divorces, by location and demographic characteristics, 1991 and trends, annual rpt, S4190–2
- Mississippi vital statistics, including births, deaths by cause, marriages, and divorces, by demographic characteristics and location, 1992 and trends, annual rpt, S4350–1
- Missouri abortions by patient characteristics, county, and region, 1992, annual rpt, S4518–1
- Montana vital statistics, including births, deaths by cause, abortion, disease, and marriage and divorce, by demographic characteristics and county, 1990-91 and trends, annual rpt, S4690–1

Abortion

Nevada vital statistics, including births, abortions, and deaths by cause, by county and demographic characteristics, 1989 and trends, annual rpt, S5075–1

New Mexico abortions by patient characteristics, 1991 and trends, annual rpt, S5605–1.1

New York State vital statistics, including population, births, deaths by cause, reportable diseases, and marriages and dissolutions, by demographic characteristics and/or location, 1990 and trends, annual rpt, S5765–1

North Dakota vital statistics, including births, deaths by cause, marriages and divorces, and abortions, by demographic characteristics and/or county, 1991 and trends, annual rpt, S6105–2

Oregon vital statistics, including abortions by patient characteristics, 1991, annual rpt, S6615–5

Rhode Island vital statistics, including population, births, deaths, marriages, and divorces, by demographic characteristics and locality, 1989 and trends, annual rpt, S6995–1

South Dakota induced abortions by patient age and race, 1991, annual rpt, S7345–1

Tennessee abortions by patient age and race, and by county and city, 1991 and trends, annual rpt, S7520–2

Tennessee statistical abstract, general data, 1992/93 annual rpt, U8710–2.17

Texas vital statistics, including births, deaths by cause, abortions, marriages, and divorces, by location and demographic characteristics, 1991 and trends, annual rpt, S7685–1

Utah vital statistics, including births by characteristics of mother and child, by location, 1990 and trends, annual rpt, S7835–1.1

Vermont vital statistics, including population, births, deaths by cause, abortions, marriages, and divorces, by location and demographic characteristics, 1991 and trends, annual rpt, S8054–1

Virginia vital statistics, including births, deaths by cause, marriages and divorces, and communicable disease, by demographic characteristics and location, 1991 and trends, annual rpt, S8225–1

Abrahamson, Shirley

"Grounds Maintenance: 1992 Salary Survey", C4725–6

Abrasive materials

Cotton and other fiber consumption in textile production, by detailed end use, 1990-92, annual rpt, A7485–1

Absenteeism

Aerospace industry injury/illness rates and lost workdays, 1986-90, annual rpt, A0250–2.5

Black American health and vital statistics data, with comparisons to whites, 1970s-91, annual compilation, C6775–2.2

Dental problems/treatment-related time lost from work or school, by demographic characteristics, 1989, article, A2623–1.502

Incidence of illness and injury, and hospitalization and mortality data, by selected demographic characteristics, 1992 annual rpt, A5173–2.4

Index by Subjects and Names

Iron and steel industry fatalities, injury/illness rate, and workdays lost, 1988-92, annual rpt, A2000–2.1

Occupational injuries, illnesses, and deaths, by industry group, with workdays lost, 1991-92 and trends, annual rpt, A8375–2.2

Occupational injuries/illnesses and deaths, and workdays lost, by detailed industry, 1991 and trends, annual rpt, A8375–4

Occupational injuries/illnesses and fatalities, lost workdays, and employee views on workplace safety, with data by State, 1992 annual rpt, R8335–1.1

Oil/gas industry occupational injury, illness, and employment data, by function, for 136 companies, 1991, annual rpt, A2575–4

School absenteeism rates, by State, 1991/92, semiannual rpt, B8500–1.7

State and local:

Hawaii school days lost, by geographic area, 1988, annual rpt, S2065–1.3

see also Truancy from school

Abu Dhabi

see Organization of Petroleum Exporting Countries

see United Arab Emirates

Accident insurance

see Property and casualty insurance

Accidental deaths

Black children and youth population, economic, health, and education data, with comparisons to whites, 1993 rpt, R3840–21

Construction industry fatal accidents, by type, 1991/92, article, U8710–1.504

Correctional instn inmate accidental deaths, by State and Canadian Province, as of June 1992, annual rpt, A1305–3

Deaths and disabling injuries from accidents, and related costs, by accident type, 1991 and trends, annual article, A8375–1.501

Deaths and disabling injuries from accidents, by detailed type, victim characteristics, circumstances, and location, 1992 and trends, annual rpt, A8375–2

Deaths and injuries from accidents, and costs, by accident type, 1991-92, article, A8375–1.504

Deaths and rates, by cause, 1993 annual fact book, A1275–1.5

Hurricane deaths and property damage caused by most serious storms since 1900, 1992 annual rpt, U6660–1.8

Injuries and deaths from accidents by type, and selected incidence and economic loss data, 1991 and trends, annual rpt, A5650–1.4

Latin America statistical abstract, general data by country, 1992 annual rpt, U6250–1.1

Lawsuit jury verdict award trends, by type of injury, 1982-92, annual rpt, C5180–1

Natural gas industry employment, payroll, and accident statistics, 1960s-91, annual rpt, A1775–3.9

Occupational injuries/illnesses and deaths, and workdays lost, by detailed industry, 1991 and trends, annual rpt, A8375–4

Oil/gas industry occupational injury, illness, and employment data, by function, for 136 companies, 1991, annual rpt, A2575–4

State social, economic, and govtl indicators, with rankings, 1993 semiannual rpt, B8500–1.9

Transportation accident fatality trends, by mode, 1992 annual rpt, R4815–1

State and local:

Alabama vital statistics, including population, births, deaths by cause, marriages and divorces, by location and demographic characteristics, 1992 and trends, annual rpt, S0175–2

Alaska fishing industry occupational deaths, by decedent characteristics, 1980-88, article, A2623–1.507

Alaska vital statistics, including births, deaths by cause, marriages, divorces, adoptions, and population, by demographic characteristics and location, 1990, annual rpt, S0315–1

Arkansas vital statistics, including births, deaths by cause, marriages, and divorces, by age, sex, race, and county, 1991 and trends, annual rpt, S0685–1

California vital statistics, including population, births, and deaths by cause, by demographic characteristics and county, 1990 and trends, annual rpt, S0865–1

Colorado vital statistics, including population, births, deaths by cause, abortion, marriage and divorce, and adoption, by demographic characteristics and location, 1990 and trends, annual rpt, S1010–1

Connecticut vital statistics, including births, deaths by cause, marriages, and divorces, by demographic characteristics and location, 1989, annual rpt, S1200–1

Delaware vital statistics, including births, deaths by cause, and marriages and dissolutions, by demographic characteristics and location, 1990, annual rpt, S1385–2

Florida deaths by selected cause, and incidence of selected communicable diseases, by county, 1992 annual rpt, S1746–1.1

Florida injuries and fatalities resulting from natural gas and electric equipment accidents, 1992 and trends, annual rpt, S1790–1

Florida vital statistics, including population, births, deaths by cause, and marriages and dissolutions, by location and demographic characteristics, 1992 and trends, annual rpt, S1745–3

Georgia vital statistics, including deaths by cause, demographic characteristics, and location, 1991 and trends, annual rpt, S1895–1.2

Hawaii data book, general data, 1992 annual rpt, S2090–1.2, S2090–1.5, S2090–1.12, S2090–1.15

Hawaii vital statistics, including births, deaths by cause, marriages, and dissolutions, by demographic characteristics and location, 1990, annual rpt, S2065–1.2

Idaho vital statistics, including births, deaths by cause, abortions, marriages, and divorces, by demographic characteristics and county, 1991 and trends, annual rpt, S2250–2

Iowa vital statistics, including population, births, deaths by cause, marriages, and divorces, by demographic characteristics and location, 1991 and trends, annual rpt, S2795–1

Index by Subjects and Names

Kansas fires by circumstances, and firefighter and citizen injuries and fatalities, 1992, annual rpt, S2925–1.1

Kansas vital statistics, including population, births, deaths by cause, abortions, marriages, and divorces, by demographic characteristics and location, 1991 and trends, annual rpt, S2975–1

Kentucky vital statistics, including births, deaths by cause, marriages and divorces, and population, by demographic characteristics and county, 1991, annual rpt, S3140–1

Louisiana vital statistics, including population, births, deaths by cause, reportable diseases, marriages, and divorces, by demographic characteristics and locality, 1989-90 and trends, annual rpt, S3295–1

Maine vital statistics, including births, deaths by cause, abortions, and marriages and divorces, by demographic characteristics and location, 1991 and trends, annual rpt, S3460–2

Maryland vital statistics, including population, births, deaths by cause, marriages, and divorces, by demographic characteristics and location, 1989 and trends, annual rpt, S3635–1

Massachusetts vital statistics, including births, deaths by cause, marriages, divorces, and population, by locality and demographic characteristics, 1990 and trends, annual rpt, S3850–1

Michigan vital statistics, including births, deaths, marriages, divorces/annulments, and communicable diseases, by location and demographic characteristics, 1990 and trends, annual rpt, S4000–3

Minnesota vital statistics, including population, births, abortions, deaths, marriages, and divorces, by location and demographic characteristics, 1991 and trends, annual rpt, S4190–2

Mississippi vital statistics, including births, deaths by cause, marriages, and divorces, by demographic characteristics and location, 1992 and trends, annual rpt, S4350–1

Missouri occupational disability and death incidents, and compensation costs, by industry and county, 1991 and trends, annual rpt, S4530–2.2

Missouri vital statistics, including population, births, deaths by cause, and marriages and divorces, by location and demographic characteristics, 1992 and trends, annual rpt, S4518–1

Montana vital statistics, including births, deaths by cause, abortion, disease, and marriage and divorce, by demographic characteristics and county, 1990-91 and trends, annual rpt, S4690–1

Nebraska vital statistics, including births, deaths, marriages, divorces, and population, by demographic characteristics and location, 1991 and trends, annual rpt, S4885–1

Nevada vital statistics, including births, abortions, and deaths by cause, by county and demographic characteristics, 1989 and trends, annual rpt, S5075–1

New Hampshire vital statistics, including population, births, deaths by cause, marriages, and divorces, by location and demographic characteristics, 1991 and trends, annual rpt, S5215–1

New Jersey vital statistics, including births, deaths, population, communicable diseases, and marriages and divorces, by demographic characteristics and location, 1990 and trends, annual rpt, S5405–1

New Mexico vital statistics, including population, births, deaths, and disease, by location and demographic characteristics, 1991 and trends, annual rpt, S5605–1

New York State statistical yearbook, general data, 1992 annual rpt, U5100–1.8

New York State vital statistics, including population, births, deaths by cause, reportable diseases, and marriages and dissolutions, by demographic characteristics and/or location, 1990 and trends, annual rpt, S5765–1

North Carolina deaths and rates, by cause and county, 1991 and trends, annual rpt, S5927–1.2

North Dakota vital statistics, including births, deaths by cause, marriages and divorces, and abortions, by demographic characteristics and/or county, 1991 and trends, annual rpt, S6105–2

Ohio vital statistics, including births, deaths by cause, marriages, divorces, and population, by demographic characteristics and location, 1991 and trends, annual rpt, S6285–1

Oklahoma tornadoes, deaths, and injuries, by county, 1950-91, annual rpt, U8130–2.1

Oregon vital statistics, including births, deaths by cause, communicable diseases, marriages, and divorces, by age, sex, race-ethnicity, and county, 1991 and trends, annual rpt, S6615–5

Rhode Island statistical almanac, general data, 1993 annual rpt, C7975–1

Rhode Island vital statistics, including population, births, deaths, marriages, and divorces, by demographic characteristics and locality, 1989 and trends, annual rpt, S6995–1

South Carolina deaths, by detailed cause, age, sex, and race, 1990, annual rpt, S7175–2

South Carolina vital statistics, including births, deaths by cause, marriages, and divorces, by age, sex, race, and location, 1990 and trends, annual rpt, S7175–1

South Dakota vital statistics, including births, deaths, marriage and divorce, and communicable disease, by demographic characteristics and county, 1991 and trends, annual rpt, S7345–1

Tennessee vital statistics, including births, deaths by cause, marriages, divorces, and population, by demographic characteristics and location, 1991 and trends, annual rpt, S7520–2

Texas vital statistics, including births, deaths by cause, abortions, marriages, and divorces, by location and demographic characteristics, 1991 and trends, annual rpt, S7685–1

Utah vital statistics, including births, deaths by cause, and population, by county and demographic characteristics, 1990 and trends, annual rpt, S7835–1

Vermont vital statistics, including population, births, deaths by cause, abortions, marriages, and divorces, by location and demographic characteristics, 1991 and trends, annual rpt, S8054–1

Accidents and accident prevention

Virginia vital statistics, including births, deaths by cause, marriages and divorces, and communicable disease, by demographic characteristics and location, 1991 and trends, annual rpt, S8225–1

Washington State vital statistics, including births, deaths by cause, and population, by demographic characteristics and location, 1991 and trends, annual rpt, S8363–1

West Virginia vital statistics, including births, deaths by cause, marriages, and divorces, by location and demographic characteristics, 1991 and trends, annual rpt, S8560–1

Wisconsin vital statistics, including population, births, deaths by cause, and marriages and dissolutions, by county and demographic characteristics, 1991 and trends, annual rpt, S8715–4

Wyoming vital statistics, including population, births, deaths by cause, marriages, and divorces, by demographic characteristics and county, 1991 and trends, annual rpt, S8920–2

see also Agricultural accidents and safety

see also Aviation accidents and safety

see also Drowning

see also Marine accidents and safety

see also Mine accidents and safety

see also Railroad accidents and safety

see also Traffic accident fatalities

Accidents and accident prevention

- Black American injury rates, with comparisons to whites, 1985 and 1989, annual compilation, C6775–2.2
- Chemical (ethylene oxide) plants involved in explosions worldwide, 1987-91, article, C5800–8.502
- Chemical hazard emergency response planning by local govts, including public notification methods, by locality, 1993 rpt, A5800–4.34
- Costs of accidental injuries, by cost component, 1986-90, annual fact book, A1275–1.5
- Health condition and preventive health care and safety practices of adults, by respondent characteristics, 1992 and trends, annual survey rpt, C8111–2
- Hospital patient discharges and length of stay, by diagnosis, type of operation, age, and region, 1991, annual rpt series, B4455–1
- Incidence of illness and injury, and hospitalization and mortality data, by selected demographic characteristics, 1992 annual rpt, A5173–2.4
- Injuries and deaths from accidents, and costs, by accident type, 1991-92, article, A8375–1.504
- Injuries and deaths from accidents, by detailed type, victim characteristics, circumstances, and location, 1992 and trends, annual rpt, A8375–2
- Injuries and deaths from accidents by type, and selected incidence and economic loss data, 1991 and trends, annual rpt, A5650–1.4
- Older population share experiencing a fall, by living arrangement, 1993 article, A1865–1.522
- Pediatrician bicycle safety counseling practices and experience with bicycle injuries among patients, 1990 survey, article, A2623–1.507

Accidents and accident prevention

Personal injury jury verdict award trends, with data by case type and for awards exceeding $1 million, 1960s-92, annual rpt, C5180–1

State and local:

- Florida injuries and fatalities resulting from natural gas and electric equipment accidents, 1992 and trends, annual rpt, S1790–1
- Louisiana traumatic brain and spinal cord injuries, by cause, 1991, annual rpt, S3345–2

see also Accidental deaths
see also Agricultural accidents and safety
see also Aviation accidents and safety
see also Drowning
see also Fires and fire prevention
see also Marine accidents and safety
see also Mine accidents and safety
see also Nuclear accidents and safety
see also Occupational health and safety
see also Poisoning and drug reaction
see also Product safety
see also Railroad accidents and safety
see also State funding for public safety
see also Traffic accident fatalities
see also Traffic accidents and safety
see also Traffic engineering

Accounting and auditing

- Airline retiree health benefits liability disclosed by new accounting requirements, for 4 carriers, 1993 article, C7000–4.504
- Construction industry finances and operations, by type of business and region, 1992-93, annual survey rpt, A4155–1
- Employment in business and industry, hiring plans for college grads, by field, salary, and degree, 1993 annual survey rpt, U3730–1
- Financial ratios and performance, for over 350 SIC 4-digit industries, FY88-92, annual rpt, A6400–3
- Museums and related instns financial structure, including donation programs, income, and expenses, by type, budget size, and governing authority, 1989/90 survey, A0750–1.3
- Operating and financial composite ratios for corporations, with establishments and receipts, for approx 200 industries, by asset size, FY90, annual rpt, C7800–1
- Plastics processing industry accounting methods used, by company sales size, 1992, annual rpt, A8920–4
- Plastics processing industry expenses included in direct selling costs, 1992 survey, biennial rpt, A8920–3
- Salaries of scientists, engineers, technicians, and other professionals, by employee and employer characteristics, 1990s and trends, biennial rpt, A3960–1
- Salary and job offers for college grads, by field of study, type of employer, and degree level, by region, interim rpt series, A3940–1
- Salary and job offers for college grads, by field of study, type of employer, and degree level, series, A3940–2
- Shopping center financial and operating data, with detail by type of tenant, US and Canada, 1991, triennial rpt, R9285–1
- Supply-demand data for accounting grads, including detail by sex, race-ethnicity, and region, 1991/92 and trends, annual rpt, A1885–1
- Transportation regulatory agency policies and practices for motor carriers and railroads, by agency, 1991/92 annual rpt, A7015–4
- Utility regulatory agency policies and practices, and industry financial and operating data, by utility type and agency, 1991/92 annual rpt, A7015–3
- Women and minorities in professional fields, detailed education and labor force data, 1991 and trends, recurring rpt, A3960–2.1

State and local:

- Arizona revenue dept tax audit billings and delinquent tax collections, FY92, annual rpt, S0515–1
- Arizona statistical abstract, general data, 1993 recurring rpt, U5850–2.24
- California business tax audits and amounts recovered, by type of tax, FY92, annual rpt, S0835–1
- Colorado State tax audits, assessments, and refunds, FY92, annual rpt, S1075–1.1
- Florida statistical abstract, general data, 1992 annual rpt, U6660–1.18
- Hawaii operations of IRS, 1989-91, annual rpt, S2090–1.9
- Idaho taxes recovered by audit, by type of tax, FY89-92, annual rpt, S2295–1
- Kansas tax audits, amounts assessed and collections, by tax type, FY91-92, annual rpt, S3020–1
- New Mexico tax dept audit activity, including expenditures and return, FY91-92 and trends, annual rpt, S5660–1
- North Carolina utility audits, by type of utility, 1990, annual rpt, S5917–2
- Ohio tax recoveries through State audits, by tax type, FY89-92, annual rpt, S6390–1.1
- South Carolina tax collections from audits and delinquent accounts, FY92, annual rpt, S7255–1.1
- South Dakota accounting firm recruiters views on tax curriculum for accounting undergraduates, and degree levels of students hired, fall 1992 survey, article, U8595–1.504
- South Dakota tax audits and assessments, FY92 and trends, annual rpt, S7380–1.1
- Texas gas utility auditing activities and violations discovered, by type, FY92, annual rpt, S7745–1
- Utah tax audit assessments, with comparison to audit costs, FY84-92, annual rpt, S7905–1

see also Depreciation

Accounts receivable

see Business assets and liabilities, general
see Business assets and liabilities, specific industry
see Credit

Achievement tests

see Educational tests

Acquired immune deficiency syndrome

- Black American AIDS cases and deaths, with comparisons to whites, 1984-91, annual compilation, C6775–2.2
- Black children and youth population, economic, health, and education data, with comparisons to whites, 1993 rpt, R3840–21
- Cases and deaths for adults and children, and adult cases by world area, 1992 annual rpt, A5173–2.4

Index by Subjects and Names

- Cases by sex and race-ethnicity, and for top 10 States/territories and metro areas, 1993 article, C4215–1.505
- Cases by sex and race-ethnicity, through June 1992, article, C4215–1.503
- Cases of AIDS per 1000,000 population, for metro and nonmetro areas, 1990/91, A4425–4
- Cases reported, with detail for children 12/under, by State, June 1981-Mar 1992, semiannual rpt, B8500–1.9
- Charitable foundation grants awarded for AIDS treatment, research, and counseling/support, 1989-91, article, C2176–1.505
- Child AIDS cases by source of exposure, as of Dec 1991, annual rpt, R3840–5.1
- College freshmen attitudes on mandatory testing to control AIDS, fall 1992, annual survey, U6215–1
- College grad new hire testing for drugs, alcohol, and AIDS, employer practices, 1992/93 annual survey rpt, U3130–1
- Condom use and concern about AIDS among sexually active young men, 1988 and 1991 surveys, article, A5160–1.504
- Correctional instn inmate deaths from AIDS, by sex, by State and Canadian Province, as of June 1992, annual rpt, A1305–3
- Costs for treatment of human immunodeficiency virus (HIV) and AIDS cases, 1993-94, article, C4215–1.503
- Death rates for human immunodeficiency virus (HIV), by race and sex, 1991, article, A8510–1.1
- Drug abuser AIDS risk sexual behavior, among injection drug users and crack smokers, May-June 1991 study, article, A2623–1.510
- Eye donors rejected for testing positive to human immunodeficiency virus (HIV), 1992, annual rpt, A4743–1
- Hispanic American AIDS cases and deaths, by sex, with comparisons to whites, 1984-91, annual compilation, C6775–3.6
- Hospital employee health care benefits, including coverage for mental health/substance abuse and AIDS, and data by region, 1992 survey, article, A1865–1.505
- Hospital patient discharges and length of stay, by diagnostic related group (DRG), payment source, age, and region, 1991, annual rpt series, B4455–3
- Insurance benefit payments for AIDS-related claims, and AIDS share of total claims, 1986-91, biennial fact book, A1325–1.2
- Japan and US health care system data, including expenditures, facilities, insurance coverage, and population health indicators, 1993 article, R5650–2.515
- Latin America mandatory AIDS and seropositivity reporting programs, by country, 1988, annual rpt, U6250–1.7
- Medical school policies regarding students with human immunodeficiency virus (HIV), 1990/91, article, A3273–8.503
- Men's disclosure of human immunodeficiency virus (HIV) infection status to male sex partners, with impact on relationship, 1992 article, A2623–1.502

Index by Subjects and Names

Acquired immune deficiency syndrome

Men's sexual behavior, including condom use, and AIDS knowledge and risks, by selected characteristics, 1991 survey, articles, A5160–1.503

Prison and jail inmate AIDS cases, deaths, separate housing, and testing, including by State or locale, 1992 annual series, R4300–1

Public health research results, including AIDS-related behavior and prevention in selected populations, 1992 articles, A2623–1.501

Public health research results, including AIDS-related behavior and prevention in selected populations, 1993 articles, A2623–1.506, A2623–1.512

Public opinion on AIDS epidemic, transmission, and prevention practices, 1992 survey and trends, annual rpt, C8111–2

Public opinion on AIDS transmission, protective methods, and behavior changes, 1987-92 surveys, A0610–1.502

Public opinion on whether AIDS may be punishment by God for immoral behavior, for US, 9 European countries, and 3 Soviet Union Republics, 1991 survey, C8915–8.1

State funding for human immunodeficiency virus (HIV) and sexually transmitted disease programs, by State, 1989, A5160–10

State use of quarantines and handling of complaints about AIDS-infected persons whose behavior increases transmission risk, by State, 1981-90, article, A2623–1.512

Western Hemisphere AIDS cases and deaths, by country, 1986-89, annual rpt, U6250–1.6

Workplace AIDS incidence, and employer testing and other policies, 1993 and trends, A2075–20.14

Youth opinions about selected social issues, by religion, 1991-93 surveys, R8780–1.510

Zambia student views on sexual behavior and treatment of persons infected with AIDS virus, by respondent characteristics, 1990 survey, article, A5160–6.503

State and local:

Alabama public health dept activities, including services provided, inspection and licensing activity, staff and finances, and vital statistics and health data, 1992 annual rpt, S0175–3

Alabama statistical abstract, general data, 1992 recurring rpt, U5680–2.8

Alaska vital statistics, including births, deaths by cause, marriages, divorces, adoptions, and population, by demographic characteristics and location, 1990, annual rpt, S0315–1

California vital statistics, including population, births, and deaths by cause, by demographic characteristics and county, 1990 and trends, annual rpt, S0865–1

Colorado public knowledge and opinions on AIDS and preventive behavior, 1990, recurring rpt, S1010–3

Colorado vital statistics, including population, births, deaths by cause, abortion, marriage and divorce, and adoption, by demographic characteristics and location, 1990 and trends, annual rpt, S1010–1

Connecticut vital statistics, including births, deaths by cause, marriages, and divorces, by demographic characteristics and location, 1989, annual rpt, S1200–1

Delaware vital statistics, including births, deaths by cause, and marriages and dissolutions, by demographic characteristics and location, 1990, annual rpt, S1385–2

Florida AIDS cases and rates, by county, 1980-92, annual rpt, U6660–1.3

Florida county data book, 1992/93 annual rpt, C6360–1

Florida deaths by selected cause, and incidence of selected communicable diseases, by county, 1992 annual rpt, S1746–1.1

Florida vital statistics, including population, births, deaths by cause, and marriages and dissolutions, by location and demographic characteristics, 1992 and trends, annual rpt, S1745–3

Georgia public knowledge and opinions on AIDS and preventive behavior, 1991, annual rpt, S1895–2

Hawaii health dept activities and services, including vital statistics and disease control, by location, 1990, annual rpt, S2065–1

Idaho vital statistics, including births, deaths by cause, abortions, marriages, and divorces, by demographic characteristics and county, 1991 and trends, annual rpt, S2250–2

Illinois statistical abstract, general data, 1992 annual rpt, U6910–2

Iowa AIDS cases and deaths, 1983-92, annual rpt, S2795–1

Kansas vital statistics, including population, births, deaths by cause, abortions, marriages, and divorces, by demographic characteristics and location, 1991 and trends, annual rpt, S2975–1

Louisiana vital statistics, including population, births, deaths by cause, reportable diseases, marriages, and divorces, by demographic characteristics and locality, 1989-90 and trends, annual rpt, S3295–1

Maine vital statistics, including births, deaths by cause, abortions, and marriages and divorces, by demographic characteristics and location, 1991 and trends, annual rpt, S3460–2

Maryland public school funding for AIDS education, by county, 1991/92, annual rpt, S3610–2.9

Maryland vital statistics, including population, births, deaths by cause, marriages, and divorces, by demographic characteristics and location, 1989 and trends, annual rpt, S3635–1

Massachusetts vital statistics, including births, deaths by cause, marriages, divorces, and population, by locality and demographic characteristics, 1990 and trends, annual rpt, S3850–1

Michigan public opinion on AIDS transmission risks, by demographic characteristics, 1991, annual rpt, S4000–4

Michigan vital statistics, including births, deaths, marriages, divorces/annulments, and communicable diseases, by location and demographic characteristics, 1990 and trends, annual rpt, S4000–3

Minnesota vital statistics, including population, births, abortions, deaths, marriages, and divorces, by location and demographic characteristics, 1991 and trends, annual rpt, S4190–2

Mississippi vital statistics, including births, deaths by cause, marriages, and divorces, by demographic characteristics and location, 1992 and trends, annual rpt, S4350–1

Missouri vital statistics, including population, births, deaths by cause, and marriages and divorces, by location and demographic characteristics, 1992 and trends, annual rpt, S4518–1

Montana vital statistics, including births, deaths by cause, abortion, disease, and marriage and divorce, by demographic characteristics and county, 1990-91 and trends, annual rpt, S4690–1

Nebraska vital statistics, including births, deaths, marriages, divorces, and population, by demographic characteristics and location, 1991 and trends, annual rpt, S4885–1

New Jersey AIDS cases by patient characteristics, and deaths, 1990 and trends, annual rpt, S5405–1

New Mexico vital statistics, including population, births, deaths, and disease, by location and demographic characteristics, 1991 and trends, annual rpt, S5605–1

New York State prison inmate deaths from AIDS in State and local facilities, 1981-91, annual rpt, S5760–3.4

New York State public knowledge about AIDS and preventive behavior, 1990, recurring rpt, S5765–3

New York State vital statistics, including population, births, deaths by cause, reportable diseases, and marriages and dissolutions, by demographic characteristics and/or location, 1990 and trends, annual rpt, S5765–1

North Carolina deaths and rates, by cause and county, 1991 and trends, annual rpt, S5927–1.2

North Dakota public knowledge and opinions on AIDS and preventive behavior, 1991, annual rpt, S6105–3

Ohio vital statistics, including births, deaths by cause, marriages, divorces, and population, by demographic characteristics and location, 1991 and trends, annual rpt, S6285–1

Oregon vital statistics, including births, deaths by cause, communicable diseases, marriages, and divorces, by age, sex, race-ethnicity, and county, 1991 and trends, annual rpt, S6615–5

Pennsylvania public knowledge and opinions on AIDS and preventive behavior, 1991, annual rpt, S6820–4

Pennsylvania statistical abstract, general data, 1992 recurring rpt, U4130–6.1

Rhode Island vital statistics, including population, births, deaths, marriages, and divorces, by demographic characteristics and locality, 1989 and trends, annual rpt, S6995–1

South Carolina communicable disease cases, by county, 1990, annual rpt, S7175–1

South Carolina deaths, by detailed cause, age, sex, and race, 1990, annual rpt, S7175–2

Acquired immune deficiency syndrome

South Dakota vital statistics, including births, deaths, marriage and divorce, and communicable disease, by demographic characteristics and county, 1991 and trends, annual rpt, S7345–1

Tennessee statistical abstract, general data, 1992/93 annual rpt, U8710–2.17

Tennessee vital statistics, including births, deaths by cause, marriages, divorces, and population, by demographic characteristics and location, 1991 and trends, annual rpt, S7520–2

Texas public knowledge and opinions on AIDS and preventive behavior, 1991, annual rpt, S7685–2

Utah public knowledge and opinions on AIDS and preventive behavior, by respondent characteristics, 1991, annual rpt, S7835–3

Utah vital statistics, including deaths by cause, 1990 and trends, annual rpt, S7835–1.1

Vermont vital statistics, including population, births, deaths by cause, abortions, marriages, and divorces, by location and demographic characteristics, 1991 and trends, annual rpt, S8054–1

Virginia vital statistics, including births, deaths by cause, marriages and divorces, and communicable disease, by demographic characteristics and location, 1991 and trends, annual rpt, S8225–1

Washington State vital statistics, including births, deaths by cause, and population, by demographic characteristics and location, 1991 and trends, annual rpt, S8363–1

West Virginia vital statistics, including births, deaths by cause, marriages, and divorces, by location and demographic characteristics, 1991 and trends, annual rpt, S8560–1

Wisconsin vital statistics, including population, births, deaths by cause, and marriages and dissolutions, by county and demographic characteristics, 1991 and trends, annual rpt, S8715–4

Wyoming vital statistics, including population, births, deaths by cause, marriages, and divorces, by demographic characteristics and county, 1991 and trends, annual rpt, S8920–2

Acquisitions, business

see Business acquisitions and mergers

ACT

see Educational tests

ACTION

see also Peace Corps

Adams, Mary

"Health Insurance Coverage in Connecticut", S1200–3

Adhesives

Financial ratios and performance, for over 350 SIC 4-digit industries, FY88-92, annual rpt, A6400–3

Plastics resin production, sales/captive use, and trade, by resin type and/or use, monthly rpt, A8920–5

Administration

see Administration of justice

see Administrative law and procedure

see Business management

see Executives and managers

see Health facilities administration

see Public administration

see School administration and staff

Administration of justice

Federal employees in law-related occupations, by sex and race-ethnicity, Sept 1991, recurring rpt, A3960–2.1

Public confidence in selected societal instns, 1972-91 surveys, annual rpt, U6395–1

State and local:

Arizona court cases and dispositions, by type of case and court, with judicial personnel and finances, by county and city, FY92, annual rpt, S0525–1

California court activity, including caseloads and dispositions, by case type and court, and location, FY92 and trends, annual rpt, S0905–1

California court cases and dispositions, by type of case and court, and location, FY92 and trends, annual rpt, S0905–2

Connecticut court caseloads and dispositions, by type of court and case, and court location, with judicial dept finances, FY91-92, biennial rpt, S1220–1

DC court cases and dispositions, by type of case, and judicial system finances, 1992 and trends, annual rpt, S1515–1

Georgia court cases and dispositions, by type of court and case, and location, with judicial dept finances and personnel, FY92, annual rpt, S1903–1

Iowa court cases, processing, and dispositions, by type of court and district, with judicial dept appropriations and personnel, 1992 and trends, annual rpt, S2815–1

Maine court cases and dispositions, by type and location, FY92 and trends, annual rpt, S3463–1

New Mexico court cases and dispositions, by type of court and case, and location, with judicial system finances and personnel, FY92, annual rpt, S5623–1

North Carolina court cases and dispositions, by type of court and case, and location, with judicial dept finances and personnel, FY91, annual rpt, S5950–1

Oklahoma court cases and dispositions, by type of court and case, with judicial system finances, by county or jurisdiction, FY92, annual rpt, S6493–1

South Carolina court cases and dispositions, by type of court and location, with judicial dept finances and employees, 1992 and trends, annual rpt, S7197–1

South Dakota court cases and dispositions by type of case, and judicial system finances and personnel, by jurisdiction, FY92 and trends, annual rpt, S7395–1

Virginia court caseloads, processing, and dispositions, by type of court and case, with judicial dept personnel and finances, by location, 1992 and trends, annual rpt, S8300–1

see also Administrative law and procedure

see also Arrest

see also Civil procedure

see also Correctional institutions

see also Courts

see also Crime and criminals

see also Crime victim compensation

see also Criminal procedure

see also Due process of law

see also Fines and settlements

see also Fugitives from justice

Index by Subjects and Names

see also Judges

see also Juries

see also Law enforcement

see also Lawyers and legal services

see also Legal aid

see also Legal arbitration and mediation

see also Pardons

see also Parole and probation

see also Pretrial detention and release

see also Sentences, criminal procedure

see also Trials

Administrative law and procedure

Chemical industry-related regulations, with associated mortality risks and costs per death averted, 1993 annual rpt, A3850–1

Federal regulatory agency costs and staff, for approx 50 agencies, FY70s-94, annual rpt, U9640–1

Transportation regulatory agency policies and practices for motor carriers and railroads, by agency, 1991/92 annual rpt, A7015–4

Utility and transportation regulatory agency activities, scope of jurisdiction, finances, and employees, by agency, 1991/92 annual rpt, A7015–2

Utility regulatory agency policies and practices, and industry financial and operating data, by utility type and agency, 1991/92 annual rpt, A7015–3

Workers compensation law coverage, benefits, and other info, by State, outlying area, and Canadian Province, 1993 annual rpt, A3840–2

State and local:

Alaska court cases and dispositions, by type of court and case, and location, with judicial dept finances and personnel, FY92 and trends, annual rpt, S0290–1

Alaska public utilities commission regulatory activities, with data by company, FY92 and trends, annual rpt, S0280–4.1

Arkansas regulatory orders issued by Public Service Commission, 1992, annual rpt, S0757–1

California public utility and transportation regulatory data, including revenue requests and rates of return by company, FY92 annual rpt, S0930–1

Colorado district court administrative review/local govt cases, by district and county, FY92, annual rpt, S1035–1.2

Colorado liquor license hearings and outcomes, FY90-92, annual rpt, S1075–1.2

Florida public utility regulatory and operating data, by company and utility type, 1992 and trends, annual rpt, S1790–1

Idaho public utility regulatory data, and commission finances, FY92, annual rpt, S2290–1

Iowa court cases, processing, and dispositions, by type of court and district, with judicial dept appropriations and personnel, 1992 and trends, annual rpt, S2815–1

Maine administrative court cases and disposition, by agency, 1983-FY92, annual rpt, S3463–1

Maryland judicial appeals from district courts and administrative agencies, by county, FY92 and trends, annual rpt, S3600–1

Index by Subjects and Names

Missouri employment security, workers compensation, and prevailing wage cases, by type and disposition, 1991-92, annual rpt, S4530–2.1

Missouri family services div case appeals and dispositions, FY92, annual rpt, S4575–2

Nebraska welfare appeals case processing, by program, FY92, annual rpt, S4957–1.2

New Mexico public assistance hearings and dispositions, monthly rpt quarterly table, S5620–2

Ohio court caseload and case disposition, by type of court and case, and location, 1992, annual rpt, S6385–1

Oklahoma welfare case appeals and disposition, by program, FY92, annual rpt, S6455–1.2

Tennessee court cases and dispositions, by type of court and case, and county, FY92, annual rpt, S7585–1

Tennessee public utility and transportation commission regulatory activities, with industry financial and operating data, 1991-92 biennial rpt, S7565–1

Texas licensing and regulation of child care facilities, administrators, and social workers, including complaint investigations, Sept 1991 and Aug 1992, annual rpt, S7695–1

Vermont public utility service dept public advocacy div caseload, June 1992, biennial rpt, S8100–1

Washington State court cases and dispositions, by type of court and case, and jurisdiction, with judicial finances and personnel, 1992 and trends, annual rpt, S8339–1

West Virginia court caseloads and dispositions, by type of court and case, and judicial circuit, 1992 and trends, annual rpt, S8537–1

West Virginia welfare program hearings, dispositions, and processing times, and child support enforcement program collections, monthly rpt, S8560–2

see also Civil procedure

see also Financial institutions regulation

see also Fines and settlements

see also Licenses and permits

see also Price regulation

see also Public administration

see also Tax laws and courts

see also Tax protests and appeals

Administrators

see Executives and managers

see School administration and staff

Adolescents

see Youth

Adoption

Catholic charity social service agency activities, clients, finances, and personnel, 1991 and trends, annual rpt, A3810–1

Statistical profiles of 50 States and DC, general data, 1993 annual almanac, C4712–1

State and local:

Alaska court cases and dispositions, by type of court and case, and location, with judicial dept finances and personnel, FY92 and trends, annual rpt, S0290–1

Alaska vital statistics, including births, deaths by cause, marriages, divorces, adoptions, and population, by demographic characteristics and location, 1990, annual rpt, S0315–1

Arizona court cases and dispositions, by type of case and court, with judicial personnel and finances, by county and city, FY92, annual rpt, S0525–1

Arkansas court caseloads and dispositions, by type of court and case, and location, FY92 and trends, annual rpt, S0647–1

Arkansas human services dept finances and operations, by program, FY91 and trends, annual rpt, S0700–2.2

Colorado court cases and dispositions, by type of court and detailed case type, FY92 and trends, annual rpt, S1035–1.2

Colorado welfare and social services expenditures and caseloads, by county and/or program, FY91, annual rpt, S1085–1

DC court cases and dispositions, by type of case, and judicial system finances, 1992 and trends, annual rpt, S1515–1

Delaware court caseloads and dispositions, by type of court and case, and by county, with judicial dept finances, FY92, annual rpt, S1360–1

Hawaii court cases and dispositions, by type of court and case, and judicial circuit, FY92 and trends, annual rpt, S2115–1.2

Hawaii data book, general data, 1992 annual rpt, S2090–1.11

Indiana court cases and dispositions by type of court and case, and location, with judicial system finances and personnel, 1992, annual rpt, S2703–1

Indiana public assistance program participation, expenditures, and services, by county, FY92 and trends, annual rpt, S2623–1

Iowa ADC and SSI program recipients, and expenditures, by county, monthly rpt, S2802–1

Kansas court caseloads and disposition, by type of court and case, and location, FY92, annual rpt, S3035–1

Massachusetts court cases and dispositions, by type of court and case, and location, FY92 and trends, annual rpt, S3807–1

Michigan court caseloads and dispositions, by type of court and case, and court location, 1992 and trends, annual rpt, S3962–1

Missouri public welfare and medical assistance recipients, expenditures, and case processing, by program and county, FY92 and trends, annual rpt, S4575–2

Nebraska court cases and dispositions, by type of court and case, and location, 1992 and trends, annual rpt, S4965–2

New Mexico court cases and dispositions, by type of court and case, and location, with judicial system finances and personnel, FY92, annual rpt, S5623–1

New York State adoptions, by sex, age, and race-ethnicity, 1991 and trends, annual rpt, S5800–2.3

North Carolina public welfare programs, cases, recipients, staff, and finances, by county, 1st half FY93, semiannual rpt, S5940–2

Ohio court caseload and case disposition, by type of court and case, and location, 1992, annual rpt, S6385–1

Oklahoma adoption and foster home care activities, FY92, annual rpt, S6455–1.2

Oklahoma court cases and dispositions, by type of court and case, with judicial system finances, by county or jurisdiction, FY92, annual rpt, S6493–1

Adult day care

Oregon public welfare caseloads, recipients, and expenditures, by program, city, county, and State region, monthly rpt, S6615–8

Pennsylvania court caseloads and dispositions, by type of court and case, and county, 1991, annual rpt, S6900–1.2

South Carolina public welfare recipients, payments, and case processing, by county and program, monthly rpt, S7252–1

South Dakota court cases and dispositions by type of case, and judicial system finances and personnel, by jurisdiction, FY92 and trends, annual rpt, S7395–1

South Dakota welfare and social services recipients and payments, by program, MSA, and county, FY92, annual rpt, S7385–1

Tennessee court cases and dispositions, by type of court and case, and county, FY92, annual rpt, S7585–1

Vermont court cases and dispositions, by type of court and case, and location, FY92 annual rpt, S8120–1

Washington State court cases and dispositions, by type of court and case, and jurisdiction, with judicial finances and personnel, 1992 and trends, annual rpt, S8339–1

Washington State public assistance clients and service costs, by client characteristics, program, and county, FY90, annual rpt, S8420–2

West Virginia court caseloads and dispositions, by type of court and case, and judicial circuit, 1992 and trends, annual rpt, S8537–1

West Virginia welfare and social service program caseloads and expenditures, by county, monthly rpt, S8560–2

Adult day care

Corporate personnel mgmt devs, including work force diversity, health care and family-related benefits, counseling services, and competitiveness, 1993 survey, B6850–6

Employer policies and views on family-related issues, including involvement in disabled and elderly care services, Mar 1992 survey, A8907–1

Food service industry sales and establishments, by market segment including adult care, 1993 annual feature, C1850–3.503

State and local:

Alabama public welfare and social service cases, recipients, and payments, by program and county, monthly rpt, S0150–1

Florida health care atlas, including manpower by occupation and health care facilities by type, by district and county, 1992 annual rpt, S1746–1.2

Kentucky Medicaid recipients and payments, by program, county, and type of medical service, monthly rpt, S3140–5

New York State expenditures for adult care services, and day care facility capacity and occupancy, by State area, 1991, annual rpt, S5800–2.3

North Carolina public welfare programs, cases, recipients, staff, and finances, by county, 1st half FY93, semiannual rpt, S5940–2

Adult day care

South Dakota social services for elderly, with recipients by race-ethnicity, FY92, annual rpt, S7385–1.1

West Virginia welfare and social service program caseloads and expenditures, by county, monthly rpt, S8560–2

Adult education

Federal budget trends, including spending by program, State, and region, FY81-94, annual rpt, R8490–11

Higher education programs for adult students availability and characteristics, 1993 annual survey, A1410–1.38

Library/info science school continuing education programs and attendance, 1991/92 and trends, annual rpt, A3235–1.5

Urban public schools adult education programs, for 47 systems, 1990/91, A4425–4

State and local:

- Alabama public school revenues by source and expenditures by object, by district, 1991/92, annual rpt, S0124–1.2
- Alaska corrections dept education program participants, FY91, annual rpt, S0287–1
- California public school adult education attendance, FY68-94, annual rpt, S0827–3
- DC enrollment in adult education programs, 1987/88-1991/92, annual rpt, S1605–2
- Delaware adult education funding, enrollment, and staff, 1991/92, annual rpt, S1430–1
- Georgia prison inmate participation in educational programs, by type, June 1992, annual rpt, S1872–1
- Illinois corrections dept admin, including inmates and characteristics, finances, and staff, FY91-93 and trends, annual rpt, S2425–1
- Kansas school district revenues by source and expenditures by object, 1990/91, annual rpt, S2945–1
- Louisiana elementary/secondary school operations, including enrollment, staff, finances, and detail by school district, 1991/92 and trends, annual rpt, S3280–1
- Maryland elementary and secondary education data, by county, 1991/92, annual rpt, S3610–2.7, S3610–2.9
- Maryland elementary and secondary education statistical summary, with data by county, 1991/92-1992/93 and trends, annual rpt, S3610–1
- Massachusetts public elementary/secondary education summary data, 1989/90-1991/92 and trends, annual rpt, S3810–3
- Michigan correctional instns educational and rehabilitation activities, by program and instn, 1991, annual rpt, S3960–1
- Mississippi vocational education enrollment and courses offered, by program, 1991/92, annual rpt, S4340–1.2
- Missouri public school finances, staff, students, and programs, detailed data, 1991/92, annual rpt, S4505–1.1
- Nevada adult diplomas and General Educational Dev (GED) certificates awarded, by school district, 1990/91, annual rpt, S5035–2
- Ohio public school enrollment, finances, special programs, and staff, 1991/92 and trends, annual rpt, S6265–2

Oklahoma school revenues and expenditures, by program, county, and district, FY92, annual rpt, S6423–1.1

Oregon public school revenues by source and fund, and expenditures by fund, function, and object, 1991/92, annual rpt, S6590–1.16

Oregon public school revenues by source and fund, and expenditures by fund, function, and object, 1992/93, annual rpt, S6590–1.17

Rhode Island education expenditures by function and source of funds, by school district, 1991/92, annual rpt, S6970–1.2

South Carolina educational enrollment, by school type or level, program, race, and location, 1991/92, annual rpt, S7145–1.3

South Carolina public and private schools, enrollment, and grads, by county, 1990/91 and trends, annual planning rpt, S7155–3.3

Tennessee public school enrollment, staff, finances, and operations, by county, city, and school district, 1991/92, annual rpt, S7490–2

Utah public schools, enrollment, attendance, personnel, and finances, by school district, 1991/92, annual rpt, S7815–1

Virginia public school enrollment, grads, finances, and staff, by county and municipality, 1991/92, annual rpt, S8190–3

West Virginia public school finances, enrollment, staff, and programs, by county, 1992/93 and trends, annual rpt, S8540–4

Wisconsin Blue Book, general data, 1993-94 biennial rpt, S8780–1.2

Wyoming penitentiary educational programs and participation, FY85-92, annual rpt, S8883–1

Wyoming public schools adult education program expenditures, by district, 1991/92, annual rpt, S8890–1.3

see also High school equivalency tests

see also Vocational education and training

Advertising

Advertising and marketing industry devs articles and special features, including data on sales, revenues, research, consumer recall, personnel, and media shares, weekly rpt, C2710–1

Agencies with multinatl clients, including countries in which they advertise, 1993 annual article, C2710–1.545

Agency income, billings by medium, employees, and offices, for leading US and/or foreign agencies, 1992 and trends, annual rpt, C2710–1.522

Auto advertising expenditures, by medium, 1990-92, annual article, C2710–3.552

Auto aftermarket natl brands and chains by advertising expenditure level, 1991, article, C2150–10.502

Auto dealer and natl campaign advertising expenditure distribution by medium, 1991, article, A8605–1.505

Auto dealer views on dealer assn and manufacturer advertising programs, including natl campaign spending levels by medium, with data by vehicle make, 1993 survey article, C2710–1.518, C2710–3.521

Auto dealership advertising expenditures by medium, by dealer sales volume, 1992, annual rpt, A7330–1

Index by Subjects and Names

Auto manufacturer advertising expenditures, by company, 1993 directory, C2710–3.552

Beverage advertising expenditures for top 10 brands, by beverage type, 1991-92, annual rpt, C4775–1.4

Broadcasting advertising industry assn chief executive salaries, for 4 assns, 1993 features, C1850–14.511

Cable TV advertising budget shares targeted to insurance industry, and types of insurance advertised, May 1993 survey, article, C1858–1.503

Cable TV advertising expenditures, for top 10 advertisers, 1st qtr 1993, article, C1850–14.523

Cable TV advertising expenditures, for top 20 industry categories, 1992, article, C1850–14.515

Cable TV advertising expenditures for top 5 advertisers in 7 product categories, biweekly rpt quarterly feature, C1858–1.502, C1858–1.508, C2965–1.505, C2965–1.511

Cable TV advertising expenditures, for top 5 advertisers, 1992, C1850–14.513

Cable TV advertising interconnect subscribers, for top 50 interconnects, June 1993, recurring feature, C1858–1.505

Cable TV advertising interconnect subscribers, for top 50 interconnects, Sept 1993, recurring feature, C1858–1.508

Cable TV advertising revenue shares from auto dealers, and use of value-added promotions, 1993 survey article, C2965–1.511

Cable TV advertising revenue shares from computer retailers, and use of value-added promotions, July 1993 survey, article, C1858–1.507

Cable TV advertising revenues, for 6 major networks, quarterly 1992, article, C1850–14.511

Cable TV advertising revenues of 17 basic cable networks and 3 representative organizations, and expenditures of top 10 advertisers, 1993 features, C1858–1.501

Cable TV network and local advertising revenues, 1992-93, C2965–1.503

Cable TV system local advertising insertion activity, views of mgmt personnel, Jan 1993 survey, C2965–1.511

Canada photographic/video products/services consumer advertising exposure and reaction, by medium and selected characteristics, 1992 survey, recurring rpt, A8695–4

Compensation data for advertising agency personnel, and employment trends, 1992 annual feature, C2710–1.505

Computer software with sales/marketing applications, advertising media used by vendors, 1990-91, annual survey article, C1200–1.502

Congressional campaign fund finances, with expenditures by item and contributions by donor type, by candidate, district, and State, 1990 elections, C2500–6

Consumer views on offensiveness of selected aspects of advertising, by sex, 1993 survey article, C1200–4.507

Convenience store industry financial and operating data, by size category, 1992 and trends, annual survey rpt, A6735–2

Index by Subjects and Names

Advertising

Corporate public image advertising practices, expenditures, and media use, 1987-92, triennial survey rpt, A3357–1

Costs for advertising in selected media, with detail by audience sex, 1993 article, A8605–1.505

Direct marketing industry devs, including advertising patterns, finances, target market characteristics, and consumer attitudes, 1992/93 annual rpt, A4620–1

Drugstore advertising shares for top 10 stationery/home office product types and brands, Aug 1992, article, C5150–2.501

Europe public opinion on political, economic, and social issues, for 9 countries and 3 Soviet Union Republics, 1991 survey, C8915–8.1

Europe public opinion on political, economic, and social issues of interest to foreign investors, for 9 countries and 3 Soviet Union Republics, 1991 survey, C8915–9

Expenditure summary for print and other media, and newsprint production and inventory, monthly rpt, A1630–4

Expenditures as percent of sales, by industry, 1992, annual survey, C1200–1.508

Expenditures for advertising as percents of sales and profits, by SIC 4-digit industry, 1993, annual article, C2710–1.537

Expenditures for advertising by medium, 1991-92, annual feature, C2710–1.525

Expenditures for advertising by top 10 advertisers, 1st qtr 1992-93, article, C2710–3.544

Expenditures for advertising of top 200 brands, by selected medium, weekly rpt quarterly feature, C2710–1.502, C2710–1.512, C2710–1.525, C2710–1.540

Expenditures for advertising of 100 leading natl advertisers, compared to earnings and sales, errata, C2710–1.502

Expenditures for advertising of 100 leading natl advertisers, compared to earnings and sales, 1991-92, annual rpt, C2710–1.547

Expenditures in newspapers and other media, and newspaper market data, 1992 annual rpt, A8610–1

Expenditures of corporations and assns, by medium, 1988-92, and top 10 advertisers for 1992, annual article, A8770–1.504

Financial performance and growth rankings for approx 1,000 top corporations, with comparisons by industry group, 1993 annual rpt, C3950–1.505

Financial ratios and performance, for over 350 SIC 4-digit industries, FY88-92, annual rpt, A6400–3

Food marketers financial and operating data, by company size and region, 1991-92, annual rpts, A4950–5

Hispanic American marketing devs, including leading advertisers and media, and market characteristics, 1992 annual features, C4575–1.502

Home furnishings retailer advertising expenditure levels, with cooperative allowances and data by medium, 1992, annual rpt, A7975–1

Home improvement industry wholesaler marketing organization advertising expenditures, for top 7 firms, 1991-92, annual feature, C5150–6.502

Home improvement store customer services offered and advertised, 1993 survey, article, C5150–6.507

Incentive programs for consumers, with advertising methods used, 1993 annual survey article, C1200–4.506

Latin America statistical abstract, general data by country, 1992 annual rpt, U6250–1.4

Liquor industry advertising expenditures, by medium, company, and brand, 1992 and trends, annual rpt, C4775–1

Magazine ad headline length, position, and background, impact on readership, 1993 article, C8950–2.501

Magazine ad size impact on readership, 1993 article, C8950–2.503

Magazine advertising page and revenue trends, by selected subject category, semimonthly rpt, C2575–1

Magazine advertising page volume, monthly rpt, A1630–5

Magazine advertising pages and revenues, by publication, weekly rpt monthly tables, C2710–1

Magazine advertising revenues and pages, for top 50 publications, 1991-92, annual feature, C2575–1.518

Magazine circulation and advertising rates, for US and Canadian publications, 1988-92, annual rpt, A3385–1

Magazine revenues, advertising pages, and circulation, for top 300 publications, 1992, annual article, C2710–1.531

Magazine revenues, circulation, advertising, and rates, for top 500 consumer and business publications, 1992, annual article, C2575–1.515

Mass media advertising expenditures by medium, 1960s-91, annual rpt, C3975–5.3

Mass media advertising revenues, by medium, 1990-92, article, C1200–1.513

Newspaper (daily) advertising revenues, by country, 1988 and 1991-92, article, A8605–1.508

Newspaper advertising expenditures compared to retail sales and consumer confidence, 1987-1st half 1992, article, A8605–1.502

Newspaper advertising expenditures, 1st qtr 1989-93, article, A8605–1.508

Newspaper advertising linage and revenues, with detail for leading publishers, 1970s-92, annual rpt, A1630–8

Newspaper advertising revenue trends by type of ad, 1986-93, A8605–1.503

Newspaper circulation, operations, and finances, US and Canada, 1940s-93, annual rpt, A8605–4

Newspaper classified, natl, and retail advertising expenditures, 1st-3rd qtrs 1992, article, A8605–1.504

Office building detailed income and expense data, and energy use, US and Canada, by building characteristics, metro area, and US region, 1991 and trends, annual rpt, A5600–2

Oil industry advertising expenditures for network and spot TV, including cable networks and syndicated programs, by company, 1991-92, annual fact book, C4680–1.507

Operating and financial composite ratios for corporations, with establishments and receipts, for approx 200 industries, by asset size, FY90, annual rpt, C7800–1

Outdoor advertising expenditures by top 100 natl advertisers, 1991-92, annual rpt, C2710–1.547

Parrots and other psittacines captive breeding info, including breeder advertising practices, 1989, annual survey rpt, R9200–14

Photographic products/services advertising, consumer awareness and reaction by media, 1993 survey, recurring rpt, A8695–2

Political advertising expenditures on local and network TV, biennially 1980-92, article, C1850–14.502

Public opinion on condom advertising for AIDS prevention, 1987 surveys, A0610–1.502

Public opinion on honesty/ethical standards of advertising practitioners, 1992 Gallup Polls and trends, C4040–1.501

Radio advertising revenue trends, Jan-Sept 1992, article, C1850–14.501

Radio audience size, leading stations and formats, and advertising rates and revenues, by market area, recurring rpt, C3165–1

Radio ownership, audience characteristics, and advertising revenues and effectiveness, with selected comparisons to other media, 1993 annual rpt, A8789–1

Restaurant industry financial and operating data, by establishment characteristics and location, 1992, annual rpt, A8200–3

Retailer Christmas season advertising budget plans, by medium, 1991-92, survey article, C1850–14.504

Supermarket bakery and deli shopper characteristics, including use of newspaper ads and circulars, 1993 annual survey article, C5225–1.508

Supermarket seafood dept sales and performance indicators, 1992 annual survey feature, C4825–3.501

Telephone Yellow Pages directory use among consumers, with detail by respondent characteristics, 1992 survey, annual rpt, A9500–2

Tobacco advertising expenditures in magazines, with detail for top 4 publications, 1981 and 1991, article, C2575–1.503

Tourism dev offices of State govts, activities, personnel, and budgets, by State, 1992 survey, annual rpt, R9375–2

Travel and tourism rankings for selected indicators, including data for top 20 States, cities, countries, businesses, and other measures, 1992 recurring rpt, R9375–6

Travel-related advertising expenditures, by travel category, and for top 24 foreign country advertisers, 1990 and trends, annual rpt, C2140–1.2

TV advertising airtime and costs for 6 Super Bowl advertisers, Jan 1993, article, C5800–7.512

TV advertising expenditures for local and spot ads, for top 5 product categories, 1991-93, article, C1850–14.526

TV advertising expenditures for top 10 broadcast TV network advertisers, 1st qtr 1992-93, C1850–14.527

TV advertising exposure value for top 19 sports event telecasts (primarily auto races), 1992, article, C2710–3.529

Advertising

TV advertising rates for a 30-second spot during 4 late-night talk shows, 1993 article, C1850–14.535

TV advertising revenues generated by 6 prime-time news magazine programs, 1992 article, C1850–14.503

TV "infomercial" program and sales trends, and rankings of top 5 programs and production companies, 1993 article, C1850–14.543

TV network advertising revenues, by daypart and program type, weekly rpt quarterly feature, C1850–14.503, C1850–14.513, C1850–14.522, C1850–14.535

TV station advertising revenue trends for total, local, and natl spot ads, weekly rpt recurring article, C1850–14.509, C1850–14.514, C1850–14.536

Wine advertising expenditures, by medium, brand, and company, 1991-92, annual rpt, C4775–2

World advertising media and marketing devs, with data for worldwide periodicals, and expenditures by top advertiser and country, 1992 annual feature, C2710–1.506

State and local:

Georgia, Atlanta area help-wanted advertising index, bimonthly rpt, U6730–2

Tennessee, Memphis area help-wanted advertising index, quarterly journal, U8710–1

Virginia newspaper advertising lineage, monthly rpt, U1120–1

Wisconsin, Milwaukee help-wanted index, monthly rpt, S8750–1

see also Labeling

see also Sales promotion

Aeronautical navigation

FAA air route facilities and services, pilot instrument ratings, and navigator certificates held, 1993 annual rpt, A5120–2

Shipment value, employment, and foreign trade, for electronics industry, by sector and product type, 1980s-92, annual rpt, A4725–1.2

see also Radar

Aeronautics

see Aviation sciences

see Space sciences

Aerospace industry

China aviation-related foreign trade value for US exports, 1989-92, article, A9315–1.504

Corporate performance ratings by executives for leading companies in 32 industries, 1993 annual survey feature, C8900–1.508

Devs and outlook for aerospace industry, with data on world airline traffic and satellite launches, 1993 annual compilation, C5800–4.513

Engineers salaries by industry group, census div, selected metro area, and years since college degree, 1993, annual survey rpt, A0685–5

Engineers salaries by industry group, census div, selected metro area, degree level, and years since college degree, 1993, annual survey rpt, A0685–3

Executive compensation and components, by industry div and major manufacturing group, 1991, annual rpt, R4105–19

Index by Subjects and Names

Financial performance and growth rankings for approx 1,000 top corporations, with comparisons by industry group, 1993 annual rpt, C3950–1.505

Financial performance of aerospace and defense industries, with data for approx 200 major US and foreign companies, FY92 and trends, annual feature, C5800–4.519

France aerospace industry export orders distribution by product type, 1991, article, C5800–4.509

Industry devs in air transport, space technology, engineering, business flying, avionics, and military aviation, weekly rpt, C5800–4

Jet aircraft worldwide inventory, orders, and deliveries, by type of aircraft, region, and individual owner/operator, 1992 and trends, annual rpt, B1582–1

Operating and financial composite ratios for corporations, with establishments and receipts, for approx 200 industries, by asset size, FY90, annual rpt, C7800–1

Plastics (thermoplastics) consumption and demand outlook, with detail by consuming sector, 1980s-2000, article, A1250–1.538

Production of civil and military aerospace products, R&D, trade, employment, and finances, with Federal funding data, 1991 and trends, annual rpt, A0250–2

Shipments of business/personal aircraft, by model, for approx 20 manufacturers, weekly rpt quarterly table, C5800–30.503, C5800–30.505, C5800–30.509

State and local:

California aerospace manufacturing employment trends, 1989-93, article, S0840–1.505

California economic condition, including population, employment and earnings, income, business activity, and taxation, 1960s-92, annual rpt, S0840–3.2

California statistical abstract, general data, 1992 annual rpt, S0840–2.8

see also Aircraft

see also Business aircraft and flying

see also Missiles and rockets

see also Satellites

see also Space programs

see also under By Industry in the "Index by Categories"

AFDC

see Aid to Families with Dependent Children

Affirmative action

see Racial discrimination

see Discrimination in employment

see Sex discrimination

AFL-CIO

Congressional voting support for 4 special interest groups, by Member and State, 1991, annual rpt, C2500–2

State and local:

Hawaii data book, general data, 1992 annual rpt, S2090–1.12

Africa

Economic condition in selected oil-rich vs oil-poor countries in Middle East and North Africa, 1991 rpt, R4105–82.1

Energy exploration, rotary drilling rigs in operation, by world area and country, monthly rpt, B4675–1

Higher education public instns, with enrollment and expenditures per student, for 12-34 countries, 1993 article, C2175–1.524

Income per capita, by country, 1987, annual rpt, C2140–1.3

Jewish population by world area, country, and US census div, State, and city, 1990-92, annual compilation, A2050–1

Military personnel hospital admissions and deaths due to selected diseases, for African troops serving in UK army, 1819-36, article, A2623–1.502

Motor vehicle world production, sales, trade, and registrations, by country, world area, manufacturer, and make, 1991 and trends, annual rpt, A0865–2.1

Natural gas reserves of 7 West African countries, 1993 article, C6985–2.504

Oil/gas deep well drilling, success ratios, and costs, by world area, 1990-92, annual article, C4420–1.503

Oil/gas seismic exploration land crews and vessels, by world area or country, quarterly press release, A8912–2

Population size and characteristics, GNP, and land area, by world region and/or country, 1993 annual data sheet, R8750–5

Refugees, resettlement, and intl aid devs, by country, 1992, annual rpt, R9372–1

Women's premarital sexual experience and childbearing, for 7 Sub-Saharan countries, 1986-89, article, A5160–6.503

see also Algeria

see also Angola

see also Benin

see also Botswana

see also Cameroon

see also Congo

see also Egypt

see also Ethiopia

see also Gabon

see also Gambia

see also Ghana

see also Ivory Coast

see also Kenya

see also Libya

see also Mauritius

see also Morocco

see also Namibia

see also Niger

see also Nigeria

see also Somalia

see also South Africa

see also Sudan

see also Tunisia

see also Zaire

see also Zambia

see also under By Foreign Country or World Area in the "Index by Categories"

African Americans

see Black Americans

Age

see Age discrimination

see Aged and aging

see Children

see Population characteristics

see Youth

see under By Age in the "Index by Categories"

Age discrimination

Index by Subjects and Names

Aged and aging

State and local:
Missouri Human Rights Commission discrimination cases and dispositions, by case type, FY92 and trends, annual rpt, S4530–2.2

Aged and aging

- Accidental deaths of persons age 55/over, by age group and accident type, 1989, annual rpt, A8375–2.1
- Advertising portrayal of older population, public opinion by age group, Aug 1992 survey, articles, C2710–1.503
- Consumers age 50/over views on 6 types of sales promotions, 1993 article, C1200–4.505
- Direct marketing industry devs, with consumer and business market characteristics, and media use patterns, 1992/93 annual rpt, A4620–1.4
- Disabled persons use of home care services, with costs, payment sources, and types of care, by selected characteristics, 1992, R4865–15
- Drug prescription and over-the-counter product use among population age 50/over, 1993 survey article, C5150–2.521
- Drugs (prescription) problems identified by pharmacists for elderly patients, and actions taken, Florida study, 1993 article, C5150–2.521
- Drugs (prescription) use, expenditures, prices, and profit trends, with data by patient characteristics and for top 20 brands, 1992 rpt, R4865–8
- Educational attainment of population age 65/over, by race-ethnicity, 1970, 1980, and 1990, B6045–1.504
- Health care expenditures of families, including insurance premiums by source of coverage, and taxes by type, by income group, 1987, R4700–20
- Health condition indicators and insurance coverage among elderly by urban-rural status and living arrangement, 1993 article, A1865–1.522
- Hospital psychiatric patient discharges and length of stay, by diagnosis, age, sex, and region, 1991, annual rpt series, B4455–2
- Japan population age 65/over as percent of population age 15-64, with comparisons to 6 other countries, 1985, 1995, and 2005, article, R5650–2.546
- Library expenditures for services for the elderly, by fund source and State, FY90-91, annual compilation, C1650–3.2
- Malnutrition risk among the elderly, New England study of residents over age 70, 1993 survey article, A2623–1.509, C2150–6.508
- Medicaid recipients age 65/over, and benefits paid, FY72-91, annual rpt, A5173–2.2
- Medical procedures and diagnostic test prevalence among elderly by race and urban-rural residence, 1986, article, A2623–1.509
- Men age 69-84 quality of life indicators, including health, finances, family, and employment, by race, 1990 survey, U3780–9
- New England elderly population smoking status correlated with dental problems, by sex, 1993 article, A2623–1.511

Physical activity levels and impact on health outcome among population age 65/over in 2 local areas and 1 State, 1982 study, article, A2623–1.512

- Population age 65/over, for 10 counties with largest increase, 1990, C4300–1.508
- Population characteristics for persons age 65/over and 85/over, by census div and State, 1990 and trends, article, B6045–1.502
- Population growth rates for persons age 65/over and 64/under, by region and metro status, decennially 1960-90, article, R8750–1.506
- Population size and selected characteristics, by region, census div, and State, 1991 and trends, annual data sheet, R8750–9
- Poverty rates for persons age 65/over, by age, sex, and race-ethnicity, 1990, article, A8510–1.1
- Prison inmates age 50/over, by State and for Federal system, Jan 1992, annual rpt, R4300–1.1
- Prison inmates age 55/over, by sex and State, June 1988-92, annual rpt, A1305–3
- Public opinion on presidential campaign candidates and issues, among voters age 65/older, Aug 1992 Gallup rpt, C4040–1.503
- Public opinion on religion importance and resources for suicide prevention, among persons age 60/over, 1993 survey feature, R8780–1.504
- Restaurant patron menu item preferences, overall and for persons age 55-64, 1991, article, A8200–1.506
- Restaurant patronage patterns and menu item preferences, for all consumers and persons age 65/over, 1992, article, A8200–1.510
- Smoking cessation success and relapse rates among population age 65/older, errata, A2623–1.501
- State social, economic, and govtl indicators, with rankings, 1993 semiannual rpt, B8500–1.1
- Women's housing issues, with data on household composition, tenure, and characteristics, 1992, A8657–5
- World population size and characteristics, GNP, and land area, by region and/or country, 1993 annual data sheet, R8750–5

State and local:

- Alabama municipal data book, general data, 1992 recurring rpt, S0121–5
- Alaska tax exemption provisions for senior citizens and disabled veterans, and State reimbursements to local areas, FY92 and trends, annual rpt, S0285–1
- Arkansas Census of Population and Housing detailed findings, 1990, U5935–7
- Arkansas senior citizens service summary, FY91, annual rpt, S0700–2.1
- California Census of Population and Housing detailed findings, 1990, S0840–9
- California individual and corporate income tax returns and property tax assistance, by income class and county, 1990 and trends, annual rpt, S0855–1
- DC statistical profile, general data, 1992 annual rpt, S1535–3.5
- Florida county data book, 1992/93 annual rpt, C6360–1

Florida population in poverty, with detail for persons age 65/over, by county, 1992, annual rpt, S1746–1.1

- Florida statistical abstract, general data, 1992 annual rpt, U6660–1.1
- Illinois traffic accidents, fatalities, and injuries, involvement of elderly drivers, 1991 and trends, annual rpt, S2540–1
- Indiana property value and tax levies, collections, credits, and deductions, by county and type, 1991, annual rpt, S2570–1.1
- Kansas statistical abstract, general data, 1991/92 annual rpt, U7095–2.2, U7095–2.6
- Louisiana job service openings and applicants, and characteristics of Job Training Partnership Act target population and insured unemployed, 1993 annual planning rpt, S3320–1.2
- Maine Census of Population and Housing summary findings, by local area, 1990, S3465–7, S3465–9
- Massachusetts probate and family court cases and dispositions, including elder abuse protection, FY92 and trends, annual rpt, S3807–1
- Missouri senior citizens tax credit claims and refunds, FY88-92, annual rpt, S4570–1.1
- Montana elderly homeowner/renter income tax credits, 1986-90, biennial rpt, S4750–1.1
- New Jersey Census of Population and Housing detailed findings, by county, 1990, S5425–19
- New Jersey domestic violence offenses involving victims over age 60, by type of offense and victim sex, 1992, annual rpt, S5430–1.4
- New York State statistical yearbook, general data, 1992 annual rpt, U5100 1.1
- Pennsylvania Census of Population and Housing detailed findings, with selected data by county and municipality, 1990, U4130–13
- Pennsylvania statistical abstract, general data, 1992 recurring rpt, U4130–6.9
- Rhode Island Census of Population and Housing detailed findings, by county and municipality, 1990, S6930–9
- South Carolina statistical abstract, general data, 1993 annual rpt, S7125–1.11
- South Dakota sales/property tax refunds for elderly and disabled, with detail by county, FY92 and trends, annual rpt, S7380–1.1
- Vermont individual income tax returns and credits, with detail for older population by county, 1991, annual rpt, S8125–1
- Washington State older drivers traffic accident involvement, 1992 and trends, annual rpt, S8428–1
- Washington State population and demographic characteristics, and housing units, by county and/or city, 1992 and trends, annual rpt, S8345–4
- Washington State senior citizen property tax exemption, applicants and amounts, by county, 1992, annual rpt, S8415–1.3

see also Adult day care

see also Age discrimination

see also Alzheimer's disease

see also Civil service pensions

Aged and aging

see also Geriatrics
see also Individual retirement arrangements
see also Medicare
see also Military benefits and pensions
see also Nursing homes
see also Old age assistance
see also Old-Age, Survivors, Disability, and Health Insurance
see also Pensions and pension funds
see also Respite care
see also Retirement
see also Retirement communities
see also Social security
see also State retirement systems
see also Supplemental Security Income
see also Veterans benefits and pensions
see also under By Age in the "Index by Categories"

Agency for International Development
Latin America statistical abstract, general data by country, 1992 annual rpt, U6250–1.28

Agribusiness
see Agriculture

Agricultural accidents and safety
Accidental deaths and disabling injuries, by detailed type, victim characteristics, circumstances, and location, 1992 and trends, annual rpt, A8375–2

State and local:
Alabama vital statistics, including population, births, deaths by cause, marriages, and divorces, by location and demographic characteristics, 1992 and trends, annual rpt, S0175–2
Idaho vital statistics, including births, deaths by cause, abortions, marriages, and divorces, by demographic characteristics and county, 1991 and trends, annual rpt, S2250–2
Iowa agriculture accidental deaths, and injuries by type, 1990-91, annual rpt, S2795–1
Missouri vital statistics, including population, births, deaths by cause, and marriages and divorces, by location and demographic characteristics, 1992 and trends, annual rpt, S4518–1
Nebraska vital statistics, including births, deaths, marriages, divorces, and population, by demographic characteristics and location, 1991 and trends, annual rpt, S4885–1
Oregon vital statistics, including births, deaths by cause, communicable diseases, marriages, and divorces, by age, sex, race-ethnicity, and county, 1991 and trends, annual rpt, S6615–5
South Carolina deaths, by detailed cause, age, sex, and race, 1990, annual rpt, S7175–2
Vermont vital statistics, including population, births, deaths by cause, abortions, marriages, and divorces, by location and demographic characteristics, 1991 and trends, annual rpt, S8054–1

Agricultural chemicals
see Fertilizers
see Pesticides

Agricultural commodities
Exports of farm products, by detailed commodity and country of destination, US and California, 1991, annual rpt, B9520–1

Futures and options contract open interest (outstanding commitments), on foreign exchanges, by commodity and exchange, monthly rpt, A5040–6
Futures and options trading volume by commodity and exchange, 1988-92, annual rpt, A5040–1
Futures and options trading volume on foreign exchanges, by commodity and exchange, monthly rpt, A5040–5
Futures contract open interest (outstanding commitments), by commodity and exchange, monthly rpt, A5040–4
Futures trading volume by commodity and exchange, monthly rpt, A5040–2
Latin America statistical abstract, general data by country, 1992 annual rpt, U6250–1.24, U6250–1.25
Options trading volume by commodity, securities index, and exchange, monthly rpt, A5040–3
Production, consumption, stocks, trade, and prices for approx 100 basic commodities, including by country and producing State, commodity yearbook for 1993, C2400–1, C2400–2

State and local:
Alabama agricultural production, marketing, and income, by county and/or commodity, and farms and acreage, 1992 and trends, annual rpt, S0090–1
Alabama county data book, general data, 1992 annual rpt, S0121–2
Alabama statistical abstract, general data, 1992 recurring rpt, U5680–2.1
Alaska agricultural production and marketing, by district and commodity, 1960s-92, annual rpt, U5750–1
Arizona agricultural production, marketing, and finances, by commodity and county, 1988-92, annual rpt, U5830–1
Arizona statistical abstract, general data, 1993 recurring rpt, U5850–2.13
Arkansas agricultural production, marketing, and finances, by commodity and county, with farms and acreage, 1992 and trends, annual rpt, U5920–1
California agricultural statistics, including production, acreage, finances, and marketing, by commodity, annual rpt series, S0850–1
California statistical abstract, general data, 1992 annual rpt, S0840–2.7
Colorado agricultural production, marketing, and finances, by commodity and/or county, with farms and acreage, 1992 and trends, annual rpt, S0985–1
Florida agricultural statistics, including production, finances, and shipment data for citrus, dairy, and other sectors, by commodity and/or county, 1993 annual rpt series, S1685–1
Georgia agricultural production, marketing, and finances, by commodity and/or county, and farms and acreage, 1991 and trends, annual rpt, S1855–1
Hawaii agricultural production and marketing, by commodity and island, 1987-91, annual rpt, S2030–1
Hawaii data book, general data, 1992 annual rpt, S2090–1.19
Illinois agricultural production, marketing, and finances, by county or commodity, and farms and farmland, 1991 and trends, annual rpt, S2390–1

Kansas agricultural production, marketing, and finances, by county and/or commodity, and farm acreage and value, 1992 and trends, annual rpt, S2915–1
Kansas statistical abstract, general data, 1991/92 annual rpt, U7095–2.15
Kentucky agricultural production, marketing, and finances, by commodity and county; and farms, acreage, and value; 1992 and trends, annual rpt, S3085–1
Louisiana agricultural production, marketing, and finances, by commodity or parish, 1985-91, annual rpt, U2740–1
Maryland statistical abstract, general data, 1993-94 biennial rpt, S3605–1.11
Michigan agricultural production, marketing, and finances, by commodity or county, 1987-91, annual rpt, S3950–1
Minnesota agricultural production, marketing, and finances, by county or commodity, and farms and acreage, 1992 and trends, annual rpt, S4130–1
Mississippi statistical abstract, general data, 1992 annual rpt, U3255–4.15
Missouri agricultural production, marketing, and finances, by commodity and/or county, and farms and acreage, 1988-92, annual rpt, S4480–1
Montana agricultural production, marketing, and finances, by commodity and county, 1991 and trends, annual rpt, S4655–1
Nebraska agricultural production, marketing, and finances, by commodity and/or county, and farms and acreage, 1991 and trends, annual rpt, S4835–1
Nevada agricultural production, marketing, and finances, by county and commodity, and farms and acreage, 1992 and trends, annual rpt, S5010–1
New Jersey agricultural production, marketing, and finances, by commodity and/or county, and farms and acreage, 1986-91, annual rpt, S5350–1
New Mexico agricultural production, marketing, and finances, by commodity and county, with farms and acreage, 1991 and trends, annual rpt, S5530–1
New York State agricultural production, marketing, and finances, by commodity and/or county, and farms and acreage, 1992 and trends, annual rpt, S5700–1
New York State statistical yearbook, general data, 1992 annual rpt, U5100–1.14
North Carolina agricultural production, marketing, and finances, by commodity and county, 1991 and trends, annual rpt, S5885–1
North Dakota agricultural production and marketing, by commodity and county, and farm finances, 1992 and trends, annual rpt, U3600–1
Ohio agricultural production, marketing, and finances, by commodity and county, with farms and acreage, 1990-91 and trends, annual rpt, S6240–1
Oklahoma agricultural production, marketing, and finances, by commodity and county, 1992 and trends, annual rpt, S6405–1
Oregon agricultural production, marketing, and finances, by commodity and/or county, with farms and acreage, 1991 and trends, annual rpt, S6575–1
Pennsylvania agricultural production, marketing, and finances, by county and commodity, and farms and acreage, 1992 and trends, annual rpt, S6760–1

Index by Subjects and Names

South Carolina statistical abstract, general data, 1993 annual rpt, S7125–1.1

South Dakota agricultural production, marketing, and finances, by commodity and county, and farms and acreage, 1992 and trends, annual rpt, S7280–1

Tennessee agricultural production and marketing, by commodity and county, with farms, acreage, and farm value, 1992 and trends, annual rpt, S7460–1

Tennessee statistical abstract, general data, 1992/93 annual rpt, U8710–2.11

Texas agricultural production, marketing, and finances, by commodity and county, and farms and farmland, 1991 and trends, annual rpt series, S7630–1

Utah agricultural production, marketing, and finances, by commodity and county, with farms and acreage, 1992 and trends, annual rpt, S7800–1

Utah statistical abstract, general data, 1993 triennial rpt, U8960–1.9

Vermont agricultural production, marketing, and finances, by commodity, with data on govt inspections and funding, 1989-90 biennial rpt, S7978–1

Washington State agricultural production, marketing, and finances, by commodity and/or county, 1992 and trends, annual rpt, S8328–1

West Virginia agricultural production, marketing, and finances, by commodity or county, 1991 and trends, annual rpt, S8510–1

Wisconsin agricultural production, marketing, and finances, by commodity and county, and farms, acreage, and sales, 1992 and trends, annual rpt, S8680–1

Wyoming agricultural production, marketing, and finances, by county and/or commodity, and farms, acreage, and value, 1992 and trends, annual rpt, S8860–1

see also Animal feed

see also Animals

see also Citrus fruits

see also Cocoa and chocolate

see also Coffee

see also Corn

see also Cotton

see also Dairy industry and products

see also Flowers and nursery products

see also Food and food industry

see also Fruit and fruit products

see also Grains and grain products

see also Gum and wood chemicals

see also Hides and skins

see also Honey and beekeeping

see also Hops

see also Livestock and livestock industry

see also Lumber industry and products

see also Meat and meat products

see also Natural fibers

see also Nuts

see also Oils, oilseeds, and fats

see also Peanuts

see also Potatoes

see also Poultry industry and products

see also Rice

see also Seeds

see also Soybeans

see also Spices and herbs

see also Sugar industry and products

see also Tea

see also Tobacco industry and products

see also Vegetables and vegetable products

see also Wheat

see also Wool and wool trade

see also under By Commodity in the "Index by Categories"

Agricultural credit

Research articles on agricultural finance, credit, investment, and related topics, 1993 annual compilation, U1380–4

Southeastern States farm real estate and non-real estate debt outstanding, 12 States, 1992/93 annual rpt, U8710–2.11

State and local:

Arizona farm real estate and other debt, by type of lender, Dec 1987-91, annual rpt, U5830–1

Arizona statistical abstract, general data, 1993 recurring rpt, U5850–2.13, U5850–2.23

Florida statistical abstract, general data, 1992 annual rpt, U6660–1.9

Missouri farm real estate debt, by type of lender, 1987-91, annual rpt, S4480–1

Montana farm/ranch property value and debt, 1990, annual rpt, S4655–1

Nebraska farm real estate debt outstanding by type of lender, 1981-90, annual rpt, S4835–1

Ohio farm debt outstanding, by type of lender, 1986-90, annual rpt, S6240–1

Oklahoma farm real estate and other debt by type of lender, 1987-91, annual rpt, S6405–1

Tennessee farm debt outstanding, by type of lender, 1987-91, annual rpt, S7460–1

Texas farm real estate debt, by type of lender, 1986-90, annual rpt, S7630–1.3

see also Agricultural production quotas and price supports

Agricultural education

Foreign students enrolled in US higher education instns, by instn, State, country of origin, and demographic characteristics, 1991/92 and trends, annual rpt, R5580–1

Salary and job offers for college grads, by field of study, type of employer, and degree level, by region, interim rpt series, A3940–1

Salary and job offers for college grads, by field of study, type of employer, and degree level, series, A3940–2

Women and minorities in professional fields, detailed education and labor force data, 1991 and trends, recurring rpt, A3960–2.3

State and local:

Maryland elementary and secondary education statistical summary, with data by county, 1991/92-1992/93 and trends, annual rpt, S3610–1

Massachusetts public elementary/secondary school enrollment by grade, by district, Oct 1992, annual rpt, S3810–4

Massachusetts public elementary/secondary school expenditures per pupil by program, by district, 1991/92, annual rpt, S3810–5

Montana income tax checkoffs, by purpose, 1987-91, biennial rpt, S4750–1.1

Pennsylvania vocational education enrollment, student characteristics, and faculty, by program and/or school, 1991/92 and trends, annual rpt, S6790–5.7

Pennsylvania vocational education 1989/90 grad employment status, by program, 1991 survey, annual rpt, S6790–5.6

Agricultural exports and imports

Agricultural energy use

Oil supply-demand, marketing, prices, finances, and employment, detailed data for US and Canada, by product, company, and location, 1993 annual fact book, C4680–1.507

Tractor performance test results, by manufacturer and model, 1983-92, annual rpt, C3450–1.502

World energy supply-demand, by fuel source and sector, by region and country, 1992/93 biennial rpt, R9455–1.7

State and local:

Arkansas public utility financial, operating, and regulatory data, by utility type and company, 1992 annual rpt, S0757–1

Wisconsin Blue Book, general data, 1993-94 biennial rpt, S8780–1.2

Wisconsin oil use, by consuming sector, 1981-90, annual rpt, S8675–3

Agricultural exports and imports

Commodity yearbook for 1993: agricultural production, acreage, stocks, marketing, and operating data, including by country and producing State, C2400–1

Commodity yearbook update: agricultural production, acreage, stocks, marketing, and operating data, including by country and producing State, Jan-Sept 1993 rpts, C2400–2

Corn and refined products supply and demand trends, US and by foreign country, 1993 annual rpt, A4200–1

Corn trade worldwide, with detail for US and selected other countries or areas, 1985/86-1992/93, annual rpt, S8680–1

Cotton and wool production by world region and country, and consumption and trade, 1950s-92, annual article, C3460–1.502

Exports of farm products, by detailed commodity and country of destination, US and California, 1991, annual rpt, B9520–1

Fig industry production, acreage, and prices in California, with US consumption and imports by country, 1950s-92, annual rpt, A3750–1

Futures trading activity on Chicago Board of Trade, with info on grain export inspections, 1992, annual rpt, B2120–1

Japan beef domestic production and imports, 1988-92, article, R5650–2.548

Japan imports of alfalfa and hay from US and other countries, 1989-91, annual rpt, S8328–1

Latin America statistical abstract, general data by country, 1992 annual rpt, U6250–1.25, U6250–1.26

Macadamia nut and ginger root imports, with nut detail by country of origin, 1991 and trends, annual rpt, S2030–1

Malt beverage and ingredients trade, by world area or country, 1970s-91, annual rpt, A3455–1.5

Meat and related products and poultry trade, production, and consumption, by country, 1990 and trends, annual rpt, A2100–1.2

Mexico citrus fruit exports to US, by fruit type, monthly 1987/88-1991/92, annual rpt, S1685–1.1

Soybean production and marketing data, including utilization, prices, and trade, with comparison to other oilseeds, 1920s-93, annual rpt, B8480–1

Agricultural exports and imports

Tobacco leaf and product exports by customs district, 1991, annual rpt, A9075–1

Wheat production, consumption, price, and trade trends, 1992 annual rpt, A7310–1

World food and agricultural policies and issues, with focus on developing countries, series, R5620–1

World trade in cereals, oils, and pulses, by country, 1977-89, biennial rpt, R9455–1.6

State and local:

Arizona agricultural exports, by commodity, FY88-92, annual rpt, U5830–1

California agricultural exports distribution by destination country or world area, 1991, annual rpt, S0840–3.1

Colorado livestock inshipments from selected States, Canada, and Mexico, 1985-92, annual rpt, S0985–1

Florida citrus fruit production, acreage, yield, and shipments, by fruit type, 1991/92 and trends, annual rpt, S1685–1.1

Florida vegetable, melon, and strawberry production, acreage, yield, shipments, and exports, 1991/92 and trends, annual rpt, S1685–1.2

Georgia agricultural export value, by commodity, 1984-91, annual rpt, S1855–1

Hawaii anthurium foreign shipments, and meat imports, 1991 and trends, annual rpt, S2030–1

Idaho economic profile, general data, 1992 recurring rpt, S2218–2.9

Illinois agricultural exports, by commodity, FY87-91, annual rpt, S2390–1

Kansas agricultural exports, by commodity, 1988-92, annual rpt, S2915–1

Kentucky and US agricultural exports, by commodity, FY91-92, annual rpt, S3085–1

Minnesota agricultural exports, by commodity, 1992, annual rpt, S4130–1

Missouri agricultural exports, by commodity, 1988-92, annual rpt, S4480–1

Montana and US agricultural exports, by commodity, 1989-91, annual rpt, S4655–1

Nebraska agricultural export value, by commodity, with comparison to 6 other States, 1988-91, annual rpt, S4835–1

New Jersey and US agricultural exports, by commodity, 1987-91, annual rpt, S5350–1

New Mexico cattle trade with Mexico and Canada, 1991, annual rpt, S5530–1

North Carolina agricultural exports, by commodity, FY88-91, annual rpt, S5885–1

North Dakota agricultural exports value, by commodity, 1989-91, annual rpt, U3600–1

Ohio and US agricultural exports, by commodity, FY88-91, annual rpt, S6240–1

Oklahoma and US agricultural exports, by commodity, 1990-92, annual rpt, S6405–1

Oregon agricultural exports, by commodity, FY89-91, annual rpt, S6575–1

Pennsylvania agricultural exports, by commodity, 1988-92, annual rpt, S6760–1

Tennessee agricultural exports, by commodity, 1989-91, annual rpt, S7460–1

Texas agricultural exports for selected leading commodities, with comparisons to other States, 1991 annual rpt, S7630–1

Vermont cattle imports from Canada and other States, and exports, 1988/89-1989/90, biennial rpt, S7978–1

Wisconsin livestock outshipments, including dairy cattle exports by country of destination, 1992 and trends, annual rpt, S8680–1

see also Public Law 480

Agricultural finance

Assets, debt, and equity of farms, by State, 1991, biennial rpt, S8780–1.2

Indonesia agricultural production trends and impacts of govt policies, for 5 major food crops, 1970s-80s, R5620–1.37

Research articles on agricultural finance, credit, investment, and related topics, 1993 annual compilation, U1380–4

State social, economic, and govtl indicators, with rankings, 1993 semiannual rpt, B8500–1.2

State and local:

Alaska farm sector balance sheet, 1986-91, annual rpt, U5750–1

Alaska property tax deferment program for farmland, acreage affected and deferred tax, by municipality, 1992 and trends, annual rpt, S0285–1

Arizona farm sector balance sheet, 1987-91, annual rpt, U5830–1

Colorado farm sector balance sheet, 1987-91, annual rpt, S0985–1

Georgia farm sector balance sheet, 1985-91, annual rpt, S1855–1

Illinois farm sector balance sheet, 1991 and trends, annual rpt, S2390–1

Kansas farm sector balance sheet, 1987-91, annual rpt, S2915–1

Kansas statistical abstract, general data, 1991/92 annual rpt, U7095–2.15

Michigan farm sector balance sheet, 1986-90, annual rpt, S3950–1

Minnesota farm sector balance sheet, 1988-92, annual rpt, S4130–1

Missouri farm sector balance sheet, 1987-91, annual rpt, S4480–1

Nebraska farm sector balance sheet, 1982-91, annual rpt, S4835–1

New Mexico farm sector balance sheet, Dec 1988-90, annual rpt, S5530–1

New York State farm sector balance sheet, 1982-91, annual rpt, S5700–1

North Dakota farm sector balance sheet, including and excluding farm households, Dec 1987-91, annual rpt, U3600–1

Ohio farm sector balance sheet compared to US, 1987-90, annual rpt, S6240–1

Oklahoma statistical abstract, general data, 1992 annual rpt, U8130–2.11

Oregon farm sector balance sheet, Dec 1986-90, annual rpt, S6575–1

Pennsylvania farm sector balance sheet, 1987-91, annual rpt, S6760–1

South Dakota farm sector balance sheet, 1989-92, annual rpt, S7280–1

Tennessee farm sector balance sheet, 1987-91, annual rpt, S7460–1

Texas farm sector balance sheet, 1986-90, annual rpt, S7630–1.3

Index by Subjects and Names

Utah farm sector balance sheet, Dec 1987-91, annual rpt, S7800–1

Vermont farm sector balance sheet, 1984-88, biennial rpt, S7978–1

Washington State farm sector balance sheet, 1987-91, annual rpt, S8328–1

Wisconsin farm sector balance sheet, 1987-91, annual rpt, S8680–1

see also Agricultural credit

see also Agricultural insurance

see also Agricultural production costs

see also Agricultural production quotas and price supports

see also Agricultural subsidies

see also Farm income

see also Property value

see also Rural cooperatives

Agricultural income

see Agricultural wages

see Farm income

Agricultural industries

see Agricultural labor

see Agricultural marketing

see Agricultural production

see Agricultural services

see Dairy industry and products

see Flowers and nursery products

see Food and food industry

see Fruit and fruit products

see Grains and grain products

see Honey and beekeeping

see Horticulture

see Livestock and livestock industry

see Meat and meat products

see Poultry industry and products

see Rural cooperatives

see Sugar industry and products

see Tobacco industry and products

see Vegetables and vegetable products

see Veterinary medicine

Agricultural insurance

Premiums written, by type of insurance or line, 1991 and trends, annual rpt, A5650–1.2

Premiums written, loss ratios, and market shares for property and casualty insurance, by line, leading company, and State, 1992 and trends, annual article, C1050–1.509

State and local:

Alabama insurance industry financial and underwriting data, by company and line of coverage, 1991, annual rpt, S0160–1

Alaska insurance industry underwriting and investment data, by company and type of insurance, with regulatory info, 1991 and trends, annual rpt, S0280–3

Arkansas farmer use of price hedging techniques, including govt programs, forward and futures contracts, and crop insurance, for 3 crops, July 1992 survey, article, U5930–1.504

Connecticut insurance industry financial and underwriting data, by company and type of insurance, 1991, annual rpt, S1222–1

Florida insurance industry financial and underwriting data, by company and line of coverage, 1991, annual rpt, S1760–1

Idaho insurance industry financial and underwriting data, by company and type of insurance, with regulatory data, 1991, annual rpt, S2260–1

Iowa insurance industry financial and underwriting data, by company and type of insurance, 1992, annual rpt, S2760–1

Index by Subjects and Names

Kansas insurance industry financial and underwriting data, by company and type of insurance, with regulatory info, 1992, annual rpt, S2990–1

Missouri insurance industry financial and underwriting data, by company and type of insurance, with regulatory info, 1992, annual rpt, S4527–1

Nebraska insurance premiums and losses by detailed line of coverage, by company, 1992, annual rpt, S4890–1

Oklahoma insurance industry financial and underwriting data, by company and type of insurance, with regulatory info, 1992, annual rpt, S6462–1

Pennsylvania insurance industry financial and underwriting data, by company and line of coverage, 1991, with FY92 regulatory info, annual rpt, S6835–1

Rhode Island insurance industry financial and underwriting data, by company and line of coverage, 1990, with FY91 regulatory info, annual rpt, S6945–2

South Dakota insurance industry financial and underwriting data, by company and type of insurance, with regulatory info, 1991-92, annual rpt, S7300–2

Utah insurance industry financial and underwriting data, by company and line of coverage, with regulatory info, 1991, annual rpt, S7845–1

West Virginia insurance industry financial and underwriting data, by company and line of coverage, with regulatory info, 1991, annual rpt, S8575–1

Wisconsin insurance industry financial and underwriting data, by company and line of coverage, with regulatory info, 1992, annual rpt, S8755–1

Agricultural labor

Appalachia agricultural workers, hours, and wage rates, 1990-91, annual rpt, S8510–1

Forecasts of natl income and product account components, employment, and financial sector activity, monthly rpt, B4950–1

North Central States farm labor force, and wage rates, 1992 and trends, annual rpt, S2390–1

Northeast region farm workers, hours, and wages, 1985-93, annual rpt, S5700–1

Northern Plains region agricultural workers, hours, and wages, 1st qtr 1989-1st qtr 1993, annual rpt, S7280–1

Southeast US farm workers, hours, and wage rates, 3 regions, 1991-92, annual rpt, S5885–1

Southeast US farm workers, hours, wages, and pay methods, 1989-92, annual rpt, S1855–1

Southern Plains region farm workers and wages, quarterly 1986-92, annual rpt, S7630–1.3

Southern Plains region farm workers and wages, quarterly 1988-92, annual rpt, S6405–1

State social, economic, and govtl indicators, with rankings, 1993 semiannual rpt, B8500–1.2

Western States farm workers, hours, and wages, 1992-93, annual rpt, S5010–1

State and local:

Alaska farm workers and wage rates, 1960s-92, annual rpt, U5750–1

Arizona economic condition, including population, employment and earnings, and business activity, by industry and locality, 1985-93, semiannual rpt, U5850–1.1

Arizona farm workers, wage rates, and hours of labor, 1988-93, annual rpt, U5830–1

Arkansas business and economic activity indicators, quarterly rpt, U5930–1

Arkansas labor force, employment, and unemployment, by MSA, county, and labor area, 1980-92, annual rpt, S0662–2

California economic condition, including population, employment and earnings, income, business activity, and taxation, 1960s-92, annual rpt, S0840–3.2

California statistical abstract, general data, 1992 annual rpt, S0840–2.3

Delaware employment projections, by county, 1990-2020, recurring rpt, S1375–3

Florida statistical abstract, general data, 1992 annual rpt, U6660–1.9

Hawaii agricultural employment, by type of work and farm, and by island, 1991 and trends, annual rpt, S2030–1

Hawaii data book, general data, 1992 annual rpt, S2090–1.19

Hawaii economic conditions, including employment, population, tourism, and construction, quarterly rpt, S2090–2

Idaho economic profile, general data, 1992 recurring rpt, S2218–2.1

Illinois statistical abstract, general data, 1992 annual rpt, U6910–2

Kansas business activity indicators, quarterly rpt, U7095–1

Kentucky economic statistics, general data, 1993 annual rpt, S3104–1

Michigan agricultural labor and wages, with comparisons to Lake States region, 1992 annual rpt, S3950–1

Minnesota farm workers, wages, and hours, Apr 1991-Apr 1993, annual rpt, S4130–1

Missouri/Iowa farm workers, hours, and wages, 1988-92, annual rpt, S4480–1

Montana employment and unemployment, earnings, and hours, by location and/or industry, quarterly rpt, S4710–1

Montana labor force planning rpt, including population, income, and employment and job openings by industry and occupation, with selected data by county, 1993-94 annual rpt, S4710–3

New Mexico agricultural employment, by county, 1980 and 1990, annual planning rpt, S5624–1

North Carolina labor force and employment by industry, by county, MSA, labor area, and planning region, 1991 and trends, annual rpt, S5917–4

Pennsylvania farm workers, wage rates, and hours of labor, 1990-92, annual rpt, S6760–1

Utah farm workers, hours, and wages, by type of worker, 1992-93, annual rpt, S7800–1

Vermont labor force by employment status, and job service openings and applicant characteristics, 1993 annual planning rpt, S8025–2.2

Washington State farm workers, hours, and wage rates, 1992-93, annual rpt, S8328–1

see also Agricultural productivity

see also Agricultural wages

Agricultural machinery and equipment

see also Farm income

see also Farm operators

see also Migrant workers

see also under By Industry in the "Index by Categories"

Agricultural land

see Farms and farmland

Agricultural machinery and equipment

Canada farm equipment retail sales volume, by equipment type, periodic rpt, C0495–1, C3450–1

Cotton and other fiber consumption in textile production of tobacco plant bed covers, 1990-92, annual rpt, A7485–1

Equipment industry operations and devs, including farm equipment retail sales, periodic rpt, C0495–1, C3450–1

Equipment on-farm inventory, sales, and foreign trade, with data by equipment type, 1993 annual feature, C3450–1.501

Financial ratios and performance, for over 350 SIC 4-digit industries, FY88-92, annual rpt, A6400–3

Injuries involving tractors and farm machinery, 1993 annual rpt, A8375–2.4

Latin America tractors in use in 20 countries compared to US, 1960s-87, annual rpt, U6250–1.2

Operating and financial composite ratios for corporations, with establishments and receipts, for approx 200 industries, by asset size, FY90, annual rpt, C7800–1

Prices paid by farmers for selected production commodities, 1982 and 1991-92, annual rpt, S3085–1

Prices paid by farmers for selected production commodities, 1986-91, annual rpt, S5350–1

Prices paid by farmers for selected production commodities, 1989-92, annual rpt, S8680–1

Tractor performance test results, by manufacturer and model, 1983-92, annual rpt, C3450–1.502

World tractor and harvester inventory, by country, 1977-89, biennial rpt, R9455–1.6

State and local:

Alabama traffic accidents, fatalities, and injuries, by circumstances, vehicle type, and driver and victim characteristics, 1992, annual rpt, S0185–1

Arizona cotton gins active, with production and charges, 1987/88-1991/92, annual rpt, U5830–1

Arizona traffic accidents, fatalities, and injuries, by vehicle type, circumstances, location, and driver and victim characteristics, 1991 and trends, annual rpt, S0530–1

Colorado property assessed valuation by detailed property type, and tax levy and revenue by local district, by county, 1991-92, annual rpt, S1055–3

Delaware traffic accidents, fatalities, and injuries, by circumstances, location, and vehicle type, and driver and victim characteristics, 1992 and trends, annual rpt, S1435–1

Florida traffic accidents, fatalities, and injuries, by vehicle type, circumstance, location, and driver and victim characteristics, 1992 and trends, annual rpt, S1750–2

Agricultural machinery and equipment

Idaho traffic accidents, fatalities, and injuries, by circumstances, location, vehicle type, and driver and victim characteristics, 1992, annual rpt, S2315–1

Illinois traffic accidents, fatalities, and injuries, by circumstances, location, and driver and victim characteristics, 1991 and trends, annual rpt, S2540–1

Indiana traffic accidents, fatalities, and injuries, by circumstances, location, and vehicle type, and driver and victim characteristics, 1992, annual rpt, S2675–1

Kansas traffic accidents, fatalities, and injuries, by vehicle type, location, circumstances, and driver and victim characteristics, 1992, annual rpt, S3040–1

Kentucky commercial and farm truck registrations, by county, 1991, annual rpt, S3104–1.3

Kentucky traffic accidents, fatalities, and injuries, by circumstances, location, vehicle type, and driver characteristics, 1992 and trends, annual rpt, S3150–2

Louisiana traffic accidents, fatalities, and injuries, by circumstances, location, and driver characteristics, 1991 and trends, annual rpt, S3345–2

Maryland traffic accidents, fatalities, and injuries, by circumstances, location, vehicle type, and driver and victim characteristics, 1992, annual rpt, S3665–4

Michigan traffic accidents, fatalities, and injuries, by vehicle type, circumstance, location, and driver and victim characteristics, 1991 and trends, annual rpt, S3997–2

Minnesota traffic accidents, fatalities, and injuries, by type of vehicle and circumstances, and driver and victim characteristics, 1992 and trends, annual rpt, S4230–2

Missouri traffic accidents, fatalities, and injuries, by circumstances, location, and driver and victim characteristics, 1992 and trends, annual rpt, S4560–1

Montana property values, by detailed property class and type, with land acreage by use, by county, 1991-92 and trends, biennial rpt, S4750–1.2

Montana traffic accidents, fatalities, and injuries, by circumstances, location, and driver and victim characteristics, 1992 and trends, annual rpt, S4705–2

Nebraska traffic accidents, fatalities, and injuries, by circumstances, location, vehicle type, and driver and victim characteristics, 1992, annual rpt, S4953–1

Nevada traffic accidents, fatalities, and injuries, by circumstances, location, and vehicle type, 1992 and trends, annual rpt, S5140–1

New Jersey fatal traffic accidents and fatalities, by vehicle type, location, and circumstances, and driver and victim characteristics, 1992 and trends, annual rpt, S5430–2

North Carolina traffic accidents, fatalities, and injuries, by circumstances, location, vehicle type, and driver and victim characteristics, 1992 and trends, annual rpt, S5990–1

North Dakota traffic accidents, fatalities, and injuries, by circumstances, location, vehicle type, and driver and victim characteristics, 1992 and trends, annual rpt, S6217–1

Ohio traffic accidents, fatalities, and injuries, by circumstances, location, driver and victim characteristics, and vehicle type, 1991 and trends, annual rpt, S6290–1

Pennsylvania traffic accidents, fatalities, and injuries, by circumstances, location, driver characteristics, and vehicle type, 1991, annual rpt, S6905–3

South Dakota traffic accidents, fatalities, and injuries, by circumstances, location, vehicle type, and driver and victim characteristics, 1992 and trends, annual rpt, S7300–3

Utah traffic accidents and fatalities by circumstances, location, driver and victim characteristics, and vehicle type, 1992 and trends, annual rpt, S7890–2

Washington State property values, by type of property and county, 1992, annual rpt, S8415–1.3

Wisconsin traffic accidents, fatalities, and injuries, by circumstances, location, vehicle type, and driver and victim characteristics, 1992 and trends, annual rpt, S8815–1

Wyoming property assessed valuations and tax levies, by property type, tax purpose, and location, 1992 and trends, annual rpt, S8990–1.2

Wyoming traffic accidents, fatalities, and injuries, by circumstances, location, vehicle type, and driver and victim characteristics, 1992 and trends, annual rpt, S9007–1

see also Lawn and garden equipment

Agricultural marketing

Commodity yearbook for 1993: agricultural production, acreage, stocks, marketing, and operating data, including by country and producing State, C2400–1

Commodity yearbook update: agricultural production, acreage, stocks, marketing, and operating data, including by country and producing State, Jan-Sept 1993 rpts, C2400–2

Corn and refined products supply and demand trends, US and by foreign country, 1993 annual rpt, A4200–1

Equipment on-farm inventory, sales, and foreign trade, with data by equipment type, 1993 annual feature, C3450–1.501

Futures trading activity on Chicago Board of Trade, with info on cash prices, supply, and disposition, by commodity, 1992 and trends, annual rpt, B2120–1

Grain futures and options trading activity on Minneapolis exchange, with production, price, and disposition data for area served, 1992 and trends, annual rpt, B6110–1

Magazine (farm) circulation, by US and Canadian publication, 6-month periods ended Dec 1992 and June 1993, semiannual rpt, A3385–3.4

Meat and poultry demand, prices, and processor operations and finances, with data on meat production, 1991 and trends, annual rpt, A2100–1.1

Soybean supply and disposition data, including farm marketings by month, 1950s-92, annual rpt, B8480–1

Index by Subjects and Names

Statistical profiles of 50 States and DC, general data, 1993 annual almanac, C4712–1

State and local:

Alabama agricultural production, marketing, and income, by county and/or commodity, and farms and acreage, 1992 and trends, annual rpt, S0090–1

Arizona agricultural production, marketing, and finances, by commodity and county, 1988-92, annual rpt, U5830–1

Arkansas agricultural production, marketing, and finances, by commodity and county, with farms and acreage, 1992 and trends, annual rpt, U5920–1

Arkansas socioeconomic trends, by MSA and/or county, 1993 annual rpt, U5935–1

California agricultural statistics, including production, acreage, finances, and marketing, by commodity, annual rpt series, S0850–1

Colorado agricultural production, marketing, and finances, by commodity and/or county, with farms and acreage, 1992 and trends, annual rpt, S0985–1

Florida agricultural statistics, including production, finances, and shipment data for citrus, dairy, and other sectors, by commodity and/or county, 1993 annual rpt series, S1685–1

Florida statistical abstract, general data, 1992 annual rpt, U6660–1.9

Georgia agricultural production, marketing, and finances, by commodity and/or county, and farms and acreage, 1991 and trends, annual rpt, S1855–1

Hawaii agricultural production and marketing, by commodity and island, 1987-91, annual rpt, S2030–1

Illinois agricultural production, marketing, and finances, by county or commodity, and farms and farmland, 1991 and trends, annual rpt, S2390–1

Kansas agricultural production, marketing, and finances, by county and/or commodity, and farm acreage and value, 1992 and trends, annual rpt, S2915–1

Kentucky agricultural production, marketing, and finances, by commodity and county; and farms, acreage, and value; 1992 and trends, annual rpt, S3085–1

Louisiana agricultural production, marketing, and finances, by commodity or parish, 1985-91, annual rpt, U2740–1

Michigan agricultural production, marketing, and finances, by commodity or county, 1987-91, annual rpt, S3950–1

Minnesota agricultural production, marketing, and finances, by county or commodity, and farms and acreage, 1992 and trends, annual rpt, S4130–1

Missouri agricultural production, marketing, and finances, by commodity and/or county, and farms and acreage, 1988-92, annual rpt, S4480–1

Montana agricultural production, marketing, and finances, by commodity and county, 1991 and trends, annual rpt, S4655–1

Nebraska agricultural production, marketing, and finances, by commodity and/or county, and farms and acreage, 1991 and trends, annual rpt, S4835–1

Nevada agricultural production, marketing, and finances, by county and commodity, and farms and acreage, 1992 and trends, annual rpt, S5010–1

Index by Subjects and Names

Agricultural prices

New Jersey agricultural production, marketing, and finances, by commodity and/or county, and farms and acreage, 1986-91, annual rpt, S5350–1

New Mexico agricultural production, marketing, and finances, by commodity and county, with farms and acreage, 1991 and trends, annual rpt, S5530–1

New York State agricultural production, marketing, and finances, by commodity and/or county, and farms and acreage, 1992 and trends, annual rpt, S5700–1

North Carolina agricultural production, marketing, and finances, by commodity and county, 1991 and trends, annual rpt, S5885–1

North Dakota agricultural production and marketing, by commodity and county, and farm finances, 1992 and trends, annual rpt, U3600–1

Ohio agricultural production, marketing, and finances, by commodity and county, with farms and acreage, 1990-91 and trends, annual rpt, S6240–1

Oklahoma agricultural production, marketing, and finances, by commodity and county, 1992 and trends, annual rpt, S6405–1

Oregon agricultural production, marketing, and finances, by commodity and/or county, with farms and acreage, 1991 and trends, annual rpt, S6575–1

Oregon economic conditions, including population, construction, income, employment, industry, and foreign trade data, 1991, annual rpt, S6585–3

Pennsylvania agricultural production, marketing, and finances, by county and commodity, and farms and acreage, 1992 and trends, annual rpt, S6760–1

South Dakota agricultural production, marketing, and finances, by commodity and county, and farms and acreage, 1992 and trends, annual rpt, S7280–1

Tennessee agricultural production and marketing, by commodity and county, with farms, acreage, and farm value, 1992 and trends, annual rpt, S7460–1

Tennessee statistical abstract, general data, 1992/93 annual rpt, U8710–2.11

Texas agricultural production, marketing, and finances, by commodity and county, and farms and farmland, 1991 and trends, annual rpt series, S7630–1

Utah agricultural production, marketing, and finances, by commodity and county, with farms and acreage, 1992 and trends, annual rpt, S7800–1

Vermont agricultural production, marketing, and finances, by commodity, with data on govt inspections and funding, 1989-90 biennial rpt, S7978–1

Washington State agricultural production, marketing, and finances, by commodity and/or county, 1992 and trends, annual rpt, S8328–1

West Virginia agricultural production, marketing, and finances, by commodity or county, 1991 and trends, annual rpt, S8510–1

Wisconsin agricultural production, marketing, and finances, by commodity and county, and farms, acreage, and sales, 1992 and trends, annual rpt, S8680–1

Wyoming agricultural production, marketing, and finances, by county and/or commodity, and farms, acreage, and value, 1992 and trends, annual rpt, S8860–1

see also Agricultural exports and imports

see also Agricultural prices

see also Agricultural production quotas and price supports

see also Agricultural stocks

see also Farm income

see also Food inspection

see also Food prices

see also Food stores

see also Futures trading

see also Market research

see also Rural cooperatives

Agricultural pests

see Pests and pest control

Agricultural prices

Commodity yearbook for 1993: agricultural production, acreage, stocks, marketing, and operating data, including by country and producing State, C2400–1

Commodity yearbook update: agricultural production, acreage, stocks, marketing, and operating data, including by country and producing State, Jan-Sept 1993 rpts, C2400–2

Economic indicator historical trends, 1900s-92, annual rpt, R9050–1.2

Fig industry production, acreage, and prices in California, with US consumption and imports by country, 1950s-92, annual rpt, A3750–1

Futures trading activity on Chicago Board of Trade, with info on cash prices, supply, and disposition, by commodity, 1992 and trends, annual rpt, B2120–1

Grain futures and options trading activity on Minneapolis exchange, with production, price, and disposition data for area served, 1992 and trends, annual rpt, B6110–1

Grain market activity on Kansas City Board of Trade, including futures volume and prices, 1992, annual rpt, B1530–1

Meat and poultry demand, prices, and processor operations and finances, with data on meat production, 1991 and trends, annual rpt, A2100–1.1

Soybean production and marketing data, including utilization, prices, and trade, with comparison to other oilseeds, 1920s-93, annual rpt, B8480–1

Wheat production, consumption, price, and trade trends, 1992 annual rpt, A7310–1

State and local:

Alabama agricultural production, marketing, and income, by county and/or commodity, and farms and acreage, 1992 and trends, annual rpt, S0090–1

Alaska agricultural production and marketing, by district and commodity, 1960s-92, annual rpt, U5750–1

Arizona agricultural production, marketing, and finances, by commodity and county, 1988-92, annual rpt, U5830–1

Arkansas agricultural production, marketing, and finances, by commodity and county, with farms and acreage, 1992 and trends, annual rpt, U5920–1

Arkansas farmer use of price hedging techniques, including govt programs, forward and futures contracts, and crop insurance, for 3 crops, July 1992 survey, article, U5930–1.504

California agricultural statistics, including production, acreage, finances, and marketing, by commodity, annual rpt series, S0850–1

Colorado agricultural production, marketing, and finances, by commodity and/or county, with farms and acreage, 1992 and trends, annual rpt, S0985–1

Florida agricultural statistics, including production, finances, and shipment data for citrus, dairy, and other sectors, by commodity and/or county, 1993 annual rpt series, S1685–1

Georgia agricultural production, marketing, and finances, by commodity and/or county, and farms and acreage, 1991 and trends, annual rpt, S1855–1

Georgia business activity indicators, bimonthly rpt, U6730–2

Georgia statistical abstract, general data, 1992-93 biennial rpt, U6730–1.3

Hawaii agricultural production and marketing, by commodity and island, 1987-91, annual rpt, S2030–1

Hawaii economic indicators, bimonthly rpt, B3500–1

Illinois agricultural production, marketing, and finances, by county or commodity, and farms and farmland, 1991 and trends, annual rpt, S2390–1

Kansas agricultural production, marketing, and finances, by county and/or commodity, and farm acreage and value, 1992 and trends, annual rpt, S2915–1

Kansas business activity indicators, quarterly rpt, U7095–1

Kentucky agricultural production, marketing, and finances, by commodity and county; and farms, acreage, and value; 1992 and trends, annual rpt, S3085–1

Louisiana agricultural production, marketing, and finances, by commodity or parish, 1985-91, annual rpt, U2740–1

Michigan agricultural production, marketing, and finances, by commodity or county, 1987-91, annual rpt, S3950–1

Minnesota agricultural production, marketing, and finances, by county or commodity, and farms and acreage, 1992 and trends, annual rpt, S4130–1

Missouri agricultural production, marketing, and finances, by commodity and/or county, and farms and acreage, 1988-92, annual rpt, S4480–1

Montana agricultural production, marketing, and finances, by commodity and county, 1991 and trends, annual rpt, S4655–1

Nebraska agricultural production, marketing, and finances, by commodity and/or county, and farms and acreage, 1991 and trends, annual rpt, S4835–1

Nevada agricultural production, marketing, and finances, by county and commodity, and farms and acreage, 1992 and trends, annual rpt, S5010–1

New Jersey agricultural production, marketing, and finances, by commodity and/or county, and farms and acreage, 1986-91, annual rpt, S5350–1

New Mexico agricultural production, marketing, and finances, by commodity and county, with farms and acreage, 1991 and trends, annual rpt, S5530–1

New York State agricultural production, marketing, and finances, by commodity and/or county, and farms and acreage, 1992 and trends, annual rpt, S5700–1

Agricultural prices

New York State index of milk prices received by farmers, quarterly rpt, S5735–2

North Carolina agricultural production, marketing, and finances, by commodity and county, 1991 and trends, annual rpt, S5885–1

North Dakota agricultural production and marketing, by commodity and county, and farm finances, 1992 and trends, annual rpt, U3600–1

Ohio agricultural production, marketing, and finances, by commodity and county, with farms and acreage, 1990-91 and trends, annual rpt, S6240–1

Oklahoma agricultural production, marketing, and finances, by commodity and county, 1992 and trends, annual rpt, S6405–1

Oregon agricultural production, marketing, and finances, by commodity and/or county, with farms and acreage, 1991 and trends, annual rpt, S6575–1

Pennsylvania agricultural production, marketing, and finances, by county and commodity, and farms and acreage, 1992 and trends, annual rpt, S6760–1

South Carolina agricultural production and finances, by commodity and county, 1991-92 and trends, annual rpt, U1075–3

South Carolina economic condition, including agriculture, finance, and govt financial data, 1970s-92, annual rpt, S7125–3.1

South Dakota agricultural production, marketing, and finances, by commodity and county, and farms and acreage, 1992 and trends, annual rpt, S7280–1

South Dakota business activity review, including selected data by city and industry, quarterly rpt, U8595–1

Tennessee agricultural production and marketing, by commodity and county, with farms, acreage, and farm value, 1992 and trends, annual rpt, S7460–1

Texas agricultural production, marketing, and finances, by commodity and county, and farms and farmland, 1991 and trends, annual rpt series, S7630–1

Utah agricultural production, marketing, and finances, by commodity and county, with farms and acreage, 1992 and trends, annual rpt, S7800–1

Utah economic and business activity review and indicators, monthly rpt, U8960–2

Vermont agricultural production, marketing, and finances, by commodity, with data on govt inspections and funding, 1989-90 biennial rpt, S7978–1

Washington State agricultural production, marketing, and finances, by commodity and/or county, 1992 and trends, annual rpt, S8328–1

West Virginia agricultural production, marketing, and finances, by commodity or county, 1991 and trends, annual rpt, S8510–1

Wisconsin agricultural production, marketing, and finances, by commodity and county, and farms, acreage, and sales, 1992 and trends, annual rpt, S8680–1

Wisconsin economic indicators, including employment and earnings by industry group, monthly rpt, S8750–1

Wyoming agricultural production, marketing, and finances, by county and/or commodity, and farms, acreage, and value, 1992 and trends, annual rpt, S8860–1

see also Agricultural production quotas and price supports

see also Food prices

Agricultural production

Commodity yearbook for 1993: agricultural production, acreage, stocks, marketing, and operating data, including by country and producing State, C2400–1

Commodity yearbook update: agricultural production, acreage, stocks, marketing, and operating data, including by country and producing State, Jan-Sept 1993 rpts, C2400–2

Corn and refined products supply and demand trends, US and by foreign country, 1993 annual rpt, A4200–1

Cotton and wool production by world region and country, and consumption and trade, 1950s-92, annual article, C3460–1.502

Crop and livestock values, and number of farms, by State, MSA, county, city, and Canadian Province, 1993 annual rpt, C3250–1

Fig industry production, acreage, and prices in California, with US consumption and imports by country, 1950s-92, annual rpt, A3750–1

Grain production and marketing trends, by commodity and State, 1992 annual rpt, B2120–1

Grain production and yield in States served by Minneapolis exchange, with area elevator receipts and shipments by mode, 1992 and trends, annual rpt, B6110–1.1

Grain production by State, 1990-92, with natl trends from 1956 and Kansas City Board of Trade market activity, annual rpt, B1530–1

Soybean production and marketing data, including utilization, prices, and trade, with comparison to other oilseeds, 1920s-93, annual rpt, B8480–1

Wheat production, consumption, price, and trade trends, 1992 annual rpt, A7310–1

State and local:

Alabama agricultural production, marketing, and income, by county and/or commodity, and farms and acreage, 1992 and trends, annual rpt, S0090–1

Alabama statistical abstract, general data, 1992 recurring rpt, U5680–2.1

Alaska agricultural production and marketing, by district and commodity, 1960s-92, annual rpt, U5750–1

Arizona agricultural production, marketing, and finances, by commodity and county, 1988-92, annual rpt, U5830–1

Arizona statistical abstract, general data, 1993 recurring rpt, U5850–2.13

Arkansas agricultural production, marketing, and finances, by commodity and county, with farms and acreage, 1992 and trends, annual rpt, U5920–1

California agricultural statistics, including production, acreage, finances, and marketing, by commodity, annual rpt series, S0850–1

California export vs total agricultural production and acreage, by commodity, 1991, annual rpt, B9520–1

Index by Subjects and Names

California statistical abstract, general data, 1992 annual rpt, S0840–2.7

Colorado agricultural production, marketing, and finances, by commodity and/or county, with farms and acreage, 1992 and trends, annual rpt, S0985–1

Florida agricultural statistics, including production, finances, and shipment data for citrus, dairy, and other sectors, by commodity and/or county, 1993 annual rpt series, S1685–1

Florida statistical abstract, general data, 1992 annual rpt, U6660–1.9

Georgia agricultural production, marketing, and finances, by commodity and/or county, and farms and acreage, 1991 and trends, annual rpt, S1855–1

Georgia county guide, general data, 1993 annual rpt, U6750–1

Georgia statistical abstract, general data, 1992-93 biennial rpt, U6730–1.4

Hawaii agricultural production and marketing, by commodity and island, 1987-91, annual rpt, S2030–1

Hawaii counties population and economic indicators, 1993 annual rpt series, B3500–2

Hawaii data book, general data, 1992 annual rpt, S2090–1.19, S2090–1.22

Hawaii economic indicators, bimonthly rpt, B3500–1

Idaho economic profile, general data, 1992 recurring rpt, S2218–2.5

Illinois agricultural production, marketing, and finances, by county or commodity, and farms and farmland, 1991 and trends, annual rpt, S2390–1

Illinois statistical abstract, general data, 1992 annual rpt, U6910–2

Kansas agricultural production, marketing, and finances, by county and/or commodity, and farm acreage and value, 1992 and trends, annual rpt, S2915–1

Kansas crop income summary, including acreage and enrollment in conservation program, 1991-93, annual article, U7095–1.501

Kansas statistical abstract, general data, 1991/92 annual rpt, U7095–2.15

Kentucky agricultural production, marketing, and finances, by commodity and county; and farms, acreage, and value; 1992 and trends, annual rpt, S3085–1

Louisiana agricultural production, marketing, and finances, by commodity or parish, 1985-91, annual rpt, U2740–1

Michigan agricultural production, marketing, and finances, by commodity or county, 1987-91, annual rpt, S3950–1

Minnesota agricultural production, marketing, and finances, by county or commodity, and farms and acreage, 1992 and trends, annual rpt, S4130–1

Mississippi statistical abstract, general data, 1992 annual rpt, U3255–4.15

Missouri agricultural production, marketing, and finances, by commodity and/or county, and farms and acreage, 1988-92, annual rpt, S4480–1

Montana agricultural production, marketing, and finances, by commodity and county, 1991 and trends, annual rpt, S4655–1

Nebraska agricultural production, marketing, and finances, by commodity and/or county, and farms and acreage, 1991 and trends, annual rpt, S4835–1

Index by Subjects and Names

Agricultural production costs

Nevada agricultural production, marketing, and finances, by county and commodity, and farms and acreage, 1992 and trends, annual rpt, S5010–1

Nevada statistical abstract, general data, 1992 biennial rpt, S5005–1.10

New Jersey agricultural production, marketing, and finances, by commodity and/or county, and farms and acreage, 1986-91, annual rpt, S5350–1

New Mexico agricultural production, marketing, and finances, by commodity and county, with farms and acreage, 1991 and trends, annual rpt, S5530–1

New York State agricultural production, marketing, and finances, by commodity and/or county, and farms and acreage, 1992 and trends, annual rpt, S5700–1

New York State statistical yearbook, general data, 1992 annual rpt, U5100–1.14

North Carolina agricultural production, marketing, and finances, by commodity and county, 1991 and trends, annual rpt, S5885–1

North Dakota agricultural production and marketing, by commodity and county, and farm finances, 1992 and trends, annual rpt, U3600–1

Ohio agricultural production, marketing, and finances, by commodity and county, with farms and acreage, 1990-91 and trends, annual rpt, S6240–1

Oklahoma agricultural production, marketing, and finances, by commodity and county, 1992 and trends, annual rpt, S6405–1

Oklahoma statistical abstract, general data, 1992 annual rpt, U8130–2.11

Oregon agricultural production, marketing, and finances, by commodity and/or county, with farms and acreage, 1991 and trends, annual rpt, S6575–1

Oregon economic conditions, including population, construction, income, employment, industry, and foreign trade data, 1991, annual rpt, S6585–3

Pennsylvania agricultural production, marketing, and finances, by county and commodity, and farms and acreage, 1992 and trends, annual rpt, S6760–1

Pennsylvania statistical abstract, general data, 1992 recurring rpt, U4130–6.8

South Carolina agricultural production and finances, by commodity and county, 1991-92 and trends, annual rpt, U1075–3

South Carolina economic activity indicators, including employment by industry div, by county, 1993 annual rpt, S7145–1.2

South Carolina economic condition, including agriculture, finance, and govt financial data, 1970s-92, annual rpt, S7125–3.1

South Carolina statistical abstract, general data, 1993 annual rpt, S7125–1.1

South Dakota agricultural production, marketing, and finances, by commodity and county, and farms and acreage, 1992 and trends, annual rpt, S7280–1

South Dakota business activity review, including selected data by city and industry, quarterly rpt, U8595–1

Tennessee agricultural production and marketing, by commodity and county, with farms, acreage, and farm value, 1992 and trends, annual rpt, S7460–1

Tennessee statistical abstract, general data, 1992/93 annual rpt, U8710–2.11

Texas agricultural production, marketing, and finances, by commodity and county, and farms and farmland, 1991 and trends, annual rpt series, S7630–1

Utah agricultural production, marketing, and finances, by commodity and county, with farms and acreage, 1992 and trends, annual rpt, S7800–1

Utah statistical abstract, general data, 1993 triennial rpt, U8960–1.9

Vermont agricultural production, marketing, and finances, by commodity, with data on govt inspections and funding, 1989-90 biennial rpt, S7978–1

Washington State agricultural production, marketing, and finances, by commodity and/or county, 1992 and trends, annual rpt, S8328–1

West Virginia agricultural production, marketing, and finances, by commodity or county, 1991 and trends, annual rpt, S8510–1

Wisconsin agricultural production, marketing, and finances, by commodity and county, and farms, acreage, and sales, 1992 and trends, annual rpt, S8680–1

Wisconsin Blue Book, general data, 1993-94 biennial rpt, S8780–1.2

Wyoming agricultural production, marketing, and finances, by county and/or commodity, and farms, acreage, and value, 1992 and trends, annual rpt, S8860–1

Wyoming penitentiary farm production and marketing, with meat sales to selected State instns, FY91-92, annual rpt, S8883–1

see also Agricultural production costs
see also Agricultural production quotas and price supports
see also Agricultural productivity
see also Agricultural stocks
see also Aquaculture
see also Fertilizers
see also Food supply
see also Foreign agriculture

Agricultural production costs

Appalachia farm production costs, by item, 1990-91, annual rpt, S8510–1

Dairy herd clinical mastitis prevalence and control efforts, with data on associated costs, Illinois and Ohio studies, 1993 articles, A3100–2.508, A3100–2.512

Economic indicator historical trends, 1900s-92, annual rpt, R9050–1.2

Southeastern States agriculture production costs for selected crops, and prices paid for fertilizer, 1993 annual rpt, S7460–1

Southeastern States farm production costs for corn and soybeans, 1989-91, annual rpt, S3085–1

Southern Delta region farm production expenses, by item, 1989-91, annual rpt, U5920–1

Veterinary services costs for dairy farmers correlated with milk production, Pennsylvania study, 1986-90, article, A3100–2.506

State and local:

Arizona agricultural production, marketing, and finances, by commodity and county, 1988-92, annual rpt, U5830–1

California economic condition, including population, employment and earnings, income, business activity, and taxation, 1960s-92, annual rpt, S0840–3.2

Colorado agricultural production, marketing, and finances, by commodity and/or county, with farms and acreage, 1992 and trends, annual rpt, S0985–1

Georgia agricultural production, marketing, and finances, by commodity and/or county, and farms and acreage, 1991 and trends, annual rpt, S1855–1

Hawaii farm production expenditures, by item, 1960-90, annual rpt, S2030–1

Illinois agricultural production, marketing, and finances, by county or commodity, and farms and farmland, 1991 and trends, annual rpt, S2390–1

Illinois statistical abstract, general data, 1992 annual rpt, U6910–2

Kansas agricultural production, marketing, and finances, by county and/or commodity, and farm acreage and value, 1992 and trends, annual rpt, S2915–1

Kentucky agricultural production, marketing, and finances, by commodity and county; and farms, acreage, and value; 1992 and trends, annual rpt, S3085–1

Louisiana farm production expenses, by item, 1985-91, annual rpt, U2740–1

Michigan agricultural production, marketing, and finances, by commodity or county, 1987-91, annual rpt, S3950–1

Minnesota agricultural production, marketing, and finances, by county or commodity, and farms and acreage, 1992 and trends, annual rpt, S4130–1

Missouri agricultural production, marketing, and finances, by commodity and/or county, and farms and acreage, 1988-92, annual rpt, S4480–1

Montana agricultural production, marketing, and finances, by commodity and county, 1991 and trends, annual rpt, S4655–1

Nebraska agricultural production, marketing, and finances, by commodity and/or county, and farms and acreage, 1991 and trends, annual rpt, S4835–1

Nevada agricultural production, marketing, and finances, by county and commodity, and farms and acreage, 1992 and trends, annual rpt, S5010–1

New Jersey agricultural production, marketing, and finances, by commodity and/or county, and farms and acreage, 1986-91, annual rpt, S5350–1

New Mexico agricultural production, marketing, and finances, by commodity and county, with farms and acreage, 1991 and trends, annual rpt, S5530–1

New York State agricultural production, marketing, and finances, by commodity and/or county, and farms and acreage, 1992 and trends, annual rpt, S5700–1

North Carolina farm production expenses, by item, 1987-91, annual rpt, S5885–1

North Dakota agricultural production and marketing, by commodity and county, and farm finances, 1992 and trends, annual rpt, U3600–1

Ohio agricultural production, marketing, and finances, by commodity and county, with farms and acreage, 1990-91 and trends, annual rpt, S6240–1

Oklahoma agricultural production, marketing, and finances, by commodity and county, 1992 and trends, annual rpt, S6405–1

Agricultural production costs

Oregon agricultural production, marketing, and finances, by commodity and/or county, with farms and acreage, 1991 and trends, annual rpt, S6575–1

Pennsylvania agricultural production, marketing, and finances, by county and commodity, and farms and acreage, 1992 and trends, annual rpt, S6760–1

South Dakota agricultural production, marketing, and finances, by commodity and county, and farms and acreage, 1992 and trends, annual rpt, S7280–1

Tennessee agricultural production costs by item, 1989-93, annual rpt, S7460–1

Texas farm income and production expense data, 1987-91, annual rpt, S7630–1.3

Utah agricultural production, marketing, and finances, by commodity and county, with farms and acreage, 1992 and trends, annual rpt, S7800–1

Utah statistical abstract, general data, 1993 triennial rpt, U8960–1.5

Vermont agricultural production, marketing, and finances, by commodity, with data on govt inspections and funding, 1989-90 biennial rpt, S7978–1

Washington State agricultural production, marketing, and finances, by commodity and/or county, 1992 and trends, annual rpt, S8328–1

West Virginia agricultural production, marketing, and finances, by commodity or county, 1991 and trends, annual rpt, S8510–1

Wisconsin agricultural production, marketing, and finances, by commodity and county, and farms, acreage, and sales, 1992 and trends, annual rpt, S8680–1

Wyoming farm production costs, 1987-91, annual rpt, S8860–1

see also Agricultural marketing

Agricultural production quotas and price supports

Crops under Govt price support, commodity yearbook for 1993, C2400–1

Crops under Govt price support, commodity yearbook Jan-Sept 1993 updates, C2400–2

Losses and price support costs of Commodity Credit Corp, by commodity, FY91 and trends, annual rpt, R9050–1.3

Payments for farm price supports, by State and region, FY82, FY88, and FY92, R8490–47

Soybean price support operations, 1940s-92, annual rpt, B8480–1

State and local:

Arkansas farmer use of price hedging techniques, including govt programs, forward and futures contracts, and crop insurance, for 3 crops, July 1992 survey, article, U5930–1.504

California milk producers minimum prices, 1992, annual rpt, S0850–1.6

Hawaii sugar industry govt support payments, 1970-91, annual rpt, S2090–1.22

Kentucky tobacco quotas and farms affected, with detail by county and district, 1993 and trends, annual rpt, S3085–1

Agricultural productivity

Commodity yearbook for 1993: agricultural production, acreage, stocks, marketing, and operating data, including by country and producing State, C2400–1

Commodity yearbook update: agricultural production, acreage, stocks, marketing, and operating data, including by country and producing State, Jan-Sept 1993 rpts, C2400–2

Corn acreage, yield, and production, by State, 1992 and trends, annual rpt, A4200–1

Cotton production and yield per acre, 1981-92, annual article, C3460–1.502

Fig industry production, acreage, and prices in California, with US consumption and imports by country, 1950s-92, annual rpt, A3750–1

Grain production and marketing trends, by commodity and State, 1992 annual rpt, B2120–1

Grain production and yield in States served by Minneapolis exchange, with area elevator receipts and shipments by mode, 1992 and trends, annual rpt, B6110–1.1

Grain production and yields by State, with Kansas City Board of Trade market activity, 1992, annual rpt, B1530–1

Latin America statistical abstract, general data by country, 1992 annual rpt, U6250–1.2, U6250–1.24

Soybean production and marketing data, including utilization, prices, and trade, with comparison to other oilseeds, 1920s-93, annual rpt, B8480–1

Wheat production, consumption, price, and trade trends, 1992 annual rpt, A7310–1

World production indexes, and yields for cereal and root/tuber crops, by country, 1978-90, biennial rpt, R9455–1.6

State and local:

Alabama agricultural production, marketing, and income, by county and/or commodity, and farms and acreage, 1992 and trends, annual rpt, S0090–1

Alaska agricultural production and marketing, by district and commodity, 1960s-92, annual rpt, U5750–1

Arizona agricultural production, marketing, and finances, by commodity and county, 1988-92, annual rpt, U5830–1

Arkansas agricultural production, marketing, and finances, by commodity and county, with farms and acreage, 1992 and trends, annual rpt, U5920–1

California dairy production, sales, marketing, and consumption, 1992 and trends, annual rpt, S0850–1.6

California field crops production, acreage, yield, and prices, by commodity and county, 1992 and trends, annual rpt, S0850–1.4

California fruit and nut production, marketing, and income, by commodity, 1983-92, annual rpt, S0850–1.1

California vegetable production, marketing, and prices, by commodity and use, 1992 and trends, annual rpt, S0850–1.3

Colorado agricultural production, marketing, and finances, by commodity and/or county, with farms and acreage, 1992 and trends, annual rpt, S0985–1

Florida agricultural statistics, including production, finances, and shipment data for citrus, dairy, and other sectors, by commodity and/or county, 1993 annual rpt series, S1685–1

Georgia agricultural production, marketing, and finances, by commodity and/or county, and farms and acreage, 1991 and trends, annual rpt, S1855–1

Index by Subjects and Names

Hawaii agricultural production and marketing, by commodity and island, 1987-91, annual rpt, S2030–1

Illinois agricultural production, marketing, and finances, by county or commodity, and farms and farmland, 1991 and trends, annual rpt, S2390–1

Kansas agricultural production, marketing, and finances, by county and/or commodity, and farm acreage and value, 1992 and trends, annual rpt, S2915–1

Kentucky agricultural production, marketing, and finances, by commodity and county; and farms, acreage, and value; 1992 and trends, annual rpt, S3085–1

Louisiana agricultural production, marketing, and finances, by commodity or parish, 1985-91, annual rpt, U2740–1

Michigan agricultural production, marketing, and finances, by commodity or county, 1987-91, annual rpt, S3950–1

Minnesota agricultural production, marketing, and finances, by county or commodity, and farms and acreage, 1992 and trends, annual rpt, S4130–1

Missouri agricultural production, marketing, and finances, by commodity and/or county, and farms and acreage, 1988-92, annual rpt, S4480–1

Montana agricultural production, marketing, and finances, by commodity and county, 1991 and trends, annual rpt, S4655–1

Nebraska agricultural production, marketing, and finances, by commodity and/or county, and farms and acreage, 1991 and trends, annual rpt, S4835–1

Nevada agricultural production, marketing, and finances, by county and commodity, and farms and acreage, 1992 and trends, annual rpt, S5010–1

New Jersey agricultural production, marketing, and finances, by commodity and/or county, and farms and acreage, 1986-91, annual rpt, S5350–1

New Mexico agricultural production, marketing, and finances, by commodity and county, with farms and acreage, 1991 and trends, annual rpt, S5530–1

New York State agricultural production, marketing, and finances, by commodity and/or county, and farms and acreage, 1992 and trends, annual rpt, S5700–1

North Carolina agricultural production, marketing, and finances, by commodity and county, 1991 and trends, annual rpt, S5885–1

North Dakota production and marketing, by commodity and county, and farm finances, 1992 and trends, annual rpt, U3600–1

Ohio agricultural production, marketing, and finances, by commodity and county, with farms and acreage, 1990-91 and trends, annual rpt, S6240–1

Oklahoma agricultural production, marketing, and finances, by commodity and county, 1992 and trends, annual rpt, S6405–1

Oregon agricultural production, marketing, and finances, by commodity and/or county, with farms and acreage, 1991 and trends, annual rpt, S6575–1

Pennsylvania agricultural production, marketing, and finances, by county and commodity, and farms and acreage, 1992 and trends, annual rpt, S6760–1

Index by Subjects and Names

Agricultural stocks

South Carolina agricultural production and finances, by commodity and county, 1991-92 and trends, annual rpt, U1075–3

South Dakota agricultural production, marketing, and finances, by commodity and county, and farms and acreage, 1992 and trends, annual rpt, S7280–1

Tennessee agricultural production and marketing, by commodity and county, with farms, acreage, and farm value, 1992 and trends, annual rpt, S7460–1

Texas agricultural production, marketing, and finances, by commodity and county, and farms and farmland, 1991 and trends, annual rpt series, S7630–1

Utah agricultural production, marketing, and finances, by commodity and county, with farms and acreage, 1992 and trends, annual rpt, S7800–1

Vermont agricultural production, marketing, and finances, by commodity, with data on govt inspections and funding, 1989-90 biennial rpt, S7978–1

Washington State agricultural production, marketing, and finances, by commodity and/or county, 1992 and trends, annual rpt, S8328–1

West Virginia agricultural production, marketing, and finances, by commodity or county, 1991 and trends, annual rpt, S8510–1

Wisconsin agricultural production, marketing, and finances, by commodity and county, and farms, acreage, and sales, 1992 and trends, annual rpt, S8680–1

Wyoming agricultural production, marketing, and finances, by county and/or commodity, and farms, acreage, and value, 1992 and trends, annual rpt, S8860–1

see also Agricultural production costs

see also Fertilizers

Agricultural quotas and price supports

see Agricultural production quotas and price supports

Agricultural research

see Agricultural sciences and research

Agricultural sciences and research

Federal USDA research budget, by program, FY92-94, article, A1250–1.525

Finance, credit, investment, and related topics, 1993 annual research compilation, U1380–4

see also Biomass energy

Agricultural services

Financial ratios and performance, for over 350 SIC 4-digit industries, FY88-92, annual rpt, A6400–3

State and local:

Florida statistical abstract, general data, 1992 annual rpt, U6660–1.9

see also Agricultural sciences and research

see also Veterinary medicine

Agricultural Stabilization and Conservation Service

see also Commodity Credit Corp.

Agricultural stocks

Coffee, Sugar, and Cocoa Exchange trading activity, with related data including deliveries and stocks by country and/or port, 1992 and trends, annual rpt, B2275–1

Commodity yearbook for 1993: agricultural production, acreage, stocks, marketing, and operating data, including by country and producing State, C2400–1

Commodity yearbook update: agricultural production, acreage, stocks, marketing, and operating data, including by country and producing State, Jan-Sept 1993 rpts, C2400–2

Corn and refined products supply and demand trends, US and by foreign country, 1993 annual rpt, A4200–1

Futures trading activity on Chicago Board of Trade, with info on cash prices, supply, and disposition, by commodity, 1992 and trends, annual rpt, B2120–1

Livestock operations and inventories, by State and foreign country, 1992 annual rpt, A2100–1

Soybean production and marketing data, including utilization, prices, and trade, with comparison to other oilseeds, 1920s-93, annual rpt, B8480–1

Wheat production, consumption, price, and trade trends, 1992 annual rpt, A7310–1

State and local:

Alabama agricultural production, marketing, and income, by county and/or commodity, and farms and acreage, 1992 and trends, annual rpt, S0090–1

Alaska agricultural production and marketing, by district and commodity, 1960s-92, annual rpt, U5750–1

Arizona agricultural production, marketing, and finances, by commodity and county, 1988-92, annual rpt, U5830–1

Arkansas agricultural production, marketing, and finances, by commodity and county, with farms and acreage, 1992 and trends, annual rpt, U5920–1

California dairy production, sales, marketing, and consumption, 1992 and trends, annual rpt, S0850–1.6

California livestock production and marketing, with comparisons to US, 1983-92, annual rpt, S0850–1.2

Colorado agricultural production, marketing, and finances, by commodity and/or county, with farms and acreage, 1992 and trends, annual rpt, S0985–1

Georgia agricultural production, marketing, and finances, by commodity and/or county, and farms and acreage, 1991 and trends, annual rpt, S1855–1

Illinois agricultural production, marketing, and finances, by county or commodity, and farms and farmland, 1991 and trends, annual rpt, S2390–1

Kansas agricultural production, marketing, and finances, by county and/or commodity, and farm acreage and value, 1992 and trends, annual rpt, S2915–1

Kentucky agricultural production, marketing, and finances, by commodity and county; and farms, acreage, and value; 1992 and trends, annual rpt, S3085–1

Michigan agricultural production, marketing, and finances, by commodity or county, 1987-91, annual rpt, S3950–1

Minnesota agricultural production, marketing, and finances, by county or commodity, and farms and acreage, 1992 and trends, annual rpt, S4130–1

Missouri agricultural production, marketing, and finances, by commodity and/or county, and farms and acreage, 1988-92, annual rpt, S4480–1

Montana agricultural production, marketing, and finances, by commodity and county, 1991 and trends, annual rpt, S4655–1

Nebraska agricultural production, marketing, and finances, by commodity and/or county, and farms and acreage, 1991 and trends, annual rpt, S4835–1

Nevada agricultural production, marketing, and finances, by county and commodity, and farms and acreage, 1992 and trends, annual rpt, S5010–1

New Jersey agricultural production, marketing, and finances, by commodity and/or county, and farms and acreage, 1986-91, annual rpt, S5350–1

New Mexico agricultural production, marketing, and finances, by commodity and county, with farms and acreage, 1991 and trends, annual rpt, S5530–1

New York State agricultural production, marketing, and finances, by commodity and/or county, and farms and acreage, 1992 and trends, annual rpt, S5700–1

North Carolina agricultural production, marketing, and finances, by commodity and county, 1991 and trends, annual rpt, S5885–1

North Dakota agricultural production and marketing, by commodity and county, and farm finances, 1992 and trends, annual rpt, U3600–1

Ohio agricultural production, marketing, and finances, by commodity and county, with farms and acreage, 1990-91 and trends, annual rpt, S6240–1

Oklahoma agricultural production, marketing, and finances, by commodity and county, 1992 and trends, annual rpt, S6405–1

Oregon agricultural production, marketing, and finances, by commodity and/or county, with farms and acreage, 1991 and trends, annual rpt, S6575–1

Pennsylvania agricultural production, marketing, and finances, by county and commodity, and farms and acreage, 1992 and trends, annual rpt, S6760–1

South Carolina agricultural production and finances, by commodity and county, 1991-92 and trends, annual rpt, U1075–3

South Dakota agricultural production, marketing, and finances, by commodity and county, and farms and acreage, 1992 and trends, annual rpt, S7280–1

Tennessee agricultural production and marketing, by commodity and county, with farms, acreage, and farm value, 1992 and trends, annual rpt, S7460–1

Texas agricultural production, marketing, and finances, by commodity and county, and farms and farmland, 1991 and trends, annual rpt series, S7630–1

Utah agricultural production, marketing, and finances, by commodity and county, with farms and acreage, 1992 and trends, annual rpt, S7800–1

Vermont agricultural production, marketing, and finances, by commodity, with data on govt inspections and funding, 1989-90 biennial rpt, S7978–1

Washington State agricultural production, marketing, and finances, by commodity and/or county, 1992 and trends, annual rpt, S8328–1

West Virginia agricultural production, marketing, and finances, by commodity or county, 1991 and trends, annual rpt, S8510–1

Agricultural stocks

Wisconsin agricultural production, marketing, and finances, by commodity and county, and farms, acreage, and sales, 1992 and trends, annual rpt, S8680–1

Wyoming agricultural production, marketing, and finances, by county and/or commodity, and farms, acreage, and value, 1992 and trends, annual rpt, S8860–1

see also Grain storage and facilities (for off-farm stocks)

Agricultural subsidies

Budget receipts and outlays of Fed Govt, by source and function, 1920s-93, annual rpt, R9050–1.3

Cash receipts from farm marketings and govt payments, by State, 1991, annual rpt, S5885–1

Commodity yearbook for 1993: agricultural production, acreage, stocks, marketing, and operating data, including by country and producing State, C2400–1

Commodity yearbook update: agricultural production, acreage, stocks, marketing, and operating data, including by country and producing State, Jan-Sept 1993 rpts, C2400–2

Economic indicator historical trends, 1900s-92, annual rpt, R9050–1.2

State and local:

Alabama farm income from marketings and govt payments, with detail by county, 1992 and trends, annual rpt, S0090–1

Arizona farm income from govt payments, with detail by program, 1987-92, annual rpt, U5830–1

Arizona statistical abstract, general data, 1993 recurring rpt, U5850–2.13

Arkansas cash receipts from farm marketings and govt payments, 1972-91, annual rpt, U5920–1

California economic condition, including population, employment and earnings, income, business activity, and taxation, 1960s-92, annual rpt, S0840–3.2

Colorado agricultural production, marketing, and finances, by commodity and/or county, with farms and acreage, 1992 and trends, annual rpt, S0985–1

Florida statistical abstract, general data, 1992 annual rpt, U6660–1.9

Georgia cash receipts from farm marketings by commodity, and govt payments, 1985-91, annual rpt, S1855–1

Hawaii farm income from marketings and govt payments, by island, 1987-91, annual rpt, S2030–1

Illinois cash receipts from farm marketings and govt payments, 1981-90, annual rpt, S2390–1

Kansas farm income from marketings and govt payments, 1952-91, annual rpt, S2915–1

Kentucky cash receipts from farm marketings and govt payments, 1950-92, annual rpt, S3085–1

Louisiana farm income from marketings and govt payments, 1985-91, annual rpt, U2740–1

Michigan income from govt agricultural programs, 1986-90, annual rpt, S3950–1

Minnesota cash receipts from farm marketings and govt payments, 1986-92, annual rpt, S4130–1

Missouri farm income from govt payments, 1987-91, annual rpt, S4480–1

Montana farm income from marketings and govt payments, with detail by county, 1991 and trends, annual rpt, S4655–1

Nebraska farm income from marketings and govt payments, 1982-91, annual rpt, S4835–1

Nevada cash receipts from farm marketings and govt payments, 1988-92, annual rpt, S5010–1

New Jersey cash receipts from farm marketings and govt payments, 1986-91, annual rpt, S5350–1

New Mexico cash receipts from farm marketings and govt payments, 1960-91, annual rpt, S5530–1

New York State farm income by source, including govt payments by program, 1982-91, annual rpt, S5700–1

North Carolina cash receipts from farm marketings and govt payments, 1987-91, annual rpt, S5885–1

North Dakota farm income and receipts from govt payments, 1989-92, annual rpt, U3600–1

Ohio and US farm income by source including Fed Govt payments, 1988-90, annual rpt, S6240–1

Oklahoma farm income from govt payments, 1988-92, annual rpt, S6405–1

Oregon farm income from marketings and govt payments, with detail for grain programs, 1987-91, annual rpt, S6575–1

Pennsylvania farm income from govt payments, with detail by county, 1940s-92, annual rpt, S6760–1

South Dakota farm income from marketing and govt payments by program, 1989-91, annual rpt, S7280–1

Tennessee farm income by source, including govt payments by program, 1987-91, annual rpt, S7460–1

Tennessee statistical abstract, general data, 1992/93 annual rpt, U8710–2.11

Texas cash receipts from farm marketings and govt payments, 1987-91, annual rpt, S7630–1.3

Utah cash receipts from farming, and govt payments, 1987-92, annual rpt, S7800–1

Vermont cash receipts from marketings and Fed Govt payments, 1984-88, biennial rpt, S7978–1

Washington State farm income by source including govt payments, 1988-92, annual rpt, S8328–1

West Virginia farm income from govt payments, 1987-91, annual rpt, S8510–1

Wisconsin farm income by source, 1987-91, annual rpt, S8680–1

Wyoming farm income by source, 1987-91, annual rpt, S8860–1

see also Agricultural production quotas and price supports

see also State funding for agriculture

Agricultural surpluses

see also Agricultural production quotas and price supports

see also Agricultural stocks

see also Food assistance

see also Public Law 480

Agricultural Trade Development and Assistance Act

see Public Law 480

Index by Subjects and Names

Agricultural transportation

see Agricultural marketing

Agricultural wages

Appalachia agricultural workers, hours, and wage rates, 1990-91, annual rpt, S8510–1

Latin America statistical abstract, general data by country, 1992 annual rpt, U6250–1.13

North Central States farm labor force, and wage rates, 1992 and trends, annual rpt, S2390–1

Northeast region farm workers, hours, and wages, 1985-93, annual rpt, S5700–1

Northern Plains region agricultural workers, hours, and wages, 1st qtr 1989-1st qtr 1993, annual rpt, S7280–1

Southeast US farm workers, hours, and wage rates, 3 regions, 1991-92, annual rpt, S5885–1

Southeast US farm workers, hours, wages, and pay methods, 1989-92, annual rpt, S1855–1

Southern Plains region farm workers and wages, quarterly 1986-92, annual rpt, S7630–1.3

Southern Plains region farm workers and wages, quarterly 1988-92, annual rpt, S6405–1

Western States farm workers, hours, and wages, 1992-93, annual rpt, S5010–1

State and local:

Alaska farm workers and wage rates, 1960s-92, annual rpt, U5750–1

Arizona economic condition, including population, employment and earnings, and business activity, by industry and locality, 1985-93, semiannual rpt, U5850–1.1

Arizona farm workers, wage rates, and hours of labor, 1988-93, annual rpt, U5830–1

Hawaii agricultural wage rates, by type of work, 1987-91, annual rpt, S2030–1

Louisiana farm production expenses, by item, 1985-91, annual rpt, U2740–1

Michigan agricultural labor and wages, with comparisons to Lake States region, 1992 annual rpt, S3950–1

Minnesota farm workers, wages, and hours, Apr 1991-Apr 1993, annual rpt, S4130–1

Missouri/Iowa farm workers, hours, and wages, 1988-92, annual rpt, S4480–1

North Dakota farm wage rates, with detail for custom work by type, 1992 and trends, annual rpt, U3600–1

Pennsylvania farm wages, and custom work rates by type of activity and State region, 1990-93, annual rpt, S6760–1

Utah farm workers, hours, and wages, by type of worker, 1992-93, annual rpt, S7800–1

Washington State farm workers, hours, and wage rates, 1992-93, annual rpt, S8328–1

Agriculture

Business failures and liabilities, by detailed industry, cause, length of operation, and location, 1991-92 and trends, annual rpt, C3150–8

Congressional campaign finances, with detailed data for individual Members, and leading contributors by type and industry, 1990 election and trends, biennial rpt, R3828–2.2

Developing countries land agricultural dev potential, by world region, 1992 rpt, R8750–2.57

Index by Subjects and Names

Operating and financial composite ratios for corporations, with establishments and receipts, for approx 200 industries, by asset size, FY90, annual rpt, C7800–1

State and local:

New Mexico economic trends and outlook, by industry div, 1982-92, annual article, U7980–1.503

see also Agricultural accidents and safety
see also Agricultural commodities
see also Agricultural credit
see also Agricultural education
see also Agricultural exports and imports
see also Agricultural finance
see also Agricultural insurance
see also Agricultural labor
see also Agricultural machinery and equipment
see also Agricultural marketing
see also Agricultural prices
see also Agricultural production
see also Agricultural production costs
see also Agricultural production quotas and price supports
see also Agricultural productivity
see also Agricultural sciences and research
see also Agricultural services
see also Agricultural subsidies
see also Agricultural wages
see also Census of Agriculture
see also Drought
see also Farm income
see also Farm operators
see also Farm population
see also Farms and farmland
see also Fertilizers
see also Food and food industry
see also Foreign agriculture
see also Forests and forestry
see also Horticulture
see also Irrigation
see also Pesticides
see also Pests and pest control
see also Rural areas
see also Soils and soil conservation
see also State funding for agriculture
see also Wildlife and wildlife conservation
see also under By Industry in the "Index by Categories"

Agriculture Department

see Department of Agriculture

AID

see Agency for International Development

Aid to blind

State and local:

Alabama public welfare and social service cases, recipients, and payments, by program and county, monthly rpt, S0150–1

Arizona statistical abstract, general data, 1993 recurring rpt, U5850–2.7

Arkansas human services dept finances and operations, including Medicaid payments by type of service, FY91 and trends, annual rpt, S0700–2.3

Colorado welfare and social services expenditures and caseloads, by county and/or program, FY91, annual rpt, S1085–1

Hawaii data book, general data, 1992 annual rpt, S2090–1.11

Idaho public welfare program expenditures and recipients, with data by county, quarterly rpt, S2250–1

Aid to disabled and handicapped persons

Illinois public assistance program cases, recipients, and payments, by program and county, FY91-92 and trends, annual rpt, S2520–2

Indiana public assistance program participation, expenditures, and services, by county, FY92 and trends, annual rpt, S2623–1

Iowa ADC and SSI program recipients, and expenditures, by county, monthly rpt, S2802–1

Kentucky AFDC and SSI recipients and payments, by county, monthly rpt, S3140–2

Kentucky Medicaid recipients and payments, by program, county, and type of medical service, monthly rpt, S3140–5

Maryland medical assistance payments and recipients, by program, type of service, location, demographic characteristics, and facility, FY92 and trends, annual rpt, S3635–3

Michigan public assistance program cases, recipients, and payments, detailed data by county, monthly rpt, S4010–1

Missouri public welfare and medical assistance recipients, expenditures, and case processing, by program and county, FY92 and trends, annual rpt, S4575–2

Montana welfare and medical assistance program cases and payments, by county and type of service, monthly rpt, S4755–1

Nebraska public welfare cases, recipients, and payments, by program and county, FY92 and trends, annual rpt, S4957–1

Oklahoma public welfare program expenditures, recipients, and services, by program and county, FY92 and trends, annual rpt, S6455–1

Pennsylvania statistical abstract, general data, 1992 recurring rpt, U4130–6.5

South Dakota welfare and social services recipients and payments, by program, MSA, and county, FY92, annual rpt, S7385–1

Tennessee statistical abstract, general data, 1992/93 annual rpt, U8710–2.18

Utah statistical abstract, general data, 1993 triennial rpt, U8960–1.6

Washington State public assistance clients and service costs, by client characteristics, program, and county, FY90, annual rpt, S8420–2

West Virginia welfare and social service program caseloads and expenditures, by county, monthly rpt, S8560–2

see also Supplemental Security Income

Aid to Dependent Children

see Aid to Families with Dependent Children

Aid to disabled and handicapped persons

Medicaid child and total recipients, expenditures, and other program characteristics, and child health summary, by State, FY91, annual rpt, A0565–1

State and local:

Alabama public welfare and social service cases, recipients, and payments, by program and county, monthly rpt, S0150–1

Arizona statistical abstract, general data, 1993 recurring rpt, U5850–2.7

Arkansas human services dept finances and operations, including Medicaid payments by type of service, FY91 and trends, annual rpt, S0700–2.3

Colorado welfare and social services expenditures and caseloads, by county and/or program, FY91, annual rpt, S1085–1

Hawaii data book, general data, 1992 annual rpt, S2090–1.11

Idaho public welfare program expenditures and recipients, with data by county, quarterly rpt, S2250–1

Illinois public assistance program cases, recipients, and payments, by program and county, FY91-92 and trends, annual rpt, S2520–2

Indiana public assistance program participation, expenditures, and services, by county, FY92 and trends, annual rpt, S2623–1

Iowa ADC and SSI program recipients, and expenditures, by county, monthly rpt, S2802–1

Kentucky AFDC and SSI recipients and payments, by county, monthly rpt, S3140–2

Kentucky Medicaid recipients and payments, by program, county, and type of medical service, monthly rpt, S3140–5

Maryland medical assistance payments and recipients, by program, type of service, location, demographic characteristics, and facility, FY92 and trends, annual rpt, S3635–3

Maryland welfare program statistics, and welfare fraud investigations, by county, monthly rpt, S3645–2

Michigan public assistance program cases, recipients, and payments, detailed data by county, monthly rpt, S4010–1

Missouri public welfare and medical assistance recipients, expenditures, and case processing, by program and county, FY92 and trends, annual rpt, S4575–2

Montana welfare and medical assistance program cases and payments, by county and type of service, monthly rpt, S4755–1

Nebraska public welfare cases, recipients, and payments, by program and county, FY92 and trends, annual rpt, S4957–1

Oklahoma public welfare program expenditures, recipients, and services, by program and county, FY92 and trends, annual rpt, S6455–1

Oregon public welfare caseloads, recipients, and expenditures, by program, city, county, and State region, monthly rpt, S6615–8

Pennsylvania statistical abstract, general data, 1992 recurring rpt, U4130–6.5

South Dakota welfare and social services recipients and payments, by program, MSA, and county, FY92, annual rpt, S7385–1

Tennessee statistical abstract, general data, 1992/93 annual rpt, U8710–2.18

Utah statistical abstract, general data, 1993 triennial rpt, U8960–1.6

Washington State public assistance clients and service costs, by client characteristics, program, and county, FY90, annual rpt, S8420–2

West Virginia welfare and social service program caseloads and expenditures, by county, monthly rpt, S8560–2

see also Supplemental Security Income

Aid to Families with Dependent Children

Aid to Families with Dependent Children

Benefits for family of 3, with trend since 1970 and comparison to fair market rent for 2-bedroom apartment, for 44 metro areas, 1992, R3834–16

- Cost-of-living increase changes for AFDC recipients, by selected State, FY94, semiannual rpt, A7955–1
- Federal budget trends, including spending by program, State, and region, FY81-94, annual rpt, R8490–11
- Income thresholds for AFDC, and Medicaid program characteristics, by State, FY91 annual rpt, A0565–1
- Low-income families and children, health and welfare indicators, with data by State and city, 1992 annual rpt, R3840–11
- Payment maximum monthly amount, by family size, for 14 States, 1991, U8850–8.5
- Payments and recipients for selected Federal entitlement programs, by State and region, early 1990s, R8490–47
- Recipients as percent of population, payments, and error rates, by State, FY92 annual rpt, S2623–1.2
- State changes in AFDC benefits, with impact on purchasing power, by State, Jan 1992-93, annual rpt, R3834–9
- State govt expenditures for AFDC and other functions, by State, FY92-93, annual rpt, A7470–4.10
- State govt expenditures for AFDC, by fund source and State, FY90-92, annual rpt, A7118–1
- State social, economic, and govtl indicators, with rankings, 1993 semiannual rpt, B8500–1.8
- Statistical profiles of 50 States and DC, general data, 1993 annual almanac, C4712–1

State and local:

- Alabama public welfare and social service cases, recipients, and payments, by program and county, monthly rpt, S0150–1
- Alaska AFDC caseloads and expenditures by region and municipality, and client self-sufficiency project survey data, 1993 article, S0320–1.503
- Arizona public assistance recipients and payments, by program, county, and district, monthly rpt, S0465–4
- Arkansas human services dept finances and operations, including Medicaid payments by type of service, FY91 and trends, annual rpt, S0700–2.3
- California public welfare cases, recipients, and expenditures, by program and county, monthly rpt, S0935–2
- Colorado welfare and social services expenditures and caseloads, by county and/or program, FY91, annual rpt, S1085–1
- DC statistical profile, general data, 1992 annual rpt, S1535–3.5
- Delaware public assistance recipients, funds available, and payments, by program, with selected data by county, monthly rpt, S1385–1
- Florida AFDC cases and payments, by district and county, FY92, annual rpt, S1717–1
- Georgia county guide, general data, 1993 annual rpt, U6750–1
- Hawaii data book, general data, 1992 annual rpt, S2090–1.11
- Idaho public welfare program expenditures and recipients, with data by county, quarterly rpt, S2250–1
- Illinois public assistance program cases, recipients, and payments, by program and county, FY91-92 and trends, annual rpt, S2520–2
- Indiana public assistance program participation, expenditures, and services, by county, FY92 and trends, annual rpt, S2623–1
- Iowa ADC and SSI program recipients, and expenditures, by county, monthly rpt, S2802–1
- Kentucky AFDC and SSI recipients and payments, by county, monthly rpt, S3140–2
- Kentucky Medicaid recipients and payments, by program, county, and type of medical service, monthly rpt, S3140–5
- Louisiana labor market info, including population receiving AFDC and food stamps, by area, 1992, annual planning rpt, S3320–1.2
- Maryland medical assistance payments and recipients, by program, type of service, location, demographic characteristics, and facility, FY92 and trends, annual rpt, S3635–3
- Maryland welfare program statistics, and welfare fraud investigations, by county, monthly rpt, S3645–2
- Michigan public assistance program cases, recipients, and payments, detailed data by county, monthly rpt, S4010–1
- Minnesota AFDC students as percent of enrollment, 1977/78-1991/92, annual rpt, S4165–1
- Minnesota public welfare program recipients and expenditures, by county, 1992, semiannual rpt, S4202–1
- Mississippi public welfare and social service cases, recipients, and payments, by program and county, FY92, annual rpt, S4357–1
- Missouri public welfare and medical assistance recipients, expenditures, and case processing, by program and county, FY92 and trends, annual rpt, S4575–2
- Montana welfare and medical assistance program cases and payments, by county and type of service, monthly rpt, S4755–1
- Nebraska public welfare cases, recipients, and payments, by program and county, FY92 and trends, annual rpt, S4957–1
- Nevada statistical abstract, general data, 1992 biennial rpt, S5005–1.2
- New Jersey public welfare cases, recipients, payments, and case processing, by program and county or city, monthly rpt, S5415–1
- New Mexico public assistance cases, expenditures, and case processing, by program and county, monthly rpt, S5620–2
- New York State and NYC ADC cases, quarterly rpt, S5735–2
- New York State public assistance and social service program statistics, by State area and source of funds, 1991 and trends, annual rpt, S5800–2

Index by Subjects and Names

- North Carolina public welfare programs, cases, recipients, staff, and finances, by county, 1st half FY93, semiannual rpt, S5940–2
- Oklahoma public welfare program expenditures, recipients, and services, by program and county, FY92 and trends, annual rpt, S6455–1
- Oregon public welfare caseloads, recipients, and expenditures, by program, city, county, and State region, monthly rpt, S6615–8
- Pennsylvania labor force planning rpt, including data on populations with employability problems, FY92 annual rpt, S6845–3.3
- Pennsylvania statistical abstract, general data, 1992 recurring rpt, U4130–6.5
- South Carolina public welfare recipients, payments, and case processing, by county and program, monthly rpt, S7252–1
- South Dakota welfare and social services recipients and payments, by program, MSA, and county, FY92, annual rpt, S7385–1
- Tennessee AFDC need standard, by component and family size, Sept 1990 and 1992, article, U8710–1.501
- Tennessee statistical abstract, general data, 1992/93 annual rpt, U8710–2.18
- Texas welfare and social services program expenditures, recipients, and fraud cases, by county and/or program, FY92 and trends, annual rpt, S7695–1
- Utah govt statistical review, fiscal and socioeconomic data, 1993 annual rpt, R9380–1.9
- Utah statistical abstract, general data, 1993 triennial rpt, U8960–1.6
- Washington State public assistance clients and service costs, by client characteristics, program, and county, FY90, annual rpt, S8420–2
- West Virginia welfare and social service program caseloads and expenditures, by county, monthly rpt, S8560–2
- Wisconsin Blue Book, general data, 1993-94 biennial rpt, S8780–1.2
- Wyoming welfare and social service recipients and expenditures, by program and county, FY92, annual rpt, S8908–1

see also Work incentive programs

AIDS

see Acquired immune deficiency syndrome

Air bases

see Military bases, posts, and reservations

Air cargo

- Agricultural exports via air and vessel, by country of destination and detailed commodity, 1991, annual rpt, B9520–1
- Airline cargo traffic, including revenues by carrier and top airports, 1992 and trends, annual rpt, A0325–5
- Airline industry devs including passenger and cargo traffic activity and fuel costs, with worldwide passenger traffic, by carrier, monthly rpt, C7000–4
- Airline mail and freight revenue ton-miles on scheduled domestic and intl flights, monthly press release, A0325–2
- Airline market activity, including traffic, financial performance, employment, and fleet composition, by US and foreign carrier, 1991-92, annual feature, C7000–4.508

Index by Subjects and Names

Air pollution

Airline traffic and financial operations, worldwide and US, 1960s-91, annual rpt, A0250–2.3

China air cargo volume, 1981-91, article, A9315–1.504

Financial performance and growth rankings for approx 1,000 top corporations, with comparisons by industry group, 1993 annual rpt, C3950–1.505

Freight carrier quality ratings by shippers, by mode and company, 1993 annual survey article, C2150–1.507

Freighter aircraft (jet) world inventory, by model and owner/operator category, 1992, annual rpt, B1582–1

Industry devs in air transport, space technology, engineering, business flying, avionics, and military aviation, weekly rpt, C5800–4

Latin America statistical abstract, general data by country, 1992 annual rpt, U6250–1.3

Logistics trends and devs, including data on costs, finances of major carriers by mode, and foreign trade, 1993 annual compilation, C2150–1.506

Mexico-Texas transportation system analysis, including bilateral trade, operations by transport mode, and data by locale, 1993 rpt, U8850–9

Regional aircraft fleets for passenger and all cargo operations, by manufacturer and type, and top models in use, 1992, annual rpt, A8795–1.1

Trends in transportation operations and finances, by mode, 1991 annual rpt, R4815–1

World airline finances and traffic, by carrier, 1993 annual feature, C7000–4.511

State and local:

Alaska air carrier landings, passengers, and freight, FY83-92, annual rpt, S0275–1

California statistical abstract, general data, 1992 annual rpt, S0840–2.11

Florida statistical abstract, general data, 1992 annual rpt, U6660–1.13

Hawaii data book, general data, 1992 annual rpt, S2090–1.18, S2090–1.24

Maryland, Baltimore-Washington Intl Airport traffic and operations by type, 1990-91, biennial rpt, S3605–1.10

New York State business activity indicators, quarterly rpt, S5735–2

Oklahoma City and Tulsa air passengers and freight, monthly rpt quarterly data, U8130–1

Oklahoma statistical abstract, general data, 1992 annual rpt, U8130–2.16

Tennessee statistical abstract, general data, 1992/93 annual rpt, U8710–2.9

Utah, Salt Lake City Intl Airport air traffic, passengers, and cargo, 1950-92, annual rpt, R9380–1.10

Utah statistical abstract, general data, 1993 triennial rpt, U8960–1.13

Wisconsin Blue Book, general data, 1993-94 biennial rpt, S8780–1.2

Air conditioning

Consumer expectations of economic conditions and change in income, and intended durable goods purchases by type, Conference Board monthly survey, R4105–4

Fuel oil dealer heating and cooling equipment sales, installations, and service, by region, 1992 annual survey, C4680–2.2

Household appliance industry manufacturing and market trends, by product type, various years 1920-94, biennial rpt, A3350–3

Life expectancy, shipments, and manufacturers market shares, for appliances by type, 1993 annual article, C2000–1.510

Sales by distributors of home appliances, by product type and State, 1992, annual rpt, A3350–2

Shipments (factory) of room air conditioners, 1992 and trends, annual rpt, A3350–4

Shipments of air conditioners/heat pumps, by size, monthly press release, A0300–1

Shipments of heating/cooling equipment, by product type, with industry review and outlook, 1992 and trends, annual rpt, C1800–1

Shipments of household appliances, by detailed product type, 1991-98, annual articles, C2000–1.503

Shipments of household appliances, by product type, with articles and special features on industry trends and devs, monthly rpt, C2000–1

Shipments of major home appliances, by type, monthly press release, A3350–1

see also Cold storage and refrigeration

Air Force

Physicians in Fed Govt, by detailed specialty and service branch, 1992, annual rpt, A2200–3.2

Post exchange and commissary sales, by product category and region, and employment, for military resale agencies, FY91 and trends, annual rpt, A2072–1

Post exchange sales, by service branch, with merchandising devs and comparisons to civilian retail trade, monthly rpt, C0500–1

Post exchange sales, retail and other, by location and store, FY92 and trends, annual rpt, A2072–2.502

see also Department of Air Force

see also National Guard

Air Force contracts and procurement

see Defense contracts and procurement

Air National Guard

see National Guard

Air navigation

see Aeronautical navigation

Air pollution

Auto fleet operating characteristics in metro areas affected by Clean Air Act clean fuel requirements, 1993 article, C1575–2.512

Auto pre-1980 model scrapping plan cost-benefit analysis, with emissions reduction and benefits, 1993 annual rpt, C6985–3.2

Chemical odor thresholds for 27 compounds, and ratings of selected odor control methods, 1993 article, C5800–8.513

Chemical use reduction and phaseout schedule under intl ozone protection treaty, for 6 ozone-harming substances, 1992 article, A1250–1.506

City govt costs to enforce Fed Govt regulations including Clean Air Act, FY93-98, A9330–12

Coal-fired boilers sulfur dioxide and nitrous oxide emission limits, for 16 countries, 1992 annual rpt, A7400–2.2

EC refinery emissions and regulation outlook, with fuel oil supply-demand data, 1990s-2010, article, C6985–1.538

Electric power (steam) plant scrubber systems to reduce sulfur, capacity by plant, 1992 annual rpt, A7400–7

Electric power plant sulfur dioxide emissions reduction methods, 1993 articles, C6985–6.510

Emission levels, by commuter transport mode, 1992 annual rpt, A2650–1.2

Emissions of pollutants in 1987 and 1991, for 4 companies with highest emissions in 1987, article, C5800–7.530

Emissions of selected pollutants by source, with detail for chemical industry, 1970 and 1980-92, annual rpt, A3850–1

Emissions of 6 pollutants, by source, selected years 1970-91, annual rpt, A8375–2.4

Emissions reduction targets for year 2000 proposed by Clinton Admin for greenhouse gases, by type and/or source, 1993 article, A1250–1.544

Energy consumption societal impacts and Govt fiscal policy issues, with related data on costs and emissions, 1993 rpt, A2575–28

Europe air pollutant emissions, by substance and country, 1992/93 biennial rpt, R9455–1.1

Fuel cell technology use potential impact on energy use and nitrogen oxide emissions, 1992 article, C5226–2.501

Industrial emission-control equipment market shares for top 10 and all other manufacturers, 1991, article, A4700–4.501

Korea (South) air pollutant emission standards for selected substances, 1994-99/beyond, article, C5800–8.510

Oil industry environmental performance, with data on toxic chemical releases, oil spills, occupational injury/illness, and corporate spending, 1990 and trends, annual rpt, A2575–27

Oil refining capacity that could be lost due to clean air legislation, by PAD district, 1992 article, C6985–1.509

Paint industry architectural and maintenance coatings proposed volatile organic compound content limits, 1993 article, A1250–1.543

Pulp and paper industry capital spending plans of US and Canadian companies, by purpose and geographic area, 1992-94, annual survey article, C3975–2.503

Railroad vs truck emissions of hydrocarbons and nitrogen oxides, 1993 article, C8400–1.509

Sources of selected air pollutants, including vehicles, stationary fuel combustion, and industrial processes, 1991, annual rpt, A0865–1.3

Southeastern cities failing to meet natl ozone standards, with number of days exceeding standards, 1988-90, annual rpt, U8710–2.12

State economic dev condition indicators, including economic performance, business vitality, growth capacity, and tax/fiscal system, by State, 1993 annual rpt, R4225–1.1

State social, economic, and govtl indicators, with rankings, 1993 semiannual rpt, B8500–1.15

Air pollution

Sulfur dioxide emission allowance bids and purchases at EPA auction, by electric utility, 1993 article, C5800-28.508

Sulfur dioxide emission allowance bids and sales at EPA auction, distribution by buyer category, 1993 article, A1250-1.519

Sulfur dioxide emission allowance sales at EPA auction, with cumulative allowances and amount and number of bids by company, Mar 1993, article, C6985-6.507

Sulfur dioxide emission allowance trading program, State regulatory issues and related data by State and major utility, 1992 rpt, A8195-12

World air pollution and atmospheric devs, with data on pollutants, by region and country, 1992/93 biennial rpt, R9455-1.4, R9455-1.7

World energy supply-demand, and carbon dioxide emissions, under 3 emission restriction scenarios, 1990s-2010, article, C6985-1.534

State and local:

California, Los Angeles area oil refinery emissions allocations, by company, 1994, 2000, and 2003, article, C6985-1.552

Florida statistical abstract, general data, 1992 annual rpt, U6660-1.8

Hawaii data book, general data, 1992 annual rpt, S2090-1.5

Hawaii environmental quality and public health control, inspection, licensing, and enforcement activities, 1990, annual rpt, S2065-1.6

New York State statistical yearbook, general data, 1992 annual rpt, U5100-1.15

Pennsylvania statistical abstract, general data, 1992 recurring rpt, U4130-6.8

see also Global climate change

see also Motor vehicle exhaust

see also Radiation

see also Radon

Air safety

see Aviation accidents and safety

Air traffic control

FAA air route facilities and services, and aviation certificates held by type, 1993 annual rpt, A5120-2

North Central States airport operations and air traffic control activities, for 8 States, 1989, annual rpt, U6910-2

Operations at top 20 FAA-operated airport traffic control towers, 1989, recurring rpt, R9375-6

see also Aviation accidents and safety

Air transportation

see Airlines

see Airports and airways

see Military aviation

Air travel

Airline commissions to travel agents, and passenger revenues, by US and foreign carrier, 1st half 1993 and trends, annual article, C7000-4.511

Airline industry devs including passenger and cargo traffic activity and fuel costs, with worldwide passenger traffic, by carrier, monthly rpt, C7000-4

Airline market activity, including traffic, financial performance, employment, and fleet composition, by US and foreign carrier, 1991-92, annual feature, C7000-4.508

Airline traffic and financial operations, worldwide and US, 1960s-91, annual rpt, A0250-2.3

Airline traffic, including passengers by carrier and top airports, 1992 and trends, annual rpt, A0325-5

Airline travel frequency, destination, and purpose, by traveler characteristics, 1992 survey and trends, annual rpt, A0325-6

Business executives ratings of ports, highways, and intl air service, with daily number of intl flights, for top 6-8 cities, 1993 article, C2150-1.504

Business traveler and trip characteristics, including purpose, and lodging, 1991, annual rpt, R9375-12

China airline passenger traffic, 1981-91, article, A9315-1.504

Cities rated as best for business by Fortune magazine, socioeconomic profiles including daily intl flights, 1992 annual article, C8900-1.501

Commuter air traffic, by carrier, monthly rpt, C7000-4

Industry devs in air transport, space technology, engineering, business flying, avionics, and military aviation, weekly rpt, C5800-4

Latin America statistical abstract, general data by country, 1992 annual rpt, U6250-1.3

Passenger traffic by transport mode, monthly rpt, R9375-1

Passenger traffic, seat miles, and load factors, for scheduled airline domestic and intl flights, monthly press release, A0325-1

Passengers boarded, and voluntary and involuntary denied boardings, by carrier, monthly rpt quarterly table, C7000-4.502, C7000-4.506

Rankings for selected travel and tourism indicators, including data for top 20 States, cities, countries, businesses, and other measures, 1992 recurring rpt, R9375-6

Regional airline passenger traffic, and top 50 companies and carriers, 1992 and trends, annual rpt, A8795-1.1

Sales industry costs, including compensation, training, and travel and related expenses, with data by metro area, 1992 and trends, annual survey, C1200-1.508

Travel trips and traveler characteristics, including mode, purpose, type of lodging, and area of destination and origin, quarterly rpt, R9375-14

Trends in transportation operations and finances, by mode, 1991 annual rpt, R4815-1

Vacation plans of consumers in US and abroad within 6 months, and travel mode, monthly rpt bimonthly table, R4105-4

World airline finances and traffic, by carrier, 1993 annual feature, C7000-4.511

World passenger jet requirements projected to 2011, by aircraft class and world region, with traffic trends and outlook, 1993 annual rpt, B3075-1

World travel and tourism trends, with traveler and trip characteristics, industry devs, and detail by country and US location, 1992 annual rpt, C2140-1

Index by Subjects and Names

State and local:

Alabama statistical abstract, general data, 1992 recurring rpt, U5680-2.16

Alaska air carrier landings, passengers, and freight, FY83-92, annual rpt, S0275-1

Arizona, Phoenix and Tucson air travel and bus ridership, 1985-93, semiannual rpt, U5850-1.2

Arizona statistical abstract, general data, 1993 recurring rpt, U5850-2.8

Florida statistical abstract, general data, 1992 annual rpt, U6660-1.13, U6660-1.19

Hawaii data book, general data, 1992 annual rpt, S2090-1.18

Illinois air passenger enplanements, by airport, 1986-90, annual rpt, U6910-2

Maryland, Baltimore-Washington Intl Airport traffic and operations by type, 1990-91, biennial rpt, S3605-1.10

Nevada passenger traffic at 2 major airports, 1980-91, annual rpt, U7920-2

Nevada statistical abstract, general data, 1992 biennial rpt, S5005-1.13

New Mexico, Albuquerque airport passenger traffic, monthly business activity rpt, U7980-1

New York State business activity indicators, quarterly rpt, S5735-2

New York State statistical yearbook, general data, 1992 annual rpt, U5100-1.13

Oklahoma City and Tulsa air passengers and freight, monthly rpt quarterly data, U8130-1

Oklahoma statistical abstract, general data, 1992 annual rpt, U8130-2.16

South Carolina statistical abstract, general data, 1993 annual rpt, S7125-1.14

Tennessee statistical abstract, general data, 1992/93 annual rpt, U8710-2.9

Utah economic and business activity review and indicators, monthly rpt, U8960-2

Utah, Salt Lake City Intl Airport air traffic, passengers, and cargo, 1950-92, annual rpt, R9380-1.10

Utah statistical abstract, general data, 1993 triennial rpt, U8960-1.13, U8960-1.17

Wisconsin Blue Book, general data, 1993-94 biennial rpt, S8780-1.2

Aircraft

Airline fleet average age, for 10 major carriers, 1993 article, C8900-1.507

Airline fleet composition and aircraft on order, by model and carrier, 1992, annual article, C7000-4.508

Airline fleet size, and flight and engine hours, by type of aircraft, Mar 1993, C5800-30.507

Airline fleet units owned, leased, and on order, by model, July 1993, and planned changes for 2nd half 1993, article, C5800-4.530

Airlines, top 19 in US/Canada ranked by number of planes, 1990, recurring rpt, R9375-6

Commonwealth of Independent States Soviet-built aircraft in airline service, by model, Dec 1992, article, C7000-4.509

Commuter aircraft market size and potential growth, 1993-2012, article, C5800-4.517

Financial ratios and performance, for over 350 SIC 4-digit industries, FY88-92, annual rpt, A6400-3

Fleet size outlook for airlines, commuter/regional carriers, and general aviation, FY93-94 and FY2004, article, C5800-4.511

Index by Subjects and Names

Airlines

Flight equipment disruptions caused by electromagnetic interference from passenger electronic devices, 1986-92, article, C5800–4.512

General aviation aircraft active, by FAA region and State, and shipments by aircraft type, 1993 annual rpt, A5120–2

General aviation aircraft shipments and net billings, by manufacturer and/or model, quarterly rpt, A5120–1

Jet aircraft order cancellations and deferrals by airline, and aircraft in storage by model, 1992 article, C7000–4.502

Jet aircraft orders from 5-6 manufacturers worldwide, by model, monthly rpt quarterly feature, C7000–4.502, C7000–4.505

Jet aircraft worldwide inventory, orders, and deliveries, by type of aircraft, region, and individual owner/operator, 1992 and trends, annual rpt, B1582–1

Orders, and fleet composition by carrier, by model, Dec 1992, annual rpt, A0325–5

Piston aircraft US and foreign manufacturers, 1980, 1986, and 1992, article, C5800–4.508

Production of civil and military aircraft, R&D, trade, employment, and finances, with Federal funding data, 1991 and trends, annual rpt, A0250–2

Regional aircraft fleets, by carrier and manufacturer, and top models in use, 1992, annual rpt, A8795–1

Regional airlines aircraft deliveries, by plane size, 1991-2010, article, C7000–4.502

Shipments of business/personal aircraft, by model, for approx 20 manufacturers, weekly rpt quarterly table, C5800–30.503, C5800–30.505, C5800–30.509

Shipments of construction/mining/farm equipment, non-electrical machinery, and aircraft/parts, quarterly 1991-94, article, C1850–4.504

Traffic and financial forecasts, and fleet acquisition and disposal plans, by US and foreign carrier, 1993 annual article, C7000–4.503

Turbine-powered aircraft in service and on order, by manufacturer and model, for over 900 airlines worldwide, Dec 1992, annual rpt, B3370–1

World airline fleet, 1992, and aircraft on order for 1993 and beyond, article, C7000–4.511

World passenger jet acquisitions, by world area, 1992-2011, article, C5800–4.507

World passenger jet requirements projected to 2011, by aircraft class and world region, with traffic trends and outlook, 1993 annual rpt, B3075–1

State and local:

Arizona statistical abstract, general data, 1993 recurring rpt, U5850–2.18

Hawaii data book, general data, 1992 annual rpt, S2090–1.18

Montana property values, by detailed property class and type, with land acreage by use, by county, 1991-92 and trends, biennial rpt, S4750–1.2

South Carolina aircraft operations by category, 1984-91, annual rpt, S7125–3.3

Tennessee statistical abstract, general data, 1992/93 annual rpt, U8710–2.9

Virginia aircraft sales/use tax revenues, FY83-92, annual rpt, S8305–1.2

Wyoming property assessed valuations and tax levies, by property type, tax purpose, and location, 1992 and trends, annual rpt, S8990–1.2

see also Aerospace industry

see also Aviation accidents and safety

see also Business aircraft and flying

see also Helicopters

see also Military aircraft

Aircraft accidents

see Aviation accidents and safety

Aircraft carriers

see Naval vessels

Aircraft insurance

see Insurance and insurance industry

Airlines

Advertising expenditures by medium for top 100 advertisers, with comparisons to earnings and sales, and detail by product type and brand, 1991-92, annual rpt, C2710–1.547

Aircraft average age, for 10 major airlines, 1993 article, C8900–1.507

Aircraft fleet size, and flight and engine hours, by aircraft type, Mar 1993, C5800–30.507

Cargo and total revenues, for leading carriers, 1992, annual article, C2150–1.506

Commuter air traffic, by carrier, monthly rpt, C7000–4

Europe airline revenues and govt ownership share, for 8 major carriers, 1992 article, C8900–1.501

Europe airline revenues and market shares, for 8 major carriers, 1991, article, C5800–4.512

Finances and operations of scheduled air carriers, summary statistics, 1992 and trends, annual rpt, A0325–5

Financial performance and growth rankings for approx 1,000 top corporations, with comparisons by industry group, 1993 annual rpt, C3950–1.505

Financial performance of aerospace and defense industries, with data for approx 200 major US and foreign companies, FY92 and trends, annual feature, C5800–4.519

Financial performance of airlines, by carrier, monthly rpt quarterly table, C7000–4.501, C7000–4.504, C7000–4.508, C7000–4.509

Financial ratios and performance, for over 350 SIC 4-digit industries, FY88-92, annual rpt, A6400–3

Food (inflight) expenditures, for 9 major carriers and all others, 1992, article, C1200–5.516

Food service expenditures, by carrier, 1st 9 months 1992 and trends, annual article, C7000–4.507

Food service industry sales trends and forecast, by market segment, 1990-93, annual feature, A8200–1.502

Freight and mail revenue ton-miles on scheduled intl and domestic flights, monthly press release, A0325–2

Hawaii-US mainland route market shares, for top 9 and all other airlines, 1990, article, B3500–1.502

Industry devs in air transport, space technology, engineering, business flying, avionics, and military aviation, weekly rpt, C5800–4

Jet aircraft worldwide inventory, orders, and deliveries, by type of aircraft, region, and individual owner/operator, 1992 and trends, annual rpt, B1582–1

Jet fleet leased vs owned, and operating lease expenses, by major carrier, 1993 annual article, C7000–4.508

Maintenance budget, employment, and contracting trends, for 38 carriers worldwide, 1992 article, C7000–4.501

Market activity including traffic, financial performance, fleet composition, and employment, by US and foreign carrier, 1991-92, annual feature, C7000–4.508

Mexico-Texas transportation system analysis, including bilateral trade, operations by transport mode, and data by locale, 1993 rpt, U8850–9

Operating and financial composite ratios for corporations, with establishments and receipts, for approx 200 industries, by asset size, FY90, annual rpt, C7800–1

Operating devs, including passenger and freight traffic, finances, on-time performance, and consumer complaints, by carrier, monthly rpt, C7000–4

Passenger traffic and operating data for world and US scheduled airlines, 1970s-91, annual rpt, C2140–1.5

Rankings for selected travel and tourism indicators, including data for top 20 States, cities, countries, businesses, and other measures, 1992 recurring rpt, R9375–6

Regional airline traffic, aircraft, subsidy payments, and services, by carrier and location, 1992 and trends, annual rpt, A8795–1

Revenues and earnings or losses, for 10 largest airlines, 1992, article, C8900–1.517

Revenues, profits, and passenger traffic, for top 50 airlines worldwide, 1991, article, C8900–1.501

Service to daily newspaper markets in US and Canada, by mode and company, 1993 annual rpt, C3250–1

Traffic and financial forecasts, and fleet acquisition and disposal plans, by US and foreign carrier, 1993 annual article, C7000–4.503

Traffic and financial operations, worldwide and US airlines, 1960s-91, annual rpt, A0250–2.3

Travel agent commissions paid by airlines, and passenger revenues, by US and foreign carrier, 1st half 1993 and trends, annual article, C7000–4.511

Trends in transportation operations and finances, by mode, 1991 annual rpt, R4815–1

Turbine-powered aircraft in service and on order, by manufacturer and model, for over 900 airlines worldwide, Dec 1992, annual rpt, B3370–1

World airline finances and traffic, by carrier, 1993 annual feature, C7000–4.511

World passenger jet requirements projected to 2011, by aircraft class and world region, with traffic trends and outlook, 1993 annual rpt, B3075–1

State and local:

Colorado property assessed valuation, by property type and county, and for regulated industries by company, 1991-92, annual rpt, S1055–3

Airlines

Hawaii data book, general data, 1992 annual rpt, S2090–1.18

Idaho economic profile, general data, 1992 recurring rpt, S2218–2.8

Montana public utility and transportation property assessments, by county and company, 1991-92, biennial rpt, S4750–1.2

New York State statistical yearbook, general data, 1992 annual rpt, U5100–1.13

North Carolina employment in trade, transportation, communications, utilities, govt, and education, by detailed occupation, 2nd qtr 1991, triennial rpt, S5917–5.2

Texas trade, transportation, and public utilities employment, by SIC 2- and 3-digit industry and detailed occupation, 2nd qtr 1991, triennial survey rpt, S7675–1.31

Washington State public service and utility companies property value, by company and county, 1992, annual rpt, S8415–1.4

Wyoming property assessed valuations and tax levies, by property type, tax purpose, and location, 1992 and trends, annual rpt, S8990–1.2

see also Aerospace industry

see also Air travel

see also Airports and airways

see also Aviation accidents and safety

see also Pilots

see also under By Industry in the "Index by Categories"

Airport Improvement Program

Federal budget trends, including spending by program, State, and region, FY81-94, annual rpt, R8490–11

State and local:

Tennessee statistical abstract, general data, 1992/93 annual rpt, U8710–2.9

Airports and airways

Cargo tons enplaned/deplaned at top 20 airports, 1992, annual article, C2150–1.506

Civil and military joint-use airports and heliports, by State, 1991, annual rpt, A0250–2.3

Civil and military joint-use landing facilities, by FAA region and State, Dec 1992, annual rpt, A5120–2.3

Construction contract awards by type of project, weekly rpt, C5800–2

Costs vs charges to airlines, by airport size category, 1992, article, C5800–4.530

EC total and business passengers, and flights and fares by airline, for 15 busiest cross-border routes, 1993 article, C7000–4.503

Financial ratios and performance, for over 350 SIC 4-digit industries, FY88-92, annual rpt, A6400–3

Financing sources used by airports worldwide, and US airport spending trends for facilities and Federal program compliance, 1993 article, C5800–4.514

Helicopters in civil aviation, production, trade, utilization, accidents, and landing facilities, 1993 annual rpt, A5190–1

Lodging industry facilities, sales, and occupancy, with top 42-100 properties in 5 market categories, 1993 annual rpt, C7000–5

Mexico-Texas transportation system analysis, including bilateral trade, operations by transport mode, and data by locale, 1993 rpt, U8850–9

Passenger and freight traffic, top 20 airports and top 30 routes, 1992, annual rpt, A0325–5

Passenger facility construction charges to airlines pending and approved by FAA, for hub airports by size class, 1993 article, C5800–4.505

Passenger traffic and aircraft movements at top 30 airports worldwide, 1991, C7000–4.501

Passenger traffic at top 32 airports worldwide, 1992, C7000–4.508

Passenger traffic at top 50 airports worldwide and for top 30 US routes, 1990 or 1991, annual rpt, C2140–1.5

Regional airline service in North America, by carrier and location, with top 50 airports, 1993 annual rpt, A8795–1.2

Regional and other daily flight departures for 10 airports with most regional flights, 1993 article, C5800–4.517

Runway incursions at 15 major airports, year ended June 1992-93, article, C5800–4.526

Sales industry costs, including compensation, training, and travel and related expenses, with data by metro area, 1992 and trends, annual survey, C1200–1.508

State and local:

Alabama county data book, general data, 1992 annual rpt, S0121–2

Alabama statistical abstract, general data, 1992 recurring rpt, U5680–2.16

Arizona statistical abstract, general data, 1993 recurring rpt, U5850–2.18

Florida statistical abstract, general data, 1992 annual rpt, U6660–1.13

Georgia statistical abstract, general data, 1992-93 biennial rpt, U6730–1.8

Hawaii data book, general data, 1992 annual rpt, S2090–1.18

Illinois air passenger enplanements, by airport, 1986-90, annual rpt, U6910–2

Maine statistical summary, general economic and social data, 1992 recurring rpt, S3434–1

Maryland statistical abstract, general data, 1993-94 biennial rpt, S3605–1.10

Mississippi statistical abstract, general data, 1992 annual rpt, U3255–4.6

New York State statistical yearbook, general data, 1992 annual rpt, U5100–1.13

Oklahoma statistical abstract, general data, 1992 annual rpt, U8130–2.16

Tennessee statistical abstract, general data, 1992/93 annual rpt, U8710–2.9

Utah, Salt Lake City Intl Airport air traffic, passengers, and cargo, 1950-92, annual rpt, R9380–1.10

Utah, Salt Lake City Intl Airport traffic, 1993 triennial rpt, U8960–1.13, U8960–1.17

Wisconsin Blue Book, general data, 1993-94 biennial rpt, S8780–1.2

see also Air traffic control

see also Airport Improvement Program

see also Aviation accidents and safety

Ajman

see United Arab Emirates

Akioka, Lorena M.

"Georgia Statistical Abstract, 1992-93", U6730–1

Index by Subjects and Names

Alabama

Agricultural production, marketing, and income, by county and/or commodity, and farms and acreage, 1992 and trends, annual rpt, S0090–1

Business activity indicators for Alabama, monthly rpt, U5680–1

County data book, general economic, social, and govtl data, 1992 annual rpt, S0121–2

Court caseloads and dispositions, by type of court and case, and location, with judicial system finances, FY92 and trends, annual rpt, S0118–1

Crimes and arrests, by offense, location, and offender characteristics, with data on law enforcement employment and assaults on officers, 1992 and trends, annual rpt, S0119–1

Economic trends and outlook, 1980s-93, annual rpt, U5680–3

Election results, by district and/or county, 1992 general election, biennial rpt, S0205–1

Elementary and secondary school enrollment, staff, pupil transportation, and finances, by district, 1991/92, annual rpt, S0124–1

Financial instns (State-chartered) financial condition, with deposits and assets by instn, FY92 annual rpt, S0110–1

Govt financial condition, including revenues by source, expenditures by function and object, and fund balances, by fund and agency, FY92, annual rpt, S0129–1

Health behavior risk factor surveillance survey results, by respondent characteristics, 1988-89, recurring rpt, S0175–6

Health dept activities, including services provided, inspection and licensing activity, staff and finances, and vital statistics and health data, 1992 annual rpt, S0175–3

Insurance industry financial and underwriting data, by company and line of coverage, 1991, annual rpt, S0160–1

Library finances, holdings, circulation, staff, and population served, by public library, FY92, annual rpt, S0180–1

Markets with daily newspapers, demographic and economic info by geographic area, US and Canada, 1993 annual rpt, C3250–1

Municipal data book, general demographic and socioeconomic data by municipality, 1992 recurring rpt, S0121–5

Oil/gas industry production, finances, exploration, and reserves, by State, 1992 and trends, annual rpt, A5425–1.1

Population size and characteristics, series, U0340–1

Statistical abstract of Alabama, detailed economic and demographic trends, 1992 recurring rpt, U5680–2

Statistical profiles of 50 States and DC, general data, 1993 annual almanac, C4712–1

Traffic accidents, fatalities, and injuries, by circumstances, vehicle type, and driver and victim characteristics, 1992, annual rpt, S0185–1

Utility and transportation regulatory agency activities, scope of jurisdiction, finances, and employees, by agency, 1991/92 annual rpt, A7015–2

Index by Subjects and Names

Alcohol abuse and treatment

Vital statistics, including population, births, deaths by cause, marriages, and divorces, by location and demographic characteristics, 1992 and trends, annual rpt, S0175–2

Welfare and social service cases, recipients, and payments, by program and county, monthly rpt, S0150–1

see also Birmingham, Ala.

see also Mobile, Ala.

see also under By City and By County in the "Index by Categories"

see also under By State in the "Index by Categories"

Alaska

- AFDC caseloads and expenditures by region and municipality, and client self-sufficiency project survey data, 1993 article, S0320–1.503
- Agricultural production and marketing, by district and commodity, 1960s-92, annual rpt, U5750–1
- Bank assets and liabilities of individual commercial and savings instns, quarterly rpt, S0280–2
- Corrections system admin, including inmate and probationer/parolee offenses and demographic characteristics, 1991 annual rpt, S0287–1
- Court cases and dispositions, by type of court and case, and location, with judicial dept finances and personnel, FY92 and trends, annual rpt, S0290–1
- Election results, and voter registration and turnout, by district and precinct, 1992 general election, biennial rpt, S0337–1
- Elementary and secondary school enrollment, staff, and finances, by school district, FY92, annual rpt, S0295–2
- Employment and unemployment, hours, and earnings, by area and/or industry, monthly rpt, S0320–1
- Fishing (crab) industry fatalities and lost vessels, with detail for selected incidents, 1992/93, article, C8900–1.516
- Fishing industry occupational deaths, by decedent characteristics, 1980-88, article, A2623–1.507
- Govt financial condition, including revenues by source, expenditures by function, fund balances, and bond obligations, FY92 and trends, annual rpt, S0275–1
- Insurance industry underwriting and investment data, by company and type of insurance, with regulatory info, 1991 and trends, annual rpt, S0280–3
- Markets with daily newspapers, demographic and economic info by geographic area, US and Canada, 1993 annual rpt, C3250–1
- Natural gas potential reserve estimates in 7 regions, Dec 1992 and trends, biennial rpt, R8765–1
- Oil and gas industry expenditures for exploration, dev, and production, contiguous US and Alaska, 1991, annual survey rpt, A2575–20
- Oil and gas supply trends and outlook under 4 economic scenarios, for onshore and offshore areas and Alaska, 1960s-2010, A2575–25
- Oil/gas industry production, finances, exploration, and reserves, by State, 1992 and trends, annual rpt, A5425–1.1

Population, housing, income, and education data, by demographic characteristics and/or locality, 1990/91 and trends, annual rpt, S0320–4

Statistical profiles of 50 States and DC, general data, 1993 annual almanac, C4712–1

Taxes by type, property values, public debt, and tax shelters, by locale, 1992 and trends, annual rpt, S0285–1

Traffic accidents, fatalities, and injuries, by vehicle type, circumstances, location, and driver and victim characteristics, 1991 and trends, annual rpt, S0360–1

Utilities financial and operating data, by utility type and company, 1991 and trends, with FY92 regulatory info, annual rpt, S0280–4

Utility and transportation regulatory agency activities, scope of jurisdiction, finances, and employees, by agency, 1991/92 annual rpt, A7015–2

Vital statistics including births, deaths by cause, marriages, divorces, adoptions, and population, by demographic characteristics and location, 1990, annual rpt, S0315–1

see also Anchorage, Alaska

see also Denali Borough, Alaska

see also Fairbanks, Alaska

see also Juneau, Alaska

see also Ketchikan, Alaska

see also Northwest Arctic Borough, Alaska

see also under By City and By County in the "Index by Categories"

see also under By State in the "Index by Categories"

Alaska Natives

see Indians

Albania

Energy intl sourcebook, with detail on oil and gas industry operations, supply-demand, and prices, for approx 80 countries, 1970s-91, annual compilation, C6985–10.2

Albert, Katherine M.

"Changing West: Corrections", A4375–13

Albuquerque, N.Mex.

- Business and economic activity indicators for New Mexico, monthly rpt, U7980–1
- Employment by industry, monthly rpt, S5624–2
- Labor force planning rpt, including employment by industry, 1992, annual rpt, S5624–1
- Tourism-related characteristics of Albuquerque, views of North Central States residents, spring 1993 survey, article, U7980–1.505

see also under By City in the "Index by Categories"

Alcohol abuse and treatment

- Catholic facilities for alcohol and drug treatment, with capacity, 1993 annual almanac, C6885–1
- Education level correlated with risk for alcohol abuse, by age group, 1980-85 studies, article, A2623–1.508
- Food marketers use of employee assistance programs, by region, 1991, annual rpt, A4950–5
- Funding by source, and client characteristics, for alcohol and drug abuse programs, by State, FY91 and trends, annual rpt, A7112–1

Higher education student use of and attitudes toward alcohol, drugs, and tobacco products, by sex and region, 1989-91 surveys, annual rpt, U4950–1

- Hospital patient admission rates and length of stay, by diagnosis and procedure, payment source, age, sex, and region, 1991, B4455–4
- Hospital patient charges and length of stay, by diagnosis and procedure, payment source, age, and region, 1991, B4455–5
- Hospital patient discharges and length of stay, by diagnosis, type of operation, age, and region, 1991, annual rpt series, B4455–1
- Hospital psychiatric patient discharges and length of stay, by diagnosis, age, sex, and region, 1991, annual rpt series, B4455–2
- Pedestrian intoxication safety and legal issues, views of traffic safety magazine readers, May/June 1993 survey, article, A8375–1.506
- Rape victim incidence of mental health, alcohol, and drug abuse problems compared to women who have never been crime victims, 1990-92 surveys, R8375–1
- Student use of and attitudes toward alcohol, drugs, and tobacco products, 1993 survey article, B6045–1.504
- Sweden, Stockholm deaths related to alcohol abuse, by sex and cause, 1987, article, A2623–1.508

State and local:

- Alabama juvenile and adult arrests, by type of offense, 1992, annual rpt, S0119–1.1
- Alabama statistical abstract, general data, 1992 recurring rpt, U5680–2.8
- Alabama vital statistics, including population, births, deaths by cause, marriages, and divorces, by location and demographic characteristics, 1992 and trends, annual rpt, S0175–2
- Alaska traffic accident pedestrian victim alcohol involvement, 1991, annual rpt, S0360–1
- Alaska vital statistics, including births, deaths by cause, marriages, divorces, adoptions, and population, by demographic characteristics and location, 1990, annual rpt, S0315–1
- Arizona arrests by offense, offender characteristics, and county, 1992, annual rpt, S0505–2.2
- Arkansas court caseloads and dispositions, by type of court and case, and location, FY92 and trends, annual rpt, S0647–1
- Arkansas crimes and arrests, by offense, victim and offender characteristics, and location, 1992 and trends, annual rpt, S0652–1
- Arkansas drug and alcohol treatment and prevention program expenditures, success rates, and client characteristics, FY91 annual rpt, S0700–2.1
- California correctional instn inmate alcohol use history, 1990, annual rpt, S0820–1
- California crimes and arrests, clearances, and arrest dispositions, with data by offense and offender characteristics, 1987-92, annual rpt, S0910–1.1
- California criminal justice system detailed data, by offense, county, age, race-ethnicity, and sex, 1991 and trends, annual rpt, S0910–2

Alcohol abuse and treatment

Index by Subjects and Names

California traffic accidents involving pedestrians, cyclists, and passengers under influence of alcohol, 1991 and trends, annual rpt, S0885–1

California vital statistics, including population, births, and deaths by cause, by demographic characteristics and county, 1990 and trends, annual rpt, S0865–1

Colorado court mental health case filings involving alcoholism, by district and county, FY92, annual rpt, S1035–1.2

Colorado crimes and arrests, by offense and location, with offender characteristics, and assaults on police, 1992, annual rpt, S1068–1

Connecticut arrests, by offense, offender characteristics, and local agency, 1992, annual rpt, S1256–1.2

Connecticut health behavior risk factor surveillance survey results, 1989-91, annual rpt, S1200–2

Connecticut traffic accident pedestrian victim alcohol involvement, 1992, annual rpt, S1275–1

Connecticut vital statistics, including births, deaths by cause, marriages, and divorces, by demographic characteristics and location, 1989, annual rpt, S1200–1

DC criminal justice system summary, including crimes and arrests, criminal procedure, prisoners, and parole, 1991 and trends, annual rpt, S1535–2

DC statistical profile, general data, 1992 annual rpt, S1535–3.5

Delaware vital statistics, including births, deaths by cause, and marriages and dissolutions, by demographic characteristics and location, 1990, annual rpt, S1385–2

Florida correctional system inmate alcohol use, by sex and race, FY92, annual rpt, S1720–1

Florida crimes and arrests, by offense, with data by victim and offender characteristics, 1992, annual rpt, S1770–1

Florida traffic accident pedestrian victim alcohol involvement, 1992, annual rpt, S1750–2

Florida vital statistics, including population, births, deaths by cause, and marriages and dissolutions, by location and demographic characteristics, 1992 and trends, annual rpt, S1745–3

Georgia alcohol/drug related deaths, by county, 1987-91, annual rpt, U6750–1

Georgia health behavior risk factor surveillance survey results, by respondent characteristics, 1991 and trends, annual rpt, S1895–2

Hawaii crimes and arrests, by offense, with data by county and victim-offender characteristics, 1992, annual rpt, S2035–1

Hawaii health behavior risk factor surveillance survey results, by respondent characteristics, 1990, annual rpt, S2065–1.4

Idaho arrests for liquor law violations, and offender alcohol use during commission of crimes, 1992, annual rpt, S2275–2

Idaho vital statistics, including births, deaths by cause, abortions, marriages, and divorces, by demographic characteristics and county, 1991 and trends, annual rpt, S2250–2

Illinois crimes and arrests, by offense, with data by location and offender characteristics, 1991, annual rpt, S2536–1

Illinois mental health facility patient population and characteristics, by facility, location, and treatment category, FY93, annual rpt, S2505–1

Iowa health behavior risk factor surveillance survey results, by respondent characteristics, 1991, annual rpt, S2795–2

Kansas court caseloads and disposition, by type of court and case, and location, FY92, annual rpt, S3035–1

Kansas crimes and arrests, by offense, with data by location, agency, and victim-offender characteristics, 1992 and trends, annual rpt, S2925–1.1

Kentucky arrests by county and offense, and law enforcement employment by agency, 1992, annual rpt, S3150–1.2

Kentucky health behavior risk factor surveillance survey results, by State area and respondent characteristics, 1988-90, annual rpt, S3140–6

Kentucky traffic accidents involving pedestrians under the influence of alcohol, 1992, annual rpt, S3150–2

Maine arrests of adults and juveniles, by offense, age, and sex, 1991, annual rpt, S3475–1.2

Maine vital statistics, including births, deaths by cause, abortions, and marriages and divorces, by demographic characteristics and location, 1991 and trends, annual rpt, S3460–2

Maryland crimes and arrests, by offense, location, and offender characteristics, with law enforcement employment and assaults on officers, 1992 and trends, annual rpt, S3665–1

Massachusetts correctional instn inmates by number of prior alcohol offenses, by instn, Jan 1992, annual rpt, S3805–1

Massachusetts health behavior risk factor surveillance survey results, by respondent characteristics, 1986-90, recurring rpt, S3850–3

Massachusetts vital statistics, including births, deaths by cause, marriages, divorces, and population, by locality and demographic characteristics, 1990 and trends, annual rpt, S3850–1

Michigan crimes and arrests, by offense, with data by location and offender characteristics, 1992 and trends, annual rpt, S3997–1

Michigan health behavior risk factor surveillance survey results, by respondent characteristics, 1991, annual rpt, S4000–4

Michigan traffic accident pedestrian victim alcohol involvement, 1991, annual rpt, S3997–2

Michigan vital statistics, including births, deaths, marriages, divorces/annulments, and communicable diseases, by location and demographic characteristics, 1990 and trends, annual rpt, S4000–3

Minnesota traffic accident fatalities involving pedestrians under the influence of alcohol, 1992 and trends, annual rpt, S4230–2

Mississippi alcohol abuse tax collections, with detail by county, FY92 and trends, annual rpt, S4435–1

Mississippi vital statistics, including births, deaths by cause, marriages, and divorces, by demographic characteristics and location, 1992 and trends, annual rpt, S4350–1

Missouri crimes and arrests, by offense and location, with victim and offender characteristics, 1991 and trends, annual rpt, S4560–2

Montana alcohol-related pedestrian and bicyclist traffic fatalities, 1992, annual rpt, S4705–2

Montana crimes and clearances, by offense and jurisdiction, 1992, annual rpt, S4705–1

Montana vital statistics, including births, deaths by cause, abortion, disease, and marriage and divorce, by demographic characteristics and county, 1990-91 and trends, annual rpt, S4690–1

Nebraska vital statistics, including births, deaths, marriages, divorces, and population, by demographic characteristics and location, 1991 and trends, annual rpt, S4885–1

Nevada health behavior risk factor surveillance survey results, by location and respondent characteristics, 1991, annual rpt, S5075–3

Nevada statistical abstract, general data, 1992 biennial rpt, S5005–1.4

New Hampshire arrests, by offense and offender age, sex, and race-ethnicity, 1991, annual rpt, S5250–2.2

New Jersey arrests for liquor law violations, and domestic violence offenses involving alcohol use, 1992, annual rpt, S5430–1

New Jersey traffic fatalities involving alcohol and drug use, including passengers and/or pedestrians, 1988-92, annual rpt, S5430–2

New Mexico vital statistics, including population, births, deaths, and disease, by location and demographic characteristics, 1991 and trends, annual rpt, S5605–1

New York State crimes and arrests by offense and demographic characteristics, and court activity and corrections, 1991 and trends, annual rpt, S5760–3

New York State health behavior risk factor surveillance survey results, by respondent characteristics, 1990, recurring rpt, S5765–3

New York State statistical yearbook, general data, 1992 annual rpt, U5100–1.11

New York State traffic accidents involving pedestrians under influence of alcohol and drugs, 1991, annual rpt, S5790–1

North Carolina alcohol use by pedestrians involved in traffic accidents, 1992, annual rpt, S5990–1

North Carolina deaths and rates, by cause and county, 1991 and trends, annual rpt, S5927–1.2

North Carolina liquor law arrests, and rape offenses with drug/alcohol influence, 1991-92, annual rpt, S5955–1

North Dakota crimes and arrests, by offense, location, and offender characteristics, and law enforcement employment, 1991 and trends, annual rpt, S6060–1

Index by Subjects and Names

Alcohol use

North Dakota health behavior risk factor surveillance survey results, by respondent characteristics, 1991 and trends, annual rpt, S6105–3

Oklahoma crimes and arrests, by offense, with victim and offender characteristics, 1990-92, annual rpt, S6465–1.1

Oklahoma traffic accident victim alcohol involvement, 1992, annual rpt, S6482–1

Oregon crimes and arrests, by offense, with data by county, local agency, and offender characteristics, 1992 and trends, annual rpt, S6603–3

Oregon vital statistics, including deaths by cause and alcohol use during pregnancy, 1991 and trends, annual rpt, S6615–5

Pennsylvania crimes and arrests, by offense, with data by location and offender characteristics, 1992 and trends, annual rpt, S6860–1

Pennsylvania traffic accidents involving pedestrians under the influence of alcohol 1991, annual rpt, S6905–3

South Carolina crimes and arrests, by detailed offense, offender characteristics, and location, 1992 and trends, annual rpt, S7205–1.2

South Carolina deaths, by detailed cause, age, sex, and race, 1990, annual rpt, S7175–2

South Carolina divorces with legal grounds of drunkenness, by county and duration of marriage, 1990, annual rpt, S7175–1

South Carolina statistical abstract, general data, 1993 annual rpt, S7125–1.10

South Dakota traffic accidents, with alcohol involvement for drivers and pedestrians, 1992 and trends, annual rpt, S7300–3

South Dakota vital statistics, including births, deaths, marriage and divorce, and communicable disease, by demographic characteristics and county, 1991 and trends, annual rpt, S7345–1

Tennessee health behavior risk factor surveillance survey results, by respondent characteristics, 1986-90, annual rpt, S7520–3

Tennessee vital statistics, including births, deaths by cause, marriages, divorces, and population, by demographic characteristics and location, 1991 and trends, annual rpt, S7520–2

Texas crimes and arrests, by offense, with data by location and offender characteristics, 1992 and trends, annual rpt, S7735–2

Texas health behavior risk factor surveillance survey results, by respondent characteristics, 1991 and trends, annual rpt, S7685–2

Utah crimes and arrests, by offense, county, and local agency, 1992 and trends, annual rpt, S7890–3

Utah health behavior risk factor surveillance survey results, by respondent characteristics, 1991, annual rpt, S7835–3

Utah traffic accidents involving pedestrians and other persons under the influence of alcohol, 1992 and trends, annual rpt, S7890–2

Vermont vital statistics, including population, births, deaths by cause, abortions, marriages, and divorces, by location and demographic characteristics, 1991 and trends, annual rpt, S8054–1

Virginia alcohol-related motor vehicle accidents, injuries, and fatalities, including pedestrian intoxication, 1991, annual rpt, S8282–1

Virginia crimes and arrests by offense, and law enforcement employment, by location and reporting agency, 1992, annual rpt, S8295–2.2

Washington State crimes and arrests, by offense, with data by location and offender characteristics, 1992 and trends, annual rpt, S8440–1

Washington State vital statistics, including births, deaths by cause, and population, by demographic characteristics and location, 1991 and trends, annual rpt, S8363–1

West Virginia crimes and arrests, by offense, location, and offender characteristics, 1990-91, annual rpt, S8610–1

West Virginia vital statistics, including births, deaths by cause, marriages, and divorces, by location and demographic characteristics, 1991 and trends, annual rpt, S8560–1

Wisconsin correctional instn admissions by inmate characteristics, including need for special services, 1991, annual rpt, S8692–1.2

Wisconsin crimes and arrests by offense, and alcohol involvement in homicides, 1992, annual rpt, S8771–1

Wyoming adult and juvenile arrests, by offense, county, and local jurisdiction, 1991, annual rpt, S8867–3.2

Wyoming prison inmate, probationer, and parolee alcohol and drug use, FY92, annual rpt, S8883–1

see also Driving while intoxicated
see also Drug abuse and treatment
see also Drug and alcohol testing

Alcohol consumption

see Alcohol use

Alcohol fuels

Auto fleet use and views on operation of flexible-fuel vehicles capable of running on methanol or gasoline, California survey, 1993 articles, A6755–1.502

Ethanol capacity operating and planned/under construction, by company and plant, 1992 article, A1250–1.501

Ethanol demand, with detail for transportation uses in California and US, 1992/93-2000/2001, article, C6985–1.533

Ethanol production and stocks, weekly rpt monthly table, C6985–1

Production of methanol, and consumption of alcohol for fuel use, commodity yearbook for 1993, C2400–1

Production of methanol, and consumption of alcohol for fuel use, commodity yearbook Jan-Sept 1993 updates, C2400–2

State and local:

Florida statistical abstract, general data, 1992 annual rpt, U6660–1.15

see also Biomass energy
see also Gasohol

Alcohol use

Beer industry production, capacity, and sales volume, including top brands and brewers, 1982-92, annual feature, C0125–2.503

Black American health and vital statistics data, with comparisons to whites, 1970s-91, annual compilation, C6775–2.2

Black children and youth population, economic, health, and education data, with comparisons to whites, 1993 rpt, R3840–21

Brewing industry financial and operating data, including consumption, trade, and taxes, 1991 and trends, annual rpt, A3455–1

Cholesterol level correlated with alcohol consumption frequency, by race and sex, 1976-80, article, A2623–1.508

College freshmen social and academic activities in past year, by sex and instn type, fall 1992, annual survey, U6215–1

Consumption of alcohol and other beverages per capita, 1979-91, annual rpt, C0125–3.1

Consumption of alcohol, by type, census div, and State, with consumer expenditures, 1960s-91, annual rpt, A3455–1.4

Consumption of distilled spirits, and consumer characteristics, 1992 and trends, annual rpt, C4775–1

Consumption of distilled spirits, wine, and beer, by State, 1991 and trends, annual rpt, A4650–3

Consumption patterns and alcoholic treatment groups in countries with history of temperance movements vs those without, 1993 article, A2623–1.508

Health condition and preventive health care and safety practices of adults, by respondent characteristics, 1992 and trends, annual survey rpt, C8111–2

High school student substance abuse as affected by junior high prevention program, 1993 article, A2623–1.508

Higher education student use of and attitudes toward alcohol, drugs, and tobacco products, by sex and region, 1989-91 surveys, annual rpt, U4950–1

Higher education student weekly alcohol consumption, by region, 1990, survey article, C2175–1.522

Hispanic American women's alcohol consumption compared to acculturation levels and other demographic characteristics, 1982-84, article, A2623–1.508

Japan and US health care system data, including expenditures, facilities, insurance coverage, and population health indicators, 1993 article, R5650–2.515

Men age 69-84 quality of life indicators, including health, finances, family, and employment, by race, 1990 survey, U3780–9

Restaurant (table service) consumption trend for alcoholic beverages, 1992, recurring rpt, A8200–11

Urban public high school drug/alcohol incidents per 1,000 students, for 47 systems, 1990/91, A4425–4

Wine market statistics, including sales, production, trade, and consumer characteristics, with data by company, brand, and geographic area, 1992 and trends, annual rpt, C4775–2

State and local:

Alabama health behavior risk factor surveillance survey results, by respondent characteristics, 1988-89, recurring rpt, S0175–6

California death rates and estimated alcohol-related mortality, by cause and demographic characteristics, 1980-89, article, A2623–1.508

Alcohol use

California health behavior risk factor surveillance survey results, by respondent characteristics, 1991 and trends, annual rpt, S0865–2

California statistical abstract, general data, 1992 annual rpt, S0840–2.11

California wine, beer, and distilled spirits consumption, and excise tax collections, FY35-92, annual rpt, S0835–1.5

Colorado health behavior risk factor surveillance survey results, by respondent characteristics, 1990, recurring rpt, S1010–3

Hawaii data book, general data, 1992 annual rpt, S2090–1.23

Michigan births by mother's alcohol use status during pregnancy, 1990, annual rpt, S4000–3

Michigan health behavior risk factor surveillance survey results, by respondent characteristics, 1991, annual rpt, S4000–4

Mississippi births by mother's alcohol use during pregnancy, by race, 1992, annual rpt, S4350–1

Missouri births by mother's drinking habits during pregnancy, by race, county, and city, 1992, annual rpt, S4518–1

Nebraska beer, alcohol, and wine gallonage and tax revenues, 1991 and trends, annual rpt, S4950–1.3

Nebraska births by mother's alcohol use during pregnancy, 1991, annual rpt, S4885–1

Pennsylvania health behavior risk factor surveillance survey results, by respondent characteristics, 1991, annual rpt, S6820–4

Tennessee births by mother's alcohol use during pregnancy, 1991, annual rpt, S7520–2

Utah births by mother's alcohol use during pregnancy, by birthweight, 1990, annual rpt, S7835–1

Utah crimes involving offender alcohol use, by offense, for 6 local agencies, 1992, annual rpt, S7890–3

Utah health behavior risk factor surveillance survey results, by respondent characteristics, 1991, annual rpt, S7835–3

Vermont births by maternal risk factors including tobacco and alcohol use during pregnancy, 1991, annual rpt, S8054–1

Virginia births by mother's alcohol and tobacco use during pregnancy, by birthweight, 1991, annual rpt, S8225–1

West Virginia births by pregnancy risk factors, including tobacco and alcohol use, by county, 1991, annual rpt, S8560–1

see also Alcohol abuse and treatment

Alcoholic beverage taxes

see Excise tax

Alcoholic beverages

see Alcohol abuse and treatment

see Alcohol use

see Alcoholic beverages licenses and fees

see Beer and breweries

see Driving while intoxicated

see Liquor and liquor industry

see Restaurants and drinking places

see Wine and winemaking

Alcoholic beverages licenses and fees

Brewers and other distillers tax payments to Federal and State govts, FY91 and trends, annual rpt, A3455–1.6

Licenses issued for alcoholic beverage operations, by type, 1984-92, annual rpt, C4775–2.2

Licenses issued for wholesale trade and other operations, by State or type of operation, 1992 and trends, annual rpt, C4775–1.2

State tax rates and collections, by tax type and State, FY02-92, annual rpt, R9050–1.5

State and local:

Alabama counties permitting and prohibiting sale of alcoholic beverages, 1992 annual rpt, S0121–2

Alabama financial condition, including revenues by source, expenditures by function and object, and fund balances, by fund and agency, FY92, annual rpt, S0129–1

California economic condition, including population, employment and earnings, income, business activity, and taxation, 1960s-92, annual rpt, S0840–3.2

Colorado liquor licenses issued by county or type, and license hearings and outcomes, FY92 and trends, annual rpt, S1075–1.2

DC statistical profile, general data, 1992 annual rpt, S1535–3.3

Florida State govt disbursements to local areas, by source of funds, FY92, annual rpt, S1717–1

Florida statistical abstract, general data, 1992 annual rpt, U6660–1.23

Kansas tax collections by tax type, and property values, with data by county, FY92 and trends, annual rpt, S3020–1

Mississippi Alcoholic Beverage Control Div operating statement, and revenue allocations to individual counties and cities, FY92 and trends, annual rpt, S4435–1

Montana revenue collections by tax type, and taxable establishments, production, and income, FY91-92 and trends, biennial rpt, S4750–1.1

Oklahoma tax revenues by source, and distribution to local govts and State funds, FY92 and trends, annual rpt, S6495–1

Pennsylvania tax collections by tax type, with data by county and industry, FY92 and trends, annual rpt, S6885–1

South Dakota tax revenues by source, and aid distributed to local areas, FY92 annual rpt, S7380–1.1

Texas financial condition, including revenues by source, expenditures by function and dept, and investments, with data for over 400 individual funds, FY92, annual rpt, S7655–2

Washington State revenues by source, and distributions by tax and locality, FY92 and trends, annual rpt, S8415–1.1

Alcoholism

see Alcohol abuse and treatment

Alfalfa

see Animal feed

see Seeds

Algeria

Energy intl sourcebook, with detail on oil and gas industry operations, supply-demand, and prices, for approx 80 countries, 1970s-91, annual compilation, C6985–10.2

Natural gas liquids US imports from Algeria, 1956-90, annual compilation, C6985–9.2

see also Organization of Petroleum Exporting Countries

see also under By Foreign Country or World Area in the "Index by Categories"

Alien workers

Chemist and chemical engineer salaries, employment status, and demographic and professional characteristics, 1993, annual rpt, A1250–4

Hires of foreign nationals and US citizens for work overseas, by employer type, 1991/92, annual survey rpt, U3130–1

Latin America immigrants to US, and temporary workers, aliens, and deportations, by country, 1992 annual rpt, U6250–1.14

Political science higher education dept faculty, including resident aliens by sex, 1991/92, annual rpt, A2617–1

Scientific/technical worker immigrant employment license ("green card") applications approved and denied, by occupation, 1992, article, A1250–1.522

Small business views on employment trends for women, minorities, immigrants, and the disabled, and related mgmt issues, 1993 survey article, C4687–1.503

State and local:

Montana wage rates for employers certified to hire alien workers, for selected occupations, quarterly rpt, S4710–1

see also Mexicans in the U.S.

Aliens

Corporate boards of directors composition, including non-US citizen members, by sex, 1991/92, B4490–2.36

Corporate boards of directors with non-US citizen members, 1991 and trends, annual survey rpt, B5000–3

Hispanic noncitizen adult population in US, with detail for 9 States, biennially 1980-90, annual rpt, A6844–1

Latin America immigrants to US, and temporary workers, aliens, and deportations, by country, 1992 annual rpt, U6250–1.14

Prison inmates who are not US citizens, by State and for Federal system, Jan 1992, annual rpt, R4300–1.1

Women and minorities in professional fields, detailed education and labor force data, 1980s-91, with historical trends, recurring rpt, A3960–2

State and local:

Hawaii data book, general data, 1992 annual rpt, S2090–1.1

Illinois crimes and arrests of alien illegal entries, 1990-91, annual rpt, S2536–1

Massachusetts correctional instn noncitizen inmates, by instn, Jan 1992, annual rpt, S3805–1

New Mexico legalized alien assistance program expenditures, monthly rpt quarterly table, S5620–2

Utah homeless shelter population characteristics, individual shelter capacity, and related housing data, 1991-92, annual rpt, S7808–2

see also Alien workers

see also Citizenship

see also Deportation

see also Foreign medical graduates

Index by Subjects and Names

see also Foreign students
see also Immigration and emigration
see also Mexicans in the U.S.

Alimony
see Child support and alimony

Allergies
Drugs (allergy) market shares, for top 5 nonprescription brands, year ended Jan 1993, article, C2710–1.518
Hospital patient discharges and length of stay, by diagnostic related group (DRG), payment source, age, and region, 1991, annual rpt series, B4455–3

State and local:
Hawaii chronic health conditions, by demographic characteristics and location, 1988, annual rpt, S2065–1.3

Allied health personnel
Compensation and productivity of allied health care professionals in group practices, by speciality, 1991, annual rpt, A6365–1
Compensation of allied health personnel in group practices, by position, 1989-92, annual rpt, B7450–2
Dental allied education enrollment, grads, and tuition, by instn, 1992/93 annual rpt, A1475–5
Dental school faculty, support personnel, and staff characteristics, by instn, 1992/93, annual rpt, A1475–4.5
HMO use of nurse practitioners, physician assistants, and nurse midwives, 1991, annual rpt, A5150–2.1
Hospital recruiting of nurses and allied health personnel, with budget, vacancies, turnover, and compensation, 1993 and trends, annual survey rpt, A6500–1
Physician assistants, with data on drug prescription-writing authority, by State, 1992 rpt, U8850–8.4

State and local:
Florida health care atlas, including manpower by occupation and health care facilities by type, by district and county, 1992 annual rpt, S1746–1.2
Florida statistical abstract, general data, 1992 annual rpt, U6660–1.20
Kentucky Medicaid recipients and payments, by program, county, and type of medical service including physicians assistants, monthly rpt, S3140–5
South Carolina statistical abstract, general data, 1993 annual rpt, S7125–1.10
see also Clinical laboratory technicians
see also Dietitians and nutritionists
see also Midwives

Alpha Publications
Health care provider spending on consulting services, 1990 and 1992, article, A1865–1.521

Alternative fuel vehicles
see Automobiles
see Electric power
see Motor fuels

Aluminum and aluminum industry
Capital spending plans for new mines and plants, by mineral and company, and mine production values, 1993 annual feature, C5226–2.503
Carbon tetrafluoride emissions by aluminum producers, atmospheric concentration, and global warming potential, 1993 article, A1250–1.535

Energy (BTU) tax proposed by Clinton Admin financial impact for aluminum manufacturers, with production and capacity data, for 5 companies, 1993-96, article, C5226–2.506
Production by world area, and US shipments by end-use market, 1991, article, C5800–8.506
Production, capacity utilization, and PPI of aluminum and other metals, monthly rpt, C7000–8
Production, consumption, stocks, trade, and prices for approx 100 basic commodities, including by country and producing State, commodity yearbook for 1993, C2400–1, C2400–2
Shipments, orders, and inventories by product class, and foreign trade of ingot, scrap, and mill products, monthly rpt, A0400–1
Supply-demand for selected metals and nonmetallic minerals, with price data, US and worldwide, 1992-93 and trends, annual feature, C5226–2.505
Supply-demand of aluminum in US and foreign countries, 1940s-92, annual rpt, A0400–2

Alzheimer's disease
Hospital patient discharges and length of stay, by diagnosis, type of operation, age, and region, 1991, annual rpt series, B4455–1

State and local:
California vital statistics, including population, births, and deaths by cause, by demographic characteristics and county, 1990 and trends, annual rpt, S0865–1
Idaho vital statistics, including births, deaths by cause, abortions, marriages, and divorces, by demographic characteristics and county, 1991 and trends, annual rpt, S2250–2
Iowa vital statistics, including population, births, deaths by cause, marriages, and divorces, by demographic characteristics and location, 1991 and trends, annual rpt, S2795–1
New Mexico vital statistics, including population, births, deaths, and disease, by location and demographic characteristics, 1991 and trends, annual rpt, S5605–1
Oregon vital statistics, including births, deaths by cause, communicable diseases, marriages, and divorces, by age, sex, race-ethnicity, and county, 1991 and trends, annual rpt, S6615–5
South Carolina deaths, by detailed cause, age, sex, and race, 1990, annual rpt, S7175–2
Vermont vital statistics, including population, births, deaths by cause, abortions, marriages, and divorces, by location and demographic characteristics, 1991 and trends, annual rpt, S8054–1

Ambulances
see Emergency medical service

Ambulatory aids
see Prosthetics and orthotics

Ambulatory surgical centers
see Surgeons and surgery

American Chemical Society
Members by demographic and employment characteristics, 1990 and trends, recurring rpt, A3960–2.3

Ancestry

American Indians
see Indians

American Medical Association
Physicians by selected specialty, 1965, 1980, and 1990, article, A1865–1.513

American Samoa
Hospital directory, with utilization, expenses, and personnel, by instn, type, and location, 1992, annual rpt, A1865–3
Judicial system salaries for judges and court administrators, by State and territory, and for Federal system, July 1993, semiannual rpt, R6600–2
Nursing programs (State-approved) for practical/vocational nurses, including admissions, enrollment, and grads, by instn, State, and territory, 1992, annual directory, A8010–5
Nursing programs (State-approved) for registered nurses, including admissions, enrollment, and grads, by instn, State, and territory, 1992, annual directory, A8010–4

Americans with Disabilities Act
see Disabled and handicapped persons

Ammonia
see Chemicals and chemical industry

Amnesties
see Pardons

Amoebiasis
see Food and waterborne diseases

Amtrak
see National Railroad Passenger Corp.

Amusement parks
Attendance at top 10 amusement parks, 1989, recurring rpt, R9375–6
Attendance at top 20 amusement parks, 1991, annual rpt, C2140–1.2
Financial ratios and performance, for over 350 SIC 4-digit industries, FY88-92, annual rpt, A6400–3
Operating and financial data, including data for US and foreign parks, miniature golf, waterparks, and games, 1992, annual rpt, A5700–1

State and local:
Ohio fair/amusement ride inspections, 1990-91, annual rpt, S6240–1

Analgesics
see Drugs
see Personal care products

Ancestry
Latin America ancestry reported by US population, by region and census div, 1980, annual rpt, U6250–1.14

State and local:
Arkansas Census of Population and Housing detailed findings, 1990, U5935–7
California Census of Population and Housing detailed findings, 1990, S0840–9
Hawaii data book, general data, 1992 annual rpt, S2090–1.1
Iowa population top 10 ancestry groups, 1990, annual rpt, S2784–3
Maryland statistical abstract, general data, 1993-94 biennial rpt, S3605–1.1
New Jersey Census of Population and Housing detailed findings, by county, 1990, S5425–19
Pennsylvania Census of Population and Housing detailed findings, with selected data by county and municipality, 1990, U4130–13
Rhode Island Census of Population and Housing detailed findings, by county and municipality, 1990, S6930–9

Anchorage, Alaska

Employment, by industry, monthly rpt, S0320–1

see also under By City in the "Index by Categories"

Andean Group

Latin America statistical abstract, general data by country, 1992 annual rpt, U6250–1.26

Andersen, Arthur, and Co.

Convenience store industry financial and operating data, by size category, 1992 and trends, annual survey rpt, A6735–1, A6735–2

North Sea offshore oil/gas exploratory drilling planned, by area, 1993, article, C6985–1.512

Public utility current and planned info mgmt system improvements, by application, 1993 survey article, C6985–6.505

Retail store credit operations, including cash vs credit sales, processing methods, and marketing techniques, 1992 annual survey, C5150–4.504

Retail store credit operations, including payment losses and loss reduction efforts, by payment method and outlet type, 1992 survey article, C5150–4.503

Wholesaler/distributor inside vs outside sales staff share of sales and allocation of time, with projections to 2000, 1993 article, C4725–5.506

Anderson, Ind.

Business conditions analysis for selected Indiana local areas, quarterly rpt semiannual feature, U2160–1.502

Anemia

see Blood diseases and disorders

see Sickle cell anemia

Anesthesiology

Income of health care specialists, public perceptions vs actual amounts, 1991-93, R4865–13

Medical school faculty and compensation, by dept, academic rank, degree, and region, 1992/93, annual rpt, A3273–2

Physician practice economic aspects, detailed data by specialty, 1991-92 and trends, annual compilation, A2200–5

Physicians by detailed specialty and location, 1992 and trends, annual rpt, A2200–3

State and local:

Kentucky Medicaid recipients and payments, by program, county, and type of medical service, monthly rpt, S3140–5

Angola

Energy intl sourcebook, with detail on oil and gas industry operations, supply-demand, and prices, for approx 80 countries, 1970s-91, annual compilation, C6985–10.2

Animal diseases and zoonoses

Birds (pet) tested for Newcastle disease in 5 States, with results and disease flowchart, 1991, article, A3100–2.503

Calf deaths and related costs, by disease, 1987/88 Colorado study, article, A3100–2.518

Dairy herd clinical mastitis prevalence and control efforts, with data on associated costs, Illinois and Ohio studies, 1993 articles, A3100–2.508, A3100–2.512

Dog congenital defects rates, for pups on sale at pet store vs dogs treated at veterinary teaching hospitals, 1970 or 1987-88, article, A3100–2.508

Dog cranial cruciate ligament rupture prevalence, by breed, sex, and neutered status, 1993 article, A3100–2.521

Dogs blastomycosis respiratory disease incidence, by region and dog characteristics, 1980-90, article, A3100–2.503

Hospital patient discharges and length of stay, by diagnosis, type of operation, age, and region, 1991, annual rpt series, B4455–1

Swine breeding stock porcine stress syndrome mutation prevalence by breed, in US, Canada, and UK, 1993 article, A3100–2.520

Swine pseudorabies virus eradication program results in 6 herds, Illinois study, 1990/91, article, A3100–2.517

State and local:

Florida vital statistics, including population, births, deaths by cause, and marriages and dissolutions, by location and demographic characteristics, 1992 and trends, annual rpt, S1745–3

Hawaii environmental quality and public health control, inspection, licensing, and enforcement activities, 1990, annual rpt, S2065–1.6

Louisiana vital statistics, including population, births, deaths by cause, reportable diseases, marriages, and divorces, by demographic characteristics and locality, 1989-90 and trends, annual rpt, S3295–1

Massachusetts vital statistics, including births, deaths by cause, marriages, divorces, and population, by locality and demographic characteristics, 1990 and trends, annual rpt, S3850–1

Mississippi vital statistics, including births, deaths by cause, marriages, and divorces, by demographic characteristics and location, 1992 and trends, annual rpt, S4350–1

Montana vital statistics, including births, deaths by cause, abortion, disease, and marriage and divorce, by demographic characteristics and county, 1990-91 and trends, annual rpt, S4690–1

New Mexico deaths hy cause, and incidence of communicable diseases, by demographic characteristics, 1991 and trends, annual rpt, S5605–1.3

New York State vital statistics, including population, births, deaths by cause, reportable diseases, and marriages and dissolutions, by demographic characteristics and/or location, 1990 and trends, annual rpt, S5765–1

Ohio vital statistics, including births, deaths by cause, marriages, divorces, and population, by demographic characteristics and location, 1991 and trends, annual rpt, S6285–1

South Carolina communicable disease cases, by county, 1990, annual rpt, S7175–1

South Carolina deaths, by detailed cause, age, sex, and race, 1990, annual rpt, S7175–2

South Dakota vital statistics, including births, deaths, marriage and divorce, and communicable disease, by demographic characteristics and county, 1991 and trends, annual rpt, S7345–1

Tennessee vital statistics, including births, deaths by cause, marriages, divorces, and population, by demographic characteristics and location, 1991 and trends, annual rpt, S7520–2

Vermont livestock tested and suspected of disease, 1988/89-1989/90, biennial rpt, S7978–1

Virginia vital statistics, including births, deaths by cause, marriages and divorces, and communicable disease, by demographic characteristics and location, 1991 and trends, annual rpt, S8225–1

Wisconsin dairy herd health problem incidence, 1992, annual rpt, S8680–1

Wisconsin vital statistics, including population, births, deaths by cause, and marriages and dissolutions, by county and demographic characteristics, 1991 and trends, annual rpt, S8715–4

see also Food and waterborne diseases

see also Rabies

see also Veterinary medicine

see also under By Disease in the "Index by Categories"

Animal feed

Appalachia prices paid by farmers for animal feeds, quarterly 1991, annual rpt, S8510–1

Exports of farm products, by detailed commodity and country of destination, US and California, 1991, annual rpt, B9520–1

Farm prices paid for selected production commodities, 1982 and 1991-92, annual rpt, S3085–1

Financial ratios and performance, for over 350 SIC 4-digit industries, FY88-92, annual rpt, A6400–3

Production, consumption, stocks, trade, and prices for approx 100 basic commodities, including by country and producing State, commodity yearbook for 1993, C2400–1, C2400–2

Soybean meal production, supply, wholesale price, and prices paid by farmers, 1950s-91, annual rpt, B8480–1

World grain fed to livestock as percent of total consumption, by country, 1970 and 1990, biennial rpt, R9455–1.6

State and local:

Alabama agricultural production, marketing, and income, by county and/or commodity, and farms and acreage, 1992 and trends, annual rpt, S0090–1

Alaska agricultural production and marketing, by district and commodity, 1960s-92, annual rpt, U5750–1

Arizona agricultural production, marketing, and finances, by commodity and county, 1988-92, annual rpt, U5830–1

Arkansas agricultural production, marketing, and finances, by commodity and county, with farms and acreage, 1992 and trends, annual rpt, U5920–1

California field crops production, acreage, yield, and prices, by commodity and county, 1992 and trends, annual rpt, S0850–1.4

Colorado agricultural production, marketing, and finances, by commodity and/or county, with farms and acreage, 1992 and trends, annual rpt, S0985–1

Florida field crop acreage, yield, production, and value, by commodity and/or county, 1992 and trends, annual rpt, S1685–1.4

Index by Subjects and Names

Animals

Georgia agricultural production, marketing, and finances, by commodity and/or county, and farms and acreage, 1991 and trends, annual rpt, S1855–1

Hawaii agricultural production and marketing, by commodity and island, 1987-91, annual rpt, S2030–1

Illinois agricultural production, marketing, and finances, by county or commodity, and farms and farmland, 1991 and trends, annual rpt, S2390–1

Kansas agricultural production, marketing, and finances, by county and/or commodity, and farm acreage and value, 1992 and trends, annual rpt, S2915–1

Kentucky agricultural production, marketing, and finances, by commodity and county; and farms, acreage, and value; 1992 and trends, annual rpt, S3085–1

Louisiana agricultural production, marketing, and finances, by commodity or parish, 1985-91, annual rpt, U2740–1

Michigan agricultural production, marketing, and finances, by commodity or county, 1987-91, annual rpt, S3950–1

Minnesota agricultural production, marketing, and finances, by county or commodity, and farms and acreage, 1992 and trends, annual rpt, S4130–1

Missouri agricultural production, marketing, and finances, by commodity and/or county, and farms and acreage, 1988-92, annual rpt, S4480–1

Montana agricultural production, marketing, and finances, by commodity and county, 1991 and trends, annual rpt, S4655–1

Nebraska agricultural production, marketing, and finances, by commodity and/or county, and farms and acreage, 1991 and trends, annual rpt, S4835–1

Nevada agricultural production, marketing, and finances, by county and commodity, and farms and acreage, 1992 and trends, annual rpt, S5010–1

New Jersey agricultural production, marketing, and finances, by commodity and/or county, and farms and acreage, 1986-91, annual rpt, S5350–1

New Mexico agricultural production, marketing, and finances, by commodity and county, with commercial feed sales by type, 1991 and trends, annual rpt, S5530–1

New York State agricultural production, marketing, and finances, by commodity and/or county, and farms and acreage, 1992 and trends, annual rpt, S5700–1

North Carolina agricultural production, marketing, and finances, by commodity and county, 1991 and trends, annual rpt, S5885–1

North Dakota agricultural production and marketing, by commodity and county, and farm finances, 1992 and trends, annual rpt, U3600–1

Ohio agricultural production, marketing, and finances, by commodity and county, with farms and acreage, 1990-91 and trends, annual rpt, S6240–1

Oklahoma agricultural production, marketing, and finances, by commodity and county, 1992 and trends, annual rpt, S6405–1

Oregon agricultural production, marketing, and finances, by commodity and/or county, with farms and acreage, 1991 and trends, annual rpt, S6575–1

Pennsylvania agricultural production, marketing, and finances, by county and commodity, and farms and acreage, 1992 and trends, annual rpt, S6760–1

South Carolina agricultural production and finances, by commodity and county, 1991-92 and trends, annual rpt, U1075–3

South Dakota agricultural production, marketing, and finances, by commodity and county, and farms and acreage, 1992 and trends, annual rpt, S7280–1

Tennessee agricultural production and marketing, by commodity and county, with farms, acreage, and farm value, 1992 and trends, annual rpt, S7460–1

Texas agricultural production, marketing, and finances, by commodity and county, and farms and farmland, 1991 and trends, annual rpt series, S7630–1

Utah agricultural production, marketing, and finances, by commodity and county, with farms and acreage, 1992 and trends, annual rpt, S7800–1

Vermont agricultural production, marketing, and finances, by commodity, with data on govt inspections and funding, 1989-90 biennial rpt, S7978–1

Washington State agricultural production, marketing, and finances, by commodity and/or county, 1992 and trends, annual rpt, S8328–1

West Virginia agricultural production, marketing, and finances, by commodity or county, 1991 and trends, annual rpt, S8510–1

Wisconsin agricultural production, marketing, and finances, by commodity and county, and farms, acreage, and sales, 1992 and trends, annual rpt, S8680–1

Wyoming agricultural production, marketing, and finances, by county and/or commodity, and farms, acreage, and value, 1992 and trends, annual rpt, S8860–1

see also Pasture and rangeland

see also Pet food and supplies

Animal oils

see Oils, oilseeds, and fats

Animals

Accidental deaths and injuries from accidents involving animals, 1992 and trends, annual rpt, A8375–2

Dog races, attendance, handle, and govt revenues, by State, 1990 and trends, annual rpt, A3363–1.2

Exports of horses, US and California, 1991, annual rpt, B9520–1

Latin America horses by country, 1947-89, annual rpt, U6250–1.24

Pet and livestock household ownership and veterinarian use, and animal populations, 1985 or 1987, annual directory, A3100–1

Pet dog and cat injuries sustained in falls, 1985-91, article, A3100–2.505

Sales of animal health products by type, 1991, article, A3100–2.516

Selenium deficiency and toxicosis cases in livestock/wildlife, by State, 1992 survey, article, A3100–2.510

Traffic accident fatalities, by type of accident, 1913-92, annual rpt, A0865–1.3

State and local:

Alabama traffic accidents involving collisions with animals, 1992, annual rpt, S0185–1

Alaska reindeer herd by sex, and meat production and sales, 1960s-92, annual rpt, U5750–1

Alaska traffic accidents involving collisions with animals, 1991, annual rpt, S0360–1

Arizona traffic accidents involving collisions with animals, 1991, annual rpt, S0530–1

Arkansas traffic accidents involving collisions with animals, 1991, annual rpt, S0692–1

Connecticut traffic accidents involving collisions with animals, 1992, annual rpt, S1275–1

Delaware traffic accidents involving collisions with animals, 1992, annual rpt, S1435–1

Florida traffic accidents involving collisions with animals, 1992, annual rpt, S1750–2

Hawaii dog licenses issued, by island, 1986-91, annual rpt, S2090–1.7

Hawaii traffic accidents involving collisions with animals, 1986, annual rpt, S2125–1

Idaho traffic accidents involving collisions with animals, 1992, annual rpt, S2315–1

Illinois traffic accidents involving collisions with animals, 1991, annual rpt, S2540–1

Indiana traffic accidents involving collisions with animals, 1992, annual rpt, S2675–1

Kansas traffic accidents involving collisions with animals, 1992, annual rpt, S3040–1

Kentucky traffic accidents involving collisions with animals, 1992, annual rpt, S3150–2

Maine traffic accidents involving collisions with animals, 1992, annual rpt, S3475–2

Maryland traffic accidents involving collisions with animals, 1992, annual rpt, S3665–4

Michigan equine operations, and inventory by breed and use, 1991 and trends, annual rpt, S3950–1

Michigan traffic accidents involving collisions with animals, 1991, annual rpt, S3997–2

Minnesota traffic accidents involving collisions with animals, 1992, annual rpt, S4230–2

Missouri cattle and calf losses to predatory animals and other causes, 1991, annual rpt, S4480–1

Missouri traffic accidents involving collisions with animals, 1992, annual rpt, S4560–1

Montana traffic accidents involving collisions with wild and domestic animals, 1992, annual rpt, S4705–2

Nebraska traffic accidents involving collisions with animals, 1992, annual rpt, S4953–1

Nevada traffic accidents involving collisions with animals, by severity, 1992, annual rpt, S5140–1

New Jersey traffic accidents involving collisions with animals, 1992 and trends, annual rpt, S5430–2

New Mexico traffic accidents involving collisions with animals, 1992, annual rpt, S5665–1

New York State lamb and sheep losses to predatory animals and other causes, 1990-92, annual rpt, S5700–1

New York State traffic accidents involving collisions with animals, 1991, annual rpt, S5790–1

North Carolina traffic accidents involving collisions with animals, 1992, annual rpt, S5990–1

Animals

North Dakota traffic accidents involving collisions with animals, 1992, annual rpt, S6217–1

Ohio livestock killed by coyotes and restitution claims paid, by species and county, FY92, annual rpt, S6240–1

Ohio traffic accidents involving collisions with animals and animal-drawn vehicles, 1991, annual rpt, S6290–1

Pennsylvania traffic accidents involving collisions with animals and horse-drawn vehicles, 1991, annual rpt, S6905–3

South Carolina traffic accidents involving collisions with animals, 1992, annual rpt, S7190–2

South Dakota traffic accidents involving collisions with animals, 1992, annual rpt, S7300–3

Utah equine inventory, with detail by breed, 1992, annual rpt, S7800–1

Utah lamb and sheep losses to predatory animals and other causes, 1992, annual rpt, S7800–1

Utah traffic accidents involving collisions with animals, 1992, annual rpt, S7890–2

Washington State motorcycle accidents involving collisions with animals, 1992, annual rpt, S8428–1

West Virginia traffic accidents involving collisions with animals, 1992, annual rpt, S8645–1

Wisconsin traffic accidents involving collisions with deer and other animals, 1992, annual rpt, S8815–1

Wyoming sheep and lamb losses to predatory animals and other causes, 1987-92, annual rpt, S8860–1

Wyoming traffic accidents involving collisions with animals, by circumstances and location, 1992, annual rpt, S9007–1

see also Animal diseases and zoonoses

see also Animal feed

see also Birds and bird conservation

see also Endangered species

see also Fish and fishing industry

see also Fishing, sport

see also Hunting and trapping

see also Livestock and livestock industry

see also Pet food and supplies

see also Poultry industry and products

see also Rabies

see also Veterinary medicine

see also Wildlife and wildlife conservation

see also Wildlife refuges

see also Zoological parks

Annexation

see Local government annexation

Anthropology

Women and minorities in professional fields, detailed education and labor force data, 1991 and trends, recurring rpt, A3960–2.3

Anthropometry

see Body measurements

Antifreeze

see Motor vehicle parts and supplies

Antimony

see Metals and metal industries

Antiques

State and local:

Mississippi antique motor vehicle license plates issued and revenue collections, FY92, annual rpt, S4435–1

Antitrust law

see also Divestiture

see also Economic concentration and diversification

Apache County, Ariz.

Oil and gas production, by field, operator, and well, monthly rpt, S0473–1

Apartheid

see Racial discrimination

see South Africa

Apartment houses

Construction contract awards by type of project, weekly rpt, C5800–2

Financial and operating detailed data for conventionally financed buildings, for US and Canada, by building type, metro area, and US region, 1991 and trends, annual rpt, A5600–1

Financial and operating detailed data for federally subsidized buildings, by building and subsidy type, building age, metro area, and region, 1991 and trends, annual rpt, A5600–5

Fuel used for heating in new multi-family buildings, by region, 1983-91, annual rpt, A1775–3.7

Homebuilder financial and operating data, including detail by location, for top 400 builders, 1993 annual feature, C1850–8.507

Housing market conditions in US regions and selected MSAs, including construction, rental vacancies, and prices, by type of housing, quarterly rpt, B5190–1

Income and expenses for apartment complex managers, and vacancy and turnover rates, by region and metro area, 1992, annual survey rpt, A6497–1

Mortgage banking trends and devs, with data on construction, home sales, and lending activity, by type of unit and instn, monthly rpt, A6450–2

Owner companies with most multi-family housing units, top 10 companies, 1993, C4300–1.508

Security access control use in multi-tenant residential facilities, 1993 feature, C1850–12.503

State and local:

Arizona building permits issued and value, by type, size, and location, monthly rpt quarterly table, U0280–1.503, U0280–1.506, U0280–1.509

Arizona statistical abstract, general data, 1993 recurring rpt, U5850–2.16

Connecticut construction activity and value, by type of structure and location, 1992 and trends, annual rpt, S1212–1

Delaware housing construction activity, with data on demolitions and mobile home sales, by locality, 1992 and trends, annual rpt, S1387–1

Florida building permits, value by county, city, and type of construction, monthly rpt, U6660–5

Florida statistical abstract, general data, 1992 annual rpt, U6660–1.2

New Jersey residential construction activity and costs, by location, 1991 and trends, annual rpt, S5425–3

Tennessee statistical abstract, general data, 1992/93 annual rpt, U8710–2.6

Utah statistical abstract, general data, 1993 triennial rpt, U8960–1.11

see also Condominiums and cooperatives

see also Rooming and boarding houses

Appalachia

Animal feed prices paid by farmers, for selected types of feed, 1st qtr 1989-2nd qtr 1993, annual rpt, S7460–1

Farm production expenditures by type, farm real estate value, and agricultural workers, hours, and wage rates, 1991 and trends, annual rpt, S8510–1

Oil and gas drilling costs, and wells and footage drilled, by State, offshore location, and type of well, 1991, annual rpt, A2575–9

Oil wells and footage drilled, and cost, 1991, annual rpt, A5425–1.2

State and local:

Maryland Appalachia Federal expenditures by function, FY91, biennial rpt, S3605–1.13

Pennsylvania funding by Appalachian Regional Commission, by program area, FY91, recurring rpt, U4130–6.2

see also under names of individual States

Apparel

see Clothing and clothing industry

Appeals

see Supreme Court

Appendicitis

see Digestive diseases

Apples

see Fruit and fruit products

Appliances

see Household appliances and equipment

Apportionment

see Congressional apportionment

Appraisals

see Property value

Apprenticeship

State and local:

California registered apprentices, by trade, race-ethnicity, and sex, 1991 and trends, annual rpt, S0840–2.3

DC statistical profile, general data, 1992 annual rpt, S1535–3.3

Appropriations

see Budget of the U.S.

see Defense budgets and appropriations

see State budgets

Aquaculture

Catfish and trout operations and sales, by selected State, 1990-92, annual rpt, S5885–1

Production volume and value, with data on FDA-approved drugs available, for selected types of animals, 1991, article, A3100–2.514

Veterinary school aquatic animal course availability, faculty, and enrollment, by instn, 1991/92, article, A3100–2.509

World aquaculture production, by species group and country, 1987-89, biennial rpt, R9455–1.7

State and local:

Alabama catfish operations, inventories, and cash receipts, 1988-93, annual rpt, S0090–1

Arkansas catfish operations, including inventory, sales, and water acreage, 1992-93 and trends, annual rpt, U5920–1

Colorado trout operations and sales, 1989-92, annual rpt, S0985–1

Hawaii aquaculture operations, acreage, production, and value, by county, 1991 and trends, annual rpt, S2090–1.19

Index by Subjects and Names

Michigan trout operations and sales, 1989-91, annual rpt, S3950–1

Minnesota trout sales, and losses by cause, 1992 and trends, annual rpt, S5700–1

Missouri catfish sales and inventory, 1991-93, annual rpt, S4480–1

Oklahoma catfish inventories and sales, 1989-93, annual rpt, S6405–1

Oregon aquaculture and mariculture production value, 1991, annual rpt, S6575–1

Pennsylvania trout and trout egg production, value, and sales, 1991-92, annual rpt, S6760–1

South Carolina statistical abstract, general data, 1993 annual rpt, S7125–1.1

Tennessee catfish and trout production and sales, 1993 annual rpt, S7460–1

Texas catfish operations and sales, 1990-92, annual rpt, S7630–1.2

Washington State trout sales and operations, 1988-92, annual rpt, S8328–1

Wisconsin trout farm operations and sales, 1989-92, annual rpt, S8680–1

Arab Republic of Egypt

see Egypt

Arabian Peninsula

see Oman

see Qatar

see Saudi Arabia

see United Arab Emirates

see Yemen

Arbitration

see Civil procedure

see Labor-management relations, general

see Labor-management relations in government

see Legal arbitration and mediation

Arbitron Co.

Cable TV advertising expenditures, for top 10 advertisers, 1st qtr 1993, article, C1850–14.523

Cable TV advertising expenditures, for top 20 industry categories, 1992, article, C1850–14.515

Cable TV advertising expenditures, for top 5 advertisers, 1992, C1850–14.513

Cable TV advertising revenues, for 6 major networks, quarterly 1992, article, C1850–14.511

Radio (public) audience and market population shares for blacks and Hispanics, for 6-13 stations, 1991, R4250–1.18

Radio audience ratings and program format, for top stations in leading metro markets, weekly rpt recurring article, C1850–14.506, C1850-14.507, C1850–14.508, C1850-14.521, C1850–14.531, C1850–14.542

Radio audience ratings for 6 news/talk format stations in 4 major cities, spring 1993, article, C1850–14.539

Radio station group owners ranked by total Arbitron rating, with stations owned and ratings, for top 25 companies, summer 1992, article, C1850–14.502

TV advertising expenditures for top 10 broadcast TV network advertisers, 1st qtr 1992-93, C1850–14.527

TV advertising expenditures for top 25 network advertisers, with detail for 4 networks, 1992, annual article, C2710–1.515

State and local:

Georgia, Atlanta participation rates for Arbitron radio listener surveys, quarterly spring 1992-spring 1993, article, C1850–14.532

Architectural barriers to the handicapped

State and local:

New York State libraries accessibility to handicapped, by library, 1991, annual rpt, S5745–2

Vermont public libraries accessibility to handicapped, FY91-92 biennial rpt, S8080–1

Architecture

Architectural devs in design and technology, with quarterly construction cost trends, monthly rpt, C5800–15

Billings of top 500 architectural and engineering design firms, 1992, annual article, C5800–2.522

Building design/construction company revenues and operations, for top 300 firms, 1991, annual feature, C1850–9.502

Design/construction contract values, for top 50 construction contractors, 1992, annual rpt, C5800–2.529

Earnings and job satisfaction of architects in settings other than private architectural practice, 1992 survey article, C5800–15.501

Operating and financial composite ratios for corporations, with establishments and receipts, for approx 200 industries, by asset size, FY90, annual rpt, C7800–1

Women and minorities in professional fields, detailed education and labor force data, 1991 and trends, recurring rpt, A3960–2.1, A3960–2.3

State and local:

Florida statistical abstract, general data, 1992 annual rpt, U6660–1.18

see also Architectural barriers to the handicapped

see also Interior design

Archives

see Government documents

Areas of Dominant Influence

see Marketing areas

Argentina

Electronics industry trade and/or production trends by product category for 33 countries, with general economic profiles, 1993 annual rpt, A4725–1.4

Energy intl sourcebook, with detail on oil and gas industry operations, supply-demand, and prices, for approx 80 countries, 1970s-91, annual compilation, C6985–10.2

Machine tool industry operating data by country and product, 1992 and trends, annual rpt, A3179–2.2

Motor vehicle world production, sales, trade, and registrations, by country, world area, manufacturer, and make, 1991 and trends, annual rpt, A0865–2.1

Nuclear reactors in operation, with capacity, electricity generation, and construction, by unit and country, 1992, annual rpt, B6800–2.2

Soybean production and marketing data, including utilization, prices, and trade, with comparison to other oilseeds, 1920s-93, annual rpt, B8480–1

Statistical abstract of Latin America, detailed social, govtl, and economic data, 1992 annual rpt, U6250–1

Arizona

Wheat supply-demand summary, 1987/88-1992/93, annual rpt, A7310–1

see also Buenos Aires, Argentina

see also under By Foreign Country or World Area in the "Index by Categories"

Arid zones

Latin America statistical abstract, general data by country, 1992 annual rpt, U6250–1.1

Arizona

Agricultural production, marketing, and finances, by commodity and county, 1988-92, annual rpt, U5830–1

Bank balance sheets and branches, individual State and natl instns, quarterly rpt, S0460–2

Business activity indicators, including housing market, population, and CPI, monthly rpt, U0280–1

Citrus fruit production and marketing data for major producing States, 1991/92 and trends, annual rpt, S1685–1.1

Copper industry operations, including production, capacity, and reserves, by company and mine, with US and intl comparisons, 1991 and trends, annual rpt, S0497–1

Copper industry State/local taxes paid by type, 1992, article, C5226–2.508

Correctional instn admin, including inmates by criminal background and demographic characteristics, FY92, annual rpt, S0464–2

Court cases and dispositions, by type of case and court, with judicial personnel and finances, by county and city, FY92, annual rpt, S0525–1

Credit union balance sheets, members, and branches, by instn, quarterly rpt, S0460–4

Crimes and arrests, by offense, county, and offender characteristics, with assaults on officers and law enforcement employment, 1992, annual rpt, S0509–2

Economic condition, including population, employment and earnings, and business activity, by industry and locality, 1985-93, semiannual rpt, U5850–1

Economic indicators for 10 Western States, including forecasts from selected organizations, monthly rpt, U0282–2

Economic indicators, including forecasts from 16 forecasting organizations, monthly rpt, U0282–1

Election results and voter registration, by county and/or district, 1992 general election, biennial rpt, S0520–1

Elementary and secondary school enrollment, staff, and finances, by school district and county, FY92 and trends, annual rpt, S0470–1

Employment and unemployment, by county and industry, with production worker hours and earnings, monthly rpt, S0465–1

Govt financial condition, including revenues by source, expenditures by function, and fund balances, FY91, annual rpt, S0450–2

Govt financial condition, including revenues by source, expenditures by function, and fund balances, FY92, annual rpt, S0450–1

Insurance industry financial and underwriting data, by company and type of insurance, with regulatory info, 1992, annual rpt, S0483–1

Arizona

Library finances, holdings, circulation, and staff, by instn and county, FY92, annual rpt, S0495–1

Markets with daily newspapers, demographic and economic info by geographic area, US and Canada, 1993 annual rpt, C3250–1

Occupational profiles, with employment and job outlook, by industry div, occupation, and county, series, S0465–2

Oil and gas production, by field, operator, and well, monthly rpt, S0473–1

Oil/gas industry production, finances, exploration, and reserves, by State, 1992 and trends, annual rpt, A5425–1.1

Savings and loan assn balance sheets and branches, individual State and natl instns, quarterly rpt, S0460–1

Statistical abstract of Arizona, detailed economic, demographic, and govtl data, 1993 recurring rpt, U5850–2

Statistical profiles of 50 States and DC, general data, 1993 annual almanac, C4712–1

Tax revenues by source, tax rates, and disbursements to local areas, FY92 and trends, annual rpt, S0515–1

Traffic accidents, fatalities, and injuries, by vehicle type, circumstances, location, and driver and victim characteristics, with economic loss data, 1991 and trends, annual rpt, S0530–1

Utility and transportation regulatory agency activities, scope of jurisdiction, finances, and employees, by agency, 1991/92 annual rpt, A7015–2

Welfare recipients and payments, by program, county, and district, monthly rpt, S0465–4

see also Apache County, Ariz.

see also Maricopa County, Ariz.

see also Phoenix, Ariz.

see also Pima County, Ariz.

see also Tucson, Ariz.

see also under By City and By County in the "Index by Categories"

see also under By State in the "Index by Categories"

Arkansas

Agricultural production, marketing, and finances, by commodity and county, with farms and acreage, 1992 and trends, annual rpt, U5920–1

Banks and other financial instns, financial condition by instn, June 1992, annual rpt, S0632–1

Business and economic activity indicators for Arkansas, quarterly rpt, U5930–1

Census of Population and Housing detailed findings, 1990, U5935–7

Court caseloads and dispositions, by type of court and case, and location, FY92 and trends, annual rpt, S0647–1

Crimes and arrests, by offense, victim and offender characteristics, and location, with law enforcement employment data, 1992 and trends, annual rpt, S0652–1

Election results, by district and/or county, 1992 general election, biennial rpt, S0775–1

Elementary and secondary school enrollment, grads, staff, and finances, by county and school, 1991/92 and trends, annual rpt, S0660–1

Govt financial condition, including revenues by source, expenditures by function and locality, and fund balances, FY91-92, biennial rpt, S0780–1

Govt financial condition, including revenues by source, expenditures by function and object, and fund balances, FY92, annual rpt, S0670–1

Higher education degrees conferred, by level, discipline, student race and sex, and instn, 1990/91 and trends, annual rpt, S0690–3

Higher education enrollment by student characteristics and geographic origins, by instn, fall 1991 and trends, annual rpt, S0690–1

Higher education finances, including revenues by source, expenditures by function, and State appropriations, by public instn, FY80s-95, biennial rpt, S0690–4

Higher education FTE enrollment, and student credit hour production by program area, by academic level and instn, 1991/92 and trends, annual rpt, S0690–2

Human services dept finances and operations, including service recipient characteristics, by program, FY91 and trends, annual rpt, S0700–2

Labor force, employment, and unemployment, by MSA, county, and labor area, 1980-92, annual rpt, S0662–2

Markets with daily newspapers, demographic and economic info by geographic area, US and Canada, 1993 annual rpt, C3250–1

Mineral (nonfuel) production, by commodity, 1991-92, annual article, U5930–1.503

Oil and gas production by field, and disposition, monthly rpt, S0737–1

Oil/gas industry production, finances, exploration, and reserves, by State, 1992 and trends, annual rpt, A5425–1.1

Socioeconomic trends for Arkansas, by MSA and/or county, 1993 annual rpt, U5935–1

Statistical profiles of 50 States and DC, general data, 1993 annual almanac, C4712–1

Traffic accidents, fatalities, and injuries, by vehicle type, circumstances, location, and driver and victim characteristics, 1991, annual rpt, S0692–1

Utility and transportation regulatory agency activities, scope of jurisdiction, finances, and employees, by agency, 1991/92 annual rpt, A7015–2

Utility financial, operating, and regulatory data, by utility type and company, 1992 annual rpt, S0757–1

Vital statistics, including births, deaths by cause, marriages, and divorces, by age, sex, race, and county, 1991 and trends, annual rpt, S0685–1

see also under By City and By County in the "Index by Categories"

see also under By State in the "Index by Categories"

Arkansas River

Freight tonnage on Arkansas River through Muskogee and Catoosa ports, monthly rpt quarterly data, U8130–1

Index by Subjects and Names

Freight traffic on Arkansas River, quarterly business activity rpt, U5930–1

Armed services

Military post exchange and commissary sales, by product category, for military resale agencies, FY91 and trends, annual rpt, A2072–1

Military post exchange and commissary sales, by service branch or region, with merchandising devs and comparisons to civilian retail trade, monthly rpt, C0500–1

Military post exchange sales, retail and other, by location and store, FY92 and trends, annual rpt, A2072–2.502

Public confidence in selected societal instns, 1993 Gallup Poll and trends, C4040–1.510, R8780–1.508

Size and structure of defense forces, by service branch and for nuclear weapons, FY90, FY93, and DOD recommendation in 1993 review of post-Cold War needs, article, C5800–4.527

State and local:

Missouri correctional instn inmate characteristics, including military service by branch, FY93, annual rpt, S4501–1

see also Air Force

see also Army

see also Coast Guard

see also Department of Defense

see also Marine Corps

see also Military personnel

see also Navy

see also Voluntary military service

Armed services reserves

see also National Guard

Arms and munitions

see Arms control and disarmament

see Arms trade

see Bombs

see Defense contracts and procurement

see Defense expenditures

see Explosives

see Firearms

see Military assistance

see Military weapons

see Missiles and rockets

see Nuclear weapons

Arms control and disarmament

College freshmen attitudes on whether nuclear disarmament is attainable, by sex and instn type, fall 1992, annual survey, U6215–1

Nuclear warhead allotments of US and Russia under strategic arms reduction treaties, 1990-93, annual rpt, C2500–2

Nuclear weapons plutonium and highly enriched uranium disposal requirements of US and Russia arms reductions, 1993 article, C5226–2.511

Public opinion in US on news items concerning US-Russia nuclear arms reduction agreement, Jan 1993 survey, C8915–1.501

Public opinion in US on selected foreign policy issues, with detail for 3 States, 1993 survey, annual rpt, A4965–1

see also Arms trade

see also Defense expenditures

Arms sales

see Arms trade

Index by Subjects and Names

Arrest

Arms trade

Aerospace industry, civil and military production, R&D, trade, employment, and finances, with Federal funding data, 1991 and trends, annual rpt, A0250–2

Communications equipment foreign trade value for defense-related equipment, with data by product type and country, 1990-92, annual rpt, A4725–1.2

Latin America military assistance from US Govt and other countries, by country, 1992 annual rpt, U6250–1.11

Public opinion on allowing sales of military equipment to developing countries, for US and 9 European countries, 1991 survey, C8915–8.1

Purchase value of US weapons for top 5 foreign countries, since Aug 1990, 1993 article, C8900–1.509

see also Military assistance

Army

Physicians in Fed Govt, by detailed specialty and service branch, 1992, annual rpt, A2200–3.2

Post exchange and commissary sales, by product category and region, and employment, for military resale agencies, FY91 and trends, annual rpt, A2072–1

Post exchange sales, by service branch, with merchandising devs and comparisons to civilian retail trade, monthly rpt, C0500–1

Post exchange sales, retail and other, by location and store, FY92 and trends, annual rpt, A2072–2.502

see also National Guard

Army bases

see Military bases, posts, and reservations

Army contracts and procurement

see Defense contracts and procurement

Arreglado, Elizabeth R.

"Top Executive Compensation, 1992 Edition", R4105–19

Arrest

Black American crime, arrest, and incarceration data, with comparisons to whites, 1970s-91, annual compilation, C6775–2.5

Black children and youth population, economic, health, and education data, with comparisons to whites, 1993 rpt, R3840–21

Latin America statistical abstract, general data by country, 1992 annual rpt, U6250–1.15

Property crime arrests, by offense and age, 1991, annual rpt, A5650–1.4

Statistical profiles of 50 States and DC, general data, 1993 annual almanac, C4712–1

State and local:

Alabama crimes and arrests, by offense, with data by location and offender characteristics, 1992 and trends, annual rpt, S0119–1

Arizona arrests by offense, offender characteristics, and county, 1992, annual rpt, S0505–2.2

Arkansas crimes and arrests, by offense, victim and offender characteristics, and location, 1992 and trends, annual rpt, S0652–1

California crimes and arrests, clearances, and arrest dispositions, with data by offense and offender characteristics, 1987-92, annual rpt, S0910–1.1

California criminal justice system detailed data, by offense, county, age, race-ethnicity, and sex, 1991 and trends, annual rpt, S0910–2

Colorado crimes and arrests, by offense and location, with offender characteristics, and assaults on police, 1992, annual rpt, S1068–1

Connecticut crimes and arrests, by offense, with data by local agency, and victim-offender characteristics, 1992, annual rpt, S1256–1

DC adult arrests for serious crimes, 1982-92, article, R5685–4.505

DC criminal justice system summary, including crimes and arrests, criminal procedure, prisoners, and parole, 1991 and trends, annual rpt, S1535–2

DC statistical profile, general data, 1992 annual rpt, S1535–3.8

Delaware crimes and arrests, by offense, county, and victim-offender characteristics, 1991 and trends, annual rpt, S1375–5

Delaware State police traffic arrests by violation, 1988-92, annual rpt, S1435–1

Florida crimes and arrests, by offense, with data by victim and offender characteristics, 1992, annual rpt, S1770–1

Hawaii crimes and arrests, by offense, with data by county and victim-offender characteristics, 1992, annual rpt, S2035–1

Idaho crimes and arrests, by offense, with data by location and offender characteristics, 1992 and trends, annual rpt, S2275–2

Illinois crimes and arrests, by offense, with data by location and offender characteristics, 1991, annual rpt, S2536–1

Kansas crimes and arrests, by offense, with data by location, agency, and victim-offender characteristics, 1992 and trends, annual rpt, S2925–1.1

Kentucky arrests by county and offense, and law enforcement employment by agency, 1992, annual rpt, S3150–1.2

Maine crimes and arrests, by offense, with data by county, reporting agency, and offender age and sex, 1991, annual rpt, S3475–1

Maryland crimes and arrests, by offense, location, and offender characteristics, with law enforcement employment and assaults on officers, 1992 and trends, annual rpt, S3665–1

Michigan arrests of intoxicated drivers, by sex, 1989-91, annual rpt, S3997–2

Michigan child/spousal support collection program bench warrants and arrests, by county, 1992, annual rpt, S3962–1.2

Michigan crimes and arrests, by offense, with data by location and offender characteristics, 1992 and trends, annual rpt, S3997–1

Minnesota arrests of drivers under the influence of alcohol, by age, 1983-92, annual rpt, S4230–2

Missouri crimes and arrests, by offense and location, with victim and offender characteristics, 1991 and trends, annual rpt, S4560–2

Montana crimes and clearances, by offense and jurisdiction, 1992, annual rpt, S4705–1

Nevada statistical abstract, general data, 1992 biennial rpt, S5005–1.4

New Hampshire arrests, by offense and offender age, sex, and race-ethnicity, 1991, annual rpt, S5250–2.2

New Jersey crimes and arrests, by offense, with data by location and offender characteristics, 1992 and trends, annual rpt, S5430–1

New York State arrests, and criminal processing and sentencing, 1991 and trends, annual rpt, S5760–3.2

North Carolina arrests by detailed offense, offender characteristics, and county, 1991-92, annual rpt, S5955–1.2

North Dakota crimes and arrests, by offense, location, and offender characteristics, and law enforcement employment, 1991 and trends, annual rpt, S6060–1

Oklahoma crimes and arrests, by offense, with victim and offender characteristics, 1990-92, annual rpt, S6465–1.1

Oregon crimes and arrests, by offense, with data by county, local agency, and offender characteristics, 1992 and trends, annual rpt, S6603–3

Pennsylvania crimes and arrests, by offense, with data by location and offender characteristics, 1992 and trends, annual rpt, S6860–1

South Carolina crimes and arrests, by offense, with data by location and victim-offender characteristics, and assaults on officers, 1992 and trends, annual rpt, S7205–1

South Carolina motor carrier regulation, including safety and hazardous materials inspections, violations, arrests, and fines, FY92 and trends, annual rpt, S7235–1

South Dakota driving while intoxicated arrests, 1986-92, annual rpt, S7300–3

Texas crimes and arrests, by offense, with data by location and offender characteristics, 1992 and trends, annual rpt, S7735–2

Utah crimes and arrests, by offense, county, and local agency, 1992 and trends, annual rpt, S7890–3

Virginia crimes and arrests, by offense, with data by location and offender characteristics, 1992, annual rpt, S8295–2

Washington State crimes and arrests, by offense, with data by location and offender characteristics, 1992 and trends, annual rpt, S8440–1

West Virginia crimes and arrests, by offense, location, and offender characteristics, 1990-91, annual rpt, S8610–1

Wisconsin crimes and arrests, by offense, offender characteristics, county, and local agency, 1992 and trends, annual rpt, S8771–1

Wyoming crimes and arrests, by offense, with data by location and victim and offender characteristics, 1991 and trends, annual rpt, S8867–3

see also Pretrial detention and release

Arson

Arson

Fires of incendiary and suspicious origin, with deaths and dollar loss, 1991, annual rpt, A5650–1.4

State and local:

- Alabama arson offenses, clearances, and damages, by type of property, 1992, annual rpt, S0119–1.1
- Arizona crimes and arrests, by offense, county, and offender characteristics, 1992, annual rpt, S0505–2
- Arkansas crimes and arrests, by offense, victim and offender characteristics, and location, 1992 and trends, annual rpt, S0652–1
- California crimes and arrests, clearances, and arrest dispositions, with data by offense and offender characteristics, 1987-92, annual rpt, S0910–1.1
- California criminal justice system detailed data, by offense, county, age, race-ethnicity, and sex, 1991 and trends, annual rpt, S0910–2
- Colorado crimes and arrests, by offense and location, with offender characteristics, and assaults on police, 1992, annual rpt, S1068–1
- Connecticut crimes and arrests, by offense, with data by local agency, and victim-offender characteristics, 1992, annual rpt, S1256–1
- DC criminal justice system summary, including crimes and arrests, criminal procedure, prisoners, and parole, 1991 and trends, annual rpt, S1535–2
- Delaware crimes and arrests, by offense, county, and victim-offender characteristics, 1991 and trends, annual rpt, S1375–5
- Florida crimes and arrests, by offense, with data by victim and offender characteristics, 1992, annual rpt, S1770–1
- Hawaii crimes and arrests, by offense, with data by county and victim-offender characteristics, 1992, annual rpt, S2035–1
- Idaho crimes and arrests, by offense, with data by location and offender characteristics, 1992 and trends, annual rpt, S2275–2
- Illinois crimes and arrests, by offense, with data by location and offender characteristics, 1991, annual rpt, S2536–1
- Kansas crimes and arrests, by offense, with data by location, agency, and victim-offender characteristics, 1992 and trends, annual rpt, S2925–1.1
- Kentucky crimes and arrests, by offense, with data by location and offender characteristics, 1992, annual rpt, S3150–1
- Maine crimes and arrests, by offense, with data by county, reporting agency, and offender age and sex, 1991, annual rpt, S3475–1
- Maryland crimes and arrests, by offense, location, and offender characteristics, with law enforcement employment and assaults on officers, 1992 and trends, annual rpt, S3665–1
- Michigan crimes and arrests, by offense, with data by location and offender characteristics, 1992 and trends, annual rpt, S3997–1
- Missouri crimes and arrests, by offense and location, with victim and offender characteristics, 1991 and trends, annual rpt, S4560–2
- Montana crimes and clearances, by offense and jurisdiction, 1992, annual rpt, S4705–1
- New Hampshire crimes and arrests, by offense, jurisdiction, and offender characteristics, 1991 and trends, annual rpt, S5250–2
- New Jersey crimes and arrests, by offense, with data by location and offender characteristics, 1992 and trends, annual rpt, S5430–1
- New York State crimes and arrests by offense and demographic characteristics, and court activity and corrections, 1991 and trends, annual rpt, S5760–3
- North Carolina crimes and arrests, by offense, with data by location and offender characteristics, 1992 and trends, annual rpt, S5955–1
- North Dakota crimes and arrests, by offense, location, and offender characteristics, and law enforcement employment, 1991 and trends, annual rpt, S6060–1
- Oklahoma crimes and arrests, by offense, with victim and offender characteristics, 1990-92, annual rpt, S6465–1.1
- Oregon crimes and arrests, by offense, with data by county, local agency, and offender characteristics, 1992 and trends, annual rpt, S6603–3
- Pennsylvania crimes and arrests, by offense, with data by location and offender characteristics, 1992 and trends, annual rpt, S6860–1
- South Carolina crimes and arrests, by detailed offense, offender characteristics, and location, 1992 and trends, annual rpt, S7205–1.2
- Tennessee fire, electrical, and manufactured housing inspections, fee revenues, and arson investigations, 1991, annual rpt, S7466–1
- Texas crimes and arrests, by offense, with data by location and offender characteristics, 1992 and trends, annual rpt, S7735–2
- Utah crimes and arrests, by offense, county, and local agency, 1992 and trends, annual rpt, S7890–3
- Virginia crimes and arrests, by offense, with data by location and offender characteristics, 1992, annual rpt, S8295–2
- Washington State crimes and arrests, by offense, with data by location and offender characteristics, 1992 and trends, annual rpt, S8440–1
- West Virginia crimes and arrests, by offense, location, and offender characteristics, 1990-91, annual rpt, S8610–1
- Wisconsin crimes and arrests, by offense, offender characteristics, county, and local agency, 1992 and trends, annual rpt, S8771–1
- Wyoming crimes and arrests, by offense, with data by location and victim and offender characteristics, 1991 and trends, annual rpt, S8867–3

Index by Subjects and Names

Art

- Shopping center financial and operating data, with detail by type of tenant, US and Canada, 1991, triennial rpt, R9285–1

State and local:

- New York State statistical yearbook, general data, 1992 annual rpt, U5100–1.10

Arteriosclerosis

- *see* Cardiovascular diseases
- *see* Cerebrovascular diseases
- *see* Circulatory diseases

Arthritis

- *see* Musculoskeletal diseases

Artificial fibers

- *see* Synthetic fibers and fabrics

Artificial organs

- *see* Medical transplants

Artificial sweeteners

- *see* Syrups and sweeteners

Arts and the humanities

- Bachelor degrees granted in the humanities, by field of study, 1980/81 and 1989/90, article, R4800–2.511
- Charitable contribution donor characteristics for arts/humanities organizations, 1993 survey article, C2176–1.507
- Charitable contributions, by type of donor and recipient, 1992 and trends, annual rpt, A0700–1
- Corporate charitable contributions, by donor characteristics and detailed type of recipient, 1991 and trends, annual rpt, R4105–8
- Corporate policies concerning charitable contributions to arts programs and other causes, 1991, recurring rpt, A3690–1
- Doctoral degree recipient characteristics, including citizenship status, source of support, field of study, and instn, 1990/91 and trends, annual rpt, R6000–7
- Employment in business and industry, hiring plans for college grads, by field, salary, and degree, 1993 annual survey rpt, U3730–1
- Foundation assets, income, and grants by type of recipient, with data for top organizations and by location, 1991 and trends, annual rpt, R4900–1
- Fundraising through united arts funds (UAFs), with fund operations, income by source, and allocations, by UAF, 1992 and trends, annual rpt, A1315–2
- Fundraising through united arts funds (UAFs), with top 10 UAFs in funds raised by source, 1992, annual article, C2176–1.513
- Salary and job offers for college grads, by field of study, type of employer, and degree level, by region, interim rpt series, A3940–1
- Salary and job offers for college grads, by field of study, type of employer, and degree level, series, A3940–2
- Southern States higher education degree conferrals, by sex, race-ethnicity, level, and selected field, by State, 1990s and trends, biennial fact book, A8945–1.3
- Women and minorities in professional fields, detailed education and labor force data, 1980s-91, with historical trends, recurring rpt, A3960–2

State and local:

Connecticut public school data, including enrollment, staff, programs, finances, and student characteristics, 1991/92, biennial rpt, S1185–3

Index by Subjects and Names

Missouri higher education student grant and academic scholarship program awards at art/music instns, FY93 and trends, annual rpt, S4520–3.2

see also Architecture

see also Art

see also Federal aid to arts and humanities

see also Foreign languages

see also Language arts

see also Motion pictures

see also Museums

see also Music

see also National Foundation on the Arts and the Humanities

see also Performing arts

see also Photography and photographic equipment

see also Social sciences

see also State funding for arts and culture

see also Theater

Aruba

see Caribbean area

Asbestos

see Asbestos contamination

see Nonmetallic minerals and mines

Asbestos contamination

City govt costs to enforce Fed Govt regulations including asbestos abatement, FY93-98, A9330–12

Construction contractor revenues, for top 20 firms specializing in asbestos abatement, 1992, annual article, C5800–2.548

Death rates from asbestos exposure in schools vs 6 other health risks, 1990, U9640–3

State and local:

Idaho deaths from asbestosis, by age, 1991, annual rpt, S2250–2

North Dakota school district mill levies for asbestos funds, by district, 1992/93, annual rpt, S6180–4

South Carolina deaths, by detailed cause, age, sex, and race, 1990, annual rpt, S7175–2

Utah correctional industries asbestos abatement program trainees and outcomes, FY92 annual rpt, S7810–1

Aseptic containers

see Packaging and containers

Asia

Advertising agency income and billings in Asia/Pacific region, for top 15 multinatl agencies, 1992, annual article, C2710–1.527

Airline financial and operating data, for Orient Airlines Assn members, FY91-92, article, C7000–4.503

Amusement park operating and financial data, including data for US and foreign parks, miniature golf, waterparks, and games, 1992, annual rpt, A5700–1

Earnings of industrial workers in Mexico and 4 Asian countries, 1991, article, C5800–7.524

Energy exploration, rotary drilling rigs in operation, by world area and country, monthly rpt, B4675–1

Executive job vacancy index, by industry, job function, and region, quarterly rpt, B5000–5

Foreign investment inflow, with detail for US and Japan investment, for 8-9 countries, FY85-92, article, R5650–2.555

Jewish population by world area, country, and US census div, State, and city, 1990-92, annual compilation, A2050–1

Liquefied natural gas trading contracts, with deliveries, prices, and countries involved, 1992 article, C6985–1.503

Lumber exports from US to Pacific Rim, by country and product type, monthly rpt, A1630–2

Lumber industry foreign trade with US, monthly rpt, A1630–1

Military commissaries of US, sales by stores in Pacific Region countries, FY92, annual feature, A2072–2.501

Motor vehicle world production, sales, trade, and registrations, by country, world area, manufacturer, and make, 1991 and trends, annual rpt, A0865–2.1

Oil refinery capacity worldwide, with data by country and company, and outlook for 1993-94, annual compilation, C6985–4.1

Oil refinery capacity worldwide, with data by country and company, and outlook for 1993-94, annual feature, C6985–1.508

Oil/gas deep well drilling, success ratios, and costs, by world area, 1990-92, annual article, C4420–1.503

Oil/gas seismic exploration land crews and vessels, by world area or country, quarterly press release, A8912–2

Polyester fiber production capacity worldwide, with shares for Asia vs other areas, 1985 and 1993, article, A1250–1.525

Population growth trends, vital statistics, and demographic and socioeconomic characteristics, series, R4500–1

Population size and characteristics, GNP, and land area, by world region and/or country, 1993 annual data sheet, R8750–5

Refugees, resettlement, and intl aid devs, by country, 1992, annual rpt, R9372–1

Securities market participation by foreign and US investors, by world area and country, quarterly rpt, A8825–2

Textile manufactured fiber industry employment, for US, Europe, and selected Asian countries, 1980-91, annual feature, C3460–1.505

Textile manufactured fiber production and capacity for 4 countries, monthly rpt semiannual survey, C3460–1.502

Tourist arrivals and daily expenditures in 6 Asian countries, 1993 article, C2710–1.549

Travel trends, including tourist arrivals and expenditures, by region and/or country, 1992 annual rpt, C2140–1.3

see also Bahrain

see also Bangladesh

see also Brunei

see also Cambodia

see also China, People's Republic

see also Hong Kong

see also India

see also Indonesia

see also Iran

see also Iraq

see also Israel

see also Japan

see also Jordan

see also Korea, South

see also Kuwait

see also Malaysia

see also Middle East

see also Mongolia

Asian Americans

see also Myanmar

see also Oman

see also Pakistan

see also Papua New Guinea

see also Philippines

see also Qatar

see also Saudi Arabia

see also Singapore

see also Southeast Asia

see also Syria

see also Taiwan

see also Thailand

see also Turkey

see also United Arab Emirates

see also Vietnam

see also Yemen

see also under By Foreign Country or World Area in the "Index by Categories"

Asian Americans

Accounting grad supply-demand, including detail by sex, race-ethnicity, and region, 1991/92 and trends, annual rpt, A1885–1

AIDS cases and deaths among children under age 13, by race-ethnicity, 1990, R3840–21

AIDS cases, by sex and race-ethnicity, through June 1992, article, C4215–1.503

Airline travel frequency, destination, and purpose, by traveler characteristics, 1992 survey and trends, annual rpt, A0325–6

American College Test (ACT) scores, by sex and race-ethnicity, 1993, annual article, C2175–1.534

American College Test (ACT) scores by student characteristics, with student views on schools and education plans, 1992 and trends, annual rpt, R1960–6

Births and fertility, by selected newborn and maternal characteristics, 1990, article, R8750–1.510

Broadcasting station seller tax deferment certificates granted by FCC for sales to minority buyers, by ethnic group, 1978-1st half 1993, article, C1850–14.537

Business establishments and gross receipts for minority-owned vs total businesses, with detail by race-ethnicity, 1987, article, C4215–1.507

Business formation rate by race-ethnicity, 1993 article, C4687–1.510

Cancer deaths among minorities, by body site and ethnic group, 1989, annual rpt, A1175–1

Catholic school enrollment by ethnic group, 1982/83 and 1991/92-1992/93, annual rpt, A7375–1

Catholic secondary school operations and finances, including enrollment by race-ethnicity and family income, 1991/92 and trends, biennial rpt, A7375–5

Chemist and chemical engineer salaries, employment status, and demographic and professional characteristics, 1993, annual rpt, A1250–4

Chemistry and chemical engineering grad starting salaries, employment status, demographic characteristics, and advanced study plans, 1991/92, annual rpt, A1250–2

Child population, and distribution by race-ethnicity, for selected cities, 1990, annual rpt, R3840–11.2

Child poverty by State and for 200 cities and 89 counties, with State and city detail by race-ethnicity, 1989 and trends, R3840–20

Asian Americans

Index by Subjects and Names

Community and junior college revenues by source and expenditures by function, and selected student characteristics, FY92, annual rpt, A6705–1

Consumer buying power survey of population, income, and sales by kind of business, by census div, State, MSA, county, and city, 1992, annual rpt, C1200–1.511

Consumer purchasing by product type, and ownership of selected electronics, for blacks, Hispanics, and Asians, 1992/93 survey, article, C2710–1.513

Corporate boards of directors with women and minority members, and board membership by sex and race-ethnicity, 1991/92, B4490–2.36

Correctional instn admin, inmates, facilities, costs, parole and probation, and staffing, for local, State, and Federal systems, 1992 annual series, R4300–1

Dental school enrollment and grads, by sex and race-ethnicity, 1992/93 annual rpt, A1475–3.1

Dental school faculty, support personnel, and staff characteristics, by instn, 1992/93, annual rpt, A1475–4.5

Dental school student attrition, by reason and student characteristics, 1991/92 and trends, annual rpt, A1475–4.4

Doctoral degree recipient characteristics, including citizenship status, source of support, field of study, and instn, 1990/91 and trends, annual rpt, R6000–7

Doctoral degrees conferred and recipient characteristics, by field, 1992, annual feature, C2175–1.535

Ecologist personal and professional characteristics, including research activity and funding, with data by field, Mar 1992 survey, recurring rpt, A4685–1

Elementary/secondary prospective teacher characteristics and opinions, survey of persons interested in alternative certification routes, 1992, R6350–7

Engineering degrees awarded, by State, instn, and field, with detail for women, minorities, and foreign students, 1991/92, annual rpt, A0685–1

Engineering program enrollment, by instn, field, and State, with detail for women, minorities, and foreign students, fall 1992, annual rpt, A0685–2

Eye bank activity in US and abroad, including donations by type, source, and donor characteristics, and data by individual bank, 1992 and trends, annual rpt, A4743–1

Foundation board trustees by sex and race-ethnicity, for 25 leading private, community, and corporate foundations, 1989 and trends, A9405–1.1

Foundation board trustees by sex and race-ethnicity, for 25 leading private, community, and corporate foundations, 1991 and trends, A9405–1.2

Foundation finances, and personnel and governing board characteristics, by organization characteristics, 1991/92, article, C2176–1.506

Geoscience enrollment and degrees awarded, by sex, race-ethnicity, and discipline, 1991/92, annual rpt, A1785–3

Health indicators, including hypertension and lung cancer rates, and cancer and

heart disease/stroke deaths, by sex and race-ethnicity, 1993 feature, C4215–1.511

Higher education degrees conferred, by level, sex, discipline, and race-ethnicity, 1990/91, recurring feature, C2175–1.523

Higher education employment, by position type and race-ethnicity, 1991/92, C2175–1.507

Higher education enrollment by race-ethnicity, by State, fall 1991, annual rpt, C2175–1.531

Higher education enrollment in historically black colleges, distribution by student race-ethnicity, 1993 article, C4215–1.509

Higher education enrollment of minority and foreign students at approx 3,100 instns, fall 1991, recurring feature, C2175–1.510

Higher education enrollment of minority and foreign students, with comparison to whites, by sex, State, and instn type, fall 1991, recurring feature, C2175–1.506

Higher education freshmen attitudes and characteristics, degree and career plans, and financial aid sources, by sex and instn type, fall 1992, annual survey, U6215–1

Higher education involvement of minorities, including enrollment and degrees awarded, by race-ethnicity, sex, and State, 1970s-91, annual rpt, A1410–10

Higher education minority student enrollment trends, 1993 annual survey, A1410–1.38

Higher education president personal and professional characteristics, 1990 and trends, recurring rpt, A1410–12

Higher education president personal and professional characteristics, 1990, article, C2175–1.533

Higher education student athlete enrollment and graduation rates, by sex, race-ethnicity, and major sport, for Natl Collegiate Athletic Assn Div I instns, 1992/93, annual rpt, A7440–4

Higher education undergrad and grad enrollment by race-ethnicity, fall 1990, article, C4215–1.508

Incarcerated mothers and their children, with data on characteristics, child caregivers, visitation, and support program use, 1991/92, A7575–4

Job Corps youth training program funding, enrollment capacity, and participants by selected characteristics, 1981-94, article, R4800–2.515

Journalism/mass communication enrollment and grads by level, by instn, sex, race-ethnicity, and field, 1990/91 and trends, annual article, A3225–1

Labor force and education data for women and minorities in professional fields, 1980s-91, with historical trends, recurring rpt, A3960–2

Law school enrollment by minority status, degrees conferred, staff, and library holdings, by instn, 1992/93 and trends, annual rpt, A0970–1

Law school grad employment and salaries, by type of employer, location, and grad characteristics, 1992 and trends, annual rpt, A6505–1

Librarians (special) salaries, by location, work setting, and personal characteristics, US and Canada, 1992 and trends, biennial survey rpt, A8965–1

Librarians at universities and research instns, by minority group and census div, FY92, annual survey, A3365–2

Library/info science school enrollment, staff and student characteristics, finances, and curricula, by school and degree program, 1991/92, annual rpt, A3235–1

Local govt land use planning commissions composition and activities, and commissioner characteristics, 1987 and trends, recurring rpt, A2615–2

Local officials in municipal and county govt, demographic profiles and job functions, 1993 annual rpt, A5800–1

Mathematics dept faculty and doctoral degree recipient characteristics, including salaries, 1991/92 and trends, annual survey, A2085–1.1

Medical school Asian vs white student performance indicators at Jefferson Medical School, including standardized test scores, 1981-92, article, A3273–8.503

Medical school programs, fees, applicants, admissions, and enrollment, with data by age, sex, minority group, and instn, 1992/93 and trends, annual rpt, A3273–10

Nursing center (community) staff and client characteristics, and services, 1990 survey, article, A8010–3.506

Nursing college deans, by race-ethnicity, 1992/93, annual rpt, A0615–2

Nursing college faculty, by race-ethnicity, 1992/93, annual rpt, A0615–1

Nursing higher education program faculty and clinic patient characteristics, 1992/93 biennial rpt, A0615–5

Nursing school enrollment and grads, by degree level, sex, race-ethnicity, and instn type and location, 1992/93 and trends, annual rpt, A0615–4

Nursing schools, programs, enrollment, student and staff characteristics, and grads, 1991 and trends, annual rpt, A8010–1

Optometry school faculty, enrollment and degrees, policies and programs, and finances, by instn, 1991/92, annual survey, A3370–2

Osteopathy college enrollment, student and faculty characteristics, and finances, 1992/93 and trends, annual rpt, A0620–1

Osteopathy student debt and career plans, by student characteristics, 1991/92 and trends, annual survey rpt, A0620–2

Pharmacy degree program applications, enrollment, and degrees conferred, by student characteristics and instn, 1990/91 and trends, annual rpt, A0630–9

Physics and astronomy bachelor degree recipients postgraduation plans and demographic characteristics, 1991/92 and trends, annual survey, A1960–3

Physics degrees awarded, by level, sex, and minority group, 1991/92, annual rpt, A1960–2.1

Planning profession employment and salaries, by type of employer, demographic and professional characteristics, and location, 1991 and trends, biennial rpt, A2615–1

Political science higher education dept faculty, by sex and race-ethnicity, 1991/92, annual rpt, A2617–1

Index by Subjects and Names

Asian Americans

Population characteristics, employment, and voting patterns for minority groups by detailed race-ethnicity, with comparisons to whites, 1980s-2040, R8750-2.58

Population of Asian/Pacific Islander origin, for top 100 zip code areas, 1992, annual rpt, C1200-1.514

Prisoners on death row, by State, sex, and race-ethnicity, 1992 and trends, annual rpt, A1305-3

Private elementary and secondary school enrollment, staff, and finances, with detail for minorities, by school type and region, 1980s-1992/93, annual rpt, A6835-3

Professional worker salaries, by employee and employer characteristics, with detail for scientists and engineers, 1990s and trends, biennial rpt, A3960-1

Psychology doctoral degree recipient employment and demographic characteristics, and finances, 1990/91, biennial survey rpt, A2620-4

Psychology grad depts, faculty characteristics, enrollment, and student aid, US and Canada, 1990/91 and trends, annual rpt, A2620-3

Public health school applicant, student, and grad characteristics, by instn, 1991/92 and trends, annual rpt, A3372-3

Public health school faculty characteristics, by instn, fall 1991, recurring rpt, A3372-1

Religious congregation characteristics, including membership, activities, staff, and finances, 1992 survey, recurring rpt, A5435-4

Restaurants/drinking places and sales, for minority-owned establishments by race-ethnicity, 1987, article, A8200-1.508

Sales workers by sex and race-ethnicity, 1990, article, C1200-1.512

Scholastic Aptitude Test (SAT) participants and/or scores, by education of parents, income, and race-ethnicity, 1992, C4215-1.501

School board members by race-ethnicity, by district enrollment size, 1992 survey rpt, A0775-5

Science and math elementary/secondary education, including student and teacher characteristics, and requirements, by State, 1991/92, biennial rpt, A4355-3

Small business owners financing sources and experience of discrimination in lending, by race-ethnicity, 1993 survey feature, C4215-1.512

Social work higher education programs, faculty and student characteristics, and student aid, with data by instn, 1992 and trends, annual rpt, A4515-1

Socioeconomic status data for blacks compared to other minority groups, 1993 annual compilation, A8510-1.1

State social, economic, and govtl indicators, with rankings, 1993 semiannual rpt, B8500-1.1, B8500-1.7

Statistical profiles of 50 States and DC, general data, 1993 annual almanac, C4712-1

Student attitudes on courses in 4 subject areas, for 8th graders by sex and race-ethnicity, 1988, R4800-2.512

Substance abuse treatment programs, funding by source, and client

characteristics, for alcohol and drug services, by State, FY91 and trends, annual rpt, A7112-1

Theological school enrollment by degree level, by sex and race-ethnicity, fall 1992 and trends, annual rpt, A3376-1

Theological seminary enrollment in Canada and US, with detail for women and minorities, 1992 and trends, annual rpt, C0105-1

TV (public) viewing habits of Asian Americans, 1992 survey, R4250-1.16

TV news coverage of Rodney King police brutality case, with reporter and source characteristics, and detail by network, Mar 1991-Apr 1992, article, R3823-1.505

TV news stories by sex and race-ethnicity of reporter or anchor, with detail by network, 1992, annual article, R3823-1.503

Urban public school performance compared to natl goals for year 2000, with data by race-ethnicity and sex, 1990/91, A4425-4

Western States higher education grad student exchange program enrollment, by race-ethnicity, for 13 States, fall 1992, annual rpt, A9385-1

Women candidates in State-level elections, outcome summaries including campaign funds raised, voting by sex, and winner's race-ethnicity, 1992, U4510-4.4

Women in elective office, by minority group, party, and govt level, 1993, annual rpt, U4510-1.66

Women professionals employment, with detail by race-ethnicity and for 3 occupations, 1990 and trends, article, R8750-1.511

Women's employment in govt, with data by race-ethnicity and State, series, U5090-1

Women's housing issues, with data on household composition, tenure, and characteristics, 1992, A8657-5

Work force and new workers, black, Hispanic, and Asian shares, 2000 article, C1200-4.509

State and local:

Alabama county data book, general data, 1992 annual rpt, S0121-2

Alabama homicide offenses, by offender and victim race-ethnicity, 1992, annual rpt, S0119-1.1

Alabama statistical abstract, general data, 1992 recurring rpt, U5680-2.3

Alaska corrections system admin, including inmate and probationer/parolee offenses and demographic characteristics, 1991 annual rpt, S0287-1

Alaska population, housing, income, and education data, by demographic characteristics and/or locality, 1990/91 and trends, annual rpt, S0320-4

Alaska public schools, enrollment, staff, and finances, by district, FY92, annual rpt, S0295-2

Alaska State court system employees, by sex and race-ethnicity, FY92, annual rpt, S0290-1

Arizona arrests and murder victims, by age, sex, and race-ethnicity, 1992, annual rpt, S0505-2

Arizona correctional instn admin, including inmates by criminal background and demographic characteristics, FY92, annual rpt, S0464-2

Arizona elementary and secondary school enrollment, by grade and race-ethnicity, 1991/92, annual rpt, S0470-1

Arizona household income and poverty rates, by race-ethnicity, 1989, article, U0280-1.502

Arizona statistical abstract, general data, 1993 recurring rpt, U5850-2.2, U5850-2.3, U5850-2.4, U5850-2.6, U5850-2.12, U5850-2.16

Arkansas Census of Population and Housing detailed findings, 1990, U5935-7

Arkansas Medicaid recipients, by race-ethnicity, FY91, annual rpt, S0700-2.3

Arkansas public school enrollment and grads, by race-ethnicity and sex, 1991/92, annual rpt, S0660-1.1

California Census of Population and Housing detailed findings, 1990, S0840-9

California judicial system employment by position, sex, and race-ethnicity, with minority utilization rates and parity targets, Jan 1993, annual rpt, S0905-1.1

California labor force planning rpt, including population characteristics, and employment by industry, 1992 annual rpt, S0830-2

California postsecondary education enrollment and degrees, by sex, race-ethnicity, and instn, 1990/91, annual series, S0827-2

California public school Asian student enrollment and number with limited English proficiency, 1987-92, annual rpt, S0825-10

California public school enrollment, grads, and staff, by race-ethnicity, 1992/93 and trends, annual rpt, S0825-9

California registered apprentices, by sex and race-ethnicity, 1987-91, annual rpt, S0840-2.3

California socioeconomic and govtl data for municipalities, counties, and school districts, 1993 annual rpt, C4712-3

California statistical abstract, general data, 1992 annual rpt, S0840-2.2

California vital statistics, including population, births, and deaths by cause, by demographic characteristics and county, 1990 and trends, annual rpt, S0865-1

Colorado homicide offenders and victims, by age, sex, and race-ethnicity, 1991-92, annual rpt, S1068-1

Colorado public school enrollment, finances, and student and staff characteristics, by locality, 1992 annual rpt series, S1000-2

Colorado vital statistics, including population, births, deaths by cause, abortion, marriage and divorce, and adoption, by demographic characteristics and location, 1990 and trends, annual rpt, S1010-1

Connecticut crimes and arrests, by offense, with data by local agency, and victim-offender characteristics, 1992, annual rpt, S1256-1

Connecticut public school data, including enrollment, staff, programs, finances, and student characteristics, 1991/92, biennial rpt, S1185-3

DC public school enrollment, by race-ethnicity, 1987/88-1991/92, annual rpt, S1605-2

Asian Americans

Index by Subjects and Names

DC statistical profile, general data, 1992 annual rpt, S1535–3.1

Delaware postsecondary instn enrollment and degrees conferred, by race-ethnicity, 1992, annual rpt, S1425–1

Delaware public and nonpublic school minority enrollment, 1991/92, annual rpt, S1430–1

Florida higher education enrollment, degree programs, staff, and finances, by State-supported instn, with student and staff characteristics, 1991/92 annual rpt, S1725–1

Florida municipal and county statistical profiles, general data, 1991 annual rpt, C4712–6

Florida statistical abstract, general data, 1992 annual rpt, U6660–1.1, U6660–1.4

Florida vital statistics, including population, births, deaths by cause, and marriages and dissolutions, by location and demographic characteristics, 1992 and trends, annual rpt, S1745–3

Georgia statistical abstract, general data, 1992-93 biennial rpt, U6730–1.1

Hawaii crimes and arrests, by offense, with data by county and victim-offender characteristics, 1992, annual rpt, S2035–1

Hawaii data book, general data, 1992 annual rpt, S2090–1.1, S2090–1.12, S2090–1.15

Hawaii health dept activities and services, including vital statistics and disease control, by location, 1990, annual rpt, S2065–1

Idaho crimes and arrests, by offense, with data by location and offender characteristics, 1992 and trends, annual rpt, S2275–2

Idaho economic profile, general data, 1992 recurring rpt, S2218–2.2

Idaho public school personnel characteristics and salaries by position, and teachers and enrollment by school district, 1992/93, annual rpt, S2225–3

Idaho vital statistics, including births, deaths by cause, abortions, marriages, and divorces, by demographic characteristics and county, 1991 and trends, annual rpt, S2250–2

Illinois corrections dept admin, including inmates and characteristics, finances, and staff, FY91-93 and trends, annual rpt, S2425–1

Illinois crimes and arrests, by offense and offender characteristics, 1990-91, annual rpt, S2536–1

Illinois higher education enrollment and degrees, by level, instn, field of instruction, and student characteristics, 1992 and trends, annual rpt, S2475–1.1

Illinois mental health facility patient population and characteristics, by facility, location, and treatment category, FY93, annual rpt, S2505–1

Illinois public school enrollment and dropouts, by race-ethnicity, 1990/91, annual rpt, S2440–1.1

Illinois statistical abstract, general data, 1992 annual rpt, U6910–2

Indiana public assistance program participation, expenditures, and services, by county, FY92 and trends, annual rpt, S2623–1

Iowa correctional instn admissions, releases, and inmate characteristics, by instn, monthly rpt, S2770–1

Iowa population share in poverty, by race-ethnicity, 1990, annual rpt, S2784–3

Kansas correctional instn inmates, by offense, demographic characteristics, and instn, FY92 and trends, annual rpt, S2940–1

Kansas crimes and arrests, with victim, offender, and law enforcement employee characteristics, 1992, annual rpt, S2925–1

Kansas statistical abstract, general data, 1991/92 annual rpt, U7095–2.2

Kentucky arrests by county and offense, and law enforcement employment by agency, 1992, annual rpt, S3150–1.2

Kentucky economic statistics, general data, 1993 annual rpt, S3104–1

Kentucky households by income group, by householder age and race-ethnicity, 1990, annual planning rpt, S3140–3

Louisiana Census of Population and Housing summary findings, by local area, 1990 and trends, U8010–4

Louisiana school district profiles, including enrollment, grads, and staff, by race-ethnicity, 1991/92, annual rpt, S3280–1.2

Maine births, by race-ethnicity and age of mother, 1991, annual rpt, S3460–2

Maine Census of Population and Housing summary findings, by local area, 1990, S3465–7, S3465–8

Maryland crimes and arrests, by offense, location, and offender characteristics, with law enforcement employment and assaults on officers, 1992 and trends, annual rpt, S3665–1

Maryland elementary and secondary education data, by county, 1991/92, annual rpt, S3610–2.3

Maryland elementary and secondary education data, by county, 1992 and trends, annual rpt, S3610–2.4

Maryland elementary and secondary education data, by county, 1992/93, annual rpt, S3610–2.8

Maryland public school enrollment and achievement test scores, by race-ethnicity and/or county, 1992, annual rpt, S3610–1

Maryland statistical abstract, general data, 1993-94 biennial rpt, S3605–1.1

Massachusetts correctional instn inmate socioeconomic characteristics and criminal background, by instn, Jan 1992 and trends, annual rpt, S3805–1

Massachusetts elementary/secondary school enrollment, by sex and race-ethnicity, Oct 1980 and 1991, annual rpt, S3810–3

Massachusetts health behavior risk factor surveillance survey results, by respondent characteristics, 1986-90, recurring rpt, S3850–3

Massachusetts municipal and county profiles, general data, 1992 annual rpt, C4712–2

Massachusetts vital statistics, including births, deaths by cause, marriages, divorces, and population, by locality and demographic characteristics, 1990 and trends, annual rpt, S3850–1

Michigan labor force planning rpt, including employment by industry, and characteristics of Job Training Partnership Act eligible population, 1993 annual rpt, S3980–1

Michigan State corrections dept employment of women, minorities, and handicapped, 1991 and trends, annual rpt, S3960–1

Michigan vital statistics, including births, deaths, marriages, divorces/annulments, and communicable diseases, by location and demographic characteristics, 1990 and trends, annual rpt, S4000–3

Minnesota enrollment distribution by race-ethnicity, and minority student shares by district and county, 1991/92 and trends, annual rpt, S4165–1

Minnesota postsecondary education finances, and enrollment by student characteristics, by type of school system, 1970s-93, biennial rpt, S4195–2.2

Minnesota vital statistics, including population, births, abortions, deaths, marriages, and divorces, by location and demographic characteristics, 1991 and trends, annual rpt, S4190–2

Mississippi statistical abstract, general data, 1992 annual rpt, U3255–4.2

Missouri correctional instn admissions, releases, and inmate characteristics, FY93, annual rpt, S4501–1

Missouri crimes and arrests, by offense and location, with victim and offender characteristics, 1991 and trends, annual rpt, S4560–2

Missouri higher education enrollment and degrees granted, by sex, race-ethnicity, and instn, 1992 and trends, annual rpt, S4520–3

Montana employment and unemployment, by race-ethnicity and county, 1990, annual planning rpt, S4710–3

Montana marriages by race-ethnicity of bride and groom, 1990-91, annual rpt, S4690–1

Montana public school enrollment by grade, and grads, by school, county, race-ethnicity, and sex, 1992 and trends, annual rpt, S4740–1

Nebraska elementary and secondary school enrollment, by race-ethnicity, school district, and county, 1992/93, annual rpt, S4865–2.5

Nevada public school enrollment and teachers, by race-ethnicity and school district, 1990/91, annual rpt, S5035–2

Nevada statistical abstract, general data, 1992 biennial rpt, S5005–1.1, S5005–1.7

New Jersey Census of Population and Housing detailed findings, by county, 1990, S5425–19

New Jersey correctional instn inmates, by offense, sentence length, demographic characteristics, and instn, Dec 1991 annual rpt, S5370–1

New Jersey crimes and arrests, by offense, with data by location and offender characteristics, 1992 and trends, annual rpt, S5430–1

New Jersey municipal and county data book, general data, 1992 annual rpt, C4712–4

New Jersey population, by race-ethnicity and age, 1990, annual rpt, S5405–1

Index by Subjects and Names

Asian Americans

New Jersey public schools, enrollment, and student and staff characteristics, and nonpublic schools and enrollment, by county, 1991/92, annual rpt, S5385–1

New Mexico elementary/secondary school enrollment by race-ethnicity, 1991/92, annual rpt, S5575–4

New Mexico labor force planning rpt, including population characteristics, and employment by industry and occupation, 1993 annual rpt, S5624–1

New Mexico public welfare recipient characteristics, by program, monthly rpt quarterly table, S5620–2

New Mexico residents in poverty, by race-ethnicity, 1979 and 1989, annual rpt, S5605–1.1

New York State arrests and juvenile corrections admissions, by race-ethnicity, 1991, annual rpt, S5760–3

New York State local jail/penitentiary inmates by offense, sentence, and demographic characteristics, by county or facility, 1991, annual rpt, S5724–2

New York State municipal and county statistical profiles, general data, 1993 annual rpt, C4712–7

New York State statistical yearbook, general data, 1992 annual rpt, U5100–1.1, U5100–1.8, U5100–1.9, U5100–1.10

North Carolina correctional instn admissions, separations, and population, with inmate characteristics, FY93, semiannual rpt, S5900–1

North Carolina crimes and arrests, by offense, with data by location and offender characteristics, 1992 and trends, annual rpt, S5955–1

North Carolina higher education degrees conferred by level, field of study, sex, race-ethnicity, and instn, 1991/92, annual rpt, U8013–1.2

North Carolina public school enrollment, by race-ethnicity, sex, and school district, 1992/93 and trends, annual rpt, S5915–1.1

North Dakota elementary and secondary school enrollment, by race-ethnicity, Sept 1992, annual directory, S6180–2

North Dakota elementary and secondary school staff characteristics and salaries, by position, region, and enrollment size, 1992/93 annual rpt, S6180–3

North Dakota higher education enrollment, by level, instn, county, and selected student characteristics, fall 1992 and trends, annual rpt, S6110–1

North Dakota local correctional instn adult and juvenile inmate characteristics, by instn, 1991 and trends, annual rpt, S6060–3

Oklahoma crimes and arrests, by offense, with data by local agency and victim and offender characteristics, 1990-92, annual rpt, S6465–1

Oklahoma public school enrollment shares by race-ethnicity, 1989 and 1992, annual rpt, S6423–2

Oklahoma statistical abstract, general data, 1992 annual rpt, U8130–2.2

Oregon crimes and arrests, by offense, with detail on bias crimes and data by victim and offender characteristics, 1992 and trends, annual rpt, S6603–3.1

Oregon elementary and secondary public school enrollment by race-ethnicity and teachers, by instn, Oct 1992, annual rpt, S6590–1.1

Oregon public high school completers, by instn, county, sex, and race-ethnicity, 1992, annual rpt, S6590–1.10

Oregon public school enrollment, by county, grade, and race-ethnicity, Oct 1992, annual rpt, S6590–1.9

Oregon vital statistics, including births, deaths by cause, communicable diseases, marriages, and divorces, by age, sex, race-ethnicity, and county, 1991 and trends, annual rpt, S6615–5

Pennsylvania Census of Population and Housing detailed findings, with selected data by county and municipality, 1990, U4130–13

Pennsylvania crimes and arrests, by offense, with data by location and offender characteristics, 1992 and trends, annual rpt, S6860–1

Pennsylvania educational statistics by level and/or type of education, series, S6790–5

Pennsylvania employment and commuting data from Census of Population and Housing, by county and municipality, 1990, C1595–16

Pennsylvania State correctional instn admin, and inmates by type of offense and demographic characteristics, 1990 and trends, annual rpt, S6782–1

Pennsylvania statistical abstract, general data, 1992 recurring rpt, U4130–6.1, U4130–6.3

Rhode Island population, by location and race-ethnicity, 1980 and 1990, annual planning rpt, S6980–3

Rhode Island public school enrollment by type of instn, grade, sex, race-ethnicity, and district, 1991/92 or fall 1992, annual rpt, S6970–1.1

South Carolina higher education enrollment and faculty, by race-ethnicity and instn, 1993 annual rpt, S7185–2

South Carolina marriages, by race-ethnicity of bride and groom, 1990, annual rpt, S7175–1

South Carolina population, by age, race-ethnicity, sex, and locality, 1990 and trends, annual planning rpt, S7155–3.1

South Carolina statistical abstract, general data, 1993 annual rpt, S7125–1.12, S7125–1.13

South Dakota elementary/secondary school enrollment and grads, by race-ethnicity, 1991/92, annual rpt, S7315–1.1

South Dakota public higher education enrollment and faculty, by race-ethnicity and instn, FY93 annual rpt, S7375–1

South Dakota social services for elderly, with recipients by race-ethnicity, FY92, annual rpt, S7385–1.1

Tennessee higher education grads and degrees conferred, by race-ethnicity, 1991/92, annual rpt, S7525–1.2

Tennessee statistical abstract, general data, 1992/93 annual rpt, U8710–2.1

Texas crimes and arrests by offender characteristics, and crimes involving bias against selected ethnic groups, 1992, annual rpt, S7735–2.2

Texas elementary and secondary education enrollment by race-ethnicity, by school, district, and county, 1991/92, annual rpt, S7670–1.1

Texas elementary/secondary education personnel, by sex and race-ethnicity, by district and county, 1991/92, annual rpt, S7670–1.3

Texas higher education enrollment and faculty, by race-ethnicity, sex, and instn, 1991/92 and trends, annual rpt, S7657–1.1

Texas Medicaid expenditures by category, and recipient characteristics and medical services received, 1975 and 1980-91, U8850–8.5

Texas nursing employment, demand outlook, earnings, and education, by selected characteristics, various years 1971-91, U8850–8.2

Texas vital statistics, including births, deaths by cause, abortions, marriages, and divorces, by location and demographic characteristics, 1991 and trends, annual rpt, S7685–1

Utah corrections inmates, parolees, and probationers, by criminal background and demographic characteristics, FY92 and trends, annual rpt, S7810–1

Utah employment by detailed occupation, and educational attainment by age group, by sex and race-ethnicity, with detail for 7 urban areas, 1990 census rpt, S7832–3.4

Utah govt statistical review, fiscal and socioeconomic data, 1993 annual rpt, R9380–1.1

Utah homeless shelter population characteristics, individual shelter capacity, and related housing data, 1991-92, annual rpt, S7808–2

Utah labor force and percent without high school diploma, by sex, age group, and/or race-ethnicity, 1990, article, U8960–2.509

Utah murder victims and offenders, by race-ethnicity, 1992, annual rpt, S7890–3

Utah personal income and household data, by location and race-ethnicity, 1990 census rpt, S7832–3.3

Utah population distribution and selected characteristics, by race-ethnicity, 1990, S7820–3.504

Utah public school enrollment, dropouts, and grads, by race-ethnicity, 1991/92, annual rpt, S7815–1.2

Utah statistical abstract, general data, 1993 triennial rpt, U8960–1.1

Vermont births, by race-ethnicity of child, mother's age, and county, 1991, annual rpt, S8054–1

Vermont elementary and secondary school enrollment by grade, sex, race-ethnicity, school, and county, 1992/93 and trends, annual rpt, S8020–1

Virginia crimes and arrests, by offense, with data by location and offender characteristics, 1992, annual rpt, S8295–2

Virginia public school dropouts by race-ethnicity and sex, by county and municipality, 1991/92, annual rpt, S8190–3

Washington State correctional instn inmate population, admissions, and releases, by demographic characteristics, quarterly rpt, S8337–1

Asian Americans

Washington State crimes and arrests, by offense, with data by location and offender characteristics, 1992 and trends, annual rpt, S8440–1

Washington State population and demographic characteristics, and housing units, by county and/or city, 1992 and trends, annual rpt, S8345–4

Washington State public assistance clients and service costs, by client characteristics, program, and county, FY90, annual rpt, S8420–2

Washington State vital statistics, including births, deaths by cause, and population, by demographic characteristics and location, 1991 and trends, annual rpt, S8363–1

West Virginia arrests and murder victims, by race-ethnicity, 1990-91, annual rpt, S8610–1.1

West Virginia higher education enrollment, degrees, faculty and student characteristics, and finances, by instn, 1992/93 and trends, annual rpt, S8533–1

West Virginia population, by race-ethnicity, 1990, annual rpt, S8560–1

Wisconsin Blue Book, general data, 1993-94 biennial rpt, S8780–1.2

Wisconsin correctional instn inmates, by criminal background and selected characteristics, series, S8692–1

Wisconsin crimes and arrests, by offense, offender characteristics, county, and local agency, 1992 and trends, annual rpt, S8771–1

Wisconsin elementary and secondary school enrollment, staff, costs, and State aid, by school district, 1992/93 and trends, annual rpt, S8795–2

Wyoming correctional instn admin, finances, inmate characteristics, and staff, and probation and parole activities, FY92 annual rpt, S8883–1

Wyoming employment and unemployment by sex and race-ethnicity, by county, 1990, S8895–1.505

Wyoming public school enrollment, by sex, race-ethnicity, school, and district, 1991/92 and trends, annual rpt, S8890–1.2

see also Pacific Islands Americans

Asotin County, Wash.

Employment by industry, monthly 1991, annual rpt, S2230–2

Asparagus

see Vegetables and vegetable products

Asphalt and tar

Commonwealth of Independent States oil refinery asphalt production capacity, by Republic and region, 1992 article, C6985–1.508

Cost indexes for construction, equipment, and labor, by type and location, weekly rpt quarterly feature, C5800–2.508

Latin America statistical abstract, general data by country, 1992 annual rpt, U6250–1.23

Oil refinery asphalt production capacity worldwide, by country, company, and US State, 1992 annual feature, C6985–1.508

Oil refinery asphalt production capacity worldwide, by country, company, and US State, 1993 annual compilation, C6985–4.1

Prices for selected building materials in approx 20 cities, weekly rpt, C5800–2

Index by Subjects and Names

State and local:

DC asphalt use in road repair, FY87-91, annual rpt, S1535–3.7

Assassination

Iraq leader Saddam Hussein possible assassination, US public opinion, June 1993 Gallup Poll, C4040–1.512

Assault

Correctional instn inmate assaults against other inmates and/or staff, by State and for Federal system, and for major jails, 1991, annual series, R4300–1

State social, economic, and govtl indicators, with rankings, 1993 semiannual rpt, B8500–1.10

State and local:

Alabama crimes and arrests, by offense, with data by location and offender characteristics, 1992 and trends, annual rpt, S0119–1

Arizona crimes and arrests, by offense, county, and offender characteristics, 1992, annual rpt, S0505–2

Arkansas crimes and arrests, by offense, victim and offender characteristics, and location, 1992 and trends, annual rpt, S0652–1

California correctional instn inmate assaults and fatalities, 1970-91, annual rpt, S0820–1

California crimes and arrests, clearances, and arrest dispositions, with data by offense and offender characteristics, 1987-92, annual rpt, S0910–1.1

California criminal justice system detailed data, by offense, county, age, race-ethnicity, and sex, 1991 and trends, annual rpt, S0910–2

Colorado crimes and arrests, by offense and location, with offender characteristics, and assaults on police, 1992, annual rpt, S1068–1

Connecticut crimes and arrests, by offense, with data by local agency, and victim-offender characteristics, 1992, annual rpt, S1256–1

DC criminal justice system summary, including crimes and arrests, criminal procedure, prisoners, and parole, 1991 and trends, annual rpt, S1535–2

Delaware crimes and arrests, by offense, county, and victim-offender characteristics, 1991 and trends, annual rpt, S1375–5

Florida crimes and arrests, by offense, with data by victim and offender characteristics, 1992, annual rpt, S1770–1

Georgia crimes and arrests, by offense, with data by location and offender characteristics, 1992 and trends, annual rpt, S1901–1

Hawaii crimes and arrests, by offense, with data by county and victim-offender characteristics, 1992, annual rpt, S2035–1

Idaho crimes and arrests, by offense, with data by location and offender characteristics, 1992 and trends, annual rpt, S2275–2

Illinois crimes and arrests, by offense, with data by location and offender characteristics, 1991, annual rpt, S2536–1

Iowa correctional instn inmate assaults on staff and other inmates, monthly rpt, S2770–1

Kansas crimes and arrests, by offense, with data by location, agency, and victim-offender characteristics, 1992 and trends, annual rpt, S2925–1.1

Kentucky crimes and arrests, by offense, with data by location and offender characteristics, 1992, annual rpt, S3150–1

Maine crimes and arrests, by offense, with data by county, reporting agency, and offender age and sex, 1991, annual rpt, S3475–1

Maryland crimes and arrests, by offense, location, and offender characteristics, with law enforcement employment and assaults on officers, 1992 and trends, annual rpt, S3665–1

Michigan crimes and arrests, by offense, with data by location and offender characteristics, 1992 and trends, annual rpt, S3997–1

Missouri crimes and arrests, by offense and location, with victim and offender characteristics, 1991 and trends, annual rpt, S4560–2

Montana crimes and clearances, by offense and jurisdiction, 1992, annual rpt, S4705–1

Nevada statistical abstract, general data, 1992 biennial rpt, S5005–1.4

New Hampshire crimes and arrests, by offense, jurisdiction, and offender characteristics, 1991 and trends, annual rpt, S5250–2

New Jersey crimes and arrests, by offense, with data by location and offender characteristics, 1992 and trends, annual rpt, S5430–1

New York State crimes and arrests by offense and demographic characteristics, and court activity and corrections, 1991 and trends, annual rpt, S5760–3

North Carolina crimes and arrests, by offense, with data by location and offender characteristics, 1992 and trends, annual rpt, S5955–1

North Dakota crimes and arrests, by offense, location, and offender characteristics, and law enforcement employment, 1991 and trends, annual rpt, S6060–1

Oklahoma crimes and arrests, by offense, with data by local agency and victim and offender characteristics, 1990-92, annual rpt, S6465–1

Oregon crimes and arrests, by offense, with data by county, local agency, and offender characteristics, 1992 and trends, annual rpt, S6603–3

Pennsylvania crimes and arrests, by offense, with data by location and offender characteristics, 1992 and trends, annual rpt, S6860–1

South Carolina crimes and arrests, by offense, with data by location and victim-offender characteristics, and assaults on officers, 1992 and trends, annual rpt, S7205–1

South Carolina deaths, by detailed cause, age, sex, and race, 1990, annual rpt, S7175–2

Index by Subjects and Names

Associations

Tennessee correctional instn incidents, including disturbances, assaults, and deaths, FY91-92, annual rpt, S7480–1

Texas crimes and arrests, by offense, with data by location and offender characteristics, 1992 and trends, annual rpt, S7735–2

Utah crimes and arrests, by offense, county, and local agency, 1992 and trends, annual rpt, S7890–3

Virginia crimes and arrests, by offense, with data by location and offender characteristics, 1992, annual rpt, S8295–2

Washington State crimes and arrests, by offense, with data by location and offender characteristics, 1992 and trends, annual rpt, S8440–1

West Virginia crimes and arrests, by offense, location, and offender characteristics, 1990-91, annual rpt, S8610–1

Wisconsin crimes and arrests, by offense, offender characteristics, county, and local agency, 1992 and trends, annual rpt, S8771–1

Wyoming crimes and arrests, by offense, with data by location and victim and offender characteristics, 1991 and trends, annual rpt, S8867–3

see also Assaults on police

Assaults on police

Black American crime, arrest, and incarceration data, with comparisons to whites, 1970s-91, annual compilation, C6775–2.5

Officers killed, by region and circumstances, 1992, annual rpt, S0119–1.2

State and local:

Alabama assaults on police, by circumstances, 1992, annual rpt, S0119–1.2

Arizona law enforcement officers assaulted, by circumstance and county, 1992, annual rpt, S0505–2.2

Arkansas law enforcement personnel assaulted and killed, 1992 and trends, annual rpt, S0652–1

California correctional instn inmate assaults on staff, 1970-91, annual rpt, S0820–1

Colorado crimes and arrests, by offense and location, with offender characteristics, and assaults on police, 1992, annual rpt, S1068–1

Connecticut crimes and arrests, law enforcement employment by sex, and assaults on officers, 1992, annual rpt, S1256–1.3

Delaware assaults on police, by circumstances, 1991, annual rpt, S1375–5

Hawaii law enforcement officers assaulted by type of weapon used and assignment, 1978-92, annual rpt, S2035–1

Idaho assaults on police officers, by activity, assignment, local agency, and county, 1992, annual rpt, S2275–2

Illinois crimes and arrests, and assaults on officers, 1991, annual rpt, S2536–1

Kansas law enforcement employees by demographic characteristics and local agency, with assaults on police by circumstance, 1992, annual rpt, S2925–1.2

Kentucky police assaults, 1992, annual rpt, S3150–1.1

Maine assaults on police officers, by circumstances and county, 1991, annual rpt, S3475–1.2

Maryland crimes and arrests, by offense, location, and offender characteristics, with law enforcement employment and assaults on officers, 1992 and trends, annual rpt, S3665–1

Michigan assaults on law enforcement officers, by circumstances, 1992 and trends, annual rpt, S3997–1

New Hampshire assaults on officers, by circumstances, weapon, and type of activity, 1991, annual rpt, S5250–2.1

New Jersey law enforcement employment, by agency, and assaults on officers, 1992 and trends, annual rpt, S5430–1.4

New York State law enforcement officers assaulted, by weapon and circumstances, 1991, annual rpt, S5760–3.3

North Carolina assaults on police, by circumstance, 1992 and trends, annual rpt, S5955–1.2

Oklahoma police assaulted, by type of assignment and activity, and time of day, 1990-92, annual rpt, S6465–1.2

Oregon crimes by offense, law enforcement employees by sex, and assaults on police, by local agency, 1992 and trends, annual rpt, S6603–3.2

Pennsylvania assaults on police officers, by State region, type of weapon used, and assignment, 1992, annual rpt, S6860–1

South Carolina police officers assaulted and killed, by detailed circumstances, 1992 annual rpt, S7205–1.1

Texas law enforcement officers assaulted and killed, 1992 and trends, annual rpt, S7735–2.2

Utah assaults on law enforcement officers, by circumstances, 1992 and trends, annual rpt, S7890–3

Virginia assaults on police, by weapon, time of day, and type of assignment, 1992, annual rpt, S8295–2.1

Washington State assaults on officers by circumstances, with assaults cleared, 1992 and trends, annual rpt, S8440–1

West Virginia police officers assaulted, 1982-91, annual rpt, S8610–1.1

Wisconsin assaults on police, by circumstances, 1992, annual rpt, S8771–1

Wyoming assaults on police, by type of weapon and circumstances, 1991, annual rpt, S8867–3.1

Assets and liabilities

see Business assets and liabilities, general

see Business assets and liabilities, specific industry

see Business inventories

see Government assets and liabilities

see Personal debt

see Wealth

Association of American Veterinary Medical Colleges

Enrollment in veterinary school academic and clinical grad programs, quinquennially 1967-92, article, A3100–2.513

Enrollment in veterinary schools by sex, program, instn, and place of residence, US and Canada, 1992/93, annual article, A3100–2.516

Association of European Airlines

Europe airline passenger and freight traffic, monthly rpt, C7000–4

Associations

Advertising expenditures of corporations and assns, by medium, 1988-92, and top 10 advertisers for 1992, annual article, A8770–1.504

Bowling (women's) assn membership and league activities, by city, State, and country, 1991/92, annual rpt, A9415–1

Bowling assn finances and membership, and bowling establishments and lanes, by State and other area, 1991/92 and trends, annual rpt, A1015–1

Broadcasting advertising industry assn chief executive salaries, for 4 assns, 1993 features, C1850–14.511

Coal industry executive views on companies and regional assns providing most leadership, Mar 1993 survey, article, C5226–1.509

Communications industries trade assn chief executive salaries, for 12 assns, 1993 feature, C1850–14.506

Elementary/secondary school superintendents membership in selected professional assns, 1992 survey rpt, A0775–5

Executive compensation in assns, by position, type, scope, budget, and census div, with personnel practices and benefit provisions, 1992, biennial rpt, A2900–3

Executive salaries in trade and professional assns, by title, 1993, annual article, C2176–1.519

Fuel oil dealer membership in trade assns, by region, 1992 annual survey, C4680–2.3

Local govt administrative assns, US and Canada, with membership, staff, and finances, 1993 annual rpt, A5800–1

Public opinion on selected special interest groups and assns, Feb-Mar 1993 Gallup Polls, C4040–1.509

Restaurant State assn staff, payroll, locations represented, and political action committee spending, for organizations in 14 States, 1993 article, C1200–5.510

State and local:

Alabama mutual aid assns and fraternal insurance companies financial data, by instn, 1991, annual rpt, S0160–1

Iowa county and State mutual insurance assns financial and underwriting data, by assn, 1992, annual rpt, S2760–1

Nebraska county mutual and intergovtl assns and motor clubs financial and insurance claim data, by assn, 1992, annual rpt, S4890–1

Tennessee county mutual fire assns financial data, by assn, 1991, annual rpt, S7466–1

Texas mutual aid assns financial and underwriting data, 1991, annual rpt, S7700–1

see also Cooperatives

see also Credit unions

see also Fraternal benefit societies

see also Labor unions

see also Lobbying and lobbying groups

see also Nonprofit organizations and foundations

see also Political action committees

see also Savings institutions

Associations

see also Tax exempt organizations
see also the "Index by Issuing Sources" for associations whose publications are covered by SRI

Asthma
see Respiratory diseases

Astronautics
see Communications satellites
see Space programs
see Space sciences

Astronomy
- Asteroids/comets in near-Earth orbit by size, with frequency and force of collisions with Earth, 1993 article, C2175–1.530
- Bachelor degree recipients postgraduation plans and demographic characteristics, 1991/92 and trends, annual survey, A1960–3
- Employment status of physics and astronomy grads, by sex, age, subfield, degree, and employer type, with salary info, 1990/91, annual rpt, A1960–1
- Enrollment and degrees awarded, by level, State, and instn, 1991/92-1992/93, annual rpt, A1960–2.3
- Enrollment and degrees awarded, by type of instn, 1991/92-1992/93 and trends, annual rpt, A1960–2.1
- Women and minorities in professional fields, detailed education and labor force data, 1991 and trends, recurring rpt, A3960–2.3

State and local:
- Hawaii, Mauna Kea and Haleakala telescopes and staff, 1991, annual rpt, S2090–1.17

Athletics
see Physical education and training
see Sports and athletics

Atlanta, Ga.
- Business activity indicators for Georgia, bimonthly rpt, U6730–2
- Discount stores shopped and store characteristics, for 3 major chains in 3 market areas, 1993 surveys and trends, articles, C5150–3.516
- Employment by industry group and income by source, forecast for Georgia and Atlanta MSA, quarterly rpt, U1880–2
- Export market awareness and promotion program involvement of small/medium-sized corporations in Atlanta metro area, 1988 survey, article, U5930–1.502
- Housing permits issued and forecast for metro Atlanta counties, quarterly rpt, U1880–2
- Printing (prepress) industry conditions for Atlanta/Miami areas, 1993 survey article, C1850–10.511
- Statistical abstract of Georgia, detailed social, govtl, and economic data, 1992-93 biennial rpt, U6730–1
- *see also* under By City in the "Index by Categories"

Atlantic Ocean
- Offshore oil and gas activity, including production, reserves, and spills, by location, 1991 and trends, annual compilation, C6985–9.4
- *see also* Caribbean area

Atomic bombs
see Nuclear weapons

Atomic energy
see Electric power plants and equipment
see Nuclear power

Atomic weapons
see Nuclear weapons

Attitudes
see Business outlook and attitude surveys
see Opinion and attitude surveys
see Political attitudes and ideology

Attorneys-at-law
see Lawyers and legal services

ATVs
see Recreational vehicles

Auctions
- Auto (used) dealer attendance at manufacturer, fleet/lease vehicle, and consignment sale auctions, 1993 article, C1575–2.511
- Auto auctions owned by 4 major chains, with hq locations, 1993 article, C2710–3.521
- Autos (used) average auction prices, by make, model, year, and region, monthly rpt, C1575–2
- Autos (used) average auction prices, for 1989-93 model year vehicles, May 1992-93, article, C2710–3.537
- Autos (used) sold through auctions, shares by vehicle source, 1992, article, C1575–2.501
- Gemstone prices paid for top 5 stones sold at an intl auction, June 1993, article, C2150–7.512
- Motor vehicle auction companies directory, with data on number of auctions held and cars sold in 1992, annual rpt, C1575–2.507

State and local:
- Florida livestock sold at auction, average price, and directory, 1993 annual rpt, S1685–1.3
- Tennessee livestock sold at auction, monthly prices by weight, 1986-92, annual rpt, S7460–1
- Texas livestock auction markets and sales, with detail by county, 1987-91, annual rpt, S7630–1.2

Audience profiles
see Media use surveys

Audiology
see Ear diseases and infections
see Hearing and hearing disorders
see Speech pathology and audiology

Audiovisual education
State and local:
- Missouri video instructional program participating instns and expenditures, 1990/91-1991/92, annual rpt, S4505–1.1
- *see also* Audiovisual equipment
- *see also* Educational broadcasting

Audiovisual equipment
- Bookstore share of audio book sales, by subject category, 1993 article, C1852–2.512
- Computer audio chip sales for personal computers, 1991-93, article, C1850–2.512
- Factory sales and shipments, foreign trade, and operating data for the electronics industry, by product category, 1980s-92, annual rpt, A4725–1
- Prices for selected types of nonprint media, 1980 and 1987-92, annual compilation, C1650–3.4
- Sales of blank audio and video cassettes, 1989-92, article, C5150–2.510

Index by Subjects and Names

- Sales, trade, and industry devs for consumer electronics, by product type, 1970s-92, annual rpt, A4725–4
- *see also* Compact disc players
- *see also* Home video and audio equipment
- *see also* Television
- *see also* Libraries (for data on library holdings by type)

Auditing
see Accounting and auditing

Austin, James
- "Does Imprisonment Reduce Crime? A Critique of 'Voodoo' Criminology", A7575–3
- "Reforming Florida's Unjust, Costly and Ineffective Sentencing Laws", A7575–5

Australia
- Airline passenger traffic market share indicators for Japan-to-Australia routes, by selected country and airline, 1993 article, C5800–4.520
- Auto industry employment and production, for 5 manufacturers, 1992 article, C2710–3.509
- Chemical production capacity for 7 major producers of petrochemicals and polymers, 1993 article, A1250–1.531
- Coal foreign trade activity, by country of origin and destination, monthly rpt, A7400–3
- Coal industry supply-demand, employment, and trade, by country, 1990-91 and trends, annual rpt, A7400–2.2
- Economic indexes for US and other industrial countries, and leading and coincident indicators, monthly rpt, U1245–1
- Economic indexes for US and selected other countries, composites of leading indicators, monthly rpt, R4105–6
- Electronics industry trade and/or production trends by product category for 33 countries, with general economic profiles, 1993 annual rpt, A4725–1.4
- Energy intl sourcebook, with detail on oil and gas industry operations, supply-demand, and prices, for approx 80 countries, 1970s-91, annual compilation, C6985–10.2
- Entertainment industry devs, including motion picture admissions, boxoffice receipts, and top 10 films in rentals, and TV and video market indicators, 1993 feature, C9380–1.523
- Eye bank activity in US and abroad, including donations by type, source, and donor characteristics, and data by individual bank, 1992 and trends, annual rpt, A4743–1
- Higher education physical plant operations, costs, employment, salaries, and energy use, by instn and region, 1991/92, recurring rpt, A3183–1
- Magazine (fashion) depiction of models wearing skin-protective clothing in summer, Australian study, 1982-91, article, A2623–1.502
- Motion picture boxoffice receipts for top 10 films, 1992, annual article, C9380–1.510
- Motor vehicle world production, sales, trade, and registrations, by country, world area, manufacturer, and make, 1991 and trends, annual rpt, A0865–2.1
- Offshore oil dev costs by system type in use, 1992, article, C6985–1.507

Index by Subjects and Names

Political attitudes of husbands and wives as affected by social background of self and spouse, 1992 article, A0610–1.501

Public opinion about Aborigine employment patterns, impacts of media campaign in a rural town, 1993 article, A0610–1.503

Restaurant provision of no-smoking areas where not mandated by law, views of owners and customers, 1993 article, A2623–1.511

Retail general merchandise chain sales, earnings, and stores, for top companies worldwide, with detail for selected areas, 1991-92, annual feature, C5150–3.516

Uranium marketing, terms of transactions for major selling-buying countries or areas, and price index and earnings data in allied industries, monthly rpt, B6800–1

Wheat supply-demand summary, 1987/88-1992/93, annual rpt, A7310–1

see also Sydney, Australia

see also under By Foreign Country or World Area in the "Index by Categories"

Austria

- Electronics industry trade and/or production trends by product category for 33 countries, with general economic profiles, 1993 annual rpt, A4725–1.4
- Energy intl sourcebook, with detail on oil and gas industry operations, supply-demand, and prices, for approx 80 countries, 1970s-91, annual compilation, C6985–10.2
- Machine tool industry operating data by country and product, 1992 and trends, annual rpt, A3179–2.2
- Motor vehicle world production, sales, trade, and registrations, by country, world area, manufacturer, and make, 1991 and trends, annual rpt, A0865–2.1

see also under By Foreign Country or World Area in the "Index by Categories"

Authors

see Writers and writing

Auto loans

see Consumer credit

Automated tellers

- Convenience stores offering special services, including automated tellers, 1992 and trends, annual survey rpt, A6735–1, A6735–2
- Shopping center financial and operating data, with detail by type of tenant, US and Canada, 1991, triennial rpt, R9285–1

State and local:

Mississippi bank electronic terminals on and off premises, 1992, annual rpt, S4325–1

Automatic funds transfer

see Electronic funds transfer

Automatic test equipment

see Instruments and measuring devices

Automation

- Auto lending operations of financial instns, including use of automated processing systems, 1992, annual rpt, A4160–2
- Bar coding labeling technology revenues worldwide, by product type, 1993, article, C5800–8.512
- Corporate sales/marketing automation issues, views of computer users and nonusers, Aug 1992 survey, article, C1200–1.504
- Electric utility automation spending, distribution by type of system, 1992, article, C5800–28.502

Automobile insurance

Factory automation market growth for 3 top products/services, and spending growth for 3 top industry groups, 1991, article, C1850–2.504

Food/beverage industry equipment purchasing plans, mgmt devs, and automation, 1993 annual survey article, C2150–6.505

Home automation system desires of consumers, and outlook for installations in new and existing homes, 1992 articles, C1850–13.501

Home automation system installations in new homes, outlook by system type, 2000, article, C1850–8.503

Hospital use of formal patient care mgmt systems, including current and planned automation level, 1993 survey, article, A1865–1.524

Industrial control and processing equipment shipments, by type, 1983-92, annual rpt, A4725–1.2

Insurance independent agency automation use and benefits, 1992 survey, article, C1050–1.501

Loan delinquent account collection efficiency indicators for automated vs manual systems, 1993 article, A6400–2.505

Machine tools (numerically controlled) US and world production, trade, and use, 1992 and trends, annual rpt, A3179–2

Pipeline/gas utility automated control and acquisition system market shares, for 8 leading and all other manufacturers, 1991, article, C6985–1.501

Retail store credit operations, including technology used for payment verification, 1992 survey article, C5150–4.503

Retailer inventory mgmt practices, including automated technology use, by retail outlet type, 1992 survey article, C5150–4.503

Sales, marketing, and customer service info technology spending, by industry, 1993 article, C1200–1.505

Telemarketing company automation levels, 1989-91, annual rpt, A4620–1.2

Textile industry automation applications, 1992 survey, article, C5226–3.502

Warehouse use of automation, 1993 articles, C2150–1.506

see also Automated tellers

see also Computer industry and products

see also Computer networks

see also Electronic funds transfer

see also Industrial robots

see also Information storage and retrieval systems

Automobile exhaust

see Air pollution

see Motor vehicle exhaust

Automobile insurance

- Collision coverage insurance claims and payments experience for autos and other vehicles, by make and series, for recent model years, 1993 annual rpt series, A5200–1
- Loss experiences in collision, personal injury, and comprehensive auto insurance coverage, special analysis rpts, series, A5200–4
- Operating costs for autos, by component, 1950-93, annual rpt, A0865–1.2
- Personal injury protection insurance claim frequencies for 1990-92 model autos and other vehicles, by make and model, annual rpt, A5200–3

Premiums, market shares, and loss ratios for passenger and commercial auto insurance, with rankings of States and 20 leading firms, 1992, annual article, C1050–1.511

Premiums written and operating ratios in property/casualty insurance, by company type and line of coverage, 1988-92, annual article, C1050–1.504

Premiums written and other detailed insurance info, including claims and payments for selected models, 1993 annual rpt, A5650–1

Premiums written, loss ratios, and market shares for property and casualty insurance, by line, leading company, and State, 1992 and trends, annual article, C1050–1.509

State social, economic, and govtl indicators, with rankings, 1993 semiannual rpt, B8500–1.11

Theft insurance claims and payments experience for 1990-92 model autos and other vehicles, by make and model, annual rpt, A5200–2

State and local:

- Alabama insurance industry financial and underwriting data, by company and line of coverage, 1991, annual rpt, S0160–1
- Alaska insurance industry underwriting and investment data, by company and type of insurance, with regulatory info, 1991 and trends, annual rpt, S0280–3
- Arizona insurance industry financial and underwriting data, by company and type of insurance, with regulatory info, 1992, annual rpt, S0483–1
- Connecticut insurance industry financial and underwriting data, by company and type of insurance, 1991, annual rpt, S1222–1
- Delaware data book, general data, 1993 annual rpt, S1375–4
- Florida insurance industry financial and underwriting data, by company and line of coverage, 1991, annual rpt, S1760–1
- Idaho insurance industry financial and underwriting data, by company and type of insurance, with regulatory data, 1991, annual rpt, S2260–1
- Iowa insurance industry financial and underwriting data, by company and type of insurance, 1992, annual rpt, S2760–1
- Kansas insurance industry financial and underwriting data, by company and type of insurance, with regulatory info, 1992, annual rpt, S2990–1
- Michigan referendum on auto insurance law changes, election results by county, Nov 1992, biennial rpt, S4020–1
- Missouri insurance industry financial and underwriting data, by company and type of insurance, with regulatory info, 1992, annual rpt, S4527–1
- Nebraska insurance premiums and losses by detailed line of coverage, by company, 1992, annual rpt, S4890–1
- New York State insurance industry devs, finances, and regulatory activity, 1990/91 and trends, annual rpt, S5770–3
- New York State insurance industry financial and underwriting data, by company and line of coverage, 1991, annual rpt, S5770–2
- Ohio uninsured driver involvement in accidents, by sex and age group, 1991, annual rpt, S6290–1

Automobile insurance

Oklahoma insurance industry financial and underwriting data, by company and type of insurance, with regulatory info, 1992, annual rpt, S6462–1

Pennsylvania insurance industry financial and underwriting data, by company and line of coverage, 1991, with FY92 regulatory info, annual rpt, S6835–1

Rhode Island insurance industry financial and underwriting data, by company and line of coverage, 1990, with FY91 regulatory info, annual rpt, S6945–2

Texas insurance dept regulatory activities, with industry financial and underwriting data by line of coverage, FY92 annual rpt, S7700–1

Utah insurance industry financial and underwriting data, by company and line of coverage, with regulatory info, 1991, annual rpt, S7845–1

West Virginia insurance industry financial and underwriting data, by company and line of coverage, with regulatory info, 1991, annual rpt, S8575–1

Wisconsin insurance industry financial and underwriting data, by company and line of coverage, with regulatory info, 1992, annual rpt, S8755–1

Automobile parking

see Parking facilities

Automobile parts and supplies

see Batteries

see Motor vehicle parts and supplies

see Tires and tire industry

Automobile rental

see Motor vehicle rental

Automobile repair and maintenance

Business activity index for auto dealer service depts, weekly rpt monthly table, C2710–3

Consumer auto maintenance market, including product purchase patterns and do-it-yourself activity, 1992 survey article, C2150–10.501

Consumer auto maintenance market, including product purchase patterns and do-it-yourself activity, 1993 annual survey feature, C2150–10.504

Consumer complaint and inquiry activity of Better Business Burs, by detailed type of business, 1992, annual rpt, A4350–1

Consumer do-it-yourself auto maintenance activity, by type and consumer characteristics, 1993 and trends, annual survey, C0125–1.506

Consumer do-it-yourself auto maintenance activity, monthly rpt, C0125–1

Corporate fleet vehicle driver maintenance habits, model preferences, and cellular telephone and credit card use, 1993 survey, article, C1575–2.509

Costs for maintenance/repair of fleet autos and light trucks, FY91-92, C1575–2.505

Costs of average insurance claim and collision repair, selected 1989-91 models, annual rpt, A5650–1.4

Dealer service dept operations and profit outlook, manager compensation, and facilities, 1993 annual survey, article, C2710–3.537

Financial ratios and performance, for over 350 SIC 4-digit industries, FY88-92, annual rpt, A6400–3

Fleet (auto) operating characteristics in metro areas affected by Clean Air Act clean fuel requirements, 1993 article, C1575–2.512

Franchise operations and finances, by type of business, 1991/92 and trends, annual rpt, A5820–1

Hispanic American career professional and business owner views on fleet repair/maintenance providers, 1993 survey, article, C4575–1.504

Mechanic views on auto quality and maintenance, and customers, Mar 1993 survey, article, C0125–1.505

Oil change outlet shares, with establishments and top chains specializing in fast service, 1992 and trends, C4680–1.503

Operating and financial composite ratios for corporations, with establishments and receipts, for approx 200 industries, by asset size, FY90, annual rpt, C7800–1

Prices of selected consumer items in approx 300 cities, quarterly rpt, A0150–1

Retail aftermarket industry devs, including auto maintenance and repair activity, monthly rpt, C2150–10

Retail aftermarket performance indicators, by product category, 1992 article, C2150–10.501

Retail aftermarket sales performance, by product group, 1993 annual feature, C0125–1.503

Sales distribution for auto aftermarket by category, 1982 and 1991, article, C5150–3.511

Service and parts depts sales, repair orders, mechanics, and service bays, for franchised new car dealerships, 1992 and trends, annual rpt, A7330–1

State and local:

Arizona statistical abstract, general data, 1993 recurring rpt, U5850–2.24

Automobile safety devices

see Motor vehicle safety devices

Automobile theft

see Motor vehicle theft

Automobile use

see Automobiles

see Commuting

see Travel and tourism

Automobiles

Alternative motor fuel use and outlook, including data on costs and by fuel type and selected country, 1993 annual rpt, C6985–3.2

Business traveler and trip characteristics, including mode, purpose, and lodging, 1991, annual rpt, R9375–12

Congressional campaign fund finances, with expenditures by item and contributions by donor type, by candidate, district, and State, 1990 elections, C2500–6

Dealership financial and operating data, including sales and employment by State, 1970s-93, annual rpt, A7330–1

Electric vs gas powered auto operating costs, and public opinion on electric car ownership, 1993 articles, C2710–3.533

Europe autos per 1,000 persons, for EC and European Free Trade Assn countries, 1993, article, C8900–1.504

Financial performance of top 3 US auto manufacturers, weekly rpt quarterly table, C2710–3.501, C2710–3.516, C2710–3.527, C2710–3.538, C2710–3.541

Fleet (auto) policies on personal use of employer vehicles, 1993 survey article, C1575–2.512

Index by Subjects and Names

Fleet manager compensation, including use of company vehicle, for full- and part-time managers, 1993 article, C1575–2.506

Flexible-fuel vehicles capable of running on methanol or gasoline, auto fleet use and views on operation, California survey, 1993 articles, A6755–1.502

Fuel consumption, mileage, and miles per gallon for average passenger auto, 1973-90, recurring rpt, S6810–3

Fuel economy, EPA estimates for 1994 model autos, by model and size group, annual feature, C2710–3.550

Homebuilder hours spent driving each day, by region, 1993 feature, C4300–1.512

Leased auto fleet characteristics, including age at replacement and annual mileage, biennially 1970-92, biennial survey article, C1575–2.503

Market area population and characteristics, households, income, and retail outlets, for 21 leading areas, 1993 feature, C2710–1.538

Market data book on production, sales, registrations, prices, options, and dealerships, with data by make and country, 1993 annual rpt, C2710–3.531

Mechanic views on domestic and import auto quality, and customer complaints, Mar 1993 survey, article, C0125–1.505

Number of cars and trucks in use, newly registered, and scrapped, 1947-92, annual rpt, C7715–2

Ownership and registration data, with fuel consumption and use, US and Canada, 1993 annual fact book, C4680–1.507

Ownership of autos in US counties and Canadian cities, 1993 annual rpt, C3250–1

Plastics processing industry auto use and expense allowance policies, 1992 survey, biennial rpt, A8920–3

Product dev costs and production requirements for new auto model programs of 3 major manufacturers, 1993 article, C8900–1.518

Production of autos worldwide, for top 20 countries and manufacturers, 1988 or 1989, recurring rpt, R9375–6

Production, sales, and market analysis, by manufacturer and make/model, with industry news and devs, weekly rpt, C2710–3

Production, sales, trade, and vehicle use, detailed data by vehicle type, State, and country, 1900s-92, annual rpt, A0865–1

Sales industry costs, including compensation, training, and travel and related expenses, with data by metro area, 1992 and trends, annual survey, C1200–1.508

Shopping center security operations, including types of security vehicles used, and auto-related crimes by center type, 1992 or 1993, articles, C5150–4.506

Statistical profiles of 50 States and DC, general data, 1993 annual almanac, C4712–1

Travel miles, fuel consumed, and registrations, 3 vehicle types, 1947-91, periodic basic data book, A2575–14.5

Travel trips and traveler characteristics, including mode, purpose, type of lodging, and area of destination and origin, quarterly rpt, R9375–14

Index by Subjects and Names

Trends in transportation operations and finances, by mode, 1991 annual rpt, R4815–1

Vacation plans of consumers in US and abroad within 6 months, and travel mode, monthly rpt bimonthly table, R4105–4

Vehicle mileage and average age, registrations, and fuel consumption, 1970-90, annual rpt, C6985–5.1

World production, sales, trade, and registrations of motor vehicles, by country, world area, manufacturer, and make, 1991 and trends, annual rpt, A0865–2

State and local:

Alabama households with no auto, by municipality, 1990, recurring rpt, S0121–5

Arkansas housing units by number of vehicles available, 1990, census rpt, U5935–7

California housing units by number of vehicles available, 1990, census rpt, S0840–9

Delaware data book, general data, 1993 annual rpt, S1375–4

Florida county data book, 1992/93 annual rpt, C6360–1

Florida statistical abstract, general data, 1992 annual rpt, U6660–1.19

Hawaii data book, general data, 1992 annual rpt, S2090–1.18

Kansas statistical abstract, general data, 1991/92 annual rpt, U7095–2.3

Maine housing units by number of vehicles available, by local area, 1990 census, S3465–9

Maryland statistical abstract, general data, 1993-94 biennial rpt, S3605–1.10

New Jersey housing units by number of vehicles available, by county, 1990, census rpt, S5425–19

Pennsylvania housing units by number of vehicles available, 1990, census rpt, U4130–13

Rhode Island housing units by number of vehicles available, by county and municipality, 1990 census, S6930–9

South Carolina statistical abstract, general data, 1993 annual rpt, S7125–1.11

Wisconsin auto use and fuel consumption, 1970-90, biennial rpt, S8780–1.2

see also Automobile insurance

see also Automobile repair and maintenance

see also Commuting

see also Drivers licenses

see also Gasoline

see also Gasoline service stations

see also Motor vehicle exhaust

see also Motor vehicle exports and imports

see also Motor vehicle fleets

see also Motor vehicle industry

see also Motor vehicle parts and supplies

see also Motor vehicle registrations

see also Motor vehicle rental

see also Motor vehicle safety devices

see also Motor vehicle sales

see also Motor vehicle theft

see also Parking facilities

see also Traffic accident fatalities

see also Traffic accidents and safety

Automotive Parts and Accessories Association

Sales distribution for auto aftermarket by category, 1982 and 1991, article, C5150–3.511

Autopsies

State and local:

Alabama deaths for which autopsies were performed, by cause of death and attendant, 1992, annual rpt, S0175–2

Colorado deaths with autopsies, by county, 1990, annual rpt, S1010–1

Maine fetal autopsies, by county, 1991, annual rpt, S3460–2

Minnesota autopsies, by cause of death, 1991, annual rpt, S4190–2

Ohio sudden infant deaths by whether autopsy performed, by county, 1991, annual rpt, S6285–1

Oregon autopsies, by county, 1991, annual rpt, S6615–5

Vermont autopsies, by certifier of death, 1991, annual rpt, S8054–1

Aviation

see Aeronautical navigation

see Aerospace industry

see Air traffic control

see Aircraft

see Airlines

see Airports and airways

see Aviation accidents and safety

see Aviation fuels

see Aviation medicine

see Aviation sciences

see Business aircraft and flying

see Civil aviation

see General aviation

see Military aviation

see Space sciences

Aviation accidents and safety

Accidental deaths and disabling injuries, by detailed type, victim characteristics, circumstances, and location, 1992 and trends, annual rpt, A8375–2

Airport runway incursions at 15 major airports, year ended June 1992-93, article, C5800–4.526

Business aircraft and helicopter accidents, with circumstances, fatalities, and model involved, weekly rpt quarterly feature, C5800–30

Business jet aircraft accidents and flight time, distribution by flight phase, 1993 feature, C5800–30.505

Commercial jet aircraft hull loss accidents worldwide by cause and flight phase, 1993 article, C7000–4.504

Commuter airline total and fatal accidents and rates, 1976-92, annual rpt, A8795–1.1

Deaths from transportation accidents, trends by mode, 1992 annual rpt, R4815–1

Fatal accidents, fatalities, and departures of scheduled air carriers, 1982-92, annual rpt, A0325–5

General aviation accident rates, total and fatal, 1972-92, annual rpt, A5120–2.3

Helicopter accidents, fatalities, and injuries, 1988-92, annual rpt, A5190–1

Injuries and deaths from accidents by type, and selected incidence and economic loss data, 1991 and trends, annual rpt, A5650–1.4

Jet aircraft accidents and fatalities worldwide, and hull loss trends and outlook, 1993 article, C5800–4.520

Jet aircraft accidents and fatalities worldwide, by circumstances, 1988-91, article, C5800–4.517

Aviation accidents and safety

State and local:

Alabama vital statistics, including population, births, deaths by cause, marriages, and divorces, by location and demographic characteristics, 1992 and trends, annual rpt, S0175–2

Alaska vital statistics, including births, deaths by cause, marriages, divorces, adoptions, and population, by demographic characteristics and location, 1990, annual rpt, S0315–1

Arkansas vital statistics, including births, deaths by cause, marriages, and divorces, by age, sex, race, and county, 1991 and trends, annual rpt, S0685–1

California vital statistics, including population, births, and deaths by cause, by demographic characteristics and county, 1990 and trends, annual rpt, S0865–1

Colorado vital statistics, including population, births, deaths by cause, abortion, marriage and divorce, and adoption, by demographic characteristics and location, 1990 and trends, annual rpt, S1010–1

Florida vital statistics, including population, births, deaths by cause, and marriages and dissolutions, by location and demographic characteristics, 1992 and trends, annual rpt, S1745–3

Idaho vital statistics, including births, deaths by cause, abortions, marriages, and divorces, by demographic characteristics and county, 1991 and trends, annual rpt, S2250–2

Iowa vital statistics, including population, births, deaths by cause, marriages, and divorces, by demographic characteristics and location, 1991 and trends, annual rpt, S2795–1

Kansas vital statistics, including population, births, deaths by cause, abortions, marriages, and divorces, by demographic characteristics and location, 1991 and trends, annual rpt, S2975–1

Louisiana vital statistics, including population, births, deaths by cause, reportable diseases, marriages, and divorces, by demographic characteristics and locality, 1989-90 and trends, annual rpt, S3295–1

Maine vital statistics, including births, deaths by cause, abortions, and marriages and divorces, by demographic characteristics and location, 1991 and trends, annual rpt, S3460–2

Maryland vital statistics, including population, births, deaths by cause, marriages, and divorces, by demographic characteristics and location, 1989 and trends, annual rpt, S3635–1

Massachusetts vital statistics, including births, deaths by cause, marriages, divorces, and population, by locality and demographic characteristics, 1990 and trends, annual rpt, S3850–1

Michigan vital statistics, including births, deaths, marriages, divorces/annulments, and communicable diseases, by location and demographic characteristics, 1990 and trends, annual rpt, S4000–3

Minnesota vital statistics, including population, births, abortions, deaths, marriages, and divorces, by location and demographic characteristics, 1991 and trends, annual rpt, S4190–2

Aviation accidents and safety

Mississippi vital statistics, including births, deaths by cause, marriages, and divorces, by demographic characteristics and location, 1992 and trends, annual rpt, S4350–1

Missouri vital statistics, including population, births, deaths by cause, and marriages and divorces, by location and demographic characteristics, 1992 and trends, annual rpt, S4518–1

Montana vital statistics, including births, deaths by cause, abortion, disease, and marriage and divorce, by demographic characteristics and county, 1990-91 and trends, annual rpt, S4690–1

Nebraska vital statistics, including births, deaths, marriages, divorces, and population, by demographic characteristics and location, 1991 and trends, annual rpt, S4885–1

Nevada vital statistics, including births, abortions, and deaths by cause, by county and demographic characteristics, 1989 and trends, annual rpt, S5075–1

Oregon vital statistics, including births, deaths by cause, communicable diseases, marriages, and divorces, by age, sex, race-ethnicity, and county, 1991 and trends, annual rpt, S6615–5

Rhode Island vital statistics, including population, births, deaths, marriages, and divorces, by demographic characteristics and locality, 1989 and trends, annual rpt, S6995–1

South Carolina deaths, by detailed cause, age, sex, and race, 1990, annual rpt, S7175–2

Tennessee vital statistics, including births, deaths by cause, marriages, divorces, and population, by demographic characteristics and location, 1991 and trends, annual rpt, S7520–2

Texas vital statistics, including births, deaths by cause, abortions, marriages, and divorces, by location and demographic characteristics, 1991 and trends, annual rpt, S7685–1

Utah vital statistics, including births and deaths by cause, by demographic characteristics and location, 1990, annual rpt, S7835–1.2

Virginia vital statistics, including births, deaths by cause, marriages and divorces, and communicable disease, by demographic characteristics and location, 1991 and trends, annual rpt, S8225–1

Washington State vital statistics, including births, deaths by cause, and population, by demographic characteristics and location, 1991 and trends, annual rpt, S8363–1

West Virginia vital statistics, including births, deaths by cause, marriages, and divorces, by location and demographic characteristics, 1991 and trends, annual rpt, S8560–1

Wisconsin vital statistics, including population, births, deaths by cause, and marriages and dissolutions, by county and demographic characteristics, 1991 and trends, annual rpt, S8715–4

Wyoming vital statistics, including population, births, deaths by cause, marriages, and divorces, by demographic characteristics and county, 1991 and trends, annual rpt, S8920–2

see also Air traffic control

Aviation Data Service Inc.

Aircraft (turbine-powered) in service and on order, by manufacturer and model, for over 900 airlines worldwide, Dec 1992, annual rpt, B3370–1

Aircraft (used) business jet and turboprop unit sales, by weight class, weekly rpt monthly feature, C5800–30

Aviation fuels

Airline fuel consumption and costs, by type of service, 1992, annual article, C7000–4.508

Airline fuel consumption and costs, monthly rpt, C7000–4

Airline fuel consumption and costs, 1977-91, annual rpt, A0250–2.3

General aviation fuel use, by aircraft type, FY87-2004, annual rpt, A5120–2.3

Latin America statistical abstract, general data by country, 1992 annual rpt, U6250–1.23

Production, exploration, drilling, refining, stock, price, and financial data for US and foreign oil and gas industry, weekly rpt, C6985–1

Production, exploration, refining, demand, finance, prices, and reserves, by State and country or world area, 1993 and trends, periodic basic data book, A2575–14.4

Sourcebook of oil and gas industry operations and finances, and world supply-demand situation, 1970s-91, annual compilation, C6985–9

Statistical compilation of oil and gas industry trends, 1993 annual rpt, C6985–4

Supply-demand by PAD district, and stocks, 1993 annual article, C6985–1.539

Supply-demand for crude oil and petroleum products, quarterly 1993, annual article, C4680–1.503

Supply-demand, marketing, prices, finances, and employment, detailed data for US and Canada, by product, company, and location, 1993 annual fact book, C4680–1.507

Supply-demand, trade, and industry exploration and operations, by product, exporting country and world area, PAD district, and State, 1993 annual feature, C6985–1.513

Supply, disposition, and stocks of refined oil products by type and/or crude oil, and refinery operations summary, monthly rpt, A2575–2

Supply of oil and refined products, including stocks, refinery operations, and imports, by PAD district and product, weekly rpt, A2575–1

World demand for jet fuel, by country and world area, 1979-89, annual compilation, C6985–10.1

State and local:

California fuel distributors sales volume and taxes assessed, by fuel type and company, FY92 and trends, annual rpt, S0835–1.4

Hawaii data book, general data, 1992 annual rpt, S2090–1.17

Hawaii fuel consumed and fuel taxes allocated, by type and use, FY91-92, annual rpt, S2120–1

New York State statistical yearbook, general data, 1992 annual rpt, U5100–1.12

Pennsylvania energy supply-demand and prices by fuel type, with electric power info by utility, 1960s-90, recurring rpt, S6810–3

Utah hwy mileage and expenditures, aviation and motor fuel consumption, and bus travel, various years 1940-92, annual rpt, R9380–1.10

Utah statistical abstract, general data, 1993 triennial rpt, U8960–1.13

see also Fuel tax

see also Kerosene

Aviation industry

see Aerospace industry

see Airlines

see Aviation accidents and safety

Aviation medicine

Physicians by detailed specialty and location, 1992 and trends, annual rpt, A2200–3

Aviation sciences

NASA R&D funding by program category, with detail for advanced subsonic transport program, 1992, article, C5800–4.505

see also Space sciences

Avionics

see Aeronautical navigation

Awards, medals, and prizes

Advertising (TV/cinema) awards won by leading agencies and/or countries, 1993 annual article, C2710–1.532, C2710–1.533

Auto fleet dealer award recipients, and top dealer sales by make, 1992, annual feature, C1575–2.508

Bowling awards, 1991/92, annual rpt, A1015–1

Industrial design awards won by leading design firms and manufacturers, 1993 and trends, annual article, C5800–7.531

Library scholarships and award recipients and donors, 1992, annual listing, C1650–3.3

Motion picture Academy Award best picture nominee films attended and preferred by public, Feb 1993 survey, C8915–1.502

Motion picture Academy Award nominations, by film and distributor, 1993, annual feature, C9380–1.514

Motion picture boxoffice receipts for films winning Academy Awards for best picture, with share received after award, 1984-91, C9380–1.520

Motion picture boxoffice receipts for films winning Academy Awards for best picture, with share received after award, 1987-91, article, C5800–7.518

Motion picture boxoffice receipts in US for foreign films winning Academy Awards, 1972-91, C9380–1.508

Motion picture rental income for films winning Academy Awards for best actor or actress but not for best picture, 1960-90, C9380–1.510

Motion picture rental income for films winning Academy Awards for best picture, 1937-91, C9380–1.509

Motor vehicle fleet safety awards issued, and recipients, by fleet type, 1991, annual rpt, A8375–3

Natl Merit Scholars freshman enrollment in top 64 higher education instns, 1992, annual feature, C2175–1.505

Index by Subjects and Names

Occupational safety/health awards earned, by industry, 1991, annual rpt, A8375–4
Quality excellence Baldrige award applicants and winners, for manufacturing and service companies, and small businesses, 1988-93, article, C1850–2.512
Quality excellence Baldrige award applicants, 1989-93, article, C1200–4.507
Quality excellence Baldrige award application rates and company views on criteria, 1993, R4105–78.32
Quality excellence Baldrige award winners, performance of hypothetical stock investments in 10 firms, 1993 article, C5800–7.550
World Culinary Olympics awards won by US and other top natl teams, 1992, article, C5150–5.501
State and local:
Florida Natl Merit and Achievement Scholar undergrad enrollment, by State-supported instn, fall 1991, annual rpt, S1725–1
see also Employee bonuses and work incentives

Babco, Eleanor L.
"Salaries of Scientists, Engineers, and Technicians: A Summary of Salary Surveys, 16th Edition", A3960–1

Bacon, Jeremy
"Corporate Boards and Corporate Governance", R4105–78.29

Bahamas
Newspaper circulation, 6-month periods ended Sept 1992 and Mar 1993, semiannual rpt, A3385–3.1
Newspaper prices per copy for daily editions, 1992, annual article, A860S–1.507

Bahrain
Energy intl sourcebook, with detail on oil and gas industry operations, supply-demand, and prices, for approx 80 countries, 1970s-91, annual compilation, C6985–10.2

Bail
see Pretrial detention and release

Bail bonds
see Surety bonds

Bain, Trevor
"Banking the Furnace: Restructuring of the Steel Industry in Eight Countries", R9260–16

Baird, Christopher
"'Prisons Pay' Studies: Research or Ideology", A7575–1.12

Baja California, Mexico
Electric power supply-demand, and utility capacities and fuel requirements, 1992-2002, annual rpt, A8630–2

Baker Hughes Inc.
Oil and gas rotary rigs active, by location, weekly rpt, C6985–1

Baker, Todd M. R.
"Professional Liability Insurance in Texas", U8850–8.8

Baking and bakery products
Consumer nutrition awareness and health concerns, with food shopping and consumption patterns, by respondent characteristics, 1993 survey, annual rpt, A4950–36

Convenience stores offering special services, including on-premises bakery, 1981-92, annual survey rpt, A6735–2
Discount wholesale membership club in-store bakery and total sales, 1991-93, article, C5225–1.509
Financial ratios and performance, for over 350 SIC 4-digit industries, FY88-92, annual rpt, A6400–3
Flour milling companies and capacity, in US by State, Canada, Mexico, and Central American and Caribbean area countries, 1993 annual directory and buyers guide, C8450–3
Food industry new product introductions, with data by product category, 1992, annual article, C2150–6.505
Military commissary sales of cookies and crackers, by region, year ended June 1992, article, C0500–1.501
Operating and financial composite ratios for corporations, with establishments and receipts, for approx 200 industries, by asset size, FY90, annual rpt, C7800–1
Restaurant practices regarding types of bread served, and on-premises baking and selling, 1991, article, C1850–3.508
Retail prices for selected consumer items in approx 300 cities, quarterly rpt, A0150–1
Sales and consumer expenditures, for food store products by type, 1991-92, annual feature, C4655–1.510
Sales volume shares by retail outlet type, for approx 300 food, drug, and other product categories, 1993 annual feature, C4655–1.504
Shopping center financial and operating data, with detail by type of tenant, US and Canada, 1991, triennial rpt, R9285–1
Supermarket bakery and deli shopper characteristics and shopping patterns, 1993 annual survey article, C5225–1.508
Supermarket bakery dept sales and performance indicators, 1992 and trends, annual article, C4655–1.505, C5225–1.504
Supermarket sales by detailed product type, 1992 and trends, annual feature, C5225–1.507
Vending machine sales by product type, and machines on location, 1992 and trends, annual rpt, C9470–1
World cookie and cracker market shares, sales growth, and consumption, for top 5-6 countries, 1993 feature, C2710–1.509
State and local:
Texas trade, transportation, and public utilities employment, by SIC 2- and 3-digit industry and detailed occupation, 2nd qtr 1991, triennial survey rpt, S7675–1.31

Balance of payments
Commodity yearbook for 1993: detailed supply-demand data, and selected indicators for futures market investors, C2400–1
Current account and trade balances, for 13 OECD countries, 1991 or 1992, article, U6910–1.501
Current account balance and components, 1991-94, annual rpt, B3520–1
Forecasts for GDP, inflation, and current account balance, for 15 countries, 1993-94, B6200–2.502

Baltimore, Md.

Japan balance of payment components, and net capital flow, weekly rpt quarterly article, R5650–2.505, R5650–2.514, R5650–2.531, R5650–2.550
Japan economic issues and devs, relations with US, and trade, balance of payments, and economic indicators, weekly rpt, R5650–2
Japan economic profile, including govt finances, industrial production, foreign trade and investments, and comparisons to US, 1988-92, annual feature, R5650–2.552
Latin America statistical abstract, general data by country, 1992 annual rpt, U6250–1.14, U6250–1.27
Securities intl transactions and net capital flow, 1982-92, annual fact book, B6625–1.1
Securities market participation by foreign and US investors, by world area and country, quarterly rpt, A8825–2
Service industries economic devs, with analysis of conditions and outlook, and comparisons to other industries, quarterly rpt, A3892–1
Transactions of US, by item, 1985-91, annual rpt, R9050–1.2
Travel receipts, expenditures, and deficits in balance of payments, for top 20 countries, 1988, R9375–6
see also Foreign exchange
see also Foreign investments
see also Foreign trade

Balance of trade
see Balance of payments
see Foreign trade

Balance sheets
see Business assets and liabilities, general
see Business assets and liabilities, specific industry
see Government assets and liabilities

Ballistic missiles
see Missiles and rockets

Baltimore, Md.
Court caseloads and dispositions, by type of court and case, FY92 and trends, annual rpt, S3600–1
Crimes and arrests, by offense, location, and offender characteristics, with law enforcement employment and assaults on officers, 1992 and trends, annual rpt, S3665–1
Elementary and secondary education data, annual rpt series, S3610–2
Elementary and secondary education statistical summary, 1991/92-1992/93 and trends, annual rpt, S3610–1
Financial condition, including revenues by source, expenditures by function, and debt obligations, FY92 and trends, annual rpt, S3618–1
Income tax (individual) returns filed, income, and State and local tax liability, 1991, annual rpt, S3685–1
Labor force, earnings, and hours data, monthly rpt, S3605–2
Library operating income and expenditures, staff, holdings, and population served, FY92, annual rpt, S3610–5
Medical assistance payments and recipients, by program, type of service, location, demographic characteristics, and facility, FY92 and trends, annual rpt, S3635–3

Baltimore, Md.

Property taxes receivable, tax rates, and fund transferrals from State and other govts, FY92 and trends, annual rpt, S3685–2

Statistical abstract of Maryland, detailed social, govtl, and economic data, 1993-94 biennial rpt, S3605–1

Vital statistics, including population, births, deaths by cause, marriages, and divorces, by demographic characteristics and location, 1989, annual rpt, S3635–1

Welfare program statistics, and welfare fraud investigations, by county, monthly rpt, S3645–2

see also under By City in the "Index by Categories"

Bangladesh

Energy intl sourcebook, with detail on oil and gas industry operations, supply-demand, and prices, for approx 80 countries, 1970s-91, annual compilation, C6985–10.2

Women's contraceptive knowledge and use, and fertility rates by age group, 1989 and trends, article, A5160–6.502

Bank deposit insurance

see Deposit insurance

Bank deposits

Black-owned enterprises financial and operating data, for top 100 firms and auto dealerships and for top 15-25 financial instns, 1992 and trends, annual feature, C4215–1.507

Deposits and commercial banks in daily newspaper markets in US and Canada, 1993 annual rpt, C3250–1

Finance company and money market fund assets, and commercial and consumer debt held, with comparisons to commercial banks, 1980-92, R4700–22

Financial performance of top 100 banks, including assets, loans, deposits, and operating ratios, 1992, annual feature, C5800–7.526

Forecast money and credit indicators, monthly rpt, B4950–1

Fortune magazine ranking of top 50-100 companies in 8 nonindustrial sectors, with financial and employment data, 1992, annual feature, C8900–1.516

Fortune magazine ranking of top 50-100 companies worldwide in 8 nonindustrial sectors, with financial and employment data, 1993 annual feature, C8900–1.522

State economic dev condition indicators, including economic performance, business vitality, growth capacity, and tax/fiscal system, by State, 1993 annual rpt, R4225–1.1

Statistical profiles of 50 States and DC, general data, 1993 annual almanac, C4712–1

Trends in bank savings/money market and time deposits, 1986-1st half 1993, article, A8825–1.508

State and local:

Alabama financial instns (State-chartered) financial condition, with deposits and assets by instn, FY92 annual rpt, S0110–1

Alabama statistical abstract, general data, 1992 recurring rpt, U5680–2.6

Alaska bank assets and liabilities of individual commercial and savings instns, quarterly rpt, S0280–2

Arizona bank balance sheets and branches, individual State and natl instns, quarterly rpt, S0460–2

Arizona statistical abstract, general data, 1993 recurring rpt, U5850–2.22

Arkansas banks and other financial instns, financial condition by instn, June 1992, annual rpt, S0632–1

Arkansas socioeconomic trends, by MSA and/or county, 1993 annual rpt, U5935–1

Arkansas State funds on deposit in banks and savings and loan assns, by type and instn, FY92, biennial rpt, S0780–1

California bank and/or savings and loan assn State govt account balances, by agency, FY92, annual rpt, S0815–1.1

California banks and trust companies, financial condition by instn, with regulatory info, Dec 1992, annual rpt, S0810–1

California economic condition, including population, employment and earnings, income, business activity, and taxation, 1960s-92, annual rpt, S0840–3.2

Colorado banks and trust companies, financial condition by instn, 1992, annual rpt, S1070–2

Colorado savings and loan assn and credit union financial condition, 1992 and trends, annual rpt, S1070–3

Connecticut banks and other financial instns, financial condition by instn, 1991 and trends, annual rpt, S1160–1

Georgia county guide, general data, 1993 annual rpt, U6750–1

Hawaii data book, general data, 1992 annual rpt, S2090–1.15

Idaho banks and other financial instns, financial condition, with data by instn and loan activity analysis, FY92 or 1991, annual rpt, S2235–1

Illinois bank and trust companies (State-chartered) financial condition and status changes, by instn, FY92, annual rpt, S2395–1

Indiana commercial bank deposits, 1980-89, annual rpt, S2570–1.1

Indiana financial instns (State-chartered) financial condition, including assets by instn arranged by city, 1991 and trends, annual rpt, S2625–1

Iowa bank and trust companies (State-chartered), financial condition by instn arranged by city, FY92 annual rpt, S2760–2

Kansas business activity indicators, quarterly rpt, U7095–1

Kansas statistical abstract, general data, 1991/92 annual rpt, U7095–2.10

Kentucky economic statistics, general data, 1993 annual rpt, S3104–1

Kentucky financial instns condition, including assets by instn and city, with regulatory info, 1992 and trends, annual rpt, S3121–1

Louisiana financial instns (State-chartered), financial condition by instn arranged by city, with regulatory info, Dec 1992, annual rpt, S3265–1

Maine banks and other financial instns, financial condition by instn, June 1992, annual rpt, S3473–2

Maine financial instn assets, deposits, and loans, by type of instn and county, 1982-92, annual rpt, S3473–1

Maryland banks and credit unions (State-chartered) financial condition by instn, with regulatory data, FY92 annual rpt, S3655–2

Michigan banks and other financial instns, financial condition by instn, with regulatory info, 1992 and trends, annual rpt, S3957–1

Minnesota bank assets and deposits, for instns held by multi-State holding companies, Dec 1991, annual rpt, S4140–3

Missouri banks and trust companies (State-chartered) financial condition, by instn, FY91-92 and trends, biennial rpt, S4502–1

Missouri State treasury investments, summary balance sheets, bonded debt, and deposits in individual banks, FY92, annual rpt, S4570–1.2

Nebraska bank demand and time deposits, 1982-91, annual rpt, S4825–1

Nevada financial instns deposits, 1983-1st half 1992, annual rpt, S5025–1

New Jersey banks and other financial instns, assets and liabilities by instn, 1992 and trends, annual rpt, S5355–1

New Mexico business and economic activity indicators, monthly rpt, U7980–1

New Mexico financial instns, financial and operating data by instn, with regulatory activities, 1992, annual rpt, S5652–1

New York State business activity indicators, quarterly rpt, S5735–2

New York State business and economic indicators, by MSA, county, and industry, 1980s-91, annual rpt, S5735–3

New York State statistical yearbook, general data, 1992 annual rpt, U5100–1.7

Oklahoma business activity indicators, monthly rpt, U8130–1

Oklahoma financial instns (State-chartered) assets and liabilities, by type of instn, with regulatory data, FY92 annual rpt, S6415–1

Oregon financial instns, financial condition by instn, Dec 1992 and trends, annual rpt, S6616–1

Pennsylvania statistical abstract, general data, 1992 recurring rpt, U4130–6.2

Rhode Island banks and other financial instns (State-chartered), assets and liabilities, by instn, 1991, annual rpt, S6945–1

Rhode Island statistical almanac, general data, 1993 annual rpt, C7975–1.1

South Carolina economic condition, including agriculture, finance, and govt financial data, 1970s-92, annual rpt, S7125–3.1

South Carolina financial instns (State-chartered) financial condition, including data by instn, FY92 annual rpt, S7165–1

South Dakota total and per capita bank deposits, 1982-91, annual rpt, S7330–1

Utah banks and other financial instns, financial condition by instn, FY93 and trends, annual rpt, S7830–1

Utah statistical abstract, general data, 1993 triennial rpt, U8960–1.15

Vermont banks and other financial instns, financial condition by instn, 1992 and trends, annual rpt, S7995–2

Index by Subjects and Names

Banks and banking

Virginia financial instns (State-chartered), financial condition by instn and instn type, Dec 1992, annual rpt, S8180–2

Washington State banks and other financial instns, financial condition by type of instn, 1992 and trends, annual rpt, S8325–1

West Virginia banks and other financial instns, composite financial condition, with selected data by instn, 1990-91, annual rpt, S8530–1

Wisconsin banks financial condition, by instn and city, with regulatory info, 1992 and trends, annual rpt, S8685–1

Wyoming State govt cash deposits in individual financial instns, and interest received, FY92 and trends, annual rpt, S9010–1

see also Certificates of deposit

see also Checking accounts

see also Deposit insurance

see also Negotiable orders of withdrawal accounts

see also Savings

Bank failures

see Business failures and closings

Bank reserves

see Banks and banking

Bankruptcy

Auto lending operations of financial instns, including bankruptcy challenges and charge-offs, 1992, annual rpt, A4160–2

Convenience store finances and number of stores, for 5 chains with bankruptcy filings, 1991-92, article, C4680–1.505

Corporations filing for Chapter 11 bankruptcy, 1980-92, and bankruptcy attorneys in 6 legal firms, 1987 and 1992, article, C5800–7.512

Discount chains filing for and emerging from bankruptcy, with number of stores, by chain, 1992-93, annual feature, C5150–3.514

Farm bankruptcy cost analyses, 1993 article, U1380–4

Filings for Chapter 11 bankruptcy by public companies, with assets of filers, 1988-May 1993, article, C2710–2.515

Foreign economic indexes, and leading and coincident indicators for US and other industrial countries, monthly rpt, U1245–1

Insurance (property/casualty) company insolvencies, 1969-92, annual article, C1050–1.504

Insurance guaranty fund assessments for property/casualty companies, with detail by State, 1991 and trends, annual rpt, A5650–1.2

Japan bankruptcies, 1990-92, article, C8900–1.505

Small corporation mgmt views on bankruptcy, and experiences with bankrupt companies, Dec 1992 survey, C4687–1.505

State and local:

Alaska insolvent insurance companies financial data, 1991, annual rpt, S0280–3

Arizona insurance companies in receivership, and guaranty fund finances, 1992, annual rpt, S0483–1

Hawaii data book, general data, 1992 annual rpt, S2090–1.4

Hawaii tax dept bankruptcy cases closed, and related amounts collected, FY92, annual rpt, S2120–1

Illinois businesses by employment size, incorporations, and bankruptcy filings, 1980s-93, S2405–2.504

Kansas statistical abstract, general data, 1991/92 annual rpt, U7095–2.8

Maryland statistical abstract, general data, 1993-94 biennial rpt, S3605–1.9

Michigan insurance companies in receivership, claims and financial data, by company, 1991, annual rpt, S3983–1

New York State insurance companies in liquidation, including claims/dividends paid and assets, 1991, annual rpt, S5770–3

Oklahoma statistical abstract, general data, 1992 annual rpt, U8130–2.15

Wyoming bankruptcies, with sales tax claims and amounts recovered, FY81-92, annual rpt, S8990–1.3

Banks and banking

Acquisitions of savings instns that have converted to stock ownership, participants, assets, and price data for 10 recent transactions, 1993 article, C3950–1.517

Aggressive business policy plans of banks, 1991-92, survey article, C8900–1.503

Assets and outstanding debt held by commercial banks compared to finance companies and other nonbank instns, 1980-92, R4700–22

Assets, equity, performance, and market value, top 50 banks worldwide, 1993 annual feature, C5800–7.535

Assets of top 12 banks worldwide, 1992, article, C5800–7.529

Black-owned enterprises financial and operating data, for top 100 firms and auto dealerships and for top 15-25 financial instns, 1992 and trends, annual feature, C4215–1.507

Charitable planning giving services offering by trust banks, 1991-93, article, C2176–1.518

Chief executive demographic and professional characteristics, attitudes, and compensation, Apr 1992 survey, annual rpt, B4490–2.33

Commercial banks in daily newspaper markets in US and Canada, 1993 annual rpt, C3250–1

Corporate performance ratings by executives for leading companies in 32 industries, 1993 annual survey feature, C8900–1.508

Direct marketing industry devs, with consumer and business market characteristics, and media use patterns, 1992/93 annual rpt, A4620–1.4

EC bank financial and/or operating ratios compared to US, for 6 countries, 1991, article, A8955–1.502

Executive compensation and components, by industry div and major manufacturing group, 1991, annual rpt, R4105–19

Failures of banks, and outlays by FDIC, by State and region, 1990-92, R8490–47

Failures of banks, healthy and failed instns absorbed through mergers, and credit outstanding by type of lender, 1992 rpt, R5025–8

Financial indicators, including assets, share of nonperforming loans, and stock performance, for 10 major banks, 1993 article, C3950–1.526

Financial performance and growth rankings for approx 1,000 top corporations, with comparisons by industry group, 1993 annual rpt, C3950–1.505

Financial performance, including assets and market capitalization, for 6 largest banks, June 1993, article, C3950–1.527

Financial performance of top 100 banks, including assets, loans, deposits, and operating ratios, 1992, annual feature, C5800–7.526

Fortune magazine ranking of top 50-100 companies in 8 nonindustrial sectors, with financial and employment data, 1992, annual feature, C8900–1.516

Fortune magazine ranking of top 50-100 companies worldwide in 8 nonindustrial sectors, with financial and employment data, 1993 annual feature, C8900–1.522

Home equity lending activity and practices of financial instns, by region, asset size, and instn type, 1992, annual rpt, A4160–3

House of Representatives Members cited for abuse of House Bank privileges, including value of largest overdrafts, and reelection status, 1988-92, annual rpt, C2500–2

Investment mgmt firms, assets and operating data for approx 900 instns, Jan 1993, annual feature, C2710–2.511

Japan bank market capitalization and investment return trends, 1993 article, C2710–2.515

Japan bank profits and nonperforming loans, for 21 leading instns, FY92, article, R5650–2.533

Latin America loan exposure of 27 US banks, 1986, annual rpt, U6250–1.28

Lending to business, including banking practices and risk analysis, and other mgmt and operation issues, monthly rpt, A6400–2

Mexico bank profit indicators, for 2 major instns, with comparisons to aggregate large US banks, 1992, C5800–7.545

Midwest business and economic conditions in metro and nonurban areas, by sector and State, bankers opinions, spring 1993 survey, semiannual rpt, B6785–1

Money and securities market activity, and related indicators, biweekly rpt, B2000–1

Mortgage banking industry aggregate financial and operating data, by lending characteristics and type of ownership, 1989 and trends, annual rpt, A6450–3

Mutual fund industry financial data, by type of investor and financial instn intermediary, 1991 and trends, annual rpt, A6025–1.2

Mutual funds investment returns, for top 5 bank proprietary vs overall funds, selected periods ended Feb 1993, C5800–7.524

Operating and financial composite ratios for corporations, with establishments and receipts, for approx 200 industries, by asset size, FY90, annual rpt, C7800–1

Public confidence in selected societal instns, 1993 Gallup Poll and trends, C4040–1.510, R8780–1.508

Public opinion on honesty/ethical standards of bankers, 1992 Gallup Polls and trends, C4040–1.501

Small business lending and services of banks, with data on organizational structure, loan delinquencies, and community dev activities, Nov 1992 survey, annual rpt, A4160–5

Banks and banking

Statistical profiles of 50 States and DC, general data, 1993 annual almanac, C4712–1

Supermarket in-store bank availability and shopper use, 1993 and trends, annual survey rpt, A4950–3

Trust instns and assets managed, approx 5,000 depts, US and Canada, 1993 annual directory, C2425–2.501

Trust/custodial master banks assets and operating data for top instns, 1993 annual directory, C2710–2.522

Trusts, master and directed, assets managed and services offered, approx 40 instns, 1992 annual directory, C2425–1.502

State and local:

Alabama county data book, general data, 1992 annual rpt, S0121–2

Alabama financial instns (State-chartered) financial condition, with deposits and assets by instn, FY92 annual rpt, S0110–1

Alabama statistical abstract, general data, 1992 recurring rpt, U5680–2.6

Alaska bank assets and liabilities of individual commercial and savings instns, quarterly rpt, S0280–2

Arizona bank balance sheets and branches, individual State and natl instns, quarterly rpt, S0460–2

Arizona statistical abstract, general data, 1993 recurring rpt, U5850–2.22

Arkansas banks and other financial instns, financial condition by instn, June 1992, annual rpt, S0632–1

California banks and trust companies, financial condition by instn, with regulatory info, Dec 1992, annual rpt, S0810–1

California economic condition, including population, employment and earnings, income, business activity, and taxation, 1960s-92, annual rpt, S0840–3.2

California statistical abstract, general data, 1992 annual rpt, S0840–2.12

Colorado banks and trust companies, financial condition by instn, 1992, annual rpt, S1070–2

Connecticut banks and other financial instns, financial condition by instn, 1991 and trends, annual rpt, S1160–1

DC FDIC-insured banks, deposits, securities, and loans, Dec 1987-91, annual rpt, S1535–3.3

Delaware financial instns, assets and branches, by instn, 1992, annual rpt, S1375–4

Florida statistical abstract, general data, 1992 annual rpt, U6660–1.17

Georgia banks and other financial instns, financial condition by instn type, and assets by instn and city, Dec 1992, annual rpt, S1865–1

Georgia statistical abstract, general data, 1992-93 biennial rpt, U6730–1.9

Hawaii data book, general data, 1992 annual rpt, S2090–1.15

Idaho banks and other financial instns, financial condition, with data by instn and loan activity analysis, FY92 or 1991, annual rpt, S2235–1

Illinois bank and trust companies (State-chartered) financial condition and status changes, by instn, FY92, annual rpt, S2395–1

Illinois statistical abstract, general data, 1992 annual rpt, U6910–2

Indiana financial instns (State-chartered) financial condition, including assets by instn arranged by city, 1991 and trends, annual rpt, S2625–1

Iowa bank and trust companies (State-chartered), financial condition by instn arranged by city, FY92 annual rpt, S2760–2

Iowa State treasury financial operations, including funds in individual banking instns, FY92, annual rpt, S2885–1

Kansas bank robberies and value of stolen property, by location, 1992, annual rpt, S2925–1.1

Kansas statistical abstract, general data, 1991/92 annual rpt, U7095–2.10

Kentucky economic statistics, general data, 1993 annual rpt, S3104–1

Kentucky financial instns condition, including assets by instn and city, with regulatory info, 1992 and trends, annual rpt, S3121–1

Louisiana financial instns (State-chartered), financial condition by instn arranged by city, with regulatory info, Dec 1992, annual rpt, S3265–1

Maine banks and other financial instns, financial condition by instn, June 1992, annual rpt, S3473–2

Maine financial instn assets, deposits, and loans, by type of instn and county, 1982-92, annual rpt, S3473–1

Maryland banks and credit unions (State-chartered) financial condition by instn, with regulatory data, FY92 annual rpt, S3655–2

Maryland statistical abstract, general data, 1993-94 biennial rpt, S3605–1.8

Michigan banks and other financial instns, financial condition by instn, with regulatory info, 1992 and trends, annual rpt, S3957–1

Minnesota financial instns (State-regulated), financial condition by instn, 1991-92, annual rpt, S4140–3

Mississippi banks and other financial instns, financial condition by instn type, and assets by bank and credit union, Dec 1992, annual rpt, S4325–1

Mississippi statistical abstract, general data, 1992 annual rpt, U3255–4.8

Missouri banks and trust companies (State-chartered) financial condition, by instn, FY91-92 and trends, biennial rpt, S4502–1

New Jersey banks and other financial instns, assets and liabilities by instn, 1992 and trends, annual rpt, S5355–1

New Mexico business and economic activity indicators, monthly rpt, U7980–1

New Mexico financial instns, financial and operating data by instn, with regulatory activities, 1992, annual rpt, S5652–1

New York State statistical yearbook, general data, 1992 annual rpt, U5100–1.5, U5100–1.7

North Carolina bank robberies by instn type, time of day, and day of week, with amount stolen, 1991-92, annual rpt, S5955–1.1

Oklahoma banks by asset size, and bank asset concentration and composition data, 1993 articles, U8130–1.502

Oklahoma business activity indicators, monthly rpt, U8130–1

Oklahoma financial instns (State-chartered) assets and liabilities, by type of instn, with regulatory data, FY92 annual rpt, S6415–1

Oklahoma statistical abstract, general data, 1992 annual rpt, U8130–2.20

Oregon financial instns, financial condition by instn, Dec 1992 and trends, annual rpt, S6616–1

Pennsylvania statistical abstract, general data, 1992 recurring rpt, U4130–6.2

Rhode Island banks and other financial instns (State-chartered), assets and liabilities, by instn, 1991, annual rpt, S6945–1

Rhode Island statistical almanac, general data, 1993 annual rpt, C7975–1.1

South Carolina economic condition, including agriculture, finance, and govt financial data, 1970s-92, annual rpt, S7125–3.1

South Carolina financial instns (State-chartered) financial condition, including data by instn, FY92 annual rpt, S7165–1

South Carolina statistical abstract, general data, 1993 annual rpt, S7125–1.2

Tennessee banks and other financial instns financial condition, by instn and city, 1992 annual rpt, S7507–1

Tennessee statistical abstract, general data, 1992/93 annual rpt, U8710–2.13

Texas banks financial performance trends, 1988-92, article, A6400–2.507

Utah banks and other financial instns, financial condition by instn, FY93 and trends, annual rpt, S7830–1

Utah statistical abstract, general data, 1993 triennial rpt, U8960–1.15

Vermont banks and other financial instns, financial condition by instn, 1992 and trends, annual rpt, S7995–2

Virginia financial instns (State-chartered), financial condition by instn and instn type, Dec 1992, annual rpt, S8180–2

Virginia tax revenues, with data on bank/trust company taxable capital, 1992, annual rpt, S8305–1.2

Washington State banks and other financial instns, financial condition by type of instn, 1992 and trends, annual rpt, S8325–1

West Virginia banks and other financial instns, composite financial condition, with selected data by instn, 1990-91, annual rpt, S8530–1

West Virginia statistical handbook, general data, 1992 annual rpt, R9385–1.8

Wisconsin banks financial condition, by instn and city, with regulatory info, 1992 and trends, annual rpt, S8685–1

Wisconsin Blue Book, general data, 1993-94 biennial rpt, S8780–1.2

see also Agricultural credit

see also Automated tellers

see also Bank deposits

see also Certificates of deposit

see also Checking accounts

see also Commercial credit

see also Consumer credit

see also Credit

see also Credit cards

see also Credit unions
see also Deposit insurance
see also Discrimination in credit
see also Electronic funds transfer
see also Eurocurrency
see also Export-Import Bank
see also Federal Reserve System
see also Financial institutions
see also Financial institutions regulation
see also Foreign exchange
see also Interest rates
see also Investment banking
see also Investment management and organizations
see also Loans
see also Money supply
see also Mortgages
see also Negotiable orders of withdrawal accounts
see also Savings
see also Savings institutions
see also under By Industry in the "Index by Categories"

Barancik, Scott
"Where Have All the Dollars Gone? A State-by-State Analysis of Income Disparities Over the 1980s", R3834–13

Barbados
Energy intl sourcebook, with detail on oil and gas industry operations, supply-demand, and prices, for approx 80 countries, 1970s-91, annual compilation, C6985–10.2

Barber and beauty shops
Customer prices for man's haircut and woman's shampoo/set in approx 300 cities, quarterly rpt, A0150–1
Financial ratios and performance, for over 350 SIC 4-digit industries, FY88-92, annual rpt, A6400–3
Shopping center financial and operating data, with detail by type of tenant, US and Canada, 1991, triennial rpt, R9285–1

Barges
Grain shipments handled by Minneapolis area elevators, by mode, 1992, annual rpt, B6110–1.1
State and local:
Oklahoma statistical abstract, general data, 1992 annual rpt, U8130–2.16

Barite
see Nonmetallic minerals and mines

Barley
see Grains and grain products

Barnes, William R.
"'All in It Together': Cities, Suburbs and Local Economic Regions", A8012–1.22
"State of America's Cities: The Ninth Annual Opinion Survey of Municipal Elected Officials", A8012–1.21

Barocas, Victor S.
"Benefit Communications: Enhancing the Employer's Investment", R4105–78.28

Bars
see Restaurants and drinking places

Barter exchange
TV syndicated program episodes available, and barter terms, by program, weekly rpt recurring table, C9380–1.511

Bartsch, Charles
"Hope and Home: Program Descriptions and Possible Changes", R8490–42

Baseball
American League player and team performance, and public attendance, 1992 and trends, annual rpt, A2068–1
Broadcasting of major league baseball, with TV and radio originators, and rights payments, by team, 1993 annual article, C1850–14.515
High school sports all-time records for boys and girls events, with school and student participation for 1991/92, annual rpt, A7830–2
Higher education student athlete enrollment and graduation rates, by sex, race-ethnicity, and major sport, for Natl Collegiate Athletic Assn Div I instns, 1992/93, annual rpt, A7440–4
Natl League player and team performance, and public attendance, 1992 and trends, annual rpt, A8015–1
Participation in 53 sports, by demographic characteristics, State, and census div, 1992, annual rpt series, A8485–3
Public opinion on disciplinary action that should be taken against Cincinnati Reds owner Marge Schott for alleged racist remarks, Dec 1992 Gallup Poll, C4040–1.506
Public opinion on proposed changes to major league baseball, Feb 1993 Gallup Poll, C4040–1.508
Public opinion on viewership of major league baseball on TV, and provisions of new network contract, May 1993 Gallup Poll, C4040–1.511
Revenues from broadcasts, and player costs, for aggregate 8 financially strongest vs 8 weakest major league teams, 1992 article, C5800–7.510
Trading cards for 6 baseball players, prices as of June 1989-93, article, C5800–7.538
TV viewers, audience share, and ratings, for All-Star Game, July 1992 and July 1993, article, C9380–1.533

Basic Education Opportunity Grants
see Pell Grant Program

Basketball
Broadcast (TV and radio) coverage of professional basketball teams, 1993/94, article, C1850–14.540
High school sports all-time records for boys and girls events, with school and student participation for 1991/92, annual rpt, A7830–2
Higher education student athlete enrollment and graduation rates, by sex, race-ethnicity, and major sport, for Natl Collegiate Athletic Assn Div I instns, 1992/93, annual rpt, A7440–4
Participation in 53 sports, by demographic characteristics, State, and census div, 1992, annual rpt series, A8485–3
Revenues by source shared and not shared with players, for Natl Basketball Assn, 1992, article, C3950–1.516

Bate, Kerry W.
"Utah's 1992 Homeless Count", S7808–2

Battered spouses
see Domestic violence

Batteries
Auto battery aftermarket sales performance, 1993 annual feature, C0125–1.503
Auto maintenance market, including consumer product purchase patterns and do-it-yourself activity, 1993 annual survey feature, C2150–10.504
Auto replacement and original battery sales volume, 1984-92, annual fact book, C4680–1.507
Market value for batteries by industry segment, including household, industrial, and govt, 1992, article, C5150–3.513
Recycling legislation provisions for auto batteries, by State, June 1992, article, C0125–1.502
Supermarket sales of nonfood products, by detailed product type, 1992, annual feature, C5225–1.508

Battleships
see Naval vessels

Bauxite
see Aluminum and aluminum industry

Bayya, Ravi
"Projections of Florida Population by County, 1992-2020", U6660–3.44

Beaches
see Seashores

Beans
see Vegetables and vegetable products

Beautification of the landscape
see Open space land programs

Beauty aids
see Cosmetics and toiletries

Beauty parlors
see Barber and beauty shops

Beck, Robert J.
"Oil Industry Outlook, 9th Edition, 1993-97", C6985–5

Beckstead, Kris
"Annual Report of Labor Market Information, 1992, Utah", S7820–10
"Utah Employers, Employment and Wages by Size, 1992", S7820–1

Bednash, Geraldine
"1992/93 Enrollment and Graduations in Baccalaureate and Graduate Programs in Nursing", A0615–4
"1992/93 Faculty Salaries in Baccalaureate and Graduate Programs in Nursing", A0615–1
"1992/93 Salaries of Deans in Baccalaureate and Graduate Programs in Nursing", A0615–2

Beecher, Janice A.
"Integrated Resource Planning for Water Utilities", A8195–11

Beef
see Meat and meat products

Beer and breweries
Advertising expenditures by medium for top 100 advertisers, with comparisons to earnings and sales, and detail by product type and brand, 1991-92, annual rpt, C2710–1.547
Consumption and sales of beverages, by type, leading company, and brand, 1992 and trends, annual rpt, C4775–1.4, C4775–2.3
Consumption of beer compared to distilled spirits and wine, by State, 1991, annual rpt, A4650–3
Financial and operating data for brewing industry, including consumption, trade, and taxes, 1991 and trends, annual rpt, A3455–1
Market shares for top 10 beer brands, and by retail outlet type, 1993 article, C5150–2.515
Operating and financial composite ratios for corporations, with establishments and receipts, for approx 200 industries, by asset size, FY90, annual rpt, C7800–1

Beer and breweries

Production, capacity, and sales volume, including top brands and brewers, 1982-92, annual feature, C0125–2.503

Retail prices for selected consumer items in approx 300 cities, quarterly rpt, A0150–1

Sales and operating data for beverage industry, by company, brand, and beverage type, 1991 and trends, annual rpt, C0125–3

Sales, consumption, and marketing devs for beverage industry, monthly rpt, C0125–2

Sales volume and market share, for top 10 brands, 1992, annual feature, C4655–1.510

Sales volume shares by retail outlet type, for approx 300 food, drug, and other product categories, 1993 annual feature, C4655–1.504

Shipments of top 10 domestic beer brands, 1992, annual article, C2710–1.507

Supermarket sales by detailed product type, 1992 and trends, annual feature, C5225–1.507

State and local:

California wine, beer, and distilled spirits consumption, and excise tax collections, FY35-92, annual rpt, S0835–1.5

Nebraska beer, alcohol, and wine gallonage and tax revenues, 1991 and trends, annual rpt, S4950–1.3

Bees and beeswax

see Honey and beekeeping

Behavioral sciences

see Anthropology

see Psychology

see Social sciences

see Sociology

Belgium

Coal industry supply-demand, employment, and trade, by country, 1990-91 and trends, annual rpt, A7400–2.2

Entertainment industry devs, including motion picture theaters and companies, boxoffice receipts, leading films, and TV and VCR use, 1993 feature, C9380–1.512

Machine tool industry operating data by country and product, 1992 and trends, annual rpt, A3179–2.2

Motor vehicle world production, sales, trade, and registrations, by country, world area, manufacturer, and make, 1991 and trends, annual rpt, A0865–2.1

Nuclear reactors in operation, with capacity, electricity generation, and construction, by unit and country, 1992, annual rpt, B6800–2.2

Steel industry employment in Belgium, for 8 companies with work force reductions, 1974-83, R9260–16

see also under By Foreign Country or World Area in the "Index by Categories"

Belman, Dale

"Truth About Public Employees: Underpaid or Overpaid?", R4700–21

Benin

Energy intl sourcebook, with detail on oil and gas industry operations, supply-demand, and prices, for approx 80 countries, 1970s-91, annual compilation, C6985–10.2

Bequests

see Gifts and private contributions

see Wills and testaments

Berenheim, Ronald E.

"Corporate Support of Dropout Prevention and Work Readiness", R4105–78.30

Berlin, Linda E.

"1992-93 Special Report on Institutional Resources and Budgets in Baccalaureate and Graduate Programs in Nursing", A0615–5

Bermuda

Newspaper circulation for 1 Bermuda publication, 6-month periods ended Sept 1992 and Mar 1993, semiannual rpt, A3385–3.1, A3385–3.3

Newspaper prices per copy for daily editions, 1992, annual article, A8605–1.507

Bernalillo County, N.Mex.

Court cases and dispositions by type of court and case, and revenues by type, FY92, annual rpt, S5623–1

Better Business Bureaus

Consumer complaint and inquiry activity of Better Business Burs, by detailed type of business, 1992, annual rpt, A4350–1

Direct marketing consumer complaints to Better Business Bureaus, and settlement rates, 1991, annual rpt, A4620–1.5

Betting

see Gambling

see Horse racing

see Pari-mutuel wagering

Beverages

Consumer purchasing of beverages in selected nonfood outlets, and soft drink sales patterns, 1993 feature, C5150–2.510

Consumption of beverages, and market shares, by beverage type, 1981-92, annual article, C0125–2.504

Corporate performance ratings by executives for leading companies in 32 industries, 1993 annual survey feature, C8900–1.508

Discount chain consumer natl brand preferences, by product category and chain, and by age group, 1993 survey, annual feature, C5150–3.521

Discount chain top-selling natl brands cited by managers, by product category, chain, and region, 1993 survey, annual feature, C5150–3.520

Discount store purchasing of selected beverage types by consumers, 1993 survey articles, C5150–3.510

Financial performance and growth rankings for approx 1,000 top corporations, with comparisons by industry group, 1993 annual rpt, C3950–1.505

Financial ratios and performance, for over 350 SIC 4-digit industries, FY88-92, annual rpt, A6400–3

Juice drink paper box container preferences, by consumer age group, 1992 survey, C1850–1.501

Mgmt salaries in food/beverage manufacturing, by selected employee characteristics, 1992 survey, annual article, C2150–6.502

Military commissary sales, by region, product type, and individual store, FY92, annual feature, A2072–2.501

Military commissary sales of top 10 beverage types, with coffee sales trend by region, 1991/92, article, C0500–1.504

Production, consumption, stocks, trade, and prices for approx 100 basic commodities, including by country and producing State, commodity yearbook for 1993, C2400–1

Production issues and devs for food and beverage industry, monthly rpt, C2150–6

Retail prices for selected consumer items in approx 300 cities, quarterly rpt, A0150–1

Sales and consumer expenditures, for food store products by type, 1991-92, annual feature, C4655–1.510

Sales and operating data for beverage industry, by company, brand, and beverage type, 1991 and trends, annual rpt, C0125–3

Sales, consumption, and marketing devs for beverage industry, monthly rpt, C0125–2

Sales volume shares by retail outlet type, for approx 300 food, drug, and other product categories, 1993 annual feature, C4655–1.504

Supermarket sales by detailed product type, 1992 and trends, annual feature, C5225–1.507

Vending machine sales by product type, and machines on location, 1992 and trends, annual rpt, C9470–1

State and local:

Florida citrus juice pack by product type, 1977/78-1991/92, annual rpt, S1685–1.1

see also Beer and breweries

see also Bottled water

see also Coffee

see also Liquor and liquor industry

see also Soft drink industry and products

see also Tea

see also Wine and winemaking

Bible

see Books and bookselling

Bibliographies

Labor market behavior, natl longitudinal surveys data users handbook and bibl, 1993 recurring rpt, U3780–2

Library and book trade reference info, including public and academic library funding, construction, and operations, by State and instn, 1992, annual compilation, C1650–3

Bicycles

Participation in 53 sports, by demographic characteristics, State, and census div, 1992, annual rpt series, A8485–3

Pediatrician bicycle safety counseling practices and experience with bicycle injuries among patients, 1990 survey, article, A2623–1.507

Shipments and imports of bicycles, by type, 1992 and trends, annual rpt, A3470–1

Shopping center financial and operating data, with detail by type of tenant, US and Canada, 1991, triennial rpt, R9285–1

Shopping center security operations, including use of selected types of security vehicles, 1993, article, C5150–4.506

Traffic accident fatalities, by type of accident, 1913-92, annual rpt, A0865–1.3

Traffic accidents, fatalities, and injuries, by vehicle type, circumstances, location, and driver and victim characteristics, 1992 and trends, annual rpt, A8375–2.3

State and local:

Alabama traffic accidents, fatalities, and injuries, by circumstances, vehicle type, and driver and victim characteristics, 1992, annual rpt, S0185–1

Alaska traffic accidents, fatalities, and injuries, by vehicle type, circumstance, location, and driver and victim characteristics, 1991 and trends, annual rpt, S0360–1

Index by Subjects and Names

Bilingual education

Arizona traffic accidents, fatalities, and injuries, by vehicle type, circumstances, location, and driver and victim characteristics, 1991 and trends, annual rpt, S0530–1

Arkansas traffic accidents, fatalities, and injuries, by vehicle type, circumstances, location, and driver and victim characteristics, 1991, annual rpt, S0692–1

California traffic accidents, fatalities, and injuries, by vehicle type, circumstances, location, and driver and victim characteristics, 1991 and trends, annual rpt, S0885–1

California traffic fatalities by type, and sex and age of victim, 1990, annual rpt, S0865–1

Connecticut traffic accidents, fatalities, and injuries, by vehicle type, circumstance, location, and driver and victim characteristics, 1992, annual rpt, S1275–1

DC statistical profile, general data, 1992 annual rpt, S1535–3.7

Delaware traffic accidents, fatalities, and injuries, by circumstances, location, and vehicle type, and driver and victim characteristics, 1992 and trends, annual rpt, S1435–1

Florida traffic accidents, fatalities, and injuries, by vehicle type, circumstance, location, and driver and victim characteristics, 1992 and trends, annual rpt, S1750–2

Hawaii data book, general data, 1992 annual rpt, S2090–1.18

Hawaii traffic accidents, injuries, and fatalities, by circumstances, location, and driver and victim characteristics, 1986 and trends, annual rpt, S2125–1

Idaho traffic accidents, fatalities, and injuries, by circumstances, location, vehicle type, and driver and victim characteristics, 1992, annual rpt, S2315–1

Illinois traffic accidents, fatalities, and injuries, by circumstances, location, and driver and victim characteristics, 1991 and trends, annual rpt, S2540–1

Indiana traffic accidents, fatalities, and injuries, by circumstances, location, and vehicle type, and driver and victim characteristics, 1992, annual rpt, S2675–1

Kansas larceny offenses and value of stolen property, by type of theft and location, 1992, annual rpt, S2925–1.1

Kansas traffic accidents, fatalities, and injuries, by vehicle type, location, circumstances, and driver and victim characteristics, 1992, annual rpt, S3040–1

Kentucky traffic accidents, fatalities, and injuries, by circumstances, location, vehicle type, and driver characteristics, 1992 and trends, annual rpt, S3150–2

Louisiana traffic accidents, fatalities, and injuries, by circumstances, location, and driver characteristics, 1991 and trends, annual rpt, S3345–2

Maine traffic accidents, fatalities, and injuries, by accident circumstances, vehicle type and make, and driver and victim characteristics, 1992, annual rpt, S3475–2

Maryland traffic accidents, fatalities, and injuries, by circumstances, location, vehicle type, and driver and victim characteristics, 1992, annual rpt, S3665–4

Michigan traffic accidents, fatalities, and injuries, by vehicle type, circumstance, location, and driver and victim characteristics, 1991 and trends, annual rpt, S3997–2

Minnesota traffic accidents, fatalities, and injuries, by type of vehicle and circumstances, and driver and victim characteristics, 1992 and trends, annual rpt, S4230–2

Missouri traffic accidents, fatalities, and injuries, by circumstances, location, and driver and victim characteristics, 1992 and trends, annual rpt, S4560–1

Montana traffic accidents, fatalities, and injuries, by circumstances, location, and driver and victim characteristics, 1992 and trends, annual rpt, S4705–2

Nebraska traffic accidents, fatalities, and injuries, by circumstances, location, vehicle type, and driver and victim characteristics, 1992, annual rpt, S4953–1

Nevada traffic accidents, fatalities, and injuries, by circumstances, location, and vehicle type, 1992 and trends, annual rpt, S5140–1

New Jersey fatal traffic accidents and fatalities, by vehicle type, location, and circumstances, and driver and victim characteristics, 1992 and trends, annual rpt, S5430–2

New Mexico traffic accidents, fatalities, and injuries, by vehicle type, circumstances, location, and driver and victim characteristics, 1992 and trends, annual rpt, S5665–1

New York State statistical yearbook, general data, 1992 annual rpt, U5100–1.13

New York State traffic accidents, fatalities, and injuries, by circumstances, location, vehicle type, and driver and victim characteristics, 1991 and trends, annual rpt, S5790–1

North Carolina traffic accidents, fatalities, and injuries, by circumstances, location, vehicle type, and driver and victim characteristics, 1992 and trends, annual rpt, S5990–1

North Dakota traffic accidents, fatalities, and injuries, by circumstances, location, vehicle type, and driver and victim characteristics, 1992 and trends, annual rpt, S6217–1

Ohio traffic accidents, fatalities, and injuries, by circumstances, location, driver and victim characteristics, and vehicle type, 1991 and trends, annual rpt, S6290–1

Oklahoma traffic accidents, fatalities, and injuries, by circumstances, location, and driver and victim characteristics, 1992 and trends, annual rpt, S6482–1

Pennsylvania traffic accidents, fatalities, and injuries, by circumstances, location, driver characteristics, and vehicle type, 1991, annual rpt, S6905–3

Rhode Island traffic accidents, fatalities, and injuries, by circumstances, community, and driver and victim characteristics, 1992, annual rpt, S7025–1

South Carolina traffic accidents, fatalities, and injuries, by circumstances, location, and driver and victim characteristics, 1992 and trends, annual rpt, S7190–2

South Dakota traffic accidents, fatalities, and injuries, by circumstances, location, vehicle type, and driver and victim characteristics, 1992 and trends, annual rpt, S7300–3

Utah traffic accidents and fatalities by circumstances, location, driver and victim characteristics, and vehicle type, 1992 and trends, annual rpt, S7890–2

Virginia traffic accidents, fatalities, and injuries, by circumstances, location, and driver and victim characteristics, 1991 and trends, annual rpt, S8282–1

Washington State traffic accidents, fatalities, and injuries, by circumstances, vehicle type, and location, with driver and victim characteristics, 1992 and trends, annual rpt, S8428–1

West Virginia traffic accidents, fatalities, and injuries, by circumstance and location, and driver and victim characteristics, 1992, annual rpt, S8645–1

Wisconsin traffic accidents, fatalities, and injuries, by circumstances, location, vehicle type, and driver and victim characteristics, 1992 and trends, annual rpt, S8815–1

Wyoming traffic accidents, fatalities, and injuries, by circumstances, location, vehicle type, and driver and victim characteristics, 1992 and trends, annual rpt, S9007–1

Bilingual education

Budget of US higher education funding, by agency and program, FY92-94, annual feature, C2175–1.516

Elementary/secondary teacher views on education policy issues and selected reform proposals, Jan-Feb 1993 survey, B6045–7

Higher education appropriations for FY94 compared to spending in FY93, by program, recurring feature, C2175–1.527, C2175–1.536

Public opinion on school problems, quality, and proposed reforms, by respondent characteristics, 1993 annual Gallup Poll, A8680–1.503

State and local:

Alaska public schools, enrollment, staff, and finances, by district, FY92, annual rpt, S0295–2

California public school limited-English-proficiency enrollment, teachers, and programs, by 1st language, grade level, and county, 1992 and trends, annual rpt, S0825–10

Connecticut bilingual education students served and funding by source and grade level, 1991/92, biennial rpt, S1185–3

DC enrollment in bilingual education programs, 1987/88-1991/92, annual rpt, S1605–2

Illinois public school students leaving bilingual programs, and bilingual students by English fluency level and native language, 1990/91, annual rpt, S2440–1.1

Kansas school district revenues by source and expenditures by object, 1990/91, annual rpt, S2945–1

Bilingual education

Maryland elementary and secondary education data, by county, 1991/92, annual rpt, S3610–2.9

Massachusetts public elementary/secondary school expenditures per pupil by program, by district, 1991/92, annual rpt, S3810–5

New Mexico elementary/secondary school statistics, including grads, student test results, and finances, by school district, 1989/90-1991/92, annual rpt, S5575–4

Oklahoma school revenues and expenditures, by program, county, and district, FY92, annual rpt, S6423–1.1

Wisconsin elementary and secondary school enrollment, staff, costs, and State aid, by school district, 1992/93 and trends, annual rpt, S8795–2

see also Compensatory education

Billings, Mont.

Unemployment insurance program new business enrollment, quarterly rpt, S4710–1

Biologic drug products

- Development of drugs using biotechnology, including FDA approvals, research by phase, and data by product type, 1989-93, article, C5150–2.521
- Development of drugs using biotechnology, with number under dev, awaiting approval, and approved, 1988-91, article, C5150–2.507
- Hospital pharmacist views on involvement in drug research activities, and impact of biotechnology drugs, 1993 survey, article, A1865–1.521
- Sales of biotechnology drugs, for 4 top-selling products in 1993 and 4 new products in 1997, article, C5800–7.528

see also Vaccination and vaccines

Biological sciences

- Medical school faculty and compensation, by dept, academic rank, degree, and region, 1992/93, annual rpt, A3273–2
- Salaries of scientists, engineers, technicians, and other professionals, by employee and employer characteristics, 1990s and trends, biennial rpt, A3960–1
- Women and minorities in professional fields, detailed education and labor force data, 1991 and trends, recurring rpt, A3960–2.3

see also Biotechnology

see also Genetics

see also Physiology

Biomass energy

- World biogas organic waste recycling project characteristics, including production capacity, for 12 major projects, 1993 article, C5800–8.507
- *State and local:*
- Florida statistical abstract, general data, 1992 annual rpt, U6660–1.15
- Hawaii data book, general data, 1992 annual rpt, S2090–1.17

see also Alcohol fuels

see also Gasohol

see also Wood fuel

Biomedical engineering

see Biotechnology

Biotechnology

Chemical and related industries production, finances, operating ratios, employment, and trade, by country, company, and chemical, 1980s-92, annual feature, A1250–1.530

Drugs based on biotechnology, sales for 4 top-selling products in 1993 and 4 new products in 1997, article, C5800–7.528

- Drugs under dev using biotechnology, including FDA approvals, research by phase, and data by product type, 1989-93, article, C5150–2.521
- Drugs under dev using biotechnology, with number awaiting approval and approved, 1988-91, article, C5150–2.507
- Financial and employment data for biotechnology industry, with detail for public companies, 1991-92, article, A6400–2.503
- Financial performance and growth rankings for approx 1,000 top corporations, with comparisons by industry group, 1993 annual rpt, C3950–1.505
- Financial performance, employment, and firms, with detail for public companies, FY92-93, annual article, A1250–1.542
- Financial performance, including income and earnings, for approx 30 biotechnology companies, 1991-92, recurring article, A1250–1.518
- Financial performance, including income and earnings, for approx 30 biotechnology companies, 3rd qtr and 1st nine months 1992, recurring article, A1250–1.504
- Financing alliances made by biotechnology companies, by alliance type and product area, 1992, article, A1250–1.537
- Formations of biotechnology companies, 1987, 1989, and 1991, C1850–6.511
- Hospital pharmacist views on involvement in drug research activities, and impact of biotechnology drugs, 1993 survey, article, A1865–1.521

Birds and bird conservation

- Newcastle disease testing of pet birds in 5 States, with test results and disease flowchart, 1991, article, A3100–2.503
- OECD known and threatened bird species, for 11 countries, 1992/93 biennial rpt, R9455 1.3
- Parrots and other psittacines captive breeding info, by detailed species, with data on bird imports, 1989-90, annual survey rpt, R9200–14

State and local:

Hawaii bird counts in Honolulu area, by species, 1987-90, annual rpt, S2090–1.5

see also Hunting and trapping

Birmingham, Ala.

Airline passenger traffic at Birmingham airport, 1985-91, recurring rpt, U5680–2.16

Birth control

see Abortion

see Contraceptives

Birth defects

Hospital patient discharges and length of stay, by diagnosis, type of operation, age, and region, 1991, annual rpt series, B4455–1

State and local:

- Alabama vital statistics, including population, births, deaths by cause, marriages, and divorces, by location and demographic characteristics, 1992 and trends, annual rpt, S0175–2
- Alaska vital statistics, including births, deaths by cause, marriages, divorces, adoptions, and population, by demographic characteristics and location, 1990, annual rpt, S0315–1
- Arkansas vital statistics, including births, deaths by cause, marriages, and divorces, by age, sex, race, and county, 1991 and trends, annual rpt, S0685–1
- California vital statistics, including population, births, and deaths by cause, by demographic characteristics and county, 1990 and trends, annual rpt, S0865–1
- Colorado vital statistics, including population, births, deaths by cause, abortion, marriage and divorce, and adoption, by demographic characteristics and location, 1990 and trends, annual rpt, S1010–1
- Connecticut vital statistics, including births, deaths by cause, marriages, and divorces, by demographic characteristics and location, 1989, annual rpt, S1200–1
- Delaware vital statistics, including births, deaths by cause, and marriages and dissolutions, by demographic characteristics and location, 1990, annual rpt, S1385–2
- Florida vital statistics, including population, births, deaths by cause, and marriages and dissolutions, by location and demographic characteristics, 1992 and trends, annual rpt, S1745–3
- Georgia vital statistics, including deaths by cause, demographic characteristics, and location, 1991 and trends, annual rpt, S1895–1.2
- Hawaii vital statistics, including births, deaths by cause, marriages, and dissolutions, by demographic characteristics and location, 1990, annual rpt, S2065–1.2
- Idaho vital statistics, including births, deaths by cause, abortions, marriages, and divorces, by demographic characteristics and county, 1991 and trends, annual rpt, S2250–2
- Iowa vital statistics, including population, births, deaths by cause, marriages, and divorces, by demographic characteristics and location, 1991 and trends, annual rpt, S2795–1
- Kansas vital statistics, including population, births, deaths by cause, abortions, marriages, and divorces, by demographic characteristics and location, 1991 and trends, annual rpt, S2975–1
- Kentucky vital statistics, including births, deaths by cause, marriages and divorces, and population, by demographic characteristics and county, 1991, annual rpt, S3140–1
- Louisiana vital statistics, including population, births, deaths by cause, reportable diseases, marriages, and divorces, by demographic characteristics and locality, 1989-90 and trends, annual rpt, S3295–1
- Maine vital statistics, including births, deaths by cause, abortions, and marriages and divorces, by demographic characteristics and location, 1991 and trends, annual rpt, S3460–2
- Maryland vital statistics, including population, births, deaths by cause, marriages, and divorces, by demographic characteristics and location, 1989 and trends, annual rpt, S3635–1
- Massachusetts vital statistics, including births, deaths by cause, marriages,

Index by Subjects and Names — Birthplace

divorces, and population, by locality and demographic characteristics, 1990 and trends, annual rpt, S3850–1

Michigan vital statistics, including births, deaths, marriages, divorces/annulments, and communicable diseases, by location and demographic characteristics, 1990 and trends, annual rpt, S4000–3

Minnesota vital statistics, including population, births, abortions, deaths, marriages, and divorces, by location and demographic characteristics, 1991 and trends, annual rpt, S4190–2

Mississippi vital statistics, including births, deaths by cause, marriages, and divorces, by demographic characteristics and location, 1992 and trends, annual rpt, S4350–1

Missouri vital statistics, including population, births, deaths by cause, and marriages and divorces, by location and demographic characteristics, 1992 and trends, annual rpt, S4518–1

Montana vital statistics, including births, deaths by cause, abortion, disease, and marriage and divorce, by demographic characteristics and county, 1990-91 and trends, annual rpt, S4690–1

Nebraska vital statistics, including births, deaths, marriages, divorces, and population, by demographic characteristics and location, 1991 and trends, annual rpt, S4885–1

Nevada vital statistics, including births, abortions, and deaths by cause, by county and demographic characteristics, 1989 and trends, annual rpt, S5075–1

New Hampshire vital statistics, including population, births, deaths by cause, marriages, and divorces, by location and demographic characteristics, 1991 and trends, annual rpt, S5215–1

New Jersey vital statistics, including births, deaths, population, communicable diseases, and marriages and divorces, by demographic characteristics and location, 1990 and trends, annual rpt, S5405–1

New Mexico vital statistics, including population, births, deaths, and disease, by location and demographic characteristics, 1991 and trends, annual rpt, S5605–1

New York State vital statistics, including population, births, deaths by cause, reportable diseases, and marriages and dissolutions, by demographic characteristics and/or location, 1990 and trends, annual rpt, S5765–1

North Dakota vital statistics, including births, deaths by cause, marriages and divorces, and abortions, by demographic characteristics and/or county, 1991 and trends, annual rpt, S6105–2

Ohio vital statistics, including births, deaths by cause, marriages, divorces, and population, by demographic characteristics and location, 1991 and trends, annual rpt, S6285–1

Oregon vital statistics, including births, deaths by cause, communicable diseases, marriages, and divorces, by age, sex, race-ethnicity, and county, 1991 and trends, annual rpt, S6615–5

Rhode Island vital statistics, including population, births, deaths, marriages, and divorces, by demographic characteristics and locality, 1989 and trends, annual rpt, S6995–1

South Carolina deaths, by detailed cause, age, sex, and race, 1990, annual rpt, S7175–2

South Carolina vital statistics, including births, deaths by cause, marriages, and divorces, by age, sex, race, and location, 1990 and trends, annual rpt, S7175–1

South Dakota vital statistics, including births, deaths, marriage and divorce, and communicable disease, by demographic characteristics and county, 1991 and trends, annual rpt, S7345–1

Tennessee vital statistics, including births, deaths by cause, marriages, divorces, and population, by demographic characteristics and location, 1991 and trends, annual rpt, S7520–2

Texas vital statistics, including births, deaths by cause, abortions, marriages, and divorces, by location and demographic characteristics, 1991 and trends, annual rpt, S7685–1

Utah vital statistics, including births, deaths by cause, and population, by county and demographic characteristics, 1990 and trends, annual rpt, S7835–1

Vermont vital statistics, including population, births, deaths by cause, abortions, marriages, and divorces, by location and demographic characteristics, 1991 and trends, annual rpt, S8054–1

Virginia vital statistics, including births, deaths by cause, marriages and divorces, and communicable disease, by demographic characteristics and location, 1991 and trends, annual rpt, S8225–1

Washington State vital statistics, including births, deaths by cause, and population, by demographic characteristics and location, 1991 and trends, annual rpt, S8363–1

West Virginia vital statistics, including births, deaths by cause, marriages, and divorces, by location and demographic characteristics, 1991 and trends, annual rpt, S8560–1

Wisconsin vital statistics, including population, births, deaths by cause, and marriages and dissolutions, by county and demographic characteristics, 1991 and trends, annual rpt, S8715–4

Wyoming vital statistics, including population, births, deaths by cause, marriages, and divorces, by demographic characteristics and county, 1991 and trends, annual rpt, S8920–2

see also under By Disease in the "Index by Categories"

Birth weight

see Birthweight

Birthing centers

State and local:

Delaware births, by type of place and attendant, and method of delivery, 1990, annual rpt, S1385–2

Florida births, by location, 1992, annual rpt, S1745–3

Florida health care atlas, including manpower by occupation and health care facilities by type, by district and county, 1992 annual rpt, S1746–1.2

Missouri births by location and selected mother and infant characteristics, 1992, annual rpt, S4518–1

New Hampshire births in birthing centers, 1987-91, annual rpt, S5215–1

South Carolina vital statistics, including births, deaths by cause, marriages, and divorces, by age, sex, race, and location, 1990 and trends, annual rpt, S7175–1

Washington State births at home and in birthing centers, by county and city, 1991, annual rpt, S8363–1

West Virginia births by location, 1991, annual rpt, S8560–1

Birthplace

Corporate CEO characteristics, compensation, and company finances, for officers of top 1,000 firms, 1993 annual feature, C5800–7.549

Northern Mariana Islands population shares by citizenship status and birthplace, 1992 rpt, B3500–1.501

State native population shares, 1990, article, B8500–2.512

Statistical profiles of 50 States and DC, general data, 1993 annual almanac, C4712–1

State and local:

Alaska marriages by participant characteristics, and adoptions by child's birthplace, 1990, annual rpt, S0315–1

Arkansas Census of Population and Housing detailed findings, 1990, U5935–7

California Census of Population and Housing detailed findings, 1990, S0840–9

Hawaii data book, general data, 1992 annual rpt, S2090–1.1

Iowa correctional instn admissions, releases, and inmate characteristics, by instn, monthly rpt, S2770–1

Louisiana Census of Population and Housing summary findings, by local area, 1990 and trends, U8010–4

Maine Census of Population and Housing summary findings, by local area, 1990, S3465–9

Maryland, births to State residents and total births, by county of residence or occurrence, 1989, annual rpt, S3635–1

Maryland statistical abstract, general data, 1993-94 biennial rpt, S3605–1.1

Missouri correctional instn admissions, releases, and inmate characteristics, FY93, annual rpt, S4501–1

Nebraska native and foreign-born population, with comparisons to Plains region, 1990, article, U7860–1.507

New Jersey Census of Population and Housing detailed findings, by county, 1990, S5425–19

Pennsylvania Census of Population and Housing detailed findings, with selected data by county and municipality, 1990, U4130–13

Pennsylvania State correctional instn admin, and inmates by type of offense and demographic characteristics, 1990 and trends, annual rpt, S6782–1

Rhode Island Census of Population and Housing detailed findings, by county and municipality, 1990, S6930–9

South Carolina statistical abstract, general data, 1993 annual rpt, S7125–1.13

Tennessee statistical abstract, general data, 1992/93 annual rpt, U8710–2.1

Vermont vital statistics, including population, births, deaths by cause, abortions, marriages, and divorces, by location and demographic characteristics, 1991 and trends, annual rpt, S8054–1

Birthplace

Wisconsin correctional instn inmates by place of birth, Dec 1991, semiannual rpt, S8692–1.5

Wisconsin correctional instn inmates by place of birth, June 1991, semiannual rpt, S8692–1.1

Births

- Black American socioeconomic status, including health, education, politics, crime, and employment, with comparisons to whites, 1993 annual compilation, C6775–2
- Child and maternal health status indicators, with data by race and State, 1992 annual rpt, R3840–5
- Developing countries family planning and child survival efforts, by country and selected demographic characteristics, 1980s-90, R8720–1
- EC Jewish population birth and death rates, for 3 countries, 1930s-90, article, A2050–1.1
- Hospital directory, with utilization, expenses, and personnel, by instn, type, and location, 1992, annual rpt, A1865–3
- Hospital patient admission rates and length of stay, by diagnosis and procedure, payment source, age, sex, and region, 1991, B4455–4
- Hospital patient charges and length of stay, by diagnosis and procedure, payment source, age, and region, 1991, B4455–5
- Labor supply trends, with births by sex and race, 1933-90, recurring rpt, A3960–2.1
- Latin America statistical abstract, general data by country, 1992 annual rpt, U6250–1.6
- Middle East population trend and demographic characteristics, by country, 1993 rpt, R8750–2.59
- Population size and selected characteristics, by region, census div, and State, 1991 and trends, annual data sheet, R8750–9
- Rates and shares of births by selected newborn and maternal characteristics, 1990, article, R8750–1.510
- State social, economic, and govtl indicators, with rankings, 1993 semiannual rpt, B8500–1.1
- Statistical profiles of 50 States and DC, general data, 1993 annual almanac, C4712–1
- Teenage mother birth rates and share of total births, by race and Hispanic ethnicity, by State, 1989 and trends, annual rpt, R3840–11
- World birth, death, population increase, and infant death rate indicators, with detail for more and less developed countries, 1993, annual feature, R8750–1.509
- World population and health indicators, with detail by region and country, 1992/93 biennial rpt, R9455–1.5
- World population size and characteristics, GNP, and land area, by region and/or country, 1993 annual data sheet, R8750–5
- World vital statistics, for top 50 countries in births, deaths, infant mortality, and life expectancy, 1992, semiannual rpt, B8500–1.16

State and local:

Alabama vital statistics, including population, births, deaths by cause, marriages, and divorces, by location and demographic characteristics, 1992 and trends, annual rpt, S0175–2

Alaska population, housing, income, and education data, by demographic characteristics and/or locality, 1990/91 and trends, annual rpt, S0320–4

Alaska vital statistics, including births, deaths by cause, marriages, divorces, adoptions, and population, by demographic characteristics and location, 1990, annual rpt, S0315–1

Arizona Indian population, education, housing, health, and employment characteristics, with detail by reservation, 1970s-91, recurring rpt, U5850–2.9

Arizona population and components of change, 1985-93, semiannual rpt, U5850–1.1

Arizona statistical abstract, general data, 1993 recurring rpt, U5850–2.3

Arkansas socioeconomic trends, by MSA and/or county, 1993 annual rpt, U5935–1

Arkansas vital statistics, including births, deaths by cause, marriages, and divorces, by age, sex, race, and county, 1991 and trends, annual rpt, S0685–1

California vital statistics, including population, births, and deaths by cause, by demographic characteristics and county, 1990 and trends, annual rpt, S0865–1

Colorado vital statistics, including population, births, deaths by cause, abortion, marriage and divorce, and adoption, by demographic characteristics and location, 1990 and trends, annual rpt, S1010–1

Connecticut vital statistics, including births, deaths by cause, marriages, and divorces, by demographic characteristics and location, 1989, annual rpt, S1200–1

DC statistical profile, general data, 1992 annual rpt, S1535–3.5

Delaware projected births and deaths, by county, 1990-2020, recurring rpt, S1375–3

Delaware vital statistics, including births, deaths by cause, and marriages and dissolutions, by demographic characteristics and location, 1990, annual rpt, S1385–2

Florida births by race and characteristics of mother, with detail for low-weight births, by county, 1990, annual rpt, S1746–1.1

Florida vital statistics, including population, births, deaths by cause, and marriages and dissolutions, by location and demographic characteristics, 1992 and trends, annual rpt, S1745–3

Georgia vital statistics, including population, births, abortions, marriages, and divorces, by demographic characteristics and location, 1991 and trends, annual rpt, S1895–1.1

Hawaii vital statistics, including births, deaths by cause, marriages, and dissolutions, by demographic characteristics and location, 1990, annual rpt, S2065–1.2

Idaho and US economic trends and forecasts, quarterly rpt, S2245–2

Idaho vital statistics, including births, deaths by cause, abortions, marriages, and divorces, by demographic characteristics and county, 1991 and trends, annual rpt, S2250–2

Illinois statistical abstract, general data, 1992 annual rpt, U6910–2

Iowa vital statistics, including population, births, deaths by cause, marriages, and divorces, by demographic characteristics and location, 1991 and trends, annual rpt, S2795–1

Kansas vital statistics, including population, births, deaths by cause, abortions, marriages, and divorces, by demographic characteristics and location, 1991 and trends, annual rpt, S2975–1

Kentucky economic statistics, general data, 1993 annual rpt, S3104–1.3

Kentucky vital statistics, including births, deaths by cause, marriages and divorces, and population, by demographic characteristics and county, 1991, annual rpt, S3140–1

Louisiana vital statistics, including population, births, deaths by cause, reportable diseases, marriages, and divorces, by demographic characteristics and locality, 1989-90 and trends, annual rpt, S3295–1

Maine vital statistics, including births, deaths by cause, abortions, and marriages and divorces, by demographic characteristics and location, 1991 and trends, annual rpt, S3460–2

Maryland vital statistics, including population, births, deaths by cause, marriages, and divorces, by demographic characteristics and location, 1989 and trends, annual rpt, S3635–1

Massachusetts vital statistics, including births, deaths by cause, marriages, divorces, and population, by locality and demographic characteristics, 1990 and trends, annual rpt, S3850–1

Michigan vital statistics, including births, deaths, marriages, divorces/annulments, and communicable diseases, by location and demographic characteristics, 1990 and trends, annual rpt, S4000–3

Minnesota vital statistics, including population, births, abortions, deaths, marriages, and divorces, by location and demographic characteristics, 1991 and trends, annual rpt, S4190–2

Mississippi vital statistics, including births, deaths by cause, marriages, and divorces, by demographic characteristics and location, 1992 and trends, annual rpt, S4350–1

Missouri live births, 1975-92, annual rpt, S4505–1.1

Missouri vital statistics, including population, births, deaths by cause, and marriages and divorces, by location and demographic characteristics, 1992 and trends, annual rpt, S4518–1

Montana births, by hospital, 1991, annual rpt, S4690–2

Montana vital statistics, including births, deaths by cause, abortion, disease, and marriage and divorce, by demographic characteristics and county, 1990-91 and trends, annual rpt, S4690–1

Nebraska vital statistics, including births, deaths, marriages, divorces, and population, by demographic characteristics and location, 1991 and trends, annual rpt, S4885–1

Births out of wedlock

Nevada vital statistics, including births, abortions, and deaths by cause, by county and demographic characteristics, 1989 and trends, annual rpt, S5075–1

New Hampshire vital statistics, including population, births, deaths by cause, marriages, and divorces, by location and demographic characteristics, 1991 and trends, annual rpt, S5215–1

New Jersey vital statistics, including births, deaths, population, communicable diseases, and marriages and divorces, by demographic characteristics and location, 1990 and trends, annual rpt, S5405–1

New Mexico population size and components of change, by county, 1990-91, article, U7980–1.503

New Mexico vital statistics, including population, births, deaths, and disease, by location and demographic characteristics, 1991 and trends, annual rpt, S5605–1

New York State vital statistics, including population, births, deaths by cause, reportable diseases, and marriages and dissolutions, by demographic characteristics and/or location, 1990 and trends, annual rpt, S5765–1

North Carolina vital statistics, including population, births, deaths, marriages, and divorces, by local area, 1991 and trends, annual rpt, S5927–1.1

North Dakota vital statistics, including births, deaths by cause, marriages and divorces, and abortions, by demographic characteristics and/or county, 1991 and trends, annual rpt, S6105–2

Ohio population by age, sex, and county, with summary components of change, quinquennially 1990-2015, recurring rpt, S6260–3

Ohio vital statistics, including births, deaths by cause, marriages, divorces, and population, by demographic characteristics and location, 1991 and trends, annual rpt, S6285–1

Oregon vital statistics, including births, deaths by cause, communicable diseases, marriages, and divorces, by age, sex, race-ethnicity, and county, 1991 and trends, annual rpt, S6615–5

Rhode Island vital statistics, including population, births, deaths, marriages, and divorces, by demographic characteristics and locality, 1989 and trends, annual rpt, S6995–1

South Carolina population and components of change, by county, 1980-90, annual planning rpt, S7155–3.1

South Carolina vital statistics, including births, deaths by cause, marriages, and divorces, by age, sex, race, and location, 1990 and trends, annual rpt, S7175–1

South Dakota vital statistics, including births, deaths, marriage and divorce, and communicable disease, by demographic characteristics and county, 1991 and trends, annual rpt, S7345–1

Tennessee vital statistics, including births, deaths by cause, marriages, divorces, and population, by demographic characteristics and location, 1991 and trends, annual rpt, S7520–2

Texas hospitals, operations, utilization, and finances, by type, ownership, size, and metro-nonmetro status, 1970s-91, U8850–8.3

Texas vital statistics, including births, deaths by cause, abortions, marriages, and divorces, by location and demographic characteristics, 1991 and trends, annual rpt, S7685–1

Utah economic and demographic trends, by county and district, 1960-91, annual rpt, S7832–2

Utah population estimates and components, including data by county, 1992 and trends, annual article, U8960–2.504

Utah vital statistics, including births, deaths by cause, and population, by county and demographic characteristics, 1990 and trends, annual rpt, S7835–1

Vermont vital statistics, including population, births, deaths by cause, abortions, marriages, and divorces, by location and demographic characteristics, 1991 and trends, annual rpt, S8054–1

Virginia births and public school enrollment, 1980-2007, annual rpt, U9080–20

Virginia vital statistics, including births, deaths by cause, marriages and divorces, and communicable disease, by demographic characteristics and location, 1991 and trends, annual rpt, S8225–1

Washington State population and components of change, 1992 and trends, annual rpt, S8345–4

Washington State vital statistics, including births, deaths by cause, and population, by demographic characteristics and location, 1991 and trends, annual rpt, S8363–1

West Virginia vital statistics, including births, deaths by cause, marriages, and divorces, by location and demographic characteristics, 1991 and trends, annual rpt, S8560–1

Wisconsin birth, death, and marriage registrations, monthly rpt, S8750–1

Wisconsin population, by age, sex, and county, with components of change, quinquennially 1990-2020, recurring rpt, S8675–4

Wisconsin vital statistics, including population, births, deaths by cause, and marriages and dissolutions, by county and demographic characteristics, 1991 and trends, annual rpt, S8715–4

Wyoming vital statistics, including population, births, deaths by cause, marriages, and divorces, by demographic characteristics and county, 1991 and trends, annual rpt, S8920–2

see also Abortion
see also Birth defects
see also Birthing centers
see also Birthplace
see also Birthweight
see also Fertility
see also Fetal deaths
see also Home births
see also Infant mortality
see also Maternity
see also Obstetrics and gynecology
see also Plural births
see also Teenage pregnancy
see also Vital statistics

Births out of wedlock

Black American health and vital statistics data, with comparisons to whites, 1970s-91, annual compilation, C6775–2.2

Black children and youth population, economic, health, and education data, with comparisons to whites, 1993 rpt, R3840–21

Child and maternal health status indicators, with data by race and State, 1992 annual rpt, R3840–5

Low-income families and children, health and welfare indicators, with data by State and city, 1992 annual rpt, R3840–11

State social, economic, and govtl indicators, with rankings, 1993 semiannual rpt, B8500–1.9

Statistical profiles of 50 States and DC, general data, 1993 annual almanac, C4712–1

State and local:

Alabama vital statistics, including population, births, deaths by cause, marriages, and divorces, by location and demographic characteristics, 1992 and trends, annual rpt, S0175–2

Alaska vital statistics, including births, deaths by cause, marriages, divorces, adoptions, and population, by demographic characteristics and location, 1990, annual rpt, S0315–1

Arizona Indian population, education, housing, health, and employment characteristics, with detail by reservation, 1970s-91, recurring rpt, U5850–2.9

Arkansas vital statistics, including births, deaths by cause, marriages, and divorces, by age, sex, race, and county, 1991 and trends, annual rpt, S0685–1

California vital statistics, including population, births, and deaths by cause, by demographic characteristics and county, 1990 and trends, annual rpt, S0865–1

Colorado vital statistics, including population, births, deaths by cause, abortion, marriage and divorce, and adoption, by demographic characteristics and location, 1990 and trends, annual rpt, S1010–1

Connecticut vital statistics, including births, deaths by cause, marriages, and divorces, by demographic characteristics and location, 1989, annual rpt, S1200–1

Delaware vital statistics, including births, deaths by cause, and marriages and dissolutions, by demographic characteristics and location, 1990, annual rpt, S1385–2

Florida births by race and characteristics of mother, with detail for low-weight births, by county, 1990, annual rpt, S1746–1.1

Florida vital statistics, including population, births, deaths by cause, and marriages and dissolutions, by location and demographic characteristics, 1992 and trends, annual rpt, S1745–3

Georgia vital statistics, including population, births, abortions, marriages, and divorces, by demographic characteristics and location, 1991 and trends, annual rpt, S1895–1.1

Hawaii vital statistics, including births, deaths by cause, marriages, and dissolutions, by demographic characteristics and location, 1990, annual rpt, S2065–1.2

Idaho vital statistics, including births, deaths by cause, abortions, marriages, and divorces, by demographic characteristics and county, 1991 and trends, annual rpt, S2250–2

Iowa vital statistics, including population, births, deaths by cause, marriages, and

Births out of wedlock

divorces, by demographic characteristics and location, 1991 and trends, annual rpt, S2795–1

- Kansas vital statistics, including population, births, deaths by cause, abortions, marriages, and divorces, by demographic characteristics and location, 1991 and trends, annual rpt, S2975–1
- Kentucky vital statistics, including births, deaths by cause, marriages and divorces, and population, by demographic characteristics and county, 1991, annual rpt, S3140–1
- Louisiana vital statistics, including population, births, deaths by cause, reportable diseases, marriages, and divorces, by demographic characteristics and locality, 1989-90 and trends, annual rpt, S3295–1
- Maine vital statistics, including births, deaths by cause, abortions, and marriages and divorces, by demographic characteristics and location, 1991 and trends, annual rpt, S3460–2
- Maryland vital statistics, including population, births, deaths by cause, marriages, and divorces, by demographic characteristics and location, 1989 and trends, annual rpt, S3635–1
- Massachusetts vital statistics, including births, deaths by cause, marriages, divorces, and population, by locality and demographic characteristics, 1990 and trends, annual rpt, S3850–1
- Minnesota vital statistics, including population, births, abortions, deaths, marriages, and divorces, by location and demographic characteristics, 1991 and trends, annual rpt, S4190–2
- Mississippi vital statistics, including births, deaths by cause, marriages, and divorces, by demographic characteristics and location, 1992 and trends, annual rpt, S4350–1
- Missouri vital statistics, including population, births, deaths by cause, and marriages and divorces, by location and demographic characteristics, 1992 and trends, annual rpt, S4518–1
- Montana vital statistics, including births, deaths by cause, abortion, disease, and marriage and divorce, by demographic characteristics and county, 1990-91 and trends, annual rpt, S4690–1
- Nebraska vital statistics, including births, deaths, marriages, divorces, and population, by demographic characteristics and location, 1991 and trends, annual rpt, S4885–1
- New Hampshire vital statistics, including population, births, deaths by cause, marriages, and divorces, by location and demographic characteristics, 1991 and trends, annual rpt, S5215–1
- New Jersey vital statistics, including births, deaths, population, communicable diseases, and marriages and divorces, by demographic characteristics and location, 1990 and trends, annual rpt, S5405–1
- New Mexico births to single mothers, by county and demographic characteristics, 1991 and trends, annual rpt, S5605–1.2
- New York State vital statistics, including population, births, deaths by cause, reportable diseases, and marriages and

dissolutions, by demographic characteristics and/or location, 1990 and trends, annual rpt, S5765–1

- North Carolina vital statistics, including population, births, deaths, marriages, and divorces, by local area, 1991 and trends, annual rpt, S5927–1.1
- North Dakota vital statistics, including births, deaths by cause, marriages and divorces, and abortions, by demographic characteristics and/or county, 1991 and trends, annual rpt, S6105–2
- Ohio vital statistics, including births, deaths by cause, marriages, divorces, and population, by demographic characteristics and location, 1991 and trends, annual rpt, S6285–1
- Oregon vital statistics, including births, deaths by cause, communicable diseases, marriages, and divorces, by age, sex, race-ethnicity, and county, 1991 and trends, annual rpt, S6615–5
- Rhode Island vital statistics, including population, births, deaths, marriages, and divorces, by demographic characteristics and locality, 1989 and trends, annual rpt, S6995–1
- South Carolina vital statistics, including births, deaths by cause, marriages, and divorces, by age, sex, race, and location, 1990 and trends, annual rpt, S7175–1
- Tennessee vital statistics, including births, deaths by cause, marriages, divorces, and population, by demographic characteristics and location, 1991 and trends, annual rpt, S7520–2
- Utah vital statistics, including births, deaths by cause, and population, by county and demographic characteristics, 1990 and trends, annual rpt, S7835–1
- Vermont vital statistics, including population, births, deaths by cause, abortions, marriages, and divorces, by location and demographic characteristics, 1991 and trends, annual rpt, S8054–1
- Virginia vital statistics, including births, deaths by cause, marriages and divorces, and communicable disease, by demographic characteristics and location, 1991 and trends, annual rpt, S8225–1
- West Virginia vital statistics, including births, deaths by cause, marriages, and divorces, by location and demographic characteristics, 1991 and trends, annual rpt, S8560–1
- Wisconsin vital statistics, including population, births, deaths by cause, and marriages and dissolutions, by county and demographic characteristics, 1991 and trends, annual rpt, S8715–4
- Wyoming vital statistics, including population, births, deaths by cause, marriages, and divorces, by demographic characteristics and county, 1991 and trends, annual rpt, S8920–2

Birthweight

- Births and fertility, by selected newborn and maternal characteristics, 1990, article, R8750–1.510
- Black American health and vital statistics data, with comparisons to whites, 1970s-91, annual compilation, C6775–2.2
- Black children and youth population, economic, health, and education data, with comparisons to whites, 1993 rpt, R3840–21

Index by Subjects and Names

- Child and maternal health status indicators, with data by race and State, 1992 annual rpt, R3840–5
- Child health and well-being indicators, with selected household characteristics, by State, 1993 annual rpt, R3832–1
- China, Shanghai low birthweight incidence correlated with paternal smoking habits and selected characteristics of mother, Oct 1986-Sept 1987, article, A2623–1.504
- Developing countries child survival efforts, with selected child and maternal health indicators, 1980s-90, R8720–1.2
- Low-income families and children, health and welfare indicators, with data by State and city, 1992 annual rpt, R3840–11
- Medicaid child and total recipients, expenditures, and other program characteristics, and child health summary, by State, FY91, annual rpt, A0565–1
- Philippines birth outcomes by maternal characteristics, 1983/84 Cebu metro area study, article, A5160–6.505
- State social, economic, and govtl indicators, with rankings, 1993 semiannual rpt, B8500–1.9
- Statistical profiles of 50 States and DC, general data, 1993 annual almanac, C4712–1
- World population and health indicators, with detail by region and country, 1992/93 biennial rpt, R9455–1.5
- World vital statistics, for top 50 countries in births, deaths, infant mortality, and life expectancy, 1992, semiannual rpt, B8500–1.16

State and local:

- Alabama vital statistics, including population, births, deaths by cause, marriages, and divorces, by location and demographic characteristics, 1992 and trends, annual rpt, S0175–2
- Alaska vital statistics, including births, deaths by cause, marriages, divorces, adoptions, and population, by demographic characteristics and location, 1990, annual rpt, S0315–1
- Arkansas vital statistics, including births, deaths by cause, marriages, and divorces, by age, sex, race, and county, 1991 and trends, annual rpt, S0685–1
- California vital statistics, including population, births, and deaths by cause, by demographic characteristics and county, 1990 and trends, annual rpt, S0865–1
- Colorado vital statistics, including population, births, deaths by cause, abortion, marriage and divorce, and adoption, by demographic characteristics and location, 1990 and trends, annual rpt, S1010–1
- Connecticut vital statistics, including births, deaths by cause, marriages, and divorces, by demographic characteristics and location, 1989, annual rpt, S1200–1
- Delaware vital statistics, including births, deaths by cause, and marriages and dissolutions, by demographic characteristics and location, 1990, annual rpt, S1385–2
- Florida births by race and characteristics of mother, with detail for low-weight births, by county, 1990, annual rpt, S1746–1.1

Index by Subjects and Names

Black Americans

Florida vital statistics, including population, births, deaths by cause, and marriages and dissolutions, by location and demographic characteristics, 1992 and trends, annual rpt, S1745–3

Georgia vital statistics, including population, births, abortions, marriages, and divorces, by demographic characteristics and location, 1991 and trends, annual rpt, S1895–1.1

Hawaii health dept activities and services, including vital statistics and disease control, by location, 1990, annual rpt, S2065–1

Idaho vital statistics, including births, deaths by cause, abortions, marriages, and divorces, by demographic characteristics and county, 1991 and trends, annual rpt, S2250–2

Iowa vital statistics, including population, births, deaths by cause, marriages, and divorces, by demographic characteristics and location, 1991 and trends, annual rpt, S2795–1

Kansas vital statistics, including population, births, deaths by cause, abortions, marriages, and divorces, by demographic characteristics and location, 1991 and trends, annual rpt, S2975–1

Kentucky vital statistics, including births, deaths by cause, marriages and divorces, and population, by demographic characteristics and county, 1991, annual rpt, S3140–1

Louisiana vital statistics, including population, births, deaths by cause, reportable diseases, marriages, and divorces, by demographic characteristics and locality, 1989-90 and trends, annual rpt, S3295–1

Maine vital statistics, including births, deaths by cause, abortions, and marriages and divorces, by demographic characteristics and location, 1991 and trends, annual rpt, S3460–2

Maryland vital statistics, including population, births, deaths by cause, marriages, and divorces, by demographic characteristics and location, 1989 and trends, annual rpt, S3635–1

Massachusetts vital statistics, including births, deaths by cause, marriages, divorces, and population, by locality and demographic characteristics, 1990 and trends, annual rpt, S3850–1

Michigan vital statistics, including births, deaths, marriages, divorces/annulments, and communicable diseases, by location and demographic characteristics, 1990 and trends, annual rpt, S4000–3

Minnesota vital statistics, including population, births, abortions, deaths, marriages, and divorces, by location and demographic characteristics, 1991 and trends, annual rpt, S4190–2

Mississippi vital statistics, including births, deaths by cause, marriages, and divorces, by demographic characteristics and location, 1992 and trends, annual rpt, S4350–1

Missouri vital statistics, including population, births, deaths by cause, and marriages and divorces, by location and demographic characteristics, 1992 and trends, annual rpt, S4518–1

Montana vital statistics, including births, deaths by cause, abortion, disease, and marriage and divorce, by demographic characteristics and county, 1990-91 and trends, annual rpt, S4690–1

Nebraska vital statistics, including births, deaths, marriages, divorces, and population, by demographic characteristics and location, 1991 and trends, annual rpt, S4885–1

Nevada vital statistics, including births, abortions, and deaths by cause, by county and demographic characteristics, 1989 and trends, annual rpt, S5075–1

New Hampshire vital statistics, including population, births, deaths by cause, marriages, and divorces, by location and demographic characteristics, 1991 and trends, annual rpt, S5215–1

New Jersey vital statistics, including births, deaths, population, communicable diseases, and marriages and divorces, by demographic characteristics and location, 1990 and trends, annual rpt, S5405–1

New Mexico births by weight, and low-weight births by county and demographic characteristics, 1991 and trends, annual rpt, S5605–1.2

New York State vital statistics, including population, births, deaths by cause, reportable diseases, and marriages and dissolutions, by demographic characteristics and/or location, 1990 and trends, annual rpt, S5765–1

North Carolina vital statistics, including population, births, deaths, marriages, and divorces, by local area, 1991 and trends, annual rpt, S5927–1.1

North Dakota vital statistics, including births, deaths by cause, marriages and divorces, and abortions, by demographic characteristics and/or county, 1991 and trends, annual rpt, S6105–2

Ohio vital statistics, including births, deaths by cause, marriages, divorces, and population, by demographic characteristics and location, 1991 and trends, annual rpt, S6285–1

Oregon vital statistics, including births, deaths by cause, communicable diseases, marriages, and divorces, by age, sex, race-ethnicity, and county, 1991 and trends, annual rpt, S6615–5

Rhode Island vital statistics, including population, births, deaths, marriages, and divorces, by demographic characteristics and locality, 1989 and trends, annual rpt, S6995–1

South Carolina vital statistics, including births, deaths by cause, marriages, and divorces, by age, sex, race, and location, 1990 and trends, annual rpt, S7175–1

South Dakota vital statistics, including births, deaths, marriage and divorce, and communicable disease, by demographic characteristics and county, 1991 and trends, annual rpt, S7345–1

Tennessee vital statistics, including births, deaths by cause, marriages, divorces, and population, by demographic characteristics and location, 1991 and trends, annual rpt, S7520–2

Texas vital statistics, including births, deaths by cause, abortions, marriages, and divorces, by location and demographic characteristics, 1991 and trends, annual rpt, S7685–1

Utah vital statistics, including births, deaths by cause, and population, by county and demographic characteristics, 1990 and trends, annual rpt, S7835–1

Vermont vital statistics, including population, births, deaths by cause, abortions, marriages, and divorces, by location and demographic characteristics, 1991 and trends, annual rpt, S8054–1

Virginia vital statistics, including births, deaths by cause, marriages and divorces, and communicable disease, by demographic characteristics and location, 1991 and trends, annual rpt, S8225–1

Washington State vital statistics, including births, deaths by cause, and population, by demographic characteristics and location, 1991 and trends, annual rpt, S8363–1

West Virginia vital statistics, including births, deaths by cause, marriages, and divorces, by location and demographic characteristics, 1991 and trends, annual rpt, S8560–1

Wisconsin vital statistics, including population, births, deaths by cause, and marriages and dissolutions, by county and demographic characteristics, 1991 and trends, annual rpt, S8715–4

Wyoming vital statistics, including population, births, deaths by cause, marriages, and divorces, by demographic characteristics and county, 1991 and trends, annual rpt, S8920–2

Bitumen

see Asphalt and tar

Black Americans

Cancer deaths among black Americans, by body site and sex, 1989, annual rpt, A1175–1

Catalog product choices among black shoppers, by sex, 1992, annual rpt, A4620–1.2

Children and youth population, economic, health, and education data, with comparisons to whites, 1993 rpt, R3840–21

Consumer buying power survey of population, income, and sales by kind of business, by census div, State, MSA, county, and city, 1992, annual rpt, C1200–1.511

Consumer purchasing by product type, and ownership of selected electronics, for blacks, Hispanics, and Asians, 1992/93 survey, article, C2710–1.513

Drugstore marketing to ethnic minorities, with related consumer indicators for blacks or by race, 1993 articles, C5150–2.518

Economic and career concerns of blacks, articles and special features, monthly rpt, C4215–1

Elected black officials, by level of govt and State, 1991, annual rpt, S7125–1.9

Elected black officials in public offices, by State, 1991, annual almanac, C4712–1

Food service black and Hispanic representation in employment and mgmt, with detail by selected occupation, 1993 articles, C5150–5.511

Higher education president personal and professional characteristics, 1990 and trends, recurring rpt, A1410–12

Labor force and education data for women and minorities in professional fields, 1980s-91, with historical trends, recurring rpt, A3960–2

Black Americans

Political, economic, and social issues related to blacks, articles and features, monthly rpt, R5685–4

Political science higher education dept faculty and salaries, with detail for blacks, 1991/92, annual rpt, A2617–1

Population characteristics, employment, and voting patterns for minority groups by detailed race-ethnicity, with comparisons to whites, 1980s-2040, R8750–2.58

Public health goals for year 2000, views of black health and political leaders on importance and amenability for change, 1993 article, A2623–1.510

Public opinion on social, political, and economic issues, detailed data, 1972-91 surveys, annual rpt, U6395–1

Racial label preferences of black population and organizations, and label usage in opinion surveys and newspapers, 1990s and trends, article, A0610–1.501

Radio (public) audience and market population shares for blacks and Hispanics, for 6-13 stations, 1991, R4250–1.18

Radio ownership, audience characteristics, and advertising revenues and effectiveness, with selected comparisons to other media, 1993 annual rpt, A8789–1

Smoking patterns and views on related community issues, 1988-89 surveys, article, A2623–1.504

Socioeconomic status, including health, education, politics, crime, and employment, with comparisons to whites, 1993 annual compilation, C6775–2

Socioeconomic status of blacks, including employment, income, education, and political data, 1993 annual compilation, A8510–1

State black shares of legislators and population, 1990 or 1992, semiannual rpt, B8500–1.1

Travel characteristics for blacks, including transport mode and trip distance and duration, 1991, article, R9375–1.501

TV (public) viewing habits of black Americans, including top-rated programs, 1992 survey, R4250–1.17

TV program ratings in black and nonblack households, for top 5 shows overall and in black households, 1st half 1992/93 season, article, C1850–14.517

Women in elective office, by minority group, party, and govt level, 1993, annual rpt, U4510–1.66

Work force and new workers, black, Hispanic, and Asian shares, 2000 article, C1200–4.509

State and local:

Alabama municipal data book, general data, 1992 recurring rpt, S0121–5

Florida black elected officials, State and local, 1990-91, annual rpt, U6660–1.21

Florida newspaper circulation of daily, weekly, and special interest newspapers, 1991, annual rpt, U6660–1.14

Georgia county guide, general data, 1993 annual rpt, U6750–1

see also Black colleges

see also Black students

see also Minority businesses

see also Racial discrimination

see also Sickle cell anemia

see also under By Race in the "Index by Categories"

Black colleges

Enrollment and degrees at traditionally black higher education instns, by field of study and sex, 1980-88, recurring rpt, A3960–2.1

Enrollment, and degrees conferred, by sex, 1988/89 or 1989, annual compilation, C6775–2.3

Enrollment by race-ethnicity and sex, for historically black colleges, 1980s-91, annual rpt, A1410–10

Enrollment distribution by student race-ethnicity, 1993 article, C4215–1.509

Freshmen attitudes and characteristics, degree and career plans, and financial aid sources, by sex and instn type, fall 1992, annual survey, U6215–1

Higher education enrollment by class level and attendance status, for historically black instns, fall 1991-92, annual rpt, A7150–5

Southern States higher education enrollment, degrees, faculty, and finances, for 15 States, 1990s and trends, biennial fact book, A8945–1

Black lung disease

State and local:

Arizona statistical abstract, general data, 1993 recurring rpt, U5850–2.7

Mississippi vital statistics, including births, deaths by cause, marriages, and divorces, by demographic characteristics and location, 1992 and trends, annual rpt, S4350–1

West Virginia vital statistics, including births, deaths by cause, marriages, and divorces, by location and demographic characteristics, 1991 and trends, annual rpt, S8560–1

see also under By Disease in the "Index by Categories"

Black market

see Underground economy

Black market currency

Latin America statistical abstract, general data by country, 1992 annual rpt, U6250–1.30

Black students

Catholic school enrollment by ethnic group, 1982/83 and 1991/92-1992/93, annual rpt, A7375–1

Catholic secondary school operations and finances, including enrollment by race-ethnicity and family income, 1991/92 and trends, biennial rpt, A7375–5

Chemistry and chemical engineering grad starting salaries, employment status, demographic characteristics, and advanced study plans, 1991/92, annual rpt, A1250–2

Community and junior college revenues by source and expenditures by function, and selected student characteristics, FY92, annual rpt, A6705–1

Dental school enrollment and grads, by sex and race-ethnicity, 1992/93 annual rpt, A1475–3.1

Doctoral degree recipient characteristics, including citizenship status, source of support, field of study, and instn, 1990/91 and trends, annual rpt, R6000–7

Elementary/secondary school experience and performance of black students, with comparisons to whites, 1993 rpt, R3840–21

Engineering degrees awarded, by State, instn, and field, with detail for women, minorities, and foreign students, 1991/92, annual rpt, A0685–1

Engineering program enrollment, by instn, field, and State, with detail for women, minorities, and foreign students, fall 1992, annual rpt, A0685–2

Higher education black student enrollment trends, 1993 annual survey, A1410–1.38

Higher education enrollment of minority and foreign students at approx 3,100 instns, fall 1991, recurring feature, C2175–1.510

Higher education enrollment of minority and foreign students, with comparison to whites, by sex, State, and instn type, fall 1991, recurring feature, C2175–1.506

Higher education freshmen attitudes and characteristics, degree and career plans, and financial aid sources, by sex and instn type, fall 1992, annual survey, U6215–1

Higher education involvement of minorities, including enrollment and degrees awarded, by race-ethnicity, sex, and State, 1970s-91, annual rpt, A1410–10

Higher education student athlete enrollment and graduation rates, by sex, race-ethnicity, and major sport, for Natl Collegiate Athletic Assn Div I instns, 1992/93, annual rpt, A7440–4

Journalism/mass communication enrollment and grads by level, by instn, sex, race-ethnicity, and field, 1990/91 and trends, annual article, A3225–1

Labor force and education data for women and minorities in professional fields, 1980s-91, with historical trends, recurring rpt, A3960–2

Law school enrollment by minority status, degrees conferred, staff, and library holdings, by instn, 1992/93 and trends, annual rpt, A0970–1

Medical school programs, fees, applicants, admissions, and enrollment, with data by age, sex, minority group, and instn, 1992/93 and trends, annual rpt, A3273–10

Nursing schools, programs, enrollment, student and staff characteristics, and grads, 1991 and trends, annual rpt, A8010–1

Optometry school faculty, enrollment and degrees, policies and programs, and finances, by instn, 1991/92, annual survey, A3370–2

Osteopathy college enrollment, student and faculty characteristics, and finances, 1992/93 and trends, annual rpt, A0620–1

Pharmacy degree program applications, enrollment, and degrees conferred, by student characteristics and instn, 1990/91 and trends, annual rpt, A0630–9

Private elementary and secondary school enrollment, staff, and finances, with detail for minorities, by school type and region, 1980s-1992/93, annual rpt, A6835–3

Southern States higher education enrollment, degrees, faculty, and finances, for 15 States, 1990s and trends, biennial fact book, A8945–1

State social, economic, and govtl indicators, with rankings, 1993 semiannual rpt, B8500–1.7

Index by Subjects and Names

Theological school enrollment by degree level, by sex and race-ethnicity, fall 1992 and trends, annual rpt, A3376–1

Theological seminary enrollment in Canada and US, with detail for women and minorities, 1992 and trends, annual rpt, C0105–1

State and local:

California postsecondary education enrollment and degrees, by sex, race-ethnicity, and instn, 1990/91, annual series, S0827–2

Connecticut public school data, including enrollment, staff, programs, finances, and student characteristics, 1991/92, biennial rpt, S1185–3

Delaware school enrollment, grads, and dropouts, by race-ethnicity, 1991/92, annual rpt, S1430–1

Florida higher education enrollment, degree programs, staff, and finances, by State-supported instn, with student and staff characteristics, 1991/92 annual rpt, S1725–1

Maryland elementary and secondary education data, by county, 1991/92, annual rpt, S3610–2.3

Maryland elementary and secondary education data, by county, 1992 and trends, annual rpt, S3610–2.4

Maryland elementary and secondary education data, by county, 1992/93, annual rpt, S3610–2.8

Minnesota enrollment distribution by race-ethnicity, and minority student shares by district and county, 1991/92 and trends, annual rpt, S4165–1

Missouri higher education enrollment and degrees granted, by sex, race-ethnicity, and instn, 1992 and trends, annual rpt, S4520–3

North Dakota higher education enrollment, by level, instn, county, and selected student characteristics, fall 1992 and trends, annual rpt, S6110–1

Pennsylvania educational statistics by level and/or type of education, series, S6790–5

see also under By Race in the "Index by Categories"

Blank, Rolf K.

"State Indicators of Science and Mathematics Education, 1993", A4355–3

Blasting agents

see Explosives

Blaustein, Saul J.

"Unemployment Insurance in the U.S.: The First Half Century", R9260–18

Blind

State and local:

Florida public library financial and operating data, including data for State braille/talking book services, FY92, annual rpt, S1800–2

Hawaii data book, general data, 1992 annual rpt, S2090–1.2

Mississippi school for the blind staff and enrollment, 1993 annual rpt, S4340–1.1

Missouri public welfare and medical assistance recipients, expenditures, and case processing, by program and county, FY92 and trends, annual rpt, S4575–2

Nevada library program for the blind, circulation and patrons served, FY92, annual rpt, S5095–1

New York State library materials for the blind, with interlibrary loans, by library and county, 1991, annual rpt, S5745–2

Oregon State library talking book and braille services and utilization, FY92, annual rpt, S6635–1

South Dakota enrollment in State school for the visually handicapped, fall 1987-92, annual rpt, S7375–1

see also Aid to blind

see also Supplemental Security Income

Blood

see also Biologic drug products

see also Blood diseases and disorders

see also Blood pressure

see also Organ and blood banks

Blood alcohol content testing

see Drug and alcohol testing

Blood diseases and disorders

Hospital patient admission rates and length of stay, by diagnosis and procedure, payment source, age, sex, and region, 1991, B4455–4

Hospital patient charges and length of stay, by diagnosis and procedure, payment source, age, and region, 1991, B4455–5

Hospital patient discharges and length of stay, by diagnosis, type of operation, age, and region, 1991, annual rpt series, B4455–1

Hospital patient discharges and length of stay, by diagnostic related group (DRG), payment source, age, and region, 1991, annual rpt series, B4455–3

State and local:

Alabama vital statistics, including population, births, deaths by cause, marriages, and divorces, by location and demographic characteristics, 1992 and trends, annual rpt, S0175–2

Arkansas vital statistics, including births, deaths by cause, marriages, and divorces, by age, sex, race, and county, 1991 and trends, annual rpt, S0685–1

California vital statistics, including population, births, and deaths by cause, by demographic characteristics and county, 1990 and trends, annual rpt, S0865–1

Colorado vital statistics, including population, births, deaths by cause, abortion, marriage and divorce, and adoption, by demographic characteristics and location, 1990 and trends, annual rpt, S1010–1

Connecticut vital statistics, including births, deaths by cause, marriages, and divorces, by demographic characteristics and location, 1989, annual rpt, S1200–1

Delaware vital statistics, including births, deaths by cause, and marriages and dissolutions, by demographic characteristics and location, 1990, annual rpt, S1385–2

Florida vital statistics, including population, births, deaths by cause, and marriages and dissolutions, by location and demographic characteristics, 1992 and trends, annual rpt, S1745–3

Georgia vital statistics, including deaths by cause, demographic characteristics, and location, 1991 and trends, annual rpt, S1895–1.2

Idaho vital statistics, including births, deaths by cause, abortions, marriages, and divorces, by demographic characteristics and county, 1991 and trends, annual rpt, S2250–2

Blood diseases and disorders

Iowa vital statistics, including population, births, deaths by cause, marriages, and divorces, by demographic characteristics and location, 1991 and trends, annual rpt, S2795–1

Louisiana vital statistics, including population, births, deaths by cause, reportable diseases, marriages, and divorces, by demographic characteristics and locality, 1989-90 and trends, annual rpt, S3295–1

Maine vital statistics, including births, deaths by cause, abortions, and marriages and divorces, by demographic characteristics and location, 1991 and trends, annual rpt, S3460–2

Maryland vital statistics, including population, births, deaths by cause, marriages, and divorces, by demographic characteristics and location, 1989 and trends, annual rpt, S3635–1

Massachusetts vital statistics, including births, deaths by cause, marriages, divorces, and population, by locality and demographic characteristics, 1990 and trends, annual rpt, S3850–1

Michigan vital statistics, including births, deaths, marriages, divorces/annulments, and communicable diseases, by location and demographic characteristics, 1990 and trends, annual rpt, S4000–3

Minnesota vital statistics, including population, births, abortions, deaths, marriages, and divorces, by location and demographic characteristics, 1991 and trends, annual rpt, S4190–2

Mississippi vital statistics, including births, deaths by cause, marriages, and divorces, by demographic characteristics and location, 1992 and trends, annual rpt, S4350–1

Montana vital statistics, including births, deaths by cause, abortion, disease, and marriage and divorce, by demographic characteristics and county, 1990-91 and trends, annual rpt, S4690–1

New Hampshire vital statistics, including population, births, deaths by cause, marriages, and divorces, by location and demographic characteristics, 1991 and trends, annual rpt, S5215–1

New Jersey vital statistics, including births, deaths, population, communicable diseases, and marriages and divorces, by demographic characteristics and location, 1990 and trends, annual rpt, S5405–1

North Dakota vital statistics, including births, deaths by cause, marriages and divorces, and abortions, by demographic characteristics and/or county, 1991 and trends, annual rpt, S6105–2

Ohio vital statistics, including births, deaths by cause, marriages, divorces, and population, by demographic characteristics and location, 1991 and trends, annual rpt, S6285–1

Oregon vital statistics, including births, deaths by cause, communicable diseases, marriages, and divorces, by age, sex, race-ethnicity, and county, 1991 and trends, annual rpt, S6615–5

Rhode Island vital statistics, including population, births, deaths, marriages, and divorces, by demographic characteristics and locality, 1989 and trends, annual rpt, S6995–1

Blood diseases and disorders

South Carolina communicable disease cases, by county, 1990, annual rpt, S7175–1

South Carolina deaths, by detailed cause, age, sex, and race, 1990, annual rpt, S7175–2

South Dakota vital statistics, including births, deaths, marriage and divorce, and communicable disease, by demographic characteristics and county, 1991 and trends, annual rpt, S7345–1

Tennessee vital statistics, including births, deaths by cause, marriages, divorces, and population, by demographic characteristics and location, 1991 and trends, annual rpt, S7520–2

Texas vital statistics, including births, deaths by cause, abortions, marriages, and divorces, by location and demographic characteristics, 1991 and trends, annual rpt, S7685–1

Utah vital statistics, including births and deaths by cause, by demographic characteristics and location, 1990, annual rpt, S7835–1.2

Vermont vital statistics, including population, births, deaths by cause, abortions, marriages, and divorces, by location and demographic characteristics, 1991 and trends, annual rpt, S8054–1

Virginia vital statistics, including births, deaths by cause, marriages and divorces, and communicable disease, by demographic characteristics and location, 1991 and trends, annual rpt, S8225–1

Washington State vital statistics, including births, deaths by cause, and population, by demographic characteristics and location, 1991 and trends, annual rpt, S8363–1

West Virginia vital statistics, including births, deaths by cause, marriages, and divorces, by location and demographic characteristics, 1991 and trends, annual rpt, S8560–1

Wisconsin vital statistics, including population, births, deaths by cause, and marriages and dissolutions, by county and demographic characteristics, 1991 and trends, annual rpt, S8715–4

see also Blood pressure

see also Septicemia

see also Sickle cell anemia

see also under By Disease in the "Index by Categories"

Blood poisoning

see Septicemia

Blood pressure

Children age 9-10 cardiovascular disease risk factor incidence, for girls by race, 1992 article, A2623–1.502

see also Hypertension

see also under By Disease in the "Index by Categories"

Blue collar workers

Construction industry wage rates, by craft and selected city, 1993, article, C5800–2.547

Construction nonunion wages and benefit levels, by craft and region, 1992, article, C5800–2.534

Plastics processing industry employment, compensation practices, and union representation, by region, 1992, annual survey rpt, A8920–2

State and local:

Arizona occupational profiles, with employment and job outlook, by industry div, occupation, and county, series, S0465–2

Maine employment, by SIC 2-digit industry and detailed occupation, triennial series, S3465–1

New Hampshire employment, by SIC 2- and 3-digit industry and detailed occupation, series, S5205–2

New Mexico employment, hours, and earnings, by labor market area and industry, monthly rpt, S5624–2

North Carolina employment in SIC 2-digit industries, by detailed occupation, triennial rpt series, S5917–5

Pennsylvania statistical abstract, general data, 1992 recurring rpt, U4130–6.3

Texas employment, by SIC 2- and 3-digit industry and detailed occupation, series, S7675–1

see also Employment and unemployment, specific industry

see also Production workers

see also under By Occupation in the "Index by Categories"

see also under name of specific industry or industry group

Blue Cross-Blue Shield

Health insurance benefit payments, by type of plan, decennially 1960-90, annual fact book, A1275–1.3

Health insurance coverage by population characteristics and location, and underwriting results by type of insurer, 1940s-90, annual rpt, A5173–2.1

HMO benefits, enrollment and utilization, staffing, finances, and relations with employers, by plan characteristics, 1990-91, annual rpt, A5150–2

Hospital patient charges and length of stay, by diagnosis and procedure, payment source, age, and region, 1991, B4455–5

Hospital patient discharges and length of stay, by diagnostic related group (DRG), payment source, age, and region, 1991, annual rpt series, B4455–3

Boarding houses

see Rooming and boarding houses

Boards of directors

Arts fundraising through united arts funds (UAFs), with fund operations, income by source, and allocations, by UAF, 1992 and trends, annual rpt, A1315–2

Chambers of commerce income, salaries and benefits, membership, staff, and operations, 1993 annual rpt, A3840–3

Compensation of corporate outside directors, by industry group, 1991-92, annual rpt, R4105–7

Corporate boards of directors composition and activities, including director time allocation, by industry sector and sales size, 1992 survey, R4105–78.29

Corporate boards of directors composition, compensation, and practices, by industry sector, 1991 and trends, annual survey rpt, B5000–3

Corporate boards of directors with women and minority members, and board membership by sex and race-ethnicity, 1991/92, B4490–2.36

Educational employee retirement plan trustee board size and authority, 1990/91, recurring rpt, A7640–18.1

Foundation board trustees by sex and race-ethnicity, for 25 leading private, community, and corporate foundations, 1989 and trends, A9405–1.1

Foundation board trustees by sex and race-ethnicity, for 25 leading private, community, and corporate foundations, 1991 and trends, A9405–1.2

Foundation finances, and personnel and governing board characteristics, by organization characteristics, 1991/92, article, C2176–1.506

Hospital CEO demographic and professional characteristics, perquisites, and views on mgmt issues, Oct 1992 survey, recurring rpt, B4490–2.35

Hospital CEO views on extent of trustee interest in natl health care reform, 1992 survey, article, A1865–1.503

Hospital CEO views on issues of greatest concern for instn trustees, 1993 survey, article, A1865–1.521

Hospital CEO views on trustee financial expertise, 1993 survey, article, A1865–1.510

Quality control and improvement, views and experience of corporate executives and outside directors, July-Aug 1992 surveys, A2800–3

Small corporation outside directors, by occupation, 1993 article, C4687–1.508

Boards of education

see School boards

Boards of trade

see Chambers of commerce

Boats and boating

Cotton and other fiber consumption in textile production, by detailed end use, 1990-92, annual rpt, A7485–1

Financial ratios and performance, for over 350 SIC 4-digit industries, FY88-92, annual rpt, A6400–3

Loan delinquency rates for approx 10 types of consumer bank loans, and repossession data, by State, quarterly rpt, A0950–1

Magazine (boating) advertising page trends, for 6 publications, 1990-Aug 1993, article, C2575–1.516

Participation in 53 sports, by demographic characteristics, State, and census div, 1992, annual rpt series, A8485–3

Recreational boat ownership, registrations, and sales, by boat type and/or State, including data for related equipment, 1992 annual rpt, A8055–1

Sales, registrations by geographic area, craft in use, and foreign trade, 1980s-92, annual feature, C2425–4

State and local:

Florida statistical abstract, general data, 1992 annual rpt, U6660–1.19

Hawaii data book, general data, 1992 annual rpt, S2090–1.7, S2090–1.18

Illinois statistical abstract, general data, 1992 annual rpt, U6910–2

Mississippi statistical abstract, general data, 1992 annual rpt, U3255–4.16

Missouri watercraft and outboard motor registrations, titles issued, and fees collected, FY88-92, annual rpt, S4570–1.1

Nevada statistical abstract, general data, 1992 biennial rpt, S5005–1.13

New York State motorboat registrations, by county and boat size, 1991, annual rpt, S5790–1

Index by Subjects and Names — Bottles

New York State statistical yearbook, general data, 1992 annual rpt, U5100–1.13, U5100–1.15

Oregon marine boating violations and arrests, 1992 and trends, annual rpt, S6603–3

Pennsylvania statistical abstract, general data, 1992 recurring rpt, U4130–6.8

South Carolina statistical abstract, general data, 1993 annual rpt, S7125–1.14

Texas trade, transportation, and public utilities employment, by SIC 2- and 3-digit industry and detailed occupation, 2nd qtr 1991, triennial survey rpt, S7675–1.31

Washington State property values, by type of property and county, 1992, annual rpt, S8415–1.3

Wyoming property assessed valuations and tax levies, by property type, tax purpose, and location, 1992 and trends, annual rpt, S8990–1.2

see also Barges

see also Ferries

see also Inland water transportation

see also Marine accidents and safety

see also Ships and shipping

Body measurements

- Children age 9-10 cardiovascular disease risk factor incidence, for girls by race, 1992 article, A2623–1.502
- Health condition and preventive health care and safety practices of adults, by respondent characteristics, 1992 and trends, annual survey rpt, C8111–2
- Philippines birth outcomes by maternal characteristics, 1983/84 Cebu metro area study, article, A5160–6.505
- Women's weight changes correlated with use of artificial sweeteners, by weight class, 1992 article, B6045–1.501
- Women's weight gain during pregnancy and retained weight after birth, by race, 1988, article, A2623–1.510
- *State and local:*
- Hawaii data book, general data, 1992 annual rpt, S2090–1.2
- *see also* Birthweight
- *see also* Obesity

Boiler and machinery insurance

see Insurance and insurance industry

Bolivia

- Energy intl sourcebook, with detail on oil and gas industry operations, supply-demand, and prices, for approx 80 countries, 1970s-91, annual compilation, C6985–10.2
- Mineral production volume and value, by type, 1991-92, article, C5226–2.509
- Statistical abstract of Latin America, detailed social, govtl, and economic data, 1992 annual rpt, U6250–1

Bombs

- *State and local:*
- Illinois crimes and arrests, by offense, with data by location and offender characteristics, 1991, annual rpt, S2536–1
- *see also* Military weapons

Bonds

see Corporate bonds

see Government securities

see Industrial revenue bonds

see Municipal bonds

see Securities

see State bonds

see Surety bonds

see Tax exempt securities

Bonuses

see Employee bonuses and work incentives

Books and bookselling

- Auto care do-it-yourself book sales performance in retail aftermarket chains, 1993 annual feature, C0125–1.503
- Auto repair manual purchasing by consumers, 1993 annual survey feature, C2150–10.504
- Bestsellers, hardcover and paperback, and copies in print, 1992, annual articles, C1852–2.509
- Bestselling books and weeks on bestseller list, 1992, annual feature, C1852–2.505
- Bible literalism, public opinion, 1972-91 surveys, annual rpt, U6395–1
- Children's book and nonbook sales performance in bookstores, by store type, Nov 1992 survey, annual article, C1852–2.506
- Direct marketing industry devs, with consumer and business market characteristics, and media use patterns, 1992/93 annual rpt, A4620–1.4
- Financial ratios and performance, for over 350 SIC 4-digit industries, FY88-92, annual rpt, A6400–3
- Latin America statistical abstract, general data by country, 1992 annual rpt, U6250–1.4
- Library and book trade reference info, including public and academic library funding, construction, and operations, by State and instn, 1992, annual compilation, C1650–3
- Presidential memoirs written by 4 former Presidents, with publisher, and contract and sales info, 1992 article, C1852–2.502
- Production, imports, translations, and prices, by subject area, various years 1977-92, annual article, C1852–2.509
- Publishers Weekly, articles and special features on publishing and bookselling activities and trade, with monthly sales trend, weekly rpt, C1852–2
- Reviews of books by specific publications, 1991-92, annual compilation, C1650–3.4
- Sales and operating data, by book publisher type and size, and subject category, 1991 and trends, annual rpt, A3274–2
- Shopping center financial and operating data, with detail by type of tenant, US and Canada, 1991, triennial rpt, R9285–1
- Stores operated by 4 leading book superstore chains, 1993 article, C5150–3.510
- Supermarket sales of nonfood products, by detailed product type, 1992, annual feature, C5225–1.508
- *State and local:*
- Hawaii University Press books and scholarly journals published, and sales, 1988-92, annual rpt, S2090–1.16
- *see also* Libraries
- *see also* Printing and publishing industry
- *see also* Textbooks
- *see also* Writers and writing

Bosnia and Herzegovina

- Public opinion in US on intl relief and military intervention in Bosnia, July/Aug 1992 Gallup Poll, C4040–1.502
- Public opinion in US on involvement in Bosnia, Feb 1993 Gallup Poll, C4040–1.509
- Public opinion in US on military intervention in Bosnia and Clinton Admin peace plan, Jan-Feb 1993 Gallup Polls, C4040–1.508
- Public opinion in US on news items concerning civil war in Bosnia, 1993 surveys, C8915–1.501, C8915–1.502, C8915–1.503, C8915–1.504, C8915–1.505
- Public opinion in US on situation in Bosnia, including possible air strikes against Serbs, May 1993 Gallup Poll, C4040–1.511

Boston, Mass.

- Court cases and dispositions, by type of court and case, FY92 and trends, annual rpt, S3807–1
- Videoconferencing substitution for air/high-speed surface travel, Boston study, 1993, 2010, and 2030, article, C5800–4.528
- *see also* under By City in the "Index by Categories"

Botanical gardens

- Operations and finances for museums and related instns, by type, budget size, governing authority, and region, 1989/90 survey, A0750–1
- World botanical gardens and membership in intl conservation organization, by country, 1991, biennial rpt, R9455–1.6
- *State and local:*
- Florida statistical abstract, general data, 1992 annual rpt, U6660–1.20
- *see also* Zoological parks

Botany

see also Botanical gardens

see also Flowers and nursery products

see also Forests and forestry

see also Fruit and fruit products

see also Horticulture

see also Plants and vegetation

see also Vegetables and vegetable products

Botswana

- Women (unmarried) receiving child support, by source and selected characteristics, 1988, article, A5160–6.503

Bottled water

- Consumption and sales of beverages, by type, leading company, and brand, 1992 and trends, annual rpt, C4775–1.4, C4775–2.3
- Consumption per capita, 1982, 1987, and 1992, article, C2150–6.504
- Industry devs, including production, consumption, and imports and exports, 1992/93 annual rpt, C0125–3.1
- Market shares and wholesale sales, for top 10 bottled water brands and total industry, 1992, article, C5150–2.515
- Sales of sparkling and still waters, by company and brand, 1991-92, annual article, C0125–2.504
- Supermarket sales by detailed product type, 1992 and trends, annual feature, C5225–1.507
- World bottled water market shares, sales growth, and consumption, for top 6 countries, 1993 feature, C2710–1.513

Bottles

see Packaging and containers

Index by Subjects and Names

Bottoms, Gene

"Making High Schools Work Through Integration of Academic and Vocational Education", A8945–33

Botulism

see Food and waterborne diseases

Boucher, Julie J.

"Statistics and Input-Output Measures for Colorado Academic Libraries, 1992", S1000–3.2

Boulder City, Nev.

Casino finances and employment, by location and gaming revenue range, FY92, annual rpt, S5062–1

Bowling

see Sports and athletics

Boycotts

Supermarket shopper involvement in personal and organized protest activity, 1993 and trends, annual survey rpt, A4950–3

State and local:

Florida, Miami convention revenue loss due to black boycott, for 5 organizations and aggregate 20 others, 1993 article, C4215–1.509

Bradley, Martin

"Churches and Church Membership in the U.S., 1990", R4985–1

Brain diseases

see Cerebrovascular diseases

see Neurological disorders

Brand names

see Generic products

see Labeling

see Product rankings

see Trademarks

see under By Individual Company or Institution in the "Index by Categories"

Brass

see Metals and metal industries

Brazil

Coal industry supply-demand, employment, and trade, by country, 1990-91 and trends, annual rpt, A7400–2.2

Coffee, Sugar, and Cocoa Exchange in US, trading activity including coffee Brazil-differential futures, 1992, annual rpt, B2275–1

Electronics industry trade and/or production trends by product category for 33 countries, with general economic profiles, 1993 annual rpt, A4725–1.4

Energy intl sourcebook, with detail on oil and gas industry operations, supply-demand, and prices, for approx 80 countries, 1970s-91, annual compilation, C6985–10.2

Energy supply-demand by fuel source, with electricity generated and costs, and nuclear plants and capacity, 1993 article, B6800–1.508

Machine tool industry operating data by country and product, 1992 and trends, annual rpt, A3179–2.2

Motor vehicle production, domestic and import sales, and sales of top 5 models, 1992, article, C2710–3.515

Motor vehicle world production, sales, trade, and registrations, by country, world area, manufacturer, and make, 1991 and trends, annual rpt, A0865–2.1

Natural gas consumption compared to other countries or world areas, and possible import sources and market characteristics, 1993 article, C6985–1.512

Nuclear reactors in operation, with capacity, electricity generation, and construction, by unit and country, 1992, annual rpt, B6800–2.2

Oil production average costs by category for State-owned company, and offshore reserves by water depth, 1993 article, C6985–2.510

Public opinion on environmental and population issues, and related church involvement, for US, Brazil, Canada, and Mexico, 1992 survey, R8780–1.504

Soybean production and marketing data, including utilization, prices, and trade, with comparison to other oilseeds, 1920s-93, annual rpt, B8480–1

Statistical abstract of Latin America, detailed social, govtl, and economic data, 1992 annual rpt, U6250–1

Wood pulp shipments and exports of leading supplying countries, and capacity of major producers, 1993 annual rpt, C3975–5.4

see also under By Foreign Country or World Area in the "Index by Categories"

Bread

see Baking and bakery products

Breast-feeding

Developing countries child survival efforts, with selected child and maternal health indicators, 1980s-90, R8720–1.2

Developing countries median duration of breast-feeding, by country, 1986-92 surveys, U2520–1.51

State and local:

Massachusetts births by characteristics of mother, including use of breast-feeding, by race-ethnicity and hospital, 1990, annual rpt, S3850–1

Breast implants

see Surgeons and surgery

Breiling, Robert E., Associates

Business aircraft and helicopter accidents, with circumstances, fatalities, and model involved, weekly rpt quarterly feature, C5800–30

Business jet aircraft accidents and flight time, distribution by flight phase, 1993 feature, C5800–30.505

Brennan, Patricia

"ARL Statistics, 1991-92", A3365–1

Bribery

see Corruption and bribery

Brick industry and products

see Building materials

see Clay industry and products

Bridges and tunnels

Construction contract awards by type of project, weekly rpt, C5800–2

Construction contracting plans for hwys and bridges, by region and State, 1993, annual feature, C5800–2.512

State economic dev condition indicators, including economic performance, business vitality, growth capacity, and tax/fiscal system, by State, 1993 annual rpt, R4225–1.1

State social, economic, and govtl indicators, with rankings, 1993 semiannual rpt, B8500–1.11

State and local:

Florida statistical abstract, general data, 1992 annual rpt, U6660–1.13

Hawaii data book, general data, 1992 annual rpt, S2090–1.18

Mississippi statistical abstract, general data, 1992 annual rpt, U3255–4.10

New York State statistical yearbook, general data, 1992 annual rpt, U5100–1.13

Texas hwy and rail bridges at Mexico ports of entry, 1993 rpt, U8850–9

Brigham, Frederick H., Jr.

"U.S. Catholic Elementary and Secondary Schools, 1992/93: Annual Statistical Report on Schools, Enrollment and Staffing", A7375–1

British Columbia Province, Canada

Paper industry strikes and capacity affected, by company and mill, 1992, annual rpt, C3975–5.2

British Commonwealth

see United Kingdom

Broadcast payments and rights

Baseball broadcasting, including TV and radio originators, and rights payments, by major league team, 1993 annual article, C1850–14.515

Football (college and professional) broadcast coverage and rights payments, by team, 1993 annual article, C1850–14.534

TV station negotiation with cable operators for retransmission rights, by affiliation, 1993 survey, article, C1850–14.530

TV station owner views on arrangements with cable operators for retransmission rights, including compensation, 1992 survey article, C2965–1.505

TV station preferred type of agreement with cable operators for retransmission rights, July 1993 survey, article, C1850–14.533

TV syndication fees for 17 situation comedy programs, 1992 article, C1850–14.503

Broadcasting

see Broadcast payments and rights

see Educational broadcasting

see Mass media

see Political broadcasting

see Public broadcasting

see Radio

see Television

Broh, Irwin, and Associates Inc.

Sporting goods purchases, by product and outlet type, census div, and purchaser characteristics, with average prices, 1992 and trends, annual survey, A8485–2

Brokers

see Futures trading

see Investment management and organizations

see Real estate business

see Stock exchanges

see Stockbrokers

Brown, Don

"Overview of the Indigent Health Care System in Texas", U8850–8.7

Brown, Jeanne C.

"1991 Estimates of the Population of Virginia Counties and Cities", U9080–9

Browne, Bortz, and Coddington Inc.

Rental equipment industry financial data, by revenue size group and region, and for Canada, 1991 and trends, annual rpt, A2665–1

Brunei

Energy intl sourcebook, with detail on oil and gas industry operations, supply-demand, and prices, for approx 80 countries, 1970s-91, annual compilation, C6985–10.2

Index by Subjects and Names

Budget of the U.S.

- Administration budget request for NSF by function, and DOD basic and applied research programs, FY94, article, C2175–1.515
- Appropriations for higher education and health in FY94 compared to spending in FY93, by program, recurring feature, C2175–1.527, C2175–1.536
- Appropriations of House and Senate, and Clinton Admin request, for NASA, NSF, and EPA, with detail for selected R&D programs, FY94, article, A1250–1.542
- Business economists forecasts of US budget deficit and Resolution Trust Corp outlays, FY93-94, article, A6650–5.501
- Business economists views on proposals for reducing spending and/or increasing revenues of Fed Govt, Jan/Feb 1993 survey, semiannual rpt, A6650–6.501
- City officials preferences for Federal budget priorities, 1992 survey, annual rpt, A8012–1.21
- Clinton Admin budget proposal, with data on spending impacts by program, deficit reduction, and tax changes, FY93-98, R3834–17
- Clinton Admin budget spending and revenue proposals, by detailed item, FY93-98, article, A3892–1.502
- Clinton Admin FY94 budget proposal summary info, including deficit reduction, military personnel reduction, natl debt increase, and page length, 1993 feature, C5800–7.525
- College freshmen support for raising taxes in order to balance budget, fall 1992, annual survey, U6215–1
- Congressional Member views on legislative priorities, Federal deficit, and tax increases, by political party, Dec 1992 survey, article, C8900–1.507
- Congressional organization, major legislative and budget actions, and agency and program appropriations, 102nd Congress, 2nd session, 1992, annual rpt, C2500–2
- Construction appropriations in FY93, and Clinton Admin requests and House committee approvals for FY94, by program, article, C5800–2.534
- Construction-related program Federal budget authority/obligation, outlays, and funding outlook, by program, 1993 article, C5800–2.517
- Construction-related program funding proposed by Clinton Admin, by agency, FY93-94, article, C5800–2.524
- Deficit estimates of Bush Admin, presidential candidate Clinton, and Congressional Budget Office, FY92 and FY96, article, C8900–1.508
- Deficit impacts of Clinton Admin budget proposal, 1993-98, article, A8813–1.501
- Deficit of Fed Govt, with outlays for interest payments, FY80-98, R9050–15.1
- Deficit of the US budget, 1989-93, article, U2160–1.502
- Deficit trends, with comparisons to CPI and Treasury bill and bond interest rates, biennially 1980-92, article, C3950–1.509
- DOE budget for FY92-93, and Clinton Admin proposal for FY94, by program, 1993 article, A1250–1.522
- Education appropriations of Fed Govt, by function and program, FY92-94, recurring feature, R4800–2.514

Building materials

- Energy tax proposals and potential effect on selected economic indicators, 1993-97, article, C6985–1.516
- EPA research budget, by program, FY92-94, article, A1250–1.526
- FCC regulatory fees for telecommunication industries under Clinton Admin proposed budget, by company category, FY94, article, C1850–14.533
- Finances of govt, including revenues by source, expenditures by function, and debt, detailed data for Federal, State, and local govts, 1993 annual rpt, R9050–1
- Forecasts for real estate industry and US economy, and housing starts and sales trends by region, monthly rpt, A7000–1
- Hard goods manufacturers views on methods for reducing Federal budget deficit, by product line, 1993 annual survey rpt, A1800–1
- Higher education funding, by agency and program, FY92-94, annual feature, C2175–1.516
- Industrial mgmt magazine reader views on who is responsible for economic problems, Federal budget deficit, and health care costs, Feb 1993 survey, article, C7000–3.510
- Information mgmt systems funding by selected govt agency and military service branch, 1987, 1992, and 1997, annual rpt, A4725–1.4
- Midwest banker opinions on Clinton Admin deficit reduction plan and health care reform, spring 1993 survey, semiannual rpt, B6785–1
- Natl Institute of Standards and Technology budget, by function, FY93 and FY97, article, A1250–1.539
- NIH budget by institute or program, FY93-94, article, A1250–1.527
- NSF budget by function and scientific field, with detail for chemical programs, FY92-94, article, A1250–1.523
- Outlays by general category, FY80 and FY92, article, R9050–3.503
- Outlays by major function, with detail for mandatory spending programs, FY80 and/or FY92, article, A1865–1.512
- Outlays for public investment programs, FY93-94 and trends, R4700–23
- Public interest in current news events, and opinion on media coverage and selected current issues, by respondent characteristics, 1993 surveys, C8915–1.504
- R&D budget authority for FY92-93, and Clinton Admin proposal for FY94, by agency and function, 1993 article, A1250–1.521
- R&D funding in Budget of US for 7 agencies in FY93, with Clinton Admin request and congressional appropriation for FY94, annual article, A1250–1.534, A1250–1.544
- Receipts by source and outlays by function, with impact of Clinton Admin proposals, FY80-98, recurring rpt, R9050–15.3
- Receipts, expenditures, surplus/deficit, and debt, FY40-92, annual rpt, R9380–1.4
- Receipts, outlay, and surplus/deficit, FY71-92, annual rpt, A3179–2.3
- Trends in Federal budget, including spending by program, State, and region, FY81-94, annual rpt, R8490–11

- Trends in outlays, receipts, and nondefense discretionary spending during current and 2 previous presidential admins, 1993 article, R9050–3.504
- USDA research budget, by program, FY92-94, article, A1250–1.525

State and local:

- California economic impact of Federal spending and tax changes, 1993-98, annual rpt, S0840–3.1
- California impact of changes in Federal revenues and expenditures under Aug 1993 Omnibus Budget Reconciliation Act (OBRA), by item, 1994-98, article, S0840–1.504

see also Defense budgets and appropriations
see also Fiscal policy
see also Public debt
see also State budgets

Budgets

- *see* Budget of the U.S.
- *see* Defense budgets and appropriations
- *see* Family budgets
- *see* Foreign budgets
- *see* State budgets

Buenaventura, Maria R. M.

"Stock Options: Motivating Through Ownership", R4105–78.31

Buenos Aires, Argentina

Motion picture theater admissions for top 10 films in Buenos Aires, 1992, article, C9380–1.519

Building abandonment

see Abandoned buildings

Building and loan associations

see Savings institutions

Building laws

- *see* Building permits
- *see* Zoning and zoning laws

Building maintenance services

see Janitorial and maintenance services

Building materials

- Consumer buying power survey of population, income, and sales by kind of business, by census div, State, MSA, county, and city, 1992, annual rpt, C1200–1.511
- Corporate performance ratings by executives for leading companies in 32 industries, 1993 annual survey feature, C8900–1.508
- Cost indexes for construction, equipment, and labor, by type and location, weekly rpt quarterly feature, C5800–2.508, C5800–2.521, C5800–2.534, C5800–2.547
- Farm prices paid for selected production commodities, 1982 and 1991-92, annual rpt, S3085–1
- Farm prices paid for selected production commodities, 1986-91, annual rpt, S5350–1
- Financial performance and growth rankings for approx 1,000 top corporations, with comparisons by industry group, 1993 annual rpt, C3950–1.505
- Financial ratios and performance, for over 350 SIC 4-digit industries, FY88-92, annual rpt, A6400–3
- Home improvement industry sales and operations, for top distributors, cooperatives, and marketing organizations, 1991-92, annual feature, C5150–6.502
- Housing construction annual buyers guide, including data on material types or brands used most frequently by builders, by product category, 1993 feature, C4300–1.506

Building materials

Oil refinery construction, operating, and materials costs, Nelson-Farrar Cost Indexes, weekly rpt monthly and quarterly tables, C6985–1

Operating and financial composite ratios for corporations, with establishments and receipts, for approx 200 industries, by asset size, FY90, annual rpt, C7800–1

Opinions of consumer hard goods manufacturers and representatives on business issues and outlook, by product line, 1992 annual survey rpt, A1800–1

PPI for construction materials, by commodity, 1987-90, annual rpt, U6660–1.11

Price trends for selected building materials, 1989-94, annual article, C1850–8.502

Prices and cost indexes for selected building materials in approx 20 cities, weekly rpt, C5800–2

Retail hardware finances and operations for hardware stores, home centers, and lumber/building material outlets, 1991 and trends, annual rpt series, A8275–1

Retail sales by outlet type, and discount chain sales in major depts, by product category, 1992, annual feature, C8130–1.507

State and local:

Maryland building materials/garden supplies industry employment and wages, by industry and occupational group, June 1991, article, S3605–2.501

New Hampshire wholesale and retail trade employment, by SIC 2-digit industry and detailed occupation, 1991, triennial rpt, S5205–2.26

North Carolina employment in trade, transportation, communications, utilities, govt, and education, by detailed occupation, 2nd qtr 1991, triennial rpt, S5917–5.2

Texas trade, transportation, and public utilities employment, by SIC 2- and 3-digit industry and detailed occupation, 2nd qtr 1991, triennial survey rpt, S7675–1.31

see also Asbestos contamination
see also Cement and concrete
see also Clay industry and products
see also Floor coverings
see also Lumber industry and products
see also Paints and varnishes
see also Stone products and quarries
see also Wall coverings

Building permits

Economic indicator trends and forecasts, with detail for approx 15 Western States, 1990s, annual rpt, B3520–1

Forecasts of economic indicators for approx 10-13 months, monthly rpt, U1880–3

Forecasts of natl income and product account components, employment, and financial sector activity, monthly rpt, B4950–1

Foreign economic indexes, and leading and coincident indicators for US and other industrial countries, monthly rpt, U1245–1

Homebuilder operations and industry devs, including housing construction and market indicators, semimonthly rpt, C1850–8

Housing market conditions in US regions and selected MSAs, including construction, rental vacancies, and prices, by type of housing, quarterly rpt, B5190–1

Housing permits issued, with comparison to mobile/manufactured home shipments, by census div and State, monthly rpt, A6325–1

Latin America statistical abstract, general data by country, 1992 annual rpt, U6250–1.7

Mortgage banking trends and devs, with data on construction, home sales, and lending activity, by type of unit and instn, monthly rpt, A6450–2

Residential building permits issued per 1,000 population, and permit trends, by State, 1992-93, article, B8500–2.523

Service sector economic activity indicators, with leading and coincident indexes and components, and detail for financial services, monthly rpt, U1245–3

State building permit trends, by State, semimonthly rpt quarterly article, B8500–2.510, B8500–2.516

Statistical profiles of 50 States and DC, general data, 1993 annual almanac, C4712–1

Western States economic indicators, including forecasts from selected organizations, for 10 States, monthly rpt, U0282–2

State and local:

Alabama statistical abstract, general data, 1992 recurring rpt, U5680–2.3

Arizona business activity indicators, including housing market, population, CPI, and industrial purchasing, monthly rpt, U0280–1

Arizona economic condition, including population, employment and earnings, and business activity, by industry and locality, 1985-93, semiannual rpt, U5850–1

Arizona economic indicators, including forecasts from 16 forecasting organizations, monthly rpt, U0282–1

Arizona statistical abstract, general data, 1993 recurring rpt, U5850–2.15

California economic condition, including population, employment and earnings, income, business activity, and taxation, 1993 annual rpt, S0840–3

California economic indicators, bimonthly rpt, S0840–1

California socioeconomic and govtl data for municipalities, counties, and school districts, 1993 annual rpt, C4712–3

California statistical abstract, general data, 1992 annual rpt, S0840–2.9

Connecticut construction activity and value, by type of structure and location, 1992 and trends, annual rpt, S1212–1

DC statistical profile, general data, 1992 annual rpt, S1535–3.3, S1535–3.4

Delaware housing construction activity, with data on demolitions and mobile home sales, by locality, 1992 and trends, annual rpt, S1387–1

Florida building permits, value by county, city, and type of construction, monthly rpt, U6660–5

Florida municipal and county statistical profiles, general data, 1991 annual rpt, C4712–6

Florida statistical abstract, general data, 1992 annual rpt, U6660–1.24

Georgia, Atlanta area housing permits issued and forecast, by county, quarterly rpt, U1880–2

Index by Subjects and Names

Georgia business activity indicators, bimonthly rpt, U6730–2

Georgia statistical abstract, general data, 1992-93 biennial rpt, U6730–1.10

Hawaii counties population and economic indicators, 1993 annual rpt series, B3500–2

Hawaii data book, general data, 1992 annual rpt, S2090–1.21

Hawaii economic conditions, including employment, population, tourism, and construction, quarterly rpt, S2090–2

Hawaii economic indicators, bimonthly rpt, B3500–1

Idaho construction activity and value, by city and county, monthly rpt, B3900–1

Illinois statistical abstract, general data, 1992 annual rpt, U6910–2

Kansas statistical abstract, general data, 1991/92 annual rpt, U7095–2.3

Maryland statistical abstract, general data, 1993-94 biennial rpt, S3605–1.12

Massachusetts municipal and county profiles, general data, 1992 annual rpt, C4712–2

Minnesota housing values authorized by building permits, 1983-92, annual rpt, S4180–1

Mississippi statistical abstract, general data, 1992 annual rpt, U3255–4.14

Missouri permit-authorized housing units and value, 1982-91, annual rpt, S4475–1

Nebraska business and economic activity indicators, monthly rpt, U7860–1

Nebraska housing units authorized, 1982-91, annual rpt, S4825–1

Nevada business and economic activity indicators, with comparisons to other Western States, 1980-91, annual rpt, U7920–2

New Jersey construction activity and costs, by location and/or building type, 1991 and trends, annual rpt, S5425–3

New Jersey economic indicators, including employment, building permits, and retail trade, monthly rpt, S5425–1

New Jersey municipal and county data book, general data, 1992 annual rpt, C4712–4

New Mexico business and economic activity indicators, monthly rpt, U7980–1

New York State business activity indicators, quarterly rpt, S5735–2

New York State municipal and county statistical profiles, general data, 1993 annual rpt, C4712–7

Oklahoma business activity indicators, monthly rpt, U8130–1

Oklahoma statistical abstract, general data, 1992 annual rpt, U8130–2.13

Oregon economic conditions, including population, construction, income, employment, industry, and foreign trade data, 1991, annual rpt, S6585–3

Pennsylvania building permits issued and value, by construction type, county, and MSA, 1992, annual article, U4110–1.506

Pennsylvania business activity indicators, monthly rpt, U4110–1

Rhode Island statistical almanac, general data, 1993 annual rpt, C7975–1.1

South Carolina economic condition, including agriculture, finance, and govt financial data, 1970s-92, annual rpt, S7125–3.1

Index by Subjects and Names

Buses

South Carolina statistical abstract, general data, 1993 annual rpt, S7125–1.11

Tennessee statistical abstract, general data, 1992/93 annual rpt, U8710–2.6

Utah economic and business activity review and indicators, monthly rpt, U8960–2

Utah statistical abstract, general data, 1993 triennial rpt, U8960–1.11

Virginia business activity indicators, by local area, monthly rpt, U1120–1

Virginia economic indicators, including new business incorporations and employment data, quarterly rpt, S8205–4

see also Zoning and zoning laws

Buildings

see Apartment houses

see Architectural barriers to the handicapped

see Architecture

see Building materials

see Building permits

see Commercial buildings

see Condominiums and cooperatives

see Construction industry

see Elevators

see Housing condition and occupancy

see Housing construction

see Housing maintenance and repair

see Housing supply and requirements

see Industrial plants and equipment

see Prefabricated buildings

see Public buildings

see State funding for capital projects

Bulgaria

Energy intl sourcebook, with detail on oil and gas industry operations, supply-demand, and prices, for approx 80 countries, 1970s-91, annual compilation, C6985–10.2

Nuclear reactors in operation, with capacity, electricity generation, and construction, by unit and country, 1992, annual rpt, B6800–2.2

Public opinion in 9 European countries and 3 Soviet Union Republics on political, economic, and social issues, 1991 survey, C8915–8

Bureau of Indian Affairs

State and local:

North Dakota enrollment and staff of BIA schools, and total Indian students, 1992/93 annual directory, S6180–2

Bureau of Labor Statistics

Employment growth projections accuracy analysis for BLS, by occupation and industry div, 1993 article, S4205–3.501

Bureau of Land Management

State and local:

Nevada administrative and conservation activities of Bur of Land Mgmt, 1992 biennial rpt, S5005–1.9

see also Minerals Management Service

Bureau of Motor Carrier Safety

see Federal Highway Administration

Bureaucracy

see Federal employees

see Government efficiency

see Public administration

see State and local employees

Burglar alarms

see Security devices

Burglary

see Motor vehicle theft

see Robbery and theft

Burial

see Cemeteries and funerals

Burma

see Myanmar

Burnham, James B.

"Changes and Challenges: The Transformation of the U.S. Steel Industry", U9640–2.15

Buses

Accidents involving fleet vehicles, and vehicles and mileage, by fleet type and company (unnamed), 1991 and trends, annual rpt, A8375–3

Business traveler and trip characteristics, including mode, purpose, and lodging, 1991, annual rpt, R9375–12

Deliveries of buses, and Federal transit bus commitments, by vehicle use or type, 1993 article, C1575–3.505

Fares in approx 300 cities, quarterly rpt, A0150–1

Financial ratios and performance, for over 350 SIC 4-digit industries, FY88-92, annual rpt, A6400–3

Fleets for top 50 private operators in US and Canada, 1993 annual feature, C1575–3.503

Inspections of buses and drivers, and number removed from service, in US/Canada, 1991-93, article, C1575–3.507

Japan bus production, 1991-92, annual data book, C2710–3.531

Mass transit industry statistics, including govt funding, vehicle purchasing, and bus production, 1992/93 annual fact book, C1575–3.501

Mass transit system finances and operations, passengers, and employment, by mode, US and Canada, 1990-91 and trends, annual rpt, A2650–1

Production, sales, trade, and vehicle use, detailed data on motor vehicle industry by vehicle type, State, and country, 1900s-92, annual rpt, A0865–1

Registrations by State and Canadian Province, fuel consumption, and mileage, 1993 annual fact book, C4680–1.507

Registrations of private/commercial buses in top 20 States, and revenues of top 10 motorcoach operators, 1989, recurring rpt, R9375–6

Regulatory agency policies and practices for motor carriers and railroads, by agency, 1991/92 annual rpt, A7015–4

Service to daily newspaper markets in US and Canada, by mode and company, 1993 annual rpt, C3250–1

Traffic accident rates, fleets, and vehicles, 1992 and trends, annual rpt, A8375–2.3

Travel miles, fuel consumed, and registrations, 3 vehicle types, 1947-91, periodic basic data book, A2575–14.5

Travel trips and traveler characteristics, including mode, purpose, type of lodging, and area of destination and origin, quarterly rpt, R9375–14

Trends in transportation operations and finances, by mode, 1991 annual rpt, R4815–1

Urban bus fleets of 100 largest transit systems in US or Canada, 1993, annual article, C1575–3.507

World production, sales, trade, and registrations of motor vehicles, by

country, world area, manufacturer, and make, 1991 and trends, annual rpt, A0865–2

State and local:

Alabama traffic accidents, fatalities, and injuries, by circumstances, vehicle type, and driver and victim characteristics, 1992, annual rpt, S0185–1

Alaska traffic accidents, fatalities, and injuries, by vehicle type, circumstance, location, and driver and victim characteristics, 1991 and trends, annual rpt, S0360–1

Arizona, Phoenix and Tucson bus ridership vs mileage, 1985-93, semiannual rpt, U5850–1.2

Arizona statistical abstract, general data, 1993 recurring rpt, U5850–2.18

Arizona traffic accidents, fatalities, and injuries, by vehicle type, circumstances, location, and driver and victim characteristics, 1991 and trends, annual rpt, S0530–1

Arkansas traffic accidents, fatalities, and injuries, by vehicle type, circumstances, location, and driver and victim characteristics, 1991, annual rpt, S0692–1

California traffic accidents, fatalities, and injuries, by vehicle type, circumstances, location, and driver and victim characteristics, 1991 and trends, annual rpt, S0885–1

Connecticut traffic accidents, fatalities, and injuries, by vehicle type, circumstance, location, and driver and victim characteristics, 1992, annual rpt, S1275–1

DC statistical profile, general data, 1992 annual rpt, S1535–3.7

Delaware traffic accidents, fatalities, and injuries, by circumstances, location, and vehicle type, and driver and victim characteristics, 1992 and trends, annual rpt, S1435–1

Florida traffic accidents, fatalities, and injuries, by vehicle type, circumstance, location, and driver and victim characteristics, 1992 and trends, annual rpt, S1750–2

Hawaii data book, general data, 1992 annual rpt, S2090–1.18

Hawaii traffic accidents, injuries, and fatalities, by circumstances, location, and driver and victim characteristics, 1986 and trends, annual rpt, S2125–1

Idaho traffic accidents, fatalities, and injuries, by circumstances, location, vehicle type, and driver and victim characteristics, 1992, annual rpt, S2315–1

Illinois traffic accidents, fatalities, and injuries, by circumstances, location, and driver and victim characteristics, 1991 and trends, annual rpt, S2540–1

Indiana traffic accidents, fatalities, and injuries, by circumstances, location, and vehicle type, and driver and victim characteristics, 1992, annual rpt, S2675–1

Kansas traffic accidents, fatalities, and injuries, by vehicle type, location, circumstances, and driver and victim characteristics, 1992, annual rpt, S3040–1

Buses

Kentucky traffic accidents, fatalities, and injuries, by circumstances, location, vehicle type, and driver characteristics, 1992 and trends, annual rpt, S3150–2

Louisiana traffic accidents, fatalities, and injuries, by circumstances, location, and driver characteristics, 1991 and trends, annual rpt, S3345–2

Maine traffic accidents, fatalities, and injuries, by accident circumstances, vehicle type and make, and driver and victim characteristics, 1992, annual rpt, S3475–2

Maryland traffic accidents, fatalities, and injuries, by circumstances, location, vehicle type, and driver and victim characteristics, 1992, annual rpt, S3665–4

Michigan traffic accidents, fatalities, and injuries, by vehicle type, circumstance, location, and driver and victim characteristics, 1991 and trends, annual rpt, S3997–2

Minnesota traffic accidents, fatalities, and injuries, by type of vehicle and circumstances, and driver and victim characteristics, 1992 and trends, annual rpt, S4230–2

Mississippi statistical abstract, general data, 1992 annual rpt, U3255–4.6

Missouri traffic accidents, fatalities, and injuries, by circumstances, location, and driver and victim characteristics, 1992 and trends, annual rpt, S4560–1

Montana traffic accidents, fatalities, and injuries, by circumstances, location, and driver and victim characteristics, 1992 and trends, annual rpt, S4705–2

Nebraska traffic accidents, fatalities, and injuries, by circumstances, location, vehicle type, and driver and victim characteristics, 1992, annual rpt, S4953–1

Nevada traffic accidents, fatalities, and injuries, by circumstances, location, and vehicle type, 1992 and trends, annual rpt, S5140–1

New Jersey fatal traffic accidents and fatalities, by vehicle type, location, and circumstances, and driver and victim characteristics, 1992 and trends, annual rpt, S5430–2

New Mexico traffic accidents, fatalities, and injuries, by vehicle type, circumstances, location, and driver and victim characteristics, 1992 and trends, annual rpt, S5665–1

North Carolina public utility financial, operating, and regulatory data, by utility type and company, 1990 and trends, annual rpt, S5917–2

North Carolina traffic accidents, fatalities, and injuries, by circumstances, location, vehicle type, and driver and victim characteristics, 1992 and trends, annual rpt, S5990–1

North Dakota traffic accidents, fatalities, and injuries, by circumstances, location, vehicle type, and driver and victim characteristics, 1992 and trends, annual rpt, S6217–1

Ohio traffic accidents, fatalities, and injuries, by circumstances, location, driver and victim characteristics, and vehicle type, 1991 and trends, annual rpt, S6290–1

Pennsylvania traffic accidents, fatalities, and injuries, by circumstances, location, driver characteristics, and vehicle type, 1991, annual rpt, S6905–3

Rhode Island traffic accidents, fatalities, and injuries, by circumstances, community, and driver and victim characteristics, 1992, annual rpt, S7025–1

South Carolina bus passengers, by company and city, 1987-91, annual rpt, S7125–1.15

South Carolina traffic accidents, fatalities, and injuries, by circumstances, location, and driver and victim characteristics, 1992 and trends, annual rpt, S7190–2

South Dakota traffic accidents, fatalities, and injuries, by circumstances, location, vehicle type, and driver and victim characteristics, 1992 and trends, annual rpt, S7300–3

Tennessee statistical abstract, general data, 1992/93 annual rpt, U8710–2.9

Texas trade, transportation, and public utilities employment, by SIC 2- and 3-digit industry and detailed occupation, 2nd qtr 1991, triennial survey rpt, S7675–1.31

Utah hwy mileage and expenditures, aviation and motor fuel consumption, and bus travel, various years 1940-92, annual rpt, R9380–1.10

Utah traffic accidents and fatalities by circumstances, location, driver and victim characteristics, and vehicle type, 1992 and trends, annual rpt, S7890–2

Virginia traffic accidents, fatalities, and injuries, by circumstances, location, and driver and victim characteristics, 1991 and trends, annual rpt, S8282–1

West Virginia traffic accidents, fatalities, and injuries, by circumstance and location, and driver and victim characteristics, 1992, annual rpt, S8645–1

Wisconsin traffic accidents, fatalities, and injuries, by circumstances, location, vehicle type, and driver and victim characteristics, 1992 and trends, annual rpt, S8815–1

Wyoming traffic accidents, fatalities, and injuries, by circumstances, location, vehicle type, and driver and victim characteristics, 1992 and trends, annual rpt, S9007–1

see also School busing

Business acquisitions and mergers

Bank acquisitions of savings instns that have converted to stock ownership, participants, assets, and price data for 10 recent transactions, 1993 article, C3950–1.517

Bank failures, and healthy and failed instns absorbed through mergers, 1930s-91, R5025–8

Broadcast industries and cable TV devs, including data on finances, advertising, ratings, and licensing, weekly rpt, C1850–14

Broadcasting stations ownership changes and transaction values, 1954-92, annual article, C1850–14.510

Coal industry acquisitions/divestitures by transaction type, 1990-92, article, C5226–1.508

Corporate acquisitions distribution by type of purchaser, by company revenue size, 1989-92, article, C4687–1.504

Index by Subjects and Names

Corporate mergers, acquisitions, and divestitures, with prices, payment methods, and characteristics of participants, 1992 and trends, annual rpt, B6020–1

Corporate mergers, acquisitions, divestitures, joint ventures, and other agreements involving US and/or foreign companies, bimonthly rpt, C4683–1

Discount chain ownership transactions, with participants and stores, 1992-93, annual feature, C5150–3.514

Drugstore chains financial performance and marketing operations, by US and Canadian company, 1993 annual feature, C5150–2.511

Employee benefit funds assets, for funds investing in buyouts/acquisitions, 1992, annual feature, C2710–2.504

Entertainment industry mergers and acquisitions, including participants and value, 3rd qtr 1992, article, C9380–1.502

Europe companies acquired by US companies, and transaction value, for top 10 transactions, 1984-92, C1575–2.506

Europe construction industry domestic and foreign mergers/acquisitions, for 23 Eastern and Western European countries, 1992 article, C5800–2.507

Europe corporate acquisitions activity by country and industry, and price and participants for top transactions, 1992 and trends, annual article, C4683–1.504

Failed merger/acquisition attempts, with participants and prices for leading failures, 1992, annual article, C4683–1.504

High-technology industry CEO characteristics, and views on mgmt issues including compensation and foreign trade, June 1992 survey, B4490–2.34

High-technology US company acquisitions by top 4 and all other foreign countries, Oct 1988-Apr 1992, C1850–2.503, C1850–6.501

Industrial distributors operations, including type of ownership and acquisition activity, 1992, annual survey, C1850–4.507

Insurance (life/health) company formations, retirements, mergers, and name changes, by company, 1992 and trends, annual article, C1050–2.506

Insurance (property/casualty) company formations, retirements, mergers, and name changes, by company, 1992 and trends, annual article, C1050–1.506

Insurance company acquisitions by foreign firms, participants, and price for major purchases of property/casualty and life/health insurers, 1988-92, article, C1050–1.503, C1050–2.503

Insurance industry corporate transactions, value, and price ratios to book value and earnings, for property/casualty and life/health insurers, 1977-91, article, C1050–1.503, C1050–2.503

Intl corporate acquisitions and value, with detail by selected country and for 19 major deals involving German firms, 1991-92 and trends, article, A5135–2.1

Leveraged buyout transactions and value, with leading participants and industries, 1992 annual feature, C4683–1.501

Media industry merger value, participants, and dates, for 5 all-time largest transactions, 1993 article, C2710–1.550

Index by Subjects and Names

Business and industry

Oil refineries sold and merged, with participants and capacity, 1991, annual fact book, C4680–1.507

Oil/gas industry mergers/acquisitions, with transaction values and summary operations, 1986-92, article, C6985–1.502

Pulp and paper industry operations and finances, US and Canada, with detail by company and product grade, and world production and trade summary, 1993 annual rpt, C3975–5

Radio station trading activity, participants, and sale prices, recurring rpt, C3165–1

Railroad mergers, and consolidations since 1982, annual rpt, A3275–8.2

Security (electronic) industry corporate acquisitions of major buyers, 1983-92, article, C1850–13.508

Security equipment dealer involvement in business acquisitions, 1988-92, article, C1850–13.506

Supermarkets opened, remodeled, and closed, including store features, dev costs, and rent, by region and sales size, 1992 and trends, annual rpt, A4950–2

Tender offer bids, prices, and outcomes, 1989-92, annual article, C4683–1.504

Utility merger regulatory policies in US and Canada, by agency, 1991/92 annual rpt, A7015–3

Venture capital-backed firms initial public offerings, and company acquisitions, selected years 1979-91, annual rpt, A8515–1

State and local:

California bank mergers, 1992, annual rpt, S0810–1

Georgia banks and other financial instns, financial condition by instn type, and assets by instn and city, Dec 1992, annual rpt, S1865–1

Maine bank acquisitions and capital injected, by instn, 1983-91, annual rpt, S3473–2

Oklahoma bank (State-chartered) mergers, FY92 annual rpt, S6415–1

Business aircraft and flying

Accidents involving business aircraft, with circumstances, fatalities, and model involved, weekly rpt quarterly feature, C5800–30

Flight hours and primary use for business aviation, with aircraft production data, 1960s-91, annual rpt, A0250–2

Issues and devs in business aviation, weekly rpt, C5800–30

Jet aircraft worldwide inventory, orders, and deliveries, by type of aircraft, region, and individual owner/operator, 1992 and trends, annual rpt, B1582–1

Shipments of business/personal aircraft, by model, for approx 20 manufacturers, weekly rpt quarterly table, C5800–30.503, C5800–30.505, C5800–30.509

Used business jet and turboprop unit sales, by weight class, weekly rpt monthly feature, C5800–30

see also General aviation

Business and industry

Accounting grad placements, by type of employer and region, 1991/92, annual rpt, A1885–1

Book publishing industry financial and operating data, by publisher type and size, and subject category, 1991 and trends, annual rpt, A3274–2

Business and economic trends, production and price indicators, and industrial mgmt activities and devs, semimonthly rpt, C7000–3

Business Week economic, business, and investment devs, with related statistical indicators, weekly rpt, C5800–7

Chambers of commerce dues and membership accounts, by type of business, 1992, annual rpt, A3840–3

Chemist and chemical engineer salaries, employment status, and demographic and professional characteristics, 1993, annual rpt, A1250–4

Congressional campaign finances, with detailed data for individual Members, and leading contributors by type and industry, 1990 election and trends, biennial rpt, R3828–2.2

Consumer expectations of economic conditions and change in income, and intended durable goods purchases by type, Conference Board monthly survey, R4105–4

Economic devs, Chemical Bank bimonthly rpt, B2000–2

Economists (business) assessments of current conditions at their companies, with industry detail, quarterly rpt, A6650–4

Economists (business) forecasts of general economic conditions, quarterly rpt, A6650–5

Food service industry sales and establishments, with growth outlook, by market segment, 1993 annual feature, C1850–3.503

Food service industry sales trends and forecast, by market segment, 1990-93, annual feature, A8200–1.502

Forbes business and corporate financial and investment devs, with related statistical indicators, biweekly rpt, C3950–1

Forecasts of economic indicators for approx 10-13 months, Georgia State Univ monthly rpt, U1880–3

Forecasts of natl income and product account components and related indicators, Georgia State Univ quarterly rpt, U1880–1

Forecasts of natl income and product account components, employment, and financial sector activity, monthly rpt, B4950–1

Forecasts of selected economic indicators, recent trends and 2-year outlook, US Chamber of Commerce quarterly rpt, A3840–6

Fortune magazine directories of largest US and foreign industrial and other corporations, and articles on business devs, biweekly rpt, C8900–1

Law school grad employment and salaries, by type of employer, location, and grad characteristics, 1992 and trends, annual rpt, A6505–1

Magazine (business) circulation, by US and Canadian publication, 6-month periods ended Dec 1992 and June 1993, semiannual rpt, A3385–3.4

Money and securities market activity, and related indicators, Chemical Bank biweekly rpt, B2000–1

Motor vehicle fleet operating and financial data, including fleets by type, registrations by make and model, and top lessors, 1970s-93, annual rpt, C1575–2.507

Public confidence in selected societal instns, 1993 Gallup Poll and trends, C4040–1.510, R8780–1.508

Public opinion on business use of personal info, including views on privacy, credit, and effects of computer use, 1992 survey and trends, annual rpt, B3280–2

R&D funding and expenditures, by source and performing sector, 1960s-93, annual rpt, R3300–1

Salaries of scientists, engineers, technicians, and other professionals, by employee and employer characteristics, 1990s and trends, biennial rpt, A3960–1

State economic dev condition indicators, including economic performance, business vitality, growth capacity, and tax/fiscal system, by State, 1993 annual rpt, R4225–1.1

Travel trips and traveler characteristics, including mode, purpose, type of lodging, and area of destination and origin, quarterly rpt, R9375–14

Traveler and trip characteristics for business travel, including mode, purpose, and lodging, 1991, annual rpt, R9375–12

Trends in business formations, failures, and bankruptcies, by region, FY92 vs FY91, article, C4687–1.511

Women and minority employment, by educational background, occupation, and type of employer, 1980s-91, with historical trends, recurring rpt, A3960–2

State and local:

Alabama business activity indicators, monthly rpt, U5680–1

Arizona business activity indicators, including housing market, population, CPI, and industrial purchasing, monthly rpt, U0280–1

Arkansas business and economic activity indicators, quarterly rpt, U5930 1

California economic condition, including population, employment and earnings, income, business activity, and taxation, 1993 annual rpt, S0840–3

California economic indicators, bimonthly rpt, S0840–1

DC statistical profile, general data, 1992 annual rpt, S1535–3.3

Florida crimes against businesses, churches, and govt, by offense, 1992, annual rpt, S1770–1

Georgia business activity indicators, bimonthly rpt, U6730–2

Hawaii business climate ratings, 1988-92, annual rpt, S2090–1.15

Hawaii economic indicators, bimonthly rpt, B3500–1

Illinois business activity indicators, quarterly rpt, U6910–1

Illinois economic and business activity indicators, including data by industry and county, bimonthly rpt, S2405–2

Indiana business conditions analysis for selected local areas, quarterly rpt semiannual feature, U2160–1.502, U2160–1.504

Indiana business review, quarterly rpt, U2160–1

Kansas business activity indicators, quarterly rpt, U7095–1

Kansas statistical abstract, general data, 1991/92 annual rpt, U7095–2.8

Business and industry

Kentucky socioeconomic devs and business indicators, series, U7138–1

Nebraska business and economic activity indicators, monthly rpt, U7860–1

Nevada business and economic activity indicators, with comparisons to other Western States, 1980-91, annual rpt, U7920–2

New Jersey economic indicators, including employment, building permits, and retail trade, monthly rpt, S5425–1

New Mexico business and economic activity indicators, monthly rpt, U7980–1

New York State business activity indicators, quarterly rpt, S5735–2

New York State statistical yearbook, general data, 1992 annual rpt, U5100–1.2

Oklahoma business activity indicators, monthly rpt, U8130–1

Pennsylvania business activity indicators, monthly rpt, U4110–1

South Dakota business activity review, including selected data by city and industry, quarterly rpt, U8595–1

Tennessee business activity indicators, quarterly journal, U8710–1

Utah economic and business activity review and indicators, monthly rpt, U8960–2

Virginia business activity indicators, by local area, monthly rpt, U1120–1

Wisconsin economic indicators, including employment and earnings by industry group, monthly rpt, S8750–1

see also Automation

see also Banks and banking

see also Better Business Bureaus

see also Business acquisitions and mergers

see also Business aircraft and flying

see also Business assets and liabilities, general

see also Business assets and liabilities, specific industry

see also Business cycles

see also Business education

see also Business ethics

see also Business expense allowances

see also Business failures and closings

see also Business firms and establishments, number

see also Business formations

see also Business income and expenses, general

see also Business income and expenses, specific industry

see also Business inventories

see also Business management

see also Business orders

see also Business outlook and attitude surveys

see also Capital investments

see also Commercial buildings

see also Commercial credit

see also Communications industries

see also Competition

see also Construction industry

see also Consultants

see also Conversion of industry

see also Corporate rankings

see also Corporations

see also Cost-of-doing-business surveys

see also Credit

see also Defense industries

see also Depreciation

see also Divestiture

see also Earnings, general

see also Earnings, specific industry

see also Economic concentration and diversification

see also Economic indicators

see also Employee benefits

see also Employment and unemployment, general

see also Employment and unemployment, specific industry

see also Executives and managers

see also Export processing zones

see also Financial institutions

see also Fish and fishing industry

see also Foreign corporations

see also Forests and forestry

see also Franchises

see also Government and business

see also Guarantees and warranties

see also Home-based offices and workers

see also Hours of labor

see also Industrial and commercial energy use

see also Industrial arts

see also Industrial capacity and utilization

see also Industrial parks

see also Industrial plants and equipment

see also Industrial production

see also Industrial production indexes

see also Industrial purchasing

see also Industrial siting

see also Input-output analysis

see also Insurance and insurance industry

see also Labor law

see also Labor-management relations, general

see also Labor mobility

see also Labor productivity

see also Labor supply and demand

see also Labor turnover

see also Labor unions

see also Manufacturing

see also Marketing

see also Mines and mineral resources

see also Minority businesses

see also Multinational corporations

see also Occupations

see also Ownership of enterprise

see also Partnerships

see also Payroll

see also Printing and publishing industry

see also Production costs

see also Productivity

see also Proprietorships

see also Public administration

see also Public utilities

see also Real estate business

see also Repair industries

see also Retail trade

see also Service industries

see also Small business

see also Trade adjustment assistance

see also Trademarks

see also Transportation and transportation equipment

see also Wholesale trade

see also Women-owned businesses

see also under By Industry in the "Index by Categories"

Business assets and liabilities, general

Accounts receivable average days outstanding, for US and 12 foreign countries, 1993 article, C4687–1.505

Building owner value of properties owned and additions, and construction in progress, top 700 owner firms, 1991, annual article, C5800–2.504

Index by Subjects and Names

Corporate CEO characteristics, compensation, and company finances, for officers of top 1,000 firms, 1993 annual feature, C5800–7.549

Corporate financial and operating composite ratios, establishments, and receipts, for approx 200 industries, by asset size, FY90, annual rpt, C7800–1

Corporate foundation assets and contributions, for US affiliates of Japanese companies, various years 1989-93, article, R5650–2.560

Corporate market value of top 1,000 firms worldwide, with related financial data, by company and country, 1993 annual feature, C5800–7.536

Corporate market value rankings of top 1,000 firms, with sales, profits, assets, and related data, by company and industry, 1993 annual feature, C5800–7.521

Employee benefit plan asset rankings of top 1,000 funds, with selected fund investment data, 1992, annual feature, C2710–2.504

Financial asset shares by sector, 1975 and 1992, article, C5800–7.511

Financial performance and growth rankings for approx 1,000 top corporations, with comparisons by industry group, 1993 annual rpt, C3950–1.505

Financial ratios and performance, for over 350 SIC 4-digit industries, FY88-92, annual rpt, A6400–3

Forbes 500 top companies in sales, profits, assets, market value, and productivity, with stock and employment data, 1992, annual rpt, C3950–1.513

Foreign investments in US, foreign companies, and US multinatls, financial data for top 100-500 in each category, 1992, annual feature, C3950–1.519

Fortune magazine ranking of top 50-100 companies in 8 nonindustrial sectors, with financial and employment data, 1992, annual feature, C8900–1.516

Fortune magazine ranking of top 50-100 companies worldwide in 8 nonindustrial sectors, with financial and employment data, 1993 annual feature, C8900–1.522

Fortune 500 largest industrial corporations, sales, financial, and stock performance data by company, 1992, annual feature, C8900–1.513

Fortune 500 largest industrial corporations worldwide, with financial and employment data, 1992, annual feature, C8900–1.520

Institutional investor assets composition, for mutual and pension funds, foreign investors, and insurance companies, 1970-2nd qtr 1992, article, A8825–1.504

Market value of top 20 companies worldwide, 1972, 1982, and 1992, article, C8900–1.514

NASDAQ typical issuing company financial profile, 1992, annual rpt, A7105–1

New York Stock Exchange activity, including stock volume and prices, credit distribution, and member firm characteristics, 1992 and trends, annual fact book, B6625–1

Pension fund assets, for top 300 funds worldwide, 1992, annual feature, C2710–2.515

Pension fund guaranteed benefit liability shares unfunded, for 50 funds with largest underfunding, 1991, article, C2710–2.502

Index by Subjects and Names

Private assets and liabilities trends, by economic sector, decennially 1950-90, U9640–2.14

Retail chain financial data and business info for approx 240 US and Canadian companies, 1991-92 and trends, annual feature, C3400–2

Venture-capital-backed company economic impact, including job creation, capital and R&D investments, and selected growth rates, 1985-91, A8515–2

State and local:

- Arizona statistical abstract, general data, 1993 recurring rpt, U5850–2.22, U5850–2.23
- Georgia statistical abstract, general data, 1992-93 biennial rpt, U6730–1.6
- Maryland statistical abstract, general data, 1993-94 biennial rpt, S3605–1.8
- Minnesota-based Fortune 500 corporation sales, assets, and net income, by company, 1991, annual rpt, S4180–1
- Nebraska public service commission regulatory activities, with financial and operating data for individual railroads and telephone companies, FY91-92 biennial rpt, S4940–1
- Oklahoma statistical abstract, general data, 1992 annual rpt, U8130–2.20
- *see also* Agricultural finance
- *see also* Bankruptcy
- *see also* Business assets and liabilities, specific industry
- *see also* Business income and expenses, general
- *see also* Business inventories
- *see also* Capital investments
- *see also* Corporate bonds
- *see also* Foreign corporations
- *see also* Foreign investments
- *see also* Industrial plants and equipment
- *see also* Investments
- *see also* Mortgages
- *see also* Operating ratios

Business assets and liabilities, specific industry

Aerospace and defense industries financial performance, with data for approx 200 major US and foreign companies, FY92 and trends, annual feature, C5800–4.519

Aerospace industry, civil and military production, R&D, trade, employment, and finances, with Federal funding data, 1991 and trends, annual rpt, A0250–2

Airline finances and operations of scheduled carriers, summary statistics, 1992 and trends, annual rpt, A0325–5

Airline retiree health benefits liability disclosed by new accounting requirements, for 4 carriers, 1993 article, C7000–4.504

Bank (master trust/custodial) assets and operating data for top instns, 1993 annual directory, C2710–2.522

Bank assets, equity, performance, and market value, top 50 instns worldwide, 1993 annual feature, C5800–7.535

Bank assets, market capitalization, and financial ratios, for 6 largest instns, June 1993, article, C3950–1.527

Bank assets, share of nonperforming loans, and stock performance, for 10 major instns, 1993 article, C3950–1.526

Bank financial performance, including assets, loans, deposits, and operating ratios, top 100 instns, 1992, annual feature, C5800–7.526

Banks and savings and loan assns, and assets, by State, 1993 annual almanac, C4712–1

Biotechnology industry summary financial performance and employment data, with detail for public companies, 1991-92, article, A6400–2.503

Brewing industry financial and operating data, including consumption, trade, and taxes, 1991 and trends, annual rpt, A3455–1

Business forms industry detailed financial and operating ratios, with summary operating data, FY91, annual rpt, A5785–3

Chemical and related industries production, finances, operating ratios, employment, and trade, by country, company, and chemical, 1980s-92, annual feature, A1250–1.530

Chemical industry finances and operations, with data by industry segment and product, 1970s-92, annual rpt, A3850–1

Chemical industry sales and operating summary for top 100 companies, 1992, annual article, A1250–1.523

Construction company finances, by region, 1992, article, C5800–2.513

Construction industry finances and operations, by type of business and region, 1992-93, annual survey rpt, A4155–1

Convenience store industry financial and operating data, by size category, 1992 and trends, annual survey rpt, A6735–1, A6735–2

Discount chain assets, for top 45 chains, 1992-93, annual feature, C5150–3.514

Drugstore (independent pharmacy) financial and operating data, by store characteristics, 1991 and trends, annual survey, B5165–1

Electric utility asset diversification, with selected comparisons to financial performance, for 35 companies, 1990 and 1992, article, A4700–4.505

Electric utility assets and liabilities, bimonthly rpt quarterly tables, A4700–4

Electric utility financial and investment performance indicators, for top 50 companies, 1991, article, C5800–28.501

Electric utility financial and operating data, by State and census div, 1991 and trends, annual rpt, A4700–1

Electric utility financial and operating ratios, by customer size class and region, 1990, annual article, A2625–1.501

Electronics company financial data and business info for approx 500 companies, 1991-92 and trends, annual rpt, C3400–4

Finance company and money market fund assets, and commercial and consumer debt held, with comparisons to commercial banks, 1980-92, R4700–22

Finance company financial and operating ratios, and loan activity, Dec 1988-92, annual article, A6400–2.506

Financial institutions, employment, and finances, and volume of printing business generated, 1992 feature, C1850–10.501

Financial instns commercial mortgage holdings, by type of instn, 2nd qtr 1992, article, A6450–2.509

Financial instns owned by blacks, with financial and employment data, 1992 and trends, annual feature, C4215–1.507

Foundation assets, and investments by type, for 10 largest organizations, Dec 1992 and trends, article, C2176–1.506

Foundation assets, income, and grants by type of recipient, with data for top organizations and by location, 1991 and trends, annual rpt, R4900–1

Foundation finances, and personnel and governing board characteristics, by organization characteristics, 1991/92, article, C2176–1.506

Foundations (community-based) asset value, grants paid, and gifts received, for top 50 organizations, 1992, annual article, C2176–1.518

Foundations (community-based) assets by type, and investment performance, 1992 and trends, article, C2176–1.522

Foundations, assets, and contributions, by organization type and census div, with top 100 organizations, FY91, annual article, C2176–1.507

Foundations, assets, gifts received, expenditures, and grants, by State and census div, 1991 and trends, annual article, C2176–1.516

Hardware finances and operations, for hardware stores, home centers, and lumber/building material outlets, 1991 and trends, annual rpt series, A8275–1

High-technology company market value, for top 10 firms, July 1993, article, C8900–1.521

High-technology experienced and inexperienced entrepreneurs use of personal vs instn equity sources, with average equity and debt, 1993 feature, C4687–1.506

HMO assets per member, by plan characteristics, 1990, annual rpt, A5150–2.3

Home furnishings retailer financial and operating data, by firm characteristics and region, 1992 and trends, annual rpt, A7975–1

Hospital industry financial and operating indicators, with detail for Medicare, by instn characteristics and location, 1988-92, annual rpt, B1880–1

Insurance (life/health) assets of top 100 firms, with A M Best Co financial ratings, 1993 annual article, C1050–2.511

Insurance (life/health) bond holdings by class and maturity period, and gross yields, by bond type, 1990-91, annual article, C1050–2.502

Insurance (life/health) capital/surplus, for top 100 companies, 1987-91, annual article, C1050–2.504

Insurance (life/health) capital/surplus, for top 100 companies, 1988-92, annual article, C1050–2.512

Insurance (life/health) company assets, for top 100 firms, 1987-91, article, C1050–2.506

Insurance (life/health) company assets, net operating gain, and return on equity, for 100 largest firms, 1992, article, C1050–2.510

Insurance (life/health) industry asset allocation and investment yields, for top 125 US and Canadian companies, 1992 and trends, annual article, C1050–2.512

Insurance (life/health) industry distribution of assets by type, 1990 and 1992, article, C1050–2.505

Business assets and liabilities, specific industry

Insurance (life/health) industry separate account performance, with top 15 firms in assets, 1991, recurring article, C1050–2.505

Insurance (property/casualty) asset composition and investment yield, for top 100 firms, 1991 and trends, annual article, C1050–1.502

Insurance (property/casualty) bond holdings value, by bond type, 1991, annual article, C1050–1.507

Insurance (property/casualty) company assets, for top 100 firms, 1987-91, article, C1050–1.505

Insurance industry assets and policyholders surplus, 1982-91, annual rpt, A5650–1.2

Investment funds investing in small business, with assets and number of companies in portfolio, for 6 funds, 1992 article, C3950–1.504

Investment mgmt firm assets managed in index funds, top firms, Dec 1992, semiannual article, C2710–2.505

Investment mgmt firm assets managed in index funds, top firms, Mar 1993, semiannual article, C2710–2.516

Investment mgmt firms, assets and operating data for approx 900 instns, Jan 1993, annual feature, C2710–2.511

Investment mgmt firms in intl investing, tax-exempt assets and operating data for top firms, 1993, annual feature, C2710–2.514

Iron and steel industry financial and operating data, 1992 and trends, annual rpt, A2000–2.1

Life insurance industry income and financial data, including investments by type of security, 1991 and trends, biennial fact book, A1325–1.4

Life insurance sales, policies in force, and assets, for top 100 US/Canadian life/health insurers, 1992, annual article, C1050–2.509

Mortgage banking industry aggregate financial and operating data, by lending characteristics and type of ownership, 1989 and trends, annual rpt, A6450–3

Mortgage insurance industry finances and performance indicators, 1988-91, annual rpt, A6455–1

Mutual fund assets and investment performance, for 273 top performing funds, 1993 recurring article, C8900–1.528

Mutual fund assets and investment performance, for 276 top performing funds, 1992 recurring article, C8900–1.511

Mutual fund assets and investment performance, 105 closed-end equity and 120 closed-end fixed-income funds, 1993 annual feature, C5800–7.517

Mutual fund assets and investment performance, 555 fixed-income funds, 1993 annual feature, C5800–7.516

Mutual fund assets and investment performance, 760 equity funds, 1993 annual feature, C5800–7.515

Mutual fund assets and investment return, for 5 funds and their namesake "clones," 1993 article, C3950–1.521

Mutual fund assets and performance, for 10 largest funds, weekly rpt recurring feature, C5800–7.523, C5800–7.533, C5800–7.549

Mutual fund assets and returns, for 10 major foreign-based funds, 1992 article, C3950–1.502

Mutual fund industry financial data, investment activity, portfolio composition, and shareholder account characteristics, 1991 and trends, annual rpt, A6025–1

Mutual fund investment performance, by fund, June 1993 and trends, annual compilation, C3950–1.522

Mutual fund mgmt company assets and market shares, for top 25 firms, Sept 1992, article, C5800–7.511

Mutual fund sales, assets, and investment activities, with data on money market and municipal bond funds, monthly rpt, A6025–5

Mutual funds (money market) financial performance and rankings of over 850 funds, with background info for investors, 1992 and trends, annual directory, C4682–2

Mutual funds financial performance and rankings of over 2,400 funds, with background info for investors, 1992 and trends, annual directory, C4682–1

Mutual funds used most by defined contribution retirement plans, rankings of top equity and income funds by assets, May 1993, semiannual article, C2710–2.517

Mutual funds used most by defined contribution retirement plans, rankings of top equity and income funds by assets, 1993 semiannual article, C2710–2.505

Natural gas industry composite assets and liabilities, by industry segment, 1970s-91, annual rpt, A1775–3.8

Nonprofit foundation assets and grants, for approx 250 foundations, 1991-92, annual rpt, A0700–1.1

Nonprofit foundation grants awarded and assets, top 50 foundations, 1991, annual feature, C2175–1.520

Nonprofit organization assets, and expenses by item, for 7 organizations, 1991, article, C2176–1.508

Office product dealer financial and operating data, by sales volume and region, 1991 and trends, annual rpt, A8110–1

Oil and gas industry financial and operating data, rankings for top 300 US and top 100 non-US companies, 1990-91, annual compilation, C6985–4.1

Oil and gas industry financial and operating data, rankings for top 300 US and top 100 non-US companies, 1991-92, annual feature, C6985–1.547

Oil industry financial and operating data for major companies, 1993 annual fact book, C4680–1.507

Oil industry income and operating data, for approx 20 major companies, 1991-92, annual article, C6985–1.533

Paper and allied products industries corporate depreciation and net worth, monthly rpt, A1630–5

Plastics industry operating and financial data, 1992 and trends, annual rpt, A8920–1.1

Plastics processing industry financial and operating ratios, by processing activity, sales size, and region, 1992, annual rpt, A8920–4

Index by Subjects and Names

Pulp, paper, and allied products financial and operating data, 1950s-92, annual rpt, A1630–6.4

Railroad (Class I) financial and operating data, with detail by company, 1982-91, annual rpt, A3275–8.2

Railroad (Class I) financial condition, operations, and employment, by company and district, 1992, annual rpt, A3275–7

Railroad operating revenues, expenses by type, and financial condition, 1920s-92, annual rpt, A3275–5.1

Real estate commingled institutional investment funds and assets, by asset type and size, Dec 1992, article, C2425–1.507

Real estate investment advisors tax-exempt and total assets by type, top 76 firms, 1993, annual feature, C2710–2.520

Real estate investment mgmt companies, pension fund and other managed assets, and investment info, by company, 1992 annual directory, C2425–1.501

Real estate investment mgmt companies, pension fund and other managed assets, and investment info, by company, 1993 annual directory, C2425–1.507

Rental equipment industry financial data, by revenue size group and region, and for Canada, 1991 and trends, annual rpt, A2665–1

Savings instn economic issues and devs, with quarterly data on financial condition by instn type and State, monthly rpt, A8813–1

Steel industry finances, operations, and employment, with data for integrated plants and mini-mills, 1970s-93, article, U2160–1.503

Supermarket industry total and leveraged buyout related debt, and sales for total and leveraged companies, 1985-91, article, C5225–1.506

Telephone local exchange carrier finances, equipment, and employment, by company, 1991 and trends, annual rpt, A9360–2

Textile and clothing companies financial data, for approx 170 firms, with industry statistical summary, 1991-92 and trends, annual rpt, C3400–5

Truck equipment distributor financial data, by company type, sales size, and rural vs metro market, FY91 and trends, annual rpt, A8505–4

Trust instns and assets managed, approx 5,000 depts, US and Canada, 1993 annual directory, C2425–2.501

Trusts, master and directed, assets managed and services offered, approx 40 instns, 1992 annual directory, C2425–1.502

State and local:

Alabama credit union assets, for top 100 instns, 1990, recurring rpt, U5680–2.6

Alabama financial instns (State-chartered) financial condition, with deposits and assets by instn, FY92 annual rpt, S0110–1

Alabama insurance industry financial and underwriting data, by company and line of coverage, 1991, annual rpt, S0160–1

Alaska bank assets and liabilities of individual commercial and savings instns, quarterly rpt, S0280–2

Alaska insurance industry underwriting and investment data, by company and type of insurance, with regulatory info, 1991 and trends, annual rpt, S0280–3

Index by Subjects and Names

Business assets and liabilities, specific industry

Arizona bank balance sheets and branches, individual State and natl instns, quarterly rpt, S0460–2

Arizona credit union balance sheets, members, and branches, by instn, quarterly rpt, S0460–4

Arizona insurance industry financial and underwriting data, by company and type of insurance, with regulatory info, 1992, annual rpt, S0483–1

Arizona savings and loan assn balance sheets and branches, individual State and natl instns, quarterly rpt, S0460–1

Arkansas banks and other financial instns, financial condition by instn, June 1992, annual rpt, S0632–1

California banks and trust companies, financial condition by instn, with regulatory info, Dec 1992, annual rpt, S0810–1

California financial instn data, including deposits and assets, by instn type, 1960-92, annual rpt, S0840–3.2

California financial instns and operating summary, 1992 annual rpt, S0840–2.12

California insurance industry financial and underwriting data, by company and type of insurance, with regulatory info, 1991, annual rpt, S0900–1

Colorado banks and trust companies, financial condition by instn, 1992, annual rpt, S1070–2

Colorado savings and loan assn and credit union financial condition, 1992 and trends, annual rpt, S1070–3

Connecticut banks and other financial instns, financial condition by instn, 1991 and trends, annual rpt, S1160–1

Connecticut insurance industry financial and underwriting data, by company and type of insurance, 1991, annual rpt, S1222–1

DC FDIC-insured banks, deposits, securities, and loans, Dec 1987-91, annual rpt, S1535–3.3

Delaware financial instns, assets and branches, by instn, 1992, annual rpt, S1375–4

Florida insurance industry financial and underwriting data, by company and line of coverage, 1991, annual rpt, S1760–1

Georgia banks and other financial instns, financial condition by instn type, and assets by instn and city, Dec 1992, annual rpt, S1865–1

Georgia commercial bank establishments and deposits, with comparisons to neighboring States, 1991 and trends, biennial rpt, U6730–1.9

Georgia credit union financial condition, including loans by type and delinquency, with comparisons to US, 1989, article, U6730–2.506

Hawaii financial instns and assets, by type of instn, 1991 and trends, annual rpt, S2090–1.15

Idaho banks and other financial instns, financial condition, with data by instn and loan activity analysis, FY92 or 1991, annual rpt, S2235–1

Idaho insurance industry financial and underwriting data, by company and type of insurance, with regulatory data, 1991, annual rpt, S2260–1

Illinois bank and trust companies (State-chartered) financial condition and status changes, by instn, FY92, annual rpt, S2395–1

Illinois bank assets and liabilities, by county and MSA, 1991, annual rpt, U6910–2

Illinois Financial Institutions Dept activities, with financial and regulatory data for credit unions, consumer lenders, and other businesses, FY91 annual rpt, S2457–2

Illinois telephone utility financial and operating data, by company, 1992, annual rpt, S2410–2

Indiana financial instns (State-chartered) financial condition, including assets by instn arranged by city, 1991 and trends, annual rpt, S2625–1

Iowa bank and trust companies (State-chartered), financial condition by instn arranged by city, FY92 annual rpt, S2760–2

Iowa insurance industry financial and underwriting data, by company and type of insurance, 1992, annual rpt, S2760–1

Kansas bank and savings and loan assn assets, 1940s-91, annual rpt, U7095–2.10

Kansas insurance industry financial and underwriting data, by company and type of insurance, with regulatory info, 1992, annual rpt, S2990–1

Kentucky financial instns condition, including assets by instn and city, with regulatory info, 1992 and trends, annual rpt, S3121–1

Louisiana financial instns (State-chartered), financial condition by instn arranged by city, with regulatory info, Dec 1992, annual rpt, S3265–1

Maine banks and other financial instns, financial condition by instn, June 1992, annual rpt, S3473–2

Maine financial instn assets, deposits, and loans, by type of instn and county, 1982-92, annual rpt, S3473–1

Maryland banks and credit unions (State-chartered) financial condition by instn, with regulatory data, FY92 annual rpt, S3655–2

Maryland insurance industry financial and underwriting data, by company and type of insurance, with regulatory info, 1991, annual rpt, S3655–1

Michigan banks and other financial instns, financial condition by instn, with regulatory info, 1992 and trends, annual rpt, S3957–1

Michigan insurance industry financial and underwriting data, by company and type of insurance, with regulatory info, 1991, annual rpt, S3983–1

Minnesota financial instns (State-regulated), financial condition by instn, 1991-92, annual rpt, S4140–3

Minnesota insurance industry financial and underwriting data, by company and line of coverage, 1991, annual rpt, S4140–4

Mississippi banks and other financial instns, financial condition by instn type, and assets by bank and credit union, Dec 1992, annual rpt, S4325–1

Mississippi financial instn assets and liabilities, 1992 annual rpt, U3255–4.8

Missouri banks and trust companies (State-chartered) financial condition, by instn, FY91-92 and trends, biennial rpt, S4502–1

Missouri insurance industry financial and underwriting data, by company and type of insurance, with regulatory info, 1992, annual rpt, S4527–1

Nebraska insurance industry financial and underwriting data, by company and line of coverage, with regulatory info, 1992, annual rpt, S4890–1

Nevada casino finances and employment, by location and gaming revenue range, FY92, annual rpt, S5062–1

New Hampshire insurance industry financial data by company, 1991, with FY92 regulatory info, annual rpt, S5220–1

New Jersey banks and other financial instns, assets and liabilities by instn, 1992 and trends, annual rpt, S5355–1

New Jersey insurance industry financial and underwriting data, by company and type of insurance, 1990, annual rpt, S5420–1

New Mexico bank and savings and loan assn assets, monthly business activity rpt, U7980–1

New Mexico financial instns, financial and operating data by instn, with regulatory activities, 1992, annual rpt, S5652–1

New York State financial instns and resources, and insurance industry financial condition, 1992 annual rpt, U5100–1.7

New York State insurance industry devs, finances, and regulatory activity, 1990/91 and trends, annual rpt, S5770–3

New York State insurance industry financial and underwriting data, by company and line of coverage, 1991, annual rpt, S5770–2

New York State public utility financial and operating data, by utility type and company, 1988-92, annual rpt, S5795–1

North Carolina public utility financial, operating, and regulatory data, by utility type and company, 1990 and trends, annual rpt, S5917–2

Oklahoma banks by asset size, and bank asset concentration and composition data, 1993 articles, U8130 1.502

Oklahoma financial instns (State-chartered) assets and liabilities, by type of instn, with regulatory data, FY92 annual rpt, S6415–1

Oklahoma insurance industry financial and underwriting data, by company and type of insurance, with regulatory info, 1992, annual rpt, S6462–1

Oregon financial instns, financial condition by instn, Dec 1992 and trends, annual rpt, S6616–1

Pennsylvania financial instns balance sheet data, by instn type, 1992 recurring rpt, U4130–6.2

Pennsylvania insurance industry financial and underwriting data, by company and line of coverage, 1991, with FY92 regulatory info, annual rpt, S6835–1

Rhode Island banks and other financial instns (State-chartered), assets and liabilities, by instn, 1991, annual rpt, S6945–1

Rhode Island financial instn assets, by type of instn, Dec 1990-91, annual rpt, C7975–1.1

Rhode Island insurance industry financial and underwriting data, by company and line of coverage, 1990, with FY91 regulatory info, annual rpt, S6945–2

South Carolina bank and savings instns financial statements, FY88-92, annual rpt, S7125–1.2

Business assets and liabilities, specific industry

South Carolina banking, savings and loan assn, and credit union financial activities, 1970-92, annual rpt, S7125–3.1

South Carolina financial instns (State-chartered) financial condition, including data by instn, FY92 annual rpt, S7165–1

South Carolina insurance industry financial and underwriting data, by company, 1991, with FY92 regulatory info, annual rpt, S7195–1

South Carolina public service commission regulatory activities, with financial and operating data for individual utilities and railroads, FY92 annual rpt, S7235–1

South Dakota insurance industry financial and underwriting data, by company and type of insurance, with regulatory info, 1991-92, annual rpt, S7300–2

Tennessee banks and other financial instns financial condition, by instn and city, 1992 annual rpt, S7507–1

Tennessee financial and insurance company finances, Dec 1990 and trends, annual rpt, U8710–2.13

Tennessee insurance industry financial and underwriting data, by company and type of insurance, with regulatory info, 1991, annual rpt, S7466–1

Texas electric utility financial and operating data, 9 largest investor-owned utilities, 1988-92, annual rpt, S7740–1

Texas hospitals, operations, utilization, and finances, by type, ownership, size, and metro-nonmetro status, 1970s-91, U8850–8.3

Texas insurance dept regulatory activities, with industry financial and underwriting data by line of coverage, FY92 annual rpt, S7700–1

Utah banks and other financial instns and operating data, by instn type, 1993 triennial rpt, U8960–1.15

Utah banks and other financial instns, financial condition by instn, FY93 and trends, annual rpt, S7830–1

Utah insurance industry financial and underwriting data, by company and line of coverage, with regulatory info, 1991, annual rpt, S7845–1

Vermont banks and other financial instns, financial condition by instn, 1992 and trends, annual rpt, S7995–2

Vermont electric utility balance sheet, by utility, 1986-91, biennial rpt, S8100–1

Vermont insurance industry financial and underwriting data, by company and type of insurance, 1991, annual rpt, S7995–1

Virginia consumer finance companies financial condition, by instn, Dec 1992, annual rpt, S8180–3

Virginia financial instns (State-chartered), financial condition by instn and instn type, Dec 1992, annual rpt, S8180–2

Washington State banks and other financial instns, financial condition by type of instn, 1992 and trends, annual rpt, S8325–1

Washington State electric utility financial and operating data, by company, 1982-91, annual rpt, S8450–1.2

Washington State natural gas utility financial and operating data, by company, 1982-91, annual rpt, S8450–1.3

Washington State telecommunication industry financial and operating data, by company, 1988-91, annual rpt, S8450–1.5

Washington State water utilities financial and operating data, by company, 1988-90, annual rpt, S8450–1.1

Washington State water utilities financial and operating data, by company, 1989-91, annual rpt, S8450–1.4

West Virginia banks and other financial instns, composite financial condition, with selected data by instn, 1990-91, annual rpt, S8530–1

West Virginia insurance industry financial and underwriting data, by company and line of coverage, with regulatory info, 1991, annual rpt, S8575–1

Wisconsin banks and savings and loan assn assets, 1992 and trends, biennial rpt, S8780–1.2

Wisconsin banks financial condition, by instn and city, with regulatory info, 1992 and trends, annual rpt, S8685–1

Wisconsin insurance industry financial and underwriting data, by company and line of coverage, with regulatory info, 1992, annual rpt, S8755–1

Wisconsin savings and loan assns and savings banks (State-chartered) financial condition, by instn, 1992 and trends, annual rpt, S8807–1

see also Agricultural finance

see also Bankruptcy

see also Business income and expenses, specific industry

see also Business inventories

see also Capital investments

see also Corporate bonds

see also Foreign corporations

see also Foreign investments

see also Industrial plants and equipment

see also Investments

see also Mortgages

see also Operating ratios

see also under By Industry in the "Index by Categories"

Business backlogs

see Business orders

Business Communications Co.

Chemical chelating agent market value, by agent type, 1988, 1993, and 1998, article, C5800–8.512

Business conventions

see Conventions

Business cycles

Capital investment growth rates during early recovery phase of business cycles, 1970-92, A1310–2.2

Chronology of business expansions and recessions since 1945, and leading indicators, 1972-92, annual rpt, A3179–2.3

Construction contract value trend during recent business cycle recovery years, by construction type, 1976, 1983, and 1992, periodic update, C5800–29

Consumer expectations of economic conditions and change in income, and intended durable goods purchases by type, Conference Board monthly survey, R4105–4

Cyclical peak and trough dates, and duration of expansion and contraction periods, 1854-1991, bimonthly rpt, S0840–1

Index by Subjects and Names

Cyclical trends for recession/recovery periods as measured by approx 70 economic indicators, quarterly rpt, U1245–2

Duration of business cycles from peak to trough, 1854-1990, annual rpt, R9050–1.2

Economists (business) short-term planning, with economic scenario being used, quarterly rpt, A6650–4

Finance company performance during economic recession and expansion periods, 1974-92, article, A6400–2.506

Forecasts of business economists for general economic conditions, quarterly rpt, A6650–5

Foreign economic growth cycle peaks and troughs, and indicator performance, selected countries, monthly rpt semiannual tables, U1245–1

Foreign economic indexes, composites of leading indicators for US and selected other countries, monthly rpt, R4105–6

GDP index at 6-30 months after beginning of economic recovery, for current and average 6 past cycles, 1993 article, C5800–7.548

Home remodeling plans of consumers as affected by economic recession, 1992 survey, article, C1850–8.505

Home remodeling plans of consumers as affected by economic recession, 1993 survey article, C5150–6.506

Interest rate business cycle peaks and troughs, with trends in price of credit, industrial production, and stock performance, 1953-92, article, C3950–1.507

Japan economic growth rates during economic expansion and contraction periods, 1951-93, article, R5650–2.538

Recession impact on corporate marketing budgets and staff, advertising media, sales, and market shares, Aug-Sept 1992 survey, A2075–20.10

Recession impact on households, unemployment, earnings, and major purchases, 1992 survey rpt, R4105–81.9

Small business views on current and expected economic conditions, survey findings, quarterly rpt, A7815–1

Unemployment insurance data for 1st year of economic recession, including unemployment, coverage, benefits, and State govt finances, 1949-91, R9260–18

Workers currently employed after losing jobs in last recessionary period, by employment type and percent change in salary, as of Jan 1992, article, C3950–1.513

World financial market devs including economic and monetary trends and forecasts for 15 industrial countries, bimonthly rpt, B6200–2

State and local:

Alabama jobs created in 2-year recovery periods following 1981/82 and 1990/91 recessions, article, U5680–1.501

Arizona trends in income, employment, and earnings, during 3 economic cycles, 1970-91, article, U0280–1.504

California employment trends during recession, with detail by industry sector and selected industry group, 1990s, annual planning rpt, S0830–2

Index by Subjects and Names

Indiana employment changes during recent business cycle, for Indianapolis and 6 other Midwest metro areas, 1990-92, article, U2160–1.502

New Jersey employment estimates, for recession peak and trough periods, Feb 1989-Sept 1992, article, S5425–1.503

Pennsylvania employment changes during recovery periods of last 5 economic recessions, 1970-93, article, S6845–1.503

see also Economic indicators

Business districts

see Central business districts

Business diversification

see Economic concentration and diversification

Business education

- Accounting grad supply-demand, including detail by sex, race-ethnicity, and region, 1991/92 and trends, annual rpt, A1885–1
- Doctoral degree recipient characteristics, including citizenship status, source of support, field of study, and instn, 1990/91 and trends, annual rpt, R6000–7
- Employment in business and industry, hiring plans for college grads, by field, salary, and degree, 1993 annual survey rpt, U3730–1
- Enrollment, faculty supply-demand, and other program and financial devs for business schools, quarterly rpt, A0605–2
- Entrepreneurship courses offered at 20 business schools, 1993 article, C5800–7.551
- Foreign students enrolled in US higher education instns, by instn, State, country of origin, and demographic characteristics, 1991/92 and trends, annual rpt, R5580–1
- Grad program characteristics, for 20 business schools ranked 21-40 in a 1992 ratings survey, article, C5800–7.531
- Grad school programs for executives, with data on revenues, enrollment, tuition, and participant characteristics, by instn, 1993 feature, C5800–7.552
- Incubator facilities and services for new rural businesses, role of State extension programs at land-grant universities, 1992 survey rpt, U2410–3
- Marketing starting salaries for college grads, 1992-93, annual survey, C1200–1.508
- Public relations education importance in business school grad programs, 1993 survey article, A8770–1.502
- Salaries of college business school faculty and admin, by rank or position, and instn control, 1992/93 and trends, annual feature, A0605–2.501
- Salaries of college business school faculty and admin, by rank or position, and instn control, 1992/93, annual rpt, A0605–1
- Salaries of scientists, engineers, technicians, and other professionals, by employee and employer characteristics, 1990s and trends, biennial rpt, A3960–1
- Salary and job offers for college grads, by field of study, type of employer, and degree level, by region, interim rpt series, A3940–1
- Salary and job offers for college grads, by field of study, type of employer, and degree level, series, A3940–2
- Southern States higher education degree conferrals, by sex, race-ethnicity, level, and selected field, by State, 1990s and trends, biennial fact book, A8945–1.3

Women and minorities in professional fields, detailed education and labor force data, 1991 and trends, recurring rpt, A3960–2.1

Women's share of tenured and tenure-track faculty at 6 business grad schools with highest and lowest shares, 1992 article, C5800–7.506

State and local:

- Iowa postsecondary enrollment, degrees, staff, and finances, by instn, 1990/91, annual rpt, S2755–1
- Maryland elementary and secondary education statistical summary, with data by county, 1991/92-1992/93 and trends, annual rpt, S3610–1
- Pennsylvania vocational education enrollment, student characteristics, and faculty, by program and/or school, 1991/92 and trends, annual rpt, S6790–5.7
- Pennsylvania vocational education 1989/90 grad employment status, by program, 1991 survey, annual rpt, S6790–5.6
- South Dakota accounting firm recruiters views on tax curriculum for accounting undergraduates, and degree levels of students hired, fall 1992 survey, article, U8595–1.504

Business efficiency

see Business management

see Labor productivity

see Operating ratios

see Productivity

Business energy use

see Industrial and commercial energy use

Business equipment and furniture

see Business machines and equipment

Business ethics

- Small corporation mgmt views on business ethics and selected practices, Sept 1992 survey, C4687–1.502
- *see also* Better Business Bureaus
- *see also* Financial disclosure

Business expense allowances

- Federal employee foreign travel allowance rates per diem, by country or city, June 1992, annual rpt, C2140–1.5
- Library/info science school faculty receiving travel funds, and amounts, by school, 1991/92, annual rpt, A3235–1.1
- Plastics processing industry auto expense allowance policies, 1992 survey, biennial rpt, A8920–3
- Sales industry costs, including compensation, training, and travel and related expenses, with data by metro area, 1992 and trends, annual survey, C1200–1.508

State and local:

Mississippi bank examiner travel expenses, 1992, annual rpt, S4325–1

Business failures and closings

- Bank failures, and healthy and failed instns absorbed through mergers, 1930s-91, R5025–8
- Bank failures and outlays by FDIC, by State and region, 1990-92, R8490–47
- Broadcast TV and radio bankruptcies or reorganizations, 1990-1st half 1993, article, C1850–14.533
- Construction contractor failures in general and special trades, weekly rpt monthly table, C5800–2
- Electronics industry business failure rates, for 3 industry segments, 1991-1st qtr 1993, article, C1850–2.508

Business failures and closings

- Foreign economic indexes, and leading and coincident indicators for US and other industrial countries, monthly rpt, U1245–1
- Incubator facilities for new business, including tenant closings, 1991, annual rpt, A7360–1
- Insurance (life/health) companies under State supervision/liquidation, 1993 and trends, annual article, C1050–2.511
- Insurance (life/health) industry insolvent companies, 1976-92, article, C1050–2.505
- Insurance (property/casualty) companies under State supervision/liquidation, 1993 and trends, annual article, C1050–1.510
- Jewelry business openings and failures, by region, monthly rpt, C2150–7
- Jewelry industry statistics on sales, marketing, trade, and employment, with customer characteristics, 1993 annual almanac, C2150–7.509
- Liabilities and number of failed businesses, by detailed industry, cause, length of operation, and location, 1991-92 and trends, annual rpt, C3150–8
- Liabilities and number of failed businesses, by industry, census div, State, and major city, monthly rpt, C3150–2
- Liabilities and number of failed businesses, by industry group, quarterly rpt, C3150–6
- Oil refineries shutdown as of Jan 1993, with distillation capacity, by company and PAD district, periodic basic data book, A2575–14.4
- Oil refineries shutdown, including crude capacity, by company, 1992-93, article, C4680–1.508
- Oil refinery shutdowns, with data on capacity, 1991, annual fact book, C4680–1.507
- Shoe manufacturing plant openings, and closings by State, 1970s-91, annual rpt, A4957–1.2
- Small business survival and failure 8 years after formation, for firms formed in 1977/78, article, C4687–1.512
- Southeastern States bank failures, by type of liquidation, 1986-89, annual rpt, U8710–2.13
- State economic dev condition indicators, including economic performance, business vitality, growth capacity, and tax/fiscal system, by State, 1993 annual rpt, R4225–1.1
- State social, economic, and govtl indicators, with rankings, 1993 semiannual rpt, B8500–1.2
- Statistical profiles of 50 States and DC, general data, 1993 annual almanac, C4712–1
- Trends in business failures, 1984-92, article, C4687–1.501
- Trends in total businesses, new incorporations/mergers, and failures, 1982-1st half 1992, C4687–1.504
- UK coal mine closures and related employment, for 31 mines, Oct 1992-Mar 1993, article, C5226–2.501
- West Coast paper and pulp mills shut down, including capacity, 1993 article, C3975–2.509

Business failures and closings

State and local:
California bank closures, and deposits, 1983-92, annual rpt, S0810–1
California insurance companies in liquidation or conservation, financial data by company, 1991 annual rpt, S0900–1
Florida statistical abstract, general data, 1992 annual rpt, U6660–1.17, U6660–1.24
Georgia financial instns in liquidation, including unpaid claims and remaining assets, 1992, annual rpt, S1865–1
Georgia statistical abstract, general data, 1992-93 biennial rpt, U6730–1.6
Hawaii data book, general data, 1992 annual rpt, S2090–1.15
Mississippi statistical abstract, general data, 1992 annual rpt, U3255–4.5
Missouri banks closing, with assets, liabilities, and deposits, by instn, FY91-92, biennial rpt, S4502–1
Nebraska insurance companies in liquidation, financial data by company, 1992, annual rpt, S4890–1
New Jersey economic indicators, including employment, building permits, and retail trade, monthly rpt, S5425–1
New Mexico business and economic activity indicators, monthly rpt, U7980–1
New York State business activity indicators, quarterly rpt, S5735–2
Oklahoma bank (State-chartered) closings, FY92 annual rpt, S6415–1
Oklahoma statistical abstract, general data, 1992 annual rpt, U8130–2.15
Rhode Island financial instns in receivership, assets and liabilities by instn, 1991, annual rpt, S6945–1
South Carolina plant closings, with employment affected, by company, 1991, annual planning rpt, S7155–3.2
South Carolina statistical abstract, general data, 1993 annual rpt, S7125–1.3
Tennessee statistical abstract, general data, 1992/93 annual rpt, U8710–2.7
Texas community hospitals closed, by type of ownership and urban-rural status, 1980-91, U8850–8.3
Texas insurance companies in liquidation, financial data by company, FY92, annual rpt, S7700 1
Utah business startups and closings, by industry div and county, 1992, annual rpt, S7820–10
Utah industrial loan corporations in liquidation, financial data for 5 instns, FY93, annual rpt, S7830–1
Utah statistical abstract, general data, 1993 triennial rpt, U8960–1.15
West Virginia failed bank finances, by instn, 1991 annual rpt, S8530–1
Wisconsin insurance companies in liquidation, financial data by company, 1992, annual rpt, S8755–1
see also Bankruptcy

Business firms and establishments, number
Advertising agency income, billings by medium, employees, and offices, for leading US and/or foreign agencies, 1992 and trends, annual rpt, C2710–1.522
Aircraft (piston) US and foreign manufacturers, 1980, 1986, and 1992, article, C5800–4.508
Alcoholic beverage on- and off-premises retail outlets, by State, 1986, annual rpt, C4775–1.4

Auto aftermarket chain sales, income, and stores, for 8 companies, 1989-91, C2150–10.501
Auto aftermarket company financial and operating data, including sales, income, stores, and inventory turns, for 8-12 public firms, 1993 article, C2150–10.508
Auto aftermarket retail and jobber stores, and warehouse distributor locations, 1980-95, article, C2150–10.501
Auto aftermarket retail sales, and number of stores and service bays, for top 100 chains, 1993 annual article, C2150–10.507
Auto auctions owned by 4 major chains, with hq locations, 1993 article, C2710–3.521
Auto dealer malls, with number of dealers, dealerships, and franchises, and new vehicle volume, 1993, article, C2710–3.552
Auto dealerships, by manufacturer, 1993 directory, C2710–3.552
Auto dealerships, including domestic and import outlets, and franchises by make, 1993 and trends, annual article, C2710–3.519
Biotechnology company finances, employment, and firms, with detail for public companies, FY92-93, annual article, A1250–1.542
Boat and related marine equipment retailers, and marina facilities, 1992, annual feature, C2425–4
Boating-related establishments, 1991-92, annual rpt, A8055–1
Book superstore outlets, for 4 leading chains, 1993 article, C5150–3.510
Book superstore sales and outlets for top 6 chains, Jan 1993, article, C1852–2.514
Bookstores and sales of 11 largest trade bookstore chains, 1991-92, article, C1852–2.516
Bookstores by type of outlet, US and Canada, 1992, annual compilation, C1650–3.4
Bowling establishments and lanes, by State and other area, 1991/92, annual rpt, A1015–1
Brewing industry financial and operating data, including consumption, trade, and taxes, 1991 and trends, annual rpt, A3455–1
Canada home improvement sales and outlets, for 4-5 leading retail chains and buying groups, 1992, articles, C5150–6.508
Chemical industry establishments, with detail by company size and State, and for exporters, 1987, annual rpt, A3850–1
Clothing (men's and boys) production, trade, and operating data, by garment type, 1960s-92, annual rpt, A3880–1
Clothing discount and off-price store sales and outlets, for top 10 chains, 1993 article, C5150–3.513
Convenience store finances and number of stores, for 5 chains with bankruptcy filings, 1991-92, article, C4680–1.505
Convenience store industry financial and operating data, by size category, 1992 and trends, annual survey rpt, A6735–1, A6735–2
Convenience stores operated or planned, by chain company, 1992-94, annual article, C4680–1.509

Index by Subjects and Names

Convenience stores with gasoline marketing operations, by chain company, census div, and State, 1992, annual article, C4680–1.502
Convenience stores with gasoline marketing operations, by chain company, census div, and State, 1993, annual article, C4680–1.510
Corporate establishments by employment size, 1991 vs 1987, article, C1200–1.513
Corporate establishments in approx 200 industries, by asset size, FY90, annual rpt, C7800–1
Corporate hqs for Fortune 500 and INC 500 firms, by State, 1992, and trends, article, B8500–2.514
Direct marketing establishments and receipts, for direct mail and catalog/mail order houses, 1987, annual rpt, A4620–1.2
Discount chain sales and merchandising, including data by dept, leading chain, and location, 1992 and trends, annual feature, C8130–1.507
Discount regional chain sales and stores, for 8 leading chains, 1993 article, C5150–3.517
Discount stores by census div and State, 1992, annual feature, C5150–3.516
Discount stores for leading chains in 3 market areas, 1992 article, C5150–3.503
Discount stores, sales, and earnings, for top chains, with detail by specialty, 1993 annual feature, C5150–3.514
Discount wholesale membership club income, stores, and sales trends, for selected leading chains, 1993 articles, C5150–3.506
Discount wholesale membership club sales and stores, for 9 major chains, 1992, annual article, C8130–1.501
Drugstore and other retail outlet pharmacies, with detail for top 24 chains, 1993 annual feature, C5150–2.511
Drugstore chains financial performance and marketing operations, by US and Canadian company, 1993 annual feature, C5150–2.511
Economic indicator historical trends, 1900s-92, annual rpt, R9050–1.2
Electric utility income and operating data, by type of company and for individual locally owned utilities, 1993 annual directory, A2625–1.501
Electrical equipment wholesalers, sales, employment, and facility size, top 250 companies, 1992, annual article, C4725–5.506
Electronics company financial data and business info for approx 500 companies, 1991-92 and trends, annual rpt, C3400–4
Environmental services firms and revenues, by industry segment, 1992, article, A1250–1.530
Europe fine chemicals producers and total capacity, with detail for 7 countries, 1992, article, A1250–1.519
Europe public relations firms with US ties, including data on worldwide offices and activities, by company, 1993 article, A8770–1.505
Financial institutions, employment, and finances, and volume of printing business generated, 1992 feature, C1850–10.501

Index by Subjects and Names

Business firms and establishments, number

Food marketers financial and operating data, by company size and region, 1991-92, annual rpts, A4950–5

Food service industry financial and operating data, for top 100 chains and companies, FY91-93, annual feature, C5150–5.509

Food service industry sales and establishments, for top 400 chains and other organizations, 1992, annual feature, C1850–3.509

Food service industry sales and establishments, with growth outlook, by market segment, 1993 annual feature, C1850–3.503

Food service industry sales, market shares, establishments, and business activity indicators, by location, 1992, annual feature, C1200–5.515

Food store industry structure, sales, operations, and business outlook, by type of store, 1993 annual rpt, C5225–1.505

Food store market shares and outlets, by company and store type, for approx 350 metro areas in US and Canada, with industry operating data, 1993 annual rpt, C3400–6

Food stores and sales, by sales size group, 1992, annual feature, C4655–1.510

Food/lodging/entertainment establishments, employment, receipts, and payroll, and volume of printing business generated, 1992 feature, C1850–10.503

Foundation assets, income, and grants by type of recipient, with data for top organizations and by location, 1991 and trends, annual rpt, R4900–1

Gasoline service stations, by State, 1993 and trends, annual article, C4680–1.505

Gasoline unattended-site retail outlets, franchises/marketers, and average transactions, for 6 retail chains, 1993 article, C4680–1.511

Gold producers (US-owned) in US, Canada, Australia, Latin America, and elsewhere, 1989-92, articles, C5226–2.506

Health care preferred provider organizations (PPOs), employee utilization, and type of sponsor or ownership, 1993 article, A1865–1.524

Home improvement industry sales and operations, for top distributors, cooperatives, and marketing organizations, 1991-92, annual feature, C5150–6.502

Home improvement industry sales and operations, for top retailers, 1992 and trends, annual feature, C5150–6.503

Home improvement industry sales and related data, by product category and for top 10 chains, 1992, article, C4725–5.507

Home improvement industry sales, stores, and other operating data, for leading foreign chains by country, 1991-92, annual feature, C5150–6.503

Hospital multifacility systems, including data by type of control, and for rural hospitals and multi-State operations, 1993 articles, A1865–1.510

Household appliance manufacturers and retail outlets, 1993 biennial rpt, A3350–3

Industrial distributor sales, branches, employment, and operating profiles, for top 50 companies, 1992, annual article, C1850–4.506

Insurance (life/health) companies by A M Best Co financial rating, 1993 and trends, annual article, C1050–2.511

Insurance (life/health) company formations, retirements, mergers, and name changes, by company, 1992 and trends, annual article, C1050–2.506

Insurance (property/casualty) companies, by A M Best Co financial rating, 1993 and trends, annual article, C1050–1.510

Insurance (property/casualty) companies, by State, 1992, annual article, C1050–1.509

Insurance (property/casualty) companies, by State, 1992, annual rpt, A5650–1.1

Insurance (property/casualty) company formations, retirements, mergers, and name changes, by company, 1992 and trends, annual article, C1050–1.506

Jewelry industry statistics on sales, marketing, trade, and employment, with customer characteristics, 1993 annual almanac, C2150–7.509

Jewelry retailers, wholesalers, and manufacturers, and new businesses by region, monthly rpt, C2150–7

Legal services establishments, employment, receipts, and payroll, and volume of printing business generated, 1992 feature, C1850–10.502

Life insurance firms and employment, 1991 and trends, biennial fact book, A1325–1.5

Liquor distillery and bottling operations, by State, 1991-92, annual rpt, C4775–1.2

Livestock slaughtering establishments, by species, 1991, annual rpt, S8510–1

Lodging chains, rooms, and establishments, with top chains worldwide, 1992 annual rpt, C2140–1.4

Machine tool industry establishments, 1991 and trends, annual rpt, A3179–2.1

Manufacturing industry trends including employment, earnings, establishments, and GSP, by State and region, 1970s-92, R8490–48

Markets with daily newspapers, demographic and economic info by geographic area, US and Canada, 1993 annual rpt, C3250–1

Meat and poultry demand, prices, and processor operations and finances, with data on meat production, 1991 and trends, annual rpt, A2100–1.1

Medical group practice characteristics, including specialties, form of organization, and location, 1991 and trends, recurring rpt, A2200–7

Metro area rankings by number of business establishments, for approx 300 metro areas, 1992, annual rpt, C1200–1.511

Mobile/manufactured home producers and manufacturing plants, monthly rpt, A6325–1

Motor vehicle auction companies directory, with number of auctions operated and cars sold, 1992, annual rpt, C1575–2.507

Motor vehicle, dealership, and related industries operating data, with data by State and industry segment, 1990s and trends, annual rpt, A0865–1.3

Motor vehicle dealership financial and operating data, including sales and employment by State, 1970s-93, annual rpt, A7330–1

Motor vehicle dealership outlets, with detail by make, 1993 annual data book, C2710–3.531

Motor vehicle parts suppliers affiliated with Japanese companies, with employment and plant square footage, 1990 and 1992-93, article, C2710–3.553

Motorcycle retail outlets, employees, and payroll, by State, 1992, annual rpt, A6485–1.1

Natural gas vehicle refueling stations by ownership class, by State and census div, Apr 1992, annual rpt, A1775–3.2

New York Stock Exchange activity, including stock volume and prices, credit distribution, and member firm characteristics, 1992 and trends, annual fact book, B6625–1

North Central States business establishments, for 9 States, 1988 and 1990, annual rpt, S6140–2

Oil and gas drilling operators and producing wells, 1973-92, annual rpt, A5425–2.1

Oil change fast service outlet establishments, with detail for top 7 chains, 1992 and trends, article, C4680–1.503

Oil supply-demand, marketing, prices, finances, and employment, detailed data for US and Canada, by product, company, and location, 1993 annual fact book, C4680–1.507

Paper and paperboard industry financial and operating data, by product, census div, and State, 1970s-95, annual rpt, A1630–6.2

Plastics product manufacturers in 9 SIC 4-digit industries, with detail for Northeast region and States, 1987, A4375–14

Public broadcasting membership income, contributors, and stations, by station type, FY91 and trends, annual rpt, R4250–1.21

Public broadcasting station revenues by source, and number of stations, by station type, FY91, annual rpt, R4250–1.20

Pulp and paper industry operations and finances, US and Canada, with detail by company and product grade, and world production and trade summary, 1993 annual rpt, C3975–5

Railroad financial and operating trends, including data by company, 1982-91, annual rpt, A3275–8

Railroad operating data, including top commodities handled, employment and wages, and retirement system, by State, 1991, annual rpt, A3275–10

Restaurant (chicken specialty) establishments by census div, 1992 annual article, C1200–5.509

Restaurant (hamburger) establishments by census div, and sales and units for top 10 chains, 1993 annual article, C1200–5.504

Restaurant (Italian food) establishments by census div, 1992, annual article, C1200–5.508

Restaurant (Mexican food) establishments by census div, and sales and/or units for top 4-5 chains, 1993 annual article, C1200–5.514

Restaurant (pizza) establishments by census div, and sales and units for top 10 chains, 1992, annual article, C1200–5.506

Business firms and establishments, number

Index by Subjects and Names

Restaurant (sandwich) establishments by census div, 1992, annual article, C1200–5.503

Restaurant (seafood) establishments by census div, 1992, article, C1200–5.516

Restaurant (steak house/saloon) establishments, for 6 leading chains, 1992 article, C5150–5.502

Restaurant franchises and sales, and franchisee fees and investment required, by leading company, 1993 annual feature, C1200–5.512

Restaurant industry expansion outlook and operating data, by census div and MSA, 1993 annual articles, C1850–3.506

Restaurant sales and units, for 50 fastest-growing chains, 1991-92, annual article, C1200–5.513

Restaurant State assn staff, payroll, locations represented, and political action committee spending, for organizations in 14 States, 1993 article, C1200–5.510

Retail chain construction activity, capital expenditures, and number of new stores, for leading firms, 1991-92, annual feature, C5150–4.503

Retail chain financial data and business info for approx 240 US and Canadian companies, 1991-92 and trends, annual rpt, C3400–2

Retail chain revenues, profits, and stores, top 100 chains, with selected data by outlet type, 1991-92, annual articles, C5150–4.508

Retail general merchandise chain sales, earnings, and stores, for top companies worldwide, with detail for selected areas, 1991-92, annual feature, C5150–3.516

Savings instn economic issues and devs, with quarterly data on financial condition by instn type and State, monthly rpt, A8813–1

Securities dealer natl assn membership, 1980-1st half 1992, recurring article, A8825–1.501

Securities dealer natl assn membership, 1980-3rd qtr 1992, recurring article, A8825–1.503

Securities dealer natl assn membership, 1987-May 1993, recurring article, A8825–1.505

Security equipment industry revenues, accounts, and operating data, for 100 leading companies, 1992, annual feature, C1850–13.507

Shoe industry production, employment, trade, marketing, and related data, by SIC 2- to 5-digit code or product type, 1992 annual rpt, A4957–1

Statistical profiles of 50 States and DC, general data, 1993 annual almanac, C4712–1

Stockbroker commissions, fees, analysts, offices, and brokers, for 18 firms, 1993 annual article, C8900–1.528

Supermarkets opened, remodeled, and closed, including store features, dev costs, and rent, by region and sales size, 1992 and trends, annual rpt, A4950–2

Telephone local exchange carrier finances, equipment, and employment, by company, 1991 and trends, annual rpt, A9360–2

Transportation companies under State agency jurisdiction, by State, 1991/92 annual rpt, A7015–4

Travel agencies, with detail by State, 1984-91, annual rpt, C2140–1.4

Trends in total businesses, new incorporations/mergers, and failures, 1982-1st half 1992, C4687–1.504

TV (public) stations, broadcasters, and programming, 1974-90, recurring rpt, R4250–1.15

Utility companies operating and/or under State agency jurisdiction, by State, 1991/92 annual rpt, A7015–3

Vending machine operating companies, by employment size, 1990-92, annual rpt, C9470–1

Venture capital industry finances and operations, 1991 and trends, annual rpt, A8515–1

Veterinary practice distribution by size, type, and ownership, 1991, article, A3100–2.514

Wineries and bottling houses, by State, Sept 1992, annual rpt, C4775–2.2

State and local:

Alabama county data book, general data, 1992 annual rpt, S0121–2

Alabama financial instns (State-chartered) financial condition, with deposits and assets by instn, FY92 annual rpt, S0110–1

Alabama insurance industry financial and underwriting data, by company and line of coverage, 1991, annual rpt, S0160–1

Alabama statistical abstract, general data, 1992 recurring rpt, U5680–2.3, U5680–2.5, U5680–2.11, U5680–2.15, U5680–2.18

Alaska insurance industry underwriting and investment data, by company and type of insurance, with regulatory info, 1991 and trends, annual rpt, S0280–3

Arizona bank balance sheets and branches, individual State and natl instns, quarterly rpt, S0460–2

Arizona credit union balance sheets, members, and branches, by instn, quarterly rpt, S0460–4

Arizona feedlots, dairy plants, and livestock slaughtering establishments, 1988-93, annual rpt, U5830–1

Arizona insurance industry financial and underwriting data, by company and type of insurance, with regulatory info, 1992, annual rpt, S0483–1

Arizona savings and loan assn balance sheets and branches, individual State and natl instns, quarterly rpt, S0460–1

Arizona statistical abstract, general data, 1993 recurring rpt, U5850–2

Arkansas banks and other financial instns, financial condition by instn, June 1992, annual rpt, S0632–1

Arkansas public utility financial, operating, and regulatory data, by utility type and company, 1992 annual rpt, S0757–1

California banks and trust companies, financial condition by instn, with regulatory info, Dec 1992, annual rpt, S0810–1

California economic condition, including population, employment and earnings, income, business activity, and taxation, 1960s-92, annual rpt, S0840–3.2

California plants reporting milk sales, by county, 1982-92, annual rpt, S0850–1.6

California public utility and transportation regulatory data, including revenue requests and rates of return by company, FY92 annual rpt, S0930–1

California statistical abstract, general data, 1992 annual rpt, S0840–2

Colorado banks and trust companies, financial condition by instn, 1992, annual rpt, S1070–2

Colorado savings and loan assn and credit union financial condition, 1992 and trends, annual rpt, S1070–3

Connecticut banks and other financial instns, financial condition by instn, 1991 and trends, annual rpt, S1160–1

Connecticut insurance industry financial and underwriting data, by company and type of insurance, 1991, annual rpt, S1222–1

DC statistical profile, general data, 1992 annual rpt, S1535–3.3

Delaware financial instns, assets and branches, by instn, 1992, annual rpt, S1375–4

Florida county data book, 1992/93 annual rpt, C6360–1

Florida insurance industry financial and underwriting data, by company and line of coverage, 1991, annual rpt, S1760–1

Florida statistical abstract, general data, 1992 annual rpt, U6660–1

Georgia banks and other financial instns, financial condition by instn type, and assets by instn and city, Dec 1992, annual rpt, S1865–1

Georgia county guide, general data, 1993 annual rpt, U6750–1

Georgia exports, by industry group and country of destination, and exporting business establishments, 1993 article, U6730–2.502

Georgia statistical abstract, general data, 1992-93 biennial rpt, U6730–1.5, U6730–1.6, U6730–1.7

Hawaii data book, general data, 1992 annual rpt, S2090–1

Idaho banks and other financial instns, financial condition, with data by instn and loan activity analysis, FY92 or 1991, annual rpt, S2235–1

Idaho economic profile, general data, 1992 recurring rpt, S2218–2.5

Idaho insurance industry financial and underwriting data, by company and type of insurance, with regulatory data, 1991, annual rpt, S2260–1

Illinois bank and trust companies (State-chartered) financial condition and status changes, by instn, FY92, annual rpt, S2395–1

Illinois businesses by employment size, incorporations, and bankruptcy filings, 1980s-93, S2405–2.504

Illinois Financial Institutions Dept activities, with financial and regulatory data for credit unions, consumer lenders, and other businesses, FY91 annual rpt, S2457–2

Illinois statistical abstract, general data, 1992 annual rpt, U6910–2

Indiana financial instns (State-chartered) financial condition, including assets by instn arranged by city, 1991 and trends, annual rpt, S2625–1

Iowa bank and trust companies (State-chartered), financial condition by instn arranged by city, FY92 annual rpt, S2760–2

Index by Subjects and Names

Business firms and establishments, number

Iowa labor force supply-demand data, including population, earnings, and employment by industry and occupation, 1993 annual rpt, S2784–3

Iowa retail sales and use tax filings data, and establishments reporting, by county and city, and by kind of business, quarterly rpt, S2860–1

Kansas agricultural product production plants, for selected commodities, 1992 and trends, annual rpt, S2915–1

Kansas statistical abstract, general data, 1991/92 annual rpt, U7095–2.8, U7095–2.10

Kentucky economic statistics, general data, 1993 annual rpt, S3104–1

Kentucky financial instns condition, including assets by instn and city, with regulatory info, 1992 and trends, annual rpt, S3121–1

Louisiana financial instns (State-chartered), financial condition by instn arranged by city, with regulatory info, Dec 1992, annual rpt, S3265–1

Maine banks and other financial instns, financial condition by instn, June 1992, annual rpt, S3473–2

Maine business establishments and employment, by establishment size, Mar 1983, 1989, and 1992, article, S3465–2.503

Maine financial instn assets, deposits, and loans, by type of instn and county, 1982-92, annual rpt, S3473–1

Maryland banks and credit unions (State-chartered) financial condition by instn, with regulatory data, FY92 annual rpt, S3655–2

Maryland insurance industry financial and underwriting data, by company and type of insurance, with regulatory info, 1991, annual rpt, S3655–1

Maryland statistical abstract, general data, 1993 94 bicnnial rpt, S3605–1

Michigan banks and other financial instns, financial condition by instn, with regulatory info, 1992 and trends, annual rpt, S3957–1

Michigan floriculture industry establishments, 1989-91, annual rpt, S3950–1

Michigan insurance industry financial and underwriting data, by company and type of insurance, with regulatory info, 1991, annual rpt, S3983–1

Minnesota financial instns (State-regulated), financial condition by instn, 1991-92, annual rpt, S4140–3

Minnesota insurance industry financial and underwriting data, by company and line of coverage, 1991, annual rpt, S4140–4

Mississippi banks and other financial instns, financial condition by instn type, and assets by bank and credit union, Dec 1992, annual rpt, S4325–1

Mississippi statistical abstract, general data, 1992 annual rpt, U3255–4.4, U3255–4.5, U3255–4.8

Mississippi wholesale and retail businesses, sales, and tax collected, by industry group, city, and county, FY92, annual rpt, S4435–1

Missouri banks and trust companies (State-chartered) financial condition, by instn, FY91-92 and trends, biennial rpt, S4502–1

Missouri insurance industry financial and underwriting data, by company and type of insurance, with regulatory info, 1992, annual rpt, S4527–1

Missouri livestock slaughtering establishments, and floriculture growers, 1988-92, annual rpt, S4480–1

Montana labor force planning rpt, including population, income, and employment and job openings by industry and occupation, with selected data by county, 1993-94 annual rpt, S4710–3

Montana revenue collections by tax type, and taxable establishments, production, and income, FY91-92 and trends, biennial rpt, S4750–1.1

Nebraska business establishments, employment, and wages, by industry, 4th qtr 1992, annual summary, S4895–2.501

Nebraska federally inspected slaughtering plants, with comparison to neighboring States, 1991 and trends, annual rpt, S4835–1

Nebraska insurance industry financial and underwriting data, by company and line of coverage, with regulatory info, 1992, annual rpt, S4890–1

Nevada business firms by industry div and/or employment size, by MSA and selected county, 2nd qtr 1992, annual rpt, S5040–4

Nevada casino finances and employment, by location and gaming revenue range, FY92, annual rpt, S5062–1

Nevada statistical abstract, general data, 1992 biennial rpt, S5005–1.6

New Jersey banks and other financial instns, assets and liabilities by instn, 1992 and trends, annual rpt, S5355–1

New Jersey foreign-owned business establishments, employment, payroll, and shipments/sales, by industry div, 1987, article, S5425–1.501

New Jersey insurance industry financial and underwriting data, by company and type of insurance, 1990, annual rpt, S5420–1

New Mexico and US retail, wholesale, and service industry establishments, sales, payroll, and employment, 1977 and 1987, U7980–1.502

New Mexico financial instns, financial and operating data by instn, with regulatory activities, 1992, annual rpt, S5652–1

New York State business and economic indicators, by MSA, county, and industry, 1980s-91, annual rpt, S5735–3

New York State establishments, employees, and payrolls, by county, labor market area, and industry, monthly rpt quarterly feature, S5775–1.501, S5775–1.502, S5775–1.504, S5775–1.505

New York State insurance industry devs, finances, and regulatory activity, 1990/91 and trends, annual rpt, S5770–3

New York State statistical yearbook, general data, 1992 annual rpt, U5100–1.2, U5100–1.5, U5100–1.7, U5100–1.9

North Carolina livestock slaughtering establishments, Jan 1991-92, annual rpt, S5885–1

North Carolina public utility financial, operating, and regulatory data, by utility type and company, 1990 and trends, annual rpt, S5917–2

Oklahoma export-related manufacturing establishments, export value, and output share and intensity, by industry group, various years 1987-89, article, U8130–1.503

Oklahoma financial instns (State-chartered) assets and liabilities, by type of instn, with regulatory data, FY92 annual rpt, S6415–1

Oklahoma statistical abstract, general data, 1992 annual rpt, U8130–2

Oregon financial instns, financial condition by instn, Dec 1992 and trends, annual rpt, S6616–1

Oregon high-technology firms and employment, 1990-91, annual rpt, S6585–3

Oregon nursery and greenhouse operations and wineries, by location, 1991, annual rpt, S6575–1

Pennsylvania insurance industry financial and underwriting data, by company and line of coverage, 1991, with FY92 regulatory info, annual rpt, S6835–1

Pennsylvania statistical abstract, general data, 1992 recurring rpt, U4130–6.2, U4130–6.9

Rhode Island banks and other financial instns (State-chartered), assets and liabilities, by instn, 1991, annual rpt, S6945–1

Rhode Island insurance industry financial and underwriting data, by company and line of coverage, 1990, with FY91 regulatory info, annual rpt, S6945–2

Rhode Island statistical almanac, general data, 1993 annual rpt, C7975–1.1

South Carolina business establishments and sales, by county, city, and industry group, 1991, annual rpt, S7255–1.3

South Carolina economic condition, including agriculture, commerce, govt finances, employment, and income, 1970s-92, annual rpt, S7125–3

South Carolina financial instns (State-chartered) financial condition, including data by instn, FY92 annual rpt, S7165–1

South Carolina insurance industry financial and underwriting data, by company, 1991, with FY92 regulatory info, annual rpt, S7195–1

South Carolina statistical abstract, general data, 1993 annual rpt, S7125–1.3, S7125–1.7

South Dakota feedlots and cattle marketed, by lot capacity, 1983-92, annual rpt, S7280–1

South Dakota insurance industry financial and underwriting data, by company and type of insurance, with regulatory info, 1991-92, annual rpt, S7300–2

Tennessee banks and other financial instns financial condition, by instn and city, 1992 annual rpt, S7507–1

Tennessee businesses and employment, by firm size, 1st qtr 1992, S7495–2.502

Tennessee employment, wages, and unemployment insurance contributions, by county and industry, 1991, annual rpt, S7495–1

Tennessee insurance industry financial and underwriting data, by company and type of insurance, with regulatory info, 1991, annual rpt, S7466–1

Business firms and establishments, number

Tennessee public utility and transportation commission regulatory activities, with industry financial and operating data, 1991-92 biennial rpt, S7565–1

Tennessee statistical abstract, general data, 1992/93 annual rpt, U8710–2

Texas insurance dept regulatory activities, with industry financial and underwriting data by line of coverage, FY92 annual rpt, S7700–1

Texas livestock slaughter plants, with comparison to other States, 1991-92, annual rpt, S7630–1.2

Texas natural gas utility financial and operating data, by city and company, 1991, with regulatory info, annual rpt, S7745–1

Utah banks and other financial instns, financial condition by instn, FY93 and trends, annual rpt, S7830–1

Utah business establishments, employment, and wages, by firm size and industry, 1992 and trends, annual rpt, S7820–10

Utah business firms, wages, and employment, by firm size, SIC 2-digit industry, and county, 1st qtr 1992, annual rpt, S7820–1

Utah govt statistical review, fiscal and socioeconomic data, 1993 annual rpt, R9380–1.9

Utah high-technology industry trends, with R&D spending, and employment of major firms, 1986-92, recurring article, U8960–2.508

Utah insurance industry financial and underwriting data, by company and line of coverage, with regulatory info, 1991, annual rpt, S7845–1

Utah statistical abstract, general data, 1993 triennial rpt, U8960–1

Vermont banks and other financial instns, financial condition by instn, 1992 and trends, annual rpt, S7995–2

Vermont insurance industry financial and underwriting data, by company and type of insurance, 1991, annual rpt, S7995–1

Virginia consumer finance companies financial condition, by instn, Dec 1992, annual rpt, S8180–3

Virginia financial instns (State-chartered), financial condition by instn and instn type, Dec 1992, annual rpt, S8180–2

Washington State banks and other financial instns, financial condition by type of instn, 1992 and trends, annual rpt, S8325–1

West Virginia banks and other financial instns, composite financial condition, with selected data by instn, 1990-91, annual rpt, S8530–1

West Virginia insurance industry financial and underwriting data, by company and line of coverage, with regulatory info, 1991, annual rpt, S8575–1

Wisconsin banks financial condition, by instn and city, with regulatory info, 1992 and trends, annual rpt, S8685–1

Wisconsin Blue Book, general data, 1993-94 biennial rpt, S8780–1.2

Wisconsin insurance industry financial and underwriting data, by company and line of coverage, with regulatory info, 1992, annual rpt, S8755–1

Wisconsin savings and loan assns and savings banks (State-chartered) financial condition, by instn, 1992 and trends, annual rpt, S8807–1

Wyoming mineral, utility, and other State-assessed producers and property values, 1991, annual rpt, S8990–1

see also Bankruptcy

see also Better Business Bureaus

see also Business acquisitions and mergers

see also Business assets and liabilities, general

see also Business assets and liabilities, specific industry

see also Business expense allowances

see also Business failures and closings

see also Business formations

see also Business income and expenses, general

see also Business income and expenses, specific industry

see also Business inventories

see also Business orders

see also Capital investments

see also Corporate rankings

see also Corporations

see also Depreciation

see also Divestiture

see also Economic concentration and diversification

see also Farms and farmland

see also Foreign corporations

see also Franchises

see also Government contracts and procurement

see also Government corporations and enterprises

see also Holding companies

see also Industrial and commercial energy use

see also Industrial capacity and utilization

see also Industrial plants and equipment

see also Industrial siting

see also Minority businesses

see also Multinational corporations

see also Operating ratios

see also Ownership of enterprise

see also Partnerships

see also Production costs

see also Proprietorships

see also Public utilities

see also Small business

see also Women-owned businesses

see also under By Individual Company or Institution in the "Index by Categories"

see also under By Industry in the "Index by Categories"

Business formations

Age of new businesses at time of venture capital financing, 1985/86-1991/92, article, C4687–1.502

Biotechnology company business formations, 1987, 1989, and 1991, C1850–6.511

Cable TV network subscribers, programming topics, and startup dates, for 33 new or proposed networks, 1992-94, article, C1850–14.524

Entrepreneur reasons for starting a business, and business success by reason, 1993 article, C4687–1.509

Foreign economic indexes, and leading and coincident indicators for US and other industrial countries, monthly rpt, U1245–1

Incorporations (new), and number of firms among top in nation, by State, 1993 annual almanac, C4712–1

Incorporations (new), by State and census div, monthly rpt, C3150–3

Index by Subjects and Names

Incubator facilities and services for new rural businesses, role of State extension programs at land-grant universities, 1992 survey rpt, U2410–3

Incubator facilities for new business, finances and operations, including services offered and tenant characteristics, 1991, annual rpt, A7360–1

Incubator facilities for new small businesses, tenants by industry sector, and types of sponsors, 1993 article, C4687–1.503

Jewelry business openings and failures, by region, monthly rpt, C2150–7

New business startups, 1954 and 1992, article, C4687–1.503

Rates of business formation by race-ethnicity and among Natl Foundation for Teaching Entrepreneurship students, 1993 article, C4687–1.510

State economic dev condition indicators, including economic performance, business vitality, growth capacity, and tax/fiscal system, by State, 1993 annual rpt, R4225–1.1

State social, economic, and govtl indicators, with rankings, 1993 semiannual rpt, B8500–1.2

Status of new businesses 8 years after startup, including voluntary termination and failure rates, 1993 article, C8900–1.523

Trends in total businesses, new incorporations/mergers, and failures, 1982-1st half 1992, C4687–1.504

State and local:

Alabama banks opened, 1981-91, annual rpt, S0110–1

Alabama business activity indicators, monthly rpt, U5680–1

California economic indicators, bimonthly rpt, S0840–1

DC statistical profile, general data, 1992 annual rpt, S1535–3.3

Florida statistical abstract, general data, 1992 annual rpt, U6660–1.24

Georgia statistical abstract, general data, 1992-93 biennial rpt, U6730–1.6

Hawaii data book, general data, 1992 annual rpt, S2090–1.15

Illinois businesses by employment size, incorporations, and bankruptcy filings, 1980s-93, S2405–2.504

Kansas business activity indicators, quarterly rpt, U7095–1

Kansas statistical abstract, general data, 1991/92 annual rpt, U7095–2.8

Massachusetts program to help unemployed start a business, impact on need for unemployment insurance benefits, 1993 article, C4687–1.507

Mississippi statistical abstract, general data, 1992 annual rpt, U3255–4.5

Missouri industrial growth, including new and expanding manufacturers, new jobs, and investment, 1982-91, annual rpt, S4475–1

Montana new businesses, by industry div and labor force area, 1990-92, annual planning rpt, S4710–3

Montana new businesses enrolling in unemployment insurance program, by MSA and labor market area, quarterly rpt, S4710–1

New Jersey economic indicators, including employment, building permits, and retail trade, monthly rpt, S5425–1

Index by Subjects and Names

New Mexico business and economic activity indicators, monthly rpt, U7980–1
New York State business activity indicators, quarterly rpt, S5735–2
Oklahoma statistical abstract, general data, 1992 annual rpt, U8130–2.15
South Carolina statistical abstract, general data, 1993 annual rpt, S7125–1.3
Tennessee statistical abstract, general data, 1992/93 annual rpt, U8710–2.7
Utah business startups and closings, by industry div and county, 1992, annual rpt, S7820–10
Utah economic and business activity review and indicators, monthly rpt, U8960–2
Utah statistical abstract, general data, 1993 triennial rpt, U8960–1.15
Virginia economic indicators, including new business incorporations and employment data, quarterly rpt, S8205–4
Washington State new business establishments, by county and industry, FY88-92, annual rpt, S8415–1.1
Wisconsin Blue Book, general data, 1993-94 biennial rpt, S8780–1.2
Wisconsin new business incorporations, monthly rpt, S8750–1

Business forms
see Office supplies

Business income and expenses, general

Advertisement "infomercial" TV programs, sales trends for products advertised, 1988-93, article, C1850–14.543
Advertising (outdoor) expenditures, for top 10 industry or product categories, 1992, recurring article, C2710–1.517
Advertising billings or expenditures on TV, for top 10 agencies and top 15 advertisers, 1991-92, annual feature, C2710–1.528
Advertising expenditures by medium for top 100 advertisers, with comparisons to earnings and sales, and detail by product type and brand, 1991-92, annual rpt, C2710–1.547
Advertising expenditures for local, spot, and syndicated TV, with detail for top 5 advertisers, 1992, article, C2710–1.516
Advertising expenditures for local, spot, syndicated, and network TV, with detail for top 10 network advertisers, 3rd qtr 1991-92, article, C2710–1.505
Advertising expenditures for top 10 advertisers, 1st qtr 1992-93, article, C2710–3.544
Advertising expenditures for top 200 brands, by selected medium, weekly rpt quarterly feature, C2710–1.502, C2710–1.512, C2710–1.525, C2710–1.540
Advertising expenditures in newspapers and other media, 1981 and 1990-91, annual rpt, A8610–1
Advertising expenditures in newspapers compared to retail sales and consumer confidence, 1987-1st half 1992, article, A8605–1.502
Advertising expenditures in newspapers, with top advertisers, and top advertising agencies in billings, 1992, C2710–1.524
Advertising expenditures of corporations and assns, by medium, 1988-92, and top 10 advertisers for 1992, annual article, A8770–1.504
Advertising expenditures on cable TV, for top 10 advertisers, 1st qtr 1993, C1850–14.523

Business income and expenses, general

Advertising expenditures on cable TV, for top 20 industry categories, 1992, article, C1850–14.515
Advertising expenditures on cable TV, for top 5 advertisers, 1992, C1850–14.513
Advertising expenditures on 4 major TV networks, for top 10 network advertisers, 1st qtr 1993, article, C2710–1.528
Advertising expenditures on 4 major TV networks, for top 10 network advertisers, 2nd qtr 1992-93, article, C2710–1.541
Advertising to enhance corporate image, company practices, expenditures, and media use, 1987-92, triennial survey rpt, A3357–1
Advertising TV expenditures for top 25 network advertisers, with detail for 4 networks, 1992, annual article, C2710–1.515
Advertising worldwide media and marketing, with data for leading periodicals, and expenditures by top advertiser and country, 1992 annual feature, C2710–1.506
Black-owned business firms, sales/receipts, employment, and payroll, by industry div and State, 1982 and/or 1987, annual compilation, C6775–2.8
Black-owned enterprises financial and operating data, for top 100 firms and auto dealerships and for top 15-25 financial instns, 1992 and trends, annual feature, C4215–1.507
Black-owned franchises, with type of business and startup costs, top 50 companies, 1993 annual article, C4215–1.510
Black-owned vs total businesses and receipts, by industry div, 1987, annual article, A8510–1.1
Business Week economic, business, and investment devs, with related statistical indicators, weekly rpt, C5800–7
Charitable contributions compared to income, 1972-92, annual rpt, A0700–1.1
Computer local-area network (LAN) operating costs, with detail for personnel costs by network size, 1993 survey article, C1850–5.513
Consumer buying power survey of population, income, and sales by product line, by State, metro area, county, and census div, 1993 annual rpt, C1200–1.514
Corporate CEO characteristics, compensation, and company finances, for officers of top 1,000 firms, 1993 annual feature, C5800–7.549
Corporate CEO compensation in 800 firms, with sales and profit data, 1993 annual article, C3950–1.515
Corporate charitable contributions, by donor characteristics and detailed type of recipient, 1991 and trends, annual rpt, R4105–8
Corporate earnings outlook and stock investment performance, approx 900 corporations, 1992 annual feature, C5800–7.509
Corporate executive compensation, with company revenues, for 20 highly paid executives in US, Germany, and Japan, 1993 article, C3950–1.516
Corporate expenditure plans for computer/info systems by component, 1993 annual survey article, C1850–5.510

Corporate expenditures on advertising, marketing, and public relations involving support for the arts, 1991-92, recurring rpt, A3690–1
Corporate financial and operating composite ratios, establishments, and receipts, for approx 200 industries, by asset size, FY90, annual rpt, C7800–1
Corporate financial losses, for 10 firms with all-time largest annual loss, 1993 article, C5800–7.517
Corporate market value of top 1,000 firms worldwide, with related financial data, by company and country, 1993 annual feature, C5800–7.536
Corporate market value rankings of top 1,000 firms, with sales, profits, assets, and related data, by company and industry, 1993 annual feature, C5800–7.521
Corporate mergers, acquisitions, and divestitures, with prices, payment methods, and characteristics of participants, 1992 and trends, annual rpt, B6020–1
Corporate mergers, acquisitions, and other agreements involving US companies, by SIC code, bimonthly rpt quarterly feature, C4683–1
Corporate productivity, employment, sales, and operating income, for 46 companies with outstanding productivity improvement, 1992 and trends, C5800–7.532
Corporate profits, taxes, dividends, and undistributed profits, 1980-92, annual rpt, A3179–2.3
Corporate R&D expenditures, and sales and profits, for approx 900 firms, 1992, annual feature, C5800–7.534
Corporate sales, earnings, and stock performance, for 100 fastest-growing companies, 1993 annual article, C8900–1.521
Corporate sales, profits, return on equity, price/earnings ratio, and earnings per share, approx 900 corporations, with industry rankings, weekly rpt quarterly article, C5800–7.503, C5800–7.519, C5800–7.528, C5800–7.541
Corporate sponsorship expenditures, by type of event, 1993, article, C2710–1.532
Corporate tax burden trends, for income and payroll taxes, with comparisons to profits, Fed Govt receipts, and GDP, FY70-93, R9050–15.2
Corporations with rapid growth, financial data for 250 firms, 1993 feature, C5800–7.551
Cost of doing business index, for 6 least and 6 most expensive States, 1993 article, C8900–1.509
Direct retail ("door-to-door") sales, with distribution by product category, 1991, article, C4215–1.501
Drug testing program employer costs, 1992, annual rpt, A2075–20.12
Economic indicator historical trends, 1900s-92, annual rpt, R9050–1.2
Economic outlook for selected indicators, recent trends and 2-year forecast, quarterly rpt, A3840–6
Electronic data interchange (EDI) use by businesses, and average expenditures, 1990-92 and 1996, article, C1850–2.511

Business income and expenses, general

Index by Subjects and Names

Employee benefit payments and employer cost/payroll ratios, by industry, detailed type of benefit, and firm size, 1991, annual rpt, A3840–1

Employee motivational training programs use, including expenditures for outdoor programs, 1993 survey article, C1200–1.503

Employee transfers and relocation policies, assistance, and costs, 1992, annual survey, B0600–1

Employer basic skills testing and training practices and costs, Jan-Mar 1993 survey, annual rpt, A2075–20.13

Export sales ranking of top 50 companies, 1992, annual feature, C8900–1.517

Financial performance and growth rankings for approx 1,000 top corporations, with comparisons by industry group, 1993 annual rpt, C3950–1.505

Financial ratios and performance, for over 350 SIC 4-digit industries, FY88-92, annual rpt, A6400–3

Forbes 500 top companies in sales, profits, assets, market value, and productivity, with stock and employment data, 1992, annual rpt, C3950–1.513

Forecasts of corporate profits and other economic indicators, monthly rpt, B4950–1

Forecasts of economic indicators for approx 10-13 months, monthly rpt, U1880–3

Forecasts of natl income and product account components and related indicators, quarterly rpt, U1880–1

Foreign economic indexes, and leading and coincident indicators for US and other industrial countries, monthly rpt, U1245–1

Foreign investments in US, foreign companies, and US multinatls, financial data for top 100-500 in each category, 1992, annual feature, C3950–1.519

Fortune magazine ranking of top 50-100 companies in 8 nonindustrial sectors, with financial and employment data, 1992, annual feature, C8900–1.516

Fortune magazine ranking of top 50-100 companies worldwide in 8 nonindustrial sectors, with financial and employment data, 1993 annual feature, C8900–1.522

Fortune 500 largest industrial corporations, sales, financial, and stock performance data by company, 1992, annual feature, C8900–1.513

Fortune 500 largest industrial corporations worldwide, with financial and employment data, 1992, annual feature, C8900–1.520

Franchise operations and finances, by type of business, 1991/92 and trends, annual rpt, A5820–1

Hiring costs and new hires, by industry, State, region, and employer characteristics, 1992 and trends, annual survey rpt, A4740–2

Hispanic American marketing devs, including leading advertisers and media, and market characteristics, 1992 annual features, C4575–1.502

Hispanic-owned business motor vehicle fleet expenditures, 1992 annual survey feature, C4575–1.501

Hispanic-owned business outlook for selected performance indicators, with data by region, monthly rpt quarterly feature, C4575–1.510

Hispanic-owned business sales and employment, for top 500 companies, 1992, annual feature, C4575–1.507

Hispanic-owned business sales and employment, for 100 fastest-growing companies, 1988-92, annual feature, C4575–1.509

Incentive programs for consumers, employees, and dealers, with expenditures by industry and incentive type, 1991-92, annual feature, C1200–4.502

Incentive programs for consumers, with methods used and expenditures for top 10 industries, 1993 annual survey article, C1200–4.506

Incentive programs for salespeople, with expenditures of top 10 user industries, 1993 survey, annual article, C1200–4.511

Incentive travel programs for sales promotion, with destinations, and expenditures of top 10 user industries, 1993 survey, annual article, C1200–4.510

Incubator facilities for new business, with revenues of present and former tenants, 1990, annual rpt, A7360–1

Industrial R&D managers outlook on expenditures, effort, personnel, and other mgmt issues, 1993, annual survey rpt, A5510–1

Logistics trends and devs, including data on costs, finances of major carriers by mode, and foreign trade, 1993 annual compilation, C2150–1.506

Manufacturing and nonmanufacturing receipts, for top 15 counties, 1992, article, C1200–1.509

Marketing costs per contact for 5 methods, 1993 article, C2575–1.509

Markets with daily newspapers, demographic and economic info by geographic area, US and Canada, 1993 annual rpt, C3250–1

Minority-owned business establishments and gross receipts compared to total US, by race-ethnicity, 1987, article, C4215–1.507

Multinatl companies sales and intl share, for 50 smaller firms, 1992, article, C5800–7.544

NASDAQ typical issuing company financial profile, 1992, annual rpt, A7105–1

New York Stock Exchange activity, including stock volume and prices, credit distribution, and member firm characteristics, 1992 and trends, annual fact book, B6625–1

Outlook of business executives on key indicators for coming qtr, with trends and data by census div, quarterly rpt, C3150–4

Packaging expenditures of top 7 manufacturers, 1992, article, C1850–1.508

Privately held corporation revenues and employment, for 400 largest firms, 1992 annual article, C3950–1.503

Recruitment costs for new college hires, by type of employer, 1992/93 annual survey rpt, U3130–1

Retail chain financial data and business info for approx 240 US and Canadian companies, 1991-92 and trends, annual rpt, C3400–2

Retail chain revenues, profits, and stores, top 100 chains, with selected data by outlet type, 1991-92, annual articles, C5150–4.508

Retail chain sales, for selected leading companies, monthly rpt, C5150–4

Retail chain store company expenditures for consulting services by type, Sept-Oct 1992 survey, article, C5150–4.504

Retail industry distribution center operating expenses, 1993 survey, C5150–4.506

Retail inventory loss prevention expenditures, by type of outlet, 1990-91, annual survey rpt, C5150–4.504

Retail mgmt info system devs, including expenses and computerized equipment use, 1992 survey, annual feature, C5150–4.501

Retail mgmt info system devs, including expenses and computerized equipment use, 1993 survey, annual feature, C5150–4.509

Retail sales by kind of business, by census div, State, MSA, county, and city, 1992, annual rpt, C1200–1.511

Retail store credit operations, including cash vs credit sales, processing methods, and marketing techniques, 1992 annual survey, C5150–4.504

Retail store credit operations, including payment losses and loss reduction efforts, by payment method and outlet type, 1992 survey article, C5150–4.503

Retail store financial performance indicators, for 98 public firms, FY92 and trends, annual rpt, B8130–4

Retailer costs for handling transactions paid with cash, checks, and debit and credit cards, 1993 article, C5225–1.507

Sales and marketing executive compensation, for top 100 executives, with company sales and profit data, 1992 annual article, C1200–1.501

Sales industry costs, including compensation, training, and travel and related expenses, with data by metro area, 1992 and trends, annual survey, C1200–1.508

Sales personnel initial training duration and costs, by company revenue size, 1990 and 1992, C4687–1.506

Service industries economic devs, with analysis of conditions and outlook, and comparisons to other industries, quarterly rpt, A3892–1

Service sector economic activity indicators, with leading and coincident indexes and components, and detail for financial services, monthly rpt, U1245–3

Small business views on current and expected economic conditions, survey findings, quarterly rpt, A7815–1

Small companies with high 5-year returns on equity, financial performance data and chief executive characteristics, for top 200 firms, 1992 annual article, C3950–1.501

Small companies with sales under $150 million, financial data for top 100 growth firms, 1993 annual article, C5800–7.529

Small companies with sales under $25 million, financial and operating data for top 100 public firms, 1992 and trends, annual feature, C4687–1.507

Small privately held companies sales, employment, and other data, for 500 fastest growing firms, 1988 and 1992, annual feature, C4687–1.512

Statistical profiles of 50 States and DC, general data, 1993 annual almanac, C4712–1

Index by Subjects and Names

Telecommunication costs as percent of total business costs or shipments value, by industry, 1992 article, U8710–1.501

Tourism receipts and travel-related industry finances, US and foreign, with detail by company, 1992 annual rpt, C2140–1

Travel expenses per diem in top 20 cities, 1991, recurring rpt, R9375–6

Travel impact on State economies, with detail by industry sector, 1990 and trends, annual rpt, R9375–7

Workers compensation costs for employers, by State, 1992 annual rpt, R8335–1.3

State and local:

Alabama business activity indicators, monthly rpt, U5680–1

Alabama statistical abstract, general data, 1992 recurring rpt, U5680–2.3, U5680–2.11, U5680–2.15, U5680–2.18

Arizona business activity indicators, including housing market, population, CPI, and industrial purchasing, monthly rpt, U0280–1

Arizona economic condition, including population, employment and earnings, and business activity, by industry and locality, 1985-93, semiannual rpt, U5850–1

Arizona net taxable sales by industry classification and county, FY92 and trends, annual rpt, S0515–1

Arizona retail sales, by kind of business and for 2 metro areas and rest of State, 1992 and trends, annual article, U0280–1.507

Arizona statistical abstract, general data, 1993 recurring rpt, U5850–2

Arkansas socioeconomic trends, by MSA and/or county, 1993 annual rpt, U5935–1

California economic condition, including population, employment and earnings, income, business activity, and taxation, 1993 annual rpt, S0840–3

California economic indicators, bimonthly rpt, S0840–1

California individual and corporate income tax returns and property tax assistance, by income class and county, 1990 and trends, annual rpt, S0855–1

California statistical abstract, general data, 1992 annual rpt, S0840–2.4, S0840–2.8, S0840–2.11

California taxable retail sales, by kind of business and county, FY92, annual rpt, S0835–1.3

Colorado retail sales and sales tax revenue, by county, city, and kind of business, FY92 and trends, annual rpt, S1075–1.5

Delaware data book, general data, 1993 annual rpt, S1375–4

Florida statistical abstract, general data, 1992 annual rpt, U6660–1

Georgia business activity indicators, bimonthly rpt, U6730–2

Georgia statistical abstract, general data, 1992-93 biennial rpt, U6730–1.6, U6730–1.7, U6730–1.8

Georgia taxable retail sales, by county, 1991, annual rpt, S1950–1.2

Hawaii counties population and economic indicators, 1993 annual rpt series, B3500–2

Hawaii data book, general data, 1992 annual rpt, S2090–1

Hawaii economic conditions, including employment, population, tourism, and construction, quarterly rpt, S2090–2

Business income and expenses, general

Hawaii economic indicators, bimonthly rpt, B3500–1

Idaho taxable sales and taxes paid, by county, FY92, annual rpt, S2295–1

Illinois economic and business activity indicators, including data by industry and county, bimonthly rpt, S2405–2

Illinois statistical abstract, general data, 1992 annual rpt, U6910–2

Iowa retail sales and use tax filings data, and establishments reporting, by county and city, and kind of business, quarterly rpt, S2860–1

Kansas service industries employment and economic growth, with comparisons to other industries, 1980s-90, article, U7095–1.502

Kansas taxable retail sales, by area and kind of business, quarterly rpt, U7095–1

Kentucky economic statistics, general data, 1993 annual rpt, S3104–1

Maine statistical summary, general economic and social data, 1992 recurring rpt, S3434–1

Maryland statistical abstract, general data, 1993-94 biennial rpt, S3605–1.5, S3605–1.10

Minnesota-based Fortune 500 corporation sales, assets, and net income, by company, 1991, annual rpt, S4180–1

Mississippi statistical abstract, general data, 1992 annual rpt, U3255–4.5, U3255–4.6, U3255–4.11, U3255–4.14

Mississippi wholesale and retail businesses, sales, and tax collected, by industry group, city, and county, FY92, annual rpt, S4435–1

Missouri retail sales by kind of business, 1982-91, annual rpt, S4475–1

Montana revenue collections by tax type, and taxable establishments, production, and income, FY91-92 and trends, biennial rpt, S4750–1.1

Nebraska business and economic activity indicators, monthly rpt, U7860–1

Nebraska public service commission regulatory activities, with financial and operating data for individual railroads and telephone companies, FY91-92 biennial rpt, S4940–1

Nebraska sales tax revenues and taxable sales, by county, city, and detailed industry, 1990-91, annual rpt, S4950–1.2

Nevada business and economic activity indicators, with comparisons to other Western States, 1980-91, annual rpt, U7920–2

Nevada, Las Vegas and Reno taxable sales, quarterly rpt, S5040–1

Nevada statistical abstract, general data, 1992 biennial rpt, S5005–1.11

New Jersey economic indicators, including employment, building permits, and retail trade, monthly rpt, S5425–1

New Mexico business and economic activity indicators, monthly rpt, U7980–1

New Mexico taxable business receipts, with detail by industry div and county, FY91-92 and trends, annual rpt, S5660–1

New York State business activity indicators, quarterly rpt, S5735–2

New York State statistical yearbook, general data, 1992 annual rpt, U5100–1.2, U5100–1.7, U5100–1.12

Ohio corporate franchise tax returns filed, income, and tax liability, by industry div, 1991, annual rpt, S6390–1.2

Oklahoma business activity indicators, monthly rpt, U8130–1

Oklahoma statistical abstract, general data, 1992 annual rpt, U8130–2.18, U8130–2.19, U8130–2.20

Pennsylvania business activity indicators, monthly rpt, U4110–1

Pennsylvania statistical abstract, general data, 1992 recurring rpt, U4130–6.2, U4130–6.9

South Carolina economic activity indicators, including employment by industry div, by county, 1993 annual rpt, S7145–1.2

South Carolina economic condition, including agriculture, commerce, govt finances, employment, and income, 1970s-92, annual rpt, S7125–3

South Carolina statistical abstract, general data, 1993 annual rpt, S7125–1.3, S7125–1.10

South Carolina taxable sales, by county, city, and industry group, 1991, annual rpt, S7255–1.3

South Dakota gross sales/use tax purchases and taxable retail sales, by county and selected city, bimonthly rpt, U8595–2

South Dakota taxable sales by locality, quarterly rpt, U8595–1

South Dakota taxable sales, by SIC 2-digit industry, FY92, annual rpt, S7380–1.1

Tennessee business activity indicators, quarterly journal, U8710–1

Tennessee economic indicator trends and forecasts, and business executives views on selected issues, 1993 annual articles, U8710–1.502

Tennessee economic indicator trends and forecasts, with data by industry div and manufacturing group, 1982-2001, annual rpt, S7560–1

Tennessee statistical abstract, general data, 1992/93 annual rpt, U8710–2.7, U8710–2.10, U8710–2.13

Utah business activity indicators, by county, 1988-91, annual feature, U8960–2.501

Utah business activity indicators, by county, 1989-92, annual feature, U8960–2.507

Utah govt statistical review, fiscal and socioeconomic data, 1993 annual rpt, R9380–1.2

Utah statistical abstract, general data, 1993 triennial rpt, U8960–1.14, U8960–1.16, U8960–1.17

Utah taxable retail sales, by county, 1986-91, annual rpt, S7905–1

Virginia taxable retail sales by kind of business, FY92, annual rpt, S8305–1.2

Virginia taxable retail sales, quarterly rpt, S8205–4

Virginia taxable sales, by kind of business and locality, 1991 and trends, annual rpt, U9080–8

see also Agricultural finance

see also Agricultural marketing

see also Agricultural production costs

see also Business assets and liabilities, general

see also Business expense allowances

see also Business income and expenses, specific industry

see also Capital investments

Business income and expenses, general

see also Cost-of-doing-business surveys
see also Depreciation
see also Economic indicators
see also Farm income
see also Foreign corporations
see also Labor costs and cost indexes
see also Operating ratios
see also Payroll
see also Production costs
see also Professionals' fees

Business income and expenses, specific industry

Advertising agencies targeting Hispanic market, revenues and billings for top 10 firms, FY91, annual article, C4575–1.502

Advertising agency income, billings by medium, employees, and offices, for leading US and/or foreign agencies, 1992 and trends, annual rpt, C2710–1.522

Aerospace and defense industries financial performance, with data for approx 200 major US and foreign companies, FY92 and trends, annual feature, C5800–4.519

Aerospace industry, civil and military production, R&D, trade, employment, and finances, with Federal funding data, 1991 and trends, annual rpt, A0250–2

Aircraft (general aviation) shipments and factory billings, 1946-92, annual rpt, A5120–2.1

Airline commissions to travel agents, and passenger revenues, by US and foreign carrier, 1st half 1993 and trends, annual article, C7000–4.511

Airline costs per seat mile for 5 carriers, and average yields for 10 short-haul routes, 1993 article, C5800–4.529

Airline expenditures on inflight meals, for 9 major carriers and all others, 1992, article, C1200–5.516

Airline finances and operations of scheduled carriers, summary statistics, 1992 and trends, annual rpt, A0325–5

Airline financial and operating data, 1986-91, annual rpt, C2140–1.5

Airline financial performance, by carrier, monthly rpt quarterly table, C7000–4.501, C7000–4.504, C7000–4.508, C7000–4.509

Airline food service expenditures, by carrier, 1st 9 months 1992 and trends, annual article, C7000–4.507

Airline fuel consumption and costs, monthly rpt, C7000–4

Airline industry financial losses, with contributing factors, 1990-92, article, C5800–4.510

Airline maintenance budget, employment, and contracting trends, for 38 carriers worldwide, 1992 article, C7000–4.501

Airline major carrier operating profit or loss, 1988-93, article, C5800–4.506

Airline market activity, including traffic, financial performance, employment, and fleet composition, by US and foreign carrier, 1991-92, annual feature, C7000–4.508

Airline operating lease expense, by major carrier, 1990-92, annual article, C7000–4.508

Airline quarterly profit or loss, 2nd qtr 1992-4th qtr 1993, article, C5800–4.521

Airline revenues and earnings or losses, for 10 largest carriers, 1992, article, C8900–1.517

Airline revenues, profits, and passenger traffic, for top 50 carriers worldwide, 1991, article, C8900–1.501

Airline summary financial, employment, and traffic data, 1977 and 1992, C5800–4.525

Airline traffic and finances worldwide, by carrier, 1993 annual feature, C7000–4.511

Airline traffic and financial forecasts, by US and foreign carrier, 1993 annual article, C7000–4.503

Airport costs vs charges to airlines, by facility size category, 1992, article, C5800–4.530

Airport spending for facilities and Federal program compliance, 1992-97, article, C5800–4.514

Ambulance company revenues, net income, and stock performance, for 4 firms, 1993 article, C3950–1.523

Amusement park operating and financial data, including data for US and foreign parks, miniature golf, waterparks, and games, 1992, annual rpt, A5700–1

Apartment building (conventionally financed) detailed income and expense ratios for US and Canada, by building type, metro area, and US region, 1991 and trends, annual rpt, A5600–1

Apartment building (federally subsidized) detailed income and expense ratios, by building and subsidy type, building age, metro area, and region, 1991 and trends, annual rpt, A5600–5

Apartment complex mgmt income and expenses, and vacancy and turnover rates, by region and metro area, 1992, annual survey rpt, A6497–1

Architectural and engineering design firm billings, for top 500 firms, 1992, annual article, C5800–2.522

Arts fundraising through united arts funds (UAFs), with fund operations, income by source, and allocations, by UAF, 1992 and trends, annual rpt, A1315–2

Auto advertising expenditures, by medium, 1990-92, annual article, C2710–3.552

Auto advertising expenditures outside US by top 10 manufacturers, and billings for auto accounts changing agencies, 1993 article, C2710–1.509

Auto aftermarket chain sales, income, and stores, for 8 companies, 1989-91, C2150–10.501

Auto aftermarket company financial and operating data, including sales, income, stores, and inventory turns, for 8-12 public firms, 1993 article, C2150–10.508

Auto aftermarket product sales, by market segment, 1992, article, C2150–10.506

Auto aftermarket retail sales, and number of stores and service bays, for top 100 chains, 1993 annual article, C2150–10.507

Auto aftermarket sales, by outlet type, 1992 and 1996, article, C4680–1.509

Auto aftermarket sales of under-car parts, by type, 1992, article, C2150–10.502

Auto industry financial performance of top 3 US auto manufacturers, weekly rpt quarterly table, C2710–3.501, C2710–3.516, C2710–3.527, C2710–3.538, C2710–3.541

Auto industry revenues and stock performance, for 3 major vehicle

manufacturers and approx 50 suppliers, weekly rpt quarterly feature, C2710–3.518, C2710–3.532, C2710–3.545

Auto insurance passenger and commercial premiums, market shares, and loss ratios, with rankings of States and 20 leading firms, 1992, annual article, C1050–1.511

Auto manufacturer advertising expenditures, by company, 1993 directory, C2710–3.552

Auto parts/supplies and repair aftermarket sales performance, by product group, 1993 annual feature, C0125–1.503

Bank assets, equity, performance, and market value, top 50 instns worldwide, 1993 annual feature, C5800–7.535

Bank financial performance, including assets, loans, deposits, and operating ratios, top 100 instns, 1992, annual feature, C5800–7.526

Basketball revenues by source shared and not shared with players, for Natl Basketball Assn, 1992, article, C3950–1.516

Battery market value by industry segment, including household, industrial, and govt, 1992, article, C5150–3.513

Beverage consumption and sales, by type, leading company, and brand, 1992 and trends, annual rpt, C4775–1.4, C4775–2.3

Beverage industry sales and operating data, by company, brand, and product type, 1991 and trends, annual rpt, C0125–3

Beverage industry sales, consumption, and marketing devs, monthly rpt, C0125–2

Biotechnology company finances, employment, and firms, with detail for public companies, FY92-93, annual article, A1250–1.542

Biotechnology company income and earnings, for approx 30 firms, 1991-92, recurring article, A1250–1.518

Biotechnology company income and earnings, for approx 30 firms, 3rd qtr and 1st nine months 1992, recurring article, A1250–1.504

Biotechnology industry summary financial performance and employment data, with detail for public companies, 1991-92, article, A6400–2.503

Boat ownership, registrations, and sales, by boat type and/or State, including data for related equipment, 1992 annual rpt, A8055–1

Boating (recreational) industry trends, including sales, foreign trade, and registrations by geographic area, 1980s-92, annual feature, C2425–4

Book publishing income and profit margin, for 16 companies, 1991-92, article, C1852–2.519

Book publishing industry financial and operating data, by publisher type and size, and subject category, 1991 and trends, annual rpt, A3274–2

Book publishing industry sales, by type of publisher, 1982-92, annual compilation, C1650–3.4

Book publishing sales, for top 11 general trade publishers, 1991-92, article, C1852–2.524

Book superstore sales and outlets for top 6 chains, Jan 1993, article, C1852–2.514

Index by Subjects and Names

Business income and expenses, specific industry

Bookstore chain income statement for aggregate 3 major chains, FY92-93, article, C1852–2.526

Bookstore chain sales, for leading companies, weekly rpt quarterly feature, C1852–2.519, C1852–2.524

Bowling assn finances and membership, and bowling establishments and lanes, by State and other area, 1991/92 and trends, annual rpt, A1015–1

Brewing industry financial and operating data, including consumption, trade, and taxes, 1991 and trends, annual rpt, A3455–1

Broadcasting (public) membership income, contributors, and stations, by station type, FY91 and trends, annual rpt, R4250–1.21

Broadcasting (public) revenues by source, by station type, FY91, annual rpt, R4250–1.20

Broadcasting (public) revenues from State sources, by State and territory, FY91, annual rpt, R4250–1.19

Broadcasting and related electronic communications companies revenues and earnings, top 100 companies, 1992, annual article, C1850–14.526

Broadcasting revenues and profits, by source, for 3 major networks, 1992, annual article, C1850–14.522

Building design/construction company revenues and operations, for top 300 firms, 1991, annual feature, C1850–9.502

Business forms industry detailed financial and operating ratios, with summary operating data, FY91, annual rpt, A5785–3

Business forms industry trends and outlook, including data by product type, 1992 annual rpt, A5785–2

Cable TV advertising revenues of 17 basic cable networks and 3 representative organizations, and expenditures of top 10 advertisers, 1993 features, C1858–1.501

Cable TV pay-per-view revenues, 1982-92, article, C1850–14.503

Candy (gummy) sales, total and for top 10 manufacturers, 1992-93, article, C2710–1.548

Catholic charity social service agency activities, clients, finances, and personnel, 1991 and trends, annual rpt, A3810–1

Cellular telephone equipment sales and subscribers, and total communications equipment market, 1985, 1991, and 1996, article, C2000–1.504

Chambers of commerce income, salaries and benefits, membership, staff, and operations, 1993 annual rpt, A3840–3

Charity gambling gross receipts and net proceeds to charity, by State, 1992, article, C2176–1.520

Charity gambling receipts, net proceeds, and State regulatory staff and finances, by State, various years FY90-92, article, C2176–1.512

Chemical and allied industries earnings, sales, and profit margins, by company, weekly rpt quarterly article, A1250–1.502, A1250–1.514, A1250–1.525, A1250–1.536

Chemical and chemical process industries, operating and technical devs, and plant and equipment costs and production indexes, monthly rpt, C5800–8

Chemical and related industries production, finances, operating ratios, employment, and trade, by country, company, and chemical, 1980s-92, annual feature, A1250–1.530

Chemical company sales and profits, for top 50 producers worldwide, 1992, annual article, A1250–1.533

Chemical industry capital and other environmental spending, for 20 firms, 1992, article, A1250–1.533

Chemical industry finances and operations, with data by industry segment and product, 1970s-92, annual rpt, A3850–1

Chemical industry R&D spending, for 27 companies, 1987-93, annual article, A1250–1.511

Chemical industry sales and operating summary for top 100 companies, 1992, annual article, A1250–1.523

Clothing (men's) sales and consumer expenditures, by outlet type, 1992, article, C5150–3.508

Clothing (women's and children's) sales, production, imports, and industry employment, hours, and earnings, by type of garment, recurring rpt, A5900–1

Clothing and shoe industries financial performance indicators for 72 companies, FY92 and trends, annual rpt, B8130–2

Communications industry expenditures, by industry segment, 1986-96, annual rpt, C3975–5.3

Computer (personal) company revenues for top 50 firms worldwide, and top 50 marketing in North America, 1991, annual article, C1850–5.503

Computer (personal) software sales, by type of program, 1991, article, C1200–1.501

Computer-aided design, manufacturing, and engineering (CAD/CAM/CAE) revenues, with market shares for 10 companies, 1992, article, C7000–7.501

Computer and business equipment revenues worldwide, by industry sector, 1990-97, annual article, C2000–1.503

Computer company advertising expenditures, for top 5 advertisers in selected media, 1st half 1992, C2710–1.502

Computer company revenues and earnings, for top 10 companies making network software, 1993 article, C8900–1.521

Computer industry advertising expenditures, for top 10 manufacturers and magazines, 1st half 1992-93, article, C2710–1.542

Computer manufacturer advertising expenditures and pages in magazines, for top 12 firms, 1st 8 months 1992-93, article, C2710–1.548

Computer manufacturer revenues from sales of Intel-based network servers, for top 4 and all other companies, 1992, article, C1850–5.522

Computer software company revenues and employment, for top 100 firms worldwide, 1992, annual article, C1850–5.520

Computer software with sales/marketing applications, vendor profit margins and revenue outlook, 1992 annual survey article, C1200–1.502

Computer systems integration consultant revenues and market shares, for top 5 companies, 1993, article, C8900–1.526

Computer/info systems companies revenues and other financial data, for top 100 firms worldwide and in North America, 1992 and trends, annual rpt, C1850–5.514

Condominium, cooperative, and planned unit dev detailed expenses, for US and Canada, by building characteristics, metro area, and US region, 1991, annual rpt, A5600–3

Construction contract values, total and foreign, with rankings of top 400 contractors, 1992, annual rpt, C5800–2.529

Construction design firms foreign billings, specialties, and work locations, for top 200 intl firms, 1992, annual article, C5800–2.538

Construction industry activities, including data on costs, materials prices, wages, financing, and contract awards, weekly rpt, C5800–2

Construction industry finances and operations, by type of business and region, 1992-93, annual survey rpt, A4155–1

Construction mgmt firm total and foreign contract values for top 100 firms, and employee compensation by position, 1992 and trends, annual article, C5800–2.533

Construction specialty firm revenues, and contract values, by specialty, for top 600 contractors, 1992, annual article, C5800–2.548

Convenience store finances and number of stores, for 5 chains with bankruptcy filings, 1991-92, article, C4680–1.505

Convenience store industry financial and operating data, by size category, 1992 and trends, annual survey rpt, A6735–1, A6735–2

Cosmetics and fragrance sales by retail outlet type, 1993 annual feature, C5150–2.515

Defense contractor military sales, and share of total sales, for top 10 contractors, 1991, article, C8900–1.509

Direct marketing billings in US and worldwide, for top direct response agencies, 1991-92, annual articles, C2710–1.535

Direct marketing industry devs, including advertising patterns, finances, target market characteristics, and consumer attitudes, 1992/93 annual rpt, A4620–1

Discount chain sales and merchandising, including data by dept, leading chain, and location, 1992 and trends, annual feature, C8130–1.507

Discount store and other outlet sales and merchandising of health and beauty aids, by product type, 1991 and trends, annual article, C5150–3.502

Discount store financial and marketing devs, biweekly rpt, C5150–3

Discount store sales and earnings, for approx 40 major companies, monthly rpt recurring feature, C8130–1

Discount store sales and productivity data for 20 depts, 1993 annual feature, C5150–3.516

Discount stores, sales, and earnings, for top chains, with detail by specialty, 1993 annual feature, C5150–3.514

Discount wholesale membership club in-store bakery and total sales, 1991-93, article, C5225–1.509

Business income and expenses, specific industry

Index by Subjects and Names

Discount wholesale membership club sales and stores, for 9 major chains, with sales summary by product category, 1992 annual article, C8130–1.501

Drug sales, for 9 chiral drugs containing molecules that can exist in mirror image forms, 1990, article, C5800–8.512

Drug wholesale company revenues, market shares, and operating ratios, for 7 major firms, 1992-93, article, C3950–1.511

Drugstore (independent pharmacy) financial and operating data, by store characteristics, 1991 and trends, annual survey, B5165–1

Drugstore and other retail outlet pharmacies and performance, 1993 annual feature, C5150–2.511

Drugstore chains financial performance and marketing operations, 1993 annual feature, C5150–2.510, C5150–2.511

Drugstore news and devs, with data on finances, operations, and marketing, biweekly rpt, C5150–2

Drugstore sales and merchandising trends, by product type and market area, 1992 annual feature, C5150–2.503

Electric utility (private vs public) revenues, by customer sector, 1990, annual article, A2625–1.501

Electric utility construction and capacity outlook, including data by region and fuel source, 1992-2001, annual feature, C5800–28.501

Electric utility demand-side mgmt programs and investment, by program type, 1992-95, article, C5800–28.502

Electric utility direct load-control budget, for 17 companies, 1993, article, C5800–28.508

Electric utility finances, sales, and capacity, 1993 annual feature, C5800–28.507

Electric utility financial and investment performance indicators, for top 50 companies, 1991, article, C5800–28.501

Electric utility financial and operating data, by State and census div, 1991 and trends, annual rpt, A4700–1

Electric utility financial and operating performance rankings, top 100 utilities, 1992, annual article, C6985–6.508

Electric utility financial and operating ratios, by customer size class and region, 1990, annual article, A2625–1.501

Electric utility income and operating data, by type of company and for individual locally owned utilities, 1993 annual directory, A2625–1.501

Electric utility income statement, bimonthly rpt quarterly tables, A4700–4

Electric utility industry construction expenditures, with detail by type of plant, 1991-95, recurring article, A4700–4.505

Electric utility revenues, sales, and distribution operating/maintenance expenses, for top 20 companies, 1990-91, article, C6985–6.501

Electrical equipment wholesaler market conditions, by geographic area, 1992 annual article, C4725–5.501

Electrical equipment wholesalers, sales, employment, and facility size, top 250 companies, 1992, annual article, C4725–5.506

Electronics company financial data and business info for approx 500 companies, 1991-92 and trends, annual rpt, C3400–4

Electronics company financial performance, for top 100 multinatl firms, 1992 annual feature, C1850–2.502

Electronics company financial performance, ranking of top 200 firms, 1992 and trends, annual feature, C1850–2.509

Electronics company revenues, funding, and employment, for 25 companies started in the recent past, 1993 recurring article, C1850–2.505

Electronics contract manufacturing sales of top 6 contractors, with selected detail by major customer, 1993 annual feature, C1850–2.510

Electronics industry factory sales and shipments, foreign trade, and operating data, by product category, 1980s-92, annual rpt, A4725–1

Electronics industry market devs, including employment, factory sales, prices, and foreign trade trends, monthly rpt, A4725–2

Electronics industry market outlook, by product category, 1989-93, annual feature, C1850–2.503

Electronics industry market trends and outlook, including product sales and shipments, employment, and leading manufacturers, monthly rpt, C1850–2

Entertainment industry devs and ticket sales, with detail for Broadway and road shows, and top films, weekly rpt, C9380–1

Environmental services firms and revenues by industry segment, with world revenues by region and/or country, 1990s, article, A1250–1.530

Financial instns performance, for 10 small/midsize instns with high returns on equity, 1992 article, C3950–1.502

Food (microwaveable) sales, 1992 and 1997, article, C2150–6.508

Food marketers financial and operating data, by company size and region, 1991-92, annual rpts, A4950–5

Food marketers mgmt info system operations, employment, and finances, for wholesalers and retailers by sales size, 1993 and trends, annual survey, A4950–7

Food private label product sales, for 7 product categories, 1992, article, C2150–6.504

Food processing industry devs, including work force reduction, finances, and employment, 1993 annual feature, C2150–6.507

Food service (institutional) financial and operating data, for leading firms by market segment, 1993 recurring feature, C1850–3.511

Food service CEO compensation, with comparisons to company performance, for top 75 executives, FY92, article, C1200–5.513

Food service industry financial and operating data, for top 100 chains and companies, FY91-93, annual feature, C5150–5.509

Food service industry health insurance coverage practices and costs, by company sales size, 1993 and trends, article, A8200–1.511

Food service industry sales and establishments, for top 400 chains and other organizations, 1992, annual feature, C1850–3.509

Food service industry sales and establishments, with growth outlook, by market segment, 1993 annual feature, C1850–3.503

Food service industry sales, market shares, establishments, and business activity indicators, by location, 1992, annual feature, C1200–5.515

Food service industry sales trends and forecast, by market segment, 1990-93, annual feature, A8200–1.502

Food service sales outlook, by industry segment and census div, 1992-93 and trends, annual feature, C5150–5.504

Food service sales, 1990-94, annual article, C5150–5.512

Food store industry structure, sales, operations, and business outlook, by type of store, 1993 annual rpt, C5225–1.505

Food store market shares and outlets, by company and store type, for approx 350 metro areas in US and Canada, with industry operating data, 1993 annual rpt, C3400–6

Food store product sales and consumer expenditures, by product type, 1991-92, annual feature, C4655–1.510

Food/lodging/entertainment establishments, employment, receipts, and payroll, and volume of printing business generated, 1992 feature, C1850–10.503

Foundation assets, income, and grants by type of recipient, with data for top organizations and by location, 1991 and trends, annual rpt, R4900–1

Foundation finances, and personnel and governing board characteristics, by organization characteristics, 1991/92, article, C2176–1.506

Foundations, assets, gifts received, expenditures, and grants, by State and census div, 1991 and trends, annual article, C2176–1.516

Fuel oil dealer sales by product, employment, computer use, and truck fleet size, by region, 1992 annual survey, C4680–2.1

Gold exploration spending of US-owned companies in US, Canada, Australia, Latin America, and elsewhere, 1989-92, articles, C5226–2.506

Greeting card sales, 1989-93, article, C4655–1.511

Hard goods manufacturers opinions on business issues and outlook, by product line, 1993 annual survey rpt, A1800–1

Hardware finances and operations, for hardware stores, home centers, and lumber/building material outlets, 1991 and trends, annual rpt series, A8275–1

Health insurance coverage by population characteristics and location, and underwriting results by type of insurer, 1940s-90, annual rpt, A5173–2.1

High-technology company sales and employment, for top 50 Hispanic-owned firms, 1992, annual article, C4575–1.510

High-technology small companies with rapid growth, employment and sales data for 25 firms, 1993 article, C5800–7.551

HMO financial data, including revenue sources and expenses by category, by plan characteristics, 1990, annual rpt, A5150–2.3

Index by Subjects and Names

Business income and expenses, specific industry

Home furnishings retailer financial and operating data, by firm characteristics and region, 1992 and trends, annual rpt, A7975–1

Home improvement industry sales and operations, for top distributors, cooperatives, and marketing organizations, 1991-92, annual feature, C5150–6.502

Home improvement industry sales and operations, for top retailers, 1992 and trends, annual feature, C5150–6.503

Home improvement industry sales and related data, by product category and for top 10 chains, 1992, article, C4725–5.507

Homebuilder financial and operating data, including detail by location, for top 400 builders, 1993 annual feature, C1850–8.507

Homebuilder operations and finances, by region and sales size group, 1992 survey, article, C4300–1.501

Hospital (public) revenues per capita, by State, 1991, article, B8500–2.518

Hospital directory, with utilization, expenses, and personnel, by instn, type, and location, 1992, annual rpt, A1865–3

Hospital financial and operating data, including ambulatory surgery and emergency service utilization, semimonthly rpt quarterly feature, A1865–1.506, A1865–1.512

Hospital industry financial and operating indicators, with detail for Medicare, by instn characteristics and location, 1988-92, annual rpt, B1880–1

Hospital pharmacy operating data, by instn type and size, and census div, 1991, annual survey, B5165–3

Hospital recruiting of nurses and allied health personnel, with budget, vacancies, turnover, and compensation, 1993 and trends, annual survey rpt, A6500–1

Household appliance industry manufacturing and market trends, by product type, various years 1920-94, biennial rpt, A3350–3

Housing construction, revenues, and closings of top 100 homebuilding companies, 1992, annual feature, C4300–1.507

Incubator facilities for new business, revenues and expenses, 1991, annual rpt, A7360–1

Industrial distributor sales, branches, employment, and operating profiles, for top 50 companies, 1992, annual article, C1850–4.506

Industrial distributor sales, employment, and inventory turns, for top 25 companies with sales of $5 million/less, 1991, annual article, C1850–4.503

Information technology company sales and employment, for 25 innovative firms, 1993 article, C8900–1.525

Insurance (accident/health) premiums and underwriting ratios, for top 300 firms, 1991, annual article, C1050–2.502

Insurance (health) administrative costs as percent of benefit payments, under current policy vs Bush Admin plan, by firm size, 1992 rpt, R4865–9

Insurance (life/health) income and expense data, for top 100 companies, 1992, annual article, C1050–2.511

Insurance (life/health) industry separate account performance, 1991, recurring article, C1050–2.505

Insurance (property/casualty) companies composite assets, income, and profitability, 1993 annual rpt, A5650–1

Insurance (property/casualty) company net premiums written, for top 100 firms, 1987-91, article, C1050–1.506

Insurance (property/casualty) income and expense data, for top 100 companies, 1992, article, C1050–1.511

Insurance (property/casualty) losses from Aug 1992 Hurricane Andrew, for 20 underwriters with greatest loss, 1992 article, C1050–1.503

Insurance (property/casualty) premiums, and expenses by category, for top 100 companies, 1991, article, C1050–1.504

Insurance (property/casualty) premiums, loss ratios, and market shares, for general liability, medical malpractice, fidelity, and surety, 1991 and trends, annual article, C1050–1.502

Insurance (property/casualty) premiums, loss ratios, and market shares, for workers compensation, 1991 and trends, annual article, C1050–1.501

Insurance (property/casualty) premiums of top 100 firms, with A M Best Co financial ratings, 1993 annual article, C1050–1.510

Insurance (property/casualty) premiums written and operating ratios, by company type and line of coverage, 1988-92, annual article, C1050–1.504

Insurance (property/casualty) premiums written by top 250 companies and groups, 1992, annual article, C1050–1.508

Insurance (property/casualty) premiums written, loss ratios, and market shares, by line, leading company, and State, 1992 and trends, annual article, C1050–1.509

Interior design industry financial and employment data, top 100 firms, 1993 annual article, C1850–7.501

Interior design industry financial and employment data, 2nd 100 largest firms, 1993 annual article, C1850–7.502

Iron and steel industry financial and operating data, 1992 and trends, annual rpt, A2000–2.1

Jewelry and watch manufacturing and marketing trends, new product dev, prices, trade, and related indicators, monthly rpt, C2150–7

Jewelry industry sales, 1st and 2nd halves 1988-92, annual article, C2150–7.507

Jewelry industry statistics on sales, marketing, trade, and employment, with customer characteristics, 1993 annual almanac, C2150–7.509

Jewelry trade assns financial performance data, for 5 organizations, 1991 or FY92, article, C2150–7.505

Legal services establishments, employment, receipts, and payroll, and volume of printing business generated, 1992 feature, C1850–10.502

Library automated system installations worldwide and in US, and vendor revenues, by vendor, 1992 and trends, annual articles, C1852–1.505, C1852–1.506

Life insurance (universal, whole, and term) sales results, for 115 companies, 1992, annual article, C1050–2.511

Life insurance annuity premium income and fund deposits of top 200 insurers, 1991, annual article, C1050–2.501

Life insurance average policy issued and in force, for 150 companies, 1981 and 1987-91, annual article, C1050–2.502

Life insurance average policyholder premiums and dividends, 10-year dividend scale comparisons, by insurer, 1993 annual article, C1050–2.510

Life insurance average policyholder premiums and dividends, 20-year dividend scale comparisons, by insurer, 1993 annual article, C1050–2.509

Life insurance individual policy sales indicators, monthly rpt, A6225–1

Life insurance industry income and financial data, including investments by type of security, 1991 and trends, biennial fact book, A1325–1.4

Life insurance premium income of top 500 US/Canadian life/health insurers, 1992 and trends, annual article, C1050–2.509

Life insurance premiums, and expenses by category, for top 100 companies, 1991, article, C1050–2.503

Life insurance sales and insurance in force, for top 25-135 issuers of ordinary, group, and industrial life policies, 1992, annual article, C1050–2.510

Life insurance variable annuity and variable life premiums/deposits, for top life/health insurers, 1992, annual article, C1050–2.512

Life insurance variable annuity fund premium income and deposits, for top life/health insurers, 1991, annual article, C1050–2.503

Liquor market statistics, including sales, consumption, trade, distillery operations, and govtl info, with data by company, brand, and location, 1992 and trends, annual rpt, C4775–1

Lodging industry facilities, sales, and occupancy, with top 42-100 properties in 5 market categories, 1993 annual rpt, C7000–5

Machine tool industry finances and ratios, 1992 and trends, annual rpt, A3179–2.1

Magazine advertising revenues, for top 5 group publishers, 1st qtr 1993, article, C2710–1.526

Magazine circulation building strategies, including cost of a new subscriber and renewal data, 1993 survey, article, C2575–1.513

Magazine revenues, advertising pages, and circulation, for top 300 publications, 1992, annual article, C2710–1.531

Magazine revenues, circulation, advertising, and rates, for top 500 consumer and business publications, 1992, annual article, C2575–1.515

Magnetic resonance imaging (MRI) machine manufacturer sales and stock performance, for 6 companies, 1992 article, C3950–1.504

Market research industry devs, including revenues and operations of leading firms, 1991-92, annual feature, C2710–1.550

Mass media advertising revenues, by medium, 1990-92, article, C1200–1.513

Mass media company revenues for leading firms, with detail by medium, 1991-92, annual feature, C2710–1.540

Business income and expenses, specific industry

Index by Subjects and Names

Mass media expenditures on TV, cable TV, and radio, 1992 and 1997, article, C1850–14.530

Mass transit industry statistics, including govt funding, vehicle purchasing, and bus production, 1992/93 annual fact book, C1575–3.501

Mass transit system finances and operations, passengers, and employment, by mode, US and Canada, 1990-91 and trends, annual rpt, A2650–1

Meat and poultry demand, prices, and processor operations and finances, with data on meat production, 1991 and trends, annual rpt, A2100–1.1

Medical group financial and operating data, by practice characteristics, 1991, annual rpt, A6365–2

Medical group physician and allied personnel compensation and productivity, by specialty, and demographic and practice characteristics, 1991, annual rpt, A6365–1

Metal heat treatment industry billings, for Michigan, Canada, and 7 regions, monthly press release, A6376–1

Military commissary supplier payments from Defense Commissary Agency, for 406 suppliers receiving $1 million/more, FY92, article, C0500–1.506

Military post exchange (Army/Air Force), sales of approx 700 top supplier companies, for year ended Jan 1993, annual feature, C0500–1.505

Military post exchange (Navy) sales of approx 200 supplier companies, and sales by Navy store and dept, FY92 and trends, annual feature, C0500–1.507

Mineral exploration activities, expenses, and staff, for foreign and domestic operations of US and Canadian companies, 1991, article, C5226–2.508

Mortgage banking industry aggregate financial and operating data, by lending characteristics and type of ownership, 1989 and trends, annual rpt, A6450–3

Mortgage banking industry computer system expenses by category, with detail for hardware by type, 1988, article, A6450–2.505

Mortgage banking industry loan production, servicing, and secondary marketing volume, revenues, and expenses, 1989-91, article, A6400–2.502

Mortgage insurance industry finances and performance indicators, 1988-91, annual rpt, A6455–1

Motion picture rental income for all-time top films, 1993 annual feature, C9380–1.514, C9380–1.525

Motion picture rental income, rankings of top all-time films, 1993 annual feature, C9380–1.509

Motion picture rental income, rankings of top films, 1992, annual feature, C9380–1.509

Motor carrier revenues, expenses, and rates of return granted by regulatory agencies, by company and State, 1991, annual rpt, A7015–4

Motor vehicle component manufacturers total and component sales, for top 13 companies worldwide, 1993 article, C2150–3.509

Motor vehicle, dealership, and related industries operating data, with data by State and industry segment, 1990s and trends, annual rpt, A0865–1.3

Motor vehicle dealership financial and operating data, including sales and employment by State, 1970s-93, annual rpt, A7330–1

Motor vehicle fleet mgmt industry maintenance/repair costs for autos and light trucks, FY91-92, C1575–2.505

Motor vehicle fleet operating and financial data, including fleets by type, registrations by make and model, and top lessors, 1970s-93, annual rpt, C1575–2.507

Motor vehicle fleet operating costs by type and region, 1991-92, article, C1575–2.508

Motor vehicle fleet operating costs for autos and light trucks, 1990-92, article, C1575–2.501

Motor vehicle industry sales, with leading dealers, 1993 annual data book, C2710–3.531

Motor vehicle production, revenues, and profits, for top 30 manufacturers worldwide, 1992, article, C8900–1.526

Motorcycle market devs, including production, sales, imports, dealer operations, and owner characteristics, 1991 and trends, annual rpt, A6485–1

Museums and related instns financial structure, including donation programs, income, and expenses, by type, budget size, and governing authority, 1989/90 survey, A0750–1.3

Musical instrument and accessory shipment volume and/or retail value, and foreign trade, by product type, 1992 and trends, annual rpt, A6848–1

Mutual fund investment performance, by fund, June 1993 and trends, annual compilation, C3950–1.522

Mutual fund sales, assets, and investment activities, with data on money market and municipal bond funds, monthly rpt, A6025–5

Natural gas distribution utility and pipeline company financial and operating data, top 500 companies, 1992, annual article, C6780–1.505

Natural gas industry composite income statement, with sales and prices by consuming sector and census div, quarterly rpt, A1775–1

Natural gas industry detailed operating and financial data, by State and census div, 1960s-91, annual rpt, A1775–3

Newspaper trends in revenues from advertising and circulation, and advertising dept costs, 1992 features, A8605–1.503

Nonprofit organization assets, and expenses by item, for 7 organizations, 1991, article, C2176–1.508

Nonprofit organization executive compensation, with comparison to organization income, by leading organization, FY91 or FY92, article, C2176–1.509

Nonprofit organizations private support, income, and services and fundraising costs, for top 400 organizations, FY91 or FY92, annual article, C2176–1.501

Office building detailed income and expense data, and energy use, US and Canada, by building characteristics, metro area, and US region, 1991 and trends, annual rpt, A5600–2

Office product dealer financial and operating data, by sales volume and region, 1991 and trends, annual rpt, A8110–1

Oil and gas drilling costs, and exploration/dev expenditures, 1973-92, annual rpt, A5425–2.2

Oil and gas independent company finances and operations, for approx 50 companies, 1991-92, semiannual article, C6985–1.504

Oil and gas industry expenditures for exploration, dev, and production, 1991 and trends, annual survey rpt, A2575–20

Oil and gas industry exploration, production, refining, demand, finance, prices, and reserves, by State and country or world area, 1992 and trends, periodic basic data book, A2575–14.3

Oil and gas industry financial and operating data, rankings for top 300 US and top 100 non-US companies, 1991-92, annual feature, C6985–1.547

Oil and gas industry intl exploration, drilling, production, refining, stock, price, and financial data, weekly rpt, C6985–1

Oil and gas industry revenues, capital spending, and cost outlook, for onshore and offshore areas and Alaska, 1990-2010, A2575–25

Oil and gas industry trends, with data by company, State, and country, 1993 annual compilation, C6985–4

Oil and gas intl supply-demand, exploration, refining, reserves, and industry finances, basic data by country and company, 1993 annual rpt, C6985–3

Oil and gas pipeline construction costs, mileage, and operating and financial data, by location and/or company, 1991 and trends, annual feature, C6985–1.504

Oil company earnings, for approx 20 companies, monthly rpt quarterly article, C4680–1.501, C4680–1.504, C4680–1.506, C4680–1.510

Oil exploration/production expenditures of US and foreign companies in US, Canada, and elsewhere, 1992-93, annual article, C6985–1.515

Oil industry environmental performance, with data on toxic chemical releases, oil spills, occupational injury/illness, and corporate spending, 1990 and trends, annual rpt, A2575–27

Oil industry financial and operating data for major companies, 1993 annual fact book, C4680–1.507

Oil industry income and operating data, for approx 20 major companies, 1991-92, annual article, C6985–1.533

Oil industry income, net profits, and selected operating data, approx 25 companies, weekly rpt quarterly article, C6985–1.520, C6985–1.534, C6985–1.545

Oil industry income, net profits, and selected operating data, approx 50 companies, 1st 9 months 1991-92, article, C6985–1.511

Oil industry revenues vs capital spending and drilling costs, 1970s-2001, annual rpt, C6985–5.2

Index by Subjects and Names

Business income and expenses, specific industry

Oil industry wellhead revenues, drilling expenditures, and taxes, 1991 and trends, annual compilation, C6985–9.3

Oil refiners net income, for top 22 companies, 1st 9 months 1991-92, article, C6985–1.507

Oil/gas industry production, finances, exploration, and reserves, by State, 1992 and trends, annual rpt, A5425–1

Olive oil sales and market shares for top 6 brands, year ended July 1993, article, C2710–1.543

Oral care product sales in food stores, for 12 manufacturers, year ended June 1993, article, C4655–1.511

Paper distribution industry financial performance, 2nd qtr 1992 and trends, article, A8140–3.501

Paper industry sales and earnings of individual companies in US and Canada, monthly rpt quarterly feature, C3975–2.502, C3975–2.503, C3975–2.505, C3975–2.506, C3975–2.508, C3975–2.511, C3975–2.512

Paperboard rigid paper box billings, 1988-92, annual article, C0125–4.504

Pharmaceutical industry financial performance for 10 major companies, and sales of top 10 prescription drugs, 1993 article, C8900–1.514

Pharmaceutical industry spending for direct-to-consumer advertising, 1987-92, article, C2710–1.509

Physician practice economic aspects, detailed data by specialty, 1991-92 and trends, annual compilation, A2200–5

Planning consultant firm revenues, 1991, biennial rpt, A2615–1

Plastics industry production and sales by resin type, consumption by end-use market, and operating characteristics, 1992 and trends, annual rpt, A8920–1

Plastics processing industry financial and operating ratios, by processing activity, sales size, and region, 1992, annual rpt, A8920–4

Plastics specialty materials manufacturer income, R&D expenditures, and stock performance, for 10 companies, 1992, article, C3950–1.511

Printing and publishing industries operations and outlook, including paper shipments and prices, monthly rpt, C1850–10

Printing company sales, employment, and equipment, for top 101 North American firms, 1993 annual feature, C1850–10.512

Public electric and gas utility sales or revenues, by service class, commodity yearbook for 1993, C2400–1

Public electric and gas utility sales or revenues, by service class, commodity yearbook Jan-Sept 1993 updates, C2400–2

Public relations firm budgets and billings, 1993 survey, annual article, A8770–1.503

Public utility expenditures for computer/info systems, software, and related services, 1990 and 1995, article, A4700–4.502

Publisher advertising revenues, for top 10 companies, 1st half 1993, C2710–1.538

Publisher advertising revenues, for top 10 companies, 1st 9 months 1992-93, C2710–1.551

Publisher advertising revenues, for top 10 companies, 1992, C2710–1.513

Publishing industry sales, 1991-93, recurring feature, C1850–10.506

Publishing industry sales, 1992-94, recurring feature, C1850–10.513

Pulp and paper industry operations and finances, US and Canada, with detail by company and product grade, and world production and trade summary, 1993 annual rpt, C3975–5

Pulp and paper mill machine maintenance operations and personnel, by region and grade, 1992 survey, recurring article, C3975–2.504

Pulp, paper, and allied products financial and operating data, 1950s-92, annual rpt, A1630–6.4

Pulp, paper, and paperboard industry production, trade, and operating data, by product class, monthly rpt, A1630–5

Radio advertising revenues, and expenditures of top advertisers, 1992 and trends, annual rpt, A8789–1

Radio audience size, leading stations and formats, and advertising rates and revenues, by market area, recurring rpt, C3165–1

Railroad (Class I) financial condition, operations, and employment, by company and district, 1992, annual rpt, A3275–7

Railroad (Class I) freight service expenditures by category, and diesel fuel consumption, with detail for 7 companies, 1991, article, C8400–1.508

Railroad (Class I) traffic, employment, finances, and equipment, by district and State, 1920s-92, annual rpt, A3275–5

Railroad costs to repair damage resulting from Midwestern floods of 1993, article, C8400–1.511

Railroad financial and operating trends, including data by company, 1982-91, annual rpt, A3275–8

Railroad financial performance and expenses, by Class I railroad and district, quarterly rpt, A3275–1

Railroad financial performance, including fuel use and costs, and returns on investment for 11 companies, 1990-93, article, C8400–1.509

Railroad operating revenues for 4 lines in Texas and for Mexico natl railroad, 1992, U8850–9

Railroad wheel tread loss (shelling/spalling) incidence and repair costs, 1987-91, article, C8400–1.505

Real estate residential brokerage firm finances and operations, with data by region and company size, 1990/91 and trends, article, A7000–1.502

Recording industry sales of Spanish-language music, for 6 leading and all other companies, 1992, article, C4575–1.508

Religious congregation characteristics, including membership, activities, staff, and finances, 1992 survey, recurring rpt, A5435–4

Religious congregation finances, and participation in charitable activities by detailed type, 1991 survey, article, C2176–1.512

Rental equipment industry financial data, by revenue size group and region, and for Canada, 1991 and trends, annual rpt, A2665–1

Restaurant (hamburger) establishments by census div, and sales and units for top 10 chains, 1993 annual article, C1200–5.504

Restaurant (Mexican food) establishments by census div, and sales and/or units for top 4-5 chains, 1993 annual article, C1200–5.514

Restaurant (Mexican food) sales, for top 5 chains, 1991, article, C1200–5.507

Restaurant (pizza) establishments by census div, and sales and units for top 10 chains, 1992, annual article, C1200–5.506

Restaurant chain sales, for 10 fastest-growing companies, 1990-93, article, C1850–3.510

Restaurant franchises and sales, and franchisee fees and investment required, by leading company, 1993 annual feature, C1200–5.512

Restaurant industry expansion outlook and operating data, by census div and MSA, 1993 annual articles, C1850–3.506

Restaurant industry financial and operating data, by establishment characteristics and location, 1992, annual rpt, A8200–3

Restaurant sales and operations of 20 organizations with outstanding marketing concepts, 1993 article, C1850–3.508

Restaurant sales and units, for 50 fastest-growing chains, 1991-92, annual article, C1200–5.513

Restaurant sales, payroll/benefits, and employment, with detail for hotel establishments, 1993 article, C5150–5.507

Restaurant sales, population age 25-44, and household income, with detail for suburban areas, 1991, article, C1200–5.501

Restaurant utility costs, by type of utility and operation, 1990-91, article, A8200–1.507

Restaurants with independent owners, sales, seating capacity, average check size, and patrons served, top 100 instns, 1992, annual article, C1850–3.505

Restaurants/drinking places and sales, for minority-owned establishments by race-ethnicity, 1987, article, A8200–1.508

Sales promotion income, for top sales promotion and promotional services agencies, 1991-92, annual feature, C2710–1.527

Savings instn economic issues and devs, with quarterly data on financial condition by instn type and State, monthly rpt, A8813–1

Securities industry analyses, with data on underwriting and trading activity, and financial trends, periodic rpt, A8825–1

Securities industry financial performance and activities, with data by type of firm, 1st 5 months 1993 and trends, recurring article, A8825–1.505

Securities industry financial performance and activities, with data by type of firm, 1992 and trends, recurring article, A8825–1.503

Security equipment industry outlook, including revenue trends, and home alarm system prices, Oct-Nov 1992 survey, annual feature, C1850–13.503

Security equipment industry revenues, accounts, and operating data, for 100 leading companies, 1992, annual feature, C1850–13.507

Business income and expenses, specific industry

Index by Subjects and Names

Shoe industry market data, including foreign trade, production, and sales, by product type, 1991 and trends, annual rpt, A4957–1.1

Shoe industry production and operating data, including trade by country, retail sales, and consumer expenditures, quarterly rpt, A4957–2

Shopping center detailed income and expense data, by building characteristics, metro area, and region, 1991, annual rpt, A5600–6

Shopping center financial and operating data, with detail by type of tenant, US and Canada, 1991, triennial rpt, R9285–1

Shopping center security operations budget, by center type, 1992, article, C5150–4.506

Snack food sales, consumption, and prices, by snack type and region, with data on industry operations and outlook, 1992 and trends, annual rpt, A8905–1

Space-related commercial revenues worldwide, by source, 1992, article, C5800–4.518

Sporting goods sales by product category, 1983-92, annual survey rpt, A8485–4

Steel industry finances, operations, and employment, with data for integrated plants and mini-mills, 1970s-93, article, U2160–1.503

Steel service center business conditions and outlook, monthly survey, A8990–2

Stockbroker income and employment, for 8 major securities firms, 1992, article, C5800–7.509

Sulfur sales, for product recovered from oil/gas processing vs mine production, 1982-91, article, C6985–1.514

Supermarket (independent) sales and operating ratios, by store type, sales size, and region, 1991, annual survey, A4950–4

Supermarket bakery dept sales and performance indicators, 1992 and trends, annual article, C4655–1.505, C5225–1.504

Supermarket deli dept sales and performance indicators, 1992 and trends, annual article, C5225–1.505

Supermarket deli dept sales and performance indicators, 1992, annual article, C4655–1.503

Supermarket fish/seafood dept sales and performance indicators, 1991, annual article, C4655–1.501

Supermarket general merchandise dept sales and performance indicators, 1992 and trends, annual article, C4655–1.509

Supermarket health and beauty aid dept sales and performance indicators, 1992 and trends, annual article, C4655–1.506

Supermarket industry total and leveraged buyout related debt, and sales for total and leveraged companies, 1985-91, article, C5225–1.506

Supermarket meat dept sales and performance indicators, 1992 and trends, annual article, C4655–1.509

Supermarket microwaveable food sales, by product category, 1st half 1992, article, C2150–6.510

Supermarket prepared food sales and performance indicators, 1992, annual article, C4655–1.508

Supermarket produce dept sales and performance indicators, 1992 and trends, annual article, C4655–1.511

Supermarket sales by detailed product type, 1992 and trends, annual feature, C5225–1.507

Supermarket sales of health/beauty care products by detailed type, year ended June 1993, article, C4655–1.511

Supermarket sales of nonfood products, by detailed product type, 1992, annual feature, C5225–1.508

Supermarket sales trends for private label products, with detail for health/beauty aid and general merchandise depts, 1993 article, C8130–1.504

Supermarkets opened, remodeled, and closed, including store features, dev costs, and rent, by region and sales size, 1992 and trends, annual rpt, A4950–2

Telephone company revenues, access lines, and vulnerability to local services competition, by major company, 1992 and trends, article, C4725–3.511

Telephone company revenues from frame relay and switched multimegabit data services, 1993-96, article, C4725–3.503

Telephone company revenues in 1992, and stock gains since 1984 breakup of AT&T, for 7 Bell regional holding companies, 1993 article, C5800–7.552

Telephone holding company finances, operations, and subsidiaries, by company, Dec 1991, annual rpt, A9360–1

Telephone local exchange carrier finances, equipment, and employment, by company, 1991 and trends, annual rpt, A9360–2

Telephone long-distance carrier revenues from toll-free ("800" number) service, for top 3 companies and all others, 1992-97, article, C1200–1.504

Telephone Yellow Pages publisher revenues and advertising agency/media buying service billings, for top 10-15 firms, 1992, article, C2710–1.546

Textile and clothing companies financial data, for approx 170 firms, with industry statistical summary, 1991-92 and trends, annual rpt, C3400–5

Textile industry economic performance indicators and outlook, with industry trends and devs, monthly rpt, C5226–3

Textile industry financial performance indicators for 32 companies, FY92 and trends, annual rpt, B8130–1

Theater (nonprofit professional) finances and operations, including revenues by source, 1992 and trends, annual survey, A9065–1

Theater (nonprofit professional) finances and operations, 1992, article, C2176–1.509

Theater receipts, attendance, and shows and weeks played, 1992/93 and trends, annual features, C9380–1.529

Tobacco advertising expenditures in magazines, with detail for top 4 publications, 1981 and 1991, article, C2575–1.503

Transportation operation and finance trends, by mode, 1992 annual rpt, R4815–1

Travel industry sales rankings for top 10-20 companies in selected industry sectors, 1992 recurring rpt, R9375–6

Truck (heavy-duty) dealership average financial results, 1988-92, annual article, C2710–3.525

Truck equipment distributor financial data, by company type, sales size, and rural vs metro market, FY91 and trends, annual rpt, A8505–4

Truck fleet financial and operating data for top 200 freight carriers, 1992 and trends, annual feature, C2150–4.504

TV (Spanish-language) network revenues, operating loss, and cash flow, for 2 major networks, 1989-92, article, C4575–1.502

TV advertising revenues generated by 6 prime-time news magazine programs, 1992 article, C1850–14.503

TV home shopping network sales, income, and homes reached, FY92, article, C5150–3.516

TV network advertising revenues, by daypart and program type, weekly rpt quarterly feature, C1850–14.503, C1850–14.513, C1850–14.522, C1850–14.535

TV network summer Olympic games broadcast rights payments, advertising revenues, and audience ratings, quadrennially 1976-96, article, C1850–14.532

TV station FCC user fees vs cash flow, by market size or per cable subscriber, 1993 article, C1850–14.534

TV station revenues, for top 20 cities, 1993, C1850–14.518

Unit investment trust sales volume and value, by trust type, maturity period, and insurance features, monthly rpt, A6025 7

Utility regulatory agency policies and practices, and industry financial and operating data, by utility type and agency, 1991/92 annual rpt, A7015–3

Vending machine sales by product type, and machines on location, 1992 and trends, annual rpt, C9470–1

Veterinarian (equine) characteristics and finances, and practice profile, 1992 survey and trends, annual article, C9480–1.503

Veterinarian fees, and average client transaction, by region and type of practice, 1993, annual survey, C9480–1.507

Veterinarian practice expenses as percent of revenues, by expenditure category and type of practice, 1990-91, annual survey article, C9480–1.501

Veterinarian practice revenue, by practice type and region, 1992, annual survey article, C9480–1.506

Veterinarians by professional characteristics and location, and financial and education summaries, 1993 annual directory, A3100–1

Veterinary clinic construction costs, by clinic type, 1992-93, annual article, C9480–1.504

Veterinary practice income, expenses by item, and financial ratios, by type of practice, 1991, biennial survey article, A3100–2.510

Video game manufacturer sales and stock performance, for 6 companies, 1993 article, C3950–1.521

Wine market statistics, including sales, production, trade, and consumer characteristics, with data by company, brand, and geographic area, 1992 and trends, annual rpt, C4775–2

Index by Subjects and Names

Business income and expenses, specific industry

Workers compensation insurance residual market underwriting loss or gain, burden, and market shares, by State, 1991 and trends, annual rpt, A0375–3

State and local:

- Alabama insurance industry financial and underwriting data, by company and line of coverage, 1991, annual rpt, S0160–1
- Alabama small loan and consumer credit licensee finances and loan analysis, Dec 1991, annual rpt, S0110–1
- Alabama statistical abstract, general data, 1992 recurring rpt, U5680–2.8
- Alaska insurance industry underwriting and investment data, by company and type of insurance, with regulatory info, 1991 and trends, annual rpt, S0280–3
- Alaska prison industry sales, FY88-91, annual rpt, S0287–1
- Alaska public utility financial and operating data, by company and utility type, 1991 and trends, with FY92 regulatory info, annual rpt, S0280–4
- Arizona insurance industry financial and underwriting data, by company and type of insurance, with regulatory info, 1992, annual rpt, S0483–1
- Arkansas public utility financial, operating, and regulatory data, by utility type and company, 1992 annual rpt, S0757–1
- California banks and trust companies, financial condition by instn, with regulatory info, Dec 1992, annual rpt, S0810–1
- California insurance industry financial and underwriting data, by company and type of insurance, with regulatory info, 1991, annual rpt, S0900–1
- California public utility and transportation regulatory data, including revenue requests and rates of return by company, FY92 annual rpt, S0930–1
- Connecticut banks and other financial instns, financial condition by instn, 1991 and trends, annual rpt, S1160–1
- Connecticut insurance industry financial and underwriting data, by company and type of insurance, 1991, annual rpt, S1222–1
- Florida insurance industry financial and underwriting data, by company and line of coverage, 1991, annual rpt, S1760–1
- Florida public utility regulatory and operating data, by company and utility type, 1992 and trends, annual rpt, S1790–1
- Georgia banks and other financial instns, financial condition by instn type, and assets by instn and city, Dec 1992, annual rpt, S1865–1
- Idaho insurance industry financial and underwriting data, by company and type of insurance, with regulatory data, 1991, annual rpt, S2260–1
- Illinois bank and trust companies (State-chartered) financial condition and status changes, by instn, FY92, annual rpt, S2395–1
- Illinois electric and gas utility sales and operating revenues, and customers served, by class of service and company, 1991-92, annual rpt series, S2410–1
- Illinois Financial Institutions Dept activities, with financial and regulatory data for credit unions, consumer lenders, and other businesses, FY91 annual rpt, S2457–2

Illinois telephone utility financial and operating data, by company, 1992, annual rpt, S2410–2

- Indiana financial instns (State-chartered) financial condition, including assets by instn arranged by city, 1991 and trends, annual rpt, S2625–1
- Iowa bank and trust companies (State-chartered), financial condition by instn arranged by city, FY92 annual rpt, S2760–2
- Iowa insurance industry financial and underwriting data, by company and type of insurance, 1992, annual rpt, S2760–1
- Kansas insurance industry financial and underwriting data, by company and type of insurance, with regulatory info, 1992, annual rpt, S2990–1
- Kentucky financial instns condition, including assets by instn and city, with regulatory info, 1992 and trends, annual rpt, S3121–1
- Maryland banks and credit unions (State-chartered) financial condition by instn, with regulatory data, FY92 annual rpt, S3655–2
- Maryland insurance industry financial and underwriting data, by company and type of insurance, with regulatory info, 1991, annual rpt, S3655–1
- Michigan banks and other financial instns, financial condition by instn, with regulatory info, 1992 and trends, annual rpt, S3957–1
- Michigan insurance industry financial and underwriting data, by company and type of insurance, with regulatory info, 1991, annual rpt, S3983–1
- Michigan prison industries sales, by factory, FY90-91, annual rpt, S3960–1
- Minnesota insurance industry financial and underwriting data, by company and line of coverage, 1991, annual rpt, S4140–4
- Mississippi small loan lender income and expense statement, Dec 1992, annual rpt, S4325–1
- Missouri banks and trust companies (State-chartered) financial condition, by instn, FY91-92 and trends, biennial rpt, S4502–1
- Missouri insurance industry financial and underwriting data, by company and type of insurance, with regulatory info, 1992, annual rpt, S4527–1
- Montana health care facility capacity, utilization, and finances, by instn, 1991, annual rpt, S4690–2
- Nebraska insurance industry financial and underwriting data, by company and line of coverage, with regulatory info, 1992, annual rpt, S4890–1
- Nevada casino finances and employment, by location and gaming revenue range, FY92, annual rpt, S5062–1
- Nevada gaming revenues and taxes, FY83-92, annual rpt, S5025–1
- New Jersey casino revenues and operations for 12 facilities, with State regulatory activities, 1992 and trends, annual rpt, S5360–1
- New Jersey insurance industry financial and underwriting data, by company and type of insurance, 1990, annual rpt, S5420–1
- New Mexico financial instns, financial and operating data by instn, with regulatory activities, 1992, annual rpt, S5652–1

New Mexico public utility operating, financial, and regulatory data, by utility type, FY92 annual rpt, S5645–1

- New York State electric utility demand-side mgmt expenditures, and resulting demand reductions, for 7 companies, 1993-94, article, C6985–6.505
- New York State insurance industry devs, finances, and regulatory activity, 1990/91 and trends, annual rpt, S5770–3
- New York State insurance industry financial and underwriting data, by company and line of coverage, 1991, annual rpt, S5770–2
- New York State public utility financial and operating data, by utility type and company, 1988-92, annual rpt, S5795–1
- North Carolina public utility financial, operating, and regulatory data, by utility type and company, 1990 and trends, annual rpt, S5917–2
- Ohio prison industries profit-loss status, FY91, annual rpt, S6370–1
- Oklahoma insurance industry financial and underwriting data, by company and type of insurance, with regulatory info, 1992, annual rpt, S6462–1
- Oregon financial instns, financial condition by instn, Dec 1992 and trends, annual rpt, S6616–1
- Pennsylvania insurance industry financial and underwriting data, by company and line of coverage, 1991, with FY92 regulatory info, annual rpt, S6835–1
- Rhode Island insurance industry financial and underwriting data, by company and line of coverage, 1990, with FY91 regulatory info, annual rpt, S6945–2
- South Carolina financial instns (State-chartered) financial condition, including data by instn, FY92 annual rpt, S7165–1
- South Carolina insurance industry financial and underwriting data, by company, 1991, with FY92 regulatory info, annual rpt, S7195–1
- South Carolina public service commission regulatory activities, with financial and operating data for individual utilities and railroads, FY92 annual rpt, S7235–1
- South Dakota insurance industry financial and underwriting data, by company and type of insurance, with regulatory info, 1991-92, annual rpt, S7300–2
- Tennessee banks and other financial instns financial condition, by instn and city, 1992 annual rpt, S7507–1
- Tennessee insurance industry financial and underwriting data, by company and type of insurance, with regulatory info, 1991, annual rpt, S7466–1
- Tennessee public utility and transportation commission regulatory activities, with industry financial and operating data, 1991-92 biennial rpt, S7565–1
- Texas electric utility financial and operating data, 9 largest investor-owned utilities, 1988-92, annual rpt, S7740–1
- Texas hospitals, operations, utilization, and finances, by type, ownership, size, and metro-nonmetro status, 1970s-91, U8850–8.3
- Texas insurance dept regulatory activities, with industry financial and underwriting data by line of coverage, FY92 annual rpt, S7700–1

Business income and expenses, specific industry

Texas natural gas utility financial and operating data, by city and company, 1991, with regulatory info, annual rpt, S7745–1

Utah banks and other financial instns, financial condition by instn, FY93 and trends, annual rpt, S7830–1

Utah high-technology industry trends, with R&D spending, and employment of major firms, 1986-92, recurring article, U8960–2.508

Utah insurance industry financial and underwriting data, by company and line of coverage, with regulatory info, 1991, annual rpt, S7845–1

Vermont banks and other financial instns, financial condition by instn, 1992 and trends, annual rpt, S7995–2

Vermont insurance industry financial and underwriting data, by company and type of insurance, 1991, annual rpt, S7995–1

Vermont public utility financial and operating data, by company, 1986-91, biennial rpt, S8100–1

Virginia banks and credit unions (State-chartered) composite income and expenses, 1991-92, annual rpt, S8180–2

Virginia finance companies composite income and expenses, Dec 1992, annual rpt, S8180–3

Washington State banks and other financial instns, financial condition by type of instn, 1992 and trends, annual rpt, S8325–1

Washington State electric utility financial and operating data, by company, 1982-91, annual rpt, S8450–1.2

Washington State natural gas utility financial and operating data, by company, 1982-91, annual rpt, S8450–1.3

Washington State telecommunication industry financial and operating data, by company, 1988-91, annual rpt, S8450–1.5

Washington State water utilitics financial and operating data, by company, 1988-90, annual rpt, S8450–1.1

Washington State water utilities financial and operating data, by company, 1989-91, annual rpt, S8450–1.4

West Virginia banks and other financial instns, composite financial condition, with selected data by instn, 1990-91, annual rpt, S8530–1

West Virginia insurance industry financial and underwriting data, by company and line of coverage, with regulatory info, 1991, annual rpt, S8575–1

Wisconsin banks financial condition, by instn and city, with regulatory info, 1992 and trends, annual rpt, S8685–1

Wisconsin insurance industry financial and underwriting data, by company and line of coverage, with regulatory info, 1992, annual rpt, S8755–1

Wisconsin railroad and urban transit system revenues, various years 1920-92, biennial rpt, S8780–1.2

Wisconsin savings and loan assns and savings banks (State-chartered) financial condition, by instn, 1992 and trends, annual rpt, S8807–1

see also Agricultural finance
see also Agricultural marketing
see also Agricultural production costs

see also Broadcast payments and rights
see also Business assets and liabilities, specific industry
see also Business expense allowances
see also Capital investments
see also Cost-of-doing-business surveys
see also Depreciation
see also Educational finance
see also Energy production costs
see also Farm income
see also Foreign corporations
see also Labor costs and cost indexes
see also Operating ratios
see also Payroll
see also Production costs
see also Professionals' fees
see also under By Industry in the "Index by Categories"
see also under name of specific commodity (for sales data)

Business inventories

Aircraft (jet) in storage, by model, Mar and Aug 1992, article, C7000–4.502

Aircraft (jet) world inventory, orders, and deliveries, by type of aircraft and individual owner/operator, 1992 and trends, annual rpt, B1582–1

Aluminum inventories, by US supplier type and foreign country, 1982-92, annual rpt, A0400–2

Aluminum shipments, orders, and inventories by product class, and foreign trade for ingot, scrap, and mill products, monthly rpt, A0400–1

Auto aftermarket company financial and operating data, including sales, income, stores, and inventory turns, for 8-12 public firms, 1993 article, C2150–10.508

Auto aftermarket retail performance indicators, by product category, 1992 article, C2150–10.501

Auto dealer inventories, monthly rpt, B4950–1

Auto domestic and import inventories, Jan 1988-Apr 1993, annual data book, C2710 3.531

Auto news and devs, with production and sales data and market analysis, US and foreign, by manufacturer and make/model, weekly rpt, C2710–3

Auto parts/supplies and repair aftermarket sales performance, by product group, 1993 annual feature, C0125–1.503

Book publishing industry financial and operating data, by publisher type and size, and subject category, 1991 and trends, annual rpt, A3274–2

Brewers operations and expenses, detailed data, 1956-90, annual rpt, A3455–1.2

Business forms industry detailed financial and operating ratios, with summary operating data, FY91, annual rpt, A5785–3

Business forms industry trends and outlook, including data by product type, 1992 annual rpt, A5785–2

Chemical industry finances and operations, with data by industry segment and product, 1970s-92, annual rpt, A3850–1

Clothing and shoe industries financial performance indicators for 72 companies, FY92 and trends, annual rpt, B8130–2

Commodity yearbook for 1993: production, stocks, trade, and prices for approx 100 agricultural and industrial materials, including by country and producing State, C2400–1

Index by Subjects and Names

Commodity yearbook update: production, stocks, trade, and prices for approx 100 basic commodities, including by country and producing State, Jan-Sept 1993 rpts, C2400–2

Computer/info processing equipment industry performance indicators, semimonthly rpt recurring feature, C1850–5

Container (fiber box) shipments by end-use industry and region, and other industry operating data, 1940s-92, annual rpt, A4875–1

Convenience store industry financial and operating data, by size category, 1992 and trends, annual survey rpt, A6735–1, A6735–2

Convenience store inventory turnover rates, by product type, 1991-92, annual fact book, C4680–1.507

Copper (refined) inventories, US and worldwide, 1985-91, annual rpt, S0497–1

Copper (refined and scrap) stocks, for mills and other users, 1972-92, annual rpt, A4175–1

Discount store sales and productivity data for 20 depts, 1993 annual feature, C5150–3.516

Distilled spirits stocks, by product type and State, 1992 and trends, annual rpt, C4775–1.2

Drugstore (independent pharmacy) financial and operating data, by store characteristics, 1991 and trends, annual survey, B5165–1

Drugstore chains financial performance and marketing operations, with sales by product type, 1993 annual feature, C5150–2.510

Drugstore profitability and inventory comparisons for 6 product categories, 1993 article, C5150–2.518

Economic outlook for selected indicators, recent trends and 2-year forecast, quarterly rpt, A3840–6

Electronics industry factory sales and shipments, foreign trade, and operating data, by product category, 1980s-92, annual rpt, A4725–1

Electronics industry market devs, including factory sales, orders, inventory, production, and operating ratios, by product category, monthly rpt, A4725–2

Electronics industry market trends and outlook, including product sales and shipments, employment, and leading manufacturers, monthly rpt, C1850–2

Europe military commissaries of US armed services, sales and inventory value, June 1992-Mar 1993, C0500–1.503

Farm machinery unit sales and inventories, periodic rpt, C0495–1, C3450–1

Financial ratios and performance, for over 350 SIC 4-digit industries, FY88-92, annual rpt, A6400–3

Food marketers financial and operating data, by company size and region, 1991-92, annual rpts, A4950–5

Food store industry structure, sales, operations, and business outlook, by type of store, 1993 annual rpt, C5225–1.505

Forecasts of economic indicators for approx 10-13 months, monthly rpt, U1880–3

Foreign economic indexes, and leading and coincident indicators for US and other industrial countries, monthly rpt, U1245–1

Index by Subjects and Names

Hardware finances and operations, for hardware stores, home centers, and lumber/building material outlets, 1991 and trends, annual rpt series, A8275–1

Home furnishings retailer financial and operating data, by firm characteristics and region, 1992 and trends, annual rpt, A7975–1

Home improvement industry sales and operations, for top distributors, cooperatives, and marketing organizations, 1991-92, annual feature, C5150–6.502

Home improvement industry sales and operations, for top retailers, 1992 and trends, annual feature, C5150–6.503

Home improvement industry sales, stores, and other operating data, for leading foreign chains by country, 1991-92, annual feature, C5150–6.503

Hospital pharmacy operating data, by instn type and size, and census div, 1991, annual survey, B5165–3

Industrial distributor sales, employment, and inventory turns, for top 25 companies with sales of $5 million/less, 1991, annual article, C1850–4.503

Iron ore production, shipments, trade, and plant inventories and consumption, US and Canada, 1992 and trends, annual rpt, A2010–3

Iron ore receipts, consumption, and inventories, and blast furnaces operating, for US and Canada, monthly rpt, A2010–1

Japan economic profile, including govt finances, industrial production, foreign trade and investments, and comparisons to US, 1988-92, annual feature, R5650–2.552

Jewelry industry purchasing plans, 1993 survey, annual article, C2150–7.507

Jewelry industry statistics on sales, marketing, trade, and employment, with customer characteristics, 1993 annual almanac, C2150–7.509

Logistics trends and devs, including data on costs, finances of major carriers by mode, and foreign trade, 1993 annual compilation, C2150–1.506

Lumber industry supply-demand, sales, trade, and employment, monthly rpt, A1630–1

Lumber production, orders, shipments, and stocks in Western regions, monthly, 1991-92, annual rpt, A9395–1

Machine tool industry employment, compensation, and operations, 1992 and trends, annual rpt, A3179–2.1

Magazine paper stocks on hand, Jan 1993, article, C2575–1.518

Manufacturing production and operating data, including equipment purchases, by selected industry, 1993 and trends, annual rpt, A3179–2.3

Manufacturing production, shipments, inventories, and new orders, quarterly rpt, S5735–2

Minerals supply-demand for selected commodities, US and worldwide, 1992-93 and trends, annual feature, C5226–2.505

Mobile/manufactured home inventories, monthly rpt, A6325–1

Motor vehicle dealership financial and operating data, including sales and employment by State, 1970s-93, annual rpt, A7330–1

Newsprint consumption by newspapers, inventories, and stock on hand, monthly rpt, A8605–1

Newsprint production, shipments, plant capacity, consumption, trade, and recycling, US and Canada, 1970s-92, annual rpt, A1630–8

Newsprint production, shipments, trade, inventory, consumption, and plant capacity, US and Canada, monthly rpt, A1630–4

Office product dealer financial and operating data, by sales volume and region, 1991 and trends, annual rpt, A8110–1

Outlook of business executives on key indicators for coming qtr, with trends and data by census div, quarterly rpt, C3150–4

Paperboard packaging devs, including containerboard inventory at fiber box plants/mills, monthly rpt, C0125–4

Potash production, inventories, and sales and exports by State, Canadian Province, and country of destination, monthly rpt, A8720–1

Potash production, inventories, sales, and exports, US and Canada, monthly rpt, A8720–2

Pulp and paper industry operations and finances, US and Canada, with detail by company and product grade, and world production and trade summary, 1993 annual rpt, C3975–5

Pulp and paper industry production, capacity, consumption, trade, and sales/earnings data, including profiles for selected companies and sectors, monthly rpt, C3975–2

Pulp, paper, and paperboard industry production, trade, and operating data, by product class, monthly rpt, A1630–5

Purchasing managers views on business conditions, monthly rpt, A6910–1

Retail industry inventory mgmt, warehousing, and distribution operations, by outlet type, 1993 survey, C5150–4.506

Retail store financial performance indicators, for 98 public firms, FY92 and trends, annual rpt, B8130–4

Retail store inventory shrinkage, and control measures, by type of outlet, 1991, annual survey rpt, C5150–4.504

Retail store perceived and actual losses from inventory shrinkage vs consumer credit, and loss reduction efforts, 1992 survey article, C5150–4.503

Retailer inventory mgmt practices, including automated technology use, by retail outlet type, 1992 survey article, C5150–4.503

Shoe industry production, employment, trade, marketing, and related data, by SIC 2- to 5-digit code or product type, 1992 annual rpt, A4957–1.2

Silver refinery production from primary materials, coins, and scrap, with disposition, stocks, prices, and industry devs, US and worldwide, bimonthly rpt, A8902–3

Small business views on current and expected economic conditions, survey findings, quarterly rpt, A7815–1

Steel service center business conditions and outlook, monthly survey, A8990–2

Business machines and equipment

Supermarket (independent) sales and operating ratios, by store type, sales size, and region, 1991, annual survey, A4950–4

Supermarkets opened, remodeled, and closed, including store features, dev costs, and rent, by region and sales size, 1992 and trends, annual rpt, A4950–2

Textile industry economic and operating performance and outlook, 1988-93, annual article, C5226–3.502

Textile industry economic performance indicators and outlook, with industry trends and devs, monthly rpt, C5226–3

Textile industry financial performance indicators for 32 companies, FY92 and trends, annual rpt, B8130–1

Truck equipment distributor financial data, by company type, sales size, and rural vs metro market, FY91 and trends, annual rpt, A8505–4

Wine production, withdrawals, and stocks or inventories, US and selected States, 1970s-92, annual rpt, C4775–2.2

Wood chemicals (naval stores) production, consumption, and trade, US and foreign, 1992 and trends, annual rpt, C6585–1

State and local:

Arizona statistical abstract, general data, 1993 recurring rpt, U5850–2.17, U5850–2.21

Georgia statistical abstract, general data, 1992-93 biennial rpt, U6730–1.6

Hawaii data book, general data, 1992 annual rpt, S2090–1.22

Idaho business inventory exemptions from sales tax, reimbursements by county, FY92, annual rpt, S2295–1

Illinois, Chicago industrial purchasing managers business activity index, bimonthly rpt, S2405–2

Ohio business property assessment data, by property class and industry, 1991 and trends, annual rpt, S6390–1.5

Pennsylvania statistical abstract, general data, 1992 recurring rpt, U4130–6.2

South Carolina merchants inventory tax exemption reimbursements to local govts, by county, 1991, annual rpt, S7127–2

Tennessee statistical abstract, general data, 1992/93 annual rpt, U8710–2.7

see also Agricultural stocks
see also Business orders
see also Coal stocks
see also Economic indicators
see also Energy stocks and inventories
see also Petroleum stocks

Business loans

see Commercial credit

Business machines and equipment

Coffee service operation equipment purchases and use, 1982 and 1990-92, annual rpt, C9470–1

Financial and operating data for office product dealers, by sales volume and region, 1991 and trends, annual rpt, A8110–1

Financial ratios and performance, for over 350 SIC 4-digit industries, FY88-92, annual rpt, A6400–3

Food retailer and wholesaler distribution centers use of batch picking conveyor systems, 1991, annual rpt, A4950–5.2

Food store industry structure, sales, operations, and business outlook, by type of store, 1993 annual rpt, C5225–1.505

Business machines and equipment

Franchise operations and finances, by type of business, 1991/92 and trends, annual rpt, A5820–1

Life expectancy, shipments, and manufacturers market shares, for appliances by type, 1993 annual article, C2000–1.510

Motors (small) shipments value, by motor type and market category, quarterly rpt, A8904–1

Operating and financial composite ratios for corporations, with establishments and receipts, for approx 200 industries, by asset size, FY90, annual rpt, C7800–1

Retail chain store expansion devs, and equipment and construction costs, by type of chain, 1993 annual articles, C5150–4.507

Sales of personal word processors and facsimile devices, 1992 and trends, annual rpt, A4725–1.1

Shipments and industry revenues for computers and other business equipment, 1990-98, annual articles, C2000–1.503

Shipments of business appliances and equipment, by product type, 1983-92, annual feature, C2000–1.505

Small companies with personal computers, facsimile machines, and cellular telephones, 1990 and 1993, article, C5800–7.551

Small corporation mgmt office technology experience and views, including whether productivity gains have justified investment, 1992 survey, article, C4687–1.506

Snack food industry use of selected types of new technology, 1991, annual rpt, A8905–1

Supermarket bakery dept equipment use, and purchasing plans, 1992-93, annual article, C5225–1.504

Supermarket bakery dept equipment use, 1992, annual article, C4655–1.505

Supermarket deli dept equipment use and purchasing plans, 1992-93, annual article, C5225–1.505

Supermarket deli dept equipment use, 1992, annual article, C4655–1.503

Supermarket produce dept equipment use, 1992, annual article, C4655 1.511

Trends in computer/office equipment industry employment and new orders, 1984-94, article, C1850–5.511

State and local:

Colorado property assessed valuation by detailed property type, and tax levy and revenue by local district, by county, 1991-92, annual rpt, S1055–3

Wyoming property assessed valuations and tax levies, by property type, tax purpose, and location, 1992 and trends, annual rpt, S8990–1.2

see also Computer industry and products
see also Electronic mail systems
see also Industrial plants and equipment
see also Office supplies
see also Telephones and telephone industry

Business management

Architectural office changes in workloads and staffing, 1993 survey article, C5800–15.503

Bank CEO demographic and professional characteristics, attitudes, and compensation, Apr 1992 survey, annual rpt, B4490–2.33

Bank loan diversification and credit concentration policies, fall 1992 survey, article, A6400–2.502

Business and economic trends, production and price indicators, and industrial mgmt activities and devs, semimonthly rpt, C7000–3

Business failures and liabilities, by detailed industry, cause, length of operation, and location, 1991-92 and trends, annual rpt, C3150–8

Communications function mgmt, activities, budget, staffing, and use of outside services, 1992 survey, R4105–78.24

Corporate business activity and mgmt trends for small corporations, monthly rpt, C4687–1

Corporate business process reengineering projects and benefits, views of chief info officers, 1991-92 surveys, article, C1850–5.517

Corporate manager views on selected mgmt issues, American Mgmt Assn research series, A2075–20

Corporate managerial trends reported by senior executives, including re-engineering, outsourcing, and restructuring, 1992 survey article, C5800–28.502

Corporate mgmt devs and related topics, series, R4105–78

Corporate performance ratings by executives for leading companies in 32 industries, 1993 annual survey feature, C8900–1.508

Electronics industry conditions and outlook, including mgmt issues, global expansion, and most promising new technologies, views of CEOs, 1992/93 survey, annual feature, C1850–2.506

Food marketers mgmt info system operations, employment, and finances, for wholesalers and retailers by sales size, 1993 and trends, annual survey, A4950–7

Food/beverage industry equipment purchasing plans, mgmt devs, and automation, 1993 annual survey article, C2150–6.505

Incubator facilities for new business, finances and operations, including services offered, 1991, annual rpt, A7360–1

Industrial R&D managers outlook on expenditures, effort, personnel, and other mgmt issues, 1993, annual survey rpt, A5510–1

Manufacturing executive views on improving company global competitiveness, including mgmt strategies and human resource issues, spring 1993 survey, U9640–4

Multinatl business implications of world events and socioeconomic devs outside the US, series, R4105–82

Quality assurance programs of North American companies, selected characteristics, 1992 annual survey rpt, B6850–2

Retailer views on "quick response" system implementation and benefits, and other technology use, 1992 survey, annual article, C5150–4.506

Self-managed work team obstacles cited by executives, 1990 survey, article, C4215–1.505

Shopping center management and leasing by owner vs outside company, 1991, triennial rpt, R9285–1

Index by Subjects and Names

see also Boards of directors
see also Consultants
see also Employee performance and appraisal
see also Executives and managers
see also Health facilities administration
see also Industrial purchasing
see also Labor-management relations, general
see also Personnel management

Business orders

Aerospace industry, civil and military production, R&D, trade, employment, and finances, with Federal funding data, 1991 and trends, annual rpt, A0250–2

Aircraft (jet) order cancellations and deferrals by airline, and aircraft in storage by model, 1992 article, C7000–4.502

Aircraft (jet) orders from 5-6 manufacturers worldwide, by model, monthly rpt quarterly feature, C7000–4.502, C7000–4.505

Aircraft (jet) world inventory, orders, and deliveries, by type of aircraft, 1992 and trends, annual rpt, B1582–1

Aircraft (passenger jet) orders and deliveries, by aircraft type, 1992-2011, annual rpt, B3075–1

Aircraft (turbine-powered) in service and on order, by manufacturer and model, for over 900 airlines worldwide, Dec 1992, annual rpt, B3370–1

Aircraft on order from airlines, by model, Dec 1992, annual rpt, A0325–5

Aircraft on order worldwide for 1993 and beyond, article, C7000–4.511

Airline fleet composition and aircraft on order, by model and carrier, 1992, annual article, C7000–4.508

Airline fleet units owned, leased, and on order, by model, July 1993, and planned changes for 2nd half 1993, article, C5800–4.530

Airline traffic and financial forecasts, and fleet acquisition and disposal plans, by US and foreign carrier, 1993 annual article, C7000–4.503

Aluminum shipments, orders, and inventories by product class, and foreign trade for ingot, scrap, and mill products, monthly rpt, A0400–1

Auto fleet acquisition plans, including vehicle replacement policy, 1992 survey article, C1575–2.502

Auto fleet acquisition plans, with factors affecting purchases, 1992 annual survey, A6755–1.501

Business and economic trends, production and price indicators, and industrial mgmt activities and devs, semimonthly rpt, C7000–3

Computer/info processing equipment industry performance indicators, semimonthly rpt recurring feature, C1850–5

Computer/office equipment industry employment and new order trends, 1984-94, article, C1850–5.511

Electric generating equipment and transformer orders, shipments, and exports, by type of equipment, 1991 annual rpt, A4700–2

Electronics industry market devs, including new and unfilled orders by product category, monthly rpt, A4725–2

Electronics industry market trends and outlook, including product sales and shipments, employment, and leading manufacturers, monthly rpt, C1850–2

Index by Subjects and Names

Forecasts of economic indicators for approx 10-13 months, monthly rpt, U1880–3

Foreign economic indexes, and leading and coincident indicators for US and other industrial countries, monthly rpt, U1245–1

France aerospace industry export orders distribution by product type, 1991, article, C5800–4.509

Freight cars and locomotives ordered and/or delivered, quarterly press release, A3275–3

Graphic arts machinery orders and shipments, monthly rpt quarterly table, C1850–10.501, C1850–10.504, C1850–10.507, C1850–10.511, C1850–10.512

Lumber industry supply-demand, sales, trade, and employment, monthly rpt, A1630–1

Lumber production, orders, shipments, and stocks in Western regions, monthly 1991-92, annual rpt, A9395–1

Machine tool production, shipments, trade, finances, orders, and use, US and worldwide, 1992 and trends, annual rpt, A3179–2

Machine tool shipments and new orders for domestic and foreign markets, and backlog, monthly press release, A3179–1

Manufacturing production and operating data, including equipment purchases, by selected industry, 1993 and trends, annual rpt, A3179–2.3

Manufacturing production, shipments, inventories, and new orders, quarterly rpt, S5735–2

Metals (primary) new orders value, monthly rpt, C7000–8

Metalworking industry devs, with machine tool orders and shipments, monthly rpt, C7000–7

Outlook of business executives on key indicators for coming qtr, with trends and data by census div, quarterly rpt, C3150–4

Pulp, paper, and paperboard industry production, trade, and operating data, by product class, monthly rpt, A1630–5

Purchasing managers views on business conditions, monthly rpt, A6910–1

Railroad freight cars and locomotives ordered and delivered, monthly rpt quarterly table, C8400–1.501, C8400–1.502, C8400–1.504, C8400–1.508, C8400–1.510

Railroad passenger cars delivered, undelivered backlog, and new orders outlook, by purchaser, 1993 annual feature, C8400–1.503

Shipbuilding govt aid programs in 6 OECD countries, and impact on US industry, 1993 recurring rpt, A8900–8

Steel service center business conditions and outlook, monthly survey, A8990–2

Toy shipments and orders received, canceled, and/or on hand, monthly rpt, A9095–2

State and local:

Illinois, Chicago industrial purchasing managers business activity index, bimonthly rpt, S2405–2

Business orders, new

see Business orders

Business orders, unfilled

see Business orders

Business outlook and attitude surveys

Advertising abroad, govt regulation, and economy impact on business, views of ad industry personnel, Nov-Dec 1992 survey, article, C2710–1.513

Advertising industry professional views on impact of Clinton Admin economic plan, Feb 1993 survey, article, C2710–1.514

Advertising media buying services, competition, and staffing, views of agency and independent service executives, 1993 annual survey articles, C2710–1.537

Architect views on industry competition and related topics, 1993 survey article, C5800–15.502

Arts program support by corporations, including reasons for not supporting and perceived benefits, 1991, recurring rpt, A3690–1

Auto dealer franchise desirability rating for top 33 makes, winter 1992-93, survey article, C2710–3.525

Auto dealer satisfaction with manufacturers, index for top 15 makes, 1991-92, survey article, C2710–3.512

Auto dealer views on dealer assn and manufacturer advertising programs, including natl campaign spending levels by medium, with data by vehicle make, 1993 survey article, C2710–1.518, C2710–3.521

Auto dealership profit expectations, 1976-93, annual rpt, A7330–1

Auto dealership service dept operations and profit outlook, and manager compensation, 1993 annual survey, article, C2710–3.537

Auto fleet acquisition plans, including safety devices, alternative fuel vehicles, and manufacturers, 1992 survey, article, C1575–2.503

Auto fleet acquisition plans, including vehicle replacement policy, 1992 survey article, C1575–2.502

Auto fleet acquisition plans, with factors affecting purchases, 1992 annual survey, A6755–1.501

Auto fleet manager views on market for used fleet vehicles, and mgmt of resale process compared to purchasing and maintenance, 1993 survey, article, C1575–2.509

Auto fleet use and views on operation of flexible-fuel vehicles capable of running on methanol or gasoline, California survey, 1993 articles, A6755–1.502

Auto fleet use of fuel credit cards, with detail for 6 oil company cards, 1993 survey article, C1575–2.505

Auto fleet vehicle driver maintenance habits, model preferences, and cellular telephone and credit card use, 1993 survey, article, C1575–2.509

Auto mechanic views on vehicle quality and maintenance, and customers, Mar 1993 survey, article, C0125–1.505

Bank (master trust/custodial) top instns for service as rated by pension executives, errata, C2710–2.507

Banker views on future competition from 8 types of financial instns, Mar 1992 survey, article, C4687–1.502

Business outlook and attitude surveys

Banks planning aggressive business policies, 1991-92, survey article, C8900–1.503

Beverage distribution operations and costs, including fleet size, maintenance, and purchase plans, 1992 survey, annual rpt, C0125–3.2

Black-owned companies top 10 problems encountered in doing business with govt agencies, 1993 article, C4215–1.503

Books (children's) and nonbook children's merchandise sales performance in bookstores, by store type, Nov 1992 survey, annual article, C1852–2.506

Broadcast news professional views on TV news programming, outlook for own TV or radio operations, and ethical issues, 1993 survey article, C1850–14.539

Cable TV operator planned methods of expanding channel capacity, 1992 survey, article, C1850–14.509

Cable TV system mgmt personnel views on selected industry topics, biweekly rpt, C1858–1, C2965–1

Cable TV system operator expansion plans, including use of digital compression and fiber optic vs coaxial cable, fall 1992 survey, article, C1850–2.508

Canada auto dealer satisfaction with manufacturers, ratings for 21 makes, 1992 survey, article, C2710–3.518

China joint ventures of US businesses, executive views on performance by location, project type, and startup year, 1991 survey, article, A9315–1.501

Coal industry executive views on industry devs and outlook, monthly rpt, C5226–1

Coal producer outlook for supply-demand and prices, and capital investments, 1993 annual survey article, C5226–1.503

College grad hiring plans by industry, with data on campus visits, starting salaries, and minority hires, 1991/92-1992/93, annual rpt, A3940–3

College grad recruiting practices and hiring trends, with data on starting salaries and layoffs, by type of employer, 1992/93 annual survey rpt, U3130–1

College grads in business and industry, hiring plans, salaries, and selected personnel practices, 1993 annual survey rpt, U3730–1

Commercial real estate market conditions and outlook, for industrial and office properties, by US metro area and selected foreign city, 1992-93, annual survey, A8916–1

Computer (mini/micro) use and market devs, 1992 survey and trends, annual article, C1850–5.502

Computer (personal) use in corporate sales depts, 1993 annual survey article, C1200–1.512

Computer software with sales/marketing applications, vendor finances, marketing methods, and customer characteristics, 1990-91, annual survey article, C1200–1.502

Computer system mgmt and technology devs, views of corporate info system officers, 1993 survey, article, C1850–5.509

Computer system purchasing and expansion plans of businesses, including data by manufacturer, 1993 survey and trends, annual article, C1850–5.513

Business outlook and attitude surveys

Index by Subjects and Names

Computer use and plans, and satisfaction with selected products, semimonthly rpt, C1850–5

Computer use and related mgmt and training issues as reported by corporate executives, 1993 survey rpt, B6850–7

Computer/info system manager outlook for 1993, including importance of selected technologies, 1992 survey, annual article, C1850–5.504

Computer/info systems expenditure plans by component, 1993 annual survey article, C1850–5.510

Concrete (ready-mixed) industry production and operating trends and outlook, by region, 1992 survey, annual article, C0125–5

Construction equipment distributor and contractor views on 1993 business outlook and marketing strategies, 1993 survey article, C1850–4.504

Construction equipment positive and negative attributes cited by contractors, for 6 manufacturers, 1993 survey article, C5800–2.519

Construction executive views on loss-control program effectiveness in controlling insurance costs, 1992 survey article, C5800–2.505

Construction industry finances and operations, by type of business and region, 1992-93, annual survey rpt, A4155–1

Corporate boards of directors composition, compensation, and practices, by industry sector, 1991 and trends, annual survey rpt, B5000–3

Corporate business process reengineering projects and benefits, views of chief info officers, 1991-92 surveys, article, C1850–5.517

Corporate CEO views on business and natl issues, including outlook by company size, 1992 annual survey, C7000–3.502

Corporate CEO views on Clinton Admin health care plan, Sept 1993 survey, article, C8900–1.527

Corporate CEO views on Clinton Admin performance, economic plan, and health care reform financing, Apr-May 1993 survey, article, C8900–1.516

Corporate CEO views on economic outlook and policies in President Clinton Admin, 1992 survey article, C8900–1.504

Corporate CEO views on outlook for company employment, wages compared to inflation, and mgmt skills needs, June 1993 survey, article, C8900–1.519

Corporate communication of benefits info to employees, including objectives, methods, and success, 1993 survey rpt, R4105–78.28

Corporate earnings forecasts of securities analysts, including 5 companies with greatest estimated increase and decrease, biweekly rpt quarterly article, C3950–1.502, C3950–1.508, C3950–1.515, C3950–1.518

Corporate executive job characteristics and attitudes, series, B4490–2

Corporate executive views on mgmt of change, July 1993 survey, article, C5800–7.546

Corporate executive views on President-elect Clinton and his proposed programs, Nov 1992 survey, C5800–7.505

Corporate manager views on selected mgmt issues, American Mgmt Assn research series, A2075–20

Corporate managerial trends reported by senior executives, including re-engineering, outsourcing, and restructuring, 1992 survey article, C5800–28.502

Corporate mgmt initiatives and guidelines on cultural/ethnic diversity of work force, and challenges to implementation, 1991-92 surveys, R4105–78.22

Corporate performance ratings by executives for leading companies in 32 industries, 1993 annual survey feature, C8900–1.508

Corporate personnel mgmt devs, including staffing practices and turnover, payroll cost control efforts, and human resources operations, 1993 survey, annual rpt, B6850–5

Corporate personnel mgmt devs, including work force diversity, health care and family-related benefits, counseling services, and competitiveness, 1993 survey, B6850–6

Corporate sales/marketing automation issues, views of computer users and nonusers, Aug 1992 survey, article, C1200–1.504

Corporate tax-deferred salary reduction 401(k) plan sponsor satisfaction with selected plan services and costs, 1993 survey article, C2710–2.510

Corporate use of selected variable pay and recognition programs, with objectives and success, by industry div, Oct 1992 survey and trends, R4105–78.27

Corporate work force outlook and related mgmt policies, views of human resources executives, Sept/Oct 1991 survey, R4105–78.21

Corporate work force reduction prevalence by industry sector, assistance provided displaced workers, and reduction effects, 1992 survey, article, C4215–1.504

Direct marketing industry devs, including advertising patterns, finances, target market characteristics, and consumer attitudes, 1992/93 annual rpt, A4620–1

Disabled workers employment provisions of Americans with Disabilities Act of 1990, business views on impact, 1992 survey, C4215–1.501

Discount buyer and vendor views on working relationship and problems, 1993 survey, annual article, C8130–1.508

Discount chain top-selling natl brands cited by managers, by product category, chain, and region, 1993 survey, annual feature, C5150–3.520

Discount chain top-selling natl brands cited by managers, errata, C5150–3.501

Discount retailer views on economic and business outlook, 1992 survey article, C8130–1.502

Economic outlook of executives, including short-term forecasts of analysts for selected industries, monthly rpt, R4105–80

Economists (business) assessments of current conditions at their companies, with industry detail, quarterly rpt, A6650–4

Economists (business) forecasts of general economic conditions, quarterly rpt, A6650–5

Economists (business) views on Govt economic policy, semiannual survey rpt, A6650–6

Electric utility commercial/industrial customer views on importance of selected service factors, 1993 survey article, C5800–28.506

Electrical equipment distributor sales forecasts, by census div and State, 1992-93, annual article, C4725–5.502

Electronic data interchange (EDI) use and/or expansion plans, and benefits cited, with detail for electronics firms, 1993 articles, C1850–2.511

Electronics industry capital spending plans, biweekly rpt semiannual article, C1850–2.505

Electronics industry conditions and outlook, including mgmt issues, global expansion, and most promising new technologies, views of CEOs, 1992/93 survey, annual feature, C1850–2.506

Electronics/computer industry sources and ratings of purchasing info, and ratings of 14 market research firms, 1993 survey article, C1850–2.511

Employee benefit plan investment strategies reported by fund executives, 1993 survey article, C2710–2.504

Employee flexible work schedules offered now and planned for 2000, by type, 1993 survey article, S0465–1.504

Employee motivational training programs use by type, with outdoor program characteristics, 1993 survey article, C1200–1.503

Employee training programs, including methods and skills needing dev, 1993 survey, annual rpt, B6850–4

Employer views on job skills worth compensation, 1993 survey article, C4215–1.503

Europe computer/info systems spending plans, by industry and application, 1993 vs 1992, survey article, C1850–2.504

Family-related policies of employers, with involvement in child, elderly, and disabled care services, and personnel mgmt views, Mar 1992 survey, A8907–1

Financial analyst views on Clinton Admin economic plan, including effects on investment performance and own strategy, Feb 1993 survey, article, C8900–1.511

Food manufacturer work force reduction impact on profits, quality, and employees, 1987-92, annual feature, C2150–6.507

Food marketers financial and operating data, by company size and region, 1991-92, annual rpts, A4950–5

Food marketers mgmt info system operations, employment, and finances, for wholesalers and retailers by sales size, 1993 and trends, annual survey, A4950–7

Food service operator kitchen equipment purchasing plans, 1993 survey article, C1850–3.512

Food service operator views regarding employee health insurance coverage, by company sales size, 1993 survey, article, A8200–1.511

Food store-brand products image trends and outlook among retailers/wholesalers, 1992 survey, article, C2710–1.508

Index by Subjects and Names

Business outlook and attitude surveys

Food store industry structure, sales, operations, and business outlook, by type of store, 1993 annual rpt, C5225–1.505

Food/beverage industry equipment purchasing plans, mgmt devs, and automation, 1993 annual survey article, C2150–6.505

Food/beverage industry new product dev influences, including industry personnel views on selected ingredients, suppliers, and dev time, 1993 annual article, C2150–6.511

Food/beverage industry packaging devs, including equipment purchase plans, partnership arrangements, and new labeling law effects, 1993 annual survey article, C2150–6.512

Food/beverage manufacturing mgmt views on job responsibilities and satisfaction, and effect of affirmative action, by sex, 1992 survey, annual article, C2150–6.502

Foundry shipments, capacity utilization, and capital investment outlook, by metal type and plant size, 1992-94, annual survey article, C7000–2.501

Freight carrier quality ratings by shippers, by mode and company, 1993 annual survey article, C2150–1.507

Fuel oil dealer operations, with heating and cooling equipment services, by region, 1992 annual survey, C4680–2

Govt policies most desired by business executives, 1992 survey article, C1850–13.501

Hard goods manufacturers and representatives opinions on business issues and outlook, by product line, 1993 annual survey rpt, A1800–1

Health care info mgmt professional views on obstacles to using computer-based patient records, 1993 survey, article, A1865–1.522

Hiring plans of employers in coming qtr, by industry div and region, quarterly rpt, B5275 1

Hispanic-owned business motor vehicle fleet characteristics and policies, 1992 annual survey feature, C4575–1.501

Hispanic-owned business outlook for selected performance indicators, with data by region, monthly rpt quarterly feature, C4575–1.510

Hispanic-owned high-technology company CEO plans, and views on espionage agencies helping business and most promising technology dev, 1993 annual article, C4575–1.510

Home automation dealer views on system features desired by consumers, 1992 articles, C1850–13.501

Homebuilder outlook for land availability and costs, with detail by region, 1993 survey, article, C1850–8.510

Homebuilder reasons for entering business, and views on job rewards and most important skills, June 1993 survey, article, C1850–8.509

Homebuilder views on environmental issues of major concern, 1992 survey, article, C1850–8.502

Homebuilder views on most significant problems for the industry, 1992-93, survey article, C1850–8.504

Homebuilder views on top industry concerns and issues, monthly rpt quarterly feature, C4300–1.501, C4300–1.507, C4300–1.510, C4300–1.511

Hospital CEO views on industry-related issues, operations, and finances, semimonthly rpt, A1865–1

Hospital patient-centered care implementation, including program characteristics and financial impact, 1992 survey, article, A1865–1.507

Hospital pharmacist views on involvement in drug research activities, and impact of biotechnology drugs, 1993 survey, article, A1865–1.521

Hospital use of contract hospitality, business, and clinical services, including contract terms, 1993 survey, annual article, A1865–1.514

Hospital views on obstacles to use of electronic medical imaging systems, 1990 and 1992 surveys, article, C1850–2.509

Hotel/motel use of computers, including perceived benefits and challenges, 1991 survey, article, C7000–6

Housing sales market conditions, views of homebuilders, monthly survey, C4300–1

Industrial distribution executives job and dept characteristics, compensation, and industry outlook, 1992 annual survey article, C2150–1.501

Industrial distribution personnel compensation, by position and selected other characteristics, 1992 survey, annual article, C1850–4.501

Industrial distributors hiring criteria for college grads, 1992 survey article, C1850–2.502

Industrial distributors operations, including type of ownership and acquisition activity, 1992, annual survey, C1850–4.507

Industrial distributors performance and importance of selected factors, views of purchasing executives, 1993 survey article, C1850–4.508

Industrial distributors ratings of employee hiring and promotion criteria, 1992 survey article, C1850–4.502

Industrial executive views on priorities for Clinton Admin, Nov 1992 survey, article, C7000–2.502

Industrial natl policy need, views of executives and manufacturing mgmt, 1993 survey article, C1850–4.506

Industrial plant operations, and performance improvement efforts, for top-rated plants, 1993 survey article, C7000–3.505

Industrial R&D managers outlook on expenditures, effort, personnel, and other mgmt issues, 1993, annual survey rpt, A5510–1

Insurance independent agency automation use and benefits, 1992 survey, article, C1050–1.501

Intellectual property protection in selected foreign countries, US multinatl corporation views, 1989 survey, R4105–82.2

Jeweler views on women's jewelry purchasing trends, 1993 survey article, C2150–7.510

Jewelry (custom-designed) demand, material sources, and sales shares, views of jewelers, Aug 1992 survey, article, C2150–7.501

Jewelry industry economic and sales outlook, 1993 survey, annual article, C2150–7.507

Jewelry retail business outlook, including staffing, merchandise selection criteria, and sales promotion, 1993, annual survey article, C2150–7.502

Jewelry retailer views on diamond grading, and importance of color, clarity, and cut to retailers and customers, 1993 survey article, C2150–7.505

Life insurance sales decline reasons, views of agents, 1990 survey, article, C1050–2.511

Logistics professionals views on continuing education programs, including benefit to own career and employer, 1993 survey, C2150–1.505

Logistics professionals views on occupational certification, 1993 survey article, C2150–1.503

Logistics professionals views on transportation and trade policy issues, Dec 1992 survey, article, C2150–1.505

Magazine advertising purchasing plans and budgets, views of media executives, 1993 survey feature, C2710–1.549

Magazine circulation building strategies, including cost of a new subscriber and renewal data, 1993 survey, article, C2575–1.513

Magazine use of desktop publishing/electronic systems for pre-press operations, including hardware and software brands used, May 1993 survey, article, C2575–1.514

Manager views on economic outlook, company budget policy, and effects on business of selected Govt policy proposals, 1993 survey article, C8900–1.510

Manufacturing executive views on improving company global competitiveness, including mgmt strategies and human resource issues, spring 1993 survey, U9640–4

Manufacturing industry natl policy desirability, views of industry executives and operations managers, 1993 survey article, C1850–12.506

Manufacturing use of "agile" production methods at midsize companies, 1993 survey article, C2150–3.509

Marketing executive views on technology use and future importance, including companies cited as top users, July/Aug 1992 survey, article, C2710–1.510

Marketing strategy future influences cited as most important by executives, Nov 1992-Jan 1993 survey, article, C2710–1.518

Metalworking industry capital spending plans, by equipment type and industry group, 1989-93, annual survey, C4080–1

Midwest business and economic conditions in metro and nonurban areas, by sector and State, bankers opinions, spring 1993 survey, semiannual rpt, B6785–1

Mining industry capital spending and capacity plans for new mines and plants, by mineral and company, 1993 annual feature, C5226–2.503

Motor vehicle sales, forecasts by 10 auto industry analysts, 1993, annual article, C2710–3.510

Motor vehicle sales, forecasts by 9 auto industry analysts, 1993-94, annual article, C2710–3.538

Mountain region printing industry devs, including sales trends and printer views on business conditions, 1992 feature, C1850–10.503

Business outlook and attitude surveys

Index by Subjects and Names

Natural gas utility expansion/maintenance expenditures, and pipe installations, 1990-93, annual article, C6780–1.501

New product dev process and significant contributing factors, 1993 survey article, C2150–6.508

News media (TV and newspaper) journalistic ethics code use, sources, and revisions, 1993 survey article, A8605–1.504

Newspaper editor views on advertiser attempts to influence editorial content, Jan 1992 survey, article, C2710–1.508

Newspaper industry capital expenditures, by item, US and Canada, 1992-93, annual article, A8605–1.507

Nuclear power plant maintenance mgmt ratings of top 15 maintenance issues, 1993 survey article, C6985–6.505

Oil and gas pipeline mileage under construction or planned in 1993, for 5 world areas, Canada, and US, annual article, C6985–1.515

Oil industry capital spending in US and Canada, by function, 1991-93, annual articles, C6985–1.517

Outlook of business executives on key indicators for coming qtr, with trends and data by census div, quarterly rpt, C3150–4

Paper distributor views on environmental concerns business effects, including customer interest in special products, 1993 survey article, A8140–3.503

Paper distributor views on total quality mgmt programs, including use, benefits, and supplier participation, 1993 survey article, A8140–3.504

Paperboard packaging equipment purchasing plans and spending trends, 1993 annual article, C0125–4.503

Pension plan mgmt views on mutual funds, and selection criteria for investments, for small business plans, 1992 annual rpt, A6025–1.1

Personnel mgmt devs, including hiring, layoffs, and health care and payroll cost control efforts, June 1992 survey, annual rpt, B6850–3

Personnel mgmt professional activities, job satisfaction, employer performance, and obstacles encountered, spring 1993 survey, A8907–2

Pharmacy operating devs, including staffing plans, price scanning, and patient counseling, by store type, 1993 survey, article, C5150–2.518

Printer views on paper supplier services and performance, and electronic prepress and output device use, 1993 survey and trends, article, A8140–3.505

Printer views on paper supplier services and performance, and paper use patterns, 1993 survey article, A8140–3.502

Printing business generated by financial institutions, with future outlook, 1992 feature, C1850–10.501

Printing business generated by food/lodging/entertainment industry, with future outlook, 1992 feature, C1850–10.503

Printing business generated by legal services industry, with future outlook, 1992 feature, C1850–10.502

Printing industry equipment purchase plans, and printer views on business conditions, monthly rpt, C1850–10

Public relations budget and staff size trends, compensation, and career attitudes, 1993 survey, annual article, A8770–1.503

Public relations challenges for 1994, corporate executives views, July/Aug 1993 survey, article, A8770–1.506

Public relations firms and depts purchasing of selected types of support services, computer software, and telecommunications, 1992 survey, article, A8770–1.501

Public relations professionals views on nature of their role in business/society, 1992 survey, article, A8770–1.501

Public utility current and planned info mgmt system improvements, by application, 1993 survey article, C6985–6.505

Pulp and paper industry capital spending plans of US and Canadian companies, by purpose and geographic area, 1992-94, annual survey article, C3975–2.503

Pulp and paper industry quality control program characteristics, 1993 survey, annual article, C3975–2.508

Purchasing managers views on business conditions, monthly rpt, A6910–1

Quality control and improvement, views and experience of corporate executives and outside directors, July-Aug 1992 surveys, A2800–3

Quality mgmt program studies, including data on mgmt and employee views on attributes, 1990s, R4105–78.32

Quality mgmt program success as seen by managers, 1993 survey article, C7000–3.508

Real estate broker ratings of market conditions and outlook in 20 States, 1992 survey article, C4300–1.501

Restaurant (table service) anticipated problems and business outlook for 1993, 1992 survey, article, A8200–1.502

Restaurant (table service) operations and menu offerings, and related consumer views and practices by demographic characteristics, 1992, recurring rpt, A8200–11

Restaurant independent owner views on business conditions, 1993 annual article, C1850–3.505

Restaurant operator plans for selected establishment changes during coming year, 1988 and 1992 surveys, C1200–5.501

Restaurant/food service mgmt compensation, characteristics, and views, including data by position, 1992 survey, annual article, C1850–3.502

Retail chain store use of consultants, by consultant and/or chain type, Sept-Oct 1992 survey, article, C5150–4.504

Retail industry inventory mgmt, warehousing, and distribution operations, by outlet type, 1993 survey, C5150–4.506

Retail store credit operations, including cash vs credit sales, processing methods, and marketing techniques, 1992 annual survey, C5150–4.504

Retail store credit operations, including payment losses and loss reduction efforts, by payment method and outlet type, 1992 survey article, C5150–4.503

Retail store inventory shrinkage, and control measures, by type of outlet, 1991, annual survey rpt, C5150–4.504

Retailer Christmas season advertising budget plans, by medium, 1991-92, survey article, C1850–14.504

Retailer inventory mgmt practices, including automated technology use, by retail outlet type, 1992 survey article, C5150–4.503

Retailer views on private label products image, benefits, promotion methods, and sales outlook vs other brands, 1993 survey article, C8130–1.504

Retailer views on "quick response" system implementation and benefits, and other technology use, 1992 survey, annual article, C5150–4.506

Retailer views on top 6 manufacturers for forming retail-supplier partnerships, 1993 survey article, C1200–4.509

Retiree health insurance corporate plan changes since 1990 and planned by 1994, 1992 article, C5800–7.505

Russia business conditions and outlook, views of enterprise executives, Feb 1993 survey, article, U2030–1.506

Sales executive ratings of corporate sales forces, by industry sector and sales function, 1993 annual survey article, C1200–1.512

Sales force recruitment practices, including selection criteria and sources of best candidates, 1993 survey, article, C1200–1.510

Sales skills considered most important by sales professionals, 1993 survey article, C1200–1.505

Sales worker incidence of reaching plateaus in productivity by age group, and mgmt views on reasons and solutions, 1993 survey article, C1200–1.509

School bus contractors business outlook, including insurance costs and impact of Clinton Admin proposals, Apr 1993 survey, annual article, C1575–1.505

Security equipment dealer purchasing from distributors, by type of equipment and company size, 1992 survey, article, C1850–13.509

Security equipment dealer purchasing outlook, by type of electronic equipment, 1993 survey article, C1850–13.504

Security equipment dealer views on outlook for selected types of monitoring technology, 1988-92, survey article, C1850–13.508

Security equipment industry outlook, including revenue trends, and home alarm system prices, Oct-Nov 1992 survey, annual feature, C1850–13.503

Security equipment industry personnel income, education, work conditions, and activities, 1993 survey, annual article, C1850–13.510

Security mgmt issues and devs, articles and special features on personnel, policies, devices, and related topics, monthly rpt, C1850–12

Security system user views on color closed-circuit TV systems, multiplexer technology, and computer system protection methods, May and Aug 1993 surveys, C1850–13.510

Self-managed work team obstacles cited by executives, 1990 survey, article, C4215–1.505

Index by Subjects and Names

Small business executives views on business conditions and problems, funding sources, and Clinton Admin economic plan, Mar 1993 survey, C5800–7.524

Small business views on current and expected economic conditions, survey findings, quarterly rpt, A7815–1

Small corporation mgmt issues and activity, with opinion data on business conditions, monthly rpt, C4687–1

Small corporations citing selected reasons for providing and not providing employee health insurance, 1993 survey feature, C4215–1.506

Snack food executive views on industry problems, challenges, and outlook, 1992, annual rpt, A8905–1

Steel service center business conditions and outlook, monthly survey, A8990–2

Stone products (sand/gravel and crushed stone) production trends and outlook, with data by region, 1992 annual article, C0125–6

Supermarket deli dept sales and performance indicators, 1992 and trends, annual article, C5225–1.505

Supermarket executive views on efficient consumer response (ECR) logistics system, 1993 survey article, C4655–1.511

Supermarket health/beauty aid merchandising practices, 1993 survey article, C5225–1.506

Supermarket health/beauty care and general merchandise product marketing devs and issues, 1992 survey article, C4655–1.502

Supermarket industry views on vendor product pricing, including every day low price concept, 1992 survey article, C4655–1.501

Supermarket meat dept views on media effect on sales, and outlook for product types and labor, 1992, annual article, C4655–1.509

Supermarket operator views on bakery and deli operations and products, including concerns about health-related incidents, 1993 survey article, C4655–1.507

Supermarket seafood dept sales and performance indicators, 1992 annual survey feature, C4825–3.501

Supermarket video cassette rental dept operations and outlook, 1993 survey article, C4655–1.508

Tax reform measures most beneficial to industry, views of manufacturing executives, 1993 survey article, C1850–4.507

Telephone toll-free ("800") number customer carrier selection criteria, 1993 survey article, C4725–3.507

Truck (heavy-/medium-duty) manufacturers ranked by desirability of franchises, dealer views, May and Nov 1992, article, C2710–3.525

TV advertising purchasing plans and budgets, views of media executives, 1993 annual survey feature, C2710–1.528

TV audience share predictions of advertising agency representatives, by network and program, 1993/94 season, annual article, C1850–14.530

TV audience shares for 38 new network series, as projected by advertising agency executives, 1993/94, annual article, C2710–1.529

TV station owner views on arrangements with cable operators for retransmission rights, including compensation, 1992 survey article, C2965–1.505

TV station preferred type of agreement with cable operators for retransmission rights, July 1993 survey, article, C1850–14.533

Veterinarian capital equipment replacement practices, including finance methods, 1992 survey article, C9480–1.502

Veterinarian outlook for client and staffing levels, income, and practice issues, 1993, survey article, C9480–1.502

Volunteer programs for employees, including methods used to encourage volunteering, obstacles, benefits, and costs, 1992 survey, article, C2176–1.511, R4105–78.26

West South Central region printing industry devs, including sales trends and printer views on business conditions, 1992 feature, C1850–10.502

State and local:

Arizona economic indicator forecasts, and views of analysts on related issues, monthly rpt, U0282–1

Arizona industrial purchasing managers views on business activity, monthly rpt, U0280–1

Georgia, Atlanta metro area small/medium-sized corporations export market awareness and promotion program involvement, 1988 survey, article, U5930–1.502

Illinois, Chicago industrial purchasing managers business activity index, bimonthly rpt, S2405–2

New York City metro area printing industry devs, including sales trends and printer views on business conditions, 1992 feature, C1850–10.501

New York State security equipment dealer views on licensing law and criminal background checks for industry personnel, Aug 1992 survey, article, C1850–13.501

Pennsylvania, suburban Philadelphia business views on alarm system purchasing, including info sources, 1991 surveys, article, C1850–13.502

South Dakota family-owned business characteristics, outlook, and views on business and family issues, 1993 survey, article, U8595–1.503

Tennessee economic indicator trends and forecasts, and business executives views on selected issues, 1993 annual articles, U8710–1.502

Business startups see Business formations

Busing see School busing

Butter see Dairy industry and products

Buttery, Thomas J. "2nd ATE Survey of Critical Issues in Teacher Education", A3375–1

Butynski, William "State Resources and Services Related to Alcohol and Other Drug Abuse Problems, FY91", A7112–1

Cable television

Advertising expenditures by medium for top 100 advertisers, with comparisons to earnings and sales, and detail by product type and brand, 1991-92, annual rpt, C2710–1.547

Advertising on cable TV, purchasing plans and budgets, views of media executives, 1993 annual survey feature, C2710–1.528

Baseball broadcasting, including TV and radio originators, and rights payments, by major league team, 1993 annual article, C1850–14.515

Basketball (professional) broadcast coverage, by team, 1993/94, article, C1850–14.540

Capital expenditures, residential subscribers, and cable miles by type, for 8 telephone and 4 cable TV companies, 1993 article, C8900–1.513

Directory of publicly owned cable TV systems, with subscribers and channels, 1993 annual feature, A2625–1.501

Elementary and secondary private and public schools with cable TV, 1989/90-1992/93, article, R4800–2.513

Expansion plans of cable system operators, including use of digital compression and fiber optic vs coaxial cable, fall 1992 survey, article, C1850–2.508

Financial ratios and performance, for over 350 SIC 4-digit industries, FY88-92, annual rpt, A6400–3

Football (college and professional) cable TV coverage, with data by network, 1993 annual article, C1850–14.534

Household market shares for top 10 and all other cable TV companies, 1993 article, C8900–1.518

Household penetration and viewership, 1991 and trends, annual rpt, A4620–1.2

Households with cable TV, by State and Nielsen market area, Sept 1993, annual rpt, B6670–2

Industry devs, including leading multiple system operators and systems, finances, advertising, and data by network and service, biweekly rpt, C1858–1, C2965–1

Industry devs, including subscribers, homes passed, number of systems, and program and network ratings, weekly rpt, C1850–14

Marketing budget shares for basic, pay, and pay-per-view cable TV, 1991-93, article, C9380–1.514

Mass media company revenues for leading firms, with detail by medium, 1991-92, annual feature, C2710–1.540

Newspaper-company owned cable TV companies among 50 largest systems, with subscribers, Dec 1992, article, A8605–1.510

Oil industry advertising expenditures for network and spot TV, including cable networks and syndicated programs, by company, 1991-92, annual fact book, C4680–1.507

Ratings and households reached, by network, weekly rpt quarterly feature, C1850–14.506, C1850–14.517, C1850–14.530, C1850–14.540

Statistical profiles of 50 States and DC, general data, 1993 annual almanac, C4712–1

Subscriber readiness to cancel if major broadcast networks are not included on system, Apr 1992 survey, article, C2710–1.533

Subscriber views on cable TV value, desirability, program quality, and service, 1991-93, survey article, C2710–1.544

Cable television

Subscribers of top 8 cable TV companies not affiliated with telephone companies, 1993 article, C4725–3.517

Utility regulatory agency policies and practices, and industry financial and operating data, by utility type and agency, 1991/92 annual rpt, A7015–3

Viewer program interests for cable TV, Mar 1993 survey, article, C2710–1.538

State and local:

Arizona statistical abstract, general data, 1993 recurring rpt, U5850–2.19

DC statistical profile, general data, 1992 annual rpt, S1535–3.3

Georgia statistical abstract, general data, 1992-93 biennial rpt, U6730–1.8

Hawaii data book, general data, 1992 annual rpt, S2090–1.16

Kansas statistical abstract, general data, 1991/92 annual rpt, U7095–2.13

Oklahoma statistical abstract, general data, 1992 annual rpt, U8130–2.17

Tennessee statistical abstract, general data, 1992/93 annual rpt, U8710–2.8

Texas trade, transportation, and public utilities employment, by SIC 2- and 3-digit industry and detailed occupation, 2nd qtr 1991, triennial survey rpt, S7675–1.31

Vermont cable TV customers and rates, by company, 1987-91, biennial rpt, S8100–1

Wyoming property assessed valuations and tax levies, by property type, tax purpose, and location, 1992 and trends, annual rpt, S8990–1.2

Cabotage

see Inland water transportation

CAD/CAM

see Computer industry and products

see Computer use

Caffeine

Soft drink caffeine-free product consumption and market shares, with detail for top 3 companies, 1988 and 1992, annual article, C0125–2.504

Soft drink caffeine-free product sales by leading brand, and shares of total market, 1987-91, annual rpt, C0125–3.1

California

Aerospace defense company plans for converting to commercial business and for leaving the State, survey of firms in Southern California, 1993 article, C5800–4.523

Agricultural exports through California ports, by detailed commodity and country of destination, with State export-related production and acreage, 1991 and trends, annual rpt, B9520–1

Agricultural statistics, including production, acreage, finances, and marketing, by commodity, annual rpt series, S0850–1

Auto fleet use and views on operation of flexible-fuel vehicles capable of running on methanol or gasoline, California survey, 1993 articles, A6755–1.502

Banks and trust companies, financial condition by instn, with regulatory info, Dec 1992, annual rpt, S0810–1

Census of Population and Housing detailed findings, 1990, S0840–9

Cigarette tax Proposition 99 mandating spending for health education and research, actual and projected expenditures by program category, FY90-94, article, A2623–1.511

Citrus fruit production and marketing data for major producing States, 1991/92 and trends, annual rpt, S1685–1.1

Correctional instn inmates, by offense, demographic characteristics, and instn, Dec 1992, semiannual rpt, S0820–2

Correctional instn inmates, with criminal background and demographic characteristics, 1991 and trends, annual rpt, S0820–1

Correctional instn populations, operating cost trends, and violent crime rate, 1981-90, A7575–3

Court activity, including caseloads and dispositions, by case type and court, and location, FY92 and trends, annual rpt, S0905–1, S0905–2

Crime rates compared with incarceration rates, for California, Wisconsin, and Minnesota, 1970s-90, A7575–1.12

Crimes and arrests, and criminal justice system data, 1987-92, annual rpt, S0910–1

Criminal justice system detailed data, by offense, county, race-ethnicity, age, and sex, 1991 and trends, annual rpt, S0910–2

Death rates and estimated alcohol-related mortality, by cause and demographic characteristics, 1980-89, article, A2623–1.508

Defense expenditures and aerospace industry job losses, with detail for selected local areas, 1992 article, C5800–4.502

Diesel fuel refining capacity, with projected impact of new State law, for 9 major refiners and aggregate independents, 1993-94, article, C6985–1.544

Diesel fuel supply under compliance with and variance from low-aromatics regulations, with detail for selected refiners, 1993-94, article, C4680–1.511

Diesel fuel wholesale prices before and after EPA low-sulfur requirements, for 6 California cities, Aug and Oct 1993, article, C6985–1.551

Economic condition, including population, employment and earnings, income, business activity, and taxation, 1993 annual rpt, S0840–3

Economic indicators for California, bimonthly rpt, S0840–1

Economic indicators for 10 Western States, including forecasts from selected organizations, monthly rpt, U0282–2

Election results, and voter registration and turnout, by district and/or county, 1992 and trends, biennial rpt, S0934–1

Electric power generating costs at best performing plants, for 6 types of energy sources, 1993 article, C6985–6.507

Elementary and secondary private schools, enrollment by grade, grads, and staff, with data by county, 1992/93 and trends, annual rpt, S0825–8

Elementary and secondary public schools, enrollment by grade, and grads, by county, 1992/93 and trends, annual rpt, S0825–7

Elementary and secondary school enrollment, grads, and staff, by race-ethnicity, 1992/93 and trends, annual rpt, S0825–9

Elementary/secondary school limited-English-proficiency enrollment,

teachers, and programs, by 1st language, grade level, and county, 1992 and trends, annual rpt, S0825–10

Employment statistics, by demographic characteristics, industry, MSA, and county, monthly rpt, S0830–1

Engineers salaries by degree level and years since college degree, for Southern California, 1993, annual survey rpt, A0685–3, A0685–5

Ethanol demand for transportation use, and methanol/methyl tertiary butyl ether imports, 1992/93-2000/2001, article, C6985–1.533

Fig industry production, acreage, and prices in California, with US consumption and imports by country, 1950s-92, annual rpt, A3750–1

Gasoline average monthly sales volume, and service station distribution by sales volume, 1993 article, C4680–1.506

Govt financial condition, including revenues by source, expenditures by agency and function, fund balances, and bonded debt, FY92 and trends, annual rpt, S0815–1

Govt general fund budget deficit reduction components, 1993 article, B8500–2.521

Health behavior risk factor surveillance survey results, by respondent characteristics, 1991 and trends, annual rpt, S0865–2

Higher education systems funding by source and expenditures by program category, with enrollment data, FY60s-94, annual rpt, S0827–3

Hospital expenditures, beds, and utilization data, with comparisons to total US, Canada, and Ontario, 1987, article, A1865–1.512

Housing (new home) shopper characteristics and design features sought, 1993 survey article, C4300–1.511

Housing (new home) shopper purchase motivations and design features sought, 1992-93 surveys, article, C1850–8.509

Immigrants distribution by county of origin, 1986-90, article, R9372–2.509

Income tax State returns, for individuals and corporations, and property tax assistance, by income class and county, 1990 and trends, annual rpt, S0855–1

Insurance industry financial and underwriting data, by company and type of insurance, with regulatory info, 1991, annual rpt, S0900–1

Labor force planning rpt, including population characteristics, and employment by industry, 1992 annual rpt, S0830–2

Library finances, staff, holdings, and services, by library type and facility, FY92, annual rpt, S0825–2

Lumber production in California redwood region, by species and county, 1984-92, annual rpt, A9395–1

Markets with daily newspapers, demographic and economic info by geographic area, US and Canada, 1993 annual rpt, C3250–1

Motion picture production starts in California vs rest of US, 1985 and 1992, article, C9380–1.540

Motor vehicle emissions requirements, 1994-2003 model years, article, C2710–3.534

Index by Subjects and Names — Campus security

Motor vehicle registrations for California and US, 1st half 1992, article, C2710–3.501

Oil and gas wells and footage drilled, by type of well, State, and offshore location, quarterly rpt, A2575–6

Oil/gas industry production, finances, exploration, and reserves, by State, 1992 and trends, annual rpt, A5425–1.1

Oil/gas production, regulatory compliance and production costs, and wellhead prices, by State region, 1993 article, C6985–1.525

Population by age, sex, race-ethnicity, and county, decennially 1990-2040, recurring rpt, S0840–4

Postsecondary education enrollment and degrees, by sex, race-ethnicity, and instn, 1990/91, annual series, S0827–2

Public opinion in US on selected foreign policy issues, with detail for 3 States, 1993 survey, annual rpt, A4965–1.2

Public opinion on public school quality and parental use of State vouchers to pay for private schools, Sept 1993 survey, C5800–7.550

School bus alternative fuel efficiency, with mileage and Btu(h) per passenger mile for 3 fuels, 1993 article, C1575–1.507

Socioeconomic and govtl data for municipalities, counties, and school districts, 1993 annual rpt, C4712–3

Statistical abstract of California, detailed social, govtl, and economic data, 1992 annual rpt, S0840–2

Statistical profiles of 50 States and DC, general data, 1993 annual almanac, C4712–1

Tax collections (excluding income tax), by locality, company, and type of tax, FY92 and trends, annual rpt, S0835–1

Traffic accidents, fatalities, and injuries, by vehicle type, circumstances, location, vehicle type, and driver and victim characteristics, 1991 and trends, annual rpt, S0885–1

Utility and transportation regulatory agency activities, scope of jurisdiction, finances, and employees, by agency, 1991/92 annual rpt, A7015–2

Utility and transportation regulatory data, including revenue requests and rates of return by company, FY92 annual rpt, S0930–1

Vital statistics, including population, births, and deaths by cause, by demographic characteristics and county, 1990 and trends, annual rpt, S0865–1

Welfare cases, recipients, and expenditures, by program and county, monthly rpt, S0935–2

Wine inventories by product type, 1971-92, annual rpt, C4775–2.2

see also Los Angeles, Calif.

see also San Diego, Calif.

see also San Francisco, Calif.

see also under By City and By County in the "Index by Categories"

see also under By State in the "Index by Categories"

Cambodia

Offshore oil/gas exploration in Gulf of Thailand, size and operator for 13 tracts licensed in Thai and Cambodian sectors, 1991-92, article, C6985–2.503

Refugee repatriated population coming from 7 Thailand camp sites, for 8 Cambodia reception centers, Mar-Nov 1992, R9372–2.502

UN peacekeeping personnel serving in Cambodia, from top 20 countries, Jan 1993, article, R5650–2.540

see also Indochinese refugees

Cambridge, Mass.

Elementary/secondary school transportation expenditures before and after parental school selection program implementation, 1978/79-1991/92, R3810–7

Camcorders

see Video recordings and equipment

Cameras

see Photography and photographic equipment

Cameroon

Energy intl sourcebook, with detail on oil and gas industry operations, supply-demand, and prices, for approx 80 countries, 1970s-91, annual compilation, C6985–10.2

Camp, Camille G.

"Corrections Yearbook, 1992", R4300–1

Camp, George M.

"Corrections Yearbook, 1992", R4300–1

Campaign funds

Congressional campaign finances, with detailed data for individual Members, and leading contributors by type and industry, 1990 election and trends, biennial rpt, R3828–2, R3828–3

Congressional campaign fund finances, with expenditures by item and contributions by donor type, by candidate, district, and State, 1990 elections, C2500–6

Violations of $25,000 contribution limit, and fines paid, for 9 individuals, 1988-90, article, C5800–7.522

Women candidates in State-level elections, outcome summaries including campaign funds raised, voting by sex, and winner's race-ethnicity, 1992, U4510–4.4

State and local:

Hawaii data book, general data, 1992 annual rpt, S2090–1.8

Hawaii tax allocations, by fund, FY91-92, annual rpt, S2120–1

Montana income tax checkoffs, by purpose, 1987-91, biennial rpt, S4750–1.1

New Jersey gubernatorial elections fund finances, FY92, annual rpt, S5455–1

Utah income tax political campaign fund checkoff, participation by political party and county, 1991 and trends, triennial rpt, U8960–1.8

see also Political action committees

Campaigns

see Elections

Camping

Participation in 53 sports, by demographic characteristics, State, and census div, 1992, annual rpt series, A8485–3

Travel trips and traveler characteristics, including mode, purpose, type of lodging, and area of destination and origin, quarterly rpt, R9375–14

State and local:

Maryland statistical abstract, general data, 1993-94 biennial rpt, S3605–1.13

New York State statistical yearbook, general data, 1992 annual rpt, U5100–1.15

Campus disorders

see Student unrest

Campus security

State and local:

Alabama crimes and arrests, by offense and location, and law enforcement employment, for State instns, 1992 and trends, annual rpt, S0119–1

Alabama statistical abstract, general data, 1992 recurring rpt, U5680–2.10

Arizona law enforcement employment by sex, by local agency, Oct 1992, annual rpt, S0505–2.2

Arkansas crimes and arrests, and law enforcement personnel by sex, by State-assisted college campus, 1992, annual rpt, S0652–1

California criminal justice system expenditures and employment, by type of agency or function, 1982-91, annual rpt, S0910–2.1

Colorado crimes and arrests, by offense and location, with offender characteristics, and assaults on police, 1992, annual rpt, S1068–1

Connecticut crimes and arrests, by offense, with data by local agency, and victim-offender characteristics, 1992, annual rpt, S1256–1

Delaware crimes reported and cleared, by reporting agency, 1988-91, annual rpt, S1375–5

Illinois criminal offenses for campus, railroad, and other special police forces, 1991, annual rpt, S2536–1

Illinois statistical abstract, general data, 1992 annual rpt, U6910–2

Kansas crimes by offense, and law enforcement employees by sex, by State-assisted higher education instn, 1992, annual rpt, S2925–1

Kentucky crimes and arrests, by offense, with data by location and offender characteristics, 1992, annual rpt, S3150–1

Maine crimes reported on individual college campuses, by offense, 1991, annual rpt, S3475–1.2

Maryland law enforcement employment by sex, criminal offenses and arrests, and assaults on police, by local agency and county, 1991-92, annual rpt, S3665–1

New Jersey crimes by offense, and law enforcement employees, by higher education instn, 1992, annual rpt, S5430–1

New York State crimes and arrests by offense and demographic characteristics, and court activity and corrections, 1991 and trends, annual rpt, S5760–3

North Carolina crimes by offense, and law enforcement employment, by local agency, 1991-92, annual rpt, S5955–1.1

Oklahoma Crime Index offenses, by county and reporting agency, 1990-92, annual rpt, S6465–1.2

Pennsylvania crimes and arrests, by offense, with data by location and offender characteristics, 1992 and trends, annual rpt, S6860–1

South Dakota public higher education instn crimes and arrests, by selected offense and instn, Aug 1991-July 1992, annual rpt, S7375–1

Campus security

Texas criminal offenses on college campuses, 1992, annual rpt, S7735–2.2

Utah crimes and arrests, by offense, county, and local agency, 1992 and trends, annual rpt, S7890–3

Virginia crimes and arrests by offense, and law enforcement employment, by location and reporting agency, 1992, annual rpt, S8295–2.2

Washington State crimes, clearances, and law enforcement employment, for university campuses, 1992, annual rpt, S8440–1

West Virginia crimes and arrests, by offense and higher education instn, 1990-91, annual rpt, S8610–1.2

Wisconsin crimes and arrests, by offense, offender characteristics, county, and local agency, 1992 and trends, annual rpt, S8771–1

Wyoming crimes and arrests, and law enforcement personnel, by jurisdiction, 1991, annual rpt, S8867–3

Canada

Abortions occurring in Maine to Canadian residents, 1991, annual rpt, S3460–2

Abortions occurring in Minnesota to Canadian residents, 1991, annual rpt, S4190–2

Abortions occurring in North Dakota to residents of 2 Canadian Provinces, 1991, annual rpt, S6105–2

Accidental deaths and disabling injuries, by detailed type, victim characteristics, circumstances, and location, 1992 and trends, annual rpt, A8375–2

Air conditioning/refrigeration wholesaler sales trend and outlook, 1992-93, annual rpt, C1800–1

Aircraft (jet) world inventory, by type of aircraft and individual owner/operator, 1992, annual rpt, B1582–1

Airports and communities in North America served by regional vs larger airlines, by carrier and location, 1993 annual rpt, A8795–1.2

Amusement park operating and financial data, including data for US and foreign parks, miniature golf, waterparks, and games, 1992, annual rpt, A5700–1

Apartment building (conventionally financed) detailed income and expense ratios for US and Canada, by building type, metro area, and US region, 1991 and trends, annual rpt, A5600–1

Art museum salaries for 37 positions, by region, population size served, and budget size, FY93, annual rpt, A3290–1

Auto dealer satisfaction with manufacturers, ratings for 21 makes, 1992 survey, article, C2710–3.518

Auto fleet acquisition plans, with factors affecting purchases, 1992 annual survey, A6755–1.501

Auto insurance financial responsibility limits, by State and Canadian Province, 1993 annual rpt, A5650–1

Auto news and devs, with production and sales data and market analysis, US and foreign, by manufacturer and make/model, weekly rpt, C2710–3

Bookstores by type of outlet, US and Canada, 1992, annual compilation, C1650–3.4

Index by Subjects and Names

Bowling (women's) assn membership and league activities, by city and Province, 1991/92, annual rpt, A9415–1

Bus (urban) fleets of 100 largest transit systems in US or Canada, 1993, annual article, C1575–3.507

Bus company fleets, for top 50 private operators in US and Canada, 1993 annual feature, C1575–3.503

Business forms manufacturing plant employment and compensation data, by region, 1992 and trends, biennial rpt, A5785–4

Catalog industry devs, including marketing methods, sales, and operating characteristics, 1992/93 annual rpt, A4620–1.5

Catholic population, clergy, and parishes, by diocese and Province, 1991, annual almanac, C6885–1

Cattle imports into Vermont from Canada and other States, 1988/89-1989/90, biennial rpt, S7978–1

Cattle trade with New Mexico, 1991, annual rpt, S5530–1

Charitable contributions of corporations, distribution by recipient type, 1991 and trends, annual rpt, A0700–1.2

Chemical and related industries production, finances, operating ratios, employment, and trade, by country, company, and chemical, 1980s-92, annual feature, A1250–1.530

Chemical industry worldwide production and trade, selected data by country and world area, 1988-92, annual feature, A1250–1.507

Church membership and contributions, by Protestant denomination, US and Canada, 1991 or 1992, annual article, C2176–1.518

Churches, membership, clergy, and contributions, by denomination, US and Canada, 1991-92, annual rpt, C0105–1

Cigarette price and consumption trends in US and Canada, 1982 and 1992, article, C5800–7.519

Coal foreign trade activity, by country of origin and destination, monthly rpt, A7400–3

Coal industry personnel earnings and employment history, US and Canada, 1993 survey article, C5226–1.507

Coal industry supply-demand, employment, and trade, by country, 1990-91 and trends, annual rpt, A7400–2.2

Coal preparation plants and capacity in US, Canada, and Mexico, by company, 1993 biennial feature, C5226–1.511

Commercial real estate market conditions and outlook, for industrial and office properties, by US metro area and selected foreign city, 1992-93, annual survey, A8916–1

Condominium, cooperative, and planned unit dev detailed expenses, for US and Canada, by building characteristics, metro area, and US region, 1991, annual rpt, A5600–3

Consumer low-calorie and reduced-fat product use, with comparisons to US, 1993 article, C2150–6.508

Consumer photographic and video equipment and supplies ownership, purchasing patterns, and use, by household characteristics, 1992 survey, recurring rpt, A8695–4

Copper smelter capacity in Canada, by company, 1991, annual rpt, S0497–1

Corporate acquisitions involving Canadian companies, with price and participants for top transactions, bimonthly rpt quarterly feature, C4683–1

Corporate employee transfers, and relocation policies, assistance, and costs, 1992, annual survey, B0600–1

Correctional instn and parole admin, summary data, 1992 annual rpt, R4300–1

Correctional instns, inmates, staff, and cost of care, by instn, US and Canada, with operating summary by State or Province, 1992, annual directory, A1305–3

Dental school admission policies, applicants, enrollment, and tuition and fees, by instn, 1992/93, annual rpt, A1475–4.1

Dental school enrollment and grads, program characteristics, and faculty, by US and Canadian instn, 1992/93, annual rpt, A1475–3

Drugstore chains financial performance and marketing operations, by US and Canadian company, 1993 annual feature, C5150–2.511

Economic indexes for US and other industrial countries, and leading and coincident indicators, monthly rpt, U1245–1

Economic indexes for US and selected other countries, composites of leading indicators, monthly rpt, R4105–6

Economic indicators, including population by Province, and imports from US of 4 fast-growing product types, 1993 article, C4687–1.505

Economic indicators, including trade with US, import shares for 8 other countries, population by Province, and employment, 1993 articles, C4687–1.508

Electric power production and capacity by fuel source, and transmission line mileage, for US and Canada, 1992 or 1993 and 2002, article, C6985–6.510

Electric power supply-demand, and utility capacities and fuel requirements, detailed data by US and Canadian region, 1992-2002, annual rpt, A8630–2

Electronics industry trade and/or production trends by product category for 33 countries, with general economic profiles, 1993 annual rpt, A4725–1.4

Energy intl sourcebook, with detail on oil and gas industry operations, supply-demand, and prices, for approx 80 countries, 1970s-91, annual compilation, C6985–10.2

Eye bank activity in US and abroad, including donations by type, source, and donor characteristics, and data by individual bank, 1992 and trends, annual rpt, A4743–1

Farm equipment inventory and retail sales, by Province and/or equipment type, 1993 annual feature, C3450–1.501

Farm equipment retail sales volume, by equipment type, periodic rpt, C0495–1, C3450–1

Flour milling companies and capacity, in US by State, Canada, Mexico, and Central American and Caribbean area countries, 1993 annual directory and buyers guide, C8450–3

Index by Subjects and Names

Canada

Food marketers financial and operating data, by company size and region, 1991-92, annual rpts, A4950–5

Food store market shares and outlets, by company and store type, for approx 350 metro areas in US and Canada, with industry operating data, 1993 annual rpt, C3400–6

General Educational Dev (GED) testing programs and results, by jurisdiction, 1992 and trends, annual rpt, A1410–16

Grain elevators and capacity in US and Canada, by type and State or Province, with ranking of top storage companies, 1993 annual directory and buyers guide, C8450–2

Hard goods US manufacturers exports to Canada and outlook for 1993, by product line, 1993 annual survey rpt, A1800–1

Hearing aid sales of US-made units by Province, quarterly rpt, A5185–1

Higher education enrollment of Canadians in North Dakota, by instn, fall 1992, annual rpt, S6110–1

Higher education physical plant operations, costs, employment, salaries, and energy use, by instn and region, 1991/92, recurring rpt, A3183–1

Higher education, 2-year college enrollment, degrees, faculty and staff, and tuition/fees, by instn and State, 1992 annual directory, A0640–1

Home improvement sales and stores, for 4-5 retail chains and buying groups, with economic indicators of interest to retailers, 1992, articles, C5150–6.508

Horse racing activity, attendance, handle, purse distribution, and govt revenue, by Province, 1990, annual rpt, A3363–1.1

Hospital expenditures, beds, and utilization data, with comparison to US, 1987, article, A1865–1.512

Ice cream and frozen dessert production, with detail by Province, 1992 and trends, annual rpt, A5825–1.2

Insurance (life/health) industry asset allocation and investment yields, for top 125 US and Canadian companies, 1992 and trends, annual article, C1050–2.512

Investment mgmt firms, assets and operating data for approx 900 instns, Jan 1993, annual feature, C2710–2.511

Iron and steel industry finances, production, shipments, materials consumption, and trade, 1992 and trends, annual rpt, A2000–2.4

Iron ore production, shipments, trade, and plant inventories and consumption, US and Canada, 1992 and trends, annual rpt, A2010–3

Iron ore receipts, consumption, and inventories, and blast furnaces operating, for US and Canada, monthly rpt, A2010–1

Iron ore shipments in US and Canada, with detail by Great Lakes port, monthly rpt, A2010–2

Latin America-Canada trade, by country, 1988-90, annual rpt, U6250–1.26

Librarians (special) salaries, by location, work setting, and personal characteristics, US and Canada, 1992 and trends, biennial survey rpt, A8965–1

Librarians at universities and research instns, salaries by sex, type of position, and instn, FY92 and trends, annual survey, A3365–2

Libraries by detailed type, 1992, annual compilation, C1650–3.4

Library (research) holdings, expenditures by type, and staff, for 120 academic and nonacademic instns, US and Canada, FY92, annual rpt, A3365–1

Library (research) holdings, staff, and expenditures, for instns in US and Canada, 1991/92, annual feature, C2175–1.511

Library/info science school enrollment, staff and student characteristics, finances, and curricula, by school and degree program, 1991/92, annual rpt, A3235–1

Life insurance company mortgage and real estate holdings, by State and outlying area, and in Canada and overseas, 1991, biennial fact book, A1325–1.4

Life insurance individual policy sales indicators, monthly rpt, A6225–2

Life insurance policy purchases and payments, and company income and assets, 1991 and trends, biennial fact book, A1325–1.7

Life insurance premium income of top 500 US/Canadian life/health insurers, 1992 and trends, annual article, C1050–2.509

Life insurance sales and insurance in force, for top 25-135 issuers of ordinary, group, and industrial life policies, 1992, annual article, C1050–2.510

Life insurance sales, policies in force, and assets, for top 100 US/Canadian life/health insurers, 1992, annual article, C1050–2.509

Local govt structure, officials, and administrative assns, 1993 annual rpt, A5800–1

Lumber industry foreign trade with US, monthly rpt, A1630–1

Lumber industry foreign trade with US, 1984-92, annual rpt, A9395–1

Lumber trade with US, and production data, by product type, monthly rpt, A1630–3

Machine tool industry operating data by country and product, 1992 and trends, annual rpt, A3179–2.2

Magazine circulation and advertising rates, for US and Canadian publications, 1988-92, annual rpt, A3385–1

Magazine circulation, by US and Canadian publication, 6-month periods ended Dec 1992 and June 1993, semiannual rpt, A3385–3.4

Manufactured fibers imports and exports, by fiber type, 1989-92, C3460–1.510

Manufacturing employees, wages, value added, and shipments, top 10 industry groups, 1987, annual rpt, C3975–5.2

Markets with daily newspapers, demographic and economic info by geographic area, US and Canada, 1993 annual rpt, C3250–1

Mass transit rail system energy efficiency ratings, for 14 systems in US and Canada, 1993 article, C1575–3.506

Mass transit rail system revenue passenger miles per vehicle hour, for 14 systems in US and Canada, 1993 article, C1575–3.505

Mass transit system finances and operations, including vehicles by type, fares, and employment, 1960s-90, annual rpt, A2650–1.2

Medical school tuition and fees, applicants, and entrants, by instn, 1992/93, annual rpt, A3273–10

Metal heat treatment industry billings, for Michigan, Canada, and 7 regions, monthly press release, A6376–1

Mineral exploration activities, expenses, and staff, for foreign and domestic operations of US and Canadian companies, 1991, article, C5226–2.508

Mortgage-backed securities issuance value, by issuer, 1987-93, article, A6450–2.508

Motion picture and TV subsidy expenditures by 2 natl organizations, by Province, FY92, article, C9380–1.503

Motor vehicle assembly plant production, by State and Canadian Province, manufacturer, model, and plant, 1993 model year, annual article, C2710–3.551

Motor vehicle production by make and manufacturer, and sales, registrations, and drivers licenses by Province, 1993 annual rpt, A0865–1.1

Motor vehicle production, plant capacity, and sales by manufacturer and/or make, 1992 and trends, annual data book, C2710–3.531

Motor vehicle unit sales per 1,000 population, 1985-92, article, C2710–3.549

Motor vehicle world production, sales, trade, and registrations, by country, world area, manufacturer, and make, 1991 and trends, annual rpt, A0865–2.1

Mutual fund sales, by State and census div, and for Canada and US territories, 1991, annual rpt, A6025–1.2

Natural gas exports to US for cogeneration plants, 1989/90-1995/96, article, C6985–1.536

Natural gas exports to US, 1990-93, annual article, C6985–1.539

Natural gas processing plants, capacity, and production, by company and Province, 1993 annual rpt, C6985–1.537

Natural gas production outlook to 2010, domestic use and foreign trade, and exports to US via 8 delivery points, 1993 article, C6985–1.529

Natural gas reserves by Province, and trade with US, 1991 and trends, annual rpt, A1775–3.1, A1775–3.2

Natural gas reserves in Western Canada, by location and stratigraphic age, 1993 article, C6985–1.546

Natural gas resources in Western Canada, by stratigraphic formation, 1993, article, C6985–1.552

Natural gas storage capacity and additions, for Western and Eastern Canada, 1986-2000, article, C6985–1.552

Natural gas trade with US, 1956-90, annual compilation, C6985–9.2

Newspaper (daily) circulation, by Canadian publication and city, 6-month periods ended Sept 1992 and Mar 1993, semiannual rpt, A3385–3.2

Newspaper (weekly) circulation, by Canadian publication and city, 6-month periods ended Sept 1992 and Mar 1993, semiannual rpt, A3385–3.3

Newspaper circulation, operations, and finances, US and Canada, 1940s-93, annual rpt, A8605–4

Canada

Index by Subjects and Names

Newspaper industry capital expenditures, by item, US and Canada, 1992-93, annual article, A8605–1.507

Newspaper prices per copy for daily editions, 1992, annual article, A8605–1.507

Newsprint production, consumption, trade, prices, and mill capacity, with data by world area, 1991-92 and trends, annual rpt, A8610–1

Newsprint production, shipments, plant capacity, consumption, trade, and recycling, US and Canada, 1970s-92, annual rpt, A1630–8

Newsprint production, shipments, trade, inventory, consumption, and plant capacity, US and Canada, monthly rpt, A1630–4

Newsprint recycling capacity, demand, and wastepaper consumption, for Northeast US and Eastern Canada, with data by mill, various years 1988-2000, A4375–15

Nuclear reactors in operation, with capacity, electricity generation, and construction, by unit and country, 1992, annual rpt, B6800–2.2

Office building detailed income and expense data, and energy use, US and Canada, by building characteristics, metro area, and US region, 1991 and trends, annual rpt, A5600–2

Oil and gas drilling and production technology devs, including drilling rigs in operation, monthly rpt, C4420–1

Oil and gas drilling rigs and active seismic exploration crews, 1970s-91, annual compilation, C6985–9.1

Oil and gas exports to US, wells by Province, and drilling activity, 1993 annual feature, C6985–1.513

Oil and gas industry trends, with data by company, State, and country, 1993 annual compilation, C6985–4

Oil and gas intl supply-demand, exploration, refining, reserves, and industry finances, basic data by country and company, 1993 annual rpt, C6985–3

Oil and gas pipeline failure rates, 1955-82, article, C6985–1.537

Oil and gas pipeline mileage under construction or planned in 1993, annual article, C6985–1.515

Oil and gas trade with US, 1987-92, article, C6985–1.544

Oil exports to US, by PAD district of receipt, weekly rpt, A2575–1

Oil industry capital spending in US and Canada, by function, 1991-93, annual articles, C6985–1.517

Oil rigs operating in Canada, total and offshore, 1980-92, annual rpt, C6985–5.2

Oil supply-demand, marketing, prices, finances, and employment, detailed data for US and Canada, 1993 annual fact book, C4680–1.507

Oil/gas seismic exploration land and marine crews, by world area, weekly rpt quarterly feature, C6985–1.515, C6985–1.521

Oil/gas seismic exploration land crews and vessels, by world area or country, quarterly press release, A8912–2

Oil/gas seismic exploration land crews and vessels, Canada and US, monthly press release, A8912–1

Oil/gas wells drilled and planned, by Province or region, 1993, annual article, C6985–1.539

Paper industry sales and earnings of individual companies in US and Canada, monthly rpt quarterly feature, C3975–2.502, C3975–2.503, C3975–2.506, C3975–2.508, C3975–2.512

Paperboard packaging industry corrugated and folding carton box plants and equipment, by census div and for Canada, 1990-92, annual article, C0125–4.501

Pipeline construction projects planned in US, Canada, and other countries, including costs, by pipeline type and company, 1993 annual feature, C6780–2.502

Planning profession employment and salaries, by type of employer, demographic and professional characteristics, and location, 1991 and trends, biennial rpt, A2615–1

Plastics and resin sales by material and major market, foreign trade, and capacity by company, 1991-92, annual feature, C5800–12.504

Plastics imports as percent of domestic demand for US-Canada bilateral trade, by selected resin, 1986 and 1992, article, A1250–1.525

Plastics resin and film/sheet trade, including percent bilateral with US, monthly rpt quarterly table, C5800–12.502, C5800–12.506, C5800–12.509, C5800–12.512

Population, income, and unemployment rate, for Manitoba and Saskatchewan Provinces, 1993 annual rpt, S6140–2

Population of Canadian areas bordering Alaska, 1991, annual rpt, S0320–4

Potash muriates and sulfates, sales and trade, US and Canada, quarterly press release, A8720–5

Potash production, inventories, and sales and exports by State, Canadian Province, and country of destination, monthly rpt, A8720–1

Potash production, inventories, sales, and exports, US and Canada, monthly rpt, A8720–2

Private elementary and secondary school enrollment, staff, and finances, by school type, 1980s-1992/93, annual rpt, A6835–3

Psychology grad dept faculty salaries, by academic rank and years in rank, 1992/93 and trends, annual rpt, A2620–1

Psychology grad depts, faculty characteristics, enrollment, and student aid, US and Canada, 1990/91 and trends, annual rpt, A2620–3

Public opinion in US, Canada, and Mexico on North American Free Trade Agreement, Aug-Sept 1992 Gallup Poll and trends, C4040–1.503

Public opinion on environmental and population issues, and related church involvement, for US, Brazil, Canada, and Mexico, 1992 survey, R8780–1.504

Pulp and paper industry capital spending plans of US and Canadian companies, by purpose and geographic area, 1992-94, annual survey article, C3975–2.503

Pulp and paper industry operations and finances, US and Canada, with detail by company and product grade, and world production and trade summary, 1993 annual rpt, C3975–5

Pulp and paper industry production, capacity, consumption, trade, and sales/earnings data, including profiles for selected companies and sectors, monthly rpt, C3975–2

Pulp and paper industry salaries, 1992 survey, annual article, C3975–2.503

Pulp, paper, and paperboard industry production, trade, and operating data, by product class, monthly rpt, A1630–5

Rental equipment industry financial data, by revenue size group and region, and for Canada, 1991 and trends, annual rpt, A2665–1

Retail chain financial data and business info for approx 240 US and Canadian companies, 1991-92 and trends, annual rpt, C3400–2

Retail general merchandise chain sales, earnings, and stores, for top companies worldwide, with detail for selected areas, 1991-92, annual feature, C5150–3.516

Salary budget increases and structure, by industry and region, and for Canada, 1993-94 and trends, annual survey rpt, A1295–1

School bus fleet rankings, top contractors in US and Canada, 1992 survey, annual article, C1575–1.501

Securities industry financial and operating trends, 1993 article, A8825–1.507

Securities market participation by foreign and US investors, by world area and country, quarterly rpt, A8825–2

Shopping center financial and operating data, with detail by type of tenant, US and Canada, 1991, triennial rpt, R9285–1

Silver market activity worldwide and in US, including production, consumption, by end use, stocks, trade, and prices, by country, 1988-92, annual rpt, B4300–1

Soybean production and marketing data, including utilization, prices, and trade, with comparison to other oilseeds, 1920s-93, annual rpt, B8480–1

Supermarkets opened, remodeled, and closed, including store features, dev costs, and rent, by region and sales size, 1992 and trends, annual rpt, A4950–2

Swine breeding stock porcine stress syndrome mutation prevalence by breed, in US, Canada, and UK, 1993 article, A3100–2.520

Textile fiber consumption and foreign trade, by fiber type, 1981-91, annual feature, C3460–1.507

Textile manufactured fibers imports and exports, by fiber type and trading partner, 1989-1st 9 months 1992, recurring feature, C3460–1.504

Textile manufactured fibers imports and exports, by fiber type and trading partner, 1989-92, recurring feature, C3460–1.506

Textile manufactured fibers imports and exports, by fiber type and trading partner, 1990-1st half 1993, recurring feature, C3460–1.512

Textile mill consumption of manufactured fibers, cotton, and wool, for selected countries, 1984-91, annual feature, C3460–1.501

Index by Subjects and Names

Theological school enrollment, staff and compensation, and finances, with data by instn, 1991/92 and trends, annual rpt, A3376–1

Tobacco product exports to US, and cigarette retail vs black market prices, 1992 article, C3950–1.503

Traffic accident deaths in selected Provinces, bimonthly rpt, A8375–1

Traffic accidents in Montana, by place of vehicle registration, 1992, annual rpt, S4705–2

Transportation regulatory agency policies and practices for motor carriers and railroads, by agency, 1991/92 annual rpt, A7015–4

Travel/tourism industry devs, including summary data on travel indicators, monthly rpt, R9375–1

Trust instns and assets managed, approx 5,000 depts, US and Canada, 1993 annual directory, C2425–2.501

Uranium marketing, terms of transactions for major selling-buying countries or areas, and price index and earnings data in allied industries, monthly rpt, B6800–1

Uranium production and reserves by company or mine, 1992 annual rpt, B6800–2.2

Utility and transportation regulatory agency activities, scope of jurisdiction, finances, and employees, by agency, 1991/92 annual rpt, A7015–2

Utility regulatory agency policies and practices, and industry financial and operating data, by utility type and agency, 1991/92 annual rpt, A7015–3

Vegetable shipments to Canada from Florida and all other States, by commodity, 1991/92, annual rpt, S1685–1.2

Veterinarians by professional characteristics and location, and financial and education summaries, 1993 annual directory, A3100–1

Veterinary school enrollment by sex, program, instn, and place of residence, US and Canada, 1992/93, annual article, A3100–2.516

Veterinary surgery teaching methods used at 27 US and Canadian veterinary schools, 1993 article, A3100–2.521

Vital events occurring in Vermont or involving Vermont residents, 1991, annual rpt, S8054–1

Wheat supply-demand summary, 1987/88-1992/93, annual rpt, A7310–1

Winter residents of Phoenix, Arizona with permanent residence in Canada, 1992/93, article, U0280–1.508

Wood panel production by grade, 1984-92, annual article, C3975–1.501

Workers compensation law coverage, benefits, and other info, by State, outlying area, and Canadian Province, 1993 annual rpt, A3840–2

State and local:

South Dakota exports to top 20 countries of destination, with detail for Canada and Mexico by commodity, 1991, article, U8595–1.502

see also British Columbia Province, Canada
see also Newfoundland Province, Canada
see also Northwest Territories, Canada
see also Ontario Province, Canada

see also Quebec Province, Canada
see also Saskatchewan Province, Canada
see also under By Foreign Country or World Area in the "Index by Categories"

Canal Zone

see Panama Canal

Canals

State and local:

New York State statistical yearbook, general data, 1992 annual rpt, U5100–1.13

see also Panama Canal

Cancer

see Carcinogens
see Neoplasms

Candy and confectionery products

Advertising expenditures by medium for top 100 advertisers, with comparisons to earnings and sales, and detail by product type and brand, 1991-92, annual rpt, C2710–1.547

Chewing gum market shares for top 3 and all other manufacturers, 1993 article, C5150–2.517

Drugstore chains financial performance and marketing operations, with sales by product type, 1993 annual feature, C5150–2.510

Financial ratios and performance, for over 350 SIC 4-digit industries, FY88-92, annual rpt, A6400–3

Military commissary candy sales, by type, year ended Mar 1993, article, C0500–1.508

Military commissary sales, by region, product type, and individual store, FY92, annual feature, A2072–2.501

Sales and consumer expenditures, for food store products by type, 1991-92, annual feature, C4655–1.510

Sales and market shares for top 10 brands, 1991-92, article, C2710–1.518

Sales and market shares for 2 major candy/confectionery manufacturers, 1991-92, article, C2710–1.513

Sales distribution for candy by outlet type, 1991-92, article, C5150–2.517

Sales of candy/mints and chewing gum at mass merchandise stores and drugstores, by product type, 1992-93, article, C5150–3.515

Sales of confectionery products by selected product type and retail outlet, 1991, article, C5150–3.505

Sales of gummy candy, total and for top 10 manufacturers, 1992-93, article, C2710–1.548

Sales of novelty candy in mass merchandise and drugstores, with top-selling brands, 1992, article, C5150–3.519

Sales volume shares by retail outlet type, for approx 300 food, drug, and other product categories, 1993 annual feature, C4655–1.504

Shopping center financial and operating data, with detail by type of tenant, US and Canada, 1991, triennial rpt, R9285–1

Supermarket sales by detailed product type, 1992 and trends, annual feature, C5225–1.507

Vending machine sales by product type, and machines on location, 1992 and trends, annual rpt, C9470–1

see also Cocoa and chocolate

Capital investments

Cans

see Packaging and containers

Capacity utilization, industrial

see Industrial capacity and utilization

Capital investments

Aerospace and defense industries financial performance, with data for approx 200 major US and foreign companies, FY92 and trends, annual feature, C5800–4.519

Aerospace industry, civil and military production, R&D, trade, employment, and finances, with Federal funding data, 1991 and trends, annual rpt, A0250–2

Aerospace/defense industry capital investments as percent of sales, for 4 major companies, 1989 and 1991, article, C5800–4.516

Airline capital expenditures and cash flow, for 7 carriers, 1991, article, C7000–4.501

Airport passenger facility construction charges to airlines pending and approved by FAA, for hub airports by size class, 1993 article, C5800–4.505

Amusement park operating and financial data, including data for US and foreign parks, miniature golf, waterparks, and games, 1992, annual rpt, A5700–1

Brewers operations and expenses, detailed data, 1956-90, annual rpt, A3455–1.2

Building owner value of properties owned and additions, and construction in progress, top 700 owner firms, 1991, annual article, C5800–2.504

Business economists forecasts of auto sales, business fixed investment, and housing starts, 1993-94, article, A6650–5.502

Cable TV fiber optics equipment expenditures, cable miles installed, and system output measures, 1988-93, articles, C2965–1.505

Chemical and related industries production, finances, operating ratios, employment, and trade, by country, company, and chemical, 1980s-92, annual feature, A1250–1.530

Chemical industry capital spending, US and worldwide, for 19 US and 6 European companies, 1988-93, annual article, A1250–1.508

Chemical industry finances and operations, with data by industry segment and product, 1970s-92, annual rpt, A3850–1

Chemical process industries capital expenditures and outlook, monthly rpt, C5800–8

Chlorine consumption, and consumer and capital investment costs of using substitutes, by end use and product, 1993 article, A1250–1.524

Coal industry executive views on highest cost component, and capital investment plans, Aug 1992 survey, article, C5226–1.503

Coal producer outlook for supply-demand and prices, and capital investments, 1993 annual survey article, C5226–1.503

Competitiveness indicators for US vs other major industrial countries, including investments, productivity, exports, and per capita GDP, 1993 annual rpt, A4475–1

Congressional testimony pertaining to investment capital formation, with supporting data on investments and govt policy, series, A1310–2

Capital investments

Convenience store investment for new urban vs rural outlets, 1992 and trends, annual survey rpt, A6735–1, A6735–2

Convenience store investment per new outlet, by object, urban vs rural, 1988-92, annual fact book, C4680–1.507

Economic indicator historical trends, 1900s-92, annual rpt, R9050–1.2

Economic outlook for selected indicators, recent trends and 2-year forecast, quarterly rpt, A3840–6

Electric utility capital spending, by function and region, and capacity addition plans, 1992-97, annual article, C6985–6.503

Electric utility construction expenditures, 1991-94, annual feature, C5800–28.507

Electric utility financial and operating data, by State and census div, 1991 and trends, annual rpt, A4700–1

Electronics industry capital spending plans, biweekly rpt semiannual article, C1850–2.505

Energy tax proposals and potential effect on selected economic indicators, 1993-97, article, C6985–1.516

Factory automation market growth for 3 top products/services, and spending growth for 3 top industry groups, 1991, article, C1850–2.504

Food service operator kitchen equipment purchasing plans, 1993 survey article, C1850–3.512

Food store industry structure, sales, operations, and business outlook, by type of store, 1993 annual rpt, C5225–1.505

Food/beverage industry equipment purchasing plans, mgmt devs, and automation, 1993 annual survey article, C2150–6.505

Foundry shipments, capacity utilization, and capital investment outlook, by metal type and plant size, 1992-94, annual survey article, C7000–2.501

France oil refinery capital outlays for unleaded gasoline projects, for 8 refineries, 1993 article, C6985–1.547

Frozen dessert industry employment, wages, and capital expenditures, 1969-92, annual rpt, A5825–1.1

Govt policy impact on investment capital formation, series, A1310–1

Gross private domestic investment component shares, 2nd qtr 1992, article, U2160–1.502

Hospital chief financial officer views on trend in access to capital, 1990-92 surveys, A1865–1.503

Hospital industry capital investment growth rate, by instn characteristics and location, 1988-92, annual rpt, B1880–1.1

Household appliance industry manufacturing and market trends, by product type, various years 1920-94, biennial rpt, A3350–3

Industrial plant and equipment investment trends, for US and 6 foreign countries, 1972-91, C7000–7.502

Industrial R&D managers outlook on expenditures, effort, personnel, and other mgmt issues, 1993, annual survey rpt, A5510–1

Iron and steel industry financial and operating data, 1992 and trends, annual rpt, A2000–2.1

Japan auto manufacturer capital investments, for 9 firms, FY93 or FY94, article, C2710–3.535

Japan economic trends, with growth in nonresidential capital stock compared to GNP, 1986-93, article, R5650–2.538

Jewelry industry statistics on sales, marketing, trade, and employment, with customer characteristics, 1993 annual almanac, C2150–7.509

Latin America statistical abstract, general data by country, 1992 annual rpt, U6250–1.29

Machine tool production, shipments, trade, finances, orders, and use, US and worldwide, 1992 and trends, annual rpt, A3179–2

Metalworking industry capital spending plans, by equipment type and industry group, 1989-93, annual survey, C4080–1

Mexico capital formation, by asset type, 1960-85, annual rpt, U6250–1.32

Mining industry capital spending plans for new mines and plants, by mineral and company, 1993 annual feature, C5226–2.503

Motor vehicle, dealership, and related industries operating data, with data by State and industry segment, 1990s and trends, annual rpt, A0865–1.3

Natural gas distribution utility and pipeline company financial and operating data, top 500 companies, 1992, annual article, C6780–1.505

Natural gas industry construction expenditures, by facility type, 1960s-95, annual rpt, A1775–3.8

Natural gas utility expansion/maintenance expenditures, and pipe installations, 1990-93, annual article, C6780–1.501

Newspaper circulation, operations, and finances, US and Canada, 1940s-93, annual rpt, A8605–4

Newspaper industry capital expenditures, by item, US and Canada, 1992-93, annual article, A8605–1.507

Norway offshore oil and gas fields under dev, with reserves and capital outlays, by field, 1993 article, C6985–1.523

Oil and gas industry capital expenditures, by industry sector and world area, 1986-92, annual compilation, C6985–10.1

Oil and gas industry capital spending trends and outlook, by expenditure category, 1970s-2001, annual rpt, C6985–5.2

Oil and gas industry exploration, production, refining, demand, finance, prices, and reserves, by State and country or world area, 1992 and trends, periodic basic data book, A2575–14.3

Oil and gas industry financial and operating data, rankings for top 300 US and top 100 non-US companies, 1991-92, annual feature, C6985–1.547

Oil and gas industry trends, with data by company, State, and country, 1993 annual compilation, C6985–4

Oil and gas pipeline construction costs, mileage, and operating and financial data, by location and/or company, 1991 and trends, annual feature, C6985–1.504

Oil industry capital expenditures, by industry segment, 1973-92, annual compilation, C6985–9.3

Index by Subjects and Names

Oil industry capital spending, by expenditure category, 1989-91, annual fact book, C4680–1.507

Oil industry capital spending in US and Canada, by function, 1991-93, annual articles, C6985–1.517

Oil industry income and operating data, for approx 20 major companies, 1991-92, annual article, C6985–1.533

Oil industry income, net profits, and selected operating data, approx 25 companies, weekly rpt quarterly article, C6985–1.534, C6985–1.545

Oil pipeline capital investments by cost item, for 5 companies (unnamed), 1991, annual rpt, C6985–3.3

Oil refineries, petrochemical processing facilities, and pipelines, construction and costs, by country and company, weekly rpt semiannual list, C6985–1.524, C6985–1.551

Oil storage tank (aboveground) cost-benefit analysis for release prevention barrier retrofitting, 1992 rpt, A2575–26

Paper and paperboard industry financial and operating data, by product, region, and State, 1992 and trends, annual rpt, A1630–6

Paper company capital spending, for 15 companies, 1990-93, article, C3975–2.509

Paperboard packaging equipment purchasing plans and spending trends, 1993 annual article, C0125–4.503

Plastics industry operating and financial data, 1992 and trends, annual rpt, A8920–1.1

Printing industry use and purchase plans for selected types of equipment, monthly rpt, C1850–10

Pulp and paper industry capital spending plans of US and Canadian companies, by purpose and geographic area, 1992-94, annual survey article, C3975–2.503

Pulp and paper industry operations and finances, US and Canada, with detail by company and product grade, and world production and trade summary, 1993 annual rpt, C3975–5

Pulp and paper industry planned expenditures for mechanical pulping projects in US and Canada, by mill, 1993 article, C3975–2.508

Pulp and paper mill environmental improvement projects of US and Canadian companies, including costs, by mill, 1993 article, C3975–2.505

Pulp, paper, and paperboard industry production, trade, and operating data, by product class, monthly rpt, A1630–5

Purchasing managers views on business conditions, monthly rpt, A6910–1

Rail transportation system upgrades needed to achieve 125 mph speeds, with costs, 1993 article, C8400–1.509

Railroad (Class I) financial and operating data, with detail by company, 1982-91, annual rpt, A3275–8.2

Railroad (Class I) financial condition, operations, and employment, by company and district, 1992, annual rpt, A3275–7

Railroad (Class I) traffic, employment, finances, and equipment, by district and State, 1920s-92, annual rpt, A3275–5

Index by Subjects and Names — Capital punishment

Railroad capital expenditures and rate of return, Class I railroads by district, quarterly rpt, A3275–1

Required capital assets to earn a dollar of annual revenue, by industry div and major manufacturing group, 1991, article, A4700–4.503

Restaurant franchises and sales, and franchisee fees and investment required, by leading company, 1993 annual feature, C1200–5.512

Retail chain construction activity, capital expenditures, and number of new stores, for leading firms, 1991-92, annual feature, C5150–4.503

Retail chain store expansion devs, and equipment and construction costs, by type of chain, 1993 annual articles, C5150–4.507

Retail mgmt info system devs, including expenses and computerized equipment use, 1992 survey, annual feature, C5150–4.501

Retail mgmt info system devs, including expenses and computerized equipment use, 1993 survey, annual feature, C5150–4.509

Service industries economic devs, with analysis of conditions and outlook, and comparisons to other industries, quarterly rpt, A3892–1

Small business capital available and required, 1993-98, article, C2425–1.504

Small business views on current and expected economic conditions, survey findings, quarterly rpt, A7815–1

State economic dev condition indicators, including economic performance, business vitality, growth capacity, and tax/fiscal system, by State, 1993 annual rpt, R4225–1.1

State social, economic, and govtl indicators, with rankings, 1993 semiannual rpt, B8500–1.15

Supermarkets opened, remodeled, and closed, including store features, dev costs, and rent, by region and sales size, 1992 and trends, annual rpt, A4950–2

Telecommunication company capital expenditures, residential subscribers, and cable miles by type, for 8 telephone and 4 cable TV companies, 1993 article, C8900–1.513

Telephone holding company finances, operations, and subsidiaries, by company, Dec 1991, annual rpt, A9360–1

Telephone industry capital expenditure plans and network profiles, by company, 1992 annual article, C4725–3.502

Telephone local exchange carrier finances, equipment, and employment, by company, 1991 and trends, annual rpt, A9360–2

Textile industry new plant/equipment expenditures, 1989-91, annual rpt, C3400–5

Transportation industries plant/equipment investment, and business outlays for transportation equipment, 1992 annual rpt, R4815–1

UK chemical industry capital spending distribution, by sector, 1992-95, article, A1250–1.520

Utility regulatory agency policies and practices, and industry financial and operating data, by utility type and agency, 1991/92 annual rpt, A7015–3

Venture-capital-backed company economic impact, including job creation, capital and R&D investments, and selected growth rates, 1985-91, A8515–2

Veterinarian capital equipment replacement practices, including finance methods, 1992 survey article, C9480–1.502

World economic trends, including fixed investment as percent of GDP for US, Europe, and selected Asian countries, 1993 annual feature, C8900–1.520

State and local:

Alabama statistical abstract, general data, 1992 recurring rpt, U5680–2.11

Arizona purchasing managers outlook for capital investments, 1984-93, annual feature, U0280–1.504

Arizona statistical abstract, general data, 1993 recurring rpt, U5850–2.14, U5850–2.17

Arkansas public utility financial, operating, and regulatory data, by utility type and company, 1992 annual rpt, S0757–1

California statistical abstract, general data, 1992 annual rpt, S0840–2.7, S0840–2.8

Florida statistical abstract, general data, 1992 annual rpt, U6660–1.12

Georgia statistical abstract, general data, 1992-93 biennial rpt, U6730–1.6

Hawaii data book, general data, 1992 annual rpt, S2090–1.20, S2090–1.22

Illinois statistical abstract, general data, 1992 annual rpt, U6910–2

Kansas statistical abstract, general data, 1991/92 annual rpt, U7095–2.8

Maine statistical summary, general economic and social data, 1992 recurring rpt, S3434–1

Maryland statistical abstract, general data, 1993-94 biennial rpt, S360S–1.10

Mississippi statistical abstract, general data, 1992 annual rpt, U3255–4.5

Missouri industrial growth, including new and expanding manufacturers, new jobs, and investment, 1982-91, annual rpt, S4475–1

New Jersey casino industry fixed asset investments, by casino, 1991-92, annual rpt, S5360–1

New Mexico manufacturing capital expenditures, by industry group, 1989 and 1991, U7980–1.504

New York State public utility financial and operating data, by utility type and company, 1988-92, annual rpt, S5795–1

New York State statistical yearbook, general data, 1992 annual rpt, U5100–1.2

North Carolina public utility financial, operating, and regulatory data, by utility type and company, 1990 and trends, annual rpt, S5917–2

Pennsylvania statistical abstract, general data, 1992 recurring rpt, U4130–6.2, U4130–6.8

South Carolina economic condition, including employment, manufacturing, and income, 1970s-92, annual rpt, S7125–3.2

South Carolina new firm investments in State, with employment, by industry and county, 1991, annual planning rpt, S7155–3.2

South Carolina statistical abstract, general data, 1993 annual rpt, S7125–1.3

South Dakota new and expanding companies and investment, 1982-92, annual rpt, S7330–1

Tennessee statistical abstract, general data, 1992/93 annual rpt, U8710–2.4, U8710–2.9, U8710–2.11

Vermont public utility financial and operating data, by company, 1986-91, biennial rpt, S8100–1

Washington State water utilities financial and operating data, by company, 1988-90, annual rpt, S8450–1.1

Washington State water utilities financial and operating data, by company, 1989-91, annual rpt, S8450–1.4

see also Depreciation

see also Economic indicators

see also Foreign investments

see also Public works

see also State funding for capital projects

Capital punishment

Black American prisoners under death sentence, incarceration time, and executions, with comparisons to whites, 1930s-90, annual compilation, C6775–2.5

College freshmen attitudes on abolishing death penalty, by sex and instn type, fall 1992, annual survey, U6215–1

Prisoners on death row by sex and race-ethnicity, and executions, by State, 1992 and trends, annual rpt, A1305–3

Prisoners with death sentences and executions by State, and death row inmates by sex and race-ethnicity, 1992 annual rpt, R4300–1.1

Prisoners with death sentences, by race-ethnicity, spring 1991, article, A8510–1.1

Prisoners with death sentences, by State, Dec 1991, annual almanac, C4712–1

Public opinion on social, political, and economic issues, detailed data, 1972-91 surveys, annual rpt, U6395–1

Public opinion on televising public executions, Feb 1993 survey and trends, C8915–11.1

State and local:

Alabama capital caseloads and dispositions, by county, FY92, annual rpt, S0118–1

Arizona statistical abstract, general data, 1993 recurring rpt, U5850–2.12

California death sentences imposed, 1987-92, annual rpt, S0910–1.1

California prisoners with death sentences, including demographic characteristics, 1991 and trends, annual rpt, S0820–1

Florida death row inmates, admissions, removals, and executions, FY83-92, annual rpt, S1720–1

Florida statistical abstract, general data, 1992 annual rpt, U6660–1.22

New Jersey State constitutional amendment on capital punishment, election results by county, Nov 1992, annual rpt, S5440–1

Oklahoma male and female death row inmates, FY91, annual rpt, S6420–1

Oklahoma statistical abstract, general data, 1992 annual rpt, U8130–2.7

Pennsylvania prisoners with death sentences, by county, age, race, and sex, 1990, annual rpt, S6782–1

South Carolina prisoners on death row, and executions, by sex and race, FY92, annual rpt, S7135–1

Tennessee statistical abstract, general data, 1992/93 annual rpt, U8710–2.19

Carbon dioxide

Carbon dioxide
see Gases

Carcinogens

Chemical carcinogenicity prediction accuracy of 8 methods, 1993 article, A1250–1.529

Environmental releases of top 25 and all other carcinogens by all industry and oil refineries, 1988-90, annual rpt, A2575–27

see also Asbestos contamination
see also Radon

Cardiovascular diseases

Alcohol consumption correlated with heart disease incidence, 1993 article, A2623–1.508

Death rates for heart disease/stroke, by sex and race-ethnicity, 1993 feature, C4215–1.511

Hospital patient admission rates and length of stay, by diagnosis and procedure, payment source, age, sex, and region, 1991, B4455–4

Hospital patient charges and length of stay, by diagnosis and procedure, payment source, age, and region, 1991, B4455–5

Hospital patient discharges and length of stay, by diagnosis, type of operation, age, and region, 1991, annual rpt series, B4455–1

Hospital patient discharges and length of stay, by diagnostic related group (DRG), payment source, age, and region, 1991, annual rpt series, B4455–3

Hospital psychiatric patients with selected physical disorders, length of stay by age, sex, and region, 1991, annual rpt series, B4455–2

Public health research results, including hypertension incidence and cardiovascular disease risk in selected populations, 1992 articles, A2623–1.502

State economic dev condition indicators, including economic performance, business vitality, growth capacity, and tax/fiscal system, by State, 1993 annual rpt, R4225–1.1

State and local:

Alabama vital statistics, including population, births, deaths by cause, marriages, and divorces, by location and demographic characteristics, 1992 and trends, annual rpt, S0175–2

Alaska vital statistics, including births, deaths by cause, marriages, divorces, adoptions, and population, by demographic characteristics and location, 1990, annual rpt, S0315–1

Arkansas vital statistics, including births, deaths by cause, marriages, and divorces, by age, sex, race, and county, 1991 and trends, annual rpt, S0685–1

California vital statistics, including population, births, and deaths by cause, by demographic characteristics and county, 1990 and trends, annual rpt, S0865–1

Colorado vital statistics, including population, births, deaths by cause, abortion, marriage and divorce, and adoption, by demographic characteristics and location, 1990 and trends, annual rpt, S1010–1

Connecticut vital statistics, including births, deaths by cause, marriages, and divorces, by demographic characteristics and location, 1989, annual rpt, S1200–1

Delaware vital statistics, including births, deaths by cause, and marriages and dissolutions, by demographic characteristics and location, 1990, annual rpt, S1385–2

Florida deaths by selected cause, and incidence of selected communicable diseases, by county, 1992 annual rpt, S1746–1.1

Florida vital statistics, including population, births, deaths by cause, and marriages and dissolutions, by location and demographic characteristics, 1992 and trends, annual rpt, S1745–3

Georgia vital statistics, including deaths by cause, demographic characteristics, and location, 1991 and trends, annual rpt, S1895–1.2

Hawaii health dept activities and services, including vital statistics and disease control, by location, 1990, annual rpt, S2065–1

Idaho vital statistics, including births, deaths by cause, abortions, marriages, and divorces, by demographic characteristics and county, 1991 and trends, annual rpt, S2250–2

Iowa vital statistics, including population, births, deaths by cause, marriages, and divorces, by demographic characteristics and location, 1991 and trends, annual rpt, S2795–1

Kansas vital statistics, including population, births, deaths by cause, abortions, marriages, and divorces, by demographic characteristics and location, 1991 and trends, annual rpt, S2975–1

Kentucky vital statistics, including births, deaths by cause, marriages and divorces, and population, by demographic characteristics and county, 1991, annual rpt, S3140–1

Louisiana vital statistics, including population, births, deaths by cause, reportable diseases, marriages, and divorces, by demographic characteristics and locality, 1989-90 and trends, annual rpt, S3295–1

Maine vital statistics, including births, deaths by cause, abortions, and marriages and divorces, by demographic characteristics and location, 1991 and trends, annual rpt, S3460–2

Maryland vital statistics, including population, births, deaths by cause, marriages, and divorces, by demographic characteristics and location, 1989 and trends, annual rpt, S3635–1

Massachusetts vital statistics, including births, deaths by cause, marriages, divorces, and population, by locality and demographic characteristics, 1990 and trends, annual rpt, S3850–1

Michigan vital statistics, including births, deaths, marriages, divorces/annulments, and communicable diseases, by location and demographic characteristics, 1990 and trends, annual rpt, S4000–3

Minnesota vital statistics, including population, births, abortions, deaths, marriages, and divorces, by location and demographic characteristics, 1991 and trends, annual rpt, S4190–2

Mississippi vital statistics, including births, deaths by cause, marriages, and divorces, by demographic characteristics and location, 1992 and trends, annual rpt, S4350–1

Missouri vital statistics, including population, births, deaths by cause, and marriages and divorces, by location and demographic characteristics, 1992 and trends, annual rpt, S4518–1

Montana vital statistics, including births, deaths by cause, abortion, disease, and marriage and divorce, by demographic characteristics and county, 1990-91 and trends, annual rpt, S4690–1

Nebraska vital statistics, including births, deaths, marriages, divorces, and population, by demographic characteristics and location, 1991 and trends, annual rpt, S4885–1

Nevada vital statistics, including births, abortions, and deaths by cause, by county and demographic characteristics, 1989 and trends, annual rpt, S5075–1

New Hampshire vital statistics, including population, births, deaths by cause, marriages, and divorces, by location and demographic characteristics, 1991 and trends, annual rpt, S5215–1

New Jersey vital statistics, including births, deaths, population, communicable diseases, and marriages and divorces, by demographic characteristics and location, 1990 and trends, annual rpt, S5405–1

New Mexico vital statistics, including population, births, deaths, and disease, by location and demographic characteristics, 1991 and trends, annual rpt, S5605–1

New York State vital statistics, including population, births, deaths by cause, reportable diseases, and marriages and dissolutions, by demographic characteristics and/or location, 1990 and trends, annual rpt, S5765–1

North Carolina deaths and rates, by cause and county, 1991 and trends, annual rpt, S5927–1.2

North Dakota vital statistics, including births, deaths by cause, marriages and divorces, and abortions, by demographic characteristics and/or county, 1991 and trends, annual rpt, S6105–2

Ohio vital statistics, including births, deaths by cause, marriages, divorces, and population, by demographic characteristics and location, 1991 and trends, annual rpt, S6285–1

Oregon vital statistics, including births, deaths by cause, communicable diseases, marriages, and divorces, by age, sex, race-ethnicity, and county, 1991 and trends, annual rpt, S6615–5

Rhode Island vital statistics, including population, births, deaths, marriages, and divorces, by demographic characteristics and locality, 1989 and trends, annual rpt, S6995–1

South Carolina deaths, by detailed cause, age, sex, and race, 1990, annual rpt, S7175–2

South Carolina vital statistics, including births, deaths by cause, marriages, and divorces, by age, sex, race, and location, 1990 and trends, annual rpt, S7175–1

South Dakota vital statistics, including births, deaths, marriage and divorce, and communicable disease, by demographic characteristics and county, 1991 and trends, annual rpt, S7345–1

Index by Subjects and Names

Tennessee vital statistics, including births, deaths by cause, marriages, divorces, and population, by demographic characteristics and location, 1991 and trends, annual rpt, S7520–2

Texas vital statistics, including births, deaths by cause, abortions, marriages, and divorces, by location and demographic characteristics, 1991 and trends, annual rpt, S7685–1

Utah vital statistics, including births, deaths by cause, and population, by county and demographic characteristics, 1990 and trends, annual rpt, S7835–1

Vermont vital statistics, including population, births, deaths by cause, abortions, marriages, and divorces, by location and demographic characteristics, 1991 and trends, annual rpt, S8054–1

Virginia vital statistics, including births, deaths by cause, marriages and divorces, and communicable disease, by demographic characteristics and location, 1991 and trends, annual rpt, S8225–1

Washington State vital statistics, including births, deaths by cause, and population, by demographic characteristics and location, 1991 and trends, annual rpt, S8363–1

West Virginia vital statistics, including births, deaths by cause, marriages, and divorces, by location and demographic characteristics, 1991 and trends, annual rpt, S8560–1

Wisconsin vital statistics, including population, births, deaths by cause, and marriages and dissolutions, by county and demographic characteristics, 1991 and trends, annual rpt, S8715–4

Wyoming vital statistics, including population, births, deaths by cause, marriages, and divorces, by demographic characteristics and county, 1991 and trends, annual rpt, S8920–2

see also Blood pressure
see also Hypertension
see also under By Disease in the "Index by Categories"

Cargo
see Air cargo
see Freight

Caribbean area

Airports and communities in North America served by regional vs larger airlines, by carrier and location, 1993 annual rpt, A8795–1.2

Flour milling companies and capacity, in US by State, Canada, Mexico, and Central American and Caribbean area countries, 1993 annual directory and buyers guide, C8450–3

Population size and characteristics, GNP, and land area, by world region and/or country, 1993 annual data sheet, R8750–5

Refugees, resettlement, and intl aid devs, by country, 1992, annual rpt, R9372–1

Securities market participation by foreign and US investors, by world area and country, quarterly rpt, A8825–2

Statistical abstract of Latin America, detailed social, govtl, and economic data, 1992 annual rpt, U6250–1

Travel trends, including tourist arrivals and expenditures, by region and/or country, 1992 annual rpt, C2140–1.3

see also Bahamas
see also Barbados
see also Bermuda
see also Caribbean refugees
see also Cuba
see also Dominican Republic
see also Haiti
see also Jamaica
see also Latin America
see also Puerto Rico
see also Trinidad and Tobago
see also U.S. Virgin Islands

Caribbean refugees

Haiti citizens (deportable) arriving in Miami, 1979-81, annual rpt, U6250–1.14

see also Cuba
see also Haiti

Carpets and rugs

Consumer expectations of economic conditions and change in income, and intended durable goods purchases by type, Conference Board monthly survey, R4105–4

Cotton and other fiber consumption in textile production, by detailed end use, 1990-92, annual rpt, A7485–1

Fiber Organon, detailed monthly and annual data on industry production, consumption, and trade, by fiber and fabric type, monthly rpt, C3460–1

Financial ratios and performance, for over 350 SIC 4-digit industries, FY88-92, annual rpt, A6400–3

Shipments by type of carpet, and trade by country, 1991 and trends, annual rpt, A3800–1

Shipments by type of carpet, 1982-93, annual article, C5226–3.503

Shipments of carpets/rugs, 1988-93, annual article, C5226–3.502

Textile fiber end-use survey, consumption and trade, by type of fiber and product, 1988-92, annual survey, C3460–1.511

Wool for carpets, foreign trade, and mill consumption, 1989-91, annual article, C3460–1.502

Carpools
see Commuting

Carson City, Nev.

Casino finances and employment, by location and gaming revenue range, FY92, annual rpt, S5062–1

Carter, Deborah J.

"Minorities in Higher Education: 11th Annual Status Report", A1410–10

Cartography

Computer geographic info systems software sales, for 4 companies, 1992, article, C5800–7.538

Cash management
see Investment management and organizations

Casinos

Revenues of top 10 casinos, 1989, recurring rpt, R9375–6

State and local:

Nevada casino finances and employment, by location and gaming revenue range, FY92, annual rpt, S5062–1

Nevada, Las Vegas construction costs of 5 new casinos, 1993 article, C5800–7.550

New Jersey casino control and revenue funds finances, FY92, annual rpt, S5455–1

Cement and concrete

New Jersey casino revenues and operations for 12 facilities, with State regulatory activities, 1992 and trends, annual rpt, S5360–1

Wisconsin State constitutional amendments on casino gambling, elections results by county, 1993-94 biennial rpt, S8780–1.3

Cassette tapes
see Audiovisual equipment
see Recording industry

Casualty insurance
see Property and casualty insurance

Cathode ray tubes
see Electronics industry and products

Catholic schools
see Parochial schools

Catholicism
see Religion

Cattle
see Dairy industry and products
see Livestock and livestock industry

CATV
see Cable television

CD-ROM technology and use

Canada photographic equipment and supplies purchasing patterns, including consumer interest in recording photos on CDs, 1992 survey, recurring rpt, A8695–4

Home computer CD-ROM drive installed base, 1991-95, C9380–1.519

Library use of CD-ROM, 1993 survey article, C1852–1.504

Photo transferring onto CDs, consumer interest and price expectations, 1993 survey, recurring rpt, A8695–2

Sales outlook for computer CD-ROM writable and read-only drives, 1993-97, article, C1850–5.507

Shipments of CD-ROM computer drives worldwide, 1991-95, article, C1850–2.509

Titles published and prices for CD-ROM serials and monographs, by subject area, 1990-92, annual compilation, C1650–3.4

Celery
see Vegetables and vegetable products

Cellular telephones
see Telephones and telephone industry

Cement and concrete

Cost indexes for construction, equipment, and labor, by type and location, weekly rpt quarterly feature, C5800–2.508, C5800–2.521, C5800–2.547

Financial performance and growth rankings for approx 1,000 top corporations, with comparisons by industry group, 1993 annual rpt, C3950–1.505

Financial ratios and performance, for over 350 SIC 4-digit industries, FY88-92, annual rpt, A6400–3

Latin America statistical abstract, general data by country, 1992 annual rpt, U6250–1.16

Operating and financial composite ratios for corporations, with establishments and receipts, for approx 200 industries, by asset size, FY90, annual rpt, C7800–1

Price averages for selected types of concrete and aggregates, 1989-93, article, C5800–2.534

Prices for selected building materials in approx 20 cities, weekly rpt, C5800–2

Production and operating trends and outlook for ready-mixed concrete industry, by

Cement and concrete

region, with data on community complaints and waste mgmt, 1992 survey, annual article, C0125–5

Production, consumption, stocks, trade, and prices for approx 100 basic commodities, including by country and producing State, commodity yearbook for 1993, C2400–1, C2400–2

State and local:

- Alabama statistical abstract, general data, 1992 recurring rpt, U5680–2.3, U5680–2.12
- California economic indicators, bimonthly rpt, S0840–1
- Hawaii data book, general data, 1992 annual rpt, S2090–1.20
- Montana cement/gypsum producers, production, and taxes paid, FY88-92, biennial rpt, S4750–1.1
- Pennsylvania statistical abstract, general data, 1992 recurring rpt, U4130–6.8

Cemeteries and funerals

- Financial ratios and performance, for over 350 SIC 4-digit industries, FY88-92, annual rpt, A6400–3
- Public opinion on honesty/ethical standards of funeral directors, 1992 Gallup Polls and trends, C4040–1.501

State and local:

- Florida deaths by disposition of remains, by race, 1980-92, annual rpt, S1745–3
- Hawaii data book, general data, 1992 annual rpt, S2090–1.2, S2090–1.6
- Michigan public welfare payments for burials, by county, monthly rpt, S4010–1
- Montana welfare and medical assistance program cases and payments, by county and type of service, monthly rpt, S4755–1
- New Jersey cemetery board trust fund trends, and licensed cemetery companies by county, 1993 annual rpt, S5355–1
- Oklahoma perpetual care cemeteries, FY92 annual rpt, S6415–1
- Oregon deaths, by disposal of remains and county, 1991, annual rpt, S6615–5
- South Carolina deaths, by burial disposition, race, and county, 1990, annual rpt, S7175–1
- Tennessee regulatory activities affecting funeral homes and cemeteries, FY91, annual rpt, S7466–1
- Vermont deaths by type of body disposition, monthly 1991, annual rpt, S8054–1
- Virginia cremations, by place of occurrence and month, 1991, annual rpt, S8225–1
- West Virginia welfare burials and expenditures, by county, monthly rpt, S8560–2

Censorship

- College freshmen attitudes on admin right to prohibit racist/sexist speech, by sex and instn type, fall 1992, annual survey, U6215–1
- Europe public opinion on political, economic, and social issues, for 9 countries and 3 Soviet Union Republics, 1991 survey, C8915–8.1
- Europe public opinion on political, economic, and social issues of interest to foreign investors, for 9 countries and 3 Soviet Union Republics, 1991 survey, C8915–9
- Public opinion on social, political, and economic issues, detailed data, 1972-91 surveys, annual rpt, U6395–1

State and local:

- Colorado public library materials challenged, by instn, 1991, annual rpt, S1000–3.1
- Kentucky public library incidents involving intellectual freedom, by county, FY92, annual rpt, S3165–1

Census divisions

see under By Census Division in the "Index by Categories"

Census of Agriculture

State and local:

- Oklahoma, Census of Agriculture findings on land area and farm operator characteristics, 1978, 1982, and 1987, annual rpt, S6405–1

Census of Manufactures

- Paper/allied products industry data from Census of Manufactures, including purchased fuel and labor costs, 1990 and/or 1991, article, A1630–5.501

Census of Population and Housing

- Minority Census of Population and Housing error rates by race-ethnicity compared to total US, by sex, 1990, R8750–2.58
- Undercount of population, by race and sex, 1990 Census and trends, annual rpt, C2500–2

State and local:

- Arkansas Census of Population and Housing detailed findings, 1990, U5935–7
- California Census of Population and Housing detailed findings, 1990, S0840–9
- Louisiana Census of Population and Housing summary findings, by local area, 1990 and trends, U8010–4
- Maine Census of Population and Housing summary findings, by local area, 1990, S3465–7, S3465–8, S3465–9
- New Jersey Census of Population and Housing detailed findings, by county, 1990, S5425–19
- New Mexico population by age, sex, county, and State region, 1980 and 1990, U7980–6
- Pennsylvania Census of Population and Housing detailed findings, with selected data by county and municipality, 1990, U4130–13
- Pennsylvania employment and commuting data from Census of Population and Housing, by county and municipality, 1990, C1595–16
- Pennsylvania housing data from Census of Population and Housing, by county and municipality, 1990, C1595–14
- Pennsylvania income data from Census of Population and Housing, by county and municipality, 1989, C1595–15
- Rhode Island Census of Population and Housing detailed findings, by county and municipality, 1990, S6930–9
- Utah population data, 1990 census rpt series, S7832–3
- Washington State Census of Population and Housing summary findings, by county, 1990, annual rpt, S8345–4

Census tracts

State and local:

- DC violent and property crimes, by census tract, 1991, annual rpt, S1535–2
- Hawaii population, by census tract, 1990 annual rpt, S2090–1.1
- Rhode Island census tract data on births, and deaths by cause, 1989, annual rpt, S6995–1

Index by Subjects and Names

Center for Healthcare Industry Performance Studies

Hospital margins and nonoperating gain ratio, 1987-91, article, A1865–1.502

Center of population

State and local:

Hawaii data book, general data, 1992 annual rpt, S2090–1.1

Centers for Disease Control and Prevention

see also National Institute for Occupational Safety and Health

Central America

- Flour milling companies and capacity, in US by State, Canada, Mexico, and Central American and Caribbean area countries, 1993 annual directory and buyers guide, C8450–3
- Jewish population by world area, country, and US census div, State, and city, 1990-92, annual compilation, A2050–1
- Population size and characteristics, GNP, and land area, by world region and/or country, 1993 annual data sheet, R8750–5
- Statistical abstract of Latin America, detailed social, govtl, and economic data, 1992 annual rpt, U6250–1

see also Caribbean area

see also Central American Common Market

see also Costa Rica

see also El Salvador

see also Guatemala

see also Honduras

see also Inter-American Development Bank

see also Latin America

see also Latin American Integration Association

see also Mexico

see also Nicaragua

see also Panama

see also South America

see also under By Foreign Country or World Area in the "Index by Categories"

Central American Common Market

Latin America statistical abstract, general data by country, 1992 annual rpt, U6250–1.26

Central business districts

- Commercial real estate market conditions and outlook, for industrial and office properties in major metro areas, 1993 annual rpt, B2800–3
- Office property rental rates, vacancy, and construction, for major metro areas, quarterly rpt, B2800–4

Central cities

- Commercial real estate market conditions and outlook, for industrial and office properties, by US metro area and selected foreign city, 1992-93, annual survey, A8916–1
- Elementary/secondary inner-city school improvement importance, and acceptability of tax increases for funding, public opinion, 1993 annual Gallup Poll, A8680–1.503
- Food store market shares and outlets, by company and store type, for approx 350 metro areas in US and Canada, with industry operating data, 1993 annual rpt, C3400–6
- Household income trends for central cities vs suburbs of 78 largest MSAs, 1979-89, A8012–1.22

Index by Subjects and Names

Cerebrovascular diseases

Lodging industry facilities, sales, and occupancy, with top 42-100 properties in 5 market categories, 1993 annual rpt, C7000–5

Unemployment rate in DC and approx 25 central cities, monthly rpt, S1527–3

see also Central business districts

see also Neighborhoods

see also Urban renewal

Centrally planned economies

Eastern Europe public opinion on political, economic, and social issues, for 5 countries and 3 Soviet Union Republics, 1991 survey, C8915–8.2

see also Albania

see also Bulgaria

see also Cambodia

see also China, People's Republic

see also Communist parties

see also Cuba

see also Czechoslovakia

see also East-West trade

see also Eastern Europe

see also Germany, East

see also Hungary

see also Poland

see also Romania

see also Soviet Union

see also Vietnam

see also Yugoslavia

Ceramic products

see Clay industry and products

Cereals

see Grains and grain products

Cerebrovascular diseases

- Hospital patient admission rates and length of stay, by diagnosis and procedure, payment source, age, sex, and region, 1991, B4455–4
- Hospital patient charges and length of stay, by diagnosis and procedure, payment source, age, and region, 1991, B4455–5
- Hospital patient discharges and length of stay, by diagnosis, type of operation, age, and region, 1991, annual rpt series, B4455–1
- Hospital patient discharges and length of stay, by diagnostic related group (DRG), payment source, age, and region, 1991, annual rpt series, B4455–3

State and local:

- Alabama vital statistics, including population, births, deaths by cause, marriages, and divorces, by location and demographic characteristics, 1992 and trends, annual rpt, S0175–2
- Alaska vital statistics, including births, deaths by cause, marriages, divorces, adoptions, and population, by demographic characteristics and location, 1990, annual rpt, S0315–1
- Arkansas vital statistics, including births, deaths by cause, marriages, and divorces, by age, sex, race, and county, 1991 and trends, annual rpt, S0685–1
- California vital statistics, including population, births, and deaths by cause, by demographic characteristics and county, 1990 and trends, annual rpt, S0865–1
- Colorado vital statistics, including population, births, deaths by cause, abortion, marriage and divorce, and adoption, by demographic characteristics and location, 1990 and trends, annual rpt, S1010–1
- Connecticut vital statistics, including births, deaths by cause, marriages, and divorces, by demographic characteristics and location, 1989, annual rpt, S1200–1
- Delaware vital statistics, including births, deaths by cause, and marriages and dissolutions, by demographic characteristics and location, 1990, annual rpt, S1385–2
- Florida deaths by selected cause, and incidence of selected communicable diseases, by county, 1992 annual rpt, S1746–1.1
- Florida vital statistics, including population, births, deaths by cause, and marriages and dissolutions, by location and demographic characteristics, 1992 and trends, annual rpt, S1745–3
- Georgia vital statistics, including deaths by cause, demographic characteristics, and location, 1991 and trends, annual rpt, S1895–1.2
- Hawaii vital statistics, including births, deaths by cause, marriages, and dissolutions, by demographic characteristics and location, 1990, annual rpt, S2065–1.2
- Idaho vital statistics, including births, deaths by cause, abortions, marriages, and divorces, by demographic characteristics and county, 1991 and trends, annual rpt, S2250–2
- Iowa vital statistics, including population, births, deaths by cause, marriages, and divorces, by demographic characteristics and location, 1991 and trends, annual rpt, S2795–1
- Kansas vital statistics, including population, births, deaths by cause, abortions, marriages, and divorces, by demographic characteristics and location, 1991 and trends, annual rpt, S2975–1
- Kentucky vital statistics, including births, deaths by cause, marriages and divorces, and population, by demographic characteristics and county, 1991, annual rpt, S3140–1
- Louisiana vital statistics, including population, births, deaths by cause, reportable diseases, marriages, and divorces, by demographic characteristics and locality, 1989-90 and trends, annual rpt, S3295–1
- Maine vital statistics, including births, deaths by cause, abortions, and marriages and divorces, by demographic characteristics and location, 1991 and trends, annual rpt, S3460–2
- Maryland vital statistics, including population, births, deaths by cause, marriages, and divorces, by demographic characteristics and location, 1989 and trends, annual rpt, S3635–1
- Massachusetts vital statistics, including births, deaths by cause, marriages, divorces, and population, by locality and demographic characteristics, 1990 and trends, annual rpt, S3850–1
- Michigan vital statistics, including births, deaths, marriages, divorces/annulments, and communicable diseases, by location and demographic characteristics, 1990 and trends, annual rpt, S4000–3
- Minnesota vital statistics, including population, births, abortions, deaths, marriages, and divorces, by location and demographic characteristics, 1991 and trends, annual rpt, S4190–2
- Mississippi vital statistics, including births, deaths by cause, marriages, and divorces, by demographic characteristics and location, 1992 and trends, annual rpt, S4350–1
- Missouri vital statistics, including population, births, deaths by cause, and marriages and divorces, by location and demographic characteristics, 1992 and trends, annual rpt, S4518–1
- Montana vital statistics, including births, deaths by cause, abortion, disease, and marriage and divorce, by demographic characteristics and county, 1990-91 and trends, annual rpt, S4690–1
- Nebraska vital statistics, including births, deaths, marriages, divorces, and population, by demographic characteristics and location, 1991 and trends, annual rpt, S4885–1
- Nevada vital statistics, including births, abortions, and deaths by cause, by county and demographic characteristics, 1989 and trends, annual rpt, S5075–1
- New Hampshire vital statistics, including population, births, deaths by cause, marriages, and divorces, by location and demographic characteristics, 1991 and trends, annual rpt, S5215–1
- New Jersey vital statistics, including births, deaths, population, communicable diseases, and marriages and divorces, by demographic characteristics and location, 1990 and trends, annual rpt, S5405–1
- New Mexico vital statistics, including population, births, deaths, and disease, by location and demographic characteristics, 1991 and trends, annual rpt, S5605–1
- New York State vital statistics, including population, births, deaths by cause, reportable diseases, and marriages and dissolutions, by demographic characteristics and/or location, 1990 and trends, annual rpt, S5765–1
- North Carolina deaths and rates, by cause and county, 1991 and trends, annual rpt, S5927–1.2
- North Dakota vital statistics, including births, deaths by cause, marriages and divorces, and abortions, by demographic characteristics and/or county, 1991 and trends, annual rpt, S6105–2
- Ohio vital statistics, including births, deaths by cause, marriages, divorces, and population, by demographic characteristics and location, 1991 and trends, annual rpt, S6285–1
- Oregon vital statistics, including births, deaths by cause, communicable diseases, marriages, and divorces, by age, sex, race-ethnicity, and county, 1991 and trends, annual rpt, S6615–5
- Rhode Island vital statistics, including population, births, deaths, marriages, and divorces, by demographic characteristics and locality, 1989 and trends, annual rpt, S6995–1
- South Carolina deaths, by detailed cause, age, sex, and race, 1990, annual rpt, S7175–2
- South Carolina vital statistics, including births, deaths by cause, marriages, and divorces, by age, sex, race, and location, 1990 and trends, annual rpt, S7175–1

Cerebrovascular diseases

South Dakota vital statistics, including births, deaths, marriage and divorce, and communicable disease, by demographic characteristics and county, 1991 and trends, annual rpt, S7345–1

Tennessee vital statistics, including births, deaths by cause, marriages, divorces, and population, by demographic characteristics and location, 1991 and trends, annual rpt, S7520–2

Texas vital statistics, including deaths by cause, abortions, marriages, and divorces, by location and demographic characteristics, 1991 and trends, annual rpt, S7685–1

Utah vital statistics, including births, deaths by cause, and population, by county and demographic characteristics, 1990 and trends, annual rpt, S7835–1

Vermont vital statistics, including population, births, deaths by cause, abortions, marriages, and divorces, by location and demographic characteristics, 1991 and trends, annual rpt, S8054–1

Virginia vital statistics, including births, deaths by cause, marriages and divorces, and communicable disease, by demographic characteristics and location, 1991 and trends, annual rpt, S8225–1

Washington State vital statistics, including births, deaths by cause, and population, by demographic characteristics and location, 1991 and trends, annual rpt, S8363–1

West Virginia vital statistics, including births, deaths by cause, marriages, and divorces, by location and demographic characteristics, 1991 and trends, annual rpt, S8560–1

Wisconsin vital statistics, including population, births, deaths by cause, and marriages and dissolutions, by county and demographic characteristics, 1991 and trends, annual rpt, S8715–4

Wyoming vital statistics, including population, births, deaths by cause, marriages, and divorces, by demographic characteristics and county, 1991 and trends, annual rpt, S8920–2

see also under By Disease in the "Index by Categories"

Certificates of deposit

Forecasts of economic indicators for approx 10-13 months, monthly rpt, U1880–3

Money and securities market activity, and related indicators, biweekly rpt, B2000–1

Money market fund asset holdings by type of investment, including bank and Eurodollar certificates of deposit, and Federal securities, monthly rpt, A6025–5

Money market funds and asset composition, including Eurodollar, bank, and other certificates of deposit, 1991 and trends, annual rpt, A6025–1

State and local:

Arkansas State funds on deposit in banks and savings and loan assns, by type and instn, FY92, biennial rpt, S0780–1

Certification

see Occupational testing and certification

CFC's

see Air pollution

see Chemicals and chemical industry

Chain stores

see Franchises

see Retail trade

Chambers of commerce

Congressional voting support for 4 special interest groups, by Member and State, 1991, annual rpt, C2500–2

Finances and operations, including income, salaries and benefits, membership, staff, and programs, 1993 annual rpt, A3840–3

Champagne

see Wine and winemaking

Chancery courts

see State courts

Charity

see Gifts and private contributions

see Nonprofit organizations and foundations

Chase Econometrics Associates

see WEFA Group

Checking accounts

Catalog orders paid by check and credit card, 1991, annual rpt, A4620–1.2

Consumer use of checks to pay for purchases, and views on business use of checking history inquiries, 1992 survey, annual rpt, B3280–2

Financial performance of top 100 banks, including assets, loans, deposits, and operating ratios, 1992, annual feature, C5800–7.526

Food store customer checks, number and average value accepted, returned, and written off, 1991-92, annual rpts, A4950–5

Retail store credit operations, including payment losses and loss reduction efforts, by payment method and outlet type, 1992 survey article, C5150–4.503

State and local:

Alaska bank assets and liabilities of individual commercial and savings instns, quarterly rpt, S0280–2

Arizona bank balance sheets and branches, individual State and natl instns, quarterly rpt, S0460–2

California economic condition, including population, employment and earnings, income, business activity, and taxation, 1960s-92, annual rpt, S0840–3.2

Colorado banks and trust companies, financial condition by instn, 1992, annual rpt, S1070–2

Connecticut banks and other financial instns, financial condition by instn, 1991 and trends, annual rpt, S1160–1

Idaho banks and other financial instns, financial condition, with data by instn and loan activity analysis, FY92 or 1991, annual rpt, S2235–1

Illinois bank and trust companies (State-chartered) financial condition and status changes, by instn, FY92, annual rpt, S2395–1

Kansas business activity indicators, quarterly rpt, U7095–1

Kentucky financial instns condition, including assets by instn and city, with regulatory info, 1992 and trends, annual rpt, S3121–1

Louisiana financial instns (State-chartered), financial condition by instn arranged by city, with regulatory info, Dec 1992, annual rpt, S3265–1

Maine financial instn assets, deposits, and loans, by type of instn and county, 1982-92, annual rpt, S3473–1

Michigan banks and other financial instns, financial condition by instn, with regulatory info, 1992 and trends, annual rpt, S3957–1

New Jersey banks and other financial instns, assets and liabilities by instn, 1992 and trends, annual rpt, S5355–1

New Mexico financial instns, financial and operating data by instn, with regulatory activities, 1992, annual rpt, S5652–1

Oklahoma business activity indicators, monthly rpt, U8130–1

Oregon financial instns, financial condition by instn, Dec 1992 and trends, annual rpt, S6616–1

Rhode Island banks and other financial instns (State-chartered), assets and liabilities, by instn, 1991, annual rpt, S6945–1

South Dakota insufficient funds check violation court cases and dispositions, FY90-92, annual rpt, S7395–1

Vermont banks and other financial instns, financial condition by instn, 1992 and trends, annual rpt, S7995–2

Virginia financial instns (State-chartered), financial condition by instn and instn type, Dec 1992, annual rpt, S8180–2

see also Negotiable orders of withdrawal accounts

Cheese

see Dairy industry and products

Chemical dependency

see Drug abuse and treatment

Chemicals and chemical industry

Australia chemical production capacity for 7 major producers of petrochemicals and polymers, 1993 article, A1250–1.531

Capital spending, US and worldwide, for 19 US and 6 European companies, 1988-93, annual article, A1250–1.508

Chicago Board of Trade futures trading in diammonium phosphate and anhydrous ammonia, 1992, annual rpt, B2120–1

Chlorinated solvents consumption, and possible substitutes and cost of substitution, by application, 1993 article, C5800–8.508

Construction cost trends for chemical process plants, Dec 1991-Dec 1992, article, C5800–2.521

Corporate performance ratings by executives for leading companies in 32 industries, 1993 annual survey feature, C8900–1.508

Czechoslovakia chemical production by product, and sales, exports, and employment of leading firms, by Republic, 1990-92, article, A1250–1.509

Earnings of US and Canadian workers in mining and allied industries, monthly rpt, B6800–1

Earnings, sales, and profit margins, for chemical and allied industries, by company, weekly rpt quarterly article, A1250–1.502, A1250–1.514, A1250–1.525, A1250–1.536

Engineers salaries by industry group, census div, selected metro area, and years since college degree, 1993, annual survey rpt, A0685–5

Engineers salaries by industry group, census div, selected metro area, degree level, and years since college degree, 1993, annual survey rpt, A0685–3

Index by Subjects and Names

Executive compensation and components, by industry div and major manufacturing group, 1991, annual rpt, R4105–19

Finances and operations for chemical industry, with data by industry segment and product, 1970s-92, annual rpt, A3850–1

Financial performance and growth rankings for approx 1,000 top corporations, with comparisons by industry group, 1993 annual rpt, C3950–1.505

Financial ratios and performance, for over 350 SIC 4-digit industries, FY88-92, annual rpt, A6400–3

Lubricants (synthetic) market volume, by product type, 1991 and 1996, article, C5800–8.509

Lubricants (synthetic) wholesale shipments value, by use category, 1991 and 1996, article, C5150–3.501

Operating and financial composite ratios for corporations, with establishments and receipts, for approx 200 industries, by asset size, FY90, annual rpt, C7800–1

Operating and technical devs for chemical and chemical process industries, and plant and equipment costs and production indexes, monthly rpt, C5800–8

Paper and pulp industry consumption of major chemicals, 1985, 1991, and 1996, annual rpt, C3975–5.4

Paper processing chemicals market by type, 1991, article, C3975–2.501

Plastics industry production and sales by resin type, consumption by end-use market, and operating characteristics, 1992 and trends, annual rpt, A8920–1

Plastics production chemical compound ingredient costs, monthly rpt quarterly table, C5800–12.501, C5800–12.505, C5800–12.508, C5800–12.511

Production, consumption, stocks, trade, and prices for approx 100 basic commodities, including by country and producing State, commodity yearbook for 1993, C2400–1, C2400–2

Production, finance, operating ratios, employment, and trade for chemical and related industries, by country, company, and chemical, 1980s-92, annual feature, A1250–1.530

Production of top 50 chemicals, 1992 and trends, annual article, A1250–1.520

Production, R&D, operating data, and finance, articles and special features, weekly rpt, A1250–1

R&D spending by chemical industry, for 27 companies, 1987-93, annual article, A1250–1.511

R&D spending in Federal, industrial, and academic sectors, with data by company and instn, 1980s-93, annual feature, A1250–1.537

Russia chlorine production and consumption at pulp/paper mills, by mill, 1990, article, C3975–2.504

Salaries and employment of chemists, by employee and employer characteristics, Mar 1993 and trends, annual article, A1250–1.532

Sales and operating summary for top 100 chemical companies, 1992, annual article, A1250–1.523

Sales and profits for top 50 chemical companies worldwide, 1992, annual article, A1250–1.533

Water treatment chemical consumption, by type, 1990 and 2000, article, C5800–8.507

Worldwide and US production and trade, selected data by country or world area, 1988-92, annual feature, A1250–1.507

State and local:

Florida statistical abstract, general data, 1992 annual rpt, U6660–1.12

Texas trade, transportation, and public utilities employment, by SIC 2- and 3-digit industry and detailed occupation, 2nd qtr 1991, triennial survey rpt, S7675–1.31

see also Adhesives
see also Explosives
see also Fertilizers
see also Food ingredients and additives
see also Gases
see also Gum and wood chemicals
see also Hazardous substances
see also Nonmetallic minerals and mines
see also Paints and varnishes
see also Pesticides
see also Petrochemicals
see also Plastics and plastics industry
see also Soap and detergent industry
see also Synthetic fibers and fabrics
see also under By Industry in the "Index by Categories"

Chemistry

Degrees awarded by sex and instn, and grad student enrollment by degree level, 1991/92 and trends, annual articles, A1250–1.535

Degrees awarded in chemistry and chemical engineering, by level, 1980/81-1990/91, annual article, A1250–1.544

Employment in business and industry, hiring plans for college grads, by field, salary, and degree, 1993 annual survey rpt, U3730–1

Grads in chemistry and chemical engineering, starting salaries, employment status, demographic characteristics, and advanced study plans, 1991/92, annual rpt, A1250–2

Salaries and employment of chemists, by employee and employer characteristics, Mar 1993 and trends, annual article, A1250–1.532

Salaries, employment status, and demographic and professional characteristics, for chemists and chemical engineers, 1993, annual rpt, A1250–4

Salaries of scientists, engineers, technicians, and other professionals, by employee and employer characteristics, 1990s and trends, biennial rpt, A3960–1

Women and minorities in professional fields, detailed education and labor force data, 1991 and trends, recurring rpt, A3960–2.3

see also Chemicals and chemical industry

Cherries

see Fruit and fruit products

Chesapeake Bay

State and local:

Maryland fish landings from Chesapeake region, by species, 1990-91, biennial rpt, S3605–1.3

Chicago, Ill.

CPI and inflation rates for Chicago and St Louis, 1978-92, annual rpt, U6910–2

Child abuse and neglect

Crimes and arrests, by offense, location, and offender characteristics, with data on assaults on officers, 1991, annual rpt, S2536–1

Economic and business indicators for Illinois, with selected data for Chicago, quarterly rpt, S2405–2

Election results for Federal offices and Governor, by State, county, major city, and party, with voter registration and turnout, 1992 and trends, biennial rpt, C2500–1

Engineers salaries by industry group, census div, selected metro area, and years since college degree, 1993, annual survey rpt, A0685–5

Engineers salaries by industry group, census div, selected metro area, degree level, and years since college degree, 1993, annual survey rpt, A0685–3

Housing starts for single-family dwellings, 1990-93, article, C1850–8.506

Mental health facility patient population and characteristics, by facility, location, and treatment category, FY93, annual rpt, S2505–1

Printing (prepress) industry conditions for Chicago metro area, 1993 survey article, C1850–10.513

Statistical pocket guide of Chicago area population, income, and market data, suspended annual rpt, C2130–1

see also under By City in the "Index by Categories"

Chicanos

see Hispanic Americans
see Mexicans in the U.S.

Chickens

see Poultry industry and products

Child abuse and neglect

Black American crime, arrest, and incarceration data, with comparisons to whites, 1970s-91, annual compilation, C6775 2.5

Cases reported by type, and fatalities, by State, 1992 and trends, annual rpt, A7456–1

Child and maternal health and welfare indicators, by State, FY90 or 1990, annual rpt, R3840–11.2

Incidence of abuse correlated with selected family characteristics that pose a risk to child dev, 1992 article, A8680–1.501

State and local:

Arkansas child day care facility complaints, and child abuse/neglect cases reported by county, 1991, annual rpt, S0700–2.2

California vital statistics, including population, births, and deaths by cause, by demographic characteristics and county, 1990 and trends, annual rpt, S0865–1

Colorado court cases and dispositions, by type of court and detailed case type, FY92 and trends, annual rpt, S1035–1.2

DC court cases and dispositions, by type of case, and judicial system finances, 1992 and trends, annual rpt, S1515–1

DC statistical profile, general data, 1992 annual rpt, S1535–3.5

Florida infant and child homicides, by age and race, 1992, annual rpt, S1745–3

Georgia county guide, general data, 1993 annual rpt, U6750–1

Georgia court cases and dispositions, by type of court and case, and location, with judicial dept finances and personnel, FY92, annual rpt, S1903–1

Child abuse and neglect

Hawaii court cases and dispositions, by type of court and case, and judicial circuit, FY92 and trends, annual rpt, S2115–1.2

Hawaii data book, general data, 1992 annual rpt, S2090–1.4

Illinois crimes and arrests, by offense, with data by location and offender characteristics, 1991, annual rpt, S2536–1

Indiana public assistance program participation, expenditures, and services, by county, FY92 and trends, annual rpt, S2623–1

Louisiana vital statistics, including population, births, deaths by cause, reportable diseases, marriages, and divorces, by demographic characteristics and locality, 1989-90 and trends, annual rpt, S3295–1

Maine court child protective cases, by district and city, 1987-FY92, annual rpt, S3463–1

Michigan child and adult protection applications and cases, by county, monthly rpt, S4010–1

Michigan court caseloads and dispositions, by type of court and case, and court location, 1992 and trends, annual rpt, S3962–1

Mississippi child abuse/neglect trust fund finances, FY92, annual rpt, S4357–1

Missouri public welfare and medical assistance recipients, expenditures, and case processing, by program and county, FY92 and trends, annual rpt, S4575–2

Montana income tax checkoffs, by purpose, 1987-91, biennial rpt, S4750–1.1

Nebraska public welfare cases, recipients, and payments, by program and county, FY92 and trends, annual rpt, S4957–1

New York State child abuse and neglect cases reported and indicated, 1981-91, annual rpt, S5800–2.3

New York State court cases and dispositions, by type of court and case, and jurisdiction, 1991, annual rpt, S5730–1

North Carolina court cases and dispositions, by type of court and case, and location, with judicial dept finances and personnel, FY91, annual rpt, S5950–1

North Carolina reported abuse and neglect, and children receiving protective services, by county, 1st half FY93, semiannual rpt, S5940–2

North Dakota cases referred to juvenile court by reason, and caseload activity by district, 1991-92, annual rpt, S6210–1

Ohio court caseload and case disposition, by type of court and case, and location, 1992, annual rpt, S6385–1

Oklahoma child abuse/neglect cases alleged and confirmed, by county, FY92, annual rpt, S6455–1.2

Oregon crimes and arrests, by offense, with data by county, local agency, and offender characteristics, 1992 and trends, annual rpt, S6603–3.1

Pennsylvania statistical abstract, general data, 1992 recurring rpt, U4130–6.5

South Carolina deaths, by detailed cause, age, sex, and race, 1990, annual rpt, S7175–2

South Dakota child abuse and neglect investigations, and substantiated and unsubstantiated cases, FY91-92, annual rpt, S7385–1.1

Texas child abuse/neglect reports investigated, FY83-92, annual rpt, S7695–1

Texas infant deaths due to abuse, by victim sex and race-ethnicity, 1991, annual rpt, S7685–1

Utah juvenile status offenses, by type and month, 1992, annual rpt, S7890–3

Utah vital statistics, including births and deaths by cause, by demographic characteristics and location, 1990, annual rpt, S7835–1.2

Washington State juvenile murder victims, including child abuse deaths, 1986-92, annual rpt, S8440–1

West Virginia child abuse cases, 1990-91, annual rpt, S8610–1.2

West Virginia court caseloads and dispositions, by type of court and case, and judicial circuit, 1992 and trends, annual rpt, S8537–1

West Virginia welfare and social service program caseloads and expenditures, by county, monthly rpt, S8560–2

Wyoming child abuse/neglect cases, and protective and preventive services clients and funding by county, FY92 and trends, annual rpt, S8908–1

Child day care

Business forms manufacturing plant use of day care programs, by region, 1992, biennial rpt, A5785–4

Corporate personnel mgmt devs, including work force diversity, health care and family-related benefits, counseling services, and competitiveness, 1993 survey, B6850–6

Ear infection incidence in children under age 6, by selected characteristics including day care setting, 1988 survey, article, A2623–1.511

Employer policies and views on family-related issues, including involvement in child care service, Mar 1992 survey, A8907–1

Financial ratios and performance, for over 350 SIC 4-digit industries, FY88-92, annual rpt, A6400–3

Food service industry sales and establishments, with growth outlook, by market segment, 1993 annual feature, C1850–3.503

Hospital (teaching) child day care services available for house staff, 1992/93, annual rpt, A3273–3

Low-income families and children, health and welfare indicators, with data by State and city, 1992 annual rpt, R3840–11

Magazine publisher employee benefits, costs, and trends, with employee ratings of health coverage, Mar/Apr 1993 survey, article, C2575–1.517

Public opinion on establishment of publicly funded child care programs, by respondent characteristics, 1993 annual Gallup Poll, A8680–1.503

Salaries, health benefits, and turnover, for child care centers in 5 States or local areas, 1992 survey, annual article, A3865–2

School districts providing child day care, by enrollment size, 1992 survey rpt, A0775–5

Staff compensation, health benefits, and turnover, in child day care centers, 1992 and trends, A3865–3

Index by Subjects and Names

Urban public school systems providing day care for "latchkey" students and infants of teenage mothers, for 47 systems, 1990/91, A4425–4

State and local:

Alabama public welfare and social service cases, recipients, and payments, by program and county, monthly rpt, S0150–1

Arkansas human services dept finances and operations, by program, FY91 and trends, annual rpt, S0700–2.2

Colorado welfare and social services expenditures and caseloads, by county and/or program, FY91, annual rpt, S1085–1

Connecticut day care center capacity, 1991/92, biennial rpt, S1185–3

DC statistical profile, general data, 1992 annual rpt, S1535–3.1, S1535–3.5

Hawaii data book, general data, 1992 annual rpt, S2090–1.11

Illinois before- and after-school programs for unsupervised children, with participants and staff, 1986/87-1990/91, annual rpt, S2440–1.4

Indiana public assistance program participation, expenditures, and services, by county, FY92 and trends, annual rpt, S2623–1

Kansas statistical abstract, general data, 1991/92 annual rpt, U7095–2.6

Michigan public assistance program cases, recipients, and payments, detailed data by county, monthly rpt, S4010–1

Missouri licensed day care homes and centers, and capacity, June 1992, annual rpt, S4575–2

Montana day care services for persons receiving welfare or job training, including children participating and expenditures, monthly rpt, S4755–1

Nebraska registered/licensed child care facilities, by State area, FY92, annual rpt, S4957–1.2

New York State child services program statistics, 1991 and trends, annual rpt, S5800–2.3

North Carolina day care subsidies, including approved centers, spaces available, and children served, by county, 1st half FY93, semiannual rpt, S5940–2

Oklahoma licensed facilities by type, and day care slots by county, FY92, annual rpt, S6455–1.2

Oregon public welfare caseloads, recipients, and expenditures, by program, city, county, and State region, monthly rpt, S6615–8

Texas welfare and social services program expenditures, recipients, and fraud cases, by county and/or program, FY92 and trends, annual rpt, S7695–1

Utah public assistance program spending and recipients, including child care, 1993 annual rpt, R9380–1.9

Washington State public assistance clients and service costs, by client characteristics, program, and county, FY90, annual rpt, S8420–2

West Virginia welfare and social service program caseloads and expenditures, by county, monthly rpt, S8560–2

Wyoming welfare and social service recipients and expenditures, by program and county, FY92, annual rpt, S8908–1

Index by Subjects and Names

Child welfare

see also Respite care

Child labor

Issues of child/youth employment, with data on number of child workers, occupational deaths and injuries, and Federal and State regulation, 1992 rpt, R8335–2

Violators of child labor laws, with fines assessed and number of minors illegally employed, 1988-92, article, C1200–5.510

State and local:

Missouri child labor law enforcement activity, FY92, annual rpt, S4530–2.1

see also Youth employment

Child mortality

- Accidental and total deaths of children and youth age 0-24, by accident type, 1989, annual rpt, A8375–2.1
- AIDS cases and deaths among children under age 13, 1991 and trends, annual rpt, A5173–2.4
- Developing countries child, postneonatal, neonatal, and infant mortality rates, by sex and country, 1980s, article, A5160–6.501
- Developing countries child survival efforts, with selected child and maternal health indicators, 1980s-90, R8720–1.2
- Developing countries fertility, family planning, sexual behavior, and child health indicators, with selected detail by demographic characteristics, 1984-92 surveys, U2520–1.51
- Health and well-being indicators, including infant and child mortality, and teen violent death rates, by State, 1993 annual rpt, R3832–1
- Latin America statistical abstract, general data by country, 1992 annual rpt, U6250–1.6
- Maltreatment fatalities, by State, 1985-92, annual rpt, A7456–1
- Rates of mortality for children under age 5, by selected country, 1990, annual rpt, R3840–11.1
- School bus loading/unloading accident fatalities, by circumstances, location, and victim age and sex, 1991 and trends, annual rpt, S3040–2
- State social, economic, and govtl indicators, with rankings, 1993 semiannual rpt, B8500–1.9
- Vietnam child and infant mortality rates before, during, and after Vietnam war, with detail by regional area, 1993 article, A2623–1.510
- Weight-for-age indicators and mortality rates among children in studies conducted in 4 countries, 1993 article, A2623–1.510
- Work-related deaths among working children, 1990 estimates, R8335–2
- World population and health indicators, with detail by region and country, 1992/93 biennial rpt, R9455–1.2, R9455–1.5

State and local:

- Georgia county guide, general data, 1993 annual rpt, U6750–1
- Georgia vital statistics, including deaths by cause, demographic characteristics, and location, 1991 and trends, annual rpt, S1895–1.2
- Indiana child fatalities from abuse and neglect, by age group, FY92 and trends, annual rpt, S2623–1.7
- Michigan vital statistics, including births, deaths, marriages, divorces/annulments,

and communicable diseases, by location and demographic characteristics, 1990 and trends, annual rpt, S4000–3

see also Infant mortality

Child support and alimony

- Botswana unmarried women receiving child support, by source and selected characteristics, 1988, article, A5160–6.503
- Child health and well-being indicators, with selected household characteristics, by State, 1993 annual rpt, R3832–1
- Payment collection rates for child support cases, by State, FY90, annual rpt, R3840–11.2
- State social, economic, and govtl indicators, with rankings, 1993 semiannual rpt, B8500–1.8
- Student aid applicant untaxed income sources, American College Testing (ACT) program, 1992, annual rpt, R1960–5

State and local:

- Alabama public welfare and social service cases, recipients, and payments, by program and county, monthly rpt, S0150–1
- Arkansas child support enforcement collections, cases, and expenditures, FY91 and trends, annual rpt, S0700–2.3
- California criminal justice system detailed data, by offense, county, age, race-ethnicity, and sex, 1991 and trends, annual rpt, S0910–2
- California individual taxable income reported by source, deductions and credits by type, and tax returns, by income class and county, 1990, annual rpt, S0855–1.1
- Colorado child support court cases, by district and county, FY92, annual rpt, S1035–1.2
- DC court cases and dispositions, by type of case, and judicial system finances, 1992 and trends, annual rpt, S1515–1
- DC statistical profile, general data, 1992 annual rpt, S1535–3.5
- Delaware family court cases and dispositions, by county and type of case, FY92, annual rpt, S1360–1
- Hawaii court cases and dispositions, by type of court and case, and judicial circuit, FY92 and trends, annual rpt, S2115–1.2
- Illinois child support enforcement collections, FY83-92, annual rpt, S2520–2
- Indiana child support collections and distribution, by county, FY92, annual rpt, S2623–1.3
- Iowa child support recoveries in ADC program, monthly rpt, S2802–1
- Iowa district court civil filings and dispositions, by case type and district, 1991-92, annual rpt, S2815–1
- Kansas court caseloads and disposition, by type of court and case, and location, FY92, annual rpt, S3035–1
- Maine court cases and dispositions, by type and location, FY92 and trends, annual rpt, S3463–1
- Massachusetts court cases and dispositions, by type of court and case, and location, FY92 and trends, annual rpt, S3807–1
- Michigan child support collections, including tax offset activity, by county, monthly rpt, S4010–1

Michigan court caseloads and dispositions, and support collection program activities and finances, 1992 and trends, annual rpt, S3962–1

- Minnesota divorces/annulments, with children involved and custody and support awards, 1991, annual rpt, S4190–2
- Mississippi public welfare and social service cases, recipients, and payments, by program and county, FY92, annual rpt, S4357–1
- Missouri divorces, by child support settlement, 1992, annual rpt, S4518–1
- New Jersey child support/paternity collections and distributions, monthly rpt, S5415–1
- New Mexico child support collections, by county, monthly rpt quarterly feature, S5620–2
- New Mexico court cases and dispositions, by type of court and case, and location, with judicial system finances and personnel, FY92, annual rpt, S5623–1
- New York State child support cases and collections, by State area, 1991, annual rpt, S5800–2.1
- North Carolina public welfare programs, cases, recipients, staff, and finances, by county, 1st half FY93, semiannual rpt, S5940–2
- Ohio court caseload and case disposition, by type of court and case, and location, 1992, annual rpt, S6385–1
- Oklahoma child support enforcement collections, AFDC and non-AFDC, FY92, annual rpt, S6455–1.2
- Oklahoma court cases and dispositions, by type of court and case, with judicial system finances, by county or jurisdiction, FY92, annual rpt, S6493–1
- Rhode Island child support collections, 1987-91, annual rpt, S6965–1
- South Carolina public welfare recipients, payments, and case processing, by county and program, monthly rpt, S7252–1
- South Dakota child support enforcement cases and collections, by local office, FY92, annual rpt, S7385–1.1
- Texas court cases and dispositions, by type of court and case, and location, FY92, annual rpt, S7703–1
- Vermont district court case activity under Uniform Reciprocal Enforcement of Support Act, by circuit, FY92 annual rpt, S8120–1
- Washington State court cases and dispositions, by type of court and case, and jurisdiction, with judicial finances and personnel, 1992 and trends, annual rpt, S8339–1
- West Virginia child support enforcement program collections, monthly rpt, S8560–2
- Wyoming child support collections by method, FY92 and trends, annual rpt, S8908–1

Child welfare

- Catholic charity social service agency activities, clients, finances, and personnel, 1991 and trends, annual rpt, A3810–1
- Catholic child residential and day care centers, and children assisted, by diocese and State, 1993 annual compilation, C4950–1

Child welfare

Catholic child welfare centers and nurseries, and children assisted, 1993 annual almanac, C6885–1

Low-income families and children, health and welfare indicators, with data by State and city, 1992 annual rpt, R3840–11

Public opinion on best US policies for improving the lives of children in US and abroad, 1993 survey, annual rpt, A4965–1

State and local:

Arkansas human services dept finances and operations, including service recipient characteristics, by program, FY91 and trends, annual rpt, S0700–2

Colorado welfare and social services expenditures and caseloads, by county and/or program, FY91, annual rpt, S1085–1

Delaware AFDC and general assistance program cases, payments, and children involved, by program, monthly rpt, S1385–1

Indiana public assistance program participation, expenditures, and services, by county, FY92 and trends, annual rpt, S2623–1

Iowa ADC and SSI program recipients, and expenditures, by county, monthly rpt, S2802–1

Michigan public assistance program cases, recipients, and payments, detailed data by county, monthly rpt, S4010–1

Minnesota public welfare program recipients and expenditures, by county, 1992, semiannual rpt, S4202–1

Missouri public welfare and medical assistance recipients, expenditures, and case processing, by program and county, FY92 and trends, annual rpt, S4575–2

Montana welfare and medical assistance program cases and payments, by county and type of service, monthly rpt, S4755–1

New York State child services program statistics, 1991 and trends, annual rpt, S5800–2.3

North Carolina public welfare programs, cases, recipients, staff, and finances, by county, 1st half FY93, semiannual rpt, S5940–2

Oklahoma public welfare program expenditures, recipients, and services, by program and county, FY92 and trends, annual rpt, S6455–1

South Carolina public welfare recipients, payments, and case processing, by county and program, monthly rpt, S7252–1

South Dakota welfare and social services recipients and payments, by program, MSA, and county, FY92, annual rpt, S7385–1

Texas child care facilities and capacity, by type of facility, and child protective service clients, FY92 annual rpt, S7695–1

Washington State public assistance clients and service costs, by client characteristics, program, and county, FY90, annual rpt, S8420–2

West Virginia welfare and social service program caseloads and expenditures, by county, monthly rpt, S8560–2

see also Adoption

see also Aid to Families with Dependent Children

see also Child abuse and neglect

see also Child day care

see also Child labor

see also Child support and alimony

see also Foster home care

see also Head Start Project

see also Missing persons and runaways

see also School lunch and breakfast programs

Childbirth

see Births

see Birthweight

see Infant mortality

see Maternity

see Midwives

see Obstetrics and gynecology

Children

Advertising cartoon character recognition and popularity among children, for 3 leading and all other characters, Nov 1992 survey, article, C2710–1.515

AIDS cases among white and Hispanic children, with detail by transmission category, 1988-91, article, A2623–1.506

Asthma incidence among children, by race-ethnicity, with detail by Hispanic ethnic origin, 1993 article, A2623–1.506

Black American AIDS cases and deaths, with detail for children and comparisons to whites, 1984-91, annual compilation, C6775–2.2

Black American socioeconomic status, including health, education, politics, crime, and employment, with comparisons to whites, 1993 annual compilation, C6775–2

Black children and youth population, economic, health, and education data, with comparisons to whites, 1993 rpt, R3840–21

Books (children's) and nonbook children's merchandise sales performance in bookstores, by store type, Nov 1992 survey, annual article, C1852–2.506

Books (children's) bestsellers, 1992, annual feature, C1852–2.509

Books (children's) sales compared to birth rate, 1985-95, article, C1852–2.518

Budget of US outlays for public investment programs by type, with intl comparisons, FY93-94 and trends, R4700–23

Cardiovascular disease risk factor incidence among girls age 9-10, by race, 1992 article, A2623–1.502

Clothing (children's) sales, by retail outlet type, 1990-92, article, C5150–3.503

Clothing (children's) sales, by retail outlet type, 1992, article, C5150–3.510

Clothing (children's) with imprinted designs, market shares by retail outlet type and design category, Apr 1992-Mar 1993, article, C5150–3.513

Computer educational networks for children, subscribers and prices for 5 networks, 1993 article, C8900–1.524

Consumer attitudes and savings practices of children age 6-17, Dec 1992-Jan 1993 survey, article, C2710–1.531

Developing countries family planning and child survival efforts, by country and selected demographic characteristics, 1980s-90, R8720–1

Developing countries fertility, family planning, sexual behavior, and child health

Index by Subjects and Names

indicators, with selected detail by demographic characteristics, 1984-92 surveys, U2520–1.51

Discipline methods used by parents of children age 11/younger, 1962 and 1992, article, R4800–2.517

Divorce caseloads and processing times by case characteristics, with domestic court judicial staff, for 16 urban jurisdictions, 1989 and/or 1990, R6600–6

Ear infection incidence in children under age 6, by selected characteristics including day care setting, 1988 survey, article, A2623–1.511

Ear tube implantation prevalence in children, by demographic characteristics and reasons for implant, 1988, article, A2623–1.509

Elementary/secondary education data, including child poverty rates, by State, 1993 biennial rpt, A4355–1

Family planning devs worldwide, with data on fertility, contraceptive use, and family size preferences, quarterly rpt, A5160–6

Food product consumption among children, for 6 product types, 1990 survey, article, C2710–1.512

Foreign-born shares of population age 17/under, for top 10 States and DC, 1990, article, R8750–1.509

Health and welfare indicators for women and children, with data by race and State, 1992 annual rpt, R3840–5

Health and well-being indicators, with selected household characteristics, by State, 1993 annual rpt, R3832–1

Health insurance coverage status of children, 1991, article, R8750–1.510

Health research results, including data on incidence of infant and children's health problems, 1993 articles, A2623–1.503

Hispanic American AIDS cases and deaths, with detail for children and comparisons to whites, 1984-91, annual compilation, C6775–3.6

Hispanic American socioeconomic status, including education, politics, income, and employment, with comparisons to whites, 1993 annual compilation, C6775–3

Incarcerated mothers and their children, with data on characteristics, child caregivers, visitation, and support program use, 1991/92, A7575–4

Latin America statistical abstract, general data by country, 1992 annual rpt, U6250–1.5

Living arrangements of children, by parents characteristics and child age and race-ethnicity, 1992, article, B6045–1.504

Living arrangements of children, by parents characteristics and child race-ethnicity, 1991, article, B6045–1.503

Living arrangements of children, by race-ethnicity, decennially 1960-90, B6045–1.502

Low-income families and children, health and welfare indicators, with data by State and city, 1992 annual rpt, R3840–11

Measles cases in preschool children, health care providers used and welfare status, in 5 metro areas, 1989-90, article, A2623–1.508

Media market areas ranked by population age 2-11, top 26 markets, 1992, annual rpt, C1200–1.514

Index by Subjects and Names

Children

Media use by children, for selected written material and radio, 1990 survey, article, C2710–1.512

Medicaid child and total recipients, expenditures, and other program characteristics, and child health summary, by State, FY91, annual rpt, A0565–1

Orthopedic internal fixation device implantation prevalence in children, and results, with detail by demographic characteristics, 1988, article, A2623–1.509

Personal injury jury verdict awards in wrongful death of children cases, 1989-92, annual rpt, C5180–1

Poor children age 5/under, with demographic and family characteristics, 1991 and trends, annual rpt, U1260–2

Population shares under age 15, for 10 States with highest and lowest shares, 1940 and 1990, B6045–1.501

Population size and selected characteristics, by region, census div, and State, 1991 and trends, annual data sheet, R8750–9

Population under 6 and 6-17 years old, approx 300 metro areas, 1992, annual rpt, C1200–1.511

Poverty among children by State and for 200 cities and 89 counties, with State and city detail by race-ethnicity, 1989 and trends, R3840–20

Poverty among white, black, and Hispanic children, 1991, R3834–15

Poverty rates for children in married-couple and female-headed families, by race and parental education level, 1982/83, article, A8510–1.1

Quality of life indicators for children based on social, economic, and environmental factors, for 239 MSAs, with detail by component county and city, 1980s-90s, R9700–2

Restaurant menu item order shares from children, 1991, article, A8200–1.505

Retail outlet preferences of consumers buying children's hard goods, 1993 article, C8130–1.511

Risk factors at home and school correlated with abuse and reading ability, and special instructional efforts correlated with drug use, 1992 article, A8680–1.501

Southern States children age 17/under lacking health insurance and eligible for Medicaid, with detail by age and family income, for 6-17 States, 1991, R9000–1

State social, economic, and govtl indicators, with rankings, 1993 semiannual rpt, B8500–1.1

Toiletry products for children, consumer interest in and retail outlets shopped, 1993 survey article, C5150–2.519

TV commercial and public network children's program audience, and syndicated episodes available, by program, 1993 articles, C1850–14.531

TV violence concerns of parents, with detail for news programs, Feb 1993 survey, C8915–11.1

Urban poverty rate compared to total US, for aggregate population age 5-17 of 47 major urban areas, 1980 and 1990, A4425–4

Video cassette unit sales, for children's prerecorded tapes, by retail outlet type, Nov/Dec 1992, article, C8130–1.505

State and local:

Alabama divorces and annulments, by number of children involved, 1992, annual rpt, S0175–2

Alabama municipal data book, general data, 1992 recurring rpt, S0121–5

Alaska divorces/annulments and number of children affected, 1990, annual rpt, S0315–1

Arkansas Census of Population and Housing detailed findings, 1990, U5935–7

Arkansas divorces, by number of children affected and county, 1991, annual rpt, S0685–1

Arkansas traffic accidents, fatalities, and injuries involving children in restraint systems, 1991, annual rpt, S0692–1

California Census of Population and Housing detailed findings, 1990, S0840–9

California library services for children, including programs and attendance, by library, FY92, annual rpt, S0825–2

California traffic deaths and injuries for children under age 3, by county, 1989-91, annual rpt, S0885–1

Connecticut marriage dissolutions, by number of children affected, 1989, annual rpt, S1200–1

Connecticut traffic accident victim use of child safety restraints, 1992, annual rpt, S1275–1

Delaware divorces, by number of children involved, 1990, annual rpt, S1385–2

Florida traffic accidents involving children with and without restraints, including injuries and fatalities, by age, 1992, annual rpt, S1750–2

Georgia prison inmates by number of children reported, FY92 annual rpt, S1872–1

Hawaii vital statistics and health services, including children affected by divorces, and various programs for children, 1990, annual rpt, S2065–1

Idaho divorces, by number of children affected, 1991, annual rpt, S2250–2

Iowa marital dissolutions, children under age 18 affected, by race, 1991, annual rpt, S2795–1

Kansas divorces and annulments, by number of children affected, 1991, annual rpt, S2975–1

Kansas traffic accidents, fatalities, and injuries involving children in safety restraint systems, 1992, annual rpt, S3040–1

Kentucky motor vehicle accident injuries and fatalities, and child safety device use, 1992, annual rpt, S3150–2

Louisiana Census of Population and Housing summary findings, by local area, 1990 and trends, U8010–4

Louisiana motor vehicle child safety restraint use, 1986-92, annual rpt, S3345–2

Maine Census of Population and Housing summary findings, by local area, 1990, S3465–9

Maryland divorces/annulments, by number of children affected, 1989, annual rpt, S3635–1

Maryland homeless children, by region and county, 1991/92, annual rpt, S3610–1

Michigan and US children involved in divorces/annulments, 1960s-90, annual rpt, S4000–3

Minnesota divorces/annulments, with children involved and custody and support awards, 1991, annual rpt, S4190–2

Mississippi characteristics of economically disadvantaged and Job Training Partnership Act eligible population, 1993/94, annual planning rpt, S4345–1.3

Mississippi divorces by cause, and number of children affected, by race, 1992, annual rpt, S4350–1

Missouri divorces, by number of children affected and custody petitioner, 1992, annual rpt, S4518–1

Montana divorces, by number of children affected, 1990-91, annual rpt, S4690–1

Montana traffic accidents, fatalities, and injuries, including child safety device use, 1992, annual rpt, S4705–2

Nebraska divorce settlements and number of children affected, 1991, annual rpt, S4885–1

New Hampshire divorces involving children, by county, and custody awards, 1987-91, annual rpt, S5215–1

New Jersey Census of Population and Housing detailed findings, by county, 1990, S5425–19

New York State traffic fatalities and injuries, by safety equipment use including child restraints, 1991, annual rpt, S5790–1

North Carolina traffic accidents child safety restraint use correlated with injury level, 1992, annual rpt, S5990–1

North Dakota children by age and/or sex, by county, Aug 1991, annual education directory, S6180–2

North Dakota divorces, by number of children affected, 1991, annual rpt, S6105–2

North Dakota traffic deaths and injuries of children age 5/under, by safety device use, 1992, annual rpt, S6217–1

Ohio divorces and annulments, by legal grounds and number of children involved, 1991, annual rpt, S6285–1

Ohio traffic accident victim use of child safety restraints, 1991, annual rpt, S6290–1

Oklahoma traffic fatalities, including child safety restraint use, 1992, annual rpt, S6482–1

Oregon marriage dissolutions, by number of children affected, 1991, annual rpt, S6615–5

Pennsylvania Census of Population and Housing detailed findings, with selected data by county and municipality, 1990, U4130–13

Rhode Island Census of Population and Housing detailed findings, by county and municipality, 1990, S6930–9

Rhode Island divorces, by county and number of children affected, 1989, S6995–1

South Carolina divorces, with number of children involved, by race and county, 1990, annual rpt, S7175–1

South Carolina traffic accident injuries and fatalities of children, by safety restraint use, 1992, annual rpt, S7190–2

South Dakota traffic accident injuries and fatalities involving children under age 5, by safety device use, 1992 and trends, annual rpt, S7300–3

Children

Texas children's hospitals capacity, use, and finances, 1989, U8850–8.3
Texas divorces by number of children affected, 1991, annual rpt, S7685–1
Utah divorces and number of children affected, 1990 and trends, annual rpt, S7835–2
Utah homeless shelter population characteristics, individual shelter capacity, and related housing data, 1991-92, annual rpt, S7808–2
Utah traffic accident injuries and fatalities of children age 0-4, by safety restraint use, 1992, annual rpt, S7890–2
Vermont divorces and children under age 18 affected, by county, 1991, annual rpt, S8054–1
Virginia divorces, by number of children involved, 1991, annual rpt, S8225–1
West Virginia divorces and annulments, by number of children affected, 1991, annual rpt, S8560–1
Wisconsin children affected by divorces, by county, 1991, annual rpt, S8715–4
Wyoming divorces/annulments by number of children affected and county, 1991, annual rpt, S8920–2
see also Abortion
see also Adoption
see also Aid to Families with Dependent Children
see also Birth defects
see also Births out of wedlock
see also Child abuse and neglect
see also Child day care
see also Child labor
see also Child mortality
see also Child support and alimony
see also Child welfare
see also Compensatory education
see also Educational enrollment
see also Elementary and secondary education
see also Fertility
see also Foster home care
see also Handicapped children
see also Head Start Project
see also Infant mortality
see also Juvenile courts and cases
see also Juvenile delinquency
see also Missing persons and runaways
see also Old-Age, Survivors, Disability, and Health Insurance
see also Parents
see also Pediatrics
see also Preschool education
see also Remedial education
see also School lunch and breakfast programs
see also Special education
see also Youth
see also Youth employment
see also under By Age in the "Index by Categories"

Chile

Energy intl sourcebook, with detail on oil and gas industry operations, supply-demand, and prices, for approx 80 countries, 1970s-91, annual compilation, C6985–10.2
Foreign investments by Chilean companies in other Latin American countries, for 8 firms, 1993 article, C5800–7.544
Motor vehicle world production, sales, trade, and registrations, by country, world area, manufacturer, and make, 1991 and trends, annual rpt, A0865–2.1

Statistical abstract of Latin America, detailed social, govtl, and economic data, 1992 annual rpt, U6250–1
see also under By Foreign Country or World Area in the "Index by Categories"

Chilton, Kenneth

"Changing Structures and Strategies: Survey of American Manufacturing Executives", U9640–4

China, Nationalist

see Taiwan

China, People's Republic

Auto import purchases under sales agreement with 3 major US manufacturers, by vehicle model, Apr 1993, article, C2710–3.525
Auto production for 6 joint venture plants operating in China, various years 1991-96, article, C2710–3.537
Chemical and related industries production, finances, operating ratios, employment, and trade, by country, company, and chemical, 1980s-92, annual feature, A1250–1.530
Coal industry supply-demand, employment, and trade, by country, 1990-91 and trends, annual rpt, A7400–2.2
Computer revenues by industry sector, 1991, article, C5800–7.505
Economic activity, including industrial and agricultural production, and foreign trade and investment, with data by commodity, 1980s-92, annual feature, A9315–1.504
Economic activity indicators for China, including trade with US and other countries, bimonthly rpt, A9315–1
Economic indicators, including population, and imports from US of 3 fast-growing product types, 1993 article, C4687–1.511
Electronics industry trade and/or production trends by product category for 33 countries, with general economic profiles, 1993 annual rpt, A4725–1.4
Energy intl sourcebook, with detail on oil and gas industry operations, supply-demand, and prices, for approx 80 countries, 1970s-91, annual compilation, C6985–10.2
Ethylene plants operating and planned, with data on capacity, construction costs, and imported equipment origins, 1993 article, C6985–1.512
Hard goods US manufacturers affected by import of goods produced by Chinese prison labor, by product line, 1993 annual survey rpt, A1800–1
Lumber and log exports from US to China and Japan, 1984-92, annual rpt, A9395–1
Machine tool industry operating data by country and product, 1992 and trends, annual rpt, A3179–2.2
Magnesium imports of US and Japan from China and Commonwealth of Independent States, with worldwide demand by application or world region, 1992-93, article, A1250–1.544
Motor vehicle world production, sales, trade, and registrations, by country, world area, manufacturer, and make, 1991 and trends, annual rpt, A0865–2.1
Nuclear power generating capacity by unit, uranium resources by Province, and uranium processing capacity by plant, 1993 article, B6800–1.509

Nuclear reactors in operation, with capacity, electricity generation, and construction, by unit and country, 1992, annual rpt, B6800–2.2
Oil and gas production by region, and offshore activity including foreign investments, 1993 annual rpt, C6985–3.1
Oil exploration joint venture contracts, with location, land area, and participating companies, 1993 article, C6985–1.550
Oil industry outlook in southeastern region, with demand by Province and coastal refinery construction projects and capacity, 1990s-2000, article, C6985–1.528
Population, births, deaths, infant deaths, and youth population as shares of world totals, 1993 article, R8750–1.508
Public opinion in US on selected foreign policy issues, with detail for 3 States, 1993 survey, annual rpt, A4965–1
Socioeconomic and infrastructure indicators, with comparisons to US, 1993 rpt, R4105–82.8
Trade value with US, with detail for Illinois exports, and US tariff rates and collections, for top 20-25 commodities, 1989-91, article, U6910–1.502
Women's fertility patterns correlated with socioeconomic characteristics, in 6 Provinces, 1987, article, A5160–6.502
see also Guangdong Province, China
see also Jiangsu Province, China
see also Shanghai, China
see also under By Foreign Country or World Area in the "Index by Categories"

Chinese Americans

see Asian Americans

Chiropractic and naturopathy

HMO benefits coverage, premiums, and rating methods used, by plan characteristics, 1991 and trends, annual rpt, A5150–2.1

State and local:

Florida county data book, 1992/93 annual rpt, C6360–1
Florida health care atlas, including manpower by occupation and health care facilities by type, by district and county, 1992 annual rpt, S1746–1.2
Florida statistical abstract, general data, 1992 annual rpt, U6660–1.20
Hawaii births, by type of attendant and race-ethnicity of child, 1990, annual rpt, S2065–1.2
Idaho live births by type of attendant, including midwife and naturopath, by county, 1991, annual rpt, S2250–2
Indiana Medicaid expenditures, by service and provider type and county, FY91-92, annual rpt, S2623–1.6
Kentucky Medicaid recipients and payments, by program, county, and type of medical service, monthly rpt, S3140–5
South Dakota medical assistance recipients and payments, by type of service, FY92, annual rpt, S7385–1.1
Texas chiropractors offices/clinics and expenditures, 1977, 1982, and 1987, U8850–8.3

Chlorine

see Gases

Index by Subjects and Names

Chlorofluorocarbons

see Air pollution
see Chemicals and chemical industry

Chocolate
see Cocoa and chocolate

Cholesterol

Alcohol consumption frequency correlated with cholesterol level, by race and sex, 1976-80, article, A2623–1.508

Children age 9-10 cardiovascular disease risk factor incidence, for girls by race, 1992 article, A2623–1.502

Consumer nutrition awareness and health concerns, with food shopping and consumption patterns, by respondent characteristics, 1993 survey, annual rpt, A4950–36

State and local:

Alabama health behavior risk factor surveillance survey results, by respondent characteristics, 1988-89, recurring rpt, S0175–6

Colorado health behavior risk factor surveillance survey results, by respondent characteristics, 1990, recurring rpt, S1010–3

Connecticut health behavior risk factor surveillance survey results, 1989-91, annual rpt, S1200–2

Georgia health behavior risk factor surveillance survey results, by respondent characteristics, 1991 and trends, annual rpt, S1895–2

Hawaii resident awareness of cholesterol levels, and health dept screening activity, 1990, annual rpt, S2065–1

Iowa health behavior risk factor surveillance survey results, by respondent characteristics, 1991, annual rpt, S2795–2

Massachusetts health behavior risk factor surveillance survey results, by respondent characteristics, 1986-90, recurring rpt, S3850–3

Michigan health behavior risk factor surveillance survey results, by respondent characteristics, 1991, annual rpt, S4000–4

Nevada health behavior risk factor surveillance survey results, by location and respondent characteristics, 1991, annual rpt, S5075–3

New York State health behavior risk factor surveillance survey results, by respondent characteristics, 1990, recurring rpt, S5765–3

North Dakota health behavior risk factor surveillance survey results, by respondent characteristics, 1991 and trends, annual rpt, S6105–3

Pennsylvania health behavior risk factor surveillance survey results, by respondent characteristics, 1991, annual rpt, S6820–4

Utah health behavior risk factor surveillance survey results, by respondent characteristics, 1991, annual rpt, S7835–3

Chromite
see Metals and metal industries

Chura, Karin M.

"1993 Small Business Banking Study: An Analysis of the September Survey", A4160–5

Church and state

High school graduation ceremony prayer acceptability, public opinion by respondent characteristics, 1993 annual Gallup Poll, A8680–1.503

Public opinion on school prayer issue and role of religion in govt, 1972-91 surveys, annual rpt, U6395–1

Churches
see Religious organizations

Cigarette tax
see Excise tax

Cigarettes and cigars
see Smoking
see Tobacco industry and products

CIM
see Automation
see Manufacturing

Cinema
see Motion pictures

Circuit courts
see State courts

Circulatory diseases

Hospital patient admission rates and length of stay, by diagnosis and procedure, payment source, age, sex, and region, 1991, B4455–4

Hospital patient charges and length of stay, by diagnosis and procedure, payment source, age, and region, 1991, B4455–5

Hospital patient discharges and length of stay, by diagnosis, type of operation, age, and region, 1991, annual rpt series, B4455–1

Hospital patient discharges and length of stay, by diagnostic related group (DRG), payment source, age, and region, 1991, annual rpt series, B4455–3

State and local:

Alabama vital statistics, including population, births, deaths by cause, marriages, and divorces, by location and demographic characteristics, 1992 and trends, annual rpt, S0175–2

Alaska vital statistics, including births, deaths by cause, marriages, divorces, adoptions, and population, by demographic characteristics and location, 1990, annual rpt, S0315–1

Arkansas vital statistics, including births, deaths by cause, marriages, and divorces, by age, sex, race, and county, 1991 and trends, annual rpt, S0685–1

California vital statistics, including population, births, and deaths by cause, by demographic characteristics and county, 1990 and trends, annual rpt, S0865–1

Colorado vital statistics, including population, births, deaths by cause, abortion, marriage and divorce, and adoption, by demographic characteristics and location, 1990 and trends, annual rpt, S1010–1

Connecticut vital statistics, including births, deaths by cause, marriages, and divorces, by demographic characteristics and location, 1989, annual rpt, S1200–1

Delaware vital statistics, including births, deaths by cause, and marriages and dissolutions, by demographic characteristics and location, 1990, annual rpt, S1385–2

Florida vital statistics, including population, births, deaths by cause, and marriages and dissolutions, by location and demographic characteristics, 1992 and trends, annual rpt, S1745–3

Georgia vital statistics, including deaths by cause, demographic characteristics, and location, 1991 and trends, annual rpt, S1895–1.2

Hawaii vital statistics, including births, deaths by cause, marriages, and dissolutions, by demographic characteristics and location, 1990, annual rpt, S2065–1.2

Idaho vital statistics, including births, deaths by cause, abortions, marriages, and divorces, by demographic characteristics and county, 1991 and trends, annual rpt, S2250–2

Iowa vital statistics, including population, births, deaths by cause, marriages, and divorces, by demographic characteristics and location, 1991 and trends, annual rpt, S2795–1

Kansas vital statistics, including population, births, deaths by cause, abortions, marriages, and divorces, by demographic characteristics and location, 1991 and trends, annual rpt, S2975–1

Kentucky vital statistics, including births, deaths by cause, marriages and divorces, and population, by demographic characteristics and county, 1991, annual rpt, S3140–1

Louisiana vital statistics, including population, births, deaths by cause, reportable diseases, marriages, and divorces, by demographic characteristics and locality, 1989-90 and trends, annual rpt, S3295–1

Maine vital statistics, including births, deaths by cause, abortions, and marriages and divorces, by demographic characteristics and location, 1991 and trends, annual rpt, S3460–2

Maryland vital statistics, including population, births, deaths by cause, marriages, and divorces, by demographic characteristics and location, 1989 and trends, annual rpt, S3635–1

Massachusetts vital statistics, including births, deaths by cause, marriages, divorces, and population, by locality and demographic characteristics, 1990 and trends, annual rpt, S3850–1

Michigan vital statistics, including births, deaths, marriages, divorces/annulments, and communicable diseases, by location and demographic characteristics, 1990 and trends, annual rpt, S4000–3

Minnesota vital statistics, including population, births, abortions, deaths, marriages, and divorces, by location and demographic characteristics, 1991 and trends, annual rpt, S4190–2

Mississippi vital statistics, including births, deaths by cause, marriages, and divorces, by demographic characteristics and location, 1992 and trends, annual rpt, S4350–1

Missouri vital statistics, including population, births, deaths by cause, and marriages and divorces, by location and demographic characteristics, 1992 and trends, annual rpt, S4518–1

Montana vital statistics, including births, deaths by cause, abortion, disease, and marriage and divorce, by demographic characteristics and county, 1990-91 and trends, annual rpt, S4690–1

Circulatory diseases

Nebraska vital statistics, including births, deaths, marriages, divorces, and population, by demographic characteristics and location, 1991 and trends, annual rpt, S4885–1

Nevada vital statistics, including births, abortions, and deaths by cause, by county and demographic characteristics, 1989 and trends, annual rpt, S5075–1

New Hampshire vital statistics, including population, births, deaths by cause, marriages, and divorces, by location and demographic characteristics, 1991 and trends, annual rpt, S5215–1

New Jersey vital statistics, including births, deaths, population, communicable diseases, and marriages and divorces, by demographic characteristics and location, 1990 and trends, annual rpt, S5405–1

New Mexico vital statistics, including population, births, deaths, and disease, by location and demographic characteristics, 1991 and trends, annual rpt, S5605–1

New York State vital statistics, including population, births, deaths by cause, reportable diseases, and marriages and dissolutions, by demographic characteristics and/or location, 1990 and trends, annual rpt, S5765–1

North Carolina deaths and rates, by cause and county, 1991 and trends, annual rpt, S5927–1.2

North Dakota vital statistics, including births, deaths by cause, marriages and divorces, and abortions, by demographic characteristics and/or county, 1991 and trends, annual rpt, S6105–2

Ohio vital statistics, including births, deaths by cause, marriages, divorces, and population, by demographic characteristics and location, 1991 and trends, annual rpt, S6285–1

Oregon vital statistics, including births, deaths by cause, communicable diseases, marriages, and divorces, by age, sex, race-ethnicity, and county, 1991 and trends, annual rpt, S6615–5

Rhode Island vital statistics, including population, births, deaths, marriages, and divorces, by demographic characteristics and locality, 1989 and trends, annual rpt, S6995–1

South Carolina deaths, by detailed cause, age, sex, and race, 1990, annual rpt, S7175–2

South Carolina vital statistics, including births, deaths by cause, marriages, and divorces, by age, sex, race, and location, 1990 and trends, annual rpt, S7175–1

South Dakota vital statistics, including births, deaths, marriage and divorce, and communicable disease, by demographic characteristics and county, 1991 and trends, annual rpt, S7345–1

Tennessee vital statistics, including births, deaths by cause, marriages, divorces, and population, by demographic characteristics and location, 1991 and trends, annual rpt, S7520–2

Texas vital statistics, including births, deaths by cause, abortions, marriages, and divorces, by location and demographic characteristics, 1991 and trends, annual rpt, S7685–1

Utah vital statistics, including births, deaths by cause, and population, by county and demographic characteristics, 1990 and trends, annual rpt, S7835–1

Vermont vital statistics, including population, births, deaths by cause, abortions, marriages, and divorces, by location and demographic characteristics, 1991 and trends, annual rpt, S8054–1

Virginia vital statistics, including births, deaths by cause, marriages and divorces, and communicable disease, by demographic characteristics and location, 1991 and trends, annual rpt, S8225–1

Washington State vital statistics, including births, deaths by cause, and population, by demographic characteristics and location, 1991 and trends, annual rpt, S8363–1

West Virginia vital statistics, including births, deaths by cause, marriages, and divorces, by location and demographic characteristics, 1991 and trends, annual rpt, S8560–1

Wisconsin vital statistics, including population, births, deaths by cause, and marriages and dissolutions, by county and demographic characteristics, 1991 and trends, annual rpt, S8715–4

Wyoming vital statistics, including population, births, deaths by cause, marriages, and divorces, by demographic characteristics and county, 1991 and trends, annual rpt, S8920–2

see also Cardiovascular diseases

see also Cerebrovascular diseases

see also under By Disease in the "Index by Categories"

Cirino, Anna M.

"Comparative Financial Statistics for Public Two-Year Colleges: FY92 National Sample", A6705–1

Cirrhosis of liver

see Digestive diseases

CIS

see Commonwealth of Independent States

Cities

Business socioeconomic profiles for 60 cities rated as best by Fortune magazine, 1992 annual article, C8900–1.501

Consumer buying power survey of population, income, and sales by kind of business, by census div, State, MSA, county, and city, 1992, annual rpt, C1200–1.511

Cost-of-living indexes and retail prices for selected consumer items in approx 300 cities, quarterly rpt, A0150–1

Elementary/secondary math and science student enrollment and new teachers, for large city school districts in 4-5 States, 1993 biennial rpt, A4355–3

Emergency food and shelter supply-demand and assisted housing availability in 28-29 cities, with data on homeless population characteristics, 1991/92, annual rpt, A9330–9

Finances of local govts, by type of govt unit, and for 52 largest cities, 1993 annual rpt, R9050–1.6

Market rankings of leading MSAs, counties, and cities, by population, income, and retail sales, 1993 annual rpt, C3250–1

Officials views on city issues and conditions, 1992 survey, annual rpt, A8012–1.21

Index by Subjects and Names

Policies and conditions in cities, Natl League of Cities surveys, series, A8012–1

Socioeconomic characteristics and geographic distribution of US and Canadian cities, 1993 annual rpt, A5800–1

Southeastern States economic and demographic indicators, for municipalities in Alabama and 4 adjacent States, 1992 recurring rpt, S0121–5

Statistical profiles of 50 States and DC, general data, 1993 annual almanac, C4712–1

Tobacco products excise tax collections, and number of counties and cities imposing, by State, FY63-92, annual rpt, A9075–2

Traffic accident deaths for 433 cities in US and Canada, 1991-92, annual rpt, A8375–2.3

World cities with 1 million/more inhabitants, with share of population, by country, 1990 and trends, biennial rpt, R9455–1.5

State and local:

Georgia statistical abstract, general data, 1992-93 biennial rpt, U6730–1.11

see also Central business districts

see also Central cities

see also City and town planning

see also Electoral districts and precincts

see also Harbors and ports

see also Local government

see also Marketing areas

see also Neighborhoods

see also Suburbs

see also Wards, city

see also under By City and By SMSA in the "Index by Categories"

see also under names of individual cities

Citizenship

Chemistry and chemical engineering grad starting salaries, employment status, demographic characteristics, and advanced study plans, 1991/92, annual rpt, A1250–2

Ecologist personal and professional characteristics, including research activity and funding, with data by field, Mar 1992 survey, recurring rpt, A4685–1

Hispanic American elected officials by office and State, with related population characteristics, 1992 annual directory, A6844–1

Latin America immigrants to US and naturalized citizens, by country, 1992 annual rpt, U6250–1.14

Northern Mariana Islands population shares by citizenship status and birthplace, 1992 rpt, B3500–1.501

Professional worker salaries, by employee and employer characteristics, with detail for scientists and engineers, 1990s and trends, biennial rpt, A3960–1

Southeastern region persons naturalized, FY85-89, annual rpt, U3255–4.1

Statistical profiles of 50 States and DC, general data, 1993 annual almanac, C4712–1

State and local:

Arkansas Census of Population and Housing detailed findings, 1990, U5935–7

California Census of Population and Housing detailed findings, 1990, S0840–9

Hawaii data book, general data, 1992 annual rpt, S2090–1.1

Maryland statistical abstract, general data, 1993-94 biennial rpt, S3605–1.1, S3605–1.9

New Jersey Census of Population and Housing detailed findings, by county, 1990, S5425–19

Pennsylvania Census of Population and Housing detailed findings, with selected data by county and municipality, 1990, U4130–13

South Carolina statistical abstract, general data, 1993 annual rpt, S7125–1.13

Tennessee statistical abstract, general data, 1992/93 annual rpt, U8710–2.1

Utah prison inmates, parolees, and probationers, by citizenship status and sex, Oct 1992, annual rpt, S7810–1

Citrus fruits

Exports of farm products, by detailed commodity and country of destination, US and California, 1991, annual rpt, B9520–1

Financial ratios and performance, for over 350 SIC 4-digit industries, FY88-92, annual rpt, A6400–3

Latin America statistical abstract, general data by country, 1992 annual rpt, U6250–1.24

Production, consumption, stocks, trade, and prices for approx 100 basic commodities, including by country and producing State, commodity yearbook for 1993, C2400–1, C2400–2

State and local:

Arizona agricultural production, marketing, and finances, by commodity and county, 1988-92, annual rpt, U5830–1

California fruit and nut production, marketing, and income, by commodity, 1983-92, annual rpt, S0850–1.1

Florida citrus fruit production, acreage, yield, and shipments, by fruit type, 1991/92 and trends, annual rpt, S1685–1.1

Hawaii agricultural production and marketing, by commodity and island, 1987-91, annual rpt, S2030–1

Texas agricultural production, marketing, and finances, by commodity and county, and farms and farmland, 1991 and trends, annual rpt series, S7630–1

City and town planning

Commissions for land use planning, composition and activities, and commissioner characteristics, 1987 and trends, recurring rpt, A2615–2

Personnel practices of public planning agencies, by jurisdiction size, 1991 survey rpt, A2615–3

City councils

see Local government

City employees

see State and local employees

City taxation

see State and local taxes

Civil Aeronautics Board

see Department of Transportation

Civil aviation

Latin America statistical abstract, general data by country, 1992 annual rpt, U6250–1.3

State and local:

Hawaii data book, general data, 1992 annual rpt, S2090–1.18

Maine employment in trade, utilities, and transportation SIC 2-digit industries, by detailed occupation, 2nd qtr 1991, triennial rpt, S3465–1.25

see also Aerospace industry

see also Air cargo

see also Air traffic control

see also Aircraft

see also Airlines

see also Airports and airways

see also Aviation accidents and safety

see also Business aircraft and flying

see also General aviation

see also Pilots

Civil courts

see Civil procedure

see Courts

see Domestic relations courts and cases

see Federal district courts

see Juvenile courts and cases

see Probate courts and cases

see Small claims courts and cases

see State courts

see Supreme Court

see Tax laws and courts

see Traffic laws and courts

Civil defense

State and local:

Arkansas financial condition, including revenues by source, expenditures by function and locality, and fund balances, FY91-92, biennial rpt, S0780–1

Civil engineering

see Bridges and tunnels

see Canals

see Dams

see Harbors and ports

see Highways, streets, and roads

see Irrigation

see Public works

see Reclamation of land

see Rivers and waterways

Civil liberties

see Censorship

see Civil rights

see Due process of law

see Electronic surveillance

see Habeas corpus

see Right of privacy

see Searches and seizures

Civil-military relations

see also Defense contracts and procurement

see also Defense industries

Civil procedure

Correctional instns under court order, by State, Dec 1992, recurring directory, A1305–1.2

Correctional instns under court order, by State, June 1992, annual rpt, A1305–3

Divorce caseload, processing time, and filings per judge, compared to other civil cases, for 11 urban jurisdictions, 1987 or 1990, R6600–6

State appellate and trial court caseloads and dispositions, by case type and State, 1991 and trends, annual rpt, R6600–1

Urban small claims and traffic court caseloads, processing, dispositions, judgments, and litigant satisfaction, for 3-12 jurisdictions, 1990, R6600–5

State and local:

Alabama court caseloads and dispositions, by type of court and case, and location, with judicial dept finances, FY92 and trends, annual rpt, S0118–1

Alaska court cases and dispositions, by type of court and case, and location, with judicial dept finances and personnel, FY92 and trends, annual rpt, S0290–1

Arizona court cases and dispositions, by type of case and court, with judicial personnel and finances, by county and city, FY92, annual rpt, S0525–1

Arkansas court caseloads and dispositions, by type of court and case, and location, FY92 and trends, annual rpt, S0647–1

California court activity, including caseloads and dispositions, by case type and court, and location, FY92 and trends, annual rpt, S0905–1

California court cases and dispositions, by type of case and court, and location, FY92 and trends, annual rpt, S0905–2

Colorado court cases and dispositions, by type of court and detailed case type, FY92 and trends, annual rpt, S1035–1.2

Connecticut court caseloads and dispositions, by type of court and case, and court location, with judicial dept finances, FY91-92, biennial rpt, S1220–1

DC court cases and dispositions, by type of case, and judicial system finances, 1992 and trends, annual rpt, S1515–1

DC statistical profile, general data, 1992 annual rpt, S1535–3.8

Delaware court caseloads and dispositions, by type of case and court, and by county, with judicial dept finances, FY92, annual rpt, S1360–1

Florida court cases and dispositions, by type of court and case, and location, 1992, annual rpt, S1805–1

Georgia court cases and dispositions, by type of court and case, and location, with judicial dept finances and personnel, FY92, annual rpt, S1903–1

Hawaii court cases and dispositions, by type of court and case, and judicial circuit, FY92 and trends, annual rpt, S2115–1.2

Hawaii data book, general data, 1992 annual rpt, S2090–1.4

Indiana court cases and dispositions by type of court and case, and location, with judicial system finances and personnel, 1992, annual rpt, S2703–1

Iowa court cases, processing, and dispositions, by type of court and district, with judicial dept appropriations and personnel, 1992 and trends, annual rpt, S2815–1

Kansas court caseloads and disposition, by type of court and case, and location, FY92, annual rpt, S3035–1

Louisiana court caseloads and dispositions, by type of court and case, and jurisdiction, 1992 and trends, annual rpt, S3375–1

Maine court cases and dispositions, by type and location, FY92 and trends, annual rpt, S3463–1

Maryland court caseloads and dispositions, by type of court and case, and county, with judicial personnel and finances, FY92 and trends, annual rpt, S3600–1

Massachusetts court cases and dispositions, by type of court and case, and location, FY92 and trends, annual rpt, S3807–1

Michigan court caseloads and dispositions, by type of court and case, and court location, 1992 and trends, annual rpt, S3962–1

Civil procedure

Nebraska court cases and dispositions, by type of court and case, and location, 1992 and trends, annual rpt, S4965–2

New Mexico court cases and dispositions, by type of court, case, and location, with judicial system finances and personnel, FY92, annual rpt, S5623–1

New York State community dispute resolution program cases and dispositions, by facility, 1990, annual rpt, U5100–1.8

New York State court cases and dispositions, by court type and location, 1991, annual rpt, S5760–3.3

New York State court cases and dispositions, by type of court and case, and jurisdiction, 1991, annual rpt, S5730–1

North Carolina court cases and dispositions, by type of court and case, and location, with judicial dept finances and personnel, FY91, annual rpt, S5950–1

North Dakota court caseloads and dispositions, by type of case and court, and location, with judicial dept finances, 1991-92, annual rpt, S6210–1

Ohio court caseload and case disposition, by type of court and case, and location, 1992, annual rpt, S6385–1

Oklahoma court cases and dispositions, by type of court and case, with judicial system finances, by county or jurisdiction, FY92, annual rpt, S6493–1

Pennsylvania court caseloads and dispositions, by type of court and case, and county, 1991, annual rpt, S6900–1.2

Pennsylvania statistical abstract, general data, 1992 recurring rpt, U4130–6.7

Rhode Island court cases and dispositions, by type of court and case, and county, 1987-91, annual rpt, S6965–1

South Carolina court cases and dispositions, by type of court and location, with judicial dept finances and employees, 1992 and trends, annual rpt, S7197–1

South Dakota court cases and dispositions by type of case, and judicial system finances and personnel, by jurisdiction, FY92 and trends, annual rpt, S7395–1

Tennessee court cases and dispositions, by type of court and case, and county, FY92, annual rpt, S7585–1

Texas court cases and dispositions, by type of court and case, and location, FY92, annual rpt, S7703–1

Vermont court cases and dispositions, by type of court and case, and location, FY92 annual rpt, S8120–1

Virginia court caseloads, processing, and dispositions, by type of court and case, with judicial dept personnel and finances, by location, 1992 and trends, annual rpt, S8300–1

Washington State court cases and dispositions, by type of court and case, and jurisdiction, with judicial finances and personnel, 1992 and trends, annual rpt, S8339–1

West Virginia court caseloads and dispositions, by type of court and case, and judicial circuit, 1992 and trends, annual rpt, S8537–1

see also Administrative law and procedure
see also Adoption
see also Bankruptcy

see also Child support and alimony
see also Claims
see also Commitment
see also Contempt of court
see also Divestiture
see also Fines and settlements
see also Government-citizen lawsuits
see also Guardianship
see also Habeas corpus
see also Judgments, civil procedure
see also Juries
see also Lawsuits
see also Legal arbitration and mediation
see also Marriage and divorce
see also Medical malpractice
see also Tax protests and appeals
see also Torts
see also Trials

Civil rights

Latin America statistical abstract, general data by country, 1992 annual rpt, U6250–1.9

Public opinion on cause of homosexuality, and homosexual civil rights, Apr 1993 Gallup Poll, C4040–1.510

Soviet Union political and economic restructuring issues, public opinion in Russia, Ukraine, and Lithuania, 1991-92 surveys, C8915–10

State and local:

DC statistical profile, general data, 1992 annual rpt, S1535–3.1

Nevada State constitutional amendment concerning voting and officeholding rights for male citizens, election results by county, 1992, biennial rpt, S5125–1

see also Age discrimination
see also Censorship
see also Discrimination against the handicapped
see also Discrimination in credit
see also Discrimination in education
see also Discrimination in employment
see also Discrimination in housing
see also Freedom of information
see also Freedom of the press
see also Racial discrimination
see also Right of privacy
see also Sex discrimination

Civil service pensions

Coverage, assets, and benefits paid, for private and govt pension and retirement programs, 1991 and trends, biennial fact book, A1325–1.3

Federal civilian retirement payments and recipients, by State and region, FY91, R8490–47

see also State retirement systems

Civil service system

see also Civil service pensions
see also Federal employees
see also State and local employees

Civil works

see Public works

Claims

Latin America claims of US banks and non-banking enterprises, by country, 1979-91, annual rpt, U6250–1.28

Local govt police liability lawsuits, claim and settlement amounts, and legal costs, by population size, census div, and/or case type, 1990/91 survey, A5800–2.113

Railroad freight loss/damage claims paid, 1982-91, annual rpt, A3275–8.2

Index by Subjects and Names

State and local:

Arizona corrections dept admin, including property and injury claims processed, FY92, annual rpt, S0464–2

Colorado water court case filings and claims, by location, FY92 and trends, annual rpt, S1035–1.2

see also Insurance and insurance industry
see also under names of specific types of insurance

Clark County, Nev.

Business and economic activity indicators for Nevada and local areas, 1980-91, annual rpt, U7920–2

Casino finances and employment, by location and gaming revenue range, FY92, annual rpt, S5062–1

Health behavior risk factor surveillance survey results for Nevada, by location and respondent characteristics, 1991, annual rpt, S5075–3

Clark Martire & Bartolomeo Inc.

Corporate chief executive views on selected business, economic, and political issues, monthly rpt recurring feature, C8900–1

Class actions

see Government-citizen lawsuits

Classifications

Insurance (life/health) companies by A M Best Co financial rating, 1993 and trends, annual article, C1050–2.511

Insurance (property/casualty) companies, by A M Best Co financial rating, 1993 and trends, annual article, C1050–1.510

State bond credit rating classifications for 41 States, July 1992, U5085–2.6

Classrooms

see Educational facilities

Clay industry and products

Financial ratios and performance, for over 350 SIC 4-digit industries, FY88-92, annual rpt, A6400–3

State and local:

Hawaii ceramic ware tested for leachable lead, 1990, annual rpt., S2065–1.6

Pennsylvania statistical abstract, general data, 1992 recurring rpt, U4130–6.8

Utah statistical abstract, general data, 1993 triennial rpt, U8960–1.10

Clean Air Act

see Air pollution

Clean Water Act

see Water pollution

Cleaning services

see Janitorial and maintenance services
see Laundry and cleaning services

Clear, Todd R.

"Does Involvement in Religion Help Prisoners Adjust to Prison?", A7575–1.11

Clemency

see also Pardons

Clergy

Catholic population, clergy, and instns, by diocese and State, 1993 annual compilation, C4950–1

Catholic population, clergy, instns, missionaries, and religious order membership, US and worldwide, 1993 annual almanac, C6885–1

Catholic public opinion on marriage for priests, ordination of women, and consultation with priests, 1971-93 surveys, R8780–1.510

Index by Subjects and Names

Catholic schools, enrollment, and teachers, by region, State, and diocese, 1992/93 and trends, annual rpt, A7375–1

Catholic secondary school salaries for lay and religious personnel, by school characteristics, 1985/86-1991/92, biennial rpt, A7375–5

Churches, membership, clergy, and contributions, by denomination, US and Canada, 1991-92, annual rpt, C0105–1

Homosexuals in clergy, public opinion, 1977-92 Gallup Polls, R8780–1.501

Latin America statistical abstract, general data by country, 1992 annual rpt, U6250–1.10

Pope John Paul II popularity in US, with comparisons to 3 predecessors, 1978-92 surveys, R8780–1.509

Public opinion on honesty/ethical standards of selected occupations, 1992 Gallup Polls and trends, C4040–1.501

Religious congregation characteristics, including membership, activities, staff, and finances, 1992 survey, recurring rpt, A5435–4

Clerical workers

Earnings index for 27 MSAs and 4 occupational groups, 1990, biennial rpt, S3605–1.6

Political science higher education dept secretarial staff, 1991/92, annual rpt, A2617–1

White-collar work force trends, including employment, earnings, and unionization, with data by occupation, sex, and educational attainment, 1990s and trends, annual rpt, A1570–1

State and local:

Arizona occupational profiles, with employment and job outlook, by industry div, occupation, and county, series, S0465–2

Maine employment, by SIC 2-digit industry and detailed occupation, triennial series, S3465–1

Maryland elementary and secondary education data, by county, 1992/93, annual rpt, S3610–2.10

New Hampshire employment, by SIC 2- and 3-digit industry and detailed occupation, series, S5205–2

North Carolina employment in SIC 2-digit industries, by detailed occupation, triennial rpt series, S5917–5

Texas employment, by SIC 2- and 3-digit industry and detailed occupation, series, S7675–1

see also Employment and unemployment, specific industry

see also under By Occupation in the "Index by Categories"

Cleverley, William O.

"1993 Almanac of Hospital Financial and Operating Indicators", B1880–1

Climate

see Global climate change

see Weather

Clinical laboratory technicians

Dental allied education enrollment, grads, and tuition, by instn, 1992/93 annual rpt, A1475–5

Dental school faculty, support personnel, and staff characteristics, by instn, 1992/93, annual rpt, A1475–4.5

Hospital recruiting of nurses and allied health personnel, with budget, vacancies, turnover, and compensation, 1993 and trends, annual survey rpt, A6500–1

Salaries of scientists, engineers, technicians, and other professionals, by employee and employer characteristics, 1990s and trends, biennial rpt, A3960–1

Women and minorities in professional fields, detailed education and labor force data, 1991 and trends, recurring rpt, A3960–2.3

State and local:

Florida health care atlas, including manpower by occupation and health care facilities by type, by district and county, 1992 annual rpt, S1746–1.2

Clinics

Developing countries family planning availability, including distance to nearest clinic for rural women age 15-49, for 10 countries, 1987-91 surveys, U2520–1.51

Nursing higher education program finances, faculty and clinical practice, and clinic/center operations, by instn characteristics, 1992/93 biennial rpt, A0615–5

School-based health clinics effect on student pregnancy rates, St Paul Minn study, 1971/72-1986/87, article, A5160–1.502

Urban public schools with health clinics, and total student visits, for 47 systems, 1990/91, A4425–4

State and local:

Arkansas human services dept finances and operations, including Medicaid payments by type of service, FY91 and trends, annual rpt, S0700–2.3

DC statistical profile, general data, 1992 annual rpt, S1535–3.5

Indiana Medicaid expenditures, by service and provider type and county, FY91-92, annual rpt, S2623–1.6

Kentucky Medicaid recipients and payments, by program, county, and type of medical service, monthly rpt, S3140–5

Maryland medical assistance payments and recipients, by program, type of service, location, demographic characteristics, and facility, FY92 and trends, annual rpt, S3635–3

Missouri public welfare and medical assistance recipients, expenditures, and case processing, by program and county, FY92 and trends, annual rpt, S4575–2

Montana welfare and medical assistance program cases and payments, by county and type of service, monthly rpt, S4755–1

Nebraska Medicaid recipients and payments, by type of service and county, FY92, annual rpt, S4957–1.2

New York State medical assistance expenditures, by State area and type of care, 1991 and trends, annual rpt, S5800–2.2

see also Clinical laboratory technicians

see also Hospitals

see also Laboratories

see also Medical examinations and tests

Clocks

see Watches and clocks

Clothing and clothing industry

Australia fashion magazine depiction of models wearing skin-protective clothing in summer, 1982-91, article, A2623–1.502

Children's clothing sales, by retail outlet type, 1990-92, article, C5150–3.503

Children's clothing sales, by retail outlet type, 1992, article, C5150–3.510

Consumer buying power survey of population, income, and sales by kind of business, by census div, State, MSA, county, and city, 1992, annual rpt, C1200–1.511

Consumer buying power survey of population, income, and sales by product line, by State, metro area, county, and census div, 1993 annual rpt, C1200–1.514

Consumer clothing purchase shares by outlet and product type, 1991, article, C8130–1.501

Consumer retail outlet types shopped for clothing, with shopper age and work class, 1993 survey article, C5150–3.516

Consumer views on clothing shopping experience, and activities cited as status symbols, 1989 and/or 1992, survey article, C8130–1.506

Corporate performance ratings by executives for leading companies in 32 industries, 1993 annual survey feature, C8900–1.508

Cotton and other fiber consumption in textile production, by detailed end use, 1990-92, annual rpt, A7485–1

Discount and off-price store sales and outlets, for top 10 chains, 1993 article, C5150–3.513

Discount chain consumer natl brand preferences, by product category and chain, and by age group, 1993 survey, annual feature, C5150–3.521

Discount chain top-selling natl brands cited by managers, by product category, chain, and region, 1993 survey, annual feature, C5150–3.520

Discount store sales and productivity data for 20 depts, 1993 annual feature, C5150–3.516

Discount store sales volume of women's clothing in 4 special sizes, by product type, 1st half 1992-93, article, C5150–3.521

Discount store shopper characteristics, use of natl vs regional discounters, and types of clothing purchased, 1990 and 1992, article, C8130–1.506

Discount stores, sales, and earnings, for top chains, with detail by specialty, 1993 annual feature, C5150–3.514

Europe retail clothing chain stores and sales, for 5 major chains, 1993 article, C2710–1.517

Financial and operating data for textile and clothing industries, including workers and retail sales, 1988-93, annual article, C5226–3.502

Financial data for approx 170 textile and clothing companies, with industry statistical summary, 1991-92 and trends, annual rpt, C3400–5

Financial performance and growth rankings for approx 1,000 top corporations, with comparisons by industry group, 1993 annual rpt, C3950–1.505

Clothing and clothing industry

Financial performance indicators for 51 clothing companies, FY92 and trends, annual rpt, B8130–2

Financial ratios and performance, for over 350 SIC 4-digit industries, FY88-92, annual rpt, A6400–3

Hosiery production, by product type, 1983-92, annual feature, C3460–1.510

Imprinted design clothing market shares by retail outlet type, by design category, Apr 1992-Mar 1993, article, C5150–3.513

Market shares by clothing product category and outlet type, 1991-94, annual article, C8130–1.509

Markets with daily newspapers, demographic and economic info by geographic area, US and Canada, 1993 annual rpt, C3250–1

Men's and boys clothing production, trade, and operating data, by garment type, 1960s-92, annual rpt, A3880–1

Men's clothing sales and consumer expenditures, by outlet type, 1992, article, C5150–3.508

Men's sweats/warm-up clothing sales by retail outlet type, 1992, article, C5150–3.510

Operating and financial composite ratios for corporations, with establishments and receipts, for approx 200 industries, by asset size, FY90, annual rpt, C7800–1

Retail chain store expansion devs, and equipment and construction costs, by type of chain, 1993 annual articles, C5150–4.507

Retail prices for selected consumer items in approx 300 cities, quarterly rpt, A0150–1

Retail sales by outlet type, and discount chain sales in major depts, by product category, 1992, annual feature, C8130–1.507

Sales and consumer expenditures, for food store products by type, 1991-92, annual feature, C4655–1.510

Shirt (sport) sales volume and value, 1991-93, article, C5150–3.518

Shopping center financial and operating data, with detail by type of tenant, US and Canada, 1991, triennial rpt, R9285–1

Sporting goods purchases, by product and outlet type, census div, and purchaser characteristics, with average prices, 1992 and trends, annual survey, A8485–2

Sporting goods sales by product category, 1983-92, annual survey rpt, A8485–4

Supermarket sales of nonfood products, by detailed product type, 1992, annual feature, C5225–1.508

Textile fiber end-use survey, consumption and trade, by type of fiber and product, 1988-92, annual survey, C3460–1.511

Textile industry economic performance indicators and outlook, with industry trends and devs, monthly rpt, C5226–3

Women's and children's garment sales, production, imports, employment, hours, and earnings, by type of garment, recurring rpt, A5900–1

Women's jeans market shares for top 8 and all other manufacturers, 1993 article, C5150–3.518

Women's sleepwear sales volume, by product type, 1st half 1992-93, article, C5150–3.521

State and local:

Florida statistical abstract, general data, 1992 annual rpt, U6660–1.12

Maine employment in trade, utilities, and transportation SIC 2-digit industries, by detailed occupation, 2nd qtr 1991, triennial rpt, S3465–1.25

North Carolina employment in trade, transportation, communications, utilities, govt, and education, by detailed occupation, 2nd qtr 1991, triennial rpt, S5917–5.2

Texas trade, transportation, and public utilities employment, by SIC 2- and 3-digit industry and detailed occupation, 2nd qtr 1991, triennial survey rpt, S7675–1.31

see also Shoes and shoe industry
see also Textile industry and fabrics
see also under By Industry in the "Index by Categories"

Clover

see Seeds

Clubs

see Membership organizations

Coal and coal mining

Consumption of fossil energy resources and electricity from hydro and nuclear power, 1960s-91, annual rpt, A1775–3.6

Degasification emissions recovered, used, and vented, for 7 major coal producing countries, 1992 article, C6985–1.507

Electric power (steam) plant operating data, including coal use, costs, and quality, by plant, utility, and location, 1991, annual rpt, A7400–7

Electric power supply-demand, and utility capacities and fuel requirements, detailed data by US and Canadian region, 1992-2002, annual rpt, A8630–2

Electric utility coal deliveries and prices for individual power plants, by utility, State, and census div, monthly rpt, A7400–9

Electric utility financial and operating data, by State and census div, 1991 and trends, annual rpt, A4700–1

Electric utility operating data, including generating capacity and efficiency, peak demand, and fuel consumption, top 100 utilities, 1992, annual article, C6985–6.512

Financial ratios and performance, for over 350 SIC 4-digit industries, FY88-92, annual rpt, A6400–3

Higher education physical plant operations, costs, employment, salaries, and energy use, by instn and region, 1991/92, recurring rpt, A3183–1

Intl energy sourcebook, with detail on oil and gas industry operations, supply-demand, and prices, for approx 80 countries, 1970s-91, annual compilation, C6985–10

Iron and steel industry consumption of materials and energy, US and Canada, 1992 and trends, annual rpt, A2000–2

Japan energy supply-demand and outlook, by fuel source, 1980s-2000, recurring article, R5650–2.536

Latin America statistical abstract, general data by country, 1992 annual rpt, U6250–1.23

Methane gas resources in coal seams, selected basins, Dec 1992, biennial rpt, R8765–1

Index by Subjects and Names

Operating and financial composite ratios for corporations, with establishments and receipts, for approx 200 industries, by asset size, FY90, annual rpt, C7800–1

Preparation plants and capacity in US, Canada, and Mexico, by company, 1993, biennial feature, C5226–1.511

Producer outlook for supply-demand and prices, and capital investments, 1993 annual survey article, C5226–1.503

Railroad coal shipments, including top 7 systems, and coal production, 1982-91, annual rpt, A3275–8.2

Revenues, shipments, prices, and reserves, for aggregate 39-46 coal companies, 1987-91, article, C5800–28.507

Sourcebook of oil and gas industry, with supply-demand comparisons to other energy types, 1991 and trends, annual compilation, C6985–9.5

Statistical profiles of 50 States and DC, general data, 1993 annual almanac, C4712–1

Supply-demand and price data for energy resources, including by country and producing State, commodity yearbook for 1993, C2400–1

Supply-demand and price data for energy resources, including by country and producing State, commodity yearbook Jan-Sept 1993 updates, C2400–2

Supply-demand by energy source and consuming sector, 1947-2010, periodic basic data book, A2575–14.1

Supply-demand for non-oil energy sources, 1970s-2010, annual rpt, C6985–5.3

Supply-demand indicators for coal, and industry devs and operations, monthly rpt, C5226–1

UK coal industry devs, including consumption trends, mine closures and related employment, and British Coal Corp output, 1992 articles, C5226–2.501

UK coal production, longwall faces, and employees, by mine and operating status, for Govt-owned company, 1991-92, article, C5226–1.510

World coal supply-demand, employment, and trade trends, by country, with summary data on world energy resources, 1992 annual rpt, A7400–2

World energy supply-demand, by fuel source and sector, by region and country, 1992/93 biennial rpt, R9455–1.3

State and local:

Alabama business activity indicators, monthly rpt, U5680–1

Alabama county data book, general data, 1992 annual rpt, S0121–2

Alabama statistical abstract, general data, 1992 recurring rpt, U5680–2.12

Arizona statistical abstract, general data, 1993 recurring rpt, U5850–2.14, U5850–2.20

Colorado property assessed valuation, and summary production data, by county, 1991-92, annual rpt, S1055–3

Florida statistical abstract, general data, 1992 annual rpt, U6660–1.15

Georgia statistical abstract, general data, 1992-93 biennial rpt, U6730–1.8

Hawaii data book, general data, 1992 annual rpt, S2090–1.17

Kentucky economic statistics, general data, 1993 annual rpt, S3104–1.1

Index by Subjects and Names — Cocaine

Maryland statistical abstract, general data, 1993-94 biennial rpt, S3605–1.10

Montana mine production and taxes assessed, by county, 1990-91, biennial rpt, S4750–1.1

New Mexico business and economic activity indicators, monthly rpt, U7980–1

New York State statistical yearbook, general data, 1992 annual rpt, U5100–1.12

North Dakota coal production, 1983-92, annual rpt, S6162–1

Ohio natural gas and electricity supply-demand by utility and consuming sector, 1992-93 and trends, annual rpt, S6355–1

Oklahoma statistical abstract, general data, 1992 annual rpt, U8130–2.12

Pennsylvania business activity indicators, monthly rpt, U4110–1

Pennsylvania energy supply-demand and prices by fuel type, with electric power info by utility, 1960s-90, recurring rpt, S6810–3

Pennsylvania statistical abstract, general data, 1992 recurring rpt, U4130–6.8

South Carolina statistical abstract, general data, 1993 annual rpt, S7125–1.8

Tennessee statistical abstract, general data, 1992/93 annual rpt, U8710–2.5, U8710–2.10

Utah economic and business activity review and indicators, monthly rpt, U8960–2

Utah statistical abstract, general data, 1993 triennial rpt, U8960–1.10

West Virginia coal mining hours and earnings, and production, monthly rpt, S8534–1

West Virginia underground and surface coal production, by county, 1982-91, annual rpt, R9385–1.7

Wyoming coal production and taxable valuation, by county, and severance and ad valorem taxes, FY91 annual rpt, S8990–1.2

see also Black lung disease
see also Coal exports and imports
see also Coal prices
see also Coal reserves
see also Coal stocks
see also Energy conservation
see also Mine accidents and safety
see also under By Industry in the "Index by Categories"

Coal exports and imports

Electric power plant coal use and costs, including imports from 4 countries, 1990-91, annual rpt, A7400–7

Electric utility coal deliveries and prices, by producing source, including imports from selected countries, monthly rpt, A7400–9

Producer outlook for supply-demand and prices, 1993 annual survey article, C5226–1.503

Supply-demand indicators for coal, and industry devs and operations, monthly rpt, C5226–1

World coal supply-demand, employment, and trade trends, by country, with summary data on world energy resources, 1992 annual rpt, A7400–2

World coal trade activity, by country of origin and destination, monthly rpt, A7400–3

State and local:

Pennsylvania coal trade, with detail by customs district and country of destination, 1982-90, recurring rpt, S6810–3

Coal prices

Bituminous coal exported overseas and to Canada, prices, and ocean freight rates, monthly rpt, A7400–3

Electric utility coal deliveries and prices for individual power plants, by utility, State, and census div, monthly rpt, A7400–9

Midwest electric utilities prices paid for Powder River Basin coal, for 15 plants, 1991, article, A4700–4.501

Producer outlook for supply-demand and prices, 1993 annual survey article, C5226–1.503

Sales price per ton for coal, 1987-91, article, C5800–28.507

Supply-demand and price data for energy resources, including by country and producing State, commodity yearbook for 1993, C2400–1

Supply-demand and price data for energy resources, including by country and producing State, commodity yearbook Jan-Sept 1993 updates, C2400–2

Supply-demand indicators for coal, and industry devs and operations, monthly rpt, C5226–1

State and local:

Pennsylvania energy supply-demand and prices by fuel type, with electric power info by utility, 1960s-90, recurring rpt, S6810–3

Tennessee statistical abstract, general data, 1992/93 annual rpt, U8710–2.5, U8710–2.10

Coal reserves

Federal Govt coal leases issued, acreage, and reserves, FY78-91, article, C5226 1.510

Latin America statistical abstract, general data by country, 1992 annual rpt, U6250–1.23

Proved reserves of natural gas, coal, and oil, with detail by State, 1960s-91, annual rpt, A1775–3.1

Trends in coal reserves, for aggregate 39 companies, 1987-91, article, C5800–28.507

World coal supply-demand, employment, and trade trends, by country, 1992 annual rpt, A7400–2

State and local:

Tennessee statistical abstract, general data, 1992/93 annual rpt, U8710–2.5

Coal slurry pipelines

see Pipelines

Coal stocks

Electric power plant coal stocks and related info, by census div and region, monthly 1991, annual rpt, A7400–7

Electric utility coal stockpiles at individual plants, by utility and State, monthly rpt, A7400–8

Supply-demand and price data for energy resources, including by country and producing State, commodity yearbook for 1993, C2400–1

Supply-demand and price data for energy resources, including by country and producing State, commodity yearbook Jan-Sept 1993 updates, C2400–2

Supply-demand indicators for coal, and industry devs and operations, monthly rpt, C5226–1

World coal supply-demand, employment, and trade trends, by country, 1992 annual rpt, A7400–2

State and local:

Pennsylvania electric utility year-end coal and petroleum stocks, 1970-90, recurring rpt, S6810–3

Tennessee statistical abstract, general data, 1992/93 annual rpt, U8710–2.5

Coast Guard

Post exchange and commissary sales, for military resale agencies, and by individual exchange, FY91 and trends, annual rpt, A2072–1

Post exchange sales, by service branch, with merchandising devs and comparisons to civilian retail trade, monthly rpt, C0500–1

Post exchange sales, retail and other, by location and store, FY92 and trends, annual rpt, A2072–2.502

see also Service academies

Coastal areas

World maritime zone and coastline length, and coastal cities share of population, by country, 1992/93 biennial rpt, R9455–1.7

see also Offshore oil and gas
see also Oil spills
see also Seashores

Coastal shipping

see Inland water transportation

Cobb County, Ga.

Housing costs attributable to govt regulations and fees, and impact on households eligible to purchase homes, for 2 local areas, 1993 article, C4300–1.510

Cocaine

Black children and youth population, economic, health, and education data, with comparisons to whites, 1993 rpt, R3840–21

Drug abuse treatment clients by substance abused, by State, FY91, annual rpt, A7112–1

Higher education student use of and attitudes toward alcohol, drugs, and tobacco products, by sex and region, 1989-91 surveys, annual rpt, U4950–1

Hospital patient admission rates and length of stay, by diagnosis and procedure, payment source, age, sex, and region, 1991, B4455–4

Hospital psychiatric patient discharges and length of stay, by diagnosis, age, sex, and region, 1991, annual rpt series, B4455–2

Latin America statistical abstract, general data by country, 1992 annual rpt, U6250–1.15

User characteristics, including criminal behavior and health condition, with comparison to nonusers, 1991 and trends, article, A2623–1.510

State and local:

Alabama arrests of adults and juveniles for drug sale and possession, by race and sex, and drug task force property seizures by locale, 1992, annual rpt, S0119–1.1

DC criminal offender drug test results, including positive tests for selected drugs, 1987-91, annual rpt, S1535–2

Cocaine

Delaware crimes and arrests, by offense, county, and victim-offender characteristics, 1991 and trends, annual rpt, S1375–5

Florida crimes and arrests, by offense, with data by victim and offender characteristics, 1992, annual rpt, S1770–1

Idaho drug-related arrests by offender characteristics, and volume of drugs seized, 1992, annual rpt, S2275–2

Illinois penalty changes for cocaine manufacture/delivery offenses, 1984-91, annual rpt, S2425–1

Oregon crimes and arrests, by offense, with data by county, local agency, and offender characteristics, 1992 and trends, annual rpt, S6603–3.1

South Carolina crimes and arrests, by detailed offense, offender characteristics, and location, 1992 and trends, annual rpt, S7205–1.2

Texas crimes and arrests, and drugs seized by detailed type, 1992, annual rpt, S7735–2.2

West Virginia drug law arrests by offender age, and drugs confiscated and value, by substance, 1990-91, annual rpt, S8610–1

Cocoa and chocolate

Futures trading on Coffee, Sugar, and Cocoa Exchange, with related data including deliveries and stocks by country and/or port, 1992 and trends, annual rpt, B2275–1

Latin America statistical abstract, general data by country, 1992 annual rpt, U6250–1.24, U6250–1.25

Production, consumption, stocks, trade, and prices for approx 100 basic commodities, including by country and producing State, commodity yearbook for 1993, C2400–1, C2400–2

World chocolate market shares, sales growth, and consumption, for top 6-8 countries, 1992 feature, C2710–1.504

see also Candy and confectionery products

Coconut oil

see Oils, oilseeds, and fats

Cody, Scott

"Number of Households and Average Household Size in Florida: Apr. 1, 1992", U6660–3.45

Coffee

Advertising expenditures by medium for top 100 advertisers, with comparisons to earnings and sales, and detail by product type and brand, 1991-92, annual rpt, C2710–1.547

Futures trading on Coffee, Sugar, and Cocoa Exchange, with related data including deliveries and stocks by country and/or port, 1992 and trends, annual rpt, B2275–1

Latin America statistical abstract, general data by country, 1992 annual rpt, U6250–1.24, U6250–1.25

Market shares for coffee by company, for regular and instant brands, 1990-92, annual article, C2710–1.531

Military commissary sales of top 10 beverage types, with coffee sales trend by region, 1991/92, article, C0500–1.504

Production, consumption, stocks, trade, and prices for approx 100 basic commodities, including by country and producing State, commodity yearbook for 1993, C2400–1, C2400–2

Restaurant (table service) coffee/espresso sales trend, 1992, recurring rpt, A8200–11

Retail prices for selected consumer items in approx 300 cities, quarterly rpt, A0150–1

Supermarket sales and market shares, for top 10 brands of soluble and ground coffee, 1992-93, C2710–1.536

Supermarket sales by detailed product type, 1992 and trends, annual feature, C5225–1.507

Vending machine sales by product type, and machines on location, 1992 and trends, annual rpt, C9470–1

State and local:

Hawaii agricultural production and marketing, by commodity and island, 1987-91, annual rpt, S2030–1

see also Caffeine

Cogeneration

see Electric power and heat cogeneration

Cognetics Inc.

Jobs created in small firms vs number lost in large firms, for low, average, and high wage categories, 1987-92, article, C8900–1.517

Cohen, Andrew

"Overview of the Indigent Health Care System in Texas", U8850–8.7

Coins and coinage

Gold coins issued, face value, gold content, and physical characteristics, by mint, for 60 issuing countries, 1992, annual rpt, A5145–1

Gold consumption shares for coinage, for top 10 and all other countries, 1991, article, C2150–7.501

Silver coins issued, face value, silver content, and physical characteristics, by mint, for 83 countries, 1992, annual rpt, A8902–2

Silver market activity worldwide and in US, including production, consumption by end use, stocks, trade, and prices, by country, 1988-92, annual rpt, B4300–1

Silver refinery production from primary materials, coins, and scrap, with disposition, stocks, prices, and industry devs, US and worldwide, bimonthly rpt, A8902–3

Silver supply-demand by country and end use, with prices, futures trading, and market analyses, 1993 and trends, annual rpt, A8902–4

see also Counterfeiting and forgery

see also Money supply

Coke

see Coal and coal mining

see Petroleum and petroleum industry

Cold storage and refrigeration

Apple holdings in cold storage, US, Pacific region, and Washington State, 1990/91-1992/93, annual rpt, S8328–1

Commodity yearbook for 1993: production, stocks, prices, and cold storage holdings of selected commodities, C2400–1

Commodity yearbook update: production, stocks, prices, and cold storage holdings of selected commodities, Jan-Sept 1993 rpts, C2400–2

Financial ratios and performance, for over 350 SIC 4-digit industries, FY88-92, annual rpt, A6400–3

Fruit and vegetable cold storage holdings for selected commodities, quarterly 1988-91, annual rpt, S6575–1

Sales and shipments of commercial refrigeration equipment, with detail by type, 1982, 1992, and 1997, article, C2000–1.509

Shipments of heating/cooling equipment, by product type, with industry review and outlook, 1992 and trends, annual rpt, C1800–1

Stocks of cherries and pickles in East North Central region and/or US, 1991 and trends, annual rpt, S3950–1

State and local:

Michigan cold storage warehouses and capacity, 1991 annual rpt, S3950–1

New York State cold storage warehouses and capacity, and apple holdings, 1992 and trends, annual rpt, S5700–1

Texas refrigerated warehouses and storage capacity, 1987, 1989, and 1991, annual rpt, S7630–1.2

Collective bargaining

see Labor-management relations, general

see Labor unions

College graduates

see Degrees, higher education

see Educational attainment

Colleges

see Black colleges

see Community colleges

see Federal aid to higher education

see Federal aid to medical education

see Higher education

see Junior colleges

see School administration and staff

see State funding for higher education

see State funding for medical education

see under By Individual Company or Institution in the "Index by Categories"

Colombia

Coal industry supply-demand, employment, and trade, by country, 1990-91 and trends, annual rpt, A7400–2.2

Energy intl sourcebook, with detail on oil and gas industry operations, supply-demand, and prices, for approx 80 countries, 1970s-91, annual compilation, C6985–10.2

Motor vehicle world production, sales, trade, and registrations, by country, world area, manufacturer, and make, 1991 and trends, annual rpt, A0865–2.1

Statistical abstract of Latin America, detailed social, govtl, and economic data, 1992 annual rpt, U6250–1

see also under By Foreign Country or World Area in the "Index by Categories"

Colorado

Agricultural production, marketing, and finances, by commodity and/or county, with farms and acreage, 1992 and trends, annual rpt, S0985–1

Banks and trust companies, financial condition by instn, Dec 1992, annual rpt, S1070–2

Calf deaths and related costs, by disease, 1987/88 Colorado study, article, A3100–2.518

Court cases and dispositions, by type of court and case, and location, with judicial dept finances, FY92 and trends, annual rpt, S1035–1

Crimes and arrests, by offense and location, with offender characteristics, and assaults on police, 1992, annual rpt, S1068–1

Index by Subjects and Names

Economic indicators for 10 Western States, including forecasts from selected organizations, monthly rpt, U0282–2

Election results and voter registration, by political party, and county and/or district, 1992, biennial rpt, S1090–1

Elementary and secondary school enrollment, finances, and student and staff characteristics, by locality, 1991 annual rpt series, S1000–4

Elementary and secondary school enrollment, finances, and student and staff characteristics, by locality, 1992 annual rpt series, S1000–2

Employment, unemployment, hours, and earnings, with job service activities, monthly rpt, S1040–4

Govt financial condition, including receipts by source, and expenditures by function, FY92 and trends, annual rpt, S0980–1

Health behavior risk factor surveillance survey results, by respondent characteristics, 1990, recurring rpt, S1010–3

Labor force planning rpt, including population, employment by industry, and job service applicants, FY94 annual rpt, S1040–3

Library finances and operations, including staff, holdings, and population served, by instn and library type, series, S1000–3

Markets with daily newspapers, demographic and economic info by geographic area, US and Canada, 1993 annual rpt, C3250–1

Motor vehicle registrations, fees, and taxes, by license plate type and/or county, 1991, annual rpt, S1075–1.4

Oil/gas industry production, finances, exploration, and reserves, by State, 1992 and trends, annual rpt, A5425–1.1

Property assessed valuation by detailed property type, and tax levy and revenue by local district, by county, 1991-92, annual rpt, S1055–3

Retail sales and sales tax revenue, by county, city, and kind of business, FY92 and trends, annual rpt, S1075–1.5

Savings and loan assn and credit union financial condition, 1992 and trends, annual rpt, S1070–3

Statistical profiles of 50 States and DC, general data, 1993 annual almanac, C4712–1

Tax revenues by type, with selected data by county and city, FY92 and trends, annual rpt, S1075–1

Utility and transportation regulatory agency activities, scope of jurisdiction, finances, and employees, by agency, 1991/92 annual rpt, A7015–2

Vital statistics, including population, births, deaths by cause, abortion, marriage and divorce, and adoption, by demographic characteristics and location, 1990 and trends, annual rpt, S1010–1

Welfare and social services expenditures and caseloads, by county and/or program, FY91, annual rpt, S1085–1

see also Colorado Springs, Colo.

see also Denver, Colo.

see also Mesa County, Colo.

see also Pueblo, Colo.

see also under By City and By County in the "Index by Categories"

see also under By State in the "Index by Categories"

Colorado River

State and local:

Arizona reservoir capacity and storage from Colorado and Gila River drainage, Apr 1989-93, annual rpt, U5830–1

Colorado Springs, Colo.

Income per capita, 1991, annual article, S1040–4.507

Columbus, Ind.

Business conditions analysis for selected Indiana local areas, quarterly rpt semiannual feature, U2160–1.502, U2160–1.504

Columbus, Ohio

Environmental regulation costs in Columbus under 13 Federal mandates, 1993-2000, U9640–3

see also under By City in the "Index by Categories"

Comdisco Medical Equipment Group

Hospital diagnostic imaging equipment age, by type of equipment, 1992, A1865–1.507

Commerce Department

see Department of Commerce

Commercial banking

see Banks and banking

Commercial buildings

Chambers of commerce income, salaries and benefits, membership, staff, and operations, 1993 annual rpt, A3840–3

Construction contract awards by type of project, weekly rpt, C5800–2

Construction contract value, by construction type and region, including floor area and number of residential units, 1992-93, annual rpt, C5800–15.501, C5800–15.504, C5800–15.507, C5800–26, C5800–29

Construction of office space, for 14 metro areas, 1993 article, C8900–1.520

Construction, vacancy, and rental rates, for office buildings in major metro areas, quarterly rpt, B2800–4

Food service industry sales trends and forecast, by market segment, 1990-93, annual feature, A8200–1.502

Investment return on commercial real estate, by property type, 1980-91, article, A6450–2.506

Office building detailed income and expense data, and energy use, US and Canada, by building characteristics, metro area, and US region, 1991 and trends, annual rpt, A5600–2

Owner companies value of buildings owned and additions, and construction in progress, top 700 firms, 1991, annual article, C5800–2.504

Property taxes as percent of gross rent in commercial buildings, for 26 metro areas, 1993 article, A6450–2.506

Real estate market conditions and outlook for office property, including inventory, vacancy, and construction, by metro area, 1992-93, annual survey, A8916–1

Real estate market conditions and outlook, including construction, vacancy, rental rates, and inventory, for major metro areas, 1993 annual rpt, B2800–3

Restaurant industry financial and operating data, by establishment characteristics and location, 1992, annual rpt, A8200–3

Commercial credit

Shopping center office tenants, financial and operating data, US and Canada, 1991, triennial rpt, R9285–1

Supermarkets opened, remodeled, and closed, including store features, dev costs, and rent, by region and sales size, 1992 and trends, annual rpt, A4950–2

Tax rates on office space in 12 cities, 1993, R9050–15.7

Value of new residential, commercial, industrial, and public construction put in place, monthly rpt, A7000–1

Vending machine sales and operations, by product and location type, 1990-92, annual rpt, C9470–1

State and local:

Arizona building permits issued and value, by type, size, and location, monthly rpt quarterly table, U0280–1.503, U0280–1.506, U0280–1.509

California commercial and industrial vacancy rates in 10 State areas or cities, bimonthly rpt, S0840–1

California nonresidential construction, and office building vacancy rates in selected areas, 1993 annual rpt, S0840–3

Colorado property assessed valuation by detailed property type, and tax levy and revenue by local district, by county, 1991-92, annual rpt, S1055–3

Connecticut construction activity and value, by type of structure and location, 1992 and trends, annual rpt, S1212–1

DC statistical profile, general data, 1992 annual rpt, S1535–3.3

Delaware data book, general data, 1993 annual rpt, S1375–4

Hawaii data book, general data, 1992 annual rpt, S2090–1.21

Kansas robberies and value of stolen property, by location and property type, 1992, annual rpt, S2925–1.1

New York City commercial building leasing activity, vacancies, rental rates, and construction, by city area, 1988-92, annual rpt, B2800–5

see also Business machines and equipment

see also Industrial plants and equipment

Commercial credit

Airlines distribution by credit rating, 1983 and 1993, article, C5800–4.519

Amusement park operating and financial data, including sources of initial funding, 1992, annual rpt, A5700–1

Bank commercial real estate loans as percent of total lending, top 100 instns, 1992, annual feature, C5800–7.526

Bank noncurrent loans/leases, and losses, by type of loan, asset size, and metro status, 1992, semiannual rpt, A6400–4

Construction company credit availability, and means of financing equipment purchases, 1993 annual survey rpt, A4155–1

Corporate merger/acquisition loan value for top 10 lending instns, 1992, article, C4683–1.504

Exporters receiving loans guaranteed by SBA, and value of guaranteed loans, 1987-92, C4687–1.506

Finance company and money market fund assets, and commercial and consumer debt held, with comparisons to commercial banks, 1980-92, R4700–22

Commercial credit

Foundry industry borrowing plans, 1992 annual survey article, C7000–2.501

Franchise company provision of financing to franchisees, by selected industry group, 1993 survey article, C4215–1.510

Hard goods manufacturers problems with financing because of lender liability for environmental problems, by product line, 1993 annual survey rpt, A1800–1

Hispanic American career professional and business owner motor vehicle fleet financing sources, 1993 survey, article, C4575–1.504

Hispanic-owned business outlook for selected performance indicators, with data by region, monthly rpt quarterly feature, C4575–1.510

Homebuilder financial and operating data, including detail by location, for top 400 builders, 1993 annual feature, C1850–8.507

Homebuilder sources for acquisition, dev, and construction loans, by region and company size, 1992 survey, article, C4300–1.501

Jewelry business credit rating changes, and claims placed with board of trade for collection, monthly rpt, C2150–7

Lending to business, including banking practices and risk analysis, and other mgmt and operation issues, monthly rpt, A6400–2

Leveraged buyout financing by top 15 commercial bank lenders, 1985-1st half 1992, C4683–1.501

Operating and financial composite ratios for corporations, with establishments and receipts, for approx 200 industries, by asset size, FY90, annual rpt, C7800–1

Restaurant (table service) operators seeking credit lines and bank loans, with approval and interest rates, 1992, recurring rpt, A8200–11

Restaurant credit application approval rates, by type of financing sought, 1992, article, C5150–5.506

SBA loan distribution by industry div, FY92, C4687–1.509

Small business lending and services of banks, with data on organizational structure, loan delinquencies, and community dev activities, Nov 1992 survey, annual rpt, A4160–5

Small business loan bank commitments distribution by loan risk rating, 1991-92, article, C4687–1.511

Small business loan risk ratings by bankers, for 10 most and least risky industries, 1993 article, C4687–1.503

Small business owners financing sources and experience of discrimination in lending, by race-ethnicity, 1993 survey feature, C4215–1.512

Small business views on current and expected economic conditions, survey findings, quarterly rpt, A7815–1

Small corporation CEO views on expected sources of capital, June 1993 survey, article, C4687–1.512

Soviet Union public opinion on allowing loans for starting businesses, for 3 Republics, 1991 survey, C8915–8.2

State economic dev condition indicators, including economic performance, business vitality, growth capacity, and tax/fiscal system, by State, 1993 annual rpt, R4225–1.1

Veterinary practice loan applications and dispositions, by veterinarian experience, 1992 survey, article, A3100–2.519

State and local:

Idaho business/industrial dev corporation financial condition, FY92, annual rpt, S2235–1

New York State business activity indicators, quarterly rpt, S5735–2

Pennsylvania statistical abstract, general data, 1992 recurring rpt, U4130–6.2

see also Corporate bonds

see also Investment banking

Commercial energy use

see Industrial and commercial energy use

Commercial finance companies

see Finance companies

Commercial law

see also Bankruptcy

see also Guarantees and warranties

see also Interstate commerce

see also Licenses and permits

see also Patents

see also Price regulation

see also Trademarks

Commercial treaties

see Trade agreements

Commissaries

see Military post exchanges and commissaries

Commissions of the Federal Government

see Federal boards, committees, and commissions

see Federal independent agencies

Commitment

State and local:

Delaware court caseloads and dispositions, by type of court and case, and by county, with judicial dept finances, FY92, annual rpt, S1360–1

Georgia probate court involuntary hospitalization cases, by county, FY92, annual rpt, S1903–1

Illinois mental health facility inpatient admissions, by legal status and instn, FY93, annual rpt, S2505–1

Massachusetts court cases and dispositions, by type of court and case, and location, FY92 and trends, annual rpt, S3807–1

North Carolina public defender and assigned counsel caseloads and costs, including State mental hospital hearings, FY91, annual rpt, S5950–1

Virginia court caseloads, processing, and dispositions, by type of court and case, with judicial dept personnel and finances, by location, 1992 and trends, annual rpt, S8300–1

see also Sentences, criminal procedure

Committees of Congress

see Congressional committees

Commodities

Production, consumption, stocks, trade, and prices for approx 100 basic commodities, including by country and producing State, commodity yearbook for 1993, C2400–1, C2400–2

see also Agricultural commodities

see also Futures trading

see also Generic products

see also Manufacturing

see also Mines and mineral resources

see also Natural resources

see also Stockpiling

Index by Subjects and Names

see also Strategic materials

see also under By Commodity in the "Index by Categories"

see also under names of specific commodities or commodity groups

Commodity Credit Corp.

Losses and price support costs of CCC, by commodity, FY91 and trends, annual rpt, R9050–1.3

Wheat inventory of CCC, 1976-92, annual rpt, A7310–1

State and local:

Arizona, Commodity Credit Corp loans granted and liquidated, 1987-91, annual rpt, U5830–1

Commodity exchanges

see Futures trading

Commodity futures

see Futures trading

Common carriers

see Airlines

see Buses

see Mobile radio

see Passenger ships

see Public utilities

see Railroads

see Ships and shipping

see Taxicabs

see Trucks and trucking industry

Common markets and free trade areas

see also Andean Group

see also Central American Common Market

see also European Community

see also Export processing zones

see also Latin American Integration Association

Common pleas courts

see State courts

Commonwealth of Independent States

Aircraft (Soviet-built) in airline service in CIS, by model, Dec 1992, article, C7000–4.509

Economic devs in CIS, monthly rpt, U2030–1

Energy intl sourcebook, with detail on oil and gas industry operations, supply-demand, and prices, for approx 80 countries, 1970s-91, annual compilation, C6985–10.2

Magnesium imports of US and Japan from China and Commonwealth of Independent States, with worldwide demand by application or world region, 1992-93, article, A1250–1.544

Motor vehicle world production, sales, trade, and registrations, by country, world area, manufacturer, and make, 1991 and trends, annual rpt, A0865–2.1

Natural gas supply-demand by Republic, price trends, and comparisons to other fuels, 1993 article, C6985–1.514, C6985–1.515

Oil and gas pipeline length and condition, with Russian production and export outlook, 1993 article, C6985–1.527

Oil and gas production and reserves in 7 CIS Republics, 1991, article, C6985–1.510

Oil and gas production, by Republic, 1990-91, annual rpt, C6985–3.1

Oil refinery capacity by process, and refined products production and consumption, by Republic and region, 1992 article, C6985–1.508

Index by Subjects and Names

Oil/gas seismic exploration land crews and vessels, by world area or country, quarterly press release, A8912–2

Population, and fertility, abortion, and contraceptive use rates, for 5 central Asian Republics, 1993 article, A5160–1.504

Population by sex, location type, Republic, and selected city, with Soviet Union economic indicators affecting foreign investment, 1985 or 1986, R4105–82.4

Public opinion in US on selected foreign policy issues, with detail for 3 States, 1993 survey, annual rpt, A4965–1

Uranium deposits by reserve classification, and resources of 4 Republics by production cost category, 1993 article, B6800–1.510

Uranium reserves in 4 CIS Republics, Jan 1991-92, article, B6790–1.502

Uranium US import quotas from 6 CIS Republics, and projected imports from Russia, 1993 article, B6790–1.501

see also Kyrgyzstan

see also Russia

see also Soviet Union

see also Ukraine

see also Uzbekistan

Commonwealth of Nations

see United Kingdom

Communicable diseases

see Animal diseases and zoonoses

see Infective and parasitic diseases

see Respiratory diseases

see Sexually transmitted diseases

Communications industries

China and US socioeconomic and infrastructure indicators comparison, 1993 rpt, R4105–82.8

Congressional campaign finances, with detailed data for individual Members, and leading contributors by type and industry, 1990 election and trends, biennial rpt, R3828–2.2

Electronics industry factory sales and shipments, foreign trade, and operating data, by product category, 1980s-92, annual rpt, A4725–1

Electronics trade, by product category, detailed type, and country, monthly rpt, A4725–3

Engineers salaries by industry group, census div, selected metro area, and years since college degree, 1993, annual survey rpt, A0685–5

Engineers salaries by industry group, census div, selected metro area, degree level, and years since college degree, 1993, annual survey rpt, A0685–3

Executive compensation and components, by industry div and major manufacturing group, 1991, annual rpt, R4105–19

Expenditures by industry segment, 1986-96, annual rpt, C3975–5.3

Financial performance and growth rankings for approx 1,000 top corporations, with comparisons by industry group, 1993 annual rpt, C3950–1.505

Financial ratios and performance, for over 350 SIC 4-digit industries, FY88-92, annual rpt, A6400–3

Latin America statistical abstract, general data by country, 1992 annual rpt, U6250–1.4, U6250–1.13, U6250–1.32

Operating and financial composite ratios for corporations, with establishments and receipts, for approx 200 industries, by asset size, FY90, annual rpt, C7800–1

Religious congregation characteristics, including radio/TV programming activity, 1992 survey, recurring rpt, A5435–4

Revenues and earnings of top 100 broadcasting and related electronic communications companies, 1992, annual article, C1850–14.526

Salaries of chief executives of 12 communications industry trade assns, 1993 feature, C1850–14.506

Sales and employment, for 25 innovative info technology companies, 1993 article, C8900–1.525

Statistical profiles of 50 States and DC, general data, 1993 annual almanac, C4712–1

Utility regulatory agency policies and practices, and industry financial and operating data, by utility type and agency, 1991/92 annual rpt, A7015–3

Women's communications industries employment opportunities, sexual harassment, and income compared to men, Dec 1992 survey, article, C2710–1.528

State and local:

Arizona economic condition, including population, employment and earnings, and business activity, by industry and locality, 1985-93, semiannual rpt, U5850–1.1

Florida statistical abstract, general data, 1992 annual rpt, U6660–1.12, U6660–1.14

Georgia statistical abstract, general data, 1992-93 biennial rpt, U6730–1.8

Hawaii data book, general data, 1992 annual rpt, S2090–1.16

Maine employment in trade, utilities, and transportation SIC 2-digit industries, by detailed occupation, 2nd qtr 1991, triennial rpt, S3465–1.25

New Mexico economic trends and outlook, by industry div, 1982-92, annual article, U7980–1.503

North Carolina employment in trade, transportation, communications, utilities, govt, and education, by detailed occupation, 2nd qtr 1991, triennial rpt, S5917–5.2

Texas trade, transportation, and public utilities employment, by SIC 2- and 3-digit industry and detailed occupation, 2nd qtr 1991, triennial survey rpt, S7675–1.31

Utah statistical abstract, general data, 1993 triennial rpt, U8960–1.13

see also Audiovisual equipment

see also Books and bookselling

see also Cable television

see also Communications satellites

see also Journalism

see also Mass media

see also Media use surveys

see also Motion pictures

see also Newspapers

see also Periodicals

see also Political broadcasting

see also Public broadcasting

see also Radio

see also Recording industry

Community-based correctional programs

see also Telecommunication

see also Telegraph

see also Telephones and telephone industry

see also Television

see also under By Industry in the "Index by Categories"

Communications satellites

Cable TV homes passed, subscribers, and finances, for telephone, cable, and direct broadcast satellite company systems, 2000, article, C1850–14.516

Low earth orbit communications satellite systems ("Big LEOS") planned by 5 companies, with number of satellites and estimated cost, 1992 article, C5800–7.504

Orbiting communications satellites current and proposed, including owners and number of transponders, 1993 annual feature, C1850–14.512

Shipment value, employment, and foreign trade, for electronics industry, by sector and product type, 1980s-92, annual rpt, A4725–1.2

TV home satellite earth station factory sales, 1986-92, annual rpt, A4725–1.1

TV home satellite earth station factory sales, 1988-92, annual rpt, A4725–4

World space flight devs and records, with launches and orbiting equipment by country, and detail for US programs, 1992 and trends, annual rpt, B9170–1

Communism

see Centrally planned economies

see Communist parties

see East-West trade

Communist countries

see Centrally planned economies

Communist parties

Eastern Europe public opinion on selected govt and societal instns, for 6 countries and 3 Soviet Union Republics, 1991 survey, C8915–8.2

Latin America Communist party membership, by country, 1940s-90, annual rpt, U6250–1.9

see also Centrally planned economies

Communities

see Neighborhoods

Community-based correctional programs

Directory of correctional instns, with inmates, staff, and cost of care, by US and Canadian instn, 1992, annual rpt, A1305–3

Directory of local jails and adult detention facilities, with use of alternative programs, by State and instn, Dec 1992, recurring rpt, A1305–1.2

Inmates and number of facilities, for programs administered and contracted by State and Federal corrections systems, 1992, annual series, R4300–1

State and local:

Alaska corrections system admin, including inmate and probationer/parolee offenses and demographic characteristics, 1991 annual rpt, S0287–1

Arizona correctional instn admin, including inmates by criminal background and demographic characteristics, FY92, annual rpt, S0464–2

Arkansas juvenile community-based program admissions, by provider, age, and sex, 1991 and trends, annual rpt, S0700–2.2

Community-based correctional programs

California correctional instn inmates, by offense, demographic characteristics, and instn, Dec 1992, semiannual rpt, S0820–2

California correctional instn inmates, with criminal background and demographic characteristics, 1991 and trends, annual rpt, S0820–1

DC statistical profile, general data, 1992 annual rpt, S1535–3.1, S1535–3.5

Delaware public opinion on criminal sentencing, prison alternatives, and related issues, Feb 1991 survey, R8825–11

Florida correctional instns, admin, and inmates by criminal background and demographic characteristics, FY92 annual rpt, S1720–1

Georgia correctional instns, admin, and inmate characteristics, FY92, annual rpt, S1872–1

Illinois corrections dept admin, including inmates and characteristics, finances, and staff, FY91-93 and trends, annual rpt, S2425–1

Kansas correctional instn inmates, by offense, demographic characteristics, and instn, FY92 and trends, annual rpt, S2940–1

Michigan correctional instns, admin, and inmates by selected demographic characteristics, 1991 and trends, annual rpt, S3960–1

Nebraska correctional instn admin, with inmates by criminal background and demographic characteristics, by instn, FY92 and trends, annual rpt, S4850–1

Oklahoma community treatment centers, and house arrest program, with participants and costs, FY91, annual rpt, S6420–1

Pennsylvania State correctional instn admin, and inmates by type of offense and demographic characteristics, 1990 and trends, annual rpt, S6782–1

South Carolina prisoner participation in work-release and other community programs, FY92, annual rpt, S7135–1

South Carolina statistical abstract, general data, 1993 annual rpt, S7125–1.5

South Dakota correctional instn admin, including inmates by criminal background and demographic characteristics, FY92 and trends, annual rpt, S7296–1

Tennessee correctional instn admin, with inmate characteristics, and corrections dept finances and staff, FY92, annual rpt, S7480–1

Washington State community-based programs for juvenile offenders, clients and costs by race-ethnicity and county, FY90, annual rpt, S8420–2

Washington State correctional instn inmate population, admissions, and releases, by demographic characteristics, quarterly rpt, S8337–1

Wisconsin correctional instn inmates, admissions, and releases, by instn and sex, FY92 and trends, annual rpt, S8692–1.6

Wisconsin correctional instn inmates, admissions, and releases, by instn and sex, 1991 and trends, annual rpt, S8692–1.4

see also Group homes

Community centers

Food service industry sales trends and forecast, by market segment, 1990-93, annual feature, A8200–1.502

State and local:

South Carolina statistical abstract, general data, 1993 annual rpt, S7125–1.10

see also Community health services

see also Mental health facilities and services

Community colleges

Appropriations for higher education, by State, instn, and function, 1993/94, annual feature, C2175–1.S38

Appropriations of tax funds for higher education, by State, instn, and function, FY92-93 and trends, annual rpt, A8970–1

Dental allied education enrollment, grads, and tuition, by instn, 1992/93 annual rpt, A1475–5

Engineering degrees awarded, by State, instn, and field, with detail for women, minorities, and foreign students, 1991/92, annual rpt, A0685–1

Engineering program enrollment, by instn, field, and State, with detail for women, minorities, and foreign students, fall 1992, annual rpt, A0685–2

Enrollment by minority status, degrees, faculty and staff, and tuition/fees, by instn and State, 1992 annual directory, A0640–1

Financial and operating data, including revenues by source, and expenditures and staff by function, and selected student characteristics, FY92, annual rpt, A6705–1

Foreign students enrolled in US higher education instns, by instn, State, country of origin, and demographic characteristics, 1991/92 and trends, annual rpt, R5580–1

Nursing schools, programs, enrollment, student and staff characteristics, and grads, 1991 and trends, annual rpt, A8010–1

Tuition/fees at 19 community colleges, 1992/93, article, B8500–2.501

State and local:

Alabama statistical abstract, general data, 1992 recurring rpt, U5680 2.4

Arizona statistical abstract, general data, 1993 recurring rpt, U5850–2.4

Arkansas higher education degrees conferred, by level, discipline, student race and sex, and instn, 1990/91 and trends, annual rpt, S0690–3

Arkansas higher education enrollment by student characteristics and geographic origins, by instn, fall 1991 and trends, annual rpt, S0690–1

Arkansas higher education finances, including revenues by source, expenditures by function, and State appropriations, by public instn, FY80s-95, biennial rpt, S0690–4

Arkansas higher education FTE enrollment, and student credit hour production by program area, by academic level and instn, 1991/92 and trends, annual rpt, S0690–2

California higher education systems funding by source and expenditures by program category, with enrollment data, FY60s-94, annual rpt, S0827–3

Index by Subjects and Names

California postsecondary education enrollment and degrees, by sex, race-ethnicity, and instn, 1990/91, annual series, S0827–2

Colorado higher education library finances and operations, and enrollment, by instn, 1992, biennial rpt, S1000–3.2

Florida community college transfers into State university system, by instn, fall 1991, annual rpt, S1725–1

Florida statistical abstract, general data, 1992 annual rpt, U6660–1.20

Hawaii data book, general data, 1992 annual rpt, S2090–1.3

Illinois higher education enrollment, degrees, staff, and finances, by public and private instn and student characteristics, 1993 annual rpt, S2475–1

Iowa postsecondary enrollment, degrees, staff, and finances, by instn, 1990/91, annual rpt, S2755–1

Kansas statistical abstract, general data, 1991/92 annual rpt, U7095–2.5

Kentucky higher education enrollment, degrees, staff, and finances, by State-supported instn, 1983-92, annual rpt, S3130–3

Maryland statistical abstract, general data, 1993-94 biennial rpt, S3605–1.2

Minnesota postsecondary education finances, and enrollment by student characteristics, by type of school system, 1970s-93, biennial rpt, S4195–2.2

Missouri higher education enrollment, degrees, libraries, staff, and finances, by instn, 1992 and trends, annual rpt, S4520–3

Nevada statistical abstract, general data, 1992 biennial rpt, S5005–1.7

New York State university system enrollment, degrees, and employment, by campus, 1992 annual rpt, U5100–1.10

North Carolina higher education enrollment, degrees, libraries, staff, and student characteristics, finances, and housing, by instn, 1992/93 and trends, annual rpt, U8013–1

Pennsylvania higher education degrees conferred, by level, sex, race-ethnicity, instn type, and field of study, 1990/91 and trends, annual rpt, S6790–5.2

Pennsylvania higher education degrees conferred, by level, sex, race-ethnicity, instn type, and field of study, 1991/92 and trends, annual rpt, S6790–5.15

Pennsylvania higher education enrollment, by student characteristics and instn, 1992 and trends, annual rpt, S6790–5.9

Pennsylvania higher education students by residence location, by academic level and instn type, 1992 and trends, biennial rpt, S6790–5.8

Pennsylvania higher education tuition/fees, and room and board charges, by instn, 1992/93 and trends, annual rpt, S6790–5.3

Tennessee higher education enrollment, finances, staff, and programs, by instn, 1992/93 and trends, annual rpt, S7525–1

Texas higher education enrollment, faculty, curricula, and finances, by instn, 1991/92 and trends, annual rpt, S7657–1

Utah higher education degrees, enrollment, staff, and finances, by public instn, with selected comparisons to instns in other States, 1993/94 annual rpt, S7895–2

West Virginia higher education enrollment, degrees, faculty and student characteristics, and finances, by instn, 1992/93 and trends, annual rpt, S8533–1

see also Junior colleges

Community development

Bank small business lending and services, with data on organizational structure, loan delinquencies, and community dev activities, Nov 1992 survey, annual rpt, A4160–5

Catholic dioceses involved in community dev programs, by type, 1991, annual rpt, A3810–1

Foundations (community-based) asset value, grants paid, and gifts received, for top 50 organizations, 1992, annual article, C2176–1.518

Foundations (community-based) assets by type, and investment performance, 1992 and trends, article, C2176–1.522

Nonprofit organization grants for community dev, with top 50 donors, 1989 and 1991, article, C2176–1.514

State and local:

Kansas county economic dev planning, including plan characteristics and funding sources, 1993 article, U7095–1.502

see also City and town planning

see also Community Development Block Grants

see also Urban renewal

Community Development Block Grants

Federal budget trends, including spending by program, State, and region, FY81-94, annual rpt, R8490–11

State and local:

DC statistical profile, general data, 1992 annual rpt, S1535–3.4

Community health services

Blood bank operating profiles, arranged by State, 1993 biennial directory, A0612–1

Developing countries family planning facilities by type, and prevalence of community-based programs, by country, 1980s, R8720–1.1

Nursing center (community) staff and client characteristics, and services, 1990 survey, article, A8010–3.506

Voluntary health agency revenues, and expenditures by function, for 39 major organizations, FY90, annual rpt, A7973–1

Zaire community-based contraceptive distribution program costs and effectiveness, 1980s, article, A5160–6.505

State and local:

DC statistical profile, general data, 1992 annual rpt, S1535–3.1, S1535–3.5

Hawaii health dept activities and services, including vital statistics and disease control, by location, 1990, annual rpt, S2065–1

Maryland medical assistance payments and recipients, by program, type of service, location, demographic characteristics, and facility, FY92 and trends, annual rpt, S3635–3

see also Home health services

see also Respite care

Community mental health centers

see Mental health facilities and services

Community service

see Volunteers

see Public service employment

see Volunteers

Commuting

Mass transit system finances and operations, passengers, and employment, by mode, US and Canada, 1990-91 and trends, annual rpt, A2650–1

Metro area average commuting times, for 14 areas with longest times, 1992 feature, C4300–1.502

Motorcycle use and user characteristics, licensed operators, and State requirements, 1992 annual rpt, A6485–1.2

Railroad commuting trends, Amtrak and other, 1992 annual rpt, R4815–1

State social, economic, and govtl indicators, with rankings, 1993 semiannual rpt, B8500–1.11

Western States travel times to work, population, and land area, for 18 urban areas, 1990, article, U0280–1.511

State and local:

Alabama county data book, general data, 1992 annual rpt, S0121–2

Arkansas Census of Population and Housing detailed findings, 1990, U5935–7

California Census of Population and Housing detailed findings, 1990, S0840–9

Florida county data book, 1992/93 annual rpt, C6360–1

Florida statistical abstract, general data, 1992 annual rpt, U6660–1.13

Georgia county guide, general data, 1993 annual rpt, U6750–1

Hawaii data book, general data, 1992 annual rpt, S2090–1.12

Idaho economic profile, general data, 1992 recurring rpt, S2218–2.7

Louisiana Census of Population and Housing summary findings, by local area, 1990 and trends, U8010–4

Maine Census of Population and Housing summary findings, by local area, 1990, S3465–9

Maryland statistical abstract, general data, 1993-94 biennial rpt, S3605–1.4

New Jersey Census of Population and Housing detailed findings, by county, 1990, S5425–19

Oklahoma commuting patterns, including interstate and international travel, and detailed data by county, 1990 and trends, S6416–2

Pennsylvania Census of Population and Housing detailed findings, with selected data by county and municipality, 1990, U4130–13

Pennsylvania employment and commuting data from Census of Population and Housing, by county and municipality, 1990, C1595–16

Pennsylvania statistical abstract, general data, 1992 recurring rpt, U4130–6.3

Rhode Island Census of Population and Housing detailed findings, by county and municipality, 1990, S6930–9

South Carolina statistical abstract, general data, 1993 annual rpt, S7125–1.15

South Dakota workers and intercounty commuters, for counties with highest rates of commuting, 1990, S7355–1.501

Tennessee commuting patterns by county, for primary counties of 5 MSAs, 1990, S7495–2.505

Tennessee statistical abstract, general data, 1992/93 annual rpt, U8710–2.9

see also Buses

see also High-speed ground transportation

see also Subways

see also Urban transportation

Compact disc information storage

see CD-ROM technology and use

Compact disc players

Sales (distributor units) of consumer electronics products by type, 1991-93, annual article, C2000–1.503

Sales to dealer volume of compact disc players, 1984-92, annual rpt, A4725–4

Compact discs

see Recording industry

Companies

see Business firms and establishments, number

see Corporations

see Foreign corporations

see Franchises

see Government corporations and enterprises

see Holding companies

see Minority businesses

see Multinational corporations

see Partnerships

see Proprietorships

see under By Individual Company or Institution in the "Index by Categories"

Comparable worth

see Discrimination in employment

see Sex discrimination

Compensation

see Earnings, general

see Earnings, specific industry

see Payroll

Compensatory education

Catholic elementary schools with students eligible and receiving Federal Chapter 1 educational assistance, by State and region, 1992/93, annual rpt, A7375–1

Elementary/secondary teacher views on education policy issues and selected reform proposals, Jan-Feb 1993 survey, B6045–7

Federal budget trends, including spending by program, State, and region, FY81-94, annual rpt, R8490–11

Higher education appropriations for FY94 compared to spending in FY93, by program, recurring feature, C2175–1.527, C2175–1.536

Southern States compensatory education funding, for 15 States, 1990, annual rpt, U6660–1.20

State social, economic, and govtl indicators, with rankings, 1993 semiannual rpt, B8500–1.6

Test scores in math and reading for 3rd and 4th grade participants of Chapter 1 compensatory education programs, 1993, article, R4800–2.522

State and local:

Connecticut public school data, including enrollment, staff, programs, finances, and student characteristics, 1991/92, biennial rpt, S1185–3

Delaware Federal educational grant awards by program, and program enrollment and employees, by county and administering agency/instn, 1991/92, annual rpt, S1430–1.5

Compensatory education

Maryland elementary and secondary education data, by county, 1991/92, annual rpt, S3610–2.9

Maryland elementary and secondary education statistical summary, with data by county, 1991/92-1992/93 and trends, annual rpt, S3610–1

Missouri Elementary and Secondary Education Act programs, students, and teachers, by grade level and subject, FY92, annual rpt, S4505–1.1

New Jersey public and nonpublic school students participating in Chapter 1 programs, by county, 1991/92, annual rpt, S5385–1

New Mexico elementary/secondary school statistics, including grads, student test results, and finances, by school district, 1989/90-1991/92, annual rpt, S5575–4

Ohio public school enrollment, finances, special programs, and staff, 1991/92 and trends, annual rpt, S6265–2

Oklahoma school revenues and expenditures, by program, county, and district, FY92, annual rpt, S6423–1.1

Pennsylvania vocational education enrollment of disadvantaged students, 1991/92, annual rpt, S6790–5.7

Pennsylvania vocational education 1989/90 grad employment status, with detail for disadvantaged students, 1991 survey, annual rpt, S6790–5.6

Rhode Island education expenditures by function and source of funds, by school district, 1991/92, annual rpt, S6970–1.2

West Virginia public school finances, enrollment, staff, and programs, by county, 1992/93 and trends, annual rpt, S8540–4

see also Bilingual education

see also Head Start Project

see also Remedial education

Competition

- Advertising media buying services, competition, and staffing, views of agency and independent service executives, 1993 annual survey articles, C2710–1.537
- Architect views on industry competition and related topics, 1993 survey article, C5800–15.502
- Banker views on future competition from 8 types of financial instns, Mar 1992 survey, article, C4687–1.502
- Construction industry anticipated future foreign and domestic competition, by type of business, 1993, annual survey rpt, A4155–1
- Corporate personnel mgmt devs, including work force diversity, health care and family-related benefits, counseling services, and competitiveness, 1993 survey, B6850–6
- Electronics industry conditions and outlook, including mgmt issues, global expansion, and most promising new technologies, views of CEOs, 1992/93 survey, annual feature, C1850–2.506
- Food store industry structure, sales, operations, and business outlook, by type of store, 1993 annual rpt, C5225–1.505
- Fuel oil and heating equipment dealer loss of business to gas conversions, 1992 annual survey, C4680–2.3
- Fuel oil customers and dealer views on competition from natural gas, by region, 1992, annual fact book, C4680–1.507

Paper industry sectors potentially affected by electronic competition, 1993 annual rpt, C3975–5.3

Supermarket health/beauty care and general merchandise product marketing devs and issues, 1992 survey article, C4655–1.502

Telephone company revenues, access lines, and vulnerability to local services competition, by major company, 1992 and trends, article, C4725–3.511

Telephone long-distance competition and regulation in local access areas, by State, 1991/92 annual rpt, A7015–3

see also Corporate rankings

see also Economic concentration and diversification

see also Foreign competition

see also Product rankings

Comprehensive Employment and Training Act *see also* Public service employment

Compulsory military service see Voluntary military service

Computer industry and products

- Advertising expenditures and pages in magazines, for top 12 computer manufacturers, 1st 8 months 1992-93, article, C2710–1.548
- Advertising expenditures for top 10 computer advertisers and magazines, 1st half 1992-93, article, C2710–1.542
- Advertising expenditures for top 5 computer companies in selected media, 1st half 1992, C2710–1.502
- Cable TV advertising revenue shares from computer retailers, and use of value-added promotions, July 1993 survey, article, C1858–1.507
- China computer revenues by industry sector, 1991, article, C5800–7.505
- China computer sales value and/or volume, and imports value, by equipment type, 1991-95, article, A9315–1.506
- Consumer buying power survey of population, income, and sales by product line, by State, metro area, county, and census div, 1993 annual rpt, C1200–1.514
- Contract revenues of 4 major computer manufacturers, 1993, article, C5800–7.528
- Corporate performance ratings by executives for leading companies in 32 industries, 1993 annual survey feature, C8900–1.508
- Design, manufacturing, and engineering (CAD/CAM/CAE) revenues, with market shares for 10 companies, 1992, article, C7000–7.501
- Design, manufacturing, and engineering (CAD/CAM/CAE) revenues worldwide, with market shares for 10 companies, 1993, article, C5800–4.513
- Direct marketing industry devs, with consumer and business market characteristics, and media use patterns, 1992/93 annual rpt, A4620–1.4
- Discount stores, sales, and earnings, for top chains, with detail by specialty, 1993 annual feature, C5150–3.514
- Engineers salaries by industry group, census div, selected metro area, and years since college degree, 1993, annual survey rpt, A0685–5
- Engineers salaries by industry group, census div, selected metro area, degree level, and years since college degree, 1993, annual survey rpt, A0685–3

Europe and Germany personal computer market shares for top 6 manufacturers, 1993 article, C5800–7.539

- Europe computer advertising expenditures, for top 15 manufacturers, with detail by country, 1992, article, C2710–1.527
- Executive compensation and components, by industry div and major manufacturing group, 1991, annual rpt, R4105–19
- Factory sales and shipments, foreign trade, and operating data for the electronics industry, by product category, 1980s-92, annual rpt, A4725–1
- Finances of top 100 computer/info systems companies worldwide and in North America, 1992 and trends, annual rpt, C1850–5.514
- Financial performance and growth rankings for approx 1,000 top corporations, with comparisons by industry group, 1993 annual rpt, C3950–1.505
- Financial ratios and performance, for over 350 SIC 4-digit industries, FY88-92, annual rpt, A6400–3
- Foreign trade in electronics, by product category, detailed type, and country, monthly rpt, A4725–3
- Geographic info systems software sales, for 4 companies, 1992, article, C5800–7.538
- Hard drive market shares worldwide, for 6 leading and all other manufacturers, 1992, article, C5800–7.527
- India computer software export revenues, for top 5 firms, FY92, article, C5800–7.511
- Japan personal computer market shares for 5 major and all other manufacturers, and use compared to selected other countries, 1993 article, C8900–1.519
- Latin America statistical abstract, general data by country, 1992 annual rpt, U6250–1.4
- Manufacturing computer-integrated systems (CIM) market outlook, by system use, 1991 and 1996, article, C1850–12.502
- Market devs in electronics industry, including employment, factory sales, prices, and foreign trade trends, monthly rpt, A4725–2
- Market trends and outlook for computers and related equipment, including sales, shipments, orders, employment, and trade, monthly rpt, C1850–2
- Marketing and manufacturing news and devs for computer and info processing industries, semimonthly rpt, C1850–5
- Mini/microcomputer use and market devs, 1992 survey and trends, annual article, C1850–5.502
- Music software shipment retail value, 1988-92, annual rpt, A6848–1
- Operating systems (advanced) copies installed and applications, for 5 systems, 1993 article, C5800–7.530
- Outlook of computer/info system managers for 1993, including importance of selected technologies, 1992 survey, annual article, C1850–5.504
- Personal computer company revenues, for top 50 firms worldwide, and top 50 marketing in North America, 1991, annual article, C1850–5.503
- Personal computer shipments, with market shares for top 10 and all other manufacturers, 1991-92, article, C5800–7.515

Index by Subjects and Names

Computer use

Personal computer unit sales, by end use sector, 1992 and 1996, article, C5800–7.544

Pipeline/gas utility automated control and acquisition system market shares, for 8 leading and all other manufacturers, 1991, article, C6985–1.501

Profit rates for computer industry, by sector, 1988 and 1992, article, C8900–1.517

Purchasing and expansion plans of businesses for computer systems, including data by manufacturer, 1993 survey and trends, annual article, C1850–5.513

Revenues and earnings of top 10 companies making network software, 1993 article, C8900–1.521

Salaries for 24 computer/info systems positions, by industry sector and location, 1993 survey, annual article, C1850–5.518

Salary ranges for 22 computer-related occupations, 1992, article, C4215–1.503

Sales (factory) of home computers, 1988-92, annual rpt, A4725–4

Sales and employment, for 25 innovative info technology companies, 1993 article, C8900–1.525

Sales of computer products, distribution by distribution channel and retail outlet type, 1991 or 1992 and 1995, article, C5150–3.507

Security methods businesses would consider to protect computers/data, Aug 1993 survey, C1850–13.510

Security methods used to protect computer-based info, 1993 feature, C1850–12.511

Shipment value of info technology products for small businesses, home offices, and general consumers, 1992-96, article, C2710–1.551

Shipments and industry revenues for computers and other business equipment, 1990-98, annual articles, C2000–1.503

Shopping center financial and operating data, with detail by type of tenant, US and Canada, 1991, triennial rpt, R9285–1

Software company revenues and employment, for top 100 firms worldwide, 1992, annual article, C1850–5.520

Software company spending for marketing, sales, and support as percent of revenues, by revenue size group, 1991-92, article, C1200–1.504

Software desktop operating system worldwide market shares, for 4 leading and all other programs, 1995, article, C5800–7.510

Software for personal computers, sales by type of program, 1991, article, C1200–1.501

Software with sales/marketing applications, installations sold and product characteristics, by vendor, 1992 annual directory, C1200–1.502

Software with sales/marketing applications, titles, vendors, and prices, 1992 and trends, article, C1200–1.506

Software with sales/marketing applications, vendor finances, marketing methods, and customer characteristics, 1990-91, annual survey article, C1200–1.502

Systems integration consultant revenues and market shares, for top 5 companies, 1993, article, C8900–1.526

see also CD-ROM technology and use
see also Computer networks
see also Computer sciences
see also Computer use
see also Economic and econometric models
see also Industrial robots
see also Information storage and retrieval systems

Computer networks

Asynchronous transfer mode (ATM) transmission technology market value for computer applications, by type, 1993-97, article, C4725–3.515

Corporate personal computer networking, 1989 and 1992-93, article, C1850–2.503

Educational networks for children, subscribers and prices for 5 networks, 1993 article, C8900–1.524

Elementary/secondary teacher use of Internet intl computer network, 1993 survey article, R4800–2.522

Hub market value, with market shares for 6 leading and all other manufacturers, 1993 article, C1850–2.504

Internet intl computer network host computers worldwide, 1988 and 1993, article, C8900–1.525

Library statewide computer network characteristics and components, dev status, and benefits, 1993 survey feature, C1852–1.511

Marketing and manufacturing devs for computer industry, including computer network use and corporate purchasing plans, semimonthly rpt, C1850–5

Mini/microcomputer use and networking, including software in use, 1992 survey and trends, annual article, C1850–5.502

Outlook of computer/info system managers for 1993, including importance of selected technologies, 1992 survey, annual article, C1850–5.504

Purchasing and expansion plans of businesses for computer systems, including data by manufacturer, 1993 survey and trends, annual article, C1850–5.513

Veterinarian computer and network info services use in home and office, by practice type, 1992 survey, articles, A3100–2.501, A3100–2.502

see also Automated tellers
see also Computer use

Computer Petroleum Corp.

Gasoline prices, by city and PAD district, weekly rpt, C6985–1

Computer sciences

Chemist and chemical engineer salaries, employment status, and demographic and professional characteristics, 1993, annual rpt, A1250–4

Employment in business and industry, hiring plans for college grads, by field, salary, and degree, 1993 annual survey rpt, U3730–1

Salaries of scientists, engineers, technicians, and other professionals, by employee and employer characteristics, 1990s and trends, biennial rpt, A3960–1

Salary and job offers for college grads, by field of study, type of employer, and degree level, by region, interim rpt series, A3940–1

Salary and job offers for college grads, by field of study, type of employer, and degree level, series, A3940–2

Women and minorities in professional fields, detailed education and labor force data, 1991 and trends, recurring rpt, A3960–2.3

Computer software

see Computer industry and products

Computer use

Architectural firm use of computers, 1993 survey, article, C5800–15.505

Chambers of commerce income, salaries and benefits, membership, staff, and operations, 1993 annual rpt, A3840–3

College grad recruiter use of commercial personnel data bases, 1993 annual survey rpt, U3730–1

Consumer ownership of home computers, and interest in computer photo imaging, 1993 survey, recurring rpt, A8695–2

Convenience store use of computerized scanning and personal computers, 1992 and trends, annual survey rpt, A6735–1, A6735–2

Corporate employee intl transfers, use of electronic data interchange (EDI) in intl shipments, 1992, annual survey, B0600–1

Corporate expenditure plans for computer/info systems by component, 1993 annual survey article, C1850–5.510

Corporate functional areas for pen-based computers, views of chief info officers, 1992 survey article, C1200–1.501

Corporate integrated logistics info systems implementation status, 1976 and 1992 surveys, article, C2150–1.507

Corporate reasons for making back-up copies of computerized data, 1992 survey article, C4687–1.504

Corporate sales dept use of personal computers, with effect on productivity, 1993 annual survey article, C1200–1.512

Corporate sales/marketing automation issues including computer applications and impacts, views of computer users and nonusers, Aug 1992 survey, article, C1200–1.504

Corporate use of computers, and related mgmt and training issues, views of executives, 1993 survey rpt, B6850–7

Direct marketing industry use of computers, for catalog and telemarketing segments, 1992/93 annual rpt, A4620–1.2

Drugstore chain stores use of scanning equipment, by chain, 1993 feature, C5150–2.512

Earnings index for 27 MSAs and 4 occupational groups, 1990, biennial rpt, S3605–1.6

Electronic data interchange (EDI) use and/or expansion plans, and benefits cited, with detail for electronics firms, 1993 articles, C1850–2.511

Electronic data interchange (EDI) use by industrial distributors, and percent of customers requiring EDI, 1992 annual survey, C1850–4.507

Elementary/secondary student computer use at school, by State, 1989, article, B8500–2.506

Elementary/secondary student shares using computers in school, by State, 1989, semiannual rpt, B8500–1.7

Computer use

Elementary/secondary teacher use of Internet intl computer network, 1993 survey article, R4800–2.522

Food marketers mgmt info system operations, employment, and finances, for wholesalers and retailers by sales size, 1993 and trends, annual survey, A4950–7

Food store industry structure, sales, operations, and business outlook, by type of store, 1993 annual rpt, C5225–1.505

Fuel oil dealer computer use, by region, 1991, annual fact book, C4680–1.507

Fuel oil dealer sales by product, employment, computer use, and truck fleet size, by region, 1992 annual survey, C4680–2.1

Games use on computers at work, and impact on productivity, as reported by info system managers, 1993 survey article, C5800–7.549

Higher education grad earnings superiority over high school grads, share attributable to computer skills, by sex, 1991, article, C8900–1.515

Higher education language faculty computer access by academic rank, and use for selected tasks, 1990/91 survey, article, C2175–1.517

Home improvement industry top distributors use of electronic data interchange (EDI), by type of product line, 1992, annual feature, C5150–6.502

Home remodeling company computer use, including types of software used, by revenue size, 1992 survey, article, C1850–8.501

Homebuilder use of personal computer software for selected applications, 1993 feature, C4300–1.506

Hospital pharmacy operating data, by instn type and size, and census div, 1991, annual survey, B5165–3

Hotel/motel use of computers, including perceived benefits and challenges, 1991 survey, article, C7000–6

Households with personal computers and modems, selected years 1982-96, article, A8605–1.509

Industrial distribution use of electronic data interchange (EDI) with carriers, vendors, and customers, 1992 article, C2150–1.502

Industrial distributor customers requiring use of electronic data interchange (EDI), 1993 survey article, C1850–4.508

Library automated system installations worldwide and in US, and vendor revenues, by vendor, 1992 and trends, annual articles, C1852–1.505, C1852–1.506

Library statewide computer network characteristics and components, dev status, and benefits, 1993 survey feature, C1852–1.511

Library/info science school income by source, and expenditures by object, by instn, 1991/92 and trends, annual rpt, A3235–1.4

Magazine use of desktop publishing/electronic systems for pre-press operations, including hardware and software brands used, May 1993 survey, article, C2575–1.514

Index by Subjects and Names

Marketing and manufacturing news and devs for computer and info processing industries, semimonthly rpt, C1850–5

Marketing executive views on technology use and future importance, including companies cited as top users, July/Aug 1992 survey, article, C2710–1.510

Medical group financial and operating data, by practice characteristics, 1991, annual rpt, A6365–2

Medical group practice characteristics, including specialties, form of organization, and location, 1991 and trends, recurring rpt, A2200–7

Metalworking industry capital spending plans, by equipment type and industry group, 1989-93, annual survey, C4080–1

Mortgage banking industry computer system expenses by category, with detail for hardware by type, 1988, article, A6450–2.505

NASDAQ quotation terminals abroad, by country, 1993 annual rpt, A7105–1

Navy tactical advanced computer costs and processor speeds, by computer generation, 1993 article, C5800–4.521

Paperboard packaging industry computer software use for plant mgmt, 1993 annual article, C0125–4.503

Personal computer vs high-performance workstation use outlook, 1993 article, C4725–3.515

Pharmacy computer software systems and computerized scanning use, 1993 survey, article, C5150–2.518

Physician use of electronic billing systems, by payment source and region, 1991-92, article, A2200–5.1

Plastics processing industry computerized system use, by company sales size, 1992, annual rpt, A8920–4

Public opinion on business use of personal info, including views on privacy, credit, and effects of computer use, 1992 survey and trends, annual rpt, B3280–2

Public relations firms and depts purchasing of selected types of support services, computer software, and telecommunications, 1992 survey, article, A8770–1.501

Public utility expenditures for computer/info systems, software, and related services, 1990 and 1995, article, A4700–4.502

Pulp and paper mill machine maintenance operations and personnel, by region and grade, 1992 survey, recurring article, C3975–2.504

Railroad (short line/regional) computer hardware and electronic data interchange (EDI) use, 1990 and 1992 surveys, article, C8400–1.505

Restaurant (table service) computer and specialized software use, by application, 1992 and trends, recurring rpt, A8200–11

Restaurant (table service) computer use, 1992 article, A8200–1.502

Retail credit operations, and participation in selected emerging technologies, by outlet type, 1992 annual survey, C5150–4.504

Retail industry inventory mgmt, warehousing, and distribution operations, by outlet type, 1993 survey, C5150–4.506

Retail mgmt info system devs, including expenses and computerized equipment use, 1992 survey, annual feature, C5150–4.501

Retail mgmt info system devs, including expenses and computerized equipment use, 1993 survey, annual feature, C5150–4.509

Retailer point-of-sale (POS) computer system installation status, generations in use, and maintenance practices, 1992 survey article, C5150–4.502

Retailer views on "quick response" system implementation and benefits, and other technology use, 1992 survey, annual article, C5150–4.506

Securities program trading shares of NYSE volume, 1989-91 and monthly 1992, annual fact book, B6625–1.1

Small corporation mgmt office technology experience and views, including whether productivity gains have justified investment, 1992 survey, article, C4687–1.506

State govt info resources mgmt, including data on budgets, staff, and organizational structure, by State, 1991, biennial rpt, A7121–1

Textile industry use of computerized information systems, 1992 survey, article, C5226–3.502

Utility and transportation regulatory agency computer use, by agency, 1991/92 annual rpt, A7015–2

Veterinarian computer and network info services use in home and office, by practice type, 1992 survey, articles, A3100–2.501, A3100–2.502

Warehouse use of selected types of computer systems, 1992 and 1994, article, C2150–1.506

Worker use of selected sources for computer assistance, 1993 article, C4687–1.503

State and local:

Arizona library on-line data base search activity and expenditures, by instn, FY92, annual rpt, S0495–1

Colorado public library finances and operations, by instn, 1991, annual rpt, S1000–3.1

DC statistical profile, general data, 1992 annual rpt, S1535–3.2

Florida electric utility customer savings from computerized fuel cost sharing, 1978-92, annual rpt, S1790–1

Iowa public library computer software expenditures and acquisitions, by library, FY92, annual rpt, S2778–1

Kentucky public library expenditures for computer equipment, microcomputers installed, and computer uses and public access, by county, FY92, annual rpt, S3165–1

Montana public library computer-related expenditures, software holdings, and online searches, by library, FY92, annual rpt, S4725–1

Nebraska public libraries, finances, holdings, circulation, staff, and population served, by instn, FY91, annual rpt, S4910–1

New Hampshire public library computer access, by city, 1991, annual rpt, S5227–1

Ohio public library holdings and circulation, including computer software, by library, 1992, annual rpt, S6320–1

Index by Subjects and Names

Utah crimes involving use of computer equipment, by offense, for 6 local agencies, 1992, annual rpt, S7890–3

Virginia public library online data base searches, by instn, FY92, annual rpt, S8275–1

see also CD-ROM technology and use
see also Computer networks

Computers in education
see Educational technology

Concrete
see Cement and concrete

Condition of health
see Health condition

Condominium timesharing
see Resort timesharing

Condominiums and cooperatives

Expenses, detailed data for US and Canada, by building characteristics, metro area, and US region, 1991, annual rpt, A5600–3

Home buyer (1st-time and repeat) profile, and transaction characteristics, including prices and financing, by region and for 18 metro areas, 1990-92, annual survey rpt, B2150–1

Sales and prices of apartment condominiums and cooperatives, by region and State, monthly rpt, A7000–2

Sales of condominiums/cooperatives, by region, quarterly rpt, B5190–1

State and local:

Arkansas Census of Population and Housing detailed findings, 1990, U5935–7

California Census of Population and Housing detailed findings, 1990, S0840–9

Colorado property assessed valuation by detailed property type, and tax levy and revenue by local district, by county, 1991-92, annual rpt, S1055–3

DC statistical profile, general data, 1992 annual rpt, S1535–3.1, S1535 3.2, S1535–3.4

Florida statistical abstract, general data, 1992 annual rpt, U6660–1.2

Hawaii counties population and economic indicators, 1993 annual rpt series, B3500–2

Hawaii data book, general data, 1992 annual rpt, S2090–1.21, S2090–1.23

Hawaii economic indicators, bimonthly rpt, B3500–1

Louisiana Census of Population and Housing summary findings, by local area, 1990 and trends, U8010–4

Maine Census of Population and Housing summary findings, by local area, 1990, S3465–9

New Jersey Census of Population and Housing detailed findings, by county, 1990, S5425–19

Pennsylvania Census of Population and Housing detailed findings, with selected data by county and municipality, 1990, U4130–13

Rhode Island Census of Population and Housing detailed findings, by county and municipality, 1990, S6930–9

see also Resort timesharing

Condoms
see Contraceptives
see Personal care products

Confectionery products
see Candy and confectionery products

Conferences

Political science higher education dept conference travel expenditures and funds, 1991/92 annual rpt, A2617–1

State and local:

Mississippi govt expenses and attendance at public welfare conferences, FY92, annual rpt, S4357–1

Congenital malformations
see Birth defects

Conglomerates
see Business acquisitions and mergers
see Economic concentration and diversification

Congo

Energy intl sourcebook, with detail on oil and gas industry operations, supply-demand, and prices, for approx 80 countries, 1970s-91, annual compilation, C6985–10.2

Congress

Black congressional caucus member sponsoring of bills, for 5 most active members, 1st 4 months 1993, article, C4215–1.511

Black elected officials, and characteristics of voting age population, with comparisons to whites, 1970s-91, annual compilation, C6775–2.4

Budget outlays of legislative branch by unit, FY70-93, annual rpt, R9050–1.3

Campaign finances, with detailed data for individual Members, and leading contributors by type and industry, 1990 election and trends, biennial rpt, R3828–2, R3828–3

Campaign fund finances in congressional races, with expenditures by detailed item and contributions by donor type, by candidate, district, and State, 1990 elections, C2500–6

Congressional organization, major legislative and budget actions, and agency and program appropriations, 102nd Congress, 2nd session, 1992, annual rpt, C2500–2

Hispanic American Members contributions from political action committees (PACs), and contribution activity of leading Hispanic PACs, 1993 article, C4575–1.511

Member views on legislative priorities, Federal deficit, and tax increases, by political party, Dec 1992 survey, article, C8900–1.507

Minority membership in Congress after Nov 1990 and 1992 elections, by race-ethnicity, article, C4215–1.504

Opinions of Representatives/Senators on seriousness of 18 public policy issues, 1993 survey feature, C4300–1.506

Public communication with Senators and Representatives, and satisfaction with Representatives job performance, Sept 1993 survey, C8915–1.505

Public confidence in selected societal instns, 1972-91 surveys, annual rpt, U6395–1

Public confidence in selected societal instns, 1993 Gallup Poll and trends, C4040–1.510, R8780–1.508

Public opinion on Clinton Admin economic plan, including support in Congress, with data by respondent characteristics, May 1993 survey and trends, C8915–7.3

Public opinion on Congress performance, Feb 1993 Gallup Poll and trends, C4040–1.509

Public opinion on performance of Congress and own Representative, 1970-92 surveys, A0610–1.501

Term limitation initiative voting results in 14 States, 1992, article, A1865–1.507

Women in US House of Representatives and Senate, by party, 1917-95, annual rpt, U4510–1.61, U4510–1.69

State and local:

California State initiative on congressional term limits, election results by county, 1992, biennial rpt, S0934–1

see also Congressional apportionment
see also Congressional committees
see also Congressional districts
see also Congressional employees
see also Congressional-executive relations
see also House of Representatives
see also Library of Congress
see also Senate

Congressional apportionment

Redistricting actions taken, and seats gained or lost following 1990 census, by State, 1993 annual rpt, C2500–2

State and local:

Florida statistical abstract, general data, 1992 annual rpt, U6660–1.21

Congressional committees

Black congressional caucus members on House committees, by committee, 1993 article, R5685–4.504

Campaign contributions to individual members of each standing committee, with detail for top contributors by type, 1990 election, biennial rpt, R3828–2.2

Congressional organization, major legislative and budget actions, and agency and program appropriations, 102nd Congress, 2nd session, 1992, annual rpt, C2500–2

Election outcomes for members of House and Senate commerce and judiciary committees, Nov 1992, article, C1850–14.502

Investment capital formation and impact of govt policies, congressional testimony rpts, series, A1310–2

Congressional districts

Hispanic American population shares in 17 congressional districts that elected Hispanic Representatives in Nov 1992, article, C4575–1.502

State and local:

Arizona statistical abstract, general data, 1993 recurring rpt, U5850–2.2

Pennsylvania statistical abstract, general data, 1992 recurring rpt, U4130–6.6

South Carolina statistical abstract, general data, 1993 annual rpt, S7125–1.9

see also Congressional apportionment
see also Electoral districts and precincts

Congressional elections
see Congressional districts
see Elections

Congressional employees

House of Representatives staff characteristics, salaries, and benefits by position, 1992 and trends, recurring rpt, R4140–1

Congressional ethics
see Political ethics

Congressional-executive relations

Congressional-executive relations
Voting support for President in Congress, 1950s-92, annual rpt, C2500–2

Congressional powers
see also Congressional-executive relations
see also Presidential powers

Connecticut
Construction activity and value, by type of structure and location, 1992 and trends, annual rpt, S1212–1
Court caseloads and dispositions, by type of court and case, and court location, with judicial dept finances, FY91-92, biennial rpt, S1220–1
Crimes and arrests, by offense, local agency, and victim-offender characteristics, with data on law enforcement employment and assaults on officers, 1992, annual rpt, S1256–1
Education dept staff and finances, by div, 1991/92, annual rpt, S1185–1
Election results and voter registration and turnout, by location, 1992 general election, biennial rpt, S1265–1
Elementary/secondary public school data, including enrollment, staff, programs, finances, and student characteristics, 1991/92, biennial rpt, S1185–3
Employment, hours, and earnings, by labor market area and industry, and selected economic indicators, monthly rpt, S1235–1
Financial instns, financial condition by instn, 1991 and trends, annual rpt, S1160–1
Govt financial condition, including revenues by source, expenditures by function, and bonded debt, FY92, annual rpt, S1170–1, S1170–2
Health behavior risk factor surveillance survey results, 1989-91, annual rpt, S1200–2
Health insurance coverage rate, by respondent characteristics and behavior risk factors, 1991 survey, S1200–3
Insurance industry financial and underwriting data, by company and type of insurance, 1991, annual rpt, S1222–1
Jai alai games played, attendance, handle, and govt revenues, for 3 States, 1990, annual rpt, A3363–1.2
Libraries, staff, holdings, circulation, and finances, by library and town, FY91, annual rpt, S1242–1
Markets with daily newspapers, demographic and economic info by geographic area, US and Canada, 1993 annual rpt, C3250–1
School district profiles, community and educational data by district and city, discontinued annual rpt, S1185–2
Statistical profiles of 50 States and DC, general data, 1993 annual almanac, C4712–1
Traffic accidents, fatalities, and injuries, by vehicle type, circumstance, location, and driver and victim characteristics, 1992, annual rpt, S1275–1
Utility and transportation regulatory agency activities, scope of jurisdiction, finances, and employees, by agency, 1991/92 annual rpt, A7015–2
Vital statistics, including births, deaths by cause, marriages, and divorces, by demographic characteristics and location, 1989, annual rpt, S1200–1

see also under By City and By County in the "Index by Categories"
see also under By State in the "Index by Categories"

Conservation areas
State and local:
Hawaii data book, general data, 1992 annual rpt, S2090–1.6, S2090–1.20
Illinois statistical abstract, general data, 1992 annual rpt, U6910–2

Conservation of natural resources
Canada corporate charitable contributions share going to environmental causes, 1985-91, annual rpt, A0700–1.2
Charitable contributions, by type of donor and recipient, 1992 and trends, annual rpt, A0700–1
Charitable contributions to 8 environmental conservation groups, 1st qtr 1992-93, article, C2176–1.511
Minority representation in environmental conservation organization membership, staff, volunteers, and boards, 1993 article, C2176–1.511
Public opinion on environmental and population issues, and related church involvement, for US, Brazil, Canada, and Mexico, 1992 survey, R8780–1.504
World resource issues and environmental devs, by region and country, 1992/93 biennial rpt, R9455–1
Youth opinions on environmental and population issues, 1992 survey, R8780–1.503

State and local:
Maryland local govt financial condition, including revenues by source, expenditures by function, and debt obligations, FY92 and trends, annual rpt, S3618–1.1

see also Birds and bird conservation
see also Conservation areas
see also Endangered species
see also Energy conservation
see also Environmental pollution and control
see also Flood control
see also Forests and forestry
see also Land use
see also National forests
see also National parks
see also Reclamation of land
see also Recycling of waste materials
see also Severance taxes
see also Soils and soil conservation
see also State funding for natural resources and conservation
see also Water resources development
see also Wilderness areas
see also Wildlife and wildlife conservation
see also Wildlife refuges

Constitutional amendments
see also State constitutional amendments

Constitutional conventions
see also State constitutional conventions

Constitutional law
see also Administrative law and procedure
see also Citizenship
see also Civil rights
see also Congressional-executive relations
see also Due process of law
see also Federal-State relations
see also Habeas corpus
see also Presidential powers
see also State constitutional amendments

see also State constitutional conventions

Construction costs
see Building permits
see Capital investments
see Construction industry
see Housing costs and financing
see State funding for capital projects

Construction industry
Activities, including data on costs, materials prices, wages, and contract awards, weekly rpt, C5800–2
Aluminum shipments by end-use market and product type, 1982-92, annual rpt, A0400–2.1
Billings of top 500 architectural and engineering design firms, 1992, annual article, C5800–2.522
Building owner value of properties owned and additions, and construction in progress, top 700 owner firms, 1991, annual article, C5800–2.504
Building systems engineer views on influence of terror threats and World Trade Center bombing on own designs and specifications, 1993 article, C1850–12.506
Business failures and liabilities, by detailed industry, cause, length of operation, and location, 1991-92 and trends, annual rpt, C3150–8
Commercial contract square footage, monthly rpt, U1245–3
Commercial real estate market conditions and outlook, for industrial and office properties, by US metro area and selected foreign city, 1992-93, annual survey, A8916–1
Commercial real estate market conditions and outlook, for industrial and office properties in major metro areas, 1993 annual rpt, B2800–3
Congressional campaign finances, with detailed data for individual Members, and leading contributors by type and industry, 1990 election and trends, biennial rpt, R3828–2.2
Contract value, by construction type and region, including floor area and number of residential units, 1992-93, annual rpt, C5800–15.501, C5800–15.504, C5800–15.507, C5800 26
Contract value, by construction type and region, including floor area and number of residential units, 1992-93, periodic update, C5800–29
Contract value, by project type, 1991-93, annual article, C5800–2.502
Contract values of top 100 construction mgmt firms, and employee compensation by position, 1992 and trends, annual article, C5800–2.533
Contract values, total and foreign, with rankings of top 400 contractors, errata, C5800–2.506
Contract values, total and foreign, with rankings of top 400 contractors, 1992, annual rpt, C5800–2.529
Cost indexes for construction, equipment, and labor, by type and location, weekly rpt quarterly feature, C5800–2.508, C5800–2.521, C5800–2.534, C5800–2.547
Discount and off-price specialty chain new and remodeled stores, with costs, 1991-92, article, C5150–3.506

Index by Subjects and Names

Construction industry

Economic indicator historical trends, 1900s-92, annual rpt, R9050–1.2

Electric power generating capacity of units under construction, by utility, 1993-2003, annual rpt, A8630–2

Electric power plants planned and under construction in 1993, by type, utility, and region, and forecast capacity for 1993-2001, annual feature, C5800–28.503

Electric power transmission facility additions/upgrades planned, by facility and region, winter 1992/93, C5800–28.504

Electric utility construction and capacity outlook, including data by region and fuel source, 1992-2001, annual feature, C5800–28.501

Electric utility industry construction expenditures, with detail by type of plant, 1991-95, recurring article, A4700–4.505

Engineers salaries by industry group, census div, selected metro area, and years since college degree, 1993, annual survey rpt, A0685–5

Engineers salaries by industry group, census div, selected metro area, degree level, and years since college degree, 1993, annual survey rpt, A0685–3

Europe construction industry domestic and foreign mergers/acquisitions, for 23 Eastern and Western European countries, 1992 article, C5800–2.507

Fatal accidents in construction industry, by type, 1991/92, article, U8710–1.504

Federal office building construction project costs and size, for 9 projects, 1992 article, C3950–1.503

Finances and operations for construction industry, by type of business and region, 1992-93, annual survey rpt, A4155–1

Finances and operations for top design/construction companies, and public sector construction activities, 1992-93 annual features, C1850–9

Financial performance and growth rankings for approx 1,000 top corporations, with comparisons by industry group, 1993 annual rpt, C3950–1.505

Financial ratios and performance, for over 350 SIC 4-digit industries, FY88-92, annual rpt, A6400–3

Food plant construction/expansion project info, cost, and employees, by company, 1992, annual feature, C2150–6.506

Forecasts of economic indicators for approx 10-13 months, monthly rpt, U1880–3

Franchise operations and finances, by type of business, 1991/92 and trends, annual rpt, A5820–1

Govt agencies construction value and activities, for top 25 Federal or State agencies, FY92, annual article, C1850–9.501

Hospital planning activity, including construction plans and influence of anticipated health care reform, 1993 survey, article, A1865–1.523

Intl construction cost indicators for selected countries and cities, with data by project and material type and wage rates, 1992 article, C5800–2.502

Intl construction design firms foreign billings, specialties, and work locations, for top 200 firms, 1992, annual article, C5800–2.538

Intl construction firms foreign and total contract values, errata, C5800–2.511

Intl construction firms foreign and total contract values, for top 225 firms, 1992, annual feature, C5800–2.542

Japan public and private construction market value and contracts awarded to US firms, and US Govt contract value won by Japanese firms, 1988-92, article, C5800–2.528

Latin America statistical abstract, general data by country, 1992 annual rpt, U6250–1.7, U6250–1.13, U6250–1.32

Library construction, costs, and funding sources, by State, city, instn, and library type, FY92 and trends, annual article, C1852–1.501

Library construction, costs, and funding sources, by State, city, instn, and library type, FY92 and trends, annual compilation, C1650–3.4

Loans closed for nonresidential construction, with related mortgage market trends and devs, monthly rpt, A6450–2

Military commissary construction contract value and completion dates, by military base, 1993 article, C0500–1.503

Military commissary construction projects approved, including planned square footage, by site, 1993 article, C0500–1.510

Museums and related instns size, renovations, and relocations, by type and governing authority, 1989/90 survey, A0750–1.1

Natural gas industry construction expenditures, by facility type, 1960s-95, annual rpt, A1775–3.8

Natural gas processing plants planned or under construction, by country or world area, 1992-93, annual article, C6985–1.537

Nuclear reactors in operation, with capacity, electricity generation, and construction, by unit and country, 1992, annual rpt, B6800–2.2

Office property rental rates, vacancy, and construction, for major metro areas, quarterly rpt, B2800–4

Office space construction, for 14 metro areas, 1993 article, C8900–1.520

Offshore oil/gas production system projects under construction or planned, by company and country, 1992 annual feature, C6985–2.501

Oil and gas drilling activity, and refinery operations including production and construction cost indexes, by country and US State, 1991 and trends, annual compilation, C6985–9.1

Oil and gas industry trends, with data by company, State, and country, 1993 annual compilation, C6985–4

Oil and gas pipeline construction, by world area, 1980-92, annual compilation, C6985–9.4

Oil and gas pipeline construction costs, mileage, and operating and financial data, by location and/or company, 1991 and trends, annual feature, C6985–1.504

Oil and gas pipeline construction planned, by world area, 1992 annual rpt, C6985–5.2

Oil and gas pipeline mileage under construction or planned in 1993, for 5 world areas, Canada, and US, annual article, C6985–1.515

Operating and financial composite ratios for corporations, with establishments and receipts, for approx 200 industries, by asset size, FY90, annual rpt, C7800–1

Pipeline construction activity and costs, by location, item, and pipe diameter, 1993 annual rpt, C6985–3.3

Pipeline construction projects planned in foreign countries, including costs, by company, 1994, annual feature, C6780–2.504

Pipeline construction projects planned in US, Canada, and other countries, including costs, by pipeline type and company, 1993 annual feature, C6780–2.502

Piping system installation costs, by project characteristics, for 33 types of corrosion-resistant piping, 1993 article, C5800–8.503

Plastics industry production and sales by resin type, consumption by end-use market, and operating characteristics, 1992 and trends, annual rpt, A8920–1

Public opinion on honesty/ethical standards of building contractors, 1992 Gallup Polls and trends, C4040–1.501

R&D facility construction costs, with cost indexes for 23 cities, 1993 article, C1850–6.504

Retail chain construction activity, capital expenditures, and number of new stores, for leading firms, 1991-92, annual feature, C5150–4.503

Retail chain store expansion devs, and equipment and construction costs, by type of chain, 1993 annual articles, C5150–4.507

Revenues of design/construction companies in 7 categories, with employment and operating summaries, top 300 firms, 1992, annual feature, C1850–9.502

Shopping center expansion and renovation costs, by building characteristics and region, 1991, annual rpt, A5600–6

Shopping center expansion plans of top 10 developers, with square footage added, and new centers, 1991-92, annual article, C5150–4.506

Shopping center renovation and expansion activity, by type and age of facility, 1993 triennial rpt, R9285–1

Specialty firm revenues, and contract values, by specialty, for top 600 contractors, 1992, annual article, C5800–2.548

Statistical profiles of 50 States and DC, general data, 1993 annual almanac, C4712–1

Supermarket construction costs and related data, 1992 and trends, annual rpt, A4950–2

Underground pipeline and utility construction industry intl devs, articles and special features, monthly rpt, C6780–2

Urban nonresidential construction cost indexes, for 21 metro areas, with cost increase by region, monthly rpt quarterly feature, C5800–15

Value of new contracts and/or construction put in place, with data by project type, State, and region, 1993 annual feature, C5800–2.512

Value of new residential, commercial, industrial, and public construction put in place, monthly rpt, A7000–1

Construction industry

Value of residential, nonresidential, and nonbuilding construction, 1991-93, article, C1850–4.501

Veterinary clinic construction costs, by clinic type, 1992-93, annual article, C9480–1.504

West Coast employment by industry div, and construction activity, for 3 States, various months 1992-93, article, A6400–2.504

State and local:

Alabama statistical abstract, general data, 1992 recurring rpt, U5680–2.3

Arizona construction industry employment and job outlook, by occupation and county, 1990-95, triennial rpt, S0465–2.34

Arizona construction industry employment distribution by occupational group, 1992 and trends, article, S0465–1.507

Arizona economic condition, including population, employment and earnings, and business activity, by industry and locality, 1985-93, semiannual rpt, U5850–1

Arizona statistical abstract, general data, 1993 recurring rpt, U5850–2.15

Arkansas business and economic activity indicators, quarterly rpt, U5930–1

Arkansas traffic accidents occurring in construction zones, 1991, annual rpt, S0692–1

California economic condition, including population, employment and earnings, income, business activity, and taxation, 1993 annual rpt, S0840–3

California economic indicators, bimonthly rpt, S0840–1

California statistical abstract, general data, 1992 annual rpt, S0840–2.9

Colorado value of construction by type, 1983-92, annual rpt, S0980–1

DC statistical profile, general data, 1992 annual rpt, S1535–3.3

Delaware data book, general data, 1993 annual rpt, S1375–4

Florida statistical abstract, general data, 1992 annual rpt, U6660–1.11

Georgia business activity indicators, bimonthly rpt, U6730–2

Georgia statistical abstract, general data, 1992-93 biennial rpt, U6730–1.10

Hawaii construction activity and cost indexes, quarterly rpt, S2090–2

Hawaii counties population and economic indicators, 1993 annual rpt series, B3500–2

Hawaii data book, general data, 1992 annual rpt, S2090–1.13, S2090–1.21

Hawaii economic indicators, bimonthly rpt, B3500–1

Illinois economic and business activity indicators, including data by industry and county, bimonthly rpt, S2405–2

Illinois statistical abstract, general data, 1992 annual rpt, U6910–2

Illinois traffic accidents, fatalities, and injuries occurring in construction work zones, 1987-91, annual rpt, S2540–1

Kentucky economic statistics, general data, 1993 annual rpt, S3104–1.1

Kentucky residential and nonresidential construction and value, 1982-91, annual rpt, S3120–1

Maine traffic accidents involving construction equipment and zones, 1992, annual rpt, S3475–2

Index by Subjects and Names

Mississippi statistical abstract, general data, 1992 annual rpt, U3255–4.14

Nevada business and economic activity indicators, with comparisons to other Western States, 1980-91, annual rpt, U7920–2

Nevada traffic accidents occurring in construction zones, 1992, annual rpt, S5140–1

New Jersey construction activity and costs, including nonresidential construction by building type and county, 1991 and trends, annual rpt, S5425–3

New Jersey economic indicators, including employment, building permits, and retail trade, monthly rpt, S5425–1

New Jersey employment in 4 nonmanufacturing industry divs, by occupation, 1987 and 1990, article, S5425–1.506

New Mexico business and economic activity indicators, monthly rpt, U7980–1

New Mexico economic trends and outlook, by industry div, 1982-92, annual article, U7980–1.503

New York City commercial building leasing activity, vacancies, rental rates, and construction, by city area, 1988-92, annual rpt, B2800–5

New York State business activity indicators, quarterly rpt, S5735–2

New York State business and economic indicators, by MSA, county, and industry, 1980s-91, annual rpt, S5735–3

New York State statistical yearbook, general data, 1992 annual rpt, U5100–1.2, U5100–1.9

Ohio traffic accidents, deaths, and injuries involving construction equipment, 1991, annual rpt, S6290–1

Oklahoma statistical abstract, general data, 1992 annual rpt, U8130–2.13

Pennsylvania business activity indicators, monthly rpt, U4110–1

Pennsylvania statistical abstract, general data, 1992 recurring rpt, U4130–6.2

South Carolina statistical abstract, general data, 1993 annual rpt, S7125–1.11

South Carolina traffic accidents occurring in construction zones, 1990-92, annual rpt, S7190–2

Tennessee business activity indicators, quarterly journal, U8710–1

Tennessee construction starts and value, 1989-92, annual rpt, S7560–1

Tennessee statistical abstract, general data, 1992/93 annual rpt, U8710–2.6

Utah business activity indicators, by county, 1988-91, annual feature, U8960–2.501

Utah business activity indicators, by county, 1989-92, annual feature, U8960–2.507

Utah economic and business activity review and indicators, monthly rpt, U8960–2

Utah statistical abstract, general data, 1993 triennial rpt, U8960–1.11

Wyoming property assessed valuations and tax levies, by property type, tax purpose, and location, 1992 and trends, annual rpt, S8990–1.2

see also Building materials
see also Building permits
see also Cement and concrete
see also Housing construction
see also Housing maintenance and repair

see also Plumbing and heating
see also Shipbuilding and repairing
see also State funding for capital projects
see also Wrecking and demolition
see also under By Industry in the "Index by Categories"

Consultants

Architectural and engineering design firm billing rates for private and govt clients, by employee position, 1993 article, C5800–2.524

Auto customer use of 3rd-party pricing and buying services, by type, 1992 survey, article, C2710–3.547

Bar admissions, including foreign legal consultants, by State, 1988-92, annual rpt, A7458–1

Chemist and chemical engineer salaries, employment status, and demographic and professional characteristics, 1993, annual rpt, A1250–4

Computer systems integration consultant revenues and market shares, for top 5 companies, 1993, article, C8900–1.526

Congressional campaign spending for consultants by leading candidates, with rankings of top consultant firms by payments received, 1990 elections, C2500–6

Corporate communications mgmt, activities, budget, staffing, and use of outside services, 1992 survey, R4105–78.24

Engineers salaries by industry group, census div, selected metro area, and years since college degree, 1993, annual survey rpt, A0685–5

Engineers salaries by industry group, census div, selected metro area, degree level, and years since college degree, 1993, annual survey rpt, A0685–3

Financial ratios and performance, for over 350 SIC 4-digit industries, FY88-92, annual rpt, A6400–3

Food marketers mgmt info system operations, including use of outside firms, 1993, annual survey, A4950–7

Health care provider spending on consulting services, 1990 and 1992, article, A1865–1.521

Interior design industry financial and employment data, top 100 firms, 1993 annual article, C1850–7.501

Interior design industry financial and employment data, 2nd 100 largest firms, 1993 annual article, C1850–7.502

Investment mgmt consultants, with data on clients and staff, 1992 annual feature, C2710–2.501

Investment mgmt firms, assets and operating data for approx 900 instns, Jan 1993, annual feature, C2710–2.511

Local govt administrative assns, consultants, and officials, US and Canada, 1993 annual directory, A5800–1

Planning profession employment and salaries, by type of employer, demographic and professional characteristics, and location, 1991 and trends, biennial rpt, A2615–1

Retail chain store use of consultants, including performance ratings and expenditures, by consultant and/or chain type, Sept-Oct 1992 survey, article, C5150–4.504

Index by Subjects and Names

Salaries of scientists, engineers, technicians, and other professionals, by employee and employer characteristics, 1990s and trends, biennial rpt, A3960–1

Small business dev center client sales and employment trend, for new and established businesses, 1991, article, C4687–1.504

Utility mgmt audit/study contract values and consultants, by utility grouped by State, 1991/92 annual rpt, A7015–3

Veterinarian practice expenses as percent of revenues, by expenditure category and type of practice, 1990-91, annual survey article, C9480–1.501

see also Government contracts and procurement

Consumer complaints

see Consumer protection

Consumer cooperatives

Discount wholesale membership club importance to food industry, views of processing industry personnel, 1993 survey article, C2150–6.511

Discount wholesale membership club in-store bakery and total sales, 1991-93, article, C5225–1.509

Discount wholesale membership club income, stores, and sales trends, for selected leading chains, 1993 articles, C5150–3.506

Discount wholesale membership club prospects, views of food store industry executives, 1993 annual rpt, C5225–1.505

Discount wholesale membership club sales and stores, for top 10 chains, 1993 annual feature, C5150–3.514

Discount wholesale membership club sales and stores, for 9 major chains, with sales summary by product category, 1992 annual article, C8130–1.501

Discount wholesale membership club stores and sales, with data by company and location, 1991-92, annual feature, C8130–1.507

Discount wholesale membership club stores, by State and census div, 1992, annual feature, C5150–3.516

Discount wholesale membership club top food and nonfood products purchased for families and business, 1992 article, C8130–1.501

Sales volume shares by retail outlet type, for approx 300 food, drug, and other product categories, 1993 annual feature, C4655–1.504

see also Rural cooperatives

Consumer credit

Auto lending and leasing operations of financial instns, 1992 and trends, annual rpt, A4160–2

Auto loan installment credit, by type of lending instn, 1980-92, annual rpt, A0865–1.2

Auto loan installment credit outstanding, by type of lending instn, 1982-92, annual rpt, A7330–1

Bank noncurrent loans/leases, and losses, by type of loan, asset size, and metro status, 1992, semiannual rpt, A6400–4

Complaint and inquiry activity of Better Business Burs, by detailed type of business, 1992, annual rpt, A4350–1

Delinquency rates for approx 10 types of bank loans, and repossession data, by State, quarterly rpt, A0950–1

Europe public opinion on political, economic, and social issues of interest to foreign investors, for 9 countries and 3 Soviet Union Republics, 1991 survey, C8915–9

Forecasts of natl income and product account components, employment, and financial sector activity, monthly rpt, B4950–1

Foreign economic indexes, and leading and coincident indicators for US and other industrial countries, monthly rpt, U1245–1

Home equity lending activity and practices of financial instns, by region, asset size, and instn type, 1992, annual rpt, A4160–3

Japan consumer credit by type, with debt vs disposable income and savings, and comparisons to US, 1970s-92, article, R5650–2.542

Life insurance (credit) policies in force and issued, for top 100 companies, 1991, annual article, C1050–2.504

Mobile/manufactured home installment credit outstanding, by type of holder, monthly rpt, A6325–1

Operating and financial composite ratios for corporations, with establishments and receipts, for approx 200 industries, by asset size, FY90, annual rpt, C7800–1

Outstanding debt held by banks, finance companies, and other financial instns, 1980-92, R4700–22

Public opinion on business use of personal info, including views on privacy, credit, and effects of computer use, 1992 survey and trends, annual rpt, B3280–2

Soviet Union public opinion on allowing borrowing for consumer purchases, for 3 Republics, 1991 survey, C8915–8.2

State and local:

Alabama small loan and consumer credit licensee finances and loan analysis, Dec 1991, annual rpt, S0110–1

Idaho banks and other financial instns, financial condition, with data by instn and loan activity analysis, FY92 or 1991, annual rpt, S2235–1

Illinois Financial Institutions Dept activities, with financial and regulatory data for credit unions, consumer lenders, and other businesses, FY91 annual rpt, S2457–2

Kentucky consumer loan company loan amounts by type of collateral, 1992, annual rpt, S3121–1

New Jersey consumer lending and interest rate trends, by type of instn and loan, 1991-92, annual rpt, S5355–1

Wisconsin consumer credit company licensing and regulatory activity, 1992 and trends, annual rpt, S8685–1

see also Credit cards

see also Credit unions

see also Discrimination in credit

see also Finance companies

see also Pawnbrokers

see also Personal debt

Consumer Expenditure Survey

Black American household expenditures by item, with comparisons to total population, 1988-89, annual compilation, C6775–2.8

Consumer Price Index

Food away from home expenditures, by household characteristics and for 26 MSAs, 1991, recurring rpt, A8200–13

Hispanic American household expenditures by item, with comparisons to total population, 1988-89, annual compilation, C6775–3.6

Consumer expenditures

see Consumer Expenditure Survey

see Personal consumption

Consumer finance companies

see Finance companies

Consumer income

see Personal and household income

Consumer Price Index

Australia CPI, price index for manufacturing materials, and mining pay index, monthly rpt, B6800–1

Beverage CPI by product type, 1980-92, annual rpt, C4775–2.3

Beverage CPI by product type, 1992 and trends, annual rpt, C4775–1

Business and economic trends, production and price indicators, and industrial mgmt activities and devs, semimonthly rpt, C7000–3

Canada CPI, and price index for industrial products, monthly rpt, B6800–1

Economic indicator historical trends, 1900s-92, annual rpt, R9050–1.2

Economic outlook for selected indicators, recent trends and 2-year forecast, quarterly rpt, A3840–6

Electricity CPI, 1968-91, annual rpt, A4700–1

Food at home and away from home CPI trends, 1982-92, annual rpts, A4950–5

Food CPI, by item, 1992, annual rpt, C5225–1.505

Food CPI for fish/seafood, poultry, beef/veal and pork, 1991-92, article, A8200–1.509

Footwear CPI compared to other items, 1969-91, annual rpt, A4957–1.1

Forecasts for GDP and CPI from Congressional Budget Office, OMB, and private companies, 4th qtr 1992-95, article, B8500–2.523

Forecasts for real estate industry and US economy, and housing starts and sales trends by region, monthly rpt, A7000–1

Forecasts of economic indicators for approx 10-13 months, monthly rpt, U1880–3

Forecasts of natl income and product account components and related indicators, quarterly rpt, U1880–1

Forecasts of natl income and product account components, employment, and financial sector activity, monthly rpt, B4950–1

Foreign CPI and PPI trends, for 6 industrial countries compared to US, 1972-92, annual rpt, A3179–2.3

Gasoline and heating oil prices compared to CPI, 1918-91, annual compilation, C6985–9.3

Germany (West) and US comparative socioeconomic statistics, 1970s-91, annual rpt, A5135–2.2

Health care expenditures, by fund source and as percent of GDP and personal consumption, and medical care CPI, 1960s-91, annual fact book, A1275–1.4

Home heating oil retail price compared to CPI, 1956-92, periodic basic data book, A2575–14.3

Consumer Price Index

Household appliance industry manufacturing and market trends, by product type, various years 1920-94, biennial rpt, A3350–3

Industrial countries leading and coincident economic index trends, monthly rpt, U1245–1

Japan economic profile, including govt finances, industrial production, foreign trade and investments, and comparisons to US, 1988-92, annual feature, R5650–2.552

Latin America statistical abstract, general data by country, 1992 annual rpt, U6250–1.18, U6250–1.31

Malt beverages producer and retail price indexes, 1972-91, annual rpt, A3455–1.3

Meat CPI and PPI, for beef/veal, pork, other meats, poultry, and fish, 1983-91, annual rpt, A2100–1.1

Medical care and other components of CPI, 1969-91, annual rpt, A5173–2.3

Medical care CPI trends, by item and location, 1983-93, annual article, B6045–1.502

North Central States CPI, by population size group, quarterly rpt, S4895–2

Productivity and related indicators, trend analysis for US and other industrial countries, 1980s-92, annual rpt, R2800–2

Purchasing power as measured by CPI, and CPI trends, 1913-91, recurring rpt, U5680–2.14

Service industries economic devs, with analysis of conditions and outlook, and comparisons to other industries, quarterly rpt, A3892–1

Shoe industry production and operating data, including trade by country, retail sales, and consumer expenditures, quarterly rpt, A4957–2

South Africa economic indicators, with CPI, PPI, mining/quarrying employment and earnings, and gold milled ore working costs, monthly rpt, B6800–1

Travel price index trends, 1989-91, annual rpt, C2140–1.2

Urban consumers CPI trends, monthly rpt, S8205–6

Urban CPI, selected cities, 1991, annual rpt, U8710–2.2

State and local:

Alaska, Anchorage CPI, with detail by major component, 1970-92, annual article, S0320–1.501

Arizona business activity indicators, including housing market, population, CPI, and industrial purchasing, monthly rpt, U0280–1

Arizona, Phoenix area CPI for all urban consumers, monthly rpt, S0465–1

Arizona, Phoenix area CPI trends and forecasts, monthly rpt, U0282–1

California economic condition, including population, employment and earnings, income, business activity, and taxation, 1993 annual rpt, S0840–3

California economic indicators, bimonthly rpt, S0840–1

California statistical abstract, general data, 1992 annual rpt, S0840–2.4

Colorado, Denver area CPI, by component, 1st half 1992, semiannual feature, S1040–4.501

Colorado, Denver area CPI, by component, 2nd half 1992, semiannual feature, S1040–4.504

Colorado, Denver-Boulder area and US CPI, 1988-92, annual planning rpt, S1040–3.1

DC CPI by item, monthly rpt bimonthly feature, S1527–3.501, S1527–3.502, S1527–3.503, S1527–3.504, S1527–3.505

Florida CPI and price level index, by county and/or major item, 1992 annual rpt, U6660–1.24

Georgia, Atlanta area CPI, with comparisons to Southern US, bimonthly rpt, U6730–2

Georgia statistical abstract, general data, 1992-93 biennial rpt, U6730–1.3

Hawaii data book, general data, 1992 annual rpt, S2090–1.7, S2090–1.14

Hawaii, Honolulu CPI, bimonthly rpt, B3500–1

Hawaii, Honolulu CPI by major item, quarterly rpt, S2090–2

Illinois, Chicago CPI, with comparison to St Louis and North Central region, 1978-92, annual rpt, U6910–2

Illinois economic and business activity indicators, including data by industry and county, bimonthly rpt, S2405–2

Kansas business activity indicators, quarterly rpt, U7095–1

Maryland statistical abstract, general data, 1993-94 biennial rpt, S3605–1.6, S3605–1.10

Michigan, Detroit area CPI, monthly rpt, S3980–2

Minnesota, Minneapolis/St Paul area CPI, quarterly rpt, S4205–3

New Jersey economic indicators, with CPI for NYC and Philadelphia metro areas, monthly rpt, S5425–1

New York State business activity indicators, quarterly rpt, S5735–2

New York State statistical yearbook, general data, 1992 annual rpt, U5100–1.2

Oklahoma statistical abstract, general data, 1992 annual rpt, U8130–2.22

Oregon economic conditions, including population, construction, income, employment, industry, and foreign trade data, 1991, annual rpt, S6585–3

Oregon, Portland-Vancouver area CPI compared with US, monthly rpt, S6592–1, S6615–2

Pennsylvania, CPI for Philadelphia and Pittsburgh, monthly rpt, U4110–1

Washington State, Seattle area CPI, monthly rpt, S8340–3

Wisconsin, Milwaukee CPI, monthly rpt, S8750–1

see also Economic indicators

Consumer protection

Airline passenger complaints, by carrier, monthly rpt, C7000–4

College freshmen attitudes on govt policies regarding consumers, by sex and instn type, fall 1992, annual survey, U6215–1

Direct marketing mgmt info, including consumer complaints and handling, and mail volume and rates, 1992/93 annual rpt, A4620–1.5

Federal regulatory agency costs and staff, for approx 50 agencies, FY70s-94, annual rpt, U9640–1

Product liability lawsuit verdicts awarded, including number exceeding $1 million, 1981-91, annual rpt, A5650–1.3

Index by Subjects and Names

Public opinion on business use of personal info, including views on privacy, credit, and effects of computer use, 1992 survey and trends, annual rpt, B3280–2

Supermarket customer shopping patterns, and views on responsibility for ensuring product safety, 1993 and trends, annual survey rpt, A4950–3

Utility and transportation regulatory agencies receipt of consumer complaints, by agency, 1991, annual rpt, A7015–2

State and local:

Alaska insurance industry consumer complaints, FY91, annual rpt, S0280–3

Alaska public utility consumer complaints, by category and utility type, FY89-92, annual rpt, S0280–4.1

Arkansas child day care facility complaints, including abuse/neglect, by facility type, 1991, annual rpt, S0700–2.2

Arkansas utility customer complaints, by type and company, 1992 and trends, annual rpt, S0757–1

California insurance industry consumer complaint statistics, 1991, annual rpt, S0900–1

California public utility and transportation regulatory data, including revenue requests and rates of return by company, FY92 annual rpt, S0930–1

DC govt consumer complaints and investigations, FY87-91, annual rpt, S1535–3.3, S1535–3.4

Florida insurance dept consumer complaints, by type and line of coverage, FY92, annual rpt, S1760–1

Florida public utility regulatory and operating data, by company and utility type, 1992 and trends, annual rpt, S1790–1

Idaho insurance industry financial and underwriting data, by company and type of insurance, with regulatory data, 1991, annual rpt, S2260–1

Idaho public utility payments to intervenor consumer groups ordered by State utilities commission, 1985-92, annual rpt, S2290–1

Illinois Financial Institutions Dept activities, with financial and regulatory data for credit unions, consumer lenders, and other businesses, FY91 annual rpt, S2457–2

Kansas insurance dept consumer assistance activities, 1988-92, annual rpt, S2990–1

Nebraska insurance dept consumer complaint investigations, by type of insurance, 1990-92, annual rpt, S4890–1

New Hampshire insurance dept consumer complaints handled, FY92, annual rpt, S5220–1

New Jersey consumer complaints regarding financial instns, by type, 1992, annual rpt, S5355–1

New Mexico financial instn consumer complaints, by type of instn, 1991-92, annual rpt, S5652–1

New Mexico public utility customer complaints, by type of utility, FY92, annual rpt, S5645–1

New York State insurance dept activity, including consumer complaint cases and dispositions, 1991, annual rpt, S5770–3

Oklahoma insurance industry consumer complaints by reason and coverage type, 1992, annual rpt, S6462–1

Index by Subjects and Names

Consumer surveys

South Carolina insurance industry consumer complaints and investigations, FY92 annual rpt, S7195–1

South Carolina public utility customer complaints, by type of company, FY92, annual rpt, S7235–1

South Dakota insurance div consumer complaint cases closed, FY91-92, annual rpt, S7300–2

Tennessee consumer complaints, by insurance line, 1991, annual rpt, S7466–1

Tennessee financial instn consumer complaints, 1992, annual rpt, S7507–1

Tennessee public utility and transportation commission regulatory activities, with industry financial and operating data, 1991-92 biennial rpt, S7565–1

Texas insurance dept regulatory activities, with industry financial and underwriting data by line of coverage, FY92 annual rpt, S7700–1

Utah insurance dept consumer complaints processed and recoveries, 1991, annual rpt, S7845–1

Vermont financial instn consumer complaints and disposition, 1992, annual rpt, S7995–2

Vermont public utility customer complaints, by utility type, 1986-92, biennial rpt, S8100–1

West Virginia insurance dept consumer complaints filed, by line of coverage and/or company, 1991, annual rpt, S8575–1

Wisconsin consumer credit licensing and regulatory activity, including complaints handled by line of business, 1992 and trends, annual rpt, S8685–1

Wisconsin insurance industry consumer complaints filed, by line of coverage, 1992 and trends, annual rpt, S8755–1

see also Better Business Bureaus

see also Food ingredients and additives

see also Food inspection

see also Government-citizen lawsuits

see also Guarantees and warranties

see also Hazardous substances

see also Labeling

see also Landlord-tenant relations

see also Lawsuits

see also Licenses and permits

see also Motor vehicle defects

see also Motor vehicle safety devices

see also Packaging and containers

see also Product safety

Consumer surveys

Advertising campaign reactions of consumers in US, UK, and France, 1993 survey article, C2710–1.529

Airline passenger views on contribution of selected factors to overall satisfaction, Sept/Nov 1992 survey, article, C5800–4.507

Airline selection factors cited by US and foreign travelers, 4th qtr 1991, C7000–4.503

Airline travel frequency, destination, and purpose, by traveler characteristics, 1992 survey and trends, annual rpt, A0325–6

Auto and truck customer sales satisfaction index, by leading model, 1992-93, annual article, C2710–3.535

Auto and truck models and/or makes with fewest problems for buyers, with summaries for US, Asian, and European manufacturers, 1993 and trends, article, C2710–3.532

Auto consumer purchase plans, views on one-price vs negotiation retailing, and perceptions of dealer profits, 1993 survey, article, C2710–3.519

Auto customer preference for US vs Japanese cars, by age, 1993 survey article, C2150–3.508

Auto customer satisfaction index after 3 years of ownership, for top 14 nameplates, 1993, article, C2710–3.517

Auto customer satisfaction index, by leading model, 1992-93, annual article, C2710–3.538

Auto dependability index after 5 years of ownership, for top 12 nameplates, 1992-93, article, C2710–3.524

Auto do-it-yourself (DIY) maintenance activity, by type and consumer characteristics, 1993 and trends, annual survey, C0125–1.506

Auto maintenance activity and product purchasing, for imported vehicle owners, 1991 and 1993 surveys, annual article, C2150–10.508

Auto maintenance market, including consumer product purchase patterns and do-it-yourself activity, 1992 survey article, C2150–10.501

Auto maintenance market, including consumer product purchase patterns and do-it-yourself activity, 1993 annual survey feature, C2150–10.504

Auto parts shopping patterns of professional installers and do-it-yourself customers, 1993 survey article, C2150–10.503

Auto problems for buyers, for 7 European manufacturers, 1993, article, C2710–3.533

Auto purchasing and plans, including makes most likely to be purchased, by age group, 1993 survey article, C2710–1.539

Auto sales process improvements desired by consumers, and preferred day for auto shopping, 1993 survey article, C2710–3.547

Auto specialty equipment purchaser characteristics, 1992 survey article, C2150–10.501

Beverage purchasing at discount stores, and for leading fruit juice brands, 1993 survey articles, C5150–3.510

Black American shopping practices, with comparisons to non-blacks, 1993 survey feature, C4215–1.510

Books as Christmas gifts, public opinion, 1990-92 surveys, article, C1852–2.503

Brand purchasing in half-off and two-for-one sales promotions under selected conditions, 1993 feature, C1200–4.508

Cable TV network quality, awareness, and viewer satisfaction, for top 10 networks, 1993 survey article, C1858–1.505

Cable TV subscriber readiness to cancel if major broadcast networks are not included on system, Apr 1992 survey, article, C2710–1.533

Cable TV subscriber views on value, desirability, program quality, and service, 1991-93, survey article, C2710–1.544

Canada photographic and video equipment and supplies ownership, purchasing patterns, and use, by household characteristics, 1992 survey, recurring rpt, A8695–4

Cellular telephone installation plans of prospective auto buyers, 1992 article, C1575–2.501

Children's consumer attitudes and savings practices, Dec 1992-Jan 1993 survey, article, C2710–1.531

Children's hard goods purchaser outlet preferences, 1993 article, C8130–1.511

Children's toiletry product interest among consumers, and retail outlets shopped, 1993 survey article, C5150–2.519

Clock market trends, including types of clocks purchased and purchase influences, 1988-92 surveys, article, C2150–7.504

Clothing purchase shares by outlet and product type, 1991, article, C8130–1.501

Clothing purchaser outlet types shopped, age, and work class, 1993 survey article, C5150–3.516

Clothing shopping enjoyment, and activities cited as status symbols, 1989 and/or 1992, survey article, C8130–1.506

Concerns and views of consumers on selected topics, series, R4105–81

Corporate logos, consumer rankings of 5 best and worst, 1993 survey article, C5800–7.547

Corporate logos, consumer rankings of 6 best and worst, spring 1993 survey, article, C2710–1.544

Cosmetics consumer views on whether products are overpackaged, 1991-93, survey article, C1850–1.506

Craft activities of households, including retail outlets shopped for needlework supplies, 1990 and/or 1992, articles, C5150–3.504

Daily time allocation by type of activity, Apr 1993 survey, article, A8200–1.509

Direct marketing industry devs, including advertising patterns, finances, target market characteristics, and consumer attitudes, 1992/93 annual rpt, A4620–1

Discount chain consumer natl brand preferences, by product category and chain, and by age group, 1993 survey, annual feature, C5150–3.521

Discount store customer service improvement methods, views of consumers, 1993 survey article, C5150–3.513

Discount store ratings and shopping patterns of consumers in 3 market areas, including expenditures, by leading chain, 1992 surveys, article, C5150–3.503

Discount stores shopped and store characteristics, for 3 major chains in 3 market areas, 1993 surveys and trends, articles, C5150–3.516

Distilled spirits consumption, and consumer characteristics and buying habits, 1992 and trends, annual rpt, C4775–1.3

Drug (over-the-counter) packaging preferences of consumers, by presence of children, 1993 survey article, C1850–1.508

Drugstore chain and brand preferences of consumers, with data by product type and region, 1992 annual survey feature, C5150–2.503

Drugstore marketing to ethnic minorities, with related consumer indicators for blacks or by race, 1993 articles, C5150–2.518

EC airline deregulation effects on industry and passenger service, business traveler expectations, 1993 survey article, C7000–4.503

Consumer surveys

Economic conditions and change in income expected by consumers, and intended durable goods purchases by type, Conference Board monthly survey, R4105–4

Economic conditions and outlook for major purchases, consumer attitudes, monthly survey, U7475–2

Electric utility customer satisfaction, including likelihood of switching utilities if offered price reduction, 1993 survey article, C5800–28.505

Environmental claims by marketers influence on consumer purchasing decisions, 1992 survey feature, C1200–4.501

Financial advisor characteristics cited as most important by clients, 1993 survey article, C2425–2.504

Floor coverings purchaser buying practices, and effect of recession on home improvement plans, 1993 survey article, C5150–6.506

Food (single-serving packaged) use by consumers, by region, 1993 survey article, C1850–1.509

Food nutrition awareness and health concerns, including shopping and consumption patterns, by respondent characteristics, 1993 survey, annual rpt, A4950–36

Food service establishment patronage patterns, including use of take-out services, monthly rpt, A8200–1

Food shopper characteristics, for households shopping wholesale membership clubs vs supermarkets, 1992 survey, article, C2710–1.511

Food shopper use of supermarkets, wholesale membership clubs, and mass merchandisers for purchases of 6 types of perishable items, 1993 survey article, C5225–1.509

Food take-out consumer characteristics, consumption patterns, and attitudes, May 1992 survey, A8200–21

Food/beverage product issues ranked as important by consumers, 1992 survey article, C2150–6.501

Gardening and landscaping activities of do-it-yourself home improvement consumers, summer 1993 survey, article, C5150–6.508

Gift product categories consumers plan to buy for 1992 holiday season, 1992 survey article, C5150–3.503

Home improvement store kitchen installation and design service use, and kitchen and bathroom remodeling activity, Apr 1993 survey, article, C5150–6.504

Home ownership attitudes and outlook of owners and renters, 1991 survey, article, A7000–1.501

Home remodeling plans of consumers as affected by economic recession, 1992 survey, article, C1850–8.505

Homeowner views on characteristics and attributes of "traditional neighborhood development" housing, 1993 survey, article, C4300–1.510

Housing market current positive aspects cited by consumers, 1993 survey article, C4300–1.509

Jewelry purchaser characteristics, for diamonds and gold, 1993 annual almanac, C2150–7.509

Index by Subjects and Names

Juice drink paper box container preferences, by consumer age group, 1992 survey, C1850–1.501

Low-calorie and reduced-fat product use, for US and Canada, 1993 article, C2150–6.508

Mail (3rd-class) reading and usefulness, 1988-91, article, C1858–1.505

Men's grocery product purchasing, with comparisons to women, by detailed product type, 1992 article, C5225–1.501

Minority consumer purchasing by product type, and ownership of selected electronics, for blacks, Hispanics, and Asians, 1992/93 survey, article, C2710–1.513

Pharmacist requirements under 1990 Omnibus Budget Reconciliation Act (OBRA) to keep Medicaid patient drug use records and offer counseling, consumer views, 1993 article, C5150–2.509

Photographic equipment and supplies, consumer ownership, purchasing patterns, and use, 1993 survey and trends, recurring rpt, A8695–2

Private label product characteristics and purchasing factors as seen by consumers, by selected characteristics, 1991 survey, article, C0125–1.504

Product packaging views and attitudes of consumers, 1993 survey, article, C1850–1.505, C1850–1.507

Product quality importance and methods used to assess quality, 1993 survey article, C1850–8.507

Recreational vehicle and travel trailer selection factors cited by owners, 1990 and 1993, survey article, C8950–2.503

Recreational vehicle owners length of time between purchases of vehicles, 1993 survey article, C8950–2.505

Restaurant (table service) operations and menu offerings, and related consumer views and practices by demographic characteristics, 1992, recurring rpt, A8200–11

Restaurant dessert operations and consumer ordering patterns, 1992 survey rpt, A8200–20

Restaurant ethnic food ordering practices of consumers, 1992 survey, C1850–3.510

Restaurant patron characteristics and attitudes, survey rpt series, A8200–8

Restaurant patronage patterns, expenditures, and food preferences, 1992 survey, recurring feature, C1850–3.501

Restaurant quality ratings among consumers, for most popular chains, 1993 annual feature, C1850–3.504

Restaurant selection factors for family meals, May 1993 survey, C1850–3.513

Restaurant smoking policy importance to consumers by own smoking status, and views on smoking acceptability in public places, 1993 survey, A8200–1.506

Retail outlet selection factors cited by consumers, by race, 1993 survey article, C4215–1.509

Retail shopping patterns and expenditures, by outlet type and demographic characteristics, 1993 annual feature, C4655–1.504

Retail shopping patterns, including outlet preference trends and buying on sale, 1993 article, C5150–4.508

Retail store customer service improvement methods, views of consumers by outlet type, 1993 survey article, C8130–1.509

Retail store shopper methods of saving money on purchases, including use of private label products, 1989-91, survey article, C8130–1.504

Snack food consumption patterns, by snack type and consumer characteristics, 1989/90 and trends, recurring rpt, A8905–2

Sporting goods purchaser characteristics, by product category, 1992, annual survey rpt, A8485–4

Sporting goods purchases, by product and outlet type, census div, and purchaser characteristics, with average prices, 1992 and trends, annual survey, A8485–2

Supermarket bakery and deli shopper characteristics and shopping patterns, 1993 annual survey article, C5225–1.508

Supermarket bakery dept shopping frequency, by shopper characteristics, 1991-92, annual article, C5225–1.504

Supermarket customer views on bakery and deli dept products, and shopping patterns, 1993 survey article, C4655–1.507

Supermarket shopper actions taken to protest food products or company policies, Jan 1991-92, article, C2150–6.504

Supermarket shopper attitudes, practices, and characteristics, 1993 annual rpt, C5225–1.505

Supermarket shopper perception of change in product variety at stores that reduced number of duplicate items carried, 1993 survey article, C5225–1.509

Supermarket shopper practices, attitudes, and expenditures, by respondent characteristics, 1993 and trends, annual survey rpt, A4950–3

Supermarket shopper readiness to switch brand and size if preferred brand/size is unavailable, by selected product type, 1993 survey article, C5225–1.507

Supermarket shopper views on quality of customer service and importance of selected factors, by respondent characteristics, 1991-92 surveys, A4950–37

Teenage girls cosmetics use and views on drugstore marketing, 1993 articles, C5150–2.508

Telephone Yellow Pages directory use among consumers, with detail by respondent characteristics, 1992 survey, annual rpt, A9500–2

Truck do-it-yourself maintenance activity by type, 1992 article, C0125–1.501

Trucks (light) accessory purchasing, and owner characteristics, 1993 annual survey feature, C2150–10.506

TV advertisement recall by consumers, top brands or companies, 1st qtr 1993 and trends, article, C2710–1.530

TV home shopper characteristics, 1993 article, C5800–7.538

TV interactive services and costs, consumer opinions, Sept 1993 survey, article, C2710–1.549

Water (bottled) purchaser reasons for purchase, 1992/93 annual rpt, C0125–3.1

Wine and other alcoholic beverage consumption, and consumer characteristics and buying habits, 1993 annual rpt, C4775–2.2

Index by Subjects and Names

Contracts

Women age 18-29 beauty product use and shopping practices, 1993 articles, C5150–2.514

Women's shopping patterns for cosmetics and fragrances, with views on store attributes, by outlet type, 1993 survey, annual feature, C5150–2.516

Women's use and shopping patterns for personal care products, with preferred outlets and brands, 1993 survey and trends, annual feature, C5150–2.515

Women's views on offensiveness of selected aspects of advertising compared to men, and use of 6 supermarket promotions, 1993 survey article, C1200–4.507

State and local:

California new home shopper purchase motivations and design features sought, 1992-93 surveys, article, C1850–8.509

Florida consumer confidence index, 1989-92, annual rpt, U6660–1.24

see also Media use surveys

see also Opinion and attitude surveys

Consumers

see Boycotts

see Consumer cooperatives

see Consumer Price Index

see Consumer protection

see Consumer surveys

see Cost of living

see Family budgets

see Food consumption

see Personal and household income

see Personal consumption

see under names of specific commodities or commodity groups

Containerboard

see Paper and paper products

Containerization

Railroad freight car loadings by commodity, piggyback carloadings, and revenue ton-miles, monthly rpt, C8400–1

Railroad freight tonnage and revenue ton-miles, including intermodal carloadings and comparison to other modes, 1920s-92, annual rpt, A3275–5.2

Containers

see Containerization

see Packaging and containers

Contempt of court

State and local:

Illinois crimes and arrests, by offense, with data by location and offender characteristics, 1991, annual rpt, S2536–1

Continental shelf

see also Coastal areas

see also Offshore oil and gas

Continuing education

see Adult education

Contraception

see Contraceptives

see Family planning

Contraceptives

Black American health and vital statistics data, with comparisons to whites, 1970s-91, annual compilation, C6775–2.2

Black children and youth population, economic, health, and education data, with comparisons to whites, 1993 rpt, R3840–21

Condom ads for AIDS prevention, public opinion, 1987 surveys, A0610–1.502

Gallbladder disease incidence correlated with oral contraceptive use, review of epidemiological studies, 1993 article, A2623–1.510

High school students sexual activity and condom use, by sex and race-ethnicity, 1993 article, C4215–1.505

Latin America fertility and contraceptive use rates, for 11 countries, 1992, article, R8750–1.504

Latin America statistical abstract, general data by country, 1992 annual rpt, U6250–1.7

Men's sexual behavior, including condom use, and AIDS knowledge and risks, by selected characteristics, 1991 survey, articles, A5160–1.503

Middle East married women age 15-49 use of contraception, by country, various years 1987-92, R8750–2.59

Policy and medical aspects of family planning, with research findings on contraceptive use, abortions, and provider facilities, bimonthly rpt, A5160–1

Policy and medical aspects of intl family planning, with data on fertility, contraceptive use, and family size preferences, quarterly rpt, A5160–6

Public school condom distribution, public opinion by respondent characteristics, 1993 annual Gallup Poll, A8680–1.503

Sales and consumer expenditures, for food store products by type, 1991-92, annual feature, C4655–1.510

Sexual behavior among adults, including extramarital sex, condom use, and impact of AIDS, by demographic characteristics, 1990 survey, article, A2623–1.512

Women's sexually transmitted disease prevention using various contraceptive methods, review of research results, 1992 article, A2623–1.501

World contraceptive use among married women, by region and country, 1993 annual data sheet, R8750–5

World contraceptive use by method, and access to affordable methods, by country, 1992/93 biennial rpt, R9455–1.5

World family planning and fertility trends, and contraceptives effectiveness, safety, and availability, by method, series, U2520–1

State and local:

Minnesota abortions, by women's age, marital status, and contraceptive use, 1991, annual rpt, S4190–2

Oregon abortions, by type of contraceptive used, 1991, annual rpt, S6615–5

Contracts

Airline maintenance budget, employment, and contracting trends, for 38 carriers worldwide, 1992 article, C7000–4.501

Architectural firm services included in basic contracts, 1993 survey article, C5800–15.506

Association executives employment contract provisions, 1992, biennial rpt, A2900–3

Computer application outside contracting market, with shares for top 5 and all other major vendors, 1991 and 1997, article, C1850–5.502

Computer manufacturer contract revenues, for 4 major firms, 1993, article, C5800–7.528

Construction industry finances and operations, by type of business and region, 1992-93, annual survey rpt, A4155–1

Corporate employee transfers, use of contracts with household goods carriers, 1992, annual survey, B0600–1

Electric utility competitive bidding project contracts signed, and capacity involved, by fuel source, as of Nov 1992, article, C6985–6.506

Electronics contract manufacturing sales of top 6 contractors, with selected detail by major customer, 1993 annual feature, C1850–2.510

Food service (institutional) financial and operating data, for leading firms by market segment, 1993 recurring feature, C1850–3.511

Higher education physical plant operations, including types of functions contracted, by instn and region, 1991/92, recurring rpt, A3183–1

Homebuilder use of subcontractors, by sales size group, 1992 survey, article, C4300–1.501

Hospital involvement in capitated contracting with physician groups, 1993, article, A1865–1.512

Hospital use of contract hospitality, business, and clinical services, including contract terms, 1993 survey, annual article, A1865–1.514

Intl construction firms foreign and total contract values, for top 225 firms, 1992, annual feature, C5800–2.542

Liquefied natural gas trade by country and outlook, and trading contracts in effect with participants, 1993 article, C6985–1.535

Plastics processing industry manufacturers sales representative contract and commission policies, 1992 survey, biennial rpt, A8920–3

Security equipment industry revenues, accounts, and operating data, for 100 leading companies, 1992, annual feature, C1850–13.507

State appellate and trial court caseloads and dispositions, by case type and State, 1991 and trends, annual rpt, R6600–1

Utility mgmt audit/study contract values and consultants, by utility grouped by State, 1991/92 annual rpt, A7015–3

State and local:

Alaska corrections service contracts and value, by program, 1991 annual rpt, S0287–1

Arizona court cases and dispositions, by type of case and court, with judicial personnel and finances, by county and city, FY92, annual rpt, S0525–1

Arkansas court caseloads and dispositions, by type of court and case, and location, FY92 and trends, annual rpt, S0647–1

Arkansas farmer use of price hedging techniques, including govt programs, forward and futures contracts, and crop insurance, for 3 crops, July 1992 survey, article, U5930–1.504

Kansas court caseloads and disposition, by type of court and case, and location, FY92, annual rpt, S3035–1

Maine court cases and dispositions, by type and location, FY92 and trends, annual rpt, S3463–1

Maryland court caseloads and dispositions, by type of court and case, and county, with judicial personnel and finances, FY92 and trends, annual rpt, S3600–1

Massachusetts court cases and dispositions, by type of court and case, and location, FY92 and trends, annual rpt, S3807–1

Contracts

Ohio court caseload and case disposition, by type of court and case, and location, 1992, annual rpt, S6385–1

see also Defense contracts and procurement

see also Escalator clauses

see also Futures trading

see also Government contracts and procurement

see also Labor-management relations, general

see also Labor-management relations in government

Contreras, Carlos A.

"Statistical Abstract of Latin America", U6250–1

Contributions

see Gifts and private contributions

Convalescent homes

see Nursing homes

Convenience stores

- Establishments operated or planned, and gasoline sales, by chain company, 1993 annual article, C4680–1.509
- Establishments, sales, and gasoline marketing, 1993 annual fact book, C4680–1.507
- Establishments with gasoline marketing operations, by chain company, census div, and State, 1992, annual article, C4680–1.502
- Establishments with gasoline marketing operations, by chain company, census div, and State, 1993, annual article, C4680–1.510
- Finances and stores of 5 chains with bankruptcy filings, 1991-92, article, C4680–1.505
- Financial and operating data for convenience store industry, by size category, 1992 and trends, annual survey rpt, A6735–1, A6735–2
- Financial ratios and performance, for over 350 SIC 4-digit industries, FY88-92, annual rpt, A6400–3
- Food service industry sales and establishments, with growth outlook, by market segment, 1993 annual feature, C1850–3.503
- Franchise operations and finances, by type of business, 1991/92 and trends, annual rpt, A5820–1
- Sales rankings by market segment, for leading food service organizations, 1992, annual feature, C1850–3.509
- Sales volume shares by retail outlet type, for approx 300 food, drug, and other product categories, 1993 annual feature, C4655–1.504
- Shopping center financial and operating data, with detail by type of tenant, US and Canada, 1991, triennial rpt, R9285–1

State and local:

Kansas robberies and value of stolen property, by location and property type, 1992, annual rpt, S2925–1.1

Conventions

- Business traveler and trip characteristics, including mode, purpose, and lodging, 1991, annual rpt, R9375–12

State and local:

- DC convention center bookings and revenues, FY83-91, annual rpt, S1535–3.3
- Florida, Miami convention revenue loss due to black boycott, for 5 organizations and aggregate 20 others, 1993 article, C4215–1.509

Hawaii data book, general data, 1992 annual rpt, S2090–1.7

see also Political conventions

see also State constitutional conventions

see also Treaties and conventions

Conversion of industry

- Defense budget for dual-use technology programs, by program type, FY93-94, article, C5800–4.515
- Defense industries conversion to nonmilitary production, with data on defense contracts and spending, top contractors, and employment by occupation, 1980s and trends, R4700–19

State and local:

California (Southern) aerospace company plans for converting from defense to commercial business, and for leaving the State, 1993 survey article, C5800–4.523

Convictions, criminal

see Sentences, criminal procedure

Cook County, Ill.

- Correctional instns, inmates, staff, and cost of care, by instn, US and Canada, with operating summary by State or Province, 1992, annual directory, A1305–3
- Election results, and voter registration trends, by county and/or district, 1992 general election, biennial rpt, S2445–1

Cook, Suzanne D.

"Tourism's Top Twenty: Fast Facts on Travel and Tourism, 1992 Edition", R9375–6

Cooke, James A.

"Traffic Management: Annual Salary Survey", C1850–11

Cooking equipment

see Household appliances and equipment

Cooking utensils

see Household supplies and utensils

Cooperatives

- Auto dealer views on dealer assn and manufacturer advertising programs, including natl campaign spending levels by medium, with data by vehicle make, 1993 survey article, C2710–1.518, C2710–3.521
- Drugstore (independent pharmacy) participation in buying groups, by census div and sales size, 1991, annual survey, B5165–1
- Electric utility income and operating data, by type of company and for individual locally owned utilities, 1993 annual directory, A2625–1.501
- Home improvement industry sales and operations, for top distributors, cooperatives, and marketing organizations, 1991-92, annual feature, C5150–6.502
- Hospitals affiliated with cooperative buying groups, 1991, annual survey, B5165–3

State and local:

Illinois telephone utility financial and operating data, by company, 1992, annual rpt, S2410–2

see also Condominiums and cooperatives

see also Consumer cooperatives

see also Rural cooperatives

see also Rural electrification

Coopers and Lybrand

- Family-owned business owner actions to ensure family succession, 1993 feature, C4687–1.509
- Hotel restaurant average check size and seat turnover, compared to all restaurants, 1993 article, C1200–5.505

Index by Subjects and Names

- Restaurant income and cost comparisons, for table service and hotel operations, 1992 feature, C1200–5.503
- Retailer inventory mgmt practices, including automated technology use, by retail outlet type, 1992 survey article, C5150–4.503
- Small corporation CEO outlook for investment in selected company functions, 1991-92, article, C4687–1.507
- Small corporation mgmt views on trends in State/local taxes and tax-related personnel, 1993 article, C4687–1.508
- Small corporation outside directors, by occupation, 1993 article, C4687–1.508
- Small corporation use of selected types of strategic business alliances, for manufacturing and service companies, June 1993 survey, article, C4687–1.512
- Soviet Union oil refined products demand, by product type, 1991, article, C6985–1.502

Copper and copper industry

- Capital spending plans for new mines and plants, by mineral and company, and mine production values, 1993 annual feature, C5226–2.503
- Latin America statistical abstract, general data by country, 1992 annual rpt, U6250–1.16, U6250–1.23, U6250–1.25
- Production, capacity utilization, and PPI of copper and other metals, monthly rpt, C7000–8
- Production, consumption, stocks, trade, and prices for approx 100 basic commodities, including by country and producing State, commodity yearbook for 1993, C2400–1, C2400–2
- Supply-demand for selected metals and nonmetallic minerals, with price data, US and worldwide, 1992-93 and trends, annual feature, C5226–2.505
- Supply of copper by source, consumption by end use, stocks, and trade, 1972-92, annual rpt, A4175–1

State and local:

- Arizona copper industry operations, including production, capacity, and reserves, by company and mine, with US and intl comparisons, 1991 and trends, annual rpt, S0497–1
- Arizona copper industry State/local taxes paid by type, 1992, article, C5226–2.508
- Arizona economic condition, including population, employment and earnings, and business activity, by industry and locality, 1985-93, semiannual rpt, U5850–1.1
- Arizona statistical abstract, general data, 1993 recurring rpt, U5850–2.14

Copyright

- Book publishing industry financial and operating data, by publisher type and size, and subject category, 1991 and trends, annual rpt, A3274–2
- Canada professional photography service consumer views on photo copyright ownership, 1992 survey, recurring rpt, A8695–4
- Multinatl corporation views on recognition and enforcement of intellectual property rights in selected countries, 1989 survey, R4105–82.2
- Theater income from royalties, 1988-92, annual survey, A9065–1

Index by Subjects and Names

Corporate bonds

State and local:

Florida State-supported universities copyright and patent applications and grants, by instn, FY92, annual rpt, S1725–1

see also Broadcast payments and rights
see also Patents
see also Trademarks

Corn

- Chicago Board of Trade futures and options trading in financial instruments and agricultural commodities, 1992, annual rpt, B2120–1
- Exports of farm products, by detailed commodity and country of destination, US and California, 1991, annual rpt, B9520–1
- Futures trading volume and prices at Kansas City Board of Trade grain market, with natl production by State, 1992, annual rpt, B1530–1
- Indonesia agricultural production trends and impacts of govt policies, for 5 major food crops, 1970s-80s, R5620–1.37
- Latin America statistical abstract, general data by country, 1992 annual rpt, U6250–1.24, U6250–1.25
- Popcorn market shares, with consumption data for microwave popcorn, for top 5-7 countries, 1993 feature, C2710–1.517
- Production, consumption, stocks, trade, and prices for approx 100 basic commodities, including by country and producing State, commodity yearbook for 1993, C2400–1, C2400–2
- Production, prices, and disposition of grain in States served by Minneapolis exchange, by commodity, 1992 and trends, annual rpt, B6110–1
- Supply and demand trends for corn and refined products, with data by State and foreign country, 1993 annual rpt, A4200–1

State and local:

- Alabama agricultural production, marketing, and income, by county and/or commodity, and farms and acreage, 1992 and trends, annual rpt, S0090–1
- Arizona agricultural production, marketing, and finances, by commodity and county, 1988-92, annual rpt, U5830–1
- Arkansas agricultural production, marketing, and finances, by commodity and county, with farms and acreage, 1992 and trends, annual rpt, U5920–1
- California field crops production, acreage, yield, and prices, by commodity and county, 1992 and trends, annual rpt, S0850–1.4
- California vegetable production, marketing, and prices, by commodity and use, 1992 and trends, annual rpt, S0850–1.3
- Colorado agricultural production, marketing, and finances, by commodity and/or county, with farms and acreage, 1992 and trends, annual rpt, S0985–1
- Florida field crop acreage, yield, production, and value, by commodity and/or county, 1992 and trends, annual rpt, S1685–1.4
- Florida vegetable, melon, and strawberry production, acreage, yield, shipments, and exports, 1991/92 and trends, annual rpt, S1685–1.2
- Georgia agricultural production, marketing, and finances, by commodity and/or county, and farms and acreage, 1991 and trends, annual rpt, S1855–1
- Hawaii agricultural production and marketing, by commodity and island, 1987-91, annual rpt, S2030–1
- Illinois agricultural production, marketing, and finances, by county or commodity, and farms and farmland, 1991 and trends, annual rpt, S2390–1
- Kansas agricultural production, marketing, and finances, by county and/or commodity, and farm acreage and value, 1992 and trends, annual rpt, S2915–1
- Kentucky agricultural production, marketing, and finances, by commodity and county; and farms, acreage, and value; 1992 and trends, annual rpt, S3085–1
- Louisiana agricultural production, marketing, and finances, by commodity or parish, 1985-91, annual rpt, U2740–1
- Michigan agricultural production, marketing, and finances, by commodity or county, 1987-91, annual rpt, S3950–1
- Minnesota agricultural production, marketing, and finances, by county or commodity, and farms and acreage, 1992 and trends, annual rpt, S4130–1
- Missouri agricultural production, marketing, and finances, by commodity and/or county, and farms and acreage, 1988-92, annual rpt, S4480–1
- Montana agricultural production, marketing, and finances, by commodity and county, 1991 and trends, annual rpt, S4655–1
- Nebraska agricultural production, marketing, and finances, by commodity and/or county, and farms and acreage, 1991 and trends, annual rpt, S4835–1
- New Jersey agricultural production, marketing, and finances, by commodity and/or county, and farms and acreage, 1986-91, annual rpt, S5350–1
- New Mexico agricultural production, marketing, and finances, by commodity and county, with farms and acreage, 1991 and trends, annual rpt, S5530–1
- New York State agricultural production, marketing, and finances, by commodity and/or county, and farms and acreage, 1992 and trends, annual rpt, S5700–1
- North Carolina agricultural production, marketing, and finances, by commodity and county, 1991 and trends, annual rpt, S5885–1
- North Dakota agricultural production and marketing, by commodity and county, and farm finances, 1992 and trends, annual rpt, U3600–1
- Ohio agricultural production, marketing, and finances, by commodity and county, with farms and acreage, 1990-91 and trends, annual rpt, S6240–1
- Oklahoma agricultural production, marketing, and finances, by commodity and county, 1992 and trends, annual rpt, S6405–1
- Oregon agricultural production, marketing, and finances, by commodity and/or county, with farms and acreage, 1991 and trends, annual rpt, S6575–1
- Pennsylvania agricultural production, marketing, and finances, by county and commodity, and farms and acreage, 1992 and trends, annual rpt, S6760–1
- South Carolina agricultural production and finances, by commodity and county, 1991-92 and trends, annual rpt, U1075–3
- South Dakota agricultural production, marketing, and finances, by commodity and county, and farms and acreage, 1992 and trends, annual rpt, S7280–1
- Tennessee agricultural production and marketing, by commodity and county, with farms, acreage, and farm value, 1992 and trends, annual rpt, S7460–1
- Texas agricultural production, marketing, and finances, by commodity and county, and farms and farmland, 1991 and trends, annual rpt series, S7630–1
- Utah agricultural production, marketing, and finances, by commodity and county, with farms and acreage, 1992 and trends, annual rpt, S7800–1
- Vermont agricultural production, marketing, and finances, by commodity, with data on govt inspections and funding, 1989-90 biennial rpt, S7978–1
- Washington State agricultural production, marketing, and finances, by commodity and/or county, 1992 and trends, annual rpt, S8328–1
- West Virginia agricultural production, marketing, and finances, by commodity or county, 1991 and trends, annual rpt, S8510–1
- Wisconsin agricultural production, marketing, and finances, by commodity and county, and farms, acreage, and sales, 1992 and trends, annual rpt, S8660–1
- Wyoming agricultural production, marketing, and finances, by county and/or commodity, and farms, acreage, and value, 1992 and trends, annual rpt, S8860–1

Coroners

State and local:

- Colorado deaths certified by coroners and physicians, by county, 1990, annual rpt, S1010–1
- Massachusetts deaths certified by medical examiners, by cause, sex, race, age, and county, 1990, annual rpt, S3850–1
- Ohio election results and voter registration, by local area, 1991-92 and trends, biennial rpt, S6380–1
- South Carolina deaths, by certifier, race, and county, 1990, annual rpt, S7175–1

Corporate bonds

- Default rate, loss, and recovery price trends for publicly traded bonds, 1970s-91, article, A6400–2.505
- Forecast corporate bond yield, quarterly rpt, U1880–1
- Forecasts of economic indicators for approx 10-13 months, monthly rpt, U1880–3
- Forecasts of natl income and product account components, employment, and financial sector activity, monthly rpt, B4950–1
- Foreign investor participation in US securities markets, by world area and country, quarterly rpt, A8825–2
- Hospital unrated long-term bond issuances and value, 1991 and 1st 10 months 1992, article, A1865–1.503
- Issues and value of bonds for financial instns, industrial companies, and utilities, 1992, article, C2710–2.507
- Life insurance industry income and financial data, including investments by type of security, 1991 and trends, biennial fact book, A1325–1.4

Corporate bonds

Money and securities market activity, and related indicators, biweekly rpt, B2000–1
Mutual fund sales, assets, and investment activities, with data on money market and municipal bond funds, monthly rpt, A6025–5
Mutual funds asset composition, by type of financial instrument and investment objective, 1991 and trends, annual rpt, A6025–1
New York Stock Exchange activity, including stock volume and prices, credit distribution, and member firm characteristics, 1992 and trends, annual fact book, B6625–1
Underwriting of corporate bonds, periodic rpt, A8825–1
Unit investment trust sales volume and value, by trust type, maturity period, and insurance features, monthly rpt, A6025–7
Utility long-term financing and yields, by type of issue and/or utility, 1991 and trends, annual rpt, A4700–1
Yields of broad investment grade bonds, 1990-July 1993, article, C2710–2.516

State and local:
Arkansas State treasurer safekeeping account balances and interest rates, by account, FY92, biennial rpt, S0780–1
see also Industrial revenue bonds

Corporate net worth
see Business assets and liabilities, general
see Business assets and liabilities, specific industry

Corporate profits
see Business income and expenses, general
see Business income and expenses, specific industry

Corporate rankings
Advertising agency employment, for top 16 firms, Oct 1991-92, annual feature, C2710–1.505
Advertising agency income and billings, for top 10-20 multinatl firms in Latin America, Europe, and Asia/Pacific, 1992, annual article, C2710–1.527
Advertising agency income, billings by medium, employees, and offices, for leading US and/or foreign agencies, 1992 and trends, annual rpt, C2710–1.522
Advertising expenditures by medium for top 100 advertisers, with comparisons to earnings and sales, and detail by product type and brand, 1991-92, annual rpt, C2710–1.547
Advertising expenditures for top 10 advertisers, 1st qtr 1992-93, article, C2710–3.544
Advertising expenditures for top 10 manufacturers of 200 leading brands, weekly rpt quarterly feature, C2710–1.502, C2710–1.512, C2710–1.525, C2710–1.540
Advertising expenditures for top 25 network TV advertisers, with detail for 4 networks, 1992, annual article, C2710–1.515
Advertising expenditures of corporations and assns, by medium, 1988-92, and top 10 advertisers for 1992, annual article, A8770–1.504
Advertising worldwide media and marketing, with data for leading periodicals, and expenditures by top advertiser and country, 1992 annual feature, C2710–1.506

Aerospace and defense industries financial performance, with data for approx 200 major US and foreign companies, FY92 and trends, annual feature, C5800–4.519
Aerospace contractors, NASA and DOD, top 30 companies, FY87-91, annual rpt, A0250–2.5
Airline (regional) passenger traffic, for top 50 companies and carriers, 1992, annual rpt, A8795–1.1
Airline intl and domestic passenger-kilometers flown by top 15 carriers worldwide, 1992, article, C5800–4.524
Airline market activity, including traffic, financial performance, employment, and fleet composition, by US and foreign carrier, 1991-92, annual feature, C7000–4.508
Airline passengers for top 50 carriers worldwide, 1991, annual rpt, C2140–1.5
Airline revenues, profits, and passenger traffic, for top 50 carriers worldwide, 1991, article, C8900–1.501
Airline service performance indicators, top 25 carriers, 1992, annual rpt, A0325–5
Airline traffic and load factors, on-time performance, and passenger complaint rates, by carrier, monthly rpt, C7000–4
Aluminum production capacity for top 20 producers, 1982-92, annual rpt, A0400–2.1
Apartment units owned by top 10 companies, 1993, C4300–1.508
Appliance manufacturers market shares, by product type, 1992, annual article, C2000–1.510
Architectural and engineering design firm billings, for top 500 firms, 1992, annual article, C5800–2.522
Auto advertising expenditures outside US by top 10 manufacturers, and billings for auto accounts changing agencies, 1993 article, C2710–1.509
Auto aftermarket retail sales, and number of stores and service bays, for top 100 chains, 1993 annual article, C2150–10.507
Auto dealer fleet vehicle sales, for top 30 dealers, 1992 article, C1575–2.501
Auto fleet dealer award recipients, and top dealer sales by make, 1992, annual feature, C1575–2.508
Auto insurance passenger and commercial premiums, market shares, and loss ratios, with rankings of States and 20 leading firms, 1992, annual article, C1050–1.511
Auto manufacturers ranked by share of passenger car market, 1973 and 1993, article, C2710–3.552
Autos and light trucks/vans in top 100 corporate fleets, 1993, annual feature, C1575–2.504
Autos and light trucks/vans in 2nd 100 largest corporate fleets, 1993, annual feature, C1575–2.506
Bank (master trust/custodial) assets and operating data for top instns, 1993 annual directory, C2710–2.522
Bank assets, equity, performance, and market value, top 50 instns worldwide, 1993 annual feature, C5800–7.535
Bank assets, for top 12 instns worldwide, 1992, article, C5800–7.529

Index by Subjects and Names

Bank assets, market capitalization, and financial ratios, for 6 largest instns, June 1993, article, C3950–1.527
Bank financial performance, including assets, loans, deposits, and operating ratios, top 100 instns, 1992, annual feature, C5800–7.526
Bank loans for corporate mergers/acquisitions, top 10 lending instns, 1992, article, C4683–1.504
Beer industry production, capacity, and sales volume, including top brands and brewers, 1982-92, annual feature, C0125–2.503
Beverage consumption and sales, by type, leading company, and brand, 1992 and trends, annual rpt, C4775–1.4, C4775–2.3
Beverage product market shares and sales, by company and/or brand, 1991 and trends, annual rpt, C0125–3.1
Black-owned enterprises financial and operating data, for top 100 firms and auto dealerships and for top 15-25 financial instns, 1992 and trends, annual feature, C4215–1.507
Black-owned franchises, with type of business and startup costs, top 50 companies, 1993 annual article, C4215–1.510
Book publishing sales, for top 11 general trade publishers, 1991-92, article, C1852–2.524
Book superstore sales and outlets for top 6 chains, Jan 1993, article, C1852–2.514
Bookstores and sales of 11 largest trade bookstore chains, 1991-92, article, C1852–2.516
Broadcast industries and cable TV devs, including data on finances, advertising, ratings, and licensing, weekly rpt, C1850–14
Broadcasting and related electronic communications companies revenues and earnings, top 100 companies, 1992, annual article, C1850–14.526
Building design/construction company revenues and operations, for top 300 firms, 1991, annual feature, C1850–9.502
Building owner value of properties owned and additions, and construction in progress, top 700 owner firms, 1991, annual article, C5800–2.504
Bus (urban) fleets of 100 largest transit systems in US or Canada, 1993, annual article, C1575–3.507
Bus company fleets, for top 50 private operators in US and Canada, 1993 annual feature, C1575–3.503
Buses/vans owned or leased by major transit systems, top 41 and all other manufacturers, 1992 annual rpt, A2650–1.2
Business Week economic, business, and investment devs, with related statistical indicators, weekly rpt, C5800–7
Cable TV advertising interconnect subscribers, for top 50 interconnects, June 1993, recurring feature, C1858–1.505
Cable TV advertising interconnect subscribers, for top 50 interconnects, Sept 1993, recurring feature, C1858–1.508
Cable TV industry devs, including leading multiple system operators and systems, finances, advertising, and data by network and service, biweekly rpt, C1858–1, C2965–1

Index by Subjects and Names

Corporate rankings

Cable TV subscribers of top 8 cable companies not affiliated with telephone companies, 1993 article, C4725–3.517

Candy (gummy) sales, total and for top 10 manufacturers, 1992-93, article, C2710–1.548

Charitable contributions of largest corporate donors (unnamed), and relation to income, 1991, annual rpt, R4105–8

Chemical and allied industries earnings, sales, and profit margins, by company, weekly rpt quarterly article, A1250–1.502, A1250–1.514, A1250–1.525, A1250–1.536

Chemical company sales and profits, for top 50 producers worldwide, 1992, annual article, A1250–1.533

Chemical industry sales and operating summary for top 100 companies, 1992, annual article, A1250–1.523

Chemical industry sales and operating summary for top 50 companies, FY68, article, A1250–1.523

Chemical producers income, profits, and assets, for top 100 companies in sales, 1992, annual feature, A1250–1.530

Clothing and shoe industries financial performance indicators for 72 companies, FY92 and trends, annual rpt, B8130–2

Coffee market shares by company, for regular and instant brands, 1990-92, annual article, C2710–1.531

Commodity exchanges ranked by futures and options contract volume, 1991-92, annual rpt, A5040–1, C2400–1

Computer (personal) company revenues for top 50 firms worldwide, and top 50 marketing in North America, 1991, annual article, C1850–5.503

Computer company advertising expenditures, for top 5 advertisers in selected media, 1st half 1992, C2710–1.502

Computer industry advertising expenditures, for top 10 manufacturers and magazines, 1st half 1992-93, article, C2710–1.542

Computer manufacturer advertising expenditures and pages in magazines, for top 12 firms, 1st 8 months 1992-93, article, C2710–1.548

Computer software company revenues and employment, for top 100 firms worldwide, 1992, annual article, C1850–5.520

Computer systems integration consultant revenues and market shares, for top 5 companies, 1993, article, C8900–1.526

Computer/info systems companies revenues and other financial data, for top 100 firms worldwide and in North America, 1992 and trends, annual rpt, C1850–5.514

Congressional campaign finances, with detailed data for individual Members, and leading contributors by type and industry, 1990 election and trends, biennial rpt, R3828–2

Construction contract values, total and foreign, with rankings of top 400 contractors, 1992, annual rpt, C5800–2.529

Construction design firms foreign billings, specialties, and work locations, for top 200 intl firms, 1992, annual article, C5800–2.538

Construction intl companies foreign and total contract values, and work locations, for top 225 firms, 1992, annual feature, C5800–2.542

Construction mgmt firm total and foreign contract values for top 100 firms, and employee compensation by position, 1992 and trends, annual article, C5800–2.533

Construction specialty firm revenues, and contract values, by specialty, for top 600 contractors, 1992, annual article, C5800–2.548

Defense Commissary Agency payments to 406 suppliers receiving $1 million/more, with ranking of top 45 suppliers, FY92, article, C0500–1.506

Defense contractor military sales, and share of total sales, for top 10 contractors, 1991, article, C8900–1.509

Defense industries conversion to nonmilitary production, with data on defense contracts and spending, top contractors, and employment by occupation, 1980s and trends, R4700–19

Direct marketing billings in US and worldwide, for top direct response agencies, 1991-92, annual articles, C2710–1.535

Direct marketing industry devs, including advertising patterns, finances, target market characteristics, and consumer attitudes, 1992/93 annual rpt, A4620–1

Discount chain sales and merchandising, including data by dept, leading chain, and location, 1992 and trends, annual feature, C8130–1.507

Discount stores, sales, and earnings, for top chains, with detail by specialty, 1993 annual feature, C5150–3.514

Discount wholesale membership club income, stores, and sales trends, for selected leading chains, 1993 articles, C5150–3.506

Drug wholesale company revenues, market shares, and operating ratios, for 7 major firms, 1992-93, article, C3950–1.511

Drugstore chain pharmacy outlets for top 24 companies, 1993, annual feature, C5150–2.511

Drugstore chains financial performance and marketing operations, by US and Canadian company, 1993 annual feature, C5150–2.511

Electric power residential costs for 12 utilities with highest and lowest rates, summer 1992, annual article, C6985–6.508

Electric power residential costs for 12 utilities with highest and lowest rates, winter 1991/92, annual article, C6985–6.502

Electric utility customers, kWh sales, and revenues, rankings of largest 20 publicly owned utilities, 1991, annual feature, A2625–1.501

Electric utility financial and investment performance indicators, for top 50 companies, 1991, article, C5800–28.501

Electric utility financial and operating performance rankings, top 100 utilities, 1992, annual article, C6985–6.508

Electric utility operating data, for top 100 utilities ranked by heat rate (Btu/kWh), 1992, annual article, C6985–6.512

Electric utility revenues, sales, and distribution operating/maintenance expenses, for top 20 companies, 1990-91, article, C6985–6.501

Electrical equipment wholesalers, sales, employment, and facility size, top 250 companies, 1992, annual article, C4725–5.506

Electronics company financial performance, for top 100 multinatl firms, 1992 annual feature, C1850–2.502

Electronics company financial performance, ranking of top 200 firms, 1992 and trends, annual feature, C1850–2.509

Electronics industry market trends and outlook, including product sales and shipments, employment, and leading manufacturers, monthly rpt, C1850–2

Employee benefit plan asset rankings of top 1,000 funds, with selected fund investment data, 1992, annual feature, C2710–2.504

Europe and worldwide computer chip sales for top 12 companies ranked by sales in Europe, 1991, article, C5800–7.508

Europe computer advertising expenditures, for top 15 manufacturers, with detail by country, 1992, article, C2710–1.527

Europe corporate acquisitions involving companies from different and same countries, price and participants for top transactions, 1992, annual article, C4683–1.504

Europe electronics industry financial performance, for top 50 companies, FY91 or FY92, annual article, C1850–2.501

Europe household appliance production, sales, and market shares, by country, product type, and manufacturer, 1991-92, annual feature, C2000–1.508

Executives ratings of corporate performance, for leading companies in 32 industries, 1993 annual survey feature, C8900–1.508

Export sales ranking of top 50 companies, 1992, annual feature, C8900–1.517

Finance company assets, for 12 leading nonbank firms, 1989-91, R4700–22

Financial data for top 100 growth companies with sales under $150 million, 1993 annual article, C5800–7.529

Financial data for 250 corporations with rapid growth, 1993 feature, C5800–7.551

Financial losses for 10 corporations with all-time largest annual loss, 1993 article, C5800–7.517

Financial performance and growth rankings for approx 1,000 top corporations, with comparisons by industry group, 1993 annual rpt, C3950–1.505

Flour milling companies and capacity, in US by State, Canada, Mexico, and Central American and Caribbean area countries, 1993 annual directory and buyers guide, C8450–3

Food service (institutional) financial and operating data, for leading firms by market segment, 1993 recurring feature, C1850–3.511

Food service industry financial and operating data, for top 100 chains and companies, FY91-93, annual feature, C5150–5.509

Food service industry sales and establishments, for top 400 chains and other organizations, 1992, annual feature, C1850–3.509

Food store market shares and outlets, by company and store type, for approx 350 metro areas in US and Canada, with industry operating data, 1993 annual rpt, C3400–6

Corporate rankings

Forbes 500 top companies in sales, profits, assets, market value, and productivity, with stock and employment data, 1992, annual rpt, C3950–1.513

Foreign investments in US, foreign companies, and US multinatls, financial data for top 100-500 in each category, 1992, annual feature, C3950–1.519

Fortune magazine ranking of top 50-100 companies in 8 nonindustrial sectors, with financial and employment data, 1992, annual feature, C8900–1.516

Fortune magazine ranking of top 50-100 companies worldwide in 8 nonindustrial sectors, with financial and employment data, 1993 annual feature, C8900–1.522

Fortune 500 largest industrial corporations, sales, financial, and stock performance data by company, 1992, annual feature, C8900–1.513

Fortune 500 largest industrial corporations worldwide, with financial and employment data, 1992, annual feature, C8900–1.520

Foundation assets, income, and grants by type of recipient, with data for top organizations and by location, 1991 and trends, annual rpt, R4900–1

Foundations, assets, and contributions, by organization type and census div, with top 100 organizations, FY91, annual article, C2176–1.507

Gasoline sales and market shares, top 15 companies, 1991-92, annual fact book, C4680–1.507

Grain elevators and capacity in US and Canada, by type and State or Province, with ranking of top storage companies, 1993 annual directory and buyers guide, C8450–2

High-technology company market value, and computer network manufacturer revenues and earnings, for 10 firms, 1993 article, C8900–1.521

High-technology small companies with rapid growth, employment and sales data for 25 firms, 1993 article, C5800–7.551

Hispanic American marketing devs, including leading advertisers and media, and market characteristics, 1992 annual features, C4575–1.502

Hispanic American professional views on work conditions at own company, with ratings of regions and top 19-20 companies and industries, 1993 survey article, C4575–1.504

Hispanic-owned business sales and employment, for top 500 companies, 1992, annual feature, C4575–1.507

Hispanic-owned business sales and employment, for 100 fastest-growing companies, 1988-92, annual feature, C4575–1.509

Hispanic-owned high-technology company sales and employment, for top 50 firms, 1992, annual article, C4575–1.510

Home improvement industry sales and operations, for top distributors, cooperatives, and marketing organizations, 1991-92, annual feature, C5150–6.502

Home improvement industry sales and operations, for top retailers, 1992 and trends, annual feature, C5150–6.503

Home improvement industry sales, stores, and other operating data, for leading foreign chains by country, 1991-92, annual feature, C5150–6.503

Homebuilder financial and operating data, including detail by location, for top 400 builders, 1993 annual feature, C1850–8.507

Housing construction, revenues, and closings of top 100 homebuilding companies, 1992, annual feature, C4300–1.507

Industrial distributor sales, branches, employment, and operating profiles, for top 50 companies, 1992, annual article, C1850–4.506

Industrial distributor sales, employment, and inventory turns, for top 25 companies with sales of $5 million/less, 1991, annual article, C1850–4.503

Insurance (accident/health) premiums and underwriting ratios, for top 300 firms, 1991, annual article, C1050–2.502

Insurance (life/health) capital/surplus, for top 100 companies, 1987-91, annual article, C1050–2.504

Insurance (life/health) capital/surplus, for top 100 companies, 1988-92, annual article, C1050–2.512

Insurance (life/health) company assets, for top 100 firms, 1987-91, article, C1050–2.506

Insurance (life/health) company assets, net operating gain, and return on equity, for 100 largest firms, 1992, article, C1050–2.510

Insurance (life/health) income and expense data, for top 100 companies, 1992, annual article, C1050–2.511

Insurance (life/health) industry asset allocation and investment yields, for top 125 US and Canadian companies, 1992 and trends, annual article, C1050–2.512

Insurance (life/health) industry separate account assets, for top 15 firms, 1991, recurring article, C1050–2.505

Insurance (property/casualty) company assets, for top 100 firms, 1987-91, article, C1050–1.505

Insurance (property/casualty) company net premiums written, for top 100 firms, 1987-91, article, C1050–1.506

Insurance (property/casualty) income and expense data, for top 100 companies, 1992, article, C1050–1.511

Insurance (property/casualty) losses from Aug 1992 Hurricane Andrew, for 20 underwriters with greatest loss, 1992 article, C1050–1.503

Insurance (property/casualty) premiums, loss ratios, and market shares, for top 20 general liability, medical malpractice, fidelity, and surety underwriters, 1991 and trends, annual article, C1050–1.502

Insurance (property/casualty) premiums, loss ratios, and market shares, for top 20 workers compensation underwriters, 1991 and trends, annual article, C1050–1.501

Insurance (property/casualty) premiums written by top 250 companies and groups, 1992, annual article, C1050–1.508

Insurance (property/casualty) premiums written, loss ratios, and market shares, by line, leading company, and State, 1992 and trends, annual article, C1050–1.509

Interior design industry financial and employment data, top 100 firms, 1993 annual article, C1850–7.501

Interior design industry financial and employment data, 2nd 100 largest firms, 1993 annual article, C1850–7.502

Index by Subjects and Names

Investment banks with black owners, value of securities issues managed, for top 13 instns, Dec 1992, article, C4215–1.507

Investment mgmt companies new business, rankings of top 10 firms in selected categories, 1992, annual feature, C2710–2.506

Investment mgmt firm assets managed in index funds, top firms, Dec 1992, semiannual article, C2710–2.505

Investment mgmt firm assets managed in index funds, top firms, Mar 1993, semiannual article, C2710–2.516

Investment mgmt firms, assets and operating data for approx 900 instns, Jan 1993, annual feature, C2710–2.511

Investment mgmt firms in intl investing, tax-exempt assets and operating data for top firms, 1993, annual feature, C2710–2.514

Investment performance of leading funds with institutional investors, by fund and type, biweekly rpt quarterly feature, C2710–2.502, C2710–2.506, C2710–2.507, C2710–2.512, C2710–2.513, C2710–2.518, C2710–2.519

Japan defense budget allocations by equipment type, procurement, and value of contracts for top 10 contractors, various periods FY82-95, article, R5650–2.518

Japan defense contract value for top 10 contractors, FY91-92, article, R5650–2.533

Latin America statistical abstract, general data by country, 1992 annual rpt, U6250–1.29

Life insurance (credit) policies in force and issued, for top 100 companies, 1991, annual article, C1050–2.504

Life insurance annuity premium income and fund deposits of top 200 insurers, 1991, annual article, C1050–2.501

Life insurance average policyholder premiums and dividends, 10-year dividend scale comparisons, by insurer, 1993 annual article, C1050–2.510

Life insurance average policyholder premiums and dividends, 20-year dividend scale comparisons, by insurer, 1993 annual article, C1050–2.509

Life insurance premium income of top 500 US/Canadian life/health insurers, 1992 and trends, annual article, C1050–2.509

Life insurance sales and insurance in force, for top 25-135 issuers of ordinary, group, and industrial life policies, 1992, annual article, C1050–2.510

Life insurance sales, policies in force, and assets, for top 100 US/Canadian life/health insurers, 1992, annual article, C1050–2.509

Life insurance variable annuity and variable life premiums/deposits, for top life/health insurers, 1992, annual article, C1050–2.512

Life insurance variable annuity fund premium income and deposits, for top life/health insurers, 1991, annual article, C1050–2.503

Liquor market statistics, including sales, consumption, trade, distillery operations, and govtl info, with data by company, brand, and location, 1992 and trends, annual rpt, C4775–1

Index by Subjects and Names

Corporate rankings

Lodging chain rooms and establishments, for top 50 firms worldwide, 1991, annual rpt, C2140–1.4

Lodging industry facilities, sales, and occupancy, with top 42-100 properties in 5 market categories, 1993 annual rpt, C7000–5

Logistics trends and devs, including data on costs, finances of major carriers by mode, and foreign trade, 1993 annual compilation, C2150–1.506

Magazine revenues, circulation, advertising, and rates, for top 500 consumer and business publications, 1992, annual article, C2575–1.515

Market research industry devs, including revenues and operations of leading firms, 1991-92, annual feature, C2710–1.550

Market value of top 100 firms in developing countries, by company, 1993 annual feature, C5800–7.536

Market value of top 1,000 firms worldwide, with related financial data, by company and country, 1993 annual feature, C5800–7.536

Market value of top 20 companies worldwide, 1972, 1982, and 1992, article, C8900–1.514

Market value rankings of top 1,000 corporations, with sales, profits, assets, and related data, by company and industry, 1993 annual feature, C5800–7.521

Mass media company revenues for leading firms, with detail by medium, 1991-92, annual feature, C2710–1.540

Meat company sales and slaughterhouse capacity, for top 20 firms, 1992 annual rpt, A2100–1.1

Mergers, acquisitions, and divestitures, with prices, payment methods, and characteristics of participants, 1992, annual rpt, D6020–1

Mergers and acquisitions, and other transactions involving US and/or foreign companies, rankings of top participants, bimonthly rpt, C4683–1

Mergers and acquisitions, top transactions and acquiring companies, 1992, annual compilation, C4683–1.504

Mining companies shares of Western world nonfuel mine production, for top 50 companies worldwide, 1991, article, C5226–2.511

Mortgage lender ranking trends based on originations and servicing volume, for top instns, 1970s-92, article, A6450–2.509

Mortgage purchasing from loan originators, with volume purchased by 78 leading instns, 1991-92, article, A6450–2.502

Motion picture distributors ranked by films released, 1987-92, article, C9380–1.507

Motion picture distributors ranked by market share, weekly rpt, C9380–1

Motor vehicle dealership rankings by sales, 1992, annual data book, C2710–3.531

Motor vehicle fleet lessors ranked by number of cars and truck managed, for top 15 companies, 1983 and 1993, C1575–2.510

Motor vehicle fleet operating and financial data, including fleets by type, registrations by make and model, and top lessors, 1970s-93, annual rpt, C1575–2.507

Motor vehicle production for top 40 manufacturers worldwide, 1990-91, annual rpt, A0865–1.1

Motor vehicle production, revenues, and profits, for top 30 manufacturers worldwide, 1992, article, C8900–1.526

Motor vehicle production worldwide, by leading manufacturer, 1990-91 and trends, annual rpt, A0865–2

Motorcycle manufacturer market share, top 6 makes, 1987-91, annual rpt, A6485–1.1

Mutual fund assets and investment performance, for 273 top performing funds, 1993 recurring article, C8900–1.528

Mutual fund assets and investment performance, for 276 top performing funds, 1992 recurring article, C8900–1.511

Mutual fund investment performance, for best and/or worst equity, and taxable and tax-free bond funds, 1992, annual feature, C5800–7.509

Mutual fund investment performance, with detail for best- and worst-performing funds in selected categories, weekly rpt recurring article, C5800–7.523, C5800–7.533, C5800–7.549

Mutual funds (money market) financial performance and rankings of over 850 funds, with background info for investors, 1992 and trends, annual directory, C4682–2

Mutual funds financial performance and rankings of over 2,400 funds, with background info for investors, 1992 and trends, annual directory, C4682–1

Mutual funds used most by defined contribution retirement plans, rankings of top equity and income funds by assets, May 1993, semiannual article, C2710–2.517

Mutual funds used most by defined contribution retirement plans, rankings of top equity and income funds by assets, 1993 semiannual article, C2710–2.505

Mutual funds used most by defined contribution retirement plans, rankings of top equity and income funds by investment performance trends, biweekly rpt quarterly feature, C2710–2.505, C2710–2.509, C2710–2.517

Mutual funds with highest and lowest tax liability, rankings of 60 funds, 1993 article, C5800–7.547

Natural gas distribution utility and pipeline company financial and operating data, top 500 companies, 1992, annual article, C6780–1.505

Natural gas throughput of top 10 interstate pipelines, 1991 and trends, article, C6780–1.502

Natural gas well completions in tight gas sands formations, for top 25 operators, cumulative through 1992, article, C6985–1.501

Newspaper advertising expenditures, with top advertisers, and top advertising agencies in billings, 1992, C2710–1.524

Newspaper circulation and newsprint consumption of 15 largest daily newspapers and companies, 1991, annual rpt, C3975–5.3

Newspapers and circulation, for top 10 publishing companies, 1992, annual rpt, A8610–1

Newspapers and circulation, for top 45 publishing companies, 6-month period ended Sept 1992, annual rpt, A1630–8

Newspapers and circulation of top 20 companies, Sept 1992, annual rpt, A8605–4

Oil and gas independent company finances and operations, for approx 50 companies, 1991-92, semiannual article, C6985–1.504

Oil and gas industry financial and operating data, rankings for top 300 US and top 100 non-US companies, 1991-92, annual feature, C6985–1.547

Oil and gas industry operations of top 20 companies, 1991 and trends, periodic basic data book, A2575–14.2, A2575–14.4, A2575–14.6

Oil and gas industry trends, with data by company, State, and country, 1993 annual compilation, C6985–4

Oil and gas lease sales in Gulf of Mexico, with top bidders, weekly rpt recurring article, C6985–1.522, C6985–1.547

Oil and gas pipeline mileage, sales, and income of top 10 companies, 1991, annual feature, C6985–1.504

Oil industry financial and operating data for major companies, 1993 annual fact book, C4680–1.507

Oil industry income and operating data, for approx 20 major companies, 1991-92, annual article, C6985–1.533

Oil industry income, net profits, and selected operating data, approx 25 companies, weekly rpt quarterly article, C6985–1.520, C6985–1.534, C6985–1.545

Oil industry income, net profits, and selected operating data, approx 50 companies, 1st 9 months 1991-92, article, C6985–1.511

Oil refineries and capacity by process, for top 10-20 companies in US, Europe, and worldwide, 1992 annual feature, C6985–1.508

Oil refiners net income, for top 22 companies, 1st 9 months 1991-92, article, C6985–1.507

Oil refining capacity, by company and plant, Jan 1992, annual fact book, C4680–1.507

Packaging expenditures of top 7 manufacturers, 1992, article, C1850–1.508

Patent activity for approx 200 US and foreign firms in 13 industries, 1992 and trends, article, C5800–7.540

Pension fund assets, for top 300 funds worldwide, 1992, annual feature, C2710–2.515

Photonics-related patents issued to top 10 manufacturers, 1992, article, C1850–6.508

Plastics production capacity for specified resins, by major company and/or world region, monthly rpt recurring table, C5800–12.502, C5800–12.504, C5800–12.506, C5800–12.509, C5800–12.510, C5800–12.512, C5800–12.513

Printing (quick) sales, employment, and establishments, for top companies, 1992 article, C1850–10.503

Printing company sales, employment, and equipment, for top 101 North American firms, 1993 annual feature, C1850–10.512

Corporate rankings

Index by Subjects and Names

Privately held corporation revenues and employment, for 400 largest firms, 1992 annual article, C3950–1.503

Productivity, employment, sales, and operating income, for 46 companies with outstanding productivity improvement, 1992 and trends, C5800–7.532

Public utility truck/van fleets, top 40 ranked by size, 1992, annual feature, C1575–2.502

Publisher advertising revenues, for top 10 companies, 1st half 1993, C2710–1.538

Publisher advertising revenues, for top 10 companies, 1st 9 months 1992-93, C2710–1.551

Publisher advertising revenues, for top 10 companies, 1992, C2710–1.513

Pulp and paper industry operations and finances, US and Canada, with detail by company and product grade, and world production and trade summary, 1993 annual rpt, C3975–5

Pulp and paper industry production, capacity, consumption, trade, and sales/earnings data, including profiles for selected companies and sectors, monthly rpt, C3975–2

R&D expenditure activity for top 10 firms, 1992, annual feature, C5800–7.534

Radio advertising expenditures for top 50 advertisers, 1992, annual rpt, A8789–1

Radio audience ratings and program format, for top stations in leading metro markets, weekly rpt recurring article, C1850–14.506, C1850–14.507, C1850–14.508, C1850–14.521, C1850–14.531, C1850–14.542

Radio audience size, leading stations and formats, and advertising rates and revenues, by market area, recurring rpt, C3165–1

Radio station group owners ranked by total Arbitron rating, with stations owned and ratings, for top 25 companies, summer 1992, article, C1850–14.502

Railroad operating revenues, employment, and track miles operated, for 13 Class I systems, 1991, annual rpt, A3275–8.2

Railroads (Class I) equipment and performance rankings for 13 companies, 1992, annual rpt, A3275–7

Real estate investment advisors tax-exempt and total assets by type, top 76 firms, 1993, annual feature, C2710–2.520

Recording industry sales of Spanish-language music, for 6 leading and all other companies, 1992, article, C4575–1.508

Recreational vehicle towables and motorhome manufacturer market shares, for top 10 companies and all others, 1992, annual article, C8950–2.502

Restaurant (fast-food) chain sales, for top 6 companies, 1990, annual rpt, C2140–1.4

Restaurant (Mexican food) establishments by census div, and sales and/or units for top 4-5 chains, 1993 annual article, C1200–5.514

Restaurant (pizza) establishments by census div, and sales and units for top 10 chains, 1992, annual article, C1200–5.506

Restaurant franchises and sales, and franchisee fees and investment required, by leading company, 1993 annual feature, C1200–5.512

Restaurant quality ratings among consumers, for most popular chains, 1993 annual feature, C1850–3.504

Restaurant sales and units, for 50 fastest-growing chains, 1991-92, annual article, C1200–5.513

Restaurants with independent owners, sales, seating capacity, average check size, and patrons served, top 100 instns, 1992, annual article, C1850–3.505

Retail chain construction activity, capital expenditures, and number of new stores, for leading firms, 1991-92, annual feature, C5150–4.503

Retail chain financial data and business info for approx 240 US and Canadian companies, 1991-92 and trends, annual rpt, C3400–2

Retail chain performance indexes and ratios, for top 38 chains, 1986-91, annual article, C5150–4.502

Retail chain revenues, profits, and stores, top 100 chains, with selected data by outlet type, 1991-92, annual articles, C5150–4.508

Retail general merchandise chain sales, earnings, and stores, for top companies worldwide, with detail for selected areas, 1991-92, annual feature, C5150–3.516

Retail store financial performance indicators, for 98 public firms, FY92 and trends, annual rpt, B8130–4

Sales and other financial and operating data for top 100 small public firms with sales under $25 million, 1992 and trends, annual feature, C4687–1.507

Sales, earnings, and stock performance, for 100 fastest-growing companies, 1993 annual article, C8900–1.521

Sales executive ratings of corporate sales forces, by industry sector and sales function, 1993 annual survey article, C1200–1.512

Sales, profits, return on equity, price/earnings ratio, and earnings per share, approx 900 corporations, with industry rankings, weekly rpt quarterly article, C5800–7.503, C5800–7.519, C5800–7.528, C5800–7.541

Sales promotion income, for top sales promotion and promotional services agencies, 1991-92, annual feature, C2710–1.527

Sales to Army/Air Force post exchange, approx 700 top supplier companies, for year ended Jan 1993, annual feature, C0500–1.505

Securities initial public offerings, performance of best and worst issues, and leading underwriters, 1993 annual article, C3950–1.517

Securities investment return and dividends per share, for 5-50 best and worst performing stocks on 3 exchanges, 1992, annual article, C8900–1.507

Securities listed on NYSE, rankings of leading stocks by trading volume and market value, 1992, annual fact book, B6625–1.1

Securities traded over-the-counter on NASDAQ market, trading volume and price performance, for over 4,500 issues, 1992 and trends, annual rpt, A7105–1

Security equipment industry revenues, accounts, and operating data, for 100 leading companies, 1992, annual feature, C1850–13.507

Small companies with high 5-year returns on equity, financial performance data and chief executive characteristics, for top 200 firms, 1992 annual article, C3950–1.501

Small privately held companies sales, employment, and other data, for 500 fastest growing firms, 1988 and 1992, annual feature, C4687–1.512

Soft drink consumption and market shares, by company and brand, and by flavor, 1985-92, annual article, C0125–2.504

Spain chemical process industry sales and employment of top 15 companies, and production capacity and utilization of major chemicals, 1991, article, C5800–8.511

Telephone company access lines and revenues, for top 150 firms, Dec 1991, annual rpt, A9360–2

Telephone Yellow Pages publisher revenues and advertising agency/media buying service billings, for top 10-15 firms, 1992, article, C2710–1.546

Tender offer prices for 10 largest bids, 1992, annual article, C4683–1.504

Textile and clothing company financial performance indicators, rankings for 18-27 leading firms, 1990-91, annual rpt, C3400–5

Textile industry financial performance indicators for 32 companies, FY92 and trends, annual rpt, B8130–1

Travel and tourism rankings for selected indicators, including data for top 20 States, cities, countries, businesses, and other measures, 1992 recurring rpt, R9375–6

Truck (heavy-/medium-duty) manufacturers ranked by desirability of franchises, dealer views, May and Nov 1992, article, C2710–3.525

Truck fleet financial and operating data for top 200 freight carriers, 1992 and trends, annual feature, C2150–4.504

TV advertising billings or expenditures, for top 10 agencies and top 15 advertisers, 1991-92, annual feature, C2710–1.528

TV advertising expenditures for top 10 network advertisers, 3rd qtr 1991-92, article, C2710–1.505

TV advertising expenditures for top 5 advertisers on local, spot, and syndicated TV, 1992, article, C2710–1.516

TV advertising expenditures on 4 major networks, for top 10 network advertisers, 1st qtr 1993, article, C2710–1.528

TV advertising expenditures on 4 major networks, for top 10 network advertisers, 2nd qtr 1992-93, article, C2710–1.541

TV prime-time programs and hours sold by top producers, 1992/93 season, annual article, C1850–14.523

TV station group owner companies ranked by market penetration, with stations owned, 1992/93, recurring article, C1850–14.516

TV station group owner companies ranked by market penetration, with stations owned, 1993 recurring article, C1850–14.524

Wine market statistics, including sales, production, trade, and consumer characteristics, with data by company, brand, and geographic area, 1992 and trends, annual rpt, C4775–2

Index by Subjects and Names

Corporations

Wine sales and market shares for top 24 wine companies, and imports, 1990-92, recurring article, C2710–1.544

State and local:

- Alabama bank assets, for top 10 instns, FY92, annual rpt, S0110–1
- Alabama credit union assets, for top 100 instns, 1990, recurring rpt, U5680–2.6
- Alaska employment for top 100 companies, with distribution by industry div, 1992, annual article, S0320–1.510
- Alaska insurance market share rankings for top firms, 1991, annual rpt, S0280–3
- Arizona copper industry operations, including production, capacity, and reserves, by company and mine, with US and intl comparisons, 1991 and trends, annual rpt, S0497–1
- Arizona employment for top 10 employers, FY91, annual rpt, S0450–2
- Arizona property/casualty insurance company financial data, for top 25 underwriters by line of coverage, 1992, annual rpt, S0483–1
- California banks ranked by assets, top 25 instns, Dec 1992, annual rpt, S0810–1
- Connecticut insurance company assets and rankings for top 10 life/health and fire/casualty firms, 1991, annual rpt, S1222–1
- DC top 10 business and nonprofit employers, 1992, annual rpt, S1535–3.3
- Florida insurance underwriting data, for top 10 insurers by line of coverage, 1991, annual rpt, S1760–1
- Georgia-based Fortune 500 firms, 1991, biennial rpt, U6730–1.6
- Georgia employment for top 50 employers, 1991, biennial rpt, U6730–1.3
- Hawaii data book, general data, 1992 annual rpt, S2090–1.15
- Idaho employment for 94 largest employers, 1992 recurring rpt, S2218–2.5
- Idaho insurance underwriting activity of top 4-20 firms, by line of business, 1991, annual rpt, S2260–1
- Illinois bank and trust companies ranked by assets, FY92, annual rpt, S2395–1
- Iowa top 10-50 employers, 1982 and 1992, annual rpt, S2784–3
- Kentucky banks and credit unions ranked by deposits, assets, and/or leverage ratios, 1992, annual rpt, S3121–1
- Kentucky employment and number of plants, for top 58 manufacturers, 1992, annual rpt, S3120–1
- Michigan insurance company financial and underwriting data, for leading insurers, 1991, annual rpt, S3983–1
- Mississippi employment and number of plants, top 25 companies, FY92 annual rpt, S4346–1
- Missouri insurance companies ranked by selected financial and underwriting measures, 1992, annual rpt, S4527–1
- Missouri top 15 employers, 1991, annual rpt, S4475–1
- Nevada assessed property values for top 10 owners, FY92, annual rpt, S5025–1
- New Jersey employment, for 50 largest employers, 1991, annual rpt, S5455–1
- New York State insurance company assets or premiums, for top 10 life, property/casualty, and auto insurers, 1990, annual rpt, U5100–1.7

Oklahoma insurance market share rankings for top 10 firms, overall and by line of coverage, 1992, annual rpt, S6462–1

- Oregon employment for top 39 private employers, FY92 annual rpt, S6603–2
- Oregon employment for top 50 employers, Sept 1992, article, S6592–1.501
- Pennsylvania insurance industry financial and underwriting data, by company and line of coverage, 1991, with FY92 regulatory info, annual rpt, S6835–1
- Pennsylvania 30 largest employers, 1991, annual rpt, S6810–4
- Pennsylvania 50 largest employers, Mar 1991, annual planning rpt, S6845–3.2
- South Carolina employment for top 44 manufacturing plants, 1990, annual rpt, S7125–1.3
- Tennessee bank financial ratios, and rank by asset size, Dec 1989, annual rpt, U8710–2.13
- Tennessee employment for top 50 companies, FY92 annual rpt, S7505–1
- Utah employment at 46 largest employers, Dec 1992, S7820–3.509
- Utah insurance industry financial and underwriting data, with top 8-20 companies by line of coverage, 1991, annual rpt, S7845–1
- Vermont financial instns ranked by assets, Dec 1992, annual rpt, S7995–2
- West Virginia insurance taxes paid by top 20 fire/casualty and life insurers, 1991, annual rpt, S8575–1
- Wisconsin insurance industry, top 12-20 companies ranked by market share, by line of coverage, 1992, annual rpt, S8755–1

see also Product rankings

Corporations

- Advertising to enhance corporate image, company practices, expenditures, and media use, 1987 92, triennial survey rpt, A3357–1
- Arts fundraising through united arts funds (UAFs), with fund operations, income by source, and allocations, by UAF, 1992 and trends, annual rpt, A1315–2
- Autos and light trucks/vans in top 100 corporate fleets, 1993 and trends, annual feature, C1575–2.504
- Autos and light trucks/vans in 2nd 100 largest corporate fleets, 1993, annual feature, C1575–2.506
- Business activity and mgmt trends for small corporations, monthly rpt, C4687–1
- Charitable contribution policies concerning arts programs and other causes, 1991, recurring rpt, A3690–1
- Charitable contributions, by type of donor and recipient, 1992 and trends, annual rpt, A0700–1
- Charitable contributions of corporations, by donor characteristics and detailed type of recipient, 1991 and trends, annual rpt, R4105–8
- Charitable contributions, with detail for education, and top 10 donor companies, errata, C2176–1.502
- Charitable contributions, with detail for education, 1992 and trends, annual article, C2176–1.520
- Computer/info systems expenditure plans by component, 1993 annual survey article, C1850–5.510

Earnings outlook and stock investment performance, approx 900 corporations, 1992 annual feature, C5800–7.509

- Eastern Europe public opinion on private corporations, with detail for selected Western companies, for 6 countries and 3 Soviet Union Republics, 1991 survey, C8915–8.2, C8915–9
- Economic indicator historical trends, 1900s-92, annual rpt, R9050–1.2
- Education involvement of corporations, including types of recipients and contribution levels by company, 1992 survey and trends, annual article, C8900–1.502
- Educational instns financial support from corporate contributions, with detail for top 10-15 instns, by instn type, 1991/92 and trends, article, C2176–1.514
- Employee transfers and relocation policies, assistance, and costs, 1992, annual survey, B0600–1
- Financial and operating composite ratios for corporations, with establishments and receipts, for approx 200 industries, by asset size, FY90, annual rpt, C7800–1
- Financial data for top 100 growth companies with sales under $150 million, 1993 annual article, C5800–7.529
- Financial data for 250 corporations with rapid growth, 1993 feature, C5800–7.551
- Financial performance and growth rankings for approx 1,000 top corporations, with comparisons by industry group, 1993 annual rpt, C3950–1.505
- Fortune magazine ranking of top 50-100 companies in 8 nonindustrial sectors, with financial and employment data, 1992, annual feature, C8900–1.516
- Fortune 500 largest industrial corporations, sales, financial, and stock performance data by company, 1992, annual feature, C8900–1.513
- Foundation assets, income, and grants by type of recipient, with data for top organizations and by location, 1991 and trends, annual rpt, R4900–1
- Higher education contributions 1982-92, and allocations for all education by program 1992, annual article, C2175–1.534
- Higher education student level of familiarity with 35 corporations, 1993 survey article, C1200–1.503
- Homebuilders distribution by corporate organization, 1993 article, C4300–1.504
- Income tax (corporate) burden according to 5 alternative measures, for 9 States, 1990, article, B8500–2.514
- Income tax data, Federal, State, and local govts, 1902-92, annual rpt, R9050–1
- Logos of corporations, consumer rankings of 5 best and worst, 1993 survey article, C5800–7.547
- Logos of corporations, consumer rankings of 6 best and worst, spring 1993 survey, article, C2710–1.544
- Market value of top 1,000 firms worldwide, with related financial data, by company and country, 1993 annual feature, C5800–7.536
- Market value rankings of top 1,000 corporations, with sales, profits, assets, and related data, by company and industry, 1993 annual feature, C5800–7.521

Corporations

Mgmt devs and related topics, series, R4105–78

Motor vehicle fleet manager earnings, and personal and professional characteristics, 1993 article, C1575–2.506

Motor vehicle fleet size, with makes and/or models used, for 7 major corporate fleets, 1993-94, article, C2710–3.553

Mutual fund industry financial data, by type of investor and financial instn intermediary, 1991 and trends, annual rpt, A6025–1.2

Performance decline indicators for 5 major corporations whose CEOs recently resigned, 1993 article, C5800–7.515

Privately held corporation revenues and employment, for 400 largest firms, 1992 annual article, C3950–1.503

Public confidence in selected societal instns, 1972-91 surveys, annual rpt, U6395–1

Public opinion on corporate handling of crises, including honesty and media reliability, 1993 survey article, A8770–1.505

R&D expenditures, and sales and profits, for approx 900 firms, 1992, annual feature, C5800–7.534

Sales, profits, return on equity, price/earnings ratio, and earnings per share, approx 900 corporations, with industry rankings, weekly rpt quarterly article, C5800–7.503, C5800–7.519, C5800–7.528, C5800–7.541

Sponsorship expenditures, by type of event, 1993, article, C2710–1.532

Sponsorship spending for events, for 13 top companies, 1992, article, C1200–1.512

State social, economic, and govtl indicators, with rankings, 1993 semiannual rpt, B8500–1.2

State/local tax burden comparisons by tax type for typical corporations in 19 States, 1993 article, B8500–2.513

Volunteer programs for employees, including methods used to encourage volunteering, obstacles, benefits, and costs, 1992 survey, article, C2176–1.511

State and local:

California corporations and taxable net income, with detail by industry, 1960-90, annual rpt, S0840–3.2

California individual and corporate income tax returns and property tax assistance, by income class and county, 1990 and trends, annual rpt, S0855–1

California library finances, staff, holdings, and services, by library type and facility, FY92, annual rpt, S0825–2

California statistical abstract, general data, 1992 annual rpt, S0840–2.4

California tax collections (excluding income tax), by locality, company, and type of tax, FY92 and trends, annual rpt, S0835–1

Colorado corporate income tax returns filed, liabilities, credits, and refunds, FY92 and trends, annual rpt, S1075–1.3

Georgia corporate income tax returns, by income class, 1990, annual rpt, S1950–1.2

Hawaii data book, general data, 1992 annual rpt, S2090–1.15

Hawaii tax collections and allocations, by type, for State and counties, FY91-92 and trends, annual rpt, S2120–1

Minnesota-based Fortune 500 corporation sales, assets, and net income, by company, 1991, annual rpt, S4180–1

Mississippi statistical abstract, general data, 1992 annual rpt, U3255–4.11

Montana corporate income tax returns filed and tax liability, by industry div, and tax credits claimed by type, FY91-92 and trends, biennial rpt, S4750–1.1

Nebraska personal and corporate income tax returns filed, tax credits and liability, and income, by county and/or income group, 1990, annual rpt, S4950–1.1

New York State statistical yearbook, general data, 1992 annual rpt, U5100–1.5

Ohio corporate franchise tax returns filed, income, and tax liability, by industry div, 1991, annual rpt, S6390–1.2

Pennsylvania corporate income and capital stock/franchise tax payments, by industry, FY88-91, annual rpt, S6885–1

South Carolina corporate income tax returns and collections, by amount of liability and industry group, FY92, annual rpt, S7255–1.2

Utah corporate franchise tax revenues, FY92 and trends, annual rpt, S7905–1

Virginia personal and corporate income tax returns filed, taxable income, and tax, 1990 or FY92 and trends, annual rpt, S8305–1.1

see also Boards of directors

see also Business acquisitions and mergers

see also Business assets and liabilities, general

see also Business assets and liabilities, specific industry

see also Business formations

see also Business income and expenses, general

see also Business income and expenses, specific industry

see also Corporate bonds

see also Corporate rankings

see also Divestiture

see also Economic concentration and diversification

see also Executives and managers

see also Foreign corporations

see also Government corporations and enterprises

see also Holding companies

see also Multinational corporations

see also Public utilities

see also Securities

see also the "Index by Issuing Sources" for corporations whose publications are covered by SRI

see also under By Individual Company or Institution in the "Index by Categories"

Correctional institutions

Administration of local, State, and Federal correctional instns, with inmates, facilities, costs, parole and probation, and staffing, 1992 annual series, R4300–1

Directory of correctional instns, with inmates, staff, and cost of care, by US and Canadian instn, 1992, annual rpt, A1305–3

Directory of local jails and adult detention facilities, with inmates, staff, and operating summary, by State and instn, Dec 1992, recurring rpt, A1305–1

State social, economic, and govtl indicators, with rankings, 1993 semiannual rpt, B8500–1.10

Index by Subjects and Names

Western States corrections data, including prisoners and capacity, and related data on population and crime, for 13 States, 1980s-90, A4375–13

State and local:

Alaska corrections system admin, including inmate and probationer/parolee offenses and demographic characteristics, 1991 annual rpt, S0287–1

Arizona correctional instn admin, including inmates by criminal background and demographic characteristics, FY92, annual rpt, S0464–2

Arkansas population in instns and other group quarters, 1990, census rpt, U5935–7

California correctional instn inmates, by offense, demographic characteristics, and instn, Dec 1992, semiannual rpt, S0820–2

California correctional instn population, parole and probation, and justice system expenditures, 1987-92, annual rpt, S0910–1.2

California criminal justice system detailed data, by offense, county, age, race-ethnicity, and sex, 1991 and trends, annual rpt, S0910–2

California population in instns and other group quarters, 1990, census rpt, S0840–9

California State agency library staff, expenditures, holdings, and activities, by library, FY92, annual rpt, S0825–2

DC criminal justice system summary, including crimes and arrests, criminal procedure, prisoners, and parole, 1991 and trends, annual rpt, S1535–2

DC statistical profile, general data, 1992 annual rpt, S1535–3.8

Delaware public opinion on criminal sentencing, prison alternatives, and related issues, Feb 1991 survey, R8825–11

Florida correctional instns, admin, and inmates by criminal background and demographic characteristics, FY92 annual rpt, S1720–1

Georgia correctional instns, admin, and inmate characteristics, FY92, annual rpt, S1872–1

Georgia statistical abstract, general data, 1992-93 biennial rpt, U6730–1.12

Illinois correctional instn education program enrollment and staff, 1990/91, annual rpt, S2440–1

Illinois corrections dept admin, including inmates and characteristics, finances, and staff, FY91-93 and trends, annual rpt, S2425–1

Illinois local correctional facility inspection results, with data on programs and inmates by sex, suspended annual rpt, S2425–2

Iowa correctional instn admissions, releases, and inmate characteristics, by instn, monthly rpt, S2770–1

Kansas correctional instn inmates, by offense, demographic characteristics, and instn, FY92 and trends, annual rpt, S2940–1

Kansas statistical abstract, general data, 1991/92 annual rpt, U7095–2.12

Maryland correctional instn education programs enrollment and completions, by instn, 1991/92, annual rpt, S3610–1

Index by Subjects and Names

Cosmetics and toiletries

Maryland local govt financial condition, including revenues by source, expenditures by function, and debt obligations, FY92 and trends, annual rpt, S3618–1.1

Maryland statistical abstract, general data, 1993-94 biennial rpt, S3605–1.9

Massachusetts correctional instn inmate socioeconomic characteristics and criminal background, by instn, Jan 1992 and trends, annual rpt, S3805–1

Michigan correctional instns, admin, and inmates by selected demographic characteristics, 1991 and trends, annual rpt, S3960–1

Missouri correctional instn admissions, releases, and inmate characteristics, FY93, annual rpt, S4501–1

Nebraska correctional instn admin, with inmates by criminal background and demographic characteristics, by instn, FY92 and trends, annual rpt, S4850–1

Nevada statistical abstract, general data, 1992 biennial rpt, S5005–1.4

New Jersey correctional instn inmates, by offense, sentence length, demographic characteristics, and instn, Dec 1991 annual rpt, S5370–1

New Jersey population in instns and other group quarters, by county, 1990, census rpt, S5425–19

New York State correctional instn inmate population and characteristics, and probation and parole, 1991 and trends, annual rpt, S5760–3.4

New York State local jail/penitentiary inmate characteristics and facility capacity, by county, 1991, annual rpt, S5724–2

New York State statistical yearbook, general data, 1992 annual rpt, U5100–1.8

North Carolina correctional instn admissions, separations, and population, with inmate characteristics, FY93, semiannual rpt, S5900–1

North Dakota local correctional instn adult and juvenile inmate characteristics, by instn, 1991 and trends, annual rpt, S6060–3

Ohio correctional instn admissions and releases, inmate characteristics, programs, finances, and staffing, FY91 and trends, annual rpt, S6370–1

Ohio public, academic, and other library finances, holdings, and staff, by library and location, 1992 and trends, annual rpt, S6320–1

Oklahoma correctional instn admin, including inmate characteristics, incarceration costs, and data by instn, FY91, annual rpt, S6420–1

Oklahoma public and institutional library holdings, circulation, finances, and staff, by facility, FY92, annual rpt, S6470–1

Pennsylvania population in instns and other group quarters, 1990, census rpt, U4130–13

Pennsylvania public and institutional library personnel, holdings, circulation, and finances, by county and facility, FY92, annual rpt, S6790–2

Pennsylvania State correctional instn admin, and inmates by type of offense and demographic characteristics, 1990 and trends, annual rpt, S6782–1

Pennsylvania vocational education enrollment, by instn type, 1991/92, annual rpt, S6790–5.7

South Carolina correctional instns, admin, and inmates by criminal offense and demographic characteristics, FY92 and trends, annual rpt, S7135–1

South Dakota correctional instn admin, including inmates by criminal background and demographic characteristics, FY92 and trends, annual rpt, S7296–1

Tennessee correctional instn admin, with inmate characteristics, and corrections dept finances and staff, FY92, annual rpt, S7480–1

Tennessee statistical abstract, general data, 1992/93 annual rpt, U8710–2.19

Texas correctional instn inmates by criminal background and demographic characteristics, FY92, annual rpt, S7660–1

Utah corrections inmates, parolees, and probationers, by criminal background and demographic characteristics, FY92 and trends, annual rpt, S7810–1

Washington State correctional instn inmate population, admissions, and releases, by demographic characteristics, quarterly rpt, S8337–1

Wisconsin Blue Book, general data, 1993-94 biennial rpt, S8780–1.2

Wisconsin correctional instn inmates, by criminal background and selected characteristics, series, S8692–1

Wyoming correctional instn admin, finances, inmate characteristics, and staff, and probation and parole activities, FY92 annual rpt, S8883–1

see also Community-based correctional programs

see also Juvenile detention and correctional institutions

see also Military prisons

see also Parole and probation

see also Prison work programs

see also Prisoners

see also State funding for corrections

Corruption and bribery

State and local:

Florida crimes and arrests, by offense, with data by victim and offender characteristics, 1992, annual rpt, S1770–1

Illinois crimes and arrests, by offense, with data by location and offender characteristics, 1991, annual rpt, S2536–1

New York State crimes and arrests by offense and demographic characteristics, and court activity and corrections, 1991 and trends, annual rpt, S5760–3

Cosby, Virginia

"Population Projections for Oklahoma, 1990-2020", S6416–1

Cosmetics and toiletries

Children's toiletry product interest among consumers, and retail outlets shopped, 1993 survey article, C5150–2.519

Discount chain consumer natl brand preferences, by product category and chain, and by age group, 1993 survey, annual feature, C5150–3.521

Discount chain top-selling natl brands cited by managers, by product category, chain, and region, 1993 survey, annual feature, C5150–3.520

Discount store sales and productivity data for 20 depts, 1993 annual feature, C5150–3.516

Drugstore artificial fingernail product sales trends, for 5 top brands, year ended June 1993, article, C5150–2.519

Drugstore chain and brand preferences of consumers, with data by product type and region, 1992 annual survey feature, C5150–2.503

Drugstore chains financial performance and marketing operations, with sales by product type, 1993 annual feature, C5150–2.510

Drugstore sales and merchandising trends, by product type and market area, 1992 annual feature, C5150–2.503

Ethnic and mass market cosmetics sales trends, by product type, 1992-93, articles, C5150–2.518

Ethnic cosmetics and hair care product sales distribution by product category, year ended July 1992-93, article, C5150–2.520

Financial ratios and performance, for over 350 SIC 4-digit industries, FY88-92, annual rpt, A6400–3

New beauty care and cosmetic product sales performance for top brands in selected categories, biweekly rpt recurring feature, C5150–2.504, C5150–2.505, C5150–2.511

Raw materials sales for personal care/cosmetics products, by ingredient and/or product type, 1990, 1993, and 1996, article, A1250–1.522

Retail prices for selected consumer items in approx 300 cities, quarterly rpt, A0150–1

Sales and consumer expenditures, for food store products by type, 1991-92, annual feature, C4655–1.510

Sales and market shares in food stores/drugstores, for 11 cosmetics marketers, year ended June 1993, article, C2710–1.546

Sales of cosmetics and fragrances by retail outlet type, 1993 annual feature, C5150–2.515

Sales of 4 types of cosmetics at supermarkets/drugstores, and consumer views on product packaging, 1993 article, C1850–1.506

Sales to general population and black consumers, distribution by outlet type, 1991, article, C5150–2.502

Sales volume shares by retail outlet type, for approx 300 food, drug, and other product categories, 1993 annual feature, C4655–1.504

Shopping center financial and operating data, with detail by type of tenant, US and Canada, 1991, triennial rpt, R9285–1

Supermarket sales of nonfood products, by detailed product type, 1992, annual feature, C5225–1.508

Teenage girls cosmetics use and views on drugstore marketing, 1993 articles, C5150–2.508

Women age 18-29 beauty product use and shopping practices, 1993 articles, C5150–2.514

Women's shopping patterns for cosmetics and fragrances, with views on store attributes, by outlet type, 1993 survey, annual feature, C5150–2.516

Cosmetics and toiletries

Women's use and shopping patterns for personal care products, with preferred outlets and brands, 1993 survey and trends, annual feature, C5150–2.515

see also Barber and beauty shops

see also Personal care products

Cost-of-doing-business surveys

- Apartment building (conventionally financed) detailed income and expense ratios for US and Canada, by building type, metro area, and US region, 1991 and trends, annual rpt, A5600–1
- Apartment building (federally subsidized) detailed income and expense ratios, by building and subsidy type, building age, metro area, and region, 1991 and trends, annual rpt, A5600–5
- Apartment complex mgmt income and expenses, and vacancy and turnover rates, by region and metro area, 1992, annual survey rpt, A6497–1
- Book publishing industry financial and operating data, by publisher type and size, and subject category, 1991 and trends, annual rpt, A3274–2
- Business forms industry detailed financial and operating ratios, with summary operating data, FY91, annual rpt, A5785–3
- Business forms manufacturing plant employment and compensation data, by region, 1992 and trends, biennial rpt, A5785–4
- Condominium, cooperative, and planned unit dev detailed expenses, for US and Canada, by building characteristics, metro area, and US region, 1991, annual rpt, A5600–3
- Drugstore (independent pharmacy) financial and operating data, by store characteristics, 1991 and trends, annual survey, B5165–1
- Food marketers mgmt info system operations, employment, and finances, for wholesalers and retailers by sales size, 1993 and trends, annual survey, A4950–7
- Hardware finances and operations, for hardware stores, home centers, and lumber/building material outlets, 1991 and trends, annual rpt series, A8275–1
- Hiring costs and new hires, by industry, State, region, and employer characteristics, 1992 and trends, annual survey rpt, A4740–2
- Home furnishings retailer financial and operating data, by firm characteristics and region, 1992 and trends, annual rpt, A7975–1
- Homebuilder operations and finances, by region and sales size group, 1992 survey, article, C4300–1.501
- Medical group financial and operating data, by practice characteristics, 1991, annual rpt, A6365–2
- Office building detailed income and expense data, and energy use, US and Canada, by building characteristics, metro area, and US region, 1991 and trends, annual rpt, A5600–2
- Office product dealer financial and operating data, by sales volume and region, 1991 and trends, annual rpt, A8110–1
- Plastics processing industry financial and operating ratios, by processing activity, sales size, and region, 1992, annual rpt, A8920–4
- Real estate residential brokerage firm finances and operations, with data by region and company size, 1990/91 and trends, article, A7000–1.502
- Rental equipment industry financial data, by revenue size group and region, and for Canada, 1991 and trends, annual rpt, A2665–1
- Restaurant industry financial and operating data, by establishment characteristics and location, 1992, annual rpt, A8200–3
- Shopping center detailed income and expense data, by building characteristics, metro area, and region, 1991, annual rpt, A5600–6
- Shopping center financial and operating data, with detail by type of tenant, US and Canada, 1991, triennial rpt, R9285–1
- Supermarket (independent) sales and operating ratios, by store type, sales size, and region, 1991, annual survey, A4950–4

Cost of education

see Educational finance

see Tuition and fees

Cost of living

- Auto operating costs by components, and weeks of median family income necessary for new car purchase, 1950s-90s, annual rpt, A0865–1.2
- Condominium and cooperative owner median monthly assessment, by building type, 1991, annual rpt, A5600–3
- Consumer attitudes on economic conditions and personal financial situation, monthly survey, U7475–2
- Foreign student living expenses, by State, 1992/93, annual rpt, R5580–1
- Household income with and without cost-of-living adjustment, and cost indexes, by census div and population size, 1991, annual article, U0280–1.501
- Indexes for cost of living in approx 300 cities, by component, quarterly rpt, A0150–1
- Indexes for housing and other costs of living in 51 metro areas, 4th qtr 1992, article, U0280–1.510
- Insurance expenditures as percent of household spending, and price indexes for property and auto and related items, 1993 annual rpt, A5650–1.3
- Labor hours required per day to earn money for taxes vs personal consumption expenditures by object, 1993, annual rpt, R9050–15.4
- Labor hours required per day to earn money for taxes vs selected other living expenditures, 1993, annual feature, R9050–3.504
- Latin America statistical abstract, general data by country, 1992 annual rpt, U6250–1.31
- Medicaid Federal grants, recipients, and benefits by type of service, with selected public health funding factors, by State and region, various years 1974-94, R8490–46
- Purchasing power of dollar, 1958-92, annual rpt, U8710–2.2
- Wealthy lifestyles, comparative prices of selected goods and services, 1976 and 1993, annual article, C3950–1.526
- Western cities cost-of-living index, by component, selected cities, monthly rpt quarterly table, S7820–3.503, S7820–3.506, S7820–3.507

State and local:

- Alaska cost-of-living indicators for selected items and local areas, with comparisons to other US cities, 1992 annual article, S0320–1.501
- Arizona cost of living and income, by city, 1991, annual article, U0280–1.501
- Delaware data book, general data, 1993 annual rpt, S1375–4
- Hawaii data book, general data, 1992 annual rpt, S2090–1.14
- Nebraska cost-of-living indicators by component, for 6 cities, with comparisons to other US cities, quarterly rpt, S4895–2
- Oregon cost-of-living index, for 4 cities and Portland metro area, 4th qtr 1991, annual rpt, S6585–3
- Tennessee cost-of-living indexes by component, for 11 metro areas, 4th qtr 1992, article, S7495–2.503

see also Consumer Price Index

see also Electric power prices

see also Energy prices

see also Escalator clauses

see also Family budgets

see also Food prices

see also Housing costs and financing

see also Inflation

see also Medical costs

see also Natural gas prices

see also Petroleum prices

see also Prices

see also Producer Price Index

see also Rent

Cost of medical care

see Medical costs

Cost of operation

see Agricultural production costs

see Business income and expenses, general

see Business income and expenses, specific industry

see Cost-of-doing-business surveys

see Operating ratios

see Production costs

Cost of production

see Agricultural production costs

see Energy production costs

see Production costs

Costa Rica

Statistical abstract of Latin America, detailed social, govtl, and economic data, 1992 annual rpt, U6250–1

Cotton

- Consumption and trade by type of fiber and product, 1988-92, annual survey, C3460–1.511
- Consumption of cotton and other fibers in textile production, by detailed end use, 1990-92, annual rpt, A7485–1
- Exports of farm products, by detailed commodity and country of destination, US and California, 1991, annual rpt, B9520–1
- Fiber Organon, detailed monthly and annual data on industry production, consumption, and trade, by fiber and fabric type, monthly rpt, C3460–1
- Latin America statistical abstract, general data by country, 1992 annual rpt, U6250–1.16, U6250–1.24, U6250–1.25
- Motor vehicle industry materials consumption, by type, 1988-91, annual rpt, A0865–1.2
- Production and acreage in 4 States, and ginning rates in 14 States, 1992, C5226–3.505

Index by Subjects and Names

Index by Subjects and Names

Production and consumption, by world region and country, and trade, 1950s-92, annual article, C3460–1.502

Production, consumption, stocks, trade, and prices for approx 100 basic commodities, including by country and producing State, commodity yearbook for 1993, C2400–1, C2400–2

Southeastern States cotton acreage harvested, bales ginned, and gins active and idle, for 6 States, 1987-90, biennial rpt, U6730–1.4

Textile mill consumption of manufactured fibers, cotton, and wool, by country, 1989-91, annual feature, C3460–1.503

World cotton supply and use, with data by selected country, 1991/92-1992/93, annual rpt, U5830–1

World demand for cotton, 1988-92, annual rpt, C3460–1.508, C3460–1.509

State and local:

Alabama agricultural production, marketing, and income, by county and/or commodity, and farms and acreage, 1992 and trends, annual rpt, S0090–1

Arizona agricultural production, marketing, and finances, by commodity and county, 1988-92, annual rpt, U5830–1

Arkansas agricultural production, marketing, and finances, by commodity and county, with farms and acreage, 1992 and trends, annual rpt, U5920–1

California field crops production, acreage, yield, and prices, by commodity and county, 1992 and trends, annual rpt, S0850–1.4

Florida field crop acreage, yield, production, and value, by commodity and/or county, 1992 and trends, annual rpt, S1685–1.4

Georgia agricultural production, marketing, and finances, by commodity and/or county, and farms and acreage, 1991 and trends, annual rpt, S1855–1

Louisiana agricultural production, marketing, and finances, by commodity or parish, 1985-91, annual rpt, U2740–1

Missouri agricultural production, marketing, and finances, by commodity and/or county, and farms and acreage, 1988-92, annual rpt, S4480–1

New Mexico agricultural production, marketing, and finances, by commodity and county, with farms and acreage, 1991 and trends, annual rpt, S5530–1

North Carolina agricultural production, marketing, and finances, by commodity and county, 1991 and trends, annual rpt, S5885–1

Oklahoma agricultural production, marketing, and finances, by commodity and county, 1992 and trends, annual rpt, S6405–1

South Carolina agricultural production and finances, by commodity and county, 1991-92 and trends, annual rpt, U1075–3

Tennessee agricultural production and marketing, by commodity and county, with farms, acreage, and farm value, 1992 and trends, annual rpt, S7460–1

Texas agricultural production, marketing, and finances, by commodity and county, and farms and farmland, 1991 and trends, annual rpt series, S7630–1

Cottonseed

see Oils, oilseeds, and fats

Council on Library Resources Inc.

Grants/contracts over $10,000 awarded by CLR, FY92, annual compilation, C1650–3.2

Counselors and counseling

Catholic charity social service agency activities, clients, finances, and personnel, 1991 and trends, annual rpt, A3810–1

Corporate personnel mgmt devs, including work force diversity, health care and family-related benefits, counseling services, and competitiveness, 1993 survey, B6850–6

Correctional instn treatment staff, by State and for Federal system, and for major jails, 1992 annual series, R4300–1

Employer policies and views on family-related issues, including involvement in counseling services, Mar 1992 survey, A8907–1

Human immunodeficiency virus (HIV) testing and posttest counseling rates, by demographic characteristics, 1989, article, A2623–1.501

Urban public school systems suicide/stress reduction programs for students, for 47 systems, 1990/91, A4425–4

State and local:

Florida health care atlas, including manpower by occupation and health care facilities by type, by district and county, 1992 annual rpt, S1746–1.2

Georgia prison inmate participation in counseling services, by type, FY92 annual rpt, S1872–1

Maryland elementary and secondary education data, by county, Oct 1992, annual rpt, S3610–2.12

Maryland elementary and secondary education data, by county, 1992/93, annual rpt, S3610–2.10

Maryland public school guidance counselor, therapist, and psychologist salaries, by county, Oct 1991, annual rpt, S3610–2.2

Maryland public school guidance counselor, therapist, and psychologist salaries, by county, Oct 1992, annual rpt, S3610–2.11

North Dakota elementary and secondary school staff characteristics and salaries, by position, region, and enrollment size, 1992/93 annual rpt, S6180–3

Utah public school personnel and salaries, by detailed position and district, 1991/92, annual rpt, S7815–1.2

Wyoming penitentiary counseling and psychological services, with inmate participation, FY92, annual rpt, S8883–1

see also Alcohol abuse and treatment

see also Clergy

see also Drug abuse and treatment

see also Social work

Counterfeiting and forgery

State and local:

Alabama juvenile and adult arrests, by type of offense, 1992, annual rpt, S0119–1.1

Arizona arrests by offense, offender characteristics, and county, 1992, annual rpt, S0505–2.2

Arkansas crimes and arrests, by offense, victim and offender characteristics, and location, 1992 and trends, annual rpt, S0652–1

Counterfeiting and forgery

California crimes and arrests, clearances, and arrest dispositions, with data by offense and offender characteristics, 1987-92, annual rpt, S0910–1.1

California criminal justice system detailed data, by offense, county, age, race-ethnicity, and sex, 1991 and trends, annual rpt, S0910–2

Colorado crimes and arrests, by offense and location, with offender characteristics, and assaults on police, 1992, annual rpt, S1068–1

Connecticut arrests, by offense, offender characteristics, and local agency, 1992, annual rpt, S1256–1.2

DC criminal justice system summary, including crimes and arrests, criminal procedure, prisoners, and parole, 1991 and trends, annual rpt, S1535–2

Florida crimes and arrests, by offense, with data by victim and offender characteristics, 1992, annual rpt, S1770–1

Hawaii crimes and arrests, by offense, with data by county and victim-offender characteristics, 1992, annual rpt, S2035–1

Idaho crimes and arrests, by offense, with data by location and offender characteristics, 1992 and trends, annual rpt, S2275–2

Illinois crimes and arrests, by offense, with data by location and offender characteristics, 1991, annual rpt, S2536–1

Kansas crimes and arrests, by offense, with data by location, agency, and victim-offender characteristics, 1992 and trends, annual rpt, S2925–1.1

Kentucky arrests by county and offense, and law enforcement employment by agency, 1992, annual rpt, S3150–1 2

Maine arrests of adults and juveniles, by offense, age, and sex, 1991, annual rpt, S3475–1.2

Maryland crimes and arrests, by offense, location, and offender characteristics, with law enforcement employment and assaults on officers, 1992 and trends, annual rpt, S3665–1

Michigan crimes and arrests, by offense, with data by location and offender characteristics, 1992 and trends, annual rpt, S3997–1

Missouri crimes and arrests, by offense and location, with victim and offender characteristics, 1991 and trends, annual rpt, S4560–2

Montana crimes and clearances, by offense and jurisdiction, 1992, annual rpt, S4705–1

New Hampshire arrests, by offense and offender age, sex, and race-ethnicity, 1991, annual rpt, S5250–2.2

New Jersey arrests by offense, age, race-ethnicity, sex, and county, 1992 and trends, annual rpt, S5430–1.2

New York State crimes and arrests by offense and demographic characteristics, and court activity and corrections, 1991 and trends, annual rpt, S5760–3

North Carolina arrests by detailed offense, offender characteristics, and county, 1991-92, annual rpt, S5955–1.2

Counterfeiting and forgery

North Dakota crimes and arrests, by offense, location, and offender characteristics, and law enforcement employment, 1991 and trends, annual rpt, S6060–1

Oklahoma crimes and arrests, by offense, with victim and offender characteristics, 1990-92, annual rpt, S6465–1.1

Oregon crimes and arrests, by offense, with data by county, local agency, and offender characteristics, 1992 and trends, annual rpt, S6603–3

Pennsylvania crimes and arrests, by offense, with data by location and offender characteristics, 1992 and trends, annual rpt, S6860–1

South Carolina crimes and arrests, by detailed offense, offender characteristics, and location, 1992 and trends, annual rpt, S7205–1.2

Texas arrests, by age, sex, race-ethnicity, and offense, 1992, annual rpt, S7735–2.2

Utah crimes and arrests, by offense, county, and local agency, 1992 and trends, annual rpt, S7890–3

Virginia crimes and arrests by offense, and law enforcement employment, by location and reporting agency, 1992, annual rpt, S8295–2.2

Washington State crimes and arrests, by offense, with data by location and offender characteristics, 1992 and trends, annual rpt, S8440–1

West Virginia crimes and arrests, by offense, location, and offender characteristics, 1990-91, annual rpt, S8610–1

Wisconsin crimes and arrests, by offense, offender characteristics, county, and local agency, 1992 and trends, annual rpt, S8771–1

Wyoming adult and juvenile arrests, by offense, county, and local jurisdiction, 1991, annual rpt, S8867–3.2

Counties

Consumer buying power survey of population, income, and sales by kind of business, by census div, State, MSA, county, and city, 1992, annual rpt, C1200–1.511

Consumer buying power survey of population, income, and sales by product line, by State, metro area, county, and census div, 1993 annual rpt, C1200–1.514

Market rankings of leading MSAs, counties, and cities, by population, income, and retail sales, 1993 annual rpt, C3250–1

Physicians, counties lacking active practitioners, with population and land area, by State, Jan 1992, annual rpt, A2200–3.1

Socioeconomic characteristics and geographic distribution of counties, 1993 annual rpt, A5800–1

Tobacco products excise tax collections, and number of counties and cities imposing, by State, FY63-92, annual rpt, A9075–2

State and local:

Alabama counties permitting and prohibiting sale of alcoholic beverages, 1992 annual rpt, S0121–2

Georgia statistical abstract, general data, 1992-93 biennial rpt, U6730–1.11

Mississippi counties with alcoholic beverage control restrictions, FY92 annual rpt, S4435–1

Nebraska demographic and economic characteristics of selected counties, monthly rpt, U7860–1

see also Local government

see also under By County in the "Index by Categories"

County courts

see State courts

County employees

see State and local employees

Coupons

see Sales promotion

Courts

Law school grad employment and salaries, by type of employer, location, and grad characteristics, 1992 and trends, annual rpt, A6505–1

see also Civil procedure

see also Contempt of court

see also Criminal procedure

see also Domestic relations courts and cases

see also Federal district courts

see also Judges

see also Judgments, civil procedure

see also Juries

see also Juvenile courts and cases

see also Parole and probation

see also Probate courts and cases

see also Sentences, criminal procedure

see also Small claims courts and cases

see also State courts

see also State funding for courts

see also Supreme Court

see also Tax laws and courts

see also Traffic laws and courts

see also Trials

Cows

see Dairy industry and products

see Livestock and livestock industry

CPI

see Consumer Price Index

Crabs

see Shellfish

Crack

see Cocaine

Cranberries

see Fruit and fruit products

Creal, Richard C.

"1992/93 Administrative Compensation Survey", A3900–1

Credit

Book publishing industry financial and operating data, by publisher type and size, and subject category, 1991 and trends, annual rpt, A3274–2

Brokerage margin account credit balances, debts, and potential purchasing power, 1992 and trends, annual fact book, B6625–1

Corporate accounts receivable collection rates by number of months outstanding, 1993, article, C4687–1.512

Hospital accounts receivable average days outstanding, 1989-92, article, A1865–1.509

Interest rate business cycle peaks and troughs, with trends in price of credit, industrial production, and stock performance, 1953-92, article, C3950–1.507

Nonfinancial sector debt, by component, compared to population and GDP, 1960-91, R9050–15.1

Outstanding market debt by type of lender, 1989, R5025–8

Service sector economic activity indicators, with leading and coincident indexes and components, and detail for financial services, monthly rpt, U1245–3

Truck equipment distributor financial data, by company type, sales size, and rural vs metro market, FY91 and trends, annual rpt, A8505–4

see also Agricultural credit

see also Business assets and liabilities, general

see also Business assets and liabilities, specific industry

see also Commercial credit

see also Commodity Credit Corp.

see also Consumer credit

see also Credit cards

see also Credit unions

see also Discrimination in credit

see also Economic indicators

see also Finance companies

see also Government assets and liabilities

see also International finance

see also Loan delinquency and default

see also Loans

see also Mortgages

see also Public debt

Credit cards

Advertising expenditures by medium for top 100 advertisers, with comparisons to earnings and sales, and detail by product type and brand, 1991-92, annual rpt, C2710–1.547

Auto fleet use of fuel credit cards, with detail for 6 oil company cards, 1993 survey article, C1575–2.505

Catalog orders paid by check and credit card, 1991, annual rpt, A4620–1.2

Convenience stores offering special services, including use of credit cards, 1992 and trends, annual survey rpt, A6735–1, A6735–2

Corporate fleet vehicle driver maintenance habits, model preferences, and cellular telephone and credit card use, 1993 survey, article, C1575–2.509

Direct marketing industry devs, with consumer and business market characteristics, and media use patterns, 1992/93 annual rpt, A4620–1.4

Food store acceptance of credit and debit cards, by type of purchase, company size, and region, 1992, annual rpt, A4950–5.4

Food store Visa credit card sales, 1990-92, article, C2710–1.507

Hispanic American households holding selected major credit cards, by income group, 1992 article, C4575–1.501

Home furnishings retailer financial and operating data, by firm characteristics and region, 1992 and trends, annual rpt, A7975–1

Home improvement stores among top 500 retailers offering private label credit cards, 1993 annual feature, C5150–6.503

Japan consumer credit by type, with debt vs disposable income and savings, and comparisons to US, 1970s-92, article, R5650–2.542

Loan delinquency rates for approx 10 types of consumer bank loans, and repossession data, by State, quarterly rpt, A0950–1

Market value and shares for 5 major credit cards, 1992, article, C2710–1.516

Index by Subjects and Names

Retail store credit operations, including cash vs credit sales, processing methods, and marketing techniques, 1992 annual survey, C5150–4.504

Retail store credit operations, including payment losses and loss reduction efforts, by payment method and outlet type, 1992 survey article, C5150–4.503

Supermarket acceptance of credit cards for purchases, and shopper use of service, 1993 and trends, annual survey rpt, A4950–3

Supermarket acceptance of credit cards, 1991 and 1993, article, C0500–1.506

State and local:

Illinois credit card deception offenses and arrests, 1990-91, annual rpt, S2536–1

Credit life insurance

see Life insurance

Credit unions

State and local:

Alabama credit union assets, for top 100 instns, 1990, recurring rpt, U5680–2.6

Arizona credit union balance sheets, members, and branches, by instn, quarterly rpt, S0460–4

California economic condition, including population, employment and earnings, income, business activity, and taxation, 1960s-92, annual rpt, S0840–3.2

Colorado savings and loan assn and credit union financial condition, 1992 and trends, annual rpt, S1070–3

Connecticut credit union (State-chartered) financial and membership data, by instn and assn type, 1991 and trends, annual rpt, S1160–1

Georgia banks and other financial instns, financial condition by instn type, and assets by instn and city, Dec 1992, annual rpt, S1865–1

Georgia credit union financial condition, including loans by type and delinquency, with comparisons to US, 1989, article, T16730–2.506

Hawaii data book, general data, 1992 annual rpt, S2090–1.15

Idaho banks and other financial instns, financial condition, with data by instn and loan activity analysis, FY92 or 1991, annual rpt, S2235–1

Illinois Financial Institutions Dept activities, with financial and regulatory data for credit unions, consumer lenders, and other businesses, FY91 annual rpt, S2457–2

Indiana financial instns (State-chartered) financial condition, including assets by instn arranged by city, 1991 and trends, annual rpt, S2625–1

Kentucky financial instns condition, including assets by instn and city, with regulatory info, 1992 and trends, annual rpt, S3121–1

Louisiana financial instns (State-chartered), financial condition by instn arranged by city, with regulatory info, Dec 1992, annual rpt, S3265–1

Maine banks and other financial instns, financial condition by instn, June 1992, annual rpt, S3473–2

Maine financial instn assets, deposits, and loans, by type of instn and county, 1982-92, annual rpt, S3473–1

Maryland banks and credit unions (State-chartered) financial condition by instn, with regulatory data, FY92 annual rpt, S3655–2

Michigan banks and other financial instns, financial condition by instn, with regulatory info, 1992 and trends, annual rpt, S3957–1

Minnesota financial instns (State-regulated), financial condition by instn, 1991-92, annual rpt, S4140–3

Mississippi banks and other financial instns, financial condition by instn type, and assets by bank and credit union, Dec 1992, annual rpt, S4325–1

Mississippi statistical abstract, general data, 1992 annual rpt, U3255–4.8

New Jersey banks and other financial instns, assets and liabilities by instn, 1992 and trends, annual rpt, S5355–1

New Mexico financial instns, financial and operating data by instn, with regulatory activities, 1992, annual rpt, S5652–1

Oklahoma financial instns (State-chartered) assets and liabilities, by type of instn, with regulatory data, FY92 annual rpt, S6415–1

Oklahoma statistical abstract, general data, 1992 annual rpt, U8130–2.20

Oregon financial instns, financial condition by instn, Dec 1992 and trends, annual rpt, S6616–1

Pennsylvania statistical abstract, general data, 1992 recurring rpt, U4130–6.2

Rhode Island banks and other financial instns (State-chartered), assets and liabilities, by instn, 1991, annual rpt, S6945–1

Rhode Island statistical almanac, general data, 1993 annual rpt, C7975–1.1

South Carolina economic condition, including agriculture, finance, and govt financial data, 1970s-92, annual rpt, S7125–3.1

Tennessee banks and other financial instns financial condition, by instn and city, 1992 annual rpt, S7507–1

Utah banks and other financial instns, financial condition by instn, FY93 and trends, annual rpt, S7830–1

Utah statistical abstract, general data, 1993 triennial rpt, U8960–1.15

Vermont banks and other financial instns, financial condition by instn, 1992 and trends, annual rpt, S7995–2

Virginia financial instns (State-chartered), financial condition by instn and instn type, Dec 1992, annual rpt, S8180–2

West Virginia banks and other financial instns, composite financial condition, with selected data by instn, 1990-91, annual rpt, S8530–1

Creech, Joseph D.

"Readiness for College: College-to-School Reporting in the SREB States", A8945–32

Crime and criminals

Analyses of special topics related to crime, delinquency, and the criminal justice system, series, A7575–1

Black American crime, arrest, and incarceration data, with comparisons to whites, 1970s-91, annual compilation, C6775–2.5

Black children and youth population, economic, health, and education data, with comparisons to whites, 1993 rpt, R3840–21

City fiscal condition, including budget trends and adjustments, and influencing factors, by region and population size, Mar-Apr 1993 survey, annual rpt, A8012–1.23

Cocaine user characteristics, including criminal behavior and health condition, with comparison to nonusers, 1991 and trends, article, A2623–1.510

Elementary/secondary school criminal activity, including student victimization rates, 1992, article, C1850–12.510

Elementary/secondary teacher views on selected measures to increase school safety, Jan-Feb 1993 survey, B6045–7

Hate crimes involving bias against selected persons or groups, by State, 1991, semiannual rpt, B8500–1.10

Higher education on-campus crime incidence and arrests by selected offense, by instn and State, 1991/92, C2175–1.506

Hispanic American crime victimization rates, with comparisons to whites, 1979-90, annual compilation, C6775–3.6

Hotel guest crime victimization experience, by type of crime, 1993 survey article, C4215–1.511

Household crime victimization rates for burglary, larceny, and motor vehicle theft, by age of victim, 1987-90, article, C1850–13.506

Japan and US violent crime rates, for murder, rape, and robbery, 1986-90, article, R5650–2.515

Liability claims citing inadequate security, distribution by type of crime, 1993 feature, C1850–12.507

Metro area poverty and unemployment level effects on crime and mortality rates, for selected offenses and causes of death, 1990, R4700–18

Mexico criminal suspects and sentenced delinquents, by sex, 1976-84, annual rpt, U6250–1.15

Property crime incidence, by offense and State, 1991 and trends, annual rpt, A5650–1.4

Public opinion on 5-year trend in local crime rate, 1993 article, C5800–7.552

Rates for property crimes, robberies, burglaries, and vehicle thefts, by State, 1993 article, C1050–1.511

Shopping center security operations, including staffing, equipment, and crime incidents, by center type, 1992-93 and trends, articles, C5150–4.506

State economic dev condition indicators, including economic performance, business vitality, growth capacity, and tax/fiscal system, by State, 1993 annual rpt, R4225–1.1

State social, economic, and govtl indicators, with rankings, 1993 semiannual rpt, B8500–1.10

Statistical profiles of 50 States and DC, general data, 1993 annual almanac, C4712–1

Trends in incarceration rates, correctional populations, and crime rates, with analysis of theory that increased imprisonment reduces crime, 1993 rpt, A7575–3

Victims of crime per 1,000 population, by demographic characteristics, 1991, article, R8750–1.505

Crime and criminals

Western States corrections data, including prisoners and capacity, and related data on population and crime, for 13 States, 1980s-90, A4375–13

State and local:

Alabama county data book, general data, 1992 annual rpt, S0121–2

Alabama crimes and arrests, by offense, with data by location and offender characteristics, 1992 and trends, annual rpt, S0119–1

Alabama municipal data book, general data, 1992 recurring rpt, S0121–5

Alabama statistical abstract, general data, 1992 recurring rpt, U5680–2.10

Arizona crimes and arrests, by offense, county, and offender characteristics, 1992, annual rpt, S0505–2

Arizona crimes involving bias against selected persons or groups, with offense characteristics, 1992, annual rpt, S0505–2.2

Arizona statistical abstract, general data, 1993 recurring rpt, U5850–2.12

Arkansas crimes and arrests, by offense, victim and offender characteristics, and location, 1992 and trends, annual rpt, S0652–1

California crimes and arrests, and criminal justice system data, 1987-92, annual rpt, S0910–1

California criminal justice system detailed data, by offense, county, age, race-ethnicity, and sex, 1991 and trends, annual rpt, S0910–2

California socioeconomic and govtl data for municipalities, counties, and school districts, 1993 annual rpt, C4712–3

California statistical abstract, general data, 1992 annual rpt, S0840–2.14

Colorado crimes and arrests, by offense and location, with offender characteristics, and assaults on police, 1992, annual rpt, S1068–1

Connecticut crimes and arrests, by offense, with data by local agency, and victim-offender characteristics, 1992, annual rpt, S1256–1

DC criminal justice system summary, including crimes and arrests, criminal procedure, prisoners, and parole, 1991 and trends, annual rpt, S1535–2

DC statistical profile, general data, 1992 annual rpt, S1535–3.8

Delaware crimes and arrests, by offense, county, and victim-offender characteristics, 1991 and trends, annual rpt, S1375–5

Delaware data book, general data, 1993 annual rpt, S1375–4

Delaware public opinion on criminal sentencing, prison alternatives, and related issues, Feb 1991 survey, R8825–11

Florida county data book, 1992/93 annual rpt, C6360–1

Florida crimes and arrests, by offense, with data by victim and offender characteristics, 1992, annual rpt, S1770–1

Florida municipal and county statistical profiles, general data, 1991 annual rpt, C4712–6

Florida serious crimes reported after passage of "habitual offender" sentencing laws, 1987-91, A7575–5

Florida statistical abstract, general data, 1992 annual rpt, U6660–1.22

Georgia county guide, general data, 1993 annual rpt, U6750–1

Georgia statistical abstract, general data, 1992-93 biennial rpt, U6730–1.12

Hawaii crimes and arrests, by offense, with data by county and victim-offender characteristics, 1992, annual rpt, S2035–1

Hawaii data book, general data, 1992 annual rpt, S2090–1.4

Idaho crimes and arrests, by offense, with data by location and offender characteristics, 1992 and trends, annual rpt, S2275–2

Idaho crimes involving bias against selected groups, 1992, annual rpt, S2275–2

Illinois crimes and arrests, by offense, with data by location and offender characteristics, 1991, annual rpt, S2536–1

Illinois State constitutional amendment on crime victims rights, election results by county, 1992, biennial rpt, S2445–1

Illinois statistical abstract, general data, 1992 annual rpt, U6910–2

Kansas crimes and arrests, by offense, with data by location, agency, and victim-offender characteristics, 1992 and trends, annual rpt, S2925–1

Kansas election results for State constitutional amendment on crime victim rights, 1992, biennial rpt, S3030–1

Kansas statistical abstract, general data, 1991/92 annual rpt, U7095–2.12

Kentucky crimes and arrests, by offense, with data by location and offender characteristics, 1992, annual rpt, S3150–1

Maine crimes and arrests, by offense, with data by county, reporting agency, and offender age and sex, 1991, annual rpt, S3475–1

Maryland crimes and arrests, by offense, location, and offender characteristics, with law enforcement employment and assaults on officers, 1992 and trends, annual rpt, S3665–1

Maryland statistical abstract, general data, 1993-94 biennial rpt, S3605–1.9

Massachusetts municipal and county profiles, general data, 1992 annual rpt, C4712–2

Michigan crimes and arrests, by offense, with data by location and offender characteristics, 1992 and trends, annual rpt, S3997–1

Mississippi statistical abstract, general data, 1992 annual rpt, U3255–4.9

Missouri crimes and arrests, by offense and location, with victim and offender characteristics, 1991 and trends, annual rpt, S4560–2

Montana crimes and clearances, by offense and jurisdiction, 1992, annual rpt, S4705–1

Nevada statistical abstract, general data, 1992 biennial rpt, S5005–1.4

New Hampshire crimes and arrests, by offense, jurisdiction, and offender characteristics, 1991 and trends, annual rpt, S5250–2

New Jersey crimes and arrests, by offense, with data by location and offender characteristics, 1992 and trends, annual rpt, S5430–1

Index by Subjects and Names

New Jersey crimes involving bias against racial, religious, or ethnic groups, with arrests and victim-offender characteristics, 1992, annual rpt, S5430–1.4

New Jersey municipal and county data book, general data, 1992 annual rpt, C4712–4

New York State crimes and arrests by offense and demographic characteristics, and court activity and corrections, 1991 and trends, annual rpt, S5760–3

New York State Federal Crime Insurance Program policies, premiums, and losses, 1990-91, annual rpt, S5770–3

New York State municipal and county statistical profiles, general data, 1993 annual rpt, C4712–7

New York State security equipment dealer views on criminal background checks for industry personnel, Aug 1992 survey, article, C1850–13.501

New York State statistical yearbook, general data, 1992 annual rpt, U5100–1.8

North Carolina crimes and arrests, by offense, with data by location and offender characteristics, 1992 and trends, annual rpt, S5955–1

North Dakota crimes and arrests, by offense, location, and offender characteristics, and law enforcement employment, 1991 and trends, annual rpt, S6060–1

Oklahoma crimes and arrests, by offense, with data by local agency and victim and offender characteristics, 1990-92, annual rpt, S6465–1

Oklahoma statistical abstract, general data, 1992 annual rpt, U8130–2.7

Oregon crimes and arrests, by offense, with data by county, local agency, and offender characteristics, 1992 and trends, annual rpt, S6603–3

Oregon crimes involving bias against selected persons or groups, with victim and offender characteristics, 1991-92, annual rpt, S6603–3.1

Pennsylvania crimes and arrests, by offense, with data by location and offender characteristics, 1992 and trends, annual rpt, S6860–1

Pennsylvania crimes involving ethnic intimidation, by victim, offender, and crime characteristics, 1992, annual rpt, S6860–1

Pennsylvania statistical abstract, general data, 1992 recurring rpt, U4130–6.7

South Carolina crime rates, by county, 1991, annual rpt, S7145–1.1

South Carolina crimes and arrests, by offense, with data by location and victim-offender characteristics, and assaults on officers, 1992 and trends, annual rpt, S7205–1

South Carolina statistical abstract, general data, 1993 annual rpt, S7125–1.5

Tennessee statistical abstract, general data, 1992/93 annual rpt, U8710–2.19

Texas crimes and arrests, by offense, with data by location and offender characteristics, 1992 and trends, annual rpt, S7735–2

Texas crimes involving bias against selected persons or groups, by victim, offender, and incident characteristics, 1992, annual rpt, S7735–2.2

Index by Subjects and Names

Texas prison inmates compared to Index crimes, by MSA, FY92, annual rpt, S7660–1

Utah crimes and arrests, by offense, county, and local agency, 1992 and trends, annual rpt, S7890–3

Virginia crimes and arrests, by offense, with data by location and offender characteristics, 1992, annual rpt, S8295–2

Washington State crimes and arrests, by offense, with data by location and offender characteristics, 1992 and trends, annual rpt, S8440–1

West Virginia crimes and arrests, by offense, location, and offender characteristics, 1990-91, annual rpt, S8610–1

Wisconsin crimes and arrests, by offense, offender characteristics, county, and local agency, 1992 and trends, annual rpt, S8771–1

Wisconsin State constitutional amendment providing rights for victims of crimes, election results by county, 1993-94 biennial rpt, S8780–1.3

Wyoming corrections dept crime victim notification program participants by county, FY92, annual rpt, S8883–1

Wyoming crimes and arrests, by offense, with data by location and victim and offender characteristics, 1991 and trends, annual rpt, S8867–3

see also Arrest
see also Arson
see also Assassination
see also Assault
see also Assaults on police
see also Bombs
see also Child abuse and neglect
see also Correctional institutions
see also Corruption and bribery
see also Counterfeiting and forgery
see also Crime victim compensation
see also Criminal investigations
see also Criminal procedure
see also Detective and protective services
see also Domestic violence
see also Driving while intoxicated
see also Drug and narcotics offenses
see also Embezzlement
see also Fraud
see also Fugitives from justice
see also Gambling
see also Homicide
see also Juvenile delinquency
see also Kidnapping
see also Law enforcement
see also Motor vehicle theft
see also Obscenity and pornography
see also Offenses against family
see also Organized crime
see also Parole and probation
see also Pretrial detention and release
see also Prisoners
see also Prostitution
see also Rape
see also Recidivism
see also Rehabilitation of criminals
see also Robbery and theft
see also Sentences, criminal procedure
see also Sex crimes
see also State funding for corrections
see also Terrorism
see also Trials

see also Vandalism

Crime victim compensation

Retail store inventory loss restitution cases and amounts recovered, by type of outlet, 1991, annual survey rpt, C5150–4.504

State and local:

Colorado crime victim restitution collections, by district, FY92, annual rpt, S1035–1.1

Colorado financial condition, including receipts by source, and expenditures by function, FY92 and trends, annual rpt, S0980–1

Connecticut courts probation activity, including restitution collected and disbursed, FY91-92, biennial rpt, S1220–1.2

DC statistical profile, general data, 1992 annual rpt, S1535–3.3

Delaware crime victim restitutions assessed and paid, by court, FY92, annual rpt, S1360–1

Georgia offender restitution payments collected, FY92, annual rpt, S1872–1

Indiana financial condition, including revenues by source, expenditures by function and object, and fund balances, by agency, FY92, annual rpt, S2570–1

Massachusetts court cases and dispositions, by type of court and case, and location, FY92 and trends, annual rpt, S3807–1

Missouri crime victim compensation applications and awards, FY83-92, annual rpt, S4530–2.2

Missouri financial condition, including fund finances, tax collections and distribution, and State treasury activity, FY92 and trends, annual rpt, S4570–1

New York State crime victim compensation claims and awards, FY68-92, annual rpt, S5760–3.4

New York State statistical yearbook, general data, 1992 annual rpt, U5100–1.8

Ohio court of claims case activity for crime victim compensation, 1992, annual rpt, S6385–1

Oklahoma juvenile service cases, and restitution paid, by county, FY92, annual rpt, S6455–1.2

Rhode Island violent crimes indemnity fund finances and claims, 1991, annual rpt, S6965–1

South Carolina juvenile offender restitution orders, FY89-92, annual rpt, S7125–1.5

Tennessee financial condition, including revenues by source, expenditures by function and object, and fund balances, FY92, annual rpt, S7505–1

Texas financial condition, including revenues by source, expenditures by function and dept, and investments, with data for over 400 individual funds, FY92, annual rpt, S7655–2.2

Wyoming correctional instn admin, finances, inmate characteristics, and staff, and probation and parole activities, FY92 annual rpt, S8883–1

Criminal courts

see Courts
see Criminal procedure
see Federal district courts
see Juvenile courts and cases
see State courts
see Supreme Court

Criminal procedure

see Traffic laws and courts

Criminal investigations

State and local:

Utah Corrections Investigation Bureau criminal cases, by type of offense, FY91-92, annual rpt, S7810–1

see also Police
see also Searches and seizures

Criminal procedure

Analyses of special topics related to crime, delinquency, and the criminal justice system, series, A7575–1

College freshmen opinions on criminal procedure, by sex and instn type, fall 1992, annual survey, U6215–1

Public confidence in selected societal instns, 1993 Gallup Poll and trends, C4040–1.510

Public opinion on criminal justice system and prosecution of police officers, Feb 1993 Gallup Poll, C4040–1.508

Public opinion on social, political, and economic issues, detailed data, 1972-91 surveys, annual rpt, U6395–1

Rape incidence, victim characteristics, and views of victims and service agency staff on related issues, 1990-92 surveys, R8375–1

State appellate and trial court caseloads and dispositions, by case type and State, 1991 and trends, annual rpt, R6600–1

State and local:

Alabama court caseloads and dispositions, by type of court and case, and location, with judicial dept finances, FY92 and trends, annual rpt, S0118–1

Alabama criminal offender dispositions including incarcerations, and prison releases, by selected offense, 1988-90, annual rpt, S0119–1.2

Alaska court cases and dispositions, by type of court and case, and location, with judicial dept finances and personnel, FY92 and trends, annual rpt, S0290–1

Arizona court cases and dispositions, by type of case and court, with judicial personnel and finances, by county and city, FY92, annual rpt, S0525–1

Arizona statistical abstract, general data, 1993 recurring rpt, U5850–2.12

Arkansas court caseloads and dispositions, by type of case and court, and location, FY92 and trends, annual rpt, S0647–1

California court activity, including caseloads and dispositions, by case type and court, and location, FY92 and trends, annual rpt, S0905–1

California court cases and dispositions, by type of case and court, and location, FY92 and trends, annual rpt, S0905–2

California crimes and arrests, and criminal justice system data, 1987-92, annual rpt, S0910–1

California criminal justice system detailed data, by offense, county, age, race-ethnicity, and sex, 1991 and trends, annual rpt, S0910–2

Colorado court cases and dispositions, by type of court and detailed case type, FY92 and trends, annual rpt, S1035–1.2

Connecticut court caseloads and dispositions, by type of court and case, and court location, with judicial dept finances, FY91-92, biennial rpt, S1220–1

Criminal procedure

DC court cases and dispositions, by type of case, and judicial system finances, 1992 and trends, annual rpt, S1515–1

DC criminal justice system summary, including crimes and arrests, criminal procedure, prisoners, and parole, 1991 and trends, annual rpt, S1535–2

DC statistical profile, general data, 1992 annual rpt, S1535–3.8

Delaware court caseloads and dispositions, by type of court and case, and by county, with judicial dept finances, FY92, annual rpt, S1360–1

Florida court cases and dispositions, by type of court and case, and location, 1992, annual rpt, S1805–1

Georgia court cases and dispositions, by type of court and case, and location, with judicial dept finances and personnel, FY92, annual rpt, S1903–1

Hawaii court cases and dispositions, by type of court and case, and judicial circuit, FY92 and trends, annual rpt, S2115–1.2

Hawaii data book, general data, 1992 annual rpt, S2090–1.4

Indiana court cases and dispositions by type of court and case, and location, with judicial system finances and personnel, 1992, annual rpt, S2703–1

Iowa court cases, processing, and dispositions, by type of court and district, with judicial dept appropriations and personnel, 1992 and trends, annual rpt, S2815–1

Kansas court caseloads and disposition, by type of court and case, and location, FY92, annual rpt, S3035–1

Louisiana court caseloads and dispositions, by type of court and case, and jurisdiction, 1992 and trends, annual rpt, S3375–1

Maine court cases and dispositions, by type and location, FY92 and trends, annual rpt, S3463–1

Maryland court caseloads and dispositions, by type of court and case, and county, with judicial personnel and finances, FY92 and trends, annual rpt, S3600–1

Massachusetts court cases and dispositions, by type of court and case, and location, FY92 and trends, annual rpt, S3807–1

Michigan court caseloads and dispositions, by type of court and case, and court location, 1992 and trends, annual rpt, S3962–1

Nebraska court cases and dispositions, by type of court and case, and location, 1992 and trends, annual rpt, S4965–2

New Mexico court cases and dispositions, by type of court and case, and location, with judicial system finances and personnel, FY92, annual rpt, S5623–1

New York State court cases and dispositions, by type of court and case, and jurisdiction, 1991, annual rpt, S5730–1

New York State crimes and arrests by offense and demographic characteristics, and court activity and corrections, 1991 and trends, annual rpt, S5760–3

New York State statistical yearbook, general data, 1992 annual rpt, U5100–1.8

North Carolina court cases and dispositions, by type of court and case, and location, with judicial dept finances and personnel, FY91, annual rpt, S5950–1

North Dakota court caseloads and dispositions, by type of case and court, and location, with judicial dept finances, 1991-92, annual rpt, S6210–1

Ohio court caseload and case disposition, by type of court and case, and location, 1992, annual rpt, S6385–1

Oklahoma court cases and dispositions, by type of court and case, with judicial system finances, by county or jurisdiction, FY92, annual rpt, S6493–1

Pennsylvania court caseloads and dispositions, by type of court and case, and county, 1991, annual rpt, S6900–1.2

Pennsylvania criminal offenders charged, and case dispositions, by offense, 1992, annual rpt, S6860–1

Pennsylvania statistical abstract, general data, 1992 recurring rpt, U4130–6.7

Rhode Island court cases and dispositions, by type of court and case, and county, 1987-91, annual rpt, S6965–1

South Carolina court cases and dispositions, by type of court and location, with judicial dept finances and employees, 1992 and trends, annual rpt, S7197–1

South Dakota court cases and dispositions by type of case, and judicial system finances and personnel, by jurisdiction, FY92 and trends, annual rpt, S7395–1

Tennessee court cases and dispositions, by type of court and case, and county, FY92, annual rpt, S7585–1

Texas court cases and dispositions, by type of court and case, and location, FY92, annual rpt, S7703–1

Vermont court cases and dispositions, by type of court and case, and location, FY92 annual rpt, S8120–1

Virginia court caseloads, processing, and dispositions, by type of court and case, with judicial dept personnel and finances, by location, 1992 and trends, annual rpt, S8300–1

Washington State court cases and dispositions, by type of court and case, and jurisdiction, with judicial finances and personnel, 1992 and trends, annual rpt, S8339–1

West Virginia court caseloads and dispositions, by type of court and case, and judicial circuit, 1992 and trends, annual rpt, S8537–1

see also Arrest

see also Capital punishment

see also Commitment

see also Fines and settlements

see also Habeas corpus

see also Juries

see also Pardons

see also Parole and probation

see also Pretrial detention and release

see also Searches and seizures

see also Sentences, criminal procedure

see also Trials

Crop insurance

see Agricultural insurance

Crops

see Agricultural production

see Animal feed

see Cotton

see Grains and grain products

see Potatoes

see Tobacco industry and products

Index by Subjects and Names

Crude oil

see Petroleum and petroleum industry

Cuba

Economic indicators, including trade and inflation, 1970s-88, U6250–1.19

Energy intl sourcebook, with detail on oil and gas industry operations, supply-demand, and prices, for approx 80 countries, 1970s-91, annual compilation, C6985–10.2

Oil production and oil in place, by field, 1993 article, C6985–1.526

Statistical abstract of Latin America, detailed social, govtl, and economic data, 1992 annual rpt, U6250–1

see also Caribbean refugees

Cuban Americans

see Hispanic Americans

Cuban refugee programs

see Caribbean refugees

Cults

see Religious cults

Cultural activities

Religious congregation characteristics, including membership, activities, staff, and finances, 1992 survey, recurring rpt, A5435–4

see also Educational exchanges

see also International cooperation in science and technology

Cultural relations

see Cultural activities

Currency

see Black market currency

see Coins and coinage

see Foreign exchange

see Money supply

see Travelers checks

Curricula

American College Test (ACT) scores by student characteristics, with student views on schools and education plans, 1992 and trends, annual rpt, R1960–6

Black American educational statistics, with comparisons to whites, 1970s-92, annual compilation, C6775–2.3

Catholic vs public school ratings for selected aspects of education and environment, public opinion by respondent characteristics, July 1992 survey, A7375–8

College grad starting salary trends by academic major, 1992/93, annual survey rpt, U3130–1

Doctoral degree recipient characteristics, including citizenship status, source of support, field of study, and instn, 1990/91 and trends, annual rpt, R6000–7

Doctoral degrees conferred and recipient characteristics, by field, 1992, annual feature, C2175–1.535

Elementary/secondary education data, with detail for mathematics including test scores and teacher preparation, by State, 1993 biennial rpt, A4355–1

Elementary/secondary prospective teacher characteristics and opinions, survey of persons interested in alternative certification routes, 1992, R6350–7

Employment in business and industry, hiring plans for college grads, by field, salary, and degree, 1993 annual survey rpt, U3730–1

Foreign students enrolled in US higher education instns, by instn, State, country of origin, and demographic characteristics, 1991/92 and trends, annual rpt, R5580–1

Index by Subjects and Names

Curricula

Foreign students enrolled in US higher education instns distribution by academic level, by field of study, 1991/92, article, A0605–2.501

High school vocational-academic program integration, pilot project evaluative data including achievement test results, student and teacher attitudes, and curricula, 1990, A8945–33

Higher education degree recipient earnings by field, and degree fields of male and female recipients, 1990, article, U7860–1.505

Higher education degrees conferred, by level, sex, discipline, and race-ethnicity, 1990/91, recurring feature, C2175–1.523

Higher education enrollment of foreign students, by instn, discipline, State, and country of origin, 1991/92, annual feature, C2175–1.501

Higher education faculty and salaries at private instns, by discipline and academic rank, 1992/93, annual rpt, A3900–4

Higher education faculty and salaries at public instns with and without collective bargaining contracts, by discipline and academic rank, 1992/93, annual rpt, A3900–5

Higher education faculty salaries, by academic rank and discipline, 1992/93, annual rpt, A0800–1, C2175–1.514

Higher education freshmen attitudes and characteristics, degree and career plans, and financial aid sources, by sex and instn type, fall 1992, annual survey, U6215–1

Hispanic American educational statistics, with comparisons to whites, 1970s-92, annual compilation, C6775–3.2

Latin America statistical abstract, general data by country, 1992 annual rpt, U6250–1.8

Library/info science school curricula, by school and degree program, 1991/92, annual rpt, A3235–1.3

Medical school curriculum committee activities and future plans, 1990 survey, article, A3273–8.505

Medical school inclusion of 38 intl health topics, with faculty ratings of topic importance, 1989/90 or June 1991, article, A3273–8.509

Minority involvement in higher education, including degrees awarded by field, race-ethnicity, sex, and State, 1970s-91, annual rpt, A1410–10

Nursing complex skills considered basic knowledge by hospital nurses, and inclusion in education programs, 1993 survey article, A8010–3.504

Nursing education gerontological curriculum content and teaching methods, for programs in Southeastern States, 1993 article, A8010–3.505

Osteopathy college student training received in special interest curricula areas, 1992/93 and trends, annual rpt, A0620–1

Public opinion on school problems, quality, and proposed reforms, by respondent characteristics, 1993 annual Gallup Poll, A8680–1.503

Salaries of new college grads, by degree level and field, 1991/92-1992/93, annual rpt, A3940–3

Salaries of professional workers, by discipline and other characteristics, with detail for scientists and engineers, 1990s and trends, biennial rpt, A3960–1

Salary and job offers for college grads, by field of study, type of employer, and degree level, by region, interim rpt series, A3940–1

Salary and job offers for college grads, by field of study, type of employer, and degree level, series, A3940–2

Southern States higher education faculty and administrator characteristics and salaries, by instn type, 1990s and trends, biennial fact book, A8945–1.5

Student attitudes on courses in 4 subject areas, for 8th graders by sex and race-ethnicity, 1988, R4800–2.512

Textbook sales by subject category, by educational level, 1990-91, annual rpt, A3274–2

Women and minorities in professional fields, detailed education and labor force data, 1980s-91, with historical trends, recurring rpt, A3960–2

State and local:

Arkansas higher education degrees conferred, by level, discipline, student race and sex, and instn, 1990/91 and trends, annual rpt, S0690–3

Arkansas higher education FTE enrollment, and student credit hour production by program area, by academic level and instn, 1991/92 and trends, annual rpt, S0690–2

Connecticut public school data, including enrollment, staff, programs, finances, and student characteristics, 1991/92, biennial rpt, S1185–3

Delaware data book, general data, 1993 annual rpt, S1375–4

Delaware postsecondary education finances, enrollment, and degrees conferred, by instn, FY94 annual rpt, S1425–1

Delaware teacher certificates issued, and employment status of education grads, by subject area, 1991/92, annual rpt, S1430–1.3

Florida higher education enrollment, degree programs, staff, and finances, by State-supported instn, with student and staff characteristics, 1991/92 annual rpt, S1725–1

Idaho economic profile, general data, 1992 recurring rpt, S2218–2.3

Illinois higher education enrollment, degrees, staff, and finances, by public and private instn and student characteristics, 1993 annual rpt, S2475–1

Iowa postsecondary enrollment, degrees, staff, and finances, by instn, 1990/91, annual rpt, S2755–1

Maine statistical summary, general economic and social data, 1992 recurring rpt, S3434–1

Massachusetts high school graduation requirements, by subject area, 1988, annual rpt, S3810–3

Minnesota postsecondary education finances, and enrollment by student characteristics, by type of school system, 1970s-93, biennial rpt, S4195–2.2

Mississippi higher education enrollment and degrees, by level and field, and finances, by State-supported instn, 1991/92, annual rpt, S4360–1

Mississippi vocational, technical, and adult education courses offered, by program, 1993 annual rpt, S4340–1.2

Missouri American College Test (ACT) scores, by participant characteristics and/or higher education instn, 1993 annual rpt, S4520–3.1

Missouri higher education degrees conferred, by level, sex, race-ethnicity, instn, and field of study, FY92 and trends, annual rpt, S4520–3.3

Missouri public school finances, staff, students, and programs, detailed data, 1991/92, annual rpt, S4505–1.1

New Jersey higher education bachelor degrees awarded and starting salaries of college grads, by field of study, 1993 annual article, S5425–1.504

New Jersey public school active, entering, and departing teachers, by subject, 1990/91, annual rpt, S5385–1.2

North Carolina higher education enrollment, degrees, libraries, staff, and student characteristics, finances, and housing, by instn, 1992/93 and trends, annual rpt, U8013–1

North Carolina public school course enrollment and classes, by course type and level, 1992/93, annual rpt, S5915–1.1

Pennsylvania higher education degrees conferred, by level, sex, race-ethnicity, instn type, and field of study, 1990/91 and trends, annual rpt, S6790–5.2

Pennsylvania higher education degrees conferred, by level, sex, race-ethnicity, instn type, and field of study, 1991/92 and trends, annual rpt, S6790–5.15

Pennsylvania public and nonpublic school enrollment, by grade, race-ethnicity, sex, and county, 1991/92 and trends, annual rpt, S6790–5.1

Pennsylvania public and nonpublic school enrollment, by grade, race-ethnicity, sex, and county, 1992/93 and trends, annual rpt, S6790–5.17

South Carolina higher education enrollment, degrees, staff, and finances, by instn, 1992 and trends, annual rpt, S7185–2

South Dakota public higher education finances, staff, enrollment, degrees, and facilities, by instn, FY93 annual rpt, S7375–1

Tennessee higher education enrollment, finances, staff, and programs, by instn, 1992/93 and trends, annual rpt, S7525–1

Tennessee statistical abstract, general data, 1992/93 annual rpt, U8710–2.16

Texas higher education credit hours and enrollment, by curriculum area and instn, 1991/92, annual rpt, S7657–1.2

Utah high school senior course-taking patterns, by subject area, 1992 and trends, annual rpt, S7815–1.1

Vermont higher education info, including degrees conferred, enrollment, and finances, by instn, 1992 annual rpt, S8035–2

West Virginia education professional certification, by field, 1991/92, annual rpt, S8540–3

West Virginia higher education enrollment and degrees conferred, by instn, 1991/92 and trends, annual rpt, S8533–1.1

West Virginia public school professional employment and certification data, by field, 1992/93 and trends, annual rpt, S8540–4

Curricula

Wyoming public secondary school instructors and salaries, by subject area and sex, 1992, annual rpt, S8890–1.2

see also Agricultural education
see also Art
see also Arts and the humanities
see also Astronomy
see also Biological sciences
see also Business education
see also Chemistry
see also Driver education
see also Earth sciences
see also Economics
see also Educational reform
see also Environmental sciences
see also Foreign languages
see also Health education
see also Home economics
see also Industrial arts
see also Journalism
see also Language arts
see also Legal education
see also Mathematics
see also Medical education
see also Military education
see also Music
see also Physical education and training
see also Physical sciences
see also Physics
see also Political science
see also Psychology
see also Scientific education
see also Social sciences
see also Social work
see also Teacher education
see also Technical education
see also Vocational education and training

Customer service

see Public relations

Customs duties

see Tariffs and foreign trade controls

Cutts, James A.

"Taxable Sales in Virginia, 1991", U9080–8
"Virginia Gross State Product, 1963-89", U9080–6

Czech Republic

- Chemical industry sales, export value, and employment, by leading firm, 1990, article, A1250–1.509
- Entertainment industry devs, including film production, theater screens, TV homes, and VCR penetration, 1993 feature, C9380–1.536
- Nuclear reactors in operation, with capacity, electricity generation, and construction, by unit and country, 1992, annual rpt, B6800–2.2

Czechoslovakia

- Chemical production by product, and sales, exports, and employment of leading firms, by Republic, 1990-92, article, A1250–1.509
- Energy intl sourcebook, with detail on oil and gas industry operations, supply-demand, and prices, for approx 80 countries, 1970s-91, annual compilation, C6985–10.2
- Foreign investment in chemical and aggregate leading industries by US and 5 European countries, 1992, article, A1250–1.520
- Motor vehicle world production, sales, trade, and registrations, by country, world area, manufacturer, and make, 1991 and trends, annual rpt, A0865–2.1

Public opinion in 9 European countries and 3 Soviet Union Republics on political, economic, and social issues, 1991 survey, C8915–8

Sulfur dioxide concentrations above selected regions of Czechoslovakia, quinquennially 1970-85, biennial rpt, R9455–1.1

see also Czech Republic
see also Slovakia

Dahomey

see Benin

Daidone, John

"Supply of Accounting Graduates and the Demand for Public Accounting Recruits, 1993", A1885–1

Dairy industry and products

- Clinical mastitis prevalence and control efforts in dairy herds, with data on associated costs, Illinois and Ohio studies, 1993 articles, A3100–2.508, A3100–2.512
- Consumer nutrition awareness and health concerns, with food shopping and consumption patterns, by respondent characteristics, 1993 survey, annual rpt, A4950–36
- Exports of farm products, by detailed commodity and country of destination, US and California, 1991, annual rpt, B9520–1
- Financial ratios and performance, for over 350 SIC 4-digit industries, FY88-92, annual rpt, A6400–3
- Food industry new product introductions, with data by product category, 1992, annual article, C2150–6.505
- Latin America statistical abstract, general data by country, 1992 annual rpt, U6250–1.16, U6250–1.24, U6250–1.25
- Livestock operations with milk cows, by State and region, 1991, annual rpt, A2100–1.1
- Milk production volume and number of dairy cows, 1992 and 2000, article, C2150–6.503
- Milk sales, by container type and size, 1989 and trends, annual rpt, C3975–5.3
- Milk sales volume share for plastic vs paperboard containers, 1973 and 1991, article, C1850–1.509
- Operating and financial composite ratios for corporations, with establishments and receipts, for approx 200 industries, by asset size, FY90, annual rpt, C7800–1
- Production, consumption, milk prices, and cows on farms, US and/or by State, 1992 and trends, annual rpt, S1685–1.3
- Production, consumption, stocks, trade, and prices for approx 100 basic commodities, including by country and producing State, commodity yearbook for 1993, C2400–1, C2400–2
- Production, income, and milk cows on farms, by State, 1992, annual rpt, S0850–1.6
- Retail prices for selected consumer items in approx 300 cities, quarterly rpt, A0150–1
- Sales and consumer expenditures, for food store products by type, 1991-92, annual feature, C4655–1.510
- Sales volume shares by retail outlet type, for approx 300 food, drug, and other product categories, 1993 annual feature, C4655–1.504

Index by Subjects and Names

- Shopping center financial and operating data, with detail by type of tenant, US and Canada, 1991, triennial rpt, R9285–1
- Supermarket product sales and market shares, for top 10 brands in 10 cheese product categories, 1991-92, C2710–1.505
- Supermarket sales by detailed product type, 1992 and trends, annual feature, C5225–1.507
- Vending machine sales by product type, and machines on location, 1992 and trends, annual rpt, C9470–1
- Veterinary services costs for dairy farmers correlated with milk production, Pennsylvania study, 1986-90, article, A3100–2.506
- Yogurt market shares, and number of coupons issued, for 2 leading brands and/or aggregate private labels, 1992-93, article, C2710–1.545

State and local:

- Alabama agricultural production, marketing, and income, by county and/or commodity, and farms and acreage, 1992 and trends, annual rpt, S0090–1
- Alaska agricultural production and marketing, by district and commodity, 1960s-92, annual rpt, U5750–1
- Arizona agricultural production, marketing, and finances, by commodity and county, 1988-92, annual rpt, U5830–1
- Arkansas agricultural production, marketing, and finances, by commodity and county, with farms and acreage, 1992 and trends, annual rpt, U5920–1
- California dairy production, sales, marketing, and consumption, 1992 and trends, annual rpt, S0850–1.6
- California livestock production and marketing, with comparisons to US, 1983-92, annual rpt, S0850–1.2
- Colorado agricultural production, marketing, and finances, by commodity and/or county, with farms and acreage, 1992 and trends, annual rpt, S0985–1
- Florida livestock, dairy, and poultry production, inventory, marketing, and finances, with detail by commodity or species, 1992 and trends, annual rpt, S1685–1.3
- Georgia agricultural production, marketing, and finances, by commodity and/or county, and farms and acreage, 1991 and trends, annual rpt, S1855–1
- Hawaii agricultural production and marketing, by commodity and island, 1987-91, annual rpt, S2030–1
- Hawaii dairy product inspections, and milk production, by location, 1990, annual rpt, S2065–1.6
- Illinois agricultural production, marketing, and finances, by county or commodity, and farms and farmland, 1991 and trends, annual rpt, S2390–1
- Kansas agricultural production, marketing, and finances, by county and/or commodity, and farm acreage and value, 1992 and trends, annual rpt, S2915–1
- Kentucky agricultural production, marketing, and finances, by commodity and county; and farms, acreage, and value; 1992 and trends, annual rpt, S3085–1
- Louisiana agricultural production, marketing, and finances, by commodity or parish, 1985-91, annual rpt, U2740–1

Index by Subjects and Names

Michigan agricultural production, marketing, and finances, by commodity or county, 1987-91, annual rpt, S3950–1

Minnesota agricultural production, marketing, and finances, by county or commodity, and farms and acreage, 1992 and trends, annual rpt, S4130–1

Missouri agricultural production, marketing, and finances, by commodity and/or county, and farms and acreage, 1988-92, annual rpt, S4480–1

Montana agricultural production, marketing, and finances, by commodity and county, 1991 and trends, annual rpt, S4655–1

Nebraska agricultural production, marketing, and finances, by commodity and/or county, and farms and acreage, 1991 and trends, annual rpt, S4835–1

Nevada agricultural production, marketing, and finances, by county and commodity, and farms and acreage, 1992 and trends, annual rpt, S5010–1

New Jersey agricultural production, marketing, and finances, by commodity and/or county, and farms and acreage, 1986-91, annual rpt, S5350–1

New Mexico agricultural production, marketing, and finances, by commodity and county, with farms and acreage, 1991 and trends, annual rpt, S5530–1

New York State dairy cows, milk and manufactured products production, and plants, 1992 and trends, annual rpt, S5700–1

New York State index of milk prices received by farmers, quarterly rpt, S5735–2

North Carolina agricultural production, marketing, and finances, by commodity and county, 1991 and trends, annual rpt, S5885–1

North Dakota agricultural production and marketing, by commodity and county, and farm finances, 1992 and trends, annual rpt, U3600–1

Ohio agricultural production, marketing, and finances, by commodity and county, with farms and acreage, 1990-91 and trends, annual rpt, S6240–1

Oklahoma agricultural production, marketing, and finances, by commodity and county, 1992 and trends, annual rpt, S6405–1

Oregon agricultural production, marketing, and finances, by commodity and/or county, with farms and acreage, 1991 and trends, annual rpt, S6575–1

Pennsylvania agricultural production, marketing, and finances, by county and commodity, and farms and acreage, 1992 and trends, annual rpt, S6760–1

South Carolina agricultural production and finances, by commodity and county, 1991-92 and trends, annual rpt, U1075–3

South Dakota agricultural production, marketing, and finances, by commodity and county, and farms and acreage, 1992 and trends, annual rpt, S7280–1

Tennessee agricultural production and marketing, by commodity and county, with farms, acreage, and farm value, 1992 and trends, annual rpt, S7460–1

Texas agricultural production, marketing, and finances, by commodity and county, and farms and farmland, 1991 and trends, annual rpt series, S7630–1

Utah agricultural production, marketing, and finances, by commodity and county, with farms and acreage, 1992 and trends, annual rpt, S7800–1

Vermont dairy production data, and industry plants and operations, 1989-90 biennial rpt, S7978–1

Washington State agricultural production, marketing, and finances, by commodity and/or county, 1992 and trends, annual rpt, S8328–1

Washington State dairy farms affected by Nov 1990 flood, with cattle deaths and economic loss, 1993 article, A3100–2.512

West Virginia agricultural production, marketing, and finances, by commodity or county, 1991 and trends, annual rpt, S8510–1

Wisconsin agricultural production, marketing, and finances, by commodity and county, and farms, acreage, and sales, 1992 and trends, annual rpt, S8680–1

Wyoming agricultural production, marketing, and finances, by county and/or commodity, and farms, acreage, and value, 1992 and trends, annual rpt, S8860–1

see also Ice cream

Dallas, Tex.

Discount stores shopped and store characteristics, for 3 major chains in 3 market areas, 1993 surveys and trends, articles, C5150–3.516

see also under By City in the "Index by Categories"

Dams

Construction cost indexes for water projects, by expenditure category, weekly rpt quarterly feature, C5800–2.534

World dams installed and under construction, and hydroelectric resources, by country, 1992/93 biennial rpt, R9455–1.7

State and local:

California statistical abstract, general data, 1992 annual rpt, S0840–2.7

Hawaii data book, general data, 1992 annual rpt, S2090–1.5

see also Reservoirs

Daniel Stern and Associates

Hospital emergency dept salaries for physician directors and staff, 1992-93, article, A1865–1.514

Daratech Inc.

Computer-aided design, manufacturing, and engineering (CAD/CAM/CAE) revenues, with market shares for 10 companies, 1992, article, C7000–7.501

Computer-aided design, manufacturing, and engineering (CAD/CAM/CAE) revenues worldwide, with market shares for 10 companies, 1993, article, C5800–4.513

Computer aided design/manufacturing (CAD/CAM) market value, with market shares for 7 companies, 1992-93, article, C1850–2.506

D'Arista, Jane W.

"Parallel Banking System", R4700–22

Data processing

see Computer industry and products

see Computer networks

see Computer sciences

see Computer use

see Information storage and retrieval systems

D.C.

Dataquest Inc.

Computer product sales distribution by distribution channel and retail outlet type, 1991 or 1992 and 1995, article, C5150–3.507

Electronics and computer industries market trends and outlook, monthly rpt, C1850–2

Europe and Germany personal computer market shares for top 6 manufacturers, 1993 article, C5800–7.539

Daval, Nicola

"ARL Statistics, 1991-92", A3365–1

Davis, Jerry S.

"NASSGP 24th Annual Survey Report, 1992/93 Academic Year", A7140–1

Day care programs

see Adult day care

see Child day care

Daylight Savings Time

Public opinion on uses for extra hour gained in time switch from daylight savings to standard, 1992 survey article, C5800–7.501

D.C.

Arrests of adults for serious crimes, 1982-92, article, R5685–4.505

Congressional appropriations for DC, and District funds approved, FY93, annual rpt, C2500–2

Court caseloads and dispositions, by type of case, and other court activity, 1992 and trends, annual rpt, S1515–1

Criminal justice system summary, including crimes and arrests, prosecutions and convictions, prisoners, and parole, 1991 and trends, annual rpt, S1535–2

Election results and turnout, and voter registration, by ward and precinct, 1992, biennial series, S1525–1

Elementary/secondary school finances, enrollment, grads, and test scores, with data by school, 1987/88-1991/92, annual rpt, S1605–2

Employment, earnings, and hours, by industry, with unemployment insurance data, monthly rpt, S1527–3

Engineers salaries by industry group, census div, selected metro area, and years since college degree, 1993, annual survey rpt, A0685–5

Engineers salaries by industry group, census div, selected metro area, degree level, and years since college degree, 1993, annual survey rpt, A0685–3

Govt financial condition, including receipts by source, expenditures by object or function, and fund balances, FY92, annual rpt, S1507–1

Labor force, employment by industry, and unemployment, for Maryland portion of DC metro area, monthly rpt, S3605–2

Markets with daily newspapers, demographic and economic info by geographic area, US and Canada, 1993, annual rpt, C3250–1

Statistical abstract of Maryland, with data for Washington MSA, 1993-94 biennial rpt, S3605–1

Statistical profile of DC, detailed social, govtl, and economic statistics, 1992 annual rpt, S1535–3

Statistical profiles of 50 States and DC, general data, 1993 annual almanac, C4712–1

D.C.

Utility and transportation regulatory agency activities, scope of jurisdiction, finances, and employees, by agency, 1991/92 annual rpt, A7015–2

see also under By City in the "Index by Categories"

see also under By State in the "Index by Categories"

de la Dehesa, Guillermo

"EMU and the Regions", R5025–9

Deaf

State and local:

Arkansas office for deaf/hearing impaired services offered and clients served, FY90, annual rpt, S0700–2

Mississippi school for the deaf staff, 1993 annual rpt, S4340–1.1

South Dakota enrollment in State school for the deaf, by level, fall 1987-92, annual rpt, S7375–1

Death penalty

see Capital punishment

Deaths

Africa military personnel hospital admissions and deaths due to selected diseases, for African troops serving in UK army, 1819-36, article, A2623–1.502

AIDS deaths in hospitals vs at home, by region and decedent characteristics, 1988 and trends, article, A2623–1.512

AIDS victims reported causes of death, including mention of AIDS on death certificates by patient characteristics, 1987-89, article, A2623–1.512

Black American socioeconomic status, including health, education, politics, crime, and employment, with comparisons to whites, 1993 annual compilation, C6775–2

Black American socioeconomic status, with comparisons to whites and data by region, 1960s-92, annual compilation, A8510–1.1

Black children and youth population, economic, health, and education data, with comparisons to whites, 1993 rpt, R3840–21

Cancer (urinary tract) death rates for men age 45-84, by age, State, and census div, 1979-89, article, B6045–1.503

Cancer incidence and mortality, including data by State, sex, and body site, 1993 and trends, annual rpt, A1175–1

Catholic population, including marriages and deaths, by diocese and State, 1993 annual compilation, C4950–1

Correctional instn admin, inmates, facilities, costs, parole and probation, and staffing, for local, State, and Federal systems, 1992 annual series, R4300–1

Correctional instn inmate deaths from natural causes, by sex, by State and Canadian Province, as of June 1992, annual rpt, A1305–3

EC Jewish population birth and death rates, for 3 countries, 1930s-90, article, A2050–1.1

Exercising population mortality rates for selected causes, by sex, 1992 article, B6045–1.501

Food-borne illness cases and fatalities, 1993 article, C2150–6.505

Latin America statistical abstract, general data by country, 1992 annual rpt, U6250–1.6

Leading causes of death by age group, 1989, B6045–1.501

Maternal mortality rates, by race, 1940-89, annual rpt, R3840–5.1

Metro area poverty and unemployment level effects on crime and mortality rates, for selected offenses and causes of death, 1990, R4700–18

Middle East death rates by country, with detail by selected cause for 3 countries, various years 1952-93, R8750–2.59

Occupational injuries/illnesses and fatalities, lost workdays, and employee views on workplace safety, with data by State, 1992 annual rpt, R8335–1.1

Older men deaths by cause, by smoking and drinking habits, race, and occupation, 1966-90, U3780–9

Population size and selected characteristics, by region, census div, and State, 1991 and trends, annual data sheet, R8750–9

Rates of death (age-adjusted) by sex, and deaths by cause, 1991 and trends, biennial fact book, A1325–1.6

Rates of death, by age, race, and sex, 1990, annual article, B6045–1.504

Rates of death, by demographic characteristics, for US and 14 other countries, 1991 and trends, article, B6045–1.503

Rates of death for leading causes, selected years 1960-90, and by State 1989, annual fact book, A1275–1.5

Rates of death for leading causes, with data by State, 1988 or 1990, annual rpt, A5173–2.4

Rates of death from cancer and heart disease/stroke, by sex and race-ethnicity, 1993 feature, C4215–1.511

State social, economic, and govtl indicators, with rankings, 1993 semiannual rpt, B8500–1.1, B8500–1.9

Statistical profiles of 50 States and DC, general data, 1993 annual almanac, C4712–1

Sweden, Stockholm deaths related to alcohol abuse, by sex and cause, 1987, article, A2623–1.508

Vitamin/mineral supplement use correlated with death rates, by sex and selected other characteristics, 1993 article, A2623–1.506

Women's deaths from AIDS and related conditions, 1988, article, A2623–1.501

Women's deaths from breast cancer correlated with occupation, by race, 1979-87, article, A2623–1.511

World birth, death, population increase, and infant death rate indicators, with detail for more and less developed countries, 1993, annual feature, R8750–1.509

World family planning programs and population socioeconomic profile, by country, 1991 rpt, R8720–1

World population and health indicators, with detail by region and country, 1992/93 biennial rpt, R9455–1.2, R9455–1.5

World population size and characteristics, GNP, and land area, by region and/or country, 1993 annual data sheet, R8750–5

World vital statistics, for top 50 countries in births, deaths, infant mortality, and life expectancy, 1992, semiannual rpt, B8500–1.16

Index by Subjects and Names

Youth death rates from leading causes, with firearm death rates by race, sex, and age, 1988 or 1989, annual rpt, R3840–11.1

State and local:

Alabama public health dept activities, including services provided, inspection and licensing activity, staff and finances, and vital statistics and health data, 1992 annual rpt, S0175–3

Alabama vital statistics, including population, births, deaths by cause, marriages, and divorces, by location and demographic characteristics, 1992 and trends, annual rpt, S0175–2

Alaska population, housing, income, and education data, by demographic characteristics and/or locality, 1990/91 and trends, annual rpt, S0320–4

Alaska vital statistics, including births, deaths by cause, marriages, divorces, adoptions, and population, by demographic characteristics and location, 1990, annual rpt, S0315–1

Alaska work-related deaths by cause, 1991, article, S0320–1.510

Arizona Indian population, education, housing, health, and employment characteristics, with detail by reservation, 1970s-91, recurring rpt, U5850–2.9

Arizona population and components of change, 1985-93, semiannual rpt, U5850–1.1

Arizona statistical abstract, general data, 1993 recurring rpt, U5850–2.3

Arkansas socioeconomic trends, by MSA and/or county, 1993 annual rpt, U5935–1

Arkansas vital statistics, including births, deaths by cause, marriages, and divorces, by age, sex, race, and county, 1991 and trends, annual rpt, S0685–1

California correctional instn inmate deaths, and fatal assaults on inmates and staff, 1991 and trends, annual rpt, S0820–1

California death rates and estimated alcohol-related mortality, by cause and demographic characteristics, 1980-89, article, A2623–1.508

California vital statistics, including population, births, and deaths by cause, by demographic characteristics and county, 1990 and trends, annual rpt, S0865–1

Colorado vital statistics, including population, births, deaths by cause, abortion, marriage and divorce, and adoption, by demographic characteristics and location, 1990 and trends, annual rpt, S1010–1

Connecticut vital statistics, including births, deaths by cause, marriages, and divorces, by demographic characteristics and location, 1989, annual rpt, S1200–1

DC statistical profile, general data, 1992 annual rpt, S1535–3.5

Delaware projected births and deaths, by county, 1990-2020, recurring rpt, S1375–3

Delaware vital statistics, including births, deaths by cause, and marriages and dissolutions, by demographic characteristics and location, 1990, annual rpt, S1385–2

Florida county data book, 1992/93 annual rpt, C6360–1

Index by Subjects and Names

Deaths

Florida deaths by selected cause, and incidence of selected communicable diseases, by county, 1992 annual rpt, S1746–1.1

Florida vital statistics, including population, births, deaths by cause, and marriages and dissolutions, by location and demographic characteristics, 1992 and trends, annual rpt, S1745–3

Georgia county guide, general data, 1993 annual rpt, U6750–1

Georgia vital statistics, including deaths by cause, demographic characteristics, and location, 1991 and trends, annual rpt, S1895–1.2

Hawaii health dept activities and services, including vital statistics and disease control, by location, 1990, annual rpt, S2065–1

Idaho and US economic trends and forecasts, quarterly rpt, S2245–2

Idaho vital statistics, including births, deaths by cause, abortions, marriages, and divorces, by demographic characteristics and county, 1991 and trends, annual rpt, S2250–2

Illinois statistical abstract, general data, 1992 annual rpt, U6910–2

Indiana deaths from top 3 causes and AIDS, by age group, 1989, article, U2160–1.501

Iowa vital statistics, including population, births, deaths by cause, marriages, and divorces, by demographic characteristics and location, 1991 and trends, annual rpt, S2795–1

Kansas vital statistics, including population, births, deaths by cause, abortions, marriages, and divorces, by demographic characteristics and location, 1991 and trends, annual rpt, S2975–1

Kentucky economic statistics, general data, 1993 annual rpt, S3104–1.3

Kentucky vital statistics, including births, deaths by cause, marriages and divorces, and population, by demographic characteristics and county, 1991, annual rpt, S3140–1

Louisiana vital statistics, including population, births, deaths by cause, reportable diseases, marriages, and divorces, by demographic characteristics and locality, 1989-90 and trends, annual rpt, S3295–1

Maine vital statistics, including births, deaths by cause, abortions, and marriages and divorces, by demographic characteristics and location, 1991 and trends, annual rpt, S3460–2

Maryland vital statistics, including population, births, deaths by cause, marriages, and divorces, by demographic characteristics and location, 1989 and trends, annual rpt, S3635–1

Massachusetts vital statistics, including births, deaths by cause, marriages, divorces, and population, by locality and demographic characteristics, 1990 and trends, annual rpt, S3850–1

Michigan vital statistics, including births, deaths, marriages, divorces/annulments, and communicable diseases, by location and demographic characteristics, 1990 and trends, annual rpt, S4000–3

Minnesota vital statistics, including population, births, abortions, deaths, marriages, and divorces, by location and demographic characteristics, 1991 and trends, annual rpt, S4190–2

Mississippi vital statistics, including births, deaths by cause, marriages, and divorces, by demographic characteristics and location, 1992 and trends, annual rpt, S4350–1

Missouri vital statistics, including population, births, deaths by cause, and marriages and divorces, by location and demographic characteristics, 1992 and trends, annual rpt, S4518–1

Montana vital statistics, including births, deaths by cause, abortion, disease, and marriage and divorce, by demographic characteristics and county, 1990-91 and trends, annual rpt, S4690–1

Nebraska vital statistics, including births, deaths, marriages, divorces, and population, by demographic characteristics and location, 1991 and trends, annual rpt, S4885–1

Nevada vital statistics, including births, abortions, and deaths by cause, by county and demographic characteristics, 1989 and trends, annual rpt, S5075–1

New Hampshire vital statistics, including population, births, deaths by cause, marriages, and divorces, by location and demographic characteristics, 1991 and trends, annual rpt, S5215–1

New Jersey vital statistics, including births, deaths, population, communicable diseases, and marriages and divorces, by demographic characteristics and location, 1990 and trends, annual rpt, S5405–1

New Mexico population size and components of change, by county, 1990-91, article, U7980–1.503

New Mexico vital statistics, including population, births, deaths, and disease, by location and demographic characteristics, 1991 and trends, annual rpt, S5605–1

New York State inmate deaths in correctional instns, by sex, 1991, recurring rpt, S5725–1.1

New York State prison inmate deaths by major cause in State and local facilities, 1991, annual rpt, S5760–3.4

New York State vital statistics, including population, births, deaths by cause, reportable diseases, and marriages and dissolutions, by demographic characteristics and/or location, 1990 and trends, annual rpt, S5765–1

North Carolina vital statistics, including population, births, deaths by cause, marriages, and divorces, by local area, 1991 and trends, annual rpt, S5927–1

North Dakota vital statistics, including births, deaths by cause, marriages and divorces, and abortions, by demographic characteristics and/or county, 1991 and trends, annual rpt, S6105–2

Ohio population by age, sex, and county, with summary components of change, quinquennially 1990-2015, recurring rpt, S6260–3

Ohio vital statistics, including births, deaths by cause, marriages, divorces, and population, by demographic characteristics and location, 1991 and trends, annual rpt, S6285–1

Oregon vital statistics, including births, deaths by cause, communicable diseases, marriages, and divorces, by age, sex, race-ethnicity, and county, 1991 and trends, annual rpt, S6615–5

Rhode Island vital statistics, including population, births, deaths, marriages, and divorces, by demographic characteristics and locality, 1989 and trends, annual rpt, S6995–1

South Carolina deaths, by detailed cause, age, sex, and race, 1990, annual rpt, S7175–2

South Carolina population and components of change, by county, 1980-90, annual planning rpt, S7155–3.1

South Carolina vital statistics, including births, deaths by cause, marriages, and divorces, by age, sex, race, and location, 1990 and trends, annual rpt, S7175–1

South Dakota vital statistics, including births, deaths, marriage and divorce, and communicable disease, by demographic characteristics and county, 1991 and trends, annual rpt, S7345–1

Tennessee correctional instn incidents, including disturbances, assaults, and deaths, FY91-92, annual rpt, S7480–1

Tennessee vital statistics, including births, deaths by cause, marriages, divorces, and population, by demographic characteristics and location, 1991 and trends, annual rpt, S7520–2

Texas vital statistics, including births, deaths by cause, abortions, marriages, and divorces, by location and demographic characteristics, 1991 and trends, annual rpt, S7685–1

Utah economic and demographic trends, by county and district, 1960-91, annual rpt, S7832–2

Utah population estimates and components, including data by county, 1992 and trends, annual article, U8960–2.504

Utah vital statistics, including births, deaths by cause, and population, by county and demographic characteristics, 1990 and trends, annual rpt, S7835–1

Vermont vital statistics, including population, births, deaths by cause, abortions, marriages, and divorces, by location and demographic characteristics, 1991 and trends, annual rpt, S8054–1

Virginia vital statistics, including births, deaths by cause, marriages and divorces, and communicable disease, by demographic characteristics and location, 1991 and trends, annual rpt, S8225–1

Washington State population and components of change, 1992 and trends, annual rpt, S8345–4

Washington State vital statistics, including births, deaths by cause, and population, by demographic characteristics and location, 1991 and trends, annual rpt, S8363–1

West Virginia vital statistics, including births, deaths by cause, marriages, and divorces, by location and demographic characteristics, 1991 and trends, annual rpt, S8560–1

Wisconsin birth, death, and marriage registrations, monthly rpt, S8750–1

Wisconsin correctional instn inmates, admissions, and releases, by instn and sex, FY92 and trends, annual rpt, S8692–1.6

Deaths

Wisconsin correctional instn inmates, admissions, and releases, by instn and sex, 1991 and trends, annual rpt, S8692–1.4

Wisconsin population, by age, sex, and county, with components of change, quinquennially 1990-2020, recurring rpt, S8675–4

Wisconsin vital statistics, including population, births, deaths by cause, and marriages and dissolutions, by county and demographic characteristics, 1991 and trends, annual rpt, S8715–4

Wyoming vital statistics, including population, births, deaths by cause, marriages, and divorces, by demographic characteristics and county, 1991 and trends, annual rpt, S8920–2

see also Accidental deaths
see also Autopsies
see also Capital punishment
see also Child mortality
see also Coroners
see also Euthanasia
see also Fetal deaths
see also Homicide
see also Infant mortality
see also Probate courts and cases
see also Suicide
see also Traffic accident fatalities
see also Vital statistics
see also War casualties
see also Wills and testaments

Debit cards
see Electronic funds transfer

Debt
see Business assets and liabilities, general
see Business assets and liabilities, specific industry
see Consumer credit
see Corporate bonds
see Credit
see Foreclosures
see Foreign debts
see Government assets and liabilities
see Government securities
see Loans
see Mortgages
see Municipal bonds
see Personal debt
see Public debt
see State bonds

Decaffeinated beverages
see Caffeine

DeComo, Robert E.
"Juveniles Taken into Custody Research Program: Estimating the Prevalence of Juvenile Custody by Race and Gender", A7575–1.13

Decontrol of prices
see Price regulation

Default
see Loan delinquency and default

Defective products
see also Motor vehicle defects

Defense
see Civil defense
see Department of Defense
see National defense

Defense budgets and appropriations

Aerospace industry, civil and military production, R&D, trade, employment, and finances, with Federal funding data, 1991 and trends, annual rpt, A0250–2

Budget authority and outlays under Bush vs Clinton Admin plans, FY93-98, R3834–17

Budget for defense R&D by service branch, FY92-94, and authority and outlays for DOD and DOE/other, FY93-98, article, C5800–4.514

Budget receipts and outlays of Fed Govt, by source and function, 1920s-93, annual rpt, R9050–1.3

Budget requests, and amounts approved by House and Senate Armed Services Committees, for 16 major procurement and R&D programs, FY94, article, C5800–4.524

Congressional organization, major legislative and budget actions, and agency and program appropriations, 102nd Congress, 2nd session, 1992, annual rpt, C2500–2

DOD budget authority and outlays under Bush and Clinton Admins, FY94-98, article, C5800–4.510

Dual-use technology program defense budget, by program type, FY93-94, article, C5800–4.515

Japan defense budget allocations by equipment type, procurement, and value of contracts for top 10 contractors, various periods FY82-95, article, R5650–2.518

Reduction effect on jobs in 10 most affected States, and current and proposed budget and armed forces, 1993 article, C8900–1.508

Science and technology funding by program area, FY93, annual rpt, A4725–1.4

State and local:

California economic impact of DOD budget cuts, 1993-98, annual rpt, S0840–3.1
see also Defense expenditures

Defense Commissary Agency

Payments to 406 DeCA suppliers receiving $1 million/more, FY92, article, C0500–1.506

Defense contracts and procurement

Aerospace industry, civil and military production, R&D, trade, employment, and finances, with Federal funding data, 1991 and trends, annual rpt, A0250–2

Aircraft (off-the-shelf) shipments and/or billings to US military, by general aviation manufacturer, quarterly rpt, A5120–1

Base closure/realignment and impact on personnel, with data on military spending and installations, by State, region, and base, 1988-93, R8490–45

Coal shipments to US military in West Germany, 1967-91, annual rpt, A7400–2.1

Commissary supplier payments from Defense Commissary Agency, for 406 suppliers receiving $1 million/more, FY92, article, C0500–1.506

Communications equipment for defense purposes, shipments, new and unfilled orders, and inventories, monthly rpt, A4725–2

Conversion of defense industries to nonmilitary production, with data on defense contracts and spending, top contractors, and employment, 1980s and trends, R4700–19

DOD contract and payroll spending, military and civilian personnel, installations, and cutbacks, by State and region, various years FY81-93, R8490–44

Hispanic-owned high-technology company defense contracting involvement, and response to reduced DOD spending, 1993 annual survey article, C4575–1.510

Japan defense budget allocations by equipment type, procurement, and value of contracts for top 10 contractors, various periods FY82-95, article, R5650–2.518

Japan defense contract value for top 10 contractors, FY91-92, article, R5650–2.533

Japan defense program planned equipment purchases, FY91-95, article, R5650–2.510

Local area rankings by DOD contract spending, for top 20 counties and/or metro areas, 1992, article, A6450–2.509

Machine tool military prime contract awards, by machine type, FY88-92, annual rpt, A3179–2.1

Navy tactical advanced computer costs and processor speeds, by computer generation, 1993 article, C5800–4.521

Prime contract awards, by region and State, FY81, FY86, and FY91, annual rpt, R8490–11

Sales (military) for top 10 defense contractors, with share of company total sales, 1991, article, C8900–1.509

Shipbuilding (naval vessel) activity in private shipyards, including contracts, deliveries, and ongoing construction, 1993 recurring rpt, A8900–6

Statistical profiles of 50 States and DC, general data, 1993 annual almanac, C4712–1

State and local:

Alaska defense contract values for top 5 contractors, 1992, article, S0320–1.511

Arizona defense contracts and value, employment, and wages, for aggregate leading contractors, 1987-92, article, S0465–1.509

California defense contract value, FY82-92, annual rpt, S0840–3.1

California DOD prime contracts, bimonthly rpt, S0840–1

California prime contract awards from DOD and NASA, FY91 and trends, annual rpt, S0840–2.8

Connecticut economic trends, including defense contract awards, FY83-92, annual rpt, S1170–2

Florida statistical abstract, general data, 1992 annual rpt, U6660–1.23

Hawaii data book, general data, 1992 annual rpt, S2090–1.10

Minnesota defense contract awards, with detail by industry and impact on employment, FY85-92, article, S4205–3.501

Mississippi statistical abstract, general data, 1992 annual rpt, U3255–4.13

New York State statistical yearbook, general data, 1992 annual rpt, U5100–1.3

Tennessee statistical abstract, general data, 1992/93 annual rpt, U8710–2.3

Defense Department
see Department of Defense

Defense expenditures

Aerospace industry, civil and military production, R&D, trade, employment, and finances, with Federal funding data, 1991 and trends, annual rpt, A0250–2

Base closure/realignment and impact on personnel, with data on military spending and installations, by State, region, and base, 1988-93, R8490–45

Index by Subjects and Names

College freshmen attitudes on military spending increase, by sex and instn type, fall 1992, annual survey, U6215–1

Conversion of defense industries to nonmilitary production, with data on defense contracts and spending, top contractors, and employment, 1980s and trends, R4700–19

DOD contract and payroll spending, military and civilian personnel, installations, and cutbacks, by State and region, various years FY81-93, R8490–44

Expenditures for defense and share of GDP, for high and low points during 4 defense "drawdowns" (World War II, Korea, Vietnam, and current), article, C5800–4.506

Federal budget trends, including spending by program, State, and region, FY81-94, annual rpt, R8490–11

Forecasts of natl income and product account components and related indicators, quarterly rpt, U1880–1

Latin America statistical abstract, general data by country, 1992 annual rpt, U6250–1.11

Public opinion on defense spending and Clinton Admin proposed cuts, Mar 1993 Gallup Poll and trends, C4040–1.510

Purchases of durable goods vs total expenditures, 1988-92, annual rpt, A3179–2.3

State defense-related product as percent of total product, for top 10 States, 1992, article, C5800–7.531

Trends in GDP and defense component, 1990-1st qtr 1993, article, A8813–1.503

State and local:

Alaska military personnel, housing arrangements, and defense expenditures, by census area and borough, 1993 article, S0320–1.511

California defense expenditures, with detail for 5 local areas, 1992 article, C5800–4.502

Georgia DOD and other Federal expenditures, by county, FY91, biennial rpt, U6730–1.11

Hawaii data book, general data, 1992 annual rpt, S2090–1.9, S2090–1.10, S2090–1.13

Hawaii defense payroll and local purchases, bimonthly rpt, B3500–1

Hawaii economic conditions, including employment, population, tourism, and construction, quarterly rpt, S2090–2

Virginia defense purchases compared to total output, by industry div and selected group, 1991, with outlook for 1997, article, S8205–4.503

Virginia DOD expenditures by category, by county and city, FY89-91, article, S8205–4.502

see also Budget of the U.S.

see also Defense budgets and appropriations

see also Defense contracts and procurement

see also Defense research

see also Military pay

Defense industries

Congressional campaign finances, with detailed data for individual Members, and leading contributors by type and industry, 1990 election and trends, biennial rpt, R3828–2.2

Electronics industry defense-related factory sales, by equipment type, 1982-91, annual rpt, A4725–1.2

Expenditures, employment, exports, and facilities for health care vs defense, 1993, article, C8900–1.515

Financial performance and growth rankings for approx 1,000 top corporations, with comparisons by industry group, 1993 annual rpt, C3950–1.505

Financial performance of aerospace and defense industries, with data for approx 200 major US and foreign companies, FY92 and trends, annual feature, C5800–4.519

Job losses from defense budget cuts, with loss outlook for 1997, for 10 States, 1993 article, C8900–1.508

Russia military-industrial complex share of production for 16 products, 1992 feature, U2030–1.503

Stock performance outlook for 8 defense contractors, 1993 article, C5800–7.546

State and local:

Maine defense-dependent employment, by industry, 1989, article, S3465–2.502

see also Aerospace industry

see also Arms trade

see also Conversion of industry

see also Defense contracts and procurement

see also Defense expenditures

see also Missiles and rockets

Defense research

Aerospace industry, civil and military production, R&D, trade, employment, and finances, with Federal funding data, 1991 and trends, annual rpt, A0250–2

Budgets and staff of 3 Federal weapons laboratories, 1993 article, C5800–7.531

Expenditures for total and/or industry R&D, with Federal funding by purpose, DOD obligations by object, and comparisons to 3 other countries, 1991 and trends, article, R5650–2.521

Federal budget for defense-related R&D, by service branch, FY92-94, article, C5800–4.514

see also Strategic Defense Initiative

Degrees, educational

see Degrees, higher education

see Educational attainment

see under By Educational Attainment in the "Index by Categories"

Degrees, higher education

Accounting grad supply-demand, including detail by sex, race-ethnicity, and region, 1991/92 and trends, annual rpt, A1885–1

Athletes with scholarships, enrollment and graduation rates, by sex, race-ethnicity, and major sport, for Natl Collegiate Athletic Assn Div I instns, 1992/93, annual rpt, A7440–4

Black American educational statistics, with comparisons to whites, 1970s-92, annual compilation, C6775–2.3

Black American higher education degrees earned, by sex and level, 1989/90, article, A8510–1.1

Black children and youth population, economic, health, and education data, with comparisons to whites, 1993 rpt, R3840–21

Business and total higher education degrees awarded, by level and sex, 1962/63-1990/91, article, A0605–2.502

Degrees, higher education

Business school doctoral degrees awarded and faculty positions filled and vacant, by field, 1991/92-1993/94, annual feature, A0605–2.502

Chemistry and chemical engineering degrees awarded, by level, sex, and instn, 1991/92 and trends, annual articles, A1250–1.535

Chemistry and chemical engineering degrees awarded, by level, 1972-91, annual feature, A1250–1.537

Chemistry and chemical engineering degrees awarded, by level, 1980/81-1990/91, annual article, A1250–1.544

Chemistry and chemical engineering grad starting salaries, employment status, demographic characteristics, and advanced study plans, 1991/92, annual rpt, A1250–2

Conferrals of bachelors and masters degrees, by sex and race-ethnicity, 1990, C4215–1.503

Conferrals of degrees by level and sex, 1992-2003, annual feature, C2175–1.504

Conferrals of degrees by level, sex, discipline, and race-ethnicity, 1990/91, recurring feature, C2175–1.523

Dental advanced education programs, enrollment, grads, and finances, by instn and State, 1992/93 annual rpt, A1475–10

Dental allied education enrollment, grads, and tuition, by instn, 1992/93 annual rpt, A1475–5

Dental school applications, enrollment, grads, and tuition/fees, by instn, 1992 and trends, annual rpt, A1475–4.2

Dental school enrollment and level of prior education for 1st-year students, and grads, by instn, 1992/93 annual rpt, A1475–3.1

Doctoral degree recipient characteristics, including citizenship status, source of support, field of study, and instn, 1990/91 and trends, annual rpt, R6000–7

Doctoral degrees conferred, and fields, for 108 instns, US and Canada, 1991/92 annual rpt, A3365–1

Doctoral degrees conferred and recipient characteristics, by field, 1992, annual feature, C2175–1.535

Earnings for persons receiving bachelors and advanced degrees by field, and degree fields of male and female recipients, 1990, article, U7860–1.505

Ecologist personal and professional characteristics, including research activity and funding, with data by field, Mar 1992 survey, recurring rpt, A4685–1

Elementary/secondary school superintendents personal and professional characteristics and views, 1992 survey rpt, A0775–5

Employment, hiring plans for college grads by industry, with data on campus visits, starting salaries, and minority hires, 1991/92-1992/93, annual rpt, A3940–3

Employment in business and industry, hiring plans for college grads, by field, salary, and degree, 1993 annual survey rpt, U3730–1

Engineering degrees awarded, by State, instn, and field, with detail for women, minorities, and foreign students, 1991/92, annual rpt, A0685–1

Freshmen attitudes and characteristics, degree and career plans, and financial aid sources, by sex and instn type, fall 1992, annual survey, U6215–1

Degrees, higher education

Freshmen attitudes and characteristics, degree and career plans, and financial aid sources, fall 1992, annual survey summary, C2175–1.505

Geoscience enrollment and degrees awarded, by sex, race-ethnicity, and discipline, 1991/92, annual rpt, A1785–3

Higher education student athlete vs total graduation rates after 6 years, by sex, race, and Natl Collegiate Athletic Assn Div I instn, summer 1991, recurring feature, C2175–1.522, C2175–1.527

Higher education, 2-year college enrollment, degrees, faculty and staff, and tuition/fees, by instn and State, 1992 annual directory, A0640–1

Hispanic American educational statistics, with comparisons to whites, 1970s-92, annual compilation, C6775–3.2

Hospital CEO views on best educational preparation for CEO position, 1992 survey, article, A1865–1.504

Humanities bachelor degrees granted, by field of study, 1980/81 and 1989/90, article, R4800–2.511

Journalism/mass communication enrollment and grads by level, by instn, sex, race-ethnicity, and field, 1990/91 and trends, annual article, A3225–1

Latin America statistical abstract, general data by country, 1992 annual rpt, U6250–1.8

Law school enrollment by minority status, degrees conferred, staff, and library holdings, by instn, 1992/93 and trends, annual rpt, A0970–1

Library school grads, placements, and salaries, by region and sex, 1991 and trends, annual compilation, C1650–3.3

Library/info science school degrees awarded, by level, sex, race-ethnicity, and instn, 1991/92, annual rpt, A3235–1.2

Mathematics dept faculty, salaries, enrollment, and degree recipient characteristics, 1991/92 and trends, annual survey, A2085–1

Medical school total and women grads, decennially 1960/61-1990/91, annual fact book, A1275–1.1

Mining engineer grads by degree level, 1980-1995/96, article, C5226–1.507

Minority involvement in higher education, including degrees awarded by field, race-ethnicity, sex, and State, 1970s-91, annual rpt, A1410–10

Nursing college deans and salaries, by personal and instn characteristics, 1992/93, annual rpt, A0615–2

Nursing grad student reasons for pursuing degrees, and employment expectations, 1993 survey article, A8010–3.503

Nursing programs (State-approved) for practical/vocational nurses, including admissions, enrollment, and grads, by instn, State, and territory, 1992, annual directory, A8010–5

Nursing programs (State-approved) for registered nurses, including admissions, enrollment, and grads, by instn, State, and territory, 1992, annual directory, A8010–4

Nursing school enrollment and grads, by degree level, sex, race-ethnicity, and instn type and location, 1992/93 and trends, annual rpt, A0615–4

Nursing schools, programs, enrollment, student and staff characteristics, and grads, 1991 and trends, annual rpt, A8010–1

Optometry school faculty, enrollment and degrees, policies and programs, and finances, by instn, 1991/92, annual survey, A3370–2

Osteopathy college enrollment, student and faculty characteristics, and finances, 1992/93 and trends, annual rpt, A0620–1

Pharmacy degree program applications, enrollment, and degrees conferred, by student characteristics and instn, 1990/91 and trends, annual rpt, A0630–9

Physics and astronomy bachelor degree recipients postgraduation plans and demographic characteristics, 1991/92 and trends, annual survey, A1960–3

Physics and astronomy enrollment and degrees, annual survey of US college depts, series, A1960–2

Physics and astronomy grads employment status, by sex, age, subfield, citizenship, degree, and employer type, with salary info, 1990/91, annual rpt, A1960–1

Political science higher education dept characteristics, including faculty, salaries, enrollment, and finances, 1991/92 annual rpt, A2617–1

Psychology doctoral degree recipient employment and demographic characteristics, and finances, 1990/91, biennial survey rpt, A2620–4

Public health school applicant, student, and grad characteristics, by instn, 1991/92 and trends, annual rpt, A3372–3

Public health school faculty characteristics, by instn, fall 1991, recurring rpt, A3372–1

Salaries of scientists, engineers, technicians, and other professionals, by employee and employer characteristics, 1990s and trends, biennial rpt, A3960–1

Salary and job offers for college grads, by field of study, type of employer, and degree level, by region, interim rpt series, A3940–1

Salary and job offers for college grads, by field of study, type of employer, and degree level, series, A3940–2

Salary trends for new grads, by degree level, 1992/93, annual survey rpt, U3130–1

Social work higher education programs, faculty and student characteristics, and student aid, with data by instn, 1992 and trends, annual rpt, A4515–1

Southern States higher education degree conferrals, by sex, race-ethnicity, level, and selected field, by State, 1990s and trends, biennial fact book, A8945–1.3

Southern States higher education enrollment, degrees, appropriations, tuition/fees, and faculty compensation, by instn type, for 15 States, 1990/91, annual rpt, A8945–31

State higher education data, including degrees awarded by level, and graduation rates at Natl Collegiate Athletic Assn Div I instns, by State, 1993 annual rpt, C2175–1.531

State social, economic, and govtl indicators, with rankings, 1993 semiannual rpt, B8500–1.13

Index by Subjects and Names

Statistical profiles of 50 States and DC, general data, 1993 annual almanac, C4712–1

Theological school enrollment, staff and compensation, and finances, with data by instn, 1991/92 and trends, annual rpt, A3376–1

Veterinarian professional characteristics for public/corporate employees, including importance of selected degrees, 1993 survey article, A3100–2.520

Women and minorities in professional fields, detailed education and labor force data, 1980s-91, with historical trends, recurring rpt, A3960–2

State and local:

Alabama statistical abstract, general data, 1992 recurring rpt, U5680–2.4

Arizona statistical abstract, general data, 1993 recurring rpt, U5850–2.4

Arkansas higher education degrees conferred, by level, discipline, student race and sex, and instn, 1990/91 and trends, annual rpt, S0690–3

California postsecondary education enrollment and degrees, by sex, race-ethnicity, and instn, 1990/91, annual series, S0827–2

DC statistical profile, general data, 1992 annual rpt, S1535–3.6

Delaware postsecondary education finances, enrollment, and degrees conferred, by instn, FY94 annual rpt, S1425–1

Florida higher education enrollment, degree programs, staff, and finances, by State-supported instn, with student and staff characteristics, 1991/92 annual rpt, S1725–1

Georgia statistical abstract, general data, 1992-93 biennial rpt, U6730–1.2

Hawaii data book, general data, 1992 annual rpt, S2090–1.3

Idaho economic profile, general data, 1992 recurring rpt, S2218–2.3

Illinois higher education enrollment and degrees, by level, instn, field of instruction, and student characteristics, 1992 and trends, annual rpt, S2475–1.1

Iowa postsecondary enrollment, degrees, staff, and finances, by instn, 1990/91, annual rpt, S2755–1

Kentucky higher education enrollment, degrees, staff, and finances, by State-supported instn, 1983-92, annual rpt, S3130–3

Maryland statistical abstract, general data, 1993-94 biennial rpt, S3605–1.2

Minnesota postsecondary degrees awarded, by level, 1977/78-1989/90, biennial rpt, S4195–2.2

Mississippi higher education enrollment and degrees, by level and field, and finances, by State-supported instn, 1991/92, annual rpt, S4360–1

Missouri higher education degrees conferred, by level, sex, race-ethnicity, instn, and field of study, FY92 and trends, annual rpt, S4520–3.3

Nevada statistical abstract, general data, 1992 biennial rpt, S5005–1.7

New Jersey higher education bachelor degrees awarded and starting salaries of college grads, by field of study, 1993 annual article, S5425–1.504

North Carolina higher education degrees conferred by level, field of study, sex, race-ethnicity, and instn, 1991/92, annual rpt, U8013–1.2

Pennsylvania elementary/secondary and higher education enrollment, grads, staff, and finances, by instn type, 1981/82-1996/97, recurring rpt, S6790–5.10

Pennsylvania higher education degrees conferred, by level, sex, race-ethnicity, instn type, and field of study, 1990/91 and trends, annual rpt, S6790–5.2

Pennsylvania higher education degrees conferred by level, sex, race-ethnicity, instn type, and field of study, 1991/92 and trends, annual rpt, S6790–5.15

South Carolina higher education degrees awarded, by sex and race, FY91, annual planning rpt, S7155–3.3

South Carolina higher education enrollment, degrees, staff, and finances, by instn, 1992 and trends, annual rpt, S7185–2

South Dakota public higher education finances, staff, enrollment, degrees, and facilities, by instn, FY93 annual rpt, S7375–1

Tennessee higher education and vocational grads and degrees conferred, by sex and race-ethnicity, 1991/92, annual rpt, S7525–1.2

Utah higher education degrees, enrollment, staff, and finances, by public instn, with selected comparisons to instns in other States, 1993/94 annual rpt, S7895–2

Utah statistical abstract, general data, 1993 triennial rpt, U8960–1.3

Vermont higher education degrees conferred, by level, field, sex, and instn, 1991/92 and trends, annual rpt, S8035–2.1

West Virginia higher education enrollment and degrees conferred, by instn, 1991/92 and trends, annual rpt, S8533–1.1

see also under By Educational Attainment in the "Index by Categories"

Delaware

Court caseloads and dispositions, by type of court and case, and by county, with judicial dept finances, FY92, annual rpt, S1360–1

Crimes and arrests, by offense, county, and victim-offender characteristics, 1991 and trends, annual rpt, S1375–5

Criminal sentencing, prison alternatives, and related issues, public opinion by respondent characteristics, Feb 1991 survey, R8825–11

Educational enrollment, grads, staff, finances, and facilities, by county, school district, and/or instn, 1991/92, annual rpt, S1430–1

Election results, by district and/or county, 1992 general election, biennial rpt, S1365–1

Employment, earnings, and hours, by locality and industry, and unemployment insurance activity, monthly rpt, S1405–2

Housing construction activity, with data on demolitions and mobile home sales, by locality, 1992 and trends, annual rpt, S1387–1

Markets with daily newspapers, demographic and economic info by geographic area, US and Canada, 1993 annual rpt, C3250–1

Population by age, sex, race, county, and city, and employment by county, 1990-2020, recurring rpt, S1375–3

Postsecondary education finances, enrollment, and degrees conferred, by instn, FY94 annual rpt, S1425–1

Statistical data book of Delaware, with social and economic data, 1993 annual rpt, S1375–4

Statistical profiles of 50 States and DC, general data, 1993 annual almanac, C4712–1

Traffic accidents, fatalities, and injuries, by circumstances, location, and vehicle type, and driver and victim characteristics, 1992 and trends, annual rpt, S1435–1

Utility and transportation regulatory agency activities, scope of jurisdiction, finances, and employees, by agency, 1991/92 annual rpt, A7015–2

Vital statistics, including births, deaths by cause, and marriages and dissolutions, by demographic characteristics and location, 1990, annual rpt, S1385–2

Welfare recipients, funds available, and payments, by program, with selected data by county, monthly rpt, S1385–1

see also Dover, Del.

see also Newark, Del.

see also Wilmington, Del.

see also under By City and By County in the "Index by Categories"

see also under By State in the "Index by Categories"

Deloitte and Touche

Advertising budget plans of retailers for Christmas season, 1991-92, survey article, C1850–14.504

Business process reengineering projects and benefits, views of corporate info officers, 1991-92 surveys, article, C1850–5.517

Computer system mgmt and technology devs, views of corporate info system officers, 1993 survey, article, C1850–5.509

Discount retailer views on economic and business outlook, 1992 survey article, C8130–1.502

Retailer views on "quick response" system implementation and benefits, and other technology use, 1992 survey, annual article, C5150–4.506

Textile industry use of computerized information systems, 1992 survey, article, C5226–3.502

DeLong, J. Bradford

"Investment Tax Credit and Economic Growth", A1310–1.16

Demand deposits

see Checking accounts

see Negotiable orders of withdrawal accounts

Democratic Party

Presidential primary election results and voter registration by county and district, by State, 1992 and trends, C2500–7

Women in State senates and houses/assemblies, by party and State, 1993 and trends, recurring rpt, U4510–1.63, U4510–1.67

Women in US House of Representatives and Senate, by party, 1917-95, annual rpt, U4510–1.61, U4510–1.69

Women State senate and house candidates and officeholders, by party and State, 1992 and trends, recurring rpt, U4510–1.64

State and local:

West Virginia election results and voter registration, by county and party, 1992 and trends, biennial rpt, S8630–1

Demography

see Population characteristics

see Population size

see Vital statistics

see under Demographic Breakdowns in the "Index by Categories"

Demolition

see Wrecking and demolition

DeMong, Richard F.

"1993 Home Lending Survey for Year End 1992", A4160–3

Demonstrations

see Public demonstrations

Denali Borough, Alaska

Population characteristics and income, with detail by local area, 1990-91, article, S0320–1.509

Denmark

Electronics industry trade and/or production trends by product category for 33 countries, with general economic profiles, 1993 annual rpt, A4725–1.4

Energy intl sourcebook, with detail on oil and gas industry operations, supply-demand, and prices, for approx 80 countries, 1970s-91, annual compilation, C6985–10.2

Machine tool industry operating data by country and product, 1992 and trends, annual rpt, A3179–2.2

Motor vehicle world production, sales, trade, and registrations, by country, world area, manufacturer, and make, 1991 and trends, annual rpt, A0865–2.1

see also under By Foreign Country or World Area in the "Index by Categories"

Dental condition

Absenteeism from work or school due to dental problems/treatment, by demographic characteristics, 1989, article, A2623–1.502

New England elderly population smoking status correlated with dental problems, by sex, 1993 article, A2623–1.511

State and local:

Hawaii data book, general data, 1992 annual rpt, S2090–1.2

Dentists and dentistry

Advanced dental education programs, enrollment, grads, and finances, by instn and State, 1992/93 annual rpt, A1475–10

Allied dental education enrollment, grads, and tuition, by instn, 1992/93 annual rpt, A1475–5

Black American practices concerning dental care, with comparisons to whites, 1981, 1986, and 1989, annual compilation, C6775–2.2

Black student enrollment in dental school, with comparison to whites, 1978/79 and 1989/90, annual compilation, C6775–2.3

Financial ratios and performance, for over 350 SIC 4-digit industries, FY88-92, annual rpt, A6400–3

Health insurance coverage and finances, and health care costs and facilities, by selected demographic characteristics, 1940s-91, annual rpt, A5173–2

Hispanic American student enrollment in dental school, with comparison to whites, 1979/80 and 1989/90, annual compilation, C6775–3.2

Dentists and dentistry

HMO benefits coverage, premiums, and rating methods used, by plan characteristics, 1991 and trends, annual rpt, A5150-2.1

Hospital patient admission rates and length of stay, by diagnosis and procedure, payment source, age, sex, and region, 1991, B4455-4

Hospital patient discharges and length of stay, by diagnosis, type of operation, age, and region, 1991, annual rpt series, B4455-1

Hospital patient discharges and length of stay, by diagnostic related group (DRG), payment source, age, and region, 1991, annual rpt series, B4455-3

Latin America statistical abstract, general data by country, 1992 annual rpt, U6250-1.7

Office visits to dentists, costs in approx 300 cities, quarterly rpt, A0150-1

Operating and financial composite ratios for corporations, with establishments and receipts, for approx 200 industries, by asset size, FY90, annual rpt, C7800-1

Public health school faculty characteristics, by instn, fall 1991, recurring rpt, A3372-1

Public opinion on honesty/ethical standards of selected occupations, 1992 Gallup Polls and trends, C4040-1.501

Schools of dentistry enrollment and grads, program characteristics, and faculty, by US and Canadian instn, 1992/93, annual rpt, A1475-3

Schools of dentistry finances, programs, and enrollment, by instn, annual rpt series, A1475-4

Statistical profiles of 50 States and DC, general data, 1993 annual almanac, C4712-1

Women and minorities in professional fields, detailed education and labor force data, 1991 and trends, recurring rpt, A3960-2.3

State and local:

Arizona statistical abstract, general data, 1993 recurring rpt, U5850-2.3

Arkansas human services dept finances and operations, including Medicaid payments by type of service, FY91 and trends, annual rpt, S0700-2.3

Florida county data book, 1992/93 annual rpt, C6360-1

Florida health care atlas, including manpower by occupation and health care facilities by type, by district and county, 1992 annual rpt, S1746-1.2

Florida statistical abstract, general data, 1992 annual rpt, U6660-1.20

Georgia statistical abstract, general data, 1992-93 biennial rpt, U6730-1.1

Hawaii data book, general data, 1992 annual rpt, S2090-1.2

Indiana Medicaid expenditures, by service and provider type and county, FY91-92, annual rpt, S2623-1.6

Kansas statistical abstract, general data, 1991/92 annual rpt, U7095-2.2

Kentucky Medicaid recipients and payments, by program, county, and type of medical service, monthly rpt, S3140-5

Maryland medical assistance payments and recipients, by program, type of service, location, demographic characteristics, and facility, FY92 and trends, annual rpt, S3635-3

Mississippi statistical abstract, general data, 1992 annual rpt, U3255-4.2

Missouri public welfare and medical assistance recipients, expenditures, and case processing, by program and county, FY92 and trends, annual rpt, S4575-2

Montana welfare and medical assistance program cases and payments, by county and type of service, monthly rpt, S4755-1

Nebraska Medicaid recipients and payments, by type of service and county, FY92, annual rpt, S4957-1.2

Nevada statistical abstract, general data, 1992 biennial rpt, S5005-1.2

New York State medical assistance expenditures, by State area and type of care, 1991 and trends, annual rpt, S5800-2.2

Oregon caseload and payments for medical service by category, monthly rpt quarterly table, S6615-8

South Carolina statistical abstract, general data, 1993 annual rpt, S7125-1.10

South Dakota medical assistance recipients and payments, by type of service, FY92, annual rpt, S7385-1.1

Tennessee statistical abstract, general data, 1992/93 annual rpt, U8710-2.17

Texas dentists offices/clinics and expenditures, 1977, 1982, and 1987, U8850-8.3

Washington State public assistance clients and service costs, by client characteristics, program, and county, FY90, annual rpt, S8420-2

see also Dental condition

Denver, Colo.

CPI by component, 1st half 1992, semiannual feature, S1040-4.501

CPI by component, 2nd half 1992, semiannual feature, S1040-4.504

Elementary and secondary school staff and salaries, and grads, by district sctting including Denver metro area, 1992 annual rpt series, S1000-2

Employment, unemployment, hours, and earnings, with job service activities, monthly rpt, S1040-4

Housing sales by price category, 1992, article, C1850-8.506

see also under By City in the "Index by Categories"

Department of Agriculture

Congressional organization, major legislative and budget actions, and agency and program appropriations, 102nd Congress, 2nd session, 1992, annual rpt, C2500-2

Research budget of USDA, by program, FY92-94, article, A1250-1.525

see also Commodity Credit Corp.

see also Farmers Home Administration

see also Rural Development Administration

Department of Air Force

Hazardous waste Air Force base site evaluation and cleanup costs by type, 1993 article, C5800-2.534

see also Air Force

see also National Guard

see also Service academies

Department of Army

see also Army

see also National Guard

see also Reserve Officers Training Corps

Index by Subjects and Names

see also Service academies

Department of Commerce

Congressional organization, major legislative and budget actions, and agency and program appropriations, 102nd Congress, 2nd session, 1992, annual rpt, C2500-2

see also Economic Development Administration

Department of Defense

Congressional organization, major legislative and budget actions, and agency and program appropriations, 102nd Congress, 2nd session, 1992, annual rpt, C2500-2

State and local:

Hawaii military and civilian DOD employment, with detail by service branch and installation, Sept 1991 and trends, annual rpt, S2090-1.10

see also Armed services

see also Defense Commissary Agency

see also Department of Air Force

see also Marine Corps

see also Under terms beginning "Defense" and "Military"

Department of Education

Congressional organization, major legislative and budget actions, and agency and program appropriations, 102nd Congress, 2nd session, 1992, annual rpt, C2500-2

Educational Resources Info Center data base records, 1960s-92, annual compilation, C1650-3.1

Department of Energy

Budget of DOE for FY92-93, and Clinton Admin proposal for FY94, by program, 1993 article, A1250-1.522

Congressional organization, major legislative and budget actions, and agency and program appropriations, 102nd Congress, 2nd session, 1992, annual rpt, C2500-2

Department of Health and Human Services

Congressional organization, major legislative and budget actions, and agency and program appropriations, 102nd Congress, 2nd session, 1992, annual rpt, C2500-2

Refugee assistance budgets for HHS and State Dept, by type of program, FY93-94, annual article, R9372-2.506

Department of Health, Education and Welfare

see Department of Education

see Department of Health and Human Services

Department of Housing and Urban Development

Appropriations by program, with number of assisted housing units by type, FY92-93, annual article, C4300-1.502

Congressional organization, major legislative and budget actions, and agency and program appropriations, 102nd Congress, 2nd session, 1992, annual rpt, C2500-2

Proposed funding for selected housing programs, and assisted housing units, FY94, annual feature, C4300-1.508

see also Government National Mortgage Association

see also Housing (FHA), HUD

Department of Interior

Congressional organization, major legislative and budget actions, and agency and program appropriations, 102nd Congress, 2nd session, 1992, annual rpt, C2500-2

see also Bureau of Indian Affairs

Index by Subjects and Names

see also Bureau of Land Management
see also Minerals Management Service

Department of Justice
Congressional organization, major legislative and budget actions, and agency and program appropriations, 102nd Congress, 2nd session, 1992, annual rpt, C2500–2

see also Immigration and Naturalization Service

Department of Labor
Congressional organization, major legislative and budget actions, and agency and program appropriations, 102nd Congress, 2nd session, 1992, annual rpt, C2500–2

see also Bureau of Labor Statistics
see also Occupational Safety and Health Administration

Department of Navy
see also Marine Corps
see also Navy
see also Service academies

Department of State
Congressional organization, major legislative and budget actions, and agency and program appropriations, 102nd Congress, 2nd session, 1992, annual rpt, C2500–2
Refugee assistance appropriations for 2 State Dept funds, FY93-94, article, R9372–2.508
Refugee assistance budgets for HHS and State Dept, by type of program, FY93-94, annual article, R9372–2.506
see also Agency for International Development

Department of Transportation
Congressional organization, major legislative and budget actions, and agency and program appropriations, 102nd Congress, 2nd session, 1992, annual rpt, C2500–2
see also Coast Guard
see also Federal Aviation Administration
see also Federal Highway Administration

Department of Treasury
Congressional organization, major legislative and budget actions, and agency and program appropriations, 102nd Congress, 2nd session, 1992, annual rpt, C2500–2
see also Internal Revenue Service

Department of Veterans Affairs
Congressional organization, major legislative and budget actions, and agency and program appropriations, 102nd Congress, 2nd session, 1992, annual rpt, C2500–2
Hearing aids issued to VA clinics by Denver Distribution Center, quarterly rpt, A5185–1
Physicians in Fed Govt, by detailed specialty and dept or service branch, 1992, annual rpt, A2200–3.2
Sales by Veterans Canteen Service, by dept, FY87-91, annual rpt, A2072–1
Sales by Veterans Canteen Service, by location and store, FY92 and trends, annual rpt, A2072–2.502

State and local:
Mississippi expenditures of VA, by object and county, 1991, annual rpt, U3255–4.13

Department stores
Clothing (men's) sales performance summary, with detail for private label, Feb-Oct 1991-92, annual rpt, A3880–1
Consumer buying power survey of population, income, and sales by kind of business, by census div, State, MSA, county, and city, 1992, annual rpt, C1200–1.511

Discount store financial and marketing devs, biweekly rpt, C5150–3
Expansion devs, and equipment and construction costs, by type of retail chain, 1993 annual articles, C5150–4.507
Financial data and business info for approx 240 US and Canadian retail chains, 1991-92 and trends, annual rpt, C3400–2
Financial performance and growth rankings for approx 1,000 top corporations, with comparisons by industry group, 1993 annual rpt, C3950–1.505
Financial ratios and performance, for over 350 SIC 4-digit industries, FY88-92, annual rpt, A6400–3
Markets with daily newspapers, demographic and economic info by geographic area, US and Canada, 1993 annual rpt, C3250–1
Military post exchange and commissary sales, by service branch or region, with merchandising devs and comparisons to civilian retail trade, monthly rpt, C0500–1
Operating and financial composite ratios for corporations, with establishments and receipts, for approx 200 industries, by asset size, FY90, annual rpt, C7800–1
Shopping center financial and operating data, with detail by type of tenant, US and Canada, 1991, triennial rpt, R9285–1
Sporting goods purchases, by product and outlet type, census div, and purchaser characteristics, with average prices, 1992 and trends, annual survey, A8485–2

State and local:
Hawaii data book, general data, 1992 annual rpt, S2090–1.23
Maine employment in trade, utilities, and transportation SIC 2-digit industries, by detailed occupation, 2nd qtr 1991, triennial rpt, S3465–1.25
New Hampshire wholesale and retail trade employment, by SIC 2-digit industry and detailed occupation, 1991, triennial rpt, S5205–2.26
Tennessee statistical abstract, general data, 1992/93 annual rpt, U8710–2.7
Texas trade, transportation, and public utilities employment, by SIC 2- and 3-digit industry and detailed occupation, 2nd qtr 1991, triennial survey rpt, S7675–1.31

Departments of Federal Government
see Federal executive departments
see under By Government Agency in the "Index by Categories"
see under name of individual department or agency

Deportation
Latin America immigrants to US, and temporary workers, aliens, and deportations, by country, 1992 annual rpt, U6250–1.14

Deposit insurance
Unit investment trust sales volume and value, by trust type, maturity period, and insurance features, monthly rpt, A6025–7

State and local:
Georgia credit union deposit insurance corporation assets and liabilities, Dec 1991-92, annual rpt, S1865–1
New Jersey public funds deposits in financial institutions, and collateral pledged for security, Dec 1992, annual rpt, S5355–1

Detective and protective services

see also Federal Deposit Insurance Corp.

Deposits
see Bank deposits
see Certificates of deposit
see Checking accounts
see Deposit insurance
see Negotiable orders of withdrawal accounts
see Savings

Depreciation
Auto operating costs, by component, 1950-93, annual rpt, A0865–1.2
Corporate alternative minimum tax impacts on capital investment costs, including data by industry and type of equipment, and comparisons to 7 other countries, 1991 rpt, A1310–4
Hospital industry physical assets depreciation rate, by instn characteristics and location, 1988-92, annual rpt, B1880–1.1
Machinery (metalworking) purchases, depreciation, and average age, for 9 manufacturing industry groups, 1973-92, annual rpt, A3179–2.3
Motor vehicle fleet vehicle depreciation costs, for autos and light trucks, 1990-92, article, C1575–2.501
Motor vehicle fleet vehicle depreciation costs, for autos and light trucks, 1991-92, annual rpt, C1575–2.507
Paper and allied products industries corporate depreciation and net worth, monthly rpt, A1630–5
Railroad (Class I) financial and operating data, with detail by company, 1982-91, annual rpt, A3275–8.2
Utility regulatory agency policies and practices, and industry financial and operating data, by utility type and agency, 1991/92 annual rpt, A7015–3

State and local:
Washington State water utilities financial and operating data, by company, 1988-90, annual rpt, S8450–1.1
Washington State water utilities financial and operating data, by company, 1989-91, annual rpt, S8450–1.4

Depressions
see Business cycles

Deregulation
see Government and business
see Price regulation

Desalination
see Saline water conversion

DeSantis, Victor S.
"Use of Council Committees in Local Governments", A5800–2.114

Desegregation of schools
see Discrimination in education

Deserts
see Arid zones

Detective and protective services
Apartment building (conventionally financed) detailed income and expense ratios for US and Canada, by building type, metro area, and US region, 1991 and trends, annual rpt, A5600–1
Apartment building (federally subsidized) detailed income and expense ratios, by building and subsidy type, building age, metro area, and region, 1991 and trends, annual rpt, A5600–5
Condominium, cooperative, and planned unit dev detailed expenses, for US and Canada, by building characteristics, metro area, and US region, 1991, annual rpt, A5600–3

Detective and protective services

Financial ratios and performance, for over 350 SIC 4-digit industries, FY88-92, annual rpt, A6400–3

Home security mechanical equipment, alarm systems, and services market value, 1980, 1991, and 1996, article, C2000–1.507

Office building detailed income and expense data, and energy use, US and Canada, by building characteristics, metro area, and US region, 1991 and trends, annual rpt, A5600–2

Security mgmt issues and devs, articles and special features on personnel, policies, devices, and related topics, monthly rpt, C1850–12

Shopping center detailed income and expense data, by building characteristics, metro area, and region, 1991, annual rpt, A5600–6

Shopping center security operations, including staffing, equipment, and crime incidents, by center type, 1992-93 and trends, articles, C5150–4.506

State and local:

- Colorado welfare and social services expenditures and caseloads, by county and/or program, FY91, annual rpt, S1085–1
- DC statistical profile, general data, 1992 annual rpt, S1535–3.5
- Illinois criminal offenses for campus, railroad, and other special police forces, 1991, annual rpt, S2536–1
- Indiana child protective service program case investigations and findings, FY92 annual rpt, S2623–1.7
- Michigan child and adult protection applications and cases, by county, monthly rpt, S4010–1
- Missouri public welfare and medical assistance recipients, expenditures, and case processing, by program and county, FY92 and trends, annual rpt, S4575–2
- New York State child and adult protective services clients and expenditures, 1991, annual rpt, S5800–2.3
- North Carolina children and adults receiving protective services, and reported child abuse and neglect, by county, 1st half FY93, semiannual rpt, S5940–2
- South Carolina public welfare recipients, payments, and case processing, by county and program, monthly rpt, S7252–1
- South Dakota welfare and social services recipients and payments, by program, MSA, and county, FY92, annual rpt, S7385–1
- Texas welfare and social services program expenditures, recipients, and fraud cases, by county and/or program, FY92 and trends, annual rpt, S7695–1
- Vermont district court petitions for protective services, by circuit, FY92 annual rpt, S8120–1
- Washington State public assistance clients and service costs, by client characteristics, program, and county, FY90, annual rpt, S8420–2
- West Virginia welfare and social service program caseloads and expenditures, by county, monthly rpt, S8560–2
- Wyoming welfare and social service recipients and expenditures, by program and county, FY92, annual rpt, S8908–1

see also Campus security

see also Security devices

Detention

see Arrest

see Correctional institutions

see Habeas corpus

see Pretrial detention and release

Detergent industry

see Soap and detergent industry

Detroit, Mich.

Election results for Federal offices and Governor, by State, county, major city, and party, with voter registration and turnout, 1992 and trends, biennial rpt, C2500–1

see also under By City in the "Index by Categories"

Developing countries

Chemical exports for developing vs developed areas, with detail for Eastern Europe, 1980, 1986, and 1991, article, A1250–1.534

Corporate market value of top 100 firms in developing countries, by company, 1993 annual feature, C5800–7.536

Family planning and child survival efforts in developing countries, with related health and maternity data, by country, 1980s-90, R8720–1

Family planning and fertility trends, and contraceptives effectiveness, safety, and availability, by method, series, U2520–1

Family planning devs worldwide, with data on fertility, contraceptive use, and family size preferences, quarterly rpt, A5160–6

Population characteristics, Asian and Pacific countries, series, R4500–1

Population size, and annual births, deaths, and natural increase, with detail for more and less developed countries, 1993-2010, R8750–1.508

Population size and characteristics, GNP, and land area, by world region and/or country, 1993 annual data sheet, R8750–5

Soviet Union economic and military aid to developing countries, with detail for selected world regions, 1950s-85, annual rpt, U6250–1.28

Statistical abstract of Latin America, detailed social, govtl, and economic data, 1992 annual rpt, U6250–1

Urban population of developing countries, and share living in informal settlements, for 13 cities, 1993 rpt, A5800–1.1

World birth, death, population increase, and infant death rate indicators, with detail for more and less developed countries, 1993, annual feature, R8750–1.509

World food and agricultural policies and issues, with focus on developing countries, series, R5620–1

World privatization of govt businesses, by method of transfer, industry sector, and natl economy type, 1980-87, R4105–82.5

World resource issues and environmental devs, by region and country, 1992/93 biennial rpt, R9455–1

see also under By Foreign Country or World Area in the "Index by Categories"

see also under names of individual countries

Dey, Eric L.

"American Freshman: National Norms for Fall 1992", U6215–1

Index by Subjects and Names

Diabetes

Hospital patient admission rates and length of stay, by diagnosis and procedure, payment source, age, sex, and region, 1991, B4455–4

Hospital patient charges and length of stay, by diagnosis and procedure, payment source, age, and region, 1991, B4455–5

Hospital patient discharges and length of stay, by diagnosis, type of operation, age, and region, 1991, annual rpt series, B4455–1

Hospital patient discharges and length of stay, by diagnostic related group (DRG), payment source, age, and region, 1991, annual rpt series, B4455–3

Netherlands forecasts of diabetes incidence through 2005, article, A2623–1.509

Women's diabetes incidence correlated with smoking status, 1976-88 study, article, A2623–1.504

State and local:

Alabama public health dept activities, including services provided, inspection and licensing activity, staff and finances, and vital statistics and health data, 1992 annual rpt, S0175–3

Alabama vital statistics, including population, births, deaths by cause, marriages, and divorces, by location and demographic characteristics, 1992 and trends, annual rpt, S0175–2

Alaska vital statistics, including births, deaths by cause, marriages, divorces, adoptions, and population, by demographic characteristics and location, 1990, annual rpt, S0315–1

Arkansas vital statistics, including births, deaths by cause, marriages, and divorces, by age, sex, race, and county, 1991 and trends, annual rpt, S0685–1

California vital statistics, including population, births, and deaths by cause, by demographic characteristics and county, 1990 and trends, annual rpt, S0865–1

Colorado health behavior risk factor surveillance survey results, by respondent characteristics, 1990, recurring rpt, S1010–3

Colorado vital statistics, including population, births, deaths by cause, abortion, marriage and divorce, and adoption, by demographic characteristics and location, 1990 and trends, annual rpt, S1010–1

Connecticut vital statistics, including births, deaths by cause, marriages, and divorces, by demographic characteristics and location, 1989, annual rpt, S1200–1

Delaware vital statistics, including births, deaths by cause, and marriages and dissolutions, by demographic characteristics and location, 1990, annual rpt, S1385–2

Florida deaths by selected cause, and incidence of selected communicable diseases, by county, 1992 annual rpt, S1746–1.1

Florida vital statistics, including population, births, deaths by cause, and marriages and dissolutions, by location and demographic characteristics, 1992 and trends, annual rpt, S1745–3

Georgia vital statistics, including deaths by cause, demographic characteristics, and location, 1991 and trends, annual rpt, S1895–1.2

Index by Subjects and Names — Diesel fuel

Hawaii health dept activities and services, including vital statistics and disease control, by location, 1990, annual rpt, S2065–1

Idaho vital statistics, including births, deaths by cause, abortions, marriages, and divorces, by demographic characteristics and county, 1991 and trends, annual rpt, S2250–2

Iowa vital statistics, including population, births, deaths by cause, marriages, and divorces, by demographic characteristics and location, 1991 and trends, annual rpt, S2795–1

Kansas vital statistics, including population, births, deaths by cause, abortions, marriages, and divorces, by demographic characteristics and location, 1991 and trends, annual rpt, S2975–1

Kentucky vital statistics, including births, deaths by cause, marriages and divorces, and population, by demographic characteristics and county, 1991, annual rpt, S3140–1

Louisiana vital statistics, including population, births, deaths by cause, reportable diseases, marriages, and divorces, by demographic characteristics and locality, 1989-90 and trends, annual rpt, S3295–1

Maine vital statistics, including births, deaths by cause, abortions, and marriages and divorces, by demographic characteristics and location, 1991 and trends, annual rpt, S3460–2

Maryland vital statistics, including population, births, deaths by cause, marriages, and divorces, by demographic characteristics and location, 1989 and trends, annual rpt, S3635–1

Massachusetts health behavior risk factor surveillance survey results, by respondent characteristics, 1986-90, recurring rpt, S3850–3

Massachusetts vital statistics, including births, deaths by cause, marriages, divorces, and population, by locality and demographic characteristics, 1990 and trends, annual rpt, S3850–1

Michigan vital statistics, including births, deaths, marriages, divorces/annulments, and communicable diseases, by location and demographic characteristics, 1990 and trends, annual rpt, S4000–3

Minnesota vital statistics, including population, births, abortions, deaths, marriages, and divorces, by location and demographic characteristics, 1991 and trends, annual rpt, S4190–2

Mississippi vital statistics, including births, deaths by cause, marriages, and divorces, by demographic characteristics and location, 1992 and trends, annual rpt, S4350–1

Missouri vital statistics, including population, births, deaths by cause, and marriages and divorces, by location and demographic characteristics, 1992 and trends, annual rpt, S4518–1

Montana vital statistics, including births, deaths by cause, abortion, disease, and marriage and divorce, by demographic characteristics and county, 1990-91 and trends, annual rpt, S4690–1

Nebraska vital statistics, including births, deaths, marriages, divorces, and population, by demographic characteristics and location, 1991 and trends, annual rpt, S4885–1

Nevada vital statistics, including births, abortions, and deaths by cause, by county and demographic characteristics, 1989 and trends, annual rpt, S5075–1

New Hampshire vital statistics, including population, births, deaths by cause, marriages, and divorces, by location and demographic characteristics, 1991 and trends, annual rpt, S5215–1

New Jersey vital statistics, including births, deaths, population, communicable diseases, and marriages and divorces, by demographic characteristics and location, 1990 and trends, annual rpt, S5405–1

New Mexico vital statistics, including population, births, deaths, and disease, by location and demographic characteristics, 1991 and trends, annual rpt, S5605–1

New York State health behavior risk factor surveillance survey results, by respondent characteristics, 1990, recurring rpt, S5765–3

New York State vital statistics, including population, births, deaths by cause, reportable diseases, and marriages and dissolutions, by demographic characteristics and/or location, 1990 and trends, annual rpt, S5765–1

North Carolina deaths and rates, by cause and county, 1991 and trends, annual rpt, S5927–1.2

North Dakota vital statistics, including births, deaths by cause, marriages and divorces, and abortions, by demographic characteristics and/or county, 1991 and trends, annual rpt, S6105–2

Ohio vital statistics, including births, deaths by cause, marriages, divorces, and population, by demographic characteristics and location, 1991 and trends, annual rpt, S6285–1

Oregon vital statistics, including births, deaths by cause, communicable diseases, marriages, and divorces, by age, sex, race-ethnicity, and county, 1991 and trends, annual rpt, S6615–5

Rhode Island vital statistics, including population, births, deaths, marriages, and divorces, by demographic characteristics and locality, 1989 and trends, annual rpt, S6995–1

South Carolina deaths, by detailed cause, age, sex, and race, 1990, annual rpt, S7175–2

South Carolina vital statistics, including births, deaths by cause, marriages, and divorces, by age, sex, race, and location, 1990 and trends, annual rpt, S7175–1

South Dakota vital statistics, including births, deaths, marriage and divorce, and communicable disease, by demographic characteristics and county, 1991 and trends, annual rpt, S7345–1

Tennessee vital statistics, including births, deaths by cause, marriages, divorces, and population, by demographic characteristics and location, 1991 and trends, annual rpt, S7520–2

Texas health behavior risk factor surveillance survey results, by respondent characteristics, 1991 and trends, annual rpt, S7685–2

Texas vital statistics, including births, deaths by cause, abortions, marriages, and divorces, by location and demographic characteristics, 1991 and trends, annual rpt, S7685–1

Utah vital statistics, including births, deaths by cause, and population, by county and demographic characteristics, 1990 and trends, annual rpt, S7835–1

Vermont vital statistics, including population, births, deaths by cause, abortions, marriages, and divorces, by location and demographic characteristics, 1991 and trends, annual rpt, S8054–1

Virginia vital statistics, including births, deaths by cause, marriages and divorces, and communicable disease, by demographic characteristics and location, 1991 and trends, annual rpt, S8225–1

Washington State vital statistics, including births, deaths by cause, and population, by demographic characteristics and location, 1991 and trends, annual rpt, S8363–1

West Virginia vital statistics, including births, deaths by cause, marriages, and divorces, by location and demographic characteristics, 1991 and trends, annual rpt, S8560–1

Wisconsin vital statistics, including population, births, deaths by cause, and marriages and dissolutions, by county and demographic characteristics, 1991 and trends, annual rpt, S8715–4

Wyoming vital statistics, including population, births, deaths by cause, marriages, and divorces, by demographic characteristics and county, 1991 and trends, annual rpt, S8920–2

see also under By Disease in the "Index by Categories"

Diamonds

see Gemstones

Diapers

see Clothing and clothing industry

see Personal care products

Dickmeyer, Nathan

"Comparative Financial Statistics for Public Two-Year Colleges: FY92 National Sample", A6705–1

Diesel fuel

- Biodiesel fuel derived from vegetable oils or animal fats, manufacturing capacity of 14 plants worldwide, 1993 article, C5800–8.504
- Europe diesel fuel quality indicators, for 8 countries or areas, 1991/92, article, C6985–1.519
- Fuel oil dealer sales by product, employment, computer use, and truck fleet size, by region, 1992 annual survey, C4680–2.1
- Low-sulfur diesel fuel supply-demand and cost outlook, and desulfurization projects and capacity by company, 1993 article, C6985–1.549
- Mass transit system energy use by source, employee compensation, and labor costs, 1970s-91, annual rpt, A2650–1.2
- Prices of diesel fuel, by selected city, July-Dec 1992, annual rpt, C1575–2.507
- Prices of diesel fuel, by selected city, monthly rpt, C1575–2
- Railroad (Class I) freight service expenditures by category, and diesel fuel consumption, with detail for 7 companies, 1991, article, C8400–1.508

Diesel fuel

Railroad diesel fuel consumption and costs, by company and district, 1992, annual rpt, A3275–7

Railroad diesel fuel consumption and costs, 1955-92, annual rpt, A3275–5.4

Supply-demand, marketing, prices, finances, and employment, detailed data for US and Canada, by product, company, and location, 1993 annual fact book, C4680–1.507

Tractor performance test results, by manufacturer and model, 1983-92, annual rpt, C3450–1.502

Truck (light, diesel-fueled) sales by manufacturer and engine size, 1989-92, article, C2710–3.515

State and local:

California diesel fuel refining capacity, with projected impact of new State law, for 9 major refiners and aggregate independents, 1993-94, article, C6985–1.544

California diesel fuel supply under compliance with and variance from low-aromatics regulations, with detail for selected refiners, 1993-94, article, C4680–1.511

California diesel fuel wholesale prices before and after EPA low-sulfur requirements, for 6 cities, Aug and Oct 1993, article, C6985–1.551

California fuel distributors sales volume and taxes assessed, by fuel type and company, FY92 and trends, annual rpt, S0835–1.4

Hawaii data book, general data, 1992 annual rpt, S2090–1.17

Hawaii fuel consumed and fuel taxes allocated, by type and use, FY91-92, annual rpt, S2120 1

North Carolina motor carrier and railroad diesel fuel purchased or used, 1970s-90, annual rpt, S5917–2

South Carolina statistical abstract, general data, 1993 annual rpt, S7125–1.8

see also Fuel oil

see also Fuel tax

see also Motor fuels

Diet

see Nutrition and malnutrition

Dieting and dietetic products

Consumer low-calorie and reduced-fat product use, for US and Canada, 1993 article, C2150–6.508

Consumer use of selected reduced-fat and fat-free products, by respondent characteristics, 1993 survey, annual rpt, A4950–36

Sales and consumer expenditures, for food store products by type, 1991-92, annual feature, C4655–1.510

Soft drink consumption and market shares, by company and brand, and by flavor, 1985-92, annual article, C0125–2.504

Soft drink diet product sales by company and/or brand, and artificial sweetener price, production, and demand, 1992/93 annual rpt, C0125–3

Soft drink vending machine sales, with diet drink share, 1990-92, annual rpt, C9470–1

Women's obesity and related activity and weight-loss indicators, by race, 1985-86, article, A2623–1.502

State and local:

Alabama health behavior risk factor surveillance survey results, by respondent characteristics, 1988-89, recurring rpt, S0175–6

California health behavior risk factor surveillance survey results, by respondent characteristics, 1991 and trends, annual rpt, S0865–2

Michigan health behavior risk factor surveillance survey results, by respondent characteristics, 1991, annual rpt, S4000–4

North Dakota health behavior risk factor surveillance survey results, by respondent characteristics, 1991 and trends, annual rpt, S6105–3

Dietitians and nutritionists

State and local:

Florida health care atlas, including manpower by occupation and health care facilities by type, by district and county, 1992 annual rpt, S1746–1.2

Montana home health service clients and visits by type of service, by agency, 1991, annual rpt, S4690–2

Diffusion indexes

Electronics industry diffusion ratios for foreign operations, by industry sector, 1993 annual feature, C1850–2.506

Purchasing managers views on business conditions, monthly rpt, A6910–1

Digestive diseases

Contraceptive (oral) use correlated with gallbladder disease, review of epidemiological studies, 1993 article, A2623–1.510

Hospital patient admission rates and length of stay, by diagnosis and procedure, payment source, age, sex, and region, 1991, B4455–4

Hospital patient charges and length of stay, by diagnosis and procedure, payment source, age, and region, 1991, B4455–5

Hospital patient discharges and length of stay, by diagnosis, type of operation, age, and region, 1991, annual rpt series, B4455–1

Hospital patient discharges and length of stay, by diagnostic related group (DRG), payment source, age, and region, 1991, annual rpt series, B4455–3

Hospital psychiatric patients with selected physical disorders, length of stay by age, sex, and region, 1991, annual rpt series, B4455–2

State and local:

Alabama vital statistics, including population, births, deaths by cause, marriages, and divorces, by location and demographic characteristics, 1992 and trends, annual rpt, S0175–2

Alaska vital statistics, including births, deaths by cause, marriages, divorces, adoptions, and population, by demographic characteristics and location, 1990, annual rpt, S0315–1

Arkansas vital statistics, including births, deaths by cause, marriages, and divorces, by age, sex, race, and county, 1991 and trends, annual rpt, S0685–1

California vital statistics, including population, births, and deaths by cause, by demographic characteristics and county, 1990 and trends, annual rpt, S0865–1

Index by Subjects and Names

Colorado vital statistics, including population, births, deaths by cause, abortion, marriage and divorce, and adoption, by demographic characteristics and location, 1990 and trends, annual rpt, S1010–1

Connecticut vital statistics, including births, deaths by cause, marriages, and divorces, by demographic characteristics and location, 1989, annual rpt, S1200–1

Florida deaths by selected cause, and incidence of selected communicable diseases, by county, 1992 annual rpt, S1746–1.1

Florida vital statistics, including population, births, deaths by cause, and marriages and dissolutions, by location and demographic characteristics, 1992 and trends, annual rpt, S1745–3

Georgia vital statistics, including deaths by cause, demographic characteristics, and location, 1991 and trends, annual rpt, S1895–1.2

Hawaii health dept activities and services, including vital statistics and disease control, by location, 1990, annual rpt, S2065–1

Idaho vital statistics, including births, deaths by cause, abortions, marriages, and divorces, by demographic characteristics and county, 1991 and trends, annual rpt, S2250–2

Iowa vital statistics, including population, births, deaths by cause, marriages, and divorces, by demographic characteristics and location, 1991 and trends, annual rpt, S2795–1

Kansas vital statistics, including population, births, deaths by cause, abortions, marriages, and divorces, by demographic characteristics and location, 1991 and trends, annual rpt, S2975–1

Kentucky vital statistics, including births, deaths by cause, marriages and divorces, and population, by demographic characteristics and county, 1991, annual rpt, S3140–1

Louisiana vital statistics, including population, births, deaths by cause, reportable diseases, marriages, and divorces, by demographic characteristics and locality, 1989-90 and trends, annual rpt, S3295–1

Maine vital statistics, including births, deaths by cause, abortions, and marriages and divorces, by demographic characteristics and location, 1991 and trends, annual rpt, S3460–2

Maryland vital statistics, including population, births, deaths by cause, marriages, and divorces, by demographic characteristics and location, 1989 and trends, annual rpt, S3635–1

Massachusetts vital statistics, including births, deaths by cause, marriages, divorces, and population, by locality and demographic characteristics, 1990 and trends, annual rpt, S3850–1

Michigan vital statistics, including births, deaths, marriages, divorces/annulments, and communicable diseases, by location and demographic characteristics, 1990 and trends, annual rpt, S4000–3

Minnesota vital statistics, including population, births, abortions, deaths, marriages, and divorces, by location and demographic characteristics, 1991 and trends, annual rpt, S4190–2

Mississippi vital statistics, including births, deaths by cause, marriages, and divorces, by demographic characteristics and location, 1992 and trends, annual rpt, S4350–1

Missouri vital statistics, including population, births, deaths by cause, and marriages and divorces, by location and demographic characteristics, 1992 and trends, annual rpt, S4518–1

Montana vital statistics, including births, deaths by cause, abortion, disease, and marriage and divorce, by demographic characteristics and county, 1990-91 and trends, annual rpt, S4690–1

Nebraska vital statistics, including births, deaths, marriages, divorces, and population, by demographic characteristics and location, 1991 and trends, annual rpt, S4885–1

Nevada vital statistics, including births, abortions, and deaths by cause, by county and demographic characteristics, 1989 and trends, annual rpt, S5075–1

New Hampshire vital statistics, including population, births, deaths by cause, marriages, and divorces, by location and demographic characteristics, 1991 and trends, annual rpt, S5215–1

New Jersey vital statistics, including births, deaths, population, communicable diseases, and marriages and divorces, by demographic characteristics and location, 1990 and trends, annual rpt, S5405–1

New Mexico vital statistics, including population, births, deaths, and disease, by location and demographic characteristics, 1991 and trends, annual rpt, S5605–1

New York State vital statistics, including population, births, deaths by cause, reportable diseases, and marriages and dissolutions, by demographic characteristics and/or location, 1990 and trends, annual rpt, S5765–1

North Carolina deaths and rates, by cause and county, 1991 and trends, annual rpt, S5927–1.2

North Dakota vital statistics, including births, deaths by cause, marriages and divorces, and abortions, by demographic characteristics and/or county, 1991 and trends, annual rpt, S6105–2

Ohio vital statistics, including births, deaths by cause, marriages, divorces, and population, by demographic characteristics and location, 1991 and trends, annual rpt, S6285–1

Oregon vital statistics, including births, deaths by cause, communicable diseases, marriages, and divorces, by age, sex, race-ethnicity, and county, 1991 and trends, annual rpt, S6615–5

Rhode Island vital statistics, including population, births, deaths, marriages, and divorces, by demographic characteristics and locality, 1989 and trends, annual rpt, S6995–1

South Carolina deaths, by detailed cause, age, sex, and race, 1990, annual rpt, S7175–2

South Carolina vital statistics, including births, deaths by cause, marriages, and divorces, by age, sex, race, and location, 1990 and trends, annual rpt, S7175–1

South Dakota vital statistics, including births, deaths, marriage and divorce, and communicable disease, by demographic characteristics and county, 1991 and trends, annual rpt, S7345–1

Tennessee vital statistics, including births, deaths by cause, marriages, divorces, and population, by demographic characteristics and location, 1991 and trends, annual rpt, S7520–2

Texas vital statistics, including births, deaths by cause, abortions, marriages, and divorces, by location and demographic characteristics, 1991 and trends, annual rpt, S7685–1

Utah vital statistics, including births, deaths by cause, and population, by county and demographic characteristics, 1990 and trends, annual rpt, S7835–1

Vermont vital statistics, including population, births, deaths by cause, abortions, marriages, and divorces, by location and demographic characteristics, 1991 and trends, annual rpt, S8054–1

Virginia vital statistics, including births, deaths by cause, marriages and divorces, and communicable disease, by demographic characteristics and location, 1991 and trends, annual rpt, S8225–1

Washington State vital statistics, including births, deaths by cause, and population, by demographic characteristics and location, 1991 and trends, annual rpt, S8363–1

West Virginia vital statistics, including births, deaths by cause, marriages, and divorces, by location and demographic characteristics, 1991 and trends, annual rpt, S8560–1

Wisconsin vital statistics, including population, births, deaths by cause, and marriages and dissolutions, by county and demographic characteristics, 1991 and trends, annual rpt, S8/15–4

Wyoming vital statistics, including population, births, deaths by cause, marriages, and divorces, by demographic characteristics and county, 1991 and trends, annual rpt, S8920–2

see also Infective and parasitic diseases

see also under By Disease in the "Index by Categories"

DiLorenzo, Thomas J.

"Unfunded Federal Mandates: Environmentalism's Achilles Heel?", U9640–3

Diphtheria

see Infective and parasitic diseases

Diplomacy

see Foreign relations

Direct marketing

Billings for top direct response agencies, US and worldwide, 1991-92, annual articles, C2710–1.535

Book mail order sales, 1990-91, annual rpt, A3274–2

Congressional campaign fund finances, with expenditures by item and contributions by donor type, by candidate, district, and State, 1990 elections, C2500–6

Consumer complaint and inquiry activity of Better Business Burs, by detailed type of business, 1992, annual rpt, A4350–1

Financial ratios and performance, for over 350 SIC 4-digit industries, FY88-92, annual rpt, A6400–3

Market devs for direct marketing industry, including advertising patterns, finances, target markets, and consumer attitudes, 1992/93 annual rpt, A4620–1

Military post exchange (Army/Air Force) mail order sales, FY92, annual rpt, A2072–2.502

Military post exchange mail order sales, US and overseas, monthly rpt, C0500–1

Mutual fund assets by method of sales, monthly rpt, A6025–5

Mutual fund sales and purchases, by investment objective and method of sales, 1991 and trends, annual rpt, A6025–1

Sales "door-to-door," with distribution by product category, 1991, article, C4215–1.501

Sporting goods purchases, by product and outlet type, census div, and purchaser characteristics, with average prices, 1992 and trends, annual survey, A8485–2

Telemarketing regulations and restrictions, by State and Canadian Province, 1991/92 annual rpt, A7015–3

TV home shopper characteristics, and subscribers, revenues, and ownership shares for 2 shopping networks, 1993 article, C5800–7.538

TV home shopping network sales, income, and homes reached, FY92, article, C5150–3.516

Directories

Appliance manufacturers and principal executives, 1993 annual article, C2000–1.510

Bank (master trust/custodial) assets and operating data for top instns, 1993 annual directory, C2710–2.522

Baseball American League player and team performance, and public attendance, 1992 and trends, annual rpt, A2068–1

Baseball Natl League player and team performance, and public attendance, 1992 and trends, annual rpt, A8015–1

Billionaire profiles and sources of wealth, for persons/families worldwide worth 1 billion/more, 1993 annual feature, C3950–1.518

Blood bank operating profiles, arranged by State, 1993 biennial directory, A0612–1

Cancer society divs and cancer centers, by State, 1993 annual rpt, A1175–1

Catholic religious organizations and publications, and facilities for elderly and handicapped, 1993 annual almanac, C6885–1

College scholarship and grant program assns directory, by State, 1992/93, annual rpt, A7140–1

Computer software with sales/marketing applications, installations sold and product characteristics, by vendor, 1992 annual directory, C1200–1.502

Correctional instns, inmates, staff, and cost of care, by instn, US and Canada, with operating summary by State or Province, 1992, annual directory, A1305–3

Dental advanced education programs, enrollment, grads, and finances, by instn and State, 1992/93 annual rpt, A1475–10

Electric utility income and operating data, by type of company and for individual locally owned utilities, 1993 annual directory, A2625–1.501

Directories

Electronics company financial data and business info for approx 500 companies, 1991-92 and trends, annual rpt, C3400–4

Flour milling companies and capacity, in US by State, Canada, Mexico, and Central American and Caribbean area countries, 1993 annual directory and buyers guide, C8450–3

Forbes profile of 400 wealthiest individuals, with info on family background, income, and assets, 1993 annual feature, C3950–1.526

Grain elevators and capacity in US and Canada, by type and State or Province, with ranking of top storage companies, 1993 annual directory and buyers guide, C8450–2

Helicopters in civil aviation, production, trade, utilization, accidents, and landing facilities, 1993 annual rpt, A5190–1

Higher education, 2-year college enrollment, degrees, faculty and staff, and tuition/fees, by instn and State, 1992 annual directory, A0640–1

Hispanic American elected officials by office and State, with related population characteristics, 1992 annual directory, A6844–1

Hospital directory, with utilization, expenses, and personnel, by instn, type, and location, 1992, annual rpt, A1865–3

Investment mgmt consultants, with data on clients and staff, 1992 annual feature, C2710–2.501

Investment mgmt firms, assets and operating data for approx 900 instns, Jan 1993, annual feature, C2710–2.511

Jails and adult detention facilities, inmates, staff, and operating summary, by State and instn, Dec 1992, recurring directory, A1305–1

Jewelry industry statistics on sales, marketing, trade, and employment, with customer characteristics, 1993 annual almanac, C2150–7.509

Law school enrollment by minority status, degrees conferred, staff, and library holdings, by instn, 1992/93 and trends, annual rpt, A0970–1

Library and book trade reference info, including public and academic library funding, construction, and operations, by State and instn, 1992, annual compilation, C1650–3

Library automated system vendors, 1993, annual directory, C1852–1.505, C1852–1.506

Local govt administrative assns, consultants, and officials, US, Canada, and overseas, 1993 annual directory, A5800–1

Military post exchange and commissary sales, by product category, for military resale agencies, FY91 and trends, annual rpt, A2072–1

Motor vehicle fleet industry directories of manufacturer and dealership personnel, lessors, and related companies, 1993 annual rpt, C1575–2.507

Mutual funds (money market) financial performance and rankings of over 850 funds, with background info for investors, 1992 and trends, annual directory, C4682–2

Mutual funds financial performance and rankings of over 2,400 funds, with background info for investors, 1992 and trends, annual directory, C4682–1

Nursing programs (State-approved) for practical/vocational nurses, including admissions, enrollment, and grads, by instn, State, and territory, 1992, annual directory, A8010–5

Nursing programs (State-approved) for registered nurses, including admissions, enrollment, and grads, by instn, State, and territory, 1992, annual directory, A8010–4

Railroad industry assn profiles, 1992 annual rpt, A3275–8

Real estate investment mgmt companies, pension fund and other managed assets, and investment info, by company, 1992 annual directory, C2425–1.501

Real estate investment mgmt companies, pension fund and other managed assets, and investment info, by company, 1993 annual directory, C2425–1.507

Religious organizations and publications, 1993 annual directory, C0105–1

Retail chain financial data and business info for approx 240 US and Canadian companies, 1991-92 and trends, annual rpt, C3400–2

State alcoholic beverage control agencies, 1991 annual directory, A3455–1

Telephone holding company finances, operations, and subsidiaries, by company, Dec 1991, annual rpt, A9360–1

Telephone Yellow Pages directory use among consumers, with detail by respondent characteristics, 1992 survey, annual rpt, A9500–2

Telephone Yellow Pages publisher revenues and advertising agency/media buying service billings, for top 10-15 firms, 1992, article, C2710–1.546

Textile and clothing companies financial data, for approx 170 firms, with industry statistical summary, 1991-92 and trends, annual rpt, C3400–5

Textile fiber product manufacturers, with plants by State and region, 1992 annual directory, C3460–1.501

Tourism dev offices of State govts, activities, personnel, and budgets, by State, 1992 survey, annual rpt, R9375–2

Trust instns and assets managed, approx 5,000 depts, US and Canada, 1993 annual directory, C2425–2.501

Trusts, master and directed, assets managed and services offered, approx 40 instns, 1992 annual directory, C2425–1.502

Veterinarians by professional characteristics and location, and financial and education summaries, 1993 annual directory, A3100–1

Workers compensation law coverage, benefits, and other info, by State, outlying area, and Canadian Province, 1993 annual rpt, A3840–2

State and local:

Alabama public libraries, finances, holdings, circulation, staff, and population served, by library, FY92, annual rpt, S0180–1

Connecticut banks and other financial instns, financial condition by instn, 1991 and trends, annual rpt, S1160–1

Florida public libraries, finances, holdings, staff, and services, by system and library, FY92, annual rpt, S1800–2

Indiana public and other library holdings, circulation, finances, and staff, by instn, 1992 or FY92, annual rpt, S2655–1

Index by Subjects and Names

Missouri public, special, and academic libraries, finances, holdings, circulation, staff, and services, by location, FY92, annual rpt, S4520–2

Nevada library and staff directories for public and academic libraries, with data on holdings, operations, and finances, FY92, annual rpt, S5095–1

New Jersey insurance industry financial and underwriting data, by company and type of insurance, 1990, annual rpt, S5420–1

Oregon financial instns, financial condition by instn, Dec 1992 and trends, annual rpt, S6616–1

Oregon library finances, staff, holdings, and services, for public, academic, and special libraries by instn, FY92 and trends, annual rpt, S6635–1

South Carolina public and institutional libraries, finances, services, holdings, and staff, by library, FY92, annual rpt, S7210–1

Texas judges and court personnel, by type of court and location, FY92 directory, annual rpt, S7703–1

Vermont banks and other financial instns, financial condition by instn, 1992 and trends, annual rpt, S7995–2

Vermont libraries, finances, resources, and circulation, by city and library, FY91-92, biennial rpt, S8080–1

West Virginia insurance industry financial and underwriting data, by company and line of coverage, with regulatory info, 1991, annual rpt, S8575–1

West Virginia public, academic, and special library operations and/or finances, by instn, 1991/92, annual rpt, S8590–1

Directors

see Boards of directors

Disability

see Disabled and handicapped persons

Disability benefits and insurance

Association executives compensation, by position, assn type, and census div, with personnel practices and benefit provisions, 1992, biennial rpt, A2900–3

Educational and public employee retirement plans with disability benefits, 1990/91, recurring rpt, A7640–18.1

Employee benefit payments and employer cost/payroll ratios, by industry, detailed type of benefit, and firm size, 1991, annual rpt, A3840–1

Higher education instn employee retirement and insurance benefits, prevalence and expenditures, by type of instn and region, 1991, biennial survey, A9025–3

Hospital (teaching) house staff disability benefits, 1992/93, annual rpt, A3273–3

Policy comparison for noncancellable disability insurance, by company, 1993 annual feature, C1050–2.504

Social Security Admin disability benefits programs, initial claims processing time and number pending, by State, FY88-93, R4865–11

Workers covered, and benefit recipients and payments, 1957-91, annual rpt, A5173–2.4

State and local:

California statistical abstract, general data, 1992 annual rpt, S0840–2.5

DC statistical profile, general data, 1992 annual rpt, S1535–3.3

Index by Subjects and Names

Idaho insurance industry financial and underwriting data, by company and type of insurance, with regulatory data, 1991, annual rpt, S2260–1

see also Black lung disease

see also Maternity benefits

see also Old-Age, Survivors, Disability, and Health Insurance

see also Workers compensation

Disability insurance

see Disability benefits and insurance

Disabled and handicapped persons

- Americans with Disabilities Act complaint filings with Equal Employment Opportunity Commission, by type, through Feb 1993, article, C5800–7.520
- Americans with Disabilities Act concerns and response of recruiting companies, 1993 annual survey rpt, U3730–1
- Americans with Disabilities Act employment-related complaints filed with Equal Employment Opportunity Commission, for top 10 States, Mar 1993, article, C1200–5.511
- Americans with Disabilities Act enforcement costs for cities, FY93-98, A9330–12
- Americans with Disabilities Act hard goods manufacturers compliance efforts and costs, by product line, 1993 annual survey rpt, A1800–1
- Americans With Disabilities Act impact, business views, 1992 survey, C4215–1.501
- Americans with Disabilities Act small corporation compliance activities and perceived impact, 1992 survey article, C4687–1.501
- Black American health and vital statistics data, with comparisons to whites, 1970s-91, annual compilation, C6775–2.2
- City fiscal condition, including perceived impact of spending to meet requirements of Americans with Disabilities Act, Mar Apr 1993 survey, annual rpt, A8012–1.23
- College grad recruiting practices and hiring trends, with data on starting salaries and layoffs, by type of employer, 1992/93 annual survey rpt, U3130–1
- Corporate employee transfers involving disabled persons, 1992, annual survey, B0600–1
- Drugs (prescription) use, expenditures, and financing methods among population age 65/older and 64/under, by patient characteristics, 1987, R4865–8
- General Educational Dev (GED) testing using special formats and accommodations, by jurisdiction, 1992, annual rpt, A1410–16
- Higher education enrollment of disabled students, by sex and type of disability, 1983-91, recurring rpt, A3960–2.1
- Higher education freshmen with physical disabilities by type, by sex and instn type, fall 1992, annual survey, U6215–1
- Home care service use by the disabled, with costs, payment sources, and types of care, by selected characteristics, 1992, R4865–15
- Law school grad employment and salaries, for grads with selected disabilities, 1992, annual rpt, A6505–1
- Library expenditures for handicapped services, by fund source and State, FY90, annual compilation, C1650–3.2

Disabled and handicapped persons

- Library State agency funding activities for Americans with Disabilities Act compliance, by State, 1992 annual rpt, A3862–1
- Mass transit agency policies regarding wheelchair restraint devices, 1993 article, C1575–3.507
- Population share needing assistance for activities of daily living, by sex and age, 1990, A8657–5
- Population share with work-preventing disabilities, by State, 1990, semiannual rpt, B8500–1.9
- Rates of disability and probable duration, by age group, 1993 article, A3100–2.505
- Scientists and engineers with physical handicaps, by field, type of disability, and employment status, 1986, recurring rpt, A3960–2.2
- Small business views on employment trends for women, minorities, immigrants, and the disabled, and related mgmt issues, 1993 survey article, C4687–1.503
- Urban public school disabled student enrollment, with comparisons to total State and US, for 47 systems, 1990/91, A4425–4

State and local:

- Arkansas Census of Population and Housing detailed findings, 1990, U5935–7
- California Census of Population and Housing detailed findings, 1990, S0840–9
- California disabled and senior citizens property tax assistance, claimants, and income, by income class, 1991 and trends, annual rpt, S0855–1.3
- Colorado job service applicant characteristics, FY93 annual planning rpt, S1040–3.2
- Georgia county guide, general data, 1993 annual rpt, U6750–1
- Hawaii data book, general data, 1992 annual rpt, S2090–1.11
- Illinois mental health facility patient population and characteristics, by facility, location, and treatment category, FY93, annual rpt, S2505–1
- Indiana property value and tax levies, collections, credits, and deductions, by county and type, 1991, annual rpt, S2570–1.1
- Kansas statistical abstract, general data, 1991/92 annual rpt, U7095–2.9
- Kentucky traffic accidents involving physically disabled persons, 1992, annual rpt, S3150–2
- Louisiana Census of Population and Housing summary findings, by local area, 1990 and trends, U8010–4
- Maine Census of Population and Housing summary findings, by local area, 1990, S3465–9
- Michigan labor force planning rpt, including characteristics of Job Training Partnership Act eligible population by State area, 1993 annual rpt, S3980–1.2
- Michigan State corrections dept employment of women, minorities, and handicapped, 1991 and trends, annual rpt, S3960–1
- Mississippi vocational education enrollment and courses offered, by program, 1991/92, annual rpt, S4340–1.2
- Missouri employment service activities for the handicapped, and occupational disability and death incidents, 1991 and trends, annual rpt, S4530–2.2
- New Jersey Census of Population and Housing detailed findings, by county, 1990, S5425–19
- Pennsylvania Census of Population and Housing detailed findings, with selected data by county and municipality, 1990, U4130–13
- Pennsylvania employment and commuting data from Census of Population and Housing, by county and municipality, 1990, C1595–16
- Pennsylvania labor force planning rpt, including data on populations with employability problems, FY92 annual rpt, S6845–3.3
- Pennsylvania vocational education enrollment, student characteristics, and faculty, by program and/or school, 1991/92 and trends, annual rpt, S6790–5.7
- Pennsylvania vocational education 1989/90 grad employment status, with detail for disabled/handicapped students, 1991 survey, annual rpt, S6790–5.6
- Rhode Island Census of Population and Housing detailed findings, by county and municipality, 1990, S6930–9
- South Carolina labor force planning rpt, detailed data on employment, hours, wages, turnover, and characteristics of job service applicants, 1992 annual rpt, S7155–3.2
- South Carolina statistical abstract, general data, 1993 annual rpt, S7125–1.7
- South Dakota sales/property tax refunds for elderly and disabled, with detail by county, FY92 and trends, annual rpt, S7380–1.1
- Texas disabled persons above and below poverty level, by age group, FY92, annual rpt, S7695–1
- Utah homeless shelter population characteristics, individual shelter capacity, and related housing data, 1991-92, annual rpt, S7808–2
- Vermont labor force by employment status, and job service openings and applicant characteristics, 1993 annual planning rpt, S8025–2.2
- Washington State noninstitutional population with disabilities, by severity and county, 1990, annual rpt, S8345–4
- Wisconsin Blue Book, general data, 1993-94 biennial rpt, S8780–1.2
- Wisconsin correctional instn inmates, by criminal background and selected characteristics, series, S8692–1

see also Adult day care

see also Aid to disabled and handicapped persons

see also Architectural barriers to the handicapped

see also Blind

see also Deaf

see also Disability benefits and insurance

see also Discrimination against the handicapped

see also Handicapped children

see also Mental retardation

see also Mobility limitations

see also Old-Age, Survivors, Disability, and Health Insurance

see also Rehabilitation of the disabled

see also Respite care

Disabled and handicapped persons

see also Sheltered workshops
see also Special education
see also Supplemental Security Income
see also Vocational rehabilitation

Disadvantaged

see Compensatory education
see Disabled and handicapped persons
see Discrimination in credit
see Discrimination in education
see Discrimination in employment
see Discrimination in housing
see Handicapped children
see Minority groups
see Poverty
see Racial discrimination
see Sex discrimination

Disarmament

see Arms control and disarmament

Disaster relief

Congressional appropriations for natural disasters and other emergency assistance, FY92, annual rpt, C2500–2

State and local:

- Alabama special disaster assistance applications and payments, monthly rpt, S0150–1
- Arkansas financial condition, including revenues by source, expenditures by function and locality, and fund balances, FY91-92, biennial rpt, S0780–1
- California financial condition, including revenues by source, expenditures by agency and function, fund balances, and bonded debt, FY92 and trends, annual rpt, S0815–1
- New Jersey Disaster Unemployment Assistance Program claims and benefits for victims of Dec 1992 storm, 1993 article, S5425–1.507
- Oklahoma school revenues and expenditures, by program, county, and district, FY92, annual rpt, S6423–1.1
- Pennsylvania statistical abstract, general data, 1992 recurring rpt, U4130–6.2
- Texas financial condition, including revenues by source, expenditures by function and dept, and investments, with data for over 400 individual funds, FY92, annual rpt, S7655–2.2

see also Food assistance

Disasters

- Damage value caused by 7 weather-related disasters occurring in 1988-93, article, C5800–7.548
- Deaths in major disasters since 1865, by category, annual rpt, A8375–2.1
- Health care instn info system readiness for disaster, 1993 survey, A1865–1.517
- Information systems organizations affected by 19 major disasters, 1983-92, article, C5150–4.502
- Insurance industry losses from natural disasters, 1977-1st half 1993, article, C5800–7.543
- Property and human losses from fires, storms, and earthquakes, with selected data by incident, 1991 and trends, annual rpt, A5650–1.4

State and local:

- South Carolina deaths, by detailed cause, age, sex, and race, 1990, annual rpt, S7175–2

see also Disaster relief
see also Drought

see also Earthquakes
see also Fires and fire prevention
see also Floods
see also Forest fires
see also Nuclear accidents and safety
see also Storms
see also Tsunamis
see also Volcanoes

Discipline

see Student discipline

Disclosure

see Financial disclosure

Discount stores

- Department discount stores operating and financial data, by size and sales dept, discontinued annual rpt, A5940–6
- Drugstore discount chain sales and stores, for leading chains, 1993 annual feature, C5150–2.511
- Expansion devs, and equipment and construction costs, by type of retail chain, 1993 annual articles, C5150–4.507
- Financial and marketing devs, biweekly rpt, C5150–3
- Financial data and business info for approx 240 US and Canadian retail chains, 1991-92 and trends, annual rpt, C3400–2
- Financial performance and growth rankings for approx 1,000 top corporations, with comparisons by industry group, 1993 annual rpt, C3950–1.505
- Markets with daily newspapers, demographic and economic info by geographic area, US and Canada, 1993 annual rpt, C3250–1
- Merchandising devs for discount stores, with data on sales and earnings of leading companies, monthly rpt, C8130–1
- Pharmacies in stores of top mass merchandise or wholesale membership club chains, 1993 annual feature, C5150–2.511
- Sales and merchandising data, including detail by dept, leading chain, and location, 1992 and trends, annual feature, C8130–1.507
- Sales and merchandising trends for health and beauty aid products, by product type, 1992 annual feature, C5150–2.503
- Sales and productivity data for 20 depts, 1993 annual feature, C5150–3.516
- Sales, earnings, and stores, for top discount chains, with detail by specialty, 1993 annual feature, C5150–3.514
- Sales volume shares by retail outlet type, for approx 300 food, drug, and other product categories, 1993 annual feature, C4655–1.504
- Shopping center financial and operating data, with detail by type of tenant, US and Canada, 1991, triennial rpt, R9285–1
- Sporting goods purchases, by product and outlet type, census div, and purchaser characteristics, with average prices, 1992 and trends, annual survey, A8485–2
- Wholesale membership club in-store bakery and total sales, 1991-93, article, C5225–1.509

Discrimination

see Age discrimination
see Discrimination against the handicapped
see Discrimination in credit
see Discrimination in education
see Discrimination in employment

see Discrimination in housing
see Racial discrimination
see Sex discrimination

Discrimination against the handicapped

State and local:

- Missouri Human Rights Commission discrimination cases and dispositions, by case type, FY92 and trends, annual rpt, S4530–2.2
- Oregon crimes involving bias against selected persons or groups, with victim and offender characteristics, 1991-92, annual rpt, S6603–3.1

see also Architectural barriers to the handicapped

Discrimination in credit

- Small business owners financing sources and experience of discrimination in lending, by race-ethnicity, 1993 survey feature, C4215–1.512

State and local:

- New York State statistical yearbook, general data, 1992 annual rpt, U5100–1.8
- Oklahoma real estate loan rejection rates for whites and minorities by income level, statewide and by MSA, 1991, article, U8130–1.504

Discrimination in education

- Black students in schools with greater than 50% and 90% minority enrollment, 1968-86, R3840–21
- Elementary/secondary school superintendents personal and professional characteristics and views, 1992 survey rpt, A0775–5
- GDP impacts of racial bias in education and employment, 1967-93, article, C4215–1.512
- Urban public school desegregation court orders, and school system desegregation plan status and scope, for 47 systems, 1990/91, A4425–4

State and local:

- New York State statistical yearbook, general data, 1992 annual rpt, U5100–1.8

see also School busing

Discrimination in employment

- Bank CEO views on existence of a "glass ceiling" for female/minority executives, April 1992 survey, annual rpt, B4490–2.33
- Eating/drinking place employment discrimination complaints filed with Equal Employment Opportunity Commission, with comparison to all industries, 1992, article, C5150–5.511
- Elementary/secondary school superintendents personal and professional characteristics and views, 1992 survey rpt, A0775–5
- Food/beverage manufacturing mgmt views on effect of affirmative action, by sex, 1992 survey, article, C2150–6.502
- GDP impacts of racial bias in education and employment, 1967-93, article, C4215–1.512
- High-technology industry CEO views on existence of a "glass ceiling" for female executives, June 1992 survey, B4490–2.34
- Hospital CEO views on existence of a "glass ceiling" for female and minority executives, June 1992 survey, B4490–2.35

Index by Subjects and Names

Diseases and disorders

Planning professional perceived discrimination in the workplace due to sex and race, 1991, biennial rpt, A2615–1

Public planning agencies with antidiscrimination personnel policies, by jurisdiction size, 1991 survey rpt, A2615–3

Researcher assessment of own employers discrimination against selected groups, 1992 survey, annual article, C1850–6.505

State and local:

California judicial system employment by position, sex, and race-ethnicity, with minority utilization rates and parity targets, Jan 1993, annual rpt, S0905–1.1

Missouri Human Rights Commission discrimination cases and dispositions, by case type, FY92 and trends, annual rpt, S4530–2.2

New York State statistical yearbook, general data, 1992 annual rpt, U5100–1.8

Discrimination in housing

Mortgage lender HUD audit results on discriminatory treatment of blacks, 1988/89, article, A8510–1.1

State and local:

Missouri Human Rights Commission discrimination cases and dispositions, by case type, FY92 and trends, annual rpt, S4530–2.2 .

New York State statistical yearbook, general data, 1992 annual rpt, U5100–1.8

Diseases and disorders

Australia, Sydney smoker and ex-smoker belief in smoking as cause for selected diseases, and reasons for continuing to smoke, 1993 article, A2623–1.504

Deaths from accidents compared with other causes, by age and sex, 1992 and trends, annual rpt, A8375–2.1

Developing countries child health indicators, including diarrhea incidence and availability and use of oral rehydration treatment, by country, 1980s-90, R8720–1.2

Developing countries child health indicators, including total and treated diarrhea incidence, and vaccination rates, by country, 1985-92 surveys, U2520–1.51

Hospital patient admission rates and length of stay, by diagnosis and procedure, payment source, age, sex, and region, 1991, B4455–4

Hospital patient charges and length of stay, by diagnosis and procedure, payment source, age, and region, 1991, B4455–5

Hospital patient discharges and length of stay, by diagnosis, type of operation, age, and region, 1991, annual rpt series, B4455–1

Hospital patient discharges and length of stay, by diagnostic related group (DRG), payment source, age, and region, 1991, annual rpt series, B4455–3

Incidence of illness and injury, and hospitalization and mortality data, by selected demographic characteristics, 1992 annual rpt, A5173–2.4

Latin America statistical abstract, general data by country, 1992 annual rpt, U6250–1.6

Men age 69-84 quality of life indicators, including health, finances, family, and employment, by race, 1990 survey, U3780–9

Metro area poverty and unemployment level effects on crime and mortality rates, for selected offenses and causes of death, 1990, R4700–18

Older population incidence of selected medical conditions, by urban-rural status, 1993 article, A1865–1.522

Research expenditures by NIH, and incidence, for cystic fibrosis, multiple sclerosis, muscular dystrophy, and scleroderma, 1993 article, C5800–7.546

State and local:

Alabama public health dept activities, including services provided, inspection and licensing activity, staff and finances, and vital statistics and health data, 1992 annual rpt, S0175–3

Alabama statistical abstract, general data, 1992 recurring rpt, U5680–2.8

Alabama vital statistics, including population, births, deaths by cause, marriages, and divorces, by location and demographic characteristics, 1992 and trends, annual rpt, S0175–2

Alaska vital statistics, including births, deaths by cause, marriages, divorces, adoptions, and population, by demographic characteristics and location, 1990, annual rpt, S0315–1

Arkansas vital statistics, including births, deaths by cause, marriages, and divorces, by age, sex, race, and county, 1991 and trends, annual rpt, S0685–1

California statistical abstract, general data, 1992 annual rpt, S0840–2.5

California vital statistics, including population, births, and deaths by cause, by demographic characteristics and county, 1990 and trends, annual rpt, S0865–1

Colorado vital statistics, including population, births, deaths by cause, abortion, marriage and divorce, and adoption, by demographic characteristics and location, 1990 and trends, annual rpt, S1010–1

Connecticut vital statistics, including births, deaths by cause, marriages, and divorces, by demographic characteristics and location, 1989, annual rpt, S1200–1

Florida deaths by cause, communicable disease incidence, and hospital utilization, 1992 annual rpt, S1746–1

Florida statistical abstract, general data, 1992 annual rpt, U6660–1.3

Florida vital statistics, including population, births, deaths by cause, and marriages and dissolutions, by location and demographic characteristics, 1992 and trends, annual rpt, S1745–3

Georgia vital statistics, including deaths by cause, demographic characteristics, and location, 1991 and trends, annual rpt, S1895–1.2

Hawaii data book, general data, 1992 annual rpt, S2090–1.2

Hawaii health dept activities and services, including vital statistics and disease control, by location, 1990, annual rpt, S2065–1

Idaho vital statistics, including births, deaths by cause, abortions, marriages, and divorces, by demographic characteristics and county, 1991 and trends, annual rpt, S2250–2

Iowa vital statistics, including population, births, deaths by cause, marriages, and divorces, by demographic characteristics and location, 1991 and trends, annual rpt, S2795–1

Kansas vital statistics, including population, births, deaths by cause, abortions, marriages, and divorces, by demographic characteristics and location, 1991 and trends, annual rpt, S2975–1

Kentucky vital statistics, including births, deaths by cause, marriages and divorces, and population, by demographic characteristics and county, 1991, annual rpt, S3140–1

Louisiana vital statistics, including population, births, deaths by cause, reportable diseases, marriages, and divorces, by demographic characteristics and locality, 1989-90 and trends, annual rpt, S3295–1

Maine vital statistics, including births, deaths by cause, abortions, and marriages and divorces, by demographic characteristics and location, 1991 and trends, annual rpt, S3460–2

Maryland vital statistics, including population, births, deaths by cause, marriages, and divorces, by demographic characteristics and location, 1989 and trends, annual rpt, S3635–1

Massachusetts vital statistics, including births, deaths by cause, marriages, divorces, and population, by locality and demographic characteristics, 1990 and trends, annual rpt, S3850–1

Michigan vital statistics, including births, deaths, marriages, divorces/annulments, and communicable diseases, by location and demographic characteristics, 1990 and trends, annual rpt, S4000–3

Minnesota vital statistics, including population, births, abortions, deaths, marriages, and divorces, by location and demographic characteristics, 1991 and trends, annual rpt, S4190–2

Mississippi vital statistics, including births, deaths by cause, marriages, and divorces, by demographic characteristics and location, 1992 and trends, annual rpt, S4350–1

Missouri vital statistics, including population, births, deaths by cause, and marriages and divorces, by location and demographic characteristics, 1992 and trends, annual rpt, S4518–1

Montana vital statistics, including births, deaths by cause, abortion, disease, and marriage and divorce, by demographic characteristics and county, 1990-91 and trends, annual rpt, S4690–1

Nebraska vital statistics, including births, deaths, marriages, divorces, and population, by demographic characteristics and location, 1991 and trends, annual rpt, S4885–1

Nevada vital statistics, including births, abortions, and deaths by cause, by county and demographic characteristics, 1989 and trends, annual rpt, S5075–1

New Hampshire vital statistics, including population, births, deaths by cause, marriages, and divorces, by location and demographic characteristics, 1991 and trends, annual rpt, S5215–1

Diseases and disorders

New Jersey vital statistics, including births, deaths, population, communicable diseases, and marriages and divorces, by demographic characteristics and location, 1990 and trends, annual rpt, S5405–1

New Mexico vital statistics, including population, births, deaths, and disease, by location and demographic characteristics, 1991 and trends, annual rpt, S5605–1

New York State statistical yearbook, general data, 1992 annual rpt, U5100–1.11

New York State vital statistics, including population, births, deaths by cause, reportable diseases, and marriages and dissolutions, by demographic characteristics and/or location, 1990 and trends, annual rpt, S5765–1

North Carolina deaths and rates, by cause and county, 1991 and trends, annual rpt, S5927–1.2

North Dakota vital statistics, including births, deaths by cause, marriages and divorces, and abortions, by demographic characteristics and/or county, 1991 and trends, annual rpt, S6105–2

Ohio vital statistics, including births, deaths by cause, marriages, divorces, and population, by demographic characteristics and location, 1991 and trends, annual rpt, S6285–1

Oregon vital statistics, including births, deaths by cause, communicable diseases, marriages, and divorces, by age, sex, race-ethnicity, and county, 1991 and trends, annual rpt, S6615–5

Rhode Island vital statistics, including population, births, deaths, marriages, and divorces, by demographic characteristics and locality, 1989 and trends, annual rpt, S6995–1

South Carolina deaths, by detailed cause, age, sex, and race, 1990, annual rpt, S7175–2

South Carolina vital statistics, including births, deaths by cause, marriages, and divorces, by age, sex, race, and location, 1990 and trends, annual rpt, S7175–1

South Dakota vital statistics, including births, deaths, marriage and divorce, and communicable disease, by demographic characteristics and county, 1991 and trends, annual rpt, S7345–1

Tennessee statistical abstract, general data, 1992/93 annual rpt, U8710–2.17

Tennessee vital statistics, including births, deaths by cause, marriages, divorces, and population, by demographic characteristics and location, 1991 and trends, annual rpt, S7520–2

Texas vital statistics, including births, deaths by cause, abortions, marriages, and divorces, by location and demographic characteristics, 1991 and trends, annual rpt, S7685–1

Utah vital statistics, including births, deaths by cause, and population, by county and demographic characteristics, 1990 and trends, annual rpt, S7835–1

Vermont vital statistics, including population, births, deaths by cause, abortions, marriages, and divorces, by location and demographic characteristics, 1991 and trends, annual rpt, S8054–1

Virginia vital statistics, including births, deaths by cause, marriages and divorces, and communicable disease, by demographic characteristics and location, 1991 and trends, annual rpt, S8225–1

Washington State vital statistics, including births, deaths by cause, and population, by demographic characteristics and location, 1991 and trends, annual rpt, S8363–1

West Virginia vital statistics, including births, deaths by cause, marriages, and divorces, by location and demographic characteristics, and trends, annual rpt, S8560–1

Wisconsin vital statistics, including population, births, deaths by cause, and marriages and dissolutions, by county and demographic characteristics, 1991 and trends, annual rpt, S8715–4

Wyoming vital statistics, including population, births, deaths by cause, marriages, and divorces, by demographic characteristics and county, 1991 and trends, annual rpt, S8920–2

see also Accidents and accident prevention

see also Acquired immune deficiency syndrome

see also Alcohol abuse and treatment

see also Allergies

see also Animal diseases and zoonoses

see also Birth defects

see also Black lung disease

see also Blood diseases and disorders

see also Blood pressure

see also Cardiovascular diseases

see also Cerebrovascular diseases

see also Circulatory diseases

see also Diabetes

see also Digestive diseases

see also Drug abuse and treatment

see also Ear diseases and infections

see also Epidemiology and epidemiologists

see also Eye diseases and defects

see also Food and waterborne diseases

see also Hearing and hearing disorders

see also Hereditary diseases

see also Hypertension

see also Immunity disorders

see also Infective and parasitic diseases

see also Mental health and illness

see also Mental retardation

see also Metabolic and endocrine diseases

see also Mobility limitations

see also Musculoskeletal diseases

see also Neoplasms

see also Neurological disorders

see also Nose and throat disorders

see also Nutrition and malnutrition

see also Obesity

see also Occupational health and safety

see also Pathology

see also Pneumonia and influenza

see also Poisoning and drug reaction

see also Rabies

see also Respiratory diseases

see also Septicemia

see also Sexually transmitted diseases

see also Sickle cell anemia

see also Skin diseases

see also Tuberculosis

see also Urogenital diseases

see also Vaccination and vaccines

see also under By Disease in the "Index by Categories"

Displaced workers

see Labor turnover

Disposable income

see Personal and household income

Distillate fuels

see Diesel fuel

see Fuel oil

see Kerosene

see Petroleum and petroleum industry

Distilled spirits

see Liquor and liquor industry

Distribution

see Industrial distribution

District courts

see Federal district courts

see State courts

District of Columbia

see D.C.

Districts

see Electoral districts and precincts

see Wards, city

Diversification of business

see Economic concentration and diversification

Divestiture

Coal industry acquisitions/divestitures by transaction type, 1990-92, article, C5226–1.508

Corporate mergers, acquisitions, and divestitures, with prices, payment methods, and characteristics of participants, 1992 and trends, annual rpt, B6020–1

Corporate mergers, acquisitions, divestitures, joint ventures, and other agreements involving US and/or foreign companies, bimonthly rpt, C4683–1

Divorce

see Marriage and divorce

Divorce courts

see Domestic relations courts and cases

Do-it-yourself stores

see Home improvement stores

Doble, John

"Punishing Criminals: The People of Delaware Consider the Options", R8825–11

Doctors

see Physicians

Documents

see Bibliographies

see Government documents

DOD

see Department of Defense

Dodson, James K. Co.

Gulf of Mexico Federal oil/gas leases relinquished by top 5 companies, 1st half 1993, article, C6985–2.509

Gulf of Mexico offshore oil and gas drilling devs, 1993 annual article, C6985–2.503

Gulf of Mexico oil/gas exploratory and dev wells drilled, 1st 8 months 1992-93, article, C6985–2.510

Gulf of Mexico oil/gas lease status, wells drilled by operator, and drilling platforms, 1993 article, C6985–2.508

Gulf of Mexico total and undrilled Federal oil/gas leases relinquished, by company, 1992, article, C6985–2.505

Dog food

see Pet food and supplies

Domestic relations

see Child abuse and neglect

see Domestic relations courts and cases

Index by Subjects and Names

see Domestic violence
see Families and households
see Marriage and divorce
see Offenses against family

Domestic relations courts and cases

Divorce caseloads and processing times by case characteristics, with domestic court judicial staff, for 16 urban jurisdictions, 1989 and/or 1990, R6600–6

State appellate and trial court caseloads and dispositions, by case type and State, 1991 and trends, annual rpt, R6600–1

State and local:

Alabama court caseloads and dispositions, by type of court and case, and location, with judicial dept finances, FY92 and trends, annual rpt, S0118–1

Alabama divorces and annulments, by legal grounds and party granted decree, 1992, annual rpt, S0175–2

Alaska court cases and dispositions, by type of court and case, and location, with judicial dept finances and personnel, FY92 and trends, annual rpt, S0290–1

Arizona court cases and dispositions, by type of case and court, with judicial personnel and finances, by county and city, FY92, annual rpt, S0525–1

Arkansas court caseloads and dispositions, by type of court and case, and location, FY92 and trends, annual rpt, S0647–1

California court cases and dispositions, by type of case and court, and location, FY92 and trends, annual rpt, S0905–1.2, S0905–2

Colorado court cases and dispositions, by type of court and detailed case type, FY92 and trends, annual rpt, S1035–1.2

Connecticut court caseloads and dispositions, by type of court and case, and court location, with judicial dept finances, FY91-92, biennial rpt, S1220–1

Connecticut family violence offenses, by injury status and presence of prior court order, 1992, annual rpt, S1256–1.3

DC court cases and dispositions, by type of case, and judicial system finances, 1992 and trends, annual rpt, S1515–1

Delaware court caseloads and dispositions, by type of court and case, and by county, with judicial dept finances, FY92, annual rpt, S1360–1

Georgia court cases and dispositions, by type of court and case, and location, with judicial dept finances and personnel, FY92, annual rpt, S1903–1

Hawaii court cases and dispositions, by type of court and case, and judicial circuit, FY92 and trends, annual rpt, S2115–1.2

Hawaii divorces and annulments, by legal grounds, 1990, annual rpt, S2065–1.2

Idaho divorces and annulments, by legal grounds, 1991, annual rpt, S2250–2

Indiana court cases and dispositions by type of court and case, and location, with judicial system finances and personnel, 1992, annual rpt, S2703–1

Iowa court cases, processing, and dispositions, by type of court and district, with judicial dept appropriations and personnel, 1992 and trends, annual rpt, S2815–1

Kansas court caseloads and disposition, by type of court and case, and location, FY92, annual rpt, S3035–1

Louisiana court caseloads and dispositions, by type of court and case, and jurisdiction, 1992 and trends, annual rpt, S3375–1

Maine court cases and dispositions, by type and location, FY92 and trends, annual rpt, S3463–1

Maryland court caseloads and dispositions, by type of court and case, and county, with judicial personnel and finances, FY92 and trends, annual rpt, S3600–1

Maryland divorces and annulments, including legal grounds, with data by location, 1989, annual rpt, S3635–1

Massachusetts court cases and dispositions, by type of court and case, and location, FY92 and trends, annual rpt, S3807–1

Michigan court caseloads and dispositions, by type of court and case, and court location, 1992 and trends, annual rpt, S3962–1

Mississippi divorces by cause, and number of children affected, by race, 1992, annual rpt, S4350–1

Missouri divorces, by type of decree and by child custody and support settlement, 1992, annual rpt, S4518–1

Montana divorces, by legal grounds, 1990-91, annual rpt, S4690–1

Nebraska court cases and dispositions, by type of court and case, and location, 1992 and trends, annual rpt, S4965–2

Nebraska divorce settlements and number of children affected, 1991, annual rpt, S4885–1

New Hampshire child custody awards in contested and uncontested divorce cases, 1987-91, annual rpt, S5215–1

New Mexico court cases and dispositions, by type of court and case, and location, with judicial system finances and personnel, FY92, annual rpt, S5623–1

New York State court cases and dispositions, by type of court and case, and jurisdiction, 1991, annual rpt, S5730–1

New York State marital dissolutions by type of decree, by county and city, 1988-90, annual rpt, S5765–1

North Carolina court cases and dispositions, by type of court and case, and location, with judicial dept finances and personnel, FY91, annual rpt, S5950–1

Ohio court caseload and case disposition, by type of court and case, and location, 1992, annual rpt, S6385–1

Ohio divorces and annulments, by legal grounds and number of children involved, 1991, annual rpt, S6285–1

Oklahoma court cases and dispositions, by type of court and case, with judicial system finances, by county or jurisdiction, FY92, annual rpt, S6493–1

Pennsylvania court caseloads and dispositions, by type of court and case, and county, 1991, annual rpt, S6900–1.2

Rhode Island court cases and dispositions, by type of court and case, and county, 1987-91, annual rpt, S6965–1

South Carolina court cases and dispositions, by type of court and location, with judicial dept finances and employees, 1992 and trends, annual rpt, S7197–1

South Carolina divorces, by legal grounds and county, 1990, annual rpt, S7175–1

Domestic violence

South Dakota court cases and dispositions by type of case, and judicial system finances and personnel, by jurisdiction, FY92 and trends, annual rpt, S7395–1

Tennessee court cases and dispositions, by type of court and case, and county, FY92, annual rpt, S7585–1

Texas court cases and dispositions, by type of court and case, and location, FY92, annual rpt, S7703–1

Vermont court cases and dispositions, by type of court and case, and location, FY92 annual rpt, S8120–1

Virginia court caseloads, processing, and dispositions, by type of court and case, with judicial dept personnel and finances, by location, 1992 and trends, annual rpt, S8300–1

Virginia divorces, by legal grounds, plaintiff, and party granted decree, 1991, annual rpt, S8225–1

Washington State court cases and dispositions, by type of court and case, and jurisdiction, with judicial finances and personnel, 1992 and trends, annual rpt, S8339–1

West Virginia court caseloads and dispositions, by type of court and case, and judicial circuit, 1992 and trends, annual rpt, S8537–1

see also Child support and alimony

Domestic violence

State and local:

Arizona court cases and dispositions, by type of case and court, with judicial personnel and finances, by county and city, FY92, annual rpt, S0525–1

California domestic violence calls for police assistance, by weapon involvement and county, 1991, annual rpt, S0910–2.2

California domestic violence calls received by police, 1987-92, annual rpt, S0910–1.2

Colorado income tax return checkoff contributions, for selected causes, FY92 and trends, annual rpt, S1075–1.3

Connecticut family violence offenses, with circumstances, participant characteristics, and arrests by jurisdiction, 1992, annual rpt, S1256–1.3

Florida crimes and arrests, by offense, with data by victim and offender characteristics, 1992, annual rpt, S1770–1

Illinois domestic violence incidents, selected characteristics and arrests, 1990-91, annual rpt, S2536–1

Maine domestic assaults, by county, type of weapon, and victim-offender characteristics, 1990-91, annual rpt, S3475–1.1

Maryland spousal assaults, by time, circumstances, county, and military installation, 1992 and trends, annual rpt, S3665–1

Montana crimes and clearances, by offense and jurisdiction, 1992, annual rpt, S4705–1

New Hampshire domestic assaults, by type of weapon and victim-offender relationship, 1991, annual rpt, S5250–2.1

New Jersey crimes involving domestic violence, by offense, locale, victim-offender relationship, and other circumstances, 1992, annual rpt, S5430–1

Domestic violence

New York State domestic violence offenses by type and victim-offender relationship, 1991, annual rpt, S5760–3.1
Oklahoma domestic abuse crimes reported, 1992, annual rpt, S6465–1.2
South Carolina domestic assault victims, by victim/offender relationship, 1991-92, annual rpt, S7205–1
Texas family violence incidents, by offender, victim, and incident characteristics, 1992, annual rpt, S7735–2.2
Texas protective services for family violence victims, by county, FY92, annual rpt, S7695–1
Utah homeless shelter population characteristics, including victims of spousal abuse, 1991-92, annual rpt, S7808–2
Vermont court petitions for relief from domestic abuse, by court, FY92 annual rpt, S8120–1
West Virginia domestic violence complaints, with victim and offender characteristics, and investigative activity, 1991, annual rpt, S8610–1.2
Wyoming domestic violence incidents, circumstances, and case dispositions, by county, 1991, annual rpt, S8867–3.2
see also Child abuse and neglect
see also Domestic relations courts and cases

Domiciliary care
see Group homes
see Home health services
see Homemaker services
see Nursing homes
see Respite care

Dominican Republic
Agricultural Dev Bank loan repayment performance, by borrower characteristics, 1993 article, U1380–4
Statistical abstract of Latin America, detailed social, govtl, and economic data, 1992 annual rpt, U6250–1
Women's childbearing and contraceptive use patterns, 1993 article, A5160–6.503

Donations
see Gifts and private contributions
see Organ and blood banks

Donnelley Marketing Information Services Inc.
Sales promotion methods used by packaged goods manufacturers, 1990 and 1992, article, C1200–4.510

Donovan, Patricia
"Testing Positive: Sexually Transmitted Disease and the Public Health Response", A5160–10

Dormitories
see Student housing

DOT
see Department of Transportation

Douglas County, Nev.
Casino finances and employment, by location and gaming revenue range, FY92, annual rpt, S5062–1

Dover, Del.
Population by age and sex, 1990-2020, recurring rpt, S1375–3

Dover, N.H.
Employment, hours, and earnings in Portsmouth-Dover-Rochester MSA, monthly rpt, S5205–1

Index by Subjects and Names

DRI/McGraw-Hill
Economic trends and forecasts for 34 indicators, 1991-95, article, U8595–1.501, U8595–1.503

Drilling
see Energy exploration and drilling
see Offshore oil and gas

Drinking places
see Restaurants and drinking places

Drinking water
see Bottled water
see Water supply and use

Driver education
Motorcycle operator education program sites, grads, instructors, and funding info, by State, 1991, annual rpt, A6485–1.2
State and local:
Alabama public school revenues by source and expenditures by object, by district, 1991/92, annual rpt, S0124–1.2
Delaware public and nonpublic school enrollment in driver education, 1991/92, annual rpt, S1430–1.6
Illinois public school driver education program participants and costs, 1979/80-1990/91, annual rpt, S2440–1.3
Kansas school district revenues by source and expenditures by object, 1990/91, annual rpt, S2945–1
Maryland elementary and secondary education data, by county, 1991/92, annual rpt, S3610–2.9
Oklahoma school revenues and expenditures, by program, county, and district, FY92, annual rpt, S6423–1.1
Wisconsin elementary and secondary school enrollment, staff, costs, and State aid, by school district, 1992/93 and trends, annual rpt, S8795–2

Drivers licenses
Canada drivers licenses by Province, 1991, annual rpt, A0865–1.1
Licensed drivers and accidents, by age group, 1991, annual rpt, A5650–1.4
Licensed drivers and registered vehicles, 1992 and trends, annual rpt, A8375–2.3
Licensed drivers, by age, sex, and State, 1992 and trends, annual rpt, A0865–1.2
Licensed drivers by sex and State, and Canadian Province, 1993 annual fact book, C4680–1.507
Licensed drivers, top 20 States, 1989, recurring rpt, R9375–6
Motorcycle operator licensing procedures, operators, and vehicle registrations, by State, 1993 annual rpt, A6490–1
Motorcycle use and user characteristics, licensed operators, and State requirements, 1992 annual rpt, A6485–1.2
Older driver age 65/over retesting, public opinion, June 1993 Gallup Poll, C4040–1.512
State social, economic, and govtl indicators, with rankings, 1993 semiannual rpt, B8500–1.11
Statistical profiles of 50 States and DC, general data, 1993 annual almanac, C4712–1
State and local:
Alabama traffic accidents, by drivers license status, 1992, annual rpt, S0185–1
Alaska licensed drivers and vehicle registrations, 1982-91, annual rpt, S0360–1

Arizona licensed drivers by age and sex, 1991, annual rpt, S0530–1
Arizona statistical abstract, general data, 1993 recurring rpt, U5850–2.18
California licensed drivers, by county, age, and sex, 1991 and trends, annual rpt, S0885–1
Colorado drivers licensing and control activity, FY92, annual rpt, S1075–1.4
DC statistical profile, general data, 1992 annual rpt, S1535–3.7
Delaware licensed drivers, with detail by sex and age, 1992 and trends, annual rpt, S1435–1
Florida county data book, 1992/93 annual rpt, C6360–1
Florida licensed drivers and vehicle registrations, 1972-92, annual rpt, S1750–2
Florida statistical abstract, general data, 1992 annual rpt, U6660–1.13
Georgia statistical abstract, general data, 1992-93 biennial rpt, U6730–1.8
Hawaii data book, general data, 1992 annual rpt, S2090–1.18
Hawaii drivers registered, by county, sex, and age group, 1986, annual rpt, S2125–1
Illinois motor vehicle accident involvement rates, and licensed drivers, by age, 1991 and trends, annual rpt, S2540–1
Kansas drivers license fees collected, 1986-91, and licensed drivers by age and class, 1991, annual rpt, S3020–1
Kansas licensed drivers, by age and sex, 1992, annual rpt, S3040–1
Kansas statistical abstract, general data, 1991/92 annual rpt, U7095–2.13
Louisiana licensed drivers by parish and age, 1991, annual rpt, S3345–2
Maine traffic accidents, fatalities, and injuries, by license type and status, 1992, annual rpt, S3475–2
Michigan licensed drivers, 1982-91, annual rpt, S3997–2
Minnesota licensed drivers by age, and alcohol-related license revocations, 1992 and trends, annual rpt, S4230–2
Missouri drivers licenses issued, and vehicle and boat registrations, by type, FY88-92, annual rpt, S4570 1.1
Missouri motor vehicle registrations and licensed drivers, with data for motorcycles, 1992, annual rpt, S4560–1
Montana traffic accidents, fatalities, and injuries, by compliance with drivers license restrictions, 1992, annual rpt, S4705–2
Nebraska licensed drivers, 1992, annual rpt, S4953–1
Nevada statistical abstract, general data, 1992 biennial rpt, S5005–1.13
New Mexico licensed drivers by sex, age, and county, and licensing activity by office, FY91-92 annual rpt, S5660–1.2
New York State licensed drivers by driver characteristics, and licenses revoked and suspended, 1991, annual rpt, S5790–1
New York State statistical yearbook, general data, 1992 annual rpt, U5100–1.13
North Carolina licensed drivers by age, 1992, annual rpt, S5990–1
North Dakota licensed drivers and accident involvement, by age and sex, 1992, annual rpt, S6217–1

Index by Subjects and Names

Driving while intoxicated

Ohio licensed drivers, and license suspensions, by sex and/or age, 1991, annual rpt, S6290–1

Oklahoma licensed drivers by sex, age, and license type, 1992 and trends, annual rpt, S6482–1

South Carolina licensed drivers by age and sex, 1992, annual rpt, S7190–2

South Carolina statistical abstract, general data, 1993 annual rpt, S7125–1.15

South Dakota licensed drivers and motorcyclists, by age and/or sex, 1992 and trends, annual rpt, S7300–3

Utah licensed drivers, by age, 1992, annual rpt, S7890–2

Virginia licensed drivers, by location, 1991, annual rpt, S8282–1

Washington State licensed drivers, with detail by age and sex, 1992 and trends, annual rpt, S8428–1

West Virginia motor vehicle licensed drivers, 1992, annual rpt, S8645–1

West Virginia statistical handbook, general data, 1992 annual rpt, R9385–1.2

Wisconsin Blue Book, general data, 1993-94 biennial rpt, S8780–1.2

Wisconsin licensed drivers, with detail by age, 1992 and trends, annual rpt, S8815–1

Driving while intoxicated

- Blood alcohol content law revision and enforcement, views of traffic safety magazine readers, 1992 survey, article, A8375–1.502
- Deterrence measures for drunk driving, views of traffic safety magazine readers, 1992 survey, article, A8375–1.501
- Fatal accident drivers by blood alcohol content and sex, 1982-90, article, A8375–1.505
- Health condition and preventive health care and safety practices of adults, by respondent characteristics, 1992 and trends, annual survey rpt, C8111–2
- Laws and other measures to deter drunk driving by State, and drunk driver accident involvement, 1993 annual rpt, A5650–1
- Traffic fatal accident alcohol involvement by driver age and vehicle type, 1982 and/or 1991, annual rpt, A8375–2.3
- Urban small claims and traffic court caseloads, processing, dispositions, judgments, and litigant satisfaction, for 3-12 jurisdictions, 1990, R6600–5
- Youth age 15-20 share of total and night drivers and driving fatalities, and juvenile blood alcohol limits in 17 States with low limits, 1993 article, A8375–1.506

State and local:

- Alabama juvenile and adult arrests, by type of offense, 1992, annual rpt, S0119–1.1
- Alabama traffic accidents, fatalities, and injuries, by circumstances, vehicle type, and driver and victim characteristics, 1992, annual rpt, S0185–1
- Alaska traffic accidents, fatalities, and injuries, by vehicle type, circumstance, location, and driver and victim characteristics, 1991 and trends, annual rpt, S0360–1
- Arizona arrests by offense, offender characteristics, and county, 1992, annual rpt, S0505–2.2

Arizona court cases and dispositions, by type of case and court, with judicial personnel and finances, by county and city, FY92, annual rpt, S0525–1

Arizona traffic accidents, fatalities, and injuries, by vehicle type, circumstances, location, and driver and victim characteristics, 1991 and trends, annual rpt, S0530–1

Arkansas court caseloads and dispositions, by type of court and case, and location, FY92 and trends, annual rpt, S0647–1

Arkansas crimes and arrests, by offense, victim and offender characteristics, and location, 1992 and trends, annual rpt, S0652–1

Arkansas traffic accidents, fatalities, and injuries, by vehicle type, circumstances, location, and driver and victim characteristics, 1991, annual rpt, S0692–1

California crimes and arrests, clearances, and arrest dispositions, with data by offense and offender characteristics, 1987-92, annual rpt, S0910–1.1

California criminal justice system detailed data, by offense, county, age, race-ethnicity, and sex, 1991 and trends, annual rpt, S0910–2

California health behavior risk factor surveillance survey results, by respondent characteristics, 1991 and trends, annual rpt, S0865–2

California traffic accidents, fatalities, and injuries, by vehicle type, circumstances, location, and driver and victim characteristics, 1991 and trends, annual rpt, S0885–1

Colorado court cases and dispositions, by type of court and detailed case type, FY92 and trends, annual rpt, S1035–1.2

Colorado crimes and arrests, by offense and location, with offender characteristics, and assaults on police, 1992, annual rpt, S1068–1

Colorado drivers license suspension activity for driving while intoxicated violations, FY92 and trends, annual rpt, S1075–1.4

Colorado health behavior risk factor surveillance survey results, by respondent characteristics, 1990, recurring rpt, S1010–3

Connecticut arrests, by offense, offender characteristics, and local agency, 1992, annual rpt, S1256–1.2

Connecticut health behavior risk factor surveillance survey results, 1989-91, annual rpt, S1200–2

Connecticut traffic accidents, fatalities, and injuries, by vehicle type, circumstance, location, and driver and victim characteristics, 1992, annual rpt, S1275–1

DC criminal justice system summary, including crimes and arrests, criminal procedure, prisoners, and parole, 1991 and trends, annual rpt, S1535–2

Delaware alcohol-related traffic accident fatalities and injuries, and arrests, 1992 and trends, annual rpt, S1435–1

Delaware crimes and arrests, by offense, county, and victim-offender characteristics, 1991 and trends, annual rpt, S1375–5

Florida crimes and arrests, by offense, with data by victim and offender characteristics, 1992, annual rpt, S1770–1

Florida traffic accidents, fatalities, and injuries, by vehicle type, circumstance, location, and driver and victim characteristics, 1992 and trends, annual rpt, S1750–2

Georgia health behavior risk factor surveillance survey results, by respondent characteristics, 1991 and trends, annual rpt, S1895–2

Hawaii crimes and arrests, by offense, with data by county and victim-offender characteristics, 1992, annual rpt, S2035–1

Hawaii health behavior risk factor surveillance survey results, by respondent characteristics, 1990, annual rpt, S2065–1.4

Hawaii traffic accidents, injuries, and fatalities, by circumstances, location, and driver and victim characteristics, 1986 and trends, annual rpt, S2125–1

Idaho crimes and arrests, by offense, with data by location and offender characteristics, 1992 and trends, annual rpt, S2275–2

Idaho traffic accidents, fatalities, and injuries, by circumstances, location, vehicle type, and driver and victim characteristics, 1992, annual rpt, S2315–1

Illinois crimes and arrests, by offense, with data by location and offender characteristics, 1991, annual rpt, S2536–1

Illinois traffic fatality driver blood alcohol concentration, by age, 1991, annual rpt, S2540–1

Indiana traffic accidents, fatalities, and injuries, by circumstances, location, and vehicle type, and driver and victim characteristics, 1992, annual rpt, S2675–1

Iowa district court criminal filings and dispositions, by case type and district, 1991-92, annual rpt, S2815–1

Iowa health behavior risk factor surveillance survey results, by respondent characteristics, 1991, annual rpt, S2795–2

Kansas crimes and arrests, by offense, with data by location, agency, and victim-offender characteristics, 1992 and trends, annual rpt, S2925–1.1

Kansas district court drunk driving caseload filings and dispositions, by district and county, FY92, annual rpt, S3035–1

Kansas traffic accidents, fatalities, and injuries, by vehicle type, location, circumstances, and driver and victim characteristics, 1992, annual rpt, S3040–1

Kentucky arrests by county and offense, and law enforcement employment by agency, 1992, annual rpt, S3150–1.2

Kentucky health behavior risk factor surveillance survey results, by State area and respondent characteristics, 1988-90, annual rpt, S3140–6

Kentucky traffic accidents, fatalities, and injuries, by circumstances, location, vehicle type, and driver characteristics, 1992 and trends, annual rpt, S3150–2

Driving while intoxicated

Louisiana traffic accidents, fatalities, and injuries, by circumstances, location, and driver characteristics, 1991 and trends, annual rpt, S3345–2

Maine arrests of adults and juveniles, by offense, age, and sex, 1991, annual rpt, S3475–1.2

Maine traffic accidents, fatalities, and injuries, by accident circumstances, vehicle type and make, and driver and victim characteristics, 1992, annual rpt, S3475–2

Maryland court caseloads and dispositions, by type of court and case, and county, with judicial personnel and finances, FY92 and trends, annual rpt, S3600–1

Maryland crimes and arrests, by offense, location, and offender characteristics, with law enforcement employment and assaults on officers, 1992 and trends, annual rpt, S3665–1

Maryland traffic accidents, fatalities, and injuries, by circumstances, location, vehicle type, and driver and victim characteristics, 1992, annual rpt, S3665–4

Massachusetts court cases and dispositions, by type of court and case, and location, FY92 and trends, annual rpt, S3807–1

Massachusetts health behavior risk factor surveillance survey results, by respondent characteristics, 1986-90, recurring rpt, S3850–3

Michigan crimes and arrests, by offense, with data by location and offender characteristics, 1992 and trends, annual rpt, S3997–1

Michigan health behavior risk factor surveillance survey results, by respondent characteristics, 1991, annual rpt, S4000–4

Michigan traffic accidents, fatalities, and injuries, by vehicle type, circumstance, location, and driver and victim characteristics, 1991 and trends, annual rpt, S3997–2

Minnesota alcohol-related traffic accident fatalities, intoxication test results, and driver arrests and license revocations, 1992 and trends, annual rpt, S4230–2

Missouri crimes and arrests, by offense and location, with victim and offender characteristics, 1991 and trends, annual rpt, S4560–2

Missouri traffic accidents, fatalities, and injuries, by circumstances, location, and driver and victim characteristics, 1992 and trends, annual rpt, S4560–1

Montana crimes and clearances, by offense and jurisdiction, 1992, annual rpt, S4705–1

Montana traffic accidents, fatalities, and injuries, by circumstances, location, and driver and victim characteristics, 1992 and trends, annual rpt, S4705–2

Nebraska traffic accidents, fatalities, and injuries, by circumstances, location, vehicle type, and driver and victim characteristics, 1992, annual rpt, S4953–1

Nevada health behavior risk factor surveillance survey results, by location and respondent characteristics, 1991, annual rpt, S5075–3

Nevada statistical abstract, general data, 1992 biennial rpt, S5005–1.4

Nevada traffic accidents, fatalities, and injuries, by circumstances, location, and vehicle type, 1992 and trends, annual rpt, S5140–1

New Hampshire arrests, by offense and offender age, sex, and race-ethnicity, 1991, annual rpt, S5250–2.2

New Jersey arrests by offense, age, race-ethnicity, sex, and county, 1992 and trends, annual rpt, S5430–1.2

New Jersey fatal traffic accidents and fatalities, by vehicle type, location, and circumstances, and driver and victim characteristics, 1992 and trends, annual rpt, S5430–2

New Mexico court cases and dispositions, by type of court and case, and location, with judicial system finances and personnel, FY92, annual rpt, S5623–1

New Mexico traffic accidents, fatalities, and injuries, by vehicle type, circumstances, location, and driver and victim characteristics, 1992 and trends, annual rpt, S5665–1

New York State crimes and arrests by offense and demographic characteristics, and court activity and corrections, 1991 and trends, annual rpt, S5760–3

New York State health behavior risk factor surveillance survey results, by respondent characteristics, 1990, recurring rpt, S5765–3

New York State traffic accidents, fatalities, and injuries, by circumstances, location, vehicle type, and driver and victim characteristics, 1991 and trends, annual rpt, S5790–1

North Carolina arrests by detailed offense, offender characteristics, and county, 1991-92, annual rpt, S5955–1.2

North Carolina traffic accidents, fatalities, and injuries, by circumstances, location, vehicle type, and driver and victim characteristics, 1992 and trends, annual rpt, S5990–1

North Dakota crimes and arrests, by offense, location, and offender characteristics, and law enforcement employment, 1991 and trends, annual rpt, S6060–1

North Dakota health behavior risk factor surveillance survey results, by respondent characteristics, 1991 and trends, annual rpt, S6105–3

North Dakota traffic accidents and circumstances, including blood alcohol content of fatalities, 1992 and trends, annual rpt, S6217–1

Ohio court caseload and case disposition, by type of court and case, and location, 1992, annual rpt, S6385–1

Ohio traffic accidents, fatalities, and injuries, by circumstances, location, driver and victim characteristics, and vehicle type, 1991 and trends, annual rpt, S6290–1

Oklahoma court cases and dispositions, by type of court and case, with judicial system finances, by county or jurisdiction, FY92, annual rpt, S6493–1

Oklahoma crimes and arrests, by offense, with victim and offender characteristics, 1990-92, annual rpt, S6465–1.1

Index by Subjects and Names

Oklahoma traffic accidents, fatalities, and injuries, by circumstances, location, and driver and victim characteristics, 1992 and trends, annual rpt, S6482–1

Oregon crimes and arrests, by offense, with data by county, local agency, and offender characteristics, 1992 and trends, annual rpt, S6603–3

Pennsylvania crimes and arrests, by offense, with data by location and offender characteristics, 1992 and trends, annual rpt, S6860–1

Pennsylvania health behavior risk factor surveillance survey results, by respondent characteristics, 1991, annual rpt, S6820–4

Pennsylvania traffic accidents, fatalities, and injuries, by circumstances, location, driver characteristics, and vehicle type, 1991, annual rpt, S6905–3

Rhode Island blood alcohol test results for drivers and victims in fatal traffic accidents, 1992, annual rpt, S7025–1

South Carolina court cases and dispositions, by type of court and location, with judicial dept finances and employees, 1992 and trends, annual rpt, S7197–1

South Carolina crimes and arrests, by detailed offense, offender characteristics, and location, 1992 and trends, annual rpt, S7205–1.2

South Carolina traffic accidents, fatalities, and injuries, by circumstances, location, and driver and victim characteristics, 1992 and trends, annual rpt, S7190–2

South Dakota driving under the influence violations and court cases, FY88-92, annual rpt, S7395–1

South Dakota traffic accidents, fatalities, and injuries, by circumstances, location, vehicle type, and driver and victim characteristics, 1992 and trends, annual rpt, S7300–3

Tennessee drunk driver victims compensation fund financial condition, FY92, annual rpt, S7505–1

Tennessee health behavior risk factor surveillance survey results, by respondent characteristics, 1986-90, annual rpt, S7520–3

Texas crimes and arrests, by offense, with data by location and offender characteristics, 1992 and trends, annual rpt, S7735–2

Texas health behavior risk factor surveillance survey results, by respondent characteristics, 1991 and trends, annual rpt, S7685–2

Utah crimes and arrests, by offense, county, and local agency, 1992 and trends, annual rpt, S7890–3

Utah health behavior risk factor surveillance survey results, by respondent characteristics, 1991, annual rpt, S7835–3

Utah traffic accidents and fatalities by circumstances, location, driver and victim characteristics, and vehicle type, 1992 and trends, annual rpt, S7890–2

Virginia crimes and arrests by offense, and law enforcement employment, by location and reporting agency, 1992, annual rpt, S8295–2.2

Virginia traffic accidents, fatalities, and injuries, by circumstances, location, and driver and victim characteristics, 1991 and trends, annual rpt, S8282–1

Index by Subjects and Names — Drowning

Washington State court cases and dispositions, by type of court and case, and jurisdiction, with judicial finances and personnel, 1992 and trends, annual rpt, S8339–1

Washington State crimes and arrests, by offense, with data by location and offender characteristics, 1992 and trends, annual rpt, S8440–1

Washington State traffic accidents, fatalities, and injuries, by circumstances, vehicle type, and location, with driver and victim characteristics, 1992 and trends, annual rpt, S8428–1

West Virginia crimes and arrests, by offense, location, and offender characteristics, 1990-91, annual rpt, S8610–1

West Virginia traffic accidents, fatalities, and injuries, by circumstance and location, and driver and victim characteristics, 1992, annual rpt, S8645–1

Wisconsin alcohol-related traffic accidents, and driver fatality blood alcohol content, by age and sex, 1992, annual rpt, S8815–1

Wisconsin Blue Book, general data, 1993-94 biennial rpt, S8780–1.2

Wisconsin crimes and arrests, by offense, offender characteristics, county, and local agency, 1992 and trends, annual rpt, S8771–1

Wyoming adult and juvenile arrests, by offense, county, and local jurisdiction, 1991, annual rpt, S8867–3.2

Wyoming traffic accidents, fatalities, and injuries, by circumstances, location, vehicle type, and driver and victim characteristics, 1992 and trends, annual rpt, S9007–1

Dropouts

see School dropouts

Drought

Ethiopia famine analysis, including household impacts and responses, drought factor, agricultural activity and markets, and intervention programs, 1980s, R5620–1.36

Western States drought-response capability summary, 1990 survey, A8195–11

Drowning

Accidental deaths and disabling injuries, by detailed type, victim characteristics, circumstances, and location, 1992 and trends, annual rpt, A8375–2

Deaths from drowning, with detail for top 10 States, 1990, B6045–1.504

State and local:

Alabama vital statistics, including population, births, deaths by cause, marriages, and divorces, by location and demographic characteristics, 1992 and trends, annual rpt, S0175–2

Alaska vital statistics, including births, deaths by cause, marriages, divorces, adoptions, and population, by demographic characteristics and location, 1990, annual rpt, S0315–1

California vital statistics, including population, births, and deaths by cause, by demographic characteristics and county, 1990 and trends, annual rpt, S0865–1

Colorado vital statistics, including population, births, deaths by cause, abortion, marriage and divorce, and adoption, by demographic characteristics and location, 1990 and trends, annual rpt, S1010–1

Connecticut vital statistics, including births, deaths by cause, marriages, and divorces, by demographic characteristics and location, 1989, annual rpt, S1200–1

Florida vital statistics, including population, births, deaths by cause, and marriages and dissolutions, by location and demographic characteristics, 1992 and trends, annual rpt, S1745–3

Georgia vital statistics, including deaths by cause, demographic characteristics, and location, 1991 and trends, annual rpt, S1895–1.2

Hawaii vital statistics, including births, deaths by cause, marriages, and dissolutions, by demographic characteristics and location, 1990, annual rpt, S2065–1.2

Idaho vital statistics, including births, deaths by cause, abortions, marriages, and divorces, by demographic characteristics and county, 1991 and trends, annual rpt, S2250–2

Iowa vital statistics, including population, births, deaths by cause, marriages, and divorces, by demographic characteristics and location, 1991 and trends, annual rpt, S2795–1

Kansas vital statistics, including population, births, deaths by cause, abortions, marriages, and divorces, by demographic characteristics and location, 1991 and trends, annual rpt, S2975–1

Kentucky vital statistics, including births, deaths by cause, marriages and divorces, and population, by demographic characteristics and county, 1991, annual rpt, S3140–1

Louisiana vital statistics, including population, births, deaths by cause, reportable diseases, marriages, and divorces, by demographic characteristics and locality, 1989-90 and trends, annual rpt, S3295–1

Maine vital statistics, including births, deaths by cause, abortions, and marriages and divorces, by demographic characteristics and location, 1991 and trends, annual rpt, S3460–2

Maryland vital statistics, including population, births, deaths by cause, marriages, and divorces, by demographic characteristics and location, 1989 and trends, annual rpt, S3635–1

Massachusetts vital statistics, including births, deaths by cause, marriages, divorces, and population, by locality and demographic characteristics, 1990 and trends, annual rpt, S3850–1

Michigan vital statistics, including births, deaths, marriages, divorces/annulments, and communicable diseases, by location and demographic characteristics, 1990 and trends, annual rpt, S4000–3

Minnesota vital statistics, including population, births, abortions, deaths, marriages, and divorces, by location and demographic characteristics, 1991 and trends, annual rpt, S4190–2

Mississippi vital statistics, including births, deaths by cause, marriages, and divorces, by demographic characteristics and location, 1992 and trends, annual rpt, S4350–1

Missouri vital statistics, including population, births, deaths by cause, and marriages and divorces, by location and demographic characteristics, 1992 and trends, annual rpt, S4518–1

Montana vital statistics, including births, deaths by cause, abortion, disease, and marriage and divorce, by demographic characteristics and county, 1990-91 and trends, annual rpt, S4690–1

Nebraska vital statistics, including births, deaths, marriages, divorces, and population, by demographic characteristics and location, 1991 and trends, annual rpt, S4885–1

Nevada vital statistics, including births, abortions, and deaths by cause, by county and demographic characteristics, 1989 and trends, annual rpt, S5075–1

New Jersey vital statistics, including births, deaths, population, communicable diseases, and marriages and divorces, by demographic characteristics and location, 1990 and trends, annual rpt, S5405–1

Ohio vital statistics, including births, deaths by cause, marriages, divorces, and population, by demographic characteristics and location, 1991 and trends, annual rpt, S6285–1

Oregon vital statistics, including births, deaths by cause, communicable diseases, marriages, and divorces, by age, sex, race-ethnicity, and county, 1991 and trends, annual rpt, S6615–5

Rhode Island vital statistics, including population, births, deaths, marriages, and divorces, by demographic characteristics and locality, 1989 and trends, annual rpt, S6995–1

South Carolina deaths, by detailed cause, age, sex, and race, 1990, annual rpt, S7175–2

South Carolina vital statistics, including births, deaths by cause, marriages, and divorces, by age, sex, race, and location, 1990 and trends, annual rpt, S7175–1

Tennessee vital statistics, including births, deaths by cause, marriages, divorces, and population, by demographic characteristics and location, 1991 and trends, annual rpt, S7520–2

Texas vital statistics, including births, deaths by cause, abortions, marriages, and divorces, by location and demographic characteristics, 1991 and trends, annual rpt, S7685–1

Utah vital statistics, including births and deaths by cause, by demographic characteristics and location, 1990, annual rpt, S7835–1.2

Vermont vital statistics, including population, births, deaths by cause, abortions, marriages, and divorces, by location and demographic characteristics, 1991 and trends, annual rpt, S8054–1

Virginia vital statistics, including births, deaths by cause, marriages and divorces, and communicable disease, by demographic characteristics and location, 1991 and trends, annual rpt, S8225–1

Washington State vital statistics, including births, deaths by cause, and population, by demographic characteristics and location, 1991 and trends, annual rpt, S8363–1

Drowning

West Virginia vital statistics, including births, deaths by cause, marriages, and divorces, by location and demographic characteristics, 1991 and trends, annual rpt, S8560–1

Wisconsin vital statistics, including population, births, deaths by cause, and marriages and dissolutions, by county and demographic characteristics, 1991 and trends, annual rpt, S8715–4

Wyoming vital statistics, including population, births, deaths by cause, marriages, and divorces, by demographic characteristics and county, 1991 and trends, annual rpt, S8920–2

Drug abuse and treatment

- AIDS risk sexual behavior among injection drug users and crack smokers, May-June 1991 study, article, A2623–1.510
- Benzodiazepine dependency potential by type of drug, overview of clinical studies, 1993 article, A2623–1.511
- Black American health and vital statistics data, with comparisons to whites, 1970s-91, annual compilation, C6775–2.2
- Catholic facilities for alcohol and drug treatment, with capacity, 1993 annual almanac, C6885–1
- Catholic vs public school ratings for selected aspects of education and environment, public opinion by respondent characteristics, July 1992 survey, A7375–8
- Child abuse/neglect fatalities involving parental substance abuse, 1990-92, annual rpt, A7456–1
- Children's drug use correlated with special instructional efforts at school, 1992 article, A8680–1.501
- Corporate drug testing practices for applicants and employees, positive result ratios, and treatment programs, Jan-Mar 1993 survey and trends, annual rpt, A2075–20.12
- Correctional instn inmate drug treatment programs and participants, by State and for major local jails, 1992 annual series, R4300–1
- Food marketers use of employee assistance programs, by region, 1991, annual rpt, A4950–5
- Funding by source and client characteristics, for alcohol and drug abuse programs, by State, FY91 and trends, annual rpt, A7112–1
- Higher education student use of and attitudes toward alcohol, drugs, and tobacco products, by sex and region, 1989-91 surveys, annual rpt, U4950–1
- HMO benefits coverage, premiums, and rating methods used, by plan characteristics, 1991 and trends, annual rpt, A5150–2.1
- Homeless population characteristics in 29 cities, 1991/92, annual rpt, A9330–9
- Hospital (community) alcohol/drug dependency service provision, 1981 and 1991, article, A1865–1.512
- Hospital employee health care benefits, including coverage for mental health/substance abuse and AIDS, and data by region, 1992 survey, article, A1865–1.505
- Hospital patient discharges and length of stay, by diagnosis, type of operation, age, and region, 1991, annual rpt series, B4455–1

Hospital patient discharges and length of stay, by diagnostic related group (DRG), payment source, age, and region, 1991, annual rpt series, B4455–3

Hospital psychiatric patient discharges and length of stay, by diagnosis, age, sex, and region, 1991, annual rpt series, B4455–2

Japan and US health care system data, including expenditures, facilities, insurance coverage, and population health indicators, 1993 article, R5650–2.515

Mexico drug use among students, by substance and region, 1976 and 1986, annual rpt, U6250–1.15

Public health research results, including drug use patterns in selected populations, 1993 articles, A2623–1.504

Rape victim incidence of mental health, alcohol, and drug abuse problems compared to women who have never been crime victims, 1990-92 surveys, R8375–1

Student use of and attitudes toward alcohol, drugs, and tobacco products, 1993 survey article, B6045–1.504

Teenage pregnant women's substance abuse correlated with risky sexual behavior, 1988/89 Northwest metro area study, article, A5160–1.501

Urban public school programs for drug education and support of students with addicted parents, and student use measures, for 47 systems, 1990/91, A4425–4

Workplace drug use by workers age 19-27, by sex and race-ethnicity, 1984, annual rpt, R8335–1.1

State and local:

- Alabama Court Referral Officer Program activities for alcohol/drug-related cases, 1988-92, annual rpt, S0118–1
- Alabama statistical abstract, general data, 1992 recurring rpt, U5680–2.8
- Arizona traffic accidents involving driver drug use, 1991, annual rpt, S0530–1
- Arkansas court caseloads and dispositions, by type of court and case, and location, FY92 and trends, annual rpt, S0647–1
- Arkansas drug and alcohol treatment and prevention program expenditures, success rates, and client characteristics, FY91 annual rpt, S0700–2.1
- California correctional instn inmate drug use history, and narcotics addict population, 1990 or 1991 and trends, annual rpt, S0820–1
- California correctional instn narcotics addicts, by offense, demographic characteristics, and instn, Dec 1992, semiannual rpt, S0820–2
- California statistical abstract, general data, 1992 annual rpt, S0840–2.5
- California vital statistics, including population, births, and deaths by cause, by demographic characteristics and county, 1990 and trends, annual rpt, S0865–1
- Connecticut courts probation activity, including drug dependency caseloads, FY91-92, biennial rpt, S1220–1.2
- Connecticut family violence offenses involving liquor/drug use, 1992, annual rpt, S1256–1.3
- DC statistical profile, general data, 1992 annual rpt, S1535–3.5
- Delaware public opinion on criminal sentencing, prison alternatives, and related issues, Feb 1991 survey, R8825–11

Index by Subjects and Names

- Delaware vital statistics, including births, deaths by cause, and marriages and dissolutions, by demographic characteristics and location, 1990, annual rpt, S1385–2
- Florida correctional system inmate narcotics use, by sex and race, FY92, annual rpt, S1720–1
- Florida health care atlas, including manpower by occupation and health care facilities by type, by district and county, 1992 annual rpt, S1746–1.2
- Florida vital statistics, including population, births, deaths by cause, and marriages and dissolutions, by location and demographic characteristics, 1992 and trends, annual rpt, S1745–3
- Georgia alcohol/drug related deaths, by county, 1987-91, annual rpt, U6750–1
- Hawaii drug/alcohol abuse treatment program admissions by client characteristics and county, and discharges by length of stay, 1990, annual rpt, S2065–1.7
- Hawaii traffic accidents involving drug use, 1986, annual rpt, S2125–1
- Idaho offender drug use during commission of crimes, by offense, 1992, annual rpt, S2275–2
- Idaho vital statistics, including births, deaths by cause, abortions, marriages, and divorces, by demographic characteristics and county, 1991 and trends, annual rpt, S2250–2
- Illinois mental health facility patient population and characteristics, by facility, location, and treatment category, FY93, annual rpt, S2505–1
- Kansas correctional instn inmates by level of substance abuse, June 1992, annual rpt, S2940–1
- Kansas court caseloads and disposition, by type of court and case, and location, FY92, annual rpt, S3035–1
- Kentucky traffic accidents involving drivers under influence of drugs, 1992, annual rpt, S3150–2
- Maine traffic accidents, fatalities, and injuries, by accident circumstances, vehicle type and make, and driver and victim characteristics, 1992, annual rpt, S3475–2
- Maine vital statistics, including births, deaths by cause, abortions, and marriages and divorces, by demographic characteristics and location, 1991 and trends, annual rpt, S3460–2
- Maryland public school funding for drug education, by county, 1991/92, annual rpt, S3610–2.9
- Massachusetts vital statistics, including births, deaths by cause, marriages, divorces, and population, by locality and demographic characteristics, 1990 and trends, annual rpt, S3850–1
- Michigan drug/alcohol abusers admitted to treatment programs, by State area, FY91, annual planning rpt, S3980–1.2
- Michigan vital statistics, including births, deaths, marriages, divorces/annulments, and communicable diseases, by location and demographic characteristics, 1990 and trends, annual rpt, S4000–3
- Minnesota traffic accidents involving drug use by drivers, 1992, annual rpt, S4230–2

Index by Subjects and Names

Mississippi vital statistics, including births, deaths by cause, marriages, and divorces, by demographic characteristics and location, 1992 and trends, annual rpt, S4350–1

Missouri traffic accidents involving drugs, 1992, annual rpt, S4560–1

Montana vital statistics, including births, deaths by cause, abortjon, disease, and marriage and divorce, by demographic characteristics and county, 1990-91 and trends, annual rpt, S4690–1

Nevada traffic accidents, fatalities, and injuries, by circumstances, location, and vehicle type, 1992 and trends, annual rpt, S5140–1

New Jersey traffic fatalities involving alcohol and drug use, 1988-92, annual rpt, S5430–2

New Mexico vital statistics, including population, births, deaths, and disease, by location and demographic characteristics, 1991 and trends, annual rpt, S5605–1

New York State statistical yearbook, general data, 1992 annual rpt, U5100–1.11

New York State traffic accidents involving drug use, 1991, annual rpt, S5790–1

North Carolina rape offenses by influence of drugs/alcohol on victim and offender, 1991-92, annual rpt, S5955–1.1

Oklahoma statistical abstract, general data, 1992 annual rpt, U8130–2.9

Oklahoma traffic accident victim drug involvement, 1992, annual rpt, S6482–1

Oregon vital statistics, including deaths by cause and drug use during pregnancy, 1991 and trends, annual rpt, S6615–5

South Carolina deaths, by detailed cause, age, sex, and race, 1990, annual rpt, S7175–2

South Carolina statistical abstract, general data, 1993 annual rpt, S7125–1.10

Tennessee vital statistics, including births, deaths by cause, marriages, divorces, and population, by demographic characteristics and location, 1991 and trends, annual rpt, S7520–2

Utah homeless shelter population characteristics, individual shelter capacity, and related housing data, 1991-92, annual rpt, S7808–2

Washington State public assistance clients and service costs, by client characteristics, program, and county, FY90, annual rpt, S8420–2

West Virginia vital statistics, including births, deaths by cause, marriages, and divorces, by location and demographic characteristics, 1991 and trends, annual rpt, S8560–1

Wisconsin correctional instn admissions by inmate characteristics, including need for special services, 1991, annual rpt, S8692–1.2

Wisconsin correctional instn inmate characteristics, by sex and instn, Dec 1991, semiannual rpt, S8692–1.5

Wyoming prison inmate, probationer, and parolee alcohol and drug use, FY92, annual rpt, S8883–1

see also Alcohol abuse and treatment
see also Cocaine
see also Drug and narcotics offenses
see also Marijuana

Drug and narcotics offenses

see also Methadone treatment
see also under By Disease in the "Index by Categories"

Drug and alcohol testing

College freshmen attitudes on drug testing in workplace, fall 1992, annual survey, U6215–1

College grad new hire testing for drugs, alcohol, and AIDS, employer practices, 1992/93 annual survey rpt, U3130–1

Construction industry use of substance abuse testing, by type of business, 1992-93, annual survey rpt, A4155–1

Corporate drug testing practices for applicants and employees, positive result ratios, and treatment programs, Jan-Mar 1993 survey and trends, annual rpt, A2075–20.12

Correctional system use of drug testing for staff, inmates, and probationers and parolees, including by State and for major local jails, 1992 annual series, R4300–1

Employer use of drug/alcohol testing in hiring, 1990s, annual survey rpt, B6850–3, B6850–5

Fire dept employment and personnel practices, including eligibility requirements and testing, by population size, metro status, and census div, 1991 survey, recurring rpt, A5800–2.116

School bus contractor and district drug testing policies for drivers, 1993 article, C1575–1.506

Traffic fatalities with high blood alcohol concentrations, 1991 and trends, annual rpt, A5650–1.4

State and local:

Arkansas blood alcohol test results for drivers involved in traffic accidents, 1991, annual rpt, S0692–1

DC criminal offender drug test results, including positive tests for selected drugs, 1987-91, annual rpt, S1535–2

DC statistical profile, general data, 1992 annual rpt, S1535–3.8

Delaware alcohol-related traffic accidents and arrests, including victim blood alcohol content test results, 1992 and trends, annual rpt, S1435–1

Illinois traffic fatality driver blood alcohol concentration, by age, 1991, annual rpt, S2540–1

Kansas breath and blood tests administered to drivers involved in traffic accidents, and results, 1992, annual rpt, S3040–1

Kentucky traffic accident fatalities, blood alcohol content of drivers, 1992, annual rpt, S3150–2

Louisiana alcohol-involved traffic accidents, including arrestee test submissions and refusals, 1991 annual rpt, S3345–2

Michigan community corrections participant drug testing results, FY85-91, annual rpt, S3960–1

Michigan drunk driver breath tests taken and refused, and results, 1991, annual rpt, S3997–2

Minnesota blood alcohol test results for persons killed in motor vehicle accidents, 1992 and trends, annual rpt, S4230–2

Montana traffic accidents, fatalities, and injuries, with driver sobriety testing results, 1992, annual rpt, S4705–2

New Jersey blood alcohol level of traffic fatalities, including passengers and pedestrians, 1988-92, annual rpt, S5430–2

North Dakota traffic accidents and circumstances, including blood alcohol content of fatalities, 1992 and trends, annual rpt, S6217–1

Ohio blood alcohol content testing of drivers involved in fatal accidents, by driver age, 1983-91, annual rpt, S6290–1

Oregon arrests for driving under the influence, and blood alcohol testing results, 1992 and trends, annual rpt, S6603–3.1

Rhode Island blood alcohol test results for drivers and victims in fatal traffic accidents, 1992, annual rpt, S7025–1

South Carolina blood alcohol testing results for persons killed in traffic accidents, by county, 1991, annual rpt, S7190–2

Tennessee corrections dept probation activity, including drug tests and outcomes, FY92, annual rpt, S7480–1

Utah alcohol-related traffic accidents, by driver blood alcohol level, 1992, annual rpt, S7890–2

Washington State blood alcohol testing results for persons involved in traffic accidents, by age, 1992, annual rpt, S8428–1

Wisconsin alcohol-related traffic accidents, and driver fatality blood alcohol content, by age and sex, 1992, annual rpt, S8815–1

Wisconsin blood alcohol content of traffic accident fatalities, by age group, 1991, biennial rpt, S8780–1.2

Wyoming parole board drug testing activity, by field office, FY92, annual rpt, S8883–1

Wyoming traffic accidents involving alcohol, including blood alcohol test results by age, 1992, annual rpt, S9007–1

Drug and narcotics offenses

City fiscal condition, including budget trends and adjustments, and influencing factors, by region and population size, Mar-Apr 1993 survey, annual rpt, A8012–1.23

Latin America drug seizures and prices, and drug offenses, by country, 1992 annual rpt, U6250–1.15

Mexico poppy and marijuana fields destroyed, and drug seizures along US border, 1992 annual rpt, U6250–1.15

State and local:

Alabama arrests of adults and juveniles for drug sale and possession, by race and sex, and drug task force property seizures by locale, 1992, annual rpt, S0119–1.1

Arizona arrests by offense, offender characteristics, and county, 1992, annual rpt, S0505–2.2

Arizona controlled substances luxury tax liens and collections, FY83-92, annual rpt, S0515–1

Arkansas crimes and arrests, by offense, victim and offender characteristics, and location, 1992 and trends, annual rpt, S0652–1

California crimes and arrests, clearances, and arrest dispositions, with data by offense and offender characteristics, 1987-92, annual rpt, S0910–1.1

California criminal justice system detailed data, by offense, county, age, race-ethnicity, and sex, 1991 and trends, annual rpt, S0910–2

Drug and narcotics offenses

Colorado crimes and arrests, by offense and location, with offender characteristics, and assaults on police, 1992, annual rpt, S1068–1

Connecticut arrests, by offense, offender characteristics, and local agency, 1992, annual rpt, S1256–1.2

DC criminal justice system summary, including crimes and arrests, criminal procedure, prisoners, and parole, 1991 and trends, annual rpt, S1535–2

DC statistical profile, general data, 1992 annual rpt, S1535–3.8

Delaware crimes and arrests, by offense, county, and victim-offender characteristics, 1991 and trends, annual rpt, S1375–5

Delaware public opinion on criminal sentencing, prison alternatives, and related issues, Feb 1991 survey, R8825–11

Florida crimes and arrests, by offense, with data by victim and offender characteristics, 1992, annual rpt, S1770–1

Hawaii crimes and arrests, by offense, with data by county and victim-offender characteristics, 1992, annual rpt, S2035–1

Idaho drug-related arrests by offender characteristics, and volume of drugs and value of property seized, 1992, annual rpt, S2275–2

Illinois crimes and arrests, by offense, with data by location and offender characteristics, 1991, annual rpt, S2536–1

Iowa correctional instn inmates by commitment crime category, by instn, monthly rpt, S2770 1

Kansas crimes and arrests, by offense, with data by location, agency, and victim-offender characteristics, 1992 and trends, annual rpt, S2925–1.1

Kentucky arrests by county and offense, and law enforcement employment by agency, 1992, annual rpt, S3150–1.2

Maine arrests of adults and juveniles, by offense, age, and sex, 1991, annual rpt, S3475 1.2

Maryland crimes and arrests, by offense, location, and offender characteristics, with law enforcement employment and assaults on officers, 1992 and trends, annual rpt, S3665–1

Massachusetts correctional instn inmates by current and prior narcotics offenses, by instn, Jan 1992, annual rpt, S3805–1

Michigan crimes and arrests, by offense, with data by location and offender characteristics, 1992 and trends, annual rpt, S3997–1

Missouri crimes and arrests, by offense and location, with victim and offender characteristics, 1991 and trends, annual rpt, S4560–2

Montana crimes and clearances, by offense and jurisdiction, 1992, annual rpt, S4705–1

New Hampshire arrests, by offense and offender age, sex, and race-ethnicity, 1991, annual rpt, S5250–2.2

New Jersey arrests for drug offenses, and domestic violence offenses involving drug use, 1992, annual rpt, S5430–1

New York State correctional instn inmates released, by criminal background, sentence, and demographic characteristics, 1991 and trends, recurring rpt series, S5725–1

New York State crimes and arrests by offense and demographic characteristics, and court activity and corrections, 1991 and trends, annual rpt, S5760–3

North Carolina arrests by detailed offense, offender characteristics, and county, 1991-92, annual rpt, S5955–1.2

North Dakota crimes and arrests, by offense, location, and offender characteristics, and law enforcement employment, 1991 and trends, annual rpt, S6060–1

Oklahoma crimes and arrests, by offense, with victim and offender characteristics, 1990-92, annual rpt, S6465–1.1

Oregon crimes and arrests, by offense, with data by county, local agency, and offender characteristics, 1992 and trends, annual rpt, S6603–3

Pennsylvania crimes and arrests, by offense, with data by location and offender characteristics, 1992 and trends, annual rpt, S6860–1

South Carolina crimes and arrests, by detailed offense, offender characteristics, and location, 1992 and trends, annual rpt, S7205–1.2

Texas crimes and arrests, and drugs seized by detailed type, 1992, annual rpt, S7735–2

Utah crimes and arrests, by offense, county, and local agency, 1992 and trends, annual rpt, S7890–3

Virginia crimes and arrests by offense, and law enforcement employment, by location and reporting agency, 1992, annual rpt, S8295–2.2

Washington State crimes and arrests, by offense, with data by location and offender characteristics, 1992 and trends, annual rpt, S8440–1

West Virginia drug law arrests by offender age, and drugs confiscated and value, by substance, 1990-91, annual rpt, S8610–1

Wisconsin crimes and arrests by offense, and drug-related homicides, 1992, annual rpt, S8771–1

Wyoming adult and juvenile arrests, by offense, county, and local jurisdiction, 1991, annual rpt, S8867–3.2

see also Cocaine

Drug industry

see Pharmaceutical industry

Drugs

Abortion pill (RU-486) availability in US, public opinion, Feb 1993 Gallup Poll, C4040–1.509

Advertising expenditures by medium for top 100 advertisers, with comparisons to earnings and sales, and detail by product type and brand, 1991-92, annual rpt, C2710–1.547

Allergy medication market shares, for top 5 nonprescription brands, year ended Jan 1993, article, C2710–1.518

Aquaculture production and value, with data on FDA-approved drugs available, for selected types of animals, 1991, article, A3100–2.514

Index by Subjects and Names

Biotechnology company financial data, including sales of drug and agricultural products, by company, 1991-92, recurring article, A1250–1.518

Cattle owner use of nonsteroidal anti-inflammatory drugs in livestock, 1992 article, A3100–2.504

Chain drugstores financial performance and marketing operations, 1993 annual feature, C5150–2.510

Chemical market value for drug industry, 1991, article, A1250–1.513

Children's pain reliever product use indexes for white vs black households, by brand, 1993 article, C5150–2.520

Chiral drug sales and patent expiration dates, for 9 drugs containing molecules that can exist in mirror image forms, 1990, article, C5800–8.512

Discount store sales and productivity data for 20 depts, 1993 annual feature, C5150–3.516

Expenditures for health care by type, and prevailing treatment charges, 1950s-91, annual rpt, A5173–2.3

FDA approved new drug products, including review time needed and prior foreign approval, by drug, 1992, article, C5150–2.507

Food store sales of total and private label analgesics and cold remedies, year ended Feb 1993, article, C2710–1.526

Generic drug market devs, including share of prescriptions, and drugstore acquisition costs, 1992 and trends, articles, C5150–2.515

Laxative sales and market shares, for top 5 brands and private label, year ended May 1993, article, C2710–1.532

Market shares for natural, synthetic, and/or semisynthetic drugs, by chemical compound type, 1982 and 1991, article, A1250–1.519

Mexico-US border communities comparative prescription drug prices, 1992 rpt, R4865–10

News and devs in retail and wholesale drug industry, with data on finances and operations, biweekly rpt, C5150–2

Older population prescription and over-the-counter drug use, 1993 survey article, C5150 2.521

Packaging preferences of consumers for over-the-counter drugs, 1993 survey, article, C1850–1.507

Packaging preferences of consumers for over-the-counter pain relievers and cough remedies, by presence of children, 1993 survey article, C1850–1.508

Prescription drug health insurance claim rate trends under traditional plans vs electronic card claim submission, 1990, article, C1050–2.506

Prescription drug performance in retail pharmacies, 1993 annual feature, C5150–2.511

Prescription drug use, expenditures, prices, and profit trends, with data by patient characteristics and for top 20 brands, 1992 rpt, R4865–8

Prescription writing authority for nurse practitioners and physician assistants, by State, 1991/92, U8850–8.4

Rankings of top 200 prescription drug brands and top 100 generic products, 1992 annual pharmacy reference guide, C5150–2.503

Index by Subjects and Names

Due process of law

Revenues, market shares, and operating ratios, for 7 major drug wholesale companies, 1992-93, article, C3950–1.511

Sales and consumer expenditures, for food store products by type, 1991-92, annual feature, C4655–1.510

Sales and inventory for prescription drugs, and independent pharmacy operating data, 1991 and trends, annual survey, B5165–1

Sales and market shares for top 10 brands in 8 health care product categories, 1992-93, C2710–1.541

Sales and year of patent expiration, for top 10 prescription drugs, 1992, article, C8900–1.514

Supermarket sales of nonfood products, by detailed product type, 1992, annual feature, C5225–1.508

State and local:

- Arkansas human services dept finances and operations, including Medicaid payments by type of service, FY91 and trends, annual rpt, S0700–2.3
- Arkansas traffic accidents involving driver prescription drug use, 1991, annual rpt, S0692–1
- Hawaii traffic accidents involving drivers under medication, 1986, annual rpt, S2125–1
- Indiana Medicaid expenditures, by service and provider type and county, FY91-92, annual rpt, S2623–1.6
- Kansas traffic accidents involving drivers taking illegal and prescription drugs, 1992, annual rpt, S3040–1
- Kentucky Medicaid recipients and payments, by program, county, and type of medical service, monthly rpt, S3140–5
- Maryland medical assistance payments and recipients, by program, type of service, location, demographic characteristics, and facility, FY92 and trends, annual rpt, S3635–3
- Missouri medical assistance cases, payments, and expenditures for prescription drugs, FY92, annual rpt, S4575–2
- Montana dangerous drug possession/storage tax collections, FY88-92, biennial rpt, S4750–1.1
- Nebraska Medicaid recipients and payments, by type of service and county, FY92, annual rpt, S4957–1.2
- New York State traffic accidents involving driver prescription drug use, 1991, annual rpt, S5790–1
- Oklahoma Medicaid payments, and expenditures for rehabilitative services, by type of service and county, FY92, annual rpt, S6455–1.2
- Oregon caseload and payments for medical service by category, monthly rpt quarterly table, S6615–8
- Pennsylvania senior citizen pharmaceutical assistance fund finances, FY92, annual rpt, S6810–4
- South Dakota medical assistance recipients and payments, by type of service, program, and county, FY92, annual rpt, S7385–1
- Texas welfare and social services program expenditures, recipients, and fraud cases, by county and/or program, FY92 and trends, annual rpt, S7695–1

Washington State public assistance clients and service costs, by client characteristics, program, and county, FY90, annual rpt, S8420–2

see also Biologic drug products *see also* Caffeine *see also* Cocaine *see also* Contraceptives *see also* Drug abuse and treatment *see also* Drug and alcohol testing *see also* Drug and narcotics offenses *see also* Drugstores *see also* Marijuana *see also* Personal care products *see also* Pharmaceutical industry *see also* Poisoning and drug reaction *see also* Vitamins and nutrients

Drugstores

- Chain drugstore top-selling products, and leading manufacturers, 1993 annual article, C5150–2.520
- Chain drugstores financial performance and marketing operations, 1993 annual feature, C5150–2.510, C5150–2.511
- Consumer buying power survey of population, income, and sales by kind of business, by census div, State, MSA, county, and city, 1992, annual rpt, C1200–1.511
- Consumer buying power survey of population, income, and sales by product line, by State, metro area, county, and census div, 1993 annual rpt, C1200–1.514
- Discount chain sales and merchandising, including data by dept, leading chain, and location, 1992 and trends, annual feature, C8130–1.507
- Discount drugstore sales and stores, for 11 leading chains, 1993 annual feature, C5150–3.514
- Expansion devs, and equipment and construction costs, by type of retail chain, 1993 annual articles, C5150–4.507
- Financial and operating data for independent pharmacies, by store characteristics, 1991 and trends, annual survey, B5165–1
- Financial data and business info for approx 240 US and Canadian retail chains, 1991-92 and trends, annual rpt, C3400–2
- Financial performance and growth rankings for approx 1,000 top corporations, with comparisons by industry group, 1993 annual rpt, C3950–1.505
- Financial ratios and performance, for over 350 SIC 4-digit industries, FY88-92, annual rpt, A6400–3
- Markets with daily newspapers, demographic and economic info by geographic area, US and Canada, 1993 annual rpt, C3250–1
- News and devs in retail and wholesale drug industry, with data on finances and operations, biweekly rpt, C5150–2
- Operating and financial composite ratios for corporations, with establishments and receipts, for approx 200 industries, by asset size, FY90, annual rpt, C7800–1
- Sales and merchandising trends, by product type and market area, 1992 annual feature, C5150–2.503
- Sales volume shares by retail outlet type, for approx 300 food, drug, and other product categories, 1993 annual feature, C4655–1.504

Shopping center financial and operating data, with detail by type of tenant, US and Canada, 1991, triennial rpt, R9285–1

State and local:

Texas trade, transportation, and public utilities employment, by SIC 2- and 3-digit industry and detailed occupation, 2nd qtr 1991, triennial survey rpt, S7675–1.31

Drunk drivers

see Driving while intoxicated

Drunkenness

see Alcohol abuse and treatment

Dry cleaning

see Laundry and cleaning services

Du Pont de Nemours and Co.

Motor vehicle most popular paint colors, 1992, recurring article, C1575–2.509

Dubai

see United Arab Emirates

Due process of law

Personal injury case litigation times, for medical malpractice and product liability cases, 1987-91, annual rpt, C5180–1

State and local:

- Alabama supreme court case processing times, FY91-92, annual rpt, S0118–1
- Alaska appellate courts case processing time, FY89-92, annual rpt, S0290–1
- Arkansas court case processing times and age of pending cases, by court type and circuit, FY92, annual rpt, S0647–1
- California court case processing times, and cases awaiting trial, FY92 and trends, annual rpt, S0905–1.2, S0905–2
- DC appeals court case processing time analysis, 1985-92, annual rpt, S1515–1
- Delaware court case processing time, by type of court and case, and by county, FY91-92, annual rpt, S1360–1
- Indiana appeals court cases pending by age of case, by judge and district, Dec 1992, annual rpt, S2703–1.1
- Iowa court cases, processing, and dispositions, by type of court and district, with judicial dept appropriations and personnel, 1992 and trends, annual rpt, S2815–1
- Kansas district court pending cases by age, FY92, annual rpt, S3035–1
- Louisiana appeals court case processing time, 1992, annual rpt, S3375–1
- Maine court case disposition time, by county, FY92 annual rpt, S3463–1
- Maryland court case processing times, by court and location, FY92 and trends, annual rpt, S3600–1
- Massachusetts court cases and dispositions, including caseload by age of case, FY92, annual rpt, S3807–1
- New York State family court case processing times, by jurisdiction, 1991, annual rpt, S5730–1
- New York State felony case processing times, 1991, annual rpt, S5760–3.2
- North Carolina court case processing time, by court type and location, FY91, annual rpt, S5950–1
- Ohio court cases pending beyond time guidelines, and dismissed for lack of speedy trial, by type of court and case, and location, 1992, annual rpt, S6385–1
- Pennsylvania court cases pending, by age of case and county, 1991, annual rpt, S6900–1.2

Due process of law

Rhode Island court case processing times, and age of pending cases, by court and county, 1987-91, annual rpt, S6965–1

South Carolina court cases and dispositions, by type of court and location, with judicial dept finances and employees, 1992 and trends, annual rpt, S7197–1

Texas court case processing times, by county, FY92, annual rpt, S7703–1

Vermont court cases pending, by age of case, FY92 annual rpt, S8120–1

Virginia court case processing time, by circuit, 1992, annual rpt, S8300–1

Washington State appeals court case processing time, 1988-92, annual rpt, S8339–1

West Virginia percent of court cases in compliance with processing time standards, by type of case, 1992 and trends, annual rpt, S8537–1

see also Civil procedure

see also Criminal procedure

Duffy, Gordon D.

"Air Conditioning, Heating, and Refrigeration News: 1993 Statistical Panorama", C1800–1

Duggan, Paula

"Regional Dimensions of the Crisis in Health Care Financing", R8490–46

"Where Have All the Dollars Gone? Regional Patterns in Entitlement Spending", R8490–47

Dumping

Japan steel sheet dumping margins in US, for 4 leading and all other companies, 1993 article, R5650–2.512, R5650–2.539

Uranium anti-dumping petition against former Soviet Union, with participating companies and ownership, and export quotas for 6 Republics, 1992 article, B6800–1.501

see also Trade adjustment assistance

Dumps

see Landfills

Duncan, James H., Jr.

"American Radio", C3165–1

DWI and DUI

see Driving while intoxicated

Dyes

see Chemicals and chemical industry

Dynamite

see Explosives

Ear diseases and infections

Children under age 6 ear infection incidence, by selected characteristics including day care setting, 1988 survey, article, A2623–1.511

Children's ear tube implantation prevalence, by demographic characteristics and reasons for implant, 1988, article, A2623–1.509

Hospital patient discharges and length of stay, by diagnosis, type of operation, age, and region, 1991, annual rpt series, B4455–1

Hospital patient discharges and length of stay, by diagnostic related group (DRG), payment source, age, and region, 1991, annual rpt series, B4455–3

Index by Subjects and Names

State and local:

California vital statistics, including population, births, and deaths by cause, by demographic characteristics and county, 1990 and trends, annual rpt, S0865–1

Massachusetts vital statistics, including births, deaths by cause, marriages, divorces, and population, by locality and demographic characteristics, 1990 and trends, annual rpt, S3850–1

Mississippi vital statistics, including deaths by cause, marriages, and divorces, by demographic characteristics and location, 1992 and trends, annual rpt, S4350–1

Montana vital statistics, including births, deaths by cause, abortion, disease, and marriage and divorce, by demographic characteristics and county, 1990-91 and trends, annual rpt, S4690–1

Tennessee vital statistics, including births, deaths by cause, marriages, divorces, and population, by demographic characteristics and location, 1991 and trends, annual rpt, S7520–2

see also under By Disease in the "Index by Categories"

Earnings, general

Black American earnings, income, and poverty data, with comparisons to whites, 1980s-91, annual compilation, C6775–2.7

Black American socioeconomic status, with comparisons to whites and data by region, 1960s-92, annual compilation, A8510–1.1

Black children and youth population, economic, health, and education data, with comparisons to whites, 1993 rpt, R3840–21

Business grad school programs for executives, average salary of participants at 20 instns, 1993 article, C5800–7.552

CEO characteristics and compensation, for small companies with rapid growth, 1993 survey article, C5800–7.551

CEO compensation measures, for top 10 executives among 100 leading natl advertisers, 1992 article, C2710–1.505

Chemist and chemical engineer salaries, employment status, and demographic and professional characteristics, 1993, annual rpt, A1250–4

Chemist employment and salaries, by degree level and industry, 1993, annual feature, A1250–1.537

Chemist salaries and employment, by employee and employer characteristics, Mar 1993 and trends, annual article, A1250–1.532

Chemistry and chemical engineering grad starting salaries, employment status, demographic characteristics, and advanced study plans, 1991/92, annual rpt, A1250–2

College grad hiring plans by industry, with data on campus visits, starting salaries, and minority hires, 1991/92-1992/93, annual rpt, A3940–3

College grad job and salary offers, by field of study, type of employer and occupation, and degree level, by region, interim rpt series, A3940–1

College grad job and salary offers, by field of study, type of employer and occupation, and degree level, series, A3940–2

College grad recruiting practices and hiring trends, with data on starting salaries and layoffs, by type of employer, 1992/93 annual survey rpt, U3130–1

College grads in business and industry, hiring plans, salaries, and selected personnel practices, 1993 annual survey rpt, U3730–1

Computer-related occupation salary ranges, for 22 occupations, 1992, article, C4215–1.503

Computer/info systems salaries for 24 positions, by industry sector and location, 1993 survey, annual article, C1850–5.518

Corporate boards of directors compensation practices and amounts, by industry group, 1991-92, annual rpt, R4105–7

Corporate boards of directors composition, compensation, and practices, by industry sector, 1991 and trends, annual survey rpt, B5000–3

Corporate CEO characteristics, compensation, and company finances, for officers of top 1,000 firms, 1993 annual feature, C5800–7.549

Corporate CEO compensation compared to company performance, for 200 executives, 1992, annual article, C8900–1.517

Corporate CEO compensation in 800 firms, with sales and profit data, 1993 annual article, C3950–1.515

Corporate CEO compensation relative to company size and performance, errata, C2710–2.501

Corporate CEO compensation shares from base pay and long-term incentives, 1985 and 1992, article, C4687–1.503

Corporate CEO views on outlook for company employment, wages compared to inflation, and mgmt skills needs, June 1993 survey, article, C8900–1.519

Corporate employees frequently transferred, salary ranges, 1992, annual survey, B0600–1

Corporate executive compensation for top executives at approx 400 companies, by industry group, 1992 and trends, annual survey, C5800–7.525

Corporate executive compensation, with company revenues, for 20 highly paid executives in US, Germany, and Japan, 1993 article, C3950–1.516

Economic dev condition indicators, including economic performance, business vitality, growth capacity, and tax/fiscal system, by State, 1993 annual rpt, R4225–1

Economic outlook for selected indicators, recent trends and 2-year forecast, quarterly rpt, A3840–6

Education impact on earnings, difference between college and high school grads by sex, 1979 and 1989, R4105–80.501

Employee wages and pension coverage as affected by job mobility, by pension plan type, 1984-85, R9260–17

Engineer compensation, by work and employee characteristics, and region and metro area, 1992, annual rpt, A8460–1

Engineering grad salaries, by discipline, 1992-93, article, C5800–8.509

Engineers salaries by industry group, census div, selected metro area, and years since college degree, 1993, annual survey rpt, A0685–5

Index by Subjects and Names

Earnings, general

Engineers salaries by industry group, census div, selected metro area, degree level, and years since college degree, 1993, annual survey rpt, A0685–3

Executive compensation, by industry div and major manufacturing group, top 5 positions, 1991, annual rpt, R4105–19

Financial employees salary trends in companies with sales up to $15 million, by position, 1993 vs 1992, C4687–1.506

Forecasts of economic indicators for approx 10-13 months, monthly rpt, U1880–3

Forecasts of natl income and product account components and related indicators, quarterly rpt, U1880–1

Forecasts of natl income and product account components, employment, and financial sector activity, monthly rpt, B4950–1

Fundraising professionals characteristics, earnings, and benefits, 1992 survey, recurring rpt, A8455–1

Grounds maintenance manager salaries, by type of employer, 1992, annual article, C4725–6

Higher education degree recipient earnings, for persons with bachelors and advanced degrees by selected field, 1990, article, U7860–1.505

Law school grad employment and salaries, by type of employer, location, and grad characteristics, 1992 and trends, annual rpt, A6505–1

Librarians (special) salaries, by location, work setting, and personal characteristics, US and Canada, 1992 and trends, biennial survey rpt, A8965–1

Logistics personnel compensation by position, 1993 annual article, C2150–1.508

Low earnings incidence among workers, 1964-90, R3834–13

Manufacturing industry trends including employment, earnings, establishments, and GSP, by State and region, 1970s-92, R8490–48

Manufacturing value added and wages per hour, for 9 States with highest and lowest values, 1991, article, B8500–2.516

Markets with daily newspapers, demographic and economic info by geographic area, US and Canada, 1993 annual rpt, C3250–1

Mathematics doctoral degree recipient characteristics, including salaries, 1991/92 and trends, annual survey, A2085–1.1

Men age 18-29 earnings, by race-ethnicity, 1973-86, annual rpt, R8335–1.1

Middle mgmt salaries for 22 positions, by industry and location, US and Canada, discontinued annual rpt, A0175–2

Mountain-Plains region average annual pay, with detail for 10 States, 1991, article, U7860–1.505

MSA earnings index for 27 areas and 4 occupational groups, 1990, biennial rpt, S3605–1.6

Office worker salaries for 40 clerical, professional, and data processing positions, by industry and location, US and Canada, discontinued annual rpt, A0175–1

Physics and astronomy grads employment status, by sex, age, subfield, citizenship, degree, and employer type, with salary info, 1990/91, annual rpt, A1960–1

Physics bachelor degree recipients starting salaries, by sex and type of employer, 1991/92, annual survey, A1960–3

Planning profession employment and salaries, by type of employer, demographic and professional characteristics, and location, 1991 and trends, biennial rpt, A2615–1

Prisoner wages received in industry and nonindustry work programs, by State and for Federal system, 1991, annual rpt, R4300–1.1

Private sector wages compared to State and local govt pay, with detail by sex and State, 1989 and trends, R4700–21

Professional worker salaries, by employee and employer characteristics, with detail for scientists and engineers, 1990s and trends, biennial rpt, A3960–1

Psychology doctoral degree recipient employment and demographic characteristics, and finances, 1990/91, biennial survey rpt, A2620–4

Public opinion on fixed salary vs incentive pay, for US, 9 European countries, and 3 Soviet Union Republics, 1991 survey, C8915–8.1, C8915–9

Purchasing power as measured by CPI and PPI, 1920-91, recurring rpt, U5680–2.14

R&D professional salaries and employment characteristics, 1993 and trends, annual article, C1850–6.509

Regional wage and personal income levels compared to total US, with detail for 10 Western States, 1991 and trends, article, U0280–1.505

Salaries for occupations with significant employment growth projected for 2005, 1993 feature, C4215–1.503

Salary ranges for selected positions, by industry or profession, 1993 article, C4215–1.503

Sales and marketing executive compensation, for top 100 executives, with company sales and profit data, 1992 annual article, C1200–1.501

Sales and marketing executives average compensation for 7 positions, 1993 survey article, C4300–1.503

Sales industry costs, including compensation, training, and travel and related expenses, with data by metro area, 1992 and trends, annual survey, C1200–1.508

Sales worker compensation methods used, by company revenue size, 1993 article, C4687–1.504

Service industries economic devs, with analysis of conditions and outlook, and comparisons to other industries, quarterly rpt, A3892–1

Service sector economic activity indicators, with leading and coincident indexes and components, and detail for financial services, monthly rpt, U1245–3

Small company chief executive compensation and stock holdings, for 200 firms with high 5-year returns on equity, 1992 annual article, C3950–1.501

Small company chief executive salaries, for top 100 firms with sales under $25 million, 1993 annual feature, C4687–1.507

Small corporation CEO compensation compared to lowest-paid full-time employee, 1993 feature, C4687–1.506

Starting salary averages, 1992, annual survey rpt, A4740–2

State social, economic, and govtl indicators, with rankings, 1993 semiannual rpt, B8500–1.2, B8500–1.13

Statistical profiles of 50 States and DC, general data, 1993 annual almanac, C4712–1

Trends in hourly wages for manufacturing and selected transportation-related industries, 1977-90, article, C7000–4.504

Trends in labor productivity vs compensation, 1950-92, article, C8900–1.515

Unemployment insurance trends, including data on unemployment, worker characteristics, coverage, benefits, and State govt finances, 1940s-90, R9260–18

Wages/salaries and benefits per hour, by company employment size, Mar 1991, C5800–7.524

White-collar work force trends, including employment, earnings, and unionization, with data by occupation, sex, and educational attainment, 1990s and trends, annual rpt, A1570–1

Women's employment and earnings, with comparisons to men, and detail by occupation and worker characteristics, 1990s and trends, annual rpt, A1570–2

State and local:

Alabama county data book, general data, 1992 annual rpt, S0121–2

Alabama statistical abstract, general data, 1992 recurring rpt, U5680–2.9, U5680–2.11

Alaska employment and unemployment, hours, and earnings, by area and/or industry, monthly rpt, S0320–1

Arizona average annual pay, by industry div, with comparisons to other Western States, 1990-91, annual article, S0465–1.502

Arizona economic condition, including population, employment and earnings, and business activity, by industry and locality, 1985-93, semiannual rpt, U5850–1.1

Arizona employment and earnings for selected leading industries, 1982-91, article, U0280–1.502

Arizona employment and unemployment, by county and industry, with production worker hours and earnings, monthly rpt, S0465–1

Arizona statistical abstract, general data, 1993 recurring rpt, U5850–2.6, U5850–2.14, U5850–2.15, U5850–2.17

Arizona trends in income, employment, and earnings, during 3 economic cycles, 1970-91, article, U0280–1.504

Arkansas population, income, and employment trends, by MSA, 1973-2040, article, U5930–1.503

Arkansas socioeconomic trends, by MSA and/or county, 1993 annual rpt, U5935–1

Arkansas vocational rehabilitation expenditures, impact on earnings and employment, and client characteristics, FY91 annual rpt, S0700–2.4

California economic condition, including population, employment and earnings, income, business activity, and taxation, 1993 annual rpt, S0840–3

California economic indicators, bimonthly rpt, S0840–1

Earnings, general

California employment statistics, by demographic characteristics, industry, MSA, and county, monthly rpt, S0830–1

California individual taxable income reported by source, deductions and credits by type, and tax returns, by income class and county, 1990, annual rpt, S0855–1.1

California statistical abstract, general data, 1992 annual rpt, S0840–2.3, S0840–2.5, S0840–2.8

Colorado employment, unemployment, hours, and earnings, with job service activities, monthly rpt, S1040–4

Connecticut employment, hours, and earnings, by labor market area and industry, and selected economic indicators, monthly rpt, S1235–1

DC annual average pay, by industry div, 1990-91, annual article, S1527–3.501

DC employment, earnings, and hours, by industry, with unemployment insurance data, monthly rpt, S1527–3

DC statistical profile, general data, 1992 annual rpt, S1535–3.3

Delaware data book, general data, 1993 annual rpt, S1375–4

Delaware employment, earnings, and hours, by locality and industry, and unemployment insurance activity, monthly rpt, S1405–2

Florida statistical abstract, general data, 1992 annual rpt, U6660–1.5, U6660–1.6

Georgia and Atlanta MSA forecast employment by industry group and income by source, quarterly rpt, U1880–2

Georgia, Atlanta summer 1996 Olympic games projected impact on State output, earnings, and employment, 1992 article, U6730–2.501

Georgia business activity indicators, bimonthly rpt, U6730–2

Georgia employment, earnings, and hours, by major industry group and MSA, monthly rpt, S1905–1

Georgia statistical abstract, general data, 1992-93 biennial rpt, U6730–1.3, U6730–1.6

Hawaii data book, general data, 1992 annual rpt, S2090–1.12, S2090–1.22

Idaho and US economic trends and forecasts, quarterly rpt, S2245–2

Idaho economic profile, general data, 1992 recurring rpt, S2218–2.1, S2218–2.5

Illinois statistical abstract, general data, 1992 annual rpt, U6910–2

Iowa labor force supply-demand data, including population, earnings, and employment by industry and occupation, 1993 annual rpt, S2784–3

Kansas business activity indicators, quarterly rpt, U7095–1

Kansas statistical abstract, general data, 1991/92 annual rpt, U7095–2.9

Kentucky economic statistics, general data, 1993 annual rpt, S3104–1

Kentucky labor force planning rpt, including population and labor force characteristics, and employment by industry, 1991 and trends, annual rpt, S3140–3

Louisiana employment, hours, and earnings, by industry and MSA, monthly rpt, S3320–2

Louisiana production workers average hours and earnings, by industry, monthly 1992, annual planning rpt, S3320–1.1

Maine employment, unemployment, and earnings, by industry group, MSA, and labor area, monthly rpt, S3465–2

Maine statistical summary, general economic and social data, 1992 recurring rpt, S3434–1

Maine wages in trade, utilities, and transportation SIC 2-digit industries, by detailed occupation, 2nd qtr 1991, triennial rpt, S3465–1.25

Maine wages of govt employees, by level and detailed occupation, May 1991 or Mar 1992, triennial rpt, S3465–1.27

Maryland labor force, employment, earnings, and hours, with data by industry and location, monthly rpt, S3605–2

Massachusetts employment, hours, and earnings, by industry and local area, with unemployment insurance claims, monthly rpt, S3808–1

Michigan employment, hours, and earnings, with detail by industry and local area, monthly rpt, S3980–2

Michigan labor force planning rpt, including population characteristics, and earnings in selected industries, 1993 annual rpt, S3980–1.1

Minnesota employment, hours, and earnings, by industry group and locality, monthly rpt, S4205–1

Mississippi income by source, county, and MSA, and wages by industry group, 1993 annual planning rpt, S4345–1.4

Mississippi statistical abstract, general data, 1992 annual rpt, U3255–4.4, U3255–4.5

Missouri employment, earnings, and hours, and employment security program activity, by industry and/or county, FY92 and trends, annual rpt, S4530–2.3

Missouri employment, earnings, and hours, by industry and MSA, monthly rpt, S4530–3

Missouri vocational rehabilitant earnings at referral and completion, FY92, annual rpt, S4505–1.1

Montana employment and unemployment, earnings, and hours, by location and/or industry, quarterly rpt, S4710–1

Montana labor force planning rpt, including population, income, and employment and job openings by industry and occupation, with selected data by county, 1993-94 annual rpt, S4710–3

Nebraska manufacturing and service worker hours and earnings, by selected industry group and locality, quarterly rpt, S4895–2

Nevada average wages by industry div, for 3 non-MSA counties, 1991, annual rpt, S5040–4

Nevada business and economic activity indicators, with comparisons to other Western States, 1980-91, annual rpt, U7920–2

Nevada employment, hours, and earnings, by industry, and unemployment by county, quarterly rpt, S5040–1

Nevada statistical abstract, general data, 1992 biennial rpt, S5005–1.5, S5005–1.6

New Hampshire employment, hours, and earnings, by industry and area, monthly rpt, S5205–1

New Jersey economic indicators, including employment, building permits, and retail trade, monthly rpt, S5425–1

New Jersey higher education bachelor degrees awarded and starting salaries of college grads, by field of study, 1993 annual article, S5425–1.504

New Mexico business and economic activity indicators, monthly rpt, U7980–1

New Mexico employment, hours, and earnings, by labor market area and industry, monthly rpt, S5624–2

New Mexico wages for selected occupations, Sept 1992, annual planning rpt, S5624–1

New York State business activity indicators, quarterly rpt, S5735–2

New York State employment, earnings, and hours, by county, selected metro area, and industry group, monthly rpt, S5775–1

New York State public assistance recipients earned income, by State area, 1991, annual rpt, S5800–2.1

New York State statistical yearbook, general data, 1992 annual rpt, U5100–1.2, U5100–1.3

North Carolina employment, hours, and earnings, by industry group, with job placements, monthly rpt, S5917–3

North Dakota employment, hours, and earnings, by industry div and/or location, monthly rpt, S6140–4

North Dakota labor force planning rpt, including population, employment, and earnings, with data by industry and county, 1993 annual rpt, S6140–2

Ohio employment, hours, and earnings, by industry and MSA, with job service and unemployment insurance activities, monthly rpt, S6270–1

Oklahoma business activity indicators, monthly rpt quarterly data, U8130–1

Oklahoma employment, hours, and earnings, by industry and MSA, with unemployment insurance and job service activities, monthly rpt, S6430–2

Oklahoma statistical abstract, general data, 1992 annual rpt, U8130–2.4, U8130–2.14

Oregon labor force and employment statistics, including data by industry, monthly rpt, S6592–1, S6615–2

Pennsylvania business activity indicators, monthly rpt, U4110–1

Pennsylvania employment, hours, and earnings, by industry, monthly rpt, S6845–1

Pennsylvania statistical abstract, general data, 1992 recurring rpt, U4130–6.2, U4130–6.3

Pennsylvania vocational education 1989/90 grad employment status, by program, 1991 survey, annual rpt, S6790–5.6

Pennsylvania wage and earnings data, by county and MSA, 1983-90, annual planning rpt, S6845–3.2

Rhode Island employment, hours, and earnings, by industry, monthly rpt, S6980–1

Rhode Island statistical almanac, general data, 1993 annual rpt, C7975–1.1

South Carolina economic activity indicators, including employment by industry div, by county, 1993 annual rpt, S7145–1.2

South Carolina economic condition, including employment, manufacturing, and income, 1970s-92, annual rpt, S7125–3.2

South Carolina employment, earnings, and hours, by industry group and locality, monthly rpt, S7155–2

Index by Subjects and Names

South Carolina labor force planning rpt, including population, employment, income, and job service activities, 1992 annual rpt, S7155–3

South Carolina statistical abstract, general data, 1993 annual rpt, S7125–1.7, S7125–1.12

South Dakota business activity review, including selected data by city and industry, quarterly rpt, U8595–1

South Dakota employment, earnings, and hours for selected industries and areas, with characteristics of unemployed and job service activities, monthly rpt, S7355–1

Tennessee economic indicator trends and forecasts, and business executives views on selected issues, 1993 annual articles, U8710–1.502

Tennessee economic indicator trends and forecasts, with data by industry div and manufacturing group, 1982-2001, annual rpt, S7560–1

Tennessee employment, hours, and earnings, by industry group and MSA, monthly rpt, S7495–2

Tennessee employment, wages, and unemployment insurance contributions, by county and industry, 1991, annual rpt, S7495–1

Tennessee statistical abstract, general data, 1992/93 annual rpt, U8710–2.2, U8710–2.3, U8710–2.4, U8710–2.11, U8710–2.20

Texas employment, hours, and earnings, by MSA and industry group, and unemployment insurance, monthly rpt, S7675–3

Utah business activity indicators, by county, 1988-91, annual feature, U8960–2.501

Utah business activity indicators, by county, 1989-92, annual feature, U8960–2.507

Utah business firms, wages, and employment, by firm size, SIC 2-digit industry, and county, 1st qtr 1992, annual rpt, S7820–1

Utah economic and demographic trends, by county and district, 1960-91, annual rpt, S7832–2

Utah employment and wages for workers born in Utah vs other States, by industry div, 3rd qtr 1992, article, S7820–3.507

Utah employment, hours, and earnings, by industry, monthly rpt, S7820–3

Utah govt statistical review, fiscal and socioeconomic data, 1993 annual rpt, R9380–1.2, R9380–1.9

Utah labor force characteristics, employment and unemployment, hours and earnings, with data by industry and locale, 1992 and trends, annual rpt, S7820–10

Utah statistical abstract, general data, 1993 triennial rpt, U8960–1.4, U8960–1.5, U8960–1.10, U8960–1.12, U8960–1.16

Vermont wages, with detail by industry, 1980-92, annual planning rpt, S8025–2.1

Virginia economic indicators, including new business incorporations and employment data, quarterly rpt, S8205–4

Virginia labor force, hours, and earnings, with data by industry group and locality, monthly rpt, S8205–6

Virginia total and per capita personal income, by local area and major source, 1980-90, annual rpt, U9080–7

Earnings, specific industry

Washington State employment, earnings, and hours, by labor market area and industry group, monthly rpt, S8340–3

West Virginia employment, unemployment, hours, and earnings, with job service activities, monthly rpt, S8534–1

West Virginia production worker hours and earnings, by industry group, 1990-91, annual planning rpt, S8534–2

West Virginia statistical handbook, general data, 1992 annual rpt, R9385–1.1, R9385–1.3

Wisconsin Blue Book, general data, 1993-94 biennial rpt, S8780–1.2

Wisconsin economic indicators, including employment and earnings by industry group, monthly rpt, S8750–1

Wyoming employment, payroll, and wages, by county, monthly rpt quarterly feature, S8895–1.502, S8895–1.504, S8895–1.506, S8895–1.508

Wyoming employment, payroll, and wages, by industry div, 1991, S8895–1.505

Wyoming employment, payroll, and wages, by industry div, 1991-92, S8895–1.509

Wyoming employment, payroll, and wages, by industry div, 3rd qtr 1991-4th qtr 1992, S8895–1.508

Wyoming mining industry employment, and production workers hours and earnings, monthly rpt, S8895–1

Wyoming payroll and wages by industry div, and personal income, with comparisons to US, 1987-92, article, S8895–1.507

Wyoming prisoner incentive pay, and work release program wages, FY92, annual rpt, S8883–1

see also Agricultural wages
see also Earnings, specific industry
see also Economic indicators
see also Educational employees pay
see also Employee benefits
see also Employee bonuses and work incentives
see also Escalator clauses
see also Farm income
see also Federal pay
see also Foreign labor conditions
see also Government pay
see also Labor costs and cost indexes
see also Military pay
see also Minimum wage
see also Payroll
see also Personal and household income
see also Professionals' fees
see also State and local employees pay
see also under By Income in the "Index by Categories"

Earnings, specific industry

Advertising agency personnel compensation and employment trends, 1992 annual feature, C2710–1.505

Aerospace industry production worker earnings, 1974-91, annual rpt, A0250–2.5

Airline compensation per flight crew member, for 9 carriers, 1992, article, C5800–4.528

Airline finances and operations of scheduled carriers, summary statistics, 1992 and trends, annual rpt, A0325–5

Amusement park operating and financial data, including data for US and foreign parks, miniature golf, waterparks, and games, 1992, annual rpt, A5700–1

Architects earnings in settings other than private architectural practice, 1992 survey article, C5800–15.501

Art museum salaries for 37 positions, by region, population size served, and budget size, FY93, annual rpt, A3290–1

Association executives compensation, by position, assn type, and census div, with personnel practices and benefit provisions, 1992, biennial rpt, A2900–3

Auto dealership service dept operations and profit outlook, and manager compensation, 1993 annual survey, article, C2710–3.537

Bank CEO demographic and professional characteristics, attitudes, and compensation, Apr 1992 survey, annual rpt, B4490–2.33

Brewing industry financial and operating data, including consumption, trade, and taxes, 1991 and trends, annual rpt, A3455–1

Broadcasting advertising industry assn chief executive salaries, for 4 assns, 1993 features, C1850–14.511

Bus charter service employment and average weekly earnings, with comparisons to intercity/rural bus transport workers, 1972, 1982, and 1990-91, article, C1575–3.504

Business forms manufacturing plant employment and compensation data, by region, 1992 and trends, biennial rpt, A5785–4

Cable TV system mgmt salaries by selected characteristics, and views on job satisfaction, Mar/Apr 1993 survey, articles, C1858–1.502

Chambers of commerce income, salaries and benefits, membership, staff, and operations, 1993 annual rpt, A3840–3

Chemical and related industries production, finances, operating ratios, employment, and trade, by country, company, and chemical, 1980s-92, annual feature, A1250–1.530

Chemical industry finances and operations, with data by industry segment and product, 1970s-92, annual rpt, A3850–1

Child day care center salaries, health benefits, and turnover, for centers in 5 States or local areas, 1992 survey, annual article, A3865–2

Child day care center staff compensation, health benefits, and turnover, 1992 and trends, A3865–3

Child day care teaching staff earnings, with comparison to 4 other occupations, 1988, annual rpt, R3840–11.1

Clothing (men's and boys) production, trade, and operating data, by garment type, 1960s-92, annual rpt, A3880–1

Clothing (women's and children's) sales, production, imports, and industry employment, hours, and earnings, by type of garment, recurring rpt, A5900–1

Coal industry personnel earnings and employment history, US and Canada, 1993 survey article, C5226–1.507

Communications industries employee income by sex and experience, Dec 1992 survey, article, C2710–1.528

Communications industries trade assn chief executive salaries, for 12 assns, 1993 feature, C1850–14.506

Earnings, specific industry

Construction industry design-related personnel and compensation by position, and engineers income by field, 1993 annual article, C5800–2.536

Construction industry wage rates, selected cities, weekly rpt quarterly feature, C5800–2.547

Construction labor wages for selected specialties, approx 20 cities, weekly rpt, C5800–2

Construction mgmt firm total and foreign contract values for top 100 firms, and employee compensation by position, 1992 and trends, annual article, C5800–2.533

Construction nonunion wages and benefit levels, by craft and region, 1992, article, C5800–2.534

Container (fiber box) shipments by end-use industry and region, and other industry operating data, 1940s-92, annual rpt, A4875–1

Direct marketing salaries by industry segment and position, 1992/93 annual rpt, A4620–1

Discount retail company executive compensation, for 75 highest-paid executives, 1992, annual feature, C5150–3.518

Electric utility mgmt salaries, by customer size and revenue class, 1992, annual article, A2625–1.501

Electronics industry market devs, including employment and wages, by sector, monthly rpt, A4725–2

Entertainment industry income, for top 40 professionals, 1992-93, annual feature, C3950–1.524

Food marketing mgmt personnel compensation, by position, by company sales size and region, year ended Mar 1993, annual survey, A4950–6

Food service CEO compensation, with comparisons to company performance, for top 75 executives, FY92, article, C1200–5.513

Food service industry wage rates for hourly employees, by position, census div, State, and selected metro area, 1992, recurring rpt, A8200–14

Food service wages and employment, for 18 positions, 1992 survey, biennial article, A8200–1.503

Food/beverage manufacturers mgmt salaries, by selected employee characteristics, 1992 survey, annual article, C2150–6.502

Foundation governing board member compensation, by organization characteristics, 1991/92, article, C2176–1.506

Foundation salaries by position, with regional differences and detail for executives by organization and position type, 1992 and/or 1993, article, C2176–1.520

Frozen dessert industry employment, wages, and capital expenditures, 1969-92, annual rpt, A5825–1.1

Health care employment and earnings, by occupation and sex, 1992, annual rpt, A1570–1, A1570–2

Health care specialist and health-related company CEO income, public perceptions vs actual amounts, by respondent characteristics, 1991-93, R4865–13

Index by Subjects and Names

High-technology industry CEO characteristics, and views on mgmt issues including compensation and foreign trade, June 1992 survey, B4490–2.34

Homebuilder average salaries and bonuses by position, by company sales size and region, 1992, C4300–1.509

Homebuilder executive compensation, incentives, and benefits, by position, 1992, annual survey article, C1850–8.508

Homebuilder operations and finances, by region and sales size group, 1992 survey, article, C4300–1.501

Hospital (teaching) house staff stipends and benefits, by region and ownership, with stipends in 37 metro areas, 1992/93 and trends, annual rpt, A3273–3

Hospital emergency dept salaries for physician directors and staff, 1992-93, article, A1865–1.514

Hospital executive and manager compensation, with detail by hospital bed-size and revenues, and use of incentives, 1993 annual article, A1865–1.521

Hospital financial and operating data, including ambulatory surgery and emergency service utilization, semimonthly rpt quarterly feature, A1865–1.506, A1865–1.512

Hospital fundraising personnel salaries, by position, sex, experience, and hospital size, 1993 and trends, annual article, C2176–1.517

Hospital industry financial and operating indicators, with detail for Medicare, by instn characteristics and location, 1988-92, annual rpt, B1880–1

Hospital recruiting of nurses and allied health personnel, with budget, vacancies, turnover, and compensation, 1993 and trends, annual survey rpt, A6500–1

Hospital vice president of medical affairs compensation, 1986-91, survey article, A1865–1.508

Household appliance manufacturing production worker hours and earnings, 1977-91, biennial rpt, A3350–3

Industrial distribution personnel compensation, by position and selected other characteristics, 1992 survey, annual article, C1850–4.501

Interior design industry financial and employment data, top 100 firms, 1993 annual article, C1850–7.501

Interior design industry financial and employment data, 2nd 100 largest firms, 1993 annual article, C1850–7.502

Investment mgmt executive compensation, for executives serving pension funds, 1993 survey article, C2710–2.513

Iron and steel industry financial and operating data, 1992 and trends, annual rpt, A2000–2.1

Iron ore mining industry employment, wages, and hours, 1983-92, annual rpt, A2010–3.3

Jewelry industry statistics on sales, marketing, trade, and employment, with customer characteristics, 1993 annual almanac, C2150–7.509

Jewelry store employee compensation, by position, 1992 annual survey article, C2150–7.501

Logistics manager salaries, by position, industry, and selected characteristics, Nov 1992 survey, annual article, C1850–11

Machine tool industry employment, compensation, and operations, 1992 and trends, annual rpt, A3179–2.1

Magazine circulation director and manager compensation, by region, sex, age, and publication characteristics, 1992 survey, annual article, C2575–1.502

Magazine compensation of ad sales personnel, by region, sex, age, and publication characteristics, 1993 survey, annual article, C2575–1.516

Magazine compensation of editorial personnel, by region, sex, age, and publication characteristics, 1993 survey, annual article, C2575–1.512

Magazine production director and manager compensation, by region, sex, age, and publication characteristics, 1993 survey, annual article, C2575–1.510

Magazine promotion dept activities, and executive characteristics and salary, Nov 1992 survey, article, C2575–1.506

Meat and poultry demand, prices, and processor operations and finances, with data on meat production, 1991 and trends, annual rpt, A2100–1.1

Medical group mgmt compensation, by demographic and practice characteristics, 1992, annual rpt, A6365–3

Medical group physician and allied personnel compensation and productivity, by specialty, and demographic and practice characteristics, 1991, annual rpt, A6365–1

Mining and allied industries, worker earnings in Canada, US, Australia, and South Africa, monthly rpt, B6800–1

Motor vehicle, dealership, and related industries operating data, with data by State and industry segment, 1990s and trends, annual rpt, A0865–1.3

Motor vehicle dealership financial and operating data, including sales and employment by State, 1970s-93, annual rpt, A7330–1

Motor vehicle fleet manager earnings, and personal and professional characteristics, 1993 article, C1575–2.506

Newspaper employee average compensation, 1991-93, article, A8605–1.503

Newspaper executive compensation, by circulation size, for 5 positions, 1993 and trends, annual survey article, A8605–1.510

Nonprofit organization executive compensation, by position, organization characteristics, and region, 1993, annual article, C2176–1.519

Nonprofit organization executive compensation, with comparison to organization income, by leading organization, FY91 or FY92, article, C2176–1.509

Nonprofit organization executive salaries, by title and organization type, 1993, annual article, C2176–1.519

Oil and gas industry employment and earnings, by industry segment, 1950s-91, annual compilation, C6985–9.5

Oil and gas industry employment and earnings, 1993 and trends, periodic basic data book, A2575–14.3

Index by Subjects and Names — Earthquakes

Oil refinery worker wages, including impact of contract negotiations, 1990-93, article, C6985–1.515

Oil/gas industry hourly wages, with comparison to all manufacturing, 1973-92, annual rpt, A5425–2.2

Osteopathy student earnings expectations, for freshmen and seniors, 1991/92, annual survey rpt, A0620–2

Paper and paperboard industry financial and operating data, by product, region, and State, 1992 and trends, annual rpt, A1630–6

Physician compensation, for 14 specialties, 1990-91, A1865–1.506

Physician compensation in group practices and HMOs, by specialty and region, 1992 survey and trends, annual rpt, B7450–2

Physician practice economic aspects, detailed data by specialty, 1991-92 and trends, annual compilation, A2200–5

Physician salaries in Japan and US, by type of employment, 1988 or 1990, article, R5650–2.515

Plastics industry operating and financial data, 1992 and trends, annual rpt, A8920–1.1

Plastics processing industry employment, compensation practices, and union representation, by region, 1992, annual survey rpt, A8920–2

Plastics processing industry salaries for managers, supervisors, salespersons, and engineers, by region, 1992, biennial rpt, A8920–3

Printing industries operating data, including hourly earnings, monthly rpt quarterly table, C1850–10.501, C1850–10.504, C1850–10.507, C1850–10.511, C1850–10.512

Printing industry salaries for 24 positions, and employee benefits offered, 1993 annual feature, C1850–10.510

Public relations compensation, by employee and company characteristics, 1993 survey, annual article, A8770–1.503

Pulp and paper industry operations, US and Canada, with financial performance by company, 1990s and trends, annual rpt, C3975–5.1

Pulp and paper industry salaries and benefits, by job characteristics, 1992 survey, annual article, C3975–2.503

Pulp, paper, and paperboard industry production, trade, and operating data, by product class, monthly rpt, A1630–5

Railroad (Class I) financial and operating data, with detail by company, 1982-91, biennial rpt, A3275–8.2

Railroad employment and earnings, by occupation, company, and district, 1992, annual rpt, A3275–7

Railroad operating data, including wages, fringe benefits, and retirement beneficiaries and payments, 1991, article, C8400–1.506

Real estate property managers characteristics and compensation, including types of property managed, 1989 surveys, recurring rpt, A5600–4

Religious organization employee salary trends at Protestant churches or ministries, 1992-93, article, C2176–1.519

Restaurant/food service mgmt compensation, characteristics, and views, including data by position, 1992 survey, annual article, C1850–3.502

Retail industry distribution center wages, by outlet type and region, 1993 survey, C5150–4.506

Screen actors earnings, by source, 1990-92, article, C9380–1.522

Security equipment industry personnel income, education, work conditions, and activities, 1993 survey, annual article, C1850–13.510

Security industry salaries for 9 positions and 7 metro areas, 1993 article, C1850–12.506

Shoe industry production and operating data, including trade by country, retail sales, and consumer expenditures, quarterly rpt, A4957–2

Shoe industry production, employment, trade, marketing, and related data, by SIC 2- to 5-digit code or product type, 1992 annual rpt, A4957–1.2

Steel industry finances, operations, and employment, with data for integrated plants and mini-mills, 1970s-93, article, U2160–1.503

Supermarket hourly wage rates, for independent and chain stores by region, 1992, annual rpt, C5225–1.505

Textbook (college) sales workers, with turnover and compensation data, 1988-91, annual rpt, A3274–2

Textile industry economic and operating performance and outlook, 1988-93, annual article, C5226–3.502

Textile industry economic performance indicators and outlook, with industry trends and devs, monthly rpt, C5226–3

Transportation employee compensation and earnings trends, by mode, 1992 annual rpt, R4815–1

TV station personnel and compensation, by position, and benefits, 1991, biennial rpt, A6635–9

Veterinarian income, by number of years since graduation and type of practice or employer, 1991, biennial survey article, A3100–2.508

Veterinarian income by selected personal and practice characteristics, 1992, annual survey article, C9480–1.506

Veterinarian income by type of employment, 1991, biennial survey article, A3100–2.506

Veterinarian money vs real income, by type of employment, biennially 1983-91, biennial article, A3100–2.512

Veterinarians by professional characteristics and location, and financial and education summaries, 1993 annual directory, A3100–1

Veterinary practice nonowner associate job characteristics and attitudes, 1992 survey, article, C9480–1.505

Veterinary school grad employment, starting salaries, benefits, and personal characteristics, by sex, 1992, annual survey article, A3100–2.504

Veterinary school grad starting salaries by type of employment, and educational debt, 1992, annual survey article, A3100–2.503

Western States bookstore employee salaries and benefits, 1992 survey, article, C1852–2.501

State and local:

Arizona and US copper industry wage data, 1991 and trends, annual rpt, S0497–1

Arizona defense contracts and value, employment, and wages, for aggregate leading contractors, 1987-92, article, S0465–1.509

Maryland building materials/garden supplies industry employment and wages, by industry and occupational group, June 1991, article, S3605–2.501

Michigan prison work program finances and prisoner wage rates, 1991, annual rpt, S3960–1

North Carolina public utility financial, operating, and regulatory data, by utility type and company, 1990 and trends, annual rpt, S5917–2

Oregon nursery and greenhouse industry workers and wages, 1991, annual rpt, S6575–1

Texas nursing employment, demand outlook, earnings, and education, by selected characteristics, various years 1971-91, U8850–8.2

West Virginia coal mining hours and earnings, and production, monthly rpt, S8534–1

see also Agricultural labor

see also Agricultural wages

see also Educational employees pay

see also Employee benefits

see also Employee bonuses and work incentives

see also Escalator clauses

see also Farm income

see also Federal pay

see also Foreign labor conditions

see also Government pay

see also Hours of labor

see also Labor costs and cost indexes

see also Military pay

see also Payroll

see also Professionals' fees

see also State and local employees pay

see also under By Industry in the "Index by Categories"

Earth sciences

Higher education geoscience enrollment and degrees awarded, by sex, race-ethnicity, and discipline, 1991/92, annual rpt, A1785–3

Salaries of scientists, engineers, technicians, and other professionals, by employee and employer characteristics, 1990s and trends, biennial rpt, A3960–1

Women and minorities in professional fields, detailed education and labor force data, 1991 and trends, recurring rpt, A3960–2.3

see also Geology

see also Hydrology

see also Oceanography

Earthquake insurance

see Property and casualty insurance

Earthquakes

Deaths in major disasters since 1865, by category, annual rpt, A8375–2.1

Latin America statistical abstract, general data by country, 1992 annual rpt, U6250–1.1

Property damage from 10 most costly earthquakes, 1949-89, annual rpt, A5650–1.4

Earthquakes

State and local:
Hawaii data book, general data, 1992 annual rpt, S2090–1.5
New York State statistical yearbook, general data, 1992 annual rpt, U5100–1.15

East Pakistan
see Bangladesh

East-West trade
China business review, including trade with US and other countries, and economic activity, bimonthly rpt, A9315–1
China trade value with US, with detail for Illinois exports, and US tariff rates and collections, for top 20-25 commodities, 1992 article, U6910–1.502
Commonwealth of Independent States, Russia and Ukraine foreign trade with US, by commodity, 1992 and 1st 5 months 1992-93, article, U2030–1.511
Eastern/Central Europe foreign trade with OECD and EC, with data by country and commodity, 1980s-90, R5025–10
EC chemical trade with Eastern Europe, with detail by trading partner for Germany, 1993 article, A1250–1.540
Latin America statistical abstract, general data by country, 1992 annual rpt, U6250–1.26
Lumber exports from US to Pacific Rim, by country and product type, monthly rpt, A1630–2
Russia and aggregate other former Soviet Republics foreign trade with US, with detail for selected commodities, 1st 9 months 1992, U2030–1.505
Russia foreign trade with US, with detail for selected commodities, 1st half 1992, U2030–1.503
Russia foreign trade with US, with detail for selected commodities, 1st 4 months 1992-93, U2030–1.510
Soviet Union foreign trade with approx 20 countries, monthly rpt recurring feature, U2030–1.502
see also Eastern Europe

Eastern Europe
Chemical and related industries production, finances, operating ratios, employment, and trade, by country, company, and chemical, 1980s-92, annual feature, A1250–1.530
Chemical exports for developing vs developed areas, with detail for Eastern Europe, 1980, 1986, and 1991, article, A1250–1.534
Chemical trade with Germany and EC, and ethylene plants and capacity, with data by country, 1993 article, A1250–1.540
Foreign investments in Eastern Europe from 7 leading countries, 12 months ended Sept 1992, article, C5800–7.511
Foreign trade between Eastern/Central Europe and OECD and EC, with data by country and commodity, 1980s-90, R5025–10
Foreign trade between Soviet Union and 5 Eastern European countries, monthly rpt recurring feature, U2030–1.503
Housing starts, with detail for 4 countries, 1992-2000, article, C4300–1.504
Motor vehicle world production, sales, trade, and registrations, by country, world area, manufacturer, and make, 1991 and trends, annual rpt, A0865–2.1

Oil refined products consumption and demand, 1990-96 and 2000, article, C6985–1.531
Public opinion in US on selected foreign policy issues, with detail for 3 States, 1993 survey, annual rpt, A4965–1
Public opinion on political, economic, and social issues, for 5 countries and 3 Soviet Union Republics, 1991 survey, C8915–8.2
Public opinion on political, economic, and social issues of interest to foreign investors, for 5 countries and 3 Soviet Union Republics, 1991 survey, C8915–9
Silver market activity worldwide and in US, including production, consumption by end use, stocks, trade, and prices, by country, 1988-92, annual rpt, B4300–1
see also Albania
see also Bulgaria
see also Commonwealth of Independent States
see also Czech Republic
see also Czechoslovakia
see also East-West trade
see also Germany, East
see also Hungary
see also Poland
see also Romania
see also Slovakia
see also Soviet Union
see also Yugoslavia

Eastern States
see Middle Atlantic States
see Northeast States
see Southeastern States

Eavesdropping
see Electronic surveillance

Eckl, Corina L.
"State Tax Actions, 1992", A7470–4.9

Ecology
see Conservation of natural resources
see Environmental pollution and control
see Environmental sciences
see Marine pollution
see State funding for natural resources and conservation
see Wildlife and wildlife conservation

Economic and econometric models
Forecasting accuracy of various econometric models, selected economic indicators, monthly rpt, B4950–1
Forecasts for GDP, prices, prime interest rate, and unemployment, 50 economists, 1992-93, annual feature, C5800–7.509
Forecasts of GDP, inflation, unemployment, and Treasury bond rates, by approx 10 organizations, monthly rpt, R4105–80
State and local:
Nebraska economic growth indicators, recurring feature, U7860–1.501, U7860–1.506
see also Input-output analysis

Economic assistance
see Economic policy
see Federal aid programs
see Federal aid to rural areas
see Federal aid to States
see International assistance
see Military assistance
see Public welfare programs
see Revenue sharing
see State funding for economic development
see State funding for local areas
see Subsidies

Index by Subjects and Names

Economic censuses
see also Census of Agriculture
see also Census of Manufactures

Economic concentration and diversification
Chemical industry top 50 firms share of total and export firms and sales, 1987, annual rpt, A3850–1
Corporate mergers, acquisitions, and other agreements involving US companies, by SIC code, bimonthly rpt quarterly feature, C4683–1
Discount store industry concentration, by company size, 1992, annual feature, C8130–1.507
Drugstore chain companies and outlets, by size group, 1982 and 1992, annual feature, C5150–2.511
Electric utility asset diversification, with selected comparisons to financial performance, for 35 companies, 1990 and 1992, article, A4700–4.505
Home improvement industry sales and operations, for top distributors, cooperatives, and marketing organizations, 1991-92, annual feature, C5150–6.502
Home improvement industry sales and operations, for top retailers, 1992 and trends, annual feature, C5150–6.503
Homebuilder (single-family) diversified activities, by company size, 1992 article, C4300–1.502
Latin America agricultural landholdings and area, by size and country, decennially 1950-70, annual rpt, U6250–1.2
Livestock slaughtering and red meat production shares for top 4-20 aggregate firms, 1980-90, annual rpt, A2100–1.1
Oil supply-demand, marketing, prices, finances, and employment, detailed data for US and Canada, by product, company, and location, 1993 annual fact book, C4680–1.507
Public utility involvement in other businesses by type, Nov 1991 survey, article, C5800–28.504
Pulp and paper industry production, capacity, consumption, trade, and sales/earnings data, including profiles for selected companies and sectors, monthly rpt, C3975–2
Radio broadcast market rank, stations owned, and operating characteristics, for multiple-station owners in 4 market areas, 1993 article, C1850–14.519
Security equipment industry revenues, for top 100 and all other firms, 1992, annual feature, C1850–13.507
Uranium production, reserves, and ownership interests, for 4 largest intl producers, by country and mine, 1990s-2003 article, B6800–1.508
State and local:
Hawaii land acreage owned by 6 largest landowners, 1989-91, annual rpt, S2090–1.6
Oklahoma banks and bank holding companies by asset size, and asset concentration by location and among top instns, 1984-90, article, U8130–1.502
see also Business acquisitions and mergers
see also Competition
see also Corporate rankings
see also Divestiture
see also Holding companies

Index by Subjects and Names

see also Joint ventures
see also Ownership of enterprise
see also Product rankings

Economic crises and depressions
see Business cycles

Economic development

Business incubator facilities and services for new rural businesses, role of State extension programs at land-grant universities, 1992 survey rpt, U2410–3

Business incubator facilities finances and operations, including services offered and tenant characteristics, 1991, annual rpt, A7360–1

EC member country commitments to 2 regional structural dev funds, by country, 1988, R5025–9

Federal budget trends, including spending by program, State, and region, FY81-94, annual rpt, R8490–11

Germany reunification issues for internatl investment, with data on population and employment, consumption, and infrastructure improvement, 1991 rpt, R4105–82.3

Latin America statistical abstract, general data by country, 1992 annual rpt, U6250–1.32

Local areas that solicit foreign investment, economic characteristics and dev goals, by population size, metro status, and census div, 1993 survey rpt, A5800–2.115

Planning profession employment and salaries, by type of employer, demographic and professional characteristics, and location, 1991 and trends, biennial rpt, A2615–1

State economic dev condition indicators, including economic performance, business vitality, growth capacity, and tax/fiscal system, by State, 1993 annual rpt, R4225–1

States use of selected business incentives, and number of enterprise zones by State, 1992 article, B8500–2.506

State and local:

Arizona economic growth positive and negative factors, views of analysts, 1990 and 1993 surveys, article, U0282–1.509

Arkansas economic dev resources existing and needed to attract new business, 1989/90 survey, article, U5930–1.501

DC statistical profile, general data, 1992 annual rpt, S1535–3.3

Maryland local govt financial condition, including revenues by source, expenditures by function, and debt obligations, FY92 and trends, annual rpt, S3618–1.1

see also Business cycles
see also Community development
see also Developing countries
see also Economic indicators
see also Job creation
see also State funding for economic development
see also Urban renewal

Economic Development Administration

Federal budget trends, including spending by program, State, and region, FY81-94, annual rpt, R8490–11

Economic indicators

Budget of US economic assumptions of Bush Admin, 1990-97, annual rpt, C2500–2

Business and economic trends, production and price indicators, and industrial mgmt activities and devs, semimonthly rpt, C7000–3

Business economists assessments of current conditions at their companies, with industry detail, quarterly rpt, A6650–4

Business economists forecasts of general economic conditions, quarterly rpt, A6650–5

Business executives expectations for coming qtr, attitudes on key indicators, with trends and data by census div, quarterly rpt, C3150–4

Business Week economic, business, and investment devs, with related statistical indicators, weekly rpt, C5800–7

Canada economic indicators, including US trade, import shares for 8 other countries, and population by Province, 1993 articles, C4687–1.508

China, Guangdong Province economic data, including foreign trade and investment, and industrial production, 1985-92, A9315–1.505

Commodity yearbook for 1993: detailed supply-demand data, and selected indicators for futures market investors, C2400–1

Commodity yearbook update: detailed supply-demand data, and selected indicators for futures market investors, Jan-Sept 1993 rpts, C2400–2

Consumer attitudes on economic conditions and personal financial situation, Univ of Michigan monthly survey, U7475–2

Consumer expectations of economic conditions and change in income, and intended durable goods purchases by type, Conference Board monthly survey, R4105–4

Cuba economic indicators, including trade and inflation, 1970s-88, U6250–1.19

Cyclical trends for recession/recovery periods as measured by approx 70 economic indicators, quarterly rpt, U1245–2

Democracy and economic performance measures for 16-20 countries, 1982-92, article, C5800–7.531

EC economic indicators relating to proposed economic unification, by country, 1992 rpt, R5025–9

Electronics industry market data, with related general economic indicators, 1993 annual rpt, A4725–1

Europe socioeconomic summaries, for EC and European Free Trade Assn countries, 1992-93, article, C8900–1.504

Forbes business and corporate financial and investment devs, with related statistical indicators, biweekly rpt, C3950–1

Forecast change in selected economic indicators if Clinton Admin economic proposals are adopted, 1993-95, article, C4215–1.505

Forecasts and trends for selected economic indicators, with detail for approx 15 Western States, 1990s, annual rpt, B3520–1

Forecasts and trends for selected indicators, 1980s-93, article, C8900–1.506

Forecasts and trends for 34 economic indicators, 1991-95, article, U8595–1.501, U8595–1.503

Economic indicators

Forecasts of economic indicators for approx 10-13 months, Georgia State Univ monthly rpt, U1880–3

Forecasts of natl income and product account components and related indicators, Georgia State Univ quarterly rpt, U1880–1

Forecasts of natl income and product account components, employment, and financial sector activity, monthly rpt, B4950–1

Forecasts of selected economic indicators, recent trends and 2-year outlook, US Chamber of Commerce quarterly rpt, A3840–6

Foreign economic indexes, composites of leading indicators for US and selected other countries, monthly rpt, R4105–6

Fortune magazine forecast of GDP, consumer prices, profits, and unemployment, 1993-94, article, C8900–1.519

Futures trading activity on Chicago Board of Trade, with info on economic indicator trends, 1992, annual rpt, B2120–1

Gross regional product and outlook, by region, 1991-93, semiannual article, C8900–1.507

Gross regional product and outlook, by region, 1992-94, semiannual article, C8900–1.520

Hard goods manufacturers and representatives forecasts for selected indicators in 1993, annual survey rpt, A1800–1

Historical trends in economic indicators, 1900s-92, annual rpt, R9050–1.2

Hungary economic indicators of interest to foreign investors, 1993 article, C4687–1.508

Industrial countries leading and coincident economic index trends, monthly rpt, U1245–1

Industrial mgmt magazine reader views on who is responsible for economic problems, Federal budget deficit, and health care costs, Feb 1993 survey, article, C7000–3.510

Japan economic indicators including GNP, inflation, unemployment, current account, and export and foreign investment regions, 1980s-93, article, C5800–7.535

Japan economic issues and devs, relations with US, and trade, balance of payments, and economic indicators, weekly rpt, R5650–2

Japan govt economic outlook, FY92-93, annual article, R5650–2.510

Jewelry and watch manufacturing and marketing trends, new product dev, prices, trade, and related indicators, monthly rpt, C2150–7

Mexico economic indicators, including US trade, and population by major city, 1993 articles, C4687–1.512

Mexico-US border area socioeconomic indicators, 1980s and trends, U6250–1.20

Midwest business and economic conditions in metro and nonurban areas, by sector and State, bankers opinions, spring 1993 survey, semiannual rpt, B6785–1

Money and securities market activity, and related indicators, Chemical Bank biweekly rpt, B2000–1

Economic indicators

Index by Subjects and Names

Oil and gas industry operations and finance, with selected economic indicators, 1993 and trends, periodic basic data book, A2575–14

Productivity and related indicators, trend analysis for US and other industrial countries, 1980s-92, annual rpt, R2800–2

Public interest in current news events, and opinion on media coverage and selected current issues, by respondent characteristics, 1993 surveys, C8915–1.501, C8915–1.502, C8915–1.503, C8915–1.504, C8915–1.505

Public opinion on natl economic conditions, 1992-93 Gallup Polls and trends, C4040–1.503, C4040–1.506, C4040–1.508

Purchasing managers views on business conditions, monthly rpt, A6910–1

Real estate business and general economic activity outlook, monthly rpt, A7000–1

Service industries economic devs, with analysis of conditions and outlook, and comparisons to other industries, quarterly rpt, A3892–1

Service sector economic activity indicators, with leading and coincident indexes and components, and detail for financial services, monthly rpt, U1245–3

Soviet Union economic devs, including industrial production, agriculture, exchange rates, and foreign trade, monthly rpt, U2030–1

Spain economic indicators compared to EC averages and convergence requirements for Europe economic unification, 1991, article, A8955–1.502

State economic and social devs relevant to policy decisions, with data by State, semimonthly rpt, B8500–2

State economic dev condition indicators, including economic performance, business vitality, growth capacity, and tax/fiscal system, by State, 1993 annual rpt, R4225–1

State economic performance indexes, by State, semimonthly rpt quarterly article, B8500–2.504, B8500–2.510, B8500–2.516, B8500–2.522

Textile industry economic performance indicators and outlook, with industry trends and devs, monthly rpt, C5226–3

Trends in selected indicators, and forecasts by approx 10 organizations, monthly rpt, R4105–80

Truck tonnage summary, and related indicators, monthly press release, A3075–1

TV news coverage of economic conditions, including evaluation of Clinton Admin plan, Jan-Mar 1993, recurring article, R3823–1.507

UK economic indicators, including US trade, import shares for 4 other countries, and population by country and city, 1993 articles, C4687–1.510

Uranium marketing activity, and selected economic indicators for major producing countries, monthly rpt, B6800–1

Venture-capital-backed company economic impact, including job creation, capital and R&D investments, and selected growth rates, 1985-91, A8515–2

Western States economic indicators, including forecasts from selected organizations, for 10 States, monthly rpt, U0282–2

World economic indicators for selected countries and world regions, 1992 and trends, annual rpt, A3179–2.3

World economic trends and outlook, 1993 annual feature, C8900–1.520

World economic trends, for 7 industrial countries, 1984-92, article, U2160–1.502

World energy statistics and other general indicators, for approx 80 countries, 1970s-91, annual compilation, C6985–10

World events and socioeconomic devs with implications for multinatl corporations, series, R4105–82

World financial market devs including economic and monetary trends and forecasts for 15 industrial countries, bimonthly rpt, B6200–2

State and local:

Alabama business activity indicators, monthly rpt, U5680–1

Alabama economic trends and outlook, 1980s-93, annual rpt, U5680–3

Arizona business activity indicators, including housing market, population, CPI, and industrial purchasing, monthly rpt, U0280–1

Arizona economic condition, including population, employment and earnings, and business activity, by industry and locality, 1985-93, semiannual rpt, U5850–1

Arizona economic indicators, including forecasts from 16 forecasting organizations, monthly rpt, U0282–1

Arkansas business and economic activity indicators, quarterly rpt, U5930–1

California economic condition, including population, employment and earnings, income, business activity, and taxation, 1993 annual rpt, S0840–3

California economic indicators, bimonthly rpt, S0840–1

California economic outlook, selected employment, income, and commercial indicators, 1992-94, annual article, S0840–1.502

Connecticut employment, hours, and earnings, by labor market area and industry, and selected economic indicators, monthly rpt, S1235–1

Florida statistical abstract, general data, 1992 annual rpt, U6660–1.24

Georgia business activity indicators, bimonthly rpt, U6730–2

Georgia county guide, general data, 1993 annual rpt, U6750–1

Hawaii counties population and economic indicators, 1993 annual rpt series, B3500–2

Hawaii economic indicators, bimonthly rpt, B3500–1

Idaho and US economic trends and forecasts, quarterly rpt, S2245–2

Illinois business activity indicators, quarterly rpt, U6910–1

Illinois economic and business activity indicators, including data by industry and county, bimonthly rpt, S2405–2

Indiana business conditions analysis for selected local areas, quarterly rpt semiannual feature, U2160–1.502, U2160–1.504

Kansas business activity indicators, quarterly rpt, U7095–1

Kansas economic outlook, with detail for selected State areas, 1993 and trends, annual articles, U7095–1.501

Kentucky economic impact of Toyota Motor Corp plant installation, including related State costs, employment, and benefits to other States, 1980s-2005, U7138–1.4

Kentucky socioeconomic devs and business indicators, series, U7138–1

Nebraska business and economic activity indicators, monthly rpt, U7860–1

Nevada business and economic activity indicators, with comparisons to other Western States, 1980-91, annual rpt, U7920–2

New Jersey economic indicators, including employment, building permits, and retail trade, monthly rpt, S5425–1

New Mexico business and economic activity indicators, monthly rpt, U7980–1

New York State business activity indicators, quarterly rpt, S5735–2

New York State business and economic indicators, by MSA, county, and industry, 1980s-91, annual rpt, S5735–3

New York State statistical yearbook, general data, 1992 annual rpt, U5100–1.2

Oklahoma business activity indicators, monthly rpt, U8130 1

Oklahoma statistical abstract, general data, 1992 annual rpt, U8130–2.22

Oregon economic conditions, including population, construction, income, employment, industry, and foreign trade data, 1991, annual rpt, S6585–3

Pennsylvania business activity indicators, monthly rpt, U4110–1

Pennsylvania economic trends and outlook for gross regional product, personal income, and employment, 1980s-93, annual article, U4110–1.504

South Carolina economic condition, including agriculture, commerce, govt finances, employment, and income, 1970s-92, annual rpt, S7125–3

South Dakota business activity review, including selected data by city and industry, quarterly rpt, U8595–1

Tennessee business activity indicators, quarterly journal, U8710–1

Tennessee economic indicator trends and forecasts, and business executives views on selected issues, 1993 annual articles, U8710–1.502

Tennessee economic indicator trends and forecasts, with data by industry div and manufacturing group, 1982-2001, annual rpt, S7560–1

Utah economic and business activity review and indicators, monthly rpt, U8960–2

Utah economic and demographic trends, by county and district, 1960-91, annual rpt, S7832–2

Virginia business activity indicators, by local area, monthly rpt, U1120–1

Virginia economic indicators, including new business incorporations and employment data, quarterly rpt, S8205–4

Wisconsin economic indicators, including employment and earnings by industry group, monthly rpt, S8750–1

see also Business and industry

Index by Subjects and Names

Education

see also Business assets and liabilities, general
see also Business cycles
see also Business income and expenses, general
see also Business inventories
see also Capital investments
see also Consumer Price Index
see also Credit
see also Diffusion indexes
see also Earnings, general
see also Economic and econometric models
see also Employment and unemployment, general
see also Foreign trade
see also Government spending
see also Gross Domestic Product
see also Gross National Product
see also Gross State Product
see also Housing construction
see also Housing costs and financing
see also Housing sales
see also Industrial capacity and utilization
see also Industrial production
see also Industrial production indexes
see also Inflation
see also Interest rates
see also Job creation
see also Job vacancy
see also Labor productivity
see also Labor turnover
see also Money supply
see also National income and product accounts
see also Personal and household income
see also Personal consumption
see also Prices
see also Producer Price Index

Economic policy

Advertising industry professional views on impact of Clinton Admin economic plan, Feb 1993 survey, article, C2710–1.514

Business economists expectations for Clinton Admin economic policy effects, Mar 1993 survey, A6650–4.503

Business economists views on Govt economic policy, semiannual survey rpt, A6650–6

Consumer attitudes on economic conditions and personal financial situation, monthly survey, U7475–2

Corporate CEO views on Clinton Admin performance, economic plan, and health care reform financing, Apr-May 1993 survey, article, C8900–1.516

Corporate CEO views on economic outlook and policies in President Clinton Admin, 1992 survey article, C8900–1.504

Corporate executive views on President-elect Clinton and his proposed programs, Nov 1992 survey, C5800–7.505

Europe public opinion on political, economic, and social issues, for 9 countries and 3 Soviet Union Republics, 1991 survey, C8915–8

Financial analyst views on Clinton Admin economic plan, including effects on investment performance and own strategy, Feb 1993 survey, article, C8900–1.511

Hispanic American leaders views on selected Clinton Admin economic policy proposals, Jan 1993 survey, article, C4575–1.505

Industrial natl policy need, views of executives and manufacturing mgmt, 1993 survey article, C1850–4.506

Public interest in current news events, and opinion on media coverage and selected current issues, by respondent characteristics, 1993 surveys, C8915–1.503

Public opinion on Clinton Admin economic plan, by respondent characteristics, Feb 1993 survey, C8915–7.1

Public opinion on Clinton Admin economic plan, including support in Congress, with data by respondent characteristics, May 1993 survey and trends, C8915–7.3

Public opinion on Clinton Admin economic priorities and plans, 1993 Gallup Polls, C4040–1.508, C4040–1.509, C4040–1.510, C4040–1.511

Public opinion on Clinton Admin priorities and plans, and Dec 1992 economic conference in Arkansas, Dec 1992 Gallup Poll, C4040–1.506

Public opinion on potential tax increases under consideration by Clinton Admin, Jan 1993 survey, C5800–7.514

Public opinion on success of Reagan Admin economic policies, Feb 1993 Gallup Poll, C4040–1.509

Small corporation mgmt views on Clinton Admin priorities and methods to help economy and small business, Jan 1993 survey, C4687–1.506

Soviet Union political and economic restructuring issues, public opinion in Russia, Ukraine, and Lithuania, 1991-92 surveys, C8915–10

TV news coverage of economic conditions, including evaluation of Clinton Admin plan, Jan-Mar 1993, recurring article, R3823–1.507

World financial market devs including economic and monetary trends and forecasts for 15 industrial countries, bimonthly rpt, B6200–2

see also Business cycles
see also Conversion of industry
see also Defense expenditures
see also Economic development
see also Employment and unemployment, general
see also Federal aid programs
see also Fiscal policy
see also Foreign economic relations
see also Foreign trade
see also Foreign trade promotion
see also Government spending
see also Inflation
see also Interest rates
see also International assistance
see also Land reform
see also Military assistance
see also Monetary policy
see also Price regulation
see also Prices
see also State funding for economic development
see also State government spending
see also Subsidies
see also Tariffs and foreign trade controls

Economic relations

see terms under Foreign economic relations

Economic sanctions

see International sanctions

Economics

Employment in business and industry, hiring plans for college grads, by field, salary, and degree, 1993 annual survey rpt, U3730–1

Salary and job offers for college grads, by field of study, type of employer, and degree level, by region, interim rpt series, A3940–1

Salary and job offers for college grads, by field of study, type of employer, and degree level, series, A3940–2

Women and minorities in professional fields, detailed education and labor force data, 1991 and trends, recurring rpt, A3960–2.3

see also Economic and econometric models
see also Economic indicators
see also Economic policy

Ecuador

Energy intl sourcebook, with detail on oil and gas industry operations, supply-demand, and prices, for approx 80 countries, 1970s-91, annual compilation, C6985–10.2

Oil production by domestic and foreign company, oil consumption, and outlays of govt-owned holding company, 1990s-2010, article, C6985–1.518

Statistical abstract of Latin America, detailed social, govtl, and economic data, 1992 annual rpt, U6250–1

see also Organization of Petroleum Exporting Countries
see also under By Foreign Country or World Area in the "Index by Categories"

Eddins, Kevin

"State of America's Cities: The Ninth Annual Opinion Survey of Municipal Elected Officials", A8012–1.21

Education

Arts fundraising through united arts funds (UAFs), with allocations to art education, by UAF, 1992, annual rpt, A1315–2

Catholic charity social service agency activities, clients, finances, and personnel, 1991 and trends, annual rpt, A3810–1

Corporate involvement in public education, including types of recipients and contribution levels by company, 1992 survey and trends, annual article, C8900–1.502

Education profession issues, trends, and research results, monthly rpt, A8680–1

Electric utility education-related partnership programs, by type of partner, 1993 article, A4700–4.501

Periodical editorial practices and characteristics, for 54 publications, 1993 recurring survey article, A8680–1.502

Public confidence in selected societal instns, 1972-91 surveys, annual rpt, U6395–1

Religious congregation characteristics, including membership, activities, staff, and finances, 1992 survey, recurring rpt, A5435–4

State and local:

Arizona statistical abstract, general data, 1993 recurring rpt, U5850–2.24

see also Adult education
see also Agricultural education
see also Audiovisual education
see also Business education
see also Compensatory education
see also Curricula
see also Degrees, higher education
see also Discrimination in education
see also Educational attainment
see also Educational broadcasting

Education

see also Educational employees pay
see also Educational enrollment
see also Educational exchanges
see also Educational facilities
see also Educational finance
see also Educational materials
see also Educational reform
see also Educational research
see also Educational technology
see also Educational tests
see also Elementary and secondary education
see also Federal aid to education
see also Federal aid to higher education
see also Federal aid to medical education
see also Federal aid to vocational education
see also Head Start Project
see also Health education
see also Higher education
see also Legal education
see also Libraries
see also Medical education
see also Military education
see also National Assessment of Educational Progress
see also Parochial schools
see also Physical education and training
see also Preschool education
see also Private schools
see also Remedial education
see also School administration and staff
see also School boards
see also School busing
see also School districts
see also School dropouts
see also School lunch and breakfast programs
see also Scientific education
see also Sex education
see also Special education
see also State funding for education
see also State funding for higher education
see also State funding for medical education
see also State funding for vocational education
see also Student aid
see also Students
see also Teacher education
see also Teachers
see also Technical education
see also Textbooks
see also Veterans education
see also Vocational education and training
see also Work-study programs

Education Consolidation and Improvement Act

State and local:

Alabama public school revenues by source and expenditures by object, by district, 1991/92, annual rpt, S0124–1.2

Education of handicapped children
see Special education

Educational attainment

Births by selected characteristics of mother, including high school and college grad status, 1989, annual rpt, R3840–5.1

Black American educational statistics, with comparisons to whites, 1970s-92, annual compilation, C6775–2.3

Black children and youth population, economic, health, and education data, with comparisons to whites, 1993 rpt, R3840–21

Economic dev condition indicators, including economic performance, business vitality, growth capacity, and tax/fiscal system, by State, 1993 annual rpt, R4225–1

Elementary/secondary education data, with detail for mathematics including test scores and teacher preparation, by State, 1993 biennial rpt, A4355–1

High school grads and college enrollment, for population age 18-24, by sex and race-ethnicity, 1970-91, annual rpt, A1410–10

High school grads, by State, 1991/92-2008/09, article, C2175–1.537

High school grads, by State, 1993/94 and 2003/2004, annual rpt, C2175–1.531

High school grads, 1992-2003, annual feature, C2175–1.504

High school graduation rates, by State, 1988, annual rpt, R3840–11.2

High school graduation rates, by State, 1993 annual rpt, R3832–1

Hispanic American educational statistics, with comparisons to whites, 1970s-92, annual compilation, C6775–3.2

Latin America statistical abstract, general data by country, 1992 annual rpt, U6250–1.8

Southern States high school grads, by State, 1971/72-2001/02, biennial fact book, A8945–1.1

State social, economic, and govtl indicators, with rankings, 1993 semiannual rpt, B8500–1.7

Statistical profiles of 50 States and DC, general data, 1993 annual almanac, C4712–1

Urban high school grads and postgraduation plans, for 47 school systems, 1990/91, A4425–4

Women and minorities in professional fields, detailed education and labor force data, 1980s-91, with historical trends, recurring rpt, A3960–2

World adult literacy rates and educational attainment, by sex and country, 1992/93 biennial rpt, R9455–1.5

Youth age 20 unemployment rates, with detail for high school grads and dropouts, by sex and race, 1963-67 and 1983-87, article, C4687–1.511

State and local:

Alabama high school grads, by race, sex, and school system, 1991/92, annual rpt, S0124–1.1

Alabama municipal data book, general data, 1992 recurring rpt, S0121–5

Alaska high school grads as percent of population over age 25, total and Native American, by borough and census area, 1980 and 1990, article, S0320–1.504

Alaska population, housing, income, and education data, by demographic characteristics and/or locality, 1990/91 and trends, annual rpt, S0320–4

Alaska public high school grads by sex and race-ethnicity, and high school completion rate for adults, by school district, 1993 annual report, S0295–2

Arizona high school grads, 1991/92, annual rpt, S0470–1

Arizona Indian population, education, housing, health, and employment characteristics, with detail by reservation, 1970s-91, recurring rpt, U5850–2.9

Arizona statistical abstract, general data, 1993 recurring rpt, U5850–2.4

Arkansas Census of Population and Housing detailed findings, 1990, U5935–7

Index by Subjects and Names

Arkansas high school grads, by county, sex, and race-ethnicity, various years 1980/81-1996/97, annual rpt, S0660–1

California Census of Population and Housing detailed findings, 1990, S0840–9

California private schools, enrollment by grade, grads, and staff, with data by county, 1992/93 and trends, annual rpt, S0825–8

California public school enrollment, grads, and staff, by race-ethnicity, 1992/93 and trends, annual rpt, S0825–9

California public schools, enrollment by grade, and grads, by county, 1992/93 and trends, annual rpt, S0825–7

California socioeconomic and govtl data for municipalities, counties, and school districts, 1993 annual rpt, C4712–3

Colorado public and/or private school enrollment and grads, by student characteristics, county, and district, 1992 and trends, annual rpt, S1000–2.1

Connecticut public school data, including enrollment, staff, programs, finances, and student characteristics, 1991/92, biennial rpt, S1185–3

DC public school finances, enrollment, grads, and test scores, with data by school, 1987/88-1991/92, annual rpt, S1605–2

DC statistical profile, general data, 1992 annual rpt, S1535–3.1, S1535–3.6

Delaware school enrollment, grads, staff, finances, and facilities, by county, school district, and/or instn, 1991/92, annual rpt, S1430–1

Florida county data book, 1992/93 annual rpt, C6360–1

Florida municipal and county statistical profiles, general data, 1991 annual rpt, C4712–6

Georgia county guide, general data, 1993 annual rpt, U6750–1

Hawaii data book, general data, 1992 annual rpt, S2090 1.3

Idaho economic profile, general data, 1992 recurring rpt, S2218–2.3

Illinois elementary and secondary school enrollment by level, and high school dropouts and grads, by county and district, 1990/91, annual rpt, S2440–1.1

Kansas public and private school grads and dropouts, by sex, 1990/91, annual rpt, S2945–1

Kentucky economic statistics, general data, 1993 annual rpt, S3104–1.3

Kentucky public school finances, staff, and enrollment, by district, 1989/90-1990/91, biennial rpt, S3110–2

Louisiana Census of Population and Housing summary findings, by local area, 1990 and trends, U8010–4

Louisiana public and private school grads, with detail by race-ethnicity and sex, 1991/92 annual rpt, S3280–1

Maine Census of Population and Housing summary findings, by local area, 1990, S3465–9

Maine high school grads, 1965-91, annual rpt, S3435–1

Maryland elementary and secondary education data, by county, 1991/92, annual rpt, S3610–2.3

Maryland public school grads and postgraduation plans, by county, 1992, annual rpt, S3610–1

Index by Subjects and Names

Maryland statistical abstract, general data, 1993-94 biennial rpt, S3605–1.2

Massachusetts high school graduation rate, and postgraduation plans of grads, 1993 annual rpt, S3810–3

Massachusetts municipal and county profiles, general data, 1992 annual rpt, C4712–2

Minnesota high school grads, by State region, 1978-2007, biennial rpt, S4195–2.2

Mississippi high school grads, by sex, 1966/67-1991/92, annual rpt, S4340–1.1

Missouri high school grads and postgraduation activities, 1991/92 annual rpt, S4505–1.1

Montana public school enrollment by grade, and grads, by school, county, race-ethnicity, and sex, 1992 and trends, annual rpt, S4740–1

Nevada public high school grads, by school district, 1990/91, annual rpt, S5035–2

New Hampshire births to women with less than 12 years of education, by county and town, 1991, annual rpt, S5215–1

New Hampshire high school grads and postgraduation activities, by school, county, and sex, 1991, annual tables, S5200–1.2

New Hampshire high school grads and postgraduation activities, by school, county, and sex, 1992, annual tables, S5200–1.15

New Jersey Census of Population and Housing detailed findings, by county, 1990, S5425–19

New Jersey public schools, enrollment, and student and staff characteristics, and nonpublic schools and enrollment, by county, 1991/92, annual rpt, S5385–1

New Mexico elementary/secondary school statistics, including grads, student test results, and finances, by school district, 1989/90-1991/92, annual rpt, S5575–4

New York State high school grads, by MSA and county, 1991, annual rpt, S5735–3

New York State municipal and county statistical profiles, general data, 1993 annual rpt, C4712–7

North Carolina public school enrollment, grads, staff, and finances, with data by race, sex, and local district, 1991/92-1992/93 and trends, annual rpt, S5915–1

North Dakota high school grads, by sex, 1991/92, annual directory, S6180–2

Ohio public school enrollment, finances, special programs, and staff, 1991/92 and trends, annual rpt, S6265–2

Oklahoma high school grads, by county and sex, 1991/92, annual rpt, S6423–1.2

Oklahoma high school graduation rate, and percent of teachers with advanced degrees by district, 1991/92 and trends , annual rpt, S6423–2

Oregon population share with bachelor's degree/higher, by county, 1990, article, S6615–2.502

Oregon private and parochial schools, enrollment, and grads, with detail by school, county, and religious affiliation, 1992/93, annual rpt, S6590–1.19

Oregon public and private high school grads, 1965/66-1996/97, annual rpt, S6590–1.8

Oregon public high school completers, by instn, county, sex, and race-ethnicity, 1992, annual rpt, S6590–1.10

Pennsylvania Census of Population and Housing detailed findings, with selected data by county and municipality, 1990, U4130–13

Pennsylvania elementary/secondary and higher education enrollment, grads, staff, and finances, by instn type, 1981/82-1996/97, recurring rpt, S6790–5.10

Pennsylvania high school grads compared to higher education freshmen enrollment, with data by race and sex, 1992 and trends, annual rpt, S6790–5.9

Pennsylvania public and nonpublic high school grads, sex, race-ethnicity, and county, 1991/92 and trends, annual rpt, S6790–5.14

Rhode Island Census of Population and Housing detailed findings, by county and municipality, 1990, S6930–9

Rhode Island grads of public, nonpublic, and State-operated high schools, by sex and instn, June 1992, annual rpt, S6970–1.1

South Carolina high school grads and postgraduation activities, by school district, 1991, annual rpt, S7145–1.3

South Carolina population characteristics, by county, 1993 annual rpt, S7145–1.1

South Carolina public and private schools, enrollment, and grads, by county, 1990/91 and trends, annual planning rpt, S7155–3.3

South Carolina statistical abstract, general data, 1993 annual rpt, S7125–1.6

South Dakota high school grads, and college attendance status, 1976-92, annual rpt, S7375–1

South Dakota public high school grads, by sex and postgraduation status, 1992, annual rpt, S7315–1.1

Tennessee public school enrollment, attendance, and grads, by county, city, and school district, 1991/92, annual rpt, S7490–2.2

Tennessee statistical abstract, general data, 1992/93 annual rpt, U8710–2.16

Utah employment by detailed occupation, and educational attainment by age group, by sex and race-ethnicity, with detail for 7 urban areas, 1990 census rpt, S7832–3.4

Utah high school grads by sex, race-ethnicity, and district, and population distribution by educational attainment, 1991/92 annual rpt, S7815–1

Utah Indian reservation population shares with high school and college degrees, by reservation, 1990, census rpt, S7832–3.3

Utah population distribution and selected characteristics, by race-ethnicity, 1990, S7820–3.504

Vermont high school grads, 1970-2004, annual rpt, S8035–2.2

Virginia public school enrollment and high school grads, with detail by school district, 1980/81-2012/2013, annual rpt, U9080–20

Virginia public school enrollment, grads, finances, and staff, by county and municipality, 1991/92, annual rpt, S8190–3

West Virginia high school grads, 1991/92, annual rpt, S8540–4

Educational employees pay

West Virginia public and private schools, enrollment, grads, and staff, by county, 1991/92, annual rpt, S8540–3

Wisconsin public high school grads, by race-ethnicity and school district, 1992 and trends, annual rpt, S8795–2

Wyoming public high school grads, by sex and district, 1992, annual rpt, S8890–1.3

see also Degrees, higher education

see also High school equivalency tests

see also Literacy and illiteracy

see also National Assessment of Educational Progress

see also School dropouts

see also under By Educational Attainment in the "Index by Categories"

Educational broadcasting

Cable TV equipped elementary and secondary schools by State, and educational programming on individual cable networks, 1993 article, C2965–1.510

Cable TV equipped public and private elementary and secondary schools, 1989/90-1992/93, article, R4800–2.513

Cable TV services in schools, activities and views of system mgmt personnel, Jan 1993 survey, article, C2965–1.510

Stations on the air and authorized, by type, weekly rpt, C1850–14

State and local:

Maryland public schools with cable TV access, and interactive TV locations, by county, Dec 1992, annual rpt, S3610–1

Educational employees pay

Business school faculty and admin salaries, by rank or position, and instn control, 1992/93 and trends, annual feature, A0605–2.501

Business school faculty and admin salaries, by rank or position, and instn control, 1992/93, annual rpt, A0605–1

Catholic secondary school operations and finances, including enrollment by race-ethnicity and family income, 1991/92 and trends, biennial rpt, A7375–5

Chemist and chemical engineer salaries, employment status, and demographic and professional characteristics, 1993, annual rpt, A1250–4

Chemistry and chemical engineering grad starting salaries, employment status, demographic characteristics, and advanced study plans, 1991/92, annual rpt, A1250–2

Elementary and secondary teacher salaries compared to GDP and manufacturing salaries, for US and 7 other countries, 1980s, A1600–4

Elementary/secondary prospective teacher characteristics and opinions, survey of persons interested in alternative certification routes, 1992, R6350–7

Elementary/secondary school superintendents salaries, 1982 and 1992, A0775–5

Elementary/secondary teacher salaries, by State, 1965/66-1990/91, annual rpt, R9050–1.6

Elementary/secondary teacher views on differential pay for locations and subjects with teacher shortages, Jan-Feb 1993 survey, B6045–7

Geoscience faculty salaries by rank and for women, with data on minority faculty members, 1991/92 and trends, annual rpt, A1785–4

Educational employees pay

Higher education administrative salaries, by position and instn type, 1992/93, annual feature, C2175–1.507

Higher education administrative salaries, for 167 positions, by instn type and budget size, 1992/93, annual rpt, A3900–1

Higher education administrative salaries in doctorate-granting public universities, approx 80 positions by region, 1992/93, annual survey rpt, U5960–1

Higher Education Chronicle, with data and articles on enrollment, finances, and faculty and salaries, weekly rpt, C2175–1

Higher education external affairs official salaries, by position and type of instn, 1992/93, article, C2176–1.505

Higher education faculty and librarian salaries, by sex and academic rank or position, 1993 annual rpt, A1570–2

Higher education faculty and salaries at private instns, by discipline and academic rank, 1992/93, annual rpt, A3900–4

Higher education faculty and salaries at public instns with and without collective bargaining contracts, by discipline and academic rank, 1992/93, annual rpt, A3900–5

Higher education faculty average salaries by rank, at approx 2,000 instns arranged by State, 1992/93, annual feature, C2175–1.516

Higher education faculty compensation and employment, detailed data by rank, sex, and instn, 1992/93 and trends, annual rpt, A0800–1

Higher education faculty salaries, by academic rank and discipline, 1992/93, annual rpt, C2175–1.514

Higher education faculty salaries, by sex and academic rank, 1975-91, annual rpt, A1570–1

Higher education instns, faculty, students, degrees, and finances, detailed data by State, 1993 annual rpt, C2175–1.531

Higher education physical plant operations, costs, employment, salaries, and energy use, by instn and region, 1991/92, recurring rpt, A3183–1

Higher education private instn salaries and benefits of chief executives and top 5 earners, and total expenditures, by instn, FY91 or FY92, article, C2175–1.519

Law school grad employment and salaries, by type of employer, location, and grad characteristics, 1992 and trends, annual rpt, A6505–1

Librarian salaries for 6 positions, for public and academic libraries by region, 1993, annual rpt, A2070–3

Librarians (special) salaries by age, sex, and census div, 1992, article, C1852–1.503

Librarians (special) salaries, by location, work setting, and personal characteristics, US and Canada, 1992 and trends, biennial survey rpt, A8965–1

Librarians at universities and research instns, salaries by sex, type of position, and instn, FY92 and trends, annual survey, A3365–2

Library (research) holdings, expenditures by type, and staff, for 120 academic and nonacademic instns, US and Canada, FY92, annual rpt, A3365–1

Library school grad placements and salaries, by region, sex, instn, and library type, with detail for minorities, 1992 and trends, annual article, C1852–1.512

Library school grads, placements, and salaries, by region and sex, 1991 and trends, annual compilation, C1650–3.3

Library/info science school enrollment, staff and student characteristics, finances, and curricula, by school and degree program, 1991/92, annual rpt, A3235–1

Mathematics dept faculty and doctoral degree recipient characteristics, including salaries, 1991/92 and trends, annual survey, A2085–1.1

Medical school faculty and compensation, by dept, academic rank, degree, and region, 1992/93, annual rpt, A3273–2

Medical school faculty physician and allied personnel compensation and productivity, by academic rank, sex, and specialty, 1991, annual rpt, A6365–5

Museums at universities employee salaries, by position, FY93, annual rpt, A3290–1

Nursing college deans and salaries, by personal and instn characteristics, 1992/93, annual rpt, A0615–2

Nursing college faculty and salaries, by personal and instn characteristics, 1992/93, annual rpt, A0615–1

Nursing higher education program finances, faculty and clinical practice, and clinic/center operations, by instn characteristics, 1992/93 biennial rpt, A0615–5

Nursing schools, programs, enrollment, student and staff characteristics, and grads, 1991 and trends, annual rpt, A8010–1

Planning profession employment and salaries, by type of employer, demographic and professional characteristics, and location, 1991 and trends, biennial rpt, A2615–1

Political science higher education dept characteristics, including faculty, salaries, enrollment, and finances, 1991/92 annual rpt, A2617–1

Principal and assistant principal salaries in elementary and secondary schools, by enrollment size and expenditure level, 1991/92-1992/93, annual rpt, A7085–2

Private elementary and secondary school enrollment, staff, and finances, with detail for minorities, by school type and region, 1980s-1992/93, annual rpt, A6835–3

Professional worker salaries, by employee and employer characteristics, with detail for scientists and engineers, 1990s and trends, biennial rpt, A3960–1

Psychology grad dept faculty salaries, by academic rank, years in rank, census div, and sex, 1992/93 and trends, annual rpt, A2620–1

Retirement plan characteristics and finances, for govt plans covering educational employees, 1990/91 and trends, recurring rpt, A7640–18

Salary and job offers for college grads, by field of study, type of employer, and degree level, by region, interim rpt series, A3940–1

Salary and job offers for college grads, by field of study, type of employer, and degree level, series, A3940–2

Social work higher education programs and faculty, with data by region, 1992 and trends, annual rpt, A4515–1.1

Index by Subjects and Names

Southeastern States instructional personnel salaries, for 12 States and US, 1990/91-1991/92, annual rpt, S4340–1.1

Southeastern States teacher average salaries, for 12 States, FY88-94, annual rpt, S7125–3.3

Southern States higher education enrollment, degrees, appropriations, tuition/fees, and faculty compensation, by instn type, for 15 States, 1990/91, annual rpt, A8945–31

Southern States higher education faculty and administrator characteristics and salaries, by instn type, 1990s and trends, biennial fact book, A8945–1.5

State social, economic, and govtl indicators, with rankings, 1993 semiannual rpt, B8500–1.7

Statistical profiles of 50 States and DC, general data, 1993 annual almanac, C4712–1

Theological school enrollment, staff and compensation, and finances, with data by instn, 1991/92 and trends, annual rpt, A3376–1

Urban public school performance compared to natl goals for year 2000, with data on students, teachers, and finances, for 47 systems, 1990/91 and trends, A4425–4

Western States higher education faculty salaries at 14 universities, by academic rank, 1991/92, biennial rpt, S5005–1.7

State and local:

Alabama public school salaries for teachers, principals, and other certified staff, by school district, 1991/92, annual rpt, S0124–1.2

Alaska public schools, enrollment, staff, and finances, by district, FY92, annual rpt, S0295–2

Arizona elementary and secondary school enrollment, staff, and finances, by school district and county, FY92 and trends, annual rpt, S0470–1

Arizona statistical abstract, general data, 1993 recurring rpt, U5850–2.4

Arkansas higher education finances, including revenues by source, expenditures by function, and State appropriations, by public instn, FY80s-95, biennial rpt, S0690–4

Arkansas public school enrollment, grads, staff, and finances, by county and school, 1991/92 and trends, annual rpt, S0660–1

California library finances, staff, holdings, and services, by library type and facility, FY92, annual rpt, S0825–2

California socioeconomic and govtl data for municipalities, counties, and school districts, 1993 annual rpt, C4712–3

Colorado library finances and operations, including staff, holdings, and population served, by instn and library type, series, S1000–3

Colorado public school enrollment, finances, and student and staff characteristics, by locality, 1991 annual rpt series, S1000–4

Colorado public school enrollment, finances, and student and staff characteristics, by locality, 1992 annual rpt series, S1000–2

Connecticut public school data, including enrollment, staff, programs, finances, and student characteristics, 1991/92, biennial rpt, S1185–3

Index by Subjects and Names

Educational enrollment

DC public school finances, enrollment, grads, and test scores, with data by school, 1987/88-1991/92, annual rpt, S1605–2

Delaware postsecondary education finances, enrollment, and degrees conferred, by instn, FY94 annual rpt, S1425–1

Delaware school enrollment, grads, staff, finances, and facilities, by county, school district, and/or instn, 1991/92, annual rpt, S1430–1

Florida municipal and county statistical profiles, general data, 1991 annual rpt, C4712–6

Georgia statistical abstract, general data, 1992-93 biennial rpt, U6730–1.2

Hawaii data book, general data, 1992 annual rpt, S2090–1.3

Idaho public school personnel characteristics and salaries by position, and teachers and enrollment by school district, 1992/93, annual rpt, S2225–3

Illinois higher education staff, salaries, student cost and aid, and finances, by instn, 1993 annual rpt, S2475–1.2

Indiana public school expenditures for salaries and employee benefits, by district and county, 1990/91, annual table, S2608–2.4

Indiana public school expenditures for salaries, by district, 1991/92, annual table, S2608–2.10

Iowa postsecondary enrollment, degrees, staff, and finances, by instn, 1990/91, annual rpt, S2755–1

Kansas school district revenues by source and expenditures by object, 1990/91, annual rpt, S2945–1

Kentucky higher education enrollment, degrees, staff, and finances, by State-supported instn, 1983-92, annual rpt, S3130–3

Kentucky public education profiles, with data by region and district, 1991/92 and trends, annual rpt, S3110–1

Kentucky public school finances, staff, and enrollment, by district, 1989/90-1990/91, biennial rpt, S3110–2

Louisiana elementary/secondary school operations, including enrollment, staff, finances, and detail by school district, 1991/92 and trends, annual rpt, S3280–1

Maine public school enrollment, facilities, staff, and finances, with selected data by county and for private schools, 1991 and trends, annual rpt, S3435–1

Maryland elementary and secondary education data, by county, annual rpt series, S3610–2

Maryland elementary and secondary education statistical summary, with data by county, 1991/92-1992/93 and trends, annual rpt, S3610–1

Maryland statistical abstract, general data, 1993-94 biennial rpt, S3605–1.2

Massachusetts municipal and county profiles, general data, 1992 annual rpt, C4712–2

Massachusetts public elementary/secondary education summary data, 1989/90-1991/92 and trends, annual rpt, S3810–3

Michigan school district financial and enrollment data, with rankings, 1991/92, annual rpt, S3965–3

Minnesota public school enrollment, staff, and finances, by district and county, 1991/92 and trends, annual rpt, S4165–1

Mississippi public school enrollment, staff and salaries, and finances, by district, 1991/92 and trends, annual rpt, S4340–1

Missouri higher education finances, including faculty salaries and library payroll, by instn, 1992 and trends, annual rpt, S4520–3.3

Missouri public school finances, staff, students, and programs, detailed data, 1991/92, annual rpt, S4505–1.1

Missouri public, special, and academic libraries, finances, holdings, circulation, staff, and services, by location, FY92, annual rpt, S4520–2

Nevada public school enrollment, test scores, teachers, and finances, by school district, 1990/91 and trends, annual rpt, S5035–2

New Hampshire public school teacher salary schedules, by professional degree level and school district, 1992/93, annual table, S5200–1.3

New Jersey public school teachers, administrators, staff, and salaries, by county, 1991/92, annual rpt, S5385–1.2

New Mexico elementary/secondary school statistics, including grads, student test results, and finances, by school district, 1989/90-1991/92, annual rpt, S5575–4

North Carolina higher education library holdings and expenditures, by type and instn, 1991/92, annual rpt, U8013–1.2

North Carolina public school enrollment, grads, staff, and finances, with data by race, sex, and local district, 1991/92-1992/93 and trends, annual rpt, S5915–1

North Dakota elementary and secondary school staff characteristics and salaries, by position, region, and enrollment size, 1992/93 annual rpt, S6180–3

North Dakota public school revenues by source, expenditures by function, mill levies, and taxable value, by district, 1992/93 annual rpt, S6180–4

Ohio public, academic, and other library finances, holdings, and staff, by library and location, 1992 and trends, annual rpt, S6320–1

Ohio public school enrollment, finances, special programs, and staff, 1991/92 and trends, annual rpt, S6265–2

Oklahoma public school performance indicators, including students and achievement, finances, and staff, by district, 1990/91-1991/92 and trends, annual rpt, S6423–2

Oklahoma public school staff salaries, by position, 1991/92, annual rpt, S6423–1.2

Oklahoma statistical abstract, general data, 1992 annual rpt, U8130–2.8

Oregon elementary and secondary education enrollment and finances, including data by school district and county, annual rpt series, S6590–1

Pennsylvania higher education faculty employment, compensation, and tenure status, by sex and type of instn, 1991/92 and trends, annual rpt, S6790–5.5

Pennsylvania higher education faculty employment, compensation, and tenure status, by sex and type of instn, 1992/93 and trends, annual rpt, S6790–5.13

Pennsylvania public school personnel and salary data, by position and district, 1992/93 and trends, annual rpt, S6790–5.12

Pennsylvania vocational education teacher salaries, by program, 1991/92, annual rpt, S6790–5.7

Rhode Island statistical almanac, general data, 1993 annual rpt, C7975–1.1

South Carolina higher education enrollment, degrees, staff, and finances, by instn, 1992 and trends, annual rpt, S7185–2

South Carolina teachers salary schedules, educational revenues by source, and expenditures by function, by school district, 1991/92, annual rpt, S7145–1.5

South Dakota public higher education finances, staff, enrollment, degrees, and facilities, by instn, FY93 annual rpt, S7375–1

South Dakota teacher salaries, by age group, education, and experience, 1991/92, annual rpt, S7315–1.2

Tennessee higher education finances, student aid and expenses, and faculty and salaries, by instn, 1992/93 and trends, annual rpt, S7525–1.2

Tennessee public school enrollment, staff, finances, and operations, by county, city, and school district, 1991/92, annual rpt, S7490–2

Texas elementary/secondary education personnel and salaries, by district and county, 1991/92, annual rpt, S7670–1.4

Texas higher education faculty salaries, by rank and instn, 1991/92 and trends, annual rpt, S7657–1.1

Utah college president salaries by instn, 1992, annual rpt, R9380–1.5

Utah higher education degrees, enrollment, staff, and finances, by public instn, with selected comparisons to instns in other States, 1993/94 annual rpt, S7895–2

Utah public schools, enrollment, attendance, personnel, and finances, by school district, 1991/92, annual rpt, S7815–1

Virginia public school enrollment, grads, finances, and staff, by county and municipality, 1991/92, annual rpt, S8190–3

West Virginia higher education faculty characteristics and salary, by instn, 1992 and trends, annual rpt, S8533–1.2

West Virginia public school finances, enrollment, staff, and programs, by county, 1992/93 and trends, annual rpt, S8540–4

West Virginia public school personnel and salaries, by position, 1991/92, annual rpt, S8540–3

Wyoming public school enrollment, staff, and finances, by county and district, 1991/92, annual rpt series, S8890–1

Educational enrollment

Black American educational statistics, with comparisons to whites, 1970s-92, annual compilation, C6775–2.3

Black children and youth population, economic, health, and education data, with comparisons to whites, 1993 rpt, R3840–21

Business grad school programs for executives, with data on revenues, enrollment, tuition, and participant characteristics, by instn, 1993 feature, C5800–7.552

Educational enrollment

Index by Subjects and Names

Business school enrollment by degree level, for top 10 instns, fall 1992, annual feature, A0605–2.501

Catholic colleges, elementary and high schools, enrollment, and teachers, by diocese and State, 1993 annual compilation, C4950–1

Catholic educational instns and enrollment, by State and diocese, 1993 annual almanac, C6885–1

Catholic schools, enrollment, and teachers, by region, State, and diocese, 1992/93 and trends, annual rpt, A7375–1

Catholic secondary school operations and finances, including enrollment by race-ethnicity and family income, 1991/92 and trends, biennial rpt, A7375–5

Chemistry grad student enrollment by degree level, fall 1987-91, annual articles, A1250–1.535

Dental advanced education programs, enrollment, grads, and finances, by instn and State, 1992/93 annual rpt, A1475–10

Dental allied education enrollment, grads, and tuition, by instn, 1992/93 annual rpt, A1475–5

Dental school admission policies, applicants, enrollment, and tuition and fees, by instn, 1992/93, annual rpt, A1475–4.1

Dental school applications, enrollment, grads, and tuition/fees, by instn, 1992 and trends, annual rpt, A1475–4.2

Dental school enrollment and level of prior education for 1st-year students, by instn, 1992/93 annual rpt, A1475–3.1

Developing countries family planning efforts, with data on socioeconomic and health conditions compared to developed countries, by country, 1980s-90, R8720–1.1

Elementary and secondary public and private school enrollment, 1900-2000, annual rpt, R9050–1.6

Elementary/secondary education data, with detail for mathematics including test scores and teacher preparation, by State, 1993 biennial rpt, A4355–1

Elementary/secondary public school enrollment and certified school library media specialists, by selected State, 1992, annual compilation, C1650–3.3

Elementary/secondary schools and enrollment in 10 largest school districts using year-round schedules, 1992/93, R4800–2.505

Engineering (mining) program enrollment by level, 1980-1992/93, article, C5226–2.507

Engineering program enrollment, by instn, field, and State, with detail for women, minorities, and foreign students, fall 1992, annual rpt, A0685–2

Europe Jewish schools, enrollment, and teachers, in France and UK, 1981/82-1991/92, article, A2050–1.1

Foreign student higher education enrollment, by instn, discipline, State, and country of origin, 1991/92, annual feature, C2175–1.501

Foreign students enrolled in US higher education instns, by instn, State, country of origin, and demographic characteristics, 1991/92 and trends, annual rpt, R5580–1

Geoscience enrollment and degrees awarded, by sex, race-ethnicity, and discipline, 1991/92, annual rpt, A1785–3

Higher Education Chronicle, with data and articles on enrollment, finances, and faculty and salaries, weekly rpt, C2175–1

Higher education enrollment and degrees by sex, and high school grads, 1992-2003, annual feature, C2175–1.504

Higher education enrollment, and physical plant facilities, by instn, 1991/92, recurring rpt, A3183–1

Higher education enrollment, by State and public instn, fall 1992, annual rpt, A7150–5

Higher education enrollment, for 108 instns, US and Canada, fall 1990, annual rpt, A3365–1

Higher education enrollment of minority and foreign students at approx 3,100 instns, fall 1991, recurring feature, C2175–1.510

Higher education enrollment of minority and foreign students, with comparison to whites, by sex, State, and instn type, fall 1991, recurring feature, C2175–1.506

Higher education instn policies and practices, including changes in faculty, enrollment, and finances, 1993 annual survey, A1410–1.38

Higher education instns, faculty, students, degrees, and finances, detailed data by State, 1993 annual rpt, C2175–1.531

Higher education instns revenues and expenses, by item, and enrollment vs population age 18-24, various years 1953/54-2003/04, annual rpt, R9050–1.4

Higher education involvement of minorities, including enrollment and degrees awarded, by race-ethnicity, sex, and State, 1970s-91, annual rpt, A1410–10

Higher education student athlete enrollment and graduation rates, by sex, race-ethnicity, and major sport, for Natl Collegiate Athletic Assn Div I instns, 1992/93, annual rpt, A7440–4

Higher education undergrad and grad enrollment by race-ethnicity, fall 1990, article, C4215–1.508

Higher education undergrad enrollment in fall 1990 vs student aid awards in 1992/93, by State, annual rpt, A7140–1

Higher education, 2-year college enrollment, degrees, faculty and staff, and tuition/fees, by instn and State, 1992 annual directory, A0640–1

Hispanic American educational statistics, with comparisons to whites, 1970s-92, annual compilation, C6775–3.2

Journalism/mass communication enrollment and grads by level, by instn, sex, race-ethnicity, and field, 1990/91 and trends, annual article, A3225–1

Latin America statistical abstract, general data by country, 1992 annual rpt, U6250–1.8

Law school enrollment by minority status, degrees conferred, staff, and library holdings, by instn, 1992/93 and trends, annual rpt, A0970–1

Library/info science school enrollment, staff and student characteristics, finances, and curricula, by school and degree program, 1991/92, annual rpt, A3235–1

Mathematics undergrad and grad enrollment trends, fall 1992, annual survey, A2085–1.2

Medical school programs, fees, applicants, admissions, and enrollment, with data by age, sex, minority group, and instn, 1992/93 and trends, annual rpt, A3273–10

Medical school total and women students and grads, decennially 1960/61-1990/91 and 1991/92, annual fact book, A1275–1.1

Natl Merit Scholars freshman enrollment in top 64 higher education instns, 1992, annual feature, C2175–1.505

Nursing programs (State-approved) for practical/vocational nurses, including admissions, enrollment, and grads, by instn, State, and territory, 1992, annual directory, A8010–5

Nursing programs (State-approved) for registered nurses, including admissions, enrollment, and grads, by instn, State, and territory, 1992, annual directory, A8010–4

Nursing school enrollment and grads, by degree level, sex, race-ethnicity, and instn type and location, 1992/93 and trends, annual rpt, A0615–4

Nursing schools, programs, enrollment, student and staff characteristics, and grads, 1991 and trends, annual rpt, A8010–1

OECD member countries spending on elementary/secondary and higher education, with data on enrollment and teachers, for 15 countries, 1987, A1600–4

Optometry school faculty, enrollment and degrees, policies and programs, and finances, by instn, 1991/92, annual survey, A3370–2

Osteopathy college enrollment, student and faculty characteristics, and finances, 1992/93 and trends, annual rpt, A0620–1

Pharmacy degree program applications, enrollment, and degrees conferred, by student characteristics and instn, 1990/91 and trends, annual rpt, A0630–9

Physics and astronomy enrollment and degrees, annual survey of US college depts, series, A1960–2

Political science higher education dept characteristics, including faculty, salaries, enrollment, and finances, 1991/92 annual rpt, A2617–1

Private elementary and secondary school enrollment, staff, and finances, with detail for minorities, by school type and region, 1980s-1992/93, annual rpt, A6835–3

Psychology grad depts, faculty characteristics, enrollment, and student aid, US and Canada, 1990/91 and trends, annual rpt, A2620–3

Public health school applicant, student, and grad characteristics, by instn, 1991/92 and trends, annual rpt, A3372–3

Religious Sunday/Sabbath schools and seminaries enrollment, with seminary student characteristics, 1991-92 and trends, annual rpt, C0105–1

Science and engineering grad students by field, US and foreign, 1991 and trends, annual feature, A1250–1.537

Index by Subjects and Names

Educational enrollment

Science and math elementary/secondary education, including student and teacher characteristics, and requirements, by State, 1991/92, biennial rpt, A4355–3

Social work higher education programs, faculty and student characteristics, and student aid, with data by instn, 1992 and trends, annual rpt, A4515–1

Southern States elementary/secondary school enrollment, and high school grads, by State, 1971/72-2001/02, biennial fact book, A8945–1.1

Southern States higher education enrollment, by type of instn, with detail for women and minorities, by State, 1978-92, biennial fact book, A8945–1.2

Southern States higher education enrollment, degrees, appropriations, tuition/fees, and faculty compensation, by instn type, for 15 States, 1990/91, annual rpt, A8945–31

Southern States higher education instns with 10,000/more students, and share of total enrollment, by instn type and State, fall 1990, A8945–27.10

State social, economic, and govtl indicators, with rankings, 1993 semiannual rpt, B8500–1.7

Statistical profiles of 50 States and DC, general data, 1993 annual almanac, C4712–1

Teacher employment, hiring, and labor turnover data, and enrollment, for 57 districts, Oct 1990-91, R6350–7

Textbook and educational material sales compared to school enrollment, by State, 1990-91 and trends, annual rpt, A3274–2

Theological school enrollment, staff and compensation, and finances, with data by instn, 1991/92 and trends, annual rpt, A3376–1

Urban public school performance compared to natl goals for year 2000, with data on students, teachers, and finances, for 47 systems, 1990/91 and trends, A4425–4

Veterinarians by professional characteristics and location, and financial and education summaries, 1993 annual directory, A3100–1

Veterinary school academic and clinical grad program enrollment, quinquennially 1967-92, article, A3100–2.513

Veterinary school aquatic animal course availability, faculty, and enrollment, by instn, 1991/92, article, A3100–2.509

Veterinary school enrollment by sex, program, instn, and place of residence, US and Canada, 1992/93, annual article, A3100–2.516

Western States higher education student exchange program enrollment and support fees, by program and instn, for 15 States, 1992/93, annual rpt, A9385–1

Women and minorities in professional fields, detailed education and labor force data, 1980s-91, with historical trends, recurring rpt, A3960–2

State and local:

Alabama elementary and secondary school enrollment, and pupil transportation, by district, 1991/92, annual rpt, S0124–1.1

Alabama statistical abstract, general data, 1992 recurring rpt, U5680–2.4

Alaska educational enrollment at elementary/secondary level, and by higher education instn, FY92 annual rpt, S0275–1

Alaska public schools, enrollment, staff, and finances, by district, FY92, annual rpt, S0295–2

Arizona elementary and secondary school enrollment, staff, and finances, by school district and county, FY92 and trends, annual rpt, S0470–1

Arizona higher education enrollment, by public instn, 1982-91, annual rpt, S0450–2

Arizona higher education instns, enrollment, and faculty, with comparisons to population, 1990, article, U0280–1.511

Arizona Indian population, education, housing, health, and employment characteristics, with detail by reservation, 1970s-91, recurring rpt, U5850–2.9

Arizona statistical abstract, general data, 1993 recurring rpt, U5850–2.4

Arkansas Census of Population and Housing detailed findings, 1990, U5935–7

Arkansas higher education enrollment by student characteristics and geographic origins, by instn, fall 1991 and trends, annual rpt, S0690–1

Arkansas higher education FTE enrollment, and student credit hour production by program area, by academic level and instn, 1991/92 and trends, annual rpt, S0690–2

Arkansas public higher education finances and enrollment, with comparisons to US and selected other States, 1990-92, article, U5930–1.502

Arkansas public higher education finances, with summary enrollment trends by instn, FY83-92, biennial rpt, S0690–4

Arkansas public school enrollment, grads, staff, and finances, by county and school, 1991/92 and trends, annual rpt, S0660–1

Arkansas socioeconomic trends, by MSA and/or county, 1993 annual rpt, U5935–1

California Census of Population and Housing detailed findings, 1990, S0840–9

California higher education systems funding by source and expenditures by program category, with enrollment data, FY60s-94, annual rpt, S0827–3

California postsecondary education enrollment and degrees, by sex, race-ethnicity, and instn, 1990/91, annual series, S0827–2

California private schools, enrollment by grade, grads, and staff, with data by county, 1992/93 and trends, annual rpt, S0825–8

California public school enrollment, grads, and staff, by race-ethnicity, 1992/93 and trends, annual rpt, S0825–9

California public school limited-English-proficiency enrollment, teachers, and programs, by 1st language, grade level, and county, 1992 and trends, annual rpt, S0825–10

California public schools, enrollment by grade, and grads, by county, 1992/93 and trends, annual rpt, S0825–7

California socioeconomic and govtl data for municipalities, counties, and school districts, 1993 annual rpt, C4712–3

California statistical abstract, general data, 1992 annual rpt, S0840–2.6

Colorado higher education library finances and operations, and enrollment, by instn, 1992, biennial rpt, S1000–3.2

Colorado public and/or private school enrollment and grads, by student characteristics, county, and district, 1992 and trends, annual rpt, S1000–2.1

Colorado public school enrollment and dropouts, by local area, 1991/92, annual planning rpt, S1040–3.1

Connecticut public school data, including enrollment, staff, programs, finances, and student characteristics, 1991/92, biennial rpt, S1185–3

DC public school finances, enrollment, grads, and test scores, with data by school, 1987/88-1991/92, annual rpt, S1605–2

DC statistical profile, general data, 1992 annual rpt, S1535–3.1, S1535–3.6

Delaware data book, general data, 1993 annual rpt, S1375–4

Delaware postsecondary education finances, enrollment, and degrees conferred, by instn, FY94 annual rpt, S1425–1

Delaware school enrollment, grads, staff, finances, and facilities, by county, school district, and/or instn, 1991/92, annual rpt, S1430–1

Florida higher education enrollment, degree programs, staff, and finances, by State-supported instn, with student and staff characteristics, 1991/92 annual rpt, S1725–1

Florida municipal and county statistical profiles, general data, 1991 annual rpt, C4712–6

Georgia county guide, general data, 1993 annual rpt, U6750–1

Georgia statistical abstract, general data, 1992-93 biennial rpt, U6730–1.2

Hawaii data book, general data, 1992 annual rpt, S2090–1.3

Idaho elementary/secondary enrollment and attendance, by school district, FY92, annual rpt, S2225 2

Idaho public and nonpublic school enrollment by grade, by school district and/or county, Sept 1992, annual rpt, S2225–1

Idaho public school personnel characteristics and salaries by position, and teachers and enrollment by school district, 1992/93, annual rpt, S2225–3

Illinois elementary and secondary school enrollment by level, and high school dropouts and grads, by county and district, 1990/91, annual rpt, S2440–1.1

Illinois higher education enrollment and degrees, by level, instn, field of instruction, and student characteristics, 1992 and trends, annual rpt, S2475–1.1

Indiana elementary and secondary school enrollment and finances, by district and county, annual rpt series, S2608–2

Iowa elementary/secondary and higher education, 1982/83-1991/92, annual rpt, S2860–4

Iowa postsecondary enrollment, degrees, staff, and finances, by instn, 1990/91, annual rpt, S2755–1

Kansas school enrollment, grads, staff, and finances, by county, school district, and/or school, 1990/91, annual rpt, S2945–1

Kentucky higher education enrollment, degrees, staff, and finances, by State-supported instn, 1983-92, annual rpt, S3130–3

Educational enrollment

Index by Subjects and Names

Kentucky labor force planning rpt, including population and labor force characteristics, and employment by industry, 1991 and trends, annual rpt, S3140–3

Kentucky public school finances, staff, and enrollment, by district, 1989/90-1990/91, biennial rpt, S3110–2

Louisiana Census of Population and Housing summary findings, by local area, 1990 and trends, U8010–4

Louisiana elementary/secondary school operations, including enrollment, staff, finances, and detail by school district, 1991/92 and trends, annual rpt, S3280–1

Maine Census of Population and Housing summary findings, by local area, 1990, S3465–9

Maine public school enrollment, facilities, staff, and finances, with selected data by county and for private schools, 1991 and trends, annual rpt, S3435–1

Maine statistical summary, general economic and social data, 1992 recurring rpt, S3434–1

Maryland elementary and secondary education data, by county, annual rpt series, S3610–2

Maryland elementary and secondary education statistical summary, with data by county, 1991/92-1992/93 and trends, annual rpt, S3610–1

Maryland statistical abstract, general data, 1993-94 biennial rpt, S3605–1.2

Massachusetts public and nonpublic elementary/secondary school enrollment, by city, 1991, annual rpt, C4712–2

Massachusetts public elementary/secondary education summary data, 1989/90-1991/92 and trends, annual rpt, S3810–3

Massachusetts public elementary/secondary school enrollment by grade, by district, Oct 1992, annual rpt, S3810–4

Michigan school district financial and enrollment data, with rankings, 1991/92, annual rpt, S3965–3

Minnesota postsecondary education finances, and enrollment by student characteristics, by type of school system, 1970s-93, bicnnial rpt, S4195 2.2

Minnesota public school enrollment, staff, and finances, by district and county, 1991/92 and trends, annual rpt, S4165–1

Mississippi higher education enrollment and degrees, by level and field, and finances, by State-supported instn, 1991/92, annual rpt, S4360–1

Mississippi public school enrollment, staff and salaries, and finances, by district, 1991/92 and trends, annual rpt, S4340–1

Missouri higher education enrollment by student characteristics and residence location, by instn, fall 1992 and trends, annual rpt, S4520–3.2

Missouri school finances, enrollment, grads, and staff, by county and school district, 1991/92, annual rpt, S4505–1

Montana educational enrollment, including data by higher education and vocational technical instn, 1983-92, annual rpt, S4653–1

Montana public school enrollment by grade, and grads, by school, county, race-ethnicity, and sex, 1992 and trends, annual rpt, S4740–1

Nebraska elementary and secondary schools, enrollment by grade, and staff, with data by school district and county, annual series, S4865–2

Nebraska elementary/secondary private school enrollment shares, for 21 counties, 1990, article, U7860–1.502

Nebraska public school finances, with data on average daily membership and resident pupils, by county and district, 1988/89, annual rpt, S4865–3

Nevada public school enrollment, test scores, teachers, and finances, by school district, 1990/91 and trends, annual rpt, S5035–2

Nevada statistical abstract, general data, 1992 biennial rpt, S5005–1.7

New Hampshire elementary and secondary education statistics, with selected data by school district, annual rpt series, S5200–1

New Jersey Census of Population and Housing detailed findings, by county, 1990, S5425–19

New Jersey municipal and county data book, general data, 1992 annual rpt, C4712–4

New Jersey public schools, enrollment, grads, and student characteristics, by county, 1991/92, annual rpt, S5385–1.1

New Mexico elementary/secondary school enrollment by grade level and race-ethnicity, 1991/92 and trends, annual rpt, S5575–4

New York State municipal and county statistical profiles, general data, 1993 annual rpt, C4712–7

North Carolina higher education enrollment, degrees, libraries, staff, and student characteristics, finances, and housing, by instn, 1992/93 and trends, annual rpt, U8013–1

North Carolina public school enrollment, grads, staff, and finances, with data by race, sex, and local district, 1991/92-1992/93 and trends, annual rpt, S5915–1

North Dakota elementary and secondary schools, enrollment, and staff, by school type and location, 1992/93 annual directory, S6180–2

North Dakota higher education enrollment, by level, instn, county, and selected student characteristics, fall 1992 and trends, annual rpt, S6110–1

Ohio public school enrollment, finances, special programs, and staff, 1991/92 and trends, annual rpt, S6265–2

Ohio school library data, including enrollment served, by higher education instn, 1991/92, annual rpt, S6320–1

Ohio special education expenditures, instructional hours, and enrollment, by service type and school district, 1991/92 and trends, annual rpt, S6265–1

Oklahoma public school finances, including property valuations, and enrollment, by county and district, 1991/92-1992/93 and trends, annual rpt, S6423–1.2

Oklahoma public school performance indicators, including students and achievement, finances, and staff, by district, 1990/91-1991/92 and trends, annual rpt, S6423–2

Oregon elementary and secondary education enrollment and finances, including data by school district and county, annual rpt series, S6590–1

Pennsylvania Census of Population and Housing detailed findings, with selected data by county and municipality, 1990, U4130–13

Pennsylvania educational statistics by level and/or type of education, series, S6790–5

Pennsylvania public and nonpublic school enrollment, 1972/73-1990/91, annual planning rpt, S6845–3.3

Rhode Island Census of Population and Housing detailed findings, by county and municipality, 1990, S6930–9

Rhode Island public school enrollment by type of instn, grade, sex, race-ethnicity, and district, 1991/92 or fall 1992, annual rpt, S6970–1.1

Rhode Island statistical almanac, general data, 1993 annual rpt, C7975–1

South Carolina average daily school membership, FY79-93, annual rpt, S7125–3.3

South Carolina educational characteristics and socioeconomic indicators, by school district and county, 1991/92, annual rpt, S7145–1

South Carolina educational enrollment by level, with detail for higher education instns, 1992 annual planning rpt, S7155–3.3

South Carolina higher education enrollment, degrees, staff, and finances, by instn, 1992 and trends, annual rpt, S7185–2

South Dakota public higher education finances, staff, enrollment, degrees, and facilities, by instn, FY93 annual rpt, S7375–1

South Dakota school enrollment, finances, grads, and staff, by district, 1991/92 and trends, annual rpt, S7315–1

Tennessee higher education enrollment, including by age, sex, race, and instn, fall 1992 and trends, annual rpt, S7525–1.1

Tennessee public school enrollment, staff, finances, and operations, by county, city, and school district, 1991/92, annual rpt, S7490–2

Texas elementary and secondary education enrollment by grade level, by district and county, 1991/92, annual rpt, S7670–1.2

Texas elementary and secondary education enrollment by race-ethnicity, by school, district, and county, 1991/92, annual rpt, S7670–1.1

Texas higher education enrollment, faculty, curricula, and finances, by instn, 1991/92 and trends, annual rpt, S7657–1

Utah govt statistical review, fiscal and socioeconomic data, 1993 annual rpt, R9380–1.8

Utah higher education degrees, enrollment, staff, and finances, by public instn, with selected comparisons to instns in other States, 1993/94 annual rpt, S7895–2

Utah public schools, enrollment, attendance, personnel, and finances, by school district, 1991/92, annual rpt, S7815–1

Utah statistical abstract, general data, 1993 triennial rpt, U8960–1.3

Vermont elementary and secondary school enrollment by grade, sex, race-ethnicity, school, and county, 1992/93 and trends, annual rpt, S8020–1

Index by Subjects and Names — Educational facilities

Vermont higher education enrollment, including students from abroad and selected neighboring States, by instn, fall 1992 and trends, annual rpt, S8035–2.2

Virginia public school enrollment and high school grads, with detail by school district, 1980/81-2012/2013, annual rpt, U9080–20

Virginia public school enrollment, grads, finances, and staff, by county and municipality, 1991/92, annual rpt, S8190–3

West Virginia higher education enrollment and degrees conferred, by instn, 1991/92 and trends, annual rpt, S8533–1.1

West Virginia public and private schools, enrollment, grads, and staff, by county, 1991/92, annual rpt, S8540–3

West Virginia public school finances, enrollment, staff, and programs, by county, 1992/93 and trends, annual rpt, S8540–4

Wisconsin Blue Book, general data, 1993-94 biennial rpt, S8780–1.2

Wisconsin elementary and secondary school enrollment, staff, costs, and State aid, by school district, 1992/93 and trends, annual rpt, S8795–2

Wyoming public school enrollment, staff, and finances, by county and district, 1991/92, annual rpt series, S8890–1

see also Educational retention rates

see also School dropouts

Educational exchanges

- Europe-US academic collaboration project grants awarded to 23 US instns from US Education Dept, 1993 article, C2175–1.538
- Federal funding for educational exchange programs, by agency, 1992, article, C2175 1.528
- Higher education instn language study abroad programs, including countries or world areas of study, 1993 annual survey, A1410–1.38
- Latin America statistical abstract, general data by country, 1992 annual rpt, U6250–1.11
- Western States higher education student exchange program enrollment and support fees, by program and instn, for 15 States, 1992/93, annual rpt, A9385–1

State and local:

- Florida university student exchange program participation, by instn, 1991/92, annual rpt, S1725–1
- Minnesota postsecondary interstate tuition reciprocity, by State and instn, 1981/82-1993/94, biennial rpt, S4195–2.2

Educational facilities

- Catholic educational instns and enrollment, by State and diocese, 1993 annual almanac, C6885–1
- Catholic vs public school ratings for selected aspects of education and environment, public opinion by respondent characteristics, July 1992 survey, A7375–8
- Community and junior college financial and operating data, including building square footage and operation/maintenance expenditures, FY92, annual rpt, A6705–1
- Construction contract awards by type of project, weekly rpt, C5800–2

Construction contract value, by construction type and region, including floor area and number of residential units, 1992-93, annual rpt, C5800–15.501, C5800–15.504, C5800–15.507, C5800–26, C5800–29

Consumer complaint and inquiry activity of Better Business Burs, by detailed type of business, 1992, annual rpt, A4350–1

Higher education instns, faculty, students, degrees, and finances, detailed data by State, 1993 annual rpt, C2175–1.531

Higher education physical plant operations, costs, employment, salaries, and energy use, by instn and region, 1991/92, recurring rpt, A3183–1

Latin America statistical abstract, general data by country, 1992 annual rpt, U6250–1.8

Private elementary and secondary school enrollment, staff, and finances, with detail for minorities, by school type and region, 1980s-1992/93, annual rpt, A6835–3

Southern States postsecondary instns, by State, 1989/90, biennial fact book, A8945–1.2

State social, economic, and govtl indicators, with rankings, 1993 semiannual rpt, B8500–1.7

Urban public school system characteristics, including number of schools and value of deferred maintenance, for 47 systems, 1990/91, A4425–4

Vending machine sales and operations, by product and location type, 1990-92, annual rpt, C9470–1

State and local:

- Alaska educational summary, FY92 annual rpt, S0275–1
- Alaska public schools, enrollment, staff, and finances, by district, FY92, annual rpt, S0295–2
- Arizona elementary and secondary school enrollment, staff, and finances, by school district and county, FY92 and trends, annual rpt, S0470–1
- Arkansas property assessments and school facilities, damaged buildings and insurance coverage, and finances, 1990/91-1991/92, annual rpt, S0660–1
- Arkansas public higher education instn buildings, and plant size and value, by instn, 1993 biennial rpt, S0690–4
- California private schools, enrollment by grade, grads, and staff, with data by county, 1992/93 and trends, annual rpt, S0825–8
- California property tax assessments and exemptions, by type of property, city, county, and company, FY93 and trends, annual rpt, S0835–1.2
- California public schools by type, by nonwhite enrollment share, 1992/93, annual rpt, S0825–9
- California public schools, enrollment by grade, and grads, by county, 1992/93 and trends, annual rpt, S0825–7
- Colorado public school revenues by source, and expenditures by category, by school district, 1990, annual rpt, S1000–4.3
- Colorado public schools, by district and county, fall 1992, annual rpt, S1000–2.1
- Connecticut public school data, including enrollment, staff, programs, finances, and student characteristics, 1991/92, biennial rpt, S1185–3

Delaware school enrollment, grads, staff, finances, and facilities, by county, school district, and/or instn, 1991/92, annual rpt, S1430–1

Florida higher education enrollment, degree programs, staff, and finances, by State-supported instn, with student and staff characteristics, 1991/92 annual rpt, S1725–1

Georgia county guide, general data, 1993 annual rpt, U6750–1

Hawaii data book, general data, 1992 annual rpt, S2090–1.3

Idaho elementary/secondary schools by type, and district finances, FY91-92, annual rpt, S2225–2

Illinois public school districts, attendance centers, and buildings under construction, by county, 1990/91, annual rpt, S2440–1.1

Iowa postsecondary enrollment, degrees, staff, and finances, by instn, 1990/91, annual rpt, S2755–1

Kansas school facilities in use and abandoned, and cost of vandalism, 1990/91, annual rpt, S2945–1

Kentucky higher education land holdings, and building square footage by use and age, by instn, fall 1992, annual rpt, S3130–3

Louisiana elementary/secondary school operations, including enrollment, staff, finances, and detail by school district, 1991/92 and trends, annual rpt, S3280–1

Maine public school enrollment, facilities, staff, and finances, with selected data by county and for private schools, 1991 and trends, annual rpt, S3435–1

Maryland elementary and secondary education data, by county, annual rpt series, S3610–2

Maryland elementary and secondary education statistical summary, with data by county, 1991/92-1992/93 and trends, annual rpt, S3610–1

Massachusetts public elementary/secondary education summary data, 1989/90-1991/92 and trends, annual rpt, S3810–3

Minnesota public school enrollment, staff, and finances, by district and county, 1991/92 and trends, annual rpt, S4165–1

Mississippi public schools, building funds, and capital improvement bond election results, 1991/92 and trends, annual rpt, S4340–1

Missouri higher education revenues by source and expenditures by function, by instn, FY92 and trends, annual rpt, S4520–3.3

Nebraska elementary and secondary schools, enrollment by grade, and staff, with data by school district and county, annual series, S4865–2

Nevada public school enrollment, test scores, teachers, and finances, by school district, 1990/91 and trends, annual rpt, S5035–2

New Hampshire school building aid, by school district, 1993/94, annual table, S5200–1.14

New Jersey public schools, enrollment, and student and staff characteristics, and nonpublic schools and enrollment, by county, 1991/92, annual rpt, S5385–1

Educational facilities

North Carolina educational capital outlay expenditures, by source of funds, 1991/92, annual rpt, S5915–1.1

North Dakota elementary and secondary schools, enrollment, and staff, by school type and location, 1992/93 annual directory, S6180–2

Ohio public school enrollment, finances, special programs, and staff, 1991/92 and trends, annual rpt, S6265–2

Oklahoma school districts, and schools by type, by county, 1990/91-1991/92, annual rpt, S6423–1.2

Oregon elementary and secondary public schools, by county, Oct 1992, annual rpt, S6590–1.5

Oregon elementary and secondary public schools, by grade level offered, 1992/93, annual rpt, S6590–1.6

Oregon elementary and secondary schools and student/teacher ratios, by school type and size, Oct 1992, annual rpt, S6590–1.7

Oregon public school revenues by source and fund, and expenditures by fund, function, and object, 1991/92, annual rpt, S6590–1.16

Oregon public school revenues by source and fund, and expenditures by fund, function, and object, 1992/93, annual rpt, S6590–1.17

Pennsylvania higher education physical plant assets and indebtedness, by instn type, FY91, annual rpt, S6790–5.4

Pennsylvania higher education physical plant assets and indebtedness, by instn type, FY92, annual rpt, S6790–5.16

Pennsylvania public and nonpublic schools in operation, 1982/83-1991/92, annual rpt, S6790–5.1

Pennsylvania public and nonpublic schools in operation, 1983/84, 1987/88, and 1992/93, annual rpt, S6790–5.17

South Carolina educational finances, and school plants, by school district, 1991/92, annual rpt, S7145–1.5

South Carolina public and private schools, enrollment, and grads, by county, 1990/91 and trends, annual planning rpt, S7155–3.3

South Dakota public higher education finances, staff, enrollment, degrees, and facilities, by instn, FY93 annual rpt, S7375–1

South Dakota school enrollment, finances, grads, and staff, by district, 1991/92 and trends, annual rpt, S7315–1

Tennessee public school enrollment, staff, finances, and operations, by county, city, and school district, 1991/92, annual rpt, S7490–2

Texas higher education physical plant investment and educational facilities, by instn, FY92 annual rpt, S7657–1.2

Utah public schools, enrollment, attendance, personnel, and finances, by school district, 1991/92, annual rpt, S7815–1

West Virginia elementary and secondary school buildings and square footage, new construction and additions, and capacity, by county, 1991/92, annual rpt, S8540–3

West Virginia elementary and secondary schools, and split-grade classrooms by county, 1993 annual rpt, S8540–4

Wisconsin elementary and secondary school enrollment, staff, costs, and State aid, by school district, 1992/93 and trends, annual rpt, S8795–2

Wyoming public schools and classrooms by type, by county and district, 1991/92 annual rpt series, S8890–1

see also Libraries

see also Student housing

see also under By Individual Company or Institution in the "Index by Categories"

Educational finance

Africa public universities, enrollment, and expenditures per student, for 12-34 countries, 1993 article, C2175–1.524

Business grad school programs for executives, with data on revenues, enrollment, tuition, and participant characteristics, by instn, 1993 feature, C5800–7.552

Catholic secondary school operations and finances, including enrollment by race-ethnicity and family income, 1991/92 and trends, biennial rpt, A7375–5

Charitable contributions, by type of donor and recipient, 1992 and trends, annual rpt, A0700–1

Community and junior college revenues by source and expenditures by function, and selected student characteristics, FY92, annual rpt, A6705–1

Competitiveness indicators for US vs other major industrial countries, including investments, productivity, exports, and per capita GDP, 1993 annual rpt, A4475–1

Contributions to educational instns, with top instns, by instn and donor type, 1991/92 and trend, article, C2176–1.514

Corporate charitable contributions, by donor characteristics and detailed type of recipient, 1991 and trends, annual rpt, R4105–8

Corporate charitable contributions, with detail for education, 1992 and trends, annual article, C2176–1.520

Corporate contributions to higher education 1982-92, and to all education by program 1992, annual article, C2175–1.534

Elementary/secondary education data, with detail for mathematics including test scores and teacher preparation, by State, 1993 biennial rpt, A4355–1

Elementary/secondary education foundation grants and value, for top 10 recipients, 1990/91, article, R4800–2.522

Elementary/secondary educational spending distribution by source of funds, 1970, 1980, and 1987, annual rpt, R3840–11.1

Elementary/secondary school parental selection, parent and general public views, and local program characteristics and results, 1992 rpt, R3810–7

Expenditures for education vs personal income, by State, FY91, annual rpt, R9380–1.8

Foundation assets, income, and grants by type of recipient, with data for top organizations and by location, 1991 and trends, annual rpt, R4900–1

Govt finances, including revenues by source, expenditures by function, and debt, detailed data for Federal, State, and local govts, 1993 annual rpt, R9050–1

Govt spending on preschool-12th grade education in US and 5 other industrialized countries, 1980s, R8335–2

Index by Subjects and Names

Higher education admissions dept activity, including trends in applications received, recruitment, staff, and budgets, 1992-93, annual rpt, A6695–1

Higher Education Chronicle, with data and articles on enrollment, finances, and faculty and salaries, weekly rpt, C2175–1

Higher education endowment fund investment composition, for large vs small instns, 1993 article, C2175–1.507

Higher education endowment funds of 419 instns, market values, June 1991-92, annual feature, C2175–1.508

Higher education expenditure per student, percent change by function and instn type, 1981-90, article, C5800–7.529

Higher education instn employee retirement and insurance benefits, prevalence and expenditures, by type of instn and region, 1991, biennial survey, A9025–3

Higher education instn endowment fund and investment pool characteristics and performance, by instn, FY92, annual survey rpt, A6705–2

Higher education instn policies and practices, including changes in faculty, enrollment, and finances, 1993 annual survey, A1410–1.38

Higher education instns, faculty, students, degrees, and finances, detailed data by State, 1993 annual rpt, C2175–1.531

Higher education physical plant operations, costs, employment, salaries, and energy use, by instn and region, 1991/92, recurring rpt, A3183–1

Higher education public instn administrative share of instructional expenditures, for 11 States, 1990, article, B8500–2.510

Higher education voluntary support, by type of instn and donor, with top recipient instns and use, 1991/92 and trends, annual feature, C2175–1.525

Latin America statistical abstract, general data by country, 1992 annual rpt, U6250–1.8

Library (research) expenditures distribution by function, selected years 1963-91, article, C2175–1.509

Library (research) holdings, expenditures by type, and staff, for 120 academic and nonacademic instns, US and Canada, FY92, annual rpt, A3365–1

Library (research) holdings, staff, and expenditures, for instns in US and Canada, 1991/92, annual feature, C2175–1.511

Library and book trade reference info, including public and academic library funding, construction, and operations, by State and instn, 1992, annual compilation, C1650–3

Library building referenda election results, by instn and location, FY92 and trends, annual article, C1852–1.508

Library construction, costs, and funding sources, by State, city, instn, and library type, FY92 and trends, annual article, C1852–1.501

Library/info science school income by source, and expenditures by object, by instn, 1991/92 and trends, annual rpt, A3235–1.4

Medical grad level education expenditures distribution by source of funding, 1991, article, A3273–8.510

Index by Subjects and Names

Educational finance

Medical school revenues by source, student aid, and staff, by instn type, 1989/90 and/or 1990/91, article, A3273–8.503

Mutual fund industry financial data, by type of investor and financial instn intermediary, 1991 and trends, annual rpt, A6025–1.2

Nursing higher education program finances, faculty and clinical practice, and clinic/center operations, by instn characteristics, 1992/93 biennial rpt, A0615–5

OECD member countries spending on elementary/secondary and higher education, with data on enrollment and teachers, for 15 countries, 1987, A1600–4

Optometry school faculty, enrollment and degrees, policies and programs, and finances, by instn, 1991/92, annual survey, A3370–2

Osteopathy college enrollment, student and faculty characteristics, and finances, 1992/93 and trends, annual rpt, A0620–1

Political science higher education dept characteristics, including faculty, salaries, enrollment, and finances, 1991/92 annual rpt, A2617–1

Private elementary and secondary school enrollment, staff, and finances, with detail for minorities, by school type and region, 1980s-1992/93, annual rpt, A6835–3

Psychology grad dept and personnel budget trends by budget category, by instn type and control, 1992/93, annual rpt, A2620–1

Public broadcasting station revenues from higher education instns, by station type, FY91, annual rpt, R4250–1.20

Public health school expenditures by object and fund source, by instn (unnamed), FY92 and trends, annual rpt, A3372–3

Public opinion on school problems, quality, and proposed reforms, by respondent characteristics, 1993 annual Gallup Poll, A8680–1.503

Public support for govt funding for parental selection of public/other schools, by respondent characteristics, July 1992 survey, A7375–8

School bus fleet operating cost reduction strategies used by district mgmt, July 1993 survey, annual article, C1575–1.507

School bus pupil transportation, accident, and expenditure statistics, by State, 1993 annual feature, C1575–1.502

Southern States higher education financial data, by State, 1970s-92, biennial fact book, A8945–1.6

Southern States teacher retirement and health insurance plan characteristics and costs as a percent of salaries, for 15 States, 1993 rpt, A8945–34

State social, economic, and govtl indicators, with rankings, 1993 semiannual rpt, B8500–1.7

Textbook sales compared to school expenditures, by State, 1990-91, annual rpt, A3274–2

Theological school enrollment, staff and compensation, and finances, with data by instn, 1991/92 and trends, annual rpt, A3376–1

Urban public school funding by source, spending by object compared to other locations, and bonded debt ratings, for 47 systems, 1990/91, A4425–4

State and local:

Alabama elementary and secondary school enrollment, staff, pupil transportation, and finances, by district, 1991/92, annual rpt, S0124–1

Alaska public schools, enrollment, staff, and finances, by district, FY92, annual rpt, S0295–2

Arizona elementary and secondary school enrollment, staff, and finances, by school district and county, FY92 and trends, annual rpt, S0470–1

Arizona elementary/secondary education revenues by source and expenditures by object, 1989/90, article, U0280–1.501

Arizona statistical abstract, general data, 1993 recurring rpt, U5850–2.4

Arkansas higher education finances, including revenues by source, expenditures by function, and State appropriations, by public instn, FY80s-95, biennial rpt, S0690–4

Arkansas public higher education finances and enrollment, with comparisons to US and selected other States, 1990-92, article, U5930–1.502

Arkansas public school enrollment, grads, staff, and finances, by county and school, 1991/92 and trends, annual rpt, S0660–1

California higher education systems funding by source and expenditures by program category, with enrollment data, FY60s-94, annual rpt, S0827–3

California library finances, staff, holdings, and services, by library type and facility, FY92, annual rpt, S0825–2

California socioeconomic and govtl data for municipalities, counties, and school districts, 1993 annual rpt, C4712–3

California statistical abstract, general data, 1992 annual rpt, S0840–2.6, S0840–2.13

Colorado library finances and operations, including staff, holdings, and population served, by instn and library type, series, S1000–3

Colorado public school revenues by source, and expenditures by category, by school district, 1990, annual rpt, S1000–4.3

Connecticut public school data, including enrollment, staff, programs, finances, and student characteristics, 1991/92, biennial rpt, S1185–3

DC public school finances, enrollment, grads, and test scores, with data by school, 1987/88-1991/92, annual rpt, S1605–2

DC statistical profile, general data, 1992 annual rpt, S1535–3.6

Delaware postsecondary education finances, enrollment, and degrees conferred, by instn, FY94 annual rpt, S1425–1

Delaware school enrollment, grads, staff, finances, and facilities, by county, school district, and/or instn, 1991/92, annual rpt, S1430–1

Florida higher education enrollment, degree programs, staff, and finances, by State-supported instn, with student and staff characteristics, 1991/92 annual rpt, S1725–1

Florida municipal and county statistical profiles, general data, 1991 annual rpt, C4712–6

Georgia county guide, general data, 1993 annual rpt, U6750–1

Georgia State-supported higher education instn assets and liabilities, revenues by source, and expenditures by function, FY92, annual rpt, S1860–1

Georgia statistical abstract, general data, 1992-93 biennial rpt, U6730–1.2

Hawaii data book, general data, 1992 annual rpt, S2090–1.3

Idaho school district revenues by source, and expenditures by function, by district and fund, FY92, annual rpt, S2225–2

Illinois higher education staff, salaries, student cost and aid, and finances, by instn, 1993 annual rpt, S2475–1.2

Illinois public school revenues and expenditures by district, with data on busing, State aid claims, and per capita costs, 1990/91, annual rpt, S2440–1.3

Indiana elementary and secondary school enrollment and finances, by district and county, annual rpt series, S2608–2

Indiana public and other library holdings, circulation, finances, and staff, by instn, 1992 or FY92, annual rpt, S2655–1

Iowa postsecondary enrollment, degrees, staff, and finances, by instn, 1990/91, annual rpt, S2755–1

Kansas school enrollment, grads, staff, and finances, by county, school district, and/or school, 1990/91, annual rpt, S2945–1

Kentucky higher education enrollment, degrees, staff, and finances, by State-supported instn, 1983-92, annual rpt, S3130–3

Kentucky public education profiles, with data by region and district, 1991/92 and trends, annual rpt, S3110–1

Kentucky public school finances, staff, and enrollment, by district, 1989/90-1990/91, biennial rpt, S3110–2

Louisiana elementary/secondary school operations, including enrollment, staff, finances, and detail by school district, 1991/92 and trends, annual rpt, S3280–1

Maine public school enrollment, facilities, staff, and finances, with selected data by county and for private schools, 1991 and trends, annual rpt, S3435–1

Maryland elementary and secondary education data, by county, annual rpt series, S3610–2

Maryland elementary and secondary education statistical summary, with data by county, 1991/92-1992/93 and trends, annual rpt, S3610–1

Maryland local govt financial condition, including revenues by source, expenditures by function, and debt obligations, FY92 and trends, annual rpt, S3618–1.1

Maryland statistical abstract, general data, 1993-94 biennial rpt, S3605–1.2

Massachusetts municipal and county profiles, general data, 1992 annual rpt, C4712–2

Massachusetts public elementary/secondary education summary data, 1989/90-1991/92 and trends, annual rpt, S3810–3

Educational finance

Massachusetts public elementary/secondary school expenditures per pupil by program, by district, 1991/92, annual rpt, S3810–5
Michigan school district financial and enrollment data, with rankings, 1991/92, annual rpt, S3965–3
Minnesota postsecondary education finances, and enrollment by student characteristics, by type of school system, 1970s-93, biennial rpt, S4195–2.2
Minnesota public school enrollment, staff, and finances, by district and county, 1991/92 and trends, annual rpt, S4165–1
Mississippi higher education enrollment and degrees, by level and field, and finances, by State-supported instn, 1991/92, annual rpt, S4360–1
Mississippi public school enrollment, staff and salaries, and finances, by district, 1991/92 and trends, annual rpt, S4340–1
Missouri higher education revenues by source and expenditures by function, by instn, FY92 and trends, annual rpt, S4520–3.3
Missouri school finances, enrollment, grads, and staff, by county and school district, 1991/92, annual rpt, S4505–1
Montana property taxes levied, by purpose and county, 1991-92, biennial rpt, S4750–1.2
Nebraska property taxes levied for education, by county, 1991, annual rpt, S4950–1.4
Nebraska public school finances, including receipts by source and disbursements by function, by county and district, 1988/89, annual rpt, S4865–3
Nevada public school enrollment, test scores, teachers, and finances, by school district, 1990/91 and trends, annual rpt, S5035–2
Nevada statistical abstract, general data, 1992 biennial rpt, S5005–1.7
New Hampshire elementary and secondary education statistics, with selected data by school district, annual rpt series, S5200–1
New Jersey municipal and county data book, general data, 1992 annual rpt, C4712–4
New Mexico elementary/secondary school statistics, including grads, student test results, and finances, by school district, 1989/90-1991/92, annual rpt, S5575–4
New York State municipal and county statistical profiles, general data, 1993 annual rpt, C4712–7
North Carolina higher education library holdings and expenditures, by type and instn, 1991/92, annual rpt, U8013–1.2
North Carolina public school enrollment, grads, staff, and finances, with data by race, sex, and local district, 1991/92-1992/93 and trends, annual rpt, S5915–1
North Dakota public school revenues by source, expenditures by function, mill levies, and taxable value, by district, 1992/93 annual rpt, S6180–4
Ohio public school enrollment, finances, special programs, and staff, 1991/92 and trends, annual rpt, S6265–2
Oklahoma public school finances, personnel, enrollment, and facilities, by county and district, 1991/92 and trends, annual rpt, S6423–1

Oklahoma public school performance indicators, including students and achievement, finances, and staff, by district, 1990/91-1991/92 and trends, annual rpt, S6423–2
Oklahoma statistical abstract, general data, 1992 annual rpt, U8130–2.8
Oregon elementary and secondary education enrollment and finances, including data by school district and county, annual rpt series, S6590–1
Oregon library finances, staff, holdings, and services, for public, academic, and special libraries by instn, FY92 and trends, annual rpt, S6635–1
Pennsylvania elementary/secondary and higher education enrollment, grads, staff, and finances, by instn type, 1981/82-1996/97, recurring rpt, S6790–5.10
Pennsylvania higher education revenues, expenditures, and endowment funds, by instn type, FY91 and trends, annual rpt, S6790–5.4
Pennsylvania higher education revenues, expenditures, and endowment funds, by instn type, FY92 and trends, annual rpt, S6790–5.16
Rhode Island education expenditures by function and source of funds, by school district, 1991/92, annual rpt, S6970–1.2
Rhode Island statistical almanac, general data, 1993 annual rpt, C7975–1
South Carolina county govt finances, including property value and tax assessments, by county, FY92, annual rpt, S7127–2
South Carolina higher education enrollment, degrees, staff, and finances, by instn, 1992 and trends, annual rpt, S7185–2
South Carolina teachers salary schedules, educational revenues by source, and expenditures by function, by school district, 1991/92, annual rpt, S7145–1.5
South Dakota property tax and valuations, by property type and locality, FY92 annual rpt, S7380–1.2
South Dakota public higher education finances, staff, enrollment, degrees, and facilities, by instn, FY93 annual rpt, S7375–1
South Dakota school enrollment, finances, grads, and staff, by district, 1991/92 and trends, annual rpt, S7315–1
Tennessee higher education finances, student aid and expenses, and faculty and salaries, by instn, 1992/93 and trends, annual rpt, S7525–1.2
Tennessee public school enrollment, staff, finances, and operations, by county, city, and school district, 1991/92, annual rpt, S7490–2
Texas higher education enrollment, faculty, curricula, and finances, by instn, 1991/92 and trends, annual rpt, S7657–1
Texas public libraries, holdings, circulation, staff, and finances, by library and location, FY91, annual rpt, S7710–1
Texas State-supported colleges and universities revenues, detailed expenditures, and fund balances, by instn, FY92, annual rpt, S7655–2.2
Utah govt statistical review, fiscal and socioeconomic data, 1993 annual rpt, R9380–1.8

Utah higher education degrees, enrollment, staff, and finances, by public instn, with selected comparisons to instns in other States, 1993/94 annual rpt, S7895–2
Utah public libraries, services, staff, and finances, by library, 1992, annual rpt, S7808–1
Utah public schools, enrollment, attendance, personnel, and finances, by school district, 1991/92, annual rpt, S7815–1
Utah statistical abstract, general data, 1993 triennial rpt, U8960–1.3
Vermont higher education revenues by source, expenditures by function, and tuition/fees, by instn, and student aid trends, 1992 annual rpt, S8035–2.3
Virginia public school enrollment, grads, finances, and staff, by county and municipality, 1991/92, annual rpt, S8190–3
Washington State tax levies, by type of taxing district, 1988-92, annual rpt, S8415–1.2
West Virginia higher education revenues by source and expenditures by function, by instn, FY92 and trends, annual rpt, S8533–1.2
West Virginia property tax levy rates, by purpose and locale, FY93, annual rpt, S8640–3
West Virginia property valuations and tax levies by property class, and levies by purpose, by county, 1992/93 and trends, annual rpt, S8640–2
West Virginia public school finances, enrollment, staff, and programs, by county, 1992/93 and trends, annual rpt, S8540–4
Wisconsin elementary and secondary school enrollment, staff, costs, and State aid, by school district, 1992/93 and trends, annual rpt, S8795–2
Wyoming public school enrollment, staff, and finances, by county and district, 1991/92, annual rpt series, S8890–1
see also Educational employees pay
see also Federal aid to education
see also Federal aid to higher education
see also Federal aid to medical education
see also Federal aid to vocational education
see also State funding for education
see also State funding for higher education
see also State funding for medical education
see also State funding for vocational education
see also Student aid
see also Tuition and fees

Educational materials

Book publishing industry financial and operating data, by publisher type and size, and subject category, 1991 and trends, annual rpt, A3274–2
Elementary/secondary education data, with detail for mathematics including test scores and teacher preparation, by State, 1993 biennial rpt, A4355–1
Franchise operations and finances, by type of business, 1991/92 and trends, annual rpt, A5820–1
Library (research) holdings, expenditures by type, and staff, for 120 academic and nonacademic instns, US and Canada, FY92, annual rpt, A3365–1
Library materials prices, and acquisition expenditures by library type and State, 1993 annual compilation, C1650–3.4

Index by Subjects and Names

Nursing higher education program finances, faculty and clinical practice, and clinic/center operations, by instn characteristics, 1992/93 biennial rpt, A0615–5

State and local:

Alabama public school revenues by source and expenditures by object, by district, 1991/92, annual rpt, S0124–1.2

Colorado public school revenues by source, and expenditures by category, by school district, 1990, annual rpt, S1000–4.3

Delaware school district expenditures for operations, materials, and health and food services, 1991/92, annual rpt, S1430–1.4

Kansas school district revenues by source and expenditures by object, 1990/91, annual rpt, S2945–1

Maryland elementary and secondary education data, by county, 1991/92 and trends, annual rpt, S3610–2.13

Maryland elementary and secondary education data, by county, 1991/92, annual rpt, S3610–2.6, S3610–2.7

Oklahoma school revenues and expenditures, by program, county, and district, FY92, annual rpt, S6423–1.1

Oregon public school revenues by source and fund, and expenditures by fund, function, and object, 1991/92, annual rpt, S6590–1.16

Oregon public school revenues by source and fund, and expenditures by fund, function, and object, 1992/93, annual rpt, S6590–1.17

South Dakota public school expenditures by function and object, 1991/92, annual rpt, S7315–1.2

Utah public school revenues by source and expenditures by object, by State fund and school district, FY92, annual rpt, S7815–1.2

West Virginia public school equipment and materials value, by county, 1991/92, annual rpt, S8540–3

Wyoming public school revenues by source, expenditures by program and object, and bonded debt, by district, 1991/92, annual rpt, S8890–1.3

see also Audiovisual education

see also Textbooks

Educational reform

Elementary/secondary prospective teacher characteristics and opinions, survey of persons interested in alternative certification routes, 1992, R6350–7

Elementary/secondary school parental selection, parent and general public views, and local program characteristics and results, 1992 rpt, R3810–7

Elementary/secondary teacher views on education policy issues and selected reform proposals, Jan-Feb 1993 survey, B6045–7

High school vocational-academic program integration, pilot project evaluative data including achievement test results, student and teacher attitudes, and curricula, 1990, A8945–33

Mathematics elementary/secondary education policies and reform efforts, by State, 1993 biennial rpt, A4355–1

Public opinion on school problems, quality, and proposed reforms, by respondent characteristics, 1993 annual Gallup Poll, A8680–1.503

Teacher education and school reform goals, views of educators, 1992 recurring survey rpt, A3375–1

State and local:

Colorado State constitutional amendments on educational vouchers and other educational reforms, election results by county, 1992, biennial rpt, S1090–1

Massachusetts elementary/secondary school reform expenditures, by program, 1986-92, annual rpt, S3810–3

Tennessee executive views on educational reform issues, 1993 annual article, U8710–1.502

Educational research

Education profession issues, trends, and research results, monthly rpt, A8680–1

Education Week, issues and devs in elementary/secondary school programs, enrollment, finances, and staff, and selected higher education issues, weekly rpt, R4800–2

Elementary/secondary school superintendents views on usefulness of educational research, 1992 survey rpt, A0775–5

Higher education appropriations for FY94 compared to spending in FY93, by program, recurring feature, C2175–1.527, C2175–1.536

Higher education research and policy review, series, A1410–1

Library/info science school income by source, and expenditures by object, by instn, 1991/92 and trends, annual rpt, A3235–1.4

Southern States use of reporting systems to track college performance of recent high school grads, for 15 States, 1992, A8945–32

see also National Assessment of Educational Progress

Educational Research Service Inc.

Principal and assistant principal salaries in elementary and secondary schools, by enrollment size and expenditure level, 1991/92-1992/93, annual rpt, A7085–2

Educational retention rates

State and local:

Arkansas higher education freshman enrollment as percent of high school grads, by county and instn, fall 1991, annual rpt, S0690–1

Delaware retention rates by grade and district, 1991/92, annual rpt, S1430–1.2

Florida higher education student progression and retention rates, by race-ethnicity and sex, 1984/85-1990/91, annual rpt, S1725–1

Georgia county guide, general data, 1993 annual rpt, U6750–1

Kentucky public education profiles, with data by region and district, 1991/92 and trends, annual rpt, S3110–1

Maine public school enrollment, facilities, staff, and finances, with selected data by county and for private schools, 1991 and trends, annual rpt, S3435–1

Maryland elementary and secondary education data, by county, 1991/92, annual rpt, S3610–2.3

Massachusetts public elementary/secondary education summary data, 1989/90-1991/92 and trends, annual rpt, S3810–3

Educational tests

Minnesota postsecondary student persistence rates to 2nd and 4th years, by type of school system, 1984 and 1987 or 1989, biennial rpt, S4195–2.2

Missouri high school grads and retention from 9th grade, 1980-92, annual rpt, S4505–1.1

North Carolina high school dropouts and retention rates, by school district, 1991/92, annual rpt, S5915–1.1

South Carolina educational enrollment, by school type or level, program, race, and location, 1991/92, annual rpt, S7145–1.3

Virginia public high school grads and 9th grade enrollment 4 years earlier, by county and municipality, 1991/92, annual rpt, S8190–3

West Virginia public school promotions, retentions, and withdrawals, by county, 1991/92, annual rpt, S8540–3

see also School dropouts

Educational technology

Computer educational networks for children, subscribers and prices for 5 networks, 1993 article, C8900–1.524

Computer use at school by elementary/secondary students, by State, 1989, article, B8500–2.506

Elementary/secondary public schools use of selected technologies, 1992 vs 1991, article, R4800–2.508

State and local:

Connecticut elementary and secondary schools with selected facilities, cable TV, and outside telecommunication, 1991/92 biennial rpt, S1185–3

Utah educational technology initiative funding by source, 1991/92, annual rpt, S7815–1.1

see also Audiovisual education

see also Educational broadcasting

Educational television

see Educational broadcasting

Educational tests

Achievement test scores worldwide for math and science, for students age 13 in 14 countries, 1990, annual rpt, R3840–11.1

American College Test (ACT) scores, by sex and race-ethnicity, 1993, annual article, C2175–1.534

American College Test (ACT) scores by student characteristics, with student views on schools and education plans, 1992 and trends, annual rpt, R1960–6

Black American educational statistics, with comparisons to whites, 1970s-92, annual compilation, C6775–2.3

Black elementary/secondary student educational test results, for math, science, and/or reading, with comparisons to whites, 1993 rpt, R3840–21

Compensatory education program 3rd and 4th grade participant math and reading test scores, 1993 article, R4800–2.522

Dental student admission test scores and pre-dental grade averages, by instn, 1992/93, annual rpt, A1475–4.1

High school vocational-academic program integration, pilot project evaluative data including achievement test results, student and teacher attitudes, and curricula, 1990, A8945–33

Higher education instns, faculty, students, degrees, and finances, detailed data by State, 1993 annual rpt, C2175–1.531

Educational tests

Higher education student athlete average scores on college entrance exams, for freshmen entering Natl Collegiate Athletic Assn Div I instns, by major sport, 1990/91-1992/93, annual rpt, A7440–4

Hispanic American educational statistics, with comparisons to whites, 1970s-92, annual compilation, C6775–3.2

Law School Admission Tests administered, 1963/64-1992/93, annual rpt, A0970–1

Medical College Admission Test (MCAT) scores of osteopathy college freshmen, 1989-92, annual rpt, A0620–1

Medical school Asian vs white student performance indicators at Jefferson Medical School, including standardized test scores, 1981-92, article, A3273–8.503

Public support for achievement tests, and use in determining grade promotion, teacher pay, and school financing, 1993 annual Gallup Poll, A8680–1.503

Scholastic Aptitude Test (SAT) participants and/or scores, by education of parents, income, and race-ethnicity, 1992, C4215–1.501

Science and math elementary/secondary education, including student and teacher characteristics, and requirements, by State, 1991/92, biennial rpt, A4355–3

Scores on math and science proficiency, college entrance, and graduate record tests, 1970s-90s, recurring rpt, A3960–2.1

Secondary school 7th grade student mathematics and reading test performance at low- vs high-poverty schools, 1991, article, R4800–2.519

Southern States use of reporting systems to track college performance of recent high school grads, for 15 States, 1992, A8945–32

State social, economic, and govtl indicators, with rankings, 1993 semiannual rpt, B8500–1.7

Statistical profiles of 50 States and DC, general data, 1993 annual almanac, C4712–1

Theological school Graduate Record Exam (GRE) scores required for admission, fall 1992, annual rpt, A3376–1

Urban public school performance compared to natl goals for year 2000, with data on students, teachers, and finances, for 47 systems, 1990/91 and trends, A4425–4

State and local:

California socioeconomic and govtl data for municipalities, counties, and school districts, 1993 annual rpt, C4712–3

Connecticut public school data, including enrollment, staff, programs, finances, and student characteristics, 1991/92, biennial rpt, S1185–3

DC public school finances, enrollment, grads, and test scores, with data by school, 1987/88-1991/92, annual rpt, S1605–2

Delaware educational assessment scores, by grade and district, 1991/92, annual rpt, S1430–1

Florida higher education undergrad and grad admission test scores, and enrollment by score level, by State-supported instn, 1991/92, annual rpt, S1725–1

Florida municipal and county statistical profiles, general data, 1991 annual rpt, C4712–6

Georgia county guide, general data, 1993 annual rpt, U6750–1

Hawaii data book, general data, 1992 annual rpt, S2090–1.3

Idaho economic profile, general data, 1992 recurring rpt, S2218–2.3

Iowa higher education freshmen mean American College Test (ACT) scores, by instn, fall 1990, annual rpt, S2755–1

Louisiana scores on American College Test (ACT) and Scholastic Aptitude Test (SAT), 1985/86-1991/92, annual rpt, S3280–1.1

Maryland elementary and secondary education statistical summary, with data by county, 1991/92-1992/93 and trends, annual rpt, S3610–1

Massachusetts public elementary/secondary education summary data, 1989/90-1991/92 and trends, annual rpt, S3810–3

Minnesota high school student scores on college entrance tests, 1980/81-1991/92, biennial rpt, S4195–2.2

Mississippi public schools student assessment and functional literacy test result trends, 1988-92, annual rpt, S4340–1

Missouri American College Test (ACT) scores, by participant characteristics and/or higher education instn, 1993 annual rpt, S4520–3.1

Missouri student performance on basic skills and college entrance tests, 1991/92 and trends, annual rpt, S4505–1.1

Nevada public school enrollment, test scores, teachers, and finances, by school district, 1990/91 and trends, annual rpt, S5035–2

New Mexico elementary/secondary school statistics, including grads, student test results, and finances, by school district, 1989/90-1991/92, annual rpt, S5575–4

New Mexico work incentive program participant actual vs tested education levels, by county, monthly rpt quarterly table, S5620–2

North Carolina higher education freshmen Scholastic Aptitude Test (SAT) scores, by instn, fall 1992 and trends, annual rpt, U8013–1.3

Oklahoma public school performance indicators, including detailed achievement test data by grade, subject area, and district, 1991/92 and trends, annual rpt, S6423–2

Oklahoma statistical abstract, general data, 1992 annual rpt, U8130–2.8

South Carolina advanced placement candidates and exams taken, by school district, 1991/92, annual rpt, S7145–1.3

South Carolina public higher education freshmen average Scholastic Aptitude Test (SAT) scores, by instn, fall 1992, annual rpt, S7185–2

South Dakota achievement and college entrance test scores, 1991/92 and trends, annual rpt, S7315–1.1

Tennessee statistical abstract, general data, 1992/93 annual rpt, U8710–2.16

Texas prison inmate achievement test results, by sex, FY92, annual rpt, S7660–1

Utah American College Testing and advanced placement participation and performance, by subject area, 1992 and trends, annual rpt, S7815–1.1

Virginia public school student assessment test scores, 4 grades, by county and municipality, 1991/92, annual rpt, S8190–3

see also High school equivalency tests

see also National Assessment of Educational Progress

see also Occupational testing and certification

Educational vouchers

see Tuition and fees

Edwards, Chris R.

"Corporate Tax Burden", R9050–15.2

"President's Fiscal Year 1994 Budget", R9050–15.3

"Price of Mobility: Gasoline Taxes in America", R9050–15.6

"Property Taxes on the Rise Again Across Nation", R9050–15.7

"Special Report: Survey of State Tax Rates and Collections", R9050–14

"Tax Freedom Day 1993", R9050–15.4

"Washington's Largest Monument: The National Debt", R9050–15.1

"1993 Federal Tax Burden by State", R9050–15.5

Eggs

see Poultry industry and products

Egypt

Energy intl sourcebook, with detail on oil and gas industry operations, supply-demand, and prices, for approx 80 countries, 1970s-91, annual compilation, C6985–10.2

El-Khawas, Elaine

"Campus Trends, 1993", A1410–1.38

El Salvador

Statistical abstract of Latin America, detailed social, govtl, and economic data, 1992 annual rpt, U6250–1

Elderly

see Aged and aging

Elections

Black Americans elected to House of Representatives, vote shares by district and State, Nov 1992, article, R5685–4.501

Black elected officials, and characteristics of voting age population, with comparisons to whites, 1970s-91, annual compilation, C6775–2.4

Black voter participation, with detail for persons age 18-24 and comparisons to whites, biennially 1972-90, R3840–21

Congressional campaign finances and results, with data by candidate, and for leading contributors by type, 1990 election and trends, biennial rpt, R3828–2

Congressional campaign finances and results, with data by candidate, State, and for leading contributors by type, 1990 election and trends, biennial rpt, R3828–3

Congressional commerce and judiciary committee members election outcomes, Nov 1992, article, C1850–14.502

Europe public opinion on political, economic, and social issues, for 9 countries and 3 Soviet Union Republics, 1991 survey, C8915–8.1

Index by Subjects and Names

Elections

Hispanic American elected officials, registered voters, and voting, with comparisons to whites, 1970s-91, annual compilation, C6775–3.3

Hispanic American leader presidential candidate preference in 1992 election, 1993 annual survey article, C4575–1.511

Hispanic American population shares in 17 congressional districts that elected Hispanic Representatives in Nov 1992, article, C4575–1.502

Hispanic American voter candidate preferences in 1992 presidential election, in 5 States, Oct 1992 survey, article, C4575–1.501

Hispanic American vs non-Hispanic voter turnout, by demographic characteristics, Nov 1992 election, article, C4575–1.511

Japan Diet Lower House political party composition, 1993 article, R5650–2.544

Latin America statistical abstract, general data by country, 1992 annual rpt, U6250–1.9

Minority voting patterns in 1992 presidential election, by race-ethnicity, 1992 rpt, R8750–2.58

Municipal official election methods, and use of initiatives, referenda, recalls, and petitions, 1991, A5800–1.1

News media personnel views on 1992 presidential election coverage, candidates, and related issues, for natl media, Oct 1992 survey, C8915–4.25

Presidential election candidate choice, by voter religion, 1976-92 surveys, R8780–1.501

Presidential election voting patterns of moderate and conservative Democrats and Independents, 1976-92, article, A8510–1.1

Presidential primary election results and voter registration by county and district, by State, 1992 and trends, C2500–7

Public opinion on candidates and issues in 1992 presidential election, and related topics, series, C8915–4

Public opinion on 1992 presidential election campaign and related events, 1992 Gallup Polls, C4040–1.501, C4040–1.502, C4040–1.503, C4040–1.504, C4040–1.505

Results of elections for Federal offices and Governor, by State, county, major city, and party, 1992 and trends, biennial rpt, C2500–1

Results of presidential, congressional, and gubernatorial elections, by State, 1992 and trends, annual rpt, C2500–2

State social, economic, and govtl indicators, with rankings, 1993 semiannual rpt, B8500–1

State tax increases, with political party of Governors and legislators before vs after subsequent elections, for 17 States, 1991-92, U5085–2.8

Statistical profiles of 50 States and DC, general data, 1993 annual almanac, C4712–1

TV news coverage of presidential campaign, 1992 article, R3823–1.501

UK public opinion poll results deviation from natl election outcome, 1992 polls, article, A0610–1.503

Voter turnout and registration trends, by race-ethnicity and/or sex, 1960s-92, U4510–1.70

Voting patterns of men vs women in natl and statewide elections, 1950s-90, U4510–1.65

Women candidates in State-level elections, outcome summaries including campaign funds raised, voting by sex, and winner's race-ethnicity, 1992, U4510–4.4

Women State senate and house candidates and officeholders, by party and State, 1992 and trends, recurring rpt, U4510–1.64

State and local:

Alabama county data book, general data, 1992 annual rpt, S0121–2

Alabama election results, by district and/or county, 1992 general election, biennial rpt, S0205–1

Alaska election results, and voter registration and turnout, by district and precinct, 1992 general election, biennial rpt, S0337–1

Arizona election results and voter registration, by county and/or district, 1992 general election, biennial rpt, S0520–1

Arizona statistical abstract, general data, 1993 recurring rpt, U5850–2.11

Arkansas election results, by district and/or county, 1992 general election, biennial rpt, S0775–1

California election results, and voter registration and turnout, by district and/or county, 1992 and trends, biennial rpt, S0934–1

California statistical abstract, general data, 1992 annual rpt, S0840–2.15

Colorado election results and voter registration, by political party, and county and/or district, 1992, biennial rpt, S1090–1

Connecticut election results and voter registration and turnout, by location, 1992 general election, biennial rpt, S1265–1

DC election results and turnout, and voter registration, by ward and precinct, 1992, biennial series, S1525–1

Delaware election results, by district and/or county, 1992 general election, biennial rpt, S1365–1

Florida county data book, 1992/93 annual rpt, C6360–1

Florida election results, by county and/or district, 1992 general election, biennial rpt, S1800–1

Florida statistical abstract, general data, 1992 annual rpt, U6660–1.21

Georgia county guide, general data, 1993 annual rpt, U6750–1

Georgia election results by county, 1992 general election, biennial rpt, S1955–1

Georgia statistical abstract, general data, 1992-93 biennial rpt, U6730–1.11

Hawaii data book, general data, 1992 annual rpt, S2090–1.8

Hawaii election results, and voter registration by sex, by district and precinct, 1992, biennial series, S2077–1

Idaho election results and voter registration, by county and/or district and precinct, 1992 general election, biennial rpt, S2305–1

Idaho school district finances, including tax levy election amounts requested and approved by district, 1991/92, annual rpt, S2225–2

Illinois election results, and voter registration trends, by county and/or district, 1992 general election, biennial rpt, S2445–1

Indiana election results, by county and district, with voter registration, 1992 primary and general elections, biennial rpt, S2702–1

Iowa election results, by county and/or district, 1992 general election, biennial rpt, S2865–1

Kansas election results, by county and district, 1992 primary and general elections, biennial rpt, S3030–1

Kansas statistical abstract, general data, 1991/92 annual rpt, U7095–2.4

Kentucky election results, by county, district, and circuit, 1992, annual rpt, S3213–1

Louisiana presidential election results, by parish and precinct, 1992 general election, quadrennial rpt, S3370–3

Maine election results, by district, county, and municipality, 1992 general election, biennial rpt, S3490–1

Maryland election results, by county and district, 1992 general election, biennial rpt, S3615–1

Maryland statistical abstract, general data, 1993-94 biennial rpt, S3605–1.13

Massachusetts election results and voter registration, by local area, 1992 and trends, biennial rpt, S3920–1

Michigan election results and voter registration, by county and/or district, 1992 general election, biennial rpt, S4020–1

Minnesota election results and voter registration, by locality, 1992 primary and general elections, biennial rpt, S4255–1

Mississippi statistical abstract, general data, 1992 annual rpt, U3255–4.13

Missouri election results and voter registration, by district and/or county, with directory of govt officials, 1992 general election, biennial rpt, S4580–1

Montana election results and voter registration, by county and/or district, 1992 general election, biennial rpt, S4760–1

Nebraska election results, and voter registration by party, by county and/or district, 1992 general and primary elections, biennial rpt, S4955–1

Nevada election results, and voter registration and turnout, by county, 1992 general election, biennial rpt, S5125–1

Nevada statistical abstract, general data, 1992 biennial rpt, S5005–1.3

New Hampshire election results, by county and locality, 1992, biennial rpt, S5255–1

New Jersey election results and voter registration, by location, 1992 general election, annual rpt, S5440–1

New Mexico election results, and voter registration by party, by location, 1992 general election, biennial rpt, S5655–1

New York State general election results by county and district, Nov 1992, biennial rpt, S5750–1

New York State statistical yearbook, general data, 1992 annual rpt, U5100–1.4

North Carolina election results, by county and/or district, 1992 general election, biennial rpt, S5920–1

Elections

North Dakota election results and historical trends, including data on ballot measures and detail by location, 1880s-1992, biennial rpt, U8080–1

North Dakota election results, by location, 1992 general election, biennial rpt, S6205–1

Ohio election results and voter registration, by local area, 1991-92 and trends, biennial rpt, S6380–1

Oklahoma election results and voter registration, by county and/or district, 1992, biennial rpt, S6425–1

Oklahoma statistical abstract, general data, 1992 annual rpt, U8130–2.6

Oregon election results and voter registration and turnout, by county and/or district, 1992 general election, biennial rpt, S6665–1

Pennsylvania statistical abstract, general data, 1992 recurring rpt, U4130–6.6

Rhode Island statistical almanac, general data, 1993 annual rpt, C7975–1.1

South Carolina statistical abstract, general data, 1993 annual rpt, S7125–1.9

South Dakota election results, and voter registration by party, by county, 1992 general election, biennial rpt, S7390–1

Tennessee election results, by district and/or county, 1992 general election, biennial rpt, S7580–1

Tennessee statistical abstract, general data, 1992/93 annual rpt, U8710–2.14

Texas election results and voter registration, by district and/or county, 1992 general election, biennial series, S7750–1

Utah election results and voter registration and turnout, by county and/or district, 1992 general election, biennial rpt, S7875–1

Utah statistical abstract, general data, 1993 triennial rpt, U8960–1.8

Virginia election results by jurisdiction, and voter registration and turnout, 1992 and Jan 1993 elections, annual rpt, S8195–1

Washington State election results and voter registration, by county and/or district, 1992 general election, annual rpt, S8425–1

West Virginia election results and voter registration, by county and party, 1992 and trends, biennial rpt, S8630–1

West Virginia public school finances, including tax levy and bond election results, bonding potential, and levy proceeds, by county, 1992/93 and trends, annual rpt, S8540–4.1

Wisconsin Blue Book, general data, 1993-94 biennial rpt, S8780–1.2, S8780–1.3

Wyoming election results by county, district, and precinct, 1992, annual rpt and govtl directory, S9000–1

see also Campaign funds
see also Electoral districts and precincts
see also Officials
see also Political action committees
see also Political broadcasting
see also Political conventions
see also Referenda
see also Voter registration

Electoral districts and precincts

Congressional campaign fund finances, with expenditures by item and contributions by donor type, by candidate, district, and State, 1990 elections, C2500–6

Index by Subjects and Names

Election results for Federal offices and Governor, by State, county, major city, and party, with voter registration and turnout, 1992 and trends, biennial rpt, C2500–1

Presidential primary election results and voter registration by county and district, by State, 1992 and trends, C2500–7

State and local:

Alabama election results, by district and/or county, 1992 general election, biennial rpt, S0205–1

Alaska election results, and voter registration and turnout, by district and precinct, 1992 general election, biennial rpt, S0337–1

Arizona election results and voter registration, by county and/or district, 1992 general election, biennial rpt, S0520–1

Arkansas election results, by district and/or county, 1992 general election, biennial rpt, S0775–1

California election results, and voter registration and turnout, by district and/or county, 1992 and trends, biennial rpt, S0934–1

Colorado election results and voter registration, by political party, and county and/or district, 1992, biennial rpt, S1090–1

Connecticut election results and voter registration and turnout, by location, 1992 general election, biennial rpt, S1265–1

DC election results and turnout, and voter registration, by ward and precinct, 1992, biennial series, S1525–1

Delaware election results, by district and/or county, 1992 general election, biennial rpt, S1365–1

Florida election results, by county and/or district, 1992 general election, biennial rpt, S1800–1

Georgia election results by county, 1992 general election, biennial rpt, S1955–1

Hawaii data book, general data, 1992 annual rpt, S2090–1.8

Hawaii election results, and voter registration by sex, by district and precinct, 1992, biennial series, S2077–1

Idaho election results and voter registration, by county and/or district and precinct, 1992 general election, biennial rpt, S2305–1

Illinois election results, and voter registration trends, by county and/or district, 1992 general election, biennial rpt, S2445–1

Indiana election results, by county and district, with voter registration, 1992 primary and general elections, biennial rpt, S2702–1

Iowa election results, by county and/or district, 1992 general election, biennial rpt, S2865–1

Kansas election results, by county and district, 1992 primary and general elections, biennial rpt, S3030–1

Kentucky election results, by county, district, and circuit, 1992, annual rpt, S3213–1

Louisiana presidential election results, by parish and precinct, 1992 general election, quadrennial rpt, S3370–3

Maine election results, by district, county, and municipality, 1992 general election, biennial rpt, S3490–1

Maryland election results, by county and district, 1992 general election, biennial rpt, S3615–1

Massachusetts election results and voter registration, by local area, 1992 and trends, biennial rpt, S3920–1

Michigan election results and voter registration, by county and/or district, 1992 general election, biennial rpt, S4020–1

Minnesota election results and voter registration, by locality, 1992 primary and general elections, biennial rpt, S4255–1

Mississippi statistical abstract, general data, 1992 annual rpt, U3255–4.13

Missouri election results and voter registration, by district and/or county, with directory of govt officials, 1992 general election, biennial rpt, S4580–1

Montana election results and voter registration, by county and/or district, 1992 general election, biennial rpt, S4760–1

Nebraska election results, and voter registration by party, by county and/or district, 1992 general and primary elections, biennial rpt, S4955–1

Nevada election results, and voter registration and turnout, by county, 1992 general election, biennial rpt, S5125–1

New Hampshire election results, by county and locality, 1992, biennial rpt, S5255–1

New Jersey election results and voter registration, by location, 1992 general election, annual rpt, S5440–1

New Mexico election results, and voter registration by party, by location, 1992 general election, biennial rpt, S5655–1

New York State general election results by county and district, Nov 1992, biennial rpt, S5750–1

New York State statistical yearbook, general data, 1992 annual rpt, U5100–1.4

North Carolina election results, by county and/or district, 1992 general election, biennial rpt, S5920–1

North Dakota election results and historical trends, including data on ballot measures and detail by location, 1880s-1992, biennial rpt, U8080–1

North Dakota election results, by location, 1992 general election, biennial rpt, S6205–1

Ohio election results and voter registration, by local area, 1991-92 and trends, biennial rpt, S6380–1

Oklahoma election results and voter registration, by county and/or district, and number of precincts by county, 1992 biennial rpt, S6425–1

Oregon election results and voter registration and turnout, by county and/or district, 1992 general election, biennial rpt, S6665–1

Pennsylvania statistical abstract, general data, 1992 recurring rpt, U4130–6.6

South Dakota election results, and voter registration by party, by county, 1992 general election, biennial rpt, S7390–1

Tennessee election results, by district and/or county, 1992 general election, biennial rpt, S7580–1

Index by Subjects and Names

Electric power

Utah election results and voter registration and turnout, by county and/or district, 1992 general election, biennial rpt, S7875–1

Virginia election results by jurisdiction, and voter registration and turnout, 1992 and Jan 1993 elections, annual rpt, S8195–1

Washington State election results and voter registration, by county and/or district, 1992 general election, annual rpt, S8425–1

West Virginia election results and voter registration, by county and party, 1992 and trends, biennial rpt, S8630–1

Wisconsin Blue Book, general data, 1993-94 biennial rpt, S8780–1.3

Wyoming election results by county, district, and precinct, 1992, annual rpt and govtl directory, S9000–1

see also Wards, city

Electric appliances

see Household appliances and equipment

Electric power

- Apartment building (conventionally financed) detailed income and expense ratios for US and Canada, by building type, metro area, and US region, 1991 and trends, annual rpt, A5600–1
- Apartment building (federally subsidized) detailed income and expense ratios, by building and subsidy type, building age, metro area, and region, 1991 and trends, annual rpt, A5600–5
- Auto operating costs for electric vs gas powered cars, and public opinion on electric car ownership, 1993 articles, C2710–3.533
- Brazil energy supply-demand by fuel source, with electricity generated and costs, and nuclear plants and capacity, 1993 article, B6800–1.508
- Business, regulatory, and technological devs concerning electric utilities, with industry financial statements, bimonthly rpt, A4700–4
- Capital spending by electric utilities, by function and region, and capacity addition plans, 1992-97, annual article, C6985–6.503
- China and US socioeconomic and infrastructure indicators comparison, 1993 rpt, R4105–82.8
- Coal imports for electric utilities, and world electricity production, by country, 1980s-91, annual rpt, A7400–2.1
- Commonwealth of Independent States electricity generation by Republic, and natural gas vs other fuel use for generation, projected to 2005, article, C6985–1.514
- Condominium, cooperative, and planned unit dev detailed expenses, for US and Canada, by building characteristics, metro area, and US region, 1991, annual rpt, A5600–3
- Consumption of fossil energy resources and electricity from hydro and nuclear power, 1960s-91, annual rpt, A1775–3.6
- Finances, sales, and capacity of electric utilities, with data by sector and region, 1993 annual feature, C5800–28.507
- Financial and operating ratios for electric utilities, by customer size class and region, 1990, annual article, A2625–1.501

Financial performance and growth rankings for approx 1,000 top corporations, with comparisons by industry group, 1993 annual rpt, C3950–1.505

Financial performance rankings of top 100 electric utilities, 1992, annual article, C6985–6.508

Generation from coal and nuclear fuels, and coal spot purchases by approx 20 utilities, monthly rpt, C5226–1

Heating equipment and appliance shipments, by type of energy consumed, quarterly rpt, A1775–1

Higher education physical plant operations, costs, employment, salaries, and energy use, by instn and region, 1991/92, recurring rpt, A3183–1

Income and operating data by type of company, and publicly owned utilities directory, US and outlying areas, 1993 annual directory, A2625–1.501

Iron and steel industry consumption of electric power, 1988-92, annual rpt, A2000–2.3

Japan energy supply-demand and outlook, by fuel source, 1980s-2000, recurring article, R5650–2.536

Latin America statistical abstract, general data by country, 1992 annual rpt, U6250–1.23

Mass transit system energy use by source, employee compensation, and labor costs, 1970s-91, annual rpt, A2650–1.2

Natural gas consumption for electric power generation, with industry sales and revenues, by State and census div, 1960s-91, annual rpt, A1775–3.4

Natural gas sales and prices, by consuming sector, monthly rpt, A1775–2

Office building detailed income and expense data, and energy use, US and Canada, by building characteristics, metro area, and US region, 1991 and trends, annual rpt, A5600–2

Operating and financial composite ratios for corporations, with establishments and receipts, for approx 200 industries, by asset size, FY90, annual rpt, C7800–1

Operating data for top 100 electric utilities, including generating capacity and efficiency, peak demand, and fuel consumption, 1992, annual article, C6985–6.512

Private vs public utility revenues and consumption, by customer sector, 1990, annual article, A2625–1.501

Shopping center detailed income and expense data, by building characteristics, metro area, and region, 1991, annual rpt, A5600–6

Sourcebook of oil and gas industry, with supply-demand comparisons to other energy types, 1991 and trends, annual compilation, C6985–9.5

State social, economic, and govtl indicators, with rankings, 1993 semiannual rpt, B8500–1.12

Statistical profiles of 50 States and DC, general data, 1993 annual almanac, C4712–1

Statistical yearbook of electric utility financial and operating data, by State and census div, 1991 and trends, annual rpt, A4700–1

Steel mill electricity consumption, for individual mini and market mills, 1992 annual feature, C7000–8.501

Sulfur dioxide emission allowance trading program, State regulatory issues and related data by State and major utility, 1992 rpt, A8195–12

Supply-demand and price data for energy resources, including by country and producing State, commodity yearbook for 1993, C2400–1

Supply-demand and price data for energy resources, including by country and producing State, commodity yearbook Jan-Sept 1993 updates, C2400–2

Supply-demand, and utility capacity and fuel requirements, detailed data by US and Canadian region, 1992-2002, annual rpt, A8630–2

Supply-demand by energy source and consuming sector, 1947-2010, periodic basic data book, A2575–14.1

Supply-demand for non-oil energy sources, 1970s-2010, annual rpt, C6985–5.3

Utility (publicly owned) trends and devs, bimonthly rpt, A2625–1

Utility industry devs, and production by region, monthly rpt, C5800–28

Utility mgmt, technology, regulatory, and operating devs, monthly rpt, C6985–6

Utility regulatory agency policies and practices, and industry financial and operating data, by utility type and agency, 1991/92 annual rpt, A7015–3

World energy supply-demand, by fuel source and sector, by region and country, 1992/93 biennial rpt, R9455–1.7

State and local:

- Alabama statistical abstract, general data, 1992 recurring rpt, U5680–2.12
- Alaska public utility financial and operating data, by company and utility type, 1991 and trends, with FY92 regulatory info, annual rpt, S0280–4
- Arizona business activity indicators, including housing market, population, CPI, and industrial purchasing, monthly rpt, U0280–1
- Arizona statistical abstract, general data, 1993 recurring rpt, U5850–2.20
- Arkansas public utility financial, operating, and regulatory data, by utility type and company, 1992 annual rpt, S0757–1
- California economic indicators, bimonthly rpt, S0840–1
- California electrical energy resources surcharge revenue, FY75-92, annual rpt, S0835–1.6
- California public utility and transportation regulatory data, including revenue requests and rates of return by company, FY92 annual rpt, S0930–1
- California statistical abstract, general data, 1992 annual rpt, S0840–2.10
- Colorado property assessed valuation, by property type and county, and for regulated industries by company, 1991-92, annual rpt, S1055–3
- Florida public utility regulatory and operating data, by company and utility type, 1992 and trends, annual rpt, S1790–1
- Florida statistical abstract, general data, 1992 annual rpt, U6660–1.15

Electric power

Georgia statistical abstract, general data, 1992-93 biennial rpt, U6730–1.8

Hawaii data book, general data, 1992 annual rpt, S2090–1.17

Idaho public utility regulatory data, and commission finances, FY92, annual rpt, S2290–1

Illinois electric utility sales and operating revenues, energy sold, and customers served, by class of service and company, 1991-92, annual rpt, S2410–1.2

Maine statistical summary, general economic and social data, 1992 recurring rpt, S3434–1

Maryland statistical abstract, general data, 1993-94 biennial rpt, S3605–1.10

Mississippi statistical abstract, general data, 1992 annual rpt, U3255–4.14

Montana electric power generated and license taxes paid, FY88-92, biennial rpt, S4750–1.1

Nevada statistical abstract, general data, 1992 biennial rpt, S5005–1.11

New Jersey economic indicators, including employment, building permits, and retail trade, monthly rpt, S5425–1

New Mexico public utility operating, financial, and regulatory data, by utility type, FY92 annual rpt, S5645–1

New York State electric power production, quarterly rpt, S5735–2

New York State public utility financial and operating data, by utility type and company, 1988-92, annual rpt, S5795–1

New York State statistical yearbook, general data, 1992 annual rpt, U5100–1.12

North Carolina public utility financial, operating, and regulatory data, by utility type and company, 1990 and trends, annual rpt, S5917–2

Ohio natural gas and electricity supply-demand by utility and consuming sector, 1992-93 and trends, annual rpt, S6355–1

Oklahoma business activity indicators, monthly rpt, U8130–1

Oklahoma statistical abstract, general data, 1992 annual rpt, U8130–2.18

Pennsylvania business activity indicators, monthly rpt, U4110–1

Pennsylvania energy supply-demand and prices by fuel type, with electric power info by utility, 1960s-90, recurring rpt, S6810–3

Pennsylvania statistical abstract, general data, 1992 recurring rpt, U4130–6.9

South Carolina economic condition, including energy and transportation data, 1970s-92, annual rpt, S7125–3.3

South Carolina public service commission regulatory activities, with financial and operating data for individual utilities and railroads, FY92 annual rpt, S7235–1

South Carolina statistical abstract, general data, 1993 annual rpt, S7125–1.8

Tennessee economic indicator trends and forecasts, with data by industry div and manufacturing group, 1982-2001, annual rpt, S7560–1

Tennessee statistical abstract, general data, 1992/93 annual rpt, U8710–2.10

Texas electric utility financial and operating data, 9 largest investor-owned utilities, 1988-92, annual rpt, S7740–1

Texas trade, transportation, and public utilities employment, by SIC 2- and 3-digit industry and detailed occupation, 2nd qtr 1991, triennial survey rpt, S7675–1.31

Utah economic and business activity review and indicators, monthly rpt, U8960–2

Utah statistical abstract, general data, 1993 triennial rpt, U8960–1.13

Vermont public utility financial and operating data, by company, 1986-91, biennial rpt, S8100–1

Virginia business activity indicators, by local area, monthly rpt, U1120–1

Virginia electric power sales, quarterly rpt, S8205–4

Washington State electric utility financial and operating data, by company, 1982-91, annual rpt, S8450–1.2

Washington State public service and utility companies property value, by company and county, 1992, annual rpt, S8415–1.4

West Virginia commercial/industrial electric power sold, monthly rpt, S8534–1

Wisconsin electric power sales, monthly rpt, S8750–1

see also Electric power and heat cogeneration

see also Electric power plants and equipment

see also Electric power prices

see also Electrical machinery and equipment

see also Hydroelectric power

see also Nuclear power

see also Rural cooperatives

see also Rural electrification

Electric power and heat cogeneration

Canada natural gas exports to US for cogeneration plants, 1989/90-1995/96, article, C6985–1.536

Capacity, operating status, and natural gas demand for cogeneration projects, by census div, Sept 1990, annual rpt, C6985–3.2

Electric power conservation

see Energy conservation

Electric power generation and capacity

see Electric power plants and equipment

Electric power plants and equipment

Brazil nuclear power plants and capacity, and uranium and enriched fuel requirements, under 3 dev plans, 1990, 2000, and 2010, article, B6800–1.508

Capacity additions, and equipment orders and shipments, with data by location and facility, 1991 annual rpt, A4700–2

Capacity of planned fossil fuel-fired electric power plants, by fuel type, 2001-2011, article, C6985–6.508

Capacity of planned fossil fuel-fired electric power plants, 2001-2011, article, C5226–1.508

China nuclear power generating capacity, by unit, 1993 article, B6800–1.509

Coal deliveries and prices for individual electric power plants, by utility, State, and census div, monthly rpt, A7400–9

Construction (industrial) contract awards, by type of plant, weekly rpt monthly table, C5800–2

Construction and capacity outlook, including data by region and fuel source, 1992-2001, annual feature, C5800–28.501

Construction expenditures of electric utility industry, with detail by type of plant, 1991-95, recurring article, A4700–4.505

Construction of electric power plants in 1993, by type, utility, and region, and forecast capacity for 1993-2001, annual feature, C5800–28.503

Costs for electric power generation by type of generating unit, 1993 article, C6985–6.504

Cuba electricity generating capacity, by fuel source, 1980s-2000, annual rpt, U6250–1.23

Finances, sales, and capacity of electric utilities, with data by sector and region, 1993 annual feature, C5800–28.507

Finland nuclear generation and capacity of operating reactors, and capacity of nonnuclear plants to be commissioned by 2000, 1993 article, B6800–1.507

Generating capacity additions not yet under construction, 1992-2001, article, C6985–6.501

Generating capacity and generation, for utilities by type and industrial plants, 1970-91, article, C6985–6.504

Generating capacity and production by fuel source, and transmission line mileage, for US and Canada, 1992 or 1993 and 2002, article, C6985–6.510

Generating unit addition plans, for combustion turbine and coal-fired units, and generation requirement outlook, 1993 article, A2625–1.502

Installed and planned generating capacity by fuel source, and transmission line mileage, by US and Canadian region, 1992-2002, annual rpt, A8630–2

Installed capacity and kWh generated, by type of company and for individual locally owned utilities, 1993 annual directory, A2625–1.501

Japan electric generation capacity by fuel source, and nuclear power plant operating rates, 1993 recurring article, R5650–2.536

Natural gas resource outlook, with cost, capacity, and pollutant emissions of gas-fired vs coal-fired and/or nuclear plants, 1993 article, C6985–1.527

Nonutility coal- or coke-fired plants entering commercial service in 1992, with generating capacity, for 8 plants, 1993 article, C5226–1.512

Nuclear power generation trends and devs, with related data on individual reactor capacity and completion status, quarterly rpt, B6790–1

Nuclear power plant (non-US) capacity factors and cumulative generation, by plant, 1993 annual feature, B6790–1.503

Nuclear power plant capability factors and gross heat rates, 1980-92, article, C6985–6.508

Nuclear power plant capacity factors and cumulative generation, by plant, 1993 annual feature, B6790–1.502

Nuclear reactors in operation, with capacity, electricity generation, and construction, by unit and country, 1992, annual rpt, B6800–2.2

Operating data for top 100 electric utilities, including generating capacity, and transmission and distribution equipment, 1992, annual article, C6985–6.512

Public opinion on electric and magnetic fields (EMF), including reaction to having high-voltage transmission lines nearby, 1987-93 surveys, article, A4700–4.503

Index by Subjects and Names

Statistical profiles of 50 States and DC, general data, 1993 annual almanac, C4712–1

Statistical yearbook of electric utility financial and operating data, by State and census div, 1991 and trends, annual rpt, A4700–1

Steam-powered plants, capacity, generation, and fuel use and costs, by fuel type, utility, and location, 1991, annual rpt, A7400–7

Steam-powered plants electricity generated and fuel use by type, by utility and State, monthly rpt, A7400–8

Sulfur dioxide emission allowance trading program, State regulatory issues and related data by State and major utility, 1992 rpt, A8195–12

Sulfur dioxide emissions reduction methods used by electric power plants, 1993 articles, C6985–6.510

Summer demand and resources, by region, June-Sept 1993, annual article, C5800–28.508

Transmission facility additions/upgrades planned, by facility and region, winter 1992/93, C5800–28.504

Transmission line mileage existing and planned in US and Canada, 1991 and 2001, article, C6985–6.506

Transmission line mileage in 1991 and additions planned for 1992-96, by voltage capacity, article, C6985–6.501

Utility industry capacity and generating data, 1933 and 1991, article, A4700–4.503

Utility industry devs, and production by region, monthly rpt, C5800–28

Utility power delivery equipment voltage level upgrades completed or planned, and system characteristics, for 20 substations, 1993 article, C6985–6.512

Waste-to-energy plants by planning or operational status, 1984-93, article, C5800–2.541

World electric power plant capacity on order outside North America, for developed and developing countries by region, 1993-2000, article, C6985–6.509

State and local:

Arizona statistical abstract, general data, 1993 recurring rpt, U5850–2.20

California electric power generating costs at best performing plants, for 6 types of energy sources, 1993 article, C6985–6.507

California statistical abstract, general data, 1992 annual rpt, S0840–2.7

Georgia statistical abstract, general data, 1992-93 biennial rpt, U6730–1.8

Hawaii data book, general data, 1992 annual rpt, S2090–1.17

Maryland electric generating capacity by fuel type and ownership class, 1987 and 1990, biennial rpt, S3605–1.10

Mississippi statistical abstract, general data, 1992 annual rpt, U3255–4.14

Nebraska electrical transmission line construction regulatory activities, FY91-92, biennial rpt, S4940–1

New York State value of electric power plants in place, by company, 1988-92, annual rpt, S5795–1

North Carolina electric power generation and capacity, by utility and type of plant, 1990 and trends, annual rpt, S5917–2

Pennsylvania energy supply-demand and prices by fuel type, with electric power info by utility, 1960s-90, recurring rpt, S6810–3

South Carolina public service commission regulatory activities, with financial and operating data for individual utilities and railroads, FY92 annual rpt, S7235–1

Tennessee statistical abstract, general data, 1992/93 annual rpt, U8710–2.10

Texas electric utility financial and operating data, 9 largest investor-owned utilities, 1988-92, annual rpt, S7740–1

Washington State electric utility financial and operating data, by company, 1982-91, annual rpt, S8450–1.2

Electric power prices

Average bills for residential and industrial/commercial sectors, 1983-92, annual feature, C5800–28.507

Household appliance average electricity costs, for 1972 and 1991 models by appliance type, 1992, biennial rpt, A3350–3

Industrial electric power and natural gas costs, by State, 1991 or 1992, article, C5800–12.512

Northeast region industrial electric power average bills, by State, 1985-91, recurring rpt, S3434–1

Rate increases requested and approved, quarterly 1992, article, A4700–4.504

Rates for public, private, and cooperative utilities, by customer sector and State, 1990, annual feature, A2625–1.501

Residential electric bills, for 10 States, 1980-91, annual rpt, S5917–2

Residential electric costs for 12 utilities with highest and lowest rates, summer 1992, annual article, C6985–6.508

Residential electric costs for 12 utilities with highest and lowest rates, winter 1991/92, annual article, C6985–6.502

Residential monthly bills, for electric power and other energy, and telephone, in approx 300 cities, quarterly rpt, A0150–1

State economic dev condition indicators, including economic performance, business vitality, growth capacity, and tax/fiscal system, by State, 1993 annual rpt, R4225–1.1

Statistical yearbook of electric utility financial and operating data, by State and census div, 1991 and trends, annual rpt, A4700–1

Trends in electric power prices by consuming sector, 1960-91, annual compilation, C6985–9.3

Utility costs for fossil fuel deliveries by type, and retail electricity prices by sector, 1973-91, annual rpt, C6985–3.4

Utility regulatory agency policies and practices, and industry financial and operating data, by utility type and agency, 1991/92 annual rpt, A7015–3

State and local:

Alaska public utility financial and operating data, by company and utility type, 1991 and trends, with FY92 regulatory info, annual rpt, S0280–4

Delaware data book, general data, 1993 annual rpt, S1375–4

Florida public utility regulatory and operating data, by company and utility type, 1992 and trends, annual rpt, S1790–1

Electrical machinery and equipment

Hawaii data book, general data, 1992 annual rpt, S2090–1.17

Idaho average residential electric and gas bill, by utility, FY92 and trends, annual rpt, S2290–1

Idaho economic profile, general data, 1992 recurring rpt, S2218–2.6

Nevada statistical abstract, general data, 1992 biennial rpt, S5005–1.11

New Mexico public utility operating, financial, and regulatory data, by utility type, FY92 annual rpt, S5645–1

New York State electric power customers, revenues, kWh sales, and average bill, by customer class, 1988-92, annual rpt, S5795–1

North Carolina public utility financial, operating, and regulatory data, by utility type and company, 1990 and trends, annual rpt, S5917–2

Pennsylvania energy supply-demand and prices by fuel type, with electric power info by utility, 1960s-90, recurring rpt, S6810–3

South Carolina economic condition, including energy and transportation data, 1970s-92, annual rpt, S7125–3.3

South Carolina public service commission regulatory activities, with financial and operating data for individual utilities and railroads, FY92 annual rpt, S7235–1

Tennessee statistical abstract, general data, 1992/93 annual rpt, U8710–2.10

Texas electric utility financial and operating data, 9 largest investor-owned utilities, 1988-92, annual rpt, S7740–1

Vermont residential typical electric bills, by utility, Dec 1992, biennial rpt, S8100–1

Electric utilities

see Electric power

see Electric power plants and equipment

see Electric power prices

see Nuclear power

see Public utilities

see Rural cooperatives

see Rural electrification

Electrical machinery and equipment

Aluminum shipments by end-use market and product type, 1982-92, annual rpt, A0400–2.1

Earnings of production workers in electric/electronic equipment industry, monthly rpt, B6800–1

Engineers salaries by industry group, census div, selected metro area, and years since college degree, 1993, annual survey rpt, A0685–5

Engineers salaries by industry group, census div, selected metro area, degree level, and years since college degree, 1993, annual survey rpt, A0685–3

Executive compensation and components, by industry div and major manufacturing group, 1991, annual rpt, R4105–19

Financial performance and growth rankings for approx 1,000 top corporations, with comparisons by industry group, 1993 annual rpt, C3950–1.505

Financial ratios and performance, for over 350 SIC 4-digit industries, FY88-92, annual rpt, A6400–3

Heavy electric power generating equipment orders, shipments, and exports, by type of equipment, 1991 annual rpt, A4700–2

Electrical machinery and equipment

Operating and financial composite ratios for corporations, with establishments and receipts, for approx 200 industries, by asset size, FY90, annual rpt, C7800–1

Plastics industry production and sales by resin type, consumption by end-use market, and operating characteristics, 1992 and trends, annual rpt, A8920–1

Sales and marketing of electrical equipment, special articles and features, monthly rpt, C4725–5

Shipment trends by selected electrical equipment type, 1991-93, article, C6985–6.501

Shipment value, employment, and foreign trade, for electronics industry, by sector and product type, 1980s-92, annual rpt, A4725–1.2

Wholesalers market conditions, by geographic area, 1992 annual article, C4725–5.501

Wholesalers, sales, employment, and facility size, top 250 companies, 1992, annual article, C4725–5.506

State and local:

- Arizona statistical abstract, general data, 1993 recurring rpt, U5850–2.17
- Florida statistical abstract, general data, 1992 annual rpt, U6660–1.12
- Texas trade, transportation, and public utilities employment, by SIC 2- and 3-digit industry and detailed occupation, 2nd qtr 1991, triennial survey rpt, S7675–1.31

see also Batteries

see also Electronics industry and products

see also Engines and motors

see also Household appliances and equipment

see also under By Industry in the "Index by Categories"

Electromagnetic radiation

see Radiation

Electronic data processing

see Computer industry and products

see Computer sciences

see Computer use

see Electronic mail systems

see Information storage and retrieval systems

Electronic funds transfer

Convenience stores offering special services, including use of debit cards, 1992 and trends, annual survey rpt, A6735–1, A6735–2

Food store acceptance of credit and debit cards, by type of purchase, company size, and region, 1992, annual rpt, A4950–5.4

Retail store credit operations, including debit card acceptance and average sales, 1992 annual survey, C5150–4.504

Retail store debit card acceptance rate, by selected store type, 1992 survey article, C5150–4.503

State and local:

Washington State automated clearinghouse transactions, 1988-92, annual rpt, S8455–1

see also Automated tellers

Electronic games

Amusement equipment in use, and revenue, by type of equipment including video games and pinball machines, 1982 and 1990-92, annual rpt, C9470–1

Computer game use at work by info system managers, and impact on productivity, 1993 survey article, C5800–7.549

Convenience stores offering special services, including video games, 1992 and trends, annual survey rpt, A6735–1, A6735–2

Sales and stock performance, for 6 video game manufacturers, 1993 article, C3950–1.521

Shipments and value, by type of toy and game, 1991-92, annual rpt, A9095–1

Electronic mail systems

Corporate executive strategic info mgmt, including communications methods and use of nonfinancial performance measures, 1992 survey, R4105–78.25

Facsimile machine complaints most frequently made by secretaries, 1993 Chicago area survey, article, C4687–1.511

Facsimile transmission portable computer modem market shares by board type, and shipments by selected specifications, 1990-97, article, C1850–2.507

Mailboxes installed, 1981-91, article, C1850–5.505

Electronic surveillance

Defense reconnaissance and surveillance system factory shipments value, 1982-91, annual rpt, A4725–1.2

Probation and parole agency use of electronic monitoring devices on supervisees, by State and for Federal system, 1992 annual rpt, R4300–1.3

Retail store use of closed-circuit TV and point-of-sale electronic monitoring systems, by annual sales size, 1991, annual survey rpt, C5150–4.504

see also Radar

Electronics industry and products

Aircraft equipment disruptions caused by electromagnetic interference from passenger electronic devices, 1986-92, article, C5800–4.512

Appliance life expectancy, sales, shipments, and manufacturers market share, by product type, 1993 annual article, C2000–1.510

Brazil electronic equipment market value, 1992 annual rpt, U6250–1.4

Broadcasting and related electronic communications companies revenues and earnings, top 100 companies, 1992, annual article, C1850–14.526

CEO views on industry conditions and outlook, including mgmt issues, global expansion, and most promising new technologies, 1992/93 survey, annual feature, C1850–2.506

Congressional campaign finances, with detailed data for individual Members, and leading contributors by type and industry, 1990 election and trends, biennial rpt, R3828–2.2

Consumer electronics distributor sales volume, by product type, 1991-93, annual article, C2000–1.503

Consumer electronics sales, trade, and industry devs, by product type, 1970s-92, annual rpt, A4725–4

Corporate performance ratings by executives for leading companies in 32 industries, 1993 annual survey feature, C8900–1.508

Discount chain consumer natl brand preferences, by product category and chain, and by age group, 1993 survey, annual feature, C5150–3.521

Discount chain top-selling natl brands cited by managers, by product category, chain, and region, 1993 survey, annual feature, C5150–3.520

Discount store sales and productivity data for 20 depts, 1993 annual feature, C5150–3.516

Discount stores, sales, and earnings, for top chains, with detail by specialty, 1993 annual feature, C5150–3.514

Display screen sales, for active matrix liquid crystal displays, 1992 and 1997, article, C1850–6.503

Engineers salaries by industry group, census div, selected metro area, and years since college degree, 1993, annual survey rpt, A0685–5

Engineers salaries by industry group, census div, selected metro area, degree level, and years since college degree, 1993, annual survey rpt, A0685–3

Europe electronics industry financial performance, for top 50 companies, FY91 or FY92, annual article, C1850–2.501

Factory sales and shipments, foreign trade, and operating data, by product category, 1980s-92, annual rpt, A4725–1

Financial data and business info for approx 500 electronics companies, 1991-92 and trends, annual rpt, C3400–4

Financial performance and growth rankings for approx 1,000 top corporations, with comparisons by industry group, 1993 annual rpt, C3950–1.505

Financial performance data for top 100 multinatl electronics companies, 1992 annual feature, C1850–2.502

Financial performance of leading defense electronics companies, FY92 and trends, annual feature, C5800–4.519

Financial performance ranking of top 200 electronics companies, 1992 and trends, annual feature, C1850–2.509

Financial ratios and performance, for over 350 SIC 4-digit industries, FY88-92, annual rpt, A6400–3

Foreign trade in electronics, by product category, detailed type, and country, monthly rpt, A4725–3

Japan electronics industry output change, by type of product, 1992, article, C8900–1.511

Market devs in electronics industry, including employment, factory sales, prices, and foreign trade trends, monthly rpt, A4725–2

Market trends and outlook for electronics industry, by product category, 1989-93, annual feature, C1850–2.503

Market trends and outlook, including product sales and shipments, employment, and leading manufacturers, monthly rpt, C1850–2

Minority consumer purchasing by product type, and ownership of selected electronics, for blacks, Hispanics, and Asians, 1992/93 survey, article, C2710–1.513

Musical instrument and accessory shipment volume and/or retail value, and foreign trade, by product type, 1992 and trends, annual rpt, A6848–1

Operating and financial composite ratios for corporations, with establishments and receipts, for approx 200 industries, by asset size, FY90, annual rpt, C7800–1

Index by Subjects and Names

Paper industry sectors potentially affected by electronic competition, and electronics-related specialty paper market volume, 1993 annual rpt, C3975–5.3

Printer views on paper supplier services and performance, and electronic prepress and output device use, 1993 survey and trends, article, A8140–3.505

R&D effectiveness measure for electronic systems dev companies, 1993 article, C1850–6.511

Retail sales by outlet type, and discount chain sales in major depts, by product category, 1992, annual feature, C8130–1.507

Revenues, funding, and employment, for 25 companies started in the recent past, 1993 recurring article, C1850–2.505

Security equipment dealer purchasing outlook, by type of equipment, 1993 survey article, C1850–13.504

Shipments of household equipment, by product type, 1983-92, annual feature, C2000–1.505

State and local:

California economic condition, including population, employment and earnings, income, business activity, and taxation, 1960s-92, annual rpt, S0840–3.2

California statistical abstract, general data, 1992 annual rpt, S0840–2.8

see also Audiovisual equipment

see also Automated tellers

see also CD-ROM technology and use

see also Compact disc players

see also Computer industry and products

see also Electronic funds transfer

see also Electronic games

see also Electronic surveillance

see also Home video and audio equipment

see also Lasers

see also Radio

see also Semiconductors

see also Television

see also Video recordings and equipment

see also under By Industry in the "Index by Categories"

Elementary and secondary education

Black American educational statistics, with comparisons to whites, 1970s-92, annual compilation, C6775–2.3

Business participation in activities involving local public school systems, 1993 feature, C4687–1.509

Catholic vs public school performance, and support for parental school selection funded by govt, public opinion by respondent characteristics, July 1992 survey, A7375–8

Corporate executive ratings of education system performance in preparation of new employees, July 1992 survey, A2800–3

Corporate-sponsored dropout prevention/work readiness programs for high school students, profiles of selected programs, 1993 rpt, R4105–78.30

Criminal activity in schools, student views on metal detector use, and proposed Federal funding for security measures, 1993 article, C1850–12.510

Education Week, issues and devs in elementary/secondary school programs, enrollment, finances, and staff, and selected higher education issues, weekly rpt, R4800–2

Elementary and secondary education

Firearm-related incidents at schools, by level, incident type, and cause, 1993 feature, C4215–1.508

Food service (institutional) financial and operating data, for leading firms by market segment, 1993 recurring feature, C1850–3.511

Food service industry sales and establishments, with growth outlook, by market segment, 1993 annual feature, C1850–3.503

Food service industry sales rankings by market segment, for leading organizations, 1992, annual feature, C1850–3.509

Food service industry sales trends and forecast, by market segment, 1990-93, annual feature, A8200–1.502

High school grade averages, and completion of recommended years in 8 subject areas, for higher education freshmen, fall 1992, annual survey, U6215–1

High school sports all-time records for boys and girls events, with school and student participation for 1991/92, annual rpt, A7830–2

Hispanic American educational statistics, with comparisons to whites, 1970s-92, annual compilation, C6775–3.2

Hours of academic activity, math, and homework, for typical elementary schools in US, Japan, and Taiwan, 1993 annual rpt, R2800–2

Latin America statistical abstract, general data by country, 1992 annual rpt, U6250–1.8

Parental school selection, parent and general public views, and local program characteristics and results, 1992 rpt, R3810–7

Public confidence in selected societal instns, 1993 Gallup Poll and trends, C4040–1.510, R8780–1.508

Public opinion on public vs private school preference if cost were not a factor, and Clinton choice of private school for daughter, Jan 1993 Gallup Poll, C4040–1.507

Public opinion on school problems, quality, and proposed reforms, by respondent characteristics, 1993 annual Gallup Poll, A8680–1.503

Public school new teacher views on teaching and quality of schools, after 2nd year of teaching, spring 1992 survey, B6045–2

Public school new teacher views on teaching, and reasons for leaving profession, spring 1992 survey, article, B6045–1.504

Public school teacher views on education policy issues and selected reform proposals, Jan-Feb 1993 survey, B6045–7

Science and math elementary/secondary education, including student and teacher characteristics, and requirements, by State, 1991/92, biennial rpt, A4355–3

State elementary/secondary education data, with detail for mathematics including test scores and teacher preparation, by State, 1993 biennial rpt, A4355–1

Statistical profiles of 50 States and DC, general data, 1993 annual almanac, C4712–1

Teenage pregnancy/parenthood education continuation program characteristics, Arizona study, 1985-89, article, A5160–1.505

Trends in education spending, teacher salaries and unionization, and test scores, 1940s-92, article, C3950–1.516

Urban public school performance compared to natl goals for year 2000, with data on students, teachers, and finances, for 47 systems, 1990/91 and trends, A4425–4

Volunteer activity of youth age 12-17, including involvement through school, 1992 survey, biennial rpt, A5435–5

State and local:

Alabama county data book, general data, 1992 annual rpt, S0121–2

Alabama elementary and secondary school enrollment, staff, pupil transportation, and finances, by district, 1991/92, annual rpt, S0124–1

Alabama statistical abstract, general data, 1992 recurring rpt, U5680–2.4

Alaska public and private schools, staff, and enrollment summary, FY92 annual rpt, S0275–1

Alaska public schools, enrollment, staff, and finances, by district, FY92, annual rpt, S0295–2

Arizona elementary and secondary school enrollment, staff, and finances, by school district and county, FY92 and trends, annual rpt, S0470–1

Arizona statistical abstract, general data, 1993 recurring rpt, U5850–2.4

Arkansas public school enrollment, grads, staff, and finances, by county and school, 1991/92 and trends, annual rpt, S0660–1

California public opinion on public school quality and parental use of State vouchers to pay for private schools, Sept 1993 survey, C5800–7.550

California public school limited-English-proficiency enrollment, teachers, and programs, by 1st language, grade level, and county, 1992 and trends, annual rpt, S0825–10

California socioeconomic and govtl data for municipalities, counties, and school districts, 1993 annual rpt, C4712–3

California statistical abstract, general data, 1992 annual rpt, S0840–2.6

Colorado public school enrollment, finances, and student and staff characteristics, by locality, 1991 annual rpt series, S1000–4

Colorado public school enrollment, finances, and student and staff characteristics, by locality, 1992 annual rpt series, S1000–2

Connecticut public school data, including enrollment, staff, programs, finances, and student characteristics, 1991/92, biennial rpt, S1185–3

DC public school finances, enrollment, grads, and test scores, with data by school, 1987/88-1991/92, annual rpt, S1605–2

DC statistical profile, general data, 1992 annual rpt, S1535–3.6

Delaware school enrollment, grads, staff, finances, and facilities, by county, school district, and/or instn, 1991/92, annual rpt, S1430–1

Florida county data book, 1992/93 annual rpt, C6360–1

Florida municipal and county statistical profiles, general data, 1991 annual rpt, C4712–6

Florida statistical abstract, general data, 1992 annual rpt, U6660–1.4, U6660–1.20

Elementary and secondary education

Georgia county guide, general data, 1993 annual rpt, U6750–1

Georgia statistical abstract, general data, 1992-93 biennial rpt, U6730–1.2

Hawaii data book, general data, 1992 annual rpt, S2090–1.3

Idaho economic profile, general data, 1992 recurring rpt, S2218–2.3

Idaho school district revenues by source, and expenditures by function, by district and fund, FY92, annual rpt, S2225–2

Illinois elementary and secondary school enrollment, staff, and finances, by county and district, 1990/91 and trends, annual rpt, S2440–1

Illinois statistical abstract, general data, 1992 annual rpt, U6910–2

Indiana elementary and secondary school enrollment and finances, by district and county, annual rpt series, S2608–2

Kansas school enrollment, grads, staff, and finances, by county, school district, and/or school, 1990/91, annual rpt, S2945–1

Kansas statistical abstract, general data, 1991/92 annual rpt, U7095–2.5

Kentucky public education profiles, with data by region and district, 1991/92 and trends, annual rpt, S3110–1

Kentucky public school finances, staff, and enrollment, by district, 1989/90-1990/91, biennial rpt, S3110–2

Louisiana elementary/secondary school operations, including enrollment, staff, finances, and detail by school district, 1991/92 and trends, annual rpt, S3280–1

Maine public school enrollment, facilities, staff, and finances, with selected data by county and for private schools, 1991 and trends, annual rpt, S3435–1

Maryland elementary and secondary education data, by county, annual rpt series, S3610–2

Maryland elementary and secondary education statistical summary, with data by county, 1991/92-1992/93 and trends, annual rpt, S3610–1

Maryland statistical abstract, general data, 1993-94 biennial rpt, S3605–1.2

Massachusetts municipal and county profiles, general data, 1992 annual rpt, C4712–2

Massachusetts public elementary/secondary education summary data, 1989/90-1991/92 and trends, annual rpt, S3810–3

Michigan school district financial and enrollment data, with rankings, 1991/92, annual rpt, S3965–3

Minnesota public school enrollment, staff, and finances, by district and county, 1991/92 and trends, annual rpt, S4165–1

Mississippi public school enrollment, staff and salaries, and finances, by district, 1991/92 and trends, annual rpt, S4340–1

Mississippi statistical abstract, general data, 1992 annual rpt, U3255–4.3

Missouri school finances, enrollment, grads, and staff, by county and school district, 1991/92, annual rpt, S4505–1

Nebraska elementary and secondary schools, enrollment by grade, and staff, with data by school district and county, annual series, S4865–2

Nevada public school enrollment, test scores, teachers, and finances, by school district, 1990/91 and trends, annual rpt, S5035–2

Nevada statistical abstract, general data, 1992 biennial rpt, S5005–1.7

New Hampshire elementary and secondary education statistics, with selected data by school district, annual rpt series, S5200–1

New Jersey municipal and county data book, general data, 1992 annual rpt, C4712–4

New Jersey public schools, enrollment, and student and staff characteristics, and nonpublic schools and enrollment, by county, 1991/92, annual rpt, S5385–1

New Mexico elementary/secondary school statistics, including grads, student test results, and finances, by school district, 1989/90-1991/92, annual rpt, S5575–4

New Mexico elementary/secondary school statistics, including students, teachers, and grads, by race-ethnicity and school district, discontinued annual rpt, S5575–2

New York State municipal and county statistical profiles, general data, 1993 annual rpt, C4712–7

New York State statistical yearbook, general data, 1992 annual rpt, U5100–1.10

North Carolina public school enrollment, grads, staff, and finances, with data by race, sex, and local district, 1991/92-1992/93 and trends, annual rpt, S5915–1

North Dakota elementary and secondary schools, enrollment, and staff, by school type and location, 1992/93 annual directory, S6180–2

Ohio public school enrollment, finances, special programs, and staff, 1991/92 and trends, annual rpt, S6265–2

Oklahoma public school finances, personnel, enrollment, and facilities, by county and district, 1991/92 and trends, annual rpt, S6423–1

Oklahoma public school performance indicators, including students and achievement, finances, and staff, by district, 1990/91-1991/92 and trends, annual rpt, S6423–2

Oklahoma statistical abstract, general data, 1992 annual rpt, U8130–2.8

Oregon elementary and secondary education enrollment and finances, including data by school district and county, annual rpt series, S6590–1

Pennsylvania elementary/secondary and higher education enrollment, grads, staff, and finances, by instn type, 1981/82-1996/97, recurring rpt, S6790–5.10

Pennsylvania public and nonpublic school enrollment, by grade, race-ethnicity, sex, and county, 1991/92 and trends, annual rpt, S6790–5.1

Pennsylvania public and nonpublic school enrollment, by grade, race-ethnicity, sex, and county, 1992/93 and trends, annual rpt, S6790–5.17

Pennsylvania public school dropout characteristics, with reasons for leaving school and subsequent activities, 1991/92 and trends, annual rpt, S6790–5.11

Index by Subjects and Names

Pennsylvania statistical abstract, general data, 1992 recurring rpt, U4130–6.4

Rhode Island educational enrollment, grads, and finances, by district or community, 1991/92 or fall 1992, annual rpt, S6970–1

Rhode Island statistical almanac, general data, 1993 annual rpt, C7975–1.1

South Carolina educational characteristics and socioeconomic indicators, by school district and county, 1991/92, annual rpt, S7145–1

South Carolina public and private schools, enrollment, and grads, by county, 1990/91 and trends, annual planning rpt, S7155–3.3

South Carolina statistical abstract, general data, 1993 annual rpt, S7125–1.6

South Dakota school enrollment, finances, grads, and staff, by district, 1991/92 and trends, annual rpt, S7315–1

Tennessee public school enrollment, staff, finances, and operations, by county, city, and school district, 1991/92, annual rpt, S7490–2

Tennessee statistical abstract, general data, 1992/93 annual rpt, U8710–2.16

Texas elementary and secondary education data, by school district and county, annual series, S7670–1

Utah public schools, enrollment, attendance, personnel, and finances, by school district, 1991/92, annual rpt, S7815–1

Utah statistical abstract, general data, 1993 triennial rpt, U8960–1.3

Virginia public school enrollment, grads, finances, and staff, by county and municipality, 1991/92, annual rpt, S8190–3

West Virginia public and private schools, enrollment, grads, and staff, by county, 1991/92, annual rpt, S8540–3

West Virginia public school finances, enrollment, staff, and programs, by county, 1992/93 and trends, annual rpt, S8540–4

West Virginia statistical handbook, general data, 1992 annual rpt, R9385–1.4

Wisconsin Blue Book, general data, 1993-94 biennial rpt, S8780–1.2

Wisconsin elementary and secondary school enrollment, staff, costs, and State aid, by school district, 1992/93 and trends, annual rpt, S8795–2

Wyoming public school enrollment, staff, and finances, by county and district, 1991/92, annual rpt series, S8890–1

see also Compensatory education

see also Curricula

see also Discrimination in education

see also Educational attainment

see also Educational broadcasting

see also Educational employees pay

see also Educational enrollment

see also Educational exchanges

see also Educational facilities

see also Educational finance

see also Educational materials

see also Educational reform

see also Educational research

see also Educational technology

see also Educational tests

see also Federal aid to education

see also Head Start Project

see also National Assessment of Educational Progress
see also Parochial schools
see also Preschool education
see also Private schools
see also Remedial education
see also School administration and staff
see also School districts
see also School lunch and breakfast programs
see also Special education
see also Student discipline
see also Students
see also Teacher education
see also Teachers
see also Truancy from school

Elementary and Secondary Education Act
State and local:
Missouri ESEA-funded programs, students, and teachers, by grade level and subject, FY92, annual rpt, S4505–1.1

Elevation
see Topography

Elevators
Condominium, cooperative, and planned unit dev detailed expenses, for US and Canada, by building characteristics, metro area, and US region, 1991, annual rpt, A5600–3
Office building detailed income and expense data, and energy use, US and Canada, by building characteristics, metro area, and US region, 1991 and trends, annual rpt, A5600–2
State and local:
Hawaii data book, general data, 1992 annual rpt, S2090–1.21
see also Grain storage and facilities

Elkhart, Ind.
Business conditions analysis for selected Indiana local areas, quarterly rpt semiannual feature, U2160–1.502, U2160–1.504

Elko County, Nev.
Casino finances and employment, by location and gaming revenue range, FY92, annual rpt, S5062–1

Ellis, Susanne D.
"Employment Survey, 1991", A1960–1
"Physics and Astronomy Enrollments and Degrees", A1960–2
"1991/92 Survey of Physics and Astronomy Bachelor's Degree Recipients", A1960–3

Elmendorf, Fritz
"1993 Small Business Banking Study: An Analysis of the September Survey", A4160–5

Embassies
see Diplomatic and consular service

Embezzlement
State and local:
Alabama juvenile and adult arrests, by type of offense, 1992, annual rpt, S0119–1.1
Arizona arrests by offense, offender characteristics, and county, 1992, annual rpt, S0505–2.2
Arkansas crimes and arrests, by offense, victim and offender characteristics, and location, 1992 and trends, annual rpt, S0652–1
Colorado crimes and arrests, by offense and location, with offender characteristics, and assaults on police, 1992, annual rpt, S1068–1
Connecticut arrests, by offense, offender characteristics, and local agency, 1992, annual rpt, S1256–1.2

DC criminal justice system summary, including crimes and arrests, criminal procedure, prisoners, and parole, 1991 and trends, annual rpt, S1535–2
Florida crimes and arrests, by offense, with data by victim and offender characteristics, 1992, annual rpt, S1770–1
Hawaii crimes and arrests, by offense, with data by county and victim-offender characteristics, 1992, annual rpt, S2035–1
Idaho crimes and arrests, by offense, with data by location and offender characteristics, 1992 and trends, annual rpt, S2275–2
Illinois crimes and arrests, by offense, with data by location and offender characteristics, 1991, annual rpt, S2536–1
Kansas crimes and arrests, by offense, with data by location, agency, and victim-offender characteristics, 1992 and trends, annual rpt, S2925–1.1
Kentucky arrests by county and offense, and law enforcement employment by agency, 1992, annual rpt, S3150–1.2
Maine arrests of adults and juveniles, by offense, age, and sex, 1991, annual rpt, S3475–1.2
Maryland crimes and arrests, by offense, location, and offender characteristics, with law enforcement employment and assaults on officers, 1992 and trends, annual rpt, S3665–1
Michigan crimes and arrests, by offense, with data by location and offender characteristics, 1992 and trends, annual rpt, S3997–1
Missouri crimes and arrests, by offense and location, with victim and offender characteristics, 1991 and trends, annual rpt, S4560 2
Montana crimes and clearances, by offense and jurisdiction, 1992, annual rpt, S4705–1
New Hampshire arrests, by offense and offender age, sex, and race-ethnicity, 1991, annual rpt, S5250–2.2
New Jersey arrests by offense, age, race-ethnicity, sex, and county, 1992 and trends, annual rpt, S5430–1.2
New York State crimes and arrests by offense and demographic characteristics, and court activity and corrections, 1991 and trends, annual rpt, S5760–3
North Carolina arrests by detailed offense, offender characteristics, and county, 1991-92, annual rpt, S5955–1.2
North Dakota crimes and arrests, by offense, location, and offender characteristics, and law enforcement employment, 1991 and trends, annual rpt, S6060–1
Oklahoma crimes and arrests, by offense, with victim and offender characteristics, 1990-92, annual rpt, S6465–1.1
Oregon crimes and arrests, by offense, with data by county, local agency, and offender characteristics, 1992 and trends, annual rpt, S6603–3
Pennsylvania crimes and arrests, by offense, with data by location and offender characteristics, 1992 and trends, annual rpt, S6860–1

South Carolina crimes and arrests, by detailed offense, offender characteristics, and location, 1992 and trends, annual rpt, S7205–1.2
Texas arrests, by age, sex, race-ethnicity, and offense, 1992, annual rpt, S7735–2.2
Utah crimes and arrests, by offense, county, and local agency, 1992 and trends, annual rpt, S7890–3
Virginia crimes and arrests by offense, and law enforcement employment, by location and reporting agency, 1992, annual rpt, S8295–2.2
Washington State crimes and arrests, by offense, with data by location and offender characteristics, 1992 and trends, annual rpt, S8440–1
West Virginia crimes and arrests, by offense, location, and offender characteristics, 1990-91, annual rpt, S8610–1
Wisconsin crimes and arrests, by offense, offender characteristics, county, and local agency, 1992 and trends, annual rpt, S8771–1
Wyoming adult and juvenile arrests, by offense, county, and local jurisdiction, 1991, annual rpt, S8867–3.2

Emergency medical service
Ambulance company revenues, net income, and stock performance, for 4 firms, 1993 article, C3950–1.523
Ambulance costs for ground vs air transport, 1993 article, C5800–4.531
Black youths age 12-17 and 18-24 cocaine-related emergency room use, with comparisons to whites and Hispanics, by sex, 1990, R3840–21
HMO benefits coverage, premiums, and rating methods used, by plan characteristics, 1991 and trends, annual rpt, A5150–2.1
Hospital emergency dept salaries for physician directors and staff, 1992-93, article, A1865–1.514
Hospital emergency dept use, by location and patient insurance coverage status, 1990 and trends, A1865–1.508
Hospital emergency dept visits for non-urgent, urgent, and emergent care, in 4 metro areas, Nov 1991, article, A1865–1.514
Hospital emergency dept visits per 1,000 population, by State, 1990, article, B8500–2.501
Hospital emergency room admissions by State, and physician charges by type of service, 1992 annual rpt, A5173–2.3
Hospital financial and operating data, including ambulatory surgery and emergency service utilization, semimonthly rpt quarterly feature, A1865–1.506, A1865–1.512
Physicians by detailed specialty and location, 1992 and trends, annual rpt, A2200–3
State social, economic, and govtl indicators, with rankings, 1993 semiannual rpt, B8500–1.9
State and local:
DC ambulance trips by city ward of emergency and hospital destination, FY91 and trends, annual rpt, S1535–3.8
Florida health care atlas, including manpower by occupation and health care facilities by type, by district and county, 1992 annual rpt, S1746–1.2

Emergency medical service

Hawaii ambulances and emergency responses, by island, 1990 annual rpt, S2065–1.3

Hawaii, Honolulu beach attendance and emergency assistance, 1992, annual rpt, S2090–1.7

Idaho emergency equipment responding to traffic accidents, and ambulance response time, 1992, annual rpt, S2315–1

Kentucky Medicaid recipients and payments, by program, county, and type of medical service, monthly rpt, S3140–5

Louisiana traffic accident ambulance and rescue unit use, and source of first aid, 1991, annual rpt, S3345–2

Maryland medical assistance payments and recipients, by program, type of service, location, demographic characteristics, and facility, FY92 and trends, annual rpt, S3635–3

Missouri medical assistance expenditures for ambulance services, by month, FY92, annual rpt, S4575–2

Montana hospital emergency outpatient visits, by instn, 1991, annual rpt, S4690–2

New York State ambulance registrations, and method of transport for traffic accident victims, 1991, annual rpt, S5790–1

West Virginia births by type of attendant, including emergency/paramedic personnel, 1991, annual rpt, S8560–1

Emergency shelters

Catholic charity social service agency activities, clients, finances, and personnel, 1991 and trends, annual rpt, A3810–1

Catholic shelters for homeless, abused, and other persons in need, 1993 annual almanac, C6885–1

Homeless shelter beds and transitional housing units, and demand, for 29 cities, 1991/92, annual rpt, A9330–9

State and local:

Alabama public welfare and social service cases, recipients, and payments, by program and county, monthly rpt, S0150–1

Arkansas human services dept finances and operations, including Medicaid payments by type of service, FY91 and trends, annual rpt, S0700–2.3

Arkansas population in emergency shelters and apparently living on the street, 1990, census rpt, U5935–7

California population in emergency shelters and apparently living on the street, 1990, census rpt, S0840–9

California public welfare cases, recipients, and expenditures, by program and county, monthly rpt, S0935–2

DC statistical profile, general data, 1992 annual rpt, S1535–3.5

New Jersey population in emergency shelters and apparently living on the street, by county, 1990, census rpt, S5425–19

New Mexico emergency shelter program expenditures, by locality, monthly rpt quarterly table, S5620–2

Pennsylvania population in emergency shelters and apparently living on the street, 1990, census rpt, U4130–13

Utah homeless shelter population characteristics, individual shelter capacity, and related housing data, 1991-92, annual rpt, S7808–2

West Virginia welfare and social service program caseloads and expenditures, by county, monthly rpt, S8560–2

see also Homeless population

Emergency vehicles

see Traffic accidents and safety (for accident data)

Emigration

see Immigration and emigration

see Refugees

Eminent domain

see Land ownership and rights

Emissions

see Air pollution

see Global climate change

see Motor vehicle exhaust

Emphysema

see Respiratory diseases

Employee benefits

Art museum employee benefits offered, FY93, annual rpt, A3290–1

Asset rankings of top 1,000 employee benefit funds, with selected fund investment data, 1992, annual feature, C2710–2.504

Association executives compensation, by position, assn type, and census div, with personnel practices and benefit provisions, 1992, biennial rpt, A2900–3

Auto fleet policies on personal use of employer vehicles, 1993 survey article, C1575–2.512

Bank CEO demographic and professional characteristics, attitudes, and compensation, Apr 1992 survey, annual rpt, B4490–2.33

Book publishing industry financial and operating data, by publisher type and size, and subject category, 1991 and trends, annual rpt, A3274–2

Business forms manufacturing plant employment and compensation data, by region, 1992 and trends, biennial rpt, A5785–4

Catholic secondary school teacher benefits, by presence of bargaining representation, 1992 biennial rpt, A7375–5

Chambers of commerce income, salaries and benefits, membership, staff, and operations, 1993 annual rpt, A3840–3

College grad new hire benefits offered by employers, 1992/93 annual survey rpt, U3130–1

Construction industry finances and operations, by type of business and region, 1992-93, annual survey rpt, A4155–1

Construction nonunion wages and benefit levels, by craft and region, 1992, article, C5800–2.534

Corporate boards of directors compensation practices and amounts, by industry group, 1991-92, annual rpt, R4105–7

Corporate boards of directors composition, compensation, and practices, by industry sector, 1991 and trends, annual survey rpt, B5000–3

Corporate communication of benefits info to employees, including objectives, methods, and success, 1993 survey rpt, R4105–78.28

Corporate employee transfers, and relocation policies, assistance, and costs, 1992, annual survey, B0600–1

Corporate personnel mgmt devs, including work force diversity, health care and

family-related benefits, counseling services, and competitiveness, 1993 survey, B6850–6

Corporate work force reduction prevalence by industry sector, assistance provided displaced workers, and reduction effects, 1992 survey, article, C4215–1.504

Corporate work force reductions, measures to avoid discharges, assistance to displaced workers, and impacts, Aug-Sept 1992 survey and trends, annual rpt, A2075–20.9

Executive benefits offered by companies, 1987 and 1991, C1200–4.501

Family-related policies of employers, with involvement in child, elderly, and disabled care services, and personnel mgmt views, Mar 1992 survey, A8907–1

Federal employee compensation and benefit costs, FY90-93, annual rpt, R9050–1.3

Fire dept employment and personnel practices, including eligibility requirements and testing, by population size, metro status, and census div, 1991 survey, recurring rpt, A5800–2.116

Fleet manager compensation, including use of company vehicle, for full- and part-time managers, 1993 article, C1575–2.506

Food marketing mgmt personnel compensation, by position, by company sales size and region, year ended Mar 1993, annual survey, A4950–6

Foundation chief executive benefits, by organization characteristics, 1991/92, article, C2176–1.506

Fundraising professionals characteristics, earnings, and benefits, 1992 survey, recurring rpt, A8455–1

Grounds maintenance manager benefits received, 1992, annual article, C4725–6

High-technology firm methods used to handle work of employees on leave, with costs as a percent of salary, 1993 article, A1250–1.524

High-technology industry CEO characteristics, and views on mgmt issues including compensation and foreign trade, June 1992 survey, B4490–2.34

Higher education faculty average salary and benefits, by position, 1992/93, C2175–1.521

Higher education faculty compensation and employment, detailed data by rank, sex, and instn, 1992/93 and trends, annual rpt, A0800–1

Higher education instn average expenditures for selected faculty benefits, by instn control, 1992/93, C2175–1.517

Higher education instn employee retirement and insurance benefits, prevalence and expenditures, by type of instn and region, 1991, biennial survey, A9025–3

Higher education private instn salaries and benefits of chief executives and top 5 earners, and total expenditures, by instn, FY91 or FY92, article, C2175–1.519

Homebuilder executive compensation, incentives, and benefits, by position, 1992, annual survey article, C1850–8.508

Homebuilder operations and finances, by region and sales size group, 1992 survey, article, C4300–1.501

Hospital (teaching) house staff benefits, by region and ownership, 1992/93, annual rpt, A3273–3

Index by Subjects and Names

Employee benefits

Hospital CEO demographic and professional characteristics, perquisites, and views on mgmt issues, Oct 1992 survey, recurring rpt, B4490–2.35

Hospital employee benefits as percent of compensation costs, by instn characteristics and location, 1988-92, annual rpt, B1880–1.2

Hospital recruiting of nurses and allied health personnel, with budget, vacancies, turnover, and compensation, 1993 and trends, annual survey rpt, A6500–1

House of Representatives staff characteristics, salaries, and benefits by position, 1992 and trends, recurring rpt, R4140–1

Industrial distribution personnel compensation, by position and selected other characteristics, 1992 survey, annual article, C1850–4.501

Investment and admin of pension funds and employee benefit plans, monthly rpt, C2425–1

Iron and steel industry financial and operating data, 1992 and trends, annual rpt, A2000–2.1

Jewelry industry statistics on sales, marketing, trade, and employment, with customer characteristics, 1993 annual almanac, C2150–7.509

Jewelry store employee benefits, 1992 annual survey article, C2150–7.501

Library/info science school faculty benefits as percent of salary, by school, 1987/88-1991/92, annual rpt, A3235–1.1

Magazine publisher employee benefits, costs, and trends, with employee ratings of health coverage, Mar/Apr 1993 survey, article, C2575–1.517

Mass transit system energy use by source, employee compensation, and labor costs, 1970s-91, annual rpt, A2650–1.2

Medical group financial and operating data, by practice characteristics, 1991, annual rpt, A6365–2

Medical group mgmt compensation, by demographic and practice characteristics, 1992, annual rpt, A6365–3

Municipal police and fire dept employment, hours, compensation, and expenditures, by census div, city, and city size, 1992, annual rpt, A5800–1.3

Nonprofit organization executive compensation, with comparison to organization income, by leading organization, FY91 or FY92, article, C2176–1.509

Nursing higher education program finances, faculty and clinical practice, and clinic/center operations, by instn characteristics, 1992/93 biennial rpt, A0615–5

Office building detailed income and expense data, and energy use, US and Canada, by building characteristics, metro area, and US region, 1991 and trends, annual rpt, A5600–2

Office employee benefits offered, by company size, industry, and region, discontinued annual rpt, A0175–5

Optometry school faculty fringe benefits, by instn, 1991/92, annual survey, A3370–2

Payments and employer cost/payroll ratios for employee benefits, by industry and detailed type of benefit, 1991, annual rpt, A3840–1

Personnel mgmt professional activities, job satisfaction, employer performance, and obstacles encountered, spring 1993 survey, A8907–2

Physician compensation in group practices and HMOs, by specialty and region, 1992 survey and trends, annual rpt, B7450–2

Planning professional benefits received and use, 1991, biennial rpt, A2615–1

Political science higher education dept characteristics, including faculty, salaries, enrollment, and finances, 1991/92 annual rpt, A2617–1

Printing industry employee benefits offered, by company size, 1993 annual feature, C1850–10.510

Private elementary and secondary school housing assistance for staff, by position, 1992/93, annual rpt, A6835–3

Psychology grad dept chair salaries and benefits, 1992/93, annual rpt, A2620–1

Public planning agency personnel practices, by jurisdiction size, 1991 survey rpt, A2615–3

Pulp and paper industry salaries and benefits, 1991-92 surveys, annual article, C3975–2.503

Railroad (Class I) financial and operating data, with detail by company, 1982-91, annual rpt, A3275–8.2

Railroad (Class I) financial condition, operations, and employment, by company and district, 1992, annual rpt, A3275–7

Railroad operating data, including top commodities handled, employment and wages, and retirement system, by State, 1991, annual rpt, A3275–10

Railroad operating data, including wages, fringe benefits, and retirement beneficiaries and payments, 1991, article, C8400–1.506

Real estate property managers characteristics and compensation, including types of property managed, 1989 surveys, recurring rpt, A5600–4

Restaurant industry financial and operating data, by establishment characteristics and location, 1992, annual rpt, A8200–3

Restaurant/food service mgmt compensation, characteristics, and views, including data by position, 1992 survey, annual article, C1850–3.502

School bus contractor outlook for insurance costs, and provision of health insurance coverage, by fleet size, Apr 1993 survey, annual article, C1575–1.505

Small business employee benefits offered, with detail for executives, at companies with 250/fewer employees, 1993 feature, C4687–1.504

Small business employee leave and unpaid parental leave policy prevalence at companies with 500/fewer employees, 1992 survey, article, C4687–1.504

Small corporation employee benefits and compensation methods, for companies with and without interest in improving quality, May 1992 survey, article, C4687–1.502

Small corporation employee health promotion programs offered, by type, 1992 survey, article, C4687–1.511

Small corporations offering employee equity incentives and 401(k) plans, by selected industry, 1992-93, survey article, C4687–1.502

Southern States higher education enrollment, degrees, appropriations, tuition/fees, and faculty compensation, by instn type, for 15 States, 1990/91, annual rpt, A8945–31

Southern States higher education faculty benefits share of salaries, by type of instn, 1991/92, biennial fact book, A8945–1.5

Sweden natl steel corporation costs of training, employment, and assistance programs for laid-off workers, by program type, 1979-83, R9260–16

Tax-deferred salary reduction 401(k) plan asset allocation and investment return trends, by type of investment option, 1992 article, C8900–1.505

Tax-deferred salary reduction 401(k) plan employee participation rates at 3 levels of company investment matching, 1992 feature, C1200–4.502

Tax-deferred salary reduction 401(k) plan employee participation rates, 1993 survey, article, C2710–2.521

Tax-deferred salary reduction 401(k) plan investment return variation factors, 1993 article, C2425–1.508

Tax-deferred salary reduction 401(k) plan sponsor satisfaction with selected plan services and costs, 1993 survey article, C2710–2.510

Tax-deferred salary reduction 401(k) plan types of fees charged and recordkeeping service providers, 1993 articles, C2710–2.505

Telephone company free or reduced rate service for employees, by State, 1991/92 annual rpt, A7015–3

Theological school enrollment, staff and compensation, and finances, with data by instn, 1991/92 and trends, annual rpt, A3376–1

TV station personnel and compensation, by position, and benefits, 1991, biennial rpt, A6635–9

Utility and other executives benefits and perquisites received, 1992 and trends, article, C5800–28.507

Veterinary school grad employment, starting salaries, benefits, and personal characteristics, by sex, 1992, annual survey article, A3100–2.504

Western States bookstore employee salaries and benefits, 1992 survey, article, C1852–2.501

State and local:

Colorado public school revenues by source, and expenditures by category, by school district, 1990, annual rpt, S1000–4.3

Connecticut public library staff, holdings, circulation, and finances, by library and town, FY91, annual rpt, S1242–1

DC statistical profile, general data, 1992 annual rpt, S1535–3.2

Delaware school district expenditures for operations, materials, and health and food services, 1991/92, annual rpt, S1430–1.4

Indiana library employee vacation and other leave, by position, 1992, annual rpt, S2655–1

Maryland elementary and secondary education data, by county, 1991/92, annual rpt, S3610–2.7

Maryland public library operating income and expenditures, staff, holdings, and population served, by county, FY92, annual rpt, S3610–5

Employee benefits

Oregon public school revenues by source and fund, and expenditures by fund, function, and object, 1991/92, annual rpt, S6590–1.16

Oregon public school revenues by source and fund, and expenditures by fund, function, and object, 1992/93, annual rpt, S6590–1.17

Pennsylvania higher education faculty employment, compensation, and tenure status, by sex and type of instn, 1991/92 and trends, annual rpt, S6790–5.5

Pennsylvania higher education faculty employment, compensation, and tenure status, by sex and type of instn, 1992/93 and trends, annual rpt, S6790–5.13

Rhode Island financial condition, including revenues by source, expenditures by function, and fund balances, FY92 and trends, annual rpt, S6930–1

South Dakota employee benefits for full- and part-time workers, 1993 article, S7355–1.502

Tennessee public school finances, by county, city, and school district, 1991/92, annual rpt, S7490–2.4

Utah fringe benefits as percent of payroll, by employer size, July 1992, annual article, S7820–3.503

Wyoming public library holdings, staff, circulation, and finances, by county, FY92, annual rpt, S8855–3

see also Disability benefits and insurance

see also Employee bonuses and work incentives

see also Employee stock ownership plans

see also Health insurance

see also Health maintenance organizations

see also Labor costs and cost indexes

see also Maternity benefits

see also Pensions and pension funds

see also Railroad Retirement System

see also State retirement systems

see also Vacations and holidays

Employee Benefits Research Institute

Employee views on value of employer-provided health insurance, 1992 survey, article, A1865–1.514

Employee bonuses and work incentives

Advertising agency personnel compensation, and employment trends, 1992 annual feature, C2710–1.505

Association executives compensation, by position, assn type, and census div, with personnel practices and benefit provisions, 1992, biennial rpt, A2900–3

Bank CEO demographic and professional characteristics, attitudes, and compensation, Apr 1992 survey, annual rpt, B4490–2.33

Bank small business loan sales and underwriting staff incentive compensation practices, Nov 1992 survey, annual rpt, A4160–5

Business forms manufacturing plant employment and compensation data, by region, 1992 and trends, biennial rpt, A5785–4

Coal industry personnel earnings and employment history, US and Canada, 1993 survey article, C5226–1.507

Construction industry finances and operations, by type of business and region, 1992-93, annual survey rpt, A4155–1

Corporate executive incentive compensation, by position, 1992, biennial rpt, B2535–1

Corporate use of bonuses based on nonfinancial performance measures, 1992 survey, R4105–78.25

Corporate use of selected variable pay and recognition programs, with objectives and success, by industry div, Oct 1992 survey and trends, R4105–78.27

Discount retail company executive compensation, for 75 highest-paid executives, 1992, annual feature, C5150–3.518

Engineers receiving bonuses/incentives, by industry group, 1990-92, annual survey rpt, A0685–3, A0685–5

Executive compensation and components, by industry div and major manufacturing group, 1991, annual rpt, R4105–19

Executive compensation for top executives at approx 400 companies, by industry group, 1992 and trends, annual survey, C5800–7.525

Food marketing mgmt personnel compensation, by position, by company sales size and region, year ended Mar 1993, annual survey, A4950–6

Food service CEO salaries and bonuses for 11 executives, FY92, article, C1200–5.513

Fundraising professionals characteristics, earnings, and benefits, 1992 survey, recurring rpt, A8455–1

Hiring referral and sign-on bonus averages, 1992 and trends, annual survey rpt, A4740–2

Homebuilder executive compensation, incentives, and benefits, by position, 1992, annual survey article, C1850–8.508

Homebuilder operations and finances, by region and sales size group, 1992 survey, article, C4300–1.501

Hospital executive and manager compensation, with detail by hospital bed-size and revenues, and use of incentives, 1993 annual article, A1865–1.521

House of Representatives staff characteristics, salaries, and benefits by position, 1992 and trends, recurring rpt, R4140–1

Incentive programs for consumers, employees, and dealers, with expenditures by industry and incentive type, 1991-92, annual feature, C1200–4.502

Incentive programs for consumers, salespeople, and dealers, issues and devs, monthly rpt, C1200–4

Incentive programs for dealers, with purpose, performance measures, and types of awards, 1993 and trends, annual survey article, C1200–4.505

Incentive programs for non-sales employees, with objectives and types of awards used, 1993 survey, annual article, C1200–4.507

Incentive programs for salespeople, with expenditures of top 10 user industries, 1993 survey, annual article, C1200–4.511

Incentive travel programs for sales promotion, with destinations, and expenditures of top 10 user industries, 1993 survey, annual article, C1200–4.510

Industrial distribution sales personnel incentive compensation, 1992 survey, annual article, C1850–4.501

Investment mgmt executive compensation, for executives serving pension funds, 1993 survey article, C2710–2.513

Local govt use of incentive pay, including methods, effectiveness, and advantages and disadvantages, 1993 rpt, A5800–1.1

Magazine circulation director and manager compensation, by region, sex, age, and publication characteristics, 1992 survey, annual article, C2575–1.502

Magazine compensation of ad sales personnel, by region, sex, age, and publication characteristics, 1993 survey, annual article, C2575–1.516

Magazine compensation of editorial personnel, by region, sex, age, and publication characteristics, 1993 survey, annual article, C2575–1.512

Magazine production director and manager compensation, by region, sex, age, and publication characteristics, 1993 survey, annual article, C2575–1.510

Payments and employer cost/payroll ratios for employee benefits, by industry and detailed type of benefit, 1991, annual rpt, A3840–1

Physician compensation in group practices and HMOs, by specialty and region, 1992 survey and trends, annual rpt, B7450–2

Plastics processing industry employment, compensation practices, and union representation, by region, 1992, annual survey rpt, A8920–2

Plastics processing industry sales representative compensation and allowance policies, 1992 survey, biennial rpt, A8920–3

Public relations compensation, by employee and company characteristics, 1993 survey, annual article, A8770–1.503

Restaurant/food service mgmt compensation, characteristics, and views, including data by position, 1992 survey, annual article, C1850–3.502

Salary budget increases and structure, by industry and region, and for Canada, 1993-94 and trends, annual survey rpt, A1295–1

Sales industry costs, including compensation, training, and travel and related expenses, with data by metro area, 1992 and trends, annual survey, C1200–1.508

Sales-related tasks perceived importance and use of incentives for performance, 1993 survey article, C4687–1.510

Small company chief executive compensation and stock holdings, for 200 firms with high 5-year returns on equity, 1992 annual article, C3950–1.501

Small corporation employee bonus types used, Apr 1993 survey, article, C4687–1.509

Small corporation mgmt views on employee motivation, including use of selected types of incentives, Oct 1992 survey, C4687–1.503

TV station personnel and compensation, by position, and benefits, 1991, biennial rpt, A6635–9

State and local:

Utah teaching career incentive program finances, 1991/92, annual rpt, S7815–1.1

see also Employee stock ownership plans

Index by Subjects and Names

Employee development

Bank small business loan staff training programs and sources, Nov 1992 survey, annual rpt, A4160–5

Basic skills testing and training practices and costs, Jan-Mar 1993 survey, annual rpt, A2075–20.13

Business grad school programs for executives, with data on revenues, enrollment, tuition, and participant characteristics, by instn, 1993 feature, C5800–7.552

College grad new employee skill deficiencies, related corporate responses, 1992/93 annual survey rpt, U3130–1

Computer use and related mgmt and training issues as reported by corporate executives, 1993 survey rpt, B6850–7

Corporate employee training policies and spending as a percent of payroll, for 8 companies with outstanding programs, 1993 article, C8900–1.511

Corporate mgmt of culturally diverse work force, with program characteristics and minority opportunity indicators, Nov 1992 survey, A2075–20.11

Corporate use of motivational training programs by type, with outdoor program characteristics, 1993 survey article, C1200–1.503

Corporate work force outlook and related mgmt policies, views of human resources executives, Sept/Oct 1991 survey, R4105–78.21

Correctional instn admin, inmates, facilities, costs, parole and probation, and staffing, for local, State, and Federal systems, 1992 annual series, R4300–1

Electronics company purchasing dept training program characteristics, 1993 survey article, C1850–2.512

Fire dept employment and personnel practices, including eligibility requirements and testing, by population size, metro status, and census div, 1991 survey, recurring rpt, A5800–2.116

Food marketer training program characteristics by position, and training budget and staff, by company size, 1991-92, annual rpts, A4950–5

Hazardous substance handling training methods used by employers, by industry sector, 1992 annual rpt, R8335–1.2

Hospital basic skills education program availability and budget, 1993 survey article, A1865–1.507

Logistics professionals views on continuing education programs, including benefit to own career and employer, 1993 survey, C2150–1.505

Personnel mgmt professional activities, job satisfaction, employer performance, and obstacles encountered, spring 1993 survey, A8907–2

Public planning agency personnel practices, by jurisdiction size, 1991 survey rpt, A2615–3

Quality assurance programs of North American companies, related employee training activities, 1992 annual survey rpt, B6850–2

Restaurant (table service) employee training methods, Sept 1992 survey, article, A8200–1.504

Restaurant (table service) employee training practices, 1992, recurring rpt, A8200–11

Sales industry costs, including compensation, training, and travel and related expenses, with data by metro area, 1992 and trends, annual survey, C1200–1.508

Sales personnel initial training duration and costs, by company revenue size, 1990 and 1992, C4687–1.506

School bus driver training period requirements, 1993 annual article, C1575–1.504

Shopping center security personnel training requirements, 1993 survey, article, C5150–4.506

Small corporation employee training provided, Apr 1993 survey, article, C4687–1.509

Supermarket fish/seafood dept employee training, 1991, annual article, C4655–1.501

Training programs of employers, including methods and skills needing dev, 1993 survey, annual rpt, B6850–4

State and local:

Wyoming penitentiary security and nonsecurity staff training, FY92, annual rpt, S8883–1

Employee-management relations in government

see Labor-management relations in government

Employee performance and appraisal

Elementary/secondary school superintendents personal and professional characteristics and views, 1992 survey rpt, A0775–5

Personnel mgmt professional activities, job satisfaction, employer performance, and obstacles encountered, spring 1993 survey, A8907–2

Physician performance ratings on selected criteria by nurses vs by other doctors, and views on use of ratings by nurses, 1993 article, A3273–8.510

Public planning agency personnel practices, by jurisdiction size, 1991 survey rpt, A2615–3

Small/midsize company use of corporate and employee performance goals, views of employees and managers, 1992 survey, article, C4687–1.505

State govt employee appraisal practices, for Southeastern and Southwestern States, 1993 article, U5930–1.502

see *also* Employee bonuses and work incentives

Employee stock ownership plans

Corporate CEO nonexercised stock options value, for 20 CEOs with largest options, 1993 article, C5800–7.525

Corporate employee stock option plans, percent of employees eligible at 9 companies with high eligibility rates, 1993 article, C5800–7.523

Corporate use of employee stock option plans, with recipient and plan characteristics, Nov/Dec 1992 survey, R4105–78.31

Small corporation mgmt views on sharing equity with employees, Oct 1992 survey, C4687–1.503

Employment and unemployment, general

AIDS progression in untreated homosexual men, including employment and mental status indicators, 1992 article, A2623–1.501

Black American socioeconomic status, including health, education, politics, crime, and employment, with comparisons to whites, 1993 annual compilation, C6775–2

Black American socioeconomic status, with comparisons to whites and data by region, 1960s-92, annual compilation, A8510–1.1

Black children and youth population, economic, health, and education data, with comparisons to whites, 1993 rpt, R3840–21

Black employment share and/or total employment in 10 industries and 16 occupations with projected high employment growth by 2005, 1993 feature, C4215–1.503

Black-owned enterprises financial and operating data, for top 100 firms and auto dealerships and for top 15-25 financial instns, 1992 and trends, annual feature, C4215–1.507

Business executives expectations for coming qtr, attitudes on key indicators, with trends and data by census div, quarterly rpt, C3150–4

Business incubator facilities operations, including employment of present and former tenants, 1991, annual rpt, A7360–1

Chemist and chemical engineer salaries, employment status, and demographic and professional characteristics, 1993, annual rpt, A1250–4

Chemist salaries and employment, by employee and employer characteristics, Mar 1993 and trends, annual article, A1250–1.532

Chemistry and chemical engineering grad starting salaries, employment status, demographic characteristics, and advanced study plans, 1991/92, annual rpt, A1250–2

Child health and well-being indicators, with selected household characteristics, by State, 1993 annual rpt, R3832–1

City officials views on city issues and conditions, including employment, 1992 survey, annual rpt, A8012–1.21

College grad hiring plans by industry, with data on campus visits, starting salaries, and minority hires, 1991/92-1992/93, annual rpt, A3940–3

College grad job and salary offers, by field of study, type of employer and occupation, and degree level, by region, interim rpt series, A3940–1

College grad job and salary offers, by field of study, type of employer and occupation, and degree level, series, A3940–2

College grad recruiting practices and hiring trends, with data on starting salaries and layoffs, by type of employer, 1992/93 annual survey rpt, U3130–1

College grads in business and industry, hiring plans, salaries, and selected personnel practices, 1993 annual survey rpt, U3730–1

Employment and unemployment, general

Index by Subjects and Names

Computer local-area network (LAN) average staff size and requirements by function, 1993 survey article, C1850–5.513

Consumer attitudes on economic conditions and personal financial situation, monthly survey, U7475–2

Corporate CEO views on outlook for company employment, wages compared to inflation, and mgmt skills needs, June 1993 survey, article, C8900–1.519

Corporate middle mgmt share of employment and layoffs, 1993 article, C4687–1.503

Corporate personnel mgmt devs, including work force diversity, health care and family-related benefits, counseling services, and competitiveness, 1993 survey, B6850–6

Corporate productivity, employment, sales, and operating income, for 46 companies with outstanding productivity improvement, 1992 and trends, C5800–7.532

Corporate revenues and hqs employment, for 9 Forbes 500 companies located in suburban or rural areas, 1992 article, C3950–1.502

Defense industries conversion to nonmilitary production, with data on defense contracts and spending, top contractors, and employment by occupation, 1980s and trends, R4700–19

Doctoral degree recipients, postdoctoral employment plans, 1990/91 and trends, annual rpt, R6000–7

Ecologist personal and professional characteristics, including research activity and funding, with data by field, Mar 1992 survey, recurring rpt, A4685–1

Economic conditions and change in employment expected by consumers, Conference Board monthly survey, R4105–4

Economic dev condition indicators, including economic performance, business vitality, growth capacity, and tax/fiscal system, by State, 1993 annual rpt, R4225–1

Economic indicator forecasts for 30 countries by approx 50 forecasting organizations, including GDP, inflation, unemployment, and interest rates, 1992-94, R4105–6.502

Economic indicator historical trends, 1900s-92, annual rpt, R9050–1.2

Economic indicator trends and forecasts, with detail for approx 15 Western States, 1990s, annual rpt, B3520–1

Economic outlook for selected indicators, recent trends and 2-year forecast, quarterly rpt, A3840–6

Employment in electrical equipment industries and selected industry divs, by geographic area, 1992, annual article, C4725–5.501

Energy (BTU) tax proposed by Clinton Admin, resulting job losses by State, 1994-98, article, R9050–3.506

Energy tax proposals and potential effect on selected economic indicators, 1993-97, article, C6985–1.516

Forbes 500 top companies in sales, profits, assets, market value, and productivity, with stock and employment data, 1992, annual rpt, C3950–1.513

Forecasts for real estate industry and US economy, and housing starts and sales trends by region, monthly rpt, A7000–1

Forecasts for unemployment rate, 50 economists, 4th qtr 1993, annual feature, C5800–7.509

Forecasts of economic indicators for approx 10-13 months, monthly rpt, U1880–3

Forecasts of GDP, inflation, unemployment, and Treasury bond rates, by approx 10 organizations, monthly rpt, R4105–80

Forecasts of natl income and product account components and related indicators, quarterly rpt, U1880–1

Forecasts of natl income and product account components, employment, and financial sector activity, monthly rpt, B4950–1

Fortune magazine ranking of top 50-100 companies in 8 nonindustrial sectors, with financial and employment data, 1992, annual feature, C8900–1.516

Fortune magazine ranking of top 50-100 companies worldwide in 8 nonindustrial sectors, with financial and employment data, 1993 annual feature, C8900–1.522

Fortune 500 largest industrial corporations employment, by company and industry, 1992, annual feature, C8900–1.513

Fortune 500 largest industrial corporations worldwide, with financial and employment data, 1992, annual feature, C8900–1.520

High-technology employment growth rates for top 10 industries, 1993 article, C1850–6.510

Hispanic American labor force and employment data, with comparisons to whites, 1980s-91, annual compilation, C6775–3.4

Hispanic American vs nonminority employment, by occupational group and sex, 1992, article, C4575–1.511

Hispanic-owned business sales and employment, for top 500 companies, 1992, annual feature, C4575–1.507

Hispanic-owned business sales and employment, for 100 fastest-growing companies, 1988-92, annual feature, C4575–1.509

Industrial R&D managers outlook on expenditures, effort, personnel, and other mgmt issues, 1993, annual survey rpt, A5510–1

Job trends by company employment size, 1987-92, article, C5800–7.551

Jobs lost or gained, for 5 cities with greatest losses and gains since June 1990, C8900–1.524

Labor force by employment status, by race, 1991-93, article, C4215–1.502

Labor market behavior, natl longitudinal surveys data users handbook and bibl, 1993 recurring rpt, U3780–2

Law school grad employment and salaries, by type of employer, location, and grad characteristics, 1992 and trends, annual rpt, A6505–1

Low-income families and children, health and welfare indicators, with data by State and city, 1992 annual rpt, R3840–11

Manufacturing and nonmanufacturing shipment value and employment, for top 25 industries, 1992, article, C1200–1.509

Manufacturing employment change, by State, Nov 1992 vs 1991, article, B8500–2.509

Manufacturing employment share, and growth compared to total employment, by State, Feb 1993, article, B8500–2.513

Manufacturing employment share, for top 20 metro areas, 1992, article, A6450–2.509

Manufacturing employment trends and shares of work force, by State, Sept 1992, article, B8500–2.504

Manufacturing employment trends by State, July 1993 vs July 1992, article, B8500–2.523

Manufacturing exports share of private sector employment, by State, 1989, article, B8500–2.508

Manufacturing industry trends including employment, earnings, establishments, and GSP, by State and region, 1970s-92, R8490–48

Manufacturing job trends, for 20 States with greatest proportion of manufacturing employment, May 1991-May 1993, C8900–1.523

Markets with daily newspapers, demographic and economic info by geographic area, US and Canada, 1993 annual rpt, C3250–1

Mathematics dept faculty, salaries, enrollment, and degree recipient characteristics, 1991/92 and trends, annual survey, A2085–1

Men age 69-84 quality of life indicators, including health, finances, family, and employment, by race, 1990 survey, U3780–9

Metro and regional employment trends, total and manufacturing, by region and for approx 50 MSAs, quarterly rpt, B5190–1

Metro area household income trends for central cities vs suburbs, and employment data, for 78 largest MSAs, 1993 rpt, A8012–1.22

Metro area low-income housing supply-demand, with data on population, and poverty and unemployment rates, for 44 metro areas, 1980s-91, R3834–16

Metro area poverty and unemployment level effects on crime and mortality rates, for selected offenses and causes of death, 1990, R4700–18

Metro area rankings by total business employment, for approx 300 metro areas, 1992, annual rpt, C1200–1.511

Metro areas with greatest projected employment growth, with current trends, 1982-2002, article, C8900–1.519

Military base proposed closures effect on total employment, by State, 1993, article, B8500–2.513

Minority population characteristics, employment, and voting patterns by detailed race-ethnicity, with comparisons to whites, 1980s-2040, R8750–2.58

Nonfarm employment, by State, quarterly rpt, U5085–1

North American Free Trade Agreement outlook for 12 major industries, with employment and Mexico trade value, by industry, 1991, article, C8900–1.513

Physics and astronomy bachelor degree recipients postgraduation plans and demographic characteristics, 1991/92 and trends, annual survey, A1960–3

Physics and astronomy grads employment status, by sex, age, subfield, citizenship, degree, and employer type, with salary info, 1990/91, annual rpt, A1960–1

Index by Subjects and Names

Employment and unemployment, general

Planning profession employment and salaries, by type of employer, demographic and professional characteristics, and location, 1991 and trends, biennial rpt, A2615–1

Poor children age 5/under, with demographic and family characteristics, 1991 and trends, annual rpt, U1260–2

Privately held corporation revenues and employment, for 400 largest firms, 1992 annual article, C3950–1.503

Professional women and minorities, detailed education and labor force data, 1980s-91, with historical trends, recurring rpt, A3960–2

Professional worker salaries and employment, by employee and employer characteristics, with detail for scientists and engineers, 1990s and trends, biennial rpt, A3960–1

Projected employment growth through 2005, and employment in 1990, by detailed occupation, article, C8900–1.519

Psychology doctoral degree recipient employment and demographic characteristics, and finances, 1990/91, biennial survey rpt, A2620–4

Public opinion on fear of losing job and other employment-related topics, May 1993 Gallup Poll, C4040–1.511

Public opinion on social, political, and economic issues, detailed data, 1972-91 surveys, annual rpt, U6395–1

Puerto Rico employment of 10 largest US companies manufacturing under IRS Code Section 936, 1993 article, C5800–7.532

Purchasing managers views on business conditions, monthly rpt, A6910–1

Researcher job search methods, 1992 survey, article, C1850–6.504

Retail industry distribution center employment, by outlet type, 1993 survey, C5150–4.506

Retail mgmt info system personnel, 1991, annual feature, C5150–4.501

Retail mgmt info system personnel, 1992, annual feature, C5150–4.509

Scientist and engineer employment, US and foreign, 1993 annual feature, A1250–1.537

Service industries economic devs, with analysis of conditions and outlook, and comparisons to other industries, quarterly rpt, A3892–1

Service sector economic activity indicators, with leading and coincident indexes and components, and detail for financial services, monthly rpt, U1245–3

Small business views on current and expected economic conditions, survey findings, quarterly rpt, A7815–1

Small companies with sales under $25 million, financial and operating data for top 100 public firms, 1992 and trends, annual feature, C4687–1.507

Small privately held companies sales, employment, and other data, for 500 fastest growing firms, 1988 and 1992, annual feature, C4687–1.512

State employment trends, by State, May 1992-93, article, B8500–2.519

State employment trends, by State, semimonthly rpt quarterly article, B8500–2.504, B8500–2.510, B8500–2.516, B8500–2.522

State employment trends, by State, 1985-92, article, B8500–2.517

State social, economic, and govtl indicators, with rankings, 1993 semiannual rpt, B8500–1.2, B8500–1.13

Statistical profiles of 50 States and DC, general data, 1993 annual almanac, C4712–1

Travel and tourism rankings for selected indicators, including data for top 20 States, cities, countries, businesses, and other measures, 1992 recurring rpt, R9375–6

Travel impact on State economies, with detail by industry sector, 1990 and trends, annual rpt, R9375–7

Trends in employment for 19 States with greatest growth and 10 with greatest decline, Nov 1992 vs 1991, article, B8500–2.507

Unemployment insurance trends, including data on unemployment, worker characteristics, coverage, benefits, and State govt finances, 1940s-90, R9260–18

Unemployment rate in DC and selected other central cities and MSAs, monthly rpt, S1527–3

Unemployment rate in 29 cities, Aug 1991-92, annual rpt, A9330–9

Unemployment rates in 10 largest States, Sept 1993, with change from Mar 1991, article, C5800–7.552

Urban public high school grads by type of postgraduation activity, for 47 systems, 1990/91, A4425–4

West Coast employment by industry div, and construction activity, for 3 States, various months 1992-93, article, A6400–2.504

Western States economic indicators, including forecasts from selected organizations, for 10 States, monthly rpt, U0282–2

White-collar work force trends, including employment, earnings, and unionization, with data by occupation, sex, and educational attainment, 1990s and trends, annual rpt, A1570–1

Workers currently employed after losing jobs in last recessionary period, by employment type and percent change in salary, as of Jan 1992, article, C3950–1.513

State and local:

Alabama business activity indicators, monthly rpt, U5680–1

Alabama county data book, general data, 1992 annual rpt, S0121–2

Alabama economic trends and outlook, 1980s-93, annual rpt, U5680–3

Alabama employment for top 20 private employers, 1991, annual rpt, S0129–1

Alabama municipal data book, general data, 1992 recurring rpt, S0121–5

Alabama statistical abstract, general data, 1992 recurring rpt, U5680–2

Alaska employment and unemployment, hours, and earnings, by area and/or industry, monthly rpt, S0320–1

Alaska employment trends and outlook, by industry div, 1991-94, annual feature, S0320–1.507

Arizona economic condition, including population, employment and earnings, and business activity, by industry and locality, 1985-93, semiannual rpt, U5850–1

Arizona economic indicators, including forecasts from 16 forecasting organizations, monthly rpt, U0282–1

Arizona economic trends and forecast, Maricopa County and statewide, monthly rpt quarterly article, U0280–1.503, U0280–1.506, U0280–1.509

Arizona employment and earnings for selected leading industries, 1982-91, article, U0280–1.502

Arizona employment and unemployment, by county and industry, with production worker hours and earnings, monthly rpt, S0465–1

Arizona employment distribution by industry div and occupational group, 1990, article, U0280–1.502

Arizona employment levels in private and public sector jobs, 1990, article, U0280–1.503

Arizona occupational profiles, with employment and job outlook, by industry div, occupation, and county, series, S0465–2

Arizona statistical abstract, general data, 1993 recurring rpt, U5850–2

Arizona temporary winter resident impact on employment by industry div, winter 1992/93, annual article, U0280–1.508

Arizona trends in income, employment, and earnings, during 3 economic cycles, 1970-91, article, U0280–1.504

Arizona unemployment rates as reported by Census Bur vs BLS and State Dept of Economic Security, by county, 1980 and 1990, article, U0280–1.511

Arkansas business and economic activity indicators, quarterly rpt, U5930–1

Arkansas Census of Population and Housing detailed findings, 1990, U5935–7

Arkansas labor force, employment, and unemployment, by MSA, county, and labor area, 1980-92, annual rpt, S0662–2

Arkansas socioeconomic trends, by MSA and/or county, 1993 annual rpt, U5935–1

California Census of Population and Housing detailed findings, 1990, S0840–9

California economic condition, including population, employment and earnings, income, business activity, and taxation, 1993 annual rpt, S0840–3

California economic indicators, bimonthly rpt, S0840–1

California employment statistics, by demographic characteristics, industry, MSA, and county, monthly rpt, S0830–1

California labor force planning rpt, including population characteristics, and employment by industry, 1992 annual rpt, S0830–2

California statistical abstract, general data, 1992 annual rpt, S0840–2.3, S0840–2.5, S0840–2.7, S0840–2.8, S0840–2.11

Colorado employment, unemployment, hours, and earnings, with job service activities, monthly rpt, S1040–4

Colorado labor force planning rpt, including population, employment by industry, and job service applicants, FY94 annual rpt, S1040–3

Connecticut employment, hours, and earnings, by labor market area and industry, and selected economic indicators, monthly rpt, S1235–1

Employment and unemployment, general

Index by Subjects and Names

DC employment, earnings, and hours, by industry, with unemployment insurance data, monthly rpt, S1527–3

DC statistical profile, general data, 1992 annual rpt, S1535–3.3

Delaware data book, general data, 1993 annual rpt, S1375–4

Delaware employment, earnings, and hours, by locality and industry, and unemployment insurance activity, monthly rpt, S1405–2

Delaware employment projections, by county, 1990-2020, recurring rpt, S1375–3

Florida county data book, 1992/93 annual rpt, C6360–1

Florida employment and unemployment, by industry div and location, monthly rpt, S1765–3

Florida statistical abstract, general data, 1992 annual rpt, U6660–1

Georgia and Atlanta MSA forecast employment by industry group and income by source, quarterly rpt, U1880–2

Georgia, Atlanta summer 1996 Olympic games projected impact on State output, earnings, and employment, 1992 article, U6730–2.501

Georgia business activity indicators, bimonthly rpt, U6730–2

Georgia county guide, general data, 1993 annual rpt, U6750–1

Georgia employment, earnings, and hours, by major industry group and MSA, monthly rpt, S1905–1

Georgia prison inmates by employment status at time of arrest, FY92 annual rpt, S1872–1

Georgia statistical abstract, general data, 1992-93 biennial rpt, U6730–1

Hawaii counties population and economic indicators, 1993 annual rpt series, B3500–2

Hawaii data book, general data, 1992 annual rpt, S2090–1

Hawaii economic conditions, including employment, population, tourism, and construction, quarterly rpt, S2090–2

Hawaii economic indicators, bimonthly rpt, B3500–1

Idaho and US economic trends and forecasts, quarterly rpt, S2245–2

Idaho economic profile, general data, 1992 recurring rpt, S2218–2.1, S2218–2.5, S2218–2.10

Idaho employment by industry, by county and labor market area, monthly 1991, annual rpt, S2230–2

Illinois business activity indicators, quarterly rpt, U6910–1

Illinois economic and business activity indicators, including data by industry and county, bimonthly rpt, S2405–2

Illinois statistical abstract, general data, 1992 annual rpt, U6910–2

Indiana business conditions analysis for selected local areas, quarterly rpt semiannual feature, U2160–1.502, U2160–1.504

Indiana labor force and employment, 1982-91, annual rpt, S2570–1.1

Iowa labor force supply-demand data, including population, earnings, and employment by industry and occupation, 1993 annual rpt, S2784–3

Kansas business activity indicators, quarterly rpt, U7095–1

Kansas statistical abstract, general data, 1991/92 annual rpt, U7095–2.8, U7095–2.9

Kentucky economic statistics, general data, 1993 annual rpt, S3104–1

Kentucky labor force planning rpt, including population and labor force characteristics, and employment by industry, 1991 and trends, annual rpt, S3140–3

Louisiana Census of Population and Housing summary findings, by local area, 1990 and trends, U8010–4

Louisiana employment, hours, and earnings, by industry and MSA, monthly rpt, S3320–2

Louisiana labor force planning rpt, including population and labor force characteristics, unemployment claimants, and data by parish and MSA, 1993 annual rpt, S3320–1

Maine Census of Population and Housing summary findings, by local area, 1990, S3465–9

Maine employment, by SIC 2-digit industry and detailed occupation, triennial series, S3465–1

Maine employment, unemployment, and earnings, by industry group, MSA, and labor area, monthly rpt, S3465–2

Maine statistical summary, general economic and social data, 1992 recurring rpt, S3434–1

Maryland labor force, employment, earnings, and hours, with data by industry and location, monthly rpt, S3605–2

Maryland statistical abstract, general data, 1993-94 biennial rpt, S3605–1

Massachusetts employment, by SIC 2- and 3-digit industry and detailed occupation, suspended series, S3808–2

Massachusetts employment, hours, and earnings, by industry and local area, with unemployment insurance claims, monthly rpt, S3808–1

Massachusetts municipal and county profiles, general data, 1992 annual rpt, C4712–2

Michigan employment, hours, and earnings, with detail by industry and local area, monthly rpt, S3980–2

Michigan labor force planning rpt, including employment by industry, and characteristics of Job Training Partnership Act eligible population, 1993 annual rpt, S3980–1

Minnesota employment, hours, and earnings, by industry group and locality, monthly rpt, S4205–1

Minnesota labor and economic trends, quarterly rpt, S4205–3

Mississippi labor force planning rpt, including population, employment, and characteristics of unemployed and disadvantaged, 1993 annual rpt, S4345–1

Mississippi statistical abstract, general data, 1992 annual rpt, U3255–4.4, U3255–4.5, U3255–4.6

Missouri employment, earnings, and hours, and employment security program activity, by industry and/or county, FY92 and trends, annual rpt, S4530–2.3

Missouri employment, earnings, and hours, by industry and MSA, monthly rpt, S4530–3

Montana employment and unemployment, earnings, and hours, by location and/or industry, quarterly rpt, S4710–1

Montana labor force planning rpt, including population, income, and employment and job openings by industry and occupation, with selected data by county, 1993-94 annual rpt, S4710–3

Nebraska business and economic activity indicators, monthly rpt, U7860–1

Nebraska employment and unemployment, by industry group and locality, quarterly rpt, S4895–2

Nevada business and economic activity indicators, with comparisons to other Western States, 1980-91, annual rpt, U7920–2

Nevada employment, hours, and earnings, by industry, and unemployment by county, quarterly rpt, S5040–1

Nevada labor force conditions and outlook, with data by industry, MSA, and county, 1992 annual rpt, S5040–4

Nevada statistical abstract, general data, 1992 biennial rpt, S5005–1.6

New Hampshire employment, by SIC 2- and 3-digit industry and detailed occupation, series, S5205–2

New Hampshire employment, hours, and earnings, by industry and area, monthly rpt, S5205–1

New Hampshire labor force and population by race, sex, and age, and employment by industry div, statewide and by county, 1992 recurring rpt, S5205–7

New Jersey Census of Population and Housing detailed findings, by county, 1990, S5425–19

New Jersey economic indicators, including employment, building permits, and retail trade, monthly rpt, S5425–1

New Jersey municipal and county data book, general data, 1992 annual rpt, C4712–4

New Mexico business and economic activity indicators, monthly rpt, U7980–1

New Mexico employment, hours, and earnings, by labor market area and industry, monthly rpt, S5624–2

New Mexico labor force planning rpt, including population characteristics, and employment by industry and occupation, 1993 annual rpt, S5624–1

New York State business activity indicators, quarterly rpt, S5735–2

New York State business and economic indicators, by MSA, county, and industry, 1980s-91, annual rpt, S5735–3

New York State employment, earnings, and hours, by county, selected metro area, and industry group, monthly rpt, S5775–1

New York State municipal and county statistical profiles, general data, 1993 annual rpt, C4712–7

New York State statistical yearbook, general data, 1992 annual rpt, U5100–1.2, U5100–1.3, U5100–1.9

North Carolina employment, hours, and earnings, by industry group, with job placements, monthly rpt, S5917–3

North Carolina employment in SIC 2-digit industries, by detailed occupation, triennial rpt series, S5917–5

North Carolina labor force and employment by industry, by county, MSA, labor area, and planning region, 1991 and trends, annual rpt, S5917–4

Index by Subjects and Names

Employment and unemployment, general

North Dakota employment, hours, and earnings, by industry div and/or location, monthly rpt, S6140–4

North Dakota labor force planning rpt, including population, employment, and earnings, with data by industry and county, 1993 annual rpt, S6140–2

Ohio employment, hours, and earnings, by industry and MSA, with job service and unemployment insurance activities, monthly rpt, S6270–1

Oklahoma business activity indicators, monthly rpt, U8130–1

Oklahoma employment, hours, and earnings, by industry and MSA, with unemployment insurance and job service activities, monthly rpt, S6430–2

Oklahoma statistical abstract, general data, 1992 annual rpt, U8130–2.3, U8130–2.13, U8130–2.14, U8130–2.15

Oklahoma unemployment rates, by county, 1991, annual rpt, S6455–1.1

Oregon economic conditions, including population, construction, income, employment, industry, and foreign trade data, 1991, annual rpt, S6585–3

Oregon employment, population, and other economic devs, discontinued biennial rpt, S6615–9

Oregon labor force and employment statistics, including data by industry, monthly rpt, S6592–1, S6615–2

Pennsylvania business activity indicators, monthly rpt, U4110–1

Pennsylvania Census of Population and Housing detailed findings, with selected data by county and municipality, 1990, U4130–13

Pennsylvania economic trends and outlook for gross regional product, personal income, and employment, 1980s-93, annual article, U4110–1.504

Pennsylvania employment and commuting data from Census of Population and Housing, by county and municipality, 1990, C1595–16

Pennsylvania employment, hours, and earnings, by industry, monthly rpt, S6845–1

Pennsylvania labor force planning rpt, including population characteristics, employment and job openings by industry and occupation, and income trends, FY92 annual rpt, S6845–3

Pennsylvania statistical abstract, general data, 1992 recurring rpt, U4130–6.2, U4130–6.3, U4130–6.8

Pennsylvania vocational education grads employment status, by field, 1992, annual rpt, S6790–5.7

Pennsylvania vocational education 1989/90 grad employment status, by program, 1991 survey, annual rpt, S6790–5.6

Rhode Island Census of Population and Housing detailed findings, by county and municipality, 1990, S6930–9

Rhode Island employment, hours, and earnings, by industry, monthly rpt, S6980–1

Rhode Island labor force planning rpt, including population, employment by industry, job openings, and characteristics of insured unemployed, 1993 annual rpt, S6980–3

Rhode Island statistical almanac, general data, 1993 annual rpt, C7975–1.1

South Carolina economic activity indicators, including employment by industry div, by county, 1993 annual rpt, S7145–1.2

South Carolina economic condition, including employment, manufacturing, and income, 1970s-92, annual rpt, S7125–3.2

South Carolina employment, earnings, and hours, by industry group and locality, monthly rpt, S7155–2

South Carolina labor force planning rpt, including population, employment, income, and job service activities, 1992 annual rpt, S7155–3

South Carolina statistical abstract, general data, 1993 annual rpt, S7125–1.1, S7125–1.3, S7125–1.7

South Dakota business activity review, including selected data by city and industry, quarterly rpt, U8595–1

South Dakota employment, earnings, and hours for selected industries and areas, with characteristics of unemployed and job service activities, monthly rpt, S7355–1

Tennessee business activity indicators, quarterly journal, U8710–1

Tennessee economic indicator trends and forecasts, and business executives views on selected issues, 1993 annual articles, U8710–1.502

Tennessee economic indicator trends and forecasts, with data by industry div and manufacturing group, 1982-2001, annual rpt, S7560–1

Tennessee employment, hours, and earnings, by industry group and MSA, monthly rpt, S7495–2

Tennessee employment, wages, and unemployment insurance contributions, by county and industry, 1991, annual rpt, S7495–1

Tennessee statistical abstract, general data, 1992/93 annual rpt, U8710–2

Texas employment, by SIC 2- and 3-digit industry and detailed occupation, series, S7675–1

Texas employment, hours, and earnings, by MSA and industry group, and unemployment insurance, monthly rpt, S7675–3

Texas labor force planning rpt, including labor force, employment by industry, income, and population, 1993 annual rpt, S7675–2

Utah business activity indicators, by county, 1988-91, annual feature, U8960–2.501

Utah business activity indicators, by county, 1989-92, annual feature, U8960–2.507

Utah business firms, wages, and employment, by firm size, SIC 2-digit industry, and county, 1st qtr 1992, annual rpt, S7820–1

Utah economic and business activity review and indicators, monthly rpt, U8960–2

Utah economic and demographic trends, by county and district, 1960-91, annual rpt, S7832–2

Utah employment and wages for workers born in Utah vs other States, by industry div, 3rd qtr 1992, article, S7820–3.507

Utah employment by detailed occupation, and educational attainment by age group, by sex and race-ethnicity, with detail for 7 urban areas, 1990 census rpt, S7832–3.4

Utah employment, hours, and earnings, by industry, monthly rpt, S7820–3

Utah govt statistical review, fiscal and socioeconomic data, 1993 annual rpt, R9380–1.1, R9380–1.2, R9380–1.9

Utah homeless shelter population characteristics, including employment status, 1991-92, annual rpt, S7808–2

Utah Indian reservation unemployment rate, by reservation, 1990, census rpt, S7832–3.3

Utah labor force characteristics, employment and unemployment, hours, and earnings, with data by industry and locale, 1992 and trends, annual rpt, S7820–10

Utah statistical abstract, general data, 1993 triennial rpt, U8960–1

Vermont labor force by employment status, and job service openings and applicant characteristics, 1993 annual planning rpt, S8025–2.2

Virginia business activity indicators, by local area, monthly rpt, U1120–1

Virginia economic indicators, including new business incorporations and employment data, quarterly rpt, S8205–4

Virginia employment and GSP, by industry div, 1989, recurring rpt, U9080–6

Virginia labor force, hours, and earnings, with data by industry group and locality, monthly rpt, S8205–6

Washington State employment, earnings, and hours, by labor market area and industry group, monthly rpt, S8340–3

Washington State population and demographic characteristics, and housing units, by county and/or city, 1992 and trends, annual rpt, S8345–4

West Virginia employment, unemployment, hours, and earnings, with job service activities, monthly rpt, S8534–1

West Virginia labor force planning rpt, including population, employment, and job service activities, with data by county and service delivery area, 1993 annual rpt, S8534–2

West Virginia statistical handbook, general data, 1992 annual rpt, R9385–1.1, R9385–1.3

Wisconsin Blue Book, general data, 1993-94 biennial rpt, S8780–1.2

Wisconsin economic indicators, including employment and earnings by industry group, monthly rpt, S8750–1

Wyoming employment by industry group and county, with unemployment insurance and job service activities, monthly rpt, S8895–1

see also Absenteeism

see also Agricultural labor

see also Alien workers

see also Blue collar workers

see also Child labor

see also Clerical workers

see also Discrimination in employment

see also Earnings, general

see also Economic indicators

see also Employee benefits

see also Employee development

see also Employee performance and appraisal

see also Employment and unemployment, specific industry

see also Employment services

see also Executives and managers

Employment and unemployment, general

see also Foreign labor conditions
see also Government employees
see also Home-based offices and workers
see also Hours of labor
see also Job creation
see also Job tenure
see also Job Training Partnership Act
see also Job vacancy
see also Labor law
see also Labor-management relations, general
see also Labor-management relations in government
see also Labor mobility
see also Labor supply and demand
see also Labor turnover
see also Manpower training programs
see also Migrant workers
see also Minority employment
see also Moonlighting
see also Occupations
see also Overtime
see also Part-time employment
see also Payroll
see also Personnel management
see also Production workers
see also Professional and technical workers
see also Public service employment
see also Retirement
see also Sales workers
see also Self-employment
see also Service workers
see also Sheltered workshops
see also Temporary and seasonal employment
see also Unemployment insurance
see also Veterans employment
see also Vocational rehabilitation
see also Volunteers
see also Women's employment
see also Work conditions
see also Work incentive programs
see also Work stoppages
see also Youth employment

Employment and unemployment, specific industry

Advertising agency income, billings by medium, employees, and offices, for leading US and/or foreign agencies, 1992 and trends, annual rpt, C2710–1.522

Advertising agency personnel compensation, and employment trends, 1992 annual feature, C2710–1.505

Advertising media buying services, competition, and staffing, views of agency and independent service executives, 1993 annual survey articles, C2710–1.537

Aerospace industry employment by sector and occupation, with distribution by census div, 1979-91, annual rpt, A0250–2.5

Airline employment for top 20 US/Canadian carriers, 1990, recurring rpt, R9375–6

Airline finances and operations of scheduled carriers, summary statistics, 1992 and trends, annual rpt, A0325–5

Airline maintenance budget, employment, and contracting trends, for 38 carriers worldwide, 1992 article, C7000–4.501

Airline market activity, including traffic, financial performance, employment, and fleet composition, by US and foreign carrier, 1991-92, annual feature, C7000–4.508

Airline summary financial, employment, and traffic data, 1977 and 1992, C5800–4.525

Amusement park operating and financial data, including data for US and foreign parks, miniature golf, waterparks, and games, 1992, annual rpt, A5700–1

Arts fundraising through united arts funds (UAFs), with UAF full- and part-time employment, by UAF, 1992, annual rpt, A1315–2

Biotechnology company finances, employment, and firms, with detail for public companies, FY92-93, annual article, A1250–1.542

Biotechnology industry summary financial performance and employment data, with detail for public companies, 1991-92, article, A6400–2.503

Blood bank operating profiles, arranged by State, 1993 biennial directory, A0612–1

Book publishing industry financial and operating data, by publisher type and size, and subject category, 1991 and trends, annual rpt, A3274–2

Brewing industry financial and operating data, including consumption, trade, and taxes, 1991 and trends, annual rpt, A3455–1

Broadcasting (public) full-time employment, with detail for women and minorities, by job category, 1977-92, recurring rpt, R4250–1.23

Brokerage firm personnel in US, New York State, NYC, and NYSE, 1992 and trends, annual fact book, B6625–1

Bus charter service employment and average weekly earnings, with comparisons to intercity/rural bus transport workers, 1972, 1982, and 1990-91, article, C1575–3.504

Business forms industry detailed financial and operating ratios, with summary operating data, FY91, annual rpt, A5785–3

Business incubator facilities finances and operations, including services offered and tenant characteristics, 1991, annual rpt, A7360–1

Catholic charity social service agency activities, clients, finances, and personnel, 1991 and trends, annual rpt, A3810–1

Chambers of commerce income, salaries and benefits, membership, staff, and operations, 1993 annual rpt, A3840–3

Chemical and related industries production, finances, operating ratios, employment, and trade, by country, company, and chemical, 1980s-92, annual feature, A1250–1.530

Chemical industry finances and operations, with data by industry segment and product, 1970s-92, annual rpt, A3850–1

Chemical process industry employment in 23 countries, 1991-92, article, C5800–8.509

Clothing (men's and boys) production, trade, and operating data, by garment type, 1960s-92, annual rpt, A3880–1

Clothing (women's and children's) sales, production, imports, and industry employment, hours, and earnings, by type of garment, recurring rpt, A5900–1

Coal mine employment and productivity, 1986-91, annual rpt, A7400–2.1

Computer industry employment and sales productivity, for 5 manufacturers, FY92, article, C1850–2.507

Computer services employment, 1988-93, article, C1850–5.508

Computer software company revenues and employment, for top 100 firms worldwide, 1992, annual article, C1850–5.520

Computer/office equipment industry employment and new order trends, 1984-94, article, C1850–5.511

Container (fiber box) shipments by end-use industry and region, and other industry operating data, 1940s-92, annual rpt, A4875–1

Convenience store employment data, 1992 and trends, annual survey rpt, A6735–1, A6735–2

Electric utility financial and operating data, by State and census div, 1991 and trends, annual rpt, A4700–1

Electrical equipment wholesaler market conditions, by geographic area, 1992 annual article, C4725–5.501

Electrical equipment wholesalers, sales, employment, and facility size, top 250 companies, 1992, annual article, C4725–5.506

Electronics company financial data and business info for approx 500 companies, 1991-92 and trends, annual rpt, C3400–4

Electronics company revenues, funding, and employment, for 25 companies started in the recent past, 1993 recurring article, C1850–2.505

Electronics industry factory sales and shipments, foreign trade, and operating data, by product category, 1980s-92, annual rpt, A4725–1

Electronics industry market devs, including employment and wages, by sector, monthly rpt, A4725–2

Financial institutions, employment, and finances, and volume of printing business generated, 1992 feature, C1850–10.501

Financial instns owned by blacks, with financial and employment data, 1992 and trends, annual feature, C4215–1.507

Food marketers financial and operating data, by company size and region, 1991, annual rpt, A4950–5.2

Food marketers mgmt info system operations, employment, and finances, for wholesalers and retailers by sales size, 1993 and trends, annual survey, A4950–7

Food plant construction/expansion project info, cost, and employees, by company, 1992, annual feature, C2150–6.506

Food processing industry devs, including work force reduction, finances, and employment, 1993 annual feature, C2150–6.507

Food service industry employee characteristics, and minority-owned establishments and sales, 1993 article, A8200–1.508

Food service industry employment and turnover rate, by type of operation, 1991, annual article, A8200–1.508

Food service industry work force, work-related injuries, and lost workdays, 1990-91, article, C1200–5.507

Food service wages and employment, for 18 positions, 1992 survey, biennial article, A8200–1.503

Food/lodging/entertainment establishments, employment, receipts, and payroll, and volume of printing business generated, 1992 feature, C1850–10.503

Index by Subjects and Names

Employment and unemployment, specific industry

Foundation finances, and personnel and governing board characteristics, by organization characteristics, 1991/92, article, C2176–1.506

Foundation full- and part-time staff, by asset size, 1992, annual rpt, R4900–1

Frozen dessert industry employment, wages, and capital expenditures, 1969-92, annual rpt, A5825–1.1

Fuel oil dealer operations, with heating and cooling equipment services, by region, 1992 annual survey, C4680–2

Hard goods manufacturers employment and outlook for 1993, by product line, annual survey rpt, A1800–1

High-technology company sales and employment, for top 50 Hispanic-owned firms, 1992, annual article, C4575–1.510

High-technology small companies with rapid growth, employment and sales data for 25 firms, 1993 article, C5800–7.551

Home improvement industry sales and operations, for top distributors, cooperatives, and marketing organizations, 1991-92, annual feature, C5150–6.502

Home improvement industry sales and operations, for top retailers, 1992 and trends, annual feature, C5150–6.503

Homebuilder financial and operating data, including detail by location, for top 400 builders, 1993 annual feature, C1850–8.507

Homebuilder operations and finances, by region and sales size group, 1992 survey, article, C4300–1.501

Hospital financial and operating data, including ambulatory surgery and emergency service utilization, semimonthly rpt quarterly feature, A1865–1.506, A1865–1.512

Household appliance industry manufacturing and market trends, by product type, various years 1920-94, biennial rpt, A3350 3

Industrial distributor sales, branches, employment, and operating profiles, for top 50 companies, 1992, annual article, C1850–4.506

Industrial distributor sales, employment, and inventory turns, for top 25 companies with sales of $5 million/less, 1991, annual article, C1850–4.503

Information technology company sales and employment, for 25 innovative firms, 1993 article, C8900–1.525

Insurance industry employment, payroll, share of GSP, and premium taxes, by State, 1992 annual rpt, A0375–2

Insurance industry employment, 1982-91, annual rpt, A5650–1.1

Interior design industry financial and employment data, top 100 firms, 1993 annual article, C1850–7.501

Interior design industry financial and employment data, 2nd 100 largest firms, 1993 annual article, C1850–7.502

Investment mgmt firms, assets and operating data for approx 900 instns, Jan 1993, annual feature, C2710–2.511

Iron and steel industry financial and operating data, 1992 and trends, annual rpt, A2000–2.1

Iron ore mining industry employment, wages, and hours, 1983-92, annual rpt, A2010–3.3

Jewelry industry statistics on sales, marketing, trade, and employment, with customer characteristics, 1993 annual almanac, C2150–7.509

Legal services establishments, employment, receipts, and payroll, and volume of printing business generated, 1992 feature, C1850–10.502

Library school grad placements and salaries, by region, sex, instn, and library type, with detail for minorities, 1992 and trends, annual article, C1852–1.512

Life insurance firms and employment, 1991 and trends, biennial fact book, A1325–1.5

Lumber industry production in Western States and counties, with acreage owned, employment, and sawmill operations, 1980s-92, annual rpt, A9395–1

Lumber industry supply-demand, sales, trade, and employment, monthly rpt, A1630–1

Machine tool industry employment, compensation, and operations, 1992 and trends, annual rpt, A3179–2.1

Market research industry devs, including revenues and operations of leading firms, 1991-92, annual feature, C2710–1.550

Mass transit system finances and operations, passengers, and employment, by mode, US and Canada, 1990-91 and trends, annual rpt, A2650–1

Meat and poultry demand, prices, and processor operations and finances, with data on meat production, 1991 and trends, annual rpt, A2100–1.1

Medical group financial and operating data, by practice characteristics, 1991, annual rpt, A6365–2

Mineral exploration activities, expenses, and staff, for foreign and domestic operations of US and Canadian companies, 1991, article, C5226–2.508

Motor vehicle, dealership, and related industries operating data, with data by State and industry segment, 1990s and trends, annual rpt, A0865–1.3

Motor vehicle dealership financial and operating data, including sales and employment by State, 1970s-93, annual rpt, A7330–1

Motor vehicle industry employment in North America, 1979 and 1991, article, C2150–3.502

Motor vehicle parts suppliers affiliated with Japanese companies, with employment and plant square footage, 1990 and 1992-93, article, C2710–3.553

Motor vehicle plant capacity, production, employment, and productivity, for 12 plants in 6 countries, 1993 article, C2150–3.504

Motorcycle retail outlets, employees, and payroll, by State, 1992, annual rpt, A6485–1.1

Museums and related instns staff and volunteers, by instn type, 1989/90 survey, A0750–1.1

Natural gas industry employment, payroll, and accident statistics, 1960s-91, annual rpt, A1775–3.9

Newspaper employment, by sex, 1960-92, annual rpt, A8605–4

Nonprofit organization employment by State, and foundation boards, officers, and staff by sex and race, 1993 annual rpt, A0700–1.1

Nonprofit organizations employment, with comparison to population, by State, 1990, article, C2176–1.505

Oil and gas industry employment and earnings, by industry segment, 1950s-91, annual compilation, C6985–9.5

Oil and gas industry employment and earnings, 1993 and trends, periodic basic data book, A2575–14.3, A2575–14.7

Oil and gas industry employment, with detail by State, 1992, annual rpt, A5425–1

Oil industry employment, by State and function, Jan 1992, annual fact book, C4680–1.507

Oil/gas employment, by industry segment, 1973-92, annual rpt, A5425–2.2

Oil/gas industry occupational injury, illness, and employment data, by function, for 136 companies, 1991, annual rpt, A2575–4

Paper and paperboard industry financial and operating data, by product, region, and State, 1992 and trends, annual rpt, A1630–6

Plastics industry operating and financial data, 1992 and trends, annual rpt, A8920–1.1

Plastics processing industry employment, compensation practices, and union representation, by region, 1992, annual survey rpt, A8920–2

Printing and publishing industries operations and outlook, including paper shipments and prices, monthly rpt, C1850–10

Printing company sales, employment, and equipment, for top 101 North American firms, 1993 annual feature, C1850–10.512

Publishing employment and productivity indicators, for 10 companies, 1992-93, article, C1852–2.521

Pulp and paper industry operations and finances, US and Canada, with detail by company and product grade, and world production and trade summary, 1993 annual rpt, C3975–5

Pulp and paper mill machine maintenance operations and personnel, by region and grade, 1992 survey, recurring article, C3975–2.504

Pulp, paper, and paperboard industry production, trade, and operating data, by product class, monthly rpt, A1630–5

Railroad (Class I) employment, by employee category, monthly rpt, C8400–1

Railroad (Class I) financial condition, operations, and employment, by company and district, 1992, annual rpt, A3275–7

Railroad employment for 4 lines in Texas and for Mexico natl railroad, 1992, U8850–9

Railroad employment, payroll, and hours, with data by occupational class and company, 1920s-92, annual rpt, A3275–5.4

Railroad financial and operating trends, including data by company, 1982-91, annual rpt, A3275–8

Railroad operating data, including top commodities handled, employment and wages, and retirement system, by State, 1991, annual rpt, A3275–10

Religious congregation characteristics, including membership, activities, staff, and finances, 1992 survey, recurring rpt, A5435–4

Employment and unemployment, specific industry

Restaurant (hamburger) employment and other operating data, for 3 low-price drive-through chains, 1993, article, C1200–5.514

Restaurant industry financial and operating data, by establishment characteristics and location, 1992, annual rpt, A8200–3

Restaurant sales, payroll/benefits, and employment, with detail for hotel establishments, 1993 article, C5150–5.507

Restaurant State assn staff, payroll, locations represented, and political action committee spending, for organizations in 14 States, 1993 article, C1200–5.510

Securities industry employment, 3rd qtr 1987-1st qtr 1992, recurring article, A8825–1.501

Securities industry employment, 3rd qtr 1987-1st qtr 1993, recurring article, A8825–1.505

Security equipment industry revenues, accounts, and operating data, for 100 leading companies, 1992, annual feature, C1850–13.507

Security operations at shopping centers, including staffing, equipment, and crime incidents, by center type, 1992-93 and trends, articles, C5150–4.506

Shipbuilding related employment impact of foreign govt subsidies, 1990-2000, recurring rpt, A8900–8

Shoe industry production and operating data, including trade by country, retail sales, and consumer expenditures, quarterly rpt, A4957–2

Shoe industry production, employment, trade, marketing, and related data, by SIC 2- to 5-digit code or product type, 1992 annual rpt, A4957–1.2

Space launch crew for 4 vehicles, and staff at 3 launch base/range operations centers, 1993 article, C5800–4.532

Steel industry finances, operations, and employment, with data for integrated plants and mini-mills, 1970s-93, article, U2160–1.503

Steel industry operating trends and devs, including profiles of 4 major companies, 1960-90, U9640–2.15

Steel industry restructuring devs, with data on production, employment, and worker assistance, and selected detail by company, for 8-12 countries, 1970s-90, R9260–16

Steel mill employment, capacity, shipments, and other operating info, for individual mini and market mills, 1992 annual feature, C7000–8.501

Stockbroker commissions, fees, analysts, offices, and brokers, for 18 firms, 1993 annual article, C8900–1.528

Stockbroker income and employment, for 8 major securities firms, 1992, article, C5800–7.509

Supermarket bakery dept full- and part-time employees, 1992, annual article, C4655–1.505, C5225–1.504

Supermarket deli dept full- and part-time employees, 1992, annual article, C4655–1.503, C5225–1.505

Supermarket employees and sales productivity, by store characteristics and region, 1992, annual rpt, C5225–1.505

Supermarket fish/seafood dept full- and part-time employees, 1991, annual article, C4655–1.501

Supermarket general merchandise dept full- and part-time employees, 1992, annual article, C4655–1.509

Supermarket health and beauty aid dept full- and part-time employees, 1992, annual article, C4655–1.506

Supermarket meat dept full- and part-time employees, 1992, annual article, C4655–1.509

Supermarket produce dept full- and part-time employees, 1992, annual article, C4655–1.511

Telecommunication operations, including number of countries with selected types of equipment, services, and staff, for 6 major carriers, 1993 article, C1850–5.520

Telephone holding company finances, operations, and subsidiaries, by company, Dec 1991, annual rpt, A9360–1

Telephone local exchange carrier finances, equipment, and employment, by company, 1991 and trends, annual rpt, A9360–2

Textile and clothing employment in US affiliates of foreign companies, 1989-90, annual rpt, C3400–5

Textile industry economic and operating performance and outlook, 1988-93, annual article, C5226–3.502

Textile industry economic performance indicators and outlook, with industry trends and devs, monthly rpt, C5226–3

Textile manufactured fiber industry employment, for US, Europe, and selected Asian countries, 1980-91, annual feature, C3460–1.505

Theater (nonprofit professional) finances and operations, including revenues by source, 1992 and trends, annual survey, A9065–1

Theater (nonprofit professional) finances and operations, 1992, article, C2176–1.509

Transportation employment trends by mode, 1992 annual rpt, R4815–1

TV station personnel and compensation, by position, and benefits, 1991, biennial rpt, A6635–9

Venture capital industry finances and operations, 1991 and trends, annual rpt, A8515–1

Veterinarians by location and type of employment, 1990 and 1992, article, A3100–2.522

Veterinarians by professional characteristics and location, and financial and education summaries, 1993 annual directory, A3100–1

Veterinary school grad employment, starting salaries, benefits, and personal characteristics, by sex, 1992, annual survey article, A3100–2.504

State and local:

Arizona and US copper industry employment data, 1991 and trends, annual rpt, S0497–1

Arizona defense contracts and value, employment, and wages, for aggregate leading contractors, 1987-92, article, S0465–1.509

California aerospace industry job losses, for 3 southern areas and rest of State, 1988-Aug 1992, article, C5800–4.502

Index by Subjects and Names

Florida insurance industry employment, 1991, annual rpt, S1760–1

Maryland building materials/garden supplies industry employment and wages, by industry and occupational group, June 1991, article, S3605–2.501

Nevada casino finances and employment, by location and gaming revenue range, FY92, annual rpt, S5062–1

Nevada mining employment by county, 1985-90, biennial rpt, S5005–1.12

New Jersey casino revenues and operations for 12 facilities, with State regulatory activities, 1992 and trends, annual rpt, S5360–1

New York State telephone access lines and employment, by company, 1988 and 1991, annual rpt, S5795–1

North Carolina public utility financial, operating, and regulatory data, by utility type and company, 1990 and trends, annual rpt, S5917–2

Oregon nursery and greenhouse industry workers and wages, 1991, annual rpt, S6575–1

Pennsylvania coal industry employment and work-related fatalities, 1960-90, recurring rpt, S6810–3

Tennessee industrial loan and thrift companies employment, 1990-91, annual rpt, S7507–1

Utah high-technology industry trends, with R&D spending, and employment of major firms, 1986-92, recurring article, U8960–2.508

Vermont telephone company employment, by company, 1986-91, biennial rpt, S8100–1

see also Agricultural labor
see also Discrimination in employment
see also Earnings, specific industry
see also Employee benefits
see also Employee development
see also Employee performance and appraisal
see also Executives and managers
see also Foreign labor conditions
see also Government employees
see also Health occupations
see also Home-based offices and workers
see also Hours of labor
see also Job creation
see also Job vacancy
see also Labor-management relations, general
see also Labor mobility
see also Labor turnover
see also Migrant workers
see also Moonlighting
see also Overtime
see also Payroll
see also Personnel management
see also Public service employment
see also Retirement
see also School administration and staff
see also Work conditions
see also Work stoppages
see also under By Industry in the "Index by Categories"
see also under By Occupation in the "Index by Categories"

Employment services

Business hiring costs by item, and new hires by source, 1992 and trends, annual survey rpt, A4740–2

Federal budget trends, including spending by program, State, and region, FY81-94, annual rpt, R8490–11

Financial ratios and performance, for over 350 SIC 4-digit industries, FY88-92, annual rpt, A6400–3

Franchise operations and finances, by type of business, 1991/92 and trends, annual rpt, A5820–1

Shopping center financial and operating data, with detail by type of tenant, US and Canada, 1991, triennial rpt, R9285–1

State and local:

Alabama public welfare and social service cases, recipients, and payments, by program and county, monthly rpt, S0150–1

California statistical abstract, general data, 1992 annual rpt, S0840–2.3

Colorado employment, unemployment, hours, and earnings, with job service activities, monthly rpt, S1040–4

Colorado job service applicant characteristics, FY93 annual planning rpt, S1040–3.2

Georgia statistical abstract, general data, 1992-93 biennial rpt, U6730–1.13

Louisiana job service openings and applicants, and characteristics of Job Training Partnership Act target population and insured unemployed, 1993 annual planning rpt, S3320–1.2

Maryland statistical abstract, general data, 1993-94 biennial rpt, S3605–1.4

Minnesota work readiness program registrants and payments, 1992, semiannual rpt, S4202–1

Mississippi job service applicants and placement activity, 1991/92, annual planning rpt, S4345–1.3

Missouri employment, earnings, and hours, and employment security program activity, by industry and/or county, FY92 and trends, annual rpt, S4530–2.3

New Hampshire job service activities, including applicant characteristics and job openings, monthly rpt, S3205–1

New Mexico job service applicants and openings, by leading occupation, 1993 annual planning rpt, S5624–1

New York State AFDC and home relief recipients participating in employment service programs, by program, 1991, annual rpt, S5800–2.1

North Carolina employment, hours, and earnings, by industry group, with job placements, monthly rpt, S5917–3

North Carolina public welfare programs, cases, recipients, staff, and finances, by county, 1st half FY93, semiannual rpt, S5940–2

Ohio job service program applicants, referrals, and openings, monthly rpt, S6270–1

Oklahoma AFDC employment program participants, and placements by county, FY92, annual rpt, S6455–1.2

Oklahoma employment, hours, and earnings, by industry and MSA, with unemployment insurance and job service activities, monthly rpt, S6430–2

Oregon public welfare caseloads, recipients, and expenditures, by program, city, county, and State region, monthly rpt, S6615–8

Pennsylvania job applicants and openings, by sex and/or occupation, FY91, annual planning rpt, S6845–3.3

Pennsylvania statistical abstract, general data, 1992 recurring rpt, U4130–6.3

South Carolina labor force planning rpt, detailed data on employment, hours, wages, turnover, and characteristics of job service applicants, 1992 annual rpt, S7155–3.2

South Carolina public welfare recipients, payments, and case processing, by county and program, monthly rpt, S7252–1

South Dakota job service applicants, placements, and openings, monthly rpt, S7355–1

Vermont labor force by employment status, and job service openings and applicant characteristics, 1993 annual planning rpt, S8025–2.2

Washington State public assistance clients and service costs, by client characteristics, program, and county, FY90, annual rpt, S8420–2

West Virginia employment, unemployment, hours, and earnings, with job service activities, monthly rpt, S8534–1

West Virginia labor force planning rpt, including population, employment, and job service activities, with data by county and service delivery area, 1993 annual rpt, S8534–2

Wyoming employment by industry group and county, with unemployment insurance and job service activities, monthly rpt, S8895–1

Encephalitis

see Infective and parasitic diseases

Endangered species

Animal and plant species threatened, by major taxa, by country, 1990, biennial rpt, R9455–1.6

City govt costs to enforce Fed Govt regulations including Endangered Species Act, FY93-98, A9330–12

OECD threatened bird and mammal species, for 11 countries, 1992/93 biennial rpt, R9455–1.3

State and local:

Hawaii endangered, threatened, and extinct fauna and flora, Dec 1990, annual rpt, S2090–1.5

Nebraska income tax return donations to endangered species fund, by county, 1990, annual rpt, S4950–1.1

see also Birds and bird conservation

Endocrine diseases

see Metabolic and endocrine diseases

Endowment funds

see Gifts and private contributions

Energy assistance

see Low-income energy assistance

Energy conservation

Appliance energy efficiency trends, by product type, 1972-91, with Govt standards for 1990-94, biennial rpt, A3350–3

College freshmen attitudes on discouraging energy consumption, by sex and instn type, fall 1992, annual survey, U6215–1

Electric and total energy shares from renewable sources, 1989, semiannual rpt, B8500–1.12

Electric utility demand-side mgmt program impact on electricity demand in 8 States, by 2000, article, C4725–5.502

Electric utility demand-side mgmt programs and investment, by program type, 1992-95, article, C5800–28.502

Energy exploration and drilling

Electric utility demand-side mgmt programs by type, by utility type, 1993 article, C6985–6.511

Fuel cell technology potential impact on energy use and nitrogen oxide emissions, 1992 article, C5226–2.501

Gasoline saved under older vehicle scrapping plan, and emissions reduction and benefits, 1993 annual rpt, C6985–3.2

Mass transit vs auto use, estimated fuel savings, 1992 annual rpt, A2650–1.2

Poland energy and economic savings potential for 8 conservation measures, 2005, biennial rpt, R9455–1.1

Utility energy conservation activities, by State and Canadian Province, 1991/92 annual rpt, A7015–3

State and local:

Alabama trucks equipped with fuel conservation equipment by type, 1987, recurring rpt, U5680–2.16

DC energy conservation program grants and residential services by type, FY87-91, annual rpt, S1535–3.4

Florida utility energy conservation expenditures and recovery factors, by selected company, 1992, annual rpt, S1790–1

Montana tax credits claimed for energy conservation, 1990-91, biennial rpt, S4750–1.1

New York State electric utility demand-side mgmt expenditures, and resulting demand reductions, for 7 companies, 1993-94, article, C6985–6.505

Vermont electric utility projected energy savings from use of demand side mgmt programs, by utility, 1995-2000, biennial rpt, S8100–1

Energy consumption

see Agricultural energy use

see Energy conservation

see Government energy use

see Housing energy use

see Industrial and commercial energy use

see Transportation energy use

see Energy resources (for total consumption)

see under names of specific types of energy

Energy exploration and drilling

Cost of drilling, and wells and footage drilled, by State, offshore location, and type of well, 1991, annual rpt, A2575–9

Deep well drilling, success ratios, and costs, by State and for offshore, 1991-92, annual article, C4420–1.502

Deep well drilling, success ratios, and costs, by world area, 1990-92, annual article, C4420–1.503

Deepwater oil/gas drilling activity, with data by company, 1993, annual feature, C6985–2.510

Financial performance and growth rankings for approx 1,000 top corporations, with comparisons by industry group, 1993 annual rpt, C3950–1.505

Financial ratios and performance, for over 350 SIC 4-digit industries, FY88-92, annual rpt, A6400–3

Intl energy sourcebook, with detail on oil and gas industry operations, supply-demand, and prices, for approx 80 countries, 1970s-91, annual compilation, C6985–10

Intl Petroleum Encyclopedia, basic data on oil and gas supply-demand, exploration,

Energy exploration and drilling

Index by Subjects and Names

refining, reserves, and industry finances, by country and company, 1993 annual rpt, C6985–3

Latin America statistical abstract, general data by country, 1992 annual rpt, U6250–1.23

Mongolia oil/gas exploratory wells drilled, seismic surveys, and contract areas available for foreign dev, 1992 article, C6985–1.506

Natural gas potential reserve estimates in 7 regions, Dec 1992 and trends, biennial rpt, R8765–1

Natural gas production, and drilling activity, results, and costs, inland and offshore, by State, 1970s-91, annual rpt, A1775–3.2

Occupational injury, illness, and employment data, by function, for 136 oil/gas companies, 1991, annual rpt, A2575–4

Offshore oil and gas industry devs, with exploration, production, and equipment trends, monthly rpt, C6985–2

Offshore oil and gas wells, reserves, and production, by country, 1990-93, annual article, C6985–2.508

Oil and gas drilling and production technology devs, including drilling rigs in operation, monthly rpt, C4420–1

Oil and gas industry expenditures for exploration, dev, and production, 1991 and trends, annual survey rpt, A2575–20

Oil and gas industry exploration, production, refining, demand, finance, prices, and reserves, by State and country or world area, 1992 and trends, periodic basic data book, A2575–14.2, A2575–14.3, A2575–14.5

Oil and gas industry intl exploration, drilling, production, refining, stock, price, and financial data, weekly rpt, C6985–1

Oil and gas industry trends, with data by company, State, and country, 1993 annual compilation, C6985–4

Oil and gas supply and drilling trends and outlook under 4 economic scenarios, for onshore and offshore areas and Alaska, 1960s-2010, A2575–25

Oil and gas supply-demand and industry operations, with trends by country and producing State, 1970s-2001, annual rpt, C6985–5

Oil and gas well completion and servicing activity summary, 1992 and trends, annual article, C4420–1.504

Oil industry capital spending in US and Canada, by function, 1991-93, annual articles, C6985–1.517

Oil industry production, reserves, and financial and operating data, for approx 20 major companies, 1991-92, annual article, C6985–1.533

Oil operating rotary rigs, 1980-92, annual feature, C5226–2.505

Oil wells and footage drilled, and rotary rig activity, with detail by State, State subregion, and Canadian Province, 1993 annual feature, C6985–1.513

Oil/gas drilling coiled tubing units in use, by tubing size and world region, 3rd-4th qtr 1992, article, C4420–1.502

Oil/gas drilling coiled tubing units in use, by world region and country, Oct 1992, article, C4420–1.501

Oil/gas industry production, finances, exploration, and reserves, by State, 1992 and trends, annual rpt, A5425–1

Oil/gas wells drilled and planned, by State and Canadian Province, 1993, annual article, C6985–1.539

Operating and financial composite ratios for corporations, with establishments and receipts, for approx 200 industries, by asset size, FY90, annual rpt, C7800–1

Rotary drilling rigs in operation, by world area and country, monthly rpt, B4675–1

Seismic crews operating, by country or world area, 1987-92, annual rpt, C6985–3.5

Seismic exploration crews and months worked, by world area and/or US State, 1960s-91, annual compilation, C6985–9.1

Seismic exploration land and marine crews, by world area, weekly rpt quarterly feature, C6985–1.515, C6985–1.521

Seismic exploration land crews and vessels, by world area or country, quarterly press release, A8912–2

Seismic exploration land crews and vessels, oil/gas, Canada and US, monthly press release, A8912–1

Sourcebook of oil and gas industry operations and finances, and world supply-demand situation, 1970s-91, annual compilation, C6985–9

Tonga oil and gas exploration activity, with seismic lines laid, 1970-88, article, C6985–1.503

Well completions, by type of well, with seismic crews, active rigs, and footage drilled, 1973-92, annual rpt, A5425–2.1

Wells and footage drilled, by type of well, State, and offshore location, quarterly rpt, A2575–6

Wells and footage drilled for exploration and dev, by month and year of completion, monthly rpt, A2575–3

State and local:

Arizona statistical abstract, general data, 1993 recurring rpt, U5850–2.14, U5850–2.20

California statistical abstract, general data, 1992 annual rpt, S0840–2.7

Mississippi statistical abstract, general data, 1992 annual rpt, U3255–4.10

New Mexico oil and gas well completions, and total footage drilled, monthly business activity rpt, U7980–1

New York State statistical yearbook, general data, 1992 annual rpt, U5100–1.12

Oklahoma statistical abstract, general data, 1992 annual rpt, U8130–2.12

Pennsylvania oil and gas exploratory and development wells and footage, 1989-90, recurring rpt, S6810–3

Tennessee statistical abstract, general data, 1992/93 annual rpt, U8710–2.5

see also Oil and gas leases

Energy exports and imports

Electric power and other energy source imports and exports, 1971-91, annual rpt, A4700–1

Electric power imports compared to domestic generation, 1971-91, article, C6985–6.504

Electric power net imports, by US and Canadian region, 1992-2002, annual rpt, A8630–2

Japan energy supply-demand and outlook, by fuel source, 1980s-2000, recurring article, R5650–2.536

Kyrgyzstan energy consumption, production, and foreign trade, by fuel source, 1990-92, article, C6985–1.520

Latin America statistical abstract, general data by country, 1992 annual rpt, U6250–1.25

Supply-demand and price data for energy resources, including by country and producing State, commodity yearbook for 1993, C2400–1

Supply-demand and price data for energy resources, including by country and producing State, commodity yearbook Jan-Sept 1993 updates, C2400–2

Uranium import forecasts from Russia, and quotas for imports from 6 Commonwealth of Independent States Republics, 1993 article, B6790–1.501

Uranium oxide deliveries to US utilities, distribution by country of origin, 1991-92, article, B6790–1.503

World energy supply-demand, by fuel source and sector, by region and country, 1992/93 biennial rpt, R9455–1.7

see also Coal exports and imports

see also Natural gas exports and imports

see also Petroleum exports and imports

Energy prices

Alternative motor fuel prices and mileages, and vehicle conversion costs, for 3-4 fuels, 1993 article, C1575–1.505

Clinton Admin proposed energy (BTU) tax effect on retail fuel prices, by fuel type and consuming sector, 1993 article, C4680–1.505

Cost-of-living indexes and retail prices for selected consumer items in approx 300 cities, quarterly rpt, A0150 1

Electric power (steam) plant operating data, including oil, gas, and coal use and costs, by plant, utility, and location, 1991, annual rpt, A7400–7

Electric utility fuel costs, by type and census div, 1990-91, article, A4700–4.501

Fossil fuel prices at steam-electric utility plants, by fuel type, 1974-91, annual rpt, C6985–5.1

Fossil fuel prices, by fuel type, 1951-91, annual compilation, C6985–9.3

Higher education physical plant operations, costs, employment, salaries, and energy use, by instn and region, 1991/92, recurring rpt, A3183–1

Railroad (Class I) financial condition, operations, and employment, by company and district, 1992, annual rpt, A3275–7

Russia oil exports to 8 former Soviet Republics, and oil and gas prices, 1993 article, U2030–1.511

Supply-demand and price data for energy resources, including by country and producing State, commodity yearbook for 1993, C2400–1

Supply-demand and price data for energy resources, including by country and producing State, commodity yearbook Jan-Sept 1993 updates, C2400–2

Tax rates for energy (BTU) tax proposed by Clinton Admin, with effects on energy prices, by fuel and/or energy type, 1993 article, C6985–1.528

Index by Subjects and Names

Energy projections

Uranium marketing, including terms of transactions for major selling-buying countries or areas, and prices for restricted vs unrestricted intl markets, monthly rpt, B6800–1

Uranium supply-demand and prices worldwide, with data by country, 1992 and trends, annual rpt, B6800–2.1

State and local:

- Florida public utility regulatory and operating data, by company and utility type, 1992 and trends, annual rpt, S1790–1
- Florida statistical abstract, general data, 1992 annual rpt, U6660–1.24
- Georgia statistical abstract, general data, 1992-93 biennial rpt, U6730–1.8
- Maryland statistical abstract, general data, 1993-94 biennial rpt, S3605–1.10
- New York State statistical yearbook, general data, 1992 annual rpt, U5100–1.12
- North Carolina public utility financial, operating, and regulatory data, by utility type and company, 1990 and trends, annual rpt, S5917–2
- Pennsylvania energy supply-demand and prices by fuel type, with electric power info by utility, 1960s-90, recurring rpt, S6810–3
- Tennessee statistical abstract, general data, 1992/93 annual rpt, U8710–2.20

see also Coal prices

see also Electric power prices

see also Gasoline

see also Natural gas prices

see also Petroleum prices

Energy production costs

- Brazil State-owned oil company average production costs, by category, 1993 article, C6985–2.510
- Commonwealth of Independent States uranium deposits by reserve classification, and resources of 4 Republics by production cost category, 1993 article, B6800–1 510
- Natural gas drilling activity, results, and costs, inland and offshore, by State, 1970s-91, annual rpt, A1775–3.2
- Natural gas storage reservoir deliverability enhancement techniques used and costs, 1993 article, C6985–1.523
- North Sea oil/gas field production costs, distribution by process, 1986, C6985–2.502
- Offshore drilling platform costs, 1993 feature, C6985–2.504
- Oil and gas deep well drilling, success ratios, and costs, by State and for offshore, 1991-92, annual article, C4420–1.502
- Oil and gas drilling activity and costs, 1990-91 and trends, annual compilation, C6985–9.1, C6985–9.3
- Oil and gas drilling costs, and exploration/dev expenditures, 1973-92, annual rpt, A5425–2.2
- Oil and gas drilling costs, and wells and footage drilled, by State, offshore location, and type of well, 1991, annual rpt, A2575–9
- Oil and gas industry expenditures for exploration, dev, and production, 1991 and trends, annual survey rpt, A2575–20
- Oil and gas industry exploration, production, refining, demand, finance, prices, and reserves, by State and country or world area, 1992 and trends, periodic basic data book, A2575–14.2

Oil and gas well completions, drilling costs vs revenues, and rig activity, 1970s-2001, annual rpt, C6985–5.2

Oil drilling costs, by State, 1991, annual rpt, A5425–1

- Oil industry exploration/production spending in US, Canada, and overseas, by company, 1991-92, annual rpt, C6985–3.5
- Oil refinery construction, operating, and materials costs, Nelson-Farrar Cost Indexes, weekly rpt monthly and quarterly tables, C6985–1
- Oil refinery operating cost indexes, 1956-92, periodic basic data book, A2575–14.4
- Oil reserves replacement and finding/dev costs by world area, and OPEC costs for maintaining production capacity, 1993 article, C6985–1.534
- Oil/gas deep well drilling, success ratios, and costs, by world area, 1990-92, annual article, C4420–1.503
- Oil/gas finding and production costs, reserve additions, and production, 1978-91, article, C6985–1.539
- World oil/gas reserve additions and replacement costs, for selected countries and world areas, 1988-92, article, C6985–1.530

State and local:

California oil/gas production, regulatory compliance and production costs, and wellhead prices, by State region, 1993 article, C6985–1.525

Energy projections

- Alternative motor fuel use and outlook, including data on costs and by fuel type and selected country, 1993 annual rpt, C6985–3.2
- Brazil nuclear power plants and capacity, and uranium and enriched fuel requirements, under 3 dev plans, 1990, 2000, and 2010, article, B6800–1.508
- China (southeast) oil demand by Province, and coastal refinery construction projects and capacity, 1990s-2000, article, C6985–1.528
- Commonwealth of Independent States natural gas supply-demand indicators, 1980s-2005, article, C6985–1.514, C6985–1.515
- Eastern Europe and former Soviet Union refined oil products consumption and demand, 1990-96 and 2000, article, C6985–1.531
- Ecuador oil production by domestic and foreign company, oil consumption, and outlays of govt-owned holding company, 1990s-2010, article, C6985–1.518
- Electric power forecast high and low demand, 1990, 2000, and 2010, article, C6985–6.505
- Electric power fossil fuel-fired plant planned capacity, by fuel type, 2001-2011, article, C6985–6.508
- Electric power fossil fuel-fired plant planned capacity, 2001-2011, article, C5226–1.508
- Electric power generating equipment orders and shipments, and capacity addition trends, with data by location and facility, 1991 annual rpt, A4700–2
- Electric power plant capacity on order outside North America, for developed and developing countries by region, 1993-2000, article, C6985–6.509

Electric power plants planned and under construction in 1993, by type, utility, and region, and forecast capacity for 1993-2001, annual feature, C5800–28.503

- Electric power production and capacity by fuel source, and transmission line mileage, for US and Canada, 1992 or 1993 and 2002, article, C6985–6.510
- Electric power summer peak demand and capacity margins, and transmission line additions, by region, 1993-2002, article, C5800–28.509
- Electric power supply-demand, and utility capacities and fuel requirements, detailed data by US and Canadian region, 1992-2002, annual rpt, A8630–2
- Electric power transmission line mileage existing and planned in US and Canada, 1991 and 2001, article, C6985–6.506
- Electric power utility and nonutility generators planned and under construction, by fuel type, utility, and State, 1992-2001, annual rpt, A7400–7
- Electric utility capacity additions and plans, by region, 1991-2001, annual feature, C5800–28.507
- Electric utility capital spending, by function and region, and capacity addition plans, 1992-97, annual article, C6985–6.503
- Electric utility construction and capacity outlook, including data by region and fuel source, 1992-2001, annual feature, C5800–28.501
- Electric utility demand-side mgmt program impact on electricity demand in 8 States, by 2000, article, C4725–5.502
- Electric utility generating capacity and transmission line planned additions, and demand projections, 1992 features, C6985–6.501, C6985–6.502
- Electric utility generating capacity of natural-gas fired combined-cycle power plants, by region, 1992-2002, article, C5800–28.509
- Electric utility generating unit addition plans and generation requirement outlook, 1993 article, A2625–1.502
- Gasoline price increases attributable to new Federal environmental, health, and safety regulations, 1995 and 2000, article, C4680–1.511
- Gulf of Mexico offshore oil and gas production and reserves, 1970s-2000, annual article, C6985–2.503
- Japan energy supply-demand and outlook, by fuel source, 1980s-2000, recurring article, R5650–2.536
- Latin America geothermal energy installed capacity, by country, 1980-2000, annual rpt, U6250–1.23
- Natural gas transmission pipeline construction mileage planned, 1993-97, article, C6780–2.503
- Norway oil and gas production, 1990-2010, article, C6985–2.506
- Nuclear fuel and uranium supply-demand devs worldwide, quarterly rpt, B6790–1
- Offshore subsea drilling trees installed, 1975-2000, C6985–2.505
- Oil and gas industry intl exploration, drilling, production, refining, stock, price, and financial data, weekly rpt, C6985–1
- Oil and gas intl supply-demand, by country or world area, 1980s-96, annual feature, C6985–1.552

Energy projections

Oil and gas supply-demand and industry operations, 1970s-2010, annual rpt, C6985–5

Oil and gas supply trends and outlook under 4 economic scenarios, for onshore and offshore areas and Alaska, 1960s-2010, A2575–25

Poland energy and economic savings potential for 8 conservation measures, 2005, biennial rpt, R9455–1.1

Russia oil and gas production and exports, selected years 1990-2010, article, C6985–1.527

Russia oil field dev, reserves, and supply-demand data, with detail for Tyumen region, 1990s-2000, articles, C6985–1.540

Russia, Siberia natural gas production forecast, for 6 fields, quinquennially 1990-2010, article, C6985–1.551

Southeast Asia offshore oil/gas fields and platforms planned, by country, 1993-97, article, C6985–2.501

Southeastern States electric power generation capacity additions, by fuel type and for 11 States, 1992-2000, article, C5800–28.506

Superconductor device sales outlook, with market shares by end use, selected years 1993-2020, article, A1250–1.528

Supply-demand by source and consuming sector, 1990-2010, periodic basic data book, A2575–14.1

Uranium enrichment Govt-owned corporation operating costs by item, production, and sales, 1991-2001, article, B6790–1.502

Uranium enrichment market shares for DOE, utility inventory utilization, and other sources, 1991-2000, annual article, B6790–1.501

Uranium production and consumption, by country or world area, 1992-96, annual feature, C5226–2.505

Uranium production, reserves, and ownership interests, for 4 largest intl producers, by country and mine, 1990s-2003 article, B6800–1.508

Uranium reprocessing commitments, and plutonium available from reprocessing, for 5 countries, 1990s-2010, article, B6790–1.502

State and local:

New York State natural gas requirements and supply, and electricity requirements by provider, projections to 2007, annual rpt, U5100–1.12

Pennsylvania nuclear-based electricity generation, by utility, 1990-2000, recurring rpt, S6810–3

Texas lignite coal production, 1980-2005, article, C5226–1.501

Vermont electric utility projected energy savings from use of demand side mgmt programs, by utility, 1995-2000, biennial rpt, S8100–1

Energy research and development

Fuel cell technology potential impact on energy use and nitrogen oxide emissions, 1992 article, C5226–2.501

Occupational injury, illness, and employment data, by function, for 136 oil/gas companies, 1991, annual rpt, A2575–4

Oil and gas research grant awards of American Chemical Society Petroleum Research Fund, by recipient, 1993 recurring feature, A1250–1.514, A1250–1.525, A1250–1.538

Oil company R&D expenditures, for 17 firms, 1981-92, article, C6985–1.536

Superconductor device sales outlook, with market shares by end use, selected years 1993-2020, article, A1250–1.528

see also Energy exploration and drilling

see also Federal funding for energy programs

see also State funding for energy programs

Energy reserves

China uranium resources, by Province, 1993 article, B6800–1.509

Commonwealth of Independent States uranium deposits by reserve classification, and resources of 4 Republics by production cost category, 1993 article, B6800–1.510

Commonwealth of Independent States uranium reserves, for 4 Republics, Jan 1991-92, article, B6790–1.502

Uranium production, reserves, and ownership interests, for 4 largest intl producers, by country and mine, 1990s-2003 article, B6800–1.508

Uranium reserves, capacity, and operating status of in situ leach mining projects, 1993 article, B6790–1.501

World energy supply-demand, by fuel source and sector, by region and country, 1992/93 biennial rpt, R9455–1.3

State and local:

Wyoming uranium reserves and resources in Green Mountain/Sheep Mountain region, by deposit, 1993 article, B6790–1.503

see also Coal reserves

see also Natural gas reserves

see also Petroleum reserves

Energy resources

Brazil energy production and consumption distribution by fuel source, 1991, article, B6800–1.508

China energy consumption shares, by fuel source, 1993 article, B6800–1.509

China energy production, 1989-92, annual article, A9315–1.504

Commonwealth of Independent States energy production, use, and trade, with detail for natural gas, by Republic, 1993 article, C6985–1.514

Congressional campaign finances, with detailed data for individual Members, and leading contributors by type and industry, 1990 election and trends, biennial rpt, R3828–2.2

Consumption by fuel source, 1991-92, annual feature, A2575–2.501

Consumption distribution by fuel type or energy source, 1st 11 months 1992, annual rpt, C1800–1

Consumption of energy, by fuel source, consuming sector, State, and census div, 1960s-91, annual rpt, A1775–3.6

Demand for major energy sources, 1991-93, annual feature, C6985–1.513

Europe energy consumption, for Spain and EC, by fuel source, 1991, article, A8955–1.503

Federal regulatory agency costs and staff, for approx 50 agencies, FY70s-94, annual rpt, U9640–1

Index by Subjects and Names

Higher education physical plant operations, costs, employment, salaries, and energy use, by instn and region, 1991/92, recurring rpt, A3183–1

Intl energy consumption and production by source, for approx 80 countries, 1970s-91, annual compilation, C6985–10

Japan energy supply-demand and outlook, by fuel source, 1980s-2000, recurring article, R5650–2.536

Kyrgyzstan energy consumption, production, and foreign trade, by fuel source, 1990-92, article, C6985–1.520

Latin America statistical abstract, general data by country, 1992 annual rpt, U6250–1.23

Societal impacts of energy consumption, and related Govt fiscal policy issues, with data on costs and emissions, 1993 rpt, A2575–28

Sourcebook of oil and gas industry, with supply-demand comparisons to other energy types, 1991 and trends, annual compilation, C6985–9.5

State social, economic, and govtl indicators, with rankings, 1993 semiannual rpt, B8500–1.12

Statistical compilation of oil and gas industry trends, 1993 annual rpt, C6985–4

Statistical profiles of 50 States and DC, general data, 1993 annual almanac, C4712–1

Supply and disposition of energy sources, 1991 and trends, annual rpt, A4700–1

Supply-demand and price data for energy resources, including by country and producing State, commodity yearbook for 1993, C2400–1

Supply-demand and price data for energy resources, including by country and producing State, commodity yearbook Jan-Sept 1993 updates, C2400–2

Supply-demand by energy source and consuming sector, 1947-2010, periodic basic data book, A2575–14.1

Tax rates and revenues under proposed energy (BTU) tax, with comparison to consumption and prices, by fuel type, 1993 article, C6985–1.518

World energy consumption by fuel source and world area, 1990, annual rpt, A7400–2.1

World energy supply-demand, by fuel source and sector, by region and country, 1992/93 biennial rpt, R9455–1.1, R9455–1.3, R9455–1.7

State and local:

Alabama statistical abstract, general data, 1992 recurring rpt, U5680–2.12

Arizona statistical abstract, general data, 1993 recurring rpt, U5850–2.20

California energy use distribution by sector, 1991, annual rpt, S0840–3.1

Florida statistical abstract, general data, 1992 annual rpt, U6660–1.15

Hawaii data book, general data, 1992 annual rpt, S2090–1.17

Louisiana energy indicators, suspended quarterly rpt, U2730–1

Nevada statistical abstract, general data, 1992 biennial rpt, S5005–1.11

New York State statistical yearbook, general data, 1992 annual rpt, U5100–1.12

Pennsylvania energy supply-demand and prices by fuel type, with electric power info by utility, 1960s-90, recurring rpt, S6810–3

Pennsylvania statistical abstract, general data, 1992 recurring rpt, U4130–6.9

South Carolina economic condition, including energy and transportation data, 1970s-92, annual rpt, S7125–3.3

Tennessee statistical abstract, general data, 1992/93 annual rpt, U8710–2.10

Utah govt statistical review, fiscal and socioeconomic data, 1993 annual rpt, R9380–1.2

Wisconsin Blue Book, general data, 1993-94 biennial rpt, S8780–1.2

Wisconsin energy consumption, by fuel source, 1981-90, annual rpt, S8675–3

see also Agricultural energy use

see also Alcohol fuels

see also Aviation fuels

see also Biomass energy

see also Coal and coal mining

see also Coal exports and imports

see also Coal prices

see also Coal reserves

see also Coal stocks

see also Diesel fuel

see also Electric power

see also Electric power and heat cogeneration

see also Electric power plants and equipment

see also Electric power prices

see also Energy conservation

see also Energy exploration and drilling

see also Energy exports and imports

see also Energy prices

see also Energy production costs

see also Energy projections

see also Energy research and development

see also Energy reserves

see also Energy stocks and inventories

see also Federal funding for energy programs

see also Fuel oil

see also Gasohol

see also Gasoline

see also Geothermal resources

see also Government energy use

see also Housing energy use

see also Hydroelectric power

see also Industrial and commercial energy use

see also Kerosene

see also Liquefied petroleum gas

see also Low-income energy assistance

see also Natural gas and gas industry

see also Natural gas exports and imports

see also Natural gas liquids

see also Natural gas prices

see also Natural gas reserves

see also Nuclear power

see also Offshore oil and gas

see also Oil shale

see also Oil spills

see also Petrochemicals

see also Petroleum and petroleum industry

see also Petroleum exports and imports

see also Petroleum prices

see also Petroleum reserves

see also Petroleum stocks

see also Solar energy

see also State funding for energy programs

see also Transportation energy use

see also Uranium

see also Water power

see also Wind energy

see also Wood fuel

Energy stocks and inventories

Fuel oil dealers with bulk plants, and storage capacity by fuel type, by region, 1992 annual survey, C4680–2.1

Natural gas storage inventory, Apr 1988-93, article, C6985–1.526

Natural gas underground storage pools and capacity, with detail by State, 1991 and trends, annual rpt, A1775–3.3

Supply-demand and price data for energy resources, including by country and producing State, commodity yearbook for 1993, C2400–1

Supply-demand and price data for energy resources, including by country and producing State, commodity yearbook Jan-Sept 1993 updates, C2400–2

State and local:

Ohio natural gas and electricity supply-demand by utility and consuming sector, 1992-93 and trends, annual rpt, S6355–1

see also Coal stocks

see also Petroleum stocks

Energy tax

see Excise tax

Engineers and engineering

Billings of top 500 architectural and engineering design firms, 1992, annual article, C5800–2.522

Building design/construction company revenues and operations, for top 300 firms, 1991, annual feature, C1850–9.502

Building systems engineer views on influence of terror threats and World Trade Center bombing on own designs and specifications, 1993 article, C1850–12.506

Chemical engineer and chemist salaries, employment status, and demographic and professional characteristics, 1993, annual rpt, A1250–4

Chemistry and chemical engineering degrees awarded, by level, sex, and instn, 1991/92 and trends, annual articles, A1250–1.535

Chemistry and chemical engineering degrees awarded, by level, 1980/81-1990/91, annual article, A1250–1.544

Chemistry and chemical engineering grad starting salaries, employment status, demographic characteristics, and advanced study plans, 1991/92, annual rpt, A1250–2

Compensation of engineers by field, and construction industry design-related personnel and salaries by position, 1993 annual article, C5800–2.536

Compensation of professional engineers, by work and employee characteristics, and region and metro area, 1992, annual rpt, A8460–1

Degrees awarded, by State, instn, and field, with detail for women, minorities, and foreign students, 1991/92, annual rpt, A0685–1

Doctoral degree recipient characteristics, including citizenship status, source of support, field of study, and instn, 1990/91 and trends, annual rpt, R6000–7

Education enrollment by instn, field, and State, with detail for women, minorities, and foreign students, fall 1992, annual rpt, A0685–2

Engines and motors

Employment in business and industry, hiring plans for college grads, by field, salary, and degree, 1993 annual survey rpt, U3730–1

Environmental engineering professional views on career and top employers, May 1993, annual survey article, C5800–2.546

Federal employment of scientists and engineers, by field and sex, 1989, article, A1250–1.523

Financial ratios and performance, for over 350 SIC 4-digit industries, FY88-92, annual rpt, A6400–3

Mining engineer grads by degree level, 1980-1995/96, article, C5226–1.507

Mining engineering higher education program enrollment, by level, 1980-1992/93, article, C5226–2.507

Public opinion on honesty/ethical standards of selected occupations, 1992 Gallup Polls and trends, C4040–1.501

R&D professional salaries and employment characteristics, 1993 and trends, annual article, C1850–6.509

R&D spending by Fed Govt for engineering research, and US and foreign engineer students and employment, 1993 annual feature, A1250–1.537

Salaries of engineering grads, by discipline, 1992-93, article, C5800–8.509

Salaries of engineers, by industry group, census div, selected metro area, and years since college degree, 1993, annual survey rpt, A0685–5

Salaries of engineers, by industry group, census div, selected metro area, degree level, and years since college degree, 1993, annual survey rpt, A0685–3

Salaries of scientists, engineers, technicians, and other professionals, by employee and employer characteristics, 1990s and trends, biennial rpt, A3960–1

Salary and job offers for college grads, by field of study, type of employer, and degree level, by region, interim rpt series, A3940–1

Salary and job offers for college grads, by field of study, type of employer, and degree level, series, A3940–2

State social, economic, and govtl indicators, with rankings, 1993 semiannual rpt, B8500–1.13

Women and minorities in professional fields, detailed education and labor force data, 1980s-91, with historical trends, recurring rpt, A3960–2

State and local:

Arizona statistical abstract, general data, 1993 recurring rpt, U5850–2.24

Florida statistical abstract, general data, 1992 annual rpt, U6660–1.18

Tennessee statistical abstract, general data, 1992/93 annual rpt, U8710–2.3

see also Architecture

see also Biotechnology

see also Technological innovations

see also Traffic engineering

Engines and motors

Aerospace industry production, sales, and trade data, for aircraft and missile engines, 1977-91, annual rpt, A0250–2

Aircraft (jet) world inventory, by individual model and engine, 1992, annual rpt, B1582–1

Engines and motors

Auto factory installations of engines by selected specifications, by manufacturer, make, and model, for 1992 model year, annual data book, C2710–3.531

Boat motors sales and ownership, 1992, annual feature, C2425–4

Boat ownership, registrations, and sales, by boat type and/or State, including data for related equipment, 1992 annual rpt, A8055–1

Financial ratios and performance, for over 350 SIC 4-digit industries, FY88-92, annual rpt, A6400–3

Small motors shipments value, by motor type and market category, quarterly rpt, A8904–1

Truck factory sales by make and diesel engine sales by manufacturer, 1991-92, annual feature, C2150–4.503

see also Electrical machinery and equipment

England

see United Kingdom

English language

see Language use and ability

Enid, Okla.

Business activity indicators for Oklahoma, monthly rpt, U8130–1

Employment by industry, monthly rpt, S6430–2

Enlistment

see Voluntary military service

Enrollment

see Educational enrollment

Enterovirus infections

see Infective and parasitic diseases

Entertainment industries

see Communications industries

Entitlement programs

see Public welfare programs

Environmental pollution and control

Auto dealership service dept manager views on impact of pollution control demands on profitability, 1993 annual survey, article, C2710–3.537

Chemical industry emissions and pollution abatement expenditure and cost trends, 1993 annual rpt, A3850–1

Chemical industry environmental spending and pollutant releases by 10-20 firms, with toxic chemical disposition summary, 1993 article, A1250–1.533

Chemical releases and transfers compared to production, and waste reduction activities of selected companies, 1992 article, A1250–1.503

Child well-being indicators based on social, economic, and environmental factors, for 239 MSAs, with detail by component county and city, 1980s-90s, R9700–2

City govt costs to enforce Fed Govt regulations including environmental laws, for 314 cities, FY93, with summary projections to FY98, A9330–12

City govt impacts of enforcing Fed Govt environmental laws, including summary cost projections, 1993 rpt, U9640–3

City officials views on issues and conditions affecting local govt, including top issues for Fed Govt to address , 1992 survey, annual rpt, A8012–1.21

College freshmen attitudes on govt policies regarding pollution control, by sex and instn type, fall 1992, annual survey, U6215–1

Consumer purchase decisions influence of marketer environmental claims, 1992 survey feature, C1200–4.501

Corporate environmental monitoring activity of company facilities, 1992 feature, C1850–12.501

Direct marketer and consumer views on environmental issues, 1992/93 annual rpt, A4620–1

Employees of environmental engineering industry views on career and top employers, May 1993, annual survey article, C5800–2.546

Energy consumption societal impacts and Govt fiscal policy issues, with related data on costs and emissions, 1993 rpt, A2575–28

Europe public opinion on political, economic, and social issues, for 9 countries and 3 Soviet Union Republics, 1991 survey, C8915–8

Europe public opinion on political, economic, and social issues of interest to foreign investors, for 9 countries and 3 Soviet Union Republics, 1991 survey, C8915–9

Expenditures for pollution abatement/control, by spending sector, 1984-90, annual rpt, A0865–1.3

Federal regulatory agency costs and staff, for approx 50 agencies, FY70s-94, annual rpt, U9640–1

Federal spending for environmental research, by agency, FY92, article, A1250–1.508

Hard goods manufacturers experience and views regarding environmental regulation and recycling, by product line, 1993 annual survey rpt, A1800–1

Homebuilder views on environmental issues of major concern, 1992 survey, article, C1850–8.502

Industrial pollution control equipment current value vs cost, for 8 countries, 1993 rpt, A1310–2.2

Japan environment-related foreign aid, including grants, loans, and technical assistance, FY89-91, article, R5650–2.541

Japan exports of water and nonvehicle air filtering/purifying equipment, with detail by major importing country, 1988-92, article, R5650–2.532

Manufacturing company environmental records and summary financial data, for 10 leading and 20 other companies rated by Fortune magazine, 1993 article, C8900–1.520

Oil industry environmental performance, with data on toxic chemical releases, oil spills, occupational injury/illness, and corporate spending, 1990 and trends, annual rpt, A2575–27

Oil industry environmental protection expenditures, 1960s-90, periodic basic data book, A2575–14.3

Oil offshore well blowouts and spills, and other polluting incidents, 1991 and trends, periodic basic data book, A2575–14.5

Paper distributor views on environmental concerns business effects, including customer interest in special products, 1993 survey article, A8140–3.503

Paper industry expenditures to comply with environmental protection regulations, 1966-93, annual rpt, A1630–6.3

Public opinion on environmental laws/protection adequacy, 1980 and 1990, article, A1865–1.505

Pulp and paper industry operations, US and Canada, with financial performance by company, 1990s and trends, annual rpt, C3975–5.1, C3975–5.2

Pulp and paper mill environmental improvement projects of US and Canadian companies, including costs, by mill, 1993 article, C3975–2.505

Pulp and paper mills subject to Clean Air Act and Clean Water Act guidelines for selected effluent subcategories, 1993 article, C3975–2.511

Pulp manufacturing environmental impacts of using virgin fiber vs recycled wastepaper, 1993 article, C3975–2.511

Religious congregation characteristics, including membership, activities, staff, and finances, 1992 survey, recurring rpt, A5435–4

State economic dev condition indicators, including economic performance, business vitality, growth capacity, and tax/fiscal system, by State, 1993 annual rpt, R4225–1.1

State social, economic, and govtl indicators, with rankings, 1993 semiannual rpt, B8500–1.15

Supermarket shopper views on responsibility for environmentally safe products, 1993 and trends, annual survey rpt, A4950–3

State and local:

DC vacant lot nuisance citations, maintenance, and liens charged, FY88-91, annual rpt, S1535–3.7

Hawaii data book, general data, 1992 annual rpt, S2090–1.5

Hawaii environmental quality and public health control, inspection, licensing, and enforcement activities, 1990, annual rpt, S2065–1.6

Mississippi sales tax diverted to cities for pollution control grant repayment, and environmental protection fees collected on fuels, FY92, annual rpt, S4435–1

Montana pollution control facility property value, by county, 1991-92, biennial rpt, S4750–1.2

New York State environmental conservation law violators and enforcement activity, FY91, annual rpt, U5100–1.15

Ohio tax exemption certificates issued and values for pollution control facilities, by type, FY92, annual rpt, S6390–1.1

Pennsylvania statistical abstract, general data, 1992 recurring rpt, U4130–6.8

Tennessee executive views on environmental issues, 1993 annual article, U8710–1.502

Tennessee pollution abatement capital expenditures and operating costs, 1989 and trends, annual rpt, U8710–2.4

Vermont environmental court cases and dispositions, by type of case, FY92 annual rpt, S8120–1

see also Air pollution

see also Environmental services industry

see also Global climate change

see also Hazardous waste and disposal

see also International cooperation in environmental sciences

see also Landfills

see also Lead poisoning and pollution

Index by Subjects and Names — Estate tax

see also Marine pollution
see also Noise
see also Oil spills
see also Pesticides
see also Radiation
see also Radioactive waste and disposal
see also Radon
see also Reclamation of land
see also Recycling of waste materials
see also Refuse and refuse disposal
see also Soil pollution
see also State funding for natural resources and conservation
see also Water pollution

Environmental Protection Agency

Hard goods manufacturers views on govt regulation, including 1992 EPA investigations and outcomes, by product line, 1993 annual survey rpt, A1800–1

Motor vehicle fuel economy for 1994 models, EPA estimates by model and size group, annual feature, C2710–3.550, C2710–3.551

Research budget of EPA, by program, FY92-94, article, A1250–1.526

Environmental sciences

Ecologist personal and professional characteristics, including research activity and funding, with data by field, Mar 1992 survey, recurring rpt, A4685–1

Higher education geoscience enrollment and degrees awarded, by sex, race-ethnicity, and discipline, 1991/92, annual rpt, A1785–3

Salaries of scientists, engineers, technicians, and other professionals, by employee and employer characteristics, 1990s and trends, biennial rpt, A3960–1

Women and minorities in professional fields, detailed education and labor force data, 1991 and trends, recurring rpt, A3960–2.3

see also Astronomy
see also Earth sciences
see also Energy research and development
see also International cooperation in environmental sciences
see also Oceanography

Environmental services industry

Engineers salaries by industry group, census div, selected metro area, and years since college degree, 1993, annual survey rpt, A0685–5

Engineers salaries by industry group, census div, selected metro area, degree level, and years since college degree, 1993, annual survey rpt, A0685–3

Financial performance and growth rankings for approx 1,000 top corporations, with comparisons by industry group, 1993 annual rpt, C3950–1.505

Revenues and number of environmental services firms by industry segment, with world revenues by region and/or country, 1990s, article, A1250–1.530

see also Environmental pollution and control
see also Hazardous waste and disposal
see also Recycling of waste materials
see also Refuse and refuse disposal

Epidemiology and epidemiologists

Public health research, monthly journal, A2623–1

Epilepsy

see Neurological disorders

Equal employment opportunity

see Discrimination in employment

Equal Rights Amendment

see Constitutional amendments

Equity courts

see State courts

Ermatinger, Kathy

"Profiles of Alaska's Public School Districts, FY92", S0295–2

Ernst and Young Co.

Biotechnology company business formations, 1987, 1989, and 1991, C1850–6.511

Biotechnology company finances, employment, and firms, with detail for public companies, FY92-93, annual article, A1250–1.542

Biotechnology industry summary financial performance and employment data, with detail for public companies, 1991-92, article, A6400–2.503

Manufacturing foreign investment projects started by 5 most active US industries, 1991, article, C1850–2.502

Plastics processing industry financial and operating ratios, by processing activity, sales size, and region, 1992, annual rpt, A8920–4

Retail mgmt info system devs, including expenses and computerized equipment use, 1992 survey, annual feature, C5150–4.501

Retail mgmt info system devs, including expenses and computerized equipment use, 1993 survey, annual feature, C5150–4.509

Retail store inventory shrinkage, and control measures, by type of outlet, 1991, annual survey rpt, C5150–4.504

Small corporation CEO views on expected sources of capital, June 1993 survey, article, C4687–1.512

Small corporation employee benefits and compensation methods, for companies with and without interest in improving quality, May 1992 survey, article, C4687–1.502

Small corporation expected funding sources for business growth, 1991-92 surveys, article, C4687–1.501

Small corporations offering employee equity incentives and 401(k) plans, by selected industry, 1992-93, survey article, C4687–1.502

TV network advertising revenues, by daypart and program type, weekly rpt quarterly feature, C1850–14.503, C1850–14.513, C1850–14.522, C1850–14.535

Erosion

see Soils and soil conservation

Escalator clauses

Educational employee retirement plan characteristics, including cost-of-living adjustment provisions, 1990/91, recurring rpt, A7640–18.1

State and local:

Hawaii, Federal employee cost of living pay adjustment compared to DC, 1990-93, annual rpt, S2090–1.14

Eskimos

see Indians

ESOPs

see Employee stock ownership plans

Estate tax

Federal tax rate trends, Sept 1916-Oct 1989, annual rpt, R9050–1.3

State receipts from death taxes credited against Federal taxes, and estate tax rates, by State, 1989 or 1992, article, B8500–2.518

State tax rates and collections, by tax type and State, FY02-92, annual rpt, R9050–1.5

State and local:

Alabama financial condition, including revenues by source, expenditures by function and object, and fund balances, by fund and agency, FY92, annual rpt, S0129–1

Arizona tax revenues by source, tax rates, and disbursements to local areas, FY92 and trends, annual rpt, S0515–1

Arkansas financial condition, including revenues by source, expenditures by function and object, and fund balances, FY92, annual rpt, S0670–1

California economic condition, including population, employment and earnings, income, business activity, and taxation, 1960s-92, annual rpt, S0840–3.2

California financial condition, including revenues by source, expenditures by agency and function, fund balances, and bonded debt, FY92 and trends, annual rpt, S0815–1

Colorado tax revenues by type, with selected data by county and city, FY92 and trends, annual rpt, S1075–1

Connecticut financial condition, including revenues by source, expenditures by function, and bonded debt, FY92, annual rpt, S1170–1

DC financial condition, including receipts by source, expenditures by object or function, and fund balances, FY92, annual rpt, S1507–1

Georgia tax revenues, by type, FY90-92, annual rpt, S1950–1.1

Hawaii tax collections and allocations, by type, for State and counties, FY91-92 and trends, annual rpt, S2120–1

Idaho tax statistics, including collections, and data by county and city, FY92 and trends, annual rpt, S2295–1

Illinois financial condition, including revenues by source, and expenditures by object, function, and agency, FY92, annual rpt, S2415–1

Kansas tax collections by tax type, and property values, with data by county, FY92 and trends, annual rpt, S3020–1

Kentucky financial condition, including revenues by source, expenditures by function and object, fund balances, and bonded debt, FY92, annual rpt, S3120–1

Maryland financial condition, including revenues by source, expenditures by function, fund balances, and bonded debt, FY92 and trends, annual rpt, S3685–2

Massachusetts tax collections by type, and distributions to local areas, FY91 and trends, annual rpt, S3917–1

Michigan financial condition, including revenues by source, expenditures by function, and fund balances, FY92 and trends, annual rpt, S3985–2

Estate tax

Missouri financial condition, including revenues and expenditures by agency, and tax collections and distribution, FY92 and trends, annual rpt, S4570–1.1

Montana revenue collections by tax type, and taxable establishments, production, and income, FY91-92 and trends, biennial rpt, S4750–1.1

Nebraska revenues from licenses, fees, and miscellaneous taxes, 1991 and trends, annual rpt, S4950–1.3

New Hampshire financial condition, with revenues by source, expenditures by function or object, and fund balances, FY92 and trends, annual rpt, S5175–1

New Mexico tax revenues and disbursements, with data by tax type, county, and city, FY91-92 and trends, annual rpt, S5660–1

North Carolina financial condition, including revenues by source, expenditures by function, fund balances, and bonded debt, FY92, annual rpt, S5897–1

Ohio taxable estates, tax returns, and collections, by estate value and county, FY92 and trends, annual rpt, S6390–1.3

Oklahoma tax revenues by source, and distribution to local govts and State funds, FY92 and trends, annual rpt, S6495–1

Oregon financial condition, including revenues by source, expenditures by function, and fund statements, FY92, annual rpt, S6603–2

Pennsylvania tax collections by tax type, with data by county and industry, FY92 and trends, annual rpt, S6885–1

South Dakota tax revenues by source, and aid distributed to local areas, FY92 annual rpt, S7380–1.1

Tennessee tax revenues by source and apportionments to counties, cities, and funds, FY91-92 and trends, biennial rpt, S7570 1

Texas financial condition, including revenues by source, expenditures by function and dept, and investments, with data for over 400 individual funds, FY92, annual rpt, S7655–2

Utah tax revenues by source, and distribution to localities and State funds, FY92 and trends, annual rpt, S7905–1

Virginia tax revenues by type, including sales tax data by county and independent city, FY92 and trends, annual rpt, S8305–1.2

Washington State revenues by source, and distributions by tax and locality, FY92 and trends, annual rpt, S8415–1.1

Wisconsin financial condition, including revenues by source, expenditures by function and object, and fund balances, FY93, annual rpt, S8675–2

Wyoming tax revenues and distributions, by type of tax, FY92 and trends, annual rpt, S8990–1.3

see also Gift tax

Estonia

Public opinion on political issues in Tallinn, Estonia during Aug 1991 Soviet coup attempt, for Estonian vs Russian-speaking residents, article, A0610–1.501

Ethanol

see Alcohol fuels

Ethics and morality

Catholic vs public school ratings for selected aspects of education and environment, public opinion by respondent characteristics, July 1992 survey, A7375–8

Europe public opinion on political, economic, and social issues, for 9 countries and 3 Soviet Union Republics, 1991 survey, C8915–8.1

Europe public opinion on political, economic, and social issues of interest to foreign investors, for 9 countries and 3 Soviet Union Republics, 1991 survey, C8915–9

News media (TV and newspaper) journalistic ethics code use, sources, and revisions, 1993 survey article, A8605–1.504

News media professional views on revealing names of rape victims and broadcasting criminal executions, 1993 survey article, C1850–14.539

Public opinion on honesty/ethical standards of selected occupations, 1992 Gallup Polls and trends, C4040–1.501

Public opinion on social, political, and economic issues, detailed data, 1972-91 surveys, annual rpt, U6395–1

Public opinion on whether US is in moral decline, by respondent characteristics, Sept 1992 Gallup Poll, C4040–1.503

Public school moral education feasibility, and support for teaching selected values, public opinion, 1993 annual Gallup Poll, A8680–1.503

see also Business ethics

see also Financial disclosure

see also Judicial ethics

see also Legal ethics

see also Medical ethics

see also Political ethics

Ethiopia

Famine analysis, including household impacts and responses, drought factor, agricultural activity and markets, and intervention programs, 1980s, R5620–1.36

Ethnic minorities

see Minority groups

Ethnic origin

see Ancestry

see Birthplace

see Minority groups

Ethylene

see Petrochemicals

Eurocurrency

Commodity yearbook for 1993: detailed supply-demand data, and selected indicators for futures market investors, C2400–1

Commodity yearbook update: detailed supply-demand data, and selected indicators for futures market investors, Jan-Sept 1993 rpts, C2400–2

Money and securities market activity, and related indicators, biweekly rpt, B2000–1

Money market fund asset holdings by type of investment, including bank and Eurodollar certificates of deposit, and Federal securities, monthly rpt, A6025–5

Eurodollars

see Eurocurrency

Europe

Advertising agency income and billings in Europe, for top 20 multinatl agencies, 1992, annual article, C2710–1.527

Advertising costs for 4 media, by country, with comparisons to US, 1992, article, C2710–1.532

Advertising expenditure outlook by medium, for 12 countries, 1993 vs 1992, article, C2710–1.513

Air pollutant emissions and forest defoliation severity, by country, 1989, biennial rpt, R9455–1.1

Air traffic projections for Western Europe, 1995-2010, article, C5800–4.501

Airline passenger and freight traffic of European carriers, monthly rpt, C7000–4

Airline revenues and govt ownership share, for 8 major carriers, 1992 article, C8900–1.501

Airline revenues and market shares, for 8 major European carriers, 1991, article, C5800–4.512

Amusement park operating and financial data, including data for US and foreign parks, miniature golf, waterparks, and games, 1992, annual rpt, A5700–1

Auto market in Europe, including buyer preferences and market shares for selected manufacturers, by country, Aug/Sept 1992 survey, article, C2710–1.523

Auto market shares and sales trends for 5 European, 2 US, and aggregate Japanese manufacturers, 1st 8 months 1993, article, C5800–7.549

Auto production in Europe for 2 major US manufacturers, for 4-6 makes, 1992, article, C2150–3.510

Auto sales in Europe, by country and/or manufacturer, weekly rpt monthly tables, C2710–3

Business acquisition transaction value for top 10 European companies acquired by US companies, 1984-92, C1575–2.506

Cellular telephone market penetration, for 11 countries, 1993 article, C2710–1.509

Chemical and related industries production, finances, operating ratios, employment, and trade, by country, company, and chemical, 1980s-92, annual feature, A1250–1.530

Chemical company earnings trends, for 12 European companies, 1st-2nd half 1992, article, A1250–1.517

Chemical industry capital spending, US and worldwide, for 19 US and 6 European companies, 1988-93, annual article, A1250–1.508

Chemical process industries capital expenditures, for US, Japan, and Europe, 1990-95, article, C5800–8.508

Chemical production outlook for 7 Western European countries, 1992-93, annual article, A1250–1.511

Chemicals (fine) producers and total capacity, with detail for 7 countries, 1992, article, A1250–1.519

Clothing retail chain stores and sales, for 5 major European chains, 1993 article, C2710–1.517

Computer (personal) market shares in Europe and Germany, for top 6 manufacturers, 1993 article, C5800–7.539

Computer advertising expenditures in Europe, for top 15 manufacturers, with detail by selected country, 1992, article, C2710–1.527

Index by Subjects and Names

Europe

Computer chip sales worldwide and in Europe, for top 12 companies ranked by European sales, 1991, article, C5800–7.508

Computer/info systems spending plans, by industry and application, 1993 vs 1992, survey article, C1850–2.504

Construction cost indicators for selected countries in Eastern and Western Europe, 1992 article, C5800–2.502

Construction industry domestic and foreign mergers/acquisitions, for 23 Eastern and Western European countries, 1992 article, C5800–2.507

Consumer socioeconomic characteristics and attitudes regarding direct mail, with data by country, 1992/93 annual rpt, A4620–1.5

Corporate acquisitions activity by country and industry, and price and participants for top transactions, 1992 and trends, annual article, C4683–1.504

Corporate acquisitions involving European companies, price and participants for top transactions, bimonthly rpt quarterly feature, C4683–1

Coupons redeemed per household, in US, Canada, and 5 European countries, 1992, article, C2710–1.549

Diesel fuel quality indicators, for 8 European countries or areas, 1991/92, article, C6985–1.519

Economic indicator trends and forecasts for Europe and 15 key industrial countries, bimonthly rpt, B6200–2

Electronic components market value in 8 European countries and rest of Europe, 1991, article, C1850–2.501

Electronics industry financial performance of top 50 European companies, FY91 or FY92, annual article, C1850–2.501

Electronics market value for 8 European countries, US, and Japan, 1992 and 1994, article, C1850–2.502

Energy exploration, rotary drilling rigs in operation, by world area and country, monthly rpt, B4675–1

Entertainment industry devs, including TV audience shares by network and/or channel in selected countries, and boxoffice receipts for top films, weekly rpt, C9380–1

Executive job vacancy index, by industry, job function, and region, quarterly rpt, B5000–5

Exports increase to US from UK, Italy, and Sweden, with top commodities, 1st half 1993 vs 1992, article, C5800–7.549

Higher education US-Europe collaboration project grants awarded to 23 US instns from US Education Dept, with European schools involved, 1993 article, C2175–1.538

Home improvement stores and sales, for 10 major chains in US and Europe, 1993 article, C5150–6.507

Household appliance production, sales, and market shares, by country, product type, and manufacturer, 1991-92, annual feature, C2000–1.508

Household appliance shipments value, for 4 types of cleaning appliances, 1987-91, article, C2000–1.505

Immigrant population from Turkey, with detail for 6 European countries, 1990, R8750–2.59

Industrial distribution costs as percent of revenue, for typical European firm, 1987 and 1992, article, C2150–1.502

Integrated circuit sales, for 5 manufacturers, 1991-92, article, C1850–2.503

Jewish population by world area, country, and US census div, State, and city, 1990-92, annual compilation, A2050–1

Methanol supply-demand outlook in North America, Europe, and worldwide, with capacity by company, 1993 article, C6985–1.522

Military commissaries of US, sales by stores in European countries, FY92, annual feature, A2072–2.501

Military commissaries of US, sales in Europe, monthly rpt, C0500–1

Motion picture subsidy activity of European Film Distribution Office (EFDO), for 12 countries, 1988-92, article, C9380–1.540

Motor fuel retail and wholesale prices, and tax rates, for gasoline and diesel by country, Apr 1992, article, C6985–1.523

Motor vehicle (sport-utility) unit sales, for 8 manufacturers and all others, 1992, article, C2150–3.506

Motor vehicle production and sales, with selected detail by manufacturer, make, and country, 1992 and trends, annual data book, C2710–3.531

Motor vehicle world production, sales, trade, and registrations, by country, world area, manufacturer, and make, 1991 and trends, annual rpt, A0865–2.1

Nuclear power generation and units, for 11 countries, 1991-92, annual rpt, B6800–2.2

Office rental rates in 8 major European cities, 1992, annual rpt, B2800–3

Oil refinery desulfurization requirements, with detail for 18 companies, 1997 and 2002, article, C6985–1.547

Oil retail outlets in 15 European countries, 1986-90, annual fact book, C4680–1.507

Oil/gas deep well drilling, success ratios, and costs, by world area, 1990-92, annual article, C4420–1.503

Oil/gas seismic exploration land crews and vessels, by world area or country, quarterly press release, A8912–2

Plastics (polyvinyl chloride) market volume and import share, 1988 and 1992, article, C5800–12.511

Plastics waste handling and recycling devs in US, Europe, and Japan, 1993 annual encyclopedia, C5800–12.503

Population shares foreign born, for US and 5 European countries, 1985 and 1990, article, C5800–7.535

Population size and characteristics, GNP, and land area, by world region and/or country, 1993 annual data sheet, R8750–5

Prenatal care use in US and 3 European countries, by demographic characteristics, 1993 article, A2623–1.503

Privatization outlook, govt ownership share and value for 25 firms likely to be privatized in 6 countries, 1993 article, C5800–7.537

Public opinion in 9 European countries and 3 Soviet Union Republics on political, economic, and social issues, 1991 survey, C8915–8

Public opinion on political, economic, and social issues of interest to foreign investors, for 5 countries and 3 Soviet Union Republics, 1991 survey, C8915–9

Public relations firms with US ties, including data on worldwide offices and activities, by company, 1993 article, A8770–1.505

Public religious beliefs and practices, and views on role of church, with comparisons to US, Hungary, and Poland, 1990 surveys, R8780–1.502

Railroad high-speed lines in service, with route length and top speed, 1993 article, C8400–1.507

Refugees, resettlement, and intl aid devs, by country, 1992, annual rpt, R9372–1

Retail general merchandise chain sales, earnings, and stores, for top companies worldwide, with detail for selected areas, 1991-92, annual feature, C5150–3.516

Scandinavia wood pulp production, shipment, and foreign trade data, by country, 1970s-91, annual rpt, C3975–5.4

Securities market participation by foreign and US investors, by world area and country, quarterly rpt, A8825–2

Semiconductor consortium (Jessi) budget, 1990-1995/96, article, C1850–2.508

Semiconductor production equipment market shares for US, Europe, and Japan, and sales of top 10 suppliers, 1991-92, article, C1850–2.509

Socioeconomic summaries, for EC and European Free Trade Assn countries, 1992-93, article, C8900–1.504

Textile manufactured fiber industry employment, for US, Europe, and selected Asian countries, 1980-91, annual feature, C3460–1.505

Textile manufactured fiber production and capacity, monthly rpt semiannual survey, C3460–1 502

Thermoplastics demand, including polypropylene foreign trade, 1980s-2000, article, A1250–1.501

Travel trends, including tourist arrivals and expenditures, by region and/or country, 1992 annual rpt, C2140–1.3

TV advertising rates and countries and households reached, for 7 pan-Europe channels, 1993 article, C2710–1.517

TV programming shares purchased from foreign sources, total and from major suppliers, for 16 European countries, 1993 article, C1850–14.508

TV viewership of govt-run and commercial TV, for 6 European countries, Nov/Dec 1992, article, C2710–1.523

Uranium reprocessing commitments, and plutonium available from reprocessing, for 5 countries, 1990s-2010, article, B6790–1.502

see also Albania

see also Austria

see also Belgium

see also Bulgaria

see also Commonwealth of Independent States

see also Czech Republic

see also Czechoslovakia

see also Denmark

see also Eastern Europe

see also Eurocurrency

see also European Community

Europe

see also Finland
see also France
see also Germany
see also Germany, East
see also Germany, West
see also Greece
see also Hungary
see also Ireland
see also Italy
see also Luxembourg
see also Netherlands
see also North Atlantic Treaty Organization
see also Norway
see also Organization for Economic Cooperation and Development
see also Poland
see also Portugal
see also Romania
see also Slovakia
see also Soviet Union
see also Spain
see also Sweden
see also Switzerland
see also United Kingdom
see also Yugoslavia
see also under By Foreign Country or World Area in the "Index by Categories"

European Community

Airline deregulation effects anticipated by business travelers, with data on major route operations and govt ownership of airlines, 1993 article, C7000–4.503

Airline fares before and after EC deregulation, by selected European route and airline, Oct 1992 and June 1993, article, C7000–4.510

Bank financial and/or operating ratios, for 6 EC countries and US, 1991, article, A8955–1.502

Chemical trade with Eastern Europe, with detail by trading partner for Germany, 1993 article, A1250–1.540

Coal production, employment, stocks, and imports of EC, 1986-91, annual rpt, A7400–2.2

Corporate intl acquisitions and value, with detail by selected country and for 19 major deals involving German firms, 1991-92 and trends, article, A5135–2.1

Economic indicators compared to convergence requirements for Europe economic unification, Spain vs EC averages, 1991, article, A8955–1.502

Economic unification issues, with comparative economic indicators and EC budget contribution and disbursement shares, by country, 1992 rpt, R5025–9

Energy consumption of Spain and EC, by fuel source, 1991, article, A8955–1.503

Environmental services revenues for 11 EC countries, 1991 and 1996, article, A1250–1.530

Foreign trade between EC and Eastern/Central Europe, with data by commodity, 1980s-90, R5025–10

Foreign trade value with US, for 5 types of commodities, 1993 article, C8900–1.516

GNP and cargo traffic shares for member countries or groups, 1993 article, C2150–6.504

Hard goods US manufacturer views on effects of Europe unification on exports, by product line, 1993 annual survey rpt, A1800–1

Import market values for top 12 EC countries, 1992, articles, C4687–1.510

Japan corporate acquisition activity in EC, with detail for 5 countries, 1988-1st half 1992, article, C4683–1.501

Jewish population, and social and demographic characteristics, for selected EC countries, 1930s-91, article, A2050–1.1

Lumber industry foreign trade with US, monthly rpt, A1630–1

Mineral and metal consumption trend, and reliance on imports, by commodity, 1993 annual feature, C5226–2.503

Motor vehicle world production, sales, trade, and registrations, by country, world area, manufacturer, and make, 1991 and trends, annual rpt, A0865–2.1

Oil refinery capacity worldwide, with data by country and company, and outlook for 1993-94, annual compilation, C6985–4.1

Oil refinery capacity worldwide, with data by country and company, and outlook for 1993-94, annual feature, C6985–1.508

Public opinion in US on policy toward European integration, with detail for 3 States, 1993 survey, annual rpt, A4965–1

Public opinion on economic unification and effects on selected industries, for 5 EC countries, 1991 survey, C8915–9

Public opinion on economic unification effects on selected industries, and possible admission of Eastern European countries, for 5 EC countries, 1991 survey, C8915–8.2

Public opinion on feminist goals, correlation with social characteristics, by sex, 1983 survey, article, A0610–1.502

Refinery emissions and regulation outlook, with fuel oil supply-demand data, 1990s-2010, article, C6985–1.538

Refugee intl aid contributions, 20 countries and EC, 1992, annual rpt, R9372–1

Steel industry production capacity and quotas, work force reductions by type, and worker assistance program costs, for 4-8 EC countries, 1970s-90, R9260–16

Textile mill consumption of manufactured fibers, cotton, and wool, for selected countries, 1984-91, annual feature, C3460–1.501

Uranium marketing, terms of transactions for major selling-buying countries or areas, and price index and earnings data in allied industries, monthly rpt, B6800–1

Video cassette rental and sales revenues, by EC country, 1991, articles, C9380–1.503

Wheat supply-demand summary, 1987/88-1992/93, annual rpt, A7310–1

European Space Agency

Columbus space station module dev contribution shares by country, 1992 article, C5800–4.503

Euthanasia

Public opinion on legalization of physician-assisted suicide in selected situations, Dec 1992 Gallup Poll, C4040–1.506

State and local:

California State initiative on physician-assisted death for the terminally ill, election results by county, 1992, biennial rpt, S0934–1

Evans, Alison

"Council of Teaching Hospitals Survey of Housestaff Stipends, Benefits, and Funding, 1992", A3273–3

Evansville, Ind.

Business conditions analysis for selected Indiana local areas, quarterly rpt semiannual feature, U2160–1.502, U2160–1.504

Exceptional children

see Handicapped children
see Special education

Exchange of persons programs

see also Educational exchanges

Exchange rates

see Foreign exchange

Excise tax

Alcoholic beverages, Federal and State excise rates, and Federal tax collections, 1992 and trends, annual rpt, C4775–1.2

Brewers and other distillers tax payments to Federal and State govts, FY91 and trends, annual rpt, A3455–1.6

Cigarette added tax burden from proposed increase to finance health care reform, by State, with natl average price and taxes, 1993 article, R9050–3.509

Cigarette added tax burden from proposed increase to finance health care reform, with detail for 8 States, 1993 article, C5800–7.549

Coal industry executive preferences for energy (BTU) vs carbon tax, Mar 1993 survey, article, C5226–1.507

Energy (BTU) tax proposals and estimated revenues, with comparison to consumption and prices, by fuel type, 1993 article, C6985–1.518

Energy (BTU) tax proposed by Clinton Admin as a percent of household income, by income level, 1993 article, R9050–3.502

Energy (BTU) tax proposed by Clinton Admin average household cost, by region, 1993 feature, C4300–1.506

Energy (BTU) tax proposed by Clinton Admin, burden per household and by economic sector, by State, 1993 article, R9050–3.505

Energy (BTU) tax proposed by Clinton Admin effect on retail fuel prices, by fuel type and consuming sector, 1993 article, C4680–1.505

Energy (BTU) tax proposed by Clinton Admin, effects on energy prices by type and on number and capacity of oil refineries by region, 1993 articles, C6985–1.528

Energy (BTU) tax proposed by Clinton Admin financial impact for aluminum manufacturers, with production and capacity data, for 5 companies, 1993-96, article, C5226–2.506

Energy (BTU) tax proposed by Clinton Admin, including impact by census div, 1993 article, C6985–1.524

Energy (BTU) tax proposed by Clinton Admin, resulting job losses by State, 1994-98, article, R9050–3.506

Energy tax options considered by Clinton Admin, total and per-household cost estimates by State and region, 1993 rpt, R8490–49

Energy tax proposals and potential effect on selected economic indicators, 1993-97, article, C6985–1.516

Index by Subjects and Names

Executives and managers

Govt finances, including revenues by source, expenditures by function, and debt, detailed data for Federal, State, and local govts, 1993 annual rpt, R9050–1

Japan and US energy taxes by type, 1993, recurring article, R5650–2.536

Northeast States cigarette excise and State sales taxes per pack, for 8 States, Jan 1993, article, R9050–3.502

Printing industry additional costs that would be generated by energy (BTU) tax proposed by Clinton Admin, 1993 article, C1850–10.507

State social, economic, and govtl indicators, with rankings, 1993 semiannual rpt, B8500–1.4

Telecommunication services tax rates, by State, 1991/92 annual rpt, A7015–3

Tobacco products taxation, by State, 1950s-92, annual rpt, A9075–2

Transportation-related revenues of Fed Govt and individual States, by type, 1990s and trends, annual rpt, A0865–1.3

Value-added tax rates and revenues for 6 industrial countries, with potential US revenues, 1993 article, C8900–1.515

Wine Federal excise tax collections and rates, and rates by State, 1993 annual rpt, C4775–2.2

State and local:

Alabama financial condition, including revenues by source, expenditures by function and object, and fund balances, by fund and agency, FY92, annual rpt, S0129–1

Alaska financial condition, including revenues by source, expenditures by function, fund balances, and bond obligations, FY92 and trends, annual rpt, S0275–1

Arizona tax revenues by source, tax rates, and disbursements to local areas, FY92 and trends, annual rpt, S0515–1

Arkansas financial condition, including revenues by source, expenditures by function and object, and fund balances, FY92, annual rpt, S0670–1

California alcoholic beverage and cigarette excise tax collections, FY92 and trends, annual rpt, S0835–1.5

California cigarette tax Proposition 99 mandating spending for health education and research, actual and projected expenditures by program category, FY90-94, article, A2623–1.511

California economic condition, including population, employment and earnings, income, business activity, and taxation, 1960s-92, annual rpt, S0840–3.2

California financial condition, including revenues by source, expenditures by agency and function, fund balances, and bonded debt, FY92 and trends, annual rpt, S0815–1

Colorado tax revenues by type, with selected data by county and city, FY92 and trends, annual rpt, S1075–1

Connecticut financial condition, including revenues by source, expenditures by function, and bonded debt, FY92, annual rpt, S1170–1

DC financial condition, including receipts by source, expenditures by object or function, and fund balances, FY92, annual rpt, S1507–1

Delaware data book, general data, 1993 annual rpt, S1375–4

Georgia tax revenues, by type and county, FY92 annual rpt, S1950–1

Hawaii data book, general data, 1992 annual rpt, S2090–1.15, S2090–1.19, S2090–1.21, S2090–1.22, S2090–1.23

Hawaii tax collections and allocations, by type, for State and counties, FY91-92 and trends, annual rpt, S2120–1

Idaho tax statistics, including collections, and data by county and city, FY92 and trends, annual rpt, S2295–1

Illinois financial condition, including revenues by source, and expenditures by object, function, and agency, FY92, annual rpt, S2415–1

Indiana financial condition, including revenues by source, expenditures by function and object, and fund balances, by agency, FY92, annual rpt, S2570–1

Kansas tax collections by tax type, and property values, with data by county, FY92 and trends, annual rpt, S3020–1

Maryland financial condition, including revenues by source, expenditures by function, fund balances, and bonded debt, FY92 and trends, annual rpt, S3685–2

Massachusetts State initiatives to establish excise taxes on tobacco and hazardous substances, election results by locality, 1992, biennial rpt, S3920–1

Massachusetts tax collections by type, and distributions to local areas, FY91 and trends, annual rpt, S3917–1

Michigan financial condition, including revenues by source, expenditures by function, and fund balances, FY92 and trends, annual rpt, S3985–2

Minnesota financial condition, including revenues by source, expenditures by function, fund balances, and bonded debt, FY92 and trends, annual rpt, S4180–1

Mississippi tax collections by type, and disbursements, with selected sales and income tax data by locality and industry, FY92 and trends, annual rpt, S4435–1

Missouri financial condition, including fund finances, tax collections and distribution, and State treasury activity, FY92 and trends, annual rpt, S4570–1

Missouri school revenues from special sales and excise taxes, by county and district, 1991/92 and trends, annual rpt, S4505–1

Montana revenue collections by tax type, and taxable establishments, production, and income, FY91-92 and trends, biennial rpt, S4750–1.1

Nebraska revenues from licenses, fees, and miscellaneous taxes, 1991 and trends, annual rpt, S4950–1.3

New Hampshire financial condition, with revenues by source, expenditures by function or object, and fund balances, FY92 and trends, annual rpt, S5175–1

New Mexico tax revenues and disbursements, with data by tax type, county, and city, FY91-92 and trends, annual rpt, S5660–1

New York State tax collections by type, FY84-93, annual rpt, S5710–1

North Carolina financial condition, including revenues by source, expenditures by function, fund balances, and bonded debt, FY92, annual rpt, S5897–1

Ohio tax revenues and collections, by tax type, with distributions and property assessments by county, and corporate taxes by industry, FY92 annual rpt, S6390–1

Oklahoma tax revenues by source, and distribution to local govts and State funds, FY92 and trends, annual rpt, S6495–1

Pennsylvania tax collections by tax type, with data by county and industry, FY92 and trends, annual rpt, S6885–1

South Dakota excise tax collections, bimonthly rpt, U8595–2

South Dakota tax revenues by source, and aid distributed to local areas, FY92 annual rpt, S7380–1.1

Tennessee tax revenues by source and apportionments to counties, cities, and funds, FY91-92 and trends, biennial rpt, S7570–1

Texas financial condition, including revenues by source, expenditures by function and dept, and investments, with data for over 400 individual funds, FY92, annual rpt, S7655–2

Utah tax revenues by source, and distribution to localities and State funds, FY92 and trends, annual rpt, S7905–1

Virginia tax revenues by type, including sales tax data by county and independent city, FY92 and trends, annual rpt, S8305–1.2

Washington State revenues by source, and distributions by tax and locality, FY92 and trends, annual rpt, S8415–1.1

Wisconsin financial condition, including revenues by source, expenditures by function and object, and fund balances, FY93, annual rpt, S8675–2

Wyoming tax revenues and distributions, by type of tax, FY92 and trends, annual rpt, S8990–1.3

see also Fuel tax
see also Sales tax
see also Tolls
see also User fees
see also Windfall profit tax

Executions

see Capital punishment

Executive clemency

see Pardons

Executive-congressional relations

see Congressional-executive relations

Executive departments

see Federal executive departments

Executive stock options

see Employee stock ownership plans

Executives and managers

Association executives compensation, by position, assn type, and census div, with personnel practices and benefit provisions, 1992, biennial rpt, A2900–3

Auto dealership service dept operations and profit outlook, and manager compensation, 1993 annual survey, article, C2710–3.537

Auto fleet corporate manager job outlook, duties, and use of outside administrative services, 1992 survey, article, C1575–2.501

Bank (master trust/custodial) operating data, including account supervisors, by instn, 1993 annual directory, C2710–2.522

Benefits offered to executives, 1987 and 1991, C1200–4.501

Executives and managers

Index by Subjects and Names

Broadcasting advertising industry assn chief executive salaries, for 4 assns, 1993 features, C1850–14.511

Business grad school programs for executives, with data on revenues, enrollment, tuition, and participant characteristics, by instn, 1993 feature, C5800–7.552

Business incubator facilities manager tenure, experience, and education, 1991, annual rpt, A7360–1

Cable TV system mgmt salaries by selected characteristics, and views on job satisfaction, Mar/Apr 1993 survey, articles, C1858–1.502

Chambers of commerce income, salaries and benefits, membership, staff, and operations, 1993 annual rpt, A3840–3

Chemist and chemical engineer salaries, employment status, and demographic and professional characteristics, 1993, annual rpt, A1250–4

Communications industries trade assn chief executive salaries, for 12 assns, 1993 feature, C1850–14.506

Compensation (incentive) for corporate executives, by position, 1992, biennial rpt, B2535–1

Compensation for top executives at approx 400 companies, by industry group, 1992 and trends, annual survey, C5800–7.525

Compensation measures for top 10 CEOs among 100 leading natl advertisers, 1992 article, C2710–1.505

Compensation of CEOs in 800 corporations, with sales and profit data, 1993 annual article, C3950–1.515

Compensation of corporate CEOs compared to company performance, for 200 executives, 1992, annual article, C8900–1.517

Compensation of top 5 executive positions, by industry div and major manufacturing group, 1991, annual rpt, R4105–19

Compensation of 20 highly paid executives, with company revenues, for US, Germany, and Japan, 1993 article, C3950–1.516

Computer game use at work by info system managers, and impact on productivity, 1993 survey article, C5800–7.549

Corporate CEO characteristics, compensation, and company finances, for officers of top 1,000 firms, 1993 annual feature, C5800–7.549

Corporate CEO views on outlook for company employment, wages compared to inflation, and mgmt skills needs, June 1993 survey, article, C8900–1.519

Corporate executive strategic info mgmt, including communications methods and use of nonfinancial performance measures, 1992 survey, R4105–78.25

Corporate middle mgmt share of employment and layoffs, and CEO compensation from base pay and long-term incentives, 1993 article, C4687–1.503

Corporate stock performance after appointment of outsider as CEO, for 10 companies, 1993 article, C5800–7.523

Corporate stock performance before and after CEO resignation/firing, for 7 companies, 1993 article, C5800–7.542

Corporate use of employee stock option plans, with recipient and plan characteristics, Nov/Dec 1992 survey, R4105–78.31

Corporate work force outlook and related mgmt policies, views of human resources executives, Sept/Oct 1991 survey, R4105–78.21

Discount retail company executive compensation, for 75 highest-paid executives, 1992, annual feature, C5150–3.518

Eastern Europe public opinion on entrepreneurs and govt enterprise managers, for 6 countries and 3 Soviet Union Republics, 1991 survey, C8915–9

Economic outlook of managers, including company budget policy and effects of selected Govt economic/trade policy proposals, 1993 survey article, C8900–1.510

Electric utility mgmt salaries, by customer size and revenue class, 1992, annual article, A2625–1.501

Electronics company executives selling stock holdings in own company, with minimum amounts received, for 6 companies, Dec 1992-Feb 1993, article, C1850–2.507

Engineer compensation, by work and employee characteristics, and region and metro area, 1992, annual rpt, A8460–1

Engineers salaries for supervisors and nonsupervisors, by industry group, census div, selected metro area, and years since college degree, 1993, annual survey rpt, A0685–5

Engineers salaries for supervisors and nonsupervisors, by industry group, census div, selected metro area, degree level, and years since college degree, 1993, annual survey rpt, A0685–3

Food marketing mgmt personnel compensation, by position, by company sales size and region, year ended Mar 1993, annual survey, A4950–6

Food service CEO compensation, with comparisons to company performance, for top 75 executives, FY92, article, C1200–5.513

Food store supervisory staff training characteristics, by position and company size, 1992, annual rpt, A4950–5.4

Food/beverage manufacturers mgmt salaries, by selected employee characteristics, 1992 survey, annual article, C2150–6.502

Foundation finances, and personnel and governing board characteristics, by organization characteristics, 1991/92, article, C2176–1.506

Fundraising professionals characteristics, earnings, and benefits, 1992 survey, recurring rpt, A8455–1

Grounds maintenance manager salaries, by type of employer, 1992, annual article, C4725–6

Health care specialist and health-related company CEO income, public perceptions vs actual amounts, by respondent characteristics, 1991-93, R4865–13

Higher education private instn salaries and benefits of chief executives and top 5 earners, and total expenditures, by instn, FY91 or FY92, article, C2175–1.519

Homebuilder executive compensation, incentives, and benefits, by position, 1992, annual survey article, C1850–8.508

Hospital CEO outlook for next career move, 1992 survey, article, A1865–1.501

Hospital CEO views on best educational preparation for CEO position, 1992 survey, article, A1865–1.504

Hospital CEO views on trustee financial expertise, 1993 survey, article, A1865–1.510

Hospital CEO views on whether own career path focused on operational experience at expense of generalist skills, 1993 survey, article, A1865–1.523

Hospital CEOs grooming a successor from senior mgmt, 1993 survey, article, A1865–1.511

Hospital chief financial officer views on educational needs and top challenges, 1993 survey, article, A1865–1.511

Hospital chief info officer responsibilities and qualifications, Nov 1992 survey, article, A1865–1.508

Hospital executive and manager compensation, with detail by hospital bed-size and revenues, and use of incentives, 1993 annual article, A1865–1.521

Hospital physician CEO personal and professional characteristics, 1993 article, A1865–1.513

Hospital vice president of medical affairs characteristics, responsibilities, and compensation trends, 1993 survey article, A1865–1.508

Industrial distribution executives job and dept characteristics, compensation, and industry outlook, 1992 annual survey article, C2150–1.501

Investment mgmt executive compensation, for executives serving pension funds, 1993 survey article, C2710–2.513

Japan corporate CEOs compensation, for 50 largest companies, 1991, article, C5800–7.525

Job characteristics and attitudes of corporate executives, series, B4490–2

Job vacancy index for executives earning $100,000/more, by industry, job function, and region, quarterly rpt, B5000–5

Laid-off executives, distribution by position type, 1992, article, C5800–7.523

Local govt use of selected types of incentive pay for managerial employees, 1993 rpt, A5800–1.1

Logistics manager salaries, by position, industry, and selected characteristics, Nov 1992 survey, annual article, C1850–11

Logistics personnel compensation by position, 1993 annual article, C2150–1.508

Magazine circulation director and manager compensation, by region, sex, age, and publication characteristics, 1992 survey, annual article, C2575–1.502

Magazine compensation of ad sales personnel, by region, sex, age, and publication characteristics, 1993 survey, annual article, C2575–1.516

Magazine compensation of editorial personnel, by region, sex, age, and publication characteristics, 1993 survey, annual article, C2575–1.512

Magazine production director and manager compensation, by region, sex, age, and publication characteristics, 1993 survey, annual article, C2575–1.510

Index by Subjects and Names

Magazine promotion dept activities, and executive characteristics and salary, Nov 1992 survey, article, C2575–1.506

Motor vehicle fleet manager earnings, and personal and professional characteristics, 1993 article, C1575–2.506

Newspaper executive compensation, by circulation size, for 5 positions, 1993 and trends, annual survey article, A8605–1.510

Nonprofit organization executive compensation, by position, organization characteristics, and region, 1993, annual article, C2176–1.519

Nonprofit organization executive compensation, with comparison to organization income and salaries in other sectors, by leading organization, FY91 or FY92, article, C2176–1.509

Nonprofit organization executive salaries, by title and organization type, 1993, annual article, C2176–1.519

Performance ratings by executives for 10 most admired CEOs of leading companies, 1993 survey feature, C8900–1.508

Plastics processing industry employment, compensation practices, and union representation, by region, 1992, annual survey rpt, A8920–2

Promotional gifts from advertisers, corporate executives reasons cited for keeping items, 1993 survey article, C1200–4.504

Public opinion on honesty/ethical standards of selected occupations, 1992 Gallup Polls and trends, C4040–1.501

Quality control and improvement, views and experience of corporate executives and outside directors, July-Aug 1992 surveys, A2800–3

Real estate property managers characteristics and compensation, including types of property managed, 1989 surveys, recurring rpt, A5600–4

Restaurant/food service mgmt compensation, characteristics, and views, including data by position, 1992 survey, annual article, C1850–3.502

Restaurant/lodging industries executives/managers, by sex and race-ethnicity, 1992, article, C5150–5.511

Salaries of scientists, engineers, technicians, and other professionals, by employee and employer characteristics, 1990s and trends, biennial rpt, A3960–1

Sales and marketing executive compensation, for top 100 executives, with company sales and profit data, 1992 annual article, C1200–1.501

Sales and marketing executives average compensation for 7 positions, 1993 survey article, C4300–1.503

Small business employee benefits offered to executives, for companies with 250/fewer employees, 1993 feature, C4687–1.504

Small companies CEO characteristics and compensation, for top growth firms, 1993 survey article, C5800–7.551

Small companies with high 5-year returns on equity, financial performance data and chief executive characteristics, for top 200 firms, 1992 annual article, C3950–1.501

Small companies with sales under $25 million, financial and operating data for top 100 public firms, 1992 and trends, annual feature, C4687–1.507

Small corporation CEO compensation compared to lowest-paid full-time employee, 1993 feature, C4687–1.506

Small, fast-growing company years in business before appointment of 1st sales director, 1992 survey, article, C4687–1.511

Steel industry CEO educational backgrounds, for 4 major companies, 1960-90, U9640–2.15

Utility and other executives benefits and perquisites received, 1992 and trends, article, C5800–28.507

White-collar work force trends, including employment, earnings, and unionization, with data by occupation, sex, and educational attainment, 1990s and trends, annual rpt, A1570–1

State and local:

Arizona occupational profiles, with employment and job outlook, by industry div, occupation, and county, series, S0465–2

Hawaii data book, general data, 1992 annual rpt, S2090–1.12

Maine employment, by SIC 2-digit industry and detailed occupation, triennial series, S3465–1

New Hampshire employment, by SIC 2- and 3-digit industry and detailed occupation, series, S5205–2

North Carolina employment in SIC 2-digit industries, by detailed occupation, triennial rpt series, S5917–5

Texas employment, by SIC 2- and 3-digit industry and detailed occupation, series, S7675–1

see also Boards of directors

see also Business outlook and attitude surveys

see also Officials

see also under By Occupation in the "Index by Categories"

Exercise

see Physical exercise

see Sports and athletics

Eximbank

see Export-Import Bank

Expense accounts

see Business expense allowances

Exploration, natural resources

see Energy exploration and drilling

see Natural resources

Explosives

State and local:

California vital statistics, including population, births, and deaths by cause, by demographic characteristics and county, 1990 and trends, annual rpt, S0865–1

Maryland vital statistics, including population, births, deaths by cause, marriages, and divorces, by demographic characteristics and location, 1989 and trends, annual rpt, S3635–1

South Carolina deaths, by detailed cause, age, sex, and race, 1990, annual rpt, S7175–2

Utah vital statistics, including births and deaths by cause, by demographic characteristics and location, 1990, annual rpt, S7835–1.2

Virginia vital statistics, including births, deaths by cause, marriages and divorces, and communicable disease, by demographic characteristics and location, 1991 and trends, annual rpt, S8225–1

Eye diseases and defects

see also Bombs

Export controls

see Tariffs and foreign trade controls

Export-Import Bank

Credit authorizations and guarantees, total and for individual commercial aircraft customers, FY91 or FY92 and trends, annual rpt, A0250–2.4

Latin America statistical abstract, general data by country, 1992 annual rpt, U6250–1.28

Export processing zones

Mexico maquiladora plants, employment, and earnings, 1965-88, annual rpt, U6250–1.16

Public opinion in US, Canada, and Mexico on North American Free Trade Agreement, Aug-Sept 1992 Gallup Poll and trends, C4040–1.503

State and local:

Hawaii foreign trade zone operations and merchandise value, FY90-92, annual rpt, S2090–1.24

Export promotion

see Foreign trade promotion

Exports and imports

see Agricultural exports and imports

see Coal exports and imports

see Energy exports and imports

see Foreign trade

see Motor vehicle exports and imports

see Natural gas exports and imports

see Petroleum exports and imports

Expropriation of alien property

World expropriation acts, and number of countries expropriating, 1960-85, annual rpt, U6250–1.29

External debt

see Foreign debts

Extinction

see Endangered species

Eye banks

see Organ and blood banks

Eye diseases and defects

Hospital patient admission rates and length of stay, by diagnosis and procedure, payment source, age, sex, and region, 1991, B4455–4

Hospital patient charges and length of stay, by diagnosis and procedure, payment source, age, and region, 1991, B4455–5

Hospital patient discharges and length of stay, by diagnosis, type of operation, age, and region, 1991, annual rpt series, B4455–1

Hospital patient discharges and length of stay, by diagnostic related group (DRG), payment source, age, and region, 1991, annual rpt series, B4455–3

State and local:

California vital statistics, including population, births, and deaths by cause, by demographic characteristics and county, 1990 and trends, annual rpt, S0865–1

Hawaii chronic health conditions, by demographic characteristics and location, 1988, annual rpt, S2065–1.3

Mississippi vital statistics, including births, deaths by cause, marriages, and divorces, by demographic characteristics and location, 1992 and trends, annual rpt, S4350–1

Tennessee vital statistics, including deaths by cause, marriages, divorces, and population, by demographic characteristics and location, 1991 and trends, annual rpt, S7520–2

Eye diseases and defects

West Virginia vital statistics, including births, deaths by cause, marriages, and divorces, by location and demographic characteristics, 1991 and trends, annual rpt, S8560–1
see also Blind
see also Optometry
see also Vision

Eyewear
see Vision

Eymonerie, Maryse, Associates
Higher education faculty average salaries by rank, at approx 2,000 instns arranged by State, 1992/93, annual feature, C2175–1.516
Higher education faculty compensation and employment, detailed data by rank, sex, and instn, 1992/93 and trends, annual rpt, A0800–1

FAA
see Federal Aviation Administration

Fabrics
see Natural fibers
see Synthetic fibers and fabrics
see Textile industry and fabrics

Facsimile equipment
see Business machines and equipment
see Electronic mail systems

Factories
see Industrial plants and equipment
see Materials handling equipment

Factory sales
see Wholesale trade

Factory workers
see Production workers

Faculty
see Faculty tenure
see Teachers

Faculty tenure
Business grad school women's share of tenured and tenure-track faculty, for 6 schools with highest and lowest shares, 1992 article, C5800–7.506
Chemist and chemical engineer salaries, employment status, and demographic and professional characteristics, 1993, annual rpt, A1250–4
Dental school faculty, support personnel, and staff characteristics, by instn, 1992/93, annual rpt, A1475–4.5
Ecologist personal and professional characteristics, including research activity and funding, with data by field, Mar 1992 survey, recurring rpt, A4685–1
Higher education faculty and tenure, by sex, race, and selected discipline, 1980s-91, with historical trends, recurring rpt, A3960–2
Higher education faculty compensation and employment, detailed data by rank, sex, and instn, 1992/93 and trends, annual rpt, A0800–1
Higher education faculty share with tenure, by position, 1992/93, C2175–1.521
Higher education instn policies and practices, including changes in faculty, enrollment, and finances, 1993 annual survey, A1410–1.38
Higher education instns, faculty, students, degrees, and finances, detailed data by State, 1993 annual rpt, C2175–1.531
Higher education president personal and professional characteristics, 1990 and trends, recurring rpt, A1410–12

Higher education president personal and professional characteristics, 1990, article, C2175–1.533
Library/info science schools faculty tenure status, by rank and sex, Jan 1993 and trends, annual rpt, A3235–1.1
Mathematics dept doctoral faculty trends by tenure status, total and for women, fall 1992, annual survey, A2085–1.2
Nursing college deans and salaries, by personal and instn characteristics, 1992/93, annual rpt, A0615–2
Nursing college faculty and salaries, by personal and instn characteristics, 1992/93, annual rpt, A0615–1
Nursing higher education program finances, faculty and clinical practice, and clinic/center operations, by instn characteristics, 1992/93 biennial rpt, A0615–5
Optometry school faculty, enrollment and degrees, policies and programs, and finances, by instn, 1991/92, annual survey, A3370–2
Political science higher education dept characteristics, including faculty, salaries, enrollment, and finances, 1991/92 annual rpt, A2617–1
Psychology grad depts, faculty characteristics, enrollment, and student aid, US and Canada, 1990/91 and trends, annual rpt, A2620–3
Public health school faculty characteristics, by instn, fall 1991, recurring rpt, A3372–1
Social work higher education programs and faculty, with data by region, 1992 and trends, annual rpt, A4515–1.1

State and local:
Florida higher education enrollment, degree programs, staff, and finances, by State-supported instn, with student and staff characteristics, 1991/92 annual rpt, S1725–1
Illinois higher education staff, salaries, student cost and aid, and finances, by instn, 1993 annual rpt, S2475–1.2
Iowa postsecondary enrollment, degrees, staff, and finances, by instn, 1990/91, annual rpt, S2755–1
Kentucky higher education enrollment, degrees, staff, and finances, by State-supported instn, 1983-92, annual rpt, S3130–3
Maryland statistical abstract, general data, 1993-94 biennial rpt, S3605–1.2
Missouri higher education faculty, by rank, tenure status, age, and instn, fall 1992 and trends, annual rpt, S4520–3.3
Pennsylvania higher education faculty employment, compensation, and tenure status, by sex and type of instn, 1991/92 and trends, annual rpt, S6790–5.5
Pennsylvania higher education faculty employment, compensation, and tenure status, by sex and type of instn, 1992/93 and trends, annual rpt, S6790–5.13
South Carolina higher education enrollment, degrees, staff, and finances, by instn, 1992 and trends, annual rpt, S7185–2
South Dakota public higher education finances, staff, enrollment, degrees, and facilities, by instn, FY93 annual rpt, S7375–1

Texas higher education enrollment and faculty, by race-ethnicity, sex, and instn, 1991/92 and trends, annual rpt, S7657–1.1
West Virginia higher education faculty characteristics and salary, by instn, 1992 and trends, annual rpt, S8533–1.2

Failed businesses
see Business failures and closings

Fair employment practices
see Discrimination in employment

Fair housing
see Discrimination in housing

Fairbanks, Alaska
Employment, by industry, monthly rpt, S0320–1
see also under By City in the "Index by Categories"

Faith
see Religion

Falkenmark, Malin
"Population and Water Resources: A Delicate Balance", R8750–2.57

Fallout
see Radiation

Families and households
Appliance ownership by households, by appliance type, 1973-92, annual article, C2000–1.510
Australia husbands and wives political attitudes as affected by social background of self and spouse, 1992 article, A0610–1.501
Black American population and demographic characteristics, with comparisons to whites, 1970s-2080, annual compilation, C6775–2.1
Black American socioeconomic status, with comparisons to whites and data by region, 1960s-92, annual compilation, A8510–1.1
Black children and youth population, economic, health, and education data, with comparisons to whites, 1993 rpt, R3840–21
Business traveler and trip characteristics, including mode, purpose, and lodging, 1991, annual rpt, R9375–12
Cable TV ratings and viewing households, for 14 basic networks, 4th qtr 1992-1st qtr 1993, C1858–1.501
Canada photographic and video equipment and supplies ownership, purchasing patterns, and use, by household characteristics, 1992 survey, recurring rpt, A8695–4
Catholic charity social service agency activities, clients, finances, and personnel, 1991 and trends, annual rpt, A3810–1
Charitable contributions, and share of households making donations, by income level, 1989, article, C2176–1.505
Child health and well-being indicators, with selected household characteristics, by State, 1993 annual rpt, R3832–1
College freshmen attitudes and characteristics, degree and career plans, and financial aid sources, by sex and instn type, fall 1992, annual survey, U6215–1
Consumer buying power survey of population, income, and sales by kind of business, by census div, State, MSA, county, and city, 1992, annual rpt, C1200–1.511
Consumer buying power survey of population, income, and sales by product

Index by Subjects and Names

Families and households

line, by State, metro area, county, and census div, 1993 annual rpt, C1200–1.514

Developing countries women married/cohabiting, by age group and country, various years 1971-90, R8720–1.1

Ecologist personal and professional characteristics, including research activity and funding, with data by field, Mar 1992 survey, recurring rpt, A4685–1

Economic indicator historical trends, 1900s-92, annual rpt, R9050–1.2

Ethiopia famine analysis, including household impacts and responses, drought factor, agricultural activity and markets, and intervention programs, 1980s, R5620–1.36

Europe appliance ownership by households, by appliance type and country, 1992, annual feature, C2000–1.508

Food away from home expenditures, by household characteristics and for 26 MSAs, 1991, recurring rpt, A8200–13

Food nutrition awareness and health concerns, including shopping, preparation, and consumption patterns, by respondent characteristics, 1992 survey, annual rpt, A4950–36

Food service industry employee characteristics, and minority-owned establishments and sales, 1993 article, A8200–1.508

Food take-out consumer characteristics, consumption patterns, and attitudes, May 1992 survey, A8200–21

Foreign-language-speaking households, for 11 languages, 1980 and 1990, article, C2710–1.526

Germany (West) and US comparative socioeconomic statistics, 1970s-91, annual rpt, A5135–2.2

Health care expenditures of families, including insurance premiums by source of coverage, and taxes by type, by income group, 1987, R4700–20

Health insurance coverage lack, and population with high out-of-pocket expenses, by State and selected characteristics, 1993, R4865–14

Higher education financial aid applicant characteristics, American College Testing (ACT) program, 1993/94, annual rpt, R1960–5

Hispanic American households with income over $35,000, by income group and leading State, 1989, article, C4575–1.501

Hispanic American population and demographic characteristics, with comparisons to whites, 1993 annual compilation, C6775–3.1

Home buyer (1st-time and repeat) profile, and transaction characteristics, including prices and financing, by region and for 18 metro areas, 1990-92, annual survey rpt, B2150–1

Homeless population characteristics, and demand among families for emergency food and shelter, for 29 cities, 1991/92, annual rpt, A9330–9

Households by housing tenure status, region, and age of household head, quarterly rpt, B5190–1

Households with children age 17/under, by type of family, 1990, article, R8750–1.504

Insurance coverage against property loss, by household tenure, 1984, 1986, and 1989, annual rpt, A5650–1.1

Kitchen uses cited by households, 1993 survey article, C4300–1.505

Life insurance purchases and ownership, by consumer and household characteristics, 1991 and trends, biennial fact book, A1325–1.1

Market area population and characteristics, households, income, and retail outlets, for 21 leading areas, 1993 feature, C2710–1.538

Markets with daily newspapers, demographic and economic info by geographic area, US and Canada, 1993 annual rpt, C3250–1

Men age 69-84 quality of life indicators, including health, finances, family, and employment, by race, 1990 survey, U3780–9

Minority population characteristics, employment, and voting patterns by detailed race-ethnicity, with comparisons to whites, 1980s-2040, R8750–2.58

Motor vehicle ownership patterns, 1977-90, annual rpt, A0865–1.3

Photographic equipment and supplies, consumer ownership, purchasing patterns, and use, 1993 survey and trends, recurring rpt, A8695–2

Poor children age 5/under, with demographic and family characteristics, 1991 and trends, annual rpt, U1260–2

Public housing authority income and expenses, resident and property characteristics, and unit vacancy and turnover rates, various years FY77-1992, A6800–2

Public housing authority operations and finances, including resident characteristics, by agency size, 1989, A6800–1

Public opinion on social, political, and economic issues, detailed data, 1972-91 surveys, annual rpt, U6395–1

Religious congregation characteristics, including membership, activities, staff, and finances, 1992 survey, recurring rpt, A5435–4

Retail outlet household preference indexes, by selected demographic characteristics, 1993 annual feature, C4655–1.504

Snack food consumption patterns, by snack type and consumer characteristics, 1989/90 and trends, recurring rpt, A8905–2

Socioeconomic profiles of consumers in top 50 MSAs ranked by supermarket sales, 1991, annual rpt, C3400–6

Sporting goods purchaser characteristics, by product category, 1992, annual survey rpt, A8485–4

Statistical profiles of 50 States and DC, general data, 1993 annual almanac, C4712–1

Stock holdings of households, as percent of total assets and compared to institutional stock holdings, 1960s-1st qtr 1993, article, A8825–1.508

Stock holdings of households vs institutional investors, 1960s-92, recurring article, A8825–1.501

Supermarket shopper practices, attitudes, and expenditures, by respondent characteristics, 1993 and trends, annual survey rpt, A4950–3

Telephone service worldwide, including access lines by type, and intl calling patterns, with comparisons to population, by world area and country, 1990-91, annual rpt, B0350–1

Travel trips and traveler characteristics, including mode, purpose, type of lodging, and area of destination and origin, quarterly rpt, R9375–14

TV and cable TV households in top 20 market areas, Nielsen vs Arbitron estimates, biweekly rpt recurring feature, C1858–1.504, C2965–1.507, C2965–1.510

TV and total households, and member population by age and sex, by market area, county, State, and/or census div, 1992/93, annual rpt, B0525–3

TV households and population by race-ethnicity, sex, and age, by market area, 1992/93, annual rpt, B0525–4

TV households by census div, State, county, Nielsen market area, and time zone, Jan 1994, annual rpt, B6670–2

Unemployment insurance trends, including data on unemployment, worker characteristics, coverage, benefits, and State govt finances, 1940s-90, R9260–18

Volunteer organization views on using families as volunteers, 1992 survey article, C2176–1.501

Women's employment and earnings trends, including number of families for whom women are sole support, 1990s and trends, annual rpt, A1570–2

Women's housing issues, with data on household composition, tenure, and characteristics, 1992, A8657–5

Youth age 12-17 charitable contributions, volunteer activity, and views on related issues, by respondent characteristics, 1992 survey, biennial rpt, A5435–5

State and local:

Alabama municipal data book, general data, 1992 recurring rpt, S0121–5

Alabama statistical abstract, general data, 1992 recurring rpt, U5680–2.13

Alaska population, housing, income, and education data, by demographic characteristics and/or locality, 1990/91 and trends, annual rpt, S0320–4

Arizona Indian population, education, housing, health, and employment characteristics, with detail by reservation, 1970s-91, recurring rpt, U5850–2.9

Arizona prisoners by number of dependents, by sex, June 1992, annual rpt, S0464–2

Arizona temporary winter residents and expenditures, and mobile home and trailer park spaces and occupancy, by local area, winter 1992/93, annual article, U0280–1.508

Arkansas Census of Population and Housing detailed findings, 1990, U5935–7

California Census of Population and Housing detailed findings, 1990, S0840–9

California socioeconomic and govtl data for municipalities, counties, and school districts, 1993 annual rpt, C4712–3

DC statistical profile, general data, 1992 annual rpt, S1535–3.1, S1535–3.4

Delaware projected households, by county, 1990-2020, recurring rpt, S1375–3

Florida county data book, 1992/93 annual rpt, C6360–1

Families and households

Florida households and average size, by county, 1980, 1990, and 1992, annual rpt, U6660–3.45

Florida statistical abstract, general data, 1992 annual rpt, U6660–1.2

Georgia county guide, general data, 1993 annual rpt, U6750–1

Georgia statistical abstract, general data, 1992-93 biennial rpt, U6730–1.1

Hawaii data book, general data, 1992 annual rpt, S2090–1.1, S2090–1.13

Illinois statistical abstract, general data, 1992 annual rpt, U6910–2

Indiana population and family characteristics, 1990, article, U2160–1.501

Kansas statistical abstract, general data, 1991/92 annual rpt, U7095–2.2, U7095–2.6

Kentucky economic statistics, general data, 1993 annual rpt, S3104–1

Louisiana Census of Population and Housing summary findings, by local area, 1990 and trends, U8010–4

Maine Census of Population and Housing summary findings, by local area, 1990, S3465–7, S3465–8, S3465–9

Massachusetts municipal and county profiles, general data, 1992 annual rpt, C4712–2

Mississippi labor force planning rpt, including population, employment, and characteristics of unemployed and disadvantaged, 1993 annual rpt, S4345–1

Nebraska northeastern counties families and households, poverty rates, and income by source, by population size, 1989, article, U7860–1.509

Nevada statistical abstract, general data, 1992 biennial rpt, S5005–1.1

New Jersey Census of Population and Housing detailed findings, by county, 1990, S5425–19

New Jersey municipal and county data book, general data, 1992 annual rpt, C4712–4

New York State juvenile corrections admissions, by household characteristics, 1991, annual rpt, S5760–3.4

New York State municipal and county statistical profiles, general data, 1993 annual rpt, C4712–7

New York State statistical yearbook, general data, 1992 annual rpt, U5100–1.1

Oklahoma statistical abstract, general data, 1992 annual rpt, U8130–2.2

Pennsylvania Census of Population and Housing detailed findings, with selected data by county and municipality, 1990, U4130–13

Pennsylvania statistical abstract, general data, 1992 recurring rpt, U4130–6.1

Rhode Island Census of Population and Housing detailed findings, by county and municipality, 1990, S6930–9

South Carolina single-parent households and female-headed families, by county, 1990, annual rpt, S7145–1.1

South Carolina statistical abstract, general data, 1993 annual rpt, S7125–1.7, S7125–1.11

South Dakota family-owned business characteristics, outlook, and views on business and family issues, 1993 survey, article, U8595–1.503

Tennessee statistical abstract, general data, 1992/93 annual rpt, U8710–2.1

Utah homeless shelter population characteristics, individual shelter capacity, and related housing data, 1991-92, annual rpt, S7808–2

Utah households, 1995-2020, annual rpt, R9380–1.1

Utah personal income and household data, by location and race-ethnicity, 1990 census rpt, S7832–3.3

Utah statistical abstract, general data, 1993 triennial rpt, U8960–1.1, U8960–1.5

see also Adoption

see also Aid to Families with Dependent Children

see also Births out of wedlock

see also Child support and alimony

see also Child welfare

see also Children

see also Domestic relations courts and cases

see also Domestic violence

see also Family budgets

see also Family planning

see also Living arrangements

see also Marriage and divorce

see also Men

see also Offenses against family

see also Personal and household income

see also Widows and widowers

see also Women

Family budgets

Expenditures of typical family by item, including Federal and State/local taxes, 1992, annual rpt, R9050–13

Health care spending per family under current law vs plans of presidential candidates Bush and Clinton, by State, 2000 and 2005, R4865–9

State and local:

Hawaii data book, general data, 1992 annual rpt, S2090–1.14

see also Financial planning

Family courts

see Domestic relations courts and cases

Family income

see Personal and household income

Family planning

Developing countries family planning and child survival efforts, by country and selected demographic characteristics, 1980s-90, R8720–1

Policy and medical aspects of family planning, with research findings on contraceptive use, abortions, and provider facilities, bimonthly rpt, A5160–1

Policy and medical aspects of intl family planning, with data on fertility, contraceptive use, and family size preferences, quarterly rpt, A5160–6

World demographic trends and population-related issues, monthly rpt, R8750–1

World family planning and fertility trends, and contraceptives effectiveness, safety, and availability, by method, series, U2520–1

State and local:

Arkansas human services dept finances and operations, including Medicaid payments by type of service, FY91 and trends, annual rpt, S0700–2.3

Hawaii health dept family health services and recipients, including school health programs, 1990 annual rpt, S2065–1.5

Index by Subjects and Names

Kentucky Medicaid recipients and payments, by program, county, and type of medical service, monthly rpt, S3140–5

Maryland medical assistance payments and recipients, by program, type of service, location, demographic characteristics, and facility, FY92 and trends, annual rpt, S3635–3

Missouri public welfare and medical assistance recipients, expenditures, and case processing, by program and county, FY92 and trends, annual rpt, S4575–2

Nebraska Medicaid recipients and payments, by type of service and county, FY92, annual rpt, S4957–1.2

New York State medical assistance expenditures, by State area and type of care, 1991 and trends, annual rpt, S5800–2.2

West Virginia welfare and social service program caseloads and expenditures, by county, monthly rpt, S8560–2

see also Abortion

see also Contraceptives

see also Sex education

see also Sexual sterilization

Famine

see Food supply

see Nutrition and malnutrition

Farm costs

see Agricultural finance

see Agricultural production costs

Farm debt

see Agricultural credit

see Agricultural finance

Farm energy use

see Agricultural energy use

Farm income

Economic indicator historical trends, 1900s-92, annual rpt, R9050–1.2

Livestock operations and inventories, cash receipts, and slaughtering plants, by animal species and State, 1992 annual rpt, A2100–1.1

Southeastern States agricultural receipts, for 7 States, 1979-89, annual rpt, S7560 1

State rankings by per capita farm income, 1991, article, B8500–2.503

Statistical profiles of 50 States and DC, general data, 1993 annual almanac, C4712–1

Tobacco crop cash receipts in 16 States, and farm value per acre compared to 7 other crops, 1991, annual rpt, A9075–1

State and local:

Alabama agricultural production, marketing, and income, by county and/or commodity, and farms and acreage, 1992 and trends, annual rpt, S0090–1

Alaska agricultural production and marketing, by district and commodity, 1960s-92, annual rpt, U5750–1

Arizona agricultural production, marketing, and finances, by commodity and county, 1988-92, annual rpt, U5830–1

Arizona economic condition, including population, employment and earnings, and business activity, by industry and locality, 1985-93, semiannual rpt, U5850–1.1

Arizona statistical abstract, general data, 1993 recurring rpt, U5850–2.13

Arkansas agricultural production, marketing, and finances, by commodity and county, with farms and acreage, 1992 and trends, annual rpt, U5920–1

Index by Subjects and Names

Farm operators

Arkansas business and economic activity indicators, quarterly rpt, U5930–1

Arkansas socioeconomic trends, by MSA and/or county, 1993 annual rpt, U5935–1

California agricultural statistics, including production, acreage, finances, and marketing, by commodity, annual rpt series, S0850–1

California economic condition, including population, employment and earnings, income, business activity, and taxation, 1960s-92, annual rpt, S0840–3.2

California individual taxable income reported by source, deductions and credits by type, and tax returns, by income class and county, 1990, annual rpt, S0855–1.1

Colorado agricultural production, marketing, and finances, by commodity and/or county, with farms and acreage, 1992 and trends, annual rpt, S0985–1

Florida livestock, dairy, and poultry production, inventory, marketing, and finances, with detail by commodity or species, 1992 and trends, annual rpt, S1685–1.3

Florida statistical abstract, general data, 1992 annual rpt, U6660–1.9

Georgia agricultural production, marketing, and finances, by commodity and/or county, and farms and acreage, 1991 and trends, annual rpt, S1855–1

Hawaii farm income from marketings and govt payments, by island, 1987-91, annual rpt, S2030–1

Idaho and US economic trends and forecasts, quarterly rpt, S2245–2

Idaho economic profile, general data, 1992 recurring rpt, S2218–2.5

Illinois agricultural production, marketing, and finances, by county or commodity, and farms and farmland, 1991 and trends, annual rpt, S2390–1

Illinois statistical abstract, general data, 1992 annual rpt, U6910–2

Iowa crop and livestock cash receipts, and govt payments, 1982-91, annual rpt, S2860–4

Kansas agricultural production, marketing, and finances, by county and/or commodity, and farm acreage and value, 1992 and trends, annual rpt, S2915–1

Kansas business activity indicators, quarterly rpt, U7095–1

Kentucky agricultural production, marketing, and finances, by commodity and county; and farms, acreage, and value; 1992 and trends, annual rpt, S3085–1

Kentucky economic statistics, general data, 1993 annual rpt, S3104–1

Louisiana agricultural production, marketing, and finances, by commodity or parish, 1985-91, annual rpt, U2740–1

Michigan agricultural production, marketing, and finances, by commodity or county, 1987-91, annual rpt, S3950–1

Minnesota agricultural production, marketing, and finances, by county or commodity, and farms and acreage, 1992 and trends, annual rpt, S4130–1

Mississippi income by source, county, and MSA, and wages by industry group, 1993 annual planning rpt, S4345–1.4

Missouri agricultural production, marketing, and finances, by commodity and/or county, and farms and acreage, 1988-92, annual rpt, S4480–1

Montana agricultural production, marketing, and finances, by commodity and county, 1991 and trends, annual rpt, S4655–1

Montana household income from farming, by income level, as reported on tax returns, 1990-91, biennial rpt, S4750–1.1

Nebraska agricultural production, marketing, and finances, by commodity and/or county, and farms and acreage, 1991 and trends, annual rpt, S4835–1

Nebraska farm and nonfarm personal income, with comparisons to neighboring States, 3rd qtr 1992, U7860–1.503

Nebraska farmer/rancher/fisherman income tax returns, and income, by county, 1990, annual rpt, S4950–1.1

Nevada agricultural production, marketing, and finances, by county and commodity, and farms and acreage, 1992 and trends, annual rpt, S5010–1

New Jersey agricultural production, marketing, and finances, by commodity and/or county, and farms and acreage, 1986-91, annual rpt, S5350–1

New Mexico agricultural production, marketing, and finances, by commodity and county, with farms and acreage, 1991 and trends, annual rpt, S5530–1

New Mexico business and economic activity indicators, monthly rpt, U7980–1

New York State agricultural production, marketing, and finances, by commodity and/or county, and farms and acreage, 1992 and trends, annual rpt, S5700–1

North Carolina agricultural production, marketing, and finances, by commodity and county, 1991 and trends, annual rpt, S5885–1

North Dakota agricultural production and marketing, by commodity and county, and farm finances, 1992 and trends, annual rpt, U3600–1

Ohio agricultural production, marketing, and finances, by commodity and county, with farms and acreage, 1990-91 and trends, annual rpt, S6240–1

Oklahoma agricultural production, marketing, and finances, by commodity and county, 1992 and trends, annual rpt, S6405–1

Oregon agricultural production, marketing, and finances, by commodity and/or county, with farms and acreage, 1991 and trends, annual rpt, S6575–1

Pennsylvania agricultural production, marketing, and finances, by county and commodity, and farms and acreage, 1992 and trends, annual rpt, S6760–1

South Carolina economic condition, including agriculture, finance, and govt financial data, 1970s-92, annual rpt, S7125–3.1

South Dakota agricultural production, marketing, and finances, by commodity and county, and farms and acreage, 1992 and trends, annual rpt, S7280–1

South Dakota business activity review, including selected data by city and industry, quarterly rpt, U8595–1

Tennessee farm income by source, 1987-91, annual rpt, S7460–1

Texas agricultural production, marketing, and finances, by commodity and county, and farms and farmland, 1991 and trends, annual rpt series, S7630–1

Utah agricultural production, marketing, and finances, by commodity and county, with farms and acreage, 1992 and trends, annual rpt, S7800–1

Utah govt statistical review, fiscal and socioeconomic data, 1993 annual rpt, R9380–1.2

Utah statistical abstract, general data, 1993 triennial rpt, U8960–1.5

Vermont agricultural production, marketing, and finances, by commodity, with data on govt inspections and funding, 1989-90 biennial rpt, S7978–1

Washington State agricultural production, marketing, and finances, by commodity and/or county, 1992 and trends, annual rpt, S8328–1

West Virginia agricultural production, marketing, and finances, by commodity or county, 1991 and trends, annual rpt, S8510–1

Wisconsin agricultural production, marketing, and finances, by commodity and county, and farms, acreage, and sales, 1992 and trends, annual rpt, S8680–1

Wisconsin economic indicators, including employment and earnings by industry group, monthly rpt, S8750–1

Wyoming agricultural production, marketing, and finances, by county and/or commodity, and farms, acreage, and value, 1992 and trends, annual rpt, S8860–1

see also Agricultural production quotas and price supports

see also Agricultural subsidies

see also Agricultural wages

Farm labor

see Agricultural labor

see Agricultural wages

see Farm operators

see Migrant workers

Farm machinery

see Agricultural machinery and equipment

Farm operators

Black American farm and farm operator characteristics, with comparisons to all farms, 1987, annual compilation, C6775–2.8

Hispanic American farm and farm operator characteristics, with comparisons to all farms, 1987, annual compilation, C6775–3.6

State and local:

Arizona statistical abstract, general data, 1993 recurring rpt, U5850–2.13

Florida county data book, 1992/93 annual rpt, C6360–1

Florida statistical abstract, general data, 1992 annual rpt, U6660–1.6, U6660–1.9

Georgia county guide, general data, 1993 annual rpt, U6750–1

Georgia statistical abstract, general data, 1992-93 biennial rpt, U6730–1.4

Hawaii data book, general data, 1992 annual rpt, S2090–1.19

Nevada statistical abstract, general data, 1992 biennial rpt, S5005–1.10

Oklahoma farm operators by age and ownership status, 1978, 1982, and 1987, annual rpt, S6405–1

South Carolina statistical abstract, general data, 1993 annual rpt, S7125–1.1

Tennessee statistical abstract, general data, 1992/93 annual rpt, U8710–2.11

Farm operators

Wisconsin Blue Book, general data, 1993-94 biennial rpt, S8780–1.2

Wisconsin dairy farmers by age group, Dec 1992, annual rpt, S8680–1

Farm population

Accidental deaths of farm residents, by accident type, and farm population, 1992 and trends, annual rpt, A8375–2.4

Latin America statistical abstract, general data by country, 1992 annual rpt, U6250–1.12

State and local:

- Arkansas Census of Population and Housing detailed findings, 1990, U5935–7
- California Census of Population and Housing detailed findings, 1990, S0840–9
- Florida statistical abstract, general data, 1992 annual rpt, U6660–1.1
- Georgia county guide, general data, 1993 annual rpt, U6750–1
- Illinois farm population, decennially 1920-90, annual rpt, S2390–1
- Montana farm and total population, 1990, annual rpt, S4655–1
- New Jersey Census of Population and Housing detailed findings, by county, 1990, S5425–19
- Oklahoma farms, and farm and total population, 1990, annual rpt, S6405–1
- Pennsylvania Census of Population and Housing detailed findings, with selected data by county and municipality, 1990, U4130–13
- Rhode Island Census of Population and Housing detailed findings, by county and municipality, 1990, S6930–9
- Tennessee statistical abstract, general data, 1992/93 annual rpt, U8710–2.11
- Utah farm vs total population, decennially 1930-90, annual rpt, S7800–1

Farm prices

see Agricultural prices

see Food prices

Farmers Home Administration

Funding for rural housing and dev, by FmHA program, FY93, article, C4300–1.502

see *also* Rural Development Administration

Farming

see Agricultural labor

see Farm income

see Farm operators

see Farm population

see Farms and farmland

see Rural cooperatives

see Agriculture and terms beginning with Agricultural

see under By Industry in the "Index by Categories"

see under By Occupation in the "Index by Categories"

Farms and farmland

Black American farm and farm operator characteristics, with comparisons to all farms, 1987, annual compilation, C6775–2.8

Commodity yearbook for 1993: agricultural production, acreage, stocks, marketing, and operating data, including by country and producing State, C2400–1

Commodity yearbook update: agricultural production, acreage, stocks, marketing, and operating data, including by country and producing State, Jan-Sept 1993 rpts, C2400–2

Hispanic American farm and farm operator characteristics, with comparisons to all farms, 1987, annual compilation, C6775–3.6

Latin America statistical abstract, general data by country, 1992 annual rpt, U6250–1.2, U6250–1.24

Number of farms, and livestock and crop values, by State, MSA, county, city, and Canadian Province, 1993 annual rpt, C3250–1

Soviet Union private farms, by Republic, Aug 1992, recurring feature, U2030–1.503

State social, economic, and govtl indicators, with rankings, 1993 semiannual rpt, B8500–1.12

Statistical profiles of 50 States and DC, general data, 1993 annual almanac, C4712–1

Value of farm real estate, by State, 1984-93, annual rpt, S5700–1

Vegetable farms financial performance and ratios, FY88-92, annual rpt, A6400–3

World cropland and irrigation, by country, 1992/93 biennial rpt, R9455–1.6

State and local:

Alabama agricultural production, marketing, and income, by county and/or commodity, and farms and acreage, 1992 and trends, annual rpt, S0090–1

Alabama county data book, general data, 1992 annual rpt, S0121–2

Alabama statistical abstract, general data, 1992 recurring rpt, U5680–2.1

Alaska farms and farmland, 1960s-92, annual rpt, U5750–1

Alaska property tax deferment program for farmland, acreage affected and deferred tax, by municipality, 1992 and trends, annual rpt, S0285–1

Arizona farms/ranches and acreage, 1988-92, annual rpt, U5830–1

Arizona statistical abstract, general data, 1993 recurring rpt, U5850–2.13

Arkansas agricultural production, marketing, and finances, by commodity and county, with farms and acreage, 1992 and trends, annual rpt, U5920–1

California agricultural statistics, including production, acreage, finances, and marketing, by commodity, annual rpt series, S0850–1

California export vs total agricultural production and acreage, by commodity, 1991, annual rpt, B9520–1

California statistical abstract, general data, 1992 annual rpt, S0840–2.7

Colorado agricultural production, marketing, and finances, by commodity and/or county, with farms and acreage, 1992 and trends, annual rpt, S0985–1

Colorado property assessed valuation by detailed property type, and tax levy and revenue by local district, by county, 1991-92, annual rpt, S1055–3

Florida county data book, 1992/93 annual rpt, C6360–1

Florida statistical abstract, general data, 1992 annual rpt, U6660–1.9

Georgia agricultural production, marketing, and finances, by commodity and/or county, and farms and acreage, 1991 and trends, annual rpt, S1855–1

Georgia county guide, general data, 1993 annual rpt, U6750–1

Georgia statistical abstract, general data, 1992-93 biennial rpt, U6730–1.4

Hawaii agricultural production and marketing, by commodity and island, 1987-91, annual rpt, S2030–1

Hawaii data book, general data, 1992 annual rpt, S2090–1.19, S2090–1.22, S2090–1.24

Illinois agricultural production, marketing, and finances, by county or commodity, and farms and farmland, 1991 and trends, annual rpt, S2390–1

Illinois statistical abstract, general data, 1992 annual rpt, U6910–2

Kansas agricultural production, marketing, and finances, by county and/or commodity, and farm acreage and value, 1992 and trends, annual rpt, S2915–1

Kansas statistical abstract, general data, 1991/92 annual rpt, U7095–2.15

Kentucky agricultural production, marketing, and finances, by commodity and county; and farms, acreage, and value; 1992 and trends, annual rpt, S3085–1

Kentucky economic statistics, general data, 1993 annual rpt, S3104–1.1

Louisiana farms by size, acreage by use, and property value, selected years 1974-91, annual rpt, U2740–1

Maryland statistical abstract, general data, 1993-94 biennial rpt, S3605–1.11

Michigan farms, acreage, and value, 1900-92, annual rpt, S3950–1

Minnesota agricultural production, marketing, and finances, by county or commodity, and farms and acreage, 1992 and trends, annual rpt, S4130–1

Missouri agricultural production, marketing, and finances, by commodity and/or county, and farms and acreage, 1988-92, annual rpt, S4480–1

Montana farms and acreage, 1910-92, annual rpt, S4655–1

Montana property values, by detailed property class and type, with land acreage by use, by county, 1991-92 and trends, biennial rpt, S4750–1.2

Nebraska agricultural acreage and value, by land use and county, 1991, annual rpt, S4950–1.4

Nebraska agricultural production, marketing, and finances, by commodity and/or county, and farms and acreage, 1991 and trends, annual rpt, S4835–1

Nevada agricultural production, marketing, and finances, by county and commodity, and farms and acreage, 1992 and trends, annual rpt, S5010–1

Nevada statistical abstract, general data, 1992 biennial rpt, S5005–1.10

New Jersey agricultural production, marketing, and finances, by commodity and/or county, and farms and acreage, 1986-91, annual rpt, S5350–1

New Mexico agricultural production, marketing, and finances, by commodity and county, with farms and acreage, 1991 and trends, annual rpt, S5530–1

New York State agricultural production, marketing, and finances, by commodity and/or county, and farms and acreage, 1992 and trends, annual rpt, S5700–1

New York State statistical yearbook, general data, 1992 annual rpt, U5100–1.14
North Carolina farms and acreage, 1988-92, annual rpt, S5885–1
North Dakota farmland, acres in conservation reserve program, and sales and average prices, by county, 1993 annual planning rpt, S6140–2
North Dakota farms and acreage, 1983-92, annual rpt, U3600–1
Ohio agricultural production, marketing, and finances, by commodity and county, with farms and acreage, 1990-91 and trends, annual rpt, S6240–1
Oklahoma farms, acreage, value, and rent, 1993 and trends, annual rpt, S6405–1
Oklahoma statistical abstract, general data, 1992 annual rpt, U8130–2.11
Oregon agricultural production, marketing, and finances, by commodity and/or county, with farms and acreage, 1991 and trends, annual rpt, S6575–1
Pennsylvania agricultural production, marketing, and finances, by county and commodity, and farms and acreage, 1992 and trends, annual rpt, S6760–1
South Carolina economic condition, including agriculture, finance, and govt financial data, 1970s-92, annual rpt, S7125–3.1
South Carolina farms and acreage, with detail by county, 1992 and trends, annual rpt, U1075–3
South Carolina property tax assessed values, by class and county, FY92, annual rpt, S7255–1.3
South Carolina statistical abstract, general data, 1993 annual rpt, S7125–1.1
South Dakota agricultural production, marketing, and finances, by commodity and county, and farms and acreage, 1992 and trends, annual rpt, S7280–1
South Dakota field crop acreage, by crop, 1991-92 and intended 1993, recurring table, U8595–1.503
South Dakota property tax and valuations, by property type and locality, FY92 annual rpt, S7380–1.2
South Dakota property value and levies, by school district, 1991/92, annual rpt, S7315–1
Tennessee agricultural production and marketing, by commodity and county, with farms, acreage, and farm value, 1992 and trends, annual rpt, S7460–1
Tennessee statistical abstract, general data, 1992/93 annual rpt, U8710–2.11
Texas agricultural production, marketing, and finances, by commodity and county, and farms and farmland, 1991 and trends, annual rpt series, S7630–1
Utah agricultural production, marketing, and finances, by commodity and county, with farms and acreage, 1992 and trends, annual rpt, S7800–1
Utah statistical abstract, general data, 1993 triennial rpt, U8960–1.9
Vermont farms and farmland, 1979-89, biennial rpt, S7978–1
Washington State farms, acreage, and value, with comparisons to other States and US, 1970s-93, annual rpt, S8328–1
West Virginia farms, acreage, and value, with selected comparisons to other Appalachian States, 1991 and trends, annual rpt, S8510–1

Wisconsin agricultural production, marketing, and finances, by commodity and county, and farms, acreage, and sales, 1992 and trends, annual rpt, S8680–1
Wisconsin farms, and farmland sales and diversion to nonagricultural use, by county, 1993-94 biennial rpt, S8780–1.2
Wyoming agricultural production, marketing, and finances, by county and/or commodity, and farms, acreage, and value, 1992 and trends, annual rpt, S8860–1
Wyoming property assessed valuations and tax levies, by property type, tax purpose, and location, 1992 and trends, annual rpt, S8990–1.2
see also Agricultural accidents and safety
see also Agricultural credit
see also Agricultural energy use
see also Agricultural exports and imports
see also Agricultural finance
see also Agricultural insurance
see also Agricultural labor
see also Agricultural machinery and equipment
see also Agricultural marketing
see also Agricultural prices
see also Agricultural production
see also Agricultural production costs
see also Agricultural production quotas and price supports
see also Agricultural productivity
see also Agricultural stocks
see also Agricultural subsidies
see also Agricultural wages
see also Farm income
see also Farm operators
see also Farm population
see also Irrigation
see also Pasture and rangeland
see also Soils and soil conservation

Fast food restaurants
see Restaurants and drinking places

Fats and oils
see Oils, oilseeds, and fats

FDA
see Food and Drug Administration

Federal advisory bodies
see Federal boards, committees, and commissions

Federal agencies
see Federal boards, committees, and commissions
see Federal employees
see Federal executive departments
see Federal independent agencies
see under By Government Agency in the "Index by Categories"
see under name of specific agency

Federal aid programs
Budget receipts and outlays of Fed Govt, by source and function, 1920s-93, annual rpt, R9050–1.3
Congressional organization, major legislative and budget actions, and agency and program appropriations, 102nd Congress, 2nd session, 1992, annual rpt, C2500–2
Expenditures of Fed Govt for selected aid programs, by type, FY93-94, article, C2176–1.510
Forecasts of natl income and product account components and related indicators, quarterly rpt, U1880–1
Refugee assistance appropriations for 2 State Dept funds, FY93-94, article, R9372–2.508

Refugee assistance budgets for HHS and State Dept, by type of program, FY93-94, annual article, R9372–2.506
Science/technology-related program Federal outlay changes proposed by Clinton Admin, by agency, 1994-98, article, A1250–1.517
Trends in Federal budget, including spending by program, State, and region, FY81-94, annual rpt, R8490–11
State and local:
Utah govt statistical review, fiscal and socioeconomic data, 1993 annual rpt, R9380–1.4
see also Agricultural credit
see also Agricultural production quotas and price supports
see also Agricultural subsidies
see also Community Development Block Grants
see also Disaster relief
see also Federal aid to arts and humanities
see also Federal aid to education
see also Federal aid to higher education
see also Federal aid to highways
see also Federal aid to housing
see also Federal aid to law enforcement
see also Federal aid to libraries
see also Federal aid to local areas
see also Federal aid to medical education
see also Federal aid to medicine
see also Federal aid to rural areas
see also Federal aid to States
see also Federal aid to transportation
see also Federal aid to vocational education
see also Federal funding for energy programs
see also Federal funding for research and development
see also Food assistance
see also Government and business
see also Medical assistance
see also Medicare
see also Public welfare programs
see also Revenue sharing
see also Subsidies
see also Tax expenditures

Federal aid to arts and humanities
Arts fundraising through united arts funds (UAFs), with fund operations, income by source, and allocations, by UAF, 1992 and trends, annual rpt, A1315–2
Budget of US higher education funding, by agency and program, FY92-94, annual feature, C2175–1.516
Museums and related instns financial structure, including donation programs, income, and expenses, by type, budget size, and governing authority, 1989/90 survey, A0750–1.3
Public broadcasting station revenues by source, and number of stations, by station type, FY91, annual rpt, R4250–1.20
Theater (nonprofit professional) finances and operations, including revenues by source, 1992 and trends, annual survey, A9065–1
State and local:
DC statistical profile, general data, 1992 annual rpt, S1535–3.6

Federal aid to business
see Government and business
see Subsidies

Federal aid to cities

Federal aid to cities
see Federal aid to local areas

Federal aid to education

Appropriations for education, by function and program, FY92-94, recurring feature, R4800–2.514

Budget of US outlays for public investment programs by type, with intl comparisons, FY93-94 and trends, R4700–23

Budget receipts and outlays of Fed Govt, by source and function, 1920s-93, annual rpt, R9050–1.3

Catholic secondary school operations and finances, including enrollment by race-ethnicity and family income, 1991/92 and trends, biennial rpt, A7375–5

Elementary/secondary disadvantaged student Federal assistance program participation and funding, 1979/80-1992/93, article, R4800–2.504

Elementary/secondary teacher views on education policy issues and selected reform proposals, Jan-Feb 1993 survey, B6045–7

Exchange (educational) program funding, by agency, 1992, article, C2175–1.528

Security program funding under proposed Safe Schools Act of 1993, FY93-94, article, C1850–12.510

Southern States compensatory education funding, for 15 States, 1990, annual rpt, U6660–1.20

Trends in Federal budget, including spending by program, State, and region, FY81-94, annual rpt, R8490–11

Urban public school performance compared to natl goals for year 2000, with data on students, teachers, and finances, for 47 systems, 1990/91 and trends, A4425–4

State and local:

Alabama elementary and secondary school enrollment, staff, pupil transportation, and finances, by district, 1991/92, annual rpt, S0124–1

Alaska public schools, enrollment, staff, and finances, by district, FY92, annual rpt, S0295–2

Arizona elementary and secondary school enrollment, staff, and finances, by school district and county, FY92 and trends, annual rpt, S0470–1

Arkansas public school revenues by source, expenditures by function and object, and indebtedness, 1991/92 and trends, annual rpt, S0660–1.3

Colorado public school revenues by source, and expenditures by category, by school district, 1990, annual rpt, S1000–4.3

Connecticut education dept staff and expenditures, by div, 1991/92, annual rpt, S1185–1

Connecticut public school data, including enrollment, staff, programs, finances, and student characteristics, 1991/92, biennial rpt, S1185–3

DC public school finances, enrollment, grads, and test scores, with data by school, 1987/88-1991/92, annual rpt, S1605–2

Delaware public education finances, govt aid by program and school district, 1991/92, annual rpt, S1430–1

Georgia statistical abstract, general data, 1992-93 biennial rpt, U6730–1.2

Idaho school district revenues by source, and expenditures by function, by district and fund, FY92, annual rpt, S2225–2

Illinois public school revenues and expenditures by district, with data on busing, State aid claims, and per capita costs, 1990/91, annual rpt, S2440–1.3

Indiana public school receipts by fund and source, by district, 1991/92, annual table, S2608–2.11

Kansas school district revenues by source and expenditures by object, 1990/91, annual rpt, S2945–1

Kentucky public education profiles, with data by region and district, 1991/92 and trends, annual rpt, S3110–1

Kentucky public school finances, staff, and enrollment, by district, 1989/90-1990/91, biennial rpt, S3110–2

Louisiana elementary/secondary school operations, including enrollment, staff, finances, and detail by school district, 1991/92 and trends, annual rpt, S3280–1

Maine public school enrollment, facilities, staff, and finances, with selected data by county and for private schools, 1991 and trends, annual rpt, S3435–1

Maryland elementary and secondary education data, by county, 1991/92 and trends, annual rpt, S3610–2.13

Maryland elementary and secondary education data, by county, 1991/92, annual rpt, S3610–2.6, S3610–2.9

Maryland elementary and secondary education statistical summary, with data by county, 1991/92-1992/93 and trends, annual rpt, S3610–1

Maryland elementary and secondary school Federal food donation value, by county, 1991/92, annual rpt, S3610–2.7

Massachusetts public elementary/secondary education summary data, 1989/90-1991/92 and trends, annual rpt, S3810–3

Michigan school district financial and enrollment data, with rankings, 1991/92, annual rpt, S3965–3

Minnesota public school enrollment, staff, and finances, by district and county, 1991/92 and trends, annual rpt, S4165–1

Mississippi public school enrollment, staff and salaries, and finances, by district, 1991/92 and trends, annual rpt, S4340–1

Missouri school finances, enrollment, grads, and staff, by county and school district, 1991/92, annual rpt, S4505–1

Nebraska public school finances, including receipts by source and disbursements by function, by county and district, 1988/89, annual rpt, S4865–3

Nevada public school enrollment, test scores, teachers, and finances, by school district, 1990/91 and trends, annual rpt, S5035–2

New Hampshire elementary and secondary school revenues by source and expenditures by function, 1991/92, annual tables, S5200–1.12

New Mexico elementary/secondary school statistics, including grads, student test results, and finances, by school district, 1989/90-1991/92, annual rpt, S5575–4

North Carolina public school enrollment, grads, staff, and finances, with data by race, sex, and local district, 1991/92-1992/93 and trends, annual rpt, S5915–1

Index by Subjects and Names

North Dakota public school revenues by source, expenditures by function, mill levies, and taxable value, by district, 1992/93 annual rpt, S6180–4

Ohio public school enrollment, finances, special programs, and staff, 1991/92 and trends, annual rpt, S6265–2

Oklahoma public school finances, personnel, enrollment, and facilities, by county and district, 1991/92 and trends, annual rpt, S6423–1

Oklahoma public school performance indicators, including students and achievement, finances, and staff, by district, 1990/91-1991/92 and trends, annual rpt, S6423–2

Oregon public school revenues by source and fund, and expenditures by fund, function, and object, 1991/92, annual rpt, S6590–1.16

Oregon public school revenues by source and fund, and expenditures by fund, function, and object, 1992/93, annual rpt, S6590–1.17

Oregon public school revenues by source, by school district and county, 1992/93, annual rpt, S6590–1.21

Rhode Island education expenditures by function and source of funds, by school district, 1991/92, annual rpt, S6970–1.2

South Carolina teachers salary schedules, educational revenues by source, and expenditures by function, by school district, 1991/92, annual rpt, S7145–1.5

South Dakota school enrollment, finances, grads, and staff, by district, 1991/92 and trends, annual rpt, S7315–1

Tennessee public school finances, by county, city, and school district, 1991/92, annual rpt, S7490–2.4

Tennessee value of food donated by USDA distributed to schools, by county, 1992/93, annual rpt, S7460–1

Utah public schools, enrollment, attendance, personnel, and finances, by school district, 1991/92, annual rpt, S7815–1

Virginia public school enrollment, grads, finances, and staff, by county and municipality, 1991/92, annual rpt, S8190–3

West Virginia public school finances, enrollment, staff, and programs, by county, 1992/93 and trends, annual rpt, S8540–4

Wisconsin elementary and secondary school enrollment, staff, costs, and State aid, by school district, 1992/93 and trends, annual rpt, S8795–2

Wyoming public school revenues by source, expenditures by program and object, and bonded debt, by district, 1991/92, annual rpt, S8890–1.3

see also Compensatory education
see also Federal aid to higher education
see also Federal aid to medical education
see also Federal aid to vocational education
see also Head Start Project
see also Pell Grant Program
see also School lunch and breakfast programs
see also Student aid
see also Veterans education

Federal aid to higher education

Appropriations for FY94 compared to spending in FY93, by program, recurring feature, C2175–1.527, C2175–1.536

Index by Subjects and Names

Federal aid to libraries

Budget of US higher education funding, by agency and program, FY92-94, annual feature, C2175–1.516

Chemicals R&D spending in Federal, industrial, and academic sectors, with data by company and instn, 1980s-93, annual feature, A1250–1.537

Congressional appropriations earmarked for projects at specific instns, FY88-93, article, C2175–1.525

DOD prime R&D contract awards to higher education instns, for top 6-10 States, 1962, 1972, and 1982, R4700–19

Europe-US academic collaboration project Education Dept grants awarded to 23 US instns, 1993 article, C2175–1.538

Higher education Fed Govt obligations, for top 100 instns, FY91, annual feature, C2175–1.528

Higher education instns, faculty, students, degrees, and finances, detailed data by State, 1993 annual rpt, C2175–1.531

Library/info science school enrollment, staff and student characteristics, finances, and curricula, by school and degree program, 1991/92, annual rpt, A3235–1

R&D higher education funding by source, by State and for US territories, FY91, annual feature, C2175–1.503

R&D higher education funding, for top 100 instns, FY91, annual feature, C2175–1.502

R&D higher education funding from Fed Govt, by State, FY90, article, B8500–2.501

Southern States higher education financial data, by State, 1970s-92, biennial fact book, A8945–1.6

Spending reductions resulting from 11 Clinton Admin proposals affecting higher education, FY94-97, C2175–1.510

State and local:

Arkansas higher education finances, including revenues by source, expenditures by function, and State appropriations, by public instn, FY80s-95, biennial rpt, S0690–4

California higher education systems funding by source and expenditures by program category, with enrollment data, FY60s-94, annual rpt, S0827–3

Florida higher education enrollment, degree programs, staff, and finances, by State-supported instn, with student and staff characteristics, 1991/92 annual rpt, S1725–1

Hawaii data book, general data, 1992 annual rpt, S2090–1.3

Illinois higher education staff, salaries, student cost and aid, and finances, by instn, 1993 annual rpt, S2475–1.2

Iowa postsecondary enrollment, degrees, staff, and finances, by instn, 1990/91, annual rpt, S2755–1

Kentucky higher education enrollment, degrees, staff, and finances, by State-supported instn, 1983-92, annual rpt, S3130–3

Maryland higher education funding, by instn and Federal agency, FY90, biennial rpt, S3605–1.2

Minnesota postsecondary education finances, and enrollment by student characteristics, by type of school system, 1970s-93, biennial rpt, S4195–2.2

Mississippi higher education enrollment and degrees, by level and field, and finances, by State-supported instn, 1991/92, annual rpt, S4360–1

Missouri higher education enrollment, degrees, libraries, staff, and finances, by instn, 1992 and trends, annual rpt, S4520–3

Pennsylvania statistical abstract, general data, 1992 recurring rpt, U4130–6.4

South Carolina higher education enrollment, degrees, staff, and finances, by instn, 1992 and trends, annual rpt, S7185–2

South Dakota public higher education finances, staff, enrollment, degrees, and facilities, by instn, FY93 annual rpt, S7375–1

Utah higher education degrees, enrollment, staff, and finances, by public instn, with selected comparisons to instns in other States, 1993/94 annual rpt, S7895–2

Vermont higher education revenues by source, expenditures by function, and tuition/fees, by instn, and student aid trends, 1992 annual rpt, S8035–2.3

see also Federal aid to medical education

see also Pell Grant Program

see also Student aid

see also Veterans education

see also Work-study programs

Federal aid to highways

Cost indexes for construction, equipment, and labor, by type and location, weekly rpt quarterly feature, C5800–2.508, C5800–2.521, C5800–2.534, C5800–2.547

Road/bridge special project funding, for 25 States, FY92, annual rpt, C2500–2

Trends in Federal budget, including spending by program, State, and region, FY93-94, annual rpt, R8490–11

State and local:

Arizona statistical abstract, general data, 1993 recurring rpt, U5850–2.18

Kansas statistical abstract, general data, 1991/92 annual rpt, U7095–2.13

see also Federal aid to transportation

Federal aid to housing

Budget of US proposed by Clinton Admin, with data on spending impacts by program, deficit reduction, and tax changes, FY93-98, R3834–17

Grants by State and region, for HOPE and HOME Federal housing assistance programs, FY92, R8490–42

HUD appropriations by program, with number of assisted housing units by type, FY92-93, annual article, C4300–1.502

HUD low-income housing additional unit commitments, 1977-92, R3834–16

Proposed funding for selected housing programs, and assisted housing units, FY94, annual feature, C4300–1.508

Trends in Federal budget, including spending by program, State, and region, FY78-93, annual rpt, R8490–11

State and local:

DC statistical profile, general data, 1992 annual rpt, S1535–3.4

see also Housing (FHA), HUD

see also Mortgages

see also Public housing

see also Rent supplements

see also Veterans housing

Federal aid to law enforcement

State and local:

Arizona court cases and dispositions, by type of case and court, with judicial personnel and finances, by county and city, FY92, annual rpt, S0525–1

Illinois corrections dept admin, including inmates and characteristics, finances, and staff, FY91-93 and trends, annual rpt, S2425–1

Ohio correctional instn admissions and releases, inmate characteristics, programs, finances, and staffing, FY91 and trends, annual rpt, S6370–1

Federal aid to libraries

Budget of US higher education funding, by agency and program, FY92-94, annual feature, C2175–1.516

Higher education appropriations for FY94 compared to spending in FY93, by program, recurring feature, C2175–1.527, C2175–1.536

Library and book trade reference info, including public and academic library funding, construction, and operations, by State and instn, 1992, annual compilation, C1650–3

Library construction, costs, and funding sources, by State, city, instn, and library type, FY92 and trends, annual article, C1852–1.501

State library agency appropriations, expenditures, salaries, and staff, by State, 1992 annual rpt, A3862–1

State and local:

Alabama public libraries, finances, holdings, circulation, staff, and population served, by library, FY92, annual rpt, S0180–1

Arizona public library holdings, circulation, finances, and staff, by instn and county, FY92, annual rpt, S0495–1

California library finances, staff, holdings, and services, by library type and facility, FY92, annual rpt, S0825–2

Colorado public library finances and operations, by instn, 1991, annual rpt, S1000–3.1

Florida public libraries, finances, holdings, staff, and services, by system and library, FY92, annual rpt, S1800–2

Idaho public library holdings, staff, services, circulation, and finances, by instn, FY92, annual rpt, S2282–1

Iowa public library finances and operations, by county, size of population served, and library, FY92, annual rpt, S2778–1

Louisiana public library finances, holdings, circulation, and personnel, by library system, FY92, annual rpt, S3275–1

Maryland public library operating income and expenditures, staff, holdings, and population served, by county, FY92, annual rpt, S3610–5

Missouri public, special, and academic libraries, finances, holdings, circulation, staff, and services, by location, FY92, annual rpt, S4520–2

Montana public library holdings, staff, circulation, and finances, by library, FY92, annual rpt, S4725–1

Nebraska public libraries, finances, holdings, circulation, staff, and population served, by instn, FY91, annual rpt, S4910–1

Nevada library and staff directories for public and academic libraries, with data on holdings, operations, and finances, FY92, annual rpt, S5095–1

Federal aid to libraries

New Hampshire public library finances and operations, by library and/or location, 1991, annual rpt, S5227–1

New Mexico public library operations and finances, by instn, FY92, annual rpt, S5627–1

New York State public library finances, staff, holdings, and services, by library and county, 1991, annual rpt, S5745–2

North Carolina public libraries, finances, holdings, and personnel, by library system, FY91, annual rpt, S5910–1

North Dakota public library finances, holdings, staff, and operations, by instn, FY91, annual rpt, S6180–5

Oklahoma public and institutional library holdings, circulation, finances, and staff, by facility, FY92, annual rpt, S6470–1

Oregon library finances, staff, holdings, and services, for public, academic, and special libraries by instn, FY92 and trends, annual rpt, S6635–1

Pennsylvania public and institutional library personnel, holdings, circulation, and finances, by county and facility, FY92, annual rpt, S6790–2

Pennsylvania statistical abstract, general data, 1992 recurring rpt, U4130–6.4

South Carolina public and institutional libraries, finances, services, holdings, and staff, by library, FY92, annual rpt, S7210–1

Texas public libraries, holdings, circulation, staff, and finances, by library and location, FY91, annual rpt, S7710–1

Virginia public library operations and finances, by instn, FY92, annual rpt, S8275–1

Washington State public libraries, finances, holdings, circulation, staff, and population served, by instn, 1992, annual rpt, S8375–1

West Virginia public, academic, and special library operations and/or finances, by instn, 1991/92, annual rpt, S8590–1

Wisconsin libraries, operations, and finances, by library type, instn, and location, 1992, annual rpt, S8795–1

Wyoming public library holdings, staff, circulation, and finances, by county, FY92, annual rpt, S8855–3

Federal aid to local areas

Capital project financing methods of local govt, by population size, metro status, and census div, 1991 survey, A5800–2.112

City fiscal condition, including budget trends and adjustments, and influencing factors, by region and population size, Mar-Apr 1993 survey, annual rpt, A8012–1.23

Govt finances, including revenues by source, expenditures by function, and debt, detailed data for Federal, State, and local govts, 1993 annual rpt, R9050–1

Housing assistance grants to local govts through HOME program, by State and region, FY92, R8490–42

Trends in Federal budget, including spending by program, State, and region, FY81 and FY93-94, annual rpt, R8490–11

State and local:

Alabama county data book, general data, 1992 annual rpt, S0121–2

California statistical abstract, general data, 1992 annual rpt, S0840–2.13

Georgia statistical abstract, general data, 1992-93 biennial rpt, U6730–1.11

Kansas local aid from Federal and State sources, by function, FY92, annual rpt, S2900–1.1

Maryland funds from Fed Govt transferred to counties, FY92, annual rpt, S3685–2

Maryland local govt financial condition, including revenues by source, expenditures by function, and debt obligations, FY92 and trends, annual rpt, S3618–1.1

Nevada compensatory payments by Fed Govt for public land tax immunity, by county, 1984-90, biennial rpt, S5005–1.8

New Jersey municipal and county data book, general data, 1992 annual rpt, C4712–4

New York State statistical yearbook, general data, 1992 annual rpt, U5100–1.6

South Carolina county govt finances, including property value and tax assessments, by county, FY92, annual rpt, S7127–2

South Carolina statistical abstract, general data, 1993 annual rpt, S7125–1.2

Tennessee statistical abstract, general data, 1992/93 annual rpt, U8710–2.15

Texas financial condition, including revenues by source, expenditures by function and dept, and investments, with data for over 400 individual funds, FY92, annual rpt, S7655–2

Utah, Federal payments in lieu of property taxes, by county, 1988-91, annual feature, U8960–2.501

Utah, Federal payments in lieu of property taxes, by county, 1989-92, annual feature, U8960–2.507

Utah govt statistical review, fiscal and socioeconomic data, 1993 annual rpt, R9380–1.6

Utah public lands by govt owner, and Federal land payments to State and local govts, with data by county, 1992 article, U8960–2.502

Washington State treasury operations, including receipts, disbursements, aid to localities, and investments, by fund, FY92, annual rpt, S8455–1

Wisconsin Blue Book, general data, 1993-94 biennial rpt, S8780–1.2

see also Community Development Block Grants

see also Federal aid to rural areas

see also Revenue sharing

Federal aid to medical education

Nursing education Federal funding appropriations for FY92-93, with reauthorized levels for FY93, article, A8010–3.502

Nursing education Federal funding for FY92, with Senate and House appropriations for FY93, recurring article, A8010–3.501

Nursing higher education program finances, faculty and clinical practice, and clinic/center operations, by instn characteristics, 1992/93 biennial rpt, A0615–5

Optometry school revenues by source, and student financial aid, by instn, 1991/92, annual survey, A3370–2

Index by Subjects and Names

Osteopathy college enrollment, student and faculty characteristics, and finances, 1992/93 and trends, annual rpt, A0620–1

Public health school research and training grants, and student aid, by instn (unnamed), FY92 and trends, annual rpt, A3372–3

Southern States higher education student aid data, by State, 1990s and trends, biennial fact book, A8945–1.4

Federal aid to medicine

Appropriations for FY94 compared to spending in FY93, by program, recurring feature, C2175–1.527, C2175–1.536

Budget receipts and outlays of Fed Govt, by source and function, 1920s-93, annual rpt, R9050–1.3

Funding of govt health care programs by source, Medicare enrollments, and Medicaid recipients, 1960s-91, annual rpt, A5173–2.2

General practice specialty choices of medical school grads, by school characteristics including Federal aid, and for top 20 schools (unnamed), 1993 articles, A2623–1.505

Natl Institute of General Medical Sciences budget, by program, FY92-93, article, A1250–1.514

NIH research expenditures, and disease incidence, for cystic fibrosis, multiple sclerosis, muscular dystrophy, and scleroderma, 1993 article, C5800–7.546

Nursing appropriations for HHS Division of Nursing, by program, FY92-93, article, A8010–3.505

Public opinion on AIDS research funding, 1987-92 surveys, A0610–1.502

Public opinion on health care issues, including govt and medical profession role, satisfaction with care and insurance, and reforms, 1975-92 surveys, A0610–1.504

Sexually transmitted disease incidence and Federal funding allocations by disease, 1992, A5160–10

Substance abuse treatment programs, funding by source, and client characteristics, for alcohol and drug services, by State, FY91 and trends, annual rpt, A7112–1

Teaching hospital house staff stipend/benefit cost funding sources, by ownership, 1992/93, annual rpt, A3273–3

Trends in Federal budget, including spending by program, State, and region, FY81-94, annual rpt, R8490–11

State and local:

Arkansas children's medical service State and Federal funding, FY89-91, annual rpt, S0700–2.3

DC statistical profile, general data, 1992 annual rpt, S1535–3.5

Texas indigent health care finances and utilization, with data by county, district, public hospital, and medical school, 1986-91, U8850–8.7

Texas State and local health depts finances, employment, and service area characteristics, FY91 and trends, U8850–8.6

see also Federal aid to medical education

see also Medicaid

Index by Subjects and Names

Federal aid to States

see also Medical assistance
see also Medicare
Federal aid to railroads
see also Federal aid to transportation
Federal aid to research and development
see Federal funding for research and development
Federal aid to rural areas
State and local:
Maryland Appalachia Federal expenditures by function, FY91, biennial rpt, S3605–1.13
see also Agricultural production quotas and price supports
see also Agricultural subsidies
see also Farmers Home Administration
Federal aid to States
Expenditures of Fed Govt by category, by State and region, FY92, annual rpt, R8490–35
Expenditures of State govts by fund source and function, by State, FY90-92, annual rpt, A7118–1
Govt finances, including revenues by source, expenditures by function, and debt, detailed data for Federal, State, and local govts, 1993 annual rpt, R9050–1
Grants to State/local govts by category, 1993 and trends, U5085–2.12
Grants to State/local govts, by State, FY92 and trends, article, B8500–2.514
Grants to States for Medicaid, hwys, and AFDC programs, by State and region, 1984 and 1991, R8490–46
Refugee assistance outlays under State Legalization Impact Assistance Grants program, with shares for 7 States, 1992, article, A1865–1.523
State social, economic, and govtl indicators, with rankings, 1993 semiannual rpt, B8500–1.6
Statistical profiles of 50 States and DC, general data, 1993 annual almanac, C4712–1
Tax revenues for Fed Govt from States compared to Federal spending in States, by State, FY91, article, B8500–2.502
Trends in Federal budget, including spending by program, State, and region, FY81-94, annual rpt, R8490–11
Trends in Federal intergovernmental transfers and outlook for grants-in-aid, selected years 1954-95, article, U7860–1.503
Western States expenditures of Fed Govt, for 9 States, 1984-91, annual article, U7980–1.503
State and local:
Alabama financial condition, including revenues by source, expenditures by function and object, and fund balances, by fund and agency, FY92, annual rpt, S0129–1
Alabama public health dept activities, including services provided, inspection and licensing activity, staff and finances, and vital statistics and health data, 1992 annual rpt, S0175–3
Alabama statistical abstract, general data, 1992 recurring rpt, U5680–2.6
Alaska financial condition, including revenues by source, expenditures by function, fund balances, and bond obligations, FY92 and trends, annual rpt, S0275–1

Arizona financial condition, including revenues by source, expenditures by function, and fund balances, FY91, annual rpt, S0450–2
Arizona financial condition, including revenues by source, expenditures by function, and fund balances, FY92, annual rpt, S0450–1
Arkansas financial condition, including revenues by source, expenditures by function and locality, and fund balances, FY91-92, biennial rpt, S0780–1
Arkansas financial condition, including revenues by source, expenditures by function and object, and fund balances, FY92, annual rpt, S0670–1
California financial condition, including revenues by source, expenditures by agency and function, fund balances, and bonded debt, FY92 and trends, annual rpt, S0815–1
California statistical abstract, general data, 1992 annual rpt, S0840–2.13
Colorado financial condition, including receipts by source, and expenditures by function, FY92 and trends, annual rpt, S0980–1
Connecticut financial condition, including revenues by source, expenditures by function, and bonded debt, FY92, annual rpt, S1170–1, S1170–2
DC financial condition, including receipts by source, expenditures by object or function, and fund balances, FY92, annual rpt, S1507–1
DC statistical profile, general data, 1992 annual rpt, S1535–3.2
Florida financial condition, including receipts by source, expenditures by function, and fund balances, FY92, annual rpt, S1717–1, S1717–3
Florida statistical abstract, general data, 1992 annual rpt, U6660–1.23
Georgia financial condition, including revenues by source, expenditures by function and object, and fund balances, FY92, annual rpt, S1860–1
Georgia statistical abstract, general data, 1992-93 biennial rpt, U6730–1.11
Hawaii data book, general data, 1992 annual rpt, S2090–1.9
Hawaii financial condition, including revenues by source, expenditures by function, and fund balances, FY92, annual rpt, S2020–1
Idaho and US economic trends and forecasts, quarterly rpt, S2245–2
Idaho financial condition, including revenues by source and expenditures by object, by agency and/or fund, FY92, annual rpt, S2215–1
Illinois financial condition, including revenues by source, and expenditures by object, function, and agency, FY92, annual rpt, S2415–1
Indiana financial condition, including revenues by source, expenditures by function and object, and fund balances, by agency, FY92, annual rpt, S2570–1
Indiana public assistance program participation, expenditures, and services, by county, FY92 and trends, annual rpt, S2623–1
Iowa financial condition, including revenues by source, expenditures by function, and bonded debt, FY92 and trends, annual rpt, S2860–4

Kansas financial condition, including revenues by source, expenditures by function and object, and fund balances, FY92, annual rpt, S2900–1
Kentucky financial condition, including revenues by source, expenditures by function and object, fund balances, and bonded debt, FY92, annual rpt, S3120–1
Louisiana financial condition, including revenues by source, expenditures by function, and fund balances, FY92 and trends, annual rpt, S3285–2
Maine financial condition, including revenues by source, expenditures by function and object, and fund balances, FY92, annual rpt, S3420–1
Maryland financial condition, including revenues by source, expenditures by function, fund balances, and bonded debt, FY92 and trends, annual rpt, S3685–2
Maryland statistical abstract, general data, 1993-94 biennial rpt, S3605–1.13
Massachusetts financial condition, including revenues by source, and expenditures by function, by fund, FY92 and trends, annual rpt, S3777–1
Michigan financial condition, including revenues by source, expenditures by function, and fund balances, FY92 and trends, annual rpt, S3985–2
Minnesota financial condition, including revenues by source, expenditures by function, fund balances, and bonded debt, FY92 and trends, annual rpt, S4180–1
Mississippi financial condition, including revenues by source, expenditures by function and object, and detail by agency, FY92 and trends, annual rpt, S4346–1
Mississippi public welfare and social service cases, recipients, and payments, by program and county, FY92, annual rpt, S4357–1
Mississippi statistical abstract, general data, 1992 annual rpt, U3255–4.13
Missouri financial condition, including fund finances, tax collections and distribution, and State treasury activity, FY92 and trends, annual rpt, S4570–1
Missouri financial condition, including revenues by source, expenditures by function, and fund balances, FY92, annual rpt, S4475–1
Montana financial condition, including revenues by source, expenditures by function, and fund balances, FY92, annual rpt, S4653–1
Nebraska financial condition, including revenues by source, expenditures by function and agency, and fund balances, FY92, annual rpt, S4825–1
Nevada financial condition, including fund revenues by source, expenditures by function, and bonded debt, FY92, annual rpt, S5025–1
Nevada statistical abstract, general data, 1992 biennial rpt, S5005–1.8
New Hampshire financial condition, with revenues by source, expenditures by function or object, and fund balances, FY92 and trends, annual rpt, S5175–1
New Jersey financial condition, including revenues by source, expenditures by function, fund balances, and bonded debt, FY92, annual rpt, S5455–1

Federal aid to States

New Mexico financial condition, including receipts by source, expenditures by agency and function, fund balances, and bonded debt, FY91, annual rpt, S5585–1

New York State financial condition, including revenues by source, expenditures by function, and fund balances, FY93, annual rpt, S5710–1

New York State public assistance and social service program statistics, by State area and source of funds, 1991 and trends, annual rpt, S5800–2

North Carolina financial condition, including revenues by source, expenditures by function, fund balances, and bonded debt, FY92, annual rpt, S5897–1

North Dakota financial condition, including revenues by source, expenditures by function, fund balances, and bonded debt, FY92, annual rpt, S6162–1

Ohio financial condition, including revenues by source, expenditures by function, and fund balances, FY92, annual rpt, S6255–1

Oklahoma financial audit narrative summary, with data on Federal expenditures by agency and program, FY91, annual rpt, S6410–1

Oklahoma financial condition, including revenues by source, expenditures by function, and fund balances, FY91, annual rpt, S6438–1

Oklahoma public welfare program expenditures, recipients, and services, by program and county, FY92 and trends, annual rpt, S6455–1

Oklahoma statistical abstract, general data, 1992 annual rpt, U8130–2.5, U8130–2.6

Oregon financial condition, including revenues by source, expenditures by function, and fund statements, FY92, annual rpt, S6603–2

Pennsylvania financial condition, including revenues by source, expenditures by function, and fund balances, FY92 and trends, annual rpt, S6810–4

Rhode Island financial condition, including revenues by source, expenditures by function, and fund balances, FY92 and trends, annual rpt, S6930–1

Rhode Island statistical almanac, general data, 1993 annual rpt, C7975–1.1

South Carolina financial condition, including receipts by source, expenditures by function, fund balances, and bonded debt, FY92, annual rpt, S7127–1

South Carolina statistical abstract, general data, 1993 annual rpt, S7125–1.2

South Dakota financial condition, including revenues by source, expenditures by function, and bonded debt, FY92, annual rpt, S7330–1

Tennessee financial condition, including revenues by source, expenditures by function and object, and fund balances, FY92, annual rpt, S7505–1

Tennessee statistical abstract, general data, 1992/93 annual rpt, U8710–2.15

Texas financial condition, including revenues by source, and Federal assistance by agency, FY92, annual rpt, S7655–3

Texas financial condition, including revenues by source, expenditures by function and dept, and investments, with data for over 400 individual funds, FY92, annual rpt, S7655–2

Utah financial condition, including revenues by source, expenditures by function and agency, and fund balances, FY92, annual rpt, S7795–1

Utah govt statistical review, fiscal and socioeconomic data, 1993 annual rpt, R9380–1.4

Vermont financial condition, including revenues by source, expenditures by function, fund balances, and bonded debt, FY92, annual rpt, S8035–1

Virginia financial condition, including revenues by source, expenditures by function, and fund balances, FY92 and trends, annual rpt, S8170–1

Virginia judicial system grants from Fed Govt, FY92, annual rpt, S8300–1

Washington State financial condition, including revenues by source, expenditures by function, fund balances, and bonded debt, FY92, annual rpt, S8345–3

Washington State revenues by source, and distributions by tax and locality, FY92 and trends, annual rpt, S8415–1.1

West Virginia statistical handbook, general data, 1992 annual rpt, R9385–1.2, R9385–1.6

Wisconsin Blue Book, general data, 1993-94 biennial rpt, S8780–1.2

Wisconsin financial condition, including revenues by source, expenditures by function and object, and fund balances, FY92, annual rpt, S8675–3

Wisconsin financial condition, including revenues by source, expenditures by function and object, and fund balances, FY93, annual rpt, S8675–2

Wyoming financial condition, including revenues by source, expenditures by function, and fund balances, FY92 and trends, annual rpt, S8875–1

see also Revenue sharing

see also Supplemental Security Income

Federal aid to transportation

Airline (regional) subsidy payments for essential air service, by carrier and location, 1993 annual rpt, A8795–1.2

Airport and Airway Trust Fund financial statement, weekly rpt recurring tables, C5800–30.502, C5800–30.504, C5800–30.508, C5800–30.512

Budget receipts and outlays of Fed Govt, by source and function, 1920s-93, annual rpt, R9050–1.3

Bus (transit) new Federal commitments, by vehicle type, FY87-91, article, C1575–3.505

Expenditures on facilities/services by transport mode, and on R&D and planning, 1992 annual rpt, R4815–1

Local transit system Federal funding for new rail starts, for 26 cities, 1993, article, C8400–1.501

Mass transit industry statistics, including govt funding, vehicle purchasing, and bus production, 1992/93 annual fact book, C1575–3.501

Mass transit system finances and operations, including govt assistance, 1976-92, annual rpt, A2650–1.1

State transit funding received per dollar contributed to Mass Transit Account, by State, 1991, C1575–3.507

Index by Subjects and Names

Trends in Federal budget, including spending by program, State, and region, FY93-94, annual rpt, R8490–11

see also Airport Improvement Program

see also Federal aid to highways

Federal aid to vocational education

Job Corps youth training program funding, enrollment capacity, and participants by selected characteristics, 1981-94, article, R4800–2.515

Southern States job training program funding, for 15 States, 1990, annual rpt, U6660–1.20

Trends in Federal budget, including spending by program, State, and region, FY81 and FY93, annual rpt, R8490–11

State and local:

Alabama elementary and secondary school enrollment, staff, pupil transportation, and finances, by district, 1991/92, annual rpt, S0124–1

Connecticut education dept staff and expenditures, by div, 1991/92, annual rpt, S1185–1

Delaware public school vocational education revenues by source, 1991/92, annual rpt, S1430–1

Louisiana education dept revenues by source and expenditures by function, 1991/92 and trends, annual rpt, S3280–1.1

Maryland elementary and secondary education data, by county, 1991/92, annual rpt, S3610–2.9

Missouri public school finances, staff, students, and programs, detailed data, 1991/92, annual rpt, S4505–1.1

Tennessee public school finances, by county, city, and school district, 1991/92, annual rpt, S7490–2.4

see also Job Training Partnership Act

Federal Aviation Administration

Aeronautics R&D budget authority and outlays, FY73-91, annual rpt, A0250–2.4

Airport and Airway Trust Fund financial statement, weekly rpt recurring tables, C5800–30.502, C5800–30.504, C5800–30.508, C5800–30.512

Federal boards, committees, and commissions

Advisory committees sponsored by HHS, NSF, and all other depts and agencies, with committee costs, FY92-93, article, A1250–1.541

Regulatory costs and staff, for approx 50 Federal agencies, FY70s-94, annual rpt, U9640–1

Transportation regulatory agency policies and practices for motor carriers and railroads, by agency, 1991/92 annual rpt, A7015–4

Utility and transportation regulatory agency activities, scope of jurisdiction, finances, and employees, by agency, 1991/92 annual rpt, A7015–2

Utility regulatory agency policies and practices, and industry financial and operating data, by utility type and agency, 1991/92 annual rpt, A7015–3

see also Federal independent agencies

Federal budget

see Budget of the U.S.

Federal buildings

see Public buildings

Index by Subjects and Names

Federal contracts
see Government contracts and procurement

Federal corporations
see Government corporations and enterprises

Federal courts
see Courts
see Federal district courts
see Supreme Court

Federal Deposit Insurance Corp.
Bank failures and outlays by FDIC, by State and region, 1990-92, R8490-47
State and local:
New Jersey insured public funds, Dec 1992, annual rpt, S5355-1

Federal district courts
Caseloads and judges for Federal district courts vs State courts, by type of case, 1991, annual rpt, R6600-1

State and local:
Hawaii data book, general data, 1992 annual rpt, S2090-1.4
Maryland statistical abstract, general data, 1993-94 biennial rpt, S3605-1.9

Federal employees
Agency regulatory costs and staff, for approx 50 Federal agencies, FY70s-94, annual rpt, U9640-1
Charitable contributions raised in annual Federal worker campaign, 1982-92, article, C2176-1.516
College grad job and salary offers, by field of study, type of employer and occupation, and degree level, by region, interim rpt series, A3940-1
College grad job and salary offers, by field of study, type of employer and occupation, and degree level, series, A3940-2
Correctional instn admin, inmates, facilities, costs, parole and probation, and staffing, for local, State, and Federal systems, 1992 annual series, R4300-1
Correctional instns, inmates, staff, and cost of care, by instn, US and Canada, with operating summary by State or Province, 1992, annual directory, A1305-3
DOD military and civilian personnel, with positions added and subtracted due to base closures, 1993 rpt, R8490-45
Employment, earnings, and payroll, by level of govt and State, Dec 1990 and trends, annual rpt, R9050-1
Employment in govt, by level and State, Oct 1991, annual rpt, R9380-1.3
Labor Dept Wage and Hour Div investigators, and time devoted to child labor law enforcement, FY83-93, R8335-2
Law school grad employment and salaries, by type of employer, location, and grad characteristics, 1992 and trends, annual rpt, A6505-1
Military (Army/Air Force) resale agency uniformed and civilian personnel, FY91, annual rpt, A2072-1
NASA and DOD employees and/or contractors, FY61-93, annual rpt, A0250-2.5
Occupational health and safety govt regulatory activities, including inspections, fines, and data by State and company, 1992 annual rpt, R8335-1.2
Physicians in Fed Govt, by detailed specialty and location, 1992 and trends, annual rpt, A2200-3

Planning profession employment and salaries, by type of employer, demographic and professional characteristics, and location, 1991 and trends, biennial rpt, A2615-1
Scientists and engineers employed by Fed Govt, by field and sex, 1989, article, A1250-1.523
State social, economic, and govtl indicators, with rankings, 1993 semiannual rpt, B8500-1.6
Unemployment insurance claims and benefits for former Federal and military personnel, monthly rpt, S7495-2
Utility and transportation regulatory agency activities, scope of jurisdiction, finances, and employees, by agency, 1991/92 annual rpt, A7015-2
Women and minority employment, by educational background, occupation, and type of employer, 1980s-91, with historical trends, recurring rpt, A3960-2

State and local:
Alaska employment and unemployment, hours, and earnings, by area and/or industry, monthly rpt, S0320-1
Arizona statistical abstract, general data, 1993 recurring rpt, U5850-2.10
DC employment, earnings, and hours, by industry, with unemployment insurance data, monthly rpt, S1527-3
Florida statistical abstract, general data, 1992 annual rpt, U6660-1.23
Georgia employment, earnings, and hours, by major industry group and MSA, monthly rpt, S1905-1
Georgia statistical abstract, general data, 1992-93 biennial rpt, U6730-1.3
Hawaii data book, general data, 1992 annual rpt, S2090-1.9, S2090-1.10, S2090-1.12
Illinois statistical abstract, general data, 1992 annual rpt, U6910-2
Kansas business activity indicators, quarterly rpt, U7095-1
Louisiana labor force, employment, and unemployment, by industry div and MSA, monthly rpt, S3320-2
Maine govt employment, by level and detailed occupation, May 1991 or Mar 1992, triennial survey, S3465-1.27
Maryland labor force, employment, earnings, and hours, with data by industry and location, monthly rpt, S3605-2
Maryland statistical abstract, general data, 1993-94 biennial rpt, S3605-1.4
Massachusetts employment, hours, and earnings, by industry and local area, with unemployment insurance claims, monthly rpt, S3808-1
Missouri employment, earnings, and hours, by industry and MSA, monthly rpt, S4530-3
Nebraska employment and unemployment, by industry group and locality, quarterly rpt, S4895-2
Nevada statistical abstract, general data, 1992 biennial rpt, S5005-1.6
New Hampshire employment, hours, and earnings, by industry and area, monthly rpt, S5205-1
New Hampshire govt and education employment by detailed occupation, 1991 or 1992, triennial rpt, S5205-2.25

Federal executive departments

New Mexico business and economic activity indicators, monthly rpt, U7980-1
New Mexico employment, hours, and earnings, by labor market area and industry, monthly rpt, S5624-2
New York State employment, earnings, and hours, by county, selected metro area, and industry group, monthly rpt, S5775-1
New York State statistical yearbook, general data, 1992 annual rpt, U5100-1.3
North Carolina employment, hours, and earnings, by industry group, with job placements, monthly rpt, S5917-3
Ohio employment, hours, and earnings, by industry and MSA, with job service and unemployment insurance activities, monthly rpt, S6270-1
Oregon labor force and employment statistics, including data by industry, monthly rpt, S6592-1, S6615-2
Pennsylvania employment, hours, and earnings, by industry, monthly rpt, S6845-1
Pennsylvania labor force planning rpt, including population characteristics, employment and job openings by industry and occupation, and income trends, FY92 annual rpt, S6845-3
South Carolina employment, earnings, and hours, by industry group and locality, monthly rpt, S7155-2
South Dakota employment, earnings, and hours for selected industries and areas, with characteristics of unemployed and job service activities, monthly rpt, S7355-1
Tennessee statistical abstract, general data, 1992/93 annual rpt, U8710-2.3
Utah economic and business activity review and indicators, monthly rpt, U8960-2
Utah statistical abstract, general data, 1993 triennial rpt, U8960-1.7
Virginia DOD military and civilian employment by service branch, by region, locale, and installation, 1991 and trends, article, S8205-4.501
Virginia labor force, hours, and earnings, with data by industry group and locality, monthly rpt, S8205-6
Wyoming employment by industry group and county, with unemployment insurance and job service activities, monthly rpt, S8895-1

see also Civil service pensions
see also Congressional employees
see also Federal pay
see also Labor-management relations in government
see also Military benefits and pensions
see also Military pay
see also Military personnel
see also Postal employees
see also Presidential appointments

Federal Energy Administration
see Department of Energy

Federal executive departments
Public confidence in selected societal instns, 1972-91 surveys, annual rpt, U6395-1
Regulatory costs and staff, for approx 50 Federal agencies, FY70s-94, annual rpt, U9640-1
see also Federal boards, committees, and commissions
see also Federal independent agencies

see also under By Government Agency in the "Index by Categories"
see also under names of individual departments or agencies

Federal expenditures
see Budget of the U.S.
see Defense expenditures
see Government spending

Federal funding for energy programs
Budget receipts and outlays of Fed Govt, by source and function, 1920s-93, annual rpt, R9050-1.3
DOE budget for FY92-93, and Clinton Admin proposal for FY94, by program, 1993 article, A1250-1.522
Trends in Federal budget, including spending by program, State, and region, FY81 and FY93, annual rpt, R8490-11

Federal funding for research and development
Academic research funding awarded to individuals, teams, and facilities, 1980 and 1989, article, A1250-1.511
Aerospace industry, civil and military production, R&D, trade, employment, and finances, with Federal funding data, 1991 and trends, annual rpt, A0250-2
Agriculture research budget of USDA, by program, FY92-94, article, A1250-1.525
Appropriations of House and Senate, and Clinton Admin request, for NASA, NSF, and EPA, with detail for selected R&D programs, FY94, article, A1250-1.542
Budget of the US Clinton Admin request for NSF by function, and DOD basic and applied research programs, FY94, article, C2175-1.515
Budget of the US R&D funding for FY92-93, and Clinton Admin proposal for FY94, by agency and function, 1993 article, A1250-1.521
Budget of the US R&D funding for 7 agencies in FY93, with Clinton Admin request and congressional appropriation for FY94, annual article, A1250-1.534, A1250-1.544
Budget of US outlays for public investment programs by type, with intl comparisons, FY93-94 and trends, R4700-23
Budget receipts and outlays of Fed Govt, by source and function, 1920s-93, annual rpt, R9050-1.3
Chemicals R&D spending in Federal, industrial, and academic sectors, with data by company and instn, 1980s-93, annual feature, A1250-1.537
DOD funding for science and technology, by program area, FY93, annual rpt, A4725-1.4
Ecologist research grant sources, and funding activity of selected Govt agencies, 1992 recurring rpt, A4685-1
Environmental research spending of Fed Govt, by agency, FY92, article, A1250-1.508
EPA research budget, by program, FY92-94, article, A1250-1.526
Expenditures for R&D, and Small Business Innovation Research (SBIR) grants, by State, 1993 annual rpt, R4225-1
Expenditures for research, by selected agency, 1981, 1987, and 1993, article, A1250-1.514
Funding and expenditures for R&D, by source and performing sector, and Federal functional category, 1960s-93, annual rpt, R3300-1

Funding for 4 large-scale science projects, 1992-93, article, C1850-6.503
Higher education Fed Govt obligations for R&D, top US and Southern instns, 1989/90 and trends, biennial fact book, A8945-1.6
Higher education Fed Govt obligations, for top 100 instns, FY91, annual feature, C2175-1.528
Higher education funding and Federal aid for R&D, for top 100 instns, FY91, annual feature, C2175-1.502
Higher education funding, by agency and program, FY92-94, annual feature, C2175-1.516
Higher education instn Fed Govt R&D obligations per capita, by State, FY90, article, B8500-2.501
Higher education R&D funding by source, by State and for US territories, FY91, annual feature, C2175-1.503
Higher education R&D program spending, by State and selected agency, FY91, annual rpt, C2175-1.531
Library-related research and research library funding, by instn and program, 1993 annual compilation, C1650-3.2
NASA R&D funding by program category, with detail for advanced subsonic transport program, 1992, article, C5800-4.505
State social, economic, and govtl indicators, with rankings, 1993 semiannual rpt, B8500-1.13
Transportation R&D and planning outlays, by Federal agency, 1992 annual rpt, R4815-1

State and local:
California higher education systems funding by source and expenditures by program category, with enrollment data, FY60s-94, annual rpt, S0827-3
Florida higher education research contract and grant funds by source and expenditures by discipline, 1991/92, annual rpt, S1725-1
Hawaii data book, general data, 1992 annual rpt, S2090-1.17
Pennsylvania statistical abstract, general data, 1992 recurring rpt, U4130-6.4
see also Defense research
see also Federal funding for energy programs
see also Federally Funded R&D Centers

Federal grants
see terms beginning with Federal aid to

Federal Highway Administration
Buses and drivers inspected and removed from service under FHWA/Commercial Vehicle Safety Alliance Roadcheck program in US/Canada, 1991-93, article, C1575-3.507

Federal Housing Administration
see Housing (FHA), HUD

Federal independent agencies
Congressional organization, major legislative and budget actions, and agency and program appropriations, 102nd Congress, 2nd session, 1992, annual rpt, C2500-2
Regulatory costs and staff, for approx 50 Federal agencies, FY70s-94, annual rpt, U9640-1
see also Environmental Protection Agency
see also Export-Import Bank
see also Federal boards, committees, and commissions

see also Federal Deposit Insurance Corp.
see also Federal Reserve System
see also Government corporations and enterprises
see also National Aeronautics and Space Administration
see also National Foundation on the Arts and the Humanities
see also National Science Foundation
see also Small Business Administration
see also Tennessee Valley Authority
see also U.S. Postal Service

Federal lands
see Government supplies and property
see Military bases, posts, and reservations
see Public lands

Federal-local relations
City govt costs to enforce Fed Govt regulations including environmental laws, for 314 cities, FY93, with summary projections to FY98, A9330-12
City officials views on issues and conditions affecting local govt, including top issues for Fed Govt to address , 1992 survey, annual rpt, A8012-1.21
Elementary/secondary teacher views on whether Fed Govt can contribute to improving educational system, Jan-Feb 1993 survey, B6045-7
Environmental regulation by cities under Federal mandates, local impact analysis including selected cost projections, 1993 rpt, U9640-3
see also Federal aid to local areas
see also Intergovernmental relations
see also Revenue sharing

Federal National Mortgage Association
Yields and interest rates for selected securities and loans, monthly rpt, A6450-2

Federal officials
see Federal employees
see Officials

Federal pay
Budget of US economic assumptions of Bush Admin, 1990-97, annual rpt, C2500-2
Chemistry and chemical engineering grad starting salaries, employment status, demographic characteristics, and advanced study plans, 1991/92, annual rpt, A1250-2
College grad job and salary offers, by field of study, type of employer and occupation, and degree level, by region, interim rpt series, A3940-1
College grad job and salary offers, by field of study, type of employer and occupation, and degree level, series, A3940-2
Congressional Member salary chronology, 1789-1991, annual rpt, C2500-2
Correctional instn admin, inmates, facilities, costs, parole and probation, and staffing, for local, State, and Federal systems, 1992 annual series, R4300-1
Earnings, employees, and payroll, by level of govt and State, Dec 1990 and trends, annual rpt, R9050-1
Engineers salaries in Fed Govt, by years since college degree, 1993, annual survey rpt, A0685-5
Expenditures of Fed Govt by category, by State and region, FY92, annual rpt, R8490-35

Index by Subjects and Names

Fertility

House of Representatives staff characteristics, salaries, and benefits by position, 1992 and trends, recurring rpt, R4140–1

Judicial system salaries for judges and court administrators, by State and territory, and for Federal system, July 1993, semiannual rpt, R6600–2

Law school grad employment and salaries, by type of employer, location, and grad characteristics, 1992 and trends, annual rpt, A6505–1

Pay schedule for Federal white collar workers, and salaries of typical positions, 1993 annual rpt, R9380–1.4

Planning profession employment and salaries, by type of employer, demographic and professional characteristics, and location, 1991 and trends, biennial rpt, A2615–1

Professional worker salaries, by employee and employer characteristics, with detail for scientists and engineers, 1990s and trends, biennial rpt, A3960–1

State social, economic, and govtl indicators, with rankings, 1993 semiannual rpt, B8500–1.6

Travel allowance rates per diem for US Govt employees, by country or foreign city, June 1992, annual rpt, C2140–1.5

Utility and transportation regulatory agency activities, scope of jurisdiction, finances, and employees, by agency, 1991/92 annual rpt, A7015–2

State and local:

California statistical abstract, general data, 1992 annual rpt, S0840–2.13

Florida statistical abstract, general data, 1992 annual rpt, U6660–1.23

Hawaii data book, general data, 1992 annual rpt, S2090–1.12, S2090–1.14

Illinois statistical abstract, general data, 1992 annual rpt, U6910–2

Maryland statistical abstract, general data, 1993-94 blennial rpt, S3605–1.13

New York State average earnings of Federal, State, and local govt employees, 1987-91, annual feature, S5775–1.501

see also Civil service pensions

see also Military benefits and pensions

see also Military pay

Federal Republic of Germany

see Germany

see Germany, West

Federal Reserve System

Money and securities market activity, and related indicators, biweekly rpt, B2000–1

Federal-State relations

State budget effect of hypothetical Federal entitlement spending limit, by State, FY94, article, B8500–2.516

see also Federal aid to States

see also Intergovernmental relations

see also Revenue sharing

Federal stockpiles

see Stockpiling

Federal trust funds

see Government trust funds

Federally Funded R&D Centers

Budgets and facilities for R&D laboratories of 6 Federal agencies, 1993 article, C5800–7.531

Chemicals R&D spending in Federal, industrial, and academic sectors, with data by company and instn, 1980s-93, annual feature, A1250–1.537

Feedlots

see Livestock and livestock industry

Feeds

see Animal feed

Feedstocks, petrochemical

see Petrochemicals

Fees

see License taxes and fees

see Professionals' fees

see Tuition and fees

see User fees

Feistritzer, C. Emily

"Who Wants To Teach?", R6350–7

Fellowships

see Student aid

Ferries

Mass transit system finances and operations, passengers, and employment, by mode, US and Canada, 1990-91 and trends, annual rpt, A2650–1

State and local:

Alaska hwy and ferry mileage, 1991-92, annual rpt, S0275–1

Fertility

Black American women fertility rates, with comparison to whites, by age group, 1990, 2000, and 2010, annual compilation, C6775–2.2

Developing countries family planning efforts, with data on socioeconomic and health conditions compared to developed countries, by country, 1980s-90, R8720–1.1

Family planning devs worldwide, with data on fertility, contraceptive use, and family size preferences, quarterly rpt, A5160–6

France Jewish European- and North-African-born population fertility rates, 1930s-71, article, A2050–1.1

Latin America statistical abstract, general data by country, 1992 annual rpt, U6250–1.6

Middle East population trend and demographic characteristics, by country, 1993 rpt, R8750–2.59

Minority population characteristics, employment, and voting patterns by detailed race-ethnicity, with comparisons to whites, 1980s-2040, R8750–2.58

Soviet Union former central Asian Republics population, and fertility, abortion, and contraceptive use rates, for 5 Republics, 1993 article, A5160–1.504

State social, economic, and govtl indicators, with rankings, 1993 semiannual rpt, B8500–1.9

World demographic trends and population-related issues, monthly rpt, R8750–1

World family planning and fertility trends, and contraceptives effectiveness, safety, and availability, by method, series, U2520–1

World population and health indicators, with detail by region and country, 1992/93 biennial rpt, R9455–1.5

World population size and characteristics, GNP, and land area, by region and/or country, 1993 annual data sheet, R8750–5

State and local:

Alabama fertility rates by race and county, 1992 and trends, annual rpt, S0175–2

Arkansas Census of Population and Housing detailed findings, 1990, U5935–7

California and US fertility rates, 1970-90, annual rpt, S0865–1

California Census of Population and Housing detailed findings, 1990, S0840–9

Colorado vital statistics, including population, births, deaths by cause, abortion, marriage and divorce, and adoption, by demographic characteristics and location, 1990 and trends, annual rpt, S1010–1

Florida fertility rates, 1974-92, annual rpt, S1745–3

Hawaii data book, general data, 1992 annual rpt, S2090–1.2

Idaho vital statistics, including births, deaths by cause, abortions, marriages, and divorces, by demographic characteristics and county, 1991 and trends, annual rpt, S2250–2

Kansas birth and fertility rates, 1951-91, annual rpt, S2975–1

Kentucky fertility rate, by county, 1991, annual rpt, S3140–1

Maryland fertility rates, by county, 1989, annual rpt, S3635–1

Michigan vital statistics, including births, deaths, marriages, divorces/annulments, and communicable diseases, by location and demographic characteristics, 1990 and trends, annual rpt, S4000–3

Minnesota vital statistics, including population, births, abortions, deaths, marriages, and divorces, by location and demographic characteristics, 1991 and trends, annual rpt, S4190–2

Mississippi fertility rates, by race, age, and county, 1992, annual rpt, S4350–1

Missouri fertility rates, by age, 1911-92, annual rpt, S4518–1

Nevada fertility and birth rates, 1980-89, annual rpt, S5075–1

New Jersey Census of Population and Housing detailed findings, by county, 1990, S5425–19

New Jersey fertility rates, 1970-90, annual rpt, S5405–1

New Mexico vital statistics, including population, births, deaths, and disease, by location and demographic characteristics, 1991 and trends, annual rpt, S5605–1

New York State fertility rate, 1970-90, annual rpt, S5765–1

Ohio population by age, sex, and county, with summary components of change, quinquennially 1990-2015, recurring rpt, S6260–3

Ohio vital statistics, including births, deaths by cause, marriages, divorces, and population, by demographic characteristics and location, 1991 and trends, annual rpt, S6285–1

Oklahoma population projections, by age, sex, and locality, with data on fertility and migration, 1990-2020, recurring rpt, S6416–1

Oregon fertility rates, 1940s-91, annual rpt, S6615–5

Pennsylvania Census of Population and Housing detailed findings, with selected data by county and municipality, 1990, U4130–13

Rhode Island Census of Population and Housing detailed findings, by county and municipality, 1990, S6930–9

Fertility

Rhode Island fertility rates by age group, 1960s-80, annual rpt, S6995–1

South Carolina vital statistics, including fertility rates, by race, 1971-90, annual rpt, S7175–1

Texas fertility rates, by age and race-ethnicity, 1990, recurring rpt, S7645–3

Texas fertility rates by age and race-ethnicity, 1991, annual rpt, S7685–1

Utah vital statistics, including births by characteristics of mother and child, by location, 1990 and trends, annual rpt, S7835–1.1

Vermont fertility rates, with detail by county and age, 1991 and trends, annual rpt, S8054–1

Washington State fertility rate, 1930s-92, annual rpt, S8345–4

West Virginia fertility rates, 1991, annual rpt, S8560–1

see also Abortion

see also Births

see also Family planning

see also Population size

Fertilizers

Chemical and related industries production, finances, operating ratios, employment, and trade, by country, company, and chemical, 1980s-92, annual feature, A1250–1.530

Chemical industry worldwide production and trade, selected data by country and world area, 1988-92, annual feature, A1250–1.507

Field crop pesticide and fertilizer use for 4 major crops, 1992, article, A1250–1.542

Financial ratios and performance, for over 350 SIC 4-digit industries, FY88-92, annual rpt, A6400–3

Latin America statistical abstract, general data by country, 1992 annual rpt, U6250–1.2, U6250–1.24

Phosphate fertilizer production distribution by type, and demand by world area, 1993 article, C5800–8.511

Potash imports, by State and country of origin, quarterly rpt, A8720–4

Potash muriates and sulfates, sales and trade, US and Canada, quarterly press release, A8720–5

Potash production, inventories, and sales and exports by State, Canadian Province, and country of destination, monthly rpt, A8720–1

Potash production, inventories, sales, and exports, US and Canada, monthly rpt, A8720–2

Prices paid by farmers for selected production commodities, 1982 and 1991-92, annual rpt, S3085–1

Prices paid by farmers for selected production commodities, 1986-91, annual rpt, S5350–1

Prices paid by farmers for selected production commodities, 1989-92, annual rpt, S8680–1

Production and consumption of fertilizers, and other financial and operating data for chemical industry, 1970s-92, annual rpt, A3850–1

Production, consumption, stocks, trade, and prices for approx 100 basic commodities, including by country and producing State, commodity yearbook for 1993, C2400–1, C2400–2

World fertilizer use, by country, 1977-89, biennial rpt, R9455–1.6

Zambia (Eastern Province) small farm fertilizer use analysis, 1980s, R5620–1.38

State and local:

Alaska fertilizer consumption, 1960s-92, annual rpt, U5750–1

Arizona fertilizer sales, and use on upland cotton, by type, 1987-92, annual rpt, U5830–1

Arkansas fertilizer consumption by type, and sales by county, 1992 and trends, annual rpt, U5920–1

Florida statistical abstract, general data, 1992 annual rpt, U6660–1.9

Georgia fertilizer consumption, by type, 1987-92, annual rpt, S1855–1

Hawaii data book, general data, 1992 annual rpt, S2090–1.19

Hawaii fertilizer consumption, by type, 1987-91, annual rpt, S2030–1

Illinois fertilizer consumption, by type and crop, 1982-91, annual rpt, S2390–1

Kansas fertilizer sales, FY66-92, annual rpt, S2915–1

Kentucky fertilizer sales and use, by type, 1991-92, annual rpt, S3085–1

Louisiana farm production expenses, by item, 1985-91, annual rpt, U2740–1

Michigan fertilizer and pesticide use, by chemical and crop, 1992 annual rpt, S3950–1

Missouri commercial fertilizer consumption, by product class, 1988-92, annual rpt, S4480–1

Montana fertilizer sales volume by type, 1986-91, annual rpt, S4655–1

Nebraska fertilizer sales and use, by county and/or type, FY91 and trends, annual rpt, S4835–1

New Jersey fertilizer consumption, FY92, annual rpt, S5350–1

New Mexico fertilizer inshipments, by type, quarterly 1991, annual rpt, S5530–1

New York State fertilizer prices and consumption, by type, 1983-92, annual rpt, S5700–1

North Carolina fertilizer shipments by county, and use by type and crop, 1991 annual rpt, S5885–1

North Dakota fertilizer consumption and use, 1988-92, annual rpt, U3600–1

Ohio fertilizer consumption and prices, and deliveries by county, 1991 and trends, annual rpt, S6240–1

Oklahoma and US consumption of commercial fertilizers, by type, 1991-92, annual rpt, S6405–1

Oregon fertilizer use, by type and crop, 1991 and trends, annual rpt, S6575–1

Pennsylvania fertilizer use, by type and crop, 1992, annual rpt, S6760–1

South Carolina fertilizer consumption, by county and type, FY92, annual rpt, U1075–3

South Dakota fertilizer consumption by type, 1986-92, annual rpt, S7280–1

Tennessee fertilizer consumption, 1946-92, annual rpt, S7460–1

Texas field crop fertilizer use, 1987-91, annual rpt, S7630–1.1

Vermont fertilizer sales and monitoring activity, 1989-90, biennial rpt, S7978–1

Washington State fertilizer use, by type and crop, 1992, annual rpt, S8328–1

West Virginia fertilizer sales, by type, 1990-91, annual rpt, S8510–1

Wisconsin fertilizer use on corn, 1992, annual rpt, S8680–1

Wyoming farm production costs and prices paid by farmers, by item, 1992 and trends, annual rpt, S8860–1

Fescue

see Seeds

Fetal deaths

Black American health and vital statistics data, with comparisons to whites, 1970s-91, annual compilation, C6775–2.2

Hospital patient admission rates and length of stay, by diagnosis and procedure, payment source, age, sex, and region, 1991, B4455–4

Latin America statistical abstract, general data by country, 1992 annual rpt, U6250–1.6

State and local:

Alabama vital statistics, including population, births, deaths by cause, marriages, and divorces, by location and demographic characteristics, 1992 and trends, annual rpt, S0175–2

Arkansas vital statistics, including births, deaths by cause, marriages, and divorces, by age, sex, race, and county, 1991 and trends, annual rpt, S0685–1

California vital statistics, including population, births, and deaths by cause, by demographic characteristics and county, 1990 and trends, annual rpt, S0865–1

Colorado vital statistics, including population, births, deaths by cause, abortion, marriage and divorce, and adoption, by demographic characteristics and location, 1990 and trends, annual rpt, S1010–1

Connecticut vital statistics, including births, deaths by cause, marriages, and divorces, by demographic characteristics and location, 1989, annual rpt, S1200–1

Delaware vital statistics, including births, deaths by cause, and marriages and dissolutions, by demographic characteristics and location, 1990, annual rpt, S1385–2

Florida vital statistics, including population, births, deaths by cause, and marriages and dissolutions, by location and demographic characteristics, 1992 and trends, annual rpt, S1745–3

Georgia vital statistics, including population, births, abortions, marriages, and divorces, by demographic characteristics and location, 1991 and trends, annual rpt, S1895–1.1

Hawaii vital statistics, including births, deaths by cause, marriages, and dissolutions, by demographic characteristics and location, 1990, annual rpt, S2065–1.2

Idaho vital statistics, including births, deaths by cause, abortions, marriages, and divorces, by demographic characteristics and county, 1991 and trends, annual rpt, S2250–2

Iowa vital statistics, including population, births, deaths by cause, marriages, and divorces, by demographic characteristics and location, 1991 and trends, annual rpt, S2795–1

Kansas vital statistics, including population, births, deaths by cause, abortions, marriages, and divorces, by demographic characteristics and location, 1991 and trends, annual rpt, S2975–1

Kentucky vital statistics, including births, deaths by cause, marriages and divorces, and population, by demographic characteristics and county, 1991, annual rpt, S3140–1

Louisiana vital statistics, including population, births, deaths by cause, reportable diseases, marriages, and divorces, by demographic characteristics and locality, 1989-90 and trends, annual rpt, S3295–1

Maine vital statistics, including births, deaths by cause, abortions, and marriages and divorces, by demographic characteristics and location, 1991 and trends, annual rpt, S3460–2

Maryland vital statistics, including population, births, deaths by cause, marriages, and divorces, by demographic characteristics and location, 1989 and trends, annual rpt, S3635–1

Massachusetts vital statistics, including births, deaths by cause, marriages, divorces, and population, by locality and demographic characteristics, 1990 and trends, annual rpt, S3850–1

Michigan vital statistics, including births, deaths, marriages, divorces/annulments, and communicable diseases, by location and demographic characteristics, 1990 and trends, annual rpt, S4000–3

Minnesota vital statistics, including population, births, abortions, deaths, marriages, and divorces, by location and demographic characteristics, 1991 and trends, annual rpt, S4190–2

Mississippi vital statistics, including births, deaths by cause, marriages, and divorces, by demographic characteristics and location, 1992 and trends, annual rpt, S4350–1

Missouri vital statistics, including population, births, deaths by cause, and marriages and divorces, by location and demographic characteristics, 1992 and trends, annual rpt, S4518–1

Montana vital statistics, including births, deaths by cause, abortion, disease, and marriage and divorce, by demographic characteristics and county, 1990-91 and trends, annual rpt, S4690–1

Nebraska vital statistics, including births, deaths, marriages, divorces, and population, by demographic characteristics and location, 1991 and trends, annual rpt, S4885–1

Nevada vital statistics, including births, abortions, and deaths by cause, by county and demographic characteristics, 1989 and trends, annual rpt, S5075–1

New Hampshire vital statistics, including population, births, deaths by cause, marriages, and divorces, by location and demographic characteristics, 1991 and trends, annual rpt, S5215–1

New Jersey vital statistics, including births, deaths, population, communicable diseases, and marriages and divorces, by demographic characteristics and location, 1990 and trends, annual rpt, S5405–1

New Mexico vital statistics, including population, births, deaths, and disease, by location and demographic characteristics, 1991 and trends, annual rpt, S5605–1

New York State vital statistics, including population, births, deaths by cause, reportable diseases, and marriages and dissolutions, by demographic characteristics and/or location, 1990 and trends, annual rpt, S5765–1

North Carolina vital statistics, including population, births, deaths, marriages, and divorces, by local area, 1991 and trends, annual rpt, S5927–1.1

North Dakota vital statistics, including births, deaths by cause, marriages and divorces, and abortions, by demographic characteristics and/or county, 1991 and trends, annual rpt, S6105–2

Ohio vital statistics, including births, deaths by cause, marriages, divorces, and population, by demographic characteristics and location, 1991 and trends, annual rpt, S6285–1

Oregon vital statistics, including births, deaths by cause, communicable diseases, marriages, and divorces, by age, sex, race-ethnicity, and county, 1991 and trends, annual rpt, S6615–5

Rhode Island vital statistics, including population, births, deaths, marriages, and divorces, by demographic characteristics and locality, 1989 and trends, annual rpt, S6995–1

South Carolina deaths, by detailed cause, age, sex, and race, 1990, annual rpt, S7175–2

South Carolina vital statistics, including births, deaths by cause, marriages, and divorces, by age, sex, race, and location, 1990 and trends, annual rpt, S7175–1

South Dakota vital statistics, including births, deaths, marriage and divorce, and communicable disease, by demographic characteristics and county, 1991 and trends, annual rpt, S7345–1

Tennessee vital statistics, including births, deaths by cause, marriages, divorces, and population, by demographic characteristics and location, 1991 and trends, annual rpt, S7520–2

Texas vital statistics, including births, deaths by cause, abortions, marriages, and divorces, by location and demographic characteristics, 1991 and trends, annual rpt, S7685–1

Utah vital statistics, including births, deaths by cause, and population, by county and demographic characteristics, 1990 and trends, annual rpt, S7835–1

Vermont vital statistics, including population, births, deaths by cause, abortions, marriages, and divorces, by location and demographic characteristics, 1991 and trends, annual rpt, S8054–1

Virginia vital statistics, including births, deaths by cause, marriages and divorces, and communicable disease, by demographic characteristics and location, 1991 and trends, annual rpt, S8225–1

Washington State vital statistics, including births, deaths by cause, and population, by demographic characteristics and location, 1991 and trends, annual rpt, S8363–1

West Virginia vital statistics, including births, deaths by cause, marriages, and divorces, by location and demographic characteristics, 1991 and trends, annual rpt, S8560–1

Wisconsin vital statistics, including population, births, deaths by cause, and marriages and dissolutions, by county and demographic characteristics, 1991 and trends, annual rpt, S8715–4

Wyoming vital statistics, including population, births, deaths by cause, marriages, and divorces, by demographic characteristics and county, 1991 and trends, annual rpt, S8920–2

see also Abortion

see also Infant mortality

FHA

see Housing (FHA), HUD

Fiber optics

Cable TV fiber optics equipment expenditures, cable miles installed, and system output measures, 1988-93, articles, C2965–1.505

Cable TV system mgmt personnel views on fiber optics technology use, July 1992 survey, article, C2965–1.501

Germany telecommunication passive optical network locations and subscribers, for 4 contractors, 1993, article, C4725–3.513

Telecommunication company miles of copper wire, coaxial cable, and/or optical fiber in use, for 8 telephone and 4 cable TV companies, 1993 article, C8900–1.513

Testing device sales for fiber optic cable, 1991-92, article, C4725–3.501

Fibers

see Natural fibers

see Synthetic fibers and fabrics

FICA

see Social security tax

Ficara, Suzanne

"New Jersey Health Statistics, 1990", S5405–1

Fidelity insurance

see Surety bonds

Field crops

see Grains and grain products

Figs

Production, acreage, and price of figs in California, with US consumption and imports by country, 1950s-92, annual rpt, A3750–1

Production, marketing, and income data for California fruit and nuts, by commodity, 1983-92, annual rpt, S0850–1.1

Filipino Americans

see Asian Americans

Films

see Motion pictures

Finance

Congressional campaign finances, with detailed data for individual Members, and leading contributors by type and industry, 1990 election and trends, biennial rpt, R3828–2.2

Economic activity leading and coincident indexes and components for financial services sector, monthly rpt, U1245–3

State and local:

New Jersey employment in 4 nonmanufacturing industry divs, by occupation, 1987 and 1990, article, S5425–1.506

Finance

see also Agricultural credit
see also Agricultural finance
see also Bankruptcy
see also Banks and banking
see also Certificates of deposit
see also Commercial credit
see also Consumer credit
see also Corporate bonds
see also Credit
see also Educational finance
see also Eurocurrency
see also Financial institutions
see also Financial institutions regulation
see also Financial planning
see also Fiscal policy
see also Foreign exchange
see also Government securities
see also Gross Domestic Product
see also Gross National Product
see also Housing costs and financing
see also Individual retirement arrangements
see also Inflation
see also Input-output analysis
see also Insurance and insurance industry
see also Interest rates
see also International finance
see also International reserves
see also Investments
see also Loans
see also Monetary policy
see also Money supply
see also Municipal bonds
see also National income and product accounts
see also New York Stock Exchange
see also Personal and household income
see also Prices
see also Securities
see also State bonds
see also Stock exchanges
see also Venture capital

Finance companies

- Assets and outstanding debt held by finance companies compared to commercial banks, with data by company, 1980-92, R4700–22
- Auto lending and leasing operations of financial instns, 1992 and trends, annual rpt, A4160–2
- Auto loan average interest rate, maturity, amount, and payment, for new and used cars, 1980-92, annual rpt, A0865–1.2
- Auto loan installment credit outstanding, by type of lending instn, 1982-92, annual rpt, A7330–1
- Financial performance and growth rankings for approx 1,000 top corporations, with comparisons by industry group, 1993 annual rpt, C3950–1.505
- Lending and financial ratios of consumer finance companies, Dec 1989-91, annual rpt, A6400–3
- Operating and financial ratios of finance companies, and loan activity, Dec 1988-92, annual article, A6400–2.506

State and local:

- Alabama financial instns (State-chartered) financial condition, with deposits and assets by instn, FY92 annual rpt, S0110–1
- Arkansas banks and other financial instns, financial condition by instn, June 1992, annual rpt, S0632–1
- California economic condition, including population, employment and earnings, income, business activity, and taxation, 1960s-92, annual rpt, S0840–3.2

Hawaii data book, general data, 1992 annual rpt, S2090–1.15

- Idaho banks and other financial instns, financial condition, with data by instn and loan activity analysis, FY92 or 1991, annual rpt, S2235–1
- Indiana financial instns (State-chartered) financial condition, including assets by instn arranged by city, 1991 and trends, annual rpt, S2625–1
- Iowa small loan companies composite financial data, loan and licensing activity, and legal actions, 1991, annual rpt, S2760–2
- Kentucky financial instns condition, including assets by instn and city, with regulatory info, 1992 and trends, annual rpt, S3121–1
- Michigan banks and other financial instns, financial condition by instn, with regulatory info, 1992 and trends, annual rpt, S3957–1
- Minnesota financial instns (State-regulated), financial condition by instn, 1991-92, annual rpt, S4140–3
- Mississippi banks and other financial instns, financial condition by instn type, and assets by bank and credit union, Dec 1992, annual rpt, S4325–1
- Missouri consumer credit lenders, and aggregate financial data, 1990-91, biennial rpt, S4502–1
- New Jersey banks and other financial instns, assets and liabilities by instn, 1992 and trends, annual rpt, S5355–1
- New Mexico financial instns, financial and operating data by instn, with regulatory activities, 1992, annual rpt, S5652–1
- Oregon financial instns, financial condition by instn, Dec 1992 and trends, annual rpt, S6616–1
- Pennsylvania statistical abstract, general data, 1992 recurring rpt, U4130–6.2
- South Carolina consumer finance company aggregate finances and loan activity, and legal actions, 1991 and trends, annual rpt, S7165–1
- South Carolina economic condition, including agriculture, finance, and govt financial data, 1970s-92, annual rpt, S7125–3.1
- Utah banks and other financial instns, financial condition by instn, FY93 and trends, annual rpt, S7830–1
- Vermont banks and other financial instns, financial condition by instn, 1992 and trends, annual rpt, S7995–2
- Virginia consumer finance companies financial condition, by instn, Dec 1992, annual rpt, S8180–3
- Virginia industrial loan assns assets by instn and composite liabilities, Dec 1991-92, annual rpt, S8180–2
- Washington State banks and other financial instns, financial condition by type of instn, 1992 and trends, annual rpt, S8325–1
- West Virginia banks and other financial instns, composite financial condition, with selected data by instn, 1990-91, annual rpt, S8530–1
- Wisconsin consumer credit licensing and regulatory activity, including complaints handled by line of business, 1992 and trends, annual rpt, S8685–1

Index by Subjects and Names

Financial crises and depressions
see Business cycles

Financial disclosure

- Utility regulatory agency policies and practices, and industry financial and operating data, by utility type and agency, 1991/92 annual rpt, A7015–3

Financial institutions

- Asset shares by financial sector, 1975 and 1992, article, C5800–7.511
- Auto lending and leasing operations of financial instns, 1992 and trends, annual rpt, A4160–2
- Black-owned enterprises financial and operating data, for top 100 firms and auto dealerships and for top 15-25 financial instns, 1992 and trends, annual feature, C4215–1.507
- Business failures and liabilities, by detailed industry, cause, length of operation, and location, 1991-92 and trends, annual rpt, C3150–8
- Competition expected by bankers from 8 types of financial instns, Mar 1992 survey, article, C4687–1.502
- Consumer complaint and inquiry activity of Better Business Burs, by detailed type of business, 1992, annual rpt, A4350–1
- Corporate performance ratings by executives for leading companies in 32 industries, 1993 annual survey feature, C8900–1.508
- Establishments, employment, and finances, and volume of printing business generated, 1992 feature, C1850–10.501
- Financial data for mutual fund industry, by type of investor and financial instn intermediary, 1985-91, annual rpt, A6025–1.2
- Fortune magazine ranking of top 50-100 companies in 8 nonindustrial sectors, with financial and employment data, 1992, annual feature, C8900–1.516
- Fortune magazine ranking of top 50-100 companies worldwide in 8 nonindustrial sectors, with financial and employment data, 1993 annual feature, C8900–1.522
- Higher education investment managers and bank custodians, by instn, FY92, annual rpt, A6705–2
- Operating and financial composite ratios for corporations, with establishments and receipts, for approx 200 industries, by asset size, FY90, annual rpt, C7800–1
- Shopping center financial and operating data, with detail by type of tenant, US and Canada, 1991, triennial rpt, R9285–1
- Small/midsize financial instns financial performance, for 10 instns with high returns on equity, 1992 article, C3950–1.502
- Statistical profiles of 50 States and DC, general data, 1993 annual almanac, C4712–1
- Stock prices, yields, and earnings per share, for 10 financial instns, Feb 1993, article, C3950–1.510

State and local:

- Arizona finance, insurance, and real estate employment and job outlook, by occupation and county, 1990-95, triennial rpt, S0465–2.36
- Arkansas banks and other financial instns, financial condition by instn, June 1992, annual rpt, S0632–1

Index by Subjects and Names

Financial statements

California banks and trust companies, financial condition by instn, with regulatory info, Dec 1992, annual rpt, S0810–1

California economic condition, including population, employment and earnings, income, business activity, and taxation, 1960s-92, annual rpt, S0840–3.2

California statistical abstract, general data, 1992 annual rpt, S0840–2.12

Connecticut banks and other financial instns, financial condition by instn, 1991 and trends, annual rpt, S1160–1

Florida statistical abstract, general data, 1992 annual rpt, U6660–1.17

Georgia banks and other financial instns, financial condition by instn type, and assets by instn and city, Dec 1992, annual rpt, S1865–1

Hawaii data book, general data, 1992 annual rpt, S2090–1.15

Idaho banks and other financial instns, financial condition, with data by instn and loan activity analysis, FY92 or 1991, annual rpt, S2235–1

Idaho economic profile, general data, 1992 recurring rpt, S2218–2.5

Illinois bank and trust companies (State-chartered) financial condition and status changes, by instn, FY92, annual rpt, S2395–1

Illinois Financial Institutions Dept activities, with financial and regulatory data for credit unions, consumer lenders, and other businesses, FY91 annual rpt, S2457–2

Indiana financial instns (State-chartered) financial condition, including assets by instn arranged by city, 1991 and trends, annual rpt, S2625–1

Kansas financial instn privilege tax collections, returns, and liability, FY92 annual rpt, S3020–1

Kentucky financial instns condition, including assets by instn and city, with regulatory info, 1992 and trends, annual rpt, S3121–1

Louisiana financial instns (State-chartered), financial condition by instn arranged by city, with regulatory info, Dec 1992, annual rpt, S3265–1

Maine banks and other financial instns, financial condition by instn, June 1992, annual rpt, S3473–2

Maine financial instn assets, deposits, and loans, by type of instn and county, 1982-92, annual rpt, S3473–1

Maryland banks and credit unions (State-chartered) financial condition by instn, with regulatory data, FY92 annual rpt, S3655–2

Maryland statistical abstract, general data, 1993-94 biennial rpt, S3605–1.8

Michigan banks and other financial instns, financial condition by instn, with regulatory info, 1992 and trends, annual rpt, S3957–1

Minnesota financial instns (State-regulated), financial condition by instn, 1991-92, annual rpt, S4140–3

Mississippi banks and other financial instns, financial condition by instn type, and assets by bank and credit union, Dec 1992, annual rpt, S4325–1

Mississippi statistical abstract, general data, 1992 annual rpt, U3255–4.8

Missouri financial instn tax collections, and disbursements to local areas, FY92 and trends, annual rpt, S4570–1.1

Nebraska personal and corporate income tax returns filed, tax credits and liability, and income, by county and/or income group, 1990, annual rpt, S4950–1.1

New Jersey banks and other financial instns, assets and liabilities by instn, 1992 and trends, annual rpt, S5355–1

New Mexico economic trends and outlook, by industry div, 1982-92, annual article, U7980–1.503

New Mexico financial instns, financial and operating data by instn, with regulatory activities, 1992, annual rpt, S5652–1

New York State statistical yearbook, general data, 1992 annual rpt, U5100–1.7

Ohio corporate franchise tax returns filed, income, and tax liability, by industry div, 1991, annual rpt, S6390–1.2

Oklahoma financial instns (State-chartered) assets and liabilities, by type of instn, with regulatory data, FY92 annual rpt, S6415–1

Oregon financial instns, financial condition by instn, Dec 1992 and trends, annual rpt, S6616–1

Pennsylvania statistical abstract, general data, 1992 recurring rpt, U4130–6.2

Rhode Island banks and other financial instns (State-chartered), assets and liabilities, by instn, 1991, annual rpt, S6945–1

Rhode Island statistical almanac, general data, 1993 annual rpt, C7975–1.1

South Carolina financial instns (State-chartered) financial condition, including data by instn, FY92 annual rpt, S7165–1

South Carolina statistical abstract, general data, 1993 annual rpt, S7125–1.2

Tennessee banks and other financial instns financial condition, by instn and city, 1992 annual rpt, S7507–1

Tennessee statistical abstract, general data, 1992/93 annual rpt, U8710–2.13

Utah banks and other financial instns, financial condition by instn, FY93 and trends, annual rpt, S7830–1

Vermont banks and other financial instns, financial condition by instn, 1992 and trends, annual rpt, S7995–2

Virginia financial instns (State-chartered), financial condition by instn and instn type, Dec 1992, annual rpt, S8180–2

Washington State banks and other financial instns, financial condition by type of instn, 1992 and trends, annual rpt, S8325–1

Washington State public depository instns summary financial data, FY91-92, annual rpt, S8455–1

West Virginia banks and other financial instns, composite financial condition, with selected data by instn, 1990-91, annual rpt, S8530–1

West Virginia statistical handbook, general data, 1992 annual rpt, R9385–1.8

see also Banks and banking

see also Credit unions

see also Federal Reserve System

see also Finance companies

see also Financial institutions regulation

see also Investment banking

see also Investment management and organizations

see also Mutual funds

see also Savings institutions

see also Stockbrokers

see also under By Industry in the "Index by Categories"

Financial institutions regulation

Bank CEO demographic and professional characteristics, attitudes, and compensation, Apr 1992 survey, annual rpt, B4490–2.33

Business economists forecasts of US budget deficit and Resolution Trust Corp outlays, FY93-94, article, A6650–5.501

Federal regulatory agency costs and staff, for approx 50 agencies, FY70s-94, annual rpt, U9640–1

Resolution Trust Corp assets, with distribution by asset category, as of Aug 1992, article, C8900–1.502

Resolution Trust Corp real estate-owned assets and book value, by type of property, June 1993, article, A6450–2.506

State and local:

Kentucky financial instns condition, including assets by instn and city, with regulatory info, 1992 and trends, annual rpt, S3121–1

Maryland banks and credit unions (State-chartered) financial condition by instn, with regulatory data, FY92 annual rpt, S3655–2

Michigan banks and other financial instns, financial condition by instn, with regulatory info, 1992 and trends, annual rpt, S3957–1

Mississippi bank regulatory info, including bank examinations, examiner salaries, and travel and training expenses, 1992, annual rpt, S4325–1

New Jersey banks and other financial instns, assets and liabilities by instn, 1992 and trends, annual rpt, S5355–1

New Mexico financial instns, financial and operating data by instn, with regulatory activities, 1992, annual rpt, S5652–1

Oklahoma financial instns (State-chartered) assets and liabilities, by type of instn, with regulatory data, FY92 annual rpt, S6415–1

Wisconsin banks financial condition, by instn and city, with regulatory info, 1992 and trends, annual rpt, S8685–1

see also Deposit insurance

Financial planning

Hospital (teaching) offering of financial planning services to house staff, 1992/93, annual rpt, A3273–3

Public opinion on most important financial advisor characteristics, 1993 survey article, C2425–2.504

see also Investment management and organizations

Financial ratios

see Operating ratios

Financial statements

see Business assets and liabilities, general

see Business assets and liabilities, specific industry

see Business income and expenses, general

see Business income and expenses, specific industry

Financial statements

see Government assets and liabilities
see Operating ratios

FIND/SVP

Home health care product market value, 1987, 1991, and 1996, A1865–1.502

Fine arts

see Art
see Arts and the humanities

Fines and settlements

- Campaign contribution $25,000 limit violations, and fines paid, for 9 individuals, 1988-90, article, C5800–7.522
- Child labor Federal law penalties assessed and collected, FY83-92, R8335–2
- Child labor law violators, with fines assessed and number of minors illegally employed, 1988-92, article, C1200–5.510
- FCC fine schedule for specific violations, 1991 and 1993, article, C1850–14.534
- Local govt police liability lawsuits, claim and settlement amounts, and legal costs, by population size, census div, and/or case type, 1990/91 survey, A5800–2.113
- Occupational health and safety govt regulatory activities, including inspections, fines, and data by State and company, 1992 annual rpt, R8335–1.2
- Personal injury case pretrial settlement amounts, for medical malpractice and product liability cases, 1993 annual rpt, C5180–1
- Urban small claims and traffic court caseloads, processing, dispositions, judgments, and litigant satisfaction, for 3-12 jurisdictions, 1990, R6600–5
- Workers compensation laws, including fines for insurance and reporting failures, by State, outlying area, and Canadian Province, 1993 annual rpt, A3840–2

State and local:

- Arkansas local court costs and fines assessed and collected, by locality, FY92, annual rpt, S0647–1
- DC statistical profile, general data, 1992 annual rpt, S1535 3.7
- Delaware truck weight enforcement stops and arrests, and related fines, 1992 and trends, annual rpt, S1435–1
- Hawaii water pollution penalties assessed and collected, by facility, 1990, annual rpt, S2065–1.6
- New York State insurance industry devs, finances, and regulatory activity, 1990/91 and trends, annual rpt, S5770–3
- South Dakota court fine receipts, with detail by county, FY88-92, annual rpt, S7395–1

see also Crime victim compensation
see also Judgments, civil procedure
see also Torts

Finland

- Electronics industry trade and/or production trends by product category for 33 countries, with general economic profiles, 1993 annual rpt, A4725–1.4
- Motor vehicle world production, sales, trade, and registrations, by country, world area, manufacturer, and make, 1991 and trends, annual rpt, A0865–2.1
- Newsprint shipments from 3 Scandinavian countries, total and to US, monthly rpt, A1630–4
- Nuclear power generation and capacity for 4 operating reactors, and capacity of nonnuclear power plants to be commissioned by 2000, 1993 article, B6800–1.507

Nuclear reactors in operation, with capacity, electricity generation, and construction, by unit and country, 1992, annual rpt, B6800–2.2

Fire departments

- Employment and personnel practices, including eligibility requirements and testing, by population size, metro status, and census div, 1991 survey, recurring rpt, A5800–2.116
- Employment, compensation, hours, and expenditures of police and fire depts, by census div, city, and city size, 1992, annual rpt, A5800–1.3
- Local govt expenditures by function and type of govt unit, and for 52 largest cities, 1993 annual rpt, R9050–1.6

State and local:

- Alaska fire depts and personnel, 1991-92, annual rpt, S0275–1
- DC statistical profile, general data, 1992 annual rpt, S1535–3.8
- Florida fire depts, and paid and volunteer firefighters, by city and county, 1991 annual rpt, C4712–6
- Maryland local govt financial condition, including revenues by source, expenditures by function, and debt obligations, FY92 and trends, annual rpt, S3618–1.1
- New York State statistical yearbook, general data, 1992 annual rpt, U5100–1.8
- South Carolina insurance dept county allocation of fire dept premium taxes, 1991, annual rpt, S7195–1

Fire insurance

see Insurance and insurance industry

Firearms

- Accidental deaths and disabling injuries, by detailed type, victim characteristics, circumstances, and location, 1992 and trends, annual rpt, A8375–2
- Black youth death and crime victimization rates, with detail for firearm incidents and comparisons to whites, by sex and age, 1993 rpt, R3840–21
- College freshmen attitudes on handgun control, by sex and instn type, fall 1992, annual survey, U6215–1
- Congressional campaign finances, with detailed data for individual Members, and leading contributors by type and industry, 1990 election and trends, biennial rpt, R3828–2.2
- Elementary/secondary school violence incidents involving guns, by school level, incident type, and cause, 1993 feature, C4215–1.508
- Participation in 53 sports, by demographic characteristics, State, and census div, 1992, annual rpt series, A8485–3
- Public opinion on laws concerning firearm sales, and gun ownership, Mar 1993 Gallup Poll and trends, C4040–1.509
- Purchases of sporting goods by product and outlet type, census div, and purchaser characteristics, with average prices, 1992 and trends, annual survey, A8485–2
- Violent crime rates involving firearms, for murder, robberies, and assault, by State, 1991, semiannual rpt, B8500–1.10
- Youth age 10-19 handgun experience and attitudes, Apr-May 1993 survey, article, R4800–2.522

Youth firearm death rates, by race, sex, and age, 1988, annual rpt, R3840–11.1

State and local:

- Alabama crimes and arrests, by offense, with data by location and offender characteristics, 1992 and trends, annual rpt, S0119–1
- Alabama vital statistics, including population, births, deaths by cause, marriages, and divorces, by location and demographic characteristics, 1992 and trends, annual rpt, S0175–2
- Alaska vital statistics, including births, deaths by cause, marriages, divorces, adoptions, and population, by demographic characteristics and location, 1990, annual rpt, S0315–1
- Arizona crimes and arrests, by offense, county, and offender characteristics, 1992, annual rpt, S0505–2
- Arkansas crimes and arrests, by offense, victim and offender characteristics, and location, 1992 and trends, annual rpt, S0652–1
- California crimes and arrests, clearances, and arrest dispositions, with data by offense and offender characteristics, 1987-92, annual rpt, S0910–1.1
- California criminal justice system detailed data, by offense, county, age, race-ethnicity, and sex, 1991 and trends, annual rpt, S0910–2
- California vital statistics, including population, births, and deaths by cause, by demographic characteristics and county, 1990 and trends, annual rpt, S0865–1
- Colorado crimes and arrests, by offense and location, with offender characteristics, and assaults on police, 1992, annual rpt, S1068–1
- Colorado vital statistics, including population, births, deaths by cause, abortion, marriage and divorce, and adoption, by demographic characteristics and location, 1990 and trends, annual rpt, S1010–1
- Connecticut crimes and arrests, by offense, with data by local agency, and victim-offender characteristics, 1992, annual rpt, S1256–1
- DC criminal justice system summary, including crimes and arrests, criminal procedure, prisoners, and parole, 1991 and trends, annual rpt, S1535–2
- Delaware crimes and arrests, by offense, county, and victim-offender characteristics, 1991 and trends, annual rpt, S1375–5
- Florida crimes and arrests, by offense, with data by victim and offender characteristics, 1992, annual rpt, S1770–1
- Florida vital statistics, including population, births, deaths by cause, and marriages and dissolutions, by location and demographic characteristics, 1992 and trends, annual rpt, S1745–3
- Georgia pistol licenses issued, by county, FY92, annual rpt, S1903–1
- Georgia vital statistics, including deaths by cause, demographic characteristics, and location, 1991 and trends, annual rpt, S1895–1.2
- Hawaii crimes and arrests, by offense, with data by county and victim-offender characteristics, 1992, annual rpt, S2035–1

Index by Subjects and Names

Firearms

Hawaii vital statistics, including births, deaths by cause, marriages, and dissolutions, by demographic characteristics and location, 1990, annual rpt, S2065–1.2

Idaho crimes and arrests, by offense, with data by location and offender characteristics, 1992 and trends, annual rpt, S2275–2

Idaho vital statistics, including births, deaths by cause, abortions, marriages, and divorces, by demographic characteristics and county, 1991 and trends, annual rpt, S2250–2

Illinois crimes and arrests, by offense, with data by location and offender characteristics, 1991, annual rpt, S2536–1

Iowa vital statistics, including population, births, deaths by cause, marriages, and divorces, by demographic characteristics and location, 1991 and trends, annual rpt, S2795–1

Kansas crimes and arrests, by offense, with data by location, agency, and victim-offender characteristics, 1992 and trends, annual rpt, S2925–1

Kentucky crimes and arrests, by offense, with data by location and offender characteristics, 1992, annual rpt, S3150–1

Kentucky vital statistics, including births, deaths by cause, marriages and divorces, and population, by demographic characteristics and county, 1991, annual rpt, S3140–1

Louisiana vital statistics, including population, births, deaths by cause, reportable diseases, marriages, and divorces, by demographic characteristics and locality, 1989-90 and trends, annual rpt, S3295–1

Maine crimes and arrests, by offense, with data by county, reporting agency, and offender age and sex, 1991, annual rpt, S3475–1

Maine vital statistics, including births, deaths by cause, abortions, and marriages and divorces, by demographic characteristics and location, 1991 and trends, annual rpt, S3460–2

Maryland crimes and arrests, by offense, location, and offender characteristics, with law enforcement employment and assaults on officers, 1992 and trends, annual rpt, S3665–1

Maryland vital statistics, including population, births, deaths by cause, marriages, and divorces, by demographic characteristics and location, 1989 and trends, annual rpt, S3635–1

Massachusetts vital statistics, including births, deaths by cause, marriages, divorces, and population, by locality and demographic characteristics, 1990 and trends, annual rpt, S3850–1

Michigan crimes and arrests, by offense, with data by location and offender characteristics, 1992 and trends, annual rpt, S3997–1

Michigan vital statistics, including births, deaths, marriages, divorces/annulments, and communicable diseases, by location and demographic characteristics, 1990 and trends, annual rpt, S4000–3

Minnesota vital statistics, including population, births, abortions, deaths, marriages, and divorces, by location and demographic characteristics, 1991 and trends, annual rpt, S4190–2

Mississippi vital statistics, including births, deaths by cause, marriages, and divorces, by demographic characteristics and location, 1992 and trends, annual rpt, S4350–1

Missouri crimes and arrests, by offense and location, with victim and offender characteristics, 1991 and trends, annual rpt, S4560–2

Missouri vital statistics, including population, births, deaths by cause, and marriages and divorces, by location and demographic characteristics, 1992 and trends, annual rpt, S4518–1

Montana crimes and clearances, by offense and jurisdiction, 1992, annual rpt, S4705–1

Montana vital statistics, including births, deaths by cause, abortion, disease, and marriage and divorce, by demographic characteristics and county, 1990-91 and trends, annual rpt, S4690–1

Nebraska vital statistics, including births, deaths, marriages, divorces, and population, by demographic characteristics and location, 1991 and trends, annual rpt, S4885–1

Nevada vital statistics, including births, abortions, and deaths by cause, by county and demographic characteristics, 1989 and trends, annual rpt, S5075–1

New Hampshire crimes and arrests, by offense, jurisdiction, and offender characteristics, 1991 and trends, annual rpt, S5250–2

New Jersey crimes and arrests, by offense, with data by location and offender characteristics, 1992 and trends, annual rpt, S5430–1

New Jersey vital statistics, including births, deaths, population, communicable diseases, and marriages and divorces, by demographic characteristics and location, 1990 and trends, annual rpt, S5405–1

New York State crimes and arrests by offense and demographic characteristics, and court activity and corrections, 1991 and trends, annual rpt, S5760–3

New York State handgun licenses issued, by county, 1982-90, annual rpt, U5100–1.8

North Carolina crimes and arrests, by offense, with data by location and offender characteristics, 1992 and trends, annual rpt, S5955–1

North Dakota crimes and arrests, by offense, location, and offender characteristics, and law enforcement employment, 1991 and trends, annual rpt, S6060–1

Ohio vital statistics, including births, deaths by cause, marriages, divorces, and population, by demographic characteristics and location, 1991 and trends, annual rpt, S6285–1

Oklahoma crimes and arrests, by offense, with data by local agency and victim and offender characteristics, 1990-92, annual rpt, S6465–1

Oregon crimes and arrests, by offense, with data by county, local agency, and offender characteristics, 1992 and trends, annual rpt, S6603–3

Oregon vital statistics, including births, deaths by cause, communicable diseases, marriages, and divorces, by age, sex, race-ethnicity, and county, 1991 and trends, annual rpt, S6615–5

Pennsylvania crimes and arrests, by offense, with data by location and offender characteristics, 1992 and trends, annual rpt, S6860–1

South Carolina crimes and arrests, by offense, with data by location and victim-offender characteristics, and assaults on officers, 1992 and trends, annual rpt, S7205–1

South Carolina deaths, by detailed cause, age, sex, and race, 1990, annual rpt, S7175–2

South Carolina prison inmates sentenced under Armed Robbery Act, FY76-92, annual rpt, S7135–1

South Carolina vital statistics, including births, deaths by cause, marriages, and divorces, by age, sex, race, and location, 1990 and trends, annual rpt, S7175–1

Tennessee vital statistics, including births, deaths by cause, marriages, divorces, and population, by demographic characteristics and location, 1991 and trends, annual rpt, S7520–2

Texas crimes and arrests, by offense, with data by location and offender characteristics, 1992 and trends, annual rpt, S7735–2

Texas vital statistics, including births, deaths by cause, abortions, marriages, and divorces, by location and demographic characteristics, 1991 and trends, annual rpt, S7685–1

Utah crimes and arrests, by offense, county, and local agency, 1992 and trends, annual rpt, S7890–3

Utah vital statistics, including births and deaths by cause, by demographic characteristics and location, 1990, annual rpt, S7835–1.2

Vermont vital statistics, including population, births, deaths by cause, abortions, marriages, and divorces, by location and demographic characteristics, 1991 and trends, annual rpt, S8054–1

Virginia crimes and arrests, by offense, with data by location and offender characteristics, 1992, annual rpt, S8295–2

Virginia vital statistics, including births, deaths by cause, marriages and divorces, and communicable disease, by demographic characteristics and location, 1991 and trends, annual rpt, S8225–1

Washington State crimes and arrests, by offense, with data by location and offender characteristics, 1992 and trends, annual rpt, S8440–1

Washington State vital statistics, including births, deaths by cause, and population, by demographic characteristics and location, 1991 and trends, annual rpt, S8363–1

West Virginia crimes and arrests, by offense, location, and offender characteristics, 1990-91, annual rpt, S8610–1

West Virginia vital statistics, including births, deaths by cause, marriages, and divorces, by location and demographic characteristics, 1991 and trends, annual rpt, S8560–1

Firearms

Wisconsin crimes and arrests, by offense, offender characteristics, county, and local agency, 1992 and trends, annual rpt, S8771–1

Wisconsin vital statistics, including population, births, deaths by cause, and marriages and dissolutions, by county and demographic characteristics, 1991 and trends, annual rpt, S8715–4

Wyoming crimes and arrests, by offense, with data by location and victim and offender characteristics, 1991 and trends, annual rpt, S8867–3

Wyoming vital statistics, including population, births, deaths by cause, marriages, and divorces, by demographic characteristics and county, 1991 and trends, annual rpt, S8920–2

see also Military weapons

Fires and fire prevention

Accidental deaths and disabling injuries, by detailed type, victim characteristics, circumstances, and location, 1992 and trends, annual rpt, A8375–2

Hospital burn patient discharges and length of stay, by age and census region, 1991, annual rpt series, B4455–1

Hospital burn patient discharges and length of stay, by payment source, age, and census region, 1991, annual rpt series, B4455–3

Motor vehicle fuel tank fire related fatalities before and after Govt standards for fuel system integrity, by location of tank, 1981-86, article, A2623–1.510

Plastic flame-retardant resin production and sales/captive use, monthly rpt, A8920–5

Property and human losses from fires, with selected data by incident, 1991 and trends, annual rpt, A5650–1.4

Telephone system fires, including incidents affecting service, by cause, 1993 article, C4725–3.510

State and local:

Alabama Fire Marshal's Office activities, 1991, annual rpt, S0160–1

Alabama vital statistics, including population, births, deaths by cause, marriages, and divorces, by location and demographic characteristics, 1992 and trends, annual rpt, S0175–2

Alaska vital statistics, including births, deaths by cause, marriages, divorces, adoptions, and population, by demographic characteristics and location, 1990, annual rpt, S0315–1

Arkansas vital statistics, including births, deaths by cause, marriages, and divorces, by age, sex, race, and county, 1991 and trends, annual rpt, S0685–1

California vital statistics, including population, births, and deaths by cause, by demographic characteristics and county, 1990 and trends, annual rpt, S0865–1

Colorado vital statistics, including population, births, deaths by cause, abortion, marriage and divorce, and adoption, by demographic characteristics and location, 1990 and trends, annual rpt, S1010–1

DC statistical profile, general data, 1992 annual rpt, S1535–3.8

Florida vital statistics, including population, births, deaths by cause, and marriages and dissolutions, by location and demographic characteristics, 1992 and trends, annual rpt, S1745–3

Georgia vital statistics, including deaths by cause, demographic characteristics, and location, 1991 and trends, annual rpt, S1895–1.2

Hawaii data book, general data, 1992 annual rpt, S2090–1.15

Hawaii vital statistics, including births, deaths by cause, marriages, and dissolutions, by demographic characteristics and location, 1990, annual rpt, S2065–1.2

Idaho fire marshal activity, including criminal cases investigated, 1991, annual rpt, S2260–1

Idaho vital statistics, including births, deaths by cause, abortions, marriages, and divorces, by demographic characteristics and county, 1991 and trends, annual rpt, S2250–2

Iowa vital statistics, including population, births, deaths by cause, marriages, and divorces, by demographic characteristics and location, 1991 and trends, annual rpt, S2795–1

Kansas fires by circumstances, and firefighter and citizen injuries and fatalities, 1992, annual rpt, S2925–1.1

Kansas vital statistics, including population, births, deaths by cause, abortions, marriages, and divorces, by demographic characteristics and location, 1991 and trends, annual rpt, S2975–1

Kentucky vital statistics, including births, deaths by cause, marriages and divorces, and population, by demographic characteristics and county, 1991, annual rpt, S3140–1

Louisiana vital statistics, including population, births, deaths by cause, reportable diseases, marriages, and divorces, by demographic characteristics and locality, 1989-90 and trends, annual rpt, S3295–1

Maine vital statistics, including births, deaths by cause, abortions, and marriages and divorces, by demographic characteristics and location, 1991 and trends, annual rpt, S3460–2

Maryland vital statistics, including population, births, deaths by cause, marriages, and divorces, by demographic characteristics and location, 1989 and trends, annual rpt, S3635–1

Massachusetts vital statistics, including births, deaths by cause, marriages, divorces, and population, by locality and demographic characteristics, 1990 and trends, annual rpt, S3850–1

Michigan vital statistics, including births, deaths, marriages, divorces/annulments, and communicable diseases, by location and demographic characteristics, 1990 and trends, annual rpt, S4000–3

Minnesota vital statistics, including population, births, abortions, deaths, marriages, and divorces, by location and demographic characteristics, 1991 and trends, annual rpt, S4190–2

Mississippi vital statistics, including births, deaths by cause, marriages, and divorces, by demographic characteristics and location, 1992 and trends, annual rpt, S4350–1

Missouri vital statistics, including population, births, deaths by cause, and marriages and divorces, by location and demographic characteristics, 1992 and trends, annual rpt, S4518–1

Montana vital statistics, including births, deaths by cause, abortion, disease, and marriage and divorce, by demographic characteristics and county, 1990-91 and trends, annual rpt, S4690–1

Nebraska vital statistics, including births, deaths, marriages, divorces, and population, by demographic characteristics and location, 1991 and trends, annual rpt, S4885–1

Nevada statistical abstract, general data, 1992 biennial rpt, S5005–1.9

Nevada vital statistics, including births, abortions, and deaths by cause, by county and demographic characteristics, 1989 and trends, annual rpt, S5075–1

New Jersey vital statistics, including births, deaths, population, communicable diseases, and marriages and divorces, by demographic characteristics and location, 1990 and trends, annual rpt, S5405–1

New York State statistical yearbook, general data, 1992 annual rpt, U5100–1.8

Ohio vital statistics, including births, deaths by cause, marriages, divorces, and population, by demographic characteristics and location, 1991 and trends, annual rpt, S6285–1

Oregon vital statistics, including births, deaths by cause, communicable diseases, marriages, and divorces, by age, sex, race-ethnicity, and county, 1991 and trends, annual rpt, S6615–5

Rhode Island statistical almanac, general data, 1993 annual rpt, C7975–1

Rhode Island vital statistics, including population, births, deaths, marriages, and divorces, by demographic characteristics and locality, 1989 and trends, annual rpt, S6995–1

South Carolina deaths, by detailed cause, age, sex, and race, 1990, annual rpt, S7175–2

South Carolina vital statistics, including births, deaths by cause, marriages, and divorces, by age, sex, race, and location, 1990 and trends, annual rpt, S7175–1

Tennessee fire, electrical, and manufactured housing inspections, fee revenues, and arson investigations, 1991, annual rpt, S7466–1

Tennessee vital statistics, including births, deaths by cause, marriages, divorces, and population, by demographic characteristics and location, 1991 and trends, annual rpt, S7520–2

Texas vital statistics, including births, deaths by cause, abortions, marriages, and divorces, by location and demographic characteristics, 1991 and trends, annual rpt, S7685–1

Utah vital statistics, including births and deaths by cause, by demographic characteristics and location, 1990, annual rpt, S7835–1.2

Vermont vital statistics, including population, births, deaths by cause, abortions, marriages, and divorces, by location and demographic characteristics, 1991 and trends, annual rpt, S8054–1

Virginia vital statistics, including births, deaths by cause, marriages and divorces, and communicable disease, by demographic characteristics and location, 1991 and trends, annual rpt, S8225–1

Washington State vital statistics, including births, deaths by cause, and population, by demographic characteristics and location, 1991 and trends, annual rpt, S8363–1

West Virginia fire protection classification ratings, by town and fire district, 1991, annual rpt, S8575–1

West Virginia vital statistics, including births, deaths by cause, marriages, and divorces, by location and demographic characteristics, 1991 and trends, annual rpt, S8560–1

Wisconsin traffic accidents involving fires, 1992, annual rpt, S8815–1

Wisconsin vital statistics, including population, births, deaths by cause, and marriages and dissolutions, by county and demographic characteristics, 1991 and trends, annual rpt, S8715–4

Wyoming vital statistics, including population, births, deaths by cause, marriages, and divorces, by demographic characteristics and county, 1991 and trends, annual rpt, S8920–2

see also Arson

see also Fire departments

see also Forest fires

see also Smoke and fire detectors

see also State funding for public safety

Fireworks

see Explosives

Fiscal policy

Energy consumption societal impacts and Govt fiscal policy issues, with related data on costs and emissions, 1993 rpt, A2575–28

Govt finances, taxation, and related issues, series, R9050–15

Govt finances, taxation, and spending policies, periodic rpt, R9050–3

Investment capital formation and impact of govt policies, series, A1310–1

Japan and US trade balances impact of fiscal policies of Japan, US, and other countries, 1980-85, article, R5650–2.528

Latin America statistical abstract, general data by country, 1992 annual rpt, U6250–1.30

State economic dev condition indicators, including economic performance, business vitality, growth capacity, and tax/fiscal system, by State, 1993 annual rpt, R4225–1.1

see also Budget of the U.S.

see also Business cycles

see also Credit

see also Government assets and liabilities

see also Government revenues

see also Income taxes

see also Inflation

see also Monetary policy

see also Prices

see also Public debt

see also State budgets

see also State government revenues

see also Subsidies

see also Tax incentives and shelters

see also Tax reform

see also Taxation

see also terms beginning with Federal aid

see also terms beginning with State funding for

Fish and fishing industry

Commercial fish stocks exploitation levels, 1990, biennial rpt, R9455–1.4

Consumer nutrition awareness and health concerns, with food shopping and consumption patterns, by respondent characteristics, 1993 survey, annual rpt, A4950–36

Consumption and consumer expenditures for meat, poultry, and fish, 1992 annual rpt, A2100–1.1

Consumption per capita of seafood, for top 10 species, 1992, article, C1850–3.513

Exports of farm products, by detailed commodity and country of destination, US and California, 1991, annual rpt, B9520–1

Financial ratios and performance, for over 350 SIC 4-digit industries, FY88-92, annual rpt, A6400–3

Japan fish/shellfish production, consumption, and trade, FY83-89, article, R5650–2.506

Latin America statistical abstract, general data by country, 1992 annual rpt, U6250–1.24, U6250–1.25

Production, consumption, stocks, trade, and prices for approx 100 basic commodities, including by country and producing State, commodity yearbook for 1993, C2400–1, C2400–2

Restaurant (seafood) establishments and customer traffic trends, with consumption of top 10 types of seafood, 1993 annual article, C1200–5.516

Restaurant patron fish/seafood ordering patterns, and consumption and price trends, 1993 article, A8200–1.509

Sales of food store products by type, with per capita consumption for top 10 types of seafood, 1992, annual feature, C4655–1.510

Statistical profiles of 50 States and DC, general data, 1993 annual almanac, C4712–1

Supermarket fish/seafood dept sales and performance indicators, 1991, annual article, C4655–1.501

Supermarket sales by detailed product type, 1992 and trends, annual feature, C5225–1.507

Supermarket seafood dept sales and performance indicators, 1992 annual survey feature, C4825–3.501

World fishing harvests, by species group and country, 1992/93 biennial rpt, R9455–1.7

State and local:

Alaska crab fishing fatalities and lost vessels, with detail for selected incidents, 1992/93, article, C8900–1.516

Alaska fishing industry occupational deaths, by decedent characteristics, 1980-88, article, A2623–1.507

Alaska, Ketchikan salmon and other fisheries catch and value, 1980-91, article, S0320–1.502

California statistical abstract, general data, 1992 annual rpt, S0840–2.7

Florida statistical abstract, general data, 1992 annual rpt, U6660–1.10

Georgia statistical abstract, general data, 1992-93 biennial rpt, U6730–1.5

Hawaii data book, general data, 1992 annual rpt, S2090–1.20

Illinois statistical abstract, general data, 1992 annual rpt, U6910–2

Louisiana fish/shellfish sales, 1982-91, annual rpt, S3285–2

Maryland statistical abstract, general data, 1993-94 biennial rpt, S3605–1.3

New Jersey seafood harvest and value, for top 10 products, 1988-92, annual rpt, S5350–1

New York State statistical yearbook, general data, 1992 annual rpt, U5100–1.15

North Carolina fish/seafood income from govt educational program, by county, 1990-91, annual rpt, S5885–1

Oregon commercial fishing landings by species and county, oyster harvest, and licensing activity, 1970s-91, annual rpt, S6575–1

Oregon referendum on restricting fishing methods on Columbia river, election results by county, 1992, biennial rpt, S6665–1

South Carolina statistical abstract, general data, 1993 annual rpt, S7125–1.1

see also Aquaculture

see also Fishing, sport

see also Shellfish

see also Wildlife and wildlife conservation

see also under By Industry in the "Index by Categories"

Fisheries

see Fish and fishing industry

Fishing, sport

Participation in 53 sports, by demographic characteristics, State, and census div, 1992, annual rpt series, A8485–3

State and local:

Georgia statistical abstract, general data, 1992-93 biennial rpt, U6730–1.5

Hawaii data book, general data, 1992 annual rpt, S2090–1.7

Illinois statistical abstract, general data, 1992 annual rpt, U6910–2

Mississippi statistical abstract, general data, 1992 annual rpt, U3255–4.16

Pennsylvania game and sport fish released by species and county, 1992 recurring rpt, U4130–6.8

Wisconsin Blue Book, general data, 1993-94 biennial rpt, S8780–1.2

see also Fish and fishing industry

see also Hunting and fishing licenses

Fissionable materials

see Radiation

see Uranium

Fixed investment

see Capital investments

Flags

see National signs and symbols

Flaxseed

see Oils, oilseeds, and fats

Fleets

see Motor vehicle fleets

Flood control

State and local:

South Carolina revenue shared with county govts, by tax or fund type, FY92, annual rpt, S7127–2

see also Dams

see also Reservoirs

Flood insurance

see Insurance and insurance industry

Floods

Floods

Deaths in major disasters since 1865, by category, annual rpt, A8375–2.1

Property loss insurance payments related to natural disasters, by location, 1991, annual rpt, A5650–1.4

Public interest in news items on 1993 Midwestern floods, by respondent characteristics, July/Aug 1993 survey, C8915–1.504

Railroad costs to repair damage resulting from Midwestern floods of 1993, article, C8400–1.511

State and local:

Washington State dairy farms affected by Nov 1990 flood, with cattle deaths and economic loss, 1993 article, A3100–2.512

see also Flood control

see also Tsunamis

Floor coverings

Auto parts/supplies and repair aftermarket sales performance, by product group, 1993 annual feature, C0125–1.503

Consumer floor covering buying practices, and effect of recession on home improvement plans, 1993 survey article, C5150–6.506

Financial ratios and performance, for over 350 SIC 4-digit industries, FY88-92, annual rpt, A6400–3

see also Carpets and rugs

Florida

Agricultural statistics, including production, finances, and shipment data for citrus, dairy, and other sectors, by commodity, 1993 annual rpt series, S1685–1

Building permits value, by county, city, and type of construction, monthly rpt, U6660–5

Children of immigrants characteristics, attitudes, and discrimination experience, 1992, survey article, R4800–2.522

Correctional instns, admin, and inmates by criminal background and demographic characteristics, FY92 annual rpt, S1720–1

County economic, social, and govtl data, 1992/93 annual rpt, C6360–1

Court cases and dispositions, by type of court and case, and location, 1992, annual rpt, S1805–1

Crimes and arrests, by offense, with victim and offender characteristics, 1992, annual rpt, S1770–1

Election results, by county and/or district, 1992 general election, biennial rpt, S1800–1

Employment and unemployment, by industry div and location, monthly rpt, S1765–3

Govt financial condition, including receipts by source, expenditures by function, and fund balances, FY92, annual rpt, S1717–1, S1717–3

Health care atlas, including births and deaths, communicable disease, manpower, and facilities and utilization, by county, 1992 annual rpt, S1746–1

Higher education enrollment, degree programs, staff, and finances, by State-supported instn, with student and staff characteristics, 1991/92 annual rpt, S1725–1

Hospitals offering 8 types of geriatrics services, 1992, article, A1865–1.519

Hurricane Andrew economic impact, including insurance payments, unemployment, and tax and lottery sales shortfalls, 1992 article, C5800–7.503

Insurance industry financial and underwriting data, by company and line of coverage, 1991, annual rpt, S1760–1

Jai alai games played, attendance, handle, and govt revenues, for 3 States, 1990, annual rpt, A3363–1.2

Library finances, holdings, staff, and services, by system and library, FY92, annual rpt, S1800–2

Markets with daily newspapers, demographic and economic info by geographic area, US and Canada, 1993 annual rpt, C3250–1

Medical malpractice insurance State joint underwriting assn (JUA) financial condition, for 11 States, 1991, annual rpt, A0375–1

Oil/gas industry production, finances, exploration, and reserves, by State, 1992 and trends, annual rpt, A5425–1.1

Population by city, county, and MSA, with components of population change, Apr 1992 and trends, annual rpt, U6660–4

Population size and household composition, series, U6660–3

Prison population impact of "habitual offender" sentencing laws, with data by circuit court and offender characteristics, 1993 rpt, A7575–5

Public opinion in US on selected foreign policy issues, with detail for 3 States, 1993 survey, annual rpt, A4965–1.2

Restaurant sales, licenses, and seats, for 3 Gulf Coast counties, 1993 article, C1850–3.507

Shopping center rents and vacancy rates in 8 metro areas, and centers under construction, 1993 article, C5150–4.508

Statistical abstract of Florida, detailed social, govtl, and economic data, 1992 annual rpt, U6660–1

Statistical profiles for Florida municipalities and counties, socioeconomic and govtl data, 1991 annual rpt, C4712–6

Statistical profiles of 50 States and DC, general data, 1993 annual almanac, C4712–1

Traffic accidents, fatalities, and injuries, by vehicle type, circumstances, location, and driver and victim characteristics, 1992 and trends, annual rpt, S1750–2

Utility and transportation regulatory agency activities, scope of jurisdiction, finances, and employees, by agency, 1991/92 annual rpt, A7015–2

Utility regulatory and operating data, by company and utility type, 1992 and trends, annual rpt, S1790–1

Vital statistics, including population, births, deaths, and marriages and dissolutions, by location and demographic characteristics, 1992 and trends, annual rpt, S1745–3

Welfare cases, recipients, and payments, by program and county, discontinued annual rpt, S1745–4

Workers compensation State employee claims, and costs by type, for HMO vs fee-for-service plans, 1993 article, C5800–2.534

see also Miami, Fla.

see also under By City and By County in the "Index by Categories"

see also under By State in the "Index by Categories"

Florists

see Flowers and nursery products

Flour

see Baking and bakery products

see Grains and grain products

Flowers and nursery products

Exports of farm products, by detailed commodity and country of destination, US and California, 1991, annual rpt, B9520–1

Financial ratios and performance, for over 350 SIC 4-digit industries, FY88-92, annual rpt, A6400–3

Shopping center financial and operating data, with detail by type of tenant, US and Canada, 1991, triennial rpt, R9285–1

Supermarket in-store floral depts and shopper use, 1993 and trends, annual survey rpt, A4950–3

Supermarket sales by detailed product type, 1992 and trends, annual feature, C5225–1.507

State and local:

Alabama agricultural production, marketing, and income, by county and/or commodity, and farms and acreage, 1992 and trends, annual rpt, S0090–1

Colorado agricultural production, marketing, and finances, by commodity and/or county, with farms and acreage, 1992 and trends, annual rpt, S0985–1

Hawaii agricultural production and marketing, by commodity and island, 1987-91, annual rpt, S2030–1

Hawaii data book, general data, 1992 annual rpt, S2090–1.19

Illinois floriculture sales, by crop, 1990-91, annual rpt, S2390–1

Kentucky agricultural production, marketing, and finances, by commodity and county; and farms, acreage, and value; 1992 and trends, annual rpt, S3085–1

Michigan agricultural production, marketing, and finances, by commodity or county, 1987-91, annual rpt, S3950–1

Minnesota agricultural production, marketing, and finances, by county or commodity, and farms and acreage, 1992 and trends, annual rpt, S4130–1

Missouri agricultural production, marketing, and finances, by commodity and/or county, and farms and acreage, 1988-92, annual rpt, S4480–1

New Jersey plant nurseries and acreage, by county, 1988-91, annual rpt, S5350–1

New York State agricultural production, marketing, and finances, by commodity and/or county, and farms and acreage, 1992 and trends, annual rpt, S5700–1

New York State statistical yearbook, general data, 1992 annual rpt, U5100–1.15

Ohio agricultural production, marketing, and finances, by commodity and county, with farms and acreage, 1990-91 and trends, annual rpt, S6240–1

Oklahoma agricultural production, marketing, and finances, by commodity and county, 1992 and trends, annual rpt, S6405–1

Oregon agricultural production, marketing, and finances, by commodity and/or county, with farms and acreage, 1991 and trends, annual rpt, S6575–1

Pennsylvania agricultural production, marketing, and finances, by county and commodity, and farms and acreage, 1992 and trends, annual rpt, S6760–1

Tennessee agricultural production and marketing, by commodity and county, with farms, acreage, and farm value, 1992 and trends, annual rpt, S7460–1

Texas trade, transportation, and public utilities employment, by SIC 2- and 3-digit industry and detailed occupation, 2nd qtr 1991, triennial survey rpt, S7675–1.31

Vermont greenhouse/nursery inspection activity, 1988-89, biennial rpt, S7978–1

Washington State agricultural production, marketing, and finances, by commodity and/or county, 1992 and trends, annual rpt, S8328–1

Wisconsin agricultural production, marketing, and finances, by commodity and county, and farms, acreage, and sales, 1992 and trends, annual rpt, S8680–1

see also Seeds

Flu

see Pneumonia and influenza

Fluorine

see Gases

Fluorspar

see Metals and metal industries

FNMA

see Federal National Mortgage Association

Food and Drug Administration

Drug new products approved by FDA, including review time needed and prior foreign approval, by drug, 1992, article, C5150–2.507

Food and food industry

Airline food service expenditures, by carrier, 1st 9 months 1992 and trends, annual article, C7000–4.507

Business devs and issues in restaurant/food service industry, with data on establishments and sales by market segment, recurring rpt, C1200–5

Compensation of food marketing mgmt personnel by position, by company sales size and region, year ended Mar 1993, annual survey, A4950–6

Consumer buying power survey of population, income, and sales by product line, by State, metro area, county, and census div, 1993 annual rpt, C1200–1.514

Consumer complaint and inquiry activity of Better Business Burs, by detailed type of business, 1992, annual rpt, A4350–1

Consumer use of single-serving packaged food, by region, 1993 survey article, C1850–1.509

Corporate performance ratings by executives for leading companies in 32 industries, 1993 annual survey feature, C8900–1.508

Discount and drugstore food product purchasing by consumers, with expenditures, by product category, 1992-93, survey article, C5150–3.515

Discount chain consumer natl brand preferences, by product category and chain, and by age group, 1993 survey, annual feature, C5150–3.521

Discount chain top-selling natl brands cited by managers, by product category, chain, and region, 1993 survey, annual feature, C5150–3.520

Discount store sales and productivity data for 20 depts, 1993 annual feature, C5150–3.516

Drugstore chains financial performance and marketing operations, with sales by product type, 1993 annual feature, C5150–2.510

Executive compensation and components, by industry div and major manufacturing group, 1991, annual rpt, R4105–19

Financial and operating data for retail and wholesale marketers, by company size and region, 1991-92, annual rpts, A4950–5

Financial and operating data for top 100 chains and companies, FY91-93, annual feature, C5150–5.509

Financial and operating devs for restaurant/food service industry, including data by company, weekly rpt, C5150–5

Financial performance and growth rankings for approx 1,000 top corporations, with comparisons by industry group, 1993 annual rpt, C3950–1.505

Financial ratios and performance, for over 350 SIC 4-digit industries, FY88-92, annual rpt, A6400–3

Industry trends and devs in food service, monthly rpt, A8200–1

Institutional food service operators financial and operating data, for leading firms by market segment, 1993 recurring feature, C1850–3.511

Mgmt info system operations of food retailers and wholesalers, including employment and finances, by company sales size, 1993 and trends, annual survey, A4950–7

Mgmt salaries in food/beverage manufacturing, by selected employee characteristics, 1992 survey, annual article, C2150–6.502

Military commissary sales, by region, product type, and individual store, FY92, annual feature, A2072–2.501

Military commissary sales of 5 types of snack food, by region, 1992, article, C0500–1.507

New product introductions, with data by product category, 1992, annual article, C2150–6.505

Operating and financial composite ratios for corporations, with establishments and receipts, for approx 200 industries, by asset size, FY90, annual rpt, C7800–1

Operations of restaurants/food service instns, including data and articles on finances, employment, companies, and customers, biweekly rpt, C1850–3

Plant construction/expansion project info, cost, and employees, by company, 1992, annual feature, C2150–6.506

Processing industry devs, including work force reduction, finances, and employment, 1993 annual feature, C2150–6.507

Production issues and devs for food and beverage industry, monthly rpt, C2150–6

Production worker employment, hours, and earnings, 1972-91, annual rpt, A3455–1.3

Promotional budgets for beef, pork, dairy, and fruits/vegetables organizations, 1993 article, C4655–1.509

Russia production of 16 food products, monthly rpt recurring feature, U2030–1.507

Sales and establishments, and growth outlook, for food service industry by market segment, 1993 annual feature, C1850–3.503

Sales and establishments, for top 400 food service chains and other organizations, 1992, annual feature, C1850–3.509

Sales and market shares for top 10 brands in 7 breakfast food product categories, 1992-93, C2710–1.536

Sales and market shares for top 10 brands in 7 sweet/snack food product categories, 1992-93, C2710–1.550

Sales trends and forecast for food service industry, by market segment, 1990-93, annual feature, A8200–1.502

Snack food consumption patterns, by snack type and consumer characteristics, 1989/90 and trends, recurring rpt, A8905–2

Snack food private label product sales in discount and drugstores, for 6 top-selling product types, 1992 or 1st qtr 1993, article, C5150–3.519

Snack food sales and market shares in supermarkets, for top 10 brands in 7 product categories, 1992-93, C2710–1.527

Snack food sales, consumption, and prices, by snack type and region, with data on industry operations and outlook, 1992 and trends, annual rpt, A8905–1

Snack food types appearing most frequently in ads with coupons, 1992, article, C2710–1.523

Vending machine sales by product type, and machines on location, 1992 and trends, annual rpt, C9470–1

State and local:

Arizona statistical abstract, general data, 1993 recurring rpt, U5850–2.17

Florida statistical abstract, general data, 1992 annual rpt, U6660–1.12

Texas trade, transportation, and public utilities employment, by SIC 2- and 3-digit industry and detailed occupation, 2nd qtr 1991, triennial survey rpt, S7675–1.31

see also Animal feed

see also Aquaculture

see also Baking and bakery products

see also Beverages

see also Candy and confectionery products

see also Cocoa and chocolate

see also Coffee

see also Cold storage and refrigeration

see also Dairy industry and products

see also Fish and fishing industry

see also Food and waterborne diseases

see also Food assistance

see also Food consumption

see also Food ingredients and additives

see also Food inspection

see also Food prices

see also Food stamp programs

see also Food stores

see also Food supply

see also Frozen foods

see also Fruit and fruit products

see also Grains and grain products

see also Honey and beekeeping

Food and food industry

see also Ice cream
see also Liquor and liquor industry
see also Livestock and livestock industry
see also Meat and meat products
see also Nuts
see also Oils, oilseeds, and fats
see also Packaging and containers
see also Peanuts
see also Pet food and supplies
see also Poultry industry and products
see also Restaurants and drinking places
see also Shellfish
see also Soft drink industry and products
see also Spices and herbs
see also Sugar industry and products
see also Syrups and sweeteners
see also Tea
see also Vegetables and vegetable products
see also under By Industry in the "Index by Categories"

Food and waterborne diseases

Cases and fatalities from food-borne illness, 1993 article, C2150–6.505
Sources of foodborne illness, 1993 article, C2150–6.511

State and local:

- California vital statistics, including population, births, and deaths by cause, by demographic characteristics and county, 1990 and trends, annual rpt, S0865–1
- Colorado vital statistics, including population, births, deaths by cause, abortion, marriage and divorce, and adoption, by demographic characteristics and location, 1990 and trends, annual rpt, S1010–1
- Florida deaths by selected cause, and incidence of selected communicable diseases, by county, 1992 annual rpt, S1746–1.1
- Florida vital statistics, including population, births, deaths by cause, and marriages and dissolutions, by location and demographic characteristics, 1992 and trends, annual rpt, S1745–3
- Hawaii communicable disease cases and deaths, by disease, 1986-90, annual rpt, S2065–1.4
- Idaho communicable disease morbidity, by county, 1991 and trends, annual rpt, S2250–2
- Louisiana vital statistics, including population, births, deaths by cause, reportable diseases, marriages, and divorces, by demographic characteristics and locality, 1989-90 and trends, annual rpt, S3295–1
- Maryland vital statistics, including population, births, deaths by cause, marriages, and divorces, by demographic characteristics and location, 1989 and trends, annual rpt, S3635–1
- Montana vital statistics, including births, deaths by cause, abortion, disease, and marriage and divorce, by demographic characteristics and county, 1990-91 and trends, annual rpt, S4690–1
- New Hampshire vital statistics, including population, births, deaths by cause, marriages, and divorces, by location and demographic characteristics, 1991 and trends, annual rpt, S5215–1
- New Mexico deaths by cause, and incidence of communicable diseases, by demographic characteristics, 1991 and trends, annual rpt, S5605–1.3
- New York State vital statistics, including population, births, deaths by cause, reportable diseases, and marriages and dissolutions, by demographic characteristics and/or location, 1990 and trends, annual rpt, S5765–1
- Oregon vital statistics, including communicable diseases by type, county, sex, and age, 1991 and trends, annual rpt, S6615–5
- South Carolina communicable disease cases, by county, 1990, annual rpt, S7175–1
- South Carolina deaths, by detailed cause, age, sex, and race, 1990, annual rpt, S7175–2
- South Dakota vital statistics, including births, deaths, marriage and divorce, and communicable disease, by demographic characteristics and county, 1991 and trends, annual rpt, S7345–1
- Tennessee vital statistics, including births, deaths by cause, marriages, divorces, and population, by demographic characteristics and location, 1991 and trends, annual rpt, S7520–2
- Texas vital statistics, including births, deaths by cause, abortions, marriages, and divorces, by location and demographic characteristics, 1991 and trends, annual rpt, S7685–1
- Utah vital statistics, including births and deaths by cause, by demographic characteristics and location, 1990, annual rpt, S7835–1.2
- Vermont vital statistics, including population, births, deaths by cause, abortions, marriages, and divorces, by location and demographic characteristics, 1991 and trends, annual rpt, S8054–1
- Virginia vital statistics, including births, deaths by cause, marriages and divorces, and communicable disease, by demographic characteristics and location, 1991 and trends, annual rpt, S8225–1
- Wisconsin vital statistics, including population, births, deaths by cause, and marriages and dissolutions, by county and demographic characteristics, 1991 and trends, annual rpt, S8715–4

see also Food inspection
see also under By Disease in the "Index by Categories"

Food assistance

- Catholic charity social service agency activities, clients, finances, and personnel, 1991 and trends, annual rpt, A3810–1
- Emergency food demand and availability summary, and local spending by source of funds, for 28 cities, 1991/92, annual rpt, A9330–9
- Ethiopia famine analysis, including household impacts and responses, drought factor, agricultural activity and markets, and intervention programs, 1980s, R5620–1.36
- Federal budget trends, including spending by program, State, and region, FY81-94, annual rpt, R8490–11
- Latin America statistical abstract, general data by country, 1992 annual rpt, U6250–1.28
- State funding for supplemental food program for women, infants, and children (WIC), and purchasing power, by State, FY92-93, annual rpt, R3834–9

Index by Subjects and Names

- State social, economic, and govtl indicators, with rankings, 1993 semiannual rpt, B8500–1.6
- World donations or receipts of cereals, oils, and milk, by country, 1977-89, biennial rpt, R9455–1.6

State and local:

- Alabama public health dept activities, including services provided, inspection and licensing activity, staff and finances, and vital statistics and health data, 1992 annual rpt, S0175–3
- Arizona school food service program meals served, expenditures, and value of donated commodities, by school district and county, 1991/92, annual rpt, S0470–1
- Arkansas human services dept finances and operations, including service recipient characteristics, by program, FY91 and trends, annual rpt, S0700–2
- DC statistical profile, general data, 1992 annual rpt, S1535–3.5
- Delaware year-round child/adult care food program meals and funding, 1991/92, annual rpt, S1430–1.4
- Hawaii nutrition education and supplemental food program for women and children, 1990, annual rpt, S2065–1.4
- Maryland elementary and secondary school Federal food donation value, by county, 1991/92, annual rpt, S3610–2.7
- Missouri food distribution program recipient groups, participants, and commodity value, FY92, annual rpt, S4575–2
- Nebraska food distributed to low-income families, amount and value of 25 commodities, FY92, annual rpt, S4957–1.1
- New York State food distribution program staples distributed, by county, FY90, annual rpt, U5100–1.11
- Oklahoma food donations value by target group, and meals served in elderly nutrition program, by county, FY92, annual rpt, S6455–1.2
- South Dakota social services for elderly, with recipients by race-ethnicity, FY92, annual rpt, S7385–1.1
- Tennessee statistical abstract, general data, 1992/93 annual rpt, U8710–2.18
- Tennessee value of food donated by USDA distributed to schools, by county, 1992/93, annual rpt, S7460–1
- Washington State public assistance clients and service costs, by client characteristics, program, and county, FY90, annual rpt, S8420–2
- Wisconsin State appropriations for food service for elderly, by school district, FY92, annual rpt, S8795–2

see also Food stamp programs
see also Public Law 480
see also School lunch and breakfast programs

Food consumption

- Beverage consumption, and market shares, by beverage type, 1981-92, annual article, C0125–2.504
- Beverage consumption and sales, by type, leading company, and brand, 1992 and trends, annual rpt, C4775–1.4, C4775–2.3
- Beverage consumption per capita, by type, 1979-91, annual rpt, C0125–3.1
- Beverage industry sales, consumption, and marketing devs, monthly rpt, C0125–2

Index by Subjects and Names

Catered market indicators, including types of food eaten at catered occasions, 1992 survey, article, A8200–1.503

Children's consumption of 6 food product types, by sex, 1990 survey, article, C2710–1.512

Citrus fruit per capita consumption by product type, 1981/82-1990/91, annual rpt, S1685–1.1

Commodity yearbook for 1993: detailed supply-demand data, and selected indicators for futures market investors, C2400–1

Commodity yearbook update: detailed supply-demand data, and selected indicators for futures market investors, Jan-Sept 1993 rpts, C2400–2

Consumer expenditure shares for food at-home and away-from-home, 1960s-91, article, C5225–1.507

Consumer expenditures for food store products by type, 1991-92, annual feature, C4655–1.510

Consumer nutrition awareness and health concerns, with food shopping and consumption patterns, by respondent characteristics, 1993 survey, annual rpt, A4950–36

Ethiopia famine analysis, including household impacts and responses, drought factor, agricultural activity and markets, and intervention programs, 1980s, R5620–1.36

Expenditure trends for food at home, by age group, 1990s, article, C5225–1.506

Fig industry production, acreage, and prices in California, with US consumption and imports by country, 1950s-92, annual rpt, A3750–1

Fish/seafood consumption and price trends, with comparisons to other meats, 1993 article, A8200–1.509

Food service product consumption trends, for 7 menu items, 1983 and 1992, article, C1850–3.503

Household expenditures for food away from home, by selected characteristics, 1991, article, A8200–1.507

Household expenditures for food away from home, by selected characteristics, 1991, recurring rpt, A8200–13

Household expenditures for food consumed at home, for approx 300 metro areas, 1992, annual rpt, C1200–1.511

Japan fish/shellfish production, consumption, and trade, FY83-89, article, R5650–2.506

Japan rice production and consumption, 1980-92, article, R5650–2.556

Latin America statistical abstract, general data by country, 1992 annual rpt, U6250–1.7

Meat and poultry consumption by product type, with data by foreign country, 1992 annual rpt, A2100–1

Meat and poultry consumption per capita, 1981-91, annual rpt, S1855–1

Meat consumption per capita, by type, 1940s-93, annual rpt, S8680–1

Meat consumption trends compared to GDP, by selected country or world area, 1989-91, article, C2400–1.1

Meat, poultry, fish, and dairy product consumption per capita, by type, 1971-92, annual rpt, S1685–1.3

Mexico food consumption, distribution by commodity group, 1993 article, C2150–6.509

Per capita consumption by major commodity, 1991 and trends, annual rpt, S6760–1

Restaurant (quick-service) operations, including most popular menu items, and patron age, use of promotions, and views on smoking, 1992, article, A8200–1.509

Restaurant ethnic food ordering practices of consumers, 1992 survey, C1850–3.510

Restaurant patron characteristics and attitudes, survey rpt series, A8200–8

Restaurant patron menu item preferences, overall and for persons age 55-64, 1991, article, A8200–1.506

Restaurant patronage patterns and menu item preferences, for all consumers and persons age 65/over, 1992, article, A8200–1.510

Restaurant patronage patterns, expenditures, and food preferences, 1992 survey, recurring feature, C1850–3.501

Restaurant/food service menu item popularity, 1993 survey, recurring article, C1850–3.514

Seafood consumption per capita, for top 10 species, 1992, article, C1200–5.516, C1850–3.513

Snack food consumption patterns, by snack type and consumer characteristics, 1989/90 and trends, recurring rpt, A8905–2

Snack food sales, consumption, and prices, by snack type and region, with data on industry operations and outlook, 1992 and trends, annual rpt, A8905–1

Soft drink consumption and market shares, by company and brand, and by flavor, 1985-92, annual article, C0125–2.504

Supermarket bakery and deli shopper characteristics, including expenditures, with comparisons to other outlet types, 1993 annual survey article, C5225–1.508

Supermarket bakery dept sales and performance indicators, 1992 and trends, annual article, C4655–1.505, C5225–1.504

Supermarket deli dept sales and performance indicators, 1992, annual article, C4655–1.503

Supermarket fish/seafood dept sales and performance indicators, 1991, annual article, C4655–1.501

Supermarket produce dept sales and performance indicators, 1992 and trends, annual article, C4655–1.511

Supermarket shopper attitudes, practices, and characteristics, 1993 annual rpt, C5225–1.505

Supermarket shopper practices, attitudes, and expenditures, by respondent characteristics, 1993 and trends, annual survey rpt, A4950–3

Take-out food consumer characteristics, consumption patterns, and attitudes, May 1992 survey, A8200–21

Traveler preferences for dining location, and views on hotel room service, 1992 survey article, C7000–6

Vegetable consumption, and restaurant patron salad ordering patterns, 1992 article, A8200–1.501

Food poisoning

Vegetarian food attitudes of consumers, including restaurant ordering practices, and reasons for choosing vegetarian items, 1991-92 surveys, article, A8200–1.511

Water (bottled) consumption per capita, 1982, 1987, and 1992, article, C2150–6.504

World per capita daily calories consumed in developed and developing countries, by country, 1985, R8720–1.1

World per capita protein consumption, by country, 1987-89, biennial rpt, R9455–1.5

State and local:

California dairy production, sales, marketing, and consumption, 1992 and trends, annual rpt, S0850–1.6

Florida statistical abstract, general data, 1992 annual rpt, U6660–1.9

Mississippi statistical abstract, general data, 1992 annual rpt, U3255–4.15

see also Alcohol use

see also Dieting and dietetic products

see also Food assistance

see also Nutrition and malnutrition

see also Restaurants and drinking places

see also Food stores (for industry sales data)

Food costs

see Food prices

Food expenditures

see Food consumption

Food for Peace Program

see Public Law 480

Food ingredients and additives

Food/beverage industry new product dev influences, including industry personnel views on selected ingredients, suppliers, and dev time, 1993 annual article, C2150–6.511

Supermarket shopper concerns about food ingredients and safety, 1993 and trends, annual survey rpt, A4950–3

see also Caffeine

see also Cholesterol

see also Vitamins and nutrients

Food inspection

Livestock slaughter and establishments under Federal inspection, with detail by State, 1992 annual rpt, A2100–1.1

Supermarket seafood dept support for mandatory inspection programs, 1992 annual survey feature, C4825–3.501

Wheat inspected for export, by variety and port, June 1991-May 1992, annual rpt, A7310–1

State and local:

Hawaii environmental quality and public health control, inspection, licensing, and enforcement activities, 1990, annual rpt, S2065–1.6

North Carolina livestock slaughtering establishments under Federal inspection, Jan 1991-92, annual rpt, S5885–1

Utah agriculture dept inspections of food and dairy establishments, and produce, 1991, annual rpt, S7800–1

Vermont agricultural production, marketing, and finances, by commodity, with data on govt inspections and funding, 1989-90 biennial rpt, S7978–1

see also Food and waterborne diseases

Food poisoning

see Food and waterborne diseases

Food prices

Food prices

Artificial sweetener prices, with comparison to sugar, by sweetener, 1992/93 annual rpt, C0125–3.2

Consumer and food industry personnel price expectations, 1993 annual rpt, C5225–1.505

Cost-of-living indexes and retail prices for selected consumer items in approx 300 cities, quarterly rpt, A0150–1

Ethiopia famine analysis, including household impacts and responses, drought factor, agricultural activity and markets, and intervention programs, 1980s, R5620–1.36

Forecast food price changes, by selected commodity, 1992-93, article, C1200–5.502

Ice cream retail price and worktime required to purchase half gallon, 1982-92, annual rpt, A5825–1.1

Latin America statistical abstract, general data by country, 1992 annual rpt, U6250–1.31

Meat and poultry wholesale and retail prices, by item, 1991 and trends, annual rpt, A2100–1.1

Restaurant menu trends, with data on entree prices, 1987 and 1992, A8200–22

Snack food sales, consumption, and prices, by snack type and region, with data on industry operations and outlook, 1992 and trends, annual rpt, A8905–1

Supermarket prices for selected grocery items in 4-7 chains in 7 metro areas, Apr 1993, article, C4655–1.507

Wholesale food prices for selected commodities, 1992-93, annual article, A8200–1.503

State and local:

Alaska cost-of-living indicators for selected items and local areas, with comparisons to other US cities, 1992 annual article, S0320–1.501

Hawaii data book, general data, 1992 annual rpt, S2090–1.14, S2090–1.22

see also Agricultural prices

see also Consumer Price Index

Food shortage

see Food supply

see Nutrition and malnutrition

Food stamp programs

Convenience stores accepting food stamps, 1992, annual survey rpt, A6735–1

Participants as percent of population, by State, FY91, annual rpt, S2623–1.4

Payments and recipients for selected Federal entitlement programs, by State and region, early 1990s, R8490–47

Poor children age 5/under in families receiving food stamps, by family type, 1990-91, annual rpt, U1260–2

State social, economic, and govtl indicators, with rankings, 1993 semiannual rpt, B8500–1.6, B8500–1.8

Statistical profiles of 50 States and DC, general data, 1993 annual almanac, C4712–1

State and local:

Alabama public welfare and social service cases, recipients, and payments, by program and county, monthly rpt, S0150–1

Arizona public assistance recipients and payments, by program, county, and district, monthly rpt, S0465–4

Arkansas human services dept finances and operations, including Medicaid payments by type of service, FY91 and trends, annual rpt, S0700–2.3

California public welfare cases, recipients, and expenditures, by program and county, monthly rpt, S0935–2

DC statistical profile, general data, 1992 annual rpt, S1535–3.5

Delaware public assistance recipients, funds available, and payments, by program, with selected data by county, monthly rpt, S1385–1

Georgia county guide, general data, 1993 annual rpt, U6750–1

Georgia statistical abstract, general data, 1992-93 biennial rpt, U6730–1.1

Hawaii data book, general data, 1992 annual rpt, S2090–1.11

Idaho public welfare program expenditures and recipients, with data by county, quarterly rpt, S2250–1

Indiana public assistance program participation, expenditures, and services, by county, FY92 and trends, annual rpt, S2623–1

Kansas statistical abstract, general data, 1991/92 annual rpt, U7095–2.6

Louisiana labor market info, including population receiving AFDC and food stamps, by area, 1992, annual planning rpt, S3320–1.2

Maryland statistical abstract, general data, 1993-94 biennial rpt, S3605–1.6

Maryland welfare program statistics, and welfare fraud investigations, by county, monthly rpt, S3645–2

Michigan public assistance program cases, recipients, and payments, detailed data by county, monthly rpt, S4010–1

Minnesota public welfare program recipients and expenditures, by county, 1992, semiannual rpt, S4202–1

Mississippi public welfare and social service cases, recipients, and payments, by program and county, FY92, annual rpt, S4357–1

Missouri public welfare and medical assistance recipients, expenditures, and case processing, by program and county, FY92 and trends, annual rpt, S4575–2

Montana welfare and medical assistance program cases and payments, by county and type of service, monthly rpt, S4755–1

Nebraska public welfare cases, recipients, and payments, by program and county, FY92 and trends, annual rpt, S4957–1

Nevada statistical abstract, general data, 1992 biennial rpt, S5005–1.2

New Jersey public welfare cases, recipients, payments, and case processing, by program and county or city, monthly rpt, S5415–1

New Mexico food stamp recipients, by county, Jan 1993, annual planning rpt, S5624–1

New Mexico public assistance cases, expenditures, and case processing, by program and county, monthly rpt, S5620–2

New York State food stamp statistics, by State area, 1991 and trends, annual rpt, S5800–2.3

North Carolina public welfare programs, cases, recipients, staff, and finances, by county, 1st half FY93, semiannual rpt, S5940–2

Oklahoma food stamp recipients and value of coupons issued, by county, FY92, annual rpt, S6455–1.2

Oregon public welfare caseloads, recipients, and expenditures, by program, city, county, and State region, monthly rpt, S6615–8

South Carolina public welfare recipients, payments, and case processing, by county and program, monthly rpt, S7252–1

South Dakota welfare and social services recipients and payments, by program, MSA, and county, FY92, annual rpt, S7385–1

Tennessee statistical abstract, general data, 1992/93 annual rpt, U8710–2.18

Texas welfare and social services program expenditures, recipients, and fraud cases, by county and/or program, FY92 and trends, annual rpt, S7695–1

Utah govt statistical review, fiscal and socioeconomic data, 1993 annual rpt, R9380–1.9

West Virginia welfare and social service program caseloads and expenditures, by county, monthly rpt, S8560–2

Wyoming welfare and social service recipients and expenditures, by program and county, FY92, annual rpt, S8908–1

Food stocks

see Agricultural stocks

see Food supply

Food stores

Advertising on grocery carts, reactions of marketing professionals and general public, Oct 1992 surveys, article, C2710–1.512

Bakery dept sales and performance indicators, 1992 and trends, annual article, C4655–1.505, C5225–1.504

Beverage off-premises market share held by grocery stores, by beverage type, 1986-91, annual rpt, C4775–1.4, C4775–2.3

Compensation of food marketing mgmt personnel by position, by company sales size and region, year ended Mar 1993, annual survey, A4950–6

Consumer buying power survey of population, income, and sales by kind of business, by census div, State, MSA, county, and city, 1992, annual rpt, C1200–1.511

Consumer buying power survey of population, income, and sales by product line, by State, metro area, county, and census div, 1993 annual rpt, C1200–1.514

Consumer household characteristics, for shoppers of wholesale membership clubs vs supermarkets, 1992 survey, article, C2710–1.511

Consumer nutrition awareness and health concerns, with food shopping and consumption patterns, by respondent characteristics, 1993 survey, annual rpt, A4950–36

Credit card (Visa) charges at food stores, 1990-92, article, C2710–1.507

Credit card acceptance by supermarkets, 1991 and 1993, article, C0500–1.506

Index by Subjects and Names — Football

Deli dept sales and performance indicators, 1992 and trends, annual article, C5225–1.505

Deli dept sales and performance indicators, 1992, annual article, C4655–1.503

Discount chain sales and merchandising, including data by dept, leading chain, and location, 1992 and trends, annual feature, C8130–1.507

Employees admitting they had eaten food without paying, stolen merchandise, and observed theft by coworkers, 1993 feature, C1850–12.502

Expansion devs, and equipment and construction costs, by type of retail chain, 1993 annual articles, C5150–4.507

Financial and operating data for retail and wholesale marketers, by company size and region, 1991-92, annual rpts, A4950–5

Financial data and business info for approx 240 US and Canadian retail chains, 1991-92 and trends, annual rpt, C3400–2

Financial performance and growth rankings for approx 1,000 top corporations, with comparisons by industry group, 1993 annual rpt, C3950–1.505

Financial ratios and performance, for over 350 SIC 4-digit industries, FY88-92, annual rpt, A6400–3

Franchise operations and finances, by type of business, 1991/92 and trends, annual rpt, A5820–1

General merchandise dept sales and performance indicators, 1992 and trends, annual article, C4655–1.509

Health and beauty aid dept sales and performance indicators, 1992 and trends, annual article, C4655–1.506

Market shares and outlets, by company and store type, for approx 350 metro areas in US and Canada, with industry operating data, 1993 annual rpt, C3400–6

Marketing in-store techniques effectiveness as seen by retailers, 1993 article, C2710–1.526

Markets with daily newspapers, demographic and economic info by geographic area, US and Canada, 1993 annual rpt, C3250–1

Meat dept sales and performance indicators, 1992 and trends, annual article, C4655–1.509

Mgmt info system operations of food retailers and wholesalers, including employment and finances, by company sales size, 1993 and trends, annual survey, A4950–7

Microwaveable food sales in supermarkets, by product category, 1st half 1992, article, C2150–6.510

Military post exchange and commissary sales, by product category, for military resale agencies, FY91 and trends, annual rpt, A2072–1

Military post exchange and commissary sales, by service branch or region, with merchandising devs and comparisons to civilian retail trade, monthly rpt, C0500–1

Operating and financial composite ratios for corporations, with establishments and receipts, for approx 200 industries, by asset size, FY90, annual rpt, C7800–1

Operating and marketing devs, monthly rpt, C5225–1

Pharmacies in stores of top supermarket chains, 1993 annual feature, C5150–2.511

Private label product merchandising trends, with retailer views, consumer practices, and supermarket sales shares, 1993 article, C8130–1.504

Private label product sales shares in supermarkets, with sales for top 15 product categories, 1992 article, C1850–1.502

Sales and consumer expenditures, for food store products by type, 1991-92, annual feature, C4655–1.510

Sales and establishments, and growth outlook, for food service industry by market segment, 1993 annual feature, C1850–3.503

Sales and market shares for private label products and top 4 brands in 6 product categories, 1992, article, C2710–1.521

Sales and merchandising trends for health and beauty aid products, by product type, 1992 annual feature, C5150–2.503

Sales, operations, business outlook, and structure of food store industry, by type of store, 1993 annual rpt, C5225–1.505

Sales volume shares by retail outlet type, for approx 300 food, drug, and other product categories, 1993 annual feature, C4655–1.504

Seafood dept sales and performance indicators, 1992 annual survey feature, C4825–3.501

Shopping center financial and operating data, with detail by type of tenant, US and Canada, 1991, triennial rpt, R9285–1

Store-brand products image trends and outlook among retailers/wholesalers, 1992 survey, article, C2710–1.508

Supermarket (independent) sales and operating ratios, by store type, sales size, and region, 1991, annual survey, A4950–4

Supermarket industry composite financial ratios, 1991/92 and trends, annual rpt, A4950–1

Supermarket industry devs, product sales, merchandising, and store finances, monthly rpt, C4655–1

Supermarket product sales and market shares, for top brands in selected product categories, weekly rpt monthly table, C2710–1

Supermarket sales by detailed product type, 1992 and trends, annual feature, C5225–1.507

Supermarket sales of nonfood products, by detailed product type, 1992, annual feature, C5225–1.508

Supermarket shopper practices, attitudes, and expenditures, by respondent characteristics, 1993 and trends, annual survey rpt, A4950–3

Supermarket shopper views on quality of customer service and importance of selected factors, by respondent characteristics, 1991-92 surveys, A4950–37

Supermarkets opened, remodeled, and closed, including store features, dev costs, and rent, by region and sales size, 1992 and trends, annual rpt, A4950–2

Take-out food consumer characteristics, consumption patterns, and attitudes, May 1992 survey, A8200–21

Women's use of 6 types of supermarket promotions, 1988 and 1992, survey article, C1200–4.507

State and local:

Hawaii data book, general data, 1992 annual rpt, S2090–1.23

Maine employment in trade, utilities, and transportation SIC 2-digit industries, by detailed occupation, 2nd qtr 1991, triennial rpt, S3465–1.25

North Carolina employment in trade, transportation, communications, utilities, govt, and education, by detailed occupation, 2nd qtr 1991, triennial rpt, S5917–5.2

Texas trade, transportation, and public utilities employment, by SIC 2- and 3-digit industry and detailed occupation, 2nd qtr 1991, triennial survey rpt, S7675–1.31

see also Convenience stores

Food supply

Fish and fishery product contribution to food supply, by country, 1986-88, biennial rpt, R9455–1.7

Latin America statistical abstract, general data by country, 1992 annual rpt, U6250–1.7

World food and agricultural policies and issues, with focus on developing countries, series, R5620–1

World per capita calories available as percent of need, by country, 1987-89, biennial rpt, R9455–1.5

see also Agricultural production

see also Agricultural stocks

see also Nutrition and malnutrition

Foot health and diseases

see Podiatry

Football

Broadcast (TV and radio) coverage and rights payments to college and professional football teams, 1993 annual article, C1850–14.534

College football bowl games, payments to participating teams, 1992/93, annual feature, C2175–1.503

High school sports all-time records for boys and girls events, with school and student participation for 1991/92, annual rpt, A7830–2

Higher education student athlete enrollment and graduation rates, by sex, race-ethnicity, and major sport, for Natl Collegiate Athletic Assn Div I instns, 1992/93, annual rpt, A7440–4

Natl Football League team revenues from local and natl sources, expenses including player costs, and profit, 1991, article, C5800–7.514

Participation in 53 sports, by demographic characteristics, State, and census div, 1992, annual rpt series, A8485–3

Super Bowl TV advertising airtime and costs for 6 advertisers, Jan 1993, article, C5800–7.512

TV Super Bowl XXVII advertising units purchased, for 15 major advertisers, Jan 1993, article, C2710–1.509

TV Super Bowl XXVII broadcast time devoted to game vs commercials, Jan 1993, article, C2710–1.512

Football

State and local:
Hawaii data book, general data, 1992 annual rpt, S2090–1.7

Footwear
see Shoes and shoe industry

Forage
see Pasture and rangeland

Forecasts
see Business outlook and attitude surveys
see Energy projections
see Population projections
see Projections and forecasts

Foreclosures
Delinquency and foreclosure rates, and residential loans serviced, by type, State, and census div and region, quarterly rpt, A6450–1
Home equity lending activity and practices of financial instns, by region, asset size, and instn type, 1992, annual rpt, A4160–3
Mortgage foreclosure rate 5-year projection, with detail for 43 metro areas or regions in rank order, 1993 article, A6450–2.509
Mortgage foreclosure rates, 1987-88 and quarterly 1989-91, article, A6450–2.505

State and local:
Arizona statistical abstract, general data, 1993 recurring rpt, U5850–2.15
Hawaii data book, general data, 1992 annual rpt, S2090–1.21
Hawaii tax dept mortgage foreclosure cases closed, and related amounts collected, FY92, annual rpt, S2120–1
Ohio court cases and dispositions involving foreclosure, by county, 1992, annual rpt, S6385–1

Foreign affairs
see Foreign relations

Foreign agriculture
China industrial and agricultural production, and foreign trade and investment, with detail for leading commodities, 1980s-92, annual feature, A9315–1.504
Citrus fruit production in selected countries, by type of fruit, 1987/88-1991/92, annual rpt, S1685–1.1
Commodity yearbook for 1993: agricultural production, acreage, stocks, marketing, and operating data, including by country, C2400–1
Commodity yearbook update: agricultural production, acreage, stocks, marketing, and operating data, including by country, Jan-Sept 1993 rpts, C2400–2
Cotton and wool production by world region and country, and consumption and trade, 1950s-92, annual article, C3460–1.502
Dominican Republic Agricultural Dev Bank loan repayment performance, by borrower characteristics, 1993 article, U1380–4
EC agricultural productivity, farmers, farmland, and distribution of common agricultural fund payments, by country, 1986-90, R5025–9
Japan rice production and consumption, 1980-92, article, R5650–2.556
Latin America statistical abstract, general data by country, 1992 annual rpt, U6250–1.2, U6250–1.12, U6250–1.24, U6250–1.32
Russia production of meat, milk, eggs, and wool, 1976-91, U2030–1.503
Soviet Union livestock inventories, monthly rpt recurring feature, U2030–1.503

Soviet Union private farms, by Republic, Aug 1992, recurring feature, U2030–1.503
Soybean production and marketing data, including utilization, prices, and trade, with comparison to other oilseeds, 1920s-93, annual rpt, B8480–1
Wheat supply-demand summary for leading producing countries, 1987/88-1992/93, annual rpt, A7310–1
World agriculture indicators, including production, equipment, livestock, and food supply, by country, 1992/93 biennial rpt, R9455–1.6
World food and agricultural policies and issues, with focus on developing countries, series, R5620–1
see also Agricultural exports and imports

Foreign assistance
see International assistance

Foreign budgets
Developing countries govt spending for health, education, and defense, with total budget and detail for family planning by program, by country, 1980s-90, R8720–1.1
GDP reductions budgeted in US and 5 European countries, 1st half 1993, article, C5800–7.505
Japan economic profile, including govt finances, industrial production, foreign trade and investments, and comparisons to US, 1988-92, annual feature, R5650–2.552
Japan govt budget outlays by function and revenues by source, FY92-93, annual article, R5650–2.510
Japan govt budget surplus as percent of GDP, with comparisons to US, Germany, and OECD, 1989-93, article, R5650–2.546
Japan govt financial condition, including account budgets, expenditures, and revenues, FY93 and trends, annual article, R5650–2.526
Japan govt general account fiscal stimulus plan and supplemental budget, and fiscal investment/loan program supplements, FY93, article, R5650–2.535
Japan govt R&D expenditures, by agency, FY92, article, C1850–6.504
Japan govt spending proposed in Apr 1993 economic stimulus plan, by function, 1993 article, C5800–7.525
Japan govt supplemental budget, and tax revenue forecasts, FY92, article, R5650–2.503
Latin America statistical abstract, general data by country, 1992 annual rpt, U6250–1.7, U6250–1.30
Mexico govt income from oil, and allocation by function, 1980-81, annual rpt, U6250–1.23
Public investment outlays share of GNP, for US, Japan, Germany, and other industrial countries, 1960-89, R4700–23
Venezuela presidential decrees compared with govt expenditures, 1958-83, U6250–1.22
World financial market devs including economic and monetary trends and forecasts for 15 industrial countries, bimonthly rpt, B6200–2

Index by Subjects and Names

Foreign competition
Coal industry executive views on foreign competitors and exporting mining technology to developing countries, Mar 1993 survey, article, C5226–1.511
Hard goods industry foreign competition, and manufacturers and representatives views on trade issues, by product line, 1993 annual survey rpt, A1800–1
Indicators of US competitiveness vs other major industrial countries, including investments, productivity, exports, and per capita GDP, 1993 annual rpt, A4475–1
Japan vs US company US market shares in construction and computer chip equipment, and motor vehicles, 1989-92, article, C5800–7.531
Manufacturing executive views on improving company global competitiveness, including mgmt strategies and human resource issues, spring 1993 survey, U9640–4
Semiconductor market trends in Japan and US, with shares for Japanese and US companies by customer and product type, 1993 article, C1850–2.509
Steel service center foreign steel competition, monthly survey, A8990–2
see also Dumping
see also Foreign trade
see also Tariffs and foreign trade controls
see also Trade adjustment assistance

Foreign corporations
Advertising agency income, billings by medium, employees, and offices, for leading US and/or foreign agencies, 1992 and trends, annual rpt, C2710–1.522
Advertising budget, and prospective and current ad agencies, for selected foreign accounts, weekly rpt recurring feature, C2710–1.504
Advertising budgets, and prospective and current ad agencies, for selected foreign accounts, weekly rpt recurring feature, C2710–1.509, C2710–1.513, C2710–1.517, C2710–1.523, C2710–1.527, C2710–1.532, C2710–1.536, C2710–1.545, C2710–1.549
Aerospace and defense industries financial performance, with data for approx 200 major US and foreign companies, FY92 and trends, annual feature, C5800–4.519
Airline industry devs including passenger and cargo traffic activity and fuel costs, with worldwide passenger traffic, by carrier, monthly rpt, C7000–4
Airline market activity, including traffic, financial performance, employment, and fleet composition, by US and foreign carrier, 1991-92, annual feature, C7000–4.508
Australia chemical production capacity for 7 major producers of petrochemicals and polymers, 1993 article, A1250–1.531
Auto news and devs, with production and sales data and market analysis, US and foreign, by manufacturer and make/model, weekly rpt, C2710–3
Bank assets, equity, performance, and market value, top 50 instns worldwide, 1993 annual feature, C5800–7.535
Bank assets, for top 12 instns worldwide, 1992, article, C5800–7.529
Canada home improvement sales and outlets, for 4-5 leading retail chains and buying groups, 1992, articles, C5150–6.508

Index by Subjects and Names

Foreign corporations

Chemical and related industries production, finances, operating ratios, employment, and trade, by country, company, and chemical, 1980s-92, annual feature, A1250–1.530

Chemical company sales and profits, for top 50 producers worldwide, 1992, annual article, A1250–1.533

Computer software company revenues and employment, for top 100 firms worldwide, 1992, annual article, C1850–5.520

Computer/info systems companies revenues and other financial data, for top 100 firms worldwide and in North America, 1992 and trends, annual rpt, C1850–5.514

Construction design firms foreign billings, specialties, and work locations, for top 200 intl firms, 1992, annual article, C5800–2.538

Construction intl companies foreign and total contract values, and work locations, for top 225 firms, 1992, annual feature, C5800–2.542

Corporate mergers, acquisitions, and divestitures, with prices, payment methods, and characteristics of participants, 1992 and trends, annual rpt, B6020–1

Czechoslovakia chemical production by product, and sales, exports, and employment of leading firms, by Republic, 1990-92, article, A1250–1.509

Europe airline revenues and govt ownership share, for 8 major carriers, 1992 article, C8900–1.501

Europe airline revenues and market shares, for 8 major carriers, 1991, article, C5800–4.512

Europe chemical company earnings trends, for 12 companies, 1st-2nd half 1992, article, A1250–1.517

Europe companies acquired by US companies, and transaction value, for top 10 transactions, 1984-92, C1575–2.506

Europe construction industry domestic and foreign mergers/acquisitions, for 23 Eastern and Western European countries, 1992 article, C5800–2.507

Europe corporate acquisitions activity by country and industry, and price and participants for top transactions, 1992 and trends, annual article, C4683–1.504

Europe electronics industry financial performance, for top 50 companies, FY91 or FY92, annual article, C1850–2.501

Europe retail clothing chain stores and sales, for 5 major chains, 1993 article, C2710–1.517

Financial data for 500 largest foreign companies, 1993 annual feature, C3950–1.519

Fortune magazine ranking of top 50-100 companies worldwide in 8 nonindustrial sectors, with financial and employment data, 1993 annual feature, C8900–1.522

Fortune 500 largest industrial corporations worldwide, with financial and employment data, 1992, annual feature, C8900–1.520

France public relations firms with US ties, including data on fees and staff, by company, 1993 article, A8770–1.503

Germany telecommunication passive optical network locations and subscribers, for 4 contractors, 1993, article, C4725–3.513

Germany vs US corporations market value and employment, for 2-3 major companies in 5 industries, 1993 article, A5135–2.1

Home improvement industry sales, stores, and other operating data, for leading foreign chains by country, 1991-92, annual feature, C5150–6.503

Home improvement stores and sales, for 10 major chains in US and Europe, 1993 article, C5150–6.507

Insurance, foreign surplus lines companies trust funds on deposit in US, by company, Dec 1991, annual rpt, S7466–1

Israel company stock performance, sales, and market value, for 14 firms traded on US exchanges, 1993 article, C3950–1.523

Italy oil refinery capacity and throughput, by company and plant, 1990-91 or 1992, article, C6985–1.523

Italy property/casualty insurance industry loss ratios for 4 lines of coverage, 1990-91, article, C1050–1.505

Japan auto manufacturer US auto parts purchases, and auto production in US and Canada compared to US firms, with selected detail by company and plant, 1993 article, R5650–2.523

Japan bank market capitalization trends for 14 major instns, Apr 1992-June 1993, article, C2710–2.515

Japan bank profits and nonperforming loans, for 21 leading instns, FY92, article, R5650–2.533

Japan defense budget allocations by equipment type, procurement, and value of contracts for top 10 contractors, various periods FY82-95, article, R5650–2.518

Japan defense contract value for top 10 contractors, FY91-92, article, R5650–2.533

Japan machine tool manufacturer sales, and income or loss, for 6 leading companies, FY93, article, C7000–7.504

Japan steel sheet dumping margins in US, for 4 leading and all other companies, 1993 article, R5650–2.512, R5650–2.539

Latin America statistical abstract, general data by country, 1992 annual rpt, U6250–1.29

Market value of top 100 firms in developing countries, by company, 1993 annual feature, C5800–7.536

Market value of top 1,000 firms worldwide, with related financial data, by company and country, 1993 annual feature, C5800–7.536

Mergers and acquisitions, and other transactions involving US and/or foreign companies, bimonthly rpt, C4683–1

Mexico bank profit indicators, for 2 major instns, with comparisons to aggregate large US banks, 1992, C5800–7.545

Mexico for-hire motor carriers, by State, 1980-92, U8850–9

NASDAQ over-the-counter securities trading volume and prices for leading foreign issues, and financial profile of typical foreign issuer, 1993 annual rpt, A7105–1

Oil and gas industry financial and operating data, rankings for top 300 US and top 100 non-US companies, 1991-92, annual feature, C6985–1.547

Oil and gas industry trends, with data by company, State, and country, 1993 annual compilation, C6985–4

Oil and gas intl supply-demand, exploration, refining, reserves, and industry finances, basic data by country and company, 1993 annual rpt, C6985–3

Oil exploration/production expenditures of US and foreign companies in US, Canada, and elsewhere, 1972-93, annual article, C6985–1.515

Oil refinery capacity worldwide, by process, with data by country, company, and US State, 1992 annual feature, C6985–1.508

Pakistan insurance industry underwriting data, with operating results for 2 major companies, 1990-91, annual article, C1050–1.504

Pension fund assets, for top 300 funds worldwide, 1992, annual feature, C2710–2.515

Plastics production capacity for specified resins, by major company and world region, monthly rpt recurring table, C5800–12.502, C5800–12.507

Pulp and paper industry operations and finances, US and Canada, with detail by company and product grade, and world production and trade summary, 1993 annual rpt, C3975–5

Retail general merchandise chain sales, earnings, and stores, for top companies worldwide, with detail for selected areas, 1991-92, annual feature, C5150–3.516

Spain chemical process industry sales and employment of top 15 companies, and production capacity and utilization of major chemicals, 1991, article, C5800–8.511

Spain insurance premiums for 10 leading underwriting groups, 1992, annual article, C1050 1.510

Spain, Madrid stock exchange performance by industry sector, and 20 leading stocks with greatest gains or losses, 1992, article, A8955–1.502

Spain market conditions for 15 industries judged to be good prospects for US investment, 1992 feature, A8955–1.501

Steel industry restructuring devs, with data on production, employment, and worker assistance, and selected detail by company, for 8-12 countries, 1970s-90, R9260–16

Telephone company stock prices and returns after privatization, for 12 foreign firms, 1993 article, C2710–2.516

Travel and tourism rankings for selected indicators, including data for top 20 States, cities, countries, businesses, and other measures, 1992 recurring rpt, R9375–6

UK oil revenue tax impact on oil companies operating in North Sea, by company, 1993-96, article, C6985–1.525

State and local:

California foreign bank offices, with financial condition, by instn and hq country, Dec 1992, annual rpt, S0810–1

Florida foreign bank offices and assets, by hq country, Dec 1990-91, annual rpt, U6660–1.17

Georgia intl bank agencies and assets in State, 1992, annual rpt, S1865–1

Foreign corporations

Hawaii data book, general data, 1992 annual rpt, S2090–1.15

Illinois, assets of foreign banks licensed in State, by instn, FY92, annual rpt, S2395–1

Maryland insurance industry financial and underwriting data, by company and type of insurance, with regulatory info, 1991, annual rpt, S3655–1

Michigan insurance industry financial and underwriting data, by company and type of insurance, with regulatory info, 1991, annual rpt, S3983–1

New Jersey insurance industry financial and underwriting data, by company and type of insurance, 1990, annual rpt, S5420–1

New York State foreign banking corporation assets and liabilities, for State chartered agencies and branches, 1988-90, annual rpt, U5100–1.7

New York State insurance industry financial and underwriting data, by company and line of coverage, 1991, annual rpt, S5770–2

Utah new corporations, by type, 1950-91, triennial rpt, U8960–1.15

Washington State banks and other financial instns, financial condition by type of instn, 1992 and trends, annual rpt, S8325–1

Wisconsin Blue Book, general data, 1993-94 biennial rpt, S8780–1.2

see also Foreign competition

see also Foreign investments

see also Multinational corporations

Foreign countries

Aircraft (turbine-powered) in service and on order, by manufacturer and model, for over 900 airlines worldwide, Dec 1992, annual rpt, B3370–1

Catholic population, clergy, instns, missionaries, and religious order membership, US and worldwide, 1993 annual almanac, C6885–1

Energy exploration, rotary drilling rigs in operation, by world area and country, monthly rpt, B4675–1

Financial market devs worldwide, including economic and monetary trends and forecasts for 15 industrial countries, bimonthly rpt, B6200–2

Hard goods US manufacturer use of foreign materials and components, by product line, 1993 annual survey rpt, A1800–1

Law school US grad employment, for grads employed in foreign areas, 1992, annual rpt, A6505–1

Motor vehicle world production, sales, trade, and registrations, by country, world area, manufacturer, and make, 1991 and trends, annual rpt, A0865–2

Oil and gas industry intl exploration, drilling, production, refining, stock, price, and financial data, weekly rpt, C6985–1

Oil and gas intl supply-demand, exploration, refining, reserves, and industry finances, basic data by country and company, 1993 annual rpt, C6985–3

Refugees, resettlement, and intl aid devs, by country, 1992, annual rpt, R9372–1

Telephone service worldwide, including access lines by type, and intl calling patterns, with comparisons to population, by world area and country, 1990-91, annual rpt, B0350–1

Travel and tourism trends in US and worldwide, with traveler and trip characteristics, and data by local area, 1992 annual rpt, C2140–1

see also Africa

see also Asia

see also Balance of payments

see also Caribbean area

see also Central America

see also Centrally planned economies

see also Developing countries

see also Eastern Europe

see also Europe

see also Foreign agriculture

see also Foreign budgets

see also Foreign competition

see also Foreign corporations

see also Foreign debts

see also Foreign economic relations

see also Foreign exchange

see also Foreign investments

see also Foreign labor conditions

see also Foreign languages

see also Foreign legislative bodies

see also Foreign medical graduates

see also Foreign relations

see also Foreign students

see also Foreign trade

see also Foreign trade promotion

see also International assistance

see also International cooperation in cultural activities

see also International cooperation in environmental sciences

see also International cooperation in science and technology

see also International finance

see also Middle East

see also North America

see also Oceania

see also South America

see also Southeast Asia

see also Treaties and conventions

see also under By Foreign Country or World Area in the "Index by Categories"

see also under names of individual countries

Foreign debts

Debt of foreign countries to US, by country and world region, FY54-92, annual rpt, R9050–1.3

Developing countries debt acquisition in exchange for conservation program funding, summary of programs in 11 countries including participating organizations, Nov 1991, biennial rpt, R9455–1.6

Latin America statistical abstract, general data by country, 1992 annual rpt, U6250–1.28, U6250–1.30, U6250–1.33

World external debt indicators, by country, 1979, 1984, and 1989, biennial rpt, R9455–1.5

see also Balance of payments

see also Public debt

Foreign economic relations

Germany and US commercial and economic trends and policies, with comparative statistics, 1993 annual compilation, A5135–2

Japan economic issues and devs, relations with US, and trade, balance of payments, and economic indicators, weekly rpt, R5650–2

Public interest in news items on Group of 7 (G-7) countries economic conference in Tokyo, July/Aug 1993 survey, C8915–1.504

Spain business activities and trade relations with US, quarterly rpt, A8955–1

see also Agricultural exports and imports

see also Arms trade

see also Balance of payments

see also Dumping

see also East-West trade

see also Eurocurrency

see also Foreign corporations

see also Foreign debts

see also Foreign exchange

see also Foreign investments

see also Foreign trade

see also Foreign trade promotion

see also International assistance

see also International finance

see also Military assistance

see also Multinational corporations

see also Tariffs and foreign trade controls

see also Trade agreements

see also Treaties and conventions

Foreign exchange

Business Week economic indicators, including exchange rates for selected currencies, weekly rpt, C5800–7

Commodity yearbook for 1993: detailed supply-demand data, and selected indicators for futures market investors, C2400–1

Commodity yearbook update: detailed supply-demand data, and selected indicators for futures market investors, Jan-Sept 1993 rpts, C2400–2

Dollar exchange rates for approx 30 countries, monthly rpt, A7400–3

Electronics manufacturer currency forwards/options purchases, for 3 companies, 1992, article, C1850–2.510

Forecasts of Federal Reserve trade-weighted index for the dollar, monthly rpt, U1880–3

Futures and options contract open interest (outstanding commitments), on foreign exchanges, by commodity and exchange, monthly rpt, A5040–6

Futures and options trading volume by commodity and exchange, 1988-92, annual rpt, A5040–1

Futures and options trading volume on foreign exchanges, by commodity and exchange, monthly rpt, A5040–5

Futures contract open interest (outstanding commitments), by commodity and exchange, monthly rpt, A5040–4

Futures trading volume by commodity and exchange, monthly rpt, A5040–2

Germany (West) and US comparative socioeconomic statistics, 1970s-91, annual rpt, A5135–2.2

Japan economic profile, including govt finances, industrial production, foreign trade and investments, and comparisons to US, 1988-92, annual feature, R5650–2.552

Japan-US exchange rate, weekly rpt quarterly table, R5650–2.506, R5650–2.519, R5650–2.541, R5650–2.558

Japan yen exchange rates with US dollar and 8 other currencies, 1992 and trends, annual article, R5650–2.511

Latin America statistical abstract, general data by country, 1992 annual rpt, U6250–1.30

Index by Subjects and Names

Foreign investments

Money and securities market activity, and related indicators, biweekly rpt, B2000–1 Options trading volume by commodity, securities index, and exchange, monthly rpt, A5040–3 World financial market devs including economic and monetary trends and forecasts for 15 industrial countries, bimonthly rpt, B6200–2

State and local:

Maryland foreign exchange licensed agents, 1990-91, annual rpt, S3655–2

see also Balance of payments

see also Eurocurrency

Foreign investments

- Asset composition for 6 institutional investor categories, 1970-2nd qtr 1992, article, A8825–1.504
- Bank (master trust/custodial) assets and operating data for top instns, 1993 annual directory, C2710–2.522
- Bank deposits, percent foreign held, top 100 instns, 1992, annual feature, C5800–7.526
- Business firms with foreign owners, by State, 1982, annual almanac, C4712–1
- Chemical and related industries production, finances, operating ratios, employment, and trade, by country, company, and chemical, 1980s-92, annual feature, A1250–1.530
- Chemical industry and total manufacturing foreign investment in US and US investment abroad, 1970 and 1980-92, annual rpt, A3850–1
- Chemical industry capital spending, US and worldwide, for 19 US and 6 European companies, 1988-93, annual article, A1250–1.508
- Chile corporate investments in other Latin American countries, for 8 firms, 1993 article, C5800–7.544
- China business review, including trade with US and other countries, and economic activity, bimonthly rpt, A9315–1
- China, Guangdong Province foreign investment contracted and utilized, 1985 and 1990-92, A9315–1.505
- China industrial and agricultural production, and foreign trade and investment, with detail for leading commodities, 1980s-92, annual feature, A9315–1.504
- China offshore oil and gas exploration activity, including foreign investments, 1982-92, annual rpt, C6985–3.1
- China oil exploration joint venture contracts, with location, land area, and participating companies, 1993 article, C6985–1.550
- Cities rated as best for business by Fortune magazine, socioeconomic profiles of top 60 metro areas, 1992 annual article, C8900–1.501
- Construction contract values, total and foreign, with rankings of top 400 contractors, 1992, annual rpt, C5800–2.529
- Construction mgmt firm total and foreign contract values for top 100 firms, and employee compensation by position, 1992 and trends, annual article, C5800–2.533
- Corporate intl acquisitions and value, with detail by selected country and for 19 major deals involving German firms, 1991-92 and trends, article, A5135–2.1
- Corporate mergers, acquisitions, and divestitures, with prices, payment methods, and characteristics of participants, 1992 and trends, annual rpt, B6020–1
- Corporate mergers, acquisitions, and other agreements involving US companies, by SIC code, bimonthly rpt quarterly feature, C4683–1
- Czechoslovakia chemical and aggregate leading industries investments of US and 5 European countries, 1992, article, A1250–1.520
- Direct foreign investment inflows, for 10 developed and 10 emerging countries, 1991, annual feature, C8900–1.520
- Direct investment abroad for 5 countries, and intracompany vs intercompany trade for US, EC, and Japan, 1993 article, C8900–1.520
- Direct investment and employment of US firms, for 10 foreign countries, 1970s-91, article, C8900–1.504
- Eastern Europe foreign investments from 7 leading countries, 12 months ended Sept 1992, article, C5800–7.511
- Eastern Europe public opinion on good vs bad influence of foreign investors, for 6 countries, 1991 survey, C8915–8.2
- EC investments between member countries and from rest of world, with data by country and industry sector, 1992 rpt, R5025–9
- Economic characteristics and dev goals of local areas that solicit foreign investment, by population size, metro status, and census div, 1993 survey rpt, A5800–2.115
- Electronics industry conditions and outlook, including mgmt issues, global expansion, and most promising new technologies, views of CEOs, 1992/93 survey, annual feature, C1850–2.506
- Employee benefit funds assets, for funds with intl investments, 1992, annual feature, C2710–2.504
- Europe companies acquired by US companies, and transaction value, for top 10 transactions, 1984-92, C1575–2.506
- Europe public opinion on political, economic, and social issues of interest to foreign investors, for 9 countries and 3 Soviet Union Republics, 1991 survey, C8915–9
- Financial data for 100 largest foreign investments in US, 1992, annual feature, C3950–1.519
- Food processing industry devs, including work force reduction, finances, and employment, 1993 annual feature, C2150–6.507
- Forecasts of natl income and product account components and related indicators, quarterly rpt, U1880–1
- Germany (West) and US comparative socioeconomic statistics, 1970s-91, annual rpt, A5135–2.2
- High-technology US company foreign acquisitions, distribution among top 4 and all other hq countries, Oct 1988-Apr 1992, C1850–2.503, C1850–6.501
- Higher education instn endowment fund and investment pool characteristics and performance, by instn, FY92, annual survey rpt, A6705–2
- Insurance company acquisitions by foreign firms, participants and price for major purchases of property/casualty and life/health insurers, 1988-92, article, C1050–1.503, C1050–2.503
- Investment mgmt firms, assets and operating data for approx 900 instns, Jan 1993, annual feature, C2710–2.511
- Investment mgmt firms in intl investing, tax-exempt assets and operating data for top firms, 1993, annual feature, C2710–2.514
- Israel high-technology market trend for US-owned companies, with sales and employment for 5 firms, 1993 article, C1850–2.503
- Japan-affiliated auto parts suppliers in US, with employment and plant square footage, 1990 and 1992-93, article, C2710–3.553
- Japan economic profile, including govt finances, industrial production, foreign trade and investments, and comparisons to US, 1988-92, annual feature, R5650–2.552
- Japan foreign direct investments, with data by industry and investing country/world area, 1950s-93, annual article, R5650–2.544
- Japan foreign investment in US, by selected industry, 1985-91, article, R5650–2.509
- Japan foreign investment rate of return on sales by world region, and overseas share of production, with detail by industry, FY84-91, article, R5650–2.559
- Japan foreign investment trends, by country and industry, FY88-Mar 1993, annual article, R5650–2.533
- Japan net capital flow, including intl securities transactions, weekly rpt quarterly article, R5650–2.505, R5650–2.514, R5650–2.531, R5650–2.550
- Japan real estate investment in Hawaii and California since 1985, with buyer, purchase price, and current value for 9 properties, 1993 article, C3950–1.517
- Japan vs US foreign investment indicators, 1993 article, C5800–7.532
- Latin America statistical abstract, general data by country, 1992 annual rpt, U6250–1.29
- Lodging chain foreign properties and rooms owned, for 45 leading chains and their subsidiaries, 1993 annual rpt, C7000–5
- Manufacturing and total foreign investment, by world region and/or country, 1991-93, annual rpt, A3179–2.3
- Manufacturing export value and employees for US operations of 4 major foreign corporations, 1992, article, C8900–1.517
- Manufacturing foreign investment projects started by 5 most active US industries, 1991, article, C1850–2.502
- Mexico auto industry investment planned by 5 foreign manufacturers, 1990s, R8490–43
- Mexico foreign-owned motor vehicle plants and employment by company, and hq countries of auto parts industry foreign participants, 1993 article, C2150–3.505
- Mexico investment of US vs other countries, by industry sector, 1929-87, U6250–1.21
- Mexico oil and gas finances of govt-owned company, and potential impact of foreign lease program, 1993 article, C6985–1.518

Foreign investments

Mineral exploration activities, expenses, and staff, for foreign and domestic operations of US and Canadian companies, 1991, article, C5226–2.508

Motion picture industry foreign investment, with outlays and gains/losses, by investor, 1993 article, C3950–1.516

Mutual fund industry financial data, investment activity, portfolio composition, and shareholder account characteristics, 1991 and trends, annual rpt, A6025–1

Mutual fund investment performance, by fund, June 1993 and trends, annual compilation, C3950–1.522

Mutual funds investing in emerging markets, returns for 10 funds with best performance for 1 and 3 years ended Sept 1993, article, C5800–7.549

New York Stock Exchange foreign securities listings and value by type, by world region, 1992, annual fact book, B6625–1.1

Oil exploration/production expenditures of US and foreign companies in US, Canada, and elsewhere, 1992-93, annual article, C6985–1.515

Oil industry capital spending in US and Canada, by function, 1991-93, annual articles, C6985–1.517

Oil industry foreign investment, by sector, 1991 and trends, annual fact book, C4680–1.507

Oil industry income, net profits, and selected operating data, approx 25 companies, weekly rpt quarterly article, C6985–1.520

Performance of leading funds with institutional investors, by fund and type, biweekly rpt quarterly feature, C2710–2.502, C2710–2.506, C2710–2.512, C2710–2.518

Petrochemical foreign ownership shares for major companies investing in US plants, for 2 product types, 1992, article, C6985–1.522

Philippines GNP, foreign investment inflow, intl aid, and trade with US and Japan, with comparisons to 7-8 other Asian countries, 1992 and trends, article, R5650–2.555

Productivity and related indicators, trend analysis for US and other industrial countries, 1980s-92, annual rpt, R2800–2

Pulp and paper industry operations and finances, US and Canada, with detail by company and product grade, and world production and trade summary, 1993 annual rpt, C3975–5

R&D spending abroad by US chemical and other companies, 1981-91, annual feature, A1250–1.537

Restaurant intl franchise units and sales, for 50 leading chains, 1991-92, annual feature, C1200–5.512

Russia oil field dev foreign participation outlook, and risk ratings for foreign investment, 1993 article, C6985–1.540

Saudi Arabia oil refining network organization, including refinery capacities and foreign ownership shares, 1993 article, C6985–1.542

Securities market participation by foreign and US investors, by world area and country, quarterly rpt, A8825–2

Securities net purchases by foreign investors in US and by US investors abroad, 1980-91, recurring article, A8825–1.501

Securities of foreign countries sold in US, with detail for public and private placements, stocks and bonds, and by country, 1981-1st half 1993, article, A8825–1.506

Soft drink foreign capital investments, for Coca Cola and Pepsi Cola in 9 emerging foreign markets, 1993 article, C5800–7.543

Southeastern States property holdings and employment of foreign owned firms, by country, 1990 and trends, annual rpt, U8710–2.20

Spain foreign trade and investment devs, by country and industry, 1991 and trends, articles, A8955–1.502

Spain population, foreign investment trends, and GDP shares, by region, 1993 feature, A8955–1.502

State social, economic, and govtl indicators, with rankings, 1993 semiannual rpt, B8500–1.2

Textile/clothing manufacturing foreign investment in US, 1990-91, annual rpt, C3400–5

State and local:

Arizona farmland holdings of foreign owners, with use, by county, Dec 1992, annual rpt, U5830–1

Florida statistical abstract, general data, 1992 annual rpt, U6660–1.9

Georgia affiliates of foreign companies, with facilities, employment, and investment, by hq country, 1991 and trends, biennial rpt, U6730–1.6

Georgia farmland holdings of foreign owners, by county, Dec 1991, annual rpt, S1855–1

Hawaii data book, general data, 1992 annual rpt, S2090–1.24

Hawaii farmland holdings of foreign owners, with detail by selected country, 1991, annual rpt, S2030–1

Illinois farmland holdings of foreign owners, by county, country, and land use, 1990, annual rpt, U6910–2

Iowa State govt investment data, including number of foreign companies deemed unacceptable due to business in South Africa, by country, FY92 annual rpt, S2885–1

Kentucky economic impact of Toyota Motor Corp plant installation, including related State costs, employment, and benefits to other States, 1980s-2005, U7138–1.4

Missouri agricultural land holdings of foreign owners, by county, Dec 1991, annual rpt, S4480–1

Nevada farmland holdings of foreign owners, by county and country, Dec 1992, annual rpt, S5010–1

Nevada foreign-owned business employment share by industry div, with comparison to US, 4th qtr 1990, article, S5040–1.501

New Jersey employment and wages in foreign-owned establishments, by industry div, 4th qtr 1990, article, S5425–1.502

New Jersey foreign-owned business establishments, employment, payroll, and shipments/sales, by industry div, 1987, article, S5425–1.501

Oklahoma and US farmland holdings of foreign owners, by country, Dec 1992, annual rpt, S6405–1

Pennsylvania foreign-owned business employment and wages, by industry div, 4th qtr 1990, article, S6845–1.501

South Carolina economic condition, including employment, manufacturing, and income, 1970s-92, annual rpt, S7125–3.2

South Carolina statistical abstract, general data, 1993 annual rpt, S7125–1.3

see also Balance of payments

see also Expropriation of alien property

see also Foreign corporations

see also Multinational corporations

Foreign labor conditions

Asia airline employment, for Orient Airlines Assn members, FY91-92, article, C7000–4.503

Australia auto industry employment and production, for 5 manufacturers, 1992 article, C2710–3.509

Auto production worker compensation in US and 15 other countries, 1991, annual rpt, A0865–1.3

Canada pulp and paper industry employment, earnings, and wage trends, 1970s-93, annual rpt, C3975–5.2

Canada, Saskatchewan Province uranium industry employment, finances, and labor productivity with comparison to Ontario, 1993 article, B6800–1.506

Chemical industry employment, for selected foreign countries, 1970 and 1980-92, annual rpt, A3850–1

Chemical process industry employment in 23 countries, 1991-92, article, C5800–8.509

China and US socioeconomic and infrastructure indicators comparison, 1993 rpt, R4105–82.8

China hard goods produced by prison labor affecting US market, views of US manufacturers, by product line, 1993 annual survey report, A1800–1

Coal industry supply-demand, employment, and trade, by country, 1990-91 and trends, annual rpt, A7400–2.2

Commodity yearbook for 1993: detailed supply-demand data, and selected indicators for futures market investors, C2400–1

Commodity yearbook update: detailed supply-demand data, and selected indicators for futures market investors, Jan-Sept 1993 rpts, C2400–2

Construction skilled and unskilled labor wage rates in Eastern and Western Europe and selected other countries, 1992 article, C5800–2.502

Corporate employment, for 500 largest companies, 1993 annual feature, C3950–1.519

Czechoslovakia chemical production by product, and sales, exports, and employment of leading firms, by Republic, 1990-92, article, A1250–1.509

EC economic indicators relating to proposed economic unification, by country, 1992 rpt, R5025–9

Economic indexes for US and other industrial countries, and leading and coincident indicators, monthly rpt, U1245–1

Index by Subjects and Names

Foreign relations

Employment abroad of US multinatl firms, and foreign compensation and unemployment data, for 10 countries, 1970s-93, article, C8900–1.504

Europe public opinion on political, economic, and social issues, for 9 countries and 3 Soviet Union Republics, 1991 survey, C8915–8.1

Europe public opinion on political, economic, and social issues of interest to foreign investors, for 9 countries and 3 Soviet Union Republics, 1991 survey, C8915–9

France public relations firms with US ties, including data on fees and staff, by company, 1993 article, A8770–1.503

Germany (West) and US comparative socioeconomic statistics, 1970s-91, annual rpt, A5135–2.2

Germany chemical industry employment and operations, including trade with Eastern Europe by country, 1992-93, article, A1250–1.540

Germany reunification issues for internatl investment, with data on population and employment, consumption, and infrastructure improvement, 1991 rpt, R4105–82.3

Home improvement industry sales, stores, and other operating data, for leading foreign chains by country, 1991, annual feature, C5150–6.503

Indonesia employment by industry sector, 1971 and 1980, R5620–1.37

Israel high-technology market trend for US-owned companies, with sales and employment for 5 firms, 1993 article, C1850–2.503

Japan academic library operations, including full- and part-time staff, by instn type, 1990, annual compilation, C1650–3.1

Japan chemical industry production, plants, employment, and leading product sales, 1991, article, C5800–8.505

Japan corporate CEOs compensation, for 50 largest companies, 1991, article, C5800–7.525

Japan corporate retirement age policies, and share of population age 55/over who are employed, 1986-92, article, R5650–2.549

Japan employee wage costs composition, 1991, article, R5650–2.512

Japan labor force by employment status, and employment and wages by industry, 1988-92, annual compilation, R5650–2.552

Japan unemployment rate and ratio of job openings to applications, 1980-92, article, R5650–2.559

Japan wage negotiation results, by industry, spring 1993, article, R5650–2.522

Labor cost per hour in US, Germany, France, UK, and Japan, 1988 and 1992, article, C5800–7.517

Labor mobility by worker sex and/or age, for Japan, Netherlands, and UK, 1993 rpt, R9260–17

Latin America statistical abstract, general data by country, 1992 annual rpt, U6250–1.12, U6250–1.13, U6250–1.18, U6250–1.29

Machine tool production, shipments, trade, finances, orders, and use, US and worldwide, 1992 and trends, annual rpt, A3179–2

Mexico foreign-owned motor vehicle plants and employment by company, and hq countries of auto parts industry foreign participants, 1993 article, C2150–3.505

Mexico industrial worker hourly earnings, with detail by industry and comparisons to US and 4 Asian countries, 1990-91, article, C5800–7.524

Mexico maquiladora plants, employment, and earnings, 1965-88, annual rpt, U6250–1.16

OECD countries labor market devs, including cost trends and unemployment, by country, bimonthly rpt, B6200–2

Persian Gulf region foreign workers and labor force share, for 6 countries, 1975 and 1990, R8750–2.59

Production worker compensation costs for 25 countries and 3 country groups, 1992, article, S0465–1.508

Productivity and related indicators, trend analysis for US and other industrial countries, 1980s-92, annual rpt, R2800–2

Shoe industry production workers compensation, US vs 7 other countries, 1981-91, annual rpt, A4957–1.2

South Africa economic indicators, with CPI, PPI, mining/quarrying employment and earnings, and gold milled ore working costs, monthly rpt, B6800–1

Spain chemical process industry sales and employment of top 15 companies, and production capacity and utilization of major chemicals, 1991, article, C5800–8.511

Spain oil refining capacity and utilization, and employment, for 3 refineries, 1993 article, A8955–1.503

Steel industry restructuring devs, with data on production, employment, and worker assistance, and selected detail by company, for 8-12 countries, 1970s-90, R9260–16

UK coal mine closures and related employment, for 31 mines, Oct 1992-Mar 1993, article, C5226–2.501

UK coal mining employees, by mine and operating status, for Govt-owned company, 1991-92, article, C5226–1.510

Unemployment rates for US, Japan, EC, and 5 European countries, 1993, article, C8900–1.526

Worker average hours and labor costs, for Germany, Japan, and US, 1993 article, C8900–1.517

World labor force, including women's share, by country, 1970s-2000, biennial rpt, R9455–1.5

Foreign languages

Book translations by source language, and translation publishing by country, 1993 annual compilation, C1650–3.4

Book translations into English from 16 foreign languages, 1987-92, annual feature, C1852–2.509

Canada French language magazine circulation and advertising rates, by publication, 1988-92, annual rpt, A3385–1

High school foreign language course enrollment trends, for 6 languages, 1985-90, R4800–2.504

Higher education instn language study abroad programs, including countries or world areas of study, 1993 annual survey, A1410–1.38

Households in which a foreign language is spoken, for 11 languages, 1980 and 1990, article, C2710–1.526

Library foreign-language materials acquisition projects Federal funding, by instn, FY92, annual compilation, C1650–3.2

Population speaking a foreign language at home, for top 50 languages, 1990 and trends, R4800–2.516

State and local:

California public school limited-English-proficiency enrollment, teachers, and programs, by 1st language, grade level, and county, 1992 and trends, annual rpt, S0825–10

Connecticut public school data, including enrollment, staff, programs, finances, and student characteristics, 1991/92, biennial rpt, S1185–3

Florida newspaper circulation of daily, weekly, and special interest newspapers, 1991, annual rpt, U6660–1.14

see also Bilingual education

Foreign legislative bodies

Eastern Europe public opinion on selected govt and societal instns, for 6 countries and 3 Soviet Union Republics, 1991 survey, C8915–8.2

Japan Diet Lower House political party composition, 1993 article, R5650–2.544, R5650–2.545

Japan Diet Upper and Lower House political party composition, Aug 1993 and trends, article, R5650–2.551

Japan Diet Upper and Lower House political party composition, Aug 1993, article, R5650–2.547

Latin America statistical abstract, general data by country, 1992 annual rpt, U6250–1.9

Foreign loans

see Export-Import Bank

see International assistance

see Military assistance

Foreign medical graduates

Dental school admission qualifications, by instn, US and Canada, 1992/93, annual rpt, A1475–3.1

Hospital recruiting of foreign nurses, with source countries, by region, 1993 and trends, annual survey rpt, A6500–1

Medical certification exam pass rates, and previous failure record, for foreign medical grads, by test type, Sept and July 1989-90, article, A3273–8.504

Physicians (foreign medical grads) by detailed specialty and location, 1992 and trends, annual rpt, A2200–3.1

Resident matching program participants, by specialty, 1993, annual article, A3273–8.507

Surgeons in residence and practice, with female and foreign medical grads by specialty and type of activity, 1993 annual fact book, A1275–1.1

Foreign military sales

see Arms trade

see Military assistance

Foreign relations

Charitable contributions, by type of donor and recipient, 1992 and trends, annual rpt, A0700–1

Europe public opinion on political, economic, and social issues, for 9 countries and 3 Soviet Union Republics, 1991 survey, C8915–8.2

Foreign relations

Japan public opinion on relations with US, among persons age 40-49 and 70/over, 1992 survey, article, C5800–7.552

Multinatl business implications of world events and socioeconomic devs outside the US, series, R4105–82

Public opinion in US on selected foreign policy issues, with detail for 3 States, 1993 survey, annual rpt, A4965–1

Public opinion on Clinton Admin handling of foreign affairs, Feb 1993 Gallup Poll, C4040–1.508

Public opinion on foreign policy issues including support for US involvement in world affairs, 1945-92 surveys, A0610–1.503

Public opinion on foreign policy issues, including US role in world affairs, Mar 1993 Gallup Poll and trends, C4040–1.510

State and local:

Tennessee executive views on intl trade and political issues, and US role in world affairs, 1993 annual article, U8710–1.502

see also Arms trade

see also Cultural activities

see also East-West trade

see also Educational exchanges

see also Food assistance

see also Foreign countries

see also Foreign debts

see also Foreign economic relations

see also Foreign students

see also Foreign trade

see also Foreign trade promotion

see also International assistance

see also International cooperation in cultural activities

see also International cooperation in environmental sciences

see also International cooperation in science and technology

see also Military assistance

see also Military intervention

see also Treaties and conventions

see also War

Foreign students

Chemistry and chemical engineering grad starting salaries, employment status, demographic characteristics, and advanced study plans, 1991/92, annual rpt, A1250–2

Community and junior college revenues by source and expenditures by function, and selected student characteristics, FY92, annual rpt, A6705–1

Dental school admission policies, applicants, enrollment, and tuition and fees, by instn, 1992/93, annual rpt, A1475–4.1

Doctoral degree recipient characteristics, including citizenship status, source of support, field of study, and instn, 1990/91 and trends, annual rpt, R6000–7

Doctoral degrees conferred and recipient characteristics, by field, 1992, annual feature, C2175–1.535

Engineering degrees awarded, by State, instn, and field, with detail for women, minorities, and foreign students, 1991/92, annual rpt, A0685–1

Engineering program enrollment, by instn, field, and State, with detail for women, minorities, and foreign students, fall 1992, annual rpt, A0685–2

Index by Subjects and Names

Enrollment in US higher education instns, by instn, State, country of origin, and selected demographic characteristics, 1991/92 and trends, annual rpt, R5580–1

Enrollment of foreign students, by higher education instn, discipline, State, and country of origin, 1991/92, annual feature, C2175–1.501

Geoscience enrollment and degrees awarded, by sex, race-ethnicity, and discipline, 1991/92, annual rpt, A1785–3

Higher education degrees conferred to nonresident aliens, by level and sex, 1990/91, recurring feature, C2175–1.523

Higher education enrollment of minority and foreign students at approx 3,100 instns, fall 1991, recurring feature, C2175–1.510

Higher education enrollment of minority and foreign students, with comparison to whites, by sex, State, and instn type, fall 1991, recurring feature, C2175–1.506

Higher education foreign student enrollment distribution by academic level, by field of study, 1991/92, article, A0605–2.501

Higher education freshmen attitudes and characteristics, degree and career plans, and financial aid sources, by sex and instn type, fall 1992, annual survey, U6215–1

Higher education instns, faculty, students, degrees, and finances, detailed data by State, 1993 annual rpt, C2175–1.531

Higher education intl student enrollment trends, 1993 annual survey, A1410–1.38

Higher education involvement of minorities, including enrollment and degrees awarded, by race-ethnicity, sex, and State, 1970s-91, annual rpt, A1410–10

Japan higher education foreign students, with detail for US students by funding source, by academic level, 1993 article, R5650–2.527

Journalism/mass communication enrollment and grads by level, by instn, sex, race-ethnicity, and field, 1990/91 and trends, annual article, A3225–1

Library/info science school foreign students and degrees awarded, by sex, instn, and country of origin, 1991/92, annual rpt, A3235–1.2

Mathematics dept faculty and doctoral degree recipient characteristics, including salaries, 1991/92 and trends, annual survey, A2085–1.1

Medical school programs, fees, applicants, admissions, and enrollment, with data by age, sex, minority group, and instn, 1992/93 and trends, annual rpt, A3273–10

Nursing school enrollment and grads, by degree level, sex, race-ethnicity, and instn type and location, 1992/93 and trends, annual rpt, A0615–4

Optometry school faculty, enrollment and degrees, policies and programs, and finances, by instn, 1991/92, annual survey, A3370–2

Pharmacy degree program applications, enrollment, and degrees conferred, by student characteristics and instn, 1990/91 and trends, annual rpt, A0630–9

Physics and astronomy bachelor degree recipients postgraduation plans and demographic characteristics, 1991/92 and trends, annual survey, A1960–3

Physics and astronomy enrollment and degrees awarded, by type of instn and census div, 1991/92-1992/93 and trends, annual rpt, A1960–2.1

Physics and astronomy grads employment status, by sex, age, subfield, citizenship, degree, and employer type, with salary info, 1990/91, annual rpt, A1960–1

Postsecondary enrollment and degrees by field of study and degree level, and student aid by sex, 1980s-91, with historical trends, recurring rpt, A3960–2

Private elementary and secondary school enrollment, staff, and finances, with detail for minorities, by school type and region, 1980s-1992/93, annual rpt, A6835–3

Public health school applicant, student, and grad characteristics, by instn, 1991/92 and trends, annual rpt, A3372–3

Science and engineering foreign grad students, by field, 1986-91, annual feature, A1250–1.537

Social work higher education programs, faculty and student characteristics, and student aid, with data by instn, 1992 and trends, annual rpt, A4515–1

Southern States higher education degree conferrals, by sex, race-ethnicity, level, and selected field, by State, 1990s and trends, biennial fact book, A8945–1.3

Theological school enrollment, staff and compensation, and finances, with data by instn, 1991/92 and trends, annual rpt, A3376–1

Veterinary school enrollment by student State or country of residence, by instn, 1992/93, annual article, A3100–2.516

State and local:

Arkansas higher education enrollment by student characteristics and geographic origins, by instn, fall 1991 and trends, annual rpt, S0690–1

California postsecondary education enrollment and degrees, by sex, race-ethnicity, and instn, 1990/91, annual series, S0827–2

Delaware postsecondary education finances, enrollment, and degrees conferred, by instn, FY94 annual rpt, S1425–1

Florida foreign students enrolled in State-supported universities, by field, instn, and country, fall 1991, annual rpt, S1725–1

Illinois higher education enrollment and degrees, by level, instn, field of instruction, and student characteristics, 1992 and trends, annual rpt, S2475–1.1

Iowa postsecondary enrollment, degrees, staff, and finances, by instn, 1990/91, annual rpt, S2755–1

Kentucky higher education enrollment, degrees, staff, and finances, by State-supported instn, 1983-92, annual rpt, S3130–3

Minnesota postsecondary education finances, and enrollment by student characteristics, by type of school system, 1970s-93, biennial rpt, S4195–2.2

Missouri higher education enrollment and degrees conferred, for nonresident aliens, by instn, 1992, annual rpt, S4520–3

North Carolina higher education enrollment, degrees, libraries, staff, and student characteristics, finances, and housing, by instn, 1992/93 and trends, annual rpt, U8013–1

Index by Subjects and Names

Foreign trade

North Dakota higher education enrollment, by level, instn, county, and selected student characteristics, fall 1992 and trends, annual rpt, S6110–1

Pennsylvania higher education degrees conferred, by level, sex, race-ethnicity, instn type, and field of study, 1990/91 and trends, annual rpt, S6790–5.2

Pennsylvania higher education degrees conferred, by level, sex, race-ethnicity, instn type, and field of study, 1991/92 and trends, annual rpt, S6790–5.15

Pennsylvania higher education enrollment, by student characteristics and instn, 1992 and trends, annual rpt, S6790–5.9

Pennsylvania higher education students by residence location, by academic level and instn type, 1992 and trends, biennial rpt, S6790–5.8

South Carolina higher education enrollment, degrees, staff, and finances, by instn, 1992 and trends, annual rpt, S7185–2

Tennessee higher education enrollment, finances, staff, and programs, by instn, 1992/93 and trends, annual rpt, S7525–1

Texas higher education enrollment and faculty, by race-ethnicity, sex, and instn, 1991/92 and trends, annual rpt, S7657–1.1

Utah higher education enrollment, by instn, fall 1992, annual rpt, S7895–2

Vermont higher education enrollment, including students from abroad and selected neighboring States, by instn, fall 1992 and trends, annual rpt, S8035–2.2

West Virginia higher education enrollment and degrees conferred, by instn, 1991/92 and trends, annual rpt, S8533–1.1

see also Foreign medical graduates

Foreign trade

Aerospace industry, civil and military production, R&D, trade, employment, and finances, with Federal funding data, 1991 and trends, annual rpt, A0250–2

Air conditioning and refrigeration equipment trade, with detail by equipment type, 1991-92, article, C2000–1.508

Air conditioning/refrigeration equipment trade, by country or world area, 1991-92, annual rpt, C1800–1

Aircraft (general aviation) exports, 1965-92, annual rpt, A5120–2.1

Aluminum exports and imports of US and foreign countries, 1982-92, annual rpt, A0400–2

Aluminum shipments, orders, and inventories by product class, and foreign trade for ingot, scrap, and mill products, monthly rpt, A0400–1

Asia household appliance import trends of US, for 7 product types from 8 source countries, 1991 vs 1987, C2000–1.502

Beer market volume and shares, for 40 leading and all other imported brands, 1985-92, annual feature, C0125–2.503

Bicycle industry shipments and imports, by type, 1992 and trends, annual rpt, A3470–1

Boating (recreational) industry trends, including sales, foreign trade, and registrations by geographic area, 1980s-92, annual feature, C2425–4

Boats (pleasure) export and import value, 1989-91, annual rpt, A8055–1

Book production, imports, translations, and prices, by subject area, various years 1977-92, annual article, C1852–2.509

Book publishing industry financial and operating data, by publisher type and size, and subject category, 1991 and trends, annual rpt, A3274–2

Book trade, by category and country of origin or destination, 1993 annual compilation, C1650–3.4

Business executives expectations for coming qtr, attitudes on key indicators, with trends and data by census div, quarterly rpt, C3150–4

Canada economic indicators, including US trade, import shares for 8 other countries, and population by Province, 1993 articles, C4687–1.508

Canada imports from US of 4 fast-growing product types, 1992-94, article, C4687–1.505

Canada lumber trade with US, and production data, by product type, monthly rpt, A1630–3

Canada manufactured fibers imports and exports, by fiber type and trading partner, 1989-1st 9 months 1992, recurring feature, C3460–1.504

Canada manufactured fibers imports and exports, by fiber type and trading partner, 1989-92, recurring feature, C3460–1.506

Canada manufactured fibers imports and exports, by fiber type and trading partner, 1990-1st half 1993, recurring feature, C3460–1.512

Canada manufactured fibers imports and exports, by fiber type, 1989-92, C3460–1.510

Canada plastic resins and film/sheet trade, including percent bilateral with US, monthly rpt quarterly table, C5800–12.502, C5800–12.506, C5800–12.509, C5800–12.512

Canada tobacco exports to US, and cigarette retail vs black market prices, 1992 article, C3950–1.503

Canada-US bilateral plastics imports as percent of domestic demand, by selected resin, 1986 and 1992, article, A1250–1.525

Carpet and rug industry shipments by type, PPI, and US trade by country, 1991 and trends, annual rpt, A3800–1

Chemical and related industries production, finances, operating ratios, employment, and trade, by country, company, and chemical, 1980s-92, annual feature, A1250–1.530

Chemical exports and imports, by trading partner and product category, 1992, article, A1250–1.521

Chemical exports for developing vs developed areas, with detail for Eastern Europe, 1980, 1986, and 1991, article, A1250–1.534

Chemical industry finances and operations, with data by industry segment and product, 1970s-92, annual rpt, A3850–1

Chemical industry worldwide production and trade, selected data by country and world area, 1988-92, annual feature, A1250–1.507

China business review, including trade with US and other countries, and economic activity, bimonthly rpt, A9315–1

China, Guangdong Province foreign trade, 1985-92, A9315–1.505

China imports, with detail for 3 fast-growing product types from the US, 1992-2018, article, C4687–1.511

China industrial and agricultural production, and foreign trade and investment, with detail for leading commodities, 1980s-92, annual feature, A9315–1.504

Cigarette exports by customs district, 1991, annual rpt, A9075–1

Clothing (men's and boys) production, trade, and operating data, by garment type, 1960s-92, annual rpt, A3880–1

Clothing (women's and children's) sales, production, imports, and industry employment, hours, and earnings, by type of garment, recurring rpt, A5900–1

Commodity yearbook for 1993: prices, stocks, production, exports, and imports, for approx 100 agricultural and industrial materials, including by producing State and country, C2400–1

Commodity yearbook update: prices, stocks, production, and trade, for approx 100 basic commodities, including by country and producing State, Jan-Sept 1993 rpts, C2400–2

Competitiveness indicators for US vs other major industrial countries, including investments, productivity, exports, and per capita GDP, 1993 annual rpt, A4475–1

Consumer electronics product imports and exports, by product type, 1982-92, annual rpt, A4725–4

Contraceptive imports and prices in developing countries, by method and country, 1980s-90, R8720–1.1

Copper exports and imports, by country of origin or destination, 1987-91, annual rpt, S0497–1

Copper supply by source, consumption by end use, stocks, and trade, 1972-92, annual rpt, A4175–1

Cuba economic indicators, including trade and inflation, 1970s-88, U6250–1.19

Czechoslovakia chemical production by product, and sales, exports, and employment of leading firms, by Republic, 1990-92, article, A1250–1.509

Deficit of US foreign trade, top 5 countries, 1993, article, C8900–1.510

Deficit value, 1987 and 1992, article, C7000–3.503

Diamond imports and polished exports, for various countries, 1991-93, article, C5226–2.510

Dye imports, with shares from Europe, Japan, and China/India, 1983 and 1991, article, A1250–1.531

Eastern Europe public opinion on sale of products made by foreign corporations, for 4 countries, 1991 survey, C8915–8.2

Economic outlook for selected indicators, recent trends and 2-year forecast, quarterly rpt, A3840–6

Electric generating equipment and transformer orders, shipments, and exports, by type of equipment, 1987-91 and scheduled for 1992-95/beyond, annual rpt, A4700–2.2

Electronics industry factory sales and shipments, foreign trade, and operating data, by product category, 1980s-92, annual rpt, A4725–1

Foreign trade

Index by Subjects and Names

Electronics industry market devs, including employment, factory sales, prices, and foreign trade trends, monthly rpt, A4725–2

Electronics trade, by product category, detailed type, and country, monthly rpt, A4725–3

Employment and percent of shipments related to exports, by State, 1989, semiannual rpt, B8500–1.2

Europe percent increase in exports to US, for UK, Italy, and Sweden, with top commodities, 1st half 1993 vs 1992, article, C5800–7.549

Europe polypropylene trade, 1986, 1991, and 1995, article, A1250–1.501

Europe polyvinyl chloride market volume and import share, 1988 and 1992, article, C5800–12.511

Europe TV programming shares purchased from foreign sources, total and from major suppliers, for 16 countries, 1993 article, C1850–14.508

Export sales ranking of top 50 companies, 1992, annual feature, C8900–1.517

Exports of the US distribution by country or world region of destination, 1992, article, C4575–1.510

Farm equipment trade, by equipment type and country, 1986-92, annual feature, C3450–1.501

Fiber Organon, detailed monthly and annual data on industry production, consumption, and trade, by fiber and fabric type, monthly rpt, C3460–1

Forecasts of economic indicators for approx 10-13 months, monthly rpt, U1880–3

Forecasts of natl income and product account components and related indicators, quarterly rpt, U1880–1

Forecasts of natl income and product account components, employment, and financial sector activity, monthly rpt, B4950–1

Forest products foreign trade by product category and at 30 leading ports, 1991-92, annual article, C3975–2.512

France aerospace industry export orders distribution by product type, 1991, article, C5800–4.509

Germany (West) and US comparative socioeconomic statistics, 1970s-91, annual rpt, A5135–2.2

Hard goods industry foreign competition, and manufacturers and representatives views on trade issues, by product line, 1993 annual survey rpt, A1800–1

Hearing aid unit sales, by type and State, and trade summary, quarterly rpt, A5185–1

Helicopters in civil aviation, production, trade, utilization, accidents, and landing facilities, 1993 annual rpt, A5190–1

High-technology industry CEO characteristics, and views on mgmt issues including compensation and foreign trade, June 1992 survey, B4490–2.34

Hispanic-owned business export revenues, with comparison to total revenues, for top 10 companies, 1992, annual feature, C4575–1.507

Household appliance industry manufacturing and market trends, by product type, various years 1920-94, biennial rpt, A3350–3

Hungary economic indicators, including value of total and selected US imports, 1993 article, C4687–1.508

Ice cream/frozen dessert exports, by country of destination, 1991-92, annual rpt, A5825–1.1

India computer software export revenues, for top 5 firms, FY92, article, C5800–7.511

Intracompany vs intercompany trade for US, EC, and Japan, 1990, article, C8900–1.520

Iran imports by country of origin, 1977 and 1990, R4105–82.7

Iron and steel industry production, trade, and materials consumption, with financial and employment data, 1992 and trends, annual rpt, A2000–2

Iron ore trade and production, by country, 1983-92, annual rpt, A2010–3.2

Japan economic issues and devs, relations with US, and trade, balance of payments, and economic indicators, weekly rpt, R5650–2

Japan economic profile, including govt finances, industrial production, foreign trade and investments, and comparisons to US, 1988-92, annual feature, R5650–2.552

Japan exports of compact cameras, 1987-92, article, C2710–1.523

Japan household appliance exports and imports, with detail by trading partner, by appliance type, 1985-91, article, C2000–1.504

Japan imports from US, for top 10 product categories, 1st 8 months 1992, article, C8900–1.502

Japan Office of Trade and Investment Ombudsman cases, by world area of origin and jurisdictional ministry, 1982-July 1993, article, R5650–2.553

Japan public and private construction market value and contracts awarded to US firms, and US Govt contract value won by Japanese firms, 1988-92, article, C5800–2.528

Japan trade, total and with US, weekly rpt quarterly feature, R5650–2.513, R5650–2.525, R5650–2.545

Japan-US trade balance, with detail for motor vehicles and parts, 1988-92, article, C2710–3.544

Jewelry and watch manufacturing and marketing trends, new product dev, prices, trade, and related indicators, monthly rpt, C2150–7

Jewelry industry statistics on sales, marketing, trade, and employment, with customer characteristics, 1993 annual almanac, C2150–7.509

Korea (South) petrochemical and thermoplastics production and foreign trade, with detail by trading partner, 1992 and trends, article, C5800–8.510

Latin America economic indicators affecting business climate, with data on motor vehicle and oil industries and detail by country, 1992 rpt, R4105–82.6

Latin America statistical abstract, general data by country, 1992 annual rpt, U6250–1.4, U6250–1.25, U6250–1.26, U6250–1.27

Lawn and garden equipment imports and exports, 1985-92, article, C2000–1.511

Liquor consumption, trade, and sales volume or shipments, by product type and State, 1991 and trends, annual rpt, A4650–3

Liquor market statistics, including sales, consumption, trade, distillery operations, and govtl info, with data by company, brand, and location, 1992 and trends, annual rpt, C4775–1

Logistics professionals views on transportation and trade policy issues, Dec 1992 survey, article, C2150–1.505

Logistics trends and devs, including data on costs, finances of major carriers by mode, and foreign trade, 1993 annual compilation, C2150–1.506

Lumber industry exports by destination, and imports from Canada and all other countries, 1984-92, annual rpt, A9395–1

Lumber industry supply-demand, sales, trade, and employment, monthly rpt, A1630–1

Machine tool and other manufacturing technology exports and imports, by country of destination and origin, and by detailed product type, monthly rpt, A3179–3

Machine tool and other manufacturing technology trade, Aug-Sept 1992 and 1st 9 months 1991-92, article, C7000–7.502

Machine tool production, shipments, trade, finances, orders, and use, US and worldwide, 1992 and trends, annual rpt, A3179–2

Machine tool shipments and new orders for domestic and foreign markets, and backlog, monthly press release, A3179–1

Machine tool world production, trade, and consumption, by country, 1991-92, annual article, C7000–7.503

Magazine paper consumption, for regular and/or recycled paper by type, North American vs overseas source, and weight, 1992-94, article, C2575–1.518

Magnesium imports of US and Japan from China and Commonwealth of Independent States, with worldwide demand by application or world region, 1992-93, article, A1250–1.544

Manufacturing exports share of private sector employment, by State, 1989, article, B8500–2.508

Manufacturing exports value per capita, by State, 1992, article, B8500–2.512

Manufacturing foreign trade balance, with detail by selected industry, 1987, R4700–19

Merchandise imports and exports by industry sector, 1970-91, and import penetration for selected manufactured goods, 1981 and 1991, R8490–48

Metalworking industries capital spending plans, including equipment purchasing from foreign sources, 1989-93, annual survey, C4080–1

Mexico air-conditioning/refrigeration equipment exports of US, for top 6 product categories, 1991, article, C2000–1.506

Mexico and US trade value, and US employment, for 12 major industries, 1991, article, C8900–1.513

Mexico economic indicators, including US trade, 1993 articles, C4687–1.512

Mexico exports value from 10 Western States, 1987 and 1992, article, U0282–2.501

Index by Subjects and Names

Foreign trade

Mexico GDP components, including shares by industry div, and services trade with US by industry group, 1980-92, article, A3892–1.504

Mexico manufactured fibers imports and exports, by fiber type, 1989-92, C3460–1.510

Mexico-Texas transportation system analysis, including bilateral trade, operations by transport mode, and data by locale, 1993 rpt, U8850–9

Mexico textile manufactured fiber imports and exports, by country of origin and destination, 1990-1st half 1993, C3460–1.512

Minerals supply-demand for selected commodities, US and worldwide, 1992 and trends, annual feature, C5226–2.505

Musical instrument and accessory shipment volume and/or retail value, and foreign trade, by product type, 1992 and trends, annual rpt, A6848–1

Newsprint production, consumption, trade, prices, and mill capacity, with data by world area, 1991-92 and trends, annual rpt, A8610–1

Newsprint production, shipments, plant capacity, consumption, trade, and recycling, US and Canada, 1970s-92, annual rpt, A1630–8

Newsprint production, shipments, trade, inventory, consumption, and plant capacity, US and Canada, monthly rpt, A1630–4

North American Free Trade Agreement devs for auto industry, with data on Mexico vehicle production and US total and auto trade with Mexico and Canada, 1980s-91, R8490–43

Oil/gas exploration and production equipment/services exports and potential market, 1991-2010, article, C6985–1.505

Paper and paperboard industry financial and operating data, by product, region, and State, 1992 and trends, annual rpt, A1630–6

Paper industry trade, by selected grade, 1990-92, article, C1850–10.504

Parrots and other psittacines captive breeding info, by detailed species, with data on bird imports, 1989-90, annual survey rpt, R9200–14

Philippines GNP, foreign investment inflow, intl aid, and trade with US and Japan, with comparisons to 7-8 other Asian countries, 1992 and trends, article, R5650–2.555

Plastics (polypropylene) foreign trade balance, by world area, 1991 and 1995, article, C6985–1.533

Plastics and resin sales by material and major market, foreign trade, and capacity by company, 1991-92, annual feature, C5800–12.504

Plastics exports and imports of resins, and semi-finished and plastics-containing goods, monthly rpt quarterly table, C5800–12.501, C5800–12.505, C5800–12.508, C5800–12.511

Plastics industry production and sales by resin type, consumption by end-use market, and operating characteristics, 1992 and trends, annual rpt, A8920–1

Plastics resin production, sales/captive use, and trade, by resin type and/or use, monthly rpt, A8920–5

Potash imports, by State and country of origin, quarterly rpt, A8720–4

Potash muriates and sulfates, sales and trade, US and Canada, quarterly press release, A8720–5

Potash production, inventories, and sales and exports by State, Canadian Province, and country of destination, monthly rpt, A8720–1

Potash production, inventories, sales, and exports, US and Canada, monthly rpt, A8720–2

Productivity and related indicators, trend analysis for US and other industrial countries, 1980s-92, annual rpt, R2800–2

Public opinion in US on selected foreign policy issues, with detail for 3 States, 1993 survey, annual rpt, A4965–1

Pulp and paper industry operations and finances, US and Canada, with detail by company and product grade, and world production and trade summary, 1993 annual rpt, C3975–5

Pulp and paper industry production, capacity, consumption, trade, and sales/earnings data, including profiles for selected companies and sectors, monthly rpt, C3975–2

Pulp, paper, and paperboard industry production, trade, and operating data, by product class, monthly rpt, A1630–5

Purchasing managers views on business conditions, monthly rpt, A6910–1

Retail industry inventory from foreign sources, by outlet type, 1993 survey, C5150–4.506

Russia foreign trade, by selected commodity, 1st 5 months 1993, article, U2030–1.509

Services and merchandise exports and imports, with detail by trading partner, 1986-92, article, A3892–1.503

Services export value for top 24 and all other industry groups, 1991, article, A3892–1.501

Shoe industry production and operating data, including trade by country, retail sales, and consumer expenditures, quarterly rpt, A4957–2

Shoe industry production, employment, trade, marketing, and related data, by SIC 2- to 5-digit code or product type, 1992 annual rpt, A4957–1

Silver market activity worldwide and in US, including production, consumption by end use, stocks, trade, and prices, by country, 1988-92, annual rpt, B4300–1

Silver supply-demand by country and end use, with prices, futures trading, and market analyses, 1993 and trends, annual rpt, A8902–4

South America heating, ventilating, and air conditioning (HVAC) market indicators, for 4 countries, 1993 article, C2000–1.503

Soviet Union and Russia foreign trade, by selected commodity, 1990-92, U2030–1.508

Soviet Union foreign trade with 5 Eastern European countries, monthly rpt recurring feature, U2030–1.503

Soviet Union imports and exports compared to US, 1986, R4105–82.4

Spain business activities and trade relations with US, quarterly rpt, A8955–1

Steel industry operating trends and devs, including profiles of 4 major companies, 1960-90, U9640–2.15

Taiwan economic indicators, monthly rpt, U1245–1

Textile and clothing industries trade summary, 1988-92, annual rpt, C3400–5

Textile fiber end-use survey, consumption and trade, by type of fiber and product, 1988-92, annual survey, C3460–1.511

Textile industry economic and operating performance and outlook, 1988-93, annual article, C5226–3.502

Textile industry economic performance indicators and outlook, with industry trends and devs, monthly rpt, C5226–3

Textile manufactured fibers production and trade, by country, 1991, annual feature, C3460–1.503

Textile manufactured fibers trade, detailed data by type and country, 1989-92, annual rpt, C3460–1.504

Trends in exports and imports, with detail for major trading partners, 1980-92, article, R5650–2.509

UK economic indicators, including US trade, import shares for 4 other countries, and population by country and city, 1993 articles, C4687–1.510

Value of total vs oil exports and imports, 1974-92, periodic basic data book, A2575–14.3

Value of US exports to and imports from Japan and EC, for 5 types of commodities, 1993 article, C8900–1.516

Wastepaper use, prices, and exports, 1970s-94, annual rpt, C3975–5.4

Water (bottled) import and export value, 1986-92 and 2001, annual rpt, C0125–3.1

Waterborne trade activity at 15-16 leading US ports, with detail for Baltimore, 1989-91, biennial rpt, S3605–1.10

Wine market statistics, including sales, production, trade, and consumer characteristics, with data by company, brand, and geographic area, 1992 and trends, annual rpt, C4775–2

Wine sales and market shares for top 24 wine companies, and imports, 1990-92, recurring article, C2710–1.544

Wood chemicals (naval stores) production, consumption, and trade, US and foreign, 1992 and trends, annual rpt, C6585–1

World financial market devs including economic and monetary trends and forecasts for 15 industrial countries, bimonthly rpt, B6200–2

World wildlife trade in live primates and parrots, cat and reptile skins, cacti, and orchids, by country, 1988, biennial rpt, R9455–1.6

World wood product production and trade, by country, 1977-89, biennial rpt, R9455–1.6

State and local:

Alabama export values for 6 countries of destination and top 5 commodities, 1990, annual rpt, U5680–3

Alabama exports trends, with detail for exports to Mexico, Latin America, and Japan, 1992 vs 1991, article, U5680–1.502

Alabama statistical abstract, general data, 1992 recurring rpt, U5680–2.7

Foreign trade

California ports foreign trade activity, by product category, 1991, annual rpt, S0840–3.1

California statistical abstract, general data, 1992 annual rpt, S0840–2.11

Florida statistical abstract, general data, 1992 annual rpt, U6660–1.13

Georgia, Atlanta metro area small/medium-sized corporations export market awareness and promotion program involvement, 1988 survey, article, U5930–1.502

Georgia exports, by industry group and country of destination, and exporting business establishments, 1993 article, U6730–2.502

Georgia statistical abstract, general data, 1992-93 biennial rpt, U6730–1.6, U6730–1.8

Hawaii data book, general data, 1992 annual rpt, S2090–1.13, S2090–1.18, S2090–1.24

Hawaii real trade-weighted exchange rate index, and GNP or GDP for 10 foreign trading partners, bimonthly rpt, B3500–1

Idaho economic profile, general data, 1992 recurring rpt, S2218–2.9

Illinois exports value, quarterly rpt, S2405–2

Illinois statistical abstract, general data, 1992 annual rpt, U6910–2

Iowa exports to top 10 countries of destination, 1991, annual rpt, S2784–3

Maine statistical summary, general economic and social data, 1992 recurring rpt, S3434–1

Maryland, Port of Baltimore imports and exports, by country, 1991, biennial rpt, S3605–1.10

New York State imports and exports, by custom district and for New York Port, 1985-88, annual feature, S5735–2

New York State statistical yearbook, general data, 1992 annual rpt, U5100–1.13

North Dakota exports, by country of destination, 1991, annual rpt, S6140–2

Oklahoma export-related manufacturing establishments, export value, and output share and intensity, by industry group, various years 1987-89, article, U8130–1.503

Oregon customs district trade, 1982-91, annual rpt, S6603–2

Oregon economic conditions, including population, construction, income, employment, industry, and foreign trade data, 1991, annual rpt, S6585–3

Pennsylvania statistical abstract, general data, 1992 recurring rpt, U4130–6.2

South Carolina economic condition, including energy and transportation data, 1970s-92, annual rpt, S7125–3.3

South Carolina statistical abstract, general data, 1993 annual rpt, S7125–1.15

South Dakota exports to top 20 countries of destination, with detail for Canada and Mexico by commodity, 1991, article, U8595–1.502

Tennessee statistical abstract, general data, 1992/93 annual rpt, U8710–2.4, U8710–2.20

Virginia ports export value, total and for 16 industries, 1989 and 1991, U1120–1.501

Washington State intl trade, by major trading partner, 1982-91, annual rpt, S8345–3

see also Agricultural exports and imports
see also Arms trade
see also Balance of payments
see also Coal exports and imports
see also Dumping
see also East-West trade
see also Economic indicators
see also Energy exports and imports
see also Export-Import Bank
see also Export processing zones
see also Foreign competition
see also Foreign exchange
see also Foreign investments
see also Foreign trade promotion
see also International assistance
see also Military assistance
see also Motor vehicle exports and imports
see also Multinational corporations
see also Natural gas exports and imports
see also Petroleum exports and imports
see also Tariffs and foreign trade controls
see also Trade adjustment assistance
see also Trade agreements

Foreign trade promotion

China business review, including trade with US and other countries, and economic activity, bimonthly rpt, A9315–1

Loans made to exporters guaranteed by SBA, 1987-92, C4687–1.506

Forensic sciences

Chemist and chemical engineer salaries, employment status, and demographic and professional characteristics, 1993, annual rpt, A1250–4

Forest fires

Deaths in major disasters since 1865, by category, annual rpt, A8375–2.1

State and local:

Georgia statistical abstract, general data, 1992-93 biennial rpt, U6730–1.5

Hawaii data book, general data, 1992 annual rpt, S2090–1.20

Maryland statistical abstract, general data, 1993-94 biennial rpt, S3605–1.3

Mississippi statistical abstract, general data, 1992 annual rpt, U3255–4.10

New York State statistical yearbook, general data, 1992 annual rpt, U5100–1.15

South Carolina statistical abstract, general data, 1993 annual rpt, S7125–1.1

Forests and forestry

Commercial forestland ownership, and timber harvested, by region, 1987, annual rpt, A1630–6.3

Europe forest defoliation, and potential harvest loss due to air pollution, by country, 1992/93 biennial rpt, R9455–1.1, R9455–1.4

Forest industries mgmt, technical devs, and manufactures data, articles and special features, bimonthly rpt, C3975–1

Latin America statistical abstract, general data by country, 1992 annual rpt, U6250–1.2, U6250–1.24

Timberland holdings of major paper companies, 1993 annual rpt, C3975–5.1

Tropical forest acreage lost in 50 countries, and selected deforestation rates, 1981-85, annual rpt, U6250–1.24

World forest and rangeland areas, with data on condition and mgmt, by region and country, 1992/93 biennial rpt, R9455–1.3, R9455–1.6

World total and protected forest land, other wooded land, and forest products production value, by world region, 1993 article, C3975–2.506

State and local:

Alabama statistical abstract, general data, 1992 recurring rpt, U5680–2.1

California statistical abstract, general data, 1992 annual rpt, S0840–2.7

Florida county data book, 1992/93 annual rpt, C6360–1

Florida statistical abstract, general data, 1992 annual rpt, U6660–1.10

Georgia county guide, general data, 1993 annual rpt, U6750–1

Georgia statistical abstract, general data, 1992-93 biennial rpt, U6730–1.5

Hawaii data book, general data, 1992 annual rpt, S2090–1.20

Illinois statistical abstract, general data, 1992 annual rpt, U6910–2

Maine statistical summary, general economic and social data, 1992 recurring rpt, S3434–1

Maryland statistical abstract, general data, 1993-94 biennial rpt, S3605–1.3

Mississippi statistical abstract, general data, 1992 annual rpt, U3255–4.10

Montana property values, by detailed property class and type, with land acreage by use, by county, 1991-92 and trends, biennial rpt, S4750–1.2

New York State statistical yearbook, general data, 1992 annual rpt, U5100–1.15

South Carolina statistical abstract, general data, 1993 annual rpt, S7125–1.1

Tennessee statistical abstract, general data, 1992/93 annual rpt, U8710–2.11

Tennessee timberland by ownership and county, and timber harvest data, 1993 annual rpt, S7460–1

Washington State property values, by type of property and county, 1992, annual rpt, S8415–1.3

Wyoming property assessed valuations and tax levies, by property type, tax purpose, and location, 1992 and trends, annual rpt, S8990–1.2

see also Forest fires
see also Gum and wood chemicals
see also Lumber industry and products
see also National forests
see also National parks
see also State forests

Forgery

see Counterfeiting and forgery

Forrer, Kathleen

"New Mexico Accountability Report, 1991/92", S5575–4

Fort Wayne, Ind.

Business conditions analysis for selected Indiana local areas, quarterly rpt semiannual feature, U2160–1.504

Fort Worth, Tex.

Discount stores shopped and store characteristics, for 3 major chains in 3 market areas, 1993 surveys and trends, articles, C5150–3.516

see also under By City in the "Index by Categories"

Foster home care

Catholic charity social service agency activities, clients, finances, and personnel, 1991 and trends, annual rpt, A3810–1

Child and maternal health and welfare indicators, by State, FY90 or 1990, annual rpt, R3840–11.2

Federal budget trends, including spending by program, State, and region, FY81-94, annual rpt, R8490–11

Index by Subjects and Names

Franchises

State social, economic, and govtl indicators, with rankings, 1993 semiannual rpt, B8500–1.8

State and local:

- Alabama public welfare and social service cases, recipients, and payments, by program and county, monthly rpt, S0150–1
- Arizona children in foster homes, and payments, monthly rpt, S0465–4
- Arkansas human services dept finances and operations, by program, FY91 and trends, annual rpt, S0700–2.2
- California public welfare cases, recipients, and expenditures, by program and county, monthly rpt, S0935–2
- Colorado welfare and social services expenditures and caseloads, by county and/or program, FY91, annual rpt, S1085–1
- Florida adult foster homes and beds, by district and county, 1992, annual rpt, S1746–1.2
- Hawaii data book, general data, 1992 annual rpt, S2090–1.11
- Indiana public assistance program participation, expenditures, and services, by county, FY92 and trends, annual rpt, S2623–1
- Kentucky Medicaid recipients and payments, by program, county, and type of medical service, monthly rpt, S3140–5
- Michigan public assistance program cases, recipients, and payments, detailed data by county, monthly rpt, S4010–1
- Mississippi public welfare and social service cases, recipients, and payments, by program and county, FY92, annual rpt, S4357–1
- Missouri public welfare and medical assistance recipients, expenditures, and case processing, by program and county, FY92 and trends, annual rpt, S4575–2
- Nebraska juvenile parolees placed in foster homes, by sex, FY92, annual rpt, S4850–1
- Nebraska public welfare recipients and expenditures, by program, FY92, annual rpt, S4957–1.1
- New York State child services program statistics, 1991 and trends, annual rpt, S5800–2.3
- North Carolina public welfare programs, cases, recipients, staff, and finances, by county, 1st half FY93, semiannual rpt, S5940–2
- Oklahoma adoption and foster home care activities, FY92, annual rpt, S6455–1.2
- Pennsylvania statistical abstract, general data, 1992 recurring rpt, U4130–6.5
- South Carolina public welfare recipients, payments, and case processing, by county and program, monthly rpt, S7252–1
- South Dakota welfare and social services recipients and payments, by program, MSA, and county, FY92, annual rpt, S7385–1
- Texas foster homes verified by dept of human services, and children in foster care, FY92 and trends, annual rpt, S7695–1
- Washington State public assistance clients and service costs, by client characteristics, program, and county, FY90, annual rpt, S8420–2

West Virginia welfare and social service program caseloads and expenditures, by county, monthly rpt, S8560–2

Wyoming welfare and social service recipients and expenditures, by program and county, FY92, annual rpt, S8908–1

Foster, J. D.

"Tax Freedom Day 1993", R9050–15.4

Foundations

see Nonprofit organizations and foundations

Foundries

- Copper supply by source, consumption by end use, stocks, and trade, 1972-92, annual rpt, A4175–1
- Financial ratios and performance, for over 350 SIC 4-digit industries, FY88-92, annual rpt, A6400–3
- Iron and steel industry consumption of materials and energy, US and Canada, 1992 and trends, annual rpt, A2000–2
- Projected shipments, capacity utilization, and capital investment in foundries, by metal type and plant size, 1992-94, annual survey article, C7000–2.501
- Trends and devs in foundry metalcasting industry, monthly rpt, C7000–2

Fowles, Richard

"Effects of Diminished Economic Opportunities on Social Stress: Heart Attacks, Stroke, and Crime", R4700–18

Fragrances

see Cosmetics and toiletries

France

- Advertising campaign reactions of consumers in US, UK, and France, 1993 survey article, C2710–1.529
- Aerospace industry export orders distribution by product type, 1991, article, C5800–4.509
- Chemical company billings, sales, employment, R&D spending, and/or contracts, errata, C5800–8.501
- Coal industry supply-demand, employment, and trade, by country, 1990-91 and trends, annual rpt, A7400–2.2
- Economic indexes for US and other industrial countries, and leading and coincident indicators, monthly rpt, U1245–1
- Economic indexes for US and selected other countries, composites of leading indicators, monthly rpt, R4105–6
- Electronics industry trade and/or production trends by product category for 33 countries, with general economic profiles, 1993 annual rpt, A4725–1.4
- Energy intl sourcebook, with detail on oil and gas industry operations, supply-demand, and prices, for approx 80 countries, 1970s-91, annual compilation, C6985–10.2
- Jewish population and characteristics, and Jewish schools, enrollment, and teachers, 1993 article, A2050–1.1
- Machine tool industry operating data by country and product, 1992 and trends, annual rpt, A3179–2.2
- Motion picture boxoffice receipts in US for 17 French films and their US remakes, 1970s-93, article, C9380–1.522
- Motion picture theater screens, for top 4-8 and all other exhibitors in Germany, Spain, France, and UK, 1992, C9380–1.531

Motor vehicle world production, sales, trade, and registrations, by country, world area, manufacturer, and make, 1991 and trends, annual rpt, A0865–2.1

- Natural gas govt-owned company operations and finances, including employment, 1990, article, C6985–1.505
- Nuclear reactors in operation, with capacity, electricity generation, and construction, by unit and country, 1992, annual rpt, B6800–2.2
- Oil refinery capacity by process, and capital outlays for unleaded gasoline projects, for selected companies, 1993 article, C6985–1.547
- Privatization potential proceeds from sale of 6 govt-owned companies in France, 1993 article, C5800–7.531
- Public opinion in 9 European countries and 3 Soviet Union Republics on political, economic, and social issues, 1991 survey, C8915–8
- Public relations firms with US ties, including data on fees and staff, by company, 1993 article, A8770–1.503
- R&D expenditures for 9 leading industry groups, 1993 article, C1850–6.509
- Shipbuilding govt aid programs in 6 OECD countries, and impact on US industry, 1993 recurring rpt, A8900–8
- Silver market activity worldwide and in US, including production, consumption by end use, stocks, trade, and prices, by country, 1988-92, annual rpt, B4300–1
- Silver supply-demand by country and end use, with prices, futures trading, and market analyses, 1993 and trends, annual rpt, A8902–4
- *see also* under By Foreign Country or World Area in the "Index by Categories"

Franchise tax

see License taxes and fees

Franchises

- Auto dealer franchise desirability rating for top 33 makes, winter 1992-93, survey article, C2710–3.525
- Auto dealer satisfaction with manufacturers, index for top 15 makes, 1991-92, survey article, C2710–3.512
- Auto dealerships, including domestic and import outlets, and franchises by make, 1993 and trends, annual article, C2710–3.519
- Black-owned franchises, with type of business and startup costs, top 50 companies, 1993 annual article, C4215–1.510
- Canada auto dealer franchises, by make, 1992-93, article, C2710–3.530
- Canada auto dealer satisfaction with manufacturers, ratings for 21 makes, 1992 survey, article, C2710–3.518
- Consumer complaint and inquiry activity of Better Business Burs concerning franchise/business opportunity companies, 1992, annual rpt, A4350–1
- Convenience store outlets, including number company- and franchise-operated, by company, 1993 annual fact book, C4680–1.507
- Food service franchise and total units for 100 largest chains, with top 64 chains ranked by franchise growth, FY93 and trends, annual feature, C5150–5.509

Franchises

Gasoline unattended-site retail outlets, franchises/marketers, and average transactions, for 6 retail chains, 1993 article, C4680–1.511

Lodging chain properties by ownership status, for leading facilities and chains, 1993 annual rpt, C7000–5

Motor vehicle dealership financial and operating data, including sales and employment by State, 1970s-93, annual rpt, A7330–1

Motor vehicle dealership outlets and sales, with detail by make, 1993 annual data book, C2710–3.531

Motorcycle retail franchised and nonfranchised outlets and operations, 1992 annual rpt, A6485–1.1

Operating and financial data for franchise industry, by type of business, 1991/92 and trends, annual rpt, A5820–1

Printing (quick) sales and establishments, for top 13 franchise companies, 1992 article, C1850–10.503

Restaurant franchises and sales, and franchisee fees and investment required, by leading company, 1993 annual feature, C1200–5.512

Restaurant minority franchisees, and minority-managed units, for 12 major chains, Sept 1993, article, C5150–5.511

Truck (heavy-/medium-duty) manufacturers ranked by desirability of franchises, dealer views, May and Nov 1992, article, C2710–3.525

Frank, David

"Agricultural Statistics and Prices for Louisiana, 1985-91", U2740–1

Fraternal benefit societies

Life insurance operating summary for fraternal benefit societies and savings banks, 1986-91, biennial fact book, A1325–1.7

State and local:

Alabama insurance industry financial and underwriting data, by company and line of coverage, 1991, annual rpt, S0160–1

Alaska insurance industry underwriting and investment data, by company and type of insurance, with regulatory info, 1991 and trends, annual rpt, S0280–3

California insurance industry financial and underwriting data, by company and type of insurance, with regulatory info, 1991, annual rpt, S0900–1

Connecticut insurance industry financial and underwriting data, by company and type of insurance, 1991, annual rpt, S1222–1

Florida insurance industry financial and underwriting data, by company and line of coverage, 1991, annual rpt, S1760–1

Georgia statistical abstract, general data, 1992-93 biennial rpt, U6730–1.9

Idaho insurance industry financial and underwriting data, by company and type of insurance, with regulatory data, 1991, annual rpt, S2260–1

Iowa insurance industry financial and underwriting data, by company and type of insurance, 1992, annual rpt, S2760–1

Kansas insurance industry financial and underwriting data, by company and type of insurance, with regulatory info, 1992, annual rpt, S2990–1

Maryland insurance industry financial and underwriting data, by company and type of insurance, with regulatory info, 1991, annual rpt, S3655–1

Michigan insurance industry financial and underwriting data, by company and type of insurance, with regulatory info, 1991, annual rpt, S3983–1

Minnesota insurance industry financial and underwriting data, by company and line of coverage, 1991, annual rpt, S4140 4

Missouri insurance industry financial and underwriting data, by company and type of insurance, with regulatory info, 1992, annual rpt, S4527–1

Nebraska insurance industry financial and underwriting data, by company and line of coverage, with regulatory info, 1992, annual rpt, S4890–1

New Jersey insurance industry financial and underwriting data, by company and type of insurance, 1990, annual rpt, S5420–1

New York State insurance industry financial and underwriting data, by company and line of coverage, 1991, annual rpt, S5770–2

Oklahoma insurance industry financial and underwriting data, by company and type of insurance, with regulatory info, 1992, annual rpt, S6462–1

Pennsylvania insurance industry financial and underwriting data, by company and line of coverage, 1991, with FY92 regulatory info, annual rpt, S6835–1

Rhode Island insurance industry financial and underwriting data, by company and line of coverage, 1990, with FY91 regulatory info, annual rpt, S6945–2

South Dakota insurance industry financial and underwriting data, by company and type of insurance, with regulatory info, 1991-92, annual rpt, S7300–2

Tennessee insurance industry financial and underwriting data, by company and type of insurance, with regulatory info, 1991, annual rpt, S7466–1

Texas insurance dept regulatory activities, with industry financial and underwriting data by line of coverage, FY92 annual rpt, S7700–1

Utah insurance industry financial and underwriting data, by company and line of coverage, with regulatory info, 1991, annual rpt, S7845–1

Vermont insurance industry financial and underwriting data, by company and type of insurance, 1991, annual rpt, S7995–1

West Virginia insurance industry financial and underwriting data, by company and line of coverage, with regulatory info, 1991, annual rpt, S8575–1

Wisconsin insurance industry financial and underwriting data, by company and line of coverage, with regulatory info, 1992, annual rpt, S8755–1

Fraud

Insurance premiums written for fidelity bonds, 1982-91, annual rpt, A5650–1.2

Motor vehicle odometer tampering prevalence by State, 1st half 1991, article, C1575–2.504

Shopping center security operations, including staffing, equipment, and crime incidents, by center type, 1992-93 and trends, articles, C5150–4.506

State and local:

Alabama juvenile and adult arrests, by type of offense, 1992, annual rpt, S0119–1.1

Arizona arrests by offense, offender characteristics, and county, 1992, annual rpt, S0505–2.2

Arkansas crimes and arrests, by offense, victim and offender characteristics, and location, 1992 and trends, annual rpt, S0652–1

California insurance dept fraudulent claims enforcement activity, including claim value by insurance type, 1991 and trends, annual rpt, S0900–1

Colorado crimes and arrests, by offense and location, with offender characteristics, and assaults on police, 1992, annual rpt, S1068–1

Connecticut arrests, by offense, offender characteristics, and local agency, 1992, annual rpt, S1256–1.2

DC criminal justice system summary, including crimes and arrests, criminal procedure, prisoners, and parole, 1991 and trends, annual rpt, S1535–2

Florida crimes and arrests, by offense, with data by victim and offender characteristics, 1992, annual rpt, S1770–1

Hawaii crimes and arrests, by offense, with data by county and victim-offender characteristics, 1992, annual rpt, S2035–1

Idaho crimes and arrests, by offense, with data by location and offender characteristics, 1992 and trends, annual rpt, S2275–2

Illinois crimes and arrests, by offense, with data by location and offender characteristics, 1991, annual rpt, S2536–1

Indiana welfare recipient fraud cases, and actions taken, FY92, annual rpt, S2623–1.8

Kansas crimes and arrests, by offense, with data by location, agency, and victim-offender characteristics, 1992 and trends, annual rpt, S2925–1.1

Kentucky arrests by county and offense, and law enforcement employment by agency, 1992, annual rpt, S3150–1.2

Maine arrests of adults and juveniles, by offense, age, and sex, 1991, annual rpt, S3475–1.2

Maryland crimes and arrests, by offense, location, and offender characteristics, with law enforcement employment and assaults on officers, 1992 and trends, annual rpt, S3665–1

Maryland medical assistance fraud investigations and recoveries, FY92, annual rpt, S3635–3

Maryland welfare program statistics, and welfare fraud investigations, by county, monthly rpt, S3645–2

Michigan crimes and arrests, by offense, with data by location and offender characteristics, 1992 and trends, annual rpt, S3997–1

Missouri crimes and arrests, by offense and location, with victim and offender characteristics, 1991 and trends, annual rpt, S4560–2

Montana crimes and clearances, by offense and jurisdiction, 1992, annual rpt, S4705–1

Montana welfare fraud investigations, convictions, and recoveries, FY91-92, biennial rpt, S4750–1.1

New Hampshire arrests, by offense and offender age, sex, and race-ethnicity, 1991, annual rpt, S5250–2.2

New Jersey arrests by offense, age, race-ethnicity, sex, and county, 1992 and trends, annual rpt, S5430–1.2

New York State crimes and arrests by offense and demographic characteristics, and court activity and corrections, 1991 and trends, annual rpt, S5760–3

New York State insurance dept fraud investigation and prosecution activity, 1991, annual rpt, S5770–3

North Carolina arrests by detailed offense, offender characteristics, and county, 1991-92, annual rpt, S5955–1.2

North Dakota crimes and arrests, by offense, location, and offender characteristics, and law enforcement employment, 1991 and trends, annual rpt, S6060–1

Oklahoma crimes and arrests, by offense, with victim and offender characteristics, 1990-92, annual rpt, S6465–1.1

Oregon crimes and arrests, by offense, with data by county, local agency, and offender characteristics, 1992 and trends, annual rpt, S6603–3

Pennsylvania crimes and arrests, by offense, with data by location and offender characteristics, 1992 and trends, annual rpt, S6860–1

South Carolina AFDC and food stamp fraud case detection and prosecution activity, by county, monthly rpt, S7252–1

South Carolina crimes and arrests, by detailed offense, offender characteristics, and location, 1992 and trends, annual rpt, S7205–1.2

Texas arrests, by age, sex, race-ethnicity, and offense, 1992, annual rpt, S7735–2.2

Texas insurance fraud cases, dispositions, penalties, and restitution, FY92, annual rpt, S7700–1

Texas welfare and social services program expenditures, recipients, and fraud cases, by county and/or program, FY92 and trends, annual rpt, S7695–1

Utah crimes and arrests, by offense, county, and local agency, 1992 and trends, annual rpt, S7890–3

Virginia crimes and arrests by offense, and law enforcement employment, by location and reporting agency, 1992, annual rpt, S8295–2.2

Washington State crimes and arrests, by offense, with data by location and offender characteristics, 1992 and trends, annual rpt, S8440–1

West Virginia court caseloads and dispositions, by type of court and case, and judicial circuit, 1992 and trends, annual rpt, S8537–1

West Virginia crimes and arrests, by offense, location, and offender characteristics, 1990-91, annual rpt, S8610–1

West Virginia welfare recipient fraud case investigations and actions taken, by State region, monthly rpt, S8560–2

Wisconsin crimes and arrests, by offense, offender characteristics, county, and local agency, 1992 and trends, annual rpt, S8771–1

Wyoming adult and juvenile arrests, by offense, county, and local jurisdiction, 1991, annual rpt, S8867–3.2

see also Counterfeiting and forgery
see also Embezzlement

Frayer, Eric R.

"Capital Improvement Financing, 1991", A5800–2.112

Freedom of information

Germany public opinion on desirability of public access to East German secret police files, 1991 survey, C8915–8.2

Public opinion on acceptability of selected uses of public access to personal info contained in govt records, 1992 survey, annual rpt, B3280–2

Utility and transportation regulatory agencies operating under freedom of info statutes, 1991/92 annual rpt, A7015–2

Freedom of the press

College freshmen attitudes on admin regulation of student publications, by sex and instn type, fall 1992, annual survey, U6215–1

Europe public opinion on political, economic, and social issues, for 9 countries and 3 Soviet Union Republics, 1991 survey, C8915–8.1

Soviet Union political and economic restructuring issues, public opinion in Russia, Ukraine, and Lithuania, 1991-92 surveys, C8915–10

see also Censorship

Freedonia Group Inc.

Cellular telephone equipment sales and subscribers, and total communications equipment market, 1985, 1991, and 1996, article, C2000–1.504

Drug/pharmaceutical product packaging demand, by package type, 1980, 1991, and 1996, article, C1850–1.503

Graphite demand by type and market, 1982, 1992, and 1997, article, C7000–8.505

Home security mechanical equipment, alarm systems, and services market value, 1980, 1991, and 1996, article, C2000–1.507

Medical device sterile packaging demand value, by package type, 1991 and 1996, article, C1850–1.502

Packaging (paper/paperboard and plastic) demand, by container type, 1980, 1991, and 1996, article, C1850–1.506

Paper (business) shipment value, by paper type, 1987, 1992, and 1997, article, A8140–3.505

Paperboard and corrugated box sales and shipment value, by end-use market or box type, 1991 and 1996, article, C0125–4.501

Plastic container demand, by container type, 1980, 1991, and 1996, article, C1850–1.501

Plastic packaging recycling volume, by plastic type, 1985, 1991, and 1996, article, C1850–1.507

Plastics demand of appliance industry, by plastic and appliance type, 1987, 1992, and 1997, article, C2000–1.509

Refrigeration commercial equipment sales and shipments, with detail by equipment type, 1982, 1992, and 1997, article, C2000–1.509

Textile dye sales by process, 1989 and 1994, article, C5800–8.505

Freelance workers

see Self-employment
see Temporary and seasonal employment

Freeways

see Highways, streets, and roads

Freight

Chemical products freight volume and value, with detail for rail and other transport modes, 1992 and trends, annual rpt, A3850–1

Coal rail freight index, monthly rpt, C5226–1

Costs of motor carrier transport for approx 150 commodities, 2 alternative measures, 1992 article, U5930–1.501

EC cargo traffic and GNP shares for member countries or groups, 1993 article, C2150–6.504

Financial performance and growth rankings for approx 1,000 top corporations, with comparisons by industry group, 1993 annual rpt, C3950–1.505

Financial ratios and performance, for over 350 SIC 4-digit industries, FY88-92, annual rpt, A6400–3

Grain futures and options trading activity on Minneapolis exchange, with production, price, and disposition data for area served, 1992 and trends, annual rpt, B6110–1

Hard goods manufacturers govt regulation experience, including assessments for undercharges by common carriers, by product line, 1993 annual survey rpt, A1800–1

Intercity freight distribution and revenues, by mode, 1982-91, annual rpt, A3275–8.1

Intercity freight ton-miles, by mode, 1950s-91, annual rpt, A0865–1.3

Interstate migration patterns indicated by household goods shipments, by State, 1992, annual press release, B0210–1, B9300–1

Iron ore shipments in US and Canada, with detail by Great Lakes port, monthly rpt, A2010–2

Latin America statistical abstract, general data by country, 1992 annual rpt, U6250–1.3

Logistics professionals views on transportation and trade policy issues, Dec 1992 survey, article, C2150–1.505

Logistics trends and devs, including data on costs, finances of major carriers by mode, and foreign trade, 1993 annual compilation, C2150–1.506

Lumber industry distribution channels, principal market areas, and transport modes, selected Western States, 1992, annual rpt, A9395–1

Mexico-Texas transportation system analysis, including bilateral trade, operations by transport mode, and data by locale, 1993 rpt, U8850–9

Oil and refined products domestic transport, by mode, 1974-89, annual rpt, C6985–5.2

Oil transported in US, by mode, 1972-91, periodic basic data book, A2575–14.5

Paper and forest products transportation data, including price trends and US and Canadian rail carloadings, 1993 annual rpt, C3975–5.1

Railroad (Class I) financial condition, operations, and employment, by company and district, 1992, annual rpt, A3275–7

Railroad (Class I) traffic, employment, finances, and equipment, by district and State, 1920s-92, annual rpt, A3275–5

Freight

Railroad financial and operating trends, including data by company, 1982-91, annual rpt, A3275–8

Railroad freight car loadings by commodity, and ton-miles, weekly press release, A3275–2

Railroad freight car loadings by commodity, piggyback carloadings, and revenue ton-miles, monthly rpt, C8400–1

Railroad operating data, including top commodities handled, employment and wages, and retirement system, by State, 1991, annual rpt, A3275–10

Ratings by shippers on quality of individual freight carriers, by mode, 1993 annual survey article, C2150–1.507

Regulatory agency policies and practices for motor carriers and railroads, by agency, 1991/92 annual rpt, A7015–4

Retail industry inventory mgmt, warehousing, and distribution operations, by outlet type, 1993 survey, C5150–4.506

Shippers switching between use of intermodal vs truck transportation, 1992 survey, article, C2150–4.502

Taiwan economic indicators, monthly rpt, U1245–1

Trends in transportation operations and finances, by mode, 1991 annual rpt, R4815–1

Truck fleet financial and operating data for top 200 freight carriers, 1992 and trends, annual feature, C2150–4.504

Truck tonnage summary, and related indicators, monthly press release, A3075–1

State and local:

Alabama statistical abstract, general data, 1992 recurring rpt, U5680–2.16

Arkansas River freight traffic, quarterly business activity rpt, U5930–1

Georgia statistical abstract, general data, 1992-93 biennial rpt, U6730–1.8

Hawaii data book, general data, 1992 annual rpt, S2090–1.18, S2090–1.24

Idaho economic profile, general data, 1992 recurring rpt, S2218–2.8

Maine employment in trade, utilities, and transportation SIC 2-digit industries, by detailed occupation, 2nd qtr 1991, triennial rpt, S3465–1.25

Mississippi statistical abstract, general data, 1992 annual rpt, U3255–4.6

Montana wheat shipments out of State, by mode, 1991-92 annual rpt, S4655–1

Nebraska railroad revenue freight by commodity, and earnings, by railroad, 1990-91, biennial rpt, S4940–1

New York State statistical yearbook, general data, 1992 annual rpt, U5100–1.13

North Carolina railroad revenue freight tonnage, by commodity, Dec 1990, annual rpt, S5917–2

Oklahoma statistical abstract, general data, 1992 annual rpt, U8130–2.16

Tennessee statistical abstract, general data, 1992/93 annual rpt, U8710–2.9

Texas trade, transportation, and public utilities employment, by SIC 2- and 3-digit industry and detailed occupation, 2nd qtr 1991, triennial survey rpt, S7675–1.31

Utah statistical abstract, general data, 1993 triennial rpt, U8960–1.13

Wisconsin Blue Book, general data, 1993-94 biennial rpt, S8780–1.2

see also Air cargo

see also Coal exports and imports

see also Containerization

see also Energy exports and imports

see also Foreign trade

see also Hazardous substances transport

see also Industrial distribution

Freight cars

see Railroad equipment and vehicles

French Antilles

see Caribbean area

French Polynesia

see Oceania

French West Indies

see Caribbean area

Fretwell, Gordon

"ARL Annual Salary Survey, 1992", A3365–2

Fringe benefits

see Employee benefits

Fritz, Sara

"Handbook of Campaign Spending: Money in the 1990 Congressional Races", C2500–6

Frost and Sullivan Inc.

Bar coding labeling technology revenues worldwide, by product type, 1993, article, C5800–8.512

Computer (personal) memory card sales, by application, 1992, 1994, and 1996, article, C1850–2.507

Computer-integrated manufacturing (CIM) open system market outlook, by system use, 1991 and 1996, article, C1850–12.502

Electronics surface-mount-technology manufacturing equipment sales, 1990-96, article, C1850–2.512

Industrial pneumatic power systems/components market value, 1992 and 1996, article, C1850 4.505

Lubricants (synthetic) market volume, by product type, 1991 and 1996, article, C5800–8.509

Lubricants (synthetic) wholesale shipments value, by use category, 1991 and 1996, article, C5150–3.501

Paper processing chemicals market by type, 1991, article, C3975–2.501

Personal care/cosmetic product raw materials sales, by ingredient and/or product type, 1990, 1993, and 1996, article, A1250–1.522

Frozen foods

Advertising expenditures by medium for top 100 advertisers, with comparisons to earnings and sales, and detail by product type and brand, 1991-92, annual rpt, C2710–1.547

Exports of farm products, by detailed commodity and country of destination, US and California, 1991, annual rpt, B9520–1

Financial ratios and performance, for over 350 SIC 4-digit industries, FY88-92, annual rpt, A6400–3

Military commissary frozen food sales, for top 10 commodities, FY92 and trends, article, C0500–1.503

Military commissary sales, by region, product type, and individual store, FY92, annual feature, A2072–2.501

Production of ice cream and frozen desserts by State, region, and country, with related industry operating info, 1992 and trends, annual rpt, A5825–1

Retail prices for selected consumer items in approx 300 cities, quarterly rpt, A0150–1

Sales and consumer expenditures, for food store products by type, 1991-92, annual feature, C4655–1.510

Sales volume shares by retail outlet type, for approx 300 food, drug, and other product categories, 1993 annual feature, C4655–1.504

Supermarket product sales and market shares, for top 10 brands in 10 frozen food product categories, 1991-92, C2710–1.501

Supermarket sales by detailed product type, 1992 and trends, annual feature, C5225–1.507

Supermarket seafood dept sales and performance indicators, 1992 annual survey feature, C4825–3.501

see also Ice cream

Fruit and fruit products

Exports of farm products, by detailed commodity and country of destination, US and California, 1991, annual rpt, B9520–1

Juice purchasing by consumers at discount stores, and leading brands, 1993 survey article, C5150–3.510

Juice vending machine sales, 1982 and 1990-92, annual rpt, C9470–1

Latin America statistical abstract, general data by country, 1992 annual rpt, U6250–1.24, U6250–1.25

Production, consumption, stocks, trade, and prices for approx 100 basic commodities, including by country and producing State, commodity yearbook for 1993, C2400–1, C2400–2

Retail prices for selected consumer items in approx 300 cities, quarterly rpt, A0150–1

Sales and consumer expenditures, for food store products by type, 1991-92, annual feature, C4655–1.510

Sales volume shares by retail outlet type, for approx 300 food, drug, and other product categories, 1993 annual feature, C4655–1.504

Supermarket produce dept sales and performance indicators, 1992 and trends, annual article, C4655–1.511

Supermarket sales by detailed product type, 1992 and trends, annual feature, C5225–1.507

State and local:

Alabama agricultural production, marketing, and income, by county and/or commodity, and farms and acreage, 1992 and trends, annual rpt, S0090–1

Arizona agricultural production, marketing, and finances, by commodity and county, 1988-92, annual rpt, U5830–1

Arkansas agricultural production, marketing, and finances, by commodity and county, with farms and acreage, 1992 and trends, annual rpt, U5920–1

California fruit and nut production, marketing, and income, by commodity, 1983-92, annual rpt, S0850–1.1

California melon production and marketing, 1992 and trends, annual rpt, S0850–1.3

Index by Subjects and Names

Fuel oil

Colorado agricultural production, marketing, and finances, by commodity and/or county, with farms and acreage, 1992 and trends, annual rpt, S0985–1

Florida vegetable, melon, and strawberry production, acreage, yield, shipments, and exports, 1991/92 and trends, annual rpt, S1685–1.2

Georgia agricultural production, marketing, and finances, by commodity and/or county, and farms and acreage, 1991 and trends, annual rpt, S1855–1

Hawaii agricultural production and marketing, by commodity and island, 1987-91, annual rpt, S2030–1

Hawaii data book, general data, 1992 annual rpt, S2090–1.13, S2090–1.22

Hawaii, Honolulu County pineapple sales, 1988-91, annual rpt, B3500–2.2

Hawaii, Maui County pineapple sales, 1988-91, annual rpt, B3500–2.3

Hawaii pineapple production and industry employment, bimonthly rpt, B3500–1

Hawaii pineapple production value, quarterly rpt, S2090–2

Illinois agricultural production, marketing, and finances, by county or commodity, and farms and farmland, 1991 and trends, annual rpt, S2390–1

Kansas agricultural production, marketing, and finances, by county and/or commodity, and farm acreage and value, 1992 and trends, annual rpt, S2915–1

Kentucky agricultural production, marketing, and finances, by commodity and county; and farms, acreage, and value; 1992 and trends, annual rpt, S3085–1

Louisiana agricultural production, marketing, and finances, by commodity or parish, 1985-91, annual rpt, U2740–1

Michigan agricultural production, marketing, and finances, by commodity or county, 1987-91, annual rpt, S3950–1

Minnesota agricultural production, marketing, and finances, by county or commodity, and farms and acreage, 1992 and trends, annual rpt, S4130–1

Missouri agricultural production, marketing, and finances, by commodity and/or county, and farms and acreage, 1988-92, annual rpt, S4480–1

Montana agricultural production, marketing, and finances, by commodity and county, 1991 and trends, annual rpt, S4655–1

New Jersey agricultural production, marketing, and finances, by commodity and/or county, and farms and acreage, 1986-91, annual rpt, S5350–1

New Mexico agricultural production, marketing, and finances, by commodity and county, with farms and acreage, 1991 and trends, annual rpt, S5530–1

New York State fruit production, marketing, and operating data, including apple processing plants, 1983-92, annual rpt, S5700–1

North Carolina agricultural production, marketing, and finances, by commodity and county, 1991 and trends, annual rpt, S5885–1

Ohio agricultural production, marketing, and finances, by commodity and county, with farms and acreage, 1990-91 and trends, annual rpt, S6240–1

Oklahoma agricultural production, marketing, and finances, by commodity and county, 1992 and trends, annual rpt, S6405–1

Oregon agricultural production, marketing, and finances, by commodity and/or county, with farms and acreage, 1991 and trends, annual rpt, S6575–1

Pennsylvania agricultural production, marketing, and finances, by county and commodity, and farms and acreage, 1992 and trends, annual rpt, S6760–1

South Carolina agricultural production and finances, by commodity and county, 1991-92 and trends, annual rpt, U1075–3

Tennessee agricultural production and marketing, by commodity and county, with farms, acreage, and farm value, 1992 and trends, annual rpt, S7460–1

Texas agricultural production, marketing, and finances, by commodity and county, and farms and farmland, 1991 and trends, annual rpt series, S7630–1

Utah agricultural production, marketing, and finances, by commodity and county, with farms and acreage, 1992 and trends, annual rpt, S7800–1

Vermont agricultural production, marketing, and finances, by commodity, with data on govt inspections and funding, 1989-90 biennial rpt, S7978–1

Washington State agricultural production, marketing, and finances, by commodity and/or county, 1992 and trends, annual rpt, S8328–1

West Virginia agricultural production, marketing, and finances, by commodity or county, 1991 and trends, annual rpt, S8510–1

Wisconsin agricultural production, marketing, and finances, by commodity and county, and farms, acreage, and sales, 1992 and trends, annual rpt, S8680–1

see also Citrus fruits

see also Figs

see also Nuts

Fuel

see Agricultural energy use

see Aviation fuels

see Biomass energy

see Coal and coal mining

see Coal exports and imports

see Coal prices

see Coal reserves

see Coal stocks

see Diesel fuel

see Energy conservation

see Energy exploration and drilling

see Energy exports and imports

see Energy prices

see Energy projections

see Energy reserves

see Energy resources

see Energy stocks and inventories

see Fuel oil

see Fuel tax

see Gasoline

see Housing energy use

see Industrial and commercial energy use

see Kerosene

see Liquefied petroleum gas

see Low-income energy assistance

see Motor fuels

see Natural gas and gas industry

see Natural gas exports and imports

see Natural gas liquids

see Natural gas prices

see Natural gas reserves

see Offshore oil and gas

see Oil shale

see Petroleum and petroleum industry

see Petroleum exports and imports

see Petroleum prices

see Petroleum reserves

see Petroleum stocks

see Transportation energy use

see Wood fuel

Fuel oil

Apartment building (conventionally financed) detailed income and expense ratios for US and Canada, by building type, metro area, and US region, 1991 and trends, annual rpt, A5600–1

Apartment building (federally subsidized) detailed income and expense ratios, by building and subsidy type, building age, metro area, and region, 1991 and trends, annual rpt, A5600–5

Condominium, cooperative, and planned unit dev detailed expenses, for US and Canada, by building characteristics, metro area, and US region, 1991, annual rpt, A5600–3

Dealer operations, including heating and cooling equipment services, by region, 1992 annual survey, C4680–2

Electric utility financial and operating data, by State and census div, 1991 and trends, annual rpt, A4700–1

Financial ratios and performance, for over 350 SIC 4-digit industries, FY88-92, annual rpt, A6400–3

Futures and options contract open interest (outstanding commitments), on foreign exchanges, by commodity and exchange, monthly rpt, A5040–6

Heating equipment and appliance shipments, by type of energy consumed, quarterly rpt, A1775–1

Imports of crude oil and refined products, by importing company, port, and country of origin, monthly rpt, A2575–12

Intl energy sourcebook, with detail on oil and gas industry operations, supply-demand, and prices, for approx 80 countries, 1970s-91, annual compilation, C6985–10

Japan energy supply-demand and outlook, by fuel source, 1980s-2000, recurring article, R5650–2.536

Latin America statistical abstract, general data by country, 1992 annual rpt, U6250–1.23

Marketing and service operations of fuel oil dealers, with related supply-demand and price data by region and State, 1993 annual fact book, C4680–1.507

Office building detailed income and expense data, and energy use, US and Canada, by building characteristics, metro area, and US region, 1991 and trends, annual rpt, A5600–2

Production, exploration, drilling, refining, stock, price, and financial data for US and foreign oil and gas industry, weekly rpt, C6985–1

Production, exploration, refining, demand, finance, prices, and reserves, by State and country or world area, 1993 periodic basic data book, A2575–14.3, A2575–14.4

Fuel oil

Refinery cost index for residual fuel oil, by PAD district, quarterly 1989-92, article, C6985–1.536

Shopping center detailed income and expense data, by building characteristics, metro area, and region, 1991, annual rpt, A5600 6

Sourcebook of oil and gas industry operations and finances, and world supply-demand situation, 1970s-91, annual compilation, C6985–9

Statistical compilation of oil and gas industry trends, 1993 annual rpt, C6985–4

Stocks of gasoline, jet kerosene, and distillate and residual fuels, monthly rpt, C4680–1

Supply-demand and price data for energy resources, including by country and producing State, commodity yearbook for 1993, C2400–1

Supply-demand and price data for energy resources, including by country and producing State, commodity yearbook Jan-Sept 1993 updates, C2400–2

Supply-demand and prices, with data by PAD district, 1993 annual article, C6985–1.539

Supply-demand for crude oil and petroleum products, quarterly 1993, annual article, C4680–1.503

Supply-demand, trade, and industry exploration and operations, by product, exporting country and world area, PAD district, and State, 1993 annual feature, C6985–1.513

Supply, disposition, and stocks of refined oil products by type and/or crude oil, and refinery operations summary, monthly rpt, A2575–2

Supply of oil and refined products, including stocks, refinery operations, and imports, by PAD district and product, weekly rpt, A2575–1

State and local:

New York State statistical yearbook, general data, 1992 annual rpt, U5100–1.12

Pennsylvania energy supply-demand and prices by fuel type, with electric power info by utility, 1960s-90, recurring rpt, S6810–3

South Carolina statistical abstract, general data, 1993 annual rpt, S7125–1.8

see also Diesel fuel

see also Kerosene

Fuel tax

Collections of fuel taxes, Federal and by State, 1992 and trends, annual fact book, C4680–1.507

Cost estimates for 4 energy tax options considered by Clinton Admin, including gasoline, BTU, and carbon taxes, and oil import fee, by State and region, 1993 rpt, R8490–49

Economic impact of 5 proposed energy taxes, 1993-97, article, C6985–1.516

Federal gasoline tax per gallon, 1932-90, article, C2710–3.535

Gasoline Federal and average State taxes per gallon, 1980-94, article, C2710–3.546

Gasoline prices and tax component, for US and 6 foreign countries, 1992 annual rpt, C2140–1.3

Gasoline tax payments as a percent of family income, by income level, 1993 article, R9050–3.502

Index by Subjects and Names

Gasoline taxes and rates, with detail by State and comparisons to 7 foreign countries, 1993 article, R9050–3.507

Gasoline taxes and rates, with detail by State and comparisons to 7 foreign countries, 1993 rpt, R9050–15.6

Govt finances, including revenues by source, expenditures by function, and debt, detailed data for Federal, State, and local govts, 1993 annual rpt, R9050–1

State gasoline tax rates, by State, Jan 1993, annual rpt, A7118–1

State social, economic, and govtl indicators, with rankings, 1993 semiannual rpt, B8500–1.4, B8500–1.11

Transportation-related revenues of Fed Govt and individual States, by type, 1990s and trends, annual rpt, A0865–1.3

State and local:

Alabama financial condition, including revenues by source, expenditures by function and object, and fund balances, by fund and agency, FY92, annual rpt, S0129–1

Alabama statistical abstract, general data, 1992 recurring rpt, U5680–2.6

Alaska financial condition, including revenues by source, expenditures by function, fund balances, and bond obligations, FY92 and trends, annual rpt, S0275–1

Arizona statistical abstract, general data, 1993 recurring rpt, U5850–2.18

Arkansas financial condition, including revenues by source, expenditures by function and object, and fund balances, FY92, annual rpt, S0670–1

Arkansas interstate motor fuel and gasoline tax refund fund transactions, FY91-92, biennial rpt, S0780–1

California economic condition, including population, employment and earnings, income, business activity, and taxation, 1960s-92, annual rpt, S0840–3.2

California financial condition, including revenues by source, expenditures by agency and function, fund balances, and bonded debt, FY92 and trends, annual rpt, S0815–1

California fuel distributors sales volume and taxes assessed, by fuel type and company, FY92 and trends, annual rpt, S0835–1.4

Colorado tax revenues by type, with selected data by county and city, FY92 and trends, annual rpt, S1075–1

DC financial condition, including receipts by source, expenditures by object or function, and fund balances, FY92, annual rpt, S1507–1

Florida State govt disbursements to local areas, by source of funds, FY92, annual rpt, S1717–1

Florida statistical abstract, general data, 1992 annual rpt, U6660–1.23

Georgia tax revenues, by type and county, FY92 annual rpt, S1950–1

Hawaii tax collections and allocations, by type, for State and counties, FY91-92 and trends, annual rpt, S2120–1

Idaho tax statistics, including collections, and data by county and city, FY92 and trends, annual rpt, S2295–1

Illinois financial condition, including revenues by source, and expenditures by object, function, and agency, FY92, annual rpt, S2415–1

Indiana financial condition, including revenues by source, expenditures by function and object, and fund balances, by agency, FY92, annual rpt, S2570–1

Kansas statistical abstract, general data, 1991/92 annual rpt, U7095–2.13

Kansas tax collections by tax type, and property values, with data by county, FY92 and trends, annual rpt, S3020–1

Maryland financial condition, including revenues by source, expenditures by function, fund balances, and bonded debt, FY92 and trends, annual rpt, S3685–2

Massachusetts tax collections by type, and distributions to local areas, FY91 and trends, annual rpt, S3917–1

Michigan financial condition, including revenues by source, expenditures by function, and fund balances, FY92 and trends, annual rpt, S3985–2

Minnesota financial condition, including revenues by source, expenditures by function, fund balances, and bonded debt, FY92 and trends, annual rpt, S4180–1

Mississippi tax collections by type, and disbursements, with selected sales and income tax data by locality and industry, FY92 and trends, annual rpt, S4435–1

Missouri financial condition, including fund finances, tax collections and distribution, and State treasury activity, FY92 and trends, annual rpt, S4570–1

Nebraska revenues from licenses, fees, and miscellaneous taxes, 1991 and trends, annual rpt, S4950–1.3

Nevada statistical abstract, general data, 1992 biennial rpt, S5005–1.11

New Hampshire financial condition, with revenues by source, expenditures by function or object, and fund balances, FY92 and trends, annual rpt, S5175–1

New Mexico tax revenues and disbursements, with data by tax type, county, and city, FY91-92 and trends, annual rpt, S5660–1

New York State tax collections by type, FY84-93, annual rpt, S5710–1

North Carolina financial condition, including revenues by source, expenditures by function, fund balances, and bonded debt, FY92, annual rpt, S5897 1

Ohio fuel tax collections, FY88-92, and distributions by county, 1992, annual rpt, S6390–1.4

Oklahoma tax revenues by source, and distribution to local govts and State funds, FY92 and trends, annual rpt, S6495–1

Pennsylvania tax collections by tax type, with data by county and industry, FY92 and trends, annual rpt, S6885–1

South Dakota tax revenues by source, and aid distributed to local areas, FY92 annual rpt, S7380–1.1

Tennessee statistical abstract, general data, 1992/93 annual rpt, U8710–2.9

Tennessee tax revenues by source and apportionments to counties, cities, and funds, FY91-92 and trends, biennial rpt, S7570–1

Texas financial condition, including revenues by source, expenditures by function and dept, and investments, with data for over 400 individual funds, FY92, annual rpt, S7655–2

Index by Subjects and Names

Furs and fur industry

Utah tax revenues by source, and distribution to localities and State funds, FY92 and trends, annual rpt, S7905–1

Washington State revenues by source, and distributions by tax and locality, FY92 and trends, annual rpt, S8415–1.1

Wisconsin Blue Book, general data, 1993-94 biennial rpt, S8780–1.2

Wisconsin financial condition, including revenues by source, expenditures by function and object, and fund balances, FY93, annual rpt, S8675–2

Wyoming State treasurer financial transactions, revenues, investments, and disbursements by local area, FY92 and trends, annual rpt, S9010–1

see also Severance taxes

Fugitives from justice

- Correctional instn admin, inmates, facilities, costs, parole and probation, and staffing, for local, State, and Federal systems, 1992 annual series, R4300–1
- Correctional instn inmate escapees, by State and Canadian Province, as of June 1992, annual rpt, A1305–3

State and local:

- California correctional instn escapes, by sex, 1970-91, annual rpt, S0820–1
- California correctional instn inmates, by offense, demographic characteristics, and instn, Dec 1992, semiannual rpt, S0820–2
- California criminal justice system detailed data, by offense, county, age, race-ethnicity, and sex, 1991 and trends, annual rpt, S0910–2.2
- DC criminal justice system summary, including crimes and arrests, criminal procedure, prisoners, and parole, 1991 and trends, annual rpt, S1535–2
- Florida correctional instn escapes and captures, FY92, annual rpt, S1770–1
- Georgia correctional instns, admin, and inmate characteristics, FY92, annual rpt, S1872–1
- Iowa correctional instn escapes and returns, by instn, monthly rpt, S2770–1
- Kansas correctional instn inmates, by offense, demographic characteristics, and instn, FY92 and trends, annual rpt, S2940–1
- Massachusetts correctional instn inmate socioeconomic characteristics and criminal background, by instn, Jan 1992 and trends, annual rpt, S3805–1
- Michigan inmate escapes from correctional instns and community programs, 1991, annual rpt, S3960–1
- Nebraska correctional instn admin, with inmates by criminal background and demographic characteristics, by instn, FY92 and trends, annual rpt, S4850–1
- New York State correctional instn escapes and abscondences, by sex, 1991, recurring rpt, S5725–1.1
- North Carolina prison escapes and captures, by crime category and instn, FY93, semiannual rpt, S5900–1
- North Dakota local correctional instn adult and juvenile inmate characteristics, by instn, 1991 and trends, annual rpt, S6060–3
- Pennsylvania State prison escapes, by instn, 1980-90, annual rpt, S6782–1

Tennessee correctional instn admin, with inmate characteristics, and corrections dept finances and staff, FY92, annual rpt, S7480–1

Wisconsin correctional instn inmates, admissions, and releases, by instn and sex, FY92 and trends, annual rpt, S8692–1.6

Wisconsin correctional instn inmates, admissions, and releases, by instn and sex, 1991 and trends, annual rpt, S8692–1.4

Wyoming correctional instn admin, finances, inmate characteristics, and staff, and probation and parole activities, FY92 annual rpt, S8883–1

Fujairah

see United Arab Emirates

Fundraising

see Campaign funds

see Gifts and private contributions

see Nonprofit organizations and foundations

Funerals

see Cemeteries and funerals

Fungicides

see Pesticides

Furnaces

see Plumbing and heating

Furniture and furnishings

- Cabinet (kitchen and bathroom) installation shares by wood type, 1993 feature, C5150–6.504
- Children's hard goods purchaser outlet preferences, 1993 article, C8130–1.511
- Consumer buying power survey of population, income, and sales by kind of business, by census div, State, MSA, county, and city, 1992, annual rpt, C1200–1.511
- Consumer buying power survey of population, income, and sales by product line, by State, metro area, county, and census div, 1993 annual rpt, C1200–1.514
- Corporate performance ratings by executives for leading companies in 32 industries, 1993 annual survey feature, C8900–1.508
- Cotton and other fiber consumption in textile production, by detailed end use, 1990-92, annual rpt, A7485–1
- Discount store sales and productivity data for 20 depts, 1993 annual feature, C5150–3.516
- Financial performance and growth rankings for approx 1,000 top corporations, with comparisons by industry group, 1993 annual rpt, C3950–1.505
- Financial ratios and performance, for over 350 SIC 4-digit industries, FY88-92, annual rpt, A6400–3
- Interstate migration patterns indicated by household goods shipments, by State, 1992, annual press release, B0210–1, B9300–1
- Kitchen cabinet wood types specified by kitchen designers, 1992 and trends, C4300–1.511
- Markets with daily newspapers, demographic and economic info by geographic area, US and Canada, 1993 annual rpt, C3250–1
- Medical group financial and operating data, by practice characteristics, 1991, annual rpt, A6365–2
- Operating and financial composite ratios for corporations, with establishments and receipts, for approx 200 industries, by asset size, FY90, annual rpt, C7800–1

Plastics industry production and sales by resin type, consumption by end-use market, and operating characteristics, 1992 and trends, annual rpt, A8920–1

Retail home furnishings industry financial and operating data, by firm characteristics and region, 1992 and trends, annual rpt, A7975–1

Shopping center financial and operating data, with detail by type of tenant, US and Canada, 1991, triennial rpt, R9285–1

Textile fiber end-use survey, consumption and trade, by type of fiber and product, 1988-92, annual survey, C3460–1.511

State and local:

- Colorado property assessed valuation by detailed property type, and tax levy and revenue by local district, by county, 1991-92, annual rpt, S1055–3
- Florida statistical abstract, general data, 1992 annual rpt, U6660–1.12
- Maine employment in trade, utilities, and transportation SIC 2-digit industries, by detailed occupation, 2nd qtr 1991, triennial rpt, S3465–1.25
- Montana property values, by detailed property class and type, with land acreage by use, by county, 1991-92 and trends, biennial rpt, S4750–1.2
- New Hampshire wholesale and retail trade employment, by SIC 2-digit industry and detailed occupation, 1991, triennial rpt, S5205–2.26
- North Carolina employment in trade, transportation, communications, utilities, govt, and education, by detailed occupation, 2nd qtr 1991, triennial rpt, S5917–5.2
- Texas trade, transportation, and public utilities employment, by SIC 2- and 3-digit industry and detailed occupation, 2nd qtr 1991, triennial survey rpt, S7675–1.31

see also Antiques

see also Business machines and equipment

see also Carpets and rugs

see also Floor coverings

see also Household appliances and equipment

see also Household supplies and utensils

see also Wall coverings

Furs and fur industry

State and local:

- Illinois mink ranches, breeding, and pelt production by color class, 1982-91, annual rpt, S2390–1
- Michigan mink ranches, and pelt production by color class, 1987-91, annual rpt, S3950–1
- Minnesota mink farms, pelts produced, and females bred, 1988-91 annual rpt, S4130–1
- New York State mink pelts produced and females bred, by color class, 1992 and trends, annual rpt, S5700–1
- Ohio mink pelts produced and females bred, by color class, 1988-91, annual rpt, S6240–1
- Oregon mink pelt production and females bred, by color, 1988-92, annual rpt, S6575–1
- Pennsylvania mink ranches, pelts produced, and females bred, 1993 and trends, annual rpt, S6760–1

Furs and fur industry

South Dakota mink ranches, pelts produced, and females bred, 1987-92, annual rpt, S7280–1

Utah mink ranches, and females bred and pelts produced, 1971-92, annual rpt, S7800–1

Washington State mink ranches, and females bred and pelts produced by color class and county, 1987-93, annual rpt, S8328–1

Wisconsin mink ranches, females bred, and pelts produced, 1988-92, annual rpt, S8680–1

see also Hides and skins

Future

see Projections and forecasts

Futures trading

- Chicago Board of Trade futures and options trading in financial instruments and agricultural commodities, 1992, annual rpt, B2120–1
- Coffee, Sugar, and Cocoa Exchange trading activity, with related data including deliveries and stocks by country and/or port, 1992 and trends, annual rpt, B2275–1
- Commodity futures investment performance and assets, for 10 largest managed funds, 1992 article, C5800–7.504
- Commodity price trends, with detail for selected commodities or groups, biweekly rpt quarterly feature, C3950–1.505, C3950–1.513, C3950–1.519, C3950–1.524
- Commodity yearbook for 1993: detailed supply-demand data, and selected indicators for futures market investors, C2400–1
- Commodity yearbook update: detailed supply-demand data, and selected indicators for futures market investors, Jan-Sept 1993 rpts, C2400–2
- Electronics manufacturer currency forwards/options purchases, for 3 companies, 1992, article, C1850–2.510
- Foreign trading volume by commodity and exchange, monthly rpt, A5040–5
- Fuel oil dealers futures trading activity, by region, 1992 annual survey, C4680–2.1
- Grain futures trading activity on Minneapolis exchange, with detailed commodity info for area served, 1992 and trends, annual rpt, B6110–1.1
- Grain market activity on Kansas City Board of Trade, including futures volume and prices, 1992 and trends, annual rpt, B1530–1
- New York Futures Exchange activities, and contract specifications, 1992, annual fact book, B6625–1.1
- Oil and gas futures prices, monthly 1991 and trends, annual compilation, C6985–9.3
- Oil contracts traded on New York Mercantile Exchange, by fuel type, 1978-91, annual rpt, C6985–5.1
- Open interest (outstanding commitments) on futures contracts, by commodity and exchange, monthly rpt, A5040–4
- Open interest (outstanding commitments) on futures contracts on foreign exchanges, by commodity and exchange, monthly rpt, A5040–6
- Silver futures trading volume and open interest, by exchange, 1970-93, annual rpt, A8902–4
- Trading volume by commodity and exchange, monthly rpt, A5040–2
- Trading volume by commodity and exchange, 1988-92, annual rpt, A5040–1

see also Options trading

Gabon

- Energy intl sourcebook, with detail on oil and gas industry operations, supply-demand, and prices, for approx 80 countries, 1970s-91, annual compilation, C6985–10.2
- Uranium mine ownership shares, 1992 annual rpt, B6800–2.2

see also Organization of Petroleum Exporting Countries

Gaines, Gale F.

"Cost of Teacher Benefits in the SREB States", A8945–34

Gallup Organization Inc.

- Advertising importance to public in 20 countries, 1993 survey article, C2710–1.549
- Airline travel frequency, destination, and purpose, by traveler characteristics, 1992 survey and trends, annual rpt, A0325–6
- Books as Christmas gifts, public opinion, 1990-92 surveys, article, C1852–2.503
- Catholic vs public school performance, and support for parental school selection funded by govt, public opinion by respondent characteristics, July 1992 survey, A7375–8
- Charitable contributions plans of general public, with views on operations and regulation of charities, July 1993 survey, article, C2176–1.520
- Congressional Member views on seriousness of 18 public policy issues, 1993 survey feature, C4300–1.506
- Elementary/secondary school problems, quality, and proposed reforms, public opinion by respondent characteristics, 1993 annual survey, A8680–1.503
- Employee leave and unpaid parental leave policy prevalence at companies with 500/fewer employees, 1992 survey, article, C4687–1.504
- Global warming and related issues, views of climate scientists, Feb 1992 survey, article, R3823–1.502
- Health care reform support among general public, Mar-Apr 1993 survey, article, A1865–1.514
- Public opinion on campaign ads influence in 1992 presidential election, by candidate, Oct 1992 survey, article, C2710–1.501
- Quality control and improvement, views and experience of corporate executives and outside directors, July-Aug 1992 surveys, A2800–3
- Religion and related social issues, public opinions and attitudes, monthly survey, R8780–1
- Volunteer activities and characteristics of teenagers vs adults, 1991, survey article, C2176–1.503
- Women's shopping patterns for cosmetics and fragrances, with views on store attributes, by outlet type, 1993 survey, annual feature, C5150–2.516
- Women's use and shopping patterns for personal care products, with preferred outlets and brands, 1993 survey and trends, annual feature, C5150–2.515

Youth age 12-17 charitable contributions, volunteer activity, and views on related issues, by respondent characteristics, 1992 survey, biennial rpt, A5435–5

Gambia

Women's contraceptive use discontinuation patterns among new family planning clinic clients in Niger and Gambia, 1992 article, A5160–6.502

Gambling

- Charity gambling gross receipts and net proceeds to charity, by State, 1992, article, C2176–1.520
- Charity gambling receipts, net proceeds, and State regulatory staff and finances, by State, various years FY90-92, article, C2176–1.512
- Public opinion on selected types of legalized gambling, and gambling behavior, Nov 1992 Gallup Poll and trends, C4040–1.506

State and local:

- Alabama juvenile and adult arrests, by type of offense, 1992, annual rpt, S0119–1.1
- Arizona arrests by offense, offender characteristics, and county, 1992, annual rpt, S0505–2.2
- Arizona State govt bingo tax collections, FY79-92, annual rpt, S0515–1
- Arkansas crimes and arrests, by offense, victim and offender characteristics, and location, 1992 and trends, annual rpt, S0652–1
- California crimes and arrests, clearances, and arrest dispositions, with data by offense and offender characteristics, 1987-92, annual rpt, S0910–1.1
- California criminal justice system detailed data, by offense, county, age, race-ethnicity, and sex, 1991 and trends, annual rpt, S0910–2
- Colorado commercial gaming property assessed valuation, by county, 1992, annual rpt, S1055 3
- Colorado crimes and arrests, by offense and location, with offender characteristics, and assaults on police, 1992, annual rpt, S1068–1
- Colorado limited stakes gaming revenues and expenditures, and distributions by fund or local area, FY92, annual rpt, S1075–1.3
- Colorado State constitutional amendments on legalized gambling, election results by county, 1992, biennial rpt, S1090–1
- Connecticut arrests, by offense, offender characteristics, and local agency, 1992, annual rpt, S1256–1.2
- DC criminal justice system summary, including crimes and arrests, criminal procedure, prisoners, and parole, 1991 and trends, annual rpt, S1535–2
- Florida crimes and arrests, by offense, with data by victim and offender characteristics, 1992, annual rpt, S1770–1
- Hawaii crimes and arrests, by offense, with data by county and victim-offender characteristics, 1992, annual rpt, S2035–1
- Idaho crimes and arrests, by offense, with data by location and offender characteristics, 1992 and trends, annual rpt, S2275–2

Index by Subjects and Names — Gasoline

Illinois crimes and arrests, by offense, with data by location and offender characteristics, 1991, annual rpt, S2536–1

Kansas crimes and arrests, by offense, with data by location, agency, and victim-offender characteristics, 1992 and trends, annual rpt, S2925–1.1

Kentucky arrests by county and offense, and law enforcement employment by agency, 1992, annual rpt, S3150–1.2

Maine arrests of adults and juveniles, by offense, age, and sex, 1991, annual rpt, S3475–1.2

Maryland crimes and arrests, by offense, location, and offender characteristics, with law enforcement employment and assaults on officers, 1992 and trends, annual rpt, S3665–1

Michigan crimes and arrests, by offense, with data by location and offender characteristics, 1992 and trends, annual rpt, S3997–1

Missouri crimes and arrests, by offense and location, with victim and offender characteristics, 1991 and trends, annual rpt, S4560–2

Montana crimes and clearances, by offense and jurisdiction, 1992, annual rpt, S4705–1

Nebraska charitable gaming tax receipts, 1990-91, annual rpt, S4950–1.3

Nevada business and economic activity indicators, with comparisons to other Western States, 1980-91, annual rpt, U7920–2

Nevada employment data for hotels/gaming/recreation industry, 1992 annual rpt, S5040–4

Nevada gaming revenues and taxes, FY83-92, annual rpt, S5025–1

Nevada, Las Vegas and Reno gaming revenues, quarterly rpt, S5040–1

Nevada statistical abstract, general data, 1992 biennial rpt, S5005–1.8

New Hampshire arrests, by offense and offender age, sex, and race-ethnicity, 1991, annual rpt, S5250–2.2

New Jersey arrests by offense, age, race-ethnicity, sex, and county, 1992 and trends, annual rpt, S5430–1.2

New York State crimes and arrests by offense and demographic characteristics, and court activity and corrections, 1991 and trends, annual rpt, S5760–3

North Carolina arrests by detailed offense, offender characteristics, and county, 1991-92, annual rpt, S5955–1.2

North Dakota crimes and arrests, by offense, location, and offender characteristics, and law enforcement employment, 1991 and trends, annual rpt, S6060–1

Oklahoma crimes and arrests, by offense, with victim and offender characteristics, 1990-92, annual rpt, S6465–1.1

Oklahoma State referendum concerning bingo and ticket games for charity, election results by county, 1992, biennial rpt, S6425–1

Oregon crimes and arrests, by offense, with data by county, local agency, and offender characteristics, 1992 and trends, annual rpt, S6603–3

Pennsylvania crimes and arrests, by offense, with data by location and offender characteristics, 1992 and trends, annual rpt, S6860–1

South Carolina crimes and arrests, by detailed offense, offender characteristics, and location, 1992 and trends, annual rpt, S7205–1.2

Texas arrests, by age, sex, race-ethnicity, and offense, 1992, annual rpt, S7735–2.2

Utah crimes and arrests, by offense, county, and local agency, 1992 and trends, annual rpt, S7890–3

Virginia crimes and arrests by offense, and law enforcement employment, by location and reporting agency, 1992, annual rpt, S8295–2.2

Washington State crimes and arrests, by offense, with data by location and offender characteristics, 1992 and trends, annual rpt, S8440–1

West Virginia crimes and arrests, by offense, location, and offender characteristics, 1990-91, annual rpt, S8610–1

Wisconsin crimes and arrests, by offense, offender characteristics, county, and local agency, 1992 and trends, annual rpt, S8771–1

Wisconsin State constitutional amendment allowing video gambling, election results by county, 1993-94 biennial rpt, S8780–1.3

Wyoming adult and juvenile arrests, by offense, county, and local jurisdiction, 1991, annual rpt, S8867–3.2

see also Casinos

see also Horse racing

see also Lotteries

see also Pari-mutuel wagering

Game

see Birds and bird conservation

see Hunting and trapping

see Wildlife and wildlife conservation

Games

see Electronic games

see Olympic games

see Toys and games

Garbage

see Landfills

see Refuse and refuse disposal

Garbett, Thomas F.

"Corporate Advertising Practices, 1992", A3357–1

Garden equipment

see Lawn and garden equipment

Gardening

see Flowers and nursery products

see Horticulture

see Lawn and garden equipment

Garment industry

see Clothing and clothing industry

Garwood, Alfred N.

"Black Americans: A Statistical Sourcebook, 1993 Edition", C6775–2

"Hispanic Americans: A Statistical Sourcebook, 1993 Edition", C6775–3

Gas appliances

see Household appliances and equipment

Gas utilities

see Natural gas and gas industry

Gas wells

see Energy exploration and drilling

Gases

Carbon dioxide pipelines in Texas/New Mexico Permian Basin region, with ownership, mileage, and throughput capacity, 1993 article, C6985–1.542

Carbon dioxide production, distribution by source, 1993 article, C5800–8.505

Chlorine consumption, and consumer and capital investment costs of using substitutes, by end use and product, 1993 article, A1250–1.524

Electronics industry worldwide market for gases, with market shares for top 5 and all other suppliers, 1992, article, C1850–2.504

Hydrogen production capacity of oil refineries worldwide, by country, company, and US State, 1992 annual feature, C6985–1.508

Hydrogen production capacity of oil refineries worldwide, by country, company, and US State, 1993 annual compilation, C6985–4.1

Hydrogen supply-demand at oil refineries, and consumption by end user, 1993 article, C6985–1.521

Industrial gas market value, by country or world region, 1991, article, C5800–8.502

Oxygen consumption in iron and steel industry, by use, US and Canada, 1988-92, annual rpt, A2000–2

Production of industrial gases and other financial and operating data for chemical industry, 1970s-92, annual rpt, A3850–1

see also Air pollution

see also Helium

see also Liquefied petroleum gas

see also Natural gas and gas industry

see also Radon

Gasohol

Consumption of gasohol by State, 1991-92, annual fact book, C4680–1.507

Use of gasohol as percent of hwy use gasoline, by State, 1991, semiannual rpt, B8500–1.11

State and local:

Colorado taxable motor fuel monthly gallonage received by distributors, FY90-92, annual rpt, S1075–1.4

Florida statistical abstract, general data, 1992 annual rpt, U6660–1.23

Montana gasohol-related property value, by county, 1991-92, biennial rpt, S4750–1.2

Nebraska revenues from licenses, fees, and miscellaneous taxes, 1991 and trends, annual rpt, S4950–1.3

South Carolina statistical abstract, general data, 1993 annual rpt, S7125–1.8

Gasoline

Convenience store gasoline sales and operating data, 1992 and trends, annual survey rpt, A6735–1, A6735–2

Convenience store gasoline sales, by chain company, 1993 annual article, C4680–1.509

Convenience stores with gasoline marketing operations, by chain company, census div, and State, 1992, annual article, C4680–1.502

Convenience stores with gasoline marketing operations, by chain company, census div, and State, 1993, annual article, C4680–1.510

Corporate fleet vehicle driver maintenance habits, model preferences, and cellular telephone and credit card use, 1993 survey, article, C1575–2.509

Gasoline

Demand for motor gasoline, monthly rpt, R9375–1

Fuel oil dealer sales by product, employment, computer use, and truck fleet size, by region, 1992 annual survey, C4680–2.1

Intl energy sourcebook, with detail on oil and gas industry operations, supply-demand, and prices, for approx 80 countries, 1970s-91, annual compilation, C6985–10

Japan energy supply-demand and outlook, by fuel source, 1980s-2000, recurring article, R5650–2.536

Oxygenates and gasoline supply-demand and outlook, 1991-97, article, C6985–1.505

Price of gasoline, 1973-92, annual rpt, A5425–2.2

Price per gallon and tax component, for US and 6 foreign countries, 1992 annual rpt, C2140–1.3

Prices by grade and region, monthly rpt, C4680–1

Prices by grade, 1975-92, annual rpt, A0865–1.3

Prices of unleaded gasoline, by selected city, July-Dec 1992, annual rpt, C1575–2.507

Prices of unleaded gasoline, by selected city, monthly rpt, C1575–2

Production, exploration, drilling, refining, stock, price, and financial data for US and foreign oil and gas industry, weekly rpt, C6985–1

Production, exploration, refining, demand, finance, prices, and reserves, by State and country or world area, 1993 and trends, periodic basic data book, A2575–14.3, A2575–14.4

Retail prices for selected consumer items in approx 300 cities, quarterly rpt, A0150–1

Sourcebook of oil and gas industry operations and finances, and world supply-demand situation, 1970s-91, annual compilation, C6985–9

State social, economic, and govtl indicators, with rankings, 1993 semiannual rpt, B8500–1.11

Statistical compilation of oil and gas industry trends, 1993 annual rpt, C6985–4

Stocks of gasoline, jet kerosene, and distillate and residual fuels, monthly rpt, C4680–1

Supply-demand and price data for energy resources, including by country and producing State, commodity yearbook for 1993, C2400–1

Supply-demand and price data for energy resources, including by country and producing State, commodity yearbook Jan-Sept 1993 updates, C2400–2

Supply-demand and prices, with data by PAD district, 1993 annual article, C6985–1.539

Supply-demand for crude oil and petroleum products, quarterly 1993, annual article, C4680–1.503

Supply-demand, marketing, prices, finances, and employment, detailed data for US and Canada, by product, company, and location, with octane averages, 1993 annual fact book, C4680–1.507

Supply-demand, trade, and industry exploration and operations, by product, exporting country and world area, PAD district, and State, 1993 annual feature, C6985–1.513

Supply, disposition, and stocks of refined oil products by type and/or crude oil, and refinery operations summary, monthly rpt, A2575–2

Supply of oil and refined products, including stocks, refinery operations, and imports, by PAD district and product, weekly rpt, A2575–1

State and local:

Alabama statistical abstract, general data, 1992 recurring rpt, U5680–2.16

Arizona statistical abstract, general data, 1993 recurring rpt, U5850–2.20

Arkansas gasoline plant intake and production, monthly rpt, S0737–1

California fuel distributors sales volume and taxes assessed, by fuel type and company, FY92 and trends, annual rpt, S0835–1.4

Colorado taxable motor fuel monthly gallonage received by distributors, FY90-92, annual rpt, S1075–1.4

Florida statistical abstract, general data, 1992 annual rpt, U6660–1.15, U6660–1.23

Hawaii data book, general data, 1992 annual rpt, S2090–1.17

Hawaii fuel consumed and fuel taxes allocated, by type and use, FY91-92, annual rpt, S2120–1

Maryland statistical abstract, general data, 1993-94 biennial rpt, S3605–1.10

Nevada statistical abstract, general data, 1992 biennial rpt, S5005–1.11

New York State statistical yearbook, general data, 1992 annual rpt, U5100–1.12

Ohio gasoline and special fuels consumption, FY88-92, annual rpt, S6390–1.4

Pennsylvania energy supply-demand and prices by fuel type, with electric power info by utility, 1960s-90, recurring rpt, S6810–3

South Carolina economic condition, including energy and transportation data, 1970s-92, annual rpt, S7125–3.3

South Carolina statistical abstract, general data, 1993 annual rpt, S7125–1.8

Tennessee economic indicator trends and forecasts, with data by industry div and manufacturing group, 1982-2001, annual rpt, S7560–1

Virginia motor vehicle registrations, mileage, and fuel consumption, 1982-91, annual rpt, S8282–1

see also Aviation fuels

see also Fuel tax

see also Gasohol

see also Gasoline service stations

see also Motor fuels

Gasoline service stations

Consumer buying power survey of population, income, and sales by kind of business, by census div, State, MSA, county, and city, 1992, annual rpt, C1200–1.511

Establishments and employment, by State, 1993 and trends, periodic basic data book, A2575–14.7

Establishments, sales, employment, and marketing trends, detailed data by company and location, 1993 annual fact book, C4680–1.507

Financial ratios and performance, for over 350 SIC 4-digit industries, FY88-92, annual rpt, A6400–3

Index by Subjects and Names

Franchise operations and finances, by type of business, 1991/92 and trends, annual rpt, A5820–1

Fuel oil dealer retail gasoline outlets and sales volume, by region, 1992 annual survey, C4680–2.3

Markets with daily newspapers, demographic and economic info by geographic area, US and Canada, 1993 annual rpt, C3250–1

Operating and financial composite ratios for corporations, with establishments and receipts, for approx 200 industries, by asset size, FY90, annual rpt, C7800–1

Receipts/sales of travel-related industries, monthly rpt, R9375–1

Retail gasoline outlets, by State, 1993 and trends, annual article, C4680–1.505

Shopping center financial and operating data, with detail by type of tenant, US and Canada, 1991, triennial rpt, R9285–1

UK service station operations, by company, with aggregate sales of non-gasoline products by type, 1989-90, annual fact book, C4680–1.507

Unattended fueling sites, franchises/marketers, and average transactions, for 6 retail chains, 1993 article, C4680–1.511

State and local:

California gasoline sales volume, and service station distribution by sales volume, 1993 article, C4680–1.506

California service stations taxable transactions vs gasoline distributions, quarterly FY92, annual rpt, S0835–1

Hawaii data book, general data, 1992 annual rpt, S2090–1.17

Kansas robberies and value of stolen property, by location and property type, 1992, annual rpt, S2925–1.1

North Carolina employment in trade, transportation, communications, utilities, govt, and education, by detailed occupation, 2nd qtr 1991, triennial rpt, S5917–5.2

Texas trade, transportation, and public utilities employment, by SIC 2- and 3-digit industry and detailed occupation, 2nd qtr 1991, triennial survey rpt, S7675–1.31

see also Automobile repair and maintenance

Gastrointestinal diseases

see Digestive diseases

GDP

see Gross Domestic Product

Gehrke, James B.

"Rough Cuts: The Continuing Decline of Defense Dollars for the Northeast-Midwest Region", R8490–44

Gemstones

Auction prices paid for top 5 gemstones sold at an intl auction, June 1993, article, C2150–7.512

Diamond (cut but unset) exports and imports, for top 8 trading partners and all others, 1st half 1993, article, C2150–7.512

Diamond (polished) exports and imports, for top 10 trading partners and all others, 1991, article, C2150–7.501

Diamond grading adequacy, and qualities important to retailer and customer, views of jewelers, 1993 survey article, C2150–7.505

Index by Subjects and Names

Diamond jewelry sales and average price, 1987-92, article, C2150-7.508

Diamond jewelry sales, 1991 and trends, article, C2150-7.503

Diamond production by country, sales of DeBeers cartel, and imports and polished exports for various countries, 1993 article, C5226-2.510

Diamond sales of DeBeers cartel, 1st half 1983-1st half 1993, recurring article, C2150-7.511

Diamond sales of DeBeers cartel, 1st-2nd half 1990-92, recurring article, C2150-7.503

Import trends for colored gemstones, 1992, article, C2150-7.508

Jewelry industry statistics on sales, marketing, trade, and employment, with customer characteristics, 1993 annual almanac, C2150-7.509

Prices at wholesale level for colored stones, pearls, and diamonds, monthly rpt quarterly feature, C2150-7

Production, consumption, stocks, trade, and prices for approx 100 basic commodities, including by country and producing State, commodity yearbook for 1993, C2400-1, C2400-2

Russia diamond production/marketing organizational structure for central govt and Sakha Province, 1993 article, C2150-7.502

State and local:

Utah statistical abstract, general data, 1993 triennial rpt, U8960-1.10

see also Jewelry

General aviation

Aircraft (business/personal) shipments by model, for approx 20 manufacturers, weekly rpt quarterly table, C5800-30.503, C5800-30.505, C5800-30.509

Aircraft production, landing facilities, pilots, and operating data, by FAA region and State, 1993 annual rpt, A5120-2

Aircraft shipments and net billings, by general aviation manufacturer and/or model, quarterly rpt, A5120-1

Flight hours and primary use for general aviation, with aircraft production data, 1960s-91, annual rpt, A0250-2

see also Business aircraft and flying

General Educational Development Test *see* High school equivalency tests

General elections *see* Elections

Generating plants *see* Electric power plants and equipment

Generic products

Drug generic product sales distribution by retail outlet type, 1992, annual feature, C5150-2.511

Drugs (generic) market devs, including share of prescriptions, and drugstore acquisition costs, 1992 and trends, articles, C5150-2.515

Drugs (prescription) top 200 brands and top 100 generic products, 1992 annual pharmacy reference guide, C5150-2.503

Genetic engineering

see Biotechnology

Genetics

Physician genetics knowledge indicators, for primary care and genetics professionals, 1991, article, A3273-8.509

see also Hereditary diseases

Genito-urinary diseases *see* Urogenital diseases

Geography

see also Cartography

see also Topography

Geology

Higher education geoscience enrollment and degrees awarded, by sex, race-ethnicity, and discipline, 1991/92, annual rpt, A1785-3

Salaries of scientists, engineers, technicians, and other professionals, by employee and employer characteristics, 1990s and trends, biennial rpt, A3960-1

Seismic crews operating, by country or world area, 1987-92, annual rpt, C6985-3.5

Women and minorities in professional fields, detailed education and labor force data, 1991 and trends, recurring rpt, A3960-2.3

Georgia

Agricultural production, marketing, and finances, by commodity and/or county, and farms and acreage, 1991 and trends, annual rpt, S1855-1

Banks and other financial instns, financial condition by instn type, and assets by instn and city, Dec 1992, annual rpt, S1865-1

Business activity indicators for Georgia, bimonthly rpt, U6730-2

Correctional instns, admin, and inmate characteristics, FY92, annual rpt, S1872-1

Counties ranked by retail sales, income, auto registrations, personal income, and property value, FY92 annual rpt, S1950-1.2

County guide for Georgia, general social, economic, and govtl data, 1993 annual rpt, U6750-1

Court cases and dispositions, by type of court and case, and location, with judicial dept finances and personnel, FY92, annual rpt, S1903-1

Crimes and arrests, by offense, with data by location and offender characteristics, 1992 and trends, annual rpt, S1901-1

Election results by county, 1992 general election, biennial rpt, S1955-1

Employment by industry group and income by source, forecast for Georgia and Atlanta MSA, quarterly rpt, U1880-2

Employment, earnings, and hours, by major industry group and MSA, monthly rpt, S1905-1

Govt financial condition, including revenues by source, expenditures by function and object, and fund balances, FY92, annual rpt, S1860-1

Health behavior risk factor surveillance survey results, by respondent characteristics, 1991 and trends, annual rpt, S1895-2

Markets with daily newspapers, demographic and economic info by geographic area, US and Canada, 1993 annual rpt, C3250-1

Olympic games projected impact on output, earnings, and employment, for Atlanta summer 1996 games, 1992 article, U6730-2.501

Gerke and Associates Inc.

Statistical abstract of Georgia, detailed social, govtl, and economic data, 1992-93 biennial rpt, U6730-1

Statistical profiles of 50 States and DC, general data, 1993 annual almanac, C4712-1

Tax revenues, by type and county, FY92 annual rpt, S1950-1

Utility and transportation regulatory agency activities, scope of jurisdiction, finances, and employees, by agency, 1991/92 annual rpt, A7015-2

Vital statistics, including population, births, abortions, deaths by cause, marriages, and divorces, by demographic characteristics and location, 1991 and trends, annual rpt, S1895-1

see also Atlanta, Ga.

see also Cobb County, Ga.

see also Savannah, Ga.

see also under By City and By County in the "Index by Categories"

see also under By State in the "Index by Categories"

Geothermal resources

Electric power supply-demand, and utility capacities and fuel requirements, detailed data by US and Canadian region, 1992-2002, annual rpt, A8630-2

Japan energy supply-demand and outlook, by fuel source, 1980s-2000, recurring article, R5650-2.536

Latin America statistical abstract, general data by country, 1992 annual rpt, U6250-1.23

Sourcebook of oil and gas industry, with supply-demand comparisons to other energy types, 1991 and trends, annual compilation, C6985-9.5

World energy supply-demand, by fuel source and sector, by region and country, 1992/93 biennial rpt, R9455-1.7

State and local:

Hawaii data book, general data, 1992 annual rpt, S2090-1.17

Nevada statistical abstract, general data, 1992 biennial rpt, S5005-1.11

Geriatrics

Drugs under dev for selected diseases affecting older adults and women, 1989-93, A1865-1.519

Hospital geriatric services availability, by census div and bed-size group, 1991 and trends, article, A1865-1.505

Hospital patient discharges and length of stay, by diagnosis, type of operation, and age, 1991, annual rpt, B4455-1.6

Nursing education gerontological curriculum content and teaching methods, for programs in Southeastern States, 1993 article, A8010-3.505

State and local:

Florida health care facilities, including geriatric residential treatment systems, by district and county, 1992, annual rpt, S1746-1.2

Florida hospitals offering 8 types of geriatric services, 1992, article, A1865-1.519

Gerke and Associates Inc.

Supermarket industry composite financial ratios, 1991/92 and trends, annual rpt, A4950-1

German Democratic Republic

German Democratic Republic
see Germany, East

Germany

Chemical industry employment and operations, including trade with Eastern Europe by country, 1992-93, article, A1250–1.540

Coal industry supply-demand, employment, and trade, by country, 1990-91 and trends, annual rpt, A7400–2.2

Computer (personal) market shares in Europe and Germany, for top 6 manufacturers, 1993 article, C5800–7.539

Corporate executive compensation, with company revenues, for 20 highly paid executives in US, Germany, and Japan, 1993 article, C3950–1.516

Economic and commercial trends and policies, with US comparative statistics, 1993 annual compilation, A5135–2

Electronics industry trade and/or production trends by product category for 33 countries, with general economic profiles, 1993 annual rpt, A4725–1.4

Energy intl sourcebook, with detail on oil and gas industry operations, supply-demand, and prices, for approx 80 countries, 1970s-91, annual compilation, C6985–10.2

Machine tool industry operating data by country and product, 1992 and trends, annual rpt, A3179–2.2

Motion picture boxoffice market shares, for German, US, and other films, 1989-92, C9380–1.540

Motion picture boxoffice receipts for top 10 German and non-German films, 1992, C9380–1.540

Motion picture theater screens, for top 4-8 and all other exhibitors in Germany, Spain, France, and UK, 1992, C9380–1.531

Natural gas supply in western Germany from domestic and selected foreign sources, and foreign reserves and supply distances to Germany, 1993 article, C6780–1.504

Nuclear reactors in operation, with capacity, electricity generation, and construction, by unit and country, 1992, annual rpt, B6800–2.2

Plastics injection molding machine production, for US, Germany, Japan, and other Far East countries, 1983-92, article, C5800–12.510

Plastics waste handling and recycling devs in US, Europe, and Japan, 1993 annual encyclopedia, C5800–12.503

Public opinion in Germany on unification, and mutual perceptions of East and West Germans, 1991 survey, C8915–9

Public opinion in US on news items concerning neo-Nazi attacks on foreigners in Germany, Jan 1993 survey, C8915–1.501

Public opinion in 9 European countries and 3 Soviet Union Republics on political, economic, and social issues, 1991 survey, C8915–8

Publishing industry academic books and periodicals published, and prices, by subject area, 1989-93, annual compilation, C1650–3.4

Recycling fees charged for packaging, by material type, 1993 article, C1850–1.508

Reunification issues for internatl investment, with data on population and employment, consumption, and infrastructure improvement, 1991 rpt, R4105–82.3

Shipbuilding govt aid programs in 6 OECD countries, and impact on US industry, 1993 recurring rpt, A8900–8

Silver market activity worldwide and in US, including production, consumption by end use, stocks, trade, and prices, by country, 1988-92, annual rpt, B4300–1

Silver supply-demand by country and end use, with prices, futures trading, and market analyses, 1993 and trends, annual rpt, A8902–4

Telecommunication restructuring, with number of locations and subscribers for 4 contractors providing passive optical network systems, 1993, article, C4725–3.513

see also Germany, East
see also Germany, West

Germany, East

Motor vehicle world production, sales, trade, and registrations, by country, world area, manufacturer, and make, 1991 and trends, annual rpt, A0865–2.1

Germany, West

Coal shipments to US military in West Germany, 1967-91, annual rpt, A7400–2.1

Economic indexes for US and other industrial countries, and leading and coincident indicators, monthly rpt, U1245–1

Economic indexes for US and selected other countries, composites of leading indicators, monthly rpt, R4105–6

Motor vehicle world production, sales, trade, and registrations, by country, world area, manufacturer, and make, 1991 and trends, annual rpt, A0865–2.1

Socioeconomic comparative statistics for US and West Germany, 1970s-91, annual rpt, A5135–2.2

see also under By Foreign Country or World Area in the "Index by Categories"

Getzels, Judith

"Planning Commission: Its Composition and Function, 1987", A2615–2

Ghana

Energy intl sourcebook, with detail on oil and gas industry operations, supply-demand, and prices, for approx 80 countries, 1970s-91, annual compilation, C6985–10.2

G.I. Bill

see Veterans education

Gift tax

Federal tax rate trends, Sept 1916-Oct 1989, annual rpt, R9050–1.3

State and local:

California financial condition, including revenues by source, expenditures by agency and function, fund balances, and bonded debt, FY92 and trends, annual rpt, S0815–1

Colorado tax revenues by type, with selected data by county and city, FY92 and trends, annual rpt, S1075–1

North Carolina financial condition, including revenues by source, expenditures by function, fund balances, and bonded debt, FY92, annual rpt, S5897–1

Virginia tax revenues by type, including sales tax data by county and independent city, FY92 and trends, annual rpt, S8305–1.2

Wisconsin financial condition, including revenues by source, expenditures by function and object, and fund balances, FY93, annual rpt, S8675–2

Gifts and private contributions

Arts fundraising through united arts funds (UAFs), with fund operations, income by source, and allocations, by UAF, 1992 and trends, annual rpt, A1315–2

Arts fundraising through united arts funds (UAFs), with top 10 UAFs in funds raised by source, 1992, annual article, C2176–1.513

Business gift-giving practices, including types of gifts and top 10 industry users, 1993 survey, annual article, C1200–4.508

Catholic charity social service agency activities, clients, finances, and personnel, 1991 and trends, annual rpt, A3810–1

Charitable contributions, by type of donor and recipient, 1992 and trends, annual rpt, A0700–1

Charitable contributions, by type of recipient, 1992, article, C2175–1.522

Church membership and finances, including contributions and benevolences, by denomination, US and Canada, 1993 annual rpt, C0105–1

Community and junior college revenues by source and expenditures by function, and selected student characteristics, FY92, annual rpt, A6705–1

Congressional campaign fund spending for gifts to constituents and donations, by candidate, district, and State, 1990 elections, C2500–6

Corporate charitable contributions, by donor characteristics and detailed type of recipient, 1991 and trends, annual rpt, R4105–8

Corporate contributions to higher education 1982-92, and to all education by program 1992, annual article, C2175–1.534

Corporate event sponsorship expenditures, for top 13 companies, 1992, article, C1200–1.512

Corporate involvement in public education, including types of recipients and contribution levels by company, 1992 survey and trends, annual article, C8900–1.502

Corporate policies concerning charitable contributions to arts programs and other causes, 1991, recurring rpt, A3690–1

Corporate spending levels for customer holiday gifts, 1993 article, C1200–1.512

Corporate sponsorship expenditures, by type of event, 1993, article, C2710–1.532

Direct marketing industry devs, with consumer and business market characteristics, and media use patterns, 1992/93 annual rpt, A4620–1.4

Elementary/secondary education foundation grants and value, for top 10 recipients, 1990/91, article, R4800–2.522

Employee contributions to non-United Way funds through on-the-job campaigns, with data for selected individual funds, 1989-92, article, C2176–1.502

Foundation assets, income, and grants by type of recipient, with data for top organizations and by location, 1991 and trends, annual rpt, R4900–1

Foundation grants awarded and assets of top 50 foundations, 1991, annual feature, C2175–1.520

Foundation grants by detailed purpose, type of recipient, and State, with detail for grants of $5.7 million/over, 1991, annual article, C2176–1.504

Higher education endowment funds of 419 instns, market values, June 1991-92, annual feature, C2175–1.508

Higher education instn gifts of $35 million/more from individuals, by instn, 1967-93, C2175–1.518, C2175–1.526

Higher education instns, faculty, students, degrees, and finances, detailed data by State, 1993 annual rpt, C2175–1.531

Higher education voluntary support, by type of instn and donor, with top recipient instns and use, 1991/92 and trends, annual feature, C2175–1.525

Hospital (teaching) house staff stipend/benefit cost funding sources, by ownership, 1992/93, annual rpt, A3273–3

Incentive programs for consumers, employees, and dealers, with expenditures by industry and incentive type, 1991-92, annual feature, C1200–4.502

Japan corporate affiliate philanthropic activity in US, for service and manufacturing operations, 1992, survey article, R5650–2.560

Library construction, costs, and funding sources, by State, city, instn, and library type, FY92 and trends, annual article, C1852–1.501

Library construction, costs, and funding sources, by State, city, instn, and library type, FY92 and trends, annual compilation, C1650–3.4

Magazine charitable contributions, with beneficiary, sponsor, and amount, for 11 publications, 1992, C2575–1.508

Museums and related instns financial structure, including donation programs, income, and expenses, by type, budget size, and governing authority, 1989/90 survey, A0750–1.3

Nonprofit organizations private support, income, and services and fundraising costs, for top 400 organizations, FY91 or FY92, annual article, C2176–1.501

Nursing higher education program finances, faculty and clinical practice, and clinic/center operations, by instn characteristics, 1992/93 biennial rpt, A0615–5

Oil and gas research grant awards of American Chemical Society Petroleum Research Fund, by recipient, 1993 recurring feature, A1250–1.514, A1250–1.525, A1250–1.538

Optometry school revenues by source, by instn, 1991/92, annual survey, A3370–2

Philanthropy trends and devs, including data on nonprofit organization activities and finances, and corporate and individual giving, biweekly rpt, C2176–1

Private elementary and secondary school enrollment, staff, and finances, with detail for minorities, by school type and region, 1980s-1992/93, annual rpt, A6835–3

Public broadcasting membership income, contributors, and stations, by station type, FY91 and trends, annual rpt, R4250–1.21

Religious congregation characteristics, including membership, activities, staff, and finances, 1992 survey, recurring rpt, A5435–4

Restaurant (table service) support of political and charitable organizations, 1991, recurring rpt, A8200–1.501

Theater (nonprofit professional) finances and operations, including revenues by source, 1992 and trends, annual survey, A9065–1

Theological school endowment revenues and assets, with detail by instn, 1992 and trends, annual rpt, A3376–1

Voluntary health agency revenues, and expenditures by function, for 39 major organizations, FY90, annual rpt, A7973–1

Women/girls program support by foundations, with comparisons to total grants, by recipient characteristics, 1990 and trends, A9405–1.2

Worldwide charitable contributions of US corporations, by recipient type and country or world area, 1990 and trends, R4105–78.23

Youth age 12-17 charitable contributions, volunteer activity, and views on related issues, by respondent characteristics, 1992 survey, biennial rpt, A5435–5

Youth donations made to church, by demographic characteristics, 1993 survey, R8780–1.509

State and local:

Arkansas higher education finances, including revenues by source, expenditures by function, and State appropriations, by public instn, FY80s-95, biennial rpt, S0690–4

California individual and corporate income tax returns and property tax assistance, by income class and county, 1990 and trends, annual rpt, S0855–1

Colorado income tax return checkoff contributions, for selected causes, FY92 and trends, annual rpt, S1075–1.3

Colorado public library finances and operations, by instn, 1991, annual rpt, S1000–3.1

Florida public libraries, finances, holdings, staff, and services, by system and library, FY92, annual rpt, S1800–2

Hawaii United Way revenues and expenses, by island, 1990-91, annual rpt, S2090–1.11

Iowa postsecondary enrollment, degrees, staff, and finances, by instn, 1990/91, annual rpt, S2755–1

Maryland public school finances, including expenditures from funds raised by students, by county, 1991/92, annual rpt, S3610–2.7

Montana income tax checkoffs, by purpose, 1987-91, biennial rpt, S4750–1.1

Oklahoma food donations, value by target population and county, FY92, annual rpt, S6455–1.2

Oregon public school revenues by source and fund, and expenditures by fund, function, and object, 1991/92, annual rpt, S6590–1.16

Oregon public school revenues by source and fund, and expenditures by fund, function, and object, 1992/93, annual rpt, S6590–1.17

Pennsylvania higher education revenues, expenditures, and endowment funds, by instn type, FY91 and trends, annual rpt, S6790–5.4

Pennsylvania higher education revenues, expenditures, and endowment funds, by instn type, FY92 and trends, annual rpt, S6790–5.16

South Carolina higher education enrollment, degrees, staff, and finances, by instn, 1992 and trends, annual rpt, S7185–2

South Carolina public welfare service volunteers and contributions, by county, monthly rpt, S7252–1

Tennessee public school finances, by county, city, and school district, 1991/92, annual rpt, S7490–2.4

Vermont higher education revenues by source, expenditures by function, and tuition/fees, by instn, and student aid trends, 1992 annual rpt, S8035–2.3

Virginia income tax return checkoff contributions to political parties and other programs, 1990, annual rpt, S8305–1.1

West Virginia public, academic, and special library operations and/or finances, by instn, 1991/92, annual rpt, S8590–1

see also Campaign funds

see also Gift tax

Gila River

State and local:

Arizona reservoir capacity and storage from Colorado and Gila River drainage, Apr 1989-93, annual rpt, U5830–1

Glass and glass industry

Bullet-resistant glass use by type of area within users facilities, 1993 survey feature, C1850–12.505

Financial ratios and performance, for over 350 SIC 4-digit industries, FY88-92, annual rpt, A6400 3

Operating and financial composite ratios for corporations, with establishments and receipts, for approx 200 industries, by asset size, FY90, annual rpt, C7800–1

Glass insurance

see Property and casualty insurance

Glass, Thomas E.

"1992 Study of the American School Superintendency", A0775–5

Global climate change

Carbon tetrafluoride emissions by aluminum producers, atmospheric concentration, and global warming potential, 1993 article, A1250–1.535

Coal industry executive views on seriousness of global warming issue, Aug 1992 survey, article, C5226–1.505

Gas emissions and other activity contributing to greenhouse effect, with data by source and country, 1992/93 biennial rpt, R9455–1.4, R9455–1.7

News media coverage of global warming issue, including threat assessment and proposed solutions, 1985-Aug 1992, article, R3823–1.502

Scientists views on global warming and related issues, Feb 1992 survey, article, R3823–1.502

Temperature trends for US/China/Soviet Union, by season, 1890-1990, article, A4700–4.501

GNMA

GNMA
see Government National Mortgage Association

GNP
see Gross National Product

Goerdt, John A.
"Divorce Courts: Case Management, Case Characteristics, and the Pace of Litigation in 16 Urban Jurisdictions", R6600–6
"Small Claims and Traffic Courts: Case Management Procedures, Case Characteristics, and Outcomes in 12 Urban Jurisdictions", R6600–5

Gold
Capital spending plans for new mines and plants, by mineral and company, and mine production values, 1993 annual feature, C5226–2.503
Chicago Board of Trade futures and options trading in financial instruments and agricultural commodities, 1992, annual rpt, B2120–1
Coinage consumption shares of gold, for top 10 countries and all others, 1991, article, C2150–7.501
Coins (gold) issued, face value, gold content, and physical characteristics, by mint, for 60 issuing countries, 1992, annual rpt, A5145–1
Jewelry (gold) sales trends, by jewelry type, 3rd qtr 1991-3rd qtr 1992, article, C2150–7.503
Jewelry gold consumption, for top 10 countries, 1988-92, article, C2150–7.510
Jewelry industry statistics on sales, marketing, trade, and employment, with customer characteristics, 1993 annual almanac, C2150–7.509
Latin America statistical abstract, general data by country, 1992 annual rpt, U6250–1.23, U6250–1.27
Production, consumption, stocks, trade, and prices for approx 100 basic commodities, including by country and producing State, commodity yearbook for 1993, C2400–1, C2400–2
Production of gold from mines in 65 countries, 1992-96, annual rpt, A5145–2
Sales distribution for gold jewelry by retail outlet type, 1992, article, C2150–7.507
South Africa economic indicators, with CPI, PPI, mining/quarrying employment and earnings, and gold milled ore working costs, monthly rpt, B6800–1
South Africa gold mining production, revenues, and costs, 1st 9 months 1992, article, C5226–2.505
Supply-demand data for gold, including consumption by end use, production by country and State, and foreign trade, 1991-92 and trends, annual almanac, C2150–7.509
World producers and exploration spending of US-owned gold companies, for operations in US, Canada, Australia, Latin America, and elsewhere, 1989-92, articles, C5226–2.506

State and local:
Arizona gold and silver recovery from copper ore, 1972-91, annual rpt, S0497–1

Gold, Steven D.
"Anatomy and Magnitude of State Tax Increases in 1992", U5085–2.9
"Impact of the Clinton Economic Plan on the States", U5085–2.10

"Local Taxes Outpace State Taxes", U5085–2.11
"State and Local Employment in the 1980s: How Did It Grow?", U5085–2.7
"State Revenue Report", U5085–1
"Trends in Federal Aid to States Since 1989: Not What Many People Assume", U5085–2.12
"What Do the 1992 Election Results Say About State Fiscal Policy?", U5085–2.8

Goldman, Sachs and Co.
Labor cost per hour in US, Germany, France, UK, and Japan, 1988 and 1992, article, C5800–7.517

Golf
Financial ratios and performance, for over 350 SIC 4-digit industries, FY88-92, annual rpt, A6400–3
Grounds maintenance manager salaries, by type of employer, 1992, annual article, C4725–6
High school sports all-time records for boys and girls events, with school and student participation for 1991/92, annual rpt, A7830–2
Miniature golf facility characteristics and operations, 1992, annual rpt, A5700–1
Participation in 53 sports, by demographic characteristics, State, and census div, 1992, annual rpt series, A8485–3
Women's share of total and professional golfers, and golf course pros/directors by sex, 1993 article, C5800–7.524

State and local:
Hawaii data book, general data, 1992 annual rpt, S2090–1.7

Gong, Gerrit W.
"China at the Crossroads", R4105–82.8

Gonorrhea
see Sexually transmitted diseases

Gonzales, Leonardo A.
"Economic Incentives and Comparative Advantage in Indonesian Food Crop Production", R5620–1.37

Gonzalez, Martin L.
"Socioeconomic Characteristics of Medical Practice, 1993", A2200–5

Gordon, Melanie B.
"Cotton Counts Its Customers: The Quantity of Cotton Consumed in Final Uses in the U.S., Revised 1990-91 and Preliminary 1992", A7485–1

Gout
see Metabolic and endocrine diseases

Government agencies
see Federal boards, committees, and commissions
see Federal executive departments
see Federal independent agencies
see Government corporations and enterprises
see Local government
see State government
see the Index by Issuing Sources for names of issuing State agencies
see under By Government Agency in the "Index by Categories"
see under name of specific Federal agency

Government and business
Air pollutant (sulfur dioxide) emission allowance bids and purchases at EPA auction, by electric utility, 1993 article, C5800–28.508
Air pollutant (sulfur dioxide) emission allowance bids and sales at EPA auction, distribution by buyer category, 1993 article, A1250–1.519

Air pollutant (sulfur dioxide) emission allowance sales at EPA auction, with cumulative allowances and amount and number of bids by company, Mar 1993, article, C6985–6.507
Air pollutant (sulfur dioxide) emission allowance trading program, State regulatory issues and related data by State and major utility, 1992 rpt, A8195–12
Alcoholic beverage sales in selected retail outlets, restrictions by State, 1992 annual rpt, C4775–1.2, C4775–2
Americans with Disabilities Act small corporation compliance activities and perceived impact, 1992 survey article, C4687–1.501
Auto and truck corporate fuel economy (CAFE) ratings, by manufacturer, 1970s-93, annual rpt, A0865–1.3
Auto cost increases due to Fed Govt safety and emissions standards, 1968-93, annual rpt, A0865–1.3
Auto fleet operating characteristics in metro areas affected by Clean Air Act clean fuel requirements, 1993 article, C1575–2.512
Bank participation in SBA and other Govt programs for small business, Nov 1992 survey, annual rpt, A4160–5
Cable TV system mgmt personnel views on new FCC technical standards, errata, C2965–1.502
Cable TV system mgmt personnel views on upcoming revision to FCC guidelines, including anticipated effects, Jan 1993 survey, article, C2965–1.508
Chambers of commerce participation in govt affairs, by govt level, 1993 annual rpt, A3840–3
Child labor regulatory activity of Federal and State govts, 1992 rpt, R8335–2
Coal industry executive views on Federal regulation fairness and agency performance, Aug 1992 survey, article, C5226–1.506
Corporate executive views on most desired govt policies, 1992 survey article, C1850–13.501
EC steel production capacity, with reductions since 1980 made voluntarily and under EC Coal and Steel Commission quotas, 1992 rpt, R9260–16
Electronics industry conditions and outlook, including mgmt issues, global expansion, and most promising new technologies, views of CEOs, 1992/93 survey, annual feature, C1850–2.506
Europe public opinion on political, economic, and social issues, for 9 countries and 3 Soviet Union Republics, 1991 survey, C8915–8.2
Europe public opinion on political, economic, and social issues of interest to foreign investors, for 9 countries and 3 Soviet Union Republics, 1991 survey, C8915–9
Family-related workplace issues, including govt role and selected legislative proposals, views of personnel mgmt, Mar 1992 survey, A8907–1
Federal regulatory agency costs and staff, for approx 50 agencies, FY70s-94, annual rpt, U9640–1
Food/beverage industry packaging devs, including equipment purchase plans, partnership arrangements, and new labeling law effects, 1993 annual survey article, C2150–6.512

Index by Subjects and Names

Government and business

Freight traffic under Federal regulation, trends by transport mode, 1992 annual rpt, R4815–1

Gasoline price increases attributable to new Federal environmental, health, and safety regulations, 1995 and 2000, article, C4680–1.511

Hard goods manufacturers and representatives views on govt regulation, including agencies responsible for problems, by product line, 1993 annual survey rpt, A1800–1

Health care reform issues and/or options, views of physicians and general public, by respondent characteristics, Mar-Apr 1993 surveys, C8915–7.2

Health insurance benefits mandated by law in each State, and State program provisions in 2 States, 1991, U8850–8.1

Health insurance low-cost "barebones" plan characteristics and persons covered, for 29 States waiving mandated benefits, 1992/93, R4865–16

Housing costs attributable to govt regulations and fees, and impact on households eligible to purchase homes, for 2 local areas, 1993 article, C4300–1.510

Japan business shares of value added, and extent of govt regulation, by industry div, Mar 1989, article, R5650–2.501

Logistics professionals views on transportation and trade policy issues, Dec 1992 survey, article, C2150–1.505

Manufacturing industry natl policy desirability, views of industry executives and operations managers, 1993 survey article, C1850–12.506

Motor vehicle crash test results for selected auto or light truck models, weekly rpt recurring feature, C2710–3.511, C2710–3.533

Motor vehicle crash tests trends, including number of vehicles crashed and percent passing, for 16 manufacturers, 1979-93, article, C2710–3.551

Motor vehicle Fed Govt safety standards, 1993 annual rpt, A0865–1.3

Motor vehicle fuel tank fire related fatalities before and after Govt standards for fuel system integrity, by location of tank, 1981-86, article, A2623–1.510

Natural gas demand outlook, with expected effects of selected energy and environmental policy proposals, 2000, article, C6985–1.527

Natural gas pipeline cost of compliance with FERC order to stop offering merchant services to end users, 1993 article, C6985–1.541

Northwest forest timber peak production compared to lumber demand outlook and Clinton Admin harvest plan, 1993 article, C1850–8.509

Occupational health and safety govt regulatory activities, including inspections, fines, and data by State and company, 1992 annual rpt, R8335–1.2

Paint industry architectural and maintenance coatings proposed volatile organic compound content limits, 1993 article, A1250–1.543

Paper industry expenditures to comply with environmental protection regulations, 1966-93, annual rpt, A1630–6.3

Personnel mgmt professional views on govt record-keeping requirement activities and job satisfaction, spring 1993 survey, A8907–2

Public opinion on govt role in business/industry, and social responsibilities, Mar 1993 Gallup Poll and trends, C4040–1.509

Regulatory policies of Fed Govt, effects on business, with related issues and devs, series, U9640–2

Security professional views on Federal standards for private security officers, 1991-92, C1850–12.503

Shipbuilding govt aid programs in 6 OECD countries, and impact on US industry, 1993 recurring rpt, A8900–8

Small corporation mgmt views on Clinton Admin priorities and methods to help economy and small business, Jan 1993 survey, C4687–1.506

State economic dev condition indicators, including economic performance, business vitality, growth capacity, and tax/fiscal system, by State, 1993 annual rpt, R4225–1.1

State govt regulatory requirements for HMOs and preferred provider organizations (PPOs), 1993 feature, A1865–1.521

States use of selected business incentives, and number of enterprise zones by State, 1992 article, B8500–2.506

Transportation regulatory agency policies and practices for motor carriers and railroads, by agency, 1991/92 annual rpt, A7015–4

TV violence and Govt regulation, opinions of advertising industry magazine readers, Oct 1993 survey, article, C2710–1.551

Utility and transportation regulatory agency activities, scope of jurisdiction, finances, and employees, by agency, 1991/92 annual rpt, A7015–2

Utility regulatory agency policies and practices, and industry financial and operating data, by utility type and agency, 1991/92 annual rpt, A7015–3

State and local:

Alaska insurance industry underwriting and investment data, by company and type of insurance, with regulatory info, 1991 and trends, annual rpt, S0280–3

Arizona insurance industry financial and underwriting data, by company and type of insurance, with regulatory info, 1992, annual rpt, S0483–1

California banks and trust companies, financial condition by instn, with regulatory info, Dec 1992, annual rpt, S0810–1

California diesel fuel supply under compliance with and variance from low-aromatics regulations, with detail for selected refiners, 1993-94, article, C4680–1.511

California govt vehicle emissions requirements, 1994-2003 model years, article, C2710–3.534

California insurance industry financial and underwriting data, by company and type of insurance, with regulatory info, 1991, annual rpt, S0900–1

California, Los Angeles area oil refinery emissions allocations, by company, 1994, 2000, and 2003, article, C6985–1.552

California oil/gas production, regulatory compliance and production costs, and wellhead prices, by State region, 1993 article, C6985–1.525

Connecticut securities broker-dealers, investment advisors, and enforcement activities, 1991 and trends, annual rpt, S1160–1

DC statistical profile, general data, 1992 annual rpt, S1535–3.3

Florida nursing home certificate of need review activity, 1973-91, annual rpt, S1746–1.2

Idaho insurance industry financial and underwriting data, by company and type of insurance, with regulatory data, 1991, annual rpt, S2260–1

Idaho Securities Bur registration and enforcement activity, FY89-92, annual rpt, S2235–1

Iowa insurance industry financial and underwriting data, by company and type of insurance, 1992, annual rpt, S2760–1

Kansas insurance industry financial and underwriting data, by company and type of insurance, with regulatory info, 1992, annual rpt, S2990–1

Louisiana financial instns (State-chartered), financial condition by instn arranged by city, with regulatory info, Dec 1992, annual rpt, S3265–1

Maryland insurance industry financial and underwriting data, by company and type of insurance, with regulatory info, 1991, annual rpt, S3655–1

Michigan insurance industry financial and underwriting data, by company and type of insurance, with regulatory info, 1991, annual rpt, S3983–1

Missouri insurance industry financial and underwriting data, by company and type of insurance, with regulatory info, 1992, annual rpt, S4527–1

Nebraska insurance industry financial and underwriting data, by company and line of coverage, with regulatory info, 1992, annual rpt, S4890–1

Nevada State constitutional amendment on State lending to and holding stock in private enterprise, election results by county, 1992, biennial rpt, S5125–1

New Hampshire insurance industry financial data by company, 1991, with FY92 regulatory info, annual rpt, S5220–1

New York State insurance industry devs, finances, and regulatory activity, 1990/91 and trends, annual rpt, S5770–3

Oklahoma insurance industry financial and underwriting data, by company and type of insurance, with regulatory info, 1992, annual rpt, S6462–1

Pennsylvania insurance industry financial and underwriting data, by company and line of coverage, 1991, with FY92 regulatory info, annual rpt, S6835–1

Rhode Island insurance industry financial and underwriting data, by company and line of coverage, 1990, with FY91 regulatory info, annual rpt, S6945–2

South Carolina insurance industry financial and underwriting data, by company, 1991, with FY92 regulatory info, annual rpt, S7195–1

South Carolina public service commission regulatory activities, with financial and operating data for individual utilities and railroads, FY92 annual rpt, S7235–1

Government and business

South Dakota insurance industry financial and underwriting data, by company and type of insurance, with regulatory info, 1991-92, annual rpt, S7300–2

Tennessee insurance industry financial and underwriting data, by company and type of insurance, with regulatory info, 1991, annual rpt, S7466–1

Texas insurance dept regulatory activities, with industry financial and underwriting data by line of coverage, FY92 annual rpt, S7700–1

Texas natural gas utility financial and operating data, by city and company, 1991, with regulatory info, annual rpt, S7745–1

Utah insurance industry financial and underwriting data, by company and line of coverage, with regulatory info, 1991, annual rpt, S7845–1

West Virginia insurance industry financial and underwriting data, by company and line of coverage, with regulatory info, 1991, annual rpt, S8575–1

Wisconsin insurance industry financial and underwriting data, by company and line of coverage, with regulatory info, 1992, annual rpt, S8755–1

see also Administrative law and procedure

see also Agricultural production quotas and price supports

see also Agricultural subsidies

see also Consultants

see also Consumer protection

see also Defense contracts and procurement

see also Defense industries

see also Financial institutions regulation

see also Government contracts and procurement

see also Government corporations and enterprises

see also Government inspections

see also Industrial revenue bonds

see also Lobbying and lobbying groups

see also Mineral leases

see also Oil and gas leases

see also Price regulation

see also Subsidies

see also Tariffs and foreign trade controls

see also Tax exempt securities

see also Tax expenditures

see also Tax incentives and shelters

see also Trade adjustment assistance

Government and the press

News media personnel views on 1992 presidential election coverage, candidates, and related issues, for natl media, Oct 1992 survey, C8915–4.25

Utility and transportation regulatory agencies public info operations and conditions for media coverage, by agency, 1991/92 annual rpt, A7015–2

Government assets and liabilities

Airport and Airway Trust Fund financial statement, weekly rpt recurring tables, C5800–30.502, C5800–30.504, C5800–30.508, C5800–30.512

Educational and public employee retirement plan characteristics and finances, with detail for selected individual plans, 1990/91 and trends, recurring rpt, A7640–18

Federal debt measures, including data on Govt assets, liabilities, interest payments, total outlays, and deficit, 1980-98, R9050–15.1

Finances of govt, including revenues by source, expenditures by function, and debt, detailed data for Federal, State, and local govts, 1993 annual rpt, R9050–1

Medical malpractice insurance State joint underwriting assn (JUA) financial condition, for 11 States, 1991, annual rpt, A0375–1

OASDI trust fund finances and beneficiaries by category, selected years FY40-92, annual rpt, R9380–1.9

Resolution Trust Corp assets, with distribution by asset category, as of Aug 1992, article, C8900–1.502

Resolution Trust Corp real estate-owned assets and book value, by type of property, June 1993, article, A6450–2.506

Silver market activity worldwide and in US, including production, consumption by end use, stocks, trade, and prices, by country, 1988-92, annual rpt, B4300–1

State govt financial solvency, based on per capita assets, debt, and pension fund surplus or deficit, by State, 1993 article, B8500–2.521

State social, economic, and govtl indicators, with rankings, 1993 semiannual rpt, B8500–1.3

State and local:

Alabama financial condition, including revenues by source, expenditures by function and object, and fund balances, by fund and agency, FY92, annual rpt, S0129–1

Alaska financial condition, including revenues by source, expenditures by function, fund balances, and bond obligations, FY92 and trends, annual rpt, S0275–1

Arizona financial condition, including revenues by source, expenditures by function, and fund balances, FY91, annual rpt, S0450–2

Arizona financial condition, including revenues by source, expenditures by function, and fund balances, FY92, annual rpt, S0450–1

Arkansas financial condition, including revenues by source, expenditures by function and object, and fund balances, FY92, annual rpt, S0670–1

California financial condition, including revenues by source, expenditures by agency and function, fund balances, and bonded debt, FY92 and trends, annual rpt, S0815–1

Colorado financial condition, including receipts by source, and expenditures by function, FY92 and trends, annual rpt, S0980–1

Connecticut financial condition, including revenues by source, expenditures by function, and bonded debt, FY92, annual rpt, S1170–1, S1170–2

DC financial condition, including receipts by source, expenditures by object or function, and fund balances, FY92, annual rpt, S1507–1

Florida defaulted loans made to public utility customers and guaranteed by Public Service Commission, June 1992, annual rpt, S1790–1

Florida financial condition, including receipts by source, expenditures by function, and fund balances, FY92, annual rpt, S1717–3

Index by Subjects and Names

Florida statistical abstract, general data, 1992 annual rpt, U6660–1.23

Georgia financial condition, including revenues by source, expenditures by function and object, and fund balances, FY92, annual rpt, S1860–1

Hawaii financial condition, including revenues by source, expenditures by function, and fund balances, FY92, annual rpt, S2020–1

Idaho financial condition, including revenues by source and expenditures by object, by agency and/or fund, FY92, annual rpt, S2215–1

Illinois financial condition, including revenues by source, and expenditures by object, function, and agency, FY92, annual rpt, S2415–1

Indiana financial condition, including revenues by source, expenditures by function and object, and fund balances, by agency, FY92, annual rpt, S2570–1

Iowa financial condition, including revenues by source, expenditures by function, and bonded debt, FY92 and trends, annual rpt, S2860–4

Iowa State treasury financial operations, including receipts, disbursements, and detailed investment activity, FY92, annual rpt, S2885–1

Kansas financial condition, including revenues by source, expenditures by function and object, and fund balances, FY92, annual rpt, S2900–1

Kentucky financial condition, including revenues by source, expenditures by function and object, fund balances, and bonded debt, FY92, annual rpt, S3120–1

Louisiana financial condition, including revenues by source, expenditures by function, and fund balances, FY92 and trends, annual rpt, S3285–2

Maine financial condition, including revenues by source, expenditures by function and object, and fund balances, FY92, annual rpt, S3420–1

Maryland financial condition, including revenues by source, expenditures by function, fund balances, and bonded debt, FY92 and trends, annual rpt, S3685–2

Massachusetts financial condition, including revenues by source, and expenditures by function, by fund, FY92 and trends, annual rpt, S3777–1

Michigan financial condition, including revenues by source, expenditures by function, and fund balances, FY92 and trends, annual rpt, S3985–2

Minnesota financial condition, including revenues by source, expenditures by function, fund balances, and bonded debt, FY92 and trends, annual rpt, S4180–1

Mississippi financial condition, including revenues by source, expenditures by function and object, and detail by agency, FY92 and trends, annual rpt, S4346–1

Mississippi statistical abstract, general data, 1992 annual rpt, U3255–4.10

Missouri financial condition, including fund finances, tax collections and distribution, and State treasury activity, FY92 and trends, annual rpt, S4570–1

Missouri financial condition, including revenues by source, expenditures by function, and fund balances, FY92, annual rpt, S4475–1

Index by Subjects and Names

Montana financial condition, including revenues by source, expenditures by function, and fund balances, FY92, annual rpt, S4653–1

Nebraska financial condition, including revenues by source, expenditures by function and agency, and fund balances, FY92, annual rpt, S4825–1

Nevada financial condition, including fund revenues by source, expenditures by function, and bonded debt, FY92, annual rpt, S5025–1

New Hampshire financial condition, with revenues by source, expenditures by function or object, and fund balances, FY92 and trends, annual rpt, S5175–1

New Jersey casino control commission assets and liabilities, FY91-92, annual rpt, S5360–1

New Jersey financial condition, including revenues by source, expenditures by function, fund balances, and bonded debt, FY92, annual rpt, S5455–1

New Jersey public funds deposits in financial institutions, and collateral pledged for security, Dec 1992, annual rpt, S5355–1

New Mexico financial condition, including receipts by source, expenditures by agency and function, fund balances, and bonded debt, FY91, annual rpt, S5585–1

New York State financial condition, including revenues by source, expenditures by function, and fund balances, FY93, annual rpt, S5710–1

North Carolina financial condition, including revenues by source, expenditures by function, fund balances, and bonded debt, FY92, annual rpt, S5897–1

North Dakota financial condition, including revenues by source, expenditures by function, fund balances, and bonded debt, FY92, annual rpt, S6162–1

Ohio financial condition, including revenues by source, expenditures by function, and fund balances, FY92, annual rpt, S6255–1

Oklahoma financial condition, including revenues by source, expenditures by function, and fund balances, FY91, annual rpt, S6438–1

Oregon financial condition, including revenues by source, expenditures by function, and fund statements, FY92, annual rpt, S6603–2

Pennsylvania financial condition, including revenues by source, expenditures by function, and fund balances, FY92 and trends, annual rpt, S6810–4

Rhode Island financial condition, including revenues by source, expenditures by function, and fund balances, FY92 and trends, annual rpt, S6930–1

South Carolina financial condition, including receipts by source, expenditures by function, fund balances, and bonded debt, FY92, annual rpt, S7127–1

South Dakota financial condition, including revenues by source, expenditures by function, fund balances, and bonded debt, FY92, annual rpt, S7330–1

Tennessee financial condition, including revenues by source, expenditures by function and object, and fund balances, FY92, annual rpt, S7505–1

Texas financial condition, including revenues by source, expenditures by function, and bonded indebtedness, FY92, annual rpt, S7655–3

Texas insurance dept finances, including fund assets and liabilities, FY92, annual rpt, S7700–1

Utah financial condition, including revenues by source, expenditures by function and agency, and fund balances, FY92, annual rpt, S7795–1

Utah public school district balance sheets, by district, FY92, annual rpt, S7815–1.2

Utah statistical abstract, general data, 1993 triennial rpt, U8960–1.7

Vermont financial condition, including revenues by source, expenditures by function, fund balances, and bonded debt, FY92, annual rpt, S8035–1

Virginia financial condition, including revenues by source, expenditures by function, and fund balances, FY92 and trends, annual rpt, S8170–1

Washington State financial condition, including revenues by source, expenditures by function, fund balances, and bonded debt, FY92, annual rpt, S8345–3

Wisconsin financial condition, including revenues by source, expenditures by function and object, and fund balances, FY92, annual rpt, S8675–3

Wisconsin financial condition, including revenues by source, expenditures by function and object, and fund balances, FY93, annual rpt, S8675–2

Wyoming financial condition, including revenues by source, expenditures by function, and fund balances, FY92 and trends, annual rpt, S8875–1

Wyoming State treasurer financial transactions, including revenues, investments, and disbursements by local area, FY92 and trends, annual rpt, S9010–1

see also Foreign debts
see also Government revenues
see also Government securities
see also Government spending
see also International reserves
see also Municipal bonds
see also Public debt
see also State bonds
see also State budgets
see also State government revenues
see also State government spending
see also U.S. savings bonds

Government bonds
see Government securities
see State bonds
see Tax exempt securities

Government buildings
see Public buildings
see State funding for capital projects

Government-citizen lawsuits

City fiscal condition, including budget trends and adjustments, and influencing factors, by region and population size, Mar-Apr 1993 survey, annual rpt, A8012–1.23

Correctional instn prisoner and class action lawsuits, by State, 1991 or 1992, annual rpt, R4300–1.1

Local govt police liability lawsuits, claim and settlement amounts, and legal costs, by population size, census div, and/or case type, 1990/91 survey, A5800–2.113

Government contracts and procurement

State and local:

DC lawsuits filed by and against District govt, FY87-91, annual rpt, S1535–3.8

Michigan State corrections dept inmate litigation by category, 1988-91, annual rpt, S3960–1

Government consultants
see Consultants
see Government contracts and procurement

Government contracts and procurement

Black-owned companies top 10 problems encountered in doing business with govt agencies, 1993 article, C4215–1.503

Correctional instn food and health services contracted and costs, by State, 1992 annual series, R4300–1

Federal expenditures by category, by State and region, FY92 and trends, annual rpt, R8490–35

Hispanic-owned business availability vs use for city govt contracts by type, and status of contract award disparity studies, for 5-10 cities, 1993 article, C4575–1.510

Hispanic-owned business Govt contracts under 8(a) set-aside program, and total Federal procurement, FY83-91, article, C4575–1.501

Hispanic-owned high-technology company characteristics, including eligibility for SBA 8(a) contracts, 1993 annual article, C4575–1.510

Hwy bid price trends, weekly rpt quarterly feature, C5800–2.508, C5800–2.521, C5800–2.534, C5800–2.547

Japan construction firm contract value for projects awarded by US Fed Govt, 1988-92, article, C5800–2.528

Japan govt public works contracts let under US-Japan Major Projects Agreement, with bids submitted and won by US firms, 1988-92, article, R5650–2.537

Minority businesses eligible for SBA contracts, and value of contracts awarded, by minority group, FY92, article, C4575–1.507

State govt info resources mgmt, including data on budgets, staff, and organizational structure, by State, 1991, biennial rpt, A7121–1

State and local:

Alaska property assessment contract revaluation costs, by contractor and municipality, 1992, annual rpt, S0285–1

California milk sales to Fed Govt, by container type and size, 1992 and trends, annual rpt, S0850–1.6

California prime contract awards from DOD and NASA, FY91 and trends, annual rpt, S0840–2.8

DC minority vs nonminority contracts awarded, and contract protests and appeals, 1992 annual rpt, S1535–3.2

Hawaii counties population and economic indicators, 1993 annual rpt series, B3500–2

Hawaii data book, general data, 1992 annual rpt, S2090–1.15, S2090–1.21

Hawaii economic conditions, including employment, population, tourism, and construction, quarterly rpt, S2090–2

Hawaii public contract awards, by level of govt and county, bimonthly rpt, B3500–1

Maryland statistical abstract, general data, 1993-94 biennial rpt, S3605–1.13

Government contracts and procurement

Nevada statistical abstract, general data, 1992 biennial rpt, S5005–1.8

New Jersey casino control commission contracts issued, by enterprise type, FY92, annual rpt, S5360–1

New York State statistical yearbook, general data, 1992 annual rpt, U5100–1.5

Oregon employment service program expenditures for contracted support services, by State region, monthly rpt, S6615–8

Pennsylvania labor surplus areas eligible for Federal procurement preference, FY92, annual planning rpt, S6845–3.3

see also Consultants

see also Defense contracts and procurement

see also Federal funding for research and development

see also Government energy use

Government corporations and enterprises

- Brazil nuclear power plants operated by govt holding company, with capacity and fuel requirements, 1990, 2000, 2010, article, B6800–1.508
- Brazil oil production average costs by category for State-owned company, and offshore reserves by water depth, 1993 article, C6985–2.510
- Europe govt-owned companies likely to be privatized, govt ownership share and value for 25 firms in 6 countries, 1993 article, C5800–7.537
- France natural gas govt-owned company operations and finances, including employment, 1990, article, C6985–1.505
- France potential proceeds from privatization of 6 govt-owned companies, 1993 article, C5800–7.531
- Latin America oil and gas industry devs and outlook, 1993 articles, C6985–1.518
- Latin America statistical abstract, general data by country, 1992 annual rpt, U6250–1.29
- Medical malpractice insurance State joint underwriting assn (JUA) financial condition, for 11 States, 1991, annual rpt, A0375–1
- Mexico natl rail and air transport systems operating data, 1993 rpt, U8850–9
- Oil industry operations of govt-owned companies in 4 Middle Eastern or Latin American countries, 1993 articles, C6985–1.542
- Peru oil production for govt-owned and 4 private companies, 1992-94, article, C6985–1.525
- Russia diamond production/marketing organizational structure for central govt and Sakha Province, 1993 article, C2150–7.502
- Russia natural gas govt-owned company operations, with former Soviet Union supply-demand, foreign trade, and pipeline mileage by Republic, 1993 article, C6985–1.551
- Sweden natl steel corporation employment at 3 plants, and costs of early retirement and employee assistance programs, 1970s-86, R9260–16
- Telephone company stock prices and returns after privatization, for 12 foreign firms, 1993 article, C2710–2.516
- UK coal output, productivity, and market share trends, for British Coal Corp, 1991/92 and trends, article, C5226–2.501

UK coal production, longwall faces, and employees, by mine and operating status, for Govt-owned company, 1991-92, article, C5226–1.510

Uranium enrichment Govt-owned corporation operating costs by item, production, and sales, 1991-2001, article, B6790–1.502

Venezuela oil fields, production, and reserves, in govt-owned production units available for private contract, 1992 article, C6985–1.506

World privatization of govt businesses, by method of transfer, industry sector, and natl economy type, 1980-87, R4105–82.5

State and local:

New York State financial condition, including revenues by source, expenditures by function, and fund balances, FY93, annual rpt, S5710–1

see also Commodity Credit Corp.

see also Export-Import Bank

see also Federal Deposit Insurance Corp.

see also Federal National Mortgage Association

see also Government National Mortgage Association

see also National Railroad Passenger Corp.

see also Tennessee Valley Authority

see also U.S. Postal Service

Government debt

see Government assets and liabilities

see Public debt

Government documents

State and local:

- Colorado higher education library finances and operations, and enrollment, by instn, 1992, biennial rpt, S1000–3.2
- DC statistical profile, general data, 1992 annual rpt, S1535–3.1
- Florida public libraries, finances, holdings, staff, and services, by system and library, FY92, annual rpt, S1800–2
- Nevada archive accessions, holdings, and research inquiries, FY92, annual rpt, S5095–1
- New York State archive accessions, holdings, and research inquiries, 1978-91, annual rpt, U5100–1.10
- North Carolina higher education library holdings and expenditures, by type and instn, 1991/92, annual rpt, U8013–1.2

see also Statistical compendia

Government efficiency

- Disability benefit programs of Social Security Admin, initial claims processing times and number pending, by State, FY88-93, R4865–11
- Europe public opinion on political, economic, and social issues, for 9 countries and 3 Soviet Union Republics, 1991 survey, C8915–8.1
- Europe public opinion on political, economic, and social issues of interest to foreign investors, for 9 countries and 3 Soviet Union Republics, 1991 survey, C8915–9
- Occupational health and safety govt regulatory activities, including fines, staff productivity, and contested citations, 1992 annual rpt, R8335–1.2
- Public housing authority operations and finances, including households waiting for units and average length of wait, by agency size, 1989, A6800–1

Index by Subjects and Names

Public interest in news items concerning Clinton Admin proposal to reform Govt operations, and opinions on likelihood of success, Sept 1993 survey, C8915–1.505

Welfare program payment error rates, for AFDC and Medicaid, by State, FY92 annual rpt, S2623–1

State and local:

- Michigan ADC, general assistance, and food stamp benefits recoupment activity, by county, monthly rpt, S4010–1
- New Mexico public assistance dept staff, cases, and efficiency measures, by program and county, monthly rpt quarterly feature, S5620–2
- Oregon food stamps issued through mail, with loss rates, monthly rpt, S6615–8
- South Carolina AFDC and food stamp benefits recovery program activity, by county, monthly rpt, S7252–1
- West Virginia public assistance agency quality control and fraud mgmt activities, monthly rpt, S8560–2
- Wyoming welfare program overpayment recovery activity, monthly FY92, annual rpt, S8908–1

Government employees

- Accounting grad placements, by type of employer and region, 1991/92, annual rpt, A1885–1
- Chemist and chemical engineer salaries, employment status, and demographic and professional characteristics, 1993, annual rpt, A1250–4
- DOD contract and payroll spending, military and civilian personnel, installations, and cutbacks, by State and region, various years FY81-93, R8490–44
- Latin America statistical abstract, general data by country, 1992 annual rpt, U6250–1.12
- Motor vehicle fleet manager earnings, and personal and professional characteristics, 1993 article, C1575–2.506
- Professional worker salaries and employment, by employee and employer characteristics, with detail for scientists and engineers, 1990s and trends, biennial rpt, A3960–1
- Women's employment in govt, with data by race-ethnicity and State, series, U5090–1

State and local:

- Arizona economic condition, including population, employment and earnings, and business activity, by industry and locality, 1985-93, semiannual rpt, U5850–1
- Arkansas Census of Population and Housing detailed findings, 1990, U5935–7
- California Census of Population and Housing detailed findings, 1990, S0840–9
- Georgia county guide, general data, 1993 annual rpt, U6750–1
- Michigan govt and private employment, by State area, 1991, annual planning rpt, S3980–1.2
- New Jersey Census of Population and Housing detailed findings, by county, 1990, S5425–19
- New Mexico economic trends and outlook, by industry div, 1982-92, annual article, U7980–1.503
- Pennsylvania Census of Population and Housing detailed findings, with selected data by county and municipality, 1990, U4130–13

Pennsylvania employment and commuting data from Census of Population and Housing, by county and municipality, 1990, C1595–16

Rhode Island Census of Population and Housing detailed findings, by county and municipality, 1990, S6930–9

see also Congressional employees

see also Federal employees

see also Military personnel

see also Postal employees

see also Public administration

see also State and local employees

Government energy use

Electric utility customers, sales, and revenues, by user sector, bimonthly rpt quarterly table, A4700–4

Electric utility financial and operating data, by State and census div, 1991 and trends, annual rpt, A4700–1

Federal Govt energy consumption, by agency and source, FY78-92, periodic basic data book, A2575–14.1

Higher education physical plant operations, costs, employment, salaries, and energy use, by instn and region, 1991/92, recurring rpt, A3183–1

Oil supply-demand, marketing, prices, finances, and employment, detailed data for US and Canada, by product, company, and location, 1993 annual fact book, C4680–1.507

State and local:

Arizona statistical abstract, general data, 1993 recurring rpt, U5850–2.20

Illinois electric and gas utility sales and operating revenues, and customers served, by class of service and company, 1991-92, annual rpt series, S2410–1

Kansas statistical abstract, general data, 1991/92 annual rpt, U7095–2.13

Mississippi statistical abstract, general data, 1992 annual rpt, U3255–4.14

New York State electric power sales, by customer class, 1988-92, annual rpt, S5795–1

South Dakota public higher education instn utility appropriation and expenditures, FY92 and trends, annual rpt, S7375–1

Utah hwy mileage and expenditures, aviation and motor fuel consumption, and bus travel, various years 1940-92, annual rpt, R9380–1.10

Utah statistical abstract, general data, 1993 triennial rpt, U8960–1.13

Washington State electric utility customers, sales, and revenues, by customer class and utility, 1982-91, annual rpt, S8450–1.2

Wyoming penitentiary utility costs for electricity, coal, fuel oil, and water, FY91-92, annual rpt, S8883–1

see also Industrial and commercial energy use

Government grants

see Community Development Block Grants

see Federal aid programs

see Federal funding for research and development

see Revenue sharing

see terms beginning with Federal aid to

see terms beginning with State funding for

Government housing

see Public housing

Government information

State govt info resources mgmt, including data on budgets, staff, and organizational structure, by State, 1991, biennial rpt, A7121–1

Utility and transportation regulatory agencies public info operations and conditions for media coverage, by agency, 1991/92 annual rpt, A7015–2

State and local:

New York State police info network entries and inquiries, 1983-90, annual rpt, U5100–1.8

see also Government documents

see also Statistical programs and activities

Government inspections

Buses and drivers inspected and removed from service under Federal Hwy Admin/Commercial Vehicle Safety Alliance Roadcheck program, 1991-93, article, C1575–3.507

Grain inspected for export, 1992, annual rpt, B2120–1

Occupational health and safety govt regulatory activities, including inspections, fines, and data by State and company, 1992 annual rpt, R8335–1.2

State and local:

Alabama public health dept activities, including services provided, inspection and licensing activity, staff and finances, and vital statistics and health data, 1992 annual rpt, S0175–3

California motor carrier roadside inspections, FY92, annual rpt, S0930–1

Colorado truck inspection activities, with detail by port of entry, FY90-92, annual rpt, S1075–1.4

DC motor vehicle inspections, FY87-91, annual rpt, S1535–3.7

Hawaii environmental quality and public health control, inspection, licensing, and enforcement activities, 1990, annual rpt, S2065–1.6

Nebraska public service commission regulatory activities, with financial and operating data for individual railroads and telephone companies, FY91-92 biennial rpt, S4940–1

New Mexico motor carrier safety inspection outcomes, and port-of-entry inspection activity and revenue collections, FY91-92 annual rpt, S5660–1

Ohio agriculture dept inspection and licensing activities, 1991, annual rpt, S6240–1

South Carolina public service commission regulatory activities, with financial and operating data for individual utilities and railroads, FY92 annual rpt, S7235–1

Tennessee fire, electrical, and manufactured housing inspections, fee revenues, and arson investigations, 1991, annual rpt, S7466–1

Texas insurance dept regulatory activities, with industry financial and underwriting data by line of coverage, FY92 annual rpt, S7700–1

Texas natural gas and hazardous liquids pipeline safety inspections, by region, FY92, annual rpt, S7745–1

see also Food inspection

Government investigations

State and local:

California insurance dept investigations, and fraudulent claim value by insurance type, 1991 and trends, annual rpt, S0900–1

California motor carrier investigations, FY92, annual rpt, S0930–1

Connecticut securities broker-dealers, investment advisors, and enforcement activities, 1991 and trends, annual rpt, S1160–1

Idaho regulated carrier investigations, FY88-92, annual rpt, S2290–1

Indiana child protective service program case investigations and findings, FY92 annual rpt, S2623–1.7

Maryland medical assistance fraud investigations and recoveries, FY92, annual rpt, S3635–3

Maryland welfare program statistics, and welfare fraud investigations, by county, monthly rpt, S3645–2

Michigan State corrections dept special investigations, by type, 1991, annual rpt, S3960–1

Montana welfare fraud and liquor investigations, FY91-92, biennial rpt, S4750–1.1

Pennsylvania insurance industry financial and underwriting data, by company and line of coverage, 1991, with FY92 regulatory info, annual rpt, S6835–1

Tennessee govt regulatory and arson investigation activity, 1991, annual rpt, S7466–1

Tennessee public utility and transportation commission regulatory activities, with industry financial and operating data, 1991-92 biennial rpt, S7565–1

Texas insurance dept regulatory activities, with industry financial and underwriting data by line of coverage, FY92 annual rpt, S7700–1

Texas licensing and regulation of child care facilities, administrators, and social workers, including complaint investigations, Sept 1991 and Aug 1992, annual rpt, S7695–1

Wyoming parole board investigations, hearings, and drug testing, FY92, annual rpt, S8883–1

see also Criminal investigations

Government lands

see Government supplies and property

see Public lands

Government loans and grants

see terms beginning with Federal aid to

see terms beginning with State funding for

Government National Mortgage Association

Yields and interest rates for selected securities and loans, monthly rpt, A6450–2

Government ownership

Europe airline revenues and govt ownership share, for 8 major carriers, 1992 article, C8900–1.501

Europe airline shares owned by govt, for 12 carriers, 1993 article, C7000–4.503

see also Government assets and liabilities

see also Government corporations and enterprises

see also Government supplies and property

see also Military bases, posts, and reservations

Government ownership

see also Military supplies and property
see also Public buildings
see also Public lands
see also Surplus government property

Government pay

Corrections operating expenditures by major category, by State and Canadian Province, as of June 1992, annual rpt, A1305–3

Mathematics doctoral degree recipient characteristics, including salaries, 1991/92 and trends, annual survey, A2085–1.1

see also Civil service pensions
see also Federal pay
see also Military benefits and pensions
see also Military pay
see also State and local employees pay

Government price control

see Price regulation

Government publications

see Government documents

Government regulation

see Administrative law and procedure
see Government and business
see Interstate commerce
see Licenses and permits
see Price regulation

Government reorganization

Municipal govt structure and election method changes proposed and approved, by size, census div, and govt and location type, 1986 and 1991, A5800–1.1

Government revenues

Airport and Airway Trust Fund financial statement, weekly rpt recurring tables, C5800–30.502, C5800–30.504, C5800–30.508, C5800–30.512

Corporate tax burden trends, for income and payroll taxes, with comparisons to profits, Fed Govt receipts, and GDP, FY70-93, R9050–15.2

Finances of govt, including revenues by source, expenditures by function, and debt, detailed data for Federal, State, and local govts, 1993 annual rpt, R9050–1

Finances of govts by level, including revenues by source and expenditures by function, FY90 and trends, annual rpt, R9380–1.3

Forecasts of natl income and product account components and related indicators, quarterly rpt, U1880–1

Forecasts of natl income and product account components, employment, and financial sector activity, monthly rpt, B4950–1

Govt finances, taxation, and spending policies, periodic rpt, R9050–3

Revenues for State/local govts, with comparisons to personal income, by State, 1993 semiannual rpt, B8500–1.3

Southern States population, personal income, and State/local revenues and expenditures, by State, 1950s-2010, biennial fact book, A8945–1.1

State/local govt revenue shares by source, 1992 and trends, article, B8500–2.512

State/local govt revenue shares by source, 1992, article, B8500–2.509

Trends in State/local govt revenues by source, 1948, 1980, and 1990, article, U7860–1.503

Utility and transportation regulatory agency activities, scope of jurisdiction, finances, and employees, by agency, 1991/92 annual rpt, A7015–2

State and local:

Arizona court revenues by type of court and source, FY92, annual rpt, S0525–1

Hawaii data book, general data, 1992 annual rpt, S2090–1.16

New York/New Jersey Port Authority operating revenues and net income, for 10 properties, 1992, article, C3950–1.511

Pennsylvania State/local govt per capita revenues by source and expenditures by function, with comparisons to US, 1989/90, article, U4110–1.505

Utah govt statistical review, fiscal and socioeconomic data, 1993 annual rpt, R9380–1.7

Utah statistical abstract, general data, 1993 triennial rpt, U8960–1.17

see also Budget of the U.S.
see also Estate tax
see also Excise tax
see also Federal aid to States
see also Foreign budgets
see also Gift tax
see also Government assets and liabilities
see also Income taxes
see also License taxes and fees
see also Local government
see also Mineral leases
see also Oil and gas leases
see also Property tax
see also Revenue sharing
see also Sales tax
see also Severance taxes
see also Social security tax
see also State and local taxes
see also State budgets
see also State government revenues
see also Tariffs and foreign trade controls
see also Tax delinquency and evasion
see also Tax expenditures
see also Taxation
see also Tolls
see also Unemployment insurance tax
see also User fees
see also Windfall profit tax
see also Withholding tax

Government securities

Chicago Board of Trade futures and options trading in financial instruments and agricultural commodities, 1992, annual rpt, B2120–1

Corrections capital expenditures budget, with funding from bond issues, by State, as of June 1992, annual rpt, A1305–3

Forecast Treasury bill and bond rates, quarterly rpt, U1880–1

Forecasts for real estate industry and US economy, and housing starts and sales trends by region, monthly rpt, A7000–1

Forecasts of economic indicators for approx 10-13 months, monthly rpt, U1880–3

Forecasts of GDP, inflation, unemployment, and Treasury bond rates, by approx 10 organizations, monthly rpt, R4105–80

Forecasts of natl income and product account components, employment, and financial sector activity, monthly rpt, B4950–1

Foreign govt bond investment return rate trends in emerging vs mature markets, and market ratings for 31 countries, 1993 article, C2710–2.520

Foreign investor participation in US securities markets, and foreign purchases by US investors, by world area and country, quarterly rpt, A8825–2

Japan govt general account deficit, including bond issues by type, FY70-93, annual article, R5650–2.526

Life insurance industry income and financial data, including investments by type of security, 1991 and trends, biennial fact book, A1325–1.4

Money and securities market activity, and related indicators, biweekly rpt, B2000–1

Money market fund asset holdings by type of investment, including bank and Eurodollar certificates of deposit, and Federal securities, monthly rpt, A6025–5

Mutual fund asset composition, by type of financial instrument and investment objective, 1991 and trends, annual rpt, A6025–1

Ownership of Federal securities, by type of investor, FY39-91, annual rpt, R9050–1.3

Return rates for US Govt fixed-income securities, in US and 5 foreign countries, Dec 1984-Sept 1992, A8825–2.501

Treasury bond (30-year) interest rate forecasts of 16 economists, year-end 1993-94, article, C8900–1.526

Unit investment trust sales volume and value, by trust type, maturity period, and insurance features, monthly rpt, A6025–7

Yields and interest rates for selected securities and loans, monthly rpt, A6450–2

State and local:

Arkansas State treasurer safekeeping account balances and interest rates, by account, FY92, biennial rpt, S0780–1

Missouri State treasury investments, summary balance sheets, bonded debt, and deposits in individual banks, FY92, annual rpt, S4570–1.2

see also Municipal bonds
see also State bonds
see also Tax exempt securities
see also U.S. savings bonds

Government spending

Correctional instn admin, inmates, facilities, costs, parole and probation, and staffing, for local, State, and Federal systems, 1992 annual series, R4300–1

Expenditures of State/local govts, with detail by selected function, by State, 1993 semiannual rpt, B8500–1.5

Federal debt measures, including data on Govt assets, liabilities, interest payments, total outlays, and deficit, 1980-98, R9050–15.1

Federal expenditure per dollar of taxes paid, and State per capita gain or loss from Federal taxes and spending, by State, FY92, article, B8500–2.521

Federal expenditures by category, by State and region, FY92 and trends, annual rpt, R8490–35

Federal regulatory agency costs and staff, for approx 50 agencies, FY70s-94, annual rpt, U9640–1

Federal tax burden and spending, by State, FY93 annual rpt, R9050–15.5

Federal tax receipts and expenditures as a percent of GNP, forecasts by qtr, monthly rpt, A7000–1

Federal taxes and spending per capita, by State, 1992, article, R9050–3.506

Finances of govt, including revenues by source, expenditures by function, and debt, detailed data for Federal, State, and local govts, 1993 annual rpt, R9050–1

Index by Subjects and Names

Finances of govts by level, including revenues by source and expenditures by function, FY90 and trends, annual rpt, R9380–1.3

Forecasts of natl income and product account components and related indicators, quarterly rpt, U1880–1

Forecasts of natl income and product account components, employment, and financial sector activity, monthly rpt, B4950–1

Govt finances, taxation, and spending policies, periodic rpt, R9050–3

Southern States population, personal income, and State/local revenues and expenditures, by State, 1950s-2010, biennial fact book, A8945–1.1

State/local govt distribution of expenditures by major function, 1992 and trends, article, B8500–2.512

Statistical profiles of 50 States and DC, general data, 1993 annual almanac, C4712–1

Utility and transportation regulatory agency activities, scope of jurisdiction, finances, and employees, by agency, 1991/92 annual rpt, A7015–2

Workplace safety and health data, including injury and death incidence, govt regulation and spending, and workers compensation, with data by State, 1992 annual rpt, R8335–1

World central govt expenditures, with detail for selected functions, by country, 1992/93 biennial rpt, R9455–1.5

State and local:

Arizona expenditures of Fed Govt, by expenditure type, FY92, annual article, U0280–1.509

Pennsylvania State/local govt per capita revenues by source and expenditures by function, with comparisons to US, 1989/90, article, U4110–1.505

Utah govt statistical review, fiscal and socioeconomic data, 1993 annual rpt, R9380–1.4, R9380–1.7

see also Agricultural production quotas and price supports

see also Agricultural subsidies

see also Budget of the U.S.

see also Defense expenditures

see also Disaster relief

see also Economic indicators

see also Federal aid programs

see also Federal aid to arts and humanities

see also Federal aid to education

see also Federal aid to higher education

see also Federal aid to highways

see also Federal aid to housing

see also Federal aid to law enforcement

see also Federal aid to libraries

see also Federal aid to local areas

see also Federal aid to medical education

see also Federal aid to medicine

see also Federal aid to rural areas

see also Federal aid to States

see also Federal aid to transportation

see also Federal aid to vocational education

see also Federal funding for energy programs

see also Federal funding for research and development

see also Federal pay

see also Foreign budgets

see also Government assets and liabilities

see also Government contracts and procurement

see also Government energy use

see also Government pay

see also International assistance

see also Local government

see also Public welfare programs

see also Revenue sharing

see also State budgets

see also State funding for agriculture

see also State funding for arts and culture

see also State funding for capital projects

see also State funding for corrections

see also State funding for courts

see also State funding for economic development

see also State funding for education

see also State funding for employment

see also State funding for energy programs

see also State funding for health and hospitals

see also State funding for higher education

see also State funding for highways and streets

see also State funding for housing

see also State funding for libraries

see also State funding for local areas

see also State funding for medical education

see also State funding for natural resources and conservation

see also State funding for parks and recreation

see also State funding for public safety

see also State funding for social welfare

see also State funding for transportation

see also State funding for vocational education

see also State government spending

see also Subsidies

Government supplies and property

Aircraft (jet) world inventory, orders, and deliveries, by type of aircraft and individual owner/operator, 1992 and trends, annual rpt, B1582–1

Motor vehicle fleet alternative fuel vehicle purchase requirements for Federal and State govts, 1992 article, C1575–2.502

Motor vehicle fleet operating and financial data, including fleets by type, registrations by make and model, and top lessors, 1970s-93, annual rpt, C1575–2.507

Motor vehicle ownership, by level of govt and State, 1991, annual rpt, A0865–1.1

Silver market activity worldwide and in US, including production, consumption by end use, stocks, trade, and prices, by country, 1988-92, annual rpt, B4300–1

State and local:

Colorado property assessed valuation by detailed property type, and tax levy and revenue by local district, by county, 1991-92, annual rpt, S1055–3

Connecticut govt property inventory by type, 1988-91, annual rpt, S1170–1

DC statistical profile, general data, 1992 annual rpt, S1535–3.2

Florida crimes against businesses, churches, and govt, by offense, 1992, annual rpt, S1770–1

Hawaii data book, general data, 1992 annual rpt, S2090–1.6

Illinois financial condition, including expenditures by agency and object, FY92, annual rpt, S2415–1.2

Government trust funds

Indiana financial condition, including revenues by source, expenditures by function and object, and fund balances, by agency, FY92, annual rpt, S2570–1.2

Maryland property federally owned and leased, 1989-90, biennial rpt, S3605–1.12

Mississippi statistical abstract, general data, 1992 annual rpt, U3255–4.6

New York State police vehicles, by agency and county, 1991, annual rpt, S5760–3.3

New York State statistical yearbook, general data, 1992 annual rpt, U5100–1.5, U5100–1.8

see also Government assets and liabilities

see also Military bases, posts, and reservations

see also Military supplies and property

see also Public buildings

see also Public lands

see also Surplus government property

Government trust funds

Airport and Airway Trust Fund financial statement, weekly rpt recurring tables, C5800–30.502, C5800–30.504, C5800–30.508, C5800–30.512

Finances of govt, including revenues by source, expenditures by function, and debt, detailed data for Federal, State, and local govts, 1993 annual rpt, R9050–1

Insurance guaranty fund assessments for property/casualty companies, with detail by State, 1991 and trends, annual rpt, A5650–1.2

OASDI trust fund finances and beneficiaries by category, selected years FY40-92, annual rpt, R9380–1.9

State social, economic, and govtl indicators, with rankings, 1993 semiannual rpt, B8500–1.3

State and local:

Alabama financial condition, including revenues by source, expenditures by function and object, and fund balances, by fund and agency, FY92, annual rpt, S0129–1

Alabama State tax collections for education trust fund, FY90-93, annual rpt, U5680–3

Alaska financial condition, including revenues by source, expenditures by function, fund balances, and bond obligations, FY92 and trends, annual rpt, S0275–1

Arizona financial condition, including revenues by source, expenditures by function, and fund balances, FY91, annual rpt, S0450–2

Arizona financial condition, including revenues by source, expenditures by function, and fund balances, FY92, annual rpt, S0450–1

Arizona insurance guaranty fund finances, 1992, annual rpt, S0483–1

Arkansas financial condition, including revenues by source, expenditures by function and object, and fund balances, FY92, annual rpt, S0670–1

California financial condition, including revenues by source, expenditures by agency and function, fund balances, and bonded debt, FY92 and trends, annual rpt, S0815–1

Colorado financial condition, including receipts by source, and expenditures by function, FY92 and trends, annual rpt, S0980–1

Government trust funds

Connecticut financial condition, including revenues by source, expenditures by function, and bonded debt, FY92, annual rpt, S1170–2

DC financial condition, including receipts by source, expenditures by object or function, and fund balances, FY92, annual rpt, S1507–1

Florida financial condition, including receipts by source, expenditures by function, and fund balances, FY92, annual rpt, S1717–1, S1717–3

Florida utility regulatory trust fund appropriations and revenues, 1992 annual rpt, S1790–1

Georgia financial condition, including revenues by source, expenditures by function and object, and fund balances, FY92, annual rpt, S1860–1

Georgia State constitutional amendments on trust funds for transportation and indigent care, election results by county, Nov 1992, biennial rpt, S1955–1

Hawaii financial condition, including revenues by source, expenditures by function, and fund balances, FY92, annual rpt, S2020–1

Idaho school district revenues by source, and expenditures by function, by district and fund, FY92, annual rpt, S2225–2

Illinois financial condition, including revenues by source, and expenditures by object, function, and agency, FY92, annual rpt, S2415–1

Indiana financial condition, including revenues by source, expenditures by function and object, and fund balances, by agency, FY92, annual rpt, S2570–1

Iowa financial condition, including revenues by source, expenditures by function, and bonded debt, FY92 and trends, annual rpt, S2860–4

Iowa State treasury financial operations, including receipts, disbursements, and detailed investment activity, FY92, annual rpt, S2885–1

Kansas financial condition, including revenues by source, expenditures by function and object, and fund balances, FY92, annual rpt, S2900–1

Kentucky financial condition, including revenues by source, expenditures by function and object, fund balances, and bonded debt, FY92, annual rpt, S3120–1

Louisiana financial condition, including revenues by source, expenditures by function, and fund balances, FY92 and trends, annual rpt, S3285–2

Maine financial condition, including revenues by source, expenditures by function and object, and fund balances, FY92, annual rpt, S3420–1

Maryland financial condition, including revenues by source, expenditures by function, fund balances, and bonded debt, FY92 and trends, annual rpt, S3685–2

Massachusetts financial condition, including revenues by source, and expenditures by function, by fund, FY92 and trends, annual rpt, S3777–1

Michigan financial condition, including revenues by source, expenditures by function, and fund balances, FY92 and trends, annual rpt, S3985–2

Minnesota financial condition, including revenues by source, expenditures by function, fund balances, and bonded debt, FY92 and trends, annual rpt, S4180–1

Mississippi financial condition, including revenues by source, expenditures by function and object, and detail by agency, FY92 and trends, annual rpt, S4346–1

Mississippi insurance guaranty fund assessments, with comparison to total US and neighboring States, 1969-89, annual rpt, U3255–4.8

Missouri financial condition, including revenues by source, expenditures by function, and fund balances, FY92, annual rpt, S4475–1

Missouri school trust fund balance sheets, for selected special education funds, FY92, annual rpt, S4505–1.1

Montana financial condition, including revenues by source, expenditures by function, and fund balances, FY92, annual rpt, S4653–1

Montana severance tax collections placed in trusts, FY91-92, biennial rpt, S4750–1.1

Nebraska financial condition, including revenues by source, expenditures by function and agency, and fund balances, FY92, annual rpt, S4825–1

Nevada financial condition, including fund revenues by source, expenditures by function, and bonded debt, FY92, annual rpt, S5025–1

New Hampshire financial condition, with revenues by source, expenditures by function or object, and fund balances, FY92 and trends, annual rpt, S5175–1

New Jersey cemetery board trust fund trends, and licensed cemetery companies by county, 1993 annual rpt, S5355–1

New Jersey financial condition, including revenues by source, expenditures by function, fund balances, and bonded debt, FY92, annual rpt, S5455–1

New Mexico financial condition, including receipts by source, expenditures by agency and function, fund balances, and bonded debt, FY91, annual rpt, S5585–1

New York State financial condition, including revenues by source, expenditures by function, and fund balances, FY93, annual rpt, S5710–1

North Carolina financial condition, including revenues by source, expenditures by function, fund balances, and bonded debt, FY92, annual rpt, S5897–1

North Dakota trust fund balances, and income vs claims analysis, FY92 and trends, annual rpt, S6162–1

Ohio financial condition, including revenues by source, expenditures by function, and fund balances, FY92, annual rpt, S6255–1

Oklahoma financial condition, including revenues by source, expenditures by function, and fund balances, FY91, annual rpt, S6438–1

Oregon financial condition, including revenues by source, expenditures by function, and fund statements, FY92, annual rpt, S6603–2

Pennsylvania financial condition, including revenues by source, expenditures by function, and fund balances, FY92 and trends, annual rpt, S6810–4

Index by Subjects and Names

Rhode Island financial condition, including revenues by source, expenditures by function, and fund balances, FY92 and trends, annual rpt, S6930–1

South Carolina financial condition, including receipts by source, expenditures by function, fund balances, and bonded debt, FY92, annual rpt, S7127–1

South Dakota financial condition, including revenues by source, expenditures by function, fund balances, and bonded debt, FY92, annual rpt, S7330–1

Tennessee financial condition, including revenues by source, expenditures by function and object, and fund balances, FY92, annual rpt, S7505–1

Texas financial condition, including revenues by source, expenditures by function, and bonded indebtedness, FY92, annual rpt, S7655–3

Texas financial condition, including revenues by source, expenditures by function and dept, and investments, with data for over 400 individual funds, FY92, annual rpt, S7655–2.2

Utah financial condition, including revenues by source, expenditures by function and agency, and fund balances, FY92, annual rpt, S7795–1

Vermont financial condition, including revenues by source, expenditures by function, fund balances, and bonded debt, FY92, annual rpt, S8035–1

Virginia financial condition, including revenues by source, expenditures by function, and fund balances, FY92 and trends, annual rpt, S8170–1

Washington State financial condition, including revenues by source, expenditures by function, fund balances, and bonded debt, FY92, annual rpt, S8345–3

Washington State treasury operations, including receipts, disbursements, aid to localities, and investments, by fund, FY92, annual rpt, S8455–1

Wisconsin financial condition, including revenues by source, expenditures by function and object, and fund balances, FY92, annual rpt, S8675–3

Wisconsin financial condition, including revenues by source, expenditures by function and object, and fund balances, FY93, annual rpt, S8675–2

Wisconsin insurance industry financial and underwriting data, by company and line of coverage, with regulatory info, 1992, annual rpt, S8755–1

Wyoming financial condition, including revenues by source, expenditures by function, and fund balances, FY92 and trends, annual rpt, S8875–1

see also Highway Trust Fund

see also Unemployment trust funds

Governors

see Officials

Graduates

see Degrees, higher education

see Educational attainment

see High school equivalency tests

Grain storage and facilities

Elevators and capacities in Minneapolis-St Paul and Duluth-Superior switching districts, and grain stocks in sites served by Minneapolis exchange, 1992, annual rpt, B6110–1.1

Index by Subjects and Names

Grains and grain products

Elevators and capacity in US and Canada, by type and State or Province, with ranking of top grain companies, 1993 annual directory and buyers guide, C8450–2

Flour milling companies grain storage facilities and capacity, 1993 annual directory and buyers guide, C8450–3

State and local:

- Alabama off-farm grain and soybean stocks, quarterly 1983-92, annual rpt, S0090–1
- Alaska on- and off-farm grain stocks, 1985-93, annual rpt, U5750–1
- Arizona grain storage facilities and capacity, and stocks on and off farms, 1988-93, annual rpt, U5830–1
- Colorado off-farm grain storage facilities, capacity, and stocks, 1992 and trends, annual rpt, S0985–1
- Georgia on- and off-farm grain stocks, and storage facilities and capacity, 1992 annual rpt, S1855–1
- Illinois off-farm grain storage capacity by county, and stocks, 1992 annual rpt, S2390–1
- Kansas commercial grain storage capacity, and off-farm stocks, 1986-92, annual rpt, S2915–1
- Kansas grain facilities and capacity serving Kansas City Board of Trade, by company, 1992 and trends, annual rpt, B1530–1
- Kentucky on- and off-farm grain stocks by commodity, and storage facilities and capacity, 1989-93, annual rpt, S3085–1
- Michigan grain storage facilities and capacity, and stocks by commodity, 1991 and trends, annual rpt, S3950–1
- Minnesota on- and off-farm grain stocks, by commodity, 1989-1st qtr 1993, annual rpt, S4130–1
- Missouri grain storage facilities and capacity, and on- and off-farm grain stocks, 1988-92, annual rpt, S4480–1
- Nebraska licensed grain warehouses, inspections, and capacity, 1952-92, biennial rpt, S4940–1
- Nebraska on- and off-farm grain stocks, quarterly 1989-92, annual rpt, S4835–1
- North Carolina off-farm grain stocks and storage capacity, 1989-91, annual rpt, S5885–1
- North Dakota farm and off-farm storage capacity and stocks, 1983-93, annual rpt, U3600–1
- Ohio commercial grain storage capacity by county, and grain stocks, 1991 annual rpt, S6240–1
- Oklahoma off-farm grain stocks, by commodity, 1988-92, annual rpt, S6405–1
- Oregon off-farm and total grain stocks, 1982-92, annual rpt, S6575–1
- Pennsylvania on- and off-farm grain stocks, 1990-92, annual rpt, S6760–1
- South Carolina off-farm grain stocks, by commodity, quarterly 1988-92, annual rpt, U1075–3
- South Dakota grain storage facilities and capacity, and stocks by commodity, 1980-92, annual rpt, S7280–1
- Tennessee on- and off-farm grain stocks, 4th qtr 1983-3rd qtr 1992, annual rpt, S7460–1
- Texas grain storage capacity and on- and off-farm grain stocks, 1987-92, annual rpt, S7630–1.1

Utah off-farm grain stocks, 1960-92, annual rpt, S7800–1

Washington State on- and off-farm grain stocks, 1983-92, annual rpt, S8328–1

Wisconsin on- and off-farm grain stocks, by commodity, 1988-93, annual rpt, S8680–1

Wyoming on- and off- farm grain stocks, and grain storage facilities and capacity, 1988-92, annual rpt, S8860–1

Grains and grain products

- Brewers grain consumption, by commodity, FY64-91, annual rpt, A3455–1.1
- Cereal (ready-to-eat) advertising expenditures and market shares for top 10 brands, 1991-92, annual rpt, C2710–1.547
- Cereal coupon advertisement shares for top 5 companies, 1991/92, article, C2710–1.511
- Cereal market shares for selected manufacturers, by world region, 1989-92, C2710–1.527
- Cereal sales for 5 major brands and aggregate private label products, year ended Mar 1993, article, C5800–7.527
- Chicago Board of Trade futures and options trading in financial instruments and agricultural commodities, 1992, annual rpt, B2120–1
- Consumer nutrition awareness and health concerns, with food shopping and consumption patterns, by respondent characteristics, 1993 survey, annual rpt, A4950–36
- Ethiopia famine analysis, including cereal production, consumption, and price trends in affected areas, 1980s, R5620–1.36
- Exports of farm products, by detailed commodity and country of destination, US and California, 1991, annual rpt, B9520–1
- Financial ratios and performance, for over 350 SIC 4-digit industries, FY88-92, annual rpt, A6400–3
- Flour milling companies and capacity, in US by State, Canada, Mexico, and Central American and Caribbean area countries, 1993 annual directory and buyers guide, C8450–3
- Futures trading volume and prices at Kansas City Board of Trade grain market, with natl production by State, 1992, annual rpt, B1530–1
- Latin America statistical abstract, general data by country, 1992 annual rpt, U6250–1.16, U6250–1.24, U6250–1.25
- Liquor industry grain consumption, by commodity, FY46-92, annual rpt, C4775–1.2
- Operating and financial composite ratios for corporations, with establishments and receipts, for approx 200 industries, by asset size, FY90, annual rpt, C7800–1
- Production, consumption, stocks, trade, and prices for approx 100 basic commodities, including by country and producing State, commodity yearbook for 1993, C2400–1, C2400–2
- Production, prices, and futures and options trading activity on Minneapolis exchange, 1992 and trends, annual rpt, B6110–1
- Railroad grain shipments, including top 9 systems, grain fleet and capacity, and grain production, 1982-91, annual rpt, A3275–8.2

Retail prices for selected consumer items in approx 300 cities, quarterly rpt, A0150–1

Sales and consumer expenditures, for food store products by type, 1991-92, annual feature, C4655–1.510

Supermarket sales trends for cereals, pasta, and rice, 1993 annual feature, C5225–1.507

World cereal production and yields, by country, 1978-90, biennial rpt, R9455–1.6

State and local:

- Alabama agricultural production, marketing, and income, by county and/or commodity, and farms and acreage, 1992 and trends, annual rpt, S0090–1
- Alaska agricultural production and marketing, by district and commodity, 1960s-92, annual rpt, U5750–1
- Arizona agricultural production, marketing, and finances, by commodity and county, 1988-92, annual rpt, U5830–1
- Arkansas agricultural production, marketing, and finances, by commodity and county, with farms and acreage, 1992 and trends, annual rpt, U5920–1
- California field crops production, acreage, yield, and prices, by commodity and county, 1992 and trends, annual rpt, S0850–1.4
- Colorado agricultural production, marketing, and finances, by commodity and/or county, with farms and acreage, 1992 and trends, annual rpt, S0985–1
- Georgia agricultural production, marketing, and finances, by commodity and/or county, and farms and acreage, 1991 and trends, annual rpt, S1855–1
- Illinois agricultural production, marketing, and finances, by county or commodity, and farms and farmland, 1991 and trends, annual rpt, S2390–1
- Kansas agricultural production, marketing, and finances, by county and/or commodity, and farm acreage and value, 1992 and trends, annual rpt, S2915–1
- Kentucky agricultural production, marketing, and finances, by commodity and county; and farms, acreage, and value; 1992 and trends, annual rpt, S3085–1
- Louisiana agricultural production, marketing, and finances, by commodity or parish, 1985-91, annual rpt, U2740–1
- Michigan agricultural production, marketing, and finances, by commodity or county, 1987-91, annual rpt, S3950–1
- Minnesota agricultural production, marketing, and finances, by county or commodity, and farms and acreage, 1992 and trends, annual rpt, S4130–1
- Missouri agricultural production, marketing, and finances, by commodity and/or county, and farms and acreage, 1988-92, annual rpt, S4480–1
- Montana agricultural production, marketing, and finances, by commodity and county, 1991 and trends, annual rpt, S4655–1
- Nebraska agricultural production, marketing, and finances, by commodity and/or county, and farms and acreage, 1991 and trends, annual rpt, S4835–1
- Nebraska grain trading regulatory activities, FY91-92, biennial rpt, S4940–1
- Nevada agricultural production, marketing, and finances, by county and commodity, and farms and acreage, 1992 and trends, annual rpt, S5010–1

Grains and grain products

New Jersey agricultural production, marketing, and finances, by commodity and/or county, and farms and acreage, 1986-91, annual rpt, S5350–1

New Mexico agricultural production, marketing, and finances, by commodity and county, with farms and acreage, 1991 and trends, annual rpt, S5530–1

New York State agricultural production, marketing, and finances, by commodity and/or county, and farms and acreage, 1992 and trends, annual rpt, S5700–1

North Carolina agricultural production, marketing, and finances, by commodity and county, 1991 and trends, annual rpt, S5885–1

North Dakota agricultural production and marketing, by commodity and county, and farm finances, 1992 and trends, annual rpt, U3600–1

Ohio agricultural production, marketing, and finances, by commodity and county, with farms and acreage, 1990-91 and trends, annual rpt, S6240–1

Oklahoma agricultural production, marketing, and finances, by commodity and county, 1992 and trends, annual rpt, S6405–1

Oregon agricultural production, marketing, and finances, by commodity and/or county, with farms and acreage, 1991 and trends, annual rpt, S6575–1

Pennsylvania agricultural production, marketing, and finances, by county and commodity, and farms and acreage, 1992 and trends, annual rpt, S6760–1

South Carolina agricultural production and finances, by commodity and county, 1991-92 and trends, annual rpt, U1075–3

South Dakota agricultural production, marketing, and finances, by commodity and county, and farms and acreage, 1992 and trends, annual rpt, S7280–1

Tennessee agricultural production and marketing, by commodity and county, with farms, acreage, and farm value, 1992 and trends, annual rpt, S7460–1

Texas agricultural production, marketing, and finances, by commodity and county, and farms and farmland, 1991 and trends, annual rpt series, S7630–1

Utah agricultural production, marketing, and finances, by commodity and county, with farms and acreage, 1992 and trends, annual rpt, S7800–1

Washington State agricultural production, marketing, and finances, by commodity and/or county, 1992 and trends, annual rpt, S8328–1

West Virginia agricultural production, marketing, and finances, by commodity or county, 1991 and trends, annual rpt, S8510–1

Wisconsin agricultural production, marketing, and finances, by commodity and county, and farms, acreage, and sales, 1992 and trends, annual rpt, S8680–1

Wyoming agricultural production, marketing, and finances, by county and/or commodity, and farms, acreage, and value, 1992 and trends, annual rpt, S8860–1

see also Animal feed

see also Baking and bakery products

see also Corn

see also Gasohol

see also Grain storage and facilities

see also Hops

see also Rice

see also Soybeans

see also Wheat

Grants and grants-in-aid

see terms beginning with Federal aid to

see terms beginning with State funding for

Grapefruits

see Citrus fruits

Grapes

see Fruit and fruit products

Graphics

see Advertising

see Art

see Audiovisual education

see Photography and photographic equipment

see Printing and publishing industry

Graphite

see Nonmetallic minerals and mines

Gravel

see Stone products and quarries

Grazing

see Pasture and rangeland

Great Britain

see United Kingdom

Great Falls, Mont.

Unemployment insurance program new business enrollment, quarterly rpt, S4710–1

Great Lakes

Grain shipments on Great Lakes, 1954-92, annual rpt, B6110–1.1

Iron ore production, shipments, trade, and plant inventories and consumption, US and Canada, 1992 and trends, annual rpt, A2010–3

Iron ore shipments in US and Canada, with detail by Great Lakes port, monthly rpt, A2010–2

State and local:

Wisconsin waterborne freight traffic by commodity, by port, 1990, biennial rpt, S8780–1.2

Great Plains

see North Central States

Grebenschikoff, Jennifer R.

"Practitioner Compensation in Group Practice and HMOs: A 1992 Report", B7450–2

Greece

Energy intl sourcebook, with detail on oil and gas industry operations, supply-demand, and prices, for approx 80 countries, 1970s-91, annual compilation, C6985–10.2

Motor vehicle world production, sales, trade, and registrations, by country, world area, manufacturer, and make, 1991 and trends, annual rpt, A0865–2.1

Greenhouse effect

see Global climate change

Greenstein, Robert

"New Direction: The Clinton Budget and Economic Plan", R3834–17

Greenwich Associates

Pension fund asset allocations, and commercial property investment returns, 1993 article, C2425–1.505

Greeting cards

see Printing and publishing industry

Index by Subjects and Names

Grocery stores

see Food stores

Gross Domestic Product

Aerospace industry sales compared to GDP, 1977-91, annual rpt, A0250–2.1

Budgeted reductions in GDP for US and 5 European countries, 1st half 1993, article, C5800–7.505

Business and economic trends, production and price indicators, and industrial mgmt activities and devs, semimonthly rpt, C7000–3

Business cycle performance of GDP index 6-30 months after beginning of recovery, for current and average 6 past cycles, 1993 article, C5800–7.548

Business cycle performance of GDP, 1948-96, U1245–2.503

Chemical industry finances and operations, with data by industry segment and product, 1970s-92, annual rpt, A3850–1

Competitiveness indicators for US vs other major industrial countries, including investments, productivity, exports, and per capita GDP, 1993 annual rpt, A4475–1

Components of GDP, 1973-92, annual rpt, A3179–2.3

Corporate tax burden trends, for income and payroll taxes, with comparisons to profits, Fed Govt receipts, and GDP, FY70-93, R9050–15.2

EC economic indicators relating to proposed economic unification, by country, 1992 rpt, R5025–9

Economic indicator forecasts for 30 countries by approx 50 forecasting organizations, including GDP, inflation, unemployment, and interest rates, 1992-94, R4105–6.502

Economic indicator trends and forecasts, with detail for approx 15 Western States, 1990s, annual rpt, B3520–1

Economic outlook for GDP, 2-year forecast by qtr, monthly rpt, A1630–4

Economic outlook for selected indicators, recent trends and 2-year forecast, quarterly rpt, A3840–6

Electronics market value compared to percent change in GDP, for 12 countries, 1991-94, article, C1850–2.506

Energy (total), and oil and gas consumption compared to GDP, 1959-92, annual compilation, C6985–4.1, C6985–9.5

Energy (total), and oil and gas consumption compared to GDP, 1959-93, annual article, C6985–1.539

Energy and oil consumption compared to GDP, 1959-92, annual rpt, C6985–5.1

Energy consumption vs GDP, 1959-93, annual feature, C6985–1.513

Energy demand/GDP ratio, 1973-92, annual rpt, A5425–2.1

Energy tax proposals and potential effect on selected economic indicators, 1993-97, article, C6985–1.516

Forecast change in GDP based on long-leading and coincident indexes, with accuracy assessment and comparisons to actual GDP, 1963/64-1992/93, U1245–2.502

Forecast changes in GDP, by component, 1991-93, article, U2160–1.502

Forecast GDP by 20 economists, 2nd qtr 1993-2nd qtr 1994, annual article, C5800–7.533

Index by Subjects and Names

Gross State Product

Forecasts for GDP and CPI from Congressional Budget Office, OMB, and private companies, 4th qtr 1992-95, article, B8500–2.523

Forecasts for GDP, 50 economists, 1992-93, annual feature, C5800–7.509

Forecasts for real estate industry and US economy, and housing starts and sales trends by region, monthly rpt, A7000–1

Forecasts of economic indicators for approx 10-13 months, monthly rpt, U1880–3

Forecasts of GDP, inflation, unemployment, and Treasury bond rates, by approx 10 organizations, monthly rpt, R4105–80

Forecasts of natl income and product account components and related indicators, quarterly rpt, U1880–1

Forecasts of natl income and product account components, employment, and financial sector activity, monthly rpt, B4950–1

Foreign economic indexes, and leading and coincident indicators for US and other industrial countries, monthly rpt, U1245–1

Foreign GDP trends by country or region, 1992-94, article, C8900–1.527

Foreign GDP trends, for EC, newly industrialized economies, and 3 countries, 1991-93, article, C8900–1.502

Germany (West) and US comparative socioeconomic statistics, 1970s-91, annual rpt, A5135–2.2

Govt finances, with US and intl GDP data including comparisons to govt expenditures and revenues, and capital formation, 1993 annual rpt, R9050–1

Health care expenditures, by fund source and as percent of GDP and personal consumption, and medical care CPI, 1960s-91, annual fact book, A1275–1.4

Health care expenditures compared with GNP and GDP, 1950-91, annual rpt, A5173–2.3

Indonesia GDP, by industry, 1970s-88, R5620–1.37

Iran GDP, 1977-92, R4105–82.7

Japan GDP, weekly rpt quarterly table, R5650–2.508, R5650–2.516, R5650–2.537, R5650–2.554

Japan GNP or GDP growth and current account balance, forecasts of 6 organizations, 1993 article, R5650–2.538

Latin America economic indicators affecting business climate, with data on motor vehicle and oil industries and detail by country, 1992 rpt, R4105–82.6

Latin America statistical abstract, general data by country, 1992 annual rpt, U6250–1.32

Meat consumption trends compared to GDP, by selected country or world area, 1989-91, article, C2400–1.1

Mexico GDP components, including shares by industry div, and services trade with US by industry group, 1980-92, article, A3892–1.504

Motor vehicle production and trade, compared to GDP, 1987-92, annual rpt, A0865–1.3

Paper production and supply in relation to GDP, 1992 and trends, annual rpt, A1630–6.1

Productivity and related indicators, trend analysis for US and other industrial countries, 1980s-92, annual rpt, R2800–2

Racial bias impact on GDP, 1967-93, article, C4215–1.512

Service industries economic devs, with analysis of conditions and outlook, and comparisons to other industries, quarterly rpt, A3892–1

Soviet Union GDP distribution by industry sector, 1985, R4105–82.4

Spain population, foreign investment trends, and GDP shares, by region, 1993 feature, A8955–1.502

Tourism receipts compared to world and US gross product, 1990 and 2000, annual rpt, C2140–1.1

Trends in GDP and components for 1992, and outlook for 1993, article, C8900–1.509

Trends in GDP and defense component, 1990-1st qtr 1993, article, A8813–1.503

Trends in GDP in current and constant dollars, by industry, with comparisons to Virginia and Southeast region GSP, 1963-89, recurring rpt, U9080–6

Trends in GDP, with detail by economic sector, 1990-94, article, C8900–1.528

Trends in GDP, 1990-2nd qtr 1993, A8813–1.505

World financial market devs including economic and monetary trends and forecasts for 15 industrial countries, bimonthly rpt, B6200–2

World GDP and population, for top 20 countries, with trends for selected other countries, 1993 annual feature, C8900–1.520

World GDP for top 20 countries, 1990, recurring rpt, R9375–6

World GDP/GNP and inflation trends and forecasts, for 31 countries and EC, 1991-93, R4105–6.501

World GDP/GNP and inflation trends and forecasts, for 31 countries and EC, 1992-94, R4105–6.503

World GNP, and GDP by sector, by country, 1989 and trends, biennial rpt, R9455–1.5

see also Economic indicators

see also Gross National Product

see also Gross State Product

Gross margins

see Operating ratios

Gross National Product

China and US socioeconomic and infrastructure indicators comparison, 1993 rpt, R4105–82.8

Components of GNP, with trends and comparison to selected foreign countries and world regions, 1929-91, annual rpt, R9050–1

Developing countries family planning efforts, with data on socioeconomic and health conditions compared to developed countries, by country, 1980s-90, R8720–1.1

EC cargo traffic and GNP shares for member countries or groups, 1993 article, C2150–6.504

Energy consumption vs GNP, 1970-92, annual compilation, C6985–4.1

Forecasts of natl income and product account components and related indicators, quarterly rpt, U1880–1

Foreign economic indexes, and leading and coincident indicators for US and other industrial countries, monthly rpt, U1245–1

Germany (West) and US comparative socioeconomic statistics, 1970s-91, annual rpt, A5135–2.2

Health care expenditures compared with GNP and GDP, 1950-91, annual rpt, A5173–2.3

Japan economic profile, including govt finances, industrial production, foreign trade and investments, and comparisons to US, 1988-92, annual feature, R5650–2.552

Japan GNP and foreign trade trends, 1980-92, article, R5650–2.546

Japan GNP, by component, weekly rpt quarterly table, R5650–2.508, R5650–2.516, R5650–2.537, R5650–2.554

Japan GNP growth forecasts of 6 organizations, FY93-94, article, R5650–2.558

Japan GNP or GDP growth and current account balance, forecasts of 6 organizations, 1993 article, R5650–2.538

Latin America statistical abstract, general data by country, 1992 annual rpt, U6250–1.32

Philippines GNP, foreign investment inflow, intl aid, and trade with US and Japan, with comparisons to 7-8 other Asian countries, 1992 and trends, article, R5650–2.555

Productivity and related indicators, trend analysis for US and other industrial countries, 1980s-92, annual rpt, R2800–2

World GDP/GNP and inflation trends and forecasts, for 31 countries and EC, 1991-93, R4105–6.501

World GDP/GNP and inflation trends and forecasts, for 31 countries and EC, 1992-94, R4105–6.503

World GNP, and GDP by sector, by country, 1989 and trends, biennial rpt, R9455–1.5

World GNP, total and per capita, for 50 countries, 1989, semiannual rpt, B8500–1.16

World population size and characteristics, GNP, and land area, by region and/or country, 1993 annual data sheet, R8750–5

see also Economic indicators

see also Gross Domestic Product

see also Gross State Product

Gross State Product

Defense expenditure share of GSP, for top 10 States, 1993 article, S0320–1.511

Defense-related product as percent of total product, for top 10 States, 1992, article, C5800–7.531

Elementary/secondary education data, including area wealth indicators, by State, 1993 biennial rpt, A4355–1

Insurance industry employment, payroll, share of GSP, and premium taxes, by State, 1992 annual rpt, A0375–2

Manufacturing industry trends including employment, earnings, establishments, and GSP, by State and region, 1970s-92, R8490–48

Southeastern States GSP, for 7 States, 1977 and 1989, annual rpt, U5680–3

Southern States GSP growth rate, for 12 States, 1979-89, article, U8710–1.502

State social, economic, and govtl indicators, with rankings, 1993 semiannual rpt, B8500–1.2

Gross State Product

Statistical profiles of 50 States and DC, general data, 1993 annual almanac, C4712–1

State and local:

California statistical abstract, general data, 1992 annual rpt, S0840–2.4

Florida statistical abstract, general data, 1992 annual rpt, U6660–1.24

Georgia statistical abstract, general data, 1992-93 biennial rpt, U6730–1.3

Hawaii data book, general data, 1992 annual rpt, S2090–1.13, S2090–1.14

Idaho economic profile, general data, 1992 recurring rpt, S2218–2.5

Illinois business activity indicators, quarterly rpt, U6910–1

Illinois economic and business activity indicators, including data by industry and county, bimonthly rpt, S2405–2

Illinois statistical abstract, general data, 1992 annual rpt, U6910–2

Kansas statistical abstract, general data, 1991/92 annual rpt, U7095–2.8

Kentucky economic statistics, general data, 1993 annual rpt, S3104–1.1

Maine statistical summary, general economic and social data, 1992 recurring rpt, S3434–1

Maryland statistical abstract, general data, 1993-94 biennial rpt, S3605–1.6

Tennessee economic indicator trends and forecasts, with data by industry div and manufacturing group, 1982-2001, annual rpt, S7560–1

Tennessee statistical abstract, general data, 1992/93 annual rpt, U8710–2.2

Texas GSP by industry div, 1983-92, annual rpt, S7655–3

Utah govt statistical review, fiscal and socioeconomic data, 1993 annual rpt, R9380–1.2

Virginia GSP in current and constant dollars, by industry, with comparisons to Southeast region GSP and US GDP, 1963-89, recurring rpt, U9080–6

West Virginia statistical handbook, general data, 1992 annual rpt, R9385–1.8

Groundwater

see Hydrology

see Rivers and waterways

see Water supply and use

Group health

see Blue Cross-Blue Shield

see Health insurance

see Health maintenance organizations

Group Health Association of America

HMO enrollment as percent of population, for top 5 States, 1992, A1865–1.515

Group homes

Catholic charity social service agency activities, clients, finances, and personnel, 1991 and trends, annual rpt, A3810–1

Directory of correctional instns, with facilities and programs, by US and Canadian instn, 1992, annual rpt, A1305–3

Juvenile corrections halfway houses, residents, and costs, by State, Jan 1992, annual rpt, R4300–1.2

Substance abuse treatment clients by type of program, by State, FY91, annual rpt, A7112–1

State and local:

Colorado welfare and social services expenditures and caseloads, by county and/or program, FY91, annual rpt, S1085–1

New York State child services program statistics, 1991 and trends, annual rpt, S5800–2.3

New York State statistical yearbook, general data, 1992 annual rpt, U5100–1.11

Washington State public assistance clients and service costs, by client characteristics, program, and county, FY90, annual rpt, S8420–2

Group quarters

Library expenditures for services for institutionalized persons, by fund source and State, FY89-90, annual compilation, C1650–3.2

State and local:

Alaska population, housing, income, and education data, by demographic characteristics and/or locality, 1990/91 and trends, annual rpt, S0320–4

Arkansas Census of Population and Housing detailed findings, 1990, U5935–7

California Census of Population and Housing detailed findings, 1990, S0840–9

California statistical abstract, general data, 1992 annual rpt, S0840–2.9

DC statistical profile, general data, 1992 annual rpt, S1535–3.1, S1535–3.4, S1535–3.5

Florida inmates/patients in govt-operated instns, by county and city, Apr 1992, annual rpt, U6660–4

Florida statistical abstract, general data, 1992 annual rpt, U6660–1.2

Hawaii data book, general data, 1992 annual rpt, S2090–1.1

Illinois statistical abstract, general data, 1992 annual rpt, U6910–2

Kentucky economic statistics, general data, 1993 annual rpt, S3104–1.3

Louisiana Census of Population and Housing summary findings, by local area, 1990 and trends, U8010–4

Maine Census of Population and Housing summary findings, by local area, 1990, S3465–7, S3465–8

New Jersey Census of Population and Housing detailed findings, by county, 1990, S5425–19

New York State statistical yearbook, general data, 1992 annual rpt, U5100–1.1

Oklahoma group quarters population by age, for selected counties, 1990, S6416–1

Pennsylvania Census of Population and Housing detailed findings, with selected data by county and municipality, 1990, U4130–13

Tennessee statistical abstract, general data, 1992/93 annual rpt, U8710–2.1

Washington State population and demographic characteristics, and housing units, by county and/or city, 1992 and trends, annual rpt, S8345–4

see also Correctional institutions

see also Group homes

see also Military housing

see also Nursing homes

see also Student housing

see also Transient housing

Index by Subjects and Names

Gruebel, Doreen

"State Indicators of Science and Mathematics Education, 1993", A4355–3

GSP

see Gross State Product

Guam

Foreign students enrolled in US higher education instns, by instn, State, country of origin, and demographic characteristics, 1991/92 and trends, annual rpt, R5580–1

Higher education enrollment, by State and public instn, fall 1992, annual rpt, A7150–5

Higher education faculty average salaries by rank, by instn, 1992/93, annual feature, C2175–1.516

Higher education faculty compensation and employment, detailed data by rank, sex, and instn, 1992/93 and trends, annual rpt, A0800–1

HMO enrollment and plans, by State and for Guam, 1991, annual rpt, A5173–2.1

Hospital directory, with utilization, expenses, and personnel, by instn, type, and location, 1992, annual rpt, A1865–3

Judicial system salaries for judges and court administrators, by State and territory, and for Federal system, July 1993, semiannual rpt, R6600–2

Mathematics proficiency results on Natl Assessment of Educational Progress test, with comparisons to classroom and teacher characteristics, 1993 biennial rpt, A4355–1

Nursing programs (State-approved) for registered nurses, including admissions, enrollment, and grads, by instn, State, and territory, 1992, annual directory, A8010–4

Substance abuse treatment programs, funding by source, and client characteristics, for alcohol and drug services, by State, FY91 and trends, annual rpt, A7112–1

Tourism indicators for Guam, including visitor shares by country of origin, and share of Japanese departing airline passengers, 1992 rpt, B3500–1.501

Trust instns and assets managed, approx 5,000 depts, US and Canada, 1993 annual directory, C2425–2.501

Guangdong Province, China

Consumer market indicators, including income, retail sales, and imports, 1983-91, article, A9315–1.501

Economic data, including foreign trade and investment, and industrial production, 1985-92, A9315–1.505

Guaranteed income

see Income maintenance

Guaranteed Student Loan Program

see Student aid

Guarantees and warranties

Motor vehicle warranty coverage characteristics and duration, by make, 1993, annual data book, C2710–3.531

see also Surety bonds

Guardianship

State and local:

Alaska court cases and dispositions, by type of court and case, and location, with judicial dept finances and personnel, FY92 and trends, annual rpt, S0290–1

Arizona court cases and dispositions, by type of case and court, with judicial personnel and finances, by county and city, FY92, annual rpt, S0525–1

Arkansas court caseloads and dispositions, by type of court and case, and location, FY92 and trends, annual rpt, S0647–1

Arkansas human services dept finances and operations, by program, FY91 and trends, annual rpt, S0700–2.2

Colorado court cases and dispositions, by type of court and detailed case type, FY92 and trends, annual rpt, S1035–1.2

DC court cases and dispositions, by type of case, and judicial system finances, 1992 and trends, annual rpt, S1515–1

Delaware court caseloads and dispositions, by type of court and case, and by county, with judicial dept finances, FY92, annual rpt, S1360–1

Florida court cases and dispositions, by type of court and case, and location, 1992, annual rpt, S1805–1

Georgia court cases and dispositions, by type of court and case, and location, with judicial dept finances and personnel, FY92, annual rpt, S1903–1

Hawaii court cases and dispositions, by type of court and case, and judicial circuit, FY92 and trends, annual rpt, S2115–1.2

Indiana court cases and dispositions by type of court and case, and location, with judicial system finances and personnel, 1992, annual rpt, S2703–1

Iowa court cases, processing, and dispositions, by type of court and district, with judicial dept appropriations and personnel, 1992 and trends, annual rpt, S2815–1

Kansas court caseloads and disposition, by type of court and case, and location, FY92, annual rpt, S3035–1

Kentucky Medicaid recipients and payments, for cases under guardianship, monthly rpt, S3140–5

Kentucky SSI recipients and payments, for cases under guardianship, monthly rpt, S3140–2

Michigan court caseloads and dispositions, by type of court and case, and court location, 1992 and trends, annual rpt, S3962–1

Nebraska court cases and dispositions, by type of court and case, and location, 1992 and trends, annual rpt, S4965–2

New Mexico court cases and dispositions, by type of court and case, and location, with judicial system finances and personnel, FY92, annual rpt, S5623–1

North Dakota court caseloads and dispositions, by type of case and court, and location, with judicial dept finances, 1991-92, annual rpt, S6210–1

Ohio court caseload and case disposition, by type of court and case, and location, 1992, annual rpt, S6385–1

Oklahoma court cases and dispositions, by type of court and case, with judicial system finances, by county or jurisdiction, FY92, annual rpt, S6493–1

South Carolina court cases and dispositions, by type of court and location, with judicial dept finances and employees, 1992 and trends, annual rpt, S7197–1

South Dakota court cases and dispositions by type of case, and judicial system finances and personnel, by jurisdiction, FY92 and trends, annual rpt, S7395–1

Tennessee court cases and dispositions, by type of court and case, and county, FY92, annual rpt, S7585–1

Vermont court cases and dispositions, by type of court and case, and location, FY92 annual rpt, S8120–1

Washington State court cases and dispositions, by type of court and case, and jurisdiction, with judicial finances and personnel, 1992 and trends, annual rpt, S8339–1

Guatemala

Energy intl sourcebook, with detail on oil and gas industry operations, supply-demand, and prices, for approx 80 countries, 1970s-91, annual compilation, C6985–10.2

Statistical abstract of Latin America, detailed social, govtl, and economic data, 1992 annual rpt, U6250–1

Gubernatorial elections

see Elections

Gubernatorial vetoes

State and local:

Wisconsin Blue Book, general data, 1993-94 biennial rpt, S8780–1

Gulf of Mexico

Offshore leasing, drilling, and production activity in Gulf of Mexico for major vs independent oil companies, 1988-93, article, C6985–1.548

Offshore oil and gas activity, including production, reserves, and spills, by location, 1991 and trends, annual compilation, C6985–9.4

Offshore oil and gas drilling devs, 1993 annual article, C6985–2.503

Offshore oil/gas exploratory and dev wells drilled, 1st 8 months 1992-93, article, C6985–2.510

Offshore oil/gas leases from Fed Govt relinquished by top 5 companies, 1st half 1993, article, C6985–2.509

Offshore oil/gas total and undrilled leases from Fed Govt relinquished, by company, 1992, article, C6985–2.505

Oil and gas drilling costs, and wells and footage drilled, by State, offshore location, and type of well, 1991, annual rpt, A2575–9

Oil and gas exploration activity, reserves, and production, 1991-92 and trends, annual rpt, C6985–3.1, C6985–3.2

Oil and gas fields, reserves, and production, by location and stratigraphic formation, 1991, article, C6985–1.508

Oil and gas lease sales, winning bidders and bids, by tract, weekly rpt recurring article, C6985–1.522, C6985–1.547

Oil refinery, ethylene, and gas processing Gulf Coast plants profitability analyses, weekly rpt monthly tables, C6985–1

Oil spills incidence and volume, 1970-91, periodic basic data book, A2575–14.5

Oil/gas exploration data, including lease status, wells drilled by operator, and Fed Govt liability for abandoned platforms or pipelines, 1993 articles, C6985–2.508

Gultiano, Socorro A.

"Trends in Female and Male Age at Marriage and Celibacy in Asia", R4500–1.64

Gum and wood chemicals

Production, consumption, stocks, trade, and prices for approx 100 basic commodities, including by country and producing State, commodity yearbook for 1993, C2400–1, C2400–2

World naval stores production, consumption, and trade, by country, with capacity of tall oil fractionating companies, 1992 and trends, annual rpt, C6585–1

Guns

see Firearms

see Military weapons

Gypsum

see Nonmetallic minerals and mines

Habeas corpus

State and local:

Arizona court cases and dispositions, by type of case and court, with judicial personnel and finances, by county and city, FY92, annual rpt, S0525–1

California court cases and dispositions, by type of case and court, and location, FY92 and trends, annual rpt, S0905–1.2, S0905–2

Colorado supreme court cases filed, by type, FY86-92, annual rpt, S1035–1.2

Georgia court cases and dispositions, by type of court and case, and location, with judicial dept finances and personnel, FY92, annual rpt, S1903–1

Hawaii court cases and dispositions, by type of court and case, and judicial circuit, FY92 and trends, annual rpt, S2115–1.2

Nebraska court cases and dispositions, by type of court and case, and location, 1992 and trends, annual rpt, S4965–2

Texas court cases and dispositions, by type of court and case, and location, FY92, annual rpt, S7703–1

Vermont court cases and dispositions, by type of court and case, and location, FY92 annual rpt, S8120–1

Virginia court caseloads, processing, and dispositions, by type of court and case, with judicial dept personnel and finances, by location, 1992 and trends, annual rpt, S8300–1

West Virginia court caseloads and dispositions, by type of court and case, and judicial circuit, 1992 and trends, annual rpt, S8537–1

see also Pretrial detention and release

Haiti

Refugees (deportable) from Haiti arriving in Miami, 1979-82, annual rpt, U6250–1.14

Statistical abstract of Latin America, detailed social, govtl, and economic data, 1992 annual rpt, U6250–1

see also Caribbean refugees

Halfway houses

see Community-based correctional programs

see Group homes

Hallucinogenic drugs

see Drug abuse and treatment

Hamilton/KSA

Hospital CEO views on relations between mgmt and medical staff, including effect of selected Medicare policies, 1992 survey, article, A1865–1.517

Hospital collaboration with other health care providers, including data by activity and partner type, 1992 survey, article, A1865–1.508

Hospital revenue shares from outpatient services and managed care plans, by region, 1992-94, article, A1865–1.505

Hand tools

see Tools

Handguns

see Firearms

Handicapped

see Blind

see Deaf

see Disabled and handicapped persons

see Discrimination against the handicapped

see Handicapped children

see Mental retardation

see Mobility limitations

see Rehabilitation of the disabled

Handicapped children

Number of alcohol- and drug-affected infants born, and disabled elementary/secondary students, 1993 article, C1575–1.507

State and local:

Alabama crippled children service caseloads, and Federal and State/local appropriations, FY87-92, annual rpt, S0124–1.1

Hawaii health dept family health services and recipients, including school health programs, 1990 annual rpt, S2065–1.5

Indiana public assistance program participation, expenditures, and services, by county, FY92 and trends, annual rpt, S2623–1

Kentucky Medicaid recipients and payments, by program, county, and type of medical service, monthly rpt, S3140–5

Virginia disabled youth by age, by county and city, Jan 1993, triennial rpt, S8190–1

see also Birth defects

see also Old-Age, Survivors, Disability, and Health Insurance

see also Respite care

see also Special education

see also Supplemental Security Income

Harbors and ports

Business executives ratings of ports, highways, and intl air service, with daily number of intl flights, for top 6-8 cities, 1993 article, C2150–1.504

Coal trade by customs district, 1988-91, annual rpt, A7400–2.1

Foreign trade volume and value handled by top 20 ports, 1992, recurring article, C2150–1.506

Forest products foreign trade by product category and at 30 leading ports, 1991-92, annual article, C3975–2.512

Iron and steel imports, by US customs district and port, 1992, annual rpt, A2000–2.2

Iron ore imports by customs district, and shipments by US and Canadian Great Lake port, 1983-92, annual rpt, A2010–3.2

Iron ore shipments in US and Canada, with detail by Great Lakes port, monthly rpt, A2010–2

Mexico-Texas transportation system analysis, including bilateral trade, operations by transport mode, and data by locale, 1993 rpt, U8850–9

Oil and refined products imports, by importing company, port, and country of origin, monthly rpt, A2575–12

Soybean exports from selected US ports and coastal areas, 1992 and trends, annual rpt, B8480–1

Tobacco leaf and product exports by customs district, 1991, annual rpt, A9075–1

Trade activity at 15-16 leading US ports, with detail for Baltimore, 1989-91, biennial rpt, S3605–1.10

Wheat inspected for export, by variety and port, June 1991-May 1992, annual rpt, A7310–1

State and local:

Alabama, Port of Mobile waterborne shipments, monthly business activity rpt, U5680–1

Alabama statistical abstract, general data, 1992 recurring rpt, U5680–2.7, U5680–2.16

California ports agricultural exports, by country and detailed commodity, 1991, annual rpt, B9520–1

Florida statistical abstract, general data, 1992 annual rpt, U6660–1.13

Georgia statistical abstract, general data, 1992-93 biennial rpt, U6730–1.8

Hawaii data book, general data, 1992 annual rpt, S2090–1.18

New York Port waterborne trade, 1985-88, annual feature, S5735–2

New York State statistical yearbook, general data, 1992 annual rpt, U5100–1.13

Oklahoma barge traffic and freight carried, by port, 1990-91, annual rpt, U8130–2.16

Pennsylvania statistical abstract, general data, 1992 recurring rpt, U4130–6.2

South Carolina State Ports Authority ocean commerce activity, FY75-92, annual rpt, S7125–3.3

South Carolina statistical abstract, general data, 1993 annual rpt, S7125–1.15

Wisconsin Blue Book, general data, 1993-94 biennial rpt, S8780–1.2

Hardware

Discount chain consumer natl brand preferences, by product category and chain, and by age group, 1993 survey, annual feature, C5150–3.521

Discount chain top-selling natl brands cited by managers, by product category, chain, and region, 1993 survey, annual feature, C5150–3.520

Discount store sales and productivity data for 20 depts, 1993 annual feature, C5150–3.516

Financial ratios and performance, for over 350 SIC 4-digit industries, FY88-92, annual rpt, A6400–3

Markets with daily newspapers, demographic and economic info by geographic area, US and Canada, 1993 annual rpt, C3250–1

Operating and financial composite ratios for corporations, with establishments and receipts, for approx 200 industries, by asset size, FY90, annual rpt, C7800–1

Opinions of consumer hard goods manufacturers and representatives on business issues and outlook, by product line, 1992 annual survey rpt, A1800–1

Retail hardware finances and operations for hardware stores, home centers, and lumber/building material outlets, 1991 and trends, annual rpt series, A8275–1

Retail sales by outlet type, and discount chain sales in major depts, by product category, 1992, annual feature, C8130–1.507

Sales and consumer expenditures, for food store products by type, 1991-92, annual feature, C4655–1.510

Shopping center financial and operating data, with detail by type of tenant, US and Canada, 1991, triennial rpt, R9285–1

State and local:

Texas trade, transportation, and public utilities employment, by SIC 2- and 3-digit industry and detailed occupation, 2nd qtr 1991, triennial survey rpt, S7675–1.31

see also Lawn and garden equipment

see also Tools

Harris County, Tex.

Election results for Federal offices and Governor, by State, county, major city, and party, with voter registration and turnout, 1992 and trends, biennial rpt, C2500–1

Harris, Louis, and Associates

Business journalism performance as rated by executives, journalists, and academics, June 1992 survey, article, A8605–1.502

Business Week surveys of public and corporate executive opinion on current issues, weekly rpt recurring feature, C5800–7

Corporate work force outlook and related mgmt policies, views of human resources executives, Sept/Oct 1991 survey, R4105–78.21

Elementary/secondary new teacher views on teaching and quality of schools, after 2nd year of teaching, spring 1992 survey, B6045–2

Elementary/secondary teacher views on education policy issues and selected reform proposals, Jan-Feb 1993 survey, B6045–7

Medical education and careers, views of college undergrads and advisors, Feb/Mar 1990 survey, article, A3273–8.506

Public opinion on business use of personal info, including views on privacy, credit, and effects of computer use, 1992 survey and trends, annual rpt, B3280–2

Secondary school student sexual harassment experience at school, for 8-11th graders, by sex, 1993 survey, article, R4800–2.519

Youth age 10-19 handgun experience and attitudes, Apr-May 1993 survey, article, R4800–2.522

Hartland-Thunberg, Penelope

"China at the Crossroads", R4105–82.8

Hartman, Eric

"North American Free Trade Agreement's Auto Text in Strategic Context", R8490–43

Hassell, Sue

"Arkansas State and County Economic Data", U5935–1

Haub, Carl

"U.S. Population Data Sheet", R8750–9

Hawaii

Agricultural production and marketing, by commodity and island, 1987-91, annual rpt, S2030–1

Court cases and dispositions, by type of court and case, with judicial system finances, FY92, annual rpt, S2115–1

Index by Subjects and Names — Head Start Project

Crimes and arrests by offense, with data by county and victim-offender characteristics, 1992, annual rpt, S2035–1

Economic conditions, including employment, population, tourism, and construction, quarterly rpt, S2090–2

Economic indicators and population for Hawaii counties, 1993 annual rpt series, B3500–2

Economic indicators for Hawaii, bimonthly rpt, B3500–1

Election results, and voter registration by sex, by district and precinct, 1992, biennial series, S2077–1

Govt financial condition, including revenues by source, expenditures by function, and fund balances, FY92, annual rpt, S2020–1

Health dept activities and services, including vital statistics and disease control, by location, 1990, annual rpt, S2065–1

Markets with daily newspapers, demographic and economic info by geographic area, US and Canada, 1993 annual rpt, C3250–1

Statistical data book of Hawaii, detailed social, govtl, and economic data, 1992 annual rpt, S2090–1

Statistical profiles of 50 States and DC, general data, 1993 annual almanac, C4712–1

Tax collections and allocations, by type, for State and counties, FY91-92 and trends, annual rpt, S2120–1

Tourists in Hawaii, by origin, 1990-92, article, C1200–4.507

Traffic accidents, injuries, and fatalities, by circumstances, location, and driver and victim characteristics, 1986 and trends, annual rpt, S2125–1

Utility and transportation regulatory agency activities, scope of jurisdiction, finances, and employees, by agency, 1991/92 annual rpt, A7015–2

Visitor arrivals and spending, 1976-91, annual rpt, C2140–1.3

see also Honolulu County, Hawaii

see also Honolulu, Hawaii

see also Kauai County, Hawaii

see also Maui County, Hawaii

see also under By City and By County in the "Index by Categories"

see also under By State in the "Index by Categories"

Hawkes, Jennifer

"Equal Employment Opportunity Data for Utah", S7832–3.4

Hay

see Animal feed

Hazardous substances

Chemical hazard emergency response planning by local govts, including public notification methods, by locality, 1993 rpt, A5800–4.34

Employee training provided for handling hazardous substances, and employer views on Govt material safety instructions, 1992 annual rpt, R8335–1.2

Methyl tertiary butyl ether (MTBE) gasoline oxygenate exposure of workers, by processing or distribution step, 1993 article, A1250–1.541

Oil industry environmental performance, with data on toxic chemical releases, oil spills, occupational injury/illness, and corporate spending, 1990 and trends, annual rpt, A2575–27

Spills of oil and hazardous substances, by source, 1983-86, periodic basic data book, A2575–14.5

State and local:

Georgia toxic chemical releases, by type and industry div, 1990 and trends, biennial rpt, U6730–1.4

Massachusetts State initiative establishing excise tax on hazardous substances, election results by locality, 1992, biennial rpt, S3920–1

Ohio State constitutional amendment on labeling of hazardous chemicals, election results by county, Nov 1992, biennial rpt, S6380–1

Oregon births by maternal risk factors including exposure to toxins, 1991, annual rpt, S6615–5

see also Air pollution

see also Asbestos contamination

see also Carcinogens

see also Hazardous substances transport

see also Hazardous waste and disposal

see also Lead poisoning and pollution

see also Motor vehicle exhaust

see also Pesticides

see also Poisoning and drug reaction

see also Product safety

see also Radiation

see also Radioactive materials

see also Soil pollution

see also Water pollution

Hazardous substances transport

Accidents, injuries, and fatalities involving hazardous materials, 1970 and 1980-92, annual rpt, A3850–1

Southeastern States truck transport of hazardous substances, by substance type, 12 States, 1987, annual rpt, U8710–2.9

State and local:

Alabama traffic accidents, by type of hazardous cargo, 1992, annual rpt, S0185–1

Alabama trucks carrying hazardous materials, and miles traveled, 1987, recurring rpt, U5680–2.16

Kentucky traffic accidents involving trucks carrying hazardous cargo, 1992, annual rpt, S3150–2

Maine traffic accidents involving hazardous substances, 1992, annual rpt, S3475–2

Missouri traffic accidents involving hazardous material releases/spills, 1992, annual rpt, S4560–1

New York State hazardous transport vehicle inspections and violations, 1991, annual rpt, S5760–3.3

South Carolina motor carrier regulation, including safety and hazardous materials inspections, violations, arrests, and fines, FY92 and trends, annual rpt, S7235–1

Texas hazardous liquids pipelines and safety inspections, by region, FY92, annual rpt, S7745–1

see also Radiation

Hazardous waste and disposal

Air Force base hazardous waste site evaluation and cleanup costs by type, 1993 article, C5800–2.534

Labor time impacts of using protective suits at hazardous waste jobsites, 1993 article, C5800–2.534

Oil industry environmental performance, with data on toxic chemical releases, oil spills, occupational injury/illness, and corporate spending, 1990 and trends, annual rpt, A2575–27

State economic dev condition indicators, including economic performance, business vitality, growth capacity, and tax/fiscal system, by State, 1993 annual rpt, R4225–1.1

State social, economic, and govtl indicators, with rankings, 1993 semiannual rpt, B8500–1.15

Superfund site cleanup liability, costs, and settlements, for 49 cities, 1993 rpt, A9330–12

Technological innovations used for hazardous waste cleanup in EPA Superfund program, by type of contaminant, Oct 1992, article, C5800–2.537

Technological innovations vs traditional methods used for hazardous waste cleanup at EPA priority sites, 1983-91, article, C5800–8.507

State and local:

California financial condition, including revenues by source, expenditures by agency and function, fund balances, and bonded debt, FY92 and trends, annual rpt, S0815–1

Georgia county guide, general data, 1993 annual rpt, U6750–1

Georgia hazardous waste generated, received from out-of-State, and processed, 1989 and trends, biennial rpt, U6730–1.4

Hawaii data book, general data, 1992 annual rpt, S2090–1.5

Hawaii hazardous waste program activities, including govt inspections, 1990, annual rpt, S2065–1.6

New Jersey hazardous site cleanup and spill compensation funds finances, FY92, annual rpt, S5455–1

New Jersey local health official views on hazardous waste site concerns and interactions with Federal and State govts, Nov 1991 survey, article, A2623–1.507

New York State hazardous waste disposal law violations, by local area, 1991, annual rpt, S5760–3.3

New York State statistical yearbook, general data, 1992 annual rpt, U5100–1.15

Pennsylvania financial condition, including revenues by source, expenditures by function, and fund balances, FY92 and trends, annual rpt, S6810–4

Tennessee hazardous waste facilities fund financial condition, FY92, annual rpt, S7505–1

Tennessee statistical abstract, general data, 1992/93 annual rpt, U8710–2.12

see also Radioactive waste and disposal

see also Radon

Head Start Project

Children age 3-5 population share enrolled in Head Start, by State, FY90, annual rpt, R3840–11.2

Enrollment and enrollment rate of children age 3-5 in Head Start programs, by State, 1993 semiannual rpt, B8500–1.7

Expenditures of Fed Govt for Head Start, and enrollment, 1988-92, article, C1575–1.503

Federal budget trends, including spending by program, State, and region, FY81-94, annual rpt, R8490–11

Head Start Project

State and local:

Alabama public school revenues by source and expenditures by object, by district, 1991/92, annual rpt, S0124–1.2

DC statistical profile, general data, 1992 annual rpt, S1535–3.5

Tennessee public school special programs, by county, city, and school district, 1991/92, annual rpt, S7490–2.3

Health and beauty aids

see Personal care products

Health care costs and expenditures

see Medical costs

Health care products

see Drugs

see Medical supplies and equipment

see Personal care products

Health care reform

- Business economists views on economic merit and political feasibility of selected reform measures, Aug 1993 survey, semiannual rpt, A6650–6.502
- College freshmen attitudes on natl health care plan, by sex and instn type, fall 1992, annual survey, U6215–1
- Corporate CEO views on Clinton Admin health care plan, Sept 1993 survey, article, C8900–1.527
- Corporate CEO views on Clinton Admin performance, economic plan, and health care reform financing, Apr-May 1993 survey, article, C8900–1.516
- Corporate executive views on President-elect Clinton and his proposed programs, Nov 1992 survey, C5800–7.505
- Corporate personnel mgmt views on mandatory employee health benefits, 1993 survey, B6850–6
- Cost for health care as percent of payroll, for companies in regional vs corporate alliances under Clinton Admin reforms, by company type, 1993 article, C5800–7.550
- Expenditure increases if private insurance coverage is extended to the uninsured, by spending category, 1993 article, C5800–7.520
- Expenditures and insurance coverage under health care plans of presidential candidates Bush and Clinton vs current law, by State, 1993-2005, R4865–9
- Funding sources for Clinton Admin health care reform plan, 1993 article, C5800–7.541
- Hard goods manufacturers and representatives views on health care reform and responsibility for excessive costs, by product line, 1993 annual survey rpt, A1800–1
- Hospital CEO demographic and professional characteristics, perquisites, and views on mgmt issues, Oct 1992 survey, recurring rpt, B4490–2.35
- Hospital CEO views on extent of trustee interest in natl health care reform, 1992 survey, article, A1865–1.503
- Hospital executive views on health care reform, including ability to address selected problems, and expected changes, 1993 survey, article, A1865–1.520
- Hospital planning activity, including construction plans and influence of anticipated health care reform, 1993 survey, article, A1865–1.523

Insurance (health) low-cost "barebones" plan characteristics and persons covered, for 29 States permitting such plans, 1992/93, R4865–16

- Midwest banker opinions on Clinton Admin deficit reduction plan and health care reform, spring 1993 survey, semiannual rpt, B6785–1
- Opinions of general public vs health professionals on priorities, including importance of ethics and alternative medicine, 1993 survey, article, A1865–1.522
- Opinions of physicians and general public on health care reform, by respondent characteristics, Mar-Apr 1993 surveys, C8915–7.2
- Public interest in current news events, and opinion on media coverage and selected current issues, by respondent characteristics, 1993 surveys, C8915–1.502, C8915–1.503, C8915–1.504, C8915–1.505
- Public opinion on financing natl health care plan, Feb-Mar 1993 Gallup Polls, C4040–1.509
- Public opinion on health care issues, including govt and medical profession role, satisfaction with care and insurance, and reforms, 1975-92 surveys, A0610–1.504
- Public opinion on health care reform, including use of natl health insurance system, 1993 survey article, A1865–1.521
- Public opinion on health care reform options following Nov 1992 presidential election, 1993 article, C5800–7.511
- Public opinion on Hillary Clinton appointment to head health care reform task force, Jan 1993 Gallup Poll, C4040–1.508
- Public opinion on priority for health care reform, May 1993 Gallup Poll, C4040–1.512
- Public support for selected health care reform proposals, Mar-Apr 1993 survey, article, A1865–1.514
- TV news coverage of health issues, including leading topics, and Clinton Admin policies, Jan-May 1993, article, R3823–1.508

State and local:

- Oklahoma State referendum concerning tax on providers to fund health care programs, election results by county, 1992, biennial rpt, S6425–1
- Tennessee executive views on health care issues, 1993 annual article, U8710–1.502

Health condition

- Black American health and vital statistics data, with comparisons to whites, 1970s-91, annual compilation, C6775–2.2
- Black children and youth population, economic, health, and education data, with comparisons to whites, 1993 rpt, R3840–21
- Child and maternal health indicators and insurance coverage, by race-ethnicity and other demographic characteristics, 1992 annual rpt, R3840–5.1
- Child illness, treatment, and malnutrition incidence in developing countries, by sex and country, 1980s, article, A5160–6.501

Cocaine user characteristics, including criminal behavior and health condition, with comparison to nonusers, 1991 and trends, article, A2623–1.510

- Consumer nutrition awareness and health concerns, with food shopping and consumption patterns, by respondent characteristics, 1993 survey, annual rpt, A4950–36
- Health and mortality-related characteristics of US, quarterly rpt, B6045–1
- Life expectancy for persons age 55/over, with detail for specific health status indicators, 1984-90, R8750–1.507
- Men age 69-84 quality of life indicators, including health, finances, family, and employment, by race, 1990 survey, U3780–9
- Nutrition labeling law changes potential impact on public health condition, by sex, 1993 article, A2623–1.507
- Older population physical activity levels and impact on health outcome in 2 local areas and 1 State, 1982 study, article, A2623–1.512
- Public health condition and preventive health care and safety practices, by respondent characteristics, 1992 and trends, annual survey rpt, C8111–2
- Public perception of personal health condition correlated with health insurance status, 1987 survey, article, A2623–1.511
- Small corporation employee health promotion programs offered, by type, 1992 survey, article, C4687–1.511
- Stress frequency and amount of sleep per night, 1983 and 1991-92 health habit surveys, article, C1200–4.506
- Youth age 10-15 health condition and health service use and sources, with data by insurance status, by race-ethnicity, 1988, article, A2623–1.509

State and local:

- Alabama health behavior risk factor surveillance survey results, by respondent characteristics, 1988-89, recurring rpt, S0175–6
- Alabama health risk behavior survey summary results, 1991, annual rpt, S0175–3
- California health behavior risk factor surveillance survey results, by respondent characteristics, 1991 and trends, annual rpt, S0865–2
- Colorado health behavior risk factor surveillance survey results, by respondent characteristics, 1990, recurring rpt, S1010–3
- Connecticut health behavior risk factor surveillance survey results, 1989-91, annual rpt, S1200–2
- Connecticut health insurance coverage rate, by respondent characteristics and behavior risk factors, 1991 survey, S1200–3
- Georgia health behavior risk factor surveillance survey results, by respondent characteristics, 1991 and trends, annual rpt, S1895–2
- Hawaii data book, general data, 1992 annual rpt, S2090–1.2
- Hawaii health dept activities and services, including vital statistics and disease control, by location, 1990, annual rpt, S2065–1

Index by Subjects and Names

Iowa health behavior risk factor surveillance survey results, by respondent characteristics, 1991, annual rpt, S2795–2

Kentucky health behavior risk factor surveillance survey results, by State area and respondent characteristics, 1988-90, annual rpt, S3140–6

Massachusetts health behavior risk factor surveillance survey results, by respondent characteristics, 1986-90, recurring rpt, S3850–3

Michigan health behavior risk factor surveillance survey results, by respondent characteristics, 1991, annual rpt, S4000–4

Nevada health behavior risk factor surveillance survey results, by location and respondent characteristics, 1991, annual rpt, S5075–3

New York State health behavior risk factor surveillance survey results, by respondent characteristics, 1990, recurring rpt, S5765–3

North Dakota health behavior risk factor surveillance survey results, by respondent characteristics, 1991 and trends, annual rpt, S6105–3

Pennsylvania health behavior risk factor surveillance survey results, by respondent characteristics, 1991, annual rpt, S6820–4

Tennessee health behavior risk factor surveillance survey results, by respondent characteristics, 1986-90, annual rpt, S7520–3

Texas health behavior risk factor surveillance survey results, by respondent characteristics, 1991 and trends, annual rpt, S7685–2

Utah health behavior risk factor surveillance survey results, by respondent characteristics, 1991, annual rpt, S7835–3

see also Absenteeism
see also Blind
see also Cholesterol
see also Deaf
see also Dental condition
see also Dieting and dietetic products
see also Disabled and handicapped persons
see also Diseases and disorders
see also Handicapped children
see also Hospitalization
see also Medical examinations and tests
see also Mental health and illness
see also Mobility limitations
see also Nutrition and malnutrition
see also Obesity
see also Occupational health and safety
see also Prenatal care
see also Vital statistics

Health education

Honduras hospital maternal education program effect on women's contraceptive use and knowledge of reproductive health, 1993 article, A5160–6.505

Magazines (health/fitness) started 1987-91, with number still published in 1992, article, C2575–1.501

Urban public school systems offering selected types of health education programs, for 47 systems, 1990/91, A4425–4

Voluntary health agency revenues, and expenditures by function, for 39 major organizations, FY90, annual rpt, A7973–1

State and local:

Connecticut public school data, including enrollment, staff, programs, finances, and student characteristics, 1991/92, biennial rpt, S1185–3

Hawaii health dept activities and services, including vital statistics and disease control, by location, 1990, annual rpt, S2065–1

see also Sex education

Health facilities administration

Compensation of medical group mgmt, by demographic and practice characteristics, 1992, annual rpt, A6365–3

Hospital CEO demographic and professional characteristics, perquisites, and views on mgmt issues, Oct 1992 survey, recurring rpt, B4490–2.35

Hospital operations, admin, and mgmt devs, semimonthly rpt, A1865–1

Hospital use of contract hospitality, business, and clinical services, including contract terms, 1993 survey, annual article, A1865–1.514

Medical group practice policies, including role of administrators in decision making, 1991, recurring rpt, A2200–7

Nursing center (community) staff and client characteristics, and services, 1990 survey, article, A8010–3.506

Physicians by detailed specialty and location, 1992 and trends, annual rpt, A2200–3

Women and minorities in professional fields, detailed education and labor force data, 1991 and trends, recurring rpt, A3960–2.3

State and local:

Florida statistical abstract, general data, 1992 annual rpt, U6660–1.20

see also Business management
see also Health planning and evaluation

Health facilities and services

Black children and youth population, economic, health, and education data, with comparisons to whites, 1993 rpt, R3840–21

Catholic facilities for health care and social services, including cancer hospitals, 1993 annual almanac, C6885–1

Catholic health care centers and utilization, by diocese and State, 1993 annual compilation, C4950–1

Charitable contributions, by type of donor and recipient, 1992 and trends, annual rpt, A0700–1

Child and maternal health indicators and insurance coverage, by race-ethnicity and other demographic characteristics, 1992 annual rpt, R3840–5.1

Construction contract awards by type of project, weekly rpt, C5800–2

Construction contract value, by construction type and region, including floor area and number of residential units, 1992-93, annual rpt, C5800–15.501, C5800–15.504, C5800–15.507, C5800–26, C5800–29

Consumer complaint and inquiry activity of Better Business Burs, by detailed type of business, 1992, annual rpt, A4350–1

Health facilities and services

Corporate charitable contributions, by donor characteristics and detailed type of recipient, 1991 and trends, annual rpt, R4105–8

Dental school undergrad student expenses, by type and instn, 1992/93, annual rpt, A1475–4.3

Dental student patient visits and screenings, by facility type, 1992/93 annual rpt, A1475–3.2

Developing countries family planning facilities by type, and prevalence of community-based programs, by country, 1980s, R8720–1

Directories of health organizations, including HMOs, surgery centers, hospices, and substance abuse programs, 1992 annual rpt, A1865–3

Elderly population receiving selected medical procedures and diagnostic tests, by race and urban-rural residence, 1986, article, A2623–1.509

Expenditures, employment, exports, and facilities for health care vs defense, 1993, article, C8900–1.515

Financial performance and growth rankings for approx 1,000 top corporations, with comparisons by industry group, 1993 annual rpt, C3950–1.505

Food marketers with health care programs, by type, 1993 annual survey, A4950–6

Food service industry sales rankings by market segment, for leading organizations, 1992, annual feature, C1850–3.509

Food service industry sales trends and forecast, by market segment, 1990-93, annual feature, A8200–1.502

Foundation assets, income, and grants by type of recipient, with data for top organizations and by location, 1991 and trends, annual rpt, R4900–1

Group practice ownership of selected medical facilities, 1991, recurring rpt, A2200–7

Latin America Catholic welfare, health, and educational instns, by country, 1982-87, annual rpt, U6250–1.10

Local govt expenditures by function and type of govt unit, and for 52 largest cities, 1993 annual rpt, R9050–1.6

Measles cases in preschool children, health care providers used and welfare status, in 5 metro areas, 1989-90, article, A2623–1.508

Medicaid child and adult recipients, and treatment use and costs, by type of service, by State, FY91, annual rpt, A0565–1

Medicaid Federal grants, recipients, and benefits by type of service, with selected public health funding factors, by State and region, various years 1974-94, R8490–46

Mexico health care services use by US residents of border communities, as reported by physicians and patients, 1992 surveys, R4865–10

Minority non-English speaking population health care provision, by type of facility, 1993, article, A1865–1.514

Mutual fund industry financial data, by type of investor and financial instn intermediary, 1991 and trends, annual rpt, A6025–1.2

Operating and financial composite ratios for corporations, with establishments and receipts, for approx 200 industries, by asset size, FY90, annual rpt, C7800–1

Health facilities and services

Physician practice characteristics, including specialty, employer type, and participation in statistical profiling programs, 1992, articles, A2200–5.1

Preferred provider organizations (PPOs) by State, and total enrollment, 1990 and trends, annual fact book, A1275–1.3

Preferred provider organizations (PPOs), employee utilization, and type of sponsor or ownership, 1993 article, A1865–1.524

Public opinion on health care concerns, including costs and insurance coverage, May 1993 Gallup Poll, C4040–1.512

Public opinion on health care cost, quality, and insurance coverage, May 1993 Gallup Poll, C4040–1.511

Public opinion on health care issues, including govt and medical profession role, satisfaction with care and insurance, and reforms, 1975-92 surveys, A0610–1.504

Religious congregation characteristics, including membership, activities, staff, and finances, 1992 survey, recurring rpt, A5435–4

Shopping center financial and operating data, with detail by type of tenant, US and Canada, 1991, triennial rpt, R9285–1

State economic dev condition indicators, including economic performance, business vitality, growth capacity, and tax/fiscal system, by State, 1993 annual rpt, R4225–1.1

State govt regulatory requirements for HMOs and preferred provider organizations (PPOs), 1993 feature, A1865–1.521

Terminally ill patients treatment decisions, views of health professionals, 1993 survey article, A2623–1.503

TV news coverage of health issues, including leading topics, and Clinton Admin policies, Jan-May 1993, article, R3823–1.508

Vending machine sales and operations, by product and location type, 1990-92, annual rpt, C9470–1

World population and health indicators, with detail by region and country, 1992/93 biennial rpt, R9455–1.5

Youth age 10-15 health condition and health service use and sources, with data by insurance status, by race-ethnicity, 1988, article, A2623–1.509

State and local:

Alabama county data book, general data, 1992 annual rpt, S0121–2

Arizona statistical abstract, general data, 1993 recurring rpt, U5850–2.24

California statistical abstract, general data, 1992 annual rpt, S0840–2.5

Delaware data book, general data, 1993 annual rpt, S1375–4

Delaware school nurse services, including screening examinations, by county, 1991/92, annual rpt, S1430–1.6

Florida health care atlas, including manpower by occupation and health care facilities by type, by district and county, 1992 annual rpt, S1746–1.2

Florida statistical abstract, general data, 1992 annual rpt, U6660–1.20

Hawaii data book, general data, 1992 annual rpt, S2090–1.2

Hawaii health dept activities and services, including vital statistics and disease control, by location, 1990, annual rpt, S2065–1

Maryland elementary and secondary education data, by county, 1991/92, annual rpt, S3610–2.6, S3610–2.7

Montana health care facility capacity, utilization, and finances, by instn, 1991, annual rpt, S4690–2

New Mexico and US health services employment by SIC 4-digit industry, 1982 and 1991, article, S5624–2.510

New Mexico births, by health facility and type of attendant, by county, 1991, annual rpt, S5605–1.4

New York State adult care facility capacity and occupancy, by State area, 1991, annual rpt, S5800–2.3

New York State local jail/penitentiary inmates temporarily housed in mental health and medical facilities, by county or facility, 1991, annual rpt, S5724–2

New York State statistical yearbook, general data, 1992 annual rpt, U5100–1.11

Oklahoma public and institutional library holdings, circulation, finances, and staff, by facility, FY92, annual rpt, S6470–1

Pennsylvania public and institutional library personnel, holdings, circulation, and finances, by county and facility, FY92, annual rpt, S6790–2

Pennsylvania statistical abstract, general data, 1992 recurring rpt, U4130–6.5

Rhode Island statistical almanac, general data, 1993 annual rpt, C7975–1

Tennessee public school finances, by county, city, and school district, 1991/92, annual rpt, S7490–2.4

Texas health care system policy research, including data on providers and finances, utilization, and insurance, series, U8850–8

Washington State public assistance clients and service costs, by client characteristics, program, and county, FY90, annual rpt, S8420–2

Wyoming penitentiary medical services, including inmate hospital visits, FY92, annual rpt, S8883 1

see also Adult day care

see also Birthing centers

see also Clinics

see also Community health services

see also Emergency medical service

see also Health care reform

see also Health facilities administration

see also Health insurance

see also Health maintenance organizations

see also Health planning and evaluation

see also Home health services

see also Hospices

see also Hospitals

see also Laboratories

see also Medical examinations and tests

see also Medical supplies and equipment

see also Mental health facilities and services

see also Military health facilities and services

see also Nursing homes

see also Oral rehydration therapy

see also Public health

see also Vaccination and vaccines

see also Veterans health facilities and services

Index by Subjects and Names

see also Medicine and terms beginning with Medical

see also terms listed under Health occupations

Health insurance

Airline retiree health benefits liability disclosed by new accounting requirements, for 4 carriers, 1993 article, C7000–4.504

Asset allocation and investment yields for top 125 US and Canadian life/health insurance companies, 1992 and trends, annual article, C1050–2.512

Association executives compensation, by position, assn type, and census div, with personnel practices and benefit provisions, 1992, biennial rpt, A2900–3

Benefit payments by life insurance companies for health insurance, and AIDS-related claims paid, 1992 biennial fact book, A1325–1.2

Benefits paid by insurance companies, and average hospitalization cost and stay by State, 1989 and/or 1990, annual rpt, A5650–1.4

Black American health and vital statistics data, with comparisons to whites, 1970s-91, annual compilation, C6775–2.2

Black children and youth population, economic, health, and education data, with comparisons to whites, 1993 rpt, R3840–21

CEOs of health insurance companies income, public perceptions vs actual amounts, with detail for 10 leading firms, 1991-93, R4865–13

Child and maternal health indicators and insurance coverage, by race-ethnicity and other demographic characteristics, 1992 annual rpt, R3840–5.1

Child coverage rates under employment-related insurance, by income and race-ethnicity, 1977, 1987, and 2000, annual rpt, R3840–11.1

Child day care center salaries, health benefits, and turnover, for centers in 5 States or local areas, 1992 survey, annual article, A3865–2

Child day care center staff compensation, health benefits, and turnover, 1992 and trends, A3865–3

Child health and well-being indicators, with selected household characteristics, by State, 1993 annual rpt, R3832–1

Children's health insurance coverage status, 1991, article, R8750–1.510

Corporate personnel mgmt devs, including hiring, layoffs, and health care and payroll cost control efforts, June 1992 survey, annual rpt, B6850–3

Cost and enrollment data by plan type, region, and industry, 1992, article, A1865–1.511

Costs of employee health insurance benefits, 10 metro areas with highest and lowest rates compared to natl average, 1992 article, C4687–1.501

Costs of group health insurance plans in 400 cities compared to natl average, 1989, B6095–1, B6095–2

Coverage and finances for health insurance, with health care costs and facilities, and demographic data, 1940s-91, annual rpt, A5173–2

Coverage, benefit payments, and premiums, by type of plan, 1990 and trends, annual fact book, A1275–1.3

Index by Subjects and Names

Health insurance

Coverage for health insurance, and health care spending, under current law vs plans of presidential candidates Bush and Clinton, by State, 1993-2005, R4865–9

Coverage status, and views on types of care which should be covered, 1992 survey, annual rpt, C8111–2

Drugs (prescription) financing methods among population age 65/older and 64/under, by patient characteristics, 1987, R4865–8

Educational employee retirement plan health insurance coverage, with detail for selected individual plans, 1990/91, recurring rpt, A7640–18

Employee benefit payments and employer cost/payroll ratios, by industry, detailed type of benefit, and firm size, 1991, annual rpt, A3840–1

Employee views on value of employer-provided health insurance, 1992 survey, article, A1865–1.514

Employer costs for indirectly subsidizing uninsured and Medicare/Medicaid patients, by industry div, 1993 article, C5800–7.520

Employer premiums for typical employee coverage as percent of natl average, by State, Mar 1992, article, B8500–2.505

Employer-provided insurance coverage, plans offered, and employee reasons for plan choice, 1993 article, A1865–1.515

Expenditures for health care, by fund source, decennially 1960-90, annual fact book, A1275–1.4

Family expenditures for insurance premiums, and population health insurance coverage, by source of coverage and income group, 1987, R4700–20

Food marketers with health care programs, by type, 1993 annual survey, A4950–6

Food service industry health insurance coverage practices and costs, by company sales size, 1993 and trends, article, A8200–1.511

Hard goods manufacturers and representatives views on health insurance costs, coverage, and issues, by product line, 1993 annual survey rpt, A1800–1

Higher education instn employee retirement and insurance benefits, prevalence and expenditures, by type of instn and region, 1991, biennial survey, A9025–3

Hispanic American health insurance coverage status, with comparison to whites and detail by provider type, 1990, annual compilation, C6775–3.6

Hospital (teaching) house staff benefits, by region and ownership, 1992/93, annual rpt, A3273–3

Hospital emergency dept use, by location and patient insurance coverage status, 1990 and trends, A1865–1.508

Hospital employee health care benefits, including coverage for mental health/substance abuse and AIDS, and data by region, 1992 survey, article, A1865–1.505

Hospital patient admission rates and length of stay, by diagnosis and procedure, payment source, age, sex, and region, 1991, B4455–4

Hospital patient charges and length of stay, by diagnosis and procedure, payment source, age, and region, 1991, B4455–5

Hospital patient discharges and length of stay, by diagnostic related group (DRG), payment source, age, and region, 1991, annual rpt series, B4455–3

Income tax revenues that would be generated if employer-paid health benefits were taxed, and benefits coverage, by income group, 1991, article, C3950–1.505

Industrial distributors providing employee health insurance, by type of plan and cost-sharing arrangement, 1992, annual survey, C1850–4.507

Japan and US health care system data, including expenditures, facilities, insurance coverage, and population health indicators, 1993 article, R5650–2.515

Jewelry store employee benefits, with health insurance premium provisions, 1992 annual survey article, C2150–7.501

Limited-benefit low-cost plan characteristics and persons covered, for 29 States waiving mandated benefits, 1992/93, R4865–16

Magazine publisher employee benefits, costs, and trends, with employee ratings of health coverage, Mar/Apr 1993 survey, article, C2575–1.517

Marketing trends and devs, and mgmt and finance topics, for life and health insurance, monthly rpt, C1050–2

Men age 69-84 private health insurance coverage, by race, 1990 survey, U3780–9

Metro areas with greatest market shares for health insurance managed care and nonmanaged care plans, including population, top 10 cities, 1992, article, A1865–1.510

Nurse practitioner services insurance coverage, by State, 1991/92, U8850–8.4

Nursing center (community) characteristics, including payment sources used by clients, 1990 survey, article, A8010–3.506

Nursing higher education program clinic patient characteristics, including insurance coverage, FY92, biennial rpt, A0615–5

Nursing home insurance adequacy as means of making care affordable to elderly, with detail by age and/or State, 1992 and 2005, R4865–12

Older population health insurance sources, for urban, suburban, and rural areas, 1993 article, A1865–1.522

Opinions of physicians and general public on health care reform, by respondent characteristics, Mar-Apr 1993 surveys, C8915–7.2

Physician use of electronic billing systems, by payment source and region, 1991-92, article, A2200–5.1

Physician visit volume forecast for HMOs vs indemnity insurance coverage, with detail by procedure, and industry or region, 1993 article, A1865–1.524

Population (non-elderly) share without health insurance coverage, by State, 1991 and trends, article, B8500–2.508

Population and workers lacking insurance coverage, by family income level or employer size class, 1991, article, C8900–1.516

Population lacking health insurance and with high out-of-pocket expenses, by State and selected characteristics, 1993, R4865–14

Population lacking health insurance, by race, 1989-91, article, C4215–1.507

Population lacking health insurance coverage, by State and region, 1989-91, R8490–46

Premium receipts and reserves of life insurance companies, by type of plan, 1991 and trends, biennial fact book, A1325–1.4

Premiums and underwriting ratios for top 300 accident/health companies, 1991, annual article, C1050–2.502

Public opinion on health care concerns, including costs and insurance coverage, May 1993 Gallup Poll, C4040–1.512

Public opinion on health care issues, including govt and medical profession role, satisfaction with care and insurance, and reforms, 1975-92 surveys, A0610–1.504

Public opinion on health care reform and satisfaction with current insurance coverage, 1993 survey article, A1865–1.521

Public perception of personal health condition correlated with health insurance status, 1987 survey, article, A2623–1.511

Retiree health insurance corporate plan changes since 1990 and planned by 1994, 1992 article, C5800–7.505

Small corporation views on health benefits, with data on uninsured population characteristics and employment size of firms not offering insurance, 1993 feature, C4215–1.506

Southern States children age 17/under lacking health insurance and eligible for Medicaid, with detail by age and family income, for 6-17 States, 1991, R9000–1

Southern States teacher retirement and health insurance plan characteristics and costs as a percent of salaries, for 15 States, 1993 rpt, A8945–34

State economic dev condition indicators, including economic performance, business vitality, growth capacity, and tax/fiscal system, by State, 1993 annual rpt, R4225–1.1

State employee health benefit plan funding patterns, coverage and HMO participation by State, and cost mgmt practices, 1993 annual article, C2425–1.506

State govt mandated benefits in each State, and State program provisions in 2 States, 1991, U8850–8.1

State, regional, and census div population shares not covered by health insurance, 1989-91, annual data sheet, R8750–9

State social, economic, and govtl indicators, with rankings, 1993 semiannual rpt, B8500–1.9

Surgery coverage denial incidence among utilization review organizations, for 21 procedures, 1990, A1865–1.506

Youth age 10-15 health condition and health service use and sources, with data by insurance status, by race-ethnicity, 1988, article, A2623–1.509

State and local:

Alabama insurance industry financial and underwriting data, by company and line of coverage, 1991, annual rpt, S0160–1

Alaska insurance industry underwriting and investment data, by company and type of insurance, with regulatory info, 1991 and trends, annual rpt, S0280–3

Health insurance

Arizona insurance industry financial and underwriting data, by company and type of insurance, with regulatory info, 1992, annual rpt, S0483–1

California insurance industry financial and underwriting data, by company and type of insurance, with regulatory info, 1991, annual rpt, S0900–1

California State initiative on basic health care coverage, election results by county, 1992, biennial rpt, S0934–1

Connecticut health insurance coverage rate, by respondent characteristics and behavior risk factors, 1991 survey, S1200–3

Connecticut health insurance coverage rate, 1991, annual rpt, S1200–2

Connecticut insurance industry financial and underwriting data, by company and type of insurance, 1991, annual rpt, S1222–1

Florida insurance industry financial and underwriting data, by company and line of coverage, 1991, annual rpt, S1760–1

Georgia statistical abstract, general data, 1992-93 biennial rpt, U6730–1.9

Hawaii data book, general data, 1992 annual rpt, S2090–1.15

Hawaii insurance coverage status of perinatal service and drug/alcohol treatment clients, 1990, annual rpt, S2065–1

Idaho insurance industry financial and underwriting data, by company and type of insurance, with regulatory data, 1991, annual rpt, S2260–1

Iowa insurance industry financial and underwriting data, by company and type of insurance, 1992, annual rpt, S2760–1

Kansas insurance industry financial and underwriting data, by company and type of insurance, with regulatory info, 1992, annual rpt, S2990–1

Maryland insurance industry financial and underwriting data, by company and type of insurance, with regulatory info, 1991, annual rpt, S3655–1

Missouri insurance industry financial and underwriting data, by company and type of insurance, with regulatory info, 1992, annual rpt, S4527–1

Nebraska insurance industry financial and underwriting data, by company and line of coverage, with regulatory info, 1992, annual rpt, S4890–1

New Jersey insurance industry financial and underwriting data, by company and type of insurance, 1990, annual rpt, S5420–1

New York State insurance industry devs, finances, and regulatory activity, 1990/91 and trends, annual rpt, S5770–3

New York State insurance industry financial and underwriting data, by company and line of coverage, 1991, annual rpt, S5770–2

North Dakota population lack of insurance, and coverage of hospital and preventive services expenses, 1991, annual rpt, S6105–3

Oklahoma insurance industry financial and underwriting data, by company and type of insurance, with regulatory info, 1992, annual rpt, S6462–1

Pennsylvania health insurance coverage, by age, 1991, annual rpt, S6820–4

Pennsylvania insurance industry financial and underwriting data, by company and line of coverage, 1991, with FY92 regulatory info, annual rpt, S6835–1

Rhode Island insurance industry financial and underwriting data, by company and line of coverage, 1990, with FY91 regulatory info, annual rpt, S6945–2

South Carolina insurance industry financial and underwriting data, by company, 1991, with FY92 regulatory info, annual rpt, S7195–1

South Dakota insurance industry financial and underwriting data, by company and type of insurance, with regulatory info, 1991-92, annual rpt, S7300–2

Tennessee insurance industry financial and underwriting data, by company and type of insurance, with regulatory info, 1991, annual rpt, S7466–1

Texas health insurance coverage, 1991, annual rpt, S7685–2

Texas insurance dept regulatory activities, with industry financial and underwriting data by line of coverage, FY92 annual rpt, S7700–1

Utah insurance industry financial and underwriting data, by company and line of coverage, with regulatory info, 1991, annual rpt, S7845–1

West Virginia insurance industry financial and underwriting data, by company and line of coverage, with regulatory info, 1991, annual rpt, S8575–1

Wisconsin insurance industry financial and underwriting data, by company and line of coverage, with regulatory info, 1992, annual rpt, S8755–1

see also Blue Cross-Blue Shield

see also Disability benefits and insurance

see also Health maintenance organizations

see also Medicaid

see also Medical assistance

see also Medicare

see also Old-Age, Survivors, Disability, and Health Insurance

see also Workers compensation

Health maintenance organizations

Drugstore (independent pharmacy) serving of HMOs, by census div and sales size, 1991, annual survey, B5165–1

Enrollment and costs, with comparisons to other health plans, and detail by region and industry, 1970s-92, article, A1865–1.511

Enrollment as percent of population, for top 5 States, 1992, A1865–1.515

Enrollment by plan type and for top 10 HMOs, and enrollment as a percent of total population by region, 1993 article, A1865–1.513

Enrollment in HMOs and number of plans by State, and HMO contracts per physician by specialty, 1991 and trends, annual fact book, A1275–1.3

Enrollment, plans, and average premiums, with data by region and State, 1991, annual rpt, A5173–2.1

Metro areas with greatest market shares for health insurance managed care and nonmanaged care plans, including population, top 10 cities, 1992, article, A1865–1.510

Operations and finances of HMOs, including benefits, enrollment and utilization, and staffing, by plan characteristics, 1990-91, annual rpt, A5150–2

Opinions of physicians and general public on health care reform, by respondent characteristics, Mar-Apr 1993 surveys, C8915–7.2

Index by Subjects and Names

Pharmaceutical cost containment methods used by HMOs, 1988 and 1991, article, A1865–1.517

Physician compensation in group practices and HMOs, by specialty and region, 1992 survey and trends, annual rpt, B7450–2

Physician group practice affiliation with HMOs, including revenue shares generated, with detail by State, 1991, recurring rpt, A2200–7

State employee health benefit plan coverage and HMO participation, by State, 1993 annual article, C2425–1.506

State and local:

Connecticut insurance industry financial and underwriting data, by company and type of insurance, 1991, annual rpt, S1222–1

Florida health care atlas, including manpower by occupation and health care facilities by type, by district and county, 1992 annual rpt, S1746–1.2

Florida statistical abstract, general data, 1992 annual rpt, U6660–1.20

Hawaii data book, general data, 1992 annual rpt, S2090–1.15

Idaho insurance industry financial and underwriting data, by company and type of insurance, with regulatory data, 1991, annual rpt, S2260–1

Iowa insurance industry financial and underwriting data, by company and type of insurance, 1992, annual rpt, S2760–1

Kansas insurance industry financial and underwriting data, by company and type of insurance, with regulatory info, 1992, annual rpt, S2990–1

Maryland insurance industry financial and underwriting data, by company and type of insurance, with regulatory info, 1991, annual rpt, S3655–1

Maryland medical assistance payments and recipients, by program, type of service, location, demographic characteristics, and facility, FY92 and trends, annual rpt, S3635–3

Michigan insurance industry financial and underwriting data, by company and type of insurance, with regulatory info, 1991, annual rpt, S3983–1

Missouri insurance industry financial and underwriting data, by company and type of insurance, with regulatory info, 1992, annual rpt, S4527–1

Nebraska insurance industry financial and underwriting data, by company and line of coverage, with regulatory info, 1992, annual rpt, S4890–1

New York State insurance industry devs, finances, and regulatory activity, 1990/91 and trends, annual rpt, S5770–3

New York State insurance industry financial and underwriting data, by company and line of coverage, 1991, annual rpt, S5770–2

Pennsylvania insurance industry financial and underwriting data, by company and line of coverage, 1991, with FY92 regulatory info, annual rpt, S6835–1

Rhode Island insurance industry financial and underwriting data, by company and line of coverage, 1990, with FY91 regulatory info, annual rpt, S6945–2

Tennessee insurance industry financial and underwriting data, by company and type of insurance, with regulatory info, 1991, annual rpt, S7466–1

Texas insurance dept regulatory activities, with industry financial and underwriting data by line of coverage, FY92 annual rpt, S7700–1

Utah insurance industry financial and underwriting data, by company and line of coverage, with regulatory info, 1991, annual rpt, S7845–1

Washington State medical assistance services in HMOs, clients and costs by county, FY90, annual rpt, S8420–2

West Virginia enrollment and financial data, by HMO, 1991, annual rpt, S8575–1

Wisconsin insurance industry financial and underwriting data, by company and line of coverage, with regulatory info, 1992, annual rpt, S8755–1

Health occupations

Compensation of medical group mgmt, by demographic and practice characteristics, 1992, annual rpt, A6365–3

Employment and earnings of health care workers, by occupation and sex, 1992, annual rpt, A1570–1, A1570–2

Employment distribution of health care professionals making career change, by new employer type, 1993 survey article, A1865–1.523

Employment in 16 fastest-growing health care occupations, 1990 and 2005, article, A1865–1.514

Employment of health care workers for top 10 States, June 1993, article, A1865–1.522

Hospital directory, with utilization, expenses, and personnel, by instn, type, and location, 1992, annual rpt, A1865–3

Hospital FTE per occupied bed, by instn characteristics and location, 1988-92, annual rpt, B1880–1

Hospital positions with highest vacancy rates, and recruitment and retention difficulties, 1991 survey, article, A1865–1.504

Medical group financial and operating data, by practice characteristics, 1991, annual rpt, A6365–2

Medical group practice characteristics, including specialties, form of organization, and location, 1991 and trends, recurring rpt, A2200–7

Psychiatric hospital FTE employment, 1981-91, article, A1865–1.512

Terminally ill patients treatment decisions, views of health professionals, 1993 survey article, A2623–1.503

Women and minorities in professional fields, detailed education and labor force data, 1980s-91, with historical trends, recurring rpt, A3960–2

Work conditions cited as source of dissatisfaction by health care professionals, 1992 survey, article, A1865–1.511

World health manpower, with detail for family planning personnel, by occupation and country, various years 1965-89, R8720–1

State and local:

Alabama county data book, general data, 1992 annual rpt, S0121–2

Alabama statistical abstract, general data, 1992 recurring rpt, U5680–2.8

Delaware data book, general data, 1993 annual rpt, S1375–4

Florida county data book, 1992/93 annual rpt, C6360–1

Florida health care atlas, including manpower by occupation and health care facilities by type, by district and county, 1992 annual rpt, S1746–1.2

Florida statistical abstract, general data, 1992 annual rpt, U6660–1.20

Illinois mental health dept employment, by facility, FY91-93, annual rpt, S2505–1

Kansas statistical abstract, general data, 1991/92 annual rpt, U7095–2.2

New Mexico and US health services employment by SIC 4-digit industry, 1982 and 1991, article, S5624–2.510

North Dakota physicians and nurses, by county, 1992, annual planning rpt, S6140–2

Oklahoma statistical abstract, general data, 1992 annual rpt, U8130–2.9

Tennessee statistical abstract, general data, 1992/93 annual rpt, U8710–2.17

Texas hospitals, operations, utilization, and finances, by type, ownership, size, and metro-nonmetro status, 1970s-91, U8850–8.3

see also Allied health personnel

see also Anesthesiology

see also Biotechnology

see also Chiropractic and naturopathy

see also Clinical laboratory technicians

see also Coroners

see also Counselors and counseling

see also Dentists and dentistry

see also Dietitians and nutritionists

see also Epidemiology and epidemiologists

see also Geriatrics

see also Health facilities administration

see also Medical education

see also Midwives

see also Nuclear medicine and radiology

see also Nurses and nursing

see also Obstetrics and gynecology

see also Occupational therapy

see also Optometry

see also Orthopedics

see also Osteopathy

see also Pathology

see also Pediatrics

see also Pharmacists and pharmacy

see also Physical therapy

see also Physicians

see also Podiatry

see also Psychiatry

see also Social work

see also Speech pathology and audiology

see also Surgeons and surgery

see also Veterinary medicine

see also Medicine and terms beginning with Medical

Health of workers

see Absenteeism

see Occupational health and safety

Health planning and evaluation

Hospital planning activity, including construction plans and influence of anticipated health care reform, 1993 survey, article, A1865–1.523

State and local:

Texas health care system policy research, including data on providers and finances, utilization, and insurance, series, U8850–8

Health statistics

see Vital statistics

Healthcare Financial Management Association

Hospital chief financial officer views on educational needs and top challenges, 1993 survey, article, A1865–1.511

Healthcare Research System

Hospital outpatient top 10 nonsurgical and surgical procedures performed, 1991, 1997, and 2002, article, A1865–1.502

Hearing aids

Sales (unit) of hearing aids, by type and State, and trade summary, quarterly rpt, A5185–1

State and local:

Maryland medical assistance payments and recipients, by program, type of service, location, demographic characteristics, and facility, FY92 and trends, annual rpt, S3635–3

Hearing and hearing disorders

Telephone equipment provisions for hearing- and speech-impaired customers, regulatory policies by State and Canadian Province, 1991/92 annual rpt, A7015–3

State and local:

Florida hearing- and speech-impaired recipients of specialized telephone equipment, FY92, annual rpt, S1790–1

Hawaii chronic health conditions, by demographic characteristics and location, 1988, annual rpt, S2065–1.3

Hawaii health dept family health services and recipients, including school health programs, 1990 annual rpt, S2065–1.5

Kentucky Medicaid recipients and payments, by program, county, and type of medical service, monthly rpt, S3140–5

Ohio special education services for hearing-handicapped children, by school district, 1991/92 and trends, annual rpt, S6265–1

see also Deaf

see also Ear diseases and infections

see also Hearing aids

see also Speech pathology and audiology

Heart diseases

see Cardiovascular diseases

Heart transplantation

see Medical transplants

Heating

see Plumbing and heating

Heating degree days

see Weather

Heating oil

see Fuel oil

Hedging

see Futures trading

Height

see Body measurements

Helicopters

Accidents involving turbine helicopters, with circumstances, fatalities, and model involved, weekly rpt quarterly feature, C5800–30

Airline fleet composition and aircraft on order, by model and carrier, 1992, annual article, C7000–4.508

Civil aviation helicopters, production, trade, utilization, accidents, and landing facilities, 1993 annual rpt, A5190–1

Regional aircraft fleets for passenger and all cargo operations, by manufacturer and type, and top models in use, 1992, annual rpt, A8795–1.1

Helicopters

Shipments of civil and military helicopters by model and company, and heliports by State, 1991 and trends, annual rpt, A0250–2

Turbine-powered aircraft in service and on order, by manufacturer and model, for over 900 airlines worldwide, Dec 1992, annual rpt, B3370–1

State and local:

Hawaii data book, general data, 1992 annual rpt, S2090–1.18

Helium

State and local:

Arizona helium production, 1959-76, monthly rpt, S0473–1

Help-wanted advertising

see Advertising

see Job vacancy

Helyar, Thelma

"Kansas Statistical Abstract, 1991-92", U7095–2

Hepatitis

see Infective and parasitic diseases

Herbicides

see Pesticides

Herbs

see Spices and herbs

Hereditary diseases

State and local:

- California vital statistics, including population, births, and deaths by cause, by demographic characteristics and county, 1990 and trends, annual rpt, S0865–1
- Florida vital statistics, including population, births, deaths by cause, and marriages and dissolutions, by location and demographic characteristics, 1992 and trends, annual rpt, S1745–3
- Idaho vital statistics, including births, deaths by cause, abortions, marriages, and divorces, by demographic characteristics and county, 1991 and trends, annual rpt, S2250–2
- Louisiana vital statistics, including population, births, deaths by cause, reportable diseases, marriages, and divorces, by demographic characteristics and locality, 1989-90 and trends, annual rpt, S3295–1
- Maine vital statistics, including births, deaths by cause, abortions, and marriages and divorces, by demographic characteristics and location, 1991 and trends, annual rpt, S3460–2
- Massachusetts vital statistics, including births, deaths by cause, marriages, divorces, and population, by locality and demographic characteristics, 1990 and trends, annual rpt, S3850–1
- Montana vital statistics, including births, deaths by cause, abortion, disease, and marriage and divorce, by demographic characteristics and county, 1990-91 and trends, annual rpt, S4690–1
- South Carolina deaths, by detailed cause, age, sex, and race, 1990, annual rpt, S7175–2
- Tennessee vital statistics, including births, deaths by cause, marriages, divorces, and population, by demographic characteristics and location, 1991 and trends, annual rpt, S7520–2
- Vermont vital statistics, including population, births, deaths by cause, abortions, marriages, and divorces, by location and demographic characteristics, 1991 and trends, annual rpt, S8054–1

West Virginia vital statistics, including births, deaths by cause, marriages, and divorces, by location and demographic characteristics, 1991 and trends, annual rpt, S8560–1

see also Birth defects

see also under By Disease in the "Index by Categories"

Heroin

see Drug abuse and treatment

see Drug and narcotics offenses

see Drugs

see Methadone treatment

Herpes

see Sexually transmitted diseases

Hewitt Associates

Health insurance provisions by employers, with employee reasons for plan choice, 1993 article, A1865–1.515

Tax-deferred salary reduction 401(k) plan employee participation rates, 1993 survey, article, C2710–2.521

Heywood, John

"Truth About Public Employees: Underpaid or Overpaid?", R4700–21

Hiam, Alexander

"Does Quality Work? A Review of Relevant Studies", R4105–78.32

Hides and skins

- Exports of farm products, by detailed commodity and country of destination, US and California, 1991, annual rpt, B9520–1
- Foreign trade and prices for meat and livestock products, with data by country, 1991 and trends, annual rpt, A2100–1
- Production, consumption, stocks, trade, and prices for approx 100 basic commodities, including by country and producing State, commodity yearbook for 1993, C2400–1, C2400–2

see also Furs and fur industry

see also Leather industry and products

High fructose corn syrup

see Syrups and sweeteners

High school equivalency tests

- General Educational Dev (GED) diploma recipients, by State, 1992, annual rpt, C2175–1.531
- General Educational Dev (GED) testing programs and results, by jurisdiction, 1992 and trends, annual rpt, A1410–16

State and local:

- Kentucky General Educational Dev (GED) diplomas issued, by State area, 1991, annual planning rpt, S3140–3
- Louisiana adult education test results, and General Equivalency Diplomas awarded, 1985/86-1991/92, annual rpt, S3280–1.1
- Maine high school equivalency diploma recipients, by age, 1971/72-1991/92, annual rpt, S3435–1
- Maryland General Educational Dev (GED) test results, by test center, FY92, annual rpt, S3610–1
- Massachusetts General Educational Dev (GED) certificates issued, 1991, annual rpt, S3810–3
- Missouri high school equivalency applications and certificates issued, 1991/92, annual rpt, S4505–1.1
- Ohio adults passing General Educational Dev (GED) test, 1989-91, annual rpt, S6265–2

West Virginia General Educational Dev (GED) diplomas issued, 1947-92, annual rpt, S8540–4.2

High school graduates

see Educational attainment

High schools

see Elementary and secondary education

High-speed ground transportation

- Europe high-speed rail lines in service, with route length and top speed, 1993 article, C8400–1.507
- Mass transit system finances and operations, passengers, and employment, by mode, US and Canada, 1990-91 and trends, annual rpt, A2650–1
- Operations of railroads and rail rapid transit, data and related articles, monthly rpt, C8400–1

High technology

see Science and technology

Higher education

- Admissions dept activity, including trends in applications received, recruitment, staff, and budgets, 1992-93, annual rpt, A6695–1
- Africa public universities, enrollment, and expenditures per student, for 12-34 countries, 1993 article, C2175–1.524
- Black American educational statistics, with comparisons to whites, 1970s-92, annual compilation, C6775–2.3
- Black children and youth population, economic, health, and education data, with comparisons to whites, 1993 rpt, R3840–21
- Catholic colleges and enrollment, by diocese and State, 1993 annual compilation, C4950–1
- Catholic educational instns and enrollment, by State and diocese, 1993 annual almanac, C6885–1
- Chemicals R&D spending in Federal, industrial, and academic sectors, with data by company and instn, 1980s-93, annual feature, A1250–1.537
- Chemistry and chemical engineering grad starting salaries, employment status, demographic characteristics, and advanced study plans, 1991/92, annual rpt, A1250–2
- Chronicle of Higher Education, with data and articles on enrollment, finances, and faculty and salaries, weekly rpt, C2175–1
- Coal industry executive views on education support and skills needed in mgmt and technical positions, Mar 1993 survey, article, C5226–1.510
- Corporate executive ratings of education system performance in preparation of new employees, July 1992 survey, A2800–3
- Drug, alcohol, and tobacco use patterns and attitudes among higher education students, by sex and region, 1989-91 surveys, annual rpt, U4950–1
- Education Week, issues and devs in elementary/secondary school programs, enrollment, finances, and staff, and selected higher education issues, weekly rpt, R4800–2
- Employers recruiting on-campus, visit plans and hiring practices, 1992/93 annual survey rpt, U3130–1
- Finances, and enrollment vs population age 18-24, by instn control, various years 1953/54-2003/04, annual rpt, R9050–1.4

Index by Subjects and Names

Higher education

Financial support of educational instns from contributions, with top instns, by instn and donor type, 1991/92 and trends, article, C2176–1.514

Food service (institutional) financial and operating data, for leading firms by market segment, 1993 recurring feature, C1850–3.511

Food service industry sales and establishments, with growth outlook, by market segment, 1993 annual feature, C1850–3.503

Food service industry sales trends and forecast, by market segment, 1990-93, annual feature, A8200–1.502

Football (college) bowl game payments to participating teams, 1992/93, annual feature, C2175–1.503

Freshmen attitudes and characteristics, degree and career plans, and financial aid sources, by sex and instn type, fall 1992, annual survey, U6215–1

Graduate students, faculty and salaries, and total enrollment, for library science compared to 4 other fields, 1993 annual rpt, A3235–1.6

High school grad college enrollment rates, by sex and race, 1980 and 1991, article, A8510–1.1

Hispanic American educational statistics, with comparisons to whites, 1970s-92, annual compilation, C6775–3.2

Japan higher education foreign students, with detail for US students by funding source, by academic level, 1993 article, R5650–2.527

Latin America statistical abstract, general data by country, 1992 annual rpt, U6250–1.8

Library (research) holdings, expenditures by type, and staff, for 120 academic and nonacademic instns, US and Canada, FY92, annual rpt, A3365–1

Library and book trade reference info, including public and academic library funding, construction, and operations, by State and instn, 1992, annual compilation, C1650–3

Library construction, costs, and funding sources, by State, city, instn, and library type, FY92 and trends, annual article, C1852–1.501

Library school grad placements and salaries, by region, sex, instn, and library type, with detail for minorities, 1992 and trends, annual article, C1852–1.512

Library/info science school enrollment, staff and student characteristics, finances, and curricula, by school and degree program, 1991/92, annual rpt, A3235–1

Mathematics dept faculty, salaries, enrollment, and degree recipient characteristics, 1991/92 and trends, annual survey, A2085–1

Minority involvement in higher education, including enrollment, and degrees awarded, by race-ethnicity, sex, and State, 1970s-91, annual rpt, A1410–10

Missouri higher education enrollment, degrees conferred, and appropriations, by instn, and coordinating board activities, annual rpt discontinued coverage, S4520–1

Physical plant operations, costs, employment, salaries, and energy use, by instn and region, 1991/92, recurring rpt, A3183–1

Psychology grad depts, faculty characteristics, enrollment, and student aid, US and Canada, 1990/91 and trends, annual rpt, A2620–3

R&D funding and expenditures, by source and performing sector, 1960s-93, annual rpt, R3300–1

Research and policy review in higher education, series, A1410–1

Social work higher education programs, faculty and student characteristics, and student aid, with data by instn, 1992 and trends, annual rpt, A4515–1

Southern States higher education enrollment, degrees, appropriations, tuition/fees, and faculty compensation, by instn type, for 15 States, 1990/91, annual rpt, A8945–31

Southern States higher education enrollment, degrees, faculty, and finances, for 15 States, 1990s and trends, biennial fact book, A8945–1

Southern States higher education-related data for 15 States, fact book update series, A8945–27

Sports intercollegiate women's program participation, and scholarship recommendations of Natl Collegiate Athletic Assn gender equity task force, by sport, 1993 rpt, A7440–6

State and land-grant university tuition/fees, and room and board charges, by type of professional program and/or instn, fall 1991-92, annual rpt, A7150–4

State higher education data, including instns, faculty, students, degrees, and finances, by State, 1993 annual rpt, C2175–1.531

State higher education participation rates by age 19, for 9 States with highest and lowest rates, 1988, article, B8500–2.510

State social, economic, and govtl indicators, with rankings, 1993 semiannual rpt, B8500–1.7

Statistical profiles of 50 States and DC, general data, 1993 annual almanac, C4712–1

Theological school enrollment, staff and compensation, and finances, with data by instn, 1991/92 and trends, annual rpt, A3376–1

Theological seminary enrollment in Canada and US, with detail for women and minorities, 1992 and trends, annual rpt, C0105–1

Urban public high school grads by type of postgraduation activity, for 47 systems, 1990/91, A4425–4

Women and minorities in professional fields, detailed education and labor force data, 1980s-91, with historical trends, recurring rpt, A3960–2

State and local:

Alabama statistical abstract, general data, 1992 recurring rpt, U5680–2.4

Arizona higher education instns, enrollment, and faculty, with comparisons to population, 1990, article, U0280–1.511

Arizona statistical abstract, general data, 1993 recurring rpt, U5850–2.4

Arkansas public higher education finances and enrollment, with comparisons to US and selected other States, 1990-92, article, U5930–1.502

California library finances, staff, holdings, and services, by library type and facility, FY92, annual rpt, S0825–2

California statistical abstract, general data, 1992 annual rpt, S0840–2.6

Colorado higher education library finances and operations, and enrollment, by instn, 1992, biennial rpt, S1000–3.2

Connecticut public high school grads and postgraduate activities, 1991, biennial rpt, S1185–3

DC statistical profile, general data, 1992 annual rpt, S1535–3.6

Delaware postsecondary education finances, enrollment, and degrees conferred, by instn, FY94 annual rpt, S1425–1

Florida county data book, 1992/93 annual rpt, C6360–1

Florida higher education enrollment, degree programs, staff, and finances, by State-supported instn, with student and staff characteristics, 1991/92 annual rpt, S1725–1

Florida municipal and county statistical profiles, general data, 1991 annual rpt, C4712–6

Florida statistical abstract, general data, 1992 annual rpt, U6660–1.4, U6660–1.14

Georgia county guide, general data, 1993 annual rpt, U6750–1

Georgia statistical abstract, general data, 1992-93 biennial rpt, U6730–1.2

Hawaii data book, general data, 1992 annual rpt, S2090–1.3

Idaho economic profile, general data, 1992 recurring rpt, S2218–2.3

Illinois higher education enrollment, degrees, staff, and finances, by public and private instn and student characteristics, 1993 annual rpt, S2475–1

Illinois statistical abstract, general data, 1992 annual rpt, U6910–2

Indiana enrollment for top 20 higher education instns, fall 1990, annual rpt, S2570–1.1

Iowa postsecondary enrollment, degrees, staff, and finances, by instn, 1990/91, annual rpt, S2755–1

Kansas statistical abstract, general data, 1991/92 annual rpt, U7095–2.5

Kentucky higher education enrollment, degrees, staff, and finances, by State-supported instn, 1983-92, annual rpt, S3130–3

Maine statistical summary, general economic and social data, 1992 recurring rpt, S3434–1

Maryland statistical abstract, general data, 1993-94 biennial rpt, S3605–1.2

Minnesota postsecondary education enrollment and finances, by type of school system, 1970s-93, biennial rpt, S4195–2

Mississippi higher education enrollment and degrees, by level and field, and finances, by State-supported instn, 1991/92, annual rpt, S4360–1

Mississippi statistical abstract, general data, 1992 annual rpt, U3255–4.3

Missouri higher education enrollment, degrees, libraries, staff, and finances, by instn, 1992 and trends, annual rpt, S4520–3

Missouri public, special, and academic libraries, finances, holdings, circulation, staff, and services, by location, FY92, annual rpt, S4520–2

Higher education

Nevada library and staff directories for public and academic libraries, with data on holdings, operations, and finances, FY92, annual rpt, S5095–1

Nevada statistical abstract, general data, 1992 biennial rpt, S5005–1.7

New Hampshire high school grads and postgraduation activities, by school, county, and sex, 1991, annual tables, S5200–1.2

New Hampshire high school grads and postgraduation activities, by school, county, and sex, 1992, annual tables, S5200–1.15

New Jersey high school grad postgraduation plans, by county, fall 1991, annual rpt, S5385–1.1

New York State high school grads and postgraduation activities, by municipality and school district, 1991, annual rpt, C4712–7

New York State statistical yearbook, general data, 1992 annual rpt, U5100–1.10

North Carolina higher education enrollment, degrees, libraries, staff, and student characteristics, finances, and housing, by instn, 1992/93 and trends, annual rpt, U8013–1

North Dakota higher education enrollment, by level, instn, county, and selected student characteristics, fall 1992 and trends, annual rpt, S6110–1

Ohio public, academic, and other library finances, holdings, and staff, by library and location, 1992 and trends, annual rpt, S6320–1

Oklahoma statistical abstract, general data, 1992 annual rpt, U8130–2.8

Oregon library finances, staff, holdings, and services, for public, academic, and special libraries by instn, FY92 and trends, annual rpt, S6635–1

Pennsylvania elementary/secondary and higher education enrollment, grads, staff, and finances, by instn type, 1981/82-1996/97, recurring rpt, S6790–5.10

Pennsylvania higher education enrollment, by student characteristics and instn, 1992 and trends, annual rpt, S6790–5.9

Pennsylvania higher education faculty employment, compensation, and tenure status, by sex and type of instn, 1991/92 and trends, annual rpt, S6790–5.5

Pennsylvania higher education faculty employment, compensation, and tenure status, by sex and type of instn, 1992/93 and trends, annual rpt, S6790–5.13

Pennsylvania higher education revenues, expenditures, and endowment funds, by instn type, FY91 and trends, annual rpt, S6790–5.4

Pennsylvania higher education revenues, expenditures, and endowment funds, by instn type, FY92 and trends, annual rpt, S6790–5.16

Pennsylvania higher education students by residence location, by academic level and instn type, 1992 and trends, biennial rpt, S6790–5.8

Pennsylvania higher education tuition/fees, and room and board charges, by instn, 1992/93 and trends, annual rpt, S6790–5.3

Pennsylvania statistical abstract, general data, 1992 recurring rpt, U4130–6.4

Rhode Island statistical almanac, general data, 1993 annual rpt, C7975–1

South Carolina college and university library finances, holdings, circulation, and staff, by instn, FY92, annual rpt, S7210–1

South Carolina high school grads entering higher education, by school district, 1991, annual rpt, S7145–1.3

South Carolina higher education enrollment, degrees, staff, and finances, by instn, 1992 and trends, annual rpt, S7185–2

South Carolina statistical abstract, general data, 1993 annual rpt, S7125–1.6

South Dakota public high school grads, by sex and postgraduation status, 1992, annual rpt, S7315–1.1

South Dakota public higher education finances, staff, enrollment, degrees, and facilities, by instn, FY93 annual rpt, S7375–1

Tennessee higher education enrollment, finances, staff, and programs, by instn, 1992/93 and trends, annual rpt, S7525–1

Tennessee statistical abstract, general data, 1992/93 annual rpt, U8710–2.16

Texas higher education enrollment, faculty, curricula, and finances, by instn, 1991/92 and trends, annual rpt, S7657–1

Utah higher education degrees, enrollment, staff, and finances, by public instn, with selected comparisons to instns in other States, 1993/94 annual rpt, S7895–2

Utah statistical abstract, general data, 1993 triennial rpt, U8960–1.3

Vermont higher education info, including degrees conferred, enrollment, and finances, by instn, 1992 annual rpt, S8035–2

West Virginia higher education enrollment, degrees, faculty and student characteristics, and finances, by instn, 1992/93 and trends, annual rpt, S8533–1

West Virginia public, academic, and special library operations and/or finances, by instn, 1991/92, annual rpt, S8590–1

West Virginia statistical handbook, general data, 1992 annual rpt, R9385–1.4

Wisconsin Blue Book, general data, 1993-94 biennial rpt, S8780–1.2

Wisconsin libraries, operations, and finances, by library type, instn, and location, 1992, annual rpt, S8795–1

see also Adult education
see also Agricultural education
see also Black colleges
see also Business education
see also Campus security
see also Community colleges
see also Curricula
see also Degrees, higher education
see also Educational attainment
see also Educational broadcasting
see also Educational employees pay
see also Educational enrollment
see also Educational exchanges
see also Educational facilities
see also Educational finance
see also Educational materials
see also Educational research
see also Educational technology
see also Educational tests
see also Faculty tenure

Index by Subjects and Names

see also Federal aid to higher education
see also Federal aid to medical education
see also Junior colleges
see also Legal education
see also Medical education
see also National Collegiate Athletic Association
see also Private schools
see also Reserve Officers Training Corps
see also School administration and staff
see also Scientific education
see also Service academies
see also State funding for higher education
see also State funding for medical education
see also Student aid
see also Student housing
see also Student unrest
see also Students
see also Teacher education
see also Teachers
see also Technical education
see also Tuition and fees
see also Veterans education
see also Vocational education and training
see also Work-study programs

Highway Trust Fund

Gasoline tax and other revenues, and grants to States, 1992, R9050–15.6

Receipts by source and disbursements by type, FY60-92, annual rpt, A0865–1.3

Receipts, expenditures, and balance in Hwy Trust Fund, FY57-96, annual rpt, R9050–1.3

State social, economic, and govtl indicators, with rankings, 1993 semiannual rpt, B8500–1.6, B8500–1.11

Highways, streets, and roads

Business executives ratings of ports, highways, and intl air service, with daily number of intl flights, for top 6-8 cities, 1993 article, C2150–1.504

Construction contract awards by type of project, weekly rpt, C5800–2

Cost indexes for construction, equipment, and labor, by type and location, weekly rpt quarterly feature, C5800–2.508, C5800–2.521, C5800–2.534, C5800–2.547

Interstate hwy mileage, top 20 States, 1989, recurring rpt, R9375–6

Latin America statistical abstract, general data by country, 1992 annual rpt, U6250–1.3

Local govt expenditures by function and type of govt unit, and for 52 largest cities, 1993 annual rpt, R9050–1.6

Lodging industry facilities, sales, and occupancy, with top 42-100 properties in 5 market categories, 1993 annual rpt, C7000–5

Mexico roadway kilometers by road type, 1980-92, and toll road dev project summaries including construction costs, 1993 rpt, U8850–9

Mileage of roads by type and State, and public expenditures on roads by State, 1993 annual rpt, A0865–1.3

Revenues, expenditures, and debt on public hwys and toll roads, by item, 1954-91, annual rpt, R9050–1.4

State economic dev condition indicators, including economic performance, business vitality, growth capacity, and tax/fiscal system, by State, 1993 annual rpt, R4225–1.1

Index by Subjects and Names

Hispanic Americans

State social, economic, and govtl indicators, with rankings, 1993 semiannual rpt, B8500–1.11

Statistical profiles of 50 States and DC, general data, 1993 annual almanac, C4712–1

Traffic volume on hwys, monthly rpt, R9375–1

State and local:

Alabama county data book, general data, 1992 annual rpt, S0121–2

Alaska hwy and ferry mileage, 1991-92, annual rpt, S0275–1

Arizona hwy traffic, 1984-91, semiannual rpt, U5850–1.1

Arizona statistical abstract, general data, 1993 recurring rpt, U5850–2.18

California roadway mileage, by type and county, Dec 1991, annual rpt, S0885–1

California statistical abstract, general data, 1992 annual rpt, S0840–2.10

DC statistical profile, general data, 1992 annual rpt, S1535–3.7

Florida county data book, 1992/93 annual rpt, C6360–1

Florida statistical abstract, general data, 1992 annual rpt, U6660–1.13

Georgia county guide, general data, 1993 annual rpt, U6750–1

Georgia statistical abstract, general data, 1992-93 biennial rpt, U6730–1.8

Hawaii data book, general data, 1992 annual rpt, S2090–1.18

Kansas robberies and value of stolen property, by location and property type, 1992, annual rpt, S2925–1.1

Kansas statistical abstract, general data, 1991/92 annual rpt, U7095–2.13

Maryland local govt financial condition, including revenues by source, expenditures by function, and debt obligations, FY92 and trends, annual rpt, S3618–1.1

Maryland statistical abstract, general data, 1993-94 biennial rpt, S3605–1.10

Michigan motor vehicle accidents, deaths and injuries, and mileage, by road type, 1991, annual rpt, S3997–2

Mississippi statistical abstract, general data, 1992 annual rpt, U3255–4.10

Nevada hwy traffic flow, 1980-91, annual rpt, U7920–2

Nevada statistical abstract, general data, 1992 biennial rpt, S5005–1.13

New Jersey interstate hwy mileage, and fatal accidents by roadway, 1992 and trends, annual rpt, S5430–2

New York State statistical yearbook, general data, 1992 annual rpt, U5100–1.13

Ohio hwy mileage, 1990-91, annual rpt, S6290–1

Oklahoma hwy miles, by type and jurisdiction, 1970-92, annual rpt, S6482–1

Oklahoma statistical abstract, general data, 1992 annual rpt, U8130–2.16

Pennsylvania statistical abstract, general data, 1992 recurring rpt, U4130–6.9

Rhode Island statistical almanac, general data, 1993 annual rpt, C7975–1.1

South Carolina statistical abstract, general data, 1993 annual rpt, S7125–1.15

Tennessee statistical abstract, general data, 1992/93 annual rpt, U8710–2.9

Utah hwy mileage and expenditures, aviation and motor fuel consumption, and bus travel, various years 1940-92, annual rpt, R9380–1.10

Utah statistical abstract, general data, 1993 triennial rpt, U8960–1.13

Washington State hwy mileage, by type of hwy, 1992, annual rpt, S8428–1

Wisconsin Blue Book, general data, 1993-94 biennial rpt, S8780–1.2

see also Federal aid to highways

see also State funding for highways and streets

see also Traffic accident fatalities

see also Traffic accidents and safety

see also Traffic engineering

see also Traffic laws and courts

see also Turnpikes

Hill, Catherine

"Converting the Cold War Economy: Investing in Industries, Workers, and Communities", R4700–19

Hines, Edward R.

"State Higher Education Appropriations, 1992/93", A8970–1

Hires

see Labor turnover

Hiring practices

see Personnel management

Hispanic Americans

- Abortion attitudes of teenage boys, by respondent characteristics, 1988 survey, article, A5160–1.505
- Accounting grad supply-demand, including detail by sex, race-ethnicity, and region, 1991/92 and trends, annual rpt, A1885–1
- Advertising devs for Hispanic market, including leading advertisers and media, and market characteristics, 1992 annual features, C4575–1.502
- AIDS cases, by sex and race-ethnicity, through June 1992, article, C4215–1.503
- AIDS deaths in hospitals vs at home, by region and decedent characteristics, 1988 and trends, article, A2623–1.512
- AIDS incidence among Hispanics, with detail by victim ethnic origin and other characteristics, 1988-91, article, A2623–1.506
- Airline travel frequency, destination, and purpose, by traveler characteristics, 1992 survey and trends, annual rpt, A0325–6
- Alcohol consumption among Hispanic women compared to acculturation levels and other demographic characteristics, 1982-84, article, A2623–1.508
- American College Test (ACT) scores, by sex and race-ethnicity, 1993, annual article, C2175–1.534
- American College Test (ACT) scores by student characteristics, with student views on schools and education plans, 1992 and trends, annual rpt, R1960–6
- Arts/humanities organization charitable contribution donor characteristics, 1993 survey article, C2176–1.507
- Asthma incidence among children, by race-ethnicity, with detail by Hispanic ethnic origin, 1993 article, A2623–1.506
- Births and fertility, by selected newborn and maternal characteristics, 1990, article, R8750–1.510
- Broadcasting station seller tax deferment certificates granted by FCC for sales to minority buyers, by ethnic group, 1978-1st half 1993, article, C1850–14.537

Business and career concerns of Hispanics, articles and features, monthly rpt, C4575–1

- Business establishments and gross receipts for minority-owned vs total businesses, with detail by race-ethnicity, 1987, article, C4215–1.507
- Business formation rate by race-ethnicity, 1993 article, C4687–1.510
- Business outlook for Hispanic-owned firms, with data by region, monthly rpt quarterly feature, C4575–1.510
- Cancer deaths among minorities, by body site and ethnic group, 1989, annual rpt, A1175–1
- Catholic school enrollment by ethnic group, 1982/83 and 1991/92-1992/93, annual rpt, A7375–1
- Catholic secondary school operations and finances, including enrollment by race-ethnicity and family income, 1991/92 and trends, biennial rpt, A7375–5
- Catholic vs public school performance, and support for parental school selection funded by govt, views of Catholics by race-ethnicity, July 1992 survey, A7375–8
- Chemist and chemical engineer salaries, employment status, and demographic and professional characteristics, 1993, annual rpt, A1250–4
- Chemistry and chemical engineering grad starting salaries, employment status, demographic characteristics, and advanced study plans, 1991/92, annual rpt, A1250–2
- Child and maternal health indicators and insurance coverage, by race-ethnicity and other demographic characteristics, 1992 annual rpt, R3840–5.1
- Child health and well-being indicators, by race-ethnicity, 1993 annual rpt, R3832–1
- Child poverty by State and for 200 cities and 89 counties, with State and city detail by race-ethnicity, 1989 and trends, R3840–20
- Children's living arrangements, by parents characteristics and child age and race-ethnicity, 1992, article, B6045–1.504
- Children's living arrangements, by parents characteristics and child race-ethnicity, 1991, article, B6045–1.503
- Children's living arrangements, by race-ethnicity, decennially 1960-90, B6045–1.502
- Cocaine user characteristics, including criminal behavior and health condition, with comparison to nonusers, 1991 and trends, article, A2623–1.510
- Community and junior college revenues by source and expenditures by function, and selected student characteristics, FY92, annual rpt, A6705–1
- Condom use and attitudes among sexually active young men, by race-ethnicity, 1988 and 1991 surveys, article, A5160–1.504
- Consumer buying power survey of population, income, and sales by kind of business, by census div, State, MSA, county, and city, 1992, annual rpt, C1200–1.511
- Consumer buying power survey of population, income, and sales by product line, by State, metro area, county, and census div, 1993 annual rpt, C1200–1.514

Hispanic Americans

Consumer purchasing by product type, and ownership of selected electronics, for blacks, Hispanics, and Asians, 1992/93 survey, article, C2710–1.513

Corporate boards of directors with women and minority members, and board membership by sex and race-ethnicity, 1991/92, B4490–2.36

Correctional instn admin, inmates, facilities, costs, parole and probation, and staffing, for local, State, and Federal systems, 1992 annual series, R4300–1

Correctional instns, inmates, staff, and cost of care, by instn, US and Canada, with operating summary by State or Province, 1992, annual directory, A1305–3

Crime victims per 1,000 population, by demographic characteristics, 1991, article, R8750–1.505

Dental problems/treatment-related time lost from work or school, by demographic characteristics, 1989, article, A2623–1.502

Dental school enrollment and grads, by sex and race-ethnicity, 1992/93 annual rpt, A1475–3.1

Dental school faculty, support personnel, and staff characteristics, by instn, 1992/93, annual rpt, A1475–4.5

Dental school student attrition, by reason and student characteristics, 1991/92 and trends, annual rpt, A1475–4.4

Displaced workers by sex, race-ethnicity, industry div, and occupation, with characteristics of new employment, 1987-92, article, S0465–1.506

Distilled spirits consumption, and consumer characteristics and buying habits, 1992 and trends, annual rpt, C4775–1.3

Doctoral degree recipient characteristics, including citizenship status, source of support, field of study, and instn, 1990/91 and trends, annual rpt, R6000–7

Doctoral degrees conferred and recipient characteristics, by field, 1992, annual feature, C2175–1.535

Drugs (prescription) use, expenditures, and financing methods among population age 65/older and 64/under, by patient characteristics, 1987, R4865–8

Earnings by sex and race-ethnicity, 1992 feature, C4215–1.502

Ecologist personal and professional characteristics, including research activity and funding, with data by field, Mar 1992 survey, recurring rpt, A4685–1

Elected Hispanic officials, by office and State, with related population characteristics, 1992 annual directory, A6844–1

Elementary/secondary prospective teacher characteristics and opinions, survey of persons interested in alternative certification routes, 1992, R6350–7

Elementary/secondary teacher views on selected school reform proposals, with data by race-ethnicity, Jan-Feb 1993 survey, B6045–7

Elementary/secondary teaching profession factors limiting minority participation, public opinion by race-ethnicity, 1993 annual Gallup Poll, A8680–1.503

Engineering degrees awarded, by State, instn, and field, with detail for women, minorities, and foreign students, 1991/92, annual rpt, A0685–1

Engineering program enrollment, by instn, field, and State, with detail for women, minorities, and foreign students, fall 1992, annual rpt, A0685–2

Eye bank activity in US and abroad, including donations by type, source, and donor characteristics, and data by individual bank, 1992 and trends, annual rpt, A4743–1

Food service black and Hispanic representation in employment and mgmt, with detail by selected occupation, 1993 articles, C5150–5.511

Food service industry employee characteristics, and minority-owned establishments and sales, 1993 article, A8200–1.508

Food service patronage patterns, by race-ethnicity, June 1992-May 1993, article, A8200–1.510

Foundation board trustees by sex and race-ethnicity, for 25 leading private, community, and corporate foundations, 1989 and trends, A9405–1.1

Foundation board trustees by sex and race-ethnicity, for 25 leading private, community, and corporate foundations, 1991 and trends, A9405–1.2

Foundation finances, and personnel and governing board characteristics, by organization characteristics, 1991/92, article, C2176–1.506

Geoscience enrollment and degrees awarded, by sex, race-ethnicity, and discipline, 1991/92, annual rpt, A1785–3

Health care specialist and health-related company CEO income, public perceptions vs actual amounts, by respondent characteristics, 1991-93, R4865–13

Health condition and preventive health care and safety practices of adults, by respondent characteristics, 1992 and trends, annual survey rpt, C8111–2

Health indicators for children and youths, including AIDS cases and deaths, and cocaine-related hospital emergency room use, by race-ethnicity, 1993 rpt, R3840–21

Health indicators, including hypertension and lung cancer rates, and cancer and heart disease/stroke deaths, by sex and race-ethnicity, 1993 feature, C4215–1.511

Health insurance coverage by population characteristics and location, and underwriting results by type of insurer, 1940s-90, annual rpt, A5173–2.1

Health insurance coverage lack, and population with high out-of-pocket expenses, by State and selected characteristics, 1993, R4865–14

High school dropouts by recency of immigration, for Hispanics vs non-Hispanics, Nov 1989, article, R4800–2.507

Higher education bachelors and masters degrees conferred, by sex and race-ethnicity, 1990, C4215–1.503

Higher education degrees conferred, by level, sex, discipline, and race-ethnicity, 1990/91, recurring feature, C2175–1.523

Higher education employment, by position type and race-ethnicity, 1991/92, C2175–1.507

Higher education enrollment by race-ethnicity, by State, fall 1991, annual rpt, C2175–1.531

Higher education enrollment in historically black colleges, distribution by student race-ethnicity, 1993 article, C4215–1.509

Higher education enrollment of minority and foreign students at approx 3,100 instns, fall 1991, recurring feature, C2175–1.510

Higher education enrollment of minority and foreign students, with comparison to whites, by sex, State, and instn type, fall 1991, recurring feature, C2175–1.506

Higher education freshmen attitudes and characteristics, degree and career plans, and financial aid sources, by sex and instn type, fall 1992, annual survey, U6215–1

Higher education involvement of minorities, including enrollment and degrees awarded, by race-ethnicity, sex, and State, 1970s-91, annual rpt, A1410–10

Higher education minority student enrollment trends, 1993 annual survey, A1410–1.38

Higher education president personal and professional characteristics, 1990 and trends, recurring rpt, A1410–12

Higher education president personal and professional characteristics, 1990, article, C2175–1.533

Higher education student athlete enrollment and graduation rates, by sex, race-ethnicity, and major sport, for Natl Collegiate Athletic Assn Div I instns, 1992/93, annual rpt, A7440–4

Higher education undergrad and grad enrollment by race-ethnicity, fall 1990, article, C4215–1.508

Homeless population characteristics in 29 cities, 1991/92, annual rpt, A9330–9

House of Representatives staff characteristics, salaries, and benefits by position, 1992 and trends, recurring rpt, R4140–1

Human immunodeficiency virus (HIV) testing and posttest counseling rates, by demographic characteristics, 1989, article, A2623–1.501

Hysterectomy prevalence by women's demographic characteristics, 1988 surveys, article, A2623–1.503

Incarcerated mothers and their children, with data on characteristics, child caregivers, visitation, and support program use, 1991/92, A7575–4

Job Corps youth training program funding, enrollment capacity, and participants by selected characteristics, 1981-94, article, R4800–2.515

Journalism/mass communication enrollment and grads by level, by instn, sex, race-ethnicity, and field, 1990/91 and trends, annual article, A3225–1

Juvenile State instn custody prevalence rates by sex, age, and race-ethnicity, for 16 States, 1991, A7575–1.13

Labor force and education data for women and minorities in professional fields, 1980s-91, with historical trends, recurring rpt, A3960–2

Labor force size, entrants, and leavers, by sex and race-ethnicity, 1990-2005, article, R8750–1.507

Index by Subjects and Names — Hispanic Americans

Labor union membership compared to total workers, by sex, race and Hispanic ethnicity, occupation, and industry div, 1991-92, article, S0465–1.505

Law school enrollment by minority status, degrees conferred, staff, and library holdings, by instn, 1992/93 and trends, annual rpt, A0970–1

Law school grad employment and salaries, by type of employer, location, and grad characteristics, 1992 and trends, annual rpt, A6505–1

Librarians (special) salaries, by location, work setting, and personal characteristics, US and Canada, 1992 and trends, biennial survey rpt, A8965–1

Librarians at universities and research instns, by minority group and census div, FY92, annual survey, A3365–2

Library/info science school enrollment, staff and student characteristics, finances, and curricula, by school and degree program, 1991/92, annual rpt, A3235–1

Local govt land use planning commissions composition and activities, and commissioner characteristics, 1987 and trends, recurring rpt, A2615–2

Local officials in municipal and county govt, demographic profiles and job functions, 1993 annual rpt, A5800–1

Low-income families and children, health and welfare indicators, with data by State and city, 1992 annual rpt, R3840–11

Low-income housing supply-demand, costs, physical conditions, and public assistance, with data by race-ethnicity, for 44 metro areas, 1980s-91, R3834–16

Market area population and characteristics, households, income, and retail outlets, for 21 leading areas, 1993 feature, C2710–1.538

Mathematics dept faculty and doctoral degree recipient characteristics, including salaries, 1991/92 and trends, annual survey, A2085–1.1

Measles cases in preschool children, health care providers used and welfare status, by race-ethnicity, 1989-90, article, A2623–1.508

Medical school programs, fees, applicants, admissions, and enrollment, with data by age, sex, minority group, and instn, 1992/93 and trends, annual rpt, A3273–10

Men's sexual behavior, including condom use, and AIDS knowledge and risks, by selected characteristics, 1991 survey, articles, A5160–1.503

Military personnel by race-ethnicity, total and women, FY90, article, R8750–1.504

Natl Assessment of Educational Progress test reading scores of students at 3 ages, by race-ethnicity, 1971-90, article, R4800–2.504

News events followed most closely by public, and opinion on media coverage and selected current issues, by respondent characteristics, recurring rpt, C8915–1

Nursing center (community) staff and client characteristics, and services, 1990 survey, article, A8010–3.506

Nursing college deans, by race-ethnicity, 1992/93, annual rpt, A0615–2

Nursing college faculty, by race-ethnicity, 1992/93, annual rpt, A0615–1

Nursing higher education program faculty and clinic patient characteristics, 1992/93 biennial rpt, A0615–5

Nursing school enrollment and grads, by degree level, sex, race-ethnicity, and instn type and location, 1992/93 and trends, annual rpt, A0615–4

Nursing schools, programs, enrollment, student and staff characteristics, and grads, 1991 and trends, annual rpt, A8010–1

Older population age 65/over educational attainment, by race-ethnicity, 1970, 1980, and 1990, B6045–1.504

Optometry school faculty, enrollment and degrees, policies and programs, and finances, by instn, 1991/92, annual survey, A3370–2

Osteopathy college enrollment, student and faculty characteristics, and finances, 1992/93 and trends, annual rpt, A0620–1

Pharmacy degree program applications, enrollment, and degrees conferred, by student characteristics and instn, 1990/91 and trends, annual rpt, A0630–9

Physics and astronomy bachelor degree recipients postgraduation plans and demographic characteristics, 1991/92 and trends, annual survey, A1960–3

Physics degrees awarded, by level, sex, and minority group, 1991/92, annual rpt, A1960–2.1

Planning profession employment and salaries, by type of employer, demographic and professional characteristics, and location, 1991 and trends, biennial rpt, A2615–1

Political science higher education dept faculty, by sex and race-ethnicity, 1991/92, annual rpt, A2617–1

Poor children age 5/under, with demographic and family characteristics, 1991 and trends, annual rpt, U1260–2

Population and elected officials in top 15-20 States and cities with largest Hispanic populations, 1980, annual rpt, U6250–1.5

Population characteristics, employment, and voting patterns for minority groups by detailed race-ethnicity, with comparisons to whites, 1980s-2040, R8750–2.58

Population of Hispanic origin, by State, 1980 and 1990, annual rpt, U6250–1.14

Poverty indicators for white population, with comparisons to blacks and Hispanics and data by State, 1990-91, R3834–15

Private elementary and secondary school enrollment, staff, and finances, with detail for minorities, by school type and region, 1980s-1992/93, annual rpt, A6835–3

Professional worker salaries, by employee and employer characteristics, with detail for scientists and engineers, 1990s and trends, biennial rpt, A3960–1

Psychology doctoral degree recipient employment and demographic characteristics, and finances, 1990/91, biennial survey rpt, A2620–4

Psychology grad depts, faculty characteristics, enrollment, and student aid, US and Canada, 1990/91 and trends, annual rpt, A2620–3

Public health school applicant, student, and grad characteristics, by instn, 1991/92 and trends, annual rpt, A3372–3

Public health school faculty characteristics, by instn, fall 1991, recurring rpt, A3372–1

Public opinion of Hispanic leaders on current issues of importance to Hispanic community, 1993 annual survey article, C4575–1.511

Public opinion on Clinton Admin economic plan, by respondent characteristics, Feb 1993 survey, C8915–7.1

Public opinion on the media and related issues, by respondent characteristics, series, C8915–11

Public school improvement outlook and funding adequacy, views of parents by race and Hispanic ethnicity, Feb 1993 survey, article, R4800–2.517

Radio (public) audience and market population shares for blacks and Hispanics, for 6-13 stations, 1991, R4250–1.18

Radio ownership, audience characteristics, and advertising revenues and effectiveness, with selected comparisons to other media, 1993 annual rpt, A8789–1

Religious congregation characteristics, including membership, activities, staff, and finances, 1992 survey, recurring rpt, A5435–4

Sales workers by sex and race-ethnicity, 1990, article, C1200–1.512

Scholastic Aptitude Test (SAT) participants and/or scores, by education of parents, income, and race-ethnicity, 1992, C4215–1.501

School district central office administrators and board members by race-ethnicity, by enrollment size, 1992 survey rpt, A0775–5

Science and math elementary/secondary education, including student and teacher characteristics, and requirements, by State, 1991/92, biennial rpt, A4355–3

Sexual activity and condom use among high school students by sex, and adolescent/adult AIDS cases, by race-ethnicity, 1993 article, C4215–1.505

Sexual behavior among heterosexuals, including data on demographic characteristics, number of partners, and condom use, 1990/91 survey, article, A5160–1.506

Sexual behavior, including condom use and incidence of multiple partners, by sex and marital status, 1991 survey, article, A5160–1.505

Small business owners financing sources and experience of discrimination in lending, by race-ethnicity, 1993 survey feature, C4215–1.512

Smoking status of men and women by occupation, and smoker characteristics, 1985 and/or 1990, article, B6045–1.501

Social work higher education programs, faculty and student characteristics, and student aid, with data by instn, 1992 and trends, annual rpt, A4515–1

Socioeconomic indicators for Mexico-US border area, 1980s and trends, U6250–1.20

Socioeconomic status data for blacks compared to other minority groups, 1993 annual compilation, A8510–1.1

Socioeconomic status, including education, politics, income, and employment, with comparisons to whites, 1993 annual compilation, C6775–3

Hispanic Americans

Southern States higher education enrollment, degrees, faculty, and finances, for 15 States, 1990s and trends, biennial fact book, A8945–1

State legislators who are Hispanic, and Hispanic shares of population, by State, 1990 or 1992, semiannual rpt, B8500–1.1

State social, economic, and govtl indicators, with rankings, 1993 semiannual rpt, B8500–1.7

Statistical profiles of 50 States and DC, general data, 1993 annual almanac, C4712–1

Student attitudes on courses in 4 subject areas, for 8th graders by sex and race-ethnicity, 1988, R4800–2.512

Substance abuse treatment programs, funding by source, and client characteristics, for alcohol and drug services, by State, FY91 and trends, annual rpt, A7112–1

Theological school enrollment by degree level, by sex and race-ethnicity, fall 1992 and trends, annual rpt, A3376–1

Theological seminary enrollment in Canada and US, with detail for women and minorities, 1992 and trends, annual rpt, C0105–1

TV (public) programming characteristics compared to 4 other networks, opinions of Hispanic viewers, 1992 survey, R4250–1.24

TV Hispanic household audience ratings, for top 15 prime-time English-language programs, Nov 1992, article, C1850–14.516

TV home shoppers vs average shoppers, TV viewing time and race-ethnicity, 1993 feature, C1850–14.514

TV households and population by race-ethnicity, sex, and age, by market area, 1992/93, annual rpt, B0525–4

TV news coverage of Rodney King police brutality case, with reporter and source characteristics, and detail by network, Mar 1991-Apr 1992, article, R3823–1.505

TV news stories by sex and race-ethnicity of reporter or anchor, with detail by network, 1992, annual article, R3823–1.503

TV Spanish-language program audience ratings, for top 10 programs among Hispanic viewers, Oct/Nov 1992, article, C2710–1.510

Urban public school performance compared to natl goals for year 2000, with data by race-ethnicity and sex, for 47 systems, 1990/91, A4425–4

Voter turnout and registration trends, by race-ethnicity and/or sex, 1960s-92, U4510–1.70

Wealthiest Hispanic individuals or families, top 50 ranked by net worth, with info on background and assets, 1993, annual feature, C4575–1.505

Western States higher education grad student exchange program enrollment, by race-ethnicity, for 13 States, fall 1992, annual rpt, A9385–1

Women candidates in State-level elections, outcome summaries including campaign funds raised, voting by sex, and winner's race-ethnicity, 1992, U4510–4.4

Women in elective office, by minority group, party, and govt level, 1993, annual rpt, U4510–1.66

Women professionals employment, with detail by race-ethnicity and for 3 occupations, 1990 and trends, article, R8750–1.511

Women's employment in govt, with data by race-ethnicity and State, series, U5090–1

Women's housing issues, with data on household composition, tenure, and characteristics, 1992, A8657–5

Women's labor force participation by race-ethnicity, and black and Hispanic earnings by sex compared to white men, 1993 annual rpt, A1570–2

Women's sexual behavior and disease risk, including data on multiple partners and condom use, by selected characteristics, 1988, article, A5160–1.501

Women's use of mammography and Pap smear tests, by demographic characteristics, 1987 survey, article, A2623–1.503

Work force and new workers, black, Hispanic, and Asian shares, 2000 article, C1200–4.509

Workplace drug use, employment in manufacturing, and earnings, by race-ethnicity, 1992 annual rpt, R8335–1.1

Youth age 10-15 health condition and health service use and sources, with data by insurance status, by race-ethnicity, 1988, article, A2623–1.509

Youth donations made to church, by demographic characteristics, 1993 survey, R8780–1.509

Youth employment shares by race and Hispanic ethnicity, among ages 15-17, 1991, R8335–2

Youth religious beliefs and approval of interracial and interfaith marriages, by respondent characteristics, 1993 survey feature, R8780–1.507

State and local:

Alabama county data book, general data, 1992 annual rpt, S0121–2

Alabama statistical abstract, general data, 1992 recurring rpt, U5680–2.13

Alaska corrections system admin, including inmate and probationer/parolee offenses and demographic characteristics, 1991 annual rpt, S0287–1

Alaska population, housing, income, and education data, by demographic characteristics and/or locality, 1990/91 and trends, annual rpt, S0320–4

Alaska public schools, enrollment, staff, and finances, by district, FY92, annual rpt, S0295–2

Arizona arrests and murder victims, by age, sex, and race-ethnicity, 1992, annual rpt, S0505–2

Arizona correctional instn admin, including inmates by criminal background and demographic characteristics, FY92, annual rpt, S0464–2

Arizona elementary and secondary school enrollment, by grade and race-ethnicity, 1991/92, annual rpt, S0470–1

Arizona household income and poverty rates, by race-ethnicity, 1989, article, U0280–1.502

Index by Subjects and Names

Arizona statistical abstract, general data, 1993 recurring rpt, U5850–2.2, U5850–2.3, U5850–2.4, U5850–2.6, U5850–2.12, U5850–2.16

Arkansas Census of Population and Housing detailed findings, 1990, U5935–7

Arkansas Medicaid recipients, by race-ethnicity, FY91, annual rpt, S0700–2.3

Arkansas public school enrollment and grads, by race-ethnicity and sex, 1991/92, annual rpt, S0660–1.1

California Census of Population and Housing detailed findings, 1990, S0840–9

California correctional instn inmates, by offense, demographic characteristics, and instn, Dec 1992, semiannual rpt, S0820–2

California correctional instn inmates, with criminal background and demographic characteristics, 1991 and trends, annual rpt, S0820–1

California crimes and arrests, clearances, and arrest dispositions, with data by offense and offender characteristics, 1987-92, annual rpt, S0910–1.1

California criminal justice system detailed data, by offense, county, age, race-ethnicity, and sex, 1991 and trends, annual rpt, S0910–2.2

California death rates and estimated alcohol-related mortality, by cause and demographic characteristics, 1980-89, article, A2623–1.508

California health behavior risk factor surveillance survey results, by respondent characteristics, 1991 and trends, annual rpt, S0865–2

California judicial system employment by position, sex, and race-ethnicity, with minority utilization rates and parity targets, Jan 1993, annual rpt, S0905–1.1

California labor force planning rpt, including population characteristics, and employment by industry, 1992 annual rpt, S0830–2

California population by age, sex, race-ethnicity, and county, decennially 1990-2040, recurring rpt, S0840–4

California postsecondary education enrollment and degrees, by sex, race-ethnicity, and instn, 1990/91, annual series, S0827–2

California public school enrollment, grads, and staff, by race-ethnicity, 1992/93 and trends, annual rpt, S0825–9

California public school Hispanic student enrollment and number with limited English proficiency, 1987-92, annual rpt, S0825–10

California registered apprentices, by sex and race-ethnicity, 1987-91, annual rpt, S0840–2.3

California socioeconomic and govtl data for municipalities, counties, and school districts, 1993 annual rpt, C4712–3

California statistical abstract, general data, 1992 annual rpt, S0840–2.2, S0840–2.5

California vital statistics, including population, births, and deaths by cause, by demographic characteristics and county, 1990 and trends, annual rpt, S0865–1

Colorado health behavior risk factor surveillance survey results, by respondent characteristics, 1990, recurring rpt, S1010–3

Index by Subjects and Names

Hispanic Americans

Colorado job service applicant characteristics, FY93 annual planning rpt, S1040–3.2

Colorado public school enrollment, finances, and student and staff characteristics, by locality, 1992 annual rpt series, S1000–2

Colorado vital statistics, including population, births, deaths by cause, abortion, marriage and divorce, and adoption, by demographic characteristics and location, 1990 and trends, annual rpt, S1010–1

Connecticut crimes and arrests, including murder victims and offenders by race-ethnicity, 1992, annual rpt, S1256–1.1

Connecticut public school data, including enrollment, staff, programs, finances, and student characteristics, 1991/92, biennial rpt, S1185–3

Connecticut vital statistics, including births, deaths by cause, marriages, and divorces, by demographic characteristics and location, 1989, annual rpt, S1200–1

DC court committee members by race-ethnicity and sex, by committee, 1992, annual rpt, S1515–1

DC public school enrollment, by race-ethnicity, 1987/88-1991/92, annual rpt, S1605–2

DC statistical profile, general data, 1992 annual rpt, S1535–3.1

Delaware births to parents of Hispanic origin, by selected characteristics, 1990, annual rpt, S1385–2

Delaware crimes and arrests, by offense, county, and victim-offender characteristics, 1991 and trends, annual rpt, S1375–5

Delaware postsecondary instn enrollment and degrees conferred, by race-ethnicity, 1992, annual rpt, S1425–1

Delaware school enrollment and dropouts, by race-ethnicity, 1991/92, annual rpt, S1430–1

Florida county data book, 1992/93 annual rpt, C6360–1

Florida higher education enrollment, degree programs, staff, and finances, by State-supported instn, with student and staff characteristics, 1991/92 annual rpt, S1725–1

Florida municipal and county statistical profiles, general data, 1991 annual rpt, C4712–6

Florida newspaper circulation of daily, weekly, and special interest newspapers, 1991, annual rpt, U6660–1.14

Florida population, by race-ethnicity, age, and county, 1990 and 1992, annual rpt, S1746–1.1

Florida statistical abstract, general data, 1992 annual rpt, U6660–1.1, U6660–1.2, U6660–1.4, U6660–1.6, U6660–1.9, U6660–1.22

Florida 8th-9th grade children of immigrants characteristics, attitudes, and discrimination experience, 1992, survey article, R4800–2.522

Georgia county guide, general data, 1993 annual rpt, U6750–1

Georgia statistical abstract, general data, 1992-93 biennial rpt, U6730–1.1, U6730–1.10

Hawaii data book, general data, 1992 annual rpt, S2090–1.1, S2090–1.12, S2090–1.15

Hawaii health dept activities and services, including vital statistics and disease control, by location, 1990, annual rpt, S2065–1

Idaho crimes and arrests, by offense, with data by location and offender characteristics, 1992 and trends, annual rpt, S2275–2

Idaho economic profile, general data, 1992 recurring rpt, S2218–2.2

Idaho public school personnel characteristics and salaries by position, and teachers and enrollment by school district, 1992/93, annual rpt, S2225–3

Idaho vital statistics, including births, deaths by cause, abortions, marriages, and divorces, by demographic characteristics and county, 1991 and trends, annual rpt, S2250–2

Illinois corrections dept admin, including inmates and characteristics, finances, and staff, FY91-93 and trends, annual rpt, S2425–1

Illinois crimes and arrests, by offense and offender characteristics, 1990-91, annual rpt, S2536–1

Illinois higher education enrollment and degrees, by level, instn, field of instruction, and student characteristics, 1992 and trends, annual rpt, S2475–1.1

Illinois mental health facility patient population and characteristics, by facility, location, and treatment category, FY93, annual rpt, S2505–1

Illinois public school enrollment and dropouts, by race-ethnicity, 1990/91, annual rpt, S2440–1.1

Indiana public assistance program participation, expenditures, and services, by county, FY92 and trends, annual rpt, S2623–1

Iowa correctional instn admissions, releases, and inmate characteristics, by instn, monthly rpt, S2770–1

Iowa population share in poverty, by race-ethnicity, 1990, annual rpt, S2784–3

Iowa postsecondary enrollment, degrees, staff, and finances, by instn, 1990/91, annual rpt, S2755–1

Kansas correctional instn inmates, by offense, demographic characteristics, and instn, FY92 and trends, annual rpt, S2940–1

Kansas crimes and arrests, with victim, offender, and law enforcement employee characteristics, 1992, annual rpt, S2925–1

Kansas statistical abstract, general data, 1991/92 annual rpt, U7095–2.2

Louisiana Census of Population and Housing summary findings, by local area, 1990 and trends, U8010–4

Louisiana school district profiles, including enrollment, grads, and staff, by race-ethnicity, 1991/92, annual rpt, S3280–1.2

Maine Census of Population and Housing summary findings, by local area, 1990, S3465–7, S3465–8

Maryland elementary and secondary education data, by county, 1991/92, annual rpt, S3610–2.3

Maryland elementary and secondary education data, by county, 1992 and trends, annual rpt, S3610–2.4

Maryland elementary and secondary education data, by county, 1992/93, annual rpt, S3610–2.8

Maryland public school enrollment and achievement test scores, by race-ethnicity and/or county, 1992, annual rpt, S3610–1

Maryland statistical abstract, general data, 1993-94 biennial rpt, S3605–1.1

Massachusetts correctional instn inmate socioeconomic characteristics and criminal background, by instn, Jan 1992 and trends, annual rpt, S3805–1

Massachusetts elementary/secondary school enrollment, by sex and race-ethnicity, Oct 1980 and 1991, annual rpt, S3810–3

Massachusetts health behavior risk factor surveillance survey results, by respondent characteristics, 1986-90, recurring rpt, S3850–3

Massachusetts municipal and county profiles, general data, 1992 annual rpt, C4712–2

Massachusetts vital statistics, including births, deaths by cause, marriages, divorces, and population, by locality and demographic characteristics, 1990 and trends, annual rpt, S3850–1

Michigan labor force planning rpt, including employment by industry, and characteristics of Job Training Partnership Act eligible population, 1993 annual rpt, S3980–1

Michigan public assistance recipients, by race-ethnicity and county, monthly rpt quarterly tables, S4010–1

Michigan State corrections dept employment of women, minorities, and handicapped, 1991 and trends, annual rpt, S3960–1

Michigan vital statistics, including births, deaths, marriages, divorces/annulments, and communicable diseases, by location and demographic characteristics, 1990 and trends, annual rpt, S4000–3

Minnesota enrollment distribution by race-ethnicity, and minority student shares by district and county, 1991/92 and trends, annual rpt, S4165–1

Minnesota postsecondary education finances, and enrollment by student characteristics, by type of school system, 1970s-93, biennial rpt, S4195–2.2

Mississippi labor force planning rpt, including population, employment, and characteristics of unemployed and disadvantaged, 1993 annual rpt, S4345–1

Mississippi statistical abstract, general data, 1992 annual rpt, U3255–4.9

Missouri births to Hispanic mothers, 1992, annual rpt, S4518–1

Missouri correctional instn admissions, releases, and inmate characteristics, FY93, annual rpt, S4501–1

Missouri higher education enrollment and degrees granted, by sex, race-ethnicity, and instn, 1992 and trends, annual rpt, S4520–3

Montana employment and unemployment, by race-ethnicity and county, 1990, annual planning rpt, S4710–3

Montana public school enrollment by grade, and grads, by school, county, race-ethnicity, and sex, 1992 and trends, annual rpt, S4740–1

Hispanic Americans

Nebraska correctional instn admin, with inmates by criminal background and demographic characteristics, by instn, FY92 and trends, annual rpt, S4850–1

Nebraska elementary and secondary school enrollment, by race-ethnicity, school district, and county, 1992/93, annual rpt, S4865–2.5

Nebraska vital statistics, including births, deaths, marriages, divorces, and population, by demographic characteristics and location, 1991 and trends, annual rpt, S4885–1

Nevada public school enrollment and teachers, by race-ethnicity and school district, 1990/91, annual rpt, S5035–2

Nevada statistical abstract, general data, 1992 biennial rpt, S5005–1.1, S5005–1.7

New Jersey arrests and racial bias crimes, by offender or victim characteristics, 1992, annual rpt, S5430–1

New Jersey Census of Population and Housing detailed findings, by county, 1990, S5425–19

New Jersey correctional instn inmates, by offense, sentence length, demographic characteristics, and instn, Dec 1991 annual rpt, S5370–1

New Jersey insured unemployed characteristics, monthly rpt, S5425–1

New Jersey municipal and county data book, general data, 1992 annual rpt, C4712–4

New Jersey public schools, enrollment, and student and staff characteristics, and nonpublic schools and enrollment, by county, 1991/92, annual rpt, S5385–1

New Jersey unemployment rates for youths and Hispanics, and by race and sex, 1991-92, annual article, S5425–1.503

New Jersey vital statistics, including births, deaths, population, communicable diseases, and marriages and divorces, by demographic characteristics and location, 1990 and trends, annual rpt, S5405–1

New Mexico elementary/secondary school enrollment by race-ethnicity, 1991/92, annual rpt, S5575–4

New Mexico labor force planning rpt, including population characteristics, and employment by industry and occupation, 1993 annual rpt, S5624–1

New Mexico population in poverty, by race-ethnicity and county, 1990, S5620–2.501

New Mexico public welfare recipient characteristics, by program, monthly rpt quarterly table, S5620–2

New Mexico vital statistics, including population, births, deaths, and disease, by location and demographic characteristics, 1991 and trends, annual rpt, S5605–1

New York State adoptions, by sex, age, and race-ethnicity, 1991 and trends, annual rpt, S5800–2.3

New York State correctional instn inmates released, by criminal background, sentence, and demographic characteristics, 1991 and trends, recurring rpt series, S5725–1

New York State crimes and arrests by offense and demographic characteristics, and court activity and corrections, 1991 and trends, annual rpt, S5760–3

New York State health behavior risk factor surveillance survey results, by respondent characteristics, 1990, recurring rpt, S5765–3

New York State local jail/penitentiary inmates by offense, sentence, and demographic characteristics, by county or facility, 1991, annual rpt, S5724–2

New York State municipal and county statistical profiles, general data, 1993 annual rpt, C4712–7

New York State statistical yearbook, general data, 1992 annual rpt, U5100–1.1, U5100–1.3, U5100–1.4, U5100–1.8, U5100–1.10, U5100–1.11

New York State total and low-weight births, fetal deaths, and abortions, by race-Hispanic ethnicity and location, 1990, annual rpt, S5765–1

North Carolina arrests by detailed offense, offender characteristics, and county, 1991-92, annual rpt, S5955–1.2

North Carolina higher education degrees conferred by level, field of study, sex, race-ethnicity, and instn, 1991/92, annual rpt, U8013–1.2

North Carolina public school enrollment, by race-ethnicity, sex, and school district, 1992/93 and trends, annual rpt, S5915–1.1

North Dakota elementary and secondary school enrollment, by race-ethnicity, Sept 1992, annual directory, S6180–2

North Dakota elementary and secondary school staff characteristics and salaries, by position, region, and enrollment size, 1992/93 annual rpt, S6180–3

North Dakota health behavior risk factor surveillance survey results, by respondent characteristics, 1991 and trends, annual rpt, S6105–3

North Dakota higher education enrollment, by level, instn, county, and selected student characteristics, fall 1992 and trends, annual rpt, S6110–1

Oklahoma correctional instn admin, including inmate characteristics, incarceration costs, and data by instn, FY91, annual rpt, S6420–1

Oklahoma crimes and arrests, by offense, with data by local agency and victim and offender characteristics, 1990-92, annual rpt, S6465–1

Oklahoma public school enrollment shares by race-ethnicity, 1989 and 1992, annual rpt, S6423–2

Oklahoma statistical abstract, general data, 1992 annual rpt, U8130–2.2, U8130–2.3, U8130–2.6

Oregon crimes and arrests, by offense, with detail on bias crimes and data by victim and offender characteristics, 1992 and trends, annual rpt, S6603–3.1

Oregon elementary and secondary public school enrollment by race-ethnicity and teachers, by instn, Oct 1992, annual rpt, S6590–1.1

Oregon public high school completers, by instn, county, sex, and race-ethnicity, 1992, annual rpt, S6590–1.10

Oregon public school enrollment, by county, grade, and race-ethnicity, Oct 1992, annual rpt, S6590–1.9

Oregon vital statistics, including births, deaths by cause, communicable diseases,

Index by Subjects and Names

marriages, and divorces, by age, sex, race-ethnicity, and county, 1991 and trends, annual rpt, S6615–5

Pennsylvania Census of Population and Housing detailed findings, with selected data by county and municipality, 1990, U4130–13

Pennsylvania crimes and arrests, by offense, with data by location and offender characteristics, 1992 and trends, annual rpt, S6860–1

Pennsylvania educational statistics by level and/or type of education, series, S6790–5

Pennsylvania employment and commuting data from Census of Population and Housing, by county and municipality, 1990, C1595–16

Pennsylvania labor force and population characteristics, FY92 annual planning rpt, S6845–3.1

Pennsylvania statistical abstract, general data, 1992 recurring rpt, U4130–6.1, U4130–6.3

Rhode Island population, by location and race-ethnicity, 1980 and 1990, annual planning rpt, S6980–3

Rhode Island public school enrollment by type of instn, grade, sex, race-ethnicity, and district, 1991/92 or fall 1992, annual rpt, S6970–1.1

South Carolina higher education enrollment and faculty, by race-ethnicity and instn, 1993 annual rpt, S7185–2

South Carolina population, by age, race-ethnicity, sex, and locality, 1990 and trends, annual planning rpt, S7155–3.1

South Carolina statistical abstract, general data, 1993 annual rpt, S7125–1.12, S7125–1.13

South Dakota elementary/secondary school enrollment and grads, by race-ethnicity, 1991/92, annual rpt, S7315–1.1

South Dakota public higher education enrollment and faculty, by race-ethnicity and instn, FY93 annual rpt, S7375–1

South Dakota social services for elderly, with recipients by race-ethnicity, FY92, annual rpt, S7385–1.1

Tennessee higher education grads and degrees conferred, by race-ethnicity, 1991/92, annual rpt, S7525–1.2

Tennessee statistical abstract, general data, 1992/93 annual rpt, U8710–2.1

Tennessee vital statistics, including births, deaths by cause, marriages, divorces, and population, by demographic characteristics and location, 1991 and trends, annual rpt, S7520–2

Texas correctional instn inmates by criminal background and demographic characteristics, FY92, annual rpt, S7660–1

Texas criminal offenders and victims by race-ethnicity and selected offense, 1992, annual rpt, S7735–2

Texas elementary and secondary education enrollment by race-ethnicity, by school, district, and county, 1991/92, annual rpt, S7670–1.1

Texas elementary/secondary education personnel, by sex and race-ethnicity, by district and county, 1991/92, annual rpt, S7670–1.3

Index by Subjects and Names

Texas health behavior risk factor surveillance survey results, by respondent characteristics, 1991 and trends, annual rpt, S7685–2

Texas higher education enrollment and faculty, by race-ethnicity, sex, and instn, 1991/92 and trends, annual rpt, S7657–1.1

Texas labor force planning rpt, including labor force, employment by industry, income, and population, 1993 annual rpt, S7675–2

Texas local health dept service area population by race-ethnicity, for 22 local areas, 1990, U8850–8.6

Texas Medicaid expenditures by category, and recipient characteristics and medical services received, 1975 and 1980-91, U8850–8.5

Texas nursing employment, demand outlook, earnings, and education, by selected characteristics, various years 1971-91, U8850–8.2

Texas population, by age, sex, race-ethnicity, and county, July 1991, annual rpt, S7645–2

Texas population, by county and race-ethnicity, 1990-2030, recurring rpt, S7645–3

Texas vital statistics, including births, deaths by cause, abortions, marriages, and divorces, by location and demographic characteristics, 1991 and trends, annual rpt, S7685–1

Utah corrections inmates, parolees, and probationers, by criminal background and demographic characteristics, FY92 and trends, annual rpt, S7810–1

Utah employment by detailed occupation, and educational attainment by age group, by sex and race-ethnicity, with detail for 7 urban areas, 1990 census rpt, S7832–3.4

Utah govt statistical review, fiscal and socioeconomic data, 1993 annual rpt, R9380–1.1

Utah homeless shelter population characteristics, individual shelter capacity, and related housing data, 1991-92, annual rpt, S7808–2

Utah labor force and percent without high school diploma, by sex, age group, and/or race-ethnicity, 1990, article, U8960–2.509

Utah labor force characteristics, employment and unemployment, hours, and earnings, with data by industry and locale, 1992 and trends, annual rpt, S7820–10

Utah personal income and household data, by location and race-ethnicity, 1990 census rpt, S7832–3.3

Utah population distribution and selected characteristics, by race-ethnicity, 1990, S7820–3.504

Utah public school enrollment, dropouts, and grads, by race-ethnicity, 1991/92, annual rpt, S7815–1.2

Utah statistical abstract, general data, 1993 triennial rpt, U8960–1.1

Utah vital statistics, including births, deaths by cause, and population, by county and demographic characteristics, 1990 and trends, annual rpt, S7835–1

Vermont elementary and secondary school enrollment by grade, sex, race-ethnicity, school, and county, 1992/93 and trends, annual rpt, S8020–1

Virginia public school dropouts by race-ethnicity and sex, by county and municipality, 1991/92, annual rpt, S8190–3

Washington State correctional instn inmate population, admissions, and releases, by demographic characteristics, quarterly rpt, S8337–1

Washington State crimes and arrests, by offense, with data by location and offender characteristics, 1992 and trends, annual rpt, S8440–1

Washington State population and demographic characteristics, and housing units, by county and/or city, 1992 and trends, annual rpt, S8345–4

Washington State public assistance clients and service costs, by client characteristics, program, and county, FY90, annual rpt, S8420–2

Washington State vital statistics, including births, deaths by cause, and population, by demographic characteristics and location, 1991 and trends, annual rpt, S8363–1

West Virginia higher education enrollment, degrees, faculty and student characteristics, and finances, by instn, 1992/93 and trends, annual rpt, S8533–1

West Virginia population, by race-ethnicity, 1990, annual rpt, S8560–1

Wisconsin Blue Book, general data, 1993-94 biennial rpt, S8780–1.2

Wisconsin correctional instn inmates, by criminal background and selected characteristics, series, S8692–1

Wisconsin elementary and secondary school enrollment, staff, costs, and State aid, by school district, 1992/93 and trends, annual rpt, S8795–2

Wisconsin vital statistics, including population, births, deaths by cause, and marriages and dissolutions, by county and demographic characteristics, 1991 and trends, annual rpt, S8715–4

Wyoming correctional instn admin, finances, inmate characteristics, and staff, and probation and parole activities, FY92 annual rpt, S8883–1

Wyoming public school enrollment, by sex, race-ethnicity, school, and district, 1991/92 and trends, annual rpt, S8890–1.2

Historic sites

Operations and finances for museums and related instns, by type, budget size, governing authority, and region, 1989/90 survey, A0750–1

State and local:

Hawaii data book, general data, 1992 annual rpt, S2090–1.7

New York State statistical yearbook, general data, 1992 annual rpt, U5100–1.15

Pennsylvania statistical abstract, general data, 1992 recurring rpt, U4130–6.8

Wisconsin Blue Book, general data, 1993-94 biennial rpt, S8780–1.2

see also Monuments and memorials

see also National parks

HIV (human immunodeficiency virus)

see Acquired immune deficiency syndrome

Hockey

High school sports all-time records for boys and girls events, with school and student participation for 1991/92, annual rpt, A7830–2

Home-based offices and workers

Participation in 53 sports, by demographic characteristics, State, and census div, 1992, annual rpt series, A8485–3

Hodgkinson, Virginia A.

"From Belief to Commitment: The Community Service Activities and Finances of Religious Congregations in the U.S., 1993 Edition", A5435–4

"Giving and Volunteering, 1992: Volunteering and Giving Among American Teenagers 12 to 17 Years of Age", A5435–5

Hogs

see Livestock and livestock industry

Hojjati, Behjat

"Fertilizer Use on Smallholder Farms in Eastern Province, Zambia", R5620–1.38

Holding companies

Mortgage banking industry aggregate financial and operating data, by lending characteristics and type of ownership, 1989 and trends, annual rpt, A6450–3

Operating and financial composite ratios for corporations, with establishments and receipts, for approx 200 industries, by asset size, FY90, annual rpt, C7800–1

Real estate holding companies financial ratios and performance, FY88-92, annual rpt, A6400–3

Telephone holding company finances, operations, and subsidiaries, by company, Dec 1991, annual rpt, A9360–1

State and local:

Connecticut bank holding companies assets, by instn, Dec 1991, annual rpt, S1160–1

Maine banks and other financial instns, financial condition by instn, June 1992, annual rpt, S3473–2

New Jersey bank assets and deposits, for individual subsidiaries of holding companies, Dec 1992, annual rpt, S5355–1

Oklahoma banks and bank holding companies by asset size, and asset concentration by location and among top instns, 1984-90, article, U8130–1.502

Oklahoma statistical abstract, general data, 1992 annual rpt, U8130–2.20

Texas insurance holding company regulatory activities, FY92, annual rpt, S7700–1

Holidays

see Vacations and holidays

Holland

see Netherlands

Holland, Marjorie M.

"Profiles of Ecologists: Results of a Survey of the Membership of the Ecological Society of America", A4685–1

Hollingsworth, J. Selwyn

"Population Changes in Alabama's Black Belt: 1880-1990", U0340–1.6

Home-based offices and workers

Computer product shipment value for small businesses, home offices, and general consumers, 1992-96, article, C2710–1.551

Population working at home, by employment type, 1988-95, article, C4687–1.502

Regional distribution of home-based businesses and home workers linked to offices by telecommunication, 1993 article, C4725–3.504

Tax deductions for home offices, number and value of claims, 1992, article, C5800–7.512

Home-based offices and workers

see also Self-employment

Home births

State and local:

Alaska births, by place of birth and type of attendant, 1990, annual rpt, S0315–1

Connecticut vital statistics, including births, deaths by cause, marriages, and divorces, by demographic characteristics and location, 1989, annual rpt, S1200–1

Delaware births, by type of place and attendant, and method of delivery, 1990, annual rpt, S1385–2

Idaho vital statistics, including births, deaths by cause, abortions, marriages, and divorces, by demographic characteristics and county, 1991 and trends, annual rpt, S2250–2

Maine vital statistics, including births, deaths by cause, abortions, and marriages and divorces, by demographic characteristics and location, 1991 and trends, annual rpt, S3460–2

Mississippi vital statistics, including births, deaths by cause, marriages, and divorces, by demographic characteristics and location, 1992 and trends, annual rpt, S4350–1

Missouri births by location and selected mother and infant characteristics, 1992, annual rpt, S4518–1

Nevada vital statistics, including births, abortions, and deaths by cause, by county and demographic characteristics, 1989 and trends, annual rpt, S5075–1

New Hampshire vital statistics, including population, births, deaths by cause, marriages, and divorces, by location and demographic characteristics, 1991 and trends, annual rpt, S5215–1

Ohio vital statistics, including births, deaths by cause, marriages, divorces, and population, by demographic characteristics and location, 1991 and trends, annual rpt, S6285–1

Rhode Island vital statistics, including population, births, deaths, marriages, and divorces, by demographic characteristics and locality, 1989 and trends, annual rpt, S6995–1

Texas births by location, 1991 and trends, annual rpt, S7685–1

Vermont vital statistics, including population, births, deaths by cause, abortions, marriages, and divorces, by location and demographic characteristics, 1991 and trends, annual rpt, S8054–1

Washington State births at home and in birthing centers, by county and city, 1991, annual rpt, S8363–1

West Virginia births by location, 1991, annual rpt, S8560–1

Home economics

State and local:

Pennsylvania vocational education enrollment, student characteristics, and faculty, by program and/or school, 1991/92 and trends, annual rpt, S6790–5.7

Pennsylvania vocational education 1989/90 grad employment status, by program, 1991 survey, annual rpt, S6790–5.6

Home equity loans

see Consumer credit

see Mortgages

Home health services

Agencies providing home health care by owner type, with top 10 services provided and patient characteristics, 1993 article, A1865–1.516

Disabled persons use of home care services, with costs, payment sources, and types of care, by selected characteristics, 1992, R4865–15

Expenditures for home health services, home health agencies by type, and hospital-based home care visits, 1993 article, A1865–1.508

Financial ratios and performance, for over 350 SIC 4-digit industries, FY88-92, annual rpt, A6400–3

HMO benefits coverage, premiums, and rating methods used, by plan characteristics, 1991 and trends, annual rpt, A5150–2.1

Hospital home health care business and services, by instn type and size, 1991, annual survey, B5165–3

Market value for home health care products, 1987, 1991, and 1996, A1865–1.502

Medicaid home health care payments per recipient, for 16 highest and 17 lowest States, FY91, article, B8500–2.511

Medicare patient use of home health care agencies, by type of service and urban-rural residence, 1987, article, A2623–1.505

State and local:

Arkansas human services dept finances and operations, including Medicaid payments by type of service, FY91 and trends, annual rpt, S0700–2.3

Florida health care atlas, including manpower by occupation and health care facilities by type, by district and county, 1992 annual rpt, S1746–1.2

Kentucky Medicaid recipients and payments, by program, county, and type of medical service, monthly rpt, S3140 5

Maryland medical assistance payments and recipients, by program, type of service, location, demographic characteristics, and facility, FY92 and trends, annual rpt, S3635–3

Missouri public welfare and medical assistance recipients, expenditures, and case processing, by program and county, FY92 and trends, annual rpt, S4575–2

Montana health care facility capacity, utilization, and finances, by instn, 1991, annual rpt, S4690–2

Montana welfare and medical assistance program cases and payments, by county and type of service, monthly rpt, S4755–1

Nebraska Medicaid recipients and payments, by type of service and county, FY92, annual rpt, S4957–1.2

New York State medical assistance expenditures, by State area and type of care, 1991 and trends, annual rpt, S5800–2.2

South Dakota medical assistance recipients and payments, by type of service, program, and county, FY92, annual rpt, S7385–1

Texas home health care facilities and expenditures, 1977, 1982, and 1987, U8850–8.3

see also Respite care

Home improvement stores

Canada home improvement sales and outlets, for 4-5 leading retail chains and buying groups, 1992, articles, C5150–6.508

Electrical contractor nonelectric products purchased at home centers, 1993 survey article, C4725–5.503

Expansion devs, and equipment and construction costs, by type of retail chain, 1993 annual articles, C5150–4.507

Finances and operations for retail hardware stores, home centers, and lumber/building material outlets, 1991 and trends, annual rpt series, A8275–1

Financial and marketing devs for home improvement stores, biweekly rpt, C5150–6

Financial performance and growth rankings for approx 1,000 top corporations, with comparisons by industry group, 1993 annual rpt, C3950–1.505

Sales and operations for top distributors, cooperatives, and marketing organizations, 1991-92, annual feature, C5150–6.502

Sales and operations for top home improvement retailers, 1992 and trends, annual feature, C5150–6.503

Sales and related data by product category and for top 10 chains, 1992, article, C4725–5.507

Sales and stores for 5 leading home improvement store chains, 1993 article, C1850–4.505

Shopping center financial and operating data, with detail by type of tenant, US and Canada, 1991, triennial rpt, R9285–1

World sales, stores, and other operating data, for leading home improvement chains by country, 1991-92, annual feature, C5150–6.503

Home security devices

see Security devices

see Smoke and fire detectors

Home video and audio equipment

Canada photographic and video equipment and supplies ownership, purchasing patterns, and use, by household characteristics, 1992 survey, recurring rpt, A8695–4

Consumer buying power survey of population, income, and sales by product line, by State, metro area, county, and census div, 1993 annual rpt, C1200–1.514

Drugstore sales shares for blank video vs audio cassette tapes, year ended Feb 1992-93, article, C5150–2.513

Factory sales and/or shipments of home video and audio equipment, by product type, 1980s-92, annual rpt, A4725–1.1

Financial ratios and performance, for over 350 SIC 4-digit industries, FY88-92, annual rpt, A6400–3

Foreign trade in electronics, by product category, detailed type, and country, monthly rpt, A4725–3

Life expectancy, shipments, and manufacturers market shares, for appliances by type, 1993 annual article, C2000–1.510

Market devs in electronics industry, including employment, factory sales, prices, and foreign trade trends, monthly rpt, A4725–2

Index by Subjects and Names — Homicide

Sales (distributor units) of consumer electronics products by type, 1991-93, annual article, C2000–1.503

Sales and consumer expenditures, for food store products by type, 1991-92, annual feature, C4655–1.510

Sales, trade, and industry devs for consumer electronics, by product type, 1970s-92, annual rpt, A4725–4

Shipments of household appliances, by product type, with articles and special features on industry trends and devs, monthly rpt, C2000–1

Shopping center financial and operating data, with detail by type of tenant, US and Canada, 1991, triennial rpt, R9285–1

Supermarket sales of nonfood products, by detailed product type, 1992, annual feature, C5225–1.508

UK audio equipment market value, 1982-92, article, C2000–1.510

State and local:

Texas trade, transportation, and public utilities employment, by SIC 2- and 3-digit industry and detailed occupation, 2nd qtr 1991, triennial survey rpt, S7675–1.31

see also Electronic games

see also Radio

see also Television

see also Video recordings and equipment

Homeless population

Characteristics of homeless population, demand for shelter, and local spending by source of funds, for 29 cities, 1991/92, annual rpt, A9330–9

Latin America internally displaced persons, by country, 1984-89, annual rpt, U6250–1.14

Urban public school systems programs for homeless children, for 47 systems, 1990/91, A4425–4

State and local:

Arkansas population in emergency shelters and apparently living on the street, 1990, census rpt, U5935–7

California population in emergency shelters and apparently living on the street, 1990, census rpt, S0840–9

Colorado income tax return checkoff contributions, for selected causes, FY92 and trends, annual rpt, S1075–1.3

DC statistical profile, general data, 1992 annual rpt, S1535–3.5

Hawaii data book, general data, 1992 annual rpt, S2090–1.21

Maryland homeless children, by region and county, 1991/92, annual rpt, S3610–1

Maryland public school funding for homeless assistance programs, by county, 1991/92, annual rpt, S3610–2.9

Maryland welfare program statistics, and welfare fraud investigations, by county, monthly rpt, S3645–2

New Jersey population in emergency shelters and apparently living on the street, by county, 1990, census rpt, S5425–19

New Mexico assistance program for the homeless, expenditures by locality, monthly rpt quarterly tables, S5620–2

Oregon emergency assistance for homeless persons, cases and expenditures by locale, monthly rpt, S6615–8

Pennsylvania population in emergency shelters and apparently living on the street, 1990, census rpt, U4130–13

Utah homeless shelter population characteristics, individual shelter capacity, and related housing data, 1991-92, annual rpt, S7808–2

see also Emergency shelters

Homeless shelters

see Emergency shelters

Homemaker services

Disabled persons use of home care services, with costs, payment sources, and types of care, by selected characteristics, 1992, R4865–15

State and local:

DC statistical profile, general data, 1992 annual rpt, S1535–3.5

Michigan public assistance program cases, recipients, and payments, detailed data by county, monthly rpt, S4010–1

South Carolina public welfare recipients, payments, and case processing, by county and program, monthly rpt, S7252–1

South Dakota welfare and social services recipients and payments, by program, MSA, and county, FY92, annual rpt, S7385–1

Washington State public assistance clients and service costs, by client characteristics, program, and county, FY90, annual rpt, S8420–2

West Virginia welfare and social service program caseloads and expenditures, by county, monthly rpt, S8560–2

Homeowner's insurance

see Property and casualty insurance

Homeownership

see Housing tenure

Homes

see terms under Housing

Homesteads

State and local:

DC statistical profile, general data, 1992 annual rpt, S1535–3.4

Hawaii native homestead acreage, leases, and applicants, by island, June 1991, annual rpt, S2090–1.6

Indiana property value and tax levies, collections, credits, and deductions, by county and type, 1991, annual rpt, S2570–1.1

Mississippi regular and elderly/disabled homestead tax exemption applications and reimbursements, by county and school district, 1989-91, annual rpt, S4435–1

Nebraska property tax revenues and actual valuation by property type, by city and/or county, 1991 and trends, annual rpt, S4950–1.4

Ohio homestead exemptions and property tax reductions, by county, 1991, annual rpt, S6390–1.5

South Carolina homestead exemption reimbursements to local govts, by county, 1991, annual rpt, S7127–2

West Virginia homestead tax-exempt property, assessed valuations by county, 1992/93, annual rpt, S8640–2

Homicide

Black American crime, arrest, and incarceration data, with comparisons to whites, 1970s-91, annual compilation, C6775–2.5

Black American health and vital statistics data, with comparisons to whites, 1970s-91, annual compilation, C6775–2.2

Black children and youth homicide death rates, with comparisons to whites, by sex and age, 1989, R3840–21

Correctional instn inmate deaths from homicides, by sex, by State and Canadian Province, as of June 1992, annual rpt, A1305–3

Death rates from homicide/legal intervention, by race and sex, 1989, article, A8510–1.1

Deaths from accidents compared with other causes, by age and sex, 1992 and trends, annual rpt, A8375–2.1

Latin America statistical abstract, general data by country, 1992 annual rpt, U6250–1.15

Public interest in news items concerning murders of tourists in Florida, by respondent characteristics, Sept 1993 survey, C8915–1.505

State social, economic, and govtl indicators, with rankings, 1993 semiannual rpt, B8500–1, B8500–1.10

State and local:

Alabama crimes and arrests, by offense, with data by location and offender characteristics, 1992 and trends, annual rpt, S0119–1

Alabama vital statistics, including population, births, deaths by cause, marriages, and divorces, by location and demographic characteristics, 1992 and trends, annual rpt, S0175–2

Alaska vital statistics, including births, deaths by cause, marriages, divorces, adoptions, and population, by demographic characteristics and location, 1990, annual rpt, S0315–1

Arizona crimes and arrests, by offense, county, and offender characteristics, 1992, annual rpt, S0505–2

Arkansas crimes and arrests, by offense, victim and offender characteristics, and location, 1992 and trends, annual rpt, S0652–1

Arkansas vital statistics, including births, deaths by cause, marriages, and divorces, by age, sex, race, and county, 1991 and trends, annual rpt, S0685–1

California crimes and arrests, clearances, and arrest dispositions, with data by offense and offender characteristics, 1987-92, annual rpt, S0910–1.1

California criminal justice system detailed data, by offense, county, age, race-ethnicity, and sex, 1991 and trends, annual rpt, S0910–2

California vital statistics, including population, births, and deaths by cause, by demographic characteristics and county, 1990 and trends, annual rpt, S0865–1

Colorado crimes and arrests, by offense and location, with offender characteristics, and assaults on police, 1992, annual rpt, S1068–1

Colorado vital statistics, including population, births, deaths by cause, abortion, marriage and divorce, and adoption, by demographic characteristics and location, 1990 and trends, annual rpt, S1010–1

Homicide

Connecticut crimes and arrests, by offense, with data by local agency, and victim-offender characteristics, 1992, annual rpt, S1256–1

Connecticut vital statistics, including births, deaths by cause, marriages, and divorces, by demographic characteristics and location, 1989, annual rpt, S1200–1

DC criminal justice system summary, including data on homicide motives, and victim-offender characteristics, 1991 and trends, annual rpt, S1535–2

Delaware crimes and arrests, by offense, county, and victim-offender characteristics, 1991 and trends, annual rpt, S1375–5

Delaware vital statistics, including births, deaths by cause, and marriages and dissolutions, by demographic characteristics and location, 1990, annual rpt, S1385–2

Florida crimes and arrests, by offense, with data by victim and offender characteristics, 1992, annual rpt, S1770–1

Florida deaths by selected cause, and incidence of selected communicable diseases, by county, 1992 annual rpt, S1746–1.1

Florida vital statistics, including population, births, deaths by cause, and marriages and dissolutions, by location and demographic characteristics, 1992 and trends, annual rpt, S1745–3

Georgia county guide, general data, 1993 annual rpt, U6750–1

Georgia crimes and arrests, by offense, with data by location and offender characteristics, 1992 and trends, annual rpt, S1901–1

Georgia vital statistics, including deaths by cause, demographic characteristics, and location, 1991 and trends, annual rpt, S1895–1.2

Hawaii crimes and arrests, by offense, with data by county and victim-offender characteristics, 1992, annual rpt, S2035–1

Hawaii health dept activities and services, including vital statistics and disease control, by location, 1990, annual rpt, S2065–1

Idaho crimes and arrests, by offense, with data by location and offender characteristics, 1992 and trends, annual rpt, S2275–2

Idaho vital statistics, including births, deaths by cause, abortions, marriages, and divorces, by demographic characteristics and county, 1991 and trends, annual rpt, S2250–2

Illinois crimes and arrests, by offense, with data by location and offender characteristics, 1991, annual rpt, S2536–1

Iowa vital statistics, including population, births, deaths by cause, marriages, and divorces, by demographic characteristics and location, 1991 and trends, annual rpt, S2795–1

Kansas crimes and arrests, by offense, with data by location, agency, and victim-offender characteristics, 1992 and trends, annual rpt, S2925–1.1

Kansas vital statistics, including population, births, deaths by cause, abortions, marriages, and divorces, by demographic characteristics and location, 1991 and trends, annual rpt, S2975–1

Kentucky crimes and arrests, by offense, with data by location and offender characteristics, 1992, annual rpt, S3150–1

Kentucky vital statistics, including births, deaths by cause, marriages and divorces, and population, by demographic characteristics and county, 1991, annual rpt, S3140–1

Louisiana vital statistics, including population, births, deaths by cause, reportable diseases, marriages, and divorces, by demographic characteristics and locality, 1989-90 and trends, annual rpt, S3295–1

Maine crimes and arrests, by offense, with data by county, reporting agency, and offender age and sex, 1991, annual rpt, S3475–1

Maine vital statistics, including births, deaths by cause, abortions, and marriages and divorces, by demographic characteristics and location, 1991 and trends, annual rpt, S3460–2

Maryland crimes and arrests, by offense, location, and offender characteristics, with law enforcement employment and assaults on officers, 1992 and trends, annual rpt, S3665–1

Maryland vital statistics, including population, births, deaths by cause, marriages, and divorces, by demographic characteristics and location, 1989 and trends, annual rpt, S3635–1

Massachusetts vital statistics, including births, deaths by cause, marriages, divorces, and population, by locality and demographic characteristics, 1990 and trends, annual rpt, S3850–1

Michigan crimes and arrests, by offense, with data by location and offender characteristics, 1992 and trends, annual rpt, S3997–1

Michigan vital statistics, including births, deaths, marriages, divorces/annulments, and communicable diseases, by location and demographic characteristics, 1990 and trends, annual rpt, S4000–3

Minnesota vital statistics, including population, births, abortions, deaths, marriages, and divorces, by location and demographic characteristics, 1991 and trends, annual rpt, S4190–2

Mississippi vital statistics, including births, deaths by cause, marriages, and divorces, by demographic characteristics and location, 1992 and trends, annual rpt, S4350–1

Missouri crimes and arrests, by offense and location, with victim and offender characteristics, 1991 and trends, annual rpt, S4560–2

Missouri vital statistics, including population, births, deaths by cause, and marriages and divorces, by location and demographic characteristics, 1992 and trends, annual rpt, S4518–1

Montana crimes and clearances, by offense and jurisdiction, 1992, annual rpt, S4705–1

Montana vital statistics, including births, deaths by cause, abortion, disease, and marriage and divorce, by demographic characteristics and county, 1990-91 and trends, annual rpt, S4690–1

Nebraska vital statistics, including births, deaths, marriages, divorces, and population, by demographic characteristics and location, 1991 and trends, annual rpt, S4885–1

Nevada statistical abstract, general data, 1992 biennial rpt, S5005–1.4

Nevada vital statistics, including births, abortions, and deaths by cause, by county and demographic characteristics, 1989 and trends, annual rpt, S5075–1

New Hampshire crimes and arrests, by offense, jurisdiction, and offender characteristics, 1991 and trends, annual rpt, S5250–2

New Hampshire vital statistics, including population, births, deaths by cause, marriages, and divorces, by location and demographic characteristics, 1991 and trends, annual rpt, S5215–1

New Jersey crimes and arrests, by offense, with data by location and offender characteristics, 1992 and trends, annual rpt, S5430–1

New Jersey vital statistics, including births, deaths, population, communicable diseases, and marriages and divorces, by demographic characteristics and location, 1990 and trends, annual rpt, S5405–1

New Mexico vital statistics, including population, births, deaths, and disease, by location and demographic characteristics, 1991 and trends, annual rpt, S5605–1

New York State crimes and arrests by offense and demographic characteristics, and court activity and corrections, 1991 and trends, annual rpt, S5760–3

New York State vital statistics, including population, births, deaths by cause, reportable diseases, and marriages and dissolutions, by demographic characteristics and/or location, 1990 and trends, annual rpt, S5765–1

North Carolina crimes and arrests, by offense, with data by location and offender characteristics, 1992 and trends, annual rpt, S5955–1

North Carolina deaths and rates, by cause and county, 1991 and trends, annual rpt, S5927–1.2

North Dakota crimes and arrests, by offense, location, and offender characteristics, and law enforcement employment, 1991 and trends, annual rpt, S6060–1

North Dakota vital statistics, including births, deaths by cause, marriages and divorces, and abortions, by demographic characteristics and/or county, 1991 and trends, annual rpt, S6105–2

Ohio vital statistics, including births, deaths by cause, marriages, divorces, and population, by demographic characteristics and location, 1991 and trends, annual rpt, S6285–1

Oklahoma crimes and arrests, by offense, with data by local agency and victim and offender characteristics, 1990-92, annual rpt, S6465–1

Oregon crimes and arrests, by offense, with data by county, local agency, and offender characteristics, 1992 and trends, annual rpt, S6603–3

Oregon vital statistics, including births, deaths by cause, communicable diseases, marriages, and divorces, by age, sex, race-ethnicity, and county, 1991 and trends, annual rpt, S6615–5

Pennsylvania crimes and arrests, by offense, with data by location and offender characteristics, 1992 and trends, annual rpt, S6860–1

Rhode Island vital statistics, including population, births, deaths, marriages, and divorces, by demographic characteristics and locality, 1989 and trends, annual rpt, S6995–1

South Carolina crimes and arrests, by offense, with data by location and victim-offender characteristics, and assaults on officers, 1992 and trends, annual rpt, S7205–1

South Carolina deaths, by detailed cause, age, sex, and race, 1990, annual rpt, S7175–2

South Carolina vital statistics, including births, deaths by cause, marriages, and divorces, by age, sex, race, and location, 1990 and trends, annual rpt, S7175–1

South Dakota vital statistics, including births, deaths, marriage and divorce, and communicable disease, by demographic characteristics and county, 1991 and trends, annual rpt, S7345–1

Tennessee vital statistics, including births, deaths by cause, marriages, divorces, and population, by demographic characteristics and location, 1991 and trends, annual rpt, S7520–2

Texas crimes and arrests, by offense, with data by location and offender characteristics, 1992 and trends, annual rpt, S7735–2

Texas vital statistics, including births, deaths by cause, abortions, marriages, and divorces, by location and demographic characteristics, 1991 and trends, annual rpt, S7685–1

Utah crimes and arrests, by offense, county, and local agency, 1992 and trends, annual rpt, S7890–3

Utah vital statistics, including births, deaths by cause, and population, by county and demographic characteristics, 1990 and trends, annual rpt, S7835–1

Vermont vital statistics, including population, births, deaths by cause, abortions, marriages, and divorces, by location and demographic characteristics, 1991 and trends, annual rpt, S8054–1

Virginia crimes and arrests, by offense, with data by location and offender characteristics, 1992, annual rpt, S8295–2

Virginia vital statistics, including births, deaths by cause, marriages and divorces, and communicable disease, by demographic characteristics and location, 1991 and trends, annual rpt, S8225–1

Washington State crimes and arrests, including number of victims in gang-related homicides, 1992 and trends, annual rpt, S8440–1

Washington State vital statistics, including births, deaths by cause, and population, by demographic characteristics and location, 1991 and trends, annual rpt, S8363–1

West Virginia crimes and arrests, by offense, location, and offender characteristics, 1990-91, annual rpt, S8610–1

West Virginia vital statistics, including births, deaths by cause, marriages, and divorces, by location and demographic characteristics, 1991 and trends, annual rpt, S8560–1

Wisconsin crimes and arrests, by offense, offender characteristics, county, and local agency, 1992 and trends, annual rpt, S8771–1

Wisconsin vital statistics, including population, births, deaths by cause, and marriages and dissolutions, by county and demographic characteristics, 1991 and trends, annual rpt, S8715–4

Wyoming crimes and arrests, by offense, with data by location and victim and offender characteristics, 1991 and trends, annual rpt, S8867–3

Wyoming vital statistics, including population, births, deaths by cause, marriages, and divorces, by demographic characteristics and county, 1991 and trends, annual rpt, S8920–2

see also Assaults on police

Homosexuality

AIDS progression in untreated homosexual men, including employment and mental status indicators, 1992 article, A2623–1.501

College freshmen attitudes on selected moral and family issues, by sex and instn type, fall 1992, annual survey, U6215–1

Human immunodeficiency virus (HIV) infection status disclosure to male sex partners, with impact on relationship, 1992 article, A2623–1.502

Magazines targeted to gay audiences, number started 1987-92, with number still published, 1993 article, C2575–1.514

Magazines targeted to gay/lesbian audience, with circulation and advertising rates, for 7 publications, 1993 feature, C2710–1.509

Public interest in news items concerning "March on Washington" demonstration, by respondent characteristics, Apr/May 1993 survey, C8915–1.503

Public interest in news items on Clinton Admin attempt to lift ban on homosexuals in the military, by respondent characteristics, Feb 1993 survey, C8915–1.502

Public opinion on barring homosexuals from teaching school, for US, 9 European countries, and 3 Soviet Union Republics, 1991 survey, C8915–8.1, C8915–9

Public opinion on cause of homosexuality, and homosexual civil rights, Apr 1993 Gallup Poll, C4040–1.510

Public opinion on homosexuality acceptability and legality, and homosexuals in clergy, June 1992 Gallup Poll and trends, R8780–1.501

Public opinion on homosexuality and Clinton Admin attempt to lift military service ban, by respondent characteristics, July/Aug 1993 survey, C8915–1.504

Public opinion on military ban on homosexuals, Jan 1993 Gallup Poll, C4040–1.508

Public opinion on social, political, and economic issues, detailed data, 1972-91 surveys, annual rpt, U6395–1

Youth opinions about selected social issues, by religion, 1991-93 surveys, R8780–1.510

State and local:

Arizona crimes involving bias against selected persons or groups, with offense characteristics, 1992, annual rpt, S0505–2.2

Colorado State constitutional amendment on minority status of homosexuals, election results by county, 1992, biennial rpt, S1090–1

Illinois crimes involving bias against selected groups, 1991, annual rpt, S2536–1

Oklahoma crimes involving bias against selected groups, with offense characteristics and offender race-ethnicity, 1992, annual rpt, S6465–1.2

Oregon State constitutional amendment on discouragement of homosexuality, election results by county, 1992, biennial rpt, S6665–1

Texas crimes involving bias against selected persons or groups, by victim, offender, and incident characteristics, 1992, annual rpt, S7735–2.2

Honduras

Statistical abstract of Latin America, detailed social, govtl, and economic data, 1992 annual rpt, U6250–1

Women's contraceptive use and knowledge of reproductive health, as affected by a hospital maternal education program, 1993 article, A5160–6.505

Honey and beekeeping

Exports of farm products, by detailed commodity and country of destination, US and California, 1991, annual rpt, B9520–1

Production, consumption, stocks, trade, and prices for approx 100 basic commodities, including by country and producing State, commodity yearbook for 1993, C2400–1, C2400–2

Production, stocks, and value, and bee colonies, US and 16 leading States, 1992, annual rpt, S6760–1

State and local:

Arizona agricultural production, marketing, and finances, by commodity and county, 1988-92, annual rpt, U5830–1

Arkansas agricultural production, marketing, and finances, by commodity and county, with farms and acreage, 1992 and trends, annual rpt, U5920–1

Colorado agricultural production, marketing, and finances, by commodity and/or county, with farms and acreage, 1992 and trends, annual rpt, S0985–1

Florida apiary production, yield, and prices, 1987-92, annual rpt, S1685–1.3

Georgia bee sales and honey production, 1991 and trends, annual rpt, S1855–1

Hawaii agricultural production and marketing, by commodity and island, 1987-91, annual rpt, S2030–1

Illinois agricultural production, marketing, and finances, by county or commodity, and farms and farmland, 1991 and trends, annual rpt, S2390–1

Honey and beekeeping

Kansas bee colonies and honey production, 1986-92, annual rpt, S2915–1

Kentucky bee colonies, and honey production and value, 1972-92, annual rpt, S3085–1

Michigan agricultural production, marketing, and finances, by commodity or county, 1987-91, annual rpt, S3950–1

Minnesota agricultural production, marketing, and finances, by county or commodity, and farms and acreage, 1992 and trends, annual rpt, S4130–1

Missouri agricultural production, marketing, and finances, by commodity and/or county, and farms and acreage, 1988-92, annual rpt, S4480–1

Montana agricultural production, marketing, and finances, by commodity and county, 1991 and trends, annual rpt, S4655–1

Nevada agricultural production, marketing, and finances, by county and commodity, and farms and acreage, 1992 and trends, annual rpt, S5010–1

New Jersey agricultural production, marketing, and finances, by commodity and/or county, and farms and acreage, 1986-91, annual rpt, S5350–1

New York State agricultural production, marketing, and finances, by commodity and/or county, and farms and acreage, 1992 and trends, annual rpt, S5700–1

North Dakota agricultural production and marketing, by commodity and county, and farm finances, 1992 and trends, annual rpt, U3600–1

Oklahoma agricultural production, marketing, and finances, by commodity and county, 1992 and trends, annual rpt, S6405–1

Oregon agricultural production, marketing, and finances, by commodity and/or county, with farms and acreage, 1991 and trends, annual rpt, S6575–1

Pennsylvania honey production, prices, value, and stocks, and bee colonies, 1974-92, annual rpt, S6760–1

South Dakota agricultural production, marketing, and finances, by commodity and county, and farms and acreage, 1992 and trends, annual rpt, S7280–1

Tennessee agricultural production and marketing, by commodity and county, with farms, acreage, and farm value, 1992 and trends, annual rpt, S7460–1

Texas honey production, prices, and stocks, 1987-91, annual rpt, S7630–1.2

Utah agricultural production, marketing, and finances, by commodity and county, with farms and acreage, 1992 and trends, annual rpt, S7800–1

Vermont apiaries and hives inspected, and hives diseased, 1989-90 biennial rpt, S7978–1

Washington State bee colonies and honey production, 1980-92, annual rpt, S8328–1

West Virginia bee colonies, and honey production and value, 1987-91, annual rpt, S8510–1

Wisconsin agricultural production, marketing, and finances, by commodity and county, and farms, acreage, and sales, 1992 and trends, annual rpt, S8680–1

Wyoming bee colonies and production, 1988-92, annual rpt, S8860–1

Hong Kong

Electronics industry trade and/or production trends by product category for 33 countries, with general economic profiles, 1993 annual rpt, A4725–1.4

Higher education physical plant operations, costs, employment, salaries, and energy use, by instn and region, 1991/92, recurring rpt, A3183–1

Hip fracture incidence rates in US and Hong Kong, by age and sex, 1988/89, article, A2623–1.507

Silver supply-demand by country and end use, with prices, futures trading, and market analyses, 1993 and trends, annual rpt, A8902–4

Honolulu County, Hawaii

Economic indicators and population, 1988-1st 3 months 1993, annual rpt, B3500–2.2

Honolulu, Hawaii

CPI, home mortgage rates, and construction cost indexes, bimonthly rpt, B3500–1

Economic conditions, including employment, population, tourism, and construction, quarterly rpt, S2090–2

Statistical data book of Hawaii, detailed social, govtl, and economic data, 1992 annual rpt, S2090–1

see also under By City in the "Index by Categories"

Hops

Malt beverage and ingredients trade, by world area or country, 1970s-91, annual rpt, A3455–1.5

State and local:

Washington State agricultural production, marketing, and finances, by commodity and/or county, 1992 and trends, annual rpt, S8328–1

Hornor, Edith R.

"Almanac of the 50 States: Basic Data Profiles with Comparative Tables", C4712–1

"California Cities, Towns, and Counties, 1993", C4712–3

"Massachusetts Municipal Profiles, 1992-93", C4712–2

"New Jersey Municipal Data Book, 1992-93 Edition", C4712–4

Hornor, Louise L.

"Florida Municipal Profiles, 1991-92", C4712–6

"New York State Municipal Profiles, 1993", C4712–7

Horse racing

Attendance at horse races compared to other professional and collegiate sports, suspended annual rpt, C2825–1

Wagering activity, attendance, purse distribution, and govt revenue, by State and Canadian Province, 1990 and trends, annual rpt, A3363–1

State and local:

California financial condition, including revenues by source, expenditures by agency and function, fund balances, and bonded debt, FY92 and trends, annual rpt, S0815–1

California State tax receipts by source, FY67-92, annual rpt, S0840–3.2

Florida racing and jai alai attendance, and pari-mutuel revenue, FY88-91, annual rpt, U6660–1.23

Indiana financial condition, including revenues by source, expenditures by function and object, and fund balances, by agency, FY92, annual rpt, S2570–1

Kentucky financial condition, including revenues by source, expenditures by function and object, fund balances, and bonded debt, FY92, annual rpt, S3120–1

New York State statistical yearbook, general data, 1992 annual rpt, U5100–1.5

Ohio horse racing wagers, tax collections and distributions, and racing days, FY92 and trends, annual rpt, S6390–1.3

Oklahoma statistical abstract, general data, 1992 annual rpt, U8130–2.21

Horses

see Animals

see Horse racing

Horticulture

Grounds maintenance manager salaries, by type of employer, 1992, annual article, C4725–6

Home gardening and landscaping activities of do-it-yourself home improvement consumers, summer 1993 survey, article, C5150–6.508

see also Flowers and nursery products

Hosiery

see Clothing and clothing industry

Hospices

AIDS deaths at home and in hospice/nursing homes, by decedent characteristics, 1988, article, A2623–1.512

State and local:

Florida health care atlas, including manpower by occupation and health care facilities by type, by district and county, 1992 annual rpt, S1746–1.2

Kentucky Medicaid recipients and payments, by program, county, and type of medical service, monthly rpt, S3140–5

Hospital administration

see Health facilities administration

Hospitalization

Admission rates and length of stay, by diagnosis and procedure, payment source, age, sex, and region, 1991, B4455–4

Admissions and patient days of care, 1980-91, article, A1865–1.501

Admissions, length of stay, operative procedures, and discharges by patient characteristics, 1990 and trends, annual fact book, A1275–1.2

Admissions to community hospitals, by bed-size group and urban-rural location, 1981 and 1991, article, A1865–1.514

Africa military personnel hospital admissions and deaths due to selected diseases, for African troops serving in UK army, 1819-36, article, A2623–1.502

Black American health and vital statistics data, with comparisons to whites, 1970s-91, annual compilation, C6775–2.2

Canada and US acute care hospital beds, inpatient days, and length of stay, with detail for Ontario and California, 1987, article, A1865–1.512

Catholic hospitals and utilization, by diocese and State, 1993 annual compilation, C4950–1

Cost of semiprivate hospital room in approx 300 cities, quarterly rpt, A0150–1

Discharges and length of stay in hospitals, by diagnosis, type of operation, age, and region, 1991, annual rpt series, B4455–1

Index by Subjects and Names

Hospitals

Discharges and length of stay in hospitals, by diagnostic related group (DRG), payment source, patient age, and region, 1991, annual rpt series, B4455–3

Financial and operating indicators for hospitals, with detail for Medicare, by instn characteristics and location, 1988-92, annual rpt, B1880–1

Health insurance coverage and finances, and health care costs and facilities, by selected demographic characteristics, 1940s-91, annual rpt, A5173–2

HMO benefits, enrollment and utilization, staffing, finances, and relations with employers, by plan characteristics, 1990-91, annual rpt, A5150–2

Medical group hospital inpatient surgical/anesthesia cases and visits/consultations, by specialty, 1991, annual rpt, A6365–1

Men age 69-84 quality of life indicators, including health, finances, family, and employment, by race, 1990 survey, U3780–9

Patient charges and length of stay, by diagnosis and procedure, payment source, age, and region, 1991, B4455–5

Physician fees and expenses, and detailed work patterns, by specialty, type of practice and location, and age, 1982-92, annual rpt, A2200–5.2

Prostate surgery procedures, costs, and hospital stay, with data by census div and State, 1991 and trends, article, B6045–1.503

Psychiatric hospital operating and utilization data, 1981-91, article, A1865–1.512

Psychiatric patients in general hospitals, discharges and length of stay by diagnosis, age, sex, and region, 1991, annual rpt series, B4455–2

Statistical profiles of 50 States and DC, general data, 1993 annual almanac, C4712–1

Stay length in hospitals, and average cost per day and stay, by State, 1990, annual rpt, A5650–1.4

Tonsillectomy/adenoidectomy procedures, costs, and hospital stay, with data by census div and State, 1991 and trends, article, B6045–1.502

Utilization, expenses, and personnel, by instn, type, and location, 1992, annual directory, A1865–3

Utilization measures for hospitals and physicians under fee-for-service vs HMO care, 1992 rpt, R4865–9

State and local:

Alabama statistical abstract, general data, 1992 recurring rpt, U5680–2.8

Arizona statistical abstract, general data, 1993 recurring rpt, U5850–2.3

DC statistical profile, general data, 1992 annual rpt, S1535–3.5

Florida hospital admissions, length of stay, and charges, for selected conditions or procedures, by county, 1990, annual rpt, S1746–1.2

Georgia county guide, general data, 1993 annual rpt, U6750–1

Georgia statistical abstract, general data, 1992-93 biennial rpt, U6730–1.1

Hawaii hospital admissions, length of stay, and occupancy, by type of care, 1990 and trends, annual rpt, S2065–1.7

Illinois mental health facility patient population and characteristics, by facility, location, and treatment category, FY93, annual rpt, S2505–1

Indiana public assistance program participation, expenditures, and services, by county, FY92 and trends, annual rpt, S2623–1

Iowa hospitalization hearings, by court district and case type, 1991-92, annual rpt, S2815–1

Kansas statistical abstract, general data, 1991/92 annual rpt, U7095–2.2

Maryland medical assistance payments and recipients, by program, type of service, location, demographic characteristics, and facility, FY92 and trends, annual rpt, S3635–3

Mississippi statistical abstract, general data, 1992 annual rpt, U3255–4.2

Missouri public welfare and medical assistance recipients, expenditures, and case processing, by program and county, FY92 and trends, annual rpt, S4575–2

Montana health care facility capacity, utilization, and finances, by instn, 1991, annual rpt, S4690–2

Montana welfare and medical assistance program cases and payments, by county and type of service, monthly rpt, S4755–1

Nebraska Medicaid recipients and payments, by type of service and county, FY92, annual rpt, S4957–1.2

Nevada statistical abstract, general data, 1992 biennial rpt, S5005–1.2

New York State hospital discharges by age group and selected diagnosis, by location, 1990, annual rpt, S5765–1

New York State statistical yearbook, general data, 1992 annual rpt, U5100–1.11

Oklahoma Medical Center, admissions and services, FY92, annual rpt, S6455–1.2

Pennsylvania statistical abstract, general data, 1992 recurring rpt, U4130–6.5

South Carolina statistical abstract, general data, 1993 annual rpt, S7125–1.10

South Dakota medical assistance recipients and payments, by type of service, program, and county, FY92, annual rpt, S7385–1

Tennessee statistical abstract, general data, 1992/93 annual rpt, U8710–2.17

Texas hospitals, operations, utilization, and finances, by type, ownership, size, and metro-nonmetro status, 1970s-91, U8850–8.3

Utah statistical abstract, general data, 1993 triennial rpt, U8960–1.2

Hospitalization insurance

see Health insurance

Hospitals

AIDS and human immunodeficiency virus (HIV) infection reporting accuracy on hospital and Medicaid records, 1993 article, A2623–1.512

AIDS case reporting completeness by hospitals in 6 selected States or cities, 1988, article, A2623–1.501

AIDS deaths in hospitals vs at home, by region and decedent characteristics, 1988 and trends, article, A2623–1.512

Blood bank collection and transfusion data, and shipments by region, 1993 annual rpt, A0612–2

Catholic hospitals and utilization, by diocese and State, 1993 annual compilation, C4950–1

CEO demographic and professional characteristics, perquisites, and views on mgmt issues, Oct 1992 survey, recurring rpt, B4490–2.35

CEOs of large hospitals income, public perceptions vs actual amounts, 1991-93, R4865–13

Characteristics of hospitals with and without psychiatric units, including teaching activity, and urban-rural location, 1991, annual rpt series, B4455–2

Characteristics of short-term hospitals, including teaching activity, and urban-rural location, 1991, B4455–4, B4455–5

Characteristics of short-term hospitals, including teaching activity, and urban-rural location, 1991, annual rpt series, B4455–3

Charitable donations to hospitals, 1987-92, article, C2176–1.513

Community hospital facilities, use, and costs, by State, 1990 and trends, annual rpt, A5173–2

Dental advanced education programs in hospitals, enrollment, grads, and finances, by instn and State, 1992/93 annual rpt, A1475–10

Facilities, beds, and selected operating data, with detail by ownership type, 1990 and trends, annual fact book, A1275–1.2

Facility directory, with utilization, expenses, and personnel, by instn, type, and location, 1992, annual rpt, A1865–3

Financial and operating indicators, with detail for Medicare, by hospital characteristics and location, 1988-92, annual rpt, B1880–1

Financial ratios and Medicaid discharge rates for academic medical center hospitals, 1987-91, article, A3273–8.511

Food service (institutional) financial and operating data, for leading firms by market segment, 1993 recurring feature, C1850–3.511

Food service industry sales and establishments, with growth outlook, by market segment, 1993 annual feature, C1850–3.503

Fundraising personnel salaries, by position, sex, experience, and hospital size, 1993 and trends, annual article, C2176–1.517

Higher education nursing program financial and other support from hospitals, 1992/93, biennial rpt, A0615–5

Japan and US health care system data, including expenditures, facilities, insurance coverage, and population health indicators, 1993 article, R5650–2.515

Latin America statistical abstract, general data by country, 1992 annual rpt, U6250–1.7

Medicaid Federal grants, recipients, and benefits by type of service, with selected public health funding factors, by State and region, various years 1974-94, R8490–46

Operating and financial composite ratios for corporations, with establishments and receipts, for approx 200 industries, by asset size, FY90, annual rpt, C7800–1

Operations, admin, and mgmt devs for hospitals, semimonthly rpt, A1865–1

Hospitals

Pharmacies in hospitals, operating data, by instn type and size, and census div, 1991, annual survey, B5165–3

Physician fees and expenses, and detailed work patterns, by specialty, type of practice and location, and age, 1982-92, annual rpt, A2200–5.2

Physician group practice affilation with hospitals, by practice characteristics, 1991, recurring rpt, A2200–7

Recruiting of nurses and allied health personnel, with budget, vacancies, turnover, and compensation, 1993 and trends, annual survey rpt, A6500–1

Regional distribution of nonfederal hospitals, by census div, 1991, annual rpt series, B4455–1

Revenues per capita for public hospitals, by State, 1991, article, B8500–2.518

State social, economic, and govtl indicators, with rankings, 1993 semiannual rpt, B8500–1.9

Statistical profiles of 50 States and DC, general data, 1993 annual almanac, C4712–1

Substance abuse treatment clients in hospital and other alcohol and drug programs, by State, FY91, annual rpt, A7112–1

Teaching hospital house staff stipends, benefits, and expenditures, by region and ownership, 1992/93 and trends, annual rpt, A3273–3

State and local:

Alabama births in hospitals, by sex and race, by instn and county, 1992, annual rpt, S0175–2

Alabama statistical abstract, general data, 1992 recurring rpt, U5680–2.8

Arizona statistical abstract, general data, 1993 recurring rpt, U5850–2.3

Arkansas human services dept finances and operations, including Medicaid payments by type of service, FY91 and trends, annual rpt, S0700 2.3

California births in hospitals by type, by county, 1990, annual rpt, S0865–1

California property tax assessments and exemptions, by type of property, city, county, and company, FY93 and trends, annual rpt, S0835–1.2

DC statistical profile, general data, 1992 annual rpt, S1535–3.1, S1535–3.5

Florida county data book, 1992/93 annual rpt, C6360–1

Florida health care atlas, including manpower by occupation and health care facilities by type, by district and county, 1992 annual rpt, S1746–1.2

Florida statistical abstract, general data, 1992 annual rpt, U6660–1.20

Georgia county guide, general data, 1993 annual rpt, U6750–1

Georgia statistical abstract, general data, 1992-93 biennial rpt, U6730–1.1

Hawaii data book, general data, 1992 annual rpt, S2090–1.6

Hawaii hospital bed capacity, by type of care and instn, 1990 annual rpt, S2065–1.7

Indiana hospitals participating in Medicaid, by county, July 1992, annual rpt, S2623–1.6

Kansas statistical abstract, general data, 1991/92 annual rpt, U7095–2.2

Kentucky Medicaid recipients and payments, by program, county, and type of medical service, monthly rpt, S3140–5

Louisiana births by race and deaths by age, by hospital of occurrence, 1989-90, annual rpt, S3295–1

Maryland hospital and nursing home deaths, by race and location, 1989, annual rpt, S3635–1

Maryland local govt financial condition, including revenues by source, expenditures by function, and debt obligations, FY92 and trends, annual rpt, S3618–1.1

Maryland medical assistance payments and recipients, by program, type of service, location, demographic characteristics, and facility, FY92 and trends, annual rpt, S3635–3

Massachusetts births, by method of delivery, characteristics of mother, and payment sources, by hospital, 1990, annual rpt, S3850–1

Mississippi statistical abstract, general data, 1992 annual rpt, U3255–4.2

Missouri public welfare and medical assistance recipients, expenditures, and case processing, by program and county, FY92 and trends, annual rpt, S4575–2

Montana health care facility capacity, utilization, and finances, by instn, 1991, annual rpt, S4690–2

Nebraska public welfare cases, recipients, and payments, by program and county, FY92 and trends, annual rpt, S4957–1

Nevada statistical abstract, general data, 1992 biennial rpt, S5005–1.2

New Hampshire births, by county and for residents of 3 neighboring States, by hospital, 1991, annual rpt, S5215–1

New York State medical assistance expenditures, by State area and type of care, 1991 and trends, annual rpt, S5800–2.2

Oklahoma Medicaid payments, and expenditures for rehabilitative services, by type of service and county, FY92, annual rpt, S6455–1.2

Oklahoma statistical abstract, general data, 1992 annual rpt, U8130–2.9

Oregon caseload and payments for medical service by category, monthly rpt quarterly table, S6615–8

Pennsylvania statistical abstract, general data, 1992 recurring rpt, U4130–6.5

South Carolina statistical abstract, general data, 1993 annual rpt, S7125–1.10

South Dakota medical assistance recipients and payments, by type of service, program, and county, FY92, annual rpt, S7385–1

Tennessee statistical abstract, general data, 1992/93 annual rpt, U8710–2.17

Texas hospitals, operations, utilization, and finances, by type, ownership, size, and metro-nonmetro status, 1970s-91, U8850–8.3

Utah statistical abstract, general data, 1993 triennial rpt, U8960–1.2

Utah vital statistics, including births and deaths, by instn and/or location, 1990, annual rpt, S7835–1.2

Vermont births and deaths by location, including individual instns, 1991, annual rpt, S8054–1

Washington State hospital cesarean section delivery rates correlated with hospital and patient characteristics, 1987, article, A2623–1.510

Washington State public assistance clients and service costs, by client characteristics, program, and county, FY90, annual rpt, S8420–2

see also Clinics

see also Emergency medical service

see also Health facilities administration

see also Health maintenance organizations

see also Hospitalization

see also Mental health facilities and services

see also Military health facilities and services

see also Nurses and nursing

see also Nursing homes

see also State funding for health and hospitals

see also Veterans health facilities and services

Hotels and motels

Almanac for lodging industry, including top chains, and selected survey results, 1993 annual rpt, C7000–6

Business traveler and trip characteristics, including mode, purpose, and lodging, 1991, annual rpt, R9375–12

Caribbean area hotel rooms and occupancy rates, by country, 1992 annual rpt, C2140–1.3

City lodging tax rates, for top 5 cities, 1993 feature, C1200–1.513

Crime victimization experience of hotel guests, by type of crime, 1993 survey article, C4215–1.511

Facilities, sales, and occupancy, with top 42-100 properties in 5 market categories, 1993 annual rpt, C7000–5

Financial performance and growth rankings for approx 1,000 top corporations, with comparisons by industry group, 1993 annual rpt, C3950–1.505

Financial ratios and performance, for over 350 SIC 4-digit industries, FY88-92, annual rpt, A6400–3

Food service industry sales and establishments, with growth outlook, by market segment, 1993 annual feature, C1850–3.503

Food service industry sales rankings by market segment, for leading organizations, 1992, annual feature, C1850–3.509

Food service industry sales trends and forecast, by market segment, 1990-93, annual feature, A8200–1.502

Food service worker wage rates, by position, 1992, recurring rpt, A8200–14

Franchise operations and finances, by type of business, 1991/92 and trends, annual rpt, A5820–1

Latin America statistical abstract, general data by country, 1992 annual rpt, U6250–1.14

Operating and financial composite ratios for corporations, with establishments and receipts, for approx 200 industries, by asset size, FY90, annual rpt, C7800–1

Operating data by world region, and establishments and rooms for top 50 chains, 1992 annual rpt, C2140–1.4

Real estate sales transactions for hotels, with prices, financing methods, and industry performance data, by region, 1991 and trends, article, A6450–2.501

Index by Subjects and Names

Hours of labor

Receipts and occupancy rate for hotels/motels, monthly rpt, R9375–1

Restaurant (hotel) average check size and seat turnover, compared to all restaurants, 1993 article, C1200–5.505

Restaurant industry financial and operating data, by establishment characteristics and location, 1992, annual rpt, A8200–3

Restaurant sales, payroll/benefits, and employment, with detail for hotel establishments, 1993 article, C5150–5.507

Sales industry costs, including compensation, training, and travel and related expenses, with data by metro area, 1992 and trends, annual survey, C1200–1.508

South Carolina accommodations tax collections, by county, FY92, annual rpt, S7255–1.2

Travel and tourism rankings for selected indicators, including data for top 20 States, cities, countries, businesses, and other measures, 1992 recurring rpt, R9375–6

Travel impact on State economies, with detail by industry sector, 1990 and trends, annual rpt, R9375–7

Travel trips and traveler characteristics, including mode, purpose, type of lodging, and area of destination and origin, quarterly rpt, R9375–14

Value trends for hotel properties, 5 metro areas with greatest gains and losses, 1991 vs 1990, C1200–5.502

State and local:

Arizona statistical abstract, general data, 1993 recurring rpt, U5850–2.24

Colorado property assessed valuation by detailed type, and tax levy and revenue by local district, by county, 1991-92, annual rpt, S1055–3

Connecticut construction activity and value, by type of structure and location, 1992 and trends, annual rpt, S1212–1

Florida statistical abstract, general data, 1992 annual rpt, U6660–1.19

Hawaii counties population and economic indicators, 1993 annual rpt series, B3500–2

Hawaii data book, general data, 1992 annual rpt, S2090–1.7, S2090–1.23, S2090–1.24

Hawaii economic conditions, including employment, population, tourism, and construction, quarterly rpt, S2090–2

Hawaii economic indicators, bimonthly rpt, B3500–1

Iowa hotel/motel tax collections, by jurisdiction, quarterly FY91, annual supplement, S2860–1.501

Iowa hotel/motel tax collections, by jurisdiction, quarterly FY92, annual supplement, S2860–1.502

Montana accommodations tax collections, FY88-92, biennial rpt, S4750–1.1

Nebraska lodging tax collections and distributions to counties, 1990-91, annual rpt, S4950–1.3

Nevada room tax collections, by county, 1980-91, annual rpt, U7920–2

Nevada statistical abstract, general data, 1992 biennial rpt, S5005–1.13

New Jersey casino revenues and operations for 12 facilities, with State regulatory activities, 1992 and trends, annual rpt, S5360–1

New Mexico lodging industry occupancy rates, monthly business activity rpt, U7980–1

South Carolina statistical abstract, general data, 1993 annual rpt, S7125–1.14

Utah statistical abstract, general data, 1993 triennial rpt, U8960–1.17

Utah tax revenues by source, and distribution to localities and State funds, FY92 and trends, annual rpt, S7905–1

Wyoming lodging tax collection and distribution by county, FY92, annual rpt, S8990–1.3

see also Casinos

Hours of labor

Advertising media buying services, competition, and staffing, views of agency and independent service executives, 1993 annual survey articles, C2710–1.537

Aerospace industry production worker regular and overtime hours, 1977-91, annual rpt, A0250–2.5

Appalachia agricultural workers, hours, and wage rates, 1990-91, annual rpt, S8510–1

Brewing industry financial and operating data, including consumption, trade, and taxes, 1991 and trends, annual rpt, A3455–1

Business forms manufacturing plant employment and compensation data, by region, 1992 and trends, biennial rpt, A5785–4

Chemical and related industries production, finances, operating ratios, employment, and trade, by country, company, and chemical, 1980s-92, annual feature, A1250–1.530

Chemical industry finances and operations, with data by industry segment and product, 1970s-92, annual rpt, A3850–1

Clothing (women's and children's) sales, production, imports, and industry employment, hours, and earnings, by type of garment, recurring rpt, A5900–1

Computer industry production workers and hours, semimonthly rpt recurring feature, C1850–5

Container (fiber box) shipments by end-use industry and region, and other industry operating data, 1940s-92, annual rpt, A4875–1

Convenience store industry financial and operating data, by size category, 1992 and trends, annual survey rpt, A6735–1, A6735–2

Corporate family-related personnel policies, including use of selected types of alternative work schedules, Mar 1992 survey, A8907–1

Corporate staffing practices, including use of part-time and home-based workers, flextime, and job-sharing, 1993 survey, annual rpt, B6850–5

Drugstore (independent pharmacy) hours worked by proprietor and pharmacists, by store characteristics, 1991 and trends, annual survey, B5165–1

Flexible work schedules offered by employers, and workers with flexible schedules by occupation and industry div, 1993 article, S0465–1.504

Food store manager hours per week, and Sundays worked and pay policy, by sales size, year ended Mar 1993, annual survey, A4950–6

Food store produce dept weekly labor hours, by company size and region, 1992, annual rpt, A4950–5.4

Forecasts of economic indicators for approx 10-13 months, monthly rpt, U1880–3

Foreign economic indexes, and leading and coincident indicators for US and other industrial countries, monthly rpt, U1245–1

Frozen dessert industry employment, wages, and capital expenditures, 1969-92, annual rpt, A5825–1.1

Fundraising professionals characteristics, earnings, and benefits, 1992 survey, recurring rpt, A8455–1

Hospital pharmacy personnel weekly hours, 1991, annual survey, B5165–3

Household appliance manufacturing production worker hours and earnings, 1977-91, biennial rpt, A3350–3

Iron and steel industry financial and operating data, 1992 and trends, annual rpt, A2000–2.1

Iron ore mining industry employment, wages, and hours, 1983-92, annual rpt, A2010–3.3

Jewelry industry statistics on sales, marketing, trade, and employment, with customer characteristics, 1993 annual almanac, C2150–7.509

Latin America statistical abstract, general data by country, 1992 annual rpt, U6250–1.12

Machine tool industry employment, compensation, and operations, 1992 and trends, annual rpt, A3179–2.1

Manufacturing workers annual hours worked and days off, for 7 countries, 1990 or 1991, article, C5800–7.539

Meat and poultry demand, prices, and processor operations and finances, with data on meat production, 1991 and trends, annual rpt, A2100–1.1

Men age 69-84 quality of life indicators, including health, finances, family, and employment, by race, 1990 survey, U3780–9

Municipal police and fire dept employment, hours, compensation, and expenditures, by census div, city, and city size, 1992, annual rpt, A5800–1.3

Northeast region farm workers, hours, and wages, 1985-93, annual rpt, S5700–1

Northern Plains region agricultural workers, hours, and wages, 1st qtr 1989-1st qtr 1993, annual rpt, S7280–1

Oil/gas industry occupational injury, illness, and employment data, by function, for 136 companies, 1991, annual rpt, A2575–4

Paper and paperboard industry financial and operating data, by product, region, and State, 1992 and trends, annual rpt, A1630–6

Paper/allied products industry data from Census of Manufactures, including purchased fuel and labor costs, 1990 and/or 1991, article, A1630–5.501

Physician fees and expenses, and detailed work patterns, by specialty, type of practice and location, and age, 1992 and trends, annual rpt, A2200–5

Prison inmate daily hours worked in prison industries, by State and for Federal system, 1992 annual rpt, R4300–1.1

Hours of labor

Probation and parole officers weekly hours, by State and for Federal system, 1992 annual rpt, R4300-1.3

Productivity and related indicators, trend analysis for US and other industrial countries, 1980s-92, annual rpt, R2800-2

Pulp and paper mill machine maintenance operations and personnel, by region and grade, 1992 survey, recurring article, C3975-2.504

Railroad (Class I) financial and operating data, with detail by company, 1982-91, annual rpt, A3275-8.2

Railroad (Class I) financial condition, operations, and employment, by company and district, 1992, annual rpt, A3275-7

Railroad employment, payroll, and hours, with data by occupational class and company, 1920s-92; annual rpt, A3275-5.4

Religious congregation characteristics, including membership, activities, staff, and finances, 1992 survey, recurring rpt, A5435-4

Semiconductor market trends, including orders, prices, and worker hours, monthly rpt, C1850-2

Service sector economic activity indicators, with leading and coincident indexes and components, and detail for financial services, monthly rpt, U1245-3

Shoe industry production and operating data, including trade by country, retail sales, and consumer expenditures, quarterly rpt, A4957-2

Shoe industry production, employment, trade, marketing, and related data, by SIC 2- to 5-digit code or product type, 1992 annual rpt, A4957-1.2

Southeast US farm workers, hours, and wage rates, 3 regions, 1991-92, annual rpt, S5885-1

Southeast US farm workers, hours, wages, and pay methods, 1989-92, annual rpt, S1855 1

Statistical profiles of 50 States and DC, general data, 1993 annual almanac, C4712-1

Textile industry economic performance indicators and outlook, with industry trends and devs, monthly rpt, C5226-3

Veterinarian (equine) characteristics and finances, and practice profile, 1992 survey and trends, annual article, C9480-1.503

Veterinarian income by selected personal and practice characteristics, 1992, annual survey article, C9480-1.506

Veterinary practice nonowner associate job characteristics and attitudes, 1992 survey, article, C9480-1.505

Western States farm workers, hours, and wages, 1992-93, annual rpt, S5010-1

Worker annual hours of labor and amount of paid vacation, for 12 industrialized countries, 1993 feature, C4215-1.507

State and local:

Alabama statistical abstract, general data, 1992 recurring rpt, U5680-2.3, U5680-2.11

Alaska employment and unemployment, hours, and earnings, by area and/or industry, monthly rpt, S0320-1

Arizona and US copper industry employment data, 1991 and trends, annual rpt, S0497-1

Arizona employment and unemployment, by county and industry, with production worker hours and earnings, monthly rpt, S0465-1

Arizona farm workers, wage rates, and hours of labor, 1988-93, annual rpt, U5830-1

Arizona statistical abstract, general data, 1993 recurring rpt, U5850-2.6, U5850-2.15, U5850-2.17

Arkansas Census of Population and Housing detailed findings, 1990, U5935-7

California Census of Population and Housing detailed findings, 1990, S0840-9

California economic condition, including population, employment and earnings, income, business activity, and taxation, 1960s-92, annual rpt, S0840-3.2

California economic indicators, bimonthly rpt, S0840-1

California employment statistics, by demographic characteristics, industry, MSA, and county, monthly rpt, S0830-1

California statistical abstract, general data, 1992 annual rpt, S0840-2.3, S0840-2.8

Colorado employment, unemployment, hours, and earnings, with job service activities, monthly rpt, S1040-4

Colorado public library staff weekly hours, 1991, annual rpt, S1000-3.1

Connecticut employment, hours, and earnings, by labor market area and industry, and selected economic indicators, monthly rpt, S1235-1

DC employment, earnings, and hours, by industry, with unemployment insurance data, monthly rpt, S1527-3

Delaware employment, earnings, and hours, by locality and industry, and unemployment insurance activity, monthly rpt, S1405-2

Georgia employment, earnings, and hours, by major industry group and MSA, monthly rpt, S1905-1

Georgia statistical abstract, general data, 1992-93 biennial rpt, U6730-1.3, U6730-1.6

Hawaii data book, general data, 1992 annual rpt, S2090-1.12, S2090-1.22

Idaho economic profile, general data, 1992 recurring rpt, S2218-2.5

Illinois statistical abstract, general data, 1992 annual rpt, U6910-2

Indiana, Northwest area hours worked, by sector, quarterly rpt semiannual feature, U2160-1.502

Indiana, Northwest area manufacturing hours worked, quarterly rpt semiannual feature, U2160-1.504

Kansas business activity indicators, quarterly rpt, U7095-1

Kentucky economic statistics, general data, 1993 annual rpt, S3104-1.1

Kentucky labor force planning rpt, including population and labor force characteristics, and employment by industry, 1991 and trends, annual rpt, S3140-3

Louisiana employment, hours, and earnings, by industry and MSA, monthly rpt, S3320-2

Louisiana production workers average hours and earnings, by industry, monthly 1992, annual planning rpt, S3320-1.1

Maine employment, unemployment, and earnings, by industry group, MSA, and labor area, monthly rpt, S3465-2

Maryland labor force, employment, earnings, and hours, with data by industry and location, monthly rpt, S3605-2

Massachusetts employment, hours, and earnings, by industry and local area, with unemployment insurance claims, monthly rpt, S3808-1

Massachusetts public library FTE employees and hours, by municipality, FY92, annual rpt, S3870-1

Michigan employment, hours, and earnings, with detail by industry and local area, monthly rpt, S3980-2

Minnesota employment, hours, and earnings, by industry group and locality, monthly rpt, S4205-1

Minnesota farm workers, wages, and hours, Apr 1991-Apr 1993, annual rpt, S4130-1

Mississippi statistical abstract, general data, 1992 annual rpt, U3255-4.4

Missouri employment, earnings, and hours, and employment security program activity, by industry and/or county, FY92 and trends, annual rpt, S4530-2.3

Missouri employment, earnings, and hours, by industry and MSA, monthly rpt, S4530-3

Missouri/Iowa farm workers, hours, and wages, 1988-92, annual rpt, S4480-1

Montana employment and unemployment, earnings, and hours, by location and/or industry, quarterly rpt, S4710-1

Montana production workers, hours, and earnings, by industry div, monthly 1991-92, annual planning rpt, S4710-3

Nebraska manufacturing and service worker hours and earnings, by selected industry group and locality, quarterly rpt, S4895-2

Nevada business and economic activity indicators, with comparisons to other Western States, 1980-91, annual rpt, U7920-2

Nevada employment, hours, and earnings, by industry, and unemployment by county, quarterly rpt, S5040-1

New Hampshire employment, hours, and earnings, by industry and area, monthly rpt, S5205-1

New Jersey Census of Population and Housing detailed findings, by county, 1990, S5425-19

New Jersey economic indicators, including employment, building permits, and retail trade, monthly rpt, S5425-1

New Mexico employment, hours, and earnings, by labor market area and industry, monthly rpt, S5624-2

New York State business activity indicators, quarterly rpt, S5735-2

New York State employment, earnings, and hours, by county, selected metro area, and industry group, monthly rpt, S5775-1

New York State statistical yearbook, general data, 1992 annual rpt, U5100-1.3

North Carolina employment, hours, and earnings, by industry group, with job placements, monthly rpt, S5917-3

North Dakota employment, hours, and earnings, by industry div and/or location, monthly rpt, S6140-4

Ohio employment, hours, and earnings, by industry and MSA, with job service and unemployment insurance activities, monthly rpt, S6270-1

Index by Subjects and Names

Index by Subjects and Names

Oklahoma business activity indicators, monthly rpt quarterly data, U8130–1
Oklahoma employment, hours, and earnings, by industry and MSA, with unemployment insurance and job service activities, monthly rpt, S6430–2
Oklahoma statistical abstract, general data, 1992 annual rpt, U8130–2.14
Oregon labor force and employment statistics, including data by industry, monthly rpt, S6592–1, S6615–2
Pennsylvania business activity indicators, monthly rpt, U4110–1
Pennsylvania Census of Population and Housing detailed findings, with selected data by county and municipality, 1990, U4130–13
Pennsylvania employment, hours, and earnings, by industry, monthly rpt, S6845–1
Pennsylvania farm workers, wage rates, and hours of labor, 1990-92, annual rpt, S6760–1
Pennsylvania manufacturing production worker hours and earnings, by MSA, 1985-91, annual planning rpt, S6845–3.2
Pennsylvania statistical abstract, general data, 1992 recurring rpt, U4130–6.2, U4130–6.3
Rhode Island employment, hours, and earnings, by industry, monthly rpt, S6980–1
Rhode Island statistical almanac, general data, 1993 annual rpt, C7975–1.1
South Carolina economic condition, including employment, manufacturing, and income, 1970s-92, annual rpt, S7125–3.2
South Carolina employment, earnings, and hours, by industry group and locality, monthly rpt, S7155–2
South Carolina labor force planning rpt, detailed data on employment, hours, wages, turnover, and characteristics of job service applicants, 1992 annual rpt, S7155–3.2
South Dakota business activity review, including selected data by city and industry, quarterly rpt, U8595–1
South Dakota employment, earnings, and hours for selected industries and areas, with characteristics of unemployed and job service activities, monthly rpt, S7355–1
Tennessee business activity indicators, quarterly journal, U8710–1
Tennessee employment, hours, and earnings, by industry group and MSA, monthly rpt, S7495–2
Tennessee manufacturing average weekly hours, 1989-92, annual rpt, S7560–1
Tennessee statistical abstract, general data, 1992/93 annual rpt, U8710–2.4
Texas employment, hours, and earnings, by MSA and industry group, and unemployment insurance, monthly rpt, S7675–3
Utah economic and business activity review and indicators, monthly rpt, U8960–2
Utah employment, hours, and earnings, by industry, monthly rpt, S7820–3
Utah farm workers, hours, and wages, by type of worker, 1992-93, annual rpt, S7800–1
Utah labor force characteristics, employment and unemployment, hours, and earnings, with data by industry and locale, 1992 and trends, annual rpt, S7820–10

Virginia economic indicators, including new business incorporations and employment data, quarterly rpt, S8205–4
Virginia labor force, hours, and earnings, with data by industry group and locality, monthly rpt, S8205–6
Virginia magistrates duty and activity hours, by locality, 1992, annual rpt, S8300–1
Washington State employment, earnings, and hours, by labor market area and industry group, monthly rpt, S8340–3
Washington State farm workers, hours, and wage rates, 1992-93, annual rpt, S8328–1
West Virginia employment, unemployment, hours, and earnings, with job service activities, monthly rpt, S8534–1
West Virginia production worker hours and earnings, by industry group, 1990-91, annual planning rpt, S8534–2
Wisconsin economic indicators, including employment and earnings by industry group, monthly rpt, S8750–1
Wyoming mining industry employment, and production workers hours and earnings, monthly rpt, S8895–1
see also Absenteeism
see also Earnings, general
see also Moonlighting
see also Overtime
see also Part-time employment

House of Representatives

Black Americans elected to House of Representatives, vote shares by district and State, Nov 1992, article, R5685–4.501
Campaign finances, with detailed data for individual Members, and leading contributors by type and industry, 1990 election and trends, biennial rpt, R3828–2
Campaign fund finances, with expenditures by detailed item and contributions by donor type, by candidate, district, and State, 1990 elections, C2500–6
Congressional organization, major legislative and budget actions, and agency and program appropriations, 102nd Congress, 2nd session, 1992, annual rpt, C2500–2
Election results for Federal offices and Governor, by State, county, major city, and party, with voter registration and turnout, 1992 and trends, biennial rpt, C2500–1
Public opinion on performance of Congress and own Representative, 1970-92 surveys, A0610–1.501
Racial/ethnic minority chairpersons of House committees, funds received from political action committees (PACs), 1992, article, C4215–1.510
Staff characteristics, salaries, and benefits by position, 1992 and trends, recurring rpt, R4140–1
Voting records of Senators and Representatives, by State and district, 1992, annual rpt, C2500–2
Voting results for 7 bills, for Members from districts with at least 15% black population, by State, 1993 article, R5685–4.503
Women elected to House of Representatives in Nov 1992, by marital status, own and children's ages, abortion views, and political party, 1992 article, C5800–7.504

Household appliances and equipment

Women in US House of Representatives and Senate, by party, 1917-95, annual rpt, U4510–1.61, U4510–1.69
see also Congressional apportionment

House trailers
see Mobile homes

Household appliances and equipment
Aluminum shipments by end-use market and product type, 1982-92, annual rpt, A0400–2.1
Automation home system desires of consumers, and outlook for installations in new and existing homes, 1992 articles, C1850–13.501
Automation home system installations in new homes, outlook by system type, 2000, article, C1850–8.503
Consumer attitudes on economic conditions and personal financial situation, monthly survey, U7475–2
Consumer buying power survey of population, income, and sales by product line, by State, metro area, county, and census div, 1993 annual rpt, C1200–1.514
Consumer expectations of economic conditions and change in income, and intended durable goods purchases by type, Conference Board monthly survey, R4105–4
Discount chain consumer natl brand preferences, by product category and chain, and by age group, 1993 survey, annual feature, C5150–3.521
Discount chain top-selling natl brands cited by managers, by product category, chain, and region, 1993 survey, annual feature, C5150–3.520
Electronics containing appliances share of shipments, for 9 appliance types, 1990 and 1995, article, C1850–2.503
Europe household appliance production, sales, and market shares, by country, product type, and manufacturer, 1991-92, annual feature, C2000–1.508
Europe household cleaning appliance shipments value, for 4 product types, 1987-91, article, C2000–1.505
Financial performance and growth rankings for approx 1,000 top corporations, with comparisons by industry group, 1993 annual rpt, C3950–1.505
Financial ratios and performance, for over 350 SIC 4-digit industries, FY88-92, annual rpt, A6400–3
Gas appliance shipments, by appliance type, 1971-91, annual rpt, A1775–3.7
Japan household appliance market penetration, production, and foreign trade, by appliance type, 1993 article, C2000–1.504
Life expectancy, shipments, and manufacturers market shares, for appliances by type, 1993 annual article, C2000–1.510
Manufacturing and market trends for home appliance industry, by product type, various years 1920-94, biennial rpt, A3350–3
Motors (small) shipments value, by motor type and market category, quarterly rpt, A8904–1
Operating and financial composite ratios for corporations, with establishments and receipts, for approx 200 industries, by asset size, FY90, annual rpt, C7800–1

Household appliances and equipment

Opinions of consumer hard goods manufacturers and representatives on business issues and outlook, by product line, 1992 annual survey rpt, A1800–1

Retail hardware sales and productivity measures for hardware stores, home centers, and lumber/building material outlets, 1991 and trends, annual rpt series, A8275–1

Retail sales by outlet type, and discount chain sales in major depts, by product category, 1992, annual feature, C8130–1.507

Sales and consumer expenditures, for food store products by type, 1991-92, annual feature, C4655–1.510

Sales by distributors of home appliances, by product type and State, 1992, annual rpt, A3350–2

Shipments (factory) of major home appliances, by type, 1992 and trends, annual rpt, A3350–4

Shipments of heating/cooling equipment, by product type, with industry review and outlook, 1992 and trends, annual rpt, C1800–1

Shipments of household appliances, by detailed product type, 1991-98, annual articles, C2000–1.503

Shipments of household appliances, by product type, with articles and special features on industry trends and devs, monthly rpt, C2000–1

Shipments of household equipment, by product type, 1983-92, annual feature, C2000–1.505

Shipments of major appliances and heating equipment, by type of energy consumed, quarterly rpt, A1775–1

Shipments of major appliances, by type of energy used, monthly rpt, A1775–2

Shipments of major home appliances, by type, monthly press release, A3350–1

Shopping center financial and operating data, with detail by type of tenant, US and Canada, 1991, triennial rpt, R9285–1

Turkey household appliance production, by type, for 7 manufacturers, 1993 feature, C2000–1.511

Washing machine home repair, minimum service charge in approx 300 cities, quarterly rpt, A0150–1

State and local:

Texas trade, transportation, and public utilities employment, by SIC 2- and 3-digit industry and detailed occupation, 2nd qtr 1991, triennial survey rpt, S7675–1.31

see also Air conditioning

see also Hardware

see also Home video and audio equipment

see also Household supplies and utensils

see also Plumbing and heating

see also Radio

see also Security devices

see also Smoke and fire detectors

see also Telephones and telephone industry

see also Television

see also Tools

see also Watches and clocks

Household assets

see Wealth

Household furnishings

see Furniture and furnishings

Household income

see Personal and household income

Household supplies and utensils

Cleaning product sales performance in auto aftermarket chains, 1993 annual feature, C0125–1.503

Discount chain consumer natl brand preferences, by product category and chain, and by age group, 1993 survey, annual feature, C5150–3.521

Discount chain top-selling natl brands cited by managers, by product category, chain, and region, 1993 survey, annual feature, C5150–3.520

Discount store sales and productivity data for 20 depts, 1993 annual feature, C5150–3.516

Drugstore chains financial performance and marketing operations, with sales by product type, 1993 annual feature, C5150–2.510

Drugstore chains top-selling products, and leading manufacturers, 1993 annual article, C5150–2.520

Drugstore light bulb sales distribution by bulb type, 1992, article, C5150–2.513

Financial ratios and performance, for over 350 SIC 4-digit industries, FY88-92, annual rpt, A6400–3

Military commissary sales, by region, product type, and individual store, FY92, annual feature, A2072–2.501

Packaging preferences of consumers for household chemicals, 1993 survey, article, C1850–1.507

Paper and paperboard shipments and consumption, by product grade and end use, 1993 annual rpt, C3975–5.3

Retail prices for selected consumer items in approx 300 cities, quarterly rpt, A0150–1

Retail sales by outlet type, and discount chain sales in major depts, by product category, 1992, annual feature, C8130–1.507

Sales and consumer expenditures, for food store products by type, 1991-92, annual feature, C4655 1.510

Sales volume shares by retail outlet type, for approx 300 food, drug, and other product categories, 1993 annual feature, C4655–1.504

Shipments of household appliances, by detailed product type, 1991-98, annual articles, C2000–1.503

Shopping center financial and operating data, with detail by type of tenant, US and Canada, 1991, triennial rpt, R9285–1

Silver supply-demand by country and end use, with prices, futures trading, and market analyses, 1993 and trends, annual rpt, A8902–4

Supermarket sales by detailed product type, 1992 and trends, annual feature, C5225–1.507

Supermarket sales of nonfood products, by detailed product type, 1992, annual feature, C5225–1.508

Tableware production, trade, and related industry data, 1993 annual almanac, C2150–7.509

see also Tools

Index by Subjects and Names

Households

see Families and households

Housewares

see Household appliances and equipment

see Household supplies and utensils

Housing

see Apartment houses

see Condominiums and cooperatives

see Discrimination in housing

see Emergency shelters

see Furniture and furnishings

see Group homes

see Group quarters

see Homesteads

see Household appliances and equipment

see Housing condition and occupancy

see Housing construction

see Housing costs and financing

see Housing energy use

see Housing maintenance and repair

see Housing sales

see Housing supply and requirements

see Housing tenure

see Living arrangements

see Low-income housing

see Military housing

see Mobile homes

see Mortgages

see Prefabricated buildings

see Public housing

see Real estate business

see Relocation

see Resort timesharing

see Retirement communities

see Rooming and boarding houses

see Second homes

see Student housing

see Transient housing

see Urban renewal

see Veterans housing

see Wrecking and demolition

Housing (FHA), HUD

Mobile/manufactured home FHA loans, monthly rpt, A6325–1

Mortgage (FHA-insured) originations, claim and nonclaim terminations, and interest rates, monthly FY78 and FY86, article, A6450–2.508

Mortgage delinquency and foreclosure rates, and residential loans serviced, by type, State, and census div and region, quarterly rpt, A6450–1

New public or assisted housing units added under 6 HUD programs, FY81 and FY87-93, A6800–2

State and local:

Hawaii data book, general data, 1992 annual rpt, S2090–1.21

Utah statistical abstract, general data, 1993 triennial rpt, U8960–1.11

Housing and Urban Development Department

see Department of Housing and Urban Development

Housing census

see Census of Population and Housing

Housing condition and occupancy

Apartment vacancies and turnover rate for conventionally financed buildings, for US and Canada, 1991 and trends, annual rpt, A5600–1

Apartment vacancies and turnover rate for federally subsidized buildings, by building and subsidy type, building age, metro area, and region, 1991 and trends, annual rpt, A5600–5

Index by Subjects and Names

Housing construction

Black American housing characteristics, by tenure, with comparisons to total population, 1985, annual compilation, C6775–2.8

Black children and youth population, economic, health, and education data, with comparisons to whites, 1993 rpt, R3840–21

Heating/cooling system characteristics of new housing units, by region, 1990-91, annual rpt, C1800–1

Hispanic American housing characteristics, by tenure, with comparisons to total population, 1985, annual compilation, C6775–3.6

Low-income housing supply-demand, costs, physical conditions, and public assistance, with data by race-ethnicity, for 44 metro areas, 1980s-91, R3834–16

Market conditions in US regions and selected MSAs, including construction, rental vacancies, and prices, by type of housing, quarterly rpt, B5190–1

Public housing authority income and expenses, resident and property characteristics, and unit vacancy and turnover rates, various years FY77-1992, A6800–2

Public housing authority operations and finances, including unit vacancy rates and need for modernization, by agency size and region, 1989, A6800–1

Size of rooms in typical house, 1986 and 1992, C4300–1.504

Statistical profiles of 50 States and DC, general data, 1993 annual almanac, C4712–1

Women's housing issues, including percent of single women living in housing built before 1950, by age and race-ethnicity, 1991, A8657–5

World population and health indicators, with detail by region and country, 1992/93 biennial rpt, R9455–1.5

State and local:

Alabama county data book, general data, 1992 annual rpt, S0121–2

Alabama municipal data book, general data, 1992 recurring rpt, S0121–5

Alabama statistical abstract, general data, 1992 recurring rpt, U5680–2.3

Arizona Indian population, education, housing, health, and employment characteristics, with detail by reservation, 1970s-91, recurring rpt, U5850–2.9

Arizona statistical abstract, general data, 1993 recurring rpt, U5850–2.16

Arkansas Census of Population and Housing detailed findings, 1990, U5935–7

California Census of Population and Housing detailed findings, 1990, S0840–9

California statistical abstract, general data, 1992 annual rpt, S0840–2.9

DC statistical profile, general data, 1992 annual rpt, S1535–3.4

Florida statistical abstract, general data, 1992 annual rpt, U6660–1.2

Georgia county guide, general data, 1993 annual rpt, U6750–1

Georgia statistical abstract, general data, 1992-93 biennial rpt, U6730–1.10

Hawaii data book, general data, 1992 annual rpt, S2090–1.21

Illinois statistical abstract, general data, 1992 annual rpt, U6910–2

Kansas statistical abstract, general data, 1991/92 annual rpt, U7095–2.3

Louisiana Census of Population and Housing summary findings, by local area, 1990 and trends, U8010–4

Maine Census of Population and Housing summary findings, by local area, 1990, S3465–7, S3465–8, S3465–9

Maryland statistical abstract, general data, 1993-94 biennial rpt, S3605–1.12

New Jersey Census of Population and Housing detailed findings, by county, 1990, S5425–19

New Jersey municipal and county data book, general data, 1992 annual rpt, C4712–4

New York State statistical yearbook, general data, 1992 annual rpt, U5100–1.9

Pennsylvania Census of Population and Housing detailed findings, with selected data by county and municipality, 1990, U4130–13

Pennsylvania housing data from Census of Population and Housing, by county and municipality, 1990, C1595–14

Pennsylvania statistical abstract, general data, 1992 recurring rpt, U4130–6.1

Rhode Island Census of Population and Housing detailed findings, by county and municipality, 1990, S6930–9

Rhode Island statistical almanac, general data, 1993 annual rpt, C7975–1.1

South Carolina statistical abstract, general data, 1993 annual rpt, S7125–1.11

Tennessee statistical abstract, general data, 1992/93 annual rpt, U8710–2.6

Utah statistical abstract, general data, 1993 triennial rpt, U8960–1.11

Washington State population and demographic characteristics, and housing units, by county and/or city, 1992 and trends, annual rpt, S8345–4

see also Abandoned buildings
see also Families and households
see also Furniture and furnishings
see also Household appliances and equipment
see also Housing energy use
see also Housing maintenance and repair
see also Housing supply and requirements
see also Housing tenure
see also Landlord-tenant relations
see also Plumbing and heating
see also Rent
see also Rent supplements
see also Second homes
see also Student housing
see also Transient housing

Housing construction

Appliance installations by builders of new housing, by product type, 1990, biennial rpt, A3350–3

Business economists forecasts of auto sales, business fixed investment, and housing starts, 1993-94, article, A6650–5.502

Buyers guide for homebuilders, including data on material types or brands used most frequently, by product category, 1993 annual feature, C4300–1.506

Carpet/rug industry shipments vs housing starts, 1970-91, annual rpt, A3800–1

Construction and market devs for housing, monthly rpt, C4300–1

Construction industry activities, including data on costs, materials prices, wages, financing, and contract awards, weekly rpt, C5800–2

Consumer complaint and inquiry activity of Better Business Burs, by detailed type of business, 1992, annual rpt, A4350–1

Contract value, by construction type and region, including floor area and number of residential units, 1992-93, annual rpt, C5800–15.501, C5800–15.504, C5800–15.507, C5800–26

Contract value, by construction type and region, including floor area and number of residential units, 1992-93, periodic update, C5800–29

Contracts awarded, and housing starts, by month, commodity yearbook for 1993, C2400–1

Contracts awarded, and housing starts, by month, commodity yearbook Jan-Sept 1993 updates, C2400–2

Eastern Europe housing starts, with detail for 4 countries, 1992-2000, article, C4300–1.504

Economic indicator historical trends, 1900s-92, annual rpt, R9050–1.2

Economic outlook for selected indicators, recent trends and 2-year forecast, quarterly rpt, A3840–6

Financial performance and growth rankings for approx 1,000 top corporations, with comparisons by industry group, 1993 annual rpt, C3950–1.505

Financial ratios and performance, for over 350 SIC 4-digit industries, FY88-92, annual rpt, A6400–3

Forecasts and trends for housing market, including starts, sales, and prices, 1989-94, annual article, A6450–2.503

Forecasts for real estate industry and US economy, and housing starts and sales trends by region, monthly rpt, A7000–1

Forecasts of economic indicators for approx 10-13 months, monthly rpt, U1880–3

Forecasts of natl income and product account components and related indicators, quarterly rpt, U1880–1

Forecasts of natl income and product account components, employment, and financial sector activity, monthly rpt, B4950–1

Foreign economic indexes, and leading and coincident indicators for US and other industrial countries, monthly rpt, U1245–1

Homebuilder executive compensation, incentives, and benefits, by position, 1992, annual survey article, C1850–8.508

Homebuilder financial and operating data, including detail by location, for top 400 builders, 1993 annual feature, C1850–8.507

Homebuilder operations and industry devs, including housing construction and market indicators, semimonthly rpt, C1850–8

Homebuilder production, revenues, and closings, for top 100 companies, 1992, annual feature, C4300–1.507

Japan economic profile, including govt finances, industrial production, foreign trade and investments, and comparisons to US, 1988-92, annual feature, R5650–2.552

Lumber industry production and trade, with construction activity and mobile home shipments, monthly rpt, A1630–1

Lumber industry softwood consumption by type of demand and supply region, and housing starts, 1984-92, annual rpt, A9395–1

Housing construction

Market conditions in US regions and selected MSAs, including construction, rental vacancies, and prices, by type of housing, quarterly rpt, B5190–1

Mortgage banking trends and devs, with data on construction, home sales, and lending activity, by type of unit and instn, monthly rpt, A6450–2

Starts and completions, new housing, quarterly rpt, A1775–1

Starts by region and leading metro area, with forecasts of industry analysts, 1993 annual article, C4300–1.503

Starts of privately owned housing units, by structure type and region, monthly rpt, A7000–2

Starts of single- and multi-family housing, 1981-93, article, C5150–6.507

Starts of single- and multi-family housing, 1987-94, annual article, C1850–8.502

Statistical profiles of 50 States and DC, general data, 1993 annual almanac, C4712–1

State and local:

Alabama statistical abstract, general data, 1992 recurring rpt, U5680–2.3

Arizona statistical abstract, general data, 1993 recurring rpt, U5850–2.15

Arkansas business and economic activity indicators, quarterly rpt, U5930–1

California economic condition, including population, employment and earnings, income, business activity, and taxation, 1993 annual rpt, S0840–3

California economic indicators, bimonthly rpt, S0840–1

California statistical abstract, general data, 1992 annual rpt, S0840–2.9

Connecticut construction activity and value, by type of structure and location, 1992 and trends, annual rpt, S1212–1

DC statistical profile, general data, 1992 annual rpt, S1535–3.4

Delaware housing construction activity, with data on demolitions and mobile home sales, by locality, 1992 and trends, annual rpt, S1387–1

Georgia statistical abstract, general data, 1992-93 biennial rpt, U6730–1.10

Hawaii data book, general data, 1992 annual rpt, S2090–1.21

Hawaii economic conditions, including employment, population, tourism, and construction, quarterly rpt, S2090–2

Idaho and US economic trends and forecasts, quarterly rpt, S2245–2

Idaho construction activity and value, by city and county, monthly rpt, B3900–1

Kansas statistical abstract, general data, 1991/92 annual rpt, U7095–2.3

Kentucky economic statistics, general data, 1993 annual rpt, S3104–1.1

Mississippi statistical abstract, general data, 1992 annual rpt, U3255–4.14

Nevada business and economic activity indicators, with comparisons to other Western States, 1980-91, annual rpt, U7920–2

New Jersey residential construction activity and costs, by location, 1991 and trends, annual rpt, S5425–3

New York State statistical yearbook, general data, 1992 annual rpt, U5100–1.9

Pennsylvania business activity indicators, monthly rpt, U4110–1

South Carolina statistical abstract, general data, 1993 annual rpt, S7125–1.11

South Dakota business activity review, including selected data by city and industry, quarterly rpt, U8595–1

Tennessee statistical abstract, general data, 1992/93 annual rpt, U8710–2.6

Utah economic and business activity review and indicators, monthly rpt, U8960–2

Utah statistical abstract, general data, 1993 triennial rpt, U8960–1.11

Wisconsin housing units authorized, 1982-91, annual rpt, S8675–3

see also Building materials

see also Building permits

see also Economic indicators

see also Energy conservation

see also Federal aid to housing

see also Housing condition and occupancy

see also Housing costs and financing

see also Housing energy use

see also Housing maintenance and repair

see also Housing supply and requirements

see also Housing tenure

see also Low-income housing

see also Mortgages

see also Prefabricated buildings

see also Property value

see also Public housing

see also Second homes

see also State funding for housing

see also Wrecking and demolition

Housing costs and financing

Black American housing characteristics, and housing affordability indicators, with comparisons to total population, 1993 annual compilation, C6775–2.8

Construction (residential) cost increases, for top 11 States, 1992 vs 1991, C4300–1.511

Corporate employee transfers, and relocation policies, assistance, and costs, 1992, annual survey, B0600–1

Cost indexes for construction, labor and materials, approx 20 cities, weekly rpt, C5800–2

Cost-of-living indexes and retail prices for selected consumer items in approx 300 cities, quarterly rpt, A0150–1

Forecasts and trends for housing market, including starts, sales, and prices, 1989-94, annual article, A6450–2.503

Forecasts and trends for housing prices, and mortgage foreclosure rate projections, for 43 metro areas or regions in rank order, 1993 article, A6450–2.509

Forecasts for real estate industry and US economy, and housing starts and sales trends by region, monthly rpt, A7000–1

Forecasts of natl income and product account components, employment, and financial sector activity, monthly rpt, B4950–1

Govt regulations and required fees impact on new home prices and households eligible to purchase homes, for 2 local areas, 1993 article, C4300–1.510

Hispanic American housing characteristics, by tenure, with comparisons to total population, 1985, annual compilation, C6775–3.6

Home buyer (1st-time and repeat) profile, and transaction characteristics, including prices and financing, by region and for 18 metro areas, 1990-92, annual survey rpt, B2150–1

Homebuilder operations and industry devs, including housing construction and market indicators, semimonthly rpt, C1850–8

Homebuilder sources for acquisition, dev, and construction loans, by region and company size, 1992 survey, article, C4300–1.501

Land acquisition, dev, and construction loan-to-value ratios, 1989 and 1992, article, C4300–1.501

Low-income housing supply-demand, costs, physical conditions, and public assistance, with data by race-ethnicity, for 44 metro areas, 1980s-91, R3834–16

Maintenance/operating cost per $100,000 of home value, by date of construction, 1993 feature, C4300–1.512

Market conditions in US and selected MSAs, including existing home sales and prices, quarterly rpt, B5190–1

Mobile/manufactured home average sales prices, by census div and State, 1980-92, A6325–1

Owner and renter views on outlook for housing prices, 1991 survey, article, A7000–1.501

Price and cost components of median-priced new house, selected years 1949-92, article, C4300–1.508

Price averages and sales for new homes, by region, 1987-91, annual rpt, S7125–1.11

Price trends for housing in 14 cities, 1st qtr 1993 vs 1992, article, B8500–2.516

Price variations for housing resulting from selected neighborhood and structural characteristics, 1991, article, C4300–1.512

Prices for typical high-income homes in 29 metro areas, 1992, article, B8500–2.518

Public housing authority operations and finances, including resident characteristics, by agency size, 1989, A6800–1

Public opinion on housing market conditions, 1992-93 surveys, article, C5800–7.529

Public opinion on trend in home value, 1990-92 surveys, article, U7475–2.501

Public opinion on trend in home value, 1990-93 surveys, article, U7475–2.504, U7475–2.505

Sales prices of new homes, by region, 1970-92, annual rpt, S7125–3.1

Single-family and condominium/cooperative housing sales, with price and affordability data, by region, State, and metro area, monthly rpt, A7000–2

State economic dev condition indicators, including economic performance, business vitality, growth capacity, and tax/fiscal system, by State, 1993 annual rpt, R4225–1.1

State and local:

Arizona business activity indicators, including housing market, population, CPI, and industrial purchasing, monthly rpt, U0280–1

Arizona statistical abstract, general data, 1993 recurring rpt, U5850–2.16

Arkansas Census of Population and Housing detailed findings, 1990, U5935–7

California Census of Population and Housing detailed findings, 1990, S0840–9

California housing median prices by State region, 1992, annual rpt, S0840–3.1

Index by Subjects and Names

Housing energy use

California median price for existing single-family homes, bimonthly rpt, S0840–1

Connecticut construction activity and value, by type of structure and location, 1992 and trends, annual rpt, S1212–1

DC statistical profile, general data, 1992 annual rpt, S1535–3.4

Delaware data book, general data, 1993 annual rpt, S1375–4

Florida county data book, 1992/93 annual rpt, C6360–1

Hawaii counties population and economic indicators, 1993 annual rpt series, B3500–2

Hawaii data book, general data, 1992 annual rpt, S2090–1.21

Hawaii economic indicators, bimonthly rpt, B3500–1

Hawaii, Oahu multiple listing service listings and sales, with selling prices, by type of property, quarterly rpt, S2090–2

Illinois statistical abstract, general data, 1992 annual rpt, U6910–2

Iowa median home value and monthly house payment, 1990, annual rpt, S2784–3

Louisiana Census of Population and Housing summary findings, by local area, 1990 and trends, U8010–4

Maine Census of Population and Housing summary findings, by local area, 1990, S3465–9

New Jersey Census of Population and Housing detailed findings, by county, 1990, S5425–19

New Jersey residential construction activity and costs, by location, 1991 and trends, annual rpt, S5425–3

New York State statistical yearbook, general data, 1992 annual rpt, U5100–1.9

Pennsylvania Census of Population and Housing detailed findings, with selected data by county and municipality, 1990, U4130–13

Pennsylvania statistical abstract, general data, 1992 recurring rpt, U4130–6.1

Rhode Island Census of Population and Housing detailed findings, by county and municipality, 1990, S6930–9

South Carolina statistical abstract, general data, 1993 annual rpt, S7125–1.11

Tennessee statistical abstract, general data, 1992/93 annual rpt, U8710–2.6

see also Economic indicators

see also Federal aid to housing

see also Housing (FHA), HUD

see also Housing sales

see also Mortgages

see also Property value

see also Rent

see also State funding for housing

Housing energy conservation

see Energy conservation

Housing energy use

Apartment building (conventionally financed) detailed income and expense ratios for US and Canada, by building type, metro area, and US region, 1991 and trends, annual rpt, A5600–1

Apartment building (federally subsidized) detailed income and expense ratios, by building and subsidy type, building age, metro area, and region, 1991 and trends, annual rpt, A5600–5

Apartment complex mgmt income and expenses, and vacancy and turnover rates, by region and metro area, 1992, annual survey rpt, A6497–1

Black American housing characteristics, including utility costs, by tenure, 1985, annual compilation, C6775–2.8

Condominium, cooperative, and planned unit dev detailed expenses, for US and Canada, by building characteristics, metro area, and US region, 1991, annual rpt, A5600–3

Consumption of electricity and natural gas, by State, 1991/92 annual rpt, A7015–3

Consumption of energy by type of home appliance, 1991 and trends, biennial rpt, A3350–3

Consumption per capita, by energy source, and fuel used for heating and cooking, 1960s-91, annual rpt, A1775–3

Electric utility (private vs public) revenues and consumption, by customer sector, 1990, annual article, A2625–1.501

Electric utility customers, sales, and revenues, by user sector, bimonthly rpt quarterly table, A4700–4

Electric utility finances, sales, and capacity, 1993 annual feature, C5800–28.507

Electric utility financial and operating data, by State and census div, 1991 and trends, annual rpt, A4700–1

Electric utility financial and operating performance rankings, top 100 utilities, 1992, annual article, C6985–6.508

Energy consumption by fuel type and sector, 1970s-2010, annual rpt, C6985–5

Fuel oil dealer operations, with heating and cooling equipment services, by region, 1992 annual survey, C4680–2

Hispanic American housing characteristics, including utility costs, by tenure, 1985, annual compilation, C6775–3.6

Japan energy supply-demand and outlook, by fuel source, 1980s-2000, recurring article, R5650–2.536

Natural gas demand, by consuming sector, 1992, 2000, and 2005, article, C6985–1.527

Natural gas industry composite income statement, with sales and prices by consuming sector and census div, quarterly rpt, A1775–1

Natural gas industry detailed operating and financial data, by State and census div, 1960s-91, annual rpt, A1775–3

Natural gas residential prices, 1973-92, annual rpt, A5425–2.2

Natural gas sales and prices, by consuming sector, monthly rpt, A1775–2

Oil supply-demand, marketing, prices, finances, and employment, detailed data for US and Canada, by product, company, and location, 1993 annual fact book, C4680–1.507

Sourcebook of oil and gas industry operations and finances, and world supply-demand situation, 1970s-91, annual compilation, C6985–9

Statistical profiles of 50 States and DC, general data, 1993 annual almanac, C4712–1

Supply-demand by energy source and consuming sector, 1947-2010, periodic basic data book, A2575–14.1

World energy supply-demand, by fuel source and sector, by region and country, 1992/93 biennial rpt, R9455–1.7

State and local:

Alabama statistical abstract, general data, 1992 recurring rpt, U5680–2.12

Alaska electric utility sales, by company and consuming sector, 1991, annual rpt, S0280–4.2

Arizona statistical abstract, general data, 1993 recurring rpt, U5850–2.20

Arkansas public utility financial, operating, and regulatory data, by utility type and company, 1992 annual rpt, S0757–1

Florida electric power and gas average residential consumption, by utility, 1992, annual rpt, S1790–1

Florida statistical abstract, general data, 1992 annual rpt, U6660–1.15

Georgia statistical abstract, general data, 1992-93 biennial rpt, U6730–1.8

Hawaii data book, general data, 1992 annual rpt, S2090–1.17

Idaho average residential electric and gas bill, by utility, FY92 and trends, annual rpt, S2290–1

Illinois electric and gas utility sales and operating revenues, and customers served, by class of service and company, 1991-92, annual rpt series, S2410–1

Maryland statistical abstract, general data, 1993-94 biennial rpt, S3605–1.10

Mississippi statistical abstract, general data, 1992 annual rpt, U3255–4.14

Nevada statistical abstract, general data, 1992 biennial rpt, S5005–1.11

New Mexico public utility operating, financial, and regulatory data, by utility type, FY92 annual rpt, S5645–1

New York State electric and gas customers, revenues, sales, and average bill, by customer class, 1988-92, annual rpt, S5795–1

New York State statistical yearbook, general data, 1992 annual rpt, U5100–1.9, U5100–1.12

North Carolina public utility financial, operating, and regulatory data, by utility type and company, 1990 and trends, annual rpt, S5917–2

Ohio natural gas and electricity supply-demand by utility and consuming sector, 1992-93 and trends, annual rpt, S6355–1

Oklahoma statistical abstract, general data, 1992 annual rpt, U8130–2.18

Pennsylvania energy supply-demand and prices by fuel type, with electric power info by utility, 1960s-90, recurring rpt, S6810–3

Pennsylvania statistical abstract, general data, 1992 recurring rpt, U4130–6.1, U4130–6.9

South Carolina economic condition, including energy and transportation data, 1970s-92, annual rpt, S7125–3.3

South Carolina public service commission regulatory activities, with financial and operating data for individual utilities and railroads, FY92 annual rpt, S7235–1

Tennessee economic indicator trends and forecasts, with data by industry div and manufacturing group, 1982-2001, annual rpt, S7560–1

Housing energy use

Tennessee statistical abstract, general data, 1992/93 annual rpt, U8710–2.10

Texas electric utility financial and operating data, 9 largest investor-owned utilities, 1988-92, annual rpt, S7740–1

Texas natural gas utility financial and operating data, by city and company, 1991, with regulatory info, annual rpt, S7745–1

Utah statistical abstract, general data, 1993 triennial rpt, U8960–1.13

Vermont public utility financial and operating data, by company, 1986-91, biennial rpt, S8100–1

Washington State electric utility customers, sales, and revenues, by customer class and utility, 1982-91, annual rpt, S8450–1.2

Washington State natural gas utilities customers and sales, by consuming sector, by utility, 1982-91, annual rpt, S8450–1.3

Wisconsin Blue Book, general data, 1993-94 biennial rpt, S8780–1.2

Wisconsin oil use, by consuming sector, 1981-90, annual rpt, S8675–3

see also Energy conservation

see also Low-income energy assistance

see also Fuel oil, Electric power, and Natural gas and gas industry (for supply, demand, and price data)

Housing inventory

see Housing supply and requirements

Housing maintenance and repair

Apartment complex mgmt income and expenses, and vacancy and turnover rates, by region and metro area, 1992, annual survey rpt, A6497–1

Consumer complaint and inquiry activity of Better Business Burs, by detailed type of business, 1992, annual rpt, A4350–1

Consumer home remodeling plans as affected by economic recession, 1992 survey, article, C1850–8.505

Deficiencies in homes being resold, with percent of resales affected and cost of repair, 1992 feature, C4300–1.501

Expenditures for remodeling projects by type, 1989-94, annual article, C1850–8.502

Expenditures for remodeling projects by type, 1989-94, article, C1850–8.507

Expenditures for residential improvements and maintenance, 1992-2000, annual article, C4300–1.503

Homebuilder financial and operating data, including detail by location, for top 400 builders, 1993 annual feature, C1850–8.507

Kitchen and bathroom remodeling activity of consumers, and use of home improvement store services, Apr 1993 survey, article, C5150–6.504

Loan delinquency rates for approx 10 types of consumer bank loans, and repossession data, by State, quarterly rpt, A0950–1

Public housing authority operations and finances, including resident characteristics, by agency size, 1989, A6800–1

Remodeling activities of builders, including average age of home and most popular projects, 1991 and 1993, article, C1850–8.510

Remodeling company computer use, including types of software used, by revenue size, 1992 survey, article, C1850–8.501

Remodeling project cost compared to resale value, for 11 types of projects, 1993 article, C4215–1.512

State and local:

Alabama statistical abstract, general data, 1992 recurring rpt, U5680–2.3

Connecticut construction activity and value, by type of structure and location, 1992 and trends, annual rpt, S1212–1

Delaware rehabilitated housing units and costs, by county and city, 1991-92, annual rpt, S1387–1

New Jersey residential construction activity and costs, by location, 1991 and trends, annual rpt, S5425–3

see also Energy conservation

see also Home improvement stores

Housing prices

see Housing costs and financing

Housing rehabilitation

see Housing maintenance and repair

see Urban renewal

Housing sales

Consumer attitudes on economic conditions and personal financial situation, monthly survey, U7475–2

Consumer expectations of economic conditions and change in income, and intended durable goods purchases by type, Conference Board monthly survey, R4105–4

Consumer views on current housing market positive aspects, 1993 survey article, C4300–1.509

First-time home buyer share of housing sales, by region, 1992, C4300–1.510

Forecasts and trends for housing market, including starts, sales, and prices, 1989-94, annual article, A6450–2.503

Forecasts for housing starts and sales, and mortgage interest rates, 4th qtr 1992-4th qtr 1994, article, C4300–1.508

Forecasts for real estate industry and US economy, and housing starts and sales trends by region, monthly rpt, A7000–1

Homebuilder financial and operating data, including detail by location, for top 400 builders, 1993 annual feature, C1850–8.507

Homebuilder operations and industry devs, including housing construction and market indicators, semimonthly rpt, C1850–8

Market conditions in US, States, and selected MSAs, including housing and condominium/cooperative sales, quarterly rpt, B5190–1

Mortgage banking trends and devs, with data on construction, home sales, and lending activity, by type of unit and instn, monthly rpt, A6450–2

New vs existing home shares of housing sales, by region, 1992, C4300–1.507

Sales of new and existing homes, 1979-93, C4300–1.504

Single-family and condominium/cooperative housing sales, with price and affordability data, by region, State, and metro area, monthly rpt, A7000–2

Statistical profiles of 50 States and DC, general data, 1993 annual almanac, C4712–1

State and local:

Arizona business activity indicators, including housing market, population, CPI, and industrial purchasing, monthly rpt, U0280–1

California new home shopper purchase motivations and design features sought, 1992-93 surveys, article, C1850–8.509

DC statistical profile, general data, 1992 annual rpt, S1535–3.4

Delaware housing construction activity, with data on demolitions and mobile home sales, by locality, 1992 and trends, annual rpt, S1387–1

Hawaii data book, general data, 1992 annual rpt, S2090–1.21

Hawaii economic indicators, bimonthly rpt, B3500–1

New York State statistical yearbook, general data, 1992 annual rpt, U5100–1.9

Pennsylvania existing home sales, monthly rpt quarterly table, U4110–1.502, U4110–1.504, U4110–1.506

Tennessee statistical abstract, general data, 1992/93 annual rpt, U8710–2.6

see also Economic indicators

Housing starts

see Housing construction

Housing stock

see Housing supply and requirements

Housing supply and requirements

Market conditions in US regions and selected MSAs, including construction, rental vacancies, and prices, by type of housing, quarterly rpt, B5190–1

Mobile/manufactured home shipments compared to housing starts and sales, monthly rpt, A6325–1

State social, economic, and govtl indicators, with rankings, 1993 semiannual rpt, B8500–1.2

Statistical profiles of 50 States and DC, general data, 1993 annual almanac, C4712–1

State and local:

Alabama statistical abstract, general data, 1992 recurring rpt, U5680–2.3

Alaska population, housing, income, and education data, by demographic characteristics and/or locality, 1990/91 and trends, annual rpt, S0320–4

Arizona Indian population, education, housing, health, and employment characteristics, with detail by reservation, 1970s-91, recurring rpt, U5850–2.9

Arizona statistical abstract, general data, 1993 recurring rpt, U5850–2.16

Arkansas Census of Population and Housing detailed findings, 1990, U5935–7

California Census of Population and Housing detailed findings, 1990, S0840–9

California socioeconomic and govtl data for municipalities, counties, and school districts, 1993 annual rpt, C4712–3

California statistical abstract, general data, 1992 annual rpt, S0840–2.9

Connecticut housing units, by type and location, 1992 and trends, annual rpt, S1212–1

DC statistical profile, general data, 1992 annual rpt, S1535–3.4

Florida county data book, 1992/93 annual rpt, C6360–1

Florida statistical abstract, general data, 1992 annual rpt, U6660–1.2

Georgia county guide, general data, 1993 annual rpt, U6750–1

Georgia statistical abstract, general data, 1992-93 biennial rpt, U6730–1.1, U6730–1.10

Hawaii data book, general data, 1992 annual rpt, S2090–1.1, S2090–1.6, S2090–1.21

Idaho and US economic trends and forecasts, quarterly rpt, S2245–2

Illinois statistical abstract, general data, 1992 annual rpt, U6910–2

Kansas statistical abstract, general data, 1991/92 annual rpt, U7095–2.3

Louisiana Census of Population and Housing summary findings, by local area, 1990 and trends, U8010–4

Maine Census of Population and Housing summary findings, by local area, 1990, S3465–7, S3465–8, S3465–9

Maryland statistical abstract, general data, 1993-94 biennial rpt, S3605–1.12

Massachusetts municipal and county profiles, general data, 1992 annual rpt, C4712–2

New Jersey Census of Population and Housing detailed findings, by county, 1990, S5425–19

New Jersey municipal and county data book, general data, 1992 annual rpt, C4712–4

New York State municipal and county statistical profiles, general data, 1993 annual rpt, C4712–7

New York State statistical yearbook, general data, 1992 annual rpt, U5100–1.9

Pennsylvania Census of Population and Housing detailed findings, with selected data by county and municipality, 1990, U4130–13

Pennsylvania housing data from Census of Population and Housing, by county and municipality, 1990, C1595–14

Pennsylvania statistical abstract, general data, 1992 recurring rpt, U4130–6.1

Rhode Island Census of Population and Housing detailed findings, by county and municipality, 1990, S6930–9

Rhode Island statistical almanac, general data, 1993 annual rpt, C7975–1.1

South Carolina statistical abstract, general data, 1993 annual rpt, S7125–1.11

Tennessee statistical abstract, general data, 1992/93 annual rpt, U8710–2.6

Utah statistical abstract, general data, 1993 triennial rpt, U8960–1.11

Washington State population and demographic characteristics, and housing units, by county and/or city, 1992 and trends, annual rpt, S8345–4

see also Building permits

see also Housing construction

see also Housing costs and financing

see also Housing sales

see also Urban renewal

see also Wrecking and demolition

Housing tenure

Black American housing characteristics, by tenure, with comparisons to total population, 1985, annual compilation, C6775–2.8

Black American population and demographic characteristics, with comparisons to whites, 1970s-2080, annual compilation, C6775–2.1

Black children and youth population, economic, health, and education data, with comparisons to whites, 1993 rpt, R3840–21

Hispanic American housing characteristics, by tenure, with comparisons to total population, 1985, annual compilation, C6775–3.6

Hispanic American population and demographic characteristics, with comparisons to whites, 1993 annual compilation, C6775–3.1

Home ownership attitudes and outlook of owners and renters, 1991 survey, article, A7000–1.501

Home ownership rates in 10 metro areas with highest and lowest rates, 1992, C4300–1.510

Home rental rates by householder age, 1982-92, article, A7000–1.503

Households by housing tenure status, region, and age of household head, quarterly rpt, B5190–1

Immigrant households, income, and home ownership rates by origin and length of US residence, and 15 cities with most new immigrants, 1993 article, C4300–1.512

Insurance coverage against property loss, by household tenure, 1984, 1986, and 1989, annual rpt, A5650–1.1

Low-income housing supply-demand, costs, physical conditions, and public assistance, with data by race-ethnicity, for 44 metro areas, 1980s-91, R3834–16

Market area population and characteristics, households, income, and retail outlets, for 21 leading areas, 1993 feature, C2710–1.538

Public housing authority operations and finances, including home ownership programs and housing sales, by agency size, 1989, A6800–1

Public opinion on willingness to make selected sacrifices in order to own a home, 1992 survey feature, C4300–1.502

Renter households with heads age 25-34, with percent qualifying for home mortgages at selected rates, 1993 article, C4300–1.510

Women's housing issues, with data on household composition, tenure, and characteristics, 1992, A8657–5

State and local:

Alabama municipal data book, general data, 1992 recurring rpt, S0121–5

Alabama statistical abstract, general data, 1992 recurring rpt, U5680–2.3

Arizona Indian population, education, housing, health, and employment characteristics, with detail by reservation, 1970s-91, recurring rpt, U5850–2.9

Arizona statistical abstract, general data, 1993 recurring rpt, U5850–2.16

Arkansas Census of Population and Housing detailed findings, 1990, U5935–7

California Census of Population and Housing detailed findings, 1990, S0840–9

California socioeconomic and govtl data for municipalities, counties, and school districts, 1993 annual rpt, C4712–3

California statistical abstract, general data, 1992 annual rpt, S0840–2.9

DC statistical profile, general data, 1992 annual rpt, S1535–3.1, S1535–3.4

Florida county data book, 1992/93 annual rpt, C6360–1

Florida statistical abstract, general data, 1992 annual rpt, U6660–1.2

Georgia county guide, general data, 1993 annual rpt, U6750–1

Hawaii data book, general data, 1992 annual rpt, S2090–1.21

Illinois statistical abstract, general data, 1992 annual rpt, U6910–2

Louisiana Census of Population and Housing summary findings, by local area, 1990 and trends, U8010–4

Maine Census of Population and Housing summary findings, by local area, 1990, S3465–7, S3465–8

Maryland statistical abstract, general data, 1993-94 biennial rpt, S3605–1.12

Massachusetts municipal and county profiles, general data, 1992 annual rpt, C4712–2

New Jersey Census of Population and Housing detailed findings, by county, 1990, S5425–19

New York State statistical yearbook, general data, 1992 annual rpt, U5100–1.9

Pennsylvania Census of Population and Housing detailed findings, with selected data by county and municipality, 1990, U4130–13

Pennsylvania statistical abstract, general data, 1992 recurring rpt, U4130–6.1

Rhode Island statistical almanac, general data, 1993 annual rpt, C7975–1.1

South Carolina household income by tenure status, by county, 1979, annual planning rpt, S7155–3.3

South Carolina statistical abstract, general data, 1993 annual rpt, S7125–1.11

Tennessee statistical abstract, general data, 1992/93 annual rpt, U8710–2.6

Utah statistical abstract, general data, 1993 triennial rpt, U8960–1.11

Vermont tax rebates to homeowners and renters, by household income class and county, 1991, annual rpt, S8125–1.2

see also Apartment houses

see also Condominiums and cooperatives

see also Housing sales

see also Rent

see also Resort timesharing

Howell, James T.

"Cotton Counts Its Customers: The Quantity of Cotton Consumed in Final Uses in the U.S., Revised 1990-91 and Preliminary 1992", A7485–1

HUD

see Department of Housing and Urban Development

Human immunodeficiency virus

see Acquired immune deficiency syndrome

Human resources management

see Personnel management

Human Resources Services Inc.

Health care professionals dissatisfaction with selected aspects of their jobs, 1992 survey, article, A1865–1.511

Human rights

see Civil rights

Human services

see Public welfare programs

see Social services

Humanities

see Arts and the humanities

see Federal aid to arts and humanities

see State funding for arts and culture

Hungary

Economic indicators of interest to foreign investors, 1993 article, C4687–1.508

Electronics industry trade and/or production trends by product category for 33 countries, with general economic profiles, 1993 annual rpt, A4725–1.4

Hungary

Energy intl sourcebook, with detail on oil and gas industry operations, supply-demand, and prices, for approx 80 countries, 1970s-91, annual compilation, C6985–10.2

Entertainment industry devs, including film production, theater screens, TV homes, and VCR penetration, 1993 feature, C9380–1.536

Motor vehicle world production, sales, trade, and registrations, by country, world area, manufacturer, and make, 1991 and trends, annual rpt, A0865–2.1

Nuclear reactors in operation, with capacity, electricity generation, and construction, by unit and country, 1992, annual rpt, B6800–2.2

Public opinion in 9 European countries and 3 Soviet Union Republics on political, economic, and social issues, 1991 survey, C8915–8

Public opinion on role of church, in Western Europe, Hungary, and Poland, 1990 surveys, R8780–1.502

Hunger

see Food assistance

see Food supply

see Nutrition and malnutrition

Hunting and fishing licenses

License revenues and holders, for top 20 States, FY89, recurring rpt, R9375–6

State social, economic, and govtl indicators, with rankings, 1993 semiannual rpt, B8500–1.12

State and local:

Arizona statistical abstract, general data, 1993 recurring rpt, U5850–2.8

California statistical abstract, general data, 1992 annual rpt, S0840–2.7

Hawaii data book, general data, 1992 annual rpt, S2090–1.7

Idaho economic profile, general data, 1992 recurring rpt, S2218–2.10

Maryland statistical abstract, general data, 1993-94 biennial rpt, S3605–1.3

Nevada statistical abstract, general data, 1992 biennial rpt, S5005–1.9

New York State statistical yearbook, general data, 1992 annual rpt, U5100–1.15

Oregon commercial fishing licensing activity, 1991, annual rpt, S6575–1

Oregon fish/game violations and arrests, 1992 and trends, annual rpt, S6603–3

Pennsylvania statistical abstract, general data, 1992 recurring rpt, U4130–6.8

South Carolina statistical abstract, general data, 1993 annual rpt, S7125–1.14

Utah statistical abstract, general data, 1993 triennial rpt, U8960–1.17

Wisconsin Blue Book, general data, 1993-94 biennial rpt, S8780–1.2

Hunting and trapping

Participation in 53 sports, by demographic characteristics, State, and census div, 1992, annual rpt series, A8485–3

State and local:

Colorado State referendum on limiting hunting of black bears, election results by county, 1992, biennial rpt, S1090–1

Florida statistical abstract, general data, 1992 annual rpt, U6660–1.10

Hawaii data book, general data, 1992 annual rpt, S2090–1.7

Illinois statistical abstract, general data, 1992 annual rpt, U6910–2

Nevada statistical abstract, general data, 1992 biennial rpt, S5005–1.9

New York State statistical yearbook, general data, 1992 annual rpt, U5100–1.15

Utah statistical abstract, general data, 1993 triennial rpt, U8960–1.17

Wisconsin Blue Book, general data, 1993-94 biennial rpt, S8780–1.2

see also Hunting and fishing licenses

Hurricanes

see Storms

Hutchison, Anthony M.

"State Budget Actions, 1992", A7470–4.10

Hydroelectric power

Capacity additions, and equipment orders and shipments, with data by location and facility, 1991 annual rpt, A4700–2

Consumption of fossil energy resources and electricity from hydro and nuclear power, 1960s-91, annual rpt, A1775–3.6

Electric power plants planned and under construction in 1993, by type, utility, and region, and forecast capacity for 1993-2001, annual feature, C5800–28.503

Finances, sales, and capacity of electric utilities, with data by sector and region, 1993 annual feature, C5800–28.507

Generating capacity developed and undeveloped, for hydroelectric power, by region, 1993 article, C6985–6.507

Interstate compacts affecting hydroelectric power dev, by river, 1991/92 annual rpt, A7015–3

Intl energy sourcebook, with detail on oil and gas industry operations, supply-demand, and prices, for approx 80 countries, 1970s-91, annual compilation, C6985–10

Japan energy supply-demand and outlook, by fuel source, 1980s-2000, recurring article, R5650–2.536

Latin America statistical abstract, general data by country, 1992 annual rpt, U6250–1.23

Operating data for top 100 electric utilities, including generating capacity by fuel source, 1992, annual article, C6985–6.512

Production by type of fuel, by State and census div, monthly rpt, A7400–8

Sourcebook of oil and gas industry, with supply-demand comparisons to other energy types, 1991 and trends, annual compilation, C6985–9.5

Statistical profiles of 50 States and DC, general data, 1993 annual almanac, C4712–1

Statistical yearbook of electric utility financial and operating data, by State and census div, 1991 and trends, annual rpt, A4700–1

Supply-demand, and utility capacity and fuel requirements, detailed data by US and Canadian region, 1992-2002, annual rpt, A8630–2

Supply-demand by energy source and consuming sector, 1947-2010, periodic basic data book, A2575–14.1

World energy supply-demand, by fuel source and sector, by region and country, 1992/93 biennial rpt, R9455–1.3, R9455–1.7

Index by Subjects and Names

State and local:

California statistical abstract, general data, 1992 annual rpt, S0840–2.7

Florida statistical abstract, general data, 1992 annual rpt, U6660–1.15

Georgia statistical abstract, general data, 1992-93 biennial rpt, U6730–1.8

Hawaii data book, general data, 1992 annual rpt, S2090–1.17

New York State public utility financial and operating data, by utility type and company, 1988-92, annual rpt, S5795–1

New York State statistical yearbook, general data, 1992 annual rpt, U5100–1.12

Pennsylvania energy supply-demand and prices by fuel type, with electric power info by utility, 1960s-90, recurring rpt, S6810–3

South Carolina statistical abstract, general data, 1993 annual rpt, S7125–1.4

Tennessee statistical abstract, general data, 1992/93 annual rpt, U8710–2.10

Utah statistical abstract, general data, 1993 triennial rpt, U8960–1.13

Washington State electric utility financial and operating data, by company, 1982-91, annual rpt, S8450–1.2

see also Electric power prices

Hydrogen

see Gases

Hydrology

Higher education geoscience enrollment and degrees awarded, by sex, race-ethnicity, and discipline, 1991/92, annual rpt, A1785–3

see also Oceanography

see also Water pollution

see also Water power

see also Water resources development

see also Water supply and use

Hydrothermal power

see Geothermal resources

Hypertension

Heart disease risk factor prevalence, by State, 1989, semiannual rpt, B8500–1.9

Hospital patient admission rates and length of stay, by diagnosis and procedure, payment source, age, sex, and region, 1991, B4455–4

Hospital patient charges and length of stay, by diagnosis and procedure, payment source, age, and region, 1991, B4455–5

Hospital patient discharges and length of stay, by diagnosis, type of operation, age, and region, 1991, annual rpt series, B4455–1

Hospital patient discharges and length of stay, by diagnostic related group (DRG), payment source, age, and region, 1991, annual rpt series, B4455–3

Incidence by sex and race, 1993 feature, C4215–1.511

Public health research results, including hypertension incidence and cardiovascular disease risk in selected populations, 1992 articles, A2623–1.502

State and local:

Alabama health behavior risk factor surveillance survey results, by respondent characteristics, 1988-89, recurring rpt, S0175–6

Alabama public health dept activities, including services provided, inspection and licensing activity, staff and finances, and vital statistics and health data, 1992 annual rpt, S0175–3

Index by Subjects and Names

Hypertension

Alabama vital statistics, including population, births, deaths by cause, marriages, and divorces, by location and demographic characteristics, 1992 and trends, annual rpt, S0175–2

Alaska vital statistics, including births, deaths by cause, marriages, divorces, adoptions, and population, by demographic characteristics and location, 1990, annual rpt, S0315–1

California health behavior risk factor surveillance survey results, by respondent characteristics, 1991 and trends, annual rpt, S0865–2

California vital statistics, including population, births, and deaths by cause, by demographic characteristics and county, 1990 and trends, annual rpt, S0865–1

Colorado health behavior risk factor surveillance survey results, by respondent characteristics, 1990, recurring rpt, S1010–3

Colorado vital statistics, including population, births, deaths by cause, abortion, marriage and divorce, and adoption, by demographic characteristics and location, 1990 and trends, annual rpt, S1010–1

Connecticut health behavior risk factor surveillance survey results, 1989-91, annual rpt, S1200–2

Connecticut vital statistics, including births, deaths by cause, marriages, and divorces, by demographic characteristics and location, 1989, annual rpt, S1200–1

Delaware vital statistics, including births, deaths by cause, and marriages and dissolutions, by demographic characteristics and location, 1990, annual rpt, S1385–2

Florida vital statistics, including population, births, deaths by cause, and marriages and dissolutions, by location and demographic characteristics, 1992 and trends, annual rpt, S1745–3

Georgia health behavior risk factor surveillance survey results, by respondent characteristics, 1991 and trends, annual rpt, S1895–2

Georgia vital statistics, including deaths by cause, demographic characteristics, and location, 1991 and trends, annual rpt, S1895–1.2

Hawaii health dept activities and services, including vital statistics and disease control, by location, 1990, annual rpt, S2065–1

Idaho vital statistics, including births, deaths by cause, abortions, marriages, and divorces, by demographic characteristics and county, 1991 and trends, annual rpt, S2250–2

Iowa health behavior risk factor surveillance survey results, by respondent characteristics, 1991, annual rpt, S2795–2

Iowa vital statistics, including population, births, deaths by cause, marriages, and divorces, by demographic characteristics and location, 1991 and trends, annual rpt, S2795–1

Kansas vital statistics, including population, births, deaths by cause, abortions, marriages, and divorces, by demographic characteristics and location, 1991 and trends, annual rpt, S2975–1

Kentucky health behavior risk factor surveillance survey results, by State area and respondent characteristics, 1988-90, annual rpt, S3140–6

Kentucky vital statistics, including births, deaths by cause, marriages and divorces, and population, by demographic characteristics and county, 1991, annual rpt, S3140–1

Louisiana vital statistics, including population, births, deaths by cause, reportable diseases, marriages, and divorces, by demographic characteristics and locality, 1989-90 and trends, annual rpt, S3295–1

Maine vital statistics, including births, deaths by cause, abortions, and marriages and divorces, by demographic characteristics and location, 1991 and trends, annual rpt, S3460–2

Maryland vital statistics, including population, births, deaths by cause, marriages, and divorces, by demographic characteristics and location, 1989 and trends, annual rpt, S3635–1

Massachusetts health behavior risk factor surveillance survey results, by respondent characteristics, 1986-90, recurring rpt, S3850–3

Massachusetts vital statistics, including births, deaths by cause, marriages, divorces, and population, by locality and demographic characteristics, 1990 and trends, annual rpt, S3850–1

Michigan health behavior risk factor surveillance survey results, by respondent characteristics, 1991, annual rpt, S4000–4

Michigan vital statistics, including births, deaths, marriages, divorces/annulments, and communicable diseases, by location and demographic characteristics, 1990 and trends, annual rpt, S4000–3

Minnesota vital statistics, including population, births, abortions, deaths, marriages, and divorces, by location and demographic characteristics, 1991 and trends, annual rpt, S4190–2

Mississippi vital statistics, including births, deaths by cause, marriages, and divorces, by demographic characteristics and location, 1992 and trends, annual rpt, S4350–1

Missouri vital statistics, including population, births, deaths by cause, and marriages and divorces, by location and demographic characteristics, 1992 and trends, annual rpt, S4518–1

Montana vital statistics, including births, deaths by cause, abortion, disease, and marriage and divorce, by demographic characteristics and county, 1990-91 and trends, annual rpt, S4690–1

Nevada health behavior risk factor surveillance survey results, by location and respondent characteristics, 1991, annual rpt, S5075–3

New Hampshire vital statistics, including population, births, deaths by cause, marriages, and divorces, by location and demographic characteristics, 1991 and trends, annual rpt, S5215–1

New Jersey vital statistics, including births, deaths, population, communicable diseases, and marriages and divorces, by demographic characteristics and location, 1990 and trends, annual rpt, S5405–1

New Mexico vital statistics, including population, births, deaths, and disease, by location and demographic characteristics, 1991 and trends, annual rpt, S5605–1

New York State health behavior risk factor surveillance survey results, by respondent characteristics, 1990, recurring rpt, S5765–3

New York State vital statistics, including population, births, deaths by cause, reportable diseases, and marriages and dissolutions, by demographic characteristics and/or location, 1990 and trends, annual rpt, S5765–1

North Carolina deaths and rates, by cause and county, 1991 and trends, annual rpt, S5927–1.2

North Dakota health behavior risk factor surveillance survey results, by respondent characteristics, 1991 and trends, annual rpt, S6105–3

North Dakota vital statistics, including births, deaths by cause, marriages and divorces, and abortions, by demographic characteristics and/or county, 1991 and trends, annual rpt, S6105–2

Ohio vital statistics, including births, deaths by cause, marriages, divorces, and population, by demographic characteristics and location, 1991 and trends, annual rpt, S6285–1

Oregon vital statistics, including births, deaths by cause, communicable diseases, marriages, and divorces, by age, sex, race-ethnicity, and county, 1991 and trends, annual rpt, S6615–5

Rhode Island vital statistics, including population, births, deaths, marriages, and divorces, by demographic characteristics and locality, 1989 and trends, annual rpt, S6995–1

South Carolina deaths, by detailed cause, age, sex, and race, 1990, annual rpt, S7175–2

South Carolina vital statistics, including births, deaths by cause, marriages, and divorces, by age, sex, race, and location, 1990 and trends, annual rpt, S7175–1

South Dakota vital statistics, including births, deaths, marriage and divorce, and communicable disease, by demographic characteristics and county, 1991 and trends, annual rpt, S7345–1

Tennessee health behavior risk factor surveillance survey results, by respondent characteristics, 1986-90, annual rpt, S7520–3

Tennessee vital statistics, including births, deaths by cause, marriages, divorces, and population, by demographic characteristics and location, 1991 and trends, annual rpt, S7520–2

Texas health behavior risk factor surveillance survey results, by respondent characteristics, 1991 and trends, annual rpt, S7685–2

Texas vital statistics, including births, deaths by cause, abortions, marriages, and divorces, by location and demographic characteristics, 1991 and trends, annual rpt, S7685–1

Utah health behavior risk factor surveillance survey results, by respondent characteristics, 1991, annual rpt, S7835–3

Hypertension

Utah vital statistics, including births and deaths by cause, by demographic characteristics and location, 1990, annual rpt, S7835–1.2

Vermont vital statistics, including population, births, deaths by cause, abortions, marriages, and divorces, by location and demographic characteristics, 1991 and trends, annual rpt, S8054–1

Virginia vital statistics, including births, deaths by cause, marriages and divorces, and communicable disease, by demographic characteristics and location, 1991 and trends, annual rpt, S8225–1

Washington State hypertension incidence and deaths, by demographic characteristics, 1991 annual rpt, S8363–1

West Virginia vital statistics, including births, deaths by cause, marriages, and divorces, by location and demographic characteristics, 1991 and trends, annual rpt, S8560–1

Wisconsin vital statistics, including population, births, deaths by cause, and marriages and dissolutions, by county and demographic characteristics, 1991 and trends, annual rpt, S8715–4

Wyoming vital statistics, including population, births, deaths by cause, marriages, and divorces, by demographic characteristics and county, 1991 and trends, annual rpt, S8920–2

see also under By Disease in the "Index by Categories"

IBM

see International Business Machines Corp.

Ice cream

- Exports of farm products, by detailed commodity and country of destination, US and California, 1991, annual rpt, B9520–1
- Production of ice cream and frozen desserts by State, region, and country, with related industry operating info, 1992 and trends, annual rpt, A5825–1
- Sales and consumer expenditures, for food store products by type, 1991-92, annual feature, C4655–1.510
- Sales trends and forecast for food service industry, by market segment, 1990-93, annual feature, A8200–1.502
- Shopping center financial and operating data, with detail by type of tenant, US and Canada, 1991, triennial rpt, R9285–1
- Supermarket sales by detailed product type, 1992 and trends, annual feature, C5225–1.507
- Vending machine sales by product type, and machines on location, 1992 and trends, annual rpt, C9470–1

State and local:

- Alaska ice cream and ice milk products production, 1988-92, annual rpt, U5750–1
- Arizona ice cream, ice milk, and sherbet production, monthly 1988-92, annual rpt, U5830–1
- Arkansas manufactured dairy product production, 1983-92, annual rpt, U5920–1
- California ice cream, ice milk, and sherbet manufactured, monthly 1982-92, annual rpt, S0850–1.6

Colorado dairy products manufactured, 1982-92, annual rpt, S0985–1

Florida livestock, dairy, and poultry production, inventory, marketing, and finances, with detail by commodity or species, 1992 and trends, annual rpt, S1685–1.3

Georgia manufactured dairy products production, 1984-91, annual rpt, S1855–1

Hawaii frozen dairy product inspections, 1990, annual rpt, S2065–1.6

Illinois dairy products manufactured, including ice cream, monthly 1982-91, annual rpt, S2390–1

Kansas dairy processing plants, and products manufactured by type, 1983-92, annual rpt, S2915–1

Michigan dairy products manufactured, monthly 1989-91, annual rpt, S3950–1

Minnesota dairy products manufactured, 1988-92, annual rpt, S4130–1

Missouri manufactured dairy product production, by type of product, 1988-92, annual rpt, S4480–1

Montana dairy products manufactured, by type, 1982-91, annual rpt, S4655–1

Nebraska manufactured dairy products production, 1986-91, annual rpt, S4835–1

New Jersey dairy products manufactured, 1986-91, annual rpt, S5350–1

New York State dairy industry production, by product type, 1983-92, annual rpt, S5700–1

North Carolina manufactured dairy products production, 1989-91, annual rpt, S5885–1

North Dakota manufactured dairy products production, by type, 1991-92, annual rpt, U3600–1

Ohio manufactured dairy products production, 1990-91, annual rpt, S6240–1

Oklahoma manufactured dairy products production, quarterly 1988-92, annual rpt, S6405–1

Oregon dairy products manufactured, including ice cream, monthly 1990-91, annual rpt, S6575–1

Pennsylvania manufactured dairy products production, by type, 1992 and trends, annual rpt, S6760–1

South Carolina production of frozen dairy products by type, 1977-92, annual rpt, U1075–3

Tennessee dairy products produced, by type, 1986-92, annual rpt, S7460–1

Texas manufactured dairy product production, 1987-91, annual rpt, S7630–1.2

Utah production of ice cream, ice milk, and sherbet, 1940-92, annual rpt, S7800–1

Washington State manufactured dairy products production, 1988-92, annual rpt, S8328–1

Wisconsin manufactured dairy products production and plants, 1992 and trends, annual rpt, S8680–1

Idaho

Banks and other financial instns, financial condition, with data by instn and loan activity analysis, FY92 or 1991, annual rpt, S2235–1

Construction activity and value, by city and county, monthly rpt, B3900–1

Crimes and arrests, by offense, location, and offender characteristics, with data on law enforcement employment and assaults on officers, 1992 and trends, annual rpt, S2275–2

Index by Subjects and Names

Economic indicators for 10 Western States, including forecasts from selected organizations, monthly rpt, U0282–2

Economic profile of Idaho, detailed social and economic data, 1992 recurring rpt, S2218–2

Economic trends and forecasts, Idaho and US, quarterly rpt, S2245–2

Educational finance, school district revenues by source, and expenditures by function, by district and fund, FY92, annual rpt, S2225–2

Election results and voter registration, by county and/or district and precinct, 1992 general election, biennial rpt, S2305–1

Elementary and secondary public and nonpublic school enrollment by grade, by school district and/or county, Sept 1992, annual rpt, S2225–1

Elementary and secondary school personnel characteristics and salaries by position, and teachers and enrollment by school district, 1992/93, annual rpt, S2225–3

Employment by industry, by county and labor market area, monthly 1991, annual rpt, S2230–2

Govt financial condition, including revenues by source and expenditures by object, by agency and/or fund, FY92, annual rpt, S2215–1

Insurance industry financial and underwriting data, by company and type of insurance, with regulatory data, 1991, annual rpt, S2260–1

Libraries (academic) staff, expenditures, and holdings, by instn, 1992, annual feature, A5370–1

Libraries (public) holdings, staff, services, circulation, and finances, by instn, FY92, annual rpt, S2282–1

Markets with daily newspapers, demographic and economic info by geographic area, US and Canada, 1993 annual rpt, C3250–1

Public opinion on top general and environmental issues for State, and positive and negative aspects of mining industry, Sept 1992 survey, article, C5226–2.506

Statistical profiles of 50 States and DC, general data, 1993 annual almanac, C4712–1

Tax statistics, including collections, and data by county and city, FY92 and trends, annual rpt, S2295–1

Traffic accidents, fatalities, and injuries, by circumstances, location, vehicle type, and driver and victim characteristics, 1992, annual rpt, S2315–1

Utilities regulatory data, and commission finances, FY92, annual rpt, S2290–1

Utility and transportation regulatory agency activities, scope of jurisdiction, finances, and employees, by agency, 1991/92 annual rpt, A7015–2

Vital statistics, including population, births, deaths by cause, abortions, marriages, and divorces, by demographic characteristics and county, 1991 and trends, annual rpt, S2250–2

Welfare program expenditures and recipients, with data by county, quarterly rpt, S2250–1

see also Lewiston, Idaho

Index by Subjects and Names

see also under By City and By County in the "Index by Categories"
see also under By State in the "Index by Categories"

Illegitimacy
see Births out of wedlock

Illinois

Agricultural production, marketing, and finances, by county or commodity, and farms and farmland, 1991 and trends, annual rpt, S2390–1

Banks and trust companies (State-chartered), financial condition and status changes, by instn, FY92, annual rpt, S2395–1

Business activity indicators for Illinois, quarterly rpt, U6910–1

Business and economic activity indicators, including data by industry and county, quarterly rpt, S2405–2

China trade value with US, with detail for Illinois exports, and US tariff rates and collections, for top 20-25 commodities, 1992 article, U6910–1.502

Corrections dept admin, including inmates and characteristics, finances, and staff, FY91-93 and trends, annual rpt, S2425–1

Corrections local facility inspection results, with data on programs and inmates by sex, suspended annual rpt, S2425–2

Crimes and arrests, by offense, location, and offender characteristics, with data on assaults on officers, 1991, annual rpt, S2536–1

Election results, and voter registration trends, by county and/or district, 1992 general election, biennial rpt, S2445–1

Elementary and secondary school enrollment, staff, and finances, by county and district, 1990/91 and trends, annual rpt, S2440–1

Financial Institutions Dept activities, with financial and regulatory data for credit unions, consumer lenders, and other businesses, FY91 annual rpt, S2457–2

Govt financial condition, including revenues by source, and expenditures by object, function, and agency, FY92, annual rpt, S2415–1

Higher education enrollment, degrees, staff, and finances, by public and private instn, and student characteristics, 1993 annual rpt, S2475–1

Libraries (public) holdings, staff, and finances, by instn, FY92, annual rpt, S2535–2

Markets with daily newspapers, demographic and economic info by geographic area, US and Canada, 1993 annual rpt, C3250–1

Mental health facility patient population and characteristics, by facility, location, and treatment category, FY93, annual rpt, S2505–1

Oil/gas industry production, finances, exploration, and reserves, by State, 1992 and trends, annual rpt, A5425–1.1

Property valuation and tax rates, by county and school district, 1990/91, annual rpt, S2440–1.3

Public assistance program cases, recipients, and payments, by program and county, FY91-92 and trends, annual rpt, S2520–2

Public opinion in US on selected foreign policy issues, with detail for 3 States, 1993 survey, annual rpt, A4965–1.2

Statistical abstract of Illinois, detailed economic, demographic, and govtl data, 1992 annual rpt, U6910–2

Statistical profiles of 50 States and DC, general data, 1993 annual almanac, C4712–1

Telephone utility financial and operating data, by company, 1992, annual rpt, S2410–2

Traffic accidents, fatalities, and injuries, by circumstances, location, and driver and victim characteristics, 1991 and trends, annual rpt, S2540–1

Utilities sales and operating revenues, and customers served, by class of service and company, 1991-92, annual rpt series, S2410–1

Utility and transportation regulatory agency activities, scope of jurisdiction, finances, and employees, by agency, 1991/92 annual rpt, A7015–2

see also Chicago, Ill.
see also Cook County, Ill.
see also under By City and By County in the "Index by Categories"
see also under By State in the "Index by Categories"

Illiteracy
see Literacy and illiteracy

Illness
see Disabled and handicapped persons
see Diseases and disorders
see Hospitalization

Immigration and emigration

Arrivals of immigrants, and ceilings, by world area of origin, 1st half FY93, R9372–2.509

Characteristics of 1992 immigrants, and immigrant share of 1992-2010 population growth by race-ethnicity, article, C5800–7.533

Child population shares born abroad, for top 10 States and DC, 1990, article, R8750–1.509

EC foreign population shares, with detail for EC vs other areas of origin, by country, 1988, R5025–9

Europe public opinion on political, economic, and social issues, for 9 countries and 3 Soviet Union Republics, 1991 survey, C8915–8.1

Hispanic American and non-Hispanic high school dropouts distribution by recency of immigration, Nov 1989, article, R4800–2.507

Home ownership rates, income, and households, for new and established immigrants by origin, and 15 cities with most new immigrants, 1993 article, C4300–1.512

Latin America immigrants to US, and temporary workers, aliens, and deportations, by country, 1992 annual rpt, U6250–1.14

Legal immigrants admitted to US, Florida, and 6 MSAs, by country/area of birth, 1990, annual rpt, U6660–1.1

Legal immigrants not covered by Immigration Reform and Control Act, from top 15 and all other countries of origin, FY91, article, R8750–1.501

Minority population characteristics, employment, and voting patterns by detailed race-ethnicity, with comparisons to whites, 1980s-2040, R8750–2.58

Population foreign born, by world region of origin, decennially 1960-90, article, R8750–1.511

Population shares foreign born, for US and 5 European countries, 1985 and 1990, article, C5800–7.535

Puerto Rican immigrants with college education, percent living in 4 leading US States, 1982-88, article, C4575–1.506

Southeastern region persons naturalized, FY85-89, annual rpt, U3255–4.1

Statistical profiles of 50 States and DC, general data, 1993 annual almanac, C4712–1

State and local:

Arkansas Census of Population and Housing detailed findings, 1990, U5935–7

California Census of Population and Housing detailed findings, 1990, S0840–9

California legal immigrants, distribution by country of origin, 1986-90, article, R9372–2.509

Florida 8th-9th grade children of immigrants characteristics, attitudes, and discrimination experience, 1992, survey article, R4800–2.522

Hawaii data book, general data, 1992 annual rpt, S2090–1.1

Hawaii economic indicators, bimonthly rpt, B3500–1

Maryland statistical abstract, general data, 1993-94 biennial rpt, S3605–1.1

New Jersey Census of Population and Housing detailed findings, by county, 1990, S5425–19

Pennsylvania Census of Population and Housing detailed findings, with selected data by county and municipality, 1990, U4130–13

Rhode Island Census of Population and Housing detailed findings, by county and municipality, 1990, S6930–9

see also Alien workers
see also Aliens
see also Deportation
see also Foreign medical graduates
see also Refugees

Immigration and Naturalization Service

Border patrol and other investigative activities, and asylum case processing, 1992 annual rpt, U6250–1.14

Refugee arrival activity worldwide, and US admission and asylum data, by country, 1992 annual feature, R9372–2.503

Immunity disorders

Hospital patient discharges and length of stay, by diagnostic related group (DRG), payment source, age, and region, 1991, annual rpt series, B4455–3

Physician (allergist/immunologist) fees and expenses, and detailed work patterns, 1991-92, article, A2200–5.1

State and local:

California vital statistics, including population, births, and deaths by cause, by demographic characteristics and county, 1990 and trends, annual rpt, S0865–1

Idaho vital statistics, including births, deaths by cause, abortions, marriages, and divorces, by demographic characteristics and county, 1991 and trends, annual rpt, S2250–2

Massachusetts vital statistics, including births, deaths by cause, marriages, divorces, and population, by locality and demographic characteristics, 1990 and trends, annual rpt, S3850–1

Immunity disorders

Mississippi vital statistics, including births, deaths by cause, marriages, and divorces, by demographic characteristics and location, 1992 and trends, annual rpt, S4350–1

Montana vital statistics, including births, deaths by cause, abortion, disease, and marriage and divorce, by demographic characteristics and county, 1990-91 and trends, annual rpt, S4690–1

South Carolina deaths, by detailed cause, age, sex, and race, 1990, annual rpt, S7175–2

Vermont vital statistics, including population, births, deaths by cause, abortions, marriages, and divorces, by location and demographic characteristics, 1991 and trends, annual rpt, S8054–1

Washington State vital statistics, including births, deaths by cause, and population, by demographic characteristics and location, 1991 and trends, annual rpt, S8363–1

West Virginia vital statistics, including births, deaths by cause, marriages, and divorces, by location and demographic characteristics, 1991 and trends, annual rpt, S8560–1

Wisconsin vital statistics, including population, births, deaths by cause, and marriages and dissolutions, by county and demographic characteristics, 1991 and trends, annual rpt, S8715–4

see also Acquired immune deficiency syndrome

see also Allergies

see also under By Disease in the "Index by Categories"

Immunology

see Vaccination and vaccines

see Immunity disorders

Import restrictions

see Tariffs and foreign trade controls

Imports

see Agricultural exports and imports

see Coal exports and imports

see Energy exports and imports

see Foreign trade

see Natural gas exports and imports

see Petroleum exports and imports

Imprisonment

see Correctional institutions

see Prisoners

Incentives

see Employee bonuses and work incentives

see Sales promotion

Income

see Business income and expenses, general

see Business income and expenses, specific industry

see Earnings, general

see Earnings, specific industry

see Farm income

see Income maintenance

see Income taxes

see National income and product accounts

see Personal and household income

see Poverty

see Professionals' fees

see Underground economy

see under By Income in the "Index by Categories"

Income maintenance

Forecasts of natl income and product account components and related indicators, quarterly rpt, U1880–1

Govt finances, including revenues by source, expenditures by function, and debt, detailed data for Federal, State, and local govts, 1993 annual rpt, R9050–1

State social, economic, and govtl indicators, with rankings, 1993 semiannual rpt, B8500–1.2, B8500–1.6

Transfer payments by State and region, 1990-91, biennial rpt, S3605–1.6

State and local:

California disabled and senior citizens property tax assistance, claimants, and income, by income class, 1991 and trends, annual rpt, S0855–1.3

DC statistical profile, general data, 1992 annual rpt, S1535–3.5

Florida county data book, 1992/93 annual rpt, C6360–1

Florida statistical abstract, general data, 1992 annual rpt, U6660–1.5

Georgia county guide, general data, 1993 annual rpt, U6750–1

Georgia statistical abstract, general data, 1992-93 biennial rpt, U6730–1.13

Idaho and US economic trends and forecasts, quarterly rpt, S2245–2

Illinois statistical abstract, general data, 1992 annual rpt, U6910–2

Kansas statistical abstract, general data, 1991/92 annual rpt, U7095–2.9

Mississippi income by source, county, and MSA, and wages by industry group, 1993 annual planning rpt, S4345–1.4

Nebraska transfer payments, by component and State area, with comparisons to total personal income, 1990-91 and trends, article, U7860–1.504

Nebraska transfer payments per capita, with share of personal income, by county, 1990, article, U7860–1.505

Pennsylvania transfer payments as percent of personal income, by county, 1991, annual article, U4110–1.506

Tennessee statistical abstract, general data, 1992/93 annual rpt, U8710–2.2, U8710–2.18

West Virginia statistical handbook, general data, 1992 annual rpt, R9385–1.6

see also Aid to blind

see also Aid to Families with Dependent Children

see also Disability benefits and insurance

see also Food stamp programs

see also Medical assistance

see also Medicare

see also Old age assistance

see also Old-Age, Survivors, Disability, and Health Insurance

see also Public welfare programs

see also Rent supplements

see also Social security

see also State funding for social welfare

see also Supplemental Security Income

see also Unemployment insurance

see also Workers compensation

Income taxes

Budget of US proposed by Clinton Admin, with data on spending impacts by program, deficit reduction, and tax changes, FY93-98, R3834–17

Collections under current and/or initial budget-formulation estimates, by State, FY93-94, semiannual rpt, A7955–1

Corporate alternative minimum tax impacts on capital investment costs, including data

by industry and type of equipment, and comparisons to 7 other countries, 1991 rpt, A1310–4

Corporate income tax and govt mineral royalty rates, for 12 countries, 1993 article, C5226–2.506

Corporate income tax returns and taxes paid, distribution by asset size group, 1989, article, R9050–3.503

Corporate State/local income tax burden according to 5 alternative measures, for 9 States, 1990, article, B8500–2.514

Corporate tax burden trends, for income and payroll taxes, with comparisons to profits, Fed Govt receipts, and GDP, FY70-93, R9050–15.2

Family income, with impact of Federal and State/local taxes and inflation, 1980-92, annual rpt, R9050–13

Federal income tax returns, income, and taxes, by income percentile, 1981 and/or 1991, annual article, R9050–3.509

Federal income tax returns, liabilities, deductions, and credits, by State and region, 1988 or 1990, R8490–47

Federal income tax top rates, 1929/30-1992/93, B2000–2.501

Govt finances, including revenues by source, expenditures by function, and debt, detailed data for Federal, State, and local govts, 1993 annual rpt, R9050–1

Health insurance employer-paid benefits coverage, and tax revenues that would be generated if benefits were taxed, by income group, 1991, article, C3950–1.505

Oil industry income tax rate and allowance trends for independent and major companies, 1950s-90, A2575–25

Public opinion on amount of taxes paid by self, big and small business, and various income groups, Mar 1993 Gallup Poll and trends, C4040–1.510

Public opinion on social, political, and economic issues, detailed data, 1972-91 surveys, annual rpt, U6395–1

Pulp, paper, and allied products financial and operating data, 1950s-92, annual rpt, A1630–6.4

Small business returns filed under Subchapter S personal tax code status, with comparison to total corporate income tax returns, 1970-90, article, C1850–4.508

State corporate income tax rates on added dollar of profit, by State, Apr 1993, article, B8500–2.512

State personal income tax rates, exemptions or credits, and deductibility of Federal taxes, by State, Jan 1993, annual rpt, R9380–1.7

State shares of upper-level income tax increases proposed by Clinton Admin, compared to population, for 10 States most and least affected, 1993 article, C8900–1.510

State social, economic, and govtl indicators, with rankings, 1993 semiannual rpt, B8500–1.4, B8500–1.6

State tax revenue from personal, corporate, and sales taxes, by State and region, quarterly rpt, U5085–1

State/local tax revenue shares, and comparison to personal income, for 3 major tax types, by State, FY91, article, B8500–2.511

Index by Subjects and Names

India

Statistical profiles of 50 States and DC, general data, 1993 annual almanac, C4712–1

Utility income tax special provisions, by State, 1991/92 annual rpt, A7015–3

State and local:

Alabama financial condition, including revenues by source, expenditures by function and object, and fund balances, by fund and agency, FY92, annual rpt, S0129–1

Alabama statistical abstract, general data, 1992 recurring rpt, U5680–2.6

Alaska financial condition, including revenues by source, expenditures by function, fund balances, and bond obligations, FY92 and trends, annual rpt, S0275–1

Arizona tax revenues by source, tax rates, and disbursements to local areas, FY92 and trends, annual rpt, S0515–1

Arkansas financial condition, including revenues by source, expenditures by function and object, and fund balances, FY92, annual rpt, S0670–1

California economic condition, including population, employment and earnings, income, business activity, and taxation, 1960s-92, annual rpt, S0840–3.2

California financial condition, including revenues by source, expenditures by agency and function, fund balances, and bonded debt, FY92 and trends, annual rpt, S0815–1

California individual and corporate income tax returns and property tax assistance, by income class and county, 1990 and trends, annual rpt, S0855–1

California statistical abstract, general data, 1992 annual rpt, S0840–2.4

Colorado tax revenues by type, with selected data by county and city, FY92 and trends, annual rpt, S1075–1

DC financial condition, including receipts by source, expenditures by object or function, and fund balances, FY92, annual rpt, S1507–1

DC statistical profile, general data, 1992 annual rpt, S1535–3.2

Delaware data book, general data, 1993 annual rpt, S1375–4

Florida statistical abstract, general data, 1992 annual rpt, U6660–1.5

Georgia county guide, general data, 1993 annual rpt, U6750–1

Georgia statistical abstract, general data, 1992-93 biennial rpt, U6730–1.3

Georgia tax revenues, by type and county, FY92 annual rpt, S1950–1

Hawaii data book, general data, 1992 annual rpt, S2090–1.9

Hawaii economic conditions, including employment, population, tourism, and construction, quarterly rpt, S2090–2

Hawaii tax collections and allocations, by type, for State and counties, FY91-92 and trends, annual rpt, S2120–1

Idaho tax statistics, including collections, and data by county and city, FY92 and trends, annual rpt, S2295–1

Illinois financial condition, including revenues by source, and expenditures by object, function, and agency, FY92, annual rpt, S2415–1

Indiana child support collections through tax intercept programs, FY87-92, annual rpt, S2623–1.3

Iowa individual income tax return filings, income, taxes paid, and credits, by income bracket, and filings by county, 1991, annual rpt, S2860–3

Kansas tax collections by tax type, and property values, with data by county, FY92 and trends, annual rpt, S3020–1

Kentucky financial condition, including revenues by source, expenditures by function and object, fund balances, and bonded debt, FY92, annual rpt, S3120–1

Maryland financial condition, including revenues by source, expenditures by function, fund balances, and bonded debt, FY92 and trends, annual rpt, S3685–2

Maryland individual income tax return filings, and income and tax liability data, by city, county, and income group, 1991, annual rpt, S3685–1

Maryland local govt financial condition, including revenues by source, expenditures by function, and debt obligations, FY92 and trends, annual rpt, S3618–1

Massachusetts tax collections by type, and distributions to local areas, FY91 and trends, annual rpt, S3917–1

Michigan child support collections, including tax offset activity, by county, monthly rpt, S4010–1

Michigan financial condition, including revenues by source, expenditures by function, and fund balances, FY92 and trends, annual rpt, S3985–2

Minnesota financial condition, including revenues by source, expenditures by function, fund balances, and bonded debt, FY92 and trends, annual rpt, S4180–1

Minnesota individual income tax return data, discontinued, S4250–1

Mississippi tax collections by type, and disbursements, with selected sales and income tax data by locality and industry, FY92 and trends, annual rpt, S4435–1

Missouri financial condition, including fund finances, tax collections and distribution, and State treasury activity, FY92 and trends, annual rpt, S4570–1

Montana revenue collections by tax type, and taxable establishments, production, and income, FY91-92 and trends, biennial rpt, S4750–1.1

Nebraska personal and corporate income tax returns filed, tax credits and liability, and income, by county and/or income group, 1990, annual rpt, S4950–1.1

New Mexico tax revenues and disbursements, with data by tax type, county, and city, FY91-92 and trends, annual rpt, S5660–1

New York State tax collections by type, FY84-93, annual rpt, S5710–1

North Carolina financial condition, including revenues by source, expenditures by function, fund balances, and bonded debt, FY92, annual rpt, S5897–1

North Carolina public utility financial, operating, and regulatory data, by utility type and company, 1990 and trends, annual rpt, S5917–2

Ohio tax revenues and collections, by tax type, with distributions and property

assessments by county, and corporate taxes by industry, FY92 annual rpt, S6390–1

Oklahoma tax revenues by source, and distribution to local govts and State funds, FY92 and trends, annual rpt, S6495–1

Oregon financial condition, including revenues by source, expenditures by function, and fund statements, FY92, annual rpt, S6603–2

Pennsylvania tax collections by tax type, with data by county and industry, FY92 and trends, annual rpt, S6885–1

South Carolina economic condition, including agriculture, finance, and govt financial data, 1970s-92, annual rpt, S7125–3.1

South Carolina income tax returns, distribution by taxable income, by county, 1991, annual rpt, S7145–1.2

South Carolina individual and corporate income tax returns, income, and liability or refunds, FY92, annual rpt, S7255–1.2

South Carolina statistical abstract, general data, 1993 annual rpt, S7125–1.12

Tennessee tax revenues by source and apportionments to counties, cities, and funds, FY91-92 and trends, biennial rpt, S7570–1

Texas natural gas gross receipt taxes paid, by company, FY92, annual rpt, S7745–1

Utah govt statistical review, fiscal and socioeconomic data, 1993 annual rpt, R9380–1.4

Utah statistical abstract, general data, 1993 triennial rpt, U8960–1.5

Utah tax revenues by source, and distribution to localities and State funds, FY92 and trends, annual rpt, S7905–1

Vermont individual State income tax returns, and property and sales tax refunds, by income class and locality, 1991, annual rpt, S8125 1

Virginia income distribution and income tax returns filed, by locality, 1990, annual rpt, U9080–1

Virginia personal and corporate income tax returns filed, taxable income, and tax, 1990 or FY92 and trends, annual rpt, S8305–1.1

West Virginia statistical handbook, general data, 1992 annual rpt, R9385–1.6

Wisconsin financial condition, including revenues by source, expenditures by function and object, and fund balances, FY93, annual rpt, S8675–2

see also Tax incentives and shelters

see also Tax protests and appeals

see also Windfall profit tax

see also Withholding tax

Incorporations, new

see Business formations

Indexes

see Bibliographies

see Consumer Price Index

see Cost of living

see Diffusion indexes

see Directories

see Industrial production indexes

see Labor costs and cost indexes

see Producer Price Index

India

Computer software export revenues for top 5 India firms, FY92, article, C5800–7.511

India

Electronics industry trade and/or production trends by product category for 33 countries, with general economic profiles, 1993 annual rpt, A4725–1.4

Energy intl sourcebook, with detail on oil and gas industry operations, supply-demand, and prices, for approx 80 countries, 1970s-91, annual compilation, C6985–10.2

Machine tool industry operating data by country and product, 1992 and trends, annual rpt, A3179–2.2

Motor vehicle world production, sales, trade, and registrations, by country, world area, manufacturer, and make, 1991 and trends, annual rpt, A0865–2.1

Nuclear reactors in operation, with capacity, electricity generation, and construction, by unit and country, 1992, annual rpt, B6800–2.2

Oil refining capacity and throughput, by company and refinery, 1993 annual rpt, C6985–3.1

Population, with persons in upper and lower middle class income segments, 1990, article, C8900–1.502

Public opinion in US on selected foreign policy issues, with detail for 3 States, 1993 survey, annual rpt, A4965–1

Silver market activity worldwide and in US, including production, consumption by end use, stocks, trade, and prices, by country, 1988-92, annual rpt, B4300–1

Silver supply-demand by country and end use, with prices, futures trading, and market analyses, 1993 and trends, annual rpt, A8902–4

Indiana

Business activity indicators for Indiana and US, quarterly rpt, U2160–1

Court cases and dispositions by type of court and case, and location, with judicial system finances and personnel, 1992, annual rpt, S2703–1

Election results, by county and district, with voter registration, 1992 primary and general elections, biennial rpt, S2702–1

Elementary and secondary school enrollment and finances, by district and county, annual rpt series, S2608–2

Financial instns (State-chartered) financial condition, including assets by instn, 1991 and trends, annual rpt, S2625–1

Govt financial condition, including revenues by source, expenditures by function and object, and fund balances, by agency, FY92, annual rpt, S2570–1

Library holdings, circulation, finances, and staff, for public and other libraries by instn, 1992 or FY92, annual rpt, S2655–1

Markets with daily newspapers, demographic and economic info by geographic area, US and Canada, 1993 annual rpt, C3250–1

Oil/gas industry production, finances, exploration, and reserves, by State, 1992 and trends, annual rpt, A5425–1.1

Property value and tax levies, collections, credits, and deductions, by county and type, 1991, annual rpt, S2570–1.1

Statistical profiles of 50 States and DC, general data, 1993 annual almanac, C4712–1

Traffic accidents, fatalities, and injuries, by circumstances, location, and vehicle type, and driver and victim characteristics, 1992, annual rpt, S2675–1

Utility and transportation regulatory agency activities, scope of jurisdiction, finances, and employees, by agency, 1991/92 annual rpt, A7015–2

Welfare program participation, expenditures, and services, by county, FY92 and trends, annual rpt, S2623–1

see also Anderson, Ind.

see also Columbus, Ind.

see also Elkhart, Ind.

see also Evansville, Ind.

see also Fort Wayne, Ind.

see also Indianapolis, Ind.

see also Kokomo, Ind.

see also Marion County, Ind.

see also South Bend, Ind.

see also under By City and By County in the "Index by Categories"

see also under By State in the "Index by Categories"

Indianapolis, Ind.

Business conditions analysis for selected Indiana local areas, quarterly rpt semiannual feature, U2160–1.502, U2160–1.504

Discount stores shopped and store characteristics, for 3 major chains in 3 market areas, 1993 surveys and trends, articles, C5150–3.516

see also under By City in the "Index by Categories"

Indians

Accounting grad supply-demand, including detail by sex, race-ethnicity, and region, 1991/92 and trends, annual rpt, A1885–1

AIDS cases and deaths among children under age 13, by race-ethnicity, 1990, R3840–21

AIDS cases, by sex and race-ethnicity, through June 1992, article, C4215–1.503

American College Test (ACT) scores, by sex and race-ethnicity, 1993, annual article, C2175–1.534

American College Test (ACT) scores by student characteristics, with student views on schools and education plans, 1992 and trends, annual rpt, R1960–6

Births and fertility, by selected newborn and maternal characteristics, 1990, article, R8750–1.510

Broadcasting station seller tax deferment certificates granted by FCC for sales to minority buyers, by ethnic group, 1978-1st half 1993, article, C1850–14.537

Business establishments and gross receipts for minority-owned vs total businesses, with detail by race-ethnicity, 1987, article, C4215–1.507

Cancer deaths among minorities, by body site and ethnic group, 1989, annual rpt, A1175–1

Catholic school enrollment by ethnic group, 1982/83 and 1991/92-1992/93, annual rpt, A7375–1

Catholic secondary school operations and finances, including enrollment by race-ethnicity and family income, 1991/92 and trends, biennial rpt, A7375–5

Chemist and chemical engineer salaries, employment status, and demographic and professional characteristics, 1993, annual rpt, A1250–4

Index by Subjects and Names

Chemistry and chemical engineering grad starting salaries, employment status, demographic characteristics, and advanced study plans, 1991/92, annual rpt, A1250–2

Child poverty by State and for 200 cities and 89 counties, with State and city detail by race-ethnicity, 1989 and trends, R3840–20

Community and junior college revenues by source and expenditures by function, and selected student characteristics, FY92, annual rpt, A6705–1

Correctional instn admin, inmates, facilities, costs, parole and probation, and staffing, for local, State, and Federal systems, 1992 annual series, R4300–1

Dental school enrollment and grads, by sex and race-ethnicity, 1992/93 annual rpt, A1475–3.1

Dental school faculty, support personnel, and staff characteristics, by instn, 1992/93, annual rpt, A1475–4.5

Dental school student attrition, by reason and student characteristics, 1991/92 and trends, annual rpt, A1475–4.4

Doctoral degree recipient characteristics, including citizenship status, source of support, field of study, and instn, 1990/91 and trends, annual rpt, R6000–7

Doctoral degrees conferred and recipient characteristics, by field, 1992, annual feature, C2175–1.535

Ecologist personal and professional characteristics, including research activity and funding, with data by field, Mar 1992 survey, recurring rpt, A4685–1

Elementary/secondary prospective teacher characteristics and opinions, survey of persons interested in alternative certification routes, 1992, R6350–7

Engineering degrees awarded, by State, instn, and field, with detail for women, minorities, and foreign students, 1991/92, annual rpt, A0685–1

Engineering program enrollment, by instn, field, and State, with detail for women, minorities, and foreign students, fall 1992, annual rpt, A0685–2

Eye bank activity in US and abroad, including donations by type, source, and donor characteristics, and data by individual bank, 1992 and trends, annual rpt, A4743–1

Foundation board trustees by sex and race-ethnicity, for 25 leading private, community, and corporate foundations, 1989 and trends, A9405–1.1

Foundation board trustees by sex and race-ethnicity, for 25 leading private, community, and corporate foundations, 1991 and trends, A9405–1.2

Foundation finances, and personnel and governing board characteristics, by organization characteristics, 1991/92, article, C2176–1.506

Geoscience enrollment and degrees awarded, by sex, race-ethnicity, and discipline, 1991/92, annual rpt, A1785–3

Health indicators, including hypertension and lung cancer rates, and cancer and heart disease/stroke deaths, by sex and race-ethnicity, 1993 feature, C4215–1.511

Index by Subjects and Names

Indians

High school students taking advanced placement exams in biology and calculus, by race-ethnicity and State, 1992, biennial rpt, A4355–3.2

Higher education degrees conferred, by level, sex, discipline, and race-ethnicity, 1990/91, recurring feature, C2175–1.523

Higher education employment, by position type and race-ethnicity, 1991/92, C2175–1.507

Higher education enrollment by race-ethnicity, by State, fall 1991, annual rpt, C2175–1.531

Higher education enrollment in historically black colleges, distribution by student race-ethnicity, 1993 article, C4215–1.509

Higher education enrollment of minority and foreign students at approx 3,100 instns, fall 1991, recurring feature, C2175–1.510

Higher education enrollment of minority and foreign students, with comparison to whites, by sex, State, and instn type, fall 1991, recurring feature, C2175–1.506

Higher education freshmen attitudes and characteristics, degree and career plans, and financial aid sources, by sex and instn type, fall 1992, annual survey, U6215–1

Higher education involvement of minorities, including enrollment and degrees awarded, by race-ethnicity, sex, and State, 1970s-91, annual rpt, A1410–10

Higher education minority student enrollment trends, 1993 annual survey, A1410–1.38

Higher education president personal and professional characteristics, 1990 and trends, recurring rpt, A1410–12

Higher education president personal and professional characteristics, 1990, article, C2175–1.533

Higher education student athlete enrollment and graduation rates, by sex, race-ethnicity, and major sport, for Natl Collegiate Athletic Assn Div I instns, 1992/93, annual rpt, A7440–4

Higher education undergrad and grad enrollment by race-ethnicity, fall 1990, article, C4215–1.508

Incarcerated mothers and their children, with data on characteristics, child caregivers, visitation, and support program use, 1991/92, A7575–4

Job Corps youth training program funding, enrollment capacity, and participants by selected characteristics, 1981-94, article, R4800–2.515

Journalism/mass communication enrollment and grads by level, by instn, sex, race-ethnicity, and field, 1990/91 and trends, annual article, A3225–1

Labor force and education data for women and minorities in professional fields, 1980s-91, with historical trends, recurring rpt, A3960–2

Latin America statistical abstract, general data by country, 1992 annual rpt, U6250–1.5

Law school enrollment by minority status, degrees conferred, staff, and library holdings, by instn, 1992/93 and trends, annual rpt, A0970–1

Law school grad employment and salaries, by type of employer, location, and grad characteristics, 1992 and trends, annual rpt, A6505–1

Librarians (special) salaries, by location, work setting, and personal characteristics, US and Canada, 1992 and trends, biennial survey rpt, A8965–1

Librarians at universities and research instns, by minority group and census div, FY92, annual survey, A3365–2

Library/info science school enrollment, staff and student characteristics, finances, and curricula, by school and degree program, 1991/92, annual rpt, A3235–1

Local govt land use planning commissions composition and activities, and commissioner characteristics, 1987 and trends, recurring rpt, A2615–2

Local officials in municipal and county govt, demographic profiles and job functions, 1993 annual rpt, A5800–1

Mathematics dept faculty and doctoral degree recipient characteristics, including salaries, 1991/92 and trends, annual survey, A2085–1.1

Medical school programs, fees, applicants, admissions, and enrollment, with data by age, sex, minority group, and instn, 1992/93 and trends, annual rpt, A3273–10

Nursing center (community) staff and client characteristics, and services, 1990 survey, article, A8010–3.506

Nursing college deans, by race-ethnicity, 1992/93, annual rpt, A0615–2

Nursing college faculty, by race-ethnicity, 1992/93, annual rpt, A0615–1

Nursing higher education program faculty and clinic patient characteristics, 1992/93 biennial rpt, A0615–5

Nursing school enrollment and grads, by degree level, sex, race-ethnicity, and instn type and location, 1992/93 and trends, annual rpt, A0615–4

Nursing schools, programs, enrollment, student and staff characteristics, and grads, 1991 and trends, annual rpt, A8010–1

Oil production and value, and oil revenues received from onshore Federal and Indian land leases, 1991 and trends, periodic basic data book, A2575–14.2

Optometry school faculty, enrollment and degrees, policies and programs, and finances, by instn, 1991/92, annual survey, A3370–2

Osteopathy college enrollment, student and faculty characteristics and finances, 1992/93 and trends, annual rpt, A0620–1

Pharmacy degree program applications, enrollment, and degrees conferred, by student characteristics and instn, 1990/91 and trends, annual rpt, A0630–9

Physics and astronomy bachelor degree recipients postgraduation plans and demographic characteristics, 1991/92 and trends, annual survey, A1960–3

Physics degrees awarded, by level, sex, and minority group, 1991/92, annual rpt, A1960–2.1

Planning profession employment and salaries, by type of employer, demographic and professional characteristics, and location, 1991 and trends, biennial rpt, A2615–1

Political science higher education dept faculty, by sex and race-ethnicity, 1991/92, annual rpt, A2617–1

Population characteristics, employment, and voting patterns for minority groups by detailed race-ethnicity, with comparisons to whites, 1980s-2040, R8750–2.58

Prisoners on death row, by State, sex, and race-ethnicity, 1992 and trends, annual rpt, A1305–3

Private elementary and secondary school enrollment, staff, and finances, with detail for minorities, by school type and region, 1980s-1992/93, annual rpt, A6835–3

Professional worker salaries, by employee and employer characteristics, with detail for scientists and engineers, 1990s and trends, biennial rpt, A3960–1

Psychology doctoral degree recipient employment and demographic characteristics, and finances, 1990/91, biennial survey rpt, A2620–4

Psychology grad depts, faculty characteristics, enrollment, and student aid, US and Canada, 1990/91 and trends, annual rpt, A2620–3

Public health school applicant, student, and grad characteristics, by instn, 1991/92 and trends, annual rpt, A3372–3

Public health school faculty characteristics, by instn, fall 1991, recurring rpt, A3372–1

Religious congregation characteristics, including membership, activities, staff, and finances, 1992 survey, recurring rpt, A5435–4

Restaurants/drinking places and sales, for minority-owned establishments by race-ethnicity, 1987, article, A8200–1.508

Scholastic Aptitude Test (SAT) participants and/or scores, by education of parents, income, and race-ethnicity, 1992, C4215–1.501

School board members by race-ethnicity, by district enrollment size, 1992 survey rpt, A0775–5

Social work higher education programs, faculty and student characteristics, and student aid, with data by instn, 1992 and trends, annual rpt, A4515–1

Socioeconomic status data for blacks compared to other minority groups, 1993 annual compilation, A8510–1.1

State social, economic, and govtl indicators, with rankings, 1993 semiannual rpt, B8500–1.1, B8500–1.7

Statistical profiles of 50 States and DC, general data, 1993 annual almanac, C4712–1

Student attitudes on courses in 4 subject areas, for 8th graders by sex and race-ethnicity, 1988, R4800–2.512

Substance abuse treatment programs, funding by source, and client characteristics, for alcohol and drug services, by State, FY91 and trends, annual rpt, A7112–1

Theological school enrollment by degree level, by sex and race-ethnicity, fall 1992 and trends, annual rpt, A3376–1

Urban public school enrollment by race-ethnicity, with comparisons to total State, for 47 systems, 1990/91, A4425–4

Western States higher education grad student exchange program enrollment, by race-ethnicity, for 13 States, fall 1992, annual rpt, A9385–1

Indians

Index by Subjects and Names

Women candidates in State-level elections, outcome summaries including campaign funds raised, voting by sex, and winner's race-ethnicity, 1992, U4510–4.4

Women in elective office, by minority group, party, and govt level, 1993, annual rpt, U4510–1.66

Women's employment in govt, with data by race-ethnicity and State, series, U5090–1

State and local:

Alabama county data book, general data, 1992 annual rpt, S0121–2

Alabama public school Federal revenues for Indian education programs, by district, FY92, annual rpt, S0124–1.2

Alabama statistical abstract, general data, 1992 recurring rpt, U5680–2.3

Alaska corrections system admin, including inmate and probationer/parolee offenses and demographic characteristics, 1991 annual rpt, S0287–1

Alaska high school grads as percent of population over age 25, total and Native American, by borough and census area, 1980 and 1990, article, S0320–1.504

Alaska population, housing, income, and education data, by demographic characteristics and/or locality, 1990/91 and trends, annual rpt, S0320–4

Alaska public schools, enrollment, staff, and finances, by district, FY92, annual rpt, S0295–2

Alaska State court system employees, by sex and race-ethnicity, FY92, annual rpt, S0290–1

Alaska vital statistics, including births, deaths by cause, marriages, divorces, adoptions, and population, by demographic characteristics and location, 1990, annual rpt, S0315–1

Arizona arrests and murder victims, by age, sex, and race-ethnicity, 1992, annual rpt, S0505–2

Arizona correctional instn admin, including inmates by criminal background and demographic characteristics, FY92, annual rpt, S0464–2

Arizona elementary and secondary school enrollment, by grade and race-ethnicity, 1991/92, annual rpt, S0470–1

Arizona household income and poverty rates, by race-ethnicity, 1989, article, U0280–1.502

Arizona Indian population, education, housing, health, and employment characteristics, with detail by reservation, 1970s-91, recurring rpt, U5850–2.9

Arizona land acreage in Indian reservations, by county, 1992, annual rpt, U5830–1

Arizona Navajo/Hopi Indian AFDC recipients and payments, monthly rpt, S0465–4

Arizona statistical abstract, general data, 1993 recurring rpt, U5850–2.2, U5850–2.3, U5850–2.4, U5850–2.6, U5850–2.12, U5850–2.16

Arkansas Census of Population and Housing detailed findings, 1990, U5935–7

Arkansas Medicaid recipients, by race-ethnicity, FY91, annual rpt, S0700–2.3

Arkansas public school enrollment and grads, by race-ethnicity and sex, 1991/92, annual rpt, S0660–1.1

Arkansas vocational rehabilitation expenditures, impact on earnings and employment, and client characteristics, FY91 annual rpt, S0700–2.4

California Census of Population and Housing detailed findings, 1990, S0840–9

California judicial system employment by position, sex, and race-ethnicity, with minority utilization rates and parity targets, Jan 1993, annual rpt, S0905–1.1

California labor force planning rpt, including population characteristics, and employment by industry, 1992 annual rpt, S0830–2

California postsecondary education enrollment and degrees, by sex, race-ethnicity, and instn, 1990/91, annual series, S0827–2

California public school enrollment, grads, and staff, by race-ethnicity, 1992/93 and trends, annual rpt, S0825–9

California registered apprentices, by sex and race-ethnicity, 1987-91, annual rpt, S0840–2.3

California socioeconomic and govtl data for municipalities, counties, and school districts, 1993 annual rpt, C4712–3

California statistical abstract, general data, 1992 annual rpt, S0840–2.2

California vital statistics, including population, births, and deaths by cause, by demographic characteristics and county, 1990 and trends, annual rpt, S0865–1

Colorado homicide offenders and victims, by age, sex, and race-ethnicity, 1991-92, annual rpt, S1068–1

Colorado job service applicant characteristics, FY93 annual planning rpt, S1040–3.2

Colorado public school enrollment, finances, and student and staff characteristics, by locality, 1992 annual rpt series, S1000–2

Colorado vital statistics, including population, births, deaths by cause, abortion, marriage and divorce, and adoption, by demographic characteristics and location, 1990 and trends, annual rpt, S1010–1

Connecticut crimes and arrests, by offense, with data by local agency, and victim-offender characteristics, 1992, annual rpt, S1256–1

Connecticut public school data, including enrollment, staff, programs, finances, and student characteristics, 1991/92, biennial rpt, S1185–3

DC public school enrollment, by race-ethnicity, 1987/88-1991/92, annual rpt, S1605–2

DC statistical profile, general data, 1992 annual rpt, S1535–3.1

Delaware postsecondary instn enrollment and degrees conferred, by race-ethnicity, 1992, annual rpt, S1425–1

Delaware public and nonpublic school minority enrollment, 1991/92, annual rpt, S1430–1

Florida higher education enrollment, degree programs, staff, and finances, by State-supported instn, with student and staff characteristics, 1991/92 annual rpt, S1725–1

Florida municipal and county statistical profiles, general data, 1991 annual rpt, C4712–6

Florida statistical abstract, general data, 1992 annual rpt, U6660–1.1, U6660–1.4

Florida vital statistics, including population, births, deaths by cause, and marriages and dissolutions, by location and demographic characteristics, 1992 and trends, annual rpt, S1745–3

Georgia statistical abstract, general data, 1992-93 biennial rpt, U6730–1.1

Hawaii crimes and arrests, by offense, with data by county and victim-offender characteristics, 1992, annual rpt, S2035–1

Hawaii data book, general data, 1992 annual rpt, S2090–1.1, S2090–1.12, S2090–1.15

Idaho crimes and arrests, by offense, with data by location and offender characteristics, 1992 and trends, annual rpt, S2275–2

Idaho economic profile, general data, 1992 recurring rpt, S2218–2.2

Idaho public school personnel characteristics and salaries by position, and teachers and enrollment by school district, 1992/93, annual rpt, S2225–3

Idaho vital statistics, including births, deaths by cause, abortions, marriages, and divorces, by demographic characteristics and county, 1991 and trends, annual rpt, S2250–2

Illinois corrections dept admin, including inmates and characteristics, finances, and staff, FY91-93 and trends, annual rpt, S2425–1

Illinois crimes and arrests, by offense and offender characteristics, 1990-91, annual rpt, S2536–1

Illinois higher education enrollment and degrees, by level, instn, field of instruction, and student characteristics, 1992 and trends, annual rpt, S2475–1.1

Illinois mental health facility patient population and characteristics, by facility, location, and treatment category, FY93, annual rpt, S2505–1

Illinois public school enrollment and dropouts, by race-ethnicity, 1990/91, annual rpt, S2440–1.1

Illinois statistical abstract, general data, 1992 annual rpt, U6910–2

Indiana public assistance program participation, expenditures, and services, by county, FY92 and trends, annual rpt, S2623–1

Iowa correctional instn admissions, releases, and inmate characteristics, by instn, monthly rpt, S2770–1

Iowa population share in poverty, by race-ethnicity, 1990, annual rpt, S2784–3

Kansas correctional instn inmates, by offense, demographic characteristics, and instn, FY92 and trends, annual rpt, S2940–1

Kansas crimes and arrests, with victim, offender, and law enforcement employee characteristics, 1992, annual rpt, S2925–1

Kansas statistical abstract, general data, 1991/92 annual rpt, U7095–2.2

Kentucky arrests by county and offense, and law enforcement employment by agency, 1992, annual rpt, S3150–1.2

Kentucky economic statistics, general data, 1993 annual rpt, S3104–1

Index by Subjects and Names — Indians

Kentucky households by income group, by householder age and race-ethnicity, 1990, annual planning rpt, S3140–3

Louisiana Census of Population and Housing summary findings, by local area, 1990 and trends, U8010–4

Louisiana school district profiles, including enrollment, grads, and staff, by race-ethnicity, 1991/92, annual rpt, S3280–1.2

Maine births by race-ethnicity of mother, and abortions by patient characteristics, 1991, annual rpt, S3460–2

Maine Census of Population and Housing findings, including detail for Indian reservations and trust lands, 1990, S3465–7, S3465–9

Maine Census of Population and Housing summary findings, by local area, 1990, S3465–8

Maine schools for Indian education, enrollment by grade, 1991/92, annual rpt, S3435–1

Maryland crimes and arrests, by offense, location, and offender characteristics, with law enforcement employment and assaults on officers, 1992 and trends, annual rpt, S3665–1

Maryland elementary and secondary education data, by county, 1991/92, annual rpt, S3610–2.3

Maryland elementary and secondary education data, by county, 1992 and trends, annual rpt, S3610–2.4

Maryland elementary and secondary education data, by county, 1992/93, annual rpt, S3610–2.8

Maryland public school enrollment by race-ethnicity and county, 1992, annual rpt, S3610–1

Maryland statistical abstract, general data, 1993-94 biennial rpt, S3605–1.1

Massachusetts correctional instn inmate socioeconomic characteristics and criminal background, by instn, Jan 1992 and trends, annual rpt, S3805–1

Massachusetts elementary/secondary school enrollment, by sex and race-ethnicity, Oct 1980 and 1991, annual rpt, S3810–3

Massachusetts municipal and county profiles, general data, 1992 annual rpt, C4712–2

Michigan labor force planning rpt, including employment by industry, and characteristics of Job Training Partnership Act eligible population, 1993 annual rpt, S3980–1

Michigan public assistance recipients, by race-ethnicity and county, monthly rpt quarterly tables, S4010–1

Michigan State corrections dept employment of women, minorities, and handicapped, 1991 and trends, annual rpt, S3960–1

Michigan vital statistics, including births, deaths, marriages, divorces/annulments, and communicable diseases, by location and demographic characteristics, 1990 and trends, annual rpt, S4000–3

Minnesota enrollment distribution by race-ethnicity, and minority student shares by district and county, 1991/92 and trends, annual rpt, S4165–1

Minnesota postsecondary education finances, and enrollment by student characteristics, by type of school system, 1970s-93, biennial rpt, S4195–2.2

Minnesota vital statistics, including population, births, abortions, deaths, marriages, and divorces, by location and demographic characteristics, 1991 and trends, annual rpt, S4190–2

Mississippi statistical abstract, general data, 1992 annual rpt, U3255–4.2

Missouri correctional instn admissions, releases, and inmate characteristics, FY93, annual rpt, S4501–1

Missouri crimes and arrests, by offense and location, with victim and offender characteristics, 1991 and trends, annual rpt, S4560–2

Missouri higher education enrollment and degrees granted, by sex, race-ethnicity, and instn, 1992 and trends, annual rpt, S4520–3

Montana employment and unemployment, by race-ethnicity and county, 1990, annual planning rpt, S4710–3

Montana land ownership distribution, including govt agencies and Indian reservations, 1983, annual rpt, S4655–1

Montana public school enrollment by grade, and grads, by school, county, race-ethnicity, and sex, 1992 and trends, annual rpt, S4740–1

Montana vital statistics, including births, deaths by cause, abortion, disease, and marriage and divorce, by demographic characteristics and county, 1990-91 and trends, annual rpt, S4690–1

Nebraska correctional instn admin, with inmates by criminal background and demographic characteristics, by instn, FY92 and trends, annual rpt, S4850–1

Nebraska elementary and secondary school enrollment, by race-ethnicity, school district, and county, 1992/93, annual rpt, S4865–2.5

Nebraska vital statistics, including births, deaths, marriages, divorces, and population, by demographic characteristics and location, 1991 and trends, annual rpt, S4885–1

Nevada public school enrollment and teachers, by race-ethnicity and school district, 1990/91, annual rpt, S5035–2

Nevada statistical abstract, general data, 1992 biennial rpt, S5005–1.1, S5005–1.7

Nevada vital statistics, including births, abortions, and deaths by cause, by county and demographic characteristics, 1989 and trends, annual rpt, S5075–1

New Hampshire arrests, by offense and offender age, sex, and race-ethnicity, 1991, annual rpt, S5250–2.2

New Jersey Census of Population and Housing detailed findings, by county, 1990, S5425–19

New Jersey correctional instn inmates, by offense, sentence length, demographic characteristics, and instn, Dec 1991 annual rpt, S5370–1

New Jersey crimes and arrests, by offense, with data by location and offender characteristics, 1992 and trends, annual rpt, S5430–1

New Jersey municipal and county data book, general data, 1992 annual rpt, C4712–4

New Jersey population, by race-ethnicity and age, 1990, annual rpt, S5405–1

New Jersey public schools, enrollment, and student and staff characteristics, and nonpublic schools and enrollment, by county, 1991/92, annual rpt, S5385–1

New Mexico elementary/secondary school enrollment by race-ethnicity, 1991/92, annual rpt, S5575–4

New Mexico labor force planning rpt, including population characteristics, and employment by industry and occupation, 1993 annual rpt, S5624–1

New Mexico public welfare recipient characteristics, by program, monthly rpt quarterly table, S5620–2

New Mexico traffic accidents, fatalities, and injuries, by Indian pueblo or reservation, 1992, annual rpt, S5665–1

New Mexico vital statistics, including population, births, deaths, and disease, by location and demographic characteristics, 1991 and trends, annual rpt, S5605–1

New York State arrests and juvenile corrections admissions, by race-ethnicity, 1991, annual rpt, S5760–3

New York State local jail/penitentiary inmates by offense, sentence, and demographic characteristics, by county or facility, 1991, annual rpt, S5724–2

New York State municipal and county statistical profiles, general data, 1993 annual rpt, C4712–7

New York State statistical yearbook, general data, 1992 annual rpt, U5100–1.1, U5100–1.8, U5100–1.10

North Carolina correctional instn admissions, separations, and population, with inmate characteristics, FY93, semiannual rpt, S5900–1

North Carolina crimes and arrests, by offense, with data by location and offender characteristics, 1992 and trends, annual rpt, S5955–1

North Carolina election results, with voter registration by party and race-ethnicity, by county, 1992, biennial rpt, S5920–1

North Carolina higher education enrollment, and degrees conferred, by race-ethnicity and instn, 1992/93 annual rpt, U8013–1

North Carolina public school enrollment, grads, staff, and finances, with data by race, sex, and local district, 1991/92-1992/93 and trends, annual rpt, S5915–1

North Dakota crimes and arrests, by offense, location, and offender characteristics, and law enforcement employment, 1991 and trends, annual rpt, S6060–1

North Dakota elementary and secondary school staff characteristics and salaries, by position, region, and enrollment size, 1992/93 annual rpt, S6180–3

North Dakota enrollment and staff of Bur of Indian Affairs schools, and total Indian students, 1992/93 annual directory, S6180–2

North Dakota higher education enrollment, by level, instn, county, and selected student characteristics, fall 1992 and trends, annual rpt, S6110–1

North Dakota local correctional instn adult and juvenile inmate characteristics, by instn, 1991 and trends, annual rpt, S6060–3

Indians

North Dakota vital statistics, including births, deaths by cause, marriages and divorces, and abortions, by demographic characteristics and/or county, 1991 and trends, annual rpt, S6105–2

Oklahoma correctional instn admin, including inmate characteristics, incarceration costs, and data by instn, FY91, annual rpt, S6420–1

Oklahoma crimes and arrests, by offense, with data by local agency and victim and offender characteristics, 1990-92, annual rpt, S6465–1

Oklahoma public school enrollment shares by race-ethnicity, 1989 and 1992, annual rpt, S6423–2

Oklahoma public welfare program recipients and payments, and recipient characteristics, by county and type of service, FY92, annual rpt, S6455–1.2

Oklahoma school revenues from Federal Indian education programs, by county and district, FY92, annual rpt, S6423–1.1

Oklahoma statistical abstract, general data, 1992 annual rpt, U8130–2.2, U8130–2.3, U8130–2.9

Oregon crimes and arrests, by offense, with detail on bias crimes and data by victim and offender characteristics, 1992 and trends, annual rpt, S6603–3.1

Oregon elementary and secondary public school enrollment by race-ethnicity and teachers, by instn, Oct 1992, annual rpt, S6590–1.1

Oregon public high school completers, by instn, county, sex, and race-ethnicity, 1992, annual rpt, S6590–1.10

Oregon public school enrollment, by county, grade, and race-ethnicity, Oct 1992, annual rpt, S6590–1.9

Oregon vital statistics, including births, deaths by cause, communicable diseases, marriages, and divorces, by age, sex, race-ethnicity, and county, 1991 and trends, annual rpt, S6615–5

Pennsylvania Census of Population and Housing detailed findings, with selected data by county and municipality, 1990, U4130–13

Pennsylvania crimes and arrests, by offense, with data by location and offender characteristics, 1992 and trends, annual rpt, S6860–1

Pennsylvania educational statistics by level and/or type of education, series, S6790–5

Pennsylvania employment and commuting data from Census of Population and Housing, by county and municipality, 1990, C1595–16

Pennsylvania State correctional instn admin, and inmates by type of offense and demographic characteristics, 1990 and trends, annual rpt, S6782–1

Pennsylvania statistical abstract, general data, 1992 recurring rpt, U4130–6.1, U4130–6.3

Rhode Island public school enrollment by type of instn, grade, sex, race-ethnicity, and district, 1991/92 or fall 1992, annual rpt, S6970–1.1

South Carolina higher education enrollment and faculty, by race-ethnicity and instn, 1993 annual rpt, S7185–2

South Carolina marriages, by race-ethnicity of bride and groom, 1990, annual rpt, S7175–1

South Carolina population, by age, race-ethnicity, sex, and locality, 1990 and trends, annual planning rpt, S7155–3.1

South Carolina statistical abstract, general data, 1993 annual rpt, S7125–1.12, S7125–1.13

South Dakota city and reservation sales/use tax revenues, FY91-92, annual rpt, S7380–1.1

South Dakota correctional instn admin, including inmates by criminal background and demographic characteristics, FY92 and trends, annual rpt, S7296–1

South Dakota public higher education enrollment and faculty, by race-ethnicity and instn, FY93 annual rpt, S7375–1

South Dakota recipients of elderly assistance and health services, FY92, annual rpt, S7385–1.1

South Dakota school enrollment, grads, and dropouts by race-ethnicity, 1991/92, annual rpt, S7315–1.1

South Dakota vital statistics, including births, deaths, marriage and divorce, and communicable disease, by demographic characteristics and county, 1991 and trends, annual rpt, S7345–1

Tennessee higher education grads and degrees conferred, by race-ethnicity, 1991/92, annual rpt, S7525–1.2

Tennessee statistical abstract, general data, 1992/93 annual rpt, U8710–2.1

Texas crimes and arrests by offender characteristics, and crimes involving bias against selected ethnic groups, 1992, annual rpt, S7735–2.2

Texas elementary and secondary education enrollment by race-ethnicity, by school, district, and county, 1991/92, annual rpt, S7670–1.1

Texas elementary/secondary education personnel, by sex and race-ethnicity, by district and county, 1991/92, annual rpt, S7670–1.3

Texas higher education enrollment and faculty, by race-ethnicity, sex, and instn, 1991/92 and trends, annual rpt, S7657–1.1

Texas Medicaid expenditures by category, and recipient characteristics and medical services received, 1975 and 1980-91, U8850–8.5

Texas vital statistics, including births, deaths by cause, abortions, marriages, and divorces, by location and demographic characteristics, 1991 and trends, annual rpt, S7685–1

Utah corrections inmates, parolees, and probationers, by criminal background and demographic characteristics, FY92 and trends, annual rpt, S7810–1

Utah employment by detailed occupation, and educational attainment by age group, by sex and race-ethnicity, with detail for 7 urban areas, 1990 census rpt, S7832–3.4

Utah govt statistical review, fiscal and socioeconomic data, 1993 annual rpt, R9380–1.1

Utah higher education enrollment, by instn, fall 1992, annual rpt, S7895–2

Utah homeless shelter population characteristics, individual shelter capacity, and related housing data, 1991-92, annual rpt, S7808–2

Index by Subjects and Names

Utah income data by race-ethnicity, and population profiles for individual Indian reservations, 1990 census rpt, S7832–3.3

Utah Indian reservation acreage, by county, 1992 article, U8960–2.502

Utah labor force and percent without high school diploma, by sex, age group, and/or race-ethnicity, 1990, article, U8960–2.509

Utah marriages and divorces, by participant characteristics and location, 1990 and trends, annual rpt, S7835–2

Utah murder victims and offenders, by race-ethnicity, 1992, annual rpt, S7890–3

Utah population distribution and selected characteristics, by race-ethnicity, 1990, S7820–3.504

Utah public school enrollment, dropouts, and grads, by race-ethnicity, 1991/92, annual rpt, S7815–1.2

Utah statistical abstract, general data, 1993 triennial rpt, U8960–1.1

Utah vital statistics, including births and deaths by cause, by demographic characteristics and location, 1990, annual rpt, S7835–1.2

Vermont births, by race-ethnicity of child, mother's age, and county, 1991, annual rpt, S8054–1

Vermont elementary and secondary school enrollment by grade, sex, race-ethnicity, school, and county, 1992/93 and trends, annual rpt, S8020–1

Virginia crimes and arrests, by offense, with data by location and offender characteristics, 1992, annual rpt, S8295–2

Virginia public school dropouts by race-ethnicity and sex, by county and municipality, 1991/92, annual rpt, S8190–3

Washington State correctional instn inmate population, admissions, and releases, by demographic characteristics, quarterly rpt, S8337–1

Washington State crimes and arrests, by offense, with data by location and offender characteristics, 1992 and trends, annual rpt, S8440–1

Washington State population and demographic characteristics, and housing units, by county and/or city, 1992 and trends, annual rpt, S8345–4

Washington State public assistance clients and service costs, by client characteristics, program, and county, FY90, annual rpt, S8420–2

Washington State vital statistics, including births, deaths by cause, and population, by demographic characteristics and location, 1991 and trends, annual rpt, S8363–1

West Virginia arrests and murder victims, by race-ethnicity, 1990-91, annual rpt, S8610–1.1

West Virginia higher education enrollment, degrees, faculty and student characteristics, and finances, by instn, 1992/93 and trends, annual rpt, S8533–1

West Virginia population, by race-ethnicity, 1990, annual rpt, S8560–1

Wisconsin Blue Book, general data, 1993-94 biennial rpt, S8780–1.2

Wisconsin correctional instn inmates, by criminal background and selected characteristics, series, S8692–1

Index by Subjects and Names

Wisconsin crimes and arrests, by offense, offender characteristics, county, and local agency, 1992 and trends, annual rpt, S8771–1

Wisconsin elementary and secondary school enrollment, staff, costs, and State aid, by school district, 1992/93 and trends, annual rpt, S8795–2

Wisconsin vital statistics, including population, births, deaths by cause, and marriages and dissolutions, by county and demographic characteristics, 1991 and trends, annual rpt, S8715–4

Wyoming correctional instn admin, finances, inmate characteristics, and staff, and probation and parole activities, FY92 annual rpt, S8883–1

Wyoming employment and unemployment by sex and race-ethnicity, by county, 1990, S8895–1.505

Wyoming Native American population, unemployment, and poverty rates, by county and/or reservation, 1990, article, S8895–1.501

Wyoming public school enrollment, by sex, race-ethnicity, school, and district, 1991/92 and trends, annual rpt, S8890–1.2

Wyoming vital statistics, including population, births, deaths by cause, marriages, and divorces, by demographic characteristics and county, 1991 and trends, annual rpt, S8920–2

see also Bureau of Indian Affairs

Indigent defense

see Legal aid

Individual retirement arrangements

Assets of retirement accounts, by investment objective and type of fund and instn, 1991 and trends, annual rpt, A6025–1

Mutual funds (money market) IRA and Keogh plan availability, for over 850 funds, 1993 annual directory, C4682–2

Mutual funds IRA and Keogh plan availability, for more than 1,200 funds, 1993 annual directory, C4682–1

Outstanding amounts in IRAs and Keogh plans, and life insurance pension plans by type, 1991 and trends, biennial fact book, A1325–1.3

Pension benefit lump sum payments disposition, including placement in savings by type, by recipient characteristics, 1980s, R9260–17

Indochina

see Cambodia

see Indochinese refugees

see Southeast Asia

see Vietnam

Indochinese refugees

Arrivals, and resettlement, with detail by country, 1992 annual feature, R9372–2.503

Cambodia repatriated refugee population coming from 7 Thailand camp sites, for 8 reception centers, Mar-Nov 1992, R9372–2.502

State and local:

Alabama public school Federal revenues for Indochinese education programs, by district, FY92, annual rpt, S0124–1.2

see also Cambodia

see also Vietnam

Indonesia

Agricultural production trends and impacts of govt policies, for 5 major food crops, 1970s-80s, R5620–1.37

Coal industry supply-demand, employment, and trade, by country, 1990-91 and trends, annual rpt, A7400–2.2

Electronics industry trade and/or production trends by product category for 33 countries, with general economic profiles, 1993 annual rpt, A4725–1.4

Energy intl sourcebook, with detail on oil and gas industry operations, supply-demand, and prices, for approx 80 countries, 1970s-91, annual compilation, C6985–10.2

Foreign trade with and assistance from Japan, 1992 and trends, article, R5650–2.534

Motor vehicle world production, sales, trade, and registrations, by country, world area, manufacturer, and make, 1991 and trends, annual rpt, A0865–2.1

see also Organization of Petroleum Exporting Countries

see also under By Foreign Country or World Area in the "Index by Categories"

Industrial accidents and safety

see Hazardous substances

see Mine accidents and safety

see Occupational health and safety

see Railroad accidents and safety

Industrial and commercial energy use

Chemical industry finances and operations, with data by industry segment and product, 1970s-92, annual rpt, A3850–1

Coal industry supply-demand, employment, and trade, by country, with summary data on world energy resources, 1992 annual rpt, A7400–2

Consumption of energy, by fuel source, consuming sector, State, and census div, 1970s-91, annual rpt, A1775–3.6

Consumption of energy for industrial purposes, with detail for chemical and oil industries, 1988-89, article, C5800–8.502

Convenience store industry financial and operating data, by size category, 1992 and trends, annual survey rpt, A6735–1, A6735–2

Electric power generated and fuel use by type, for individual steam plants by utility and State, monthly rpt, A7400–8

Electric power supply-demand, and utility capacities and fuel requirements, detailed data by US and Canadian region, 1992-2002, annual rpt, A8630–2

Electric utility (private vs public) revenues and consumption, by customer sector, 1990, annual article, A2625–1.501

Electric utility customers, sales, and revenues, by user sector, bimonthly rpt quarterly table, A4700–4

Electric utility finances, sales, and capacity, 1993 annual feature, C5800–28.507

Electric utility financial and operating data, by State and census div, 1991 and trends, annual rpt, A4700–1

Electric utility fuel consumption, by type and census div, 1990-91, article, A4700–4.501

Electric utility operating data, including generating capacity and efficiency, peak demand, and fuel consumption, top 100 utilities, 1992, annual article, C6985–6.512

Industrial and commercial energy use

Energy consumption by fuel type and sector, 1970s-2010, annual rpt, C6985–5

Fuel oil dealer operations, with heating and cooling equipment services, by region, 1992 annual survey, C4680–2

Higher education physical plant operations, costs, employment, salaries, and energy use, by instn and region, 1991/92, recurring rpt, A3183–1

Iron and steel industry consumption of materials and energy, US and Canada, 1992 and trends, annual rpt, A2000–2

Japan energy supply-demand and outlook, by fuel source, 1980s-2000, recurring article, R5650–2.536

Manufacturing energy consumption per dollar of value added, by industry group, 1993 article, C7000–3.507

Natural gas demand, by consuming sector, 1992, 2000, and 2005, article, C6985–1.527

Natural gas industrial prices, 1973-92, annual rpt, A5425–2.2

Natural gas industry composite income statement, with sales and prices by consuming sector and census div, quarterly rpt, A1775–1

Natural gas industry detailed operating and financial data, by State and census div, 1960s-91, annual rpt, A1775–3

Natural gas sales and prices, by consuming sector, monthly rpt, A1775–2

Northeast region industrial electric power average bills, by State, 1985-91, recurring rpt, S3434–1

Office building detailed income and expense data, and energy use, US and Canada, by building characteristics, metro area, and US region, 1991 and trends, annual rpt, A5600–2

Oil supply-demand, marketing, prices, finances, and employment, detailed data for US and Canada, by product, company, and location, 1993 annual fact book, C4680–1.507

Paper/allied products industry data from Census of Manufactures, including purchased fuel and labor costs, 1990 and/or 1991, article, A1630–5.501

Pulp and paper industry energy use, by fuel type, 1972 and 1987-91, annual rpt, A1630–6.3

Pulp and paper industry operations, US and Canada, with financial performance by company, 1990s and trends, annual rpt, C3975–5.1, C3975–5.2

Restaurant industry financial and operating data, by establishment characteristics and location, 1992, annual rpt, A8200–3

Restaurant utility costs, by type of utility and operation, 1990-91, article, A8200–1.507

Shopping center detailed income and expense data, by building characteristics, metro area, and region, 1991, annual rpt, A5600–6

Shopping center financial and operating data, with detail by type of tenant, US and Canada, 1991, triennial rpt, R9285–1

Sourcebook of oil and gas industry operations and finances, and world supply-demand situation, 1970s-91, annual compilation, C6985–9

Statistical profiles of 50 States and DC, general data, 1993 annual almanac, C4712–1

Industrial and commercial energy use

Steel mill electricity consumption, for individual mini and market mills, 1992 annual feature, C7000-8.501

Supermarket energy costs and increases, 1993 annual rpt, C5225-1.505

Supply-demand by energy source and consuming sector, 1947-2010, periodic basic data book, A2575-14.1

World energy supply-demand, by fuel source and sector, by region and country, 1992/93 biennial rpt, R9455-1.7

State and local:

- Alabama statistical abstract, general data, 1992 recurring rpt, U5680-2.12
- Alaska electric utility sales, by company and consuming sector, 1991, annual rpt, S0280-4.2
- Arizona statistical abstract, general data, 1993 recurring rpt, U5850-2.20
- Arkansas public utility financial, operating, and regulatory data, by utility type and company, 1992 annual rpt, S0757-1
- Florida statistical abstract, general data, 1992 annual rpt, U6660-1.15
- Georgia statistical abstract, general data, 1992-93 biennial rpt, U6730-1.6, U6730-1.8
- Hawaii data book, general data, 1992 annual rpt, S2090-1.17
- Illinois electric and gas utility sales and operating revenues, and customers served, by class of service and company, 1991-92, annual rpt series, S2410-1
- Maryland statistical abstract, general data, 1993-94 biennial rpt, S3605-1.10
- Mississippi statistical abstract, general data, 1992 annual rpt, U3255-4.14
- Nevada statistical abstract, general data, 1992 biennial rpt, S5005-1.11
- New Jersey economic indicators, including employment, building permits, and retail trade, monthly rpt, S5425-1
- New York State electric and gas customers, revenues, sales, and average bill, by customer class, 1988-92, annual rpt, S5795-1
- New York State statistical yearbook, general data, 1992 annual rpt, U5100-1.12
- North Carolina public utility financial, operating, and regulatory data, by utility type and company, 1990 and trends, annual rpt, S5917-2
- Ohio natural gas and electricity supply-demand by utility and consuming sector, 1992-93 and trends, annual rpt, S6355-1
- Oklahoma business activity indicators, monthly rpt, U8130-1
- Oklahoma statistical abstract, general data, 1992 annual rpt, U8130-2.18
- Pennsylvania business activity indicators, monthly rpt, U4110-1
- Pennsylvania energy supply-demand and prices by fuel type, with electric power info by utility, 1960s-90, recurring rpt, S6810-3
- Pennsylvania statistical abstract, general data, 1992 recurring rpt, U4130-6.9
- South Carolina economic condition, including energy and transportation data, 1970s-92, annual rpt, S7125-3.3
- South Carolina public service commission regulatory activities, with financial and operating data for individual utilities and railroads, FY92 annual rpt, S7235-1

Tennessee business activity indicators, quarterly journal, U8710-1

Tennessee economic indicator trends and forecasts, with data by industry div and manufacturing group, 1982-2001, annual rpt, S7560-1

Tennessee statistical abstract, general data, 1992/93 annual rpt, U8710-2.10

Texas natural gas utility financial and operating data, by city and company, 1991, with regulatory info, annual rpt, S7745-1

Utah statistical abstract, general data, 1993 triennial rpt, U8960-1.13

Vermont public utility financial and operating data, by company, 1986-91, biennial rpt, S8100-1

Washington State electric utility customers, sales, and revenues, by customer class and utility, 1982-91, annual rpt, S8450-1.2

Washington State natural gas utilities customers and sales, by consuming sector, by utility, 1982-91, annual rpt, S8450-1.3

West Virginia commercial/industrial electric power sold, monthly rpt, S8534-1

Wisconsin Blue Book, general data, 1993-94 biennial rpt, S8780-1.2

Wisconsin oil use, by consuming sector, 1981-90, annual rpt, S8675-3

see also Agricultural energy use

see also Government energy use

Industrial arts

State and local:

Pennsylvania vocational education enrollment, student characteristics, and faculty, by program and/or school, 1991/92 and trends, annual rpt, S6790-5.7

Pennsylvania vocational education 1989/90 grad employment status, by program, 1991 survey, annual rpt, S6790-5.6

Industrial capacity and utilization

Alternative fuel (biodiesel) derived from vegetable oils or animal fats, manufacturing capacity of 14 plants worldwide, 1993 article, C5800-8.504

Aluminum industry production, capacity, and manufacturing cost per pound, for 5 companies, 1993 article, C5226-2.506

Aluminum production capacity for top 20 producers, 1982-92, annual rpt, A0400-2.1

Australia chemical production capacity for 7 major producers of petrochemicals and polymers, 1993 article, A1250-1.531

Beer industry production, capacity, and sales volume, including top brands and brewers, 1982-92, annual feature, C0125-2.503

Biogas organic waste recycling project characteristics, including production capacity, for 12 major projects worldwide, 1993 article, C5800-8.507

Business and economic trends, production and price indicators, and industrial mgmt activities and devs, semimonthly rpt, C7000-3

Business forms industry trends and outlook, including data by product type, 1992 annual rpt, A5785-2

Carbon dioxide pipelines in Texas/New Mexico Permian Basin region, with ownership, mileage, and throughput capacity, 1993 article, C6985-1.542

Index by Subjects and Names

Cellulosic fiber production and capacity, 1981-92, article, A1250-1.505

Chemical (ethoxylation) plant new capacity worldwide, by company, 1992 article, C5800-8.502

Chemical and chemical process industries, operating and technical devs, and plant and equipment costs and production indexes, monthly rpt, C5800-8

Chemical industry finances and operations, with data by industry segment and product, 1970s-92, annual rpt, A3850-1

Chemical industry methyl tertiary butyl ether (MTBE) capacity, and polyethylene capacity additions, by company and plant, 1993 articles, A1250-1.541

China (southeast) oil demand by Province, and coastal refinery construction projects and capacity, 1990s-2000, article, C6985-1.528

China ethylene plants operating and planned, with data on capacity, construction costs, and imported equipment origins, 1993 article, C6985-1.512

China nuclear power generating capacity by unit, uranium resources by Province, and uranium processing capacity by plant, 1993 article, B6800-1.509

Coal industry executive views on current operating capacity, Aug 1992 survey, article, C5226-1.502

Coal longwall mining operations, by company and location, 1993, annual article, C5226-1.504

Coal preparation plants and capacity in US, Canada, and Mexico, by company, 1993 biennial feature, C5226-1.511

Coal producer outlook for supply-demand and prices, and capital investments, 1993 annual survey article, C5226-1.503

Commonwealth of Independent States oil refinery capacity by process, and refined products production and consumption, by Republic and region, 1992 article, C6985-1.508

EC steel industry production capacity, with reductions since 1980 made voluntarily and under EC Coal and Steel Commission quotas, 1992 rpt, R9260-16

Economic indicator historical trends, 1900s-92, annual rpt, R9050-1.2

Ethanol capacity operating and planned/under construction, by company and plant, 1992 article, A1250-1.501

Europe plastic bottle recycler capacity, for 9 companies, 1993 annual encyclopedia, C5800-12.503

Flour milling companies and capacity, in US by State, Canada, Mexico, and Central American and Caribbean area countries, 1993 annual directory and buyers guide, C8450-3

Forecasts for real estate industry and US economy, and housing starts and sales trends by region, monthly rpt, A7000-1

Forecasts of economic indicators for approx 10-13 months, monthly rpt, U1880-3

Forecasts of natl income and product account components and related indicators, quarterly rpt, U1880-1

Forecasts of natl income and product account components, employment, and financial sector activity, monthly rpt, B4950-1

Index by Subjects and Names

Industrial capacity and utilization

Foundry shipments, capacity utilization, and capital investment outlook, by metal type and plant size, 1992-94, annual survey article, C7000–2.501

France oil refinery capacity by process, for 13 refineries, Dec 1992, article, C6985–1.547

High fructose corn syrup shipments, and production capacity and utilization, 1979-91, annual rpt, C0125–3.2

Iran oil production and/or capacity, by onshore and offshore field, 1992-93, article, C6985–1.502

Italy oil refinery capacity and throughput, by company and plant, Jan 1992, article, C6985–1.523

Korea (South) thermoplastics production capacity, by resin, May 1993, article, C5800–8.510

Latin America statistical abstract, general data by country, 1992 annual rpt, U6250–1.23

Manufacturing production and operating data, including equipment purchases, by selected industry, 1993 and trends, annual rpt, A3179–2.3

Metals (primary) capacity utilization rates, with detail for aluminum, steel, and copper, monthly rpt, C7000–8

Metalworking industries capital spending plans and plant operating rates, 1989-93, annual survey, C4080–1

Methanol supply-demand outlook in North America, Europe, and worldwide, with capacity by company, 1993 article, C6985–1.522

Minerals supply-demand for selected commodities, US and worldwide, 1992 and trends, annual feature, C5226–2.505

Mining industry planned capacity of individual mines and plants, 1993 annual feature, C5226–2.503

Motor vehicle assembly plant capacity and production, by manufacturer and plant, for US and Canada, 1992, annual data book, C2710–3.531

Motor vehicle plant capacity, production, employment, and productivity, for 12 plants in 6 countries, 1993 article, C2150–3.504

Motor vehicle/parts industry capacity utilization, with comparison to total manufacturing, 1970-92, annual rpt, A0865–1.3

Natural gas (dry) production, capacity, and utilization, 1982-93, article, C6985–1.526

Natural gas processing plants, capacity, and production, by company, State, and country, 1993 annual rpt, C6985–1.537

Natural gas underground storage pools and capacity, with detail by State, 1991 and trends, annual rpt, A1775–3.3

Newsprint (recycled) mills and capacity, 1992-95, article, A8605–1.501

Newsprint production, consumption, trade, prices, and mill capacity, with data by world area, 1991-92 and trends, annual rpt, A8610–1

Newsprint production, shipments, plant capacity, consumption, trade, and recycling, US and Canada, 1970s-92, annual rpt, A1630–8

Newsprint production, shipments, trade, inventory, consumption, and plant capacity, US and Canada, monthly rpt, A1630–4

Newsprint recycling capacity, demand, and wastepaper consumption, for Northeast US and Eastern Canada, with data by mill, various years 1988-2000, A4375–15

Nuclear reactors in operation, with capacity, electricity generation, and construction, by unit and country, 1992, annual rpt, B6800–2.2

Nylon fiber production capacity, by country or world area, 1992, article, A1250–1.534

Oil and gas drilling activity, and refinery operations including production and construction cost indexes, by country and US State, 1991 and trends, annual compilation, C6985–9.1

Oil and gas industry trends, with data by company, State, and country, 1993 annual compilation, C6985–4

Oil and gas intl supply-demand, exploration, refining, reserves, and industry finances, basic data by country and company, 1993 annual rpt, C6985–3

Oil and gas supply-demand and industry operations, 1970s-2001, annual rpt, C6985–5

Oil refineries shutdown, including crude capacity, by company, 1992-93, article, C4680–1.508

Oil refinery capacity and utilization, by PAD district, weekly rpt, A2575–1

Oil refinery capacity and utilization, monthly rpt, A2575–2

Oil refinery capacity and utilization rate, 1982-93, annual article, C6985–1.539

Oil refinery capacity, for 10 plants up for sale, Aug 1993, article, C4680–1.510

Oil refinery capacity worldwide, by process, with data by country, company, and US State, 1992 annual feature, C6985–1.508

Oil refinery operable capacity and utilization, by PAD district and subarea, weekly rpt, C6985–1

Oil refinery runs and capacity utilization, by PAD district, 1983-93, annual feature, C6985–1.513

Oil refinery utilization rates, commodity yearbook Jan-Sept 1993 updates, C2400–2

Oil refinery utilization rates, monthly 1983-Sept 1992, commodity yearbook, C2400–1

Oil refining and gas processing capacity, throughput, and utilization rate, by country or world area, 1970s-91, annual compilation, C6985–10

Oil refining and gas processing world capacities and utilization, with US data by PAD district and State, 1993 and trends, periodic basic data book, A2575–14.4

Oil refining and storage capacities, and plant shutdowns, individual US and Canadian oil companies, 1993 annual fact book, C4680–1.507

Paper, paperboard, and wood pulp industry capacity and material consumption, by grade and census div, 1970s-95, annual rpt, A1630–7

Paper, paperboard, and wood pulp production capacity, by grade and census div, 1970s-95, annual rpt, A1630–6

Paperboard mill capacity by product type, 1990-95, annual article, C0125–4.504

Plastics (degradable) production capacity and costs, for 13 companies, 1993 annual encyclopedia, C5800–12.503

Plastics (polyethylene terephthalate) reclamation capacity, for 3 integrated fiber manufacturers, 1993 article, C5800–12.513

Plastics and resin sales by material and major market, foreign trade, and capacity by company, 1991-92, annual feature, C5800–12.504

Plastics manufacturing capacity and utilization rates, by product, 1992 and trends, annual rpt, A8920–1.2

Plastics processing capacity for consumer waste and industrial scrap, by resin, 1990, A4375–14

Plastics production capacity for specified resins, by major company and/or world region, monthly rpt recurring table, C5800–12.502, C5800–12.504, C5800–12.506, C5800–12.507, C5800–12.509, C5800–12.510, C5800–12.512, C5800–12.513

Plastics/rubber and all manufacturing plant capacity utilization rates, monthly rpt quarterly table, C5800–12.501, C5800–12.505, C5800–12.508, C5800–12.511

Pulp and paper capacity trends and outlook, by grade, 1982-95, annual article, C3975–2.504

Pulp and paper industry operations and finances, US and Canada, with detail by company and product grade, and world production and trade summary, 1993 annual rpt, C3975–5

Pulp and paper industry production and other operating trends and outlook, 1993 annual article, C3975–2.503

Pulp and paper industry production, capacity, consumption, trade, and sales/earnings data, including profiles for selected companies and sectors, monthly rpt, C3975–2

Pulp, paper, and paperboard industry production, trade, and operating data, by product class, monthly rpt, A1630–5

Railroad freight car fleet capacity, 1982-91, annual rpt, A3275–8.2

Rubber (synthetic) capacity, by resin, 1983 and 1993, article, A1250–1.524

Saudi Arabia oil refining network organization, including refinery capacities and foreign ownership shares, 1993 article, C6985–1.542

Southeastern States oil refineries operable and crude capacity, for 10 States, 1991, annual rpt, U8710–2.10

Soybean crush and share of capacity, weekly 1989-92, annual rpt, B2120–1

Spain chemical process industry sales and employment of top 15 companies, and production capacity and utilization of major chemicals, 1991, article, C5800–8.511

Spain oil refinery distillation capacity and crude runs to stills, by company and refinery, 1991, article, C6985–1.522

Spain oil refining capacity and utilization, and employment, for 3 refineries, 1993 article, A8955–1.503

Steel industry operating trends and devs, including profiles of 4 major companies, 1960-90, U9640–2.15

Steel ingot capacity utilization, commodity yearbook Jan-Sept 1993 updates, C2400–2

Industrial capacity and utilization

Steel ingot capacity utilization, monthly 1984-Oct 1992, commodity yearbook, C2400–1

Steel mill employment, capacity, shipments, and other operating info, for individual mini and market mills, 1992 annual feature, C7000–8.501

Steel production and capacity utilization, monthly 1988-92, annual rpt, A2000–2.3

Sulfur (oil-based) recovery plant capacity and production, by company and country, Jan 1993, annual feature, C6985–1.537

Tall oil fractionating capacity of US and foreign companies, 1992, annual rpt, C6585–1

Textile industry economic performance indicators and outlook, with industry trends and devs, monthly rpt, C5226–3

Textile manufactured fiber production and capacity, monthly rpt semiannual survey, C3460–1.502, C3460–1.507

Textile manufactured fiber production, capacity, and utilization rates, by fiber type, 1982-92, annual article, C3460–1.503

Textile manufactured fiber production capacity by product type and country or world region, Mar 1993 and Dec 1994, annual rpt, C3460–1.508, C3460–1.509

Textile manufactured fiber production capacity, by product type and country or world region, 1980-94, annual feature, C3460–1.510

Textile mill and clothing industry capacity utilization rates, 1990-92, annual rpt, C3400–5

Trinidad and Tobago oil refinery capacity by process and refinery, 1991, article, C6985–1.518

Uranium conversion and enrichment suppliers, and fuel fabrication facilities, with plant capacities, 1992 annual rpt, B6800–2.1

Uranium conversion capacity and 1993 commitments, for 5 suppliers worldwide, article, B6800–1.504

Uranium reserves, capacity, and operating status of in situ leach mining projects, 1993 article, B6790–1.501

State and local:

Alaska oil pipelines property value, revenues, and throughput, with detail by company, 1991 and trends, annual rpt, S0280–4

Arizona copper industry operations, including production, capacity, and reserves, by company and mine, with US and intl comparisons, 1991 and trends, annual rpt, S0497–1

California diesel fuel refining capacity, with projected impact of new State law, for 9 major refiners and aggregate independents, 1993-94, article, C6985–1.544

Hawaii data book, general data, 1992 annual rpt, S2090–1.22

Tennessee statistical abstract, general data, 1992/93 annual rpt, U8710–2.5

Washington State refrigerated storage space and capacity, biennially 1985-91, annual rpt, S8328–1

see also Electric power plants and equipment

Industrial distribution

Aluminum shipments for general line distributors, by product type, 1982-92, annual rpt, A0400–2.1

Electronics distributor revenues and financial ratios, for 4 companies, 1992, article, C1850–2.505

Executives in industrial distribution, job and dept characteristics, compensation, and industry outlook, 1992 annual survey article, C2150–1.501

Hiring criteria for college grads cited by industrial distributors, 1992 survey article, C1850–2.502

Home improvement industry sales and operations, for top distributors, cooperatives, and marketing organizations, 1991-92, annual feature, C5150–6.502

Lumber industry distribution channels, principal market areas, and transport modes, selected Western States, 1992, annual rpt, A9395–1

Mgmt of physical distribution of industrial goods, including inventory control, materials handling, and traffic, monthly rpt, C2150–1

Operating and marketing devs for industrial distributors, monthly rpt, C1850–4

Operations of industrial distributors, 1990-91, annual survey, C1850–4.507

Purchasing managers views on business conditions, monthly rpt, A6910–1

Sales, branches, employment, and operating profiles, for top 50 industrial distributors, 1992, annual article, C1850–4.506

Semiconductor market value, for distributors vs contract manufacturers, 1989-92, article, C1850–2.506

Small distributor sales, employment, and inventory turns, for top 25 companies with sales of $5 million/less, 1991, annual article, C1850–4.503

Supermarket executive views on efficient consumer response (ECR) logistics system, 1993 survey article, C4655–1.511

see also Freight

see also Warehouses

Industrial location

see Industrial siting

Industrial management

see Business management

Industrial parks

Real estate market conditions and outlook for industrial property, including inventory, vacancy, prices, and construction costs, by metro area, 1992-93, annual survey, A8916–1

State and local:

Hawaii data book, general data, 1992 annual rpt, S2090–1.22

Maine industrial park acreage and prices, by site, 1992 recurring rpt, S3434–1

Industrial plants and equipment

Aluminum plants in operation, by ingot and mill product category, 1992 and trends, annual rpt, A0400–2.1

Auto assembly plant shutdowns, with production losses, by plant, weekly rpt, C2710–3

Auto assembly plants producing models with fewest problems for buyers, for top 3 North American plants, 1992, article, C2710–3.532

Blast furnaces in operation, Canada and US by State, monthly 1991-92, annual rpt, A2010–3

Index by Subjects and Names

Chemical and chemical process industries, operating and technical devs, and plant and equipment costs and production indexes, monthly rpt, C5800–8

Coal preparation plants and capacity in US, Canada, and Mexico, by company, 1993 biennial feature, C5226–1.511

Commonwealth of Independent States natural gas processing plants, by site, 1993 article, C6985–1.514

Construction contract awards by type of project, weekly rpt, C5800–2

Construction contract value, by construction type and region, including floor area and number of residential units, 1992-93, annual rpt, C5800–15.501, C5800–15.504, C5800–15.507, C5800–26, C5800–29

Container (fiber box) shipments by end-use industry and region, and other industry operating data, 1940s-92, annual rpt, A4875–1

Eastern Europe ethylene plants and capacity, by country, 1993 article, A1250–1.540

Electronics company financial data and business info for approx 500 companies, 1991-92 and trends, annual rpt, C3400–4

Electronics surface-mount-technology manufacturing equipment sales, 1990-96, article, C1850–2.512

Electronics trade, by product category, detailed type, and country, monthly rpt, A4725–3

Emission-control equipment market shares for top 10 and all other manufacturers, 1991, article, A4700–4.501

Equipment industry operations and devs, including farm equipment retail sales, periodic rpt, C0495–1, C3450–1

Financial performance and growth rankings for approx 1,000 top corporations, with comparisons by industry group, 1993 annual rpt, C3950–1.505

Financial ratios and performance, for over 350 SIC 4-digit industries, FY88-92, annual rpt, A6400–3

Flour milling companies and capacity, in US by State, Canada, Mexico, and Central American and Caribbean area countries, 1993 annual directory and buyers guide, C8450–3

Food plant construction/expansion project info, cost, and employees, by company, 1992, annual feature, C2150–6.506

Food/beverage industry equipment purchasing plans, mgmt devs, and automation, 1993 annual survey article, C2150–6.505

Foreign economic indexes, and leading and coincident indicators for US and other industrial countries, monthly rpt, U1245–1

Gulf of Mexico oil/gas lease status, wells drilled by operator, and drilling platforms installed and removed, 1993 articles, C6985–2.508

Hard goods manufacturer plant/equipment purchase and expansion plans in 1993, by product line, annual survey rpt, A1800–1

Ice cream and frozen dessert plants, 1965-92, annual rpt, A5825–1.1

Iron and steel industry production, trade, and materials consumption, with financial and employment data, 1992 and trends, annual rpt, A2000–2

Index by Subjects and Names

Industrial plants and equipment

Iron ore receipts, consumption, and inventories, and blast furnaces operating, for US and Canada, monthly rpt, A2010–1

Japan-affiliated auto parts suppliers in US, with employment and plant square footage, 1990 and 1992-93, article, C2710–3.553

Japan auto manufacturer US auto parts purchases, and auto production in US and Canada compared to US firms, with selected detail by company and plant, 1993 article, R5650–2.523

Lumber industry production in Western States and counties, with acreage owned, employment, and sawmill operations, 1980s-92, annual rpt, A9395–1

Machine tool production, shipments, trade, finances, orders, and use, US and worldwide, 1992 and trends, annual rpt, A3179–2

Manufacturing new plants announced, per million residents, by State, 1990-92, article, B8500–2.509

Metal (primary) manufacturing plants, by type and State, 1993, annual article, C7000–8.504

Mexico maquiladora plants, employment, and earnings, 1965-88, annual rpt, U6250–1.16

Mexico maquiladora plants, for 6 Texas-Mexico twin city areas, 1993 rpt, U8850–9

Mexico oil and gas equipment imports from US, and tariffs and phaseout schedule under North American Free Trade Agreement, 1993 article, C6985–1.544

Mexico original auto equipment supplier plants and locations, with major products and customers, by company, 1993 article, C2710–3.550

Mobile/manufactured home producers and manufacturing plants, monthly rpt, A6325–1

Motor vehicle assembly plant production, by State and Canadian Province, manufacturer, model, and plant, 1993 model year, annual article, C2710–3.551

Motor vehicle plant die change operations, efficiency scores for teams at 9 plants, 1992 annual article, C2150–3.501

Natural gas distribution utility and pipeline company financial and operating data, top 500 companies, 1992, annual article, C6780–1.505

Natural gas industry plant value, by function and type of company, 1970s-91, annual rpt, A1775–3.8

Natural gas processing plants, capacity, and production, by company, State, and country, 1993 annual rpt, C6985–1.537

Offshore drilling platforms installed and removed from Federal waters, 1953-90, annual compilation, C6985–9.4

Offshore oil/gas drilling rigs under contract and idle worldwide, errata, C6985–1.506

Offshore well coiled tubing servicing units, by world area, 1993 chart, C6985–2.503

Oil and gas drilling activity, and refinery operations including production and construction cost indexes, by country and US State, 1991 and trends, annual compilation, C6985–9.1

Oil and gas industry exploration, production, refining, demand, finance, prices, and

reserves, by State and country or world area, 1993 and trends, periodic basic data book, A2575–14.4

Oil and gas industry trends, with data by company, State, and country, 1993 annual compilation, C6985–4

Oil and gas intl supply-demand, exploration, refining, reserves, and industry finances, basic data by country and company, 1993 annual rpt, C6985–3

Oil refineries, petrochemical processing facilities, and pipelines, construction and costs, by country and company, weekly rpt semiannual list, C6985–1.524, C6985–1.551

Oil refinery capacity worldwide, by process, with data by country, company, and US State, 1992 annual feature, C6985–1.508

Oil refinery construction, operating, and materials costs, Nelson-Farrar Cost Indexes, weekly rpt monthly and quarterly tables, C6985–1

Oil refinery, ethylene, and gas processing plants profitability analyses, Gulf Coast, other US, and foreign, weekly rpt monthly tables, C6985–1

Oil/gas well tubular goods cost per deep well drilled, by State and for offshore, 1991-92, annual article, C4420–1.502

Paper and paperboard mills and machines by capacity and grade, machines by age, and shutdowns, 1992 annual rpt, A1630–7

Paper, paperboard, wood pulp, and recovered paper production and mills, and pulpwood production, by State and census div, 1991, article, A1630–5.502

Paperboard packaging industry corrugated and folding carton box plants and equipment, by census div and for Canada, 1990-92, annual article, C0125–4.501

Performance improvement efforts and selected operating data for top-rated industrial plants, 1993 survey article, C7000–3.505

Pipe/valve/fitting distributor sales trends, 1st half 1992, article, C1850–4.501

Plastics industry production and sales by resin type, consumption by end-use market, and operating characteristics, 1992 and trends, annual rpt, A8920–1

Plastics injection molding machine production, for US, Germany, Japan, and other Far East countries, 1983-92, article, C5800–12.510

Pneumatic power systems/components market value, 1992 and 1996, article, C1850–4.505

Printing and publishing industries operations and outlook, including paper shipments and prices, monthly rpt, C1850–10

Printing company sales, employment, and equipment, for top 101 North American firms, 1993 annual feature, C1850–10.512

Pulp and paper industry operations and finances, US and Canada, with detail by company and product grade, and world production and trade summary, 1993 annual rpt, C3975–5

Pulp and paper mill machine maintenance operations and personnel, by region and grade, 1992 survey, recurring article, C3975–2.504

Real estate market conditions and outlook for industrial property, including

inventory, vacancy, prices, and construction costs, by metro area, 1992-93, annual survey, A8916–1

Real estate market conditions and outlook, including space, rent, transactions, and prices, for major metro areas, 1993 annual rpt, B2800–3

Rental rates and other property data for industrial and high-technology facilities, for major metro areas by region, mid-1993, annual rpt, B2800–6

Semiconductor production equipment market shares for US, Europe, and Japan, and sales of top 10 suppliers, 1991-92, article, C1850–2.509

Shipments of industrial control and processing equipment, by type, 1982-91, annual rpt, A4725–1.2

Soft drink manufacturing plants, by State, 1981-91, annual rpt, C0125–3.1

South Africa uranium production facilities by company, with other activities, operating status, and 1992 production, article, B6800–1.505

Southeastern States oil refineries operable and crude capacity, for 10 States, 1991, annual rpt, U8710–2.10

Steel industry finances, operations, and employment, with data for integrated plants and mini-mills, 1970s-93, article, U2160–1.503

Steel industry operating trends and devs, including profiles of 4 major companies, 1960-90, U9640–2.15

Steel mill employment, capacity, shipments, and other operating info, for individual mini and market mills, 1992 annual feature, C7000–8.501

Sulfur (oil-based) recovery plant capacity and production, by company and country, Jan 1993, annual feature, C6985–1.537

Telephone local exchange carrier finances, equipment, and employment, by company, 1991 and trends, annual rpt, A9360–2

Textile fiber end-use survey, consumption and trade, by type of fiber and product, 1988-92, annual survey, C3460–1.511

Textile fiber product manufacturers, with plants by State and region, 1992 annual directory, C3460–1.501

Textile machinery in place, by detailed type, with detail by selected State, June 1983 and 1988, annual rpt, A3800–1

Utility regulatory agency policies and practices, and industry financial and operating data, by utility type and agency, 1991/92 annual rpt, A7015–3

Value of equipment compared to costs, for selected manufacturing and pollution control equipment, for 8 countries, 1993 rpt, A1310–2.2

Vending machine sales and operations, by product and location type, 1990-92, annual rpt, C9470–1

Waste fuel boiler/industrial furnace applications to EPA for continued use, by region, May 1992, article, C5800–8.505

State and local:

Alabama new and expanded industrial plants, capital invested, and jobs created, 1955-90, recurring rpt, U5680–2.11

Alaska public utility financial and operating data, by company and utility type, 1991 and trends, with FY92 regulatory info, annual rpt, S0280–4

Industrial plants and equipment

Arizona building permits issued and value, by type, size, and location, monthly rpt quarterly table, U0280–1.503, U0280–1.506, U0280–1.509

Colorado property assessed valuation by detailed property type, and tax levy and revenue by local district, by county, 1991-92, annual rpt, S1055–3

Georgia statistical abstract, general data, 1992-93 biennial rpt, U6730–1.6

Hawaii data book, general data, 1992 annual rpt, S2090–1.17, S2090–1.22

Illinois telephone utility financial and operating data, by company, 1992, annual rpt, S2410–2

Kentucky economic impact of Toyota Motor Corp plant installation, including related State costs, employment, and benefits to other States, 1980s-2005, U7138–1.4

Kentucky employment and number of plants, for top 58 manufacturers, 1992, annual rpt, S3120–1

Mississippi employment and number of plants, top 25 companies, FY92 annual rpt, S4346–1

Montana property values, by detailed property class and type, with land acreage by use, by county, 1991-92 and trends, biennial rpt, S4750–1.2

North Carolina public utility financial, operating, and regulatory data, by utility type and company, 1990 and trends, annual rpt, S5917–2

Ohio business property assessment data, by property class and industry, 1991 and trends, annual rpt, S6390–1.5

South Carolina statistical abstract, general data, 1993 annual rpt, S7125–1.3

Tennessee new and expanded plants, investment, and job creation, 1982-91, annual rpt, S7505–1

Tennessee telephone, natural gas, and water companies average plant value, 1987-91, biennial rpt, S7565–1

Texas gas utility plants in service by type, and pipeline miles, by company, 1991, annual rpt, S7745–1

Utah statistical abstract, general data, 1993 triennial rpt, U8960–1.12

Washington State natural gas utility financial and operating data, by company, 1982-91, annual rpt, S8450–1.3

Washington State property values, by type of property and county, 1992, annual rpt, S8415–1.3

Washington State telecommunication industry financial and operating data, by company, 1988-91, annual rpt, S8450–1.5

Washington State water utilities financial and operating data, by company, 1988-90, annual rpt, S8450–1.1

Washington State water utilities financial and operating data, by company, 1989-91, annual rpt, S8450–1.4

Wyoming property assessed valuations and tax levies, by property type, tax purpose, and location, 1992 and trends, annual rpt, S8990–1.2

see also Automation

see also Business firms and establishments, number

see also Business machines and equipment

see also Capital investments

see also Depreciation

see also Electric power plants and equipment

see also Foundries

see also Grain storage and facilities

see also Industrial capacity and utilization

see also Industrial parks

see also Industrial robots

see also Industrial siting

see also Materials handling equipment

see also Natural gas pipelines

see also Pipelines

see also Railroad equipment and vehicles

see also Warehouses

Industrial pollution

see Air pollution

see Environmental pollution and control

see Lead poisoning and pollution

see Marine pollution

see Noise

see Radiation

see Refuse and refuse disposal

see Water pollution

Industrial production

Business Week industrial production indicators, for selected industries, weekly rpt, C5800–7

China, Guangdong Province industrial production, with detail by enterprise ownership type, 1985-92, A9315–1.505

China industrial and agricultural production, and foreign trade and investment, with detail for leading commodities, 1980s-92, annual feature, A9315–1.504

China industrial production, with detail by enterprise ownership type, 1978 and 1990, R4105–82.8

Commodity yearbook for 1993: production, stocks, trade, and prices for approx 100 agricultural and industrial materials, including by country and producing State, C2400–1

Commodity yearbook update: production, stocks, trade, and prices for approx 100 basic commodities, including by country and producing State, Jan-Sept 1993 rpts, C2400–2

Japan electronics industry output change, by type of product, 1992, article, C8900–1.511

Japan foreign investment rate of return on sales by world region, and overseas share of production, with detail by industry, FY84-91, article, R5650–2.559

Latin America statistical abstract, general data by country, 1992 annual rpt, U6250–1.16

Purchasing managers views on business conditions, monthly rpt, A6910–1

Soviet Union industrial production by commodity, monthly rpt recurring feature, U2030–1.507

Soviet Union selected industrial production measures compared to US, 1985 or 1986, R4105–82.4

Spain industrial production distribution by industry group, for Catalonia and Aragon regions, 1992 articles, A8955–1.501

Statistical profiles of 50 States and DC, general data, 1993 annual almanac, C4712–1

Steel industry finances, operations, and employment, with data for integrated plants and mini-mills, 1970s-93, article, U2160–1.503

Steel industry restructuring devs, with data on production, employment, and worker

Index by Subjects and Names

assistance, and selected detail by company, for 8-12 countries, 1970s-90, R9260–16

State and local:

Alabama economic trends and outlook, 1980s-93, annual rpt, U5680–3

Arizona statistical abstract, general data, 1993 recurring rpt, U5850–2.17

Arkansas business and economic activity indicators, quarterly rpt, U5930–1

Arkansas socioeconomic trends, by MSA and/or county, 1993 annual rpt, U5935–1

California statistical abstract, general data, 1992 annual rpt, S0840–2.7, S0840–2.8

Florida statistical abstract, general data, 1992 annual rpt, U6660–1.12

Georgia statistical abstract, general data, 1992-93 biennial rpt, U6730–1.6

Hawaii data book, general data, 1992 annual rpt, S2090–1.22

Illinois statistical abstract, general data, 1992 annual rpt, U6910–2

Kansas statistical abstract, general data, 1991/92 annual rpt, U7095–2.8

Kentucky economic statistics, general data, 1993 annual rpt, S3104–1.1

Maine statistical summary, general economic and social data, 1992 recurring rpt, S3434–1

Maryland statistical abstract, general data, 1993-94 biennial rpt, S3605–1.3, S3605–1.4

Tennessee statistical abstract, general data, 1992/93 annual rpt, U8710–2.4

Utah govt statistical review, fiscal and socioeconomic data, 1993 annual rpt, R9380–1.2

Utah statistical abstract, general data, 1993 triennial rpt, U8960–1.12

see also Business inventories

see also Business orders

see also Economic indicators

see also Industrial capacity and utilization

see also Industrial production indexes

see also Industrial purchasing

see also Labor productivity

see also Production workers

see also Productivity

see also under names of specific industry groups and industries

Industrial production indexes

Business Week index of industrial production, weekly rpt, C5800–7

Chemical and chemical process industries, operating and technical devs, and plant and equipment costs and production indexes, monthly rpt, C5800–8

Chemical and related industries production, finances, operating ratios, employment, and trade, by country, company, and chemical, 1980s-92, annual feature, A1250–1.530

Chemical industry finances and operations, with data by industry segment and product, 1970s-92, annual rpt, A3850–1

Computer/info processing equipment industry performance indicators, semimonthly rpt recurring feature, C1850–5

Economic outlook for selected industries, recent trends and 2-year forecast, quarterly rpt, A3840–6

Electric utility weekly output index, 1981-91, annual rpt, A4700–1

Electronics industry market trends and outlook, including product sales and shipments, employment, and leading manufacturers, monthly rpt, C1850–2

Energy tax proposals and potential effect on selected economic indicators, 1993-97, article, C6985–1.516

Forecasts for real estate industry and US economy, and housing starts and sales trends by region, monthly rpt, A7000–1

Forecasts of economic indicators for approx 10-13 months, monthly rpt, U1880–3

Forecasts of natl income and product account components and related indicators, quarterly rpt, U1880–1

Forecasts of natl income and product account components, employment, and financial sector activity, monthly rpt, B4950–1

Foreign economic indexes, and leading and coincident indicators for US and other industrial countries, monthly rpt, U1245–1

Germany (West) and US comparative socioeconomic statistics, 1970s-91, annual rpt, A5135–2.2

Interest rate business cycle peaks and troughs, with trends in price of credit, industrial production, and stock performance, 1953-92, article, C3950–1.507

Japan economic profile, including govt finances, industrial production, foreign trade and investments, and comparisons to US, 1988-92, annual feature, R5650–2.552

Latin America statistical abstract, general data by country, 1992 annual rpt, U6250–1.16

Malt beverage seasonal production and withdrawal indexes, 1992, annual rpt, A3455–1.1

Metals (primary) production index, monthly rpt, C7000–8

Oil and gas drilling activity, and refinery operations including production and construction cost indexes, by country and US State, 1991 and trends, annual compilation, C6985–9.1

Oil and gas industry production indexes, 1960-91, annual compilation, C6985–9.5

Printing/publishing and related industries production indexes, monthly rpt quarterly table, C1850–10.502, C1850–10.505, C1850–10.508, C1850–10.510

Shoe industry production, employment, trade, marketing, and related data, by SIC 2- to 5-digit code or product type, 1992 annual rpt, A4957–1.2

Steel service center production index, quarterly 1991-94, article, C1850–4.504

Textile and clothing industries production indexes, 1990-92, annual rpt, C3400–5

Textile industry economic performance indicators and outlook, with industry trends and devs, monthly rpt, C5226–3

Trends in industrial production indexes for selected industries, 1972-93, annual rpt, A3179–2.3

State and local:

Connecticut employment, hours, and earnings, by labor market area and industry, and selected economic indicators, monthly rpt, S1235–1

New York State business activity indicators, quarterly rpt, S5735–2

Pennsylvania business activity indicators, monthly rpt, U4110–1

see also Labor productivity

Industrial purchasing

Business conditions reported by purchasing managers, monthly rpt, A6910–1

Cost, time, and quality factors for typical vs "world class" companies, 1992 article, C5800–7.505

Electronics company purchasing dept training program characteristics, 1993 survey article, C1850–2.512

Paperboard packaging equipment purchasing plans and spending trends, 1993 annual article, C0125–4.503

State and local:

Arizona industrial purchasing managers views on business activity, monthly rpt, U0280–1

Illinois, Chicago industrial purchasing managers business activity index, bimonthly rpt, S2405–2

see also Business orders

see also Wholesale trade

Industrial relations

see Labor-management relations, general

see Work stoppages

Industrial revenue bonds

State and local:

DC statistical profile, general data, 1992 annual rpt, S1535–3.3

Kansas statistical abstract, general data, 1991/92 annual rpt, U7095–2.11

Industrial robots

Foreign trade in machine tools including robots and parts, monthly rpt, A3179–3

Metalworking industry capital spending plans, by equipment type and industry group, 1989-93, annual survey, C4080–1

Shipments and net new orders, 1983-92, annual rpt, A3179–2.1

Shipments of robots and robot components, by type, 1984-91, annual rpt, A4725–1.2

Industrial siting

Cities rated as best for business by Fortune magazine, socioeconomic profiles of top 60 metro areas, 1992 annual article, C8900–1.501

Corporate revenues and hqs employment, for 9 Forbes 500 companies located in suburban or rural areas, 1992 article, C3950–1.502

Real estate market conditions and outlook for industrial property, including inventory, vacancy, prices, and construction costs, by metro area, 1992-93, annual survey, A8916–1

Real estate market conditions and outlook, including space, rent, transactions, and prices, for major metro areas, 1993 annual rpt, B2800–3

Selection factors importance ratings among businesses, 1991/92 survey, article, U0280–1.510

Textile fiber product manufacturers, with plants by State and region, 1992 annual directory, C3460–1.501

State and local:

Arkansas economic dev resources existing and needed to attract new business, 1989/90 survey, article, U5930–1.501

Delaware data book, general data, 1993 annual rpt, S1375–4

Indiana manufacturing firm site location factor analysis, 1986-89, article, U2160–1.501

Mississippi new and expanded industry employment and investment, by company, 1991, annual rpt, U3255–4.5

South Carolina new and expanded plants, investment, and jobs created, 1971-92, annual rpt, S7125–3.2

South Carolina new firm investments in State, with employment, by industry and county, 1991, annual planning rpt, S7155–3.2

see also Industrial parks

Industrial standards

see also Quality control and testing

see also Weights and measures

Industrial workers

see Production workers

Industry

see terms listed under Business and industry

see under By Industry in the "Index by Categories"

Industry conversion

see Conversion of industry

Infant health

see Pediatrics

see Prenatal care

Infant mortality

Black American health and vital statistics data, with comparisons to whites, 1970s-91, annual compilation, C6775–2.2

Black children and youth population, economic, health, and education data, with comparisons to whites, 1993 rpt, R3840–21

Child and maternal health status indicators, with data by race and State, 1992 annual rpt, R3840–5

Japan and US health care system data, including expenditures, facilities, insurance coverage, and population health indicators, 1993 article, R5650–2.515

Latin America statistical abstract, general data by country, 1992 annual rpt, U6250–1.6

Low-income families and children, health and welfare indicators, with data by State and city, 1992 annual rpt, R3840–11

Medicaid child and total recipients, expenditures, and other program characteristics, and child health summary, by State, FY91, annual rpt, A0565–1

Number of infant deaths attributable to 9 leading causes, 1993 feature, C4215–1.511

Rates of infant mortality, by sex and race, 1989, article, A8510–1.1

State economic dev condition indicators, including economic performance, business vitality, growth capacity, and tax/fiscal system, by State, 1993 annual rpt, R4225–1.1

State social, economic, and govtl indicators, with rankings, 1993 semiannual rpt, B8500–1.9

Statistical profiles of 50 States and DC, general data, 1993 annual almanac, C4712–1

Sudden infant death syndrome mortality rates, by race, census div, and State, 1980 and 1988, article, B6045–1.502

Sweden infant mortality rates, by cause and characteristics of mother, 1983-86, article, A2623–1.503

Infant mortality

Sweden sudden infant death syndrome incidence correlated with mother's smoking habits and other characteristics, errata, A2623–1.501

Urban (large city) infant mortality rate compare to total US, 1987, A4425–4

World birth, death, population increase, and infant death rate indicators, with detail for more and less developed countries, 1993, annual feature, R8750–1.509

World population and health indicators, with detail by region and country, 1992/93 biennial rpt, R9455–1.2, R9455–1.5

World population size and characteristics, GNP, and land area, by region and/or country, 1993 annual data sheet, R8750–5

World vital statistics, for top 50 countries in births, deaths, infant mortality, and life expectancy, 1992, semiannual rpt, B8500–1.16

State and local:

- Alabama vital statistics, including population, births, deaths by cause, marriages, and divorces, by location and demographic characteristics, 1992 and trends, annual rpt, S0175–2
- Alaska vital statistics, including births, deaths by cause, marriages, divorces, adoptions, and population, by demographic characteristics and location, 1990, annual rpt, S0315–1
- Arizona Indian population, education, housing, health, and employment characteristics, with detail by reservation, 1970s-91, recurring rpt, U5850–2.9
- Arkansas vital statistics, including births, deaths by cause, marriages, and divorces, by age, sex, race, and county, 1991 and trends, annual rpt, S0685–1
- California vital statistics, including population, births, and deaths by cause, by demographic characteristics and county, 1990 and trends, annual rpt, S0865–1
- Colorado vital statistics, including population, births, deaths by cause, abortion, marriage and divorce, and adoption, by demographic characteristics and location, 1990 and trends, annual rpt, S1010–1
- Connecticut vital statistics, including births, deaths by cause, marriages, and divorces, by demographic characteristics and location, 1989, annual rpt, S1200–1
- DC statistical profile, general data, 1992 annual rpt, S1535–3.5
- Delaware vital statistics, including births, deaths by cause, and marriages and dissolutions, by demographic characteristics and location, 1990, annual rpt, S1385–2
- Florida vital statistics, including population, births, deaths by cause, and marriages and dissolutions, by location and demographic characteristics, 1992 and trends, annual rpt, S1745–3
- Georgia vital statistics, including deaths by cause, demographic characteristics, and location, 1991 and trends, annual rpt, S1895–1.2
- Hawaii health dept activities and services, including vital statistics and disease control, by location, 1990, annual rpt, S2065–1
- Idaho vital statistics, including births, deaths by cause, abortions, marriages, and divorces, by demographic characteristics and county, 1991 and trends, annual rpt, S2250–2
- Illinois statistical abstract, general data, 1992 annual rpt, U6910–2
- Iowa vital statistics, including population, births, deaths by cause, marriages, and divorces, by demographic characteristics and location, 1991 and trends, annual rpt, S2795–1
- Kansas vital statistics, including population, births, deaths by cause, abortions, marriages, and divorces, by demographic characteristics and location, 1991 and trends, annual rpt, S2975–1
- Kentucky vital statistics, including births, deaths by cause, marriages and divorces, and population, by demographic characteristics and county, 1991, annual rpt, S3140–1
- Louisiana vital statistics, including population, births, deaths by cause, reportable diseases, marriages, and divorces, by demographic characteristics and locality, 1989-90 and trends, annual rpt, S3295–1
- Maine vital statistics, including births, deaths by cause, abortions, and marriages and divorces, by demographic characteristics and location, 1991 and trends, annual rpt, S3460–2
- Maryland vital statistics, including population, births, deaths by cause, marriages, and divorces, by demographic characteristics and location, 1989 and trends, annual rpt, S3635–1
- Massachusetts vital statistics, including births, deaths by cause, marriages, divorces, and population, by locality and demographic characteristics, 1990 and trends, annual rpt, S3850–1
- Michigan vital statistics, including births, deaths, marriages, divorces/annulments, and communicable diseases, by location and demographic characteristics, 1990 and trends, annual rpt, S4000–3
- Minnesota vital statistics, including population, births, abortions, deaths, marriages, and divorces, by location and demographic characteristics, 1991 and trends, annual rpt, S4190–2
- Mississippi vital statistics, including births, deaths by cause, marriages, and divorces, by demographic characteristics and location, 1992 and trends, annual rpt, S4350–1
- Missouri vital statistics, including population, births, deaths by cause, and marriages and divorces, by location and demographic characteristics, 1992 and trends, annual rpt, S4518–1
- Montana vital statistics, including births, deaths by cause, abortion, disease, and marriage and divorce, by demographic characteristics and county, 1990-91 and trends, annual rpt, S4690–1
- Nebraska vital statistics, including births, deaths, marriages, divorces, and population, by demographic characteristics and location, 1991 and trends, annual rpt, S4885–1
- Nevada vital statistics, including births, abortions, and deaths by cause, by county and demographic characteristics, 1989 and trends, annual rpt, S5075–1
- New Hampshire vital statistics, including population, births, deaths by cause, marriages, and divorces, by location and demographic characteristics, 1991 and trends, annual rpt, S5215–1
- New Jersey vital statistics, including births, deaths, population, communicable diseases, and marriages and divorces, by demographic characteristics and location, 1990 and trends, annual rpt, S5405–1
- New Mexico vital statistics, including population, births, deaths, and disease, by location and demographic characteristics, 1991 and trends, annual rpt, S5605–1
- New York State vital statistics, including population, births, deaths by cause, reportable diseases, and marriages and dissolutions, by demographic characteristics and/or location, 1990 and trends, annual rpt, S5765–1
- North Carolina vital statistics, including population, births, deaths by cause, marriages, and divorces, by local area, 1991 and trends, annual rpt, S5927–1
- North Dakota vital statistics, including births, deaths by cause, marriages and divorces, and abortions, by demographic characteristics and/or county, 1991 and trends, annual rpt, S6105–2
- Ohio vital statistics, including births, deaths by cause, marriages, divorces, and population, by demographic characteristics and location, 1991 and trends, annual rpt, S6285–1
- Oregon vital statistics, including births, deaths by cause, communicable diseases, marriages, and divorces, by age, sex, race-ethnicity, and county, 1991 and trends, annual rpt, S6615–5
- Rhode Island vital statistics, including population, births, deaths, marriages, and divorces, by demographic characteristics and locality, 1989 and trends, annual rpt, S6995–1
- South Carolina deaths, by detailed cause, age, sex, and race, 1990, annual rpt, S7175–2
- South Carolina vital statistics, including births, deaths by cause, marriages, and divorces, by age, sex, race, and location, 1990 and trends, annual rpt, S7175–1
- South Dakota vital statistics, including births, deaths, marriage and divorce, and communicable disease, by demographic characteristics and county, 1991 and trends, annual rpt, S7345–1
- Tennessee vital statistics, including births, deaths by cause, marriages, divorces, and population, by demographic characteristics and location, 1991 and trends, annual rpt, S7520–2
- Texas vital statistics, including births, deaths by cause, abortions, marriages, and divorces, by location and demographic characteristics, 1991 and trends, annual rpt, S7685–1
- Utah vital statistics, including births, deaths by cause, and population, by county and demographic characteristics, 1990 and trends, annual rpt, S7835–1
- Vermont vital statistics, including population, births, deaths by cause, abortions, marriages, and divorces, by location and demographic characteristics, 1991 and trends, annual rpt, S8054–1

Index by Subjects and Names

Infective and parasitic diseases

Virginia vital statistics, including births, deaths by cause, marriages and divorces, and communicable disease, by demographic characteristics and location, 1991 and trends, annual rpt, S8225–1

Washington State vital statistics, including births, deaths by cause, and population, by demographic characteristics and location, 1991 and trends, annual rpt, S8363–1

West Virginia vital statistics, including births, deaths by cause, marriages, and divorces, by location and demographic characteristics, 1991 and trends, annual rpt, S8560–1

Wisconsin vital statistics, including population, births, deaths by cause, and marriages and dissolutions, by county and demographic characteristics, 1991 and trends, annual rpt, S8715–4

Wyoming vital statistics, including population, births, deaths by cause, marriages, and divorces, by demographic characteristics and county, 1991 and trends, annual rpt, S8920–2

see also Fetal deaths

Infants

see Children

Infective and parasitic diseases

- Childhood preventable disease cases, and State and/or intl immunization rates, 1992 annual rpt, R3840–5.1
- Childhood preventable disease cases for 4 diseases, 1980s-91, annual rpt, R3840–11.1
- Eye donors rejected for testing positive to selected infective diseases, 1992, annual rpt, A4743–1
- Hospital (teaching) training and policies on infection control for house staff, 1992/93, annual rpt, A3273–3
- Hospital patient admission rates and length of stay, by diagnosis and procedure, payment source, age, sex, and region, 1991, B4455–4
- Hospital patient charges and length of stay, by diagnosis and procedure, payment source, age, and region, 1991, B4455–5
- Hospital patient discharges and length of stay, by diagnosis, type of operation, age, and region, 1991, annual rpt series, B4455–1
- Hospital patient discharges and length of stay, by diagnostic related group (DRG), payment source, age, and region, 1991, annual rpt series, B4455–3
- Measles cases in preschool children, health care providers used and welfare status, in 5 metro areas, 1989-90, article, A2623–1.508
- State economic dev condition indicators, including economic performance, business vitality, growth capacity, and tax/fiscal system, by State, 1993 annual rpt, R4225–1.1

State and local:

- Alabama public health dept activities, including services provided, inspection and licensing activity, staff and finances, and vital statistics and health data, 1992 annual rpt, S0175–3
- Alabama vital statistics, including population, births, deaths by cause, marriages, and divorces, by location and demographic characteristics, 1992 and trends, annual rpt, S0175–2

Arkansas vital statistics, including births, deaths by cause, marriages, and divorces, by age, sex, race, and county, 1991 and trends, annual rpt, S0685–1

California vital statistics, including population, births, and deaths by cause, by demographic characteristics and county, 1990 and trends, annual rpt, S0865–1

Colorado vital statistics, including population, births, deaths by cause, abortion, marriage and divorce, and adoption, by demographic characteristics and location, 1990 and trends, annual rpt, S1010–1

Connecticut vital statistics, including births, deaths by cause, marriages, and divorces, by demographic characteristics and location, 1989, annual rpt, S1200–1

DC tuberculosis, venereal disease, and AIDS new cases, 1987-91, annual rpt, S1535–3.5

Florida deaths by selected cause, and incidence of selected communicable diseases, by county, 1992 annual rpt, S1746–1.1

Florida vital statistics, including population, births, deaths by cause, and marriages and dissolutions, by location and demographic characteristics, 1992 and trends, annual rpt, S1745–3

Georgia vital statistics, including deaths by cause, demographic characteristics, and location, 1991 and trends, annual rpt, S1895–1.2

Hawaii health dept activities and services, including vital statistics and disease control, by location, 1990, annual rpt, S2065–1

Idaho vital statistics, including births, deaths by cause, abortions, marriages, and divorces, by demographic characteristics and county, 1991 and trends, annual rpt, S2230–2

Iowa vital statistics, including population, births, deaths by cause, marriages, and divorces, by demographic characteristics and location, 1991 and trends, annual rpt, S2795–1

Kansas vital statistics, including population, births, deaths by cause, abortions, marriages, and divorces, by demographic characteristics and location, 1991 and trends, annual rpt, S2975–1

Kentucky vital statistics, including births, deaths by cause, marriages and divorces, and population, by demographic characteristics and county, 1991, annual rpt, S3140–1

Louisiana vital statistics, including population, births, deaths by cause, reportable diseases, marriages, and divorces, by demographic characteristics and locality, 1989-90 and trends, annual rpt, S3295–1

Maine vital statistics, including births, deaths by cause, abortions, and marriages and divorces, by demographic characteristics and location, 1991 and trends, annual rpt, S3460–2

Maryland vital statistics, including population, births, deaths by cause, marriages, and divorces, by demographic characteristics and location, 1989 and trends, annual rpt, S3635–1

Massachusetts vital statistics, including births, deaths by cause, marriages, divorces, and population, by locality and demographic characteristics, 1990 and trends, annual rpt, S3850–1

Michigan vital statistics, including births, deaths, marriages, divorces/annulments, and communicable diseases, by location and demographic characteristics, 1990 and trends, annual rpt, S4000–3

Minnesota vital statistics, including population, births, abortions, deaths, marriages, and divorces, by location and demographic characteristics, 1991 and trends, annual rpt, S4190–2

Mississippi vital statistics, including births, deaths by cause, marriages, and divorces, by demographic characteristics and location, 1992 and trends, annual rpt, S4350–1

Missouri vital statistics, including population, births, deaths by cause, and marriages and divorces, by location and demographic characteristics, 1992 and trends, annual rpt, S4518–1

Montana vital statistics, including births, deaths by cause, abortion, disease, and marriage and divorce, by demographic characteristics and county, 1990-91 and trends, annual rpt, S4690–1

New Hampshire vital statistics, including population, births, deaths by cause, marriages, and divorces, by location and demographic characteristics, 1991 and trends, annual rpt, S5215–1

New Jersey vital statistics, including births, deaths, population, communicable diseases, and marriages and divorces, by demographic characteristics and location, 1990 and trends, annual rpt, S5405–1

New Mexico vital statistics, including population, births, deaths, and disease, by location and demographic characteristics, 1991 and trends, annual rpt, S5605 1

New York State vital statistics, including population, births, deaths by cause, reportable diseases, and marriages and dissolutions, by demographic characteristics and/or location, 1990 and trends, annual rpt, S5765–1

North Dakota vital statistics, including births, deaths by cause, marriages and divorces, and abortions, by demographic characteristics and/or county, 1991 and trends, annual rpt, S6105–2

Ohio vital statistics, including births, deaths by cause, marriages, divorces, and population, by demographic characteristics and location, 1991 and trends, annual rpt, S6285–1

Oregon vital statistics, including births, deaths by cause, communicable diseases, marriages, and divorces, by age, sex, race-ethnicity, and county, 1991 and trends, annual rpt, S6615–5

Rhode Island vital statistics, including population, births, deaths, marriages, and divorces, by demographic characteristics and locality, 1989 and trends, annual rpt, S6995–1

South Carolina deaths, by detailed cause, age, sex, and race, 1990, annual rpt, S7175–2

South Carolina vital statistics, including births, deaths by cause, marriages, and divorces, by age, sex, race, and location, 1990 and trends, annual rpt, S7175–1

South Dakota vital statistics, including births, deaths, marriage and divorce, and communicable disease, by demographic characteristics and county, 1991 and trends, annual rpt, S7345–1

Tennessee statistical abstract, general data, 1992/93 annual rpt, U8710–2.17

Tennessee vital statistics, including births, deaths by cause, marriages, divorces, and population, by demographic characteristics and location, 1991 and trends, annual rpt, S7520–2

Texas vital statistics, including births, deaths by cause, abortions, marriages, and divorces, by location and demographic characteristics, 1991 and trends, annual rpt, S7685–1

Utah vital statistics, including births, deaths by cause, and population, by county and demographic characteristics, 1990 and trends, annual rpt, S7835–1

Vermont vital statistics, including population, births, deaths by cause, abortions, marriages, and divorces, by location and demographic characteristics, 1991 and trends, annual rpt, S8054–1

Virginia vital statistics, including births, deaths by cause, marriages and divorces, and communicable disease, by demographic characteristics and location, 1991 and trends, annual rpt, S8225–1

Washington State vital statistics, including births, deaths by cause, and population, by demographic characteristics and location, 1991 and trends, annual rpt, S8363–1

West Virginia vital statistics, including births, deaths by cause, marriages, and divorces, by location and demographic characteristics, 1991 and trends, annual rpt, S8560–1

Wisconsin vital statistics, including population, births, deaths by cause, and marriages and dissolutions, by county and demographic characteristics, 1991 and trends, annual rpt, S8715 4

Wyoming vital statistics, including population, births, deaths by cause, marriages, and divorces, by demographic characteristics and county, 1991 and trends, annual rpt, S8920–2

see also Acquired immune deficiency syndrome

see also Animal diseases and zoonoses

see also Food and waterborne diseases

see also Pneumonia and influenza

see also Rabies

see also Sexually transmitted diseases

see also Tuberculosis

see also Vaccination and vaccines

see also under By Disease in the "Index by Categories"

Inflation

Business and economic trends, production and price indicators, and industrial mgmt activities and devs, semimonthly rpt, C7000–3

Consumer attitudes on economic conditions and personal financial situation, monthly survey, U7475–2

Consumer expectations of economic conditions and change in income, and intended durable goods purchases by type, Conference Board monthly survey, R4105–4

Cuba economic indicators, including trade and inflation, 1970s-88, U6250–1.19

Economic indicator historical trends, 1900s-92, annual rpt, R9050–1.2

Family income, with impact of Federal and State/local taxes and inflation, 1980-92, annual rpt, R9050–13

Forecasts for real estate industry and US economy, and housing starts and sales trends by region, monthly rpt, A7000–1

Forecasts of GDP, inflation, unemployment, and Treasury bond rates, by approx 10 organizations, monthly rpt, R4105–80

Latin America statistical abstract, general data by country, 1992 annual rpt, U6250–1.30, U6250–1.31

Railroad cost inflation indexes, 1982-91, annual rpt, A3275–8.2

Rates of inflation compared with 4 types of interest rates, 1960s-93, article, U0280–1.509

Rates of inflation in US and selected other countries, monthly rpt, R4105–6

World financial market devs including economic and monetary trends and forecasts for 15 industrial countries, bimonthly rpt, B6200–2

State and local:

Arizona and natl economic analysts views on natl inflation factors, 1993 recurring survey article, U0282–1.505, U0282–1.512

Illinois, Chicago inflation rate, with comparison to St Louis and North Central region, 1979-91, annual rpt, U6910–2

see also Consumer Price Index

see also Cost of living

see also Economic indicators

see also Family budgets

see also Food prices

see also Interest rates

see also Monetary policy

see also Money supply

see also Price regulation

see also Prices

see also Producer Price Index

Influenza

see Pneumonia and influenza

Information access

see Freedom of information

see Information storage and retrieval systems

Information services

Corporate executive strategic info mgmt, including communications methods and use of nonfinancial performance measures, 1992 survey, R4105–78.25

HMO info types available and requested by employers, by plan characteristics, 1991, annual rpt, A5150–2.3

Library and book trade reference info, including public and academic library funding, construction, and operations, by State and instn, 1992, annual compilation, C1650–3

Library and info service activities and devs, articles and book reviews, semimonthly rpt, C1852–1

State and local:

DC statistical profile, general data, 1992 annual rpt, S1535–3.8

see also Government information

see also Information storage and retrieval systems

see also Libraries

see also Microforms

see also Research

Information storage and retrieval systems

Chemical Abstracts, number of papers covered, by country of origin and specialty area, 1970s-92, annual feature, A1250–1.537

Corporate info system investment shares by type of application, 1991, annual rpt, A4620–1.5

Disasters affecting info systems organizations, 1983-92, article, C5150–4.502

Educational Resources Info Center data base records, 1960s-92, annual compilation, C1650–3.1

Federal Library and Info Network (FEDLINK) service accounts and payments, FY92, annual compilation, C1650–3.1

Food marketers use of electronic scanner data, by purpose, responsible employee, and company characteristics, 1992, annual rpt, A4950–5.4

Health care info mgmt professional views on obstacles to using computer-based patient records, 1993 survey, article, A1865–1.522

Health care instn info system readiness for disaster, 1993 survey, A1865–1.517

Hospital CEO views on strategic mgmt goals and info system support, 1992 survey, article, A1865–1.503

Hospital chief info officer responsibilities and qualifications, Nov 1992 survey, article, A1865–1.508

Nurse views on hospital patient care practices and outlook, and impact of clinical info systems, 1993 survey, article, A1865–1.520

Oil industry use of document imaging systems, by application, 1992 survey article, C6985–1.502

Public utility current and planned info mgmt system improvements, by application, 1993 survey article, C6985–6.505

State and local:

New York State police info network entries and inquiries, 1983-90, annual rpt, U5100–1.8

see also CD-ROM technology and use

see also Computer industry and products

see also Computer networks

see also Computer use

see also Electronic mail systems

see also Microforms

see also Statistical programs and activities

Inforum Inc.

Metro areas with greatest market shares for health insurance managed care and nonmanaged care plans, including population, top 10 cities, 1992, article, A1865–1.510

Infrastructure

see Public works

Inheritance

see Probate courts and cases

see Wills and testaments

Inheritance tax

see Estate tax

Injuries

see Accidents and accident prevention

see Agricultural accidents and safety

see Aviation accidents and safety

Index by Subjects and Names

see Marine accidents and safety
see Mine accidents and safety
see Occupational health and safety
see Railroad accidents and safety
see Spinal cord injuries
see Traffic accidents and safety

Ink industry
see Chemicals and chemical industry
see Printing and publishing industry

Inland water transportation
Financial ratios and performance, for over 350 SIC 4-digit industries, FY88-92, annual rpt, A6400–3
Iron ore shipments in US and Canada, with detail by Great Lakes port, monthly rpt, A2010–2
Mexico-Texas transportation system analysis, including bilateral trade, operations by transport mode, and data by locale, 1993 rpt, U8850–9
Trends in transportation operations and finances, by mode, 1991 annual rpt, R4815–1

State and local:
Alabama statistical abstract, general data, 1992 recurring rpt, U5680–2.16
Arkansas River freight traffic, quarterly business activity rpt, U5930–1
Georgia statistical abstract, general data, 1992-93 biennial rpt, U6730–1.8
Maryland statistical abstract, general data, 1993-94 biennial rpt, S3605–1.10
New York State statistical yearbook, general data, 1992 annual rpt, U5100–1.13
Oklahoma, Muskogee and Catoosa ports water freight traffic, monthly rpt quarterly data, U8130–1
Oklahoma statistical abstract, general data, 1992 annual rpt, U8130–2.16
Wisconsin Blue Book, general data, 1993-94 biennial rpt, S8780–1.2
see also Barges
see also Rivers and waterways
see also Under names of specific rivers and waterways

Inner cities
see Central cities

Inoculation
see Vaccination and vaccines

Inorganic chemicals
see Chemicals and chemical industry

Input Corp.
Computer application outside contracting market, with shares for top 5 and all other major vendors, 1991 and 1997, article, C1850–5.502
Electronic data interchange (EDI) market value, 1991-92 and 1997, article, C1850–5.506

Input-output analysis
State and local:
Idaho input-output analysis multipliers by major industry group, 1993 article, S2245–2.501

Insecticides
see Pesticides

Insects
see Animal diseases and zoonoses
see Honey and beekeeping
see Infective and parasitic diseases
see Pests and pest control

Inspection of industrial products
see Quality control and testing

Installment credit
see Consumer credit

Institutional population
see Group quarters

Instructional materials
see Educational materials

Instruments and measuring devices
Automatic test equipment industry financial performance, and market shares for leading firms, 1993 article, C1850–2.503
Engineers salaries by industry group, census div, selected metro area, and years since college degree, 1993, annual survey rpt, A0685–5
Engineers salaries by industry group, census div, selected metro area, degree level, and years since college degree, 1993, annual survey rpt, A0685–3
Executive compensation and components, by industry div and major manufacturing group, 1991, annual rpt, R4105–19
Fiber optic cable testing device sales, 1991-92, article, C4725–3.501
Financial ratios and performance, for over 350 SIC 4-digit industries, FY88-92, annual rpt, A6400–3
Market devs in electronics industry, including employment, factory sales, prices, and foreign trade trends, monthly rpt, A4725–2
Operating and financial composite ratios for corporations, with establishments and receipts, for approx 200 industries, by asset size, FY90, annual rpt, C7800–1
Shipment value, employment, and foreign trade, for electronics industry, by sector and product type, 1980s-92, annual rpt, A4725–1.2
Telecommunication T-1/T-3 high-capacity systems monitoring equipment market value, 1992-97, article, C4725–3.514

State and local:
Florida statistical abstract, general data, 1992 annual rpt, U6660–1.12
see also Radar
see also Scientific equipment and apparatus
see also Watches and clocks
see also under By Industry in the "Index by Categories"

Instruments, musical
see Musical instruments

Insurance and insurance industry
Asset composition for 6 institutional investor categories, 1970-2nd qtr 1992, article, A8825–1.504
Black-owned enterprises financial and operating data, for top 100 firms and auto dealerships and for top 15-25 financial instns, 1992 and trends, annual feature, C4215–1.507
Business failures and liabilities, by detailed industry, cause, length of operation, and location, 1991-92 and trends, annual rpt, C3150–8
Cable TV advertising budget shares targeted to insurance industry, and types of insurance advertised, May 1993 survey, article, C1858–1.503
Construction company insurance coverage practices, by type of business, 1993, annual survey rpt, A4155–1
Construction executive views on loss-control program effectiveness in controlling insurance costs, 1992 survey article, C5800–2.505

Insurance and insurance industry

Consumer complaint and inquiry activity of Better Business Burs, by detailed type of business, 1992, annual rpt, A4350–1
Corporate directors compensation and insurance benefits for outside board members, 1991-92, annual rpt, R4105–7
Direct marketing industry devs, with consumer and business market characteristics, and media use patterns, 1992/93 annual rpt, A4620–1.4
Economic role of insurance industry, including employment, payroll, share of GSP, and premium taxes, by State, 1992 annual rpt, A0375–2
Employer payments for employee insurance coverage by type, 1990, annual rpt, A5173–2.1
Executive compensation and components, by industry div and major manufacturing group, 1991, annual rpt, R4105–19
Financial instn insurance requirements for home equity loans, by region, asset size, and instn type, 1992, annual rpt, A4160–3
Financial performance and growth rankings for approx 1,000 top corporations, with comparisons by industry group, 1993 annual rpt, C3950–1.505
Financial ratios and performance, for over 350 SIC 4-digit industries, FY88-92, annual rpt, A6400–3
Flood insurance govt program policies in force, by State, 1991, annual rpt, A5650–1.3
Guaranteed investment contract (GIC) performance indexes, biweekly rpt quarterly feature, C2710–2.504, C2710–2.510, C2710–2.517
Household expenditures for personal insurance/pensions, for approx 300 metro areas, 1992, annual rpt, C1200–1.511
Investment mgmt firms, assets and operating data for approx 900 instns, Jan 1993, annual feature, C2710–2.511
Marketing trends and devs, and mgmt and finance topics, for life and health insurance, monthly rpt, C1050–2
Marketing trends and devs, and mgmt and finance topics, for property and casualty insurance, monthly rpt, C1050–1
Mexico insurance premiums value by line of coverage, 1992, article, C1050–1.507, C1050–2.507
Mortgage (FHA-insured) originations, claim and nonclaim terminations, and interest rates, monthly FY78 and FY86, article, A6450–2.508
Mortgage insurance industry finances and performance indicators, 1988-91, annual rpt, A6455–1
Mutual fund industry financial data, by type of investor and financial instn intermediary, 1991 and trends, annual rpt, A6025–1.2
Operating and financial composite ratios for corporations, with establishments and receipts, for approx 200 industries, by asset size, FY90, annual rpt, C7800–1
Pakistan insurance industry underwriting data, with operating results for 2 major companies, 1990-91, annual article, C1050–1.504
Premiums and underwriting ratios for top 300 accident/health companies, 1991, annual article, C1050–2.502

Insurance and insurance industry

Public opinion on honesty/ethical standards of insurance sales workers, 1992 Gallup Polls and trends, C4040–1.501

Shopping center financial and operating data, with detail by type of tenant, US and Canada, 1991, triennial rpt, R9285–1

Shopping center insurance costs per square foot, by type of center, 1992 article, C5150–4.503

Spain insurance premiums for 10 leading underwriting groups, 1992, annual article, C1050–1.510

Supermarket insurance cost increases, for independent and chain stores, 1992, annual rpt, C5225–1.505

Transportation insurance coverage of household goods during employee transfers, 1992, annual survey, B0600–1

Truck fleet financial and operating data for top 200 freight carriers, 1992 and trends, annual feature, C2150–4.504

Trucking insurance coverage and filing requirements, by State, 1991/92 annual rpt, A7015–4

World insurance premiums, for life and non-life business, top 10 countries, 1990, annual rpt, A5650–1.1

State and local:

Alabama insurance industry financial and underwriting data, by company and line of coverage, 1991, annual rpt, S0160–1

Alaska insurance industry underwriting and investment data, by company and type of insurance, with regulatory info, 1991 and trends, annual rpt, S0280–3

Arizona finance, insurance, and real estate employment and job outlook, by occupation and county, 1990-95, triennial rpt, S0465–2.36

Arizona insurance industry financial and underwriting data, by company and type of insurance, with regulatory info, 1992, annual rpt, S0483–1

Arizona statistical abstract, general data, 1993 recurring rpt, U5850–2.23

California insurance industry financial and underwriting data, by company and type of insurance, with regulatory info, 1991, annual rpt, S0900–1

California taxable insurance premiums, and tax assessments, by company, 1992 and trends, annual rpt, S0835–1.6

Connecticut insurance industry financial and underwriting data, by company and type of insurance, 1991, annual rpt, S1222–1

Florida insurance industry financial and underwriting data, by company and line of coverage, 1991, annual rpt, S1760–1

Florida statistical abstract, general data, 1992 annual rpt, U6660–1.17

Hawaii data book, general data, 1992 annual rpt, S2090–1.15

Idaho financial instn consumer loan activity, including insurance coverage, 1991, annual rpt, S2235–1

Idaho insurance industry financial and underwriting data, by company and type of insurance, with regulatory data, 1991, annual rpt, S2260–1

Illinois real estate title insurer finances, and premiums written by county, 1989 and/or 1990, annual rpt, S2457–2

Iowa credit insurance loan activity, 1991, annual rpt, S2760–2

Iowa insurance industry financial and underwriting data, by company and type of insurance, 1992, annual rpt, S2760–1

Kansas insurance industry financial and underwriting data, by company and type of insurance, with regulatory info, 1992, annual rpt, S2990–1

Maryland insurance industry financial and underwriting data, by company and type of insurance, with regulatory info, 1991, annual rpt, S3655–1

Michigan insurance industry financial and underwriting data, by company and type of insurance, with regulatory info, 1991, annual rpt, S3983–1

Minnesota insurance industry financial and underwriting data, by company and line of coverage, 1991, annual rpt, S4140–4

Missouri insurance industry financial and underwriting data, by company and type of insurance, with regulatory info, 1992, annual rpt, S4527–1

Nebraska insurance industry financial and underwriting data, by company and line of coverage, with regulatory info, 1992, annual rpt, S4890–1

New Hampshire insurance industry financial data by company, 1991, with FY92 regulatory info, annual rpt, S5220–1

New Jersey insurance industry financial and underwriting data, by company and type of insurance, 1990, annual rpt, S5420–1

New Mexico economic trends and outlook, by industry div, 1982-92, annual article, U7980–1.503

New York State insurance fraud arrests, indictments, dispositions, and sentences, 1987-91, annual rpt, S5760–3.3

New York State insurance industry devs, finances, and regulatory activity, 1990/91 and trends, annual rpt, S5770–3

New York State insurance industry financial and underwriting data, by company and line of coverage, 1991, annual rpt, S5770–2

New York State insurance industry premiums and loss ratios, by company and line of coverage, discontinued annual rpt, S5770–1

New York State statistical yearbook, general data, 1992 annual rpt, U5100–1.7

Oklahoma insurance industry financial and underwriting data, by company and type of insurance, with regulatory info, 1992, annual rpt, S6462–1

Oklahoma statistical abstract, general data, 1992 annual rpt, U8130–2.20

Oregon population educational attainment, health and life insurance coverage, rent, and poverty, 1990 and 1992, article, S6592–1.502

Pennsylvania insurance industry financial and underwriting data, by company and line of coverage, 1991, with FY92 regulatory info, annual rpt, S6835–1

Pennsylvania insurance premium tax collections, by type of coverage or tax, FY90-92, annual rpt, S6885–1

Pennsylvania statistical abstract, general data, 1992 recurring rpt, U4130–6.2

Rhode Island insurance industry financial and underwriting data, by company and line of coverage, 1990, with FY91 regulatory info, annual rpt, S6945–2

South Carolina economic condition, including agriculture, finance, and govt financial data, 1970s-92, annual rpt, S7125–3.1

South Carolina insurance industry financial and underwriting data, by company, 1991, with FY92 regulatory info, annual rpt, S7195–1

South Dakota insurance industry financial and underwriting data, by company and type of insurance, with regulatory info, 1991-92, annual rpt, S7300–2

Tennessee insurance industry financial and underwriting data, by company and type of insurance, with regulatory info, 1991, annual rpt, S7466–1

Tennessee public school finances, by county, city, and school district, 1991/92, annual rpt, S7490–2.4

Tennessee statistical abstract, general data, 1992/93 annual rpt, U8710–2.13

Texas insurance dept regulatory activities, with industry financial and underwriting data by line of coverage, FY92 annual rpt, S7700–1

Utah insurance industry financial and underwriting data, by company and line of coverage, with regulatory info, 1991, annual rpt, S7845–1

Utah public school revenues by source and expenditures by object, by State fund and school district, FY92, annual rpt, S7815–1.2

Utah tax revenues by source, and distribution to localities and State funds, FY92 and trends, annual rpt, S7905–1

Vermont insurance industry financial and underwriting data, by company and type of insurance, 1991, annual rpt, S7995–1

Virginia insurance industry financial and underwriting data, by company and line of coverage, annual rpt discontinued coverage, S8180–1

West Virginia insurance industry financial and underwriting data, by company and line of coverage, with regulatory info, 1991, annual rpt, S8575–1

Wisconsin insurance industry financial and underwriting data, by company and line of coverage, with regulatory info, 1992, annual rpt, S8755–1

see also Agricultural insurance

see also Automobile insurance

see also Deposit insurance

see also Disability benefits and insurance

see also Employee benefits

see also Federal Deposit Insurance Corp.

see also Health insurance

see also Life insurance

see also Medicare

see also Old-Age, Survivors, Disability, and Health Insurance

see also Property and casualty insurance

see also Surety bonds

see also Unemployment insurance

see also Workers compensation

see also under By Industry in the "Index by Categories"

Integrated Circuit Engineering Corp.

Semiconductor metal-oxide gate array sales worldwide, 1993-97, article, C1850–2.507

Semiconductor sales for top 10 companies worldwide, 1992, article, C1850–2.503

World merchant integrated circuit package sales, 1991 and 1996, article, C1850–2.501

Integrated circuits
see Electronics industry and products
see Semiconductors

Intellectual property
see Copyright
see Patents
see Trademarks

Intelligence levels

State and local:

Georgia prison population by intelligence quotient (IQ) and education level, FY92 annual rpt, S1872–1

Hawaii, measured intelligence of developmental disability clients and Waimano Training School and Hospital residents, FY90 and trends, annual rpt, S2065–1.5

Missouri correctional instn inmate intelligence test scores, FY93, annual rpt, S4501–1

Texas prison inmates by intelligence quotient (IQ) and achievement test scores, by sex, FY92, annual rpt, S7660–1

Intelligence services

Hispanic-owned high-technology company CEO views on use of Govt intelligence agencies on behalf of business, 1993 annual article, C4575–1.510

see also Detective and protective services

Inter-American Development Bank

Latin America statistical abstract, general data by country, 1992 annual rpt, U6250–1.28

Interactive media
see Telecommunication

Interest groups
see Associations
see Lobbying and lobbying groups
see Membership organizations
see Political action committees

Interest rates

Business and economic trends, production and price indicators, and industrial mgmt activities and devs, semimonthly rpt, C7000–3

Business cycle interest rate peaks and troughs, with trends in price of credit, industrial production, and stock performance, 1953-92, article, C3950–1.507

Business economists forecasts of general economic conditions, quarterly rpt, A6650–5

Business loan short- and long-term rates, 1971-92, annual rpt, A3179–2.3

Business Week economic, business, and investment devs, with related statistical indicators, weekly rpt, C5800–7

Canada life insurance policy interest rate changes, monthly rpt, A6225–2

Chicago Board of Trade futures and options trading in financial instruments and agricultural commodities, 1992, annual rpt, B2120–1

Commodity yearbook for 1993: detailed supply-demand data, and selected indicators for futures market investors, C2400–1

Commodity yearbook update: detailed supply-demand data, and selected indicators for futures market investors, Jan-Sept 1993 rpts, C2400–2

Consumer attitudes on economic conditions and personal financial situation, monthly survey, U7475–2

Consumer expectations of economic conditions and change in income, and intended durable goods purchases by type, Conference Board monthly survey, R4105–4

Economic indicator forecasts for 30 countries by approx 50 forecasting organizations, including GDP, inflation, unemployment, and interest rates, 1992-94, R4105–6.502

Economic indicator historical trends, 1900s-92, annual rpt, R9050–1.2

Economic indicator trends and forecasts, with detail for approx 15 Western States, 1990s, annual rpt, B3520–1

Economic outlook for selected indicators, recent trends and 2-year forecast, quarterly rpt, A3840–6

Forecast interest rates, by type, quarterly rpt, U1880–1

Forecasts for prime rate, 50 economists, 4th qtr 1993, annual feature, C5800–7.509

Forecasts for real estate industry and US economy, and housing starts and sales trends by region, monthly rpt, A7000–1

Forecasts of economic indicators for approx 10-13 months, monthly rpt, U1880–3

Forecasts of natl income and product account components, employment, and financial sector activity, monthly rpt, B4950–1

Futures and options trading in interest rates, 1988-92, annual rpt, A5040–1

Home equity lending activity and practices of financial instns, by region, asset size, and instn type, 1992, annual rpt, A4160–3

Housing market trends and outlook, including mortgage originations and interest rates, 1989-94, annual article, A6150 2.503

Inflation rates compared with 4 types of interest rates, 1960s-93, article, U0280–1.509

Insurance flexible-premium retirement annuity policy 5-year performance, including interest rates, by company, 1988-92, annual article, C1050–2.507

Japan economic profile, including govt finances, industrial production, foreign trade and investments, and comparisons to US, 1988-92, annual feature, R5650–2.552

Latin America statistical abstract, general data by country, 1992 annual rpt, U6250–1.31

Life insurance (universal) policy 5-year performance, including interest rates, by company, 1988-92, annual article, C1050–2.511

Life insurance policy interest rate ranges, monthly rpt, A6225–1

Life insurance single-premium deferred annuity policy 5-year performance, including interest rates, by company, 1987-91, annual article, C1050–2.501

Loan and selected security rates, by type, monthly rpt, A6450–2

Money and securities market activity, and related indicators, biweekly rpt, B2000–1

Mortgage securities activity, including yields and conventional loan rates, quarterly rpt, B5190–1

Productivity and related indicators, trend analysis for US and other industrial countries, 1980s-92, annual rpt, R2800–2

Railroad interest rates on new equipment, and interest charges on long-term debt, 1982-91, annual rpt, A3275–8.2

Restaurant (table service) operators seeking credit lines and bank loans, with approval and interest rates, 1992, recurring rpt, A8200–11

Small business views on current and expected economic conditions, survey findings, quarterly rpt, A7815–1

Treasury bond (30-year) interest rate forecasts of 16 economists, year-end 1993-94, article, C8900–1.526

World financial market devs including economic and monetary trends and forecasts for 15 industrial countries, bimonthly rpt, B6200–2

State and local:

Arizona economic analysts outlook for oil prices and mortgage interest rates, 1993 annual survey article, U0282–1.507

Arizona, Maricopa County mortgage rates, monthly rpt, U0280–1

Arkansas State treasurer safekeeping account balances and interest rates, by account, FY92, biennial rpt, S0780–1

South Carolina economic condition, including agriculture, finance, and govt financial data, 1970s-92, annual rpt, S7125–3.1

West Virginia floating mortgage rate ceilings, Dec 1990-91, annual rpt, S8530–1

Intergovernmental relations

Municipal and county govt structure, public services, finances, and intergovtl relations, 1993 annual rpt, A5800–1

see also Federal-local relations
see also Federal-State relations
see also State-local relations

Intergovernmental tax relations
see Revenue sharing
see State and local taxes

Interindustry transactions
see Input-output analysis

Interior Department
see Department of Interior

Interior design

Financial and operating data for top interior design companies, 1993 annual features, C1850–7

Internal Revenue Service

Hard goods manufacturers views on govt regulation, including 1992 IRS audits and outcomes, by product line, 1993 annual survey rpt, A1800–1

Tax exempt organizations registered, and applications approved and denied, by type of organization, 1991 and/or 1992, annual article, C2176–1.517

State and local:

Hawaii operations of IRS, 1989-91, annual rpt, S2090–1.9

International agencies
see International organizations

International agreements
see Trade agreements
see Treaties and conventions

International assistance

China private sector industrial project dev costs, for 10 projects being considered by Intl Finance Corp, 1993 article, A9315–1.504

International assistance

Congressional appropriations for foreign aid vs Bush Admin requests, by program, FY93, annual rpt, C2500–2

Developing countries family planning program funding by source, by country, 1980s-90, R8720–1.1

Europe public opinion on political, economic, and social issues, for 9 countries and 3 Soviet Union Republics, 1991 survey, C8915–8.1

Foundation assets, income, and grants by type of recipient, with data for top organizations and by location, 1991 and trends, annual rpt, R4900–1

Grants and credits to foreign areas from US by program, by country and world region, 1946-90, annual rpt, R9050–1.3

Infrastructure dev share of OECD countries foreign assistance, for 11 donor countries, 1991, article, C5800–2.527

Japan economic dev loans to China, distribution by industry or purpose, as of Oct 1992, article, A9315–1.504

Japan environment-related foreign aid, including grants, loans, and technical assistance, FY89-91, article, R5650–2.541

Japan foreign aid contributions, by type and recipient region and country, 1987-91, annual article, R5650–2.507

Japan foreign dev aid, including distribution by recipient region, 1988-97, article, C5800–2.545

Japan foreign trade with and assistance to Indonesia, 1992 and trends, article, R5650–2.534

Latin America statistical abstract, general data by country, 1992 annual rpt, U6250–1.28

Middle East, West Bank territories financial aid 10-year outlook by aid source, 1993 article, C5800–7.547

OECD Dev Assistance Committee contributions, by member and recipient country, 1987-91, annual article, R5650–2.507

OECD Dev Assistance Committee contributions, by member country, 1988-92, annual article, R5650–2.550

Philippines GNP, foreign investment inflow, intl aid, and trade with US and Japan, with comparisons to 7-8 other Asian countries, 1992 and trends, article, R5650–2.555

Public opinion in US on selected foreign policy issues, with detail for 3 States, 1993 survey, annual rpt, A4965–1

Refugee intl aid contributions, 20 countries and EC, 1992, annual rpt, R9372–1

Religious congregation characteristics, including membership, activities, staff, and finances, 1992 survey, recurring rpt, A5435–4

Russia financial aid by purpose, public opinion in US, Mar 1993 Gallup Poll, C4040–1.510

Russia intl aid by type under program proposed by Group of 7 (G-7) countries, and additional aid from 3 countries, 1993 article, R5650–2.524, R5650–2.530

UN voting support for US and Soviet Union stances, and US aid received, for 50 countries, 1992 annual rpt, U6250–1.9

World official dev assistance received or granted, total and as percent of GNP, by country, 1989 and trends, biennial rpt, R9455–1.5

see also Disaster relief
see also Export-Import Bank
see also Food assistance
see also Military assistance
see also Public Law 480
see also Refugees

International Bank for Reconstruction and Development
see also International Finance Corp.

International Business Machines Corp.
Corporate customer areas of dissatisfaction with IBM products and service, 1993 survey article, C1850–2.508

International conferences, congresses and conventions
see Conferences

International cooperation in conservation
see also International cooperation in environmental sciences

International cooperation in cultural activities
Museum exhibition collaboration and loans inside and outside US, by museum type, 1989/90 survey, A0750–1.2
see also Cultural activities
see also Educational exchanges

International cooperation in environmental sciences
World conventions concerning the environment, with participation by country, 1991, biennial rpt, R9455–1.7

International cooperation in science and technology
Europe semiconductor consortium (Jessi) budget, 1990-1995/96, article, C1850–2.508
Latin America statistical abstract, general data by country, 1992 annual rpt, U6250–1.28
see also European Space Agency
see also International cooperation in environmental sciences
see also Technology transfer

International corporations
see Foreign corporations
see Multinational corporations

International crime
see also Drug and narcotics offenses

International Data Corp.
China computer revenues by industry sector, 1991, article, C5800–7.505
Computer (personal) shipment value shares for top 4 and all other manufacturers, 1st qtr 1992-93, article, C1850–2.511
Computer (personal) shipments, with market shares for top 10 and all other manufacturers, 1991-92, article, C5800–7.515

International debts
see Foreign debts

International economic relations
see Balance of payments
see Foreign debts
see Foreign economic relations
see Foreign investments
see Foreign trade
see International finance
see Multinational corporations

International finance
Currency holdings of central banks, distribution by type of currency, 1991, annual feature, C8900–1.520
Futures and options contract open interest (outstanding commitments), on foreign exchanges, by commodity and exchange, monthly rpt, A5040–6

Futures and options trading volume on foreign exchanges, by commodity and exchange, monthly rpt, A5040–5
Latin America statistical abstract, general data by country, 1992 annual rpt, U6250–1.28, U6250–1.29
World financial market devs including economic and monetary trends and forecasts for 15 industrial countries, bimonthly rpt, B6200–2
see also Balance of payments
see also Eurocurrency
see also Export-Import Bank
see also Foreign debts
see also Foreign economic relations
see also Foreign exchange
see also Foreign investments
see also Inter-American Development Bank
see also International Monetary Fund
see also International reserves
see also Multinational corporations
see also Organization for Economic Cooperation and Development
see also Special Drawing Rights

International Finance Corp.
China private sector industrial project dev costs, for 10 projects being considered by Intl Finance Corp, 1993 article, A9315–1.504

International Iron and Steel Institute
Consumption of steel worldwide, with detail by selected country or world area, 1990-93, 1995, and 2000, annual article, C7000–8.502
Steelworks yields, by type of product and/or process, 1992 article, C7000–8.502

International labor
see Foreign labor conditions

International law
see also Aliens
see also Citizenship
see also Expropriation of alien property
see also Passports and visas
see also Treaties and conventions

International Monetary Fund
Latin America statistical abstract, general data by country, 1992 annual rpt, U6250–1.28
see also Special Drawing Rights

International organizations
Europe Film Distribution Office (EFDO) motion picture subsidy activity in 12 countries, 1988-92, article, C9380–1.540
Latin America statistical abstract, general data by country, 1992 annual rpt, U6250–1.28
see also Inter-American Development Bank
see also International Finance Corp.
see also International Monetary Fund
see also North Atlantic Treaty Organization
see also Organization for Economic Cooperation and Development
see also United Nations

International relations
see Foreign economic relations
see Foreign relations
see United Nations

International relief
see International assistance

International reserves
Latin America statistical abstract, general data by country, 1992 annual rpt, U6250–1.27
see also Special Drawing Rights

Index by Subjects and Names

International sanctions
see also Boycotts

International trade
see Balance of payments
see Foreign exchange
see Foreign investments
see Foreign trade
see Multinational corporations
see Ships and shipping
see Trade agreements

International transactions
see Balance of payments
see Foreign debts
see Foreign economic relations
see Foreign exchange
see Foreign trade
see International finance

International trusteeships
see also Trust Territory of the Pacific Islands

Interstate agreements
see Interstate compacts

Interstate commerce
State and local:
Hawaii-US mainland trade, 1992 annual rpt, S2090–1.17, S2090–1.18, S2090–1.19, S2090–1.24
Kansas livestock inshipments, by State of origin, 1987-91, annual rpt, U7095–2.15
Oklahoma statistical abstract, general data, 1992 annual rpt, U8130–2.18
see also Buses
see also Freight
see also Inland water transportation
see also Natural gas pipelines
see also Pipelines
see also Railroads
see also Ships and shipping
see also Transportation and transportation equipment
see also Trucks and trucking industry

Interstate compacts
Correctional instn inmate exchanges, and parolee and probationer supervision, interstate compacts by State, 1991, annual series, R4300–1
Hydroelectric power dev interstate compacts, by river, 1991/92 annual rpt, A7015–3
Optometry school students enrolled under State contract agreements, by instn, 1991/92, annual survey, A3370–2
Western States higher education student exchange program enrollment and support fees, by program and instn, for 15 States, 1992/93, annual rpt, A9385–1

State and local:
Arizona corrections dept admin, including parole and probation activity under interstate compacts, FY92, annual rpt, S0464–2
Arkansas juvenile and child placement interstate compact activities, FY91, annual rpt, S0700–2.2
Colorado domestic relations court cases under Uniform Reciprocal Support Act, by district and county, FY92, annual rpt, S1035–1.2
Connecticut courts probation activity, including interstate compact caseloads, FY91-92, biennial rpt, S1220–1.2
DC juvenile interstate compact case activity, 1992 and trends, annual rpt, S1515–1
Iowa correctional instn admissions and releases under interstate compacts, by instn, monthly rpt, S2770–1

Kansas parole and probation interstate compact cases, by sending and receiving State, June 1992, annual rpt, S2940–1
Missouri child placement interstate compact activities, FY92, annual rpt, S4575–2
Nebraska juvenile parolee placements through interstate compact services, by sex, FY92, annual rpt, S4850–1
Oklahoma juvenile service cases under interstate compact, by county, FY92, annual rpt, S6455–1.2
Wisconsin correctional instn inmates and release caseloads under interstate compact, 1991 and trends, annual rpt, S8692–1.4
Wisconsin probation and parole cases under interstate compacts, FY92 and trends, annual rpt, S8692–1.6

Interstate highways
see Highways, streets, and roads

Interstate relations
see also Interstate compacts

InterStudy
HMO enrollment by plan type and for top 10 HMOs, and enrollment as a percent of total population by region, 1993 article, A1865–1.513

Inventions
see also Patents
see also Technological innovations
see also Technology transfer

Inventories
see Agricultural stocks
see Business inventories
see Energy stocks and inventories
see Stockpiling

Investigations
see Criminal investigations
see Government investigations

Investment banking
Black-owned investment bank value of securities managed, for top 13 instns, Dec 1992, article, C4215–1.507
Corporate merger/acquisition advisors, number of deals in selected industries handled by top 6-10 firms, Oct 1991-Sept 1992, annual compilation, C4683–1.502
Corporate merger/acquisition fees paid to financial advisors, 1988-92, article, C4683–1.502
Corporate mergers/acquisitions, activity handled by leading financial advisors, 1992, annual compilation, C4683–1.503
Securities initial public offerings and value, and funds raised, for top 10 underwriters, 1992, article, C4687–1.507
Securities initial public offerings, performance of best and worst issues, and leading underwriters, 1993 annual article, C3950–1.517
Securities initial public offerings, performance of leading issues and underwriters, biweekly rpt quarterly feature, C3950–1.507, C3950–1.520, C3950–1.527
see also Commercial credit
see also Investment management and organizations

Investment management and organizations
Acquisitions of 15 investment advisors, participants and price for 15 transactions, 1992/93, article, C4683–1.506
Assets and operating data for approx 900 investment mgmt firms, Jan 1993, annual feature, C2710–2.511

Investment management and organizations

Assets managed in index funds by top firms, Dec 1992, semiannual article, C2710–2.505
Assets managed in index funds by top firms, Mar 1993, semiannual article, C2710–2.516
Employee benefit plans, top investment managers, consultants, and trustees/custodians used by 1,000 largest funds, 1992, annual feature, C2710–2.504
Financial performance and growth rankings for approx 1,000 top corporations, with comparisons by industry group, 1993 annual rpt, C3950–1.505
Higher education instn endowment fund and investment pool characteristics and performance, by instn, FY92, annual survey rpt, A6705–2
Institutional fund mgmt and investment trends and devs, biweekly rpt, C2710–2
Intl investment mgmt firms, tax-exempt assets and operating data for top firms, 1993, annual feature, C2710–2.514
Japan social security system coverage, finances, and mgmt of fund investments, by type of program, 1993 article, R5650–2.549
Leveraged buyout activity of top 20 financial advisors, 1985-1st half 1992, C4683–1.501
New business of investment mgmt companies, rankings of top 10 firms in selected categories, 1992, annual feature, C2710–2.506
Operating and financial composite ratios for corporations, with establishments and receipts, for approx 200 industries, by asset size, FY90, annual rpt, C7800–1
Pension fund and employee benefit plan investment and admin, monthly rpt, C2425–1
Performance of leading funds with institutional investors, by fund and type, biweekly rpt quarterly feature, C2710–2.502, C2710–2.506, C2710–2.507, C2710–2.512, C2710–2.513, C2710–2.518, C2710–2.519
Performance of leading funds with institutional investors, errata, C2710–2.501
Real estate investment advisors tax-exempt and total assets by type, top 76 firms, 1993, annual feature, C2710–2.520
Real estate investment mgmt companies, pension fund and other managed assets, and investment info, by company, 1992 annual directory, C2425–1.501
Real estate investment mgmt companies, pension fund and other managed assets, and investment info, by company, 1993 annual directory, C2425–1.507
Return on investment portfolios recommended by 42 advisory newsletters, 1993 article, C3950–1.522
Securities industry financial performance and activities, with data by type of firm, 1st 5 months 1993 and trends, recurring article, A8825–1.505
Securities industry financial performance and activities, with data by type of firm, 1992 and trends, recurring article, A8825–1.503
Small business investment company fund performance, assets, and number of companies in portfolio, for 6 funds, 1992 article, C3950–1.504

Investment management and organizations

Index by Subjects and Names

Stock performance data for 8 mutual fund mgmt companies, 1993 article, C3950–1.523

Unit investment trust sales volume and value, by trust type, maturity period, and insurance features, monthly rpt, A6025–7

State and local:

Minnesota financial instns (State-regulated), financial condition by instn, 1991-92, annual rpt, S4140–3

Rhode Island banks and other financial instns (State-chartered), assets and liabilities, by instn, 1991, annual rpt, S6945–1

Wyoming State treasurer financial transactions, including managed investment yields and cost-benefit analysis, FY92, annual rpt, S9010–1

see also Financial planning
see also Investment banking
see also Mutual funds
see also Stockbrokers

Investments

Billionaire profiles and sources of wealth, for persons/families worldwide worth 1 billion/more, 1993 annual feature, C3950–1.518

Billionaire profiles and sources of wealth, for 101 wealthiest persons/families worldwide, 1993 annual feature, C8900–1.518

Business Week economic, business, and investment devs, with related statistical indicators, weekly rpt, C5800–7

Congressional testimony pertaining to investment capital formation, with supporting data on investments and govt policy, series, A1310–2

Economic outlook for selected indicators, recent trends and 2-year forecast, quarterly rpt, A3840–6

Educational employee retirement plan investment income and portfolio composition, 1990/91 and trends, recurring rpt, A7640–18.1

Employee benefit plan asset rankings of top 1,000 funds, with selected fund investment data, 1992, annual feature, C2710–2.504

Forbes business and corporate financial and investment devs, with related statistical indicators, biweekly rpt, C3950–1

Forbes profile of 400 wealthiest individuals, with info on family background, income, and assets, 1993 annual feature, C3950–1.526

Forecasts of natl income and product account components and related indicators, quarterly rpt, U1880–1

Forecasts of natl income and product account components, employment, and financial sector activity, monthly rpt, B4950–1

Foundation assets, and investments by type, for 10 largest organizations, Dec 1992 and trends, article, C2176–1.506

Foundation finances, and personnel and governing board characteristics, by organization characteristics, 1991/92, article, C2176–1.506

Foundations (community-based) assets by type, and investment performance, 1992 and trends, article, C2176–1.522

Germany (West) and US comparative socioeconomic statistics, 1970s-91, annual rpt, A5135–2.2

Govt policy impact on investment capital formation, series, A1310–1

Higher education endowment fund investment composition, for large vs small instns, 1993 article, C2175–1.507

Higher education endowment funds of 419 instns, market values, June 1991-92, annual feature, C2175–1.508

Higher education instn endowment fund and investment pool characteristics and performance, by instn, FY92, annual survey rpt, A6705–2

Hispanic American 50 wealthiest individuals or families, with info on background, assets, and net worth, 1993, annual feature, C4575–1.505

Hospital investment policies, Aug 1992 survey, article, A1865–1.501

Household income from investments vs hourly wages, percent change for 4 income groups, 1979-89, R3834–13

Household wealth and income data by income level, including assets by type and detail by age group, 1989 and trends, R4700–17

Institutional fund mgmt and investment trends and devs, biweekly rpt, C2710–2

Insurance (life/health) industry asset allocation and investment yields, for top 125 US and Canadian companies, 1992 and trends, annual article, C1050–2.512

Insurance (life/health) industry separate account performance, 1991, recurring article, C1050–2.505

Insurance (property/casualty) asset composition and investment yield, for top 100 firms, 1991 and trends, annual article, C1050–1.502

Insurance (property/casualty) investment income and holdings by type, 1991 and trends, annual rpt, A5650–1.2

Latin America statistical abstract, general data by country, 1992 annual rpt, U6250–1.32

Life insurance industry income and financial data, including investments by type of security, 1991 and trends, biennial fact book, A1325–1.4

Medical malpractice insurance State joint underwriting assn (JUA) financial condition, for 11 States, 1991, annual rpt, A0375–1

Money and securities market activity, and related indicators, biweekly rpt, B2000–1

Mutual fund industry financial data, investment activity, portfolio composition, and shareholder account characteristics, 1991 and trends, annual rpt, A6025–1

Natl trends in savings and investment by sector, and household assets and liabilities, 1960s-92, annual rpt, R9050–1.2

Oil/gas property purchaser investment preferences and purchase methods, Oct 1992 survey, article, C6985–1.513

Outlook for personal and institutional investments, and economic indicators, 1993 annual features, C5800–7.509

Pension fund investment in 3 housing-related categories vs all other assets, for public and private funds, 2nd qtr 1992, C4300–1.505

Performance of leading funds with institutional investors, by fund and type, biweekly rpt quarterly feature, C2710–2.502, C2710–2.506,

C2710–2.507, C2710–2.512, C2710–2.513, C2710–2.518, C2710–2.519

Private equity funds raised for business investment, for North America, Europe, and Asia/Pacific region, 1986-91, C4687–1.505

Real estate commercial property investment return, by property type, 1980-91, article, A6450–2.506

Real estate commercial property investment return, 1986-92, article, C2425–1.505

Real estate investment trust returns and dividend yields, by property type, 1993 recurring feature, C8900–1.506, C8900–1.518

Return rates over 1-20 year periods, for 12 types of investments, 1993 article, C3950–1.518

Tax-deferred salary reduction 401(k) plan asset allocation and investment return trends, by type of investment option, 1992 article, C8900–1.505

Tax-deferred salary reduction 401(k) plan investment return variation factors, 1993 article, C2425–1.508

Trends in growth rates for 9 investment types, 1960s-90s, article, C8900–1.507

Trust fund admin and estate planning, analyses of trust portfolios, investments, and economic outlook, monthly rpt, C2425–2

State and local:

Alabama financial condition, including revenues by source, expenditures by function and object, and fund balances, by fund and agency, FY92, annual rpt, S0129–1

Alaska bank assets and liabilities of individual commercial and savings instns, quarterly rpt, S0280–2

Alaska financial condition, including revenues by source, expenditures by function, fund balances, and bond obligations, FY92 and trends, annual rpt, S0275–1

Alaska insurance industry underwriting and investment data, by company and type of insurance, with regulatory info, 1991 and trends, annual rpt, S0280–3

Arizona financial condition, including revenues by source, expenditures by function, and fund balances, FY91, annual rpt, S0450–2

Arkansas financial condition, including revenues by source, expenditures by function and locality, and fund balances, FY91-92, biennial rpt, S0780–1

Arkansas financial condition, including revenues by source, expenditures by function and object, and fund balances, FY92, annual rpt, S0670–1

California banks and trust companies, financial condition by instn, with regulatory info, Dec 1992, annual rpt, S0810–1

California financial condition, including revenues by source, expenditures by agency and function, fund balances, and bonded debt, FY92 and trends, annual rpt, S0815–1

California insurance industry financial and underwriting data, by company and type of insurance, with regulatory info, 1991, annual rpt, S0900–1

Index by Subjects and Names

Investments

Colorado banks and trust companies, financial condition by instn, 1992, annual rpt, S1070–2

Colorado financial condition, including receipts by source, and expenditures by function, FY92 and trends, annual rpt, S0980–1

Colorado savings and loan assn and credit union financial condition, 1992 and trends, annual rpt, S1070–3

Connecticut banks and other financial instns, financial condition by instn, 1991 and trends, annual rpt, S1160–1

Connecticut financial condition, including revenues by source, expenditures by function, and bonded debt, FY92, annual rpt, S1170–2

DC financial condition, including receipts by source, expenditures by object or function, and fund balances, FY92, annual rpt, S1507–1

Florida financial condition, including receipts by source, expenditures by function, and fund balances, FY92, annual rpt, S1717–3

Hawaii data book, general data, 1992 annual rpt, S2090–1.15

Hawaii financial condition, including revenues by source, expenditures by function, and fund balances, FY92, annual rpt, S2020–1

Illinois financial condition, including revenues by source, and expenditures by object, function, and agency, FY92, annual rpt, S2415–1

Indiana financial condition, including revenues by source, expenditures by function and object, and fund balances, by agency, FY92, annual rpt, S2570–1

Iowa financial condition, including revenues by source, expenditures by function, and bonded debt, FY92 and trends, annual rpt, S2860–4

Iowa insurance industry financial and underwriting data, by company and type of insurance, 1992, annual rpt, S2760–1

Iowa State treasury financial operations, including receipts, disbursements, and detailed investment activity, FY92, annual rpt, S2885–1

Kansas financial condition, including revenues by source, expenditures by function and object, and fund balances, FY92, annual rpt, S2900–1

Kentucky financial condition, including revenues by source, expenditures by function and object, fund balances, and bonded debt, FY92, annual rpt, S3120–1

Kentucky financial instns condition, including assets by instn and city, with regulatory info, 1992 and trends, annual rpt, S3121–1

Louisiana financial condition, including revenues by source, expenditures by function, and fund balances, FY92 and trends, annual rpt, S3285–2

Louisiana financial instns (State-chartered), financial condition by instn arranged by city, with regulatory info, Dec 1992, annual rpt, S3265–1

Maryland banks and credit unions (State-chartered) financial condition by instn, with regulatory data, FY92 annual rpt, S3655–2

Maryland financial condition, including revenues by source, expenditures by function, fund balances, and bonded debt, FY92 and trends, annual rpt, S3685–2

Maryland insurance industry financial and underwriting data, by company and type of insurance, with regulatory info, 1991, annual rpt, S3655–1

Massachusetts financial condition, including revenues by source, and expenditures by function, by fund, FY92 and trends, annual rpt, S3777–1

Michigan banks and other financial instns, financial condition by instn, with regulatory info, 1992 and trends, annual rpt, S3957–1

Michigan financial condition, including revenues by source, expenditures by function, and fund balances, FY92 and trends, annual rpt, S3985–2

Minnesota financial condition, including revenues by source, expenditures by function, fund balances, and bonded debt, FY92 and trends, annual rpt, S4180–1

Mississippi financial condition, including revenues by source, expenditures by function and object, and detail by agency, FY92 and trends, annual rpt, S4346–1

Missouri financial condition, including revenues by source, expenditures by function, and fund balances, FY92, annual rpt, S4475–1

Missouri State treasury investments, summary balance sheets, bonded debt, and deposits in individual banks, FY92, annual rpt, S4570–1.2

Montana financial condition, including revenues by source, expenditures by function, and fund balances, FY92, annual rpt, S4653–1

Nebraska financial condition, including revenues by source, expenditures by function and agency, and fund balances, FY92, annual rpt, S4825–1

Nevada financial condition, including fund revenues by source, expenditures by function, and bonded debt, FY92, annual rpt, S5025–1

New Hampshire financial condition, with revenues by source, expenditures by function or object, and fund balances, FY92 and trends, annual rpt, S5175–1

New Jersey banks and other financial instns, assets and liabilities by instn, 1992 and trends, annual rpt, S5355–1

New Jersey financial condition, including revenues by source, expenditures by function, fund balances, and bonded debt, FY92, annual rpt, S5455–1

New Mexico financial condition, including receipts by source, expenditures by agency and function, fund balances, and bonded debt, FY91, annual rpt, S5585–1

New Mexico financial instns, financial and operating data by instn, with regulatory activities, 1992, annual rpt, S5652–1

New York State financial condition, including revenues by source, expenditures by function, and fund balances, FY93, annual rpt, S5710–1

New York State insurance industry devs, finances, and regulatory activity, 1990/91 and trends, annual rpt, S5770–3

New York State insurance industry financial and underwriting data, by company and line of coverage, 1991, annual rpt, S5770–2

North Carolina financial condition, including revenues by source, expenditures by function, fund balances, and bonded debt, FY92, annual rpt, S5897–1

North Dakota financial condition, including revenues by source, expenditures by function, fund balances, and bonded debt, FY92, annual rpt, S6162–1

Ohio financial condition, including revenues by source, expenditures by function, and fund balances, FY92, annual rpt, S6255–1

Ohio intangible property tax collections, by county, 1992 and trends, annual rpt, S6390–1.4

Oklahoma financial condition, including revenues by source, expenditures by function, and fund balances, FY91, annual rpt, S6438–1

Oregon financial condition, including revenues by source, expenditures by function, and fund statements, FY92, annual rpt, S6603–2

Oregon financial instns, financial condition by instn, Dec 1992 and trends, annual rpt, S6616–1

Pennsylvania financial condition, including revenues by source, expenditures by function, and fund balances, FY92 and trends, annual rpt, S6810–4

Rhode Island financial condition, including revenues by source, expenditures by function, and fund balances, FY92 and trends, annual rpt, S6930–1

South Carolina financial condition, including receipts by source, expenditures by function, fund balances, and bonded debt, FY92, annual rpt, S7127–1

South Carolina financial instns (State-chartered) financial condition, including data by instn, FY92 annual rpt, S7165–1

South Dakota financial condition, including revenues by source, expenditures by function, fund balances, and bonded debt, FY92, annual rpt, S7330–1

Tennessee financial condition, including revenues by source, expenditures by function and object, and fund balances, FY92, annual rpt, S7505–1

Texas financial condition, including revenues by source, expenditures by function, and bonded indebtedness, FY92, annual rpt, S7655–3

Texas financial condition, including revenues by source, expenditures by function and dept, and investments, with data for over 400 individual funds, FY92, annual rpt, S7655–2

Utah banks and other financial instns, financial condition by instn, FY93 and trends, annual rpt, S7830–1

Utah financial condition, including revenues by source, expenditures by function and agency, and fund balances, FY92, annual rpt, S7795–1

Utah statistical abstract, general data, 1993 triennial rpt, U8960–1.15

Vermont banks and other financial instns, financial condition by instn, 1992 and trends, annual rpt, S7995–2

Vermont financial condition, including revenues by source, expenditures by function, fund balances, and bonded debt, FY92, annual rpt, S8035–1

Investments

Virginia consumer finance companies financial condition, by instn, Dec 1992, annual rpt, S8180–3

Virginia financial condition, including revenues by source, expenditures by function, and fund balances, FY92 and trends, annual rpt, S8170–1

Virginia financial instns (State-chartered), financial condition by instn and instn type, Dec 1992, annual rpt, S8180–2

Washington State financial condition, including revenues by source, expenditures by function, fund balances, and bonded debt, FY92, annual rpt, S8345–3

Washington State treasury operations, including receipts, disbursements, aid to localities, and investments, by fund, FY92, annual rpt, S8455–1

West Virginia banks and other financial instns, composite financial condition, with selected data by instn, 1990-91, annual rpt, S8530–1

Wisconsin banks financial condition, by instn and city, with regulatory info, 1992 and trends, annual rpt, S8685–1

Wisconsin financial condition, including revenues by source, expenditures by function and object, and fund balances, FY92, annual rpt, S8675–3

Wisconsin savings and loan assns and savings banks (State-chartered) financial condition, by instn, 1992 and trends, annual rpt, S8807–1

Wyoming financial condition, including revenues by source, expenditures by function, and fund balances, FY92 and trends, annual rpt, S8875–1

Wyoming State treasurer financial transactions, including revenues, investments, and disbursements by local area, FY92 and trends, annual rpt, S9010–1

see also Capital investments

see also Corporate bonds

see also Financial planning

see also Foreign investments

see also Futures trading

see also Government securities

see also Individual retirement arrangements

see also Investment management and organizations

see also Loans

see also Mortgages

see also Mutual funds

see also New York Stock Exchange

see also Options trading

see also Securities

see also Stock exchanges

see also Venture capital

Iowa

Banks and trust companies (State-chartered), financial condition by instn and city, FY92 annual rpt, S2760–2

Correctional instn admissions, releases, and inmate characteristics, by instn, monthly rpt, S2770–1

Court cases, processing, and dispositions, by type of court and district, with judicial dept appropriations and personnel, 1992 and trends, annual rpt, S2815–1

Election results, by county and/or district, 1992 general election, biennial rpt, S2865–1

Govt financial condition, including revenues by source, expenditures by function, and bonded debt, FY92 and trends, annual rpt, S2860–4

Health behavior risk factor surveillance survey results, by respondent characteristics, 1991, annual rpt, S2795–2

Income tax (individual) return filings, income, credits, and taxes paid, by income bracket, and filings by county, 1991, annual rpt, S2860–3

Insurance industry financial and underwriting data, by company and type of insurance, 1992, annual rpt, S2760–1

Labor force supply-demand data, including population, earnings, and employment by industry and occupation, 1993 annual rpt, S2784–3

Libraries (public) finances and operations, by county, size of population served, and library, FY92, annual rpt, S2778–1

Markets with daily newspapers, demographic and economic info by geographic area, US and Canada, 1993 annual rpt, C3250–1

Postsecondary enrollment, degrees, staff, and finances, by instn, 1990/91, annual rpt, S2755–1

Retail sales and use tax filings, and establishments reporting, by county and city, and by kind of business, quarterly rpt, S2860–1

Statistical profiles of 50 States and DC, general data, 1993 annual almanac, C4712–1

Treasury financial operations, including receipts, disbursements, and detailed investment activity, FY92, annual rpt, S2885–1

Utility and transportation regulatory agency activities, scope of jurisdiction, finances, and employees, by agency, 1991/92 annual rpt, A7015–2

Vital statistics, including population, births, deaths by cause, marriages, and divorces, by demographic characteristics and location, 1991 and trends, annual rpt, S2795–1

Welfare ADC and SSI program caseloads, recipients, and expenditures, by county, monthly rpt, S2802–1

see also under By City and By County in the "Index by Categories"

see also under By State in the "Index by Categories"

IQ

see Intelligence levels

Iran

Energy intl sourcebook, with detail on oil and gas industry operations, supply-demand, and prices, for approx 80 countries, 1970s-91, annual compilation, C6985–10.2

GDP, and imports by country of origin, 1970s-92, R4105–82.7

Oil production and/or capacity, by onshore and offshore field, 1992-93, article, C6985–1.502

see also Organization of Petroleum Exporting Countries

see also under By Foreign Country or World Area in the "Index by Categories"

Iraq

Energy intl sourcebook, with detail on oil and gas industry operations, supply-demand, and prices, for approx 80 countries, 1970s-91, annual compilation, C6985–10.2

Public opinion in US on military action against Iraq, Jan 1993 Gallup Poll, C4040–1.507

Public opinion in US on resumption of military action against Iraq, including impact on reelection of President Bush, July-Aug 1992 Gallup Polls, C4040–1.502

Public opinion in US on resumption of military action against Iraq, July 1992 Gallup Poll and trends, C4040–1.501

Public opinion in US on whether to assassinate Saddam Hussein, and missile attack on Iraq intelligence hq, June 1993 Gallup Poll, C4040–1.512

see also Organization of Petroleum Exporting Countries

see also under By Foreign Country or World Area in the "Index by Categories"

Ireland

Abortions obtained by Irish women in England, patient characteristics and contraceptive use by marital status, 1988-90, article, A5160–1.501

Motor vehicle sales, for top 30 models, 1st half 1992, article, C2710–3.502

Motor vehicle world production, sales, trade, and registrations, by country, world area, manufacturer, and make, 1991 and trends, annual rpt, A0865–2.1

Iron and steel industry

Appliance industry steel shipments received, 1991-93, article, C2000–1.509

Capital spending plans for new mines and plants, by mineral and company, and mine production values, 1993 annual feature, C5226–2.503

Construction steel prices in approx 20 cities, and shipments, weekly rpt, C5800–2

Consumption, inventories, and receipts of iron ore, and blast furnaces operating, for US and Canada, monthly rpt, A2010–1

Consumption of steel worldwide, with detail by selected country or world area, 1990-93, 1995, and 2000, annual article, C7000–8.502

Cost indexes for construction, equipment, and labor, by type and location, weekly rpt quarterly feature, C5800–2.521

Electric arc steel furnace efficiency indicators, 1990 compared to 1965, article, C1850–6.508

Finances, operations, and employment for steel industry, with data for integrated plants and mini-mills, 1970s-93, article, U2160–1.503

Financial performance and growth rankings for approx 1,000 top corporations, with comparisons by industry group, 1993 annual rpt, C3950–1.505

Financial ratios and performance, for over 350 SIC 4-digit industries, FY88-92, annual rpt, A6400–3

Foundry metalcasting trends and devs, monthly rpt, C7000–2

Industrial steel service center business conditions and outlook, monthly survey, A8990–2

Index by Subjects and Names

Italy

Japan exports of autos and steel, weekly rpt quarterly table, R5650–2.506, R5650–2.519, R5650–2.541, R5650–2.558

Japan steel sheet dumping margins in US, for 4 leading and all other companies, 1993 article, R5650–2.512, R5650–2.539

Latin America statistical abstract, general data by country, 1992 annual rpt, U6250–1.16, U6250–1.23, U6250–1.25

Mill (mini and market) employment, capacity, shipments, and other operating info, by individual firm, 1992 annual feature, C7000–8.501

Natural gas utility use of steel pipe, by State, 1991, annual rpt, A1775–3.3

Oil industry tubular goods shipments, trade, and use, 1983-92, annual article, C6985–1.504

Oil industry tubular goods supply, 1980-90, annual rpt, C6985–5.2

Operating and financial composite ratios for corporations, with establishments and receipts, for approx 200 industries, by asset size, FY90, annual rpt, C7800–1

Operating, financial, and technological devs, and production data, monthly rpt, C7000–8

Operating trends and devs of steel industry, including profiles of 4 major companies, 1960-90, U9640–2.15

Production, consumption, stocks, trade, and prices for approx 100 basic commodities, including by country and producing State, commodity yearbook for 1993, C2400–1, C2400–2

Production index for steel service centers, quarterly 1991-94, article, C1850–4.504

Production of crude steel, by country and world area, monthly rpt, A7400–3

Production of iron ore, by country, 1982-91, article, C5226–2.502

Production of iron ore, shipments, trade, and plant inventories and consumption, US and Canada, 1992 and trends, annual rpt, A2010–3

Production of raw steel, by country, 1986-91, annual rpt, A7400–2.1

Production, trade, and materials consumption, with financial and employment data, 1992 and trends, annual rpt, A2000–2

Restructuring devs for steel industry, with data on production, employment, and worker assistance, and selected detail by company, for 8 countries, 1970s-90, R9260–16

Shipments of iron ore in US and Canada, with detail by Great Lakes port, monthly rpt, A2010–2

Supply-demand for selected metals and nonmetallic minerals, with price data, US and worldwide, 1992-93 and trends, annual feature, C5226–2.505

State and local:

Indiana, Northwest area steel employment trends and outlook, quarterly rpt semiannual feature, U2160–1.502

Indiana, Northwest area steel industry employment and operating trends and outlook, quarterly rpt semiannual feature, U2160–1.504

Pennsylvania business activity indicators, monthly rpt, U4110–1

Utah statistical abstract, general data, 1993 triennial rpt, U8960–1.10

Irrigation

Latin America statistical abstract, general data by country, 1992 annual rpt, U6250–1.2

World irrigated areas as percent of total cropland, by country, 1977-89, biennial rpt, R9455–1.6

State and local:

Arizona statistical abstract, general data, 1993 recurring rpt, U5850–2.13

Arkansas electric utility customers and sales, for power used in irrigation, by company, 1991, annual rpt, S0757–1

Arkansas land area, farms, and irrigated acreage, by county, 1987, annual rpt, U5920–1

California farm property value, and irrigated and other land, 1993, annual rpt, S0850–1.5

California statistical abstract, general data, 1992 annual rpt, S0840–2.7

Colorado agricultural acreage, production, and yields, by irrigation status, commodity, and county, 1992 and trends, annual rpt, S0985–1

Florida county data book, 1992/93 annual rpt, C6360–1

Florida statistical abstract, general data, 1992 annual rpt, U6660–1.9

Georgia county guide, general data, 1993 annual rpt, U6750–1

Georgia irrigated vs nonirrigated corn acreage, yield, and production, 1984-91, annual rpt, S1855–1

Hawaii data book, general data, 1992 annual rpt, S2090–1.19

Kansas irrigated acreage and production, by crop, county, and district, 1991-92, annual rpt, S2915–1

Montana irrigated and nonirrigated acreage, yield, and production, by major crop and county, 1991 and trends, annual rpt, S4655–1

Montana irrigated farmland acreage and value, by county, 1991-92, biennial rpt, S4750–1.2

Nebraska irrigated cropland acreage and value, by county, 1991, annual rpt, S4950–1.4

Nebraska irrigation wells registered and irrigated acreage, by county and/or crop, 1987-91, annual rpt, S4835–1

New Mexico irrigated cropland, and water sources, by county, 1985-91, annual rpt, S5530–1

North Dakota irrigated wheat, barley, and corn acreage, yield, and production, by county, 1992 and trends, annual rpt, U3600–1

Oklahoma irrigated acreage, by county and crop, 1992, annual rpt, S6405–1

Oregon irrigated wheat acreage and production, by county, 1990-91, annual rpt, S6575–1

South Carolina statistical abstract, general data, 1993 annual rpt, S7125–1.4

South Dakota agricultural production, marketing, and finances, by commodity and county, and farms and acreage, 1992 and trends, annual rpt, S7280–1

Texas irrigated acreage and production for selected crops, by district and county, 1990-91, annual rpt, S7630–1.1

Utah agricultural production, marketing, and finances, by commodity and county, with farms and acreage, 1992 and trends, annual rpt, S7800–1

Washington State irrigated wheat and barley acreage, production, and yield, by county and State district, 1991-92, annual rpt, S8328–1

Wyoming agricultural production, marketing, and finances, by county and/or commodity, and farms, acreage, and value, 1992 and trends, annual rpt, S8860–1

Wyoming property assessed valuations and tax levies, by property type, tax purpose, and location, 1992 and trends, annual rpt, S8990–1.2

see also Dams

see also Reservoirs

IRS

see Internal Revenue Service

Irwin, John

"Does Imprisonment Reduce Crime? A Critique of 'Voodoo' Criminology", A7575–3

Israel

Congressional campaign finances in US, including contributions from pro-Israel political action committees, 1990 election and trends, biennial rpt, R3828–2.2

Economic indicators for Israel and West Bank territories, and 10-year outlook for financial aid to territories by source, 1993 article, C5800–7.547

Electronics industry trade and/or production trends by product category for 33 countries, with general economic profiles, 1993 annual rpt, A4725–1.4

Energy intl sourcebook, with detail on oil and gas industry operations, supply-demand, and prices, for approx 80 countries, 1970s-91, annual compilation, C6985–10.2

High-technology market trend for US-owned companies, with sales and employment for 5 firms and labor force share with technical background, 1993 article, C1850–2.503

Public opinion in US on news items concerning Israeli expulsion of Muslim fundamentalists, Jan 1993 survey, C8915–1.501

Stock performance, sales, and market value, for 14 Israeli companies traded on US exchanges, 1993 article, C3950–1.523

see also under By Foreign Country or World Area in the "Index by Categories"

Italy

Coal industry supply-demand, employment, and trade, by country, 1990-91 and trends, annual rpt, A7400–2.2

Economic indexes for US and other industrial countries, and leading and coincident indicators, monthly rpt, U1245–1

Economic indexes for US and selected other countries, composites of leading indicators, monthly rpt, R4105–6

Electronics industry trade and/or production trends by product category for 33 countries, with general economic profiles, 1993 annual rpt, A4725–1.4

Energy intl sourcebook, with detail on oil and gas industry operations, supply-demand, and prices, for approx 80 countries, 1970s-91, annual compilation, C6985–10.2

Italy

Entertainment industry devs, including motion picture theater screens, admissions, and receipts, films released, and TV and home video markets, 1992 feature, C9380–1.506

Insurance (property/casualty) industry loss ratios for 4 lines of coverage, 1990-91, article, C1050–1.505

Insurance (property/casualty) industry portfolio shares by line of coverage, 1992, article, C1050–1.511

Machine tool industry operating data by country and product, 1992 and trends, annual rpt, A3179–2.2

Motion picture boxoffice receipts for top 10 Italian and non-Italian films, 1992/93, C9380–1.539

Motor vehicle world production, sales, trade, and registrations, by country, world area, manufacturer, and make, 1991 and trends, annual rpt, A0865–2.1

Oil refinery capacity and throughput, by company and plant, 1990-91 or 1992, article, C6985–1.523

Public opinion in 9 European countries and 3 Soviet Union Republics on political, economic, and social issues, 1991 survey, C8915–8

Shipbuilding govt aid programs in 6 OECD countries, and impact on US industry, 1993 recurring rpt, A8900–8

Silver supply-demand by country and end use, with prices, futures trading, and market analyses, 1993 and trends, annual rpt, A8902–4

see also under By Foreign Country or World Area in the "Index by Categories"

Ivory Coast

Energy intl sourcebook, with detail on oil and gas industry operations, supply-demand, and prices, for approx 80 countries, 1970s-91, annual compilation, C6985–10.2

Jahn, Dawn A.

"Texas Medicaid Program", U8850–8.5

Jai alai

see Pari-mutuel wagering

Jails

see Correctional institutions

see Pretrial detention and release

see State funding for corrections

Jamaica

Horse racing activity, attendance, handle, purse distribution, and govt revenue, 1990, annual rpt, A3363–1.1

Janitorial and maintenance services

Apartment building (conventionally financed) detailed income and expense ratios for US and Canada, by building type, metro area, and US region, 1991 and trends, annual rpt, A5600–1

Apartment building (federally subsidized) detailed income and expense ratios, by building and subsidy type, building age, metro area, and region, 1991 and trends, annual rpt, A5600–5

Condominium, cooperative, and planned unit dev detailed expenses, for US and Canada, by building characteristics, metro area, and US region, 1991, annual rpt, A5600–3

Financial ratios and performance, for over 350 SIC 4-digit industries, FY88-92, annual rpt, A6400–3

Franchise operations and finances, by type of business, 1991/92 and trends, annual rpt, A5820–1

Grounds maintenance manager salaries, by type of employer, 1992, annual article, C4725–6

Higher education physical plant operations, costs, employment, salaries, and energy use, by instn and region, 1991/92, recurring rpt, A3183–1

Office building detailed income and expense data, and energy use, US and Canada, by building characteristics, metro area, and US region, 1991 and trends, annual rpt, A5600–2

Shopping center detailed income and expense data, by building characteristics, metro area, and region, 1991, annual rpt, A5600–6

Janowitz, Barbara

"Theatre Facts 92", A9065–1

Japan

Agricultural imports of alfalfa and hay from US and other countries, 1989-91, annual rpt, S8328–1

Airline passenger traffic market share indicators for Japan-to-Australia routes, by selected country and airline, 1993 article, C5800–4.520

Airline weekly average flights to 5 locations in Japan, for 2 Japanese and 5 US carriers, 1993, article, C7000–4.507

Auto market shares in Japan, and models produced by size class, for 6-9 manufacturers, 1991 or 1992, article, C2710–3.520

Auto news and devs, with production and sales data and market analysis, US and foreign, by manufacturer and make/model, weekly rpt, C2710–3

Bank market capitalization and investment return trends in Japan, 1993 article, C2710–2.515

Bankruptcies in Japan, 1990-92, article, C8900–1.505

Camera (compact) exports, 1987-92, article, C2710–1.523

Chemical and related industries production, finances, operating ratios, employment, and trade, by country, company, and chemical, 1980s-92, annual feature, A1250–1.530

Chemical industry production, plants, employment, and leading product sales, 1991, article, C5800–8.505

Chemical industry worldwide production and trade, selected data by country and world area, 1988-92, annual feature, A1250–1.507

Chemical process industries capital expenditures, for US, Japan, and Europe, 1990-95, article, C5800–8.508

China economic dev loans from Japan, distribution by industry or purpose, as of Oct 1992, article, A9315–1.504

Coal foreign trade activity, by country of origin and destination, monthly rpt, A7400–3

Coal industry supply-demand, employment, and trade, by country, 1990-91 and trends, annual rpt, A7400–2.2

Computer (personal) market shares for 5 major and all other manufacturers, and use compared to selected other countries, 1993 article, C8900–1.519

Index by Subjects and Names

Construction market value of public and private projects and contracts awarded to US firms, and US Govt contract value won by Japanese firms, 1988-92, article, C5800–2.528

Corporate acquisitions overseas by Japanese companies, including activity in US and Europe, 1988-92, article, C4683–1.501

Corporate CEOs compensation for 50 largest companies in Japan, 1991, article, C5800–7.525

Corporate executive compensation, with company revenues, for 20 highly paid executives in US, Germany, and Japan, 1993 article, C3950–1.516

Corporate R&D expenditures, 1991-92, C1850–2.504

Economic indexes for US and other industrial countries, and leading and coincident indicators, monthly rpt, U1245–1

Economic indexes for US and selected other countries, composites of leading indicators, monthly rpt, R4105–6

Economic indicator trends, including semiconductor sales, 1990-92, article, C1850–2.501

Economic indicators including GNP, inflation, unemployment, current account, and export and foreign investment regions, 1980s-93, article, C5800–7.535

Economic issues and devs, relations with US, and trade, balance of payments, and related economic indicators, weekly rpt, R5650–2

Electronics industry output change, by type of product, 1992, article, C8900–1.511

Electronics industry trade and/or production trends by product category for 33 countries, with general economic profiles, 1993 annual rpt, A4725–1.4

Energy intl sourcebook, with detail on oil and gas industry operations, supply-demand, and prices, for approx 80 countries, 1970s 91, annual compilation, C6985–10.2

Energy supply-demand and outlook, by fuel source, 1980s-2000, recurring article, R5650–2.536

Entertainment industry devs, including motion picture theaters, attendance, and receipts, film releases and exports, and TV and VCR household penetration, 1993 feature, C9380–1.541

Exports from US and Japanese parent companies to their foreign affiliates, 1990, article, C5800–7.536

Foreign dev aid, including distribution by recipient region, 1988-97, article, C5800–2.545

Foreign investment in Latin America, by country and industry div, 1992 annual rpt, U6250–1.29

Foreign investment indicators for Japan vs US, 1993 article, C5800–7.532

Foreign Official Dev Assistance commitments, by type of aid and recipient country, 1987-91, annual article, R5650–2.507

Foreign trade value with US, for 5 types of commodities, 1993 article, C8900–1.516

Govt spending proposed in Apr 1993 economic stimulus plan, by function, 1993 article, C5800–7.525

Index by Subjects and Names

Job creation

Hawaii tourism and direct investment from Japan, 1992 annual rpt, S2090–1.7, S2090–1.24

Hawaii 1st-time vs repeat visits by Japanese travelers, 1992, article, B3500–1.503

Household appliance market penetration, production, and foreign trade, by appliance type, 1993 article, C2000–1.504

Imports from US, for top 10 product categories, 1st 8 months 1992, article, C8900–1.502

Insurance (property/casualty) direct premiums written in Japan by Japanese and foreign insurers, by line of coverage, FY92, recurring article, C1050–1.510

Library facilities, staff, and operations in higher education instns by type, 1990, annual compilation, C1650–3.1

Lumber and log exports from US to China and Japan, 1984-92, annual rpt, A9395–1

Lumber product imports, with share from US, and housing market indicators, monthly rpt, A1630–2

Machine tool industry operating data by country and product, 1992 and trends, annual rpt, A3179–2.2

Machine tool manufacturer sales, and income or loss, for 6 leading companies, FY93, article, C7000–7.504

Magnesium imports of US and Japan from China and Commonwealth of Independent States, with worldwide demand by application or world region, 1992-93, article, A1250–1.544

Market shares in US for Japan vs US companies in construction and computer chip equipment, and motor vehicles, 1989-92, article, C5800–7.531

Mineral and metal consumption trend, and reliance on imports, by commodity, 1993 annual feature, C5226–2.503

Motion picture boxoffice receipts for top 10 Japanese and non-Japanese films, 1992, C9380–1.541

Motion picture rental income, by distributor, 1991 and 1st 9 months 1992, article, C9380–1.502

Motion picture rental shares by distributor, and top 10 foreign films ranked by rentals, 1992, article, C9380–1.526

Motor vehicle production, sales, and exports, with data by manufacturer, 1993 annual data book, C2710–3.531

Motor vehicle world production, sales, trade, and registrations, by country, world area, manufacturer, and make, 1991 and trends, annual rpt, A0865–2.1

Natural gas liquids US exports to Japan, 1956-90, annual compilation, C6985–9.2

Nuclear reactors in operation, with capacity, electricity generation, and construction, by unit and country, 1992, annual rpt, B6800–2.2

Patent applications in Japan for top 10 companies, 1987-91, C1850–6.506

Petrochemical Asian capacity shares for Japan, for 4 product types, 1983, 1986, and 1992, article, C6985–1.522

Plastics injection molding machine production, for US, Germany, Japan, and other Far East countries, 1983-92, article, C5800–12.510

Plastics waste handling and recycling devs in US, Europe, and Japan, 1993 annual encyclopedia, C5800–12.503

Public opinion in Japan on US-Japan relations, for persons age 40-49 and 70/over, 1992 survey, article, C5800–7.552

R&D expenditures of Japanese govt, by agency, FY92, article, C1850–6.504

R&D spending by companies, 1991-92, C1850–6.502

Real estate investment in Hawaii and California since 1985, with buyer, purchase price, and current value for 9 properties, 1993 article, C3950–1.517

Research scientists from US working in Japan, and from Japan working in US, 1989, article, C1850–6.505

Retail general merchandise chain sales, earnings, and stores, for top companies worldwide, with detail for selected areas, 1991-92, annual feature, C5150–3.516

Semiconductor market trends in Japan and US, with shares for Japanese and US companies by customer and product type, 1993 article, C1850–2.509

Semiconductor production equipment market shares for US, Europe, and Japan, and sales of top 10 suppliers, 1991-92, article, C1850–2.509

Shipbuilding govt aid programs in 6 OECD countries, and impact on US industry, 1993 recurring rpt, A8900–8

Silver market activity worldwide and in US, including production, consumption by end use, stocks, trade, and prices, by country, 1988-92, annual rpt, B4300–1

Silver supply-demand by country and end use, with prices, futures trading, and market analyses, 1993 and trends, annual rpt, A8902–4

Site selection factors for Japanese firms opening plants in US, 1992 article, U5930–1.501

Steel industry employment reductions, by type, for 5 Japanese companies, 1980s, R9260–16

Textile mill consumption of manufactured fibers, cotton, and wool, for selected countries, 1984-91, annual feature, C3460–1.501

Tire volume recycled and abandoned, with detail by recycled tire use, 1991, article, C2150–3.503

Uranium reprocessing commitments, and plutonium available from reprocessing, for 5 countries, 1990s-2010, article, B6790–1.502

Work hours vs time off, 1970s-92, article, C2710–1.536

see also By Foreign Country or World Area in the "Index by Categories"

Japanese Americans

see Asian Americans

Jet fuel

see Aviation fuels

Jewelers Board of Trade

Business openings and failures, by region, and credit claims placed for collection, monthly rpt, C2150–7

Jewelry

Discount store sales and productivity data for 20 depts, 1993 annual feature, C5150–3.516

Financial ratios and performance, for over 350 SIC 4-digit industries, FY88-92, annual rpt, A6400–3

Manufacturing and marketing statistics, including sales, trade, and industry operations, 1993 annual almanac, C2150–7.509

Manufacturing and marketing trends, new product dev, prices, trade, and related indicators, monthly rpt, C2150–7

Production, foreign trade, and consumption of synthetic jewelry, 1990-92, article (in Spanish), A8955–1.503

Retail jewelry store employee compensation by position, 1992 annual survey article, C2150–7.501

Retail sales by outlet type, and discount chain sales in major depts, by product category, 1992, annual feature, C8130–1.507

Retailer business outlook, including staffing, merchandise selection criteria, and sales promotion, 1993, annual survey article, C2150–7.502

Shopping center financial and operating data, with detail by type of tenant, US and Canada, 1991, triennial rpt, R9285–1

Silver supply-demand by country and end use, with prices, futures trading, and market analyses, 1993 and trends, annual rpt, A8902–4

see also Gemstones

Jewish populations

see Minority groups

see Religion

Jha, Dayanatha

"Fertilizer Use on Smallholder Farms in Eastern Province, Zambia", R5620–1.38

Jiangsu Province, China

Town-village enterprise joint ventures with foreign partners, summary profile, 1992, article, A9315–1.501

Job creation

Economic analysts ratings of 10 proposals for promoting job growth in the next 4 years, 1993 survey article, U0282–1.503

Midsize company new jobs, distribution by industry div, 1993 article, C8900–1.517

Venture-capital-backed company economic impact, including job creation, capital and R&D investments, and selected growth rates, 1985-91, A8515–2

Western States natural gas pipeline project construction spending, jobs created, and property tax benefits, for 4 States, 1992 article, C6780–2.501

State and local:

Alabama jobs created in 2-year recovery periods following 1981/82 and 1990/91 recessions, article, U5680–1.501

Alabama new and expanded industrial plants, capital invested, and jobs created, 1955-90, recurring rpt, U5680–2.11

Kansas statistical abstract, general data, 1991/92 annual rpt, U7095–2.8

Minnesota new jobs added, by industry div and for 12 fastest-growing industries, Mar 1991-Mar 1993, article, S4205–3.501

Mississippi statistical abstract, general data, 1992 annual rpt, U3255–4.5

Missouri industrial growth, including new and expanding manufacturers, new jobs, and investment, 1982-91, annual rpt, S4475–1

South Carolina new and expanded plants, investment, and jobs created, 1971-92, annual rpt, S7125–3.2

Job creation

South Carolina new firm investments in State, with jobs created, by industry and county, 1991, annual planning rpt, S7155–3.2

Job discrimination

see Discrimination in employment

Job openings

see Job vacancy

Job placement

see Employment services

Job satisfaction

see Work conditions

Job tenure

- Corporate CEO tenure and compensation, for 800 firms, 1993 annual article, C3950–1.515
- Higher education president personal and professional characteristics, 1990 and trends, recurring rpt, A1410–12
- Higher education president personal and professional characteristics, 1990, article, C2175–1.533
- Hospital CEO demographic and professional characteristics, perquisites, and views on mgmt issues, Oct 1992 survey, recurring rpt, B4490–2.35
- House of Representatives staff characteristics, salaries, and benefits by position, 1992 and trends, recurring rpt, R4140–1
- Pension benefits and coverage as affected by job tenure and mobility, with data by plan type and worker characteristics, 1993 rpt, R9260–17
- State and local govt vs private sector employee job tenure and wages, 1983 and 1989, R4700–21
- Veterinary practice nonowner associate length of employment in 1st position, 1992 survey, article, C9480–1.505

State and local:

- Kansas law enforcement employees by demographic characteristics and local agency, with assaults on police by circumstance, 1992, annual rpt, S2925–1.2
- Texas appellate and trial judge demographic characteristics, Sept 1992, annual rpt, S7703–1

see also Labor mobility

see also Labor turnover

Job training

see Employee development

see Job Training Partnership Act

see Manpower training programs

see Vocational education and training

Job Training Partnership Act

- Federal budget trends, including spending by program, State, and region, FY81-94, annual rpt, R8490–11
- State social, economic, and govtl indicators, with rankings, 1993 semiannual rpt, B8500–1.6

State and local:

- Alabama public school revenues by source and expenditures by object, by district, 1991/92, annual rpt, S0124–1.2
- Colorado labor force planning rpt, including population, employment by industry, and job service applicants, FY94 annual rpt, S1040–3
- DC statistical profile, general data, 1992 annual rpt, S1535–3.3
- Louisiana job service openings and applicants, and characteristics of Job

Training Partnership Act target population and insured unemployed, 1993 annual planning rpt, S3320–1.2

- Maryland elementary and secondary education data, by county, 1991/92, annual rpt, S3610–2.9
- Michigan labor force planning rpt, including employment by industry, and characteristics of Job Training Partnership Act eligible population, 1993 annual rpt, S3980–1
- Mississippi characteristics of economically disadvantaged and Job Training Partnership Act eligible population, 1993/94, annual planning rpt, S4345–1.3
- Oklahoma JTPA funding for youth summer employment programs, by service delivery area, 1993, article, S6430–2.502
- Oklahoma JTPA participants, and completers and number entering employment, by program, Dec 1992, article, S6430–2.501
- Oklahoma JTPA participants, and completers and number entering employment, monthly rpt, S6430–2
- South Carolina JTPA participants, terminations, employment, and wages, by program, 1990/91, annual planning rpt, S7155–3.1
- West Virginia JTPA program performance data and client characteristics, monthly rpt, S8534–1

see also Public service employment

Job vacancy

- Business school doctoral degrees awarded and faculty positions filled and vacant, by field, 1991/92-1993/94, annual feature, A0605–2.502
- College grad recruiting practices and hiring trends, with data on starting salaries and layoffs, by type of employer, 1992/93 annual survey rpt, U3130–1
- College grads in business and industry, hiring plans, salaries, and selected personnel practices, 1993 annual survey rpt, U3730–1
- Elementary/secondary teaching positions unfilled per 1,000 teachers, with detail by location type, 1983, A4425–4
- Executive job vacancy index, by industry, job function, and region, quarterly rpt, B5000–5
- Hispanic-owned business outlook for selected performance indicators, with data by region, monthly rpt quarterly feature, C4575–1.510
- Hospital recruiting of nurses and allied health personnel, with budget, vacancies, turnover, and compensation, 1993 and trends, annual survey rpt, A6500–1
- Library/info science schools faculty appointments and vacancies, by instn, 1991/92, annual rpt, A3235–1.1
- Nursing schools, programs, enrollment, student and staff characteristics, and grads, 1991 and trends, annual rpt, A8010–1
- Small business views on current and expected economic conditions, survey findings, quarterly rpt, A7815–1

State and local:

- Alaska job openings and hourly wages for positions advertised with State employment service, by occupation, July 1991-92, article, S0320–1.505

Arizona occupational profiles, with employment and job outlook, by industry div, occupation, and county, series, S0465–2

- Georgia, Atlanta area help-wanted advertising index, bimonthly rpt, U6730–2
- Georgia employment and job openings, by detailed occupation, 1990-2005, article, U6730–2.504
- Georgia statistical abstract, general data, 1992-93 biennial rpt, U6730–1.3
- Iowa labor force supply-demand data, including population, earnings, and employment by industry and occupation, 1993 annual rpt, S2784–3
- Kentucky job openings and employment in fastest-growing occupations, 1987-2000, annual planning rpt, S3140–3
- Louisiana job service openings and applicants, and characteristics of Job Training Partnership Act target population and insured unemployed, 1993 annual planning rpt, S3320–1.2
- Michigan projected job openings, by occupation, 1988-2000, annual planning rpt, S3980–1.2
- Mississippi labor force planning rpt, including population, employment, and characteristics of unemployed and disadvantaged, 1993 annual rpt, S4345–1
- Missouri employment, earnings, and hours, and employment security program activity, by industry and/or county, FY92 and trends, annual rpt, S4530–2.3
- Montana labor force planning rpt, including population, income, and employment and job openings by industry and occupation, with selected data by county, 1993-94 annual rpt, S4710–3
- Nevada employment and job opening outlook for 6 rapidly growing occupations, through 1996, article, S5040–1.502
- New Hampshire job service activities, including applicant characteristics and job openings, monthly rpt, S5205–1
- New Mexico job applicants and openings, by occupation, 1993 annual planning rpt, S5624–1
- North Dakota employment outlook for approx 30 occupations with most growth, decline, and openings, 1988-2000, article, S6140–4.502
- Ohio job service program applicants, referrals, and openings, monthly rpt, S6270–1
- Oklahoma job service applicants, openings, and placements, monthly rpt, S6430–2
- Pennsylvania corrections dept staff and job openings, by position and instn, 1990, annual rpt, S6782–1
- Pennsylvania job openings by occupation, FY91, annual planning rpt, S6845–3.3
- Rhode Island labor force planning rpt, including population, employment by industry, job openings, and characteristics of insured unemployed, 1993 annual rpt, S6980–3
- South Carolina employment, with annual job openings due to job creation and worker separations, by occupation, 1990-2000, S7155–2.501
- South Carolina labor force planning rpt, including population, employment, income, and job service activities, 1992 annual rpt, S7155–3

Index by Subjects and Names — Judges

South Dakota job service applicants, placements, and openings, monthly rpt, S7355–1

Tennessee, Memphis area help-wanted advertising index, quarterly journal, U8710–1

Tennessee, Memphis area help-wanted advertising index, 1989-92, annual rpt, S7560–1

Texas hospital and public health nurse job vacancy rates, by position and/or urban-rural status, 1992 rpt, U8850–8.2

Utah summer job openings, by industry div, 1993, annual article, S7820–3.505

Vermont labor force by employment status, and job service openings and applicant characteristics, 1993 annual planning rpt, S8025–2.2

West Virginia employment, unemployment, hours, and earnings, with job service activities, monthly rpt, S8534–1

West Virginia labor force planning rpt, including population, employment, and job service activities, with data by county and service delivery area, 1993 annual rpt, S8534–2

West Virginia public schools unfilled teaching positions, by subject area and county, 1992/93, annual rpt, S8540–4.2

Wisconsin economic indicators, including employment and earnings by industry group, monthly rpt, S8750–1

Wyoming employment by industry group and county, with unemployment insurance and job service activities, monthly rpt, S8895–1

see also Labor turnover

Jobs

see Employee performance and appraisal

see Employment and unemployment, general

see Employment and unemployment, specific industry

see Job creation

see Job tenure

see Job Training Partnership Act

see Job vacancy

see Labor supply and demand

see Labor turnover

see Occupational testing and certification

see Occupations

see Public service employment

see Self-employment

see Temporary and seasonal employment

see Veterans employment

see Women's employment

see Work conditions

see Youth employment

see under By Occupation in the "Index by Categories"

Johnson, Arlene A.

"Availability of a Quality Work Force", R4105–78.21

Johnson, Kurt A.

"1991 Psittacine Captive Breeding Survey: A Survey of Private Aviculture in the U.S.", R9200–14

Joint ventures

Cable TV system mgmt personnel views on alternate access and personal communications services, including joint ventures with telephone companies, Jan 1993 survey, article, C2965–1.509

China auto production, for 6 foreign joint venture plants, various years 1991-96, article, C2710–3.537

China business review, including trade with US and other countries, and economic activity, bimonthly rpt, A9315–1

China oil exploration joint venture contracts, with location, land area, and participating companies, 1993 article, C6985–1.550

Hospital collaboration with other health care providers, including data by activity and partner type, 1992 survey, article, A1865–1.508

Hungary joint ventures with foreign corporations, 1993 article, C4687–1.508

Motor vehicle assembly plant ownership, for 4 North American joint ventures, 1993 annual data book, C2710–3.531

Pulp and paper industry operations, US and Canada, with financial performance by company, 1990s and trends, annual rpt, C3975–5.6

Religious congregation involvement in joint ventures with nonprofit, for-profit, and govt organizations, 1992 survey, recurring rpt, A5435–4

Semiconductor production equipment market shares for US, Europe, and Japan, and for joint ventures, 1991-92, article, C1850–2.509

Jordan

Energy intl sourcebook, with detail on oil and gas industry operations, supply-demand, and prices, for approx 80 countries, 1970s-91, annual compilation, C6985–10.2

Journalism

Actions against journalists worldwide, including killings, detentions, attacks, legal actions, expulsions, and censorship, 1991-92, article, A8605–1.506

Broadcast news professional views on TV news programming, outlook for own TV or radio operations, and ethical issues, 1993 survey article, C1850–14.539

Business journalism performance as rated by executives, journalists, and academics, June 1992 survey, article, A8605–1.502

Current event and issue coverage by TV and print news media, analysis of selected topics, bimonthly rpt, R3823–1

Grads of journalism school, by employment status, 1988-91, annual rpt, A8605–4

Higher education journalism/mass communication enrollment and grads by level, by instn, sex, race-ethnicity, and field, 1990/91 and trends, annual article, A3225–1

Professional ethics code use, sources, and revisions, for newspaper and TV news journalists, 1993 survey article, A8605–1.504

Public interest in current news events, and opinion on media coverage, recurring rpt, C8915–1

Public opinion on credibility of selected news media organizations, reporters, and public figures, 1985, 1989, and 1993 surveys, C8915–1.502

Public opinion on fairness of media coverage of Clinton Admin and Hillary Clinton, with detail by respondent characteristics, June 1993 survey, C8915–7.4

Public opinion on honesty/ethical standards of selected occupations, 1992 Gallup Polls and trends, C4040–1.501

Public opinion on issues concerning politics and the press, by respondent characteristics, series, C8915–4

Public opinion on TV and newspaper journalist concern for self-interest vs public interest, Aug 1992 survey, A8605–1.505

Public opinion on TV violence and overall quality, with detail for entertainment and news shows, by respondent characteristics, Feb 1993 survey, C8915–11.1

Public recall of news events, correlation with media use, education, and other variables, 1989 surveys, article, A0610–1.503

Radio as source of news compared with other media, 1993 annual rpt, A8789–1

see also Freedom of the press

see also Government and the press

see also Newspapers

JTPA

see Job Training Partnership Act

Judaism

see Religion

Judges

Federal judgeships, with detail for black, Hispanic, and Asian appointees, 1976-92, article, C4215–1.505

Judgeships (Federal) presidential appointments, with detail for women, blacks, and Hispanics, 1963-92, annual rpt, C2500–2

Salaries for judges and court administrators, by State and territory, and for Federal system, July 1993, semiannual rpt, R6600–2

State court judges/justices by court level, by State, 1991, annual rpt, R6600–1

Statistical profiles of 50 States and DC, general data, 1993 annual almanac, C4712–1

Urban domestic relations court judicial staff size and views on divorce case mgmt problems, for 16 jurisdictions, 1989 and/or 1990, R6600–6

Urban small claims and traffic court judicial staff, and litigant satisfaction with court judges, for 3-12 jurisdictions, 1990, R6600–5

State and local:

Alabama election results, by district and/or county, 1992 general election, biennial rpt, S0205–1

Alabama judges by type of court, FY92, annual rpt, S0118–1

Alaska election results, and voter registration and turnout, by district and precinct, 1992 general election, biennial rpt, S0337–1

Alaska judges compared to population, by city and judicial district, FY92, annual rpt, S0290–1

Arizona court cases and dispositions, by type of case and court, with judicial personnel and finances, by county and city, FY92, annual rpt, S0525–1

Arizona election results and voter registration, by county and/or district, 1992 general election, biennial rpt, S0520–1

Arizona statistical abstract, general data, 1993 recurring rpt, U5850–2.12

Arkansas court caseloads and dispositions, by type of court and case, and location, FY92 and trends, annual rpt, S0647–1

Arkansas election results, by district and/or county, 1992 general election, biennial rpt, S0775–1

Judges

California criminal justice system expenditures and employment, by type of agency or function, 1982-91, annual rpt, S0910–2.1

California election results, and voter registration and turnout, by district and/or county, 1992 and trends, biennial rpt, S0934–1

California judgeships, by location and type of court, FY92 and trends, annual rpt, S0905–1.2, S0905–2

Colorado election results and voter registration, by political party, and county and/or district, 1992, biennial rpt, S1090–1

Connecticut election results and voter registration and turnout, by location, 1992 general election, biennial rpt, S1265–1

Connecticut judicial dept personnel and finances, FY91-92, biennial rpt, S1220–1.1

Florida election results, by county and/or district, 1992 general election, biennial rpt, S1800–1

Georgia court cases and dispositions, by type of court and case, and location, with judicial dept finances and personnel, FY92, annual rpt, S1903–1

Georgia election results by county, 1992 general election, biennial rpt, S1955–1

Hawaii data book, general data, 1992 annual rpt, S2090–1.4

Illinois election results, and voter registration trends, by county and/or district, 1992 general election, biennial rpt, S2445–1

Indiana caseload data for individual supreme and appeals court judges, and trial judges by county, 1992, annual rpt, S2703–1

Indiana election results, by county and district, with voter registration, 1992 primary and general elections, biennial rpt, S2702–1

Iowa court cases, processing, and dispositions, by type of court and district, with judicial dept appropriations and personnel, 1992 and trends, annual rpt, S2815–1

Iowa election results, by county and/or district, 1992 general election, biennial rpt, S2865–1

Kansas election results, by county and district, 1992 primary and general elections, biennial rpt, S3030–1

Kentucky election results, by county, district, and circuit, 1992, annual rpt, S3213–1

Louisiana justices and judges by type of court, and court caseloads, 1992, annual rpt, S3375–1

Maine election results, by district, county, and municipality, 1992 general election, biennial rpt, S3490–1

Maryland election results, by county and district, 1992 general election, biennial rpt, S3615–1

Maryland judicial appointments and caseloads, by county, FY92, annual rpt, S3600–1

Michigan election results and voter registration, by county and/or district, 1992 general election, biennial rpt, S4020–1

Michigan judges and workloads, 1992 and trends, annual rpt, S3962–1.1

Minnesota election results and voter registration, by locality, 1992 primary and general elections, biennial rpt, S4255–1

Mississippi statistical abstract, general data, 1992 annual rpt, U3255–4.13

Missouri election results and voter registration, by district and/or county, with directory of govt officials, 1992 general election, biennial rpt, S4580–1

Montana election results and voter registration, by county and/or district, 1992 general election, biennial rpt, S4760–1

Nebraska election results, and voter registration by party, by county and/or district, 1992 general and primary elections, biennial rpt, S4955–1

Nevada election results, and voter registration and turnout, by county, 1992 general election, biennial rpt, S5125–1

New Mexico court cases and dispositions, by type of court and case, and location, with judicial system finances and personnel, FY92, annual rpt, S5623–1

New Mexico election results, and voter registration by party, by location, 1992 general election, biennial rpt, S5655–1

New York State general election results by county and district, Nov 1992, biennial rpt, S5750–1

New York State judges by court, 1991, annual rpt, S5730–1

North Carolina court cases and dispositions, by type of court and case, and location, with judicial dept finances and personnel, FY91, annual rpt, S5950–1

North Carolina election results, by county and/or district, 1992 general election, biennial rpt, S5920–1

North Dakota election results and historical trends, including data on ballot measures and detail by location, 1880s-1992, biennial rpt, U8080–1

North Dakota election results, by location, 1992 general election, biennial rpt, S6205–1

North Dakota judges, by type of court, 1992, annual rpt, S6210–1

Ohio court judges and workloads, by county or court, 1992, annual rpt, S6385–1

Ohio election results and voter registration, by local area, 1991-92 and trends, biennial rpt, S6380–1

Oklahoma election results and voter registration, by county and/or district, 1992, biennial rpt, S6425–1

Oklahoma judges by court type and district, with population and cases per judge by district, FY92, annual rpt, S6493–1.1

Oregon election results and voter registration and turnout, by county and/or district, 1992 general election, biennial rpt, S6665–1

Pennsylvania judges and justices, by court type and district, 1991, annual rpt, S6900–1

Rhode Island judicial system personnel, by court, 1991, annual rpt, S6965–1

South Carolina court cases and dispositions, by type of court and location, with judicial dept finances and employees, 1992 and trends, annual rpt, S7197–1

Tennessee judges and caseloads, by district, FY92 annual rpt, S7585–1.1

Index by Subjects and Names

Tennessee statistical abstract, general data, 1992/93 annual rpt, U8710–2.14

Texas election results and voter registration, by district and/or county, 1992 general election, biennial series, S7750–1

Texas judges, assignments, compensation, and demographic characteristics, FY92 annual rpt, S7703–1

Utah election results and voter registration and turnout, by county and/or district, 1992 general election, biennial rpt, S7875–1

Virginia court caseloads, processing, and dispositions, by type of court and case, with judicial dept personnel and finances, by location, 1992 and trends, annual rpt, S8300–1

Washington State court cases and dispositions, by type of court and case, and jurisdiction, with judicial finances and personnel, 1992 and trends, annual rpt, S8339–1

Washington State election results and voter registration, by county and/or district, 1992 general election, annual rpt, S8425–1

West Virginia election results and voter registration, by county and party, 1992 and trends, biennial rpt, S8630–1

Wisconsin Blue Book, general data, 1993-94 biennial rpt, S8780–1

Wyoming election results by county, district, and precinct, 1992, annual rpt and govtl directory, S9000–1

see also Judicial ethics

Judgments, civil procedure

Urban small claims and traffic court caseloads, processing, dispositions, judgments, and litigant satisfaction, for 3-12 jurisdictions, 1990, R6600–5

State and local:

California motor carrier investigations, disciplinary actions, and fines assessed, FY92, annual rpt, S0930–1

Delaware court caseloads and dispositions, by type of court and case, and by county, with judicial dept finances, FY92, annual rpt, S1360–1

Florida product liability insurance claim lawsuits and judgments, 1989-91, annual rpt, S1760–1

Indiana court cases and dispositions by type of court and case, and location, with judicial system finances and personnel, 1992, annual rpt, S2703–1

Kansas personal injury case outcomes, including top jury awards by county, FY92, annual rpt, S3035–1

New York State court cases and dispositions, by type of court and case, and jurisdiction, 1991, annual rpt, S5730–1

Rhode Island court cases and dispositions, by type of court and case, and county, 1987-91, annual rpt, S6965–1

Texas court cases and dispositions, by type of court and case, and location, FY92, annual rpt, S7703–1

Vermont court cases and dispositions, by type of court and case, and location, FY92 annual rpt, S8120–1

see also Child support and alimony

see also Fines and settlements

Index by Subjects and Names

Judicial ethics

State and local:

New Mexico judicial standards commission cases and dispositions, FY92, annual rpt, S5623–1

North Dakota judicial misconduct complaints and dispositions, 1992, annual rpt, S6210–1

Oklahoma judicial complaints activity, FY82-92, annual rpt, S6493–1.1

Pennsylvania Judicial Inquiry and Review Board activities, 1991, annual rpt, S6900–1.1

South Carolina grievances and disciplinary measures against judges, 1992 and trends, annual rpt, S7197–1

Judiciary

see Courts and terms listed under Courts

Juneau, Alaska

Economic profile including employment by industry div and population characteristics, 1993 article, S0320–1.512

Junior colleges

Administrative salaries in higher education, by position and instn type, 1992/93, annual feature, C2175–1.507

Administrative salaries in higher education, for 167 positions, by instn type and budget size, 1992/93, annual rpt, A3900–1

Appropriations of tax funds for higher education, by State, instn, and function, FY92-93 and trends, annual rpt, A8970–1

Chronicle of Higher Education, with data and articles on enrollment, finances, and faculty and salaries, weekly rpt, C2175–1

Dental allied education enrollment, grads, and tuition, by instn, 1992/93 annual rpt, A1475–5

Engineering degrees awarded, by State, instn, and field, with detail for women, minorities, and foreign students, 1991/92, annual rpt, A0685–1

Engineering program enrollment, by instn, field, and State, with detail for women, minorities, and foreign students, fall 1992, annual rpt, A0685–2

Enrollment by minority status, degrees, faculty and staff, and tuition/fees, by instn and State, 1992 annual directory, A0640–1

Financial and operating data, including revenues by source, and expenditures and staff by function, and selected student characteristics, FY92, annual rpt, A6705–1

Foreign students enrolled in US higher education instns, by instn, State, country of origin, and demographic characteristics, 1991/92 and trends, annual rpt, R5580–1

Freshmen attitudes and characteristics, degree and career plans, and financial aid sources, by sex and instn type, fall 1992, annual survey, U6215–1

Higher education student use of and attitudes toward alcohol, drugs, and tobacco products, by sex and region, 1989-91 surveys, annual rpt, U4950–1

President personal and professional characteristics, 1990 and trends, recurring rpt, A1410–12

Southern States higher education enrollment, degrees, appropriations, tuition/fees, and faculty compensation, by instn type, for 15 States, 1990/91, annual rpt, A8945–31

Southern States higher education enrollment, degrees, faculty, and finances, for 15 States, 1990s and trends, biennial fact book, A8945–1

Western States higher education tuition/fees, by resident status, State, and public instn, with State-funded student aid summaries, 1992/93 and trends, annual rpt, A9385–3

State and local:

Alabama statistical abstract, general data, 1992 recurring rpt, U5680–2.4

Arkansas higher education degrees conferred, by level, discipline, student race and sex, and instn, 1990/91 and trends, annual rpt, S0690–3

Arkansas higher education enrollment by student characteristics and geographic origins, by instn, fall 1991 and trends, annual rpt, S0690–1

Arkansas higher education finances, including revenues by source, expenditures by function, and State appropriations, by public instn, FY80s-95, biennial rpt, S0690–4

Arkansas higher education FTE enrollment, and student credit hour production by program area, by academic level and instn, 1991/92 and trends, annual rpt, S0690–2

Georgia State-supported higher education instn assets and liabilities, by instn, FY92, annual rpt, S1860–1

Georgia statistical abstract, general data, 1992-93 biennial rpt, U6730–1.2

Iowa postsecondary enrollment, degrees, staff, and finances, by instn, 1990/91, annual rpt, S2755–1

Missouri higher education enrollment, degrees, libraries, staff, and finances, by instn, 1992 and trends, annual rpt, S4520–3

North Carolina higher education enrollment, degrees, libraries, staff, and student characteristics, finances, and housing, by instn, 1992/93 and trends, annual rpt, U8013–1

Pennsylvania higher education degrees conferred, by level, sex, race-ethnicity, instn type, and field of study, 1990/91 and trends, annual rpt, S6790–5.2

Pennsylvania higher education degrees conferred, by level, sex, race-ethnicity, instn type, and field of study, 1991/92 and trends, annual rpt, S6790–5.15

Pennsylvania higher education students by residence location, by academic level and instn type, 1992 and trends, biennial rpt, S6790–5.8

Pennsylvania higher education tuition/fees, and room and board charges, by instn, 1992/93 and trends, annual rpt, S6790–5.3

South Carolina higher education enrollment, degrees, staff, and finances, by instn, 1992 and trends, annual rpt, S7185–2

Texas higher education enrollment, faculty, curricula, and finances, by instn, 1991/92 and trends, annual rpt, S7657–1

West Virginia higher education enrollment, degrees, faculty and student characteristics, and finances, by instn, 1992/93 and trends, annual rpt, S8533–1

see *also* Community colleges

Juries

Medical professional liability case jury awards, quinquennially 1970-90, annual fact book, A1275–1.5

Personal injury and medical malpractice verdicts awarded, including number exceeding $1 million, 1991 and trends, annual rpt, A5650–1.3

Personal injury jury verdict award trends, with data by case type and for awards exceeding $1 million, 1960s-92, annual rpt, C5180–1

State and local:

Alabama jury trials and expenses, by location, FY88-92, annual rpt, S0118–1

Alaska court cases and dispositions, by type of court and case, and location, with judicial dept finances and personnel, FY92 and trends, annual rpt, S0290–1

Arizona court cases and dispositions, by type of case and court, with judicial personnel and finances, by county and city, FY92, annual rpt, S0525–1

California court cases and dispositions, by type of case and court, and location, FY92 and trends, annual rpt, S0905–1.2, S0905–2

Colorado court cases and dispositions, by type of court and detailed case type, FY92 and trends, annual rpt, S1035–1.2

DC courts juror utilization, 1992 and trends, annual rpt, S1515–1

DC statistical profile, general data, 1992 annual rpt, S1535–3.8

Delaware court caseloads and dispositions, by type of court and case, and by county, with judicial dept finances, FY92, annual rpt, S1360–1

Florida court cases and dispositions, by type of court and case, and location, 1992, annual rpt, S1805–1

Hawaii court cases and dispositions, by type of court and case, and judicial circuit, FY92 and trends, annual rpt, S2115–1.2

Indiana court cases and dispositions by type of case, and location, with judicial system finances and personnel, 1992, annual rpt, S2703–1

Iowa court cases, processing, and dispositions, by type of court and district, with judicial dept appropriations and personnel, 1992 and trends, annual rpt, S2815–1

Kansas court caseloads and disposition, by type of court and case, and location, FY92, annual rpt, S3035–1

Louisiana court caseloads and dispositions, by type of court and case, and jurisdiction, 1992 and trends, annual rpt, S3375–1

Maine court cases and dispositions, by type and location, FY92 and trends, annual rpt, S3463–1

Maryland court caseloads and dispositions, by type of court and case, and county, with judicial personnel and finances, FY92 and trends, annual rpt, S3600–1

Maryland State constitutional amendments on civil jury size and awards, election results by county, 1992, biennial rpt, S3615–1

Massachusetts court cases and dispositions, including jury dept activities, 1992 and trends, annual rpt, S3807–1

Juries

Michigan court caseloads and dispositions, by type of court and case, and court location, 1992 and trends, annual rpt, S3962–1

North Carolina court cases and dispositions, by type of court and case, and location, with judicial dept finances and personnel, FY91, annual rpt, S5950–1

Ohio court caseload and case disposition, by type of court and case, and location, 1992, annual rpt, S6385–1

Oklahoma court cases and dispositions, by type of court and case, with judicial system finances, by county or jurisdiction, FY92, annual rpt, S6493–1

Pennsylvania jurors and jury trials, fees incurred, and related jury activities, by county, 1991, annual rpt, S6900–1.2

South Carolina court cases and dispositions, by type of court and location, with judicial dept finances and employees, 1992 and trends, annual rpt, S7197–1

South Dakota court cases and dispositions by type of case, and judicial system finances and personnel, by jurisdiction, FY92 and trends, annual rpt, S7395–1

Texas court cases and dispositions, by type of court and case, and location, FY92, annual rpt, S7703–1

Vermont court cases and dispositions, by type of court and case, and location, FY92 annual rpt, S8120–1

Virginia court caseloads, processing, and dispositions, by type of court and case, with judicial dept personnel and finances, by location, 1992 and trends, annual rpt, S8300–1

Washington State court cases and dispositions, by type of court and case, and jurisdiction, with judicial finances and personnel, 1992 and trends, annual rpt, S8339–1

Jurisdiction

see Administration of justice

see Administrative law and procedure

see Courts

see Law

Justice Department

see Department of Justice

Juvenile courts and cases

State appellate and trial court caseloads and dispositions, by case type and State, 1991 and trends, annual rpt, R6600–1

State and local:

Alabama county data book, general data, 1992 annual rpt, S0121–2

Alabama court caseloads and dispositions, by type of court and case, and location, with judicial dept finances, FY92 and trends, annual rpt, S0118–1

Alaska court cases and dispositions, by type of court and case, and location, with judicial dept finances and personnel, FY92 and trends, annual rpt, S0290–1

Arizona court cases and dispositions, by type of case and court, with judicial personnel and finances, by county and city, FY92, annual rpt, S0525–1

Arkansas court caseloads and dispositions, by type of court and case, and location, FY92 and trends, annual rpt, S0647–1

California court cases and dispositions, by type of case and court, and location, FY92 and trends, annual rpt, S0905–1.2, S0905–2

California crimes and arrests, clearances, and arrest dispositions, with data by offense and offender characteristics, 1987-92, annual rpt, S0910–1.1

Colorado court cases and dispositions, by type of court and detailed case type, FY92 and trends, annual rpt, S1035–1.2

Connecticut court caseloads and dispositions, by type of court and case, and court location, with judicial dept finances, FY91-92, biennial rpt, S1220–1

DC court cases and dispositions, by type of case, and judicial system finances, 1992 and trends, annual rpt, S1515–1

DC criminal justice system summary, including crimes and arrests, criminal procedure, prisoners, and parole, 1991 and trends, annual rpt, S1535–2

DC statistical profile, general data, 1992 annual rpt, S1535–3.8

Delaware court caseloads and dispositions, by type of court and case, and by county, with judicial dept finances, FY92, annual rpt, S1360–1

Florida court cases and dispositions, by type of court and case, and location, 1992, annual rpt, S1805–1

Georgia county guide, general data, 1993 annual rpt, U6750–1

Georgia court cases and dispositions, by type of court and case, and location, with judicial dept finances and personnel, FY92, annual rpt, S1903–1

Hawaii court cases and dispositions, by type of court and case, and judicial circuit, FY92 and trends, annual rpt, S2115–1.2

Hawaii juvenile arrests and police disposition of cases, 1992, annual rpt, S2035–1

Indiana court cases and dispositions by type of court and case, and location, with judicial system finances and personnel, 1992, annual rpt, S2703–1

Indiana welfare dept juvenile wards, and population, by county, 1990 or June 1992, annual rpt, S2623–1.7

Iowa court cases, processing, and dispositions, by type of court and district, with judicial dept appropriations and personnel, 1992 and trends, annual rpt, S2815–1

Kansas court caseloads and disposition, by type of court and case, and location, FY92, annual rpt, S3035–1

Louisiana court caseloads and dispositions, by type of court and case, and jurisdiction, 1992 and trends, annual rpt, S3375–1

Maine court cases and dispositions, by type and location, FY92 and trends, annual rpt, S3463–1

Maryland court caseloads and dispositions, by type of court and case, and county, with judicial personnel and finances, FY92 and trends, annual rpt, S3600–1

Massachusetts court cases and dispositions, by type of court and case, and location, FY92 and trends, annual rpt, S3807–1

Michigan court caseloads and dispositions, by type of court and case, and court location, 1992 and trends, annual rpt, S3962–1

Mississippi statistical abstract, general data, 1992 annual rpt, U3255–4.9

Montana juvenile justice system activity, 1992, annual rpt, S4705–1

Nebraska court cases and dispositions, by type of court and case, and location, 1992 and trends, annual rpt, S4965–2

New Mexico court cases and dispositions, by type of court and case, and location, with judicial system finances and personnel, FY92, annual rpt, S5623–1

New York State court cases and dispositions, by type of court and case, and jurisdiction, 1991, annual rpt, S5730–1

North Carolina court cases and dispositions, by type of court and case, and location, with judicial dept finances and personnel, FY91, annual rpt, S5950–1

North Dakota cases referred to juvenile court by reason, and caseload activity by district, 1991-92, annual rpt, S6210–1

North Dakota local correctional instn adult and juvenile inmate characteristics, by instn, 1991 and trends, annual rpt, S6060–3

Ohio court caseload and case disposition, by type of court and case, and location, 1992, annual rpt, S6385–1

Oklahoma court cases and dispositions, by type of court and case, with judicial system finances, by county or jurisdiction, FY92, annual rpt, S6493–1

Oklahoma juvenile arrest case dispositions, 1990-92, annual rpt, S6465–1.1

Pennsylvania court caseloads and dispositions, by type of court and case, and county, 1991, annual rpt, S6900–1.2

Rhode Island court cases and dispositions, by type of court and case, and county, 1987-91, annual rpt, S6965–1

South Carolina court cases and dispositions, by type of court and location, with judicial dept finances and employees, 1992 and trends, annual rpt, S7197–1

South Dakota court cases and dispositions by type of case, and judicial system finances and personnel, by jurisdiction, FY92 and trends, annual rpt, S7395–1

Tennessee court cases and dispositions, by type of court and case, and county, FY92, annual rpt, S7585–1

Texas court cases and dispositions, by type of court and case, and location, FY92, annual rpt, S7703–1

Vermont court cases and dispositions, by type of court and case, and location, FY92 annual rpt, S8120–1

Virginia court caseloads, processing, and dispositions, by type of court and case, with judicial dept personnel and finances, by location, 1992 and trends, annual rpt, S8300–1

Virginia juvenile arrests and case dispositions, 1992, annual rpt, S8295–2.2

Washington State court cases and dispositions, by type of court and case, and jurisdiction, with judicial finances and personnel, 1992 and trends, annual rpt, S8339–1

West Virginia court caseloads and dispositions, by type of court and case, and judicial circuit, 1992 and trends, annual rpt, S8537–1

Juvenile delinquency

Analyses of special topics related to crime, delinquency, and the criminal justice system, series, A7575–1

Black American crime, arrest, and incarceration data, with comparisons to whites, 1970s-91, annual compilation, C6775–2.5

Black children and youth population, economic, health, and education data, with comparisons to whites, 1993 rpt, R3840–21

Child health and well-being indicators, with selected household characteristics, by State, 1993 annual rpt, R3832–1

Directory of local jails and adult detention facilities, with inmates, staff, and operating summary, by State and instn, Dec 1992, recurring rpt, A1305–1

Prevention program funding in 8 States, 1992 annual rpt, R4300–1.2

State social, economic, and govtl indicators, with rankings, 1993 semiannual rpt, B8500–1.10

Statistical profiles of 50 States and DC, general data, 1993 annual almanac, C4712–1

Urban public school systems crime/gang prevention programs, for 47 systems, 1990/91, A4425–4

State and local:

Alabama crimes and arrests, by offense, with data by location and offender characteristics, 1992 and trends, annual rpt, S0119–1

Arizona arrests by offense, offender characteristics, and county, 1992, annual rpt, S0505–2.2

Arkansas crimes and arrests, by offense, victim and offender characteristics, and location, 1992 and trends, annual rpt, S0652–1

Arkansas juvenile arrests and court contacts, and correctional facility placements, 1991 and trends, annual rpt, S0700–2.2

California crimes and arrests, clearances, and arrest dispositions, with data by offense and offender characteristics, 1987-92, annual rpt, S0910–1.1

California criminal justice system detailed data, by offense, county, age, race-ethnicity, and sex, 1991 and trends, annual rpt, S0910–2

Colorado crimes and arrests, by offense and location, with offender characteristics, and assaults on police, 1992, annual rpt, S1068–1

Connecticut crimes and arrests, by offense, with data by local agency, and victim-offender characteristics, 1992, annual rpt, S1256–1

DC criminal justice system summary, including crimes and arrests, criminal procedure, prisoners, and parole, 1991 and trends, annual rpt, S1535–2

DC statistical profile, general data, 1992 annual rpt, S1535–3.8

Delaware crimes and arrests, by offense, county, and victim-offender characteristics, 1991 and trends, annual rpt, S1375–5

Florida crimes and arrests, by offense, with data by victim and offender characteristics, 1992, annual rpt, S1770–1

Hawaii crimes and arrests, by offense, with data by county and victim-offender characteristics, 1992, annual rpt, S2035–1

Idaho crimes and arrests, by offense, with data by location and offender characteristics, 1992 and trends, annual rpt, S2275–2

Illinois crimes and arrests, by offense, with data by location and offender characteristics, 1991, annual rpt, S2536–1

Kansas crimes and arrests, by offense, with data by location, agency, and victim-offender characteristics, 1992 and trends, annual rpt, S2925–1.1

Kentucky arrests by county and offense, and law enforcement employment by agency, 1992, annual rpt, S3150–1.2

Maine crimes and arrests, by offense, with data by county, reporting agency, and offender age and sex, 1991, annual rpt, S3475–1

Maryland crimes and arrests, by offense, location, and offender characteristics, with law enforcement employment and assaults on officers, 1992 and trends, annual rpt, S3665–1

Michigan crimes and arrests, by offense, with data by location and offender characteristics, 1992 and trends, annual rpt, S3997–1

Mississippi juvenile rehabilitation expenditures, and caseloads and clients served by county, FY92, annual rpt, S4357–1

Mississippi statistical abstract, general data, 1992 annual rpt, U3255–4.9

Missouri crimes and arrests, by offense and location, with victim and offender characteristics, 1991 and trends, annual rpt, S4560–2

Montana juvenile justice system activity, including data by offense, 1992, annual rpt, S4705–1

Nebraska public welfare recipients and expenditures, by program, FY92, annual rpt, S4957–1.1

New Hampshire arrests, by offense and offender age, sex, and race-ethnicity, 1991, annual rpt, S5250–2.2

New Jersey crimes and arrests, by offense, with data by location and offender characteristics, 1992 and trends, annual rpt, S5430–1

New York State correctional instn inmates released, by criminal background, sentence, and demographic characteristics, 1991 and trends, recurring rpt series, S5725–1

New York State crimes and arrests by offense and demographic characteristics, and court activity and corrections, 1991 and trends, annual rpt, S5760–3

North Carolina crimes and arrests, by offense, with data by location and offender characteristics, 1992 and trends, annual rpt, S5955–1

North Dakota crimes and arrests, by offense, location, and offender characteristics, and law enforcement employment, 1991 and trends, annual rpt, S6060–1

Oklahoma crimes and arrests, by offense, with victim and offender characteristics, 1990-92, annual rpt, S6465–1.1

Oklahoma juvenile service cases, and restitution paid, by county, FY92, annual rpt, S6455–1.2

Oregon crimes and arrests, by offense, with data by county, local agency, and offender characteristics, 1992 and trends, annual rpt, S6603–3

Pennsylvania crimes and arrests, by offense, with data by location and offender characteristics, 1992 and trends, annual rpt, S6860–1

South Carolina crimes and arrests, by offense, with data by location and victim-offender characteristics, and assaults on officers, 1992 and trends, annual rpt, S7205–1

Texas arrests, by age, sex, race-ethnicity, and offense, 1992, annual rpt, S7735–2.2

Utah juvenile offenses by detailed offense type, by month, 1992, annual rpt, S7890–3

Virginia crimes and arrests, by offense, with data by location and offender characteristics, 1992, annual rpt, S8295–2

Washington State crimes and arrests, by offense, with data by location and offender characteristics, 1992 and trends, annual rpt, S8440–1

Washington State public assistance clients and service costs, by client characteristics, program, and county, FY90, annual rpt, S8420–2

West Virginia crimes and arrests, by offense, location, and offender characteristics, 1990-91, annual rpt, S8610–1

Wisconsin crimes and arrests, by offense, offender characteristics, county, and local agency, 1992 and trends, annual rpt, S8771–1

Wyoming crimes and arrests, by offense, with data by location and victim and offender characteristics, 1991 and trends, annual rpt, S8867–3

Wyoming juvenile parole and probation activity, including supervisee characteristics, FY92, annual rpt, S8883–1

see also Juvenile courts and cases
see also Juvenile detention and correctional institutions
see also Missing persons and runaways
see also School dropouts
see also Truancy from school

Juvenile detention and correctional institutions

Administration of juvenile corrections instns, with population, facilities, costs, and staffing, by State, 1992 annual rpt, R4300–1.2

Black youths in custody, with comparisons to whites, by sex, age, instn type, and childhood living arrangements, 1985-89, R3840–21

Directory of correctional instns, with inmates, staff, and cost of care, by US and Canadian instn, 1992, annual rpt, A1305–3

Population in public juvenile facilities, by race-ethnicity, 1989, article, A8510–1.1

State instn inmate prevalence rates by sex, age, and race-ethnicity, for 16 States, 1991, A7575–1.13

Juvenile detention and correctional institutions

State and local:

- Arkansas juvenile detention center and community program admissions, by age and sex, 1989-91, annual rpt, S0700–2.2
- California correctional instn population, parole and probation, and justice system expenditures, 1987-92, annual rpt, S0910–1.2
- DC statistical profile, general data, 1992 annual rpt, S1535–3.8
- Illinois corrections dept admin, including inmates and characteristics, finances, and staff, FY91-93 and trends, annual rpt, S2425–1
- Kansas correctional instn inmates, by offense, demographic characteristics, and instn, FY92 and trends, annual rpt, S2940–1
- Nebraska correctional instn admin, with inmates by criminal background and demographic characteristics, by instn, FY92 and trends, annual rpt, S4850–1
- New Jersey correctional instn inmates, by offense, sentence length, demographic characteristics, and instn, Dec 1991 annual rpt, S5370–1
- New York State correctional instn inmate population and characteristics, and probation and parole, 1991 and trends, annual rpt, S5760–3.4
- North Carolina correctional instn admissions, separations, and population, with inmate characteristics, FY93, semiannual rpt, S5900–1
- North Dakota local correctional instn adult and juvenile inmate characteristics, by instn, 1991 and trends, annual rpt, S6060–3
- Oklahoma State treatment centers and programs for juveniles, resident population movement by instn, FY92, annual rpt, S6455–1.2
- South Carolina statistical abstract, general data, 1993 annual rpt, S7125–1.5
- South Dakota correctional instn admin, including inmates by criminal background and demographic characteristics, FY92 and trends, annual rpt, S7296–1
- Washington State public assistance clients and service costs, by client characteristics, program, and county, FY90, annual rpt, S8420–2

Kagan, Paul, Associates

- Cable TV system marketing budget shares for basic, pay, and pay-per-view, 1991-93, article, C9380–1.514
- Video cassette (prerecorded) sales, 1993-2000, article, C5150–3.514

Kammholz, Craig D.

"Hope and Home: Program Descriptions and Possible Changes", R8490–42

Kampuchea

see Cambodia

Kansas

- Agricultural production, marketing, and finances, by county or commodity, and farm acreage and value, 1992 and trends, annual rpt, S2915–1
- Business activity indicators for Kansas, quarterly rpt, U7095–1
- Correctional instn inmates by offense, demographic characteristics, and instn, and parolee characteristics, FY92 and trends, annual rpt, S2940–1
- Court caseloads and disposition, by type of court and case, and location, FY92, annual rpt, S3035–1
- Crimes and arrests, by offense, location, and victim-offender characteristics, with law enforcement employment and assaults on police, 1992 and trends, annual rpt, S2925–1
- Economic outlook, with detail for selected State areas, 1993 and trends, annual articles, U7095–1.501
- Election results, by county and district, 1992 primary and general elections, biennial rpt, S3030–1
- Elementary and secondary school enrollment, grads, staff, and finances, by county, school district, and/or school, 1990/91, annual rpt, S2945–1
- Govt financial condition, including revenues by source, expenditures by function and object, and fund balances, FY92, annual rpt, S2900–1
- Insurance industry financial and underwriting data, by company and type of insurance, with regulatory info, 1992, annual rpt, S2990–1
- Markets with daily newspapers, demographic and economic info by geographic area, US and Canada, 1993 annual rpt, C3250–1
- Medical malpractice insurance State joint underwriting assn (JUA) financial condition, for 11 States, 1991, annual rpt, A0375–1
- Oil/gas industry production, finances, exploration, and reserves, by State, 1992 and trends, annual rpt, A5425–1.1
- Statistical abstract of Kansas, detailed social, govtl, and economic data, 1991/92 annual rpt, U7095–2
- Statistical profiles of 50 States and DC, general data, 1993 annual almanac, C4712–1
- Tax collections by tax type, property values, and other Revenue Dept info, with data by county, FY92 and trends, annual rpt, S3020–1
- Traffic accidents, fatalities, and injuries, by vehicle type, location, circumstances, and driver and victim characteristics, 1992, annual rpt, S3040–1
- Utility and transportation regulatory agency activities, scope of jurisdiction, finances, and employees, by agency, 1991/92 annual rpt, A7015–2
- Vital statistics, including population, births, deaths, abortions, marriages, and divorces, by demographic characteristics and location, 1991 and trends, annual rpt, S2975–1

see also Kansas City, Kans.

see also under By City and By County in the "Index by Categories"

see also under By State in the "Index by Categories"

Kansas City, Kans.

- Economic indicators including CPI, employment, and retail sales, quarterly rpt, U7095–1

Kansas City, Mo.

- Employment, hours, and earnings, by industry, monthly rpt, S4530–3
- Grain market activity, including futures volume and prices, at Kansas City Board of Trade, 1992, annual rpt, B1530–1

see also under By City in the "Index by Categories"

Kaplan, Ann E.

"Giving USA 1993 Edition: The Annual Report on Philanthropy for the Year 1992", A0700–1

Kaplan, Samuel R.

- "Virginia Personal Income, 1980-90", U9080–7
- "1990 Virginia AGI: Distribution of Virginia Adjusted Gross Income by Income Class and Locality", U9080–1

Kauai County, Hawaii

- Economic indicators and population, 1987-1st 11 months 1992, annual rpt, B3500–2.1

Kearney, A. T., Inc.

- Europe industrial distribution costs as percent of revenue, for typical firm, 1987 and 1992, article, C2150–1.502

Kellner, Irwin L.

"Economic Report", B2000–2

Kennedy, Carolyn M. R.

"Personnel Practices in Planning Offices", A2615–3

Kennedy Group

- Hospital CEO views on strategic mgmt goals and info system support, 1992 survey, article, A1865–1.503

Kentucky

- Agricultural production, marketing, and finances, by commodity and county, with farm characteristics, 1992 and trends, annual rpt, S3085–1
- Crimes and arrests, by offense, location, and offender characteristics, with data on law enforcement employment and assaults on officers, 1992, annual rpt, S3150–1
- Economic statistics for Kentucky, detailed data, 1993 annual rpt, S3104–1
- Election results, by county, district, and circuit, 1992, annual rpt, S3213–1
- Elementary and secondary school finances, staff, and enrollment, 1989/90-1990/91, biennial rpt, S3110–2
- Elementary/secondary education profiles, with data by region and district, 1991/92 and trends, annual rpt, S3110–1
- Financial condition, including revenues by source, expenditures by function and object, fund balances, and bonded debt, FY92, annual rpt, S3120–1
- Financial instns condition, including assets by instn and city, with regulatory info, 1992 and trends, annual rpt, S3121–1
- Health behavior risk factor surveillance survey results, by State area and respondent characteristics, 1988-90, annual rpt, S3140–6
- Higher education enrollment, degrees, staff, and finances, by State-supported instn, 1983-92, annual rpt, S3130–3
- Labor force planning rpt, including population and labor force characteristics, and employment by industry, 1991 and trends, annual rpt, S3140–3
- Library (public) finances and operations, by county, FY92, annual rpt, S3165–1
- Markets with daily newspapers, demographic and economic info by geographic area, US and Canada, 1993 annual rpt, C3250–1
- Medicaid recipients and payments, by program, county, and type of medical service, monthly rpt, S3140–5

Oil/gas industry production, finances, exploration, and reserves, by State, 1992 and trends, annual rpt, A5425–1.1

Socioeconomic devs and business indicators for Kentucky, series, U7138–i

Statistical profiles of 50 States and DC, general data, 1993 annual almanac, C4712–1

Traffic accidents, fatalities, and injuries, by circumstances, location, vehicle type, and driver characteristics, 1992 and trends, annual rpt, S3150–2

Utility and transportation regulatory agency activities, scope of jurisdiction, finances, and employees, by agency, 1991/92 annual rpt, A7015–2

Vital statistics, including births, deaths by cause, marriages and divorces, and population, by demographic characteristics and county, 1991, annual rpt, S3140–1

Welfare recipients and payments, for AFDC and SSI programs, monthly rpt, S3140–2

Whiskey stocks of Kentucky distillers, by company, 1991-92, annual rpt, C4775–1.2

see also Scott County, Ky.

see also under By City and By County in the "Index by Categories"

see also under By State in the "Index by Categories"

Kenya

Student sexual experience, for elementary, secondary, and vocational students, by selected characteristics, 1989, article, A5160–6.505

Keogh plans

see Individual retirement arrangements

Kerosene

Japan energy supply-demand and outlook, by fuel source, 1980s-2000, recurring article, R5650–2.536

Latin America statistical abstract, general data by country, 1992 annual rpt, U6250–1.23

Production, exploration, refining, demand, finance, prices, and reserves, by State and country or world area, 1993 and trends, periodic basic data book, A2575–14.4

Sourcebook of oil and gas industry operations and finances, and world supply-demand situation, 1970s-91, annual compilation, C6985–9

Statistical compilation of oil and gas industry trends, 1993 annual rpt, C6985–4

Stocks of gasoline, jet kerosene, and distillate and residual fuels, monthly rpt, C4680–1

Supply-demand by PAD district, and stocks, 1993 annual article, C6985–1.539

Supply-demand, marketing, prices, finances, and employment, detailed data for US and Canada, by product, company, and location, 1993 annual fact book, C4680–1.507

Supply-demand, trade, and industry exploration and operations, by product, exporting country and world area, PAD district, and State, 1993 annual feature, C6985–1.513

World demand for kerosene, by country and world region, 1986-89, annual compilation, C6985–10.1

State and local:

New York State statistical yearbook, general data, 1992 annual rpt, U5100–1.12

Pennsylvania energy supply-demand and prices by fuel type, with electric power info by utility, 1960s-90, recurring rpt, S6810–3

Ketchikan, Alaska

Economic profile including employment by industry div, fishing and tourism industry indicators, and census data on population and housing, 1990-91 and trends, article, S0320–1.502

Kidder, Peabody and Co.

Oil refineries for sale, with current owner and crude capacity, 1993 article, C6985–1.539

Kidnapping

State and local:

California crimes and arrests, clearances, and arrest dispositions, with data by offense and offender characteristics, 1987-92, annual rpt, S0910–1.1

California criminal justice system detailed data, by offense, county, age, race-ethnicity, and sex, 1991 and trends, annual rpt, S0910–2

Connecticut family offenses involving kidnapping, with arrests by jurisdiction, 1992, annual rpt, S1256–1.3

Florida crimes and arrests, by offense, with data by victim and offender characteristics, 1992, annual rpt, S1770–1

Idaho crimes and arrests, by offense, with data by location and offender characteristics, 1992 and trends, annual rpt, S2275–2

Illinois crimes and arrests, by offense, with data by location and offender characteristics, 1991, annual rpt, S2536–1

New York State crimes and arrests by offense and demographic characteristics, and court activity and corrections, 1991 and trends, annual rpt, S5760–3

Oregon crimes and arrests, by offense, with data by county, local agency, and offender characteristics, 1992 and trends, annual rpt, S6603–3

Kidney diseases

see Urogenital diseases

Kindergarten

see Preschool education

King, Gail B.

"Fact Book on Theological Education for the Academic Year 1992/93", A3376–1

Kirschman, David R.

"Practitioner Compensation in Group Practice and HMOs: A 1992 Report", B7450–2

Kitchen utensils and appliances

see Household appliances and equipment

see Household supplies and utensils

Klein, Christina

"1980s: A Decade of Debt?", U9640–2.14

Klepper, Anne

"Corporate Contributions, 1991", R4105–8

"Global Contributions of U.S. Corporations", R4105–78.23

Kline and Co.

Chemicals (custom) worldwide sales by end use, and chemical market values for drug and pesticide industries, 1991, article, A1250–1.513

Knapp, John L.

"Taxable Sales in Virginia, 1991", U9080–8

"Virginia Gross State Product, 1963-89", U9080–6

Knit fabrics

see Textile industry and fabrics

Knopf, Leigh W.

"Supply of Accounting Graduates and the Demand for Public Accounting Recruits, 1993", A1885–1

Knoxville, Tenn.

Univ of Tennessee athletics economic impact on Knoxville MSA, 1992 article, U8710–1.501

Kohlenberg, Elizabeth

"DSHS County Data Report, FY90, Washington State", S8420–2

Kohout, Jessica

"Characteristics of Graduate Departments of Psychology, 1990/91", A2620–3

"1991 Doctorate Employment Survey", A2620–4

"1992/93 Faculty Salaries in Graduate Departments of Psychology", A2620–1

Kokomo, Ind.

Business conditions analysis for selected Indiana local areas, quarterly rpt semiannual feature, U2160–1.502

Korea, South

Chemical and related industries production, finances, operating ratios, employment, and trade, by country, company, and chemical, 1980s-92, annual feature, A1250–1.530

Coal industry supply-demand, employment, and trade, by country, 1990-91 and trends, annual rpt, A7400–2.2

Economic indexes for US and other industrial countries, and leading and coincident indicators, monthly rpt, U1245–1

Economic indexes for US and selected other countries, composites of leading indicators, monthly rpt, R4105–6

Electronics industry trade and/or production trends by product category for 33 countries, with general economic profiles, 1993 annual rpt, A4725–1.4

Machine tool industry operating data by country and product, 1992 and trends, annual rpt, A3179–2.2

Motor vehicle production, exports, domestic and import sales, and sales of top 3 models, 1992, article, C2710–3.515

Motor vehicle production, sales, and exports, with selected detail by vehicle type and make, 1992 and trends, annual data book, C2710–3.531

Motor vehicle world production, sales, trade, and registrations, by country, world area, manufacturer, and make, 1991 and trends, annual rpt, A0865–2.1

Nuclear power generation and/or capacity, for reactors operating and planned, 1993 article, B6800–1.503

Nuclear reactors in operation, with capacity, electricity generation, and construction, by unit and country, 1992, annual rpt, B6800–2.2

Petrochemical and thermoplastics production and foreign trade, with detail by trading partner, 1992 and trends, article, C5800–8.510

Petrochemical production and consumption trends, by product type, 1992 vs 1991, article, C6985–1.522

Korea, South

Shipbuilding govt aid programs in 6 OECD countries, and impact on US industry, 1993 recurring rpt, A8900–8

Silver supply-demand by country and end use, with prices, futures trading, and market analyses, 1993 and trends, annual rpt, A8902–4

Stock mutual fund market capitalization, price, asset value, and premium/discount trends, for 16 funds, 1993 article, C3950–1.508

see also under By Foreign Country or World Area in the "Index by Categories"

Kraft linerboard

see Paper and paper products

Krugman, Paul

"EMU and the Regions", R5025–9

Kuwait

Energy intl sourcebook, with detail on oil and gas industry operations, supply-demand, and prices, for approx 80 countries, 1970s-91, annual compilation, C6985–10.2

Oil active drilling rigs capacity and other specifications, by rig, 1993 article, C6985–1.520

see also Organization of Petroleum Exporting Countries

see also under By Foreign Country or World Area in the "Index by Categories"

Kyrgyzstan

Energy consumption, production, and foreign trade, by fuel source, 1990-92, article, C6985–1.520

Labeling

Auto aftermarket retailers stocking private label products in selected categories, 1992 article, C2150–10.501

Auto parts purchasing activity of do-it-yourself consumers, including buying of natl vs store brands, 1993, annual survey, C0125–1.506

Bar coding labeling technology revenues worldwide, by product type, 1993, article, C5800–8.512

Clothing (men's) department store sales performance summary, with detail for private label, Feb-Oct 1991-92, annual rpt, A3880 1

Consumer views on product label environmental claims, 1993 survey, article, C1850–1.505

Discount chain consumer natl brand preferences, by product category and chain, and by age group, 1993 survey, annual feature, C5150–3.521

Discount chain top-selling natl brands cited by managers, by product category, chain, and region, 1993 survey, annual feature, C5150–3.520

Drugstore private label product sales, for top 20 product categories, 1993 article, C5150–2.521

Drugstore private label shares of sales, for 10 top-selling product categories, 3rd qtr 1992, article, C5150–2.502

Food private label product sales, for 7 product categories, 1992, article, C2150–6.504

Food shopper use of nutrition and ingredient info on product labels, and views on label clarity, 1993 survey, annual rpt, A4950–36

Food store-brand products image trends and outlook among retailers/wholesalers, 1992 survey, article, C2710–1.508

Food store sales and market shares, for private label products and top 4 brands in 6 product categories, 1992, article, C2710–1.521

Food store sales of total and private label analgesics and cold remedies, year ended Feb 1993, article, C2710–1.526

Food/beverage industry packaging devs, including equipment purchase plans, partnership arrangements, and new labeling law effects, 1993 annual survey article, C2150–6.512

Hard goods manufacturers use of "made in USA" labels, and views on improper use on imported goods, by product line, 1993 annual survey rpt, A1800–1

Nutrition labeling law changes potential impact on public health condition, by sex, 1993 article, A2623–1.507

Oil and gasoline brands marketed by US and Canadian companies, 1993 annual fact book, C4680–1.507

Private label product characteristics and purchasing factors as seen by consumers, by selected characteristics, 1991 survey, article, C0125–1.504

Private label product market shares in selected product categories, by selected country, 1988-93, C2710–1.536

Private label product merchandising trends, with retailer views, consumer practices, and supermarket sales shares, 1993 article, C8130–1.504

Private label product sales, for 19 product categories, 1993 article, C5150–3.505

Private label product sales in food, mass merchandise, and drugstores, with detail for top 14 product categories, year ended May 1993, article, C5150–3.519

Private label product sales in food, mass merchandise, and drugstores, 1992, article, C5150–2.521

Snack food consumer vs nonconsumer use of package health/nutrition info, 1980/81, 1984/85, and 1989/90, recurring rpt, A8905–2

Snack food industry use of selected health and nutrition-related claims on labels, by snack type, 1991, annual rpt, A8905–1

Snack food private label product sales in discount and drugstores, for 6 top-selling product types, 1992 or 1st qtr 1993, article, C5150–3.519

Supermarket health/beauty aid product sales shares for private label brands, 1986 and 1991-92, article, C5225–1.502

Supermarket private label brand sales shares, and sales for top 15 private label product categories, 1992 article, C1850–1.502

Supermarket produce dept change in use of branded products, 1992, annual article, C4655–1.511

Supermarket sales of private label products, by product category, 1992, annual feature, C5225–1.507

Supermarket shopper reading of food product labels, and types of info sought, 1993, annual survey rpt, A4950–3

State and local:

Ohio State constitutional amendment on labeling of hazardous chemicals, election results by county, Nov 1992, biennial rpt, S6380–1

see also Generic products

see also Trademarks

Labor

see Agricultural labor

see Employment and unemployment, general

see Employment and unemployment, specific industry

see Foreign labor conditions

see Job creation

see Job tenure

see Labor costs and cost indexes

see Labor law

see Labor-management relations, general

see Labor mobility

see Labor productivity

see Labor supply and demand

see Labor turnover

see Labor unions

Labor costs and cost indexes

Auto manufacturers union labor costs by component, for domestic vs Japanese-owned companies, 1993 article, C2150–3.509

Chemical industry finances and operations, with data by industry segment and product, 1970s-92, annual rpt, A3850–1

Compensation costs for employers, by region, metro-nonmetro status, and industry sector, 1989-90, annual rpt, U8710–2.3

Convenience store industry financial and operating data, by size category, 1992 and trends, annual survey rpt, A6735–1, A6735–2

Economic indicator historical trends, 1900s-92, annual rpt, R9050–1.2

Economic outlook for selected indicators, recent trends and 2-year forecast, quarterly rpt, A3840–6

Forecasts of natl income and product account components and related indicators, quarterly rpt, U1880–1

Foreign economic indexes, and leading and coincident indicators for US and other industrial countries, monthly rpt, U1245–1

Germany (West) and US comparative socioeconomic statistics, 1970s-91, annual rpt, A5135–2.2

Industrial labor cost per hour in US, Germany, France, UK, and Japan, 1988 and 1992, article, C5800–7.517

Japan employee wage costs composition, 1991, article, R5650–2.512

Library cost indexes for personnel compensation, for higher education instns, FY76-91, annual compilation, C1650–3.4

Manufacturing productivity and labor cost indicators, US and foreign, 1993 and trends, annual rpt, A3179–2.3

Mass transit system energy use by source, employee compensation, and labor costs, 1970s-91, annual rpt, A2650–1.2

OECD countries labor market devs, including cost trends and unemployment, by country, bimonthly rpt, B6200–2

Oil and gas pipeline construction costs, mileage, and operating and financial data, by location and/or company, 1991 and trends, annual feature, C6985–1.504

Oil and gas pipeline construction costs, mileage, and operating and financial data, by State and/or company, 1993 annual compilation, C6985–4.1

Oil refinery operating cost indexes, including labor, weekly rpt monthly tables, C6985–1

Paper/allied products industry data from Census of Manufactures, including purchased fuel and labor costs, 1990 and/or 1991, article, A1630–5.501

Production worker compensation costs for 25 countries and 3 country groups, 1992, article, S0465–1.508

Productivity and related indicators, trend analysis for US and other industrial countries, 1980s-92, annual rpt, R2800–2

Railroad cost recovery index, including labor, 1939-92, annual rpt, A3275–5.4

Regional employment cost indexes for private industry, and Western region compensation costs by component, Mar 1993 and trends, article, S1040–4.508

Regional employment cost indexes for private industry, and Western region compensation costs by component, 1992 and trends, article, S1040–4.503

Shoe industry production, employment, trade, marketing, and related data, by SIC 2- to 5-digit code or product type, 1992 annual rpt, A4957–1.2

Supermarket bakery dept sales and performance indicators, 1992 and trends, annual article, C4655–1.505, C5225–1.504

Supermarket deli dept sales and performance indicators, 1992, annual article, C4655–1.503, C5225–1.505

Supermarket fish/seafood dept sales and performance indicators, 1991, annual article, C4655–1.501

Supermarket general merchandise dept sales and performance indicators, 1992 and trends, annual article, C4655–1.509

Supermarket health and beauty aid dept sales and performance indicators, 1992 and trends, annual article, C4655–1.506

Supermarket meat dept sales and performance indicators, 1992 and trends, annual article, C4655–1.509

Supermarket prepared food sales and performance indicators, 1992, annual article, C4655–1.508

Supermarket produce dept sales and performance indicators, 1992 and trends, annual article, C4655–1.511

Warehouse operating costs by type as a percent of sales, with detail for labor components, 1988-91, article, C2150–1.504

see also Employee benefits

see also Labor productivity

see also Payroll

see also Social security tax

see also Unemployment insurance tax

see also Workers compensation

Labor Department

see Department of Labor

Labor force

see Employment and unemployment, general

see Employment and unemployment, specific industry

see Foreign labor conditions

see Labor supply and demand

Labor law

Child labor Federal law violations and enforcement activity, FY83-92, R8335–2

City govt costs to enforce Fed Govt regulations including Fair Labor Standards Act, FY93-98, A9330–12

Labor-management relations, general

Catholic secondary schools with teacher bargaining representation, 1985/86-1991/92, biennial rpt, A7375–5

Coal industry executive views on utility stockpiling prior to labor contract negotiations, Aug 1992 survey, article, C5226–1.503

Higher education faculty and salaries at public instns with and without collective bargaining contracts, by discipline and academic rank, 1992/93, annual rpt, A3900–5

Medical education instn court cases, with detail for selected administrative, clinical, and research issues, 1950-91, article, A3273–8.503

Oil refinery worker wages, including impact of contract negotiations, 1990-93, article, C6985–1.515

State and local:

California statistical abstract, general data, 1992 annual rpt, S0840–2.3

Missouri labor and industrial relations dept activity, with data on work injuries, worker rights, and labor force, FY92 and trends, annual rpt, S4530–2

see also Absenteeism

see also Employee benefits

see also Employee performance and appraisal

see also Escalator clauses

see also Labor-management relations in government

see also Labor unions

see also Pensions and pension funds

see also Personnel management

see also Work stoppages

Labor-management relations in government

Elementary/secondary school superintendents personal and professional characteristics and views, 1992 survey rpt, A0775–5

Police collective bargaining experience of city govts, including negotiator, methods, 3rd-party interference, and union tactics, by region, 1992, A5800–1.1

State and local:

DC statistical profile, general data, 1992 annual rpt, S1535–3.2

Hawaii State and county govt employees in collective bargaining units, 1989-91, annual rpt, S2090–1.12

Tennessee corrections dept employee grievances and disposition, FY92, annual rpt, S7480–1

see also Work stoppages

Labor mobility

Coal industry personnel earnings and employment history, US and Canada, 1993 survey article, C5226–1.507

Corporate employee transfers, and relocation policies, assistance, and costs, 1992, annual survey, B0600–1

Elementary/secondary public and private school teachers changing schools, with reason for move, 1993 feature, R4800–2.506

Elementary/secondary teachers staying at same school, changing schools, and leaving teaching, by school level and highest degree earned, 1988/89, R4800–2.502

Pension benefits and coverage as affected by job tenure and mobility, with data by plan type and worker characteristics, 1993 rpt, R9260–17

Labor productivity

State and local:

Hawaii data book, general data, 1992 annual rpt, S2090–1.12

see also Job tenure

see also Labor turnover

see also Migrant workers

see also Migration

see also Relocation

Labor productivity

Business forms industry detailed financial and operating ratios, with summary operating data, FY91, annual rpt, A5785–3

Chemical and related industries production, finances, operating ratios, employment, and trade, by country, company, and chemical, 1980s-92, annual feature, A1250–1.530

Chemical industry finances and operations, with data by industry segment and product, 1970s-92, annual rpt, A3850–1

Coal industry supply-demand, employment, and trade, by country, with summary data on world energy resources, 1992 annual rpt, A7400–2

Coal longwall mining labor productivity, by height of seam, 1991, annual article, C5226–1.504

Competitiveness indicators for US vs other major industrial countries, including investments, productivity, exports, and per capita GDP, 1993 annual rpt, A4475–1

Computer (personal) use in corporate sales depts, with effect on productivity, 1993 annual survey article, C1200–1.512

Computer game use at work by info system managers, and impact on productivity, 1993 survey article, C5800–7.549

Corporate productivity, employment, sales, and operating income, for 46 companies with outstanding productivity improvement, 1992 and trends, C5800–7.532

Economic outlook for selected indicators, recent trends and 2-year forecast, quarterly rpt, A3840–6

Electronics industry market devs, including sales per employee, by product category, monthly rpt, A4725–2

Food marketers financial and operating data, by company size and region, 1991-92, annual rpts, A4950–5

Germany (West) and US comparative socioeconomic statistics, 1970s-91, annual rpt, A5135–2.2

Hazardous waste protective suit use impact on available work time, 1993 article, C5800–2.534

Home furnishings retailer financial and operating data, by firm characteristics and region, 1992 and trends, annual rpt, A7975–1

Hospital industry financial and operating indicators, with detail for Medicare, by instn characteristics and location, 1988-92, annual rpt, B1880–1

Household appliance industry manufacturing and market trends, by product type, various years 1920-94, biennial rpt, A3350–3

Iron and steel industry financial and operating data, 1992 and trends, annual rpt, A2000–2.1

Japan economic profile, including govt finances, industrial production, foreign

Labor productivity

trade and investments, and comparisons to US, 1988-92, annual feature, R5650–2.552

Layoffs impact on worker productivity and profits, 1993 article, C7000–3.503

Manufacturing productivity and labor cost indicators, US and foreign, 1993 and trends, annual rpt, A3179–2.3

Manufacturing value added and wages per hour, for 9 States with highest and lowest values, 1991, article, B8500–2.516

Motor vehicle industry labor productivity in North America, for 27 truck and 29 auto plants, 1992, article, C2150–3.503

Motor vehicle plant capacity, production, employment, and productivity, for 12 plants in 6 countries, 1993 article, C2150–3.504

Office product dealers sales and profits per employee and store space, by region, 1991, annual rpt, A8110–1

Publishing employment and productivity indicators, for 10 companies, 1992-93, article, C1852–2.521

Pulp and paper industry operations, US and Canada, with financial performance by company, 1990s and trends, annual rpt, C3975–5.1

Pulp, paper, and paperboard industry production, trade, and operating data, by product class, monthly rpt, A1630–5

Pulp/paper mills hourly output, 1950-92, annual rpt, A1630–6.3

Railroad (Class I) financial and operating data, with detail by company, 1982-91, annual rpt, A3275–8.2

Sales per employee of large vs small companies, for 6 industries in which smaller companies outperform larger ones, 1993 article, C5800–7.551

Shoe industry production and operating data, including trade by country, retail sales, and consumer expenditures, quarterly rpt, A4957–2

Shoe industry production, employment, trade, marketing, and related data, by SIC 2- to 5-digit code or product type, 1992 annual rpt, A4957–1.2

Supermarket deli dept sales and performance indicators, 1992, annual article, C5225–1.505

Trends in labor productivity vs compensation, 1950-92, article, C8900–1.515

Truck equipment distributor financial data, by company type, sales size, and rural vs metro market, FY91 and trends, annual rpt, A8505–4

World productivity and related indicators, trend analysis for US and other industrial countries, 1980s-92, annual rpt, R2800–2

State and local:

Arizona and US copper industry employment and productivity data, 1970-91, annual rpt, S0497–1

Delaware data book, general data, 1993 annual rpt, S1375–4

Kentucky economic statistics, general data, 1993 annual rpt, S3104–1.1

Pennsylvania statistical abstract, general data, 1992 recurring rpt, U4130–6.8

South Carolina employment, earnings, and hours, by industry group and locality, monthly rpt, S7155–2

Index by Subjects and Names

Tennessee economic indicator trends and forecasts, with data by industry div and manufacturing group, 1982-2001, annual rpt, S7560–1

Tennessee statistical abstract, general data, 1992/93 annual rpt, U8710–2.5

Utah statistical abstract, general data, 1993 triennial rpt, U8960–1.10

see also Employee performance and appraisal

see also Government efficiency

see also Industrial production indexes

see also Labor costs and cost indexes

see also Production costs

Labor supply and demand

Black American share of labor force and labor turnover, with comparisons to other racial-ethnic groups, 1975, 1990, and 2005, article, A8510–1.1

Cities rated as best for business by Fortune magazine, socioeconomic profiles of top 60 metro areas, 1992 annual article, C8900–1.501

College grad hiring plans by industry, with data on campus visits, starting salaries, and minority hires, 1991/92-1992/93, annual rpt, A3940–3

Corporate personnel mgmt devs, including staffing practices and turnover, payroll cost control efforts, and human resources operations, 1993 survey, annual rpt, B6850–5

Corporate work force outlook and related mgmt policies, views of human resources executives, Sept/Oct 1991 survey, R4105–78.21

Food store recruitment difficulties, by type of position, 1991-92, annual rpts, A4950–5

Hospital staff shortage trends by census div, and vacancy and recruitment data for selected types, 1991 survey, article, A1865–1.504

Hospital worker shortage trends reported by urban and rural facilities, 1991 survey, article, A1865–1.501

Jobs created in small firms vs number lost in large firms, for low, average, and high wage categories, 1987-92, article, C8900–1.517

Projected labor force, entrants, and leavers, by sex and race-ethnicity, 1990-2005, article, R8750–1.507

Restaurant (table service) operator views on number and qualifications of job applicants, and hiring standards, 1992, recurring rpt, A8200–11

Women and minorities in professional fields, detailed education and labor force data, 1980s-91, with historical trends, recurring rpt, A3960–2

State and local:

California labor force planning rpt, including population characteristics, and employment by industry, 1992 annual rpt, S0830–2

Colorado labor force planning rpt, including population, employment by industry, and job service applicants, FY94 annual rpt, S1040–3

Delaware data book, general data, 1993 annual rpt, S1375–4

Hawaii data book, general data, 1992 annual rpt, S2090–1.12

Iowa labor force supply-demand data, including population, earnings, and employment by industry and occupation, 1993 annual rpt, S2784–3

Kentucky labor force planning rpt, including population and labor force characteristics, and employment by industry, 1991 and trends, annual rpt, S3140–3

Louisiana labor force planning rpt, including population and labor force characteristics, unemployment claimants, and data by parish and MSA, 1993 annual rpt, S3320–1

Michigan labor force planning rpt, including employment by industry, and characteristics of Job Training Partnership Act eligible population, 1993 annual rpt, S3980–1

Mississippi labor force planning rpt, including population, employment, and characteristics of unemployed and disadvantaged, 1993 annual rpt, S4345–1

Montana labor force planning rpt, including population, income, and employment and job openings by industry and occupation, with selected data by county, 1993-94 annual rpt, S4710–3

New Hampshire labor force planning rpt, including population, employment, wages, and job service activities, by labor market area and MSA, discontinued annual rpt, S5205–6

New Mexico labor force planning rpt, including population characteristics, and employment by industry and occupation, 1993 annual rpt, S5624–1

North Dakota labor force planning rpt, including population, employment, and earnings, with data by industry and county, 1993 annual rpt, S6140–2

Pennsylvania labor force planning rpt, including population characteristics, employment and job openings by industry and occupation, and income trends, FY92 annual rpt, S6845–3

Pennsylvania statistical abstract, general data, 1992 recurring rpt, U4130–6.2

Rhode Island labor force planning rpt, including population, employment by industry, job openings, and characteristics of insured unemployed, 1993 annual rpt, S6980–3

South Carolina labor force planning rpt, including population, employment, income, and job service activities, 1992 annual rpt, S7155–3

Texas labor force planning rpt, including labor force, employment by industry, income, and population, 1993 annual rpt, S7675–2

Vermont labor force planning rpt, including population, employment by industry, and job service applicant characteristics, 1993 annual rpt, S8025–2

West Virginia labor force planning rpt, including population, employment, and job service activities, with data by county and service delivery area, 1993 annual rpt, S8534–2

see also Absenteeism

see also Agricultural labor

see also Alien workers

see also Blue collar workers

see also Child labor

see also Clerical workers

see also Employee benefits

see also Employee development

see also Employment and unemployment, general

Index by Subjects and Names

Labor turnover

see also Employment and unemployment, specific industry
see also Federal aid to vocational education
see also Federal employees
see also Foreign labor conditions
see also Health occupations
see also Hours of labor
see also Job creation
see also Job tenure
see also Job vacancy
see also Labor law
see also Labor-management relations, general
see also Labor mobility
see also Labor productivity
see also Labor turnover
see also Labor unions
see also Manpower training programs
see also Migrant workers
see also Occupational health and safety
see also Occupational testing and certification
see also Occupations
see also Professional and technical workers
see also Retirement
see also Sales workers
see also State and local employees
see also State funding for employment
see also State funding for vocational education
see also Temporary and seasonal employment
see also Veterans employment
see also Vocational education and training
see also Women's employment
see also Youth employment

Labor turnover

- Accounting firm staff turnover, and new grad recruitment and hires, by firm size, 1993 annual rpt, A1885–1
- Business forms manufacturing plant labor turnover rates, by region, 1992, biennial rpt, A5785–4
- Chemists employment terminations by 6 companies, Oct 1990-Dec 1991, recurring article, A1250–1.507
- Chemists employment terminations by 7 companies, 1990-92, recurring article, A1250–1.536
- Child day care center salaries, health benefits, and turnover, for centers in 5 States or local areas, 1992 survey, annual article, A3865–2
- Child day care center staff compensation, health benefits, and turnover, 1992 and trends, A3865–3
- College grad hiring plans by industry, with data on campus visits, starting salaries, and minority hires, 1991/92-1992/93, annual rpt, A3940–3
- College grad recruiting practices and hiring trends, with data on starting salaries and layoffs, by type of employer, 1992/93 annual survey rpt, U3130–1
- Corporate personnel mgmt devs, including hiring, layoffs, and health care and payroll cost control efforts, June 1992 survey, annual rpt, B6850–3
- Corporate personnel mgmt devs, including staffing practices and turnover, payroll cost control efforts, and human resources operations, 1993 survey, annual rpt, B6850–5
- Corporate work force reduction prevalence by industry sector, assistance provided displaced workers, and reduction effects, 1992 survey, article, C4215–1.504
- Corporate work force reductions, measures to avoid discharges, assistance to displaced workers, and impacts, Aug-Sept 1992 survey and trends, annual rpt, A2075–20.9
- Correctional instn admin, inmates, facilities, costs, parole and probation, and staffing, for local, State, and Federal systems, 1992 annual series, R4300–1
- Correctional instns, inmates, staff, and cost of care, by instn, US and Canada, with operating summary by State or Province, 1992, annual directory, A1305–3
- Defense industries job losses from budget cuts, with loss outlook for 1997, for 10 States, 1993 article, C8900–1.508
- Displaced workers by sex, race-ethnicity, industry div, and occupation, with characteristics of new employment, 1987-92, article, S0465–1.506
- Elementary and secondary teacher hiring and turnover, including applicants, vacant positions, and teacher reasons for leaving, for 57 districts, Oct 1990-91, R6350–7
- Executives laid off, distribution by position type, 1992, article, C5800–7.523
- Food processing industry devs, including work force reduction, finances, and employment, 1993 annual feature, C2150–6.507
- Food service industry employment and turnover rate, by type of operation, 1991, annual article, A8200–1.508
- Health care professionals making career changes, distribution by type of new employer, 1993 article, A1865–1.523
- Higher education instn administrators turnover rate by position, for public and private instns by type, 1984/85-1991/92, C2175–1.508
- Higher education instn presidents turnover rate, for public and private instns by type, 1984/85-1991/92, C2175–1.504
- Hiring costs and new hires, by industry, State, region, and employer characteristics, 1992 and trends, annual survey rpt, A4740–2
- Hiring plans of employers in coming qtr, by industry div and region, quarterly rpt, B5275–1
- Hospital recruiting of nurses and allied health personnel, with budget, vacancies, turnover, and compensation, 1993 and trends, annual survey rpt, A6500–1
- Jewelry store changes in staffing levels, 1992 annual survey article, C2150–7.501
- Jewelry store staffing changes, 1992 survey, annual almanac, C2150–7.509
- Layoffs announced by corportions, with distribution by industry, 1st half 1993, article, C8900–1.521
- Layoffs announced by top 10 industries, 1st 7 months 1993, article, C8900–1.524
- Layoffs impact on worker productivity and profits, 1993 article, C7000–3.503
- Mathematics dept faculty attrition rates, positions open, and new hires by sex, fall 1992, annual survey, A2085–1.2
- Nursing higher education program faculty resigning and retiring, by selected characteristics, 1991/92, biennial rpt, A0615–5
- Office employee turnover in US and Canada, by region, metro area, type of business, office size, and reason, discontinued biennial rpt, A0175–4
- Pension benefits and coverage as affected by job tenure and mobility, with data by plan type and worker characteristics, 1993 rpt, R9260–17
- Plastics processing industry sales representative turnover rates, 1992 survey, biennial rpt, A8920–3
- Political science higher education dept characteristics, including faculty, salaries, enrollment, and finances, 1991/92 annual rpt, A2617–1
- Profits before and after layoffs, for 5 major companies with work force reductions since 1985, 1992 article, C5800–7.506
- Public awareness of announced layoffs, by company or industry involved, Jan 1993 survey, C8915–1.501
- Reductions in work force at 7 major companies, 1992 article, C5800–7.507
- Restaurant (table service) hourly kitchen and service employee turnover trend, 1992, recurring rpt, A8200–11
- Restaurant industry financial and operating data, by establishment characteristics and location, 1992, annual rpt, A8200–3
- Sales industry labor turnover rates by industry, and salaries for new college hires, 1992 annual survey, C1200–1.508
- Small corporation mgmt views on trends in State/local taxes and tax-related personnel, 1993 article, C4687–1.508
- Southeastern States mass layoffs, by industry div, 1991, article, S7495–2.501
- Teachers with 2 years public school experience likelihood of leaving profession in next 5 years, and reasons cited, spring 1992 survey, B6045–2
- Teachers with 2 years public school experience likelihood of leaving profession in next 5 years, and reasons, spring 1992 survey, article, B6045–1.504
- Textbook (college) sales workers, with turnover and compensation data, 1988-91, annual rpt, A3274–2

State and local:

- Arizona occupational profiles, with employment and job outlook, by industry div, occupation, and county, series, S0465–2
- California aerospace industry job losses, for 3 southern areas and rest of State, 1988-Aug 1992, article, C5800–4.502
- Colorado public school teacher turnover rate, by district, fall 1992, annual rpt, S1000–2.2
- Georgia public school data, including attrition rates of certified staff, by county and city, 1986-91, annual rpt, U6750–1
- Idaho public school personnel characteristics and salaries by position, and teachers and enrollment by school district, 1992/93, annual rpt, S2225–3
- Maine mass layoffs, with number of employees separated and initial unemployment insurance claimants, quarterly 1989-92, article, S3465–2.505
- Michigan public assistance applications approved and denied, and cases closed, by reason and county, monthly rpt quarterly tables, S4010–1
- Missouri public school administrators and teachers turnover, 1991/92, annual rpt, S4505–1.1
- Montana layoffs, workers affected, and unemployment insurance claims, by industry div, quarterly rpt, S4710–1

Labor turnover

North Dakota elementary and secondary school new and re-entry staff, by position and previous employment, 1992/93 annual rpt, S6180–3

Pennsylvania public school personnel terminations, by reason, 1992/93, annual rpt, S6790–5.12

South Carolina educational employees and training, by school district, 1991/92, annual rpt, S7145–1.4

South Carolina labor force planning rpt, including population, employment, income, and job service activities, 1992 annual rpt, S7155–3

South Dakota public higher education staff turnover rates, by position and instn, FY92, annual rpt, S7375–1

Tennessee layoffs, workers affected, and unemployment insurance claims, by industry div and reason, with claimant characteristics, 1st half 1992, article, S7495–2.501

Tennessee statistical abstract, general data, 1992/93 annual rpt, U8710–2.3

Utah labor force characteristics, including new hires by industry and county, 1992 and trends, annual rpt, S7820–10

West Virginia nonreturning public school teachers and administrators, by reason, subject area, and county, 1992/93, annual rpt, S8540–4.2

Wyoming penitentiary staff separations, and reasons for leaving, FY91-92, annual rpt, S8883–1

see also Job tenure

see also Job vacancy

Labor unions

Black American labor force and employment data, with comparisons to whites, 1970s-91, annual compilation, C6775–2.6

Business forms manufacturing plant employment and compensation data, by region, 1992 and trends, biennial rpt, A5785–4

Congressional campaign finances, with detailed data for individual Members, and leading contributors by type and industry, 1990 election and trends, biennial rpt, R3828–2.2

Construction industry finances and operations, by type of business and region, 1992-93, annual survey rpt, A4155–1

Eastern Europe public opinion on selected govt and societal instns, for 6 countries and 3 Soviet Union Republics, 1991 survey, C8915–8.2

Elementary/secondary prospective teacher characteristics and opinions, survey of persons interested in alternative certification routes, 1992, R6350–7

Elementary/secondary teacher unionization, and education assns dues and revenues, 1993 article, C3950–1.516

Employee benefit plan asset rankings of top 1,000 funds, with selected fund investment data, 1992, annual feature, C2710–2.504

Europe public opinion on political, economic, and social issues of interest to foreign investors, for 9 countries and 3 Soviet Union Republics, 1991 survey, C8915–9

Hard goods manufacturers employee unionization status, by product line, 1993 annual survey rpt, A1800–1

Higher education physical plant operations, costs, employment, salaries, and energy use, by instn and region, 1991/92, recurring rpt, A3183–1

Hispanic American labor force and employment data, with comparisons to whites, 1980s-91, annual compilation, C6775–3.4

Hospital CEO views on union activity trends in their facilities, 1993 survey, A1865–1.519

Membership compared to total workers, by sex, race and Hispanic ethnicity, occupation, and industry div, 1991-92, article, S0465–1.505

Membership of 10 largest labor unions, 1981 and 1991, article, C8900–1.508

Mutual fund industry financial data, by type of investor and financial instn intermediary, 1991 and trends, annual rpt, A6025–1.2

NLRB election success rates for unions, by industry group and census div, and for public utility plants by employment size, 1985-90, article, C6985–6.506

Paper industry labor union membership, US and Canada, by union, 1993 annual rpt, C3975–5.1, C3975–5.2

Pension benefits and coverage as affected by job tenure and mobility, with data by plan type and worker characteristics, 1993 rpt, R9260–17

Plastics processing industry employment, compensation practices, and union representation, by region, 1992, annual survey rpt, A8920–2

Police collective bargaining experience of city govts, including negotiator, methods, 3rd-party interference, and union tactics, by region, 1992, A5800–1.1

Public confidence in selected societal instns, 1993 Gallup Poll and trends, C4040–1.510, R8780–1.508

Public opinion on honesty/ethical standards of selected occupations, 1992 Gallup Polls and trends, C4040–1.501

Pulp and paper mill machine maintenance operations and personnel, by region and grade, 1992 survey, recurring article, C3975–2.504

School bus fleet union and non-union share of work force, 1993, annual article, C1575–1.507

State social, economic, and govtl indicators, with rankings, 1993 semiannual rpt, B8500–1.14

Statistical profiles of 50 States and DC, general data, 1993 annual almanac, C4712–1

Supermarket clerk and meat cutter unionization, 1985-92, annual rpt, C5225–1.505

White-collar work force trends, including employment, earnings, and unionization, with data by occupation, sex, and educational attainment, 1990s and trends, annual rpt, A1570–1

Women's employment and earnings, with comparisons to men, and detail by occupation and worker characteristics, 1990s and trends, annual rpt, A1570–2

State and local:

Arizona statistical abstract, general data, 1993 recurring rpt, U5850–2.5

California statistical abstract, general data, 1992 annual rpt, S0840–2.3

Connecticut public library employee unionization, FY91, annual rpt, S1242–1

Delaware data book, general data, 1993 annual rpt, S1375–4

Georgia statistical abstract, general data, 1992-93 biennial rpt, U6730–1.3

Hawaii data book, general data, 1992 annual rpt, S2090–1.12

Idaho economic profile, general data, 1992 recurring rpt, S2218–2.1

Maine statistical summary, general economic and social data, 1992 recurring rpt, S3434–1

New Jersey labor organizations registered with casino control commission, 1992 and trends, annual rpt, S5360–1

Tennessee statistical abstract, general data, 1992/93 annual rpt, U8710–2.4

see also AFL-CIO

see also Labor-management relations, general

see also United Auto Workers

Laboratories

Financial ratios and performance, for over 350 SIC 4-digit industries, FY88-92, annual rpt, A6400–3

Medical group financial and operating data, by practice characteristics, 1991, annual rpt, A6365–2

Operating and financial composite ratios for corporations, with establishments and receipts, for approx 200 industries, by asset size, FY90, annual rpt, C7800–1

R&D laboratory budgets and facilities or staff, for 6 Federal agencies, 3 weapons laboratories, and 2 corporations, 1993 article, C5800–7.531

State and local:

Florida health care atlas, including manpower by occupation and health care facilities by type, by district and county, 1992 annual rpt, S1746–1.2

Missouri public welfare and medical assistance recipients, expenditures, and case processing, by program and county, FY92 and trends, annual rpt, S4575–2

Nebraska Medicaid recipients and payments, by type of service and county, FY92, annual rpt, S4957–1.2

Utah State Chemical Laboratory agriculture-related analyses, by type, 1992, annual rpt, S7800–1

see also Clinical laboratory technicians

Lakes and lakeshores

Latin America statistical abstract, general data by country, 1992 annual rpt, U6250–1.1

State and local:

Hawaii data book, general data, 1992 annual rpt, S2090–1.5

Mississippi statistical abstract, general data, 1992 annual rpt, U3255–4.16

Wisconsin Blue Book, general data, 1993-94 biennial rpt, S8780–1.2

see also Great Lakes

see also National parks

see also Reservoirs

see also Water resources development

see also Water supply and use

Lamb

see Meat and meat products

Index by Subjects and Names

Lamps
see Household appliances and equipment

Land
see Farms and farmland
see Homesteads
see Land area
see Land ownership and rights
see Land reform
see Land use
see Local government annexation
see Open space land programs
see Public lands
see Real estate business
see Reclamation of land
see Soil pollution
see Soils and soil conservation

Land area
Acreage by State, including Federal and State lands, 1991, annual rpt, A6485–1.2
Germany (West) and US comparative socioeconomic statistics, 1970s-91, annual rpt, A5135–2.2
Latin America statistical abstract, general data by country, 1992 annual rpt, U6250–1.1
Municipal govt annexation activity, and population and land area affected, by city, State, and census div, 1980-91, A5800–1.2
State, regional, and census div land area, 1991 annual data sheet, R8750–9
Statistical profiles of 50 States and DC, general data, 1993 annual almanac, C4712–1
Western States population and land area in urban and rural areas, for 12 States, 1990, article, U0280–1.502
World land area and use, by country, 1992/93 biennial rpt, R9455–1.5
World population size and characteristics, GNP, and land area, by region and/or country, 1993 annual data sheet, R8750–5

State and local:
Alabama county data book, general data, 1992 annual rpt, S0121–2
Alabama statistical abstract, general data, 1992 recurring rpt, U5680–2.13
Arizona Indian population, education, housing, health, and employment characteristics, with detail by reservation, 1970s-91, recurring rpt, U5850–2.9
Arizona statistical abstract, general data, 1993 recurring rpt, U5850–2.1, U5850–2.2, U5850–2.8
Arkansas land area, farms, and irrigated acreage, by county, 1987, annual rpt, U5920–1
California socioeconomic and govtl data for municipalities, counties, and school districts, 1993 annual rpt, C4712–3
California statistical abstract, general data, 1992 annual rpt, S0840–2.1
DC statistical profile, general data, 1992 annual rpt, S1535–3.1
Florida county data book, 1992/93 annual rpt, C6360–1
Florida land area by county, 1990, annual rpt, U6660–4
Florida municipal and county statistical profiles, general data, 1991 annual rpt, C4712–6
Florida statistical abstract, general data, 1992 annual rpt, U6660–1.1, U6660–1.8

Georgia county guide, general data, 1993 annual rpt, U6750–1
Georgia statistical abstract, general data, 1992-93 biennial rpt, U6730–1.1, U6730–1.4
Hawaii data book, general data, 1992 annual rpt, S2090–1.1, S2090–1.5, S2090–1.6, S2090–1.20
Idaho economic profile, general data, 1992 recurring rpt, S2218–2.2
Illinois statistical abstract, general data, 1992 annual rpt, U6910–2
Kansas statistical abstract, general data, 1991/92 annual rpt, U7095–2.2
Kentucky economic statistics, general data, 1993 annual rpt, S3104–1
Maine land area and population density, by local area, 1990 census rpt, S3465–7
Maine statistical summary, general economic and social data, 1992 recurring rpt, S3434–1
Maryland land area, by county and taxing jurisdiction, 1993 annual rpt, S3618–1.2
Maryland statistical abstract, general data, 1993-94 biennial rpt, S3605–1.1
Massachusetts municipal and county profiles, general data, 1992 annual rpt, C4712–2
Mississippi statistical abstract, general data, 1992 annual rpt, U3255–4.16
Nevada land area, with distribution by owner and farm use, 1992 annual rpt, S5010–1
Nevada statistical abstract, general data, 1992 biennial rpt, S5005–1.9
New Hampshire land area, by county and city, 1993 biennial rpt, S5255–1
New Jersey crimes, population and land area, and law enforcement personnel by sex, by county and municipality, 1992 and trends, annual rpt, S5430–1.3
New Jersey municipal and county data book, general data, 1992 annual rpt, C4712–4
New York State municipal and county statistical profiles, general data, 1993 annual rpt, C4712–7
New York State statistical yearbook, general data, 1992 annual rpt, U5100–1.1, U5100–1.15
Oklahoma statistical abstract, general data, 1992 annual rpt, U8130–2.1
Pennsylvania statistical abstract, general data, 1992 recurring rpt, U4130–6.1
South Carolina land area, by county, 1993 annual rpt, S7145–1.5
South Carolina statistical abstract, general data, 1993 annual rpt, S7125–1.4
Tennessee statistical abstract, general data, 1992/93 annual rpt, U8710–2.1, U8710–2.12
Utah land area by county, 1990, annual article, U8960–2.504
Utah population and land area by county, 1990, annual rpt, S7835–1.1
Utah statistical abstract, general data, 1993 triennial rpt, U8960–1.1, U8960–1.17
Virginia land area, by county and independent city, 1991, annual rpt, S8305–1.3
Wisconsin Blue Book, general data, 1993-94 biennial rpt, S8780–1.2
see also Farms and farmland
see also Land ownership and rights

Land ownership and rights

see also Land use

Land ownership and rights
Foreign-owned farmland as percent of all privately owned agricultural land, by State, Dec 1991, semiannual rpt, B8500–1.12
Forestland (commercial) ownership, including Federal, forest industry, and other private, for selected Western States, Jan 1992, annual rpt, A9395–1
Forestland owned by commercial forest industry, and timber harvest, by region, 1987, annual rpt, A1630–6.3
Latin America statistical abstract, general data by country, 1992 annual rpt, U6250–1.2
Northwest region, Washington State/Oregon timberland distribution by ownership, 1993 article, C3975–2.511
Timberland holdings of major paper companies, 1993 annual rpt, C3975–5.1

State and local:
Alabama statistical abstract, general data, 1992 recurring rpt, U5680–2.1
Arizona court case filings and dispositions, including eminent domain, by county, FY92, annual rpt, S0525–1
Arizona land ownership distribution, including govt agencies, Indian reservations, and foreign agricultural holdings, 1992, annual rpt, U5830–1
Arizona statistical abstract, general data, 1993 recurring rpt, U5850–2.8
California court case filings and dispositions, including eminent domain, FY92 and trends, annual rpt, S0905–1.2, S0905–2
California statistical abstract, general data, 1992 annual rpt, S0840–2.7
Florida county data book, 1992/93 annual rpt, C6360–1
Florida statistical abstract, general data, 1992 annual rpt, U6660–1.9
*Georgia county guide, general data, 1993 annual rpt, U6750–1
Hawaii data book, general data, 1992 annual rpt, S2090–1.6
Maryland statistical abstract, general data, 1993-94 biennial rpt, S3605–1.3
Missouri agricultural land holdings of foreign owners, by county, Dec 1991, annual rpt, S4480–1
Montana land ownership distribution, including govt agencies and Indian reservations, 1983, annual rpt, S4655–1
Nebraska court eminent domain cases and dispositions, by county and district, 1991, annual rpt, S4965–2
Nevada statistical abstract, general data, 1992 biennial rpt, S5005–1.9
Texas court cases and dispositions, by type of court and case, and location, FY92, annual rpt, S7703–1
Utah statistical abstract, general data, 1993 triennial rpt, U8960–1.9
Washington State court cases and dispositions, by type of court and case, and jurisdiction, with judicial finances and personnel, 1992 and trends, annual rpt, S8339–1

see also Government supplies and property
see also Homesteads
see also Public lands
see also Real estate business

Land reclamation

Land reclamation
see Reclamation of land

Land reform
Latin America statistical abstract, general data by country, 1992 annual rpt, U6250–1.2

Land surveying
see Land area

Land tax
see Property tax

Land use
Homebuilder outlook for land availability and costs, with detail by region, 1993 survey, article, C1850–8.510
Latin America statistical abstract, general data by country, 1992 annual rpt, U6250–1.2
Local govt land use planning commissions composition and activities, and commissioner characteristics, 1987 and trends, recurring rpt, A2615–2
State social, economic, and govtl indicators, with rankings, 1993 semiannual rpt, B8500–1.12
World land area and use, by country, 1992/93 biennial rpt, R9455–1.5

State and local:
Alabama county data book, general data, 1992 annual rpt, S0121–2
Arizona farmland holdings of foreign owners, with use, by county, Dec 1992, annual rpt, U5830–1
DC statistical profile, general data, 1992 annual rpt, S1535–3.1, S1535–3.2
Florida statistical abstract, general data, 1992 annual rpt, U6660–1.8, U6660–1.9
Georgia statistical abstract, general data, 1992-93 biennial rpt, U6730–1.4
Hawaii data book, general data, 1992 annual rpt, S2090–1.6
Hawaii land court cases and dispositions, FY92, annual rpt, S2115–1.2
Massachusetts land court cases and dispositions, FY92 and trends, annual rpt, S3807–1
Montana property values, by detailed property class and type, with land acreage by use, by county, 1991-92 and trends, biennial rpt, S4750–1.2
Oklahoma statistical abstract, general data, 1992 annual rpt, U8130–2.1
South Carolina statistical abstract, general data, 1993 annual rpt, S7125–1.1
Wyoming property assessed valuations and tax levies, by property type, tax purpose, and location, 1992 and trends, annual rpt, S8990–1.2

see also City and town planning
see also Farms and farmland
see also Forests and forestry
see also Industrial siting
see also Land ownership and rights
see also Land reform
see also Mines and mineral resources
see also Pasture and rangeland
see also Public lands
see also Reclamation of land
see also Relocation
see also Zoning and zoning laws

Landfills
State landfills, tipping fees, and remaining capacity, and percent of waste landfilled, by State, 1991, semiannual rpt, B8500–1.15

Landlord-tenant relations
Urban small claims and traffic court caseloads, processing, dispositions, judgments, and litigant satisfaction, for 3-12 jurisdictions, 1990, R6600–5

State and local:
DC court cases and dispositions, by type of case, and judicial system finances, 1992 and trends, annual rpt, S1515–1
Delaware justice of the peace court cases and disposition, by jurisdiction, FY92, annual rpt, S1360–1
Maryland court caseloads and dispositions, by type of court and case, and county, with judicial personnel and finances, FY92 and trends, annual rpt, S3600–1

Landscape protection
see Environmental pollution and control
see Land use
see Open space land programs

Language
see Language arts
see Language use and ability

Language arts
Women and minorities in professional fields, detailed education and labor force data, 1991 and trends, recurring rpt, A3960–2.3

State and local:
Connecticut public school data, including enrollment, staff, programs, finances, and student characteristics, 1991/92, biennial rpt, S1185–3

Language use and ability
Canada photographic and video equipment and supplies ownership, purchases, and use by household characteristics and language spoken, 1992 survey, recurring rpt, A8695–4
Child health and well-being indicators, with selected household characteristics, by State, 1993 annual rpt, R3832–1
College freshmen attitudes and characteristics, including whether native English speaker and speaking other languages at home, fall 1992, annual survey, U6215–1
Foreign student enrollment in college intensive English language programs, by sex, State, instn, and country of origin, 1991/92 and trends, annual rpt, R5580–1
General Educational Dev (GED) testing in English, Spanish, and French, by jurisdiction, 1992, annual rpt, A1410–16
Spanish-language speakers and English-speaking ability, for 11 States, 1990, article, C4575–1.508
Urban public school students with limited English proficiency, with number of languages spoken and comparisons to State and US, for 47 systems, 1990/91, A4425–4

State and local:
Alaska population speaking Native American language at home, by village and cultural-linguistic area, 1990, annual rpt, S0320–4
Arkansas population speaking foreign language at home, and English-speaking ability, 1990, census rpt, U5935–7
California population speaking foreign language at home, and English-speaking ability, 1990, census rpt, S0840–9
California public school limited-English-proficiency enrollment,

teachers, and programs, by 1st language, grade level, and county, 1992 and trends, annual rpt, S0825–10
Florida statistical abstract, general data, 1992 annual rpt, U6660–1.1
Hawaii population, by language spoken at home and English-speaking ability, 1990, annual rpt, S2090–1.1
Louisiana population speaking English and selected foreign languages at home, by local area, 1980 and 1990, census rpt, U8010–4
Maine population speaking foreign language at home, and English-speaking ability, by local area, 1990 census rpt, S3465–9
Maryland limited-English-proficiency students, by region, 1992/93 annual rpt, S3610–1
Massachusetts elementary/secondary students in linguistic minorities and with limited English proficiency, Oct 1980 and 1991, annual rpt, S3810–3
Michigan population with limited English proficiency, by State area, 1980, annual planning rpt, S3980–1.2
New Jersey population speaking foreign language at home, and English-speaking ability, by county, 1990, census rpt, S5425–19
Pennsylvania population speaking foreign language at home, and English-speaking ability, 1990, census rpt, U4130–13
Rhode Island limited-English-proficiency students receiving services, by school district, June 1992, annual rpt, S6970–1.1
Rhode Island population speaking foreign language at home, and English-speaking ability, by county and municipality, 1990 census rpt, S6930–9
South Carolina statistical abstract, general data, 1993 annual rpt, S7125–1.13
Washington State English language training program for refugees, clients and costs by county, FY90, annual rpt, S8420–2
Washington State population, by language spoken at home and English speaking ability, by county, 1990, annual rpt, S8345–4

see also Compensatory education
see also Foreign languages
see also Language arts
see also Literacy and illiteracy
see also Reading ability and habits
see also Writers and writing

LANs
see Computer networks

Laos
see also Indochinese refugees

Laramie County, Wyo.
Employment by industry group, monthly rpt, S8895–1

Larceny
see Motor vehicle theft
see Robbery and theft

Lard
see Oils, oilseeds, and fats

Las Cruces, N.Mex.
Business and economic activity indicators for New Mexico, monthly rpt, U7980–1
Employment by industry, monthly rpt, S5624–2

Index by Subjects and Names

Law enforcement

Las Vegas, Nev.

Casino construction costs for 5 new facilities, 1993 article, C5800–7.550

Casino finances and employment, by location and gaming revenue range, FY92, annual rpt, S5062–1

Employment, hours, and earnings, by industry, quarterly rpt, S5040–1

Housing construction permits issued, Feb 1989-93, article, C1850–8.506

Labor force conditions and outlook, with data by industry, 1992 annual rpt, S5040–4

Lasers

Metalworking industry capital spending plans, by equipment type and industry group, 1989-93, annual survey, C4080–1

Sales of commercial lasers, by type and application, 1993 and trends, annual rpt, A4725–1.2

see also Compact disc players

Latin America

Advertising agency income and billings in Latin America, for top 10 multinatl agencies, 1992, annual article, C2710–1.527

Airline US carrier revenues and traffic capacity for Latin American routes, for 5 airlines, 1st half 1992, article, C7000–4.503

Books purchased by US libraries, with average cost, by Latin American source country or area, FY91-92, annual compilation, C1650–3.4

Economic indicators affecting business climate, with data on motor vehicle and oil industries and detail by country, 1992 rpt, R4105–82.6

Energy exploration, rotary drilling rigs in operation, by world area and country, monthly rpt, B4675–1

Executive job vacancy index, by industry, job function, and region, quarterly rpt, B5000–5

Fertility and contraceptive use rates, for 11 countries, 1992, article, R8750–1.504

Home video market indicators for 8 Latin American countries, 1993 feature, C9380–1.519

Oil and gas industry devs and outlook, 1993 articles, C6985–1.518

Oil/gas deep well drilling, success ratios, and costs, by world area, 1990-92, annual article, C4420–1.503

Population size and characteristics, GNP, and land area, by world region and/or country, 1993 annual data sheet, R8750–5

Refugees, resettlement, and intl aid devs, by country, 1992, annual rpt, R9372–1

Statistical abstract of Latin America, detailed social, govtl, and economic data, 1992 annual rpt, U6250–1

Stock exchange profiles for 6 South American countries and Mexico, with market capitalization, trading volume, and return rates, 1993 articles, C2710–2.507

Youth sexual experience, by sex, for selected Latin American cities and countries, 1985-91 surveys, U2520–1.51

see also Argentina

see also Bolivia

see also Brazil

see also Caribbean area

see also Central America

see also Chile

see also Colombia

see also Costa Rica

see also Cuba

see also Dominican Republic

see also Ecuador

see also El Salvador

see also Guatemala

see also Haiti

see also Honduras

see also Mexico

see also Nicaragua

see also Panama

see also Paraguay

see also Peru

see also South America

see also Uruguay

see also Venezuela

Latin American Free Trade Association

see Latin American Integration Association

Latin American Integration Association

Latin America statistical abstract, general data by country, 1992 annual rpt, U6250–1.26

Laughlin, Nev.

Casino finances and employment, by location and gaming revenue range, FY92, annual rpt, S5062–1

Laundry and cleaning services

Dry cleaning costs for man's suit in approx 300 cities, quarterly rpt, A0150–1

Financial ratios and performance, for over 350 SIC 4-digit industries, FY88-92, annual rpt, A6400–3

Franchise operations and finances, by type of business, 1991/92 and trends, annual rpt, A5820–1

Shopping center financial and operating data, with detail by type of tenant, US and Canada, 1991, triennial rpt, R9285–1

see also Janitorial and maintenance services

Laundry equipment

see Household appliances and equipment

Lav, Iris J.

"States and the Poor: How Budget Decisions Affected Low Income People in 1992", R3834–9

Law

Alcoholic beverage promotion laws, by State, Feb 1992, annual rpt, C4775–1.2

Book publishing industry financial and operating data, by publisher type and size, and subject category, 1991 and trends, annual rpt, A3274–2

Wine tasting and promotion laws, by State, 1993 annual rpt, C4775–2.2

State and local:

California law libraries, finances, staff, and holdings, by library, FY92, annual rpt, S0825–2

DC statistical profile, general data, 1992 annual rpt, S1535–3.1

Maryland State law library usage, FY92, annual rpt, S3600–1

see also Administration of justice

see also Administrative law and procedure

see also Building permits

see also Courts

see also Due process of law

see also Financial institutions regulation

see also Government-citizen lawsuits

see also Labor law

see also Law enforcement

see also Lawyers and legal services

see also Legal aid

see also Legal education

see also State constitutional amendments

see also State constitutional conventions

see also U.S. statutes

see also Zoning and zoning laws

see also under specific subject matter of laws

Law enforcement

Statistical profiles of 50 States and DC, general data, 1993 annual almanac, C4712–1

State and local:

Alabama crimes and arrests, by offense and location, with data on law enforcement employment and assaults on officers, 1992 and trends, annual rpt, S0119–1

Alabama statistical abstract, general data, 1992 recurring rpt, U5680–2.10

Arizona crimes and arrests, by offense, county, and offender characteristics, with assaults on officers and law enforcement employment, 1992, annual rpt, S0505–2

Arizona statistical abstract, general data, 1993 recurring rpt, U5850–2.12

Arkansas crimes and arrests, and law enforcement personnel by sex, by agency and county, 1992, annual rpt, S0652–1

Arkansas traffic accidents, by county and investigating agency, 1991, annual rpt, S0692–1

California crimes and arrests, and criminal justice system data, 1987-92, annual rpt, S0910–1

California criminal justice system detailed data, by offense, county, age, race-ethnicity, and sex, 1991 and trends, annual rpt, S0910–2

Colorado crimes and arrests, by offense and location, with offender characteristics, and assaults on police, 1992, annual rpt, S1068–1

Connecticut crimes and arrests, law enforcement employment by sex, and assaults on officers, 1992, annual rpt, S1256–1

Florida county data book, 1992/93 annual rpt, C6360–1

Florida statistical abstract, general data, 1992 annual rpt, U6660–1.22

Hawaii data book, general data, 1992 annual rpt, S2090–1.4

Idaho crimes and arrests, law enforcement employees by sex, and assaults on officers, by local agency and county, 1992, annual rpt, S2275–2

Illinois crimes and arrests, and assaults on officers, 1991, annual rpt, S2536–1

Illinois statistical abstract, general data, 1992 annual rpt, U6910–2

Kansas law enforcement employees by demographic characteristics and local agency, with assaults on police by circumstance, 1992, annual rpt, S2925–1.2

Kansas statistical abstract, general data, 1991/92 annual rpt, U7095–2.12

Kentucky crimes and arrests, law enforcement employment, and assaults on police, 1992, annual rpt, S3150–1

Louisiana law enforcement employment, by agency type, 1991 annual rpt, S3345–2

Maryland law enforcement employment by sex, criminal offenses and arrests, and assaults on police, by local agency and county, 1991-92, annual rpt, S3665–1

Law enforcement

Michigan crimes and arrests, by offense, with law enforcement employment and assaults on officers, 1992 and trends, annual rpt, S3997–1

Mississippi statistical abstract, general data, 1992 annual rpt, U3255–4.9

Nevada traffic accidents, by investigating agency, 1992, annual rpt, S5140–1

New Jersey crimes and arrests, law enforcement employment, and assaults on officers, 1992 and trends, annual rpt, S5430–1

New York State law enforcement expenditures, and employment by sex, county, and local agency, 1991, annual rpt, S5760–3.3

New York State statistical yearbook, general data, 1992 annual rpt, U5100–1.8

North Carolina law enforcement employment by local agency and sex, and assaults on police, 1991-92, annual rpt, S5955–1

North Dakota crimes and arrests, by offense, and law enforcement employment by sex, 1991 and trends, annual rpt, S6060–1

Oklahoma criminal offenses, by law enforcement agency, police employment by sex, and assaults on officers, 1990-92, annual rpt, S6465–1.2

Oregon crimes by offense, law enforcement employees by sex, and assaults on police, by local agency, 1992 and trends, annual rpt, S6603–3.2

Pennsylvania crimes and arrests, by offense, location, and offender characteristics, with law enforcement employment, 1992 and trends, annual rpt, S6860–1

South Carolina crimes and arrests, by offense, with data by location and victim-offender characteristics, and assaults on officers, 1992 and trends, annual rpt, S7205–1

Tennessee statistical abstract, general data, 1992/93 annual rpt, U8710–2.19

Texas crimes and arrests, law enforcement employment, and assaults on officers, with data by reporting agency, 1992, annual rpt, S7735–2.2

Utah crimes and arrests, and law enforcement employment by county and local agency, 1992, annual rpt, S7890–3

Virginia crimes and arrests by offense, and law enforcement employment, by location and reporting agency, 1992, annual rpt, S8295–2.2

Washington State crimes, clearances, and law enforcement employment, by reporting agency, with assaults on officers, 1992 and trends, annual rpt, S8440–1

West Virginia crimes and arrests, by offense, location, and offender characteristics, with data on law enforcement employment, 1990-91, annual rpt, S8610–1

Wisconsin law enforcement employees by local agency, and assaults on police by circumstances, 1992, annual rpt, S8771–1

Wyoming crimes and arrests, and law enforcement personnel, by jurisdiction, 1991, annual rpt, S8867–3

see also Administration of justice

see also Administrative law and procedure

see also Arrest

see also Campus security

see also Correctional institutions

see also Courts

see also Crime and criminals

see also Criminal investigations

see also Criminal procedure

see also Electronic surveillance

see also Federal aid to law enforcement

see also Forensic sciences

see also Juvenile delinquency

see also Organized crime

see also Police

see also Pretrial detention and release

see also Riots and disorders

see also Searches and seizures

see also Sheriffs

see also State funding for corrections

see also State funding for public safety

see also State police

see also Traffic laws and courts

Law schools

see Legal education

Lawn and garden equipment

Consumer expenditures and retail sales, for lawn/garden products, 1992 and trends, article, C5150–6.508

Discount store sales and productivity data for 20 depts, 1993 annual feature, C5150–3.516

Financial ratios and performance, for over 350 SIC 4-digit industries, FY88-92, annual rpt, A6400–3

Foreign trade in lawn and garden equipment, 1985-92, article, C2000–1.511

Life expectancy, shipments, and manufacturers market shares, for appliances by type, 1993 annual article, C2000–1.510

Opinions of consumer hard goods manufacturers and representatives on business issues and outlook, by product line, 1992 annual survey rpt, A1800–1

Retail hardware sales and productivity measures for hardware stores, home centers, and lumber/building material outlets, 1991 and trends, annual rpt series, A8275–1

Retail sales by outlet type, and discount chain sales in major depts, by product category, 1992, annual feature, C8130–1.507

Shipments of household appliances, by detailed product type, 1991-98, annual articles, C2000–1.503

Shipments of household equipment, by product type, 1983-92, annual feature, C2000–1.505

Shipments of selected types of outdoor power equipment, 1991-94, article, C5150–3.515

Shipments of walk-behind and rider lawn mowers, 1990-94, article, C5150–6.508

State and local:

Maryland building materials/garden supplies industry employment and wages, by industry and occupational group, June 1991, article, S3605–2.501

Lawnmowers

see Lawn and garden equipment

Lawrence, Steven

"Foundation Giving: Yearbook of Facts and Figures on Private, Corporate and Community Foundations", R4900–1

Index by Subjects and Names

Lawsuits

Hard goods manufacturer legal actions against foreign patent/trademark infringement, and pending liability suits, by product line, 1993 annual survey rpt, A1800–1

Liability claims citing inadequate security, distribution by type of crime, 1993 feature, C1850–12.507

Medical education instn court cases, with detail for selected administrative, clinical, and research issues, 1950-91, article, A3273–8.503

Personal injury and medical malpractice verdicts awarded, including number exceeding $1 million, 1991 and trends, annual rpt, A5650–1.3

Personal injury jury verdict award trends, with data by case type and for awards exceeding $1 million, 1960s-92, annual rpt, C5180–1

Product liability verdicts awarded, including number exceeding $1 million, 1981-91, annual rpt, A5650–1.3

see also Government-citizen lawsuits

Lawton, Okla.

Business activity indicators for Oklahoma, monthly rpt, U8130–1

Employment by industry, monthly rpt, S6430–2

Lawyers and legal services

Bankruptcy attorneys in 6 legal firms, 1987 and 1992, article, C5800–7.512

Bar exam results and admissions, by State and territory, 1992 and trends, annual rpt, A7458–1

Condominium, cooperative, and planned unit dev detailed expenses, for US and Canada, by building characteristics, metro area, and US region, 1991, annual rpt, A5600–3

Congressional campaign finances, with detailed data for individual Members, and leading contributors by type and industry, 1990 election and trends, biennial rpt, R3828–2.2

Divorce caseloads and processing times by case characteristics, with domestic court judicial staff, for 16 urban jurisdictions, 1989 and/or 1990, R6600–6

Employment and salaries of law school grads, by employer type, location, and grad characteristics, 1992 and trends, annual rpt, A6505–1

Establishments, employment, receipts, and payroll, and volume of printing business generated, 1992 feature, C1850–10.502

Financial ratios and performance, for over 350 SIC 4-digit industries, FY88-92, annual rpt, A6400–3

Law school enrollment by minority status, degrees conferred, staff, and library holdings, by instn, 1992/93 and trends, annual rpt, A0970–1

Local govt police liability lawsuits, claim and settlement amounts, and legal costs, by population size, census div, and/or case type, 1990/91 survey, A5800–2.113

Number of lawyers compared to population, for US and 5 other countries, 1993 article, C2425–2.503

Operating and financial composite ratios for corporations, with establishments and receipts, for approx 200 industries, by asset size, FY90, annual rpt, C7800–1

Index by Subjects and Names

Planning profession employment and salaries, by type of employer, demographic and professional characteristics, and location, 1991 and trends, biennial rpt, A2615–1

Public opinion on honesty/ethical standards of selected occupations, 1992 Gallup Polls and trends, C4040–1.501

Shopping center financial and operating data, with detail by type of tenant, US and Canada, 1991, triennial rpt, R9285–1

State appellate court lawyer support personnel, by State, 1991, annual rpt, R6600–1

State social, economic, and govtl indicators, with rankings, 1993 semiannual rpt, B8500–1.1

Statistical profiles of 50 States and DC, general data, 1993 annual almanac, C4712–1

Urban small claims litigant use of attorneys and correlation with case outcome, and small claims and traffic court attorney costs, 1990, R6600–5

State and local:

Alaska lawyers compared to population, by city and judicial district, FY92, annual rpt, S0290–1

Arizona statistical abstract, general data, 1993 recurring rpt, U5850–2.24

California county law libraries finances and operations, including attorneys served, by county, FY92, annual rpt, S0825–2

California criminal justice system expenditures and employment, by type of agency or function, 1982-91, annual rpt, S0910–2.1

DC bar applications, admissions, and disciplinary actions, 1985-92, annual rpt, S1515–1

Florida county data book, 1992/93 annual rpt, C6360–1

Florida statistical abstract, general data, 1992 annual rpt, U6660–1.22

Georgia election results for district attorneys, by county and district, Nov 1992, biennial rpt, S1955–1

Hawaii data book, general data, 1992 annual rpt, S2090–1.4

Indiana bar examination review petitions handled by supreme court, 1992, annual rpt, S2703–1.1

Maryland bar exam results, with detail by in-State school of graduation, FY92 and trends, annual rpt, S3600–1

New Mexico bar exam results, FY92, annual rpt, S5623–1

New York State attorney registrations and retainer statements, 1991, annual rpt, S5730–1

Oklahoma statistical abstract, general data, 1992 annual rpt, U8130–2.7

South Carolina bar exam results, 1977-92, annual rpt, S7197–1

see also Judges

see also Legal aid

see also Legal education

see also Legal ethics

Layoffs

see Labor turnover

Lazere, Edward B.

"Place to Call Home: The Low Income Housing Crisis in 44 Major Metropolitan Areas", R3834–16

Lead and lead industry

Capital spending plans for new mines and plants, by mineral and company, and mine production values, 1993 annual feature, C5226–2.503

Latin America statistical abstract, general data by country, 1992 annual rpt, U6250–1.23, U6250–1.25

Production, consumption, stocks, trade, and prices for approx 100 basic commodities, including by country and producing State, commodity yearbook for 1993, C2400–1, C2400–2

see also Lead poisoning and pollution

Lead poisoning and pollution

Calcium supplement lead content, by type of supplement, 1993 article, A2623–1.510

City govt costs to enforce Fed Govt regulations including lead paint abatement, FY93-98, A9330–12

Factory worker disease and mortality related to lead exposure, research results summary, 1992 article, A2623–1.502

State and local:

Hawaii ceramic ware tested for leachable lead, 1990, annual rpt., S2065–1.6

Leading indicators

see Economic indicators

Leading National Advertisers Inc.

Advertising expenditures of corporations and assns, by medium, 1988-92, and top 10 advertisers for 1992, annual article, A8770–1.504

Magazine advertising revenues, for top 5 group publishers, 1st qtr 1993, article, C2710–1.526

Publisher advertising revenues, for top 10 companies, 1992, C2710–1.513

Tobacco advertising expenditures in magazines, with detail for top 4 publications, 1981 and 1991, article, C2575–1.503

Leasing

see Mineral leases

see Oil and gas leases

see Rental industries

Leather industry and products

Employment, hours, and earnings, by State, 1984-91, annual rpt, A4957–1.2

Financial ratios and performance, for over 350 SIC 4-digit industries, FY88-92, annual rpt, A6400–3

Operating and financial composite ratios for corporations, with establishments and receipts, for approx 200 industries, by asset size, FY90, annual rpt, C7800–1

Production, consumption, stocks, trade, and prices for approx 100 basic commodities, including by country and producing State, commodity yearbook for 1993, C2400–1, C2400–2

Shopping center financial and operating data, with detail by type of tenant, US and Canada, 1991, triennial rpt, R9285–1

State and local:

Florida statistical abstract, general data, 1992 annual rpt, U6660–1.12

Wyoming valuation of saddles/harnesses, by county, 1992, annual rpt, S8990–1.2

see also Hides and skins

see also Shoes and shoe industry

see also under By Industry in the "Index by Categories"

Legal arbitration and mediation

Ledebur, Larry C.

"'All in It Together': Cities, Suburbs and Local Economic Regions", A8012–1.22

Lee Hecht Harrison

Health care professionals making career changes, distribution by type of new employer, 1993 article, A1865–1.523

Leeward and Windward Islands

see Caribbean area

Legal aid

Law school grad employment and salaries, by type of employer, location, and grad characteristics, 1992 and trends, annual rpt, A6505–1

State and local:

Arkansas public defender caseload and dispositions, by court and case type, FY92, annual rpt, S0647–1

DC statistical profile, general data, 1992 annual rpt, S1535–3.8

Indiana court cases and dispositions by type of court and case, and location, with judicial system finances and personnel, 1992, annual rpt, S2703–1

North Carolina public defender and assigned counsel caseloads and costs, including State mental hospital hearings, FY91, annual rpt, S5950–1

Oklahoma expenditures on legal representation for indigents, FY89-92, annual rpt, S6493–1.1

Rhode Island prepaid legal service corporations, financial summary, 1990, annual rpt, S6945–2

South Carolina public defenders office finances and personnel, with detail by county, FY83-93, annual rpt, S7197–1

South Dakota expenditures for court-appointed attorneys/public defenders, by county, FY92, annual rpt, S7395–1

Virginia court indigent defense costs, by district, FY92, annual rpt, S8300–1

see also Lawyers and legal services

Legal arbitration and mediation

Small claims court mediation caseloads, and litigant satisfaction with fairness compared to trial, for 3-5 urban jurisdictions, 1990, R6600–5

State and local:

Arizona court cases and dispositions, by type of case and court, with judicial personnel and finances, by county and city, FY92, annual rpt, S0525–1

DC court mediation program caseloads and outcome, 1986-92, annual rpt, S1515–1

Delaware superior and family court arbitration activity, FY91-92, annual rpt, S1360–1

Indiana court cases and dispositions by type of court and case, and location, with judicial system finances and personnel, 1992, annual rpt, S2703–1

Maine court cases and dispositions, by type and location, FY92 and trends, annual rpt, S3463–1

Michigan court caseloads and dispositions, by type of court and case, and court location, 1992 and trends, annual rpt, S3962–1

New York State court cases and dispositions, by type of court and case, and jurisdiction, 1991, annual rpt, S5730–1

Legal arbitration and mediation

New York State no-fault auto insurance arbitration case dispositions, 1989-91, annual rpt, S5770–3

North Carolina court arbitration and child custody/visitation mediation activity, by location, FY91, annual rpt, S5950–1

Pennsylvania court caseloads and dispositions, including arbitration, by county, 1991, annual rpt, S6900–1.2

Texas alternative dispute resolution center caseloads, by center, FY92, annual rpt, S7703–1

Legal education

Law school enrollment by minority status, degrees conferred, staff, and library holdings, by instn, 1992/93 and trends, annual rpt, A0970–1

Southern States higher education degree conferrals, by sex, race-ethnicity, level, and selected field, by State, 1990s and trends, biennial fact book, A8945–1.3

Southern States higher education enrollment, degrees, appropriations, tuition/fees, and faculty compensation, by instn type, for 15 States, 1990/91, annual rpt, A8945–31

State and land-grant university tuition/fees, and room and board charges, by type of professional program and/or instn, fall 1991-92, annual rpt, A7150–4

Western States higher education student exchange program enrollment and support fees, by program and instn, for 15 States, 1992/93, annual rpt, A9385–1

Women and minorities in professional fields, detailed education and labor force data, 1991 and trends, recurring rpt, A3960–2.1

Women's share of law school enrollment, 1960s-91, annual rpt, A1570–2

State and local:

California postsecondary education enrollment and degrees, by sex, race-ethnicity, and instn, 1990/91, annual series, S0827–2

DC statistical profile, general data, 1992, annual rpt, S1535–3.6

Georgia judicial continuing education and certification seminar attendance, FY92, annual rpt, S1903–1

Illinois higher education enrollment, degrees, staff, and finances, by public and private instn and student characteristics, 1993 annual rpt, S2475–1

Texas appellate and trial judge demographic characteristics, Sept 1992, annual rpt, S7703–1

Legal ethics

State and local:

Arizona supreme court bar disciplinary and judicial conduct cases filed and disposed, FY92, annual rpt, S0525–1

California attorney disciplinary proceedings filed with State supreme court, FY83-92, annual rpt, S0905–1.2

DC bar disciplinary actions, 1985-92, annual rpt, S1515–1

Indiana supreme court disposition of disciplinary matters, 1992, annual rpt, S2703–1.1

Iowa lawyer disciplinary proceedings of State supreme court, 1977-92, annual rpt, S2815–1

Maryland complaints and disciplinary actions against lawyers, FY88-92, annual rpt, S3600–1

North Dakota attorney misconduct complaints and dispositions, 1992, annual rpt, S6210–1

Ohio attorney disciplinary cases and dispositions, 1992, annual rpt, S6385–1

Pennsylvania legal disciplinary board actions, and client security fund awards, 1991 and trends, annual rpt, S6900–1.1

Rhode Island legal disciplinary board complaints received and actions, 1991, annual rpt, S6965–1

South Carolina grievances and disciplinary measures against attorneys, 1992 and trends, annual rpt, S7197–1

West Virginia court caseloads and dispositions, by type of court and case, and judicial circuit, 1992 and trends, annual rpt, S8537–1

see also Judicial ethics

Legal profession

see Lawyers and legal services

Legislative bodies

see Congress

see Foreign legislative bodies

see House of Representatives

see Senate

see State legislatures

Lehman Brothers Inc.

Cable TV multiple system operator subscriber base overlaps with telephone company service areas, for 9 cable and 8 telephone companies, 1993 article, C1850–14.541

Leisure activities

see Recreation

Lemons

see Citrus fruits

Lennon, Todd M.

"Statistics on Social Work Education in the U.S.: 1992", A4515–1

Leonard, Paul A.

"New Direction: The Clinton Budget and Economic Plan", R3834–17

"Place to Call Home: The Low Income Housing Crisis in 44 Major Metropolitan Areas", R3834–16

Leprosy

see Infective and parasitic diseases

LeRoy, David

"Do Members Use Public Television Differently? An Exploratory Study", R4250–1.22

LeRoy, Judith

"Do Members Use Public Television Differently? An Exploratory Study", R4250–1.22

Letter carriers

see Postal employees

Lettuce

see Vegetables and vegetable products

Leukemia

see Neoplasms

Level of education

see Degrees, higher education

see Educational attainment

Leveraged buyouts

see Business acquisitions and mergers

Levin, Martha

"U.S. Schools of Public Health Data Report on Applicants, New Enrollments, and Students, Fall 1992, and Graduates and Expenditures, 1991/92, with Trends Analysis for 1974/75 Through Fall 1992", A3372–3

"U.S. Schools of Public Health: Data Report on Faculty, 1991-92", A3372–1

Lewiston, Idaho

Waterborne shipments through Port of Lewiston, 1975-91, recurring rpt, S2218–2.8

Lewiston, Maine

Employment, unemployment, and earnings, by industry, MSA, and labor area, monthly rpt, S3465–2

Liability insurance

see Property and casualty insurance

Liability lawsuits

see Lawsuits

Libby, Lori B.

"Capital Improvement Financing, 1991", A5800–2.112

Librarians

Elementary/secondary public school enrollment and certified school library media specialists, by selected State, 1992, annual compilation, C1650–3.3

Employment of library school grads, and salaries, by region and sex, 1991 and trends, annual compilation, C1650–3.3

Research library holdings, expenditures by type, and staff, for 120 academic and nonacademic instns, US and Canada, FY92, annual rpt, A3365–1

Salaries and placements of library school grads, by region, sex, instn, and library type, with detail for minorities, 1992 and trends, annual article, C1852–1.512

Salaries by sex, and women's employment shares, for university librarians, FY93, annual rpt, A1570–2

Salaries for 6 librarian positions, for public and academic libraries by region, 1993, annual rpt, A2070–3

Salaries of librarians at universities and research instns, by sex, race-ethnicity, type of position, and instn, FY92 and trends, annual survey, A3365–2

Salaries of special librarians, by location, work setting, and personal characteristics, US and Canada, 1992 and trends, biennial survey rpt, A8965–1

State and local:

Arizona public library holdings, circulation, finances, and staff, by instn and county, FY92, annual rpt, S0495–1

California library finances, staff, holdings, and services, by library type and facility, FY92, annual rpt, S0825–2

Colorado library finances and operations, including staff, holdings, and population served, by instn and library type, series, S1000–3

Connecticut public library staff, holdings, circulation, and finances, by library and town, FY91, annual rpt, S1242–1

Florida public libraries, finances, holdings, staff, and services, by system and library, FY92, annual rpt, S1800–2

Hawaii data book, general data, 1992 annual rpt, S2090–1.3

Idaho academic library staff, expenditures, and holdings, by instn, 1992, annual feature, A5370–1

Idaho public library holdings, staff, services, circulation, and finances, by instn, FY92, annual rpt, S2282–1

Indiana public and other library holdings, circulation, finances, and staff, by instn, 1992 or FY92, annual rpt, S2655–1

Index by Subjects and Names

Libraries

Iowa public library finances and operations, by county, size of population served, and library, FY92, annual rpt, S2778–1

Louisiana public library finances, holdings, circulation, and personnel, by library system, FY92, annual rpt, S3275–1

Maryland elementary and secondary education data, by county, 1992/93, annual rpt, S3610–2.10

Maryland public library operating income and expenditures, staff, holdings, and population served, by county, FY92, annual rpt, S3610–5

Maryland public school librarian salaries, by county, Oct 1991, annual rpt, S3610–2.2

Maryland public school librarian salaries, by county, Oct 1992, annual rpt, S3610–2.11

Minnesota public library holdings, staff, services, circulation, and finances, by library, 1991, annual rpt, S4165–2

Montana public library holdings, staff, circulation, and finances, by library, FY92, annual rpt, S4725–1

New Jersey public library finances, holdings, circulation, and staff, by county and library, 1991, annual rpt, S5385–2

New York State public library finances, staff, holdings, and services, by library and county, 1991, annual rpt, S5745–2

North Carolina public libraries, finances, holdings, and personnel, by library system, FY91, annual rpt, S5910–1

North Dakota public library finances, holdings, staff, and operations, by instn, FY91, annual rpt, S6180–5

Ohio public, academic, and other library finances, holdings, and staff, by library and location, 1992 and trends, annual rpt, S6320–1

Oklahoma public and institutional library holdings, circulation, finances, and staff, by facility, FY92, annual rpt, S6470–1

Oregon library finances, staff, holdings, and services, for public, academic, and special libraries by instn, FY92 and trends, annual rpt, S6635–1

Pennsylvania public and institutional library personnel, holdings, circulation, and finances, by county and facility, FY92, annual rpt, S6790–2

South Carolina public and institutional libraries, finances, services, holdings, and staff, by library, FY92, annual rpt, S7210–1

Texas public libraries, holdings, circulation, staff, and finances, by library and location, FY91, annual rpt, S7710–1

Utah higher education degrees, enrollment, staff, and finances, by public instn, with selected comparisons to instns in other States, 1993/94 annual rpt, S7895–2

Virginia public library operations and finances, by instn, FY92, annual rpt, S8275–1

Washington State public libraries, finances, holdings, circulation, staff, and population served, by instn, 1992, annual rpt, S8375–1

Wisconsin libraries, operations, and finances, by library type, instn, and location, 1992, annual rpt, S8795–1

Wyoming public library holdings, staff, circulation, and finances, by county, FY92, annual rpt, S8855–3

Libraries

Automated system installations worldwide and in US, and vendor revenues, by vendor, 1992 and trends, annual articles, C1852–1.505, C1852–1.506

Construction of public and academic libraries, costs, and funding sources, by State, city, and instn, FY92 and trends, annual article, C1852–1.501

Japan academic library facilities, staff, and operations, by instn type, 1990, annual compilation, C1650–3.1

Latin America statistical abstract, general data by country, 1992 annual rpt, U6250–1.8

Law school enrollment by minority status, degrees conferred, staff, and library holdings, by instn, 1992/93 and trends, annual rpt, A0970–1

Library and book trade reference info, including public and academic library funding, construction, and operations, by State and instn, 1992, annual compilation, C1650–3

Library and info service activities and devs, articles and book reviews, semimonthly rpt, C1852–1

Library/info science school enrollment, staff and student characteristics, finances, and curricula, by school and degree program, 1991/92, annual rpt, A3235–1

Optometry school library operating and financial data, by instn, 1991/92, annual survey, A3370–2

Periodical subscription prices, by subject area, and by country or world region of origin, 1993 and trends, annual article, C1852–1.506

Research library expenditures distribution by function, selected years 1963-91, article, C2175–1.509

Research library holdings, expenditures by type, and staff, for 120 academic and nonacademic instns, US and Canada, FY92, annual rpt, A3365–1

Research library holdings, staff, and expenditures, for instns in US and Canada, 1991/92, annual feature, C2175–1.511

Salaries and placements of library school grads, by region, sex, instn, and library type, with detail for minorities, 1992 and trends, annual article, C1852–1.512

Southern States higher education instn library collections, staff, and expenditures, for 26 instns, 1990/91 and trends, biennial fact book, A8945–1.6

State library agency appropriations, expenditures, salaries, and staff, by State, 1992 annual rpt, A3862–1

Theological school library holdings, by instn, 1992/93 annual rpt, A3376–1

Utility and transportation regulatory agency library facilities and holdings, by agency, 1991/92 annual rpt, A7015–2

State and local:

Alabama county data book, general data, 1992 annual rpt, S0121–2

Alabama public libraries, finances, holdings, circulation, staff, and population served, by library, FY92, annual rpt, S0180–1

Alabama State law library utilization, FY89-92, annual rpt, S0118–1

Arizona public library holdings, circulation, finances, and staff, by instn and county, FY92, annual rpt, S0495–1

Arkansas academic library holdings and expenditures, by instn, FY87-92, with funding recommendations through FY95, biennial rpt, S0690–4

California library finances, staff, holdings, and services, by library type and facility, FY92, annual rpt, S0825–2

California socioeconomic and govtl data for municipalities, counties, and school districts, 1993 annual rpt, C4712–3

California statistical abstract, general data, 1992 annual rpt, S0840–2.6

Colorado library finances and operations, including staff, holdings, and population served, by instn and library type, series, S1000–3

Connecticut public library staff, holdings, circulation, and finances, by library and town, FY91, annual rpt, S1242–1

DC statistical profile, general data, 1992 annual rpt, S1535–3.6

Florida public libraries, finances, holdings, staff, and services, by system and library, FY92, annual rpt, S1800–2

Florida statistical abstract, general data, 1992 annual rpt, U6660–1.20

Georgia correctional instns library holdings and users, FY92 annual rpt, S1872–1

Georgia county guide, general data, 1993 annual rpt, U6750–1

Hawaii data book, general data, 1992 annual rpt, S2090–1.3

Idaho academic library staff, expenditures, and holdings, by instn, 1992, annual feature, A5370–1

Idaho public library holdings, staff, services, circulation, and finances, by instn, FY92, annual rpt, S2282–1

Illinois public library holdings, staff, and finances, by instn, FY92, annual rpt, S2535–2

Indiana public and other library holdings, circulation, finances, and staff, by instn, 1992 or FY92, annual rpt, S2655–1

Iowa public library finances and operations, by county, size of population served, and library, FY92, annual rpt, S2778–1

Kentucky public library finances and operations, by county, FY92, annual rpt, S3165–1

Louisiana public library finances, holdings, circulation, and personnel, by library system, FY92, annual rpt, S3275–1

Maryland local govt financial condition, including revenues by source, expenditures by function, and debt obligations, FY92 and trends, annual rpt, S3618–1.1

Maryland public library operating income and expenditures, staff, holdings, and population served, by county, FY92, annual rpt, S3610–5

Maryland school and public library facilities, finances, staff, and/or circulation, by county, 1991/92, annual rpt, S3610–1

Maryland State law library usage, FY92, annual rpt, S3600–1

Massachusetts municipal and county profiles, general data, 1992 annual rpt, C4712–2

Massachusetts public library finances, holdings, and circulation, by municipality, FY92, annual rpt, S3870–1

Minnesota library info exchange program activities, 1993 biennial rpt, S4195–2.2

Libraries

Index by Subjects and Names

Minnesota public library holdings, staff, services, circulation, and finances, by library, 1991, annual rpt, S4165–2

Mississippi statistical abstract, general data, 1992 annual rpt, U3255–4.3

Missouri higher education library holdings by type, and expenditures by function, by instn, FY92, annual rpt, S4520–3.3

Missouri public, special, and academic libraries, finances, holdings, circulation, staff, and services, by location, FY92, annual rpt, S4520–2

Montana public library holdings, staff, circulation, and finances, by library, FY92, annual rpt, S4725–1

Nebraska public libraries, finances, holdings, circulation, staff, and population served, by instn, FY91, annual rpt, S4910–1

Nevada library and staff directories for public and academic libraries, with data on holdings, operations, and finances, FY92, annual rpt, S5095–1

New Hampshire public library finances and operations, by library and/or location, 1991, annual rpt, S5227–1

New Jersey municipal and county data book, general data, 1992 annual rpt, C4712–4

New Jersey public library finances, holdings, circulation, and staff, by county and library, 1991, annual rpt, S5385–2

New Mexico public library operations and finances, by instn, FY92, annual rpt, S5627–1

New York State public library finances, staff, holdings, and services, by library and county, 1991, annual rpt, S5745–2

New York State statistical yearbook, general data, 1992 annual rpt, U5100–1.10

North Carolina higher education library holdings and expenditures, by type and instn, 1991/92, annual rpt, U8013–1.2

North Carolina public libraries, finances, holdings, and personnel, by library system, FY91, annual rpt, S5910–1

North Dakota public library finances, holdings, staff, and operations, by instn, FY91, annual rpt, S6180–5

Ohio public, academic, and other library finances, holdings, and staff, by library and location, 1992 and trends, annual rpt, S6320–1

Oklahoma public and institutional library holdings, circulation, finances, and staff, by facility, FY92, annual rpt, S6470–1

Oklahoma school revenues and expenditures, by program, county, and district, FY92, annual rpt, S6423–1.1

Oklahoma statistical abstract, general data, 1992 annual rpt, U8130–2.21

Oregon library finances, staff, holdings, and services, for public, academic, and special libraries by instn, FY92 and trends, annual rpt, S6635–1

Pennsylvania public and institutional library personnel, holdings, circulation, and finances, by county and facility, FY92, annual rpt, S6790–2

Pennsylvania statistical abstract, general data, 1992 recurring rpt, U4130–6.4

South Carolina public and institutional libraries, finances, services, holdings, and staff, by library, FY92, annual rpt, S7210–1

Tennessee statistical abstract, general data, 1992/93 annual rpt, U8710–2.16

Texas public libraries, holdings, circulation, staff, and finances, by library and location, FY91, annual rpt, S7710–1

Utah higher education library staff, expenditures, and holdings, by instn, FY92 and trends, annual rpt, S7895–2

Utah public libraries, services, staff, and finances, by library, 1992, annual rpt, S7808–1

Vermont libraries, finances, resources, and circulation, by city and library, FY91-92, biennial rpt, S8080–1

Virginia public library operations and finances, by instn, FY92, annual rpt, S8275–1

Washington State public libraries, finances, holdings, circulation, staff, and population served, by instn, 1992, annual rpt, S8375–1

West Virginia public, academic, and special library operations and/or finances, by instn, 1991/92, annual rpt, S8590–1

Wisconsin Blue Book, general data, 1993-94 biennial rpt, S8780–1.2

Wisconsin libraries, operations, and finances, by library type, instn, and location, 1992, annual rpt, S8795–1

Wyoming property assessed valuations and tax levies, by property type, tax purpose, and location, 1992 and trends, annual rpt, S8990–1.2

Wyoming public library holdings, staff, circulation, and finances, by county, FY92, annual rpt, S8855–3

see also Federal aid to libraries

see also Librarians

see also Library of Congress

see also Medical libraries

see also State funding for libraries

Library of Congress

Salaries of librarians in nonuniversity research libraries, FY92-93, annual survey, A3365–2

Libya

Energy intl sourcebook, with detail on oil and gas industry operations, supply-demand, and prices, for approx 80 countries, 1970s-91, annual compilation, C6985–10.2

see also Organization of Petroleum Exporting Countries

see also under By Foreign Country or World Area in the "Index by Categories"

License taxes and fees

Apartment building (conventionally financed) detailed income and expense ratios for US and Canada, by building type, metro area, and US region, 1991 and trends, annual rpt, A5600–1

Apartment building (federally subsidized) detailed income and expense ratios, by building and subsidy type, building age, metro area, and region, 1991 and trends, annual rpt, A5600–5

Auto operating costs, by component, 1950-93, annual rpt, A0865–1.2

Charity gambling receipts, net proceeds, and State regulatory staff and finances, by State, various years FY90-92, article, C2176–1.512

Govt finances, including revenues by source, expenditures by function, and debt, detailed data for Federal, State, and local govts, 1993 annual rpt, R9050–1

Housing costs attributable to govt regulations and fees, and impact on households eligible to purchase homes, for 2 local areas, 1993 article, C4300–1.510

Life insurance industry taxes paid, by type of tax, 1947-91, biennial fact book, A1325–1.4

Motorcycle operator licensing procedures, operators, and vehicle registrations, by State, 1993 annual rpt, A6490–1

Office building detailed income and expense data, and energy use, US and Canada, by building characteristics, metro area, and US region, 1991 and trends, annual rpt, A5600–2

Pari-mutuel wagering activity, attendance, purse distribution, and govt revenue, by State and Canadian Province, 1990 and trends, annual rpt, A3363–1

Transportation regulatory agency policies and practices for motor carriers and railroads, by agency, 1991/92 annual rpt, A7015–4

Transportation-related revenues of Fed Govt and individual States, by type, 1990s and trends, annual rpt, A0865–1.3

Truck fleet financial and operating data for top 200 freight carriers, 1992 and trends, annual feature, C2150–4.504

Utility and transportation regulatory agency activities, scope of jurisdiction, finances, and employees, by agency, 1991/92 annual rpt, A7015–2

State and local:

Alabama financial condition, including revenues by source, expenditures by function and object, and fund balances, by fund and agency, FY92, annual rpt, S0129–1

Alabama Insurance Dept receipts by type, and disbursements, FY91, annual rpt, S0160–1

Alaska financial condition, including revenues by source, expenditures by function, fund balances, and bond obligations, FY92 and trends, annual rpt, S0275–1

Alaska insurance industry underwriting and investment data, by company and type of insurance, with regulatory info, 1991 and trends, annual rpt, S0280–3

Arizona insurance industry financial and underwriting data, by company and type of insurance, with regulatory info, 1992, annual rpt, S0483–1

Arizona State govt bingo tax collections, FY79-92, annual rpt, S0515–1

Arizona statistical abstract, general data, 1993 recurring rpt, U5850–2.18

Arkansas financial condition, including revenues by source, expenditures by function and object, and fund balances, FY92, annual rpt, S0670–1

California economic condition, including population, employment and earnings, income, business activity, and taxation, 1960s-92, annual rpt, S0840–3.2

California financial condition, including revenues by source, expenditures by agency and function, fund balances, and bonded debt, FY92 and trends, annual rpt, S0815–1

California insurance industry financial and underwriting data, by company and type of insurance, with regulatory info, 1991, annual rpt, S0900–1

Index by Subjects and Names

License taxes and fees

Colorado tax revenues by type, with selected data by county and city, FY92 and trends, annual rpt, S1075–1

Connecticut Banking Dept receipts and expenditures, FY91, annual rpt, S1160–1

Connecticut financial condition, including revenues by source, expenditures by function, and bonded debt, FY92, annual rpt, S1170–1, S1170–2

DC financial condition, including receipts by source, expenditures by object or function, and fund balances, FY92, annual rpt, S1507–1

Florida county data book, 1992/93 annual rpt, C6360–1

Florida State govt disbursements to local areas, by source of funds, FY92, annual rpt, S1717–1

Georgia tax revenues, by type and county, FY92 annual rpt, S1950–1

Hawaii tax collections and allocations, by type, for State and counties, FY91-92 and trends, annual rpt, S2120–1

Idaho financial condition, including revenues by source and expenditures by object, by agency and/or fund, FY92, annual rpt, S2215–1

Idaho insurance industry financial and underwriting data, by company and type of insurance, with regulatory data, 1991, annual rpt, S2260–1

Idaho tax statistics, including collections, and data by county and city, FY92 and trends, annual rpt, S2295–1

Illinois financial condition, including revenues by source, and expenditures by object, function, and agency, FY92, annual rpt, S2415–1

Illinois Financial Institutions Dept activities, with financial and regulatory data for credit unions, consumer lenders, and other businesses, FY91 annual rpt, S2457–2

Indiana court cases and dispositions by type of court and case, and location, with judicial system finances and personnel, 1992, annual rpt, S2703–1

Indiana financial condition, including revenues by source, expenditures by function and object, and fund balances, by agency, FY92, annual rpt, S2570–1

Iowa insurance industry financial and underwriting data, by company and type of insurance, 1992, annual rpt, S2760–1

Kansas insurance industry financial and underwriting data, by company and type of insurance, with regulatory info, 1992, annual rpt, S2990–1

Kansas tax collections by tax type, and property values, with data by county, FY92 and trends, annual rpt, S3020–1

Kentucky financial condition, including revenues by source, expenditures by function and object, fund balances, and bonded debt, FY92, annual rpt, S3120–1

Maryland financial condition, including revenues by source, expenditures by function, fund balances, and bonded debt, FY92 and trends, annual rpt, S3685–2

Maryland insurance industry financial and underwriting data, by company and type of insurance, with regulatory info, 1991, annual rpt, S3655–1

Maryland local govt financial condition, including revenues by source, expenditures by function, and debt obligations, FY92 and trends, annual rpt, S3618–1

Massachusetts tax collections by type, and distributions to local areas, FY91 and trends, annual rpt, S3917–1

Michigan financial condition, including revenues by source, expenditures by function, and fund balances, FY92 and trends, annual rpt, S3985–2

Michigan Insurance Bur taxes and fees collected, FY91, annual rpt, S3983–1

Michigan motor vehicle registrations by vehicle type, and total revenue, by county, 1991, annual rpt, S3997–2

Minnesota financial condition, including revenues by source, expenditures by function, fund balances, and bonded debt, FY92 and trends, annual rpt, S4180–1

Mississippi statistical abstract, general data, 1992 annual rpt, U3255–4.6

Mississippi tax collections by type, and disbursements, with selected sales and income tax data by locality and industry, FY92 and trends, annual rpt, S4435–1

Missouri financial condition, including fund finances, tax collections and distribution, and State treasury activity, FY92 and trends, annual rpt, S4570–1

Missouri insurance industry financial and underwriting data, by company and type of insurance, with regulatory info, 1992, annual rpt, S4527–1

Montana revenue collections by tax type, and taxable establishments, production, and income, FY91-92 and trends, biennial rpt, S4750–1.1

Nebraska insurance industry financial and underwriting data, by company and line of coverage, with regulatory info, 1992, annual rpt, S4890–1

Nebraska public service commission regulatory activities, with financial and operating data for individual railroads and telephone companies, FY91-92 biennial rpt, S4940–1

Nebraska revenues from licenses, fees, and miscellaneous taxes, 1991 and trends, annual rpt, S4950–1.3

New Hampshire financial condition, with revenues by source, expenditures by function or object, and fund balances, FY92 and trends, annual rpt, S5175–1

New Hampshire insurance industry financial data by company, 1991, with FY92 regulatory info, annual rpt, S5220–1

New Mexico tax revenues and disbursements, with data by tax type, county, and city, FY91-92 and trends, annual rpt, S5660–1

New York State tax collections by type, FY84-93, annual rpt, S5710–1

North Carolina financial condition, including revenues by source, expenditures by function, fund balances, and bonded debt, FY92, annual rpt, S5897–1

North Carolina public utility financial, operating, and regulatory data, by utility type and company, 1990 and trends, annual rpt, S5917–2

Oklahoma statistical abstract, general data, 1992 annual rpt, U8130–2.5, U8130–2.16

Oklahoma tax revenues by source, and distribution to local govts and State funds, FY92 and trends, annual rpt, S6495–1

Oregon banking regulatory section revenues and expenditures, 1992, annual rpt, S6616–1

Oregon financial condition, including revenues by source, expenditures by function, and fund statements, FY92, annual rpt, S6603–2

Pennsylvania insurance industry financial and underwriting data, by company and line of coverage, 1991, with FY92 regulatory info, annual rpt, S6835–1

Pennsylvania tax collections by tax type, with data by county and industry, FY92 and trends, annual rpt, S6885–1

Rhode Island financial condition, including revenues by source, expenditures by function, and fund balances, FY92 and trends, annual rpt, S6930–1

Rhode Island insurance industry financial and underwriting data, by company and line of coverage, 1990, with FY91 regulatory info, annual rpt, S6945–2

South Carolina county govt finances, including property value and tax assessments, by county, FY92, annual rpt, S7127–2

South Carolina insurance industry financial and underwriting data, by company, 1991, with FY92 regulatory info, annual rpt, S7195–1

South Carolina statistical abstract, general data, 1993 annual rpt, S7125–1.14

South Dakota insurance industry financial and underwriting data, by company and type of insurance, with regulatory info, 1991-92, annual rpt, S7300–2

South Dakota tax revenues by source, and aid distributed to local areas, FY92 annual rpt, S7380–1.1

Tennessee financial instns dept revenues and expenditures, FY92, annual rpt, S7507–1

Tennessee insurance industry financial and underwriting data, by company and type of insurance, with regulatory info, 1991, annual rpt, S7466–1

Tennessee public utility and transportation commission regulatory activities, with industry financial and operating data, 1991-92 biennial rpt, S7565–1

Tennessee tax revenues by source and apportionments to counties, cities, and funds, FY91-92 and trends, biennial rpt, S7570–1

Texas financial condition, including revenues by source, expenditures by function and dept, and investments, with data for over 400 individual funds, FY92, annual rpt, S7655–2

Texas insurance dept regulatory activities, with industry financial and underwriting data by line of coverage, FY92 annual rpt, S7700–1

Utah financial instns dept regulatory fee receipts, by type of instn, FY93, annual rpt, S7830–1

Utah insurance industry financial and underwriting data, by company and line of coverage, with regulatory info, 1991, annual rpt, S7845–1

Utah statistical abstract, general data, 1993 triennial rpt, U8960–1.17

Utah tax revenues by source, and distribution to localities and State funds, FY92 and trends, annual rpt, S7905–1

Vermont financial instns, financial condition by instn, and Banking Div receipts, FY91-92, annual rpt, S7995–2

License taxes and fees

Vermont insurance dept receipts and disbursements, FY91-92, annual rpt, S7995–1

Washington State revenues by source, and distributions by tax and locality, FY92 and trends, annual rpt, S8415–1.1

West Virginia insurance industry financial and underwriting data, by company and line of coverage, with regulatory info, 1991, annual rpt, S8575–1

Wisconsin Blue Book, general data, 1993-94 biennial rpt, S8780–1.2

Wisconsin financial condition, including revenues by source, expenditures by function and object, and fund balances, FY93, annual rpt, S8675–2

Wisconsin insurance industry financial and underwriting data, by company and line of coverage, with regulatory info, 1992, annual rpt, S8755–1

Licensed products see Trademarks

Licenses and permits

- Aviation certificates issued and held, by certificate type, 1993 annual rpt, A5120–2
- Broadcasting stations on the air and authorized by type, weekly rpt, C1850–14
- Mexico motor carrier operating permits granted to established, informal, and new operators, 1989-92, U8850–9
- Nuclear reactor licensing, construction, and operating status, by unit and utility, 1992, annual rpt, B6800–2.2
- Oil and gas well permit applications, for 6 Southwestern States, monthly 1983-91, annual compilation, C6985–9.1
- Transportation regulatory agency policies and practices for motor carriers and railroads, by agency, 1991/92 annual rpt, A7015–4
- TV station broadcast license renewal requests, and number challenged by competing applicants, since Oct 1991, 1993 feature, C1850–14.518
- Utility regulatory agency policies and practices, and industry financial and operating data, by utility type and agency, 1991/92 annual rpt, A7015–3

State and local:

- Alabama public health dept activities, including services provided, inspection and licensing activity, staff and finances, and vital statistics and health data, 1992 annual rpt, S0175–3
- Alaska insurance industry underwriting and investment data, by company and type of insurance, with regulatory info, 1991 and trends, annual rpt, S0280–3
- California insurance industry financial and underwriting data, by company and type of insurance, with regulatory info, 1991, annual rpt, S0900–1
- California licensed financial instns, by type, 1987-92, annual rpt, S0810–1
- California public utility and transportation regulatory data, including revenue requests and rates of return by company, FY92 annual rpt, S0930–1
- California sales/use tax collections and permits, and tax revenue distributions to localities, FY92 and trends, annual rpt, S0835–1.3

Florida statistical abstract, general data, 1992 annual rpt, U6660–1.2

- Georgia marriage licenses and pistol licenses issued, by county, FY92, annual rpt, S1903–1
- Hawaii data book, general data, 1992 annual rpt, S2090–1.7, S2090–1.21
- Hawaii environmental quality and public health control, inspection, licensing, and enforcement activities, 1990, annual rpt, S2065–1.6
- Idaho insurance industry financial and underwriting data, by company and type of insurance, with regulatory data, 1991, annual rpt, S2260–1
- Illinois Financial Institutions Dept activities, with financial and regulatory data for credit unions, consumer lenders, and other businesses, FY91 annual rpt, S2457–2
- Kentucky financial instns condition, including assets by instn and city, with regulatory info, 1992 and trends, annual rpt, S3121–1
- Maryland insurance industry financial and underwriting data, by company and type of insurance, with regulatory info, 1991, annual rpt, S3655–1
- Michigan insurance industry financial and underwriting data, by company and type of insurance, with regulatory info, 1991, annual rpt, S3983–1
- Missouri licensed day care homes and centers, and capacity, June 1992, annual rpt, S4575–2
- Nebraska insurance agent licensing activity, 1992, annual rpt, S4890–1
- Nebraska public service commission regulatory activities, with financial and operating data for individual railroads and telephone companies, FY91-92 biennial rpt, S4940–1
- Nebraska State constitutional amendment on local control of liquor licensing, election results by county, Nov 1992, biennial rpt, S4955–1
- New Hampshire insurance industry financial data by company, 1991, with FY92 regulatory info, annual rpt, S5220–1
- New Jersey casino revenues and operations for 12 facilities, with State regulatory activities, 1992 and trends, annual rpt, S5360–1
- New York State insurance industry devs, finances, and regulatory activity, 1990/91 and trends, annual rpt, S5770–3
- New York State motorboat and snowmobile registrations, by county, 1991, annual rpt, S5790–1
- New York State security equipment dealer views on licensing law and criminal background checks for industry personnel, Aug 1992 survey, article, C1850–13.501
- New York State statistical yearbook, general data, 1992 annual rpt, U5100–1.5, U5100–1.8
- North Carolina motor passenger carriers franchised, by company and scope of operation, Dec 1990, annual rpt, S5917–2
- Oklahoma insurance agent, broker, bail bond, and company licensing activity, 1992, annual rpt, S6462–1
- Oregon securities regulatory section licensing activity, 1992, annual rpt, S6616–1

Index by Subjects and Names

- Pennsylvania statistical abstract, general data, 1992 recurring rpt, U4130–6.8
- Rhode Island insurance industry financial and underwriting data, by company and line of coverage, 1990, with FY91 regulatory info, annual rpt, S6945–2
- South Carolina coin-operated device license sales, FY92, annual rpt, S7255–1.2
- South Carolina insurance agent licensing and exams, FY92, annual rpt, S7195–1
- South Carolina motor carrier certification and licensing activity, FY92, annual rpt, S7235–1
- South Dakota insurance industry financial and underwriting data, by company and type of insurance, with regulatory info, 1991-92, annual rpt, S7300–2
- Tennessee financial instn State charters and licensees, by type, 1992 annual rpt, S7507–1
- Texas insurance dept regulatory activities, with industry financial and underwriting data by line of coverage, FY92 annual rpt, S7700–1
- Texas licensing and regulation of child care facilities, FY92 annual rpt, S7695–1
- Utah insurance industry financial and underwriting data, by company and line of coverage, with regulatory info, 1991, annual rpt, S7845–1
- Vermont agricultural production, marketing, and finances, by commodity, with data on govt inspections and funding, 1989-90 biennial rpt, S7978–1
- West Virginia insurance agent licensing and examination activity, with testing results for individual pre-licensing schools, 1990-91, annual rpt, S8575–1
- Wisconsin Blue Book, general data, 1993-94 biennial rpt, S8780–1.2
- Wisconsin consumer credit company licensing and regulatory activity, 1992 and trends, annual rpt, S8685–1

see also Alcoholic beverages licenses and fees

see also Building permits

see also Drivers licenses

see also Franchises

see also Hunting and fishing licenses

see also License taxes and fees

see also Motor vehicle registrations

see also Occupational testing and certification

see also Severance taxes

Life care communities see Retirement communities

Life expectancy

- Black American health and vital statistics data, with comparisons to whites, 1970s-91, annual compilation, C6775–2.2
- Black American socioeconomic status, with comparisons to whites and data by region, 1960s-92, annual compilation, A8510–1.1
- Death rates and life expectancy, by age, race, and sex, 1900-92, annual article, B6045–1.504
- Developing countries family planning efforts, with data on socioeconomic and health conditions compared to developed countries, by country, 1980s-90, R8720–1.1
- Expectation of life at birth, by sex and race, decennially 1960-90, annual fact book, A1275–1.5

Index by Subjects and Names — Life insurance

Expectation of life at birth, by sex and race, 1980-89, annual rpt, A5173–2.4

Expectation of life at birth, 1900-91, and at selected ages, 1988-91, by race and/or sex, biennial fact book, A1325–1.6

Health status effect on life expectancy for persons age 55/over, 1984-90, R8750–1.507

Japan and US health care system data, including expenditures, facilities, insurance coverage, and population health indicators, 1993 article, R5650–2.515

Latin America statistical abstract, general data by country, 1992 annual rpt, U6250–1.6

State social, economic, and govtl indicators, with rankings, 1993 semiannual rpt, B8500–1.9

Statistical profiles of 50 States and DC, general data, 1993 annual almanac, C4712–1

World population and health indicators, with detail by region and country, 1992/93 biennial rpt, R9455–1.5

World population size and characteristics, GNP, and land area, by region and/or country, 1993 annual data sheet, R8750–5

World vital statistics, for top 50 countries in births, deaths, infant mortality, and life expectancy, 1992, semiannual rpt, B8500–1.16

State and local:

California life expectancy at birth and age 65, by sex, 1919-90, annual rpt, S0865–1

Colorado life expectancy by race-ethnicity, age, and sex, with years of potential life lost by cause of death, 1990, annual rpt, S1010–1

Florida life expectancy, by race and sex, 1919-92, annual rpt, S1745–3

Hawaii data book, general data, 1992 annual rpt, S2090–1.2

Maine causes of death resulting in most years of potential life lost, by sex, 1991, annual rpt, S3460–2

Michigan resident life expectancy at birth, by sex and race, 1990 and trends, annual rpt, S4000–3

Missouri life expectancy tables, by sex, 1992, annual rpt, S4518–1

New Mexico life expectancy, by age, sex, and race-ethnicity, 1989-91, annual rpt, S5605–1.3

Oklahoma survival ratios, by sex and age group, 1980-2010, recurring rpt, S6416–1

South Carolina statistical abstract, general data, 1993 annual rpt, S7125–1.16

Texas life expectancy by sex and race-ethnicity, 1991 and trends, annual rpt, S7685–1

Texas survival rates, by age, sex, and race-ethnicity, 1989/90, recurring rpt, S7645–3

Washington State life expectancy, by age, 1991, annual rpt, S8363–1

Wyoming causes of death resulting in most years of potential life lost, 1991, annual rpt, S8920–2

Life insurance

Asset allocation and investment yields for top 125 US and Canadian life/health insurance companies, 1992 and trends, annual article, C1050–2.512

Association executives compensation, by position, assn type, and census div, with personnel practices and benefit provisions, 1992, biennial rpt, A2900–3

Canada life insurance individual policy sales indicators, monthly rpt, A6225–2

Capital/surplus of top 100 life/health insurers, 1987-91, annual article, C1050–2.504

Capital/surplus of top 100 life/health insurers, 1988-92, annual article, C1050–2.512

Charitable remainder trust promotion by life insurance companies, 1991-93, article, C2176–1.518

Company formations, retirements, mergers, and name changes, by company, 1992 and trends, annual article, C1050–2.506

Corporate performance ratings by executives for leading companies in 32 industries, 1993 annual survey feature, C8900–1.508

Credit life insurance policies in force and issued, for top 100 companies, 1991, annual article, C1050–2.504

Dividends and premiums for average life policies, 10-year dividend scale comparisons, by insurer, 1993 annual article, C1050–2.510

Dividends and premiums for average life policies, 20-year dividend scale comparisons, by insurer, 1993 annual article, C1050–2.509

Employee benefit payments and employer cost/payroll ratios, by industry, detailed type of benefit, and firm size, 1991, annual rpt, A3840–1

Flexible-premium retirement annuity policy 5-year performance, by company, 1988-92, annual article, C1050–2.507

Fortune magazine ranking of top 50-100 companies in 8 nonindustrial sectors, with financial and employment data, 1992, annual feature, C8900–1.516

Fortune magazine ranking of top 50-100 companies worldwide in 8 nonindustrial sectors, with financial and employment data, 1993 annual feature, C8900–1.522

Higher education instn employee retirement and insurance benefits, prevalence and expenditures, by type of instn and region, 1991, biennial survey, A9025–3

Income and expense data for top 100 life/health insurance companies, 1992, annual article, C1050–2.511

Marketing trends and devs, and mgmt and finance topics, for life and health insurance, monthly rpt, C1050–2

Operating and financial composite ratios for corporations, with establishments and receipts, for approx 200 industries, by asset size, FY90, annual rpt, C7800–1

Policy average size issued and in force, for 150 companies, 1981 and 1987-91, annual article, C1050–2.502

Policy lapse ratios, for 150 companies, 1987-91, annual article, C1050–2.502

Policy purchases and ownership, payments, and company operations, life insurance industry fact book, 1991 and trends, biennial rpt, A1325–1

Premium income and deposits for variable annuity funds of top life/health insurers, 1991, annual article, C1050–2.503

Premium income and fund deposits from annuities, for top 200 insurers, 1991, annual article, C1050–2.501

Premium income of top 500 US/Canadian life/health insurers, 1992 and trends, annual article, C1050–2.509

Premium income/deposits for variable annuity and variable life funds of top life/health insurers, 1992, annual article, C1050–2.512

Sales and insurance in force, for top 25-135 issuers of ordinary, group, and industrial life policies, 1992, annual article, C1050–2.510

Sales indicators for individual life insurance policies, monthly rpt, A6225–1

Sales, policies in force, and assets, for top 100 US/Canadian life/health insurance companies, 1992, annual article, C1050–2.509

Single-premium deferred annuity policy comparisons, by company, 1992 annual article, C1050–2.501

Single-premium deferred annuity policy 5-year performance, by company, 1987-91, annual article, C1050–2.501

Universal life insurance policy 5-year performance, by company, 1988-92, annual article, C1050–2.511

Universal, whole, and term life insurance sales results, for 115 companies, 1992, annual article, C1050–2.511

Widow quality of life indicators for survivors of older men surveyed in 1966, including insurance benefits, by race, 1990 survey, U3780–9

State and local:

Alabama insurance industry financial and underwriting data, by company and line of coverage, 1991, annual rpt, S0160–1

Alaska insurance industry underwriting and investment data, by company and type of insurance, with regulatory info, 1991 and trends, annual rpt, S0280–3

Arizona insurance industry financial and underwriting data, by company and type of insurance, with regulatory info, 1992, annual rpt, S0483–1

Arizona statistical abstract, general data, 1993 recurring rpt, U5850–2.23

California insurance industry financial and underwriting data, by company and type of insurance, with regulatory info, 1991, annual rpt, S0900–1

Connecticut insurance industry financial and underwriting data, by company and type of insurance, 1991, annual rpt, S1222–1

Connecticut savings bank life insurance issuances, by instn, 1991, annual rpt, S1160–1

Florida insurance industry financial and underwriting data, by company and line of coverage, 1991, annual rpt, S1760–1

Georgia statistical abstract, general data, 1992-93 biennial rpt, U6730–1.9

Hawaii data book, general data, 1992 annual rpt, S2090–1.15

Idaho insurance industry financial and underwriting data, by company and type of insurance, with regulatory data, 1991, annual rpt, S2260–1

Iowa insurance industry financial and underwriting data, by company and type of insurance, 1992, annual rpt, S2760–1

Kansas insurance industry financial and underwriting data, by company and type of insurance, with regulatory info, 1992, annual rpt, S2990–1

Life insurance

Kansas statistical abstract, general data, 1991/92 annual rpt, U7095–2.10
Maryland insurance industry financial and underwriting data, by company and type of insurance, with regulatory info, 1991, annual rpt, S3655–1
Maryland statistical abstract, general data, 1993-94 biennial rpt, S3605–1.8
Michigan insurance industry financial and underwriting data, by company and type of insurance, with regulatory info, 1991, annual rpt, S3983–1
Minnesota insurance industry financial and underwriting data, by company and line of coverage, 1991, annual rpt, S4140–4
Mississippi statistical abstract, general data, 1992 annual rpt, U3255–4.8
Missouri insurance industry financial and underwriting data, by company and type of insurance, with regulatory info, 1992, annual rpt, S4527–1
Nebraska insurance industry financial and underwriting data, by company and line of coverage, with regulatory info, 1992, annual rpt, S4890–1
New Hampshire insurance industry financial data by company, 1991, with FY92 regulatory info, annual rpt, S5220–1
New Jersey insurance industry financial and underwriting data, by company and type of insurance, 1990, annual rpt, S5420–1
New York State insurance industry devs, finances, and regulatory activity, 1990/91 and trends, annual rpt, S5770–3
New York State insurance industry financial and underwriting data, by company and line of coverage, 1991, annual rpt, S5770–2
Oklahoma insurance industry financial and underwriting data, by company and type of insurance, with regulatory info, 1992, annual rpt, S6462–1
Oklahoma statistical abstract, general data, 1992 annual rpt, U8130–2.20
Pennsylvania insurance industry financial and underwriting data, by company and line of coverage, 1991, with FY92 regulatory info, annual rpt, S6835–1
Rhode Island insurance industry financial and underwriting data, by company and line of coverage, 1990, with FY91 regulatory info, annual rpt, S6945–2
South Carolina insurance industry financial and underwriting data, by company, 1991, with FY92 regulatory info, annual rpt, S7195–1
South Dakota insurance industry financial and underwriting data, by company and type of insurance, with regulatory info, 1991-92, annual rpt, S7300–2
Tennessee insurance industry financial and underwriting data, by company and type of insurance, with regulatory info, 1991, annual rpt, S7466–1
Texas insurance dept regulatory activities, with industry financial and underwriting data by line of coverage, FY92 annual rpt, S7700–1
Utah insurance industry financial and underwriting data, by company and line of coverage, with regulatory info, 1991, annual rpt, S7845–1
Utah statistical abstract, general data, 1993 triennial rpt, U8960–1.15

Vermont insurance industry financial and underwriting data, by company and type of insurance, 1991, annual rpt, S7995–1
West Virginia insurance industry financial and underwriting data, by company and line of coverage, with regulatory info, 1991, annual rpt, S8575–1
Wisconsin insurance industry financial and underwriting data, by company and line of coverage, with regulatory info, 1992, annual rpt, S8755–1
see also Old-Age, Survivors, Disability, and Health Insurance
see also Servicepersons life insurance programs

Light
see also Fiber optics
see also Lasers

Light bulbs
see Household supplies and utensils

Lighthouses and lightships
State and local:
Hawaii data book, general data, 1992 annual rpt, S2090–1.18

Lighting equipment
see Electrical machinery and equipment
see Household appliances and equipment

Lima, Peru
Women's contraceptive use in experimental program providing in-hospital family planning services for postpartum women, 1988/89 study, article, A5160–6.503

Lime
see Fertilizers
see Nonmetallic minerals and mines

Lincoln, Nebr.
Employment, hours, and earnings, by selected industry group and locality, quarterly rpt, S4895–2

Linden, Fabian
"Availability of a Quality Work Force", R4105–78.21
"Consumer Confidence Survey", R4105–4
"Special Consumer Survey Reports", R4105–81

Lindgren, John II., Jr.
"1993 Home Lending Survey for Year End 1992", A4160–3

Lindquist, Victor R.
"Northwestern Lindquist-Endicott Report, 1993: A National Survey of 258 Well-Known Business and Industrial Organizations", U3730–1

Linens
see Household supplies and utensils

LINK Resources Corp.
Computer (personal) and modem ownership by households, selected years 1982-96, article, A8605–1.509
Home-based workers, by type, 1988-95, article, C4687–1.502

Lipper Analytical Services Inc.
Mutual fund assets and investment return, for 5 funds and their namesake "clones," 1993 article, C3950–1.521
Mutual fund assets and returns, for 10 major foreign-based funds, 1992 article, C3950–1.502
Mutual fund investment returns and assets, for 50 funds selected on basis of long-term performance, 1993 annual article, C4215–1.505
Mutual funds investing in State and natl municipal bonds, and assets, 1991-92, article, C8900–1.509

Index by Subjects and Names

Liquefied natural gas
see Natural gas and gas industry

Liquefied petroleum gas
Financial ratios and performance, for over 350 SIC 4-digit industries, FY88-92, annual rpt, A6400–3
Fuel oil dealer sales by product, employment, computer use, and truck fleet size, by region, 1992 annual survey, C4680–2.1
Imports of LPG, by PAD district, weekly rpt, A2575–1
Japan energy supply-demand and outlook, by fuel source, 1980s-2000, recurring article, R5650–2.536
Latin America statistical abstract, general data by country, 1992 annual rpt, U6250–1.23
Natural gas processing plant capacity and production by product, by country, State, and Canadian Province, Jan 1992, annual rpt, C6985–3.5
Operating and financial detailed data, for natural gas industry, by State and census div, 1960s-91, annual rpt, A1775–3
Russia, Tyumen region gas processing by plant, and liquefied petroleum gas production and demand, 1993 article, C6985–1.540
Sourcebook of oil and gas industry operations and finances, and world supply-demand situation, 1970s-91, annual compilation, C6985–9
Statistical compilation of oil and gas industry trends, 1993 annual rpt, C6985–4
Supply-demand, marketing, prices, finances, and employment, detailed data for US and Canada, by product, company, and location, 1993 annual fact book, C4680–1.507
Supply-demand, trade, and industry exploration and operations, by product, exporting country and world area, PAD district, and State, 1993 annual feature, C6985–1.513
State and local:
California fuel distributors sales volume and taxes assessed, by fuel type and company, FY92 and trends, annual rpt, S0835–1.4
Hawaii data book, general data, 1992 annual rpt, S2090–1.17
Hawaii fuel consumed and fuel taxes allocated, by type and use, FY91-92, annual rpt, S2120–1
Mississippi consumption of motor fuel and liquefied compressed gas on hwys, and taxes collected, monthly FY92, annual rpt, S4435–1
New York State statistical yearbook, general data, 1992 annual rpt, U5100–1.12
Pennsylvania energy supply-demand and prices by fuel type, with electric power info by utility, 1960s-90, recurring rpt, S6810–3

Liquidations
see Business failures and closings

Liquor and liquor industry
Beverage consumption and sales, by type, leading company, and brand, 1992 and trends, annual rpt, C4775–2.3
Convenience stores selling alcoholic beverages and lottery tickets, by company size, 1993, annual article, C4680–1.510

Index by Subjects and Names

Distilled spirits consumption, trade, and sales volume or shipments, by product type and State, 1991 and trends, annual rpt, A4650–3

Financial ratios and performance, for over 350 SIC 4-digit industries, FY88-92, annual rpt, A6400–3

Govt revenues, State and local, from liquor stores, 1993 annual rpt, R9050–1

Market statistics, including sales, consumption, trade, distillery operations, and govtl info, with data by company, brand, and location, 1992 and trends, annual rpt, C4775–1

Operating and financial composite ratios for corporations, with establishments and receipts, for approx 200 industries, by asset size, FY90, annual rpt, C7800–1

Production, consumption, stocks, trade, and prices for approx 100 basic commodities, including by country and producing State, commodity yearbook for 1993, C2400–1, C2400–2

Retail prices for selected consumer items in approx 300 cities, quarterly rpt, A0150–1

Sales and consumer expenditures, for food store products by type, 1991-92, annual feature, C4655–1.510

Sales, consumption, and marketing devs for beverage industry, monthly rpt, C0125–2

Sales for top 35 brands, 1990-91, annual rpt, C0125–3.1

Sales for top 36 brands, 1991-92, annual article, C2710–1.513

Shipments and per capita consumption of alcoholic beverages, by type, census div, and State, 1981-91, annual rpt, A3455–1.4

Shopping center financial and operating data, with detail by type of tenant, US and Canada, 1991, triennial rpt, R9285–1

State and local:

Pennsylvania State-owned liquor store fund finances, FY92, annual rpt, S6810–4

Texas trade, transportation, and public utilities employment, by SIC 2- and 3-digit industry and detailed occupation, 2nd qtr 1991, triennial survey rpt, S7675–1.31

see also Alcohol abuse and treatment

see also Alcohol use

see also Alcoholic beverages licenses and fees

see also Beer and breweries

see also Wine and winemaking

Literacy and illiteracy

Developing countries family planning efforts, with data on socioeconomic and health conditions compared to developed countries, by country, 1980s-90, R8720–1.1

Grants awarded by Natl Institute for Literacy, with amount and recipient, 1992, annual compilation, C1650–3.1

Hard goods manufacturers opinions on need for Federal action on student competence and worker literacy, 1993 annual survey rpt, A1800–1

Jail literacy programs and participants, for 90 local systems, 1992 annual rpt, R4300–1.4

Latin America statistical abstract, general data by country, 1992 annual rpt, U6250–1.8

Library grants from Fed Govt for literacy programs, by instn and State, FY92, annual compilation, C1650–3.2

Middle East population trend and demographic characteristics, by country, 1993 rpt, R8750–2.59

State economic dev condition indicators, including economic performance, business vitality, growth capacity, and tax/fiscal system, by State, 1993 annual rpt, R4225–1.1

State social, economic, and govtl indicators, with rankings, 1993 semiannual rpt, B8500–1

World adult literacy rates, by sex and country, 1970 and 1990, biennial rpt, R9455–1.5

State and local:

California public library expenditures on literacy programs, by instn, FY92, annual rpt, S0825–2

Georgia prison inmate participation in educational programs, by type, June 1992, annual rpt, S1872–1

Hawaii data book, general data, 1992 annual rpt, S2090–1.3

Mississippi public schools student assessment and functional literacy test result trends, 1988-92, annual rpt, S4340–1

New York State local jail/penitentiary inmates by literacy status, by sex and county or facility, 1991, annual rpt, S5724–2

Literature

see Books and bookselling

see Language arts

Lithuania

Nuclear reactors in operation, with capacity, electricity generation, and construction, by unit and country, 1992, annual rpt, B6800–2.2

Public opinion in Russia, Ukraine, and Lithuania on political and economic issues and devs, 1991-92 surveys, C8915–10

Public opinion in 9 European countries and 3 Soviet Union Republics on political, economic, and social issues, 1991 survey, C8915–8

Litter

see Refuse and refuse disposal

Liver diseases

see Digestive diseases

Livestock and livestock industry

Calf deaths and related costs, by disease, 1987/88 Colorado study, article, A3100–2.518

Drugs (nonsteroidal anti-inflammatory) use in cattle, 1992 article, A3100–2.504

Ethiopia famine analysis, including livestock inventories and sales in affected areas, 1980s, R5620–1.36

Exports of farm products, by detailed commodity and country of destination, US and California, 1991, annual rpt, B9520–1

Feedlots and beef cattle operations, financial statements and performance ratios, FY88-92, annual rpt, A6400–3

Latin America statistical abstract, general data by country, 1992 annual rpt, U6250–1.24

Production, consumption, stocks, trade, and prices for approx 100 basic commodities, including by country and producing State, commodity yearbook for 1993, C2400–1, C2400–2

Soviet Union livestock inventories, monthly rpt recurring feature, U2030–1.503

Supply-demand of meat and poultry, and livestock and packing industries finances and operations, 1991 and trends, annual rpt, A2100–1

Swine breeding stock porcine stress syndrome mutation prevalence by breed, in US, Canada, and UK, 1993 article, A3100–2.520

Veterinary caseloads, including farms served and animals per farm, by livestock and practice type, 1991, survey article, A3100–2.518

World livestock population by species, by country, 1978-90, biennial rpt, R9455–1.6

State and local:

Alabama agricultural production, marketing, and income, by county and/or commodity, and farms and acreage, 1992 and trends, annual rpt, S0090–1

Alaska agricultural production and marketing, by district and commodity, 1960s-92, annual rpt, U5750–1

Arizona agricultural production, marketing, and finances, by commodity and county, 1988-92, annual rpt, U5830–1

Arkansas agricultural production, marketing, and finances, by commodity and county, with farms and acreage, 1992 and trends, annual rpt, U5920–1

California livestock production and marketing, with comparisons to US, 1983-92, annual rpt, S0850–1.2

Colorado agricultural production, marketing, and finances, by commodity and/or county, with farms and acreage, 1992 and trends, annual rpt, S0985–1

Georgia agricultural production, marketing, and finances, by commodity and/or county, and farms and acreage, 1991 and trends, annual rpt, S1855–1

Hawaii agricultural production and marketing, by commodity and island, 1987-91, annual rpt, S2030–1

Hawaii counties population and economic indicators, 1993 annual rpt series, B3500–2

Illinois agricultural production, marketing, and finances, by county or commodity, and farms and farmland, 1991 and trends, annual rpt, S2390–1

Kansas agricultural production, marketing, and finances, by county and/or commodity, and farm acreage and value, 1992 and trends, annual rpt, S2915–1

Kentucky agricultural production, marketing, and finances, by commodity and county; and farms, acreage, and value; 1992 and trends, annual rpt, S3085–1

Louisiana agricultural production, marketing, and finances, by commodity or parish, 1985-91, annual rpt, U2740–1

Michigan agricultural production, marketing, and finances, by commodity or county, 1987-91, annual rpt, S3950–1

Minnesota agricultural production, marketing, and finances, by county or commodity, and farms and acreage, 1992 and trends, annual rpt, S4130–1

Missouri agricultural production, marketing, and finances, by commodity and/or county, and farms and acreage, 1988-92, annual rpt, S4480–1

Livestock and livestock industry

Montana agricultural production, marketing, and finances, by commodity and county, 1991 and trends, annual rpt, S4655–1

Montana property values, by detailed property class and type, with land acreage by use, by county, 1991-92 and trends, biennial rpt, S4750–1.2

Nebraska agricultural production, marketing, and finances, by commodity and/or county, and farms and land, 1991 and trends, annual rpt, S4835–1

Nevada agricultural production, marketing, and finances, by county and commodity, and farms and acreage, 1992 and trends, annual rpt, S5010–1

New Jersey agricultural production, marketing, and finances, by commodity and/or county, and farms and acreage, 1986-91, annual rpt, S5350–1

New Mexico agricultural production, marketing, and finances, by commodity and county, with farms and acreage, 1991 and trends, annual rpt, S5530–1

New York State agricultural production, marketing, and finances, by commodity and/or county, and farms and acreage, 1992 and trends, annual rpt, S5700–1

North Carolina agricultural production, marketing, and finances, by commodity and county, 1991 and trends, annual rpt, S5885–1

North Dakota agricultural production and marketing, by commodity and county, and farm finances, 1992 and trends, annual rpt, U3600–1

Ohio agricultural production, marketing, and finances, by commodity and county, with farms and acreage, 1990-91 and trends, annual rpt, S6240–1

Oklahoma agricultural production, marketing, and finances, by commodity and county, 1992 and trends, annual rpt, S6405–1

Oregon agricultural production, marketing, and finances, by commodity and/or county, with farms and acreage, 1991 and trends, annual rpt, S6575–1

Pennsylvania agricultural production, marketing, and finances, by county and commodity, and farms and acreage, 1992 and trends, annual rpt, S6760–1

South Carolina agricultural production and finances, by commodity and county, 1991-92 and trends, annual rpt, U1075–3

South Carolina economic condition, including agriculture, finance, and govt financial data, 1970s-92, annual rpt, S7125–3.1

South Dakota agricultural prices received by farmers, by commodity, quarterly rpt, U8595–1

South Dakota agricultural production, marketing, and finances, by commodity and county, and farms and acreage, 1992 and trends, annual rpt, S7280–1

Tennessee agricultural production and marketing, by commodity and county, with farms, acreage, and farm value, 1992 and trends, annual rpt, S7460–1

Texas agricultural production, marketing, and finances, by commodity and county, and farms and farmland, 1991 and trends, annual rpt series, S7630–1

Utah agricultural production, marketing, and finances, by commodity and county, with farms and acreage, 1992 and trends, annual rpt, S7800–1

Vermont agricultural production, marketing, and finances, by commodity, with data on govt inspections and funding, 1989-90 biennial rpt, S7978–1

Washington State agricultural production, marketing, and finances, by commodity and/or county, 1992 and trends, annual rpt, S8328–1

West Virginia agricultural production, marketing, and finances, by commodity or county, 1991 and trends, annual rpt, S8510–1

Wisconsin agricultural production, marketing, and finances, by commodity and county, and farms, acreage, and sales, 1992 and trends, annual rpt, S8680–1

Wyoming agricultural production, marketing, and finances, by county and/or commodity, and farms, acreage, and value, 1992 and trends, annual rpt, S8860–1

see also Animal diseases and zoonoses

see also Animal feed

see also Dairy industry and products

see also Food and waterborne diseases

see also Hides and skins

see also Meat and meat products

see also Poultry industry and products

see also Veterinary medicine

Living arrangements

Black children and youth population, economic, health, and education data, with comparisons to whites, 1993 rpt, R3840–21

Children of incarcerated mothers, by type of primary caregiver, 1991/92, A7575–4

Children's living arrangements, by parents characteristics and child age and race-ethnicity, 1992, article, B6045–1.504

Children's living arrangements, by parents characteristics and child race-ethnicity, 1991, article, B6045–1.503

Children's living arrangements, by race-ethnicity, decennially 1960-90, B6045–1.502

Children's living arrangements, by race, 1991, article, A8510–1.1

Developing countries urban population, and share living in informal settlements, for 13 cities, 1993 rpt, A5800–1.1

Disabled persons use of home care services, with costs, payment sources, and types of care, by selected characteristics, 1992, R4865–15

Population age 20-24 living arrangements, 1991, article, R8750–1.501

Solitary living population, by age and sex, 1990, 1995, and 2000, article, C4655–1.506

Women's housing issues, with data on household composition, tenure, and characteristics, 1992, A8657–5

State and local:

Nebraska living arrangements of children receiving State-financed social services, FY91-92, annual rpt, S4957–1.1

New York State SSI recipients by eligibility category and living arrangements, 1991, annual rpt, S5800–2.3

New York State statistical yearbook, general data, 1992 annual rpt, U5100–1.1

Oregon adolescent suicide attempts, by age and living arrangement, 1991, annual rpt, S6615–5

West Virginia child welfare recipient living arrangements, by State area, monthly rpt, S8560–2

Wisconsin juvenile correctional instn inmate living arrangements upon release, FY92, annual rpt, S7296–1

see also Families and households

see also Foster home care

see also Group quarters

see also Homeless population

see also Housing condition and occupancy

see also Retirement communities

see also Rooming and boarding houses

see also Transient housing

Living standard

see Cost of living

see Family budgets

see Personal and household income

see Quality of life

Loan companies

see Finance companies

Loan delinquency and default

Auto lending and leasing operations of financial instns, 1992 and trends, annual rpt, A4160–2

Bank assets, share of nonperforming loans, and stock performance, for 10 major instns, 1993 article, C3950–1.526

Bank consumer loans, delinquency rates for approx 10 types of loans, and repossession data, by State, quarterly rpt, A0950–1

Bank financial performance, including assets, loans, deposits, and operating ratios, top 100 instns, 1992, annual feature, C5800–7.526

Bank noncurrent loans/leases, and losses, by type of loan, asset size, and metro status, 1992, semiannual rpt, A6400–4

Bank small business lending and services, with data on organizational structure, loan delinquencies, and community dev activities, Nov 1992 survey, annual rpt, A4160–5

Boat loan vs overall delinquency rate, 1991, annual feature, C2425–4

Collection efficiency indicators for delinquent loans, for automated vs manual systems, 1993 article, A6400–2.505

Finance company financial and operating ratios, and loan activity, Dec 1988-92, annual article, A6400–2.506

Higher education student Federal loan default rates, by State, and for top 50 lenders and top 10 guarantee agencies, 1991, article, C2175–1.532

Home equity lending activity and practices of financial instns, by region, asset size, and instn type, 1992, annual rpt, A4160–3

Mobile/manufactured home loan delinquency rates and repossessions, monthly rpt, A6325–1

Mortgage (commercial) delinquency and foreclosure rates, quarterly 1991-92, article, A6450–2.506

Mortgage delinquency and foreclosure rates, and residential loans serviced, by type, State, and census div and region, quarterly rpt, A6450–1

Mortgages held by life/health insurance companies, by loan performance status, 1991-92, article, C1050–2.508

Student federally guaranteed loan default rates, with detail for proprietary school students, 1988-91, article, C2175–1.528

Index by Subjects and Names

Loans

State and local:

California financial instn delinquent loans, charge-offs, and recoveries, by loan type, 1988-92, annual rpt, S0810–1

Idaho banks and other financial instns, financial condition, with data by instn and loan activity analysis, FY92 or 1991, annual rpt, S2235–1

Illinois Financial Institutions Dept activities, with financial and regulatory data for credit unions, consumer lenders, and other businesses, FY91 annual rpt, S2457–2

Iowa small loan companies composite financial data, loan and licensing activity, and legal actions, 1991, annual rpt, S2760–2

Maine bank loans outstanding, and overdue loans as percent of total, 1988-91, annual rpt, S3473–2

South Carolina consumer finance company aggregate finances and loan activity, and legal actions, 1991 and trends, annual rpt, S7165–1

South Dakota student loan default rates, by public instn, FY92, annual rpt, S7375–1

Texas student loan program accounts by status, FY92, annual rpt, S7657–1.3

Vermont and US student Stafford loan default rates, FY87-92, annual rpt, S8035–2.3

Virginia finance companies delinquent accounts, by instn type, Dec 1992, annual rpt, S8180–3

see also Foreclosures

Loans

Bank financial performance, including assets, loans, deposits, and operating ratios, top 100 instns, 1992, annual feature, C5800–7.526

Black-owned enterprises financial and operating data, for top 100 firms and auto dealerships and for top 15-25 financial instns, 1992 and trends, annual feature, C4215–1.507

Forecasts of natl income and product account components, employment, and financial sector activity, monthly rpt, B4950–1

Fortune magazine ranking of top 50-100 companies in 8 nonindustrial sectors, with financial and employment data, 1992, annual feature, C8900–1.516

Fortune magazine ranking of top 50-100 companies worldwide in 8 nonindustrial sectors, with financial and employment data, 1993 annual feature, C8900–1.522

Insurance (life/health) industry asset allocation and investment yields, for top 125 US and Canadian companies, 1992 and trends, annual article, C1050–2.512

Land acquisition, dev, and construction loan-to-value ratios, 1989 and 1992, article, C4300–1.501

Life insurance company policyholder loans, 1890-1991, biennial fact book, A1325–1.4

Money and securities market activity, and related indicators, biweekly rpt, B2000–1

State economic dev condition indicators, including economic performance, business vitality, growth capacity, and tax/fiscal system, by State, 1993 annual rpt, R4225–1.1

State and local:

Alabama small loan and consumer credit licensee finances and loan analysis, Dec 1991, annual rpt, S0110–1

Arizona bank balance sheets and branches, individual State and natl instns, quarterly rpt, S0460–2

Arizona statistical abstract, general data, 1993 recurring rpt, U5850–2.15

Arkansas banks and other financial instns, financial condition by instn, June 1992, annual rpt, S0632–1

California banks and trust companies, financial condition by instn, with regulatory info, Dec 1992, annual rpt, S0810–1

California economic condition, including population, employment and earnings, income, business activity, and taxation, 1960s-92, annual rpt, S0840–3.2

Colorado banks and trust companies, financial condition by instn, 1992, annual rpt, S1070–2

Colorado savings and loan assn and credit union financial condition, 1992 and trends, annual rpt, S1070–3

Connecticut banks and other financial instns, financial condition by instn, 1991 and trends, annual rpt, S1160–1

DC statistical profile, general data, 1992 annual rpt, S1535–3.3

Georgia credit union financial condition, including loans by type and delinquency, with comparisons to US, 1989, article, U6730–2.506

Hawaii data book, general data, 1992 annual rpt, S2090–1.15

Hawaii economic indicators, bimonthly rpt, B3500–1

Idaho banks and other financial instns, financial condition, with data by instn and loan activity analysis, FY92 or 1991, annual rpt, S2235–1

Illinois bank and trust companies (State-chartered) financial condition and status changes, by instn, FY92, annual rpt, S2395–1

Illinois Financial Institutions Dept activities, with financial and regulatory data for credit unions, consumer lenders, and other businesses, FY91 annual rpt, S2457–2

Indiana financial instns (State-chartered) financial condition, including assets by instn arranged by city, 1991 and trends, annual rpt, S2625–1

Iowa financial instn loan activity, FY92 annual rpt, S2760–2

Kansas statistical abstract, general data, 1991/92 annual rpt, U7095–2.10

Kentucky financial instns condition, including assets by instn and city, with regulatory info, 1992 and trends, annual rpt, S3121–1

Louisiana financial instns (State-chartered), financial condition by instn arranged by city, with regulatory info, Dec 1992, annual rpt, S3265–1

Maine banks and other financial instns, financial condition by instn, June 1992, annual rpt, S3473–2

Maine financial instn assets, deposits, and loans, by type of instn and county, 1982-92, annual rpt, S3473–1

Maryland banks and credit unions (State-chartered) financial condition by instn, with regulatory data, FY92 annual rpt, S3655–2

Michigan banks and other financial instns, financial condition by instn, with regulatory info, 1992 and trends, annual rpt, S3957–1

Minnesota motor vehicle and insurance premium finance company activity, 1990-91, annual rpt, S4140–3

Mississippi statistical abstract, general data, 1992 annual rpt, U3255–4.14

Missouri banks and trust companies (State-chartered) financial condition, by instn, FY91-92 and trends, biennial rpt, S4502–1

New Jersey banks and other financial instns, assets and liabilities by instn, 1992 and trends, annual rpt, S5355–1

New Mexico business and economic activity indicators, monthly rpt, U7980–1

New Mexico financial instns, financial and operating data by instn, with regulatory activities, 1992, annual rpt, S5652–1

New York State statistical yearbook, general data, 1992 annual rpt, U5100–1.7

Oklahoma financial instns (State-chartered) assets and liabilities, by type of instn, with regulatory data, FY92 annual rpt, S6415–1

Oregon financial instns, financial condition by instn, Dec 1992 and trends, annual rpt, S6616–1

Pennsylvania statistical abstract, general data, 1992 recurring rpt, U4130–6.2

Rhode Island banks and other financial instns (State-chartered), assets and liabilities, by instn, 1991, annual rpt, S6945–1

South Carolina economic condition, including agriculture, finance, and govt financial data, 1970s-92, annual rpt, S7125–3.1

South Carolina financial instns (State-chartered) financial condition, including data by instn, FY92 annual rpt, S7165–1

Tennessee banks and other financial instns financial condition, by instn and city, 1992 annual rpt, S7507–1

Utah banks and other financial instns, financial condition by instn, FY93 and trends, annual rpt, S7830–1

Utah statistical abstract, general data, 1993 triennial rpt, U8960–1.15

Vermont banks and other financial instns, financial condition by instn, 1992 and trends, annual rpt, S7995–2

Virginia consumer finance companies financial condition, by instn, Dec 1992, annual rpt, S8180–3

Virginia financial instns (State-chartered), financial condition by instn and instn type, Dec 1992, annual rpt, S8180–2

Washington State banks and other financial instns, financial condition by type of instn, 1992 and trends, annual rpt, S8325–1

West Virginia banks and other financial instns, composite financial condition, with selected data by instn, 1990-91, annual rpt, S8530–1

Wisconsin banks financial condition, by instn and city, with regulatory info, 1992 and trends, annual rpt, S8685–1

Wisconsin savings and loan assns and savings banks (State-chartered) financial condition, by instn, 1992 and trends, annual rpt, S8807–1

Loans

see also Agricultural credit
see also Commercial credit
see also Consumer credit
see also Credit unions
see also Discrimination in credit
see also Export-Import Bank
see also Federal aid programs
see also Finance companies
see also Foreclosures
see also Foreign debts
see also Government assets and liabilities
see also Interest rates
see also International assistance
see also Loan delinquency and default
see also Military assistance
see also Mortgages
see also Pawnbrokers
see also Public debt
see also Student aid
see also terms beginning with Federal aid to, Federal funding for, or State funding for

Lobbying and lobbying groups

Congressional campaign finances, with detailed data for individual Members, and leading contributors by type and industry, 1990 election and trends, biennial rpt, R3828–2.2

Congressional voting support for 4 special interest groups, by Member and State, 1991, annual rpt, C2500–2

Hard goods representatives views on business lobby performance in 1991, by product line, 1993 annual survey rpt, A1800–1

Mexico lobbyists in US income from Mexican Govt, for 8 major Hispanic firms or individuals, 1991-93, article, C4575–1.510

Religious congregation lobbying activity, and views on lobbying importance and related laws, 1992 survey, recurring rpt, A5435–4

see also Political action committees

Lobsters

see Shellfish

Local-area networks

see Computer networks

Local-Federal relations

see Federal-local relations

Local government

Activities and structure, finances, and employment, for local govt, series, A5800–2, A5800–4

Arts fundraising through united arts funds (UAFs), with fund operations, income by source, and allocations, by UAF, 1992 and trends, annual rpt, A1315–2

City fiscal condition, including budget trends and adjustments, and influencing factors, by region and population size, Mar-Apr 1993 survey, annual rpt, A8012–1.23

City govt costs to enforce Fed Govt regulations including environmental laws, for 314 cities, FY93, with summary projections to FY98, A9330–12

Environmental regulation by cities under Federal mandates, local impact analysis including selected cost projections, 1993 rpt, U9640–3

Govt finances, including revenues by source, expenditures by function, and debt, detailed data for Federal, State, and local govts, 1993 annual rpt, R9050–1

Index by Subjects and Names

Health dept expenditures and State funding, by State and territory, FY89, annual rpt, A5173–2.2

Hispanic American municipal officials, 1984-92, and total vs Hispanic population of 35 cities with Hispanic mayors as of 1993, article, C4575–1.511

Hospital (teaching) house staff stipend/benefit cost funding sources, by ownership, 1992/93, annual rpt, A3273–3

Latin America statistical abstract, general data by country, 1992 annual rpt, U6250–1.9

Library construction, costs, and funding sources, by State, city, instn, and library type, FY92 and trends, annual article, C1852–1.501

Municipal and county govt structure, public services, finances, and intergovtl relations, 1993 annual rpt, A5800–1

Officials views on city issues and conditions, including top issues for Fed Govt to address, 1992 survey, annual rpt, A8012–1.21

Policies and conditions in cities, Natl League of Cities surveys, series, A8012–1

Public housing authorities, units managed by type, and vacancy and turnover rates, by agency size, 1988-91, A6800–2

Public housing authority operations and finances, including resident characteristics, by agency size, 1989, A6800–1

Recycling curbside program operations, funding, and recycled materials, municipal official views and summary program characteristics, July 1991 survey, B0230–2

Social, economic, and govtl indicators, with rankings by State, 1993 semiannual rpt, B8500–1

Statistical profiles of 50 States and DC, general data, 1993 annual almanac, C4712–1

Substance abuse treatment programs, funding by source, and client characteristics, for alcohol and drug services, by State, FY91 and trends, annual rpt, A7112–1

Theater (nonprofit professional) finances and operations, including revenues by source, 1992 and trends, annual survey, A9065–1

Units of local govt, total and per 100,000 population, by State, 1993 article, B8500–2.508

Urban public school performance compared to natl goals for year 2000, with data on students, teachers, and finances, for 47 systems, 1990/91 and trends, A4425–4

State and local:

Alabama county data book, general data, 1992 annual rpt, S0121–2

Alabama elementary and secondary school enrollment, staff, pupil transportation, and finances, by district, 1991/92, annual rpt, S0124–1

Alabama public libraries, finances, holdings, circulation, staff, and population served, by library, FY92, annual rpt, S0180–1

Alaska public schools, enrollment, staff, and finances, by district, FY92, annual rpt, S0295–2

Arizona public library holdings, circulation, finances, and staff, by instn and county, FY92, annual rpt, S0495–1

Arizona statistical abstract, general data, 1993 recurring rpt, U5850–2.10, U5850–2.12

California socioeconomic and govtl data for municipalities, counties, and school districts, 1993 annual rpt, C4712–3

California statistical abstract, general data, 1992 annual rpt, S0840–2.13

Colorado public library finances and operations, by instn, 1991, annual rpt, S1000–3.1

Colorado public school revenues by source, and expenditures by category, by school district, 1990, annual rpt, S1000–4.3

DC council legislative activity, 1992 annual rpt, S1535–3.1

Florida municipal and county statistical profiles, general data, 1991 annual rpt, C4712–6

Florida public libraries, finances, holdings, staff, and services, by system and library, FY92, annual rpt, S1800–2

Florida statistical abstract, general data, 1992 annual rpt, U6660–1.21, U6660–1.23

Georgia statistical abstract, general data, 1992-93 biennial rpt, U6730–1.11

Hawaii data book, general data, 1992 annual rpt, S2090–1.8, S2090–1.9

Idaho public library holdings, staff, services, circulation, and finances, by instn, FY92, annual rpt, S2282–1

Illinois public library holdings, staff, and finances, by instn, FY92, annual rpt, S2535–2

Illinois public school revenues and expenditures by district, with data on busing, State aid claims, and per capita costs, 1990/91, annual rpt, S2440–1.3

Indiana court cases and dispositions by type of court and case, and location, with judicial system finances and personnel, 1992, annual rpt, S2703–1

Indiana public assistance program participation, expenditures, and services, by county, FY92 and trends, annual rpt, S2623–1

Iowa public library finances and operations, by county, size of population served, and library, FY92, annual rpt, S2778–1

Kansas county economic dev planning, including plan characteristics and funding sources, 1993 article, U7095–1.502

Kansas statistical abstract, general data, 1991/92 annual rpt, U7095–2.11

Kentucky public library finances and operations, by county, FY92, annual rpt, S3165–1

Louisiana public library finances, holdings, circulation, and personnel, by library system, FY92, annual rpt, S3275–1

Maryland elementary and secondary education data, by county, 1991/92, annual rpt, S3610–2.9

Maryland local govt financial condition, including revenues by source, expenditures by function, and debt obligations, FY92 and trends, annual rpt, S3618–1

Maryland public library operating income and expenditures, staff, holdings, and population served, by county, FY92, annual rpt, S3610–5

Maryland statistical abstract, general data, 1993-94 biennial rpt, S3605–1.7

Index by Subjects and Names — Local taxation

Massachusetts municipal and county profiles, general data, 1992 annual rpt, C4712–2

Massachusetts public library finances, holdings, and circulation, by municipality, FY92, annual rpt, S3870–1

Michigan school district financial and enrollment data, with rankings, 1991/92, annual rpt, S3965–3

Minnesota public library holdings, staff, services, circulation, and finances, by library, 1991, annual rpt, S4165–2

Mississippi public school enrollment, staff and salaries, and finances, by district, 1991/92 and trends, annual rpt, S4340–1

Mississippi statistical abstract, general data, 1992 annual rpt, U3255–4.13

Missouri higher education revenues by source and expenditures by function, by instn, FY92 and trends, annual rpt, S4520–3.3

Montana public library holdings, staff, circulation, and finances, by library, FY92, annual rpt, S4725–1

Nebraska local govt units and employment, by type of governing unit, 1957 and/or 1987, article, U7860–1.502

Nebraska public libraries, finances, holdings, circulation, staff, and population served, by instn, FY91, annual rpt, S4910–1

Nevada public school enrollment, test scores, teachers, and finances, by school district, 1990/91 and trends, annual rpt, S5035–2

Nevada statistical abstract, general data, 1992 biennial rpt, S5005–1.8

New Hampshire elementary and secondary school revenues by source and expenditures by function, 1991/92, annual data, tables, S5200–1.12

New Hampshire public library finances and operations, by library and/or location, 1991, annual rpt, S5227–1

New Jersey local health official views on hazardous waste site concerns and interactions with Federal and State govts, Nov 1991 survey, article, A2623–1.507

New Jersey municipal and county data book, general data, 1992 annual rpt, C4712–4

New Mexico public library operations and finances, by instn, FY92, annual rpt, S5627–1

New York State municipal and county statistical profiles, general data, 1993 annual rpt, C4712–7

New York State public library finances, staff, holdings, and services, by library and county, 1991, annual rpt, S5745–2

New York State social services local admin expenditures and staff, by program, 1991 and trends, annual rpt, S5800–2.3

New York State statistical yearbook, general data, 1992 annual rpt, U5100–1.4, U5100–1.6

North Carolina public libraries, finances, holdings, and personnel, by library system, FY91, annual rpt, S5910–1

North Carolina public school enrollment, grads, staff, and finances, with data by race, sex, and local district, 1991/92-1992/93 and trends, annual rpt, S5915–1

North Dakota public library finances, holdings, staff, and operations, by instn, FY91, annual rpt, S6180–5

Ohio business property tax collections and assessments, by type of subdivision and county, 1991 and trends, annual rpt, S6390–1.5

Ohio public, academic, and other library finances, holdings, and staff, by library and location, 1992 and trends, annual rpt, S6320–1

Oklahoma public and institutional library holdings, circulation, finances, and staff, by facility, FY92, annual rpt, S6470–1

Oklahoma statistical abstract, general data, 1992 annual rpt, U8130–2.5

Oregon library finances, staff, holdings, and services, for public, academic, and special libraries by instn, FY92 and trends, annual rpt, S6635–1

Oregon public school revenues by source and fund, and expenditures by fund, function, and object, 1991/92, annual rpt, S6590–1.16

Oregon public school revenues by source and fund, and expenditures by fund, function, and object, 1992/93, annual rpt, S6590–1.17

Oregon public school revenues by source, by school district and county, 1992/93, annual rpt, S6590–1.21

Pennsylvania public and institutional library personnel, holdings, circulation, and finances, by county and facility, FY92, annual rpt, S6790–2

Pennsylvania statistical abstract, general data, 1992 recurring rpt, U4130–6.6

Rhode Island education expenditures by function and source of funds, by school district, 1991/92, annual rpt, S6970–1.2

Rhode Island statistical almanac, general data, 1993 annual rpt, C7975–1

South Carolina county govt finances, including property value and tax assessments, by county, FY92, annual rpt, S7127–2

South Carolina statistical abstract, general data, 1993 annual rpt, S7125–1.2, S7125–1.9

South Dakota school enrollment, finances, grads, and staff, by district, 1991/92 and trends, annual rpt, S7315–1

South Dakota tax revenues by source, aid distributed to local areas, and property tax valuations, FY92 annual rpt, S7380–1

Tennessee statistical abstract, general data, 1992/93 annual rpt, U8710–2.14, U8710–2.15

Texas indigent health care finances and utilization, with data by county, district, public hospital, and medical school, 1986-91, U8850–8.7

Texas public libraries, holdings, circulation, staff, and finances, by library and location, FY91, annual rpt, S7710–1

Texas State and local health depts finances, employment, and service area characteristics, FY91 and trends, U8850–8.6

Utah govt statistical review, fiscal and socioeconomic data, 1993 annual rpt, R9380–1.6

Utah public lands by govt owner, and Federal land payments to State and local govts, with data by county, 1992 article, U8960–2.502

Utah public libraries, services, staff, and finances, by library, 1992, annual rpt, S7808–1

Utah statistical abstract, general data, 1993 triennial rpt, U8960–1.7

Vermont libraries, finances, resources, and circulation, by city and library, FY91-92, biennial rpt, S8080–1

Virginia public library operations and finances, by instn, FY92, annual rpt, S8275–1

Virginia public school enrollment, grads, finances, and staff, by county and municipality, 1991/92, annual rpt, S8190–3

Washington State local govt investment pool participation and performance, with detail by local area, FY92 and trends, annual rpt, S8455–1

Washington State public libraries, finances, holdings, circulation, staff, and population served, by instn, 1992, annual rpt, S8375–1

West Virginia public, academic, and special library operations and/or finances, by instn, 1991/92, annual rpt, S8590–1

West Virginia public school finances, enrollment, staff, and programs, by county, 1992/93 and trends, annual rpt, S8540–4

West Virginia statistical handbook, general data, 1992 annual rpt, R9385–1.6

Wisconsin Blue Book, general data, 1993-94 biennial rpt, S8780–1.2

Wisconsin libraries, operations, and finances, by library type, instn, and location, 1992, annual rpt, S8795–1

Wyoming public library holdings, staff, circulation, and finances, by county, FY92, annual rpt, S8855–3

see also City and town planning

see also Community centers

see also Federal aid to local areas

see also Federal-local relations

see also Fire departments

see also Local government annexation

see also Municipal bonds

see also Police

see also School districts

see also Sheriffs

see also Special districts

see also State and local employees

see also State and local employees pay

see also State and local taxes

see also State funding for local areas

see also State-local relations

see also Zoning and zoning laws

Local government annexation

Municipal govt annexation activity, and population and land area affected, by city, State, and census div, 1980-91, A5800–1.2

State and local:

Oklahoma school district annexations or consolidations since 1946, by county, annual rpt, S6423–1.2

Washington State local govt annexations, by county and city, Apr 1990-92, annual rpt, S8345–4

Local government bonds

see Municipal bonds

Local government debt

see Government assets and liabilities

see Public debt

Local taxation

see State and local taxes

Location of industries

Location of industries
see Industrial siting
Lockouts
see Labor-management relations, general
see Work stoppages
Lodging
see Hotels and motels
see Rooming and boarding houses
Logistics
Certification of logistics personnel, including perceived benefits, views of industry professionals, 1993 survey article, C2150–1.503
Finances and other operating data for logistics, including major carriers by mode, and foreign trade, 1993 annual compilation, C2150–1.506
Retail industry inventory mgmt, warehousing, and distribution operations, by outlet type, 1993 survey, C5150–4.506
Salaries of logistics managers, by position, industry, and selected characteristics, Nov 1992 survey, annual article, C1850–11
see also Industrial distribution
see also Military supplies and property
Long-term care
see Aged and aging
see Nursing homes
Los Angeles, Calif.
CPI for California and 2 major cities, bimonthly rpt, S0840–1
Election results for Federal offices and Governor, by State, county, major city, and party, with voter registration and turnout, 1992 and trends, biennial rpt, C2500–1
Oil refinery emissions allocations, by company, 1994, 2000, and 2003, article, C6985–1.552
Riots following Rodney King police brutality case verdict, TV news coverage characteristics, Apr-May 1992, article, R3823–1.506
Statistical abstract of California, detailed social, govtl, and economic data, 1992 annual rpt, S0840–2
see also under By City in the "Index by Categories"
Lotteries
Advertising budget and agency for lotteries, by State, FY92, article, C2710–1.526
Convenience stores offering special services, including lottery ticket sales, 1992 and trends, annual survey rpt, A6735–1, A6735–2
Convenience stores selling alcoholic beverages and lottery tickets, by company size, 1993, annual article, C4680–1.510
Public opinion on selected types of legalized gambling, and lottery ticket expenditures, Nov 1992 Gallup Poll and trends, C4040–1.506
State govt net lottery revenue per capita and as percent of total revenues, for 17 States, FY85 and FY91, article, B8500–2.521
State social, economic, and govtl indicators, with rankings, 1993 semiannual rpt, B8500–1.4
State and local:
Arizona financial condition, including revenues by source, expenditures by function, and fund balances, FY91, annual rpt, S0450–2

Arizona financial condition, including revenues by source, expenditures by function, and fund balances, FY92, annual rpt, S0450–1
California financial condition, including revenues by source, expenditures by agency and function, fund balances, and bonded debt, FY92 and trends, annual rpt, S0815–1
California higher education system revenues by source, including State lottery, FY70-94, annual rpt, S0827–3
Colorado financial condition, including receipts by source, and expenditures by function, FY92 and trends, annual rpt, S0980–1
Colorado State lottery sales, and distributions by fund, FY92 and trends, annual rpt, S1075–1.3
Connecticut financial condition, including revenues by source, expenditures by function, and bonded debt, FY92, annual rpt, S1170–2
DC financial condition, including receipts by source, expenditures by object or function, and fund balances, FY92, annual rpt, S1507–1
DC statistical profile, general data, 1992 annual rpt, S1535–3.2
Florida financial condition, including receipts by source, expenditures by function, and fund balances, FY92, annual rpt, S1717–1, S1717–3
Florida statistical abstract, general data, 1992 annual rpt, U6660–1.23
Georgia State constitutional amendment on lottery, election results by county, Nov 1992, biennial rpt, S1955–1
Idaho financial condition, including revenues by source and expenditures by object, by agency and/or fund, FY92, annual rpt, S2215–1
Illinois financial condition, including revenues by source, and expenditures by object, function, and agency, FY92, annual rpt, S2415–1
Indiana financial condition, including revenues by source, expenditures by function and object, and fund balances, by agency, FY92, annual rpt, S2570–1
Iowa financial condition, including revenues by source, expenditures by function, and bonded debt, FY92 and trends, annual rpt, S2860–4
Kentucky financial condition, including revenues by source, expenditures by function and object, fund balances, and bonded debt, FY92, annual rpt, S3120–1
Louisiana financial condition, including revenues by source, expenditures by function, and fund balances, FY92 and trends, annual rpt, S3285–2
Maine financial condition, including revenues by source, expenditures by function and object, and fund balances, FY92, annual rpt, S3420–1
Maryland financial condition, including revenues by source, expenditures by function, fund balances, and bonded debt, FY92 and trends, annual rpt, S3685–2
Massachusetts financial condition, including revenues by source, and expenditures by function, by fund, FY92 and trends, annual rpt, S3777–1

Michigan financial condition, including revenues by source, expenditures by function, and fund balances, FY92 and trends, annual rpt, S3985–2
Minnesota financial condition, including revenues by source, expenditures by function, fund balances, and bonded debt, FY92 and trends, annual rpt, S4180–1
Missouri financial condition, including revenues by source, expenditures by function, and fund balances, FY92, annual rpt, S4475–1
Montana financial condition, including revenues by source, expenditures by function, and fund balances, FY92, annual rpt, S4653–1
Nebraska State constitutional amendments on State lottery system, election results by county, 1992, biennial rpt, S4955–1
New Jersey financial condition, including revenues by source, expenditures by function, fund balances, and bonded debt, FY92, annual rpt, S5455–1
New York State financial condition, including revenues by source, expenditures by function, and fund balances, FY93, annual rpt, S5710–1
New York State statistical yearbook, general data, 1992 annual rpt, U5100–1.5, U5100–1.6
Ohio financial condition, including revenues by source, expenditures by function, and fund balances, FY92, annual rpt, S6255–1
Oregon financial condition, including revenues by source, expenditures by function, and fund statements, FY92, annual rpt, S6603–2
Pennsylvania financial condition, including revenues by source, expenditures by function, and fund balances, FY92 and trends, annual rpt, S6810–4
Pennsylvania lottery sales by type of game, prizes, and revenue use by program, FY82-92, annual rpt, S6885–1
Pennsylvania statistical abstract, general data, 1992 recurring rpt, U4130–6.6
Rhode Island financial condition, including revenues by source, expenditures by function, and fund balances, FY92 and trends, annual rpt, S6930–1
South Dakota financial condition, including revenues by source, expenditures by function, fund balances, and bonded debt, FY92, annual rpt, S7330–1
South Dakota State measure to repeal video lottery, election results by county, 1992, biennial rpt, S7390–1
Texas financial condition, including revenues by source, expenditures by function, and bonded indebtedness, FY92, annual rpt, S7655–3
Texas financial condition, including revenues by source, expenditures by function and dept, and investments, with data for over 400 individual funds, FY92, annual rpt, S7655–2
Vermont financial condition, including revenues by source, expenditures by function, fund balances, and bonded debt, FY92, annual rpt, S8035–1
Virginia financial condition, including revenues by source, expenditures by function, and fund balances, FY92 and trends, annual rpt, S8170–1

Index by Subjects and Names

Washington State financial condition, including revenues by source, expenditures by function, fund balances, and bonded debt, FY92, annual rpt, S8345–3

Wisconsin financial condition, including revenues by source, expenditures by function and object, and fund balances, FY92, annual rpt, S8675–3

Wisconsin financial condition, including revenues by source, expenditures by function and object, and fund balances, FY93, annual rpt, S8675–2

Wisconsin State constitutional amendments on State lottery, election results by county, 1993-94 biennial rpt, S8780–1.3

Louisiana

Agricultural production, marketing, and finances, by commodity or parish, 1985-91, annual rpt, U2740–1

Census of Population and Housing summary findings, by local area, 1990 and trends, U8010–4

Court caseloads and dispositions, by type of court and case, and jurisdiction, 1992 and trends, annual rpt, S3375–1

Election results, by parish and precinct, 1992 presidential election, quadrennial rpt, S3370–3

Elementary and secondary school operations, including enrollment, staff, finances, and detail by school district, 1991/92 and trends, annual rpt, S3280–1

Employment, hours, and earnings, by industry and MSA, monthly rpt, S3320–2

Energy indicators for Louisiana, suspended quarterly rpt, U2730–1

Financial instns (State-chartered), financial condition by instn arranged by city, with regulatory info, Dec 1992, annual rpt, S3265–1

Govt financial condition, including revenues by source, expenditures by function, and fund balances, FY92 and trends, annual rpt, S3285–2

Labor force planning rpt, including population and labor force characteristics, unemployment claimants, and data by parish and MSA, 1993 annual rpt, S3320–1

Library finances, holdings, circulation, and personnel, by library system, FY92, annual rpt, S3275–1

Markets with daily newspapers, demographic and economic info by geographic area, US and Canada, 1993 annual rpt, C3250–1

Oil and gas wells and footage drilled, by type of well, State, and offshore location, quarterly rpt, A2575–6

Oil/gas industry production, finances, exploration, and reserves, by State, 1992 and trends, annual rpt, A5425–1.1

Statistical profiles of 50 States and DC, general data, 1993 annual almanac, C4712–1

Traffic accidents, fatalities, and injuries, by circumstances, location, and driver characteristics, 1991 and trends, annual rpt, S3345–2

Utility and transportation regulatory agency activities, scope of jurisdiction, finances, and employees, by agency, 1991/92 annual rpt, A7015–2

Vital statistics, including population, births, deaths by cause, reportable diseases, marriages, and divorces, by demographic characteristics and locality, 1989-90 and trends, annual rpt, S3295–1

see also under By City and By County in the "Index by Categories"

see also under By State in the "Index by Categories"

Low-income energy assistance

Federal budget trends, including spending by program, State, and region, FY81-94, annual rpt, R8490–11

State and local:

Arkansas human services dept finances and operations, including Medicaid payments by type of service, FY91 and trends, annual rpt, S0700–2.3

DC statistical profile, general data, 1992 annual rpt, S1535–3.4

Missouri public welfare and medical assistance recipients, expenditures, and case processing, by program and county, FY92 and trends, annual rpt, S4575–2

Montana low-income energy assistance cases and payments, by county, monthly rpt, S4755–1

Nebraska households receiving low-income energy assistance, FY92 and trends, annual rpt, S4957–1

New Mexico low-income energy assistance cases and payments, by county monthly rpt quarterly table, S5620–2

New York State home energy assistance program statistics, by State area, FY91, annual rpt, S5800–2.3

North Carolina public welfare programs, cases, recipients, staff, and finances, by county, 1st half FY93, semiannual rpt, S5940–2

Ohio home heating energy credit program assistance, by county, winter 1991/92, annual rpt, S6390–1.3

South Dakota low-income energy assistance clients and payments, by MSA and county, FY92, annual rpt, S7385–1.2

Wyoming welfare and social service recipients and expenditures, by program and county, FY92, annual rpt, S8908–1

Low-income housing

Apartment complex mgmt income and expenses, and vacancy and turnover rates, for subsidized properties by region and selected metro area, 1992, annual survey rpt, A6497–1

Availability indicators for assisted housing in 28 cities, 1991/92, annual rpt, A9330–9

Catholic charity social service agency activities, clients, finances, and personnel, 1991 and trends, annual rpt, A3810–1

Federal housing program funding, and assisted units, FY94, annual feature, C4300–1.508

HUD appropriations by program, with number of assisted housing units by type, FY92-93, annual article, C4300–1.502

Supply-demand, costs, physical conditions, and public assistance, with data by race-ethnicity, for 44 metro areas, 1992 rpt, R3834–16

State and local:

DC statistical profile, general data, 1992 annual rpt, S1535–3.1, S1535–3.4

Utah, Salt Lake County low-income rental units, and rates by type of unit, 1987 and 1991-92, annual rpt, S7808–2

Lumber industry and products

see also Public housing

see also Rent supplements

LPG

see Liquefied petroleum gas

Lumber industry and products

Canada lumber trade with US, and production data, by product type, monthly rpt, A1630–3

Corporate performance ratings by executives for leading companies in 32 industries, 1993 annual survey feature, C8900–1.508

Cost indexes for construction, equipment, and labor, by type and location, weekly rpt quarterly feature, C5800–2.534, C5800–2.547

Financial and operating data of paper and paperboard industry, by product, region, and State, 1992 and trends, annual rpt, A1630–6

Financial performance and growth rankings for approx 1,000 top corporations, with comparisons by industry group, 1993 annual rpt, C3950–1.505

Financial ratios and performance, for over 350 SIC 4-digit industries, FY88-92, annual rpt, A6400–3

Foreign trade of forest products by product category and at 30 leading ports, 1991-92, annual article, C3975–2.512

Forest industries mgmt, technical devs, and manufactures data, articles and special features, bimonthly rpt, C3975–1

Homebuilder use of 5 types of wood vs all others for luxury-market kitchen cabinets, 1990-92, annual feature, C4300–1.506

Kitchen cabinet wood types specified by kitchen designers, 1992 and trends, C4300–1.511

Latin America statistical abstract, general data by country, 1992 annual rpt, U6250–1.24, U6250–1.25

Markets with daily newspapers, demographic and economic info by geographic area, US and Canada, 1993 annual rpt, C3250–1

Northwest forest timber peak production compared to lumber demand outlook and Clinton Admin harvest plan, 1993 article, C1850–8.509

Operating and financial composite ratios for corporations, with establishments and receipts, for approx 200 industries, by asset size, FY90, annual rpt, C7800–1

Pacific Rim region lumber exports from US, by country and product type, monthly rpt, A1630–2

Panel (wood) production for US and Canada, by grade, 1983-92, annual article, C3975–1.501

Prices for framing lumber, 1987-93, article, C4300–1.511

Prices for selected building materials in approx 20 cities, weekly rpt, C5800–2

Production, consumption, stocks, trade, and prices for approx 100 basic commodities, including by country and producing State, commodity yearbook for 1993, C2400–1, C2400–2

Production in Western States and counties, with acreage owned, employment, and sawmill operations, 1980s-92, annual rpt, A9395–1

Pulp and paper industry production, capacity, consumption, trade, and sales/earnings data, including profiles for selected companies and sectors, monthly rpt, C3975–2

Lumber industry and products

Retail hardware finances and operations for hardware stores, home centers, and lumber/building material outlets, 1991 and trends, annual rpt series, A8275–1

- Salaries and benefits in pulp/paper industry, by job characteristics, 1992 survey, annual article, C3975–2.503
- Supply-demand and prices for timber products, 1950s-2040, annual rpt, C3975–5.1
- Supply-demand, sales, trade, and employment, monthly rpt, A1630–1
- World wood product production and trade, by country, 1977-89, biennial rpt, R9455–1.6

State and local:

- Alabama cash receipts from farm forest products and nonfarm commercial timber, by county, 1991-92, annual rpt, S0090–1
- Alabama county data book, general data, 1992 annual rpt, S0121–2
- Alabama statistical abstract, general data, 1992 recurring rpt, U5680–2.1
- California timber harvest value, production, and yield tax and reserve fund rates and revenues, 1991 and trends, annual rpt, S0835–1.2
- Florida statistical abstract, general data, 1992 annual rpt, U6660–1.10, U6660–1.12
- Georgia statistical abstract, general data, 1992-93 biennial rpt, U6730–1.5
- Hawaii data book, general data, 1992 annual rpt, S2090–1.20
- Idaho economic profile, general data, 1992 recurring rpt, S2218–2.5
- Louisiana timber value delivered to mills, 1982-91, annual rpt, S3285–2
- Maryland statistical abstract, general data, 1993-94 biennial rpt, S3605–1.3
- Mississippi statistical abstract, general data, 1992 annual rpt, U3255–4.10
- New York State statistical yearbook, general data, 1992 annual rpt, U5100–1.15
- North Carolina forest products income from govt educational program, by county, 1990-91, annual rpt, S5885–1
- Oregon economic conditions, including population, construction, income, employment, industry, and foreign trade data, 1991, annual rpt, S6585–3
- Oregon lumber/wood products industry job losses, 1989-95, article, S6615–2.503
- South Carolina statistical abstract, general data, 1993 annual rpt, S7125–1.1
- Tennessee statistical abstract, general data, 1992/93 annual rpt, U8710–2.11
- Texas trade, transportation, and public utilities employment, by SIC 2- and 3-digit industry and detailed occupation, 2nd qtr 1991, triennial survey rpt, S7675–1.31
- Utah timber production volume and value from natl forests, 1960-92, triennial rpt, U8960–1.9
- Washington State timber excise tax distributions, by county, FY92, annual rpt, S8415–1.1

see also Forests and forestry
see also Gum and wood chemicals
see also Paper and paper products
see also Wood fuel
see also under By Industry in the "Index by Categories"

Lung diseases

see Black lung disease
see Pneumonia and influenza
see Respiratory diseases
see Tuberculosis

Luxembourg

- Entertainment industry devs, including motion picture theaters and funding, and TV and VCR use, 1993 feature, C9380–1.512
- Motor vehicle world production, sales, trade, and registrations, by country, world area, manufacturer, and make, 1991 and trends, annual rpt, A0865–2.1

Luxury tax

see Excise tax

Lynch, Mary J.

"ALA Survey of Librarian Salaries, 1993", A2070–3

Machine tools

see Machines and machinery industry
see Tools

Machines and machinery industry

- Aluminum shipments by end-use market and product type, 1982-92, annual rpt, A0400–2.1
- Capital spending plans for machinery industries, by equipment type and industry group, 1989-93, annual survey, C4080–1
- Construction equipment positive and negative attributes cited by contractors, for 6 manufacturers, 1993 survey article, C5800–2.519
- Construction machinery sales and inventory indexes, weekly rpt monthly tables, C5800–2
- Corporate performance ratings by executives for leading companies in 32 industries, 1993 annual survey feature, C8900–1.508
- Cost indexes for construction, equipment, and labor, by type and location, weekly rpt quarterly feature, C5800–2.508, C5800–2.534, C5800–2.547
- Engineers salaries by industry group, census div, selected metro area, and years since college degree, 1993, annual survey rpt, A0685–5
- Engineers salaries by industry group, census div, selected metro area, degree level, and years since college degree, 1993, annual survey rpt, A0685–3
- Executive compensation and components, by industry div and major manufacturing group, 1991, annual rpt, R4105–19
- Financial performance and growth rankings for approx 1,000 top corporations, with comparisons by industry group, 1993 annual rpt, C3950–1.505
- Financial ratios and performance, for over 350 SIC 4-digit industries, FY88-92, annual rpt, A6400–3
- Machine tool and other manufacturing technology exports and imports, by country of destination and origin, and by detailed product type, monthly rpt, A3179–3
- Machine tool production, shipments, trade, finances, orders, and use, US and worldwide, 1992 and trends, annual rpt, A3179–2
- Machine tool shipments and new orders for domestic and foreign markets, and backlog, monthly press release, A3179–1

- Machine tool world production, trade, and consumption, by country, 1991-92, annual article, C7000–7.503
- Metalworking industry devs, with machine tool orders and shipments, monthly rpt, C7000–7
- Operating and financial composite ratios for corporations, with establishments and receipts, for approx 200 industries, by asset size, FY90, annual rpt, C7800–1
- Plastics production machinery sales and shipments, 1986-92, annual rpt, A8920–1.3
- Shipments of construction/mining/farm equipment, non-electrical machinery, and aircraft/parts, quarterly 1991-94, article, C1850–4.504

State and local:

- Arizona statistical abstract, general data, 1993 recurring rpt, U5850–2.17
- Florida statistical abstract, general data, 1992 annual rpt, U6660–1.12
- Texas trade, transportation, and public utilities employment, by SIC 2- and 3-digit industry and detailed occupation, 2nd qtr 1991, triennial survey rpt, S7675–1.31
- Wyoming property assessed valuations and tax levies, by property type, tax purpose, and location, 1992 and trends, annual rpt, S8990–1.2

see also Agricultural machinery and equipment
see also Electrical machinery and equipment
see also Engines and motors
see also Hardware
see also Industrial plants and equipment
see also Tools
see also Vending machines and stands
see also under By Industry in the "Index by Categories"

Mackey, Scott R.

"State Programs to Assist Distressed Local Governments", A7470–4.13
"State Tax Actions, 1992", A7470–4.9

Madrid, Spain

- Exports through Madrid, by destination country or area, 1991, article (in Spanish), A8955–1.501
- Foreign trade value by product type, trade volume by industry sector, and export distribution by country, 1991 and trends, article, A8955 1.502

Mafia

see Organized crime

Magazines

see Periodicals

Magistrate courts

see State courts

Magistrates

see Judges

Magnesium

see Metals and metal industries

Mail

see Electronic mail systems
see Postal service
see U.S. Postal Service

Mail order

see Direct marketing

Maine

- Banks and other financial instns, financial condition by instn, June 1992, annual rpt, S3473–2
- Census of Population and Housing summary findings, by local area, 1990, S3465–7, S3465–8, S3465–9

Index by Subjects and Names — Manufacturing

Court cases and dispositions, by type and location, FY92 and trends, annual rpt, S3463–1

Crimes and arrests, by offense, location, and offender age and sex, with data on law enforcement employment and assaults on officers, 1991, annual rpt, S3475–1

Election results, by district, county, and municipality, 1992 general election, biennial rpt, S3490–1

Elementary and secondary school enrollment, facilities, staff, and finances, with selected data by county and for private schools, 1991 and trends, annual rpt, S3435–1

Employment, by SIC 2-digit industry and detailed occupation, triennial series, S3465–1

Employment, unemployment, and earnings, by industry, MSA, and labor area, monthly rpt, S3465–2

Financial instn assets, deposits, and loans, by type of instn and county, 1982-92, annual rpt, S3473–1

Govt financial condition, including revenues by source, expenditures by function and object, and fund balances, FY92, annual rpt, S3420–1

Markets with daily newspapers, demographic and economic info by geographic area, US and Canada, 1993 annual rpt, C3250–1

Statistical profiles of 50 States and DC, general data, 1993 annual almanac, C4712–1

Statistical summary of Maine, general economic and social data, 1992 recurring rpt, S3434–1

Traffic accidents, fatalities, and injuries, by accident circumstances, vehicle type and make, and driver and victim characteristics, 1992, annual rpt, S3475 2

Utility and transportation regulatory agency activities, scope of jurisdiction, finances, and employees, by agency, 1991/92 annual rpt, A7015–2

Vital statistics, including births, deaths by cause, abortions, marriages, divorces, and population, by demographic characteristics and/or location, 1991 and trends, annual rpt, S3460–2

see also Lewiston, Maine

see also Portland, Maine

see also under By City and By County in the "Index by Categories"

see also under By State in the "Index by Categories"

Maintenance services

see Janitorial and maintenance services

Maize

see Corn

Makinson, Larry

"Cash Constituents of Congress", R3828–3

"Open Secrets: Encyclopedia of Congressional Money and Politics", R3828–2

Malaria

see Infective and parasitic diseases

Malaysia

Electronics industry trade and/or production trends by product category for 33 countries, with general economic profiles, 1993 annual rpt, A4725–1.4

Energy intl sourcebook, with detail on oil and gas industry operations, supply-demand, and prices, for approx 80 countries, 1970s-91, annual compilation, C6985–10.2

Machine tool industry operating data by country and product, 1992 and trends, annual rpt, A3179–2.2

Motor vehicle world production, sales, trade, and registrations, by country, world area, manufacturer, and make, 1991 and trends, annual rpt, A0865–2.1

Malnutrition

see Nutrition and malnutrition

Malpractice

see Lawsuits

see Medical malpractice

see Property and casualty insurance

Malt

see Grains and grain products

Malt beverages

see Beer and breweries

Mammography

Women's use of mammography and Pap smear tests, by demographic characteristics, 1987 survey, article, A2623–1.503

State and local:

Alabama health behavior risk factor surveillance survey results, by respondent characteristics, 1988-89, recurring rpt, S0175–6

Colorado health behavior risk factor surveillance survey results, by respondent characteristics, 1990, recurring rpt, S1010–3

Connecticut health behavior risk factor surveillance survey results, 1989-91, annual rpt, S1200–2

Iowa health behavior risk factor surveillance survey results, by respondent characteristics, 1991, annual rpt, S2795–2

Massachusetts health behavior risk factor surveillance survey results, by respondent characteristics, 1986-90, recurring rpt, S3850–3

Michigan health behavior risk factor surveillance survey results, by respondent characteristics, 1991, annual rpt, S4000–4

Nevada health behavior risk factor surveillance survey results, by location and respondent characteristics, 1991, annual rpt, S5075–3

New York State health behavior risk factor surveillance survey results, by respondent characteristics, 1990, recurring rpt, S5765–3

North Dakota health behavior risk factor surveillance survey results, by respondent characteristics, 1991 and trends, annual rpt, S6105–3

Pennsylvania health behavior risk factor surveillance survey results, by respondent characteristics, 1991, annual rpt, S6820–4

Texas health behavior risk factor surveillance survey results, by respondent characteristics, 1991 and trends, annual rpt, S7685–2

Utah health behavior risk factor surveillance survey results, by respondent characteristics, 1991, annual rpt, S7835–3

Management

see Business management

see Consultants

see Executives and managers

see Government efficiency

see Labor-management relations, general

see Labor-management relations in government

Management consultants

see Consultants

Manchester, N.H.

Employment, hours, and earnings, and job service applicant characteristics, monthly rpt, S5205–1

Manganese

see Metals and metal industries

Manned space flight

see Space programs

Manpower

see Labor supply and demand

Manpower training programs

Federal budget trends, including spending by program, State, and region, FY81-94, annual rpt, R8490–11

Job Corps youth training program funding, enrollment capacity, and participants by selected characteristics, 1981-94, article, R4800–2.515

State and local:

DC statistical profile, general data, 1992 annual rpt, S1535–3.3

Indiana AFDC and food stamp recipient training/employment service program participation and expenditures, by type of aid, FY92 annual rpt, S2623–1.5

Missouri employment, earnings, and hours, and employment security program activity, by industry and/or county, FY92 and trends, annual rpt, S4530–2.3

New York State AFDC and home relief recipients participating in employment service programs, by program, 1991, annual rpt, S5800–2.1

Utah job training for displaced homemakers and single parents, program participants, 1991/92, annual rpt, S7815–1.1

see also Apprenticeship

see also Employee development

see also Federal aid to vocational education

see also Job Training Partnership Act

see also Military training

see also Scientific education

see also Vocational education and training

see also Vocational rehabilitation

see also Work incentive programs

Manslaughter

see Homicide

Manufactured housing

see Mobile homes

see Prefabricated buildings

Manufacturing

Business executives expectations for coming qtr, attitudes on key indicators, with trends and data by census div, quarterly rpt, C3150–4

Business failures and liabilities, by detailed industry, cause, length of operation, and location, 1991-92 and trends, annual rpt, C3150–8

Canada manufacturing employees, wages, value added, and shipments, top 10 industry groups, 1987, annual rpt, C3975–5.2

Chemist and chemical engineer salaries, employment status, and demographic and professional characteristics, 1993, annual rpt, A1250–4

Manufacturing

Index by Subjects and Names

Cities rated as best for business by Fortune magazine, socioeconomic profiles of top 60 metro areas, 1992 annual article, C8900–1.501

College grad job and salary offers, by field of study, type of employer and occupation, and degree level, by region, interim rpt series, A3940–1

College grad job and salary offers, by field of study, type of employer and occupation, and degree level, series, A3940–2

Earnings, sales, and profit margins, for chemical and allied industries, by company, weekly rpt quarterly article, A1250–1.502, A1250–1.514, A1250–1.525, A1250–1.536

Economic indicator historical trends, 1900s-92, annual rpt, R9050–1.2

Employment shares in manufacturing, and growth compared to total employment, by State, Feb 1993, article, B8500–2.513

Employment shares in manufacturing, and manufacturing employment trends, by State, Sept 1992, article, B8500–2.504

Employment shares in manufacturing, for top 20 metro areas, 1992, article, A6450–2.509

Employment trends in metro and regional areas, total and manufacturing, by region and for approx 50 MSAs, quarterly rpt, B5190–1

Engineers salaries by industry group, census div, selected metro area, and years since college degree, 1993, annual survey rpt, A0685–5

Engineers salaries by industry group, census div, selected metro area, degree level, and years since college degree, 1993, annual survey rpt, A0685–3

Environmental records and summary financial data for 10 leading and 20 other manufacturers rated by Fortune magazine, 1993 article, C8900–1.520

Executive compensation and components, by industry div and major manufacturing group, 1991, annual rpt, R4105–19

Export value of manufactured goods per capita, by State, 1992, article, B8500–2.512

Financial ratios and performance, for over 350 SIC 4-digit industries, FY88-92, annual rpt, A6400–3

Foreign competitiveness of US manufacturing companies, including related mgmt strategies and human resource issues, executive views, spring 1993 survey, U9640–4

Foreign economic indexes, and leading and coincident indicators for US and other industrial countries, monthly rpt, U1245–1

Fortune 500 largest industrial corporations, sales, financial, and stock performance data by company, 1992, annual feature, C8900–1.513

Fortune 500 largest industrial corporations worldwide, with financial and employment data, 1992, annual feature, C8900–1.520

Germany (West) and US comparative socioeconomic statistics, 1970s-91, annual rpt, A5135–2.2

Japan corporate affiliate philanthropic activity in US, for service and manufacturing operations, 1992, survey article, R5650–2.560

Japan manufacturing operating rates, and employment and wages, by industry, 1988-92, annual compilation, R5650–2.552

Job trends in manufacturing, for 20 States with greatest proportion of manufacturing employment, May 1991-May 1993, C8900–1.523

Korea (South) manufacturing and mining earnings and employee-days, 1986-91, annual rpt, A7400–2.2

Latin America statistical abstract, general data by country, 1992 annual rpt, U6250–1.12, U6250–1.13, U6250–1.32

Men age 18-29 employment in manufacturing, by race-ethnicity and education, 1973 and 1986, annual rpt, R8335–1.1

Midsize manufacturing companies use of "agile" production methods, 1993 survey article, C2150–3.509

Operating and financial composite ratios for corporations, with establishments and receipts, for approx 200 industries, by asset size, FY90, annual rpt, C7800–1

Production and operating data, including equipment purchases, by selected industry, 1993 and trends, annual rpt, A3179–2.3

Production, consumption, stocks, trade, and prices for approx 100 basic commodities, including by country and producing State, commodity yearbook for 1993, C2400–1, C2400–2

Productivity and related indicators, trend analysis for US and other industrial countries, 1980s-92, annual rpt, R2800–2

Quality control and improvement, views and experience of corporate executives and outside directors, July-Aug 1992 surveys, A2800–3

R&D spending by selected industry group, 1991, annual rpt, C3975–5.1

Shipment forecasts for selected manufacturing industries, 1993 article, C7000–3.504

Shipment values and employment for top 25 manufacturing industries, and top 15 counties in manufacturing receipts, 1992, article, C1200–1.509

Shipment values for 25 largest SIC 4-digit manufacturing industries, 1993, annual rpt, A8920–1.1

Statistical profiles of 50 States and DC, general data, 1993 annual almanac, C4712–1

Trends in manufacturing industry indicators, with data by State and region and comparisons to other countries, 1993 rpt, R8490–48

Value added and wages per hour, for 9 States with highest and lowest values, 1991, article, B8500–2.516

State and local:

Alabama county data book, general data, 1992 annual rpt, S0121–2

Alabama statistical abstract, general data, 1992 recurring rpt, U5680–2.11

Arizona economic condition, including population, employment and earnings, and business activity, by industry and locality, 1985-93, semiannual rpt, U5850–1

Arizona statistical abstract, general data, 1993 recurring rpt, U5850–2.5, U5850–2.17

Arkansas business and economic activity indicators, quarterly rpt, U5930–1

Arkansas socioeconomic trends, by MSA and/or county, 1993 annual rpt, U5935–1

California economic condition, including population, employment and earnings, income, business activity, and taxation, 1993 annual rpt, S0840–3

California economic indicators, bimonthly rpt, S0840–1

California employment in selected manufacturing industry groups, 1992 and trends, annual planning rpt, S0830–2

California statistical abstract, general data, 1992 annual rpt, S0840–2.8

Delaware data book, general data, 1993 annual rpt, S1375–4

Florida statistical abstract, general data, 1992 annual rpt, U6660–1.12

Georgia business activity indicators, bimonthly rpt, U6730–2

Georgia statistical abstract, general data, 1992-93 biennial rpt, U6730–1.3, U6730–1.6

Hawaii data book, general data, 1992 annual rpt, S2090–1.22, S2090–1.24

Idaho and US economic trends and forecasts, quarterly rpt, S2245–2

Idaho economic profile, general data, 1992 recurring rpt, S2218–2.1, S2218–2.5, S2218–2.9

Illinois statistical abstract, general data, 1992 annual rpt, U6910–2

Iowa labor force supply-demand data, including population, earnings, and employment by industry and occupation, 1993 annual rpt, S2784–3

Kansas business activity indicators, quarterly rpt, U7095–1

Kansas statistical abstract, general data, 1991/92 annual rpt, U7095–2.8

Kentucky economic statistics, general data, 1993 annual rpt, S3104–1

Kentucky labor force planning rpt, including population and labor force characteristics, and employment by industry, 1991 and trends, annual rpt, S3140–3

Louisiana employment, hours, and earnings, by industry and MSA, monthly rpt, S3320–2

Maine employment, unemployment, and earnings, by industry group, MSA, and labor area, monthly rpt, S3465–2

Maine statistical summary, general economic and social data, 1992 recurring rpt, S3434–1

Maryland statistical abstract, general data, 1993-94 biennial rpt, S3605–1.4

Mississippi statistical abstract, general data, 1992 annual rpt, U3255–4.5

Missouri employment, earnings, and hours, by industry and MSA, monthly rpt, S4530–3

Missouri industrial growth, including new and expanding manufacturers, new jobs, and investment, 1982-91, annual rpt, S4475–1

Nebraska employment and unemployment, by industry group and locality, quarterly rpt, S4895–2

New Jersey economic indicators, including employment, building permits, and retail trade, monthly rpt, S5425–1

Index by Subjects and Names — Marijuana

New Mexico economic trends and outlook, by industry div, 1982-92, annual article, U7980–1.503

New Mexico manufacturing employment, payroll, value added, shipments, and capital expenditures, by industry group, 1989 and 1991, U7980–1.504

New York State statistical yearbook, general data, 1992 annual rpt, U5100–1.2, U5100–1.3

North Carolina employment, hours, and earnings, by industry group, with job placements, monthly rpt, S5917–3

North Dakota employment, hours, and earnings, by industry div and/or location, monthly rpt, S6140–4

Oklahoma export-related manufacturing establishments, export value, and output share and intensity, by industry group, various years 1987-89, article, U8130–1.503

Oklahoma statistical abstract, general data, 1992 annual rpt, U8130–2.14

Pennsylvania business activity indicators, monthly rpt, U4110–1

Pennsylvania employment, hours, and earnings, by industry, monthly rpt, S6845–1

Pennsylvania labor force planning rpt, including population characteristics, employment and job openings by industry and occupation, and income trends, FY92 annual rpt, S6845–3

Pennsylvania statistical abstract, general data, 1992 recurring rpt, U4130–6.2

Rhode Island statistical almanac, general data, 1993 annual rpt, C7975–1.1

South Carolina economic condition, including employment, manufacturing, and income, 1970s-92, annual rpt, S7125–3.2

South Carolina employment, earnings, and hours, by industry group and locality, monthly rpt, S7155–2

South Carolina property tax assessed values, by class and county, FY92, annual rpt, S7255–1.3

South Carolina statistical abstract, general data, 1993 annual rpt, S7125–1.3

Tennessee business activity indicators, quarterly journal, U8710–1

Tennessee economic indicator trends and forecasts, and business executives views on selected issues, 1993 annual articles, U8710–1.502

Tennessee economic indicator trends and forecasts, with data by industry div and manufacturing group, 1982-2001, annual rpt, S7560–1

Tennessee statistical abstract, general data, 1992/93 annual rpt, U8710–2.4

Utah statistical abstract, general data, 1993 triennial rpt, U8960–1.12

Virginia economic indicators, including new business incorporations and employment data, quarterly rpt, S8205–4

Virginia labor force, hours, and earnings, with data by industry group and locality, monthly rpt, S8205–6

Washington State employment, earnings, and hours, by labor market area and industry group, monthly rpt, S8340–3

West Virginia employment, unemployment, hours, and earnings, with job service activities, monthly rpt, S8534–1

Wisconsin Blue Book, general data, 1993-94 biennial rpt, S8780–1.2

Wisconsin economic indicators, including employment and earnings by industry group, monthly rpt, S8750–1

see also Aerospace industry
see also Aircraft
see also Aluminum and aluminum industry
see also Business machines and equipment
see also Cement and concrete
see also Census of Manufactures
see also Chemicals and chemical industry
see also Clay industry and products
see also Clothing and clothing industry
see also Copper and copper industry
see also Electrical machinery and equipment
see also Electronics industry and products
see also Food and food industry
see also Furniture and furnishings
see also Furs and fur industry
see also Glass and glass industry
see also Gum and wood chemicals
see also Household appliances and equipment
see also Industrial capacity and utilization
see also Industrial plants and equipment
see also Industrial production
see also Instruments and measuring devices
see also Iron and steel industry
see also Leather industry and products
see also Lumber industry and products
see also Machines and machinery industry
see also Metals and metal industries
see also Motor vehicle industry
see also Paints and varnishes
see also Paper and paper products
see also Petroleum and petroleum industry
see also Pharmaceutical industry
see also Plastics and plastics industry
see also Printing and publishing industry
see also Production workers
see also Rubber and rubber industry
see also Ships and shipping
see also Sporting goods
see also Stone products and quarries
see also Textile industry and fabrics
see also Tires and tire industry
see also Tobacco industry and products
see also Toys and games
see also Transportation and transportation equipment
see also under By Industry in the "Index by Categories"

Maple syrup
see Syrups and sweeteners

Marble
see Stone products and quarries

Margarine
see Oils, oilseeds, and fats

Mariana Islands
see Guam
see Northern Mariana Islands

Maricopa County, Ariz.

Business activity indicators, including housing market, population, and CPI, monthly rpt, U0280–1

Employment, and production worker hours and earnings, by industry, monthly rpt, S0465–1

Labor force by employment status, and employment by industry div, 1992-94, annual feature, S0465–1.505

Marijuana

College freshmen attitudes on marijuana legalization, by sex and instn type, fall 1992, annual survey, U6215–1

Drug abuse treatment clients by substance abused, by State, FY91, annual rpt, A7112–1

High school student substance abuse as affected by junior high prevention program, 1993 article, A2623–1.508

Higher education student use of and attitudes toward alcohol, drugs, and tobacco products, by sex and region, 1989-91 surveys, annual rpt, U4950–1

Hospital psychiatric patient discharges and length of stay, by diagnosis, age, sex, and region, 1991, annual rpt series, B4455–2

Latin America statistical abstract, general data by country, 1992 annual rpt, U6250–1.15

State and local:

Alabama arrests of adults and juveniles for drug sale and possession, by race and sex, and drug task force property seizures by locale, 1992, annual rpt, S0119–1.1

Arizona arrests by offense, offender characteristics, and county, 1992, annual rpt, S0505–2.2

Arkansas crimes and arrests, by offense, victim and offender characteristics, and location, 1992 and trends, annual rpt, S0652–1

California crimes and arrests, clearances, and arrest dispositions, with data by offense and offender characteristics, 1987-92, annual rpt, S0910–1.1

California criminal justice system detailed data, by offense, county, age, race-ethnicity, and sex, 1991 and trends, annual rpt, S0910–2

DC criminal justice system summary, including crimes and arrests, criminal procedure, prisoners, and parole, 1991 and trends, annual rpt, S1535 2

Florida crimes and arrests, by offense, with data by victim and offender characteristics, 1992, annual rpt, S1770–1

Hawaii crimes and arrests, by offense, with data by county and victim-offender characteristics, 1992, annual rpt, S2035–1

Hawaii marijuana plants confiscated and value, by county, 1991, annual rpt, S2090–1.4

Idaho drug-related arrests by offender characteristics, and volume of drugs seized, 1992, annual rpt, S2275–2

Illinois crimes and arrests, by offense, with data by location and offender characteristics, 1991, annual rpt, S2536–1

Kansas crimes and arrests, by offense, with data by location, agency, and victim-offender characteristics, 1992 and trends, annual rpt, S2925–1.1

Kentucky arrests by county and offense, and law enforcement employment by agency, 1992, annual rpt, S3150–1.2

Maine arrests of adults and juveniles, by offense, age, and sex, 1991, annual rpt, S3475–1.2

Maryland crimes and arrests, by offense, location, and offender characteristics, with law enforcement employment and assaults on officers, 1992 and trends, annual rpt, S3665–1

Marijuana

New Hampshire arrests, by offense and offender age, sex, and race-ethnicity, 1991, annual rpt, S5250–2.2

New York State crimes and arrests by offense and demographic characteristics, and court activity and corrections, 1991 and trends, annual rpt, S5760–3

North Carolina arrests by detailed offense, offender characteristics, and county, 1991-92, annual rpt, S5955–1.2

Oklahoma crimes and arrests, by offense, with victim and offender characteristics, 1990-92, annual rpt, S6465–1.1

Oregon crimes and arrests, by offense, with data by county, local agency, and offender characteristics, 1992 and trends, annual rpt, S6603–3.1

Pennsylvania crimes and arrests, by offense, with data by location and offender characteristics, 1992 and trends, annual rpt, S6860–1

South Carolina crimes and arrests, by detailed offense, offender characteristics, and location, 1992 and trends, annual rpt, S7205–1.2

Texas crimes and arrests, and drugs seized by detailed type, 1992, annual rpt, S7735–2.2

Utah crimes and arrests, by offense, county, and local agency, 1992 and trends, annual rpt, S7890–3

Virginia crimes and arrests by offense, and law enforcement employment, by location and reporting agency, 1992, annual rpt, S8295–2.2

West Virginia drug law arrests by offender age, and drugs confiscated and value, by substance, 1990-91, annual rpt, S8610–1

Wisconsin crimes and arrests, by offense, offender characteristics, county, and local agency, 1992 and trends, annual rpt, S8771–1

Marine accidents and safety

Accidental deaths and disabling injuries, by detailed type, victim characteristics, circumstances, and location, 1992 and trends, annual rpt, A8375–2

Deaths from transportation accidents, trends by mode, 1992 annual rpt, R4815–1

Oil/gas industry occupational injury, illness, and employment data, by function, for 136 companies, 1991, annual rpt, A2575–4

Recreational boating accidents, and fatalities, 1987-91, annual feature, C2425–4

State and local:

Alabama vital statistics, including population, births, deaths by cause, marriages, and divorces, by location and demographic characteristics, 1992 and trends, annual rpt, S0175–2

Alaska crab fishing fatalities and lost vessels, with detail for selected incidents, 1992/93, article, C8900–1.516

Alaska vital statistics, including births, deaths by cause, marriages, divorces, adoptions, and population, by demographic characteristics and location, 1990, annual rpt, S0315–1

Arkansas vital statistics, including births, deaths by cause, marriages, and divorces, by age, sex, race, and county, 1991 and trends, annual rpt, S0685–1

California vital statistics, including population, births, and deaths by cause, by demographic characteristics and county, 1990 and trends, annual rpt, S0865–1

Colorado vital statistics, including population, births, deaths by cause, abortion, marriage and divorce, and adoption, by demographic characteristics and location, 1990 and trends, annual rpt, S1010–1

Florida accidental deaths by type, including underwater diving fatalities, 1960-92, annual rpt, S1745–3

Georgia vital statistics, including deaths by cause, demographic characteristics, and location, 1991 and trends, annual rpt, S1895–1.2

Hawaii data book, general data, 1992 annual rpt, S2090–1.7, S2090–1.18

Idaho vital statistics, including births, deaths by cause, abortions, marriages, and divorces, by demographic characteristics and county, 1991 and trends, annual rpt, S2250–2

Iowa vital statistics, including population, births, deaths by cause, marriages, and divorces, by demographic characteristics and location, 1991 and trends, annual rpt, S2795–1

Kansas vital statistics, including population, births, deaths by cause, abortions, marriages, and divorces, by demographic characteristics and location, 1991 and trends, annual rpt, S2975–1

Louisiana vital statistics, including population, births, deaths by cause, reportable diseases, marriages, and divorces, by demographic characteristics and locality, 1989-90 and trends, annual rpt, S3295–1

Maine vital statistics, including births, deaths by cause, abortions, and marriages and divorces, by demographic characteristics and location, 1991 and trends, annual rpt, S3460–2

Maryland vital statistics, including population, births, deaths by cause, marriages, and divorces, by demographic characteristics and location, 1989 and trends, annual rpt, S3635–1

Massachusetts vital statistics, including births, deaths by cause, marriages, divorces, and population, by locality and demographic characteristics, 1990 and trends, annual rpt, S3850–1

Michigan vital statistics, including births, deaths, marriages, divorces/annulments, and communicable diseases, by location and demographic characteristics, 1990 and trends, annual rpt, S4000–3

Minnesota vital statistics, including population, births, abortions, deaths, marriages, and divorces, by location and demographic characteristics, 1991 and trends, annual rpt, S4190–2

Mississippi vital statistics, including births, deaths by cause, marriages, and divorces, by demographic characteristics and location, 1992 and trends, annual rpt, S4350–1

Missouri vital statistics, including population, births, deaths by cause, and marriages and divorces, by location and demographic characteristics, 1992 and trends, annual rpt, S4518–1

Montana vital statistics, including births, deaths by cause, abortion, disease, and marriage and divorce, by demographic characteristics and county, 1990-91 and trends, annual rpt, S4690–1

Nebraska vital statistics, including births, deaths, marriages, divorces, and population, by demographic characteristics and location, 1991 and trends, annual rpt, S4885–1

Nevada vital statistics, including births, abortions, and deaths by cause, by county and demographic characteristics, 1989 and trends, annual rpt, S5075–1

Oregon vital statistics, including births, deaths by cause, communicable diseases, marriages, and divorces, by age, sex, race-ethnicity, and county, 1991 and trends, annual rpt, S6615–5

Rhode Island vital statistics, including population, births, deaths, marriages, and divorces, by demographic characteristics and locality, 1989 and trends, annual rpt, S6995–1

South Carolina deaths, by detailed cause, age, sex, and race, 1990, annual rpt, S7175–2

Tennessee vital statistics, including births, deaths by cause, marriages, divorces, and population, by demographic characteristics and location, 1991 and trends, annual rpt, S7520–2

Texas vital statistics, including births, deaths by cause, abortions, marriages, and divorces, by location and demographic characteristics, 1991 and trends, annual rpt, S7685–1

Utah vital statistics, including births and deaths by cause, by demographic characteristics and location, 1990, annual rpt, S7835–1.2

Virginia vital statistics, including births, deaths by cause, marriages and divorces, and communicable disease, by demographic characteristics and location, 1991 and trends, annual rpt, S8225–1

Washington State vital statistics, including births, deaths by cause, and population, by demographic characteristics and location, 1991 and trends, annual rpt, S8363–1

West Virginia vital statistics, including births, deaths by cause, marriages, and divorces, by location and demographic characteristics, 1991 and trends, annual rpt, S8560–1

Wisconsin vital statistics, including population, births, deaths by cause, and marriages and dissolutions, by county and demographic characteristics, 1991 and trends, annual rpt, S8715–4

Wyoming vital statistics, including population, births, deaths by cause, marriages, and divorces, by demographic characteristics and county, 1991 and trends, annual rpt, S8920–2

see also Drowning

see also Oil spills

see also Salvage

Marine bases

see Military bases, posts, and reservations

Marine Corps

Post exchange sales, by service branch, with merchandising devs and comparisons to civilian retail trade, monthly rpt, C0500–1

Post exchange sales, retail and other, by location and store, FY92 and trends, annual rpt, A2072–2.502

Marine Corps personnel
see Military personnel

Marine insurance
see Insurance and insurance industry

Marine pollution
State and local:
Hawaii beach water quality samplings and results, by beach, 1990, annual rpt, S2065–1.6
see also Oil spills

Marine resources
Latin America seaweed production, by country, 1970-88, annual rpt, U6250–1.24
World marine oils and fats production and disposition, by type, 1988/89-1992/93, annual rpt, B8480–1
see also Coastal areas
see also Fish and fishing industry
see also Offshore oil and gas
see also Oil spills
see also Shellfish
see also Water resources development

Marine resources conservation
see also Marine pollution

Marine safety
see Marine accidents and safety

Marion County, Ind.
Court cases and dispositions by type of court and case, and location, with judicial system finances and personnel, 1992, annual rpt, S2703–1

Marital status
see Marriage and divorce
see Widows and widowers
see under By Marital Status in the "Index by Categories"

Maritime academies
see Service academies

Maritime industry
see Ships and shipping

Mark, David E.
"Foreign Business Activity in the Former U.S.S.R.", R4105–82.4
"Gulf War", R4105–82.1

Market Facts Inc.
Cable TV subscriber views on value, desirability, program quality, and service, 1991-93, survey article, C2710–1.544
Canada photographic and video equipment and supplies ownership, purchasing patterns, and use, by household characteristics, 1992 survey, recurring rpt, A8695–4

Market Intelligence Research Co.
Electronic chip (fuzzy logic) sales worldwide, 1990-94, article, C1850–2.501
Microscope (scanning probe) sales distribution by application and world region, 1992 article, C1850–6.501
Microscope (visible light) sales, by end use, 1992, 1995, and 1998, article, C1850–6.501

Market research
Advertising and marketing industry devs articles and special features, including data on sales, revenues, research, consumer recall, personnel, and media shares, weekly rpt, C2710–1
Advertising to enhance corporate image, company practices, expenditures, and media use, 1987-92, triennial survey rpt, A3357–1

Direct marketer use of selected types of market research, 1992/93 annual rpt, A4620–1
Electronics/computer industry sources and ratings of purchasing info, and ratings of 14 market research firms, 1993 survey article, C1850–2.511
Incentive programs for consumers, with methods used to test consumer premium preferences, 1993 annual survey article, C1200–4.506
Radio audience ratings for 11 program formats, Arbitron vs Strategic Radio Research data, summer 1992, article, C1850–14.505
Radio audience ratings for 12 stations, Arbitron vs Strategic Radio Research data, summer 1992, article, C1850–14.502
Revenues and operations for leading market research firms, and industry devs, 1991-92, annual feature, C2710–1.550
Sales and marketing mgmt, issues and devs, including product sales, and demographic and socioeconomic profiles for major market areas, monthly rpt, C1200–1
Small business use of selected methods to obtain customer feedback, 1992 survey, C4687–1.503
Tourism dev offices of State govts, activities, personnel, and budgets, by State, 1992 survey, annual rpt, R9375–2
see also Consumer surveys
see also Media use surveys

Market shares
see Business income and expenses, specific industry
see Corporate rankings
see Economic concentration and diversification
see Product rankings
see Under names of specific industries and product types

Marketing
Auto aftermarket retail performance indicators, by product category, 1992 article, C2150–10.501
Auto dealer views on dealer assn and manufacturer advertising programs, including natl campaign spending levels by medium, with data by vehicle make, 1993 survey article, C2710–1.518, C2710–3.521
Bank small business lending and services, with data on organizational structure, loan delinquencies, and community dev activities, Nov 1992 survey, annual rpt, A4160–5
Book publishing industry financial and operating data, by publisher type and size, and subject category, 1991 and trends, annual rpt, A3274–2
Business-to-business marketing expenditure distribution by marketing vehicle, 1993 article, C2575–1.507
Cable TV system marketing budget shares for basic, pay, and pay-per-view, 1991-93, article, C9380–1.514
Chemist and chemical engineer salaries, employment status, and demographic and professional characteristics, 1993, annual rpt, A1250–4
Construction equipment distributor and contractor views on 1993 business outlook and marketing strategies, 1993 survey article, C1850–4.504

Corporate CEO workweek time spent on sales/marketing, by company sales size, 1992 survey, C4687–1.505
Corporate expenditures on advertising, marketing, and public relations involving support for the arts, 1991-92, recurring rpt, A3690–1
Cost per contact for 5 marketing methods, 1993 article, C2575–1.509
Discount chain manager views on influence in marketing decisions and product categories, 1993 survey, annual feature, C5150–3.520
Discount chain sales and merchandising, including data by dept, leading chain, and location, 1992 and trends, annual feature, C8130–1.507
Discount store financial and marketing devs, biweekly rpt, C5150–3
Discount store general merchandising devs, articles and special features, monthly rpt, C8130–1
Executive views on most important factors influencing future marketing strategy, Nov 1992-Jan 1993 survey, article, C2710–1.518
Financial instn home equity loan marketing media use, 1992, annual rpt, A4160–3
Food industry new product introductions, with data by product category, 1992, annual article, C2150–6.505
Food store operating and marketing devs, monthly rpt, C5225–1
Food/beverage industry new product dev influences, including industry personnel views on selected ingredients, suppliers, and dev time, 1993 annual article, C2150–6.511
Fuel oil dealer marketing techniques, by region, 1992 annual survey, C4680–2.3
Home improvement store financial and marketing devs, biweekly rpt, C5150–6
Homebuilder quality features marketing practices, 1993 survey, article, C1850–8.507
Homebuilder use of model homes, trailers, and off-site offices for sales purposes, 1993 survey article, C4300–1.503
Homebuilder use of selected marketing programs related to model homes, 1993 survey article, C4300–1.510
Liquor market statistics, including sales, consumption, trade, distillery operations, and govtl info, with data by company, brand, and location, 1992 and trends, annual rpt, C4775–1
Magazine circulation building strategies, including cost of a new subscriber and renewal data, 1993 survey, article, C2575–1.513
Medical group financial and operating data, by practice characteristics, 1991, annual rpt, A6365–2
New product dev process and significant contributing factors, 1993 articles, C2150–6.508
New product introductions, 1989-92, C5150–2.505
Oil industry capital spending in US and Canada, by function, 1991-93, annual articles, C6985–1.517
Oil supply-demand, marketing, prices, finances, and employment, detailed data for US and Canada, by product, company, and location, 1993 annual fact book, C4680–1.507

Marketing

Recession impact on corporate marketing budgets and staff, advertising media, sales, and market shares, Aug-Sept 1992 survey, A2075–20.10

Retail store credit operations, including cash vs credit sales, processing methods, and marketing techniques, 1992 annual survey, C5150–4.504

Sales and marketing mgmt, issues and devs, including product sales, and demographic and socioeconomic profiles for major market areas, monthly rpt, C1200–1

Sales executive ratings of corporate sales forces, by industry sector and sales function, 1993 annual survey article, C1200–1.512

Selling costs, including personnel compensation and training, and travel and related expenses, 1992 and trends, annual survey, C1200–1.508

Shoe industry market data, including foreign trade, production, and sales, by product type, 1991 and trends, annual rpt, A4957–1.1

Shopping center detailed income and expense data, by building characteristics, metro area, and region, 1991, annual rpt, A5600–6

Sporting goods purchases, by product and outlet type, census div, and purchaser characteristics, with average prices, 1992 and trends, annual survey, A8485–2

Supermarket health/beauty aid merchandising practices, 1993 survey article, C5225–1.506

Supermarket industry devs, product sales, merchandising, and store finances, monthly rpt, C4655–1

Supermarket shopper views on quality of customer service and importance of selected factors, by respondent characteristics, 1991-92 surveys, A4950–37

Technology use and future importance to marketing, executive views, July/Aug 1992 survey, article, C2710–1.510

Wine market statistics, including sales, production, trade, and consumer characteristics, with data by company, brand, and geographic area, 1992 and trends, annual rpt, C4775–2

see also Advertising

see also Agricultural marketing

see also Competition

see also Consumer credit

see also Consumer protection

see also Consumer surveys

see also Credit

see also Direct marketing

see also Economic concentration and diversification

see also Foreign competition

see also Industrial distribution

see also Labeling

see also Market research

see also Marketing areas

see also Packaging and containers

see also Price regulation

see also Prices

see also Retail trade

see also Sales promotion

see also Sales workers

see also Shopping centers

see also Wholesale trade

Marketing areas

Consumer buying power survey of population, income, and sales by kind of business, by census div, State, MSA, county, and city, 1992, annual rpt, C1200–1.511

Demographic and economic info on daily newspaper markets, by geographic area, US and Canada, 1993 annual rpt, C3250–1

Food store industry sales and operations, for 52 market areas, with rankings, 1992, annual rpt, C5225–1.505

Food store market shares and outlets, by company and store type, for approx 350 metro areas in US and Canada, with industry operating data, 1993 annual rpt, C3400–6

Media market area population, effective buying income, and retail sales, by State, 1992, annual rpt, C1200–1.514

Population and characteristics, households, income, and retail outlets, for 21 leading media market areas, 1993 feature, C2710–1.538

Radio audience ratings and program format, for top stations in leading metro markets, weekly rpt recurring article, C1850–14.506, C1850–14.507, C1850–14.508, C1850–14.521, C1850–14.531, C1850–14.542

Radio audience size, leading stations and formats, and advertising rates and revenues, by market area, recurring rpt, C3165–1

TV and total households, and member population by age and sex, by market area, county, State, and/or census div, 1992/93, annual rpt, B0525–3

TV households and population by race-ethnicity, sex, and age, by market area, 1992/93, annual rpt, B0525–4

TV households and ranking among top 100 market areas, for 46 areas changing rank, 1992/93-1993/94, C1850–14.538

TV households by census div, State, county, Nielsen market area, and time zone, Jan 1994, annual rpt, B6670–2

Marketing quotas

see Agricultural production quotas and price supports

Marks, Joseph L.

"SREB Fact Book on Higher Education, 1992", A8945–1

Markusen, Ann

"Converting the Cold War Economy: Investing in Industries, Workers, and Communities", R4700–19

Marriage and divorce

Asia population age at 1st marriage, by sex and country, 1890s-1980s, R4500–1.64

Black youth age 15-19 and 20-24 marriage trends, with comparisons to whites, by sex, 1970, 1980, and/or 1991, R3840–21

Catholic population, including marriages and deaths, by diocese and State, 1993 annual compilation, C4950–1

Catholic public opinion on marriage for priests, 1971-93 surveys, R8780–1.510

College freshmen social and academic expectations, by sex and instn type, fall 1992, annual survey, U6215–1

Developing countries median age of women at 1st marriage, and percent married before age 20, by country, 1985-92 surveys, U2520–1.51

Interracial married couples, 1980, 1990, and 1991, annual compilation, C6775–2.1

Latin America statistical abstract, general data by country, 1992 annual rpt, U6250–1.6

Public opinion on desirability of wives being employed vs keeping house, US, 9 European countries, and 3 Soviet Union Republics, 1991 survey, C8915–8.1, C8915–9

Race and Hispanic ethnicity of husbands and wives, Mar 1991, annual compilation, C6775–3.1

State social, economic, and govtl indicators, with rankings, 1993 semiannual rpt, B8500–1.1

Statistical profiles of 50 States and DC, general data, 1993 annual almanac, C4712–1

Women's marriage rates, by age, race, and education, 1985, article, A8510–1.1

Youth approval of interracial and interfaith marriages, by respondent characteristics, 1993 survey feature, R8780–1.507

Youth opinions about selected social issues, by religion, 1991-93 surveys, R8780–1.510

State and local:

Alabama vital statistics, including population, births, deaths by cause, marriages, and divorces, by location and demographic characteristics, 1992 and trends, annual rpt, S0175–2

Alaska vital statistics, including births, deaths by cause, marriages, divorces, adoptions, and population, by demographic characteristics and location, 1990, annual rpt, S0315–1

Arkansas vital statistics, including births, deaths by cause, marriages, and divorces, by age, sex, race, and county, 1991 and trends, annual rpt, S0685–1

Colorado vital statistics, including population, births, deaths by cause, abortion, marriage and divorce, and adoption, by demographic characteristics and location, 1990 and trends, annual rpt, S1010–1

Connecticut vital statistics, including births, deaths by cause, marriages, and divorces, by demographic characteristics and location, 1989, annual rpt, S1200–1

DC marriage bur activities, 1985-92, annual rpt, S1515–1

Delaware vital statistics, including births, deaths by cause, and marriages and dissolutions, by demographic characteristics and location, 1990, annual rpt, S1385–2

Florida vital statistics, including population, births, deaths by cause, and marriages and dissolutions, by location and demographic characteristics, 1992 and trends, annual rpt, S1745–3

Georgia marriage licenses issued, by county, FY92, annual rpt, S1903–1

Georgia vital statistics, including population, births, abortions, marriages, and divorces, by demographic characteristics and location, 1991 and trends, annual rpt, S1895–1.1

Hawaii vital statistics, including births, deaths by cause, marriages, and dissolutions, by demographic characteristics and location, 1990, annual rpt, S2065–1.2

Index by Subjects and Names

Maryland

Idaho vital statistics, including births, deaths by cause, abortions, marriages, and divorces, by demographic characteristics and county, 1991 and trends, annual rpt, S2250–2

Illinois statistical abstract, general data, 1992 annual rpt, U6910–2

Iowa vital statistics, including population, births, deaths by cause, marriages, and divorces, by demographic characteristics and location, 1991 and trends, annual rpt, S2795–1

Kansas vital statistics, including population, births, deaths by cause, abortions, marriages, and divorces, by demographic characteristics and county, 1991 and trends, annual rpt, S2975–1

Kentucky vital statistics, including births, deaths by cause, marriages and divorces, and population, by demographic characteristics and county, 1991, annual rpt, S3140–1

Louisiana vital statistics, including population, births, deaths by cause, reportable diseases, marriages, and divorces, by demographic characteristics and locality, 1989-90 and trends, annual rpt, S3295–1

Maine vital statistics, including births, deaths by cause, abortions, and marriages and divorces, by demographic characteristics and location, 1991 and trends, annual rpt, S3460–2

Maryland vital statistics, including population, births, deaths by cause, marriages, and divorces, by demographic characteristics and location, 1989 and trends, annual rpt, S3635–1

Massachusetts vital statistics, including births, deaths by cause, marriages, divorces, and population, by locality and demographic characteristics, 1990 and trends, annual rpt, S3850–1

Michigan vital statistics, including births, deaths, marriages, divorces/annulments, and communicable diseases, by location and demographic characteristics, 1990 and trends, annual rpt, S4000–3

Minnesota vital statistics, including population, births, abortions, deaths, marriages, and divorces, by location and demographic characteristics, 1991 and trends, annual rpt, S4190–2

Mississippi vital statistics, including births, deaths by cause, marriages, and divorces, by demographic characteristics and location, 1992 and trends, annual rpt, S4350–1

Missouri vital statistics, including population, births, deaths by cause, and marriages and divorces, by location and demographic characteristics, 1992 and trends, annual rpt, S4518–1

Montana vital statistics, including births, deaths by cause, abortion, disease, and marriage and divorce, by demographic characteristics and county, 1990-91 and trends, annual rpt, S4690–1

Nebraska vital statistics, including births, deaths, marriages, divorces, and population, by demographic characteristics and location, 1991 and trends, annual rpt, S4885–1

Nevada marriages and divorces, by county, 1989, annual rpt, S5075–1

New Hampshire vital statistics, including population, births, deaths by cause, marriages, and divorces, by location and demographic characteristics, 1991 and trends, annual rpt, S5215–1

New Jersey vital statistics, including births, deaths, population, communicable diseases, and marriages and divorces, by demographic characteristics and location, 1990 and trends, annual rpt, S5405–1

New Mexico marriages and divorces, 1980-91, annual rpt, S5605–1.1

New York State vital statistics, including population, births, deaths by cause, reportable diseases, and marriages and dissolutions, by demographic characteristics and/or location, 1990 and trends, annual rpt, S5765–1

North Carolina vital statistics, including population, births, deaths, marriages, and divorces, by local area, 1991 and trends, annual rpt, S5927–1.1

North Dakota vital statistics, including births, deaths by cause, marriages and divorces, and abortions, by demographic characteristics and/or county, 1991 and trends, annual rpt, S6105–2

Ohio vital statistics, including births, deaths by cause, marriages, divorces, and population, by demographic characteristics and location, 1991 and trends, annual rpt, S6285–1

Oregon vital statistics, including births, deaths by cause, communicable diseases, marriages, and divorces, by age, sex, race-ethnicity, and county, 1991 and trends, annual rpt, S6615–5

Rhode Island vital statistics, including population, births, deaths, marriages, and divorces, by demographic characteristics and locality, 1989 and trends, annual rpt, S6995–1

South Carolina vital statistics, including births, deaths by cause, marriages, and divorces, by age, sex, race, and location, 1990 and trends, annual rpt, S7175–1

South Dakota vital statistics, including births, deaths, marriage and divorce, and communicable disease, by demographic characteristics and county, 1991 and trends, annual rpt, S7345–1

Tennessee statistical abstract, general data, 1992/93 annual rpt, U8710–2.17

Tennessee vital statistics, including births, deaths by cause, marriages, divorces, and population, by demographic characteristics and location, 1991 and trends, annual rpt, S7520–2

Texas vital statistics, including births, deaths by cause, abortions, marriages, and divorces, by location and demographic characteristics, 1991 and trends, annual rpt, S7685–1

Utah marriages and divorces, by participant characteristics and location, 1990 and trends, annual rpt, S7835–2

Utah vital statistics, including marriages and divorces/annulments, 1990 and trends, annual rpt, S7835–1.1

Vermont vital statistics, including population, births, deaths by cause, abortions, marriages, and divorces, by location and demographic characteristics, 1991 and trends, annual rpt, S8054–1

Virginia vital statistics, including births, deaths by cause, marriages and divorces, and communicable disease, by demographic characteristics and location, 1991 and trends, annual rpt, S8225–1

Washington State marriages and divorces, 1950-90, annual rpt, S8345–4

West Virginia vital statistics, including births, deaths by cause, marriages, and divorces, by location and demographic characteristics, 1991 and trends, annual rpt, S8560–1

Wisconsin birth, death, and marriage registrations, monthly rpt, S8750–1

Wisconsin vital statistics, including population, births, deaths by cause, and marriages and dissolutions, by county and demographic characteristics, 1991 and trends, annual rpt, S8715–4

Wyoming vital statistics, including population, births, deaths by cause, marriages, and divorces, by demographic characteristics and county, 1991 and trends, annual rpt, S8920–2

see also Births out of wedlock

see also Child support and alimony

see also Domestic relations courts and cases

see also Families and households

see also Vital statistics

see also Widows and widowers

see also under By Marital Status in the "Index by Categories"

Marshall Islands

see Trust Territory of the Pacific Islands

Martin, Julia H.

"1991 Estimates of the Population of Virginia Counties and Cities", U9080–9

Martin, Rose Marie

"New Jersey Health Statistics, 1990", S5405–1

Maryland

Banks and credit unions (State-chartered) financial condition by instn, with regulatory data, FY92 annual rpt, S3655–2

Court caseloads and dispositions, by type of court and case, and county, with judicial personnel and finances, FY92 and trends, annual rpt, S3600–1

Crimes and arrests, by offense, location, and offender characteristics, with law enforcement employment and assaults on officers, 1992 and trends, annual rpt, S3665–1

Election results, by county and district, 1992 general election, biennial rpt, S3615–1

Elementary and secondary education data, by county, annual rpt series, S3610–2

Elementary and secondary education statistical summary, with data by county, 1991/92-1992/93 and trends, annual rpt, S3610–1

Govt financial condition, including revenues by source, expenditures by function, fund balances, and bonded debt, FY92 and trends, annual rpt, S3685–2

Income tax (individual) returns filed, and income and tax liability data, by city, county, and income group, 1991, annual rpt, S3685–1

Insurance industry financial and underwriting data, by company and type of insurance, with regulatory info, 1991, annual rpt, S3655–1

Maryland

Labor force, employment, earnings, and hours, with data by industry and location, monthly rpt, S3605–2

Library operating income and expenditures, staff, holdings, and population served, by county, FY92, annual rpt, S3610–5

Local govt financial condition, including revenues by source, expenditures by function, and debt obligations, FY92 and trends, annual rpt, S3618–1

Markets with daily newspapers, demographic and economic info by geographic area, US and Canada, 1993 annual rpt, C3250–1

Medical assistance payments and recipients, by program, type of service, location, demographic characteristics, and facility, FY92 and trends, annual rpt, S3635–3

Oil/gas industry production, finances, exploration, and reserves, by State, 1992 and trends, annual rpt, A5425–1.1

Rabies cases in animals, and dispositions of infected animals, by species, 1981-87, article, A3100–2.504

Rabies cases in cats and raccoons, and human exposure from cats, 1983-92, article, A3100–2.515

Statistical abstract of Maryland, detailed social, govtl, and economic data, 1993-94 biennial rpt, S3605–1

Statistical profiles of 50 States and DC, general data, 1993 annual almanac, C4712–1

Traffic accidents, fatalities, and injuries, by circumstances, location, vehicle type, and driver and victim characteristics, 1992, annual rpt, S3665–4

Utility and transportation regulatory agency activities, scope of jurisdiction, finances, and employees, by agency, 1991/92 annual rpt, A7015–2

Vital statistics, including population, births, deaths by cause, marriages, and divorces, by demographic characteristics and location, 1989 and trends, annual rpt, S3635–1

Vocational rehabilitation case activity, by county and disability, 1992, annual rpt, S3610–1

Welfare program statistics, and welfare fraud investigations, by county, monthly rpt, S3645–2

see also Baltimore, Md.

see also under By City and By County in the "Index by Categories"

see also under By State in the "Index by Categories"

Mass media

Advertising agency income, billings by medium, employees, and offices, for leading US and/or foreign agencies, 1992 and trends, annual rpt, C2710–1.522

Advertising costs for selected media, with detail by audience sex, 1993 article, A8605–1.505

Advertising expenditure increase, by medium, 1993, article, C2710–1.505

Advertising expenditures at natl and local levels, by medium, 1993, article, C2710–1.506

Advertising expenditures by medium for top 100 advertisers, with comparisons to earnings and sales, and detail by product type and brand, 1991-92, annual rpt, C2710–1.547

Advertising expenditures by medium, 1965-91, annual rpt, C3975–5.3

Advertising expenditures by medium, 1991-92, annual feature, C2710–1.525

Advertising expenditures of corporations and assns, by medium, 1988-92, and top 10 advertisers for 1992, annual article, A8770–1.504

Advertising media buying services, competition, and staffing, views of agency and independent service executives, 1993 annual survey articles, C2710–1.537

Advertising revenues for mass media, by medium, 1990-92, article, C1200–1.513

Advertising to enhance corporate image, company practices, expenditures, and media use, 1987-92, triennial survey rpt, A3357–1

Audience characteristics and advertising effectiveness of radio compared with other media, 1993 annual rpt, A8789–1

Auto advertising expenditures, by medium, 1990-92, annual article, C2710–3.552

Auto dealer and natl campaign advertising expenditure distribution by medium, 1991, article, A8605–1.505

Auto dealer views on dealer assn and manufacturer advertising programs, including natl campaign spending levels by medium, with data by vehicle make, 1993 survey article, C2710–1.518, C2710–3.521

Auto dealership advertising expenditures by medium, by dealer sales volume, 1992, annual rpt, A7330–1

Broadcast industries and cable TV devs, including data on finances, advertising, ratings, and licensing, weekly rpt, C1850–14

Broadcasting revenues and profits, by source, for 3 major networks, 1992, annual article, C1850–14.522

Canada photographic/video products/services consumer advertising exposure and reaction, by medium and selected characteristics, 1992 survey, recurring rpt, A8695–4

Current event and issue coverage by TV and print news media, analysis of selected topics, bimonthly rpt, R3823–1

Developing countries women's views on family planning messages, and TV and radio ownership rates, by country, 1985-92 surveys, U2520–1.51

Direct marketing industry devs, including advertising patterns, finances, target market characteristics, and consumer attitudes, 1992/93 annual rpt, A4620–1

Europe advertising costs for 4 media, by country, with comparisons to US, 1992, article, C2710–1.532

Europe advertising expenditure outlook by medium, for 12 countries, 1993 vs 1992, article, C2710–1.513

Europe public opinion on political, economic, and social issues of interest to foreign investors, for 9 countries and 3 Soviet Union Republics, 1991 survey, C8915–9

Hispanic American marketing devs, including leading advertisers and media, and market characteristics, 1992 annual features, C4575–1.502

Liquor industry advertising expenditures, by medium, company, and brand, 1992 and trends, annual rpt, C4775–1

Index by Subjects and Names

News media personnel views on 1992 presidential election coverage, candidates, and related issues, for natl media, Oct 1992 survey, C8915–4.25

Photographic products/services advertising, consumer awareness and reaction by media, 1993 survey, recurring rpt, A8695–2

Public opinion on corporate handling of crises, including honesty and media reliability, 1993 survey article, A8770–1.505

Public opinion on the media and related issues, by respondent characteristics, series, C8915–11

Public opinion on whether media are too critical of President Clinton, and treatment compared to Bush, June 1993 Gallup Poll, C4040–1.512

Public relations firms and depts purchasing of selected types of media-related services, 1992 survey, article, A8770–1.501

Rape victim and service agency staff views on withholding victim names in media, 1990-92 surveys, R8375–1

Revenues and earnings of top 100 broadcasting and related electronic communications companies, 1992, annual article, C1850–14.526

Revenues for leading media companies, with detail by medium, 1991-92, annual feature, C2710–1.540

Wine advertising expenditures, by medium, brand, and company, 1991-92, annual rpt, C4775–2

see also Media use surveys

see also Motion pictures

see also Newspapers

see also Periodicals

see also Public broadcasting

see also Radio

see also Television

Mass transit

see Airlines

see Buses

see National Railroad Passenger Corp.

see Railroads

see Subways

see Urban transportation

Massachusetts

Correctional instn inmate characteristics and criminal background, by instn, Jan 1992 and trends, annual rpt, S3805–1

Court cases and dispositions, by type of court and case, and location, FY92 and trends, annual rpt, S3807–1

Election results and voter registration, by local area, 1992 and trends, biennial rpt, S3920–1

Elementary/secondary education summary data, 1989/90-1991/92 and trends, annual rpt, S3810–3

Elementary/secondary school enrollment by grade, by district, Oct 1992, annual rpt, S3810–4

Elementary/secondary school expenditures per pupil by program, by district, 1991/92, annual rpt, S3810–5

Employment, by SIC 2- and 3-digit industry and detailed occupation, suspended series, S3808–2

Employment, hours, and earnings, by industry and local area, with unemployment insurance claims, monthly rpt, S3808–1

Index by Subjects and Names

Maternity

Govt financial condition, including revenues by source, and expenditures by function, by fund, FY92 and trends, annual rpt, S3777–1

Health behavior risk factor surveillance survey results, by respondent characteristics, 1986-90, recurring rpt, S3850–3

Libraries (public) finances, holdings, and circulation, by municipality, FY92, annual rpt, S3870–1

Markets with daily newspapers, demographic and economic info by geographic area, US and Canada, 1993 annual rpt, C3250–1

Medical malpractice insurance State joint underwriting assn (JUA) financial condition, for 11 States, 1991, annual rpt, A0375–1

Statistical profiles for Massachusetts municipalities and counties, socioeconomic and govtl data, 1992 annual rpt, C4712–2

Statistical profiles of 50 States and DC, general data, 1993 annual almanac, C4712–1

Tax collections by type, and distributions to local areas, FY91 and trends, annual rpt, S3917–1

Unemployment insurance benefit needs as affected by program to help unemployed start a business, 1993 article, C4687–1.507

Utility and transportation regulatory agency activities, scope of jurisdiction, finances, and employees, by agency, 1991/92 annual rpt, A7015–2

Vital statistics, including births, deaths by cause, marriages, divorces, and population, by locality and demographic characteristics, 1990 and trends, annual rpt, S3850–1

see also Boston, Mass.

see also Cambridge, Mass.

see also under By City and By County in the "Index by Categories"

see also under By State in the "Index by Categories"

Materials handling equipment

Shipments of conveyors/systems, 1970-91, article, C2150–1.506

Maternity

Africa women's premarital sexual experience and childbearing, for 7 Sub-Saharan countries, 1986-89, article, A5160–6.503

Births and fertility, by selected newborn and maternal characteristics, 1990, article, R8750–1.510

Black American health and vital statistics data, with comparisons to whites, 1970s-91, annual compilation, C6775–2.2

Child health and well-being indicators, including percent of births to women with selected risk factors, by State, 1990, annual rpt, R3832–1

Death (maternal) rates by race, 1970-90, R3840–21

Developing countries family planning and child survival efforts, by country and selected demographic characteristics, 1980s-90, R8720–1

Dominican Republic women's childbearing and contraceptive use patterns, 1993 article, A5160–6.503

Expenditures for health care by type, and prevailing treatment charges, 1950s-91, annual rpt, A5173–2.3

Health and welfare indicators for women and children, with data by race and State, 1992 annual rpt, R3840–5

Hospital patient admission rates and length of stay, by diagnosis and procedure, payment source, age, sex, and region, 1991, B4455–4

Hospital patient charges and length of stay, by diagnosis and procedure, payment source, age, and region, 1991, B4455–5

Latin America statistical abstract, general data by country, 1992 annual rpt, U6250–1.6

Low-income families and children, health and welfare indicators, with data by State and city, 1992 annual rpt, R3840–11

Philippines birth outcomes by maternal characteristics, 1983/84 Cebu metro area study, article, A5160–6.505

Public health research results concerning perinatal condition of mothers and infants, 1993 articles, A2623–1.510

Sexual behavior of unmarried women with unplanned pregnancies, by selected characteristics, 1989/90 Baltimore study, A5160–1.506

Unintended pregnancy risk and eligibility for subsidized family planning services among women age 13-44, by State, 1990, article, A5160–1.502

World population and health indicators, with detail by region and country, 1992/93 biennial rpt, R9455–1.5

State and local:

Alabama vital statistics, including population, births, deaths by cause, marriages, and divorces, by location and demographic characteristics, 1992 and trends, annual rpt, S0175–2

Alaska vital statistics, including births, deaths by cause, marriages, divorces, adoptions, and population, by demographic characteristics and location, 1990, annual rpt, S0315–1

Arkansas vital statistics, including births, deaths by cause, marriages, and divorces, by age, sex, race, and county, 1991 and trends, annual rpt, S0685–1

California vital statistics, including population, births, and deaths by cause, by demographic characteristics and county, 1990 and trends, annual rpt, S0865–1

Colorado vital statistics, including population, births, deaths by cause, abortion, marriage and divorce, and adoption, by demographic characteristics and location, 1990 and trends, annual rpt, S1010–1

Connecticut vital statistics, including births, deaths by cause, marriages, and divorces, by demographic characteristics and location, 1989, annual rpt, S1200–1

Delaware vital statistics, including births, deaths by cause, and marriages and dissolutions, by demographic characteristics and location, 1990, annual rpt, S1385–2

Florida vital statistics, including population, births, deaths by cause, and marriages and dissolutions, by location and demographic characteristics, 1992 and trends, annual rpt, S1745–3

Georgia vital statistics, including population, births, abortions, deaths by cause, marriages, and divorces, by demographic characteristics and location, 1991 and trends, annual rpt, S1895–1

Hawaii vital statistics, including births, deaths by cause, marriages, and dissolutions, by demographic characteristics and location, 1990, annual rpt, S2065–1.2

Idaho vital statistics, including births, deaths by cause, abortions, marriages, and divorces, by demographic characteristics and county, 1991 and trends, annual rpt, S2250–2

Iowa vital statistics, including population, births, deaths by cause, marriages, and divorces, by demographic characteristics and location, 1991 and trends, annual rpt, S2795–1

Kansas vital statistics, including population, births, deaths by cause, abortions, marriages, and divorces, by demographic characteristics and location, 1991 and trends, annual rpt, S2975–1

Kentucky vital statistics, including births, deaths by cause, marriages and divorces, and population, by demographic characteristics and county, 1991, annual rpt, S3140–1

Louisiana vital statistics, including population, births, deaths by cause, reportable diseases, marriages, and divorces, by demographic characteristics and locality, 1989-90 and trends, annual rpt, S3295–1

Maine vital statistics, including births, deaths by cause, abortions, and marriages and divorces, by demographic characteristics and location, 1991 and trends, annual rpt, S3460–2

Maryland vital statistics, including population, births, deaths by cause, marriages, and divorces, by demographic characteristics and location, 1989 and trends, annual rpt, S3635–1

Massachusetts vital statistics, including births, deaths by cause, marriages, divorces, and population, by locality and demographic characteristics, 1990 and trends, annual rpt, S3850–1

Michigan vital statistics, including births, deaths, marriages, divorces/annulments, and communicable diseases, by location and demographic characteristics, 1990 and trends, annual rpt, S4000–3

Minnesota vital statistics, including population, births, abortions, deaths, marriages, and divorces, by location and demographic characteristics, 1991 and trends, annual rpt, S4190–2

Mississippi vital statistics, including births, deaths by cause, marriages, and divorces, by demographic characteristics and location, 1992 and trends, annual rpt, S4350–1

Missouri vital statistics, including population, births, deaths by cause, and marriages and divorces, by location and demographic characteristics, 1992 and trends, annual rpt, S4518–1

Montana vital statistics, including births, deaths by cause, abortion, disease, and marriage and divorce, by demographic characteristics and county, 1990-91 and trends, annual rpt, S4690–1

Maternity

Nebraska vital statistics, including births, deaths, marriages, divorces, and population, by demographic characteristics and location, 1991 and trends, annual rpt, S4885–1

Nevada vital statistics, including births, abortions, and deaths by cause, by county and demographic characteristics, 1989 and trends, annual rpt, S5075–1

New Hampshire vital statistics, including population, births, deaths by cause, marriages, and divorces, by location and demographic characteristics, 1991 and trends, annual rpt, S5215–1

New Jersey vital statistics, including births, deaths, population, communicable diseases, and marriages and divorces, by demographic characteristics and location, 1990 and trends, annual rpt, S5405–1

New Mexico vital statistics, including population, births, deaths, and disease, by location and demographic characteristics, 1991 and trends, annual rpt, S5605–1

New York State vital statistics, including population, births, deaths by cause, reportable diseases, and marriages and dissolutions, by demographic characteristics and/or location, 1990 and trends, annual rpt, S5765–1

North Dakota vital statistics, including births, deaths by cause, marriages and divorces, and abortions, by demographic characteristics and/or county, 1991 and trends, annual rpt, S6105–2

Ohio vital statistics, including births, deaths by cause, marriages, divorces, and population, by demographic characteristics and location, 1991 and trends, annual rpt, S6285–1

Oregon vital statistics, including births, deaths by cause, communicable diseases, marriages, and divorces, by age, sex, race-ethnicity, and county, 1991 and trends, annual rpt, S6615–5

Rhode Island vital statistics, including population, births, deaths, marriages, and divorces, by demographic characteristics and locality, 1989 and trends, annual rpt, S6995–1

South Carolina deaths, by detailed cause, age, sex, and race, 1990, annual rpt, S7175–2

South Carolina vital statistics, including births, deaths by cause, marriages, and divorces, by age, sex, race, and location, 1990 and trends, annual rpt, S7175–1

South Dakota vital statistics, including births, deaths, marriage and divorce, and communicable disease, by demographic characteristics and county, 1991 and trends, annual rpt, S7345–1

Tennessee vital statistics, including births, deaths by cause, marriages, divorces, and population, by demographic characteristics and location, 1991 and trends, annual rpt, S7520–2

Texas vital statistics, including births, deaths by cause, abortions, marriages, and divorces, by location and demographic characteristics, 1991 and trends, annual rpt, S7685–1

Utah vital statistics, including births, deaths by cause, and population, by county and demographic characteristics, 1990 and trends, annual rpt, S7835–1

Vermont vital statistics, including population, births, deaths by cause, abortions, marriages, and divorces, by location and demographic characteristics, 1991 and trends, annual rpt, S8054–1

Virginia vital statistics, including births, deaths by cause, marriages and divorces, and communicable disease, by demographic characteristics and location, 1991 and trends, annual rpt, S8225–1

Washington State vital statistics, including births, deaths by cause, and population, by demographic characteristics and location, 1991 and trends, annual rpt, S8363–1

West Virginia vital statistics, including births, deaths by cause, marriages, and divorces, by location and demographic characteristics, 1991 and trends, annual rpt, S8560–1

Wisconsin vital statistics, including population, births, deaths by cause, and marriages and dissolutions, by county and demographic characteristics, 1991 and trends, annual rpt, S8715–4

Wyoming vital statistics, including population, births, deaths by cause, marriages, and divorces, by demographic characteristics and county, 1991 and trends, annual rpt, S8920–2

see also Birth defects

see also Birthing centers

see also Births

see also Births out of wedlock

see also Birthweight

see also Breast-feeding

see also Family planning

see also Fertility

see also Fetal deaths

see also Home births

see also Infant mortality

see also Maternity benefits

see also Midwives

see also Obstetrics and gynecology

see also Plural births

see also Prenatal care

see also Teenage pregnancy

Maternity benefits

Business forms manufacturing plant use of maternity leave benefits, by region, 1992, biennial rpt, A5785–4

Family-related policies of employers, with involvement in child, elderly, and disabled care services, and personnel mgmt views, Mar 1992 survey, A8907–1

House of Representatives staff characteristics, salaries, and benefits by position, 1992 and trends, recurring rpt, R4140–1

Psychiatry residency program maternity and paternity leave policies, 1991/92 survey, article, A3273–8.511

State and local:

Arkansas human services dept finances and operations, including Medicaid payments by type of service, FY91 and trends, annual rpt, S0700–2.3

Maryland medical assistance payments and recipients, by program, type of service, location, demographic characteristics, and facility, FY92 and trends, annual rpt, S3635–3

Michigan public assistance program cases, recipients, and payments, detailed data by county, monthly rpt, S4010–1

South Carolina medical assistance program for pregnant women and children, applications and dispositions by county, monthly rpt, S7252–1

Washington State public assistance clients and service costs, by client characteristics, program, and county, FY90, annual rpt, S8420–2

West Virginia welfare and social service program caseloads and expenditures, by county, monthly rpt, S8560–2

Maternity homes

see also Births out of wedlock

Mathematic models and modeling

see also Economic and econometric models

Mathematics

Achievement test scores worldwide for math and science, for students age 13 in 14 countries, 1990, annual rpt, R3840–11.1

Black elementary/secondary students taking selected math courses, and educational test results, with comparisons to whites, 1993 rpt, R3840–21

Elementary/secondary education data, with detail for mathematics including test scores and teacher preparation, by State, 1993 biennial rpt, A4355–1

Elementary/secondary science and math education, including student and teacher characteristics, and requirements, by State, 1991/92, biennial rpt, A4355–3

Elementary/secondary students with math teachers emphasizing algebra and geometry, by State, 1990, article, R4800–2.522

Employer basic skills testing and training practices and costs, Jan-Mar 1993 survey, annual rpt, A2075–20.13

Employment in business and industry, hiring plans for college grads, by field, salary, and degree, 1993 annual survey rpt, U3730–1

Higher education math dept faculty, salaries, enrollment, and degree recipient characteristics, 1991/92 and trends, annual survey, A2085–1

Natl Assessment of Educational Progress mathematics test results, for public vs private school students, 1990, article, U8710–1.503

Public school student distribution and mathematics proficiency ratings by frequency of changing schools in past 2 years, by region, 1992, R4800–2.520

Salaries of scientists, engineers, technicians, and other professionals, by employee and employer characteristics, 1990s and trends, biennial rpt, A3960–1

Urban public school student performance on standardized reading and mathematics tests, for 47 systems, 1990/91, A4425–4

Women and minorities in professional fields, detailed education and labor force data, 1991 and trends, recurring rpt, A3960–2.3

State and local:

Connecticut public school data, including enrollment, staff, programs, finances, and student characteristics, 1991/92, biennial rpt, S1185–3

see also Computer sciences

Maui County, Hawaii

Economic indicators and population, 1988-1st half 1993, annual rpt, B3500–2.3

Mauritius

Motor vehicle world production, sales, trade, and registrations, by country, world area, manufacturer, and make, 1991 and trends, annual rpt, A0865–2.1

Mayors
see Officials

McCann-Erickson Inc.
Advertising expenditures at natl and local levels, by medium, 1993, article, C2710–1.506
Advertising expenditures by medium, 1991-92, annual feature, C2710–1.525
Advertising revenues for mass media, by medium, 1990-92, article, C1200–1.513

McClure, Donald E.
"1992 Annual AMS-MAA Survey", A2085–1

McCormick, Jennifer
"State Revenue Report", U5085–1
"Trends in Federal Aid to States Since 1989: Not What Many People Assume", U5085–2.12

McGillivray, Alice V.
"America Votes 20: A Handbook of Contemporary American Election Statistics", C2500–1
"Presidential Primaries and Caucuses, 1992: A Handbook of Election Statistics", C2500–7

McGlynn, Anita
"United Arts Fundraising 1992", A1315–2

McGonagle, Sara R.
"Mid-Level Practitioners: Their Role in Providing Quality Health Care", U8850–8.4

McKenzie, Richard B.
"1980s: A Decade of Debt?", U9640–2.14

Measles
see Infective and parasitic diseases

Measures
see Instruments and measuring devices
see Weights and measures

Meat and meat products
Consumer nutrition awareness and health concerns, with food shopping and consumption patterns, by respondent characteristics, 1993 survey, annual rpt, A4950–36
Exports of farm products, by detailed commodity and country of destination, US and California, 1991, annual rpt, B9520–1
Financial and operating ratios of the meat packing industry, discontinued annual rpt, A2100–2
Financial ratios and performance, for over 350 SIC 4-digit industries, FY88-92, annual rpt, A6400–3
Food store meat dept personnel, marketing practices, and sales by product type, 1991, annual rpt, A4950–5
Japan beef domestic production and imports, 1988-92, article, R5650–2.548
Latin America statistical abstract, general data by country, 1992 annual rpt, U6250–1.16, U6250–1.25
Military commissary sales, by region, product type, and individual store, FY92, annual feature, A2072–2.501
Operating and financial composite ratios for corporations, with establishments and receipts, for approx 200 industries, by asset size, FY90, annual rpt, C7800–1

Production, consumption, stocks, trade, and prices for approx 100 basic commodities, including by country and producing State, commodity yearbook for 1993, C2400–1, C2400–2
Retail prices for selected consumer items in approx 300 cities, quarterly rpt, A0150–1
Sales and consumer expenditures, for food store products by type, 1991-92, annual feature, C4655–1.510
Sales volume shares by retail outlet type, for approx 300 food, drug, and other product categories, 1993 annual feature, C4655–1.504
Supermarket meat dept sales and performance indicators, 1992 and trends, annual article, C4655–1.509
Supermarket product sales and market shares, for top 10 brands in 5 processed meat categories, 1991-92, C2710–1.513
Supermarket sales by detailed product type, 1992 and trends, annual feature, C5225–1.507
Supply-demand of meat and poultry, and livestock and packing industries finances and operations, 1991 and trends, annual rpt, A2100–1
Swine slaughtered, tuberculosis-infected carcass incidence, and carcass value and loss, 1976-88, article, A3100–2.519

State and local:
Alaska agricultural production and marketing, by district and commodity, 1960s-92, annual rpt, U5750–1
Arizona livestock slaughtering establishments, and red meat production, 1988-93, annual rpt, U5830–1
Arkansas agricultural production, marketing, and finances, by commodity and county, with farms and acreage, 1992 and trends, annual rpt, U5920–1
California livestock slaughtered under govt inspection, by species, 1983-92, annual rpt, S0850–1.2
Colorado livestock slaughtered, by species and month, 1987-92, annual rpt, S0985–1
Florida livestock, dairy, and poultry production, inventory, marketing, and finances, with detail by commodity or species, 1992 and trends, annual rpt, S1685–1.3
Georgia red meat production, 1984-91, annual rpt, S1855–1
Hawaii beef, pork, and poultry marketings by island, and supplies from mainland and foreign sources, 1991 and trends, annual rpt, S2030–1
Illinois agricultural production, marketing, and finances, by county or commodity, and farms and farmland, 1991 and trends, annual rpt, S2390–1
Kansas livestock slaughter, feedlots, and red meat production, 1992 and trends, annual rpt, S2915–1
Kentucky agricultural production, marketing, and finances, by commodity and county; and farms, acreage, and value; 1992 and trends, annual rpt, S3085–1
Louisiana agricultural production, marketing, and finances, by commodity or parish, 1985-91, annual rpt, U2740–1
Michigan agricultural production, marketing, and finances, by commodity or county, 1987-91, annual rpt, S3950–1

Minnesota agricultural production, marketing, and finances, by county or commodity, and farms and acreage, 1992 and trends, annual rpt, S4130–1
Missouri agricultural production, marketing, and finances, by commodity and/or county, and farms and acreage, 1988-92, annual rpt, S4480–1
Montana livestock slaughtered, and red meat production, 1983-91, annual rpt, S4655–1
Nebraska agricultural production, marketing, and finances, by commodity and/or county, and farms and acreage, 1991 and trends, annual rpt, S4835–1
Nevada agricultural production, marketing, and finances, by county and commodity, and farms and acreage, 1992 and trends, annual rpt, S5010–1
New Jersey livestock slaughtered, by month, 1990-91, annual rpt, S5350–1
New Mexico livestock slaughtered, 1987-91, annual rpt, S5530–1
New York State agricultural production, marketing, and finances, by commodity and/or county, and farms and acreage, 1992 and trends, annual rpt, S5700–1
North Carolina livestock slaughter, and number of slaughtering establishments, various years 1990-92, annual rpt, S5885–1
Ohio agricultural production, marketing, and finances, by commodity and county, with farms and acreage, 1990-91 and trends, annual rpt, S6240–1
Oklahoma agricultural production, marketing, and finances, by commodity and county, 1992 and trends, annual rpt, S6405–1
Pennsylvania agricultural production, marketing, and finances, by county and commodity, and farms and acreage, 1992 and trends, annual rpt, S6760–1
South Carolina red meat production and poultry slaughter, 1991-92, annual rpt, U1075–3
South Dakota agricultural production, marketing, and finances, by commodity and county, and farms and acreage, 1992 and trends, annual rpt, S7280–1
Tennessee livestock slaughtering establishments, and red meat production, 1986-93, annual rpt, S7460–1
Texas agricultural production, marketing, and finances, by commodity and county, and farms and farmland, 1991 and trends, annual rpt series, S7630–1
Utah livestock slaughtered, monthly business activity rpt, U8960–2
Vermont licensed meat handling establishments, and production and condemnation, 1989-90 biennial rpt, S7978–1
Washington State livestock slaughtered, 1992 and trends, annual rpt, S8328–1
West Virginia commercial livestock slaughtered, by species, 1982-91, annual rpt, S8510–1
Wisconsin agricultural production, marketing, and finances, by commodity and county, and farms, acreage, and sales, 1992 and trends, annual rpt, S8680–1
Wyoming agricultural production, marketing, and finances, by county and/or commodity, and farms, acreage, and value, 1992 and trends, annual rpt, S8860–1

Meat and meat products

see also Food and waterborne diseases
see also Oils, oilseeds, and fats

Medals

see Awards, medals, and prizes

Media use surveys

Black American public TV viewing habits, including top-rated programs, 1992 survey, R4250–1.17

Broadcast industries and cable TV devs, including data on finances, advertising, ratings, and licensing, weekly rpt, C1850–14

Cable TV industry devs, including leading multiple system operators and systems, finances, advertising, and data by network and service, biweekly rpt, C1858–1, C2965–1

Children reading selected written material, and listening to radio, by sex, 1990 survey, article, C2710–1.512

Consumer use of TV and other media, 1992/93 annual rpt, A4620–1.2

Energy publications deemed most helpful by fuel oil dealers, by publication and region, 1992 annual survey, C4680–2.3

Hours of media use per capita, trends by medium, 1987-91, article, C9380–1.504

News events followed most closely by public, and opinion on media coverage and selected current issues, by respondent characteristics, recurring rpt, C8915–1

Newspaper pages and sections read, 1989-92, article, C2710–1.537

Newspaper readers, and sections read, by sex, 1993 annual rpt, A8605–4

Newspaper readership among men vs women, biennially 1986-92, article, A8605–1.507

Newspaper readership by sex, 1992-93, article, A8605–1.511

Public recall of news events, correlation with media use, education, and other variables, 1989 surveys, article, A0610–1.503

Radio ownership, audience characteristics, and advertising revenues and effectiveness, with selected comparisons to other media, 1993 annual rpt, A8789–1

TV (public) viewing habits of members vs general public, 1992 survey rpt, R4250–1.22

TV viewership among public leaders/experts, with detail for public TV, 1992 survey rpt, R8825–10.2

State and local:

Hawaii data book, general data, 1992 annual rpt, S2090–1.16

Mediation

see Legal arbitration and mediation

Medicaid

AIDS and human immunodeficiency virus (HIV) infection reporting accuracy on hospital and Medicaid records, 1993 article, A2623–1.512

Child and maternal health and welfare indicators, by State, FY90 or 1990, annual rpt, R3840–11.2

Child and total recipients, expenditures, and other Medicaid program characteristics, and child health summary, by State, FY91, annual rpt, A0565–1

Drugs (prescription) financing methods among population age 65/older and 64/under, by patient characteristics, 1987, R4865–8

Expenditures of State govts by fund source and function, by State, FY90-92, annual rpt, A7118–1

Federal budget trends, including spending by program, State, and region, FY81-94, annual rpt, R8490–11

Federal grants, recipients, and benefits by type of service, with selected public health funding factors, by State and region, various years 1974-94, R8490–46

Federal share of Medicaid cost, by State, FY93, article, B8500–2.514

Funding of govt health care programs by source, Medicare enrollments, and Medicaid recipients, 1960s-91, annual rpt, A5173–2.2

HMO benefits, enrollment and utilization, staffing, finances, and relations with employers, by plan characteristics, 1990-91, annual rpt, A5150–2

Home health care payments per recipient, for 16 highest and 17 lowest States, FY91, article, B8500–2.511

Hospital Medicaid share of discharges, and average length of stay, by instn characteristics and location, 1988-92, annual rpt, B1880–1.3

Hospital Medicaid share of discharges, for academic medical centers, 1987-91, article, A3273–8.511

Hospital patient admission rates and length of stay, by diagnosis and procedure, payment source, age, sex, and region, 1991, B4455–4

Hospital patient charges and length of stay, by diagnosis and procedure, payment source, age, and region, 1991, B4455–5

Hospital patient discharges and length of stay, by diagnostic related group (DRG), payment source, age, and region, 1991, annual rpt series, B4455–3

Payment error rates, by State, FY90-91, annual rpt, S2623–1.6

Payments and recipients for selected Federal entitlement programs, by State and region, early 1990s, R8490–47

Pharmacist requirements under 1990 Omnibus Budget Reconciliation Act (OBRA) to keep Medicaid patient drug use records and offer counseling, consumer views, 1993 article, C5150–2.509

Physician group practice participation in Medicaid, with detail by State, 1991, recurring rpt, A2200–7

Population (non-elderly) share covered by Medicaid, for 8 States with highest and lowest rates, 1991, article, B8500–2.508

Pregnancy services expansion efforts, including eligibility, outreach activities, and obstetrician reimbursement, by State, 1993 article, A5160–1.506

Recipients and expenditures, by basis of eligibility and type of service, FY81 and/or FY90, annual rpt, R3840–5.1

Recipients as percent of population in poverty, by State, FY90, article, B8500–2.501

Recipients, payments by type of service, and Federal and State expenditures by State, 1993 annual fact book, A1275–1.5

Southern States children age 17/under lacking health insurance and eligible for Medicaid, with detail by age and family income, for 6-17 States, 1991, R9000–1

Southern States Federal Medicaid funding, for 15 States, 1990, annual rpt, U6660–1.20

State govt actual vs budgeted change in Medicaid spending, by State, FY92, article, B8500–2.507

State govt expenditures for Medicaid and other functions, by State, FY92-93, annual rpt, A7470–4.10

State Medicaid funding from general fund and aggregate other funds, 1989-92, U5085–2.12

State Medicaid matching funds from sources other than general fund as a percent of Federal Medicaid grants, by State, FY93, article, B8500–2.509

State rankings by percent change in Medicaid appropriations, FY93, article, B8500–2.506

State social, economic, and govtl indicators, with rankings, 1993 semiannual rpt, B8500–1.6, B8500–1.9

Statistical profiles of 50 States and DC, general data, 1993 annual almanac, C4712–1

State and local:

Alabama public welfare and social service cases, recipients, and payments, by program and county, monthly rpt, S0150–1

Arkansas human services dept finances and operations, including Medicaid payments by type of service, FY91 and trends, annual rpt, S0700–2.3

DC statistical profile, general data, 1992 annual rpt, S1535–3.5

Florida persons eligible for Medicaid, and Medicaid expenditures, by county, 1992, annual rpt, S1746–1.1

Georgia county guide, general data, 1993 annual rpt, U6750–1

Idaho public welfare program expenditures and recipients, with data by county, quarterly rpt, S2250–1

Indiana public assistance program participation, expenditures, and services, by county, FY92 and trends, annual rpt, S2623–1

Kentucky Medicaid recipients and payments, by program, county, and type of medical service, monthly rpt, S3140–5

Michigan public assistance program cases, recipients, and payments, detailed data by county, monthly rpt, S4010–1

Mississippi public welfare and social service cases, recipients, and payments, by program and county, FY92, annual rpt, S4357–1

Montana health care facility capacity, utilization, and finances, by instn, 1991, annual rpt, S4690–2

Montana Medicaid fraud investigations, FY91-92, biennial rpt, S4750–1.1

Montana welfare and medical assistance program cases and payments, by county and type of service, monthly rpt, S4755–1

Nebraska public welfare cases, recipients, and payments, by program and county, FY92 and trends, annual rpt, S4957–1

Nevada statistical abstract, general data, 1992 biennial rpt, S5005–1.2

New Mexico public assistance cases, expenditures, and case processing, by program and county, monthly rpt, S5620–2

Index by Subjects and Names

Medical costs

North Carolina public welfare programs, cases, recipients, staff, and finances, by county, 1st half FY93, semiannual rpt, S5940–2

Oklahoma public welfare program expenditures, recipients, and services, by program and county, FY92 and trends, annual rpt, S6455–1

Oklahoma statistical abstract, general data, 1992 annual rpt, U8130–2.10

Pennsylvania statistical abstract, general data, 1992 recurring rpt, U4130–6.5

South Carolina public welfare recipients, payments, and case processing, by county and program, monthly rpt, S7252–1

Tennessee Medicaid expenditures and recipients, including spending by funding source, FY87-93, annual rpt, S7560–1

Tennessee Medicaid recipients and payments by eligibility category, and expenditures by funding source, early FY90s and trends, article, U8710–1.502

Tennessee statistical abstract, general data, 1992/93 annual rpt, U8710–2.18

Texas Medicaid expenditures by category, and recipient characteristics and medical services received, 1975 and 1980-91, U8850–8.5

Texas population eligible for Medicaid, by county, FY92, annual rpt, S7695–1

West Virginia Medicaid case quality control activity, monthly rpt, S8560–2

Wyoming Medicaid recipients and payments, by county and category, monthly FY92, annual rpt, S8908–1

Medical assistance

Drugstore (independent pharmacy) prescription activity covered by Medicaid and other 3rd-party programs, by store characteristics, 1991 and trends, annual survey, B5165–1

Expenditures for health and medical care by source of funds and program, 1960s-91, annual rpt, R9050–1.1

Japan and US health care system data, including expenditures, facilities, insurance coverage, and population health indicators, 1993 article, R5650–2.515

Voluntary health agency revenues, and expenditures by function, for 39 major organizations, FY90, annual rpt, A7973–1

State and local:

Arizona public assistance recipients and payments, by program, county, and district, monthly rpt, S0465–4

Arkansas human services dept finances and operations, including Medicaid payments by type of service, FY91 and trends, annual rpt, S0700–2.3

Colorado welfare and social services expenditures and caseloads, by county and/or program, FY91, annual rpt, S1085–1

DC statistical profile, general data, 1992 annual rpt, S1535–3.5

Hawaii data book, general data, 1992 annual rpt, S2090–1.11

Idaho public welfare program expenditures and recipients, with data by county, quarterly rpt, S2250–1

Illinois public assistance program cases, recipients, and payments, by program and county, FY91-92 and trends, annual rpt, S2520–2

Indiana expenditures and/or cases for selected medical assistance programs, by county, FY92 annual rpt, S2623–1.8

Louisiana births occurring in charity hospitals, by race, 1978-90, annual rpt, S3295–1

Maryland medical assistance payments and recipients, by program, type of service, location, demographic characteristics, and facility, FY92 and trends, annual rpt, S3635–3

Maryland welfare program statistics, and welfare fraud investigations, by county, monthly rpt, S3645–2

Massachusetts births, by payment sources for prenatal and hospital care, 1990, annual rpt, S3850–1

Michigan public assistance program cases, recipients, and payments, detailed data by county, monthly rpt, S4010–1

Minnesota public welfare program recipients and expenditures, by county, 1992, semiannual rpt, S4202–1

Missouri public welfare and medical assistance recipients, expenditures, and case processing, by program and county, FY92 and trends, annual rpt, S4575–2

Montana welfare and medical assistance program cases and payments, by county and type of service, monthly rpt, S4755–1

New York State public assistance and social service program statistics, by State area and source of funds, 1991 and trends, annual rpt, S5800–2

New York State statistical yearbook, general data, 1992 annual rpt, U5100–1.11

Oklahoma public welfare program expenditures, recipients, and services, by program and county, FY92 and trends, annual rpt, S6455–1

Oregon caseload and payments for medical service by category, monthly 1pt quarterly table, S6615–8

Pennsylvania statistical abstract, general data, 1992 recurring rpt, U4130–6.5

South Carolina public welfare recipients, payments, and case processing, by county and program, monthly rpt, S7252–1

South Dakota medical assistance recipients and payments, by county and type of service, FY92, annual rpt, S7385–1

Tennessee statistical abstract, general data, 1992/93 annual rpt, U8710–2.18

Texas hospitals, operations, utilization, and finances, by type, ownership, size, and metro-nonmetro status, 1970s-91, U8850–8.3

Texas indigent health care finances and utilization, with data by county, district, public hospital, and medical school, 1986-91, U8850–8.7

Texas welfare and social services program expenditures, recipients, and fraud cases, by county and/or program, FY92 and trends, annual rpt, S7695–1

Utah govt statistical review, fiscal and socioeconomic data, 1993 annual rpt, R9380–1.9

Utah statistical abstract, general data, 1993 triennial rpt, U8960–1.6

Washington State public assistance clients and service costs, by client characteristics, program, and county, FY90, annual rpt, S8420–2

West Virginia welfare and social service program caseloads and expenditures, by county, monthly rpt, S8560–2

Wisconsin Blue Book, general data, 1993-94 biennial rpt, S8780–1.2

see also Maternity benefits

see also Medicaid

see also Medicare

see also State funding for health and hospitals

Medical centers

see Hospitals

see Military health facilities and services

see Veterans health facilities and services

Medical costs

Abortion costs in selected developing countries, 1989, R8720–1.1

Accident medical costs, by type of accident, 1992, annual rpt, A8375–2.1

AIDS and human immunodeficiency virus (HIV) treatment costs, 1993-94, article, C4215–1.503

City fiscal condition, including perceived impact of spending for health care services, Mar-Apr 1993 survey, annual rpt, A8012–1.23

Cost-of-living indexes and retail prices for selected consumer items in approx 300 cities, quarterly rpt, A0150–1

Developing countries family planning service costs, by contraceptive method and service type, for 13 countries, 1980s, article, A5160–6.502

Disabled persons use of home care services, with costs, payment sources, and types of care, by selected characteristics, 1992, R4865–15

Drugs (prescription) use, expenditures, prices, and profit trends, with data by patient characteristics and for top 20 brands, 1992 rpt, R4865–8

Electric utility industry employee health care costs, with comparisons to revenue and expenses, 1991 and 2000, article, A4700–4.505

Expenditures and insurance coverage under health care plans of presidential candidates Bush and Clinton vs current law, by State, 1993-2005, R4865–9

Expenditures for health care, and/or medical care CPI, for US and 14 OECD countries, 1960s-91, annual fact book, A1275–1.4

Expenditures for health care, by category, 1970-90, article, C5150–2.521

Expenditures for health care, with detail by expenditure category, 1970s-93, annual article, B6045–1.502

Eye bank activity, including processing fees, 1992, annual rpt, A4743–1

Family expenditures for health care, including insurance premiums by source of coverage, and taxes by type, by income group, 1987, R4700–20

Hard goods manufacturers and representatives views on health care reform and responsibility for excessive costs, by product line, 1993 annual survey rpt, A1800–1

Health care vs defense expenditures, employment, exports, and facilities, with detail for health care expenditures by type, 1993, article, C8900–1.515

Health insurance coverage and finances, and health care costs and facilities, by selected demographic characteristics, 1940s-91, annual rpt, A5173–2

Medical costs

HMO benefits, enrollment and utilization, staffing, finances, and relations with employers, by plan characteristics, 1990-91, annual rpt, A5150–2

Home health services expenditures, 1987-93, article, A1865–1.508

Hospital costs per day and per stay by State, and health care expenditures by payment source and item, 1990, annual rpt, A5650–1

Hospital expenditures for acute care facilities in US and Canada, with detail for California and Ontario, 1987, article, A1865–1.512

Hospital industry financial and operating indicators, with detail for Medicare, by instn characteristics and location, 1988-92, annual rpt, B1880–1

Hospital patient charges and length of stay, by diagnosis and procedure, payment source, age, and region, 1991, B4455–5

Hospital use of formal program to control rising pharmaceutical costs, 1993 survey article, A1865–1.505

Hospital vs home care costs for 6 conditions, 1993 feature, A1865–1.519

Household expenditures for health care, for approx 300 metro areas, 1992, annual rpt, C1200–1.511

Industrial mgmt magazine reader views on who is responsible for economic problems, Federal budget deficit, and health care costs, Feb 1993 survey, article, C7000–3.510

Japan and US health care system data, including expenditures, facilities, insurance coverage, and population health indicators, 1993 article, R5650–2.515

Mexico-US border communities comparative physician fees, 1992 rpt, R4865–10

Opinions of physicians and general public on health care reform, by respondent characteristics, Mar-Apr 1993 surveys, C8915–7.2

Physician fees and expenses, and detailed work patterns, by specialty, type of practice and location, and age, 1982-92, annual rpt, A2200–5.2

Population with high out-of-pocket medical expenses, by State, source of insurance, and selected characteristics, 1993, R4865–14

Prostate surgery procedures, costs, and hospital stay, with data by census div and State, 1991 and trends, article, B6045–1.503

Public opinion on health care concerns, including costs and insurance coverage, May 1993 Gallup Poll, C4040–1.512

Public opinion on health care issues, including govt and medical profession role, satisfaction with care and insurance, and reforms, 1975-92 surveys, A0610–1.504

Sexually transmitted disease early detection and treatment costs vs treatment costs for subsequent illnesses, for gonorrhea and chlamydia, 1990, A5160–10

Statistical profiles of 50 States and DC, general data, 1993 annual almanac, C4712–1

Tonsillectomy/adenoidectomy procedures, costs, and hospital stay, with data by census div and State, 1991 and trends, article, B6045–1.502

TV news coverage of health issues, including leading topics, and Clinton Admin policies, Jan-May 1993, article, R3823–1.508

Widow nonreimbursed medical expenses for husband in year preceding his death, by race, 1990 survey, U3780–9

State and local:

Alabama statistical abstract, general data, 1992 recurring rpt, U5680–2.8

Arizona statistical abstract, general data, 1993 recurring rpt, U5850–2.3

Arkansas prescription drug and nursing home cost trends, 1982-91, annual rpt, S0700–2.3

California births by payment source for prenatal care and delivery, 1990, annual rpt, S0865–1

California individual taxable income reported by source, deductions and credits by type, and tax returns, by income class and county, 1990, annual rpt, S0855–1.1

Connecticut health care cost influence on population receiving care, by health insurance coverage, 1991 survey, S1200–3

Delaware data book, general data, 1993 annual rpt, S1375–4

Florida hospital admissions, length of stay, and charges, for selected conditions or procedures, by county, 1990, annual rpt, S1746–1.2

Florida statistical abstract, general data, 1992 annual rpt, U6660–1.20

Georgia statistical abstract, general data, 1992-93 biennial rpt, U6730–1.1

Hawaii data book, general data, 1992 annual rpt, S2090–1.2

Idaho economic profile, general data, 1992 recurring rpt, S2218–2.7

Nevada statistical abstract, general data, 1992 biennial rpt, S5005–1.2

New York State births by payment source, by location, 1990, annual rpt, S5765–1

Oklahoma statistical abstract, general data, 1992 annual rpt, U8130–2.9

South Carolina statistical abstract, general data, 1993 annual rpt, S7125–1.10

Texas indigent health care finances and utilization, with data by county, district, public hospital, and medical school, 1986-91, U8850–8.7

see also Health insurance

see also Medicaid

see also Medical assistance

see also Medicare

Medical education

Black student enrollment in medical school, with comparison to whites, 1978/79 and 1989/90, annual compilation, C6775–2.3

Dental advanced education programs, enrollment, grads, and finances, by instn and State, 1992/93 annual rpt, A1475–10

Dental allied education enrollment, grads, and tuition, by instn, 1992/93 annual rpt, A1475–5

Dental school enrollment and grads, program characteristics, and faculty, by US and Canadian instn, 1992/93, annual rpt, A1475–3

Dental school programs, enrollment, and finances by instn, annual rpt series, A1475–4

Faculty and compensation in medical school preclinical depts, 1992/93, annual rpt, A0800–1

Faculty and compensation in medical schools, by dept, academic rank, degree, and region, 1991/92, annual rpt, A3273–2

Faculty physician and allied personnel compensation and productivity at medical schools, by academic rank, sex, and specialty, 1991, annual rpt, A6365–5

Finances of medical schools, with revenues, student aid, and staff, by instn type, 1989/90 and/or 1990/91, article, A3273–8.503

General practice specialty choices of medical school grads, by school characteristics including Federal aid, and for top 20 schools (unnamed), 1993 articles, A2623–1.505

Hispanic American student enrollment in medical school, with comparison to whites, 1979/80 and 1989/90, annual compilation, C6775–3.2

Hospital financial and operating indicators by teaching status, and intern/resident cost per FTE, by instn characteristics and location, 1988-92, annual rpt, B1880–1

Hospitals by selected characteristics including teaching activity, 1991, B4455–4, B4455–5

Hospitals by selected characteristics including teaching activity, 1991, annual rpt series, B4455–1, B4455–3

Hospitals with and without psychiatric units, by selected characteristics including teaching activity, 1991, annual rpt series, B4455–2

Nurse views on managed health care topics appropriate for undergraduate nursing curriculums, Jan 1993 survey, article, A1865–1.517

Nursing college deans and salaries, by personal and instn characteristics, 1992/93, annual rpt, A0615–2

Nursing college faculty and salaries, by personal and instn characteristics, 1992/93, annual rpt, A0615–1

Nursing educational and professional trends and devs, monthly rpt, A8010–3

Nursing higher education program finances, faculty and clinical practice, and clinic/center operations, by instn characteristics, 1992/93 biennial rpt, A0615–5

Nursing programs (State-approved) for practical/vocational nurses, including admissions, enrollment, and grads, by instn, State, and territory, 1992, annual directory, A8010–5

Nursing programs (State-approved) for registered nurses, including admissions, enrollment, and grads, by instn, State, and territory, 1992, annual directory, A8010–4

Nursing school enrollment and grads, by degree level, sex, race-ethnicity, and instn type and location, 1992/93 and trends, annual rpt, A0615–4

Nursing schools, programs, enrollment, student and staff characteristics, and grads, 1991 and trends, annual rpt, A8010–1

Optometry school faculty, enrollment and degrees, policies and programs, and finances, by instn, 1991/92, annual survey, A3370–2

Index by Subjects and Names

Medical examinations and tests

Osteopathy college enrollment, student and faculty characteristics, and finances, 1992/93 and trends, annual rpt, A0620–1

Osteopathy student debt and career plans, by student characteristics, 1991/92 and trends, annual survey rpt, A0620–2

Pharmacy degree program applications, enrollment, and degrees conferred, by student characteristics and instn, 1990/91 and trends, annual rpt, A0630–9

Physician resident matching program participants, by specialty, 1993, annual article, A3273–8.507

Physicians by detailed specialty and location, 1992 and trends, annual rpt, A2200–3

Professional issues and devs in medical education, monthly rpt, A3273–8

Programs, fees, applicants, admissions, and enrollment, with data by age, sex, minority group, and instn, 1992/93 and trends, annual rpt, A3273–10

Public health school applicant, student, and grad characteristics, by instn, 1991/92 and trends, annual rpt, A3372–3

Public health school faculty characteristics, by instn, fall 1991, recurring rpt, A3372–1

Residents in surgery by specialty, and medical schools, students, and grads, 1993 annual fact book, A1275–1.1

Salary and job offers for college grads, by field of study, type of employer, and degree level, by region, interim rpt series, A3940–1

Salary and job offers for college grads, by field of study, type of employer, and degree level, series, A3940–2

Southern States higher education enrollment, degrees, appropriations, tuition/fees, and faculty compensation, by instn type, for 15 States, 1990/91, annual rpt, A8945–31

Southern States higher education enrollment, degrees, faculty, and finances, for 15 States, 1990s and trends, biennial fact book, A8945–1

State and land-grant university tuition/fees, and room and board charges, by type of professional program and/or instn, fall 1991-92, annual rpt, A7150–4

Teaching hospital house staff stipends, benefits, and expenditures, by region and ownership, 1992/93 and trends, annual rpt, A3273–3

Veterinarian practice expenses as percent of revenues, by expenditure category and type of practice, 1990-91, annual survey article, C9480–1.501

Veterinarians by professional characteristics and location, and financial and education summaries, 1993 annual directory, A3100–1

Veterinary school academic and clinical grad program enrollment, quinquennially 1967-92, article, A3100–2.513

Veterinary school aquatic animal course availability, faculty, and enrollment, by instn, 1991/92, article, A3100–2.509

Veterinary school enrollment by sex, program, instn, and place of residence, US and Canada, 1992/93, annual article, A3100–2.516

Veterinary school grad employment, starting salaries, benefits, and personal characteristics, by sex, 1992, annual survey article, A3100–2.504

Veterinary school grad starting salaries by type of employment, and educational debt, 1992, annual survey article, A3100–2.503

Veterinary surgery teaching methods used at 27 US and Canadian veterinary schools, 1993 article, A3100–2.521

Voluntary health agency revenues, and expenditures by function, for 39 major organizations, FY90, annual rpt, A7973–1

Western States higher education student exchange program enrollment and support fees, by program and instn, for 15 States, 1992/93, annual rpt, A9385–1

Women and minorities in professional fields, detailed education and labor force data, 1980s-91, with historical trends, recurring rpt, A3960–2

Women's share of medical school enrollment, 1960s-93, annual rpt, A1570–2

State and local:

California postsecondary education enrollment and degrees, by sex, race-ethnicity, and instn, 1990/91, annual series, S0827–2

Florida health care program enrollment and completers in postsecondary instns, by program, 1991, annual rpt, S1746–1.2

Florida higher education enrollment, degree programs, staff, and finances, by State-supported instn, with student and staff characteristics, 1991/92 annual rpt, S1725–1

Illinois higher education enrollment, degrees, staff, and finances, by public and private instn and student characteristics, 1993 annual rpt, S2475–1

Iowa postsecondary enrollment, degrees, staff, and finances, by instn, 1990/91, annual rpt, S2755–1

Minnesota medical student loan program participation and loan status, 1993 biennial rpt, S4195–2.2

Mississippi higher education enrollment and degrees, by level and field, and finances, by State-supported instn, 1991/92, annual rpt, S4360–1

Missouri student grant and academic scholarship program awards at allied health care education instns, FY93 and trends, annual rpt, S4520–3.2

New York State statistical yearbook, general data, 1992 annual rpt, U5100–1.10

Pennsylvania vocational education enrollment, student characteristics, and faculty, by program and/or school, 1991/92 and trends, annual rpt, S6790–5.7

Pennsylvania vocational education 1989/90 grad employment status, by program, 1991 survey, annual rpt, S6790–5.6

South Carolina higher education enrollment, degrees, staff, and finances, by instn, 1992 and trends, annual rpt, S7185–2

Texas higher education enrollment, faculty, curricula, and finances, by instn, 1991/92 and trends, annual rpt, S7657–1

Texas indigent health care finances and utilization, with data by county, district, public hospital, and medical school, 1986-91, U8850–8.7

Texas nursing employment, demand outlook, earnings, and education, by selected characteristics, various years 1971-91, U8850–8.2

Utah higher education degrees, enrollment, staff, and finances, by public instn, with selected comparisons to instns in other States, 1993/94 annual rpt, S7895–2

see also Federal aid to medical education

see also Foreign medical graduates

see also Medical research

see also State funding for medical education

Medical equipment

see Medical supplies and equipment

Medical ethics

Health care reform priorities of general public vs health professionals, including importance of ethics and alternative medicine, 1993 survey article, A1865–1.522

see also Euthanasia

see also Medical malpractice

Medical examinations and tests

AIDS incidence in the workplace by region and industry, and employer testing and other policies, 1993 and trends, A2075–20.14

AIDS testing, including confidentiality, notification, and testing of selected groups, public opinion, 1987-91 surveys, A0610–1.502

AIDS testing of prison and jail inmates, and positive cases, including by State or locale, 1992 annual series, R4300–1

AIDS testing site awareness among adults, with analysis by demographic characteristics, 1990 survey, article, A2623–1.506

College freshmen attitudes on mandatory testing to control AIDS, fall 1992, annual survey, U6215–1

College grad new hire testing for drugs, alcohol, and AIDS, employer practices, 1992/93 annual survey rpt, U3130–1

Corporate employee screening and testing practices, including drug use and AIDS, 1993 annual survey rpt, U3730–1

Fire dept employment and personnel practices, including eligibility requirements and testing, by population size, metro status, and census div, 1991 survey, recurring rpt, A5800–2.116

Health condition and preventive health care and safety practices of adults, by respondent characteristics, 1992 and trends, annual survey rpt, C8111–2

High-technology patient procedures overuse, recommendations of health care professionals, 1993 survey article, A1865–1.522

HMO benefits coverage, premiums, and rating methods used, by plan characteristics, 1991 and trends, annual rpt, A5150–2.1

Hospital diagnostic imaging procedures performed monthly, by bed-size group, 1989-92, survey article, A1865–1.523

Hospital patient admission rates and length of stay, by diagnosis and procedure, payment source, age, sex, and region, 1991, B4455–4

Hospital patient charges and length of stay, by diagnosis and procedure, payment source, age, and region, 1991, B4455–5

Medical examinations and tests

Human immunodeficiency virus (HIV) testing and posttest counseling rates, by demographic characteristics, 1989, article, A2623–1.501

Outpatient procedures likely to be performed in nonhospital settings, 1993 article, A1865–1.518

Pregnancy home test kit market shares, for top 5 and all other brands, 1992, articles, C5150–2.511

Smoking status reported by cessation program participants correlated with biochemical testing results, 1993 article, A2623–1.511

Women's use of mammography and Pap smear tests, by demographic characteristics, 1987 survey, article, A2623–1.503

State and local:

Alabama infant condition at birth, Apgar scores by demographic characteristics, 1992, annual rpt, S0175–2

Arkansas human services dept finances and operations, including Medicaid payments by type of service, FY91 and trends, annual rpt, S0700–2.3

Colorado births by 5-minute Apgar scores, by age and race-ethnicity of mother, 1990, annual rpt, S1010–1

Colorado health behavior risk factor surveillance survey results, by respondent characteristics, 1990, recurring rpt, S1010–3

Connecticut health behavior risk factor surveillance survey results, 1989-91, annual rpt, S1200–2

Delaware births by Apgar score at 1 and 5 minutes, 1990, annual rpt, S1385–2

Delaware school nurse services, including screening examinations, by county, 1991/92, annual rpt, S1430–1.6

Hawaii health dept activities and services, including vital statistics and disease control, by location, 1990, annual rpt, S2065–1

Idaho live births and Apgar scores, 1991, annual rpt, S2250–2

Iowa health behavior risk factor surveillance survey results, by respondent characteristics, 1991, annual rpt, S2795–2

Kentucky Medicaid recipients and payments, by program, county, and type of medical service, monthly rpt, S3140–5

Massachusetts health behavior risk factor surveillance survey results, by respondent characteristics, 1986-90, recurring rpt, S3850–3

Michigan health behavior risk factor surveillance survey results, by respondent characteristics, 1991, annual rpt, S4000–4

Nevada health behavior risk factor surveillance survey results, by location and respondent characteristics, 1991, annual rpt, S5075–3

New Jersey births, by Apgar score and selected maternal characteristics, 1990, annual rpt, S5405–1

New York State health behavior risk factor surveillance survey results, by respondent characteristics, 1990, recurring rpt, S5765–3

Pennsylvania health behavior risk factor surveillance survey results, by respondent characteristics, 1991, annual rpt, S6820–4

Texas health behavior risk factor surveillance survey results, by respondent characteristics, 1991 and trends, annual rpt, S7685–2

Utah births, by birthweight and Apgar score, 1990, annual rpt, S7835–1.2

Utah health behavior risk factor surveillance survey results, by respondent characteristics, 1991, annual rpt, S7835–3

Utah human immunodeficiency virus (HIV) victim sexual partner notification program results, including HIV testing outcome for partners, 1988-90, article, A2623–1.512

Virginia births, with Apgar scores by race and sex of infant and age of mother, 1991, annual rpt, S8225–1

Wyoming infant condition at birth, as indicated by 1- and 5-minute Apgar scores, 1991, annual rpt, S8920–2

see also Autopsies

see also Drug and alcohol testing

see also Mammography

see also X-rays

Medical facilities and services

see Health facilities and services

Medical instruments

see Instruments and measuring devices

see Medical supplies and equipment

Medical insurance

see Blue Cross-Blue Shield

see Health insurance

see Health maintenance organizations

Medical libraries

Librarians at universities and research instns, salaries by sex, type of position, and instn, FY92 and trends, annual survey, A3365–2

Natl Library of Medicine collection and services, FY92, annual compilation, C1650–3.1

State and local:

California library finances, staff, holdings, and services, by library type and facility, FY92, annual rpt, S0825–2

Medical malpractice

Costs of tort cases, with detail for medical malpractice and comparisons to 10 other countries, 1991, article, A1865–1.503

Jury awards in medical professional liability cases, quinquennially 1970-90, annual fact book, A1275–1.5

Lawsuit verdicts awarded, including number exceeding $1 million, 1982-91, annual rpt, A5650–1.3

Personal injury jury verdict award trends, with data by case type and for awards exceeding $1 million, 1960s-92, annual rpt, C5180–1

Physician medical malpractice claim rates, by specialty and census div, 1985-91, annual rpt, A2200–5.1

State and local:

Arizona superior court medical malpractice cases, by county, FY92, annual rpt, S0525–1

Kansas medical malpractice cases, FY92, annual rpt, S3035–1

Maine medical malpractice court claims filed and dispositions, by county, 1987-91, annual rpt, S3463–1

Massachusetts court cases and dispositions, by type of court and case, and location, FY92 and trends, annual rpt, S3807–1

Index by Subjects and Names

New Mexico court cases and dispositions, by type of court and case, and location, with judicial system finances and personnel, FY92, annual rpt, S5623–1

Texas physicians insured against professional liability, with data on premiums and claims, and detail by specialty and/or age, sex, and city, 1978-91, U8850–8.8

Virginia medical malpractice review panel activity, including claims by detailed specialty, July 1976-Dec 1992, annual rpt, S8300–1

see also Property and casualty insurance (for data on malpractice insurance)

Medical personnel

see Health occupations

Medical research

Cancer research funding by American Cancer Society, by recipient instn, FY92, annual rpt, A1175–1

Chemical carcinogenicity prediction accuracy of 8 methods, 1993 article, A1250–1.529

Court cases involving medical education instn/faculty research issues by type, 1950-91, article, A3273–8.503

Drugs under dev for selected diseases affecting older adults and women, 1989-93, A1865–1.519

Expenditures for health care by type, and prevailing treatment charges, 1950s-91, annual rpt, A5173–2.3

Eye bank activity in US and abroad, including donations by type, source, and donor characteristics, and data by individual bank, 1992 and trends, annual rpt, A4743–1

Faculty physician and allied personnel compensation at medical schools, by specialty and percent of time spent on research, 1991, annual rpt, A6365–5

Federal appropriations for FY94 compared to spending in FY93, by program, recurring feature, C2175–1.527, C2175–1.536

Foundations supporting medical research, grants awarded and assets for top 10 organizations, FY90 or FY91, article, C2176–1.513

Funding distribution by source for health-related R&D, 1992, article, A3273–8.510

General practice specialty choices of medical school grads compared to research funding levels, for top 20 schools (unnamed), 1993 article, A2623–1.505

Journal article multiple author incidence, for 2 radiation oncology publications, with data by author country and instn, 1983-87, article, A3273–8.502

Natl Institute of General Medical Sciences budget, by program, FY92-93, article, A1250–1.514

Pharmaceutical industry clinical studies incorporating health economic analyses, 1988-94, article, A1865–1.517

Physicians by detailed specialty and location, 1992 and trends, annual rpt, A2200–3

Public health school research and training grants, by fund source and instn (unnamed), FY92, annual rpt, A3372–3

Voluntary health agency revenues, and expenditures by function, for 39 major organizations, FY90, annual rpt, A7973–1

see also Biotechnology
see also Genetics
see also Laboratories

Medical supplies and equipment

Cotton and other fiber consumption in textile production, by detailed end use, 1990-92, annual rpt, A7485–1

Dental school undergrad student expenses, by type and instn, 1992/93, annual rpt, A1475–4.3

Electronic medical equipment market value, with trends by equipment type, 1992 and 1997, article, C1850–2.512

Electronic medical imaging systems use obstacles cited by hospitals, 1990 and 1992 surveys, article, C1850–2.509

Expenditures for health care by type, and prevailing treatment charges, 1950s-91, annual rpt, A5173–2.3

Finances and operating data for medical groups, by practice characteristics, 1991, annual rpt, A6365–2

Financial performance and growth rankings for approx 1,000 top corporations, with comparisons by industry group, 1993 annual rpt, C3950–1.505

Financial ratios and performance, for over 350 SIC 4-digit industries, FY88-92, annual rpt, A6400–3

Foreign trade in electromedical equipment, by product category, detailed type, and country, monthly rpt, A4725–3

HMO benefits coverage, premiums, and rating methods used, by plan characteristics, 1991 and trends, annual rpt, A5150–2.1

Hospital diagnostic imaging equipment age, by type of equipment, 1992, A1865–1.507

Magnetic resonance imaging (MRI) machine manufacturer sales and stock performance, for 6 companies, 1992 article, C3950–1.504

Market devs in electronics industry, including employment, factory sales, prices, and foreign trade trends, monthly rpt, A4725–2

Operating and financial composite ratios for corporations, with establishments and receipts, for approx 200 industries, by asset size, FY90, annual rpt, C7800–1

Physician fees and expenses, and detailed work patterns, by specialty, type of practice and location, and age, 1982-92, annual rpt, A2200–5.2

Shipment value, employment, and foreign trade, for electronics industry, by sector and product type, 1980s-92, annual rpt, A4725–1.2

Sterile packaging for medical devices, demand value by package type, 1991 and 1996, article, C1850–1.502

Veterinarian practice expenses as percent of revenues, by expenditure category and type of practice, 1990-91, annual survey article, C9480–1.501

State and local:

Florida hospital equipment in acute care facilities, by selected equipment type, 1992, annual rpt, S1746–1.2

Indiana Medicaid expenditures, by service and provider type and county, FY91-92, annual rpt, S2623–1.6

Kentucky Medicaid recipients and payments, by program, county, and type of medical service, monthly rpt, S3140–5

Maryland medical assistance payments and recipients, by program, type of service, location, demographic characteristics, and facility, FY92 and trends, annual rpt, S3635–3

Missouri public welfare and medical assistance recipients, expenditures, and case processing, by program and county, FY92 and trends, annual rpt, S4575–2

Montana welfare and medical assistance program cases and payments, by county and type of service, monthly rpt, S4755–1

New York State medical assistance expenditures, by State area and type of care, 1991 and trends, annual rpt, S5800–2.2

see also Biologic drug products
see also Drugs
see also Hearing aids
see also Instruments and measuring devices
see also Oral rehydration therapy
see also Prosthetics and orthotics
see also X-rays

Medical technicians

see Allied health personnel
see Clinical laboratory technicians
see Health occupations

Medical technology

see Medical examinations and tests
see Medical research
see Medical supplies and equipment

Medical transplants

HMO benefits coverage, premiums, and rating methods used, by plan characteristics, 1991 and trends, annual rpt, A5150–2.1

Hospital patient discharges and length of stay, by diagnosis, type of operation, age, and region, 1991, annual rpt series, B4455–1

Hospital patient discharges and length of stay, by diagnostic related group (DRG), payment source, age, and region, 1991, annual rpt series, B4455–3

Number of transplant operations, by type, 1985-91, annual fact book, A1275–1.2

Organ transplants and persons waiting for transplants, by organ, 1992 annual rpt, A5173–2.4

see also Organ and blood banks

Medicare

Expenditures and use of procedures determined as overpriced in Omnibus Budget Reconciliation Act of 1987, with comparison to other expenditures, 1986-89, article, A2623–1.505

Funding of govt health care programs by source, Medicare enrollments, and Medicaid recipients, 1960s-91, annual rpt, A5173–2.2

HMO benefits, enrollment and utilization, staffing, finances, and relations with employers, by plan characteristics, 1990-91, annual rpt, A5150–2

Home health care agency use by Medicare patients, by type of service and urban-rural residence, 1987, article, A2623–1.505

Hospital CEO views on relations between mgmt and medical staff, including effect of selected Medicare policies, 1992 survey, article, A1865–1.517

Hospital industry financial and operating indicators, with detail for Medicare, by instn characteristics and location, 1988-92, annual rpt, B1880–1

Hospital patient admission rates and length of stay, by diagnosis and procedure, payment source, age, sex, and region, 1991, B4455–4

Hospital patient charges and length of stay, by diagnosis and procedure, payment source, age, and region, 1991, B4455–5

Hospital patient discharges and length of stay, by diagnostic related group (DRG), payment source, age, and region, 1991, annual rpt series, B4455–3

Nursing higher education programs receiving Medicare pass-through funds from hospitals, 1992/93, biennial rpt, A0615–5

Opinions of physicians and general public on health care reform, by respondent characteristics, Mar-Apr 1993 surveys, C8915–7.2

Payments and recipients for selected Federal entitlement programs, by State and region, early 1990s, R8490–47

Physician group practice participation in Medicare, including revenue shares generated, with detail by State, 1991, recurring rpt, A2200–7

Physician participation by specialty and State, recipient enrollment and payments, and Federal outlays, 1970s-92, annual fact book, A1275–1.5

Public opinion on health care issues, including govt and medical profession role, satisfaction with care and insurance, and reforms, 1975-92 surveys, A0610–1.504

Railroad Retirement System Medicare tax rates and base earnings, Jan 1982-93, annual rpt, A3275–8.2

State social, economic, and govtl indicators, with rankings, 1993 semiannual rpt, B8500–1.9

Statistical profiles of 50 States and DC, general data, 1993 annual almanac, C4712 1

State and local:

Alabama statistical abstract, general data, 1992 recurring rpt, U5680–2.8

Arizona statistical abstract, general data, 1993 recurring rpt, U5850–2.7

Florida statistical abstract, general data, 1992 annual rpt, U6660–1.7

Hawaii data book, general data, 1992 annual rpt, S2090–1.11

Kentucky Medicare recipients and payments qualifying for Medicaid, by county and type of service, monthly rpt, S3140–5

Maryland medical assistance payments and recipients, by program, type of service, location, demographic characteristics, and facility, FY92 and trends, annual rpt, S3635–3

Montana health care facility capacity, utilization, and finances, by instn, 1991, annual rpt, S4690–2

Nevada statistical abstract, general data, 1992 biennial rpt, S5005–1.2

Oklahoma statistical abstract, general data, 1992 annual rpt, U8130–2.10

Pennsylvania statistical abstract, general data, 1992 recurring rpt, U4130–6.5

South Carolina statistical abstract, general data, 1993 annual rpt, S7125–1.10

Tennessee statistical abstract, general data, 1992/93 annual rpt, U8710–2.18

Utah statistical abstract, general data, 1993 triennial rpt, U8960–1.6

Medicare

Washington State public assistance clients and service costs, by client characteristics, program, and county, FY90, annual rpt, S8420–2

see also Old-Age, Survivors, Disability, and Health Insurance

Medicine

- Book publishing industry financial and operating data, by publisher type and size, and subject category, 1991 and trends, annual rpt, A3274–2
- Congressional campaign finances, with detailed data for individual Members, and leading contributors by type and industry, 1990 election and trends, biennial rpt, R3828–2.2
- Public confidence in selected societal instns, 1993 Gallup Poll and trends, C4040–1.510, R8780–1.508
- *see also* Anesthesiology
- *see also* Aviation medicine
- *see also* Biologic drug products
- *see also* Biotechnology
- *see also* Chiropractic and naturopathy
- *see also* Dentists and dentistry
- *see also* Diseases and disorders
- *see also* Drugs
- *see also* Epidemiology and epidemiologists
- *see also* Federal aid to medical education
- *see also* Federal aid to medicine
- *see also* Geriatrics
- *see also* Health condition
- *see also* Health education
- *see also* Health facilities administration
- *see also* Health facilities and services
- *see also* Health insurance
- *see also* Health maintenance organizations
- *see also* Health occupations
- *see also* Hospitals
- *see also* Medicaid
- *see also* Medical assistance
- *see also* Medical costs
- *see also* Medical education
- *see also* Medical ethics
- *see also* Medical examinations and tests
- *see also* Medical libraries
- *see also* Medical research
- *see also* Medical supplies and equipment
- *see also* Medical transplants
- *see also* Medicare
- *see also* Nurses and nursing
- *see also* Optometry
- *see also* Osteopathy
- *see also* Pathology
- *see also* Pediatrics
- *see also* Pharmaceutical industry
- *see also* Pharmacists and pharmacy
- *see also* Physicians
- *see also* Physiology
- *see also* Podiatry
- *see also* Preventive medicine
- *see also* Psychiatry
- *see also* Public health
- *see also* State funding for health and hospitals
- *see also* State funding for medical education
- *see also* Surgeons and surgery
- *see also* Vaccination and vaccines
- *see also* Veterinary medicine

Melons

see Fruit and fruit products

Membership organizations

Auto aftermarket jobber wholesale buying patterns, including product sources and use of distribution groups, 1993 article, C2150–10.504

Auto aftermarket warehouse distributor membership, for 15 programmed distribution groups, 1993 article, C2150–10.505

Book club sales and membership, 1990-91, annual rpt, A3274–2

- College freshmen interest in joining fraternities and sororities, by sex and instn type, fall 1992, annual survey, U6215–1
- Ecologist personal and professional characteristics, including membership in various professional organizations, Mar 1992 survey, recurring rpt, A4685–1
- Financial ratios and performance, for over 350 SIC 4-digit industries, FY88-92, annual rpt, A6400–3
- Food marketing industry "share groups," membership and facilitating organization for 15 groups, 1993 article, C4655–1.508
- Food service worker wage rates for clubs, by position, 1992, recurring rpt, A8200–14
- Operating and financial composite ratios for corporations, with establishments and receipts, for approx 200 industries, by asset size, FY90, annual rpt, C7800–1
- Shopping center merchants assn participation, by building characteristics, region, and metro area, 1991, annual rpt, A5600–6

State and local:

- Florida statistical abstract, general data, 1992 annual rpt, U6660–1.20
- *see also* Associations
- *see also* Fraternal benefit societies
- *see also* Nonprofit organizations and foundations

Memorials

see Monuments and memorials

Memphis, Tenn.

- Help-wanted advertising index, quarterly journal, U8710–1
- Help-wanted advertising index, 1989-92, annual rpt, S7560–1
- *see also under* By City in the "Index by Categories"

Men

- Abortion attitudes of teenage boys, by respondent characteristics, 1988 survey, article, A5160–1.505
- Cancer (urinary tract) death rates for men age 45-84, by age, State, and census div, 1979-89, article, B6045–1.503
- Clothing (men's) sales and consumer expenditures, by outlet type, 1992, article, C5150–3.508
- Clothing (men's) with imprinted designs, market shares by retail outlet type and design category, Apr 1992-Mar 1993, article, C5150–3.513
- Clothing (men's and boys) production and operating data, and population projections, 1993 annual rpt, A3880–1
- Clothing (men's sweats/warm-up) sales by retail outlet type, 1992, article, C5150–3.510
- Condom use and attitudes among sexually active young men, by race-ethnicity, 1988 and 1991 surveys, article, A5160–1.504
- Consumer purchases by men, shares and value for 7 household items, 1992 article, C5800–7.502
- Europe public opinion on quality of life for men vs women, for 9 countries and 3 Soviet Union Republics, 1991 survey, C8915–8.1, C8915–9
- Grocery product purchasing by men, with comparisons to women, by detailed product type, 1992 article, C5225–1.501
- Higher education freshmen attitudes and characteristics, degree and career plans, and financial aid sources, by sex and instn type, fall 1992, annual survey, U6215–1
- Human immunodeficiency virus (HIV) infection status disclosure to male sex partners, with impact on relationship, 1992 article, A2623–1.502
- Magazine circulation and advertising pages, for 5 men's magazines, 1st 6-8 months 1993, article, C2710–1.546
- Nursing schools, programs, enrollment, student and staff characteristics, and grads, 1991 and trends, annual rpt, A8010–1
- Nursing student (male) reasons for career choice and intended specialty, 1993 survey article, A8010–3.503
- Older population shares who are male, for persons age 65/over and 85/over, by census div and State, 1990, article, B6045–1.502
- Popularity ranking of selected world figures, 1991-92, R8780–1.506
- Popularity ratings of selected world figures, 1991-92, annual Gallup Poll, C4040–1.506
- Prostate surgery procedures, costs, and hospital stay, with data by census div and State, 1991 and trends, article, B6045–1.503
- Quality of life indicators for men age 69-84, including health, finances, family, and employment, by race, 1990 survey, U3780–9
- Sexual behavior of men, including condom use, and AIDS knowledge and risks, by selected characteristics, 1991 survey, articles, A5160–1.503
- Shoe sales by retail outlet type, for women's and men's shoes, 1991-92, article, C5150–3.515
- TV audience ratings among men, for 5 major sporting event telecasts, 1991/92, article, C9380–1.508
- TV audience ratings for 3 network morning news programs among men age 35-49, June/July 1992-93, article, C9380–1.535
- Youth AIDS and sex education among males age 15-19 impact on sexual behavior and condom use, errata, A5160–1.502
- Youth contraception and paternity attitudes and behavior among males age 15-19, correlation with selected characteristics, 1988 survey, article, A5160–1.502

State and local:

South Carolina male teachers, by school district, 1991/92, annual rpt, S7145–1.4

see also Families and households

see also Sex discrimination

see also under By Sex in the "Index by Categories"

Meningitis, aseptic

see Infective and parasitic diseases

Mental health and illness

- AIDS progression in untreated homosexual men, including employment and mental status indicators, 1992 article, A2623–1.501
- College freshmen self-rating of emotional health and self-confidence, by sex and instn type, fall 1992, annual survey, U6215–1

Mental health and illness

Corporate personnel mgmt devs, including work force diversity, health care and family-related benefits, counseling services, and competitiveness, 1993 survey, B6850–6

Correctional instn inmates in mental health treatment programs, by State, Jan 1992, annual series, R4300–1

Depression incidence among blacks and whites by selected demographic characteristics, 1984 survey, article, A2623–1.504

Depression incidence by period of birth and sex, 1993 article, A2623–1.507

Health condition and preventive health care and safety practices of adults, by respondent characteristics, 1992 and trends, annual survey rpt, C8111–2

Homeless population characteristics in 29 cities, 1991/92, annual rpt, A9330–9

Hospital employee health care benefits, including coverage for mental health/substance abuse and AIDS, and data by region, 1992 survey, article, A1865–1.505

Hospital patient admission rates and length of stay, by diagnosis and procedure, payment source, age, sex, and region, 1991, B4455–4

Hospital patient charges and length of stay, by diagnosis and procedure, payment source, age, and region, 1991, B4455–5

Hospital patient discharges and length of stay, by diagnosis, type of operation, age, and region, 1991, annual rpt series, B4455–1

Hospital patient discharges and length of stay, by diagnostic related group (DRG), payment source, age, and region, 1991, annual rpt series, B4455–3

Hospital psychiatric patient discharges and length of stay, by diagnosis, age, sex, and region, 1991, annual rpt series, B4455–2

Men age 69-84 quality of life indicators, including health, finances, family, and employment, by race, 1990 survey, U3780–9

Mexico, Tijuana female maquiladora worker characteristics and incidence of psychological problems, 1990 study, article, A2623–1.503

Rape victim incidence of mental health, alcohol, and drug abuse problems compared to women who have never been crime victims, 1990-92 surveys, R8375–1

Stress frequency and amount of sleep per night, 1983 and 1991-92 health habit surveys, article, C1200–4.506

State and local:

Alaska probate court cases and dispositions, including sanity hearings, by location, FY92, annual rpt, S0290–1

Arizona superior court mental health hearings, by county, FY92, annual rpt, S0525–1

Arkansas court caseloads and dispositions, by type of court and case, and location, FY92 and trends, annual rpt, S0647–1

Arkansas vital statistics, including births, deaths by cause, marriages, and divorces, by age, sex, race, and county, 1991 and trends, annual rpt, S0685–1

California court cases and dispositions, by type of case and court, and location, FY92 and trends, annual rpt, S0905–1.2, S0905–2

California statistical abstract, general data, 1992 annual rpt, S0840–2.5

California vital statistics, including population, births, and deaths by cause, by demographic characteristics and county, 1990 and trends, annual rpt, S0865–1

Colorado court cases and dispositions, by type of court and detailed case type, FY92 and trends, annual rpt, S1035–1.2

DC court cases and dispositions, by type of case, and judicial system finances, 1992 and trends, annual rpt, S1515–1

Florida vital statistics, including population, births, deaths by cause, and marriages and dissolutions, by location and demographic characteristics, 1992 and trends, annual rpt, S1745–3

Georgia vital statistics, including deaths by cause, demographic characteristics, and location, 1991 and trends, annual rpt, S1895–1.2

Hawaii health dept activities and services, including vital statistics and disease control, by location, 1990, annual rpt, S2065–1

Idaho vital statistics, including births, deaths by cause, abortions, marriages, and divorces, by demographic characteristics and county, 1991 and trends, annual rpt, S2250–2

Illinois mental health facility patient population and characteristics, by facility, location, and treatment category, FY93, annual rpt, S2505–1

Indiana court cases and dispositions by type of court and case, and location, with judicial system finances and personnel, 1992, annual rpt, S2703–1

Kansas court caseloads and disposition, by type of court and case, and location, FY92, annual rpt, S3035–1

Maine court cases and dispositions, by type and location, FY92 and trends, annual rpt, S3463–1

Maine vital statistics, including births, deaths by cause, abortions, and marriages and divorces, by demographic characteristics and location, 1991 and trends, annual rpt, S3460–2

Massachusetts vital statistics, including births, deaths by cause, marriages, divorces, and population, by locality and demographic characteristics, 1990 and trends, annual rpt, S3850–1

Michigan court caseloads and dispositions, by type of court and case, and court location, 1992 and trends, annual rpt, S3962–1

Michigan vital statistics, including births, deaths, marriages, divorces/annulments, and communicable diseases, by location and demographic characteristics, 1990 and trends, annual rpt, S4000–3

Minnesota vital statistics, including population, births, abortions, deaths, marriages, and divorces, by location and demographic characteristics, 1991 and trends, annual rpt, S4190–2

Mississippi vital statistics, including births, deaths by cause, marriages, and divorces, by demographic characteristics and location, 1992 and trends, annual rpt, S4350–1

Missouri public welfare and medical assistance recipients, expenditures, and case processing, by program and county, FY92 and trends, annual rpt, S4575–2

Montana vital statistics, including births, deaths by cause, abortion, disease, and marriage and divorce, by demographic characteristics and county, 1990-91 and trends, annual rpt, S4690–1

Nebraska vital statistics, including births, deaths, marriages, divorces, and population, by demographic characteristics and location, 1991 and trends, annual rpt, S4885–1

New Mexico court cases and dispositions, by type of court and case, and location, with judicial system finances and personnel, FY92, annual rpt, S5623–1

North Dakota court caseloads and dispositions, by type of case and court, and location, with judicial dept finances, 1991-92, annual rpt, S6210–1

Ohio court caseload and case disposition, by type of court and case, and location, 1992, annual rpt, S6385–1

Oklahoma court cases and dispositions, by type of court and case, with judicial system finances, by county or jurisdiction, FY92, annual rpt, S6493–1

Oregon vital statistics, including births, deaths by cause, communicable diseases, marriages, and divorces, by age, sex, race-ethnicity, and county, 1991 and trends, annual rpt, S6615–5

South Carolina deaths, by detailed cause, age, sex, and race, 1990, annual rpt, S7175–2

South Dakota court cases and dispositions by type of case, and judicial system finances and personnel, by jurisdiction, FY92 and trends, annual rpt, S7395–1

South Dakota medical assistance recipients and payments, by type of service, FY92, annual rpt, S7385–1.1

Tennessee court cases and dispositions, by type of court and case, and county, FY92, annual rpt, S7585–1

Tennessee vital statistics, including births, deaths by cause, marriages, divorces, and population, by demographic characteristics and location, 1991 and trends, annual rpt, S7520–2

Texas court cases and dispositions, by type of court and case, and location, FY92, annual rpt, S7703–1

Utah homeless shelter population characteristics, individual shelter capacity, and related housing data, 1991-92, annual rpt, S7808–2

Vermont court cases and dispositions, by type of court and case, and location, FY92 annual rpt, S8120–1

Vermont vital statistics, including population, births, deaths by cause, abortions, marriages, and divorces, by location and demographic characteristics, 1991 and trends, annual rpt, S8054–1

Washington State court cases and dispositions, by type of court and case, and jurisdiction, with judicial finances and personnel, 1992 and trends, annual rpt, S8339–1

Washington State vital statistics, including births, deaths by cause, and population, by demographic characteristics and location, 1991 and trends, annual rpt, S8363–1

West Virginia court caseloads and dispositions, by type of court and case, and judicial circuit, 1992 and trends, annual rpt, S8537–1

Mental health and illness

West Virginia vital statistics, including births, deaths by cause, marriages, and divorces, by location and demographic characteristics, 1991 and trends, annual rpt, S8560–1

Wisconsin correctional instn admissions by inmate characteristics, including need for special services, 1991, annual rpt, S8692–1.2

Wisconsin vital statistics, including population, births, deaths by cause, and marriages and dissolutions, by county and demographic characteristics, 1991 and trends, annual rpt, S8715–4

see also Alzheimer's disease
see also Commitment
see also Mental health facilities and services
see also Mental retardation
see also Neurological disorders
see also Psychiatry
see also Psychology
see also Sheltered workshops
see also under By Disease in the "Index by Categories"

Mental health facilities and services

Costs for selected types of psychiatric treatment or psychotherapy, 1989, annual rpt, A5173–2.3

HMO benefits coverage, premiums, and rating methods used, by plan characteristics, 1991 and trends, annual rpt, A5150–2.1

Hospital directory, with utilization, expenses, and personnel, by instn, type, and location, 1992, annual rpt, A1865–3

Medical school student mental health service availability, Oct 1991 survey, article, A3273–8.506

Nursing home resident mental health care use, by resident and home characteristics, and provider type, 1985/86 survey, article, A2623–1.505

Psychiatric hospital operating and utilization data, and psychiatric services at community hospitals, 1981-91, article, A1865–1.512

Psychiatric patients in general hospitals, discharges and length of stay by diagnosis, age, sex, and region, 1991, annual rpt series, B4455–2

State and local:

Alabama statistical abstract, general data, 1992 recurring rpt, U5680–2.8

Arkansas mental health program clients served, by age, race, county, and facility, FY91, annual rpt, S0700–2.4

Arkansas population in instns and other group quarters, 1990, census rpt, U5935–7

California correctional system inmates in State hospitals, by offense and demographic characteristics, Dec 1992, semiannual rpt, S0820–2

California population in instns and other group quarters, 1990, census rpt, S0840–9

California State hospital admissions, population, deaths, and discharges, by county and/or instn, FY91-92, annual rpt, S0840–2.5

DC statistical profile, general data, 1992 annual rpt, S1535–3.5

Florida health care atlas, including manpower by occupation and health care facilities by type, by district and county, 1992 annual rpt, S1746–1.2

Hawaii data book, general data, 1992 annual rpt, S2090–1.2

Hawaii psychiatric facility capacity, admissions, and length of stay, by county and/or facility, 1990 and trends, annual rpt, S2065–1.7

Illinois mental health facility patient population and characteristics, by facility, location, and treatment category, FY93, annual rpt, S2505–1

Indiana Medicaid-certified cases and payments for mental health facilities, FY91-92, annual rpt, S2623–1.6

Kentucky Medicaid recipients and payments, by program, county, and type of medical service, monthly rpt, S3140–5

Maryland medical assistance payments and recipients, by program, type of service, location, demographic characteristics, and facility, FY92 and trends, annual rpt, S3635–3

Maryland psychiatric instn inpatients, treatments, admissions, and releases, FY80-91, biennial rpt, S3605–1.2

Montana welfare and medical assistance program cases and payments, by county and type of service, monthly rpt, S4755–1

Nebraska Medicaid recipients and payments, by type of service and county, FY92, annual rpt, S4957–1.2

New Jersey population in instns and other group quarters, by county, 1990, census rpt, S5425–19

New York State statistical yearbook, general data, 1992 annual rpt, U5100–1.11

North Carolina public defender and assigned counsel caseloads and costs, including State mental hospital hearings, FY91, annual rpt, S5950–1

Oklahoma statistical abstract, general data, 1992 annual rpt, U8130–2.9

Pennsylvania population in instns and other group quarters, 1990, census rpt, U4130–13

South Carolina statistical abstract, general data, 1993 annual rpt, S7125–1.10

South Dakota medical assistance recipients and payments, by type of service, FY92, annual rpt, S7385–1.1

Washington State deaths in psychiatric facilities, 1991, annual rpt, S8363–1

Washington State public assistance clients and service costs, by client characteristics, program, and county, FY90, annual rpt, S8420–2

Wisconsin Blue Book, general data, 1993-94 biennial rpt, S8780–1.2

see also Group homes

Mental retardation

Hospital patient discharges and length of stay, by diagnosis, type of operation, age, and region, 1991, annual rpt series, B4455–1

State and local:

California vital statistics, including population, births, and deaths by cause, by demographic characteristics and county, 1990 and trends, annual rpt, S0865–1

DC court cases and dispositions, by type of case, and judicial system finances, 1992 and trends, annual rpt, S1515–1

Florida vital statistics, including population, births, deaths by cause, and marriages and dissolutions, by location and demographic characteristics, 1992 and trends, annual rpt, S1745–3

Hawaii health dept family health services and recipients, including school health programs, 1990 annual rpt, S2065–1.5

Idaho vital statistics, including births, deaths by cause, abortions, marriages, and divorces, by demographic characteristics and county, 1991 and trends, annual rpt, S2250–2

Indiana Medicaid-certified mentally retarded care cases and expenditures, FY91-92, annual rpt, S2623–1.6

Maine vital statistics, including births, deaths by cause, abortions, and marriages and divorces, by demographic characteristics and location, 1991 and trends, annual rpt, S3460–2

Massachusetts vital statistics, including births, deaths by cause, marriages, divorces, and population, by locality and demographic characteristics, 1990 and trends, annual rpt, S3850–1

Mississippi vital statistics, including births, deaths by cause, marriages, and divorces, by demographic characteristics and location, 1992 and trends, annual rpt, S4350–1

Nebraska Medicaid recipients and payments, by type of service and county, FY92, annual rpt, S4957–1.2

New York State statistical yearbook, general data, 1992 annual rpt, U5100–1.11

South Carolina deaths, by detailed cause, age, sex, and race, 1990, annual rpt, S7175–2

South Carolina statistical abstract, general data, 1993 annual rpt, S7125–1.10

South Dakota medical assistance recipients and payments, by type of service, FY92, annual rpt, S7385–1.1

Tennessee vital statistics, including births, deaths by cause, marriages, divorces, and population, by demographic characteristics and location, 1991 and trends, annual rpt, S7520–2

Washington State public assistance clients and service costs, by client characteristics, program, and county, FY90, annual rpt, S8420–2

West Virginia vital statistics, including births, deaths by cause, marriages, and divorces, by location and demographic characteristics, 1991 and trends, annual rpt, S8560–1

Wisconsin vital statistics, including population, births, deaths by cause, and marriages and dissolutions, by county and demographic characteristics, 1991 and trends, annual rpt, S8715–4

Merchandising

see Marketing

Merchant marine

see Ships and shipping

Mercury

see Metals and metal industries

Mergers

see Business acquisitions and mergers

Merski, Paul G.

"Special Report: Value of Typical American Family's 1992 Income Eroded by Taxes and Inflation", R9050–13

Merva, Mary

"Effects of Diminished Economic Opportunities on Social Stress: Heart Attacks, Stroke, and Crime", R4700–18

Index by Subjects and Names

Mesa County, Colo.

Labor force, employment by industry div, and unemployment, monthly 1990-91, article, S1040–4.502

Metabolic and endocrine diseases

- Hospital patient admission rates and length of stay, by diagnosis and procedure, payment source, age, sex, and region, 1991, B4455–4
- Hospital patient charges and length of stay, by diagnosis and procedure, payment source, age, and region, 1991, B4455–5
- Hospital patient discharges and length of stay, by diagnosis, type of operation, age, and region, 1991, annual rpt series, B4455–1
- Hospital patient discharges and length of stay, by diagnostic related group (DRG), payment source, age, and region, 1991, annual rpt series, B4455–3
- Hospital psychiatric patients with selected physical disorders, length of stay by age, sex, and region, 1991, annual rpt series, B4455–2

State and local:

- Arkansas vital statistics, including births, deaths by cause, marriages, and divorces, by age, sex, race, and county, 1991 and trends, annual rpt, S0685–1
- California vital statistics, including population, births, and deaths by cause, by demographic characteristics and county, 1990 and trends, annual rpt, S0865–1
- Florida vital statistics, including population, births, deaths by cause, and marriages and dissolutions, by location and demographic characteristics, 1992 and trends, annual rpt, S1745–3
- Georgia vital statistics, including deaths by cause, demographic characteristics, and location, 1991 and trends, annual rpt, S1895–1.2
- Idaho vital statistics, including births, deaths by cause, abortions, marriages, and divorces, by demographic characteristics and county, 1991 and trends, annual rpt, S2250–2
- Iowa vital statistics, including population, births, deaths by cause, marriages, and divorces, by demographic characteristics and location, 1991 and trends, annual rpt, S2795–1
- Maine vital statistics, including births, deaths by cause, abortions, and marriages and divorces, by demographic characteristics and location, 1991 and trends, annual rpt, S3460–2
- Massachusetts vital statistics, including births, deaths by cause, marriages, divorces, and population, by locality and demographic characteristics, 1990 and trends, annual rpt, S3850–1
- Michigan vital statistics, including births, deaths, marriages, divorces/annulments, and communicable diseases, by location and demographic characteristics, 1990 and trends, annual rpt, S4000–3
- Minnesota vital statistics, including population, births, abortions, deaths, marriages, and divorces, by location and demographic characteristics, 1991 and trends, annual rpt, S4190–2
- Mississippi vital statistics, including births, deaths by cause, marriages, and divorces, by demographic characteristics and location, 1992 and trends, annual rpt, S4350–1

Montana vital statistics, including births, deaths by cause, abortion, disease, and marriage and divorce, by demographic characteristics and county, 1990-91 and trends, annual rpt, S4690–1

- Oregon vital statistics, including births, deaths by cause, communicable diseases, marriages, and divorces, by age, sex, race-ethnicity, and county, 1991 and trends, annual rpt, S6615–5
- South Carolina deaths, by detailed cause, age, sex, and race, 1990, annual rpt, S7175–2
- Tennessee vital statistics, including births, deaths by cause, marriages, divorces, and population, by demographic characteristics and location, 1991 and trends, annual rpt, S7520–2
- Vermont vital statistics, including population, births, deaths by cause, abortions, marriages, and divorces, by location and demographic characteristics, 1991 and trends, annual rpt, S8054–1
- Washington State vital statistics, including births, deaths by cause, and population, by demographic characteristics and location, 1991 and trends, annual rpt, S8363–1
- West Virginia vital statistics, including births, deaths by cause, marriages, and divorces, by location and demographic characteristics, 1991 and trends, annual rpt, S8560–1
- Wisconsin vital statistics, including population, births, deaths by cause, and marriages and dissolutions, by county and demographic characteristics, 1991 and trends, annual rpt, S8715–4

see also Diabetes

see also Immunity disorders

see also Nutrition and malnutrition

see also under By Disease in the "Index by Categories"

Metals and metal industries

- Capital spending plans for metalworking industries, by equipment type and industry group, 1989-93, annual survey, C4080–1
- Capital spending plans for new mines and plants, by mineral and company, and mine production values, 1993 annual feature, C5226–2.503
- Corporate performance ratings by executives for leading companies in 32 industries, 1993 annual survey feature, C8900–1.508
- Earnings of US and Canadian workers in mining and allied industries, monthly rpt, B6800–1
- Engineers salaries by industry group, census div, selected metro area, and years since college degree, 1993, annual survey rpt, A0685–5
- Engineers salaries by industry group, census div, selected metro area, degree level, and years since college degree, 1993, annual survey rpt, A0685–3
- Executive compensation and components, by industry div and major manufacturing group, 1991, annual rpt, R4105–19
- Financial performance and growth rankings for approx 1,000 top corporations, with comparisons by industry group, 1993 annual rpt, C3950–1.505
- Financial ratios and performance, for over 350 SIC 4-digit industries, FY88-92, annual rpt, A6400–3
- Futures and options contract open interest (outstanding commitments), on foreign exchanges, by commodity and exchange, monthly rpt, A5040–6
- Futures and options trading volume by commodity and exchange, 1988-92, annual rpt, A5040–1
- Futures and options trading volume on foreign exchanges, by commodity and exchange, monthly rpt, A5040–5
- Futures contract open interest (outstanding commitments), by commodity and exchange, monthly rpt, A5040–4
- Futures trading volume by commodity and exchange, monthly rpt, A5040–2
- Indium refinery production and capacity, and reserves, by country or world area, 1991, article, C5226–2.505
- Industrial metal heat treatment billings, for Michigan, Canada, and 7 regions, monthly press release, A6376–1
- Inventory-consumption ratios for aluminum, copper, lead, and zinc, 1981-93, article, R4105–80.502
- Jewelry and watch manufacturing and marketing trends, new product dev, prices, trade, and related indicators, monthly rpt, C2150–7
- Latin America statistical abstract, general data by country, 1992 annual rpt, U6250–1.16, U6250–1.23
- Magnesium imports of US and Japan from China and Commonwealth of Independent States, with worldwide demand by application or world region, 1992-93, article, A1250–1.544
- Metalworking industry devs, with machine tool orders and shipments, monthly rpt, C7000–7
- Motor vehicle industry materials consumption, by type, 1980-93, annual rpt, A0865–1.2
- Operating and financial composite ratios for corporations, with establishments and receipts, for approx 200 industries, by asset size, FY90, annual rpt, C7800–1
- Operating and financial data for metals and nonmetallic minerals industries, with articles and special features, monthly rpt, C5226–2
- Options trading volume by commodity, securities index, and exchange, monthly rpt, A5040–3
- Platinum supply by world area, and demand by end use, 1990-92, article, C5226–2.511
- Platinum supply-demand and price data, 1992 and trends, annual almanac, C2150–7.509
- Platinum use in jewelry, for Japan, Europe, North America, and rest of Western world, 1991, article, C2150–7.507
- Primary metal industries operating, financial, and technological devs, monthly rpt, C7000–8
- Production, consumption, stocks, trade, and prices for approx 100 basic commodities, including by country and producing State, commodity yearbook for 1993, C2400–1, C2400–2
- Shipments of metal powder, 1981-90, article, C2710–3.514
- Supply-demand for selected metals and nonmetallic minerals, with price data, US and worldwide, 1992-93 and trends, annual feature, C5226–2.505

Metals and metal industries

World production, consumption, and reserves of selected metals, by country, 1990 and trends, biennial rpt, R9455–1.7

State and local:

- Arizona statistical abstract, general data, 1993 recurring rpt, U5850–2.14, U5850–2.17
- Colorado property assessed valuation, and summary production data, by county, 1991-92, annual rpt, S1055–3
- Florida statistical abstract, general data, 1992 annual rpt, U6660–1.12
- Texas trade, transportation, and public utilities employment, by SIC 2- and 3-digit industry and detailed occupation, 2nd qtr 1991, triennial survey rpt, S7675–1.31
- Utah statistical abstract, general data, 1993 triennial rpt, U8960–1.10

see also Abrasive materials
see also Aluminum and aluminum industry
see also Copper and copper industry
see also Foundries
see also Gold
see also Hardware
see also Iron and steel industry
see also Lead and lead industry
see also Lead poisoning and pollution
see also Scrap metals
see also Silver
see also Stockpiling
see also Tin and tin industry
see also Uranium
see also Zinc and zinc industry
see also under By Industry in the "Index by Categories"

Meteorology

see also Weather

Methadone treatment

- Drug abuse treatment clients by substance abused and type of program, by State, FY91, annual rpt, A7112–1

State and local:

- Washington State public assistance clients and service costs, by client characteristics, program, and county, FY90, annual rpt, S8420–2

Methane

see Natural gas and gas industry

Methanol

see Alcohol fuels

Methodology

- Labor market behavior, natl longitudinal surveys data users handbook and bibl, 1993 recurring rpt, U3780–2
- Public opinion devs, with results of social, economic, and political surveys, and polling methodology, quarterly rpt, A0610–1

see also Classifications
see also Economic and econometric models

Metrication

see Weights and measures

Metropolitan areas

see Central cities
see Metropolitan Statistical Areas
see Suburbs
see Urban areas
see under By City, By SMSA or MSA, and By Urban-Rural and Metro-Nonmetro in the "Index by Categories"

Metropolitan Statistical Areas

- Child well-being indicators based on social, economic, and environmental factors, for 239 MSAs, with detail by component county and city, 1980s-90s, R9700–2
- Consumer buying power survey of population, income, and sales by kind of business, by census div, State, MSA, county, and city, 1992, annual rpt, C1200–1.511
- Consumer buying power survey of population, income, and sales by product line, by State, metro area, county, and census div, 1993 annual rpt, C1200–1.514
- Food store market shares and outlets, by company and store type, for approx 350 metro areas in US and Canada, with industry operating data, 1993 annual rpt, C3400–6
- Market rankings of leading MSAs, counties, and cities, by population, income, and retail sales, 1993 annual rpt, C3250–1
- Poverty and unemployment level effects on crime and mortality rates in major MSAs, for selected offenses and causes of death, 1990, R4700–18
- Sales industry costs, including compensation, training, and travel and related expenses, with data by metro area, 1992 and trends, annual survey, C1200–1.508

see also Central business districts
see also Central cities
see also Marketing areas
see also Suburbs
see also under By SMSA or MSA in the "Index by Categories"

Mexican Americans

see Hispanic Americans
see Mexicans in the U.S.

Mexicans in the U.S.

- Immigrants to US, and temporary workers, aliens, and deportations, 1992 annual rpt, U6250–1.14
- Socioeconomic indicators for Mexico-US border area, 1980s and trends, U6250–1.20

see also Hispanic Americans

Mexico

- Air conditioning/refrigeration equipment exports from US to Mexico, for top 6 product categories, 1991, article, C2000–1.506
- Airline traffic trends, and aircraft, for Mexico and US carriers, 1993 article, C7000–4.503
- Airports and communities in North America served by regional vs larger airlines, by carrier and location, 1993 annual rpt, A8795–1.2
- Auto original equipment supplier plants in Mexico, with locations, and major products and customers, by company, 1993 article, C2710–3.550
- Auto parts market value and imports, 1993 article, C2710–3.541
- Bank profit indicators, for 2 Mexican and aggregate large US banks, 1992, article, C5800–7.545
- Border crossings between Mexico and 6 Arizona cities, 1985-93, semiannual rpt, U5850–1.1
- Cattle trade with New Mexico, 1991, annual rpt, S5530–1
- Citrus fruit exports to US, by fruit type, monthly 1987/88-1991/92, annual rpt, S1685–1.1
- Coal preparation plants and capacity in US, Canada, and Mexico, by company, 1993 biennial feature, C5226–1.511
- Commercial real estate market conditions and outlook, for industrial and office properties, by US metro area and selected foreign city, 1992-93, annual survey, A8916–1
- Copper smelter capacity in Mexico, by company, 1991, annual rpt, S0497–1
- Drugstore outlets for top 11 Mexican chains, 1993 annual feature, C5150–2.511
- Earnings of industrial workers in Mexico, with detail by industry and comparisons to US and 4 Asian countries, 1990-91, article, C5800–7.524
- Economic indicators, including US trade, and population by major city, 1993 articles, C4687–1.512
- Economic trends, including GDP components and services trade with US by industry group, 1980-92, article, A3892–1.504
- Electronics industry trade and/or production trends by product category for 33 countries, with general economic profiles, 1993 annual rpt, A4725–1.4
- Energy intl sourcebook, with detail on oil and gas industry operations, supply-demand, and prices, for approx 80 countries, 1970s-91, annual compilation, C6985–10.2
- Exports value from 10 Western States to Mexico, 1987 and 1992, article, U0282–2.501
- Flour milling companies and capacity, in US by State, Canada, Mexico, and Central American and Caribbean area countries, 1993 annual directory and buyers guide, C8450–3
- Food consumption, distribution by commodity group, 1993 article, C2150–6.509
- Foreign investments in Mexico for US vs other countries, by sector, 1929-87, U6250–1.21
- Foreign trade value with US, for 12 major industries, 1991, article, C8900–1.513
- Hard goods US manufacturers exports to Mexico, and expected effects of US-Mexico trade agreement, by product line, 1993 annual survey rpt, A1800–1
- Health care services in Mexico, use by US residents of border communities as reported by physicians and patients, 1992 surveys, R4865–10
- Home improvement sales, and economic indicators of interest to retailers, with selected data for 5 cities, 1993 articles, C5150–6.508
- Horse racing activity, attendance, handle, purse distribution, and govt revenue, 1990, annual rpt, A3363–1.1
- Insurance premiums value by line of coverage, 1992, article, C1050–1.507, C1050–2.507
- Lobbyists (Hispanic) for Mexican interests in US, with income from Mexican Govt for top 8 firms or individuals, 1991-93, article, C4575–1.510
- Motor vehicle assembly cost by component for Mexico and US, and unit sales per 1,000 population in Mexico, US, and Canada, 1993 article, C2710–3.549
- Motor vehicle exports of Mexico to rest of Western Hemisphere, by country or world region, 1991-92, article, C2710–3.553

Index by Subjects and Names

Microforms

Motor vehicle industry trade with US, and auto production and planned foreign investment by manufacturer, with related North American Free Trade Agreement devs, 1992 rpt, R8490–43

Motor vehicle industry trade with US, foreign-owned plants and employment, and economic indicator trends, 1993 article, C2150–3.505

Motor vehicle production for domestic and export markets, for top 5 and all other manufacturers, 1990-91, R4105–82.6

Motor vehicle sales, and domestic and export production, for 5 manufacturers, weekly rpt monthly tables, C2710–3

Motor vehicle sales, and domestic and export production, with detail for 5 manufacturers, 1991-92, annual data book, C2710–3.531

Motor vehicle world production, sales, trade, and registrations, by country, world area, manufacturer, and make, 1991 and trends, annual rpt, A0865–2.1

Natural gas exports to US, 1990-93, annual feature, C6985–1.513, C6985–1.539

Natural gas trade with US, 1956-90, annual compilation, C6985–9.2

North American Free Trade Agreement, public interest in news items and opinions on related issues, by respondent characteristics, Sept 1993 survey, C8915–1.505

North American Free Trade Agreement, US public support and desired conditions, with detail for 3 States, 1993 survey, annual rpt, A4965–1

Nuclear reactors in operation, with capacity, electricity generation, and construction, by unit and country, 1992, annual rpt, B6800–2.2

Oil and gas and equipment trade with US, and energy tariffs and phaseout schedule under North American Free Trade Agreement, 1993 article, C6985–1.544

Oil and gas finances of govt-owned company, and potential impact of foreign lease program, 1993 article, C6985–1.518

Oil and gas pipeline kilometers, by product type, 1991, article, C6985–1.542

Oil industry operations of govt-owned company, including finances, production, and refining capacity, 1993 article, C6985–1.542

Oil/gas seismic exploration land and marine crews, by world area, weekly rpt quarterly feature, C6985–1.515, C6985–1.521

Oil/gas seismic exploration land crews and vessels, by world area or country, quarterly press release, A8912–2

Plastics and resin sales by material and major market, foreign trade, and capacity by company, 1991-92, annual feature, C5800–12.504

Public opinion in US, Canada, and Mexico on North American Free Trade Agreement, Aug-Sept 1992 Gallup Poll and trends, C4040–1.503

Public opinion on environmental and population issues, and related church involvement, for US, Brazil, Canada, and Mexico, 1992 survey, R8780–1.504

Retail general merchandise chain sales, earnings, and stores, for top companies worldwide, with detail for selected areas, 1991-92, annual feature, C5150–3.516

Silver market activity worldwide and in US, including production, consumption by end use, stocks, trade, and prices, by country, 1988-92, annual rpt, B4300–1

Socioeconomic indicators for Mexico-US border area, 1980s and trends, U6250–1.20

Statistical abstract of Latin America, detailed social, govtl, and economic data, 1992 annual rpt, U6250–1

Textile fiber consumption and foreign trade, by fiber type, 1980s-92, C3460–1.510

Textile manufactured fiber imports and exports, by country of origin and destination, 1990-1st half 1993, C3460–1.512

Textile mill consumption of manufactured fibers, cotton, and wool, for selected countries, 1984-91, annual feature, C3460–1.501

Transportation system for Mexico-Texas trade, including data on infrastructure and operations by transport mode, 1993 rpt, U8850–9

Travel/tourism industry devs, including summary data on travel indicators, monthly rpt, R9375–1

State and local:

South Dakota exports to top 20 countries of destination, with detail for Canada and Mexico by commodity, 1991, article, U8595–1.502

see also Baja California, Mexico

see also Gulf of Mexico

see also Mexicans in the U.S.

see also Tijuana, Mexico

see also under By Foreign Country or World Area in the "Index by Categories"

Meyer, Laurence H., and Associates

Forecasts for real estate industry and US economy, and housing starts and sales trends by region, monthly rpt, A7000–1

Miami, Fla.

Convention revenue loss due to black boycott, for 5 organizations and aggregate 20 others, 1993 article, C4215–1.509

Haiti citizens (deportable) arriving in Miami, 1979-81, annual rpt, U6250–1.14

Printing (prepress) industry conditions for Atlanta/Miami areas, 1993 survey article, C1850–10.511

Statistical abstract of Florida, detailed social, govtl, and economic data, 1992 annual rpt, U6660–1

see also under By City in the "Index by Categories"

Michigan

Agricultural production, marketing, and finances, by commodity or county, and farms and acreage, 1987-91, annual rpt, S3950–1

Correctional instns, admin, and inmates by selected demographic characteristics, 1991 and trends, annual rpt, S3960–1

Court caseloads and dispositions, by type of court and case, and court location, 1992 and trends, annual rpt, S3962–1

Crimes and arrests, by offense, location, and offender characteristics, with law enforcement employment and assaults on officers, 1992 and trends, annual rpt, S3997–1

Election results and voter registration, by county and/or district, 1992 general election, biennial rpt, S4020–1

Employment, hours, and earnigns, with detail by industry and local area, monthly rpt, S3980–2

Financial instns, financial condition by type and instn, with regulatory info, 1992 and trends, annual rpt, S3957–1

General Educational Dev (GED) testing programs and results in Michigan prisons, 1992, annual rpt, A1410–16

Govt financial condition, including revenues by source, expenditures by function, and fund balances, FY92 and trends, annual rpt, S3985–2

Health behavior risk factor surveillance survey results, by respondent characteristics, 1991, annual rpt, S4000–4

Insurance industry financial and underwriting data, by company and type of insurance, with regulatory info, 1991, annual rpt, S3983–1

Labor force planning rpt, including employment by industry, and characteristics of Job Training Partnership Act eligible population, 1993 annual rpt, S3980–1

Markets with daily newspapers, demographic and economic info by geographic area, US and Canada, 1993 annual rpt, C3250–1

Metal heat treatment industry billings, for Michigan, Canada, and 7 regions, monthly press release, A6376–1

Oil/gas industry production, finances, exploration, and reserves, by State, 1992 and trends, annual rpt, A5425–1.1

School district financial and enrollment data, with rankings, 1991/92, annual rpt, S3965–3

Statistical profiles of 50 States and DC, general data, 1993 annual almanac, C4712–1

Traffic accidents, fatalities, and injuries, by vehicle type, circumstance, location, and driver and victim characteristics, 1991 and trends, annual rpt, S3997–2

Utility and transportation regulatory agency activities, scope of jurisdiction, finances, and employees, by agency, 1991/92 annual rpt, A7015–2

Vital statistics, including births, deaths, marriages, divorces/annulments, communicable diseases, and population, by location and demographic characteristics, 1990 and trends, annual rpt, S4000–3

Welfare program cases, recipients, and payments, detailed data by county, monthly rpt, S4010–1

see also Detroit, Mich.

see also under By City and By County in the "Index by Categories"

see also under By State in the "Index by Categories"

Microcomputers

see Computer industry and products

Microfilm

see Microforms

Microforms

Law school enrollment by minority status, degrees conferred, staff, and library holdings, by instn, 1992/93 and trends, annual rpt, A0970–1

Library (research) holdings, expenditures by type, and staff, for 120 academic and nonacademic instns, US and Canada, FY92, annual rpt, A3365–1

Microforms

Library materials prices, and acquisition expenditures by library type and State, 1993 annual compilation, C1650–3.4

Optometry school library holdings, by instn, 1991/92, annual survey, A3370–2

State and local:

Alabama public libraries, finances, holdings, circulation, staff, and population served, by library, FY92, annual rpt, S0180–1

Arizona public library holdings, circulation, finances, and staff, by instn and county, FY92, annual rpt, S0495–1

California library finances, staff, holdings, and services, by library type and facility, FY92, annual rpt, S0825–2

Colorado higher education library finances and operations, and enrollment, by instn, 1992, biennial rpt, S1000–3.2

Florida public libraries, finances, holdings, staff, and services, by system and library, FY92, annual rpt, S1800–2

Idaho academic library staff, expenditures, and holdings, by instn, 1992, annual feature, A5370–1

Indiana public and other library holdings, circulation, finances, and staff, by instn, 1992 or FY92, annual rpt, S2655–1

Iowa public library finances and operations, by county, size of population served, and library, FY92, annual rpt, S2778–1

Missouri public, special, and academic libraries, finances, holdings, circulation, staff, and services, by location, FY92, annual rpt, S4520–2

Montana public library holdings, staff, circulation, and finances, by library, FY92, annual rpt, S4725–1

New York State university system library holdings, 1988/89, annual rpt, U5100–1.10

North Carolina higher education library holdings and expenditures, by type and instn, 1991/92, annual rpt, U8013–1.2

Ohio public, academic, and other library finances, holdings, and staff, by library and location, 1992 and trends, annual rpt, S6320–1

Oregon library finances, staff, holdings, and services, for public, academic, and special libraries by instn, FY92 and trends, annual rpt, S6635–1

South Carolina public and institutional libraries, finances, services, holdings, and staff, by library, FY92, annual rpt, S7210–1

Texas public libraries, holdings, circulation, staff, and finances, by library and location, FY91, annual rpt, S7710–1

Virginia public library operations and finances, by instn, FY92, annual rpt, S8275–1

Micronesia Federated States

General Educational Dev (GED) testing programs and results, by jurisdiction, 1992 and trends, annual rpt, A1410–16

see also Guam

see also Trust Territory of the Pacific Islands

Microwave ovens

see Household appliances and equipment

Middle Atlantic States

College grad job and salary offers, by field of study, type of employer, occupation, and degree level, interim rpt, A3940–1.2

High school grads for Pennsylvania and 6 neighboring States, 1987/88 and 1991/92, annual rpt, S6790–5.14

Higher education faculty salaries by instn type, for Pennsylvania and 6 neighboring States, 1991/92, annual rpt, S6790–5.5

Housing units by primary heating fuel, for 14 New England and Middle Atlantic States, 1990, article, C4680–1.501

see also Appalachia

see also under By Region in the "Index by Categories"

see also under names of individual States

Middle East

Economic condition in selected oil-rich vs oil-poor countries in Middle East and North Africa, 1991 rpt, R4105–82.1

Economic indicators for Israel and West Bank territories, and 10-year outlook for financial aid to territories by source, 1993 article, C5800–7.547

Energy exploration, rotary drilling rigs in operation, by world area and country, monthly rpt, B4675–1

Fertility lifetime rates, for 16 countries, 1993 article, R8750–1.506

Jordan River basin water supply and use, and population, for West Bank and 3 countries, 1990s and 2025, R8750–2.57

Offshore oil and gas reserves and production, for 12 Middle East countries, 1992, article, C6985–2.505

Oil/gas deep well drilling, success ratios, and costs, by world area, 1990-92, annual article, C4420–1.503

Oil/gas seismic exploration land crews and vessels, by world area or country, quarterly press release, A8912–2

Petrochemical capacity and world market share, by chemical, 1991 and 2000, article, A1250–1.501

Population trends and demographic characteristics in the Middle East, by country, 1993 rpt, R8750–2.59

Public interest in US in news items concerning peace accords between Israel and Palestine Liberation Organization, by respondent characteristics, Sept 1993 survey, C8915–1.505

Public opinion in US on Persian Gulf war, Nov 1990-Jan 1991, with analysis of polling issues, 1993 article, A0610–1.502

Refugees, resettlement, and intl aid devs, by country, 1992, annual rpt, R9372–1

see also Bahrain

see also Egypt

see also Iran

see also Iraq

see also Israel

see also Jordan

see also Kuwait

see also Oman

see also Organization of Petroleum Exporting Countries

see also Persian Gulf

see also Qatar

see also Saudi Arabia

see also Syria

see also Turkey

see also United Arab Emirates

see also Yemen

see also under By Foreign Country or World Area in the "Index by Categories"

Midwestern States

see North Central States

Index by Subjects and Names

Midwives

State and local:

Alabama births and fetal deaths by type of attendant, by sex and/or race, 1992, annual rpt, S0175–2

Alaska births, by place of birth and type of attendant, 1990, annual rpt, S0315–1

Arkansas births by location and type of attendant, 1991, annual rpt, S0685–1

Delaware births, by type of place and attendant, and method of delivery, 1990, annual rpt, S1385–2

Florida live births by type of attendant, race, and county, 1992 and trends, annual rpt, S1745–3

Hawaii births, by type of attendant and race-ethnicity of child, 1990, annual rpt, S2065–1.2

Idaho live births by type of attendant, including midwife and naturopath, by county, 1991, annual rpt, S2250–2

Kentucky births in and out of hospitals, by type of attendant and county, 1991, annual rpt, S3140–1

Kentucky Medicaid recipients and payments, by program, county, and type of medical service, monthly rpt, S3140–5

Louisiana live births by type of attendant, by race, sex, and locality, 1989-90, annual rpt, S3295–1

Maryland births, by type of attendant, and location, 1989, annual rpt, S3635–1

Mississippi births and fetal deaths by type of attendant and race, 1992, annual rpt, S4350–1

Missouri births by type of attendant, by race of mother, 1992, annual rpt, S4518–1

Nevada births by type of attendant and county, 1989, annual rpt, S5075–1

New Mexico births by type of attendant and individual facility, 1991 and trends, annual rpt, S5605–1

North Carolina births, by type of attendant and local area, 1991 and trends, annual rpt, S5927–1.1

North Dakota births by type of attendant, 1991, annual rpt, S6105–2

Oregon births, by type of attendant and county, 1991, annual rpt, S6615–5

South Carolina births by race, type of attendant, and county, 1990, annual rpt, S7175–1

Texas births by type of attendant, 1991 and trends, annual rpt, S7685–1

Utah births by type of attendant and location, 1990, annual rpt, S7835–1.2

Vermont births by type of attendant and facility, 1991, annual rpt, S8054–1

Washington State births by type of attendant, 1991, annual rpt, S8363–1

West Virginia births by type of attendant, 1991, annual rpt, S8560–1

Migrant workers

State and local:

Alaska public school enrollment for children of migrant workers, by district, FY92, annual rpt, S0295–2

Arkansas natl migrant data bank fund transactions, FY91-92, biennial rpt, S0780–1

California statistical abstract, general data, 1992 annual rpt, S0840–2.3

Connecticut migrant education program participation, 1991/92, biennial rpt, S1185–3

Index by Subjects and Names

Delaware Federal educational grant awards by program, and program enrollment and employees, by county and administering agency/instn, 1991/92, annual rpt, S1430–1.5

Florida statistical abstract, general data, 1992 annual rpt, U6660–1.9

Maryland public school funding for migrant worker assistance programs, by county, 1991/92, annual rpt, S3610–2.9

Ohio public school enrollment, finances, special programs, and staff, 1991/92 and trends, annual rpt, S6265–2

South Carolina labor force planning rpt, detailed data on employment, hours, wages, turnover, and characteristics of job service applicants, 1992 annual rpt, S7155–3.2

Utah migrant education program participants, summer 1992, annual rpt, S7815–1.1

Migration

Interstate migration patterns indicated by household goods shipments, by State, 1992, annual press release, B0210–1, B9300–1

Residential move date recall accuracy for husbands and wives, Belgium study, 1993 article, A0610–1.503

State migration patterns, with native population share by State, and residence changes in past 5 years including between selected States, 1990, article, B8500–2.512

State, regional, and census div internal and international migration per 1,000 population, 1990/91, annual data sheet, R8750–9

State social, economic, and govtl indicators, with rankings, 1993 semiannual rpt, B8500–1

World demographic trends and population-related issues, monthly rpt, R8750–1

State and local:

Alabama county data book, general data, 1992 annual rpt, S0121–2

Alabama population trends by race, with detail for 20 counties comprising Black Belt region, 1880-1990, U0340–1.6

Alaska population, housing, income, and education data, by demographic characteristics and/or locality, 1990/91 and trends, annual rpt, S0320–4

Arizona and Maricopa County population and migration, quarterly 1990-92, article, U0280–1.505

Arizona migration and population trends, with detail for 2 urban and total nonurban areas, FY61-95, annual article, U0280–1.504

Arizona, Phoenix area temporary winter resident characteristics, including expenditures, dwelling type, and region of residence, 1992/93, article, U0280–1.508

Arizona population and components of change, 1985-93, semiannual rpt, U5850–1.1

Arizona temporary winter residents and expenditures, and mobile home and trailer park spaces and occupancy, by local area, winter 1992/93, annual article, U0280–1.508

Arkansas socioeconomic trends, by MSA and/or county, 1993 annual rpt, U5935–1

Arkansas 1990 population by place of residence in 1985, census rpt, U5935–7

California economic condition, including population, employment and earnings, income, business activity, and taxation, 1960s-92, annual rpt, S0840–3.2

California statistical abstract, general data, 1992 annual rpt, S0840–2.2

California 1990 population by place of residence in 1985, census rpt, S0840–9

Colorado net migration, decennially 1930-90, annual rpt, S1010–1

Delaware projected net migration, by county, 1990-2020, recurring rpt, S1375–3

Florida county data book, 1992/93 annual rpt, C6360–1

Florida net migration, by county, Apr 1990-92, annual rpt, U6660–4

Florida statistical abstract, general data, 1992 annual rpt, U6660–1.1

Georgia county guide, general data, 1993 annual rpt, U6750–1

Georgia statistical abstract, general data, 1992-93 biennial rpt, U6730–1.1

Hawaii data book, general data, 1992 annual rpt, S2090–1.1, S2090–1.21

Idaho and US economic trends and forecasts, quarterly rpt, S2245–2

Illinois population and migration trends, 1970-92, S2405–2.501

Kansas statistical abstract, general data, 1991/92 annual rpt, U7095–2.2

Kentucky economic statistics, general data, 1993 annual rpt, S3104–1.3

Louisiana 1990 population by place of residence in 1985, by local area, census rpt, U8010–4

Maine 1990 population in different place of residence in 1985, by local area, census rpt, S3465–9

Maryland statistical abstract, general data, 1993-94 biennial rpt, S3605–1.1

Michigan net migration, by county, 1980-90, annual rpt, S4000–3

Nebraska population and migration rates, with detail by age group and county, 1980-90, article, U7860–1.508

Nevada business and economic activity indicators, with comparisons to other Western States, 1980-91, annual rpt, U7920–2

New Hampshire population and components of change, 1970-91, annual rpt, S5215–1

New Jersey 1990 population by place of residence in 1985, by county, census rpt, S5425–19

New Mexico population and components of change, 1990-91, annual rpt, S5605–1.1

New Mexico population size and components of change, by county, 1990-91, article, U7980–1.503

Ohio population by age, sex, and county, with summary components of change, quinquennially 1990-2015, recurring rpt, S6260–3

Oklahoma population projections, by age, sex, and locality, with data on fertility and migration, 1990-2020, recurring rpt, S6416–1

Oregon population by county and place of residence in 1990 vs 1985, article, S6592–1.501

Pennsylvania 1990 population by place of residence in 1985, census rpt, U4130–13

Military bases, posts, and reservations

Rhode Island 1990 population by place of residence in 1985, by county and municipality, census rpt, S6930–9

South Carolina population and components of change, by county, 1980-90, annual planning rpt, S7155–3.1

South Carolina statistical abstract, general data, 1993 annual rpt, S7125–1.13

Tennessee statistical abstract, general data, 1992/93 annual rpt, U8710–2.1

Texas migration rates, and population projections under 3 migration scenarios, by county, age, sex, and race-ethnicity, 1980s-2030, recurring rpt, S7645–3

Utah economic and demographic trends, by county and district, 1960-91, annual rpt, S7832–2

Utah govt statistical review, fiscal and socioeconomic data, 1993 annual rpt, R9380–1.1

Utah population estimates and components, including data by county, 1992 and trends, annual article, U8960–2.504

Utah statistical abstract, general data, 1993 triennial rpt, U8960–1.1

Virginia population and net migration, by local area, 1990-91, annual rpt, U9080–9

Washington State population and components of change, 1992 and trends, annual rpt, S8345–4

West Virginia population and components of change, 1940-91, annual rpt, S8560–1

Wisconsin population and components of change, 1940-91, annual rpt, S8715–4

Wisconsin population, by age, sex, and county, with components of change, quinquennially 1990-2020, recurring rpt, S8675–4

see also Immigration and emigration

see also Labor mobility

see also Migrant workers

see also Relocation

Militarization of space

see Strategic Defense Initiative

Military academies

see Service academies

Military aircraft

Latin America statistical abstract, general data by country, 1992 annual rpt, U6250–1.11

Production of civil and military aircraft, R&D, trade, employment, and finances, with Federal funding data, 1991 and trends, annual rpt, A0250–2

see also Helicopters

Military appropriations

see Defense budgets and appropriations

Military assistance

Latin America statistical abstract, general data by country, 1992 annual rpt, U6250–1.28

see also Arms trade

Military aviation

State and local:

Florida statistical abstract, general data, 1992 annual rpt, U6660–1.13

see also Military aircraft

Military bases, posts, and reservations

Air Force base hazardous waste site evaluation and cleanup costs by type, 1993 article, C5800–2.534

Closures compared to total bases, by service branch, 1988, 1991, and 1993, article, C5800–2.520

Military bases, posts, and reservations

Construction project appropriations vs Bush Admin requests, by service branch, FY93, annual rpt, C2500–2

Employment change resulting from proposed military base closures, by State, 1993, article, B8500–2.513

Installations by service branch, and closures/realignments and impact on personnel, by State, region, and base, 1988-93, R8490–45

Installations by service branch, and military construction expenditures, by State and region, FY89 or 1991, R8490–44

State and local:

California Fed Govt library staff, expenditures, holdings, and activities, by library, FY92, annual rpt, S0825–2

California military base closures, with impact on employment, 1993 annual rpt, S0840–3.1

Maryland assaults against spouses, by military installation, 1992, annual rpt, S3665–1

New Jersey vital events occurring on military posts, 1990, annual rpt, S5405–1

North Carolina postsecondary enrollment at military bases, fall 1992 and trends, annual rpt, U8013–1.1

Virginia DOD military and civilian employment by service branch, by region, locale, and installation, 1991 and trends, article, S8205–4.501

see also Military clubs and messes

see also Military housing

see also Military post exchanges and commissaries

Military benefits and pensions

Recipients and payments of military retirement benefits, by State and region, 1992, R8490–47

State and local:

Hawaii data book, general data, 1992 annual rpt, S2090–1.10

see also Veterans benefits and pensions

Military clubs and messes

Food service (institutional) financial and operating data, for leading firms by market segment, 1993 recurring feature, C1850–3.511

Food service industry sales and establishments, with growth outlook, by market segment, 1993 annual feature, C1850–3.503

Food service industry sales rankings by market segment, for leading organizations, 1992, annual feature, C1850–3.509

Food service industry sales trends and forecast, by market segment, 1990-93, annual feature, A8200–1.502

Military contracts and procurement

see Defense contracts and procurement

Military dependents

State and local:

Hawaii data book, general data, 1992 annual rpt, S2090–1.1, S2090–1.2, S2090–1.3, S2090–1.10

Military education

Latin America statistical abstract, general data by country, 1992 annual rpt, U6250–1.11

see also Military training

see also Reserve Officers Training Corps

see also Service academies

Military expenditures

see Defense expenditures

see Military assistance

Military health facilities and services

State and local:

Maryland births, by type of hospital, attendant, and location, 1988, annual rpt, S3635–1

Oklahoma statistical abstract, general data, 1992 annual rpt, U8130–2.9

see also Veterans health facilities and services

Military housing

State and local:

Alaska military personnel, housing arrangements, and defense expenditures, by census area and borough, 1993 article, S0320–1.511

Arkansas population in instns and other group quarters, 1990, census rpt, U5935–7

California population in instns and other group quarters, 1990, census rpt, S0840–9

Hawaii data book, general data, 1992 annual rpt, S2090–1.10

New Jersey population in instns and other group quarters, by county, 1990, census rpt, S5425–19

Pennsylvania population in instns and other group quarters, 1990, census rpt, U4130–13

Military intervention

Bosnia air strikes by US military, public opinion in US, May 1993 Gallup Poll, C4040–1.511

Bosnia peace plan of Clinton Admin, and US military intervention, public opinion in US, Jan-Feb 1993 Gallup Polls, C4040–1.508

Iraq military intervention resumption by US, public opinion in US, July 1992 Gallup Poll and trends, C4040–1.501

Iraq bombing for UN resolution violations, public opinion in US, Jan 1993 Gallup Poll, C4040–1.507

Iraq intelligence hq missile attack by US, public opinion in US, June 1993 Gallup Poll, C4040–1.512

Iraq military action resumption by US, public opinion in US including impact on reelection of President Bush, July-Aug 1992 Gallup Polls, C4040–1.502

see also War

Military pay

Base closure/realignment and impact on personnel, with data on military spending and installations, by State, region, and base, 1988-93, R8490–45

Chemistry and chemical engineering grad starting salaries, employment status, demographic characteristics, and advanced study plans, 1991/92, annual rpt, A1250–2

DOD contract and payroll spending, military and civilian personnel, installations, and cutbacks, by State and region, various years FY81-93, R8490–44

Law school grad employment and salaries, by type of employer, location, and grad characteristics, 1992 and trends, annual rpt, A6505–1

Metro area rankings by DOD wages/salaries per capita, for top 20 areas, 1992, article, A6450–2.509

State social, economic, and govtl indicators, with rankings, 1993 semiannual rpt, B8500–1.6

State and local:

Hawaii economic conditions, including employment, population, tourism, and construction, quarterly rpt, S2090–2

Illinois statistical abstract, general data, 1992 annual rpt, U6910–2

Military pensions

see Military benefits and pensions

Military personnel

Active duty personnel by race-ethnicity, total and women, FY90, article, R8750–1.504

Africa military personnel hospital admissions and deaths due to selected diseases, for African troops serving in UK army, 1819-36, article, A2623–1.502

Base closure/realignment and impact on personnel, with data on military spending and installations, by State, region, and base, 1988-93, R8490–45

Black youth on active military duty, with comparisons to whites and detail by sex, June 1988, R3840–21

Cambodia peacekeeping personnel serving in UN forces from top 20 countries, Jan 1993, article, R5650–2.540

Catholic population, clergy, and instns, by diocese and State, 1993 annual compilation, C4950–1

Defense budget, and armed forces by service branch, under current levels and proposed reductions, 1993 article, C8900–1.508

DOD contract and payroll spending, military and civilian personnel, installations, and cutbacks, by State and region, various years FY81-93, R8490–44

Federal payments to States as affected by hypothetical military personnel reductions, by State, 1993 article, B8500–2.516

General Educational Dev (GED) testing programs and results, by jurisdiction, 1992 and trends, annual rpt, A1410–16

Homosexuals in the military, public opinion on ending the ban, Jan 1993 Gallup Poll, C4040–1.508

Latin America statistical abstract, general data by country, 1992 annual rpt, U6250–1.11

Law school grad employment and salaries, by type of employer, location, and grad characteristics, 1992 and trends, annual rpt, A6505–1

Post exchange/commissary closures proposed and affected military personnel, by base, 1993 article, C0500–1.508

Public interest in news items concerning Clinton Admin decision to allow women military personnel to serve in combat roles, Apr/May 1993 survey, C8915–1.503

Public interest in news items on Clinton Admin attempt to lift ban on homosexuals in the military, by respondent characteristics, Feb 1993 survey, C8915–1.502

Public opinion on homosexuality and Clinton Admin attempt to lift military service ban, by respondent characteristics, July/Aug 1993 survey, C8915–1.504

Respiratory problems reported by US military personnel stationed in Saudi Arabia, with detail by sleeping accommodations, 1990/91 study, article, A2623–1.511

Index by Subjects and Names

State social, economic, and govtl indicators, with rankings, 1993 semiannual rpt, B8500-1.6

Statistical profiles of 50 States and DC, general data, 1993 annual almanac, C4712-1

State and local:

- Alaska military personnel, housing arrangements, and defense expenditures, by census area and borough, 1993 article, S0320-1.511
- Alaska population by military status, by borough and census area, 1990-91, annual rpt, S0320-4
- California military base closures, with impact on employment, 1993 annual rpt, S0840-3.1
- Hawaii data book, general data, 1992 annual rpt, S2090-1.1, S2090-1.2, S2090-1.10, S2090-1.21
- Hawaii economic indicators, bimonthly rpt, B3500-1
- Hawaii military population by county and island, births by race-ethnicity of child, and reported sexually transmitted diseases by type, 1990 and trends, annual rpt, S2065-1
- Illinois statistical abstract, general data, 1992 annual rpt, U6910-2
- Maryland statistical abstract, general data, 1993-94 biennial rpt, S3605-1.4
- New York State statistical yearbook, general data, 1992 annual rpt, U5100-1.3
- Oregon ex-service personnel unemployment claims filed, 1st qtr 1989-3rd qtr 1993, article, S6592-1.503
- South Carolina statistical abstract, general data, 1993 annual rpt, S7125-1.7
- Tennessee statistical abstract, general data, 1992/93 annual rpt, U8710-2.1, U8710-2.3
- Virginia DOD military and civilian employment by service branch, by region, locale, and installation, 1991 and trends, article, S8205 4.501
- Washington State military personnel, by county, 1980 and 1990-92, annual rpt, S8345-4

see also Coast Guard

see also Military benefits and pensions

see also Military dependents

see also Military pay

see also Retired military personnel

see also Veterans

see also Voluntary military service

Military policy

see Arms trade

see Military assistance

see National defense

Military post exchanges and commissaries

Operations and sales performance of military commissary and post exchange systems, quarterly rpt, A2072-2

Sales by service branch, location, and store, FY92 and trends, annual rpt, A2072-2.502

Sales for military resale agencies, by product category, FY91 and trends, annual rpt, A2072-1

Sales in military commissaries, by region, product type, and individual store, FY92, annual feature, A2072-2.501

Sales in military post exchange and commissary systems, by service branch or region, with merchandising devs and comparisons to civilian retail trade, monthly rpt, C0500-1

Sales to Army/Air Force post exchange, approx 700 top supplier companies, for year ended Jan 1993, annual feature, C0500-1.505

Sales to Navy post exchange, for approx 200 supplier companies, and sales by Navy store and dept, FY92 and trends, annual feature, C0500-1.507

State and local:

Hawaii data book, general data, 1992 annual rpt, S2090-1.23

Military prisons

Directory of correctional instns, with inmates, staff, and cost of care, by instn, 1992, annual rpt, A1305-3

Military research

see Defense research

Military science

see also Arms control and disarmament

see also Civil defense

see also Logistics

Military service

see Armed services

see Voluntary military service

Military service academies

see Service academies

Military supplies and property

Operating and financial composite ratios for corporations, with establishments and receipts, for approx 200 industries, by asset size, FY90, annual rpt, C7800-1

State and local:

Hawaii data book, general data, 1992 annual rpt, S2090-1.10

see also Arms trade

see also Defense contracts and procurement

see also Logistics

see also Military assistance

see also Military bases, posts, and reservations

see also Military vehicles

see also Military weapons

see also Naval vessels

Military training

Latin America statistical abstract, general data by country, 1992 annual rpt, U6250-1.11

see also Military education

see also Reserve Officers Training Corps

see also Service academies

Military vehicles

State and local:

Arizona traffic accidents, fatalities, and injuries, by vehicle type, circumstances, location, and driver and victim characteristics, 1991 and trends, annual rpt, S0530-1

Florida traffic accidents, fatalities, and injuries, by vehicle type, circumstance, location, and driver and victim characteristics, 1992 and trends, annual rpt, S1750-2

Indiana traffic accidents, fatalities, and injuries, by circumstances, location, and vehicle type, and driver and victim characteristics, 1992, annual rpt, S2675-1

Minnesota traffic accidents, fatalities, and injuries, by type of vehicle and circumstances, and driver and victim characteristics, 1992 and trends, annual rpt, S4230-2

North Carolina traffic accidents, fatalities, and injuries, by circumstances, location, vehicle type, and driver and victim characteristics, 1992 and trends, annual rpt, S5990-1

Mine accidents and safety

South Carolina traffic accidents, fatalities, and injuries, by circumstances, location, and driver and victim characteristics, 1992 and trends, annual rpt, S7190-2

see also Naval vessels

Military weapons

Conventional forces in Europe, for US, NATO, Soviet Union, and Eastern Europe, prior to and after Conventional Forces in Europe (CFE) treaty, 1991, annual rpt, C2500-2

Defense budget, and armed forces by service branch, under current levels and proposed reductions, 1993 article, C8900-1.508

Federal funding for major weapons programs, by program, FY93, annual rpt, C2500-2

Soviet Union or Russia weapons production, by weapon category, 1990-92, article, C5800-4.522

see also Arms trade

see also Defense contracts and procurement

see also Defense expenditures

see also Military aircraft

see also Military assistance

see also Military vehicles

see also Missiles and rockets

see also Nuclear weapons

Militia

see National Guard

Milk and milk products

see Dairy industry and products

Milling

see Grains and grain products

Millionaires

see Wealth

Milwaukee, Wis.

CPI and help-wanted index for Milwaukee, monthly rpt, S8750-1

Crime (violent) levels in Milwaukee, Wis and St Paul, Minn, 1991, A7575-1.12

Educational attainment of parents with children in Milwaukee public schools, and in private schools under school selection program, by sex, 1989/90-1990/91, R3810-7

see also under By City in the "Index by Categories"

Mine accidents and safety

Accidental deaths and disabling injuries, by detailed type, victim characteristics, circumstances, and location, 1992 and trends, annual rpt, A8375-2

Coal industry executive views on attainability of Fed Govt goal of zero mine fatalities, Aug 1992 survey, article, C5226-1.506

State and local:

Alabama vital statistics, including population, births, deaths by cause, marriages, and divorces, by location and demographic characteristics, 1992 and trends, annual rpt, S0175-2

Iowa vital statistics, including population, births, deaths by cause, marriages, and divorces, by demographic characteristics and location, 1991 and trends, annual rpt, S2795-1

Pennsylvania coal industry employment and work-related fatalities, 1960-90, recurring rpt, S6810-3

Pennsylvania statistical abstract, general data, 1992 recurring rpt, U4130-6.8

see also Black lung disease

Mineral leases

Mineral leases

Coal leases issued by Fed Govt, including acreage, sales, royalties, and reserves, with data for 10 States, FY91 and trends, article, C5226–1.510

Federal land proposed royalty effects on employment, govt revenues, and financial performance of selected companies, with royalty rates in 12 countries, 1993 article, C5226–2.506

Revenue disbursements from Federal offshore mineral leases, by fund, 1971-90, annual compilation, C6985–9.4

State and local:

Nevada statistical abstract, general data, 1992 biennial rpt, S5005–1.12

Texas financial condition, including revenues by source, expenditures by function and dept, and investments, with data for over 400 individual funds, FY92, annual rpt, S7655–2.2

Utah mineral lease funding allocations to higher education instns, 1986/87-1992/93, annual rpt, S7895–2

Utah public lands by govt owner, and Federal land payments to State and local govts, with data by county, 1992 article, U8960–2.502

Wyoming State treasurer financial transactions, including revenues, investments, and disbursements by local area, FY92 and trends, annual rpt, S9010–1

see also Oil and gas leases

see also Severance taxes

Mineral resources

see Mines and mineral resources

Mineral supplements

see Vitamins and nutrients

Mineral water

see Bottled water

Minerals Management Service

Oil/gas offshore platforms installed and removed in Gulf of Mexico, bonding requirements, and Minerals Management Service liability for abandoned equipment, 1993 article, C6985–2.508

Mines and mineral resources

Business failures and liabilities, by detailed industry, cause, length of operation, and location, 1991-92 and trends, annual rpt, C3150–8

Capital spending plans for new mines and plants, by mineral and company, and mine production values, 1993 annual feature, C5226–2.503

Corporate performance ratings by executives for leading companies in 32 industries, 1993 annual survey feature, C8900–1.508

Earnings of US, Australian, and Canadian workers in mining and allied industries, monthly rpt, B6800–1

Exploration activities, expenses, and staff, for foreign and domestic operations of US and Canadian mining companies, 1991, article, C5226–2.508

Fortune 500 largest industrial corporations, sales, financial, and stock performance data by company, 1992, annual feature, C8900–1.513

Fortune 500 largest industrial corporations worldwide, with financial and employment data, 1992, annual feature, C8900–1.520

Latin America statistical abstract, general data by country, 1992 annual rpt, U6250–1.23, U6250–1.32

Manganese ore imports for use in iron and steel industry, by country of origin, 1988-92, annual rpt, A2000–2.3

Operating and financial composite ratios for corporations, with establishments and receipts, for approx 200 industries, by asset size, FY90, annual rpt, C7800–1

Operating and financial data for metals and nonmetallic minerals industries, with articles and special features, monthly rpt, C5226–2

Production, consumption, stocks, trade, and prices for approx 100 basic commodities, including by country and producing State, commodity yearbook for 1993, C2400–1, C2400–2

Statistical profiles of 50 States and DC, general data, 1993 annual almanac, C4712–1

Supply-demand for selected metals and nonmetallic minerals, with price data, US and worldwide, 1992-93 and trends, annual feature, C5226–2.505

Supply-demand situation for selected minerals, 1982-92, annual feature, A1250–1.530

State and local:

Alabama county data book, general data, 1992 annual rpt, S0121–2

Alabama statistical abstract, general data, 1992 recurring rpt, U5680–2.12

Arizona economic condition, including population, employment and earnings, and business activity, by industry and locality, 1985-93, semiannual rpt, U5850–1

Arizona mineral production and value, by mineral type, 1991 and trends, annual rpt, S0497–1

Arizona mining industry employment and job outlook by occupation and county, 1990-95, triennial rpt, S0465–2.33

Arizona statistical abstract, general data, 1993 recurring rpt, U5850–2.14

Arkansas nonfuel mineral production, by commodity, 1991-92, annual article, U5930–1.503

California statistical abstract, general data, 1992 annual rpt, S0840–2.7

Colorado property assessed valuation, and summary production data, by county, 1991-92, annual rpt, S1055–3

Florida statistical abstract, general data, 1992 annual rpt, U6660–1.10

Georgia statistical abstract, general data, 1992-93 biennial rpt, U6730–1.5

Hawaii data book, general data, 1992 annual rpt, S2090–1.20

Idaho economic profile, general data, 1992 recurring rpt, S2218–2.5

Kansas statistical abstract, general data, 1991/92 annual rpt, U7095–2.16

Kansas tax collections by tax type, and property values, with data by county, FY92 and trends, annual rpt, S3020–1

Kentucky economic statistics, general data, 1993 annual rpt, S3104–1.1

Missouri mineral production, by commodity and company, FY92 and trends, annual rpt, S4530–2.1

Montana mine production and taxes paid, by county, 1990-91, biennial rpt, S4750–1.1

Nebraska property tax revenues and actual valuation by property type, by city and/or county, 1991 and trends, annual rpt, S4950–1.4

Index by Subjects and Names

Nevada statistical abstract, general data, 1992 biennial rpt, S5005–1.8, S5005–1.12

New Jersey employment in 4 nonmanufacturing industry divs, by occupation, 1987 and 1990, article, S5425–1.506

New Mexico economic trends and outlook, by industry div, 1982-92, annual article, U7980–1.503

New Mexico tax revenues and disbursements, by detailed tax type, and property valuation data, FY91-92 and trends, annual rpt, S5660–1.2

New York State statistical yearbook, general data, 1992 annual rpt, U5100–1.2

Pennsylvania statistical abstract, general data, 1992 recurring rpt, U4130–6.8

South Dakota State measure on gold/silver surface mining regulation, election results by county, 1992, biennial rpt, S7390–1

Tennessee statistical abstract, general data, 1992/93 annual rpt, U8710–2.5

Utah govt statistical review, fiscal and socioeconomic data, 1993 annual rpt, R9380–1.2

Utah statistical abstract, general data, 1993 triennial rpt, U8960–1.10

Utah tax revenues by source, and distribution to localities and State funds, FY92 and trends, annual rpt, S7905–1

Wyoming mineral production tax assessments, by county, 1992, annual rpt, S8890–1.1

Wyoming minerals production and taxable valuation, by county, and severance and ad valorem taxes, FY92 annual rpt, S8990–1.2

Wyoming mining industry employment, and production workers hours and earnings, monthly rpt, S8895–1

Wyoming State govt mineral trust fund revenues by source, FY75-92, annual rpt, S8875–1

see also Aluminum and aluminum industry

see also Cement and concrete

see also Clay industry and products

see also Coal and coal mining

see also Copper and copper industry

see also Gases

see also Gemstones

see also Gold

see also Industrial production

see also Iron and steel industry

see also Lead and lead industry

see also Metals and metal industries

see also Mine accidents and safety

see also Mineral leases

see also Natural gas and gas industry

see also Nonmetallic minerals and mines

see also Offshore oil and gas

see also Oil shale

see also Petroleum and petroleum industry

see also Severance taxes

see also Silver

see also Stockpiling

see also Stone products and quarries

see also Strategic materials

see also Tin and tin industry

see also Uranium

see also Zinc and zinc industry

see also under By Industry in the "Index by Categories"

Index by Subjects and Names

Minimum income

see Income maintenance

Minimum wage

Black American workers paid hourly rates at or below minimum wage, with comparison to whites, 1992, annual compilation, C6775–2.6

Hispanic American workers paid hourly rates at or below minimum wage, with comparison to whites, 1992, annual compilation, C6775–3.4

Latin America statistical abstract, general data by country, 1992 annual rpt, U6250–1.13

State social, economic, and govtl indicators, with rankings, 1993 semiannual rpt, B8500–1.14

Women's employment and earnings, with comparisons to men, and detail by occupation and worker characteristics, 1990s and trends, annual rpt, A1570–2

Workers (minimum wage) distribution by family income level, 1993 article, C8900–1.512

State and local:

DC statistical profile, general data, 1992 annual rpt, S1535–3.3

Hawaii data book, general data, 1992 annual rpt, S2090–1.12

Mining

see Mines and mineral resources

Mink

see Furs and fur industry

Minneapolis, Minn.

Crime (violent) levels in Milwaukee, Wis and St Paul, Minn, 1991, A7575–1.12

Grain futures and options trading activity on Minneapolis exchange, with production, price, and disposition data for area served, 1992 and trends, annual rpt, B6110–1

Printing (prepress) industry conditions for Minneapolis/St Paul area, 1993 survey article, C1830–10.509

see also under By City in the "Index by Categories"

Minnesota

Agricultural production, marketing, and finances, by county or commodity, and farms and acreage, 1992 and trends, annual rpt, S4130–1

Crime rates compared with incarceration rates, for California, Wisconsin, and Minnesota, 1970s-90, A7575–1.12

Election results and voter registration, by locality, 1992 primary and general elections, biennial rpt, S4255–1

Elementary and secondary school enrollment, staff, and finances, by district and county, 1991/92 and trends, annual rpt, S4165–1

Employment, hours, and earnings, by industry group and locality, monthly rpt, S4205–1

Financial instns (State-regulated), financial condition by instn, 1991-92, annual rpt, S4140–3

Govt financial condition, including revenues by source, expenditures by function, fund balances, and bonded debt, FY92 and trends, annual rpt, S4180–1

Grain futures and options trading activity on Minneapolis exchange, with production, price, and disposition data for area served, 1992 and trends, annual rpt, B6110–1

Income tax (individual) return data, discontinued annual rpt, S4250–1

Insurance industry financial and underwriting data, by company and line of coverage, 1991, annual rpt, S4140–4

labor and economic trends, quarterly rpt, S4205–3

Libraries, holdings, staff, services, circulation, and finances, by public library, 1991, annual rpt, S4165–2

Markets with daily newspapers, demographic and economic info by geographic area, US and Canada, 1993 annual rpt, C3250–1

Postsecondary education enrollment and finance, by type of school system, 1970s-93, biennial rpt, S4195–2

Statistical profiles of 50 States and DC, general data, 1993 annual almanac, C4712–1

Traffic accidents, fatalities, and injuries, by type of vehicle and circumstances, and driver and victim characteristics, 1992 and trends, annual rpt, S4230–2

Utilities financial and operating data, discontinued biennial rpt, S4235–1

Utility and transportation regulatory agency activities, scope of jurisdiction, finances, and employees, by agency, 1991/92 annual rpt, A7015–2

Vital statistics, including population, births, abortions, deaths, marriages, and divorces, by location and demographic characteristics, 1991 and trends, annual rpt, S4190–2

Welfare program recipients and expenditures, by county, 1992, semiannual rpt, S4202–1

see also Minneapolis, Minn.

see also St. Paul, Minn.

see also under By City and By County in the "Index by Categories"

see also under By State in the "Index by Categories"

Minority businesses

Black-owned business firms, sales/receipts, employment, and payroll, by industry div and State, 1982 and/or 1987, annual compilation, C6775–2.8

Black-owned businesses and receipts, by industry div, 1987, annual article, A8510–1.1

Black-owned companies top 10 problems encountered in doing business with govt agencies, 1993 article, C4215–1.503

Black-owned enterprises financial and operating data, for top 100 firms and auto dealerships and for top 15-25 financial instns, 1992 and trends, annual feature, C4215–1.507

Black-owned franchises, with type of business and startup costs, top 50 companies, 1993 annual article, C4215–1.510

Broadcasting station seller tax deferment certificates granted by FCC for sales to minority buyers, by ethnic group, 1978-1st half 1993, article, C1850–14.537

Construction industry financial performance, for minority-owned companies, 1992-93, annual survey rpt, A4155–1

Hispanic-owned business activities, including finances and operations of top firms, monthly rpt, C4575–1

Minority employment

Hispanic-owned business availability vs use for city govt contracts by type, and status of contract award disparity studies, for 5-10 cities, 1993 article, C4575–1.510

Hispanic-owned business motor vehicle fleet characteristics and policies, 1992 annual survey feature, C4575–1.501

Hispanic-owned business outlook for selected performance indicators, with data by region, monthly rpt quarterly feature, C4575–1.510

Hispanic-owned business sales and employment, for top 500 companies, 1992, annual feature, C4575–1.507

Hispanic-owned business sales and employment, for 100 fastest-growing companies, 1988-92, annual feature, C4575–1.509

Hispanic-owned high-technology company sales and employment, for top 50 firms, 1992, annual article, C4575–1.510

Investment banks with black owners, value of securities issues managed, for top 13 instns, Dec 1992, article, C4215–1.507

Investment mgmt firms owned by minorities/women, 1993 annual feature, C2710–2.511

Number and gross receipts of minority-owned vs total businesses, with detail by race-ethnicity, 1987, article, C4215–1.507

Number of minority-owned firms, with comparison to population size, by detailed race-ethnicity, 1982 adn 1987, R8750–2.58

Restaurant minority franchisees, and minority-managed units, for 12 major chains, Sept 1993, article, C5150–5.511

Restaurants/drinking places and sales, for minority-owned establishments by race-ethnicity, 1987, article, A8200–1.508

SBA contract value awarded to minority-owned businesses, with total eligible businesses, by minority group, FY92, article, C4575–1.507

Statistical profiles of 50 States and DC, general data, 1993 annual almanac, C4712–1

State and local:

Florida statistical abstract, general data, 1992 annual rpt, U6660–1.9

Hawaii data book, general data, 1992 annual rpt, S2090–1.15

Kansas statistical data, general data, 1991/92 annual rpt, U7095–2.8

Kentucky economic statistics, general data, 1993 annual rpt, S3104–1.1

New York State contracts awarded to minority- and women-owned business, 1992 annual rpt, U5100–1.5

Pennsylvania statistical abstract, general data, 1992 recurring rpt, U4130–6.2

see also Minority employment

see also Women-owned businesses

Minority employment

Business minority employment levels among firms in minority communities, by owner race, 1993 article, C4215–1.510

Catholic charity agency minority personnel, 1991 and trends, annual rpt, A3810–1

Chemist salaries and employment, by employee and employer characteristics, Mar 1993 and trends, annual article, A1250–1.532

Minority employment

College grad hiring plans by industry, with data on campus visits, starting salaries, and minority hires, 1991/92-1992/93, annual rpt, A3940–3

College grad recruiting practices and hiring trends, with data on starting salaries and layoffs, by type of employer, 1992/93 annual survey rpt, U3130–1

Corporate mgmt of culturally diverse work force, with program characteristics and minority opportunity indicators, Nov 1992 survey, A2075–20.11

Corporate minority employment levels, and mgmt programs for dealing with diverse work force, 1991 survey, article, C1200–4.509

Elementary/secondary school superintendents personal and professional characteristics and views, 1992 survey rpt, A0775–5

Food service black and Hispanic representation in employment and mgmt, with detail by selected occupation, 1993 articles, C5150–5.511

Geoscience faculty salaries by rank and for women, with data on minority faculty members, 1991/92 and trends, annual rpt, A1785–4

Hospital CEO demographic and professional characteristics, perquisites, and views on mgmt issues, Oct 1992 survey, recurring rpt, B4490–2.35

Labor force and education data for women and minorities in professional fields, 1980s-91, with historical trends, recurring rpt, A3960–2

Law school grad employment and salaries, by type of employer, location, and grad characteristics, 1992 and trends, annual rpt, A6505–1

Librarians at universities and research instns, and salaries, for minorities by sex, position, and experience, FY92, annual survey, A3365–2

Library school grad placements and salaries, by region, sex, instn, and library type, with detail for minorities, 1992 and trends, annual article, C1852–1.512

Newspaper employment of minorities and women, 1992-93, annual rpt, A8605–4

Newspaper journalists minority shares, for 50 leading publications, 1992-93, article, A8605–1.507

Private elementary and secondary school enrollment, staff, and finances, with detail for minorities, by school type and region, 1980s-1992/93, annual rpt, A6835–3

Public broadcasting full-time employment, with detail for women and minorities, by job category, 1977-92, recurring rpt, R4250–1.23

Science and math elementary/secondary education, including student and teacher characteristics, and requirements, by State, 1991/92, biennial rpt, A4355–3

Small business views on employment trends for women, minorities, immigrants, and the disabled, and related mgmt issues, 1993 survey article, C4687–1.503

Urban public school teachers, and minority teacher share, for 47 systems, 1990/91, A4425–4

State and local:

Alabama public health dept minority employment compared to labor market, by occupational category, 1991-92, annual rpt, S0175–3

Louisiana job service openings and applicants, and characteristics of Job Training Partnership Act target population and insured unemployed, 1993 annual planning rpt, S3320–1.2

Mississippi labor force planning rpt, including population, employment, and characteristics of unemployed and disadvantaged, 1993 annual rpt, S4345–1

Oklahoma statistical abstract, general data, 1992 annual rpt, U8130–2.3

Rhode Island labor force planning rpt, including population, employment by industry, job openings, and characteristics of insured unemployed, 1993 annual rpt, S6980–3

South Carolina labor force planning rpt, detailed data on employment, hours, wages, turnover, and characteristics of job service applicants, 1992 annual rpt, S7155–3.2

see also Asian Americans
see also Black Americans
see also Hispanic Americans
see also Indians
see also Pacific Islands Americans
see also under By Race in the "Index by Categories"

Minority groups

Community problems viewed as most important by blacks, Hispanics, and Asian Americans, 1993 survey article, R4800–2.518

Congress minority membership after Nov 1990 and 1992 elections, by race-ethnicity, article, C4215–1.504

Consumer promotions targeted to minority groups, corporate use, 1991-92, annual rpt, A4620–1.2

Corporate boards of directors composition, compensation, and practices, by industry sector, 1991 and trends, annual survey rpt, B5000–3

Corporate boards of directors with women and minority members, and board membership by sex and race-ethnicity, 1991/92, B4490–2.36

Elementary/secondary minority student participation in advanced placement math and science tests, by State, 1991/92, biennial rpt, A4355–3.1

Elementary/secondary teacher views on education policy issues and selected reform proposals, with data by school minority composition, Jan-Feb 1993 survey, B6045–7

Elementary/secondary teaching profession factors limiting minority participation, public opinion by race-ethnicity, 1993 annual Gallup Poll, A8680–1.503

Environmental nonprofit organization minority representation in membership, staff, volunteers, and boards, 1993 article, C2176–1.511

Europe public opinion on political, economic, and social issues, for 9 countries and 3 Soviet Union Republics, 1991 survey, C8915–8.1

Federal judgeship presidential appointments, with detail for women, blacks, and Hispanics, 1963-92, annual rpt, C2500–2

Index by Subjects and Names

Fundraising professionals characteristics, earnings, and benefits, 1992 survey, recurring rpt, A8455–1

Health care facilities providing care to minority non-English speaking population, by type of facility, 1993, article, A1865–1.514

Higher education administrative salaries, for 167 positions, by minority status and instn type, 1992/93, annual rpt, A3900–1

Higher education admission applications received from total and minority students, 1992-93, annual rpt, A6695–1

Higher education enrollment shares for minorities, by State, fall 1991, annual rpt, C2175–1.531

Higher education instn policies and practices, including changes in faculty, enrollment, and finances, 1993 annual survey, A1410–1.38

Higher education involvement of minorities, including enrollment and degrees awarded, by race-ethnicity, sex, and State, 1970s-91, annual rpt, A1410–10

Higher education, 2-year college minority enrollment, by instn and State, Oct 1990-91, annual directory, A0640–1

House of Representatives racial/ethnic minority committee chairperson funds received from political action committees, 1992, article, C4215–1.510

Jewish population by world area, country, and US census div, State, and city, 1990-92, annual compilation, A2050–1

Jewish vs total population shares making charitable contributions, by age and income level, 1993 annual rpt, A0700–1.2

Judgeships (Federal), with detail for black, Hispanic, and Asian appointees, 1976-92, article, C4215–1.505

Law school enrollment by minority status, degrees conferred, staff, and library holdings, by instn, 1992/93 and trends, annual rpt, A0970–1

Library grants from Fed Govt for Indian/Hawaiian Native programs, by State, FY92, annual compilation, C1650–3.2

Medical school applicants and acceptance rates for underrepresented minorities vs others, by academic achievement group, 1978-91, article, A3273–8.501

Medical school grad plans for practicing in socioeconomically deprived areas, and specialty certification, for minority and nonminority grads, 1982-92, article, A3273–8.507

Middle East population distribution by ethnic group, 1993 rpt, R8750–2.59

Museums and related instns with cultural/ethnic focus for collections or audience, 1989/90 survey, A0750–1.1

Optometry school students receiving minority grants/scholarships, by instn, 1991/92, annual survey, A3370–2

Osteopathy student debt and career plans, by student characteristics, 1991/92 and trends, annual survey rpt, A0620–2

Physics degrees awarded, by level, sex, and minority group, 1991/92, annual rpt, A1960–2.1

Population characteristics, employment, and voting patterns for minority groups by detailed race-ethnicity, with comparisons to whites, 1980s-2040, R8750–2.58

Index by Subjects and Names

Mississippi

Population share by age group, 1992 and 2025, article, R8750–1.506

Population size and selected characteristics, by region, census div, and State, 1991 and trends, annual data sheet, R8750–9

Professional women and minorities, detailed education and labor force data, 1980s-91, with historical trends, recurring rpt, A3960–2

Public estimates of black, Hispanic, and Jewish shares of population, and correlations with respondent characteristics and perceptions, 1991 survey, article, A0610–1.504

Soviet Union political and economic restructuring issues, public opinion in Russia, Ukraine, and Lithuania, 1991-92 surveys, C8915–10

Women (single) minority households, by ethnic group and urban-rural location, 1992, A8657–5

State and local:

California vital statistics, including population, births, and deaths by cause, by demographic characteristics and county, 1990 and trends, annual rpt, S0865–1

Florida higher education goals for increasing minority enrollment and employment, by instn, 1987-92, annual rpt, S1725–1

Hawaii data book, general data, 1992 annual rpt, S2090–1.1, S2090–1.12

Kansas statistical abstract, general data, 1991/92 annual rpt, U7095–2.12

Oklahoma public school minority shares of enrollment, by district, 1991/92 and trends, annual rpt, S6423–2

Pennsylvania public school minority teachers and students, 1983/84, 1987/88, and 1992/93, annual rpt, S6790–5.12

Rhode Island statistical almanac, general data, 1993 annual rpt, C7975–1.1

see also Ancestry

see also Asian Americans

see also Black Americans

see also Civil rights

see also Hispanic Americans

see also Indians

see also Minority businesses

see also Minority employment

see also Pacific Islands Americans

see also Racial discrimination

Minority students

see Black students

see Minority groups

Minors

see Youth

Mints

see Spices and herbs

Miscarriage

see Fetal deaths

Missiles and rockets

Aerospace industry, civil and military production, R&D, trade, employment, and finances, with Federal funding data, 1991 and trends, annual rpt, A0250–2

see also Space programs

Missing persons and runaways

State and local:

Arizona arrests by offense, offender characteristics, and county, 1992, annual rpt, S0505–2.2

Arkansas crimes and arrests, by offense, victim and offender characteristics, and location, 1992 and trends, annual rpt, S0652–1

California criminal justice system detailed data, by offense, county, age, race-ethnicity, and sex, 1991 and trends, annual rpt, S0910–2.2

Colorado crimes and arrests, by offense and location, with offender characteristics, and assaults on police, 1992, annual rpt, S1068–1

Connecticut runaway arrests by jurisdiction, and missing persons reported by month, 1992, annual rpt, S1256–1

DC juvenile court case activity, including referrals by offense and age, 1992 and trends, annual rpt, S1515–1

Hawaii crimes and arrests, by offense, with data by county and victim-offender characteristics, 1992, annual rpt, S2035–1

Idaho crimes and arrests, by offense, with data by location and offender characteristics, 1992 and trends, annual rpt, S2275–2

Illinois crimes and arrests, by offense, with data by location and offender characteristics, 1991, annual rpt, S2536–1

Kansas crimes and arrests, by offense, with data by location, agency, and victim-offender characteristics, 1992 and trends, annual rpt, S2925–1.1

Kentucky arrests by county and offense, and law enforcement employment by agency, 1992, annual rpt, S3150–1.2

Maine arrests of adults and juveniles, by offense, age, and sex, 1991, annual rpt, S3475–1.2

Maryland crimes and arrests, by offense, location, and offender characteristics, with law enforcement employment and assaults on officers, 1992 and trends, annual rpt, S3665–1

Michigan crimes and arrests, by offense, with data by location and offender characteristics, 1992 and trends, annual rpt, S3997–1

Missouri crimes and arrests, by offense and location, with victim and offender characteristics, 1991 and trends, annual rpt, S4560–2

New Hampshire arrests, by offense and offender age, sex, and race-ethnicity, 1991, annual rpt, S5250–2.2

New Jersey arrests by offense, age, race-ethnicity, sex, and county, 1992 and trends, annual rpt, S5430–1.2

New York State juvenile arrests, by offense and demographic characteristics, 1991, annual rpt, S5760–3.2

North Carolina arrests by detailed offense, offender characteristics, and county, 1991-92, annual rpt, S5955–1.2

North Dakota crimes and arrests, by offense, location, and offender characteristics, and law enforcement employment, 1991 and trends, annual rpt, S6060–1

Oklahoma crimes and arrests, by offense, with victim and offender characteristics, 1990-92, annual rpt, S6465–1.1

Oregon crimes and arrests, by offense, with data by county, local agency, and offender characteristics, 1992 and trends, annual rpt, S6603–3

Pennsylvania crimes and arrests, by offense, with data by location and offender characteristics, 1992 and trends, annual rpt, S6860–1

South Carolina crimes and arrests, by detailed offense, offender characteristics, and location, 1992 and trends, annual rpt, S7205–1.2

Texas arrests, by age, sex, race-ethnicity, and offense, 1992, annual rpt, S7735–2.2

Utah crimes and arrests, by offense, county, and local agency, 1992 and trends, annual rpt, S7890–3

Utah homeless shelter population characteristics, individual shelter capacity, and related housing data, 1991-92, annual rpt, S7808–2

Virginia crimes and arrests by offense, and law enforcement employment, by location and reporting agency, 1992, annual rpt, S8295–2.2

Washington State crimes and arrests, by offense, with data by location and offender characteristics, 1992 and trends, annual rpt, S8440–1

West Virginia crimes and arrests, by offense, location, and offender characteristics, 1990-91, annual rpt, S8610–1

Wisconsin crimes and arrests, by offense, offender characteristics, county, and local agency, 1992 and trends, annual rpt, S8771–1

Wyoming adult and juvenile arrests, by offense, county, and local jurisdiction, 1991, annual rpt, S8867–3.2

Missions and missionaries

Catholic missionaries from US including by world region and sponsoring organization, and male religious order world membership, 1993 annual almanac, C6885–1

Catholic population, clergy, and instns, by diocese and State, 1993 annual compilation, C4950–1

Latin America statistical abstract, general data by country, 1992 annual rpt, U6250–1.10

Mississippi

Banks and other financial instns, financial condition by instn type, and assets by bank and credit union, Dec 1992, annual rpt, S4325–1

Elementary and secondary school enrollment, staff, salaries, and finances, by school district, 1991/92 and trends, annual rpt, S4340–1

Govt financial condition, including revenues by source, expenditures by function and object, and detail by agency, FY92 and trends, annual rpt, S4346–1

Higher education enrollment and degrees, by level and field, and finances, by State-supported instn, 1991/92, annual rpt, S4360–1

Labor force planning rpt, including population, employment, and characteristics of unemployed and disadvantaged, 1993 annual rpt, S4345–1

Markets with daily newspapers, demographic and economic info by geographic area, US and Canada, 1993 annual rpt, C3250–1

Natural gas production and reserves in Black Warrior basin, 1992 article, C6985–1.505

Oil/gas industry production, finances, exploration, and reserves, by State, 1992 and trends, annual rpt, A5425–1.1

Mississippi

Socioeconomic data, including income by county, and wages by industry group, 1993 annual planning rpt, S4345–1.4

Statistical abstract of Mississippi, detailed demographic, social, govtl, and economic data, 1992 annual rpt, U3255–4

Statistical profiles of 50 States and DC, general data, 1993 annual almanac, C4712–1

Tax collections by type, and disbursements, with selected sales and income tax data by locality and industry, FY92 and trends, annual rpt, S4435–1

Utility and transportation regulatory agency activities, scope of jurisdiction, finances, and employees, by agency, 1991/92 annual rpt, A7015–2

Vital statistics, including births, deaths by cause, marriages, and divorces, by demographic characteristics and location, 1992 and trends, annual rpt, S4350–1

Welfare and social service cases, recipients, and payments, by program and county, FY92, annual rpt, S4357–1

see also under By City and By County in the "Index by Categories"

see also under By State in the "Index by Categories"

Missouri

Agricultural production, marketing, and finances, by commodity and/or county, and farms and acreage, 1982-92, annual rpt, S4480–1

Banks and trust companies (State-chartered), financial condition by instn, FY91-92 and trends, biennial rpt, S4502–1

Correctional instn admissions, releases, and inmate characteristics, FY93, annual rpt, S4501–1

Crimes and arrests, by offense and location, with victim and offender characteristics, 1991 and trends, annual rpt, S4560–2

Election results, by district and/or county, with directory of govt officials, 1992 general election, biennial rpt, S4580–1

Elementary and secondary school finances, enrollment, grads, and staff, by county and school district, 1991/92, annual rpt, S4505–1

Employment, earnings, and hours, by industry and MSA, monthly rpt, S4530–3

Govt financial condition, including fund finances, tax collections and distribution, and State treasury activity, FY92 and trends, annual rpt, S4570–1

Govt financial condition, including revenues by source, expenditures by function, and fund balances, FY92, annual rpt, S4475–1

Higher education enrollment, degrees conferred, and appropriations, by instn, and coordinating board activities, annual rpt discontinued coverage, S4520–1

Higher education enrollment, degrees, libraries, staff, and finances, by instn, 1992 and trends, annual rpt, S4520–3

Insurance industry financial and underwriting data, by company and line of coverage, with regulatory info, 1992, annual rpt, S4527–1

Labor and industrial relations dept activity, with data on work injuries, worker rights, and labor force, FY92 and trends, annual rpt, S4530–2

Libraries, finances, holdings, circulation, staff, and services, for public, special, and academic libraries, by location, FY92, annual rpt, S4520–2

Markets with daily newspapers, demographic and economic info by geographic area, US and Canada, 1993 annual rpt, C3250–1

Oil/gas industry production, finances, exploration, and reserves, by State, 1992 and trends, annual rpt, A5425–1.1

Statistical profiles of 50 States and DC, general data, 1993 annual almanac, C4712–1

Traffic accidents, fatalities, and injuries, by circumstances, location, and driver and victim characteristics, 1992 and trends, annual rpt, S4560–1

Utility and transportation regulatory agency activities, scope of jurisdiction, finances, and employees, by agency, 1991/92 annual rpt, A7015–2

Vital statistics, including births, deaths by cause, and marriages and divorces, by location and demographic characteristics, 1992 and trends, annual rpt, S4518–1

Welfare and medical assistance recipients, expenditures, and case processing, by program and county, FY92 and trends, annual rpt, S4575–2

see also Kansas City, Mo.

see also Springfield, Mo.

see also St. Louis, Mo.

see also under By City and By County in the "Index by Categories"

see also under By State in the "Index by Categories"

Mobile, Ala.

Foreign trade shipped through Port of Mobile, by leading commodity and country, 1992 recurring rpt, U5680–2.7

Waterborne freight and passenger traffic at Mobile Harbor, 1951-89, recurring rpt, U5680–2.16

Waterborne shipments at Port of Mobile, monthly business activity rpt, U5680–1

see also under By City in the "Index by Categories"

Mobile homes

Financial ratios and performance, for over 350 SIC 4-digit industries, FY88-92, annual rpt, A6400–3

Forecasts of natl income and product account components, employment, and financial sector activity, monthly rpt, B4950–1

Homebuilder financial and operating data, including detail by location, for top 400 builders, 1993 annual feature, C1850–8.507

Loan delinquency rates for approx 10 types of consumer bank loans, and repossession data, by State, quarterly rpt, A0950–1

Lumber industry production and trade, with construction activity and mobile home shipments, monthly rpt, A1630–1

Number of mobile homes, and share of total homes, by State, 1990, article, C5150–6.501

Production, shipments, and financing, with data by State and census div, monthly rpt, A6325–1

Recreational vehicle dealer marketing and mgmt devs, with data on shipments and sales, by vehicle type, monthly rpt, C8950–2

Shipments, and placements by region, 1984-92, annual rpt, A9395–1

Shipments forecast for mobile homes, monthly rpt, A7000–1

Shipments of manufactured housing, July and 1st 7 months 1991-92, article, C1850–8.501

Shipments of mobile homes, quarterly rpt, A1775–1

State and local:

Arizona mobile home shipments, monthly rpt quarterly table, U0280–1.503, U0280–1.506, U0280–1.509

Arizona statistical abstract, general data, 1993 recurring rpt, U5850–2.16

Arizona temporary winter residents and expenditures, and mobile home and trailer park spaces and occupancy, by local area, winter 1992/93, annual article, U0280–1.508

Arkansas Census of Population and Housing detailed findings, 1990, U5935–7

California Census of Population and Housing detailed findings, 1990, S0840–9

California statistical abstract, general data, 1992 annual rpt, S0840–2.9

Colorado property assessed valuation by detailed property type, and tax levy and revenue by local district, by county, 1991-92, annual rpt, S1055–3

Connecticut construction activity and value, by type of structure and location, 1992 and trends, annual rpt, S1212–1

Delaware housing construction activity, with data on demolitions and mobile home sales, by locality, 1992 and trends, annual rpt, S1387–1

Florida county data book, 1992/93 annual rpt, C6360–1

Florida statistical abstract, general data, 1992 annual rpt, U6660–1.2, U6660–1.11

Georgia county guide, general data, 1993 annual rpt, U6750–1

Idaho construction activity and value, by city and county, monthly rpt, B3900–1

Maryland statistical abstract, general data, 1993-94 biennial rpt, S3605–1.12

Montana property values, by detailed property class and type, with land acreage by use, by county, 1991-92 and trends, biennial rpt, S4750–1.2

Nebraska mobile home values, by county, 1991, annual rpt, S4950–1.4

New Jersey Census of Population and Housing detailed findings, by county, 1990, S5425–19

Pennsylvania Census of Population and Housing detailed findings, with selected data by county and municipality, 1990, U4130–13

South Dakota mobile homes, assessed value, and property taxes paid, by county, FY92 annual rpt, S7380–1.2

Tennessee manufactured housing inspections and licensing revenues, 1991, annual rpt, S7466–1

Tennessee statistical abstract, general data, 1992/93 annual rpt, U8710–2.6, U8710–2.9

Texas trade, transportation, and public utilities employment, by SIC 2- and 3-digit industry and detailed occupation, 2nd qtr 1991, triennial survey rpt, S7675–1.31

Index by Subjects and Names

Utah statistical abstract, general data, 1993 triennial rpt, U8960–1.11

Mobile radio

Fuel oil dealer 2-way radio use, 1992 annual survey, C4680–2.1

Security professional use of pagers, 1993 feature, C1850–12.502

Shipment value, employment, and foreign trade, for electronics industry, by sector and product type, 1980s-92, annual rpt, A4725–1.2

Utility regulatory agency policies and practices, and industry financial and operating data, by utility type and agency, 1991/92 annual rpt, A7015–3

State and local:

Colorado mobile radio communications companies property assessed valuation, by company, 1991-92, annual rpt, S1055–3

Tennessee public utility and transportation commission regulatory activities, with industry financial and operating data, 1991-92 biennial rpt, S7565–1

Mobility

see Labor mobility

see Migration

see Mobility limitations

Mobility limitations

Accidents involving injuries causing activity restrictions, by type of accident, 1991, annual rpt, A8375–2.1

Black American health and vital statistics data, with comparisons to whites, 1970s-91, annual compilation, C6775–2.2

Incidence of illness and injury, and hospitalization and mortality data, by selected demographic characteristics, 1992 annual rpt, A5173–2.4

Men age 69-84 quality of life indicators, including health, finances, family, and employment, by race, 1990 survey, U3780–9

State and local:

Arkansas Census of Population and Housing detailed findings, 1990, U5935–7

California Census of Population and Housing detailed findings, 1990, S0840–9

Hawaii data book, general data, 1992 annual rpt, S2090–1.2, S2090–1.11

Hawaii population activity limitation status due to chronic illness, by age, sex, and income, 1988, annual rpt, S2065–1.3

Kansas statistical abstract, general data, 1991/92 annual rpt, U7095–2.6

Louisiana Census of Population and Housing summary findings, by local area, 1990 and trends, U8010–4

Maine Census of Population and Housing summary findings, by local area, 1990, S3465–9

New Jersey Census of Population and Housing detailed findings, by county, 1990, S5425–19

Rhode Island Census of Population and Housing detailed findings, by county and municipality, 1990, S6930–9

South Carolina statistical abstract, general data, 1993 annual rpt, S7125–1.7

see also Disabled and handicapped persons

Mobs

see Riots and disorders

Models

see Economic and econometric models

Mohair

see Wool and wool trade

Molasses

see Syrups and sweeteners

Molybdenum

see Metals and metal industries

Monetary policy

World financial market devs including economic and monetary trends and forecasts for 15 industrial countries, bimonthly rpt, B6200–2

see also Credit

see also Fiscal policy

see also Foreign exchange

see also Money supply

Money market funds

see Mutual funds

Money supply

Economic indexes for Australia, Taiwan, and New Zealand, monthly rpt, U1245–1

Economic indicator historical trends, 1900s-92, annual rpt, R9050–1.2

Forecasts of economic indicators for approx 10-13 months, monthly rpt, U1880–3

Forecasts of natl income and product account components and related indicators, quarterly rpt, U1880–1

Japan economic profile, including govt finances, industrial production, foreign trade and investments, and comparisons to US, 1988-92, annual feature, R5650–2.552

Latin America statistical abstract, general data by country, 1992 annual rpt, U6250–1.30

Money and securities market activity, and related indicators, biweekly rpt, B2000–1

Service sector economic activity indicators, with leading and coincident indexes and components, and detail for financial services, monthly rpt, U1245–3

see also Black market currency

see also Coins and coinage

see also Counterfeiting and forgery

see also Credit

see also Economic indicators

see also Eurocurrency

see also Foreign exchange

see also Inflation

see also Interest rates

see also Savings

Mongolia

Oil and gas lease sales offerings, with area location and size, Mar 1993, article, C6985–1.527

Oil/gas exploratory wells drilled, seismic surveys, and contract areas available for foreign dev, 1992 article, C6985–1.506

Monopolies and cartels

see also Economic concentration and diversification

see also Organization of Arab Petroleum Exporting Countries

see also Organization of Petroleum Exporting Countries

Montana

Agricultural production, marketing, and finances, by commodity and county, and farms and acreage, 1991 and trends, annual rpt, S4655–1

Crimes and clearances, by offense and jurisdiction, 1992, annual rpt, S4705–1

Election results and voter registration, by county and/or district, 1992 general election, biennial rpt, S4760–1

Monuments and memorials

Elementary and secondary public school enrollment by grade, and grads, by school, county, race-ethnicity, and sex, 1992 and trends, annual rpt, S4740–1

Employment and unemployment, earnings, and hours, by location and/or industry, quarterly rpt, S4710–1

Financial condition, including revenues by source, expenditures by function, and fund balances, FY92, annual rpt, S4653–1

Health care facility capacity, utilization, and finances, by instn, 1991, annual rpt, S4690–2

Labor force planning rpt, including population, income, and employment and job openings by industry and occupation, with selected data by county, 1993-94 annual rpt, S4710–3

Library holdings, staff, circulation, and finances, by public library, FY92, annual rpt, S4725–1

Markets with daily newspapers, demographic and economic info by geographic area, US and Canada, 1993 annual rpt, C3250–1

Oil/gas industry production, finances, exploration, and reserves, by State, 1992 and trends, annual rpt, A5425–1.1

Statistical profiles of 50 States and DC, general data, 1993 annual almanac, C4712–1

Tax collections by type, and property value by county, FY91-92 and trends, biennial rpt, S4750–1

Traffic accidents, fatalities, and injuries, by circumstances, location, and driver and victim characteristics, 1992 and trends, annual rpt, S4705–2

Utility and transportation regulatory agency activities, scope of jurisdiction, finances, and employees, by agency, 1991/92 annual rpt, A7015–2

Vital statistics, including population, births, deaths, disease, and marriage and divorce, by demographic characteristics and county, 1990-91 and trends, annual rpt, S4690–1

Welfare and medical assistance program cases and payments, by county and type of service, monthly rpt, S4755–1

see also Billings, Mont.

see also Great Falls, Mont.

see also under By City and By County in the "Index by Categories"

see also under By State in the "Index by Categories"

Montclair, N.J.

Elementary/secondary school parental selection program, parents use of selected sources of info about schools, by income level, 1989/90, R3810–7

Montoya, Pia

"Arizona Statistical Abstract: 1993 Data Handbook", U5850–2

Monuments and memorials

State and local:

Colorado income tax return checkoff contributions for veterans memorial, FY89-92, annual rpt, S1075–1.3

DC statistical profile, general data, 1992 annual rpt, S1535–3.3

Florida statistical abstract, general data, 1992 annual rpt, U6660–1.19

Illinois statistical abstract, general data, 1992 annual rpt, U6910–2

Monuments and memorials

Utah statistical abstract, general data, 1993 triennial rpt, U8960–1.17
see also National parks

Moonlighting
Multiple jobholders, by sex and occupational group, 1991, annual rpt, A1570–1
State and local:
Hawaii data book, general data, 1992 annual rpt, S2090–1.12

Moore, Barbara H.
"Police Salaries, 1992", A5800–4.32

Morality
see Ethics and morality

Morbidity
see Deaths
see Diseases and disorders

Morgan Stanley and Co.
Europe govt-owned companies likely to be privatized, govt ownership share and value for 25 firms in 6 countries, 1993 article, C5800–7.537
Foreign stock market performance, with data for selected major corporations, biweekly rpt quarterly feature, C3950–1.506, C3950–1.512, C3950–1.521, C3950–1.525
Stock market performance in 16 countries, 1992, annual article, C8900–1.507

Morningstar Inc.
Mutual fund assets and investment performance, 105 closed-end equity and 120 closed-end fixed-income funds, 1993 annual feature, C5800–7.517
Mutual fund assets and investment performance, 555 fixed-income funds, 1993 annual feature, C5800–7.516
Mutual fund assets and investment performance, 760 equity funds, 1993 annual feature, C5800–7.515
Mutual fund investment performance, with detail for best- and worst-performing funds in selected categories, weekly rpt recurring article, C5800–7.523, C5800–7.549
Mutual funds pretax and after-tax return trends and tax liability for 50 largest funds, and ranking of 30 funds with highest and lowest liability, 1993 article, C5800–7.547
Thailand investing mutual fund returns, assets, and other financial data, for 8 funds, 1993 article, C3950–1.527

Morocco
Energy intl sourcebook, with detail on oil and gas industry operations, supply-demand, and prices, for approx 80 countries, 1970s-91, annual compilation, C6985–10.2

Morris, Dwight
"Handbook of Campaign Spending: Money in the 1990 Congressional Races", C2500–6

Morris, Marya
"Planners' Salaries and Employment Trends, 1991", A2615–1

Mortality
see Child mortality
see Deaths
see Fetal deaths
see Homicide
see Infant mortality
see Life expectancy
see Suicide
see Vital statistics

Mortgages
Approval rates for mortgages, by neighborhood characteristics and applicant race-ethnicity and income level, 1990, article, A8510–1.1
Bank commercial real estate loans as percent of total lending, top 100 instns, 1992, annual feature, C5800–7.526
Bank noncurrent loans/leases, and losses, by type of loan, asset size, and metro status, 1992, semiannual rpt, A6400–4
Banking (mortgage) industry aggregate financial and operating data, by lending characteristics and type of ownership, 1989 and trends, annual rpt, A6450–3
Banking (mortgage) industry loan production, servicing, and secondary marketing volume, revenues, and expenses, 1989-91, article, A6400–2.502
Banking trends and devs for mortgage market, with data on construction, home sales, and lending activity, by type of unit and instn, monthly rpt, A6450–2
Canada Govt-insured mortgage-backed securities issuance value, by issuer, 1987-93, article, A6450–2.508
Chicago Board of Trade futures and options trading in mortgage-backed securities, 1992, annual rpt, B2120–1
Commercial real estate market conditions, including mortgage availability and sources for industrial properties, by metro area, 1992 annual survey, A8916–1
Delinquency and foreclosure rates, and residential loans serviced, by type, State, and census div and region, quarterly rpt, A6450–1
Employee benefit funds assets, for funds investing in mortgages, 1992, annual feature, C2710–2.504
Forecasts of natl income and product account components, employment, and financial sector activity, monthly rpt, B4950–1
Futures and options trading in mortgage-backed securities, by exchange, 1988-92, annual rpt, A5040–1
Home buyer (1st-time and repeat) profile, and transaction characteristics, including prices and financing, by region and for 18 metro areas, 1990-92, annual survey rpt, B2150–1
Home equity lending activity and practices of financial instns, by region, asset size, and instn type, 1992, annual rpt, A4160–3
Housing affordability, mortgage rate and average monthly payment, monthly rpt, A7000–2
Housing market conditions, including mortgage securities activity and commitment rates, quarterly rpt, B5190–1
Housing market trends and outlook, including mortgage originations and interest rates, 1989-94, annual article, A6450–2.503
Insurance (life/health) industry asset allocation and investment yields, for top 125 US and Canadian companies, 1992 and trends, annual article, C1050–2.512
Insurance (life/health) industry mortgage holding shares performing vs nonperforming, and top 50 firms aggregate share of nonperforming holdings, 1992, article, C1050–2.505

Investment mgmt firms, assets and operating data for approx 900 instns, Jan 1993, annual feature, C2710–2.511
Life insurance industry income and financial data, including investments by type of security, 1991 and trends, biennial fact book, A1325–1.4
Life/health insurance industry mortgage holdings by loan performance status, and performing loans by property type, 1991 and/or 1992, article, C1050–2.508
Loan servicing expense, income, and productivity trends, 1980-91, annual article, A6450–2.504
Mortgage insurance industry finances and performance indicators, 1988-91, annual rpt, A6455–1
Renter households with heads age 25-34, with percent qualifying for home mortgages at selected rates, 1993 article, C4300–1.510
Securities (mortgage-backed) holdings, by investor type, 1991, article, C2710–2.502
Securities value backed by commercial mortgages, and securitization rates for commercial vs residential mortgages, 1992 article, A7000–1.501
Veterinarian practice expenses as percent of revenues, by expenditure category and type of practice, 1990-91, annual survey article, C9480–1.501

State and local:
Arizona economic analysts outlook for oil prices and mortgage interest rates, 1993 annual survey article, U0282–1.507
Arizona, Maricopa County mortgage rates, monthly rpt, U0280–1
Arizona statistical abstract, general data, 1993 recurring rpt, U5850–2.15, U5850–2.16, U5850–2.23
Arkansas Census of Population and Housing detailed findings, 1990, U5935–7
California Census of Population and Housing detailed findings, 1990, S0840–9
California economic condition, including population, employment and earnings, income, business activity, and taxation, 1960s-92, annual rpt, S0840–3.2
Colorado savings and loan assn and credit union financial condition, 1992 and trends, annual rpt, S1070–3
Florida statistical abstract, general data, 1992 annual rpt, U6660–1.17
Hawaii data book, general data, 1992 annual rpt, S2090–1.21
Hawaii, Honolulu conventional mortgage rates, bimonthly rpt, B3500–1
Kansas statistical abstract, general data, 1991/92 annual rpt, U7095–2.10
Kentucky mortgage loan company and broker licenses, 1992, annual rpt, S3121–1
Louisiana Census of Population and Housing summary findings, by local area, 1990 and trends, U8010–4
Maine Census of Population and Housing summary findings, by local area, 1990, S3465–9
Maine financial instn assets, deposits, and loans, by type of instn and county, 1982-92, annual rpt, S3473–1
Maine mortgage loans originated and secondary market sales, with sales by purchaser type, 1990-91, annual rpt, S3473–2

Index by Subjects and Names — Motor fuels

Mississippi statistical abstract, general data, 1992 annual rpt, U3255–4.8

New Jersey banks and other financial instns, assets and liabilities by instn, 1992 and trends, annual rpt, S5355–1

New Jersey Census of Population and Housing detailed findings, by county, 1990, S5425–19

New Jersey mortgage guaranty insurance financial and underwriting data, by company, 1990, annual rpt, S5420–1

New York State statistical yearbook, general data, 1992 annual rpt, U5100–1.9

Oklahoma real estate loan rejection rates for whites and minorities by income level, statewide and by MSA, 1991, article, U8130–1.504

Pennsylvania Census of Population and Housing detailed findings, with selected data by county and municipality, 1990, U4130–13

Rhode Island Census of Population and Housing detailed findings, by county and municipality, 1990, S6930–9

South Carolina economic condition, including agriculture, finance, and govt financial data, 1970s-92, annual rpt, S7125–3.1

Tennessee statistical abstract, general data, 1992/93 annual rpt, U8710–2.6

Utah statistical abstract, general data, 1993 triennial rpt, U8960–1.11, U8960–1.15

Vermont Home Mortgage Guarantee Board finances and loan guarantees outstanding, and real estate lending by banks, FY92, annual rpt, S7995–2

West Virginia floating mortgage rate ceilings, Dec 1990-91, annual rpt, S8530–1

Wisconsin savings and loan assns and savings banks (State-chartered) financial condition, by instn, 1992 and trends, annual rpt, S8807–1

see also Agricultural credit

see also Foreclosures

Morticians

see Cemeteries and funerals

Moslems

see Religion

Motels

see Hotels and motels

Mothers

see Aid to Families with Dependent Children

see Births

see Breast-feeding

see Child day care

see Families and households

see Fertility

see Maternity

see Maternity benefits

see Parents

see Teenage pregnancy

see Women

Motion Picture Export Association of America

Motion picture rental income for US releases in top 15 foreign countries, 1990-92, annual feature, C9380–1.530

Motion pictures

Academy Award best picture nominee films attended and preferred by public, Feb 1993 survey, C8915–1.502

Advertising expenditures by medium for top 100 advertisers, with comparisons to earnings and sales, and detail by product type and brand, 1991-92, annual rpt, C2710–1.547

Advertising in theaters and on rental video tapes, reactions of marketing professionals and general public, Oct 1992 surveys, article, C2710–1.512

Boxoffice receipts for films winning Academy Award for best picture, with share received after award, 1987-91, article, C5800–7.518

Cable TV classic movie network subscribers, ownership, and titles available, for 3 networks, 1993 article, C1850–14.535

Financial performance and growth rankings for approx 1,000 top corporations, with comparisons by industry group, 1993 annual rpt, C3950–1.505

Financial ratios and performance, for over 350 SIC 4-digit industries, FY88-92, annual rpt, A6400–3

Foreign investment in US motion picture companies, with outlays and gains/losses, by investor, 1993 article, C3950–1.516

Foreign motion picture productions, boxoffice receipts, rental income, and top films in selected countries, weekly rpt, C9380–1

Latin America statistical abstract, general data by country, 1992 annual rpt, U6250–1.4

Operating and financial composite ratios for corporations, with establishments and receipts, for approx 200 industries, by asset size, FY90, annual rpt, C7800–1

Prices of selected consumer items in approx 300 cities, quarterly rpt, A0150–1

Production releases by type of distributor, and films not released, production years 1984-92, annual article, C9380–1.526

Production starts, by company, weekly rpt recurring feature, C9380–1

Public opinion on motion picture quality, and Academy Award nominees, Mar 1993 Gallup Poll, C4040–1.509

Shopping center financial and operating data, with detail by type of tenant, US and Canada, 1991, triennial rpt, R9285–1

Studio acreage and sound stages, for 6 major motion picture producers in Los Angeles Calif, 1993 article, C9380–1.532

Ticket sales and industry devs, for theater and film, with detail for Broadway and road shows, and top films, weekly rpt, C9380–1

State and local:

Arizona statistical abstract, general data, 1993 recurring rpt, U5850–2.24

California motion picture production employment trends, 1989-93, article, S0840–1.505

DC expenditures of motion picture/TV industry, 1987-91, annual rpt, S1535–3.3

Hawaii data book, general data, 1992 annual rpt, S2090–1.23

Wyoming property valuations for cinema/theater equipment, by county, 1992, annual rpt, S8990–1.2

Motor bus lines

see Buses

Motor carriers

see Trucks and trucking industry

Motor fuels

Alternative fuel motor vehicle acquisition plans of motor vehicle fleets, 1992 survey, article, C1575–2.503

Alternative fuel motor vehicle testing plans of auto fleets, by fuel and fleet type, 1993, C1575–2.504

Alternative fuel prices and mileages, and vehicle conversion costs, for 3-4 fuels, 1993 article, C1575–1.505

Alternative fuel use and outlook, including data on costs and by fuel type and selected country, 1993 annual rpt, C6985–3.2

Alternative fuel vehicle acquisition plans of motor vehicle fleets, 1992 annual survey, A6755–1.501

Alternative fuel vehicle purchase requirements for govt and private fleets, 1992 article, C1575–2.502

Auto fleet operations, including bulk fuel purchases by type, in metro areas affected by Clean Air Act clean fuel requirements, 1993 article, C1575–2.512

Europe gasoline and diesel retail and wholesale prices, and tax rates, by country, Apr 1992, article, C6985–1.523

Latin America statistical abstract, general data by country, 1992 annual rpt, U6250–1.23

Mass transit bus fleet distribution by fuel type, 1991, annual fact book, C1575–3.501

Natural gas vehicle refueling stations by ownership class, by State and census div, Apr 1992, annual rpt, A1775–3.2

School bus fleet use of buses with gasoline vs diesel engines, 1986 and 1993, annual article, C1575–1.507

State and local:

California school bus alternative fuel efficiency, with mileage and Btu(h) per passenger mile for 3 fuels, 1993 article, C1575–1.507

Colorado taxable motor fuel monthly gallonage received by distributors, FY90-92, annual rpt, S1075–1.4

Florida statistical abstract, general data, 1992 annual rpt, U6660–1.15

Georgia statistical abstract, general data, 1992-93 biennial rpt, U6730–1.8

Kansas statistical abstract, general data, 1991/92 annual rpt, U7095–2.13

Mississippi motor fuel consumption and taxes assessed, monthly FY92, annual rpt, S4435–1

Ohio gasoline and special fuels consumption, FY88-92, annual rpt, S6390–1.4

Oklahoma statistical abstract, general data, 1992 annual rpt, U8130–2.16

South Carolina economic condition, including energy and transportation data, 1970s-92, annual rpt, S7125–3.3

Tennessee statistical abstract, general data, 1992/93 annual rpt, U8710–2.9

Utah hwy mileage and expenditures, aviation and motor fuel consumption, and bus travel, various years 1940-92, annual rpt, R9380–1.10

Utah statistical abstract, general data, 1993 triennial rpt, U8960–1.13

Wisconsin motor fuel gallons taxed, monthly rpt, S8750–1

see also Alcohol fuels

Motor fuels

see also Aviation fuels
see also Diesel fuel
see also Fuel tax
see also Gasohol
see also Gasoline

Motor homes

see Recreational vehicles

Motor oil

see Motor vehicle parts and supplies
see Petroleum and petroleum industry

Motor transportation

see Automobiles
see Buses
see Motor vehicle industry
see Motorcycles
see Taxicabs
see Traffic accidents and safety
see Trucks and trucking industry

Motor vehicle defects

Auto industry performance indicators for 3 major manufacturers, 1970s-92, annual article, C2150–3.506

Truck accidents involving vehicle defects, by type, 1984-88, article, C1575–2.511

State and local:

- Alabama traffic accidents, by contributing vehicle defect, 1992, annual rpt, S0185–1
- Alaska traffic accidents, by contributing vehicle defect, 1991, annual rpt, S0360–1
- California traffic accidents involving defective vehicle brakes and other equipment, 1991, annual rpt, S0885–1
- Connecticut traffic accidents involving vehicle mechanical failures, 1992, annual rpt, S1275–1
- Idaho traffic accidents, with vehicle defects involved by type, 1992, annual rpt, S2315–1
- Kentucky traffic accidents involving vehicle defects, with detail for trucks, 1992, annual rpt, S3150–2
- Maine traffic accidents, fatalities, and injuries involving vehicle defects, by type, 1992, annual rpt, S3475–2
- Minnesota traffic accidents involving vehicle defects, 1992, annual rpt, S4230–2
- Missouri traffic accidents involving vehicle defects, 1992, annual rpt, S4560–1
- Montana traffic accidents, fatalities, and injuries, by type of vehicle defect, 1992, annual rpt, S4705–2
- New Mexico traffic accidents involving vehicle defects, 1986-92, annual rpt, S5665–1
- New York State traffic accidents involving vehicular defects, 1991, annual rpt, S5790–1
- North Carolina traffic accidents, vehicle defects involved by type, 1992, annual rpt, S5990–1
- Pennsylvania traffic accidents, fatalities, and injuries involving vehicle defects, by type, 1991, annual rpt, S6905–3
- Rhode Island traffic accidents, by type of vehicle mechanical failure, 1992, annual rpt, S7025–1
- South Carolina traffic accidents involving motor vehicles with mechanical defects, 1992, annual rpt, S7190–2
- Utah traffic accidents involving vehicle defects, 1992, annual rpt, S7890–2
- Virginia traffic accidents, by type of vehicle and defect, 1991, annual rpt, S8282–1
- Washington State traffic accidents, by type of vehicle defect, 1988-92, annual rpt, S8428–1

Wisconsin traffic accidents involving vehicle defects, 1992, annual rpt, S8815–1

Wyoming traffic accidents involving vehicle defects, 1992, annual rpt, S9007–1

Motor vehicle exhaust

Emission standards, and reduction programs progress, 1993 annual rpt, A0865–1.3

State and local:

California govt vehicle emissions requirements, 1994-2003 model years, article, C2710–3.534

Colorado motor vehicle emissions program licenses and collections, FY92, annual rpt, S1075–1.4

Motor vehicle exports and imports

- Auto and light truck trade, with detail by trading partner, weekly rpt quarterly table, C2710–3.513, C2710–3.524, C2710–3.539
- Auto parts trade by major trading partner, and Japanese manufacturers purchases of US parts by type for US and Japanese operations, 1993 article, R5650–2.523
- Brazil motor vehicle exports, 1982-88, annual rpt, U6250–1.16
- Imported motor vehicle sales, 1982-92, annual rpt, A7330–1
- Japan auto exports to US voluntary quotas, by manufacturer, FY81-93, article, R5650–2.531
- Japan auto sales in US, with comparison to domestic manufacturers, 1985-92, annual article, R5650–2.511
- Japan exports of autos and steel, weekly rpt quarterly table, R5650–2.506, R5650–2.519, R5650–2.541, R5650–2.558
- Japan motor vehicle trade with US, and auto registrations by domestic and import make, 1987-92, article, R5650–2.543
- Market data book, with data on intl trade by selected country and US classification of specific vehicles as domestic vs imports, 1993 annual rpt, C2710–3.531
- Mexico auto parts imports, 1991 and 1995, and US market share, 1993 article, C2710–3.541
- Mexico-US bilateral auto imports and exports, 1983-92, article, C2150–3.505
- Motorcycle imports of US, by engine size and trends, annual rpt, A6485–1.1
- North American Free Trade Agreement devs for auto industry, with data on US trade with Mexico and Canada in cars, trucks, and parts, 1986-91, R8490–43
- Production, sales, trade, and vehicle use, detailed data by vehicle type, State, and country, 1900s-92, annual rpt, A0865–1
- Registrations (new), including imports, by make and model, monthly rpt, C7715–3
- Sales and inventory data for imported autos and light trucks, weekly rpt, C2710–3
- World auto market devs, with data on foreign trade for North America, Europe, Brazil, Japan, and Korea, 1991-92, article, C2710–3.515
- World production, sales, trade, and registrations of motor vehicles, by country, world area, manufacturer, and make, 1991 and trends, annual rpt, A0865–2

Motor vehicle fleets

- Accidents involving fleet vehicles, and vehicles and mileage, by fleet type and company (unnamed), 1991 and trends, annual rpt, A8375–3
- Acquisition plans, including vehicle replacement policy, 1992 survey article, C1575–2.502
- Acquisition plans, with factors affecting purchases, 1992 annual survey, A6755–1.501
- Auto dealership fleet sales, for top 10 sellers of 35 domestic and import makes, 1992, annual data book, C2710–3.531
- Autos and light trucks/vans in top 100 corporate fleets, 1993 and trends, annual feature, C1575–2.504
- Autos and light trucks/vans in 2nd 100 largest corporate fleets, 1993, annual feature, C1575–2.506
- Bus (urban) fleets of 100 largest transit systems in US or Canada, 1993, annual article, C1575–3.507
- Bus company fleets, for top 50 private operators in US and Canada, 1993 annual feature, C1575–3.503
- Corporate auto fleet size, with makes and/or models used, for 7 major fleets, 1993-94, article, C2710–3.553
- Fleet admin trends and activities, monthly rpt, A6755–1
- Fuel oil dealer truck fleet and purchasing plans, by region, 1992 annual survey, C4680–2
- Hispanic American career professional and business owner views on fleet composition, and financing and maintenance/repair sources, 1993 survey, article, C4575–1.504
- Hispanic-owned business fleet characteristics and policies, 1992 annual survey feature, C4575–1.501
- Mexico motor carrier fleet by vehicle class and model year, and trucks and trailers by State, various years 1980-92, U8850–9
- Mgmt and operations devs for auto and truck fleets, monthly rpt, C1575–2
- Operating and financial data, including fleets by type, registrations by make and model, and top lessors, 1970s-93, annual rpt, C1575–2.507
- Personal use policies for employer-owned fleet vehicles, 1993 survey article, C1575–2.512
- Probation and parole agencies govt vehicle fleets, by State, 1992 annual rpt, R4300–1.3
- Public utility truck/van fleets, for top 40 companies, 1992, annual feature, C1575–2.502
- Registrations of fleet vehicles and total autos, by manufacturer and make, weekly rpt quarterly feature, C2710–3.507, C2710–3.521, C2710–3.536, C2710–3.546
- Rental auto company fleet size, and auto manufacturers shares of ownership and vehicles, for 8 rental companies, 1993 article, C2710–3.521
- Traffic accident rates, fleets, and vehicles, by fleet type, 1992 and trends, annual rpt, A8375–2.3
- Truck fleet financial and operating data for top 200 freight carriers, 1992 and trends, annual feature, C2150–4.504

Index by Subjects and Names

Trucks and other commercial vehicles fleet mgmt and operations, monthly rpt, C2150–4

Vehicles in fleets by type of use, and fleet registrations by manufacturer, 1992 and trends, annual rpt, A0865–1.2

Vending machine operator vehicles by type, 1990-92, annual rpt, C9470–1

State and local:

Wyoming penitentiary vehicles and use, FY92, annual rpt, S8883–1

see also Motor vehicle rental

Motor vehicle industry

Advertising agency changes for 11 auto manufacturers, including billings involved, 1991-92, article, C2710–1.501

Advertising expenditures by medium for top 100 advertisers, with comparisons to earnings and sales, and detail by product type and brand, 1991-92, annual rpt, C2710–1.547

Advertising expenditures of auto dealers and natl campaigns, distribution by medium, 1991, article, A8605–1.505

Advertising expenditures outside US by top 10 auto manufacturers, and billings for auto advertisers changing agencies, 1993 article, C2710–1.509

Advertising programs of dealer assns and manufacturers, views of dealers, with detail by vehicle make, 1993 survey article, C2710–1.518

Auto and supplier industries trends and activities, monthly rpt, C2150–3

Brazil motor vehicle production, by vehicle type, 1982-88, annual rpt, U6250–1.16

Characteristics of 1993 model year autos and other vehicles, by make, annual rpt, A5200–5

China auto production, for 6 foreign joint venture plants, various years 1991-96, article, C2710–3.537

Corporate performance ratings by executives for leading companies in 32 industries, 1993 annual survey feature, C8900–1.508

Cotton and other fiber consumption in textile production, by detailed end use, 1990-92, annual rpt, A7485–1

Electronics demand value of auto industry, with detail for chips, 1980s-96, article, C1850–2.501

Financial performance and growth rankings for approx 1,000 top corporations, with comparisons by industry group, 1993 annual rpt, C3950–1.505

Financial performance of auto industry, with revenues and stock prices for 3 major manufacturers and approx 50 suppliers, weekly rpt quarterly feature, C2710–3.518, C2710–3.532, C2710–3.545

Financial ratios and performance, for over 350 SIC 4-digit industries, FY88-92, annual rpt, A6400–3

Forecasts of natl income and product account components, employment, and financial sector activity, monthly rpt, B4950–1

Latin America economic indicators affecting business climate, with data on motor vehicle and oil industries and detail by country, 1992 rpt, R4105–82.6

Manufacturing machines and number of different models made in typical auto factory, 1900s-2000, annual rpt, R2800–2

Market data book on production, sales, registrations, prices, options, and dealerships, with data by make and country, 1993 annual rpt, C2710–3.531

Mexico foreign-owned motor vehicle plants and employment by company, and hq countries of auto parts industry foreign participants, 1993 article, C2150–3.505

Mexico motor vehicle sales, and domestic and export production, for 5 manufacturers, weekly rpt monthly tables, C2710–3

North American Free Trade Agreement devs for auto industry, with data on Mexico vehicle production and US total and auto trade with Mexico and Canada, 1980s-91, R8490–43

Operating and financial composite ratios for corporations, with establishments and receipts, for approx 200 industries, by asset size, FY90, annual rpt, C7800–1

Production of cars and trucks in US and Canada, with detail by manufacturer, and by assembly plant for Japanese-owned firms, 1992 and trends, article, R5650–2.523

Production, sales, and market analysis, by manufacturer and make/model, with industry news and devs, weekly rpt, C2710–3

Production, sales, trade, and vehicle use, detailed data by vehicle type, State, and country, 1900s-92, annual rpt, A0865–1

Raw materials used in cars, total weight, and distribution by material type, 1990 and 2000, article, C5800–12.513

Worker hand/wrist disorder cases among auto plant employees, 1985-86, article, A2623–1.501

World motor vehicle manufacturer production, revenues, and profits, for top 30 companies, 1992, article, C8900–1.526

World motor vehicle production trends and market shares, for selected countries, 1988-92, annual rpt, A3179–2.3

World production, sales, trade, and registrations of motor vehicles, by country, world area, manufacturer, and make, 1991 and trends, annual rpt, A0865–2

State and local:

Delaware unemployment insurance claims, for auto and other industries, monthly rpt, S1405–2

New Hampshire wholesale and retail trade employment, by SIC 2-digit industry and detailed occupation, 1991, triennial rpt, S5205–2.26

Texas trade, transportation, and public utilities employment, by SIC 2- and 3-digit industry and detailed occupation, 2nd qtr 1991, triennial survey rpt, S7675–1.31

see also Automobile repair and maintenance

see also Automobiles

see also Buses

see also Motor vehicle defects

see also Motor vehicle exhaust

see also Motor vehicle exports and imports

see also Motor vehicle fleets

see also Motor vehicle parts and supplies

see also Motor vehicle registrations

see also Motor vehicle safety devices

Motor vehicle parts and supplies

see also Motor vehicle sales

see also Motorcycles

see also Recreational vehicles

see also Trucks and trucking industry

Motor vehicle parts and supplies

Antifreeze sales, by type, 1991-92, annual fact book, C4680–1.507

Audio systems for autos, sales and trade, 1982-92, annual rpt, A4725–4

Auto aftermarket industry devs, including auto maintenance and repair activity, monthly rpt, C2150–10

Auto aftermarket retail performance indicators, by product category, 1992 article, C2150–10.501

Auto aftermarket retail sales, and number of stores and service bays, for top 100 chains, 1993 annual article, C2150–10.507

Auto aftermarket sales, by outlet type, 1992 and 1996, article, C4680–1.509

Auto and supplier industries trends and activities, monthly rpt, C2150–3

Auto dealer reimbursement rates paid by 14 manufacturers for parts used in warranty repairs, 1993 article, C2710–3.518

Auto dealer reimbursement rates paid by 7 manufacturers for parts used in warranty repairs, 1992 article, C2710–3.503

Consumer auto maintenance market, including product purchase patterns and do-it-yourself activity, 1992 survey article, C2150–10.501

Consumer auto maintenance market, including product purchase patterns and do-it-yourself activity, 1993 annual survey feature, C2150–10.504

Corporate fleet vehicle driver maintenance habits, model preferences, and cellular telephone and credit card use, 1993 survey, article, C1575–2.509

Dealership parts and service dept sales, and parts inventory, 1992 and trends, annual rpt, A7330–1

Discount chain consumer natl brand preferences, by product category and chain, and by age group, 1993 survey, annual feature, C5150–3.521

Discount chain top-selling natl brands cited by managers, by product category, chain, and region, 1993 survey, annual feature, C5150–3.520

Discount store sales and productivity data for 20 depts, 1993 annual feature, C5150–3.516

Discount stores, sales, and earnings, for top chains, with detail by specialty, 1993 annual feature, C5150–3.514

Do-it-yourself sales and marketing trends and devs for auto aftermarket parts/supplies, monthly rpt, C0125–1

Factory installations of options and equipment on 1992 autos, by manufacturer, make, and model, annual data book, C2710–3.531

Farm prices paid for selected production commodities, 1982 and 1991-92, annual rpt, S3085–1

Farm prices paid for selected production commodities, 1986-91, annual rpt, S5350–1

Financial performance and growth rankings for approx 1,000 top corporations, with comparisons by industry group, 1993 annual rpt, C3950–1.505

Motor vehicle parts and supplies

Financial ratios and performance, for over 350 SIC 4-digit industries, FY88-92, annual rpt, A6400–3

Foreign auto parts trade by major trading partner, and Japanese manufacturers purchases of US parts by type for US and Japanese operations, 1993 article, R5650–2.523

Installation, shipments, and trade of selected items, 1980s-92, annual rpt, A0865–1

Japan-affiliated auto parts suppliers in US, with employment and plant square footage, 1990 and 1992-93, article, C2710–3.553

Japan auto manufacturer expenditures for US parts/materials, for 5 companies, FY92 and FY94, article, C2710–3.533

Mexico auto parts market value and imports, 1993 article, C2710–3.541

Mexico original auto equipment supplier plants and locations, with major products and customers, by company, 1993 article, C2710–3.550

Motor oil sales, by retail outlet type, 1992, article, C8130–1.505

Motorcycle industry retail sales of parts/accessories, for franchised and nonfranchised outlets, 1991, annual rpt, A6485–1.1

Original equipment supplier North American sales of top 50 firms, with worldwide sales and components made, 1991-92, annual data book, C2710–3.531

Radios (auto) factory sales, 1987-92, annual rpt, A4725–1.1

Radios (auto) in use, and listener characteristics, 1993 annual rpt, A8789–1

Retail aftermarket sales performance, by product group, 1993 annual feature, C0125–1.503

Retail hardware sales and productivity measures for hardware stores, home centers, and lumber/building material outlets, 1991 and trends, annual rpt series, A8275–1

Retail sales by outlet type, and discount chain sales in major depts, by product category, 1992, annual feature, C8130–1.507

Sales and consumer expenditures, for food store products by type, 1991-92, annual feature, C4655–1.510

Sales distribution for auto aftermarket by category, 1982 and 1991, article, C5150–3.511

Sales volume shares by retail outlet type, for approx 300 food, drug, and other product categories, 1993 annual feature, C4655–1.504

School bus body sales, by type, 1975-92, annual feature, C1575–1.502

Shopping center financial and operating data, with detail by type of tenant, US and Canada, 1991, triennial rpt, R9285–1

Supermarket sales of nonfood products, by detailed product type, 1992, annual feature, C5225–1.508

UK service station operations, by company, with aggregate sales of non-gasoline products by type, 1989-90, annual fact book, C4680–1.507

State and local:

Georgia prices paid by farmers for selected items, 1986-91, annual rpt, S1855–1

Kansas larceny offenses and value of stolen property, by type of theft and location, 1992, annual rpt, S2925–1.1

Mississippi lubricating oil consumption and taxes collected, monthly FY92, annual rpt, S4435–1

see also Batteries

see also Engines and motors

see also Mobile radio

see also Tires and tire industry

Motor vehicle registrations

Fleet auto registrations by model, by size class, 1992-93 models, annual feature, C1575–2.510

Fleet light truck, sport/utility, and van registrations, by model, 1st half 1992-93 model years, annual feature, C1575–2.510

Fleet operating and financial data, including registrations by model and make, 1992 and trends, annual rpt, C1575–2.507

Insurance loss exposure by number of vehicles per square mile, by vehicle type, 1990-92 model years, A5200–4.31

Japan motor vehicle trade with US, and auto registrations by domestic and import make, 1987-92, article, R5650 2.543

Latin America statistical abstract, general data by country, 1992 annual rpt, U6250–1.3

Market data book on production, sales, registrations, prices, options, and dealerships, with data by make and country, 1993 annual rpt, C2710–3.531

Motorcycle market devs, including production, sales, imports, dealer operations, and owner characteristics, 1991 and trends, annual rpt, A6485–1

Motorcycle operator licensing procedures, operators, and vehicle registrations, by State, 1993 annual rpt, A6490–1

Motorcycle registrations, accidents, and fatalities, by State, 1991, annual rpt, A6490–2

New auto registrations, with detail for vehicle fleets by type, by manufacturer and make, weekly rpt quarterly feature, C2710–3 507, C2710–3.521, C2710–3.536, C2710–3.546

New car and truck registrations, with detail by State, 1992 and trends, annual rpt, A7330–1

New motor vehicle registrations, including imports, by make and model, monthly rpt, C7715–3

Number of cars and trucks in use, newly registered, and scrapped, 1947-92, annual rpt, C7715–2

Registered vehicles and licensed drivers, 1992 and trends, annual rpt, A8375–2.3

Registrations and thefts of motor vehicles, 1982-91, annual rpt, A5650–1.4

Registrations by vehicle type, by State and Canadian Province, 1993 annual fact book, C4680–1.507

Registrations in top 20 States and countries, 1988 or 1989, recurring rpt, R9375–6

Registrations, travel miles, and fuel consumed, 3 vehicle types, 1947-91, periodic basic data book, A2575–14.5

Rental fleet vehicle registrations under buy-back programs of 11 manufacturers, 1990-93, C1575–2.503

Index by Subjects and Names

Sourcebook of oil and gas industry, with comparisons to vehicle registrations and use, 1960s-91, annual compilation, C6985–9.5

State social, economic, and govtl indicators, with rankings, 1993 semiannual rpt, B8500–1.11

Statistical profiles of 50 States and DC, general data, 1993 annual almanac, C4712–1

World motor vehicle registrations, by region and country, 1989 and trends, annual rpt, C2140–1.5

World passenger car and total vehicle registrations, by country, 1991, annual rpt, A8375–2.3

World production, sales, trade, and registrations of motor vehicles, by country, world area, manufacturer, and make, 1991 and trends, annual rpt, A0865–2

World registrations and production of motor vehicles, by vehicle type, country, and US State, 1900s-92, annual rpt, A0865–1.1

State and local:

Alabama county data book, general data, 1992 annual rpt, S0121–2

Alabama new passenger car registrations, monthly business activity rpt, U5680–1

Alabama statistical abstract, general data, 1992 recurring rpt, U5680–2.16

Alaska licensed drivers and vehicle registrations, 1982-91, annual rpt, S0360–1

Arizona motor vehicle registrations, by vehicle type, 1991 and trends, annual rpt, S0530–1

Arizona statistical abstract, general data, 1993 recurring rpt, U5850–2.18

California economic indicators, bimonthly rpt, S0840–1

California motor vehicle registrations and licensed drivers, by county, 1991 and trends, annual rpt, S0885–1

California motor vehicle registrations, with comparison to US, 1st half 1992, article, C2710–3.501

California new auto and truck registrations, and taxable sales of new car dealers, quarterly FY92, annual rpt, S0835–1

Colorado motor vehicle fees, taxes, and registrations, by license plate type and/or county, 1991, annual rpt, S1075–1.4

Connecticut new auto registrations, monthly rpt, S1235–1

DC statistical profile, general data, 1992 annual rpt, S1535–3.7

Delaware vehicle registrations, 1992 and trends, annual rpt, S1435–1

Florida county data book, 1992/93 annual rpt, C6360–1

Florida licensed drivers and vehicle registrations, 1972-92, annual rpt, S1750–2

Florida statistical abstract, general data, 1992 annual rpt, U6660–1.13

Georgia auto registrations by county, and motor vehicle tags sold by vehicle type, FY92 annual rpt, S1950–1.2

Georgia county guide, general data, 1993 annual rpt, U6750–1

Georgia statistical abstract, general data, 1992-93 biennial rpt, U6730–1.8

Hawaii data book, general data, 1992 annual rpt, S2090–1.18

Index by Subjects and Names

Motor vehicle safety devices

Hawaii motor vehicle registrations, by county and type of vehicle, 1986, annual rpt, S2125–1

Illinois motor vehicle registrations, 1982-91, annual rpt, S2540–1

Kansas motor vehicle registrations, by vehicle type and county, 1991 and trends, annual rpt, S3020–1

Kansas statistical abstract, general data, 1991/92 annual rpt, U7095–2.13

Kentucky economic statistics, general data, 1993 annual rpt, S3104–1.3

Kentucky motor vehicle registrations, by vehicle type, 1992, annual rpt, S3150–2

Louisiana registered vehicles, by parish, 1991, annual rpt, S3345–2

Maryland statistical abstract, general data, 1993-94 biennial rpt, S3605–1.10

Michigan motor vehicle registrations, by vehicle type and county, 1991 and trends, annual rpt, S3997–2

Minnesota motor vehicle registrations, by vehicle type, 1983-92, annual rpt, S4230–2

Mississippi motor vehicle registrations by county, and tag fees and taxes by vehicle type, FY92 annual rpt, S4435–1

Mississippi statistical abstract, general data, 1992 annual rpt, U3255–4.6

Missouri motor vehicle and boat registrations, by vehicle type, FY88-92, annual rpt, S4570–1.1

Missouri motor vehicle registrations and licensed drivers, with data for motorcycles, 1992, annual rpt, S4560–1

Nebraska registered vehicles, 1992, annual rpt, S4953–1

Nevada statistical abstract, general data, 1992 biennial rpt, S5005–1.13

New Jersey economic indicators, including employment, building permits, and retail trade, monthly rpt, S5425–1

New Mexico motor vehicle registrations and fees by county, and registering activity by office, FY91-92 annual rpt, S5660–1.2

New Mexico motor vehicle registrations, with detail for motorcycles, 1983-92, annual rpt, S5665–1

New York State business activity indicators, quarterly rpt, S5735–2

New York State business and economic indicators, by MSA, county, and industry, 1980s-91, annual rpt, S5735–3

New York State motor vehicle registrations, by vehicle type and county, 1991, annual rpt, S5790–1

New York State statistical yearbook, general data, 1992 annual rpt, U5100–1.13

North Carolina motor vehicle registrations, 1940-92, annual rpt, S5990–1

Ohio vehicle registrations, by county, 1991, annual rpt, S6290–1

Oklahoma registered vehicles, 1960-92, annual rpt, S6482–1

Oklahoma statistical abstract, general data, 1992 annual rpt, U8130–2.16

Pennsylvania business activity indicators, monthly rpt, U4110–1

Pennsylvania statistical abstract, general data, 1992 recurring rpt, U4130–6.9

South Carolina economic condition, including energy and transportation data, 1970s-92, annual rpt, S7125–3.3

South Carolina motor vehicle registrations, by county, 1992 and trends, annual rpt, S7190–2

South Carolina statistical abstract, general data, 1993 annual rpt, S7125–1.15

South Dakota motor vehicle registrations, 1961-92, annual rpt, S7300–3

Tennessee economic indicator trends and forecasts, with data by industry div and manufacturing group, 1982-2001, annual rpt, S7560–1

Tennessee statistical abstract, general data, 1992/93 annual rpt, U8710–2.9

Utah business activity indicators, by county, 1988-91, annual feature, U8960–2.501

Utah business activity indicators, by county, 1989-92, annual feature, U8960–2.507

Utah statistical abstract, general data, 1993 triennial rpt, U8960–1.13

Virginia economic indicators, including new business incorporations and employment data, quarterly rpt, S8205–4

Virginia motor vehicle registrations, mileage, and fuel consumption, 1982-91, annual rpt, S8282–1

Washington State motor vehicle registrations, 1992 and trends, annual rpt, S8428–1

West Virginia motor vehicle registrations, monthly rpt, S8534–1

West Virginia motor vehicle registrations, 1992, annual rpt, S8645–1

West Virginia statistical handbook, general data, 1992 annual rpt, R9385–1.2

Wisconsin Blue Book, general data, 1993-94 biennial rpt, S8780–1.2

Wisconsin economic indicators, including employment and earnings by industry group, monthly rpt, S8750–1

Wisconsin total vehicle and motorcycle registrations, 1992 and trends, annual rpt, S8815–1

see also Motor vehicle sales

Motor vehicle rental

Auto and truck lease fleet composition and operations, biennially 1970-92, biennial survey article, C1575–2.503

Auto lending and leasing operations of financial instns, 1992 and trends, annual rpt, A4160–2

Auto rental company fleet size, and auto manufacturers shares of ownership and vehicles, for 8 rental companies, 1993 article, C2710–3.521

Autos and light trucks/vans in top 100 corporate fleets, 1993 and trends, annual feature, C1575–2.504

Autos and light trucks/vans in 2nd 100 largest corporate fleets, 1993, annual feature, C1575–2.506

Autos leased as percent of all new deliveries, and distribution by size/market segment, 1992 and trends, article, C2710–3.544

Business traveler and trip characteristics, including mode, purpose, and lodging, 1991, annual rpt, R9375–12

Financial ratios and performance, for over 350 SIC 4-digit industries, FY88-92, annual rpt, A6400–3

Fleet operating and financial data, including top lessors, 1970s-93, annual rpt, C1575–2.507

Fleet vehicle lessors ranked by number of cars and trucks managed, for top 15 companies, 1983 and 1993, C1575–2.510

Leases for motor vehicles reaching term, with dispositions, 1991-92, article, C2710–3.537

Registrations of vehicles sold to rental companies under buy-back programs of 11 manufacturers, 1990-93, C1575–2.503

Sales industry costs, including compensation, training, and travel and related expenses, with data by metro area, 1992 and trends, annual survey, C1200–1.508

Sales of top 10 car rental companies, 1989, recurring rpt, R9375–6

Sales of vehicles to rental companies under buy-back programs of 7 auto manufacturers, 1993-94, article, C2710–3.552

Travel trips and traveler characteristics, including mode, purpose, type of lodging, and area of destination and origin, quarterly rpt, R9375–14

Worldwide locations and fleet size for top 12 auto rental companies, 1992 annual rpt, C2140–1.5

State and local:

Hawaii data book, general data, 1992 annual rpt, S2090–1.18

see also Motor vehicle fleets

Motor vehicle safety

see Motor vehicle defects

see Motor vehicle safety devices

see Traffic accidents and safety

Motor vehicle safety devices

Airbag availability in 1993 model year autos, by make, annual rpt, A5200–5

Auto factory installations of airbags, automatic seat belts, and antilock brakes on 1992 models, by manufacturer, make, and model, annual data book, C2710–3.531

Auto fleet acquisition plans, including inclusion of airbags and antilock brakes, 1992 survey, article, C1575–2.503

Auto fleet acquisition plans, with factors affecting purchases, 1992 annual survey, A6755–1.501

Driver fatalities in frontal impact accidents, for autos equipped with airbags vs seat belts only, 1985-91, article, A2623–1.507

Federal motor vehicle safety standards, 1993 annual rpt, A0865–1.3

Health condition and preventive health care and safety practices of adults, by respondent characteristics, 1992 and trends, annual survey rpt, C8111–2

Mass transit agency policies regarding wheelchair restraint devices, 1993 article, C1575–3.507

Mechanic views on most important devices or improvements affecting auto safety, Mar 1993 survey, article, C0125–1.505

Motorcycle use and user characteristics, licensed operators, and State requirements, 1992 annual rpt, A6485–1.2

Seat belt use and enforcement, views of traffic safety magazine readers, Mar/Apr 1993 survey, article, A8375–1.505

Seat belt use laws, by country, 1993 annual rpt, A0865–1.3

Seat belt use laws by State, including effective date and provisions, 1993 annual rpt, A5650–1

Seat belt use rate, 1982-92, article, A8375–1.503

Use rates for driver and child restraints, 1983-92, annual rpt, A8375–2.3

Motor vehicle safety devices

State and local:

Alabama safety equipment use in traffic accidents, 1992, annual rpt, S0185–1

Alabama seat belt use patterns, by demographic characteristics, 1988-89, recurring rpt, S0175–6

Alaska safety device use in traffic accidents, by type of device and injury status, 1991, annual rpt, S0360–1

Arizona traffic accident driver and passenger restraint use, and motorcycle helmet use, 1991, annual rpt, S0530–1

Arkansas safety device use in traffic accidents, 1991, annual rpt, S0692–1

California seat belt use patterns, and views on mandatory driver side airbags, 1991 annual rpt, S0865–2

California traffic accidents, including victim use of safety devices, by county and city, 1991, annual rpt, S0885–1

Colorado seat belt use patterns, by sex and age, 1990, recurring rpt, S1010–3

Connecticut seat belt use patterns, 1989-91, annual rpt, S1200–2

Connecticut traffic accident victim safety device use, 1992, annual rpt, S1275–1

Delaware motorcycle accidents by helmet use, and accident victim seat belt usage, 1992 and trends, annual rpt, S1435 1

Florida safety device use in traffic accidents, by type of device and injury status, 1992, annual rpt, S1750–2

Georgia seat belt use patterns, by respondent characteristics, 1991 and trends, annual rpt, S1895–2

Hawaii seat belt use patterns, by demographic characteristics, 1990, annual rpt, S2065–1.4

Idaho safety equipment use in traffic accidents, 1992, annual rpt, S2315–1

Illinois seat belt use rates before and after enactment of seat belt law, 1985-92, annual rpt, S2540–1

Iowa seat belt use patterns, by demographic characteristics, 1991, annual rpt, S2795–2

Kansas traffic accident victim safety device use, 1992, annual rpt, S3040–1

Kentucky safety device use in traffic accidents, including child restraints, 1992, annual rpt, S3150–2

Kentucky seat belt use patterns, by State area and respondent characteristics, 1988-90, annual rpt, S3140–6

Louisiana seat belt and child restraint use, 1986-92, annual rpt, S3345–2

Maine traffic accidents, injuries, and fatalities, with use of safety equipment, 1992, annual rpt, S3475–2

Massachusetts seat belt use patterns, by demographic characteristics, 1986-90, recurring rpt, S3850–3

Michigan motor vehicle accidents by occupant safety restraint use, 1991 and trends, annual rpt, S3997–2

Michigan seat belt use patterns, by demographic characteristics, 1991, annual rpt, S4000–4

Minnesota safety restraint use, including in traffic accidents, 1992 and trends, annual rpt, S4230–2

Missouri traffic accident driver and passenger restraint use, and motorcyclist helmet use, 1992, annual rpt, S4560–1

Montana traffic accidents, fatalities, and injuries, including safety device use by type, 1992, annual rpt, S4705–2

Nevada seat belt use by drivers involved in traffic accidents, 1992, annual rpt, S5140–1

Nevada seat belt use patterns, by demographic characteristics, 1991, annual rpt, S5075–3

New Jersey safety restraint use in fatal traffic accidents, by type of device, 1992, annual rpt, S5430–2

New Mexico seat belt and motorcycle helmet use in traffic accidents, 1992 and trends, annual rpt, S5665–1

New York State seat belt use patterns, by respondent characteristics, 1990, recurring rpt, S5765–3

New York State traffic fatalities and injuries, by safety equipment used, 1991, annual rpt, S5790–1

North Carolina seat belt and child restraint use in traffic accidents, 1992, annual rpt, S5990–1

North Dakota seat belt use patterns, by respondent characteristics, 1991 and trends, annual rpt, S6105–3

North Dakota traffic accident fatalities and injuries, with safety devices in use, 1992, annual rpt, S6217–1

Ohio traffic accident victim use of safety restraints, child restraints, and motorcycle helmets, 1991, annual rpt, S6290–1

Oklahoma seat belt and motorcycle helmet use in traffic accidents, 1992, annual rpt, S6482–1

Pennsylvania safety restraint use in traffic accidents, by type of device and severity of injury, 1991, annual rpt, S6905–3

Pennsylvania seat belt use patterns, 1991, annual rpt, S6820–4

Rhode Island traffic accident victims, by seat belt and motorcycle helmet use, 1991, annual rpt, S7025–1

South Carolina traffic accidents and/or injuries by safety device use, 1992, annual rpt, S7190–2

South Dakota traffic fatalities and injuries, and seat belt and motorcycle helmet use by age, 1992 and trends, annual rpt, S7300–3

Tennessee seat belt use patterns, by demographic characteristics, 1986-90, annual rpt, S7520–3

Texas seat belt use patterns, by sex, 1982-91, annual rpt, S7685–2

Utah safety device use in traffic accidents, for all motor vehicles and motorcycles, 1992, annual rpt, S7890–2

Utah seat belt use patterns, by respondent characteristics, 1991, annual rpt, S7835–3

Virginia safety device use in traffic accidents, 1991, annual rpt, S8282–1

Washington State safety device use in traffic accidents, by type of vehicle, location, and occupant characteristics, 1992 and trends, annual rpt, S8428–1

West Virginia seat belt use in traffic accidents, 1992, annual rpt, S8645–1

Wisconsin safety device use in traffic accidents, 1992, annual rpt, S8815–1

Wyoming traffic accidents, fatalities, and injuries, with safety device use, 1992 and trends, annual rpt, S9007–1

Index by Subjects and Names

Motor vehicle sales

Auto and truck sales and market share summary, with data by vehicle type, manufacturer, and leading make and model, 1st qtr 1992-93, C2150–3.507

Auto dealer fleet vehicle sales, for top 30 dealers, 1992 article, C1575–2.501

Auto dealership sales per outlet, by make, 1988-92, annual article, C2710–3.520

Auto dealerships, including domestic and import outlets, and franchises by make, 1993 and trends, annual article, C2710–3.519

Auto fleet acquisition plans, including vehicle replacement policy, 1992 survey article, C1575–2.502

Auto fleet acquisition plans, with factors affecting purchases, 1992 annual survey, A6755–1.501

Auto lending and leasing operations of financial instns, 1992 and trends, annual rpt, A4160–2

Auto news and devs, with production and sales data and market analysis, US and foreign, by manufacturer and make/model, weekly rpt, C2710–3

Auto sales and leases, distribution by region, 1993 feature, C1575–2.505

Auto sales volume, quarterly 1991-94, article, C1850–4.504

Auto sales, with market shares by size class, model years 1976-90, periodic basic data book, A2575–14.5

Black-owned enterprises financial and operating data, for top 100 firms and auto dealerships and for top 15-25 financial instns, 1992 and trends, annual feature, C4215–1.507

Bus manufacturer deliveries by use, and Federal transit bus commitments by vehicle type, 1993 article, C1575–3.505

Business economists forecasts of auto sales, business fixed investment, and housing starts, 1993-94, article, A6650–5.502

Cable TV advertising revenue shares from auto dealers, and use of value-added promotions, 1993 survey article, C2965–1.511

Canada new car and commercial vehicle sales, 1990-92, annual fact book, C4680–1.507

Consumer attitudes on economic conditions and personal financial situation, monthly survey, U7475–2

Consumer buying power survey of population, income, and sales by kind of business, by census div, State, MSA, county, and city, 1992, annual rpt, C1200–1.511

Consumer complaint and inquiry activity of Better Business Burs, by detailed type of business, 1992, annual rpt, A4350–1

Consumer expectations of economic conditions and change in income, and intended durable goods purchases by type, Conference Board monthly survey, R4105–4

Consumer new auto purchasing and plans, including makes most likely to be purchased, by age group, 1993 survey article, C2710–1.539

Dealership financial and operating data, including sales and employment by State, 1970s-93, annual rpt, A7330–1

Index by Subjects and Names

Motor vehicle theft

Dealership operating data, including establishments, sales, employment, and payroll by State, 1990s and trends, annual rpt, A0865–1.3

Economic outlook for selected indicators, recent trends and 2-year forecast, quarterly rpt, A3840–6

Europe auto market, including buyer preferences and market shares for selected manufacturers, by country, Aug/Sept 1992 survey, article, C2710–1.523

Europe auto market shares and sales trends for 5 European, 2 US, and aggregate Japanese manufacturers, 1st 8 months 1993, article, C5800–7.549

Europe auto sales, by country and/or manufacturer, weekly rpt monthly tables, C2710–3

Europe sport-utility vehicle unit sales, for 8 manufacturers and all others, 1992, article, C2150–3.506

Financial ratios and performance, for over 350 SIC 4-digit industries, FY88-92, annual rpt, A6400–3

Fleet dealer award recipients, and top dealer sales by make, 1992, annual feature, C1575–2.508

Fleet manager views on market for used fleet vehicles, and mgmt of resale process compared to purchasing and maintenance, 1993 survey, article, C1575–2.509

Forecasts of auto and truck sales by 10 auto industry analysts, 1993, annual article, C2710–3.510

Forecasts of auto and truck sales by 9 auto industry analysts, 1993-94, annual article, C2710–3.538

Forecasts of economic indicators for approx 10-13 months, monthly rpt, U1880–3

Forecasts of natl income and product account components and related indicators, quarterly rpt, U1880–1

Forecasts of natl income and product account components, employment, and financial sector activity, monthly rpt, B4950–1

Franchise operations and finances, by type of business, 1991/92 and trends, annual rpt, A5820–1

Imported auto and truck sales and stocks, weekly rpt monthly tables, C2710–3

Japan auto sales in US, with comparison to domestic manufacturers, 1985-92, annual article, R5650–2.511

Latin America economic indicators affecting business climate, with data on motor vehicle and oil industries and detail by country, 1992 rpt, R4105–82.6

Lease companies associated with new auto dealerships, biennially 1970-92, biennial survey article, C1575–2.503

Loan delinquency rates for approx 10 types of consumer bank loans, and repossession data, by State, quarterly rpt, A0950–1

Luxury car market shares for 10 most popular colors, 1993 feature, C8900–1.516

Market data book on production, sales, registrations, prices, options, and dealerships, with data by make and country, 1993 annual rpt, C2710–3.531

Markets with daily newspapers, demographic and economic info by geographic area, US and Canada, 1993 annual rpt, C3250–1

Mexico motor vehicle sales, and domestic and export production, for 5 manufacturers, weekly rpt monthly tables, C2710–3

Motorcycle market devs, including production, sales, imports, dealer operations, and owner characteristics, 1991 and trends, annual rpt, A6485–1

North America light vehicle sales, percent changes for US, Canada, and Mexico, 1985-2000, article, C2150–3.505

North America sales of domestic, import, and transplant vehicles, 1979 and 1991, article, C2150–3.502

Number of car and light trucks sold, by make and for top 10 vehicles, 1992-93 model years, annual article, C2710–3.551

Operating and financial composite ratios for corporations, with establishments and receipts, for approx 200 industries, by asset size, FY90, annual rpt, C7800–1

Public opinion on honesty/ethical standards of selected occupations, 1992 Gallup Polls and trends, C4040–1.501

Recreational vehicle dealer marketing and mgmt devs, with data on shipments and sales, by vehicle type, monthly rpt, C8950–2

Sales of autos and trucks/buses, commodity yearbook Jan-Sept 1993 updates, C2400–2

Sales of autos and trucks/buses, 1982-92, commodity yearbook, C2400–1

Sports car 2-seat model sales, for 15 models, 1992, article, C2150–3.505

Trends in auto sales vs real disposable income, 1950-92, article, A6400–2.501

Truck (heavy-duty) dealership average financial results, 1988-92, annual article, C2710–3.525

Truck (light) US sales of Japanese vs US manufacturers, by vehicle type, size class, and model, 1989-92, article, R5650–2.529

Truck factory and retail sales, by vehicle type, weight, and make, 1970s-92, annual feature, C2150–4.503

Truck sales by manufacturer and gross vehicle weight class, 1991-92, article, C2150–1.506

Used auto dealer attendance at 3 types of vehicle auctions, and optional equipment effect on car resale value, 1993 article, C1575–2.511

Used auto dealer vehicle sources and types of resale customers, with resale value of selected optional equipment, 1991, article, C1575–2.506

Used autos average auction prices, by make, model, year, and region, monthly rpt, C1575–2

Used autos sold through auctions, shares by vehicle source, 1992, article, C1575–2.501

Wholesale and retail sales trends, with data by model and for Canada by Province, 1992 and trends, annual rpt, A0865–1.1

World production, sales, trade, and registrations of motor vehicles, by country, world area, manufacturer, and make, 1991 and trends, annual rpt, A0865–2

State and local:

Hawaii economic indicators, bimonthly rpt, B3500–1

Maine employment in trade, utilities, and transportation SIC 2-digit industries, by detailed occupation, 2nd qtr 1991, triennial rpt, S3465–1.25

Nebraska sales tax revenues and taxable sales, by county, city, and detailed industry, 1990-91, annual rpt, S4950–1.2

North Carolina employment in trade, transportation, communications, utilities, govt, and education, by detailed occupation, 2nd qtr 1991, triennial rpt, S5917–5.2

Texas trade, transportation, and public utilities employment, by SIC 2- and 3-digit industry and detailed occupation, 2nd qtr 1991, triennial survey rpt, S7675–1.31

Utah economic and business activity review and indicators, monthly rpt, U8960–2

Utah new car sales, by US manufacturer and for imports, 1989-92, annual rpt, R9380–1.10

Virginia business activity indicators, by local area, monthly rpt, U1120–1

see also Motor vehicle registrations

Motor vehicle salvage

see Salvage

Motor vehicle theft

Insurance claim and payment experience for theft of 1990-92 model autos and other vehicles, by make and model, annual rpt, A5200–2

Insurance claim frequency and loss payments for theft, by number of vehicles per square mile and vehicle type, 1990-92 model years, A5200–4.31

Latin America statistical abstract, general data by country, 1992 annual rpt, U6250–1.15

State social, economic, and govtl indicators, with rankings, 1993 semiannual rpt, B8500–1.10

Thefts of motor vehicles, by State, with related insurance claim info, 1993 annual rpt, A5650–1.4

Thefts of motor vehicles, with detail by State, 1991 and trends, annual rpt, A0865–1.2

State and local:

Alabama crimes and arrests, by offense, with data by location and offender characteristics, 1992 and trends, annual rpt, S0119–1

Arizona crimes and arrests, by offense, county, and offender characteristics, 1992, annual rpt, S0505–2

Arkansas crimes and arrests, by offense, victim and offender characteristics, and location, 1992 and trends, annual rpt, S0652–1

California crimes and arrests, clearances, and arrest dispositions, with data by offense and offender characteristics, 1987-92, annual rpt, S0910–1.1

California criminal justice system detailed data, by offense, county, age, race-ethnicity, and sex, 1991 and trends, annual rpt, S0910–2

Colorado crimes and arrests, by offense and location, with offender characteristics, and assaults on police, 1992, annual rpt, S1068–1

Motor vehicle theft

Connecticut crimes and arrests, by offense, with data by local agency, and victim-offender characteristics, 1992, annual rpt, S1256–1

DC criminal justice system summary, including crimes and arrests, criminal procedure, prisoners, and parole, 1991 and trends, annual rpt, S1535–2

Delaware crimes and arrests, by offense, county, and victim-offender characteristics, 1991 and trends, annual rpt, S1375–5

Florida crimes and arrests, by offense, with data by victim and offender characteristics, 1992, annual rpt, S1770–1

Georgia crimes and arrests, by offense, with data by location and offender characteristics, 1992 and trends, annual rpt, S1901–1

Hawaii crimes and arrests, by offense, with data by county and victim-offender characteristics, 1992, annual rpt, S2035–1

Idaho crimes and arrests, by offense, with data by location and offender characteristics, 1992 and trends, annual rpt, S2275–2

Illinois crimes and arrests, by offense, with data by location and offender characteristics, 1991, annual rpt, S2536–1

Kansas crimes and arrests, by offense, with data by location, agency, and victim-offender characteristics, 1992 and trends, annual rpt, S2925–1.1

Kentucky crimes and arrests, by offense, with data by location and offender characteristics, 1992, annual rpt, S3150–1

Maine crimes and arrests, by offense, with data by county, reporting agency, and offender age and sex, 1991, annual rpt, S3475–1

Maryland crimes and arrests, by offense, location, and offender characteristics, with law enforcement employment and assaults on officers, 1992 and trends, annual rpt, S3665–1

Michigan crimes and arrests, by offense, with data by location and offender characteristics, 1992 and trends, annual rpt, S3997–1

Missouri crimes and arrests, by offense and location, with victim and offender characteristics, 1991 and trends, annual rpt, S4560–2

Montana crimes and clearances, by offense and jurisdiction, 1992, annual rpt, S4705–1

Nevada statistical abstract, general data, 1992 biennial rpt, S5005–1.4

New Hampshire crimes and arrests, by offense, jurisdiction, and offender characteristics, 1991 and trends, annual rpt, S5250–2

New Jersey crimes and arrests, by offense, with data by location and offender characteristics, 1992 and trends, annual rpt, S5430–1

New York State crimes and arrests by offense and demographic characteristics, and court activity and corrections, 1991 and trends, annual rpt, S5760–3

North Carolina crimes and arrests, by offense, with data by location and offender characteristics, 1992 and trends, annual rpt, S5955–1

North Dakota crimes and arrests, by offense, location, and offender characteristics, and law enforcement employment, 1991 and trends, annual rpt, S6060–1

Oklahoma crimes and arrests, by offense, with data by local agency and victim and offender characteristics, 1990-92, annual rpt, S6465–1

Oregon crimes and arrests, by offense, with data by county, local agency, and offender characteristics, 1992 and trends, annual rpt, S6603–3

Pennsylvania crimes and arrests, by offense, with data by location and offender characteristics, 1992 and trends, annual rpt, S6860–1

South Carolina crimes and arrests, by offense, with data by location and victim-offender characteristics, and assaults on officers, 1992 and trends, annual rpt, S7205–1

Texas crimes and arrests, by offense, with data by location and offender characteristics, 1992 and trends, annual rpt, S7735–2

Utah crimes and arrests, by offense, county, and local agency, 1992 and trends, annual rpt, S7890–3

Virginia crimes and arrests, by offense, with data by location and offender characteristics, 1992, annual rpt, S8295–2

Washington State crimes and arrests, by offense, with data by location and offender characteristics, 1992 and trends, annual rpt, S8440–1

West Virginia crimes and arrests, by offense, location, and offender characteristics, 1990-91, annual rpt, S8610–1

Wisconsin crimes and arrests, by offense, offender characteristics, county, and local agency, 1992 and trends, annual rpt, S8771–1

Wyoming crimes and arrests, by offense, with data by location and victim and offender characteristics, 1991 and trends, annual rpt, S8867–3

Motorcycles

Financial ratios and performance, for over 350 SIC 4-digit industries, FY88-92, annual rpt, A6400–3

Licensing procedures for motorcycle operators, by State, with number of vehicles and operators, 1993 annual rpt, A6490–1

Market devs, including production, sales, imports, dealer operations, and owner characteristics, 1991 and trends, annual rpt, A6485–1

Registrations by State and Canadian Province, fuel consumption, and mileage, 1993 annual fact book, C4680–1.507

Traffic accidents, fatalities, and injuries, by vehicle type, circumstances, location, and driver and victim characteristics, 1992 and trends, annual rpt, A8375–2.3

Traffic accidents, fatalities, and registrations for motorcycles, by State, 1991, annual rpt, A6490–2

Index by Subjects and Names

State and local:

Alabama traffic accidents, fatalities, and injuries, by circumstances, vehicle type, and driver and victim characteristics, 1992, annual rpt, S0185–1

Alaska traffic accidents, fatalities, and injuries, by vehicle type, circumstance, location, and driver and victim characteristics, 1991 and trends, annual rpt, S0360–1

Arizona traffic accidents, fatalities, and injuries, by vehicle type, circumstances, location, and driver and victim characteristics, 1991 and trends, annual rpt, S0530–1

Arkansas traffic accidents, fatalities, and injuries, by vehicle type, circumstances, location, and driver and victim characteristics, 1991, annual rpt, S0692–1

California traffic accidents, fatalities, and injuries, by vehicle type, circumstances, location, and driver and victim characteristics, 1991 and trends, annual rpt, S0885–1

California traffic fatalities by type, and sex and age of victim, 1990, annual rpt, S0865–1

Connecticut traffic accidents, fatalities, and injuries, by vehicle type, circumstance, location, and driver and victim characteristics, 1992, annual rpt, S1275–1

Delaware traffic accidents, fatalities, and injuries, by circumstances, location, and vehicle type, and driver and victim characteristics, 1992 and trends, annual rpt, S1435–1

Florida traffic accidents, fatalities, and injuries, by vehicle type, circumstance, location, and driver and victim characteristics, 1992 and trends, annual rpt, S1750–2

Hawaii traffic accidents, injuries, and fatalities, by circumstances, location, and driver and victim characteristics, 1986 and trends, annual rpt, S2125–1

Idaho traffic accidents, fatalities, and injuries, by circumstances, location, vehicle type, and driver and victim characteristics, 1992, annual rpt, S2315–1

Illinois traffic accidents, fatalities, and injuries, by circumstances, location, and driver and victim characteristics, 1991 and trends, annual rpt, S2540–1

Indiana traffic accidents, fatalities, and injuries, by circumstances, location, and vehicle type, and driver and victim characteristics, 1992, annual rpt, S2675–1

Kansas traffic accidents, fatalities, and injuries, by vehicle type, location, circumstances, and driver and victim characteristics, 1992, annual rpt, S3040–1

Kentucky traffic accidents, fatalities, and injuries, by circumstances, location, vehicle type, and driver characteristics, 1992 and trends, annual rpt, S3150–2

Louisiana motorcycle accidents, with rider helmet usage, and injuries and deaths, 1991 and trends, annual rpt, S3345–2

Maine traffic accidents, fatalities, and injuries, by accident circumstances, vehicle type and make, and driver and victim characteristics, 1992, annual rpt, S3475–2

Maryland traffic accidents, fatalities, and injuries, by circumstances, location, vehicle type, and driver and victim characteristics, 1992, annual rpt, S3665–4

Michigan traffic accidents, fatalities, and injuries, by vehicle type, circumstance, location, and driver and victim characteristics, 1991 and trends, annual rpt, S3997–2

Minnesota traffic accidents, fatalities, and injuries, by type of vehicle and circumstances, and driver and victim characteristics, 1992 and trends, annual rpt, S4230–2

Missouri traffic accidents, fatalities, and injuries, by circumstances, location, and driver and victim characteristics, 1992 and trends, annual rpt, S4560–1

Montana traffic accidents, fatalities, and injuries, by circumstances, location, and driver and victim characteristics, 1992 and trends, annual rpt, S4705–2

Nebraska traffic accidents, fatalities, and injuries, by circumstances, location, vehicle type, and driver and victim characteristics, 1992, annual rpt, S4953–1

Nevada traffic accidents, fatalities, and injuries, by circumstances, location, and vehicle type, 1992 and trends, annual rpt, S5140–1

New Jersey fatal traffic accidents and fatalities, by vehicle type, location, and circumstances, and driver and victim characteristics, 1992 and trends, annual rpt, S5430–2

New Mexico traffic accidents, fatalities, and injuries, by vehicle type, circumstances, location, and driver and victim characteristics, 1992 and trends, annual rpt, S5665–1

New York State statistical yearbook, general data, 1992 annual rpt, U5100–1.13

New York State traffic accidents, fatalities, and injuries, by circumstances, location, vehicle type, and driver and victim characteristics, 1991 and trends, annual rpt, S5790–1

North Carolina traffic accidents, fatalities, and injuries, by circumstances, location, vehicle type, and driver and victim characteristics, 1992 and trends, annual rpt, S5990–1

North Dakota traffic accidents, fatalities, and injuries, by circumstances, location, vehicle type, and driver and victim characteristics, 1992 and trends, annual rpt, S6217–1

Ohio motorcycle accidents, injuries, and fatalities, with data on helmet use, 1991, annual rpt, S6290–1

Oklahoma motorcycle registrations, accidents, injuries, and fatalities, 1992 and trends, annual rpt, S6482–1

Pennsylvania traffic accidents, fatalities, and injuries, by circumstances, location, driver characteristics, and vehicle type, 1991, annual rpt, S6905–3

Rhode Island traffic accidents, fatalities, and injuries, by circumstances, community, and driver and victim characteristics, 1992, annual rpt, S7025–1

South Carolina traffic accidents, fatalities, and injuries, by circumstances, location, and driver and victim characteristics, 1992 and trends, annual rpt, S7190–2

South Dakota traffic accidents, fatalities, and injuries, by circumstances, location, vehicle type, and driver and victim characteristics, 1992 and trends, annual rpt, S7300–3

Tennessee statistical abstract, general data, 1992/93 annual rpt, U8710–2.9

Utah traffic accidents and fatalities by circumstances, location, driver and victim characteristics, and vehicle type, 1992 and trends, annual rpt, S7890–2

Virginia traffic accidents, fatalities, and injuries, by circumstances, location, and driver and victim characteristics, 1991 and trends, annual rpt, S8282–1

Washington State traffic accidents, fatalities, and injuries, by circumstances, vehicle type, and location, with driver and victim characteristics, 1992 and trends, annual rpt, S8428–1

West Virginia traffic accidents, fatalities, and injuries, by circumstance and location, and driver and victim characteristics, 1992, annual rpt, S8645–1

Wisconsin Blue Book, general data, 1993-94 biennial rpt, S8780–1.2

Wisconsin traffic accidents, fatalities, and injuries, by circumstances, location, vehicle type, and driver and victim characteristics, 1992 and trends, annual rpt, S8815–1

Wyoming traffic accidents, fatalities, and injuries, by circumstances, location, vehicle type, and driver and victim characteristics, 1992 and trends, annual rpt, S9007–1

Motors

see Engines and motors

Moulder, Evelina R.

"Fire Personnel Practices", A5800–2.116

"Local Government Infrastructure Financing", A5800–4.33

"Soliciting Foreign Business To Meet Economic Development Goals", A5800–2.115

Mountain-Plains States

see Western States

see under By Region in the "Index by Categories"

Mountains

see Topography

Movie industry

see Motion pictures

Mowers

see Lawn and garden equipment

MRCA Information Services

Clothing (children's) sales, by retail outlet type, 1992, article, C5150–3.510

Clothing (women's jeans) market shares for top 8 and all other manufacturers, 1993 article, C5150–3.518

Clothing (women's sleepwear) sales volume, by product type, 1st half 1992-93, article, C5150–3.521

Clothing market shares by outlet type and product category, 1991-94, annual article, C8130–1.509

Shoe sales by retail outlet type, for women's and men's shoes, 1991-92, article, C5150–3.515

Shoes (women's) sales volume by retail outlet type, 1990-92, article, C5150–3.511

Watch sales and prices, by retail outlet type, 1992, article, C5150–3.516

Multinational corporations

Advertising agencies with multinatl clients, including countries in which they advertise, 1993 annual article, C2710–1.545

Advertising agency income and billings, for top 10-20 multinatl firms in Latin America, Europe, and Asia/Pacific, 1992, annual article, C2710–1.527

Advertising agency income, billings by medium, employees, and offices, for leading US and/or foreign agencies, 1992 and trends, annual rpt, C2710–1.522

Chemical industry Intl Organization for Standardization (ISO 9000) registrations of US and non-US facilities, for 27 companies, 1992/93, article, A1250–1.516

Construction industry financial performance, for US subsidiaries of foreign companies, 1992-93, annual survey rpt, A4155–1

Electronics company financial performance, for top 100 multinatl firms, 1992 annual feature, C1850–2.502

Electronics industry conditions and outlook, including mgmt issues, global expansion, and most promising new technologies, views of CEOs, 1992/93 survey, annual feature, C1850–2.506

Europe public relations firms with US ties, including data on worldwide offices and activities, by company, 1993 article, A8770–1.505

Exports from US and foreign parent companies to their foreign affiliates, with detail for Japan, 1990, article, C5800–7.536

Financial data for 100 largest US multinatls, and for major subsidiaries of foreign companies, 1992, annual feature, C3950–1.519

Franchise operations abroad, by country and type of business, 1991, annual rpt, A5820–1

Japan corporate affiliate philanthropic activity in US, for service and manufacturing operations, 1992, survey article, R5650–2.560

Latin America statistical abstract, general data by country, 1992 annual rpt, U6250–1.29

Market research company intl revenues, for top 25 firms, 1991-92, annual feature, C2710–1.550

Plastics processing industry involvement in intl operations, by company sales size, 1992, annual rpt, A8920–4

Profits (foreign) of US companies, distribution by country or world region, 1991, article, C5800–7.546

Sales and intl share of sales, for 50 smaller multinatl firms, 1992, article, C5800–7.544

Services sales to foreign persons by foreign affiliates of US companies, by country and industry, 1986-90, article, A3892–1.501

State social, economic, and govtl indicators, with rankings, 1993 semiannual rpt, B8500–1.2

Multinational corporations

Telecommunication operations, including number of countries with selected types of equipment, services, and staff, for 6 major carriers, 1993 article, C1850–5.520

World events and socioeconomic devs outside the US with implications for multinatl corporations, series, R4105–82

Multiple births

see Plural births

Mulvey, Patrick J.

"Employment Survey, 1991", A1960–1

"1991/92 Survey of Physics and Astronomy Bachelor's Degree Recipients", A1960–3

Municipal bonds

- Capital project financing methods of local govt, by population size, metro status, and census div, 1991 survey, A5800–2.112
- Chicago Board of Trade futures and options trading in financial instruments and agricultural commodities, 1992, annual rpt, B2120–1
- Forecasts of economic indicators for approx 10-13 months, monthly rpt, U1880–3
- Govt finances, including revenues by source, expenditures by function, and debt, detailed data for Federal, State, and local govts, 1993 annual rpt, R9050–1
- Hospital tax-exempt bond issuance value, with detail by purpose, 1989-92, article, A1865–1.507
- Infrastructure financing methods used by local govts, with bond marketing methods, by locality, 1991 survey, A5800–4.33
- Investment in municipal bonds, by type, year-end 1992, article, C8900–1.513
- Money and securities market activity, and related indicators, biweekly rpt, B2000–1
- Mutual fund industry financial data, investment activity, portfolio composition, and shareholder account characteristics, 1991 and trends, annual rpt, A6025–1
- Mutual fund investment performance, by fund, June 1993 and trends, annual compilation, C3950–1.522
- Mutual fund sales, assets, and investment activities, with data on money market and municipal bond funds, monthly rpt, A6025–5
- Mutual funds investing in State and natl municipal bonds, and assets, 1991-92, article, C8900–1.509
- Underwriting of municipal issues, periodic rpt, A8825–1
- Unit investment trust sales volume and value, by trust type, maturity period, and insurance features, monthly rpt, A6025–7
- Urban school system distribution by general purpose municipal bond rating, and bonded debt ratings for individual systems, for 47 systems, 1992 rpt, A4425–4

State and local:

- Arkansas State treasurer safekeeping account balances and interest rates, by account, FY92, biennial rpt, S0780–1
- Colorado public school revenues by source, and expenditures by category, by school district, 1990, annual rpt, S1000–4.3
- Illinois school bond and tax referenda election outcomes, 1985/86-1990/91, and bonds issued and outstanding, FY91, annual rpt, S2440–1.3
- Kansas statistical abstract, general data, 1991/92 annual rpt, U7095–2.11
- Louisiana school system indebtedness, including bonds sold and redeemed, by school district, 1991/92, annual rpt, S3280–1.2
- Maryland counties bond ratings, Sept 1992, annual rpt, S3618–1.2
- Maryland elementary and secondary education data, by county, 1991/92, annual rpt, S3610–2.7
- Michigan school district financial and enrollment data, with rankings, 1991/92, annual rpt, S3965–3
- Missouri public school finances, staff, students, and programs, detailed data, 1991/92, annual rpt, S4505–1.1
- New Jersey municipal and county data book, general data, 1992 annual rpt, C4712–4
- Pennsylvania statistical abstract, general data, 1992 recurring rpt, U4130–6.6
- West Virginia public school finances, including tax levy and bond election results, bonding potential, and levy proceeds, by county, 1992/93 and trends, annual rpt, S8540–4.1
- Wyoming public school enrollment, staff, and finances, by county and district, 1991/92, annual rpt series, S8890–1

see also Industrial revenue bonds

Municipal courts

see State courts

Municipal employees

see State and local employees

Municipal government

see Local government

Municipal taxation

see State and local taxes

Municipal transportation

see Urban transportation

Murder

see Homicide

Musculoskeletal diseases

- Auto plant worker hand/wrist disorder cases, 1985-86, article, A2623–1.501
- Hip fracture incidence rates in US and Hong Kong, by age and sex, 1988/89, article, A2623–1.507
- Hospital patient admission rates and length of stay, by diagnosis and procedure, payment source, age, sex, and region, 1991, B4455–4
- Hospital patient charges and length of stay, by diagnosis and procedure, payment source, age, and region, 1991, B4455–5
- Hospital patient discharges and length of stay, by diagnosis, type of operation, age, and region, 1991, annual rpt series, B4455–1
- Hospital patient discharges and length of stay, by diagnostic related group (DRG), payment source, age, and region, 1991, annual rpt series, B4455–3
- Hospital psychiatric patients with selected physical disorders, length of stay by age, sex, and region, 1991, annual rpt series, B4455–2
- Occupations correlated with musculoskeletal disability incidence in men and women, 1992 article, A2623–1.501

State and local:

- Alabama vital statistics, including population, births, deaths by cause, marriages, and divorces, by location and demographic characteristics, 1992 and trends, annual rpt, S0175–2
- Arkansas vital statistics, including births, deaths by cause, marriages, and divorces, by age, sex, race, and county, 1991 and trends, annual rpt, S0685–1
- California vital statistics, including population, births, and deaths by cause, by demographic characteristics and county, 1990 and trends, annual rpt, S0865–1
- Florida vital statistics, including population, births, deaths by cause, and marriages and dissolutions, by location and demographic characteristics, 1992 and trends, annual rpt, S1745–3
- Georgia vital statistics, including deaths by cause, demographic characteristics, and location, 1991 and trends, annual rpt, S1895–1.2
- Hawaii health dept activities and services, including vital statistics and disease control, by location, 1990, annual rpt, S2065–1
- Idaho vital statistics, including births, deaths by cause, abortions, marriages, and divorces, by demographic characteristics and county, 1991 and trends, annual rpt, S2250–2
- Maine vital statistics, including births, deaths by cause, abortions, and marriages and divorces, by demographic characteristics and location, 1991 and trends, annual rpt, S3460–2
- Massachusetts vital statistics, including births, deaths by cause, marriages, divorces, and population, by locality and demographic characteristics, 1990 and trends, annual rpt, S3850–1
- Michigan vital statistics, including births, deaths, marriages, divorces/annulments, and communicable diseases, by location and demographic characteristics, 1990 and trends, annual rpt, S4000–3
- Minnesota vital statistics, including population, births, abortions, deaths, marriages, and divorces, by location and demographic characteristics, 1991 and trends, annual rpt, S4190–2
- Mississippi vital statistics, including births, deaths by cause, marriages, and divorces, by demographic characteristics and location, 1992 and trends, annual rpt, S4350–1
- Montana vital statistics, including births, deaths by cause, abortion, disease, and marriage and divorce, by demographic characteristics and county, 1990-91 and trends, annual rpt, S4690–1
- Oregon vital statistics, including births, deaths by cause, communicable diseases, marriages, and divorces, by age, sex, race-ethnicity, and county, 1991 and trends, annual rpt, S6615–5
- South Carolina deaths, by detailed cause, age, sex, and race, 1990, annual rpt, S7175–2
- Tennessee vital statistics, including births, deaths by cause, marriages, divorces, and population, by demographic characteristics and location, 1991 and trends, annual rpt, S7520–2
- Vermont vital statistics, including population, births, deaths by cause, abortions, marriages, and divorces, by location and demographic characteristics, 1991 and trends, annual rpt, S8054–1

Washington State vital statistics, including births, deaths by cause, and population, by demographic characteristics and location, 1991 and trends, annual rpt, S8363–1

West Virginia vital statistics, including births, deaths by cause, marriages, and divorces, by location and demographic characteristics, 1991 and trends, annual rpt, S8560–1

Wisconsin vital statistics, including population, births, deaths by cause, and marriages and dissolutions, by county and demographic characteristics, 1991 and trends, annual rpt, S8715–4

see also Mobility limitations

see also Podiatry

see also under By Disease in the "Index by Categories"

Museums

Fundraising through united arts funds (UAFs), with allocations to museums, by UAF, 1992, annual rpt, A1315–2

Operations and finances for museums and related instns, by type, budget size, governing authority, and region, 1989/90 survey, A0750–1

Salaries for 37 art museum positions, by region, population size served, and budget size, with employee benefits offered, FY93, annual rpt, A3290–1

State and local:

DC statistical profile, general data, 1992 annual rpt, S1535–3.3

Florida statistical abstract, general data, 1992 annual rpt, U6660–1.20

Hawaii data book, general data, 1992 annual rpt, S2090–1.7

New York State statistical yearbook, general data, 1992 annual rpt, U5100–1.10

Pennsylvania statistical abstract, general data, 1992 recurring rpt, U4130–6.8

Mushrooms

see Vegetables and vegetable products

Music

Concert tour receipts for top 20 performers, Mar-June 1993, annual feature, C9380–1.534

Jukebox operating data, including type of equipment in use, 1993 annual rpt, C9470–1

Radio audience size, leading stations and formats, and advertising rates and revenues, by market area, recurring rpt, C3165–1

Shopping center financial and operating data, with detail by type of tenant, US and Canada, 1991, triennial rpt, R9285–1

State and local:

Hawaii data book, general data, 1992 annual rpt, S2090–1.7

see also Musical instruments

Musical instruments

College freshmen activities in past year, including playing of musical instruments, by sex and instn type, fall 1992, annual rpt, U6215–1

Electronic musical instrument domestic consumption and/or foreign trade, by type, 1983-91, annual article, A4725–1.1

Financial ratios and performance, for over 350 SIC 4-digit industries, FY88-92, annual rpt, A6400–3

Shipment volume and retail value, and foreign trade, by type of instrument, 1992 and trends, annual rpt, A6848–1

Muskogee, Okla.

Business activity indicators for Oklahoma, monthly rpt, U8130–1

Mutual funds

Asset composition for 6 institutional investor categories, 1970-2nd qtr 1992, article, A8825–1.504

Assets and investment performance, for 273 top performing funds, 1993 recurring article, C8900–1.528

Assets and investment performance, for 276 top performing funds, 1992 recurring article, C8900–1.511

Assets and investment performance, 105 closed-end equity and 120 closed-end fixed-income funds, 1993 annual feature, C5800–7.517

Assets and investment performance, 555 fixed-income funds, 1993 annual feature, C5800–7.516

Assets and investment performance, 760 equity funds, 1993 annual feature, C5800–7.515

Assets and investment return, for 5 mutual funds and their namesake "clones," 1993 article, C3950–1.521

Assets and market shares for top 25 mutual fund mgmt firms, Sept 1992, article, C5800–7.511

Assets of mutual funds under mgmt, 1990-Mar 1993, article, C2710–2.516

Business Week economic, business, and investment devs, with related statistical indicators, weekly rpt, C5800–7

Direct marketing industry devs, with consumer and business market characteristics, and media use patterns, 1992/93 annual rpt, A4620–1.4

Equity funds value of closings and funds raised, for 13 private buy-out, mezzanine, and special situation funds, 1993 article, C2710–2.511

Equity purchases by mutual funds and pension funds, 1960s-90s, article, C2710–2.514

Finance company and money market fund assets, and commercial and consumer debt held, with comparisons to commercial banks, 1980-92, R4700–22

Financial data, investment activity, and shareholder account characteristics, 1991 and trends, annual rpt, A6025–1

Financial performance of over 2,400 mutual funds, with rankings of top funds and background info for investors, 1992 and trends, annual directory, C4682–1

Foreign-based funds assets and returns, for 10 major funds, 1992 article, C3950–1.502

Investment performance for approx 1,000 established stock/balanced, taxable bond, and municipal bond funds, 1993 annual article, C3950–1.508

Investment performance for best and/or worst equity, and taxable and tax-free bond funds, 1992, annual feature, C5800–7.509

Investment performance for equity, bond, and balanced funds, 1992 and trends, article, C2710–2.508

Investment performance of best- and worst-performing funds, biweekly rpt semiannual feature, C3950–1.501, C3950–1.514

Investment performance of mutual funds, by fund, June 1993 and trends, annual compilation, C3950–1.522

Investment performance, with detail for best- and worst-performing funds in selected categories, weekly rpt recurring article, C5800–7.523, C5800–7.533, C5800–7.549

Investment returns and assets, for 50 mutual funds selected on basis of long-term performance, 1993 annual article, C4215–1.505

Investment returns before vs after taxes and tax liability for 50 largest funds, and ranking of 30 funds with highest and lowest liability, 1993 article, C5800–7.547

Korea (South) stock fund market capitalization, price, asset value, and premium/discount trends, for 16 funds, 1993 article, C3950–1.508

Money market funds financial performance and rankings, for over 850 funds, with background info for investors, 1992 and trends, annual directory, C4682–2

Municipal bond funds and assets, for State and natl funds, 1991-92, article, C8900–1.509

Retirement plan (defined benefit) mutual funds most often used, rankings by assets and investment performance, errata, C2710–2.507

Retirement plan (defined benefit) mutual funds most often used, rankings by assets, May 1993, semiannual article, C2710–2.517

Retirement plan (defined benefit) mutual funds most often used, rankings by assets, 1993 semiannual article, C2710–2.505

Retirement plan (defined benefit) mutual funds most often used, rankings by investment performance trends, biweekly rpt quarterly feature, C2710–2.505, C2710–2.509, C2710–2.517

Sales and asset trends, periodic rpt, A8825–1

Sales, assets, and investment activity of mutual funds, with data on money market and municipal bond funds, monthly rpt, A6025–5

Spain mutual fund assets and corporate affiliation, for top 5 managers, 1993 article, A8955–1.503

Thailand investing mutual fund returns, assets, and other financial data, for 8 funds, 1993 article, C3950–1.527

Mutual savings banks

see Savings institutions

Myanmar

Energy intl sourcebook, with detail on oil and gas industry operations, supply-demand, and prices, for approx 80 countries, 1970s-91, annual compilation, C6985–10.2

Oil and gas production and potential yield, and leased acreage by company and basin, 1992 article, C6985–1.506

Mycoses

see Infective and parasitic diseases

Namibia

Uranium mine ownership shares, 1992 annual rpt, B6800–2.2

Naphtha

Naphtha
see Petroleum and petroleum industry

Narcotics
see Drug abuse and treatment
see Drug and narcotics offenses
see Drugs

NASA
see National Aeronautics and Space Administration

NASDAQ
see Stock exchanges

Nashua, N.H.
Employment, hours, and earnings, and job service applicant characteristics, monthly rpt, S5205–1

National Aeronautics and Space Administration
Aerospace industry, civil and military production, R&D, trade, employment, and finances, with Federal funding data, 1991 and trends, annual rpt, A0250–2
Cost of 6 space projects that failed or fell short of expectations, 1993 feature, C8900–1.524
Prime contract awards, by region and State, FY92, annual rpt, R8490–11
Procurement expenditures, with detail for top 25 contractors, 1988, R4700–19
R&D funding by program category, with detail for advanced subsonic transport program, 1992, article, C5800–4.505

State and local:
California prime contract awards from DOD and NASA, FY91 and trends, annual rpt, S0840–2.8

National Assessment of Educational Progress
Mathematics proficiency results on Natl Assessment of Educational Progress tests, for public vs private school students, 1990, article, U8710–1.503
Mathematics test results, by race-ethnicity and State, 1993 biennial rpt, A4355–3
Mathematics test scores, with detail by topic and classroom characteristics including teacher preparation level, by State, 1993 biennial rpt, A4355–1
Reading scores of students at 3 ages, by race-ethnicity, 1971-90, article, R4800–2.504
Reading test score gains for students age 9, 13, and 17, with detail for disadvantaged urban students, 1988/89 vs 1970/71, A4425–4

National Association of Blue Shield Plans
see Blue Cross-Blue Shield

National Association of Hosiery Manufacturers
Hosiery production, by product type, 1983-92, annual feature, C3460–1.510

National Bureau of Standards
see National Institute of Standards and Technology

National Collegiate Athletic Association
Revenues and expenditures of NCAA, 1992/93-1993/94, annual feature, C2175–1.534

National commissions
see Federal boards, committees, and commissions
see Federal independent agencies

National Conference of States on Building Codes and Standards
Mobile/manufactured home production, shipments, and financing, with data by State and census div, monthly rpt, A6325–1

National debt
see Government assets and liabilities
see Public debt

National defense
Eastern Europe public opinion on defense spending and policy, for 4 countries, 1991 survey, C8915–8.2
Public opinion on whether US is in military decline, by respondent characteristics, Sept 1992 Gallup Poll, C4040–1.503
see also Armed services
see also Arms control and disarmament
see also Civil defense
see also Defense budgets and appropriations
see also Defense contracts and procurement
see also Defense expenditures
see also Defense industries
see also Defense research
see also Department of Defense
see also Foreign relations
see also Military aircraft
see also Military assistance
see also Military aviation
see also Military bases, posts, and reservations
see also Military education
see also Military health facilities and services
see also Military housing
see also Military pay
see also Military personnel
see also Military prisons
see also Military supplies and property
see also Military training
see also Military vehicles
see also Military weapons
see also National Guard
see also Naval vessels
see also Service academies
see also Strategic Defense Initiative
see also Strategic materials

National Endowment for the Arts
see National Foundation on the Arts and the Humanities

National Endowment for the Humanities
see National Foundation on the Arts and the Humanities

National Family Opinion Inc.
see NFO Research Inc.

National forests
Statistical profiles of 50 States and DC, general data, 1993 annual almanac, C4712–1
Timber volume under contract and awaiting harvest in natl forests, 1983-92, A1630–1.501

State and local:
Arizona statistical abstract, general data, 1993 recurring rpt, U5850–2.8
California statistical abstract, general data, 1992 annual rpt, S0840–2.7
Florida statistical abstract, general data, 1992 annual rpt, U6660–1.10
Georgia statistical abstract, general data, 1992-93 biennial rpt, U6730–1.5
Mississippi statistical abstract, general data, 1992 annual rpt, U3255–4.10
Oklahoma statistical abstract, general data, 1992 annual rpt, U8130–2.1
South Carolina revenue shared with county govts, by tax or fund type, FY92, annual rpt, S7127–2
Tennessee statistical abstract, general data, 1992/93 annual rpt, U8710–2.12
Utah public lands by govt owner, and Federal land payments to State and local govts, with data by county, 1992 article, U8960–2.502

Utah timber production volume and value from natl forests, 1960-92, triennial rpt, U8960–1.9
see also Wilderness areas

National Foundation on the Arts and the Humanities
Library grants awarded by NEH, and legislative appropriations, 1993 annual compilation, C1650–3.2

National Gardening Association
Lawn/garden product sales, and consumer expenditures on gardening activities, 1992 and trends, article, C5150–6.508

National goals
see National plans and goals

National Guard
Members of Natl Guard per 10,000 population, by State, 1991, article, B8500–2.514
Personnel in Army Natl Guard, and planned reductions, by State and region, FY91-93, R8490–44

State and local:
Hawaii data book, general data, 1992 annual rpt, S2090–1.10

National income and product accounts
Corporate profits compared to natl income, FY80-92, recurring rpt, R9050–15.2
Forecasts of natl income and product account components and related indicators, quarterly rpt, U1880–1
Forecasts of natl income and product account components, employment, and financial sector activity, monthly rpt, B4950–1
Govt finances, including revenues by source, expenditures by function, and debt, detailed data for Federal, State, and local govts, 1993 annual rpt, R9050–1
Latin America statistical abstract, general data by country, 1992 annual rpt, U6250–1.32
see also Economic indicators
see also Gross Domestic Product
see also Gross National Product

National Institute for Occupational Safety and Health
Health hazard evaluations conducted by NIOSH, with summary detail for selected hazard types, FY81-91, annual rpt, R8335–1.2

National Institute of Standards and Technology
Budget of US for NIST, by function, FY93 and FY97, article, A1250–1.539

National Institutes of Health
Budget of Natl Institute of General Medical Sciences, by program, FY92-93, article, A1250–1.514
Budget of US for NIH, by institute or program, FY93-94, article, A1250–1.527

National Kitchen and Bath Association
Kitchen cabinet wood types specified by kitchen designers, 1992 and trends, C4300–1.511

National Merit Scholarship Corp.
Freshman enrollment of Natl Merit Scholars in top 64 higher education instns, 1992, annual feature, C2175–1.505

National monuments
see Monuments and memorials

National parks
Statistical profiles of 50 States and DC, general data, 1993 annual almanac, C4712–1

Index by Subjects and Names

Travel and tourism rankings for selected indicators, including data for top 20 States, cities, countries, businesses, and other measures, 1992 recurring rpt, R9375–6

Travel indicators, including visits to natl parks monthly rpt, R9375–1

State and local:

Arizona statistical abstract, general data, 1993 recurring rpt, U5850–2.8

California statistical abstract, general data, 1992 annual rpt, S0840–2.1

Florida statistical abstract, general data, 1992 annual rpt, U6660–1.19

Hawaii data book, general data, 1992 annual rpt, S2090–1.7

Maine statistical summary, general economic and social data, 1992 recurring rpt, S3434–1

New Mexico State and natl park visits, monthly business activity rpt, U7980–1

Pennsylvania statistical abstract, general data, 1992 recurring rpt, U4130–6.8

Tennessee statistical abstract, general data, 1992/93 annual rpt, U8710–2.12

Utah statistical abstract, general data, 1993 triennial rpt, U8960–1.17

see also National forests

see also Wilderness areas

see also Wildlife refuges

see also Yellowstone National Park

National Petroleum Council

Gasoline price increases attributable to new Federal environmental, health, and safety regulations, 1995 and 2000, article, C4680–1.511

Natural gas proved reserves, and conventional and nonconventional resources, Jan 1991, article, C6985–1.509

National planning

see Economic policy

see Fiscal policy

see National plans and goals

National plans and goals

Black American health and political leaders views on public health goals for year 2000, 1993 article, A2623–1.510

China oil and gas production, with percent of natl energy plan met, by region, 1991-92, annual rpt, C6985–3.1

Elementary/secondary education natl goals for year 2000, public opinion on importance, 1993 annual Gallup Poll, A8680–1.503

Pakistan family planning program targets for population control and contraceptive provision, 1977-93, article, A5160–6.501

Urban public school performance compared to natl goals for year 2000, with data on students, teachers, and finances, for 47 systems, 1990/91 and trends, A4425–4

State and local:

New Jersey status for 29 natl health objectives, 1990, annual rpt, S5405–1

see also Economic policy

National Railroad Passenger Corp.

Passenger traffic, monthly rpt, R9375–1

Trends in transportation operations and finances, by mode, 1991 annual rpt, R4815–1

State and local:

New York State Amtrak ridership, 1975-89, annual rpt, U5100–1.13

National Science Foundation

Budget of NSF by function and scientific field, with detail for chemical programs, FY92-94, article, A1250–1.523

National security

see National defense

National signs and symbols

Southern States display of Confederate flags on capitol buildings, public opinion, Dec 1992 Gallup Poll, C4040–1.506

National Wildlife Refuge System

see Wildlife refuges

Nationality

see Citizenship

Nationalization

see Government ownership

Native Americans

see Indians

Nativity

see Birthplace

NATO

see North Atlantic Treaty Organization

Natrona County, Wyo.

Employment by industry group, monthly rpt, S8895–1

Natural disasters

see Disasters

see Drought

see Earthquakes

see Floods

see Forest fires

see Storms

Natural fibers

Carpet and rug industry shipments by type, PPI, and US trade by country, 1991 and trends, annual rpt, A3800–1

Clothing (women's and children's) garments imported, by type and fabric, recurring rpt, A5900–1

Consumption and trade by type of fiber and product, 1988-92, annual survey, C3460–1.511

Paper, paperboard, and wood pulp industry capacity and material consumption, by grade and census div, 1970s-95, annual rpt, A1630–7

Production, consumption, and trade, detailed data by fiber and fabric type, monthly rpt, C3460–1

Production, consumption, stocks, trade, and prices for approx 100 basic commodities, including by country and producing State, commodity yearbook for 1993, C2400–1, C2400–2

see also Cotton

see also Paper and paper products

see also Silk

see also Wool and wool trade

Natural gas and gas industry

Apartment building (conventionally financed) detailed income and expense ratios for US and Canada, by building type, metro area, and US region, 1991 and trends, annual rpt, A5600–1

Apartment building (federally subsidized) detailed income and expense ratios, by building and subsidy type, building age, metro area, and region, 1991 and trends, annual rpt, A5600–5

Coalbed degasification emissions recovered, used, and vented, for 7 major coal producing countries, 1992 article, C6985–1.507

Commonwealth of Independent States natural gas supply-demand by Republic,

Natural gas and gas industry

price trends, and comparisons to other fuels, 1993 article, C6985–1.514, C6985–1.515

Condominium, cooperative, and planned unit dev detailed expenses, for US and Canada, by building characteristics, metro area, and US region, 1991, annual rpt, A5600–3

Distribution utility operations, and pipeline facilities construction, articles and special features, monthly rpt, C6780–1

Electric power (steam) plant operating data, including oil and gas use and costs, by plant, utility, and location, 1991, annual rpt, A7400–7

Electric power supply-demand, and utility capacities and fuel requirements, detailed data by US and Canadian region, 1992-2002, annual rpt, A8630–2

Electric utility financial and operating data, by State and census div, 1991 and trends, annual rpt, A4700–1

Electric utility fuel consumption for 7 natural-gas-fired combined-cycle power plants, 1993 article, C5800–28.509

Electric utility gas deliveries and prices, monthly rpt, A7400–9

Electric utility operating data, including generating capacity and efficiency, peak demand, and fuel consumption, top 100 utilities, 1992, annual article, C6985–6.512

Expenditures for exploration, dev, and production, 1991 and trends, annual survey rpt, A2575–20

Expenditures of gas utilities on expansion and maintenance, 1990-93, annual article, C6780–1.501

Financial and operating data for top 500 gas distribution utilities and pipeline companies, 1992, annual article, C6780–1.505

Financial performance and growth rankings for approx 1,000 top corporations, with comparisons by industry group, 1993 annual rpt, C3950–1.505

France natural gas govt-owned company operations and finances, including employment, 1990, article, C6985–1.505

Fuel oil and heating equipment dealer loss of business to gas conversions, 1992 annual survey, C4680–2.3

Higher education physical plant operations, costs, employment, salaries, and energy use, by instn and region, 1991/92, recurring rpt, A3183–1

Income composite statement, with sales and prices by consuming sector and census div, quarterly rpt, A1775–1

Intl energy sourcebook, with detail on oil and gas industry operations, supply-demand, and prices, for approx 80 countries, 1970s-91, annual compilation, C6985–10

Intl Petroleum Encyclopedia, basic data on oil and gas supply-demand, exploration, refining, reserves, and industry finances, by country and company, 1993 annual rpt, C6985–3

Japan energy supply-demand and outlook, by fuel source, 1980s-2000, recurring article, R5650–2.536

Latin America statistical abstract, general data by country, 1992 annual rpt, U6250–1.23

Natural gas and gas industry

Occupational injury, illness, and employment data, by function, for 136 oil/gas companies, 1991, annual rpt, A2575–4

Office building detailed income and expense data, and energy use, US and Canada, by building characteristics, metro area, and US region, 1991 and trends, annual rpt, A5600–2

Operating and financial composite ratios for corporations, with establishments and receipts, for approx 200 industries, by asset size, FY90, annual rpt, C7800–1

Operating and financial detailed data, for natural gas industry, by State and census div, 1960s-91, annual rpt, A1775–3

Processing plants, capacity, and production, by company, State, and country, 1993 annual rpt, C6985–1.537

Production and drilling technology devs, including oil and gas drilling rigs in operation, monthly rpt, C4420–1

Production, exploration, drilling, refining, stock, price, and financial data for US and foreign oil and gas industry, weekly rpt, C6985–1

Production, exploration, refining, demand, finance, prices, and reserves, by State and country or world area, 1993 and trends, periodic basic data book, A2575–14

Production, finances, exploration, reserves, and other data for oil/gas industry, by State, 1992 and trends, annual rpt, A5425–1

Production in US, Canada, and selected world areas, and US home heating devs, 1993 annual fact book, C4680–1.507

Russia natural gas govt-owned company operations, with former Soviet Union supply-demand, foreign trade, and pipeline mileage by Republic, 1993 article, C6985–1.551

Russia, Tyumen region gas processing by plant, and liquefied petroleum gas production and demand, 1993 article, C6985–1.540

Sales and prices of natural gas by consuming sector, with related data, monthly rpt, A1775–2

Shopping center detailed income and expense data, by building characteristics, metro area, and region, 1991, annual rpt, A5600–6

Sourcebook of oil and gas industry operations and finances, and world supply-demand situation, 1970s-91, annual compilation, C6985–9

State social, economic, and govtl indicators, with rankings, 1993 semiannual rpt, B8500–1.12

Statistical compilation of oil and gas industry trends, 1993 annual rpt, C6985–4

Statistical profiles of 50 States and DC, general data, 1993 annual almanac, C4712–1

Supply-demand and price data for energy resources, including by country and producing State, commodity yearbook for 1993, C2400–1

Supply-demand and price data for energy resources, including by country and producing State, commodity yearbook Jan-Sept 1993 updates, C2400–2

Supply-demand outlook and industry operations, with trends by country and producing State, 1970s-2010, annual rpt, C6985–5

Supply-demand, prices, and finance, oil and gas industry, 1973-92, annual rpt, A5425–2

Supply-demand, trade, and industry exploration and operations, by product, exporting country and world area, PAD district, and State, 1993 annual feature, C6985–1.513

Supply-demand, trade, and prices, with selected data by State, PAD district, and country, 1993 annual article, C6985–1.539

Supply trends and outlook under 4 economic scenarios, for onshore and offshore areas and Alaska, 1960s-2010, A2575–25

Utility regulatory agency policies and practices, and industry financial and operating data, by utility type and agency, 1991/92 annual rpt, A7015–3

World energy supply-demand, by fuel source and sector, by region and country, 1992/93 biennial rpt, R9455–1.3

World oil and gas production, by country, 1986-91, annual rpt, A7400–2.1

State and local:

Alabama business activity indicators, monthly rpt, U5680–1

Alabama county data book, general data, 1992 annual rpt, S0121–2

Alabama statistical abstract, general data, 1992 recurring rpt, U5680–2.12

Alaska public utility financial and operating data, by company and utility type, 1991 and trends, with FY92 regulatory info, annual rpt, S0280–4

Arizona oil and gas production, by field, operator, and well, monthly rpt, S0473–1

Arizona statistical abstract, general data, 1993 recurring rpt, U5850–2.14, U5850–2.20

Arkansas oil and gas production by field, and disposition, monthly rpt, S0737–1

Arkansas public utility financial, operating, and regulatory data, by utility type and company, 1992 annual rpt, S0757–1

California public utility and transportation regulatory data, including revenue requests and rates of return by company, FY92 annual rpt, S0930–1

California statistical abstract, general data, 1992 annual rpt, S0840–2.7

Colorado property assessed valuation, and summary production data, by county and/or company, 1991-92, annual rpt, S1055–3

Florida public utility regulatory and operating data, by company and utility type, 1992 and trends, annual rpt, S1790–1

Florida statistical abstract, general data, 1992 annual rpt, U6660–1.15

Georgia statistical abstract, general data, 1992-93 biennial rpt, U6730–1.8

Hawaii data book, general data, 1992 annual rpt, S2090–1.17

Idaho public utility regulatory data, and commission finances, FY92, annual rpt, S2290–1

Illinois gas utility sales and operating revenues, energy sold, and customers served, by class of service and company, 1991-92, annual rpt, S2410–1.1

Kansas oil and gas production, by county, 1991, annual rpt, S3020–1

Kansas statistical abstract, general data, 1991/92 annual rpt, U7095–2.16

Louisiana energy indicators, suspended quarterly rpt, U2730–1

Maryland statistical abstract, general data, 1993-94 biennial rpt, S3605–1.10

Mississippi statistical abstract, general data, 1992 annual rpt, U3255–4.10, U3255–4.14

Montana oil and gas production and taxes paid, by county, 1990-91, biennial rpt, S4750–1.1

Nevada statistical abstract, general data, 1992 biennial rpt, S5005–1.11

New Mexico business and economic activity indicators, monthly rpt, U7980–1

New Mexico public utility operating, financial, and regulatory data, by utility type, FY92 annual rpt, S5645–1

New York State natural gas sales, quarterly rpt, S5735–2

New York State public utility financial and operating data, by utility type and company, 1988-92, annual rpt, S5795–1

New York State statistical yearbook, general data, 1992 annual rpt, U5100–1.12

North Carolina public utility financial, operating, and regulatory data, by utility type and company, 1990 and trends, annual rpt, S5917–2

North Dakota gas production, 1983-92, annual rpt, S6162–1

Ohio natural gas and electricity supply-demand by utility and consuming sector, 1992-93 and trends, annual rpt, S6355–1

Oklahoma business activity indicators, monthly rpt, U8130–1

Oklahoma statistical abstract, general data, 1992 annual rpt, U8130–2.12, U8130–2.18

Pennsylvania energy supply-demand and prices by fuel type, with electric power info by utility, 1960s-90, recurring rpt, S6810–3

Pennsylvania statistical abstract, general data, 1992 recurring rpt, U4130–6.9

South Carolina economic condition, including energy and transportation data, 1970s-92, annual rpt, S7125–3.3

South Carolina public service commission regulatory activities, with financial and operating data for individual utilities and railroads, FY92 annual rpt, S7235–1

South Carolina statistical abstract, general data, 1993 annual rpt, S7125–1.8

Tennessee public utility and transportation commission regulatory activities, with industry financial and operating data, 1991-92 biennial rpt, S7565–1

Tennessee statistical abstract, general data, 1992/93 annual rpt, U8710–2.5, U8710–2.10

Texas natural gas utility financial and operating data, by city and company, 1991, with regulatory info, annual rpt, S7745–1

Texas trade, transportation, and public utilities employment, by SIC 2- and 3-digit industry and detailed occupation, 2nd qtr 1991, triennial survey rpt, S7675–1.31

Utah economic and business activity review and indicators, monthly rpt, U8960–2

Utah statistical abstract, general data, 1993 triennial rpt, U8960–1.10, U8960–1.13

Vermont public utility financial and operating data, by company, 1986-91, biennial rpt, S8100–1

Washington State natural gas utility financial and operating data, by company, 1982-91, annual rpt, S8450–1.3

Washington State public service and utility companies property value, by company and county, 1992, annual rpt, S8415–1.4

West Virginia oil and gas production, 1981-90, annual rpt, R9385–1.7

Wyoming natural gas production and taxable valuation, by county, and severance and ad valorem taxes, FY92 annual rpt, S8990–1.2

see also Energy exploration and drilling
see also Liquefied petroleum gas
see also Natural gas exports and imports
see also Natural gas liquids
see also Natural gas pipelines
see also Natural gas prices
see also Natural gas reserves
see also Offshore oil and gas
see also Oil and gas leases

Natural gas exports and imports

Asia-Pacific region liquefied natural gas trading contracts, with deliveries, prices, and countries involved, 1992 article, C6985–1.503

Canada natural gas exports to US for cogeneration plants, 1989/90-1995/96, article, C6985–1.536

Canada natural gas production outlook to 2010, domestic use and foreign trade, and exports to US via 8 delivery points, 1993 article, C6985–1.529

Commonwealth of Independent States natural gas exports and imports, with detail by Republic and trading partner, 1993 article, C6985–1.514

Exports and imports of natural gas for US and selected other countries, 1970s-91, annual rpt, A1775–3.2

Germany natural gas supply from domestic and selected foreign sources, 1992, article, C6780–1.504

Imports, exports, production, and other industry trends, 1950-92, annual rpt, A5425–1.1

Intl energy sourcebook, including natural gas exports and imports, for selected countries, 1980-91, annual compilation, C6985–10.2

Liquefied natural gas imports, and natural gas trade through pipelines and tankers, by country, 1980s-91, annual rpt, C6985–3.3

Liquefied natural gas trade by country and outlook, and trading contracts in effect with participants, 1993 article, C6985–1.535

Outlook for natural gas production, trade, and prices, 1970s-2001, annual rpt, C6985–5.2

Production, exploration, refining, demand, finance, prices, and reserves, by State and country or world area, 1993 and trends, periodic basic data book, A2575–14.6

Soviet Union former Republics natural gas imports and exports, by Republic and selected trading partners, 1992, article, C6985–1.551

Statistical compilation of oil and gas industry trends, 1993 annual rpt, C6985–4

Supply-demand data, including natural gas imports and exports, 1973-92, annual rpt, A5425–2.1

Supply-demand, trade, and industry exploration and operations, by product, exporting country and world area, PAD district, and State, 1993 annual feature, C6985–1.513

Supply of natural gas, including Canadian exports, 1992, 2000, and 2005, article, C6985–1.527

World oil, gas, and refined product stocks, trade, and consumption, by country and world area, 1991 and trends, annual compilation, C6985–9.2

Natural gas liquids

Crude oil, natural gas, and gas liquids reserves and reserves/production ratios, 1973-92, annual rpt, A5425–2.1

Intl energy sourcebook, with detail on oil and gas industry operations, supply-demand, and prices, for approx 80 countries, 1970s-91, annual compilation, C6985–10

Japan energy supply-demand and outlook, by fuel source, 1980s-2000, recurring article, R5650–2.536

Norway offshore reserves of oil, gas, and natural gas liquids, for 5 new fields, with operator and location, 1993 article, C6985–2.509

Operating and financial detailed data, for natural gas industry, by State and census div, 1960s-91, annual rpt, A1775–3

Processing plants, capacity, and production, by company, State, and country, 1993 annual rpt, C6985–1.537

Production and reserves of natural gas liquids, gas processed, and tanker fleet, 1992 annual rpt, C6985–5

Production, exploration, drilling, refining, stock, price, and financial data for US and foreign oil and gas industry, weekly rpt, C6985–1

Production, exploration, refining, demand, finance, prices, and reserves, by State and country or world area, 1993 and trends, periodic basic data book, A2575–14.4, A2575–14.6

Production, finances, exploration, reserves, and other data for oil/gas industry, by State, 1992 and trends, annual rpt, A5425–1

Production, reserves, and financial and operating data, for approx 20 major oil companies, 1991-92, annual article, C6985–1.533

Reserves of crude oil, natural gas, and gas liquids, 1991-92, annual article, C6985–1.549

Sourcebook of oil and gas industry operations and finances, and world supply-demand situation, 1970s-91, annual compilation, C6985–9

Statistical compilation of oil and gas industry trends, 1993 annual rpt, C6985–4

Supply-demand for crude oil and petroleum products, quarterly 1993, annual article, C4680–1.503

Supply-demand, trade, and industry exploration and operations, by product, exporting country and world area, PAD district, and State, 1993 annual feature, C6985–1.513

Supply, disposition, and stocks of refined oil products by type and/or crude oil, and refinery operations summary, monthly rpt, A2575–2

State and local:

Alabama statistical abstract, general data, 1992 recurring rpt, U5680–2.12

Natural gas pipelines

Construction costs, mileage, and operating and financial data, by location and/or company, 1991 and trends, annual feature, C6985–1.504

Construction mileage of natural gas transmission pipeline planned, 1993-97, article, C6780–2.503

Construction mileage planned, 1993-97, article, C6985–1.535

Construction of gas and other pipeline facilities, and gas utility operations, articles and special features, monthly rpt, C6780–1

Construction of oil and gas pipelines, mileage planned or underway in 1993, for 5 world areas, Canada, and US, annual article, C6985–1.515

Construction of pipelines, by country and company, weekly rpt semiannual list, C6985–1.524, C6985–1.551

Construction projects planned in foreign countries, for oil, gas, and product pipelines, by company, 1994, annual feature, C6780–2.504

FERC order stopping natural gas pipelines from offering merchant services to end users, costs of compliance for pipelines, 1993 article, C6985–1.541

Financial and operating data for top 500 gas distribution utilities and pipeline companies, 1992, annual article, C6780–1.505

Financial performance and growth rankings for approx 1,000 top corporations, with comparisons by industry group, 1993 annual rpt, C3950–1.505

Foreign pipeline mileage, by country, 1989, annual rpt, A1775–3.2

Installation of new and replacement pipelines by gas utilities, 1990-93, annual article, C6780–1.501

Mileage operating and under construction, and transmission expenses, 1993 annual rpt, C6985–3.3

Miles of gas pipelines by type, and compressor stations, 1991 and trends, periodic basic data book, A2575–14.5

Occupational injury, illness, and employment data, by function, for 136 oil/gas companies, 1991, annual rpt, A2575–4

Oil and gas industry trends, with data by company, State, and country, 1993 annual compilation, C6985–4

Production of natural gas by interstate natural gas pipeline companies, and distribution, revenues, and pipelines installed, by State, 1960s-91, annual rpt, A1775–3

Russia natural gas govt-owned company operations, with former Soviet Union supply-demand, foreign trade, and pipeline mileage by Republic, 1993 article, C6985–1.551

Natural gas pipelines

Southwest US natural gas prices, approx 15 pipelines in 4 States, weekly rpt monthly table, C6985–1

Utility regulatory agency policies and practices, and industry financial and operating data, by utility type and agency, 1991/92 annual rpt, A7015–3

Western States natural gas pipeline project construction spending, jobs created, and property tax benefits, for 4 States, 1992 article, C6780–2.501

State and local:

Arizona statistical abstract, general data, 1993 recurring rpt, U5850–2.20

Arkansas oil and gas production by field, and disposition, monthly rpt, S0737–1

Colorado property assessed valuation, by property type and county, and for regulated industries by company, 1991-92, annual rpt, S1055–3

South Carolina public service commission regulatory activities, with financial and operating data for individual utilities and railroads, FY92 annual rpt, S7235–1

Tennessee public utility and transportation commission regulatory activities, with industry financial and operating data, 1991-92 biennial rpt, S7565–1

Texas gas utility plants in service by type, and pipeline miles, by company, 1991, annual rpt, S7745–1

Utah statistical abstract, general data, 1993 triennial rpt, U8960–1.13

Natural gas prices

Commonwealth of Independent States natural gas supply-demand, and price trends, 1993 article, C6985–1.515

Electric utility gas deliveries and prices, monthly rpt, A7400–9

Industrial electric power and natural gas costs, by State, 1991 or 1992, article, C5800–12.512

OECD natural gas prices, by consumer sector and selected member country, 1978-89, annual compilation, C6985–10.1

Outlook for natural gas production, trade, and prices, 1970s-2001, annual rpt, C6985–5.2

Price averages, by consuming sector and census div, quarterly rpt, A1775–1

Prices by consuming sector and region, monthly rpt, A1775–2

Prices of natural gas in major producing States, 1992 and trends, annual rpt, A5425–1

Production, exploration, refining, demand, finance, prices, and reserves, by State and country or world area, 1993 periodic basic data book, A2575–14.3, A2575–14.6

Retail and wellhead prices, and residential gas bills and consumption, by sector, State, and census div, 1960s-92, annual rpt, A1775–3.5

Southwest US natural gas prices, approx 15 pipelines in 4 States, weekly rpt monthly table, C6985–1

Statistical compilation of oil and gas industry trends, 1993 annual rpt, C6985–4

Utility regulatory agency policies and practices, and industry financial and operating data, by utility type and agency, 1991/92 annual rpt, A7015–3

Wellhead and consumer prices, 1925-91, annual rpt, C6985–3.4

Wellhead and delivered commercial natural gas average prices, 1976-92, annual feature, C6985–1.513

Wellhead and end-use prices by consuming sector, 1973-92, annual rpt, A5425–2.2

Wellhead, import, spot market, retail, and wholesale prices, for oil, gas, and refined products, 1991 and trends, annual compilation, C6985–9.3

State and local:

Alaska public utility financial and operating data, by company and utility type, 1991 and trends, with FY92 regulatory info, annual rpt, S0280–4

Delaware data book, general data, 1993 annual rpt, S1375–4

Florida public utility regulatory and operating data, by company and utility type, 1992 and trends, annual rpt, S1790–1

Georgia statistical abstract, general data, 1992-93 biennial rpt, U6730–1.8

Hawaii data book, general data, 1992 annual rpt, S2090–1.17

Idaho average residential electric and gas bill, by utility, FY92 and trends, annual rpt, S2290–1

Idaho economic profile, general data, 1992 recurring rpt, S2218–2.6

New Mexico public utility operating, financial, and regulatory data, by utility type, FY92 annual rpt, S5645–1

New York State natural gas customers, revenues, sales, and average bill, by customer class, 1988-92, annual rpt, S5795–1

Ohio natural gas prices, by consuming sector, 1972-91, annual rpt, S6355–1

Oklahoma statistical abstract, general data, 1992 annual rpt, U8130–2.12, U8130–2.18

Pennsylvania energy supply-demand and prices by fuel type, with electric power info by utility, 1960s-90, recurring rpt, S6810–3

South Carolina economic condition, including energy and transportation data, 1970s-92, annual rpt, S7125–3.3

Tennessee statistical abstract, general data, 1992/93 annual rpt, U8710–2.10

Texas natural gas utility financial and operating data, by city and company, 1991, with regulatory info, annual rpt, S7745–1

Natural gas reserves

Africa (West) natural gas reserves, for 7 countries, 1993 article, C6985–2.504

Canada (Western) natural gas reserves, by location and stratigraphic age, 1993 article, C6985–1.546

Canada (Western) natural gas resources, by stratigraphic formation, 1993, article, C6985–1.552

Canada, Newfoundland offshore oil and gas resources discovered, by field, 1993 article, C6985–1.552

Commonwealth of Independent States natural gas reserves, by Republic, 1993 article, C6985–1.514

Commonwealth of Independent States oil and gas production and reserves, for 7 Republics, 1991, article, C6985–1.510

Crude oil, natural gas, and gas liquids reserves, 1991-92, annual article, C6985–1.549

Index by Subjects and Names

Gulf of Mexico offshore oil and gas production and reserves, 1970s-2000, annual article, C6985–2.503

Gulf of Mexico oil and gas fields, reserves, and production, by location and stratigraphic formation, 1991, article, C6985–1.508

Gulf of Mexico oil and gas reserves, 1960s-90, annual compilation, C6985–9.4

Intl energy sourcebook, with detail on oil and gas industry operations, supply-demand, and prices, for approx 80 countries, 1970s-91, annual compilation, C6985–10

Intl Petroleum Encyclopedia, basic data on oil and gas supply-demand, exploration, refining, reserves, and industry finances, by country and company, 1993 annual rpt, C6985–3

Latin America statistical abstract, general data by country, 1992 annual rpt, U6250–1.23

Middle East offshore oil and gas reserves and production, for 12 countries, 1992, article, C6985–2.505

New and total reserves of oil and gas, by State, 1992 and trends, annual rpt, A5425–1.1

Norway offshore oil and gas fields under dev, with reserves and capital outlays, by field, 1993 article, C6985–1.523

Norway offshore reserves of oil, gas, and natural gas liquids, for 5 new fields, with operator and location, 1993 article, C6985–2.509

Oil and gas industry trends, with data by company, State, and country, 1993 annual compilation, C6985–4

Potential natural gas reserves in 7 regions, Dec 1992 and trends, biennial rpt, R8765–1

Potential natural gas resources from field gas, coalbed methane, and proved reserves, 1990 and 1992, biennial article, C6985–1.534

Production, exploration, refining, demand, finance, prices, and reserves, by State and country or world area, 1993 and trends, periodic basic data book, A2575–14.2, A2575–14.6

Production, reserves, and financial and operating data, for approx 20 major oil companies, 1991-92, annual article, C6985–1.533

Proved reserves, and conventional and nonconventional resources, Jan 1991, article, C6985–1.509

Proved reserves of natural gas, coal, and oil, with detail by State, 1960s-91, annual rpt, A1775–3.1

Recoverable resources by region and category, with supply-demand outlook to 2005, 1993 article, C6985–1.527

Reserves of crude oil, natural gas, and gas liquids, 1973-92, annual rpt, A5425–2.1

Reserves of liquids and natural gas, rankings for top 300 US and top 100 non-US oil and gas companies, 1991-92, annual feature, C6985–1.547

Supply-demand outlook and industry operations, with trends by country and producing State, 1970s-2010, annual rpt, C6985–5

UK offshore gas field dev in southern North Sea, with operator, reserves, and production rate, 1993 article, C6985–2.505

World natural gas proved reserves, by country and world region, Jan 1993, annual feature, C6985–1.509

World natural gas reserves and supply distances to Germany, by selected country or area, Jan 1993, article, C6780–1.504

World oil and gas reserves, by country and US State, 1940s-92, annual compilation, C6985–9.1

World reserves by country, Dec 1992, annual article, C6985–1.537

World reserves, with OPEC, OECD, and former Soviet Union shares, 1992, article, A1250–1.540

State and local:

New York State statistical yearbook, general data, 1992 annual rpt, U5100–1.12

Pennsylvania natural gas industry proven and stored recoverable reserves, 1988-90, recurring rpt, S6810–3

Natural resources

Congressional campaign finances, with detailed data for individual Members, and leading contributors by type and industry, 1990 election and trends, biennial rpt, R3828–2.2

Executives in energy/natural resource industry, compensation and components, 1991, annual rpt, R4105–19

Foundation assets, income, and grants by type of recipient, with data for top organizations and by location, 1991 and trends, annual rpt, R4900–1

State and local:

Colorado property assessed valuation, and summary production data, by county, 1991-92, annual rpt, S1055–3

Virginia income tax return checkoff contributions to recreation/conservation fund, 1990, annual rpt, S8305–1.1

West Virginia courts natural resources case filings and dispositions, 1992, annual rpt, S8537–1

see also Conservation of natural resources

see also Energy resources

see also Fish and fishing industry

see also Forests and forestry

see also Geothermal resources

see also Marine resources

see also Mines and mineral resources

see also Plants and vegetation

see also Reclamation of land

see also Severance taxes

see also State funding for energy programs

see also State funding for natural resources and conservation

see also Strategic materials

see also Water power

see also Water resources development

see also Water supply and use

Naturalization

see Citizenship

Naturopathy

see Chiropractic and naturopathy

Naval bases

see Military bases, posts, and reservations

Naval contracts and procurement

see Defense contracts and procurement

Naval stores

see Gum and wood chemicals

Naval vessels

Latin America statistical abstract, general data by country, 1992 annual rpt, U6250–1.11

Shipbuilding (naval vessel) activity in private shipyards, including contracts, deliveries, and ongoing construction, 1993 recurring rpt, A8900–6

Navigation

Financial ratios and performance, for over 350 SIC 4-digit industries, FY88-92, annual rpt, A6400–3

Shipment value, employment, and foreign trade, for electronics industry, by sector and product type, 1980s-92, annual rpt, A4725–1.2

see also Aeronautical navigation

see also Lighthouses and lightships

see also Marine accidents and safety

see also Radar

Navy

Computer costs and processor speed, for Navy tactical advanced computers by generation, 1993 article, C5800–4.521

Physicians in Fed Govt, by detailed specialty and service branch, 1992, annual rpt, A2200–3.2

Post exchange and commissary sales, by product category, for military resale agencies, FY89-91, annual rpt, A2072–1

Post exchange sales, by service branch, with merchandising devs and comparisons to civilian retail trade, monthly rpt, C0500–1

Post exchange sales, retail and other, by location and store, FY92 and trends, annual rpt, A2072–2.502

see also Marine Corps

see also Naval vessels

Near East

see Middle East

Nebraska

Agricultural production, marketing, and finances, by commodity and/or county, and farms and acreage, 1991 and trends, annual rpt, S4835–1

Business and economic activity indicators, monthly rpt, U7860–1

Correctional instn admin, with inmates by criminal background and demographic characteristics, by instn, FY92 and trends, annual rpt, S4850–1

Court cases and dispositions, by type of court and case, and location, 1992 and trends, annual rpt, S4965–2

Election results, and voter registration by party, by county and/or district, 1992 general and primary elections, biennial rpt, S4955–1

Elementary and secondary schools, enrollment by grade, and staff, with data by school district and county, annual series, S4865–2

Elementary/secondary school finances, including receipts by source and disbursements by function, by county and district, 1988/89, annual rpt, S4865–3

Employment, hours, and earnings, by selected industry group and locality, quarterly rpt, S4895–2

Govt financial condition, including revenues by source, expenditures by function and agency, and fund balances, FY92, annual rpt, S4825–1

Insurance industry financial and underwriting data, by company and line of coverage, with regulatory info, 1992, annual rpt, S4890–1

Library finances, holdings, circulation, staff, and population served, by instn, FY91, annual rpt, S4910–1

Markets with daily newspapers, demographic and economic info by geographic area, US and Canada, 1993 annual rpt, C3250–1

Oil/gas industry production, finances, exploration, and reserves, by State, 1992 and trends, annual rpt, A5425–1.1

Regulatory activities of public service commission, with financial and operating data for individual railroads and telephone companies, FY91-92 biennial rpt, S4940–1

Statistical handbook of Nebraska, discontinued biennial rpt, S4855–1

Statistical profiles of 50 States and DC, general data, 1993 annual almanac, C4712–1

Tax revenues by type, tax rates and exemptions, and aid distribution to local areas, with data by county and city, 1991, annual rpt, S4950–1

Traffic accidents, fatalities, and injuries, by circumstances, location, vehicle type, and driver and victim characteristics, 1992, annual rpt, S4953–1

Utility and transportation regulatory agency activities, scope of jurisdiction, finances, and employees, by agency, 1991/92 annual rpt, A7015–2

Vital statistics, including births, deaths, marriages, divorces, and population, by demographic characteristics and location, 1991 and trends, annual rpt, S4885–1

Welfare cases, recipients, and payments, by program and county, FY92 and trends, annual rpt, S4957–1

see also Lincoln, Nebr.

see also Omaha, Nebr.

see also under By City and By County in the "Index by Categories"

see also under By State in the "Index by Categories"

Neff, Peter J.

"Washington's Largest Monument: The National Debt", R9050–15.1

Negotiable orders of withdrawal accounts

State and local:

Maine financial instn assets, deposits, and loans, by type of instn and county, 1982-92, annual rpt, S3473–1

Negotiations

see Labor-management relations, general

see Labor-management relations in government

see Legal arbitration and mediation

see Treaties and conventions

Negroes

see Black Americans

Neighborhoods

Homeowner views on characteristics and attributes of "traditional neighborhood development" housing, 1993 survey, article, C4300–1.510

State and local:

Hawaii, Oahu neighborhood characteristics, 1992 annual rpt, S2090–1.1, S2090–1.8

see also Census tracts

see also Wards, city

Nelson, F. Howard

"International Comparison of Public Spending on Education", A1600–4

Neoplasms

Index by Subjects and Names

Neoplasms

Black American health and vital statistics data, with comparisons to whites, 1970s-91, annual compilation, C6775–2.2

Catholic facilities for health care and social services, including cancer hospitals, 1993 annual almanac, C6885–1

Contraceptive (oral) use correlation with risks of ovarian, endometrial, cervical, and breast cancers, 1993 article, A5160–1.502

Deaths from cancer, and lung cancer rates, by race-ethnicity and sex, 1993 feature, C4215–1.511

Hospital patient admission rates and length of stay, by diagnosis and procedure, payment source, age, sex, and region, 1991, B4455–4

Hospital patient charges and length of stay, by diagnosis and procedure, payment source, age, and region, 1991, B4455–5

Hospital patient discharges and length of stay, by diagnosis, type of operation, age, and region, 1991, annual rpt series, B4455–1

Hospital patient discharges and length of stay, by diagnostic related group (DRG), payment source, age, and region, 1991, annual rpt series, B4455–3

Hospitals with accredited cancer treatment programs, 1985-92, article, A1865–1.503

Incidence and related deaths, including data by State, sex, and body site, 1993 and trends, annual rpt, A1175–1

Public opinion on possibility of cure for cancer, June 1993 Gallup Poll, C4040–1.512

State economic dev condition indicators, including economic performance, business vitality, growth capacity, and tax/fiscal system, by State, 1993 annual rpt, R4225–1.1

Urinary tract cancer death rates for men age 45-84, by age, State, and census div, 1979-89, article, B6045–1.503

Water chlorination exposure correlated with cancer risk, errata, A2623–1.511

Women's deaths from breast cancer correlated with occupation, by race, 1979-87, article, A2623–1.511

State and local:

Alabama vital statistics, including population, births, deaths by cause, marriages, and divorces, by location and demographic characteristics, 1992 and trends, annual rpt, S0175–2

Alaska vital statistics, including births, deaths by cause, marriages, divorces, adoptions, and population, by demographic characteristics and location, 1990, annual rpt, S0315–1

Arkansas vital statistics, including births, deaths by cause, marriages, and divorces, by age, sex, race, and county, 1991 and trends, annual rpt, S0685–1

California vital statistics, including population, births, and deaths by cause, by demographic characteristics and county, 1990 and trends, annual rpt, S0865–1

Colorado vital statistics, including population, births, deaths by cause, abortion, marriage and divorce, and adoption, by demographic characteristics and location, 1990 and trends, annual rpt, S1010–1

Connecticut vital statistics, including births, deaths by cause, marriages, and divorces, by demographic characteristics and location, 1989, annual rpt, S1200–1

Delaware vital statistics, including births, deaths by cause, and marriages and dissolutions, by demographic characteristics and location, 1990, annual rpt, S1385–2

Florida deaths by selected cause, and incidence of selected communicable diseases, by county, 1992 annual rpt, S1746–1.1

Florida vital statistics, including population, births, deaths by cause, and marriages and dissolutions, by location and demographic characteristics, 1992 and trends, annual rpt, S1745–3

Georgia vital statistics, including deaths by cause, demographic characteristics, and location, 1991 and trends, annual rpt, S1895–1.2

Hawaii health dept activities and services, including vital statistics and disease control, by location, 1990, annual rpt, S2065–1

Idaho vital statistics, including births, deaths by cause, abortions, marriages, and divorces, by demographic characteristics and county, 1991 and trends, annual rpt, S2250–2

Iowa vital statistics, including population, births, deaths by cause, marriages, and divorces, by demographic characteristics and location, 1991 and trends, annual rpt, S2795–1

Kansas vital statistics, including population, births, deaths by cause, abortions, marriages, and divorces, by demographic characteristics and location, 1991 and trends, annual rpt, S2975–1

Kentucky vital statistics, including births, deaths by cause, marriages and divorces, and population, by demographic characteristics and county, 1991, annual rpt, S3140–1

Louisiana vital statistics, including population, births, deaths by cause, reportable diseases, marriages, and divorces, by demographic characteristics and locality, 1989-90 and trends, annual rpt, S3295–1

Maine vital statistics, including births, deaths by cause, abortions, and marriages and divorces, by demographic characteristics and location, 1991 and trends, annual rpt, S3460–2

Maryland vital statistics, including population, births, deaths by cause, marriages, and divorces, by demographic characteristics and location, 1989 and trends, annual rpt, S3635–1

Massachusetts vital statistics, including births, deaths by cause, marriages, divorces, and population, by locality and demographic characteristics, 1990 and trends, annual rpt, S3850–1

Michigan vital statistics, including births, deaths, marriages, divorces/annulments, and communicable diseases, by location and demographic characteristics, 1990 and trends, annual rpt, S4000–3

Minnesota vital statistics, including population, births, abortions, deaths, marriages, and divorces, by location and demographic characteristics, 1991 and trends, annual rpt, S4190–2

Mississippi vital statistics, including births, deaths by cause, marriages, and divorces, by demographic characteristics and location, 1992 and trends, annual rpt, S4350–1

Missouri vital statistics, including population, births, deaths by cause, and marriages and divorces, by location and demographic characteristics, 1992 and trends, annual rpt, S4518–1

Montana vital statistics, including births, deaths by cause, abortion, disease, and marriage and divorce, by demographic characteristics and county, 1990-91 and trends, annual rpt, S4690–1

Nebraska vital statistics, including births, deaths, marriages, divorces, and population, by demographic characteristics and location, 1991 and trends, annual rpt, S4885–1

Nevada vital statistics, including births, abortions, and deaths by cause, by county and demographic characteristics, 1989 and trends, annual rpt, S5075–1

New Hampshire vital statistics, including population, births, deaths by cause, marriages, and divorces, by location and demographic characteristics, 1991 and trends, annual rpt, S5215–1

New Jersey vital statistics, including births, deaths, population, communicable diseases, and marriages and divorces, by demographic characteristics and location, 1990 and trends, annual rpt, S5405–1

New Mexico vital statistics, including population, births, deaths, and disease, by location and demographic characteristics, 1991 and trends, annual rpt, S5605–1

New York State health behavior risk factor surveillance survey results, by respondent characteristics, 1990, recurring rpt, S5765–3

New York State vital statistics, including population, births, deaths by cause, reportable diseases, and marriages and dissolutions, by demographic characteristics and/or location, 1990 and trends, annual rpt, S5765–1

North Carolina deaths and rates, by cause and county, 1991 and trends, annual rpt, S5927–1.2

North Dakota vital statistics, including births, deaths by cause, marriages and divorces, and abortions, by demographic characteristics and/or county, 1991 and trends, annual rpt, S6105–2

Ohio vital statistics, including births, deaths by cause, marriages, divorces, and population, by demographic characteristics and location, 1991 and trends, annual rpt, S6285–1

Oregon vital statistics, including births, deaths by cause, communicable diseases, marriages, and divorces, by age, sex, race-ethnicity, and county, 1991 and trends, annual rpt, S6615–5

Rhode Island vital statistics, including population, births, deaths, marriages, and divorces, by demographic characteristics and locality, 1989 and trends, annual rpt, S6995–1

South Carolina deaths, by detailed cause, age, sex, and race, 1990, annual rpt, S7175–2

South Carolina vital statistics, including births, deaths by cause, marriages, and divorces, by age, sex, race, and location, 1990 and trends, annual rpt, S7175–1

South Dakota vital statistics, including births, deaths, marriage and divorce, and communicable disease, by demographic characteristics and county, 1991 and trends, annual rpt, S7345–1

Tennessee vital statistics, including births, deaths by cause, marriages, divorces, and population, by demographic characteristics and location, 1991 and trends, annual rpt, S7520–2

Texas vital statistics, including births, deaths by cause, abortions, marriages, and divorces, by location and demographic characteristics, 1991 and trends, annual rpt, S7685–1

Utah vital statistics, including births, deaths by cause, and population, by county and demographic characteristics, 1990 and trends, annual rpt, S7835–1

Vermont vital statistics, including population, births, deaths by cause, abortions, marriages, and divorces, by location and demographic characteristics, 1991 and trends, annual rpt, S8054–1

Virginia vital statistics, including births, deaths by cause, marriages and divorces, and communicable disease, by demographic characteristics and location, 1991 and trends, annual rpt, S8225–1

Washington State vital statistics, including births, deaths by cause, and population, by demographic characteristics and location, 1991 and trends, annual rpt, S8363–1

West Virginia vital statistics, including births, deaths by cause, marriages, and divorces, by location and demographic characteristics, 1991 and trends, annual rpt, S8560–1

Wisconsin vital statistics, including population, births, deaths by cause, and marriages and dissolutions, by county and demographic characteristics, 1991 and trends, annual rpt, S8715–4

Wyoming vital statistics, including population, births, deaths by cause, marriages, and divorces, by demographic characteristics and county, 1991 and trends, annual rpt, S8920–2

see also Carcinogens

see also Mammography

see also under By Disease in the "Index by Categories"

Nephritis and nephrosis

see Urogenital diseases

Nervous system

see Neurological disorders

Netherlands

Coal industry supply-demand, employment, and trade, by country, 1990-91 and trends, annual rpt, A7400–2.2

Commercial real estate market conditions and outlook, for industrial and office properties, by US metro area and selected foreign city, 1992-93, annual survey, A8916–1

Diabetes incidence forecasts through 2005, article, A2623–1.509

Electronics industry trade and/or production trends by product category for 33 countries, with general economic profiles, 1993 annual rpt, A4725–1.4

Energy intl sourcebook, with detail on oil and gas industry operations, supply-demand, and prices, for approx 80 countries, 1970s-91, annual compilation, C6985–10.2

Motor vehicle world production, sales, trade, and registrations, by country, world area, manufacturer, and make, 1991 and trends, annual rpt, A0865–2.1

Nuclear reactors in operation, with capacity, electricity generation, and construction, by unit and country, 1992, annual rpt, B6800–2.2

Silver supply-demand by country and end use, with prices, futures trading, and market analyses, 1993 and trends, annual rpt, A8902–4

Networks

see Computer networks

see Information storage and retrieval systems

see Public broadcasting

see Radio

see Television

Neurological disorders

Hospital patient admission rates and length of stay, by diagnosis and procedure, payment source, age, sex, and region, 1991, B4455–4

Hospital patient charges and length of stay, by diagnosis and procedure, payment source, age, and region, 1991, B4455–5

Hospital patient discharges and length of stay, by diagnosis, type of operation, age, and region, 1991, annual rpt series, B4455–1

Hospital patient discharges and length of stay, by diagnostic related group (DRG), payment source, age, and region, 1991, annual rpt series, B4455–3

State and local:

Arkansas vital statistics, including births, deaths by cause, marriages, and divorces, by age, sex, race, and county, 1991 and trends, annual rpt, S0685–1

California vital statistics, including population, births, and deaths by cause, by demographic characteristics and county, 1990 and trends, annual rpt, S0865–1

Florida vital statistics, including population, births, deaths by cause, and marriages and dissolutions, by location and demographic characteristics, 1992 and trends, annual rpt, S1745–3

Georgia vital statistics, including deaths by cause, demographic characteristics, and location, 1991 and trends, annual rpt, S1895–1.2

Idaho vital statistics, including births, deaths by cause, abortions, marriages, and divorces, by demographic characteristics and county, 1991 and trends, annual rpt, S2250–2

Iowa vital statistics, including population, births, deaths by cause, marriages, and divorces, by demographic characteristics and location, 1991 and trends, annual rpt, S2795–1

Louisiana traumatic brain and spinal cord injuries, by cause, 1991, annual rpt, S3345–2

Maine vital statistics, including births, deaths by cause, abortions, and marriages and divorces, by demographic characteristics and location, 1991 and trends, annual rpt, S3460–2

Massachusetts vital statistics, including births, deaths by cause, marriages, divorces, and population, by locality and demographic characteristics, 1990 and trends, annual rpt, S3850–1

Michigan vital statistics, including births, deaths, marriages, divorces/annulments, and communicable diseases, by location and demographic characteristics, 1990 and trends, annual rpt, S4000–3

Minnesota vital statistics, including population, births, abortions, deaths, marriages, and divorces, by location and demographic characteristics, 1991 and trends, annual rpt, S4190–2

Mississippi vital statistics, including births, deaths by cause, marriages, and divorces, by demographic characteristics and location, 1992 and trends, annual rpt, S4350–1

Montana vital statistics, including births, deaths by cause, abortion, disease, and marriage and divorce, by demographic characteristics and county, 1990-91 and trends, annual rpt, S4690–1

Oregon vital statistics, including births, deaths by cause, communicable diseases, marriages, and divorces, by age, sex, race-ethnicity, and county, 1991 and trends, annual rpt, S6615–5

Rhode Island vital statistics, including population, births, deaths, marriages, and divorces, by demographic characteristics and locality, 1989 and trends, annual rpt, S6995–1

South Carolina deaths, by detailed cause, age, sex, and race, 1990, annual rpt, S7175–2

Tennessee vital statistics, including births, deaths by cause, marriages, divorces, and population, by demographic characteristics and location, 1991 and trends, annual rpt, S7520–2

Vermont vital statistics, including population, births, deaths by cause, abortions, marriages, and divorces, by location and demographic characteristics, 1991 and trends, annual rpt, S8054–1

Washington State vital statistics, including births, deaths by cause, and population, by demographic characteristics and location, 1991 and trends, annual rpt, S8363–1

West Virginia vital statistics, including births, deaths by cause, marriages, and divorces, by location and demographic characteristics, 1991 and trends, annual rpt, S8560–1

Wisconsin vital statistics, including population, births, deaths by cause, and marriages and dissolutions, by county and demographic characteristics, 1991 and trends, annual rpt, S8715–4

see also Alzheimer's disease

see also Mental health and illness

see also Rabies

see also under By Disease in the "Index by Categories"

Nevada

Agricultural production, marketing, and finances, by county and commodity, and farms and acreage, 1992 and trends, annual rpt, S5010–1

Business and economic activity indicators, with comparisons to other Western States, 1980-91, annual rpt, U7920–2

Nevada

Casino finances and employment, by location and gaming revenue range, FY92, annual rpt, S5062–1

Economic indicators for 10 Western States, including forecasts from selected organizations, monthly rpt, U0282–2

Election results, and voter registration and turnout, by county, 1992 general election, biennial rpt, S5125–1

Elementary and secondary school enrollment, test scores, teachers, and finances, by school district, 1990/91 and trends, annual rpt, S5035–2

Employment, hours, and earnings, by industry, and unemployment by county, quarterly rpt, S5040–1

Govt financial condition, including fund revenues by source, expenditures by function, and bonded debt, FY92, annual rpt, S5025–1

Health behavior risk factor surveillance survey results, by location and respondent characteristics, 1991, annual rpt, S5075–3

Labor force conditions and outlook, with data by industry, MSA, and county, 1992 annual rpt, S5040–4

Library and staff directory for public and academic libraries, with data on holdings, operations, and finances, FY92, annual rpt, S5095–1

Markets with daily newspapers, demographic and economic info by geographic area, US and Canada, 1993 annual rpt, C3250–1

Oil/gas industry production, finances, exploration, and reserves, by State, 1992 and trends, annual rpt, A5425–1.1

Statistical abstract of Nevada, detailed social, govtl, and economic data, 1992 biennial rpt, S5005–1

Statistical profiles of 50 States and DC, general data, 1993 annual almanac, C4712–1

Traffic accidents, fatalities, and injuries, by circumstances, location, and vehicle type, 1992 and trends, annual rpt, S5140–1

Utility and transportation regulatory agency activities, scope of jurisdiction, finances, and employees, by agency, 1991/92 annual rpt, A7015–2

Vital statistics, including births, abortions, and deaths by cause, by county and demographic characteristics, 1989 and trends, annual rpt, S5075–1

see also Boulder City, Nev.
see also Carson City, Nev.
see also Clark County, Nev.
see also Douglas County, Nev.
see also Elko County, Nev.
see also Las Vegas, Nev.
see also Laughlin, Nev.
see also Reno, Nev.
see also Sparks, Nev.
see also Washoe County, Nev.
see also under By City and By County in the "Index by Categories"
see also under By State in the "Index by Categories"

New businesses

see Business formations

New England

see Northeast States

New Guinea

see Papua New Guinea

New Hampshire

Crimes and arrests, by offense, jurisdiction, and offender characteristics, 1991 and trends, annual rpt, S5250–2

Election results, by county and locality, 1992, biennial rpt, S5255–1

Elementary and secondary education statistics, with selected data by school district, annual rpt series, S5200–1

Employment, by SIC 2- and 3-digit industry and detailed occupation, series, S5205–2

Employment, unemployment, hours, and earnings, by industry and area, monthly rpt, S5205–1

Govt financial condition, with revenues by source, expenditures by function or object, and fund balances, FY92 and trends, annual rpt, S5175–1

Insurance industry financial data by company, 1991, with FY92 regulatory info, annual rpt, S5220–1

Labor force and population by race, sex, and age, and employment by industry div, statewide and by county, 1992 recurring rpt, S5205–7

Labor force planning rpt, including population, employment, socioeconomic conditions, and job service activities, by county, discontinued annual rpt, S5205–3

Labor force planning rpt, including population, employment, wages, and job service activities, by labor market area and MSA, discontinued annual rpt, S5205–6

Libraries (public) finances and operations, by library and/or location, 1991, annual rpt, S5227–1

Markets with daily newspapers, demographic and economic info by geographic area, US and Canada, 1993 annual rpt, C3250–1

Medical malpractice insurance State joint underwriting assn (JUA) financial condition, for 11 States, 1991, annual rpt, A0375–1

Statistical profiles of 50 States and DC, general data, 1993 annual almanac, C4712–1

Utility and transportation regulatory agency activities, scope of jurisdiction, finances, and employees, by agency, 1991/92 annual rpt, A7015–2

Vital statistics, including population, births, deaths by cause, marriages, and divorces, by location and demographic characteristics, 1991 and trends, annual rpt, S5215–1

see also Dover, N.H.
see also Manchester, N.H.
see also Nashua, N.H.
see also Portsmouth, N.H.
see also Rochester, N.H.
see also under By City and By County in the "Index by Categories"
see also under By State in the "Index by Categories"

New Jersey

Agricultural production, marketing, and finances, by commodity and/or county, and farms and acreage, 1986-91, annual rpt, S5350–1

Casino revenues and operations for 12 facilities, with State regulatory activities, 1992 and trends, annual rpt, S5360–1

Census of Population and Housing detailed findings, by county, 1990, S5425–19

Construction activity and costs, by location, 1991 and trends, annual rpt, S5425–3

Correctional instn inmates, by offense, sentence length, demographic characteristics, and instn, Dec 1991, annual rpt, S5370–1

Crimes and arrests, by offense, location, and offender characteristics, with law enforcement employment and assaults on officers, 1992 and trends, annual rpt, S5430–1

Economic indicators for New Jersey, including employment, building permits, and retail trade, monthly rpt, S5425–1

Election results and voter registration, by location, 1992 general election, annual rpt, S5440–1

Elementary and secondary public schools, enrollment, and student and staff characteristics, and nonpublic schools and enrollment, by county, 1991/92, annual rpt, S5385–1

Financial instns assets and liabilities, by instn, 1992 and trends, annual rpt, S5355–1

Govt financial condition, including revenues by source, expenditures by function, fund balances, and bonded debt, FY92, annual rpt, S5455–1

Hazardous waste site concerns and interactions with Federal and State govts, views of local health officials, Nov 1991 surveys, article, A2623–1.507

Higher education bachelor degrees awarded and starting salaries of college grads, by field of study, 1993 annual article, S5425–1.504

Insurance industry financial and underwriting data, by company and type of insurance, 1990, annual rpt, S5420–1

Library (public) finances, holdings, circulation, and staff, by county and library, 1991, annual rpt, S5385–2

Markets with daily newspapers, demographic and economic info by geographic area, US and Canada, 1993 annual rpt, C3250–1

Statistical data book for New Jersey municipalities and counties, general socioeconomic and govtl data, 1992 annual rpt, C4712–4

Statistical profiles of 50 States and DC, general data, 1993 annual almanac, C4712–1

Traffic accidents involving fatalities, by vehicle type, location, and circumstances, and driver and victim characteristics, 1992 and trends, annual rpt, S5430–2

Utility and transportation regulatory agency activities, scope of jurisdiction, finances, and employees, by agency, 1991/92 annual rpt, A7015–2

Vital statistics, including births, deaths, population, communicable diseases, and marriages and divorces, by demographic characteristics and location, 1990 and trends, annual rpt, S5405–1

Welfare cases, recipients, payments, and case processing, by program and county or city, monthly rpt, S5415–1

see also Montclair, N.J.
see also Turnersville, N.J.

Index by Subjects and Names

New York State

see also under By City and By County in the "Index by Categories"

see also under By State in the "Index by Categories"

New Mexico

Agricultural production, marketing, and finances, by commodity and county, with farms and acreage, 1991 and trends, annual rpt, S5530–1

Business and economic activity indicators for New Mexico, monthly rpt, U7980–1

Court cases and dispositions, by type of court and case, and location, with judicial system finances and personnel, FY92, annual rpt, S5623–1

Economic indicators for 10 Western States, including forecasts from selected organizations, monthly rpt, U0282–2

Election results, and voter registration by party, by location, 1992 general election, biennial rpt, S5655–1

Elementary/secondary school statistics, including grads, student test results, and finances, by school district, 1989/90-1991/92, annual rpt, S5575–4

Elementary/secondary school statistics, including students, teachers, and grads, by race-ethnicity and school district, discontinued annual rpt, S5575–2

Employment, hours, and earnings, by labor market area and industry, monthly rpt, S5624–2

Financial instns, financial and operating data by instn, with regulatory activities, 1992, annual rpt, S5652–1

Govt financial condition, including receipts by source, expenditures by agency and function, fund balances, and bonded debt, FY91, annual rpt, S5585–1

Labor force planning rpt, with population, employment by industry and occupation, and job applicants and openings, 1993 annual rpt, S5624–1

Library operations and finances, by instn, FY92, annual rpt, S5627–1

Markets with daily newspapers, demographic and economic info by geographic area, US and Canada, 1993 annual rpt, C3250–1

Oil and gas wells and footage drilled, by type of well, State, and offshore location, quarterly rpt, A2575–6

Oil/gas industry production, finances, exploration, and reserves, by State, 1992 and trends, annual rpt, A5425–1.1

Population by age, sex, county, and State region, 1980 and 1990, U7980–6

Public assistance cases, expenditures, and case processing, by program and county, monthly rpt, S5620–2

Statistical profiles of 50 States and DC, general data, 1993 annual almanac, C4712–1

Tax revenues and disbursements, with data by tax type, county, and city, FY91-92 and trends, annual rpt, S5660–1

Traffic accidents, fatalities, and injuries, by vehicle type, circumstances, location, and driver and victim characteristics, 1992 and trends, annual rpt, S5665–1

Utilities operating, financial, and regulatory data, by utility type, FY92 annual rpt, S5645–1

Utility and transportation regulatory agency activities, scope of jurisdiction, finances, and employees, by agency, 1991/92 annual rpt, A7015–2

Vital statistics, including population, births, deaths, and diseases, by location and demographic characteristics, 1991 and trends, annual rpt, S5605–1

see also Albuquerque, N.Mex.

see also Bernalillo County, N.Mex.

see also Las Cruces, N.Mex.

see also Santa Fe, N.Mex.

see also under By City and By County in the "Index by Categories"

see also under By State in the "Index by Categories"

New orders

see Business orders

New product introductions

see Marketing

New York City

Commercial building leasing activity, vacancies, rental rates, and construction, by city area, 1988-92, annual rpt, B2800–5

Correctional instn inmates released in New York State, by region of commitment, 1991 and trends, recurring rpt series, S5725–1

Correctional instns, inmates, staff, and cost of care, by instn, US and Canada, with operating summary by State or Province, 1992, annual directory, A1305–3

Court cases and dispositions, by type of court and case, and jurisdiction, 1991, annual rpt, S5730–1

CPI for NYC and Philadelphia metro areas, monthly rpt, S5425–1

Criminal justice activities, including crimes and arrests by offense and demographic characteristics, and court activity and corrections, 1991 and trends, annual rpt, S5760–3

Election results by borough, Nov 1992, biennial rpt, S5750–1

Election results for Federal offices and Governor, by State, county, major city, and party, with voter registration and turnout, 1992 and trends, biennial rpt, C2500–1

Elementary/secondary student reading performance in district with parental school selection compared to citywide results, 1972/73-1991/92, R3810–7

Employment, earnings, and hours, by industry group, monthly rpt, S5775–1

Engineers salaries by industry group, census div, selected metro area, and years since college degree, 1993, annual survey rpt, A0685–5

Engineers salaries by industry group, census div, selected metro area, degree level, and years since college degree, 1993, annual survey rpt, A0685–3

Health behavior risk factor surveillance survey results, 1990, recurring rpt, S5765–3

Hispanic American population by country of ethnic origin, and non-Hispanic population, 1980 and 1990, article, C4575–1.506

Money and securities market activity, and related indicators, biweekly rpt, B2000–1

Port Authority of New York/New Jersey operating revenues and net income, for 10 properties, 1992, article, C3950–1.511

Port of New York waterborne trade and air traffic, 1985-88, annual feature, S5735–2

Printing (prepress) industry conditions for NYC area, 1993 survey article, C1850–10.507

Printing industry devs, including sales trends and printer views on business conditions, 1992 feature, C1850–10.501

Public assistance and social service program statistics, by source of funds, 1991 and trends, annual rpt, S5800–2

Statistical yearbook of New York State, detailed social, govtl, and economic data, 1992 annual rpt, U5100–1

Traffic accidents, fatalities, and injuries, by circumstances, location, vehicle type, and driver and victim characteristics, 1991, annual rpt, S5790–1

Vital statistics, including population, births, deaths by cause, reportable diseases, and marriages and dissolutions, by demographic characteristics and/or location, 1990 and trends, annual rpt, S5765–1

see also under By City in the "Index by Categories"

New York State

Agricultural production, marketing, and finances, by commodity and/or county, and farms and acreage, 1992 and trends, annual rpt, S5700–1

Business activity indicators for New York State, quarterly rpt, S5735–2

Business and economic indicators, by MSA, county, and industry, 1980s-91, annual rpt, S5735–3

Child labor law violations reported by teenagers, 1988 survey, R8335–2

Correctional instn inmate characteristics for local jails/penitentiaries, by county, with facility capacity, 1991, annual rpt, S5724–2

Correctional instn inmates released, by criminal background, sentence, and demographic characteristics, 1991 and trends, recurring rpt series, S5725–1

Court cases and dispositions, by type of court and case, and jurisdiction, 1991, annual rpt, S5730–1

Criminal justice activities, including crimes and arrests by offense and demographic characteristics, and court activity and corrections, 1991 and trends, annual rpt, S5760–3

Election results by county and district, Nov 1992, biennial rpt, S5750–1

Electric utility demand-side mgmt expenditures, and resulting demand reductions, for 7 companies, 1993-94, article, C6985–6.505

Employment, earnings, and hours, by county, selected metro area, and industry group, monthly rpt, S5775–1

Fiscal conditions for New York and selected other States, including tax revenues, expenditures, and taxation of corporate profits, 1992 article, A8825–1.502

Govt financial condition, including revenues by source, expenditures by function, and fund balances, FY93, annual rpt, S5710–1

Health behavior risk factor surveillance survey results, by respondent characteristics, 1990, recurring rpt, S5765–3

Insurance industry devs, finances, and regulatory activity, 1990/91 and trends, annual rpt, S5770–3

New York State

Insurance industry financial and underwriting data, by company and line of coverage, 1991, annual rpt, S5770–2

Insurance industry premiums and loss ratios, by company and line of coverage, discontinued annual rpt, S5770–1

Juveniles incarcerated at State instns, with 1st-time admissions and custody prevalence rates, by sex, age, and race-ethnicity, 1991, A7575–1.13

Library finances, staff, holdings, and services, by library and county, 1991, annual rpt, S5745–2

Markets with daily newspapers, demographic and economic info by geographic area, US and Canada, 1993 annual rpt, C3250–1

Medical malpractice insurance State joint underwriting assn (JUA) financial condition, for 11 States, 1991, annual rpt, A0375–1

Oil/gas industry production, finances, exploration, and reserves, by State, 1992 and trends, annual rpt, A5425–1.1

Public assistance and social service program statistics, by State area and source of funds, 1991 and trends, annual rpt, S5800–2

Security equipment dealer views on State licensing law and criminal background checks for industry personnel, Aug 1992 survey, article, C1850–13.501

Statistical profiles for New York State municipalities and counties, socioeconomic and govtl data, 1993 annual rpt, C4712–7

Statistical profiles of 50 States and DC, general data, 1993 annual almanac, C4712–1

Statistical yearbook of New York State, detailed social, govtl, and economic data, 1992 annual rpt, U5100–1

Traffic accidents, fatalities, and injuries, by circumstances, location, vehicle type, and driver and victim characteristics, 1991 and trends, annual rpt, S5790–1

Utility and transportation regulatory agency activities, scope of jurisdiction, finances, and employees, by agency, 1991/92 annual rpt, A7015–2

Utility financial and operating data, by utility type and company, 1988-92, annual rpt, S5795–1

Vital statistics, including population, births, deaths by cause, reportable diseases, and marriages and dissolutions, by demographic characteristics and/or location, 1990 and trends, annual rpt, S5765–1

see also New York City

see also Niagara Falls, N.Y.

see also under By City and By County in the "Index by Categories"

see also under By State in the "Index by Categories"

New York Stock Exchange

Composite index and average daily volume, biweekly rpt, B2000–1

Securities listed and trading activities, 1940s-90, annual rpt, U5100–1.7

Trading activity on NYSE, including stock volume and prices, credit distribution, and member firm characteristics, 1992 and trends, annual fact book, B6625–1

Trading activity, with data on member firms and performance, periodic rpt, A8825–1

Trading volume, 1990-July 1993, article, C2710–2.516

see also Stock exchanges

see also Stockbrokers

see also the "Index by Issuing Sources" for publications covered by SRI

New Zealand

Economic indexes for US and other industrial countries, and leading and coincident indicators, monthly rpt, U1245–1

Economic indexes for US and selected other countries, composites of leading indicators, monthly rpt, R4105–6

Energy intl sourcebook, with detail on oil and gas industry operations, supply-demand, and prices, for approx 80 countries, 1970s-91, annual compilation, C6985–10.2

Higher education physical plant operations, costs, employment, salaries, and energy use, by instn and region, 1991/92, recurring rpt, A3183–1

Motor vehicle world production, sales, trade, and registrations, by country, world area, manufacturer, and make, 1991 and trends, annual rpt, A0865–2.1

see also under By Foreign Country or World Area in the "Index by Categories"

Newark, Del.

Population by age and sex, 1990-2020, recurring rpt, S1375–3

Newell, Charldean

"Financial Aspects of Police Liability", A5800–2.113

Newfoundland Province, Canada

Offshore oil and gas resources discovered, by field, 1993 article, C6985–1.552

Newman, Richard W.

"Annual Report of Labor Market Information, 1992, Utah", S7820–10

"Utah Employers, Employment and Wages by Size, 1992", S7820–1

News media

see Journalism

see Mass media

see Newspapers

see Periodicals

see Radio

see Television

Newspapers

Advertiser attempts to influence editorial content of newspapers, Jan 1992 survey of editors, article, C2710–1.508

Advertising expenditures by medium for top 100 advertisers, with comparisons to earnings and sales, and detail by product type and brand, 1991-92, annual rpt, C2710–1.547

Advertising expenditures in newspapers, with top advertisers, and top advertising agencies in billings, 1992, C2710–1.524

Advertising insert circulation and revenues, 1975-91, annual rpt, A4620–1.2

Canada daily newspaper circulation, by publication and city, 6-month periods ended Sept 1992 and Mar 1993, semiannual rpt, A3385–3.2

Capital expenditures by item, for US and Canadian newspapers, 1992-93, annual article, A8605–1.507

Catholic newspapers and circulation in US and Canada, 1992, annual almanac, C6885–1

Circulation for daily and Sunday editions of top 100 newspapers, 6-month period ended Mar 1993, semiannual article, C2710–1.526

Circulation for daily and Sunday editions of top 100 newspapers, 6-month period ended Sept 1992, semiannual article, C2710–1.502

Circulation for leading publications worldwide, and newsprint consumption, 1992 annual rpt, A8610–1

Circulation of daily newspapers in US and Canadian markets, 1993 annual rpt, C3250–1

Circulation of US and Canadian weekly newspapers, by publication and city, 6-month periods ended Sept 1992 and Mar 1993, semiannual rpt, A3385–3.3

Circulation of US daily newspapers, by publication and city, 6-month periods ended Sept 1992 and Mar 1993, semiannual rpt, A3385–3.1

Circulation, operations, and finances, US and Canada, 1940s-93, annual rpt, A8605–4

Circulation per household, and newsprint production and consumption data, US and Canada, monthly rpt, A1630–4

Consumption of newsprint by newspapers, with data for top 15 publications and companies, 1991 and trends, annual rpt, C3975–5.3

Consumption of newsprint by region and State, and circulation and advertising data, 1970s-92, annual rpt, A1630–8

Current event and issue coverage by TV and print news media, analysis of selected topics, bimonthly rpt, R3823–1

Executive compensation, by circulation size, for 5 positions, 1993 and trends, annual survey article, A8605–1.510

Financial ratios and performance, for over 350 SIC 4-digit industries, FY88-92, annual rpt, A6400–3

Latin America statistical abstract, general data by country, 1992 annual rpt, U6250–1.4

Mass media company revenues for leading firms, with detail by medium, 1991-92, annual feature, C2710–1.540

Operating and financial composite ratios for corporations, with establishments and receipts, for approx 200 industries, by asset size, FY90, annual rpt, C7800–1

Prices of selected consumer items in approx 300 cities, quarterly rpt, A0150–1

Prices per copy for daily newspapers, by State, 1992, annual article, A8605–1.507

Public confidence in selected societal instns, 1993 Gallup Poll and trends, C4040–1.510, R8780–1.508

Public opinion on govt policy as affected by *New York Times* stories from selected sources, 1993 article, A0610–1.503

Publishing devs and practices in newspaper industry, articles and features, monthly rpt, A8605–1

Readership of newspaper pages and selected sections, 1989-92, article, C2710–1.537

Statistical profiles of 50 States and DC, general data, 1993 annual almanac, C4712–1

World sales of newspapers per 1,000 inhabitants, and advertising revenues, by country, 1988 and 1991-92, article, A8605–1.508

Index by Subjects and Names

Nielsen, A. C., Co.

State and local:

Alabama county data book, general data, 1992 annual rpt, S0121–2

Alabama statistical abstract, general data, 1992 recurring rpt, U5680–2.2

Arizona statistical abstract, general data, 1993 recurring rpt, U5850–2.19

Florida statistical abstract, general data, 1992 annual rpt, U6660–1.14

Georgia statistical abstract, general data, 1992-93 biennial rpt, U6730–1.8

Hawaii data book, general data, 1992 annual rpt, S2090–1.16

Kansas statistical abstract, general data, 1991/92 annual rpt, U7095–2.13

Maryland statistical abstract, general data, 1993-94 biennial rpt, S3605–1.8

Mississippi statistical abstract, general data, 1992 annual rpt, U3255–4.7

Oklahoma statistical abstract, general data, 1992 annual rpt, U8130–2.17

Rhode Island *Providence Journal-Bulletin* circulation, by city and county, FY92, annual rpt, C7975–1.1

Tennessee statistical abstract, general data, 1992/93 annual rpt, U8710–2.8

Utah statistical abstract, general data, 1993 triennial rpt, U8960–1.13

Virginia newspaper advertising lineage, monthly rpt, U1120–1

see also Journalism

see also Newsprint

Newsprint

Consumption and prices, and newspaper industry operating data, 1970-92, annual rpt, A8605–4

Consumption by newspapers, inventories, and stock on hand, monthly rpt, A8605–1

Latin America statistical abstract, general data by country, 1992 annual rpt, U6250–1.4, U6250–1.24

Price trends for newsprint on East and West Coasts, 1991-93, article, A8605–1.503

Production, capacity, consumption, prices, and foreign trade, including data by world area, 1993 annual rpt, C3975–5.3

Production, consumption, stocks, trade, and prices for approx 100 basic commodities, including by country and producing State, commodity yearbook for 1993, C2400–1, C2400–2

Production, consumption, trade, prices, and mill capacity, 1991-92 and trends, annual rpt, A8610–1

Production, shipments, plant capacity, consumption, trade, and recycling, US and Canada, 1970s-92, annual rpt, A1630–8

Production, shipments, trade, inventory, consumption, and plant capacity, US and Canada, monthly rpt, A1630–4

Recycled newsprint capacity and mills, 1992-95, article, A8605–1.501

Recycled newsprint production capacity, demand, and wastepaper consumption, for Northeast US and Eastern Canada, with data by State and company, various years 1988-2000, A4375–15

NFO Research Inc.

Consumer expectations of economic conditions and change in income, and intended durable goods purchases by type, Conference Board monthly survey, R4105–4

Consumer views on selected topics, series, R4105–81

Diamond jewelry sales and average price, 1987-92, article, C2150–7.508

Photographic equipment and supplies, consumer ownership, purchasing patterns, and use, 1993 survey and trends, recurring rpt, A8695–2

Restaurant patronage patterns, expenditures, and food preferences, 1992 survey, recurring feature, C1850–3.501

Restaurant quality ratings among consumers, for most popular chains, 1993 annual feature, C1850–3.504

Niagara Falls, N.Y.

Visitors, hotel rooms and occupancy rate, and unemployment rate, for Ontario and New York sides of Niagara Falls, 1993 article, C5800–7.544

Nicaragua

Statistical abstract of Latin America, detailed social, govtl, and economic data, 1992 annual rpt, U6250–1

Nickel

see Metals and metal industries

Nielsen, A. C., Co.

Baked goods (cookies and crackers) market shares, sales growth, and consumption, for top 5-6 countries, 1993 feature, C2710–1.509

Bottled water market shares, sales growth, and consumption, for top 6 countries, 1993 feature, C2710–1.513

Cable TV advertising expenditures for top 5 advertisers in 7 product categories, biweekly rpt quarterly feature, C1858–1.502, C1858–1.508, C2965–1.505, C2965–1.511

Cable TV audience ratings, for all-cartoon network vs 12 major networks, Dec 1992-Jan 1993, article, C1850–14.511

Cable TV viewership rankings in 7 audience demographic group categories, for 15 networks, 1993 feature, C1858–1.503

Cable TV viewership rankings in 7 audience demographic group categories, for 15 networks, 2nd qtr 1993, C1858–1.506

Candy sales and market shares, for top 10 brands, 1991-92, article, C2710–1.518

Candy/confectionery sales and market shares, for 2 major manufacturers, 1991-92, article, C2710–1.513

Cereal market shares for selected manufacturers, by world region, 1989-92, C2710–1.527

Chocolate market shares, sales growth, and consumption, for top 6-8 countries, 1992 feature, C2710–1.504

Confectionery product sales by selected product type and retail outlet, 1991, article, C5150–3.505

Drugstore light bulb sales distribution by bulb type, 1992, article, C5150–2.513

Drugstore sales and merchandising trends, by product type and market area, 1992 annual feature, C5150–2.503

Ethnic hair care product market shares by retail outlet type, 1992, article, C5150–3.513

Hair care product sales trends, for top 10 brands in drugstores, with comparisons to mass merchandise and food/drug stores, year ended June 1993, articles, C5150–2.519

Health and beauty aid product sales shares for drugstores, grocery stores, and mass merchandisers, 1991 and trends, annual article, C5225–1.501

Health and beauty aid sales and merchandising in discount stores and other outlets, by product type, 1991 and trends, annual article, C5150–3.502

Lotion (hand/body) market shares, for top 9 brands and private label, 1993 article, C2710–1.530

Market area population and characteristics, households, income, and retail outlets, for 21 leading areas, 1993 feature, C2710–1.538

Men's consumer purchase shares and value, for 7 household items, 1992 article, C5800–7.502

Men's grocery product purchasing, with comparisons to women, by detailed product type, 1992 article, C5225–1.501

Popcorn market shares, with consumption data for microwave popcorn, for top 5-7 countries, 1993 feature, C2710–1.517

Private label product market shares in selected product categories, by selected country, 1988-93, C2710–1.536

Sales volume shares by retail outlet type, for approx 300 food, drug, and other product categories, 1993 annual feature, C4655–1.504

Soft drink sales volume shares by retail outlet type, 1991-92, article, C8130–1.506

Supermarket product sales and market shares, for top brands in selected product categories, weekly rpt monthly table, C2710–1

Toothbrush market shares, for top 9 brands and private label, year ended Apr 1993, article, C2710–1 530

TV (public) viewing habits of members vs general public, 1992 survey rpt, R4250–1.22

TV audience ratings among men, for 5 major sporting event telecasts, 1991/92, article, C9380–1.508

TV audience ratings and shares for President Clinton's budget presentation, in 12 cities, Aug 1993, article, C9380–1.536

TV audience ratings, by network, fall 1991-92 seasons, C9380–1.503

TV audience ratings, by network, Nov 1991-92, article, C9380–1.505

TV audience ratings by sex, for 3 major networks, 1992/93, article, C9380–1.523

TV audience ratings for sign-on to sign-off period and late news programs, for 6-7 stations in top 3 metro markets, May 1993, article, C1850–14.523

TV audience ratings for sign-on to sign-off period and late news programs, for 6-7 stations in top 5 metro markets, Feb 1993, article, C1850–14.515

TV audience ratings for 3 network morning news programs among men age 35-49, June/July 1992-93, article, C9380–1.535

TV Hispanic household audience ratings, for top 15 prime-time English-language programs, Nov 1992, article, C1850–14.516

TV households and ranking among top 100 market areas, for 46 areas changing rank, 1992/93-1993/94, C1850–14.538

Nielsen, A. C., Co.

TV local news program audience ratings, with data for top stations, 1992 articles, C1850–14.501, C1850–14.502, C1850–14.503

TV out-of-home viewing impact on ratings for all network TV and 13 leading programs, Oct-Nov 1992, article, C2710–1.519

TV Saturday morning audience ratings and shares, with detail for children age 2-11, by program and network, July 1993, article, C1850–14.531

TV Spanish-language program audience ratings, for top 10 programs among Hispanic viewers, Oct/Nov 1992, article, C2710–1.510

TV Spanish-language program audience ratings, for top 20 programs among Hispanic viewers, Oct/Nov 1992, article, C4575–1.504

TV syndicated program audience ratings and shares for top 20 programs, May 1993, article, C1850–14.528

TV syndicated program audience ratings and shares for 18 programs, May 1993, article, C1850–14.525

TV syndicated program audience ratings and shares for 4-10 programs in 6 categories, Feb 1992-93, C1850–14.519

TV syndicated program audience ratings, for 13 new programs, Sept 1993, recurring feature, C1850–14.540

TV syndicated program audience ratings, for 17 new programs, May 1992-93, recurring article, C1850–14.524

TV syndicated program audience ratings, for 19 new programs, Feb 1992-93, recurring article, C1850–14.514

TV syndicated program audience shares and ratings, by daypart and audience characteristics, Nov 1991-92, article, C9380–1.511

TV tabloid news magazine program ratings, for 3 programs, 1991/92-1992/93, article, C1850–14.535

Vaginal antifungal product over-the-counter sales distribution by retail outlet type, 1st 8 months 1992, article, C5150–2.502

Niemuth, N. J.

"Primary Copper Industry of Arizona in 1991", S0497–1

Niger

Uranium mine ownership shares, 1992 annual rpt, B6800–2.2

Women's contraceptive use discontinuation patterns among new family planning clinic clients in Niger and Gambia, 1992 article, A5160–6.502

Nigeria

Energy intl sourcebook, with detail on oil and gas industry operations, supply-demand, and prices, for approx 80 countries, 1970s-91, annual compilation, C6985–10.2

Population characteristics and sexual behavior of truck drivers and women selling goods along the road, May or June 1991, article, A5160–6.504

see also Organization of Petroleum Exporting Countries

see also under By Foreign Country or World Area in the "Index by Categories"

Nitrogen

see Gases

Noise

Motor vehicle noise standards of Fed Govt and 8 States, 1993 annual rpt, A0865–1.3

Non-ferrous metals industry

see Aluminum and aluminum industry

see Copper and copper industry

see Lead and lead industry

see Metals and metal industries

see Tin and tin industry

see Zinc and zinc industry

Nonmetallic minerals and mines

Capital spending plans for new mines and plants, by mineral and company, and mine production values, 1993 annual feature, C5226–2.503

Financial ratios and performance, for over 350 SIC 4-digit industries, FY88-92, annual rpt, A6400–3

Graphite demand by type and market, 1982, 1992, and 1997, article, C7000–8.505

Latin America statistical abstract, general data by country, 1992 annual rpt, U6250–1.23

Operating and financial composite ratios for corporations, with establishments and receipts, for approx 200 industries, by asset size, FY90, annual rpt, C7800–1

Operating and financial data for metals and nonmetallic minerals industries, with articles and special features, monthly rpt, C5226–2

Production, consumption, stocks, trade, and prices for approx 100 basic commodities, including by country and producing State, commodity yearbook for 1993, C2400–1, C2400–2

Sulfur (oil-based) recovery plant capacity and production, by company and country, Jan 1992, annual compilation, C6985–4.1

Sulfur (oil-based) recovery plant capacity and production, by company and country, Jan 1993, annual feature, C6985–1.537

Sulfur mined and recovered production worldwide, and supply-demand outlook, 1980s-2000, article, C6985–1.546

Sulfur production and reserves, by country, 1991 92, article, C5226–2.508

Sulfur recovery from oil refineries and natural gas plants vs mine production, and sales by PAD district, 1982-91, article, C6985–1.514

Supply-demand for selected metals and nonmetallic minerals, with price data, US and worldwide, 1992-93 and trends, annual feature, C5226–2.505

State and local:

Arizona mineral production and value, by mineral type, 1991 and trends, annual rpt, S0497–1

Colorado property assessed valuation, and summary production data, by county, 1991-92, annual rpt, S1055–3

Florida statistical abstract, general data, 1992 annual rpt, U6660–1.12

Kansas statistical abstract, general data, 1991/92 annual rpt, U7095–2.16

Maryland statistical abstract, general data, 1993-94 biennial rpt, S3605–1.3

Mississippi statistical abstract, general data, 1992 annual rpt, U3255–4.10

South Carolina statistical abstract, general data, 1993 annual rpt, S7125–1.1

Utah statistical abstract, general data, 1993 triennial rpt, U8960–1.10

Wyoming mineral production and taxable valuation, by county, and severance and ad valorem taxes, FY92 annual rpt, S8990–1.2

see also Cement and concrete

see also Clay industry and products

see also Coal and coal mining

see also Fertilizers

see also Gases

see also Gemstones

see also Mine accidents and safety

see also Natural gas and gas industry

see also Offshore oil and gas

see also Oil shale

see also Petroleum and petroleum industry

see also Phosphate

see also Potash

see also Stockpiling

see also Stone products and quarries

see also Strategic materials

see also under By Industry in the "Index by Categories"

Nonmetropolitan areas

see Rural areas

see under By Urban-Rural and Metro-Nonmetro in the "Index by Categories"

Nonprofit organizations and foundations

Arts fundraising through united arts funds (UAFs), with fund operations, income by source, and allocations, by UAF, 1992 and trends, annual rpt, A1315–2

Assets and contributions of foundations, by organization type and census div, with top 100 organizations, FY91, annual article, C2176–1.507

Cancer incidence and mortality data, with American Cancer Society activities and funding, 1993 and trends, annual rpt, A1175–1

Catholic charity social service agency activities, clients, finances, and personnel, 1991 and trends, annual rpt, A3810–1

Charitable contributions, by type of donor and recipient, 1992 and trends, annual rpt, A0700–1

College grad job and salary offers, by field of study, type of employer and occupation, and degree level, by region, interim rpt series, A3940–1

College grad job and salary offers, by field of study, type of employer and occupation, and degree level, series, A3940–2

Consumer complaint and inquiry activity of Better Business Burs, by detailed type of business, 1992, annual rpt, A4350–1

Corporate charitable foundations, with income and payout data, 1991 and trends, annual rpt, R4105–8

Direct marketing industry devs, with consumer and business market characteristics, and media use patterns, 1992/93 annual rpt, A4620–1.4

Elementary/secondary education foundation grants and value, for top 10 recipients, 1990/91, article, R4800–2.522

Executive compensation at nonprofit organizations, by position, organization characteristics, and region, 1993, annual article, C2176–1.519

Executive salaries at nonprofit organizations, by title and organization type, 1993, annual article, C2176–1.519

Index by Subjects and Names

North Carolina

Finances for top 400 nonprofit organizations, including income and fundraising costs, FY91 or FY92, annual article, C2176–1.501

Finances of foundations, including assets, income, and grants by type of recipient, with data by location, 1991 and trends, annual rpt, R4900–1

Fundraising professionals characteristics, earnings, and benefits, 1992 survey, recurring rpt, A8455–1

Grants awarded and assets of top 50 foundations, 1991, annual feature, C2175–1.520

Grants from foundations by detailed purpose, type of recipient, and State, with detail for grants of $5.7 million/over, 1991, annual article, C2176–1.504

Health voluntary agency revenues, and expenditures by function, for 39 major organizations, FY90, annual rpt, A7973–1

HMO benefits, enrollment and utilization, staffing, finances, and relations with employers, by plan characteristics, 1990-91, annual rpt, A5150–2

Hospital (teaching) house staff stipends and benefits, by region and ownership, 1992/93, annual rpt, A3273–3

Investment returns for endowments/foundations compared to stock and bond indexes, biweekly rpt quarterly feature, C2710–2.503, C2710–2.509, C2710–2.513

Japan corporate affiliate charitable foundations in US, with assets and contributions, by company, various years 1989-93, article, R5650–2.560

Jewelry trade assns financial performance data, for 5 organizations, 1991 or FY92, article, C2150–7.505

Law school grad employment and salaries, by type of employer, location, and grad characteristics, 1992 and trends, annual rpt, A6505–1

Mass transit systems, including nonprofit providers of service to elderly/disabled, by State, 1992 annual rpt, A2650–1.1

Museums and related instns operations and finances, by type, budget size, governing authority, and region, 1989/90 survey, A0750–1

Mutual fund industry financial data, by type of investor and financial instn intermediary, 1991 and trends, annual rpt, A6025–1.2

Nursing higher education funding by source, and foundations and use of funds, FY92, biennial rpt, A0615–5

Philanthropy trends and devs, including data on nonprofit organization activities and finances, and corporate and individual giving, biweekly rpt, C2176–1

Planning profession employment and salaries, by type of employer, demographic and professional characteristics, and location, 1991 and trends, biennial rpt, A2615–1

Public broadcasting station revenues by source, and number of stations, by station type, FY91, annual rpt, R4250–1.20

R&D funding and expenditures, by source and performing sector, 1960s-93, annual rpt, R3300–1

Refugees resettled in US under voluntary agency sponsorship, with detail for 12 top agencies, FY92, R9372–2.505

Salaries of scientists, engineers, technicians, and other professionals, by employee and employer characteristics, 1990s and trends, biennial rpt, A3960–1

State govt regulation of charities, religious congregation views on strengthening laws, 1992 survey, recurring rpt, A5435–4

Telephone rate reduction policies of State and Canadian Province regulatory agencies, 1991/92 annual rpt, A7015–3

Theater (nonprofit professional) finances and operations, including revenues by source, 1992 and trends, annual survey, A9065–1

Urban League National Education Initiative population served, and opinions of students and parents, 1991 survey, article, A8510–1.1

Women and minorities involvement in philanthropic operations and support, series, A9405–1

Youth age 12-17 charitable contributions, volunteer activity, and views on related issues, by respondent characteristics, 1992 survey, biennial rpt, A5435–5

State and local:

Arkansas nonprofit financial organization finances, June 1992, annual rpt, S0632–1

California library finances, staff, holdings, and services, by library type and facility, FY92, annual rpt, S0825–2

California property tax assessments and exemptions, by type of property, city, county, and company, FY93 and trends, annual rpt, S0835–1.2

Colorado property assessed valuation by detailed property type, and tax levy and revenue by local district, by county, 1991 92, annual rpt, S1055–3

DC statistical profile, general data, 1992 annual rpt, S1535–3.3

Georgia statistical abstract, general data, 1992-93 biennial rpt, U6730–1.13

Hawaii data book, general data, 1992 annual rpt, S2090–1.11

Illinois statistical abstract, general data, 1992 annual rpt, U6910–2

New York State charitable annuity societies insurance finances and underwriting activity, 1991, annual rpt, S5770–2

New York State charitable annuity societies insurance finances, 1990 and trends, annual rpt, S5770–3

Tennessee nonprofit hospital and medical assns financial data, by assn, 1991, annual rpt, S7466–1

Texas hospitals, operations, utilization, and finances, by type, ownership, size, and metro-nonmetro status, 1970s-91, U8850–8.3

Utah new corporations, by type, 1950-91, triennial rpt, U8960–1.15

see also Fraternal benefit societies

see also Political action committees

see also Religious organizations

Norman, Donald A.

"Energy Prices and Externalities", A2575–28

North America

Computer (personal) North American unit sales and revenues, for top 25 companies, 1991, article, C1850–2.504

Free trade agreement devs for auto industry, with data on Mexico vehicle production and US total and auto trade with Mexico and Canada, 1980s-91, R8490–43

Jewish population by world area, country, and US census div, State, and city, 1990-92, annual compilation, A2050–1

Methanol supply-demand outlook in North America, Europe, and worldwide, with capacity by company, 1993 article, C6985–1.522

Motor vehicle exports for top 5 North American manufacturers, 1991-92, article, C2710–3.515

Motor vehicle industry labor productivity, for 27 truck and 29 auto plants, 1992, article, C2150–3.503

Newsprint production, shipments, plant capacity, consumption, trade, and recycling, US and Canada, 1970s-92, annual rpt, A1630–8

Newsprint production, shipments, trade, inventory, consumption, and plant capacity, US and Canada, monthly rpt, A1630–4

Population size and characteristics, GNP, and land area, by world region and/or country, 1993 annual data sheet, R8750–5

Refugees, resettlement, and intl aid devs, by country, 1992, annual rpt, R9372–1

see also Canada

see also Caribbean area

see also Central America

see also Gulf of Mexico

see also Mexico

see also under By Foreign Country or World Area in the "Index by Categories"

North Atlantic Treaty Organization

Public opinion in US on selected foreign policy issues, with detail for 3 States, 1993 survey, annual rpt, A4965–1

North Carolina

Agricultural production, marketing, and finances, by commodity and county, 1991 and trends, annual rpt, S5885–1

Correctional instn admissions, separations, and population, with inmate characteristics, FY93, semiannual rpt, S5900–1

Court cases and dispositions, by type of court and case, and location, with judicial dept finances and personnel, FY91, annual rpt, S5950–1

Crimes and arrests, by offense, location, and offender characteristics, with data on law enforcement employment and assaults on officers, 1992 and trends, annual rpt, S5955–1

Election results and voter registration, by county and/or district, 1992 general election, biennial rpt, S5920–1

Elementary and secondary public school enrollment, grads, staff, and finances, with data by race, sex, and local district, 1991/92-1992/93 and trends, annual rpt, S5915–1

Employment and labor force, by industry, county, MSA, labor area, and planning region, 1991 and trends, annual rpt, S5917–4

Employment, hours, and earnings, by industry group, with job placements, monthly rpt, S5917–3

North Carolina

Employment in SIC 2-digit industries, by detailed occupation, triennial rpt series, S5917–5

Govt financial condition, including revenues by source, expenditures by function, fund balances, and bonded debt, FY92, annual rpt, S5897–1

Higher education enrollment, degrees, libraries, staff, and student characteristics, finances, and housing, by instn, 1992/93 and trends, annual rpt, U8013–1

Libraries (public) finances, holdings, and personnel, by library system, FY91, annual rpt, S5910–1

Markets with daily newspapers, demographic and economic info by geographic area, US and Canada, 1993 annual rpt, C3250–1

Public welfare programs, cases, recipients, staff, and finances, by county, 1st half FY93, semiannual rpt, S5940–2

Statistical profiles of 50 States and DC, general data, 1993 annual almanac, C4712–1

Traffic accidents, fatalities, and injuries, by circumstances, location, vehicle type, and driver and victim characteristics, 1992 and trends, annual rpt, S5990–1

Utility and transportation regulatory agency activities, scope of jurisdiction, finances, and employees, by agency, 1991/92 annual rpt, A7015–2

Utility regulatory, financial, and operating data, by utility type and company, with commission finances, 1990 and trends, annual rpt, S5917–2

Vital statistics, including population, births, deaths by cause, marriages, and divorces, by local area, 1991 and trends, annual rpt, S5927–1

see also under By City and By County in the "Index by Categories"

see also under By State in the "Index by Categories"

North Central States

Agricultural labor and wages, for Lake States region, 1990-92, annual rpt, S3950–1

Agricultural workers, hours, and wages, for Northern Plains region, 1st qtr 1989-1st qtr 1993, annual rpt, S7280–1

Airport operations and air traffic control activities, for 8 States, 1989, annual rpt, U6910–2

Business and economic conditions in metro and nonurban areas, by sector and State, bankers opinions, spring 1993 survey, semiannual rpt, B6785–1

Business establishments, and wages by industry div, for 9 North Central States, 1993 annual rpt, S6140–2

College grad job and salary offers, by field of study, type of employer, occupation, and degree level, interim rpt, A3940–1.3

CPI for North Central region, by population size group, quarterly rpt, S4895–2

Economic trends analysis for Midwest region, 1992 article, A6400–2.501

Farm labor and wage rates, and expenditures for selected items, 1992 annual rpt, S2390–1

Grain futures and options trading activity on Minneapolis exchange, with production, price, and disposition data for area served, 1992 and trends, annual rpt, B6110–1

Higher education tuition/fees, for public instns in 8 States, FY89-92, annual rpt, S7375–1

Hospital patient discharges and length of stay, by diagnosis, type of operation, and age, 1991, annual rpt, B4455–1.3

Hospital patient discharges and length of stay, by diagnostic related group (DRG), payment source, and age, 1991, annual rpt, B4455–3.3

Hospital psychiatric patient discharges and length of stay, by diagnosis, age, and sex, 1991, annual rpt, B4455–2.3

Income (personal), for 7 Midwest States, quarterly rpt, U8595–1

Low-income housing supply-demand, costs, physical conditions, and public assistance, for 10 North Central metro areas, 1992 rpt, R3834–16.3

Public interest in news items on 1993 Midwestern floods, by respondent characteristics, July/Aug 1993 survey, C8915–1.504

see also under By Region in the "Index by Categories"

see also under names of individual States

North Dakota

Agricultural production and marketing, by commodity and county, and farm finances, 1992 and trends, annual rpt, U3600–1

Correctional instns (local), characteristics of inmates by instn, 1991 and trends, annual rpt, S6060–3

Court caseloads and dispositions, by type of case and court, and location, 1991-92, annual rpt, S6210–1

Crimes and arrests, by offense, location, and offender characteristics, and law enforcement employment, 1991 and trends, annual rpt, S6060–1

Election results and historical trends, including data on ballot measures and detail by location, 1880s-1992, biennial rpt, U8080–1

Election results, by location, 1992 general election, biennial rpt, S6205–1

Elementary and secondary revenues by source, expenditures by function, mill levies, and taxable value, by school district, 1992/93 annual rpt, S6180–4

Elementary and secondary school staff characteristics and salaries, by position, region, and enrollment size, 1992/93 annual rpt, S6180–3

Elementary and secondary schools, enrollment, and staff, by school type and location, with county census of children, 1992/93 annual directory, S6180–2

Employment, hours, and earnings, by industry div and/or location, monthly rpt, S6140–4

Govt financial condition, including revenues by source, expenditures by function, fund balances, and bonded debt, FY92, annual rpt, S6162–1

Health behavior risk factor surveillance survey results, by respondent characteristics, 1991 and trends, annual rpt, S6105–3

Higher education enrollment, by level, instn, county, and selected student characteristics, fall 1992 and trends, annual rpt, S6110–1

Labor force planning rpt, including population, employment, and earnings, with data by industry and county, 1993 annual rpt, S6140–2

Library finances, holdings, staff, and operations, by instn, FY91, annual rpt, S6180–5

Markets with daily newspapers, demographic and economic info by geographic area, US and Canada, 1993 annual rpt, C3250–1

Oil/gas industry production, finances, exploration, and reserves, by State, 1992 and trends, annual rpt, A5425–1.1

Statistical profiles of 50 States and DC, general data, 1993 annual almanac, C4712–1

Traffic accidents, fatalities, and injuries, by circumstances, location, vehicle type, and driver and victim characteristics, 1992 and trends, annual rpt, S6217–1

Utility and transportation regulatory agency activities, scope of jurisdiction, finances, and employees, by agency, 1991/92 annual rpt, A7015–2

Vital statistics, including population, births, deaths by cause, marriages and divorces, and abortions, by demographic characteristics and/or county, 1991 and trends, annual rpt, S6105–2

see also under By City and By County in the "Index by Categories"

see also under By State in the "Index by Categories"

North Sea

Offshore oil and gas activity, including production, reserves, and spills, by location, 1991 and trends, annual compilation, C6985–9.4

Oil and gas reserves planned for dev using floating production systems, by field, 1992 article, C6985–1.507

Oil/gas deep well drilling, success ratios, and costs, by world area, 1990-92, annual article, C4420–1.503

Oil/gas drilling platforms and floating structures under construction, planned, and under study, 1993-2000, article, C6985–2.509

Oil/gas exploratory drilling planned in North Sea, by area, 1993, article, C6985–1.512

Oil/gas field production costs, distribution by process, 1986, C6985–2.502

UK offshore gas field dev in southern North Sea, with operator, reserves, and production rate, 1993 article, C6985–2.505

UK offshore oil/gas wells drilled, and fields by operating status, 1991-97, article, C6985–1.546

UK oil revenue tax impact on oil companies operating in North Sea, by company, 1993-96, article, C6985–1.525

Northeast States

Cigarette excise and State sales taxes per pack, for 8 Northeast States, Jan 1993, article, R9050–3.502

College grad job and salary offers, by field of study, type of employer, occupation, and degree level, interim rpt, A3940–1.1

Elderly population smoking status correlated with dental problems, by sex, 1993 article, A2623–1.511

Index by Subjects and Names

Electric bills of typical industrial consumer, by New England State, 1985-91, recurring rpt, S3434–1

Employment, unemployment, and labor force in 5 New England States, monthly rpt, S3465–2

Farm workers, hours, and wages, 1985-93, annual rpt, S5700–1

Farms and average size, and production expenses by item, 1989 and trends, biennial rpt, S7978–1

Hospital patient discharges and length of stay, by diagnosis, type of operation, and age, 1991, annual rpt, B4455–1.2

Hospital patient discharges and length of stay, by diagnostic related group (DRG), payment source, and age, 1991, annual rpt, B4455–3.2

Hospital psychiatric patient discharges and length of stay, by diagnosis, age, and sex, 1991, annual rpt, B4455–2.2

Housing units by primary heating fuel, for 14 New England and Middle Atlantic States, 1990, article, C4680–1.501

Low-income housing supply-demand, costs, physical conditions, and public assistance, for 9 Northeast metro areas, 1992 rpt, R3834–16.2

Newsprint recycling capacity, demand, and wastepaper consumption, for Northeast US and Eastern Canada, with data by mill, various years 1988-2000, A4375–15

Plastics sales per capita, recycling collection methods, and manufacturers, for Northeast region and/or States, 1992 rpt, A4375–14

Unemployment rates, for Vermont, New England, and US, 1980-92, annual planning rpt, S8025–2.2

see also Appalachia

see also under By Region in the "Index by Categories"

see also under names of individual States

Northern Mariana Islands

Judicial system salaries for judges and court administrators, by State and territory, and for Federal system, July 1993, semiannual rpt, R6600–2

Population shares by citizenship status and birthplace, 1992 rpt, B3500–1.501

Northwest Arctic Borough, Alaska

Economic profile, including employment by industry div and population characteristics, 1993 article, S0320–1.512

Northwest Territories, Canada

Oil/gas exploration licenses issued for Northwest Territories, by region, 1993 article, C6985–2.510

Norway

Energy intl sourcebook, with detail on oil and gas industry operations, supply-demand, and prices, for approx 80 countries, 1970s-91, annual compilation, C6985–10.2

Motor vehicle world production, sales, trade, and registrations, by country, world area, manufacturer, and make, 1991 and trends, annual rpt, A0865–2.1

Newsprint shipments from 3 Scandinavian countries, total and to US, monthly rpt, A1630–4

Offshore oil and gas fields under dev, with reserves and capital outlays, by field, 1993 article, C6985–1.523

Offshore oil/gas exploration and production wells drilled, 1966-91, annual rpt, C6985–3.2

Offshore reserves of oil, gas, and natural gas liquids, for 5 new fields, with operator and location, 1993 article, C6985–2.509

Oil and gas production trends and projections, and petroleum resources by status, 1993 article, C6985–2.506

Oil and gas reserves of major fields, and pipeline ownership of 2nd largest oil company, 1993 article, C6985–1.537

see also under By Foreign Country or World Area in the "Index by Categories"

Nose and throat disorders

Hospital patient admission rates and length of stay, by diagnosis and procedure, payment source, age, sex, and region, 1991, B4455–4

Hospital patient charges and length of stay, by diagnosis and procedure, payment source, age, and region, 1991, B4455–5

Hospital patient discharges and length of stay, by diagnosis, type of operation, age, and region, 1991, annual rpt series, B4455–1

Hospital patient discharges and length of stay, by diagnostic related group (DRG), payment source, age, and region, 1991, annual rpt series, B4455–3

Tonsillectomy/adenoidectomy procedures, costs, and hospital stay, with data by census div and State, 1991 and trends, article, B6045–1.502

see also under By Disease in the "Index by Categories"

Notifiable diseases

see Infective and parasitic diseases

NOW accounts

see Negotiable orders of withdrawal accounts

NPD Research Inc.

Children's clothing sales, by retail outlet type, 1990-92, article, C5150–3.503

Children's hard goods purchaser outlet preferences, 1993 article, C8130–1.511

Clothing (men's) sales and consumer expenditures, by outlet type, 1992, article, C5150–3.508

Clothing (men's sweats/warm-up) sales by retail outlet type, 1992, article, C5150–3.510

Clothing (sport shirt) sales volume and value, 1991-93, article, C5150–3.518

Clothing with imprinted designs, market shares by retail outlet type and design category, Apr 1992-Mar 1993, article, C5150–3.513

Daily time allocation by type of activity, Apr 1993 survey, article, A8200–1.509

Discount store sales volume of women's clothing in 4 special sizes, by product type, 1st half 1992-93, article, C5150–3.521

Discount store shopper characteristics, use of natl vs regional discounters, and types of clothing purchased, 1990 and 1992, article, C8130–1.506

Food service product consumption trends, for 7 menu items, 1983 and 1992, article, C1850–3.503

Marketing strategy future influences cited as most important by executives, Nov 1992-Jan 1993 survey, article, C2710–1.518

Nuclear power

Restaurant customer traffic and check size trends, by type of operation, 1992 and trends, annual article, A8200–1.507

Restaurant patron coupon use, for 12 types of establishments with most frequent use, 1992, article, A8200–1.503

Restaurant patronage patterns, monthly rpt quarterly feature, A8200–1.503, A8200–1.508

Restaurant take-out market shares for carry out, drive-through, and delivery services, 1991, annual article, C1200–5.501

Toy shipments and orders received, canceled, and/or on hand, monthly rpt, A9095–2

NSF

see National Science Foundation

Nuclear accidents and safety

Insurance (liability and property) premiums written for nuclear accidents, 1957-91, annual rpt, A5650–1.2

Japan nuclear reactor safety inspections and reported incidence of problems, 1987-92, recurring article, R5650–2.536

see also Radiation

Nuclear explosives and explosions

see also Radiation

Nuclear fallout

see Radiation

Nuclear industries

see Nuclear power

Nuclear medicine and radiology

Hospital diagnostic imaging equipment age, by type of equipment, 1992, A1865–1.507

Hospital diagnostic imaging procedures performed monthly, by bed-size group, 1989-92, survey article, A1865–1.523

Hospital patient discharges and length of stay, by diagnostic related group (DRG), payment source, age, and region, 1991, annual rpt series, B4455–3

Income of radiologists, public perceptions vs actual amounts, 1991-93, R4865–13

Medical group financial and operating data, by practice characteristics, 1991, annual rpt, A6365–2

Medical school faculty and compensation, by dept, academic rank, degree, and region, 1992/93, annual rpt, A3273–2

Physician practice economic aspects, detailed data by specialty, 1991-92 and trends, annual compilation, A2200–5

Physicians by detailed specialty and location, 1992 and trends, annual rpt, A2200–3

State and local:

Florida health care atlas, including manpower by occupation and health care facilities by type, by district and county, 1992 annual rpt, S1746–1.2

see also X-rays

Nuclear power

Brazil nuclear power plants and capacity, and uranium and enriched fuel requirements, under 3 dev plans, 1990, 2000, and 2010, article, B6800–1.508

Capability factors and gross heat rates for nuclear power plants, 1980-92, article, C6985–6.508

Capacity additions, and equipment orders and shipments, with data by location and facility, 1991 annual rpt, A4700–2

China nuclear power generating capacity, by unit, 1993 article, B6800–1.509

Nuclear power

Consumption of fossil energy resources and electricity from hydro and nuclear power, 1960s-91, annual rpt, A1775–3.6

Decommissioning funding requirements for pressurized and boiling-water reactors, 1993 article, A4700–4.505

Electric power (steam) plants, capacity, generation, and fuel use and costs, by fuel type, utility, and location, 1991, annual rpt, A7400–7

Electric power plants planned and under construction in 1993, by type, utility, and region, and forecast capacity for 1993-2001, annual feature, C5800–28.503

Electric power production by type of fuel, by State and census div, monthly rpt, A7400–8

Finances, sales, and capacity of electric utilities, with data by sector and region, 1993 annual feature, C5800–28.507

Finland nuclear power generation and capacity, for 4 operating reactors, 1993 article, B6800–1.507

Intl energy sourcebook, with detail on oil and gas industry operations, supply-demand, and prices, for approx 80 countries, 1970s-91, annual compilation, C6985–10

Japan energy supply-demand and outlook, by fuel source, 1980s-2000, recurring article, R5650–2.536

Korea (South) nuclear power generation and/or capacity, for reactors operating and planned, 1993 article, B6800–1.503

Latin America statistical abstract, general data by country, 1992 annual rpt, U6250–1.23

Operating data for top 100 electric utilities, including generating capacity by fuel source, 1992, annual article, C6985–6.512

Plant maintenance issues most important to mgmt, and top factors adversely affecting capacity, 1993 survey article, C6985–6.505

Sourcebook of oil and gas industry, with supply-demand comparisons to other energy types, 1991 and trends, annual compilation, C6985–9.5

State performance incentive programs for nuclear power plants, by State, 1991/92 annual rpt, A7015–3

State social, economic, and govtl indicators, with rankings, 1993 semiannual rpt, B8500–1.12

Statistical profiles of 50 States and DC, general data, 1993 annual almanac, C4712–1

Statistical yearbook of electric utility financial and operating data, by State and census div, 1991 and trends, annual rpt, A4700–1

Supply-demand, and utility capacity and fuel requirements, detailed data by US and Canadian region, 1992-2002, annual rpt, A8630–2

Supply-demand by energy source and consuming sector, 1947-2010, periodic basic data book, A2575–14.1

Supply-demand for non-oil energy sources, 1970s-2010, annual rpt, C6985–5.3

Supply-demand trends and devs in nuclear power generation and fuel processing worldwide, with related data on individual reactor capacity and completion status, quarterly rpt, B6790–1

Sweden nuclear power generation and capacity, for 12 operating reactors, 1993 article, B6800–1.506

World energy supply-demand, by fuel source and sector, by region and country, 1992/93 biennial rpt, R9455–1.3, R9455–1.7

World nuclear power industry devs, including reactor construction and operating status by country and company, 1992 and trends, annual rpt, B6800–2

State and local:

Florida statistical abstract, general data, 1992 annual rpt, U6660–1.15

Georgia statistical abstract, general data, 1992-93 biennial rpt, U6730–1.8

New York State public utility financial and operating data, by utility type and company, 1988-92, annual rpt, S5795–1

New York State statistical yearbook, general data, 1992 annual rpt, U5100–1.12

Ohio natural gas and electricity supply-demand by utility and consuming sector, 1992-93 and trends, annual rpt, S6355–1

Oregon ballot measures on nuclear power plant operation, election results by county, 1992, biennial rpt, S6665–1

Pennsylvania energy supply-demand and prices by fuel type, with electric power info by utility, 1960s-90, recurring rpt, S6810–3

Tennessee statistical abstract, general data, 1992/93 annual rpt, U8710–2.10

Washington State electric utility financial and operating data, by company, 1982-91, annual rpt, S8450–1.2

see also Nuclear accidents and safety

see also Nuclear weapons

see also Radiation

see also Radioactive waste and disposal

see also Uranium

Nuclear radiation

see Radiation

Nuclear war

see War

Nuclear weapons

Defense forces structure, by service branch and for nuclear weapons, FY90, FY93, and DOD recommendation in 1993 review of post-Cold War needs, article, C5800–4.527

Soviet Union nuclear missiles and bombers in 3 Republics other than Russia, and number of warheads, 1993 article, C5800–4.504

see also Arms control and disarmament

see also Missiles and rockets

Numismatics

see Coins and coinage

Nursery products

see Flowers and nursery products

Nursery school

see Preschool education

Nurses and nursing

Colleges of nursing deans and salaries, by personal and instn characteristics, 1992/93, annual rpt, A0615–2

Colleges of nursing enrollment and grads, by degree level, sex, race-ethnicity, and instn type and location, 1992/93 and trends, annual rpt, A0615–4

Colleges of nursing faculty and salaries, by personal and instn characteristics, 1992/93, annual rpt, A0615–1

Drug prescription writing authority for nurse practitioners and physician assistants, by State, 1991/92, U8850–8.4

Educational and professional trends and devs in nursing, monthly rpt, A8010–3

Higher education nursing program finances, faculty and clinical practice, and clinic/center operations, by instn characteristics, 1992/93 biennial rpt, A0615–5

HMO benefits coverage, premiums, and rating methods used, by plan characteristics, 1991 and trends, annual rpt, A5150–2.1

Hospital incidents related to shortage of nurses, 1993, article, A1865–1.518

Hospital patient care practices and outlook, and impact of clinical info systems, views of nurses, 1993 survey, article, A1865–1.520

Hospital recruiting of nurses and allied health personnel, with budget, vacancies, turnover, and compensation, 1993 and trends, annual survey rpt, A6500–1

Japan and US health care system data, including expenditures, facilities, insurance coverage, and population health indicators, 1993 article, R5650–2.515

Latin America statistical abstract, general data by country, 1992 annual rpt, U6250–1.7

Managed health care topics seen as appropriate for undergraduate education among managed care nurses, Jan 1993 survey, article, A1865–1.517

Physician performance ratings on selected criteria by nurses vs by other doctors, and views on use of ratings by nurses, 1993 article, A3273–8.510

Practical/vocational nursing State-approved programs, including admissions, enrollment, and grads, by instn, State, and territory, 1992, annual directory, A8010–5

Registered nursing State-approved programs, including admissions, enrollment, and grads, by instn, State, and territory, 1992, annual directory, A8010–4

Salaries of scientists, engineers, technicians, and other professionals, by employee and employer characteristics, 1990s and trends, biennial rpt, A3960–1

Schools of nursing, programs, enrollment, student and staff characteristics, and grads, 1991 and trends, annual rpt, A8010–1

Southern States nursing school enrollment, with shares for blacks and Hispanics, 1989/90 and trends, biennial fact book, A8945–1.2

State social, economic, and govtl indicators, with rankings, 1993 semiannual rpt, B8500–1.9

Suicides among nurses by age, and correlation with smoking status, 1976-88, article, A2623–1.504

Women and minorities in professional fields, detailed education and labor force data, 1991 and trends, recurring rpt, A3960–2.3

World population and health indicators, with detail by region and country, 1992/93 biennial rpt, R9455–1.5

Index by Subjects and Names

Nutrition and malnutrition

State and local:

Arkansas higher education degrees conferred, by level, discipline, student race and sex, and instn, 1990/91 and trends, annual rpt, S0690–3

Delaware school nurse services, including screening examinations, by county, 1991/92, annual rpt, S1430–1.6

Florida county data book, 1992/93 annual rpt, C6360–1

Florida health care atlas, including manpower by occupation and health care facilities by type, by district and county, 1992 annual rpt, S1746–1.2

Florida statistical abstract, general data, 1992 annual rpt, U6660–1.20

Hawaii data book, general data, 1992 annual rpt, S2090–1.2

Kentucky Medicaid recipients and payments, by program, county, and type of medical service, monthly rpt, S3140–5

Montana home health service clients and visits by type of service, by agency, 1991, annual rpt, S4690–2

Nevada statistical abstract, general data, 1992 biennial rpt, S5005–1.2

New York State statistical yearbook, general data, 1992 annual rpt, U5100–1.10

North Carolina nurse education scholarship program participants and awards, by instn, 1991/92, annual rpt, U8013–1.3

South Carolina statistical abstract, general data, 1993 annual rpt, S7125–1.10

Texas nursing employment, demand outlook, earnings, and education, by selected characteristics, various years 1971-91, U8850–8.2

Virginia nursing school administrator and hospital executive views on nursing graduate skills, 1992 survey, article, A1865–1.503

see also Midwives

Nursing homes

Black American residents of nursing homes, with comparisons to whites, 1977 and 1985, annual compilation, C6775–2.2

Catholic facilities for elderly and handicapped persons, by type and State, 1993 annual almanac, C6885–1

Drugstore (independent pharmacy) serving of long-term care facilities, by census div and sales size, 1991, annual survey, B5165–1

Financial ratios and performance, for over 350 SIC 4-digit industries, FY88-92, annual rpt, A6400–3

Food service industry sales and establishments, with growth outlook, by market segment, 1993 annual feature, C1850–3.503

Insurance adequacy as means of making nursing home care affordable to elderly, with detail by age and/or State, 1992 and 2005, R4865–12

Mental health care use by nursing home residents, by resident and home characteristics, and provider type, 1985/86 survey, article, A2623–1.505

Operating and financial composite ratios for corporations, with establishments and receipts, for approx 200 industries, by asset size, FY90, annual rpt, C7800–1

Restraint use on nursing home residents correlated with resident characteristics and staff care time, 1993 article, A2623–1.505

State social, economic, and govtl indicators, with rankings, 1993 semiannual rpt, B8500–1.9

State and local:

Alabama statistical abstract, general data, 1992 recurring rpt, U5680–2.8

Arkansas human services dept finances and operations, including Medicaid payments by type of service, FY91 and trends, annual rpt, S0700–2.3

Arkansas population in instns and other group quarters, 1990, census rpt, U5935–7

California population in instns and other group quarters, 1990, census rpt, S0840–9

DC statistical profile, general data, 1992 annual rpt, S1535–3.5

Florida county data book, 1992/93 annual rpt, C6360–1

Florida nursing homes, beds, occupancy, and State certificate of need review activity, with data by district and county, 1992 annual rpt, S1746–1.2

Florida statistical abstract, general data, 1992 annual rpt, U6660–1.2, U6660–1.20

Georgia county guide, general data, 1993 annual rpt, U6750–1

Hawaii long-term care facility capacity, admissions, and length of stay, by county and/or facility, 1990 and trends, annual rpt, S2065–1.7

Indiana public assistance program participation, expenditures, and services, by county, FY92 and trends, annual rpt, S2623–1

Kansas statistical abstract, general data, 1991/92 annual rpt, U7095–2.2

Kentucky Medicaid recipients and payments, by program, county, and type of medical service, monthly rpt, S3140–5

Louisiana deaths by age, place of occurrence, and locality, 1989-90, annual rpt, S3295–1

Maryland hospital and nursing home deaths, by race and location, 1989, annual rpt, S3635–1

Maryland medical assistance payments and recipients, by program, type of service, location, demographic characteristics, and facility, FY92 and trends, annual rpt, S3635–3

Mississippi statistical abstract, general data, 1992 annual rpt, U3255–4.2

Missouri public welfare and medical assistance recipients, expenditures, and case processing, by program and county, FY92 and trends, annual rpt, S4575–2

Montana health care facility capacity, utilization, and finances, by instn, 1991, annual rpt, S4690–2

Montana welfare and medical assistance program cases and payments, by county and type of service, monthly rpt, S4755–1

Nebraska public welfare cases, recipients, and payments, by program and county, FY92 and trends, annual rpt, S4957–1

New Jersey population in instns and other group quarters, by county, 1990, census rpt, S5425–19

New York State medical assistance expenditures, by State area and type of care, 1991 and trends, annual rpt, S5800–2.2

New York State nursing home-related indictments, dispositions, and convictions, 1990-91, annual rpt, S5760–3.2

North Carolina public welfare programs, cases, recipients, staff, and finances, by county, 1st half FY93, semiannual rpt, S5940–2

Oklahoma statistical abstract, general data, 1992 annual rpt, U8130–2.9

Pennsylvania population in instns and other group quarters, 1990, census rpt, U4130–13

Pennsylvania statistical abstract, general data, 1992 recurring rpt, U4130–6.5

South Carolina public welfare recipients, payments, and case processing, by county and program, monthly rpt, S7252–1

South Dakota medical assistance recipients and payments, by type of service, program, and county, FY92, annual rpt, S7385–1

Tennessee statistical abstract, general data, 1992/93 annual rpt, U8710–2.17

Texas nursing/personal care facilities and expenditures, 1977, 1982, and 1987, U8850–8.3

Texas welfare and social services program expenditures, recipients, and fraud cases, by county and/or program, FY92 and trends, annual rpt, S7695–1

Utah vital statistics, including births and deaths, by instn and/or location, 1990, annual rpt, S7835–1.2

Washington State deaths in nursing homes, 1991, annual rpt, S8363–1

Washington State public assistance clients and service costs, by client characteristics, program, and county, FY90, annual rpt, S8420–2

West Virginia welfare and social service program caseloads and expenditures, by county, monthly rpt, S8560–2

Wyoming SSI recipients in nursing homes, by county, FY92, annual rpt, S8908–1

Nuskey, Sharon

"German Reunification", R4105–82.3

"Latin America: A Region in Transition", R4105–82.6

"Privatization", R4105–82.5

"Uruguay Round of GATT", R4105–82.2

Nutrition and malnutrition

Child mortality correlated with weight category, review of studies in 4 countries, 1993 article, A2623–1.510

Consumer nutrition awareness and health concerns, with food shopping and consumption patterns, by respondent characteristics, 1993 survey, annual rpt, A4950–36

Developing countries family planning and child survival efforts, by country and selected demographic characteristics, 1980s-90, R8720–1

Elderly population risk of malnutrition, New England study of residents over age 70, 1993 survey article, A2623–1.509, C2150–6.508

Ethiopia famine analysis, including household impacts and responses, drought factor, agricultural activity and markets, and intervention programs, 1980s, R5620–1.36

Food store use of selected methods to provide nutritional info, including fruit and vegetable nutrition awareness programs, 1992, annual rpt, A4950–5

Nutrition and malnutrition

Health condition and preventive health care and safety practices of adults, by respondent characteristics, 1992 and trends, annual survey rpt, C8111–2

Hospital patient discharges and length of stay, by diagnosis, type of operation, age, and region, 1991, annual rpt series, B4455–1

Hospital patients with diagnoses of eating disorders, length of stay by age, sex, and region, 1991, annual rpt, B4455–2

Labeling law changes potential impact on public health condition, by sex, 1993 article, A2623–1.507

Latin America statistical abstract, general data by country, 1992 annual rpt, U6250–1.7, U6250–1.12

Restaurant menu practices, including items offered, and info on nutrition, ingredients, and preparation, 1987 and 1992, A8200–22

Supermarket shopper views on healthiness of diet and food nutritional content, 1993 and trends, annual survey rpt, A4950–3

Urban public school systems nutrition education programs, for 47 systems, 1990/91, A4425–4

Vegetarian food attitudes of consumers, including restaurant ordering practices, and reasons for choosing vegetarian items, 1991-92 surveys, article, A8200–1.511

Women's calorie intake during pregnancy and lactation, by race and poverty status, 1985-86 study, article, A2623–1.510

World population and health indicators, with detail by region and country, 1992/93 biennial rpt, R9455–1.5

State and local:

Alabama vital statistics, including population, births, deaths by cause, marriages, and divorces, by location and demographic characteristics, 1992 and trends, annual rpt, S0175–2

California vital statistics, including population, births, and deaths by cause, by demographic characteristics and county, 1990 and trends, annual rpt, S0865–1

Colorado health behavior risk factor surveillance survey results, by respondent characteristics, 1990, recurring rpt, S1010–3

Colorado vital statistics, including population, births, deaths by cause, abortion, marriage and divorce, and adoption, by demographic characteristics and location, 1990 and trends, annual rpt, S1010–1

Florida vital statistics, including population, births, deaths by cause, and marriages and dissolutions, by location and demographic characteristics, 1992 and trends, annual rpt, S1745–3

Hawaii hunger indicators, by age, 1992, annual rpt, S2090–1.2

Hawaii nutrition education and supplemental food program for women and children, 1990, annual rpt, S2065–1.4

Idaho vital statistics, including births, deaths by cause, abortions, marriages, and divorces, by demographic characteristics and county, 1991 and trends, annual rpt, S2250–2

Iowa health behavior risk factor surveillance survey results, by respondent characteristics, 1991, annual rpt, S2795–2

Louisiana vital statistics, including population, births, deaths by cause, reportable diseases, marriages, and divorces, by demographic characteristics and locality, 1989-90 and trends, annual rpt, S3295–1

Maine vital statistics, including births, deaths by cause, abortions, and marriages and divorces, by demographic characteristics and location, 1991 and trends, annual rpt, S3460–2

Maryland vital statistics, including population, births, deaths by cause, marriages, and divorces, by demographic characteristics and location, 1989 and trends, annual rpt, S3635–1

Massachusetts vital statistics, including births, deaths by cause, marriages, divorces, and population, by locality and demographic characteristics, 1990 and trends, annual rpt, S3850–1

Michigan vital statistics, including births, deaths, marriages, divorces/annulments, and communicable diseases, by location and demographic characteristics, 1990 and trends, annual rpt, S4000–3

Minnesota vital statistics, including population, births, abortions, deaths, marriages, and divorces, by location and demographic characteristics, 1991 and trends, annual rpt, S4190–2

Mississippi vital statistics, including births, deaths by cause, marriages, and divorces, by demographic characteristics and location, 1992 and trends, annual rpt, S4350–1

Montana vital statistics, including births, deaths by cause, abortion, disease, and marriage and divorce, by demographic characteristics and county, 1990-91 and trends, annual rpt, S4690–1

New Hampshire vital statistics, including population, births, deaths by cause, marriages, and divorces, by location and demographic characteristics, 1991 and trends, annual rpt, S5215–1

New Jersey vital statistics, including births, deaths, population, communicable diseases, and marriages and divorces, by demographic characteristics and location, 1990 and trends, annual rpt, S5405–1

New York State health behavior risk factor surveillance survey results, by respondent characteristics, 1990, recurring rpt, S5765–3

North Dakota vital statistics, including births, deaths by cause, marriages and divorces, and abortions, by demographic characteristics and/or county, 1991 and trends, annual rpt, S6105–2

Ohio vital statistics, including births, deaths by cause, marriages, divorces, and population, by demographic characteristics and location, 1991 and trends, annual rpt, S6285–1

Oregon vital statistics, including deaths by cause, communicable diseases, marriages, and divorces, by age, sex, race-ethnicity, and county, 1991 and trends, annual rpt, S6615–5

Rhode Island vital statistics, including population, births, deaths, marriages, and divorces, by demographic characteristics and locality, 1989 and trends, annual rpt, S6995–1

South Carolina deaths, by detailed cause, age, sex, and race, 1990, annual rpt, S7175–2

Tennessee vital statistics, including births, deaths by cause, marriages, divorces, and population, by demographic characteristics and location, 1991 and trends, annual rpt, S7520–2

Texas vital statistics, including births, deaths by cause, abortions, marriages, and divorces, by location and demographic characteristics, 1991 and trends, annual rpt, S7685–1

Utah vital statistics, including births and deaths by cause, by demographic characteristics and location, 1990, annual rpt, S7835–1.2

Vermont vital statistics, including population, births, deaths by cause, abortions, marriages, and divorces, by location and demographic characteristics, 1991 and trends, annual rpt, S8054–1

Virginia vital statistics, including births, deaths by cause, marriages and divorces, and communicable disease, by demographic characteristics and location, 1991 and trends, annual rpt, S8225–1

Washington State vital statistics, including births, deaths by cause, and population, by demographic characteristics and location, 1991 and trends, annual rpt, S8363–1

West Virginia vital statistics, including births, deaths by cause, marriages, and divorces, by location and demographic characteristics, 1991 and trends, annual rpt, S8560–1

Wisconsin vital statistics, including population, births, deaths by cause, and marriages and dissolutions, by county and demographic characteristics, 1991 and trends, annual rpt, S8715–4

see also Birthweight

see also Breast-feeding

see also Dieting and dietetic products

see also Dietitians and nutritionists

see also Food assistance

see also Food consumption

see also Food ingredients and additives

see also Food supply

see also Obesity

see also School lunch and breakfast programs

see also Vitamins and nutrients

see also under By Disease in the "Index by Categories"

Nuts

Exports of farm products, by detailed commodity and country of destination, US and California, 1991, annual rpt, B9520–1

Pecan production, price, and value, US and 7 Southeastern States, 1989-91, annual rpt, U3255–4.15

Snack food consumption patterns, by snack type and consumer characteristics, 1989/90 and trends, recurring rpt, A8905–2

Snack food sales, consumption, and prices, by snack type and region, with data on industry operations and outlook, 1992 and trends, annual rpt, A8905–1

Supermarket sales by detailed product type, 1992 and trends, annual feature, C5225–1.507

Index by Subjects and Names

Obstetrics and gynecology

State and local:
Alabama agricultural production, marketing, and income, by county and/or commodity, and farms and acreage, 1992 and trends, annual rpt, S0090–1
Arizona agricultural production, marketing, and finances, by commodity and county, 1988-92, annual rpt, U5830–1
Arkansas agricultural production, marketing, and finances, by commodity and county, with farms and acreage, 1992 and trends, annual rpt, U5920–1
California fruit and nut production, marketing, and income, by commodity, 1983-92, annual rpt, S0850–1.1
Florida pecan production and prices for improved and native/seedling varieties, 1982-92, annual rpt, S1685–1.4
Georgia agricultural production, marketing, and finances, by commodity and/or county, and farms and acreage, 1991 and trends, annual rpt, S1855–1
Hawaii agricultural production and marketing, by commodity and island, 1987-91, annual rpt, S2030–1
Louisiana agricultural production, marketing, and finances, by commodity or parish, 1985-91, annual rpt, U2740–1
New Mexico agricultural production, marketing, and finances, by commodity and county, with farms and acreage, 1991 and trends, annual rpt, S5530–1
North Carolina agricultural production, marketing, and finances, by commodity and county, 1991 and trends, annual rpt, S5885–1
Oklahoma agricultural production, marketing, and finances, by commodity and county, 1992 and trends, annual rpt, S6405–1
Oregon agricultural production, marketing, and finances, by commodity and/or county, with farms and acreage, 1991 and trends, annual rpt, S6575–1
Texas agricultural production, marketing, and finances, by commodity and county, and farms and farmland, 1991 and trends, annual rpt series, S7630–1
Washington State agricultural production, marketing, and finances, by commodity and/or county, 1992 and trends, annual rpt, S8328–1
see also Oils, oilseeds, and fats
see also Peanuts

NYSE
see New York Stock Exchange
see the "Index by Issuing Sources" for publications covered by SRI

OAPEC
see Organization of Arab Petroleum Exporting Countries

OASDHI
see Old-Age, Survivors, Disability, and Health Insurance

Oats
see Grains and grain products

Obesity
Heart disease risk factor prevalence, by State, 1989, semiannual rpt, B8500–1.9
Hospital patient discharges and length of stay, by diagnosis, type of operation, age, and region, 1991, annual rpt series, B4455–1

Hospital patient discharges and length of stay, by diagnostic related group (DRG), payment source, age, and region, 1991, annual rpt series, B4455–3
Women's obesity and related activity and weight-loss indicators, by race, 1985-86, article, A2623–1.502

State and local:
Alabama health behavior risk factor surveillance survey results, by respondent characteristics, 1988-89, recurring rpt, S0175–6
California health behavior risk factor surveillance survey results, by respondent characteristics, 1991 and trends, annual rpt, S0865–2
California vital statistics, including population, births, and deaths by cause, by demographic characteristics and county, 1990 and trends, annual rpt, S0865–1
Colorado health behavior risk factor surveillance survey results, by respondent characteristics, 1990, recurring rpt, S1010–3
Connecticut health behavior risk factor surveillance survey results, 1989-91, annual rpt, S1200–2
Florida vital statistics, including population, births, deaths by cause, and marriages and dissolutions, by location and demographic characteristics, 1992 and trends, annual rpt, S1745–3
Georgia health behavior risk factor surveillance survey results, by respondent characteristics, 1991 and trends, annual rpt, S1895–2
Hawaii health behavior risk factor surveillance survey results, by respondent characteristics, 1990, annual rpt, S2065–1.4
Idaho vital statistics, including births, deaths by cause, abortions, marriages, and divorces, by demographic characteristics and county, 1991 and trends, annual rpt, S2250–2
Iowa health behavior risk factor surveillance survey results, by respondent characteristics, 1991, annual rpt, S2795–2
Kentucky health behavior risk factor surveillance survey results, by State area and respondent characteristics, 1988-90, annual rpt, S3140–6
Maine vital statistics, including births, deaths by cause, abortions, and marriages and divorces, by demographic characteristics and location, 1991 and trends, annual rpt, S3460–2
Massachusetts health behavior risk factor surveillance survey results, by respondent characteristics, 1986-90, recurring rpt, S3850–3
Massachusetts vital statistics, including births, deaths by cause, marriages, divorces, and population, by locality and demographic characteristics, 1990 and trends, annual rpt, S3850–1
Michigan health behavior risk factor surveillance survey results, by respondent characteristics, 1991, annual rpt, S4000–4
Michigan vital statistics, including births, deaths, marriages, divorces/annulments, and communicable diseases, by location and demographic characteristics, 1990 and trends, annual rpt, S4000–3

Mississippi vital statistics, including births, deaths by cause, marriages, and divorces, by demographic characteristics and location, 1992 and trends, annual rpt, S4350–1
Nevada health behavior risk factor surveillance survey results, by location and respondent characteristics, 1991, annual rpt, S5075–3
North Dakota health behavior risk factor surveillance survey results, by respondent characteristics, 1991 and trends, annual rpt, S6105–3
Pennsylvania health behavior risk factor surveillance survey results, by respondent characteristics, 1991, annual rpt, S6820–4
South Carolina deaths, by detailed cause, age, sex, and race, 1990, annual rpt, S7175–2
Tennessee health behavior risk factor surveillance survey results, by respondent characteristics, 1986-90, annual rpt, S7520–3
Texas health behavior risk factor surveillance survey results, by respondent characteristics, 1991 and trends, annual rpt, S7685–2
Utah health behavior risk factor surveillance survey results, by respondent characteristics, 1991, annual rpt, S7835–3
Vermont vital statistics, including population, births, deaths by cause, abortions, marriages, and divorces, by location and demographic characteristics, 1991 and trends, annual rpt, S8054–1
West Virginia vital statistics, including births, deaths by cause, marriages, and divorces, by location and demographic characteristics, 1991 and trends, annual rpt, S8560–1
see also Dieting and dietetic products
see also under By Disease in the "Index by Categories"

Obscenity and pornography
State and local:
California crimes and arrests, clearances, and arrest dispositions, with data by offense and offender characteristics, 1987-92, annual rpt, S0910–1.1
California criminal justice system detailed data, by offense, county, age, race-ethnicity, and sex, 1991 and trends, annual rpt, S0910–2
Idaho crimes and arrests, by offense, with data by location and offender characteristics, 1992 and trends, annual rpt, S2275–2
Illinois crimes and arrests, by offense, with data by location and offender characteristics, 1991, annual rpt, S2536–1

Obstetrics and gynecology
Developing countries births assisted by trained attendant, and prenatal care and low birthweight rates, by country, 1985, R8720–1.2
Developing countries births assisted by trained attendant, and prenatal care and tetanus vaccination rates, by country, 1984-92 surveys, U2520–1.51
Hospital patient admission rates and length of stay, by diagnosis and procedure, payment source, age, sex, and region, 1991, B4455–4

Obstetrics and gynecology

Hospital patient charges and length of stay, by diagnosis and procedure, payment source, age, and region, 1991, B4455–5

Hospital patient discharges and length of stay, by diagnosis, type of operation, age, and region, 1991, annual rpt series, B4455–1

Hospital patient discharges and length of stay, by diagnostic related group (DRG), payment source, age, and region, 1991, annual rpt series, B4455–3

Medicaid reimbursement for obstetrical services, by State, FY86-92, article, A5160–1.506

Medical school faculty and compensation, by dept, academic rank, degree, and region, 1992/93, annual rpt, A3273–2

Physician practice economic aspects, detailed data by specialty, 1991-92 and trends, annual compilation, A2200–5

Physicians by detailed specialty and location, 1992 and trends, annual rpt, A2200–3

State and local:

Colorado births by types of obstetric procedures during pregnancy, monthly 1990, annual rpt, S1010–1

Mississippi births by types of obstetric procedures during pregnancy, by race, 1992, annual rpt, S4350–1

Nebraska births by type of obstetric procedures during pregnancy, 1991, annual rpt, S4885–1

Tennessee births by types of obstetric procedures during pregnancy, 1991, annual rpt, S7520–2

Vermont births by type of obstetric procedures during pregnancy, 1991, annual rpt, S8054–1

Washington State births by type of delivery and obstetric procedure used, 1991, annual rpt, S8363–1

see also Maternity

Occupational health and safety

Accidental work-related deaths and disabling injuries, with detail for auto accidents, 1991, annual rpt, C1575–2.507

Aerospace industry injury/illness rates and lost workdays, 1986-90, annual rpt, A0250–2.5

Auto plant worker hand/wrist disorder cases, 1985-86, article, A2623–1.501

Business forms manufacturing plant safety program use, and production hours lost from accidents, 1991-92, biennial rpt, A5785–4

Chemical industry and total manufacturing occupational injury/illness cases and lost workdays, 1970 and 1980-92, annual rpt, A3850–1

Electric utility injury/illness rates per 100 employees, by customer size class and region, 1990, annual article, A2625–1.501

Federal regulatory agency costs and staff, for approx 50 agencies, FY70s-94, annual rpt, U9640–1

Food service industry work force, work-related injuries, and lost workdays, 1990-91, article, C1200–5.507

Hazardous waste protective suit use impact on available work time, 1993 article, C5800–2.534

Injuries and deaths from accidents by type, and selected incidence and economic loss data, 1991 and trends, annual rpt, A5650–1.4

Injuries, illnesses, and deaths, by industry group, with workdays lost, 1991-92 and trends, annual rpt, A8375–2.2

Injuries/illnesses and deaths, and workdays lost, by detailed industry, 1991 and trends, annual rpt, A8375–4

Injury and illness incidence and lost workdays by industry div, 1989-90 and trends, annual rpt, A5173–2.4

Iron and steel industry fatalities, injury/illness rate, and workdays lost, 1988-92, annual rpt, A2000–2.1

Meat and poultry processing injury and illness incidence, with lost workdays, 1980-90, annual rpt, A2100–1.1

Natural gas industry employment, payroll, and accident statistics, 1960s-91, annual rpt, A1775–3.9

Oil industry environmental performance, with data on toxic chemical releases, oil spills, occupational injury/illness, and corporate spending, 1990 and trends, annual rpt, A2575–27

Oil industry injury frequency rates, by sector, 1980-92, periodic basic data book, A2575–14.7

Oil/gas industry occupational injury, illness, and employment data, by function, for 136 companies, 1991, annual rpt, A2575–4

South Africa industrial accident rates, for 5 industries, 1993 article, C5226–2.505

Toxic substance exposures reported to poison control centers, by type of exposure and substance, 1988, article, A2623–1.507

Workplace safety and health data, including injury and death incidence, govt regulation and spending, and workers compensation, with data by State, 1992 annual rpt, R8335–1

Youth work-related deaths, and injuries by age and selected industry, 1990, R8335–2

State and local:

Alaska work-related deaths by cause, 1991, article, S0320–1.510

California statistical abstract, general data, 1992 annual rpt, S0840–2.3

DC occupational injuries/illnesses, and disability fund finances, FY87-91, annual rpt, S1535–3.3

Florida statistical abstract, general data, 1992 annual rpt, U6660–1.7

Hawaii data book, general data, 1992 annual rpt, S2090–1.12

Iowa occupational injury/illness rate, by industry div, 1990-91, annual rpt, S2784–3

Missouri occupational disability and death incidents, and compensation costs, by industry and county, 1991 and trends, annual rpt, S4530–2.2

New York State statistical yearbook, general data, 1992 annual rpt, U5100–1.3

Rhode Island industrial and manufacturing accidental deaths, by age, 1989, annual rpt, S6995–1

South Carolina statistical abstract, general data, 1993 annual rpt, S7125–1.7

West Virginia workers compensation accidents reported by county, and program finances, FY83-92, annual rpt, R9385–1.2

Index by Subjects and Names

see also Accidental deaths
see also Agricultural accidents and safety
see also Assaults on police
see also Black lung disease
see also Lead poisoning and pollution
see also Mine accidents and safety
see also Occupational therapy
see also Radiation
see also Workers compensation

Occupational Safety and Health Administration

Hard goods manufacturers views on govt regulation, including 1992 OSHA inspections and outcomes, by product line, 1993 annual survey rpt, A1800–1

Workplace safety and health data, including injury and death incidence, govt regulation and spending, and workers compensation, with data by State, 1992 annual rpt, R8335–1

Occupational testing and certification

Accountants taking and passing certified public accountant exam, 1982-92, annual rpt, A1885–1

Bar admissions, 1963/64-1992/93, annual rpt, A0970–1

Bar exam results and admissions, by State and territory, 1992 and trends, annual rpt, A7458–1

Elementary/secondary education data, with detail for mathematics including test scores and teacher preparation, by State, 1993 biennial rpt, A4355–1

Elementary/secondary prospective teacher characteristics and opinions, survey of persons interested in alternative certification routes, 1992, R6350–7

Elementary/secondary teacher views on use of teacher competency testing and alternative certification methods, Jan-Feb 1993 survey, B6045–7

Employer basic skills testing and training practices and costs, Jan-Mar 1993 survey, annual rpt, A2075–20.13

Employer use of job skills and personality/aptitude testing in hiring, 1991-92, annual survey rpt, B6850–3, B6850–5

Fire dept employment and personnel practices, including eligibility requirements and testing, by population size, metro status, and census div, 1991 survey, recurring rpt, A5800–2.116

Logistics professionals views on occupational certification, 1993 survey article, C2150–1.503

Medical certification exam pass rates, and previous failure record, for foreign medical grads, by test type, Sept and July 1989-90, article, A3273–8.504

Physician medical certificates issued, by specialty, 1982-91, annual fact book, A1275–1.1

Physicians by detailed specialty, location, age, sex, and board certification status, 1992 and trends, annual rpt, A2200–3.1

Real estate appraisers by certification type, 1993 article, C4300–1.505

Science and math elementary/secondary education, including student and teacher characteristics, and requirements, by State, 1991/92, biennial rpt, A4355–3

Urban public school teacher certification rates for mathematics, English, and science, for 47 systems, 1990/91, A4425–4

Index by Subjects and Names

Occupations

State and local:

Alaska insurance licensing examination activity, 1991, annual rpt, S0280–3

California statistical abstract, general data, 1992 annual rpt, S0840–2.11

Colorado public school staff and salaries, by selected characteristics, county, and district, fall 1992 and trends, annual rpt, S1000–2.2

DC licensed professionals, by profession, 1987-91, annual rpt, S1535–3.3, S1535–3.4

Delaware teacher certificates issued, and employment status of education grads, by subject area, 1991/92, annual rpt, S1430–1.3

Georgia statistical abstract, general data, 1992-93 biennial rpt, U6730–1.2

Illinois elementary and secondary school staff, by sex and county, with data on certification, 1990/91, annual rpt, S2440–1.2

Indiana bar examination review petitions handled by supreme court, 1992, annual rpt, S2703–1.1

Kansas insurance agent/broker certifications issued, 1983-92, annual rpt, S2990–1

Maryland bar exam results, with detail by in-State school of graduation, FY92 and trends, annual rpt, S3600–1

Missouri public school administrators and teachers certificates issued, 1991/92, annual rpt, S4505–1.1

New Mexico bar exam results, FY92, annual rpt, S5623–1

New York State insurance license examination results, 1990-91, annual rpt, S5770–3

New York State statistical yearbook, general data, 1992 annual rpt, U5100–1.3

North Dakota bar examinations and outcomes, 1992, annual rpt, S6210–1

North Dakota elementary and secondary school staff by position and certification status, by region, 1992/93 annual rpt, S6180–3

Pennsylvania bar examinees and results, 1991, annual rpt, S6900–1.1

South Carolina bar exam results, 1977-92, annual rpt, S7197–1

Tennessee State boards certification activity, by occupation, FY91, annual rpt, S7466–1

Texas appellate and trial judges licensed to practice law, Sept 1992, annual rpt, S7703–1

Texas financial condition, including revenues by source, expenditures by function and dept, and investments, with data for over 400 individual funds, FY92, annual rpt, S7655–2.2

Texas social worker and child care administrator certification activity, Sept 1991 and Aug 1992, annual rpt, S7695–1

West Virginia education professional certificates issued, by county, field, and/or instn, 1991/92, annual rpt, S8540–3

West Virginia public school staff specialization permits issued, by subject area and county, 1988/89-1992/93, annual rpt, S8540–4.3

Occupational therapy

HMO benefits coverage, premiums, and rating methods used, by plan characteristics, 1991 and trends, annual rpt, A5150–2.1

Hospital recruiting of nurses and allied health personnel, with budget, vacancies, turnover, and compensation, 1993 and trends, annual survey rpt, A6500–1

State and local:

Florida county data book, 1992/93 annual rpt, C6360–1

Florida health care atlas, including manpower by occupation and health care facilities by type, by district and county, 1992 annual rpt, S1746–1.2

Florida statistical abstract, general data, 1992 annual rpt, U6660–1.20

Hawaii health dept family health services and recipients, including school health programs, 1990 annual rpt, S2065–1.5

Kentucky Medicaid recipients and payments, by program, county, and type of medical service, monthly rpt, S3140–5

Montana home health service clients and visits by type of service, by agency, 1991, annual rpt, S4690–2

see also Vocational rehabilitation

Occupational training

see Employee development

see Vocational education and training

Occupations

Black American 8th grade student expected adult occupations, with comparison to whites, 1988, annual compilation, C6775–2.3

College freshmen attitudes and characteristics, degree and career plans, and financial aid sources, by sex and instn type, fall 1992, annual survey, U6215–1

Employment growth projections accuracy analysis for BLS, by occupation and industry div, 1993 article, S4205–3.501

Europe public opinion on preferred occupation for own child, for 9 countries and 3 Soviet Union Republics, 1991 survey, C8915–8.1

Hispanic American 8th grade student expected adult occupations, with comparison to whites, 1988, annual compilation, C6775–3.2

Public opinion on honesty/ethical standards of selected occupations, 1992 Gallup Polls and trends, C4040–1.501

Public opinion on political careers for their son or daughter, June 1993 Gallup Poll, C4040–1.512

Public opinion on social, political, and economic issues, detailed data, 1972-91 surveys, annual rpt, U6395–1

Social prestige ratings among general public, for 77 occupations, 1989, survey article, C7000–3.509

Women and minorities in professional fields, detailed education and labor force data, 1980s-91, with historical trends, recurring rpt, A3960–2

State and local:

Arizona occupational profiles, with employment and job outlook, by industry div, occupation, and county, series, S0465–2

Colorado labor force planning rpt, including population, employment by industry, and job service applicants, FY94 annual rpt, S1040–3

Georgia county guide, general data, 1993 annual rpt, U6750–1

Hawaii data book, general data, 1992 annual rpt, S2090–1.12

Iowa employment and job openings by leading occupation and occupational group, 1992 and 2000, annual rpt, S2784–3

Kentucky job openings and employment in fastest-growing occupations, 1987-2000, annual planning rpt, S3140–3

Maine employment, by SIC 2-digit industry and detailed occupation, triennial series, S3465–1

Michigan employment projections by occupation, 1988-2000, annual planning rpt, S3980–1.2

Mississippi labor force planning rpt, including population, employment, and characteristics of unemployed and disadvantaged, 1993 annual rpt, S4345–1

Montana labor force planning rpt, including population, income, and employment and job openings by industry and occupation, with selected data by county, 1993-94 annual rpt, S4710–3

Nevada employment and job opening outlook for 6 rapidly growing occupations, through 1996, article, S5040–1.502

New Hampshire employment, by SIC 2- and 3-digit industry and detailed occupation, series, S5205–2

New Mexico labor force planning rpt, including population characteristics, and employment by industry and occupation, 1993 annual rpt, S5624–1

North Carolina employment in SIC 2-digit industries, by detailed occupation, triennial rpt series, S5917–5

Pennsylvania labor force planning rpt, including population characteristics, employment and job openings by industry and occupation, and income trends, FY92 annual rpt, S6845–3

Rhode Island labor force planning rpt, including population, employment by industry, job openings, and characteristics of insured unemployed, 1993 annual rpt, S6980–3

South Carolina labor force planning rpt, including population, employment, income, and job service activities, 1992 annual rpt, S7155–3

Texas employment, by SIC 2- and 3-digit industry and detailed occupation, series, S7675–1

West Virginia labor force planning rpt, including population, employment, and job service activities, with data by county and service delivery area, 1993 annual rpt, S8534–2

see also Agricultural labor

see also Apprenticeship

see also Blue collar workers

see also Clerical workers

see also Consultants

see also Employee development

see also Employment and unemployment, specific industry

see also Engineers and engineering

see also Executives and managers

see also Federal employees

see also Health occupations

see also Job tenure

see also Judges

see also Lawyers and legal services

see also Librarians

see also Migrant workers

Occupations

see also Military personnel
see also Occupational testing and certification
see also Pilots
see also Production workers
see also Professional and technical workers
see also Sales workers
see also Scientists and technicians
see also Service workers
see also State and local employees
see also Teachers
see also Vocational education and training
see also Vocational rehabilitation
see also Work conditions
see also Writers and writing
see also under By Occupation in the "Index by Categories"

Ocean liners
see Passenger ships

Ocean pollution
see Marine pollution

Ocean resources
see Marine resources

Oceania
- Energy exploration, rotary drilling rigs in operation, by world area and country, monthly rpt, B4675–1
- Jewish population by world area, country, and US census div, State, and city, 1990-92, annual compilation, A2050–1
- Lumber exports from US to Pacific Rim, by country and product type, monthly rpt, A1630–2
- Motor vehicle world production, sales, trade, and registrations, by country, world area, manufacturer, and make, 1991 and trends, annual rpt, A0865–2.1
- Population growth trends, vital statistics, and demographic and socioeconomic characteristics, series, R4500–1
- Population size and characteristics, GNP, and land area, by world region and/or country, 1993 annual data sheet, R8750–5
- Travel trends, including tourist arrivals and expenditures, by region and/or country, 1992 annual rpt, C2140–1.3

see also Australia
see also New Zealand
see also Papua New Guinea
see also Tonga
see also Trust Territory of the Pacific Islands
see also under By Foreign Country or World Area in the "Index by Categories"

Oceanography
- Higher education geoscience enrollment and degrees awarded, by sex, race-ethnicity, and discipline, 1991/92, annual rpt, A1785–3

see also Marine pollution
see also Marine resources
see also Navigation

OECD
see Organization for Economic Cooperation and Development

Off-road vehicles
see Recreational vehicles

Offenses against family
State and local:
- Alabama juvenile and adult arrests, by type of offense, 1992, annual rpt, S0119–1.1
- Arizona arrests by offense, offender characteristics, and county, 1992, annual rpt, S0505–2.2

Arkansas crimes and arrests, by offense, victim and offender characteristics, and location, 1992 and trends, annual rpt, S0652–1

Colorado crimes and arrests, by offense and location, with offender characteristics, and assaults on police, 1992, annual rpt, S1068–1

Connecticut arrests, by offense, offender characteristics, and local agency, 1992, annual rpt, S1256–1.2

DC criminal justice system summary, including crimes and arrests, criminal procedure, prisoners, and parole, 1991 and trends, annual rpt, S1535–2

Hawaii crimes and arrests, by offense, with data by county and victim-offender characteristics, 1992, annual rpt, S2035–1

Idaho crimes and arrests, by offense, with data by location and offender characteristics, 1992 and trends, annual rpt, S2275–2

Kansas crimes and arrests, by offense, with data by location, agency, and victim-offender characteristics, 1992 and trends, annual rpt, S2925–1.1

Kentucky arrests by county and offense, and law enforcement employment by agency, 1992, annual rpt, S3150–1.2

Maine arrests of adults and juveniles, by offense, age, and sex, 1991, annual rpt, S3475–1.2

Maryland crimes and arrests, by offense, location, and offender characteristics, with law enforcement employment and assaults on officers, 1992 and trends, annual rpt, S3665–1

Michigan crimes and arrests, by offense, with data by location and offender characteristics, 1992 and trends, annual rpt, S3997–1

Missouri crimes and arrests, by offense and location, with victim and offender characteristics, 1991 and trends, annual rpt, S4560–2

Montana crimes and clearances, by offense and jurisdiction, 1992, annual rpt, S4705–1

New Hampshire arrests, by offense and offender age, sex, and race-ethnicity, 1991, annual rpt, S5250–2.2

New Jersey arrests by offense, age, race-ethnicity, sex, and county, 1992 and trends, annual rpt, S5430–1.2

New York State crimes and arrests by offense and demographic characteristics, and court activity and corrections, 1991 and trends, annual rpt, S5760–3

North Carolina arrests by detailed offense, offender characteristics, and county, 1991-92, annual rpt, S5955–1.2

North Dakota crimes and arrests, by offense, location, and offender characteristics, and law enforcement employment, 1991 and trends, annual rpt, S6060–1

Oklahoma crimes and arrests, by offense, with victim and offender characteristics, 1990-92, annual rpt, S6465–1.1

Oregon crimes and arrests, by offense, with data by county, local agency, and offender characteristics, 1992 and trends, annual rpt, S6603–3

Index by Subjects and Names

Pennsylvania crimes and arrests, by offense, with data by location and offender characteristics, 1992 and trends, annual rpt, S6860–1

South Carolina crimes and arrests, by detailed offense, offender characteristics, and location, 1992 and trends, annual rpt, S7205–1.2

Texas arrests, by age, sex, race-ethnicity, and offense, 1992, annual rpt, S7735–2.2

Utah crimes and arrests, by offense, county, and local agency, 1992 and trends, annual rpt, S7890–3

Virginia crimes and arrests by offense, and law enforcement employment, by location and reporting agency, 1992, annual rpt, S8295–2.2

Washington State crimes and arrests, by offense, with data by location and offender characteristics, 1992 and trends, annual rpt, S8440–1

West Virginia crimes and arrests, by offense, location, and offender characteristics, 1990-91, annual rpt, S8610–1

Wisconsin crimes and arrests, by offense, offender characteristics, county, and local agency, 1992 and trends, annual rpt, S8771–1

Wyoming adult and juvenile arrests, by offense, county, and local jurisdiction, 1991, annual rpt, S8867–3.2

see also Child abuse and neglect
see also Domestic relations courts and cases
see also Domestic violence

Office automation
see Automation
see Word processing equipment

Office buildings
see Commercial buildings
see Public buildings
see Work conditions

Office furniture and equipment
see Business machines and equipment

Office supplies
- Business card use trends, for 15 cities, 1987-92, article, C4687–1.505
- Business forms industry detailed financial and operating ratios, with summary operating data, FY91, annual rpt, A5785–3
- Business forms industry trends and outlook, including data by product type, 1992 annual rpt, A5785–2
- Business forms manufacturing plant employment and compensation data, by region, 1992 and trends, biennial rpt, A5785–4
- Discount store sales and productivity data for 20 depts, 1993 annual feature, C5150–3.516
- Discount stores, sales, and earnings, for top chains, with detail by specialty, 1993 annual feature, C5150–3.514
- Drugstore advertising shares for top 10 stationery/home office product types and brands, Aug 1992, article, C5150–2.501
- Financial and operating data for office product dealers, by sales volume and region, 1991 and trends, annual rpt, A8110–1
- Financial performance and growth rankings for approx 1,000 top corporations, with comparisons by industry group, 1993 annual rpt, C3950–1.505

Index by Subjects and Names

Officials

Financial ratios and performance, for over 350 SIC 4-digit industries, FY88-92, annual rpt, A6400–3

Paper and paperboard shipments and consumption, by product grade and end use, 1993 annual rpt, C3975–5.3

Shopping center financial and operating data, with detail by type of tenant, US and Canada, 1991, triennial rpt, R9285–1

Office workers

see Clerical workers

Official publications

see Government documents

Officials

- Black elected officials, and characteristics of voting age population, with comparisons to whites, 1970s-91, annual compilation, C6775–2.4
- Black elected officials, by office, govt level, and State, Jan 1993, annual article, R5685–4.505
- Black elected officials, by office, govt level, and State or city, Jan 1992 and trends, annual article, R5685–4.502
- City govt policies and conditions, with views of local officials, Natl League of Cities surveys, series, A8012–1
- City officials views on issues and conditions affecting local govt, including top issues for Fed Govt to address , 1992 survey, annual rpt, A8012–1.21
- Election results for Federal offices and Governor, by State, county, major city, and party, with voter registration and turnout, 1992 and trends, biennial rpt, C2500–1
- Europe public opinion on political, economic, and social issues, for 9 countries and 3 Soviet Union Republics, 1991 survey, C8915–8.1
- Governor salaries in 10 States with highest and lowest pay, 1992 article, C5800–7.506
- Governors approval ratings, with tax policy and economic indicators, for 26 Governors, 1993 article, B8500–2.520
- Governors approval ratings, with tax policy indicators, for 16 Governors, 1993, article, B8500–2.513
- Hispanic American elected officials by office and State, with related population characteristics, 1992 annual directory, A6844–1
- Hispanic American elected officials in top 15-20 States and cities with largest Hispanic populations, 1980, annual rpt, U6250–1.5
- Hispanic American elected officials, registered voters, and voting, with comparisons to whites, 1970s-91, annual compilation, C6775–3.3
- Hispanic American municipal officials, 1984-92, and total vs Hispanic population of 35 cities with Hispanic mayors as of 1993, article, C4575–1.511
- Local officials in municipal and county govt, demographic profiles, compensation, and job functions, 1993 annual rpt, A5800–1
- Public opinion on honesty/ethical standards of selected occupations, 1992 Gallup Polls and trends, C4040–1.501
- Public opinion on social, political, and economic issues, detailed data, 1972-91 surveys, annual rpt, U6395–1

Recycling curbside program operations, funding, and recycled materials, municipal official views and summary program characteristics, July 1991 survey, B0230–2

Recycling program obstacles cited by municipal officials, 1993 survey article, C1850–1.505

- Secretary of State James Baker leaving office to run President Bush's reelection campaign, public opinion, July/Aug 1992 Gallup Poll, C4040–1.502
- State tax increases, with political party of Governors and legislators before vs after subsequent elections, for 17 States, 1991-92, U5085–2.8
- Statistical profiles of 50 States and DC, general data, 1993 annual almanac, C4712–1
- Term limitation initiative voting results in 14 States, 1992, article, A1865–1.507
- Utility and transportation regulatory agency activities, scope of jurisdiction, finances, and employees, by agency, 1991/92 annual rpt, A7015–2
- Vice President Al Gore favorability ratings among general public, Apr 1993 Gallup Poll and trends, C4040–1.510
- Vice President Dan Quayle's qualification for presidency and job performance, Jan 1993 Gallup Poll and trends, C4040–1.507
- Vice President Dan Quayle's qualification for presidency and retention on 1992 ballot, July 1992 Gallup Poll and trends, C4040–1.501
- Women elected to House of Representatives in Nov 1992, by marital status, own and children's ages, abortion views, and political party, 1992 article, C5800–7.504
- Women in elective office, news and statistics, series, U4510–4
- Women officials in Federal, State, and local govt offices, fact sheet series, U4510–1

State and local:

- Alabama election results, by district and/or county, 1992 general election, biennial rpt, S0205–1
- Alaska election results, and voter registration and turnout, by district and precinct, 1992 general election, biennial rpt, S0337–1
- Arizona election results and voter registration, by county and/or district, 1992 general election, biennial rpt, S0520–1
- Arizona State constitutional amendment on term limitations, election results by county, 1992 general election, biennial rpt, S0520–1
- Arkansas election results, by district and/or county, 1992 general election, biennial rpt, S0775–1
- Arkansas State constitutional amendment on limiting elected official terms of office, election results by county, Nov 1992, biennial rpt, S0775–1
- California election results, and voter registration and turnout, by district and/or county, 1992 and trends, biennial rpt, S0934–1
- Colorado election results and voter registration, by political party, and county and/or district, 1992, biennial rpt, S1090–1

Connecticut election results and voter registration and turnout, by location, 1992 general election, biennial rpt, S1265–1

- DC election results and turnout, and voter registration, by ward and precinct, 1992, biennial series, S1525–1
- DC statistical profile, general data, 1992 annual rpt, S1535–3.1
- Delaware election results, by district and/or county, 1992 general election, biennial rpt, S1365–1
- Florida election results, by county and/or district, 1992 general election, biennial rpt, S1800–1
- Florida referendum on limiting elected official terms of office, election results by county, 1992, biennial rpt, S1800–1
- Florida statistical abstract, general data, 1992 annual rpt, U6660–1.21
- Georgia election results by county, 1992 general election, biennial rpt, S1955–1
- Hawaii data book, general data, 1992 annual rpt, S2090–1.8, S2090–1.9
- Hawaii election results, and voter registration by sex, by district and precinct, 1992, biennial series, S2077–1
- Idaho election results and voter registration, by county and/or district and precinct, 1992 general election, biennial rpt, S2305–1
- Illinois election results, and voter registration trends, by county and/or district, 1992 general election, biennial rpt, S2445–1
- Indiana election results, by county and district, with voter registration, 1992 primary and general elections, biennial rpt, S2702–1
- Iowa election results, by county and/or district, 1992 general election, biennial rpt, S2865–1
- Kansas election results, by county and district, 1992 primary and general elections, biennial rpt, S3030–1
- Kentucky election results, by county, district, and circuit, 1992, annual rpt, S3213–1
- Maine election results, by district, county, and municipality, 1992 general election, biennial rpt, S3490–1
- Maryland election results, by county and district, 1992 general election, biennial rpt, S3615–1
- Massachusetts election results and voter registration, by local area, 1992 and trends, biennial rpt, S3920–1
- Massachusetts municipal and county profiles, general data, 1992 annual rpt, C4712–2
- Michigan election results and voter registration, by county and/or district, 1992 general election, biennial rpt, S4020–1
- Michigan referendum to limit elected official terms of office, election results by county, Nov 1992, biennial rpt, S4020–1
- Minnesota election results and voter registration, by locality, 1992 primary and general elections, biennial rpt, S4255–1
- Mississippi statistical abstract, general data, 1992 annual rpt, U3255–4.13
- Missouri election results and voter registration, by district and/or county, with directory of govt officials, 1992 general election, biennial rpt, S4580–1

Officials

Montana election results and voter registration, by county and/or district, 1992 general election, biennial rpt, S4760–1

Nebraska election results, and voter registration by party, by county and/or district, 1992 general and primary elections, biennial rpt, S4955–1

Nebraska State constitutional amendment on term limits, election results by county, Nov 1992, biennial rpt, S4955–1

Nevada election results, and voter registration and turnout, by county, 1992 general election, biennial rpt, S5125–1

New Hampshire election results, by county and locality, 1992, biennial rpt, S5255–1

New Jersey election results and voter registration, by location, 1992 general election, annual rpt, S5440–1

New Jersey local health official views on hazardous waste site concerns and interactions with Federal and State govts, Nov 1991 survey, article, A2623–1.507

New Mexico election results, and voter registration by party, by location, 1992 general election, biennial rpt, S5655–1

New York State general election results by county and district, Nov 1992, biennial rpt, S5750–1

North Carolina election results, by county and/or district, 1992 general election, biennial rpt, S5920–1

North Dakota election results and historical trends, including data on ballot measures and detail by location, 1880s-1992, biennial rpt, U8080–1

North Dakota election results, by location, 1992 general election, biennial rpt, S6205–1

North Dakota State measure on Federal term limitations, election results by county, 1992, biennial rpt, S6205–1

Ohio election results and voter registration, by local area, 1991-92 and trends, biennial rpt, S6380–1

Ohio State constitutional amendment on limiting elected official terms of office, election results by county, Nov 1992, biennial rpt, S6380–1

Oklahoma election results and voter registration, by county and/or district, 1992, biennial rpt, S6425–1

Oregon election results and voter registration and turnout, by county and/or district, 1992 general election, biennial rpt, S6665–1

Oregon State constitutional amendment on term limitations for elected officials, election results by county, 1992, biennial rpt, S6665–1

Pennsylvania statistical abstract, general data, 1992 recurring rpt, U4130–6.6

Rhode Island statistical almanac, general data, 1993 annual rpt, C7975–1

South Dakota election results, and voter registration by party, by county, 1992 general election, biennial rpt, S7390–1

South Dakota State constitutional amendment on term limitations, election results by county, 1992, biennial rpt, S7390–1

Tennessee election results, by district and/or county, 1992 general election, biennial rpt, S7580–1

Tennessee statistical abstract, general data, 1992/93 annual rpt, U8710–2.14

Texas election results and voter registration, by district and/or county, 1992 general election, biennial series, S7750–1

Utah election results and voter registration and turnout, by county and/or district, 1992 general election, biennial rpt, S7875–1

Utah State govt salaries of top officials, 1992, annual rpt, R9380–1.5

Virginia election results by jurisdiction, and voter registration and turnout, 1992 and Jan 1993 elections, annual rpt, S8195–1

Washington State election results and voter registration, by county and/or district, 1992 general election, annual rpt, S8425–1

West Virginia election results and voter registration, by county and party, 1992 and trends, biennial rpt, S8630–1

Wisconsin Blue Book, general data, 1993-94 biennial rpt, S8780–1

Wyoming election results by county, district, and precinct, 1992, annual rpt and govtl directory, S9000–1

Wyoming initiative on term limits, election results by county and precinct, Nov 1992, biennial rpt, S9000–1

see also Congressional employees

see also Executives and managers

see also Federal employees

see also State and local employees

Offshore mineral resources

see also Offshore oil and gas

Offshore oil and gas

Deep well drilling, success ratios, and costs, by State and for offshore, 1991-92, annual article, C4420–1.502

Deep well drilling, success ratios, and costs, by world area, 1990-92, annual article, C4420–1.503

Deepwater oil/gas drilling activity, with data by company, 1993, annual feature, C6985–2.510

Drilling activity and costs, 1992 and trends, annual rpt, A5425–1.2

Drilling and production technology devs, including drilling rigs in operation, monthly rpt, C4420–1

Drilling costs, and wells and footage drilled, by State, offshore location, and type of well, 1991, annual rpt, A2575–9

Expenditures for onshore and offshore exploration, dev, and production, 1991, annual survey rpt, A2575–20

Exploration, production, and equipment trends, and industry devs, monthly rpt, C6985–2

Gulf of Mexico offshore drilling devs, 1993 annual article, C6985–2.503

Gulf of Mexico offshore oil and gas lease sales, winning bidders and bids, by tract, weekly rpt recurring article, C6985–1.522, C6985–1.547

Intl energy sourcebook, with detail on oil and gas industry operations, supply-demand, and prices, for approx 80 countries, 1970s-91, annual compilation, C6985–10

Intl Petroleum Encyclopedia, basic data on oil and gas supply-demand, exploration, refining, reserves, and industry finances, by country and company, 1993 annual rpt, C6985–3

Index by Subjects and Names

Latin America statistical abstract, general data by country, 1992 annual rpt, U6250–1.23

Natural gas potential reserve estimates in 7 regions, Dec 1992 and trends, biennial rpt, R8765–1

Natural gas production, and drilling activity, results, and costs, inland and offshore, by State, 1970s-91, annual rpt, A1775–3.2

North Sea oil and gas reserves planned for dev using floating production systems, and Australia fixed vs floating system costs, 1992 article, C6985–1.507

Oil and gas pipeline construction costs, mileage, and operating and financial data, by location and/or company, 1991 and trends, annual feature, C6985–1.504

Production, exploration, drilling, refining, stock, price, and financial data for US and foreign oil and gas industry, weekly rpt, C6985–1

Production, exploration, refining, demand, finance, prices, and reserves, by State and country or world area, 1993 and trends, periodic basic data book, A2575–14

Rotary drilling rigs in operation, by world area and country, monthly rpt, B4675–1

Seismic exploration land crews and vessels, by world area or country, quarterly press release, A8912–2

Seismic exploration land crews and vessels, oil/gas, Canada and US, monthly press release, A8912–1

Sourcebook of oil and gas industry operations and finances, and world supply-demand situation, 1970s-91, annual compilation, C6985–9

Statistical compilation of oil and gas industry trends, 1993 annual rpt, C6985–4

Supply trends and outlook under 4 economic scenarios, for onshore and offshore areas and Alaska, 1960s-2010, A2575–25

Wells and footage, and drilling activity, onshore and offshore, 1983-93, annual feature, C6985–1.513

Wells and footage drilled, by type of well, State, and offshore location, quarterly rpt, A2575–6

World offshore oil and gas production and reserves, by country, 1980 and/or 1990, biennial rpt, R9455–1.7

World offshore oil and gas wells, reserves, and production, by country, 1990-93, annual article, C6985–2.508

see also Oil spills

O'Hare, William P.

"America's Minorities - The Demographics of Diversity", R8750–2.58

Ohio

Agricultural production, marketing, and finances, by commodity and county, with farms and acreage; and Dept of Agriculture finances and operations; 1990-91 and trends, annual rpt, S6240–1

Correctional instn admissions and releases, inmate characteristics, programs, finances, and staffing, FY91 and trends, annual rpt, S6370–1

Court caseload and case disposition, by type of court and case, and location, 1992, annual rpt, S6385–1

Election results and voter registration, by local area, 1991-92 and trends, biennial rpt, S6380–1

Elementary and secondary public school enrollment, finances, special programs, and staff, 1991/92 and trends, annual rpt, S6265–2

Employment, hours, and earnings, by industry and MSA, with job service and unemployment insurance activities, monthly rpt, S6270–1

Energy supply-demand by electricity and natural gas utility and consuming sector, 1992-93 and trends, annual rpt, S6355–1

Govt financial condition, including revenues by source, expenditures by function, and fund balances, FY92, annual rpt, S6255–1

Library finances, holdings, and staff, for public, academic, and other libraries, by library and location, 1992 and trends, annual rpt, S6320–1

Markets with daily newspapers, demographic and economic info by geographic area, US and Canada, 1993 annual rpt, C3250–1

Oil/gas industry production, finances, exploration, and reserves, by State, 1992 and trends, annual rpt, A5425–1.1

Population by age, sex, and county, with summary components of change, quinquennially 1990-2015, recurring rpt, S6260–3

Special education expenditures, instructional hours, and enrollment, by service type and school district, 1991/92 and trends, annual rpt, S6265–1

Statistical profiles of 50 States and DC, general data, 1993 annual almanac, C4712–1

Tax revenues and collections, by tax type, with distributions and property assessments by county, and corporate taxes by industry, FY92 annual rpt, S6390–1

Traffic accidents, fatalities, and injuries, by circumstances, location, driver and victim characteristics, and vehicle type, 1991 and trends, annual rpt, S6290–1

Utility and transportation regulatory agency activities, scope of jurisdiction, finances, and employees, by agency, 1991/92 annual rpt, A7015–2

Vital statistics, including births, deaths by cause, marriages, divorces, and population, by demographic characteristics and/or location, 1991 and trends, annual rpt, S6285–1

see also Columbus, Ohio

see also under By City and By County in the "Index by Categories"

see also under By State in the "Index by Categories"

Oil

see Aviation fuels

see Diesel fuel

see Fuel oil

see Gasoline

see Kerosene

see Offshore oil and gas

see Oil and gas leases

see Oil shale

see Oil spills

see Oils, oilseeds, and fats

see Petroleum and petroleum industry

see Petroleum exports and imports

see Petroleum prices

see Petroleum reserves

Oil and gas leases

Canada, Northwest Territories, oil/gas exploration licenses issued, by region, 1993 article, C6985–2.510

Federal onshore leases, acreage leased, and royalties, by State, 1991, annual rpt, A5425–1.1

Gulf of Mexico Federal oil/gas leases relinquished by top 5 companies, 1st half 1993, article, C6985–2.509

Gulf of Mexico leasing, drilling, and production activity for major vs independent oil companies, 1988-93, article, C6985–1.548

Gulf of Mexico offshore leases by status including drilled, undrilled, and relinquished, for major and independent firms, Nov 1992, annual article, C6985–2.503

Gulf of Mexico offshore oil and gas lease sales, winning bidders and bids, by tract, weekly rpt recurring article, C6985–1.522, C6985–1.547

Gulf of Mexico oil/gas lease status, wells drilled by operator, and drilling platforms, 1993 article, C6985–2.508

Gulf of Mexico total and undrilled Federal oil/gas leases relinquished, by company, 1992, article, C6985–2.505

Investment size and purchase method preferences of oil/gas property purchasers, Oct 1992 survey, article, C6985–1.513

Mexico oil and gas finances of govt-owned company, and potential impact of foreign lease program, 1993 article, C6985–1.518

Mongolia lease sale offerings, with area location and size, Mar 1993, article, C6985–1.527

Myanmar oil and gas production and potential yield, and leased acreage by company and basin, 1992 article, C6985–1.506

Offshore lease bonus spending plans by oil industry, 1991-93, annual article, C6985–1.517

Offshore tracts and acreage leased by Fed Govt, and bonuses paid, 1954-90, annual compilation, C6985–9.4

Production, exploration, and refining activity for oil and gas, by State and country or world area, 1991 and trends, periodic basic data book, A2575–14.2, A2575–14.5, A2575–14.7

Revenues for oil and gas companies from leases, and exploration and dev expenditures, 1991 and trends, annual survey rpt, A2575–20

State and local:

Nevada statistical abstract, general data, 1992 biennial rpt, S5005–1.12

Texas financial condition, including revenues by source, expenditures by function and dept, and investments, with data for over 400 individual funds, FY92, annual rpt, S7655–2.2

see also Severance taxes

Oil heating equipment

see Plumbing and heating

Oil shale

State and local:

Colorado property assessed valuation, and summary production data, by county, 1991-92, annual rpt, S1055–3

Oil spills

Incidence and volume of oil and other hazardous substance spills by source, 1991 and trends, periodic basic data book, A2575–14.5

Major oil spills of 10,000 gallons/more, 1978-92, article, C1850–6.512

Number and/or volume of spills by size, source, and type of petroleum product, 1980-90, annual rpt, A2575–27

Pipeline accidents and failure rates, US and Canada, and accident probability rates, 1993 article, C6985–1.537

Storage tank (aboveground) cost-benefit analysis for release prevention barrier retrofitting, 1992 rpt, A2575–26

Well blowout prevention equipment failure rates, 1993 article, C6985–1.533

Well blowouts and associated financial loss, by operator and location, 1960-91, article, C6985–1.532

World tanker spills, and US offshore blowouts and spillage, 1970-90, annual compilation, C6985–9.4

Oil wells

see Energy exploration and drilling

Oils, oilseeds, and fats

Alternative fuel (biodiesel) derived from vegetable oils or animal fats, manufacturing capacity of 14 plants worldwide, 1993 article, C5800–8.504

Chicago Board of Trade futures and options trading in financial instruments and agricultural commodities, 1992, annual rpt, B2120–1

Consumer nutrition awareness and health concerns, with food shopping and consumption patterns, by respondent characteristics, 1993 survey, annual rpt, A4950–36

Exports of farm products, by detailed commodity and country of destination, US and California, 1991, annual rpt, B9520–1

Latin America statistical abstract, general data by country, 1992 annual rpt, U6250–1.24, U6250–1.25

Meat and related products and poultry trade, production, and consumption, by country, 1990 and trends, annual rpt, A2100–1.2

Olive oil sales trends, and market shares for top 6 brands, 1993 article, C2710–1.543

Production and marketing data for soybeans, including utilization, prices, and trade, with comparison to other oilseeds, 1920s-93, annual rpt, B8480–1

Production, consumption, stocks, trade, and prices for approx 100 basic commodities, including by country and producing State, commodity yearbook for 1993, C2400–1, C2400–2

Production, prices, and disposition of oils and/or oilseeds in States served by Minneapolis exchange, 1992 and trends, annual rpt, B6110–1

Retail prices for selected consumer items in approx 300 cities, quarterly rpt, A0150–1

Sales and consumer expenditures, for food store products by type, 1991-92, annual feature, C4655–1.510

Sales volume shares by retail outlet type, for approx 300 food, drug, and other product categories, 1993 annual feature, C4655–1.504

Oils, oilseeds, and fats

Supermarket sales by detailed product type, 1992 and trends, annual feature, C5225–1.507

State and local:

- Arizona agricultural production, marketing, and finances, by commodity and county, 1988-92, annual rpt, U5830–1
- Arkansas agricultural production, marketing, and finances, by commodity and county, with farms and acreage, 1992 and trends, annual rpt, U5920–1
- California field crops production, acreage, yield, and prices, by commodity and county, 1992 and trends, annual rpt, S0850–1.4
- Colorado sunflowers acreage, production, and yields, by county, 1991-92, annual rpt, S0985–1
- Kansas agricultural production, marketing, and finances, by county and/or commodity, and farm acreage and value, 1992 and trends, annual rpt, S2915–1
- Louisiana agricultural production, marketing, and finances, by commodity or parish, 1985-91, annual rpt, U2740–1
- Minnesota agricultural production, marketing, and finances, by county or commodity, and farms and acreage, 1992 and trends, annual rpt, S4130–1
- New Mexico agricultural production, marketing, and finances, by commodity and county, with farms and acreage, 1991 and trends, annual rpt, S5530–1
- North Dakota agricultural production and marketing, by commodity and county, and farm finances, 1992 and trends, annual rpt, U3600–1
- South Dakota agricultural production, marketing, and finances, by commodity and county, and farms and acreage, 1992 and trends, annual rpt, S7280–1
- Tennessee agricultural production and marketing, by commodity and county, with farms, acreage, and farm value, 1992 and trends, annual rpt, S7460–1
- Texas agricultural production, marketing, and finances, by commodity and county, and farms and farmland, 1991 and trends, annual rpt series, S7630–1

see also Animal feed

see also Corn

see also Peanuts

see also Soybeans

Oklahoma

- Agricultural production, marketing, and finances, by commodity and county, 1992 and trends, annual rpt, S6405–1
- Business activity indicators for Oklahoma, monthly rpt, U8130–1
- Commuting patterns of workers and residents, including interstate and international travel, and detailed data by county, 1990 and trends, S6416–2
- Correctional instn admin, including inmate characteristics, staff, incarceration costs, and data by instn, FY91, annual rpt, S6420–1
- Court cases and dispositions, by type of court and case, with judicial system finances, by county or jurisdiction, FY92, annual rpt, S6493–1
- Crimes and arrests, by offense, with data by local agency and victim and offender characteristics, 1990-92, annual rpt, S6465–1

Election results and voter registration, by county and/or district, 1992, biennial rpt, S6425–1

- Elementary and secondary school finances, personnel, enrollment, and facilities, by county and district, 1991/92 and trends, annual rpt, S6423–1
- Elementary/secondary school performance indicators, including students and achievement, finances, and staff, by district, 1990/91-1991/92 and trends, annual rpt, S6423–2
- Employment, hours, and earnings, by industry and MSA, with unemployment insurance and job service activities, monthly rpt, S6430–2
- Financial instns (State-chartered) assets and liabilities, by type of instn, with regulatory data, FY92 annual rpt, S6415–1
- Govt financial audit narrative summary, with data on Federal expenditures by agency and program, FY91, annual rpt, S6410–1
- Govt financial condition, including revenues by source, expenditures by function, and fund balances, FY91, annual rpt, S6438–1
- Insurance industry financial and underwriting data, by company and type of insurance, with regulatory info, 1992, annual rpt, S6462–1
- Library (public and institutional) holdings, circulation, finances, and staff, by facility, FY92, annual rpt, S6470–1
- Markets with daily newspapers, demographic and economic info by geographic area, US and Canada, 1993 annual rpt, C3250–1
- Oil/gas industry production, finances, exploration, and reserves, by State, 1992 and trends, annual rpt, A5425–1.1
- Population projections by age, sex, and locality, with data on fertility and migration, 1990-2020, recurring rpt, S6416–1
- Statistical abstract of Oklahoma, detailed social, economic, and govtl data, 1992 annual rpt, U8130–2
- Statistical profiles of 50 States and DC, general data, 1993 annual almanac, C4712–1
- Tax revenues by source, and distribution to local govts and State funds, FY92 and trends, annual rpt, S6495–1
- Traffic accidents, fatalities, and injuries, by circumstances, location, and driver and victim characteristics, 1992 and trends, annual rpt, S6482–1
- Utility and transportation regulatory agency activities, scope of jurisdiction, finances, and employees, by agency, 1991/92 annual rpt, A7015–2
- Welfare program expenditures, recipients, and services, by program and county, FY92 and trends, annual rpt, S6455–1

see also Enid, Okla.

see also Lawton, Okla.

see also Muskogee, Okla.

see also Oklahoma City, Okla.

see also Tulsa, Okla.

see also under By City and By County in the "Index by Categories"

see also under By State in the "Index by Categories"

Index by Subjects and Names

Oklahoma City, Okla.

- Business activity indicators for Oklahoma, monthly rpt, U8130–1
- Employment, hours, and earnings, by industry, monthly rpt, S6430–2
- Statistical abstract of Oklahoma, detailed social, economic, and govtl data, 1992 annual rpt, U8130–2

see also under By City in the "Index by Categories"

Old age

see Aged and aging

Old age assistance

- Catholic charity social service agency activities, clients, finances, and personnel, 1991 and trends, annual rpt, A3810–1
- Medicaid child and total recipients, expenditures, and other program characteristics, and child health summary, by State, FY91, annual rpt, A0565–1
- Participation rates in public assistance programs, for older population living in urban, suburban, and rural areas, 1993 article, A1865–1.522

State and local:

- Alabama public welfare and social service cases, recipients, and payments, by program and county, monthly rpt, S0150–1
- Arizona statistical abstract, general data, 1993 recurring rpt, U5850–2.7
- Arkansas human services dept finances and operations, including Medicaid payments by type of service, FY91 and trends, annual rpt, S0700–2.3
- Colorado welfare and social services expenditures and caseloads, by county and/or program, FY91, annual rpt, S1085–1
- Hawaii data book, general data, 1992 annual rpt, S2090–1.11
- Idaho public welfare program expenditures and recipients, with data by county, quarterly rpt, S2250–1
- Illinois public assistance program cases, recipients, and payments, by program and county, FY91-92 and trends, annual rpt, S2520–2
- Indiana public assistance program participation, expenditures, and services, by county, FY92 and trends, annual rpt, S2623–1
- Iowa ADC and SSI program recipients, and expenditures, by county, monthly rpt, S2802–1
- Kentucky AFDC and SSI recipients and payments, by county, monthly rpt, S3140–2
- Kentucky Medicaid recipients and payments, by program, county, and type of medical service, monthly rpt, S3140–5
- Maryland medical assistance payments and recipients, by program, type of service, location, demographic characteristics, and facility, FY92 and trends, annual rpt, S3635–3
- Michigan public assistance program cases, recipients, and payments, detailed data by county, monthly rpt, S4010–1
- Mississippi public welfare and social service cases, recipients, and payments, by program and county, FY92, annual rpt, S4357–1
- Missouri public welfare and medical assistance recipients, expenditures, and case processing, by program and county, FY92 and trends, annual rpt, S4575–2

Index by Subjects and Names — Operating ratios

Montana welfare and medical assistance program cases and payments, by county and type of service, monthly rpt, S4755–1

Nebraska public welfare cases, recipients, and payments, by program and county, FY92 and trends, annual rpt, S4957–1

Oklahoma public welfare program expenditures, recipients, and services, by program and county, FY92 and trends, annual rpt, S6455–1

Oregon public welfare caseloads, recipients, and expenditures, by program, city, county, and State region, monthly rpt, S6615–8

Pennsylvania senior citizen pharmaceutical assistance fund finances, FY92, annual rpt, S6810–4

Pennsylvania statistical abstract, general data, 1992 recurring rpt, U4130–6.5

South Dakota welfare and social services recipients and payments, by program, MSA, and county, FY92, annual rpt, S7385–1

Tennessee statistical abstract, general data, 1992/93 annual rpt, U8710–2.18

Utah statistical abstract, general data, 1993 triennial rpt, U8960–1.6

Washington State public assistance clients and service costs, by client characteristics, program, and county, FY90, annual rpt, S8420–2

West Virginia welfare and social service program caseloads and expenditures, by county, monthly rpt, S8560–2

see also Supplemental Security Income

Old-Age, Survivors, Disability, and Health Insurance

Contributions to OASDHI fund, and number of workers, by State and region, 1990, R8490–47

Coverage, assets, and benefits paid, for private and govt pension and retirement programs, 1991 and trends, biennial fact book, A1325–1.3

Finances and beneficiaries by category, selected years FY40-92, annual rpt, R9380–1.9

Govt finances, including revenues by source, expenditures by function, and debt, detailed data for Federal, State, and local govts, 1993 annual rpt, R9050–1

State social, economic, and govtl indicators, with rankings, 1993 semiannual rpt, B8500–1.8

State and local:

Arizona statistical abstract, general data, 1993 recurring rpt, U5850–2.7

Georgia county guide, general data, 1993 annual rpt, U6750–1

Georgia statistical abstract, general data, 1992-93 biennial rpt, U6730–1.13

Hawaii data book, general data, 1992 annual rpt, S2090–1.11

Utah statistical abstract, general data, 1993 triennial rpt, U8960–1.6

see also Medicare

see also Social security tax

Olefins

see Petrochemicals

Oleomargarine

see Oils, oilseeds, and fats

Olive oil

see Oils, oilseeds, and fats

Olives

see Fruit and fruit products

Olympic games

Cable TV system plans to offer 1996 summer Olympic games on pay-per-view service, Jan 1993 survey, article, C1858–1.501

Financial profits or losses for summer Olympic games, by host city, 1976-92, and funds raised to date for Atlanta, Ga 1996 games, article, C8900–1.514

Fundraising expected guarantees and amounts obtained to date, by source, for 1996 summer Olympics in Atlanta, 1993 article, C5800–7.526

TV network summer Olympic games broadcast rights payments, advertising revenues, and audience ratings, quadrennially 1976-96, article, C1850–14.532

State and local:

Colorado income tax return checkoff contributions, for selected causes, FY92 and trends, annual rpt, S1075–1.3

Georgia, Atlanta summer 1996 Olympic games projected impact on State output, earnings, and employment, 1992 article, U6730–2.501

Virginia income tax return checkoff contributions to US Olympic Committee, 1990, annual rpt, S8305–1.1

Omaha, Nebr.

Employment, hours, and earnings, by selected industry group and locality, quarterly rpt, S4895–2

see also under By City in the "Index by Categories"

Oman

Energy intl sourcebook, with detail on oil and gas industry operations, supply-demand, and prices, for approx 80 countries, 1970s-91, annual compilation, C6985–10.2

Omdahl, Lloyd

"North Dakota Votes", U8080–1

Omran, Abdel R.

"Middle East Population Puzzle", R8750–2.59

Onions

see Vegetables and vegetable products

Ontario Province, Canada

Hospital expenditures, beds, and utilization data, with comparisons to California and total US and Canada, 1987, article, A1865–1.512

Niagara Falls area visitors, hotel rooms and occupancy rate, and unemployment rate, 1993 article, C5800–7.544

OPEC

see Organization of Petroleum Exporting Countries

Open housing

see Discrimination in housing

Open space land programs

State and local:

Maryland statistical abstract, general data, 1993-94 biennial rpt, S3605–1.13

see also Community Development Block Grants

Opera

see Performing arts

Operating costs

see Agricultural production costs

see Business income and expenses, general

see Business income and expenses, specific industry

see Cost-of-doing-business surveys

see Operating ratios

see Production costs

Operating ratios

Advertising expenditures as percents of sales and profits, by SIC 4-digit industry, 1993, annual article, C2710–1.537

Advertising/promotional expenditures as percent of sales, by industry, 1992, annual survey, C1200–1.508

Aerospace and defense industries financial performance, with data for approx 200 major US and foreign companies, FY92 and trends, annual feature, C5800–4.519

Aerospace industry income statement and operating ratios, 1970s-91, annual rpt, A0250–2.5

Aerospace/defense industry capital investments as percent of sales, for 4 major companies, 1989 and 1991, article, C5800–4.516

Airline costs per seat mile for 5 carriers, and average yields for 10 short-haul routes, 1993 article, C5800–4.529

Airline finances and operations of scheduled carriers, summary statistics, 1992 and trends, annual rpt, A0325–5

Airline industry devs including passenger and cargo traffic activity and fuel costs, with worldwide passenger traffic, by carrier, monthly rpt, C7000–4

Airline market activity, including traffic, financial performance, employment, and fleet composition, by US and foreign carrier, 1991-92, annual feature, C7000–4.508

Airline passenger traffic, seat miles, and load factor, for scheduled domestic and intl flights, monthly press release, A0325–1

Airline traffic and finances worldwide, by carrier, 1993 annual feature, C7000–4.511

Airline traffic indicators worldwide, including load factors, 1971-2011, annual rpt, B3075–1

Amusement park operating and financial data, including data for US and foreign parks, miniature golf, waterparks, and games, 1992, annual rpt, A5700–1

Apartment building (conventionally financed) detailed income and expense ratios for US and Canada, by building type, metro area, and US region, 1991 and trends, annual rpt, A5600–1

Apartment building (federally subsidized) detailed income and expense ratios, by building and subsidy type, building age, metro area, and region, 1991 and trends, annual rpt, A5600–5

Apartment complex mgmt income and expenses, and vacancy and turnover rates, by region and metro area, 1992, annual survey rpt, A6497–1

Auto aftermarket retail performance indicators, by product category, 1992 article, C2150–10.501

Auto industry performance indicators for 3 major manufacturers, 1970s-92, annual article, C2150–3.506

Operating ratios

Auto insurance passenger and commercial premiums, market shares, and loss ratios, with rankings of States and 20 leading firms, 1992, annual article, C1050–1.511

Auto parts/supplies and repair aftermarket sales performance, by product group, 1993 annual feature, C0125–1.503

Bank assets, equity, performance, and market value, top 50 instns worldwide, 1993 annual feature, C5800–7.535

Bank assets, market capitalization, and financial ratios, for 6 largest instns, June 1993, article, C3950–1.527

Bank financial and/or operating ratios, for 6 EC countries and US, 1991, article, A8955–1.502

Bank financial performance, including assets, loans, deposits, and operating ratios, top 100 instns, 1992, annual feature, C5800–7.526

Bank noncurrent loans/leases, and losses, by type of loan, asset size, and metro status, 1992, semiannual rpt, A6400–4

Biotechnology company income and earnings, for approx 30 firms, 1991-92, recurring article, A1250–1.518

Book publishing income and profit margin, for 16 companies, 1991-92, article, C1852 2.519

Book publishing industry financial and operating data, by publisher type and size, and subject category, 1991 and trends, annual rpt, A3274–2

Brewers operations and expenses, detailed data, 1956-90, annual rpt, A3455–1.2

Business forms industry detailed financial and operating ratios, with summary operating data, FY91, annual rpt, A5785–3

Business forms industry trends and outlook, including data by product type, 1992 annual rpt, A5785–2

Chemical and allied industries earnings, sales, and profit margins, by company, weekly rpt quarterly article, A1250–1.502, A1250–1.514, A1250–1.525, A1250–1.536

Chemical and related industries production, finances, operating ratios, employment, and trade, by country, company, and chemical, 1980s-92, annual feature, A1250–1.530

Chemical company sales and profits, for top 50 producers worldwide, 1992, annual article, A1250–1.533

Chemical industry finances and operations, with data by industry segment and product, 1970s-92, annual rpt, A3850–1

Chemical industry sales and operating summary for top 100 companies, 1992, annual article, A1250–1.523

China joint ventures of US businesses, return on investment by location, project type, and startup year, 1991 survey, article, A9315–1.501

Clothing (men's and boys) production, trade, and operating data, by garment type, 1960s-92, annual rpt, A3880–1

Clothing and shoe industries financial performance indicators for 72 companies, FY92 and trends, annual rpt, B8130–2

Computer-aided design and manufacturing (CAD/CAM) software debt-equity ratios, for 7 companies, 1992 article, C1850–2.502

Computer industry profit rates, by industry sector, 1988 and 1992, article, C8900–1.517

Computer software company spending for marketing, sales, and support as percent of revenues, by revenue size group, 1991-92, article, C1200–1.504

Computer software with sales/marketing applications, vendor profit margins and revenue outlook, 1992 annual survey article, C1200–1.502

Construction company finances, by region, 1992, article, C5800–2.513

Construction industry finances and operations, by type of business and region, 1992-93, annual survey rpt, A4155–1

Convenience store gasoline and nongasoline profit margins, 1985-92, annual fact book, C4680–1.507

Convenience store industry financial and operating data, by size category, 1992 and trends, annual survey rpt, A6735–1, A6735–2

Corporate charitable contributions, by donor characteristics and detailed type of recipient, 1991 and trends, annual rpt, R4105–8

Corporate charitable contributions to education as percent of income, 1982-92, annual article, C2175–1.534

Corporate financial and operating composite ratios, establishments, and receipts, for approx 200 industries, by asset size, FY90, annual rpt, C7800–1

Corporate financial ratios for companies completing leveraged recapitalizations during 1985-89, article, C4683–1.501

Corporate market value of top 1,000 firms worldwide, with related financial data, by company and country, 1993 annual feature, C5800–7.536

Corporate market value rankings of top 1,000 firms, with sales, profits, assets, and related data, by company and industry, 1993 annual feature, C5800–7.521

Corporate R&D expenditures, and sales and profits, for approx 900 firms, 1992, annual feature, C5800–7.534

Corporate sales, profits, return on equity, price/earnings ratio, and earnings per share, approx 900 corporations, with industry rankings, weekly rpt quarterly article, C5800–7.503, C5800–7.519, C5800–7.528, C5800–7.541

Corporate stock investment performance and earnings outlook, approx 900 companies, 1992 annual feature, C5800–7.509

Corporations with rapid growth, financial data for 250 firms, 1993 feature, C5800–7.551

Discount chain rankings by selected financial ratios, for top 45-53 chains, 1992-93, annual feature, C5150–3.514

Discount store sales and productivity data for 20 depts, 1993 annual feature, C5150–3.516

Drug wholesale company revenues, market shares, and operating ratios, for 7 major firms, 1992-93, article, C3950–1.511

Drugs (prescription) profits as percent of sales, for manufacturers of top 20 brands used by patients age 65/over and 64/under, 1985-91, R4865–8

Index by Subjects and Names

Drugstore (independent pharmacy) financial and operating data, by store characteristics, 1991 and trends, annual survey, B5165–1

Drugstore chains financial performance and marketing operations, 1993 annual feature, C5150–2.510

Electric utility financial and investment performance indicators, for top 50 companies, 1991, article, C5800–28.501

Electric utility financial and operating data, by State and census div, 1991 and trends, annual rpt, A4700–1

Electric utility financial and operating ratios, by customer size class and region, 1990, annual article, A2625–1.501

Electric utility operating data, including generating capacity and efficiency, peak demand, and fuel consumption, top 100 utilities, 1992, annual article, C6985–6.512

Electric utility rate of return on equity, with level of asset diversification, for 6 top-performing utilities, 1992, article, A4700–4.505

Electric utility State/local taxes/contributions as percent of revenues, for public and private utilities by region, 1990, article, A2625–1.501

Electronics company financial data and business info for approx 500 companies, 1991-92 and trends, annual rpt, C3400–4

Electronics company financial performance, for top 100 multinatl firms, 1992 annual feature, C1850–2.502

Electronics company financial performance, ranking of top 200 firms, 1992 and trends, annual feature, C1850–2.509

Electronics distributor revenues and financial ratios, for 4 companies, 1992, article, C1850–2.505

Electronics industry market devs, including factory sales, orders, inventory, production, and operating ratios, by product category, monthly rpt, A4725–2

Employee benefit payments and employer cost/payroll ratios, by industry, detailed type of benefit, and firm size, 1991, annual rpt, A3840–1

Europe electronics industry financial performance, for top 50 companies, FY91 or FY92, annual article, C1850–2.501

Europe industrial distribution costs as percent of revenue, for typical firm, 1987 and 1992, article, C2150–1.502

Finance company financial and operating ratios, and loan activity, Dec 1988-92, annual article, A6400–2.506

Financial instns performance, for 10 small/midsize instns with high returns on equity, 1992 article, C3950–1.502

Financial performance and growth rankings for approx 1,000 top corporations, with comparisons by industry group, 1993 annual rpt, C3950–1.505

Financial ratios and performance, for over 350 SIC 4-digit industries, FY88-92, annual rpt, A6400–3

Food marketers financial and operating data, by company size and region, 1991-92, annual rpts, A4950–5

Food marketers mgmt info system operations, employment, and finances, for wholesalers and retailers by sales size, 1993 and trends, annual survey, A4950–7

Index by Subjects and Names

Operating ratios

Food processing industry devs, including work force reduction, finances, and employment, 1993 annual feature, C2150-6.507

Food store industry structure, sales, operations, and business outlook, by type of store, 1993 annual rpt, C5225-1.505

Forbes 500 companies net profit margins and dividend payout ratios, 1992, annual feature, C3950-1.513

Foreign economic indexes, and leading and coincident indicators for US and other industrial countries, monthly rpt, U1245-1

Fortune magazine ranking of top 50-100 companies in 8 nonindustrial sectors, with financial and employment data, 1992, annual feature, C8900-1.516

Fortune 500 largest industrial corporations, sales, financial, and stock performance data by company, 1992, annual feature, C8900-1.513

Fortune 500 largest industrial corporations worldwide, with financial and employment data, 1992, annual feature, C8900-1.520

Gulf coast oil refinery profit margins, 1975-91, annual compilation, C6985-9.1

Hardware finances and operations, for hardware stores, home centers, and lumber/building material outlets, 1991 and trends, annual rpt series, A8275-1

Higher education instn endowment fund and investment pool characteristics and performance, by instn, FY92, annual survey rpt, A6705-2

HMO financial data, including revenue sources and expenses by category, by plan characteristics, 1990, annual rpt, A5150-2.3

Home equity lending activity and practices of financial instns, by region, asset size, and instn type, 1992, annual rpt, A4160-3

Home furnishings retailer financial and operating data, by firm characteristics and region, 1992 and trends, annual rpt, A7975-1

Home improvement industry sales and operations, for top distributors, cooperatives, and marketing organizations, 1991-92, annual feature, C5150-6.502

Home improvement industry sales and related data, by product category and for top 10 chains, 1992, article, C4725-5.507

Homebuilder operations and finances, by region and sales size group, 1992 survey, article, C4300-1.501

Hospital (teaching) house staff benefit to stipend expenditure ratios, by region and ownership, 1992/93, annual rpt, A3273-3

Hospital debt service ratios, by bond rating category, 1991, A1865-1.502

Hospital financial and operating data, including ambulatory surgery and emergency service utilization, semimonthly rpt quarterly feature, A1865-1.506, A1865-1.512

Hospital financial ratios, for academic medical centers, 1987-91, article, A3273-8.511

Hospital financial trends, including revenue margins, semimonthly rpt quarterly feature, A1865-1.501, A1865-1.507, A1865-1.513, A1865-1.519

Hospital industry financial and operating indicators, with detail for Medicare, by instn characteristics and location, 1988-92, annual rpt, B1880-1

Hospital margins and nonoperating gain ratio, 1987-91, article, A1865-1.502

Ice cream/frozen dessert industry profitability and efficiency ratios, 1984 and 1988-92, annual rpt, A5825-1.1

Industrial R&D managers outlook on expenditures, effort, personnel, and other mgmt issues, 1993, annual survey rpt, A5510-1

Insurance (accident/health) premiums and underwriting ratios, for top 300 firms, 1991, annual article, C1050-2.502

Insurance (life/health) company assets, net operating gain, and return on equity, for 100 largest firms, 1992, article, C1050-2.510

Insurance (life/health) industry asset allocation and investment yields, for top 125 US and Canadian companies, 1992 and trends, annual article, C1050-2.512

Insurance (life/health) industry profitability, leverage, and liquidity ratios, 1988-92, annual article, C1050-2.511

Insurance (property/casualty) companies profitability ratios, 1991 and trends, annual rpt, A5650-1

Insurance (property/casualty) industry profitability, leverage, and liquidity ratios, 1987-92, annual article, C1050-1.510

Insurance (property/casualty) premium-expense ratios for top 100 companies, 1991, article, C1050-1.504

Insurance (property/casualty) premiums, loss ratios, and market shares, for general liability, medical malpractice, fidelity, and surety, 1991 and trends, annual article, C1050-1.502

Insurance (property/casualty) premiums, loss ratios, and market shares, for workers compensation, 1991 and trends, annual article, C1050-1.501

Insurance (property/casualty) premiums written and operating ratios, by company type and line of coverage, 1988-92, annual article, C1050-1.504

Insurance (property/casualty) premiums written, loss ratios, and market shares, by line, leading company, and State, 1992 and trends, annual article, C1050-1.509

Italy property/casualty insurance industry loss ratios for 4 lines of coverage, 1990-91, article, C1050-1.505

Japan corporate R&D expenditures to sales ratios, by industry, FY80, FY85, and FY90-91, annual article, R5650-2.557

Japan foreign investment rate of return on sales by world region, and overseas share of production, with detail by industry, FY84-91, article, R5650-2.559

Jeweler advertising/promotion expenditures as percent of net sales, by store type, 1992, article, C2150-7.511

Latin America airline passenger load factors, by country, 1970s-88, annual rpt, U6250-1.3

Library (research) holdings, expenditures by type, and staff, for 120 academic and nonacademic instns, US and Canada, FY92, annual rpt, A3365-1

Life insurance industry income and financial data, including investments by type of security, 1991 and trends, biennial fact book, A1325-1.4

Life insurance policy lapse ratios, for 150 companies, 1987-91, annual article, C1050-2.502

Life insurance premium-expense ratios for top 100 companies, 1991, article, C1050-2.503

Lodging industry facilities, sales, and occupancy, with top 42-100 properties in 5 market categories, 1993 annual rpt, C7000-5

Lodging industry operating data by world region, 1982-90, annual rpt, C2140-1.4

Logistics trends and devs, including data on costs, finances of major carriers by mode, and foreign trade, 1993 annual compilation, C2150-1.506

Machine tool industry finances and ratios, 1992 and trends, annual rpt, A3179-2.1

Medical group financial and operating data, by practice characteristics, 1991, annual rpt, A6365-2

Medical group physician and allied personnel compensation to production ratios, by specialty, 1991, annual rpt, A6365-1

Mexico bank profit indicators, for 2 major instns, with comparisons to aggregate large US banks, 1992, C5800-7.545

Mortgage banking industry aggregate financial and operating data, by lending characteristics and type of ownership, 1989 and trends, annual rpt, A6450-3

Mortgage insurance industry finances and performance indicators, 1988-91, annual rpt, A6455-1

Motor carrier rates of return granted by regulatory agencies, by company and State, 1991, annual rpt, A7015-4

Motor vehicle dealership financial and operating data, including sales and employment by State, 1970s-93, annual rpt, A7330-1

Mutual fund sales, assets, and investment activities, with data on money market and municipal bond funds, monthly rpt, A6025-5

Mutual funds (money market) financial performance and rankings of over 850 funds, with background info for investors, 1992 and trends, annual directory, C4682-2

Mutual funds financial performance and rankings of over 2,400 funds, with background info for investors, 1992 and trends, annual directory, C4682-1

Natural gas industry operating ratios, by industry segment, 1970s-91, annual rpt, A1775-3.8

Office building detailed income and expense data, and energy use, US and Canada, by building characteristics, metro area, and US region, 1991 and trends, annual rpt, A5600-2

Office product dealer financial and operating data, by sales volume and region, 1991 and trends, annual rpt, A8110-1

Oil and gas deep well drilling, success ratios, and costs, by State and for offshore, 1991-92, annual article, C4420-1.502

Oil and gas industry exploration, production, refining, demand, finance, prices, and reserves, by State and country or world area, 1992 and trends, periodic basic data book, A2575-14.3

Operating ratios

Oil and gas industry financial and operating data, rankings for top 300 US and top 100 non-US companies, 1990-91, annual compilation, C6985–4.1

Oil and gas industry intl exploration, drilling, production, refining, stock, price, and financial data, weekly rpt, C6985–1

Oil industry income and operating data, for approx 20 major companies, 1991-92, annual article, C6985–1.533

Oil industry income, net profits, and selected operating data, approx 25 companies, weekly rpt quarterly article, C6985–1.534, C6985–1.545

Oil industry rate of return, with comparison to all manufacturing, 1973-91, annual rpt, A5425–1.2

Oil industry returns on capital employed, for 10 major companies vs industry average, 1985-91, article, C6985–1.502

Oil refinery cash operating margins, 1975-91, annual rpt, C6985–5.2

Paper distribution industry financial performance, 2nd qtr 1992 and trends, article, A8140–3.501

Paper/allied products industry sales, profits, and balance sheet data, monthly rpt recurring table, A1630–5

Paperboard folding carton industry profit margins, 1988-92, article, C0125–4.502

Plastics industry operating and financial data, 1992 and trends, annual rpt, A8920–1.1

Plastics processing industry financial and operating ratios, by processing activity, sales size, and region, 1992, annual rpt, A8920–4

Pulp and paper industry operations, US and Canada, with financial performance by company, 1990s and trends, annual rpt, C3975–5.1

Pulp and paper mill machine maintenance operations and personnel, by region and grade, 1992 survey, recurring article, C3975–2.504

Pulp, paper, and allied products financial and operating data, 1950s-92, annual rpt, A1630–6.4

Railroad (Class I) financial and operating data, with detail by company, 1982-91, annual rpt, A3275–8.2

Railroad (Class I) financial condition, operations, and employment, by company and district, 1992, annual rpt, A3275–7

Railroad (Class I) traffic, employment, finances, and equipment, by district and State, 1920s-92, annual rpt, A3275–5

Railroad financial performance and expenses, by Class 1 railroad and district, quarterly rpt, A3275–1

Railroad financial performance, including fuel use and costs, and returns on investment for 11 companies, 1990-93, article, C8400–1.509

Real estate residential brokerage firm finances and operations, with data by region and company size, 1990/91 and trends, article, A7000–1.502

Rental equipment industry financial data, by revenue size group and region, and for Canada, 1991 and trends, annual rpt, A2665–1

Restaurant (hamburger) operating data, for 3 low-price drive-through chains, 1993, article, C1200–5.514

Restaurant industry financial and operating data, by establishment characteristics and location, 1992, annual rpt, A8200–3

Retail chain financial data and business info for approx 240 US and Canadian companies, 1991-92 and trends, annual rpt, C3400–2

Retail chain performance indexes and ratios, for top 38 chains, 1986-91, annual article, C5150–4.502

Retail chain revenues, profits, and stores, top 100 chains, with selected data by outlet type, 1991-92, annual articles, C5150–4.508

Retail industry distribution center operating expenses as percent of sales, 1993 survey, C5150–4.506

Retail mgmt info system devs, including expenses and computerized equipment use, 1992 survey, annual feature, C5150–4.501

Retail mgmt info system devs, including expenses and computerized equipment use, 1993 survey, annual feature, C5150–4.509

Retail store financial performance indicators, for 98 public firms, FY92 and trends, annual rpt, B8130–4

Retail store inventory shrinkage, and control measures, by type of outlet, 1991, annual survey rpt, C5150–4.504

Return on equity before and after layoffs, for 5 major companies with work force reductions since 1985, 1992 article, C5800–7.506

Savings instn economic issues and devs, with quarterly data on financial condition by instn type and State, monthly rpt, A8813–1

Service sector profitability and productivity ratios for top companies worldwide, in 5-6 industries, 1993 annual feature, C8900–1.522

Small companies with high 5-year returns on equity, financial performance data and chief executive characteristics, for top 200 firms, 1992 annual article, C3950–1.501

Small companies with sales under $150 million, financial data for top 100 growth firms, 1993 annual article, C5800–7.529

Steel industry operating trends and devs, including profiles of 4 major companies, 1960-90, U9640–2.15

Supermarket (independent) sales and operating ratios, by store type, sales size, and region, 1991, annual survey, A4950–4

Supermarket bakery dept sales and performance indicators, 1992 and trends, annual article, C4655–1.505, C5225–1.504

Supermarket deli dept sales and performance indicators, 1992, annual article, C4655–1.503, C5225–1.505

Supermarket fish/seafood dept sales and performance indicators, 1991, annual article, C4655–1.501

Supermarket general merchandise dept sales and performance indicators, 1992 and trends, annual article, C4655–1.509

Supermarket health and beauty aid dept sales and performance indicators, 1992 and trends, annual article, C4655–1.506

Supermarket industry composite financial ratios, 1991/92 and trends, annual rpt, A4950–1

Index by Subjects and Names

Supermarket meat dept sales and performance indicators, 1992 and trends, annual article, C4655–1.509

Supermarket prepared food sales and performance indicators, 1992, annual article, C4655–1.508

Supermarket produce dept sales and performance indicators, 1992 and trends, annual article, C4655–1.511

Textile and clothing companies financial data, for approx 170 firms, with industry statistical summary, 1991-92 and trends, annual rpt, C3400–5

Textile industry economic and operating performance and outlook, 1988-93, annual article, C5226–3.502

Textile industry economic performance indicators and outlook, with industry trends and devs, monthly rpt, C5226–3

Textile industry financial performance indicators for 32 companies, FY92 and trends, annual rpt, B8130–1

Transportation cost ratios for approx 150 commodities, 2 alternative measures, 1992 article, U5930–1.501

Truck (heavy-duty) dealership average financial results, 1988-92, annual article, C2710–3.525

Truck equipment distributor financial data, by company type, sales size, and rural vs metro market, FY91 and trends, annual rpt, A8505–4

Truck fleet financial and operating data for top 200 freight carriers, 1992 and trends, annual feature, C2150–4.504

Utility industry rates of return granted by regulatory agencies, by utility and State, 1991/92 annual rpt, A7015–3

Venture capital industry finances and operations, 1991 and trends, annual rpt, A8515–1

Veterinarian practice expenses as percent of revenues, by expenditure category and type of practice, 1990-91, annual survey article, C9480–1.501

Veterinary practice income, expenses by item, and financial ratios, by type of practice, 1991, biennial survey article, A3100–2.510

Warehouse operating costs as percent of sales, by expense category, 1988-91, article, C2150–1.504

State and local:

Alabama statistical abstract, general data, 1992 recurring rpt, U5680–2.11

Arkansas banks capital to asset ratios, by instn, June 1992, annual rpt, S0632–1

Arkansas public utility financial, operating, and regulatory data, by utility type and company, 1992 annual rpt, S0757–1

California banks and trust companies, financial condition by instn, with regulatory info, Dec 1992, annual rpt, S0810–1

California public utility and transportation regulatory data, including revenue requests and rates of return by company, FY92 annual rpt, S0930–1

Colorado savings and loan assn and credit union financial condition, 1992 and trends, annual rpt, S1070–3

Connecticut banks and other financial instns, financial condition by instn, 1991 and trends, annual rpt, S1160–1

Index by Subjects and Names

Florida insurance industry financial and underwriting data, by company and line of coverage, 1991, annual rpt, S1760–1

Georgia credit union financial condition, including loans by type and delinquency, with comparisons to US, 1989, article, U6730–2.506

Hawaii hotel occupancy rates by island, bimonthly rpt, B3500–1

Idaho credit union delinquency and capital ratio trends, 1989-92, annual rpt, S2235–1

Idaho insurance industry financial and underwriting data, by company and type of insurance, with regulatory data, 1991, annual rpt, S2260–1

Illinois Financial Institutions Dept activities, with financial and regulatory data for credit unions, consumer lenders, and other businesses, FY91 annual rpt, S2457–2

Indiana financial instns (State-chartered) financial condition, including assets by instn arranged by city, 1991 and trends, annual rpt, S2625–1

Iowa bank and trust companies (State-chartered), financial condition by instn arranged by city, FY92 annual rpt, S2760–2

Kansas fire/casualty insurers premium and loss ratios, by line of coverage and company, 1992, annual rpt, S2990–1

Kentucky financial instns condition, including assets by instn and city, with regulatory info, 1992 and trends, annual rpt, S3121–1

Louisiana financial instns (State-chartered), financial condition by instn arranged by city, with regulatory info, Dec 1992, annual rpt, S3265–1

Maryland credit unions (State-chartered) financial ratios, 1990-91, annual rpt, S3655–2

Michigan banks and other financial instns, financial condition by instn, with regulatory info, 1992 and trends, annual rpt, S3957–1

Minnesota insurance industry financial and underwriting data, by company and line of coverage, 1991, annual rpt, S4140–4

Missouri banks and trust companies (State-chartered) financial condition, by instn, FY91-92 and trends, biennial rpt, S4502–1

Missouri insurance industry financial and underwriting data, by company and type of insurance, with regulatory info, 1992, annual rpt, S4527–1

Nevada casino finances and employment, by location and gaming revenue range, FY92, annual rpt, S5062–1

New Mexico lodging industry occupancy rates, monthly business activity rpt, U7980–1

New York State public utility financial and operating data, by utility type and company, 1988-92, annual rpt, S5795–1

North Carolina public utility financial, operating, and regulatory data, by utility type and company, 1990 and trends, annual rpt, S5917–2

Oklahoma financial instns (State-chartered) assets and liabilities, by type of instn, with regulatory data, FY92 annual rpt, S6415–1

Oregon banks financial operations, 1988-92, annual rpt, S6616–1

Pennsylvania insurance industry financial and underwriting data, by company and line of coverage, 1991, with FY92 regulatory info, annual rpt, S6835–1

South Carolina financial instns (State-chartered) financial condition, including data by instn, FY92 annual rpt, S7165–1

Tennessee banks and other financial instns financial condition, by instn and city, 1992 annual rpt, S7507–1

Tennessee insurance industry financial and underwriting data, by company and type of insurance, with regulatory info, 1991, annual rpt, S7466–1

Tennessee statistical abstract, general data, 1992/93 annual rpt, U8710–2.13

Texas banks financial performance trends, 1988-92, article, A6400–2.507

Texas electric utility financial and operating data, 9 largest investor-owned utilities, 1988-92, annual rpt, S7740–1

Utah and US auto insurance loss ratios, 1987-92, annual rpt, S7845–1

Virginia banks (State-chartered) financial and operating ratios, by asset size, 1992, annual rpt, S8180–2

Virginia finance companies financial ratios, by instn type, 1992, annual rpt, S8180–3

Washington State banks and other financial instns, financial condition by type of instn, 1992 and trends, annual rpt, S8325–1

Washington State electric utility financial and operating data, by company, 1982-91, annual rpt, S8450–1.2

Washington State natural gas utility financial and operating data, by company, 1982-91, annual rpt, S8450–1.3

Washington State water utilities financial and operating data, by company, 1988-90, annual rpt, S8450–1.1

Washington State water utilities financial and operating data, by company, 1989-91, annual rpt, S8450–1.4

Wisconsin banks financial condition, by instn and city, with regulatory info, 1992 and trends, annual rpt, S8685–1

Wisconsin insurance industry financial and underwriting data, by company and line of coverage, with regulatory info, 1992, annual rpt, S8755–1

Wisconsin savings and loan assns and savings banks (State-chartered) financial condition, by instn, 1992 and trends, annual rpt, S8807–1

see also Cost-of-doing-business surveys

see also Industrial capacity and utilization

see also Labor productivity

see also Productivity

Opinion and attitude surveys

Abortion attitudes of teenage boys, by respondent characteristics, 1988 survey, article, A5160–1.505

Abortion legality support as affected by survey question formulation, with detail for 6 States, Sept/Oct 1989 survey, article, A5160–1.504

Activities important to all adults vs self-described "workaholics," leisure time trend, and work vs vacation time in 12 countries, 1993 survey feature, C4215–1.507

Advertising importance to public in 20 countries, 1993 survey article, C2710–1.549

Advertising portrayal of older population, public opinion by age group, Aug 1992 survey, articles, C2710–1.503

Advertising recall, and response to ads in selected unusual media, marketing professionals vs general public, Oct 1992 surveys, article, C2710–1.512

AIDS fears and impact on sexual behavior, by sex and age, 1990 survey, article, A2623–1.512

AIDS stigmatizing attitudes and beliefs prevalence among general public, with detail by race and sex, 1990/91 surveys, article, A2623–1.506

AIDS testing site awareness among adults, with analysis by demographic characteristics, 1990 survey, article, A2623–1.506

AIDS transmission, protective measures, and behavior changes, public opinion, 1987-92 surveys, A0610–1.502

Alienation Index trends, 1972-92, article, C5800–7.511

American College Test (ACT) scores by student characteristics, with student views on schools and education plans, 1992 and trends, annual rpt, R1960–6

Architects job satisfaction in settings other than private architectural practice, 1992 survey article, C5800–15.501

Australia restaurant provision of no-smoking areas where not mandated by law, views of owners and customers, 1993 article, A2623–1.511

Australia, Sydney smoker and ex-smoker belief in smoking as cause for selected diseases, and reasons for continuing to smoke, 1993 article, A2623–1.504

Auto (electric) ownership incentives, perceived advantages, and desired features, public opinion, Apr 1993 survey, article, C2710–3.533

Bartender views on day of the week when most job-related complaints are heard from patrons, 1993 survey feature, C1850–3.509

Black American health and political leaders views on public health goals for year 2000, 1993 article, A2623–1.510

Burglary (home) prevention, and preferred entry method and time of day, views of incarcerated burglars, 1993 survey article, C1850–13.505

Catholic vs public school performance, and support for parental school selection funded by govt, public opinion by respondent characteristics, July 1992 survey, A7375–8

Charitable contributions plans of affluent business owners as affected by 1993 tax laws, 1993 survey article, C2176–1.519

Charitable contributions plans of general public, with views on operations and regulation of charities, July 1993 survey, article, C2176–1.520

Charitable donors of $50,000 or more familiarity with and interest in selected contribution strategies, 1993 survey article, C2176–1.519

Charitable organization donor views on change in support needs for liberal causes, 1992-93 surveys, article, C2176–1.512

Opinion and attitude surveys

Index by Subjects and Names

City govt policies and conditions, with views of local officials, Natl League of Cities surveys, series, A8012–1

City officials views on issues and conditions affecting local govt, including top issues for Fed Govt to address , 1992 survey, annual rpt, A8012–1.21

College administrator views on own instn practices and policies, faculty recruitment factors, and status of women, 1993 annual survey, A1410–1.38

College freshmen attitudes and characteristics, degree and career plans, and financial aid sources, by sex and instn type, fall 1992, annual survey, U6215–1

College freshmen attitudes and characteristics, degree and career plans, and financial aid sources, fall 1992, annual survey summary, C2175–1.505

College student level of familiarity with 35 corporations, 1993 survey article, C1200–1.503

College student use of and attitudes toward alcohol, drugs, and tobacco products, by sex and region, 1989-91 surveys, annual rpt, U4950–1

Communications industries conditions for women, employee views by sex, Dec 1992 survey, article, C2710–1.528

Condom use and attitudes among sexually active young men, by race-ethnicity, 1988 and 1991 surveys, article, A5160–1.504

Corporate handling of crises, including honesty and media reliability, public opinion, 1993 survey article, A8770–1.505

Crime rate local trend in past 5 years, public opinion, 1993 article, C5800–7.552

Developing countries fertility, family planning, sexual behavior, and child health indicators, with selected detail by demographic characteristics, 1984-92 surveys, U2520–1.51

Divorce case mgmt problems cited by judges, quasi-judicial staff, and court managers in 16 urban jurisdictions, 1992 rpt, R6600–6

Drunk driving blood alcohol content laws, views of traffic safety magazine readers, 1992 survey, article, A8375–1.502

Drunk driving deterrence measures, views of traffic safety magazine readers, 1992 survey, article, A8375–1.501

Economic status self-assessment of public, 1977, 1987, and 1992, article, C8900–1.505

Electric and magnetic fields (EMF) hazards and nearby high-voltage transmission lines, public opinion, 1987-93 surveys, article, A4700–4.503

Elementary/secondary new teacher views on teaching and quality of schools, after 2nd year of teaching, spring 1992 survey, B6045–2

Elementary/secondary new teacher views on teaching, and reasons for leaving profession, spring 1992 survey, article, B6045–1.504

Elementary/secondary prospective teacher characteristics and opinions, survey of persons interested in alternative certification routes, 1992, R6350–7

Elementary/secondary school parental selection, and quality of Catholic vs public school education, public views, Aug 1992 survey, annual rpt, A7375–1

Elementary/secondary school parental selection, parent and general public views, and local program characteristics and results, 1992 rpt, R3810–7

Elementary/secondary school problems, quality, and proposed reforms, public opinion by respondent characteristics, 1993 annual Gallup Poll, A8680–1.503

Elementary/secondary school superintendents personal and professional characteristics and views, 1992 survey rpt, A0775–5

Elementary/secondary student views on school use of metal detectors to reduce violence, 1993 survey article, C1850–12.510

Elementary/secondary teacher views on education policy issues and selected reform proposals, Jan-Feb 1993 survey, B6045–7

Employee satisfaction with and views on importance of selected job aspects, 1973-92 surveys, article, C4687–1.501

Environmental engineering professional views on career and top employers, May 1993, annual survey article, C5800–2.546

Environmental laws/protection adequacy, public opinion, 1980 and 1990, article, A1865–1.505

Europe public opinion on political, economic, and social issues, for 9 countries and 3 Soviet Union Republics, 1991 survey, C8915–8

Europe public opinion on political, economic, and social issues of interest to foreign investors, for 9 countries and 3 Soviet Union Republics, 1991 survey, C8915–9

Foreign policy issues including support for US involvement in world affairs, 1945-92 surveys, A0610–1.503

Foreign policy, public opinion on selected issues, with detail for 3 States, 1993 survey, annual rpt, A4965–1

Gallup Poll public attitude surveys, results and sample characteristics, monthly rpt, C4040–1

General Social Surveys, opinions on social, political, and economic issues, detailed data, 1972-91 surveys, annual rpt, U6395–1

Global warming and related issues, views of climate scientists, Feb 1992 survey, article, R3823–1.502

Health care issues, including govt and medical profession role, satisfaction with care and insurance, and reforms, 1975-92 surveys, A0610–1.504

Health care professionals dissatisfaction with selected aspects of their jobs, 1992 survey, article, A1865–1.511

Health care reform issues and/or options, views of physicians and general public, by respondent characteristics, Mar-Apr 1993 surveys, C8915–7.2

Health care reform issues, including natl insurance system desirability and satisfaction with current coverage, 1993 survey article, A1865–1.521

Health care reform options, public opinion following Nov 1992 presidential election, 1993 article, C5800–7.511

Health care reform priorities of general public vs health professionals, including importance of ethics and alternative medicine, 1993 survey article, A1865–1.522

Health care reform support among general public, Mar-Apr 1993 survey, article, A1865–1.514

Health care specialist and health-related company CEO income, public perceptions vs actual amounts, by respondent characteristics, 1991-93, R4865–13

Health condition and preventive health care and safety practices of adults, by respondent characteristics, 1992 and trends, annual survey rpt, C8111–2

Health insurance benefit value to employees, 1992 survey, article, A1865–1.514

Health professional views on treatment decisions for patients near end of life, 1993 survey article, A2623–1.503

Hispanic American elected officials views on top 3 issues facing Hispanic community, 1992, annual rpt, A6844–1

Hispanic American leaders views on current issues of importance to Hispanic community, 1993 annual survey article, C4575–1.511

Hispanic American leaders views on selected Clinton Admin economic policy proposals, Jan 1993 survey, article, C4575–1.505

Hispanic American professionals views on work conditions at own company, with ratings of regions and top 19-20 companies and industries, 1993 survey article, C4575–1.504

Hispanic American views on characteristics of public TV vs 4 other networks, 1992 survey, R4250–1.24

Hispanic American views on natl problems and economy, and 1992 presidential candidate preferences in 5 States, Oct 1992 survey, article, C4575–1.501

Home ownership, public opinion on willingness to make selected sacrifices, 1992 survey feature, C4300–1.502

Housing market conditions, public opinion, 1992-93 surveys, article, C5800–7.529

Industrial mgmt magazine reader views on job enjoyment and problems, 1992 survey article, C7000–3.501

Industrial mgmt magazine reader views on who is responsible for economic problems, Federal budget deficit, and health care costs, Feb 1993 survey, article, C7000–3.510

Investors views on economic conditions and Clinton Admin priorities, 1993 survey article, C5800–7.514

Japan public image in US, with data on US attitudes toward the Japanese by race, 1993 survey article, R5650–2.520

Japan public opinion on relations with US, among persons age 40-49 and 70/over, 1992 survey, article, C5800–7.552

Journalist (TV and newspaper) concern for self-interest vs public interest, public opinion, Aug 1992 survey, A8605–1.505

Loyalty between companies and employees, views of industrial mgmt magazine readers, 1993 survey article, C7000–3.506

Magazine publisher employee benefits, costs, and trends, with employee ratings of health coverage, Mar/Apr 1993 survey, article, C2575–1.517

Medical education and careers, views of college undergrads and advisors, Feb/Mar 1990 survey, article, A3273–8.506

Index by Subjects and Names

Opinion and attitude surveys

Medical school inclusion of 38 intl health topics, with faculty ratings of topic importance, 1989/90 or June 1991, article, A3273–8.509

Men age 69-84 quality of life indicators, including health, finances, family, and employment, by race, 1990 survey, U3780–9

Men's sexual behavior, including condom use, and AIDS knowledge and risks, by selected characteristics, 1991 survey, articles, A5160–1.503

Midwest banker opinions on Clinton Admin deficit reduction plan and health care reform, spring 1993 survey, semiannual rpt, B6785–1

Minority groups views on most important problems for their communities, by race-ethnicity, 1993 survey, article, R4800–2.518

Motor vehicle seat belt use and enforcement, views of traffic safety magazine readers, Mar/Apr 1993 survey, article, A8375–1.505

Municipal govt ethics policies and concerns, views of personnel directors, 1992 survey, A5800–1.1

News events followed most closely by public, and opinion on media coverage and selected current issues, by respondent characteristics, recurring rpt, C8915–1

Nurse views on hospital patient care practices and outlook, and impact of clinical info systems, 1993 survey, article, A1865–1.520

Nurse views on managed health care topics appropriate for undergraduate nursing curriculums, Jan 1993 survey, article, A1865–1.517

Nursing complex skills considered basic knowledge by hospital nurses, and inclusion in education programs, 1993 survey article, A8010–3.504

Nursing grad student reasons for pursuing degrees, and employment expectations, 1993 survey article, A8010–3.503

Nursing student (male) reasons for career choice and intended specialty, 1993 survey article, A8010–3.503

Occupational injuries/illnesses and fatalities, lost workdays, and employee views on workplace safety, with data by State, 1992 annual rpt, R8335–1.1

Occupations social prestige ratings among general public, for 77 occupations, 1989, survey article, C7000–3.509

Parent expectations of their 8th grade children's ultimate educational attainment, 1988, article, R4800–2.509

Pedestrian intoxication safety and legal issues, views of traffic safety magazine readers, May/June 1993 survey, article, A8375–1.506

Personal info use by business, including views on privacy, credit, and effects of computer use, 1992 survey and trends, annual rpt, B3280–2

President Clinton job performance approval ratings, Jan-Apr 1993 surveys, article, C5800–7.526

President Clinton job performance overall and on economy during 1st 100 days in office, public opinion, Apr 1993 survey, article, C5800–7.527

Psychology doctorate recipient employment characteristics, including views on work conditions, 1990/91, biennial survey rpt, A2620–4

Public opinion devs, with results of social, economic, and political surveys, and polling methodology, quarterly rpt, A0610–1

Public opinion on the media and related issues, by respondent characteristics, series, C8915–11

Public school improvement outlook and funding adequacy, views of parents by race and Hispanic ethnicity, Feb 1993 survey, article, R4800–2.517

Puerto Rico statehood, commonwealth status, or independence, public opinion in Puerto Rico and US, 1989-92 surveys, article, C4575–1.506

Rape incidence, victim characteristics, and views of victims and service agency staff on related issues, 1990-92 surveys, R8375–1

Recycling curbside program impact on trash collection costs, public opinion, 1992 survey article, C1850–1.501

Recycling curbside program operations, funding, and recycled materials, municipal official views and summary program characteristics, July 1991 survey, B0230–2

Recycling curbside programs, State legislator views on operations, funding, and recycled materials, July 1991 survey, B0230–1

Recycling program obstacles cited by municipal officials, 1993 survey article, C1850–1.505

Religion and related social issues, public opinions and attitudes, monthly survey, R8780–1

Researcher employment situation, including job satisfaction and employer characteristics, 1992 survey, annual article, C1850–6.505

Restaurant patron rights, views of consumers, operators, and critics, 1992-93 surveys, article, C1850–3.511

Russia public opinion on political and economic issues, 1992 article, U2030–1.504

Smoking status reported by cessation program participants correlated with biochemical testing results, 1993 article, A2623–1.511

Soviet Union political and economic restructuring issues, public opinion in Russia, Ukraine, and Lithuania, 1991-92 surveys, C8915–10

State Governors approval ratings, with tax policy and economic indicators, for 26 Governors, 1993 article, B8500–2.520

State Governors approval ratings, with tax policy indicators, for 16 Governors, 1993, article, B8500–2.513

Student attitudes on courses in 4 subject areas, for 8th graders by sex and race-ethnicity, 1988, R4800–2.512

Student use of and attitudes toward alcohol, drugs, and tobacco products, 1993 survey article, B6045–1.504

Tax increases under consideration by Clinton Admin, public opinion, Jan 1993 survey, C5800–7.514

Teacher education and school reform goals, views of educators, 1992 recurring survey rpt, A3375–1

Telephone answering machines advantages vs disadvantages, public opinion, 1993 survey article, C1200–4.505

Time spent in work/commute, with family, and in physical activity, actual vs desired, 1992 survey feature, C1200–4.501

Traffic safety magazine reader views on driver vision standards, road signs and signals, and road safety costs for elderly drivers, Nov/Dec 1992 survey, article, A8375–1.503

Traffic safety magazine reader views on police pursuits, Jan/Feb 1993 survey, article, A8375–1.504

Traveler preferences for dining location, and views on hotel room service, 1992 survey article, C7000–6

TV (public) coverage and important natl issues, views of leaders and general public, 1992 series, R8825–10

TV violence and Govt regulation, opinions of advertising industry magazine readers, Oct 1993 survey, article, C2710–1.551

Urban League National Education Initiative population served, and opinions of students and parents, 1991 survey, article, A8510–1.1

Urban small claims and/or traffic court litigant satisfaction with case processing and outcome, mediation, and police and court officials, for 3-4 jurisdictions, 1990, R6600–5

Volunteer organization views on using families as volunteers, 1992 survey article, C2176–1.501

Women's concerns and views on income vs cost of living, 1992 feature, C4215–1.502

Work force diversity mgmt program effect on worker ratings of quality of work life, 1993 survey article, C1850–2.511

Work-related issues, public opinion, 1993 survey article, C5800–7.545

Youth age 10-19 handgun experience and attitudes, Apr-May 1993 survey, article, R4800–2.522

Youth age 12-17 charitable contributions, volunteer activity, and views on related issues, by respondent characteristics, 1992 survey, biennial rpt, A5435–5

Youth social concerns, 1993 survey article, C2710–1.541

Zambia student views on sexual behavior and treatment of persons infected with AIDS virus, by respondent characteristics, 1990 survey, article, A5160–6.503

State and local:

Alabama health behavior risk factor surveillance survey results, by respondent characteristics, 1988-89, recurring rpt, S0175–6

Arkansas economic dev resources existing and needed to attract new business, 1989/90 survey, article, U5930–1.501

California health behavior risk factor surveillance survey results, by respondent characteristics, 1991 and trends, annual rpt, S0865–2

California public opinion on public school quality and parental use of State vouchers to pay for private schools, Sept 1993 survey, C5800–7.550

Colorado health behavior risk factor surveillance survey results, by respondent characteristics, 1990, recurring rpt, S1010–3

Opinion and attitude surveys

Connecticut health behavior risk factor surveillance survey results, 1989-91, annual rpt, S1200–2

Delaware public opinion on criminal sentencing, prison alternatives, and related issues, Feb 1991 survey, R8825–11

Florida 8th-9th grade children of immigrants characteristics, attitudes, and discrimination experience, 1992, survey article, R4800–2.522

Georgia health behavior risk factor surveillance survey results, by respondent characteristics, 1991 and trends, annual rpt, S1895–2

Hawaii health behavior risk factor surveillance survey results, by respondent characteristics, 1990, annual rpt, S2065–1.4

Idaho public opinion on top general and environmental issues for State, and positive and negative aspects of mining industry, Sept 1992 survey, article, C5226–2.506

Iowa health behavior risk factor surveillance survey results, by respondent characteristics, 1991, annual rpt, S2795–2

Kentucky health behavior risk factor surveillance survey results, by State area and respondent characteristics, 1988-90, annual rpt, S3140–6

Massachusetts health behavior risk factor surveillance survey results, by respondent characteristics, 1986-90, recurring rpt, S3850–3

Michigan health behavior risk factor surveillance survey results, by respondent characteristics, 1991, annual rpt, S4000–4

Nevada health behavior risk factor surveillance survey results, by location and respondent characteristics, 1991, annual rpt, S5075–3

New Jersey local health official views on hazardous waste site concerns and interactions with Federal and State govts, Nov 1991 survey, article, A2623–1.507

New Mexico, Albuquerque characteristics, and vacation site selection criteria, views of North Central States residents, spring 1993 survey, article, U7980–1.505

New Mexico parents opinions on quality of public education, 1991/92 survey, annual rpt, S5575–4

New York State health behavior risk factor surveillance survey results, by respondent characteristics, 1990, recurring rpt, S5765–3

North Dakota health behavior risk factor surveillance survey results, by respondent characteristics, 1991 and trends, annual rpt, S6105–3

Oklahoma public library use and collection quality, public views by library, FY92 annual rpt, S6470–1

Pennsylvania health behavior risk factor surveillance survey results, by respondent characteristics, 1991, annual rpt, S6820–4

South Dakota accounting firm recruiters views on tax curriculum for accounting undergraduates, and degree levels of students hired, fall 1992 survey, article, U8595–1.504

Tennessee health behavior risk factor surveillance survey results, by respondent characteristics, 1986-90, annual rpt, S7520–3

Texas health behavior risk factor surveillance survey results, by respondent characteristics, 1991 and trends, annual rpt, S7685–2

Texas public health administrator views on whether State legislature should set standard eligibility requirements for indigent care, FY90 survey, U8850–8.7

Utah health behavior risk factor surveillance survey results, by respondent characteristics, 1991, annual rpt, S7835–3

see also Business outlook and attitude surveys

see also Consumer surveys

see also Market research

see also Political attitudes and ideology

Opinion Research Corp.

Supermarket shopper practices, attitudes, and expenditures, by respondent characteristics, 1993 and trends, annual survey rpt, A4950–3

Opium

see Drug abuse and treatment

see Drug and narcotics offenses

see Drugs

Optical instruments

see Instruments and measuring devices

see Optometry

Options trading

Chicago Board of Trade futures and options trading in financial instruments and agricultural commodities, 1992, annual rpt, B2120–1

Coffee, Sugar, and Cocoa Exchange trading activity, with related data including deliveries and stocks by country and/or port, 1992 and trends, annual rpt, B2275–1

Commodity yearbook for 1993: detailed supply-demand data, and options trading activity by exchange, C2400–1

Electronics manufacturer currency forwards/options purchases, for 3 companies, 1992, article, C1850–2.510

Foreign trading volume by commodity and exchange, monthly rpt, A5040–5

Grain market activity on Kansas City Board of Trade, including options volume, prices, and open interest, 1992 and trends, annual rpt, B1530–1

New York Stock Exchange options trading activities, and contract specifications, 1992, annual fact book, B6625–1.1

Open interest (outstanding commitments) on options contracts on foreign exchanges, by commodity and exchange, monthly rpt, A5040–6

Trading volume by commodity and exchange, 1988-92, annual rpt, A5040–1

Trading volume by commodity, securities index, and exchange, monthly rpt, A5040–3

Wheat options trading activity on Minneapolis exchange, 1992 and trends, annual rpt, B6110–1.1

see also Futures trading

Optometry

Medical group financial and operating data, by practice characteristics, 1991, annual rpt, A6365–2

Schools of optometry faculty, enrollment and degrees, policies and programs, and finances, by instn, 1991/92, annual survey, A3370–2

Shopping center financial and operating data, with detail by type of tenant, US and Canada, 1991, triennial rpt, R9285–1

Women and minorities in professional fields, detailed education and labor force data, 1991 and trends, recurring rpt, A3960–2.3

State and local:

Florida county data book, 1992/93 annual rpt, C6360–1

Florida health care atlas, including manpower by occupation and health care facilities by type, by district and county, 1992 annual rpt, S1746–1.2

Florida statistical abstract, general data, 1992 annual rpt, U6660–1.20

Indiana Medicaid expenditures, by service and provider type and county, FY91-92, annual rpt, S2623–1.6

Kentucky Medicaid recipients and payments, by program, county, and type of medical service, monthly rpt, S3140–5

Maryland medical assistance payments and recipients, by program, type of service, location, demographic characteristics, and facility, FY92 and trends, annual rpt, S3635–3

Minnesota optometry and osteopathy student loan program participants and loan status, FY82-92, biennial rpt, S4195–2.2

Missouri public welfare and medical assistance recipients, expenditures, and case processing, by program and county, FY92 and trends, annual rpt, S4575–2

South Carolina statistical abstract, general data, 1993 annual rpt, S7125–1.10

South Dakota medical assistance recipients and payments, by type of service, FY92, annual rpt, S7385–1.1

Texas optometrists offices/clinics and expenditures, 1977, 1982, and 1987, U8850–8.3

see also Vision

Oral rehydration therapy

World population and health indicators, with detail by region and country, 1992/93 biennial rpt, R9455–1.5

Oranges

see Citrus fruits

Orchestras

see Music

Orders

see Business orders

Ordnance

see Military supplies and property

see Military weapons

Oregon

Agricultural production, marketing, and finances, by commodity and/or county, with farms and acreage, 1991 and trends, annual rpt, S6575–1

Banks and other financial instns, financial condition by instn, Dec 1992 and trends, annual rpt, S6616–1

Crimes and arrests, by offense, with data by local agency and offender characteristics, and law enforcement employees and assaults on officers, 1992 and trends, annual rpt, S6603–3

Index by Subjects and Names — Osteopathy

Economic conditions, including population, construction, income, employment, industry, and foreign trade data, 1991, annual rpt, S6585–3

Economic indicators for 10 Western States, including forecasts from selected organizations, monthly rpt, U0282–2

Election results and voter registration and turnout, by county and/or district, 1992 general election, biennial rpt, S6665–1

Elementary and secondary education enrollment and finances, including data by school district and county, annual rpt series, S6590–1

Employment, population, and other economic devs, discontinued biennial rpt, S6615–9

Fishing (commercial) landings by species and county, oyster harvest, and licensing activity, 1970s-91, annual rpt, S6575–1

Govt financial condition, including revenues by source, expenditures by function, and fund statements, FY92, annual rpt, S6603–2

Labor force and employment statistics, including data by industry, monthly rpt, S6592–1, S6615–2

Library finances, staff, holdings, and services, for public, academic, and special libraries by instn, FY92 and trends, annual rpt, S6635–1

Markets with daily newspapers, demographic and economic info by geographic area, US and Canada, 1993 annual rpt, C3250–1

Oil/gas industry production, finances, exploration, and reserves, by State, 1992 and trends, annual rpt, A5425–1.1

Population by county and place of residence in 1990 vs 1985, article, S6592–1.501

Statistical profiles of 50 States and DC, general data, 1993 annual almanac, C4712–1

Utility and transportation regulatory agency activities, scope of jurisdiction, finances, and employees, by agency, 1991/92 annual rpt, A7015–2

Vital statistics, including births, deaths by cause, communicable diseases, marriages, and divorces, by age, sex, race-ethnicity, and county, 1991 and trends, annual rpt, S6615–5

Welfare caseloads, recipients, and expenditures, by program, city, county, and State region, monthly rpt, S6615–8

see also Portland, Oreg.

see also Salem, Oreg.

see also under By City and By County in the "Index by Categories"

see also under By State in the "Index by Categories"

Organ and blood banks

Blood bank collection and transfusion data, and shipments by region, 1993 annual rpt, A0612–2

Community blood bank operating profiles, by instn arranged by State, 1993 biennial directory, A0612–1

Donated organs by type, by race of donor, 1990, article, C4215–1.501

Eye bank activity in US and abroad, including donations by type, source, and donor characteristics, and data by individual bank, 1992 and trends, annual rpt, A4743–1

Organ transplants

see Medical transplants

Organic chemicals

see Chemicals and chemical industry

Organization for Economic Cooperation and Development

Education spending in US and 14 other OECD member countries, with related data on enrollment and teachers, 1987, A1600–4

Export value from OECD to Eastern/Central Europe, with data by OECD country, 1990, R5025–10

Financial market devs worldwide, including economic and monetary trends and forecasts for OECD countries, bimonthly rpt, B6200–2

Foreign Dev Assistance Committee contributions, by member and recipient country, 1987-91, annual article, R5650–2.507

Foreign Dev Assistance Committee contributions, by member country, 1988-92, annual article, R5650–2.550

Health care expenditures as percent of GDP and per capita, for 15 OECD countries, 1970, 1980, and 1990, annual fact book, A1275–1.4

Infrastructure dev share of OECD countries foreign assistance, for 11 donor countries, 1991, article, C5800–2.527

Oil and gas industry intl exploration, drilling, production, refining, stock, price, and financial data, weekly rpt, C6985–1

Oil and refined product stocks, by selected member country, 1970s-91, annual compilation, C6985–10.1

Oil, gas, and refined product stocks, trade, and consumption, by country, 1991 and trends, annual compilation, C6985–9.2

Oil stocks, by OECD country, 1980-91, annual rpt, C6985–5.1

Travel and tourism trends in US and worldwide, with traveler and trip characteristics, and data by local area, 1992 annual rpt, C2140–1

Organization of Arab Petroleum Exporting Countries

Oil imports of US, by OAPEC member country, Sept 1973-Apr 1974, periodic basic data book, A2575–14.4

Organization of Petroleum Exporting Countries

Oil and gas industry operations and supply-demand data, by member country, 1970s-92, annual compilation, C6985–10.3

Oil and gas industry supply-demand, including production, quotas, and US and OECD imports, weekly rpt, C6985–1

Oil and gas sourcebook, with industry operations and finances, and world supply-demand situation, 1970s-91, annual compilation, C6985–9

Oil imports of US from OPEC, OAPEC, and Persian Gulf sources, 1973-92, annual rpt, A5425–2.1

Oil production and prices, by member country, 1992 and trends, annual compilation, C6985–4.1

Oil production and reserves in 7 Commonwealth of Independent States Republics and 12 OPEC countries, 1991, article, C6985–1.510

Oil production by member country, 1st qtr 1992-93, with current quotas, annual article, C6985–1.539

Oil production, exploration, refining, demand, finance, prices, and reserves, by State and country or world area, 1993 and trends, periodic basic data book, A2575–14.7

Oil supply-demand worldwide, with OPEC production quotas, capacity, reserves, and exports, 1970s-2010, annual rpt, C6985–5

see also under By Foreign Country or World Area in the "Index by Categories"

Organized crime

State and local:

New York State organized crime task force indictments, dispositions, and convictions, 1990-91, annual rpt, S5760–3.2

Organized labor

see Labor unions

Oriental Americans

see Asian Americans

see Pacific Islands Americans

Orthopedic impairments

see Mobility limitations

see Orthopedics

see Podiatry

see Prosthetics and orthotics

Orthopedics

Hospital patient discharges and length of stay, by diagnosis, type of operation, age, and region, 1991, annual rpt series, B4455–1

Medical school faculty and compensation, by dept, academic rank, degree, and region, 1992/93, annual rpt, A3273–2

Physicians by detailed specialty and location, 1992 and trends, annual rpt, A2200–3

see also Mobility limitations

see also Podiatry

see also Prosthetics and orthotics

Orthotics

see Prosthetics and orthotics

Ortiz, Thomas C.

"Texas Medicaid Program", U8850–8.5

Osteopathy

Colleges of osteopathy, enrollment, student and faculty characteristics, and finances, 1992/93 and trends, annual rpt, A0620–1

Student debt and career plans, by selected characteristics, 1991/92, annual survey rpt, A0620–2

Women and minorities in professional fields, detailed education and labor force data, 1991 and trends, recurring rpt, A3960–2.3

State and local:

Florida health care atlas, including manpower by occupation and health care facilities by type, by district and county, 1992 annual rpt, S1746–1.2

Florida live births by type of attendant, race, and county, 1992 and trends, annual rpt, S1745–3

Florida statistical abstract, general data, 1992 annual rpt, U6660–1.20

Kansas statistical abstract, general data, 1991/92 annual rpt, U7095–2.2

Minnesota optometry and osteopathy student loan program participants and loan status, FY82-92, biennial rpt, S4195–2.2

Osteopathy

Oregon births, by type of attendant and county, 1991, annual rpt, S6615–5

Texas doctors of osteopathy offices/clinics and expenditures, 1977, 1982, and 1987, U8850–8.3

Ostry, Sylvia

"Threat of Managed Trade to Transforming Economies", R5025–10

Outdoor advertising

see Advertising

Outdoor power equipment

see Lawn and garden equipment

Outdoor Power Equipment Institute

Lawn mower shipments, for walk-behind and rider mowers, 1990-94, article, C5150–6.508

Shipments of selected types of outdoor power equipment, 1991-94, article, C5150–3.515

Outlying areas

see American Samoa
see Guam
see Panama Canal
see Puerto Rico
see Territories of the U.S.
see Trust Territory of the Pacific Islands
see U.S. Virgin Islands

Output of labor

see Labor productivity

Over-the-counter drugs

see Drugs
see Personal care products

Over-the-counter stocks

see Securities
see Stock exchanges

Overtime

Aerospace industry production worker regular and overtime hours, 1977-91, annual rpt, A0250–2.5

Business forms manufacturing plant employment and compensation data, by region, 1992 and trends, biennial rpt, A5785 4

Container (fiber box) shipments by end-use industry and region, and other industry operating data, 1940s-92, annual rpt, A4875–1

Food store manager hours per week, and Sundays worked and pay policy, by sales size, year ended Mar 1993, annual survey, A4950–6

Foreign overtime index, Australia and Japan, monthly rpt, U1245–1

Iron and steel industry financial and operating data, 1992 and trends, annual rpt, A2000–2.1

Plastics processing industry employment, compensation practices, and union representation, by region, 1992, annual survey rpt, A8920–2

Railroad employment and earnings, by occupation, company, and district, 1992, annual rpt, A3275–7

Shoe industry production, employment, trade, marketing, and related data, by SIC 2- to 5-digit code or product type, 1992 annual rpt, A4957–1.2

State and local:

California economic indicators, bimonthly rpt, S0840–1

California statistical abstract, general data, 1992 annual rpt, S0840–2.3

New York State employment, earnings, and hours, by county, selected metro area, and industry group, monthly rpt, S5775–1

Wisconsin economic indicators, including employment and earnings by industry group, monthly rpt, S8750–1

Wyoming penitentiary staff monthly overtime hours worked, FY91-92, annual rpt, S8883–1

Overweight

see Obesity

Ownership of enterprise

Auto rental company fleet size, and auto manufacturers shares of ownership and vehicles, for 8 rental companies, 1993 article, C2710–3.521

Cable TV classic movie network subscribers, ownership, and titles available, for 3 networks, 1993 article, C1850–14.535

Cable TV subscribers for 13 major companies owned by newspaper companies, Dec 1992, article, A8605–1.510

Construction industry finances and operations, by type of business and region, 1992-93, annual survey rpt, A4155–1

Eastern Europe public opinion on private and/or govt operation of selected enterprises, for 4 countries and 3 Soviet Union Republics, 1991 survey, C8915–8.2

Europe public opinion on political, economic, and social issues of interest to foreign investors, for 9 countries and 3 Soviet Union Republics, 1991 survey, C8915–9

Family-owned business owner actions to ensure family succession, 1993 feature, C4687–1.509

Family-owned business owner concerns about ownership succession, 1992, survey article, C4687–1.507

Food store industry sales and operations, independents vs chains, 1992 and trends, annual rpt, C5225–1.505

Food store sales for chains vs independents, 1992, annual feature, C4655–1.510

Food wholesaler financial and operating data, by affiliation, size, and region, 1991-92, annual rpts, A4950–5

Hardware retail store composite finances and operations, by type of ownership, 1991, annual rpt, A8275–1.1

Health care preferred provider organizations (PPOs), employee utilization, and type of sponsor or ownership, 1993 article, A1865–1.524

HMO benefits, enrollment and utilization, staffing, finances, and relations with employers, by plan characteristics, 1990-91, annual rpt, A5150–2

Homebuilder financial and operating data, including detail by location, for top 400 builders, 1993 annual feature, C1850–8.507

Hospital directory, with utilization, expenses, and personnel, by instn, type, and location, 1992, annual rpt, A1865–3

Hospital Medicare financial and operating indicators, by type of instn ownership and control, 1988-92, annual rpt, B1880–1.3

Industrial distributors operations, including type of ownership and acquisition activity, 1992, annual survey, C1850–4.507

Medical group practice characteristics, including specialties, form of organization, and location, 1991 and trends, recurring rpt, A2200–7

Index by Subjects and Names

Mortgage banking industry aggregate financial and operating data, by lending characteristics and type of ownership, 1989 and trends, annual rpt, A6450–3

Newspaper family ownership or control, circulation, and dailies published, for top 25 newspaper groups, 1992 article, A8605–1.501

Office product dealers by type of business organization, by region, 1991, annual rpt, A8110–1

Radio station group owners ranked by total Arbitron rating, with stations owned and ratings, for top 25 companies, summer 1992, article, C1850–14.502

Railroads and operating data by ownership arrangement, and ownership shares of specified rail systems, 1991, annual rpt, A3275–8

Restaurant industry financial and operating data, by establishment characteristics and location, 1992, annual rpt, A8200–3

Restaurants with independent owners, sales, seating capacity, average check size, and patrons served, top 100 instns, 1992, annual article, C1850–3.505

Shopping center financial and operating data, with detail by type of tenant, US and Canada, 1991, triennial rpt, K9285–1

Shopping centers by owner type, by building characteristics, region, and metro area, 1991, annual rpt, A5600–6

Small business survival under original and new owners 8 years after formation, for firms formed in 1977/78, article, C4687–1.512

Soviet Union oil industry ownership structure following Nov 1992 reorganization, 1992 article, C6985–1.507

Supermarket ownership/lease arrangements for new and existing stores, by type and region, 1992, annual rpt, A4950–2

TV station group owner companies ranked by market penetration, with stations owned, 1992/93, recurring article, C1850–14.516

TV station group owner companies ranked by market penetration, with stations owned, 1993 recurring article, C1850–14.524

Veterinary practice distribution by size, type, and ownership, 1991, article, A3100–2.514

State and local:

Mississippi statistical abstract, general data, 1992 annual rpt, U3255–4.5

Oklahoma farm operators by ownership status, and foreign-owned agricultural land by owner country, 1992 annual rpt, S6405–1

Tennessee statistical abstract, general data, 1992/93 annual rpt, U8710–2.7, U8710–2.11

Texas hospitals, operations, utilization, and finances, by type, ownership, size, and metro-nonmetro status, 1970s-91, U8850–8.3

see also Business acquisitions and mergers
see also Consumer cooperatives
see also Cooperatives
see also Corporations
see also Divestiture
see also Employee stock ownership plans

Index by Subjects and Names

see also Foreign corporations
see also Franchises
see also Government corporations and enterprises
see also Government ownership
see also Holding companies
see also Minority businesses
see also Multinational corporations
see also Partnerships
see also Proprietorships
see also Rural cooperatives
see also Securities
see also Self-employment
see also Women-owned businesses

Oxygen
see Gases

Ozone depletion
see Air pollution

Pace Consultants Inc.
Oil refining margins in key US and foreign processing centers, weekly rpt monthly table, C6985–1

Pace Group
HMO State regulatory requirements, 1993 article, A1865–1.521

Pacific Islands Americans
Births and fertility, by selected newborn and maternal characteristics, 1990, article, R8750–1.510
Optometry school faculty, enrollment and degrees, policies and programs, and finances, by instn, 1991/92, annual survey, A3370–2
Population characteristics, employment, and voting patterns for minority groups by detailed race-ethnicity, with comparisons to whites, 1980s-2040, R8750–2.58

State and local:
Arkansas Census of Population and Housing detailed findings, 1990, U5935–7
California Census of Population and Housing detailed findings, 1990, S0840–9
California labor force planning rpt, including population characteristics, and employment by industry, 1992 annual rpt, S0830–2
California public school enrollment, grads, and staff, by race-ethnicity, 1992/93 and trends, annual rpt, S0825–9
California socioeconomic and govtl data for municipalities, counties, and school districts, 1993 annual rpt, C4712–3
California vital statistics, including population, births, and deaths by cause, by demographic characteristics and county, 1990 and trends, annual rpt, S0865–1
Florida statistical abstract, general data, 1992 annual rpt, U6660–1.1
Florida vital statistics, including population, births, deaths by cause, and marriages and dissolutions, by location and demographic characteristics, 1992 and trends, annual rpt, S1745–3
Georgia statistical abstract, general data, 1992-93 biennial rpt, U6730–1.1
Hawaii crimes and arrests, by offense, with data by county and victim-offender characteristics, 1992, annual rpt, S2035–1
Hawaii data book, general data, 1992 annual rpt, S2090–1.1, S2090–1.6, S2090–1.12, S2090–1.15

Hawaii health dept activities and services, including vital statistics and disease control, by location, 1990, annual rpt, S2065–1
Maryland statistical abstract, general data, 1993-94 biennial rpt, S3605–1.1
New Hampshire arrests, by offense and offender age, sex, and race-ethnicity, 1991, annual rpt, S5250–2.2
New Jersey Census of Population and Housing detailed findings, by county, 1990, S5425–19
Oregon vital statistics, including births, deaths by cause, communicable diseases, marriages, and divorces, by age, sex, race-ethnicity, and county, 1991 and trends, annual rpt, S6615–5
Pennsylvania Census of Population and Housing detailed findings, with selected data by county and municipality, 1990, U4130–13
South Carolina statistical abstract, general data, 1993 annual rpt, S7125–1.13
Utah public school enrollment, dropouts, and grads, by race-ethnicity and district, 1991/92, annual rpt, S7815–1.2
Washington State vital statistics, including births, deaths by cause, and population, by demographic characteristics and location, 1991 and trends, annual rpt, S8363–1
Wisconsin Blue Book, general data, 1993-94 biennial rpt, S8780–1.2

Pacific Northwest
see Western States

Pacific Ocean
Offshore oil and gas activity, including production, reserves, and spills, by location, 1991 and trends, annual compilation, C6985–9.4
Oil spills incidence and volume, 1970-91, periodic basic data book, A2575–14.5
see also Oceania

Pacific Rim
see Asia
see Oceania

Pacific States
see Western States

Packaging and containers
Aluminum shipments by end use, and can reclamation, 1982-92, annual rpt, A0400–2.1
Beer bottle and can production, 1960s-91, annual rpt, A3455–1.1
Beverage (soft drinks and beer) sales by type of package, and closures by type, 1992/93 annual rpt, C0125–3.2
Coffee cup (paper and plastic) purchases by vending companies, 1982 and 1990-92, annual rpt, C9470–1
Consumer views and attitudes concerning product packaging, 1993 survey, article, C1850–1.505, C1850–1.507
Financial performance and growth rankings for approx 1,000 top corporations, with comparisons by industry group, 1993 annual rpt, C3950–1.505
Financial ratios and performance, for over 350 SIC 4-digit industries, FY88-92, annual rpt, A6400–3
Food (take-out) consumer characteristics and attitudes, including importance of environmentally safe packaging to purchase decision, May 1992 survey, A8200–21

Packaging and containers

Food/beverage industry packaging devs, including equipment purchase plans, partnership arrangements, and new labeling law effects, 1993 annual survey article, C2150–6.512
Operating and financial composite ratios for corporations, with establishments and receipts, for approx 200 industries, by asset size, FY90, annual rpt, C7800–1
Package engineering devs and industry activities, monthly rpt, C1850–1
Paper and paperboard industry financial and operating data, by product, region, and State, 1992 and trends, annual rpt, A1630–6
Paper and paperboard shipments and consumption, by product grade and end use, 1993 annual rpt, C3975–5.3, C3975–5.4
Paperboard packaging devs, including consumption, shipments, and inventories, monthly rpt, C0125–4
Paperboard packaging equipment purchasing plans and spending trends, 1993 annual article, C0125–4.503
Paperboard packaging industry corrugated and folding carton box plants and equipment, by census div and for Canada, 1990-92, annual article, C0125–4.501
Paperboard packaging industry supply-demand trends, by sector and product grade, 1985-95, annual article, C0125–4.504
Plastics industry production and sales by resin type, consumption by end-use market, and operating characteristics, 1992 and trends, annual rpt, A8920–1
Production, consumption, stocks, trade, and prices for approx 100 basic commodities, including by country and producing State, commodity yearbook for 1993, C2400–1, C2400–2
Pulp and paper industry production, capacity, consumption, trade, and sales/earnings data, including profiles for selected companies and sectors, monthly rpt, C3975–2
Pulp, paper, and paperboard industry production, trade, and operating data, by product class, monthly rpt, A1630–5
Recycling economic viability of selected types of containers, views of municipal officials, July 1991 survey, B0230–2
Recycling economic viability of selected types of containers, views of State legislators, July 1991 survey, B0230–1
Shipments of fiber box containers by end-use industry and region, and other industry operating data, 1940s-92, annual rpt, A4875–1
Supermarket meat dept packaging types used, 1992, annual article, C4655–1.509
Supermarket shopper concerns regarding packaging recyclability, and effect on purchases, 1993 and trends, annual survey rpt, A4950–3

State and local:
California milk sales, by type of trade, and container type and size, 1992, annual rpt, S0850–1.6
Massachusetts State initiative on packaging reduction and use of recyclable material, election results by locality, 1992, biennial rpt, S3920–1

Packaging and containers

see also Containerization
see also Labeling

PACs
see Political action committees

Pagano, Michael A.
"City Fiscal Conditions in 1993", A8012–1.23

Paging systems
see Mobile radio

PaineWebber Group Inc.
Motor vehicle component manufacturers total and component sales, for top 13 companies worldwide, 1993 article, C2150–3.509

Tampon product market value, with shares for top 4 and all other manufacturers, 1992, article, C2710–1.513

Paints and varnishes
Auto parts/supplies and repair aftermarket sales performance, by product group, 1993 annual feature, C0125–1.503

Chemical and related industries production, finances, operating ratios, employment, and trade, by country, company, and chemical, 1980s-92, annual feature, A1250–1.530

Financial ratios and performance, for over 350 SIC 4-digit industries, FY88-92, annual rpt, A6400–3

Motor vehicle most popular paint colors, 1992, recurring article, C1575–2.509

Operating and financial composite ratios for corporations, with establishments and receipts, for approx 200 industries, by asset size, FY90, annual rpt, C7800–1

Opinions of consumer hard goods manufacturers and representatives on business issues and outlook, by product line, 1992 annual survey rpt, A1800–1

Production, consumption, stocks, trade, and prices for approx 100 basic commodities, including by country and producing State, commodity yearbook for 1993, C2400–1, C2400–2

Retail hardware sales and productivity measures for hardware stores, home centers, and lumber/building material outlets, 1991 and trends, annual rpt series, A8275–1

Sales and operations for top 58 paint store chains, 1991-92, annual feature, C5150–6.503

Shipments of paint coating industry, and additives demand, by product type, 1993 annual article, A1250–1.543

Shipments of paint coating industry, and materials demand, by product type, errata, A1250–1.506

Pakistan
Electronics industry trade and/or production trends by product category for 33 countries, with general economic profiles, 1993 annual rpt, A4725–1.4

Energy intl sourcebook, with detail on oil and gas industry operations, supply-demand, and prices, for approx 80 countries, 1970s-91, annual compilation, C6985–10.2

Family planning program access, targets, and success measures, 1992 article, A5160–6.501

Insurance industry underwriting data, with operating results for 2 major companies, 1990-91, annual article, C1050–1.504

Motor vehicle world production, sales, trade, and registrations, by country, world area, manufacturer, and make, 1991 and trends, annual rpt, A0865–2.1

Public opinion in US on selected foreign policy issues, with detail for 3 States, 1993 survey, annual rpt, A4965–1

Palau
see Trust Territory of the Pacific Islands

Panama
Statistical abstract of Latin America, detailed social, govtl, and economic data, 1992 annual rpt, U6250–1
see also Panama Canal

Panama Canal
Coal and other mineral fuel shipments through Panama Canal, 1986-91, annual rpt, A7400–2.1

Paper and paper products
Capital spending plans of US and Canadian pulp and paper industry, by purpose and geographic area, 1992-94, annual survey article, C3975–2.503

Container (fiber box) shipments by end-use industry and region, and other industry operating data, 1940s-92, annual rpt, A4875–1

Discount chain consumer natl brand preferences, by product category and chain, and by age group, 1993 survey, annual feature, C5150–3.521

Discount chain top-selling natl brands cited by managers, by product category, chain, and region, 1993 survey, annual feature, C5150–3.520

Drugstore chains financial performance and marketing operations, with sales by product type, 1993 annual feature, C5150–2.510

Executive compensation and components, by industry div and major manufacturing group, 1991, annual rpt, R4105–19

Financial and operating data of paper and paperboard industry, by product, region, and State, 1992 and trends, annual rpt, A1630–6

Financial performance and growth rankings for approx 1,000 top corporations, with comparisons by industry group, 1993 annual rpt, C3950–1.505

Financial ratios and performance, for over 350 SIC 4-digit industries, FY88-92, annual rpt, A6400–3

Greeting card sales, with detail by outlet type, occasion, and holiday, 1989-93, article, C4655–1.511

Japan paper/paperboard exports and imports, 1980-92, article, R5650–2.517

Juice drink paper box container preferences, by consumer age group, 1992 survey, C1850–1.501

Latin America statistical abstract, general data by country, 1992 annual rpt, U6250–1.24, U6250–1.25

Magazine paper consumption, for regular and/or recycled paper by type, North American vs overseas source, and weight, 1992-94, article, C2575–1.518

Municipal waste composition by type of nondurable goods, with recycling rates for paper products, 1990, annual rpt, A4620–1.1

Operating and financial composite ratios for corporations, with establishments and receipts, for approx 200 industries, by asset size, FY90, annual rpt, C7800–1

Index by Subjects and Names

Operations and finances of US and Canada pulp and paper industry, with detail by company and product grade, and world production and trade summary, 1993 annual rpt, C3975–5

Packaging (paper/paperboard) demand, by container type, 1980, 1991, and 1996, article, C1850–1.506

Paperboard packaging devs, including consumption, shipments, and inventories, monthly rpt, C0125–4

Paperboard packaging equipment purchasing plans and spending trends, 1993 annual article, C0125–4.503

Paperboard packaging industry supply-demand trends, by sector and product grade, 1985-95, annual article, C0125–4.504

Prices for 2 uncoated paper grades, 1990-93, article, C2575–1.503

Printing and publishing industries operations and outlook, including paper shipments and prices, monthly rpt, C1850–10

Printing company financial and operating data, including share of revenues from paper sales, for top 101 North American firms, 1993 annual feature, C1850–10.512

Production capacity and material consumption for pulp and paper industry, by grade and census div, 1970s-95, annual rpt, A1630–7

Production capacity trends and outlook for pulp and paper by grade, 1982-95, annual article, C3975–2.504

Production, consumption, stocks, trade, and prices for approx 100 basic commodities, including by country and producing State, commodity yearbook for 1993, C2400–1, C2400–2

Pulp and paper industry production and other operating trends and outlook, 1993 annual article, C3975–2.503

Pulp and paper industry production, capacity, consumption, trade, and sales/earnings data, including profiles for selected companies and sectors, monthly rpt, C3975–2

Pulp, paper, and paperboard industry production, trade, and operating data, by product class, monthly rpt, A1630–5

Retail sales by outlet type, and discount chain sales in major depts, by product category, 1992, annual feature, C8130–1.507

Russia bleached pulp and chlorine production, by pulp/paper mill, 1990, article, C3975–2.504

Salaries and benefits in pulp/paper industry, by job characteristics, 1992 survey, annual article, C3975–2.503

Sales and consumer expenditures, for food store products by type, 1991-92, annual feature, C4655–1.510

Sales and earnings of individual paper companies in US and Canada, monthly rpt quarterly feature, C3975–2.502, C3975–2.503, C3975–2.505, C3975–2.506, C3975–2.508, C3975–2.511, C3975–2.512

Sales volume shares by retail outlet type, for approx 300 food, drug, and other product categories, 1993 annual feature, C4655–1.504

Supermarket sales and market shares, for top 5-10 brands in 8 paper product categories, 1992-93, C2710–1.532

Supermarket sales by detailed product type, 1992 and trends, annual feature, C5225–1.507

Supermarket sales of nonfood products, by detailed product type, 1992, annual feature, C5225–1.508

Supply-demand and price data for paper grades used in magazines, 1991-94, annual article, C2575–1.501

Wholesale paper industry business activity, sales and performance trends, and mgmt devs, monthly rpt, A8140–3

State and local:

Alabama business activity indicators, monthly rpt, U5680–1

Florida statistical abstract, general data, 1992 annual rpt, U6660–1.12

Texas trade, transportation, and public utilities employment, by SIC 2- and 3-digit industry and detailed occupation, 2nd qtr 1991, triennial survey rpt, S7675–1.31

see also Newsprint

see also Office supplies

see also under By Industry in the "Index by Categories"

Paper gold

see Special Drawing Rights

Paperback books

see Books and bookselling

Papua New Guinea

Energy intl sourcebook, with detail on oil and gas industry operations, supply-demand, and prices, for approx 80 countries, 1970s-91, annual compilation, C6985–10.2

Parades

State and local:

DC scheduled public events and attendance, 1991, annual rpt, S1535–3.6

Paraguay

Statistical abstract of Latin America, detailed social, govtl, and economic data, 1992 annual rpt, U6250–1

Paranormal phenomena

see Supernatural phenomena

Paraplegia

see Spinal cord injuries

Paraprofessionals

see also Allied health personnel

Pardons

Correctional instn admin, with inmate characteristics and movements, by State and for Federal system, 1992 annual rpt, R4300–1.1

Public opinion on news items concerning President Bush pardon of Caspar Weinberger and others involved in Iran-Contra affair, Jan 1993 survey, C8915–1.501

Public opinion on President Bush pardon of Caspar Weinberger for involvement in Iran-Contra affair, Dec 1992 Gallup Poll, C4040–1.506

see also Parole and probation

Parents

Catholic vs public school performance, and support for parental school selection funded by govt, public opinion by respondent characteristics, July 1992 survey, A7375–8

Child abuse/neglect fatalities involving parental substance abuse, 1990-92, annual rpt, A7456–1

College freshmen parental characteristics, by sex and instn type, fall 1992, annual survey, U6215–1

Discipline methods used by parents of children age 11/younger, 1962 and 1992, article, R4800–2.517

Educational attainment parents expect for their 8th grade children, 1988, article, R4800–2.509

Elementary/secondary school parent involvement importance, and desirability of parental school selection, public opinion, 1993 annual Gallup Poll, A8680–1.503

Elementary/secondary school parental selection, parent and general public views, and local program characteristics and results, 1992 rpt, R3810–7

Elementary/secondary teacher views on parental involvement programs and level of parent control over school selection, Jan-Feb 1993 survey, B6045–7

Incarcerated mothers and their children, with data on characteristics, child caregivers, visitation, and support program use, 1991/92, A7575–4

Magazine (parenting) advertising pages and revenues, for 4 publications, 1989-92, article, C2575–1.508

Public school improvement outlook and funding adequacy, views of parents by race and Hispanic ethnicity, Feb 1993 survey, article, R4800–2.517

School-related activities of parents of 8th grade students, by school type, 1988, survey article, R4800–2.501

TV violence concerns of parents, with detail for news programs, Feb 1993 survey, C8915–11.1

Urban League National Education Initiative population served, and opinions of students and parents, 1991 survey, article, A8510–1.1

Urban public school systems with parental school selection, and with parenting programs for teenagers and adults, for 47 systems, 1990/91, A4425–4

Volunteer activity of youth age 12-17, with comparison to volunteer activities of parents, 1992 survey, biennial rpt, A5435–5.3

State and local:

Indiana child support activities, including location of absent parents in and out of State, FY92 annual rpt, S2623–1.3

Missouri Parents as Teachers program, including funding, families served, and educational level of participants, 1988/89-1991/92, annual rpt, S4505–1.1

New Mexico parents opinions on quality of public education, 1991/92 survey, annual rpt, S5575–4

see also Adoption

see also Children

see also Maternity benefits

Pari-mutuel wagering

State social, economic, and govtl indicators, with rankings, 1993 semiannual rpt, B8500–1.4

State tax rates and collections, by tax type and State, FY02-92, annual rpt, R9050–1.5

Wagering activity, attendance, purse distribution, and govt revenue, by State and Canadian Province, 1990 and trends, annual rpt, A3363–1

State and local:

Florida racing and jai alai attendance, and pari-mutuel revenue, FY88-91, annual rpt, U6660–1.23

Florida State govt disbursements to local areas, by source of funds, FY92, annual rpt, S1717–1

Massachusetts tax collections by type, and distributions to local areas, FY91 and trends, annual rpt, S3917–1

Nebraska revenues from licenses, fees, and miscellaneous taxes, 1991 and trends, annual rpt, S4950–1.3

New York State statistical yearbook, general data, 1992 annual rpt, U5100–1.5

Utah pari-mutuel wagering initiative voting results, by county, Nov 1992 election, biennial rpt, S7875–1

Washington State revenues by source, and distributions by tax and locality, FY92 and trends, annual rpt, S8415–1.1

Wisconsin financial condition, including revenues by source, expenditures by function and object, and fund balances, FY93, annual rpt, S8675–2

Wisconsin State constitutional amendment allowing pari-mutuel betting, election results by county, 1993-94 biennial rpt, S8780–1.3

see also Horse racing

Parking facilities

Apartment building (conventionally financed) detailed income and expense ratios for US and Canada, by building type, metro area, and US region, 1991 and trends, annual rpt, A5600–1

Apartment building (federally subsidized) detailed income and expense ratios, by building and subsidy type, building age, metro area, and region, 1991 and trends, annual rpt, A5600–5

Condominium, cooperative, and planned unit dev detailed expenses, for US and Canada, by building characteristics, metro area, and US region, 1991, annual rpt, A5600–3

Convenience stores offering special services, including parking, 1987-92, annual survey rpt, A6735–2

Office building detailed income and expense data, and energy use, US and Canada, by building characteristics, metro area, and US region, 1991 and trends, annual rpt, A5600–2

Shopping center financial and operating data, with detail by type of tenant, US and Canada, 1991, triennial rpt, R9285–1

State and local:

DC parking enforcement program operations and finances, FY87-91, annual rpt, S1535–3.7

Parkinson's disease

see Hereditary diseases

Parks

State and local:

DC statistical profile, general data, 1992 annual rpt, S1535–3.6

Maryland law enforcement employment by sex, criminal offenses and arrests, and assaults on police, by local agency including park police, 1991-92, annual rpt, S3665–1

Parks

see also Amusement parks
see also National parks
see also State funding for parks and recreation
see also State parks

Parochial schools

- Catholic educational instns and enrollment, by State and diocese, and teachers, 1993 annual almanac, C6885–1
- Catholic private elementary and high schools and enrollment, by diocese and State, 1993 annual compilation, C4950–1
- Catholic schools, enrollment, and teachers, by region, State, and diocese, 1992/93 and trends, annual rpt, A7375–1
- Catholic secondary school operations and finances, including enrollment by race-ethnicity and family income, 1991/92 and trends, biennial rpt, A7375–5
- Catholic vs public school performance, and support for parental school selection funded by govt, public opinion by respondent characteristics, July 1992 survey, A7375–8
- Latin America statistical abstract, general data by country, 1992 annual rpt, U6250–1.10
- Public opinion on social, political, and economic issues, detailed data, 1972-91 surveys, annual rpt, U6395–1

State and local:

- California church-affiliated elementary/secondary schools and enrollment, by denomination, 1992/93, annual rpt, S0825–8
- DC statistical profile, general data, 1992 annual rpt, S1535–3.6
- Delaware nonpublic school enrollment, attendance, staff, and transportation costs, by instn, 1991/92, annual rpt, S1430–1.8
- Hawaii data book, general data, 1992 annual rpt, S2090–1.3
- Illinois nonpublic school enrollment, by affiliation, 1990/91, annual rpt, S2440–1.1
- New Hampshire public and nonpublic elementary/secondary school enrollment, by grade and school type, fall 1991, annual table, S5200–1.1
- New Hampshire public and nonpublic elementary/secondary school enrollment, by grade and school type, fall 1992, annual table, S5200–1.9
- Oregon private and parochial schools, enrollment, and grads, with detail by school, county, and religious affiliation, 1992/93, annual rpt, S6590–1.19
- Pennsylvania public and nonpublic school enrollment, by grade, race-ethnicity, sex, and county, 1991/92 and trends, annual rpt, S6790–5.1
- Pennsylvania public and nonpublic school enrollment, by grade, race-ethnicity, sex, and county, 1992/93 and trends, annual rpt, S6790–5.17
- Rhode Island Catholic school enrollment by grade and city, and grads by sex and instn, 1992, annual rpt, S6970–1.1
- Utah private school enrollment, by race-ethnicity, sex, and instn, Oct 1991, annual rpt, S7815–1.2
- West Virginia public and private schools, enrollment, grads, and staff, by county, 1991/92, annual rpt, S8540–3

Parole and probation

- Correctional instn admin, inmates, facilities, costs, parole and probation, and staffing, for local, State, and Federal systems, 1992 annual series, R4300–1
- Correctional instns, inmates, staff, and cost of care, by instn, US and Canada, with operating summary by State or Province, 1992, annual directory, A1305–3

State and local:

- Alaska corrections system admin, including inmate and probationer/parolee offenses and demographic characteristics, 1991 annual rpt, S0287–1
- Arizona adult and juvenile probation activity, by county, FY92, annual rpt, S0525–1
- California correctional instn inmates, by offense, demographic characteristics, and instn, Dec 1992, semiannual rpt, S0820–2
- California correctional instn inmates, with criminal background and demographic characteristics, 1991 and trends, annual rpt, S0820–1
- California correctional instn population, parole and probation, and justice system expenditures, 1987-92, annual rpt, S0910–1.2
- California criminal justice system detailed data, by offense, county, age, race-ethnicity, and sex, 1991 and trends, annual rpt, S0910–2
- California felon parolees by sex, 1988-90, annual planning rpt, S0830–2
- Colorado juvenile and adult probation activity, FY92 and trends, annual rpt, S1035–1.2
- Connecticut probation activity, including probationers by status, FY91-92, biennial rpt, S1220–1.2
- DC court cases and dispositions, by type of case, and judicial system finances, 1992 and trends, annual rpt, S1515 1
- DC criminal justice system summary, including crimes and arrests, criminal procedure, prisoners, and parole, 1991 and trends, annual rpt, S1535–2
- DC statistical profile, general data, 1992 annual rpt, S1535–3.8
- Delaware public opinion on criminal sentencing, prison alternatives, and related issues, Feb 1991 survey, R8825–11
- Florida correctional instns, admin, and inmates by criminal background and demographic characteristics, FY92 annual rpt, S1720–1
- Florida county data book, 1992/93 annual rpt, C6360–1
- Florida court cases and dispositions, by type of court and case, and location, 1992, annual rpt, S1805–1
- Florida "habitual offender" sentencing laws effect on prison population, with data by circuit court and offender characteristics, 1993 rpt, A7575–5
- Florida statistical abstract, general data, 1992 annual rpt, U6660–1.22
- Georgia correctional instns, admin, and inmate characteristics, FY92, annual rpt, S1872–1
- Hawaii court cases and dispositions, including adult and juvenile probation activities, FY92, annual rpt, S2115–1.2

Index by Subjects and Names

- Hawaii data book, general data, 1992 annual rpt, S2090–1.4
- Illinois corrections dept admin, including inmates and characteristics, finances, and staff, FY91-93 and trends, annual rpt, S2425–1
- Illinois crimes and arrests, by offense, with data by location and offender characteristics, 1991, annual rpt, S2536–1
- Iowa correctional instn admissions, releases, and inmate characteristics, by instn, monthly rpt, S2770–1
- Kansas correctional instn inmates, by offense, demographic characteristics, and instn, FY92 and trends, annual rpt, S2940–1
- Massachusetts court cases and dispositions, including adult and juvenile probation activities and finances, 1992 and trends, annual rpt, S3807–1
- Michigan correctional instns, admin, and inmates by selected demographic characteristics, 1991 and trends, annual rpt, S3960–1
- Michigan labor force planning rpt, including characteristics of Job Training Partnership Act eligible population by State area, 1993 annual rpt, S3980–1.2
- Nebraska correctional instn admin, with inmates by criminal background and demographic characteristics, by instn, FY92 and trends, annual rpt, S4850–1
- Nevada statistical abstract, general data, 1992 biennial rpt, S5005–1.4
- New York State correctional instn inmates released on parole, by criminal background, sentence, and demographic characteristics, 1991 and trends, recurring rpt, S5725–1.1
- New York State crimes and arrests by offense and demographic characteristics, and court activity and corrections, 1991 and trends, annual rpt, S5760–3
- New York State statistical yearbook, general data, 1992 annual rpt, U5100–1.8
- North Carolina correctional instn admissions, separations, and population, with inmate characteristics, FY93, semiannual rpt, S5900–1
- North Dakota local correctional instn adult and juvenile inmate characteristics, by instn, 1991 and trends, annual rpt, S6060–3
- Ohio correctional instn admissions and releases, inmate characteristics, programs, finances, and staffing, FY91 and trends, annual rpt, S6370–1
- Oklahoma correctional instn admin, including inmate characteristics, incarceration costs, and data by instn, FY91, annual rpt, S6420–1
- Pennsylvania State correctional instn admin, and inmates by type of offense and demographic characteristics, 1990 and trends, annual rpt, S6782–1
- Pennsylvania statistical abstract, general data, 1992 recurring rpt, U4130–6.7
- South Carolina correctional instns, admin, and inmates by criminal offense and demographic characteristics, FY92 and trends, annual rpt, S7135–1
- South Carolina statistical abstract, general data, 1993 annual rpt, S7125–1.5

Index by Subjects and Names

Part-time employment

Tennessee correctional instn admin, with inmate characteristics, and corrections dept finances and staff, FY92, annual rpt, S7480–1

Texas correctional instn inmates by criminal background and demographic characteristics, FY92, annual rpt, S7660–1

Utah corrections inmates, parolees, and probationers, by criminal background and demographic characteristics, FY92 and trends, annual rpt, S7810–1

Washington State correctional instn inmate population, admissions, and releases, by demographic characteristics, quarterly rpt, S8337–1

Washington State juvenile parole program clients and costs, by race-ethnicity and county, FY90, annual rpt, S8420–2

Wisconsin correctional instn inmates, by criminal background and selected characteristics, series, S8692–1

Wyoming correctional instn admin, finances, inmate characteristics, and staff, and probation and parole activities, FY92 annual rpt, S8883–1

see also Pardons

Part-time employment

Arts fundraising through united arts funds (UAFs), with UAF full- and part-time employment, by UAF, 1992, annual rpt, A1315–2

Benefits for part-time employees, percent of companies providing any and 3 selected types, 1991, annual rpt, A3840–1

Black American labor force and employment data, with comparisons to whites, 1970s-91, annual compilation, C6775–2.6

Black children and youth population, economic, health, and education data, with comparisons to whites, 1993 rpt, R3840–21

Blood bank operating profiles, arranged by State, 1993 biennial directory, A0612–1

Chemist and chemical engineer salaries, employment status, and demographic and professional characteristics, 1993, annual rpt, A1250–4

Chemist salaries and employment, by employee and employer characteristics, Mar 1993 and trends, annual article, A1250–1.532

Community and junior college part-time staff by function, FY92, annual rpt, A6705–1

Convenience store full- vs part-time employment, 1992, annual survey rpt, A6735–1

Dental school full- and part-time faculty positions, by instn and type of dept, US and Canada, 1992, annual rpt, A1475–3.2

Food service industry employment and turnover rate, by type of operation, 1991, annual article, A8200–1.508

Food store use of part- and full-time employees, and turnover rates, 1991, annual rpt, A4950–5.2

Germany (West) part-time employment, monthly rpt, U1245–1

Hard goods manufacturers part-time employment, by product line, 1993 annual survey rpt, A1800–1

Higher education instn use of part-time faculty, 1993 annual survey, A1410–1.38

Higher education, 2-year college full- and part-time faculty, by instn and State, Oct 1991, annual directory, A0640–1

Hispanic American labor force and employment data, with comparisons to whites, 1980s-91, annual compilation, C6775–3.4

Home improvement industry sales and operations, for top retailers, 1992 and trends, annual feature, C5150–6.503

Hospital use of full- vs part-time nurses, by region, 1993 and trends, annual survey rpt, A6500–1

Law school enrollment by minority status, degrees conferred, staff, and library holdings, by instn, 1992/93 and trends, annual rpt, A0970–1

Library/info science school part-time faculty and support staff, including students, by school, 1991/92, annual rpt, A3235–1.1

Museums and related instns full- and part-time staff and volunteers, by instn type, 1989/90 survey, A0750–1.1

Nursing schools, programs, enrollment, student and staff characteristics, and grads, 1991 and trends, annual rpt, A8010–1

Optometry school part-time tenured faculty, by instn, 1991/92, annual survey, A3370–2

Political science higher education dept characteristics, including faculty, salaries, enrollment, and finances, 1991/92 annual rpt, A2617–1

Psychology doctoral degree recipient employment and demographic characteristics, and finances, 1990/91, biennial survey rpt, A2620–4

Public health school faculty characteristics, by instn, fall 1991, recurring rpt, A3372–1

Religious congregation characteristics, including membership, activities, staff, and finances, 1992 survey, recurring rpt, A5435–4

Restaurant industry financial and operating data, by establishment characteristics and location, 1992, annual rpt, A8200–3

Shopping center security operations, including staffing, equipment, and crime incidents, by center type, 1992-93 and trends, articles, C5150–4.506

Statistical profiles of 50 States and DC, general data, 1993 annual almanac, C4712–1

Supermarket bakery dept full- and part-time employees, 1992, annual article, C4655–1.505, C5225–1.504

Supermarket deli dept full- and part-time employees, 1992, annual article, C4655–1.503, C5225–1.505

Supermarket fish/seafood dept full- and part-time employees, 1991, annual article, C4655–1.501

Supermarket general merchandise dept full- and part-time employees, 1992, annual article, C4655–1.509

Supermarket health and beauty aid dept full- and part-time employees, 1992, annual article, C4655–1.506

Supermarket meat dept full- and part-time employees, 1992, annual article, C4655–1.509

Supermarket produce dept full- and part-time employees, 1992, annual article, C4655–1.511

Teachers at preschool, elementary, and secondary levels, percent employed part-time, for selected OECD member countries, 1986, A1600–4

Women's employment and earnings, with comparisons to men, and detail by occupation and worker characteristics, 1990s and trends, annual rpt, A1570–2

State and local:

California labor force planning rpt, including population characteristics, and employment by industry, 1992 annual rpt, S0830–2

California private school full- and part-time teachers, 1987/88-1992/93, annual rpt, S0825–8

California public school full- and part-time staff, by race-ethnicity, 1992/93, annual rpt, S0825–9

Maryland postsecondary education part-time faculty, by instn, fall 1991, biennial rpt, S3605–1.2

Mississippi part-time employment for economic reasons, by race and sex, 1993/94, annual planning rpt, S4345–1.3

North Dakota elementary and secondary school part-time staff, by college attended, 1992/93 annual rpt, S6180–3

North Dakota full- and part-time employment shares by sex, for 8 metro areas, 1993 annual planning rpt, S6140–2

North Dakota part-time employment distribution by industry sector, 1991/92, article, S6140–4.503

Oregon employment service client placements in full- and part-time employment, monthly rpt, S6615–8

Pennsylvania higher education full- and part-time employment, by occupational activity and type of instn, 1991/92, annual rpt, S6790–5.5, S6790–5.13

Pennsylvania public school personnel and salary data, by position and district, 1992/93 and trends, annual rpt, S6790–5.12

Pennsylvania vocational education 1989/90 grad employment status, by program, 1991 survey, annual rpt, S6790–5.6

South Carolina labor force planning rpt, detailed data on employment, hours, wages, turnover, and characteristics of job service applicants, 1992 annual rpt, S7155–3.2

South Dakota employee benefits for full- and part-time workers, 1993 article, S7355–1.502

Tennessee statistical abstract, general data, 1992/93 annual rpt, U8710–2.20

Texas higher education part-time faculty, by race-ethnicity, sex, and instn, fall 1991, annual rpt, S7657–1.1

Texas nursing employment, demand outlook, earnings, and education, by selected characteristics, various years 1971-91, U8850–8.2

Utah labor force characteristics, employment and unemployment, hours, and earnings, with data by industry and locale, 1992 and trends, annual rpt, S7820–10

Vermont labor force by full- or part-time status, 1992, annual planning rpt, S8025–2.2

West Virginia higher education faculty characteristics and salary, by instn, 1992 and trends, annual rpt, S8533–1.2

see also Temporary and seasonal employment

Particleboard

see Lumber industry and products

Partnerships

Biotechnology companies involved in financing alliances, by alliance type and product area, 1992, article, A1250–1.537

Economic indicator historical trends, 1900s-92, annual rpt, R9050–1.2

Food/beverage industry packaging devs, including equipment purchase plans, partnership arrangements, and new labeling law effects, 1993 annual survey article, C2150–6.512

Investment limited partnership returns, biweekly rpt quarterly feature, C2710–2.507, C2710–2.514

Retailer views on top 6 manufacturers for forming retail-supplier partnerships, 1993 survey article, C1200–4.509

Small corporation use of selected types of strategic business alliances, for manufacturing and service companies, June 1993 survey, article, C4687–1.512

State and local:

Alabama statistical abstract, general data, 1992 recurring rpt, U5680–2.15

Arizona statistical abstract, general data, 1993 recurring rpt, U5850–2.21

California partnership/small corporation income tax returns filed, and profits or losses, by income class, 1990, annual rpt, S0855–1.1

Florida statistical abstract, general data, 1992 annual rpt, U6660–1.16

Hawaii data book, general data, 1992 annual rpt, S2090–1.15

see also Joint ventures

Passenger ships

Cruise line capacity, by company, 1991, annual rpt, C2140–1.5

Cruise line passengers and advertising expenditures, for top 10-20 companies worldwide, 1992 recurring rpt, R9375–6

Cruise ships capacity and per diem cost, by ship, 1993 feature, C1200–4.503

Passports and visas

Foreign students enrolled in US higher education instns, by instn, State, country of origin, and demographic characteristics, 1991/92 and trends, annual rpt, R5580–1

State and local:

Hawaii data book, general data, 1992 annual rpt, S2090–1.7

Pasture and rangeland

Grazing condition of pastures/ranges, commodity yearbook for 1993, C2400–1

Grazing condition of pastures/ranges, commodity yearbook Jan-Sept 1993 updates, C2400–2

Latin America statistical abstract, general data by country, 1992 annual rpt, U6250–1.2

State and local:

Arizona pasture/range feed condition, 1988-92, annual rpt, U5830–1

California rangeland condition, 1983-92, annual rpt, S0850–1.2

Colorado pasture/range feed condition, Apr-Dec 1968-92, annual rpt, S0985–1

Colorado property assessed valuation by detailed property type, and tax levy and revenue by local district, by county, 1991-92, annual rpt, S1055–3

Georgia cropland and pasture cash rents, 1977-92, annual rpt, S1855–1

Kansas pasture rental and condition, 1989-93, annual rpt, S2915–1

Mississippi statistical abstract, general data, 1992 annual rpt, U3255–4.10

Missouri farmland rent per acre, by land use, 1989-93, annual rpt, S4480–1

Montana property values, by detailed property class and type, with land acreage by use, by county, 1991-92 and trends, biennial rpt, S4750–1.2

Nebraska agricultural acreage and value, by land use and county, 1991, annual rpt, S4950–1.4

Nebraska pasture/range condition, Apr-Nov 1965-92, annual rpt, S4835–1

Nevada range/pasture condition, 1976-93, annual rpt, S5010–1

New Jersey pasture condition, 1986-91, annual rpt, S5350–1

New Mexico range/pasture condition, 1982-91, annual rpt, S5530–1

New York State pasture condition, May-Nov 1983-92, annual rpt, S5700–1

North Dakota farm pasture rent per acre and grazing rates, 1993 annual rpt, U3600–1

Oklahoma pasture/range condition, May-Nov 1988-92, annual rpt, S6405–1

South Dakota farmland cash rents, by land use, 1983-93, annual rpt, S7280–1

Tennessee pasture condition, May-Nov 1983-92, annual rpt, S7460–1

Texas pasture/rangeland condition, May 1987-Nov 1991, annual rpt, S7630–1.2

West Virginia pasture condition, monthly 1982-91, annual rpt, S8510–1

Wyoming pasture cash rents, and grazing fees for cattle on private land, 1970s-93, annual rpt, S8860–1

Wyoming property assessed valuations and tax levies, by property type, tax purpose, and location, 1992 and trends, annual rpt, S8990–1.2

Patents

Business incubator facilities tenant patent activity, 1991, annual rpt, A7360–1

Chemical industry and total manufacturing patents granted by US, with detail by industry segment and recipient type and country, 1970 and 1980-92, annual rpt, A3850–1

Corporate patent activity for approx 200 US and foreign firms in 13 industries, 1992 and trends, article, C5800–7.540

Economic dev condition indicators, including economic performance, business vitality, growth capacity, and tax/fiscal system, by State, 1993 annual rpt, R4225–1

Foreign resident receipt of US patents, for top 50 countries, 1992, semiannual rpt, B8500–1.16

Hard goods manufacturers legal actions concerning patent/trademark infringement by foreign firms, by product line, 1993 annual survey rpt, A1800–1

Higher education instns ranked by number of patents received, for top 22 instns, 1992, article, C2175–1.512

Issuances of patents in US, for top 10 countries, 1991-92, C1850–6.507

Issuances of patents to major chemical and drug companies, and to US and foreign holders, 1982-92, annual feature, A1250–1.537

Issuances of patents to US recipients by type and to foreign recipients, 1981 and 1991, article, C5800–7.511

Issuances of US patents to persons/firms in 15 leading and all other foreign countries, FY91-92, article, A1250–1.515

Japan patent applications of top 10 companies, 1987-91, C1850–6.506

Photonics-related patents issued to top 10 manufacturers, 1992, article, C1850–6.508

State social, economic, and govtl indicators, with rankings, 1993 semiannual rpt, B8500–1.13

State and local:

Florida State-supported universities copyright and patent applications and grants, by instn, FY92, annual rpt, S1725–1

Hawaii, patents granted to residents, FY84-91, annual rpt, S2090–1.17

Tennessee statistical abstract, general data, 1992/93 annual rpt, U8710–2.20

see also Trademarks

Pathology

Medical school faculty and compensation, by dept, academic rank, degree, and region, 1992/93, annual rpt, A3273–2

Physician practice economic aspects, detailed data by specialty, 1991-92 and trends, annual compilation, A2200–5

Physicians by detailed specialty and location, 1992 and trends, annual rpt, A2200–3

see also Medical examinations and tests

Pawnbrokers

State and local:

Alabama pawn shop licensees, Dec 1992, annual rpt, S0110–1

Indiana pawnbrokers aggregate earnings statement, and loan analysis, 1990-91, annual rpt, S2625–1

Oregon pawnbrokers directory and aggregate loan data, Dec 1992, annual rpt, S6616–1

Pennsylvania statistical abstract, general data, 1992 recurring rpt, U4130–6.2

Pawtucket, R.I.

Employment by industry, Jan 1991-July 1993, annual rpt, S6980–3

Payment-in-Kind Program, USDA

see Agricultural production quotas and price supports

Payroll

Aerospace industry payroll, 1979-91, annual rpt, A0250–2.5

Airline finances and operations of scheduled carriers, summary statistics, 1992 and trends, annual rpt, A0325–5

Amusement park operating and financial data, including data for US and foreign parks, miniature golf, waterparks, and games, 1992, annual rpt, A5700–1

Apartment building (conventionally financed) detailed income and expense ratios for US and Canada, by building type, metro area, and US region, 1991 and trends, annual rpt, A5600–1

Apartment building (federally subsidized) detailed income and expense ratios, by building and subsidy type, building age, metro area, and region, 1991 and trends, annual rpt, A5600–5

Apartment complex mgmt income and expenses, and vacancy and turnover rates, by region and metro area, 1992, annual survey rpt, A6497–1

Index by Subjects and Names

Payroll

Black-owned business firms, sales/receipts, employment, and payroll, by industry div and State, 1982 and/or 1987, annual compilation, C6775–2.8

Book publishing industry financial and operating data, by publisher type and size, and subject category, 1991 and trends, annual rpt, A3274–2

Brewers operations and expenses, detailed data, 1956-90, annual rpt, A3455–1.2

Business forms industry detailed financial and operating ratios, with summary operating data, FY91, annual rpt, A5785–3

Chambers of commerce income, salaries and benefits, membership, staff, and operations, 1993 annual rpt, A3840–3

Clothing (women's and children's) sales, production, imports, and industry employment, hours, and earnings, by type of garment, recurring rpt, A5900–1

Condominium, cooperative, and planned unit dev detailed expenses, for US and Canada, by building characteristics, metro area, and US region, 1991, annual rpt, A5600–3

Congressional campaign fund finances, with expenditures by item and contributions by donor type, by candidate, district, and State, 1990 elections, C2500–6

Corporate personnel mgmt devs, including hiring, layoffs, and health care and payroll cost control efforts, June 1992 survey, annual rpt, B6850–3

Corporate personnel mgmt devs, including staffing practices and turnover, payroll cost control efforts, and human resources operations, 1993 survey, annual rpt, B6850–5

Corporate tax burden trends, for income and payroll taxes, with comparisons to profits, Fed Govt receipts, and GDP, FY70-93, R9050–15.2

Corporate use of selected variable pay and recognition programs, with objectives and success, by industry div, Oct 1992 survey and trends, R4105–78.27

Costs for employee compensation, by region and metro-nonmetro status, 1989-90, annual rpt, U8710–2.3

Drugstore (independent pharmacy) financial and operating data, by store characteristics, 1991 and trends, annual survey, B5165–1

Employee benefit payments and employer cost/payroll ratios, by industry, detailed type of benefit, and firm size, 1991, annual rpt, A3840–1

Financial institutions, employment, and finances, and volume of printing business generated, 1992 feature, C1850–10.501

Food store labor expenses as a percent of sales, by company size and region, 1991-92, annual rpts, A4950–5

Food/lodging/entertainment establishments, employment, receipts, and payroll, and volume of printing business generated, 1992 feature, C1850–10.503

Forecasts of natl income and product account components and related indicators, quarterly rpt, U1880–1

Frozen dessert industry employment, wages, and capital expenditures, 1969-92, annual rpt, A5825–1.1

Hard goods manufacturers outlook for wage costs in 1993, by product line, annual survey rpt, A1800–1

Hardware finances and operations, for hardware stores, home centers, and lumber/building material outlets, 1991 and trends, annual rpt series, A8275–1

Home furnishings retailer financial and operating data, by firm characteristics and region, 1992 and trends, annual rpt, A7975–1

Hospital (teaching) expenditures for house staff stipends and benefits, by region and ownership, 1992/93, annual rpt, A3273–3

Hospital directory, with utilization, expenses, and personnel, by instn, type, and location, 1992, annual rpt, A1865–3

Hospital pharmacy operating data, by instn type and size, and census div, 1991, annual survey, B5165–3

Insurance industry employment, payroll, share of GSP, and premium taxes, by State, 1992 annual rpt, A0375–2

Iron and steel industry financial and operating data, 1992 and trends, annual rpt, A2000–2.1

Jewelry industry statistics on sales, marketing, trade, and employment, with customer characteristics, 1993 annual almanac, C2150–7.509

Legal services establishments, employment, receipts, and payroll, and volume of printing business generated, 1992 feature, C1850–10.502

Mass transit system energy use by source, employee compensation, and labor costs, 1970s-91, annual rpt, A2650–1.2

Medical group financial and operating data, by practice characteristics, 1991, annual rpt, A6365–2

Motor vehicle, dealership, and related industries operating data, with data by State and industry segment, 1990s and trends, annual rpt, A0865–1.3

Motor vehicle dealership financial and operating data, including sales and employment by State, 1970s-93, annual rpt, A7330–1

Motorcycle retail outlets, employees, and payroll, by State, 1992, annual rpt, A6485–1.1

Museums and related instns financial structure, including donation programs, income, and expenses, by type, budget size, and governing authority, 1989/90 survey, A0750–1.3

Natural gas industry employment, payroll, and accident statistics, 1960s-91, annual rpt, A1775–3.9

Newspaper payroll as percent of total revenue for newspapers of 50,000-100,000 circulation, 1986 and 1991, A8605–1.504

Office building detailed income and expense data, and energy use, US and Canada, by building characteristics, metro area, and US region, 1991 and trends, annual rpt, A5600–2

Office product dealer financial and operating data, by sales volume and region, 1991 and trends, annual rpt, A8110–1

Paper and paperboard industry financial and operating data, by product, region, and State, 1992 and trends, annual rpt, A1630–6

Paper/allied products industry data from Census of Manufactures, including purchased fuel and labor costs, 1990 and/or 1991, article, A1630–5.501

Personnel mgmt professional activities, job satisfaction, employer performance, and obstacles encountered, spring 1993 survey, A8907–2

Physician fees and expenses, and detailed work patterns, by specialty, type of practice location, and age, 1982-92, annual rpt, A2200–5.2

Railroad (Class I) financial and operating data, with detail by company, 1982-91, annual rpt, A3275–8.2

Railroad (Class I) traffic, employment, finances, and equipment, by district and State, 1920s-92, annual rpt, A3275–5

Railroad operating data, including top commodities handled, employment and wages, and retirement system, by State, 1991, annual rpt, A3275–10

Restaurant industry financial and operating data, by establishment characteristics and location, 1992, annual rpt, A8200–3

Restaurant State assn staff, payroll, locations represented, and political action committee spending, for organizations in 14 States, 1993 article, C1200–5.510

Salary budget increases and structure, by industry and region, and for Canada, 1993-94 and trends, annual survey rpt, A1295–1

Shopping center detailed income and expense data, by building characteristics, metro area, and region, 1991, annual rpt, A5600–6

Small business views on current and expected economic conditions, survey findings, quarterly rpt, A7815–1

Statistical profiles of 50 States and DC, general data, 1993 annual almanac, C4712–1

Supermarket (independent) sales and operating ratios, by store type, sales size, and region, 1991, annual survey, A4950–4

Travel and tourism rankings for selected indicators, including data for top 20 States, cities, countries, businesses, and other measures, 1992 recurring rpt, R9375–6

Travel impact on State economies, with detail by industry sector, 1990 and trends, annual rpt, R9375–7

Truck fleet financial and operating data for top 200 freight carriers, 1992 and trends, annual feature, C2150–4.504

Unemployment insurance trends, including data on unemployment, worker characteristics, coverage, benefits, and State govt finances, 1940s-90, R9260–18

Veterinarian practice expenses as percent of revenues, by expenditure category and type of practice, 1990-91, annual survey article, C9480–1.501

Western States employee compensation costs, by component, Mar 1992, article, S1040–4.503

Western States employee compensation costs, by component, Mar 1993, article, S1040–4.508

Payroll

State and local:

Alabama statistical abstract, general data, 1992 recurring rpt, U5680-2.3, U5680-2.5, U5680-2.11, U5680-2.15, U5680-2.18

Arizona statistical abstract, general data, 1993 recurring rpt, U5850-2.14, U5850-2.15, U5850-2.17, U5850-2.21, U5850-2.24

Arkansas socioeconomic trends, by MSA and/or county, 1993 annual rpt, U5935-1

California statistical abstract, general data, 1992 annual rpt, S0840-2.3, S0840-2.8, S0840-2.11

Florida statistical abstract, general data, 1992 annual rpt, U6660-1

Georgia statistical abstract, general data, 1992-93 biennial rpt, U6730-1.3, U6730-1.5, U6730-1.6, U6730-1.7

Hawaii data book, general data, 1992 annual rpt, S2090-1.15, S2090-1.21, S2090-1.22, S2090-1.23

Illinois statistical abstract, general data, 1992 annual rpt, U6910-2

Indiana, Northwest area payroll trends and outlook for selected industry sectors, quarterly rpt semiannual feature, U2160-1.504

Kansas service industries employment and economic growth, with comparisons to other industries, 1980s-90, article, U7095-1.502

Kansas statistical abstract, general data, 1991/92 annual rpt, U7095-2.8

Maryland statistical abstract, general data, 1993-94 biennial rpt, S3605-1.4, S3605-1.5, S3605-1.10

Mississippi statistical abstract, general data, 1992 annual rpt, U3255-4.4

Montana health care facility capacity, utilization, and finances, by instn, 1991, annual rpt, S4690-2

Nevada casino finances and employment, by location and gaming revenue range, FY92, annual rpt, S5062-1

Nevada statistical abstract, general data, 1992 biennial rpt, S5005-1.6

New Jersey foreign-owned business establishments, employment, payroll, and shipments/sales, by industry div, 1987, article, S5425-1.501

New Mexico and US retail, wholesale, and service industry establishments, sales, payroll, and employment, 1977 and 1987, U7980-1.502

New Mexico manufacturing payroll, by industry group, 1989 and 1991, U7980-1.504

New York State establishments, employees, and payrolls, by county, labor market area, and industry, monthly rpt quarterly feature, S5775-1.501, S5775-1.502, S5775-1.504, S5775-1.505

New York State statistical yearbook, general data, 1992 annual rpt, U5100-1.2, U5100-1.3, U5100-1.9

Oklahoma statistical abstract, general data, 1992 annual rpt, U8130-2.3, U8130-2.13, U8130-2.14, U8130-2.15

Oregon covered employment, payroll, and average earnings, by county and industry, 1991, article, S6615-2.502

Pennsylvania business activity indicators, monthly rpt, U4110-1

Pennsylvania statistical abstract, general data, 1992 recurring rpt, U4130-6.2

South Carolina statistical abstract, general data, 1993 annual rpt, S7125-1.3

Tennessee statistical abstract, general data, 1992/93 annual rpt, U8710-2.4, U8710-2.7, U8710-2.11, U8710-2.12

Utah business activity indicators, by county, 1988-91, annual feature, U8960-2.501

Utah business activity indicators, by county, 1989-92, annual feature, U8960-2.507

Utah business firms, wages, and employment, by firm size, SIC 2-digit industry, and county, 1st qtr 1992, annual rpt, S7820-1

Utah govt statistical review, fiscal and socioeconomic data, 1993 annual rpt, R9380-1.9

Utah payroll wages, by county and planning district, 1991-92, S7820-3.506

Utah statistical abstract, general data, 1993 triennial rpt, U8960-1.12, U8960-1.14, U8960-1.16

Wyoming employment, payroll, and wages, by county, monthly rpt quarterly feature, S8895-1.502, S8895-1.504, S8895-1.506, S8895-1.508

Wyoming employment, payroll, and wages, by industry div, 1991, S8895-1.505

Wyoming employment, payroll, and wages, by industry div, 1991-92, S8895-1.509

Wyoming employment, payroll, and wages, by industry div, 3rd qtr 1991-4th qtr 1992, S8895-1.508

Wyoming payroll and wages by industry div, and personal income, with comparisons to US, 1987-92, article, S8895-1.507

see also Agricultural wages

see also Earnings, general

see also Earnings, specific industry

see also Educational employees pay

see also Federal pay

see also Government pay

see also Labor costs and cost indexes

see also Military pay

see also Social security tax

see also State and local employees pay

see also Unemployment insurance tax

Payroll tax

see Social security tax

see Unemployment insurance tax

Peace Corps

Latin America Peace Corps budget, offices, and volunteers, with comparisons to worldwide data, 1960s-92, annual rpt, U6250-1.28

Peanuts

Production, consumption, stocks, trade, and prices for approx 100 basic commodities, including by country and producing State, commodity yearbook for 1993, C2400-1, C2400-2

State and local:

Alabama agricultural production, marketing, and income, by county and/or commodity, and farms and acreage, 1992 and trends, annual rpt, S0090-1

Florida field crop acreage, yield, production, and value, by commodity and/or county, 1992 and trends, annual rpt, S1685-1.4

Georgia agricultural production, marketing, and finances, by commodity and/or county, and farms and acreage, 1991 and trends, annual rpt, S1855-1

New Mexico agricultural production, marketing, and finances, by commodity and county, with farms and acreage, 1991 and trends, annual rpt, S5530-1

North Carolina agricultural production, marketing, and finances, by commodity and county, 1991 and trends, annual rpt, S5885-1

Oklahoma agricultural production, marketing, and finances, by commodity and county, 1992 and trends, annual rpt, S6405-1

South Carolina agricultural production and finances, by commodity and county, 1991-92 and trends, annual rpt, U1075-3

Texas agricultural production, marketing, and finances, by commodity and county, and farms and farmland, 1991 and trends, annual rpt series, S7630-1

Peas

see Vegetables and vegetable products

Pecans

see Nuts

Peck, Charles A.

"Stock Options: Motivating Through Ownership", R4105-78.31

"Variable Pay: Nontraditional Programs for Motivation and Reward", R4105-78.27

Pedestrians

Intoxicated pedestrian safety and legal issues, views of traffic safety magazine readers, May/June 1993 survey, article, A8375-1.506

Traffic accident fatalities, by type of accident, 1913-92, annual rpt, A0865-1.3

Traffic accidents, fatalities, and injuries, by vehicle type, circumstances, location, and driver and victim characteristics, 1992 and trends, annual rpt, A8375-2.3

State and local:

Alabama traffic accidents, fatalities, and injuries, by circumstances, vehicle type, and driver and victim characteristics, 1992, annual rpt, S0185-1

Alaska traffic accidents, fatalities, and injuries, by vehicle type, circumstance, location, and driver and victim characteristics, 1991 and trends, annual rpt, S0360-1

Arizona traffic accidents, fatalities, and injuries, by vehicle type, circumstances, location, and driver and victim characteristics, 1991 and trends, annual rpt, S0530-1

Arkansas traffic accidents, fatalities, and injuries, by vehicle type, circumstances, location, and driver and victim characteristics, 1991, annual rpt, S0692-1

California traffic accidents, fatalities, and injuries, by vehicle type, circumstances, location, and driver and victim characteristics, 1991 and trends, annual rpt, S0885-1

California traffic fatalities by type, and sex and age of victim, 1990, annual rpt, S0865-1

Connecticut traffic accidents, fatalities, and injuries, by vehicle type, circumstance, location, and driver and victim characteristics, 1992, annual rpt, S1275-1

Delaware traffic accidents, fatalities, and injuries, by circumstances, location, and vehicle type, and driver and victim characteristics, 1992 and trends, annual rpt, S1435-1

Index by Subjects and Names — Pennsylvania

Florida traffic accidents, fatalities, and injuries, by vehicle type, circumstance, location, and driver and victim characteristics, 1992 and trends, annual rpt, S1750–2

Hawaii traffic accidents, injuries, and fatalities, by circumstances, location, and driver and victim characteristics, 1986 and trends, annual rpt, S2125–1

Idaho traffic accidents, fatalities, and injuries, by circumstances, location, vehicle type, and driver and victim characteristics, 1992, annual rpt, S2315–1

Illinois traffic accidents, fatalities, and injuries, by circumstances, location, and driver and victim characteristics, 1991 and trends, annual rpt, S2540–1

Indiana traffic accidents, fatalities, and injuries, by circumstances, location, and vehicle type, and driver and victim characteristics, 1992, annual rpt, S2675–1

Kansas traffic accidents, fatalities, and injuries, by vehicle type, location, circumstances, and driver and victim characteristics, 1992, annual rpt, S3040–1

Kentucky traffic accidents, fatalities, and injuries, by circumstances, location, vehicle type, and driver characteristics, 1992 and trends, annual rpt, S3150–2

Louisiana traffic accidents, fatalities, and injuries, by circumstances, location, and driver characteristics, 1991 and trends, annual rpt, S3345–2

Maine traffic accidents, fatalities, and injuries, by accident circumstances, vehicle type and make, and driver and victim characteristics, 1992, annual rpt, S3475–2

Maryland traffic accidents, fatalities, and injuries, by circumstances, location, vehicle type, and driver and victim characteristics, 1992, annual rpt, S3665–4

Michigan traffic accidents, fatalities, and injuries, by vehicle type, circumstance, location, and driver and victim characteristics, 1991 and trends, annual rpt, S3997–2

Minnesota traffic accidents, fatalities, and injuries, by type of vehicle and circumstances, and driver and victim characteristics, 1992 and trends, annual rpt, S4230–2

Missouri traffic accidents, fatalities, and injuries, by circumstances, location, and driver and victim characteristics, 1992 and trends, annual rpt, S4560–1

Montana traffic accidents, fatalities, and injuries, by circumstances, location, and driver and victim characteristics, 1992 and trends, annual rpt, S4705–2

Nebraska traffic accidents, fatalities, and injuries, by circumstances, location, vehicle type, and driver and victim characteristics, 1992, annual rpt, S4953–1

Nevada traffic accidents, fatalities, and injuries, by circumstances, location, and vehicle type, 1992 and trends, annual rpt, S5140–1

New Jersey fatal traffic accidents and fatalities, by vehicle type, location, and circumstances, and driver and victim characteristics, 1992 and trends, annual rpt, S5430–2

New Mexico traffic accidents, fatalities, and injuries, by vehicle type, circumstances, location, and driver and victim characteristics, 1992 and trends, annual rpt, S5665–1

New York State traffic accidents, fatalities, and injuries, by circumstances, location, vehicle type, and driver and victim characteristics, 1991 and trends, annual rpt, S5790–1

North Carolina traffic accidents, fatalities, and injuries, by circumstances, location, vehicle type, and driver and victim characteristics, 1992 and trends, annual rpt, S5990–1

North Dakota traffic accidents, fatalities, and injuries, by circumstances, location, vehicle type, and driver and victim characteristics, 1992 and trends, annual rpt, S6217–1

Ohio traffic accidents, fatalities, and injuries, by circumstances, location, driver and victim characteristics, and vehicle type, 1991 and trends, annual rpt, S6290–1

Oklahoma traffic accidents, fatalities, and injuries, by circumstances, location, and driver and victim characteristics, 1992 and trends, annual rpt, S6482–1

Pennsylvania traffic accidents, fatalities, and injuries, by circumstances, location, driver characteristics, and vehicle type, 1991, annual rpt, S6905–3

Rhode Island traffic accidents, fatalities, and injuries, by circumstances, community, and driver and victim characteristics, 1992, annual rpt, S7025–1

South Carolina traffic accidents, fatalities, and injuries, by circumstances, location, and driver and victim characteristics, 1992 and trends, annual rpt, S7190–2

South Dakota traffic accidents, fatalities, and injuries, by circumstances, location, vehicle type, and driver and victim characteristics, 1992 and trends, annual rpt, S7300–3

Texas pedestrian traffic from Mexico, by port of entry, 1993 rpt, U8850–9

Utah traffic accidents and fatalities by circumstances, location, driver and victim characteristics, and vehicle type, 1992 and trends, annual rpt, S7890–2

Virginia traffic accidents, fatalities, and injuries, by circumstances, location, and driver and victim characteristics, 1991 and trends, annual rpt, S8282–1

Washington State traffic accidents, fatalities, and injuries, by circumstances, vehicle type, and location, with driver and victim characteristics, 1992 and trends, annual rpt, S8428–1

West Virginia traffic accidents, fatalities, and injuries, by circumstance and location, and driver and victim characteristics, 1992, annual rpt, S8645–1

Wisconsin traffic accidents, fatalities, and injuries, by circumstances, location, vehicle type, and driver and victim characteristics, 1992 and trends, annual rpt, S8815–1

Wyoming traffic accidents, fatalities, and injuries, by circumstances, location, vehicle type, and driver and victim characteristics, 1992 and trends, annual rpt, S9007–1

Pediatrics

Bicycle safety counseling practices and experience with bicycle injuries among patients of pediatricians, 1990 survey, article, A2623–1.507

Hospital patient discharges and length of stay, by diagnosis, type of operation, and age, 1991, annual rpt, B4455–1.7

Hospital patient discharges and length of stay, by diagnostic related group (DRG), payment source, age, and region, 1991, annual rpt series, B4455–3

Hospital psychiatric patient discharges and length of stay, by diagnosis, age, sex, and region, 1991, annual rpt series, B4455–2

Medical school faculty and compensation, by dept, academic rank, degree, and region, 1992/93, annual rpt, A3273–2

Physician practice economic aspects, detailed data by specialty, 1991-92 and trends, annual compilation, A2200–5

Physicians by detailed specialty and location, 1992 and trends, annual rpt, A2200–3

Pell Grant Program

Higher education freshmen attitudes and characteristics, degree and career plans, and financial aid sources, by sex and instn type, fall 1992, annual survey, U6215–1

Southern States higher education student aid data, by State, 1990s and trends, biennial fact book, A8945–1.4

State and local:

North Carolina higher education student costs, admissions, housing, and financial aid, by instn, 1992/93 annual rpt, U8013–1.3

Utah higher education degrees, enrollment, staff, and finances, by public instn, with selected comparisons to instns in other States, 1993/94 annual rpt, S7895–2

Pelvic inflammatory disease

see Urogenital diseases

Penalties

see Fines and settlements

see Judgments, civil procedure

see Sentences, criminal procedure

Pennsylvania

Agricultural production, marketing, and finances, by county and commodity, and farms and acreage, 1992 and trends, annual rpt, S6760–1

Business activity indicators for Pennsylvania, monthly rpt, U4110–1

Census of Population and Housing detailed findings, with selected data by county and municipality, 1990, U4130–13

Census of Population and Housing employment and commuting data, by county and municipality, 1990, C1595–16

Census of Population and Housing housing data, by county and municipality, 1990, C1595–14

Census of Population and Housing income data, by county and municipality, 1989, C1595–15

Correctional instn admin, and inmates by type of offense and demographic characteristics, for State prisons, 1990 and trends, annual rpt, S6782–1

Court caseloads and dispositions, by type of court and case, and county, with judicial system finances, 1991, annual rpt, S6900–1

Pennsylvania

Crimes and arrests, by offense, location, and offender characteristics, with law enforcement employment and assaults on officers, 1992 and trends, annual rpt, S6860–1

Educational statistics by level and/or type of education, series, S6790–5

Employment, hours, and earnings, by industry and/or location, monthly rpt, S6845–1

Energy supply-demand and prices by fuel type, with electric power info by utility, 1960s-90, recurring rpt, S6810–3

Govt financial condition, including revenues by source, expenditures by function, and fund balances, FY92 and trends, annual rpt, S6810–4

Health behavior risk factor surveillance survey results, by respondent characteristics, 1991, annual rpt, S6820–4

Insurance industry financial and underwriting data, by company and line of coverage, 1991, with FY92 regulatory info, annual rpt, S6835–1

Labor force planning rpt, including population characteristics, employment and job openings by industry and occupation, and income trends, FY92 annual rpt, S6845–3

Library (public and institutional) personnel, holdings, circulation, and finances, by county and facility, FY92, annual rpt, S6790–2

Markets with daily newspapers, demographic and economic info by geographic area, US and Canada, 1993 annual rpt, C3250–1

Medical malpractice insurance State joint underwriting assn (JUA) financial condition, for 11 States, 1991, annual rpt, A0375–1

Oil/gas industry production, finances, exploration, and reserves, by State, 1992 and trends, annual rpt, A5425–1.1

Statistical abstract of Pennsylvania, detailed social, govtl, and economic data, 1992 recurring rpt, U4130–6

Statistical profiles of 50 States and DC, general data, 1993 annual almanac, C4712–1

Tax collections by tax type, with data by county and industry, FY92 and trends, annual rpt, S6885–1

Traffic accidents, fatalities, and injuries, by circumstances, location, driver characteristics, and vehicle type, 1991, annual rpt, S6905–3

Utility and transportation regulatory agency activities, scope of jurisdiction, finances, and employees, by agency, 1991/92 annual rpt, A7015–2

Veterinary services costs for dairy farmers correlated with milk production, Pennsylvania study, 1986-90, article, A3100–2.506

see also Philadelphia, Pa.

see also Pittsburgh, Pa.

see also under By City and By County in the "Index by Categories"

see also under By State in the "Index by Categories"

Pensions and pension funds

Asset composition for 6 institutional investor categories, 1970-2nd qtr 1992, article, A8825–1.504

Asset rankings of top 1,000 employee benefit funds, with selected fund investment data, 1992, annual feature, C2710–2.504

Assets of top 300 pension funds worldwide, 1992, annual feature, C2710–2.515

Association executives compensation, by position, assn type, and census div, with personnel practices and benefit provisions, 1992, biennial rpt, A2900–3

Canada top pension funds asset allocation among bonds and Canadian vs foreign equities, 1991-92, article, A8825–1.507

Corporate directors retirement benefits for outside board members, 1992, annual rpt, R4105–7

Coverage, assets, and benefits paid, for private and govt pension and retirement programs, 1991 and trends, biennial fact book, A1325–1.3

Employee benefit payments and employer cost/payroll ratios, by industry, detailed type of benefit, and firm size, 1991, annual rpt, A3840–1

Hard goods manufacturers pension costs, by product line, 1993 annual survey rpt, A1800–1

Higher education instn employee retirement and insurance benefits, prevalence and expenditures, by type of instn and region, 1991, biennial survey, A9025–3

Household expenditures for personal insurance/pensions, for approx 300 metro areas, 1992, annual rpt, C1200–1.511

Institutional fund mgmt and investment trends and devs, biweekly rpt, C2710–2

Investment and admin of pension funds and employee benefit plans, monthly rpt, C2425–1

Investment in 3 housing-related categories vs all other assets, for public and private pension funds, 2nd qtr 1992, C4300–1.505

Investment portfolio characteristics and performance of pension funds, 4th qtr 1992, semiannual feature, C3950–1.509

Japan social security system coverage, finances, and mgmt of fund investments, by type of program, 1993 article, R5650–2.549

Labor mobility effect on pension benefits, with data by plan type and worker characteristics, 1993 rpt, R9260–17

Medical group physician and allied personnel retirement benefits, by specialty and practice characteristics, 1991, annual rpt, A6365–1

Mutual fund industry conditions, with data on pension plan investment practices and disposition of preretirement payouts, 1992 annual rpt, A6025–1.1

Real estate investment mgmt companies, pension fund and other managed assets, and investment info, by company, 1992 annual directory, C2425–1.501

Real estate investment mgmt companies, pension fund and other managed assets, and investment info, by company, 1993 annual directory, C2425–1.507

Widow quality of life indicators for survivors of older men surveyed in 1966, including pension benefits, by race, 1990 survey, U3780–9

Index by Subjects and Names

State and local:

California individual taxable income reported by source, deductions and credits by type, and tax returns, by income class and county, 1990, annual rpt, S0855–1.1

Maryland local govt pension systems, cost and actuarial info, by jurisdiction, FY92, annual rpt, S3618–1.1

Montana individual retirement benefits excluded from taxation, 1987-91, biennial rpt, S4750–1.1

New York State insurance industry devs, finances, and regulatory activity, 1990/91 and trends, annual rpt, S5770–3

New York State insurance industry financial and underwriting data, by company and line of coverage, 1991, annual rpt, S5770–2

South Dakota employee benefits for full- and part-time workers, 1993 article, S7355–1.502

see also Civil service pensions

see also Military benefits and pensions

see also Old-Age, Survivors, Disability, and Health Insurance

see also Railroad Retirement System

see also Social security

see also State retirement systems

see also Veterans benefits and pensions

People's Republic of China

see China, People's Republic

Per capita income

see Personal and household income

Perez, Arturo

"State Fiscal Outlook for 1993", A7470–4.11

"State Fiscal Update: Feb. 1993", A7470–4.12

"State Fiscal Update: Mar. 1993.", A7470–4.14

Performing arts

Amusement park operating and financial data, including payment rates for entertainers at selected US and foreign parks, 1992, annual rpt, A5700–1

Entertainment industry devs, including production activity, ticket sales, and marketing, weekly rpt, C9380–1

Fundraising through united arts funds (UAFs), with allocations to performing arts by type, by UAF, 1992, annual rpt, A1315–2

Hispanic American entertainers income, for top 20 individuals, 1992-93, annual article, C4575–1.508

Income for 40 highest paid entertainment industry professionals, 1992-93, annual feature, C3950–1.524

State and local:

Hawaii data book, general data, 1992 annual rpt, S2090–1.7

see also Motion pictures

see also Music

see also Theater

Periodicals

Advertisement size impact on readership, 1993 article, C8950–2.503

Advertising expenditures by medium for top 100 advertisers, with comparisons to earnings and sales, and detail by product type and brand, 1991-92, annual rpt, C2710–1.547

Advertising headline length, position, and background, impact on readership, 1993 article, C8950–2.501

Index by Subjects and Names

Advertising page volume for magazines, monthly rpt, A1630–5

Advertising pages and revenues for consumer magazines, by publication, weekly rpt monthly tables, C2710–1

Advertising purchasing plans and views of media executives, 1993 survey feature, C2710–1.549

Advertising rate changes for magazines, 1989-94, article, C2710–1.544

Advertising revenues and pages, for top 50 magazines, 1991-92, annual feature, C2575–1.518

Australia fashion magazine depiction of models wearing skin-protective clothing in summer, 1982-91, article, A2623–1.502

Catholic magazines and circulation in US and Canada, 1993 annual almanac, C6885–1

Circulation and advertising rates, for US and Canadian publications, 1988-92, annual rpt, A3385–1

Circulation by world area, for 16 worldwide publications, 1990-91, annual feature, C2710–1.506

Circulation for top 200 consumer magazines and top 10 nonpaid circulation magazines, 1st half 1993, semiannual article, C2710–1.541

Circulation for top 200 consumer magazines and top 12 nonpaid circulation magazines, 2nd half 1992, semiannual article, C2710–1.514

Circulation of US and Canadian magazines, by publication, 6-month periods ended Dec 1992 and June 1993, semiannual rpt, A3385–3.4

Circulation performance for top 50-100 magazines, 1991-92, annual feature, C2575–1.518

Comic book superheroes, and death of Superman, public opinion, Nov 1992 Gallup Poll, C4040–1.505

Compensation of magazine ad sales personnel, by region, sex, age, and publication characteristics, 1993 survey, annual article, C2575–1.516

Compensation of magazine circulation directors and managers, by region, sex, age, and publication characteristics, 1992 survey, annual article, C2575–1.502

Compensation of magazine editorial personnel, by region, sex, age, and publication characteristics, 1993 survey, annual article, C2575–1.512

Compensation of magazine production directors and managers, by region, sex, age, and publication characteristics, 1993 survey, annual article, C2575–1.510

Computer manufacturer advertising expenditures and pages in magazines, for top 12 firms, 1st 8 months 1992-93, article, C2710–1.548

Corporate magazines, including readership, for 10 publications, 1993 article, C1200–1.509

Direct marketing industry devs, with consumer and business market characteristics, and media use patterns, 1992/93 annual rpt, A4620–1.4

Education journal editorial practices and characteristics, for 54 publications, 1993 recurring survey article, A8680–1.502

Elementary/secondary prospective teacher characteristics, including frequently read

magazines, survey of persons interested in alternative certification routes, 1992, R6350–7

Energy publications deemed most helpful by fuel oil dealers, by publication and region, 1992 annual survey, C4680–2.3

Financial ratios and performance, for over 350 SIC 4-digit industries, FY88-92, annual rpt, A6400–3

Latin America scientific articles published in intl journals, by country, 1973-84, annual rpt, U6250–1.4

Mass media company revenues for leading firms, with detail by medium, 1991-92, annual feature, C2710–1.540

Operating and financial composite ratios for corporations, with establishments and receipts, for approx 200 industries, by asset size, FY90, annual rpt, C7800–1

Paper consumption trends by grade, and circulation of 39 magazines using recycled paper, 1993 annual rpt, C3975–5.3

Publishing industry devs for magazines, including data on circulation, advertising, and finances, semimonthly rpt, C2575–1

Revenues, advertising pages, and circulation, for top 300 periodicals, 1992, annual article, C2710–1.531

Revenues, circulation, advertising, and rates, for top 500 consumer and business magazines, 1992, annual article, C2575–1.515

Sales and consumer expenditures, for food store products by type, 1991-92, annual feature, C4655–1.510

Subscription prices for periodicals and serial services, by subject area, 1977 and 1990-93, annual compilation, C1650–3.4

Subscription prices for periodicals, by subject area, and by country or world region of origin, 1993 and trends, annual article, C1852–1.506

Supermarket sales of nonfood products, by detailed product type, 1992, annual feature, C5225–1.508

Veterinary journal error rates of reference citations made in articles, for 6 major journals, 1990, article, A3100–2.507

State and local:

Arizona statistical abstract, general data, 1993 recurring rpt, U5850–2.19

Georgia statistical abstract, general data, 1992-93 biennial rpt, U6730–1.8

Hawaii data book, general data, 1992 annual rpt, S2090–1.16

see also Newspapers

see also Libraries (for data on library holdings by type)

Permits

see Drivers licenses

see Hunting and fishing licenses

see License taxes and fees

see Licenses and permits

see Occupational testing and certification

see Severance taxes

Perquisites

see Employee benefits

see Employee bonuses and work incentives

Persian Gulf

Oil and refined products exports via Strait of Hormuz, 1991, annual rpt, C6985–5.1

Oil imports of US from OPEC, OAPEC, and Persian Gulf sources, 1973-92, annual rpt, A5425–2.1

Personal and household income

see also Middle East

Personal and household income

Africa income per capita, by country, 1987, annual rpt, C2140–1.3

Athletes earnings from product endorsements, for top 5 earners, 1993 article, C5800–7.550

Black American earnings, income, and poverty data, with comparisons to whites, 1980s-91, annual compilation, C6775–2.7

Black American socioeconomic status, with comparisons to whites and data by region, 1960s-92, annual compilation, A8510–1.1

Boats registered compared to effective buying income, by State, 1993 annual feature, C2425–4

Charitable contributions compared to income, 1972-92, annual rpt, A0700–1.1

Child health and well-being indicators, with selected household characteristics, by State, 1993 annual rpt, R3832–1

Children age 5/under in poverty, with data on family income levels and sources, 1990-91, annual rpt, U1260–2

China, Guangdong Province per capita income, 1983-91, article, A9315–1.501

China, Guangdong Province per capita income, 1985-92, A9315–1.505

Consumer attitudes on economic conditions and personal financial situation, monthly survey, U7475–2

Consumer buying power survey of population, income, and sales by kind of business, by census div, State, MSA, county, and city, 1992, annual rpt, C1200–1.511

Consumer buying power survey of population, income, and sales by product line, by State, metro area, county, and census div, 1993 annual rpt, C1200–1.514

Consumer expectations of economic conditions and change in income, and intended durable goods purchases by type, Conference Board monthly survey, R4105–4

Consumer socioeconomic profiles, for top 50 MSAs ranked by supermarket sales, 1991, annual rpt, C3400–6

Cost-of-living indexes, and adjustment impact on household income, by census div and population size, 1991, annual article, U0280–1.501

Ecologist personal and professional characteristics, including research activity and funding, with data by field, Mar 1992 survey, recurring rpt, A4685–1

Economic indicator historical trends, 1900s-92, annual rpt, R9050–1.2

Economic indicator trends and forecasts, with detail for approx 15 Western States, 1990s, annual rpt, B3520–1

Economic outlook for selected indicators, recent trends and 2-year forecast, quarterly rpt, A3840–6

Elementary/secondary education data, including area wealth indicators, by State, 1993 biennial rpt, A4355–1

Ethiopia famine analysis, including household impacts and responses, drought factor, agricultural activity and markets, and intervention programs, 1980s, R5620–1.36

Family income, with impact of Federal and State/local taxes and inflation, 1980-92, annual rpt, R9050–13

Personal and household income

Federal income tax returns, income, and taxes, by income percentile, 1981 and/or 1991, annual article, R9050–3.509

Food away from home expenditures, by household characteristics and for 26 MSAs, 1991, recurring rpt, A8200–13

Forecasts of economic indicators for approx 10-13 months, monthly rpt, U1880–3

Forecasts of natl income and product account components and related indicators, quarterly rpt, U1880–1

Forecasts of natl income and product account components, employment, and financial sector activity, monthly rpt, B4950–1

Foreign economic indexes, and leading and coincident indicators for US and other industrial countries, monthly rpt, U1245–1

Health care expenditures compared to disposable income, 1950-91, annual rpt, A5173–2.3

Higher education financial aid applicant characteristics, American College Testing (ACT) program, 1993/94, annual rpt, R1960–5

Hispanic American entertainers income, for top 20 individuals, 1992-93, annual article, C4575–1.508

Hispanic American income and poverty data, with comparisons to whites, 1980s-91, annual compilation, C6775–3.5

Hispanic American marketing devs, including leading advertisers and media, and market characteristics, 1992 annual features, C4575–1.502

Hispanic American professional athlete income, for top individuals by sport, 1993 article, C4575–1.508

Home buyer (1st-time and repeat) profile, and transaction characteristics, including prices and financing, by region and for 18 metro areas, 1990-92, annual survey rpt, B2150–1

Household wealth and income data by income level, including assets by type and detail by age group, 1989 and trends, R4700–17

Immigrant households, income, and home ownership rates by origin and length of US residence, and 15 cities with most new immigrants, 1993 article, C4300–1.512

Income comparisons among upper, middle, and lower income groups, by State, 1979-89, R3834–13, R3834–14

Income comparisons between top and bottom quintiles, by State, late 1980s, article, B8500–2.506

Japan consumer credit by type, with debt vs disposable income and savings, and comparisons to US, 1970s-92, article, R5650–2.542

Latin America statistical abstract, general data by country, 1992 annual rpt, U6250–1.13

Life insurance benefit payments, by payment method and characteristics of beneficiaries and insured, 1940s-91, biennial fact book, A1325–1.2

Life insurance compared with disposable income per household, 1930-91, biennial fact book, A1325–1.1

Market area population and characteristics, households, income, and retail outlets, for 21 leading areas, 1993 feature, C2710–1.538

Men age 69-84 quality of life indicators, including health, finances, family, and employment, by race, 1990 survey, U3780–9

Metro area household income trends for central cities vs suburbs, and employment data, for 78 largest MSAs, 1993 rpt, A8012–1.22

Metro area median income and housing costs for owners and renters, for 44 metro areas, 1992 rpt, R3834–16

Minority population characteristics, employment, and voting patterns by detailed race-ethnicity, with comparisons to whites, 1980s-2040, R8750–2.58

Money income by race, 1990-93, article, C4215–1.502

New England per capita income by State, with comparison to other regions, 1988-92, annual rpt, S6980–3

North Central States household income, for 7 States, 1990, annual rpt, S2784–3

Per capita income by State, 1989-91, R8490–46

Population size and selected characteristics, by region, census div, and State, 1991 and trends, annual data sheet, R8750–9

Public housing resident characteristics, including income and sources, 1988, A6800–1

Public housing resident characteristics, including income sources, 1991, A6800–2

Public opinion on social, political, and economic issues, detailed data, 1972-91 surveys, annual rpt, U6395–1

Rankings of MSAs, and leading cities and counties, by disposable personal and household income, 1993 annual rpt, C3250–1

Regional wage and personal income levels compared to total US, with detail for 10 Western States, 1991 and trends, article, U0280–1.505

Russia population distribution by monthly income, Aug 1992, U2030–1.504

Shareholders of NYSE member firms, by demographic characteristics and metro area, 1970s-90, annual fact book, B6625–1.1

Southern States population, personal income, and State/local revenues and expenditures, by State, 1950s-2010, biennial fact book, A8945–1.1

State economic dev condition indicators, including economic performance, business vitality, growth capacity, and tax/fiscal system, by State, 1993 annual rpt, R4225–1.1

State household income trends, by State, 1980 and 1990, article, U8960–2.505

State per capita income trends, by State, 1987-92, article, B8500–2.517

State personal income trends, by State, semimonthly rpt quarterly article, B8500–2.504, B8500–2.510, B8500–2.516, B8500–2.522

State rankings by personal income growth, 1991 vs 1982, semiannual rpt, U5850–1

State social, economic, and govtl indicators, with rankings, 1993 semiannual rpt, B8500–1.2

State tax collections and rates, with comparison to personal income, by State, FY81-93, R9050–14

Index by Subjects and Names

States with highest and lowest personal income, ranking of 20 States, 1991, annual rpt, C2140–1.2

Statistical profiles of 50 States and DC, general data, 1993 annual almanac, C4712–1

Tax reform proposed by Clinton Admin effect on disposable income of high-income households, by income level, 1993 article, C2710–3.547

TV cable basic and premium subscribers and nonsubscribers median household income, 1992/93, C2710–1.520

Western States economic indicators, including forecasts from selected organizations, for 10 States, monthly rpt, U0282–2

Western States per capita income in selected States, 1982 and 1986-91, annual article, U7980–1.503

Western States total and per capita personal income, by State, 1988-91, U7980–1.501

Women (single) age 65/over and total households with income less than $10,000, by race-ethnicity or age, Mar 1992, A8657–5

Women's views on income vs cost of living, and earnings by sex and race-ethnicity, 1992 feature, C4215–1.502

State and local:

Alabama county data book, general data, 1992 annual rpt, S0121–2

Alabama economic trends and outlook, 1980s-93, annual rpt, U5680–3

Alabama municipal data book, general data, 1992 recurring rpt, S0121–5

Alabama statistical abstract, general data, 1992 recurring rpt, U5680–2.9

Alaska population, housing, income, and education data, by demographic characteristics and/or locality, 1990/91 and trends, annual rpt, S0320–4

Alaska total and per capita personal income, 1982-91, annual rpt, S0275–1

Arizona economic indicators, including forecasts from 16 forecasting organizations, monthly rpt, U0282–1

Arizona economic trends and forecast, monthly rpt quarterly article, U0280–1.503, U0280–1.506, U0280–1.509

Arizona household and family income, with detail by source and race-ethnicity, 1989, article, U0280–1.502

Arizona Indian population, education, housing, health, and employment characteristics, with detail by reservation, 1970s-91, recurring rpt, U5850–2.9

Arizona personal income trends, with detail by source, 1960s-92, articles, S0465–1.503

Arizona, Phoenix area temporary winter resident characteristics, including expenditures, dwelling type, and region of residence, 1992/93, article, U0280–1.508

Arizona statistical abstract, general data, 1993 recurring rpt, U5850–2.6

Arizona trends in income, employment, and earnings, during 3 economic cycles, 1970-91, article, U0280–1.504

Arkansas business and economic activity indicators, quarterly rpt, U5930–1

Arkansas Census of Population and Housing detailed findings, 1990, U5935–7

Index by Subjects and Names

Personal and household income

Arkansas socioeconomic trends, by MSA and/or county, 1993 annual rpt, U5935–1

California Census of Population and Housing detailed findings, 1990, S0840–9

California economic condition, including population, employment and earnings, income, business activity, and taxation, 1993 annual rpt, S0840–3

California economic indicators, bimonthly rpt, S0840–1

California individual and corporate income tax returns and property tax assistance, by income class and county, 1990 and trends, annual rpt, S0855–1

California personal income by component, bimonthly rpt quarterly feature, S0840–1.501, S0840–1.503, S0840–1.505

California socioeconomic and govtl data for municipalities, counties, and school districts, 1993 annual rpt, C4712–3

California statistical abstract, general data, 1992 annual rpt, S0840–2.4

Colorado per capita income, by county, and for Colorado Springs and Pueblo, 1991 and trends, annual article, S1040–4.507

Colorado personal income per capita, by county and selected other area, 1985-90, annual planning rpt, S1040–3

Connecticut employment, hours, and earnings, by labor market area and industry, and selected economic indicators, monthly rpt, S1235–1

DC statistical profile, general data, 1992 annual rpt, S1535–3.1

DC total and per capita personal income, with comparisons to Maryland and Virginia, 1988-92, article, S1527–3.504

Florida county data book, 1992/93 annual rpt, C6360–1

Florida statistical abstract, general data, 1992 annual rpt, U6660–1.5

Georgia and Atlanta MSA forecast employment by industry group and income by source, quarterly rpt, U1880–2

Georgia business activity indicators, bimonthly rpt, U6730–2

Georgia county guide, general data, 1993 annual rpt, U6750–1

Georgia personal income, tax returns, and taxes paid, with detail by income class and county, FY92 annual rpt, S1950–1

Georgia statistical abstract, general data, 1992-93 biennial rpt, U6730–1.3

Hawaii data book, general data, 1992 annual rpt, S2090–1.13

Hawaii economic conditions, including employment, population, tourism, and construction, quarterly rpt, S2090–2

Hawaii economic indicators, bimonthly rpt, B3500–1

Idaho and US economic trends and forecasts, quarterly rpt, S2245–2

Idaho economic profile, general data, 1992 recurring rpt, S2218–2.5

Illinois business activity indicators, quarterly rpt, U6910–1

Illinois economic and business activity indicators, including data by industry and county, bimonthly rpt, S2405–2

Illinois statistical abstract, general data, 1992 annual rpt, U6910–2

Indiana per capita income, 1980-89, annual rpt, S2570–1.1

Indiana per capita personal income, by MSA and for metro vs nonmetro areas, 1991, U2160–1.504

Indiana population and family characteristics, 1990, article, U2160–1.501

Iowa individual income tax return filings, income, taxes paid, and credits, by income bracket, and filings by county, 1991, annual rpt, S2860–3

Kansas business activity indicators, quarterly rpt, U7095–1

Kansas statistical abstract, general data, 1991/92 annual rpt, U7095–2.9

Kansas total and disposable personal income, with comparisons to 5 neighboring States, 1987-91, annual rpt, S3020–1

Kentucky economic statistics, general data, 1993 annual rpt, S3104–1

Louisiana Census of Population and Housing summary findings, by local area, 1990 and trends, U8010–4

Louisiana total and per capita personal income, by parish, 1989-91, annual planning rpt, S3320–1.1

Maine Census of Population and Housing summary findings, by local area, 1990, S3465–9

Maryland individual income tax return filings, and income and tax liability data, by city, county, and income group, 1991, annual rpt, S3685–1

Maryland statistical abstract, general data, 1993-94 biennial rpt, S3605–1.6

Massachusetts municipal and county profiles, general data, 1992 annual rpt, C4712–2

Michigan personal income per capita, by county, 1980 and 1990, annual planning rpt, S3980–1.2

Minnesota income comparisons to higher education costs and student aid, 1970s-93, biennial rpt, S4195–2.2

Mississippi income by source, county, and MSA, and wages by industry group, 1993 annual planning rpt, S4345–1.4

Mississippi statistical abstract, general data, 1992 annual rpt, U3255–4.4

Mississippi taxpayers, taxable income, and gross tax, by county, FY92, annual rpt, S4435–1

Missouri total and per capita income, 1982-91, annual rpt, S4475–1

Montana labor force planning rpt, including population, income, and employment and job openings by industry and occupation, with selected data by county, 1993-94 annual rpt, S4710–3

Nebraska farm and nonfarm personal income, with comparisons to neighboring States, 3rd qtr 1992, U7860–1.503

Nebraska northeastern counties families and households, poverty rates, and income by source, by population size, 1989, article, U7860–1.509

Nebraska personal income and tax liability, by county, 1990, annual rpt, S4950–1

Nebraska, Plains States, and US personal and per capita income, 1982-91, annual rpt, S4825–1

Nevada business and economic activity indicators, with comparisons to other Western States, 1980-91, annual rpt, U7920–2

Nevada income trends by county, 1992 annual rpt, S5040–4

Nevada statistical abstract, general data, 1992 biennial rpt, S5005–1.5

New Hampshire per capita income, by county, 1987-90, recurring rpt, S5205–7

New Jersey Census of Population and Housing detailed findings, by county, 1990, S5425–19

New Jersey municipal and county data book, general data, 1992 annual rpt, C4712–4

New Jersey personal income, with comparisons to selected other States and detail by county, 1991-92 and trends, recurring feature, S5425–1.506

New Mexico and US personal income by source, monthly rpt quarterly feature, S5624–2.503, S5624–2.505

New Mexico business and economic activity indicators, monthly rpt, U7980–1

New Mexico income and tax data, 1990-91 and trends, annual rpt, S5660–1

New Mexico per capita income, with detail by county, 1991 and trends, annual rpt, S5605–1.1

New Mexico personal and family income, by county, 1989-90, annual planning rpt, S5624–1

New Mexico personal income by county and MSA, 1990-91, S5624–2.508

New York State business activity indicators, quarterly rpt, S5735–2

New York State business and economic indicators, by MSA, county, and industry, 1980s-91, annual rpt, S5735–3

New York State municipal and county statistical profiles, general data, 1993 annual rpt, C4712–7

New York State statistical yearbook, general data, 1992 annual rpt, U5100–1.3, U5100–1.5

North Carolina personal income by county, 1990, annual rpt, S5915–1.1

Ohio individual income tax returns filed, income, and tax liability, by income class and county, 1990, annual rpt, S6390–1.3

Oklahoma per capita income, by county, 1990, annual rpt, S6455–1.1

Oklahoma statistical abstract, general data, 1992 annual rpt, U8130–2.4

Oregon economic conditions, including population, construction, income, employment, industry, and foreign trade data, 1991, annual rpt, S6585–3

Oregon median family income, by county, 1989, article, S6615–2.502

Pennsylvania Census of Population and Housing detailed findings, with selected data by county and municipality, 1990, U4130–13

Pennsylvania economic trends and outlook for gross regional product, personal income, and employment, 1980s-93, annual article, U4110–1.504

Pennsylvania income data from Census of Population and Housing, by county and municipality, 1989, C1595–15

Pennsylvania individual income tax returns, and taxable income by source, by income class and county, 1990 and trends, annual rpt, S6885–1

Pennsylvania personal income, by county, 1970-90, annual planning rpt, S6845–3.2

Personal and household income

Pennsylvania personal income, by type, industry div, MSA, and county, 1993 annual article, U4110–1.506

Pennsylvania personal income, monthly rpt quarterly table, U4110–1.502, U4110–1.504

Pennsylvania statistical abstract, general data, 1992 recurring rpt, U4130–6.3

Rhode Island Census of Population and Housing detailed findings, by county and municipality, 1990, S6930–9

Rhode Island statistical almanac, general data, 1993 annual rpt, C7975–1.1

South Carolina economic activity indicators, including employment by industry div, by county, 1993 annual rpt, S7145–1.2

South Carolina economic condition, including agriculture, commerce, govt finances, employment, and income, 1970s-92, annual rpt, S7125–3

South Carolina personal, household, and family income, by county, 1992 annual planning rpt, S7155–3.3

South Carolina statistical abstract, general data, 1993 annual rpt, S7125–1.12

South Dakota business activity review, including selected data by city and industry, quarterly rpt, U8595–1

Tennessee business activity indicators, quarterly journal, U8710–1

Tennessee economic indicator trends and forecasts, and business executives views on selected issues, 1993 annual articles, U8710–1.502

Tennessee economic indicator trends and forecasts, with data by industry div and manufacturing group, 1982-2001, annual rpt, S7560–1

Tennessee per capita income, by county and MSA, 1990-91, recurring article, S7495–2.507

Tennessee statistical abstract, general data, 1992/93 annual rpt, U8710–2.2, U8710–2.20

Texas per capita income, by county and MSA, 1985 and 1990, annual planning rpt, S7675–2

Utah business activity indicators, by county, 1988-91, annual feature, U8960–2.501

Utah business activity indicators, by county, 1989-92, annual feature, U8960–2.507

Utah economic and business activity review and indicators, monthly rpt, U8960–2

Utah economic and demographic trends, by county and district, 1960-91, annual rpt, S7832–2

Utah govt statistical review, fiscal and socioeconomic data, 1993 annual rpt, R9380–1.2

Utah individual income tax returns and adjusted gross income, by income class and county, 1991, annual rpt, S7905–1

Utah personal income and household data, by location and race-ethnicity, 1990 census rpt, S7832–3.3

Utah personal income, by source, industry, and county, 1993 annual article, U8960–2.506

Utah personal income, with detail by source and county, 1992 annual article, S7820–3.501

Utah statistical abstract, general data, 1993 triennial rpt, U8960–1.5

Vermont per capita income, with detail by county, 1980-92, annual planning rpt, S8025–2.1

Virginia educational finances by source and program, and local area revenue base, by county and municipality, 1991/92, annual rpt, S8190–3

Virginia income distribution and income tax returns filed, by locality, 1990, annual rpt, U9080–1

Virginia personal income, statewide and for 3 MSAs, quarterly 1992-94, U1120–1.502, U1120–1.504

Virginia total and per capita personal income, by local area and major source, 1980-90, annual rpt, U9080–7

Washington State per capita and household income, by race-ethnicity and/or county, 1989-90, annual rpt, S8345–4

West Virginia per capita income, by county, 1989, annual rpt, S8560–1

West Virginia per capita personal income, by county and metro-nonmetro status, 1989-90, annual planning rpt, S8534–2

West Virginia statistical handbook, general data, 1992 annual rpt, R9385–1.1, R9385–1.6

Wisconsin Blue Book, general data, 1993-94 biennial rpt, S8780–1.2

Wyoming payroll and wages by industry div, and personal income, with comparisons to US, 1987-92, article, S8895–1.507

see also Child support and alimony
see also Earnings, general
see also Economic indicators
see also Family budgets
see also Financial planning
see also under By Income in the "Index by Categories"

Personal budgets
see Family budgets
see Financial planning

Personal care products

Advertising expenditures by medium for top 100 advertisers, with comparisons to earnings and sales, and detail by product type and brand, 1991-92, annual rpt, C2710–1.547

Beauty care and cosmetics new product sales performance for top brands in selected categories, biweekly rpt recurring feature, C5150–2.504, C5150–2.505, C5150–2.510

Condom sales shares for food vs drug stores, 12 months ended Feb 1992-93, articles, C5150–2.511

Consumer buying power survey of population, income, and sales by product line, by State, metro area, county, and census div, 1993 annual rpt, C1200–1.514

Contact lens care product market value, with shares by product and retail outlet type, 1987-95, article, C5150–2.513

Corporate performance ratings by executives for leading companies in 32 industries, 1993 annual survey feature, C8900–1.508

Diapers (disposable) couponed advertisement shares for top 3 and all other manufacturers, 1991/92, article, C2710–1.517

Discount chain consumer natl brand preferences, by product category and chain, and by age group, 1993 survey, annual feature, C5150–3.521

Discount chain top-selling natl brands cited by managers, by product category, chain, and region, 1993 survey, annual feature, C5150–3.520

Index by Subjects and Names

Discount store and other outlet sales and merchandising of health and beauty aids, by product type, 1991 and trends, annual article, C5150–3.502

Discount store sales and productivity data for 20 depts, 1993 annual feature, C5150–3.516

Drugstore chain and brand preferences of consumers, with data by product type and region, 1992 annual survey feature, C5150–2.503

Drugstore chains financial performance and marketing operations, with sales by product type, 1993 annual feature, C5150–2.510

Drugstore chains top-selling over-the-counter products, year ended June 1993, article, C5150–2.521

Drugstore chains top-selling products, and leading manufacturers, 1993 annual article, C5150–2.520

Drugstore health and beauty aid product sales, for 26 fastest-growing product categories, 1992, article, C5150–2.505

Drugstore sales and merchandising trends, by product type and market area, 1992 annual feature, C5150–2.503

Drugstore sales of oral care and other dental-related products, by product type, years ended July 1991-92, articles, C5150–2.502

Electric personal care appliance shipments, by product type, 1983-92, annual feature, C2000–1.505

Ethnic beauty care product sales distribution by product type, 1991-92, article, C5150–2.506

Ethnic cosmetics and hair care product sales distribution by product category, year ended July 1992-93, article, C5150–2.520

Ethnic hair care product market shares by retail outlet type, 1992, article, C5150–3.513

Financial performance and growth rankings for approx 1,000 top corporations, with comparisons by industry group, 1993 annual rpt, C3950–1.505

First aid product, antiseptic, and elastic/health support product sales, year ended Apr 1993, article, C5150–2.515

Food store health/beauty aid product sales as percent of total, by company size and region, 1991-92, annual rpts, A4950–5

Franchise operations and finances, by type of business, 1991/92 and trends, annual rpt, A5820–1

Hair care product sales trends, for top 10 brands in drugstores, with comparisons to mass merchandise and food/drug stores, year ended June 1993, articles, C5150–2.519

Health/beauty aid sales trends by product category and outlet type, 1992, article, A2072–2.501

Life expectancy, shipments, and manufacturers market shares, for appliances by type, 1993 annual article, C2000–1.510

Lotion (hand/body) market shares, for top 9 brands and private label, 1993 article, C2710–1.530

Military commissary sales, by region, product type, and individual store, FY92, annual feature, A2072–2.501

Index by Subjects and Names

Personal consumption

Military commissary sales of health/beauty aids, by region, 1991-92, article, C0500–1.509

Oral care product sales trends by product type and manufacturer, year ended June 1993 vs 1992, article, C4655–1.511

Packaging preferences of consumers for personal care products, 1993 survey, article, C1850–1.507

Paper and paperboard shipments and consumption, by product grade and end use, 1993 annual rpt, C3975–5.3

Raw materials sales for personal care/cosmetics products, by ingredient and/or product type, 1990, 1993, and 1996, article, A1250–1.522

Retail prices for selected consumer items in approx 300 cities, quarterly rpt, A0150–1

Retail sales by outlet type, and discount chain sales in major depts, by product category, 1992, annual feature, C8130–1.507

Sales and consumer expenditures, for food store products by type, 1991-92, annual feature, C4655–1.510

Sales and market shares for top 10 brands in 8 health care product categories, 1992-93, C2710–1.541

Sales shares for drugstores, grocery stores, and mass merchandisers, 1991 and trends, annual article, C5225–1.501

Sales volume shares by retail outlet type, for approx 300 food, drug, and other product categories, 1993 annual feature, C4655–1.504

Shipments of household appliances, by detailed product type, 1991-98, annual articles, C2000–1.503

Skin care medicated product use indexes for white vs black households, by brand, 1993 article, C5150–2.520

Sun care product sales distribution by product type, 1993 articles, C5150–2.511

Sunglasses sales and prices, by retail outlet type, 1992, article, C5150–3.516

Sunscreen promotional spending for 4 manufacturers, 1992-93, article, C2710–1.550

Supermarket health and beauty aid dept sales and performance indicators, 1992 and trends, annual article, C4655–1.506

Supermarket health/beauty aid merchandising practices, 1993 survey article, C5225–1.506

Supermarket health/beauty aid product sales shares for private label brands, 1986 and 1991-92, article, C5225–1.502

Supermarket health/beauty care and general merchandise product marketing devs and issues, 1992 survey article, C4655–1.502

Supermarket private label share of health/beauty aid sales, with detail for top 10 product categories, 1993 article, C8130–1.504

Supermarket sales and market shares, for top 10 brands in 8 personal care product categories, 1992-93, C2710–1.523

Supermarket sales and market shares, for top 5-10 brands in selected personal care paper product categories, 1992-93, C2710–1.532

Supermarket sales by detailed product type, 1992 and trends, annual feature, C5225–1.507

Supermarket sales growth for health/beauty aid products by type, monthly rpt quarterly article, C5225–1.503, C5225–1.505, C5225–1.507, C5225–1.510

Supermarket sales of health/beauty care products by detailed type, year ended June 1993, article, C4655–1.511

Supermarket sales of nonfood products, by detailed product type, 1992, annual feature, C5225–1.508

Tampon product market value, with shares for top 4 and all other manufacturers, 1992, article, C2710–1.513

Toothbrush market shares, for top 9 brands and private label, year ended Apr 1993, article, C2710–1.530

Toothpaste promotional advertisements for 4 companies, 1st half 1992-93, article, C2710–1.540

Women age 18-29 beauty product use and shopping practices, 1993 articles, C5150–2.514

Women's use and shopping patterns for personal care products, with preferred outlets and brands, 1993 survey and trends, annual feature, C5150–2.515

State and local:

New York State cancer prevention behavior, including regular use of sunscreen, by respondent characteristics, 1989, recurring rpt, S5765–3

see also Contraceptives

see also Cosmetics and toiletries

see also Drugs

see also Vitamins and nutrients

Personal consumption

Asia tourist arrivals and daily expenditures in 6 countries, 1993 article, C2710–1.549

Auto purchase expenditures as percent of household income, 1973, 1983, and 1993, article, C2710–3.537

Boating-related expenditures, including purchases of boats and accessories by State, 1992 annual rpt, A8055–1

Book expenditure trends and outlook, for consumer and professional/educational books by type, 1987-97, article, C1852–2.520

Canada photographic and video equipment and supplies ownership, purchasing patterns, and use, by household characteristics, 1992 survey, recurring rpt, A8695–4

China consumer ownership of selected products, 1985 and 1990, article, A9315–1.501

Christmas spending plans of consumers, by region, age, and income, Nov 1992 survey, annual rpt, R4105–81.10

Commodity yearbook for 1993: detailed supply-demand data, and selected indicators for futures market investors, C2400–1

Commodity yearbook update: detailed supply-demand data, and selected indicators for futures market investors, Jan-Sept 1993 rpts, C2400–2

Consumer buying power survey of population, income, and sales by kind of business, by census div, State, MSA, county, and city, 1992, annual rpt, C1200–1.511

Consumer buying power survey of population, income, and sales by product

line, by State, metro area, county, and census div, 1993 annual rpt, C1200–1.514

Consumer expenditures for food store nonfood products by type, 1991-92, annual feature, C4655–1.510

Direct marketing industry devs, including advertising patterns, finances, target market characteristics, and consumer attitudes, 1992/93 annual rpt, A4620–1

Discount store expenditures of consumers, by selected characteristics, 1993 article, C5150–3.509

Discount store expenditures of households, by dept, 1992 and trends, annual feature, C8130–1.507

Discount store ratings and shopping patterns of consumers in 3 market areas, including expenditures, by leading chain, 1992 surveys, article, C5150–3.503

Drugs (prescription) use, expenditures, prices, and profit trends, with data by patient characteristics and for top 20 brands, 1992 rpt, R4865–8

Drugstore marketing to ethnic minorities, with related consumer indicators for blacks or by race, 1993 articles, C5150–2.518

Economic conditions and outlook for major purchases, consumer attitudes, monthly survey, U7475–2

Economic indicator historical trends, 1900s-92, annual rpt, R9050–1.2

Economic outlook for selected indicators, recent trends and 2-year forecast, quarterly rpt, A3840–6

Energy tax proposals and potential effect on selected economic indicators, 1993-97, article, C6985–1.516

Expenditures for autos and fuel compared to other items, 1989-92, annual fact book, C1680 1.507

Food away from home expenditures of consumers, by age group, 1991, article, C1200–5.516

Forecasts of economic indicators for approx 10-13 months, monthly rpt, U1880–3

Forecasts of natl income and product account components and related indicators, quarterly rpt, U1880–1

Forecasts of natl income and product account components, employment, and financial sector activity, monthly rpt, B4950–1

Foreign student living expenses, by State, 1992/93, annual rpt, R5580–1

Germany (West) and US comparative socioeconomic statistics, 1970s-91, annual rpt, A5135–2.2

Health care and other personal consumption expenditures, by item, 1950s-91, annual rpt, A5173–2.3

Health care expenditures, by fund source and as percent of GDP and personal consumption, and medical care CPI, 1960s-91, annual fact book, A1275–1.4

Hispanic American consumer expenditures, by category, 1985/86 and 1989/90-1990/91, article, C4575–1.505

Hispanic American consumer expenditures for entertainment, by type, 1992, article, C4575–1.508

Hispanic American household ownership of selected luxury items, by region, 1991, article, C4575–1.501

Personal consumption

Household average expenditures for retail goods, rankings by State, 1990, biennial rpt, S3605–1.6

Jeweler views on women's jewelry purchasing trends, 1993 survey article, C2150–7.510

Latin America statistical abstract, general data by country, 1992 annual rpt, U6250–1.14, U6250–1.32

Life insurance purchases and ownership, by consumer and household characteristics, 1991 and trends, biennial fact book, A1325–1.1

Men's consumer purchase shares and value, for 7 household items, 1992 article, C5800–7.502

Minority consumer purchasing by product type, and ownership of selected electronics, for blacks, Hispanics, and Asians, 1992/93 survey, article, C2710–1.513

Pension benefit lump sum payments disposition, including use for purchases/expenditures, by recipient characteristics, 1980s, R9260–17

Photographic equipment and supplies, consumer ownership, purchasing patterns, and use, 1993 survey and trends, recurring rpt, A8695–2

Reading materials expenditures, for books and magazines/newspapers, 1991-93, recurring feature, C1850–10.506

Reading materials expenditures, for books and magazines/newspapers, 1992-94, recurring feature, C1850–10.513

Retail shopping patterns and expenditures, by outlet type and demographic characteristics, 1993 annual feature, C4655–1.504

Service industries economic devs, with analysis of conditions and outlook, and comparisons to other industries, quarterly rpt, A3892–1

Service sector economic activity indicators, with leading and coincident indexes and components, and detail for financial services, monthly rpt, U1245–3

Shoe expenditures compared to other items, 1964-91, annual rpt, A4957–1.1

Shoe industry production and operating data, including trade by country, retail sales, and consumer expenditures, quarterly rpt, A4957–2

Sporting goods purchaser characteristics, by product category, 1992, annual survey rpt, A8485–4

Sporting goods purchases, by product and outlet type, census div, and purchaser characteristics, with average prices, 1992 and trends, annual survey, A8485–2

Transportation and new auto expenditures compared to expenditures on other items, 1960s-92, annual rpt, A0865–1.2

Travel and tourism trends in US and worldwide, with traveler and trip characteristics, and data by local area, 1992 annual rpt, C2140–1

Travel impact on State economies, with detail by industry sector, 1990 and trends, annual rpt, R9375–7

Women's use and shopping patterns for personal care products, with preferred outlets and brands, 1993 survey and trends, annual feature, C5150–2.515

Youth expenditures distribution by product category, 1993 survey, article, C5150–3.518

Youth expenditures, 1986-92, article, C2710–1.541

State and local:

Arizona, Phoenix area temporary winter resident characteristics, including expenditures, dwelling type, and region of residence, 1992/93, article, U0280–1.508

Arizona temporary winter residents and expenditures, and mobile home and trailer park spaces and occupancy, by local area, winter 1992/93, annual article, U0280–1.508

California travel-related expenditures, by type of business, 1991 and trends, annual rpt, S0840–3

Hawaii data book, general data, 1992 annual rpt, S2090–1.7, S2090–1.13

Hawaii economic conditions, including employment, population, tourism, and construction, quarterly rpt, S2090–2

Maryland statistical abstract, general data, 1993-94 biennial rpt, S3605–1.5, S3605–1.6

Oregon travel-related expenditures and employment, by type of business, 1990, annual rpt, S6585–3

South Carolina statistical abstract, general data, 1993 annual rpt, S7125–1.14

see also Alcohol use

see also Consumer Expenditure Survey

see also Economic indicators

see also Family budgets

see also Food consumption

see also Housing energy use

see also Media use surveys

Personal debt

Doctoral degree recipients and debt, by recipient characteristics, 1990/91, annual rpt, R6000–7

Household assets and debts by type, by household composition, 1989, article, C4215–1.502

Household debt compared to assets by type, 1962, 1983, and 1989, R4700–17

Natl trends in savings and investment by sector, and household assets and liabilities, 1960s-92, annual rpt, R9050–1.2

Optometry school 1st-year student and grads educational indebtedness, by instn, 1991/92, annual survey, A3370–2

Osteopathy student debt and career plans, by student characteristics, 1991/92 and trends, annual survey rpt, A0620–2

Private assets and liabilities trends, by economic sector, decennially 1950-90, U9640–2.14

Psychology doctoral degree recipient employment and demographic characteristics, and finances, 1990/91, biennial survey rpt, A2620–4

Veterinary school grad starting salaries by type of employment, and educational debt, 1992, annual survey article, A3100–2.503

State and local:

Maine installment and real estate debt, by county and State area, 1982-92, annual rpt, S3473–1

Minnesota debt prorate companies composite financial statement, Dec 1990-91, annual rpt, S4140–3

South Dakota public higher education grad loan debt, by instn, 1991/92, annual rpt, S7375–1

Vermont debt counseling agency caseloads, client trust account activity, and creditor fees, Dec 1992, annual rpt, S7995–2

see also Consumer credit

see also Loans

see also Mortgages

Personal injury protection

see Automobile insurance

Personal property

see Housing tenure

see Land ownership and rights

see Ownership of enterprise

see Personal debt

see Property

see Savings

see Wealth

Personal wealth

see Wealth

Personnel management

AIDS incidence in the workplace by region and industry, and employer testing and other policies, 1993 and trends, A2075–20.14

Association executives compensation, by position, assn type, and census div, with personnel practices and benefit provisions, 1992, biennial rpt, A2900–3

College grad hiring plans by industry, with data on campus visits, starting salaries, and minority hires, 1991/92-1992/93, annual rpt, A3940–3

College grad recruiting practices and hiring trends, with data on starting salaries and layoffs, by type of employer, 1992/93 annual survey rpt, U3130–1

College grad recruitment and hiring practices, 1993 annual survey rpt, U3730–1

Computer local-area network (LAN) manager expectations for trend in staffing levels, 1992 survey, article, C1850–5.523

Computer use and related mgmt and training issues as reported by corporate executives, 1993 survey rpt, B6850–7

Corporate communication of benefits info to employees, including objectives, methods, and success, 1993 survey rpt, R4105–78.28

Corporate communications mgmt, activities, budget, staffing, and use of outside services, 1992 survey, R4105–78.24

Corporate human resources devs, including skill needs and testing for new hires, and work force diversity nature and mgmt, 1993 survey, annual rpt, B6850–4

Corporate mgmt initiatives and guidelines on cultural/ethnic diversity of work force, and challenges to implementation, 1991-92 surveys, R4105–78.22

Corporate mgmt of culturally diverse work force, with program characteristics and minority opportunity indicators, Nov 1992 survey, A2075–20.11

Corporate minority employment levels, and mgmt programs for dealing with diverse work force, 1991 survey, article, C1200–4.509

Corporate personnel mgmt devs, including hiring, layoffs, and health care and payroll cost control efforts, June 1992 survey, annual rpt, B6850–3

Corporate personnel mgmt devs, including staffing practices and turnover, payroll cost control efforts, and human resources operations, 1993 survey, annual rpt, B6850–5

Corporate personnel mgmt devs, including work force diversity, health care and family-related benefits, counseling services, and competitiveness, 1993 survey, B6850–6

Corporate personnel mgmt professional activities, job satisfaction, employer performance, and obstacles encountered, spring 1993 survey, A8907–2

Corporate use of selected variable pay and recognition programs, with objectives and success, by industry div, Oct 1992 survey and trends, R4105–78.27

Corporate work force outlook and related mgmt policies, views of human resources executives, Sept/Oct 1991 survey, R4105–78.21

Corporate work force reduction prevalence by industry sector, assistance provided displaced workers, and reduction effects, 1992 survey, article, C4215–1.504

Corporate work force reductions, measures to avoid discharges, assistance to displaced workers, and impacts, Aug-Sept 1992 survey and trends, annual rpt, A2075–20.9

Family-related policies of employers, with involvement in child, elderly, and disabled care services, and personnel mgmt views, Mar 1992 survey, A8907–1

Fire dept employment and personnel practices, including eligibility requirements and testing, by population size, metro status, and census div, 1991 survey, recurring rpt, A5800–2.116

Flexible work schedules offered by employers, and workers with flexible schedules by occupation and industry div, 1993 article, S0465–1.504

Food marketer recruiting methods, employee dev expenditures, and personnel mgmt practices, by region, 1991, annual rpt, A4950–5

Food wholesale distributor operations, including importance of selected personnel mgmt issues, by region, 1992, annual rpt, A4950–5.4

High-technology firm methods used to handle work of employees on leave, with costs as a percent of salary, 1993 article, A1250–1.524

Hiring costs and new hires, by industry, State, region, and employer characteristics, 1992 and trends, annual survey rpt, A4740–2

Hospital recruiting of nurses and allied health personnel, with budget, vacancies, turnover, and compensation, 1993 and trends, annual survey rpt, A6500–1

Incentive award criteria most commonly used by employers, 1992 annual feature, C1200–4.502

Industrial distributors hiring criteria for college grads, 1992 survey article, C1850–2.502

Industrial distributors ratings of employee hiring and promotion criteria, 1992 survey article, C1850–4.502

Jewelry retail business outlook, including staffing plans, 1993, annual survey article, C2150–7.502

Municipal govt ethics policies and concerns, views of personnel directors, 1992 survey, A5800–1.1

Psychology grad dept personnel budget trend, and effects on faculty hiring, teaching load, and salary increases, 1992/93, annual rpt, A2620–1

Public planning agency personnel practices, by jurisdiction size, 1991 survey rpt, A2615–3

Quality assurance programs of North American companies, role of human resource depts, 1992 annual survey rpt, B6850–2

Recession impact on corporate marketing budgets and staff, advertising media, sales, and market shares, Aug-Sept 1992 survey, A2075–20.10

Sales force recruitment practices, including selection criteria and sources of best candidates, 1993 survey, article, C1200–1.510

Small business CEO views on top 7 human resource mgmt concerns, 1993 survey article, C4687–1.510

Small business mgmt of diverse work force, challenges and methods, 1993 survey article, C4687–1.503

Small corporation use of flextime, job sharing, leased employees, and home-based/telecommuting workers, Mar 1993 survey, article, C4687–1.512

State and local:

Hawaii data book, general data, 1992 annual rpt, S2090–1.9

see also Employee performance and appraisal

Peru

Energy intl sourcebook, with detail on oil and gas industry operations, supply-demand, and prices, for approx 80 countries, 1970s-91, annual compilation, C6985–10.2

Motor vehicle world production, sales, trade, and registrations, by country, world area, manufacturer, and make, 1991 and trends, annual rpt, A0865–2.1

Oil production for govt-owned and 4 private companies, 1992-94, article, C6985–1.525

Statistical abstract of Latin America, detailed social, govtl, and economic data, 1992 annual rpt, U6250–1

see also Lima, Peru

see also under By Foreign Country or World Area in the "Index by Categories"

Pesticides

Chemical and related industries production, finances, operating ratios, employment, and trade, by country, company, and chemical, 1980s-92, annual feature, A1250–1.530

Chemical market value for pesticide industry, 1991, article, A1250–1.513

Field crop pesticide and fertilizer use for 4 major crops, 1992, article, A1250–1.542

Methyl bromide use by application, 1990, article, A1250–1.512

Prices paid by farmers for selected production commodities, 1982 and 1991-92, annual rpt, S3085–1

Sales and consumer expenditures, for food store products by type, 1991-92, annual feature, C4655–1.510

World pesticide market value, by region or country, 1990-91, article, A1250–1.501

World pesticide use, by country, 1975-84, biennial rpt, R9455–1.6

State and local:

Arizona pesticide sales, and use on lettuce, by type, 1993 annual rpt, U5830–1

Hawaii data book, general data, 1992 annual rpt, S2090–1.19

Hawaii food and milk products examined for pesticide residues, 1990, annual rpt, S2065–1.6

Kentucky pesticide use on corn and soybean crops, 1992, annual rpt, S3085–1

Michigan fertilizer and pesticide use, by chemical and crop, 1992 annual rpt, S3950–1

Missouri herbicide and insecticide use, by product type, 1991-92, annual rpt, S4480–1

Nevada pesticide use and acres treated, by detailed application, 1992, annual rpt, S5010–1

North Carolina pesticide use, by type, for selected crops, 1991, annual rpt, S5885–1

Oregon pesticide use, by type and crop, 1991, annual rpt, S6575–1

Pennsylvania pesticide use, by type and crop, 1992, annual rpt, S6760–1

Vermont pesticide sales and monitoring activity, including wells sampled, 1988-90, biennial rpt, S7978–1

Washington State pesticide use, by type and crop, 1992, annual rpt, S8328–1

Wisconsin pesticide use on corn, 1992, annual rpt, S8680–1

Pests and pest control

Condominium, cooperative, and planned unit dev detailed expenses, for US and Canada, by building characteristics, metro area, and US region, 1991, annual rpt, A5600–3

Financial ratios and performance, for over 350 SIC 4-digit industries, FY88-92, annual rpt, A6400–3

Lice treatment product market shares, including top 5 brands, year ended May 1993, article, C5150–2.517

State and local:

Hawaii environmental quality and public health control, inspection, licensing, and enforcement activities, 1990, annual rpt, S2065–1.6

see also Animal diseases and zoonoses

see also Pesticides

Pet food and supplies

Advertising expenditures by medium for top 100 advertisers, with comparisons to earnings and sales, and detail by product type and brand, 1991-92, annual rpt, C2710–1.547

Military commissary sales, by region, product type, and individual store, FY92, annual feature, A2072–2.501

Sales and consumer expenditures, for food store products by type, 1991-92, annual feature, C4655–1.510

Sales of pet food and supplies in drugstores and discount stores, by product type, 1991/92, article, C5150–3.505

Sales volume shares by retail outlet type, for approx 300 food, drug, and other product categories, 1993 annual feature, C4655–1.504

Shopping center financial and operating data, with detail by type of tenant, US and Canada, 1991, triennial rpt, R9285–1

Pet food and supplies

Supermarket product sales and market shares, for top 10 brands in 7 pet food categories, 1992-93, C2710–1.517

Supermarket sales by detailed product type, 1992 and trends, annual feature, C5225–1.507

Supermarket sales of nonfood products, by detailed product type, 1992, annual feature, C5225–1.508

Peterson, Jane A.

"Local Housing Authorities in the 1990s", A6800–2

Petrochemicals

Capital spending of oil industry in US and Canada, by function, 1991-93, annual articles, C6985–1.517

China ethylene plants operating and planned, with data on capacity, construction costs, and imported equipment origins, 1993 article, C6985–1.512

Commonwealth of Independent States oil refinery capacity by process, and refined products production and consumption, by Republic and region, 1992 article, C6985–1.508

Construction of petrochemical processing facilities, by country and company, weekly rpt semiannual list, C6985–1.524, C6985–1.551

Ethylene capacity, by country and world area, 1980-90, annual compilation, C6985–10

Ethylene plants under dev and capacity, by process and company, 1993 article, C5800–8.508

Gulf Coast ethylene plant variable and cash operating margins, by feedstock type, weekly rpt monthly table, C6985–1

Imports of crude oil and refined products, by importing company, port, and country of origin, monthly rpt, A2575–12

Korea (South) petrochemical and thermoplastics production and foreign trade, with detail by trading partner, 1992 and trends, article, C5800–8.510

Methanol supply-demand outlook in North America, Europe, and worldwide, with capacity by company, 1993 article, C6985–1.522

Middle East petrochemical capacity and world market share, by chemical, 1991 and 2000, article, A1250–1.501

Occupational injury, illness, and employment data, by function, for 136 oil/gas companies, 1991, annual rpt, A2575–4

Oil company earnings from chemicals, by company, weekly rpt quarterly article, A1250–1.514

Oxygenates and gasoline inventories, supply, and consumption, Oct 1992-Feb 1993, article, C6985–1.507

Oxygenates supply-demand and outlook, 1991-97, article, C6985–1.505

Soviet Union petrochemical shortages anticipated, by product category, 1990, 1995, and 2000, article, C6985–1.540

Statistical compilation of oil and gas industry trends, 1993 annual rpt, C6985–4

Styrene demand, distribution by country or world region, 1991 and 2000, article, C6985–1.505

World oxygenate capacity by country and company, 1992 annual feature, C6985–1.508

World petrochemical data, including foreign ownership of US plants, Japanese capacity, and South Korean production and use, 1992 and trends, article, C6985–1.522

Petroleum and petroleum industry

Capital outlays in US and Canada, by function, 1991-93, annual articles, C6985–1.517

Chemical and related industries production, finances, operating ratios, employment, and trade, by country, company, and chemical, 1980s-92, annual feature, A1250–1.530

China (southeast) oil demand by Province, and coastal refinery construction projects and capacity, 1990s-2000, article, C6985–1.528

Commonwealth of Independent States oil refinery capacity by process, and refined products production and consumption, by Republic and region, 1992 article, C6985–1.508

Construction of refineries, by country and company, weekly rpt semiannual list, C6985–1.524, C6985 1.551

Consumption of fossil energy resources and electricity from hydro and nuclear power, 1960s-91, annual rpt, A1775–3.6

Corporate performance ratings by executives for leading companies in 32 industries, 1993 annual survey feature, C8900–1.508

Earnings of approx 20 oil companies, monthly rpt quarterly article, C4680–1.501, C4680–1.504, C4680–1.506, C4680–1.510

Earnings, sales, and profit margins, for chemical and allied industries, by company, weekly rpt quarterly article, A1250–1.502, A1250–1.514, A1250–1.525, A1250–1.536

Electric power (steam) plant operating data, including oil and gas use and costs, by plant, utility, and location, 1991, annual rpt, A7400–7

Electric power supply-demand, and utility capacities and fuel requirements, detailed data by US and Canadian region, 1992-2002, annual rpt, A8630–2

Electric utility oil deliveries and prices, monthly rpt, A7400–9

Electric utility operating data, including generating capacity and efficiency, peak demand, and fuel consumption, top 100 utilities, 1992, annual article, C6985–6.512

Employee benefit funds assets, for funds investing in oil/gas programs, 1992, annual feature, C2710–2.504

Engineers salaries by industry group, census div, selected metro area, and years since college degree, 1993, annual survey rpt, A0685–5

Engineers salaries by industry group, census div, selected metro area, degree level, and years since college degree, 1993, annual survey rpt, A0685–3

Environmental performance, including toxic chemical releases, oil spills, occupational injury/illness, and corporate spending, 1990 and trends, annual rpt, A2575–27

Index by Subjects and Names

Expenditures for exploration, dev, and production, 1991 and trends, annual survey rpt, A2575–20

Exploration/production expenditures of US and foreign oil companies in US, Canada, and elsewhere, 1992-93, annual article, C6985–1.515

Financial and operating data, rankings for top 300 US and top 100 non-US oil and gas companies, 1991-92, annual feature, C6985–1.547

Financial performance and growth rankings for approx 1,000 top corporations, with comparisons by industry group, 1993 annual rpt, C3950–1.505

Financial ratios and performance, for over 350 SIC 4-digit industries, FY88-92, annual rpt, A6400–3

Futures and options trading volume by commodity and exchange, 1988-92, annual rpt, A5040–1

Futures and options trading volume on foreign exchanges, by commodity and exchange, monthly rpt, A5040–5

Futures contract open interest (outstanding commitments), by commodity and exchange, monthly rpt, A5040–4

Futures trading volume by commodity and exchange, monthly rpt, A5040–2

Higher education physical plant operations, costs, employment, salaries, and energy use, by instn and region, 1991/92, recurring rpt, A3183–1

Independent oil and gas company finances and operations, for approx 50 companies, 1991-92, semiannual article, C6985–1.504

Intl energy sourcebook, with detail on oil and gas industry operations, supply-demand, and prices, for approx 80 countries, 1970s-91, annual compilation, C6985–10

Intl Petroleum Encyclopedia, basic data on oil and gas supply-demand, exploration, refining, reserves, and industry finances, by country and company, 1993 annual rpt, C6985–3

Japan energy supply-demand and outlook, by fuel source, 1980s-2000, recurring article, R5650–2.536

Latin America economic indicators affecting business climate, with data on motor vehicle and oil industries and detail by country, 1992 rpt, R4105–82.6

Latin America oil and gas industry devs and outlook, 1993 articles, C6985–1.518

Latin America statistical abstract, general data by country, 1992 annual rpt, U6250–1.23

Lubricating oil sales, foreign trade, stocks, and supplies, 1993 annual fact book, C4680–1.507

Marketing news and industry devs for oil industry, articles and special features, with data on gasoline prices and product stocks, monthly rpt, C4680–1

Mass transit system energy use by source, employee compensation, and labor costs, 1970s-91, annual rpt, A2650–1.2

Occupational injury, illness, and employment data, by function, for 136 oil/gas companies, 1991, annual rpt, A2575–4

Operating and financial composite ratios for corporations, with establishments and receipts, for approx 200 industries, by asset size, FY90, annual rpt, C7800–1

Index by Subjects and Names

Petroleum exports and imports

Options trading volume by commodity, securities index, and exchange, monthly rpt, A5040–3

Production and drilling technology devs, including oil and gas drilling rigs in operation, monthly rpt, C4420–1

Production, exploration, drilling, refining, stock, price, and financial data for US and foreign oil and gas industry, weekly rpt, C6985–1

Production, exploration, refining, demand, finance, prices, and reserves, by State and country or world area, 1993 and trends, periodic basic data book, A2575–14

Production, finances, exploration, reserves, and other data for oil/gas industry, by State, 1992 and trends, annual rpt, A5425–1

Refinery capacity changes, by PAD district and company, discontinued annual rpt, A2575–7

Russia oil and gas industry devs, including foreign investment and supply-demand indicators, 1993 articles, C6985–1.540

Sourcebook of oil and gas industry operations and finances, and world supply-demand situation, 1970s-91, annual compilation, C6985–9

Spain oil refining capacity and utilization, and employment, for 3 refineries, 1993 article, A8955–1.503

State social, economic, and govtl indicators, with rankings, 1993 semiannual rpt, B8500–1.12

Statistical compilation of oil and gas industry trends, 1993 annual rpt, C6985–4

Statistical profiles of 50 States and DC, general data, 1993 annual almanac, C4712–1

Stock and summary financial performance, for 8 largest oil companies worldwide, 1992 article, C3950 1.501

Storage tank (aboveground) cost-benefit analysis for release prevention barrier retrofitting, 1992 rpt, A2575–26

Sulfur (oil-based) recovery plant capacity and production, by company and country, Jan 1993, annual feature, C6985–1.537

Supply-demand and price data for energy resources, including by country and producing State, commodity yearbook for 1993, C2400–1

Supply-demand and price data for energy resources, including by country and producing State, commodity yearbook Jan-Sept 1993 updates, C2400–2

Supply-demand for crude oil and petroleum products, quarterly 1993, annual article, C4680–1.503

Supply-demand, marketing, prices, finances, and employment, detailed data for US and Canada, by product, company, and location, 1993 annual fact book, C4680–1.507

Supply-demand outlook and industry operations, with trends by country and producing State, 1970s-2010, annual rpt, C6985–5

Supply-demand outlook for oil, gas, and refined products, 1993, annual article, C6985–1.504

Supply-demand, prices, and finance, oil and gas industry, 1973-92, annual rpt, A5425–2

Supply-demand, trade, and industry exploration and operations, by product, exporting country and world area, PAD district, and State, 1993 annual feature, C6985–1.513

Supply-demand, trade, prices, and exploration activity, with selected data by State, PAD district, and country, 1993 annual article, C6985–1.539

Supply, disposition, and stocks of refined oil products by type and/or crude oil, and refinery operations summary, monthly rpt, A2575–2

Supply of oil and refined products, including stocks, refinery operations, and imports, by PAD district and product, weekly rpt, A2575–1

Supply trends and outlook under 4 economic scenarios, for onshore and offshore areas and Alaska, 1960s-2010, A2575–25

Transportation consumption of petroleum, and shipments of crude oil and refined products, by transport mode, 1992 annual rpt, R4815–1

World energy supply-demand, by fuel source and sector, by region and country, 1992/93 biennial rpt, R9455–1.3

World oil and gas production, by country, 1986-91, annual rpt, A7400–2.1

World oil refinery capacity, by process, with data by country, company, and US State, 1992 annual feature, C6985–1.508

World oil reserves and production, by country, company, and field, 1992 annual feature, C6985–1.509

State and local:

Alabama business activity indicators, monthly rpt, U5680–1

Alabama county data book, general data, 1992 annual rpt, S0121–2

Alabama statistical abstract, general data, 1992 recurring rpt, U5680–2.12

Arizona oil and gas production, by field, operator, and well, monthly rpt, S0473–1

Arizona statistical abstract, general data, 1993 recurring rpt, U5850–2.20

Arkansas oil and gas production by field, and disposition, monthly rpt, S0737–1

California economic indicators, bimonthly rpt, S0840–1

California statistical abstract, general data, 1992 annual rpt, S0840–2.7

Colorado property assessed valuation, and summary production data, by county and/or company, 1991-92, annual rpt, S1055–3

Florida statistical abstract, general data, 1992 annual rpt, U6660–1.15

Georgia statistical abstract, general data, 1992-93 biennial rpt, U6730–1.8

Hawaii data book, general data, 1992 annual rpt, S2090–1.17

Kansas oil and gas production, by county, 1991, annual rpt, S3020–1

Kansas statistical abstract, general data, 1991/92 annual rpt, U7095–2.16

Louisiana energy indicators, suspended quarterly rpt, U2730–1

Mississippi statistical abstract, general data, 1992 annual rpt, U3255–4.10

Montana oil and gas production and taxes paid, by county, 1990-91, biennial rpt, S4750–1.1

Nevada statistical abstract, general data, 1992 biennial rpt, S5005–1.11

New Mexico business and economic activity indicators, monthly rpt, U7980–1

New Mexico oil and gas production and tax collections, 1985/86-1991/92, annual rpt, S5660–1.1

New York State statistical yearbook, general data, 1992 annual rpt, U5100–1.12

North Dakota oil production, 1982-91, annual rpt, S6162–1

Ohio natural gas and electricity supply-demand by utility and consuming sector, 1992-93 and trends, annual rpt, S6355–1

Oklahoma business activity indicators, monthly rpt, U8130–1

Oklahoma statistical abstract, general data, 1992 annual rpt, U8130–2.12

Pennsylvania energy supply-demand and prices by fuel type, with electric power info by utility, 1960s-90, recurring rpt, S6810–3

Tennessee statistical abstract, general data, 1992/93 annual rpt, U8710–2.5, U8710–2.10

Texas trade, transportation, and public utilities employment, by SIC 2- and 3-digit industry and detailed occupation, 2nd qtr 1991, triennial survey rpt, S7675–1.31

Utah economic and business activity review and indicators, monthly rpt, U8960–2

Utah statistical abstract, general data, 1993 triennial rpt, U8960–1.10

West Virginia oil and gas production, 1981-90, annual rpt, R9385–1.7

Wyoming oil production and taxable valuation, by county, and severance and ad valorem taxes, FY92 annual rpt, S8990–1.2

see also Asphalt and tar

see also Aviation fuels

see also Diesel fuel

see also Energy exploration and drilling

see also Fuel oil

see also Gasoline

see also Gasoline service stations

see also Kerosene

see also Liquefied petroleum gas

see also Motor fuels

see also Natural gas and gas industry

see also Offshore oil and gas

see also Oil and gas leases

see also Oil shale

see also Oil spills

see also Organization of Petroleum Exporting Countries

see also Petrochemicals

see also Petroleum exports and imports

see also Petroleum prices

see also Petroleum reserves

see also Petroleum stocks

see also Pipelines

see also Strategic Petroleum Reserve

see also Windfall profit tax

see also under By Industry in the "Index by Categories"

Petroleum conservation

see Energy conservation

Petroleum exports and imports

Coal industry executive views on oil import dependence, Aug 1992 survey, article, C5226–1.504

Petroleum exports and imports

Forecasts of natl income and product account components and related indicators, quarterly rpt, U1880–1

Imports and exports of oil, and refiner cost for imported crude oil, 1992 and trends, annual rpt, A5425–1

Imports of crude oil and refined products, by importing company, port, and country of origin, monthly rpt, A2575–12

Imports of oil into US, by country, 1960-91, recurring rpt, S6810–3

Intl energy sourcebook, with detail on oil and gas industry operations, supply-demand, and prices, for approx 80 countries, 1970s-91, annual compilation, C6985–10

Intl Petroleum Encyclopedia, basic data on oil and gas supply-demand, by country and company, 1993 annual rpt, C6985–3

Japan crude oil imports, weekly rpt quarterly table, R5650–2.506, R5650–2.519, R5650–2.541, R5650–2.558

Latin America statistical abstract, general data by country, 1992 annual rpt, U6250–1.23, U6250–1.25

Production, exploration, drilling, refining, stock, price, and financial data for US and foreign oil and gas industry, weekly rpt, C6985–1

Production, exploration, refining, demand, finance, prices, and reserves, by State and country or world area, 1993 and trends, periodic basic data book, A2575–14.3, A2575–14.4, A2575–14.7

Russia oil and gas production and exports, selected years 1990-2010, article, C6985–1.527

Russia oil exports to 8 former Soviet Republics, and oil and gas prices, 1993 article, U2030–1.511

Sourcebook of oil and gas industry operations and finances, and world supply-demand situation, 1970s-91, annual compilation, C6985–9

Statistical compilation of oil and gas industry trends, 1993 annual rpt, C6985–4

Supply-demand for crude oil and petroleum products, quarterly 1993, annual article, C4680–1.503

Supply-demand for oil and selected products, including by world area of origin, 1973-92, annual rpt, A5425 2.1

Supply-demand, marketing, prices, finances, and employment, detailed data for US and Canada, by product, company, and location, 1993 annual fact book, C4680–1.507

Supply-demand outlook and industry operations, with trends by country and producing State, 1970s-2010, annual rpt, C6985–5

Supply-demand, trade, and industry exploration and operations, by product, exporting country and world area, PAD district, and State, 1993 annual feature, C6985–1.513

Supply-demand, trade, and prices, with selected data by State, PAD district, and country, 1993 annual article, C6985–1.539

Supply, disposition, and stocks of refined oil products by type and/or crude oil, and refinery operations summary, monthly rpt, A2575–2

Index by Subjects and Names

Supply of oil and refined products, including stocks, refinery operations, and imports, by PAD district and product, weekly rpt, A2575–1

State and local:

Hawaii data book, general data, 1992 annual rpt, S2090–1.17

Petroleum prices

Airline fuel consumption and costs, by type of service, 1992, annual article, C7000–4.508

Airline fuel consumption and costs, monthly rpt, C7000–4

Crude oil prices in major producing States, 1992 and trends, annual rpt, A5425–1

Crude oil wellhead and import, No 2 fuel oil wholesale, and unleaded gasoline pump prices, 1976-92, annual feature, C6985–1.513

Electric utility oil deliveries and prices, monthly rpt, A7400–9

Income, production, and price data for selected oil companies, 1st 9 months 1991-92, article, C6985–1.511

Independent oil and gas company product production and prices, for approx 50 companies, 1991-92, semiannual article, C6985–1.504

Intl energy sourcebook, with detail on oil and gas industry operations, supply-demand, and prices, for approx 80 countries, 1970s-91, annual compilation, C6985–10

Intl Petroleum Encyclopedia, basic data on oil and gas supply-demand, exploration, refining, reserves, and industry finances, by country and company, 1993 annual rpt, C6985–3.4

Japan imported oil prices, and wholesale and consumer oil product price indexes, 1980-92, recurring article, R5650–2.536

Latin America statistical abstract, general data by country, 1992 annual rpt, U6250–1.25

Production, exploration, drilling, refining, stock, price, and financial data for US and foreign oil and gas industry, weekly rpt, C6985–1

Production, exploration, refining, demand, finance, prices, and reserves, by State and country or world area, 1992 and trends, periodic basic data book, A2575–14.3

Railroad fuel prices, 1982-91, annual rpt, A3275–8.2

Refined products and imported crude prices, 1991-93, article, C4680–1.502

Statistical compilation of oil and gas industry trends, 1993 annual rpt, C6985–4

Supply-demand and price data for energy resources, including by country and producing State, commodity yearbook for 1993, C2400–1

Supply-demand and price data for energy resources, including by country and producing State, commodity yearbook Jan-Sept 1993 updates, C2400–2

Supply-demand outlook and industry operations, with trends by country and producing State, 1970s-2010, annual rpt, C6985–5

Supply-demand, trade, and prices, with selected data by State, PAD district, and country, 1993 annual article, C6985–1.539

Trends in oil and refined product prices, 1973-92, annual rpt, A5425–2.2

Wellhead, import, spot market, retail, and wholesale prices, for oil, gas, and refined products, 1991 and trends, annual compilation, C6985–9.3

World crude oil and refined product prices, by product, country, and selected spot market, 1993 annual fact book, C4680–1.507

State and local:

Arizona economic analysts outlook for oil prices and mortgage interest rates, 1993 annual survey article, U0282–1.507

Oklahoma statistical abstract, general data, 1992 annual rpt, U8130–2.12

Pennsylvania energy supply-demand and prices by fuel type, with electric power info by utility, 1960s-90, recurring rpt, S6810–3

South Carolina statistical abstract, general data, 1993 annual rpt, S7125–1.8

Tennessee statistical abstract, general data, 1992/93 annual rpt, U8710–2.10

see also Gasoline

Petroleum reserves

Brazil offshore oil reserves by water depth, 1993 article, C6985–2.510

Canada, Newfoundland offshore oil and gas resources discovered, by field, 1993 article, C6985–1.552

Commonwealth of Independent States oil and gas production and reserves, for 7 Republics, 1991, article, C6985–1.510

Crude oil, natural gas, and gas liquids reserves and reserves/production ratios, 1973-92, annual rpt, A5425–2.1

Crude oil, natural gas, and gas liquids reserves, 1991-92, annual article, C6985–1.549

Cuba oil production and oil in place, by field, 1993 article, C6985–1.526

Gulf of Mexico offshore oil and gas production and reserves, 1970s-2000, annual article, C6985–2.503

Gulf of Mexico oil and gas fields, reserves, and production, by location and stratigraphic formation, 1991, article, C6985–1.508

Gulf of Mexico oil and gas reserves, 1960s-90, annual compilation, C6985–9.4

Intl energy sourcebook, with detail on oil and gas industry operations, supply-demand, and prices, for approx 80 countries, 1970s-91, annual compilation, C6985–10

Intl Petroleum Encyclopedia, basic data on oil and gas supply-demand, exploration, refining, reserves, and industry finances, by country and company, 1993 annual rpt, C6985–3

Latin America statistical abstract, general data by country, 1992 annual rpt, U6250–1.23

Middle East offshore oil and gas reserves and production, for 12 countries, 1992, article, C6985–2.505

New and total reserves of oil and gas, by State, 1992 and trends, annual rpt, A5425–1.1

North Sea oil and gas reserves planned for dev using floating production systems, by field, 1992 article, C6985–1.507

Norway offshore oil and gas fields under dev, with reserves and capital outlays, by field, 1993 article, C6985–1.523

Norway offshore reserves of oil, gas, and natural gas liquids, for 5 new fields, with operator and location, 1993 article, C6985–2.509

Norway petroleum resources by status, Feb 1993, article, C6985–2.506

Offshore oil/gas subsea reserves, wells completed, and expected production, by field in 5 world regions, for projects due onstream in 1993/94, article, C6985–2.507

Oil and gas industry trends, with data by company, State, and country, 1993 annual compilation, C6985–4

Production, exploration, refining, demand, finance, prices, and reserves, by State and country or world area, 1993 and trends, periodic basic data book, A2575–14.2, A2575–14.7

Production, reserves, and financial and operating data, for approx 20 major oil companies, 1991-92, annual article, C6985–1.533

Proved reserves of natural gas, coal, and oil, with detail by State, 1960s-91, annual rpt, A1775–3.1

Reserves of liquids and natural gas, rankings for top 300 US and top 100 non-US oil and gas companies, 1991-92, annual feature, C6985–1.547

Reserves remaining, and production and wells, for major fields by State and area, 1992, annual feature, C6985–1.513

Reserves remaining, and production and wells, for specific major oil fields, with comparisons to US totals, 1992 or Jan 1993, article, C6985–1.549

Russia oil field dev, reserves, and supply-demand data, with detail for Tyumen region, 1990s-2000, articles, C6985–1.540

Southeast Asia offshore oil/gas field reserves and production, for largest fields in operation/planned, 1992 article, C6985–2.501

Uzbekistan oil reserves by field, 1993 article, C6985–1.541

World crude oil reserves and production data, for OPEC vs non-OPEC, 1993 article, C6985–1.534

World crude oil reserves, by world area and country, 1982-92, annual fact book, C4680–1.507

World offshore oil and gas wells, reserves, and production, by country, 1990-93, annual article, C6985–2.508

World offshore oil/gas fields developed in past 15 years with reserves of 5-20 million barrels, by world area, 1993 article, C6985–2.509

World oil and gas production, prices, stocks, reserves, and consumption, by country, 1970s-92, annual rpt, C6985–5.1

World oil and gas reserves, by country and US State, 1940s-92, annual compilation, C6985–9.1

World oil reserves and production, by country, company, and field, 1992 annual feature, C6985–1.509

World oil reserves, by region, 1979-92, annual rpt, A5425–1.2

World oil/gas reserve additions and replacement costs, for selected countries and world areas, 1988-92, article, C6985–1.530

State and local:

New York State statistical yearbook, general data, 1992 annual rpt, U5100–1.12

see also Natural gas reserves

see also Strategic Petroleum Reserve

Petroleum stocks

Gasoline and oxygenates inventories, supply, and consumption, Oct 1992-Feb 1993, article, C6985–1.507

Japan energy supply-demand and outlook, by fuel source, 1980s-2000, recurring article, R5650–2.536

Marketing news and industry devs for oil industry, articles and special features, with data on gasoline prices and product stocks, monthly rpt, C4680–1

OECD oil and refined product stocks, by selected member country, 1970s-91, annual compilation, C6985–10.1

Production, exploration, drilling, refining, stock, price, and financial data for US and foreign oil and gas industry, weekly rpt, C6985–1

Production, exploration, refining, demand, finance, prices, and reserves, by State and country or world area, 1993 and trends, periodic basic data book, A2575–14.4

Refined products, crude oil, and natural gas stocks, 1983-93, annual feature, C6985–1.513

Statistical compilation of oil and gas industry trends, 1993 annual rpt, C6985–4

Supply-demand and price data for energy resources, including by country and producing State, commodity yearbook for 1993, C2400–1

Supply-demand and price data for energy resources, including by country and producing State, commodity yearbook Jan-Sept 1993 updates, C2400–2

Supply-demand for crude oil and petroleum products, quarterly 1993, annual article, C4680–1.503

Supply-demand, marketing, prices, finances, and employment, detailed data for US and Canada, by product, company, and location, 1993 annual fact book, C4680–1.507

Supply-demand, trade, and prices, with selected data by State, PAD district, and country, 1993 annual article, C6985–1.539

Supply, disposition, and stocks of refined oil products by type and/or crude oil, and refinery operations summary, monthly rpt, A2575–2

Supply of oil and refined products, including stocks, refinery operations, and imports, by PAD district and product, weekly rpt, A2575–1

World oil and gas production, prices, stocks, reserves, and consumption, by country, 1970s-92, annual rpt, C6985–5.1

World oil, gas, and refined product stocks, trade, and consumption, by country and world area, 1991 and trends, annual compilation, C6985–9.2

State and local:

Arkansas oil stocks at refineries and pipelines, monthly rpt, S0737–1

Pennsylvania electric utility year-end coal and petroleum stocks, 1970-90, recurring rpt, S6810–3

Petry Television

Syndicated TV program audience shares and ratings, by daypart and audience characteristics, Nov 1991-92, article, C9380–1.511

Syndicated TV program episodes available, by program, weekly rpt recurring table, C9380–1.511

Petrzelka, Peggy

"Cooperative Extension Services' Role in Business Incubator Educational Programs", U2410–3

Pets

see Animals

see Pet food and supplies

Pharmaceutical industry

Advertising direct-to-consumer spending by pharmaceutical industry, 1987-92, article, C2710–1.509

Advertising expenditures by medium for top 100 advertisers, with comparisons to earnings and sales, and detail by product type and brand, 1991-92, annual rpt, C2710–1.547

CEOs of drug companies income, public perceptions vs actual amounts, with detail for 3 leading firms, 1991-93, R4865–13

Chemical and related industries production, finances, operating ratios, employment, and trade, by country, company, and chemical, 1980s-92, annual feature, A1250–1.530

Corporate performance ratings by executives for leading companies in 32 industries, 1993 annual survey feature, C8900–1.508

Development projects for drugs to treat selected diseases in older adults and women, 1989-93, article, A1865–1.519

Earnings, sales, and profit margins, for chemical and allied industries, by company, weekly rpt quarterly article, A1250–1.502, A1250–1.514, A1250–1.525, A1250–1.536

Financial performance and growth rankings for approx 1,000 top corporations, with comparisons by industry group, 1993 annual rpt, C3950–1.505

Financial performance of 10 major companies, and sales of top 10 prescription drugs, 1993 article, C8900–1.514

Financial ratios and performance, for over 350 SIC 4-digit industries, FY88-92, annual rpt, A6400–3

HMO pharmaceutical cost containment methods, and pharmaceutical industry cost-related studies, 1993 article, A1865–1.517

Hospital use of formal program to control rising pharmaceutical costs, 1993 survey article, A1865–1.505

News and devs in retail and wholesale drug industry, with data on finances and operations, biweekly rpt, C5150–2

Operating and financial composite ratios for corporations, with establishments and receipts, for approx 200 industries, by asset size, FY90, annual rpt, C7800–1

Packaging demand for drug/pharmaceutical products, by package type, 1980, 1991, and 1996, article, C1850–1.503

R&D contracts between pharmaceutical companies and academic medical instns, with value, duration, and research area, for 11 major contracts, 1993 article, C2175–1.513

Pharmaceutical industry

Stock prices, yields, and earnings per share, for 8 pharmaceutical companies, July 1993, article, C3950–1.523

State and local:

Texas trade, transportation, and public utilities employment, by SIC 2- and 3-digit industry and detailed occupation, 2nd qtr 1991, triennial survey rpt, S7675–1.31

see also Biologic drug products
see also Drugs
see also Drugstores
see also Pharmacists and pharmacy

Pharmaceutical Manufacturers Assn

Drugs under dev for selected diseases affecting older adults and women, 1989-93, A1865–1.519

Pharmacists and pharmacy

- Consumer views on pharmacist requirements under 1990 Omnibus Budget Reconciliation Act (OBRA) to keep Medicaid patient drug use records and offer counseling, 1993 article, C5150–2.509
- Degree program applications, enrollment, and degrees conferred, by student characteristics and instn, 1990/91 and trends, annual rpt, A0630–9
- Discount stores with prescription depts, by region, 1986-91, annual article, C5150–3.502
- Drugstore and other retail outlet pharmacies and performance, with detail for top 24 chains, 1993 annual feature, C5150–2.511
- Financial and operating data for independent pharmacies, by store characteristics, 1991 and trends, annual survey, B5165–1
- Food store pharmacy staff training characteristics, by position and company size, 1992, annual rpt, A4950–5.4
- HMO benefits, enrollment and utilization, staffing, finances, and relations with employers, by plan characteristics, 1990-91, annual rpt, A5150–2
- Hospital pharmacist views on involvement in drug research activities, and impact of biotechnology drugs, 1993 survey, article, A1865–1.521
- Hospital pharmacy operating data, by instn type and size, and census div, 1991, annual survey, B5165–3
- Hospital recruiting of nurses and allied health personnel, with budget, vacancies, turnover, and compensation, 1993 and trends, annual survey rpt, A6500–1
- Intervention by pharmacists in problems with prescriptions and over-the-counter drug use, 1993 article, C5150–2.515
- Medical school faculty and compensation, by dept, academic rank, degree, and region, 1992/93, annual rpt, A3273–2
- Older patient prescription drug problems identified by pharmacists, and actions taken, Florida study, 1993 article, C5150–2.521
- Operating devs for pharmacies, including staffing plans, price scanning, and patient counseling, by store type, 1993 survey, article, C5150–2.518
- Public opinion on honesty/ethical standards of selected occupations, 1992 Gallup Polls and trends, C4040–1.501

Salaries of scientists, engineers, technicians, and other professionals, by employee and employer characteristics, 1990s and trends, biennial rpt, A3960–1

- Supermarket in-store pharmacies and sales, 1992, annual article, C4655–1.506
- Supermarket in-store prescription drug counter availability and shopper use, 1993 and trends, annual survey rpt, A4950–3
- Women and minorities in professional fields, detailed education and labor force data, 1991 and trends, recurring rpt, A3960–2.3

State and local:

- Florida county data book, 1992/93 annual rpt, C6360–1
- Florida health care atlas, including manpower by occupation and health care facilities by type, by district and county, 1992 annual rpt, S1746–1.2
- Florida statistical abstract, general data, 1992 annual rpt, U6660–1.20
- Hawaii data book, general data, 1992 annual rpt, S2090–1.2
- Maryland medical assistance payments and recipients, by program, type of service, location, demographic characteristics, and facility, FY92 and trends, annual rpt, S3635–3
- South Carolina statistical abstract, general data, 1993 annual rpt, S7125–1.10

see also Drugs
see also Drugstores

Philadelphia, Pa.

- Alarm system purchasing by businesses, including info sources used, 1991 suburban Philadelphia surveys, article, C1850–13.502
- Burglary (commercial) incidence correlated with alarm use and other precautions, 1989-91 suburban Philadelphia study, article, C1850–13.506
- Correctional instns, inmates, staff, and cost of care, by instn, US and Canada, with operating summary by State or Province, 1992, annual directory, A1305–3
- Court caseloads and dispositions in municipal courts, 1991 and trends, annual rpt, S6900–1.2
- CPI for NYC and Philadelphia metro areas, monthly rpt, S5425–1
- CPI for Philadelphia, monthly rpt, U4110–1
- Crimes and arrests, by offense and location, with law enforcement employment and assaults on officers, 1992, annual rpt, S6860–1
- Election results for Federal offices and Governor, by State, county, major city, and party, with voter registration and turnout, 1992 and trends, biennial rpt, C2500–1
- Residential building lot average price, 1987 and 1992, article, C1850–8.506
- Statistical abstract of Pennsylvania, detailed social, govtl, and economic data, 1992 recurring rpt, U4130–6

see also under By City in the "Index by Categories"

Philanthropy

see Gifts and private contributions
see Nonprofit organizations and foundations

Index by Subjects and Names

Philippine Americans

see Asian Americans

Philippines

- Birth outcomes by maternal characteristics, 1983/84 Cebu metro area study, article, A5160–6.505
- Electronics industry trade and/or production trends by product category for 33 countries, with general economic profiles, 1993 annual rpt, A4725–1.4
- Energy intl sourcebook, with detail on oil and gas industry operations, supply-demand, and prices, for approx 80 countries, 1970s-91, annual compilation, C6985–10.2
- Foreign direct investment inflow, intl aid, and trade with US and Japan, with GNP and comparisons to 7-8 other Asian countries, 1992 and trends, article, R5650–2.555
- Motor vehicle world production, sales, trade, and registrations, by country, world area, manufacturer, and make, 1991 and trends, annual rpt, A0865–2.1

Phillips, K. A.

"Primary Copper Industry of Arizona in 1991", S0497–1

Philosophy

see Arts and the humanities

Phoenix, Ariz.

- Business activity indicators, including housing market, population, and CPI, monthly rpt, U0280–1
- CPI for all urban consumers, monthly rpt, S0465–1
- CPI trends and forecasts, monthly rpt, U0282–1
- Economic condition, including employment and sales, by industry, 1985-93, semiannual rpt, U5850–1.2
- Home buyer (1st-time) distribution by housing price category, 1993 article, C1850–8.506
- Housing prices and appreciation rate, by community, 1981-92, annual article, U0280–1.506
- Housing sales and prices, appreciation rate, and affordability, by community, 1992, annual article, U0280–1.507

see also under By City in the "Index by Categories"

Phonograph

see Home video and audio equipment

Phonograph records

see Recording industry

Phosphate

- Capital spending plans for new mines and plants, by mineral and company, and mine production values, 1993 annual feature, C5226–2.503
- Fertilizer (phosphate) production distribution by type, and demand by world area, 1993 article, C5800–8.511
- Latin America statistical abstract, general data by country, 1992 annual rpt, U6250–1.23
- Production, consumption, stocks, trade, and prices for approx 100 basic commodities, including by country and producing State, commodity yearbook for 1993, C2400–1, C2400–2
- Production of phosphate rock worldwide, by country, 1987-91, article, C5226–2.504
- Supply-demand for selected metals and nonmetallic minerals, with price data, US and worldwide, 1992-93 and trends, annual feature, C5226–2.505

Index by Subjects and Names

Physical therapy

State and local:
Florida statistical abstract, general data, 1992 annual rpt, U6660–1.10

Photography and photographic equipment

- Camera unit sales, by camera type, 1987-91, article, C8130–1.505
- Canada photographic and video equipment and supplies ownership, purchasing patterns, and use, by household characteristics, 1992 survey, recurring rpt, A8695–4
- Consumer ownership, purchasing patterns, and use of photographic equipment and supplies, 1993 survey and trends, recurring rpt, A8695–2
- Convenience stores offering special services, including film processing, 1992 and trends, annual survey rpt, A6735–1, A6735–2
- Direct marketing industry devs, with consumer and business market characteristics, and media use patterns, 1992/93 annual rpt, A4620–1.4
- Discount chain consumer natl brand preferences, by product category and chain, and by age group, 1993 survey, annual feature, C5150–3.521
- Discount chain top-selling natl brands cited by managers, by product category, chain, and region, 1993 survey, annual feature, C5150–3.520
- Discount store sales and productivity data for 20 depts, 1993 annual feature, C5150–3.516
- Drugstore chain and brand preferences of consumers, with data by product type and region, 1992 annual survey feature, C5150–2.503
- Drugstore chains financial performance and marketing operations, with sales by product type, 1993 annual feature, C5150–2.510
- Financial performance and growth rankings for approx 1,000 top corporations, with comparisons by industry group, 1993 annual rpt, C3950–1.505
- Financial ratios and performance, for over 350 SIC 4-digit industries, FY88-92, annual rpt, A6400–3
- Japan exports of compact cameras, 1987-92, article, C2710–1.523
- Operating and financial composite ratios for corporations, with establishments and receipts, for approx 200 industries, by asset size, FY90, annual rpt, C7800–1
- Photofinishing market shares by outlet type, 1st qtr 1992-93, article, C8130–1.510
- Photofinishing market shares by outlet type, 1st qtr 1993, article, C5150–2.516
- Retail market value for photography-related business, by market segment, 1992, article, C5150–2.516
- Retail sales by outlet type, and discount chain sales in major depts, by product category, 1992, annual feature, C8130–1.507
- Sales and consumer expenditures, for food store products by type, 1991-92, annual feature, C4655–1.510
- Shopping center financial and operating data, with detail by type of tenant, US and Canada, 1991, triennial rpt, R9285–1
- Silver consumption by country and end use, 1993 annual rpt, A8902–4

Supermarket sales of nonfood products, by detailed product type, 1992, annual feature, C5225–1.508

PHS

see Public Health Service

Physical characteristics

see Body measurements

Physical education and training

State and local:

Connecticut public school data, including enrollment, staff, programs, finances, and student characteristics, 1991/92, biennial rpt, S1185–3

see also Health education

see also Physical exercise

see also Sports and athletics

Physical exercise

- Death rates for selected causes among exercising population, by sex, 1992 article, B6045–1.501
- Health condition and preventive health care and safety practices of adults, by respondent characteristics, 1992 and trends, annual survey rpt, C8111–2
- Heart disease risk factor prevalence, by State, 1989, semiannual rpt, B8500–1.9
- Older population physical activity levels and impact on health outcome in 2 local areas and 1 State, 1982 study, article, A2623–1.512
- Participation in 53 sports, by demographic characteristics, State, and census div, 1992, annual rpt series, A8485–3
- Video cassette unit sales, for sports and sports/fitness tapes, 1988-92, article, C8130–1.503
- Women's obesity and related activity and weight-loss indicators, by race, 1985-86, article, A2623–1.502

State and local:

- Alabama health behavior risk factor surveillance survey results, by respondent characteristics, 1988-89, recurring rpt, S0175–6
- California health behavior risk factor surveillance survey results, by respondent characteristics, 1991 and trends, annual rpt, S0865–2
- Colorado health behavior risk factor surveillance survey results, by respondent characteristics, 1990, recurring rpt, S1010–3
- Connecticut health behavior risk factor surveillance survey results, 1989-91, annual rpt, S1200–2
- Georgia health behavior risk factor surveillance survey results, by respondent characteristics, 1991 and trends, annual rpt, S1895–2
- Hawaii health behavior risk factor surveillance survey results, by respondent characteristics, 1990, annual rpt, S2065–1.4
- Iowa health behavior risk factor surveillance survey results, by respondent characteristics, 1991, annual rpt, S2795–2
- Kentucky health behavior risk factor surveillance survey results, by State area and respondent characteristics, 1988-90, annual rpt, S3140–6
- Massachusetts health behavior risk factor surveillance survey results, by respondent characteristics, 1986-90, recurring rpt, S3850–3
- Michigan health behavior risk factor surveillance survey results, by respondent characteristics, 1991, annual rpt, S4000–4
- Nevada health behavior risk factor surveillance survey results, by location and respondent characteristics, 1991, annual rpt, S5075–3
- New York State health behavior risk factor surveillance survey results, by respondent characteristics, 1990, recurring rpt, S5765–3
- North Dakota health behavior risk factor surveillance survey results, by respondent characteristics, 1991 and trends, annual rpt, S6105–3
- Pennsylvania health behavior risk factor surveillance survey results, by respondent characteristics, 1991, annual rpt, S6820–4
- Tennessee health behavior risk factor surveillance survey results, by respondent characteristics, 1986-90, annual rpt, S7520–3
- Texas health behavior risk factor surveillance survey results, by respondent characteristics, 1991 and trends, annual rpt, S7685–2
- Utah health behavior risk factor surveillance survey results, by respondent characteristics, 1991, annual rpt, S7835–3

see also Sports and athletics

Physical features

see Topography

Physical sciences

- Doctoral degree recipient characteristics, including citizenship status, source of support, field of study, and instn, 1990/91 and trends, annual rpt, R6000–7
- Higher education geoscience enrollment and degrees awarded, by sex, race-ethnicity, and discipline, 1991/92, annual rpt, A1785–3
- R&D spending in physical sciences by Federal and academic sectors, 1993 annual feature, A1250–1.537
- Salaries of scientists, engineers, technicians, and other professionals, by employee and employer characteristics, 1990s and trends, biennial rpt, A3960–1
- Women and minorities in professional fields, detailed education and labor force data, 1991 and trends, recurring rpt, A3960–2.3

see also Astronomy

see also Chemistry

see also Earth sciences

see also Environmental sciences

see also Mathematics

see also Oceanography

see also Physics

Physical therapy

- HMO benefits coverage, premiums, and rating methods used, by plan characteristics, 1991 and trends, annual rpt, A5150–2.1
- Hospital patient admission rates and length of stay, by diagnosis and procedure, payment source, age, sex, and region, 1991, B4455–4
- Hospital patient charges and length of stay, by diagnosis and procedure, payment source, age, and region, 1991, B4455–5

Physical therapy

Hospital recruiting of nurses and allied health personnel, with budget, vacancies, turnover, and compensation, 1993 and trends, annual survey rpt, A6500–1

Medical group financial and operating data, by practice characteristics, 1991, annual rpt, A6365–2

Women and minorities in professional fields, detailed education and labor force data, 1991 and trends, recurring rpt, A3960–2.3

State and local:

Florida county data book, 1992/93 annual rpt, C6360–1

Florida health care atlas, including manpower by occupation and health care facilities by type, by district and county, 1992 annual rpt, S1746–1.2

Florida statistical abstract, general data, 1992 annual rpt, U6660–1.20

Hawaii health dept family health services and recipients, including school health programs, 1990 annual rpt, S2065–1.5

Kentucky Medicaid recipients and payments, by program, county, and type of medical service, monthly rpt, S3140–5

Maryland medical assistance payments and recipients, by program, type of service, location, demographic characteristics, and facility, FY92 and trends, annual rpt, S3635–3

Montana home health service clients and visits by type of service, by agency, 1991, annual rpt, S4690–2

South Carolina statistical abstract, general data, 1993 annual rpt, S7125–1.10

Physically handicapped

see Blind

see Deaf

see Disabled and handicapped persons

Physician assistants

see Allied health personnel

Physician Executive Management Center

Hospital physician CEO personal and professional characteristics, 1993 article, A1865–1.513

Hospital vice president of medical affairs characteristics, responsibilities, and compensation trends, 1993 survey article, A1865–1.508

Physicians

Black American practices concerning physician care, with comparisons to whites, 1984 and 1990, annual compilation, C6775–2.2

Compensation and productivity of physicians in group practices, by speciality, and demographic and practice characteristics, 1991, annual rpt, A6365–1

Compensation of physicians, for 14 specialties, 1990-91, A1865–1.506

Compensation of physicians in group practices and HMOs, by speciality and region, 1992 survey and trends, annual rpt, B7450–2

Credit ratings and employment of 9 physician groups rated by Standard & Poors Corp, 1993 article, A1865–1.516

Economic aspects of physician medical practice, detailed data by specialty, 1991-92 and trends, annual compilation, A2200–5

Financial ratios and performance, for over 350 SIC 4-digit industries, FY88-92, annual rpt, A6400–3

General practice specialty choices of medical school grads, by school characteristics including Federal aid, and for top 20 schools (unnamed), 1993 articles, A2623–1.505

Genetics knowledge indicators for primary care physicians and genetics professionals, 1991, article, A3273–8.509

Group practice characteristics, including specialties, forms of organization, and location, 1991 and trends, recurring rpt, A2200–7

Group practice financial and operating data, by practice characteristics, 1991, annual rpt, A6365–2

Health care reform issues and/or options, views of physicians and general public, by respondent characteristics, Mar-Apr 1993 surveys, C8915–7.2

Health insurance coverage and finances, and health care costs and facilities, by selected demographic characteristics, 1940s-91, annual rpt, A5173–2

HMO staffing of primary care physicians, and compensation methods used, 1991, annual rpt, A5150–2.1

Hospital CEO views on relations between mgmt and medical staff, including effect of selected Medicare policies, 1992 survey, article, A1865–1.517

Hospital CEO views on trends in tension with medical staff, 1993 survey, article, A1865–1.513

Hospital emergency dept salaries for physician directors and staff, 1992-93, article, A1865–1.514

Hospital executive views on health care reform, including ability to address selected problems, and expected changes, 1993 survey, article, A1865–1.520

Hospital physician CEO personal and professional characteristics, 1993 article, A1865–1.513

Hospital primary care physician recruitment trends, and impact of Medicare payment scale on partnerships, 1993 survey article, A1865–1.508

Internal medicine specialty residency training and general practice selection, by sex, 1993 article, A3273–8.505

Internist performance ratings on selected criteria by nurses vs by other doctors, and views on use of ratings by nurses, 1993 article, A3273–8.510

Japan and US health care system data, including expenditures, facilities, insurance coverage, and population health indicators, 1993 article, R5650–2.515

Latin America statistical abstract, general data by country, 1992 annual rpt, U6250–1.7

Medical liability claims per 100 physicians by physician practice type, and Medicare participation by specialty and State, 1993 annual fact book, A1275–1.5

Medical school faculty and compensation, by dept, academic rank, degree, and region, 1992/93, annual rpt, A3273–2

Medical school faculty physician and allied personnel compensation and productivity, by academic rank, sex, and specialty, 1991, annual rpt, A6365–5

Mexico health care services use by US residents of border communities, as reported by physicians and patients, 1992 surveys, R4865–10

Index by Subjects and Names

Office visits to physicians, costs in approx 300 cities, quarterly rpt, A0150–1

Operating and financial composite ratios for corporations, with establishments and receipts, for approx 200 industries, by asset size, FY90, annual rpt, C7800–1

Patient visit volume forecast for HMOs vs indemnity insurance coverage, with detail by procedure, and industry or region, 1993 article, A1865–1.524

Pharmaceutical formularies used by managed health care organizations to contain costs, physician opinions, 1993 article, A1865–1.517

Public health school faculty characteristics, by instn, fall 1991, recurring rpt, A3372–1

Public opinion on health care issues, including govt and medical profession role, satisfaction with care and insurance, and reforms, 1975-92 surveys, A0610–1.504

Public opinion on honesty/ethical standards of selected occupations, 1992 Gallup Polls and trends, C4040–1.501

Resident specialty choices, matches, and attrition, for medical school grads by sex and race-ethnicity, errata, A3273–8.501

Rural vs nonrural area background and practice plans of medical school grads, with data by sex, 1993 article, A3273–8.505

Socioeconomically deprived area practice location and specialty certification plans of minority and nonminority medical school grads, 1982-92, article, A3273–8.507

Socioeconomically deprived area practice location plans of entering vs graduating medical students, 1987 and 1991, A3273–8.501

Specialty certification plans of medical school grads, 1985-92, article, A3273–8.501

State social, economic, and govtl indicators, with rankings, 1993 semiannual rpt, B8500–1.9

Statistical profiles of 50 States and DC, general data, 1993 annual almanac, C4712–1

Supply, finances, operative procedures, practice specialties, and education, surgeons and all physicians, 1993 annual fact book, A1275–1

Supply of general practice physicians and medical school grads, by specialty area, 1993 article, A3273–8.504

Supply of physicians, by detailed specialty and location, 1992 and trends, annual rpt, A2200–3

Supply of physicians by selected specialty, 1965, 1980, and 1990, article, A1865–1.513

Supply of physicians, by specialty, 1986, 1995, 2000, and 2020, article, A1865–1.511

Teaching hospital house staff stipends, benefits, and expenditures, by region and ownership, 1992/93 and trends, annual rpt, A3273–3

Utilization measures for hospitals and physicians under fee-for-service vs HMO care, 1992 rpt, R4865–9

Women and minorities in professional fields, detailed education and labor force data, 1991 and trends, recurring rpt, A3960–2.3

World population and health indicators, with detail by region and country, 1992/93 biennial rpt, R9455–1.5

State and local:

Alabama statistical abstract, general data, 1992 recurring rpt, U5680–2.8

Arizona statistical abstract, general data, 1993 recurring rpt, U5850–2.3

Arkansas human services dept finances and operations, including Medicaid payments by type of service, FY91 and trends, annual rpt, S0700–2.3

Colorado health care practices, including type of physician seen for last checkup, by sex, 1990, recurring rpt, S1010–3

Florida county data book, 1992/93 annual rpt, C6360–1

Florida physician supply by specialty, and shortages by population group or facility, by county, 1992 annual rpt, S1746–1.2

Florida statistical abstract, general data, 1992 annual rpt, U6660–1.20

Georgia county guide, general data, 1993 annual rpt, U6750–1

Georgia statistical abstract, general data, 1992-93 biennial rpt, U6730–1.1

Hawaii data book, general data, 1992 annual rpt, S2090–1.2

Indiana Medicaid expenditures, by service and provider type and county, FY91-92, annual rpt, S2623–1.6

Kansas statistical abstract, general data, 1991/92 annual rpt, U7095–2.2

Kentucky Medicaid recipients and payments, by program, county, and type of medical service, monthly rpt, S3140–5

Maryland medical assistance payments and recipients, by program, type of service, location, demographic characteristics, and facility, FY92 and trends, annual rpt, S3635–3

Maryland statistical abstract, general data, 1993-94 biennial rpt, S3605–1.2

Mississippi statistical abstract, general data, 1992 annual rpt, U3255–4.2

Missouri public welfare and medical assistance recipients, expenditures, and case processing, by program and county, FY92 and trends, annual rpt, S4575–2

Montana welfare and medical assistance program cases and payments, by county and type of service, monthly rpt, S4755–1

Nebraska Medicaid recipients and payments, by type of service and county, FY92, annual rpt, S4957–1.2

Nevada statistical abstract, general data, 1992 biennial rpt, S5005–1.2

New York State medical assistance expenditures, by State area and type of care, 1991 and trends, annual rpt, S5800–2.2

Oklahoma Medicaid payments, and expenditures for rehabilitative services, by type of service and county, FY92, annual rpt, S6455–1.2

Oklahoma statistical abstract, general data, 1992 annual rpt, U8130–2.9

Oregon caseload and payments for medical service by category, monthly rpt quarterly table, S6615–8

South Carolina statistical abstract, general data, 1993 annual rpt, S7125–1.10

South Dakota medical assistance recipients and payments, by type of service, program, and county, FY92, annual rpt, S7385–1

Tennessee statistical abstract, general data, 1992/93 annual rpt, U8710–2.17

Texas physician offices/clinics and expenditures, 1977, 1982, and 1987, U8850–8.3

Utah statistical abstract, general data, 1993 triennial rpt, U8960–1.2

Washington State public assistance clients and service costs, by client characteristics, program, and county, FY90, annual rpt, S8420–2

see also Anesthesiology

see also Coroners

see also Foreign medical graduates

see also Geriatrics

see also Medical ethics

see also Medical malpractice

see also Nuclear medicine and radiology

see also Obstetrics and gynecology

see also Orthopedics

see also Osteopathy

see also Pathology

see also Pediatrics

see also Psychiatry

see also Surgeons and surgery

Physics

Bachelor degree recipients postgraduation plans and demographic characteristics, 1991/92 and trends, annual survey, A1960–3

Employment status of physics and astronomy grads, by sex, age, subfield, degree, and employer type, with salary info, 1990/91, annual rpt, A1960–1

Enrollment and degrees awarded, by level, State, and instn, 1991/92-1992/93, annual rpt, A1960–2.2

Enrollment and degrees awarded, by type of instn and census div, 1991/92-1992/93 and trends, annual rpt, A1960–2.1

Salaries of scientists, engineers, technicians, and other professionals, by employee and employer characteristics, 1990s and trends, biennial rpt, A3960–1

Women and minorities in professional fields, detailed education and labor force data, 1991 and trends, recurring rpt, A3960–2.3

see also Weights and measures

Physiology

Medical school faculty and compensation, by dept, academic rank, degree, and region, 1992/93, annual rpt, A3273–2

Salaries of scientists, engineers, technicians, and other professionals, by employee and employer characteristics, 1990s and trends, biennial rpt, A3960–1

Pickup trucks

see Trucks and trucking industry

Pierce, Matthew D.

"State Initiatives to Establish Basic Health Insurance Plans", U8850–8.1

Piggyback freight

see Containerization

Pigments

see Chemicals and chemical industry

see Paints and varnishes

Pigs

see Livestock and livestock industry

Pilots

Airline employment summary, by position, 1982 and 1991-92, annual rpt, A0325–5

Airline pilots, and compensation per flight crew member, for 9 carriers, 1992, article, C5800–4.528

Certificates issued and held by pilots, and active pilots, 1993 annual rpt, A5120–2

Certified airmen, by type of license, 1987-91, annual rpt, A0250–2.3

Flight instructors and pilots, by FAA region and State, Dec 1992, annual rpt, A5120–2.2

State and local:

Hawaii data book, general data, 1992 annual rpt, S2090–1.18

Tennessee statistical abstract, general data, 1992/93 annual rpt, U8710–2.9

Pima County, Ariz.

Business activity indicators, including housing market, population, and CPI, monthly rpt, U0280–1

Employment, and production worker hours and earnings, by industry, monthly rpt, S0465–1

Labor force by employment status, and employment by industry div, 1992-94, annual feature, S0465–1.505

Pipelines

Accidents and failure rates for US and Canadian pipelines, and accident probability rates, 1993 article, C6985–1.537

Carbon dioxide pipelines in Texas/New Mexico Permian Basin region, with ownership, mileage, and throughput capacity, 1993 article, C6985–1.542

Commonwealth of Independent States oil and gas pipeline length, age, and failure rate with distribution by cause, 1993 article, C6985–1.527

Computer control and acquisition systems for pipelines/gas utilities, market shares for 8 leading and all other manufacturers, 1991, article, C6985–1.501

Construction activity and costs for pipelines, by location, item, and pipe diameter, 1993 annual rpt, C6985–3.3

Construction costs, mileage, and operating and financial data, by location and/or company, 1991 and trends, annual feature, C6985–1.504

Construction of gas and other pipeline facilities, and gas utility operations, articles and special features, monthly rpt, C6780–1

Construction of oil and gas pipelines, mileage planned or underway in 1993, for 5 world areas, Canada, and US, annual article, C6985–1.515

Construction of pipelines, by country and company, weekly rpt semiannual list, C6985–1.524, C6985–1.551

Construction projects planned in foreign countries, for oil, gas, and product pipelines, by company, 1994, annual feature, C6780–2.504

Construction projects planned in US, Canada, and other countries, by pipeline type and company, 1993 annual feature, C6780–2.502

Financial and operating data for top 500 gas distribution utilities and pipeline companies, 1992, annual article, C6780–1.505

Mexico oil and gas pipeline kilometers, by product type, 1991, article, C6985–1.542

Occupational injury, illness, and employment data, by function, for 136 oil/gas companies, 1991, annual rpt, A2575–4

Pipelines

Oil and gas industry trends, with data by company, State, and country, 1993 annual compilation, C6985–4

Oil and gas pipeline construction by world area, and US capital expenditures and interstate mileage, 1992 annual rpt, C6985–5.2

Oil and gas pipeline mileage and construction, and products transported, 1970s-91, annual compilation, C6985–9.4

Oil industry capital spending in US and Canada, by function, 1991-93, annual articles, C6985–1.517

Oil transported in US, by mode, and oil and gas pipeline mileage, 1991 and trends, periodic basic data book, A2575–14.5

Operating and financial composite ratios for corporations, with establishments and receipts, for approx 200 industries, by asset size, FY90, annual rpt, C7800–1

Polypropylene coated pipeline projects, and quality rankings of polypropylene vs other anti-corrosion coatings, 1992 article, C6985–1.507

Subsea pipeline projects, with length, product carried, and status, 1992-94, article, C6985–2.503

Trends in transportation operations and finances, by mode, 1991 annual rpt, R4815–1

Underground pipeline and utility construction industry intl devs, articles and special features, monthly rpt, C6780–2

Utility regulatory agency policies and practices, and industry financial and operating data, by utility type and agency, 1991/92 annual rpt, A7015–3

World pipeline construction mileage scheduled for 1993/beyond, by world area, 1993 annual rpt, C6985–3.3

State and local:

Alaska oil pipelines property value, revenues, and throughput, with detail by company, 1991 and trends, annual rpt, S0280–4

Arkansas oil and gas production by field, and disposition, monthly rpt, S0737–1

Colorado property assessed valuation, by property type and county, and for regulated industries by company, 1991-92, annual rpt, S1055–3

Montana public utility and transportation property assessments, by county and company, 1991-92, biennial rpt, S4750–1.2

Texas hazardous liquids pipelines and safety inspections, by region, FY92, annual rpt, S7745–1

Texas trade, transportation, and public utilities employment, by SIC 2- and 3-digit industry and detailed occupation, 2nd qtr 1991, triennial survey rpt, S7675–1.31

Washington State public service and utility companies property value, by company and county, 1992, annual rpt, S8415–1.4

Wyoming property assessed valuations and tax levies, by property type, tax purpose, and location, 1992 and trends, annual rpt, S8990–1.2

see also Natural gas pipelines

see also under By Industry in the "Index by Categories"

Pistols

see Firearms

Pittsburgh, Pa.

Court caseloads and dispositions in magistrate court, 1991, annual rpt, S6900–1.2

CPI for Pittsburgh, monthly rpt, U4110–1

Crimes and arrests, by offense and location, with law enforcement employment and assaults on officers, 1992, annual rpt, S6860–1

Statistical abstract of Pennsylvania, detailed social, govtl, and economic data, 1992 recurring rpt, U4130–6

see also under By City in the "Index by Categories"

Place of birth

see Birthplace

Planned parenthood

see Contraceptives

see Family planning

Planning

see City and town planning

see Economic policy

see Health planning and evaluation

see National plans and goals

Plants and equipment

see Business firms and establishments, number

see Capital investments

see Electric power plants and equipment

see Industrial plants and equipment

Plants and vegetation

Mangrove loss in selected tropical countries, 1992/93 biennial rpt, R9455–1.4

World plant taxa known and rare/threatened, and botanical gardens and membership in intl conservation organization, by country, 1991, biennial rpt, R9455–1.6

State and local:

Hawaii data book, general data, 1992 annual rpt, S2090–1.5, S2090–1.20

see also Farms and farmland

see also Flowers and nursery products

see also Forests and forestry

see also Horticulture

see also Pasture and rangeland

see also Vegetables and vegetable products

Plastic surgery

see Surgeons and surgery

Plastics and plastics industry

Appliance industry demand for plastics, by plastic and appliance type, 1987, 1992, and 1997, article, C2000–1.509

Canada-US bilateral plastics imports as percent of domestic demand, by selected resin, 1986 and 1992, article, A1250–1.525

Chemical and related industries production, finances, operating ratios, employment, and trade, by country, company, and chemical, 1980s-92, annual feature, A1250–1.530

Container (plastic) demand, by container type, 1980, 1991, and 1996, article, C1850–1.501

Employment, compensation practices, and union representation, in plastics processing industry, by region, 1992, annual survey rpt, A8920–2

Executive compensation and components, by industry div and major manufacturing group, 1991, annual rpt, R4105–19

Index by Subjects and Names

Financial and operating ratios for plastics processing industry, by processing activity, sales size, and region, 1992, annual rpt, A8920–4

Financial ratios and performance, for over 350 SIC 4-digit industries, FY88-92, annual rpt, A6400–3

Income, R&D expenditures, and stock performance, for 10 major plastics specialty materials manufacturers, 1992, article, C3950–1.511

Korea (South) petrochemical and thermoplastics production and foreign trade, with detail by trading partner, 1992 and trends, article, C5800–8.510

Motor vehicle industry materials consumption, by type, 1980-93, annual rpt, A0865–1.2

Motor vehicle plastic content average weight per car, selected years 1970-93, article, C2710–3.552

Natural gas utility industry plastic pipe used, by State, 1991, annual rpt, A1775–3.3

Operating and financial composite ratios for corporations, with establishments and receipts, for approx 200 industries, by asset size, FY90, annual rpt, C7800–1

Packaging (plastic) demand, by container type, 1980, 1991, and 1996, article, C1850–1.506

Packaging (plastic) recycling volume, by plastic type, 1985, 1991, and 1996, article, C1850–1.507

Polyethylene capacity additions, by company and plant, 1993-95, article, A1250–1.541

Polypropylene foreign trade balance, by world area, 1991 and 1995, article, C6985–1.533

Polystyrene sales volume, by end use, 1992, article, A1250–1.528

Production and sales by resin type, consumption by end-use market, and operating characteristics, 1992 and trends, annual rpt, A8920–1

Production, consumption, stocks, trade, and prices for approx 100 basic commodities, including by country and producing State, commodity yearbook for 1993, C2400–1, C2400–2

Production of plastics and other financial and operating data for chemical industry, 1970s-92, annual rpt, A3850–1

Production of plastics and synthetic fibers, by type, 1992 and trends, annual article, A1250–1.520

Production, sales/captive use, and trade, by resin type and/or use, monthly rpt, A8920–5

Production, trade, prices, and other plastics industry devs, monthly rpt, C5800–12

Recycling analysis, with data on sales and recycling volume, recovery costs, and collection methods, by resin or product type, 1990, A4375–14

Salaries for plastics processing industry managers, supervisors, salespersons, and engineers, by region, and related policies, 1992, biennial rpt, A8920–3

Sales of plastics and resin by material and major market, foreign trade, and capacity by company, 1991-92, annual feature, C5800–12.504

Thermoplastics consumption and demand outlook, with detail by consuming sector, 1980s-2000, article, A1250–1.538

Index by Subjects and Names — Plural births

Waste handling and recycling devs in US, Europe, and Japan, 1993 annual encyclopedia, C5800–12.503

Worldwide and US production and trade, selected data by country or world area, 1988-92, annual feature, A1250–1.507

see also Petrochemicals

Platinum

see Metals and metal industries

Plumbing and heating

- Eastern States housing units by primary heating fuel, for 14 New England and Middle Atlantic States, 1990, article, C4680–1.501
- Finances and operations for retail hardware stores, home centers, and lumber/building material outlets, 1991 and trends, annual rpt series, A8275–1
- Financial ratios and performance, for over 350 SIC 4-digit industries, FY88-92, annual rpt, A6400–3
- Fuel oil dealer heating and cooling equipment sales, installations, and service, by region, 1992 annual survey, C4680–2.2
- Heat pump/air conditioner shipments, by size, monthly press release, A0300–1
- Heating equipment and appliance shipments, by type of energy consumed, quarterly rpt, A1775–1
- Home heating devs in US and Canada, and shipments or installations of heating equipment by type, 1993 annual fact book, C4680–1.507
- Home heating equipment, shipments of gas units, and residences by type of heating system and region, 1970s-91, annual rpt, A1775–3.7
- Housing construction annual buyers guide, including data on material types or brands used most frequently by builders, by product category, 1993 feature, C4300–1.506
- Housing units by heating equipment and heating and cooking fuel used, 1950s-91, periodic basic data book, A2575–14.7
- Life expectancy, shipments, and manufacturers market shares, for appliances by type, 1993 annual article, C2000–1.510
- Office building detailed income and expense data, and energy use, US and Canada, by building characteristics, metro area, and US region, 1991 and trends, annual rpt, A5600–2
- Operating and financial composite ratios for corporations, with establishments and receipts, for approx 200 industries, by asset size, FY90, annual rpt, C7800–1
- Opinions of consumer hard goods manufacturers and representatives on business issues and outlook, by product line, 1992 annual survey rpt, A1800–1
- Piping system installation costs, by project characteristics, for 33 types of corrosion-resistant piping, 1993 article, C5800–8.503
- Shipments of gas, electric, and oil central heating equipment by type, monthly rpt, A5100–1
- Shipments of heating/cooling equipment, by product type, with industry review and outlook, 1992 and trends, annual rpt, C1800–1

Shipments of household appliances, by detailed product type, 1991-98, annual articles, C2000–1.503

Shipments of household appliances, by product type, with articles and special features on industry trends and devs, monthly rpt, C2000–1

Shipments of household equipment, by product type, 1983-92, annual feature, C2000–1.505

Shopping center detailed income and expense data, by building characteristics, metro area, and region, 1991, annual rpt, A5600–6

State and local:

- Alabama municipal data book, general data, 1992 recurring rpt, S0121–5
- Arizona statistical abstract, general data, 1993 recurring rpt, U5850–2.16
- Arkansas housing units plumbing facilities completeness, and heating fuels used, 1990, census rpt, U5935–7
- California housing units plumbing facilities completeness, and heating fuels used, 1990, census rpt, S0840–9
- Florida statistical abstract, general data, 1992 annual rpt, U6660–1.15
- Hawaii data book, general data, 1992 annual rpt, S2090–1.17
- Iowa heating fuels used in housing, 1990, annual rpt, S2784–3
- Kansas statistical abstract, general data, 1991/92 annual rpt, U7095–2.3
- Louisiana housing units by type of heating fuel used and local area, 1990, census rpt, U8010–4
- Maine housing units lacking complete plumbing facilities, and heating fuels used, by local area, 1990 census rpt, S3465–9
- Maryland statistical abstract, general data, 1993-94 biennial rpt, S3605–1.12
- New Jersey housing units plumbing facilities completeness, and heating fuels used, by county, 1990, census rpt, S5425–19
- New York State statistical yearbook, general data, 1992 annual rpt, U5100–1.9
- Pennsylvania and US housing units, by type of heating fuel used, 1970, 1980, and 1990, recurring rpt, S6810–3
- Pennsylvania housing units lacking complete plumbing facilities, by county and municipality, 1990, census rpt, C1595–14
- Pennsylvania housing units plumbing facilities completeness, and heating fuels used, 1990, census rpt, U4130–13
- Rhode Island housing units lacking complete plumbing facilities, and heating fuels used, by county and municipality, 1990 census rpt, S6930–9
- South Carolina statistical abstract, general data, 1993 annual rpt, S7125–1.8, S7125–1.11
- Washington State housing units by type of heating fuel used, by county, 1990, annual rpt, S8345–4

see also Air conditioning

see also Energy conservation

see also Fuel oil

see also Housing energy use

Plums and prunes

see Fruit and fruit products

Plural births

Hospital patient admission rates and length of stay, by diagnosis and procedure, payment source, age, sex, and region, 1991, B4455–4

State and local:

- Alabama vital statistics, including population, births, deaths by cause, marriages, and divorces, by location and demographic characteristics, 1992 and trends, annual rpt, S0175–2
- California vital statistics, including population, births, and deaths by cause, by demographic characteristics and county, 1990 and trends, annual rpt, S0865–1
- Colorado vital statistics, including population, deaths by cause, abortion, marriage and divorce, and adoption, by demographic characteristics and location, 1990 and trends, annual rpt, S1010–1
- Connecticut vital statistics, including births, deaths by cause, marriages, and divorces, by demographic characteristics and location, 1989, annual rpt, S1200–1
- Delaware vital statistics, including births, deaths by cause, and marriages and dissolutions, by demographic characteristics and location, 1990, annual rpt, S1385–2
- Florida vital statistics, including population, births, deaths by cause, and marriages and dissolutions, by location and demographic characteristics, 1992 and trends, annual rpt, S1745–3
- Hawaii vital statistics, including births, deaths by cause, marriages, and dissolutions, by demographic characteristics and location, 1990, annual rpt, S2065–1.2
- Iowa vital statistics, including population, births, deaths by cause, marriages, and divorces, by demographic characteristics and location, 1991 and trends, annual rpt, S2795–1
- Kansas fetal deaths by plurality, 1991, annual rpt, S2975–1
- Kentucky vital statistics, including births, deaths by cause, marriages and divorces, and population, by demographic characteristics and county, 1991, annual rpt, S3140–1
- Maryland vital statistics, including population, births, deaths by cause, marriages, and divorces, by demographic characteristics and location, 1989 and trends, annual rpt, S3635–1
- Massachusetts vital statistics, including births, deaths by cause, marriages, divorces, and population, by locality and demographic characteristics, 1990 and trends, annual rpt, S3850–1
- Michigan vital statistics, including births, deaths, marriages, divorces/annulments, and communicable diseases, by location and demographic characteristics, 1990 and trends, annual rpt, S4000–3
- Minnesota vital statistics, including population, births, abortions, deaths, marriages, and divorces, by location and demographic characteristics, 1991 and trends, annual rpt, S4190–2
- Missouri vital statistics, including population, births, deaths by cause, and marriages and divorces, by location and demographic characteristics, 1992 and trends, annual rpt, S4518–1
- Montana vital statistics, including births, deaths by cause, abortion, disease, and marriage and divorce, by demographic characteristics and county, 1990-91 and trends, annual rpt, S4690–1

Plural births

New Hampshire vital statistics, including population, births, deaths by cause, marriages, and divorces, by location and demographic characteristics, 1991 and trends, annual rpt, S5215–1

Ohio vital statistics, including births, deaths by cause, marriages, divorces, and population, by demographic characteristics and location, 1991 and trends, annual rpt, S6285–1

Rhode Island vital statistics, including population, births, deaths, marriages, and divorces, by demographic characteristics and locality, 1989 and trends, annual rpt, S6995–1

South Carolina fetal/neonatal deaths occurring in multiple pregnancies, 1990, annual rpt, S7175–2

Utah vital statistics, including births and deaths by cause, by demographic characteristics and location, 1990, annual rpt, S7835–1.2

Vermont vital statistics, including population, births, deaths by cause, abortions, marriages, and divorces, by location and demographic characteristics, 1991 and trends, annual rpt, S8054–1

Virginia vital statistics, including births, deaths by cause, marriages and divorces, and communicable disease, by demographic characteristics and location, 1991 and trends, annual rpt, S8225–1

Washington State vital statistics, including births, deaths by cause, and population, by demographic characteristics and location, 1991 and trends, annual rpt, S8363–1

Wisconsin vital statistics, including population, births, deaths by cause, and marriages and dissolutions, by county and demographic characteristics, 1991 and trends, annual rpt, S8715–4

Pneumonia and influenza

- Hospital patient admission rates and length of stay, by diagnosis and procedure, payment source, age, sex, and region, 1991, B4455–4
- Hospital patient charges and length of stay, by diagnosis and procedure, payment source, age, and region, 1991, B4455–5
- Hospital patient discharges and length of stay, by diagnosis, type of operation, age, and region, 1991, annual rpt series, B4455–1
- Hospital patient discharges and length of stay, by diagnostic related group (DRG), payment source, age, and region, 1991, annual rpt series, B4455–3

State and local:

- Alabama vital statistics, including population, births, deaths by cause, marriages, and divorces, by location and demographic characteristics, 1992 and trends, annual rpt, S0175–2
- Alaska vital statistics, including births, deaths by cause, marriages, divorces, adoptions, and population, by demographic characteristics and location, 1990, annual rpt, S0315–1
- Arkansas vital statistics, including births, deaths by cause, marriages, and divorces, by age, sex, race, and county, 1991 and trends, annual rpt, S0685–1
- California vital statistics, including population, births, and deaths by cause, by demographic characteristics and county, 1990 and trends, annual rpt, S0865–1

Colorado vital statistics, including population, births, deaths by cause, abortion, marriage and divorce, and adoption, by demographic characteristics and location, 1990 and trends, annual rpt, S1010–1

Connecticut vital statistics, including births, deaths by cause, marriages, and divorces, by demographic characteristics and location, 1989, annual rpt, S1200–1

Delaware vital statistics, including births, deaths by cause, and marriages and dissolutions, by demographic characteristics and location, 1990, annual rpt, S1385–2

Florida deaths by selected cause, and incidence of selected communicable diseases, by county, 1992 annual rpt, S1746–1.1

Florida vital statistics, including population, births, deaths by cause, and marriages and dissolutions, by location and demographic characteristics, 1992 and trends, annual rpt, S1745–3

Georgia vital statistics, including deaths by cause, demographic characteristics, and location, 1991 and trends, annual rpt, S1895–1.2

Hawaii vital statistics, including births, deaths by cause, marriages, and dissolutions, by demographic characteristics and location, 1990, annual rpt, S2065–1.2

Idaho vital statistics, including births, deaths by cause, abortions, marriages, and divorces, by demographic characteristics and county, 1991 and trends, annual rpt, S2250–2

Iowa vital statistics, including population, births, deaths by cause, marriages, and divorces, by demographic characteristics and location, 1991 and trends, annual rpt, S2795–1

Kansas vital statistics, including population, births, deaths by cause, abortions, marriages, and divorces, by demographic characteristics and location, 1991 and trends, annual rpt, S2975–1

Kentucky vital statistics, including births, deaths by cause, marriages and divorces, and population, by demographic characteristics and county, 1991, annual rpt, S3140–1

Louisiana vital statistics, including population, births, deaths by cause, reportable diseases, marriages, and divorces, by demographic characteristics and locality, 1989-90 and trends, annual rpt, S3295–1

Maine vital statistics, including births, deaths by cause, abortions, and marriages and divorces, by demographic characteristics and location, 1991 and trends, annual rpt, S3460–2

Maryland vital statistics, including population, births, deaths by cause, marriages, and divorces, by demographic characteristics and location, 1989 and trends, annual rpt, S3635–1

Massachusetts vital statistics, including births, deaths by cause, marriages, divorces, and population, by locality and demographic characteristics, 1990 and trends, annual rpt, S3850–1

Index by Subjects and Names

Michigan vital statistics, including births, deaths, marriages, divorces/annulments, and communicable diseases, by location and demographic characteristics, 1990 and trends, annual rpt, S4000–3

Minnesota vital statistics, including population, births, abortions, deaths, marriages, and divorces, by location and demographic characteristics, 1991 and trends, annual rpt, S4190–2

Mississippi vital statistics, including births, deaths by cause, marriages, and divorces, by demographic characteristics and location, 1992 and trends, annual rpt, S4350–1

Missouri vital statistics, including population, births, deaths by cause, and marriages and divorces, by location and demographic characteristics, 1992 and trends, annual rpt, S4518–1

Montana vital statistics, including births, deaths by cause, abortion, disease, and marriage and divorce, by demographic characteristics and county, 1990-91 and trends, annual rpt, S4690–1

Nebraska vital statistics, including births, deaths, marriages, divorces, and population, by demographic characteristics and location, 1991 and trends, annual rpt, S4885–1

Nevada vital statistics, including births, abortions, and deaths by cause, by county and demographic characteristics, 1989 and trends, annual rpt, S5075–1

New Hampshire vital statistics, including population, births, deaths by cause, marriages, and divorces, by location and demographic characteristics, 1991 and trends, annual rpt, S5215–1

New Jersey vital statistics, including births, deaths, population, communicable diseases, and marriages and divorces, by demographic characteristics and location, 1990 and trends, annual rpt, S5405–1

New Mexico vital statistics, including population, births, deaths, and disease, by location and demographic characteristics, 1991 and trends, annual rpt, S5605–1

New York State vital statistics, including population, births, deaths by cause, reportable diseases, and marriages and dissolutions, by demographic characteristics and/or location, 1990 and trends, annual rpt, S5765–1

North Carolina deaths and rates, by cause and county, 1991 and trends, annual rpt, S5927–1.2

North Dakota vital statistics, including births, deaths by cause, marriages and divorces, and abortions, by demographic characteristics and/or county, 1991 and trends, annual rpt, S6105–2

Ohio vital statistics, including births, deaths by cause, marriages, divorces, and population, by demographic characteristics and location, 1991 and trends, annual rpt, S6285–1

Oregon vital statistics, including births, deaths by cause, communicable diseases, marriages, and divorces, by age, sex, race-ethnicity, and county, 1991 and trends, annual rpt, S6615–5

Rhode Island vital statistics, including population, births, deaths, marriages, and divorces, by demographic characteristics and locality, 1989 and trends, annual rpt, S6995–1

South Carolina deaths, by detailed cause, age, sex, and race, 1990, annual rpt, S7175–2

South Carolina vital statistics, including births, deaths by cause, marriages, and divorces, by age, sex, race, and location, 1990 and trends, annual rpt, S7175–1

South Dakota vital statistics, including births, deaths, marriage and divorce, and communicable disease, by demographic characteristics and county, 1991 and trends, annual rpt, S7345–1

Tennessee vital statistics, including births, deaths by cause, marriages, divorces, and population, by demographic characteristics and location, 1991 and trends, annual rpt, S7520–2

Texas vital statistics, including births, deaths by cause, abortions, marriages, and divorces, by location and demographic characteristics, 1991 and trends, annual rpt, S7685–1

Utah vital statistics, including births, deaths by cause, and population, by county and demographic characteristics, 1990 and trends, annual rpt, S7835–1

Vermont vital statistics, including population, births, deaths by cause, abortions, marriages, and divorces, by location and demographic characteristics, 1991 and trends, annual rpt, S8054–1

Virginia vital statistics, including births, deaths by cause, marriages and divorces, and communicable disease, by demographic characteristics and location, 1991 and trends, annual rpt, S8225–1

Washington State vital statistics, including births, deaths by cause, and population, by demographic characteristics and location, 1991 and trends, annual rpt, S8363–1

West Virginia vital statistics, including births, deaths by cause, marriages, and divorces, by location and demographic characteristics, 1991 and trends, annual rpt, S8560–1

Wisconsin vital statistics, including population, births, deaths by cause, and marriages and dissolutions, by county and demographic characteristics, 1991 and trends, annual rpt, S8715–4

Wyoming vital statistics, including population, births, deaths by cause, marriages, and divorces, by demographic characteristics and county, 1991 and trends, annual rpt, S8920–2

see also under By Disease in the "Index by Categories"

Podiatry

HMO benefits coverage, premiums, and rating methods used, by plan characteristics, 1991 and trends, annual rpt, A5150–2.1

Women and minorities in professional fields, detailed education and labor force data, 1991 and trends, recurring rpt, A3960–2.3

State and local:

Florida health care atlas, including manpower by occupation and health care facilities by type, by district and county, 1992 annual rpt, S1746–1.2

Florida statistical abstract, general data, 1992 annual rpt, U6660–1.20

Indiana Medicaid expenditures, by service and provider type and county, FY91-92, annual rpt, S2623–1.6

Kentucky Medicaid recipients and payments, by program, county, and type of medical service, monthly rpt, S3140–5

Maryland medical assistance payments and recipients, by program, type of service, location, demographic characteristics, and facility, FY92 and trends, annual rpt, S3635–3

Missouri public welfare and medical assistance recipients, expenditures, and case processing, by program and county, FY92 and trends, annual rpt, S4575–2

Poisoning and drug reaction

Accidental deaths and disabling injuries, by detailed type, victim characteristics, circumstances, and location, 1992 and trends, annual rpt, A8375–2

Hospital patient discharges and length of stay, by diagnosis, type of operation, age, and region, 1991, annual rpt series, B4455–1

Hospital patient discharges and length of stay, by diagnostic related group (DRG), payment source, age, and region, 1991, annual rpt series, B4455–3

Occupational and environmental exposures to toxic substances reported to poison control centers, by type of exposure and substance, 1988, article, A2623–1.507

State and local:

Alabama vital statistics, including population, births, deaths by cause, marriages, and divorces, by location and demographic characteristics, 1992 and trends, annual rpt, S0175–2

Alaska vital statistics, including births, deaths by cause, marriages, divorces, adoptions, and population, by demographic characteristics and location, 1990, annual rpt, S0315–1

Arkansas vital statistics, including births, deaths by cause, marriages, and divorces, by age, sex, race, and county, 1991 and trends, annual rpt, S0685–1

California vital statistics, including population, births, and deaths by cause, by demographic characteristics and county, 1990 and trends, annual rpt, S0865–1

Colorado vital statistics, including population, births, deaths by cause, abortion, marriage and divorce, and adoption, by demographic characteristics and location, 1990 and trends, annual rpt, S1010–1

Delaware vital statistics, including births, deaths by cause, and marriages and dissolutions, by demographic characteristics and location, 1990, annual rpt, S1385–2

Florida vital statistics, including population, births, deaths by cause, and marriages and dissolutions, by location and demographic characteristics, 1992 and trends, annual rpt, S1745–3

Georgia vital statistics, including deaths by cause, demographic characteristics, and location, 1991 and trends, annual rpt, S1895–1.2

Hawaii vital statistics, including births, deaths by cause, marriages, and dissolutions, by demographic characteristics and location, 1990, annual rpt, S2065–1.2

Idaho vital statistics, including births, deaths by cause, abortions, marriages, and

divorces, by demographic characteristics and county, 1991 and trends, annual rpt, S2250–2

Iowa vital statistics, including population, births, deaths by cause, marriages, and divorces, by demographic characteristics and location, 1991 and trends, annual rpt, S2795–1

Kansas vital statistics, including population, births, deaths by cause, abortions, marriages, and divorces, by demographic characteristics and location, 1991 and trends, annual rpt, S2975–1

Louisiana vital statistics, including population, births, deaths by cause, reportable diseases, marriages, and divorces, by demographic characteristics and locality, 1989-90 and trends, annual rpt, S3295–1

Maine vital statistics, including births, deaths by cause, abortions, and marriages and divorces, by demographic characteristics and location, 1991 and trends, annual rpt, S3460–2

Maryland vital statistics, including population, births, deaths by cause, marriages, and divorces, by demographic characteristics and location, 1989 and trends, annual rpt, S3635–1

Massachusetts vital statistics, including births, deaths by cause, marriages, divorces, and population, by locality and demographic characteristics, 1990 and trends, annual rpt, S3850–1

Michigan vital statistics, including births, deaths, marriages, divorces/annulments, and communicable diseases, by location and demographic characteristics, 1990 and trends, annual rpt, S4000–3

Minnesota vital statistics, including population, births, abortions, deaths, marriages, and divorces, by location and demographic characteristics, 1991 and trends, annual rpt, S4190–2

Mississippi vital statistics, including births, deaths by cause, marriages, and divorces, by demographic characteristics and location, 1992 and trends, annual rpt, S4350–1

Missouri vital statistics, including population, births, deaths by cause, and marriages and divorces, by location and demographic characteristics, 1992 and trends, annual rpt, S4518–1

Montana vital statistics, including births, deaths by cause, abortion, disease, and marriage and divorce, by demographic characteristics and county, 1990-91 and trends, annual rpt, S4690–1

Nebraska vital statistics, including births, deaths, marriages, divorces, and population, by demographic characteristics and location, 1991 and trends, annual rpt, S4885–1

Nevada vital statistics, including births, abortions, and deaths by cause, by county and demographic characteristics, 1989 and trends, annual rpt, S5075–1

New Jersey vital statistics, including births, deaths, population, communicable diseases, and marriages and divorces, by demographic characteristics and location, 1990 and trends, annual rpt, S5405–1

Ohio vital statistics, including births, deaths by cause, marriages, divorces, and

Poisoning and drug reaction

population, by demographic characteristics and location, 1991 and trends, annual rpt, S6285–1

- Oregon vital statistics, including births, deaths by cause, communicable diseases, marriages, and divorces, by age, sex, race-ethnicity, and county, 1991 and trends, annual rpt, S6615–5
- Rhode Island vital statistics, including population, births, deaths, marriages, and divorces, by demographic characteristics and locality, 1989 and trends, annual rpt, S6995–1
- South Carolina deaths, by detailed cause, age, sex, and race, 1990, annual rpt, S7175–2
- South Carolina vital statistics, including births, deaths by cause, marriages, and divorces, by age, sex, race, and location, 1990 and trends, annual rpt, S7175–1
- Tennessee vital statistics, including births, deaths by cause, marriages, divorces, and population, by demographic characteristics and location, 1991 and trends, annual rpt, S7520–2
- Texas vital statistics, including births, deaths by cause, abortions, marriages, and divorces, by location and demographic characteristics, 1991 and trends, annual rpt, S7685–1
- Utah vital statistics, including births and deaths by cause, by demographic characteristics and location, 1990, annual rpt, S7835–1.2
- Vermont vital statistics, including population, births, deaths by cause, abortions, marriages, and divorces, by location and demographic characteristics, 1991 and trends, annual rpt, S8054–1
- Virginia vital statistics, including births, deaths by cause, marriages and divorces, and communicable disease, by demographic characteristics and location, 1991 and trends, annual rpt, S8225–1
- Washington State vital statistics, including births, deaths by cause, and population, by demographic characteristics and location, 1991 and trends, annual rpt, S8363–1
- West Virginia vital statistics, including births, deaths by cause, marriages, and divorces, by location and demographic characteristics, 1991 and trends, annual rpt, S8560–1
- Wisconsin vital statistics, including population, births, deaths by cause, and marriages and dissolutions, by county and demographic characteristics, 1991 and trends, annual rpt, S8715–4
- Wyoming vital statistics, including population, births, deaths by cause, marriages, and divorces, by demographic characteristics and county, 1991 and trends, annual rpt, S8920–2
- *see also* Food and waterborne diseases
- *see also* Lead poisoning and pollution
- *see also* Pesticides
- *see also* under By Disease in the "Index by Categories"

Poland

- Coal industry supply-demand, employment, and trade, by country, 1990-91 and trends, annual rpt, A7400–2.2
- Electronics industry trade and/or production trends by product category for 33 countries, with general economic profiles, 1993 annual rpt, A4725–1.4

Energy and economic savings potential for 8 conservation measures, 2005, biennial rpt, R9455–1.1

- Energy intl sourcebook, with detail on oil and gas industry operations, supply-demand, and prices, for approx 80 countries, 1970s-91, annual compilation, C6985–10.2
- Entertainment industry devs, including film production, theater screens, TV homes, and VCR penetration, 1993 feature, C9380–1.536
- Motor vehicle world production, sales, trade, and registrations, by country, world area, manufacturer, and make, 1991 and trends, annual rpt, A0865–2.1
- Public opinion in 9 European countries and 3 Soviet Union Republics on political, economic, and social issues, 1991 survey, C8915–8
- Public opinion on role of church, in Western Europe, Hungary, and Poland, 1990 surveys, R8780–1.502

Police

- Eastern Europe public opinion on selected govt and societal instns, for 6 countries and 3 Soviet Union Republics, 1991 survey, C8915–8.2
- Elementary/secondary teacher support for using additional police in high-crime areas near schools, Jan-Feb 1993 survey, B6045–7
- Employment, compensation, hours, and expenditures of police and fire depts, by census div, city, and city size, 1992, annual rpt, A5800–1.3
- Liability lawsuits against local govt due to police actions, with claim and settlement amounts, and legal costs, 1990/91 survey, A5800–2.113
- Local govt expenditures by function and type of govt unit, and for 52 largest cities, 1993 annual rpt, R9050–1.6
- Motor vehicle fleet operating and financial data, including fleets by type, registrations by make and model, and top lessors, 1970s-93, annual rpt, C1575–2.507
- Municipal govts experience with police collective bargaining, including negotiator, methods, 3rd-party interference, and union tactics, by region, 1992, A5800–1.1
- Municipal police personnel salaries, by position and city, 1992, recurring rpt, A5800–4.32
- Public confidence in selected societal instns, 1993 Gallup Poll and trends, C4040–1.510, R8780–1.508
- Public opinion on honesty/ethical standards of selected occupations, 1992 Gallup Polls and trends, C4040–1.501
- Public opinion on news items concerning 2nd Rodney King police brutality trial and Los Angeles riots after 1st trial, by race-ethnicity, Apr/May 1993 survey, C8915–1.503
- Public opinion on police officer prosecution and job performance, Feb 1993 Gallup Poll, C4040–1.508
- Pursuits by police, traffic safety magazine reader views, Jan/Feb 1993 survey, article, A8375–1.504
- Shopping center security operations, including sharing of crime info with police, and use of on- and off-duty officers, by center type, 1993, articles, C5150–4.506

Index by Subjects and Names

- State social, economic, and govtl indicators, with rankings, 1993 semiannual rpt, B8500–1.10
- Traffic accident rates, fleets, and vehicles, 1992 and trends, annual rpt, A8375–2.3
- Traffic court litigant satisfaction with police treatment, and officers scheduled to appear in court, for 3-12 urban jurisdictions, 1990, R6600–5
- TV news coverage of Los Angeles riots following Rodney King police brutality case verdict, with source characteristics, and detail by network, Apr-May 1992, article, R3823–1.506
- TV news coverage of Rodney King police brutality case, with reporter and source characteristics, and detail by network, Mar 1991-Apr 1992, article, R3823–1.505

State and local:

- Alabama crimes and arrests, by offense and location, with data on law enforcement employment and assaults on officers, 1992 and trends, annual rpt, S0119–1
- Alabama statistical abstract, general data, 1992 recurring rpt, U5680–2.10
- Alaska police compared to population, by city and judicial district, FY92, annual rpt, S0290–1
- Arizona law enforcement employment by sex, by local agency, Oct 1992, annual rpt, S0505–2.2
- Arkansas crimes and arrests, and law enforcement personnel by sex, by agency and county, 1992, annual rpt, S0652–1
- California criminal justice system expenditures and employment, and citizen complaints against officers, 1987-92, annual rpt, S0910–1.2
- California criminal justice system expenditures and employment, by type of agency or function, 1982-91, annual rpt, S0910–2.1
- California socioeconomic and govtl data for municipalities, counties, and school districts, 1993 annual rpt, C4712–3
- Connecticut crimes and arrests, and law enforcement employment by sex, 1992, annual rpt, S1256–1
- DC police misconduct complaints received, FY91, annual rpt, S1535–3.8
- Florida municipal and county statistical profiles, general data, 1991 annual rpt, C4712–6
- Hawaii data book, general data, 1992 annual rpt, S2090–1.4
- Idaho crimes and arrests, law enforcement employees by sex, and assaults on officers, by local agency and county, 1992, annual rpt, S2275–2
- Illinois crimes and arrests, by offense, with data by location and offender characteristics, 1991, annual rpt, S2536–1
- Kansas law enforcement employees by demographic characteristics and local agency, with assaults on police by circumstance, 1992, annual rpt, S2925–1.2
- Kentucky crimes and arrests, law enforcement employment, and assaults on police, 1992, annual rpt, S3150–1
- Maine crimes reported, law enforcement employment, and assaults on officers, by reporting agency and/or county, 1991, annual rpt, S3475–1.2

Index by Subjects and Names — Political broadcasting

Maryland law enforcement employment by sex, criminal offenses and arrests, and assaults on police, by local agency and county, 1991-92, annual rpt, S3665–1

Maryland local govt financial condition, including revenues by source, expenditures by function, and debt obligations, FY92 and trends, annual rpt, S3618–1.1

Massachusetts municipal and county profiles, general data, 1992 annual rpt, C4712–2

Michigan crimes and arrests, by offense, with officers killed by dept type, 1992 and trends, annual rpt, S3997–1

Mississippi statistical abstract, general data, 1992 annual rpt, U3255–4.9

Missouri crimes and arrests, by offense and location, with victim and offender characteristics, 1991 and trends, annual rpt, S4560–2

New Jersey crimes and arrests, law enforcement employment, and assaults on officers, 1992 and trends, annual rpt, S5430–1

New Jersey municipal and county data book, general data, 1992 annual rpt, C4712–4

New York State crimes and arrests by offense and demographic characteristics, and court activity and corrections, 1991 and trends, annual rpt, S5760–3

New York State municipal and county statistical profiles, general data, 1993 annual rpt, C4712–7

North Carolina law enforcement employment by local agency and sex, and assaults on police, 1991-92, annual rpt, S5955–1

North Dakota crimes and arrests, by offense, location, and offender characteristics, and law enforcement employment, 1991 and trends, annual rpt, S6060–1

Oklahoma criminal offenses, by law enforcement agency, police employment by sex, and assaults on officers, 1990-92, annual rpt, S6465–1.2

Oregon crimes by offense, law enforcement employees by sex, and assaults on police, by local agency, 1992 and trends, annual rpt, S6603–3.2

Pennsylvania crimes and arrests, by offense, location, and offender characteristics, with law enforcement employment, 1992 and trends, annual rpt, S6860–1

Texas crimes and arrests, law enforcement employment, and assaults on officers, with data by reporting agency, 1992, annual rpt, S7735–2.2

Utah law enforcement employment, by county and local agency, 1992, annual rpt, S7890–3

Virginia crimes and arrests by offense, and law enforcement employment, by location and reporting agency, 1992, annual rpt, S8295–2.2

Washington State crimes and clearances, and law enforcement employment, by reporting agency, 1992, annual rpt, S8440–1

West Virginia crimes and arrests by offense, agency type, and county, with data on law enforcement employment and assaults on officers, 1990-91, annual rpt, S8610–1

Wisconsin crimes and arrests, by offense, offender characteristics, county, and local agency, 1992 and trends, annual rpt, S8771–1

Wisconsin traffic accidents, including citations issued and police response times, 1992, annual rpt, S8815–1

Wyoming crimes and arrests, and law enforcement personnel, by jurisdiction, 1991, annual rpt, S8867–3

see also Assaults on police

see also Detective and protective services

see also Federal aid to law enforcement

see also Law enforcement

see also Sheriffs

see also State police

Political action committees

Chambers of commerce income, salaries and benefits, membership, staff, and operations, 1993 annual rpt, A3840–3

Congressional campaign finances, with detailed data for individual Members, and leading contributors by type and industry, 1990 election and trends, biennial rpt, R3828–2, R3828–3

Congressional campaign fund finances, with expenditures by item and contributions by donor type, by candidate, district, and State, 1990 elections, C2500–6

Hispanic American Congress Members campaign contributions from PACs, and contribution activity of leading Hispanic PACs, 1993 article, C4575–1.511

Racial/ethnic minority chairpersons of House committees, funds received from PACs, 1992, article, C4215–1.510

Restaurant industry PAC contributions to 14 congressional campaigns, with election outcome, 1992, article, C1200–5.502

Restaurant State assn staff, payroll, locations represented, and political action committee spending, for organizations in 14 States, 1993 article, C1200–5.510

Women's PACs funds raised and candidates supported, for 42 organizations, 1992, U4510–4.4

Political attitudes and ideology

Australia husbands and wives political attitudes as affected by social background of self and spouse, 1992 article, A0610–1.501

College freshmen attitudes and characteristics, degree and career plans, and financial aid sources, by sex and instn type, fall 1992, annual survey, U6215–1

Congressional Member views on legislative priorities, Federal deficit, and tax increases, by political party, Dec 1992 survey, article, C8900–1.507

Congressional Member views on seriousness of 18 public policy issues, 1993 survey feature, C4300–1.506

Congressional voting support for measures favored by Americans for Democratic Action and American Conservative Union, by Member, 1991, annual rpt, C2500–2

Conservative coalition voting patterns in House and Senate, and partisan votes cast, 1969-92, annual rpt, C2500–2

Eastern Europe public opinion on political and economic reforms, for 9 countries and 3 Soviet Union Republics, 1991 survey, C8915–8.2

Elementary/secondary school superintendents personal and professional characteristics and views, 1992 survey rpt, A0775–5

Estonia, Tallinn public political opinions during Aug 1991 Soviet coup attempt, for Estonian vs Russian-speaking residents, article, A0610–1.501

Europe public opinion on political, economic, and social issues of interest to foreign investors, for 9 countries and 3 Soviet Union Republics, 1991 survey, C8915–9

Gallup Poll public attitude surveys, results and sample characteristics, monthly rpt, C4040–1

Gender comparisons of voting patterns, party affiliation, presidential performance ratings, and opinions on issues, 1950s-92, U4510–1.65

Hard goods manufacturers and representatives views on selected public policy issues, by product line, 1993 annual survey rpt, A1800–1

Health care specialist and health-related company CEO income, public perceptions by political ideology, 1991-93, R4865–13

Hispanic American leaders views on current issues of importance to Hispanic community, 1993 annual survey article, C4575–1.511

Presidential election voting patterns of moderate and conservative Democrats and Independents, 1976-92, article, A8510–1.1

Public opinion on Clinton Admin policies and actions, by respondent characteristics, series, C8915–7

Public opinion on issues concerning politics and the press, by respondent characteristics, series, C8915–4

Public opinion on performance of Congress and own Representative, 1970-92 surveys, A0610–1.501

Public opinion on social, political, and economic issues, detailed data, 1972-91 surveys, annual rpt, U6395–1

Public vs party leaders political views, analysis of attitudinal constraints and stability, 1992 article, A0610–1.501

Soviet Union political and economic restructuring issues, public opinion in Russia, Ukraine, and Lithuania, 1991-92 surveys, C8915–10

Venezuela business and govt leader views on presidential power, 1987, U6250–1.22

Political broadcasting

Public opinion on campaign ads influence in 1992 presidential election, by candidate, Oct 1992 survey, article, C2710–1.501

Public opinion on helpfulness of televised debates and campaign ads in 1992 presidential election, Nov 1992 survey, C8915–4.24

Public opinion on televised debates in 1992 presidential campaign, Oct 1992 Gallup Polls, C4040–1.504

TV local and network political advertising expenditures, biennially 1980-92, article, C1850–14.502

TV programming hours pre-empted by paid political ads and election-night coverage, by network, Nov 1992, article, C9380–1.512

Political campaign funds

Political campaign funds
see Campaign funds
Political candidates
see Elections
Political conventions
Presidential candidate support before vs after natl political conventions, 1960-92 election years, C4040–1.502
Public opinion on 1992 presidential candidates, impact of Democratic natl convention, July 1992 Gallup Poll, C4040–1.501
State and local:
West Virginia primary election of delegates to the Democratic and Republican Natl conventions, 1992, biennial rpt, S8630–1
Political ethics
House of Representatives Members cited for abuse of House Bank privileges, including value of largest overdrafts, and reelection status, 1988-92, annual rpt, C2500–2
Municipal govt ethics policies and concerns, views of personnel directors, 1992 survey, A5800–1.1
Public interest in news items on embezzlement charges against Congressman Dan Rostenkowski, July/Aug 1993 survey, C8915–1.504
Senator honoraria amounts kept by 67 Senators, 1990-91, annual rpt, C2500–2
see also Corruption and bribery
see also Lobbying and lobbying groups
Political parties
Congressional campaign finances, including political party expenditures on top 50 candidates and payments to consultants by type, 1990 elections, C2500–6
Congressional campaign finances, with detailed data for individual Members, and leading contributors by type and industry, 1990 election and trends, biennial rpt, R3828–2
Congressional Member views on legislative priorities, Federal deficit, and tax increases, by political party, Dec 1992 survey, article, C8900–1.507
Conservative coalition voting patterns in House and Senate, and partisan votes cast, 1969-92, annual rpt, C2500–2
Election results for Federal offices and Governor, by State, county, major city, and party, with voter registration and turnout, 1992 and trends, biennial rpt, C2500–1
Europe public opinion on political, economic, and social issues, for 9 countries and 3 Soviet Union Republics, 1991 survey, C8915–8
Hispanic American Congress Members contributions from political action committees (PACs), and contribution activity of leading Hispanic PACs, 1993 article, C4575–1.511
Hispanic American elected officials by office and State, with related population characteristics, 1992 annual directory, A6844–1
House of Representatives staff characteristics, salaries, and benefits by position, 1992 and trends, recurring rpt, R4140–1
Japan Diet Lower House political party composition, 1993 article, R5650–2.544, R5650–2.545

Japan Diet Upper and Lower House political party composition, Aug 1993 and trends, article, R5650–2.551
Japan Diet Upper and Lower House political party composition, Aug 1993, article, R5650–2.547
Latin America statistical abstract, general data by country, 1992 annual rpt, U6250–1.9
News events followed most closely by public, and opinion on media coverage and selected current issues, by respondent characteristics, recurring rpt, C8915–1
Public opinion on Clinton Admin policies and actions, by respondent political party affiliation, series, C8915–7
Public opinion on most important natl issues, views of leaders/experts by political party, 1992 series, R8825–10
Public opinion on party best able to handle major problems, 1992-93 Gallup Polls and trends, C4040–1.507
Public opinion on party perceived better for peace and prosperity, 1992 Gallup Polls and trends, C4040–1.501, C4040–1.504
Public opinion on party perceived better for prosperity, 1993 Gallup Polls and trends, C4040–1.509
Public opinion on relative importance of changing political control of presidency vs Congress, Aug 1992 Gallup Poll, C4040–1.502
Public opinion on Republican vs Democratic parties, May 1993 survey and trends, C8915–7.3
Public political party affiliation, by sex, 1983-92, U4510–1.65
Public political party affiliation, 1992 Gallup Polls and trends, C4040–1.501
State and local:
Arizona statistical abstract, general data, 1993 recurring rpt, U5850–2.11
California election results, and voter registration and turnout, by district and/or county, 1992 and trends, biennial rpt, S0934–1
Colorado election results and voter registration, by political party, and county and/or district, 1992, biennial rpt, S1090–1
DC election results and turnout, and voter registration, by ward and precinct, 1992, biennial series, S1525–1
Hawaii data book, general data, 1992 annual rpt, S2090–1.8
Illinois election results, and voter registration trends, by county and/or district, 1992 general election, biennial rpt, S2445–1
Kansas election results and voter registration, by party and county, 1992 primary and general elections, biennial rpt, S3030–1
Massachusetts election results and voter registration, by local area, 1992 and trends, biennial rpt, S3920–1
Mississippi statistical abstract, general data, 1992 annual rpt, U3255–4.13
Nebraska election results, and voter registration by party, by county and/or district, 1992 general and primary elections, biennial rpt, S4955–1
New Hampshire election results, by county and locality, 1992, biennial rpt, S5255–1

New Mexico election results, and voter registration by party, by location, 1992 general election, biennial rpt, S5655–1
North Carolina election results, with voter registration by party and race-ethnicity, by county, 1992, biennial rpt, S5920–1
North Dakota election results and historical trends, including data on ballot measures and detail by location, 1880s-1992, biennial rpt, U8080–1
Ohio election results and voter registration, by local area, 1991-92 and trends, biennial rpt, S6380–1
Oklahoma voter registration by party, by county, Nov 1992, biennial rpt, S6425–1
Oregon election results and voter registration and turnout, by county and/or district, 1992 general election, biennial rpt, S6665–1
Pennsylvania statistical abstract, general data, 1992 recurring rpt, U4130–6.6
South Dakota election results, and voter registration by party, by county, 1992 general election, biennial rpt, S7390–1
Utah election historical results, legislature membership, and income tax return checkoff contributions, by party, 1993 triennial rpt, U8960–1.8
Virginia income tax return checkoff contributions to political parties and other programs, 1990, annual rpt, S8305–1.1
West Virginia election results and voter registration, by county and party, 1992 and trends, biennial rpt, S8630–1
Wisconsin Blue Book, general data, 1993-94 biennial rpt, S8780–1.1
see also Communist parties
see also Democratic Party
see also Political conventions
see also Republican Party
Political rights
see Civil rights
Political science
Higher education dept characteristics, including faculty, salaries, enrollment, and finances, 1991/92 annual rpt, A2617–1
Salaries of scientists, engineers, technicians, and other professionals, by employee and employer characteristics, 1990s and trends, biennial rpt, A3960–1
Women and minorities in professional fields, detailed education and labor force data, 1991 and trends, recurring rpt, A3960–2.3

Polls
see Elections
see Opinion and attitude surveys
see Political attitudes and ideology
Pollution
see Air pollution
see Environmental pollution and control
see Global climate change
see Marine pollution
see Noise
see Radiation
see Soil pollution
see Water pollution
Poor
see Poverty
Popcorn
see Corn
Population census
see Census of Population and Housing

Index by Subjects and Names

Population characteristics

Asia and Pacific countries population characteristics, series, R4500–1

Black American socioeconomic status, including employment, income, education, and political data, 1993 annual compilation, A8510–1

Black American socioeconomic status, including health, education, politics, crime, and employment, with comparisons to whites, 1993 annual compilation, C6775–2

Child health and well-being indicators, with selected household characteristics, by State, 1993 annual rpt, R3832–1

Child well-being indicators based on social, economic, and environmental factors, for 239 MSAs, with detail by component county and city, 1980s-90s, R9700–2

China and US socioeconomic and infrastructure indicators comparison, 1993 rpt, R4105–82.8

China population characteristics for 6 Provinces, including urban-rural residence, minority shares, women's education, and living standard, 1987, article, A5160–6.502

Consumer buying power survey of population, income, and sales by product line, by State, metro area, county, and census div, 1993 annual rpt, C1200–1.514

Direct marketing industry devs, with consumer and business market characteristics, and media use patterns, 1992/93 annual rpt, A4620–1.4

Distilled spirits consumption, and consumer characteristics and buying habits, 1992 and trends, annual rpt, C4775–1.3

Germany reunification issues for internatl investment, with data on population and employment, consumption, and infrastructure improvement, 1991 rpt, R4105–82.3

Hispanic American marketing devs, including leading advertisers and media, and market characteristics, 1992 annual features, C4575–1.502

Hispanic American population by country of ethnic origin, 1990, article, C4575–1.511

Hispanic American socioeconomic status, including education, politics, income, and employment, with comparisons to whites, 1993 annual compilation, C6775–3

Home buyer (1st-time) median age, 1984-92, article, A7000–1.503

Latin America statistical abstract, 1992 annual rpt, U6250–1

Low-income families and children, health and welfare indicators, with data by State and city, 1992 annual rpt, R3840–11

Market area population and characteristics, households, income, and retail outlets, for 21 leading areas, 1993 feature, C2710–1.538

Mexico-US border area socioeconomic indicators, 1980s and trends, U6250–1.20

Population size and selected characteristics, by region, census div, and State, 1991 and trends, annual data sheet, R8750–9

State social, economic, and govtl indicators, with rankings, 1993 semiannual rpt, B8500–1

State statistical profiles, detailed social, economic, and govtl data for 50 States and DC, 1993 annual almanac, C4712–1

Wine and other alcoholic beverage consumption, and consumer characteristics and buying habits, 1993 annual rpt, C4775–2.2

World demographic topics, series, R8750–2

State and local:

Alabama population size and characteristics, series, U0340–1

Alabama statistical abstract, general data, 1992 recurring rpt, U5680–2

Alaska, Denali Borough population characteristics and income, with detail by local area, 1990-91, article, S0320–1.509

Alaska, Juneau population socioeconomic characteristics, 1990, article, S0320–1.512

Alaska, Northwest Arctic Borough population characteristics and income, with detail by local area, 1990, article, S0320–1.512

Alaska population, housing, income, and education data, by demographic characteristics and/or locality, 1990/91 and trends, annual rpt, S0320–4

Arizona statistical abstract, general data, 1993 recurring rpt, U5850–2

Arkansas Census of Population and Housing detailed findings, 1990, U5935–7

California Census of Population and Housing detailed findings, 1990, S0840–9

California statistical abstract, general data, 1992 annual rpt, S0840–2

DC statistical profile, general data, 1992 annual rpt, S1535–3

Florida county data book, 1992/93 annual rpt, C6360–1

Florida population and household composition, series, U6660–3

Florida statistical abstract, general data, 1992 annual rpt, U6660–1

Georgia county guide, general data, 1993 annual rpt, U6750–1

Georgia statistical abstract, general data, 1992-93 biennial rpt, U6730–1

Hawaii data book, general data, 1992 annual rpt, S2090–1

Idaho economic profile, general data, 1992 recurring rpt, S2218–2

Illinois statistical abstract, general data, 1992 annual rpt, U6910–2

Indiana population and family characteristics, 1990, article, U2160–1.501

Kansas statistical abstract, general data, 1991/92 annual rpt, U7095–2

Louisiana Census of Population and Housing summary findings, by local area, 1990 and trends, U8010–4

Maine Census of Population and Housing summary findings, by local area, 1990, S3465–7, S3465–9

Maryland statistical abstract, general data, 1993-94 biennial rpt, S3605–1

Mississippi statistical abstract, general data, 1992 annual rpt, U3255–4

Nevada statistical abstract, general data, 1992 biennial rpt, S5005–1

New Jersey Census of Population and Housing detailed findings, by county, 1990, S5425–19

New York State statistical yearbook, general data, 1992 annual rpt, U5100–1

Oklahoma statistical abstract, general data, 1992 annual rpt, U8130–2

Pennsylvania Census of Population and Housing detailed findings, with selected data by county and municipality, 1990, U4130–13

Pennsylvania statistical abstract, general data, 1992 recurring rpt, U4130–6

Rhode Island Census of Population and Housing detailed findings, by county and municipality, 1990, S6930–9

Rhode Island statistical almanac, general data, 1993 annual rpt, C7975–1.1

South Carolina educational characteristics and socioeconomic indicators, by school district and county, 1991/92, annual rpt, S7145–1

South Carolina statistical abstract, general data, 1993 annual rpt, S7125–1

Tennessee statistical abstract, general data, 1992/93 annual rpt, U8710–2

Utah population distribution and selected characteristics, by race-ethnicity, 1990, S7820–3.504

Utah statistical abstract, general data, 1993 triennial rpt, U8960–1

West Virginia statistical handbook, general data, 1992 annual rpt, R9385–1

Wisconsin Blue Book, general data, 1993-94 biennial rpt, S8780–1

see also Aged and aging

see also Ancestry

see also Birthplace

see also Body measurements

see also Children

see also Disabled and handicapped persons

see also Earnings, general

see also Educational attainment

see also Educational enrollment

see also Employment and unemployment, general

see also Families and households

see also Fertility

see also Health condition

see also Homeless population

see also Housing condition and occupancy

see also Labor supply and demand

see also Living arrangements

see also Marriage and divorce

see also Men

see also Migration

see also Minority groups

see also Nutrition and malnutrition

see also Occupations

see also Personal and household income

see also Personal consumption

see also Population projections

see also Population size

see also Poverty

see also Vital statistics

see also Wealth

see also Women

see also Youth

see also under Geographic, Economic, and Demographic Breakdowns in the "Index by Categories"

Population projections

Age distribution of population, by sex, 1991, 2000, and 2080, annual rpt, A4957–1.1

Age structure of population, decennially 1970-2040, article, U0280–1.507

Black American population and demographic characteristics, with comparisons to whites, 1970s-2080, annual compilation, C6775–2.1

Consumer buying power survey of population, income, and sales by product

Population projections

line, by State, metro area, county, and census div, 1993 annual rpt, C1200–1.514

Counties with greatest population growth outlook in 21 leading media market areas, 1992-97, C2710–1.538

Hispanic American population, by age and sex, quinquennially 1995-2010, annual compilation, C6775–3.1

Immigrant share of population growth by race-ethnicity, 1992-2010, article, C5800–7.533

Japan population age 65/over as percent of population age 15-64, with comparisons to 6 other countries, 1985, 1995, and 2005, article, R5650–2.546

Latin America population by country projected to 2025, annual rpt, U6250–1.5

Male population by age, quinquennially 1995-2025, annual rpt, A3880–1

Metro area population growth rates for 5 fastest- and slowest-growing metro areas, 1990-2010, C4300–1.508

Middle East population trend and demographic characteristics, by country, 1993 rpt, R8750–2.59

Minority population characteristics, employment, and voting patterns by detailed race-ethnicity, with comparisons to whites, 1980s-2040, R8750–2.58

Minority population share, by age group, 1992 and 2025, article, R8750–1.506

Older population age 65/older ratio to population age 15-64, change in 7 industrial countries, 1985-2015, article, B6200–2.502

Projected population by age, to 2050, annual rpt, R9050–1.2

Projected population by State, region, and census div, 2010, annual data sheet, R8750–9

Projected population by State, 2000 and 2010, annual almanac, C4712–1

Racial-ethnic population distribution, 1990, 2000, and 2010, article, A8510 1.1

Solitary living population, by age and sex, 1990, 1995, and 2000, article, C4655–1.506

Southern States population, personal income, and State/local revenues and expenditures, by State, 1950s-2010, biennial fact book, A8945–1.1

Urban share of population worldwide and in more vs less developed regions, 1970-2015, R8750–1.503

Water supply outlook, population per million cubic meters in selected world areas and countries, 1990 and 2025, article, R8750–1.502

World population by country and/or region, outlook to 2025, biennial rpt, R9455–1.2, R9455–1.5

World population projections for top 50 countries, 2000, 2010, and 2020, semiannual rpt, B8500–1.16

World population projections to 2025, by region and country, 1993 annual data sheet, R8750–5

World population size, and annual births, deaths, and natural increase, by world area and/or country, 1993-2010, R8750–1.508

World population size in developing vs developed countries, with detail for women age 15-49, and birth and death rates, by country, 1960-2005, R8720–1.1

World population urban share, with detail for developing and developed countries, 1950-2025, article, R8750–1.505

World water resources supply-demand conditions and outlook, with population size and growth factors, by region and selected country, 1992 rpt, R8750–2.57

State and local:

Alabama population by age group, 1990, 2000, and 2015, article, U5680–1.503

Alabama population, by MSA, 1995-2040, recurring rpt, U5680–2.13

Arizona population by county, 1985-2040, semiannual rpt, U5850–1

Arizona population projected to 2005, by county, 1993 recurring rpt, U5850–2.2

Arizona population projections by economic analysts, 1992, 1995, and 2000, annual article, U0282–1.501

Arizona population projections under 4 economic scenarios, with detail for 2 urban and total nonurban areas, decennially 1980-2010, annual article, U0280–1.504

Arkansas population, income, and employment trends, by MSA, 1973-2040, article, U5930–1.503

California population by age, sex, race-ethnicity, and county, decennially 1990-2040, recurring rpt, S0840–4

California population by county, 2000, annual rpt, C4712–3

Delaware population, by age, sex, race, and locality, 1990-2020, recurring rpt, S1375–3

Delaware population, by county and for Wilmington, selected years 1970-2010, annual rpt, S1385–2

Florida population by age, sex, and race, by county, 1990, 1992, and quinquennially 1995-2010, annual rpt, U6660–3.46

Florida population by age, sex, and race, by county, 1990-91 and quinquennially 1995-2010, annual rpt, U6660–3.43

Florida population by county, 1930s-2000, annual rpt, C6360–1

Florida population by county, 1980-2000, annual rpt, S1746–1.1

Florida population projected to 2020, by age, sex, race, and county, annual rpt, U6660–1.1

Florida population projections, by county, 1992 and quinquennially 1995-2020, annual rpt, U6660–3.44

Georgia population by county, projected to 2010, biennial rpt, U6730–1.1

Georgia population by county, 1930s-2000, annual rpt, U6750–1

Kansas population by county, age, and sex, with detail for persons aged 65/over, projections to 2030, annual rpt, U7095–2.2

Kentucky population, by county and district, 1990-2020, annual rpt, S3104–1

Maryland population trends, with projections to 2010, biennial rpt, S3605–1.1

Massachusetts population by city and county, 1970s-2000, annual rpt, C4712–2

Nevada population by county, 1992-93 and 1997, annual rpt, S5040–4

Nevada population projected to 1997, biennial rpt, S5005–1.1

New Hampshire population by race, sex, and age, by county, 1990 and 1995, recurring rpt, S5205–7

New Mexico population, by county and age, quinquennially 1990-2020, annual planning rpt, S5624–1

New Mexico population projections by county and age group, 2000, 2010, and 2020, annual rpt, S5605–1

New York State population projected to 2010, by county, annual rpt, U5100–1.1

Ohio population by age, sex, and county, with summary components of change, quinquennially 1990-2015, recurring rpt, S6260–3

Oklahoma population projections, by age, sex, and locality, with data on fertility and migration, 1990-2020, recurring rpt, S6416–1

Pennsylvania population, by age, sex, and county, 1980-2000, recurring rpt, U4130–6.1

Rhode Island population by age group, projections for 2000, annual planning rpt, S6980–3

South Carolina population, by age, MSA, and county, with projections to 2010, annual rpt, S7125–1.13

South Carolina population, by age, sex, race, and county, projections through 2000, annual planning rpt, S7155–3.3

Tennessee population, by age, sex, race, and county, 1990-2010, recurring rpt, S7560–2

Tennessee population projections by age, sex, and county metro status, 1990-2010, article, U8710–1.501

Texas population, by county and race-ethnicity, 1990-2030, recurring rpt, S7645–3

Utah population by county and district, projected to 2020, triennial rpt, U8960–1.1

Utah total and school-age population, 1995-2020, annual rpt, R9380–1.1

Virginia population trends and projections by location, 1980-2000, recurring rpt, S8205–7

Wisconsin population, by age, sex, and county, with components of change, quinquennially 1990-2020, recurring rpt, S8675–4

see also Population size

Population size

Age distribution of population, by census div and State, Apr 1990, article, B6045–1.501

Asia and Pacific countries population characteristics, series, R4500–1

Beer "dry" areas post-prohibition population, by State, 1982-91, annual rpt, A3455–1.6

Black American population, with comparison to whites, selected years 1790-1990, with projections to 2080, annual compilation, C6775–2.1

Boats registered compared to population, by State, 1993 annual feature, C2425–4

Canada economic indicators, including US trade, import shares for 8 other countries, and population by Province, 1993 articles, C4687–1.508

Canada population by Province, 1993 article, C4687–1.505

Catholic population, clergy, instns, missionaries, and religious order membership, US and worldwide, 1993 annual almanac, C6885–1

Index by Subjects and Names

Index by Subjects and Names

Population size

Children and total State population, and Medicaid program characteristics, by State, FY91 annual rpt, A0565–1

China population, 1993 article, C4687–1.511

Cities rated as best for business by Fortune magazine, socioeconomic profiles of top 60 metro areas, 1992 annual article, C8900–1.501

Commonwealth of Independent States region population by sex, urban vs rural status, Republic, and selected city, 1986, R4105–82.4

Consumer buying power survey of population, income, and sales by kind of business, by census div, State, MSA, county, and city, 1992, annual rpt, C1200–1.511

Consumer buying power survey of population, income, and sales by product line, by State, metro area, county, and census div, 1993 annual rpt, C1200–1.514

Developing countries family planning efforts, with data on socioeconomic and health conditions compared to developed countries, by country, 1980s-90, R8720–1.1

Drinking age population, by major metro area and State, 1991-92, annual rpt, C4775–1.3, C4775–2.2

EC population and GDP trends, with detail for 4 countries, 1986-90, R5025–9

Economic indicator historical trends, 1900s-92, annual rpt, R9050–1.2

Europe socioeconomic summaries, for EC and European Free Trade Assn countries, 1992-93, article, C8900–1.504

Germany (West) and US comparative socioeconomic statistics, 1970s-91, annual rpt, A5135–2.2

Hispanic American adults, with detail for noncitizens and selected States, biennially 1980-90, annual rpt, A6844–1

Hispanic American and total population, decennially 1960-90, article, C4575–1.507

Hispanic American population and demographic characteristics, with comparisons to whites, 1993 annual compilation, C6775–3.1

Hispanic American population in top 15-20 States and cities, 1980, annual rpt, U6250–1.5

Hispanic American population trends, and shares by country of ethnic origin, 1993 article, C4575–1.511

Hispanic American vs total population, for 35 cities with Hispanic mayors as of 1993, article, C4575–1.511

India population, with persons in upper and lower middle class income segments, 1990, article, C8900–1.502

Jewish population by world area, country, and US census div, State, and city, 1990-92, annual compilation, A2050–1

Latin America statistical abstract, general data by country, 1992 annual rpt, U6250–1.1, U6250–1.5, U6250–1.17

Markets with daily newspapers, demographic and economic info by geographic area, US and Canada, 1993 annual rpt, C3250–1

Metro areas with greatest market shares for health insurance managed care and nonmanaged care plans, including population, top 10 cities, 1992, article, A1865–1.510

Mexico economic indicators, including population by major city, 1993 articles, C4687–1.512

Municipal govt annexation activity, and population and land area affected, by city, State, and census div, 1980-91, A5800–1.2

Public opinion on environmental and population issues, and related church involvement, for US, Brazil, Canada, and Mexico, 1992 survey, R8780–1.504

Racial-ethnic group populations, 1985, 1991, and 2000, article, C2150–6.504

Refugees, resettlement, and intl aid devs, by country, 1992, annual rpt, R9372–1

Southern States population, personal income, and State/local revenues and expenditures, by State, 1950s-2010, biennial fact book, A8945–1.1

Soviet Union former central Asian Republics population, and fertility, abortion, and contraceptive use rates, for 5 Republics, 1993 article, A5160–1.504

Spain population, foreign investment trends, and GDP shares, by region, 1993 feature, A8955–1.502

State rankings by population size and annual change, by State, 1992, article, B8500–2.508

State, regional, and census div population size and density, 1991 annual data sheet, R8750–9

State social, economic, and govtl indicators, with rankings, 1993 semiannual rpt, B8500–1.1

Statistical profiles of 50 States and DC, general data, 1993 annual almanac, C4712–1

Urban school system service area population, and enrollment as a percent of population age 5-17, for 47 systems, 1990/91, A4425–4

Western States corrections data, including prisoners and capacity, and related data on population and crime, for 13 States, 1980s-90, A4375–13

Western States economic indicators, including forecasts from selected organizations, for 10 States, monthly rpt, U0282–2

Western States population and land area in urban and rural areas, for 12 States, 1990, article, U0280–1.502

Western States population, for approx 15 States, 1991-94, annual rpt, B3520–1

World demographic topics, series, R8750–2

World demographic trends and population-related issues, monthly rpt, R8750–1

World population and growth, for top 50 countries, 1993 semiannual rpt, B8500–1.16

World population and health indicators, with detail by region and country, 1992/93 biennial rpt, R9455–1.2, R9455–1.5

World population size and characteristics, GNP, and land area, by region and/or country, 1993 annual data sheet, R8750–5

World telephone service, including access lines by type, and intl calling patterns, with comparisons to population, by area and country, 1990-91, annual rpt, B0350–1

Youth opinions on environmental and population issues, 1992 survey, R8780–1.503

State and local:

Alabama county data book, general data, 1992 annual rpt, S0121–2

Alabama municipal data book, general data, 1992 recurring rpt, S0121–5

Alabama population size and characteristics, series, U0340–1

Alabama statistical abstract, general data, 1992 recurring rpt, U5680–2.10, U5680–2.13

Alabama vital statistics, including population, births, deaths by cause, marriages, and divorces, by location and demographic characteristics, 1992 and trends, annual rpt, S0175–2

Alaska population, housing, income, and education data, by demographic characteristics and/or locality, 1990/91 and trends, annual rpt, S0320–4

Alaska population, with detail by borough and city, 1992 and trends, annual rpt, S0285–1

Alaska vital statistics, including births, deaths by cause, marriages, divorces, adoptions, and population, by demographic characteristics and location, 1990, annual rpt, S0315–1

Arizona and Maricopa County population, monthly rpt, U0280–1

Arizona economic condition, including population, employment and earnings, and business activity, by industry and locality, 1985-93, semiannual rpt, U5850–1

Arizona economic indicators, including forecasts from 16 forecasting organizations, monthly rpt, U0282–1

Arizona Indian population, education, housing, health, and employment characteristics, with detail by reservation, 1970s-91, recurring rpt, U5850–2.9

Arizona population trends and projections, for 2 urban and total nonurban areas, 1960s-2010, annual article, U0280–1.504

Arizona statistical abstract, general data, 1993 recurring rpt, U5850–2.2

Arkansas Census of Population and Housing detailed findings, 1990, U5935–7

Arkansas population, by race, 1920-91, annual rpt, S0685–1

Arkansas population, per capita income, and economic vitality index, by county and/or metro area, 1980s-90, article, U5930–1.501

Arkansas socioeconomic trends, by MSA and/or county, 1993 annual rpt, U5935–1

California adult and juvenile population, 1992 and trends, annual rpt, S0910–1.2

California Census of Population and Housing detailed findings, 1990, S0840–9

California economic condition, including population, employment and earnings, income, business activity, and taxation, 1993 annual rpt, S0840–3

California labor force planning rpt, including population characteristics, and employment by industry, 1992 annual rpt, S0830–2

California population by age, sex, race-ethnicity, and county, decennially 1990-2040, recurring rpt, S0840–4

Population size

California population by county, July 1990, annual rpt, S0855–1.1

California population by county, 1991 and trends, annual rpt, S0885–1

California socioeconomic and govtl data for municipalities, counties, and school districts, 1993 annual rpt, C4712–3

California statistical abstract, general data, 1992 annual rpt, S0840–2.2, S0840–2.9

California vital statistics, including population, births, and deaths by cause, by demographic characteristics and county, 1990 and trends, annual rpt, S0865–1

Colorado labor force planning rpt, including population, employment by industry, and job service applicants, FY94 annual rpt, S1040–3

Colorado population by county, 1980, 1990, and July 1991, annual rpt, S1075–1

Colorado vital statistics, including population, births, deaths by cause, abortion, marriage and divorce, and adoption, by demographic characteristics and location, 1990 and trends, annual rpt, S1010–1

Connecticut population, by locality, age, and sex, 1989, annual rpt, S1200–1

DC statistical profile, general data, 1992 annual rpt, S1535–3.1

Delaware population, by age, sex, race, and locality, 1990-2020, recurring rpt, S1375–3

Delaware population, by county and for Wilmington, selected years 1970-2010, annual rpt, S1385–2

Florida county data book, 1992/93 annual rpt, C6360–1

Florida municipal and county statistical profiles, general data, 1991 annual rpt, C4712–6

Florida population and household composition, series, U6660–3

Florida population, by city, county, and MSA, Apr 1992 and trends, annual rpt, U6660–4

Florida population, by race-ethnicity, age, and county, 1990 and 1992, annual rpt, S1746–1.1

Florida statistical abstract, general data, 1992 annual rpt, U6660–1.1

Florida vital statistics, including population, births, deaths by cause, and marriages and dissolutions, by location and demographic characteristics, 1992 and trends, annual rpt, S1745–3

Georgia county guide, general data, 1993 annual rpt, U6750–1

Georgia statistical abstract, general data, 1992-93 biennial rpt, U6730–1.1, U6730–1.11

Georgia vital statistics, including population, births, abortions, deaths by cause, marriages, and divorces, by demographic characteristics and location, 1991 and trends, annual rpt, S1895–1

Hawaii civilian and military population, by county and island, 1980 and 1989-90, annual rpt, S2065–1.2

Hawaii counties population and economic indicators, 1993 annual rpt series, B3500–2

Hawaii data book, general data, 1992 annual rpt, S2090–1.1

Hawaii economic indicators, bimonthly rpt, B3500–1

Idaho and US economic trends and forecasts, quarterly rpt, S2245–2

Idaho economic profile, general data, 1992 recurring rpt, S2218–2.2

Idaho population, by county, city, race-ethnicity, age, and sex, 1990 and trends, annual rpt, S2250–2

Illinois population and migration trends, 1970-92, S2405–2.501

Illinois statistical abstract, general data, 1992 annual rpt, U6910–2

Indiana population, with detail by age group, 1981-91, annual rpt, S2570–1.1

Iowa labor force supply-demand data, including population, earnings, and employment by industry and occupation, 1993 annual rpt, S2784–3

Iowa vital statistics, including population, births, deaths by cause, marriages, and divorces, by demographic characteristics and location, 1991 and trends, annual rpt, S2795–1

Kansas population, by selected county, 1989-90, annual articles, U7095–1.501

Kansas statistical abstract, general data, 1991/92 annual rpt, U7095–2.2

Kansas vital statistics, including population, births, deaths by cause, abortions, marriages, and divorces, by demographic characteristics and location, 1991 and trends, annual rpt, S2975–1

Kentucky economic statistics, general data, 1993 annual rpt, S3104–1

Kentucky labor force planning rpt, including population and labor force characteristics, and employment by industry, 1991 and trends, annual rpt, S3140–3

Kentucky vital statistics, including births, deaths by cause, marriages and divorces, and population, by demographic characteristics and county, 1991, annual rpt, S3140–1

Louisiana Census of Population and Housing summary findings, by local area, 1990 and trends, U8010–4

Louisiana labor force planning rpt, including population and labor force characteristics, unemployment claimants, and data by parish and MSA, 1993 annual rpt, S3320–1

Louisiana population by parish, 1980, 1990, and 1992, annual rpt, S3280–1.1

Louisiana vital statistics, including population, births, deaths by cause, reportable diseases, marriages, and divorces, by demographic characteristics and locality, 1989-90 and trends, annual rpt, S3295–1

Maine Census of Population and Housing summary findings, by local area, 1990, S3465–7, S3465–8, S3465–9

Maine population, by age, sex, and county, 1991 and trends, annual rpt, S3460–2

Maine statistical summary, general economic and social data, 1992 recurring rpt, S3434–1

Maryland population, by county and taxing jurisdiction, 1993 annual rpt, S3618–1.2

Maryland statistical abstract, general data, 1993-94 biennial rpt, S3605–1.1

Maryland vital statistics, including population, births, deaths by cause, marriages, and divorces, by demographic characteristics and location, 1989 and trends, annual rpt, S3635–1

Index by Subjects and Names

Massachusetts municipal and county profiles, general data, 1992 annual rpt, C4712–2

Massachusetts vital statistics, including births, deaths by cause, marriages, divorces, and population, by locality and demographic characteristics, 1990 and trends, annual rpt, S3850–1

Michigan labor force planning rpt, including population characteristics, and earnings in selected industries, 1993 annual rpt, S3980–1.1

Michigan population, by age, sex, race, and county, 1990 and trends, annual rpt, S4000–3

Minnesota population, by age, sex, and county, 1991, annual rpt, S4190–2

Mississippi labor force planning rpt, including population, employment, and characteristics of unemployed and disadvantaged, 1993 annual rpt, S4345–1

Mississippi population, by age, sex, race, and location, 1990, annual rpt, S4350–1

Mississippi statistical abstract, general data, 1992 annual rpt, U3255–4.1, U3255–4.13

Missouri population by city, 1980 and 1990, biennial rpt, S4580–1

Missouri urban vs rural population, decennially 1900-90, annual rpt, S4475–1

Missouri vital statistics, including population, births, deaths by cause, and marriages and divorces, by location and demographic characteristics, 1992 and trends, annual rpt, S4518–1

Montana labor force planning rpt, including population, income, and employment and job openings by industry and occupation, with selected data by county, 1993-94 annual rpt, S4710–3

Montana population, with detail by county, 1990-91 and trends, annual rpt, S4690–1

Nebraska population and migration rates, with detail by age group and county, 1980-90, article, U7860–1.508

Nebraska population, with comparison to US, 1940-91, annual rpt, S4825–1

Nebraska vital statistics, including births, deaths, marriages, divorces, and population, by demographic characteristics and location, 1991 and trends, annual rpt, S4885–1

Nevada business and economic activity indicators, with comparisons to other Western States, 1980-91, annual rpt, U7920–2

Nevada population, by county, 1980-89, annual rpt, S5075–1

Nevada population by county, 1992-93 and 1997, annual rpt, S5040–4

Nevada statistical abstract, general data, 1992 biennial rpt, S5005–1.1

New Hampshire labor force and population by race, sex, and age, and employment by industry div, statewide and by county, 1992 recurring rpt, S5205–7

New Hampshire population, by county and city, 1970, 1980, and 1990, biennial rpt, S5255–1

New Hampshire vital statistics, including population, births, deaths by cause, marriages, and divorces, by location and demographic characteristics, 1991 and trends, annual rpt, S5215–1

Index by Subjects and Names — Population size

New Jersey Census of Population and Housing detailed findings, by county, 1990, S5425–19

New Jersey crimes, population and land area, and law enforcement personnel by sex, by county and municipality, 1992 and trends, annual rpt, S5430–1.3

New Jersey municipal and county data book, general data, 1992 annual rpt, C4712–4

New Jersey population, by race-ethnicity, sex, age, and county, 1990, annual rpt, S5405–1

New Mexico labor force planning rpt, including population characteristics, and employment by industry and occupation, 1993 annual rpt, S5624–1

New Mexico population by age, sex, county, and State region, 1980 and 1990, U7980–6

New Mexico population size and components of change, by county, 1990-91, article, U7980–1.503

New Mexico vital statistics, including population, births, deaths, and disease, by location and demographic characteristics, 1991 and trends, annual rpt, S5605–1

New York City Hispanic population by country of ethnic origin, and non-Hispanic population, 1980 and 1990, article, C4575–1.506

New York State business and economic indicators, by MSA, county, and industry, 1980s-91, annual rpt, S5735–3

New York State municipal and county statistical profiles, general data, 1993 annual rpt, C4712–7

New York State population, including data for major cities, decennially 1930-90, annual rpt, S5710–1

New York State statistical yearbook, general data, 1992 annual rpt, U5100–1.1

New York State vital statistics, including population, births, deaths by cause, reportable diseases, and marriages and dissolutions, by demographic characteristics and/or location, 1990 and trends, annual rpt, S5765–1

North Carolina vital statistics, including population, births, deaths, marriages, and divorces, by local area, 1991 and trends, annual rpt, S5927–1.1

North Dakota labor force planning rpt, including population, employment, and earnings, with data by industry and county, 1993 annual rpt, S6140–2

North Dakota population, by county, 1991, annual rpt, S6105–2

Ohio vital statistics, including births, deaths by cause, marriages, divorces, and population, by demographic characteristics and location, 1991 and trends, annual rpt, S6285–1

Oklahoma population by county, 1990-92, annual rpt, S6465–1.2

Oklahoma statistical abstract, general data, 1992 annual rpt, U8130–2.2

Oregon economic conditions, including population, construction, income, employment, industry, and foreign trade data, 1991, annual rpt, S6585–3

Oregon population, by age, sex, county, and city, 1991 and trends, annual rpt, S6615–5

Oregon population by county, July 1991-92, article, S6615–2.502

Pennsylvania Census of Population and Housing detailed findings, with selected data by county and municipality, 1990, U4130–13

Pennsylvania labor force and population characteristics, FY92 annual planning rpt, S6845–3.1

Pennsylvania statistical abstract, general data, 1992 recurring rpt, U4130–6.1, U4130–6.6

Rhode Island Census of Population and Housing detailed findings, by county and municipality, 1990, S6930–9

Rhode Island labor force planning rpt, including population, employment by industry, job openings, and characteristics of insured unemployed, 1993 annual rpt, S6980–3

Rhode Island statistical almanac, general data, 1993 annual rpt, C7975–1.1

Rhode Island vital statistics, including population, births, deaths, marriages, and divorces, by demographic characteristics and locality, 1989 and trends, annual rpt, S6995–1

South Carolina population, by age, race-ethnicity, sex, and locality, 1990 and trends, annual planning rpt, S7155–3

South Carolina population, by race, age, and county, 1990 and trends, annual rpt, S7175–1

South Carolina population characteristics, by county, 1993 annual rpt, S7145–1.1

South Carolina statistical abstract, general data, 1993 annual rpt, S7125–1.4, S7125–1.9, S7125–1.11, S7125–1.13

Tennessee economic indicator trends and forecasts, with data by industry div and manufacturing group, 1982-2001, annual rpt, S7560–1

Tennessee population, by age, sex, race, and county, 1990-2010, recurring rpt, S7560–2

Tennessee population by race, county, and city, 1991 and trends, annual rpt, S7520–2

Tennessee statistical abstract, general data, 1992/93 annual rpt, U8710–2.1, U8710–2.20

Texas labor force planning rpt, including labor force, employment by industry, income, and population, 1993 annual rpt, S7675–2

Texas population, by age, sex, and race-ethnicity, 1990, recurring rpt, S7645–3

Texas population, by age, sex, race-ethnicity, and county, July 1991, annual rpt, S7645–2

Texas population by city, town, and county, 1980 and 1990-91, annual rpt, S7645–1

Utah business activity indicators, by county, 1988-91, annual feature, U8960–2.501

Utah business activity indicators, by county, 1989-92, annual feature, U8960–2.507

Utah economic and demographic trends, by county and district, 1960-91, annual rpt, S7832–2

Utah govt statistical review, fiscal and socioeconomic data, 1993 annual rpt, R9380–1.1

Utah libraries and population served, by county and library, 1992, annual rpt, S7808–1

Utah population by urban-rural status and/or county, 1990 and 1992, annual rpt, S7800–1

Utah population data, 1990 census rpt series, S7832–3

Utah population estimates and components, including data by county, 1992 and trends, annual article, U8960–2.504

Utah statistical abstract, general data, 1993 triennial rpt, U8960–1.1

Utah vital statistics, including population by county, 1990 and trends, annual rpt, S7835–1.1

Vermont population, by age, sex, and locality, 1991 and trends, annual planning rpt, S8025–2.1

Vermont population, by town, 1990, biennial rpt, S8080–1

Vermont vital statistics, including population, births, deaths by cause, abortions, marriages, and divorces, by location and demographic characteristics, 1991 and trends, annual rpt, S8054–1

Virginia population and net migration, by local area, 1990-91, annual rpt, U9080–9

Virginia population by location, 1980 and 1990, recurring rpt, S8205–7

Virginia population by race and location, 1991 and trends, annual rpt, S8225–1

Virginia youth population by age, by county and city, with summary by sex and detail for disabled youth, Jan 1993, triennial rpt, S8190–1

Washington State population and demographic characteristics, and housing units, by county and/or city, 1992 and trends, annual rpt, S8345–4

Washington State vital statistics, including births, deaths by cause, and population, by demographic characteristics and location, 1991 and trends, annual rpt, S8363–1

West Virginia labor force planning rpt, including population, employment, and job service activities, with data by county and service delivery area, 1993 annual rpt, S8534–2

West Virginia population, by county and demographic characteristics, 1920s-90, annual rpt, S8560–1

West Virginia statistical handbook, general data, 1992 annual rpt, R9385–1.1, R9385–1.6, R9385–1.8

Wisconsin Blue Book, general data, 1993-94 biennial rpt, S8780–1.1, S8780–1.2

Wisconsin population, by age, sex, and county, with components of change, quinquennially 1990-2020, recurring rpt, S8675–4

Wisconsin population by county, Jan 1992, annual rpt, S8675–2.1

Wisconsin vital statistics, including population, births, deaths by cause, and marriages and dissolutions, by county and demographic characteristics, 1991 and trends, annual rpt, S8715–4

Wyoming vital statistics, including population, births, deaths by cause, marriages, and divorces, by demographic characteristics and county, 1991 and trends, annual rpt, S8920–2

see also Center of population
see also Family planning
see also Farm population
see also Fertility

Population size

see also Group quarters
see also Population projections
see also Vital statistics

Pork
see Meat and meat products

Pornography
see Obscenity and pornography

Porter, Edward D.
"U.S. Petroleum Supply: History, Prospects, and Policy Implications", A2575–25

Portland, Maine
Employment, unemployment, and earnings, by industry, MSA, and labor area, monthly rpt, S3465–2
see also under By City in the "Index by Categories"

Portland, Oreg.
CPI for Portland-Vancouver area compared with US, monthly rpt, S6592–1, S6615–2
see also under By City in the "Index by Categories"

Ports
see Harbors and ports

Portsmouth, N.H.
Employment, hours, and earnings in Portsmouth-Dover-Rochester MSA, monthly rpt, S5205–1

Portugal
Motor vehicle world production, sales, trade, and registrations, by country, world area, manufacturer, and make, 1991 and trends, annual rpt, A0865–2.1
see also under By Foreign Country or World Area in the "Index by Categories"

Postal employees
USPS employees and facilities, 1987-91, annual rpt, A4620–1.5

Postal service
Air carrier service traffic and revenues, by source, 1970-91, annual rpt, A0250–2.3
Airline mail and freight revenue ton-miles on scheduled domestic and intl flights, monthly press release, A0325–2
Consumer reading of and reactions to 3rd-class mail, 1988-91, article, C1858–1.505
Latin America statistical abstract, general data by country, 1992 annual rpt, U6250–1.3
Newspaper use of selected delivery methods and 3rd-class mail discounts for nonsubscriber/total-market products, fall 1992 survey, article, A8605–1.509
Security methods used by organization mail rooms to screen mail/parcels, 1993 feature, C1850–12.504
Shopping center financial and operating data, with detail by type of tenant, US and Canada, 1991, triennial rpt, R9285–1
Supermarket in-store postal service availability and shopper use, 1993 and trends, annual survey rpt, A4950–3

State and local:
Hawaii data book, general data, 1992 annual rpt, S2090–1.18
Maryland Baltimore-Washington Intl Airport traffic and operations by type, 1990-91, biennial rpt, S3605–1.10
South Dakota business activity review, including selected data by city and industry, quarterly rpt, U8595–1
Utah, Salt Lake City Intl Airport air traffic, passengers, and cargo, 1950-92, annual rpt, R9380–1.10

see also Direct marketing
see also Electronic mail systems
see also Postal employees
see also U.S. Postal Service
see also Zip codes

Potash
Capital spending plans for new mines and plants, by mineral and company, and mine production values, 1993 annual feature, C5226–2.503
Imports of potash, by State and country of origin, quarterly rpt, A8720–4
Production, consumption, stocks, trade, and prices for approx 100 basic commodities, including by country and producing State, commodity yearbook for 1993, C2400–1, C2400–2
Production, inventories, and sales and exports by State, Canadian Province, and country of destination, monthly rpt, A8720–1
Production, inventories, sales, and exports, US and Canada, monthly rpt, A8720–2
Sales and trade of potash muriates and sulfates, US and Canada, quarterly press release, A8720–5
Supply-demand for selected metals and nonmetallic minerals, with price data, US and worldwide, 1992-93 and trends, annual feature, C5226–2.505

Potatoes
Exports of farm products, by detailed commodity and country of destination, US and California, 1991, annual rpt, B9520–1
Latin America statistical abstract, general data by country, 1992 annual rpt, U6250–1.24
Production, consumption, stocks, trade, and prices for approx 100 basic commodities, including by country and producing State, commodity yearbook for 1993, C2400–1, C2400–2
Retail prices for selected consumer items in approx 300 cities, quarterly rpt, A0150–1

State and local:
Alabama agricultural production, marketing, and income, by county and/or commodity, and farms and acreage, 1992 and trends, annual rpt, S0090–1
Alaska agricultural production and marketing, by district and commodity, 1960s-92, annual rpt, U5750–1
Arizona agricultural production, marketing, and finances, by commodity and county, 1988-92, annual rpt, U5830–1
California field crops production, acreage, yield, and prices, by commodity and county, 1992 and trends, annual rpt, S0850–1.4
California vegetable production, marketing, and prices, by commodity and use, 1992 and trends, annual rpt, S0850–1.3
Colorado agricultural production, marketing, and finances, by commodity and/or county, with farms and acreage, 1992 and trends, annual rpt, S0985–1
Florida field crop acreage, yield, production, and value, by commodity and/or county, 1992 and trends, annual rpt, S1685–1.4
Florida vegetable, melon, and strawberry production, acreage, yield, shipments, and exports, 1991/92 and trends, annual rpt, S1685–1.2

Georgia agricultural production, marketing, and finances, by commodity and/or county, and farms and acreage, 1991 and trends, annual rpt, S1855–1
Hawaii agricultural production and marketing, by commodity and island, 1987-91, annual rpt, S2030–1
Illinois agricultural production, marketing, and finances, by county or commodity, and farms and farmland, 1991 and trends, annual rpt, S2390–1
Louisiana agricultural production, marketing, and finances, by commodity or parish, 1985-91, annual rpt, U2740–1
Michigan agricultural production, marketing, and finances, by commodity or county, 1987-91, annual rpt, S3950–1
Minnesota agricultural production, marketing, and finances, by county or commodity, and farms and acreage, 1992 and trends, annual rpt, S4130–1
Montana agricultural production, marketing, and finances, by commodity and county, 1991 and trends, annual rpt, S4655–1
Nebraska agricultural production, marketing, and finances, by commodity and/or county, and farms and acreage, 1991 and trends, annual rpt, S4835–1
Nevada agricultural production, marketing, and finances, by county and commodity, and farms and acreage, 1992 and trends, annual rpt, S5010–1
New Jersey agricultural production, marketing, and finances, by commodity and/or county, and farms and acreage, 1986-91, annual rpt, S5350–1
New Mexico agricultural production, marketing, and finances, by commodity and county, with farms and acreage, 1991 and trends, annual rpt, S5530–1
New York State agricultural production, marketing, and finances, by commodity and/or county, and farms and acreage, 1992 and trends, annual rpt, S5700–1
North Carolina agricultural production, marketing, and finances, by commodity and county, 1991 and trends, annual rpt, S5885–1
North Dakota agricultural production and marketing, by commodity and county, and farm finances, 1992 and trends, annual rpt, U3600–1
Ohio agricultural production, marketing, and finances, by commodity and county, with farms and acreage, 1990-91 and trends, annual rpt, S6240–1
Oregon agricultural production, marketing, and finances, by commodity and/or county, with farms and acreage, 1991 and trends, annual rpt, S6575–1
Pennsylvania agricultural production, marketing, and finances, by county and commodity, and farms and acreage, 1992 and trends, annual rpt, S6760–1
Texas agricultural production, marketing, and finances, by commodity and county, and farms and farmland, 1991 and trends, annual rpt series, S7630–1
Utah agricultural production, marketing, and finances, by commodity and county, with farms and acreage, 1992 and trends, annual rpt, S7800–1
Washington State agricultural production, marketing, and finances, by commodity and/or county, 1992 and trends, annual rpt, S8328–1

Index by Subjects and Names

Poverty

Wisconsin agricultural production, marketing, and finances, by commodity and county, and farms, acreage, and sales, 1992 and trends, annual rpt, S8680–1

Wyoming agricultural production, marketing, and finances, by county and/or commodity, and farms, acreage, and value, 1992 and trends, annual rpt, S8860–1

Poultry industry and products

Consumer nutrition awareness and health concerns, with food shopping and consumption patterns, by respondent characteristics, 1993 survey, annual rpt, A4950–36

Exports of farm products, by detailed commodity and country of destination, US and California, 1991, annual rpt, B9520–1

Financial ratios and performance, for over 350 SIC 4-digit industries, FY88-92, annual rpt, A6400–3

Latin America statistical abstract, general data by country, 1992 annual rpt, U6250–1.24

Production, consumption, stocks, trade, and prices for approx 100 basic commodities, including by country and producing State, commodity yearbook for 1993, C2400–1, C2400–2

Restaurant (chicken specialty) establishments by census div, and trends in fast-food patron orders for chicken, 1993 annual article, C1200–5.509

Retail prices for selected consumer items in approx 300 cities, quarterly rpt, A0150–1

Sales and consumer expenditures, for food store products by type, 1991-92, annual feature, C4655–1.510

Supply-demand of meat and poultry, and livestock and packing industries finances and operations, 1991 and trends, annual rpt, A2100–1

State and local:

Alabama agricultural production, marketing, and income, by county and/or commodity, and farms and acreage, 1992 and trends, annual rpt, S0090–1

Alaska agricultural production and marketing, by district and commodity, 1960s-92, annual rpt, U5750–1

Arizona agricultural production, marketing, and finances, by commodity and county, 1988-92, annual rpt, U5830–1

Arkansas agricultural production, marketing, and finances, by commodity and county, with farms and acreage, 1992 and trends, annual rpt, U5920–1

California livestock production and marketing, with comparisons to US, 1983-92, annual rpt, S0850–1.2

Colorado agricultural production, marketing, and finances, by commodity and/or county, with farms and acreage, 1992 and trends, annual rpt, S0985–1

Florida livestock, dairy, and poultry production, inventory, marketing, and finances, with detail by commodity or species, 1992 and trends, annual rpt, S1685–1.3

Georgia agricultural production, marketing, and finances, by commodity and/or county, and farms and acreage, 1991 and trends, annual rpt, S1855–1

Hawaii agricultural production and marketing, by commodity and island, 1987-91, annual rpt, S2030–1

Illinois agricultural production, marketing, and finances, by county or commodity, and farms and farmland, 1991 and trends, annual rpt, S2390–1

Kansas agricultural production, marketing, and finances, by county and/or commodity, and farm acreage and value, 1992 and trends, annual rpt, S2915–1

Kentucky agricultural production, marketing, and finances, by commodity and county; and farms, acreage, and value; 1992 and trends, annual rpt, S3085–1

Louisiana agricultural production, marketing, and finances, by commodity or parish, 1985-91, annual rpt, U2740–1

Michigan agricultural production, marketing, and finances, by commodity or county, 1987-91, annual rpt, S3950–1

Minnesota agricultural production, marketing, and finances, by county or commodity, and farms and acreage, 1992 and trends, annual rpt, S4130–1

Missouri agricultural production, marketing, and finances, by commodity and/or county, and farms and acreage, 1988-92, annual rpt, S4480–1

Montana agricultural production, marketing, and finances, by commodity and county, 1991 and trends, annual rpt, S4655–1

Nebraska agricultural production, marketing, and finances, by commodity and/or county, and farms and acreage, 1991 and trends, annual rpt, S4835–1

Nevada agricultural production, marketing, and finances, by county and commodity, and farms and acreage, 1992 and trends, annual rpt, S5010–1

New Jersey agricultural production, marketing, and finances, by commodity and/or county, and farms and acreage, 1986-91, annual rpt, S5350–1

New Mexico agricultural production, marketing, and finances, by commodity and county, with farms and acreage, 1991 and trends, annual rpt, S5530–1

New York State agricultural production, marketing, and finances, by commodity and/or county, and farms and acreage, 1992 and trends, annual rpt, S5700–1

North Carolina agricultural production, marketing, and finances, by commodity and county, 1991 and trends, annual rpt, S5885–1

North Dakota agricultural production and marketing, by commodity and county, and farm finances, 1992 and trends, annual rpt, U3600–1

Ohio agricultural production, marketing, and finances, by commodity and county, with farms and acreage, 1990-91 and trends, annual rpt, S6240–1

Oklahoma agricultural production, marketing, and finances, by commodity and county, 1992 and trends, annual rpt, S6405–1

Oregon agricultural production, marketing, and finances, by commodity and/or county, with farms and acreage, 1991 and trends, annual rpt, S6575–1

Pennsylvania agricultural production, marketing, and finances, by county and commodity, and farms and acreage, 1992 and trends, annual rpt, S6760–1

South Carolina agricultural production and finances, by commodity and county, 1991-92 and trends, annual rpt, U1075–3

South Dakota agricultural production, marketing, and finances, by commodity and county, and farms and acreage, 1992 and trends, annual rpt, S7280–1

Tennessee agricultural production and marketing, by commodity and county, with farms, acreage, and farm value, 1992 and trends, annual rpt, S7460–1

Texas agricultural production, marketing, and finances, by commodity and county, and farms and farmland, 1991 and trends, annual rpt series, S7630–1

Utah agricultural production, marketing, and finances, by commodity and county, with farms and acreage, 1992 and trends, annual rpt, S7800–1

Vermont agricultural production, marketing, and finances, by commodity, with data on govt inspections and funding, 1989-90 biennial rpt, S7978–1

Washington State agricultural production, marketing, and finances, by commodity and/or county, 1992 and trends, annual rpt, S8328–1

West Virginia agricultural production, marketing, and finances, by commodity or county, 1991 and trends, annual rpt, S8510–1

Wisconsin agricultural production, marketing, and finances, by commodity and county, and farms, acreage, and sales, 1992 and trends, annual rpt, S8680–1

Wyoming agricultural production, marketing, and finances, by county and/or commodity, and farms, acreage, and value, 1992 and trends, annual rpt, S8860–1

see also Animal diseases and zoonoses

see also Animal feed

Poverty

Black American earnings, income, and poverty data, with comparisons to whites, 1980s-91, annual compilation, C6775–2.7

Black American socioeconomic status, with comparisons to whites and data by region, 1960s-92, annual compilation, A8510–1.1

Black child poverty rates, with comparisons to whites and detail by State, county, and major city, 1993 rpt, R3840–21

Child health and well-being indicators, with selected household characteristics, by State, 1993 annual rpt, R3832–1

Child poverty by State and for 200 cities and 89 counties, with State and city detail by race-ethnicity, 1989 and trends, R3840-20

Children age 5/under in poverty, with demographic and family characteristics, 1991 and trends, annual rpt, U1260–2

City poverty rate, for 29 cities, 1990, annual rpt, A9330–9

Economic indicator historical trends, 1900s-92, annual rpt, R9050–1.2

Educational test peformance in mathematics and reading, for 7th grade students at low- vs high-poverty schools, 1991, article, R4800–2.519

Elementary/secondary education data, including child poverty rates, by State, 1993 biennial rpt, A4355–1

Families and children with low income, health and welfare indicators, 1992 annual rpt, R3840–11

Hispanic American income and poverty data, with comparisons to whites, 1980s-91, annual compilation, C6775–3.5

Poverty

Latin America statistical abstract, general data by country, 1992 annual rpt, U6250–1.12

Metro area low-income housing supply-demand, with data on population, and poverty and unemployment rates, for 44 metro areas, 1980s-91, R3834–16

Metro area poverty and unemployment level effects on crime and mortality rates, for selected offenses and causes of death, 1990, R4700–18

Minority population characteristics, employment, and voting patterns by detailed race-ethnicity, with comparisons to whites, 1980s-2040, R8750–2.58

Population living in poverty, by State and region, 1980 and 1990, R8490–46

Population size and selected characteristics, by region, census div, and State, 1991 and trends, annual data sheet, R8750–9

Public opinion on social, political, and economic issues, detailed data, 1972-91 surveys, annual rpt, U6395–1

Southeastern States poverty levels, for 7 States, 1990, annual rpt, U5680–3

Southern States children age 17/under lacking health insurance and eligible for Medicaid, with detail by age and family income, for 6-17 States, 1991, R9000–1

State economic dev condition indicators, including economic performance, business vitality, growth capacity, and tax/fiscal system, by State, 1993 annual rpt, R4225–1.1

State social, economic, and govtl indicators, with rankings, 1993 semiannual rpt, B8500–1.1

Statistical profiles of 50 States and DC, general data, 1993 annual almanac, C4712–1

Urban public school students living in poverty, with comparisons to State, and US poverty rate for youths age 5-17, for 47 systems, 1990/91 and trends, A4425–4

White population poverty indicators, with comparisons to blacks and Hispanics and data by State, 1990-91, R3834–15

Women's calorie intake during pregnancy and lactation, by race and poverty status, 1985-86 study, article, A2623–1.510

Women's sexual behavior and disease risk, including data on multiple partners and condom use, by selected characteristics, 1988, article, A5160–1.501

State and local:

Alabama county data book, general data, 1992 annual rpt, S0121–2

Alabama municipal data book, general data, 1992 recurring rpt, S0121–5

Alabama statistical abstract, general data, 1992 recurring rpt, U5680–2.9

Alaska population, housing, income, and education data, by demographic characteristics and/or locality, 1990/91 and trends, annual rpt, S0320–4

Alaska public school enrollment of children living in poverty, by district, FY92, annual rpt, S0295–2

Arizona Indian population, education, housing, health, and employment characteristics, with detail by reservation, 1970s-91, recurring rpt, U5850–2.9

Arizona poverty rates by age group and race-ethnicity, 1989, article, U0280–1.502

Arizona statistical abstract, general data, 1993 recurring rpt, U5850–2.6

Arkansas Census of Population and Housing detailed findings, 1990, U5935–7

California Census of Population and Housing detailed findings, 1990, S0840–9

California socioeconomic and govtl data for municipalities, counties, and school districts, 1993 annual rpt, C4712–3

California statistical abstract, general data, 1992 annual rpt, S0840–2.4

Colorado total and low-income population, by age and local area, 1990, annual planning rpt, S1040–3.1

DC statistical profile, general data, 1992 annual rpt, S1535–3.1, S1535–3.5

Florida county data book, 1992/93 annual rpt, C6360–1

Florida population in poverty, with detail for persons age 65/over, by county, 1992, annual rpt, S1746–1.1

Florida statistical abstract, general data, 1992 annual rpt, U6660–1.5

Georgia county guide, general data, 1993 annual rpt, U6750–1

Hawaii data book, general data, 1992 annual rpt, S2090–1.13

Illinois elementary/secondary school enrollment of low-income students, by county, 1990/91, annual rpt, S2440–1.1

Iowa population share in poverty, by race-ethnicity, 1990, annual rpt, S2784–3

Kansas statistical abstract, general data, 1991/92 annual rpt, U7095–2.6

Kentucky economic statistics, general data, 1993 annual rpt, S3104–1

Kentucky economically disadvantaged student shares of enrollment, by region and district, 1991/92 and trends, annual rpt, S3110–1

Kentucky labor force planning rpt, including population and labor force characteristics, and employment by industry, 1991 and trends, annual rpt, S3140–3

Louisiana Census of Population and Housing summary findings, by local area, 1990 and trends, U8010–4

Louisiana job service openings and applicants, and characteristics of Job Training Partnership Act target population and insured unemployed, 1993 annual planning rpt, S3320–1.2

Maine Census of Population and Housing summary findings, by local area, 1990, S3465–9

Maryland statistical abstract, general data, 1993-94 biennial rpt, S3605–1.6

Massachusetts elementary/secondary students from low-income families, Oct 1991, annual rpt, S3810–3

Massachusetts municipal and county profiles, general data, 1992 annual rpt, C4712–2

Michigan labor force planning rpt, including employment by industry, and characteristics of Job Training Partnership Act eligible population, 1993 annual rpt, S3980–1

Mississippi characteristics of economically disadvantaged and Job Training Partnership Act eligible population, 1993/94, annual planning rpt, S4345–1.3

Nebraska northeastern counties families and households, poverty rates, and income by source, by population size, 1989, article, U7860–1.509

Nebraska poverty levels, including data for children, elderly, and female-headed households, 1990, annual rpt, S4957–1

New Jersey Census of Population and Housing detailed findings, by county, 1990, S5425–19

New Jersey municipal and county data book, general data, 1992 annual rpt, C4712–4

New Mexico individuals and families in poverty, by selected characteristics, 1989, annual planning rpt, S5624–1

New Mexico population and families in poverty, by race-ethnicity or county, 1990 and trends, annual rpt, S5605–1

New Mexico population in poverty, by race-ethnicity and county, 1990, S5620–2.501

New Mexico poverty rates by county, 1990, S5624–2.505

New York State municipal and county statistical profiles, general data, 1993 annual rpt, C4712–7

North Dakota population living in poverty, by sex, county, and State region, 1993 annual planning rpt, S6140–2

Oklahoma poverty rates, with detail for children, elderly, and female-headed families, by county, 1990, annual rpt, S6455–1.1

Oregon population educational attainment, health and life insurance coverage, rent, and poverty, 1990 and 1992, article, S6592–1.502

Oregon population in poverty, by county, monthly rpt, S6615–8

Pennsylvania Census of Population and Housing detailed findings, with selected data by county and municipality, 1990, U4130–13

Pennsylvania income data from Census of Population and Housing, by county and municipality, 1989, C1595–15

Pennsylvania labor force planning rpt, including data on populations with employability problems, FY92 annual rpt, S6845–3.3

Pennsylvania statistical abstract, general data, 1992 recurring rpt, U4130–6.3

Rhode Island Census of Population and Housing detailed findings, by county and municipality, 1990, S6930–9

South Carolina families in poverty, by family characteristics and county, 1989/90, annual rpt, S7145–1.2

South Carolina individuals and families in poverty, by county, 1979, annual planning rpt, S7155–3.3

South Carolina statistical abstract, general data, 1993 annual rpt, S7125–1.12

Tennessee statistical abstract, general data, 1992/93 annual rpt, U8710–2.2

Texas disabled persons above and below poverty level, by age group, FY92, annual rpt, S7695–1

Utah Indian reservation poverty rate, by reservation, 1990, census rpt, S7832–3.3

Utah population distribution and selected characteristics, by race-ethnicity, 1990, S7820–3.504

Utah statistical abstract, general data, 1993 triennial rpt, U8960–1.5

Washington State population and demographic characteristics, and housing units, by county and/or city, 1992 and trends, annual rpt, S8345–4

Index by Subjects and Names

West Virginia economically disadvantaged population, by county and age group, 1991, annual planning rpt, S8534–2

Wyoming Native American population, unemployment, and poverty rates, by county and/or reservation, 1990, article, S8895–1.501

see also Homeless population
see also Income maintenance
see also Literacy and illiteracy
see also Nutrition and malnutrition
see also Public welfare programs
see also under By Income in the "Index by Categories"

Power, J. D., and Associates

Airline passenger views on contribution of selected factors to overall satisfaction, Sept/Nov 1992 survey, article, C5800–4.507

Auto and truck customer sales satisfaction index, by leading model, 1992-93, annual article, C2710–3.535

Auto and truck models and/or makes with fewest problems for buyers, with summaries for US, Asian, and European manufacturers, 1993 and trends, article, C2710–3.532

Auto customer satisfaction index after 3 years of ownership, for top 14 nameplates, 1993, article, C2710–3.517

Auto customer satisfaction index, by leading model, 1992-93, annual article, C2710–3.538

Auto customer use of 3rd-party pricing and buying services, by type, 1992 survey, article, C2710–3.547

Auto dealer malls, with number of dealers, dealerships, and franchises, and new vehicle volume, 1993, article, C2710–3.552

Auto dealer satisfaction index for top 15 makes, 1991-92, survey article, C2710–3.512

Auto dependability index after 5 years of ownership, for top 12 nameplates, 1992-93, article, C2710–3.524

Auto problems for buyers, for 7 European manufacturers, 1993 article, C2710–3.533

Power plants
see Electric power plants and equipment

Power resources
see Energy resources

PPI
see Producer Price Index

Prayer in schools
see Church and state
see Elementary and secondary education

Precincts
see Electoral districts and precincts

Precious metals
see Gold
see Silver

Precious stones
see Gemstones

Precipitation
see Weather

Predatory animals
see Animals

Prefabricated buildings

Homebuilder financial and operating data, including detail by location, for top 400 builders, 1993 annual feature, C1850–8.507

Preferred provider arrangements
see Health facilities and services
see Health insurance

Pregnancy
see Abortion
see Maternity
see Teenage pregnancy

Prematurity
see Birthweight

Prenatal care

Black American health and vital statistics data, with comparisons to whites, 1970s-91, annual compilation, C6775–2.2

Black children and youth population, economic, health, and education data, with comparisons to whites, 1993 rpt, R3840–21

Catholic charity social service agency activities, clients, finances, and personnel, 1991 and trends, annual rpt, A3810–1

Child and maternal health status indicators, with data by race and State, 1992 annual rpt, R3840–5

Developing countries births assisted by trained attendant, prenatal care, and tetanus vaccination rates for pregnant women, by country, 1984-92 surveys, U2520–1.51

Developing countries child survival efforts, with selected child and maternal health indicators, 1980s-90, R8720–1.2

Europe prenatal care levels by demographic characteristics, for 3 countries, with comparisons to US, 1993 article, A2623–1.503

HMO benefits coverage, premiums, and rating methods used, by plan characteristics, 1991 and trends, annual rpt, A5150–2.1

Low-income families and children, health and welfare indicators, with data by State and city, 1992 annual rpt, R3840–11

Medicaid child and total recipients, expenditures, and other program characteristics, and child health summary, by State, FY91, annual rpt, A0565–1

Medicaid pregnancy services expansion efforts, including eligibility, outreach activities, and obstetrician reimbursement, by State, 1993 article, A5160–1.506

Obstacles to prenatal care in a rural area with a community-based program for low-income women, 1988-90 Oregon study, article, A5160–1.502

Philippines birth outcomes by maternal characteristics, 1983/84 Cebu metro area study, article, A5160–6.505

State social, economic, and govtl indicators, with rankings, 1993 semiannual rpt, B8500–1.9

State and local:

Alabama births by level of prenatal care, characteristics of mother, and county, 1992, annual rpt, S0175–2

Alabama public health dept activities, including services provided, inspection and licensing activity, staff and finances, and vital statistics and health data, 1992 annual rpt, S0175–3

Alaska births by level of prenatal care received, 1990, annual rpt, S0315–1

California vital statistics, including population, births, and deaths by cause, by demographic characteristics and county, 1990 and trends, annual rpt, S0865–1

Colorado births and infant deaths, by level of prenatal care and mother characteristics, 1990, annual rpt, S1010–1

Connecticut births by timing and adequacy of prenatal care, by race-ethnicity and birthweight, 1989, annual rpt, S1200–1

Delaware births by adequacy of prenatal care, birthweight, and maternal characteristics, 1990, annual rpt, S1385–2

Florida births by onset of prenatal care, by race and county, 1992, annual rpt, S1745–3

Hawaii health dept activities and services, including vital statistics and disease control, by location, 1990, annual rpt, S2065–1

Idaho live births, by level of prenatal care, education of mother, and county, 1991, annual rpt, S2250–2

Kansas births by month prenatal care began, with detail for teenage mothers, 1991, annual rpt, S2975–1

Kentucky births and stillbirths, by onset of prenatal care, 1991, annual rpt, S3140–1

Maine births and fetal deaths by level of prenatal care, by county, 1991, annual rpt, S3460–2

Maryland births by level of prenatal care, birthweight, and race, 1989 and trends, annual rpt, S3635–1

Massachusetts births with adequate prenatal care, and care payment sources, 1990 and trends, annual rpt, S3850–1

Michigan births, and fetal and infant deaths, by level of prenatal care, 1990, annual rpt, S4000–3

Minnesota births by level of prenatal care, by age of mother, county, and city, 1991, annual rpt, S4190–2

Mississippi births and fetal deaths by presence and/or timing of prenatal care, by race, 1992, annual rpt, S4350–1

Missouri births by level of prenatal care, by race, county, and city, 1992, annual rpt, S4518–1

Nebraska births by level of prenatal care, 1991, annual rpt, S4885–1

Nevada births by county, and complications and infant deaths, by level of prenatal care, 1989, annual rpt, S5075–1

New Hampshire births to women with no or late prenatal care, by county and town, 1991, annual rpt, S5215–1

New Jersey births by Apgar score and onset of prenatal care, 1990, annual rpt, S5405–1

New Mexico births and infant deaths, by level of prenatal care, 1991 and trends, annual rpt, S5605–1

New York State births by race and level of prenatal care, 1990, annual rpt, S5765–1

North Dakota births, and infant and fetal deaths, by level of prenatal care and race of mother, 1991, annual rpt, S6105–2

Ohio births and fetal deaths, by level of prenatal care, 1991, annual rpt, S6285–1

Oregon births, by level of prenatal care and characteristics of mother, 1991 and trends, annual rpt, S6615–5

Rhode Island births, by level of prenatal care and census tract, 1989, annual rpt, S6995–1

Prenatal care

South Carolina births by onset and level of prenatal care, by county and race, 1990, annual rpt, S7175–1

South Dakota births by level of prenatal care and characteristics of mother, 1991, annual rpt, S7345–1

Tennessee births by level of prenatal care and race, 1991, annual rpt, S7520–2

Texas births by onset and level of prenatal care, by race-ethnicity and location, 1991, annual rpt, S7685–1

Utah births by level of prenatal care and location, 1990, annual rpt, S7835–1.2

Vermont births by level of prenatal care received by mother, 1991, annual rpt, S8054–1

Virginia vital statistics, including births, deaths by cause, marriages and divorces, and communicable disease, by demographic characteristics and location, 1991 and trends, annual rpt, S8225–1

Washington State births by level of prenatal care and age of mother, 1991, annual rpt, S8363–1

West Virginia births by level of prenatal care, by characteristics of mother and county, 1991, annual rpt, S8560–1

Wisconsin births by level of prenatal care, 1991, annual rpt, S8715–4

Wyoming births by onset of prenatal care, age and education of mother, and county, 1991, annual rpt, S8920–2

Preschool education

- Black American educational statistics, with comparisons to whites, 1970s-92, annual compilation, C6775–2.3
- Catholic schools, enrollment, and teachers, by region, State, and diocese, 1992/93 and trends, annual rpt, A7375–1
- Hispanic American educational statistics, with comparisons to whites, 1970s-92, annual compilation, C6775–3.2
- Latin America statistical abstract, general data by country, 1992 annual rpt, U6250–1.8
- Public opinion on tax-supported assistance for parents unable to afford preschool, by respondent characteristics, 1993 annual Gallup Poll, A8680–1.503
- Urban public school system preschool student-teacher ratios and public assistance enrollment share, and 1st grader preparation, for 47 systems, 1990/91, A4425–4

State and local:

- Alabama elementary and secondary school enrollment, staff, pupil transportation, and finances, by district, 1991/92, annual rpt, S0124–1
- Arkansas enrollment in preprimary school, 1990, census rpt, U5935–7
- Arkansas public and private school enrollment and grads, by county, 1991/92, annual rpt, S0660–1.1
- California enrollment in preprimary school, 1990, census rpt, S0840–9
- California private schools, enrollment by grade, grads, and staff, with data by county, 1992/93 and trends, annual rpt, S0825–8
- California public school enrollment, grads, and staff, by race-ethnicity, 1992/93 and trends, annual rpt, S0825–9
- California public schools, enrollment by grade, and grads, by county, 1992/93 and trends, annual rpt, S0825–7

Colorado public and/or private school enrollment and grads, by student characteristics, county, and district, 1992 and trends, annual rpt, S1000–2.1

Connecticut public school data, including enrollment, staff, programs, finances, and student characteristics, 1991/92, biennial rpt, S1185–3

Delaware school enrollment, grads, staff, finances, and facilities, by county, school district, and/or instn, 1991/92, annual rpt, S1430–1

Idaho public and nonpublic school enrollment by grade, by school district and/or county, Sept 1992, annual rpt, S2225–1

Illinois elementary and secondary school enrollment by level, and high school dropouts and grads, by county and district, 1990/91, annual rpt, S2440–1.1

Indiana elementary and secondary school enrollment and finances, by district and county, annual rpt series, S2608–2

Louisiana enrollment in preprimary school, by local area, 1980 and 1990, census rpt, U8010–4

Maine enrollment in preprimary school, by local area, 1990 census rpt, S3465–9

Maine public school enrollment, facilities, staff, and finances, with selected data by county and for private schools, 1991 and trends, annual rpt, S3435–1

Maryland elementary and secondary education data, by county, 1992 and trends, annual rpt, S3610–2.4

Maryland elementary and secondary education data, by county, 1992/93, annual rpt, S3610–2.10

Maryland elementary and secondary education statistical summary, with data by county, 1991/92-1992/93 and trends, annual rpt, S3610–1

Massachusetts public elementary/secondary education summary data, 1989/90-1991/92 and trends, annual rpt, S3810–3

Massachusetts public elementary/secondary school enrollment by grade, by district, Oct 1992, annual rpt, S3810–4

Massachusetts public elementary/secondary school expenditures per pupil by program, by district, 1991/92, annual rpt, S3810–5

Minnesota public school enrollment, staff, and finances, by district and county, 1991/92 and trends, annual rpt, S4165–1

Mississippi public school enrollment, staff and salaries, and finances, by district, 1991/92 and trends, annual rpt, S4340–1

Missouri early childhood education programs, including kindergarten enrollment, 1985/86-1991/92, annual rpt, S4505–1.1

Montana public school enrollment by grade, and grads, by school, county, race-ethnicity, and sex, 1992 and trends, annual rpt, S4740–1

Nebraska elementary and secondary schools, enrollment by grade, and staff, with data by school district and county, annual series, S4865–2

New Hampshire school enrollment by level, by district, 1991/92, annual table, S5200–1.11

New Jersey enrollment in preprimary school, by county, 1990, census rpt, S5425–19

Index by Subjects and Names

New Jersey public schools, enrollment, and student and staff characteristics, and nonpublic schools and enrollment, by county, 1991/92, annual rpt, S5385–1

Oklahoma school revenues and expenditures, by program, county, and district, FY92, annual rpt, S6423–1.1

Oregon elementary and secondary education enrollment and finances, including data by school district and county, annual rpt series, S6590–1

Pennsylvania enrollment in preprimary school, 1990, census rpt, U4130–13

Pennsylvania public and nonpublic school enrollment, by grade, race-ethnicity, sex, and county, 1991/92 and trends, annual rpt, S6790–5.1

Pennsylvania public and nonpublic school enrollment, by grade, race-ethnicity, sex, and county, 1992/93 and trends, annual rpt, S6790–5.17

Rhode Island enrollment in preprimary school, by county and municipality, 1990 census rpt, S6930–9

Rhode Island public school enrollment by type of instn, grade, sex, race-ethnicity, and district, 1991/92 or fall 1992, annual rpt, S6970–1.1

South Carolina educational enrollment, by school type or level, program, race, and location, 1991/92, annual rpt, S7145–1.3

South Dakota public and nonpublic school enrollment, by grade level, 1991/92, annual rpt, S7315–1.1

Tennessee public school enrollment, attendance, and grads, by county, city, and school district, 1991/92, annual rpt, S7490–2.2

Texas elementary and secondary education enrollment by grade level, by district and county, 1991/92, annual rpt, S7670–1.2

Utah public school enrollment by demographic characteristics and district, 1991/92, annual rpt, S7815–1.2

Vermont elementary and secondary school enrollment by grade, sex, race-ethnicity, school, and county, 1992/93 and trends, annual rpt, S8020–1

West Virginia public and private schools, enrollment, grads, and staff, by county, 1991/92, annual rpt, S8540–3

West Virginia public school finances, enrollment, staff, and programs, by county, 1992/93 and trends, annual rpt, S8540–4

Wisconsin elementary and secondary school enrollment, staff, costs, and State aid, by school district, 1992/93 and trends, annual rpt, S8795–2

see also Head Start Project

Prescription drugs

see Drugs

Presidency of the U.S.

- Advertising industry professional views on impact of Clinton Admin economic plan, Feb 1993 survey, article, C2710–1.514
- Books written by 4 former Presidents, with publisher, and contract and sales info, 1992 article, C1852–2.502
- Corporate CEO views on Clinton Admin performance, economic plan, and health care reform financing, Apr-May 1993 survey, article, C8900–1.516
- Corporate executive views on President-elect Clinton and his proposed programs, Nov 1992 survey, C5800–7.505

Education reform effectiveness of President Clinton vs President Bush, public opinion by respondent characteristics, 1993 annual Gallup Poll, A8680–1.503

Gallup polling surveys of public views on presidential performance and policies, by respondent characteristics, monthly rpt, C4040–1

Industrial executive views on priorities for Clinton Admin, Nov 1992 survey, article, C7000–2.502

News media personnel views on 1992 presidential election coverage, candidates, and related issues, for natl media, Oct 1992 survey, C8915–4.25

Public confidence in selected societal instns, 1993 Gallup Poll and trends, C4040–1.510, R8780–1.508

Public interest in current news events, and opinion on media coverage and selected current issues, by respondent characteristics, 1993 surveys, C8915–1.502, C8915–1.504, C8915–1.505

Public opinion on Clinton Admin policies and actions, by respondent characteristics, series, C8915–7

Public opinion on performance of Presidents Reagan and Bush, by sex, 1981-92, U4510–1.65

Public opinion on President Clinton job performance, Jan-Apr 1993 surveys, article, C5800–7.526

Public opinion on President Clinton job performance overall and on economy during 1st 100 days in office, Apr 1993 survey, article, C5800–7.527

Public opinion on President-elect Clinton's priorities, attributes, and likely influence from selected groups, Jan 1993 survey, C8915–1.501

Public opinion on 1992 presidential campaign, Nov 1992 survey, C8915–4.24

Stock market performance during presidential admins since 1889, for 6 admins with largest gains and losses in S&P 500, 1992 article, C5800–7.505

Stock market performance during 1st 4 months of Clinton Admin and 8 previous admins, 1993 article, C5800–7.535

TV audience ratings and shares for President Clinton's budget presentation, in 12 cities, Aug 1993, article, C9380–1.536

TV news coverage of President Bush, including evaluations of policies, 1989-93, article, R3823–1.504

TV news coverage of presidential transition from Bush to Clinton, including issues, individuals, and evaluations, Nov 1992-Jan 1993, article, R3823–1.504

TV news coverage of 1st 6 months of Clinton Admin, including evaluations of individuals, issues, and agencies, and comparisons to Bush Admin, 1993 article, R3823–1.509

see also Congressional-executive relations

see also Presidential appointments

see also Presidential families

see also Presidential powers

see also Presidential vetoes

Presidential advisory bodies

see Federal boards, committees, and commissions

Presidential appointments

Clinton Admin presidential appointments and confirmations compared to same periods of Reagan and Carter Admins, as of June 1993, article, C8900–1.520

Hispanic American vs total Clinton Admin appointees confirmed by Senate, as of Sept 1993, C4575–1.511

Judgeships in Federal courts, with detail for black, Hispanic, and Asian appointees, 1976-92, article, C4215–1.505

Public interest in current news events, and opinion on media coverage and selected current issues, by respondent characteristics, 1993 surveys, C8915–1.502

Public opinion on Clinton Admin transition and cabinet appointments, Dec 1992-Jan 1993 Gallup Polls, C4040–1.507

Public opinion on Clinton and Bush Admins cabinet appointments, Dec 1992 Gallup Poll, C4040–1.506

Public opinion on Clinton appointment of David Gergen, and nomination and withdrawal of Lani Guinier, June 1993 Gallup Poll, C4040–1.512

Public opinion on controversy surrounding Clinton Attorney General nominee Kimba Wood, Feb 1993 Gallup Poll, C4040–1.508

Public opinion on controversy surrounding Clinton Attorney General nominee Zoe Baird, Jan 1993 Gallup Poll, C4040–1.507

Public opinion on news items concerning President-elect Clinton's cabinet and other appointments, Jan 1993 survey, C8915–1.501

Presidential commissions

see Federal boards, committees, and commissions

Presidential-congressional relations

see Congressional-executive relations

Presidential elections

see Elections

Presidential families

Public opinion on fairness of media coverage of Clinton Admin and Hillary Clinton, with detail by respondent characteristics, June 1993 survey, C8915–7.4

Public opinion on Hillary Clinton, including her appointment to head health care reform task force, Jan 1993 Gallup Poll, C4040–1.508

Public opinion on Hillary Clinton, 1992-93 Gallup Polls and trends, C4040–1.505, C4040–1.510, C4040–1.511, C4040–1.512

Presidential powers

Venezuela presidential decrees, by admin, purpose, and ministry, and business and govt leader views on presidential power, 1992 rpt, U6250–1.22

see also Congressional-executive relations

see also Pardons

see also Presidential appointments

see also Presidential vetoes

Presidential vetoes

Vetoes cast by President Bush, with congressional override outcomes, 1989-92, annual rpt, C2500–2

see also Gubernatorial vetoes

Presley, Cheryl A.

"Alcohol and Drugs on American College Campuses", U4950–1

Press

see Journalism

Pressure groups

see Lobbying and lobbying groups

Pretrial detention and release

Jail pretrial population and average length of stay, for 90 local systems, Jan 1992, annual rpt, R4300–1.4

State and local:

Connecticut defendants by bail disposition, and confined defendants by duration of confinement, FY91-92, biennial rpt, S1220–1.2

DC statistical profile, general data, 1992 annual rpt, S1535–3.8

Florida correctional system detainees under pretrial intervention, FY92 annual rpt, S1720–1

Maine superior court bail review cases, 1987-FY92, annual rpt, S3463–1

New York State local jail/penitentiary inmates by offense, sentence, and demographic characteristics, by county or facility, 1991, annual rpt, S5724–2

North Dakota local correctional instn adult and juvenile inmate characteristics, by instn, 1991 and trends, annual rpt, S6060–3

Tennessee correctional instn admin, with inmate characteristics, and corrections dept finances and staff, FY92, annual rpt, S7480–1

see also Habeas corpus

Preventive medicine

Health condition and preventive health care and safety practices of adults, by respondent characteristics, 1992 and trends, annual survey rpt, C8111–2

Medical school faculty and compensation, by dept, academic rank, degree, and region, 1992/93, annual rpt, A3273–2

Physicians by detailed specialty and location, 1992 and trends, annual rpt, A2200–3

Substance abuse prevention vs treatment, expenditures by State, FY91, annual rpt, A7112–1

State and local:

Alabama health behavior risk factor surveillance survey results, by respondent characteristics, 1988-89, recurring rpt, S0175–6

Colorado health behavior risk factor surveillance survey results, by respondent characteristics, 1990, recurring rpt, S1010–3

Hawaii health screening activity, and mammogram use by age group and race-ethnicity, 1990, annual rpt, S2065–1

Kentucky Medicaid recipients and payments, by program, county, and type of medical service, monthly rpt, S3140–5

Maryland medical assistance payments and recipients, by program, type of service, location, demographic characteristics, and facility, FY92 and trends, annual rpt, S3635–3

Massachusetts health behavior risk factor surveillance survey results, by respondent characteristics, 1986-90, recurring rpt, S3850–3

Preventive medicine

Missouri medical assistance expenditures for early and periodic medical screening, by month, FY92, annual rpt, S4575–2

Montana welfare and medical assistance program cases and payments, by county and type of service, monthly rpt, S4755–1

Nebraska Medicaid recipients and payments, by type of service and county, FY92, annual rpt, S4957–1.2

New York State health behavior risk factor surveillance survey results, by respondent characteristics, 1990, recurring rpt, S5765–3

North Dakota health behavior risk factor surveillance survey results, by respondent characteristics, 1991 and trends, annual rpt, S6105–3

Pennsylvania health behavior risk factor surveillance survey results, by respondent characteristics, 1991, annual rpt, S6820–4

South Dakota medical assistance recipients and payments, by type of service, FY92, annual rpt, S7385–1.1

Utah health behavior risk factor surveillance survey results, by respondent characteristics, 1991, annual rpt, S7835–3

see also Health maintenance organizations *see also* Occupational health and safety *see also* Vaccination and vaccines

Price indexes

see Consumer Price Index see Producer Price Index

Price regulation

- Electric power price rate increases requested and approved, quarterly 1992, article, A4700–4.504
- Motor carrier rate interstate discounts, including percent of shipments discounted, and comparisons to Texas intrastate shipments, 1993 rpt, U8850–9
- Transportation regulatory agency policies and practices for motor carriers and railroads, by agency, 1991/92 annual rpt, A7015–4
- Utility regulatory agency policies and practices, and industry financial and operating data, by utility type and agency, 1991/92 annual rpt, A7015–3

State and local:

- Alaska public utilities commission regulatory activities, with data by company, FY92 and trends, annual rpt, S0280–4.1
- Arkansas public utility financial, operating, and regulatory data, by utility type and company, 1992 annual rpt, S0757–1
- California public utility and transportation regulatory data, including revenue requests and rates of return by company, FY92 annual rpt, S0930–1
- Florida public utility regulatory and operating data, by company and utility type, 1992 and trends, annual rpt, S1790–1
- Nebraska public service commission regulatory activities, with financial and operating data for individual railroads and telephone companies, FY91-92 biennial rpt, S4940–1
- New Mexico public utility operating, financial, and regulatory data, by utility type, FY92 annual rpt, S5645–1

North Carolina public utility financial, operating, and regulatory data, by utility type and company, 1990 and trends, annual rpt, S5917–2

Tennessee public utility and transportation commission regulatory activities, with industry financial and operating data, 1991-92 biennial rpt, S7565–1

see also Agricultural production quotas and price supports

Prices

- Business executives expectations for coming qtr, attitudes on key indicators, with trends and data by census div, quarterly rpt, C3150–4
- Business Week economic indicators, including prices for selected commodities, weekly rpt, C5800–7
- Coffee, Sugar, and Cocoa Exchange trading activity, with related data including deliveries and stocks by country and/or port, 1992 and trends, annual rpt, B2275–1
- Commodity price trends, with detail for selected commodities or groups, biweekly rpt quarterly feature, C3950–1.505, C3950–1.513, C3950–1.519, C3950–1.524
- Commodity yearbook for 1993: prices, stocks, production, exports, and imports, for approx 100 agricultural and industrial materials, including by producing State and country, C2400–1
- Commodity yearbook update: prices, stocks, production, and trade, for approx 100 basic commodities, including by country and producing State, Jan-Sept 1993 rpts, C2400–2
- Construction industry activities, including data on costs, materials prices, wages, financing, and contract awards, weekly rpt, C5800–2
- Consumer attitudes on economic conditions and personal financial situation, monthly survey, U7475–2
- Consumer price trends, for Canada, Japan, and 4 European countries, 1976-92, article, A6450–2.503
- Consumer price trends for selected goods and services, 1953, 1973, and 1993, C8900–1.526
- Europe public opinion on political, economic, and social issues of interest to foreign investors, for 9 countries and 3 Soviet Union Republics, 1991 survey, C8915–9
- Forecasts for price changes, 50 economists, 1992-93, annual feature, C5800–7.509
- Germany (East vs West) prices of selected food and nonfood items, 1988, R4105–82.3
- Hispanic-owned business outlook for selected performance indicators, with data by region, monthly rpt quarterly feature, C4575–1.510
- Latin America statistical abstract, general data by country, 1992 annual rpt, U6250–1.31
- Purchasing managers views on business conditions, monthly rpt, A6910–1
- Retail prices for selected consumer items in approx 300 cities, quarterly rpt, A0150–1
- Russia price trends, Jan-May 1993, U2030–1.510

Securities traded over-the-counter on NASDAQ market, trading volume and price performance, for over 4,500 issues, 1992 and trends, annual rpt, A7105–1

- Small business views on current and expected economic conditions, survey findings, quarterly rpt, A7815–1
- Steel industry finances, operations, and employment, with data for integrated plants and mini-mills, 1970s-93, article, U2160–1.503
- Supermarket industry views on vendor product pricing, including every day low price concept, 1992 survey article, C4655–1.501
- Travel price index trends, by component, monthly rpt, R9375–1
- Vending machine sales by product type, with shares by price group, 1992 and trends, annual rpt, C9470–1
- Wealthy lifestyles, comparative prices of selected goods and services, 1976 and 1993, annual article, C3950–1.526
- World commodity prices and price indexes, by selected commodity, 1975-89, biennial rpt, R9455–1.5
- World financial market devs including economic and monetary trends and forecasts for 15 industrial countries, bimonthly rpt, B6200–2

State and local:

Illinois, Chicago industrial purchasing managers business activity index, bimonthly rpt, S2405–2

see also Agricultural prices

see also Agricultural production quotas and price supports

see also Coal prices

see also Consumer Price Index

see also Dumping

see also Economic indicators

see also Electric power prices

see also Energy prices

see also Family budgets

see also Food prices

see also Housing costs and financing

see also Inflation

see also Medical costs

see also Natural gas prices

see also Petroleum prices

see also Price regulation

see also Producer Price Index

see also under names of specific commodities, services, or industries

Primates

see Animals

Princeton Survey Research Associates

News events followed most closely by public, and opinion on media coverage and selected current issues, by respondent characteristics, recurring rpt, C8915–1

Printing and publishing industry

- Advertising revenues for top 10 publishing companies, 1st half 1993, C2710–1.538
- Advertising revenues for top 10 publishing companies, 1st 9 months 1992-93, C2710–1.551
- Advertising revenues for top 10 publishing companies, 1992, C2710–1.513
- Business forms industry trends and outlook, including data by product type, 1992 annual rpt, A5785–2
- Business forms manufacturing plant employment and compensation data, by region, 1992 and trends, biennial rpt, A5785–4

Corporate performance ratings by executives for leading companies in 32 industries, 1993 annual survey feature, C8900–1.508

Financial performance and growth rankings for approx 1,000 top corporations, with comparisons by industry group, 1993 annual rpt, C3950–1.505

Financial ratios and performance, for over 350 SIC 4-digit industries, FY88-92, annual rpt, A6400–3

Foundations publishing annual rpts and other publications, by organization characteristics, 1992 and trends, annual rpt, R4900–1

Franchise operations and finances, by type of business, 1991/92 and trends, annual rpt, A5820–1

Graphic arts mgmt, including data on printing and publishing industries operations and outlook, monthly rpt, C1850–10

Latin America statistical abstract, general data by country, 1992 annual rpt, U6250–1.4, U6250–1.10

Library and book trade reference info, including public and academic library funding, construction, and operations, by State and instn, 1992, annual compilation, C1650–3

Operating and financial composite ratios for corporations, with establishments and receipts, for approx 200 industries, by asset size, FY90, annual rpt, C7800–1

Paper and paperboard shipments and consumption, by product grade and end use, 1993 annual rpt, C3975–5.3

Paper distribution industry business activity, sales and performance trends, and mgmt devs, monthly rpt, A8140–3

Paper supplier services and performance, and electronic prepress and output device use, 1993 survey and trends, article, A8140–3.505

Paper supplier services and performance, and paper use patterns, views of printers, 1993 survey article, A8140–3.502

Public relations firms and depts purchasing of selected types of support services, computer software, and telecommunications, 1992 survey, article, A8770–1.501

Publishers Weekly, articles and special features on publishing and bookselling activities and trade, with monthly sales trend, weekly rpt, C1852–2

Religious congregation characteristics, including membership, activities, staff, and finances, 1992 survey, recurring rpt, A5435–4

Salaries for 24 printing industry positions, and employee benefits offered, 1993 annual feature, C1850–10.510

Sales, employment, and equipment, for top 101 North American firms, 1993 annual feature, C1850–10.512

Supermarket sales of nonfood products, by detailed product type, 1992, annual feature, C5225–1.508

Trading cards for 6 baseball players, prices as of June 1989-93, article, C5800–7.538

State and local:

Arizona statistical abstract, general data, 1993 recurring rpt, U5850–2.17

Florida statistical abstract, general data, 1992 annual rpt, U6660–1.12

Hawaii University Press books and scholarly journals published, and sales, 1988-92, annual rpt, S2090–1.16

see also Books and bookselling

see also Copyright

see also Newspapers

see also Periodicals

see also Textbooks

see also Writers and writing

see also under By Industry in the "Index by Categories"

Prison sentences

see Sentences, criminal procedure

Prison work programs

Directory of correctional instns, with facilities and programs, by US and Canadian instn, 1992, annual rpt, A1305–3

Directory of local jails and adult detention facilities, with use of work release programs, by State and instn, Dec 1992, recurring rpt, A1305–1.2

Inmates assigned to work programs, with wages received, by State and for Federal system, 1992 annual series, R4300–1

State and local:

California correctional inmates in work camps and work furlough programs, 1991, annual rpt, S0820–1

Florida correctional instns, admin, and inmates by criminal background and demographic characteristics, FY92 annual rpt, S1720–1

Georgia correctional instns, admin, and inmate characteristics, FY92, annual rpt, S1872–1

Iowa correctional instn work release revocations and inmates returned, by instn, monthly rpt, S2770–1

Kansas correctional instn inmates, by offense, demographic characteristics, and instn, FY92 and trends, annual rpt, S2940–1

Michigan prison work program finances and prisoner wage rates, 1991 annual rpt, S3960–1

Nebraska correctional instn admin, with inmates by criminal background and demographic characteristics, by instn, FY92 and trends, annual rpt, S4850–1

North Carolina correctional instn admissions, separations, and population, with inmate characteristics, FY93, semiannual rpt, S5900–1

Ohio prison industries participants and finances, FY91, annual rpt, S6370–1

Oklahoma correctional inmates participating in public works programs, monthly FY91, annual rpt, S6420–1

Oregon State corrections industries financial statements, FY92, annual rpt, S6603–2

South Carolina prison work credit program participants, FY92, annual rpt, S7135–1

Utah correctional industries workers and finances, with inmate participation compared to other leading States, FY92 annual rpt, S7810–1

Washington State correctional instn inmate population, admissions, and releases, by demographic characteristics, quarterly rpt, S8337–1

Wyoming penitentiary industry and laundry operations, and inmates in work release program, FY92, annual rpt, S8883–1

Prisoner early release programs

see Rehabilitation of criminals

Prisoners

Black American crime, arrest, and incarceration data, with comparisons to whites, 1970s-91, annual compilation, C6775–2.5

Burglary (home) prevention, and preferred entry method and time of day, views of incarcerated burglars, 1993 survey article, C1850–13.505

Correctional inmates and expenditures, by State, 1993-94 biennial rpt, S8780–1.2

Correctional instn admin, inmates, facilities, costs, parole and probation, and staffing, for local, State, and Federal systems, 1992 annual series, R4300–1

Directory of correctional instns, with inmates, staff, and cost of care, by US and Canadian instn, 1992, annual rpt, A1305–3

Directory of local jails and adult detention facilities, with inmates, staff, and operating summary, by State and instn, Dec 1992, recurring rpt, A1305–1

General Educational Dev (GED) testing programs and results in Federal and Michigan correctional instns, 1992, annual rpt, A1410–16

Latin America statistical abstract, general data by country, 1992 annual rpt, U6250–1.15

Mothers incarcerated and their children, with data on characteristics, child caregivers, visitation, and support program participation, 1991/92, A7575–4

Religious involvement correlation with adjustment to incarceration, 1992 rpt, A7575–1.11

State incarceration rates and trends in prisoners sentenced to 1 year/more, by State, 1993 article, B8500–2.520

State social, economic, and govtl indicators, with rankings, 1993 semiannual rpt, B8500–1.10

Statistical profiles of 50 States and DC, general data, 1993 annual almanac, C4712–1

Trends in incarceration rates, correctional populations, and crime rates, with analysis of theory that increased imprisonment reduces crime, 1993 rpt, A7575–3

Western States corrections data, including prisoners and capacity, and related data on population and crime, for 13 States, 1980s-90, A4375–13

State and local:

Alabama criminal offender dispositions including incarcerations, and prison releases, by selected offense, 1988-90, annual rpt, S0119–1.2

Alaska correctional instn inmates, by facility, 1991-92, annual rpt, S0275–1

Alaska corrections system admin, including inmate and probationer/parolee offenses and demographic characteristics, 1991 annual rpt, S0287–1

Arizona correctional instn admin, including inmates by criminal background and demographic characteristics, FY92, annual rpt, S0464–2

Arizona statistical abstract, general data, 1993 recurring rpt, U5850–2.12

California adults and juveniles held under local supervision, by type of facility, 1982-91, annual rpt, S0910–2.1

Prisoners

California correctional instn inmates, by offense, demographic characteristics, and instn, Dec 1992, semiannual rpt, S0820–2

California correctional instn inmates, with criminal background and demographic characteristics, 1991 and trends, annual rpt, S0820–1

California correctional instn population, parole and probation, and justice system expenditures, 1987-92, annual rpt, S0910–1.2

California felons newly received and paroled, by sex, and inmates in detention facilities, 1988-90, annual planning rpt, S0830–2

DC criminal justice system summary, including crimes and arrests, criminal procedure, prisoners, and parole, 1991 and trends, annual rpt, S1535–2

DC statistical profile, general data, 1992 annual rpt, S1535–3.8

Delaware drug offenders admitted to correctional facilities, 1986-91, annual rpt, S1375–5

Florida correctional instns, admin, and inmates by criminal background and demographic characteristics, FY92 annual rpt, S1720–1

Florida county data book, 1992/93 annual rpt, C6360–1

Florida "habitual offender" sentencing laws effect on prison population, with data by circuit court and offender characteristics, 1993 rpt, A7575–5

Florida statistical abstract, general data, 1992 annual rpt, U6660–1.22

Georgia correctional instns, admin, and inmate characteristics, FY92, annual rpt, S1872–1

Hawaii data book, general data, 1992 annual rpt, S2090–1.4

Illinois corrections dept admin, including inmates and characteristics, finances, and staff, FY91-93 and trends, annual rpt, S2425–1

Illinois statistical abstract, general data, 1992 annual rpt, U6910–2

Iowa correctional instn admissions, releases, and inmate characteristics, by instn, monthly rpt, S2770–1

Kansas correctional instn inmates, by offense, demographic characteristics, and instn, FY92 and trends, annual rpt, S2940–1

Kentucky prison releases, by State area, 1991, annual planning rpt, S3140–3

Massachusetts correctional instn inmate socioeconomic characteristics and criminal background, by instn, Jan 1992 and trends, annual rpt, S3805–1

Michigan correctional instns, admin, and inmates by selected demographic characteristics, 1991 and trends, annual rpt, S3960–1

Michigan labor force planning rpt, including characteristics of Job Training Partnership Act eligible population by State area, 1993 annual rpt, S3980–1.2

Mississippi statistical abstract, general data, 1992 annual rpt, U3255–4.9

Missouri correctional instn admissions, releases, and inmate characteristics, FY93, annual rpt, S4501–1

Nebraska correctional instn admin, with inmates by criminal background and demographic characteristics, by instn, FY92 and trends, annual rpt, S4850–1

New Jersey correctional instn inmates, by offense, sentence length, demographic characteristics, and instn, Dec 1991 annual rpt, S5370–1

New York State correctional instn inmate population and characteristics, and probation and parole, 1991 and trends, annual rpt, S5760–3.4

New York State correctional instn inmates released, by criminal background, sentence, and demographic characteristics, 1991 and trends, recurring rpt series, S5725–1

New York State local jail/penitentiary inmates by offense, sentence, and demographic characteristics, by county or facility, 1991, annual rpt, S5724–2

North Carolina correctional instn admissions, separations, and population, with inmate characteristics, FY93, semiannual rpt, S5900–1

North Dakota local correctional instn adult and juvenile inmate characteristics, by instn, 1991 and trends, annual rpt, S6060–3

Ohio correctional instn admissions and releases, inmate characteristics, programs, finances, and staffing, FY91 and trends, annual rpt, S6370–1

Oklahoma correctional instn admin, including inmate characteristics, incarceration costs, and data by instn, FY91, annual rpt, S6420–1

Oklahoma statistical abstract, general data, 1992 annual rpt, U8130–2.7

Pennsylvania State correctional instn admin, and inmates by type of offense and demographic characteristics, 1990 and trends, annual rpt, S6782–1

South Carolina correctional instns, admin, and inmates by criminal offense and demographic characteristics, FY92 and trends, annual rpt, S7135–1

South Carolina statistical abstract, general data, 1993 annual rpt, S7125–1.5

South Dakota correctional instn admin, including inmates by criminal background and demographic characteristics, FY92 and trends, annual rpt, S7296–1

Tennessee correctional instn admin, with inmate characteristics, and corrections dept finances and staff, FY92, annual rpt, S7480–1

Texas correctional instn inmates by criminal background and demographic characteristics, FY92, annual rpt, S7660–1

Utah corrections inmates, parolees, and probationers, by criminal background and demographic characteristics, FY92 and trends, annual rpt, S7810–1

Washington State correctional instn inmate population, admissions, and releases, by demographic characteristics, quarterly rpt, S8337–1

Wisconsin correctional instn inmates, by criminal background and selected characteristics, series, S8692–1

Wyoming correctional instn admin, finances, inmate characteristics, and staff, and probation and parole activities, FY92 annual rpt, S8883–1

Index by Subjects and Names

see also Community-based correctional programs

see also Fugitives from justice

see also Parole and probation

see also Prison work programs

Prisons

see Correctional institutions

see Prisoners

see Sentences, criminal procedure

see State funding for corrections

Privacy

see Right of privacy

Private branch exchanges

see Telephones and telephone industry

Private clubs and societies

see Membership organizations

Private labels

see Labeling

Private schools

Black American educational statistics, with comparisons to whites, 1970s-92, annual compilation, C6775–2.3

Business school faculty and admin salaries, by rank or position, and instn control, 1992/93, annual rpt, A0605–1

Catholic colleges, elementary and high schools, enrollment, and teachers, by diocese and State, 1993 annual compilation, C4950–1

Charitable contributions distribution by donor type for independent elementary and secondary schools, 1991, annual rpt, A0700–1.2

Costs to students of aggregate tuition, room, board, and fees, for 8 major private instns, 1993/94 and trends, article, C8900–1.514

Elementary and secondary private school enrollment, staff, and finances, by school type and region, 1980s-1992/93, annual rpt, A6835–3

Elementary/secondary private school endowments, for top 9 instns, 1993 article, R4800–2.521

Elementary/secondary school parental selection, parent and general public views, and local program characteristics and results, 1992 rpt, R3810–7

Enrollment in private schools, with comparison to public schools, 1982-2003, annual rpt, A7375–1

Enrollment in public and private elementary and secondary schools, 1900-2000, annual rpt, R9050–1.6

Europe Jewish schools, enrollment, and teachers, in France and UK, 1981/82-1991/92, article, A2050–1.1

Financial support of educational instns from contributions, with top instns, by instn and donor type, 1991/92 and trends, article, C2176–1.514

Foreign students enrolled in US higher education instns, by instn, State, country of origin, and demographic characteristics, 1991/92 and trends, annual rpt, R5580–1

Higher education administrative salaries, for 167 positions, by instn type and budget size, 1992/93, annual rpt, A3900–1

Higher education admissions dept activity, including trends in applications received, recruitment, staff, and budgets, 1992-93, annual rpt, A6695–1

Higher education faculty and salaries at private instns, by discipline and academic rank, 1992/93, annual rpt, A3900–4

Index by Subjects and Names

Private schools

Higher education president personal and professional characteristics, 1990 and trends, recurring rpt, A1410–12

Higher education private instn salaries and benefits of chief executives and top 5 earners, and total expenditures, by instn, FY91 or FY92, article, C2175–1.519

Higher education, 2-year college enrollment, degrees, faculty and staff, and tuition/fees, by instn and State, 1992 annual directory, A0640–1

Hispanic American educational statistics, with comparisons to whites, 1970s-92, annual compilation, C6775–3.2

Mathematics proficiency results on Natl Assessment of Educational Progress tests, for public vs private school students, 1990, article, U8710–1.503

Medical school revenues by source, student aid, and staff, by instn type, 1989/90 and/or 1990/91, article, A3273–8.503

Nursing schools, programs, enrollment, student and staff characteristics, and grads, 1991 and trends, annual rpt, A8010–1

OECD member countries share of elementary and secondary students in private schools, 1986, A1600–4

Political science higher education dept characteristics, including faculty, salaries, enrollment, and finances, 1991/92 annual rpt, A2617–1

Psychology grad depts, faculty characteristics, enrollment, and student aid, US and Canada, 1990/91 and trends, annual rpt, A2620–3

Public opinion on desirability of govt tuition payments and regulation for private elementary/secondary schools, 1993 annual Gallup Poll, A8680–1.503

Southern States higher education enrollment, degrees, faculty, and finances, for 15 States, 1990s and trends, biennial fact book, A8945 1

Statistical profiles of 50 States and DC, general data, 1993 annual almanac, C4712–1

Women and minorities in professional fields, detailed education and labor force data, 1980s-91, with historical trends, recurring rpt, A3960–2

State and local:

Alaska public and private schools, staff, and enrollment summary, FY92 annual rpt, S0275–1

Arizona private school enrollment by grade, and facilities, by county, 1991/92, annual rpt, S0470–1

Arkansas enrollment in private schools, by level, 1990, census rpt, U5935–7

Arkansas higher education degrees conferred, by level, discipline, student race and sex, and instn, 1990/91 and trends, annual rpt, S0690–3

Arkansas higher education enrollment by student characteristics and geographic origins, by instn, fall 1991 and trends, annual rpt, S0690–1

Arkansas public and private school enrollment and grads, by county, 1991/92, annual rpt, S0660–1.1

California enrollment in private schools, by level, 1990, census rpt, S0840–9

California postsecondary education enrollment and degrees, by sex, race-ethnicity, and instn, 1990/91, annual series, S0827–2

California private schools, enrollment by grade, grads, and staff, with data by county, 1992/93 and trends, annual rpt, S0825–8

California public and private school enrollment, by county, 1992/93 and trends, annual rpt, S0825–7

California statistical abstract, general data, 1992 annual rpt, S0840–2.6

Colorado property assessed valuation by detailed property type, and tax levy and revenue by local district, by county, 1991-92, annual rpt, S1055–3

Colorado public and/or private school enrollment and grads, by student characteristics, county, and district, 1992 and trends, annual rpt, S1000–2.1

Connecticut private schools and enrollment, 1991/92 biennial rpt, S1185–3

DC statistical profile, general data, 1992 annual rpt, S1535–3.1, S1535–3.6

Delaware postsecondary education finances, enrollment, and degrees conferred, by instn, FY94 annual rpt, S1425–1

Delaware school enrollment, grads, staff, finances, and facilities, by county, school district, and/or instn, 1991/92, annual rpt, S1430–1

Georgia statistical abstract, general data, 1992-93 biennial rpt, U6730–1.2

Hawaii data book, general data, 1992 annual rpt, S2090–1.3, S2090–1.6

Idaho public and nonpublic school enrollment by grade, by school district and/or county, Sept 1992, annual rpt, S2225–1

Illinois higher education enrollment, degrees, staff, and finances, by public and private instn and student characteristics, 1993 annual rpt, S2475–1

Illinois private school enrollment and staff, by county, 1990/91, annual rpt, S2440–1

Indiana enrollment in private schools, by grade and instn, 1992/93, annual table, S2608–2.7

Iowa postsecondary enrollment, degrees, staff, and finances, by instn, 1990/91, annual rpt, S2755–1

Kansas private school enrollment, attendance, and teachers, by instn, 1990/91, annual rpt, S2945–1

Louisiana enrollment in private schools, by level and local area, 1980 and 1990, census rpt, U8010–4

Louisiana nonpublic schools, enrollment, and grads, by school district, 1991/92, with outlook for 1995/96, annual rpt, S3280–1.2

Maine elementary/secondary students enrolled in private schools, by local area, 1990 census rpt, S3465–9

Maine public school enrollment, facilities, staff, and finances, with selected data by county and for private schools, 1991 and trends, annual rpt, S3435–1

Maryland elementary and secondary education statistical summary, with data by county, 1991/92-1992/93 and trends, annual rpt, S3610–1

Maryland elementary and secondary student transfers between public and nonpublic schools, by county, 1991/92, annual rpt, S3610–2.3

Massachusetts nonpublic school enrollment, Oct 1980 and 1991, annual rpt, S3810–3

Minnesota postsecondary education finances, and enrollment by student characteristics, by type of school system, 1970s-93, biennial rpt, S4195–2.2

Missouri higher education enrollment, degrees, libraries, staff, and finances, by instn, 1992 and trends, annual rpt, S4520–3

Nebraska elementary and secondary schools, enrollment by grade, and staff, with data by school district and county, annual series, S4865–2

Nebraska elementary/secondary private school enrollment shares, for 21 counties, 1990, article, U7860–1.502

Nevada enrollment in private schools, 1990-91, annual rpt, S5035–2

New Hampshire public and nonpublic elementary/secondary school enrollment, by grade and school type, fall 1991, annual table, S5200–1.1

New Hampshire public and nonpublic elementary/secondary school enrollment, by grade and school type, fall 1992, annual table, S5200–1.9

New Jersey enrollment in private schools, by level and county, 1990, census rpt, S5425–19

New Jersey nonpublic schools and enrollment, by county, 1991/92, annual rpt, S5385–1.3

North Dakota elementary and secondary schools, enrollment, and staff, by school type and location, 1992/93 annual directory, S6180–2

Ohio nonpublic schools by type, 1991/92, annual rpt, S6265–2

Oklahoma private/parochial elementary and high schools, by county, 1990/91-1991/92, annual rpt, S6423–1.2

Oregon private and parochial schools, enrollment, and grads, with detail by school, county, and religious affiliation, 1992/93, annual rpt, S6590–1.19

Oregon public and private high school grads, 1965/66-1996/97, annual rpt, S6590–1.8

Pennsylvania elementary/secondary and higher education enrollment, grads, staff, and finances, by instn type, 1981/82-1996/97, recurring rpt, S6790–5.10

Pennsylvania enrollment in private schools, by level, 1990, census rpt, U4130–13

Pennsylvania higher education students by residence location, by academic level and instn type, 1992 and trends, biennial rpt, S6790–5.8

Pennsylvania public and nonpublic high school grads, sex, race-ethnicity, and county, 1991/92 and trends, annual rpt, S6790–5.14

Pennsylvania public and nonpublic school enrollment, by grade, race-ethnicity, sex, and county, 1991/92 and trends, annual rpt, S6790–5.1

Pennsylvania public and nonpublic school enrollment, by grade, race-ethnicity, sex, and county, 1992/93 and trends, annual rpt, S6790–5.17

Rhode Island elementary/secondary students enrolled in private schools, by county and municipality, 1990 census rpt, S6930–9

Rhode Island independent school enrollment by grade and city, and grads by sex and instn, 1992, annual rpt, S6970–1.1

Private schools

South Carolina educational enrollment, by school type or level, program, race, and location, 1991/92, annual rpt, S7145–1.3

South Carolina higher education enrollment, degrees, staff, and finances, by instn, 1992 and trends, annual rpt, S7185–2

South Carolina public and private schools, enrollment, and grads, by county, 1990/91 and trends, annual planning rpt, S7155–3.3

South Dakota nonpublic schools, staff, enrollment, and dropouts, 1991/92, annual rpt, S7315–1.1

Tennessee higher education enrollment and tuition, by instn, 1992/93, annual rpt, S7525–1

Tennessee statistical abstract, general data, 1992/93 annual rpt, U8710–2.16

Utah higher education and private elementary and secondary enrollment, by private instn, 1993 triennial rpt, U8960–1.3

Utah higher education degrees awarded, by level and instn, 1982/83-1991/92, annual rpt, S7895–2

Utah private school enrollment, by race-ethnicity, sex, and instn, Oct 1991, annual rpt, S7815–1.2

Vermont elementary and secondary school enrollment by grade, sex, race-ethnicity, school, and county, 1992/93 and trends, annual rpt, S8020–1

Vermont higher education info, including degrees conferred, enrollment, and finances, by instn, 1992 annual rpt, S8035–2

West Virginia higher education enrollment and degrees conferred, by instn, 1991/92 and trends, annual rpt, S8533–1.1

West Virginia math/science compensatory education program enrollments in public and private schools, by county, FY93, annual rpt, S8540–4.3

West Virginia public and private schools, enrollment, grads, and staff, by county, 1991/92, annual rpt, S8540–3

Wisconsin private schools, and enrollment by school district, 1990/91-1992/93, annual rpt, S8795–2

see also Parochial schools

Privatization

see Government corporations and enterprises

Prizes

see Awards, medals, and prizes

Probate courts and cases

State and local:

Alaska court cases and dispositions, by type of court and case, and location, with judicial dept finances and personnel, FY92 and trends, annual rpt, S0290–1

Arizona court cases and dispositions, by type of case and court, with judicial personnel and finances, by county and city, FY92, annual rpt, S0525–1

Arkansas court caseloads and dispositions, by type of court and case, and location, FY92 and trends, annual rpt, S0647–1

California court cases and dispositions, by type of case and court, and location, FY92 and trends, annual rpt, S0905–1.2, S0905–2

Colorado court cases and dispositions, by type of court and detailed case type, FY92 and trends, annual rpt, S1035–1.2

DC court cases and dispositions, by type of case, and judicial system finances, 1992 and trends, annual rpt, S1515–1

Delaware court caseloads and dispositions, by type of court and case, and by county, with judicial dept finances, FY92, annual rpt, S1360–1

Florida court cases and dispositions, by type of court and case, and location, 1992, annual rpt, S1805–1

Georgia court cases and dispositions, by type of court and case, and location, with judicial dept finances and personnel, FY92, annual rpt, S1903–1

Hawaii court cases and dispositions, by type of court and case, and judicial circuit, FY92 and trends, annual rpt, S2115–1.2

Indiana court cases and dispositions by type of court and case, and location, with judicial system finances and personnel, 1992, annual rpt, S2703–1

Iowa court cases, processing, and dispositions, by type of court and district, with judicial dept appropriations and personnel, 1992 and trends, annual rpt, S2815–1

Kansas court caseloads and disposition, by type of court and case, and location, FY92, annual rpt, S3035–1

Massachusetts court cases and dispositions, by type of court and case, and location, FY92 and trends, annual rpt, S3807–1

Michigan court caseloads and dispositions, by type of court and case, and court location, 1992 and trends, annual rpt, S3962–1

Nebraska court cases and dispositions, by type of court and case, and location, 1992 and trends, annual rpt, S4965–2

New Mexico court cases and dispositions, by type of court and case, and location, with judicial system finances and personnel, FY92, annual rpt, S5623–1

New York State court cases and dispositions, by type of court and case, and jurisdiction, 1991, annual rpt, S5730–1

North Carolina court cases and dispositions, by type of court and case, and location, with judicial dept finances and personnel, FY91, annual rpt, S5950–1

North Dakota court caseloads and dispositions, by type of case and court, and location, with judicial dept finances, 1991-92, annual rpt, S6210–1

Ohio court caseload and case disposition, by type of court and case, and location, 1992, annual rpt, S6385–1

Oklahoma court cases and dispositions, by type of court and case, with judicial system finances, by county or jurisdiction, FY92, annual rpt, S6493–1

Pennsylvania court caseloads and dispositions, by type of court and case, and county, 1991, annual rpt, S6900–1.2

South Carolina court cases and dispositions, by type of court and location, with judicial dept finances and employees, 1992 and trends, annual rpt, S7197–1

South Dakota court cases and dispositions by type of case, and judicial system finances and personnel, by jurisdiction, FY92 and trends, annual rpt, S7395–1

Tennessee court cases and dispositions, by type of court and case, and county, FY92, annual rpt, S7585–1

Texas court cases and dispositions, by type of court and case, and location, FY92, annual rpt, S7703–1

Vermont court cases and dispositions, by type of court and case, and location, FY92 annual rpt, S8120–1

Washington State court cases and dispositions, by type of court and case, and jurisdiction, with judicial finances and personnel, 1992 and trends, annual rpt, S8339–1

Probation

see Parole and probation

Processed foods

see Food and food industry

Procurement

see Business orders

see Defense contracts and procurement

see Government contracts and procurement

see Industrial purchasing

Producer Price Index

Aerospace industry price deflators, by SIC 4-digit code, 1972-91, annual rpt, A0250–2.1

Australia CPI, price index for manufacturing materials, and mining pay index, monthly rpt, B6800–1

Canada CPI, and price index for industrial products, monthly rpt, B6800–1

Carpet and rug industry shipments by type, PPI, and US trade by country, 1991 and trends, annual rpt, A3800–1

Chemical and chemical process industries, operating and technical devs, and plant and equipment costs and production indexes, monthly rpt, C5800–8

Chemical industry finances and operations, with data by industry segment and product, 1970s-92, annual rpt, A3850–1

Chemicals and allied products industries price indexes, 1982-92, annual feature, A1250–1.530

Construction materials PPI, by commodity, 1987-90, annual rpt, U6660 1.11

Container (fiber box) shipments by end-use industry and region, and other industry operating data, 1940s-92, annual rpt, A4875–1

Distilled spirits supplier and alcoholic beverage price indexes, 1992 and trends, annual rpt, C4775–1

Economic indicator historical trends, 1900s-92, annual rpt, R9050–1.2

Electronics PPI, by product type, monthly rpt, A4725–2

Energy PPI for coal, gas fuels, electric power, and crude and refined oil, 1971-91, annual rpt, A4700–1

Forecasts of economic indicators for approx 10-13 months, monthly rpt, U1880–3

Forecasts of natl income and product account components and related indicators, quarterly rpt, U1880–1

Forecasts of natl income and product account components, employment, and financial sector activity, monthly rpt, B4950–1

Foreign CPI and PPI trends, for 6 industrial countries compared to US, 1972-92, annual rpt, A3179–2.3

Foreign economic indexes, and leading and coincident indicators for US and other industrial countries, monthly rpt, U1245–1

Product rankings

Germany (West) and US comparative socioeconomic statistics, 1970s-91, annual rpt, A5135–2.2

Household appliance industry manufacturing and market trends, by product type, various years 1920-94, biennial rpt, A3350–3

Japan economic profile, including govt finances, industrial production, foreign trade and investments, and comparisons to US, 1988-92, annual feature, R5650–2.552

Latin America statistical abstract, general data by country, 1992 annual rpt, U6250–1.31

Machine tools PPI, for selected materials and components, 1992 and trends, annual rpt, A3179–2

Malt beverages producer and retail price indexes, 1972-91, annual rpt, A3455–1.3

Meat CPI and PPI, for beef/veal, pork, other meats, poultry, and fish, 1983-91, annual rpt, A2100–1.1

Metals (primary) PPI, with detail for aluminum, copper, and steel, monthly rpt, C7000–8

Oil production equipment price indexes, by item, 1991 and trends, periodic basic data book, A2575–14.3

Printing and related industries PPI, monthly rpt quarterly table, C1850–10.502, C1850–10.505, C1850–10.508, C1850–10.510

Pulp and paper industry operations and finances, US and Canada, with detail by company and product grade, and world production and trade summary, 1993 annual rpt, C3975–5

Pulp, paper, and allied products PPI, by detailed item, 1985-92, annual rpt, A1630–6.4

Pulp, paper, and paperboard industry production, trade, and operating data, by product class, monthly rpt, A1630–5

Purchasing power as measured by PPI, and PPI trends, 1913-91, recurring rpt, U5680–2.14

Semiconductor market trends, including orders, prices, and worker hours, monthly rpt, C1850–2

Shoe industry market data, including foreign trade, production, and sales, by product type, 1991 and trends, annual rpt, A4957–1.1

South Africa economic indicators, with CPI, PPI, mining/quarrying employment and earnings, and gold milled ore working costs, monthly rpt, B6800–1

Textile industry economic and operating performance and outlook, 1988-93, annual article, C5226–3.502

Textile industry economic performance indicators and outlook, with industry trends and devs, monthly rpt, C5226–3

Trends in PPI, 1946-91, annual compilation, C6985–9.5

Wine and other alcoholic beverages PPI, 1970-92, annual rpt, C4775–2.2

see also Economic indicators

Product development

see Research and development

Product rankings

Advertising expenditures for top 200 brands, by selected medium, weekly rpt quarterly feature, C2710–1.502, C2710–1.512, C2710–1.525, C2710–1.540

Aircraft (regional) fleets and top models in use, 1992, annual rpt, A8795–1.1

Auto and truck customer sales satisfaction index, by leading model, 1992-93, annual article, C2710–3.535

Auto and truck models and/or makes with fewest problems for buyers, with summaries for US, Asian, and European manufacturers, 1993 and trends, article, C2710–3.532

Auto and truck sales and market share summary, with data by vehicle type, manufacturer, and leading make and model, 1st qtr 1992-93, C2150–3.507

Auto customer satisfaction index after 3 years of ownership, for top 14 nameplates, 1993, article, C2710–3.517

Auto customer satisfaction index, by leading model, 1992-93, annual article, C2710–3.538

Auto dealer franchise desirability rating for top 33 makes, winter 1992-93, survey article, C2710–3.525

Auto dealer satisfaction with manufacturers, index for top 15 makes, 1991-92, survey article, C2710–3.512

Auto dealership sales per outlet, by make, 1988-92, annual article, C2710–3.520

Auto dependability index after 5 years of ownership, for top 12 nameplates, 1992-93, article, C2710–3.524

Auto insurance collision coverage experiences, rankings of best and worst makes/series by claim frequency, for recent model years, 1993 annual rpt series, A5200–1

Auto insurance personal injury protection claim frequencies for makes with highest and lowest rates, 1990-92 models, annual rpt, A5200–3

Auto insurance theft coverage experiences, rankings of best and worst 1990-92 model autos and other vehicles, annual rpt, A5200–2

Auto makes ranked by consumer preference and willingness to consider for next purchase, 1993 survey, article, C2710–3.519

Auto problems for buyers, for 7 European manufacturers, 1993 article, C2710–3.533

Beer industry production, capacity, and sales volume, including top brands and brewers, 1982-92, annual feature, C0125–2.503

Beer shipments, for top 10 domestic brands, 1992, annual article, C2710–1.507

Beverage consumption and sales, by type, leading company, and brand, 1992 and trends, annual rpt, C4775–1.4, C4775–2.3

Beverage market shares, for top 10 soft drink, bottled water, and beer brands, 1992, article, C5150–2.515

Beverage product market shares and sales, by company and/or brand, 1991 and trends, annual rpt, C0125–3.1

Book industry bestsellers and weeks on bestseller list, 1992, annual feature, C1852–2.505

Book industry bestsellers, hardcover and paperback, and copies in print, 1992, annual articles, C1852–2.509

Canada auto dealer satisfaction with manufacturers, ratings for 21 makes, 1992 survey, article, C2710–3.518

Canada consumer photographic equipment and supplies purchasing patterns, with distribution of film purchases by brand, 1992 survey, recurring rpt, A8695–4

Candy sales and market shares, for top 10 brands, 1991-92, article, C2710–1.518

Coffee market shares by company, for regular and instant brands, 1990-92, annual article, C2710–1.531

Consumer photographic and video equipment ownership and use, including film and 1-use camera brands preferred, 1993 survey, recurring rpt, A8695–2

Discount chain consumer natl brand preferences, by product category and chain, and by age group, 1993 survey, annual feature, C5150–3.521

Discount chain top-selling natl brands cited by managers, by product category, chain, and region, 1993 survey, annual feature, C5150–3.520

Drugs (prescription) sales and year of patent expiration, for top 10 products, 1992, article, C8900–1.514

Drugs (prescription) top 100 brands in sales, 1992, annual feature, C5150–2.511

Drugs (prescription) top 200 brands and top 100 generic products, 1992 annual pharmacy reference guide, C5150–2.503

Drugstore chain and brand preferences of consumers, with data by product type and region, 1992 annual survey feature, C5150–2.503

Drugstore chains top-selling over-the-counter products, year ended June 1993, article, C5150–2.521

Drugstore chains top-selling products, and leading manufacturers, 1993 annual article, C5150–2.520

Entertainment industry devs and ticket sales, with detail for Broadway and road shows, and top films, weekly rpt, C9380 1

Hair care product sales trends, for top 10 brands in drugstores, with comparisons to mass merchandise and food/drug stores, year ended June 1993, articles, C5150–2.519

Liquor market statistics, including sales, consumption, trade, distillery operations, and govtl info, with data by company, brand, and location, 1992 and trends, annual rpt, C4775–1

Liquor sales for top 36 brands, 1991-92, annual article, C2710–1.513

Magazine advertising pages and revenues, for top 100 publications, weekly rpt monthly table, C2710–1

Magazine circulation, for top 200 consumer publications and top 10 nonpaid circulation magazines, 1st half 1993, semiannual article, C2710–1.541

Magazine circulation, for top 200 consumer publications and top 12 nonpaid circulation magazines, 2nd half 1992, semiannual article, C2710–1.514

Magazine circulation, for top 50-100 publications, 1991-92, annual feature, C2575–1.518

Magazine revenues, advertising pages, and circulation, for top 300 publications, 1992, annual article, C2710–1.531

Magazine revenues, circulation, advertising, and rates, for top 500 consumer and business publications, 1992, annual article, C2575–1.515

Product rankings

Motion picture foreign productions, boxoffice receipts, rental income, and top films in selected countries, weekly rpt, C9380–1

Motion picture rental income, rankings of top all-time films, 1993 annual feature, C9380–1.509, C9380–1.514

Motion picture rental income, rankings of top films, 1992, annual feature, C9380–1.509

Motor vehicle industry car and truck sales, by make and for top 10 vehicles, 1992-93 model years, annual article, C2710–3.551

Motor vehicle production and sales, with leading models, 1993 annual data book, C2710–3.531

Motor vehicle sales per dealer, for leading makes, weekly rpt monthly table, C2710–3

Newspaper circulation and newsprint consumption of 15 largest daily newspapers and companies, 1991, annual rpt, C3975–5.3

Newspaper circulation for daily and Sunday editions of top 100 papers, 6-month period ended Mar 1993, semiannual article, C2710–1.526

Newspaper circulation for daily and Sunday editions of top 100 papers, 6-month period ended Sept 1992, semiannual article, C2710–1.502

Newspaper circulation, for top publications worldwide, with US newsprint consumption, 1991-92, annual rpt, A8610–1

Soft drink consumption and market shares, by company and brand, and by flavor, 1985-92, annual article, C0125–2.504

Sporting goods purchases, by product and outlet type, census div, and purchaser characteristics, with average prices, 1992 and trends, annual survey, A8485–2

Supermarket product sales and market shares, for top brands in selected product categories, weekly rpt monthly table, C2710–1

TV audience shares and ratings for made-for-TV movies, Sept 1991-Aug 1992, annual feature, C9380–1.511

TV prime-time special audience ratings and share, for top shows broadcast Sept 1991-Aug 1992, annual feature, C9380–1.511

TV prime-time, syndicated, and cable program ratings and audience, by program, weekly rpt, C1850–14

Wine market statistics, including sales, advertising expenditures, and trade, for leading brands, 1992 and trends, annual rpt, C4775–2

Women's use and shopping patterns for personal care products, with preferred outlets and brands, 1993 survey and trends, annual feature, C5150–2.515

State and local:

Hawaii motor vehicle top makes registered, 1990-91, annual rpt, S2090–1.18

see also Corporate rankings

Product safety

Injuries involving selected consumer products, by product category, 1991, annual rpt, A8375–2.4

Personal injury jury verdict award trends, with data by case type and for awards exceeding $1 million, 1960s-92, annual rpt, C5180–1

Seafood safety concerns of supermarket customers as reported by store managers, 1992 survey article, C4655–1.501

Supermarket customer shopping patterns, and views on product safety, 1993 and trends, annual survey rpt, A4950–3

State and local:

Florida product liability insurance claim lawsuits and judgments, 1989-91, annual rpt, S1760–1

Massachusetts court cases and dispositions involving product liability, FY92, annual rpt, S3807–1

Ohio court cases and dispositions involving product liability, by county, 1992, annual rpt, S6385–1

see also Food ingredients and additives

see also Food inspection

see also Motor vehicle safety devices

see also Poisoning and drug reaction

see also Quality control and testing

Production

see Agricultural production

see Industrial production

see Industrial production indexes

see Production costs

see Productivity

Production capacity

see Industrial capacity and utilization

Production costs

Chemical and chemical process industries, operating and technical devs, and plant and equipment costs and production indexes, monthly rpt, C5800–8

Chemical ingredients used in plastics production, costs, monthly rpt quarterly table, C5800–12.501, C5800–12.505, C5800–12.508, C5800–12.511

Copper production costs, by item, 1983-91, annual rpt, S0497–1

Household appliance industry manufacturing and market trends, by product type, various years 1920-94, biennial rpt, A3350–3

Motion picture negative/print/advertising costs, 1983-92, C9380–1.518

Motor vehicle assembly cost by component, for Mexico and US, 1993 article, C2710–3.549

Paper and paperboard industry financial and operating data, by product, region, and State, 1992 and trends, annual rpt, A1630–6

Paper and pulp production costs in selected countries, 1993 annual rpt, C3975–5.3, C3975–5.4

South Africa economic indicators, with CPI, PPI, mining/quarrying employment and earnings, and gold milled ore working costs, monthly rpt, B6800–1

Western States plastics processing plant operating costs, by item, in 16 metro areas, 1993 article, C5800–12.512

State and local:

Arizona statistical abstract, general data, 1993 recurring rpt, U5850–2.14

Georgia statistical abstract, general data, 1992-93 biennial rpt, U6730–1.6

Hawaii data book, general data, 1992 annual rpt, S2090–1.22

Illinois statistical abstract, general data, 1992 annual rpt, U6910–2

Kansas statistical abstract, general data, 1991/92 annual rpt, U7095–2.8

Pennsylvania statistical abstract, general data, 1992 recurring rpt, U4130–6.2

see also Agricultural production costs

see also Capital investments

see also Energy production costs

see also Labor costs and cost indexes

see also Operating ratios

Production workers

Aerospace industry employment and payroll, and production worker hours and earnings, 1970s-91, annual rpt, A0250–2.5

Brewing industry financial and operating data, including consumption, trade, and taxes, 1991 and trends, annual rpt, A3455–1

Business forms manufacturing plant employment and compensation data, by region, 1992 and trends, biennial rpt, A5785–4

Chemical and related industries production, finances, operating ratios, employment, and trade, by country, company, and chemical, 1980s-92, annual feature, A1250–1.530

Chemical industry finances and operations, with data by industry segment and product, 1970s-92, annual rpt, A3850–1

Clothing (men's and boys) production, trade, and operating data, by garment type, 1960s-92, annual rpt, A3880–1

Clothing (women's and children's) sales, production, imports, and industry employment, hours, and earnings, by type of garment, recurring rpt, A5900–1

Compensation costs for production workers in 25 countries and 3 country groups, 1992, article, S0465–1.508

Computer industry production workers and hours, semimonthly rpt recurring feature, C1850–5

Earnings index for 27 MSAs and 4 occupational groups, 1990, biennial rpt, S3605–1.6

Earnings of production workers, by State and region, 1979 and 1992, R8490–48

Electronics industry factory sales and shipments, foreign trade, and operating data, by product category, 1980s-92, annual rpt, A4725–1

Electronics industry market devs, including employment and wages, by sector, monthly rpt, A4725–2

Electronics industry market trends and outlook, including product sales and shipments, employment, and leading manufacturers, monthly rpt, C1850–2

Frozen dessert industry employment, wages, and capital expenditures, 1969-92, annual rpt, A5825–1.1

Household appliance industry manufacturing and market trends, by product type, various years 1920-94, biennial rpt, A3350–3

Iron ore mining industry employment, wages, and hours, 1983-92, annual rpt, A2010–3.3

Jewelry industry statistics on sales, marketing, trade, and employment, with customer characteristics, 1993 annual almanac, C2150–7.509

Machine tool industry employment, compensation, and operations, 1992 and trends, annual rpt, A3179–2.1

Index by Subjects and Names — Productivity

Meat and poultry demand, prices, and processor operations and finances, with data on meat production, 1991 and trends, annual rpt, A2100–1.1

Motor vehicle/equipment production workers and earnings, with selected intl comparisons, 1970-92, annual rpt, A0865–1.3

Oil and gas industry employment and earnings, by industry segment, 1950s-91, annual compilation, C6985–9.5

Paper and paperboard industry financial and operating data, by product, region, and State, 1992 and trends, annual rpt, A1630–6

Plastics industry operating and financial data, 1992 and trends, annual rpt, A8920–1.1

Pulp and paper industry operations, US and Canada, with financial performance by company, 1990s and trends, annual rpt, C3975–5.1

Pulp, paper, and paperboard industry production, trade, and operating data, by product class, monthly rpt, A1630–5

Shoe industry production and operating data, including trade by country, retail sales, and consumer expenditures, quarterly rpt, A4957–2

Shoe industry production, employment, trade, marketing, and related data, by SIC 2- to 5-digit code or product type, 1992 annual rpt, A4957–1.2

State social, economic, and govtl indicators, with rankings, 1993 semiannual rpt, B8500–1.2

Statistical profiles of 50 States and DC, general data, 1993 annual almanac, C4712–1

Textile and clothing production employment, by industry sector, 1990-92, annual rpt, C3400–5

Textile industry economic and operating performance and outlook, 1988-93, annual article, C5226–3.502

Textile industry economic performance indicators and outlook, with industry trends and devs, monthly rpt, C5226–3

State and local:

Alabama statistical abstract, general data, 1992 recurring rpt, U5680–2.11

Arizona and US copper industry employment data, 1991 and trends, annual rpt, S0497–1

Arizona employment and unemployment, by county and industry, with production worker hours and earnings, monthly rpt, S0465–1

Arizona statistical abstract, general data, 1993 recurring rpt, U5850–2.14, U5850–2.17

California economic condition, including population, employment and earnings, income, business activity, and taxation, 1960s-92, annual rpt, S0840–3.2

California employment statistics, by demographic characteristics, industry, MSA, and county, monthly rpt, S0830–1

California statistical abstract, general data, 1992 annual rpt, S0840–2.3, S0840–2.8

Connecticut employment, hours, and earnings, by labor market area and industry, and selected economic indicators, monthly rpt, S1235–1

DC employment, earnings, and hours, by industry, with unemployment insurance data, monthly rpt, S1527–3

Delaware employment, earnings, and hours, by locality and industry, and unemployment insurance activity, monthly rpt, S1405–2

Georgia statistical abstract, general data, 1992-93 biennial rpt, U6730–1.6

Hawaii data book, general data, 1992 annual rpt, S2090–1.22

Illinois statistical abstract, general data, 1992 annual rpt, U6910–2

Kansas statistical abstract, general data, 1991/92 annual rpt, U7095–2.8

Louisiana employment, hours, and earnings, by industry and MSA, monthly rpt, S3320–2

Louisiana production workers average hours and earnings, by industry, monthly 1992, annual planning rpt, S3320–1.1

Maine employment, unemployment, and earnings, by industry group, MSA, and labor area, monthly rpt, S3465–2

Maryland labor force, employment, earnings, and hours, with data by industry and location, monthly rpt, S3605–2

Maryland statistical abstract, general data, 1993-94 biennial rpt, S3605–1.4

Massachusetts employment, hours, and earnings, by industry and local area, with unemployment insurance claims, monthly rpt, S3808–1

Michigan employment, hours, and earnings, with detail by industry and local area, monthly rpt, S3980–2

Minnesota employment, hours, and earnings, by industry group and locality, monthly rpt, S4205–1

Missouri employment, earnings, and hours, by industry and MSA, monthly rpt, S4530–3

Montana employment and unemployment, earnings, and hours, by location and/or industry, quarterly rpt, S4710–1

Montana production workers, hours, and earnings, by industry div, monthly 1991-92, annual planning rpt, S4710–3

New Hampshire employment, hours, and earnings, by industry and area, monthly rpt, S5205–1

New Jersey economic indicators, including employment, building permits, and retail trade, monthly rpt, S5425–1

New York State employment, earnings, and hours, by county, selected metro area, and industry group, monthly rpt, S5775–1

New York State statistical yearbook, general data, 1992 annual rpt, U5100–1.2, U5100–1.3

North Carolina employment, hours, and earnings, by industry group, with job placements, monthly rpt, S5917–3

Ohio employment, hours, and earnings, by industry and MSA, with job service and unemployment insurance activities, monthly rpt, S6270–1

Oregon labor force and employment statistics, including data by industry, monthly rpt, S6592–1, S6615–2

Pennsylvania employment, hours, and earnings, by industry, monthly rpt, S6845–1

Pennsylvania manufacturing production worker hours and earnings, by MSA, 1985-91, annual planning rpt, S6845–3.2

Pennsylvania statistical abstract, general data, 1992 recurring rpt, U4130–6.2

Rhode Island employment, hours, and earnings, by industry, monthly rpt, S6980–1

South Carolina employment, earnings, and hours, by industry group and locality, monthly rpt, S7155–2

South Dakota employment, earnings, and hours for selected industries and areas, with characteristics of unemployed and job service activities, monthly rpt, S7355–1

Tennessee economic indicator trends and forecasts, with data by industry div and manufacturing group, 1982-2001, annual rpt, S7560–1

Tennessee employment, hours, and earnings, by industry group and MSA, monthly rpt, S7495–2

Tennessee statistical abstract, general data, 1992/93 annual rpt, U8710–2.4, U8710–2.11

Texas employment, hours, and earnings, by MSA and industry group, and unemployment insurance, monthly rpt, S7675–3

Utah employment, hours, and earnings, by industry, monthly rpt, S7820–3

Utah statistical abstract, general data, 1993 triennial rpt, U8960–1.12

Virginia economic indicators, including new business incorporations and employment data, quarterly rpt, S8205–4

Virginia labor force, hours, and earnings, with data by industry group and locality, monthly rpt, S8205–6

Washington State employment, earnings, and hours, by labor market area and industry group, monthly rpt, S8340–3

West Virginia employment, unemployment, hours, and earnings, with job service activities, monthly rpt, S8534–1 •

West Virginia production worker hours and earnings, by industry group, 1990-91, annual planning rpt, S8534–2

Wisconsin economic indicators, including employment and earnings by industry group, monthly rpt, S8750–1

Wyoming mining industry employment, and production workers hours and earnings, monthly rpt, S8895–1

see also Employment and unemployment, specific industry

Productivity

Auto industry performance indicators for 3 major manufacturers, 1970s-92, annual article, C2150–3.506

Business forms industry detailed financial and operating ratios, with summary operating data, FY91, annual rpt, A5785–3

Chemical and chemical process industries, operating and technical devs, and plant and equipment costs and production indexes, monthly rpt, C5800–8

Computer industry employment and sales productivity, for 5 manufacturers, FY92, article, C1850–2.507

Container (fiber box) shipments by end-use industry and region, and other industry operating data, 1940s-92, annual rpt, A4875–1

Convenience store industry financial and operating data, by size category, 1992 and trends, annual survey rpt, A6735–1, A6735–2

Productivity

Discount store sales and productivity data for 20 depts, 1993 annual feature, C5150–3.516

Discount store sales productivity and space allocations, 1992 and trends, annual feature, C8130–1.507

Drugstore (independent pharmacy) sales per hour and square foot, by store characteristics, 1991 and trends, annual survey, B5165–1

Economic indicator historical trends, 1900s-92, annual rpt, R9050–1.2

Electronics company financial performance, ranking of top 200 firms, 1992 and trends, annual feature, C1850–2.509

Food marketers financial and operating data, by company size and region, 1991-92, annual rpts, A4950–5

Forbes 500 top companies in sales, profits, assets, market value, and productivity, with stock and employment data, 1992, annual rpt, C3950–1.513

Forecasts of natl income and product account components and related indicators, quarterly rpt, U1880–1

Hardware finances and operations, for hardware stores, home centers, and lumber/building material outlets, 1991 and trends, annual rpt series, A8275–1

Home furnishings retailer financial and operating data, by firm characteristics and region, 1992 and trends, annual rpt, A7975–1

Home improvement industry sales and operations, for top retailers, 1992 and trends, annual feature, C5150–6.503

Hospital pharmacy operating data, by instn type and size, and census div, 1991, annual survey, B5165–3

Mass transit rail system revenue passenger miles per vehicle hour, for 14 systems in US and Canada, 1993 article, C1575–3.505

Medical group physician and allied personnel compensation and productivity, by specialty, and demographic and practice characteristics, 1991, annual rpt, A6365–1

Medical school faculty physician and allied personnel compensation and productivity, by academic rank, sex, and specialty, 1991, annual rpt, A6365–5

Motor vehicle plant die change operations, efficiency scores for teams at 9 plants, 1992 annual article, C2150–3.501

Office product dealers sales and profits per employee and store space, by region, 1991, annual rpt, A8110–1

Plastics industry operating and financial data, 1992 and trends, annual rpt, A8920–1.1

Plastics processing industry financial and operating ratios, by processing activity, sales size, and region, 1992, annual rpt, A8920–4

Printing industries operating data, including productivity, monthly rpt quarterly table, C1850–10.501, C1850–10.504, C1850–10.507, C1850–10.511

Railroad financial and operating trends, including data by company, 1982-91, annual rpt, A3275–8

Railroad revenue ton-miles generated, per hour, car, gallon of fuel, and employee, 1920s-92, annual rpt, A3275–5.2

Restaurant industry financial and operating data, by establishment characteristics and location, 1992, annual rpt, A8200–3

Shopping center financial and operating data, with detail by type of tenant, US and Canada, 1991, triennial rpt, R9285–1

Small corporation mgmt office technology experience and views, including whether productivity gains have justified investment, 1992 survey, article, C4687–1.506

Steel industry finances, operations, and employment, with data for integrated plants and mini-mills, 1970s-93, article, U2160–1.503

Steel industry restructuring devs, with data on production, employment, and worker assistance, and selected detail by company, for 8-12 countries, 1970s-90, R9260–16

Steelworks yields, by type of product and/or process, 1992 article, C7000–8.502

Supermarket (independent) sales and operating ratios, by store type, sales size, and region, 1991, annual survey, A4950–4

Supermarket bakery dept sales and performance indicators, 1992 and trends, annual article, C4655–1.505, C5225–1.504

Supermarket deli dept sales and performance indicators, 1992, annual article, C4655–1.503

Supermarket employees and sales productivity, by store characteristics and region, 1992, annual rpt, C5225–1.505

Supermarket fish/seafood dept sales and performance indicators, 1991, annual article, C4655–1.501

Supermarket general merchandise dept sales and performance indicators, 1992 and trends, annual article, C4655–1.509

Supermarket health and beauty aid dept sales and performance indicators, 1992 and trends, annual article, C4655–1.506

Supermarket meat dept sales and performance indicators, 1992 and trends, annual article, C4655–1.509

Supermarket prepared food sales and performance indicators, 1992, annual article, C4655–1.508

Supermarket produce dept sales and performance indicators, 1992 and trends, annual article, C4655–1.511

World productivity and related indicators, trend analysis for US and other industrial countries, 1980s-92, annual rpt, R2800–2

State and local:

Alabama statistical abstract, general data, 1992 recurring rpt, U5680–2.18

see also Agricultural productivity

see also Government efficiency

see also Industrial capacity and utilization

see also Industrial production indexes

see also Labor productivity

Professional and technical workers

Employment in business and industry, hiring plans for college grads, by field, salary, and degree, 1993 annual survey rpt, U3730–1

Israel labor force share with technical background, with detail for immigrants, 1993 article, C1850–2.503

Magazine use of desktop publishing/electronic systems for pre-press

Index by Subjects and Names

operations, including staffing patterns and freelance fees, May 1993 survey, article, C2575–1.514

Planning profession employment and salaries, by type of employer, demographic and professional characteristics, and location, 1991 and trends, biennial rpt, A2615–1

Public planning agency personnel practices, by jurisdiction size, 1991 survey rpt, A2615–3

Pulp and paper industry salaries and benefits, by job characteristics, 1992 survey, annual article, C3975–2.503

Salaries of scientists, engineers, technicians, and other professionals, by employee and employer characteristics, 1990s and trends, biennial rpt, A3960–1

Salary and job offers for college grads, by field of study, type of employer, and degree level, by region, interim rpt series, A3940–1

Salary and job offers for college grads, by field of study, type of employer, and degree level, series, A3940–2

White-collar work force trends, including employment, earnings, and unionization, with data by occupation, sex, and educational attainment, 1990s and trends, annual rpt, A1570–1

Women and minorities in professional fields, detailed education and labor force data, 1980s-91, with historical trends, recurring rpt, A3960–2

Women professionals employment, with detail by race-ethnicity and for 3 occupations, 1990 and trends, article, R8750–1.511

State and local:

Arizona occupational profiles, with employment and job outlook, by industry div, occupation, and county, series, S0465 2

California statistical abstract, general data, 1992 annual rpt, S0840–2.11

DC licensed professionals, by profession, 1987-91, annual rpt, S1535–3.3

Maine employment, by SIC 2-digit industry and detailed occupation, triennial series, S3465–1

New Hampshire employment, by SIC 2- and 3-digit industry and detailed occupation, series, S5205–2

New York State statistical yearbook, general data, 1992 annual rpt, U5100–1.3

North Carolina employment in SIC 2-digit industries, by detailed occupation, triennial rpt series, S5917–5

Texas employment, by SIC 2- and 3-digit industry and detailed occupation, series, S7675–1

see also Consultants

see also Employment and unemployment, specific industry

see also Engineers and engineering

see also Executives and managers

see also Health occupations

see also Librarians

see also Pilots

see also Scientists and technicians

see also under By Occupation in the "Index by Categories"

see also under names of specific professions

Index by Subjects and Names

Projections and forecasts

Professional associations
see Associations

Professional Ethics
see Business ethics
see Ethics and morality
see Judicial ethics
see Legal ethics
see Medical ethics
see Political ethics

Professionals' fees
Architectural and engineering design firm billing rates for private and govt clients, by employee position, 1993 article, C5800–2.524
Developing countries family planning service fees, and payments to health personnel, by country, 1980s-90, R8720–1.1
Financial advisor fees paid by companies involved in mergers/acquisitions, 1988-92, article, C4683–1.502
Health insurance coverage and finances, and health care costs and facilities, by selected demographic characteristics, 1940s-91, annual rpt, A5173–2
Interior design industry financial and employment data, top 100 firms, 1993 annual article, C1850–7.501
Interior design industry financial and employment data, 2nd 100 largest firms, 1993 annual article, C1850–7.502
Magazine use of desktop publishing/electronic systems for pre-press operations, including staffing patterns and freelance fees, May 1993 survey, article, C2575–1.514
Medicaid reimbursement of physicians for obstetric services, by State, FY86-92, article, A5160–1.506
Medical group financial and operating data, by practice characteristics, 1991, annual rpt, A6365–2
Physician fees and expenses, and detailed work patterns, by specialty, type of practice and location, and age, 1992 and trends, annual rpt, A2200–5
Stockbroker commissions, fees, analysts, offices, and brokers, for 18 firms, 1993 annual article, C8900–1.528
Veterinarian (equine) characteristics and finances, and practice profile, 1992 survey and trends, annual article, C9480–1.503
Veterinarian fees, and average client transaction, by region and type of practice, 1993, annual survey, C9480–1.507

Profits
see Business income and expenses, general
see Business income and expenses, specific industry
see Farm income
see Operating ratios

Prohibition
see Alcoholic beverages licenses and fees

Project listings
see Directories

Projections and forecasts
Air cargo freight and mail volume outlook, 1991-2005, article, C7000–4.503
Air traffic and aircraft fleet size, with detail by route or carrier type, FY93-94 and FY2004, article, C5800–4.511
Aircraft (commuter) market size and potential growth, 1993-2012, article, C5800–4.517

Aircraft (jet) acquisitions worldwide, by world area, 1992-2011, article, C5800–4.507
Aircraft (regional) deliveries by seating capacity, 1993-2012, annual rpt, A8795–1.1
Aircraft deliveries to regional airlines, by plane size, 1991-2010, article, C7000–4.502
Airline intl passengers, with detail by selected route, 1980, 1990, and 2001, article, C5800–4.513
Airline passenger jet requirements projected to 2011, by aircraft class and world region, with traffic trends and outlook, 1993 annual rpt, B3075–1
Airline passenger traffic for US and Europe, 1990-2005, C7000–4.506
Airline traffic and fleet forecasts for scheduled carriers, FY93-2004, annual rpt, A0325–5
Airport spending for facilities and Federal program compliance, 1992-97, article, C5800–4.514
Alcohol demand for manufactured products, 1991 and 1996, article, A1250–1.511
Appliance industry demand for plastics, by plastic and appliance type, 1987, 1992, and 1997, article, C2000–1.509
Appliance industry shipments, by product type, 1991-98, annual articles, C2000–1.503
Auto aftermarket growth distribution by type of distribution channel, 1992-96, article, C0125–1.507
Auto aftermarket sales, by outlet type, 1992 and 1996, article, C4680–1.509
Auto sales projections by natl dealer assn, 1993-2000, article, C2710–3.536
Aviation (general) aircraft active and use, fuel consumption, and pilots, forecasts to 2004, annual rpt, A5120–2.3
Beverage container closures by type, 1991 and 1996, annual rpt, C0125–3.2
Black American consumer expenditures, 2000, articles, C5150–2.518
Black American fertility rates, and life expectancy, with comparisons to whites, projections to 2010, annual compilation, C6775–2.2
Black American labor force participation, by sex, with comparison to whites, 1995, 2000, and 2005, annual compilation, C6775–2.6
Book expenditure trends and outlook, for consumer and professional/educational books by type, 1987-97, article, C1852–2.520
Budget of US economic assumptions of Bush Admin, 1990-97, annual rpt, C2500–2
Bus manufacturer deliveries, by use, 1992-98, article, C1575–3.505
Business forms industry trends and outlook, including data by product type, 1992 annual rpt, A5785–2
Cable TV homes passed, subscribers, and finances, for telephone, cable, and direct broadcast satellite company systems, 2000, article, C1850–14.516
Cellular telephone equipment sales and subscribers, and total communications equipment market, 1985, 1991, and 1996, article, C2000–1.504
Cellular telephone/personal communication services subscribers, 1993-2005, article, C4725–3.515

Chemical chelating agent market value, by agent type, 1988, 1993, and 1998, article, C5800–8.512
Chemical process industries capital expenditures and outlook, monthly rpt, C5800–8
China imports from US of 3 fast-growing product types, 1992-2018, article, C4687–1.511
City govt costs to enforce Fed Govt regulations including environmental laws, for 314 cities, FY93, with summary projections to FY98, A9330–12
Computer (personal) and modem ownership by households, selected years 1982-96, article, A8605–1.509
Computer (personal) unit sales, by end use sector, 1992 and 1996, article, C5800–7.544
Computer application outside contracting market, with shares for top 5 and all other major vendors, 1991 and 1997, article, C1850–5.502
Computer CD-ROM writable and read-only drive sales, 1993-97, article, C1850–5.507
Computer-integrated manufacturing (CIM) open system market outlook, by system use, 1991 and 1996, article, C1850–12.502
Computer open on-line transaction processing system revenues, 1992-96, article, C1850–5.520
Computer product shipment value for small businesses, home offices, and general consumers, 1992-96, article, C2710–1.551
Computer-related market forecast for asynchronous transfer mode (ATM) transmission technology, and predicted use of personal computers vs workstations, 1993 article, C4725–3.515
Construction new project value outlook, by type of project, 1992-97, annual article, C5800–2.512
Consumer buying power survey of population, income, and sales by product line, by State, metro area, county, and census div, 1993 annual rpt, C1200–1.514
Cyclical trends for recession/recovery periods as measured by approx 70 economic indicators, quarterly rpt, U1245–2
Defense budget authority and outlays, for DOD and DOE/other, FY93-98, article, C5800–4.514
Defense industries job losses from budget cuts, with loss outlook for 1997, for 10 States, 1993 article, C8900–1.508
Distilled spirits sales and consumption, by product type, 1997, annual rpt, C4775–1.1
DOD budget authority and outlays under Bush and Clinton Admins, FY94-98, article, C5800–4.510
Drug/pharmaceutical product packaging demand, by package type, 1980, 1991, and 1996, article, C1850–1.503
Eastern Europe housing starts, with detail for 4 countries, 1992-2000, article, C4300–1.504
Economic indicator changes if Clinton Admin economic proposals are adopted, 1993-95, article, C4215–1.505

Projections and forecasts

Economic indicator forecast for natl income and product account components, employment, and financial sector activity, monthly rpt, B4950–1

Economic indicator forecasts for GDP, inflation, unemployment, and Treasury bond rates, by approx 10 forecasting organizations, monthly rpt, R4105–80

Economic indicator trends and forecasts, with detail for approx 15 Western States, 1990s, annual rpt, B3520–1

Economic outlook for selected indicators, recent trends and 2-year forecast, US Chamber of Commerce quarterly rpt, A3840–6

Economic trends and forecasts for 34 indicators, 1991-95, article, U8595–1.501, U8595–1.503

Electric utility industry employee health care costs, with comparisons to revenue and expenses, 1991 and 2000, article, A4700–4.505

Electronic data interchange (EDI) market value, 1991-92 and 1997, article, C1850–5.506

Electronic data interchange (EDI) use by businesses, and average expenditures, 1990-92 and 1996, article, C1850–2.511

Electronics industry market trends and outlook, including product sales and shipments, employment, and leading manufacturers, monthly rpt, C1850–2

Elementary/secondary enrollment in public and private schools, and teachers, 1982-2003, annual rpt, A7375–1

Employment by industry div and major industry group, 1975, 1990, and 2005, article, A3892–1.503

Employment forecasts by occupational group, with detail for white-collar, growing, and declining occupations, 2005, annual rpt, A1570–1

Employment growth projections accuracy analysis for BLS, by occupation and industry div, 1993 article, S4205–3.501

Employment in 1990 and growth through 2005, by detailed occupation, article, C8900–1.519

Employment in 2005, with current earnings and black employment share, for 16 fast-growing occupations, 1993 feature, C4215–1.503

Employment trends and outlook, for 10 metro areas with greatest projected growth, 1982-2002, article, C8900–1.519

Environmental regulation by cities under Federal mandates, local impact analysis including selected cost projections, 1993 rpt, U9640–3

Environmental services revenues by world region and selected country, 1991 and 1996, article, A1250–1.530

Europe air traffic projections, 1995-2010, article, C5800–4.501

Europe auto sales, with market shares for Japanese, US, and European manufacturers, 1990 and 1997, article, C2710–3.507

Europe thermoplastics demand, including polypropylene foreign trade, 1980s-2000, article, A1250–1.501

Federal budget deficit estimates of Bush Admin, presidential candidate Clinton, and Congressional Budget Office, FY92 and FY96, article, C8900–1.508

Federal budget expenditure outlook by major category, FY93-98, article, R9050–3.504

Federal debt measures, including data on Govt assets, liabilities, interest payments, total outlays, and deficit, 1980-98, R9050–15.1

Federal entitlement outlays for 12 programs, FY91, with projected change through FY97, R8490–47

Federal funding for info systems, by selected govt agency and military service branch, 1987, 1992, and 1997, annual rpt, A4725–1.4

Federal receipts by source and outlays by function, with impact of Clinton Admin proposals, FY80-98, recurring rpt, R9050–15.3

Federal tax revenue changes resulting from FY94 Federal budget, FY94-93, article, R9050–3.508

Food (microwaveable) sales, 1992 and 1997, article, C2150–6.508

Food service sales outlook to 2000, annual feature, C1850–3.503

Fortune magazine forecast of GDP, consumer prices, profits, and unemployment, 1993-94, article, C8900–1.519

GDP forecasts by 20 economists, 2nd qtr 1993-2nd qtr 1994, annual article, C5800–7.533

Govt finance statistics, including related projections for labor force and OASDHI taxes to 2000, annual rpt, R9050–1

Graphite demand by type and market, 1982, 1992, and 1997, article, C7000–8.505

Health care employment for 16 fastest-growing occupations, and outlook for minorities in work force, 1990 and 2005, article, A1865–1.514

Health care expenditures, and number of physicians, osteopaths, and dentists, 1950-2000, annual rpt, A5173–2

Health care spending and insurance coverage under current law vs plans of presidential candidates Bush and Clinton, by State, 1993-2005, R4865–9

Heating equipment shipments by type, 1991-95, annual feature, A5100–1

Helicopter market shares by weight class and type of use, 1990-99, annual rpt, A5190–1

High school grads by race-ethnicity and region, 1985/86-1994/95, annual rpt, A1410–10

High school grads, by State, 1991/92-2008/09, article, C2175–1.537

High school grads, by State, 1993/94 and 2003/2004, annual rpt, C2175–1.531

Higher education costs as percent of median family income, 1970s-2001/02, biennial fact book, A8945–1.4

Higher education enrollment and degrees by sex, and high school grads, 1992-2003, annual feature, C2175–1.504

Hispanic American labor force participation, by sex, with comparison to whites, 1995, 2000, and 2005, annual compilation, C6775–3.4

Home automation system installations in new and existing homes, by system type, 2000, article, C1850–13.501

Home automation system installations in new homes, outlook by system type, 2000, article, C1850–8.503

Index by Subjects and Names

Home health care product market value, 1987, 1991, and 1996, A1865–1.502

Home improvement industry retail sales to consumers and professionals, 1992-97, annual feature, C5150–6.503

Home security mechanical equipment, alarm systems, and services market value, 1980, 1991, and 1996, article, C2000–1.507

Home security system installations, 1988, 1992, and 1997, article, C1850–13.502

Hospital outpatient top 10 nonsurgical and surgical procedures performed, 1991, 1997, and 2002, article, A1865–1.502

Household appliance manufacturer sales, for 4 small appliance categories, 1982-2000, article, C2000–1.501

Housing market forecasts by region and leading metro area, and short-term outlook of industry analysts, 1993 annual article, C4300–1.503

Industrial pneumatic power systems/components market value, 1992 and 1996, article, C1850–4.505

Japan GNP growth forecast, 1988-2000, article, R5650–2.538

Jet aircraft fatal accidents worldwide resulting in hull loss, 1980s-2010, article, C5800–4.520

Labor force data, with selected detail by race-ethnicity and occupation, 1975, 1990, and 2005, article, A8510–1.1

Labor force distribution by age group, and retirees, 1985 and 2000, annual rpt, R8335–1.1

Labor force participation rates, by sex and age, 1975, 1990, and 2005, annual rpt, A1570–2

Labor force size, entrants, and leavers, by sex and race-ethnicity, 1990-2005, article, R8750–1.507

Latin America fertility rates, by selected country, 1970s-2020, annual rpt, U6250–1.6

Latin America labor force, by country and sex, projections to 2000, annual rpt, U6250–1.12

Latin America Protestants, by country, projections for 2000, annual rpt, U6250–1.10

Logistics 3rd-party market indicators, 1992, 1996, and 2000, article, C2150–1.506

Lubricants (synthetic) market volume, by product type, 1991 and 1996, article, C5800–8.509

Lubricants (synthetic) wholesale shipments value, by use category, 1991 and 1996, article, C5150–3.501

Mass media expenditures on TV, cable TV, and radio, 1992 and 1997, article, C1850–14.530

Medical device sterile packaging demand value, by package type, 1991 and 1996, article, C1850–1.502

Medical waste generation and treatment cost trends and outlook, 1993 article, A1865–1.505

Middle East petrochemical capacity and world market share, by chemical, 1991 and 2000, article, A1250–1.501

Milk production volume and number of dairy cows, 1992 and 2000, article, C2150–6.503

Mining engineer grads by degree level, 1980-1995/96, article, C5226–1.507

Index by Subjects and Names

Mining-related employment losses and change in govt revenues resulting from proposed mineral royalty for Federal lands, 1995-2004, article, C5226–2.506

Minority shares of work force and new workers, for blacks, Hispanics, and Asians, 2000, article, C1200–4.509

Mortgage foreclosure rate 5-year projection, with detail for 43 metro areas or regions in rank order, 1993 article, A6450–2.509

Motor vehicle industry weight of raw materials used in cars, by material type, 1990 and 2000, article, C5800–12.513

Natl income and product account components and related indicators forecast, Georgia State Univ quarterly rpt, U1880–1

Netherlands forecasts of diabetes incidence through 2005, article, A2623–1.509

Newsprint recycling capacity, demand, and wastepaper consumption, for Northeast US and Eastern Canada, with data by mill, various years 1988-2000, A4375–15

North America light motor vehicle sales, percent changes for US, Canada, and Mexico, 1985-2000, article, C2150–3.505

Nursing home insurance adequacy as means of making care affordable to elderly, with detail by age and/or State, 1992 and 2005, R4865–12

Packaging (paper/paperboard and plastic) demand, by container type, 1980, 1991, and 1996, article, C1850–1.506

Paper (business) shipment value, by paper type, 1987, 1992, and 1997, article, A8140–3.505

Paper (computer) sales, 1991-97, article, A8140–3.505

Paper (printing/writing) production and supply by grade, and demand by end use, 1970s-2002, article, C3975–2.503

Paper (uncoated mechanical) capacity by world area, with scheduled changes by company, 1989-95, annual rpt, A8610–1

Paper and paperboard production trends and outlook, by grade, 1989-97, annual article, C3975–2.503

Paper and paperboard US and worldwide supply-demand outlook through 2000, annual rpt, C3975–5.3, C3975–5.5

Paper and paperboard use of pulp substitutes/de-inked fiber, 1970s-2000, article, C3975–2.508

Paper, paperboard, and wood pulp industry capacity and material consumption, by grade and census div, 1970s-95, annual rpt, A1630–7

Paperboard and corrugated box sales and shipment value, by end-use market or box type, 1991 and 1996, article, C0125–4.501

Pension benefits as affected by labor mobility, 1987 and 2000, R9260–17

Personal income, by State, 1990-2000, annual almanac, C4712–1

Physician supply by specialty, 1986, 1995, 2000, and 2020, article, A1865–1.511

Plastic container demand, by container type, 1980, 1991, and 1996, article, C1850–1.501

Plastic packaging recycling volume, by plastic type, 1985, 1991, and 1996, article, C1850–1.507

Plastics (thermoplastics) consumption and demand outlook, with detail by consuming sector, 1980s-2000, article, A1250–1.538

Plastics recycling outlook in US and Europe, for year 2000, annual encyclopedia, C5800–12.503

Radiochemical market value, 1991 and 1996, article, C1850–6.505

Railroad passenger cars delivered, undelivered backlog, and new orders outlook, by purchaser, 1993 annual feature, C8400–1.503

Railroad transit system operating/capital costs, 1990 and 2000, annual fact book, C1575–3.501

Real estate closed-end investment funds and liquidity maturities, 1990-2005, article, C2710–2.520

Refrigeration commercial equipment sales and shipments, with detail by equipment type, 1982, 1992, and 1997, article, C2000–1.509

Retirement median age trends, by sex, 2000-2005, article, R8750–1.505

Rubber supply-demand outlook worldwide, with synthetic rubber consumption by resin, 1980s-97, article, A1250–1.524

Satellite revenue outlook from TV, business, and telephone industry, by world region, 1992-98, article, C1850–14.529

Scientific equipment or instruments market value outlook, for selected equipment types, monthly rpt, C1850–6

Shipbuilding (naval vessel) activity in private shipyards, with actual and projected deliveries, monthly 1988-98, recurring rpt, A8900–6

Shipbuilding related employment impact of foreign govt subsidies, 1990-2000, recurring rpt, A8900–8

Silver mine production for 60 countries, 1992-96, annual rpt, A8902–1

Silver production by country, 1992-96, annual rpt, A8902–4

Small business capital available and required, 1993-98, article, C2425–1.504

Southeastern States timber acreage by ownership class, for 6 States, 1980s-2040, biennial rpt, U6730–1.5

Southern States elementary/secondary school enrollment, and high school grads, by State, 1971/72-2001/02, biennial fact book, A8945–1.1

Space station costs by component, by funding and technology option, FY94-98 and post-FY98, article, C5800–4.530

Steel consumption worldwide, with detail by selected country or world area, 1990-93, 1995, and 2000, annual article, C7000–8.502

Styrene demand, distribution by country or world region, 1991 and 2000, article, C6985–1.505

Sulfur production and consumption worldwide, 1989-96 and 2000, article, C6985–1.546

Tax-deferred salary reduction 401(k) plan recordkeeping service market shares by provider type, 1992 and 1997, article, C2710–2.505

Tax levels as measured by date average taxpayer earns enough to pay yearly taxes, 1960-98, annual feature, R9050–3.504

Teacher employment outlook compared to selected other occupations, 1988 and 2000, R6350–7

Projections and forecasts

Telecommunication T-1/T-3 high-capacity systems monitoring equipment market value, 1992-97, article, C4725–3.514

Teleconferencing equipment and network/services market value worldwide for audio, video, and multimedia sectors, 1992-96, article, C7000–4.510

Telephone company revenues from frame relay and switched multimegabit data services, 1993-96, article, C4725–3.503

Telephone long-distance carrier revenues from toll-free ("800" number) service, for top 3 companies and all others, 1992-97, article, C1200–1.504

Telephone pay-per-call ("900" numbers) revenues, 1989-95, annual rpt, A4620–1.2

Timber products supply-demand, 1950s-2040, annual rpt, C3975–5.1

Tort case cost as percent of economic output, 1991 and 2000, article, C1850–12.504

Tourism receipts worldwide and in US, and US spending for intl tourism, projections through 2000, annual rpt, C2140–1.1

Treasury bond (30-year) interest rate forecasts of 16 economists, year-end 1993-94, article, C8900–1.526

TV unit sales projections, for high-definition TV (HDTV) vs digital TV (DTV), biennially 1994-2000, article, C1850–2.506

Video cassette (prerecorded) sales, 1993-2000, article, C5150–3.514

Videoconferencing substitution for air/high-speed surface travel, Boston, Mass study, 1993, 2010, and 2030, article, C5800–4.528

Warehouse operations outlook, including use of automation, 1990s-2000, article, C2150–1.506

Water (bottled) production, consumption, and imports and exports, 1970s-92 and 2001, annual rpt, C0125–3.1

Water treatment chemical consumption, by type, 1990 and 2000, article, C5800–8.507

Western States prison construction costs, for 13 States, 1990-2000, A4375–13

Wholesaler/distributor inside vs outside sales staff share of sales and allocation of time, with projections to 2000, 1993 article, C4725–5.506

Wholesaler/distributor market shares by company size, 2000, article, C4725–5.504

Wine sales volume and consumption, by product type and State, projections to 1997, annual rpt, C4775–2.1

World labor force growth rates, by country, 1975-2000, biennial rpt, R9455–1.5

State and local:

Alabama employment and income, by industry div and MSA, 1970s-2040, recurring rpt, U5680–2.5, U5680–2.9

Arkansas population, income, and employment trends, by MSA, 1973-2040, article, U5930–1.503

Arkansas public school enrollment by grade, and grads, 1980/81-1996/97, annual rpt, S0660–1.2

California economic impact of Federal spending and tax changes, 1993-98, annual rpt, S0840–3.1

Projections and forecasts

Colorado employment by occupation and industry div, with projections to 2005, FY94 annual planning rpt, S1040–3

Colorado employment growth by occupation, 1992-97, article, S1040–4.506

Delaware employment projections, by county, 1990-2020, recurring rpt, S1375–3

Florida health practitioners by type and service area, 1990 and 2005, annual rpt, S1746–1.2

Georgia and Atlanta MSA forecast employment by industry group and income by source, quarterly rpt, U1880–2

Georgia employment and job openings, by detailed occupation, 1990-2005, article, U6730–2.504

Georgia employment and job openings, by industry div and occupation, projected to 2005, biennial rpt, U6730–1.3

Hawaii, Oahu leasehold condominium/cooperative projects and units up for renegotiation and termination through 2050/beyond, annual rpt, S2090–1.21

Idaho and US economic trends and forecasts, quarterly rpt, S2245–2

Iowa employment by occupation and selected manufacturing industry group, 1992 and 2000, annual rpt, S2784–3

Kentucky economic impact of Toyota Motor Corp plant installation, including related State costs, employment, and benefits to other States, 1980s-2005, U7138–1.4

Kentucky job openings and employment in fastest-growing occupations, 1987-2000, annual planning rpt, S3140–3

Louisiana employment projections by occupation and industry div, 2000, annual planning rpt, S3320–1.2

Louisiana public and nonpublic school enrollment and grads, by school district, 1991/92-1995/96, annual rpt, S3280–1.2

Michigan employment projections by occupation, 1988-2000, annual planning rpt, S3980–1.2

Minnesota high school grads, and higher education enrollment, 1970s-2007, biennial rpt, S4195 2.2

Mississippi employment and job growth by industry and occupation projected to 2005, annual planning rpt, S4345–1.2

Montana labor force planning rpt, with employment and job opening projections to 1997, annual rpt, S4710–3

Nebraska elementary and secondary school projected enrollment, by grade, 1993-2002, annual rpt, S4865–2.3

Nevada employment and job opening outlook for 6 rapidly growing occupations, through 1996, article, S5040–1.502

New Hampshire labor force and unemployment projections by county, through FY93 or FY95, recurring rpt, S5205–7

New Mexico employment by industry and occupation, 1988 and 2000, annual planning rpt, S5624–1

New York City commercial building vacancy rates, 1992-95, annual rpt, B2800–5

North Carolina public school enrollment and grads, by local district, projections to 1997/98 or 2002, annual rpt, S5915–1.1

North Dakota employment outlook for approx 30 occupations with most growth, decline, and openings, 1988-2000, article, S6140–4.502

Ohio public school enrollment, 1992/93-2001/2002, annual rpt, S6265–2

Oklahoma employment, by county and MSA, quinquennially 1995-2010, annual rpt, U8130–2.3

Oregon elementary and secondary public school enrollment and average daily membership, by grade, 1989/90-1996/97, annual rpt, S6590–1.12

Oregon public and private high school grads, 1965/66-1996/97, annual rpt, S6590–1.8

Pennsylvania elementary/secondary and higher education enrollment, grads, staff, and finances, by instn type, 1981/82-1996/97, recurring rpt, S6790–5.10

Rhode Island job openings by detailed occupation, 1985-95, annual planning rpt, S6980–3

South Carolina education and employment projections, 1993 annual rpt, S7125–1.6, S7125–1.7

South Carolina employment and/or job openings by industry div and occupation, 1990-2000, S7155–2.501

South Carolina employment by industry div, 1991 and 2005, S7155–2.502

South Carolina employment projections by industry and occupation, through 2000, annual planning rpt, S7155–3.3

Tennessee economic indicator trends and forecasts, with data by industry div and manufacturing group, 1982-2001, annual rpt, S7560–1

Tennessee housing demand by county, 1989-2000, annual rpt, U8710–2.6

Texas nursing employment demand, by position and degree type, 2000, U8850–8.2

Utah higher education enrollment, by instn, 1977/78-2001/2002, annual rpt, S7895–2

Utah public school enrollment, 1993/94-1997/98, annual rpt, S7815–1.1

Utah total and school-age population, households, and employment, 1995-2020, annual rpt, R9380–1.1

Vermont high school grads, 1970-2004, annual rpt, S8035–2.2

Virginia defense purchases compared to total output, by industry div and selected group, 1991, with outlook for 1997, article, S8205–4.503

Virginia public school enrollment and high school grads, with detail by school district, 1980/81-2012/2013, annual rpt, U9080–20

Washington State health status goals and projections for the year 2000, 1991 annual rpt, S8363–1

West Virginia employment and job openings by occupation, 1990-2000, annual planning rpt, S8534–2

Wisconsin employment forecast, by industry, monthly rpt quarterly article, S8750–1.501, S8750–1.502, S8750–1.503, S8750–1.504

see also Business outlook and attitude surveys

see also Energy projections

see also Population projections

Index by Subjects and Names

Projectors

see Audiovisual equipment

Propaganda

see also Political broadcasting

Propane

see Liquefied petroleum gas

Property

Corporate charitable contributions of property/equipment and other noncash items, by industry group, 1991, annual rpt, R4105–8

Europe public opinion on political, economic, and social issues of interest to foreign investors, for 9 countries and 3 Soviet Union Republics, 1991 survey, C8915–9

Germany (East vs West) household ownership of selected items, 1988, R4105–82.3

see also Business assets and liabilities, general

see also Business assets and liabilities, specific industry

see also Educational facilities

see also Farms and farmland

see also Government supplies and property

see also Housing tenure

see also Land ownership and rights

see also Land use

see also Military bases, posts, and reservations

see also Military supplies and property

see also Mortgages

see also Property and casualty insurance

see also Property damage and loss

see also Property tax

see also Property value

see also Public buildings

see also Public lands

see also Real estate business

see also Rent

see also Robbery and theft

see also Surplus government property

see also Vacant and abandoned property

see also Wealth

Property and casualty insurance

Apartment building (conventionally financed) detailed income and expense ratios for US and Canada, by building type, metro area, and US region, 1991 and trends, annual rpt, A5600–1

Apartment building (federally subsidized) detailed income and expense ratios, by building and subsidy type, building age, metro area, and region, 1991 and trends, annual rpt, A5600–5

Apartment complex mgmt income and expenses, and vacancy and turnover rates, by region and metro area, 1992, annual survey rpt, A6497–1

Assets composition and investment yield for top 100 property/casualty insurance firms, 1991 and trends, annual article, C1050–1.502

Bond holdings value, by bond type, 1991, annual article, C1050–1.507

Company formations, retirements, mergers, and name changes, by company, 1992 and trends, annual article, C1050–1.506

Condominium, cooperative, and planned unit dev detailed expenses, for US and Canada, by building characteristics, metro area, and US region, 1991, annual rpt, A5600–3

Index by Subjects and Names

Crime insurance premiums written, and Federal Crime Insurance program policies in force, by State, 1991, annual rpt, A5650–1

Hard goods product liability insurance premium and coverage trends, by product line, 1993 annual survey rpt, A1800–1

Hospital professional liability insurance cost per discharge, by instn characteristics and location, 1988-92, annual rpt, B1880–1.2

Italy property/casualty insurance industry loss ratios for 4 lines of coverage, 1990-91, article, C1050–1.505

Italy property/casualty insurance industry portfolio shares by line of coverage, 1992, article, C1050–1.511

Japan direct premiums written by Japanese and foreign insurers, by line of coverage, FY92, recurring article, C1050–1.510

Marketing trends and devs, and mgmt and finance topics, for property and casualty insurance, monthly rpt, C1050–1

Medical group financial and operating data, by practice characteristics, 1991, annual rpt, A6365–2

Medical liability insurance claims and costs, with data by physician specialty, 1985-90, annual fact book, A1275–1.5

Medical malpractice insurance State joint underwriting assn (JUA) financial condition, for 11 States, 1991, annual rpt, A0375–1

Medical malpractice premium reductions under proposed tort reform, 1993-2000, R4865–9

Natural disaster insurance losses, 1977-1st half 1993, article, C5800–7.543

Office building detailed income and expense data, and energy use, US and Canada, by building characteristics, metro area, and US region, 1991 and trends, annual rpt, A5600–2

Operating and financial composite ratios for corporations, with establishments and receipts, for approx 200 industries, by asset size, FY90, annual rpt, C7800–1

Operations and finances of property/casualty insurance industries, with related accident, disaster, and crime incidence data, 1991 and trends, annual rpt, A5650–1

Physician practice economic aspects, detailed data by specialty, 1991-92 and trends, annual compilation, A2200–5

Premiums, loss ratios, and market shares, for general liability, medical malpractice, fidelity, and surety, 1991 and trends, annual article, C1050–1.502

Premiums written and operating ratios, by insurance company type and line of coverage, 1988-92, annual article, C1050–1.504

Premiums written by top 250 property/casualty insurance companies and groups, 1992, annual article, C1050–1.508

Premiums written, loss ratios, and market shares for property and casualty insurance, by line, leading company, and State, 1992 and trends, annual article, C1050–1.509

Restaurant industry financial and operating data, by establishment characteristics and location, 1992, annual rpt, A8200–3

School bus insurance claim frequencies for leading types of accidents, 1993 article, C1575–1.504

Shopping center detailed income and expense data, by building characteristics, metro area, and region, 1991, annual rpt, A5600–6

State and local:

Alabama insurance industry financial and underwriting data, by company and line of coverage, 1991, annual rpt, S0160–1

Alaska insurance industry underwriting and investment data, by company and type of insurance, with regulatory info, 1991 and trends, annual rpt, S0280–3

Arizona insurance industry financial and underwriting data, by company and type of insurance, with regulatory info, 1992, annual rpt, S0483–1

Arkansas public school property value, buildings damaged and economic loss, and insurance coverage, 1990/91-1991/92, annual rpt, S0660–1.2

California insurance industry financial and underwriting data, by company and type of insurance, with regulatory info, 1991, annual rpt, S0900–1

Connecticut insurance industry financial and underwriting data, by company and type of insurance, 1991, annual rpt, S1222–1

Florida insurance industry financial and underwriting data, by company and line of coverage, 1991, annual rpt, S1760–1

Georgia statistical abstract, general data, 1992-93 biennial rpt, U6730–1.9

Idaho insurance industry financial and underwriting data, by company and type of insurance, with regulatory data, 1991, annual rpt, S2260–1

Iowa insurance industry financial and underwriting data, by company and type of insurance, 1992, annual rpt, S2760–1

Kansas insurance industry financial and underwriting data, by company and type of insurance, with regulatory info, 1992, annual rpt, S2990–1

Maryland insurance industry financial and underwriting data, by company and type of insurance, with regulatory info, 1991, annual rpt, S3655–1

Michigan insurance industry financial and underwriting data, by company and type of insurance, with regulatory info, 1991, annual rpt, S3983–1

Minnesota insurance industry financial and underwriting data, by company and line of coverage, 1991, annual rpt, S4140–4

Missouri insurance industry financial and underwriting data, by company and type of insurance, with regulatory info, 1992, annual rpt, S4527–1

Nebraska insurance industry financial and underwriting data, by company and line of coverage, with regulatory info, 1992, annual rpt, S4890–1

New Hampshire insurance industry financial data by company, 1991, with FY92 regulatory info, annual rpt, S5220–1

New Jersey insurance industry financial and underwriting data, by company and type of insurance, 1990, annual rpt, S5420–1

New York State insurance industry devs, finances, and regulatory activity, 1990/91 and trends, annual rpt, S5770–3

Property damage and loss

New York State insurance industry financial and underwriting data, by company and line of coverage, 1991, annual rpt, S5770–2

Oklahoma insurance industry financial and underwriting data, by company and type of insurance, with regulatory info, 1992, annual rpt, S6462–1

Pennsylvania insurance industry financial and underwriting data, by company and line of coverage, 1991, with FY92 regulatory info, annual rpt, S6835–1

Rhode Island insurance industry financial and underwriting data, by company and line of coverage, 1990, with FY91 regulatory info, annual rpt, S6945–2

South Carolina insurance industry financial and underwriting data, by company, 1991, with FY92 regulatory info, annual rpt, S7195–1

South Dakota insurance industry financial and underwriting data, by company and type of insurance, with regulatory info, 1991-92, annual rpt, S7300–2

Tennessee insurance industry financial and underwriting data, by company and type of insurance, with regulatory info, 1991, annual rpt, S7466–1

Texas insurance dept regulatory activities, with industry financial and underwriting data by line of coverage, FY92 annual rpt, S7700–1

Texas physicians insured against professional liability, with data on premiums and claims, and detail by specialty and/or age, sex, and city, 1978-91, U8850–8.8

Utah insurance industry financial and underwriting data, by company and line of coverage, with regulatory info, 1991, annual rpt, S7845–1

Vermont insurance industry financial and underwriting data, by company and type of insurance, 1991, annual rpt, S7995–1

Virginia liability claims and payments for public officials and law enforcement personnel, FY91-92, annual rpt, S8170–1

West Virginia insurance industry financial and underwriting data, by company and line of coverage, with regulatory info, 1991, annual rpt, S8575–1

Wisconsin insurance industry financial and underwriting data, by company and line of coverage, with regulatory info, 1992, annual rpt, S8755–1

Wisconsin local govt property insurance fund finances and claims, FY83-92, annual rpt, S8675–3

see also Automobile insurance

Property damage and loss

Accidents and natural disasters, property damages by type, 1991 and trends, annual rpt, A5650–1.4

Accidents and related circumstances, including property loss in fires and motor vehicle accidents, 1991 or 1992, annual rpt, A8375–2

Auto insurance collision coverage experiences for autos and other vehicles, by make and series, for recent model years, 1993 annual rpt series, A5200–1

Auto insurance loss experiences, special analysis rpts, series, A5200–4

Business establishment and total insured damages in 1992 Los Angeles riots and Hurricane Andrew, 1992 article, C1200–5.502

Property damage and loss

Fleet vehicle accidents, injuries and fatalities, and property damage, 4th qtr 1992, recurring feature, C1575–2.505

Hurricane deaths and property damage caused by most serious storms since 1900, 1992 annual rpt, U6660–1.8

Oil/gas well blowouts and associated financial loss, by operator and location, 1960-91, article, C6985–1.532

Railroad freight loss/damage claims paid, 1982-91, annual rpt, A3275–8.2

Railroad freight loss/damage claims, 1920s-92, annual rpt, A3275–5.4

Retail store inventory shrinkage, and control measures, by type of outlet, 1991, annual survey rpt, C5150–4.504

Weather-related disaster damage value, for 7 events occurring in 1988-93, article, C5800–7.548

State and local:

Alabama traffic accidents involving property damage, by circumstances and location, 1992, annual rpt, S0185–1

Alabama, value of property stolen, recovered, and damaged by arson, by type of property, 1992, annual rpt, S0119–1.1

Alaska traffic accidents involving property damage, with damage values, 1991 and trends, annual rpt, S0360–1

Arizona traffic accidents involving property damage, by circumstances and location, 1991, annual rpt, S0530–1

Arizona, value of property stolen and recovered, and damaged by arson, by property type, 1992, annual rpt, S0505–2.1

Arkansas school property damaged and economic loss, and insurance coverage, 1990/91-1991/92, annual rpt, S0660–1.2

Arkansas traffic accidents involving property damage, by circumstances and location, and damage costs by vehicle type, 1991, annual rpt, S0692–1

Arkansas, value of property stolen, recovered, and damaged by arson, by type, 1992 and trends, annual rpt, S0652–1

California property value damaged by arson, by type of property, 1991, annual rpt, S0910–2.2

California traffic accidents involving property damage, by location and road type, 1991, annual rpt, S0885–1

California, value of property stolen, recovered, and damaged by arson, by property type, 1987-92, annual rpt, S0910–1.1

Colorado, value of property stolen and recovered, and arson damage, by property type, 1992, annual rpt, S1068–1

Connecticut traffic accidents involving property damage, 1992, annual rpt, S1275–1

Connecticut, value of property stolen, recovered, and damaged, by offense, 1992, annual rpt, S1256–1

Delaware traffic accidents involving property damage, by circumstance and location, 1992 and trends, annual rpt, S1435–1

Delaware, value of property stolen and recovered, by type and offense characteristics, 1988-91, annual rpt, S1375–5

Florida traffic accidents involving property damage, 1991, annual rpt, S1750–2

Florida, value of property stolen and recovered, by property type, 1992, annual rpt, S1770–1

Hawaii data book, general data, 1992 annual rpt, S2090–1.5, S2090–1.15, S2090–1.18

Hawaii traffic accidents involving property damage, by county, 1986, annual rpt, S2125–1

Hawaii, value of stolen and recovered property by type, and arson damage, by county, 1992, annual rpt, S2035–1

Idaho traffic accidents involving property damage, with detail by value size group, 1992, annual rpt, S2315–1

Idaho, value of property stolen and recovered, and damaged by vandalism, 1992, annual rpt, S2275–2

Illinois traffic accidents involving property damage, by vehicle type, 1991 and trends, annual rpt, S2540–1

Indiana traffic accidents involving property damage, by circumstances and location, 1992, annual rpt, S2675–1

Kansas, value of property stolen and recovered, by type of item, location, and offense, 1992, annual rpt, S2925–1.1

Kentucky traffic accidents involving property damage, by circumstances and location, and economic costs of accidents, 1992, annual rpt, S3150–2

Kentucky, value of property stolen and recovered, by property type, 1992, annual rpt, S3150–1.1

Maine traffic accidents, and estimated value of property damage, 1992, annual rpt, S3475–2

Maine, value of property stolen and recovered, by county and type of property, 1990-91, annual rpt, S3475–1.1

Maryland property stolen and recovered, and damaged by arson, 1992 and trends, annual rpt, S3665–1

Maryland statistical abstract, general data, 1993-94 biennial rpt, S3605–1.3

Maryland traffic accidents involving property damage, by circumstances and location, 1992, annual rpt, S3665–4

Michigan traffic accidents involving property damage, by vehicle type, circumstance, and location, 1991, annual rpt, S3997–2

Michigan, value of property stolen and recovered, by property type and offense, 1992 and trends, annual rpt, S3997–1

Minnesota traffic accidents involving property damage, and estimated losses, 1992, annual rpt, S4230–2

Missouri crimes by offense, with value of property stolen or damaged, 1991, annual rpt, S4560–2

Missouri traffic accidents involving property damage, by circumstances and driver age, 1992, annual rpt, S4560–1

Montana traffic accidents involving property damage, by circumstances and location, 1992, annual rpt, S4705–2

Montana, value of property loss and recovery, by offense, 1992, annual rpt, S4705–1

Nebraska traffic accidents involving property damage, by circumstances, 1992, annual rpt, S4953–1

Nevada traffic accidents involving property damage, by circumstances and location, 1992 and trends, annual rpt, S5140–1

New Hampshire, value of property stolen, recovered, and destroyed by arson, by property type, 1991, annual rpt, S5250–2.1

New Jersey, value of property stolen, recovered, and damaged, by county and/or property type, 1992, annual rpt, S5430–1

New Mexico traffic accidents involving property damage, by location and circumstances, 1992, annual rpt, S5665–1

New York State traffic accidents involving property damage, by circumstances and location, 1991 and trends, annual rpt, S5790–1

New York State, value of stolen and recovered property, by offense and type, 1991, annual rpt, S5760–3.1

North Carolina traffic accidents involving property damage, by circumstances and location, 1992 and trends, annual rpt, S5990–1

North Carolina, value of property stolen and recovered, by offense and property type, 1991-92, annual rpt, S5955–1

North Dakota traffic accidents involving property damage, by circumstances and location, 1992 and trends, annual rpt, S6217–1

North Dakota value of stolen and recovered property, by property type and offense, 1991 and trends, annual rpt, S6060–1

Ohio livestock killed by coyotes and restitution claims paid, by species and county, FY92, annual rpt, S6240–1

Ohio traffic accidents involving property damage, by circumstances and location, with economic loss, 1991 and trends, annual rpt, S6290–1

Oklahoma traffic accidents involving property damage, and value of damaged property, 1992 and trends, annual rpt, S6482–1

Oklahoma, value of stolen and recovered property, and arson damage, 1990-92, annual rpt, S6465–1

Oregon, value of property stolen and recovered, for selected offenses, 1992, annual rpt, S6603–3.1

Pennsylvania traffic accidents involving property damage, by circumstances and location, 1991, annual rpt, S6905–3

Pennsylvania, value of items stolen and recovered, and damaged by arson, by property type, 1992, annual rpt, S6860–1

Rhode Island statistical almanac, general data, 1993 annual rpt, C7975–1

Rhode Island traffic accidents involving property damage, by circumstances and community, 1992, annual rpt, S7025–1

South Carolina traffic accidents involving property damage, with economic loss, by circumstances and location, 1992, annual rpt, S7190–2

South Dakota traffic accidents involving property damage, by circumstances and location, 1992 and trends, annual rpt, S7300–3

Texas property stolen and destroyed by arson, by property type, 1992, annual rpt, S7735–2.1

Index by Subjects and Names

Property tax

Utah traffic accidents involving property damage, by circumstances, 1992, annual rpt, S7890–2

Utah, value of stolen and recovered property by type, and arson damage, 1992, annual rpt, S7890–3

Virginia traffic accidents involving property damage, and economic cost, 1991 and trends, annual rpt, S8282–1

Virginia, value of property stolen, recovered, and damaged, by offense and property type, 1991-92, annual rpt, S8295–2

Washington State dairy farms affected by Nov 1990 flood, with cattle deaths and economic loss, 1993 article, A3100–2.512

Washington State traffic accidents involving property damage, and economic loss, 1988-92, annual rpt, S8428–1

Washington State value of stolen and recovered property, by type, 1992, annual rpt, S8440–1

West Virginia traffic accidents involving property damage, and economic loss, by county, 1992, annual rpt, S8645–1

West Virginia, value of property stolen, by offense, and arson damage loss, 1990-91, annual rpt, S8610–1

Wisconsin traffic accidents involving property damage, with economic losses, 1992, annual rpt, S8815–1

Wisconsin, value of property stolen and recovered, by property type and local agency, 1992, annual rpt, S8771–1

Wyoming traffic accidents involving property damage, with economic costs, 1992 and trends, annual rpt, S9007–1

Wyoming, value of property stolen and recovered property, and damaged by arson, by property type and/or jurisdiction, 1991, annual rpt, S8867–3.1

see also Robbery and theft

see also Shoplifting

Property tax

Apartment building (conventionally financed) detailed income and expense ratios for US and Canada, by building type, metro area, and US region, 1991 and trends, annual rpt, A5600–1

Apartment building (federally subsidized) detailed income and expense ratios, by building and subsidy type, building age, metro area, and region, 1991 and trends, annual rpt, A5600–5

Apartment complex mgmt income and expenses, and vacancy and turnover rates, by region and metro area, 1992, annual survey rpt, A6497–1

Commercial building property taxes as percent of gross rent, for 26 metro areas, 1993 article, A6450–2.506

Condominium, cooperative, and planned unit dev detailed expenses, for US and Canada, by building characteristics, metro area, and US region, 1991, annual rpt, A5600–3

Govt finances, including revenues by source, expenditures by function, and debt, detailed data for Federal, State, and local govts, 1993 annual rpt, R9050–1

Municipal govt use of property tax increment financing for infrastructure dev, with revenues vs project costs, and complaints, 1993 rpt, A5800–1.1

Office building detailed income and expense data, and energy use, US and Canada, by building characteristics, metro area, and US region, 1991 and trends, annual rpt, A5600–2

Property tax relief benefits under "circuit-breaker" and other tax-relief programs, for selected metro areas, 1992, R3834–16

Restaurant industry financial and operating data, by establishment characteristics and location, 1992, annual rpt, A8200–3

Shopping center detailed income and expense data, by building characteristics, metro area, and region, 1991, annual rpt, A5600–6

State social, economic, and govtl indicators, with rankings, 1993 semiannual rpt, B8500–1.4

State/local property tax collections, by State, FY80 and FY91, recurring article, R9050–3.508

State/local property tax collections, with detail by State and type of govt unit, 1960s-93, R9050–15.7

State/local tax revenue shares, and comparison to personal income, for 3 major tax types, by State, FY91, article, B8500–2.511

Western States natural gas pipeline project construction spending, jobs created, and property tax benefits, for 4 States, 1992 article, C6780–2.501

State and local:

Alabama financial condition, including revenues by source, expenditures by function and object, and fund balances, by fund and agency, FY92, annual rpt, S0129–1

Alabama municipal data book, general data, 1992 recurring rpt, S0121–5

Alaska financial condition, including revenues by source, expenditures by function, fund balances, and bond obligations, FY92 and trends, annual rpt, S0275–1

Alaska State and local taxation, including taxes by type, property values, public debt, and tax shelters, by locale, 1992 and trends, annual rpt, S0285–1

Arizona tax revenues by source, tax rates, and disbursements to local areas, FY92 and trends, annual rpt, S0515–1

Arkansas homeowner property tax relief fund transactions, FY91-92, biennial rpt, S0780–1

California community college system local property tax revenues, FY92, annual rpt, S0827–3

California disabled and senior citizens property tax assistance, claimants, and income, by income class, 1991 and trends, annual rpt, S0855–1.3

California economic condition, including population, employment and earnings, income, business activity, and taxation, 1960s-92, annual rpt, S0840–3.2

California property tax assessments and exemptions, by type of property, city, county, and company, FY93 and trends, annual rpt, S0835–1.2

Colorado property assessed valuation by detailed property type, and tax levy and revenue by local district, by county, 1991-92, annual rpt, S1055–3

Colorado public school revenues by source, and expenditures by category, by school district, 1990, annual rpt, S1000–4.3

DC financial condition, including receipts by source, expenditures by object or function, and fund balances, FY92, annual rpt, S1507–1

DC statistical profile, general data, 1992 annual rpt, S1535–3.2

Delaware data book, general data, 1993 annual rpt, S1375–4

Delaware school district assessed real estate valuations, and tax rates and levies, 1991/92, annual rpt, S1430–1.4

Florida county data book, 1992/93 annual rpt, C6360–1

Florida municipal and county statistical profiles, general data, 1991 annual rpt, C4712–6

Florida statistical abstract, general data, 1992 annual rpt, U6660–1.9, U6660–1.20, U6660–1.23

Georgia county guide, general data, 1993 annual rpt, U6750–1

Georgia tax revenues, by type and county, FY92 annual rpt, S1950–1

Idaho tax statistics, including collections, and data by county and city, FY92 and trends, annual rpt, S2295–1

Illinois farm assets, debt, and taxes levied on real estate, 1982-91, annual rpt, S2390–1

Illinois property valuation and tax rates, by county and district, 1990/91, annual rpt, S2440–1.3

Indiana assessed property value and tax rates, by district, 1991/92, annual table, S2608–2.3

Indiana financial condition, including revenues by source, expenditures by function and object, and fund balances, by agency, FY92, annual rpt, S2570–1

Indiana public and other library holdings, circulation, finances, and staff, by instn, 1992 or FY92, annual rpt, S2655–1

Kansas tax collections by tax type, and property values, with data by county, FY92 and trends, annual rpt, S3020–1

Kentucky financial condition, including revenues by source, expenditures by function and object, fund balances, and bonded debt, FY92, annual rpt, S3120–1

Louisiana farm production expenses, by item, 1985-91, annual rpt, U2740–1

Maine statistical summary, general economic and social data, 1992 recurring rpt, S3434–1

Maryland local govt financial condition, including revenues by source, expenditures by function, and debt obligations, FY92 and trends, annual rpt, S3618–1

Maryland property valuations, taxes, and tax delinquencies, FY83-92, annual rpt, S3685–2

Massachusetts municipal and county profiles, general data, 1992 annual rpt, C4712–2

Massachusetts tax collections by type, and distributions to local areas, FY91 and trends, annual rpt, S3917–1

Minnesota property tax capacity rates, by school district and county, 1991/92, annual rpt, S4165–1

Mississippi property tax assessments and levies by type, by county and school district, 1991/92, annual rpt, S4340–1.3

Property tax

Mississippi statistical abstract, general data, 1992 annual rpt, U3255–4.3

Mississippi tax collections by type, and disbursements, with selected sales and income tax data by locality and industry, FY92 and trends, annual rpt, S4435–1

Missouri school finances, enrollment, grads, and staff, by county and school district, 1991/92, annual rpt, S4505–1

Montana property taxes levied, by purpose and county, 1991-92, biennial rpt, S4750–1.2

Nebraska farm real estate value and taxes, 1950-92, annual rpt, S4835–1

Nebraska property tax revenues and actual valuation by property type, by city and/or county, 1991 and trends, annual rpt, S4950–1.4

Nevada property tax levy and rates, FY84-93, annual rpt, S5025–1

Nevada statistical abstract, general data, 1992 biennial rpt, S5005–1.12

New Hampshire financial condition, with revenues by source, expenditures by function or object, and fund balances, FY92 and trends, annual rpt, S5175–1

New Hampshire public school property valuation and tax rates, by school district, 1991/92, annual tables, S5200–1.13

New Hampshire public school property valuation and tax rates, by school district, 1992, annual tables, S5200–1.17

New Jersey farm property value and taxes, 1986-92, annual rpt, S5350–1

New Jersey financial condition, including revenues by source, and finances of property tax relief fund, FY92, annual rpt, S5455–1

New Jersey municipal and county data book, general data, 1992 annual rpt, C4712–4

New Mexico tax revenues and disbursements, with data by tax type, county, and city, FY91-92 and trends, annual rpt, S5660–1

New York State statistical yearbook, general data, 1992 annual rpt, U5100–1.6

North Carolina public utility financial, operating, and regulatory data, by utility type and company, 1990 and trends, annual rpt, S5917–2

North Dakota farm property tax rates, 1984-93, annual rpt, U3600–1

North Dakota public school revenues by source, expenditures by function, mill levies, and taxable value, by district, 1992/93 annual rpt, S6180–4

Ohio intangible personal property delinquent taxes distributed to libraries, by county, 1992, annual rpt, S6320–1

Ohio tax revenues and collections, by tax type, with distributions and property assessments by county, and corporate taxes by industry, FY92 annual rpt, S6390–1

Oregon school tax data, by school district, 1992/93, annual rpt, S6590–1.20, S6590–1.21

Rhode Island statistical almanac, general data, 1993 annual rpt, C7975–1

South Carolina county govt finances, including property value and tax assessments, by county, FY92, annual rpt, S7127–2

South Carolina property tax assessed values, by class and county, FY92, annual rpt, S7255–1.3

South Carolina property tax assessments and revenue, by school district, 1991/92, annual rpt, S7145–1.5

South Dakota property value and levies, by school district, 1991/92, annual rpt, S7315–1

South Dakota tax revenues by source, aid distributed to local areas, and property tax valuations, FY92 annual rpt, S7380–1

Tennessee farm real estate taxes levied, 1981-91, annual rpt, S7460–1

Tennessee public school finances, including tax rates, by county, city, and school district, 1991/92, annual rpt, S7490–2.3

Tennessee statistical abstract, general data, 1992/93 annual rpt, U8710–2.11, U8710–2.15

Texas indigent health care finances, including hospital district tax levies, by county, district, and public hospital, 1986-90, U8850–8.7

Texas public library finances, including maximum property tax for libraries by county, FY91 annual rpt, S7710–1

Utah business activity indicators, by county, 1988-91, annual feature, U8960–2.501

Utah business activity indicators, by county, 1989-92, annual feature, U8960–2.507

Utah govt statistical review, fiscal and socioeconomic data, 1993 annual rpt, R9380–1.11

Utah statistical abstract, general data, 1993 triennial rpt, U8960–1.7

Utah tax revenues by source, and distribution to localities and State funds, FY92 and trends, annual rpt, S7905–1

Vermont individual State income tax returns, and property and sales tax refunds, by income class and locality, 1991, annual rpt, S8125–1

Virginia property assessed values and taxes, by property type, county, and independent city, 1991 and trends, annual rpt, S8305–1.3

Washington State tax revenue by source and county, with property tax rates and assessed valuation, FY92 and trends, annual rpt, S8415–1

West Virginia property tax levy rates, by purpose and locale, FY93, annual rpt, S8640–3

West Virginia property valuations and tax levies by property class, and levies by purpose, by county, 1992/93 and trends, annual rpt, S8640–2

West Virginia statistical handbook, general data, 1992 annual rpt, R9385–1.5

Wisconsin Blue Book, general data, 1993-94 biennial rpt, S8780–1

Wisconsin libraries, operations, and finances, by library type, instn, and location, 1992, annual rpt, S8795–1

Wisconsin property tax relief and shared revenue payments, by county, FY93, annual rpt, S8675–2.1

Wisconsin property values and taxes, by school district, 1992/93, annual rpt, S8795–2

Wyoming property assessed valuations and tax levies, by property type, tax purpose, and location, 1992 and trends, annual rpt, S8990–1.2

Index by Subjects and Names

Wyoming property valuations, tax levies, and bonded debt, by county and school district, 1992 and trends, annual rpt, S8890–1.1

Property value

China sales price per square foot of property offered in Hong Kong, for 9 Chinese cities, 1st qtr 1993, article, A9315–1.506

Commercial real estate market conditions and outlook, for industrial and office properties, by US metro area and selected foreign city, 1992-93, annual survey, A8916–1

Commercial real estate market conditions and outlook, for industrial and office properties in major metro areas, 1993 annual rpt, B2800–3

Farm property value, for 7 Southeastern States, 1988-93, annual rpt, U5920–1

Farm real estate values, by State, 1960-93, annual rpt, S6760–1

Farm real estate values, by State, 1984-93, annual rpt, S5700–1

Farm real estate values, by State, 1986-93, annual rpt, S5010–1

Homebuilder outlook for land availability and costs, with detail by region, 1993 survey, article, C1850–8.510

Japan real estate investment in Hawaii and California since 1985, with buyer, purchase price, and current value for 9 properties, 1993 article, C3950–1.517

Latin America statistical abstract, general data by country, 1992 annual rpt, U6250–1.7

Locally assessed property value distribution by property type, decennially 1956-86, A5800–1.1

Natural gas distribution utility and pipeline company financial and operating data, top 500 companies, 1992, annual article, C6780–1.505

State social, economic, and govtl indicators, with rankings, 1993 semiannual rpt, B8500–1.12

State and local:

Alabama assessed valuation of taxable property by type, 1983-92, annual rpt, S0129–1

Alabama county data book, general data, 1992 annual rpt, S0121–2

Alabama municipal data book, general data, 1992 recurring rpt, S0121–5

Alabama statistical abstract, general data, 1992 recurring rpt, U5680–2.1, U5680–2.3

Alaska farm property value, by State region, 1987, annual rpt, U5750–1

Alaska oil pipelines property value and revenues, with detail by company, 1991 and trends, annual rpt, S0280–4

Alaska State and local taxation, including taxes by type, property values, public debt, and tax shelters, by locale, 1992 and trends, annual rpt, S0285–1

Arizona Indian population, education, housing, health, and employment characteristics, with detail by reservation, 1970s-91, recurring rpt, U5850–2.9

Arizona property assessment, by county and selected industry, 1991-92, annual rpt, S0515–1

Arizona statistical abstract, general data, 1993 recurring rpt, U5850–2.13, U5850–2.16

Index by Subjects and Names

Property value

Arkansas Census of Population and Housing detailed findings, 1990, U5935–7

Arkansas property assessments and school facilities value, 1991/92 and trends, annual rpt, S0660–1

Arkansas socioeconomic trends, by MSA and/or county, 1993 annual rpt, U5935–1

California Census of Population and Housing detailed findings, 1990, S0840–9

California economic condition, including population, employment and earnings, income, business activity, and taxation, 1960s-92, annual rpt, S0840–3.2

California farm property value, and irrigated and other land, 1993, annual rpt, S0850–1.5

California property tax assessments and exemptions, by type of property, city, county, and company, FY93 and trends, annual rpt, S0835–1.2

California socioeconomic and govtl data for municipalities, counties, and school districts, 1993 annual rpt, C4712–3

California statistical abstract, general data, 1992 annual rpt, S0840–2.9

Colorado property assessed valuation by detailed property type, and tax levy and revenue by local district, by county, 1991-92, annual rpt, S1055–3

Connecticut govt property value, by agency, June 1991, annual rpt, S1170–1

DC commercial, residential, and tax exempt properties with highest assessed values, July 1992, annual rpt, S1507–1

DC statistical profile, general data, 1992 annual rpt, S1535–3.1, S1535–3.2

Delaware data book, general data, 1993 annual rpt, S1375–4

Delaware school district assessed real estate valuations, and tax rates and levies, 1991/92, annual rpt, S1430 1.4

Florida municipal and county statistical profiles, general data, 1991 annual rpt, C4712–6

Florida statistical abstract, general data, 1992 annual rpt, U6660–1.2, U6660–1.8, U6660–1.9, U6660–1.20, U6660–1.23

Georgia farm property value, 1964-92, annual rpt, S1855–1

Georgia general property and public utilities assessed values, FY92 annual rpt, S1950–1.2

Georgia statistical abstract, general data, 1992-93 biennial rpt, U6730–1.10

Hawaii data book, general data, 1992 annual rpt, S2090–1.21

Idaho construction activity and value, by city and county, monthly rpt, B3900–1

Idaho residential property assessment to market value ratios, 1970s-91, annual rpt, S2295–1

Idaho school district finances, including property value by district, FY92, annual rpt, S2225–2

Illinois farm real estate value, 1983-92, annual rpt, S2390–1

Illinois property valuation and tax rates, by county and district, 1990/91, annual rpt, S2440–1.3

Indiana assessed property value and tax rates, by district, 1991/92, annual table, S2608–2.3

Indiana property value and tax levies, collections, credits, and deductions, by county and type, 1991, annual rpt, S2570–1.1

Indiana public and other library holdings, circulation, finances, and staff, by instn, 1992 or FY92, annual rpt, S2655–1

Kansas agricultural production, marketing, and finances, by county and/or commodity, and farm acreage and value, 1992 and trends, annual rpt, S2915–1

Kansas statistical abstract, general data, 1991/92 annual rpt, U7095–2.3, U7095–2.5, U7095–2.11, U7095–2.15

Kansas tax collections by tax type, and property values, with data by county, FY92 and trends, annual rpt, S3020–1

Kentucky economic statistics, general data, 1993 annual rpt, S3104–1.1

Kentucky farm real estate value per acre compared to neighboring States, 1993 and trends, annual rpt, S3085–1

Kentucky property values, 1982-91, annual rpt, S3120–1

Louisiana Census of Population and Housing summary findings, by local area, 1990 and trends, U8010–4

Louisiana farm property value, selected years 1974-87, annual rpt, U2740–1

Maine Census of Population and Housing summary findings, by local area, 1990, S3465–7, S3465–8

Maryland assessed valuation, by local area, FY92, annual rpt, S3618–1.1

Maryland elementary and secondary education data, by county, 1991/92 and trends, annual rpt, S3610–2.13

Maryland elementary and secondary education data, by county, 1991/92, annual rpt, S3610–2.6

Maryland property valuations, taxes, and tax delinquencies, FY83-92, annual rpt, S3685–2

Maryland public school appropriations compared to assessed property value, 1991/92, annual rpt, S3610–2.9

Maryland statistical abstract, general data, 1993-94 biennial rpt, S3605–1.12

Massachusetts municipal and county profiles, general data, 1992 annual rpt, C4712–2

Michigan farm real estate value, and cash rent, 1900-92, annual rpt, S3950–1

Michigan school district financial and enrollment data, with rankings, 1991/92, annual rpt, S3965–3

Minnesota assessed property valuations, 1983-92, annual rpt, S4180–1

Minnesota farmland value per acre, by crop district, 1979-92, annual rpt, S4130–1

Mississippi property assessments, by type of property and county, 1991 and trends, annual rpt, S4435–1

Mississippi statistical abstract, general data, 1992 annual rpt, U3255–4.14

Missouri assessed property valuation, by county, 1992 annual rpt, S4520–2

Missouri farm real estate value, 1986-93, annual rpt, S4480–1

Missouri property assessed and actual value, 1982-91, annual rpt, S4475–1

Missouri school finances, enrollment, grads, and staff, by county and school district, 1991/92, annual rpt, S4505–1

Montana farm/ranch property value and debt, 1990, annual rpt, S4655–1

Montana property values, by detailed property class and type, with land acreage by use, by county, 1991-92 and trends, biennial rpt, S4750–1.2

Nebraska farm real estate value and taxes, 1950-92, annual rpt, S4835–1

Nebraska property tax revenues and actual valuation by property type, by city and/or county, 1991 and trends, annual rpt, S4950–1.4

Nevada statistical abstract, general data, 1992 biennial rpt, S5005–1.8, S5005–1.12

Nevada taxable property assessed value, with detail for 10 largest property owners, FY92 annual rpt, S5025–1

New Hampshire public school property valuation and tax rates, by school district, 1991/92, annual tables, S5200–1.13

New Hampshire public school property valuation and tax rates, by school district, 1992, annual tables, S5200–1.16, S5200–1.17

New Jersey Census of Population and Housing detailed findings, by county, 1990, S5425–19

New Jersey farm property value, 1986-92, annual rpt, S5350–1

New Jersey municipal and county data book, general data, 1992 annual rpt, C4712–4

New Mexico tax revenues and disbursements, by detailed tax type, and property valuation data, FY91-92 and trends, annual rpt, S5660–1.2

New York State municipal and county statistical profiles, general data, 1993 annual rpt, C4712–7

New York State statistical yearbook, general data, 1992 annual rpt, U5100 1.5, U5100–1.6, U5100–1.9

North Carolina assessed property values, 1983-92, annual rpt, S5897–1

North Carolina farm property value per acre, 1988-92, annual rpt, S5885–1

North Dakota farm property value, 1984-93, annual rpt, U3600–1

North Dakota public school revenues by source, expenditures by function, mill levies, and taxable value, by district, 1992/93 annual rpt, S6180–4

Ohio farm real estate value and cash rent, 1987-92, annual rpt, S6240–1

Ohio public school district property valuation, FY88-92, annual rpt, S6265–2

Ohio tax revenues and collections, by tax type, with distributions and property assessments by county, and corporate taxes by industry, FY92 annual rpt, S6390–1

Oklahoma farm real estate value, 1989-93, annual rpt, S6405–1

Oklahoma public school finances, including property valuations, and enrollment, by county and district, 1991/92-1992/93 and trends, annual rpt, S6423–1.2

Oklahoma statistical abstract, general data, 1992 annual rpt, U8130–2.5

Oregon property assessed value by school district, 1992/93, annual rpt, S6590–1.3

Oregon taxable property value and tax levies, by school district and county, 1992/93, annual rpt, S6590–1.21

Property value

Pennsylvania Census of Population and Housing detailed findings, with selected data by county and municipality, 1990, U4130–13

Pennsylvania housing data from Census of Population and Housing, by county and municipality, 1990, C1595–14

Pennsylvania statistical abstract, general data, 1992 recurring rpt, U4130–6.1, U4130–6.6

Rhode Island statistical almanac, general data, 1993 annual rpt, C7975–1

South Carolina county govt finances, including property value and tax assessments, by county, FY92, annual rpt, S7127–2

South Carolina farm real estate value, 1980-92, annual rpt, S7125–3.1

South Carolina property tax assessed values, by class and county, FY92, annual rpt, S7255–1.3

South Carolina property tax assessments and revenue, by school district, 1991/92, annual rpt, S7145–1.5

South Carolina statistical abstract, general data, 1993 annual rpt, S7125–1.1, S7125–1.11

South Dakota farm real estate value, 1983-93, annual rpt, S7280–1

South Dakota property tax and valuations, by property type and locality, FY92 annual rpt, S7380–1.2

South Dakota property value and levies, by school district, 1991/92, annual rpt, S7315–1

Tennessee agricultural production and marketing, by commodity and county, with farms, acreage, and farm value, 1992 and trends, annual rpt, S7460–1

Tennessee public school site, building, and equipment values, by county, city, and school district, 1991/92, annual rpt, S7490–2.3

Tennessee public utility and/or transportation property assessed valuations, 1877/78-1992, biennial rpt, S7565–1

Tennessee statistical abstract, general data, 1992/93 annual rpt, U8710–2.6, U8710–2.11, U8710–2.15

Texas farm real estate property values, 1987-92, annual rpt, S7630–1.3

Utah business activity indicators, by county, 1988-91, annual feature, U8960–2.501

Utah business activity indicators, by county, 1989-92, annual feature, U8960–2.507

Utah economic and demographic trends, by county and district, 1960-91, annual rpt, S7832–2

Utah farmland and building values, by county, 1987, annual rpt, S7800–1

Utah govt statistical review, fiscal and socioeconomic data, 1993 annual rpt, R9380–1.11

Utah property taxes and assessed values, by class of property and county, 1991, annual rpt, S7905–1

Utah public school revenues by source and expenditures by object, by State fund and school district, FY92, annual rpt, S7815–1.2

Utah statistical abstract, general data, 1993 triennial rpt, U8960–1.7, U8960–1.11

Virginia educational finances by source and program, and local area revenue base, by county and municipality, 1991/92, annual rpt, S8190–3

Virginia property assessed values and taxes, by property type, county, and independent city, 1991 and trends, annual rpt, S8305–1.3

Washington State corporate assessed property value, for top 10 firms, FY92, annual rpt, S8345–3

Washington State farm value, with comparisons to neighboring States and US, 1985-93, annual rpt, S8328–1

Washington State local property assessed value, by public library, 1992, annual rpt, S8375–1

Washington State tax revenue by source and county, with property tax rates and assessed valuation, FY92 and trends, annual rpt, S8415–1

West Virginia property valuations and tax levies by property class, and levies by purpose, by county, 1992/93 and trends, annual rpt, S8640–2

West Virginia public school buildings, grounds, and equipment values, by county, 1991/92, annual rpt, S8540–3

West Virginia statistical handbook, general data, 1992 annual rpt, R9385–1.5

West Virginia taxable property assessed valuations, by county, FY93, annual rpt, S8540–4.1

Wisconsin Blue Book, general data, 1993-94 biennial rpt, S8780–1.2

Wisconsin farm real estate value, 1988-93, annual rpt, S8680–1

Wisconsin property assessed and equalized values, 1983-92, annual rpt, S8675–3

Wisconsin property values and taxes, by school district, 1992/93, annual rpt, S8795–2

Wyoming farm real estate value, 1984-93, annual rpt, S8860–1

Wyoming public school enrollment, staff, and finances, by county and district, 1991/92, annual rpt series, S8890–1

Wyoming tax collections and distribution, and property valuation, with data by property type and location, FY92 and trends, annual rpt, S8990–1

Propositions

see Referenda

Proprietorships

Drugstore (independent pharmacy) financial and operating data, by store characteristics, 1991 and trends, annual survey, B5165–1

Economic indicator historical trends, 1900s-92, annual rpt, R9050–1.2

State and local:

Alabama statistical abstract, general data, 1992 recurring rpt, U5680–2.15

Arizona statistical abstract, general data, 1993 recurring rpt, U5850–2.21

Florida statistical abstract, general data, 1992 annual rpt, U6660–1.6, U6660–1.16

Hawaii data book, general data, 1992 annual rpt, S2090–1.15

Illinois nonfarm proprietors, 1987-92, S2405–2.504

Prosthetics and orthotics

Children's orthopedic internal fixation device implantation prevalence, and results, with detail by demographic characteristics, 1988, article, A2623–1.509

Index by Subjects and Names

HMO benefits coverage, premiums, and rating methods used, by plan characteristics, 1991 and trends, annual rpt, A5150–2.1

Hospital patient admission rates and length of stay, by diagnosis and procedure, payment source, age, sex, and region, 1991, B4455–4

Hospital patient charges and length of stay, by diagnosis and procedure, payment source, age, and region, 1991, B4455–5

Prostitution

State and local:

Alabama juvenile and adult arrests, by type of offense, 1992, annual rpt, S0119–1.1

Arizona arrests by offense, offender characteristics, and county, 1992, annual rpt, S0505–2.2

Arkansas crimes and arrests, by offense, victim and offender characteristics, and location, 1992 and trends, annual rpt, S0652–1

California crimes and arrests, clearances, and arrest dispositions, with data by offense and offender characteristics, 1987-92, annual rpt, S0910–1.1

California criminal justice system detailed data, by offense, county, age, race-ethnicity, and sex, 1991 and trends, annual rpt, S0910–2

Colorado crimes and arrests, by offense and location, with offender characteristics, and assaults on police, 1992, annual rpt, S1068–1

Connecticut arrests, by offense, offender characteristics, and local agency, 1992, annual rpt, S1256–1.2

DC criminal justice system summary, including crimes and arrests, criminal procedure, prisoners, and parole, 1991 and trends, annual rpt, S1535–2

Florida crimes and arrests, by offense, with data by victim and offender characteristics, 1992, annual rpt, S1770–1

Hawaii crimes and arrests, by offense, with data by county and victim-offender characteristics, 1992, annual rpt, S2035–1

Idaho crimes and arrests, by offense, with data by location and offender characteristics, 1992 and trends, annual rpt, S2275–2

Illinois crimes and arrests, by offense, with data by location and offender characteristics, 1991, annual rpt, S2536–1

Kansas crimes and arrests, by offense, with data by location, agency, and victim-offender characteristics, 1992 and trends, annual rpt, S2925–1.1

Kentucky arrests by county and offense, and law enforcement employment by agency, 1992, annual rpt, S3150–1.2

Maine arrests of adults and juveniles, by offense, age, and sex, 1991, annual rpt, S3475–1.2

Maryland crimes and arrests, by offense, location, and offender characteristics, with law enforcement employment and assaults on officers, 1992 and trends, annual rpt, S3665–1

Michigan crimes and arrests, by offense, with data by location and offender characteristics, 1992 and trends, annual rpt, S3997–1

Missouri crimes and arrests, by offense and location, with victim and offender characteristics, 1991 and trends, annual rpt, S4560–2

Montana crimes and clearances, by offense and jurisdiction, 1992, annual rpt, S4705–1

New Hampshire arrests, by offense and offender age, sex, and race-ethnicity, 1991, annual rpt, S5250–2.2

New Jersey arrests by offense, age, race-ethnicity, sex, and county, 1992 and trends, annual rpt, S5430–1.2

New York State crimes and arrests by offense and demographic characteristics, and court activity and corrections, 1991 and trends, annual rpt, S5760–3

North Carolina arrests by detailed offense, offender characteristics, and county, 1991-92, annual rpt, S5955–1.2

North Dakota crimes and arrests, by offense, location, and offender characteristics, and law enforcement employment, 1991 and trends, annual rpt, S6060–1

Oklahoma crimes and arrests, by offense, with victim and offender characteristics, 1990-92, annual rpt, S6465–1.1

Oregon crimes and arrests, by offense, with data by county, local agency, and offender characteristics, 1992 and trends, annual rpt, S6603–3

Pennsylvania crimes and arrests, by offense, with data by location and offender characteristics, 1992 and trends, annual rpt, S6860–1

South Carolina crimes and arrests, by detailed offense, offender characteristics, and location, 1992 and trends, annual rpt, S7205–1.2

Texas arrests, by age, sex, race-ethnicity, and offense, 1992, annual rpt, S7735–2.2

Utah crimes and arrests, by offense, county, and local agency, 1992 and trends, annual rpt, S7890–3

Virginia crimes and arrests by offense, and law enforcement employment, by location and reporting agency, 1992, annual rpt, S8295–2.2

Washington State crimes and arrests, by offense, with data by location and offender characteristics, 1992 and trends, annual rpt, S8440–1

West Virginia crimes and arrests, by offense, location, and offender characteristics, 1990-91, annual rpt, S8610–1

Wisconsin crimes and arrests, by offense, offender characteristics, county, and local agency, 1992 and trends, annual rpt, S8771–1

Wyoming adult and juvenile arrests, by offense, county, and local jurisdiction, 1991, annual rpt, S8867–3.2

Protective services

see Detective and protective services

see Security devices

Protestantism

see Religion

Protests

see Public demonstrations

Providence, R.I.

Employment by industry, Jan 1991-July 1993, annual rpt, S6980–3

Statistical almanac of Rhode Island, economic, govtl, and social reference info and statistics, 1993 annual rpt, C7975–1

Psychiatric care

see Mental health facilities and services

Psychiatry

Maternity and paternity leave policies of psychiatry residency programs, 1991/92 survey, article, A3273–8.511

Medical school faculty and compensation, by dept, academic rank, degree, and region, 1992/93, annual rpt, A3273–2

Physician practice economic aspects, detailed data by specialty, 1991-92 and trends, annual compilation, A2200–5

Physicians by detailed specialty and location, 1992 and trends, annual rpt, A2200–3

see also Counselors and counseling

Psychological disorders

see Mental health and illness

Psychology

Doctoral degree recipient employment and demographic characteristics, and finances, 1990/91, biennial survey rpt, A2620–4

Grad psychology dept faculty salaries, by academic rank, years in rank, census div, and sex, 1992/93 and trends, annual rpt, A2620–1

Grad psychology depts, faculty characteristics, enrollment, and student aid, US and Canada, 1990/91 and trends, annual rpt, A2620–3

Salaries of scientists, engineers, technicians, and other professionals, by employee and employer characteristics, 1990s and trends, biennial rpt, A3960–1

Women and minorities in professional fields, detailed education and labor force data, 1991 and trends, recurring rpt, A3960–2.3

State and local:

Florida county data book, 1992/93 annual rpt, C6360–1

Florida health care atlas, including manpower by occupation and health care facilities by type, by district and county, 1992 annual rpt, S1746–1.2

Florida statistical abstract, general data, 1992 annual rpt, U6660–1.20

South Carolina statistical abstract, general data, 1993 annual rpt, S7125–1.10

see also Counselors and counseling

Public administration

Catholic dioceses involvement in public policy implementation, by govt level, 1991, annual rpt, A3810–1

Transportation regulatory agency policies and practices for motor carriers and railroads, by agency, 1991/92 annual rpt, A7015–4

Utility and transportation regulatory agency activities, scope of jurisdiction, finances, and employees, by agency, 1991/92 annual rpt, A7015–2

Utility regulatory agency policies and practices, and industry financial and operating data, by utility type and agency, 1991/92 annual rpt, A7015–3

see also Administrative law and procedure

see also Federal boards, committees, and commissions

see also Federal employees

see also Federal executive departments

see also Federal independent agencies

see also Government and business

see also Government assets and liabilities

see also Government efficiency

see also Government revenues

see also Government spending

see also Government supplies and property

see also Labor-management relations in government

see also Local government

see also Officials

see also Public debt

see also School administration and staff

see also School boards

see also State and local employees

see also State budgets

see also State government

see also State government revenues

see also State government spending

Public assistance

see Public welfare programs

Public broadcasting

Broadcast industries and cable TV devs, including data on finances, advertising, ratings, and licensing, weekly rpt, C1850–14

Contributions of $1,000/more, with comparison to value of total contributions, for 7 public broadcasting stations, 1991-93, article, C2176–1.522

Corporate underwriting of public TV, 1987-92, triennial survey rpt, A3357–1

Revenues for public broadcasting stations, and data on general system operations and audience, series, R4250–1

TV (public) coverage of natl issues, views of leaders and general public, 1992 series, R8825–10

State and local:

New York State statistical yearbook, general data, 1992 annual rpt, U5100–1.10

see also Educational broadcasting

Public buildings

Construction contract awards and new plans, by type of project, weekly rpt, C5800–2

Construction value and activities of top 25 Federal or State govt agencies, FY92, annual article, C1850–9.501

Federal office building construction project costs and size, for 9 projects, 1992 article, C3950–1.503

Library construction, costs, and funding sources, by State, city, instn, and library type, FY92 and trends, annual article, C1852–1.501

Library construction, costs, and funding sources, by State, city, instn, and library type, FY92 and trends, annual compilation, C1650–3.4

Museums and related instns size, renovations, and relocations, by type and governing authority, 1989/90 survey, A0750–1.1

USPS employees and facilities, 1987-91, annual rpt, A4620–1.5

Value of new residential, commercial, industrial, and public construction put in place, monthly rpt, A7000–1

Vending machine sales and operations, by product and location type, 1990-92, annual rpt, C9470–1

State and local:

Connecticut construction activity and value, by type of structure and location, 1992 and trends, annual rpt, S1212–1

see also Community centers

Public buildings

see also Educational facilities
see also Military bases, posts, and reservations
see also State funding for capital projects

Public contracts
see Defense contracts and procurement
see Government contracts and procurement

Public debt

City fiscal condition, including budget trends and adjustments, and influencing factors, by region and population size, Mar-Apr 1993 survey, annual rpt, A8012-1.23

Federal debt measures, including data on Govt assets, liabilities, interest payments, total outlays, and deficit, 1980-98, R9050-15.1

Forecasts of natl income and product account components and related indicators, quarterly rpt, U1880-1

Forecasts of natl income and product account components, employment, and financial sector activity, monthly rpt, B4950-1

Govt finances, including revenues by source, expenditures by function, and debt, detailed data for Federal, State, and local govts, 1993 annual rpt, R9050-1

Latin America economic indicators affecting business climate, with data on motor vehicle and oil industries and detail by country, 1992 rpt, R4105-82.6

OECD Govts deficit financing and borrowing summaries for current fiscal year, for 12-15 countries, 1993 feature, B6200-2.502

OECD Govts gross debt as percent of GDP, by country, 1980s and 1991-94, B6200-2.503

OECD Govts net public debt as percent of GDP, for 14 countries, 1980s-94, article, B6200-2.502

State govt financial solvency, based on per capita assets, debt, and pension fund surplus or deficit, by State, 1993 article, B8500-2.521

State social, economic, and govtl indicators, with rankings, 1993 semiannual rpt, B8500-1.3

State/local govt per capita value of long term securities issued, by State, 1992, article, B8500-2.514

Statistical profiles of 50 States and DC, general data, 1993 annual almanac, C4712-1

World long-term public debt, with share of GNP, by country, 1979, 1984, and 1989, biennial rpt, R9455-1.5

State and local:

Alabama financial condition, including revenues by source, expenditures by function and object, and fund balances, by fund and agency, FY92, annual rpt, S0129-1

Alaska financial condition, including revenues by source, expenditures by function, fund balances, and bond obligations, FY92 and trends, annual rpt, S0275-1

Alaska State and local taxation, including taxes by type, property values, public debt, and tax shelters, by locale, 1992 and trends, annual rpt, S0285-1

Arizona financial condition, including revenues by source, expenditures by function, and fund balances, FY91, annual rpt, S0450-2

Arizona public school bonds outstanding, by school district and county, FY92, annual rpt, S0470-1

Arizona statistical abstract, general data, 1993 recurring rpt, U5850-2.10

Arkansas financial condition, including revenues by source, expenditures by function and object, and fund balances, FY92, annual rpt, S0670-1

Arkansas public school revenues by source, expenditures by function and object, and indebtedness, 1991/92 and trends, annual rpt, S0660-1.3

California financial condition, including revenues by source, expenditures by agency and function, fund balances, and bonded debt, FY92 and trends, annual rpt, S0815-1

California statistical abstract, general data, 1992 annual rpt, S0840-2.13

Colorado financial condition, including receipts by source, and expenditures by function, FY92 and trends, annual rpt, S0980-1

Connecticut financial condition, including revenues by source, expenditures by function, and bonded debt, FY92, annual rpt, S1170-1, S1170-2

DC financial condition, including receipts by source, expenditures by object or function, and fund balances, FY92, annual rpt, S1507-1

Delaware data book, general data, 1993 annual rpt, S1375-4

Delaware school enrollment, grads, staff, finances, and facilities, by county, school district, and/or instn, 1991/92, annual rpt, S1430-1

Florida financial condition, including receipts by source, expenditures by function, and fund balances, FY92, annual rpt, S1717-3

Florida statistical abstract, general data, 1992 annual rpt, U6660-1.23

Georgia financial condition, including revenues by source, expenditures by function and object, and fund balances, FY92, annual rpt, S1860-1

Hawaii data book, general data, 1992 annual rpt, S2090-1.9

Hawaii financial condition, including revenues by source, expenditures by function, and fund balances, FY92, annual rpt, S2020-1

Idaho school district finances, including bonded debt by district, FY92, annual rpt, S2225-2

Indiana public school indebtedness, by category and district, June 1992, annual table, S2608-2.12

Iowa financial condition, including revenues by source, expenditures by function, and bonded debt, FY92 and trends, annual rpt, S2860-4

Kansas financial condition, including revenues by source, expenditures by object, and revenue bond indebtedness, FY92, annual rpt, S2900-1.1

Kentucky financial condition, including revenues by source, expenditures by function and object, fund balances, and bonded debt, FY92, annual rpt, S3120-1

Louisiana financial condition, including revenues by source, expenditures by function, and fund balances, FY92 and trends, annual rpt, S3285-2

Index by Subjects and Names

Maine financial condition, including revenues by source, expenditures by function and object, and fund balances, FY92, annual rpt, S3420-1

Maryland elementary and secondary education data, by county, 1991/92, annual rpt, S3610-2.7

Maryland financial condition, including revenues by source, expenditures by function, fund balances, and bonded debt, FY92 and trends, annual rpt, S3685-2

Maryland local govt financial condition, including revenues by source, expenditures by function, and debt obligations, FY92 and trends, annual rpt, S3618-1.1

Massachusetts financial condition, including revenues by source, and expenditures by function, by fund, FY92 and trends, annual rpt, S3777-1

Massachusetts municipal and county profiles, general data, 1992 annual rpt, C4712-2

Michigan financial condition, including revenues by source, expenditures by function, and fund balances, FY92 and trends, annual rpt, S3985-2

Minnesota financial condition, including revenues by source, expenditures by function, fund balances, and bonded debt, FY92 and trends, annual rpt, S4180-1

Minnesota public school enrollment, staff, and finances, by district and county, 1991/92 and trends, annual rpt, S4165-1

Mississippi financial condition, including revenues by source, expenditures by function and object, and detail by agency, FY92 and trends, annual rpt, S4346-1

Missouri financial condition, including fund finances, tax collections and distribution, and State treasury activity, FY92 and trends, annual rpt, S4570-1

Missouri financial condition, including revenues by source, expenditures by function, and fund balances, FY92, annual rpt, S4475-1

Montana financial condition, including revenues by source, expenditures by function, and fund balances, FY92, annual rpt, S4653-1

Nebraska financial condition, including revenues by source, expenditures by function and agency, and fund balances, FY92, annual rpt, S4825-1

Nevada financial condition, including fund revenues by source, expenditures by function, and bonded debt, FY92, annual rpt, S5025-1

New Hampshire financial condition, with revenues by source, expenditures by function or object, and fund balances, FY92 and trends, annual rpt, S5175-1

New Jersey financial condition, including revenues by source, expenditures by function, fund balances, and bonded debt, FY92, annual rpt, S5455-1

New Jersey municipal and county data book, general data, 1992 annual rpt, C4712-4

New York State financial condition, including revenues by source, expenditures by function, and fund balances, FY93, annual rpt, S5710-1

New York State municipal and county statistical profiles, general data, 1993 annual rpt, C4712-7

New York State statistical yearbook, general data, 1992 annual rpt, U5100–1.5, U5100–1.6

North Carolina financial condition, including revenues by source, expenditures by function, fund balances, and bonded debt, FY92, annual rpt, S5897–1

North Dakota financial condition, including revenues by source, expenditures by function, fund balances, and bonded debt, FY92, annual rpt, S6162–1

Ohio financial condition, including revenues by source, expenditures by function, and fund balances, FY92, annual rpt, S6255–1

Oklahoma financial condition, including revenues by source, expenditures by function, and fund balances, FY91, annual rpt, S6438–1

Oklahoma statistical abstract, general data, 1992 annual rpt, U8130–2.5

Oregon financial condition, including revenues by source, expenditures by function, and fund statements, FY92, annual rpt, S6603–2

Pennsylvania financial condition, including revenues by source, expenditures by function, and fund balances, FY92 and trends, annual rpt, S6810–4

Pennsylvania statistical abstract, general data, 1992 recurring rpt, U4130–6.6

Rhode Island financial condition, including revenues by source, expenditures by function, and fund balances, FY92 and trends, annual rpt, S6930–1

Rhode Island statistical almanac, general data, 1993 annual rpt, C7975–1.1

South Carolina financial condition, including receipts by source, expenditures by function, fund balances, and bonded debt, FY92, annual rpt, S7127–1

South Dakota financial condition, including revenues by source, expenditures by function, fund balances, and bonded debt, FY92, annual rpt, S7330–1

Tennessee financial condition, including revenues by source, expenditures by function and object, and fund balances, FY92, annual rpt, S7505–1

Tennessee public school finances, including bonded debt, by county, city, and school district, 1991/92, annual rpt, S7490–2

Texas financial condition, including revenues by source, expenditures by function, and bonded indebtedness, FY92, annual rpt, S7655–3

Texas financial condition, including revenues by source, expenditures by function and dept, and investments, with data for over 400 individual funds, FY92, annual rpt, S7655–2

Utah financial condition, including revenues by source, expenditures by function and agency, and fund balances, FY92, annual rpt, S7795–1

Utah public school revenues by source and expenditures by object, by State fund and school district, FY92, annual rpt, S7815–1.2

Utah statistical abstract, general data, 1993 triennial rpt, U8960–1.3, U8960–1.7

Vermont financial condition, including revenues by source, expenditures by function, fund balances, and bonded debt, FY92, annual rpt, S8035–1

Virginia financial condition, including revenues by source, expenditures by function, and fund balances, FY92 and trends, annual rpt, S8170–1

Washington State financial condition, including revenues by source, expenditures by function, fund balances, and bonded debt, FY92, annual rpt, S8345–3

Washington State treasury operations, including receipts, disbursements, aid to localities, and investments, by fund, FY92, annual rpt, S8455–1

West Virginia statistical handbook, general data, 1992 annual rpt, R9385–1.2, R9385–1.6

Wisconsin Blue Book, general data, 1993-94 biennial rpt, S8780–1.2

Wisconsin financial condition, including revenues by source, expenditures by function and object, and fund balances, FY92, annual rpt, S8675–3

Wyoming financial condition, including revenues by source, expenditures by function, and fund balances, FY92 and trends, annual rpt, S8875–1

see also Government assets and liabilities

see also Government securities

see also Municipal bonds

see also State bonds

see also State budgets

see also U.S. savings bonds

Public defenders

see Legal aid

Public demonstrations

Homosexual "March on Washington" demonstration, public interest in news items by respondent characteristics, Apr/May 1993 survey, C8915–1.503

State and local:

Illinois crimes and arrests, by offense, with data by location and offender characteristics, 1991, annual rpt, S2536–1

see also Parades

see also Riots and disorders

see also Student unrest

Public documents

see Government documents

Public finance

see Budget of the U.S.

see Fiscal policy

see Government assets and liabilities

see Government revenues

see Government securities

see Government spending

see Monetary policy

see Public debt

see State budgets

see State government revenues

see State government spending

see Taxation

Public health

Chemical hazard emergency response planning by local govts, including public notification methods, by locality, 1993 rpt, A5800–4.34

Developing countries contraceptive use, including use of govt vs nongovt supply sources, by country, 1985-92 surveys, U2520–1.51

Developing countries family planning efforts, with distribution of contraceptive users by method and use of govt vs selected nongovt sources, by country, 1986-90, R8720–1.1

Faculty of public health schools, characteristics by instn, fall 1991, recurring rpt, A3372–1

Latin America statistical abstract, general data by country, 1992 annual rpt, U6250–1.7

Physicians by detailed specialty and location, 1992 and trends, annual rpt, A2200–3

Research on public health issues and devs, monthly journal, A2623–1

Schools of public health applicant, student, and grad characteristics, and school expenditures, by instn, 1991/92 and trends, annual rpt, A3372–3

State and local:

Alabama public health dept activities, including services provided, inspection and licensing activity, staff and finances, and vital statistics and health data, 1992 annual rpt, S0175–3

Hawaii health dept activities and services, including vital statistics and disease control, by location, 1990, annual rpt, S2065–1

Maryland local govt financial condition, including revenues by source, expenditures by function, and debt obligations, FY92 and trends, annual rpt, S3618–1.1

Tennessee statistical abstract, general data, 1992/93 annual rpt, U8710–2.18

Texas public health nurses, earnings, and job vacancy rates, with selected detail by degree or position type, 1992 rpt, U8850–8.2

Texas State and local health depts finances, employment, and service area characteristics, FY91 and trends, U8850–8.6

see also Accidents and accident prevention

see also Air pollution

see also Birth defects

see also Carcinogens

see also Child abuse and neglect

see also Child welfare

see also Community health services

see also Diseases and disorders

see also Environmental pollution and control

see also Epidemiology and epidemiologists

see also Food inspection

see also Hazardous substances

see also Health care reform

see also Health condition

see also Health education

see also Health facilities administration

see also Health insurance

see also Health maintenance organizations

see also Health occupations

see also Infant mortality

see also Lead poisoning and pollution

see also Medical assistance

see also Medical costs

see also Medical education

see also Medical research

see also Medical supplies and equipment

see also Medical transplants

see also Medicine

see also Mental health facilities and services

see also Noise

see also Occupational health and safety

see also Pesticides

see also Pests and pest control

see also Poisoning and drug reaction

Public health

see also Preventive medicine
see also Radiation
see also Refuse and refuse disposal
see also Sewage and wastewater systems
see also Soil pollution
see also State funding for health and hospitals
see also State funding for public safety
see also Vaccination and vaccines
see also Vital statistics
see also Water pollution
see also Water supply and use

Public Health Service

Physicians in PHS, by detailed specialty, 1992, annual rpt, A2200–3.2
see also Food and Drug Administration
see also National Institutes of Health

Public housing

Apartment building (federally subsidized) detailed income and expense ratios, by building and subsidy type, building age, metro area, and region, 1991 and trends, annual rpt, A5600–5

Local public housing authority income and expenses, resident and property characteristics, and unit vacancy and turnover rates, various years FY77-1992, A6800–2

Local public housing authority operations and finances, including resident characteristics, by agency size, 1989, A6800–1

State and local:

Connecticut construction activity and value, by type of structure and location, 1992 and trends, annual rpt, S1212–1

DC statistical profile, general data, 1992 annual rpt, S1535–3.1, S1535–3.4

Hawaii data book, general data, 1992 annual rpt, S2090–1.21

New Jersey residential construction activity and costs, by location, 1991 and trends, annual rpt, S5425–3

Virginia income tax return checkoff contributions to State housing program, 1990, annual rpt, S8305–1.1

see also Emergency shelters

Public lands

Acreage by State, including Federal and State lands, 1991, annual rpt, A6485–1.2

Broadcast tower current and proposed Federal land lease rates, for radio or TV stations in 6 cities, 1993 article, C1850–14.534

Forestland (commercial) ownership, including Federal, forest industry, and other private, for selected Western States, Jan 1992, annual rpt, A9395–1

Oil production and value, and oil revenues received from onshore Federal and Indian land leases, 1991 and trends, periodic basic data book, A2575–14.2

State social, economic, and govtl indicators, with rankings, 1993 semiannual rpt, B8500–1.12

Statistical profiles of 50 States and DC, general data, 1993 annual almanac, C4712–1

State and local:

Alaska public recreational areas by type, and acreage, 1991-92, annual rpt, S0275–1

Arizona land ownership distribution including govt agencies, and public land grazing fees, 1993 annual rpt, U5830–1

Arizona statistical abstract, general data, 1993 recurring rpt, U5850–2.8

California statistical abstract, general data, 1992 annual rpt, S0840–2.1

Connecticut govt property inventory by type, 1988-91, annual rpt, S1170–1

Hawaii data book, general data, 1992 annual rpt, S2090–1.6, S2090–1.10

Mississippi statistical abstract, general data, 1992 annual rpt, U3255–4.16

Nevada statistical abstract, general data, 1992 biennial rpt, S5005–1.9

New York State statistical yearbook, general data, 1992 annual rpt, U5100–1.5, U5100–1.15

South Carolina statistical abstract, general data, 1993 annual rpt, S7125–1.1

Tennessee statistical abstract, general data, 1992/93 annual rpt, U8710–2.12

Utah public lands by govt owner, and Federal land payments to State and local govts, with data by county, 1992 article, U8960–2.502

see also Government supplies and property
see also Homesteads
see also Mineral leases
see also National forests
see also National parks
see also Oil and gas leases
see also Public buildings
see also State forests
see also State parks
see also Wilderness areas
see also Wildlife refuges

Public Law 480

Soybean, cottonseed, and sunflowerseed oil exports under PL 480, 1950s-92, annual rpt, B8480–1

Public libraries

see Libraries

Public opinion

see Business outlook and attitude surveys
see Consumer surveys
see Opinion and attitude surveys
see Political attitudes and ideology

Public ownership

see Government ownership

Public relations

Cable TV operator local promotion campaign activities and budget, Jan 1992 survey, C2965–1.507

Chambers of commerce income, salaries and benefits, membership, staff, and operations, 1993 annual rpt, A3840–3

Coal industry executive views on industry public image, by region, Mar 1993 survey, article, C5226–1.507

Compensation of public relations personnel, by employee and company characteristics, with budget and staff size trends and career attitudes, 1993 survey, annual article, A8770–1.503

Corporate communications mgmt, activities, budget, staffing, and use of outside services, 1992 survey, R4105–78.24

Corporate expenditures on advertising, marketing, and public relations involving support for the arts, 1991-92, recurring rpt, A3690–1

Customer satisfaction with service over the telephone, by selected industry, 1993 article, C4687–1.508

Home improvement store customer services offered and advertised, 1993 survey, article, C5150–6.507

Public relations practices and trends in business and govt, monthly rpt, A8770–1

Retail store customer service improvement methods, views of consumers by outlet type, 1993 survey article, C8130–1.509

Small corporation mgmt views on obligations to society, and socially responsible activities of own company, Feb 1993 survey, C4687–1.507

Tourism dev offices of State govts, activities, personnel, and budgets, by State, 1992 survey, annual rpt, R9375–2

see also Advertising

Public schools

see Community colleges
see Elementary and secondary education
see Higher education
see terms beginning with School

Public service employment

Public interest in news items concerning National Service Act, awarding student aid for community service work, by respondent characteristics, Sept 1993 survey, C8915–1.505

Public opinion on Clinton Admin proposal to award student aid for public service, 1993 annual Gallup Poll, A8680–1.503

State and local:

South Carolina juvenile offender community service restitution orders, FY89-92, annual rpt, S7125–1.5

see also Job Training Partnership Act

Public services

see Community centers
see Community health services
see Fire departments
see Police
see Public utilities
see Sewage and wastewater systems
see Social services
see Water supply and use

Public transportation

see Subways
see Urban transportation

Public utilities

Business failures and liabilities, by detailed industry, cause, length of operation, and location, 1991-92 and trends, annual rpt, C3150–8

Computer control and acquisition systems for pipelines/gas utilities, market shares for 8 leading and all other manufacturers, 1991, article, C6985–1.501

Computer/info systems, software, and related services expenditures, 1990 and 1995, article, A4700–4.502

Construction contract awards by type of project, weekly rpt, C5800–2

Construction contract value, by construction type and region, including floor area and number of residential units, 1992-93, annual rpt, C5800–15.501, C5800–15.504, C5800–15.507, C5800–26, C5800–29

Corporate performance ratings by executives for leading companies in 32 industries, 1993 annual survey feature, C8900–1.508

Diversification activities of gas/electric utilities, Nov 1991 survey, article, C5800–28.504

Engineers salaries by industry group, census div, selected metro area, and years since college degree, 1993, annual survey rpt, A0685–5

Index by Subjects and Names

Public utilities

Engineers salaries by industry group, census div, selected metro area, degree level, and years since college degree, 1993, annual survey rpt, A0685–3

Executive benefits and perquisites offered by utility companies, 1992, article, C5800–28.507

Executive compensation and components, by industry div and major manufacturing group, 1991, annual rpt, R4105–19

Financing (long-term) and yields, by type of issue and/or utility, 1991 and trends, annual rpt, A4700–1

Fortune magazine ranking of top 50-100 companies in 8 nonindustrial sectors, with financial and employment data, 1992, annual feature, C8900–1.516

Fortune magazine ranking of top 50-100 companies worldwide in 8 nonindustrial sectors, with financial and employment data, 1993 annual feature, C8900–1.522

Govt revenues, State and local, from public utilities, 1993 annual rpt, R9050–1

Info mgmt system current and planned improvements, by application, 1993 survey article, C6985–6.505

Labor union success rates in NLRB elections, by industry group and census div, and for public utility plants by employment size, 1985-90, article, C6985–6.506

Latin America statistical abstract, general data by country, 1992 annual rpt, U6250–1.32

Motor vehicle fleet manager earnings, and personal and professional characteristics, 1993 article, C1575–2.506

Motor vehicle fleet operating and financial data, including fleets by type, registrations by make and model, and top lessors, 1970s-93, annual rpt, C1575–2.507

Natural gas utility pipeline mileage and distribution services, pipeline breakage risk, and number of customers, for 21 utilities, 1991, article, C6780–1.503

Operating and financial composite ratios for corporations, with establishments and receipts, for approx 200 industries, by asset size, FY90, annual rpt, C7800–1

Regulatory agency activities, scope of jurisdiction, finances, and employees, by agency, 1991/92 annual rpt, A7015–2

Regulatory agency policies and practices, and industry financial and operating data, by utility type and agency, 1991/92 annual rpt, A7015–3

Residential electric and gas meters in daily newspaper markets in US and Canada, 1993 annual rpt, C3250–1

State utility commission conservation, demand-side mgmt, and least-cost planning programs for electric and gas utilities, 1991 rpt, A8195–11

Truck/van fleets, for top 40 utilities, 1992, annual feature, C1575–2.502

Underground pipeline and utility construction industry intl devs, articles and special features, monthly rpt, C6780–2

State and local:

Alaska public utility financial and operating data, by company and utility type, 1991 and trends, with FY92 regulatory info, annual rpt, S0280–4

Arizona economic condition, including population, employment and earnings, and business activity, by industry and locality, 1985-93, semiannual rpt, U5850–1.1

Arkansas public utility financial, operating, and regulatory data, by utility type and company, 1992 annual rpt, S0757–1

California property tax assessments and exemptions, by type of property, city, county, and company, FY93 and trends, annual rpt, S0835–1.2

California public utility and transportation regulatory data, including revenue requests and rates of return by company, FY92 annual rpt, S0930–1

California statistical abstract, general data, 1992 annual rpt, S0840–2.10

Colorado property assessed valuation, by property type and county, and for regulated industries by company, 1991-92, annual rpt, S1055–3

DC utility regulation and consumer complaints, 1987-91, annual rpt, S1535–3.4

Delaware school district expenditures for operations, materials, and health and food services, 1991/92, annual rpt, S1430–1.4

Florida public utility regulatory and operating data, by company and utility type, 1992 and trends, annual rpt, S1790–1

Florida statistical abstract, general data, 1992 annual rpt, U6660–1.15

Georgia property tax collected and public utilities assessed value, by class of property, FY92 annual rpt, S1950–1.2

Idaho public utility regulatory data, and commission finances, FY92, annual rpt, S2290–1

Illinois electric and gas utility sales and operating revenues, and customers served, by class of service and company, 1991-92, annual rpt series, S2410–1

Maine employment in trade, utilities, and transportation SIC 2-digit industries, by detailed occupation, 2nd qtr 1991, triennial rpt, S3465–1.25

Minnesota public utility financial and operating data, discontinued biennial rpt, S4235–1

Mississippi public utilities tax assessments, by company and county, 1991 and trends, annual rpt, S4435–1

Montana public utility and transportation property assessments, by county and company, 1991-92, biennial rpt, S4750–1.2

Nebraska property tax revenues and actual valuation by property type, by city and/or county, 1991 and trends, annual rpt, S4950–1.4

Nebraska public service commission regulatory activities, with financial and operating data for individual railroads and telephone companies, FY91-92 biennial rpt, S4940–1

New Mexico economic trends and outlook, by industry div, 1982-92, annual article, U7980–1.503

New Mexico public utility operating, financial, and regulatory data, by utility type, FY92 annual rpt, S5645–1

New Mexico tax revenues and disbursements, by detailed tax type, and property valuation data, FY91-92 and trends, annual rpt, S5660–1.2

New York State public utility financial and operating data, by utility type and company, 1988-92, annual rpt, S5795–1

New York State statistical yearbook, general data, 1992 annual rpt, U5100–1.12

North Carolina employment in trade, transportation, communications, utilities, govt, and education, by detailed occupation, 2nd qtr 1991, triennial rpt, S5917–5.2

North Carolina public utility financial, operating, and regulatory data, by utility type and company, 1990 and trends, annual rpt, S5917–2

Ohio natural gas and electricity supply-demand by utility and consuming sector, 1992-93 and trends, annual rpt, S6355–1

Ohio public utility excise taxes and property assessments, by type of utility, 1987-91, annual rpt, S6390–1.4

Oklahoma statistical abstract, general data, 1992 annual rpt, U8130–2.18

Pennsylvania statistical abstract, general data, 1992 recurring rpt, U4130–6.9

South Carolina property tax assessed values, by class and county, FY92, annual rpt, S7255–1.3

South Carolina public service commission regulatory activities, with financial and operating data for individual utilities and railroads, FY92 annual rpt, S7235–1

South Carolina statistical abstract, general data, 1993 annual rpt, S7125–1.8

South Dakota property tax and valuations, by property type and locality, FY92 annual rpt, S7380–1.2

Tennessee public utility and transportation commission regulatory activities, with industry financial and operating data, 1991-92 biennial rpt, S7565–1

Texas trade, transportation, and public utilities employment, by SIC 2- and 3-digit industry and detailed occupation, 2nd qtr 1991, triennial survey rpt, S7675–1.31

Utah statistical abstract, general data, 1993 triennial rpt, U8960–1.13

Vermont public utility financial and operating data, by company, 1986-91, biennial rpt, S8100–1

Virginia public service corporation assessed values and tax levies, by county and independent city, 1991, annual rpt, S8305–1.3

Washington State regulated utilities financial and operating data, by company, annual rpt series, S8450–1

Washington State tax revenue by source and county, with property tax rates and assessed valuation, FY92 and trends, annual rpt, S8415–1

West Virginia property valuations and tax levies by property class, and levies by purpose, by county, 1992/93 and trends, annual rpt, S8640–2

Wyoming property assessed valuations and tax levies, by property type, tax purpose, and location, 1992 and trends, annual rpt, S8990–1.2

Wyoming property valuations, tax levies, and bonded debt, by county and school district, 1992 and trends, annual rpt, S8890–1.1

Public utilities

see also Buses
see also Electric power
see also Electric power plants and equipment
see also Electric power prices
see also Natural gas and gas industry
see also Natural gas prices
see also Railroads
see also Refuse and refuse disposal
see also Rural cooperatives
see also Rural electrification
see also Sewage and wastewater systems
see also Subways
see also Telephones and telephone industry
see also Water supply and use
see also under By Industry in the "Index by Categories"

Public welfare programs

Benefits (maximum) paid for AFDC, general assistance, and SSI, by State, with population shares receiving AFDC and food stamps in selected States, 1993 article, B8500–2.515

Black American disabled workers receiving public assistance by program, with comparisons to whites, 1989, annual compilation, C6775–2.2

Black American earnings, income, and poverty data, with comparisons to whites, 1980s-91, annual compilation, C6775–2.7

Child health and well-being indicators, with AFDC/food stamp benefits as a percent of poverty income threshold, by State, 1993 annual rpt, R3832–1

Children enrolled in early childhood education programs, percent receiving public assistance, urban vs total US, 1990, A4425–4

Europe public opinion on political, economic, and social issues, for 9 countries and 3 Soviet Union Republics, 1991 survey, C8915–8.1

Europe public opinion on political, economic, and social issues of interest to foreign investors, for 9 countries and 3 Soviet Union Republics, 1991 survey, C8915–9

Federal expenditures by category, by State and region, FY92 and trends, annual rpt, R8490–35

Govt finances, including revenues by source, expenditures by function, and debt, detailed data for Federal, State, and local govts, 1993 annual rpt, R9050–1

Hispanic American income and poverty data, with comparisons to whites, 1980s-91, annual compilation, C6775–3.5

Latin America Catholic welfare, health, and educational instns, by country, 1982-87, annual rpt, U6250–1.10

Latin America statistical abstract, general data by country, 1992 annual rpt, U6250–1.7

Measles cases in preschool children, health care providers used and welfare status, in 5 metro areas, 1989-90, article, A2623–1.508

Minority population characteristics, employment, and voting patterns by detailed race-ethnicity, with comparisons to whites, 1980s-2040, R8750–2.58

Participation in assistance and social insurance programs among whites, blacks, and Hispanics, 1991, R3834–15

Poor children age 5/under in families receiving welfare benefits, by family type, 1990-91, annual rpt, U1260–2

Poverty population share with incomes raised above poverty level by govt benefit payments, by age, 1990, annual rpt, R3840–11.1

Public opinion on social, political, and economic issues, detailed data, 1972-91 surveys, annual rpt, U6395–1

State budget effect of hypothetical Federal entitlement spending limit, by State, FY94, article, B8500–2.516

State social, economic, and govtl indicators, with rankings, 1993 semiannual rpt, B8500–1.8

Statistical profiles of 50 States and DC, general data, 1993 annual almanac, C4712–1

Student aid applicant untaxed income sources, American College Testing (ACT) program, 1992, annual rpt, R1960–5

State and local:

Alabama county data book, general data, 1992 annual rpt, S0121–2

Alabama public welfare and social service cases, recipients, and payments, by program and county, monthly rpt, S0150–1

Arizona public assistance recipients and payments, by program, county, and district, monthly rpt, S0465–4

Arizona statistical abstract, general data, 1993 recurring rpt, U5850–2.7

Arkansas Census of Population and Housing detailed findings, 1990, U5935–7

Arkansas human services dept finances and operations, including service recipient characteristics, by program, FY91 and trends, annual rpt, S0700–2

California Census of Population and Housing detailed findings, 1990, S0840–9

California public assistance recipients by program and selected characteristics, 1988-90, annual planning rpt, S0830–2

California public welfare cases, recipients, and expenditures, by program and county, monthly rpt, S0935 2

California statistical abstract, general data, 1992 annual rpt, S0840–2.5

Colorado welfare and social services expenditures and caseloads, by county and/or program, FY91, annual rpt, S1085 1

DC statistical profile, general data, 1992 annual rpt, S1535–3.5

Delaware public assistance recipients, funds available, and payments, by program, with selected data by county, monthly rpt, S1385–1

Florida county data book, 1992/93 annual rpt, C6360–1

Florida public welfare cases, recipients, and payments, by program and county, discontinued annual rpt, S1745–4

Florida statistical abstract, general data, 1992 annual rpt, U6660–1.7

Georgia county guide, general data, 1993 annual rpt, U6750–1

Hawaii data book, general data, 1992 annual rpt, S2090–1.11

Hawaii economic indicators, bimonthly rpt, B3500–1

Idaho public welfare program expenditures and recipients, with data by county, quarterly rpt, S2250–1

Illinois public assistance program cases, recipients, and payments, by program and county, FY91-92 and trends, annual rpt, S2520–2

Illinois statistical abstract, general data, 1992 annual rpt, U6910–2

Indiana public assistance program participation, expenditures, and services, by county, FY92 and trends, annual rpt, S2623–1

Iowa ADC and SSI program recipients, and expenditures, by county, monthly rpt, S2802–1

Maryland statistical abstract, general data, 1993-94 biennial rpt, S3605–1.6

Maryland welfare program statistics, and welfare fraud investigations, by county, monthly rpt, S3645–2

Massachusetts municipal and county profiles, general data, 1992 annual rpt, C4712–2

Michigan public assistance program cases, recipients, and payments, detailed data by county, monthly rpt, S4010–1

Michigan welfare registrants, by sex, age, and race-ethnicity, June 1992, annual planning rpt, S3980–1.2

Minnesota public welfare program recipients and expenditures, by county, 1992, semiannual rpt, S4202–1

Mississippi population eligible for Job Training Partnership Act, by welfare status, 1993/94, annual planning rpt, S4345–1.3

Mississippi public welfare and social service cases, recipients, and payments, by program and county, FY92, annual rpt, S4357–1

Mississippi statistical abstract, general data, 1992 annual rpt, U3255–4.12

Missouri births to mothers receiving welfare, by program, race, county, and city, 1992, annual rpt, S4518–1

Missouri public welfare and medical assistance recipients, expenditures, and case processing, by program and county, FY92 and trends, annual rpt, S4575–2

Montana welfare and medical assistance program cases and payments, by county and type of service, monthly rpt, S4755–1

Montana welfare fraud investigations, convictions, and recoveries, FY91-92, biennial rpt, S4750–1.1

Nebraska public welfare cases, recipients, and payments, by program and county, FY92 and trends, annual rpt, S4957–1

Nevada statistical abstract, general data, 1992 biennial rpt, S5005–1.2, S5005–1.8

New Jersey Census of Population and Housing detailed findings, by county, 1990, S5425–19

New Jersey municipal and county data book, general data, 1992 annual rpt, C4712–4

New Jersey public welfare cases, recipients, payments, and case processing, by program and county or city, monthly rpt, S5415–1

New Mexico public assistance cases, expenditures, and case processing, by program and county, monthly rpt, S5620–2

New York State and NYC home relief cases, quarterly rpt, S5735–2

New York State municipal and county statistical profiles, general data, 1993 annual rpt, C4712–7

New York State public assistance and social service program statistics, by State area and source of funds, 1991 and trends, annual rpt, S5800–2

New York State statistical yearbook, general data, 1992 annual rpt, U5100–1.11

North Carolina public welfare programs, cases, recipients, staff, and finances, by county, 1st half FY93, semiannual rpt, S5940–2

Oklahoma public welfare program expenditures, recipients, and services, by program and county, FY92 and trends, annual rpt, S6455–1

Oklahoma statistical abstract, general data, 1992 annual rpt, U8130–2.10

Oregon public welfare caseloads, recipients, and expenditures, by program, city, county, and State region, monthly rpt, S6615–8

Pennsylvania Census of Population and Housing detailed findings, with selected data by county and municipality, 1990, U4130–13

Pennsylvania income data from Census of Population and Housing, by county and municipality, 1989, C1595–15

Pennsylvania labor force planning rpt, including data on populations with employability problems, FY92 annual rpt, S6845–3.3

Pennsylvania statistical abstract, general data, 1992 recurring rpt, U4130–6.5

South Carolina public welfare recipients, payments, and case processing, by county and program, monthly rpt, S7252–1

South Carolina statistical abstract, general data, 1993 annual rpt, S7125–1.10

South Dakota welfare and social services recipients and payments, by program, MSA, and county, FY92, annual rpt, S7385 1

Tennessee statistical abstract, general data, 1992/93 annual rpt, U8710–2.18, U8710–2.20

Texas local health dept operations, with data on public assistance participation of service area population, for 22 local areas, 1980s, U8850–8.6

Texas welfare and social services program expenditures, recipients, and fraud cases, by county and/or program, FY92 and trends, annual rpt, S7695–1

Utah govt statistical review, fiscal and socioeconomic data, 1993 annual rpt, R9380–1.9

Utah statistical abstract, general data, 1993 triennial rpt, U8960–1.6

Virginia public welfare cases, recipients, and expenditures, by program, county, and city, suspended quarterly rpt, S8293–2

Washington State public assistance clients and service costs, by client characteristics, program, and county, FY90, annual rpt, S8420–2

West Virginia statistical handbook, general data, 1992 annual rpt, R9385–1.2

West Virginia welfare and social service program caseloads and expenditures, by county, monthly rpt, S8560–2

Wyoming welfare and social service recipients and expenditures, by program and county, FY92, annual rpt, S8908–1

see also Aid to blind

see also Aid to disabled and handicapped persons

see also Aid to Families with Dependent Children

see also Child day care

see also Child welfare

see also Disability benefits and insurance

see also Disaster relief

see also Food assistance

see also Food stamp programs

see also Foster home care

see also Homemaker services

see also Income maintenance

see also Legal aid

see also Low-income energy assistance

see also Maternity benefits

see also Medicaid

see also Medical assistance

see also Medicare

see also Old age assistance

see also Public service employment

see also Rent supplements

see also School lunch and breakfast programs

see also Social security

see also Social services

see also Social work

see also State funding for social welfare

see also Supplemental Security Income

see also Vocational rehabilitation

see also Work incentive programs

Public works

Budget of US outlays for public investment programs by type, with intl comparisons, FY93-94 and trends, R4700–23

City officials views on city issues and conditions, including ability to pay for needed public works, 1992 survey, annual rpt, A8012–1.21

Construction contract value, by construction type and region, including floor area and number of residential units, 1992-93, annual rpt, C5800–15.501, C5800–15.504, C5800–15.507, C5800–26, C5800–29

Construction project value ready to begin if Federal funding becomes available, by project type, 1993 article, C5800–2.514

Japan govt budgeted outlays for public works projects, FY92-93, annual article, R5650–2.510

Japan govt public works contracts let under US-Japan Major Projects Agreement, with bids submitted and won by US firms, 1988-92, article, R5650–2.537

Local govt capital improvement financing methods, by population size, metro status, and census div, 1991 survey, A5800–2.112

Local govt infrastructure financing methods used, including developer impact fees by purpose, with bond marketing methods, by locality, 1991 survey, A5800–4.33

Municipal govt use of property tax increment financing for infrastructure dev, with revenues vs project costs, and complaints, 1993 rpt, A5800–1.1

OECD foreign dev assistance share targeted for infrastructure improvements, for 11 OECD donor countries, 1991, article, C5800–2.527

State and local:

Maryland local govt financial condition, including revenues by source, expenditures by function, and debt obligations, FY92 and trends, annual rpt, S3618–1.1

see also Bridges and tunnels

see also Dams

see also Federal aid to highways

see also Highways, streets, and roads

see also Public buildings

see also Public service employment

see also Reservoirs

see also State funding for capital projects

see also Turnpikes

Publishers Information Bureau

Magazine (fashion) advertising pages, for 4 leading publications, 1st half 1991-93, article, C2710–1.527

Magazine advertising pages and revenues, for top 100 publications, weekly rpt monthly table, C2710–1

Publishing industry

see Printing and publishing industry

Pubs

see Restaurants and drinking places

Pueblo, Colo.

Income per capita, 1991, annual article, S1040–4.507

Puerto Ricans

see Hispanic Americans

see Puerto Rico

Puerto Rico

Accidental deaths, by State and type, 1992, annual rpt, A8375–2.1

AIDS cases, for top 10 States/territories, 1993 article, C4215–1.505

Aircraft civil and military joint-use facilities, by State and selected territory, 1991, annual rpt, A0250–2.3

Airports and communities in North America served by regional vs larger airlines, by carrier and location, 1993 annual rpt, A8795–1.2

Blood bank operating profiles, arranged by State, 1993 biennial directory, A0612–1

Cancer incidence and mortality, including data by State, sex, and body site, 1993 and trends, annual rpt, A1175–1

Court caseloads and dispositions by type of court and case, 1991 and trends, annual rpt, R6600–1

Dental advanced education programs, enrollment, grads, and finances, by instn and State, 1992/93 annual rpt, A1475–10

Dental allied education enrollment, grads, and tuition, by instn, 1992/93 annual rpt, A1475–5

Dental school enrollment and grads, program characteristics, and faculty, by US and Canadian instn, 1992/93, annual rpt, A1475–3

Dental school programs, enrollment, and finances by instn, annual rpt series, A1475–4

Discount stores and membership wholesale clubs, 1992, annual feature, C5150–3.516

Doctoral degree recipient characteristics, including citizenship status, source of support, field of study, and instn, 1990/91 and trends, annual rpt, R6000–7

Drug abuse incidence by population demographic and health characteristics, 1987, article, A2623–1.504

Employment of 10 largest US companies manufacturing in Puerto Rico under IRS Code Section 936, 1993 article, C5800–7.532

Engineering degrees awarded, by State, instn, and field, with detail for women, minorities, and foreign students, 1991/92, annual rpt, A0685–1

Puerto Rico

Engineering program enrollment, by instn, field, and State, with detail for women, minorities, and foreign students, fall 1992, annual rpt, A0685–2

Fiscal outlook of State legislative officers, including forecast revenues and expenditures compared to budgeted levels, by State, FY93, annual rpt, A7470–4.11

Flour milling companies and capacity, in US by State, Canada, Mexico, and Central American and Caribbean area countries, 1993 annual directory and buyers guide, C8450–3

Food store market shares and outlets, by company and store type, for approx 350 metro areas in US and Canada, with industry operating data, 1993 annual rpt, C3400–6

Foreign students enrolled in US higher education instns, by instn, State, country of origin, and demographic characteristics, 1991/92 and trends, annual rpt, R5580–1

Foundations and finances, FY91, annual rpt, R4900–1

Foundations, assets, and contributions, FY91, annual article, C2176–1.507

General fund balance data, including trends in appropriations for selected functions, by State, FY91-93, annual rpt, A7470–4.10

Higher education enrollment, by State and public instn, fall 1992, annual rpt, A7150–5

Higher education faculty average salaries by rank, by instn, 1992/93, annual feature, C2175–1.516

Higher education faculty compensation and employment, detailed data by rank, sex, and instn, 1992/93 and trends, annual rpt, A0800–1

Higher education State-administered student aid awards, by program and State, 1992/93 and trends, annual rpt, A7140–1

Higher education tuition/fees by instn, 1992/93-1993/94, annual feature, C2175–1.535

Horse racing activity, attendance, handle, purse distribution, and govt revenue, 1990, annual rpt, A3363–1.1

Hospital directory, with utilization, expenses, and personnel, by instn, type, and location, 1992, annual rpt, A1865–3

Immigrants with college education from Puerto Rico, percent living in 4 leading US States, 1982-88, article, C4575–1.506

Jewelry industry statistics on sales, marketing, trade, and employment, with customer characteristics, 1993 annual almanac, C2150–7.509

Judicial system salaries for judges and court administrators, by State and territory, and for Federal system, July 1993, semiannual rpt, R6600–2

Law school enrollment by minority status, degrees conferred, staff, and library holdings, by instn, 1992/93 and trends, annual rpt, A0970–1

Life insurance company mortgage and real estate holdings, by State and outlying area, 1991, biennial fact book, A1325–1.4

Loan delinquency rates for approx 10 types of consumer bank loans, and repossession data, by State, quarterly rpt, A0950–1

Markets with daily newspapers, demographic and economic info by geographic area, US and Canada, 1993 annual rpt, C3250–1

Medical school programs, fees, applicants, admissions, and enrollment, with data by age, sex, minority group, and instn, 1992/93 and trends, annual rpt, A3273–10

Mortgage delinquency and foreclosure rates, and residential loans serviced, by type, State, and census div and region, quarterly rpt, A6450–1

Motor vehicle world production, sales, trade, and registrations, by country, world area, manufacturer, and make, 1991 and trends, annual rpt, A0865–2.1

Newspaper circulation, 6-month periods ended Sept 1992 and Mar 1993, semiannual rpt, A3385–3.1

Nursing programs (State-approved) for practical/vocational nurses, including admissions, enrollment, and grads, by instn, State, and territory, 1992, annual directory, A8010–5

Nursing programs (State-approved) for registered nurses, including admissions, enrollment, and grads, by instn, State, and territory, 1992, annual directory, A8010–4

Optometry school faculty, enrollment and degrees, policies and programs, and finances, by instn, 1991/92, annual survey, A3370–2

Physicians by detailed specialty and location, 1992 and trends, annual rpt, A2200–3

Public health school applicant, student, and grad characteristics, by instn, 1991/92 and trends, annual rpt, A3372–3

Public health school faculty characteristics, by instn, fall 1991, recurring rpt, A3372–1

Public opinion on Puerto Rico statehood, commonwealth status, or independence, in Puerto Rico and US, 1989-92 surveys, article, C4575–1.506

Rabies cases in wild and domestic animals and humans, 1992 annual article, A3100–2.504

Science courses in high school, percent of students taking biology, chemistry, and physics, 1991/92, article, A1250–1.534

Social work higher education programs, faculty and student characteristics, and student aid, with data by instn, 1992 and trends, annual rpt, A4515–1

Student aid expenditures, 1991/92-1992/93, annual feature, C2175–1.515

Substance abuse treatment programs, funding by source, and client characteristics, for alcohol and drug services, by State, FY91 and trends, annual rpt, A7112–1

Tax changes enacted, with impact on revenues, FY93 and trends, by State, annual rpt, A7470–4.9

Traffic accident deaths, bimonthly rpt, A8375–1

Transportation regulatory agency policies and practices for motor carriers and railroads, by agency, 1991/92 annual rpt, A7015–4

Trust instns and assets managed, approx 5,000 depts, US and Canada, 1993 annual directory, C2425–2.501

Unemployment insurance trends, including data on unemployment, worker characteristics, coverage, benefits, and State govt finances, 1940s-90, R9260–18

Utility and transportation regulatory agency activities, scope of jurisdiction, finances, and employees, by agency, 1991/92 annual rpt, A7015–2

Utility regulatory agency policies and practices, and industry financial and operating data, by utility type and agency, 1991/92 annual rpt, A7015–3

Veterinarians by location and type of employment, 1990 and 1992, article, A3100–2.522

State and local:

Oklahoma commuting patterns, including interstate and international travel, and detailed data by county, 1990 and trends, S6416–2

Pulmonary diseases

see Respiratory diseases

Pulp

see Lumber industry and products

see Paper and paper products

Purchasing

see Business orders

see Defense contracts and procurement

see Government contracts and procurement

see Industrial purchasing

Purchasing power

see Earnings, general

see Personal and household income

Qatar

Energy intl sourcebook, with detail on oil and gas industry operations, supply-demand, and prices, for approx 80 countries, 1970s-91, annual compilation, C6985–10.2

see also Organization of Petroleum Exporting Countries

Quality control and testing

Chemical industry Intl Organization for Standardization (ISO 9000) registrations of US and non-US facilities, for 27 companies, 1992/93, article, A1250–1.516

Computer system interoperability tests passed, for 5 open systems, 1992 article, C1850–2.502

Construction industry finances and operations, by type of business and region, 1992-93, annual survey rpt, A4155–1

Corporate applicants and winners, for Baldrige quality excellence award, including manufacturing and service companies, and small businesses, 1988-93, article, C1850–2.512

Corporate applicants for Baldrige quality excellence award, 1989-93, article, C1200–4.507

Corporate executive and outside director quality control and improvement experience and views, July-Aug 1992 surveys, A2800–3

Corporate quality assurance programs in North America, selected characteristics, 1992 annual survey rpt, B6850–2

Corporate quality mgmt program studies, including data on mgmt and employee views on attributes, 1990s, R4105–78.32

Corporate total quality mgmt program success as seen by managers, 1993 survey article, C7000–3.508

Index by Subjects and Names

Corporate winners of Baldrige quality excellence award, performance of hypothetical stock investments in 10 firms, 1993 article, C5800–7.550

Food marketers mgmt info system operations, including use of benchmarking evaluations, 1993, annual survey, A4950–7

Industrial distributors use of quality control programs, and certification methods used with suppliers and customers, 1993 annual survey article, C2150–1.507

Industrial R&D activities and quality assurance, articles and special features, monthly rpt, C1850–6

Jewelry retailer views on diamond grading, and importance of color, clarity, and cut to retailers and customers, 1993 survey article, C2150–7.505

Library State agency total quality mgmt activities, by State, 1992 annual rpt, A3862–1

Oil/gas well blowout prevention equipment failure rates, 1993 article, C6985–1.533

Paper distributor views on total quality mgmt programs, including use, benefits, and supplier participation, 1993 survey article, A8140–3.504

Pulp and paper industry quality control program characteristics, 1993 survey, annual article, C3975–2.508

Small corporation employee benefits and compensation methods, for companies with and without interest in improving quality, May 1992 survey, article, C4687–1.502

see also Food inspection

Quality of life

Activities important to all adults vs self-described "workaholics," leisure time trend, and work vs vacation time in 12 countries, 1993 survey feature, C4215–1.507

Child well-being indicators based on social, economic, and environmental factors, for 239 MSAs, with detail by component county and city, 1980s-90s, R9700–2

City officials views on community conditions, including most important and difficult problems, 1992 survey, annual rpt, A8012–1.21

Elementary/secondary prospective teacher satisfaction with selected aspects of life, survey of persons interested in alternative certification routes, 1992, R6350–7

Europe Jewish population, with social and demographic characteristics, for 10-12 countries, 1930s-91, article, A2050–1.1

Europe public opinion on political, economic, and social issues, for 9 countries and 3 Soviet Union Republics, 1991 survey, C8915–8

Europe public opinion on political, economic, and social issues of interest to foreign investors, for 9 countries and 3 Soviet Union Republics, 1991 survey, C8915–9

Hispanic American leaders views on current issues of importance to Hispanic community, 1993 annual survey article, C4575–1.511

Latin America statistical abstract, general data by country, 1992 annual rpt, U6250–1.7, U6250–1.12

Men age 69-84 quality of life indicators, including health, finances, family, and employment, by race, 1990 survey, U3780–9

Public opinion on computer use contribution to quality of life and threat to privacy, 1992 survey and trends, annual rpt, B3280–2

Public opinion on social, political, and economic issues, detailed data, 1972-91 surveys, annual rpt, U6395–1

Public satisfaction with natl situation, and future outlook, Jan 1993 Gallup Poll, C4040–1.507

Public satisfaction with natl situation and personal life, Sept 1992 Gallup Poll and trends, C4040–1.503

Public satisfaction with natl situation, 1993 Gallup Polls and trends, C4040–1.508, C4040–1.511

Soviet Union political and economic restructuring issues, public opinion in Russia, Ukraine, and Lithuania, 1991-92 surveys, C8915–10

Standard of living indicators for US and 3 Asian countries, 1993 annual feature, C8900–1.520

State economic dev condition indicators, including economic performance, business vitality, growth capacity, and tax/fiscal system, by State, 1993 annual rpt, R4225–1.1

Time spent in work/commute, with family, and in physical activity, actual vs desired, 1992 survey feature, C1200–4.501

State and local:

Hawaii data book, general data, 1992 annual rpt, S2090–1.11

see also Living arrangements

Quarries and stone products

see Stone products and quarries

Quasi-official agencies

see Government corporations and enterprises

see National Railroad Passenger Corp.

Quebec Province, Canada

Life insurance policy sales and premiums, monthly rpt semiannual supplement, A6225–2

Questionnaires

see Consumer surveys

see Opinion and attitude surveys

see Political attitudes and ideology

see Statistical programs and activities

Quits

see Labor turnover

Rabies

Cases of rabies in animals, distribution by census div, 1st 11 months 1992, article, A3100–2.506

Cases of rabies in wild and domestic animals and humans, by State, 1992 annual article, A3100–2.504

Costs for rabies control/prevention, and cost-benefit analysis for vaccinating wild raccoons, New Jersey study, 1992 article, A3100–2.504

State and local:

Louisiana vital statistics, including population, births, deaths by cause, reportable diseases, marriages, and divorces, by demographic characteristics and locality, 1989-90 and trends, annual rpt, S3295–1

Racial discrimination

Maryland rabies cases in animals, including dispositions of infected animals, by species, 1981-87, article, A3100–2.504

Maryland rabies cases in cats and raccoons, and human exposure from cats, 1983-92, article, A3100–2.515

New Mexico deaths by cause, and incidence of communicable diseases, by demographic characteristics, 1991 and trends, annual rpt, S5605–1.3

South Carolina communicable disease cases, by county, 1990, annual rpt, S7175–1

South Dakota vital statistics, including births, deaths, marriage and divorce, and communicable disease, by demographic characteristics and county, 1991 and trends, annual rpt, S7345–1

see also under By Disease in the "Index by Categories"

Race/ethnic groups

see Asian Americans

see Black Americans

see Hispanic Americans

see Indians

see Minority groups

see Pacific Islands Americans

see Racial discrimination

see under By Race in the "Index by Categories"

Racial discrimination

Anti-Semitic public opinion trends, 1964, 1981, and 1992 surveys, article, A0610–1.504

Australia public perceptions of Aborigine employment patterns, impacts of media campaign in a small rural town, 1993 article, A0610–1.503

College freshmen attitudes on racial discrimination, fall 1992, annual survey, U6215–1

Eating/drinking place employment discrimination complaints filed with Equal Employment Opportunity Commission, with comparison to all industries, 1992, article, C5150–5.511

Elementary/secondary school superintendents personal and professional characteristics and views, 1992 survey rpt, A0775–5

GDP impacts of racial bias in education and employment, 1967-93, article, C4215–1.512

Public opinion on judicial bias against blacks, and Federal prosecution of Los Angeles police officers in Rodney King brutality case, Apr 1993 Gallup Poll, C4040–1.510

Public opinion on race relations and discrimination, Feb 1993 Gallup Poll, C4040–1.508

State and local:

Arizona crimes involving bias against selected persons or groups, with offense characteristics, 1992, annual rpt, S0505–2.2

Florida 8th-9th grade children of immigrants characteristics, attitudes, and discrimination experience, 1992, survey article, R4800–2.522

Idaho crimes involving bias against selected groups, 1992, annual rpt, S2275–2

Illinois crimes involving bias against selected groups, 1991, annual rpt, S2536–1

Missouri Human Rights Commission discrimination cases and dispositions, by case type, FY92 and trends, annual rpt, S4530–2.2

Racial discrimination

New Jersey crimes involving bias against racial, religious, or ethnic groups, with arrests and victim-offender characteristics, 1992, annual rpt, S5430–1.4

Oklahoma crimes involving bias against selected groups, with offense characteristics and offender race-ethnicity, 1992, annual rpt, S6465–1.2

Oklahoma real estate loan rejection rates for whites and minorities by income level, statewide and by MSA, 1991, article, U8130–1.504

Oregon crimes involving bias against selected persons or groups, with victim and offender characteristics, 1991-92, annual rpt, S6603–3.1

Pennsylvania crimes involving ethnic intimidation, by victim, offender, and crime characteristics, 1992, annual rpt, S6860–1

Texas crimes involving bias against selected persons or groups, by victim, offender, and incident characteristics, 1992, annual rpt, S7735–2.2

Racketeering

see Organized crime

Radar

Shipment value, employment, and foreign trade, for electronics industry, by sector and product type, 1980s-92, annual rpt, A4725–1.2

State and local:

Delaware State police traffic arrests by violation, 1988-92, annual rpt, S1435–1

Radiation

Monitoring instruments and radiation detection devices shipments, 1982-91, annual rpt, A4725–1.2

Public opinion on electric and magnetic fields (EMF), including reaction to having high-voltage transmission lines nearby, 1987-93 surveys, article, A4700–4.503

State and local:

Hawaii State radiation program inspection and licensing activity, 1990, annual rpt, S2065–1.6

see also Nuclear accidents and safety

see also Nuclear medicine and radiology

see also Radioactive materials

see also Radioactive waste and disposal

see also Radon

see also Uranium

see also X-rays

Radio

Advertising expenditures by medium for top 100 advertisers, with comparisons to earnings and sales, and detail by product type and brand, 1991-92, annual rpt, C2710–1.547

Audience age 12/over and 25-54, for top 15 radio networks, fall 1992 and trends, semiannual article, C1850–14.514

Audience age 12/over, for top 15 radio networks, spring 1993 and trends, semiannual article, C1850–14.538

Audience characteristics, and advertising revenues and effectiveness, with selected comparisons to other media, 1993 annual rpt, A8789–1

Audience ratings and program format, for top stations in leading metro markets, weekly rpt recurring article, C1850–14.506, C1850–14.507, C1850–14.508, C1850–14.521, C1850–14.531, C1850–14.542

Audience shares by listening location, by daypart, May 1992-Apr 1993, C2710–1.534

Audience size, leading stations and formats, and advertising rates and revenues, by market area, recurring rpt, C3165–1

Baseball broadcasting, including TV and radio originators, and rights payments, by major league team, 1993 annual article, C1850–14.515

Basketball (professional) broadcast coverage, by team, 1993/94, article, C1850–14.540

Broadcast industries and cable TV devs, including data on finances, advertising, ratings, and licensing, weekly rpt, C1850–14

Factory sales and shipments, foreign trade, and operating data for the electronics industry, by product category, 1980s-92, annual rpt, A4725–1

Financial ratios and performance, for over 350 SIC 4-digit industries, FY88-92, annual rpt, A6400–3

Football (college and professional) broadcast coverage and rights payments, by team, 1993 annual article, C1850–14.534

Latin America statistical abstract, general data by country, 1992 annual rpt, U6250–1.4

Mass media company revenues for leading firms, with detail by medium, 1991-92, annual feature, C2710–1.540

Public broadcasting station revenues, and data on general system operations and audience, series, R4250–1

Sales, trade, and industry devs for consumer electronics, by product type, 1970s-92, annual rpt, A4725–4

Spanish-language radio advertising billings, for top 10 stations and 4 market representative firms, 1991-92, annual article, C4575–1.502

Station group owners ranked by total Arbitron rating, with stations owned and ratings, for top 25 companies, summer 1992, article, C1850–14.502

Station ownership changes and transaction value, 1954-92, annual article, C1850–14.510

Stations in operation, AM, FM, and educational FM, 1988-92, annual rpt, A4725–4

Stations on the air and authorized, by type, weekly rpt, C1850–14

Statistical profiles of 50 States and DC, general data, 1993 annual almanac, C4712–1

Talk show listening habits, Sept 1993 survey, C8915–1.505

State and local:

Alabama county data book, general data, 1992 annual rpt, S0121–2

Alabama statistical abstract, general data, 1992 recurring rpt, U5680–2.2

Arizona statistical abstract, general data, 1993 recurring rpt, U5850–2.19

Georgia statistical abstract, general data, 1992-93 biennial rpt, U6730–1.8

Hawaii data book, general data, 1992 annual rpt, S2090–1.16

Kansas statistical abstract, general data, 1991/92 annual rpt, U7095–2.13

Mississippi statistical abstract, general data, 1992 annual rpt, U3255–4.7

Oklahoma statistical abstract, general data, 1992 annual rpt, U8130–2.17

Tennessee statistical abstract, general data, 1992/93 annual rpt, U8710–2.8

Utah statistical abstract, general data, 1993 triennial rpt, U8960–1.13

see also Broadcast payments and rights

see also Educational broadcasting

see also Mobile radio

see also Political broadcasting

see also Recording industry

Radioactive materials

Chemical (radiochemical) market value, 1991 and 1996, article, C1850–6.505

Nuclear weapons plutonium and highly enriched uranium disposal requirements of US and Russia arms reductions, 1993 article, C5226–2.511

see also Radioactive waste and disposal

see also Radon

see also Uranium

Radioactive waste and disposal

State and local:

Michigan low-level radioactive waste authority financial condition, FY92, annual rpt, S3985–2

Radiology

see Nuclear medicine and radiology

Radon

State and local:

Michigan household radon testing awareness and practices, by demographic characteristics, 1991, annual rpt, S4000–4

New York State public awareness of radon, including cancer risk, by selected characteristics, 1990, recurring rpt, S5765–3

Railroad accidents and safety

Accidental deaths and disabling injuries, by detailed type, victim characteristics, circumstances, and location, 1992 and trends, annual rpt, A8375–2

Deaths from transportation accidents, trends by mode, 1992 annual rpt, R4815–1

Public interest in news items concerning Sept 1993 Amtrak train accident in Alabama, by respondent characteristics, Sept 1993 survey, C8915–1.505

Regulatory agency activities, including railroad safety program staff and costs, 1991/92 annual rpt, A7015–4

Traffic accident fatalities, by type of accident, 1913-92, annual rpt, A0865–1.3

State and local:

Alabama traffic accidents, fatalities, and injuries, by circumstances, vehicle type, and driver and victim characteristics, 1992, annual rpt, S0185–1

Alabama vital statistics, including population, births, deaths by cause, marriages, and divorces, by location and demographic characteristics, 1992 and trends, annual rpt, S0175–2

Arizona traffic accidents, fatalities, and injuries, by vehicle type, circumstances, location, and driver and victim characteristics, 1991 and trends, annual rpt, S0530–1

Arkansas traffic accidents, fatalities, and injuries, by vehicle type, circumstances, location, and driver and victim characteristics, 1991, annual rpt, S0692–1

Index by Subjects and Names

Railroad accidents and safety

Arkansas vital statistics, including births, deaths by cause, marriages, and divorces, by age, sex, race, and county, 1991 and trends, annual rpt, S0685–1

California rail crossing and other related accidents, fatalities, and injuries, and State funding for crossing protection, FY92 annual rpt, S0930–1

California vital statistics, including population, births, and deaths by cause, by demographic characteristics and county, 1990 and trends, annual rpt, S0865–1

Colorado vital statistics, including population, births, deaths by cause, abortion, marriage and divorce, and adoption, by demographic characteristics and location, 1990 and trends, annual rpt, S1010–1

Connecticut traffic accidents, fatalities, and injuries, by vehicle type, circumstance, location, and driver and victim characteristics, 1992, annual rpt, S1275–1

Delaware traffic accidents, fatalities, and injuries, by circumstances, location, and vehicle type, and driver and victim characteristics, 1992 and trends, annual rpt, S1435–1

Florida traffic accidents, fatalities, and injuries, by vehicle type, circumstance, location, and driver and victim characteristics, 1992 and trends, annual rpt, S1750–2

Florida vital statistics, including population, births, deaths by cause, and marriages and dissolutions, by location and demographic characteristics, 1992 and trends, annual rpt, S1745–3

Idaho traffic accidents, fatalities, and injuries, by circumstances, location, vehicle type, and driver and victim characteristics, 1992, annual rpt, S2315–1

Idaho vital statistics, including births, deaths by cause, abortions, marriages, and divorces, by demographic characteristics and county, 1991 and trends, annual rpt, S2250–2

Illinois traffic accidents, fatalities, and injuries, by circumstances, location, and driver and victim characteristics, 1991 and trends, annual rpt, S2540–1

Indiana traffic accidents, fatalities, and injuries, by circumstances, location, and vehicle type, and driver and victim characteristics, 1992, annual rpt, S2675–1

Iowa vital statistics, including population, births, deaths by cause, marriages, and divorces, by demographic characteristics and location, 1991 and trends, annual rpt, S2795–1

Kansas traffic accidents, fatalities, and injuries, by vehicle type, location, circumstances, and driver and victim characteristics, 1992, annual rpt, S3040–1

Kentucky traffic accidents, fatalities, and injuries, by circumstances, location, vehicle type, and driver characteristics, 1992 and trends, annual rpt, S3150–2

Louisiana traffic accidents, fatalities, and injuries, by circumstances, location, and driver characteristics, 1991 and trends, annual rpt, S3345–2

Louisiana vital statistics, including population, births by cause, reportable diseases, marriages, and divorces, by demographic characteristics and locality, 1989-90 and trends, annual rpt, S3295–1

Maine traffic accidents, fatalities, and injuries, by accident circumstances, vehicle type and make, and driver and victim characteristics, 1992, annual rpt, S3475–2

Maine vital statistics, including births, deaths by cause, abortions, and marriages and divorces, by demographic characteristics and location, 1991 and trends, annual rpt, S3460–2

Maryland traffic accidents, fatalities, and injuries, by circumstances, location, vehicle type, and driver and victim characteristics, 1992, annual rpt, S3665–4

Maryland vital statistics, including population, births, deaths by cause, marriages, and divorces, by demographic characteristics and location, 1989 and trends, annual rpt, S3635–1

Massachusetts vital statistics, including births, deaths by cause, marriages, divorces, and population, by locality and demographic characteristics, 1990 and trends, annual rpt, S3850–1

Michigan traffic accidents, fatalities, and injuries, by vehicle type, circumstance, location, and driver and victim characteristics, 1991 and trends, annual rpt, S3997–2

Michigan vital statistics, including births, deaths, marriages, divorces/annulments, and communicable diseases, by location and demographic characteristics, 1990 and trends, annual rpt, S4000–3

Minnesota traffic accidents, fatalities, and injuries, by type of vehicle and circumstances, and driver and victim characteristics, 1992 and trends, annual rpt, S4230–2

Minnesota vital statistics, including population, births, abortions, deaths, marriages, and divorces, by location and demographic characteristics, 1991 and trends, annual rpt, S4190–2

Mississippi vital statistics, including births, deaths by cause, marriages, and divorces, by demographic characteristics and location, 1992 and trends, annual rpt, S4350–1

Missouri traffic accidents, fatalities, and injuries, by circumstances, location, and driver and victim characteristics, 1992 and trends, annual rpt, S4560–1

Missouri vital statistics, including population, births, deaths by cause, and marriages and divorces, by location and demographic characteristics, 1992 and trends, annual rpt, S4518–1

Montana traffic accidents, fatalities, and injuries, by circumstances, location, and driver and victim characteristics, 1992 and trends, annual rpt, S4705–2

Montana vital statistics, including births, deaths by cause, abortion, disease, and marriage and divorce, by demographic characteristics and county, 1990-91 and trends, annual rpt, S4690–1

Nebraska traffic accidents, fatalities, and injuries, by circumstances, location, vehicle type, and driver and victim characteristics, 1992, annual rpt, S4953–1

Nebraska vital statistics, including births, deaths, marriages, divorces, and population, by demographic characteristics and location, 1991 and trends, annual rpt, S4885–1

Nevada traffic accidents, fatalities, and injuries, by circumstances, location, and vehicle type, 1992 and trends, annual rpt, S5140–1

Nevada vital statistics, including births, abortions, and deaths by cause, by county and demographic characteristics, 1989 and trends, annual rpt, S5075–1

New Jersey fatal traffic accidents and fatalities, by vehicle type, location, and circumstances, and driver and victim characteristics, 1992 and trends, annual rpt, S5430–2

New Mexico traffic accidents, fatalities, and injuries, by vehicle type, circumstances, location, and driver and victim characteristics, 1992 and trends, annual rpt, S5665–1

New York State traffic accidents, fatalities, and injuries, by circumstances, location, vehicle type, and driver and victim characteristics, 1991 and trends, annual rpt, S5790–1

North Carolina hwy railroad grade crossings, and accident injuries and fatalities, 1970s-90, annual rpt, S5917–2

North Carolina traffic accidents, fatalities, and injuries, by circumstances, location, vehicle type, and driver and victim characteristics, 1992 and trends, annual rpt, S5990–1

North Dakota traffic accidents, fatalities, and injuries, by circumstances, location, vehicle type, and driver and victim characteristics, 1992 and trends, annual rpt, S6217–1

Ohio traffic accidents, fatalities, and injuries, by circumstances, location, driver and victim characteristics, and vehicle type, 1991 and trends, annual rpt, S6290–1

Oregon vital statistics, including births, deaths by cause, communicable diseases, marriages, and divorces, by age, sex, race-ethnicity, and county, 1991 and trends, annual rpt, S6615–5

Pennsylvania traffic accidents, fatalities, and injuries, by circumstances, location, driver characteristics, and vehicle type, 1991, annual rpt, S6905–3

Rhode Island vital statistics, including population, births, deaths, marriages, and divorces, by demographic characteristics and locality, 1989 and trends, annual rpt, S6995–1

South Carolina deaths, by detailed cause, age, sex, and race, 1990, annual rpt, S7175–2

South Carolina traffic accidents, fatalities, and injuries, by circumstances, location, and driver and victim characteristics, 1992 and trends, annual rpt, S7190–2

South Carolina vital statistics, including births, deaths by cause, marriages, and divorces, by age, sex, race, and location, 1990 and trends, annual rpt, S7175–1

Railroad accidents and safety

South Dakota traffic accidents, fatalities, and injuries, by circumstances, location, vehicle type, and driver and victim characteristics, 1992 and trends, annual rpt, S7300–3

Tennessee accident rpts and safety inspections, 1991-92, biennial rpt, S7565–1

Tennessee vital statistics, including births, deaths by cause, marriages, divorces, and population, by demographic characteristics and location, 1991 and trends, annual rpt, S7520–2

Texas vital statistics, including births, deaths by cause, abortions, marriages, and divorces, by location and demographic characteristics, 1991 and trends, annual rpt, S7685–1

Utah traffic accidents and fatalities by circumstances, location, driver and victim characteristics, and vehicle type, 1992 and trends, annual rpt, S7890–2

Utah vital statistics, including births and deaths by cause, by demographic characteristics and location, 1990, annual rpt, S7835–1.2

Virginia traffic accidents, fatalities, and injuries, by circumstances, location, and driver and victim characteristics, 1991 and trends, annual rpt, S8282–1

Virginia vital statistics, including births, deaths by cause, marriages and divorces, and communicable disease, by demographic characteristics and location, 1991 and trends, annual rpt, S8225–1

West Virginia traffic accidents, fatalities, and injuries, by circumstance and location, and driver and victim characteristics, 1992, annual rpt, S8645–1

West Virginia vital statistics, including births, deaths by cause, marriages, and divorces, by location and demographic characteristics, 1991 and trends, annual rpt, S8560–1

Wisconsin traffic accidents, fatalities, and injuries, by circumstances, location, vehicle type, and driver and victim characteristics, 1992 and trends, annual rpt, S8815–1

Wisconsin vital statistics, including population, births, deaths by cause, and marriages and dissolutions, by county and demographic characteristics, 1991 and trends, annual rpt, S8715–4

Wyoming traffic accidents, fatalities, and injuries, by circumstances, location, vehicle type, and driver and victim characteristics, 1992 and trends, annual rpt, S9007–1

Wyoming vital statistics, including population, births, deaths by cause, marriages, and divorces, by demographic characteristics and county, 1991 and trends, annual rpt, S8920–2

Railroad equipment and vehicles

Fleet composition and ownership, capacity, and use, Class I railroads, 1992, annual rpt, A3275–7

Fleet composition, costs, utilization, and capacity, 1982-91, annual rpt, A3275–8.2

Freight car inventory and cost, locomotives, and track, with detail by railroad, 1920s-92, annual rpt, A3275–5

Freight cars and locomotives ordered and delivered, monthly rpt quarterly table, C8400–1.501, C8400–1.502, C8400–1.504, C8400–1.508, C8400–1.510

Freight cars and locomotives ordered and/or delivered, quarterly press release, A3275–3

Latin America statistical abstract, general data by country, 1992 annual rpt, U6250–1.3

Mass transit rail cars by type, for top 10 systems, 1992/93 annual fact book, C1575–3.501

Mass transit system finances and operations, passengers, and employment, by mode, US and Canada, 1990-91 and trends, annual rpt, A2650–1

Mexico-Texas transportation system analysis, including bilateral trade, operations by transport mode, and data by locale, 1993 rpt, U8850–9

Passenger cars delivered, undelivered backlog, and new orders outlook, by purchaser, 1993 annual feature, C8400–1.503

Track mileage, by State, 1991, annual rpt, A3275–10

Wheel tread loss (shelling/spalling) incidence and repair costs, 1987-91, article, C8400–1.505

Wooden railroad tie trade, quarterly rpt, A1630–1

State and local:

California tax assessments and levies of private cars, with detail by nonrailroad company, FY93 and trends, annual rpt, S0835–1.2

North Carolina railroad property book values, 1970s-90, annual rpt, S5917–2

Wyoming tax collections and distribution, and property valuation, with data by property type and location, FY92 and trends, annual rpt, S8990–1

Railroad Retirement System

Beneficiaries and benefits paid, by State, 1991, annual rpt, A3275–10

Coverage, assets, and benefits paid, for private and govt pension and retirement programs, 1991 and trends, biennial fact book, A1325–1.3

Railroad operating data, including wages, fringe benefits, and retirement beneficiaries and payments, 1991, article, C8400–1.506

Tax rates and base earnings of Railroad Retirement System, Jan 1982-93, annual rpt, A3275–8.2

Railroads

Business traveler and trip characteristics, including mode, purpose, and lodging, 1991, annual rpt, R9375–12

Financial and operating trends, including data by company, 1982-91, annual rpt, A3275–8

Financial, operating, and employment data for Class I railroads, by company and district, 1992, annual rpt, A3275–7

Financial performance and growth rankings for approx 1,000 top corporations, with comparisons by industry group, 1993 annual rpt, C3950–1.505

Financial performance of Class I railroads, including return on property investment, by district and company, quarterly rpt, A3275–1

Index by Subjects and Names

Latin America statistical abstract, general data by country, 1992 annual rpt, U6250–1.3

Logistics trends and devs, including data on costs, finances of major carriers by mode, and foreign trade, 1993 annual compilation, C2150–1.506

Mass transit industry statistics, including govt funding, vehicle purchasing, and bus production, 1992/93 annual fact book, C1575–3.501

Mass transit rail system energy efficiency ratings, for 14 systems in US and Canada, 1993 article, C1575–3.506

Mass transit rail system revenue passenger miles per vehicle hour, for 14 systems in US and Canada, 1993 article, C1575–3.505

Mass transit system finances and operations, passengers, and employment, by mode, US and Canada, 1990-91 and trends, annual rpt, A2650–1

Mexico-Texas transportation system analysis, including bilateral trade, operations by transport mode, and data by locale, 1993 rpt, U8850–9

Operating and financial composite ratios for corporations, with establishments and receipts, for approx 200 industries, by asset size, FY90, annual rpt, C7800–1

Operating summaries for railroads, including top commodities handled, employment and wages, and retirement system, by State, 1991, annual rpt, A3275–10

Operations of railroads and rail rapid transit, data and related articles, monthly rpt, C8400–1

Regulatory agency policies and practices for motor carriers and railroads, by agency, 1991/92 annual rpt, A7015–4

Service to daily newspaper markets in US and Canada, by mode and company, 1993 annual rpt, C3250–1

Traffic, employment, finances, and equipment of Class I railroads, with detail by company, 1920s-92, annual rpt, A3275–5

Travel trips and traveler characteristics, including mode, purpose, type of lodging, and area of destination and origin, quarterly rpt, R9375–14

Trends in transportation operations and finances, by mode, 1991 annual rpt, R4815–1

State and local:

Arizona statistical abstract, general data, 1993 recurring rpt, U5850–2.18

Colorado property assessed valuation, by property type and county, and for regulated industries by company, 1991-92, annual rpt, S1055–3

Florida statistical abstract, general data, 1992 annual rpt, U6660–1.13

Hawaii data book, general data, 1992 annual rpt, S2090–1.18

Idaho economic profile, general data, 1992 recurring rpt, S2218–2.8

Mississippi statistical abstract, general data, 1992 annual rpt, U3255–4.6

Montana public utility and transportation property assessments, by county and company, 1991-92, biennial rpt, S4750–1.2

Nebraska property tax revenues and actual valuation by property type, by city and/or county, 1991 and trends, annual rpt, S4950–1.4

Nebraska public service commission regulatory activities, with financial and operating data for individual railroads and telephone companies, FY91-92 biennial rpt, S4940–1

North Carolina public utility financial, operating, and regulatory data, by utility type and company, 1990 and trends, annual rpt, S5917–2

Oklahoma statistical abstract, general data, 1992 annual rpt, U8130–2.16

South Carolina public service commission regulatory activities, with financial and operating data for individual utilities and railroads, FY92 annual rpt, S7235–1

South Carolina track mileage operated, by railroad, 1987-91, annual rpt, S7125–1.15

South Dakota property tax and valuations, by property type and locality, FY92 annual rpt, S7380–1.2

Tennessee statistical abstract, general data, 1992/93 annual rpt, U8710–2.9

Texas railroad employment, by detailed occupation, May 1991, triennial survey rpt, S7675–1.29

Utah statistical abstract, general data, 1993 triennial rpt, U8960–1.13

Washington State public service and utility companies property value, by company and county, 1992, annual rpt, S8415–1.4

Wisconsin Blue Book, general data, 1993-94 biennial rpt, S8780–1.2

Wisconsin State constitutional amendment authorizing bonding/funding for improvements of railways, election results by county, 1993-94 biennial rpt, S8780–1.3

see also Freight

see also High-speed ground transportation

see also National Railroad Passenger Corp.

see also Railroad accidents and safety

see also Railroad equipment and vehicles

see also Railroad Retirement System

see also Subways

see also under By Industry in the "Index by Categories"

Rainfall

see Weather

Raisins

see Fruit and fruit products

Rangeland

see Pasture and rangeland

Rankings

see Corporate rankings

see Product rankings

Rape

Incidence of rape, victim characteristics, and views of victims and service agency staff on related issues, 1990-92 surveys, R8375–1

Latin America statistical abstract, general data by country, 1992 annual rpt, U6250–1.15

State social, economic, and govtl indicators, with rankings, 1993 semiannual rpt, B8500–1.10

State and local:

Alabama crimes and arrests, by offense, with data by location and offender characteristics, 1992 and trends, annual rpt, S0119–1

Arizona crimes and arrests, by offense, county, and offender characteristics, 1992, annual rpt, S0505–2

Arkansas crimes and arrests, by offense, victim and offender characteristics, and location, 1992 and trends, annual rpt, S0652–1

California crimes and arrests, clearances, and arrest dispositions, with data by offense and offender characteristics, 1987-92, annual rpt, S0910–1.1

California criminal justice system detailed data, by offense, county, age, race-ethnicity, and sex, 1991 and trends, annual rpt, S0910–2

Colorado crimes and arrests, by offense and location, with offender characteristics, and assaults on police, 1992, annual rpt, S1068–1

Connecticut crimes and arrests, by offense, with data by local agency, and victim-offender characteristics, 1992, annual rpt, S1256–1

DC criminal justice system summary, including crimes and arrests, criminal procedure, prisoners, and parole, 1991 and trends, annual rpt, S1535–2

Delaware crimes and arrests, by offense, county, and victim-offender characteristics, 1991 and trends, annual rpt, S1375–5

Florida crimes and arrests, by offense, with data by victim and offender characteristics, 1992, annual rpt, S1770–1

Georgia crimes and arrests, by offense, with data by location and offender characteristics, 1992 and trends, annual rpt, S1901–1

Hawaii crimes and arrests, by offense, with data by county and victim-offender characteristics, 1992, annual rpt, S2035–1

Idaho crimes and arrests, by offense, with data by location and offender characteristics, 1992 and trends, annual rpt, S2275–2

Illinois crimes and arrests, by offense, with data by location and offender characteristics, 1991, annual rpt, S2536–1

Kansas crimes and arrests, by offense, with data by location, agency, and victim-offender characteristics, 1992 and trends, annual rpt, S2925–1.1

Kentucky crimes and arrests, by offense, with data by location and offender characteristics, 1992, annual rpt, S3150–1

Maine crimes and arrests, by offense, with data by county, reporting agency, and offender age and sex, 1991, annual rpt, S3475–1

Maryland crimes and arrests, by offense, location, and offender characteristics, with law enforcement employment and assaults on officers, 1992 and trends, annual rpt, S3665–1

Michigan crimes and arrests, by offense, with data by location and offender characteristics, 1992 and trends, annual rpt, S3997–1

Missouri crimes and arrests, by offense and location, with victim and offender characteristics, 1991 and trends, annual rpt, S4560–2

Montana crimes and clearances, by offense and jurisdiction, 1992, annual rpt, S4705–1

Nevada statistical abstract, general data, 1992 biennial rpt, S5005–1.4

New Hampshire crimes and arrests, by offense, jurisdiction, and offender characteristics, 1991 and trends, annual rpt, S5250–2

New Jersey crimes and arrests, by offense, with data by location and offender characteristics, 1992 and trends, annual rpt, S5430–1

New York State crimes and arrests by offense and demographic characteristics, and court activity and corrections, 1991 and trends, annual rpt, S5760–3

North Carolina crimes and arrests, by offense, with data by location and offender characteristics, 1992 and trends, annual rpt, S5955–1

North Dakota crimes and arrests, by offense, location, and offender characteristics, and law enforcement employment, 1991 and trends, annual rpt, S6060–1

Oklahoma crimes and arrests, by offense, with data by local agency and victim and offender characteristics, 1990-92, annual rpt, S6465–1

Oregon crimes and arrests, by offense, with data by county, local agency, and offender characteristics, 1992 and trends, annual rpt, S6603–3

Pennsylvania crimes and arrests, by offense, with data by location and offender characteristics, 1992 and trends, annual rpt, S6860–1

South Carolina crimes and arrests, by offense, with data by location and victim-offender characteristics, and assaults on officers, 1992 and trends, annual rpt, S7205–1

Texas crimes and arrests, by offense, with data by location and offender characteristics, 1992 and trends, annual rpt, S7735–2

Utah crimes and arrests, by offense, county, and local agency, 1992 and trends, annual rpt, S7890–3

Virginia crimes and arrests, by offense, with data by location and offender characteristics, 1992, annual rpt, S8295–2

Washington State crimes and arrests, by offense, with data by location and offender characteristics, 1992 and trends, annual rpt, S8440–1

West Virginia crimes and arrests, by offense, location, and offender characteristics, 1990-91, annual rpt, S8610–1

Wisconsin crimes and arrests, by offense, offender characteristics, county, and local agency, 1992 and trends, annual rpt, S8771–1

Wyoming crimes and arrests, by offense, with data by location and victim and offender characteristics, 1991 and trends, annual rpt, S8867–3

Rapid City, S.Dak.

Employment, earnings, and hours for selected industries and areas, monthly rpt, S7355–1

Rapid transit

see Buses

see High-speed ground transportation

see Subways

Rapid transit

see Urban transportation

Ras al-Khaimah

see United Arab Emirates

Rasell, Edith

"Impact of Health Care Financing on Family Budgets", R4700–20

Raw materials

see Stockpiling

see Strategic materials

Reactors

see Electric power plants and equipment

see Nuclear power

Reading ability and habits

- Black children and youth population, economic, health, and education data, with comparisons to whites, 1993 rpt, R3840–21
- Children's reading ability correlated with selected family characteristics that pose a risk to child dev, 1992 article, A8680–1.501
- Employer basic skills testing and training practices and costs, Jan-Mar 1993 survey, annual rpt, A2075–20.13
- Job Corps youth training program funding, enrollment capacity, and participants by selected characteristics, 1981-94, article, R4800–2.515
- Leisure activities, including types of materials read, 1990-92 study, article, A8605–1.507
- Natl Assessment of Educational Progress test reading scores of students at 3 ages, by race-ethnicity, 1971-90, article, R4800–2.504
- Urban public school student performance on standardized reading and mathematics tests, for 47 systems, 1990/91, A4425–4

State and local:

- Georgia prison population by reading ability and education level, FY92 annual rpt, S1872–1
- Iowa correctional instn admissions, releases, and inmate characteristics, by instn, monthly rpt, S2770–1
- New York City elementary/secondary student reading performance in district with parental school selection compared to citywide results, 1972/73-1991/92, R3810–7
- Ohio correctional instn admissions and releases, inmate characteristics, programs, finances, and staffing, FY91 and trends, annual rpt, S6370–1

see also Literacy and illiteracy

Real estate

see Apartment houses

see Commercial buildings

see Condominiums and cooperatives

see Farms and farmland

see Government supplies and property

see Homesteads

see Housing condition and occupancy

see Housing construction

see Housing sales

see Housing supply and requirements

see Housing tenure

see Industrial plants and equipment

see Land area

see Land ownership and rights

see Land reform

see Land use

see Landlord-tenant relations

see Military bases, posts, and reservations

see Mortgages

see Open space land programs

see Property

see Property value

see Public buildings

see Public lands

see Real estate business

see Reclamation of land

see Second homes

see Shopping centers

Real estate business

- Appraisers (real estate), by certification type, 1993 article, C4300–1.505
- Broker ratings of real estate market conditions and outlook in 20 States, 1992 survey article, C4300–1.501
- Business failures and liabilities, by detailed industry, cause, length of operation, and location, 1991-92 and trends, annual rpt, C3150–8
- Commercial real estate market conditions and outlook, for industrial and office properties, by US metro area and selected foreign city, 1992-93, annual survey, A8916–1
- Commercial real estate market conditions and outlook, for industrial and office properties in major metro areas, 1993 annual rpt, B2800–3
- Congressional campaign finances, with detailed data for individual Members, and leading contributors by type and industry, 1990 election and trends, biennial rpt, R3828–2.2
- Consumer complaint and inquiry activity of Better Business Burs, by detailed type of business, 1992, annual rpt, A4350–1
- Employee benefit funds assets, for funds investing in real estate equity, 1992, annual feature, C2710–2.504
- Executive views on commercial real estate market and business location conditions in 32 metro areas, discontinued annual survey rpt, B2800–1
- Financial ratios and performance, for over 350 SIC 4-digit industries, FY88-92, annual rpt, A6400–3
- Forecasts for real estate industry and US economy, and housing starts and sales trends by region, monthly rpt, A7000–1
- Franchise operations and finances, by type of business, 1991/92 and trends, annual rpt, A5820–1
- Higher education instn endowment fund and investment pool characteristics and performance, by instn, FY92, annual survey rpt, A6705–2
- Hotel real estate sales transactions, with prices, financing methods, and industry performance data, by region, 1991 and trends, article, A6450–2.501
- Insurance (life/health) industry asset allocation and investment yields, for top 125 US and Canadian companies, 1992 and trends, annual article, C1050–2.512
- Investment advisors in real estate, tax-exempt and total assets by type, top76 firms, annual feature, C2710–2.520
- Investment funds (closed-end real estate) and liquidity maturities, 1990-2005, article, C2710–2.520
- Investment institutional commingled real estate funds and assets, by asset type and size, Dec 1992, article, C2425–1.507
- Investment mgmt companies, pension fund and other managed assets, and investment info, by company, 1992 annual directory, C2425–1.501
- Investment mgmt companies, pension fund and other managed assets, and investment info, by company, 1993 annual directory, C2425–1.507
- Investment mgmt firms, assets and operating data for approx 900 instns, Jan 1993, annual feature, C2710–2.511
- Investment performance of leading funds with institutional investors, biweekly rpt quarterly feature, C2710–2.506
- Investment return on commercial properties, 1986-92, article, C2425–1.505
- Investment return on commercial real estate, by property type, 1980-91, article, A6450–2.506
- Investment trust returns and dividend yields, by property type, 1993 recurring feature, C8900–1.506, C8900–1.518
- Investment trust securities offerings by type, 1982-92, article, C2425–1.503
- Life insurance industry income and financial data, including investments by type of security, 1991 and trends, biennial fact book, A1325–1.4
- Lot (vacant) supply and absorption rate, for 15 metro areas, 1993 article, C4300–1.511
- Market outlook for real estate in top 13 metro areas, as rated by institutional investors, 1993, article, C4300–1.505
- Operating and financial composite ratios for corporations, with establishments and receipts, for approx 200 industries, by asset size, FY90, annual rpt, C7800–1
- Property managers characteristics and compensation, including types of property managed, 1989 surveys, recurring rpt, A5600–4
- Public opinion on honesty/ethical standards of selected occupations, 1992 Gallup Polls and trends, C4040–1.501
- Shopping center financial and operating data, with detail by type of tenant, US and Canada, 1991, triennial rpt, R9285–1

State and local:

- Arizona finance, insurance, and real estate employment and job outlook, by occupation and county, 1990-95, triennial rpt, S0465–2.36
- Arizona, Phoenix and Tucson real estate sales, 1985-93, semiannual rpt, U5850–1.2
- Arizona statistical abstract, general data, 1993 recurring rpt, U5850–2.23
- Florida statistical abstract, general data, 1992 annual rpt, U6660–1.17
- Hawaii data book, general data, 1992 annual rpt, S2090–1.15, S2090–1.21
- Hawaii, Oahu multiple listing service listings and sales, with selling prices, by type of property, quarterly rpt, S2090–2
- Illinois real estate title insurer finances, and premiums written by county, 1989 and/or 1990, annual rpt, S2457–2
- New Mexico economic trends and outlook, by industry div, 1982-92, annual article, U7980–1.503
- New York State statistical yearbook, general data, 1992 annual rpt, U5100–1.9
- Utah, Salt Lake City real estate sales, by type, 1970-92, triennial rpt, U8960–1.11

Recreation

Washington State real estate sales volume and value, and excise taxes, FY83-92, annual rpt, S8415–1.1

Wisconsin agricultural land sales, with detail by county, 1988-92, annual rpt, S8680–1

Wisconsin Blue Book, general data, 1993-94 biennial rpt, S8780–1.2

see also Housing construction

see also Housing costs and financing

see also Housing sales

see also Mortgages

see also Property value

see also Rent

see also under By Industry in the "Index by Categories"

Real property

see Property

Real property tax

see Property tax

Receivables

see Credit

Recession

see Business cycles

Recidivism

Black American crime, arrest, and incarceration data, with comparisons to whites, 1970s-91, annual compilation, C6775–2.5

Correctional instn admin, inmates, facilities, costs, parole and probation, and staffing, for local, State, and Federal systems, 1992 annual series, R4300–1

State and local:

- Arizona correctional instn admin, including inmates by criminal background and demographic characteristics, FY92, annual rpt, S0464–2
- California correctional instn inmates, by offense, demographic characteristics, and instn, Dec 1992, semiannual rpt, S0820–2
- California correctional instn inmates, with criminal background and demographic characteristics, 1991 and trends, annual rpt, S0820–1
- Florida correctional instns, admin, and inmates by criminal background and demographic characteristics, FY92 annual rpt, S1720–1
- Florida "habitual offender" sentencing laws effect on prison population, with data by circuit court and offender characteristics, 1993 rpt, A7575–5
- Georgia correctional instns, admin, and inmate characteristics, FY92, annual rpt, S1872–1
- Kansas correctional instn inmates, by offense, demographic characteristics, and instn, FY92 and trends, annual rpt, S2940–1
- Massachusetts correctional instn inmate socioeconomic characteristics and criminal background, by instn, Jan 1992 and trends, annual rpt, S3805–1
- Michigan parolees returned to prison, by original and new offense, 1987, annual rpt, S3960–1
- Missouri correctional instn admissions, releases, and inmate characteristics, FY93, annual rpt, S4501–1
- Nebraska correctional instn admin, with inmates by criminal background and demographic characteristics, by instn, FY92 and trends, annual rpt, S4850–1

New York State correctional instn inmate population and characteristics, and probation and parole, 1991 and trends, annual rpt, S5760–3.4

New York State correctional instn inmates released, by criminal background, sentence, and demographic characteristics, 1991 and trends, recurring rpt series, S5725–1

New York State local jail/penitentiary inmates by offense, sentence, and demographic characteristics, by county or facility, 1991, annual rpt, S5724–2

Texas correctional instn inmates by criminal background and demographic characteristics, FY92, annual rpt, S7660–1

Utah prison inmates criminal background, and correctional industries cost savings from reduced recidivism, FY92 annual rpt, S7810–1

Wisconsin correctional instn inmates, by criminal background and selected characteristics, series, S8692–1

Wyoming correctional instn admin, finances, inmate characteristics, and staff, and probation and parole activities, FY92 annual rpt, S8883–1

Reclamation of land

World forest area by type, and extent of deforestation and reforestation, by region and country, 1980s, biennial rpt, R9455–1.6

see also Irrigation

Recording industry

Direct marketing industry devs, with consumer and business market characteristics, and media use patterns, 1992/93 annual rpt, A4620–1.4

Market value of CDs, cassettes, and albums in US/abroad, 1988, 1991, and 1995, article, C1850–2.502

Spanish-language music sales, for 6 leading and all other recording companies, 1992, article, C4575–1.508

see also Audiovisual equipment

see also Video recordings and equipment

Recreation

Amusement equipment in use, and revenue, by type of equipment including video games and pinball machines, 1982 and 1990-92, annual rpt, C9470–1

Apartment building (conventionally financed) detailed income and expense ratios for US and Canada, by building type, metro area, and US region, 1991 and trends, annual rpt, A5600–1

Apartment building (federally subsidized) detailed income and expense ratios, by building and subsidy type, building age, metro area, and region, 1991 and trends, annual rpt, A5600–5

Black Americans preferred leisure activities, 1993 survey feature, C4215–1.510

Black 8th grade student participation in extracurricular activities by type, with comparisons to whites, 1988, R3840–21

Condominium, cooperative, and planned unit dev detailed expenses, for US and Canada, by building characteristics, metro area, and US region, 1991, annual rpt, A5600–3

Consumer complaint and inquiry activity of Better Business Burs concerning entertainment industries, 1992, annual rpt, A4350–1

Craft activities of households, including retail outlets shopped for needlework supplies, 1990 and/or 1992, articles, C5150–3.504

Economic impact of travel on States, with detail by industry sector, 1990 and trends, annual rpt, R9375–7

Financial ratios and performance, for over 350 SIC 4-digit industries, FY88-92, annual rpt, A6400–3

Food service industry sales and establishments, with growth outlook, by market segment, 1993 annual feature, C1850–3.503

Food service industry sales rankings by market segment, for leading organizations, 1992, annual feature, C1850–3.509

Food service industry sales trends and forecast, by market segment, 1990-93, annual feature, A8200–1.502

Franchise operations and finances, by type of business, 1991/92 and trends, annual rpt, A5820–1

Hispanic American consumer expenditures for entertainment, by type, 1992, article, C4575–1.508

Leisure hours and top activities, by day of the week, 1990-92 study, article, A8605–1.507

Motorcycle use and user characteristics, licensed operators, and State requirements, 1992 annual rpt, A6485–1.2

Operating and financial composite ratios for corporations, with establishments and receipts, for approx 200 industries, by asset size, FY90, annual rpt, C7800–1

Prices of selected consumer items in approx 300 cities, quarterly rpt, A0150–1

Shopping center arcade/amusement and hobby store tenants, financial and operating data, US and Canada, 1991, triennial rpt, R9285–1

Travel and tourism rankings for selected indicators, including data for top 20 States, cities, countries, businesses, and other measures, 1992 recurring rpt, R9375–6

State and local:

- Alabama county data book, general data, 1992 annual rpt, S0121–2
- Alaska public recreational areas by type, and acreage, 1991-92, annual rpt, S0275–1
- Arizona statistical abstract, general data, 1993 recurring rpt, U5850–2.8
- Arizona visitors to parks and other recreational areas, by site, 1985-93, semiannual rpt, U5850–1.1
- California statistical abstract, general data, 1992 annual rpt, S0840–2.1
- DC statistical profile, general data, 1992 annual rpt, S1535–3.1, S1535–3.6
- Florida statistical abstract, general data, 1992 annual rpt, U6660–1.19
- Georgia prison inmate participation in recreational activities, by type, FY92 annual rpt, S1872–1
- Hawaii data book, general data, 1992 annual rpt, S2090–1.7
- Idaho economic profile, general data, 1992 recurring rpt, S2218–2.10
- Illinois statistical abstract, general data, 1992 annual rpt, U6910–2
- Maryland local govt financial condition, including revenues by source,

Recreation

expenditures by function, and debt obligations, FY92 and trends, annual rpt, S3618–1.1

Maryland statistical abstract, general data, 1993-94 biennial rpt, S3605–1.13

Michigan employment in amusement/recreation industries, 1st half 1991-93, article, S3980–2.502

Mississippi statistical abstract, general data, 1992 annual rpt, U3255–4.10, U3255–4.16

New Mexico economic trends and outlook, by industry div, 1982-92, annual article, U7980–1.503

New York State statistical yearbook, general data, 1992 annual rpt, U5100–1.5, U5100–1.15

Pennsylvania statistical abstract, general data, 1992 recurring rpt, U4130–6.8

South Carolina statistical abstract, general data, 1993 annual rpt, S7125–1.14

Tennessee statistical abstract, general data, 1992/93 annual rpt, U8710–2.12

Utah statistical abstract, general data, 1993 triennial rpt, U8960–1.17

Vermont court cases involving snowmobiles, boating, and fish/game, FY92 annual rpt, S8120–1

Wisconsin Blue Book, general data, 1993-94 biennial rpt, S8780–1.2

Wyoming penitentiary recreation facilities, and inmate participation in selected activities, FY92 annual rpt, S8883–1

see also Amusement parks
see also Boats and boating
see also Camping
see also Fishing, sport
see also Horse racing
see also Hunting and trapping
see also Motion pictures
see also National forests
see also National parks
see also Parks
see also Recreational vehicles
see also Resort timesharing
see also Sporting goods
see also Sports and athletics
see also State funding for parks and recreation
see also Travel and tourism
see also Wilderness areas
see also Winter sports

Recreational boating
see Boats and boating

Recreational community centers
see Community centers

Recreational vehicles

All-terrain vehicle (ATV) and moped sales, imports, and use, 1991 and trends, annual rpt, A6485–1

Collision coverage insurance claims and payments experience for autos and other vehicles, by make and series, for recent model years, 1993 annual rpt series, A5200–1

Dealer marketing and mgmt devs, with data on RV shipments and sales, by vehicle type, monthly rpt, C8950–2

Financial performance and growth rankings for approx 1,000 top corporations, with comparisons by industry group, 1993 annual rpt, C3950–1.505

Financial ratios and performance, for over 350 SIC 4-digit industries, FY88-92, annual rpt, A6400–3

Loan delinquency rates for approx 10 types of consumer bank loans, and repossession data, by State, quarterly rpt, A0950–1

Participation in 53 sports, by demographic characteristics, State, and census div, 1992, annual rpt series, A8485–3

Personal injury protection insurance claim frequencies for 1990-92 model autos and other vehicles, by make and model, annual rpt, A5200–3

Sales of RVs by type, 1991-93, annual rpt, A8485–2

Sales of RVs, 1983-92, annual survey rpt, A8485–4

Shipments of RVs, and production by State, by vehicle type, 1992 and trends, annual rpt, A0865–1.1

Shipments of RVs, by type, weekly rpt recurring table, C2710–3

Shipments of RVs, by type, 1988-92, annual data book, C2710–3.531

Theft insurance claims and payments experience for 1990-92 model autos and other vehicles, by make and model, annual rpt, A5200–2

State and local:

Alabama traffic accidents, fatalities, and injuries, by circumstances, vehicle type, and driver and victim characteristics, 1992, annual rpt, S0185–1

Alaska traffic accidents, fatalities, and injuries, by vehicle type, circumstance, location, and driver and victim characteristics, 1991 and trends, annual rpt, S0360–1

Arizona temporary winter residents and expenditures, and mobile home and trailer park spaces and occupancy, by local area, winter 1992/93, annual article, U0280–1.508

Arizona traffic accidents, fatalities, and injuries, by vehicle type, circumstances, location, and driver and victim characteristics, 1991 and trends, annual rpt, S0530–1

Arkansas traffic accidents, fatalities, and injuries, by vehicle type, circumstances, location, and driver and victim characteristics, 1991, annual rpt, S0692–1

Connecticut traffic accidents, fatalities, and injuries, by vehicle type, circumstance, location, and driver and victim characteristics, 1992, annual rpt, S1275–1

Florida statistical abstract, general data, 1992 annual rpt, U6660–1.2

Florida traffic accidents, fatalities, and injuries, by vehicle type, circumstance, location, and driver and victim characteristics, 1992 and trends, annual rpt, S1750–2

Idaho traffic accidents, fatalities, and injuries, by circumstances, location, vehicle type, and driver and victim characteristics, 1992, annual rpt, S2315–1

Indiana snowmobile accidents, fatalities, and injuries, 1992, annual rpt, S2675–1

Maine traffic accidents, fatalities, and injuries, by accident circumstances, vehicle type and make, and driver and victim characteristics, 1992, annual rpt, S3475–2

Maryland traffic accidents, fatalities, and injuries, by circumstances, location, vehicle type, and driver and victim characteristics, 1992, annual rpt, S3665–4

Michigan traffic accidents, fatalities, and injuries, by vehicle type, circumstance, location, and driver and victim characteristics, 1991 and trends, annual rpt, S3997–2

Minnesota traffic accidents, fatalities, and injuries, by type of vehicle and circumstances, and driver and victim characteristics, 1992 and trends, annual rpt, S4230–2

Missouri all-terrain vehicle registrations and fees collected, FY88-92, annual rpt, S4570–1.1

Missouri traffic accidents, fatalities, and injuries, by circumstances, location, and driver and victim characteristics, 1992 and trends, annual rpt, S4560–1

Montana traffic accidents, fatalities, and injuries, by circumstances, location, and driver and victim characteristics, 1992 and trends, annual rpt, S4705–2

Nebraska traffic accidents, fatalities, and injuries, by circumstances, location, vehicle type, and driver and victim characteristics, 1992, annual rpt, S4953–1

Nevada traffic accidents, fatalities, and injuries, by circumstances, location, and vehicle type, 1992 and trends, annual rpt, S5140–1

New Jersey fatal traffic accidents and fatalities, by vehicle type, location, and circumstances, and driver and victim characteristics, 1992 and trends, annual rpt, S5430–2

New York State motorboat and snowmobile registrations, by county, 1991, annual rpt, S5790–1

New York State snowmobile registrations, by county, 1986-89, annual rpt, U5100–1.15

North Dakota traffic accidents, fatalities, and injuries, by circumstances, location, vehicle type, and driver and victim characteristics, 1992 and trends, annual rpt, S6217–1

Ohio traffic accidents, fatalities, and injuries, by circumstances, location, driver and victim characteristics, and vehicle type, 1991 and trends, annual rpt, S6290–1

Pennsylvania traffic accidents, fatalities, and injuries, by circumstances, location, driver characteristics, and vehicle type, 1991, annual rpt, S6905–3

Rhode Island traffic accidents, fatalities, and injuries, by circumstances, community, and driver and victim characteristics, 1991, annual rpt, S7025–1

South Dakota traffic accidents, fatalities, and injuries, by circumstances, location, vehicle type, and driver and victim characteristics, 1992 and trends, annual rpt, S7300–3

Texas trade, transportation, and public utilities employment, by SIC 2- and 3-digit industry and detailed occupation, 2nd qtr 1991, triennial survey rpt, S7675–1.31

Virginia traffic accidents, fatalities, and injuries, by circumstances, location, and driver and victim characteristics, 1991 and trends, annual rpt, S8282–1

Index by Subjects and Names

Referenda

Wisconsin traffic accidents, fatalities, and injuries, by circumstances, location, vehicle type, and driver and victim characteristics, 1992 and trends, annual rpt, S8815–1

Wyoming traffic accidents, fatalities, and injuries, by circumstances, location, vehicle type, and driver and victim characteristics, 1992 and trends, annual rpt, S9007–1

see also Boats and boating

Recruiting

see Personnel management

Recycling of waste materials

- Auto battery recycling legislation provisions, by State, June 1992, article, C0125–1.502
- Beverage and total aluminum, steel, glass, and plastic container recycling rates, 1991, article, C0125–2.501
- Catalog industry use of recycled paper, 1990, annual rpt, A4620–1.2
- Curbside recycling program operations, funding, and recycled materials, views of municipal officials and summary program characteristics, July 1991 survey, B0230–2
- Curbside recycling program operations, funding, and recycled materials, views of State legislators, July 1991 survey, B0230–1
- Food marketers solid waste recycling/composting by material type, and stores used as community collection centers, 1991, annual rpt, A4950–5
- Germany recycling fees charged for packaging, by material type, 1993 article, C1850–1.508
- Hard goods manufacturers recycled material use and advertising, by product line, 1993 annual survey rpt, A1800–1
- Magazine paper consumption, for regular and/or recycled paper by type, North American vs overseas source, and weight, 1992-94, article, C2575–1.518
- Municipal officials rankings of obstacles to local recycling programs, 1993 survey article, C1850–1.505
- Municipal solid waste recycling rates, by type of material, 1992, article, C1850–3.501
- Newspaper recycling rates, and recycled end products, 1980s-92, annual rpt, A8605–4
- Newspaper volume recycled in US and exported, monthly rpt, A1630–4
- Newsprint (recycled) mills and capacity, 1992-95, article, A8605–1.501
- Newsprint production, shipments, plant capacity, consumption, trade, and recycling, US and Canada, 1970s-92, annual rpt, A1630–8
- Newsprint recycling capacity, demand, and wastepaper consumption, for Northeast US and Eastern Canada, with data by mill, various years 1988-2000, A4375–15
- Newsprint recycling mills capacity and wastepaper demand, by US and Canadian mill, 1992 annual rpt, A8610–1
- Oil re-refiner plant capacities, by company, Jan 1993, annual fact book, C4680–1.507
- Packaging recycling rate, quinquennially 1970-90, article, C1850–1.504
- Paper (coated) recycled products, with percent of content from waste, by manufacturer, 1993 annual feature, C2575–1.518

Paper and paperboard industry recycling data, including mills, production, consumption, and wastepaper foreign trade, 1993 annual rpt, C3975–5

- Paper and paperboard use of pulp substitutes/de-inked fiber, 1970s-2000, article, C3975–2.508
- Paper, paperboard, and wood pulp industry capacity and material consumption, by grade and census div, 1970s-95, annual rpt, A1630–7
- Paper products recycling rates, by type of product, 1990, annual rpt, A4620–1.1
- Paper/paperboard supply and recovery volume, selected years 1970-92, article, C3975–2.507
- Plants converting waste to energy, by planning or operational status, 1984-93, article, C5800–2.541
- Plastic packaging recycling volume, by plastic type, 1985, 1991, and 1996, article, C1850–1.507
- Plastics reclamation and production capacity for recycled polyethylene terephthalate, by major company, 1993 features, C5800–12.513
- Plastics recycling analysis, with data on sales and recycling volume, recovery costs, and collection methods, by resin or product type, 1990, A4375–14
- Plastics waste handling and recycling devs in US, Europe, and Japan, 1993 annual encyclopedia, C5800–12.503
- Public opinion on curbside recycling impact on trash collection costs, 1992 survey article, C1850–1.501
- Silver refinery production from primary materials, coins, and scrap, with disposition, stocks, prices, and industry devs, US and worldwide, bimonthly rpt, A8902–3
- State social, economic, and govtl indicators, with rankings, 1993 semiannual rpt, B8500–1.15
- Sulfur mined and recovered production worldwide, and supply-demand outlook, 1980s-2000, article, C6985–1.546
- Sulfur recovery from oil refineries and natural gas plants vs mine production, and sales by PAD district, 1982-91, article, C6985–1.514
- Uranium reprocessing commitments, and plutonium available from reprocessing, for 5 countries, 1990s-2010, article, B6790–1.502
- Wastepaper recovery, consumption, trade, and utilization rate, 1992 and trends, annual rpt, A1630–6

State and local:

- Florida statistical abstract, general data, 1992 annual rpt, U6660–1.8
- Georgia State constitutional amendment on loan for solid waste recycling, election results by county, Nov 1992, biennial rpt, S1955–1
- Hawaii recycling campaign schools participating, materials collected, earnings, and savings, 1990, annual rpt, S2065–1.6
- Massachusetts State initiative on packaging reduction and use of recyclable material, election results by locality, 1992, biennial rpt, S3920–1
- New Jersey waste recycling fund finances, FY92, annual rpt, S5455–1

see also Biomass energy *see also* Salvage *see also* Scrap metals

Referenda

- Congressional term limitation initiative election results, for 14 States, Nov 1992, annual rpt, C2500–2
- Congressional term limitation initiative voting results in 14 States, 1992, article, A1865–1.507
- Library building referenda election results, by instn and location, FY92 and trends, annual article, C1852–1.508
- Municipal govt use of initiatives, referenda, recalls, and petitions, by population size, census div, and location and govt type, 1991, A5800–1.1
- Packaging-related referenda results for 3 States, Nov 1992, article, C1850–1.503
- Russia voter referendum, public opinion in US on media coverage by respondent characteristics, Apr/May 1993 survey, C8915–1.503
- State and municipal bond election outcomes, 1950-91, annual rpt, R9050–1.4

State and local:

- Alaska election results, and voter registration and turnout, by district and precinct, 1992 general election, biennial rpt, S0337–1
- Arizona election results and voter registration, by county and/or district, 1992 general election, biennial rpt, S0520–1
- California election results, and voter registration and turnout, by district and/or county, 1992 and trends, biennial rpt, S0934–1
- California public opinion on Proposition 174 allowing parents to use State vouchers to pay for private schools, Sept 1993 survey, C5800–7.550
- DC election results and turnout, and voter registration, by ward and precinct, 1990, biennial series, S1525–1
- Delaware school district referenda and outcomes, 1991/92, annual rpt, S1430–1.4
- Florida election results, by county and/or district, 1992 general election, biennial rpt, S1800–1
- Hawaii election results, and voter registration by sex, by district and precinct, 1992, biennial series, S2077–1
- Idaho election results and voter registration, by county and/or district and precinct, 1992 general election, biennial rpt, S2305–1
- Illinois election results, and voter registration trends, by county and/or district, 1992 general election, biennial rpt, S2445–1
- Illinois school bond and tax referenda election outcomes, 1985/86-1990/91, annual rpt, S2440–1.3
- Maine election results, by district, county, and municipality, 1992 general election, biennial rpt, S3490–1
- Maryland election results, by county and district, 1992 general election, biennial rpt, S3615–1
- Massachusetts election results and voter registration, by local area, 1992 and trends, biennial rpt, S3920–1

Referenda

Michigan election results and voter registration, by county and/or district, 1992 general election, biennial rpt, S4020–1

Mississippi public school capital improvement bond election results, by district, 1991/92, annual rpt, S4340–1.2

Missouri election results and voter registration, by district and/or county, with directory of govt officials, 1992 general election, biennial rpt, S4580–1

Montana election results and voter registration, by county and/or district, 1992 general election, biennial rpt, S4760–1

Nebraska election results, and voter registration by party, by county and/or district, 1992 general and primary elections, biennial rpt, S4955–1

Nevada election results, and voter registration and turnout, by county, 1992 general election, biennial rpt, S5125–1

New Jersey election results and voter registration, by location, 1992 general election, annual rpt, S5440–1

New Mexico election results, and voter registration by party, by location, 1992 general election, biennial rpt, S5655–1

New York State general election results by county and district, Nov 1992, biennial rpt, S5750–1

New York State statistical yearbook, general data, 1992 annual rpt, U5100–1.4

North Dakota election results and historical trends, including data on ballot measures and detail by location, 1880s-1992, biennial rpt, U8080–1

North Dakota election results, by location, 1992 general election, biennial rpt, S6205–1

Oklahoma election results and voter registration, by county and/or district, 1992, biennial rpt, S6425–1

Oregon election results and voter registration and turnout, by county and/or district, 1992 general election, biennial rpt, S6665–1

Oregon school district financial election outcomes, by district, 1992, annual rpt, S6590–1.15

Rhode Island statistical almanac, general data, 1993 annual rpt, C7975–1.1

South Dakota election results, and voter registration by party, by county, 1992 general election, biennial rpt, S7390–1

Utah election results and voter registration and turnout, by county and/or district, 1992 general election, biennial rpt, S7875–1

Washington State election results and voter registration, by county and/or district, 1992 general election, annual rpt, S8425–1

Wisconsin Blue Book, general data, 1993-94 biennial rpt, S8780–1

Wyoming election results by county, district, and precinct, 1992, annual rpt and govtl directory, S9000–1

see also State constitutional amendments

Reform schools

see Juvenile detention and correctional institutions

Refrigeration

see Air conditioning

see Cold storage and refrigeration

see Household appliances and equipment

Refugees

- Arrivals of refugees by world region of origin and State of resettlement, 1991, semiannual rpt, B8500–1.8
- Asylum application processing staff, and claims filed, for US and 8 foreign countries, 1993 article, R9372–2.507
- Catholic charity social service agency activities, clients, finances, and personnel, 1991 and trends, annual rpt, A3810–1
- Federal outlays for refugee assistance under State Legalization Impact Assistance Grants program, with shares for 7 States, 1992, article, A1865–1.523
- Latin America country of asylum for refugees worldwide, 1983-89, annual rpt, U6250–1.14
- Resettlement activity worldwide, with US admission and asylum data, by country, 1992 annual feature, R9372–2.503
- Resettlement, movement, and intl aid devs, by country, 1992, annual rpt, R9372–1
- Resettlement of refugees in US, related policies, programs, devs, and statistics, monthly rpt, R9372–2
- Statistical profiles of 50 States and DC, general data, 1993 annual almanac, C4712–1

State and local:

- Alabama public welfare and social service cases, recipients, and payments, by program and county, monthly rpt, S0150–1
- Arizona refugee resettlement program recipients and payments, monthly rpt, S0465–4
- Arkansas human services dept finances and operations, including Medicaid payments by type of service, FY91 and trends, annual rpt, S0700–2.3
- California public welfare cases, recipients, and expenditures, by program and county, monthly rpt, S0935–2
- DC refugee resettlement cases, by world area of origin, 1987-91, annual rpt, S1535–3.5
- Hawaii refugee arrivals with selected health problems, FY90, annual rpt, S2065–1.4
- Maryland public school funding for refugee assistance programs, by county, 1991/92, annual rpt, S3610–2.9
- Maryland welfare program statistics, and welfare fraud investigations, by county, monthly rpt, S3645–2
- Missouri public welfare and medical assistance recipients, expenditures, and case processing, by program and county, FY92 and trends, annual rpt, S4575–2
- New Mexico refugee resettlement program expenditures, monthly rpt quarterly table, S5620–2
- New York State refugee resettlement program expenditures, 1991, annual rpt, S5800–2.1
- Oklahoma school revenues and expenditures, by program, county, and district, FY92, annual rpt, S6423–1.1
- South Dakota medical and social services recipients and payments, by program, FY92, annual rpt, S7385–1.1

Utah aid to refugees, 1993 annual rpt, R9380–1.9

Washington State public assistance clients and service costs, by client characteristics, program, and county, FY90, annual rpt, S8420–2

see also Caribbean refugees

see also Indochinese refugees

Refuse and refuse disposal

- Chemical industry hazardous and nonhazardous waste generated, and mgmt methods used, 1990, article, A1250–1.503
- City fiscal condition, including budget trends and adjustments, and influencing factors, by region and population size, Mar-Apr 1993 survey, annual rpt, A8012–1.23
- City govt costs to enforce Fed Govt regulations including solid waste disposal, FY93-98, A9330–12
- Coal industry executive views on desirability of ash haulback agreements, Mar 1993 survey, article, C5226–1.511
- Condominium, cooperative, and planned unit dev detailed expenses, for US and Canada, by building characteristics, metro area, and US region, 1991, annual rpt, A5600–3
- Cost comparison for long-distance transporting of solid waste by truck vs rail, 1993 article, C8400–1.504
- Financial ratios and performance, for over 350 SIC 4-digit industries, FY88-92, annual rpt, A6400–3
- Food marketers solid waste disposal practices and recycling programs, by type of material, by region, 1991, annual rpt, A4950–5.2
- Housing construction typical waste composition, 1993 article, C4300–1.507
- Industrial waste fuel boiler/furnace applications to EPA for continued use, by region, May 1992, article, C5800–8.505
- Japan abandoned and recycled scrap tire volume, with detail by recycled tire use, 1991, article, C2150–3.503
- Medical waste generation and treatment cost trends and outlook, 1993 article, A1865–1.505
- Municipal waste composition, by type of material, 1990, annual rpt, A8920–1.3
- Municipal waste composition by type of nondurable goods, 1990, A4620–1.1
- OECD municipal waste generated, composition, and disposal methods, by country, 1992/93 biennial rpt, R9455–1.7
- Office building detailed income and expense data, and energy use, US and Canada, by building characteristics, metro area, and US region, 1991 and trends, annual rpt, A5600–2
- Plastics waste handling and recycling devs in US, Europe, and Japan, 1993 annual encyclopedia, C5800–12.503
- Product packaging waste concerns of consumers, including importance to purchasing decisions, 1993 survey, article, C1850–1.505
- Pulp and paper industry capital spending plans of US and Canadian companies, by purpose and geographic area, 1992-94, annual survey article, C3975–2.503

Regulatory authority of State utility commissions over motor carriers engaged in garbage collection, by State, 1991/92 annual rpt, A7015–4

Shopping center detailed income and expense data, by building characteristics, metro area, and region, 1991, annual rpt, A5600–6

Solid waste mgmt practices in State districts, as reported by legislators, July 1991 survey, B0230–1

State social, economic, and govtl indicators, with rankings, 1993 semiannual rpt, B8500–1.15

State and local:

Alaska public utility financial and operating data, by company and utility type, 1991 and trends, with FY92 regulatory info, annual rpt, S0280–4

DC statistical profile, general data, 1992 annual rpt, S1535–3.7

Florida statistical abstract, general data, 1992 annual rpt, U6660–1.8

Hawaii data book, general data, 1992 annual rpt, S2090–1.5

Hawaii litter control and recycling activities, and citations for littering, 1990, annual rpt, S2065–1.6

Maryland local govt financial condition, including revenues by source, expenditures by function, and debt obligations, FY92 and trends, annual rpt, S3618–1.1

Nebraska litter fee receipts, 1990-91, annual rpt, S4950–1.3

New York State statistical yearbook, general data, 1992 annual rpt, U5100–1.15

North Dakota State measure to establish waste disposal fees, election results by county, 1992, biennial rpt, S6205–1

Pennsylvania statistical abstract, general data, 1992 recurring rpt, U4130–6.8

South Dakota State measure on proposed solid waste facility, election results by county, 1992, biennial rpt, S7390–1

see also Air pollution

see also Hazardous waste and disposal

see also Landfills

see also Marine pollution

see also Radioactive waste and disposal

see also Recycling of waste materials

see also Sewage and wastewater systems

see also Water pollution

Regions of the U.S.

see Middle Atlantic States

see North Central States

see Northeast States

see Southeastern States

see Southwestern States

see Western States

see under By Region and By Census Division in the "Index by Categories"

see under By State in the "Index by Categories"

see under names of individual States

Regions of the world

see Africa

see Asia

see Atlantic Ocean

see Caribbean area

see Central America

see Eastern Europe

see Europe

see Gulf of Mexico

see Latin America

see Middle East

see North America

see North Sea

see Oceania

see Pacific Ocean

see South America

see Southeast Asia

see under By Foreign Country or World Area in the "Index by Categories"

Regulatory agencies

see Administrative law and procedure

Rehabilitation

see Rehabilitation of criminals

see Rehabilitation of the disabled

see Vocational rehabilitation

Rehabilitation of criminals

State and local:

California correctional inmates in State rehabilitation center program, 1991, annual rpt, S0820–1

DC statistical profile, general data, 1992 annual rpt, S1535–3.8

Florida "habitual offender" sentencing laws effect on prison population, with data by circuit court and offender characteristics, 1993 rpt, A7575–5

Georgia corrections dept operations and costs, FY92, annual rpt, S1872–1

Illinois corrections dept admin, including inmates and characteristics, finances, and staff, FY91-93 and trends, annual rpt, S2425–1

Michigan correctional instns educational and rehabilitation activities, by program and instn, 1991, annual rpt, S3960–1

Wyoming correctional instn admin, finances, inmate characteristics, and staff, and probation and parole activities, FY92 annual rpt, S8883–1

see also Community-based correctional programs

see also Pardons

see also Parole and probation

see also Prison work programs

see also Recidivism

Rehabilitation of housing

see Housing maintenance and repair

Rehabilitation of narcotics addicts

see Drug abuse and treatment

see Methadone treatment

Rehabilitation of the disabled

Catholic facilities for elderly and handicapped persons, by type and State, 1993 annual almanac, C6885–1

Federal budget trends, including spending by program, State, and region, FY81-94, annual rpt, R8490–11

State and local:

Arkansas human services dept finances and operations, by program, FY91 and trends, annual rpt, S0700–2.2

California statistical abstract, general data, 1992 annual rpt, S0840–2.5

Colorado welfare and social services expenditures and caseloads, by county and/or program, FY91, annual rpt, S1085–1

Florida health care atlas, including manpower by occupation and health care facilities by type, by district and county, 1992 annual rpt, S1746–1.2

Kentucky Medicaid recipients and payments, by program, county, and type of medical service, monthly rpt, S3140–5

Missouri public welfare and medical assistance recipients, expenditures, and case processing, by program and county, FY92 and trends, annual rpt, S4575–2

Oklahoma public welfare program expenditures, recipients, and services, by program and county, FY92 and trends, annual rpt, S6455–1

Texas rehabilitation hospitals capacity, use, and finances, 1989, U8850–8.3

Washington State public assistance clients and service costs, by client characteristics, program, and county, FY90, annual rpt, S8420–2

see also Sheltered workshops

see also Vocational rehabilitation

Relief

see Disaster relief

see International assistance

see Public welfare programs

see Refugees

see State funding for social welfare

Religion

Anti-Semitic public opinion trends, 1964, 1981, and 1992 surveys, article, A0610–1.504

Arts/humanities organization charitable contribution donor characteristics, 1993 survey article, C2176–1.507

Book publishing industry financial and operating data, by publisher type and size, and subject category, 1991 and trends, annual rpt, A3274–2

Books (religious) bestsellers, 1992, annual feature, C1852–2.509

Catholic vs public school performance, and support for parental school selection, views of general public and Catholics, July 1992 survey, A7375–8

College freshmen attitudes and characteristics, degree and career plans, and financial aid sources, by sex and instn type, fall 1992, annual survey, U6215–1

Europe public opinion on political, economic, and social issues, for 9 countries and 3 Soviet Union Republics, 1991 survey, C8915–8.1

Europe public opinion on political, economic, and social issues of interest to foreign investors, for 9 countries and 3 Soviet Union Republics, 1991 survey, C8915–9

High school graduation ceremony prayer acceptability, public opinion by respondent religious affiliation, 1993 annual Gallup Poll, A8680–1.503

Higher education president personal and professional characteristics, 1990 and trends, recurring rpt, A1410–12

Higher education presidents religious preference and religious order membership, 1990, article, C2175–1.533

Jewish population by world area, country, and US census div, State, and city, 1990-92, annual compilation, A2050–1

Latin America statistical abstract, general data by country, 1992 annual rpt, U6250–1.10

Magazine (religious) circulation, by US and Canadian publication, 6-month periods ended Dec 1992 and June 1993, semiannual rpt, A3385–3.4

Men's sexual behavior, including condom use, and AIDS knowledge and risks, by selected characteristics, 1991 survey, articles, A5160–1.503

Religion

Prisoner religious involvement correlation with adjustment to incarceration, 1992 rpt, A7575–1.11

Public attitudes on religion and related social issues, monthly survey, R8780–1

Public opinion on religious issues, including church/synagogue membership and attendance trends, June 1993 Gallup Poll and trends, C4040–1.512

Public opinion on religious preference and commitment compared to views on abortion, Mar 1993 Gallup Poll and trends, C4040–1.510

Public opinion on social, political, and economic issues, detailed data, 1972-91 surveys, annual rpt, U6395–1

Radio audience size, leading stations and formats, and advertising rates and revenues, by market area, recurring rpt, C3165–1

World religious preferences in 19 countries, 1991-92 surveys, R8780–1.503

Youth age 12-17 charitable contributions, volunteer activity, and views on related issues, by respondent characteristics, 1992 survey, biennial rpt, A5435–5

State and local:

Georgia county guide, general data, 1993 annual rpt, U6750–1

Georgia prison inmates use of chaplaincy services, and participation in religious worship by denomination, FY92 annual rpt, S1872–1

Hawaii data book, general data, 1992 annual rpt, S2090–1.1

Iowa correctional instn inmates by religious affiliation, by instn, monthly rpt, S2770–1

Missouri correctional instn inmate characteristics, including religious preference, FY93, annual rpt, S4501–1

Missouri Human Rights Commission discrimination cases and dispositions, by case type, FY92 and trends, annual rpt, S4530–2.2

Pennsylvania prison inmates by religious affiliation, 1980 and 1990, annual rpt, S6782–1

Utah marriages, by religious affiliation of officiant, 1990 and trends, annual rpt, S7835–2

Utah prison inmates, parolees, and probationers, by religious affiliation and sex, Oct 1992, annual rpt, S7810–1

see also Clergy

see also Missions and missionaries

see also Parochial schools

see also Religious cults

see also Religious organizations

Religious cults

Public opinion on Branch Davidian religious cult siege/fire in Waco, Tex and role of Federal authorities, Apr 1993 Gallup Poll, C4040–1.510

Public opinion on news items concerning Branch Davidian religious cult siege/fire in Waco, Tex, by respondent characteristics, Apr/May 1993 survey, C8915–1.503

Religious organizations

Catholic charity social service agency activities, clients, finances, and personnel, 1991 and trends, annual rpt, A3810–1

Catholic population, clergy, and instns, by diocese and State, 1993 annual compilation, C4950–1

Catholic population, clergy, instns, missionaries, and religious order membership, US and worldwide, 1993 annual almanac, C6885–1

Charitable activities and finances of religious congregations, 1991 survey, article, C2176–1.512

Charitable contributions, by type of donor and recipient, 1992 and trends, annual rpt, A0700–1

Church attendance and membership trends, monthly survey, R8780–1

Churches and membership, by denomination, census div, State, and county, 1990, R4985–1

Churches, membership, clergy, and contributions, by denomination, US and Canada, 1991-92, annual rpt, C0105–1

Congregation characteristics, including membership, activities, staff, and finances, 1992 survey, recurring rpt, A5435–4

Eastern Europe public opinion on selected govt and societal instns, for 6 countries and 3 Soviet Union Republics, 1991 survey, C8915–8.2

Europe public opinion on political, economic, and social issues of interest to foreign investors, for 9 countries and 3 Soviet Union Republics, 1991 survey, C8915–9

Foundation assets, income, and grants by type of recipient, with data for top organizations and by location, 1991 and trends, annual rpt, R4900–1

Higher education administrative salaries, for 167 positions, by instn type and budget size, 1992/93, annual rpt, A3900–1

Hospital (teaching) house staff stipends and benefits, by region and ownership, 1992/93, annual rpt, A3273–3

Mutual fund industry financial data, by type of investor and financial instn intermediary, 1991 and trends, annual rpt, A6025–1.2

Nursing college deans and salaries, by personal and instn characteristics, 1992/93, annual rpt, A0615–2

Nursing college faculty and salaries, by personal and instn characteristics, 1992/93, annual rpt, A0615–1

Nursing school enrollment and grads, by degree level, sex, race-ethnicity, and instn type and location, 1992/93 and trends, annual rpt, A0615–4

Protestant church membership and contributions, by denomination, US and Canada, 1991 or 1992, annual article, C2176–1.518

Protestant church/ministry employee salary trends, 1992-93, article, C2176–1.519

Public confidence in selected societal instns, 1972-91 surveys, annual rpt, U6395–1

Public confidence in selected societal instns, 1993 Gallup Poll and trends, C4040–1.510, R8780–1.508

Theological school enrollment, staff and compensation, and finances, with data by instn, 1991/92 and trends, annual rpt, A3376–1

Utility rate reduction policies of State and Canadian Province regulatory agencies, 1991/92 annual rpt, A7015–3

Index by Subjects and Names

State and local:

California property tax assessments and exemptions, by type of property, city, county, and company, FY93 and trends, annual rpt, S0835–1.2

California seminary and Bible college enrollment and degrees, by sex, race-ethnicity, and instn, 1990/91, annual series, S0827–2

Colorado property assessed valuation by detailed property type, and tax levy and revenue by local district, by county, 1991-92, annual rpt, S1055–3

Florida crimes against businesses, churches, and govt, by offense, 1992, annual rpt, S1770–1

Hawaii data book, general data, 1992 annual rpt, S2090–1.6

Illinois crimes involving bias against selected groups, 1991, annual rpt, S2536–1

Illinois theological school enrollment, degrees, and finances, by instn, 1993 annual rpt, S2475–1

Iowa Bible college enrollment and operating data, 1990/91, annual rpt, S2755–1

North Carolina Bible colleges and theological seminaries enrollment, degrees, staff, and student aid, by instn, 1992/93 and trends, annual rpt, U8013–1

Oklahoma crimes involving bias against selected groups, with offense characteristics and offender race-ethnicity, 1992, annual rpt, S6465–1.2

Pennsylvania degrees conferred by theological seminaries, by level, 1990/91 and trends, annual rpt, S6790–5.2

Pennsylvania degrees conferred by theological seminaries, by level, 1991/92 and trends, annual rpt, S6790–5.15

Pennsylvania higher education faculty employment, compensation, and tenure status, by sex and type of instn, 1991/92 and trends, annual rpt, S6790–5.5

Pennsylvania higher education faculty employment, compensation, and tenure status, by sex and type of instn, 1992/93 and trends, annual rpt, S6790–5.13

Pennsylvania higher education revenues, expenditures, and endowment funds, by instn type, FY91 and trends, annual rpt, S6790–5.4

Pennsylvania higher education revenues, expenditures, and endowment funds, by instn type, FY92 and trends, annual rpt, S6790–5.16

Pennsylvania theological seminary enrollment, by sex, minority and foreign status, student level, and instn, 1992 and trends, annual rpt, S6790–5.9

Pennsylvania theological seminary enrollment, by student residence location and academic level, 1992 and trends, biennial rpt, S6790–5.8

Pennsylvania tuition/fees, and room and board charges, for theological seminaries by instn, 1992/93, annual rpt, S6790–5.3

see also Clergy

see also Missions and missionaries

Relocation

Corporate employee transfers, and relocation policies, assistance, and costs, 1992, annual survey, B0600–1

Corporate new hire relocation assistance rates and costs, 1983-92, annual survey rpt, A4740–2

Index by Subjects and Names

Rent

Plastics processing industry employee relocation expense policies, 1992 survey, biennial rpt, A8920–3

see also Labor mobility

see also Migration

see also Urban renewal

Remedial education

Hospital basic skills education program availability and budget, 1993 survey article, A1865–1.507

Mathematics remedial course undergrad enrollment rates, fall 1992, annual survey, A2085–1.2

State and local:

Missouri Elementary and Secondary Education Act programs, students, and teachers, by grade level and subject, FY92, annual rpt, S4505–1.1

Virginia public school enrollment, grads, finances, and staff, by county and municipality, 1991/92, annual rpt, S8190–3

see also Compensatory education

Remodeling

see Housing maintenance and repair

Renal disorders

see Urogenital diseases

Renewable energy

see Alcohol fuels

see Biomass energy

see Geothermal resources

see Hydroelectric power

see Water power

see Wind energy

see Wood fuel

Reno, Nev.

Casino finances and employment, by location and gaming revenue range, FY92, annual rpt, S5062–1

Employment by industry, quarterly rpt, S5040–1

Labor force conditions and outlook, with data by industry, 1992 annual rpt, S5040–4

Rent

Apartment building (conventionally financed) detailed income and expense ratios for US and Canada, by building type, metro area, and US region, 1991 and trends, annual rpt, A5600–1

Apartment building (federally subsidized) detailed income and expense ratios, by building and subsidy type, building age, metro area, and region, 1991 and trends, annual rpt, A5600–5

Apartment complex mgmt income and expenses, and vacancy and turnover rates, by region and metro area, 1992, annual survey rpt, A6497–1

Apartment monthly rent in approx 300 cities, quarterly rpt, A0150–1

Business incubator facilities finances and operations, including services offered and tenant characteristics, 1991, annual rpt, A7360–1

Commercial real estate market conditions and outlook, for industrial and office properties, by US metro area and selected foreign city, 1992-93, annual survey, A8916–1

Commercial real estate market conditions and outlook, for industrial and office properties in major metro areas, 1993 annual rpt, B2800–3

Congressional campaign fund finances, with expenditures by item and contributions by donor type, by candidate, district, and State, 1990 elections, C2500–6

Convenience store industry financial and operating data, by size category, 1992 and trends, annual survey rpt, A6735–1, A6735–2

Costs of rent compared to household and minimum wage income, by State or major city, 1992 annual rpt, R3840–11

Drugstore (independent pharmacy) financial and operating data, by store characteristics, 1991 and trends, annual survey, B5165–1

Farm, cropland, and pasture rent per acre, 32 States, 1993, annual rpt, S6760–1

Home furnishings retailer financial and operating data, by firm characteristics and region, 1992 and trends, annual rpt, A7975–1

Industrial and high-technology facilities availability, rental rates, and sale prices, for major metro areas by region, mid-1993, annual rpt, B2800–6

Low-income housing supply-demand, costs, physical conditions, and public assistance, with data by race-ethnicity, for 44 metro areas, 1980s-91, R3834–16

Office building detailed income and expense data, and energy use, US and Canada, by building characteristics, metro area, and US region, 1991 and trends, annual rpt, A5600–2

Office property rental rates, vacancy, and construction, for major metro areas, quarterly rpt, B2800–4

Restaurant industry financial and operating data, by establishment characteristics and location, 1992, annual rpt, A8200–3

Shopping center detailed income and expense data, by building characteristics, metro area, and region, 1991, annual rpt, A5600–6

Shopping center financial and operating data, with detail by type of tenant, US and Canada, 1991, triennial rpt, R9285–1

Supermarkets opened, remodeled, and closed, including store features, dev costs, and rent, by region and sales size, 1992 and trends, annual rpt, A4950–2

State and local:

Alabama statistical abstract, general data, 1992 recurring rpt, U5680–2.3

Alaska tax exemption provisions for senior citizens and disabled veterans, and State reimbursements to local areas, FY92 and trends, annual rpt, S0285–1

Arizona income tax credits by type, and claimants, FY89-92, annual rpt, S0515–1

Arizona Indian population, education, housing, health, and employment characteristics, with detail by reservation, 1970s-91, recurring rpt, U5850–2.9

Arizona statistical abstract, general data, 1993 recurring rpt, U5850–2.16

Arkansas Census of Population and Housing detailed findings, 1990, U5935–7

California Census of Population and Housing detailed findings, 1990, S0840–9

California individual and corporate income tax returns and property tax assistance, by income class and county, 1990 and trends, annual rpt, S0855–1

California socioeconomic and govtl data for municipalities, counties, and school districts, 1993 annual rpt, C4712–3

California statistical abstract, general data, 1992 annual rpt, S0840–2.9

Delaware data book, general data, 1993 annual rpt, S1375–4

Delaware school district expenditures for operations, materials, and health and food services, 1991/92, annual rpt, S1430–1.4

Florida county data book, 1992/93 annual rpt, C6360–1

Florida statistical abstract, general data, 1992 annual rpt, U6660–1.2

Georgia cropland and pasture cash rents, 1977-92, annual rpt, S1855–1

Georgia statistical abstract, general data, 1992-93 biennial rpt, U6730–1.10

Hawaii data book, general data, 1992 annual rpt, S2090–1.21

Illinois farmland rent per acre, by land use, 1983-92, annual rpt, S2390–1

Illinois statistical abstract, general data, 1992 annual rpt, U6910–2

Kansas farm rent, 1983-93, annual rpt, S2915–1

Kansas statistical abstract, general data, 1991/92 annual rpt, U7095–2.3

Kentucky economic statistics, general data, 1993 annual rpt, S3104–1.1

Kentucky farm, cropland, and pasture cash rent per acre compared to neighboring States, 1980-93, annual rpt, S3085–1

Louisiana Census of Population and Housing summary findings, by local area, 1990 and trends, U8010–4

Louisiana farm production expenses, by item, 1985-91, annual rpt, U2740–1

Maine Census of Population and Housing summary findings, by local area, 1990, S3465–7, S3465–8, S3465–9

Maryland property federally owned and leased, 1989-90, biennial rpt, S3605–1.12

Maryland statistical abstract, general data, 1993-94 biennial rpt, S3605–1.12

Massachusetts municipal and county profiles, general data, 1992 annual rpt, C4712–2

Michigan farm real estate cash rent, 1960-92, annual rpt, S3950–1

Missouri farmland rent per acre, by land use, 1989-93, annual rpt, S4480–1

Nebraska farmland rental rates, by State district and type of land, 1992, annual rpt, S4835–1

New Jersey Census of Population and Housing detailed findings, by county, 1990, S5425–19

New Jersey municipal and county data book, general data, 1992 annual rpt, C4712–4

New York City commercial building leasing activity, vacancies, rental rates, and construction, by city area, 1988-92, annual rpt, B2800–5

New York State municipal and county statistical profiles, general data, 1993 annual rpt, C4712–7

New York State statistical yearbook, general data, 1992 annual rpt, U5100–1.9

North Carolina farm and cropland rent per acre, 1988-92, annual rpt, S5885–1

North Dakota farm rents per acre, by land use and county, 1993 and trends, annual rpt, U3600–1

Rent

Ohio farm real estate value and cash rent, 1987-92, annual rpt, S6240–1

Oklahoma cropland and pasture cash rent per acre compared to adjacent States, 1989-93, annual rpt, S6405–1

Oregon population educational attainment, health and life insurance coverage, rent, and poverty, 1990 and 1992, article, S6592–1.502

Pennsylvania Census of Population and Housing detailed findings, with selected data by county and municipality, 1990, U4130–13

Pennsylvania housing data from Census of Population and Housing, by county and municipality, 1990, C1595–14

Pennsylvania statistical abstract, general data, 1992 recurring rpt, U4130–6.1

Rhode Island Census of Population and Housing detailed findings, by county and municipality, 1990, S6930–9

Rhode Island statistical almanac, general data, 1993 annual rpt, C7975–1.1

South Carolina statistical abstract, general data, 1993 annual rpt, S7125–1.11

South Dakota farmland cash rents, by land use, 1983-93, annual rpt, S7280–1

Tennessee farm and cropland rent per acre, 1981-93, annual rpt, S7460–1

Tennessee statistical abstract, general data, 1992/93 annual rpt, U8710–2.6

Texas farm cropland and pasture cash rents, 1987-92, annual rpt, S7630–1.3

Utah homeless shelter population characteristics, individual shelter capacity, and related housing data, 1991-92, annual rpt, S7808–2

Utah statistical abstract, general data, 1993 triennial rpt, U8960–1.11

Utah taxable transient room rent revenues, by county, 1987-91, annual rpt, S7905–1

Wisconsin farmland rent per acre, 1988-93, annual rpt, S8680–1

Wyoming cropland and pasture cash rents, 1984-93, annual rpt, S8860–1

see also Housing tenure

see also Landlord-tenant relations

see also Motor vehicle rental

see also Rent supplements

see also Rental industries

Rent supplements

State and local:

DC statistical profile, general data, 1992 annual rpt, S1535–3.4

Rental housing

see Apartment houses

see Housing tenure

Rental industries

Airline fleet units owned, leased, and on order, by model, July 1993, and planned changes for 2nd half 1993, article, C5800–4.530

Airline jet fleet leased vs owned, and operating lease expenses, by major carrier, 1993 annual article, C7000–4.508

Airline jet plane leasing activity, by company, 1992, annual rpt, B1582–1

Canada household distribution by number of video cassettes rented and average price paid, 1986 and 1992 surveys, recurring rpt, A8695–4

Convenience stores offering special services, including video cassette rentals, 1992 and trends, annual survey rpt, A6735–1, A6735–2

Financial data for equipment rental industry, by revenue size group and region, and for Canada, 1991 and trends, annual rpt, A2665–1

Financial ratios and performance, for over 350 SIC 4-digit industries, FY88-92, annual rpt, A6400–3

Franchise operations and finances, by type of business, 1991/92 and trends, annual rpt, A5820–1

Motion picture rental income for all-time top films, 1993 annual feature, C9380–1.514, C9380–1.525

Motion picture rental income for US releases in top 15 foreign countries, 1990-92, annual feature, C9380–1.530

Motion picture rental income, rankings of top all-time films, 1993 annual feature, C9380–1.509

Motion picture rental income, rankings of top films, 1992, annual feature, C9380–1.509

Railroad fleet composition and ownership, by company, 1992, annual rpt, A3275–7

Supermarket video cassette rental dept operations and outlook, 1993 survey article, C4655–1.508

Video cassette rental market devs, including film revenues and VCR ownership in US and abroad, weekly rpt, C9380–1

State and local:

Hawaii data book, general data, 1992 annual rpt, S2090–1.23

see also Motor vehicle rental

see also under By Industry in the "Index by Categories"

Renter households

see Housing tenure

Renz, Loren

"Foundation Giving: Yearbook of Facts and Figures on Private, Corporate and Community Foundations", R4900–1

Reorganization of government

see Government reorganization

Repair industries

Canada photographic and/or video equipment repair service actual and likely use by consumers, 1992 survey, recurring rpt, A8695–4

Clothes washing machine home repair, minimum service charge in approx 300 cities, quarterly rpt, A0150–1

Financial ratios and performance, for over 350 SIC 4-digit industries, FY88-92, annual rpt, A6400–3

Fuel oil dealer heating and cooling equipment sales, installations, and service, by region, 1992 annual survey, C4680–2.2

Office building detailed income and expense data, and energy use, US and Canada, by building characteristics, metro area, and US region, 1991 and trends, annual rpt, A5600–2

Operating and financial composite ratios for corporations, with establishments and receipts, for approx 200 industries, by asset size, FY90, annual rpt, C7800–1

Photographic equipment and supplies, consumer ownership, purchasing patterns, and use, 1993 survey and trends, recurring rpt, A8695–2

Shopping center detailed income and expense data, by building characteristics, metro area, and region, 1991, annual rpt, A5600–6

Shopping center financial and operating data, with detail by type of tenant, US and Canada, 1991, triennial rpt, R9285–1

State and local:

Arizona statistical abstract, general data, 1993 recurring rpt, U5850–2.24

Florida statistical abstract, general data, 1992 annual rpt, U6660–1.18

see also Automobile repair and maintenance

see also Housing maintenance and repair

see also Shipbuilding and repairing

Repossession

see Loan delinquency and default

Republic of China

see Taiwan

Republic of Congo

see Congo

Republic of Korea

see Korea, South

Republic of South Africa

see South Africa

Republican Party

Presidential primary election results and voter registration by county and district, by State, 1992 and trends, C2500–7

Women in State senates and houses/assemblies, by party and State, 1993 and trends, recurring rpt, U4510–1.63, U4510–1.67

Women in US House of Representatives and Senate, by party, 1917-95, annual rpt, U4510–1.61, U4510–1.69

Women State senate and house candidates and officeholders, by party and State, 1992 and trends, recurring rpt, U4510–1.64

State and local:

West Virginia election results and voter registration, by county and party, 1992 and trends, biennial rpt, S8630–1

Research

Chemical Abstracts, number of papers covered, by country of origin and specialty area, 1970s-92, annual feature, A1250–1.537

Chemist and chemical engineer salaries, employment status, and demographic and professional characteristics, 1993, annual rpt, A1250–4

Ecologist personal and professional characteristics, including research activity and funding, with data by field, Mar 1992 survey, recurring rpt, A4685–1

Employment situation for researchers, including job satisfaction and employer characteristics, 1992 survey, annual article, C1850–6.505

Foreign scholars teaching/researching at US universities, for top 12-13 instns and countries of origin, 1991/92, article, C2175–1.502

Job search methods of researchers, 1992 survey, article, C1850–6.504

Librarians at universities and research instns, salaries by sex, type of position, and instn, FY92 and trends, annual survey, A3365–2

Library (research) holdings, staff, and expenditures, for instns in US and Canada, 1991/92, annual feature, C2175–1.511

Museums and related instns use by researchers, and findings published, by type, budget size, and governing authority, 1989/90 survey, A0750–1.2

Nursing higher education program finances, faculty and clinical practice, and clinic/center operations, by instn characteristics, 1992/93 biennial rpt, A0615–5

Salaries of scientists, engineers, technicians, and other professionals, by employee and employer characteristics, 1990s and trends, biennial rpt, A3960–1

State and local:

California higher education systems funding by source and expenditures by program category, with enrollment data, FY60s-94, annual rpt, S0827–3

Florida higher education research contract and grant funds by source and expenditures by discipline, 1991/92, annual rpt, S1725–1

Missouri higher education revenues by source and expenditures by function, by instn, FY92 and trends, annual rpt, S4520–3.3

see also Agricultural sciences and research
see also Consumer surveys
see also Defense research
see also Educational research
see also Energy research and development
see also Federal funding for research and development
see also Market research
see also Medical research
see also Opinion and attitude surveys
see also Research and development
see also Statistical programs and activities
see also under specific academic and scientific disciplines

Research and development

Aerospace industry, civil and military production, R&D, trade, employment, and finances, with Federal funding data, 1991 and trends, annual rpt, A0250–2

Biotechnology company finances, employment, and firms, with detail for public companies, FY92-93, annual article, A1250–1.542

Chemical and related industries production, finances, operating ratios, employment, and trade, by country, company, and chemical, 1980s-92, annual feature, A1250–1.530

Chemical engineering R&D expenditures of 50 major companies, errata, C5800–8.502

Chemical industry finances and operations, with data by industry segment and product, 1970s-92, annual rpt, A3850–1

Chemical industry R&D spending, for 27 companies, 1987-93, annual article, A1250–1.511

Chemicals R&D spending in Federal, industrial, and academic sectors, with data by company and instn, 1980s-93, annual feature, A1250–1.537

Chemist and chemical engineer salaries, employment status, and demographic and professional characteristics, 1993, annual rpt, A1250–4

Competitiveness indicators for US vs other major industrial countries, including investments, productivity, exports, and per capita GDP, 1993 annual rpt, A4475–1

Corporate R&D expenditures, and sales and profits, for approx 900 firms, 1992, annual feature, C5800–7.534

Cost index for performing R&D, by sector, 1960-93, annual rpt, R3300–1

EC expenditures for R&D as a percent of GDP, by country, 1980s, R5025–9

Economic dev condition indicators, including economic performance, business vitality, growth capacity, and tax/fiscal system, by State, 1993 annual rpt, R4225–1

Engineers salaries by industry group, census div, selected metro area, and years since college degree, 1993, annual survey rpt, A0685–5

Engineers salaries by industry group, census div, selected metro area, degree level, and years since college degree, 1993, annual survey rpt, A0685–3

Expenditures for total and/or industry R&D, with Federal funding by purpose, DOD obligations by object, and comparisons to 3 other countries, 1991 and trends, article, R5650–2.521

Financial ratios and performance, for over 350 SIC 4-digit industries, FY88-92, annual rpt, A6400–3

Food/beverage industry new product dev influences, including industry personnel views on selected ingredients, suppliers, and dev time, 1993 annual article, C2150–6.511

Funding and expenditures for R&D, by source and performing sector, 1960s-93, annual rpt, R3300–1

Funding for R&D by source, expenditures by function, and budget trends by industry div, 1992-93, annual article, C1850–6.503

High-technology industry CEO characteristics, and views on mgmt issues including compensation and foreign trade, June 1992 survey, B4490–2.34

Higher education funding and Federal aid for R&D, for top 100 instns, FY91, annual feature, C2175–1.502

Higher education instns, faculty, students, degrees, and finances, detailed data by State, 1993 annual rpt, C2175–1.531

Higher education R&D funding by source, by State and for US territories, FY91, annual feature, C2175–1.503

Hispanic-owned high-technology company R&D share of budget, and new product dev and cooperative research activities, 1993 annual article, C4575–1.510

Industrial R&D activities and quality assurance, articles and special features, monthly rpt, C1850–6

Industrial R&D managers outlook on expenditures, effort, personnel, and other mgmt issues, 1993, annual survey rpt, A5510–1

Japan corporate R&D expenditures, 1991-92, C1850–2.504

Japan R&D expenditures, by funding and performing sector, govt agency, and industry, FY70s-93, annual article, R5650–2.557

Latin America statistical abstract, general data by country, 1992 annual rpt, U6250–1.8

Manufacturing industries private and Fed Govt funding for R&D, with detail by selected industry, 1989, R4700–19

Motor vehicle manufacturer R&D expenditures, 1981-92, annual rpt, A0865–1.3

Motor vehicle new model dev costs and production requirements, for 3 major manufacturers, 1993 article, C8900–1.518

New product dev process and significant contributing factors, 1993 articles, C2150–6.508

Oil industry environmental performance, with data on toxic chemical releases, oil spills, occupational injury/illness, and corporate spending, 1990 and trends, annual rpt, A2575–27

Paper industry expenditures on R&D, 1966-91, annual rpt, A1630–6.3

Paper industry R&D spending, by company, with comparisons to other manufacturing sectors, 1993 annual rpt, C3975–5.1

Pharmaceutical companies R&D contracts with academic medical instns, with value, duration, and research area, for 11 major contracts, 1993 article, C2175–1.513

Plastics specialty materials manufacturer income, R&D expenditures, and stock performance, for 10 companies, 1992, article, C3950–1.511

Salaries, and employment characteristics of R&D professionals, 1993 and trends, annual article, C1850–6.509

Salaries of scientists, engineers, technicians, and other professionals, by employee and employer characteristics, 1990s and trends, biennial rpt, A3960–1

Shipbuilding govt aid programs in 6 OECD countries, and impact on US industry, 1993 recurring rpt, A8900–8

Venture-capital-backed company economic impact, including job creation, capital and R&D investments, and selected growth rates, 1985-91, A8515–2

State and local:

Hawaii data book, general data, 1992 annual rpt, S2090–1.17

Tennessee statistical abstract, general data, 1992/93 annual rpt, U8710–2.20

Utah high-technology industry trends, with R&D spending, and employment of major firms, 1986-92, recurring article, U8960–2.508

see also Agricultural sciences and research
see also Defense research
see also Energy research and development
see also Federal funding for research and development
see also Federally Funded R&D Centers
see also Technological innovations

Research and Forecasts Inc.

Corporate policies concerning charitable contributions to arts programs and other causes, 1991, recurring rpt, A3690–1

Reserve Officers Training Corps

State and local:

Alabama public school revenues from ROTC program, by district, FY92, annual rpt, S0124–1.2

Reservoirs

State and local:

Arizona reservoir capacity and storage, Apr 1989-93, annual rpt, U5830–1

Arizona statistical abstract, general data, 1993 recurring rpt, U5850–2.1

California statistical abstract, general data, 1992 annual rpt, S0840–2.7

Kansas indebtedness for water storage in Federal reservoirs, FY92, annual rpt, S2900–1.1

Reservoirs

Nevada statistical abstract, general data, 1992 biennial rpt, S5005–1.9

Residential energy conservation *see* Energy conservation

Residential energy use *see* Housing energy use

Residual oil *see* Fuel oil *see* Petroleum and petroleum industry

Resins *see* Chemicals and chemical industry *see* Gum and wood chemicals *see* Plastics and plastics industry

Resolution Trust Corporation *see* Financial institutions regulation

Resort timesharing *State and local:* Hawaii timesharing properties and units, by county, Oct 1990, annual rpt, S2090–1.21

Resorts *see* Hotels and motels

Resource Data International Inc. Coal supply-demand indicators, including utility purchases, monthly rpt, C5226–1

Respiratory diseases

Asthma incidence among children, by race-ethnicity, with detail by Hispanic ethnic origin, 1993 article, A2623–1.506

Hospital patient admission rates and length of stay, by diagnosis and procedure, payment source, age, sex, and region, 1991, B4455–4

Hospital patient charges and length of stay, by diagnosis and procedure, payment source, age, and region, 1991, B4455–5

Hospital patient discharges and length of stay, by diagnosis, type of operation, age, and region, 1991, annual rpt series, B4455–1

Hospital patient discharges and length of stay, by diagnostic related group (DRG), payment source, age, and region, 1991, annual rpt series, B4455–3

Hospital psychiatric patients with selected physical disorders, length of stay by age, sex, and region, 1991, annual rpt series, B4455–2

Military personnel stationed in Saudi Arabia, respiratory problems reported, with detail by sleeping accommodations, 1990/91 study, article, A2623–1.511

State and local:

Alabama vital statistics, including population, births, deaths by cause, marriages, and divorces, by location and demographic characteristics, 1992 and trends, annual rpt, S0175–2

Alaska vital statistics, including births, deaths by cause, marriages, divorces, adoptions, and population, by demographic characteristics and location, 1990, annual rpt, S0315–1

Arkansas vital statistics, including births, deaths by cause, marriages, and divorces, by age, sex, race, and county, 1991 and trends, annual rpt, S0685–1

California vital statistics, including population, births, and deaths by cause, by demographic characteristics and county, 1990 and trends, annual rpt, S0865–1

Colorado vital statistics, including population, births, deaths by cause, abortion, marriage and divorce, and adoption, by demographic characteristics and location, 1990 and trends, annual rpt, S1010–1

Connecticut vital statistics, including births, deaths by cause, marriages, and divorces, by demographic characteristics and location, 1989, annual rpt, S1200–1

Delaware vital statistics, including births, deaths by cause, and marriages and dissolutions, by demographic characteristics and location, 1990, annual rpt, S1385–2

Florida deaths by selected cause, and incidence of selected communicable diseases, by county, 1992 annual rpt, S1746–1.1

Florida vital statistics, including population, births, deaths by cause, and marriages and dissolutions, by location and demographic characteristics, 1992 and trends, annual rpt, S1745–3

Georgia vital statistics, including deaths by cause, demographic characteristics, and location, 1991 and trends, annual rpt, S1895–1.2

Hawaii health dept activities and services, including vital statistics and disease control, by location, 1990, annual rpt, S2065–1

Idaho vital statistics, including births, deaths by cause, abortions, marriages, and divorces, by demographic characteristics and county, 1991 and trends, annual rpt, S2250–2

Iowa vital statistics, including population, births, deaths by cause, marriages, and divorces, by demographic characteristics and location, 1991 and trends, annual rpt, S2795–1

Kansas vital statistics, including population, births, deaths by cause, abortions, marriages, and divorces, by demographic characteristics and location, 1991 and trends, annual rpt, S2975–1

Kentucky vital statistics, including births, deaths by cause, marriages and divorces, and population, by demographic characteristics and county, 1991, annual rpt, S3140–1

Louisiana vital statistics, including population, births, deaths by cause, reportable diseases, marriages, and divorces, by demographic characteristics and locality, 1989-90 and trends, annual rpt, S3295–1

Maine vital statistics, including births, deaths by cause, abortions, and marriages and divorces, by demographic characteristics and location, 1991 and trends, annual rpt, S3460–2

Maryland vital statistics, including population, births, deaths by cause, marriages, and divorces, by demographic characteristics and location, 1989 and trends, annual rpt, S3635–1

Massachusetts vital statistics, including births, deaths by cause, marriages, divorces, and population, by locality and demographic characteristics, 1990 and trends, annual rpt, S3850–1

Michigan vital statistics, including births, deaths, marriages, divorces/annulments, and communicable diseases, by location and demographic characteristics, 1990 and trends, annual rpt, S4000–3

Minnesota vital statistics, including population, births, abortions, deaths, marriages, and divorces, by location and demographic characteristics, 1991 and trends, annual rpt, S4190–2

Mississippi vital statistics, including births, deaths by cause, marriages, and divorces, by demographic characteristics and location, 1992 and trends, annual rpt, S4350–1

Missouri vital statistics, including population, births, deaths by cause, and marriages and divorces, by location and demographic characteristics, 1992 and trends, annual rpt, S4518–1

Montana vital statistics, including births, deaths by cause, abortion, disease, and marriage and divorce, by demographic characteristics and county, 1990-91 and trends, annual rpt, S4690–1

Nebraska vital statistics, including births, deaths, marriages, divorces, and population, by demographic characteristics and location, 1991 and trends, annual rpt, S4885–1

Nevada vital statistics, including births, abortions, and deaths by cause, by county and demographic characteristics, 1989 and trends, annual rpt, S5075–1

New Hampshire vital statistics, including population, births, deaths by cause, marriages, and divorces, by location and demographic characteristics, 1991 and trends, annual rpt, S5215–1

New Jersey vital statistics, including births, deaths, population, communicable diseases, and marriages and divorces, by demographic characteristics and location, 1990 and trends, annual rpt, S5405–1

New Mexico vital statistics, including population, births, deaths, and disease, by location and demographic characteristics, 1991 and trends, annual rpt, S5605–1

New York State vital statistics, including population, births, deaths by cause, reportable diseases, and marriages and dissolutions, by demographic characteristics and/or location, 1990 and trends, annual rpt, S5765–1

North Carolina deaths and rates, by cause and county, 1991 and trends, annual rpt, S5927–1.2

North Dakota vital statistics, including births, deaths by cause, marriages and divorces, and abortions, by demographic characteristics and/or county, 1991 and trends, annual rpt, S6105–2

Ohio vital statistics, including births, deaths by cause, marriages, divorces, and population, by demographic characteristics and location, 1991 and trends, annual rpt, S6285–1

Oregon vital statistics, including births, deaths by cause, communicable diseases, marriages, and divorces, by age, sex, race-ethnicity, and county, 1991 and trends, annual rpt, S6615–5

Rhode Island vital statistics, including population, births, deaths, marriages, and divorces, by demographic characteristics and locality, 1989 and trends, annual rpt, S6995–1

South Carolina deaths, by detailed cause, age, sex, and race, 1990, annual rpt, S7175–2

South Carolina vital statistics, including births, deaths by cause, marriages, and divorces, by age, sex, race, and location, 1990 and trends, annual rpt, S7175–1

Index by Subjects and Names

Restaurants and drinking places

South Dakota vital statistics, including births, deaths, marriage and divorce, and communicable disease, by demographic characteristics and county, 1991 and trends, annual rpt, S7345–1

Tennessee vital statistics, including births, deaths by cause, marriages, divorces, and population, by demographic characteristics and location, 1991 and trends, annual rpt, S7520–2

Texas vital statistics, including births, deaths by cause, abortions, marriages, and divorces, by location and demographic characteristics, 1991 and trends, annual rpt, S7685–1

Utah vital statistics, including births, deaths by cause, and population, by county and demographic characteristics, 1990 and trends, annual rpt, S7835–1

Vermont vital statistics, including population, births, deaths by cause, abortions, marriages, and divorces, by location and demographic characteristics, 1991 and trends, annual rpt, S8054–1

Virginia vital statistics, including births, deaths by cause, marriages and divorces, and communicable disease, by demographic characteristics and location, 1991 and trends, annual rpt, S8225–1

Washington State vital statistics, including births, deaths by cause, and population, by demographic characteristics and location, 1991 and trends, annual rpt, S8363–1

West Virginia vital statistics, including births, deaths by cause, marriages, and divorces, by location and demographic characteristics, 1991 and trends, annual rpt, S8560–1

Wisconsin vital statistics, including population, births, deaths by cause, and marriages and dissolutions, by county and demographic characteristics, 1991 and trends, annual rpt, S8715–4

Wyoming vital statistics, including population, births, deaths by cause, marriages, and divorces, by demographic characteristics and county, 1991 and trends, annual rpt, S8920–2

see also Allergies
see also Black lung disease
see also Pneumonia and influenza
see also Tuberculosis
see also under By Disease in the "Index by Categories"

Respite care

State and local:

Missouri public welfare and medical assistance recipients, expenditures, and case processing, by program and county, FY92 and trends, annual rpt, S4575–2

South Dakota respite care recipients and payments, FY92, annual rpt, S7385–1.1

Rest homes

see Nursing homes

Restaurants and drinking places

Amusement park food and/or beverage operations, including sales share of revenues, 1992, annual rpt, A5700–1

Australia restaurant provision of no-smoking areas where not mandated by law, views of owners and customers, 1993 article, A2623–1.511

Business devs and issues in restaurant/food service industry, with data on establishments and sales by market segment, recurring rpt, C1200–5

Consumer buying power survey of population, income, and sales by kind of business, by census div, State, MSA, county, and city, 1992, annual rpt, C1200–1.511

Consumer ratings of restaurants, for most popular chains, 1993 annual feature, C1850–3.504

Consumer restaurant patronage patterns, expenditures, and food preferences, 1992 survey, recurring feature, C1850–3.501

Customer characteristics and attitudes, survey rpt series, A8200–8

Dessert operations of restaurants and consumer ordering patterns, 1992 survey rpt, A8200–20

Establishments, top 20 restaurant chains worldwide, 1991, recurring rpt, R9375–6

Expansion outlook and operating data for restaurants, by census div and MSA, 1993 annual articles, C1850–3.506

Fast food restaurant advertising expenditures and market shares, for top 10 chains, 1991-92, annual rpt, C2710–1.547

Financial and operating data, by establishment characteristics and location, 1992, annual rpt, A8200–3

Financial and operating data for top 100 chains and companies, FY91-93, annual feature, C5150–5.509

Financial and operating devs for restaurant/food service industry, including data by company, weekly rpt, C5150–5

Financial performance and growth rankings for approx 1,000 top corporations, with comparisons by industry group, 1993 annual rpt, C3950–1.505

Financial ratios and performance, for over 350 SIC 4-digit industries, FY88-92, annual rpt, A6400–3

Franchise operations and finances, by type of business, 1991/92 and trends, annual rpt, A5820–1

Franchise restaurants and sales, and franchisee fees and investment required, by leading company, 1993 annual feature, C1200–5.512

Household expenditures for food away from home, by selected characteristics, 1991, recurring rpt, A8200–13

Independently owned restaurant sales, seating capacity, average check size, and patrons served, top 100 instns, 1992, annual article, C1850–3.505

Industry trends and devs in food service, monthly rpt, A8200–1

Markets with daily newspapers, demographic and economic info by geographic area, US and Canada, 1993 annual rpt, C3250–1

Menu item popularity, 1993 survey, recurring article, C1850–3.514

Menu practices, including items offered, and info on nutrition, ingredients, and preparation, 1987 and 1992, A8200–22

Operating and financial composite ratios for corporations, with establishments and receipts, for approx 200 industries, by asset size, FY90, annual rpt, C7800–1

Operations of restaurants/food service instns, including data and articles on finances, employment, companies, and customers, biweekly rpt, C1850–3

Prices of selected consumer items in approx 300 cities, quarterly rpt, A0150–1

Receipts/sales of travel-related industries, monthly rpt, R9375–1

Sales and establishments, and growth outlook, for food service industry by market segment, 1993 annual feature, C1850–3.503

Sales and establishments, for top 400 food service chains and other organizations, 1992, annual feature, C1850–3.509

Sales by type of establishment, 1992-93, annual rpt, A5825–1.1

Sales for food stores vs restaurants, 1992, annual feature, C4655–1.510

Sales industry costs, including compensation, training, and travel and related expenses, with data by metro area, 1992 and trends, annual survey, C1200–1.508

Sales, market shares, establishments, and business activity indicators, by location, 1992, annual feature, C1200–5.515

Sales of top 6 fast-food restaurant chains, 1990, annual rpt, C2140–1.4

Sales trends and forecast for food service industry, by market segment, 1990-93, annual feature, A8200–1.502

Shopping center financial and operating data, with detail by type of tenant, US and Canada, 1991, triennial rpt, R9285–1

Shopping center food court tenants, sales, and income-expense analysis, by building characteristics and region, 1991, annual rpt, A5600–6

Supermarkets with eating areas, and area operations and performance, 1992, annual article, C4655–1.508

Table service restaurant operations and menu offerings, and related consumer views and practices by demographic characteristics, 1992, recurring rpt, A8200–11

Take-out food consumer characteristics, consumption patterns, and attitudes, May 1992 survey, A8200–21

Travel impact on State economies, with detail by industry sector, 1990 and trends, annual rpt, R9375–7

Wages for food service industry hourly workers, by position, census div, State, and selected metro area, 1992, recurring rpt, A8200–14

State and local:

Florida statistical abstract, general data, 1992 annual rpt, U6660–1.19

Hawaii data book, general data, 1992 annual rpt, S2090–1.23

Hawaii environmental quality and public health control, inspection, licensing, and enforcement activities, 1990, annual rpt, S2065–1.6

Maine employment in trade, utilities, and transportation SIC 2-digit industries, by detailed occupation, 2nd qtr 1991, triennial rpt, S3465–1.25

Michigan employment in eating/drinking places, 1st half 1991-93, article, S3980–2.502

Nevada casino finances and employment, by location and gaming revenue range, FY92, annual rpt, S5062–1

New Hampshire wholesale and retail trade employment, by SIC 2-digit industry and detailed occupation, 1991, triennial rpt, S5205–2.26

North Carolina employment in trade, transportation, communications, utilities,

SRI 1993 585

govt, and education, by detailed occupation, 2nd qtr 1991, triennial rpt, S5917–5.2

Texas trade, transportation, and public utilities employment, by SIC 2- and 3-digit industry and detailed occupation, 2nd qtr 1991, triennial survey rpt, S7675–1.31

see also Military clubs and messes

Restitution

see Crime victim compensation

Retail auctions

see Auctions

Retail trade

Advertising expenditures and market shares for top 10 retailers, 1991-92, annual rpt, C2710–1.547

Auto aftermarket retail performance indicators, by product category, 1992 article, C2150–10.501

Auto parts/supplies aftermarket do-it-yourself sales and marketing trends and devs, monthly rpt, C0125–1

Auto parts/supplies and repair aftermarket sales performance, by product group, 1993 annual feature, C0125–1.503

Beverage industry sales, consumption, and marketing devs, monthly rpt, C0125–2

Book publishing industry financial and operating data, by publisher type and size, and subject category, 1991 and trends, annual rpt, A3274–2

Bookstores by type of outlet, US and Canada, 1992, annual compilation, C1650–3.4

Business executives expectations for coming qtr, attitudes on key indicators, with trends and data by census div, quarterly rpt, C3150–4

Business failures and liabilities, by detailed industry, cause, length of operation, and location, 1991-92 and trends, annual rpt, C3150–8

Canada photographic and video equipment and supplies purchasing patterns, by type of outlet and consumer characteristics, 1992 survey, recurring rpt, A8695–4

China consumer goods sales by region, 1990, with Guangdong Province trends from 1983, articles, A9315–1.501

Christmas holiday season sales gain for 12 retail companies, 1992, article, C5800–7.510

Christmas retail sales trends and outlook, 1992-93, article, C5150–3.517

Clothing (women's and children's) sales, production, imports, and industry employment, hours, and earnings, by type of garment, recurring rpt, A5900–1

Commonwealth of Independent States retail trade trends, by member country, 1991-92, U2030–1.502

Computer-related equipment use, and mgmt info system finances, 1992 survey, annual feature, C5150–4.501

Computer-related equipment use, and mgmt info system finances, 1993 survey, annual feature, C5150–4.509

Construction activity, capital expenditures, and number of new stores, for leading retail chains, 1991-92, annual feature, C5150–4.503

Consumer buying power survey of population, income, and sales by kind of business, by census div, State, MSA, county, and city, 1992, annual rpt, C1200–1.511

Consumer buying power survey of population, income, and sales by product line, by State, metro area, county, and census div, 1993 annual rpt, C1200–1.514

Consumer complaint and inquiry activity of Better Business Burs, by detailed type of business, 1992, annual rpt, A4350–1

Consumer expectations of economic conditions and change in income, and intended durable goods purchases by type, Conference Board monthly survey, R4105–4

Consumer retail outlet selection factors, by race, 1993 survey article, C4215–1.509

Corporate performance ratings by executives for leading companies in 32 industries, 1993 annual survey feature, C8900–1.508

Credit operations of retail outlets, including cash vs credit sales, processing methods, and marketing techniques, 1992 annual survey, C5150–4.504

Equipment industry operations and devs, including farm equipment retail sales, periodic rpt, C0495–1, C3450–1

Executive compensation and components, by industry div and major manufacturing group, 1991, annual rpt, R4105–19

Expansion devs, and equipment and construction costs, by type of retail chain, 1993 annual articles, C5150–4.507

Financial data and business info for approx 240 US and Canadian retail chains, 1991-92 and trends, annual rpt, C3400–2

Financial performance and growth rankings for approx 1,000 top corporations, with comparisons by industry group, 1993 annual rpt, C3950–1.505

Financial performance indicators for 98 public retailers, FY92 and trends, annual rpt, B8130–4

Financial ratios and performance, for over 350 SIC 4-digit industries, FY88-92, annual rpt, A6400–3

Food service industry sales and establishments, with growth outlook, by market segment, 1993 annual feature, C1850–3.503

Food service industry sales rankings by market segment, for leading organizations, 1992, annual feature, C1850–3.509

Forecasts of economic indicators for approx 10-13 months, monthly rpt, U1880–3

Forecasts of natl income and product account components, employment, and financial sector activity, monthly rpt, B4950–1

Foreign economic indexes, and leading and coincident indicators for US and other industrial countries, monthly rpt, U1245–1

Foreign general merchandise retail chain sales, earnings, and stores, for top companies worldwide, with detail for selected areas, 1991-92, annual feature, C5150–3.516

Fortune magazine ranking of top 50-100 companies in 8 nonindustrial sectors, with financial and employment data, 1992, annual feature, C8900–1.516

Fortune magazine ranking of top 50-100 companies worldwide in 8 nonindustrial sectors, with financial and employment data, 1993 annual feature, C8900–1.522

Hardware finances and operations, for hardware stores, home centers, and lumber/building material outlets, 1991 and trends, annual rpt series, A8275–1

Home furnishings retailer financial and operating data, by firm characteristics and region, 1992 and trends, annual rpt, A7975–1

Household appliance retail outlets and sales, by type, 1987, biennial rpt, A3350–3

Inventory mgmt, warehousing, and distribution operations, by retail outlet type, 1993 survey, C5150–4.506

Inventory shrinkage, and control measures, by type of outlet, 1991, annual survey rpt, C5150–4.504

Jewelry and watch manufacturing and marketing trends, new product dev, prices, trade, and related indicators, monthly rpt, C2150–7

Jewelry industry statistics on sales, marketing, trade, and employment, with customer characteristics, 1993 annual almanac, C2150–7.509

Jewelry retail business outlook, including staffing, merchandise selection criteria, and sales promotion, 1993, annual survey article, C2150–7.502

Licensed product sales, by product category and property type, 1992, article, C5150–2.521

Licensed product sales, by product category, 1990-91, annual article, C8130–1.507

Licensed product sales, by product category, 1992, article, C5150–3.513

Liquor consumption, trade, and sales volume or shipments, by product type and State, 1991 and trends, annual rpt, A4650–3

Liquor market statistics, including sales, consumption, trade, distillery operations, and govtl info, with data by company, brand, and location, 1992 and trends, annual rpt, C4775–1

Magazine retail sales, with market share by outlet type, and comparison to other newsstand sales, 1978-92, article, C2575–1.518

Market area population and characteristics, households, income, and retail outlets, for 21 leading areas, 1993 feature, C2710–1.538

Market shares for discount, specialty, and department stores, 1992, article, C5150–3.514

Markets with daily newspapers, demographic and economic info by geographic area, US and Canada, 1993 annual rpt, C3250–1

Merchandising and financial devs of retail chain stores, monthly rpt, C5150–4

Musical instrument and accessory shipment volume and/or retail value, and foreign trade, by product type, 1992 and trends, annual rpt, A6848–1

Office building detailed income and expense data, and energy use, US and Canada, by building characteristics, metro area, and US region, 1991 and trends, annual rpt, A5600–2

Operating and financial composite ratios for corporations, with establishments and receipts, for approx 200 industries, by asset size, FY90, annual rpt, C7800–1

Pet store puppies rates of congenital defects, by type, 1987-88 study, article, A3100–2.508

Index by Subjects and Names

Retail trade

Photographic equipment and supplies, consumer ownership, purchasing patterns, and use, 1993 survey and trends, recurring rpt, A8695–2

Revenues, profits, and stores, top 100 retail chains, with selected data by outlet type, 1991-92, annual articles, C5150–4.508

Sales by kind of business, 1991-92, article, U6730–2.503

Sales for food stores vs other retail outlets, 1992 and trends, annual feature, C4655–1.510

Sales volume shares by retail outlet type, for approx 300 food, drug, and other product categories, 1993 annual feature, C4655–1.504

Shoe industry market data, including foreign trade, production, and sales, by product type, 1991 and trends, annual rpt, A4957–1.1

Shoe industry production and operating data, including trade by country, retail sales, and consumer expenditures, quarterly rpt, A4957–2

Sporting goods purchases, by product and outlet type, census div, and purchaser characteristics, with average prices, 1992 and trends, annual survey, A8485–2

State retail sales trends, by selected State, semimonthly rpt quarterly article, B8500–2.510

State social, economic, and govtl indicators, with rankings, 1993 semiannual rpt, B8500–1.2

Statistical profiles of 50 States and DC, general data, 1993 annual almanac, C4712–1

Suppliers named as best by retailers for forming retail-supplier partnerships, top 6 manufacturers, 1993 survey article, C1200–4.509

Travel impact on State economics, with detail by industry sector, 1990 and trends, annual rpt, R9375–7

Western States economic indicators, including forecasts from selected organizations, for 10 States, monthly rpt, U0282–2

State and local:

Alabama business activity indicators, monthly rpt, U5680–1

Alabama county data book, general data, 1992 annual rpt, S0121–2

Alabama statistical abstract, general data, 1992 recurring rpt, U5680–2.15

Arizona business activity indicators, including housing market, population, CPI, and industrial purchasing, monthly rpt, U0280–1

Arizona economic condition, including population, employment and earnings, and business activity, by industry and locality, 1985-93, semiannual rpt, U5850–1

Arizona economic indicators, including forecasts from 16 forecasting organizations, monthly rpt, U0282–1

Arizona retail sales, by kind of business and for 2 metro areas and rest of State, 1992 and trends, annual article, U0280–1.507

Arizona statistical abstract, general data, 1993 recurring rpt, U5850–2.21

Arkansas socioeconomic trends, by MSA and/or county, 1993 annual rpt, U5935–1

California economic condition, including population, employment and earnings, income, business activity, and taxation, 1993 annual rpt, S0840–3

California economic indicators, bimonthly rpt, S0840–1

California milk sales, by sector, type of trade, and container type and size, 1992 and trends, annual rpt, S0850–1.6

California statistical abstract, general data, 1992 annual rpt, S0840–2.11

California taxable retail sales, by kind of business and county, FY92, annual rpt, S0835–1.3

Colorado retail sales and sales tax revenue, by county, city, and kind of business, FY92 and trends, annual rpt, S1075–1.5

Connecticut economic trends, including retail sales, FY83-92, annual rpt, S1170–2

Florida statistical abstract, general data, 1992 annual rpt, U6660–1.16, U6660–1.24

Georgia business activity indicators, bimonthly rpt, U6730–2

Georgia county guide, general data, 1993 annual rpt, U6750–1

Georgia statistical abstract, general data, 1992-93 biennial rpt, U6730–1.7

Georgia taxable retail sales, by county, 1991, annual rpt, S1950–1.2

Hawaii data book, general data, 1992 annual rpt, S2090–1.23

Idaho taxable sales and taxes paid, by county, FY92, annual rpt, S2295–1

Illinois business activity indicators, quarterly rpt, U6910–1

Illinois economic and business activity indicators, including data by industry and county, bimonthly rpt, S2405–2

Illinois retail sales, by business and location type, 1991-92, article, U6910–1.501

Illinois retail sales trends, by location type and MSA, 3rd qtr 1991-92, article, U6910–1.502

Illinois statistical abstract, general data, 1992 annual rpt, U6910–2

Iowa labor force supply-demand data, including population, earnings, and employment by industry and occupation, 1993 annual rpt, S2784–3

Iowa retail sales and use tax filings data, and establishments reporting, by county and city, and by kind of business, quarterly rpt, S2860–1

Kansas statistical abstract, general data, 1991/92 annual rpt, U7095–2.8

Kansas taxable retail sales, by area and kind of business, quarterly rpt, U7095–1

Kentucky economic statistics, general data, 1993 annual rpt, S3104–1.3

Maine employment in trade, utilities, and transportation SIC 2-digit industries, by detailed occupation, 2nd qtr 1991, triennial rpt, S3465–1.25

Maine statistical summary, general economic and social data, 1992 recurring rpt, S3434–1

Maryland statistical abstract, general data, 1993-94 biennial rpt, S3605–1.5

Mississippi retail businesses, sales, and tax collected, by industry group, city, and county, FY92, annual rpt, S4435–1

Mississippi statistical abstract, general data, 1992 annual rpt, U3255–4.5

Missouri retail sales by kind of business, 1982-91, annual rpt, S4475–1

Nebraska business and economic activity indicators, monthly rpt, U7860–1

Nebraska sales tax revenues and taxable sales, by county, city, and detailed industry, 1990-91, annual rpt, S4950–1.2

Nevada, Las Vegas and Reno taxable sales, quarterly rpt, S5040–1

Nevada statistical abstract, general data, 1992 biennial rpt, S5005–1.6, S5005–1.8

New Hampshire wholesale and retail trade employment, by SIC 2-digit industry and detailed occupation, 1991, triennial rpt, S5205–2.26

New Jersey economic indicators, including employment, building permits, and retail trade, monthly rpt, S5425–1

New Mexico business and economic activity indicators, monthly rpt, U7980–1

New Mexico economic trends and outlook, by industry div, 1982-92, annual article, U7980–1.503

New York State business activity indicators, quarterly rpt, S5735–2

New York State statistical yearbook, general data, 1992 annual rpt, U5100–1.2

North Carolina employment in trade, transportation, communications, utilities, govt, and education, by detailed occupation, 2nd qtr 1991, triennial rpt, S5917–5.2

Ohio retail sales, 1982-91, annual rpt, S6255–1

Oklahoma business activity indicators, monthly rpt, U8130–1

Oklahoma statistical abstract, general data, 1992 annual rpt, U8130–2.19

Pennsylvania business activity indicators, monthly rpt, U4110–1

Pennsylvania statistical abstract, general data, 1992 recurrnng rpt, U4130–6.2

Rhode Island statistical almanac, general data, 1993 annual rpt, C7975–1.1

South Carolina economic activity indicators, including employment by industry div, by county, 1993 annual rpt, S7145–1.2

South Carolina statistical abstract, general data, 1993 annual rpt, S7125–1.3

South Dakota business activity review, including selected data by city and industry, quarterly rpt, U8595–1

Tennessee economic indicator trends and forecasts, with data by industry div and manufacturing group, 1982-2001, annual rpt, S7560–1

Tennessee statistical abstract, general data, 1992/93 annual rpt, U8710–2.7

Texas trade, transportation, and public utilities employment, by SIC 2- and 3-digit industry and detailed occupation, 2nd qtr 1991, triennial survey rpt, S7675–1.31

Utah business activity indicators, by county, 1988-91, annual feature, U8960–2.501

Utah business activity indicators, by county, 1989-92, annual feature, U8960–2.507

Utah economic and demographic trends, by county and district, 1960-91, annual rpt, S7832–2

Utah statistical abstract, general data, 1993 triennial rpt, U8960–1.14

Utah taxable retail sales, by city and county, FY92, annual rpt, R9380–1.6

Retail trade

Utah taxable retail sales by county, 1986-91, annual rpt, S7905–1

Virginia business activity indicators, by local area, monthly rpt, U1120–1

Virginia educational finances by source and program, and local area revenue base, by county and municipality, 1991/92, annual rpt, S8190–3

Virginia taxable retail sales by kind of business, FY92, annual rpt, S8305–1.2

Virginia taxable retail sales, quarterly rpt, S8205–4

Virginia taxable sales, by kind of business and locality, 1991 and trends, annual rpt, U9080–8

West Virginia statistical handbook, general data, 1992 annual rpt, R9385–1.8

see also Advertising

see also Auctions

see also Consumer credit

see also Consumer protection

see also Convenience stores

see also Credit cards

see also Department stores

see also Direct marketing

see also Discount stores

see also Drugstores

see also Food stores

see also Franchises

see also Gasoline service stations

see also Home improvement stores

see also Labeling

see also Military post exchanges and commissaries

see also Motor vehicle sales

see also Packaging and containers

see also Pawnbrokers

see also Restaurants and drinking places

see also Sales promotion

see also Sales workers

see also Shoplifting

see also Shopping centers

see also Vending machines and stands

see also Warehouses

see also Wholesale trade

see also under By Industry in the "Index by Categories"

see also Under names of specific commodities or industries for sales by outlet type

Retired military personnel

Post exchange/commissary closures and affected military retirees, by base, 1993, C0500–1.504

Post exchange/commissary closures and affected military retirees, by base, 1994, C0500–1.505

Post exchange/commissary closures and affected military retirees, errata, C0500–1.505

Post exchange/commissary closures proposed and affected military retirees, by base, 1993 article, C0500–1.508

State and local:

Hawaii data book, general data, 1992 annual rpt, S2090–1.10

see also Military benefits and pensions

see also Veterans

Retirement

Association executives compensation, by position, assn type, and census div, with personnel practices and benefit provisions, 1992, biennial rpt, A2900–3

Canada annuity sales activity for retirement savings plans, monthly rpt quarterly supplement, A6225–2

Construction industry employee benefits offered, including selected post-retirement benefits, by type of business, 1993, annual survey rpt, A4155–1

Corporate work force outlook and related mgmt policies, including early retirement program use, Sept/Oct 1991 survey, R4105–78.21

Fire dept mandatory retirement policies, by population size, metro status, and census div, 1991 survey, recurring rpt, A5800–2.116

Health insurance corporate plans for retirees, changes since 1990 and planned by 1994, 1992 article, C5800–7.505

Insurance flexible-premium retirement annuity policy 5-year performance, by company, 1988-92, annual article, C1050–2.507

Japan corporate retirement age policies, and share of population age 55/over who are employed, 1986-92, article, R5650–2.549

Medical school use of faculty retirement benefits and early retirement programs, 1991 survey, article, A3273–8.502

Public concern about being able to afford retirement at a reasonable age, May 1993 Gallup Poll, C4040–1.511

Small/midsize business reasons for dropping employee retirement plans, 1993 survey article, C4687–1.510

Sweden natl steel corporation costs of early retirement program to reduce work force, 1978-84, R9260–16

Trends in retirement duration, and age at start of retirement and Social Security benefits, by sex, 1950-2005, article, R8750–1.505

State and local:

Arizona statistical abstract, general data, 1993 recurring rpt, U5850–2.7

Texas retired judges assigned to courts of appeals, with number of opinions written, by type, FY92, annual rpt, S7703–1

see also Civil service pensions

see also Individual retirement arrangements

see also Military benefits and pensions

see also Old-Age, Survivors, Disability, and Health Insurance

see also Pensions and pension funds

see also Railroad Retirement System

see also Retired military personnel

see also Retirement communities

see also State retirement systems

Retirement communities

State and local:

Arizona life care company finances, 1992, annual rpt, S0483–1

Florida adult congregate living facilities and beds, by district and county, 1992, annual rpt, S1746–1.2

Florida homes for the aging, residential units, by district and city, 1992, annual rpt, U6660–1.2

Retirement plans

see Pensions and pension funds

Reubi, Marie

"Current Award Trends in Personal Injury, 1993 Edition", C5180–1

Revenue sharing

Govt finances, including revenues by source, expenditures by function, and debt, detailed data for Federal, State, and local govts, 1993 annual rpt, R9050–1

State and local:

Arizona tax revenues by source, tax rates, and disbursements to local areas, FY92 and trends, annual rpt, S0515–1

Florida State govt disbursements to local areas, by source of funds, FY92, annual rpt, S1717–1

Indiana financial condition, including revenues by source, expenditures by function and object, and fund balances, by agency, FY92, annual rpt, S2570–1

Maryland local govt financial condition, including revenues by source, expenditures by function, and debt obligations, FY92 and trends, annual rpt, S3618–1.1

South Carolina county govt finances, including property value and tax assessments, by county, FY92, annual rpt, S7127–2

Texas financial condition, including revenues by source, expenditures by function and dept, and investments, with data for over 400 individual funds, FY92, annual rpt, S7655–2

Utah public lands by govt owner, and Federal land payments to State and local govts, with data by county, 1992 article, U8960–2.502

Wisconsin financial condition, including revenues by source, expenditures by function and object, and fund balances, FY93, annual rpt, S8675–2

see also State funding for local areas

Rheumatism

see Musculoskeletal diseases

Rhode Island

Banks and other financial instns (State-chartered), assets and liabilities by instn, 1991, annual rpt, S6945–1

Census of Population and Housing detailed findings, by county and municipality, 1990, S6930–9

Court cases and dispositions, by type of court and case, and county, 1987-91, annual rpt, S6965–1

Educational enrollment, grads, and finances, by district or community, 1991/92 or fall 1992, annual rpt, S6970–1

Employment, hours, and earnings, by industry, monthly rpt, S6980–1

Govt financial condition, including revenues by source, expenditures by function, and fund balances, FY92 and trends, annual rpt, S6930–1

Insurance industry financial and underwriting data, by company and line of coverage, 1990, with FY91 regulatory info, annual rpt, S6945–2

Jai alai games played, attendance, handle, and govt revenues, for 3 States, 1990, annual rpt, A3363–1.2

Labor force planning rpt, including population, employment by industry, job openings, and characteristics of insured unemployed, 1993 annual rpt, S6980–3

Markets with daily newspapers, demographic and economic info by geographic area, US and Canada, 1993 annual rpt, C3250–1

Medical malpractice insurance State joint underwriting assn (JUA) financial condition, for 11 States, 1991, annual rpt, A0375–1

Plastic waste and recycling, by resin and/or season, 1990 study, A4375–14
Statistical almanac of Rhode Island, economic, govtl, and social reference info and statistics, 1993 annual rpt, C7975–1
Statistical profiles of 50 States and DC, general data, 1993 annual almanac, C4712–1
Traffic accidents, fatalities, and injuries, by circumstances, community, and driver and victim characteristics, 1992, annual rpt, S7025–1
Utility and transportation regulatory agency activities, scope of jurisdiction, finances, and employees, by agency, 1991/92 annual rpt, A7015–2
Vital statistics, including population, births, deaths, marriages, and divorces, by demographic characteristics and locality, 1989 and trends, annual rpt, S6995–1
see also Pawtucket, R.I.
see also Providence, R.I.
see also under By City and By County in the "Index by Categories"
see also under By State in the "Index by Categories"

Rhodesia
see Zimbabwe

Rice
Exports of farm products, by detailed commodity and country of destination, US and California, 1991, annual rpt, B9520–1
Indonesia agricultural production trends and impacts of govt policies, for 5 major food crops, 1970s-80s, R5620–1.37
Japan rice production and consumption, 1980-92, article, R5650–2.556
Latin America statistical abstract, general data by country, 1992 annual rpt, U6250–1.24, U6250–1.25
Production, consumption, stocks, trade, and prices for approx 100 basic commodities, including by country and producing State, commodity yearbook for 1993, C2400–1, C2400–2

State and local:
Arkansas agricultural production, marketing, and finances, by commodity and county, with farms and acreage, 1992 and trends, annual rpt, U5920–1
California field crops production, acreage, yield, and prices, by commodity and county, 1992 and trends, annual rpt, S0850–1.4
Louisiana agricultural production, marketing, and finances, by commodity or parish, 1985-91, annual rpt, U2740–1
Missouri agricultural production, marketing, and finances, by commodity and/or county, and farms and acreage, 1988-92, annual rpt, S4480–1
Texas agricultural production, marketing, and finances, by commodity and county, and farms and farmland, 1991 and trends, annual rpt series, S7630–1

Richardson, Gary
"1992 Idaho Public Utilities Commission Annual Report", S2290–1

Rickettsioses
see Infective and parasitic diseases

Ries, Paula
"Summary Report, 1991: Doctorate Recipients from U.S. Universities", R6000–7

Rifles
see Firearms

Right of privacy
Higher education admissions dept keeping of records on subjective info about students, with impact of Education Dept privacy ruling, 1992, annual rpt, A6695–1
Public opinion on business use of personal info, including views on privacy, credit, and effects of computer use, 1992 survey and trends, annual rpt, B3280–2
Rape victim and service agency staff views on proposed privacy laws, including impact on rape reporting to police, 1990-92 surveys, R8375–1
Telephone subscriber privacy rights for conversations and records, by regulatory agency, 1991/92 annual rpt, A7015–3
see also Electronic surveillance

Right to counsel
see also Legal aid

Riots and disorders
Property insured losses in 10 most costly civil disorders, 1965-92, annual rpt, A5650–1.1
Public opinion on Los Angeles riots after Rodney King police brutality trial, Feb 1993 Gallup Poll, C4040–1.508
Public opinion on whether news items concerning 1992 Los Angeles riots encouraged participation in the riots, Apr/May 1993 survey, C8915–1.503
TV news coverage of Los Angeles riots following Rodney King police brutality case verdict, with source characteristics and detail by network, Apr-May 1992, article, R3823–1.506

State and local:
California, Los Angeles riots total insured and business establishment damages, 1992, article, C1200–5.502
Illinois crimes and arrests, by offense, with data by location and offender characteristics, 1991, annual rpt, S2536–1
Tennessee correctional instn incidents, including disturbances, assaults, and deaths, FY91-92, annual rpt, S7480–1

Ritchie, Sarah
"Credit Rating Changes: An Indicator of State Fiscal Stress", U5085–2.6
"State and Local Employment in the 1980s: How Did It Grow?", U5085–2.7

Rivers and waterways
Freight volume on 10 shallow draft waterways, 1989, U8850–9
Latin America statistical abstract, general data by country, 1992 annual rpt, U6250–1.1
Water quality indicators for selected rivers, 1992/93 biennial rpt, R9455–1.7

State and local:
Alabama waterborne freight traffic, by major river and commodity, 1992 recurring rpt, U5680–2.16
Hawaii data book, general data, 1992 annual rpt, S2090–1.5
Illinois statistical abstract, general data, 1992 annual rpt, U6910–2
Maryland statistical abstract, general data, 1993-94 biennial rpt, S3605–1.10
Oklahoma statistical abstract, general data, 1992 annual rpt, U8130–2.1
Pennsylvania statistical abstract, general data, 1992 recurring rpt, U4130–6.8

Tennessee statistical abstract, general data, 1992/93 annual rpt, U8710–2.9
see also Arkansas River
see also Bridges and tunnels
see also Canals
see also Chesapeake Bay
see also Colorado River
see also Dams
see also Floods
see also Gila River
see also Great Lakes
see also Harbors and ports
see also Lakes and lakeshores
see also Tennessee River
see also Water pollution
see also Water resources development
see also Water supply and use

Roads
see Highways, streets, and roads

Roback, Gene
"Physician Characteristics and Distribution in the U.S., 1993 Edition", A2200–3

Robbery and theft
Corporate info protection programs and attempted theft experience, 1992 feature, C1850–12.501
Home burglary prevention, and preferred entry method and time of day, views of incarcerated burglars, 1993 survey article, C1850–13.505
Retail store inventory shrinkage, and control measures, by type of outlet, 1991, annual survey rpt, C5150–4.504
State social, economic, and govtl indicators, with rankings, 1993 semiannual rpt, B8500–1.10
Supermarket employee theft value, 1989-91, article, C4655–1.502
Supermarket employees admitting they had eaten food without paying, stolen merchandise, and observed theft by coworkers, 1993 feature, C1850–12.502

State and local:
Alabama crimes and arrests, by offense, with data by location and offender characteristics, 1992 and trends, annual rpt, S0119–1
Arizona crimes and arrests, by offense, county, and offender characteristics, 1992, annual rpt, S0505–2
Arkansas crimes and arrests, by offense, victim and offender characteristics, and location, 1992 and trends, annual rpt, S0652–1
California crimes and arrests, clearances, and arrest dispositions, with data by offense and offender characteristics, 1987-92, annual rpt, S0910–1.1
California criminal justice system detailed data, by offense, county, age, race-ethnicity, and sex, 1991 and trends, annual rpt, S0910–2
Colorado crimes and arrests, by offense and location, with offender characteristics, and assaults on police, 1992, annual rpt, S1068–1
Connecticut crimes and arrests, by offense, with data by local agency, and victim-offender characteristics, 1992, annual rpt, S1256–1
DC criminal justice system summary, including crimes and arrests, criminal procedure, prisoners, and parole, 1991 and trends, annual rpt, S1535–2

Robbery and theft

Delaware crimes and arrests, by offense, county, and victim-offender characteristics, 1991 and trends, annual rpt, S1375–5

Florida crimes and arrests, by offense, with data by victim and offender characteristics, 1992, annual rpt, S1770–1

Georgia crimes and arrests, by offense, with data by location and offender characteristics, 1992 and trends, annual rpt, S1901–1

Hawaii crimes and arrests, by offense, with data by county and victim-offender characteristics, 1992, annual rpt, S2035–1

Idaho crimes and arrests, by offense, with data by location and offender characteristics, 1992 and trends, annual rpt, S2275–2

Illinois crimes and arrests, by offense, with data by location and offender characteristics, 1991, annual rpt, S2536–1

Kansas crimes and arrests, by offense, with data by location, agency, and victim-offender characteristics, 1992 and trends, annual rpt, S2925–1.1

Kentucky crimes and arrests, by offense, with data by location and offender characteristics, 1992, annual rpt, S3150–1

Maine crimes and arrests, by offense, with data by county, reporting agency, and offender age and sex, 1991, annual rpt, S3475–1

Maryland crimes and arrests, by offense, location, and offender characteristics, with law enforcement employment and assaults on officers, 1992 and trends, annual rpt, S3665–1

Michigan crimes and arrests, by offense, with data by location and offender characteristics, 1992 and trends, annual rpt, S3997–1

Missouri crimes and arrests, by offense and location, with victim and offender characteristics, 1991 and trends, annual rpt, S4560–2

Montana crimes and clearances, by offense and jurisdiction, 1992, annual rpt, S4705–1

Nevada statistical abstract, general data, 1992 biennial rpt, S5005–1.4

New Hampshire crimes and arrests, by offense, jurisdiction, and offender characteristics, 1991 and trends, annual rpt, S5250–2

New Jersey crimes and arrests, by offense, with data by location and offender characteristics, 1992 and trends, annual rpt, S5430–1

New York State crimes and arrests by offense and demographic characteristics, and court activity and corrections, 1991 and trends, annual rpt, S5760–3

North Carolina crimes and arrests, by offense, with data by location and offender characteristics, 1992 and trends, annual rpt, S5955–1

North Dakota crimes and arrests, by offense, location, and offender characteristics, and law enforcement employment, 1991 and trends, annual rpt, S6060–1

Oklahoma crimes and arrests, by offense, with data by local agency and victim and offender characteristics, 1990-92, annual rpt, S6465–1

Oregon crimes and arrests, by offense, with data by county, local agency, and offender characteristics, 1992 and trends, annual rpt, S6603–3

Pennsylvania crimes and arrests, by offense, with data by location and offender characteristics, 1992 and trends, annual rpt, S6860–1

Pennsylvania, suburban Philadelphia commercial burglary incidence correlated with alarm use and other precautions, 1989-91 study, article, C1850–13.506

South Carolina crimes and arrests, by offense, with data by location and victim-offender characteristics, and assaults on officers, 1992 and trends, annual rpt, S7205–1

Texas crimes and arrests, by offense, with data by location and offender characteristics, 1992 and trends, annual rpt, S7735–2

Utah crimes and arrests, by offense, county, and local agency, 1992 and trends, annual rpt, S7890–3

Virginia crimes and arrests, by offense, with data by location and offender characteristics, 1992, annual rpt, S8295–2

Washington State crimes and arrests, by offense, with data by location and offender characteristics, 1992 and trends, annual rpt, S8440–1

West Virginia crimes and arrests, by offense, location, and offender characteristics, 1990-91, annual rpt, S8610–1

Wisconsin crimes and arrests, by offense, offender characteristics, county, and local agency, 1992 and trends, annual rpt, S8771–1

Wyoming crimes and arrests, by offense, with data by location and victim and offender characteristics, 1991 and trends, annual rpt, S8867–3

see also Motor vehicle theft
see also Security devices
see also Shoplifting

Robotics

see Automation
see Industrial robots

Rochester, N.H.

Employment, hours, and earnings in Portsmouth-Dover-Rochester MSA, monthly rpt, S5205–1

Rocket fuel

see Missiles and rockets
see Synthetic fuels

Rockets

see Missiles and rockets

Roen, Olive

"Nurses in Texas: Nurse Aides to Advanced Nurse Practitioners, 1971-91", U8850–8.2

Romania

Energy intl sourcebook, with detail on oil and gas industry operations, supply-demand, and prices, for approx 80 countries, 1970s-91, annual compilation, C6985–10.2

Nuclear reactors in operation, with capacity, electricity generation, and construction, by unit and country, 1992, annual rpt, B6800–2.2

Index by Subjects and Names

Rooming and boarding houses

State and local:

Florida statistical abstract, general data, 1992 annual rpt, U6660–1.2

Utah, Salt Lake City single occupancy housing units and rates, by facility, 1992 annual rpt, S7808–2

Roper Organization

Business participation in activities involving local public school systems, 1993 feature, C4687–1.509

Cable TV viewer program interests, Mar 1993 survey, article, C2710–1.538

Journalist (TV and newspaper) concern for self-interest vs public interest, public opinion, Aug 1992 survey, A8605–1.505

Older population portrayal in advertising, public opinion by age group, Aug 1992 survey, articles, C2710–1.503

Public opinion on personal economic status, 1977, 1987, and 1992, article, C8900–1.505

Public opinion on uses for extra hour gained in time switch from daylight savings to standard, 1992 survey article, C5800–7.501

Rose, Kenneth

"Public Utility Commission Implementation of the Clean Air Act's Allowance Trading Program", A8195–12

Ross, John A.

"Family Planning and Child Survival Programs as Assessed in 1991", R8720–1

Ross, Marlene

"American College President: A 1993 Edition", A1410–12

ROTC

see Reserve Officers Training Corps

Roudi, Farzaneh

"Middle East Population Puzzle", R8750–2.59

Royalties

see Broadcast payments and rights
see Copyright
see Mineral leases
see Oil and gas leases
see Patents

Rubber and rubber industry

Chemical and related industries production, finances, operating ratios, employment, and trade, by country, company, and chemical, 1980s-92, annual feature, A1250–1.530

Corporate performance ratings by executives for leading companies in 32 industries, 1993 annual survey feature, C8900–1.508

Financial ratios and performance, for over 350 SIC 4-digit industries, FY88-92, annual rpt, A6400–3

Motor vehicle industry materials consumption, by type, 1980-93, annual rpt, A0865–1.2

Operating and financial composite ratios for corporations, with establishments and receipts, for approx 200 industries, by asset size, FY90, annual rpt, C7800–1

Production, consumption, stocks, trade, and prices for approx 100 basic commodities, including by country and producing State, commodity yearbook for 1993, C2400–1, C2400–2

Shoe industry production, employment, trade, marketing, and related data, by SIC 2- to 5-digit code or product type, 1992 annual rpt, A4957–1

Synthetic rubber consumption by type, for 4 world regions, 1992 and 1997, article, C5800–8.504

World supply-demand outlook for rubber, with synthetic rubber capacity and consumption by resin, 1980s-97, article, A1250–1.524

State and local:

Florida statistical abstract, general data, 1992 annual rpt, U6660–1.12

see also Tires and tire industry

see also under By Industry in the "Index by Categories"

Rubella

see Infective and parasitic diseases

Rugs

see Carpets and rugs

Runaways

see Missing persons and runaways

Runzheimer Intl.

Auto fleet operating characteristics in metro areas affected by Clean Air Act clean fuel requirements, 1993 article, C1575–2.512

Business travel costs trends, by type of expense, 1992-94, article, C1200–1.513

Gasoline (unleaded) price per gallon, 1972-92, C1575–2.506

Home prices for typical high-income homes in 29 metro areas, 1992, article, B8500–2.518

Rural areas

Business incubator facilities and services for new rural businesses, role of State extension programs at land-grant universities, 1992 survey rpt, U2410–3

China town-village enterprises export trends, and joint venture profile including foreign partner countries, 1992 article, A9315–1.501

Developing countries family planning availability, including distance to nearest clinic for rural women age 15-49, for 10 countries, 1987-91 surveys, U2520–1.51

Hospitals in rural areas, with detail for instns in multihospital systems, 1989, article, A1865–1.510

Hospitals in rural communities, with facilities and utilization data, 1982-90, annual fact book, A1275–1.2

Latin America statistical abstract, general data by country, 1992 annual rpt, U6250–1.5

Magazines (country lifestyle) started 1987-91, with number still published in 1992, article, C2575–1.503

Magazines (country lifestyle) subscribers, price, and reader age and income, for 7 publications, 1993 article, C2575–1.507

Population share in rural areas, with detail on farm population trends, by State, 1980-90, semiannual rpt, B8500–1.1

State economic dev condition disparity between urban and rural areas, by State, 1993 annual rpt, R4225–1

State and local:

Nevada health behavior risk factor surveillance survey results, by location and respondent characteristics, 1991, annual rpt, S5075–3

North Dakota 1-room rural schools, enrollment, and staff, 1992/93 annual directory, S6180–2

Oklahoma Index crimes by offense and property stolen, for rural areas, 1990-92, annual rpt, S6465–1.2

Texas births and deaths in rural areas and selected cities, by county, 1991, annual rpt, S7685–1

see also Farm income

see also Farm population

see also Farms and farmland

see also Federal aid to rural areas

see also Migrant workers

see also Rural cooperatives

see also Rural electrification

see also Soil pollution

see also Soils and soil conservation

see also under Agriculture and terms beginning with Agricultural

see also under By Urban-Rural and Metro-Nonmetro in the "Index by Categories"

Rural cooperatives

Southeastern States rural cooperatives, membership, and net business, for 6 States, 1985 and 1989, biennial rpt, U6730–1.4

Statistical yearbook of electric utility financial and operating data, by State and census div, 1991 and trends, annual rpt, A4700–1

Telephone local exchange carrier finances, equipment, and employment, by company, 1991 and trends, annual rpt, A9360–2

State and local:

Colorado rural electric and telephone cooperatives assessed property value, by company, 1991-92, annual rpt, S1055–3

Florida public utility regulatory and operating data, by company and utility type, 1992 and trends, annual rpt, S1790–1

Florida statistical abstract, general data, 1992 annual rpt, U6660–1.15

Montana rural cooperative taxes paid and property values, 1990-91 and trends, biennial rpt, S4750–1

New Mexico public utility operating, financial, and regulatory data, by utility type, FY92 annual rpt, S5645–1

Tennessee statistical abstract, general data, 1992/93 annual rpt, U8710–2.10

Vermont public utility financial and operating data, by company, 1986-91, biennial rpt, S8100–1

Wyoming rural electrification cooperatives taxable valuation, by county, 1992, annual rpt, S8990–1.2

see also Rural electrification

Rural Development Administration

Federal budget trends, including spending by program, State, and region, FY81-94, annual rpt, R8490–11

see also Farmers Home Administration

Rural electric cooperatives

see Rural cooperatives

see Rural electrification

Rural electrification

Statistical yearbook of electric utility financial and operating data, by State and census div, 1991 and trends, annual rpt, A4700–1

State and local:

Florida public utility regulatory and operating data, by company and utility type, 1992 and trends, annual rpt, S1790–1

Florida statistical abstract, general data, 1992 annual rpt, U6660–1.15

New Mexico public utility operating, financial, and regulatory data, by utility type, FY92 annual rpt, S5645–1

Tennessee statistical abstract, general data, 1992/93 annual rpt, U8710–2.10

Vermont public utility financial and operating data, by company, 1986-91, biennial rpt, S8100–1

Wyoming rural electrification cooperatives taxable valuation, by county, 1992, annual rpt, S8990–1.2

see also Rural cooperatives

see also Tennessee Valley Authority

Russia

Diamond production/marketing organizational structure for Russia and Sakha Province govt, 1993 article, C2150–7.502

Economic devs in Russia, monthly rpt, U2030–1

Electronics industry trade and/or production trends by product category for 33 countries, with general economic profiles, 1993 annual rpt, A4725–1.4

Intl aid to Russia by type under program proposed by Group of 7 (G-7) countries, and additional aid from 3 countries, 1993 article, R5650–2.524, R5650–2.530

Natural gas govt-owned company operations, with former Soviet Union supply-demand, foreign trade, and pipeline mileage by Republic, 1993 article, C6985–1.551

Nuclear reactors in operation, with capacity, electricity generation, and construction, by unit and country, 1992, annual rpt, B6800–2.2

Nuclear warhead allotments of US and Russia under strategic arms reduction treaties, 1990-93, annual rpt, C2500–2

Nuclear weapons plutonium and highly enriched uranium disposal requirements of US and Russia arms reductions, 1993 article, C5226–2.511

Oil (crude) deliveries from govt and free market sources, by production assn, 4th qtr 1992, article, C6985–1.506

Oil and gas industry devs, including foreign investment and supply-demand indicators, 1993 articles, C6985–1.540

Oil and gas production, and exports to Commonwealth of Independent States members and other countries, selected years 1990-2010, article, C6985–1.527

Oil industry ownership structure in Russia following Nov 1992 reorganization, 1992 article, C6985–1.507

Oil refined products demand, by product type, 1991, article, C6985–1.502

Population, with detail for far eastern areas and cities close to Alaska, 1990, annual rpt, S0320–4

Public opinion in Russia, Ukraine, and Lithuania on political and economic issues and devs, by respondent characteristics, 1991-92 surveys, C8915–10

Public opinion in US on news items concerning political situation in Russia, by respondent characteristics, 1993 surveys, C8915–1.503, C8915–1.505

Public opinion in US on news items concerning US-Russia nuclear arms reduction agreement, Jan 1993 survey, C8915–1.501

Russia

Public opinion in US on power struggle between Russian President Boris Yeltsin and Russian Congress, Mar 1993 Gallup Poll, C4040–1.509

Public opinion in US on selected foreign policy issues, with detail for 3 States, 1993 survey, annual rpt, A4965–1

Public opinion in 9 European countries and 3 Soviet Union Republics on political, economic, and social issues, 1991 survey, C8915–8

Pulp and paper mill production of bleached pulp and chlorine, by mill, 1990, article, C3975–2.504

Weapons production in Soviet Union or Russia, by weapon category, 1990-92, article, C5800–4.522

Ryan McGinn Samples Research Inc.

Coal industry executive views on industry devs and outlook, monthly rpt, C5226–1

Rye

see Grains and grain products

Sachs Group

Health care outpatient procedures likely to be performed in nonhospital settings, 1993 article, A1865–1.518

Physician visit volume forecast for HMOs vs indemnity insurance coverage, with detail by procedure, and industry or region, 1993 article, A1865–1.524

Safety

see Accidents and accident prevention *see* Aviation accidents and safety *see* Law enforcement *see* Marine accidents and safety *see* Mine accidents and safety *see* Motor vehicle safety devices *see* Occupational health and safety *see* Product safety *see* Railroad accidents and safety *see* State funding for public safety *see* Traffic accidents and safety

Sailing

see Boats and boating

Sailors

see Military personnel

Salaries

see Agricultural wages *see* Earnings, general *see* Earnings, specific industry *see* Educational employees pay *see* Federal pay *see* Government pay *see* Minimum wage *see* Payroll *see* State and local employees pay

Salem, Oreg.

Discount store ratings and shopping patterns of consumers in 3 market areas, including expenditures, by leading chain, 1992 surveys, article, C5150–3.503

Sales, business

see Business income and expenses, general *see* Business income and expenses, specific industry *see* Farm income

Sales finance companies

see Finance companies

Sales promotion

Airline frequent flier program characteristics and members, for 13 foreign carriers, 1993 article, C7000–4.508

Auto dealership service dept operations and profit outlook, and manager compensation, 1993 annual survey, article, C2710–3.537

Auto news and devs, with production and sales data and market analysis, US and foreign, by manufacturer and make/model, weekly rpt, C2710–3

Beverage sales promotion practices of soft drink bottlers and beer wholesalers, including discount deal characteristics, 1991, survey article, C0125–2.502

Book publishing industry financial and operating data, by publisher type and size, and subject category, 1991 and trends, annual rpt, A3274–2

Business gift-giving practices, including types of gifts and top 10 industry users, 1993 survey, annual article, C1200–4.508

Cereal coupon advertisement shares for top 5 companies, 1991/92, article, C2710–1.511

Cigarette advertisements containing coupons/other promotions, shares for 4 major and all other companies, 1991-92, article, C2710–1.536

Consumer complaint and inquiry activity of Better Business Burs concerning coupon book promotions, 1992, annual rpt, A4350–1

Coupon value issued for top 10 product categories, 1992, article, C1200–4.506

Coupons redeemed per household, in US, Canada, and 5 European countries, 1992, article, C2710–1.549

Diapers (disposable) couponed advertisement shares for top 3 and all other manufacturers, 1991/92, article, C2710–1.517

Direct marketing industry devs, including advertising patterns, finances, target market characteristics, and consumer attitudes, 1992/93 annual rpt, A4620–1

Effectiveness of 10 in-store merchandising techniques, for hardware, home center, and lumber stores, 1993 article, C4725–5.506

Food (take-out) consumer characteristics and attitudes, including importance of coupons to decision to use take-out services, May 1992 survey, A8200–21

Food promotion budgets for beef, pork, dairy, and fruits/vegetables organizations, 1993 article, C4655–1.509

Food store in-store marketing techniques effectiveness, retailer views, 1993 article, C2710–1.526

Incentive programs for consumers, employees, and dealers, with expenditures by industry and incentive type, 1991-92, annual feature, C1200–4.502

Incentive programs for consumers, salespeople, and dealers, issues and devs, monthly rpt, C1200–4

Incentive programs for consumers, with methods used and expenditures for top 10 industries, 1993 annual survey article, C1200–4.506

Incentive programs for dealers, with purpose, performance measures, and types of awards, 1993 and trends, annual survey article, C1200–4.505

Incentive programs for salespeople, with expenditures of top 10 user industries, 1993 survey, annual article, C1200–4.511

Incentive travel programs for sales promotion, with destinations, and expenditures of top 10 user industries, 1993 survey, annual article, C1200–4.510

Income for top sales promotion and promotional services agencies, 1991-92, annual feature, C2710–1.527

Jeweler advertising/promotion expenditures as percent of net sales, by store type, 1992, article, C2150–7.511

Jewelry retail business outlook, including staffing, merchandise selection criteria, and sales promotion, 1993, annual survey article, C2150–7.502

Liquor industry promotion laws, by State, 1992, annual rpt, C4775–1.2

Magazine promotion dept activities, and executive characteristics and salary, Nov 1992 survey, article, C2575–1.506

Military commissary coupon redemptions, by region, FY92, C0500–1.502

Military commissary coupon redemptions, by region, FY92, annual feature, A2072–2.501

Photofinishing promotion use by consumers, with detail by outlet type, 1993 survey, recurring rpt, A8695–2

Restaurant (quick-service) operations, including most popular menu items, and patron age, use of promotions, and views on smoking, 1992, article, A8200–1.509

Restaurant dessert operations and consumer ordering patterns, 1992 survey rpt, A8200–20

Restaurant patron coupon use, for 12 types of establishments with most frequent use, 1992, article, A8200–1.503

Sales and marketing mgmt, issues and devs, including product sales, demographic and socioeconomic profiles for major market areas, monthly rpt, C1200–1

Shopping center merchants promotional funds assessments for mgmt and tenants, US and Canada, 1991, triennial rpt, R9285–1

Snack food industry promotion/advertising activities and perceived effectiveness, 1991-92, annual rpt, A8905–1

Snack food types appearing most frequently in ads with coupons, 1992, article, C2710–1.523

Soft drink coupons issued by top 5 companies, 1991-92, article, C2710–1.532

Sunscreen promotional spending for 4 manufacturers, 1992-93, article, C2710–1.550

Supermarket bakery and deli shopper characteristics, including use of coupons, 1993 annual survey article, C5225–1.508

Supermarket bakery dept sales promotions, 1992, annual article, C4655–1.505, C5225–1.504

Supermarket deli dept merchandising techniques and advertising media use, 1992, annual article, C5225–1.505

Supermarket deli dept sales promotions, 1992, annual article, C4655–1.503

Supermarket general merchandise dept sales promotion media use, 1992, annual article, C4655–1.509

Supermarket health and beauty aid dept sales promotions, 1992, annual article, C4655–1.506

Index by Subjects and Names

Sales tax

Supermarket health/beauty aid merchandising practices, 1993 survey article, C5225–1.506

Supermarket industry views on vendor product pricing, including every day low price concept, 1992 survey article, C4655–1.501

Supermarket meat dept use of in-store sales promotions, and advertising media, 1992, annual article, C4655–1.509

Supermarket prepared food sales and performance indicators, 1992, annual article, C4655–1.508

Supermarket produce dept sales promotions, 1992, annual article, C4655–1.511

Supermarket sales promotion techniques, 1993 annual rpt, C5225–1.505

Supermarket seafood dept sales and performance indicators, 1992 annual survey feature, C4825–3.501

Supermarket shopper practices, attitudes, and expenditures, by respondent characteristics, 1993 and trends, annual survey rpt, A4950–3

Toothpaste promotional advertisements for 4 companies, 1st half 1992-93, article, C2710–1.540

Yogurt market shares, and number of coupons issued, for 2 leading brands and/or aggregate private labels, 1992-93, article, C2710–1.545

see also Advertising

see also Sales workers

Sales tax

Collections under current and/or initial budget-formulation estimates, by State, FY93-94, semiannual rpt, A7955–1

Govt finances, including revenues by source, expenditures by function, and debt, detailed data for Federal, State, and local govts, 1993 annual rpt, R9050–1

Household sales tax expenditures as a percent of annual and lifetime income, by income category, 1989, article, C8900–1.513

State social, economic, and govtl indicators, with rankings, 1993 semiannual rpt, B8500–1.4

State tax revenue from personal, corporate, and sales taxes, by State and region, quarterly rpt, U5085–1

State/local tax revenue shares, and comparison to personal income, for 3 major tax types, by State, FY91, article, B8500–2.511

Telecommunication services tax rates, by State, 1991/92 annual rpt, A7015–3

Tobacco products taxation, by State, 1950s-92, annual rpt, A9075–2

Trends in State, county, and city sales tax rates, 1981-92, C4687–1.503

State and local:

Alabama financial condition, including revenues by source, expenditures by function and object, and fund balances, by fund and agency, FY92, annual rpt, S0129–1

Alabama municipal data book, general data, 1992 recurring rpt, S0121–5

Alabama statistical abstract, general data, 1992 recurring rpt, U5680–2.6

Alaska State and local taxation, including taxes by type, property values, public debt, and tax shelters, by locale, 1992 and trends, annual rpt, S0285–1

Arizona net taxable sales and sales tax collected, by county and industry classification, FY92 and trends, annual rpt, S0515–1

Arizona statistical abstract, general data, 1993 recurring rpt, U5850–2.21

Arkansas financial condition, including revenues by source, expenditures by function and object, and fund balances, FY92, annual rpt, S0670–1

Arkansas local sales/use tax trust fund finances, FY91-92, biennial rpt, S0780–1

California economic condition, including population, employment and earnings, income, business activity, and taxation, 1960s-92, annual rpt, S0840–3.2

California financial condition, including revenues by source, expenditures by agency and function, fund balances, and bonded debt, FY92 and trends, annual rpt, S0815–1

California sales/use tax collections and permits, and tax revenue distributions to localities, FY92 and trends, annual rpt, S0835–1.3

Colorado tax revenues by type, with selected data by county and city, FY92 and trends, annual rpt, S1075–1

Connecticut financial condition, including revenues by source, expenditures by function, and bonded debt, FY92, annual rpt, S1170–1, S1170–2

DC financial condition, including receipts by source, expenditures by object or function, and fund balances, FY92, annual rpt, S1507–1

DC statistical profile, general data, 1992 annual rpt, S1535–3.2

Florida State govt disbursements to local areas, by source of funds, FY92, annual rpt, S1717–1

Florida statistical abstract, general data, 1992 annual rpt, U6660–1.23, U6660–1.24

Georgia tax revenues, by type and county, FY92 annual rpt, S1950–1

Hawaii tax collections and allocations, by type, for State and counties, FY91-92 and trends, annual rpt, S2120–1

Idaho tax statistics, including collections, and data by county and city, FY92 and trends, annual rpt, S2295–1

Illinois financial condition, including revenues by source, and expenditures by object, function, and agency, FY92, annual rpt, S2415–1

Iowa retail sales and use tax filings data, and establishments reporting, by county and city, and by kind of business, quarterly rpt, S2860–1

Kansas retail sales and tax activity trends, by urban-rural area and county, 1980-91, article, U7095–1.502

Kansas statistical abstract, general data, 1991/92 annual rpt, U7095–2.8

Kansas tax collections by tax type, and property values, with data by county, FY92 and trends, annual rpt, S3020–1

Kentucky financial condition, including revenues by source, expenditures by function and object, fund balances, and bonded debt, FY92, annual rpt, S3120–1

Maryland financial condition, including revenues by source, expenditures by function, fund balances, and bonded debt, FY92 and trends, annual rpt, S3685–2

Maryland sales and service tax rates, by commodity and county, FY92, annual rpt, S3618–1.2

Maryland statistical abstract, general data, 1993-94 biennial rpt, S3605–1.7

Massachusetts tax collections by type, and distributions to local areas, FY91 and trends, annual rpt, S3917–1

Michigan financial condition, including revenues by source, expenditures by function, and fund balances, FY92 and trends, annual rpt, S3985–2

Minnesota financial condition, including revenues by source, expenditures by function, fund balances, and bonded debt, FY92 and trends, annual rpt, S4180–1

Mississippi statistical abstract, general data, 1992 annual rpt, U3255–4.5

Mississippi tax collections by type, and disbursements, with selected sales and income tax data by locality and industry, FY92 and trends, annual rpt, S4435–1

Missouri financial condition, including fund finances, tax collections and distribution, and State treasury activity, FY92 and trends, annual rpt, S4570–1

Missouri school revenues from special sales and excise taxes, by county and district, 1991/92 and trends, annual rpt, S4505–1

Nebraska sales tax revenues and taxable sales, by county, city, and detailed industry, 1990-91, annual rpt, S4950–1.2

Nevada financial condition, including fund revenues by source, expenditures by function, and bonded debt, FY92, annual rpt, S5025–1

New York State tax collections by type, FY84-93, annual rpt, S5710–1

North Carolina financial condition, including revenues by source, expenditures by function, fund balances, and bonded debt, FY92, annual rpt, S5897–1

Ohio tax revenues and collections, by tax type, with distributions and property assessments by county, and corporate taxes by industry, FY92 annual rpt, S6390–1

Oklahoma sales tax rate change impact on taxable sales in 4 metro areas, 1992 article, U8130–1.501

Oklahoma statistical abstract, general data, 1992 annual rpt, U8130–2.5

Oklahoma tax revenues by source, and distribution to local govts and State funds, FY92 and trends, annual rpt, S6495–1

Oregon financial condition, including revenues by source, expenditures by function, and fund statements, FY92, annual rpt, S6603–2

Pennsylvania tax collections by tax type, with data by county and industry, FY92 and trends, annual rpt, S6885–1

South Carolina business establishments, sales, and sales/use tax collections, by county and/or city, FY92, annual rpt, S7255–1.3

South Carolina economic condition, including agriculture, finance, and govt financial data, 1970s-92, annual rpt, S7125–3.1

South Dakota gross sales/use tax purchases and taxable retail sales, by county and selected city, bimonthly rpt, U8595–2

South Dakota tax revenues by source, and aid distributed to local areas, FY92 annual rpt, S7380–1.1

Sales tax

Tennessee statistical abstract, general data, 1992/93 annual rpt, U8710–2.15

Tennessee tax revenues by source and apportionments to counties, cities, and funds, FY91-92 and trends, biennial rpt, S7570–1

Texas financial condition, including revenues by source, expenditures by function and dept, and investments, with data for over 400 individual funds, FY92, annual rpt, S7655–2

Utah business activity indicators, by county, 1988-91, annual feature, U8960–2.501

Utah business activity indicators, by county, 1989-92, annual feature, U8960–2.507

Utah govt statistical review, fiscal and socioeconomic data, 1993 annual rpt, R9380–1.6

Utah tax revenues by source, and distribution to localities and State funds, FY92 and trends, annual rpt, S7905–1

Vermont individual State income tax returns, and property and sales tax refunds, by income class and locality, 1991, annual rpt, S8125–1

Virginia educational finances by source and program, and local area revenue base, by county and municipality, 1991/92, annual rpt, S8190–3

Virginia tax revenues by type, including sales tax data by county and independent city, FY92 and trends, annual rpt, S8305–1.2

Washington State revenues by source, and distributions by tax and locality, FY92 and trends, annual rpt, S8415–1.1

Wisconsin financial condition, including revenues by source, expenditures by function and object, and fund balances, FY93, annual rpt, S8675–2

Wyoming sales and use tax revenue by industry div and/or retail sector, by county, FY81-92, annual rpt, S8855–1

Wyoming tax revenues and distributions, by type of tax, FY92 and trends, annual rpt, S8990–1.3

see also Excise tax

see also Fuel tax

Sales workers

Bank small business loan sales and underwriting staff incentive compensation practices, Nov 1992 survey, annual rpt, A4160–5

Compensation averages for 7 sales and marketing executive positions, 1993 survey article, C4300–1.503

Compensation methods used for sales workers, by company revenue size, 1992 article, C4687–1.504

Composition of sales employment, by sex and race-ethnicity, 1990, article, C1200–1.512

Corporate sales executives ratings of sales forces, by industry sector and sales function, 1993 annual survey article, C1200–1.512

Food store sales representatives and manufacturer services, views of industry personnel, 1993 annual rpt, C5225–1.505

Homebuilder sales force composition, and compensation methods, by region and sales size group, 1992 survey, article, C4300–1.501

Homebuilder sales worker compensation plans used, 1993 survey article, C4300–1.509

Hours devoted to selected tasks by sales workers in typical week, 1993 feature, C4687–1.509

Incentive programs for consumers, employees, and dealers, with expenditures by industry and incentive type, 1991-92, annual feature, C1200–4.502

Incentive programs for salespeople, with expenditures of top 10 user industries, 1993 survey, annual article, C1200–4.511

Incentive travel programs for sales promotion, with destinations, and expenditures of top 10 user industries, 1993 survey, annual article, C1200–4.510

Incentives provided to sales workers for selected tasks, and perceived importance of each task, 1993 survey article, C4687–1.510

Job skills considered most important by sales professionals, 1993 survey article, C1200–1.505

Job skills considered most important for long-term success by small corporation sales personnel, 1992 survey article, C4687–1.502

Magazine compensation of ad sales personnel, by region, sex, age, and publication characteristics, 1993 survey, annual article, C2575–1.516

Plastics processing industry sales representative compensation and allowance policies, 1992 survey, biennial rpt, A8920–3

Productivity plateaus, sales manager views on incidence by age group, reasons, and solutions, 1993 survey article, C1200–1.509

Real estate residential brokerage firm finances and operations, with data by region and company size, 1990/91 and trends, article, A7000–1.502

Recruitment practices for sales professionals, including selection criteria and sources of best candidates, 1993 survey, article, C1200–1.510

Selling costs, including personnel compensation and training, and travel and related expenses, 1992 and trends, annual survey, C1200–1.508

Textbook (college) sales workers, with turnover and compensation data, 1988-91, annual rpt, A3274–2

Training duration and costs for new sales personnel, by company revenue size, 1990 and 1992, C4687–1.506

TV station personnel and compensation, by position, and benefits, 1991, biennial rpt, A6635–9

Wholesaler/distributor inside vs outside sales staff share of sales and allocation of time, with projections to 2000, 1993 article, C4725–5.506

State and local:

Arizona occupational profiles, with employment and job outlook, by industry div, occupation, and county, series, S0465–2

Maine employment, by SIC 2-digit industry and detailed occupation, triennial series, S3465–1

New Hampshire employment, by SIC 2- and 3-digit industry and detailed occupation, series, S5205–2

North Carolina employment in SIC 2-digit industries, by detailed occupation, triennial rpt series, S5917–5

Texas employment, by SIC 2- and 3-digit industry and detailed occupation, series, S7675–1

see also Employment and unemployment, specific industry

see also under By Occupation in the "Index by Categories"

Salmonella

see Food and waterborne diseases

Solomon Bros. Inc.

Bond market value in top 7 foreign countries, 1st half 1993, A8825–2.503

Corporate bond issues and value, for financial instns, industrial companies, and utilities, 1992, article, C2710–2.507

Oil exploration/production expenditures of US and foreign companies in US, Canada, and elsewhere, 1992-93, annual article, C6985–1.515

Oil exploration/production spending plans in US, Canada, and elsewhere, Dec 1992 and June 1993, article, C6985–1.538

Securities (Govt) return rates, for fixed-income US instruments in US and 5 foreign countries, Dec 1984-Sept 1992, A8825–2.501

Salt

see Nonmetallic minerals and mines

Salt Lake City, Utah

Air traffic, passengers, and cargo through Salt Lake City Intl Airport, 1950-92, annual rpt, R9380–1.10

Housing single occupancy units and rates in Salt Lake City, by facility, 1992 annual rpt, S7808–2

Statistical abstract of Utah, detailed social, govtl, and economic data, 1993 triennial rpt, U8960–1

see also under By City in the "Index by Categories"

Salt Lake County, Utah

Homeless shelter capacity and population characteristics for Utah, with detail for selected counties, 1991-92, annual rpt, S7808–2

Salvage

Financial ratios and performance, for over 350 SIC 4-digit industries, FY88-92, annual rpt, A6400–3

Motor vehicle scrappage rates after 10 years, for 1966, 1971, 1976, and 1981 model year vehicles, article, C2710–3.537

Motor vehicles in use, newly registered, and scrapped, 1947-92, annual rpt, C7715–2

Motor vehicles retired from use, 1957-92, annual rpt, A0865–1.2

Vehicles in use by age, new vehicle registrations, and scrappage, 1992 and trends, annual rpt, A7330–1

see also Recycling of waste materials

see also Scrap metals

Samoa

see American Samoa

Samuels, Barbara N.

"Public Health System in Texas", U8850–8.6

San Diego, Calif.

Housing costs attributable to govt regulations and fees, and impact on households eligible to purchase homes, for 2 local areas, 1993 article, C4300–1.510

Statistical abstract of California, detailed social, govtl, and economic data, 1992 annual rpt, S0840–2

Index by Subjects and Names

see also under By City in the "Index by Categories"

San Francisco, Calif.

CPI for California and 2 major cities, bimonthly rpt, S0840–1

Engineers salaries by industry group, census div, selected metro area, and years since college degree, 1993, annual survey rpt, A0685–5

Engineers salaries by industry group, census div, selected metro area, degree level, and years since college degree, 1993, annual survey rpt, A0685–3

Statistical abstract of California, detailed social, govtl, and economic data, 1992 annual rpt, S0840–2

see also under By City in the "Index by Categories"

Sand and gravel

see Stone products and quarries

Sanders, Welford

"Planning Commission: Its Composition and Function, 1987", A2615–2

Sanitary districts

see Special districts

Sanitary engineering

see Plumbing and heating

see Refuse and refuse disposal

see Sewage and wastewater systems

Santa Fe, N.Mex.

Business and economic activity indicators for New Mexico, monthly rpt, U7980–1

Employment by labor market area and industry, monthly rpt, S5624–2

Saskatchewan Province, Canada

Uranium industry employment, finances, and labor productivity with comparison to Ontario, 1993 article, B6800–1.506

Satellites

Revenue outlook for satellites from TV, business, and telephone industry, by world region, 1992-98, article, C1850–14.529

World civil satellite launches, by launch vehicle, 1991-92, article, C5800–4.513

World launchings of spacecraft attaining orbit, by country, with US space program devs, 1991 and trends, annual rpt, A0250–2.2

World space flight devs and records, with launches and orbiting equipment by country, and detail for US programs, 1992 and trends, annual rpt, B9170–1

see also Communications satellites

see also Space programs

Saudi Arabia

Energy intl sourcebook, with detail on oil and gas industry operations, supply-demand, and prices, for approx 80 countries, 1970s-91, annual compilation, C6985–10.2

Higher education physical plant operations, costs, employment, salaries, and energy use, by instn and region, 1991/92, recurring rpt, A3183–1

Oil refining network organization, including refinery capacities and foreign ownership shares, 1993 article, C6985–1.542

Respiratory problems reported by US military personnel stationed in Saudi Arabia, with detail by sleeping accommodations, 1990/91 study, article, A2623–1.511

see also Organization of Petroleum Exporting Countries

see also under By Foreign Country or World Area in the "Index by Categories"

Savannah, Ga.

Statistical abstract of Georgia, detailed social, govtl, and economic data, 1992-93 biennial rpt, U6730–1

see also under By City in the "Index by Categories"

Savings

Children's incidence of saving for college and auto, Dec 1992-Jan 1993 survey, article, C2710–1.531

College freshmen attitudes and characteristics, degree and career plans, and financial aid sources, by sex and instn type, fall 1992, annual survey, U6215–1

Deposits and instns in daily newspaper markets in US and Canada, 1993 annual rpt, C3250–1

Forecasts of economic indicators for approx 10-13 months, monthly rpt, U1880–3

Forecasts of natl income and product account components and related indicators, quarterly rpt, U1880–1

Forecasts of natl income and product account components, employment, and financial sector activity, monthly rpt, B4950–1

GDP savings and investment component shares for US and 5 other countries, 1973-90, A1310–2.2

Germany (West) and US comparative socioeconomic statistics, 1970s-91, annual rpt, A5135–2.2

Japan consumer credit by type, with debt vs disposable income and savings, and comparisons to US, 1970s-92, article, R5650–2.542

Japan personal savings rate, with comparisons to US, Germany, and OECD, 1989-92, article, R5650–2.546

Natl trends in savings and investment by sector, and household assets and liabilities, 1960s-92, annual rpt, R9050–1.2

Pension benefit lump sum payments disposition, including placement in savings by type, by recipient characteristics, 1980s, R9260–17

Productivity and related indicators, trend analysis for US and other industrial countries, 1980s-92, annual rpt, R2800–2

State and local:

Arkansas State funds on deposit in banks and savings and loan assns, by type and instn, FY92, biennial rpt, S0780–1

California economic condition, including population, employment and earnings, income, business activity, and taxation, 1960s-92, annual rpt, S0840–3.2

Colorado banks and trust companies, financial condition by instn, 1992, annual rpt, S1070–2

Colorado savings and loan assn and credit union financial condition, 1992 and trends, annual rpt, S1070–3

Connecticut banks and other financial instns, financial condition by instn, 1991 and trends, annual rpt, S1160–1

Hawaii data book, general data, 1992 annual rpt, S2090–1.15

Idaho banks and other financial instns, financial condition, with data by instn and loan activity analysis, FY92 or 1991, annual rpt, S2235–1

Illinois Financial Institutions Dept activities, with financial and regulatory data for credit unions, consumer lenders, and other businesses, FY91 annual rpt, S2457–2

Indiana financial instns (State-chartered) financial condition, including assets by instn arranged by city, 1991 and trends, annual rpt, S2625–1

Kansas savings and loan assn deposits, quarterly rpt, U7095–1

Louisiana financial instns (State-chartered), financial condition by instn arranged by city, with regulatory info, Dec 1992, annual rpt, S3265–1

Michigan banks and other financial instns, financial condition by instn, with regulatory info, 1992 and trends, annual rpt, S3957–1

Mississippi statistical abstract, general data, 1992 annual rpt, U3255–4.14

New Jersey banks and other financial instns, assets and liabilities by instn, 1992 and trends, annual rpt, S5355–1

New Mexico financial instns, financial and operating data by instn, with regulatory activities, 1992, annual rpt, S5652–1

New Mexico savings and loan assn assets and deposits, monthly business activity rpt, U7980–1

New York State savings in savings banks, quarterly rpt, S5735–2

New York State statistical yearbook, general data, 1992 annual rpt, U5100–1.7

Oklahoma financial instns (State-chartered) assets and liabilities, by type of instn, with regulatory data, FY92 annual rpt, S6415–1

Oregon financial instns, financial condition by instn, Dec 1992 and trends, annual rpt, S6616–1

Rhode Island banks and other financial instns (State-chartered), assets and liabilities, by instn, 1991, annual rpt, S6945–1

South Carolina economic condition, including agriculture, finance, and govt financial data, 1970s-92, annual rpt, S7125–3.1

South Carolina financial instns (State-chartered) financial condition, including data by instn, FY92 annual rpt, S7165–1

Utah banks and other financial instns, financial condition by instn, FY93 and trends, annual rpt, S7830–1

Utah savings in savings and loan assns, monthly business activity rpt, U8960–2

Utah statistical abstract, general data, 1993 triennial rpt, U8960–1.15

Vermont banks and other financial instns, financial condition by instn, 1992 and trends, annual rpt, S7995–2

Virginia financial instns (State-chartered), financial condition by instn and instn type, Dec 1992, annual rpt, S8180–2

Wisconsin savings and loan assns and savings banks (State-chartered) financial condition, by instn, 1992 and trends, annual rpt, S8807–1

see also Bank deposits

see also Certificates of deposit

see also Deposit insurance

see also Individual retirement arrangements

see also Negotiable orders of withdrawal accounts

Savings bonds

Savings bonds
see U.S. savings bonds

Savings institutions
Black-owned enterprises financial and operating data, for top 100 firms and auto dealerships and for top 15-25 financial instns, 1992 and trends, annual feature, C4215–1.507

Corporate performance ratings by executives for leading companies in 32 industries, 1993 annual survey feature, C8900–1.508

Deposits of savings instns affiliated with 5 major finance companies, Dec 1991, R4700–22

Economic issues and devs affecting savings instns, with quarterly data on financial condition by instn type and State, monthly rpt, A8813–1

Establishments and deposits of savings instns in daily newspaper markets in US and Canada, 1993 annual rpt, C3250–1

Financial performance and growth rankings for approx 1,000 top corporations, with comparisons by industry group, 1993 annual rpt, C3950–1.505

Fortune magazine ranking of top 50-100 companies in 8 nonindustrial sectors, with financial and employment data, 1992, annual feature, C8900–1.516

Fortune magazine ranking of top 50-100 companies worldwide in 8 nonindustrial sectors, with financial and employment data, 1993 annual feature, C8900–1.522

Home equity lending activity and practices of financial instns, by region, asset size, and instn type, 1992, annual rpt, A4160–3

Life insurance operating summary for fraternal benefit societies and savings banks, 1986-91, biennial fact book, A1325–1.7

Operating and financial composite ratios for corporations, with establishments and receipts, for approx 200 industries, by asset size, FY90, annual rpt, C7800–1

Statistical profiles of 50 States and DC, general data, 1993 annual almanac, C4712–1

State and local:

Alaska bank assets and liabilities of individual commercial and savings instns, quarterly rpt, S0280–2

Arizona savings and loan assn balance sheets and branches, individual State and natl instns, quarterly rpt, S0460–1

Arizona statistical abstract, general data, 1993 recurring rpt, U5850–2.22

California economic condition, including population, employment and earnings, income, business activity, and taxation, 1960s-92, annual rpt, S0840–3.2

Colorado savings and loan assn and credit union financial condition, 1992 and trends, annual rpt, S1070–3

Connecticut banks and other financial instns, financial condition by instn, 1991 and trends, annual rpt, S1160–1

Hawaii data book, general data, 1992 annual rpt, S2090–1.15

Idaho banks and other financial instns, financial condition, with data by instn and loan activity analysis, FY92 or 1991, annual rpt, S2235–1

Indiana financial instns (State-chartered) financial condition, including assets by instn arranged by city, 1991 and trends, annual rpt, S2625–1

Kansas statistical abstract, general data, 1991/92 annual rpt, U7095–2.10

Kentucky financial instns condition, including assets by instn and city, with regulatory info, 1992 and trends, annual rpt, S3121–1

Louisiana financial instns (State-chartered), financial condition by instn arranged by city, with regulatory info, Dec 1992, annual rpt, S3265–1

Maine banks and other financial instns, financial condition by instn, June 1992, annual rpt, S3473–2

Maine financial instn assets, deposits, and loans, by type of instn and county, 1982-92, annual rpt, S3473–1

Michigan banks and other financial instns, financial condition by instn, with regulatory info, 1992 and trends, annual rpt, S3957–1

Minnesota financial instns (State-regulated), financial condition by instn, 1991-92, annual rpt, S4140–3

Mississippi statistical abstract, general data, 1992 annual rpt, U3255–4.14

New Jersey banks and other financial instns, assets and liabilities by instn, 1992 and trends, annual rpt, S5355–1

New Mexico financial instns, financial and operating data by instn, with regulatory activities, 1992, annual rpt, S5652–1

New Mexico savings and loan assn assets and deposits, monthly business activity rpt, U7980–1

Oklahoma financial instns (State-chartered) assets and liabilities, by type of instn, with regulatory data, FY92 annual rpt, S6415–1

Oklahoma statistical abstract, general data, 1992 annual rpt, U8130–2.20

Oregon financial instns, financial condition by instn, Dec 1992 and trends, annual rpt, S6616–1

Pennsylvania statistical abstract, general data, 1992 recurring rpt, U4130–6.2

Rhode Island banks and other financial instns (State-chartered), assets and liabilities, by instn, 1991, annual rpt, S6945–1

Rhode Island statistical almanac, general data, 1993 annual rpt, C7975–1.1

South Carolina economic condition, including agriculture, finance, and govt financial data, 1970s-92, annual rpt, S7125–3.1

South Carolina financial instns (State-chartered) financial condition, including data by instn, FY92 annual rpt, S7165–1

Utah banks and other financial instns, financial condition by instn, FY93 and trends, annual rpt, S7830–1

Utah statistical abstract, general data, 1993 triennial rpt, U8960–1.15

Vermont banks and other financial instns, financial condition by instn, 1992 and trends, annual rpt, S7995–2

Virginia financial instns (State-chartered), financial condition by instn and instn type, Dec 1992, annual rpt, S8180–2

Washington State banks and other financial instns, financial condition by type of instn, 1992 and trends, annual rpt, S8325–1

West Virginia banks and other financial instns, composite financial condition, with selected data by instn, 1990-91, annual rpt, S8530–1

Wisconsin savings and loan assns and savings banks (State-chartered) financial condition, by instn, 1992 and trends, annual rpt, S8807–1

see also Negotiable orders of withdrawal accounts

see also Savings

Savings insurance
see Deposit insurance

SBA
see Small Business Administration

Scammon, Richard M.
"America Votes 20: A Handbook of Contemporary American Election Statistics", C2500–1

Scandinavia
see Europe
see under names of specific countries

Schafer, Todd
"Still Neglecting Public Investment: The FY94 Budget Outlook", R4700–23

Scheetz, L. Patrick
"Recruiting Trends, 1992-93: A Study of Businesses, Industries, and Governmental Agencies Employing New College Graduates", U3130–1

Schell, Steven D.
"Where Have All the Dollars Gone? Regional Patterns in Entitlement Spending", R8490–47

Schlesinger, Tom
"Parallel Banking System", R4700–22

Scholarships
see Student aid

Scholastic Aptitude Test
see Educational tests

Schonfeld and Associates
Advertising expenditures as percents of sales and profits, by SIC 4-digit industry, 1993, annual article, C2710–1.537

School administration and staff
Bus driver training period and fingerprint background check requirements, 1993 annual article, C1575–1.504

Catholic secondary school lay principals, by enrollment size and region, 1985/86-1991/92, biennial rpt, A7375–5

Community and junior college staff by function, FY92, annual rpt, A6705–1

Dental advanced education program directors by full-time and certification status, 1992/93 annual rpt, A1475–10

Dental school faculty, support personnel, and staff characteristics, by instn, 1992/93, annual rpt, A1475–4.5

Elementary/secondary public school principals, teachers, and other staff, 1919/20-1990/91, R4800–2.518

Elementary/secondary school principals and assistant principals by previous position, 1966, 1981, and 1992, R4800–2.511

Elementary/secondary school principals and superintendents, 1992 recurring rpt, A3960–2.2

Higher education admissions dept activity, including trends in applications received, recruitment, staff, and budgets, 1992-93, annual rpt, A6695–1

Higher education employment, by position type and race-ethnicity, 1991/92, C2175–1.507

Index by Subjects and Names

School administration and staff

Higher education employment, by position type, 1989/90 and 1991/92, recurring article, C2175–1.504

Higher education instn administrators turnover rate by position, for public and private instns by type, 1984/85-1991/92, C2175–1.508

Higher education instn employee retirement and insurance benefits, prevalence and expenditures, by type of instn and region, 1991, biennial survey, A9025–3

Higher education instn policies and practices, including changes in faculty, enrollment, and finances, 1993 annual survey, A1410–1.38

Higher education instn presidents turnover rate, for public and private instns by type, 1984/85-1991/92, C2175–1.504

Higher education physical plant operations, costs, employment, salaries, and energy use, by instn and region, 1991/92, recurring rpt, A3183–1

Higher education president personal and professional characteristics, 1990 and trends, recurring rpt, A1410–12

Higher education president personal and professional characteristics, 1990, article, C2175–1.533

Higher education, 2-year college enrollment, degrees, faculty and staff, and tuition/fees, by instn and State, 1992 annual directory, A0640–1

Law school enrollment by minority status, degrees conferred, staff, and library holdings, by instn, 1992/93 and trends, annual rpt, A0970–1

Law school grad employment and salaries, by type of employer, location, and grad characteristics, 1992 and trends, annual rpt, A6505–1

Library (research) holdings, expenditures by type, and staff, for 120 academic and nonacademic instns, US and Canada, FY92, annual rpt, A3365–1

Library (research) holdings, staff, and expenditures, for instns in US and Canada, 1991/92, annual feature, C2175–1.511

Library/info science school enrollment, staff and student characteristics, finances, and curricula, by school and degree program, 1991/92, annual rpt, A3235–1

Medical school medicine dept chairmen article publishing activity, 1979-90, article, A3273–8.510

Medical school revenues by source, student aid, and staff, by instn type, 1989/90 and/or 1990/91, article, A3273–8.503

Nursing college deans and salaries, by personal and instn characteristics, 1992/93, annual rpt, A0615–2

Nursing schools, programs, enrollment, student and staff characteristics, and grads, 1991 and trends, annual rpt, A8010–1

Optometry school library staff, by instn, 1991/92, annual survey, A3370–2

Planning profession employment and salaries, by type of employer, demographic and professional characteristics, and location, 1991 and trends, biennial rpt, A2615–1

Principal career plans for near future, 1966, 1981, and 1992, R4800–2.514

Private elementary and secondary school enrollment, staff, and finances, with detail for minorities, by school type and region, 1980s-1992/93, annual rpt, A6835–3

Salary and job offers for college grads, by field of study, type of employer, and degree level, by region, interim rpt series, A3940–1

Salary and job offers for college grads, by field of study, type of employer, and degree level, series, A3940–2

Southern States higher education faculty and administrator characteristics and salaries, by instn type, 1990s and trends, biennial fact book, A8945–1.5

State social, economic, and govtl indicators, with rankings, 1993 semiannual rpt, B8500–1.7

Superintendents personal and professional characteristics and views, 1992 survey rpt, A0775–5

Theological school enrollment, staff and compensation, and finances, with data by instn, 1991/92 and trends, annual rpt, A3376–1

Urban public school performance compared to natl goals for year 2000, with data on students, teachers, and finances, for 47 systems, 1990/91 and trends, A4425–4

Women college presidents, by type of instn and race-ethnicity, 1970s-91, recurring rpt, A3960–2.2

Women elected officials, including State school superintendents, by State, 1993, recurring rpt, U4510–1.62, U4510–1.73

State and local:

Alabama public school teacher, principal, and other staff positions, by school district, 1991/92, annual rpt, S0124–1.2

Alaska public schools, enrollment, staff, and finances, by district, FY92, annual rpt, S0295–2

Alaska school teachers and admin personnel, FY92 annual rpt, S0275–1

Arizona elementary and secondary school enrollment, staff, and finances, by school district and county, FY92 and trends, annual rpt, S0470–1

Arkansas public school staff, by sex and position, 1990/91-1991/92, annual rpt, S0660–1.2

California library finances, staff, holdings, and services, by library type and facility, FY92, annual rpt, S0825–2

California private school administrators and teachers, 1987/88-1992/93, annual rpt, S0825–8

California public school enrollment, grads, and staff, by race-ethnicity, 1992/93 and trends, annual rpt, S0825–9

California statistical abstract, general data, 1992 annual rpt, S0840–2.6

Colorado election results for school board members and university regents, by district and county, 1992, biennial rpt, S1090–1

Colorado public school staff and salaries, by selected characteristics, county, and district, fall 1992 and trends, annual rpt, S1000–2.2

Connecticut public school data, including enrollment, staff, programs, finances, and student characteristics, 1991/92, biennial rpt, S1185–3

Delaware school enrollment, grads, staff, finances, and facilities, by county, school district, and/or instn, 1991/92, annual rpt, S1430–1

Florida higher education enrollment, degree programs, staff, and finances, by State-supported instn, with student and staff characteristics, 1991/92 annual rpt, S1725–1

Georgia county guide, general data, 1993 annual rpt, U6750–1

Georgia State constitutional amendment on selection of school boards and superintendents, election results by county, Nov 1992, biennial rpt, S1955–1

Georgia statistical abstract, general data, 1992-93 biennial rpt, U6730–1.2

Hawaii data book, general data, 1992 annual rpt, S2090–1.3

Idaho academic library staff, expenditures, and holdings, by instn, 1992, annual feature, A5370–1

Idaho public school personnel characteristics and salaries by position, and teachers and enrollment by school district, 1992/93, annual rpt, S2225–3

Idaho school administrators, teachers, and other staff, FY91-92, annual rpt, S2225–2

Illinois election results for university trustees and regional school superintendents, by county, 1992, biennial rpt, S2445–1

Illinois elementary and secondary school staff, by sex and county, with data on certification, 1990/91, annual rpt, S2440–1.2

Illinois higher education staff, salaries, student cost and aid, and finances, by instn, 1993 annual rpt, S2475–1.2

Indiana election results for State superintendent of public instruction, by county, 1992, biennial rpt, S2702–1

Iowa postsecondary enrollment, degrees, staff, and finances, by instn, 1990/91, annual rpt, S2755–1

Kansas school enrollment, grads, staff, and finances, by county, school district, and/or school, 1990/91, annual rpt, S2945–1

Kentucky election results for superintendent of public instruction, by county, 1991, annual rpt, S3213–1

Kentucky higher education enrollment, degrees, staff, and finances, by State-supported instn, 1983-92, annual rpt, S3130–3

Kentucky public school finances, staff, and enrollment, by district, 1989/90-1990/91, biennial rpt, S3110–2

Louisiana elementary/secondary school operations, including enrollment, staff, finances, and detail by school district, 1991/92 and trends, annual rpt, S3280–1

Maine educational services employment, by detailed occupation, Apr 1991, triennial survey, S3465–1.26

Maryland elementary and secondary education data, by county, Oct 1992, annual rpt, S3610–2.12

Maryland elementary and secondary education data, by county, 1992/93, annual rpt, S3610–2.8, S3610–2.10

Maryland elementary and secondary education statistical summary, with data by county, 1991/92-1992/93 and trends, annual rpt, S3610–1

School administration and staff

Maryland statistical abstract, general data, 1993-94 biennial rpt, S3605–1.4

Massachusetts public elementary/secondary education summary data, 1989/90-1991/92 and trends, annual rpt, S3810–3

Michigan election results for State university officials, by county, 1992 general election, biennial rpt, S4020–1

Minnesota public school enrollment, staff, and finances, by district and county, 1991/92 and trends, annual rpt, S4165–1

Mississippi public school enrollment, staff and salaries, and finances, by district, 1991/92 and trends, annual rpt, S4340–1

Missouri higher education employees by occupational category, by instn, fall 1992, annual rpt, S4520–3.3

Missouri public, special, and academic libraries, finances, holdings, circulation, staff, and services, by location, FY92, annual rpt, S4520–2

Missouri school finances, enrollment, grads, and staff, by county and school district, 1991/92, annual rpt, S4505–1

Nebraska election results for higher education officials, by county, 1992 primary and general elections, biennial rpt, S4955–1

Nebraska elementary and secondary schools, enrollment by grade, and staff, with data by school district and county, annual series, S4865–2

Nevada election results for higher education officials, by county, 1992, biennial rpt, S5125–1

New Hampshire govt and education employment by detailed occupation, 1991 or 1992, triennial rpt, S5205–2.25

New Jersey public school teachers, administrators, staff, and salaries, by county, 1991/92, annual rpt, S5385–1.2

North Carolina employment in trade, transportation, communications, utilities, govt, and education, by detailed occupation, 2nd qtr 1991, triennial rpt, S5917–5.2

North Carolina public school enrollment, grads, staff, and finances, with data by race, sex, and local district, 1991/92-1992/93 and trends, annual rpt, S5915–1

North Dakota elementary and secondary school staff characteristics and salaries, by position, region, and enrollment size, 1992/93 annual rpt, S6180–3

North Dakota elementary and secondary schools, enrollment, and staff, by school type and location, 1992/93 annual directory, S6180–2

Ohio public, academic, and other library finances, holdings, and staff, by library and location, 1992 and trends, annual rpt, S6320–1

Ohio public school staff experience and education data, 1991/92 and trends, annual rpt, S6265–2

Oregon elementary and secondary public school personnel by position, by county, Oct 1991, annual rpt, S6590–1.2

Pennsylvania elementary/secondary and higher education enrollment, grads, staff, and finances, by instn type, 1981/82-1996/97, recurring rpt, S6790–5.10

Pennsylvania public school personnel and salary data, by position and district, 1992/93 and trends, annual rpt, S6790–5.12

South Carolina educational employees and training, by school district, 1991/92, annual rpt, S7145–1.4

South Carolina higher education enrollment, degrees, staff, and finances, by instn, 1992 and trends, annual rpt, S7185–2

South Dakota public higher education finances, staff, enrollment, degrees, and facilities, by instn, FY93 annual rpt, S7375–1

South Dakota school enrollment, finances, grads, and staff, by district, 1991/92 and trends, annual rpt, S7315–1

Tennessee public school staff, by position, county, city, and school district, 1991/92 annual rpt, S7490–2.1

Tennessee statistical abstract, general data, 1992/93 annual rpt, U8710–2.16

Texas educational employment, by SIC 3-digit industry and detailed occupation, Apr 1991, triennial survey rpt, S7675–1.28

Texas elementary/secondary education personnel and salaries, by district and county, 1991/92, annual rpt, S7670–1.4

Texas elementary/secondary education personnel, by sex and race-ethnicity, by district and county, 1991/92, annual rpt, S7670–1.3

Utah higher education degrees, enrollment, staff, and finances, by public instn, with selected comparisons to instns in other States, 1993/94 annual rpt, S7895–2

Utah public school personnel and salaries, by detailed position and district, 1991/92, annual rpt, S7815–1.2

Virginia public school enrollment, grads, finances, and staff, by county and municipality, 1991/92, annual rpt, S8190–3

West Virginia public and private schools, enrollment, grads, and staff, by county, 1991/92, annual rpt, S8540–3

West Virginia public school finances, enrollment, staff, and programs, by county, 1992/93 and trends, annual rpt, S8540–4

Wisconsin elementary and secondary school enrollment, staff, costs, and State aid, by school district, 1992/93 and trends, annual rpt, S8795–2

Wyoming public school enrollment, staff, and finances, by county and district, 1991/92, annual rpt series, S8890–1

see also Campus security

see also Counselors and counseling

see also Educational employees pay

see also Educational finance

see also School boards

see also School districts

see also Teachers

School boards

Catholic secondary school board size and lay members, 1992 biennial rpt, A7375–5

Elementary/secondary school superintendents personal and professional characteristics and views, 1992 survey rpt, A0775–5

Urban public school board size, with member selection method and term length, for 47 school systems, 1990/91, A4425–4

Index by Subjects and Names

State and local:

Colorado election results for school board members and university regents, by district and county, 1992, biennial rpt, S1090–1

DC election results and turnout, and voter registration, by ward and precinct, 1992, biennial series, S1525–1

Georgia statistical abstract, general data, 1992-93 biennial rpt, U6730–1.2

Hawaii election results for State board of education, by district and precinct, 1992, biennial series, S2077–1

Kansas election results for State board of education, by district and county, 1992, biennial rpt, S3030–1

Maryland local govt financial condition, including revenues by source, expenditures by function, and debt obligations, FY92 and trends, annual rpt, S3618–1.1

Michigan election results for State board of education, by county, 1992 general election, biennial rpt, S4020–1

Mississippi school board members, by district type, 1993 annual rpt, S4340–1.1

Nebraska election results for State board of education, by county, 1992 primary and general elections, biennial rpt, S4955–1

Nevada election results, and voter registration and turnout, by county, 1992 general election, biennial rpt, S5125–1

New Mexico election results for State board of education, by location, 1992 general election, biennial rpt, S5655–1

Tennessee public school staff, by position, county, city, and school district, 1991/92 annual rpt, S7490–2.1

Utah election results for school board members, by county, 1992 general election, biennial rpt, S7875–1

School buildings

see Educational facilities

School busing

Accident fatalities during school bus loading/unloading, by circumstances, location, and victim age and sex, 1991 and trends, annual rpt, S3040–2

Accidents involving school buses, by type and State, 1991/92, annual rpt, A8375–2.3

College freshmen attitudes on busing to achieve racial integration, by sex and instn type, fall 1992, annual survey, U6215–1

Financial ratios and performance, for over 350 SIC 4-digit industries, FY88-92, annual rpt, A6400–3

Fleet mgmt and operating trends, articles and special features, bimonthly rpt, C1575–1

Fleet operating data for school districts, including worker unionization and transportation director pay, July 1993 survey, annual article, C1575–1.507

Fleet rankings of top 50 contractors, with data on pupils transported and districts under contract, for top 50 contractors, 1993, article, C1575–1.505

Fleet rankings of top 74 school districts and 26 contractors, with pupils transported, 1992 survey, annual article, C1575–1.501

Funding and operations issues, including training requirements and use of fingerprint background check for drivers, 1993 annual article, C1575–1.504

Index by Subjects and Names

School busing

Pupil transportation, accident, and expenditure statistics, by State, 1993 annual feature, C1575–1.502

Registrations, ownership, and use of school buses, by State, 1991/92, annual rpt, A0865–1.1

State and local:

Alabama elementary and secondary school enrollment, and pupil transportation, by district, 1991/92, annual rpt, S0124–1.1

Alabama traffic accidents, fatalities, and injuries, by circumstances, vehicle type, and driver and victim characteristics, 1992, annual rpt, S0185–1

Alaska traffic accidents, fatalities, and injuries, by vehicle type, circumstance, location, and driver and victim characteristics, 1991 and trends, annual rpt, S0360–1

Arizona traffic accidents involving school buses, with pupil transportation data, 1987/88-1990/91, annual rpt, S0530–1

Arkansas public school bus expenditures, pupils transported, and accidents, 1991/92 and trends, annual rpt, S0660–1

Arkansas traffic accidents, fatalities, and injuries, by vehicle type, circumstances, location, and driver and victim characteristics, 1991, annual rpt, S0692–1

California traffic accidents, fatalities, and injuries, by vehicle type, circumstances, location, and driver and victim characteristics, 1991 and trends, annual rpt, S0885–1

Colorado public school revenues by source, and expenditures by category, by school district, 1990, annual rpt, S1000–4.3

Connecticut traffic accidents, fatalities, and injuries, by vehicle type, circumstance, location, and driver and victim characteristics, 1992, annual rpt, S1275–1

Delaware public and nonpublic student transportation and costs, 1991/92, annual rpt, S1430–1

Delaware traffic accidents, fatalities, and injuries, by circumstances, location, and vehicle type, and driver and victim characteristics, 1992 and trends, annual rpt, S1435–1

Florida traffic accidents, fatalities, and injuries, by vehicle type, circumstance, location, and driver and victim characteristics, 1992 and trends, annual rpt, S1750–2

Georgia statistical abstract, general data, 1992-93 biennial rpt, U6730–1.2

Idaho funding for student transportation, by school district, FY92, annual rpt, S2225–2

Idaho traffic accidents, fatalities, and injuries, by circumstances, location, vehicle type, and driver and victim characteristics, 1992, annual rpt, S2315–1

Illinois public school revenues and expenditures by district, with data on busing, State aid claims, and per capita costs, 1990/91, annual rpt, S2440–1.3

Illinois traffic accidents, fatalities, and injuries, by circumstances, location, and driver and victim characteristics, 1991 and trends, annual rpt, S2540–1

Indiana public school funding for transportation, by district, 1991/92, annual table, S2608–2.2, S2608–2.11

Indiana traffic accidents, fatalities, and injuries, by circumstances, location, and vehicle type, and driver and victim characteristics, 1992, annual rpt, S2675–1

Kansas pupil transportation services and costs, with data by school district, 1990/91, annual rpt, S2945–1

Kansas traffic accidents, fatalities, and injuries, by vehicle type, location, circumstances, and driver and victim characteristics, 1992, annual rpt, S3040–1

Kentucky public school finances, staff, and enrollment, by district, 1989/90-1990/91, biennial rpt, S3110–2

Kentucky traffic accidents, fatalities, and injuries, by circumstances, location, vehicle type, and driver characteristics, 1992 and trends, annual rpt, S3150–2

Louisiana traffic accidents, fatalities, and injuries, by circumstances, location, and driver characteristics, 1991 and trends, annual rpt, S3345–2

Maine students transported by municipal and private vehicles, 1990/91, annual rpt, S3435–1

Maine traffic accidents, fatalities, and injuries, by accident circumstances, vehicle type and make, and driver and victim characteristics, 1992, annual rpt, S3475–2

Maryland elementary and secondary education data, by county, 1991/92, annual rpt, S3610–2.6, S3610–2.7, S3610–2.9

Maryland elementary and secondary education statistical summary, with data by county, 1991/92-1992/93 and trends, annual rpt, S3610–1

Maryland traffic accidents, fatalities, and injuries, by circumstances, location, vehicle type, and driver and victim characteristics, 1992, annual rpt, S3665–4

Massachusetts, Cambridge elementary/secondary school transportation expenditures before and after parental school selection program implementation, 1978/79-1991/92, R3810–7

Michigan traffic accidents, fatalities, and injuries, by vehicle type, circumstance, location, and driver and victim characteristics, 1991 and trends, annual rpt, S3997–2

Minnesota public school enrollment, staff, and finances, by district and county, 1991/92 and trends, annual rpt, S4165–1

Minnesota traffic accidents, fatalities, and injuries, by type of vehicle and circumstances, and driver and victim characteristics, 1992 and trends, annual rpt, S4230–2

Mississippi school transportation vehicles in use, mileage traveled, and accidents, fatalities, and injuries, 1991/92, annual rpt, S4340–1.2

Missouri school finances, enrollment, grads, and staff, by county and school district, 1991/92, annual rpt, S4505–1

Missouri traffic accidents, fatalities, and injuries, by circumstances, location, and driver and victim characteristics, 1992 and trends, annual rpt, S4560–1

Montana traffic accidents, fatalities, and injuries, by circumstances, location, and driver and victim characteristics, 1992 and trends, annual rpt, S4705–2

Nebraska traffic accidents, fatalities, and injuries, by circumstances, location, vehicle type, and driver and victim characteristics, 1992, annual rpt, S4953–1

Nevada expenditures for student transportation, by school district, FY89-91, annual rpt, S5035–2

Nevada traffic accidents, fatalities, and injuries, by circumstances, location, and vehicle type, 1992 and trends, annual rpt, S5140–1

New Jersey fatal traffic accidents and fatalities, by vehicle type, location, and circumstances, and driver and victim characteristics, 1992 and trends, annual rpt, S5430–2

New York State traffic accidents, fatalities, and injuries, by circumstances, location, vehicle type, and driver and victim characteristics, 1991 and trends, annual rpt, S5790–1

North Carolina public school buses, costs, and miles, by local district, 1991/92, annual rpt, S5915–1.1

North Carolina traffic accidents, fatalities, and injuries, by circumstances, location, vehicle type, and driver and victim characteristics, 1992 and trends, annual rpt, S5990–1

North Dakota public school revenues by source, expenditures by function, mill levies, and taxable value, by district, 1992/93 annual rpt, S6180 1

North Dakota traffic accidents, fatalities, and injuries, by circumstances, location, vehicle type, and driver and victim characteristics, 1992 and trends, annual rpt, S6217–1

Ohio public school pupils transported, mileage, and costs, 1987/88-1991/92, annual rpt, S6265–2

Ohio traffic accidents, fatalities, and injuries, by circumstances, location, driver and victim characteristics, and vehicle type, 1991 and trends, annual rpt, S6290–1

Oregon public school revenues by source and fund, and expenditures by fund, function, and object, 1991/92, annual rpt, S6590–1.16

Oregon public school revenues by source and fund, and expenditures by fund, function, and object, 1992/93, annual rpt, S6590–1.17

Pennsylvania traffic accidents, fatalities, and injuries, by circumstances, location, driver characteristics, and vehicle type, 1991, annual rpt, S6905–3

Rhode Island education expenditures by function and source of funds, by school district, 1991/92, annual rpt, S6970–1.2

Rhode Island statistical almanac, general data, 1993 annual rpt, C7975–1.1

Rhode Island traffic accidents, fatalities, and injuries, by circumstances, community, and driver and victim characteristics, 1991, annual rpt, S7025–1

School busing

South Carolina teachers salary schedules, educational revenues by source, and expenditures by function, by school district, 1991/92, annual rpt, S7145–1.5

South Carolina traffic accidents, fatalities, and injuries, by circumstances, location, and driver and victim characteristics, 1992 and trends, annual rpt, S7190–2

South Dakota school enrollment, finances, grads, and staff, by district, 1991/92 and trends, annual rpt, S7315–1

Tennessee public school enrollment, staff, finances, and operations, by county, city, and school district, 1991/92, annual rpt, S7490–2

Texas trade, transportation, and public utilities employment, by SIC 2- and 3-digit industry and detailed occupation, 2nd qtr 1991, triennial survey rpt, S7675–1.31

Utah school buses and drivers, pupils transported, and transportation finances, 1991/92, annual rpt, S7815–1.2

Utah traffic accidents and fatalities by circumstances, location, driver and victim characteristics, and vehicle type, 1992 and trends, annual rpt, S7890–2

Virginia public school enrollment, grads, finances, and staff, by county and municipality, 1991/92, annual rpt, S8190–3

Virginia traffic accidents, fatalities, and injuries, by circumstances, location, and driver and victim characteristics, 1991 and trends, annual rpt, S8282–1

Washington State traffic accidents, fatalities, and injuries, by circumstances, vehicle type, and location, with driver and victim characteristics, 1992 and trends, annual rpt, S8428–1

West Virginia public school finances, enrollment, staff, and programs, by county, 1992/93 and trends, annual rpt, S8540–4

West Virginia school buses, operators, passengers, and mileage, by county, 1991/92, annual rpt, S8540–3

Wisconsin elementary and secondary school enrollment, staff, costs, and State aid, by school district, 1992/93 and trends, annual rpt, S8795–2

Wisconsin traffic accidents, fatalities, and injuries, by circumstances, location, vehicle type, and driver and victim characteristics, 1992 and trends, annual rpt, S8815–1

Wyoming public school transportation expenditures, mileage, buses, and students transported, by district, 1991/92, annual rpt, S8890–1.3

Wyoming traffic accidents, fatalities, and injuries, by circumstances, location, vehicle type, and driver and victim characteristics, 1992 and trends, annual rpt, S9007–1

School desegregation

see Discrimination in education

see School busing

School districts

Bus fleet rankings, top 74 school districts, 1992 survey, annual article, C1575–1.501

Characteristics of school districts, including selected programs, enrollment trends, and central staff size and race-sex composition, 1992 survey rpt, A0775–5

Enrollment in top 100 school districts, fall 1990, R4800–2.518

Expenditures per pupil, for 10 top and bottom school districts, by State, 1987/88, annual rpt, R3840–11.2

Finances of local govts, by type of govt unit, and for 52 largest cities, 1993 annual rpt, R9050–1.6

Number of independent school districts, 1942-92, article, R4800–2.510

Public opinion on parity of education funding and quality among school districts in own State, 1993 annual Gallup Poll, A8680–1.503

Schools and enrollment in 10 largest districts using year-round schedules, 1992/93, R4800–2.505

State social, economic, and govtl indicators, with rankings, 1993 semiannual rpt, B8500–1.7

Teacher employment, hiring, and labor turnover data, for 57 districts, Oct 1990-91, R6350–7

Urban public school performance compared to natl goals for year 2000, with data on students, teachers, and finances, for 47 systems, 1990/91 and trends, A4425–4

State and local:

Alabama elementary and secondary school enrollment, staff, pupil transportation, and finances, by district, 1991/92, annual rpt, S0124–1

Alaska population, housing, income, and education data, by demographic characteristics and/or locality, 1990/91 and trends, annual rpt, S0320–4

Alaska public schools, enrollment, staff, and finances, by district, FY92, annual rpt, S0295–2

Arizona elementary and secondary school enrollment, staff, and finances, by school district and county, FY92 and trends, annual rpt, S0470–1

Arizona statistical abstract, general data, 1993 recurring rpt, U5850–2.10

Arkansas public school enrollment, grads, staff, and finances, by county and school, 1991/92 and trends, annual rpt, S0660–1

California socioeconomic and govtl data for municipalities, counties, and school districts, 1993 annual rpt, C4712–3

California statistical abstract, general data, 1992 annual rpt, S0840–2.13

Colorado property assessed valuation by detailed property type, and tax levy and revenue by local district, by county, 1991-92, annual rpt, S1055–3

Colorado public school enrollment, finances, and student and staff characteristics, by locality, 1991 annual rpt series, S1000–4

Colorado public school enrollment, finances, and student and staff characteristics, by locality, 1992 annual rpt series, S1000–2

Delaware data book, general data, 1993 annual rpt, S1375–4

Delaware school enrollment, grads, staff, finances, and facilities, by county, school district, and/or instn, 1991/92, annual rpt, S1430–1

Florida State govt disbursements to local areas, FY92, annual rpt, S1717–1

Florida statistical abstract, general data, 1992 annual rpt, U6660–1.21

Georgia statistical abstract, general data, 1992-93 biennial rpt, U6730–1.2

Index by Subjects and Names

Idaho public and nonpublic school enrollment by grade, by school district and/or county, Sept 1992, annual rpt, S2225–1

Idaho public school personnel characteristics and salaries by position, and teachers and enrollment by school district, 1992/93, annual rpt, S2225–3

Idaho school district revenues by source, and expenditures by function, by district and fund, FY92, annual rpt, S2225–2

Illinois elementary and secondary school enrollment, staff, and finances, by county and district, 1990/91 and trends, annual rpt, S2440–1

Illinois statistical abstract, general data, 1992 annual rpt, U6910–2

Indiana elementary and secondary school enrollment and finances, by district and county, annual rpt series, S2608–2

Kansas school enrollment, grads, staff, and finances, by county, school district, and/or school, 1990/91, annual rpt, S2945–1

Kentucky public education profiles, with data by region and district, 1991/92 and trends, annual rpt, S3110–1

Kentucky public school finances, staff, and enrollment, by district, 1989/90-1990/91, biennial rpt, S3110–2

Louisiana elementary/secondary school operations, including enrollment, staff, finances, and detail by school district, 1991/92 and trends, annual rpt, S3280–1

Massachusetts municipal and county profiles, general data, 1992 annual rpt, C4712–2

Massachusetts public elementary/secondary education summary data, 1989/90-1991/92 and trends, annual rpt, S3810–3

Massachusetts public elementary/secondary school enrollment by grade, by district, Oct 1992, annual rpt, S3810–4

Massachusetts public elementary/secondary school expenditures per pupil by program, by district, 1991/92, annual rpt, S3810–5

Massachusetts tax collections by type, and distributions to local areas, FY91 and trends, annual rpt, S3917–1

Michigan school district financial and enrollment data, with rankings, 1991/92, annual rpt, S3965–3

Minnesota public school enrollment, staff, and finances, by district and county, 1991/92 and trends, annual rpt, S4165–1

Mississippi public school enrollment, staff and salaries, and finances, by district, 1991/92 and trends, annual rpt, S4340–1

Mississippi statistical abstract, general data, 1992 annual rpt, U3255–4.3

Missouri school finances, enrollment, grads, and staff, by county and school district, 1991/92, annual rpt, S4505–1

Nebraska elementary and secondary schools, enrollment by grade, and staff, with data by school district and county, annual series, S4865–2

Nebraska public school finances, including receipts by source and disbursements by function, by county and district, 1988/89, annual rpt, S4865–3

Nevada public school enrollment, test scores, teachers, and finances, by school district, 1990/91 and trends, annual rpt, S5035–2

Index by Subjects and Names

School dropouts

New Hampshire elementary and secondary education statistics, with selected data by school district, annual rpt series, S5200–1

New Jersey municipal and county data book, general data, 1992 annual rpt, C4712–4

New Jersey public schools, enrollment, grads, and student characteristics, by county, 1991/92, annual rpt, S5385–1.1

New Mexico elementary/secondary school statistics, including grads, student test results, and finances, by school district, 1989/90-1991/92, annual rpt, S5575–4

New York State municipal and county statistical profiles, general data, 1993 annual rpt, C4712–7

New York State statistical yearbook, general data, 1992 annual rpt, U5100–1.10

North Carolina public school enrollment, grads, staff, and finances, with data by race, sex, and local district, 1991/92-1992/93 and trends, annual rpt, S5915–1

North Dakota elementary and secondary schools, enrollment, and staff, by school type and location, 1992/93 annual directory, S6180–2

North Dakota public school revenues by source, expenditures by function, mill levies, and taxable value, by district, 1992/93 annual rpt, S6180–4

Ohio business property tax collections and assessments, by type of subdivision and county, 1991 and trends, annual rpt, S6390–1.5

Ohio public school enrollment, finances, special programs, and staff, 1991/92 and trends, annual rpt, S6265–2

Ohio school district income tax collections, and levies by district, FY92 annual rpt, S6390–1.3

Ohio special education expenditures, instructional hours, and enrollment, by service type and school district, 1991/92 and trends, annual rpt, S6265–1

Oklahoma public school finances, personnel, enrollment, and facilities, by county and district, 1991/92 and trends, annual rpt, S6423–1

Oklahoma public school performance indicators, including students and achievement, finances, and staff, by district, 1990/91-1991/92 and trends, annual rpt, S6423–2

Oregon elementary and secondary education enrollment and finances, including data by school district and county, annual rpt series, S6590–1

Pennsylvania school district distribution by dropout rate, 1991/92, annual rpt, S6790–5.11

Rhode Island educational enrollment, grads, and finances, by district or community, 1991/92 or fall 1992, annual rpt, S6970–1

South Carolina county govt finances, including property value and tax assessments, by county, FY92, annual rpt, S7127–2

South Carolina educational characteristics and socioeconomic indicators, by school district and county, 1991/92, annual rpt, S7145–1

South Carolina statistical abstract, general data, 1993 annual rpt, S7125–1.9

South Dakota property tax and valuations, by property type and locality, FY92 annual rpt, S7380–1.2

South Dakota school enrollment, finances, grads, and staff, by district, 1991/92 and trends, annual rpt, S7315–1

Tennessee public school enrollment, staff, finances, and operations, by county, city, and school district, 1991/92, annual rpt, S7490–2

Tennessee statistical abstract, general data, 1992/93 annual rpt, U8710–2.14

Texas criminal offenses reported by school district police depts, 1992, annual rpt, S7735–2.2

Texas elementary and secondary education data, by school district and county, annual series, S7670–1

Utah govt statistical review, fiscal and socioeconomic data, 1993 annual rpt, R9380–1.6, R9380–1.11

Utah payments to counties and school districts from Natl forest revenue sharing program, by county, 1991, article, U8960–2.502

Utah public schools, enrollment, attendance, personnel, and finances, by school district, 1991/92, annual rpt, S7815–1

Utah statistical abstract, general data, 1993 triennial rpt, U8960–1.3

Vermont individual income tax returns, income, and taxes, by school district, 1991, annual rpt, S8125–1.2

Virginia public school enrollment and high school grads, with detail by school district, 1980/81-2012/2013, annual rpt, U9080–20

Washington State tax levies, by type of taxing district, 1988-92, annual rpt, S8415 1.2

Wisconsin Blue Book, general data, 1993-94 biennial rpt, S8780–1.2

Wisconsin elementary and secondary school enrollment, staff, costs, and State aid, by school district, 1992/93 and trends, annual rpt, S8795–2

Wyoming public school enrollment, staff, and finances, by county and district, 1991/92, annual rpt series, S8890–1

see also School boards

School dropouts

Black American educational statistics, with comparisons to whites, 1970s-92, annual compilation, C6775–2.3

Black children and youth population, economic, health, and education data, with comparisons to whites, 1993 rpt, R3840–21

Dental school enrollment and yearly attrition rates, 1974/75-1990/91, annual rpt, A1475–4.2

Dental school student attrition, by reason and student characteristics, 1991/92 and trends, annual rpt, A1475–4.4

High school dropout rates among youth age 16-19, for 5 States with lowest and highest rates, 1990, annual rpt, S2784–3

High school dropout rates among youth age 16-24, by race and sex, 1991, article, A8510–1.1

High school dropout rates, by State, 1990, annual rpt, C2175–1.531

Hispanic American and non-Hispanic high school dropouts distribution by recency of immigration, Nov 1989, article, R4800–2.507

Hispanic American educational statistics, with comparisons to whites, 1970s-92, annual compilation, C6775–3.2

Labor supply trends, including high school dropouts by sex, race, and age group, 1970 and 1989, recurring rpt, A3960–2.1

Latin America statistical abstract, general data by country, 1992 annual rpt, U6250–1.8

Low-income families and children, health and welfare indicators, with data by State and city, 1992 annual rpt, R3840–11

Optometry school student withdrawals or dismissals, by instn, 1991/92, annual survey, A3370–2

Southern States elementary/secondary school dropout rate, by State, 1990, biennial fact book, A8945–1.1

Urban public school performance compared to natl goals for year 2000, with data on students, teachers, and finances, for 47 systems, 1990/91 and trends, A4425–4

State and local:

Alabama public school dropouts, by race, sex, and school system, 1991/92, annual rpt, S0124–1.1

Arizona school dropouts by grade, 1991/92, annual rpt, S0470–1

Arizona youth not in school/not graduated by labor force status, by county, 1990, recurring rpt, U5850–2.4

Colorado high school dropout rates, by county and district, 1991/92, annual rpt, S1000–2.1

Colorado public school enrollment and dropouts, by local area, 1991/92, annual planning rpt, S1040–3.1

Delaware secondary school dropouts by grade, county, district, race-ethnicity, and sex, 1991/92 and trends, annual rpt, S1430–1

Georgia county guide, general data, 1993 annual rpt, U6750–1

Georgia statistical abstract, general data, 1992-93 biennial rpt, U6730–1.2

Illinois elementary and secondary school enrollment by level, and high school dropouts and grads, by county and district, 1990/91, annual rpt, S2440–1.1

Kansas public and private school grads and dropouts, by sex, 1990/91, annual rpt, S2945–1

Louisiana job service openings and applicants, and characteristics of Job Training Partnership Act target population and insured unemployed, 1993 annual planning rpt, S3320–1.2

Louisiana public school dropouts, by grade level and parish, 1991/92, annual rpt, S3280–1.1

Maine public school enrollment, facilities, staff, and finances, with selected data by county and for private schools, 1991 and trends, annual rpt, S3435–1

Maryland elementary and secondary education data, by county, 1991/92, annual rpt, S3610–2.3

Maryland public high school dropouts, by county, 1991/92, annual rpt, S3610–1

Massachusetts public elementary/secondary education summary data, 1989/90-1991/92 and trends, annual rpt, S3810–3

School dropouts

Michigan labor force planning rpt, including characteristics of Job Training Partnership Act eligible population by State area, 1993 annual rpt, S3980–1.2

Mississippi school dropouts by grade level, 1990/91-1991/92, annual rpt, S4340–1.1

Missouri public school finances, staff, students, and programs, detailed data, 1991/92, annual rpt, S4505–1.1

Nevada public school enrollment, test scores, teachers, and finances, by school district, 1990/91 and trends, annual rpt, S5035–2

New Mexico high school enrollment and dropouts, by sex, race-ethnicity, and county, 1991/92, annual planning rpt, S5624–1

North Carolina high school dropouts and retention rates, by school district, 1991/92, annual rpt, S5915–1.1

Oklahoma public school performance indicators, including students and achievement, finances, and staff, by district, 1990/91-1991/92 and trends, annual rpt, S6423–2

Pennsylvania elementary/secondary and higher education enrollment, grads, staff, and finances, by instn type, 1981/82-1996/97, recurring rpt, S6790–5.10

Pennsylvania labor force planning rpt, including data on populations with employability problems, FY92 annual rpt, S6845–3.3

Pennsylvania public school dropout characteristics, with reasons for leaving school and subsequent activities, 1991/92 and trends, annual rpt, S6790–5.11

South Carolina educational enrollment, by school type or level, program, race, and location, 1991/92, annual rpt, S7145–1.3

South Carolina public and private schools, enrollment, and grads, by county, 1990/91 and trends, annual planning rpt, S7155 3.3

South Dakota high school dropouts, by sex and race-ethnicity, 1991/92, annual rpt, S7315–1.1

Tennessee statistical abstract, general data, 1992/93 annual rpt, U8710–2.16

Utah labor force and percent without high school diploma, by sex, age group, and/or race-ethnicity, 1990, article, U8960–2.509

Utah public school dropouts, by race-ethnicity, sex, grade, and district, 1991/92, annual rpt, S7815–1.2

Virginia public school enrollment, grads, finances, and staff, by county and municipality, 1991/92, annual rpt, S8190–3

Wisconsin Blue Book, general data, 1993-94 biennial rpt, S8780–1.2

Wyoming public school dropout rate, by district, 1991/92, annual rpt, S8890–1.3

see also Educational enrollment

see also Educational retention rates

School enrollment

see Educational enrollment

School finance

see Educational finance

School lunch and breakfast programs

State social, economic, and govtl indicators, with rankings, 1993 semiannual rpt, B8500–1.8

Urban public school students eligible for free/reduced price lunches, with comparisons to total State and US, for 47 systems, 1990/91, A4425–4

State and local:

Alabama public school revenues by source and expenditures by object, by district, 1991/92, annual rpt, S0124–1.2

Arizona school food service program meals served, expenditures, and value of donated commodities, by school district and county, 1991/92, annual rpt, S0470–1

Arkansas human services dept finances and operations, including service recipient characteristics, by program, FY91 and trends, annual rpt, S0700–2

Arkansas school food service finances and meals served, 1990/91-1991/92, annual rpt, S0660–1.2

Colorado public school revenues by source, and expenditures by category, by school district, 1990, annual rpt, S1000–4.3

Connecticut public school student participation levels in reduced/free meal programs, 1991/92, biennial rpt, S1185–3

Delaware school district expenditures for operations, materials, and health and food services, 1991/92, annual rpt, S1430–1.4

Florida statistical abstract, general data, 1992 annual rpt, U6660–1.4

Georgia county guide, general data, 1993 annual rpt, U6750–1

Georgia statistical abstract, general data, 1992-93 biennial rpt, U6730–1.1

Idaho school district revenues by source, and expenditures by function, by district and fund, FY92, annual rpt, S2225–2

Kansas school district revenues by source and expenditures by object, 1990/91, annual rpt, S2945–1

Louisiana public and nonpublic school food service meals served and funding by source, by school district, 1991/92, annual rpt, S3280–1.2

Maine public school enrollment, facilities, staff, and finances, with selected data by county and for private schools, 1991 and trends, annual rpt, S3435–1

Maryland elementary and secondary education data, by county, 1991/92, annual rpt, S3610–2.9

Maryland elementary and secondary education statistical summary, with data by county, 1991/92-1992/93 and trends, annual rpt, S3610–1

Missouri public school finances, staff, students, and programs, detailed data, 1991/92, annual rpt, S4505–1.1

Nevada public school enrollment, test scores, teachers, and finances, by school district, 1990/91 and trends, annual rpt, S5035–2

New Mexico elementary/secondary school statistics, including grads, student test results, and finances, by school district, 1989/90-1991/92, annual rpt, S5575–4

Oklahoma school lunch program eligibility rates, by district, 1991/92 and trends, annual rpt, S6423–2

Oklahoma school revenues and expenditures, by program, county, and district, FY92, annual rpt, S6423–1.1

Oregon public school revenues by source and fund, and expenditures by fund, function, and object, 1991/92, annual rpt, S6590–1.16

Index by Subjects and Names

Oregon public school revenues by source and fund, and expenditures by fund, function, and object, 1992/93, annual rpt, S6590–1.17

South Carolina expenditures for pupil food service, and students eligible for free or reduced-price lunches, by school district, 1993 annual rpt, S7145–1

Tennessee public school finances, by county, city, and school district, 1991/92, annual rpt, S7490–2.4

Texas financial condition, including revenues by source, expenditures by function and dept, and investments, with data for over 400 individual funds, FY92, annual rpt, S7655–2.2

Utah public schools, enrollment, attendance, personnel, and finances, by school district, 1991/92, annual rpt, S7815–1

Virginia public school enrollment, grads, finances, and staff, by county and municipality, 1991/92, annual rpt, S8190–3

West Virginia child nutrition program operations, with meals served by category and expenditures by source of funds, 1993 rpt, S8540–4.3

Wisconsin elementary and secondary school enrollment, staff, costs, and State aid, by school district, 1992/93 and trends, annual rpt, S8795–2

Wyoming public school students eligible for free and reduced-fee lunches, by district, fall 1992, annual rpt, S8890–1.2

School prayer

see Church and state

Schools

see Black colleges

see Community colleges

see Educational facilities

see Junior colleges

see Parochial schools

see Private schools

see terms beginning with School

see terms listed under Education

Schultz, Craig

"1992 U.S. House of Representatives Employment Practices: A Study of Staff Salary, Tenure, Demographics and Benefits", R4140–1

Schultz, George

"Fuel Oil News: The Oil Heating Industry: 1992", C4680–2

Science and technology

Book publishing industry financial and operating data, by publisher type and size, and subject category, 1991 and trends, annual rpt, A3274–2

Federal outlays for science/technology-related programs, changes proposed by Clinton Admin, by agency, 1994-98, article, A1250–1.517

Foreign acquisitions of US high-technology firms, distribution among top 4 and all other hq countries, Oct 1988-Apr 1992, C1850–2.503, C1850–6.501

Foundation assets, income, and grants by type of recipient, with data for top organizations and by location, 1991 and trends, annual rpt, R4900–1

High-technology employment indicators, by State, 1989, semiannual rpt, B8500–1.13

High-technology experienced and inexperienced entrepreneurs use of personal vs instn equity sources, with average equity and debt, 1993 feature, C4687–1.506

Index by Subjects and Names

Scientists and technicians

High-technology industry CEO characteristics, and views on mgmt issues including compensation and foreign trade, June 1992 survey, B4490–2.34

High-technology small companies with rapid growth, employment and sales data for 25 firms, 1993 article, C5800–7.551

Hispanic-owned high-technology company sales and employment, for top 50 firms, 1992, annual article, C4575–1.510

Israel high-technology market trend for US-owned companies, with sales and employment for 5 firms, 1993 article, C1850–2.503

Latin America scientific articles published in intl journals, by country, 1973-84, annual rpt, U6250–1.4

Market value of top 10 high-technology companies, July 1993, article, C8900–1.521

Museums and related instns operations and finances, by type, budget size, governing authority, and region, 1989/90 survey, A0750–1

State and local:

California high-technology employment trends, by industry, 1993, annual rpt, S0840–3.1

Hawaii data book, general data, 1992 annual rpt, S2090–1.17

Idaho high-technology employment, by industry, 1988 and 1991, recurring rpt, S2218–2.5

Oregon high-technology firms and employment, 1990-91, annual rpt, S6585–3

Pennsylvania advanced technology center funding under govt partnership program, FY92, recurring rpt, U4130–6.2

Utah high-technology industry trends, with R&D spending, and employment of major firms, 1986-92, recurring article, U8960–2.508

see also Agricultural sciences and research
see also Astronomy
see also Aviation sciences
see also Biological sciences
see also Biotechnology
see also CD-ROM technology and use
see also Chemistry
see also Defense research
see also Earth sciences
see also Educational research
see also Educational technology
see also Energy research and development
see also Engineers and engineering
see also Environmental sciences
see also Epidemiology and epidemiologists
see also Federal funding for research and development
see also Federally Funded R&D Centers
see also Genetics
see also International cooperation in science and technology
see also Mathematics
see also Medical research
see also Medicine
see also Oceanography
see also Physical sciences
see also Physics
see also Psychology
see also Research
see also Research and development
see also Scientific education

see also Scientific equipment and apparatus
see also Scientists and technicians
see also Social sciences
see also Space programs
see also Space sciences
see also Technological innovations
see also Technology transfer

Scientific education

Achievement test scores worldwide for math and science, for students age 13 in 14 countries, 1990, annual rpt, R3840–11.1

Black elementary/secondary students taking selected science courses, and educational test results, with comparisons to whites, 1993 rpt, R3840–21

Chemist and chemical engineer salaries, employment status, and demographic and professional characteristics, 1993, annual rpt, A1250–4

Chemistry and chemical engineering degrees awarded, by level, sex, and instn, 1991/92 and trends, annual articles, A1250–1.535

Chemistry and chemical engineering grad starting salaries, employment status, demographic characteristics, and advanced study plans, 1991/92, annual rpt, A1250–2

Doctoral degree recipient characteristics, including citizenship status, source of support, field of study, and instn, 1990/91 and trends, annual rpt, R6000–7

Ecologist personal and professional characteristics, including research activity and funding, with data by field, Mar 1992 survey, recurring rpt, A4685–1

Elementary/secondary science and math education, including student and teacher characteristics, and requirements, by State, 1991/92, biennial rpt, A4355–3

Foreign students enrolled in US higher education instns, by instn, State, country of origin, and demographic characteristics, 1991/92 and trends, annual rpt, R5580–1

Geoscience faculty salaries by rank and for women, with data on minority faculty members, 1991/92 and trends, annual rpt, A1785–4

High school student shares taking biology, chemistry, and physics by graduation, by State, 1991/92, article, A1250–1.534

Higher education geoscience enrollment and degrees awarded, by sex, race-ethnicity, and discipline, 1991/92, annual rpt, A1785–3

Physics and astronomy bachelor degree recipients postgraduation plans and demographic characteristics, 1991/92 and trends, annual survey, A1960–3

Physics and astronomy enrollment and degrees, annual survey of US college depts, series, A1960–2

Physics and astronomy grads employment status, by sex, age, subfield, citizenship, degree, and employer type, with salary info, 1990/91, annual rpt, A1960–1

Salaries of scientists, engineers, technicians, and other professionals, by employee and employer characteristics, 1990s and trends, biennial rpt, A3960–1

Salary and job offers for college grads, by field of study, type of employer, and degree level, by region, interim rpt series, A3940–1

Salary and job offers for college grads, by field of study, type of employer, and degree level, series, A3940–2

Southern States higher education degree conferrals, by sex, race-ethnicity, level, and selected field, by State, 1990s and trends, biennial fact book, A8945–1.3

State economic dev condition indicators, including economic performance, business vitality, growth capacity, and tax/fiscal system, by State, 1993 annual rpt, R4225–1.1

State social, economic, and govtl indicators, with rankings, 1993 semiannual rpt, B8500–1.13

Women and minorities in professional fields, detailed education and labor force data, 1980s-91, with historical trends, recurring rpt, A3960–2

State and local:

Connecticut public school data, including enrollment, staff, programs, finances, and student characteristics, 1991/92, biennial rpt, S1185–3

Utah high school math/science education program graduates and college attendance, 1992, annual rpt, S7815–1.1

see also Technical education

Scientific equipment and apparatus

Corporate performance ratings by executives for leading companies in 32 industries, 1993 annual survey feature, C8900–1.508

Electronics industry factory sales and shipments, foreign trade, and operating data, by product category, 1980s-92, annual rpt, A4725–1

Financial ratios and performance, for over 350 SIC 4-digit industries, FY88-92, annual rpt, A6400–3

Market value outlook for selected types of scientific equipment or instruments, monthly rpt, C1850–6

see also Medical supplies and equipment

Scientific research

see Research

Scientists and technicians

Aerospace employment by sector and occupation, with detail for engineers/scientists, 1970s-91, annual rpt, A0250–2.5

Chemical and related industries production, finances, operating ratios, employment, and trade, by country, company, and chemical, 1980s-92, annual feature, A1250–1.530

Chemical industry and total manufacturing R&D scientist/engineer employment, 1970 and 1980-92, annual rpt, A3850–1

Chemist and chemical engineer salaries, employment status, and demographic and professional characteristics, 1993, annual rpt, A1250–4

Chemists employment terminations by 6 companies, Oct 1990-Dec 1991, recurring article, A1250–1.507

Chemists employment terminations by 7 companies, 1990-92, recurring article, A1250–1.536

Defense industries conversion to nonmilitary production, with data on defense contracts and spending, top contractors, and employment by occupation, 1980s and trends, R4700–19

Ecologist personal and professional characteristics, including research activity and funding, with data by field, Mar 1992 survey, recurring rpt, A4685–1

Scientists and technicians

Employment of scientists and engineers, US and foreign, 1993 annual feature, A1250–1.537

Federal employment of scientists and engineers, by field and sex, 1989, article, A1250–1.523

Global warming and related issues, views of climate scientists, Feb 1992 survey, article, R3823–1.502

Hospital pharmacy personnel weekly hours and annual payroll, 1991, annual survey, B5165–3

Immigrant employment license ("green card") applications approved and denied for scientific or technical workers, by occupation, 1992, article, A1250–1.522

Japan scientists working in US, and US scientists working in Japan, 1989, article, C1850–6.505

Latin America statistical abstract, general data by country, 1992 annual rpt, U6250–1.8

Salaries, and employment characteristics of R&D professionals, 1993 and trends, annual article, C1850–6.509

Salaries of chemists, by sex, degree level, and employer type, Mar 1992, annual rpt, A1570–2

Salaries of scientists, engineers, and chemists, by sex, 1989 or 1991, annual rpt, A1570–1

Salaries of scientists, engineers, technicians, and other professionals, by employee and employer characteristics, 1990s and trends, biennial rpt, A3960–1

State economic dev condition indicators, including economic performance, business vitality, growth capacity, and tax/fiscal system, by State, 1993 annual rpt, R4225–1.1

State social, economic, and govtl indicators, with rankings, 1993 semiannual rpt, B8500–1.13

Women and minorities in professional fields, detailed education and labor force data, 1980s-91, with historical trends, recurring rpt, A3960–2

State and local:

Tennessee statistical abstract, general data, 1992/93 annual rpt, U8710–2.3

see also under specific scientific disciplines

Scott County, Ky.

Auto assembly plant installation of Toyota Motor Corp economic impact for Kentucky, 5 other States, and total US, 1980s-2005, U7138–1.4

Scrap metals

Aluminum scrap consumption, recovery, and trade, 1940s-92, annual rpt, A0400–2

Aluminum shipments, orders, and inventories by product class, and foreign trade for ingot, scrap, and mill products, monthly rpt, A0400–1

Auto recycled ferrous and nonferrous metals shares of average vehicle composition, 1991, annual rpt, A0865–1.2

Copper supply by source, consumption by end use, stocks, and trade, 1972-92, annual rpt, A4175–1

Iron and steel industry scrap trade, and consumption by type of furnace, 1992 and trends, annual rpt, A2000–2

Motor vehicles in use, newly registered, and scrapped, 1947-92, annual rpt, C7715–2

Production, consumption, stocks, trade, and prices for approx 100 basic commodities, including by country and producing State, commodity yearbook for 1993, C2400–1, C2400–2

Silver refinery production from primary materials, coins, and scrap, with disposition, stocks, prices, and industry devs, US and worldwide, bimonthly rpt, A8902–3

Silver supply-demand by country and end use, with prices, futures trading, and market analyses, 1993 and trends, annual rpt, A8902–4

Wholesale scrap metal dealers financial performance and ratios, FY88-92, annual rpt, A6400–3

Sea pollution

see Marine pollution

Seafood

see Fish and fishing industry

see Shellfish

Searches and seizures

State and local:

Alabama drug task force property seizures, by type and locale, 1992, annual rpt, S0119–1.1

Idaho police seizures of illegal drugs and property involved in drug offenses, by type, 1992, annual rpt, S2275–2

Iowa court search warrant applications and seized property hearings, 1991-92, annual rpt, S2815–1

North Dakota State measure on stopping/searching of vehicles, election results by county, 1992, biennial rpt, S6205–1

Texas drug seizures by law enforcement agencies, by type of substance, 1992, annual rpt, S7735–2.2

Seashores

Coastline mileage, by State and territory, 1993 annual feature, C2425–4

Statistical profiles of 50 States and DC, general data, 1993 annual almanac, C4712–1

Women's topless sunbathing on public beaches, public opinion on legality, July/Aug 1992 Gallup Poll, C4040–1.502

State and local:

Florida statistical abstract, general data, 1992 annual rpt, U6660–1.8

Hawaii beach water quality samplings and results, by beach, 1990, annual rpt, S2065–1.6

Hawaii data book, general data, 1992 annual rpt, S2090–1.5, S2090–1.7

see also National parks

Seasonal and summer employment

see Temporary and seasonal employment

Seat belts

see Motor vehicle safety devices

Seattle, Wash.

CPI for Seattle area, monthly rpt, S8340–3

Economic impact of cutbacks at Boeing Corp on Seattle area, 1991-94, annual rpt, B3520–1

see also under By City in the "Index by Categories"

Second homes

State and local:

Maine housing units used for seasonal or recreational purposes, by local area, 1990 census rpt, S3465–7

Index by Subjects and Names

Maryland statistical abstract, general data, 1993-94 biennial rpt, S3605–1.13

see also Resort timesharing

Secondary education

see Elementary and secondary education

Secretaries

see Clerical workers

Securities

Aerospace and defense industries financial performance, with data for approx 200 major US and foreign companies, FY92 and trends, annual feature, C5800–4.519

Ambulance company revenues, net income, and stock performance, for 4 firms, 1993 article, C3950–1.523

American depositary receipt (ADR) capital raised, distribution by issuer country, 1st half 1993, article, C2710–2.519

Auto industry revenues and stock performance, for 3 major vehicle manufacturers and approx 50 suppliers, weekly rpt quarterly feature, C2710–3.518, C2710–3.532, C2710–3.545

Bank assets, share of nonperforming loans, and stock performance, for 10 major instns, 1993 article, C3950–1.526

Business Week investment indicators, including major stock indexes, and best and worst performing industries and companies, weekly rpt, C5800–7

Canada Govt-insured mortgage-backed securities issuance value, by issuer, 1987-93, article, A6450–2.508

Chemical industry stock dividends, prices, and price/earnings ratios, by company, 1988-91, annual feature, A1250–1.530

Chemical industry stock performance, for 30 companies, 1992, article, A1250–1.510

Chicago Board of Trade futures and options trading in financial instruments and agricultural commodities, 1992, annual rpt, B2120–1

Commercial mortgage securities issuances value, 1987-92, article, A6450–2.506

Commodity yearbook for 1993: detailed supply-demand data, and selected indicators for futures market investors, C2400–1

Commodity yearbook update: detailed supply-demand data, and selected indicators for futures market investors, Jan-Sept 1993 rpts, C2400–2

Computer disk drive manufacturer stock performance and earnings outlook, for 5 companies, 1993 article, C1850–2.508

Consumer expectations of economic conditions and change in income, and intended durable goods purchases by type, Conference Board monthly survey, R4105–4

Corporate acquisition impact on stock prices, and merger/acquisition premiums paid, 1993 annual compilation, C4683–1.502

Corporate CEO compensation in 800 firms, including stock gains and ownership, 1993 annual article, C3950–1.515

Corporate directors stock compensation practices for outside board members, 1991, annual rpt, R4105–7

Corporate dividend yield trends for 10 companies with large increases, 1992 vs 1991, article, C4215–1.506

Index by Subjects and Names

Securities

Corporate dividend yields and payout ratios, for selected industries and companies, biweekly rpt quarterly feature, C3950-1.504, C3950-1.510, C3950-1.517, C3950-1.523

Corporate market value of top 1,000 firms worldwide, with related financial data, by company and country, 1993 annual feature, C5800-7.536

Corporate market value rankings of top 1,000 firms, with sales, profits, assets, and related data, by company and industry, 1993 annual feature, C5800-7.521

Corporate mergers, acquisitions, and divestitures, with prices, payment methods, and characteristics of participants, 1992 and trends, annual rpt, B6020-1

Corporate sales, earnings, and stock performance, for 100 fastest-growing companies, 1993 annual article, C8900-1.521

Corporate sales, profits, return on equity, price/earnings ratio, and earnings per share, approx 900 corporations, with industry rankings, weekly rpt quarterly article, C5800-7.503, C5800-7.519, C5800-7.528, C5800-7.541

Corporate stock investment performance and earnings outlook, approx 900 companies, 1992 annual feature, C5800-7.509

Corporate stock price premiums for publicly held companies shortly before acquisition announcements, bimonthly rpt quarterly feature, C4683-1

Corporate stock prices at offering and recent dates, for 26 major firms going public during 1991-92, article, C3950-1.503

Corporations with rapid growth, financial data for 250 firms, 1993 feature, C5800-7.551

Discount store initial public stock offerings, and amount raised, by chain, 1992-93, annual feature, C5150-3.514

Dividend trends for S&P 500, 1991-92, article, C5800-7.512

Dividends declared, Jan-June 1991-93, article, C2710-2.516

Dow Jones Industrials price, and earnings outlook through 1994, for 30 stocks, article, C3950-1.527

Drugstore chains financial performance and marketing operations, by US and Canadian company, 1993 annual feature, C5150-2.511

Economic indicator historical trends, 1900s-92, annual rpt, R9050-1.2

Electric utility common stock performance, for utilities with diversified vs nondiversified assets, 1986/87-1989/90, article, A4700-4.505

Electric utility financial and investment performance indicators, for top 50 companies, 1991, article, C5800-28.501

Electric utility shares outstanding, stock dividends, and earnings per share, bimonthly rpt quarterly tables, A4700-4

Electronics company executives selling stock holdings in own company, with minimum amounts received, for 6 companies, Dec 1992-Feb 1993, article, C1850-2.507

Electronics company financial data and business info for approx 500 companies, 1991-92 and trends, annual rpt, C3400-4

Employee benefit plan asset rankings of top 1,000 funds, with selected fund investment data, 1992, annual feature, C2710-2.504

Entertainment company stock prices, by industry sector, weekly rpt, C9380-1

Entertainment industry securities issues, for 5 companies, 3rd qtr 1992, article, C9380-1.502

Executive compensation via restricted stock and stock option plans, by industry div, 1991, annual rpt, R4105-19

Financial instns performance, for 10 small/midsize instns with high returns on equity, 1992 article, C3950-1.502

Financial performance and activities of securities industry, with data by type of firm, 1st 5 months 1993 and trends, recurring article, A8825-1.505

Financial performance and activities of securities industry, with data by type of firm, 1992 and trends, recurring article, A8825-1.503

Food service CEO compensation, including stock option grants and value for 15 executives, FY92, article, C1200-5.513

Food service initial public stock offerings and prices, for 12 companies, 1992, C5150-5.503

Forbes investment indicators, including major stock indexes, and best and worst performing companies, biweekly rpt, C3950-1

Forbes 500 top companies in sales, profits, assets, market value, and productivity, with stock and employment data, 1992, annual rpt, C3950-1.513

Forecasts of economic indicators for approx 10-13 months, monthly rpt, U1880-3

Foreign economic indexes, and leading and coincident indicators for US and other industrial countries, monthly rpt, U1245-1

Foreign investor participation in US securities markets, and foreign purchases by US investors, by world area and country, quarterly rpt, A8825-2

Foreign stocks performance, for 100 traded on US exchanges, and 500 largest foreign companies, 1993 annual feature, C3950-1.519

Fortune magazine ranking of top 50-100 companies in 8 nonindustrial sectors, with financial and employment data, 1992, annual feature, C8900-1.516

Fortune 500 largest industrial corporations, sales, financial, and stock performance data by company, 1992, annual feature, C8900-1.513

Futures and options contract open interest (outstanding commitments), on foreign exchanges, by commodity and exchange, monthly rpt, A5040-6

Futures and options trading volume by commodity and exchange, 1988-92, annual rpt, A5040-1

Futures and options trading volume on foreign exchanges, by commodity and exchange, monthly rpt, A5040-5

Futures contract open interest (outstanding commitments), by commodity and exchange, monthly rpt, A5040-4

Futures trading volume by commodity and exchange, monthly rpt, A5040-2

Higher education instn endowment fund and investment pool characteristics and performance, by instn, FY92, annual survey rpt, A6705-2

Hispanic American households holding stock, by income group, 1992 article, C4575-1.501

Industry analyses, with data on underwriting and trading activity, and financial trends, periodic rpt, A8825-1

Initial public offerings, by value and company revenue size class, 1989-1st half 1992, C4687-1.504

Initial public offerings of stock for corporate restructuring purposes, by company, 1992, article, C4683-1.504

Initial public offerings, performance of best and worst issues, and leading underwriters, 1993 annual article, C3950-1.517

Initial public offerings, performance of leading issues and underwriters, biweekly rpt quarterly feature, C3950-1.507, C3950-1.520, C3950-1.527

Insurance (life/health) bond holdings by class and maturity period, and gross yields, by bond type, 1990-91, annual article, C1050-2.502

Insurance (life/health) industry asset allocation and investment yields, for top 125 US and Canadian companies, 1992 and trends, annual article, C1050-2.512

Insurance (property/casualty) bond holdings value, by bond type, 1991, annual article, C1050-1.507

Interest rate business cycle peaks and troughs, with trends in price of credit, industrial production, and stock performance, 1953-92, article, C3950-1.507

Investment banks with black owners, value of securities issues managed, for top 13 instns, Dec 1992, article, C4215-1.507

Investment mgmt firms, assets and operating data for approx 900 instns, Jan 1993, annual feature, C2710-2.511

Investment performance indexes for growth and value stocks, 1978-92, article, C2425-1.508

Investment performance of selected stock indexes, biweekly rpt quarterly feature, C2710-2.502, C2710-2.507, C2710-2.514

Investment performance rankings for over 1,000 top stocks, and comparisons by industry groups, 1993 annual rpt, C3950-1.505

Investment performance trends for non-US and global equities, through June 1993, C2710-2.520

Investment return and dividends per share, for 5-50 best and worst performing stocks on 3 exchanges, 1992, annual article, C8900-1.507

Investment return for 6 "blue chip" stocks vs S&P 500, 1982-92, article, C8900-1.503

Investment return of companies most and least admired by executives, 1982-92, annual article, C8900-1.508

Investment return rate for Standard & Poor's 500 stock index, 1990-92 and trends, article, C8900-1.511

Investment return rates by stock capitalization size, 1925-91, article, C2425-1.508

Securities

Investment returns for portfolios with low, medium, and high equity holdings, biweekly rpt quarterly feature, C2710–2.503, C2710–2.509

Israel company stock performance, sales, and market value, for 14 firms traded on US exchanges, 1993 article, C3950–1.523

Japan foreign direct investment, including equity capital and loans/bonds, FY51-92, annual article, R5650–2.544

Japan net capital flow, including intl securities transactions, weekly rpt quarterly article, R5650–2.505, R5650–2.514, R5650–2.531, R5650–2.550

Leveraged buyout transactions and value, with leading participants and industries, 1992 annual feature, C4683–1.501

Life insurance industry income and financial data, including investments by type of security, 1991 and trends, biennial fact book, A1325–1.4

Mass media company stock price trends, for leading firms, 1992-93, annual feature, C2710–1.540

Money and securities market activity, and related indicators, biweekly rpt, B2000–1

Mortgage (commercial) backed securities value, and securitization rates for commercial vs residential mortgages, 1992 article, A7000–1.501

Mutual fund industry financial data, investment activity, portfolio composition, and shareholder account characteristics, 1991 and trends, annual rpt, A6025–1

Mutual fund mgmt company stock performance data, for 8 firms, 1993 article, C3950–1.523

NASDAQ over-the-counter market securities trading volume and price performance, for over 4,500 issues, 1992 and trends, annual rpt, A7105–1

New York Stock Exchange activity, including stock volume and prices, credit distribution, and member firm characteristics, 1992 and trends, annual fact book, B6625–1

Oil company stock and summary financial performance, for 8 largest firms worldwide, 1992 article, C3950–1.501

Oil-related contracts traded on New York Mercantile Exchange, and types of organizations involved in trading, 1992 article, C6985–1.502

Options trading volume by commodity, securities index, and exchange, monthly rpt, A5040–3

Pension fund and mutual fund equity purchases, 1960s-90s, article, C2710–2.514

Pension fund portfolio characteristics and investment performance, 4th qtr 1992, semiannual feature, C3950–1.509

Presidential admins with largest gains and losses in S&P 500 performance, for 6 admins since 1889, 1992 article, C5800–7.505

Presidential admins 1st 4 months, change in S&P 500 performance for Clinton and 8 previous admins, 1993 article, C5800–7.535

Railroad (Class I) financial and operating data, with detail by company, 1982-91, annual rpt, A3275–8.2

Railroad shareholder equity and rate of return on equity, 1960s-92, annual rpt, A3275–5.1

Real estate investment trust securities offerings by type, 1982-92, article, C2425–1.503

Restaurant company stock price change, for 10 firms with greatest declines and gains, 1993 article, C5150–5.505, C5150–5.508, C5150–5.513

Restaurant company stock prices, for 10 firms with greatest declines and gains, Nov 1991-92, C5150–5.503

Retail chain financial data and business info for approx 240 US and Canadian companies, 1991-92 and trends, annual rpt, C3400–2

Service industries economic devs, with analysis of conditions and outlook, and comparisons to other industries, quarterly rpt, A3892–1

Service sector economic activity indicators, with leading and coincident indexes and components, and detail for financial services, monthly rpt, U1245–3

Small companies with high 5-year returns on equity, financial performance data and chief executive characteristics, for top 200 firms, 1992 annual article, C3950–1.501

Small companies with sales under $150 million, financial data for top 100 growth firms, 1993 annual article, C5800–7.529

Small companies with sales under $25 million, financial and operating data for top 100 public firms, 1992 and trends, annual feature, C4687–1.507

Small company earnings per share outlook of security analysts, for 18-80 companies, 1992-93, article, C3950–1.504

Telephone holding company finances, operations, and subsidiaries, by company, Dec 1991, annual rpt, A9360–1

Telephone local exchange carrier finances, equipment, and employment, by company, 1991 and trends, annual rpt, A9360–2

Textile and clothing companies financial data, for approx 170 firms, with industry statistical summary, 1991-92 and trends, annual rpt, C3400–5

Unit investment trust sales volume and value, by trust type, maturity period, and insurance features, monthly rpt, A6025–7

Utility long-term financing and yields, by type of issue and/or utility, 1991 and trends, annual rpt, A4700–1

Utility securities regulatory policies in US and Canada, by agency, 1991/92 annual rpt, A7015–3

Venture capital-backed firms initial public offerings, and company acquisitions, selected years 1979-91, annual rpt, A8515–1

Video game manufacturer sales and stock performance, for 6 companies, 1993 article, C3950–1.521

State and local:

Arkansas banks and other financial instns, financial condition by instn, June 1992, annual rpt, S0632–1

Arkansas State treasurer safekeeping account balances and interest rates, by account, FY92, biennial rpt, S0780–1

California insurance industry securities on deposit, FY82-91, annual rpt, S0900–1

Index by Subjects and Names

Colorado savings and loan assn and credit union financial condition, 1992 and trends, annual rpt, S1070–3

Connecticut securities broker-dealers, investment advisors, and enforcement activities, 1991 and trends, annual rpt, S1160–1

Idaho Securities Bur registration and enforcement activity, FY89-92, annual rpt, S2235–1

Illinois bank and trust companies (State-chartered) financial condition and status changes, by instn, FY92, annual rpt, S2395–1

Kansas insurance industry securities on deposit, by type and company, Dec 1992, annual rpt, S2990–1

Kentucky financial instns condition, including assets by instn and city, with regulatory info, 1992 and trends, annual rpt, S3121–1

Missouri insurance industry securities on deposit, by type and company, 1992 and trends, annual rpt, S4527–1

Nebraska insurance industry securities on deposit, by company, 1992, annual rpt, S4890–1

New York State statistical yearbook, general data, 1992 annual rpt, U5100–1.7

North Carolina public utility financial, operating, and regulatory data, by utility type and company, 1990 and trends, annual rpt, S5917–2

Oklahoma statistical abstract, general data, 1992 annual rpt, U8130–2.15

Oregon financial instns financial condition, and securities regulatory section activity, 1992, annual rpt, S6616–1

Tennessee regulatory activities affecting securities and brokers/dealers, 1986-91, annual rpt, S7466–1

Texas electric utility financial and operating data, 9 largest investor-owned utilities, 1988-92, annual rpt, S7740–1

Texas State treasurer securities on deposit, by fund account, FY92, annual rpt, S7655–2.1

Utah insurance industry securities on deposit, by company, Dec 1991, annual rpt, S7845–1

Utah statistical abstract, general data, 1993 triennial rpt, U8960–1.15

see also Corporate bonds

see also Employee stock ownership plans

see also Government securities

see also Municipal bonds

see also Mutual funds

see also New York Stock Exchange

see also Options trading

see also Public debt

see also State bonds

see also Stockbrokers

see also Tax exempt securities

see also U.S. savings bonds

Securities Data Co.

Hospital tax-exempt bond issuance value, with detail by purpose, 1989-92, article, A1865–1.507

Hospital unrated long-term bond issuances and value, 1991 and 1st 10 months 1992, article, A1865–1.503

Index by Subjects and Names

Senior citizens

Securities exchange
see New York Stock Exchange
see Stock exchanges

Security devices

Auto antitheft device availability in 1993 model year vehicles, by make, annual rpt, A5200–5

Auto fleet acquisition plans, including antitheft device installation, 1992 survey, article, C1575–2.503

Auto security system sales performance, 1993 annual survey, C0125–1.503

Dealer personnel income, education, work conditions, and activities,1993 survey, annual article, C1850–13.510

Home security mechanical equipment, alarm systems, and services market value, 1980, 1991, and 1996, article, C2000–1.507

Home security system sales, 1985-92, annual rpt, A4725–1.1

Life expectancy, shipments, and manufacturers market shares, for appliances by type, 1993 annual article, C2000–1.510

Management issues and devs for security depts, including data on device use and expenditures, monthly rpt, C1850–12

Museums and related instns use of intrusion and fire detection systems, by instn type and budget size, 1989/90 survey, A0750–1.1

Operating and financial devs for the security equipment industry, monthly rpt, C1850–13

Outlook for security equipment industry, including revenue trends, and home alarm system prices, Oct-Nov 1992 survey, annual feature, C1850–13.503

Retail store inventory shrinkage, and control measures, by type of outlet, 1991, annual survey rpt, C5150–4.504

Revenues, accounts, and operating data, for 100 leading security equipment companies, 1992, annual feature, C1850–13.507

Shipments of household appliances, by detailed product type, 1991-98, annual articles, C2000–1.503

Shopping center security operations, including staffing, equipment, and crime incidents, by center type, 1992-93 and trends, articles, C5150–4.506

see also Smoke and fire detectors

Sedatives
see Drug abuse and treatment
see Drugs

Seeds

Exports of farm products, by detailed commodity and country of destination, US and California, 1991, annual rpt, B9520–1

Financial ratios and performance, for over 350 SIC 4-digit industries, FY88-92, annual rpt, A6400–3

State and local:

Arizona agricultural production, marketing, and finances, by commodity and county, 1988-92, annual rpt, U5830–1

California field crops production, acreage, yield, and prices, by commodity and county, 1992 and trends, annual rpt, S0850–1.4

Hawaii agricultural production and marketing, by commodity and island, 1987-91, annual rpt, S2030–1

Minnesota agricultural production, marketing, and finances, by county or commodity, and farms and acreage, 1992 and trends, annual rpt, S4130–1

Nevada agricultural production, marketing, and finances, by county and commodity, and farms and acreage, 1992 and trends, annual rpt, S5010–1

North Dakota agricultural production and marketing, by commodity and county, and farm finances, 1992 and trends, annual rpt, U3600–1

Oklahoma agricultural production, marketing, and finances, by commodity and county, 1992 and trends, annual rpt, S6405–1

Oregon agricultural production, marketing, and finances, by commodity and/or county, with farms and acreage, 1991 and trends, annual rpt, S6575–1

South Dakota agricultural production, marketing, and finances, by commodity and county, and farms and acreage, 1992 and trends, annual rpt, S7280–1

Vermont commercial and agricultural seed inspection activity, 1988/89-1989/90, biennial rpt, S7978–1

Washington State agricultural production, marketing, and finances, by commodity and/or county, 1992 and trends, annual rpt, S8328–1

see also Oils, oilseeds, and fats

Segregation
see Discrimination in education
see Discrimination in housing
see School busing

Seizures
see Searches and seizures

Selective service
see also Voluntary military service

Self-employment

Black American labor force and employment data, with comparisons to whites, 1970s-91, annual compilation, C6775–2.6

Law school grad employment and salaries, by type of employer, location, and grad characteristics, 1992 and trends, annual rpt, A6505–1

Physician practice economic aspects, detailed data by specialty, 1991-92 and trends, annual compilation, A2200–5

Retirement plans for self-employed, accounts and assets, by investment objective, 1991 and trends, annual rpt, A6025–1

State and local:

Arkansas Census of Population and Housing detailed findings, 1990, U5935–7

California Census of Population and Housing detailed findings, 1990, S0840–9

Delaware employment projections, by county, 1990-2020, recurring rpt, S1375–3

Hawaii economic conditions, including employment, population, tourism, and construction, quarterly rpt, S2090–2

Hawaii self-employed (nonfarm), bimonthly rpt, B3500–1

Massachusetts municipal and county profiles, general data, 1992 annual rpt, C4712–2

New Jersey Census of Population and Housing detailed findings, by county, 1990, S5425–19

New Jersey municipal and county data book, general data, 1992 annual rpt, C4712–4

Pennsylvania Census of Population and Housing detailed findings, with selected data by county and municipality, 1990, U4130–13

Pennsylvania employment and commuting data from Census of Population and Housing, by county and municipality, 1990, C1595–16

Rhode Island Census of Population and Housing detailed findings, by county and municipality, 1990, S6930–9

Vermont labor force by employment status, and job service openings and applicant characteristics, 1993 annual planning rpt, S8025–2.2

see also Home-based offices and workers
see also Proprietorships

Semiconductors

Electronics industry market trends and outlook, including product sales and shipments, employment, and leading manufacturers, monthly rpt, C1850–2

Europe and worldwide computer chip sales for top 12 companies ranked by sales in Europe, 1991, article, C5800–7.508

Europe semiconductor consortium (Jessi) budget, 1990-1995/96, article, C1850–2.508

Sales of semiconductor production equipment, 1992-94, C1850–6.510

Shipments and foreign trade of solid state electronics products, by detailed product type, 1991 and trends, annual rpt, A4725–1.3

State/local tax effective rates for typical Massachusetts vs California company semiconductor manufacturing plant, for 5 States, 1993 article, B8500–2 514

Senate

Campaign finances, with detailed data for individual Members, and leading contributors by type and industry, 1990 election and trends, biennial rpt, R3828–2

Campaign fund finances, with expenditures by detailed item and contributions by donor type, by candidate, district, and State, 1990 elections, C2500–6

Congressional organization, major legislative and budget actions, and agency and program appropriations, 102nd Congress, 2nd session, 1992, annual rpt, C2500–2

Election results for Federal offices and Governor, by State, county, major city, and party, with voter registration and turnout, 1992 and trends, biennial rpt, C2500–1

Voting records of Senators and Representatives, by State and district, 1992, annual rpt, C2500–2

Women in US House of Representatives and Senate, by party, 1917-95, annual rpt, U4510–1.61, U4510–1.69

State and local:

Oregon Senator Bob Packwood sexual misconduct charges and investigation, public opinion, Dec 1992 Gallup Poll, C4040–1.506

Senior citizens
see Aged and aging

Sentences, criminal procedure

Sentences, criminal procedure

Correctional instn admin, inmates, facilities, costs, parole and probation, and staffing, for local, State, and Federal systems, 1992 annual series, R4300–1

State trends in prisoners sentenced to 1 year/more, by State, Dec 1992 vs 1991, article, B8500–2.520

Workplace environmental and safety law violators incarcerated, 1991, annual rpt, R8335–1.2

State and local:

Arizona correctional instn admin, including inmates by criminal background and demographic characteristics, FY92, annual rpt, S0464–2

Arkansas law enforcement officers killed, and disposition of offenders, 1981-92, annual rpt, S0652–1

California crimes and arrests, clearances, and arrest dispositions, with data by offense and offender characteristics, 1987-92, annual rpt, S0910–1.1

California criminal justice system detailed data, by offense, county, age, race-ethnicity, and sex, 1991 and trends, annual rpt, S0910–2

California prison commitments per 100 convictions, and average sentence, by crime, 1977-92, annual rpt, S0905–1.1

DC statistical profile, general data, 1992 annual rpt, S1535–3.8

Delaware public opinion on criminal sentencing, prison alternatives, and related issues, Feb 1991 survey, R8825–11

Florida correctional instns, admin, and inmates by criminal background and demographic characteristics, FY92 annual rpt, S1720–1

Florida "habitual offender" sentencing laws effect on prison population, with data by circuit court and offender characteristics, 1993 rpt, A7575–5

Georgia correctional instns, admin, and inmate characteristics, FY92, annual rpt, S1872–1

Georgia superior court sentence review panel caseload, FY92 and trends, annual rpt, S1903–1

Hawaii data book, general data, 1992 annual rpt, S2090–1.4

Illinois changes in selected sentencing laws, impact on prison population, 1992 annual rpt, S2425–1

Illinois statistical abstract, general data, 1992 annual rpt, U6910–2

Iowa correctional instn admissions, releases, and inmate characteristics, by instn, monthly rpt, S2770–1

Kansas correctional instn inmates, by offense, demographic characteristics, and instn, FY92 and trends, annual rpt, S2940–1

Massachusetts correctional instn inmate socioeconomic characteristics and criminal background, by instn, Jan 1992 and trends, annual rpt, S3805–1

Michigan correctional instns, admin, and inmates by selected demographic characteristics, 1991 and trends, annual rpt, S3960–1

Missouri correctional instn admissions, releases, and inmate characteristics, FY93, annual rpt, S4501–1

Nebraska correctional instn admin, with inmates by criminal background and demographic characteristics, by instn, FY92 and trends, annual rpt, S4850–1

New Jersey correctional instn inmates, by offense, sentence length, demographic characteristics, and instn, Dec 1991 annual rpt, S5370–1

New York State correctional instn inmates released, by criminal background, sentence, and demographic characteristics, 1991 and trends, recurring rpt series, S5725–1

New York State crimes and arrests by offense and demographic characteristics, and court activity and corrections, 1991 and trends, annual rpt, S5760–3

New York State local jail/penitentiary inmates by offense, sentence, and demographic characteristics, by county or facility, 1991, annual rpt, S5724–2

North Carolina correctional instn admissions, separations, and population, with inmate characteristics, FY93, semiannual rpt, S5900–1

North Dakota local correctional instn adult and juvenile inmate characteristics, by instn, 1991 and trends, annual rpt, S6060–3

Oklahoma correctional instn admin, including inmate characteristics, incarceration costs, and data by instn, FY91, annual rpt, S6420–1

Pennsylvania State correctional instn admin, and inmates by type of offense and demographic characteristics, 1990 and trends, annual rpt, S6782–1

South Carolina correctional instns, admin, and inmates by criminal offense and demographic characteristics, FY92 and trends, annual rpt, S7135–1

South Dakota correctional instn admin, including inmates by criminal background and demographic characteristics, FY92 and trends, annual rpt, S7296–1

Tennessee correctional instn admin, with inmate characteristics, and corrections dept finances and staff, FY92, annual rpt, S7480–1

Texas correctional instn inmates by criminal background and demographic characteristics, FY92, annual rpt, S7660–1

Texas court cases and dispositions, by type of court and case, and location, FY92, annual rpt, S7703–1

Washington State court cases and dispositions, by type of court and case, and jurisdiction, with judicial finances and personnel, 1992 and trends, annual rpt, S8339–1

Wisconsin correctional instn inmates, by criminal background and selected characteristics, series, S8692–1

Wyoming correctional instn admin, finances, inmate characteristics, and staff, and probation and parole activities, FY92 annual rpt, S8883–1

see also Capital punishment

see also Fines and settlements

see also Pardons

see also Parole and probation

Index by Subjects and Names

Separation of powers

see also Congressional-executive relations

Septicemia

Hospital patient admission rates and length of stay, by diagnosis and procedure, payment source, age, sex, and region, 1991, B4455–4

Hospital patient charges and length of stay, by diagnosis and procedure, payment source, age, and region, 1991, B4455–5

Hospital patient discharges and length of stay, by diagnosis, type of operation, age, and region, 1991, annual rpt series, B4455–1

Hospital patient discharges and length of stay, by diagnostic related group (DRG), payment source, age, and region, 1991, annual rpt series, B4455–3

State and local:

Alabama vital statistics, including population, births, deaths by cause, marriages, and divorces, by location and demographic characteristics, 1992 and trends, annual rpt, S0175–2

Alaska vital statistics, including births, deaths by cause, marriages, divorces, adoptions, and population, by demographic characteristics and location, 1990, annual rpt, S0315–1

Arkansas vital statistics, including births, deaths by cause, marriages, and divorces, by age, sex, race, and county, 1991 and trends, annual rpt, S0685–1

California vital statistics, including population, births, and deaths by cause, by demographic characteristics and county, 1990 and trends, annual rpt, S0865–1

Colorado vital statistics, including population, births, deaths by cause, abortion, marriage and divorce, and adoption, by demographic characteristics and location, 1990 and trends, annual rpt, S1010–1

Connecticut vital statistics, including births, deaths by cause, marriages, and divorces, by demographic characteristics and location, 1989, annual rpt, S1200–1

Delaware vital statistics, including births, deaths by cause, and marriages and dissolutions, by demographic characteristics and location, 1990, annual rpt, S1385–2

Florida vital statistics, including population, births, deaths by cause, and marriages and dissolutions, by location and demographic characteristics, 1992 and trends, annual rpt, S1745–3

Hawaii vital statistics, including births, deaths by cause, marriages, and dissolutions, by demographic characteristics and location, 1990, annual rpt, S2065–1.2

Idaho vital statistics, including births, deaths by cause, abortions, marriages, and divorces, by demographic characteristics and county, 1991 and trends, annual rpt, S2250–2

Kentucky vital statistics, including births, deaths by cause, marriages and divorces, and population, by demographic characteristics and county, 1991, annual rpt, S3140–1

Louisiana vital statistics, including population, births, deaths by cause, reportable diseases, marriages, and

Index by Subjects and Names — Service industries

divorces, by demographic characteristics and locality, 1989-90 and trends, annual rpt, S3295–1

Maine vital statistics, including births, deaths by cause, abortions, and marriages and divorces, by demographic characteristics and location, 1991 and trends, annual rpt, S3460–2

Maryland vital statistics, including population, births, deaths by cause, marriages, and divorces, by demographic characteristics and location, 1989 and trends, annual rpt, S3635–1

Michigan vital statistics, including births, deaths, marriages, divorces/annulments, and communicable diseases, by location and demographic characteristics, 1990 and trends, annual rpt, S4000–3

Minnesota vital statistics, including population, births, abortions, deaths, marriages, and divorces, by location and demographic characteristics, 1991 and trends, annual rpt, S4190–2

Montana vital statistics, including births, deaths by cause, abortion, disease, and marriage and divorce, by demographic characteristics and county, 1990-91 and trends, annual rpt, S4690–1

Nebraska vital statistics, including births, deaths, marriages, divorces, and population, by demographic characteristics and location, 1991 and trends, annual rpt, S4885–1

New Hampshire vital statistics, including population, births, deaths by cause, marriages, and divorces, by location and demographic characteristics, 1991 and trends, annual rpt, S5215–1

New Jersey vital statistics, including births, deaths, population, communicable diseases, and marriages and divorces, by demographic characteristics and location, 1990 and trends, annual rpt, S5405 1

New Mexico vital statistics, including population, births, deaths, and disease, by location and demographic characteristics, 1991 and trends, annual rpt, S5605–1

North Carolina deaths and rates, by cause and county, 1991 and trends, annual rpt, S5927–1.2

North Dakota vital statistics, including births, deaths by cause, marriages and divorces, and abortions, by demographic characteristics and/or county, 1991 and trends, annual rpt, S6105–2

Ohio vital statistics, including births, deaths by cause, marriages, divorces, and population, by demographic characteristics and location, 1991 and trends, annual rpt, S6285–1

Oregon vital statistics, including births, deaths by cause, communicable diseases, marriages, and divorces, by age, sex, race-ethnicity, and county, 1991 and trends, annual rpt, S6615–5

Rhode Island vital statistics, including population, births, deaths, marriages, and divorces, by demographic characteristics and locality, 1989 and trends, annual rpt, S6995–1

South Carolina deaths, by detailed cause, age, sex, and race, 1990, annual rpt, S7175–2

South Carolina vital statistics, including births, deaths by cause, marriages, and divorces, by age, sex, race, and location, 1990 and trends, annual rpt, S7175–1

South Dakota vital statistics, including births, deaths, marriage and divorce, and communicable disease, by demographic characteristics and county, 1991 and trends, annual rpt, S7345–1

Tennessee vital statistics, including births, deaths by cause, marriages, divorces, and population, by demographic characteristics and location, 1991 and trends, annual rpt, S7520–2

Texas vital statistics, including births, deaths by cause, abortions, marriages, and divorces, by location and demographic characteristics, 1991 and trends, annual rpt, S7685–1

Utah vital statistics, including births, deaths by cause, and population, by county and demographic characteristics, 1990 and trends, annual rpt, S7835–1

Vermont vital statistics, including population, births, deaths by cause, abortions, marriages, and divorces, by location and demographic characteristics, 1991 and trends, annual rpt, S8054–1

Virginia vital statistics, including births, deaths by cause, marriages and divorces, and communicable disease, by demographic characteristics and location, 1991 and trends, annual rpt, S8225–1

Washington State vital statistics, including births, deaths by cause, and population, by demographic characteristics and location, 1991 and trends, annual rpt, S8363–1

West Virginia vital statistics, including births, deaths by cause, marriages, and divorces, by location and demographic characteristics, 1991 and trends, annual rpt, S8560–1

Wisconsin vital statistics, including population, births, deaths by cause, and marriages and dissolutions, by county and demographic characteristics, 1991 and trends, annual rpt, S8715–4

Wyoming vital statistics, including population, births, deaths by cause, marriages, and divorces, by demographic characteristics and county, 1991 and trends, annual rpt, S8920–2

Serbia

Public opinion in US on news items concerning debate over using US air strikes against Serbian forces in Bosnia, by respondent characteristics, Apr/May 1993 survey, C8915–1.503

Service academies

Appropriations for higher education, by State, instn, and function, 1993/94, annual feature, C2175–1.538

Higher education enrollment of minority and foreign students at approx 3,100 instns, fall 1991, recurring feature, C2175–1.510

State and local:

California Maritime Academy funding, FY66-94, annual rpt, S0827–3

Service industries

Business executives expectations for coming qtr, attitudes on key indicators, with trends and data by census div, quarterly rpt, C3150–4

Business failures and liabilities, by detailed industry, cause, length of operation, and location, 1991-92 and trends, annual rpt, C3150–8

College grad job and salary offers, by field of study, type of employer and occupation, and degree level, by region, interim rpt series, A3940–1

College grad job and salary offers, by field of study, type of employer and occupation, and degree level, series, A3940–2

Computer services employment, and types of services outsourced by companies, 1993 article, C1850–5.508

Congressional campaign fund finances, including expenditures for lawyers/accountants, by candidate, district, and State, 1990 elections, C2500–6

Consumer complaint and inquiry activity of Better Business Burs, by detailed type of business, 1992, annual rpt, A4350–1

Corporate performance ratings by executives for leading companies in 32 industries, 1993 annual survey feature, C8900–1.508

Economic activity leading and coincident indexes and components for service sector, monthly rpt, U1245–3

Economic devs in service industries, with analysis of conditions and outlook, and comparisons to other industries, quarterly rpt, A3892–1

Engineers salaries by industry group, census div, selected metro area, and years since college degree, 1993, annual survey rpt, A0685–5

Engineers salaries by industry group, census div, selected metro area, degree level, and years since college degree, 1993, annual survey rpt, A0685–3

Executive compensation and components, by industry div and major manufacturing group, 1991, annual rpt, R4105–19

Financial performance and growth rankings for approx 1,000 top corporations, with comparisons by industry group, 1993 annual rpt, C3950–1.505

Financial ratios and performance, for over 350 SIC 4-digit industries, FY88-92, annual rpt, A6400–3

Fortune magazine ranking of top 50-100 companies in 8 nonindustrial sectors, with financial and employment data, 1992, annual feature, C8900–1.516

Fortune magazine ranking of top 50-100 companies worldwide in 8 nonindustrial sectors, with financial and employment data, 1993 annual feature, C8900–1.522

Hospital use of contract hospitality, business, and clinical services, including contract terms, 1993 survey, annual article, A1865–1.514

Japan corporate affiliate philanthropic activity in US, for service and manufacturing operations, 1992, survey article, R5650–2.560

Japan-US foreign trade in nonfactor services, 1991, annual article, R5650–2.502

Japan-US foreign trade in nonfactor services, 1992, annual article, R5650–2.561

Office building detailed income and expense data, and energy use, US and Canada, by building characteristics, metro area, and US region, 1991 and trends, annual rpt, A5600–2

Oil and gas well completion and servicing activity summary, 1992 and trends, annual article, C4420–1.504

Service industries

Operating and financial composite ratios for corporations, with establishments and receipts, for approx 200 industries, by asset size, FY90, annual rpt, C7800–1

Public relations firms and depts purchasing of selected types of support services, computer software, and telecommunications, 1992 survey, article, A8770–1.501

Quality control and improvement, views and experience of corporate executives and outside directors, July-Aug 1992 surveys, A2800–3

Shipment values and employment for top 25 nonmanufacturing or service industries, and top 15 counties in related receipts, 1992, article, C1200–1.509

Shopping center detailed income and expense data, by building characteristics, metro area, and region, 1991, annual rpt, A5600–6

Shopping center financial and operating data, with detail by type of tenant, US and Canada, 1991, triennial rpt, R9285–1

Statistical profiles of 50 States and DC, general data, 1993 annual almanac, C4712–1

World exports of commercial services, for top 20 countries, 1988, R4105–82.2

State and local:

- Arizona economic condition, including population, employment and earnings, and business activity, by industry and locality, 1985-93, semiannual rpt, U5850–1
- Arizona service industries employment and job outlook, by occupation and county, 1990-95, triennial rpt, S0465–2.35
- Arizona statistical abstract, general data, 1993 recurring rpt, U5850–2.24
- Arkansas socioeconomic trends, by MSA and/or county, 1993 annual rpt, U5935–1
- California employment in selected service industry groups, 1992 and trends, annual planning rpt, S0830–2
- California service industries employment, by industry group, 1992-93, annual rpt, S0840–3.1
- California statistical abstract, general data, 1992 annual rpt, S0840–2.11
- Florida statistical abstract, general data, 1992 annual rpt, U6660–1.18
- Georgia statistical abstract, general data, 1992-93 biennial rpt, U6730–1.7
- Hawaii data book, general data, 1992 annual rpt, S2090–1.23
- Illinois statistical abstract, general data, 1992 annual rpt, U6910–2
- Iowa retail sales and use tax filings data, and establishments reporting, by county and city, and by kind of business, quarterly rpt, S2860–1
- Kansas service industries employment and economic growth, with comparisons to other industries, 1980s-90, article, U7095–1.502
- Kentucky economic statistics, general data, 1993 annual rpt, S3104–1.3
- Maryland statistical abstract, general data, 1993-94 biennial rpt, S3605–1.5
- Mississippi statistical abstract, general data, 1992 annual rpt, U3255–4.5
- Nebraska employment and unemployment, by industry group and locality, quarterly rpt, S4895–2

New Jersey casino service industry establishments and revenues, by firm location including counties, FY92, annual rpt, S5360–1

New Jersey economic indicators, including employment, building permits, and retail trade, monthly rpt, S5425–1

New Jersey employment in 4 nonmanufacturing industry divs, by occupation, 1987 and 1990, article, S5425–1.506

New Mexico and US retail, wholesale, and service industry establishments, sales, payroll, and employment, 1977 and 1987, U7980–1.502

New Mexico economic trends and outlook, by industry div, 1982-92, annual article, U7980–1.503

New York State statistical yearbook, general data, 1992 annual rpt, U5100–1.2

North Dakota employment, by SIC 2-digit service industry, 1980 and 1990, article, S6140–4.501

Pennsylvania statistical abstract, general data, 1992 recurring rpt, U4130–6.2

South Carolina statistical abstract, general data, 1993 annual rpt, S7125–1.3

South Dakota business activity review, including selected data by city and industry, quarterly rpt, U8595–1

Tennessee statistical abstract, general data, 1992/93 annual rpt, U8710–2.7

Utah statistical abstract, general data, 1993 triennial rpt, U8960–1.16

see also Accounting and auditing
see also Advertising
see also Automobile repair and maintenance
see also Barber and beauty shops
see also Child day care
see also Consultants
see also Detective and protective services
see also Elementary and secondary education
see also Environmental services industry
see also Franchises
see also Gasoline service stations
see also Health facilities and services
see also Higher education
see also Hotels and motels
see also Information services
see also Janitorial and maintenance services
see also Labor unions
see also Laundry and cleaning services
see also Lawyers and legal services
see also Legal aid
see also Motion pictures
see also Motor vehicle rental
see also Museums
see also Nonprofit organizations and foundations
see also Public administration
see also Rental industries
see also Repair industries
see also Service workers
see also Travel agencies
see also Education and terms beginning with Educational
see also under By Industry in the "Index by Categories"

Service stations
see Gasoline service stations

Service workers

State and local:

Arizona occupational profiles, with employment and job outlook, by industry div, occupation, and county, series, S0465–2

Index by Subjects and Names

Maine employment, by SIC 2-digit industry and detailed occupation, triennial series, S3465–1

New Hampshire employment, by SIC 2- and 3-digit industry and detailed occupation, series, S5205–2

North Carolina employment in SIC 2-digit industries, by detailed occupation, triennial rpt series, S5917–5

Texas employment, by SIC 2- and 3-digit industry and detailed occupation, series, S7675–1

see also Employment and unemployment, specific industry
see also Health occupations
see also Police
see also Service industries

Servicemen's families
see Military dependents

Servicepersons life insurance programs

Policies in force and payments, 1941-91, biennial fact book, A1325–1.7

Set-aside programs

see Agricultural production quotas and price supports
see Defense contracts and procurement
see Small business

Settlements
see Fines and settlements

Severance taxes

Oil industry severance/production taxes paid, by State, 1970-90, annual compilation, C6985–9.3

Oil/gas industry severance tax payments, by State, 1992 and trends, annual rpt, A5425–1

Oil/gas industry severance taxes paid, 1973-92, annual rpt, A5425–2.2

State social, economic, and govtl indicators, with rankings, 1993 semiannual rpt, B8500–1.4

State tax rates and collections, by tax type and State, FY02-92, annual rpt, R9050–1.5

UK oil revenue tax impact on oil companies operating in North Sea, by company, 1993-96, article, C6985–1.525

State and local:

- Alabama financial condition, including revenues by source, expenditures by function and object, and fund balances, by fund and agency, FY92, annual rpt, S0129–1
- Alaska financial condition, including revenues by source, expenditures by function, fund balances, and bond obligations, FY92 and trends, annual rpt, S0275–1
- Alaska oil/gas tax revenues, by locale, 1992, annual rpt, S0285–1
- Arizona minerals severance tax collections, FY83-91, annual rpt, S0497–1
- Arizona tax revenues by source, tax rates, and disbursements to local areas, FY92 and trends, annual rpt, S0515–1
- Arkansas financial condition, including revenues by source, expenditures by function and object, and fund balances, FY92, annual rpt, S0670–1
- Arkansas severance tax county aid fund revenues, by county, FY91-92, biennial rpt, S0780–1
- Colorado tax revenues by type, with selected data by county and city, FY92 and trends, annual rpt, S1075–1

Index by Subjects and Names

Sex crimes

Florida State govt disbursements to local areas, by source of funds, FY92, annual rpt, S1717–1

Kansas tax collections by tax type, and property values, with data by county, FY92 and trends, annual rpt, S3020–1

Kentucky financial condition, including revenues by source, expenditures by function and object, fund balances, and bonded debt, FY92, annual rpt, S3120–1

Michigan financial condition, including revenues by source, expenditures by function, and fund balances, FY92 and trends, annual rpt, S3985–2

Mississippi statistical abstract, general data, 1992 annual rpt, U3255–4.10

Mississippi tax collections by type, and disbursements, with selected sales and income tax data by locality and industry, FY92 and trends, annual rpt, S4435–1

Montana revenue collections by tax type, and taxable establishments, production, and income, FY91-92 and trends, biennial rpt, S4750–1.1

Nebraska revenues from licenses, fees, and miscellaneous taxes, 1991 and trends, annual rpt, S4950–1.3

New Mexico tax revenues and disbursements, with data by tax type, county, and city, FY91-92 and trends, annual rpt, S5660–1

Ohio severance tax collections, by resource, FY89-92, annual rpt, S6390–1.5

Oklahoma tax revenues by source, and distribution to local govts and State funds, FY92 and trends, annual rpt, S6495–1

Oregon financial condition, including revenues by source, expenditures by function, and fund statements, FY92, annual rpt, S6603–2

South Dakota tax revenues by source, and aid distributed to local areas, FY92 annual rpt, S7380–1.1

Tennessee tax revenues by source and apportionments to counties, cities, and funds, FY91-92 and trends, biennial rpt, S7570–1

Texas financial condition, including revenues by source, expenditures by function and dept, and investments, with data for over 400 individual funds, FY92, annual rpt, S7655–2

Utah tax revenues by source, and distribution to localities and State funds, FY92 and trends, annual rpt, S7905–1

Wyoming mineral production and taxable valuation, by county, and severance and ad valorem taxes, FY92 annual rpt, S8990–1.2

Wyoming State treasurer financial transactions, including revenues, investments, and disbursements by local area, FY92 and trends, annual rpt, S9010–1

Sewage and wastewater systems

City fiscal condition, including budget trends and adjustments, and influencing factors, by region and population size, Mar-Apr 1993 survey, annual rpt, A8012–1.23

Construction contract awards by type of project, weekly rpt, C5800–2

Developing countries population access to safe drinking water and sanitation services, by urban-rural status and country, 1988-90, R8720–1.2

Federal budget trends, including spending by program, State, and region, FY81-94, annual rpt, R8490–11

Higher education physical plant operations, costs, employment, salaries, and energy use, by instn and region, 1991/92, recurring rpt, A3183–1

Latin America statistical abstract, general data by country, 1992 annual rpt, U6250–1.6

State economic dev condition indicators, including economic performance, business vitality, growth capacity, and tax/fiscal system, by State, 1993 annual rpt, R4225–1.1

State social, economic, and govtl indicators, with rankings, 1993 semiannual rpt, B8500–1.15

Utility regulatory agency policies and practices, and industry financial and operating data, by utility type and agency, 1991/92 annual rpt, A7015–3

World population share served by wastewater treatment in 23 OECD countries, and percent of sewage treated in 7 world regions, 1992/93 biennial rpt, R9455–1.4

World population shares with access to sanitation services, by urban-rural status and country, 1992/93 biennial rpt, R9455–1.5

State and local:

Alabama municipal data book, general data, 1992 recurring rpt, S0121–5

Alaska public utility financial and operating data, by company and utility type, 1991 and trends, with FY92 regulatory info, annual rpt, S0280–4

Alaska senior citizen tax deferment for sewer/water system assessments, by municipality, FY92, annual rpt, S0285–1

Arizona statistical abstract, general data, 1993 recurring rpt, U5850–2.16

Arkansas Census of Population and Housing detailed findings, 1990, U5935–7

California Census of Population and Housing detailed findings, 1990, S0840–9

DC statistical profile, general data, 1992 annual rpt, S1535–3.7

Florida statistical abstract, general data, 1992 annual rpt, U6660–1.8

Florida water and sewer dept regulatory activities, 1992, annual rpt, S1790–1

Hawaii data book, general data, 1992 annual rpt, S2090–1.5

Hawaii environmental quality and public health control, inspection, licensing, and enforcement activities, 1990, annual rpt, S2065–1.6

Kansas statistical abstract, general data, 1991/92 annual rpt, U7095–2.3

Louisiana Census of Population and Housing summary findings, by local area, 1990 and trends, U8010–4

Maine Census of Population and Housing summary findings, by local area, 1990, S3465–9

New Jersey Census of Population and Housing detailed findings, by county, 1990, S5425–19

New Jersey municipal and county data book, general data, 1992 annual rpt, C4712–4

New Mexico public utility operating, financial, and regulatory data, by utility type, FY92 annual rpt, S5645–1

North Carolina public utility financial, operating, and regulatory data, by utility type and company, 1990 and trends, annual rpt, S5917–2

Pennsylvania Census of Population and Housing detailed findings, with selected data by county and municipality, 1990, U4130–13

Pennsylvania housing data from Census of Population and Housing, by county and municipality, 1990, C1595–14

Pennsylvania statistical abstract, general data, 1992 recurring rpt, U4130–6.1, U4130–6.8, U4130–6.9

Rhode Island Census of Population and Housing detailed findings, by county and municipality, 1990, S6930–9

South Carolina public service commission regulatory activities, with financial and operating data for individual utilities and railroads, FY92 annual rpt, S7235–1

Texas trade, transportation, and public utilities employment, by SIC 2- and 3-digit industry and detailed occupation, 2nd qtr 1991, triennial survey rpt, S7675–1.31

Sex

see Homosexuality

see Men

see Sex crimes

see Sex discrimination

see Sex education

see Sexual behavior

see Sexual sterilization

see Women

see under By Sex in the "Index by Categories"

Sex crimes

State and local:

Alabama juvenile and adult arrests, by type of offense, 1992, annual rpt, S0119–1.1

Arizona arrests by offense, offender characteristics, and county, 1992, annual rpt, S0505–2.2

Arkansas child sexual abuse cases, by county, FY91, annual rpt, S0700–2.2

Arkansas crimes and arrests, by offense, victim and offender characteristics, and location, 1992 and trends, annual rpt, S0652–1

California crimes and arrests, clearances, and arrest dispositions, with data by offense and offender characteristics, 1987-92, annual rpt, S0910–1.1

California criminal justice system detailed data, by offense, county, age, race-ethnicity, and sex, 1991 and trends, annual rpt, S0910–2

Colorado crimes and arrests, by offense and location, with offender characteristics, and assaults on police, 1992, annual rpt, S1068–1

Connecticut crimes and arrests, by offense, with data by local agency, and victim-offender characteristics, 1992, annual rpt, S1256–1

DC criminal justice system summary, including crimes and arrests, criminal procedure, prisoners, and parole, 1991 and trends, annual rpt, S1535–2

Florida crimes and arrests, by offense, with data by victim and offender characteristics, 1992, annual rpt, S1770–1

Sex crimes

Hawaii crimes and arrests, by offense, with data by county and victim-offender characteristics, 1992, annual rpt, S2035–1

Idaho crimes and arrests, by offense, with data by location and offender characteristics, 1992 and trends, annual rpt, S2275–2

Illinois crimes and arrests, by offense, with data by location and offender characteristics, 1991, annual rpt, S2536–1

Indiana child abuse and neglect cases by county and victim and perpetrator characteristics, FY92 annual rpt, S2623–1.7

Kansas crimes and arrests, by offense, with data by location, agency, and victim-offender characteristics, 1992 and trends, annual rpt, S2925–1.1

Kentucky arrests by county and offense, and law enforcement employment by agency, 1992, annual rpt, S3150–1.2

Maine arrests of adults and juveniles, by offense, age, and sex, 1991, annual rpt, S3475–1.2

Maryland crimes and arrests, by offense, location, and offender characteristics, with law enforcement employment and assaults on officers, 1992 and trends, annual rpt, S3665–1

Massachusetts correctional instn inmates by current and prior sex offenses, by instn, Jan 1992, annual rpt, S3805–1

Michigan crimes and arrests, by offense, with data by location and offender characteristics, 1992 and trends, annual rpt, S3997–1

Missouri crimes and arrests, by offense and location, with victim and offender characteristics, 1991 and trends, annual rpt, S4560–2

Montana crimes and clearances, by offense and jurisdiction, 1992, annual rpt, S4705–1

New Hampshire arrests, by offense and offender age, sex, and race-ethnicity, 1991, annual rpt, S5250–2.2

New Jersey arrests by offense, age, race-ethnicity, sex, and county, 1992 and trends, annual rpt, S5430–1.2

New York State crimes and arrests by offense and demographic characteristics, and court activity and corrections, 1991 and trends, annual rpt, S5760–3

North Carolina arrests by detailed offense, offender characteristics, and county, 1991-92, annual rpt, S5955–1.2

North Dakota crimes and arrests, by offense, location, and offender characteristics, and law enforcement employment, 1991 and trends, annual rpt, S6060–1

Oklahoma crimes and arrests, by offense, with victim and offender characteristics, 1990-92, annual rpt, S6465–1.1

Oregon crimes and arrests, by offense, with data by county, local agency, and offender characteristics, 1992 and trends, annual rpt, S6603–3

Pennsylvania crimes and arrests, by offense, with data by location and offender characteristics, 1992 and trends, annual rpt, S6860–1

South Carolina crimes and arrests, by offense, with data by location and victim-offender characteristics, and assaults on officers, 1992 and trends, annual rpt, S7205–1

Texas arrests, by age, sex, race-ethnicity, and offense, 1992, annual rpt, S7735–2.2

Utah crimes and arrests, by offense, county, and local agency, 1992 and trends, annual rpt, S7890–3

Virginia crimes and arrests by offense, and law enforcement employment, by location and reporting agency, 1992, annual rpt, S8295–2.2

Washington State crimes and arrests, by offense, with data by location and offender characteristics, 1992 and trends, annual rpt, S8440–1

West Virginia crimes and arrests, by offense, location, and offender characteristics, 1990-91, annual rpt, S8610–1

Wisconsin crimes and arrests, by offense, offender characteristics, county, and local agency, 1992 and trends, annual rpt, S8771–1

Wyoming adult and juvenile arrests, by offense, county, and local jurisdiction, 1991, annual rpt, S8867–3.2

see also Prostitution

see also Rape

Sex discrimination

Communications industries conditions for women, including opportunities and sexual harassment, Dec 1992 survey, article, C2710–1.528

Elementary/secondary school superintendents personal and professional characteristics and views, 1992 survey rpt, A0775–5

Employer use of formal sexual harassment policies, by type of employer, 1992/93 annual survey rpt, U3130–1

Equal Employment Opportunity Commission sexual harassment complaints received, 1987-92, article, C1850–2.507

High-technology industry CEO views on existence of a "glass ceiling" for female executives, June 1992 survey, B4490–2.34

Public planning agencies with sexual harassment personnel policies, by jurisdiction size, 1991 survey rpt, A2615–3

Secondary school student sexual harassment experience at school, for 8-11th graders, by sex, 1993 survey, article, R4800–2.519

State and local:

Iowa State constitution equal rights amendment, election results by county, 1992, biennial rpt, S2865–1

Missouri Human Rights Commission discrimination cases and dispositions, by case type, FY92 and trends, annual rpt, S4530–2.2

Oregon Senator Bob Packwood sexual misconduct charges and investigation, public opinion, Dec 1992 Gallup Poll, C4040–1.506

Sex education

Public opinion on AIDS info in sex education courses, 1987-92 surveys, A0610–1.502

State and local:

Maryland public school funding for AIDS education, by county, 1991/92, annual rpt, S3610–2.9

Sexual assault

see Rape

see Sex crimes

Sexual behavior

Adult sexual behavior, including extramarital sex, condom use, and impact of AIDS, by demographic characteristics, 1990 survey, article, A2623–1.512

Africa women's premarital sexual experience and childbearing, for 7 Sub-Saharan countries, 1986-89, article, A5160–6.503

Black children and youth population, economic, health, and education data, with comparisons to whites, 1993 rpt, R3840–21

College freshmen attitudes on selected moral and family issues, by sex and instn type, fall 1992, annual survey, U6215–1

Developing countries fertility, family planning, sexual behavior, and child health indicators, with selected detail by demographic characteristics, 1984-92 surveys, U2520–1.51

Drug abuser AIDS risk sexual behavior, among injection drug users and crack smokers, May-June 1991 study, article, A2623–1.510

Heterosexuals with multiple sexual partners, including demographic characteristics, number of partners, and condom use, 1990/91 survey, article, A5160–1.506

High school students sexual activity and condom use, by sex and race-ethnicity, 1993 article, C4215–1.505

Hispanic Americans sexual activity with multiple partners, and condom use, with comparisons to whites, by sex and/or marital status, 1991 survey, article, A5160–1.505

Hospital patients with psychiatric diagnoses related to sexual behavior, length of stay by age, sex, and region, 1991, annual rpt series, B4455–2

Kenya elementary, secondary, and vocational students sexual experience, by selected characteristics, 1989, article, A5160–6.505

Magazines (sexually oriented) started 1987-91, with number still published in 1993, article, C2575–1.507

Men's sexual behavior, including condom use, and AIDS knowledge and risks, by selected characteristics, 1991 survey, articles, A5160–1.503

Population shares engaging in sex with multiple partners and strangers, by selected characteristics, 1988-90 surveys, article, A5160–1.503

Public opinion on social, political, and economic issues, detailed data, 1972-91 surveys, annual rpt, U6395–1

Teenage pregnant women's substance abuse correlated with risky sexual behavior, 1988/89 Northwest metro area study, article, A5160–1.501

Women (unmarried) with unplanned pregnancies, sexual behavior by selected characteristics, 1989/90 Baltimore study, article, A5160–1.506

Women's number of sexual partners, by marital status, 1993 rpt, A5160–10

Sexually transmitted diseases

Women's sexual behavior and disease risk, including data on multiple partners and condom use, by selected characteristics, 1988, article, A5160–1.501

Zambia student views on sexual behavior and treatment of persons infected with AIDS virus, by respondent characteristics, 1990 survey, article, A5160–6.503

see also Contraceptives

see also Family planning

see also Homosexuality

see also Obscenity and pornography

see also Sex crimes

Sexual harassment

see Sex discrimination

see Work conditions

Sexual sterilization

Developing countries family planning efforts, with data on socioeconomic and health conditions compared to developed countries, by country, 1980s-90, R8720–1.1

Developing countries fertility, family planning, sexual behavior, and child health indicators, with selected detail by demographic characteristics, 1984-92 surveys, U2520–1.51

Developing countries sexual sterilization prevalence and interest among women, by country, 1993 article, A5160–6.503

Hospital patient discharges and length of stay, by diagnosis, type of operation, age, and region, 1991, annual rpt series, B4455–1

Women's use of sterilization and other contraceptive methods after childbirth, in 25 developing countries, 1980s, article, A5160–6.501

World contraceptive use and access, including sexual sterilization, by country, 1992/93 biennial rpt, R9455–1.5

Sexually transmitted diseases

Black children and youth population, economic, health, and education data, with comparisons to whites, 1993 rpt, R3840–21

Hospital patient discharges and length of stay, by diagnosis, type of operation, age, and region, 1991, annual rpt series, B4455–1

Incidence, risks, and govt spending for selected sexually transmitted diseases, 1993 rpt, A5160–10

Urban public school systems sexually transmitted disease prevention programs, for 47 systems, 1990/91, A4425–4

Women (unmarried) with unplanned pregnancies, behavior regarding sexually transmitted disease risk, by selected characteristics, 1989/90 Baltimore study, article, A5160–1.506

Women's sexual behavior and disease risk, including data on multiple partners and condom use, by selected characteristics, 1988, article, A5160–1.501

Women's sexually transmitted disease prevention using various contraceptive methods, review of research results, 1992 article, A2623–1.501

State and local:

Alabama public health dept activities, including services provided, inspection and licensing activity, staff and finances, and vital statistics and health data, 1992 annual rpt, S0175–3

Alabama vital statistics, including population, births, deaths by cause, marriages, and divorces, by location and demographic characteristics, 1992 and trends, annual rpt, S0175–2

Arkansas vital statistics, including births, deaths by cause, marriages, and divorces, by age, sex, race, and county, 1991 and trends, annual rpt, S0685–1

California vital statistics, including population, births, and deaths by cause, by demographic characteristics and county, 1990 and trends, annual rpt, S0865–1

Colorado vital statistics, including population, births, deaths by cause, abortion, marriage and divorce, and adoption, by demographic characteristics and location, 1990 and trends, annual rpt, S1010–1

Connecticut vital statistics, including births, deaths by cause, marriages, and divorces, by demographic characteristics and location, 1989, annual rpt, S1200–1

Florida deaths by selected cause, and incidence of selected communicable diseases, by county, 1992 annual rpt, S1746–1.1

Florida vital statistics, including population, births, deaths by cause, and marriages and dissolutions, by location and demographic characteristics, 1992 and trends, annual rpt, S1745–3

Georgia county guide, general data, 1993 annual rpt, U6750–1

Hawaii health dept activities and services, including vital statistics and disease control, by location, 1990, annual rpt, S2065–1

Idaho vital statistics, including births, deaths by cause, abortions, marriages, and divorces, by demographic characteristics and county, 1991 and trends, annual rpt, S2250–2

Iowa vital statistics, including population, births, deaths by cause, marriages, and divorces, by demographic characteristics and location, 1991 and trends, annual rpt, S2795–1

Kansas vital statistics, including population, births, deaths by cause, abortions, marriages, and divorces, by demographic characteristics and location, 1991 and trends, annual rpt, S2975–1

Louisiana vital statistics, including population, births, deaths by cause, reportable diseases, marriages, and divorces, by demographic characteristics and locality, 1989-90 and trends, annual rpt, S3295–1

Maine vital statistics, including births, deaths by cause, abortions, and marriages and divorces, by demographic characteristics and location, 1991 and trends, annual rpt, S3460–2

Maryland vital statistics, including population, births, deaths by cause, marriages, and divorces, by demographic characteristics and location, 1989 and trends, annual rpt, S3635–1

Massachusetts vital statistics, including births, deaths by cause, marriages, divorces, and population, by locality and demographic characteristics, 1990 and trends, annual rpt, S3850–1

Michigan vital statistics, including births, deaths, marriages, divorces/annulments, and communicable diseases, by location and demographic characteristics, 1990 and trends, annual rpt, S4000–3

Minnesota vital statistics, including population, births, abortions, deaths, marriages, and divorces, by location and demographic characteristics, 1991 and trends, annual rpt, S4190–2

Mississippi vital statistics, including births, deaths by cause, marriages, and divorces, by demographic characteristics and location, 1992 and trends, annual rpt, S4350–1

Missouri vital statistics, including population, births, deaths by cause, and marriages and divorces, by location and demographic characteristics, 1992 and trends, annual rpt, S4518–1

Montana vital statistics, including births, deaths by cause, abortion, disease, and marriage and divorce, by demographic characteristics and county, 1990-91 and trends, annual rpt, S4690–1

New Hampshire vital statistics, including population, births, deaths by cause, marriages, and divorces, by location and demographic characteristics, 1991 and trends, annual rpt, S5215–1

New Jersey vital statistics, including births, deaths, population, communicable diseases, and marriages and divorces, by demographic characteristics and location, 1990 and trends, annual rpt, S5405–1

New Mexico vital statistics, including population, births, deaths, and disease, by location and demographic characteristics, 1991 and trends, annual rpt, S5605–1

New York State vital statistics, including population, births, deaths by cause, reportable diseases, and marriages and dissolutions, by demographic characteristics and/or location, 1990 and trends, annual rpt, S5765–1

Ohio vital statistics, including births, deaths by cause, marriages, divorces, and population, by demographic characteristics and location, 1991 and trends, annual rpt, S6285–1

Oregon vital statistics, including births, deaths by cause, communicable diseases, marriages, and divorces, by age, sex, race-ethnicity, and county, 1991 and trends, annual rpt, S6615–5

Rhode Island vital statistics, including population, births, deaths, marriages, and divorces, by demographic characteristics and locality, 1989 and trends, annual rpt, S6995–1

South Carolina deaths, by detailed cause, age, sex, and race, 1990, annual rpt, S7175–2

South Carolina vital statistics, including births, deaths by cause, marriages, and divorces, by age, sex, race, and location, 1990 and trends, annual rpt, S7175–1

South Dakota vital statistics, including births, deaths, marriage and divorce, and communicable disease, by demographic characteristics and county, 1991 and trends, annual rpt, S7345–1

Tennessee vital statistics, including births, deaths by cause, marriages, divorces, and population, by demographic characteristics and location, 1991 and trends, annual rpt, S7520–2

Sexually transmitted diseases

Texas vital statistics, including births, deaths by cause, abortions, marriages, and divorces, by location and demographic characteristics, 1991 and trends, annual rpt, S7685–1

Vermont vital statistics, including population, births, deaths by cause, abortions, marriages, and divorces, by location and demographic characteristics, 1991 and trends, annual rpt, S8054–1

Virginia vital statistics, including births, deaths by cause, marriages and divorces, and communicable disease, by demographic characteristics and location, 1991 and trends, annual rpt, S8225–1

West Virginia vital statistics, including births, deaths by cause, marriages, and divorces, by location and demographic characteristics, 1991 and trends, annual rpt, S8560–1

Wisconsin vital statistics, including population, births, deaths by cause, and marriages and dissolutions, by county and demographic characteristics, 1991 and trends, annual rpt, S8715–4

see also Acquired immune deficiency syndrome

see also under By Disease in the "Index by Categories"

Shale oil

see Oil shale

Shampoo

see Personal care products

Shanghai, China

Birthweight of infants correlated with paternal smoking habits and selected characteristics of mother, Oct 1986-Sept 1987, article, A2623–1.504

Shapiro, Isaac

"Where Have All the Dollars Gone? A State-by-State Analysis of Income Disparities Over the 1980s", R3834–13

Shapiro, Leo J., and Associates Inc.

Beverage purchasing at discount stores, and for leading fruit juice brands, 1993 survey articles, C5150–3.510

Children's toiletry product interest among consumers, and retail outlets shopped, 1993 survey article, C5150–2.519

Discount chain consumer natl brand preferences, by product category and chain, and by age group, 1993 survey, annual feature, C5150–3.521

Discount chain top-selling natl brands cited by managers, by product category, chain, and region, 1993 survey, annual feature, C5150–3.520

Drugstore chain and brand preferences of consumers, with data by product type and region, 1992 annual survey feature, C5150–2.503

Food purchasing in discount and drugstores, by product category, 1992-93, survey article, C5150–3.515

Pharmacist requirements under 1990 Omnibus Budget Reconciliation Act (OBRA) to keep Medicaid patient drug use records and offer counseling, consumer views, 1993 article, C5150–2.509

Retail chain store expansion devs, and equipment and construction costs, by type of chain, 1993 annual articles, C5150–4.507

Retail chain store use of consultants, Sept-Oct 1992 survey, article, C5150–4.504

Sharjah

see United Arab Emirates

Shearson Lehman Brothers Inc.

Supermarket industry total and leveraged buyout related debt, and sales for total and leveraged companies, 1985-91, article, C5225–1.506

Sheep

see Livestock and livestock industry

see Wool and wool trade

Shellfish

Exports of farm products, by detailed commodity and country of destination, US and California, 1991, annual rpt, B9520–1

State and local:

Alaska crab fishing fatalities and lost vessels, with detail for selected incidents, 1992/93, article, C8900–1.516

California statistical abstract, general data, 1992 annual rpt, S0840–2.7

Georgia statistical abstract, general data, 1992-93 biennial rpt, U6730–1.5

Maryland statistical abstract, general data, 1993-94 biennial rpt, S3605–1.3

New Jersey seafood harvest and value, for top 10 products, 1988-92, annual rpt, S5350–1

South Carolina statistical abstract, general data, 1993 annual rpt, S7125–1.1

see also Fish and fishing industry

Sheltered workshops

State and local:

Missouri special education programs, including sheltered workshops and financing, 1991/92, annual rpt, S4505–1.1

Sheriffs

State and local:

Alabama crimes and arrests, by offense and location, with data on law enforcement employment and assaults on officers, 1992 and trends, annual rpt, S0119–1

Arizona law enforcement employment by sex, by local agency, Oct 1992, annual rpt, S0505–2.2

Arkansas crimes and arrests, and law enforcement personnel by sex, by agency and county, 1992, annual rpt, S0652–1

California criminal justice system expenditures and employment, by function, 1987-92, annual rpt, S0910–1.2

California criminal justice system expenditures and employment, by type of agency or function, 1982-91, annual rpt, S0910–2.1

Colorado crimes and arrests, by offense and location, with offender characteristics, and assaults on police, 1992, annual rpt, S1068–1

Idaho crimes and arrests, law enforcement employees by sex, and assaults on officers, by local agency and county, 1992, annual rpt, S2275–2

Illinois crimes and arrests, by offense, with data by location and offender characteristics, 1991, annual rpt, S2536–1

Kansas law enforcement employees by demographic characteristics and local agency, with assaults on police by circumstance, 1992, annual rpt, S2925–1.2

Kentucky crimes and arrests, law enforcement employment, and assaults on police, 1992, annual rpt, S3150–1

Maine crimes reported, law enforcement employment, and assaults on officers, by reporting agency and/or county, 1991, annual rpt, S3475–1.2

Maine election results, by district, county, and municipality, 1992 general election, biennial rpt, S3490–1

Maryland law enforcement employment by sex, criminal offenses and arrests, and assaults on police, by local agency and county, 1991-92, annual rpt, S3665–1

Michigan crimes and arrests, by offense, with officers killed by dept type, 1992 and trends, annual rpt, S3997–1

Missouri crimes and arrests, by offense and location, with victim and offender characteristics, 1991 and trends, annual rpt, S4560–2

New Hampshire election results, by county and locality, 1992, biennial rpt, S5255–1

New Hampshire Index crimes reported, by agency and county, 1991, annual rpt, S5250–2.2

New Jersey election results and voter registration, by location, 1992 general election, annual rpt, S5440–1

New Jersey law enforcement employment, by agency, and assaults on officers, 1992 and trends, annual rpt, S5430–1.4

New York State crimes and arrests by offense and demographic characteristics, and court activity and corrections, 1991 and trends, annual rpt, S5760–3

North Carolina crimes by offense, and law enforcement employment, by local agency, 1991-92, annual rpt, S5955–1.1

North Dakota crimes and arrests, by offense, location, and offender characteristics, and law enforcement employment, 1991 and trends, annual rpt, S6060–1

Ohio election results and voter registration, by local area, 1991-92 and trends, biennial rpt, S6380–1

Oklahoma Crime Index offenses, by county and reporting agency, 1990-92, annual rpt, S6465–1.2

Oregon crimes by offense, law enforcement employees by sex, and assaults on police, by local agency, 1992 and trends, annual rpt, S6603–3.2

Pennsylvania crimes and arrests, by offense, location, and offender characteristics, with law enforcement employment, 1992 and trends, annual rpt, S6860–1

Texas crimes and arrests, law enforcement employment, and assaults on officers, with data by reporting agency, 1992, annual rpt, S7735–2.2

Utah law enforcement employment, by county and local agency, 1992, annual rpt, S7890–3

Virginia crimes and arrests by offense, and law enforcement employment, by location and reporting agency, 1992, annual rpt, S8295–2.2

Washington State crimes and clearances, and law enforcement employment, by reporting agency, 1992, annual rpt, S8440–1

West Virginia crimes and arrests by offense, agency type, and county, with data on law enforcement employment and assaults on officers, 1990-91, annual rpt, S8610–1

Wisconsin crimes and arrests, by offense, offender characteristics, county, and local agency, 1992 and trends, annual rpt, S8771–1

Wyoming crimes and arrests, and law enforcement personnel, by jurisdiction, 1991, annual rpt, S8867–3

Shigellosis

see Food and waterborne diseases

Shipbuilding and repairing

Financial ratios and performance, for over 350 SIC 4-digit industries, FY88-92, annual rpt, A6400–3

Govt aid programs in 6 OECD shipbuilding countries, and impact on US industry, 1993 recurring rpt, A8900–8

Operating and financial composite ratios for corporations, with establishments and receipts, for approx 200 industries, by asset size, FY90, annual rpt, C7800–1

Shipments

see Under names of specific industries

Ships and shipping

Financial ratios and performance, for over 350 SIC 4-digit industries, FY88-92, annual rpt, A6400–3

Latin America statistical abstract, general data by country, 1992 annual rpt, U6250–1.3

Logistics trends and devs, including data on costs, finances of major carriers by mode, and foreign trade, 1993 annual compilation, C2150–1.506

Mexico-Texas transportation system analysis, including bilateral trade, operations by transport mode, and data by locale, 1993 rpt, U8850–9

Offshore oil/gas support vessel fleet characteristics, by company, 1993 annual article, C6985–2.505

Oil/gas seismic exploration land crews and vessels, by world area or country, quarterly press release, A8912–2

Oil/gas seismic exploration land crews and vessels, Canada and US, monthly press release, A8912–1

Operating and financial composite ratios for corporations, with establishments and receipts, for approx 200 industries, by asset size, FY90, annual rpt, C7800–1

Trends in transportation operations and finances, by mode, 1991 annual rpt, R4815–1

World waterborne oil and dry cargo volume handled, by country, 1986-88, biennial rpt, R9455–1.7

State and local:

Alabama statistical abstract, general data, 1992 recurring rpt, U5680–2.7

Georgia statistical abstract, general data, 1992-93 biennial rpt, U6730–1.8

Hawaii data book, general data, 1992 annual rpt, S2090–1.18, S2090–1.24

Idaho economic profile, general data, 1992 recurring rpt, S2218–2.8

Maine employment in trade, utilities, and transportation SIC 2-digit industries, by detailed occupation, 2nd qtr 1991, triennial rpt, S3465–1.25

North Carolina employment in trade, transportation, communications, utilities, govt, and education, by detailed occupation, 2nd qtr 1991, triennial rpt, S5917–5.2

Texas trade, transportation, and public utilities employment, by SIC 2- and 3-digit industry and detailed occupation, 2nd qtr 1991, triennial survey rpt, S7675–1.31

Washington State public service and utility companies property value, by company and county, 1992, annual rpt, S8415–1.4

see also Barges

see also Boats and boating

see also Foreign trade

see also Freight

see also Harbors and ports

see also Inland water transportation

see also Marine accidents and safety

see also Naval vessels

see also Navigation

see also Oil spills

see also Passenger ships

see also Service academies

see also Shipbuilding and repairing

see also Tanker ships

Shoes and shoe industry

Athletic shoe advertising expenditures and market shares for top 10 brands, 1991-92, annual rpt, C2710–1.547

Consumer buying power survey of population, income, and sales by product line, by State, metro area, county, and census div, 1993 annual rpt, C1200–1.514

Cotton and other fiber consumption in textile production, by detailed end use, 1990-92, annual rpt, A7485–1

Financial data and business info for approx 240 US and Canadian retail chains, 1991-92 and trends, annual rpt, C3400–2

Financial performance indicators for 21 shoe companies, FY92 and trends, annual rpt, B8130–2

Financial ratios and performance, for over 350 SIC 4-digit industries, FY88-92, annual rpt, A6400–3

Operating and financial composite ratios for corporations, with establishments and receipts, for approx 200 industries, by asset size, FY90, annual rpt, C7800–1

Production and average price of footwear, commodity yearbook Jan-Sept 1993 updates, C2400–2

Production and average price of footwear, Jan 1982-Mar 1992, commodity yearbook, C2400–1

Production and operating data, including trade by country, retail sales, and consumer expenditures, quarterly rpt, A4957–2

Production, employment, trade, marketing, and related data for footwear industry, by SIC 2- to 5-digit code or product type, 1992 annual rpt, A4957–1

Sales of women's and men's shoes by retail outlet type, 1991-92, article, C5150–3.515

Shopping center financial and operating data, with detail by type of tenant, US and Canada, 1991, triennial rpt, R9285–1

Sporting goods purchaser characteristics, by product category, 1992, annual survey rpt, A8485–4

Sporting goods purchases, by product and outlet type, census div, and purchaser characteristics, with average prices, 1992 and trends, annual survey, A8485–2

Women's nonathletic shoes sales volume, by retail outlet type, 1990-92, article, C5150–3.511

State and local:

Texas trade, transportation, and public utilities employment, by SIC 2- and 3-digit industry and detailed occupation, 2nd qtr 1991, triennial survey rpt, S7675–1.31

Shoplifting

Shopping center security operations, including staffing, equipment, and crime incidents, by center type, 1992-93 and trends, articles, C5150–4.506

State and local:

Alabama larceny offenses and value of stolen property, by type of offense, 1992, annual rpt, S0119–1.1

Arizona larceny offenses by detailed type, with value of property stolen, 1992, annual rpt, S0505–2.1

Arkansas crimes and arrests, by offense, victim and offender characteristics, and location, 1992 and trends, annual rpt, S0652–1

California crimes and arrests, clearances, and arrest dispositions, with data by offense and offender characteristics, 1987-92, annual rpt, S0910–1.1

California larceny/theft offenses by detailed type, 1982-91, annual rpt, S0910–2.1

Connecticut larceny offenses and value of stolen property, by type of offense, 1992, annual rpt, S1256–1.1

Florida crimes and arrests, by offense, with data by victim and offender characteristics, 1992, annual rpt, S1770–1

Hawaii crimes and arrests, by offense, with data by county and victim-offender characteristics, 1992, annual rpt, S2035–1

Idaho crimes and arrests, by offense, with data by location and offender characteristics, 1992 and trends, annual rpt, S2275–2

Kansas larceny offenses and value of stolen property, by type of theft and location, 1992, annual rpt, S2925–1.1

Kentucky crimes and value of property stolen, by type of larceny offense, 1992, annual rpt, S3150–1.1

Maine larceny offenses and stolen property value, by offense type, 1990-91, annual rpt, S3475–1.1

Maryland larceny offenses by type, 1992, annual rpt, S3665–1

Michigan larceny offenses by detailed type, 1992 and trends, annual rpt, S3997–1

Missouri crimes and arrests, by offense and location, with victim and offender characteristics, 1991 and trends, annual rpt, S4560–2

New Hampshire larceny offenses and value stolen, by offense type, 1991, annual rpt, S5250–2.1

New Jersey crimes and arrests, by offense, with data by location and offender characteristics, 1992 and trends, annual rpt, S5430–1

New York State larceny offenses and value of stolen property, by type of offense, 1991, annual rpt, S5760–3.1

North Carolina crimes by offense, and law enforcement employment, by local agency, 1991-92, annual rpt, S5955–1.1

Shoplifting

North Dakota crimes and arrests, by offense, location, and offender characteristics, and law enforcement employment, 1991 and trends, annual rpt, S6060–1

Oklahoma crimes and arrests, by offense, with victim and offender characteristics, 1990-92, annual rpt, S6465–1.1

Oregon crimes and arrests, by offense, with data by county, local agency, and offender characteristics, 1992 and trends, annual rpt, S6603–3.1

Pennsylvania crimes and arrests, by offense, with data by location and offender characteristics, 1992 and trends, annual rpt, S6860–1

South Carolina larceny offenses by detailed type, 1991-92, annual rpt, S7205–1.1

Texas theft offenses and value of property stolen, by offense type, 1992, annual rpt, S7735–2.1

Utah crimes and arrests, by offense, county, and local agency, 1992 and trends, annual rpt, S7890–3

Virginia larceny offenses by detailed type, with value of property stolen, 1991-92, annual rpt, S8295–2.1

Washington State crimes and arrests, by offense, with data by location and offender characteristics, 1992 and trends, annual rpt, S8440–1

West Virginia larceny offenses and value stolen, by offense type, 1990-91, annual rpt, S8610–1.1

Wisconsin theft offenses by detailed type, with value of property stolen, 1992, annual rpt, S8771–1

Wyoming larceny offenses and value of stolen property, by offense type, 1991, annual rpt, S8867–3.1

Shopping centers

- Drugstore (independent pharmacy) financial and operating data, by store characteristics, 1991 and trends, annual survey, D5165–1
- Expansion plans of top 10 shopping center developers, with square footage added, and new centers, 1991-92, annual article, C5150–4.506
- Financial and operating data, with detail by type of tenant, US and Canada, 1991, triennial rpt, R9285–1
- Hardware finances and operations, for hardware stores, home centers, and lumber/building material outlets, by type of location, 1991, annual rpt series, A8275–1
- Income and expense data for shopping centers, by building characteristics, metro area, and region, 1991, annual rpt, A5600–6
- Insurance costs per square foot, by type of center, 1992 article, C5150–4.503
- Restaurant industry financial and operating data, by establishment characteristics and location, 1992, annual rpt, A8200–3
- Restaurants (table service) in shopping centers, finances and operations, with comparison to non-center establishments, 1991, article, A8200–1.505
- Sales per square foot, and square footage per capita, 1987-92, article, C5150–4.508
- Security operations at shopping centers, including staffing, equipment, and crime incidents, by center type, 1992-93 and trends, articles, C5150–4.506

Security personnel in shopping centers use of selected tools/equipment, 1993 article, C1850–12.511

Security vehicle types used by shopping centers/malls, 1993 feature, C1850–12.508

Urban shopping centers and retail stores in daily newspaper markets in US and Canada, by company, 1993 annual rpt, C3250–1

State and local:

Florida shopping center rents and vacancy rates in 8 metro areas, and centers under construction, 1993 article, C5150–4.508

Hawaii data book, general data, 1992 annual rpt, S2090–1.23

Shrimp

see Shellfish

Shuptrine, Sarah C.

"Uninsured Children in the South", R9000–1

Sibson and Co.

- Food marketing mgmt personnel compensation, by position, by company sales size and region, year ended Mar 1993, annual survey, A4950–6
- Sales and marketing executive compensation, for top 100 executives, with company sales and profit data, 1992 annual article, C1200–1.501

Sick, Gary

"Islamic Fundamentalism", R4105–82.7

Sickle cell anemia

- Hospital patient admission rates and length of stay, by diagnosis and procedure, payment source, age, sex, and region, 1991, B4455–4
- Hospital patient charges and length of stay, by diagnosis and procedure, payment source, age, and region, 1991, B4455–5
- Hospital patient discharges and length of stay, by diagnosis, type of operation, age, and region, 1991, annual rpt series, B4455–1

State and local:

South Carolina deaths, by detailed cause, age, sex, and race, 1990, annual rpt, S7175–2

see *also* under By Disease in the "Index by Categories"

Sickness

see Absenteeism

see Diseases and disorders

see Health condition

see Hospitalization

Signs and symbols

see National signs and symbols

Silicon

see Nonmetallic minerals and mines

Silk

- Deliveries of raw silk, and mill consumption, 1970s-92, annual article, C3460–1.505
- Futures trading in silk and dried cocoon on foreign exchanges, monthly rpt, A5040–5
- Imports of textiles and fibers by type, 1978-92, annual feature, C3460–1.506
- Open interest on futures contracts in silk and dried cocoon on foreign exchanges, monthly rpt, A5040–6
- Production, consumption, stocks, trade, and prices for approx 100 basic commodities, including by country and producing State, commodity yearbook for 1993, C2400–1, C2400–2

Index by Subjects and Names

World demand for silk, 1988-92, annual rpt, C3460–1.508, C3460–1.509

Silver

- Chicago Board of Trade futures and options trading in financial instruments and agricultural commodities, 1992, annual rpt, B2120–1
- Coins (silver) issued, face value, silver content, and physical characteristics, by mint, for 83 countries, 1992, annual rpt, A8902–2
- Jewelry industry statistics on sales, marketing, trade, and employment, with customer characteristics, 1993 annual almanac, C2150–7.509
- Latin America statistical abstract, general data by country, 1992 annual rpt, U6250–1.23
- Market activity worldwide and in US, including production, consumption by end use, stocks, trade, and prices, by country, 1988-92, annual rpt, B4300–1
- Production, consumption, stocks, trade, and prices for approx 100 basic commodities, including by country and producing State, commodity yearbook for 1993, C2400–1, C2400–2
- Production of silver mines, for 60 countries, 1992-96, annual rpt, A8902–1
- Refinery production of silver from primary materials, coins, and scrap, with disposition, stocks, prices, and industry devs, US and worldwide, bimonthly rpt, A8902–3
- Supply-demand by country and end use, with prices, scrap recovery, futures trading, and market analyses, 1993 and trends, annual rpt, A8902–4
- Supply-demand data for silver, including mining by State, 1992 and trends, annual almanac, C2150–7.509
- Supply-demand for selected metals and nonmetallic minerals, with price data, US and worldwide, 1992-93 and trends, annual feature, C5226–2.505

State and local:

Arizona gold and silver recovery from copper ore, 1972-91, annual rpt, S0497–1

Simmons Market Research Bureau

- Children reading selected written material, and listening to radio, by sex, 1990 survey, article, C2710–1.512
- Children's consumption of 6 food product types, by sex, 1990 survey, article, C2710–1.512
- Household use indexes for medicated skin care and children's pain reliever products, by brand, for white vs black households, 1993 article, C5150–2.520
- Newspaper pages and sections readership, 1989-92, article, C2710–1.537
- Newspaper readership among men vs women, biennially 1986-92, article, A8605–1.507
- Newspaper readership by sex, 1992-93, article, A8605–1.511

Singapore

- Electronics industry trade and/or production trends by product category for 33 countries, with general economic profiles, 1993 annual rpt, A4725–1.4
- Machine tool industry operating data by country and product, 1992 and trends, annual rpt, A3179–2.2

Index by Subjects and Names

Singer, Allen M.

"1993 Annual Statistical Report", A0620–1

Sioux Falls, S.Dak.

Employment, earnings, and hours for selected industries and areas, monthly rpt, S7355–1

Skiing

Participation in 53 sports, by demographic characteristics, State, and census div, 1992, annual rpt series, A8485–3

State and local:

- Idaho economic profile, general data, 1992 recurring rpt, S2218–2.10
- Maine ski areas, 1992 recurring rpt, S3434–1
- Utah statistical abstract, general data, 1993 triennial rpt, U8960–1.17

Skin diseases

- Hospital patient admission rates and length of stay, by diagnosis and procedure, payment source, age, sex, and region, 1991, B4455–4
- Hospital patient charges and length of stay, by diagnosis and procedure, payment source, age, and region, 1991, B4455–5
- Hospital patient discharges and length of stay, by diagnosis, type of operation, age, and region, 1991, annual rpt series, B4455–1
- Hospital patient discharges and length of stay, by diagnostic related group (DRG), payment source, age, and region, 1991, annual rpt series, B4455–3

State and local:

- Arkansas vital statistics, including births, deaths by cause, marriages, and divorces, by age, sex, race, and county, 1991 and trends, annual rpt, S0685–1
- California vital statistics, including population, births, and deaths by cause, by demographic characteristics and county, 1990 and trends, annual rpt, S0865–1
- Florida vital statistics, including population, births, deaths by cause, and marriages and dissolutions, by location and demographic characteristics, 1992 and trends, annual rpt, S1745–3
- Georgia vital statistics, including deaths by cause, demographic characteristics, and location, 1991 and trends, annual rpt, S1895–1.2
- Hawaii chronic health conditions, by demographic characteristics and location, 1988, annual rpt, S2065–1.3
- Hawaii health dept activities and services, including vital statistics and disease control, by location, 1990, annual rpt, S2065–1
- Idaho vital statistics, including births, deaths by cause, abortions, marriages, and divorces, by demographic characteristics and county, 1991 and trends, annual rpt, S2250–2
- Maine vital statistics, including births, deaths by cause, abortions, and marriages and divorces, by demographic characteristics and location, 1991 and trends, annual rpt, S3460–2
- Massachusetts vital statistics, including births, deaths by cause, marriages, divorces, and population, by locality and demographic characteristics, 1990 and trends, annual rpt, S3850–1
- Michigan vital statistics, including births, deaths, marriages, divorces/annulments, and communicable diseases, by location and demographic characteristics, 1990 and trends, annual rpt, S4000–3
- Minnesota vital statistics, including population, births, abortions, deaths, marriages, and divorces, by location and demographic characteristics, 1991 and trends, annual rpt, S4190–2
- Mississippi vital statistics, including births, deaths by cause, marriages, and divorces, by demographic characteristics and location, 1992 and trends, annual rpt, S4350–1
- Montana vital statistics, including births, deaths by cause, abortion, disease, and marriage and divorce, by demographic characteristics and county, 1990-91 and trends, annual rpt, S4690–1
- Oregon vital statistics, including births, deaths by cause, communicable diseases, marriages, and divorces, by age, sex, race-ethnicity, and county, 1991 and trends, annual rpt, S6615–5
- South Carolina deaths, by detailed cause, age, sex, and race, 1990, annual rpt, S7175–2
- Tennessee vital statistics, including births, deaths by cause, marriages, divorces, and population, by demographic characteristics and location, 1991 and trends, annual rpt, S7520–2
- Washington State vital statistics, including births, deaths by cause, and population, by demographic characteristics and location, 1991 and trends, annual rpt, S8363–1
- West Virginia vital statistics, including births, deaths by cause, marriages, and divorces, by location and demographic characteristics, 1991 and trends, annual rpt, S8560–1
- Wisconsin vital statistics, including population, births, deaths by cause, and marriages and dissolutions, by county and demographic characteristics, 1991 and trends, annual rpt, S8715–4

see also Allergies

see also under By Disease in the "Index by Categories"

Slot machines

see Casinos

see Gambling

Slovakia

- Chemical industry sales, export value, and employment, by leading firm, 1990 or 1992, article, A1250–1.509
- Nuclear reactors in operation, with capacity, electricity generation, and construction, by unit and country, 1992, annual rpt, B6800–2.2

Sludge

see Sewage and wastewater systems

Slum clearance

see Urban renewal

Slums

see Central cities

Small business

- Bank small business lending and services, with data on organizational structure, loan delinquencies, and community dev activities, Nov 1992 survey, annual rpt, A4160–5
- Business activity and mgmt trends for small corporations, monthly rpt, C4687–1
- Capital availability and requirements for small companies, 1993-98, article, C2425–1.5G4

Small Business Administration

- CEO characteristics and compensation, for top growth companies, 1993 survey article, C5800–7.551
- Computer product shipment value for small businesses, home offices, and general consumers, 1992-96, article, C2710–1.551
- Earnings per share outlook of security analysts, for 18-80 small companies, 1992-93, article, C3950–1.504
- Economic conditions, survey of small business views on current situation and expectations, quarterly rpt, A7815–1
- Executives of small businesses views on business conditions and problems, funding sources, and Clinton Admin economic plan, Mar 1993 survey, C5800–7.524
- Financial data for top 100 growth companies with sales under $150 million, 1993 annual article, C5800–7.529
- Financial performance data and chief executive characteristics, for 200 small companies with high 5-year returns on equity, 1992 annual article, C3950–1.501
- Financing sources of small business owners and experience of discrimination in lending, by race-ethnicity, 1993 survey feature, C4215–1.512
- Health insurance employee benefits, small firms reasons for providing and not providing, 1993 survey feature, C4215–1.506
- High-technology small companies with rapid growth, employment and sales data for 25 firms, 1993 article, C5800–7.551
- Income tax returns filed under Subchapter S personal tax code status, with comparison to total corporate income tax returns, 1970-90, article, C1850–4.508
- Investment performance, assets, and number of companies in portfolio, for 6 funds investing in small business, 1992 article, C3950–1.504
- Office equipment ownership among small businesses, for personal computers, facsimile machines, and cellular telephones, 1990 and 1993, article, C5800–7.551
- Pension plan admin in small businesses, including investment strategies, mutual fund types used, and manager selection criteria, 1992 annual rpt, A6025–1.1
- Privately held small companies sales, employment, and other data, for 500 fastest growing firms, 1988 and 1992, annual feature, C4687–1.512
- State economic dev condition indicators, including economic performance, business vitality, growth capacity, and tax/fiscal system, by State, 1993 annual rpt, R4225–1.1

State and local:

- Hawaii data book, general data, 1992 annual rpt, S2090–1.15
- Utah small business dev program, with awards granted, economic impact, and profiles of 10 recipient companies, 1992 article, U8960–2.503

see also Franchises

see also Venture capital

Small Business Administration

Bank participation in SBA and other Govt programs for small business, Nov 1992 survey, annual rpt, A4160–5

Small Business Administration

Federal budget trends, including spending by program, State, and region, FY81-94, annual rpt, R8490–11

Hispanic-owned high-technology company characteristics, including eligibility for SBA 8(a) contracts and use of SBA loans, 1993 annual survey article, C4575–1.510

Loan distribution by industry div, FY92, C4687–1.509

Minority businesses eligible for SBA contracts, and value of contracts awarded, by minority group, FY92, article, C4575–1.507

Minority-owned business set-aside program participants, by race-ethnicity, 1991-92, article, A8510–1.1

Small claims courts and cases

Urban small claims and traffic court caseloads, processing, dispositions, judgments, and litigant satisfaction, for 3-12 jurisdictions, 1990, R6600–5

State and local:

- Alabama court caseloads and dispositions, by type of court and case, and location, with judicial dept finances, FY92 and trends, annual rpt, S0118–1
- Alaska court cases and dispositions, by type of court and case, and location, with judicial dept finances and personnel, FY92 and trends, annual rpt, S0290–1
- Arizona court cases and dispositions, by type of case and court, with judicial personnel and finances, by county and city, FY92, annual rpt, S0525–1
- Arkansas court caseloads and dispositions, by type of court and case, and location, FY92 and trends, annual rpt, S0647–1
- California court cases and dispositions, by type of case and court, and location, FY92 and trends, annual rpt, S0905–1.2, S0905–2
- Colorado court cases and dispositions, by type of court and detailed case type, FY92 and trends, annual rpt, S1035–1.2
- Connecticut court caseloads and dispositions, by type of court and case, and court location, with judicial dept finances, FY91-92, biennial rpt, S1220–1
- DC court cases and dispositions, by type of case, and judicial system finances, 1992 and trends, annual rpt, S1515–1
- Hawaii court cases and dispositions, by type of court and case, and judicial circuit, FY92 and trends, annual rpt, S2115–1.2
- Indiana court cases and dispositions by type of court and case, and location, with judicial system finances and personnel, 1992, annual rpt, S2703–1
- Iowa court cases, processing, and dispositions, by type of court and district, with judicial dept appropriations and personnel, 1992 and trends, annual rpt, S2815–1
- Kansas court caseloads and disposition, by type of court and case, and location, FY92, annual rpt, S3035–1
- Maine court cases and dispositions, by type and location, FY92 and trends, annual rpt, S3463–1
- Massachusetts court cases and dispositions, by type of court and case, and location, FY92 and trends, annual rpt, S3807–1
- Michigan court caseloads and dispositions, by type of court and case, and court location, 1992 and trends, annual rpt, S3962–1
- Nebraska court cases and dispositions, by type of court and case, and location, 1992 and trends, annual rpt, S4965–2
- New York State court cases and dispositions, by type of court and case, and jurisdiction, 1991, annual rpt, S5730–1
- North Dakota court caseloads and dispositions, by type of case and court, and location, with judicial dept finances, 1991-92, annual rpt, S6210–1
- Ohio court caseload and case disposition, by type of court and case, and location, 1992, annual rpt, S6385–1
- Oklahoma court cases and dispositions, by type of court and case, with judicial system finances, by county or jurisdiction, FY92, annual rpt, S6493–1
- Rhode Island court cases and dispositions, by type of court and case, and county, 1987-91, annual rpt, S6965–1
- South Dakota court cases and dispositions by type of case, and judicial system finances and personnel, by jurisdiction, FY92 and trends, annual rpt, S7395–1
- Texas court cases and dispositions, by type of court and case, and location, FY92, annual rpt, S7703–1
- Vermont court cases and dispositions, by type of court and case, and location, FY92 annual rpt, S8120–1
- Washington State court cases and dispositions, by type of court and case, and jurisdiction, with judicial finances and personnel, 1992 and trends, annual rpt, S8339–1

Small loan companies

see Finance companies

SMG Marketing Group

Home health care agencies by type of ownership, with top 10 services provided and patient characteristics, 1993 article, A1865–1.516

Smith, Brian W.

"Insurance Industry: A Key Player in the U.S. Economy", A0375–2

Smith, Frank A.

"Transportation in America, 10th Edition", R4815–1

Smith International Inc.

Oil and gas rotary rig drilling activity, by type of rig and well depth, weekly rpt, C6985–1

Smith, Linda

"Equal Employment Opportunity Data for Utah", S7832–3.4

Smith, Stanley K.

- "Number of Households and Average Household Size in Florida: Apr. 1, 1992", U6660–3.45
- "Population Projections by Age, Sex, and Race for Florida and Its Counties, 1991-2010", U6660–3.43
- "Population Projections by Age, Sex, and Race for Florida and Its Counties, 1992-2010", U6660–3.46
- "Projections of Florida Population by County, 1992-2020", U6660–3.44

Smith, William C., Jr.

"Report on Medical School Faculty Salaries, 1992/93", A3273–2

Smog

see Air pollution

Smoke and fire detectors

- Dealer fire alarm revenues and costs by category, and security system dealer reasons for not bidding on fire alarm projects, 1991 study, article, C1850–13.507
- Health condition and preventive health care and safety practices of adults, by respondent characteristics, 1992 and trends, annual survey rpt, C8111–2
- Museums and related instns fire detector use and maintenance, by instn type and budget size, 1989/90 survey, A0750–1.1
- Security professional plans to purchase addressable fire detection systems that track detector condition, 1993 survey feature, C1850–12.505

State and local:

Pennsylvania, suburban Philadelphia business views on alarm system purchasing, including info sources, 1991 surveys, article, C1850–13.502

Smoking

- Australia, Sydney smoker and ex-smoker belief in smoking as cause for selected diseases, and reasons for continuing to smoke, 1993 article, A2623–1.504
- Black American smokers and cigarette consumption, by sex and age, with comparisons to whites, 1965-91, annual compilation, C6775–2.2
- Black children and youth population, economic, health, and education data, with comparisons to whites, 1993 rpt, R3840–21
- China, Shanghai low birthweight incidence correlated with paternal smoking habits and selected characteristics of mother, Oct 1986-Sept 1987, article, A2623–1.504
- Cigarette consumption, total and per capita, 1865-92, annual rpt, A9075–2
- Cigarette price and consumption trends in US and Canada, 1982 and 1992, article, C5800–7.519
- College freshmen social and academic activities in past year, by sex and instn type, fall 1992, annual survey, U6215–1
- Health condition and preventive health care and safety practices of adults, by respondent characteristics, 1992 and trends, annual survey rpt, C8111–2
- Heart disease risk factor prevalence, by State, 1989, semiannual rpt, B8500–1.9
- High school student substance abuse as affected by junior high prevention program, 1993 article, A2623–1.508
- Hospital patients with psychiatric diagnosis of tobacco use disorder, length of stay by age, sex, and region, 1991, annual rpt series, B4455–2
- Japan and US health care system data, including expenditures, facilities, insurance coverage, and population health indicators, 1993 article, R5650–2.515
- Men age 69-84 quality of life indicators, including health, finances, family, and employment, by race, 1990 survey, U3780–9
- Nicotine patch advertising expenditures and market shares for top 4 brands, 1991-92, annual rpt, C2710–1.547
- Public health research results, including smoking incidence and intervention programs in selected populations, 1993 articles, A2623–1.511

Index by Subjects and Names

Social security

Public health research results, including smoking patterns and education program effectiveness in selected populations, 1993 articles, A2623–1.504

Restaurant (quick-service) operations, including most popular menu items, and patron age, use of promotions, and views on smoking, 1992, article, A8200–1.509

Restaurant smoking policy importance to consumers, and views on smoking acceptability in restaurants and other public places, by selected characteristics, Jan 1993 survey, A8200–8.15

Restaurant smoking policy importance to consumers by own smoking status, and views on smoking acceptability in restaurants and other public places, 1993 survey, A8200–1.506

Smoker characteristics, including smoking status of men and women by occupation, 1992 articles, B6045–1.501

Sweden infant mortality rates, by cause and characteristics of mother, 1983-86, article, A2623–1.503

Workplace smoking restrictions impact on smoking habits of workers by sex, 1989-90 Washington State study, article, A2623–1.509

State and local:

Alabama health behavior risk factor surveillance survey results, by respondent characteristics, 1988-89, recurring rpt, S0175–6

California cigarette consumption per capita, FY60-92, annual rpt, S0835–1.5

California health behavior risk factor surveillance survey results, by respondent characteristics, 1991 and trends, annual rpt, S0865–2

Colorado health behavior risk factor surveillance survey results, by respondent characteristics, 1990, recurring rpt, S1010–3

Connecticut health behavior risk factor surveillance survey results, 1989-91, annual rpt, S1200–2

Georgia health behavior risk factor surveillance survey results, by respondent characteristics, 1991 and trends, annual rpt, S1895–2

Hawaii population smoking prevalence by demographic characteristics, 1990, annual rpt, S2065–1.4

Iowa health behavior risk factor surveillance survey results, by respondent characteristics, 1991, annual rpt, S2795–2

Kentucky health behavior risk factor surveillance survey results, by State area and respondent characteristics, 1988-90, annual rpt, S3140–6

Massachusetts health behavior risk factor surveillance survey results, by respondent characteristics, 1986-90, recurring rpt, S3850–3

Michigan births and fetal deaths, by mother's smoking status during pregnancy, 1990, annual rpt, S4000–3

Michigan health behavior risk factor surveillance survey results, by respondent characteristics, 1991, annual rpt, S4000–4

Mississippi births by mother's tobacco use during pregnancy, by race, 1992, annual rpt, S4350–1

Missouri births by mother's smoking habits during pregnancy, by race, county, and city, 1992, annual rpt, S4518–1

Nebraska births by mother's tobacco use during pregnancy, including correlation with birthweight, 1991, annual rpt, S4885–1

Nevada health behavior risk factor surveillance survey results, by location and respondent characteristics, 1991, annual rpt, S5075–3

New York State health behavior risk factor surveillance survey results, by respondent characteristics, 1990, recurring rpt, S5765–3

North Carolina births to mothers who smoked, by local area, 1991, annual rpt, S5927–1.1

North Dakota health behavior risk factor surveillance survey results, by respondent characteristics, 1991 and trends, annual rpt, S6105–3

Oregon vital statistics, including tobacco use during pregnancy and tobacco-related deaths, by county, 1991, annual rpt, S6615–5

Pennsylvania health behavior risk factor surveillance survey results, by respondent characteristics, 1991, annual rpt, S6820–4

Tennessee births by mother's tobacco use during pregnancy, by race, 1991, annual rpt, S7520–2

Tennessee health behavior risk factor surveillance survey results, by respondent characteristics, 1986-90, annual rpt, S7520–3

Texas health behavior risk factor surveillance survey results, by respondent characteristics, 1991 and trends, annual rpt, S7685–2

Utah births by mother's tobacco use during pregnancy, by birthweight, 1990, annual rpt, S7835–1

Utah health behavior risk factor surveillance survey results, by respondent characteristics, 1991, annual rpt, S7835–3

Vermont births by maternal risk factors including tobacco and alcohol use during pregnancy, 1991, annual rpt, S8054–1

Virginia births by mother's alcohol and tobacco use during pregnancy, by birthweight, 1991, annual rpt, S8225–1

Washington State births by mother's smoking habits during pregnancy, 1991, annual rpt, S8363–1

West Virginia births by pregnancy risk factors, including tobacco and alcohol use, by county, 1991, annual rpt, S8560–1

Wyoming births to women who smoked during pregnancy, by age and county, 1989-91, annual rpt, S8920–2

see also Tobacco industry and products

SMSA

see Metropolitan Statistical Areas

Smuggling

see also Drug and narcotics offenses

Snack foods

see Food and food industry

Snowmobiles

see Recreational vehicles

Soap and detergent industry

Financial ratios and performance, for over 350 SIC 4-digit industries, FY88-92, annual rpt, A6400–3

Laundry detergent advertising expenditures and market shares for top 10 brands, 1991-92, annual rpt, C2710–1.547

Operating and financial composite ratios for corporations, with establishments and receipts, for approx 200 industries, by asset size, FY90, annual rpt, C7800–1

Retail prices for selected consumer items in approx 300 cities, quarterly rpt, A0150–1

Sales and consumer expenditures, for food store products by type, 1991-92, annual feature, C4655–1.510

Sales volume shares by retail outlet type, for approx 300 food, drug, and other product categories, 1993 annual feature, C4655–1.504

Supermarket sales by detailed product type, 1992 and trends, annual feature, C5225–1.507

Surfactant consumption by end-use market and detergent type, 1990, annual article, A1250–1.511

Social indicators

see Quality of life

see under names of specific indicators

Social sciences

Doctoral degree recipient characteristics, including citizenship status, source of support, field of study, and instn, 1990/91 and trends, annual rpt, R6000–7

Salaries of scientists, engineers, technicians, and other professionals, by employee and employer characteristics, 1990s and trends, biennial rpt, A3960–1

Salary and job offers for college grads, by field of study, type of employer, and degree level, by region, interim rpt series, A3940–1

Salary and job offers for college grads, by field of study, type of employer, and degree level, series, A3940–2

Women and minorities in professional fields, detailed education and labor force data, 1991 and trends, recurring rpt, A3960–2.3

State and local:

Connecticut public school data, including enrollment, staff, programs, finances, and student characteristics, 1991/92, biennial rpt, S1185–3

see also Anthropology

see also Economics

see also Political science

see also Psychology

see also Sociology

Social security

Black American social security benefit recipients and payments, with comparisons to whites, 1980, 1985, and 1990, annual compilation, C6775–2.8

Disability benefit programs of Social Security Admin, initial claims processing times and number pending, by State, FY88-93, R4865–11

Income per capita from Social Security, payment trends, and hypothetical impact of military personnel reduction, by State, 1993 article, B8500–2.516

Income tax on 85% of benefits as proposed by Clinton Admin, impacts by income level, 1993 rpt, R3834–17

Social security

Japan social security system coverage, finances, and mgmt of fund investments, by type of program, 1993 article, R5650–2.549

Latin America statistical abstract, general data by country, 1992 annual rpt, U6250–1.7

Payments and contributions for selected social insurance programs, by State, 1940s-92, annual rpt, R9050–1.1

Payments and recipients for selected Federal entitlement programs, by State and region, early 1990s, R8490–47

Recipient age at 1st Social Security benefit payment, by sex, 1950-89, article, R8750–1.505

Statistical profiles of 50 States and DC, general data, 1993 annual almanac, C4712–1

Steel industry restructuring devs, with data on production, employment, and worker assistance, and selected detail by company, for 8-12 countries, 1970s-90, R9260–16

State and local:

Arizona statistical abstract, general data, 1993 recurring rpt, U5850–2.7

Florida statistical abstract, general data, 1992 annual rpt, U6660–1.7

Hawaii data book, general data, 1992 annual rpt, S2090–1.11

Nevada statistical abstract, general data, 1992 biennial rpt, S5005–1.2

New York State municipal and county statistical profiles, general data, 1993 annual rpt, C4712–7

Tennessee statistical abstract, general data, 1992/93 annual rpt, U8710–2.18

see also Aid to Families with Dependent Children

see also Health insurance

see also Health maintenance organizations

see also Income maintenance

see also Medicaid

see also Medical assistance

see also Medicare

see also Old-Age, Survivors, Disability, and Health Insurance

see also Social security tax

see also Supplemental Security Income

see also Unemployment insurance

see also Workers compensation

Social security tax

Employee benefit payments and employer cost/payroll ratios, by industry, detailed type of benefit, and firm size, 1991, annual rpt, A3840–1

Family income, with impact of Federal and State/local taxes and inflation, 1980-92, annual rpt, R9050–13

Federal and State/local social insurance/payroll taxes paid by businesses, FY80-92, article, R9050–3.503

Higher education instn employee retirement and insurance benefits, prevalence and expenditures, by type of instn and region, 1991, biennial survey, A9025–3

Payments and contributions for selected social insurance programs, by State, 1940s-92, annual rpt, R9050–1.1

State and local:

Maryland elementary and secondary education data, by county, 1991/92, annual rpt, S3610–2.7

Social services

Catholic charity social service agency activities, clients, finances, and personnel, 1991 and trends, annual rpt, A3810–1

Catholic social services centers and utilization, by diocese and State, 1993 annual compilation, C4950–1

Charitable contributions, by type of donor and recipient, 1992 and trends, annual rpt, A0700–1

Federal budget trends, including spending by program, State, and region, FY81-94, annual rpt, R8490–11

Financial ratios and performance, for over 350 SIC 4-digit industries, FY88-92, annual rpt, A6400–3

Foundation assets, income, and grants by type of recipient, with data for top organizations and by location, 1991 and trends, annual rpt, R4900–1

Incarcerated mothers and their children, with data on characteristics, child caregivers, visitation, and support program use, 1991/92, A7575–4

Operating and financial composite ratios for corporations, with establishments and receipts, for approx 200 industries, by asset size, FY90, annual rpt, C7800–1

Public housing authority operations and finances, including types of services provided to residents, 1989, A6800–1

Public opinion on whether public schools should provide selected services to students, by respondent characteristics, 1993 annual Gallup Poll, A8680–1.503

Rape service agency characteristics, and staff views on proposed privacy laws and criminal justice system performance, 1990-92 surveys, R8375–1

Religious congregation characteristics, including membership, activities, staff, and finances, 1992 survey, recurring rpt, A5435–4

Religious congregation finances, and participation in charitable activities by detailed type, 1991 survey, article, C2176–1.512

State and local:

Alabama county data book, general data, 1992 annual rpt, S0121–2

Alabama public welfare and social service cases, recipients, and payments, by program and county, monthly rpt, S0150–1

Arizona statistical abstract, general data, 1993 recurring rpt, U5850–2.24

Arkansas human services dept finances and operations, including service recipient characteristics, by program, FY91 and trends, annual rpt, S0700–2

California higher education finances, including expenditures on public service programs, FY60s-94, annual rpt, S0827–3

Colorado welfare and social services expenditures and caseloads, by county and/or program, FY91, annual rpt, S1085–1

Florida statistical abstract, general data, 1992 annual rpt, U6660–1.20

Illinois public assistance program cases, recipients, and payments, by program and county, FY91-92 and trends, annual rpt, S2520–2

Indiana public assistance program participation, expenditures, and services, by county, FY92 and trends, annual rpt, S2623–1

Index by Subjects and Names

Maryland local govt financial condition, including revenues by source, expenditures by function, and debt obligations, FY92 and trends, annual rpt, S3618–1.1

Michigan public assistance program cases, recipients, and payments, detailed data by county, monthly rpt, S4010–1

Mississippi public welfare and social service cases, recipients, and payments, by program and county, FY92, annual rpt, S4357–1

Missouri public welfare and medical assistance recipients, expenditures, and case processing, by program and county, FY92 and trends, annual rpt, S4575–2

Montana social services program cases, by county and type of service, monthly rpt quarterly tables, S4755–1

Nebraska public welfare cases, recipients, and payments, by program and county, FY92 and trends, annual rpt, S4957–1

North Carolina public welfare programs, cases, recipients, staff, and finances, by county, 1st half FY93, semiannual rpt, S5940–2

Oklahoma public welfare program expenditures, recipients, and services, by program and county, FY92 and trends, annual rpt, S6455–1

South Carolina public welfare recipients, payments, and case processing, by county and program, monthly rpt, S7252–1

South Dakota welfare and social services recipients and payments, by program, MSA, and county, FY92, annual rpt, S7385–1

Texas welfare and social services program expenditures, recipients, and fraud cases, by county and/or program, FY92 and trends, annual rpt, S7695–1

Utah govt statistical review, fiscal and socioeconomic data, 1993 annual rpt, R9380–1.9

Washington State public assistance clients and service costs, by client characteristics, program, and county, FY90, annual rpt, S8420–2

West Virginia welfare and social service program caseloads and expenditures, by county, monthly rpt, S8560–2

see also Adult day care

see also Child day care

see also Child welfare

see also Community health services

see also Disaster relief

see also Emergency shelters

see also Foster home care

see also Homemaker services

see also Legal aid

see also Respite care

see also School lunch and breakfast programs

see also Social work

see also Vocational rehabilitation

see also Work incentive programs

Social work

Higher education programs, faculty and student characteristics, and student aid, with data by instn, 1992 and trends, annual rpt, A4515–1

Women and minorities in professional fields, detailed education and labor force data, 1991 and trends, recurring rpt, A3960–2.3

State and local:
Florida health care atlas, including manpower by occupation and health care facilities by type, by district and county, 1992 annual rpt, S1746–1.2
Kentucky Medicaid recipients and payments, by program, county, and type of medical service, monthly rpt, S3140–5
Montana home health service clients and visits by type of service, by agency, 1991, annual rpt, S4690–2
Texas social worker certification activity, and certified personnel, Sept 1991 and Aug 1992, annual rpt, S7695–1
see also Counselors and counseling
see also Homemaker services
see also Social services

Sociology

Women and minorities in professional fields, detailed education and labor force data, 1991 and trends, recurring rpt, A3960–2.3

Sodium

see Nonmetallic minerals and mines

Soft drink industry and products

Advertising expenditures by medium for top 100 advertisers, with comparisons to earnings and sales, and detail by product type and brand, 1991-92, annual rpt, C2710–1.547

Consumption and market shares by company and brand, and by flavor, 1985-92, annual article, C0125–2.504

Consumption and sales of beverages, by type, leading company, and brand, 1992 and trends, annual rpt, C4775–1.4, C4775–2.3

Convenience stores offering special services, including fountain drinks, 1981-92, annual survey rpt, A6735–2

Coupons issued by top 5 soft drink companies, 1991-92, article, C2710–1.532

Financial ratios and performance, for over 350 SIC 4-digit industries, FY88-92, annual rpt, A6400–3

Foreign capital investments for Coca Cola and Pepsi Cola in 9 emerging foreign markets, 1993 article, C5800–7.543

Franchise operations and finances, by type of business, 1991/92 and trends, annual rpt, A5820–1

Market shares for top 10 soft drink brands, 1992, article, C5150–2.515

Operating and financial composite ratios for corporations, with establishments and receipts, for approx 200 industries, by asset size, FY90, annual rpt, C7800–1

Retail prices for selected consumer items in approx 300 cities, quarterly rpt, A0150–1

Sales and consumer expenditures, for food store products by type, 1991-92, annual feature, C4655–1.510

Sales and operating data for beverage industry, by company, brand, and beverage type, 1991 and trends, annual rpt, C0125–3

Sales, consumption, and marketing devs for beverage industry, monthly rpt, C0125–2

Sales volume shares by retail outlet type, for approx 300 food, drug, and other product categories, 1993 annual feature, C4655–1.504

Sales volume shares for carbonated beverages by retail outlet type, 1991-92, article, C8130–1.506

Supermarket sales by detailed product type, 1992 and trends, annual feature, C5225–1.507

Vending machine sales by product type, and machines on location, 1992 and trends, annual rpt, C9470–1

Software

see Computer industry and products

Soil pollution

Oil industry environmental performance, with data on toxic chemical releases, oil spills, occupational injury/illness, and corporate spending, 1990 and trends, annual rpt, A2575–27

World soil degradation, by cause and region, 1992/93 biennial rpt, R9455–1.3, R9455–1.6

Soils and soil conservation

Erosion of farmland by wind and water, by State, 1987, semiannual rpt, B8500–1.12

Latin America statistical abstract, general data by country, 1992 annual rpt, U6250–1.2

World land area by climate class, including land with no soil constraints, and soil degradation by cause, by country and/or region, 1992/93 biennial rpt, R9455–1.6

State and local:

Hawaii data book, general data, 1992 annual rpt, S2090–1.19

North Dakota farmland in conservation reserve program, by county, 1993 annual rpt, S6140–2

Tennessee farm tillage practices, by crop and/or district, 1988-92, annual rpt, S7460–1

see also Flood control
see also Irrigation
see also Reclamation of land
see also Soil pollution

Solar energy

Direct solar radiation per year, by zone, 1993 article, C6985–6.507

Shipments of solar collectors and photovoltaic cells/modules, 1986-90, annual rpt, C1800–1

State and local:

Florida statistical abstract, general data, 1992 annual rpt, U6660–1.15

Hawaii data book, general data, 1992 annual rpt, S2090–1.17

Soldiers

see Military personnel

Soldiers pay and allowances

see Military pay

Solid waste

see Landfills
see Recycling of waste materials
see Refuse and refuse disposal
see Sewage and wastewater systems

Somalia

Charitable organizations aiding Somalia, including expenditures and personnel, for selected organizations, 1993 article, C2176–1.504

Public opinion in US on deployment of US forces in Somalia, Dec 1992 Gallup Poll, C4040–1.506

Public opinion in US on news items concerning deployment of US forces in Somalia, by respondent characteristics, 1993 surveys, C8915–1.501, C8915–1.502

Sorghums

see Grains and grain products

South Africa

Coal industry supply-demand, employment, and trade, by country, 1990-91 and trends, annual rpt, A7400–2.2

Economic indicators, with CPI, PPI, mining/quarrying employment and earnings, and gold milled ore working costs, monthly rpt, B6800–1

Educational employee retirement plans divesting investment holdings in South Africa, 1990/91, recurring rpt, A7640–18.1

Gold mining production, revenues, and costs, and occupational accident rates for mining and 4 other industries, 1st 9 months 1992, article, C5226–2.505

Investment performance of US stock portfolios excluding companies doing business in South Africa, biweekly rpt quarterly feature, C2710–2.502, C2710–2.507, C2710–2.514

Motor vehicle world production, sales, trade, and registrations, by country, world area, manufacturer, and make, 1991 and trends, annual rpt, A0865–2.1

Nuclear reactors in operation, with capacity, electricity generation, and construction, by unit and country, 1992, annual rpt, B6800–2.2

Uranium production facilities by company, with other activities, operating status, and 1992 production, article, B6800–1.505

Uranium production, with detail by mine, 1991-92, annual rpt, B6800–2.2

South America

Heating, ventilating, and air conditioning (HVAC) market indicators for 4 South American countries, 1993 article, C2000–1.503

Jewish population by world area, country, and US census div, State, and city, 1990-92, annual compilation, A2050–1

Motor vehicle production and sales, for 6 Central and South American countries, 1992, article, C2710–3.553

Motor vehicle world production, sales, trade, and registrations, by country, world area, manufacturer, and make, 1991 and trends, annual rpt, A0865–2.1

Oil/gas seismic exploration land crews and vessels, by world area or country, quarterly press release, A8912–2

Population size and characteristics, GNP, and land area, by world region and/or country, 1993 annual data sheet, R8750–5

Statistical abstract of Latin America, detailed social, govtl, and economic data, 1992 annual rpt, U6250–1

see also Andean Group
see also Argentina
see also Bolivia
see also Brazil
see also Central America
see also Chile
see also Colombia
see also Ecuador
see also Inter-American Development Bank
see also Latin America
see also Latin American Integration Association
see also Paraguay

South America

see also Peru
see also Suriname
see also Uruguay
see also Venezuela
see also under By Foreign Country or World Area in the "Index by Categories"

South Bend, Ind.

Business conditions analysis for selected Indiana local areas, quarterly rpt semiannual feature, U2160–1.502, U2160–1.504

South Carolina

- Agricultural production and finances, by commodity and county, 1991-92 and trends, annual rpt, U1075–3
- Correctional instns, admin, and inmates by criminal offense and demographic characteristics, FY92 and trends, annual rpt, S7135–1
- County govt finances, including property value and tax assessments, by county, FY92, annual rpt, S7127–2
- Court cases and dispositions, by type of court and location, with judicial dept finances and employees, 1992 and trends, annual rpt, S7197–1
- Crimes and arrests, by offense, with data by location and victim-offender characteristics, and assaults on officers, 1992 and trends, annual rpt, S7205–1
- Deaths by detailed cause, age, sex, and race, 1990, annual rpt, S7175–2
- Economic condition, including agriculture, commerce, govt finances, employment, and income, 1970s-92, annual rpt, S7125–3
- Educational characteristics and socioeconomic indicators, by school district and county, 1991/92, annual rpt, S7145–1
- Employment, and earnings and hours, by industry group and locality, monthly rpt, S7155–2
- Financial instns (State-chartered) financial condition, including data by instn, FY92 annual rpt, S7165–1
- Govt financial condition, including receipts by source, expenditures by function, fund balances, and bonded debt, FY92, annual rpt, S7127–1
- Higher education enrollment, degrees, staff, and finances, by instn, 1992 and trends, annual rpt, S7185–2
- Insurance industry financial and underwriting data, by company, 1991, with FY92 regulatory info, annual rpt, S7195–1
- Labor force planning rpt, including population, employment, income, and job service activities, 1992 annual rpt, S7155–3
- Libraries, finances, services, holdings, and staff, by public and institutional library, FY92, annual rpt, S7210–1
- Markets with daily newspapers, demographic and economic info by geographic area, US and Canada, 1993 annual rpt, C3250–1
- Medical malpractice insurance State joint underwriting assn (JUA) financial condition, for 11 States, 1991, annual rpt, A0375–1
- Public service commission regulatory activities, with financial and operating data for individual utilities and railroads, FY92 annual rpt, S7235–1
- Statistical abstract of South Carolina, detailed social, economic, and govtl data, 1993 annual rpt, S7125–1
- Statistical profiles of 50 States and DC, general data, 1993 annual almanac, C4712–1
- Tax returns and collections, property assessments, and taxable sales, with data by county and industry group, FY92, annual rpt, S7255–1
- Traffic accidents, fatalities, and injuries, by circumstances, location, and driver and victim characteristics, 1992 and trends, annual rpt, S7190–2
- Utility and transportation regulatory agency activities, scope of jurisdiction, finances, and employees, by agency, 1991/92 annual rpt, A7015–2
- Vital statistics, including population, births, deaths by cause, marriages, and divorces, by age, sex, race, and location, 1990 and trends, annual rpt, S7175–1
- Welfare recipients, payments, and case processing, by county and program, monthly rpt, S7252–1
- *see also* under By City and By County in the "Index by Categories"
- *see also* under By State in the "Index by Categories"

South Dakota

- Agricultural production, marketing, and finances, by commodity and county, with farms and acreage, 1992 and trends, annual rpt, S7280–1
- Business activity review for South Dakota, including selected data by city and industry, quarterly rpt, U8595–1
- Correctional instn admin, including inmates by criminal background and demographic characteristics, FY92 and trends, annual rpt, S7296–1
- Court cases and dispositions by type of case, and judicial system finances and personnel, by jurisdiction, FY92 and trends, annual rpt, S7395–1
- Election results, and voter registration by party, by county, 1992 general election, biennial rpt, S7390–1
- Elementary and secondary school enrollment, finances, grads, and staff, by district, 1991/92 and trends, annual rpt, S7315–1
- Employment, earnings, and hours for selected industries and areas, with characteristics of unemployed and job service activities, monthly rpt, S7355–1
- Govt financial condition, including revenues by source, expenditures by function, fund balances, and bonded debt, FY92, annual rpt, S7330–1
- Higher education finances, staff, enrollment, degrees, and facilities, by public instn, FY93 annual rpt, S7375–1
- Insurance industry financial and underwriting data, by company and type of insurance, with regulatory info, 1991-92, annual rpt, S7300–2
- Markets with daily newspapers, demographic and economic info by geographic area, US and Canada, 1993 annual rpt, C3250–1
- Oil/gas industry production, finances, exploration, and reserves, by State, 1992 and trends, annual rpt, A5425–1.1

Index by Subjects and Names

- Sales (taxable retail) and gross sales/use tax purchases, by county and selected city, bimonthly rpt, U8595–2
- Statistical profiles of 50 States and DC, general data, 1993 annual almanac, C4712–1
- Tax revenues by source, aid distributed to local areas, and property tax valuations, FY92 annual rpt, S7380–1
- Traffic accidents, fatalities, and injuries, by circumstances, location, vehicle type, and driver and victim characteristics, 1992 and trends, annual rpt, S7300–3
- Utility and transportation regulatory agency activities, scope of jurisdiction, finances, and employees, by agency, 1991/92 annual rpt, A7015–2
- Vital statistics, including births, deaths, marriage and divorce, and communicable disease, by demographic characteristics and county, 1991 and trends, annual rpt, S7345–1
- Welfare and social services recipients and payments, by program, MSA, and county, FY92, annual rpt, S7385–1
- *see also* Rapid City, S.Dak.
- *see also* Sioux Falls, S.Dak.
- *see also* under By City and By County in the "Index by Categories"
- *see also* under By State in the "Index by Categories"

South Pacific region

see Oceania

South West Africa

see Namibia

Southeast Asia

- Offshore oil/gas fields and platforms planned, by country, and reserves and production for largest fields, 1992 article, C6985–2.501
- *see also* Cambodia
- *see also* Indochinese refugees
- *see also* Indonesia
- *see also* Malaysia
- *see also* Myanmar
- *see also* Papua New Guinea
- *see also* Thailand
- *see also* Vietnam

Southeastern States

- Agriculture production costs for selected crops, and prices paid for fertilizer, 1993 annual rpt, S7460–1
- Children age 17/under lacking health insurance and eligible for Medicaid, with detail by age and family income, for 6-17 States, 1991, R9000–1
- Economic and demographic indicators for counties adjacent to Alabama, in Florida, Georgia, Mississippi, and Tennessee, 1992 annual rpt, S0121–2
- Economic indicators, including GSP, poverty, and income, for 7 States, 1992 annual rpt, U5680–3
- Economic indicators, including income, population, and teacher salaries, for 12 States, 1970s-92, annual rpt, S7125–3
- Economic trends for Tennessee and neighboring States, including agricultural receipts, GSP, and employment, 1979-90, annual rpt, S7560–1
- Education dept use of reporting systems to track college performance of recent high school grads, for 15 Southern States, 1992, A8945–32

Index by Subjects and Names — Soybeans

Electric power generation capacity additions in Southeast region, by fuel type and for 11 States, 1992-2000, article, C5800–28.506

Elementary and secondary school expenditures and staff salaries, for 12 Southeastern States and US, 1990/91-1991/92, annual rpt, S4340–1.1

Farm production costs for corn and soybeans, 1989-91, annual rpt, S3085–1

Farm property value, for 7 Southeastern States, 1988-93, annual rpt, U5920–1

Farm workers, hours, and wage rates, 1992 annual rpt, S1855–1

Farm workers, hours, and wage rates, 3 Southeastern regions, 1991-92, annual rpt, S5885–1

GSP in current and constant dollars, by industry, for Southeast region and Virginia, with comparison to US GDP, 1963-89, recurring rpt, U9080–6

Higher education enrollment, degrees, appropriations, tuition/fees, and faculty compensation, by instn type, for 15 States, 1990/91, annual rpt, A8945–31

Higher education enrollment, degrees, faculty, and finances, for 15 Southern States, 1990s and trends, biennial fact book, A8945–1

Higher education grad job and salary offers, by field of study, type of employer, occupation, and degree level, interim rpt, A3940–1.5

Higher education-related data for 15 Southern States, fact book update series, A8945–27

Hospital patient discharges and length of stay, by diagnosis, type of operation, and age, 1991, annual rpt, B4455–1.4

Hospital patient discharges and length of stay, by diagnostic related group (DRG), payment source, and age, 1991, annual rpt, B4455–3.4

Hospital psychiatric patient discharges and length of stay, by diagnosis, age, and sex, 1991, annual rpt, B4455–2.4

Layoffs in Southeastern States, by industry div, 1991, article, S7495–2.501

Low-income housing supply-demand, costs, physical conditions, and public assistance, for 14 Southern metro areas, 1992 rpt, R3834–16.4

Municipality economic and demographic data for areas in 4 States adjacent to Alabama, 1992 recurring rpt, S0121–5

Nursing education gerontological curriculum content and teaching methods, for programs in Southeastern States, 1993 article, A8010–3.505

Public opinion on Southern States flying of confederate flags on capitol buildings, Dec 1992 Gallup Poll, C4040–1.506

State govt employee appraisal practices, for Southeastern and Southwestern States, 1993 article, U5930–1.502

Statistical abstract of Georgia, with comparisons to neighboring States, 1992-93 biennial rpt, U6730–1

Statistical abstract of Mississippi, detailed social, govtl, and economic data, with comparisons to neighboring States, 1992 annual rpt, U3255–4

Statistical abstract of South Carolina, with comparisons to other Southeastern States, 1993 annual rpt, S7125–1

Statistical abstract of Tennessee, detailed social, govtl, and economic data, with comparisons to neighboring States, 1992/93 annual rpt, U8710–2

Teacher retirement and health insurance plan characteristics and costs as a percent of salaries, for 15 States, 1993 rpt, A8945–34

Telephone local residential service rates for 11 States, 1989, article, U8710–1.501

see also Appalachia

see also under By Region in the "Index by Categories"

see also under names of individual States

Southwestern States

Carbon dioxide pipelines in Texas/New Mexico Permian Basin region, with ownership, mileage, and throughput capacity, 1993 article, C6985–1.542

College grad job and salary offers, by field of study, type of employer, occupation, and degree level, interim rpt, A3940–1.6

Employment trends by industry div, for 6 Southwestern States, Mar and July 1992-93, S5624–2.510

Employment trends by industry div, for 6 Southwestern States, Mar 1992-93, S5624–2.507

Employment trends for 6 Southwestern States, June 1991-93, S5624–2.509

Hospital patient discharges and length of stay, by diagnosis, type of operation, and age, 1991, annual rpt, B4455–1.4

Hospital patient discharges and length of stay, by diagnostic related group (DRG), payment source, and age, 1991, annual rpt, B4455–3.4

Hospital psychiatric patient discharges and length of stay, by diagnosis, age, and sex, 1991, annual rpt, B4455–2.4

Natural gas prices, approx 15 pipelines in 4 States, weekly rpt monthly table, C6985–1

Pay (annual average) by industry div, for 8 Southwestern States, 1990-91, article, S5624–2.501

Printing industry devs, including sales trends and printer views on business conditions, 1992 feature, C1850–10.502

Socioeconomic indicators for Mexico-US border area, 1980s and trends, U6250–1.20

State govt employee appraisal practices, for Southeastern and Southwestern States, 1993 article, U5930–1.502

Statistical abstract of Arizona, with comparisons to other Southwestern States, 1993 recurring rpt, U5850–2

Statistical abstract of Oklahoma, with comparisons to other Southwestern States, 1992 annual rpt, U8130–2

Unemployment rates in 6 Southwestern States, 1991-92, article, S5624–2.505

see also under By Region in the "Index by Categories"

see also under names of individual States

Soviet Union

Coal industry supply-demand, employment, and trade, by country, 1990-91 and trends, annual rpt, A7400–2.2

Economic and military aid to developing countries, with detail for selected world regions, 1950s-85, annual rpt, U6250–1.28

Economic conditions affecting foreign investment, including population, GDP, industrial production measures, and foreign trade, 1985 or 1986, R4105–82.4

Economic devs in former Soviet Union, including industrial production, agriculture, exchange rates, and foreign trade, monthly rpt, U2030–1

Energy production and consumption in former Soviet Republics, by fuel type, 1990, annual rpt, C6985–5.1

Jewish population by world area, country, and US census div, State, and city, 1990-92, annual compilation, A2050–1

Natural gas supply-demand, pipeline mileage, and foreign trade, by Republic, 1993 article, C6985–1.551

Nuclear missiles and bombers in 3 Republics other than Russia, and number of warheads, 1993 article, C5800–4.504

Oil enhanced recovery areas active and production, by process type, 1990, annual rpt, C6985–3.5

Oil enhanced recovery operations and production, by process type, 1990, annual compilation, C6985–4.1

Oil refined products consumption and demand, 1990-96 and 2000, article, C6985–1.531

Political, economic, cultural, and population issues relating to Republics and ethnic groups, discontinued quarterly rpt, U1520–1

Public opinion in Russia, Ukraine, and Lithuania on Soviet Union political, economic, and social issues, 1991 survey, C8915–8.2

UN voting support for US and Soviet Union stances, and US aid received, for 50 countries, 1992 annual rpt, U6250–1.9

Uranium anti-dumping petition against former Soviet Union, with participating companies and ownership, and export quotas for 6 Republics, 1992 article, B6800–1.501

Weapons production in Soviet Union or Russia, by weapon category, 1990-92, article, C5800–4.522

see also Commonwealth of Independent States

see also Estonia

see also Kyrgyzstan

see also Lithuania

see also Russia

see also Ukraine

see also Uzbekistan

see also under By Foreign Country or World Area in the "Index by Categories"

Soybeans

Chicago Board of Trade futures and options trading in financial instruments and agricultural commodities, 1992, annual rpt, B2120–1

Futures trading volume and prices at Kansas City Board of Trade grain market, with natl production by State, 1992, annual rpt, B1530–1

Indonesia agricultural production trends and impacts of govt policies, for 5 major food crops, 1970s-80s, R5620–1.37

Latin America statistical abstract, general data by country, 1992 annual rpt, U6250–1.25

Production and marketing data for soybeans, including utilization, prices, and trade, with comparison to other oilseeds, 1920s-93, annual rpt, B8480–1

Soybeans

Production, consumption, stocks, trade, and prices for approx 100 basic commodities, including by country and producing State, commodity yearbook for 1993, C2400–1, C2400–2

Production, prices, and disposition of grain in States served by Minneapolis exchange, by commodity, 1992 and trends, annual rpt, B6110–1

State and local:

Alabama agricultural production, marketing, and income, by county and/or commodity, and farms and trends, annual rpt, S0090–1

Arkansas agricultural production, marketing, and finances, by commodity and county, with farms and acreage, 1992 and trends, annual rpt, U5920–1

Florida field crop acreage, yield, production, and value, by commodity and/or county, 1992 and trends, annual rpt, S1685–1.4

Georgia agricultural production, marketing, and finances, by commodity and/or county, and farms and acreage, 1991 and trends, annual rpt, S1855–1

Illinois agricultural production, marketing, and finances, by county or commodity, and farms and farmland, 1991 and trends, annual rpt, S2390–1

Kansas agricultural production, marketing, and finances, by county and/or commodity, and farm acreage and value, 1992 and trends, annual rpt, S2915–1

Kentucky agricultural production, marketing, and finances, by commodity and county; and farms, acreage, and value; 1992 and trends, annual rpt, S3085–1

Louisiana agricultural production, marketing, and finances, by commodity or parish, 1985-91, annual rpt, U2740–1

Michigan agricultural production, marketing, and finances, by commodity or county, 1987-91, annual rpt, S3950–1

Minnesota agricultural production, marketing, and finances, by county or commodity, and farms and acreage, 1992 and trends, annual rpt, S4130–1

Missouri agricultural production, marketing, and finances, by commodity and/or county, and farms and acreage, 1988-92, annual rpt, S4480–1

Nebraska agricultural production, marketing, and finances, by commodity and/or county, and farms and acreage, 1991 and trends, annual rpt, S4835–1

New Jersey agricultural production, marketing, and finances, by commodity and/or county, and farms and acreage, 1986-91, annual rpt, S5350–1

New York State agricultural production, marketing, and finances, by commodity and/or county, and farms and acreage, 1992 and trends, annual rpt, S5700–1

North Carolina agricultural production, marketing, and finances, by commodity and county, 1991 and trends, annual rpt, S5885–1

North Dakota agricultural production and marketing, by commodity and county, and farm finances, 1992 and trends, annual rpt, U3600–1

Ohio agricultural production, marketing, and finances, by commodity and county, with farms and acreage, 1990-91 and trends, annual rpt, S6240–1

Oklahoma agricultural production, marketing, and finances, by commodity and county, 1992 and trends, annual rpt, S6405–1

Pennsylvania agricultural production, marketing, and finances, by county and commodity, and farms and acreage, 1992 and trends, annual rpt, S6760–1

South Carolina agricultural production and finances, by commodity and county, 1991-92 and trends, annual rpt, U1075–3

South Dakota agricultural production, marketing, and finances, by commodity and county, and farms and acreage, 1992 and trends, annual rpt, S7280–1

Tennessee agricultural production and marketing, by commodity and county, with farms, acreage, and farm value, 1992 and trends, annual rpt, S7460–1

Texas agricultural production, marketing, and finances, by commodity and county, and farms and farmland, 1991 and trends, annual rpt series, S7630–1

Wisconsin agricultural production, marketing, and finances, by commodity and county, and farms, acreage, and sales, 1992 and trends, annual rpt, S8680–1

Space programs

Cost and performance measures for 4-5 NASA space station design options, 1993 article, C5800–4.521

Cost of 6 space projects that failed or fell short of expectations, 1993 feature, C8900–1.524

European Space Agency Columbus space station dev contribution shares by country, 1992 article, C5800–4.503

Launch cost and payload comparisons for 2 current and 2 future spacecraft vehicles, 1993 article, C5800–7.533

Launch crew and days on pad for 4 vehicles, and staff at 3 launch base/range operations centers, 1993 article, C5800–4.532

Revenues for commercial space related business worldwide, by source, 1992, article, C5800–4.518

Space station costs by component, by funding and technology option, FY94-98 and post-FY98, article, C5800–4.530

World launchings of spacecraft attaining orbit, by country, with US space program devs, 1991 and trends, annual rpt, A0250–2.2

World space flight devs and records, with launches and orbiting equipment by country, and detail for US programs, 1992 and trends, annual rpt, B9170–1

see also Communications satellites

see also Satellites

see also Strategic Defense Initiative

Space sciences

World space flight devs and records, with launches and orbiting equipment by country, and detail for US programs, 1992 and trends, annual rpt, B9170–1

see also Communications satellites

see also Satellites

see also Space programs

Spain

Business activities and trade relations with US, quarterly rpt, A8955–1

Chemical process industry sales and employment of top 15 companies, and production capacity and utilization of major chemicals, 1991, article, C5800–8.511

Index by Subjects and Names

Coal industry supply-demand, employment, and trade, by country, 1990-91 and trends, annual rpt, A7400–2.2

Electronics industry trade and/or production trends by product category for 33 countries, with general economic profiles, 1993 annual rpt, A4725–1.4

Energy intl sourcebook, with detail on oil and gas industry operations, supply-demand, and prices, for approx 80 countries, 1970s-91, annual compilation, C6985–10.2

Entertainment industry devs, including motion picture production and admissions, TV, and VCRs, 1993 feature, C9380–1.542

Insurance premiums for 10 leading underwriting groups, 1992, annual article, C1050–1.510

Machine tool industry operating data by country and product, 1992 and trends, annual rpt, A3179–2.2

Motion picture boxoffice receipts for top 10 Spanish and non-Spanish films in 1992, and top 10 films in 1st 4 months 1993, C9380–1.542

Motion picture theater screens, for top 4-8 and all other exhibitors in Germany, Spain, France, and UK, 1992, C9380–1.531

Motor vehicle world production, sales, trade, and registrations, by country, world area, manufacturer, and make, 1991 and trends, annual rpt, A0865–2.1

Nuclear reactors in operation, with capacity, electricity generation, and construction, by unit and country, 1992, annual rpt, B6800–2.2

Oil refinery distillation capacity and crude runs to stills, by company and refinery, 1991, article, C6985–1.522

Public opinion in 9 European countries and 3 Soviet Union Republics on political, economic, and social issues, 1991 survey, C8915–8

Shipbuilding govt aid programs in 6 OECD countries, and impact on US industry, 1993 recurring rpt, A8900–8

see also Madrid, Spain

Spanish heritage Americans

see Hispanic Americans

Spar, Michael A.

"Projections of Educational Statistics to 2012", U9080–20

Sparks, Nev.

Casino finances and employment, by location and gaming revenue range, FY92, annual rpt, S5062–1

Special districts

Finances of local govts, by type of govt unit, and for 52 largest cities, 1993 annual rpt, R9050–1.6

State and local:

Arizona statistical abstract, general data, 1993 recurring rpt, U5850–2.10

California statistical abstract, general data, 1992 annual rpt, S0840–2.13

Colorado property assessed valuation by detailed property type, and tax levy and revenue by local district, by county, 1991-92, annual rpt, S1055–3

Florida statistical abstract, general data, 1992 annual rpt, U6660–1.21, U6660–1.23

Index by Subjects and Names

Special education

Georgia statistical abstract, general data, 1992-93 biennial rpt, U6730–1.11

Idaho property taxing districts, by type, 1992, annual rpt, S2295–1

South Carolina county govt finances, including property value and tax assessments, by county, FY92, annual rpt, S7127–2

South Carolina statistical abstract, general data, 1993 annual rpt, S7125–1.9

Tennessee statistical abstract, general data, 1992/93 annual rpt, U8710–2.14

Utah govt statistical review, fiscal and socioeconomic data, 1993 annual rpt, R9380–1.6, R9380–1.11

Washington State tax levies, by type of taxing district, 1988-92, annual rpt, S8415–1.2

see also Central business districts

see also Congressional districts

see also Conservation areas

see also Electoral districts and precincts

see also School districts

Special Drawing Rights

Latin America statistical abstract, general data by country, 1992 annual rpt, U6250–1.30

Special education

- Black children and youth population, economic, health, and education data, with comparisons to whites, 1993 rpt, R3840–21
- Budget of US funding for handicapped education programs, FY92-94, annual feature, C2175–1.516
- Catholic schools for the handicapped, and enrollment, by diocese and State, 1993 annual compilation, C4950–1
- Catholic vs public school ratings for selected aspects of education and environment, public opinion by respondent characteristics, July 1992 survey, A7375–8
- Federal budget trends, including spending by program, State, and region, FY81-94, annual rpt, R8490–11
- Higher education appropriations for FY94 compared to spending in FY93, by program, recurring feature, C2175–1.527, C2175–1.536
- OECD member countries special education students and teachers, 1986, A1600–4
- School bus route average number of special education students, and disabled students and Federal funding, 1993 article, C1575–1.507
- State social, economic, and govtl indicators, with rankings, 1993 semiannual rpt, B8500–1.7

State and local:

- Alabama public school revenues by source and expenditures by object, by district, 1991/92, annual rpt, S0124–1.2
- Alaska public schools, enrollment, staff, and finances, by district, FY92, annual rpt, S0295–2
- Arizona special education expenditures by program type, by county and school district, 1991/92, annual rpt, S0470–1
- Arkansas public school enrollment, grads, staff, and finances, by county and school, 1991/92 and trends, annual rpt, S0660–1
- California public school limited-English-proficiency enrollment, teachers, and programs, by 1st language, grade level, and county, 1992 and trends, annual rpt, S0825–10

California public schools by type, by nonwhite enrollment share, 1992/93, annual rpt, S0825–9

- Colorado public and/or private school enrollment and grads, by student characteristics, county, and district, 1992 and trends, annual rpt, S1000–2.1
- Connecticut public school data, including enrollment, staff, programs, finances, and student characteristics, 1991/92, biennial rpt, S1185–3
- DC public school finances, enrollment, grads, and test scores, with data by school, 1987/88-1991/92, annual rpt, S1605–2
- Delaware special and vocational education programs funding and enrollment, 1991/92, annual rpt, S1430–1
- Georgia prison inmate participation in educational programs, by type, June 1992, annual rpt, S1872–1
- Illinois elementary and secondary school enrollment, staff, and finances, by county and district, 1990/91 and trends, annual rpt, S2440–1
- Indiana elementary and secondary school enrollment and finances, by district and county, annual rpt series, S2608–2
- Kansas school district revenues by source and expenditures by object, 1990/91, annual rpt, S2945–1
- Kentucky public school finances, staff, and enrollment, by district, 1989/90-1990/91, biennial rpt, S3110–2
- Louisiana elementary/secondary school operations, including enrollment, staff, finances, and detail by school district, 1991/92 and trends, annual rpt, S3280–1
- Maine public school enrollment, facilities, staff, and finances, with selected data by county and for private schools, 1991 and trends, annual rpt, S3435–1
- Maryland elementary and secondary education data, by county, annual rpt series, S3610–2
- Maryland elementary and secondary education statistical summary, with data by county, 1991/92-1992/93 and trends, annual rpt, S3610–1
- Massachusetts public elementary/secondary education summary data, 1989/90-1991/92 and trends, annual rpt, S3810–3
- Massachusetts public elementary/secondary school expenditures per pupil by program, by district, 1991/92, annual rpt, S3810–5
- Minnesota public school enrollment, staff, and finances, by district and county, 1991/92 and trends, annual rpt, S4165–1
- Mississippi public school enrollment, staff and salaries, and finances, by district, 1991/92 and trends, annual rpt, S4340–1
- Missouri public school finances, staff, students, and programs, detailed data, 1991/92, annual rpt, S4505–1.1
- Nebraska elementary and secondary schools, enrollment by grade, and staff, with data by school district and county, annual series, S4865–2
- Nevada public school enrollment, test scores, teachers, and finances, by school district, 1990/91 and trends, annual rpt, S5035–2
- Nevada statistical abstract, general data, 1992 biennial rpt, S5005–1.7

New Hampshire public and nonpublic elementary/secondary school enrollment, by grade and school type, fall 1991, annual table, S5200–1.1

- New Hampshire public and nonpublic elementary/secondary school enrollment, by grade and school type, fall 1992, annual table, S5200–1.9
- New Jersey public schools, enrollment, and student and staff characteristics, and nonpublic schools and enrollment, by county, 1991/92, annual rpt, S5385–1
- New Mexico special education enrollment trends, and funding by school district, 1991/92 annual rpt, S5575–4
- North Carolina public school enrollment, grads, staff, and finances, with data by race, sex, and local district, 1991/92-1992/93 and trends, annual rpt, S5915–1
- North Dakota elementary and secondary schools, enrollment, and staff, by school type and location, 1992/93 annual directory, S6180–2
- Ohio public school enrollment, finances, special programs, and staff, 1991/92 and trends, annual rpt, S6265–2
- Ohio special education expenditures, instructional hours, and enrollment, by service type and school district, 1991/92 and trends, annual rpt, S6265–1
- Oklahoma special education enrollment, 1972/73-1991/92, annual rpt, S6423–1.2
- Oklahoma special education student enrollment shares, 1991/92 and trends, annual rpt, S6423–2
- Oregon special education expenditures, by program, 1991/92, annual rpt, S6590–1.16
- Oregon special education expenditures, by program, 1992/93, annual rpt, S6590–1.17
- Pennsylvania public and nonpublic school enrollment, by grade, race-ethnicity, sex, and county, 1991/92 and trends, annual rpt, S6790–5.1
- Pennsylvania public school dropout characteristics, with reasons for leaving school and subsequent activities, 1991/92 and trends, annual rpt, S6790–5.11
- Rhode Island educational enrollment, grads, and finances, by district or community, 1991/92 or fall 1992, annual rpt, S6970–1
- South Carolina educational characteristics and socioeconomic indicators, by school district and county, 1991/92, annual rpt, S7145–1
- South Dakota school enrollment, finances, grads, and staff, by district, 1991/92 and trends, annual rpt, S7315–1
- Tennessee public school enrollment, staff, finances, and operations, by county, city, and school district, 1991/92, annual rpt, S7490–2
- Utah public schools, enrollment, attendance, personnel, and finances, by school district, 1991/92, annual rpt, S7815–1
- Virginia public school enrollment and high school grads, with detail by school district, 1980/81-2012/2013, annual rpt, U9080–20
- Virginia public school enrollment, grads, finances, and staff, by county and municipality, 1991/92, annual rpt, S8190–3

Special education

West Virginia public and private schools, enrollment, grads, and staff, by county, 1991/92, annual rpt, S8540–3

West Virginia public school finances, enrollment, staff, and programs, by county, 1992/93 and trends, annual rpt, S8540–4

Wisconsin elementary and secondary school enrollment, staff, costs, and State aid, by school district, 1992/93 and trends, annual rpt, S8795–2

Wyoming public school enrollment, staff, and finances, by county and district, 1991/92, annual rpt series, S8890–1

see also Remedial education

Special elections

see Elections

Speech pathology and audiology

- HMO benefits coverage, premiums, and rating methods used, by plan characteristics, 1991 and trends, annual rpt, A5150–2.1
- Hospital patients with diagnosis of stammering/stuttering, length of stay by age, sex, and region, 1991, annual rpt, B4455–2
- Women and minorities in professional fields, detailed education and labor force data, 1991 and trends, recurring rpt, A3960–2.3

State and local:

- Florida health care atlas, including manpower by occupation and health care facilities by type, by district and county, 1992 annual rpt, S1746–1.2
- Indiana Medicaid expenditures, by service and provider type and county, FY91-92, annual rpt, S2623–1.6
- Missouri public welfare and medical assistance recipients, expenditures, and case processing, by program and county, FY92 and trends, annual rpt, S4575–2
- Montana home health service clients and visits by type of service, by agency, 1991, annual rpt, S4690–2

see also Ear diseases and infections

Speed limit

see Traffic laws and courts

Spendable earnings

see Earnings, general

Spices and herbs

- Exports of farm products, by detailed commodity and country of destination, US and California, 1991, annual rpt, B9520–1
- Production, consumption, stocks, trade, and prices for approx 100 basic commodities, including by country and producing State, commodity yearbook for 1993, C2400–1, C2400–2
- Restaurant menu practices, including herbs and spices mentioned in entree descriptions, 1987 and 1992, A8200–22
- Sales and consumer expenditures, for food store products by type, 1991-92, annual feature, C4655–1.510
- Sales volume shares by retail outlet type, for approx 300 food, drug, and other product categories, 1993 annual feature, C4655–1.504
- Supermarket sales by detailed product type, 1992 and trends, annual feature, C5225–1.507

State and local:

- Hawaii agricultural production and marketing, by commodity and island, 1987-91, annual rpt, S2030–1
- Michigan spearmint acreage, yield, and production, 1987-91, annual rpt, S3950–1
- Nevada garlic and onion production, prices, and value, 1983-92, annual rpt, S5010–1
- New Mexico chile pepper production, acreage by county, yield and value, 1991 and trends, annual rpt, S5530–1
- Oregon peppermint acreage and production, 1990-91, annual rpt, S6575–1
- Washington State agricultural production, marketing, and finances, by commodity and/or county, 1992 and trends, annual rpt, S8328–1
- Wisconsin mint for oil production, 1988-92, annual rpt, S8660–1

Spinal cord injuries

- Hospital patient admission rates and length of stay, by diagnosis and procedure, payment source, age, sex, and region, 1991, B4455–4
- Hospital patient charges and length of stay, by diagnosis and procedure, payment source, age, and region, 1991, B4455–5
- Hospital patient discharges and length of stay, by diagnostic related group (DRG), payment source, age, and region, 1991, annual rpt series, B4455–3
- Lawsuit jury verdict award trends, by type of injury, 1982-92, annual rpt, C5180–1

State and local:

Louisiana traumatic brain and spinal cord injuries, by cause, 1991, annual rpt, S3345–2

Sporting goods

- Discount chain consumer natl brand preferences, by product category and chain, and by age group, 1993 survey, annual feature, C5150–3.521
- Discount chain top-selling natl brands cited by managers, by product category, chain, and region, 1993 survey, annual feature, C5150–3.520
- Discount store sales and productivity data for 20 depts, 1993 annual feature, C5150–3.516
- Discount stores, sales, and earnings, for top chains, with detail by specialty, 1993 annual feature, C5150–3.514
- Financial ratios and performance, for over 350 SIC 4-digit industries, FY88-92, annual rpt, A6400–3
- Purchaser characteristics, by product category, 1992, annual survey rpt, A8485–4
- Purchases of sporting goods by product and outlet type, census div, and purchaser characteristics, with average prices, 1992 and trends, annual survey, A8485–2
- Retail hardware sales and productivity measures for hardware stores, home centers, and lumber/building material outlets, 1991 and trends, annual rpt series, A8275–1
- Sales of sporting goods by product category, 1983-92, annual survey rpt, A8485–4
- Sales of sporting goods by type, 1991-93, annual survey, A8485–2
- Sales of top 20 sporting goods product categories, 1989, recurring rpt, R9375–6
- Shopping center financial and operating data, with detail by type of tenant, US and Canada, 1991, triennial rpt, R9285–1

Tennis ball prices in approx 300 cities, quarterly rpt, A0150–1

Watercraft sales, for personal equipment other than boats, 1988-92, annual feature, C2425–4

State and local:

Wyoming property valuations for recreational equipment, by county, 1992, annual rpt, S8990–1.2

see also Bicycles

see also Boats and boating

see also Recreational vehicles

Sports and athletics

- Attendance at horse races compared to other professional and collegiate sports, suspended annual rpt, C2825–1
- Bowling (women's) assn membership and league activities, by city, State, and country, 1991/92, annual rpt, A9415–1
- Bowling assn finances and membership, and bowling establishments and lanes, by State and other area, 1991/92 and trends, annual rpt, A1015–1
- Cable TV pay-per-view sports packages, including number of games and prices, for 11 professional teams, 1993 article, C1850–14.522
- College athletic assn (NCAA) revenues and expenditures, 1992/93-1993/94, annual feature, C2175–1.534
- Corporate sponsors for 15 types of sports/athletic events, 1993 feature, C1200–4.508
- Endorsement earnings and products endorsed, for top 5 athletes, 1993 article, C5800–7.550
- Financial ratios and performance, for over 350 SIC 4-digit industries, FY88-92, annual rpt, A6400–3
- Franchise expansion entry fees in professional baseball, basketball, and hockey, 1993 article, C5800–7.525
- High school sports all-time records for boys and girls events, with school and student participation for 1991/92, annual rpt, A7830–2
- Higher education freshmen activity plans, by sex and instn type, fall 1992, annual survey, U6215–1
- Higher education intercollegiate women's sports participation, and scholarship recommendations of Natl Collegiate Athletic Assn gender equity task force, by sport, 1993 rpt, A7440–6
- Higher education student athlete enrollment and graduation rates, by sex, race-ethnicity, and major sport, for Natl Collegiate Athletic Assn Div I instns, 1992/93, annual rpt, A7440–4
- Higher education student athlete vs total graduation rates after 6 years, by sex, race, and Natl Collegiate Athletic Assn Div I instn, summer 1991, recurring feature, C2175–1.522, C2175–1.527
- Hispanic American professional athlete income, for top individuals by sport, 1993 article, C4575–1.508
- Injuries and participants, by type of sport, 1993 annual rpt, A8375–2.4
- Jai alai games played, attendance, handle, and govt revenues, for 3 States, 1990, annual rpt, A3363–1.2
- Participants and attendance at top 9-20 sports, 1989, recurring rpt, R9375–6

Index by Subjects and Names

Participation in boating-related and selected other sports and recreational activities, 1993 annual feature, C2425–4

Participation in 53 sports, by demographic characteristics, State, and census div, 1992, annual rpt series, A8485–3

Public opinion on favorite spectator sports, Sept 1992 Gallup Poll and trends, C4040–1.504

Public opinion on legalized betting on professional sports, Nov 1992 Gallup Poll and trends, C4040–1.506

Sales of merchandise licensed by professional and collegiate sports leagues, 1992, article, C0500–1.507

Soccer World Cup tournament revenues by source, 1994, article, C5800–7.543

TV advertising exposure value for top 19 sports event telecasts (primarily auto races), 1992, article, C2710–3.529

TV audience ratings among men, for 5 major sporting event telecasts, 1991/92, article, C9380–1.508

TV sports viewing hours of households, for network, syndicated, and cable programs, 1985 and 1992, article, C2710–1.548

Video cassette unit sales, for sports and sports/fitness tapes, 1988-92, article, C8130–1.503

Water skiing and boating participation, 1991-92, annual rpt, A8055–1

State and local:

- Arkansas intercollegiate athletics revenues by source and expenditures by function, by public instn, FY92 and trends, biennial rpt, S0690–4
- Hawaii data book, general data, 1992 annual rpt, S2090–1.7
- Tennessee, Knoxville MSA economic impact of Univ of Tennessee athletics, 1992 article, U8710–1.501
- Tennessee regulatory activities affecting boxing and racing, FY91, annual rpt, S7466–1

see also Baseball

see also Basketball

see also Bicycles

see also Boats and boating

see also Football

see also Golf

see also Hockey

see also Horse racing

see also National Collegiate Athletic Association

see also Olympic games

see also Physical exercise

see also Skiing

see also Sporting goods

see also Swimming

see also Tennis

see also Winter sports

Springfield, Mo.

Employment, hours, and earnings, by industry, monthly rpt, S4530–3

Squatters

see Living arrangements

St. Louis, Mo.

CPI and inflation rates for Chicago and St Louis, 1978-92, annual rpt, U6910–2

Discount store ratings and shopping patterns of consumers in 3 market areas, including expenditures, by leading chain, 1992 surveys, article, C5150–3.503

Employment, hours, and earnings, by industry, monthly rpt, S4530–3

see also under By City in the "Index by Categories"

St. Paul, Minn.

Printing (prepress) industry conditions for Minneapolis/St Paul area, 1993 survey article, C1850–10.509

Standard & Poor's Corp.

Airline capital expenditures and cash flow, for 7 carriers, 1991, article, C7000–4.501

Building owner value of properties owned and additions, and construction in progress, top 700 owner firms, 1991, annual article, C5800–2.504

Corporate financial losses, for 10 firms with all-time largest annual loss, 1993 article, C5800–7.517

Corporate market value rankings of top 1,000 firms, with sales, profits, assets, and related data, by company and industry, 1993 annual feature, C5800–7.521

Corporate R&D expenditures, and sales and profits, for approx 900 firms, 1992, annual feature, C5800–7.534

Corporate sales, profits, return on equity, price/earnings ratio, and earnings per share, approx 900 corporations, with industry rankings, weekly rpt quarterly article, C5800–7.503, C5800–7.519, C5800–7.528, C5800–7.541

Corporations with rapid growth, financial data for 250 firms, 1993 feature, C5800–7.551

Dividend trends for S&P 500, 1991-92, article, C5800–7.512

Hospital debt service ratios, by bond rating category, 1991, A1865–1.502

Hospital industry financial ratios, by S&P bond rating, 1988-92, annual rpt, B1880–1

Physician group credit ratings, and employment, for 9 groups rated by S&P, 1993 article, A1865–1.516

Presidential admins with largest gains and losses in S&P 500 performance, for 6 admins since 1889, 1992 article, C5800–7.505

Sales growth for 10 companies outperforming 5-year average of S&P Industrial Index firms, 1992 article, C5800–7.502

Sales per employee of large vs small companies, for 6 industries in which smaller companies outperform larger ones, 1993 article, C5800–7.551

Small companies with sales under $150 million, financial data for top 100 growth firms, 1993 annual article, C5800–7.529

Stock dividends declared, Jan-June 1991-93, article, C2710–2.516

Standard Metropolitan Statistical Areas

see Metropolitan Statistical Areas

see under By SMSA or MSA in the "Index by Categories"

Standard of living

see Cost of living

see Family budgets

see Personal and household income

see Quality of life

Standards

see Quality control and testing

see Weights and measures

Standards Bureau

see National Institute of Standards and Technology

State and local employees

State and local employees

- Authorized FTE positions in State general funds, by State, FY92-94, semiannual rpt, A7955–1
- Charity gambling receipts, net proceeds, and State regulatory staff and finances, by State, various years FY90-92, article, C2176–1.512
- Child labor inspectors and specialists, by State, 1992, R8335–2
- City fiscal condition, including budget trends and adjustments, and influencing factors, by region and population size, Mar-Apr 1993 survey, annual rpt, A8012–1.23
- College grad job and salary offers, by field of study, type of employer and occupation, and degree level, by region, interim rpt series, A3940–1
- College grad job and salary offers, by field of study, type of employer and occupation, and degree level, series, A3940–2
- Correctional instn admin, inmates, facilities, costs, parole and probation, and staffing, for local, State, and Federal systems, 1992 annual series, R4300–1
- Correctional instns, inmates, staff, and cost of care, by instn, US and Canada, with operating summary by State or Province, 1992, annual directory, A1305–3
- Employees, earnings, and payroll, by level of govt and State, Oct 1991 and trends, annual rpt, R9050–1
- Employment composition of State and local govts, by function, 1990 and trends, U5085–2.7
- Employment in govt, by level and State, Oct 1991, annual rpt, R9380–1.3
- Employment of State and/or local govts, with comparison to private sector, by State, Nov 1992 vs 1991, article, B8500–2.508
- Employment of State/local govt per 10,000 population, with detail for corrections and hwy depts, by State, Oct 1991, semiannual rpt, B8500–1
- Employment trends in State/local govt, including number per 10,000 population, by State, Oct 1990-91, article, B8500–2.502
- Health benefit plan funding patterns, coverage and HMO participation by State, and cost mgmt practices, 1993 annual article, C2425–1.506
- Info resources mgmt in State govts, including data on budgets, staff, and organizational structure, by State, 1991, biennial rpt, A7121–1
- Jails and adult detention facilities, inmates, staff, and operating summary, by State and instn, Dec 1992, recurring directory, A1305–1
- Law school grad employment and salaries, by type of employer, location, and grad characteristics, 1992 and trends, annual rpt, A6505–1
- Library State agency appropriations, expenditures, salaries, and staff, by State, 1992 annual rpt, A3862–1
- Municipal police and fire dept employment, hours, compensation, and expenditures, by census div, city, and city size, 1992, annual rpt, A5800–1.3

State and local employees

Occupational health and safety govt regulatory activities, including inspections, fines, and data by State and company, 1992 annual rpt, R8335–1.2

Planning profession employment and salaries, by type of employer, demographic and professional characteristics, and location, 1991 and trends, biennial rpt, A2615–1

Public housing authority average staff size, by agency size, 1988, A6800–1

Public housing authority operations, including staff size for 22 local agencies, 1993 rpt, A6800–2

Public planning agency personnel practices, by jurisdiction size, 1991 survey rpt, A2615–3

Statistical profiles of 50 States and DC, general data, 1993 annual almanac, C4712–1

Tourism dev offices of State govts, activities, personnel, and budgets, by State, 1992 survey, annual rpt, R9375–2

Utility and transportation regulatory agency activities, scope of jurisdiction, finances, and employees, by agency, 1991/92 annual rpt, A7015–2

Women's employment in low-paying State/local govt jobs, with data by race-ethnicity and State, 1990, U5090–1.3

State and local:

Alabama law enforcement employees, sworn and civilian, by sex and location, 1992, annual rpt, S0119–1.2

Alabama public health dept activities, including services provided, inspection and licensing activity, staff and finances, and vital statistics and health data, 1992 annual rpt, S0175–3

Alabama public libraries, finances, holdings, circulation, staff, and population served, by library, FY92, annual rpt, S0180–1

Alabama statistical abstract, general data, 1992 recurring rpt, U5680–2.10

Alaska corrections system admin, including inmate and probationer/parolee offenses and demographic characteristics, 1991 annual rpt, S0287–1

Alaska employment and unemployment, hours, and earnings, by area and/or industry, monthly rpt, S0320–1

Alaska property tax appraisers and workloads, by municipality, 1992, annual rpt, S0285–1

Alaska State court system employees, by sex and race-ethnicity, FY92, annual rpt, S0290–1

Alaska State govt employees, by category, June 1992, annual rpt, S0275–1

Arizona court cases and dispositions, by type of case and court, with judicial personnel and finances, by county and city, FY92, annual rpt, S0525–1

Arizona law enforcement employment by sex, by local agency, Oct 1992, annual rpt, S0505–2.2

Arizona public library holdings, circulation, finances, and staff, by instn and county, FY92, annual rpt, S0495–1

Arizona statistical abstract, general data, 1993 recurring rpt, U5850–2.10, U5850–2.12

Arkansas law enforcement personnel by sex, by agency and county, 1992, annual rpt, S0652–1

Arkansas Public Service Commission staff, 1992, annual rpt, S0757–1

California criminal justice and law enforcement employment, by type of agency, 1987-92, annual rpt, S0910–1.2

California criminal justice system expenditures and employment, by type of agency or function, 1982-91, annual rpt, S0910–2.1

California judicial employment, by court type and location, FY92 and trends, annual rpt, S0905–2

California judicial employment, by demographic characteristics and court, FY92 annual rpt, S0905–1

California library finances, staff, holdings, and services, by library type and facility, FY92, annual rpt, S0825–2

California State Banking Dept personnel, 1992, annual rpt, S0810–1

California statistical abstract, general data, 1992 annual rpt, S0840–2.3

Colorado library finances and operations, including staff, holdings, and population served, by instn and library type, series, S1000–3

Connecticut crimes and arrests, law enforcement employment by sex, and assaults on officers, 1992, annual rpt, S1256–1.3

Connecticut education dept staff and expenditures, by div, 1991/92, annual rpt, S1185–1

Connecticut judicial dept personnel and finances, FY91-92, biennial rpt, S1220–1.1

Connecticut public library staff, holdings, circulation, and finances, by library and town, FY91, annual rpt, S1242–1

DC courts authorized positions, and court reporter staffing and transcript production, 1992 annual rpt, S1515–1

DC employment, earnings, and hours, by industry, with unemployment insurance data, monthly rpt, S1527–3

DC statistical profile, general data, 1992 annual rpt, S1535–3.2

Florida corrections dept staff, by region, FY92 annual rpt, S1720–1

Florida public libraries, finances, holdings, staff, and services, by system and library, FY92, annual rpt, S1800–2

Florida statistical abstract, general data, 1992 annual rpt, U6660–1.23

Georgia employment, earnings, and hours, by major industry group and MSA, monthly rpt, S1905–1

Georgia statistical abstract, general data, 1992-93 biennial rpt, U6730–1.3

Hawaii data book, general data, 1992 annual rpt, S2090–1.3, S2090–1.4, S2090–1.9, S2090–1.12

Hawaii judges and other judicial system personnel, FY92, annual rpt, S2115–1.1

Hawaii tax dept staffing, FY90-92, annual rpt, S2120–1

Idaho crimes and arrests, law enforcement employees by sex, and assaults on officers, by local agency and county, 1992, annual rpt, S2275–2

Idaho finance dept staffing and finances, FY92, annual rpt, S2235–1

Idaho public library holdings, staff, services, circulation, and finances, by instn, FY92, annual rpt, S2282–1

Index by Subjects and Names

Illinois corrections dept admin, including inmates and characteristics, finances, and staff, FY91-93 and trends, annual rpt, S2425–1

Illinois public assistance dept staff, FY91-92, annual rpt, S2520–2

Illinois public library holdings, staff, and finances, by instn, FY92, annual rpt, S2535–2

Illinois statistical abstract, general data, 1992 annual rpt, U6910–2

Indiana court personnel, by position and court, 1992, annual rpt, S2703–1.2

Indiana public and other library holdings, circulation, finances, and staff, by instn, 1992 or FY92, annual rpt, S2655–1

Indiana public welfare dept child support div and county agencies employment, FY84-91, annual rpt, S2623–1.3

Iowa public library finances and operations, by county, size of population served, and library, FY92, annual rpt, S2778–1

Kansas business activity indicators, quarterly rpt, U7095–1

Kansas law enforcement employees by demographic characteristics and local agency, with assaults on police by circumstance, 1992, annual rpt, S2925–1.2

Kansas statistical abstract, general data, 1991/92 annual rpt, U7095–2.11, U7095–2.12

Kentucky arrests by county and offense, and law enforcement employment by agency, 1992, annual rpt, S3150–1.2

Kentucky public library finances and operations, by county, FY92, annual rpt, S3165–1

Louisiana labor force, employment, and unemployment, by industry div and MSA, monthly rpt, S3320–2

Louisiana public library finances, holdings, circulation, and personnel, by library system, FY92, annual rpt, S3275–1

Maine govt employment, by level and detailed occupation, May 1991 or Mar 1992, triennial survey, S3465–1.27

Maine law enforcement employment, by sex and county, 1991, annual rpt, S3475–1.2

Maryland court finances and personnel, by court level and judicial agency, FY92, annual rpt, S3600–1

Maryland crimes and arrests, by offense, location, and offender characteristics, with law enforcement employment and assaults on officers, 1992 and trends, annual rpt, S3665–1

Maryland labor force, employment, earnings, and hours, with data by industry and location, monthly rpt, S3605–2

Maryland public library operating income and expenditures, staff, holdings, and population served, by county, FY92, annual rpt, S3610–5

Maryland statistical abstract, general data, 1993-94 biennial rpt, S3605–1.4

Massachusetts employment, hours, and earnings, by industry and local area, with unemployment insurance claims, monthly rpt, S3808–1

Massachusetts public library employment and hours, by municipality, FY92, annual rpt, S3870–1

Michigan child/spousal support collection program activities and staff, by county, 1992, annual rpt, S3962–1.2

Index by Subjects and Names

State and local employees

Michigan law enforcement officers, 1990-92, annual rpt, S3997–1

Michigan State corrections dept employment, by sex, race-ethnicity, and instn, 1991 and trends, annual rpt, S3960–1

Minnesota public library holdings, staff, services, circulation, and finances, by library, 1991, annual rpt, S4165–2

Mississippi statistical abstract, general data, 1992 annual rpt, U3255–4.9

Missouri employment, earnings, and hours, by industry and MSA, monthly rpt, S4530–3

Missouri family services div employees, FY92, annual rpt, S4575–2

Missouri public, special, and academic libraries, finances, holdings, circulation, staff, and services, by location, FY92, annual rpt, S4520–2

Montana public library holdings, staff, circulation, and finances, by library, FY92, annual rpt, S4725–1

Nebraska correctional instn admin, with inmates by criminal background and demographic characteristics, by instn, FY92 and trends, annual rpt, S4850–1

Nebraska employment and unemployment, by industry group and locality, quarterly rpt, S4895–2

Nebraska govt employment, with detail for local govt by type of governing unit, and data by county, 1993 article, U7860–1.502

Nebraska public libraries, finances, holdings, circulation, staff, and population served, by instn, FY91, annual rpt, S4910–1

Nevada library and staff directories for public and academic libraries, with data on holdings, operations, and finances, FY92, annual rpt, S5095–1

Nevada statistical abstract, general data, 1992 biennial rpt, S5005 1.8

New Hampshire employment, hours, and earnings, by industry and area, monthly rpt, S5205–1

New Hampshire govt and education employment by detailed occupation, 1991 or 1992, triennial rpt, S5205–2.25

New Hampshire insurance dept employees, FY90-92, annual rpt, S5220–1

New Hampshire public library finances and operations, by library and/or location, 1991, annual rpt, S5227–1

New Jersey casino control commission employment, FY89-94, annual rpt, S5360–1

New Jersey crimes and arrests, law enforcement employment, and assaults on officers, 1992 and trends, annual rpt, S5430–1

New Mexico business and economic activity indicators, monthly rpt, U7980–1

New Mexico employment, hours, and earnings, by labor market area and industry, monthly rpt, S5624–2

New Mexico public assistance dept staff, cases, and efficiency measures, by county, monthly rpt quarterly feature, S5620–2

New Mexico public library operations and finances, by instn, FY92, annual rpt, S5627–1

New York State employment, earnings, and hours, by county, selected metro area, and industry group, monthly rpt, S5775–1

New York State law enforcement employment, by sex, county, and local agency, 1991, annual rpt, S5760–3.3

New York State public library finances, staff, holdings, and services, by library and county, 1991, annual rpt, S5745–2

New York State social service program admin staff, by State area, 1991, annual rpt, S5800–2.3

New York State statistical yearbook, general data, 1992 annual rpt, U5100–1.3, U5100–1.5, U5100–1.6, U5100–1.8, U5100–1.10

North Carolina court cases and dispositions, by type of court and case, and location, with judicial dept finances and personnel, FY91, annual rpt, S5950–1

North Carolina employment, hours, and earnings, by industry group, with job placements, monthly rpt, S5917–3

North Carolina employment in trade, transportation, communications, utilities, govt, and education, by detailed occupation, 2nd qtr 1991, triennial rpt, S5917–5.2

North Carolina govt positions funded, by agency, FY83-92, annual rpt, S5897–1

North Carolina law enforcement officers by sex, and civilian employees, by local agency, 1991-92, annual rpt, S5955–1.1

North Carolina public libraries, finances, holdings, and personnel, by library system, FY91, annual rpt, S5910–1

North Carolina public welfare programs, cases, recipients, staff, and finances, by county, 1st half FY93, semiannual rpt, S5940–2

North Dakota law enforcement employment by sex, 1991, annual rpt, S6060–1

North Dakota public library finances, holdings, staff, and operations, by instn, FY91, annual rpt, S6180–5

Ohio correctional instn admissions and releases, inmate characteristics, programs, finances, and staffing, FY91 and trends, annual rpt, S6370–1

Ohio Dept of Taxation employment, FY92, annual rpt, S6390–1.1

Ohio employment, hours, and earnings, by industry and MSA, with job service and unemployment insurance activities, monthly rpt, S6270–1

Ohio public, academic, and other library finances, holdings, and staff, by library and location, 1992 and trends, annual rpt, S6320–1

Oklahoma correctional instn staff, by instn, FY91, annual rpt, S6420–1

Oklahoma law enforcement employees, sworn and civilian, by sex, 1992, annual rpt, S6465–1.2

Oklahoma public and institutional library holdings, circulation, finances, and staff, by facility, FY92, annual rpt, S6470–1

Oklahoma public welfare program employment and payroll, by program, FY92, annual rpt, S6455–1

Oklahoma statistical abstract, general data, 1992 annual rpt, U8130–2.3

Oregon crimes by offense, law enforcement employees by sex, and assaults on police, by local agency, 1992 and trends, annual rpt, S6603–3.2

Oregon labor force and employment statistics, including data by industry, monthly rpt, S6592–1, S6615–2

Oregon library finances, staff, holdings, and services, for public, academic, and special libraries by instn, FY92 and trends, annual rpt, S6635–1

Pennsylvania corrections dept staff and job openings, by position and instn, 1990, annual rpt, S6782–1

Pennsylvania employment, hours, and earnings, by industry, monthly rpt, S6845–1

Pennsylvania labor force planning rpt, including population characteristics, employment and job openings by industry and occupation, and income trends, FY92 annual rpt, S6845–3

Pennsylvania police employment, sworn and civilian, by sex and county, 1992, annual rpt, S6860–1

Pennsylvania public and institutional library personnel, holdings, circulation, and finances, by county and facility, FY92, annual rpt, S6790–2

Pennsylvania statistical abstract, general data, 1992 recurring rpt, U4130–6.4, U4130–6.6

Rhode Island judicial system personnel, by court, 1991, annual rpt, S6965–1

Rhode Island statistical almanac, general data, 1993 annual rpt, C7975–1

South Carolina correctional instns, admin, and inmates by criminal offense and demographic characteristics, FY92 and trends, annual rpt, S7135–1

South Carolina court cases and dispositions, by type of court and location, with judicial dept finances and employees, 1992 and trends, annual rpt, S7197–1

South Carolina employment, earnings, and hours, by industry group and locality, monthly rpt, S7155–2

South Carolina statistical abstract, general data, 1993 annual rpt, S7125–1.5, S7125–1.7

South Dakota correctional instn admin, including inmates by criminal background and demographic characteristics, FY92 and trends, annual rpt, S7296–1

South Dakota court cases and dispositions by type of case, and judicial system finances and personnel, by jurisdiction, FY92 and trends, annual rpt, S7395–1

South Dakota employment, earnings, and hours for selected industries and areas, with characteristics of unemployed and job service activities, monthly rpt, S7355–1

Tennessee correctional instn admin, with inmate characteristics, and corrections dept finances and staff, FY92, annual rpt, S7480–1

Tennessee employment, wages, and unemployment insurance contributions, by county and industry, 1991, annual rpt, S7495–1

Tennessee statistical abstract, general data, 1992/93 annual rpt, U8710–2.3, U8710–2.16

Texas human services dept licensing staff by function, Sept 1991 and Aug 1992, annual rpt, S7695–1

Texas law enforcement employment, sworn and civilian, by sex, Oct 1992, annual rpt, S7735–2.2

Texas public libraries, holdings, circulation, staff, and finances, by library and location, FY91, annual rpt, S7710–1

State and local employees

Texas State and local govt employment, by detailed occupation, May 1991, triennial survey rpt, S7675–1.30

Texas State and local health depts finances, employment, and service area characteristics, FY91 and trends, U8850–8.6

Utah economic and business activity review and indicators, monthly rpt, U8960–2

Utah law enforcement employment, by county and local agency, 1992, annual rpt, S7890–3

Utah public libraries, services, staff, and finances, by library, 1992, annual rpt, S7808–1

Utah statistical abstract, general data, 1993 triennial rpt, U8960–1.7

Utah tax commission employment, FY92 annual rpt, S7905–1

Virginia court caseloads, processing, and dispositions, by type of court and case, with judicial dept personnel and finances, by location, 1992 and trends, annual rpt, S8300–1

Virginia crimes and arrests by offense, and law enforcement employment, by location and reporting agency, 1992, annual rpt, S8295–2.2

Virginia labor force, hours, and earnings, with data by industry group and locality, monthly rpt, S8205–6

Washington State court cases and dispositions, by type of court and case, and jurisdiction, with judicial finances and personnel, 1992 and trends, annual rpt, S8339–1

Washington State crimes and clearances, and law enforcement employment, by reporting agency, 1992, annual rpt, S8440–1

Washington State govt employees, by function, FY83-92, annual rpt, S8345–3

Washington State public libraries, finances, holdings, circulation, staff, and population served, by instn, 1992, annual rpt, S8375–1

West Virginia law enforcement employees, sworn and civilian, by sex and type of agency, 1990-91, annual rpt, S8610–1.1

West Virginia public, academic, and special library operations and/or finances, by instn, 1991/92, annual rpt, S8590–1

Wisconsin Blue Book, general data, 1993-94 biennial rpt, S8780–1.2

Wisconsin law enforcement employees, by sex and local agency, 1992, annual rpt, S8771–1

Wisconsin libraries, operations, and finances, by library type, instn, and location, 1992, annual rpt, S8795–1

Wyoming correctional instn admin, finances, inmate characteristics, and staff, and probation and parole activities, FY92 annual rpt, S8883–1

Wyoming employment by industry group and county, with unemployment insurance and job service activities, monthly rpt, S8895–1

Wyoming law enforcement personnel by sex, county, and local jurisdiction, 1991, annual rpt, S8867–3.2

Wyoming public library holdings, staff, circulation, and finances, by county, FY92, annual rpt, S8855–3

Wyoming State employees, by agency July 1991-92, annual rpt, S8875–1

see also Fire departments

see also Judges

see also Labor-management relations in government

see also Librarians

see also Police

see also School administration and staff

see also Sheriffs

see also State and local employees pay

see also State police

see also State retirement systems

see also Teachers

State and local employees pay

Chemistry and chemical engineering grad starting salaries, employment status, demographic characteristics, and advanced study plans, 1991/92, annual rpt, A1250–2

City fiscal condition, including budget trends and adjustments, and influencing factors, by region and population size, Mar-Apr 1993 survey, annual rpt, A8012–1.23

College grad job and salary offers, by field of study, type of employer and occupation, and degree level, by region, interim rpt series, A3940–1

College grad job and salary offers, by field of study, type of employer and occupation, and degree level, series, A3940–2

Compensation changes for govt employees, by State, FY94, semiannual rpt, A7955–1

Correctional instn admin, inmates, facilities, costs, parole and probation, and staffing, for local, State, and Federal systems, 1992 annual series, R4300–1

County govt officials salaries, by position, region, and county size, July 1992 and trends, annual rpt, A5800–1.3

Earnings, employees, and payroll, by level of govt and State, Oct 1991 and trends, annual rpt, R9050–1

Earnings of State/local employees, by State, Oct 1991, semiannual rpt, B8500–1.5

Engineers salaries in State and local govt, by years since college degree, 1993, annual survey rpt, A0685–5

Governor salaries in 10 States with highest and lowest pay, 1992 article, C5800–7.506

Incentive pay use by local govts, including methods, effectiveness, and advantages and disadvantages, 1993 rpt, A5800–1.1

Jails and adult detention facilities expenditures, by State and instn, Dec 1992, recurring directory, A1305–1.2

Judicial system salaries for judges and court administrators, by State and territory, and for Federal system, July 1993, semiannual rpt, R6600–2

Law school grad employment and salaries, by type of employer, location, and grad characteristics, 1992 and trends, annual rpt, A6505–1

Librarian salaries for 6 positions, for public and academic libraries by region, 1993, annual rpt, A2070–3

Library school grads, placements, and salaries, by region and sex, 1991 and trends, annual compilation, C1650–3.3

Library State agency appropriations, expenditures, salaries, and staff, by State, 1992 annual rpt, A3862–1

Index by Subjects and Names

Municipal govt officials salaries, by position, region, form of govt, and city size, July 1992 and trends, annual rpt, A5800–1.3

Municipal police and fire dept employment, hours, compensation, and expenditures, by census div, city, and city size, 1992, annual rpt, A5800–1.3

Municipal police personnel salaries, by position and city, 1992, recurring rpt, A5800–4.32

Planning commissioner compensation, for city and county land use commissions, 1987, recurring rpt, A2615–2

Planning profession employment and salaries, by type of employer, demographic and professional characteristics, and location, 1991 and trends, biennial rpt, A2615–1

Police officers salary share paid by shopping centers they patrol, 1993, article, C5150–4.506

Private sector wages compared to State and local govt pay, with detail by sex and State, 1989 and trends, R4700–21

Professional worker salaries, by employee and employer characteristics, with detail for scientists and engineers, 1990s and trends, biennial rpt, A3960–1

School district transportation director salaries, by fleet size and location type, 1993, annual article, C1575–1.507

Statistical profiles of 50 States and DC, general data, 1993 annual almanac, C4712–1

Utility and transportation regulatory agency activities, scope of jurisdiction, finances, and employees, by agency, 1991/92 annual rpt, A7015–2

State and local:

Alabama public libraries, finances, holdings, circulation, staff, and population served, by library, FY92, annual rpt, S0180–1

Arizona public library holdings, circulation, finances, and staff, by instn and county, FY92, annual rpt, S0495–1

Arizona statistical abstract, general data, 1993 recurring rpt, U5850–2.10, U5850–2.12

California library finances, staff, holdings, and services, by library type and facility, FY92, annual rpt, S0825–2

California State Banking Dept compensation, by employee, Dec 1992, annual rpt, S0810–1

Connecticut public library staff, holdings, circulation, and finances, by library and town, FY91, annual rpt, S1242–1

DC statistical profile, general data, 1992 annual rpt, S1535–3.2

Florida public libraries, finances, holdings, staff, and services, by system and library, FY92, annual rpt, S1800–2

Florida statistical abstract, general data, 1992 annual rpt, U6660–1.23

Hawaii data book, general data, 1992 annual rpt, S2090–1.9, S2090–1.12

Idaho public library finances, including director salaries, by library, FY92, annual rpt, S2282–1

Illinois financial condition, including expenditures by agency and object, FY92, annual rpt, S2415–1.2

Illinois public library holdings, staff, and finances, by instn, FY92, annual rpt, S2535–2

Index by Subjects and Names

Illinois statistical abstract, general data, 1992 annual rpt, U6910–2

Indiana court cases and dispositions by type of court and case, and location, with judicial system finances and personnel, 1992, annual rpt, S2703–1

Indiana financial condition, including revenues by source, expenditures by function and object, and fund balances, by agency, FY92, annual rpt, S2570–1.2

Indiana public and other library holdings, circulation, finances, and staff, by instn, 1992 or FY92, annual rpt, S2655–1

Iowa public library finances and operations, by county, size of population served, and library, FY92, annual rpt, S2778–1

Kentucky public library finances and operations, by county, FY92, annual rpt, S3165–1

Louisiana public library finances, holdings, circulation, and personnel, by library system, FY92, annual rpt, S3275–1

Maryland public library operating income and expenditures, staff, holdings, and population served, by county, FY92, annual rpt, S3610–5

Massachusetts public library finances, holdings, and circulation, by municipality, FY92, annual rpt, S3870–1

Minnesota public library holdings, staff, services, circulation, and finances, by library, 1991, annual rpt, S4165–2

Mississippi bank examiner salaries, and travel and training expenses, 1992, annual rpt, S4325–1

Mississippi human services dept salaries for highest-paid positions, FY92, annual rpt, S4357–1

Missouri public, special, and academic libraries, finances, holdings, circulation, staff, and services, by location, FY92, annual rpt, S4520–2

Missouri State Finance Division compensation, by employee, FY91-92 biennial rpt, S4502–1

Montana public library holdings, staff, circulation, and finances, by library, FY92, annual rpt, S4725–1

Nebraska public libraries, finances, holdings, circulation, staff, and population served, by instn, FY91, annual rpt, S4910–1

New Hampshire public library finances and operations, by library and/or location, 1991, annual rpt, S5227–1

New Hampshire State govt and judicial salary schedules, 1992, biennial rpt, S5255–1

New Jersey public library finances, holdings, circulation, and staff, by county and library, 1991, annual rpt, S5385–2

New Mexico public library operations and finances, by instn, FY92, annual rpt, S5627–1

New York State average earnings of Federal, State, and local govt employees, 1987-91, annual feature, S5775–1.501

New York State public library finances, staff, holdings, and services, by library and county, 1991, annual rpt, S5745–2

North Carolina court cases and dispositions, by type of court and case, and location, with judicial dept finances and personnel, FY91, annual rpt, S5950–1

North Carolina public libraries, finances, holdings, and personnel, by library system, FY91, annual rpt, S5910–1

North Dakota public library finances, holdings, staff, and operations, by instn, FY91, annual rpt, S6180–5

Ohio Dept of Taxation expenditures for personal service and maintenance/equipment, FY92, annual rpt, S6390–1.1

Ohio public, academic, and other library finances, holdings, and staff, by library and location, 1992 and trends, annual rpt, S6320–1

Oklahoma public and institutional library holdings, circulation, finances, and staff, by facility, FY92, annual rpt, S6470–1

Oklahoma statistical abstract, general data, 1992 annual rpt, U8130–2.3

Oregon library finances, staff, holdings, and services, for public, academic, and special libraries by instn, FY92 and trends, annual rpt, S6635–1

Pennsylvania public and institutional library personnel, holdings, circulation, and finances, by county and facility, FY92, annual rpt, S6790–2

Rhode Island statistical almanac, general data, 1993 annual rpt, C7975–1

South Carolina public and institutional libraries, finances, services, holdings, and staff, by library, FY92, annual rpt, S7210–1

South Carolina statistical abstract, general data, 1993 annual rpt, S7125–1.7

Tennessee employment, wages, and unemployment insurance contributions, by county and industry, 1991, annual rpt, S7495–1

Tennessee statistical abstract, general data, 1992/93 annual rpt, U8710–2.3

Texas financial condition, including revenues by source, expenditures by function and dept, and investments, with data for over 400 individual funds, FY92, annual rpt, S7655–2.2

Texas judicial salaries and supplemental compensation, FY92 annual rpt, S7703–1

Texas public libraries, holdings, circulation, staff, and finances, by library and location, FY91, annual rpt, S7710–1

Utah public libraries, services, staff, and finances, by library, 1992, annual rpt, S7808–1

Utah State govt salary schedule, and salaries of top officials, 1993 annual rpt, R9380–1.5

Utah statistical abstract, general data, 1993 triennial rpt, U8960–1.7

Virginia court caseloads, processing, and dispositions, by type of court and case, with judicial dept personnel and finances, by location, 1992 and trends, annual rpt, S8300–1

Virginia public library operations and finances, by instn, FY92, annual rpt, S8275–1

Washington State public library salaries by position, 1993, annual rpt, S8375–1

Washington State Revenue Dept expenditures for employee salaries, FY68-92, annual rpt, S8415–1.1

West Virginia public, academic, and special library operations and/or finances, by instn, 1991/92, annual rpt, S8590–1

Wisconsin Blue Book, general data, 1993-94 biennial rpt, S8780–1.1, S8780–1.2

State and local taxes

Wisconsin libraries, operations, and finances, by library type, instn, and location, 1992, annual rpt, S8795–1

Wyoming public library holdings, staff, circulation, and finances, by county, FY92, annual rpt, S8855–3

see also Civil service pensions

see also Educational employees pay

see also State retirement systems

State and local taxes

Burden of State taxes for families with $100,000 vs $25,000 incomes, by State, 1991, article, B8500–2.515

Changes enacted in State taxes, with change as a percent of total revenue, by State, 1992, annual rpt, U5085–2.9

City fiscal condition, including budget trends and adjustments, and influencing factors, by region and population size, Mar-Apr 1993 survey, annual rpt, A8012–1.23

Corporate State/local tax burden comparisons by tax type, for 19 States, 1993 article, B8500–2.513

Economic dev condition indicators, including economic performance, business vitality, growth capacity, and tax/fiscal system, by State, 1993 annual rpt, R4225–1.1

Electric utility State/local taxes/contributions as percent of revenues, for public and private utilities by region, 1990, article, A2625–1.501

Environmental regulation costs under Federal mandates, including related local user fees/taxes, by city population size, 1987 and 2000, U9640–3

Family income, with impact of Federal and State/local taxes and inflation, 1980-92, annual rpt, R9050–13

Fiscal conditions for New York and selected other States, including tax revenues, expenditures, and taxation of corporate profits, 1992 article, A8825–1.502

Forecasts of natl income and product account components, employment, and financial sector activity, monthly rpt, B4950–1

Govt finances, including revenues by source, expenditures by function, and debt, detailed data for Federal, State, and local govts, 1993 annual rpt, R9050–1

Govt finances, taxation, and related issues, series, R9050–15

Govt finances, taxation, and spending policies, periodic rpt, R9050–3

Increases in State taxes generating 5%/more increase in revenues, by State, 1990-92, article, B8500–2.515

Increases in State taxes, with political party of Governors and legislators before vs after subsequent elections, for 17 States, 1991-92, U5085–2.8

Increases or decreases in selected State taxes, for 12 States with largest changes, 1992, annual rpt, R3834–9

Insurance industry premium tax payments, by State, 1991, annual rpt, A5650–1.2

Lodging tax rates, for 5 cities with highest rates, 1993 feature, C1200–1.513

Meal and lodging tax rates, by metro area, 1992, annual survey, C1200–1.508

Oil/gas industry contribution to tax revenues, for 11 oil-producing States, FY87-90, article, C6985–1.550

State and local taxes

Pari-mutuel wagering activity, attendance, purse distribution, and govt revenue, by State and Canadian Province, 1990 and trends, annual rpt, A3363–1

Payments of State/local taxes, FY91, and rates by type of tax, Jan 1993, by State, annual rpt, R9380–1.7

Ratings of States in balanced use of 3 major taxes for revenues, FY90, article, B8500–2.504

Revenue impacts of State tax changes, by tax type and State, FY93 and trends, annual rpt, A7470–4.9

Revenue share from property, sales, or income tax, for States receiving less than 20% of revenues from that tax type, FY90, article, B8500–2.505

Revenue shares and/or growth for State vs local taxes, with local revenues per $100 personal income by tax type, 1991 and trends, U5085–2.11

Revenues from State personal, corporate, and sales taxes, by State and region, quarterly rpt, U5085–1

Revenues from State taxes, by State, 4th qtr 1992 vs 1991, article, B8500–2.509

Revenues from State taxes per capita, by State, 1991, annual rpt, S4950–1

Revenues from taxes, and tax rates, with data by tax type and comparisons to personal income, by State, FY81-93, R9050–14

Revenues per capita and as percent of personal income, by State, FY91, article, B8500–2.511

Revenues per capita and compared to personal income, and tax burden and capacity, by State, 1993 semiannual rpt, B8500–1.4

Semiconductor manufacturing plant effective State/local tax rates for typical Massachusetts vs California company plants, for 5 States, 1993 article, B8500–2.514

Small corporation mgmt views on trends in State/local taxes and tax-related personnel, 1993 article, C4687–1.508

Southern States population, personal income, and State/local revenues and expenditures, by State, 1950s-2010, biennial fact book, A8945–1.1

Transportation-related revenues of Fed Govt and individual States, by type, 1990s and trends, annual rpt, A0865–1.3

Travel-generated tax revenues, top 20 States, 1990, recurring rpt, R9375–6

Trends in total State taxable resources, by State and region, 1987-89, R8490–46

State and local:

Alabama county data book, general data, 1992 annual rpt, S0121–2

Alabama financial condition, including revenues by source, expenditures by function and object, and fund balances, by fund and agency, FY92, annual rpt, S0129–1

Alabama municipal data book, general data, 1992 recurring rpt, S0121–5

Alabama public school revenues by source and expenditures by object, by district, 1991/92, annual rpt, S0124–1.2

Alabama State tax revenue trends and forecast, FY90-93, annual rpt, U5680–3

Alabama statistical abstract, general data, 1992 recurring rpt, U5680–2.6

Alaska financial condition, including revenues by source, expenditures by function, fund balances, and bond obligations, FY92 and trends, annual rpt, S0275–1

Alaska State and local taxation, including taxes by type, property values, public debt, and tax shelters, by locale, 1992 and trends, annual rpt, S0285–1

Arizona copper industry State/local taxes paid by type, 1992, article, C5226–2.508

Arizona financial condition, including revenues by source, expenditures by function, and fund balances, FY91, annual rpt, S0450–2

Arizona financial condition, including revenues by source, expenditures by function, and fund balances, FY92, annual rpt, S0450–1

Arizona revenues and economic analysts outlook for economic impact of 7 proposed tax changes, 1993 article, U0282–1.508

Arizona statistical abstract, general data, 1993 recurring rpt, U5850–2.10

Arizona tax revenues by source, tax rates, and disbursements to local areas, FY92 and trends, annual rpt, S0515–1

Arkansas financial condition, including revenues by source, expenditures by function and locality, and fund balances, FY91-92, biennial rpt, S0780–1

Arkansas financial condition, including revenues by source, expenditures by function and object, and fund balances, FY92, annual rpt, S0670–1

Arkansas public higher education finances, with per capita tax revenues and capacity compared to US and selected States, 1990-92, article, U5930–1.502

Arkansas public school revenues by source, expenditures by function and object, and indebtedness, 1991/92 and trends, annual rpt, S0660–1.3

California economic condition, including population, employment and earnings, income, business activity, and taxation, 1960s-92, annual rpt, S0840–3.2

California financial condition, including revenues by source, expenditures by agency and function, fund balances, and bonded debt, FY92 and trends, annual rpt, S0815–1

California tax collections (excluding income tax), by locality, company, and type of tax, FY92 and trends, annual rpt, S0835–1

Colorado financial condition, including receipts by source, and expenditures by function, FY92 and trends, annual rpt, S0980–1

Colorado tax revenues by type, with selected data by county and city, FY92 and trends, annual rpt, S1075–1

Connecticut financial condition, including revenues by source, expenditures by function, and bonded debt, FY92, annual rpt, S1170–1, S1170–2

Connecticut public libraries income from local taxes, by library and town, FY91, annual rpt, S1242–1

DC financial condition, including receipts by source, expenditures by object or function, and fund balances, FY92, annual rpt, S1507–1

Index by Subjects and Names

DC statistical profile, general data, 1992 annual rpt, S1535–3.2

Delaware data book, general data, 1993 annual rpt, S1375–4

Florida financial condition, including receipts by source, expenditures by function, and fund balances, FY92, annual rpt, S1717–1, S1717–3

Florida statistical abstract, general data, 1992 annual rpt, U6660–1.19, U6660–1.23

Georgia financial condition, including revenues by source, expenditures by function and object, and fund balances, FY92, annual rpt, S1860–1

Georgia tax revenues, by type and county, FY92 annual rpt, S1950–1

Hawaii counties population and economic indicators, 1993 annual rpt series, B3500–2

Hawaii data book, general data, 1992 annual rpt, S2090–1.9

Hawaii economic conditions, including employment, population, tourism, and construction, quarterly rpt, S2090–2

Hawaii economic indicators, bimonthly rpt, B3500–1

Hawaii financial condition, including revenues by source, expenditures by function, and fund balances, FY92, annual rpt, S2020–1

Hawaii tax collections and allocations, by type, for State and counties, FY91-92 and trends, annual rpt, S2120–1

Idaho economic profile, general data, 1992 recurring rpt, S2218–2.4, S2218–2.10

Idaho financial condition, including revenues by source and expenditures by object, by agency and/or fund, FY92, annual rpt, S2215–1

Idaho income and excise tax structures and analysis of losses due to inflation, 1993 article, S2245–2.501

Idaho insurance premium taxes collected, 1987-91, annual rpt, S2260–1

Idaho school district revenues by source, and expenditures by function, by district and fund, FY92, annual rpt, S2225–2

Idaho tax statistics, including collections, and data by county and city, FY92 and trends, annual rpt, S2295–1

Illinois financial condition, including revenues by source, and expenditures by object, function, and agency, FY92, annual rpt, S2415–1

Illinois public library holdings, staff, and finances, by instn, FY92, annual rpt, S2535–2

Illinois statistical abstract, general data, 1992 annual rpt, U6910–2

Illinois tax revenues, by source, 1988-94, article, U6910–1.503

Illinois tax revenues, with detail for income and sales taxes, quarterly rpt, U6910–1

Indiana financial condition, including revenues by source, expenditures by function and object, and fund balances, by agency, FY92, annual rpt, S2570–1

Iowa financial condition, including revenues by source, expenditures by function, and bonded debt, FY92 and trends, annual rpt, S2860–4

Iowa retail sales and use tax filings data, and establishments reporting, by county and city, and by kind of business, quarterly rpt, S2860–1

Index by Subjects and Names

State and local taxes

Kansas business activity indicators, quarterly rpt, U7095–1

Kansas financial condition, including revenues by source, expenditures by function and object, and fund balances, FY92, annual rpt, S2900–1

Kansas school district revenues by source and expenditures by object, 1990/91, annual rpt, S2945–1

Kansas statistical abstract, general data, 1991/92 annual rpt, U7095–2.9

Kansas tax collections by tax type, and property values, with data by county, FY92 and trends, annual rpt, S3020–1

Kentucky economic impact of Toyota Motor Corp plant installation, including related State costs, employment, and benefits to other States, 1980s-2005, U7138–1.4

Kentucky financial condition, including revenues by source, expenditures by function and object, fund balances, and bonded debt, FY92, annual rpt, S3120–1

Louisiana financial condition, including revenues by source, expenditures by function, and fund balances, FY92 and trends, annual rpt, S3285–2

Louisiana school district profiles, including enrollment, grads, and staff, by race-ethnicity, 1991/92, annual rpt, S3280–1.2

Maine financial condition, including revenues by source, expenditures by function and object, and fund balances, FY92, annual rpt, S3420–1

Maine statistical summary, general economic and social data, 1992 recurring rpt, S3434–1

Maryland financial condition, including revenues by source, expenditures by function, fund balances, and bonded debt, FY92 and trends, annual rpt, S3685–2

Maryland local govt financial condition, including revenues by source, expenditures by function, and debt obligations, FY92 and trends, annual rpt, S3618–1

Maryland statistical abstract, general data, 1993-94 biennial rpt, S3605–1.7

Massachusetts financial condition, including revenues by source, and expenditures by function, by fund, FY92 and trends, annual rpt, S3777–1

Massachusetts tax collections by type, and distributions to local areas, FY91 and trends, annual rpt, S3917–1

Michigan financial condition, including revenues by source, expenditures by function, and fund balances, FY92 and trends, annual rpt, S3985–2

Minnesota financial condition, including revenues by source, expenditures by function, fund balances, and bonded debt, FY92 and trends, annual rpt, S4180–1

Mississippi financial condition, including revenues by source, expenditures by function and object, and detail by agency, FY92 and trends, annual rpt, S4346–1

Mississippi statistical abstract, general data, 1992 annual rpt, U3255–4.11

Mississippi tax collections by type, and disbursements, with selected sales and income tax data by locality and industry, FY92 and trends, annual rpt, S4435–1

Missouri financial condition, including fund finances, tax collections and distribution, and State treasury activity, FY92 and trends, annual rpt, S4570–1

Missouri financial condition, including revenues by source, expenditures by function, and fund balances, FY92, annual rpt, S4475–1

Missouri public, special, and academic libraries, finances, holdings, circulation, staff, and services, by location, FY92, annual rpt, S4520–2

Montana financial condition, including revenues by source, expenditures by function, and fund balances, FY92, annual rpt, S4653–1

Montana public library holdings, staff, circulation, and finances, by library, FY92, annual rpt, S4725–1

Montana tax collections by tax type, and property value by county, FY91-92 and trends, biennial rpt, S4750–1

Nebraska financial condition, including revenues by source, expenditures by function and agency, and fund balances, FY92, annual rpt, S4825–1

Nebraska tax revenues by type, tax rates and exemptions, and aid distribution to local areas, with data by county and city, 1991, annual rpt, S4950–1

Nevada financial condition, including fund revenues by source, expenditures by function, and bonded debt, FY92, annual rpt, S5025–1

Nevada statistical abstract, general data, 1992 biennial rpt, S5005–1.8

New Hampshire financial condition, with revenues by source, expenditures by function or object, and fund balances, FY92 and trends, annual rpt, S5175–1

New Jersey casino revenues and operations for 12 facilities, with State regulatory activities, 1992 and trends, annual rpt, S5360–1

New Jersey financial condition, including revenues by source, expenditures by function, fund balances, and bonded debt, FY92, annual rpt, S5455–1

New Jersey municipal and county data book, general data, 1992 annual rpt, C4712–4

New Jersey public library finances, holdings, circulation, and staff, by county and library, 1991, annual rpt, S5385–2

New Mexico financial condition, including receipts by source, expenditures by agency and function, fund balances, and bonded debt, FY91, annual rpt, S5585–1

New Mexico tax revenues and disbursements, with data by tax type, county, and city, FY91-92 and trends, annual rpt, S5660–1

New York State financial condition, including revenues by source, expenditures by function, and fund balances, FY93, annual rpt, S5710–1

New York State municipal and county statistical profiles, general data, 1993 annual rpt, C4712–7

New York State statistical yearbook, general data, 1992 annual rpt, U5100–1.5

North Carolina financial condition, including revenues by source, expenditures by function, fund balances, and bonded debt, FY92, annual rpt, S5897–1

North Carolina public utility financial, operating, and regulatory data, by utility type and company, 1990 and trends, annual rpt, S5917–2

North Carolina supplemental tax receipts for education, by school district, 1991/92, annual rpt, S5915–1.1

North Dakota financial condition, including revenues by source, expenditures by function, fund balances, and bonded debt, FY92, annual rpt, S6162–1

Ohio financial condition, including revenues by source, expenditures by function, and fund balances, FY92, annual rpt, S6255–1

Ohio tax revenues and collections, by tax type, with distributions and property assessments by county, and corporate taxes by industry, FY92 annual rpt, S6390–1

Oklahoma financial condition, including revenues by source, expenditures by function, and fund balances, FY91, annual rpt, S6438–1

Oklahoma public school finances, including property valuations, and enrollment, by county and district, 1991/92-1992/93 and trends, annual rpt, S6423–1.2

Oklahoma statistical abstract, general data, 1992 annual rpt, U8130–2.5

Oklahoma tax revenues by source, and distribution to local govts and State funds, FY92 and trends, annual rpt, S6495–1

Oregon financial condition, including revenues by source, expenditures by function, and fund statements, FY92, annual rpt, S6603–2

Pennsylvania financial condition, including revenues by source, expenditures by function, and fund balances, FY92 and trends, annual rpt, S6810–4

Pennsylvania insurance premium tax collections, FY92, annual rpt, S6835–1

Pennsylvania statistical abstract, general data, 1992 recurring rpt, U4130–6.2, U4130–6.6

Pennsylvania tax collections by tax type, with data by county and industry, FY92 and trends, annual rpt, S6885–1

Rhode Island financial condition, including revenues by source, expenditures by function, and fund balances, FY92 and trends, annual rpt, S6930–1

Rhode Island statistical almanac, general data, 1993 annual rpt, C7975–1.1

South Carolina county govt finances, including property value and tax assessments, by county, FY92, annual rpt, S7127–2

South Carolina economic condition, including agriculture, finance, and govt financial data, 1970s-92, annual rpt, S7125–3.1

South Carolina financial condition, including receipts by source, expenditures by function, fund balances, and bonded debt, FY92, annual rpt, S7127–1

South Carolina public service commission regulatory activities, with financial and operating data for individual utilities and railroads, FY92 annual rpt, S7235–1

South Carolina statistical abstract, general data, 1993 annual rpt, S7125–1.2, S7125–1.14

South Carolina tax returns and collections, property assessments, and taxable sales, with data by county and industry group, FY92, annual rpt, S7255–1

State and local taxes

Index by Subjects and Names

South Carolina teachers salary schedules, educational revenues by source, and expenditures by function, by school district, 1991/92, annual rpt, S7145–1.5

South Dakota financial condition, including revenues by source, expenditures by function, fund balances, and bonded debt, FY92, annual rpt, S7330–1

South Dakota tax revenues by source, aid distributed to local areas, and property tax valuations, FY92 annual rpt, S7380–1

Tennessee financial condition, including revenues by source, expenditures by function and object, and fund balances, FY92, annual rpt, S7505–1

Tennessee, Knoxville MSA economic impact of Univ of Tennessee athletics, 1992 article, U8710–1.501

Tennessee public school finances, by county, city, and school district, 1991/92, annual rpt, S7490–2.4

Tennessee statistical abstract, general data, 1992/93 annual rpt, U8710–2.12, U8710–2.15, U8710–2.20

Tennessee tax revenues by source and apportionments to counties, cities, and funds, FY91-92 and trends, biennial rpt, S7570–1

Texas financial condition, including revenues by source, expenditures by function, and bonded indebtedness, FY92, annual rpt, S7655–3

Texas financial condition, including revenues by source, expenditures by function and dept, and investments, with data for over 400 individual funds, FY92, annual rpt, S7655–2

Utah economic and business activity review and indicators, monthly rpt, U8960–2

Utah financial condition, including revenues by source, expenditures by function and agency, and fund balances, FY92, annual rpt, S7795–1

Utah govt statistical review, fiscal and socioeconomic data, 1993 annual rpt, R9380–1.4, R9380–1.6, R9380–1.7

Utah public school revenues by source and expenditures by object, by State fund and school district, FY92, annual rpt, S7815–1.2

Utah statistical abstract, general data, 1993 triennial rpt, U8960–1.7

Utah tax revenues by source, and distribution to localities and State funds, FY92 and trends, annual rpt, S7905–1

Vermont financial condition, including revenues by source, expenditures by function, fund balances, and bonded debt, FY92, annual rpt, S8035–1

Vermont individual State income tax returns, and property and sales tax refunds, by income class and locality, 1991, annual rpt, S8125–1

Vermont libraries, finances, resources, and circulation, by city and library, FY91-92, biennial rpt, S8080–1

Virginia financial condition, including revenues by source, expenditures by function, and fund balances, FY92 and trends, annual rpt, S8170–1

Virginia tax revenues by type, county, and independent city, FY92 and trends, annual rpt, S8305–1

Washington State financial condition, including revenues by source, expenditures by function, fund balances, and bonded debt, FY92, annual rpt, S8345–3

Washington State tax revenue by source and county, with property tax rates and assessed valuation, FY92 and trends, annual rpt, S8415–1

West Virginia insurance taxes paid by top 20 fire/casualty and life insurers, and by excess line brokers, 1991, annual rpt, S8575–1

West Virginia public school finances, including tax levy and bond election results, bonding potential, and levy proceeds, by county, 1992/93 and trends, annual rpt, S8540–4.1

West Virginia statistical handbook, general data, 1992 annual rpt, R9385–1.1, R9385–1.6

Wisconsin financial condition, including revenues by source, expenditures by function and object, and fund balances, FY92, annual rpt, S8675–3

Wisconsin financial condition, including revenues by source, expenditures by function and object, and fund balances, FY93, annual rpt, S8675–2

Wyoming financial condition, including revenues by source, expenditures by function, and fund balances, FY92 and trends, annual rpt, S8875–1

Wyoming general fund revenues by tax type, FY83-92, annual rpt, S8855–1

Wyoming public library holdings, staff, circulation, and finances, by county, FY92, annual rpt, S8855–3

Wyoming public school enrollment, staff, and finances, by county and district, 1991/92, annual rpt series, S8890–1

Wyoming tax collections and distribution, and property valuation, with data by property type and location, FY92 and trends, annual rpt, S8990–1

see also Estate tax
see also Excise tax
see also Fuel tax
see also Gift tax
see also Income taxes
see also License taxes and fees
see also Property tax
see also Revenue sharing
see also Sales tax
see also Severance taxes
see also Tax reform
see also Withholding tax

State bonds

Construction industry capital from State/municipal bonds, and construction bond sales by function, weekly rpt, C5800–2

Credit rating trends for State bonds, 1962-92, U5085–2.6

Expenditures of State govts by fund source and function, by State, FY90-92, annual rpt, A7118–1

Govt finances, including revenues by source, expenditures by function, and debt, detailed data for Federal, State, and local govts, 1993 annual rpt, R9050–1

Mutual fund sales, assets, and investment activities, with data on money market and municipal bond funds, monthly rpt, A6025–5

Unit investment trust sales volume and value, by trust type, maturity period, and insurance features, monthly rpt, A6025–7

State and local:

Alabama financial condition, including revenues by source, expenditures by function and object, and fund balances, by fund and agency, FY92, annual rpt, S0129–1

Alaska financial condition, including revenues by source, expenditures by function, fund balances, and bond obligations, FY92 and trends, annual rpt, S0275–1

Arizona financial condition, including revenues by source, expenditures by function, and fund balances, FY91, annual rpt, S0450–2

Arizona financial condition, including revenues by source, expenditures by function, and fund balances, FY92, annual rpt, S0450–1

Arkansas financial condition, including revenues by source, expenditures by function and locality, and fund balances, FY91-92, biennial rpt, S0780–1

Arkansas financial condition, including revenues by source, expenditures by function and object, and fund balances, FY92, annual rpt, S0670–1

California financial condition, including revenues by source, expenditures by agency and function, fund balances, and bonded debt, FY92 and trends, annual rpt, S0815–1

California higher education systems funding by source and expenditures by program category, with enrollment data, FY60s-94, annual rpt, S0827–3

Colorado financial condition, including receipts by source, and expenditures by function, FY92 and trends, annual rpt, S0980–1

Connecticut financial condition, including revenues by source, expenditures by function, and bonded debt, FY92, annual rpt, S1170 1, S1170–2

DC statistical profile, general data, 1992 annual rpt, S1535–3.2

Delaware data book, general data, 1993 annual rpt, S1375–4

Florida financial condition, including receipts by source, expenditures by function, and fund balances, FY92, annual rpt, S1717–3

Georgia financial condition, including revenues by source, expenditures by function and object, and fund balances, FY92, annual rpt, S1860–1

Hawaii financial condition, including revenues by source, expenditures by function, and fund balances, FY92, annual rpt, S2020–1

Illinois financial condition, including revenues by source, and expenditures by object, function, and agency, FY92, annual rpt, S2415–1

Indiana long-term obligation fund balance, FY92, annual rpt, S2570–1.1

Iowa financial condition, including revenues by source, expenditures by function, and bonded debt, FY92 and trends, annual rpt, S2860–4

Kansas financial condition, including revenues by source, expenditures by object, and revenue bond indebtedness, FY92, annual rpt, S2900–1.1

Index by Subjects and Names — State budgets

Kentucky financial condition, including revenues by source, expenditures by function and object, fund balances, and bonded debt, FY92, annual rpt, S3120–1

Louisiana financial condition, including revenues by source, expenditures by function, and fund balances, FY92 and trends, annual rpt, S3285–2

Maine financial condition, including revenues by source, expenditures by function and object, and fund balances, FY92, annual rpt, S3420–1

Maryland financial condition, including revenues by source, expenditures by function, fund balances, and bonded debt, FY92 and trends, annual rpt, S3685–2

Massachusetts financial condition, including revenues by source, and expenditures by function, by fund, FY92 and trends, annual rpt, S3777–1

Michigan financial condition, including revenues by source, expenditures by function, and fund balances, FY92 and trends, annual rpt, S3985–2

Minnesota financial condition, including revenues by source, expenditures by function, fund balances, and bonded debt, FY92 and trends, annual rpt, S4180–1

Mississippi financial condition, including revenues by source, expenditures by function and object, and detail by agency, FY92 and trends, annual rpt, S4346–1

Missouri financial condition, including revenues by source, expenditures by function, and fund balances, FY92, annual rpt, S4475–1

Missouri State treasury investments, summary balance sheets, bonded debt, and deposits in individual banks, FY92, annual rpt, S4570–1.2

Montana financial condition, including revenues by source, expenditures by function, and fund balances, FY92, annual rpt, S4653–1

Nebraska financial condition, including revenues by source, expenditures by function and agency, and fund balances, FY92, annual rpt, S4825–1

Nevada financial condition, including fund revenues by source, expenditures by function, and bonded debt, FY92, annual rpt, S5025–1

New Hampshire elementary and secondary school revenues by source and expenditures by function, 1991/92, annual tables, S5200–1.12

New Hampshire financial condition, with revenues by source, expenditures by function or object, and fund balances, FY92 and trends, annual rpt, S5175–1

New Jersey financial condition, including revenues by source, expenditures by function, fund balances, and bonded debt, FY92, annual rpt, S5455–1

New Mexico financial condition, including receipts by source, expenditures by agency and function, fund balances, and bonded debt, FY91, annual rpt, S5585–1

New York State financial condition, including revenues by source, expenditures by function, and fund balances, FY93, annual rpt, S5710–1

North Carolina financial condition, including revenues by source, expenditures by function, fund balances, and bonded debt, FY92, annual rpt, S5897–1

North Dakota financial condition, including revenues by source, expenditures by function, fund balances, and bonded debt, FY92, annual rpt, S6162–1

Ohio financial condition, including revenues by source, expenditures by function, and fund balances, FY92, annual rpt, S6255–1

Oklahoma financial condition, including revenues by source, expenditures by function, and fund balances, FY91, annual rpt, S6438–1

Oregon financial condition, including revenues by source, expenditures by function, and fund statements, FY92, annual rpt, S6603–2

Pennsylvania financial condition, including revenues by source, expenditures by function, and fund balances, FY92 and trends, annual rpt, S6810–4

Pennsylvania statistical abstract, general data, 1992 recurring rpt, U4130–6.2, U4130–6.6

Rhode Island financial condition, including revenues by source, expenditures by function, and fund balances, FY92 and trends, annual rpt, S6930–1

South Carolina bonded debt, and revenue bond coverage, FY92 and trends, annual rpt, S7127–1

South Dakota financial condition, including revenues by source, expenditures by function, fund balances, and bonded debt, FY92, annual rpt, S7330–1

South Dakota school enrollment, finances, grads, and staff, by district, 1991/92 and trends, annual rpt, S7315–1

Tennessee financial condition, including revenues by source, expenditures by function and object, and fund balances, FY92, annual rpt, S7505–1

Texas financial condition, including revenues by source, expenditures by function, and bonded indebtedness, FY92, annual rpt, S7655–3

Texas financial condition, including revenues by source, expenditures by function and dept, and investments, with data for over 400 individual funds, FY92, annual rpt, S7655–2

Utah financial condition, including revenues by source, expenditures by function and agency, and fund balances, FY92, annual rpt, S7795–1

Utah public school bond status, by district, FY92, annual rpt, S7815–1.2

Vermont financial condition, including revenues by source, expenditures by function, fund balances, and bonded debt, FY92, annual rpt, S8035–1

Virginia election results, with voting on State bond issues, by county and independent city, 1992, annual rpt, S8195–1

Virginia financial condition, including revenues by source, expenditures by function, and fund balances, FY92 and trends, annual rpt, S8170–1

Washington State financial condition, including revenues by source, expenditures by function, fund balances, and bonded debt, FY92, annual rpt, S8345–3

Washington State treasury operations, including receipts, disbursements, aid to localities, and investments, by fund, FY92, annual rpt, S8455–1

West Virginia statistical handbook, general data, 1992 annual rpt, R9385–1.2

Wisconsin financial condition, including revenues by source, expenditures by tax function and object, and fund balances, FY92, annual rpt, S8675–3

Wyoming financial condition, including revenues by source, expenditures by function, and fund balances, FY92 and trends, annual rpt, S8875–1

Wyoming State treasurer financial transactions, including revenues, investments, and disbursements by local area, FY92 and trends, annual rpt, S9010–1

see also Municipal bonds

State budgets

Balances compared to expenditures, and percent changes in revenues and expenditures, by State, FY93, article, B8500–2.506

Balances/reserve funds as percent of spending, by State, FY93, semiannual rpt, B8500–1.3

Budgeted changes in revenues and spending, including expected changes from tax reforms, by State, FY93, article, B8500–2.502

Fiscal issues for State govts, including budget balances, revenues, and expenditures, with data by State, series, A7470–4

General fund expenditure changes proposed by Governors, by State, FY94, article, B8500–2.513

General fund revenues, expenditures, and balances, and budget stabilization funds, by State, FY92-94 and trends, semiannual rpt, A7955–1

Govt finances, including revenues by source, expenditures by function, and debt, detailed data for Federal, State, and local govts, 1993 annual rpt, R9050–1

Public assistance program State funding and tax changes, by State, with analysis of impact on the poor, FY92-93, annual rpt, R3834–9

Tourism dev offices of State govts, activities, personnel, and budgets, by State, 1992 survey, annual rpt, R9375–2

Travel and tourism rankings for selected indicators, including data for top 20 States, cities, countries, businesses, and other measures, 1992 recurring rpt, R9375–6

Travel promotion office budgets by State, FY92, annual rpt, C2140–1.2

Trends in State funding for education compared to non-education categories, by State, FY94 vs FY93, article, B8500–2.519

State and local:

Alabama State govt actual vs budgeted revenues and expenditures, for general and special education funds, FY92, annual rpt, S0129–1

Alaska State govt actual vs budgeted revenues and expenditures, FY92, annual rpt, S0275–1

Arizona State govt appropriated vs actual revenues and expenditures, FY92, annual rpt, S0450–1

Arizona State govt budgeted vs actual revenues and expenditures, FY91, annual rpt, S0450–2

State budgets

Arkansas govt budgeted vs actual revenues and expenditures, FY92, annual rpt, S0670–1

California general fund budget reduction components, 1993 article, B8500–2.521

California State govt budgeted vs actual revenues and expenditures, FY92, annual rpt, S0815–1.1

Colorado State govt budgeted vs actual revenues by source and expenditures by function, FY92, annual rpt, S0980–1

Connecticut general and transportation fund appropriations vs expenditures, by function and object, FY92, annual rpt, S1170–1

Connecticut State budgeted vs actual revenues by source and expenditures by function, FY92, annual rpt, S1170–2

DC financial condition, including actual vs budgeted revenues and expenditures, FY92, annual rpt, S1507–1

Delaware data book, general data, 1993 annual rpt, S1375–4

Florida State govt appropriations and disbursements, by agency and detailed fund account, FY92, annual rpt, S1717–1

Florida State govt budgeted vs actual revenues and expenditures, FY92, annual rpt, S1717–3

Hawaii budgeted vs actual revenues and expenditures, FY92, annual rpt, S2020–1

Idaho State budget and appropriations, by dept, FY93, annual rpt, S2215–1

Illinois State govt budgeted vs actual revenues and expenditures, and appropriations vs warrants issued by function, object, and agency, FY92, annual rpt, S2415–1

Indiana financial condition, including appropriations, allotments, and expenditures by detailed account, and budgeted vs actual revenues and expenditures, FY92, annual rpt, S2570–1

Iowa State govt actual vs budgeted revenues and expenditures, FY92, annual rpt, S2860–4

Kentucky State govt actual vs budgeted revenues and expenditures, by fund and agency, FY91, annual rpt, S3120–1

Louisiana State govt actual vs budgeted revenues by source and expenditures by function, FY92, annual rpt, S3285–2

Maine State govt budgeted vs actual revenues by source and expenditures by function, FY92, annual rpt, S3420–1

Maryland State govt budgeted vs actual revenues and expenditures, FY92, and FY93 appropriations, annual rpt, S3685–2

Massachusetts State govt actual vs budgeted revenues by source and expenditures by function, by fund, FY92, annual rpt, S3777–1

Michigan State govt actual vs budgeted revenues by source and expenditures by function, by fund, FY92, annual rpt, S3985–2

Minnesota State govt budgeted vs actual revenues by source and expenditures by function, FY92, annual rpt, S4180–1

Mississippi govt financial condition, including budgeted vs actual revenues and expenditures, FY92, annual rpt, S4346–1

Missouri govt budgeted vs actual revenues by source and expenditures by function, FY92, annual rpt, S4475–1

Montana State govt budgeted vs actual revenues and expenditures, by fund, agency, and program, FY92, annual rpt, S4653–1

Nebraska State govt budgeted vs actual revenues and expenditures, by fund type, FY92, annual rpt, S4825–1

Nevada State govt actual vs budgeted revenues and expenditures, FY92, annual rpt, S5025–1

New Hampshire govt budgeted vs actual revenues by source and expenditures by function, FY92, annual rpt, S5175–1

New Jersey State govt budgeted vs actual revenues and expenditures, by fund, FY92, annual rpt, S5455–1

New York State budgeted vs actual receipts and disbursements, FY93, annual rpt, S5710–1

New York State statistical yearbook, general data, 1992 annual rpt, U5100–1.5

North Carolina budgeted vs actual revenues by source and expenditures by function, FY92, annual rpt, S5897–1

North Dakota budgeted vs actual revenues by source, and expenditures by function, FY91-93, annual rpt, S6162–1

Ohio govt budgeted vs actual revenues by source and expenditures by function, FY92, annual rpt, S6255–1

Oklahoma budgeted vs actual revenues and expenditures, FY91, annual rpt, S6438–1

Oregon budgeted vs actual revenues and expenditures, FY92, annual rpt, S6603–2

Pennsylvania govt budgeted vs actual revenues and expenditures, FY92, annual rpt, S6810–4

Rhode Island State govt budgeted vs actual revenues and expenditures, FY92, annual rpt, S6930–1

South Carolina budgeted vs actual revenues by source, expenditures by object, and fund balances, FY92, annual rpt, S7127–1

South Dakota budgeted vs actual general and Federal expenditures, by dept, FY92, annual rpt, S7330–1

Tennessee State govt budgeted vs actual revenues and expenditures, by fund, FY92, annual rpt, S7505–1

Texas State govt budgeted vs actual revenues and expenditures, FY92, annual rpt, S7655–3

Utah State govt budgeted vs actual revenues by source and expenditures by function, FY92, annual rpt, S7795–1

Utah statistical abstract, general data, 1993 triennial rpt, U8960–1.17

Virginia State govt general and special funds budgeted vs actual revenues and expenditures, FY92, annual rpt, S8170–1

Washington State govt budgeted vs actual revenues by source and expenditures by function, FY92, annual rpt, S8345–3

Wisconsin Blue Book, general data, 1993-94 biennial rpt, S8780–1.2

Wisconsin State govt actual vs budgeted revenues and expenditures, FY92, annual rpt, S8675–3

Wisconsin State govt actual vs budgeted revenues and expenditures, FY93, annual rpt, S8675–2

Wyoming State govt budgeted vs actual revenues and expenditures, FY92 annual rpt, S8875–1

Index by Subjects and Names

see also Budget of the U.S.

see also Government assets and liabilities

see also State government revenues

see also State government spending

State constitutional amendments

State and local:

Arizona election results and voter registration, by county and/or district, 1992 general election, biennial rpt, S0520–1

Arkansas election results, by district and/or county, 1992 general election, biennial rpt, S0775–1

California election results, and voter registration and turnout, by district and/or county, 1992 and trends, biennial rpt, S0934–1

Colorado election results and voter registration, by political party, and county and/or district, 1992, biennial rpt, S1090–1

Connecticut election results and voter registration and turnout, by location, 1992 general election, biennial rpt, S1265–1

Georgia election results by county, 1992 general election, biennial rpt, S1955–1

Hawaii election results, and voter registration by sex, by district and precinct, 1992, biennial series, S2077–1

Idaho election results and voter registration, by county and/or district and precinct, 1992 general election, biennial rpt, S2305–1

Illinois election results, and voter registration trends, by county and/or district, 1992 general election, biennial rpt, S2445–1

Iowa election results, by county and/or district, 1992 general election, biennial rpt, S2865–1

Kansas election results, by county and district, 1992 primary and general elections, biennial rpt, S3030–1

Kentucky election results, by county, district, and circuit, 1992, annual rpt, S3213–1

Maine election results, by district, county, and municipality, 1992 general election, biennial rpt, S3490–1

Maryland election results, by county and district, 1992 general election, biennial rpt, S3615–1

Missouri election results and voter registration, by district and/or county, with directory of govt officials, 1992 general election, biennial rpt, S4580–1

Nebraska election results, and voter registration by party, by county and/or district, 1992 general and primary elections, biennial rpt, S4955–1

New Hampshire election results, by county and locality, 1992, biennial rpt, S5255–1

New Jersey election results and voter registration, by location, 1992 general election, annual rpt, S5440–1

New Mexico election results, and voter registration by party, by location, 1992 general election, biennial rpt, S5655–1

North Dakota election results and historical trends, including data on ballot measures and detail by location, 1880s-1992, biennial rpt, U8080–1

North Dakota election results, by location, 1992 general election, biennial rpt, S6205–1

Ohio election results and voter registration, by local area, 1991-92 and trends, biennial rpt, S6380–1

Oklahoma election results and voter registration, by county and/or district, 1992, biennial rpt, S6425–1

Oregon election results and voter registration and turnout, by county and/or district, 1992 general election, biennial rpt, S6665–1

South Dakota election results, and vter registration by party, by county, 1992 general election, biennial rpt, S7390–1

Virginia election results by jurisdiction, and voter registration and turnout, 1992 and Jan 1993 elections, annual rpt, S8195–1

West Virginia election results and voter registration, by county and party, 1992 and trends, biennial rpt, S8630–1

Wisconsin Blue Book, general data, 1993-94 biennial rpt, S8780–1, S8780–1.3

Wyoming election results by county, district, and precinct, 1992, annual rpt and govtl directory, S9000–1

State constitutional conventions

State and local:

Alaska referendum on State constitutional convention, election results by district and precinct, 1992, biennial rpt, S0337–1

State courts

Caseloads and dispositions for State appellate and trial courts, by case type and State, 1991 and trends, annual rpt, R6600–1

Salaries for judges and court administrators, by State and territory, and for Federal system, July 1993, semiannual rpt, R6600–2

Statistical profiles of 50 States and DC, general data, 1993 annual almanac, C4712–1

State and local:

Alabama court caseloads and dispositions, by type of court and case, and location, with judicial dept finances, FY92 and trends, annual rpt, S0118–1

Alaska court cases and dispositions, by type of court and case, and location, with judicial dept finances and personnel, FY92 and trends, annual rpt, S0290–1

Arizona court cases and dispositions, by type of case and court, with judicial personnel and finances, by county and city, FY92, annual rpt, S0525–1

Arkansas court caseloads and dispositions, by type of court and case, and location, FY92 and trends, annual rpt, S0647–1

California court activity, including caseloads and dispositions, by case type and court, and location, FY92 and trends, annual rpt, S0905–1

California court cases and dispositions, by type of case and court, and location, FY92 and trends, annual rpt, S0905–2

California criminal justice system detailed data, by offense, county, age, race-ethnicity, and sex, 1991 and trends, annual rpt, S0910–2

Colorado court cases and dispositions, by type of court and case, and location, with judicial dept finances, FY92 and trends, annual rpt, S1035–1

DC court cases and dispositions, by type of case, and judicial system finances, 1992 and trends, annual rpt, S1515–1

DC statistical profile, general data, 1992 annual rpt, S1535–3.8

Delaware court caseloads and dispositions, by type of court and case, and by county, with judicial dept finances, FY92, annual rpt, S1360–1

Florida court cases and dispositions, by type of court and case, and location, 1992, annual rpt, S1805–1

Georgia court cases and dispositions, by type of court and case, and location, with judicial dept finances and personnel, FY92, annual rpt, S1903–1

Georgia statistical abstract, general data, 1992-93 biennial rpt, U6730–1.12

Hawaii court cases and dispositions, by type of court and case, with judicial system finances, FY92, annual rpt, S2115–1

Hawaii data book, general data, 1992 annual rpt, S2090–1.4

Indiana court cases and dispositions by type of court and case, and location, with judicial system finances and personnel, 1992, annual rpt, S2703–1

Iowa court cases, processing, and dispositions, by type of court and district, with judicial dept appropriations and personnel, 1992 and trends, annual rpt, S2815–1

Kansas court caseloads and disposition, by type of court and case, and location, FY92, annual rpt, S3035–1

Louisiana court caseloads and dispositions, by type of court and case, and jurisdiction, 1992 and trends, annual rpt, S3375–1

Maine court cases and dispositions, by type and location, FY92 and trends, annual rpt, S3463–1

Maryland court caseloads and dispositions, by type of court and case, and county, with judicial personnel and finances, FY92 and trends, annual rpt, S3600–1

Maryland statistical abstract, general data, 1993-94 biennial rpt, S3605–1.9

Massachusetts court cases and dispositions, by type of court and case, and location, FY92 and trends, annual rpt, S3807–1

Michigan court caseloads and dispositions, by type of court and case, and court location, 1992 and trends, annual rpt, S3962–1

Mississippi statistical abstract, general data, 1992 annual rpt, U3255–4.13

Nebraska court cases and dispositions, by type of court and case, and location, 1992 and trends, annual rpt, S4965–2

New Mexico court cases and dispositions, by type of court and case, and location, with judicial system finances and personnel, FY92, annual rpt, S5623–1

New York State court cases and dispositions, by court type and location, 1991, annual rpt, S5760–3.3

New York State court cases and dispositions, by type of court and case, and jurisdiction, 1991, annual rpt, S5730–1

New York State statistical yearbook, general data, 1992 annual rpt, U5100–1.8

North Carolina court cases and dispositions, by type of court and case, and location, with judicial dept finances and personnel, FY91, annual rpt, S5950–1

North Dakota court caseloads and dispositions, by type of case and court, and location, with judicial dept finances, 1991-92, annual rpt, S6210–1

Ohio court caseload and case disposition, by type of court and case, and location, 1992, annual rpt, S6385–1

Oklahoma court cases and dispositions, by type of court and case, with judicial system finances, by county or jurisdiction, FY92, annual rpt, S6493–1

Pennsylvania court caseloads and dispositions, by type of court and case, and county, with judicial system finances, 1991, annual rpt, S6900–1

Rhode Island court cases and dispositions, by type of court and case, and county, 1987-91, annual rpt, S6965–1

South Carolina court cases and dispositions, by type of court and location, with judicial dept finances and employees, 1992 and trends, annual rpt, S7197–1

South Carolina statistical abstract, general data, 1993 annual rpt, S7125–1.5

South Dakota court cases and dispositions by type of case, and judicial system finances and personnel, by jurisdiction, FY92 and trends, annual rpt, S7395–1

Tennessee court cases and dispositions, by type of court and case, and county, FY92, annual rpt, S7585–1

Texas court cases and dispositions, by type of court and case, and location, FY92, annual rpt, S7703–1

Vermont court cases and dispositions, by type of court and case, and location, FY92 annual rpt, S8120–1

Virginia court caseloads, processing, and dispositions, by type of court and case, with judicial dept personnel and finances, by location, 1992 and trends, annual rpt, S8300–1

Washington State court cases and dispositions, by type of court and case, and jurisdiction, with judicial finances and personnel, 1992 and trends, annual rpt, S8339–1

West Virginia court caseloads and dispositions, by type of court and case, and judicial circuit, 1992 and trends, annual rpt, S8537–1

see also Domestic relations courts and cases

see also Juvenile courts and cases

see also Probate courts and cases

see also Small claims courts and cases

see also State funding for courts

see also Traffic laws and courts

State courts of appeals

see State courts

State Department

see Department of State

State expenditures

see State government spending

see terms beginning State funding for

State forests

State and local:

New York State statistical yearbook, general data, 1992 annual rpt, U5100–1.5, U5100–1.15

West Virginia statistical handbook, general data, 1992 annual rpt, R9385–1.7

Wisconsin Blue Book, general data, 1993-94 biennial rpt, S8780–1.2

State funding for agriculture

Index by Subjects and Names

State funding for agriculture

State and local:

Alabama financial condition, including revenues by source, expenditures by function and object, and fund balances, by fund and agency, FY92, annual rpt, S0129–1

Alaska financial condition, including revenues by source, expenditures by function, fund balances, and bond obligations, FY92 and trends, annual rpt, S0275–1

Arkansas financial condition, including revenues by source, expenditures by function and locality, and fund balances, FY91-92, biennial rpt, S0780–1

California financial condition, including revenues by source, expenditures by agency and function, fund balances, and bonded debt, FY92 and trends, annual rpt, S0815–1

Connecticut financial condition, including revenues by source, expenditures by function, and bonded debt, FY92, annual rpt, S1170–1

Florida financial condition, including receipts by source, expenditures by function, and fund balances, FY92, annual rpt, S1717–1, S1717–3

Georgia financial condition, including revenues by source, expenditures by function and object, and fund balances, FY92, annual rpt, S1860–1

Idaho financial condition, including revenues by source and expenditures by object, by agency and/or fund, FY92, annual rpt, S2215–1

Indiana financial condition, including revenues by source, expenditures by function and object, and fund balances, by agency, FY92, annual rpt, S2570–1

Iowa financial condition, including revenues by source, expenditures by function, and bonded debt, FY92 and trends, annual rpt, S2860–4

Iowa State treasury financial operations, including receipts, disbursements, and detailed investment activity, FY92, annual rpt, S2885–1

Kentucky financial condition, including revenues by source, expenditures by function and object, fund balances, and bonded debt, FY92, annual rpt, S3120–1

Louisiana financial condition, including revenues by source, expenditures by function, and fund balances, FY92 and trends, annual rpt, S3285–2

Maine financial condition, including revenues by source, expenditures by function and object, and fund balances, FY92, annual rpt, S3420–1

Mississippi financial condition, including revenues by source, expenditures by function and object, and detail by agency, FY92 and trends, annual rpt, S4346–1

Missouri financial condition, including revenues and expenditures by agency, and tax collections and distribution, FY92 and trends, annual rpt, S4570–1.1

Missouri financial condition, including revenues by source, expenditures by function, and fund balances, FY92, annual rpt, S4475–1

Montana financial condition, including revenues by source, expenditures by function, and fund balances, FY92, annual rpt, S4653–1

New Jersey Agriculture Dept revenues by source, FY92, annual rpt, S5350–1

New Jersey financial condition, including revenues by source, expenditures by function, fund balances, and bonded debt, FY92, annual rpt, S5455–1

North Carolina financial condition, including revenues by source, expenditures by function, fund balances, and bonded debt, FY92, annual rpt, S5897–1

North Dakota financial condition, including revenues by source, expenditures by function, fund balances, and bonded debt, FY92, annual rpt, S6162–1

Rhode Island financial condition, including revenues by source, expenditures by function, and fund balances, FY92 and trends, annual rpt, S6930–1

Tennessee financial condition, including revenues by source, expenditures by function and object, and fund balances, FY92, annual rpt, S7505–1

Texas financial condition, including revenues by source, expenditures by function and dept, and investments, with data for over 400 individual funds, FY92, annual rpt, S7655–2.2

Utah financial condition, including revenues by source, expenditures by function and agency, and fund balances, FY92, annual rpt, S7795–1

Vermont agricultural production, marketing, and finances, by commodity, with data on govt inspections and funding, 1989-90 biennial rpt, S7978–1

Wisconsin financial condition, including revenues by source, expenditures by function and object, and fund balances, FY92, annual rpt, S8675–3

Wisconsin financial condition, including revenues by source, expenditures by function and object, and fund balances, FY93, annual rpt, S8675–2

see also Under State government spending for general State financial and budget data

State funding for arts and culture

Arts fundraising through united arts funds (UAFs), with fund operations, income by source, and allocations, by UAF, 1992 and trends, annual rpt, A1315–2

Museums and related instns financial structure, including donation programs, income, and expenses, by type, budget size, and governing authority, 1989/90 survey, A0750–1.3

Public broadcasting revenues from State sources, by State and territory, FY91, annual rpt, R4250–1.19

Public broadcasting station revenues by source, and number of stations, by station type, FY91, annual rpt, R4250–1.20

Theater (nonprofit professional) finances and operations, including revenues by source, 1992 and trends, annual survey, A9065–1

State and local:

Arizona financial condition, including revenues by source, expenditures by function, and fund balances, FY91, annual rpt, S0450–2

Arkansas financial condition, including revenues by source, expenditures by function and locality, and fund balances, FY91-92, biennial rpt, S0780–1

California financial condition, including revenues by source, expenditures by agency and function, fund balances, and bonded debt, FY92 and trends, annual rpt, S0815–1

Connecticut financial condition, including revenues by source, expenditures by function, and bonded debt, FY92, annual rpt, S1170–1

DC statistical profile, general data, 1992 annual rpt, S1535–3.6

Florida statistical abstract, general data, 1992 annual rpt, U6660–1.20

Illinois financial condition, including revenues by source, and expenditures by object, function, and agency, FY92, annual rpt, S2415–1

Indiana financial condition, including revenues by source, expenditures by function and object, and fund balances, by agency, FY92, annual rpt, S2570–1

Iowa State treasury financial operations, including receipts, disbursements, and detailed investment activity, FY92, annual rpt, S2885–1

Kentucky financial condition, including revenues by source, expenditures by function and object, fund balances, and bonded debt, FY92, annual rpt, S3120–1

Maine financial condition, including revenues by source, expenditures by function and object, and fund balances, FY92, annual rpt, S3420–1

Missouri financial condition, including revenues by source, expenditures by function, and fund balances, FY92, annual rpt, S4475–1

Montana financial condition, including revenues by source, expenditures by function, and fund balances, FY92, annual rpt, S4653–1

Nevada financial condition, including fund revenues by source, expenditures by function, and bonded debt, FY92, annual rpt, S5025–1

New Jersey financial condition, including revenues by source, expenditures by function, fund balances, and bonded debt, FY92, annual rpt, S5455–1

New York State financial condition, including revenues by source, expenditures by function, and fund balances, FY93, annual rpt, S5710–1

New York State statistical yearbook, general data, 1992 annual rpt, U5100–1.10

North Carolina financial condition, including revenues by source, expenditures by function, fund balances, and bonded debt, FY92, annual rpt, S5897–1

North Dakota financial condition, including revenues by source, expenditures by function, fund balances, and bonded debt, FY92, annual rpt, S6162–1

Oklahoma financial condition, including revenues by source, expenditures by function, and fund balances, FY91, annual rpt, S6438–1

Tennessee statistical abstract, general data, 1992/93 annual rpt, U8710–2.20

Texas financial condition, including revenues by source, expenditures by function and dept, and investments, with data for over 400 individual funds, FY92, annual rpt, S7655–2.2

Index by Subjects and Names

State funding for capital projects

Virginia financial condition, including revenues by source, expenditures by function, and fund balances, FY92 and trends, annual rpt, S8170–1

Wisconsin financial condition, including revenues by source, expenditures by function and object, and fund balances, FY92, annual rpt, S8675–3

Wisconsin financial condition, including revenues by source, expenditures by function and object, and fund balances, FY93, annual rpt, S8675–2

Wyoming financial condition, including revenues by source, expenditures by function, and fund balances, FY92 and trends, annual rpt, S8875–1

see also Under State government spending for general State financial and budget data

State funding for buildings

see State funding for capital projects see State funding for health and hospitals see State funding for housing see State funding for libraries

State funding for capital projects

Expenditures of State govts by fund source and function, by State, FY90-92, annual rpt, A7118–1

Expenditures of State/local govts, with detail by selected function, by State, 1993 semiannual rpt, B8500–1.5

Govt finances, including revenues by source, expenditures by function, and debt, detailed data for Federal, State, and local govts, 1993 annual rpt, R9050–1

Library construction, costs, and funding sources, by State, city, instn, and library type, FY92 and trends, annual compilation, C1650–3.4

Local govt capital improvement financing methods, by population size, metro status, and census div, 1991 survey, A5800 2.112

State and local:

Alabama financial condition, including revenues by source, expenditures by function and object, and fund balances, by fund and agency, FY92, annual rpt, S0129–1

Alaska financial condition, including revenues by source, expenditures by function, fund balances, and bond obligations, FY92 and trends, annual rpt, S0275–1

Arizona financial condition, including revenues by source, expenditures by function, and fund balances, FY91, annual rpt, S0450–2

Arizona financial condition, including revenues by source, expenditures by function, and fund balances, FY92, annual rpt, S0450–1

Arkansas financial condition, including revenues by source, expenditures by function and locality, and fund balances, FY91-92, biennial rpt, S0780–1

Arkansas financial condition, including revenues by source, expenditures by function and object, and fund balances, FY92, annual rpt, S0670–1

Arkansas higher education finances, including revenues by source, expenditures by function, and State appropriations, by public instn, FY80s-95, biennial rpt, S0690–4

California financial condition, including revenues by source, expenditures by agency and function, fund balances, and bonded debt, FY92 and trends, annual rpt, S0815–1

California higher education systems funding by source and expenditures by program category, with enrollment data, FY60s-94, annual rpt, S0827–3

Colorado financial condition, including receipts by source, and expenditures by function, FY92 and trends, annual rpt, S0980–1

Connecticut financial condition, including revenues by source, expenditures by function, and bonded debt, FY92, annual rpt, S1170–1, S1170–2

DC financial condition, including receipts by source, expenditures by object or function, and fund balances, FY92, annual rpt, S1507–1

DC statistical profile, general data, 1992 annual rpt, S1535–3.2

Delaware postsecondary education requests and appropriations for capital projects, by instn, FY76-96, annual rpt, S1425–1

Delaware school construction and maintenance funding, by school district and project, FY92 and trends, annual rpt, S1430–1.7

Florida correctional instns, admin, and inmates by criminal background and demographic characteristics, FY92 annual rpt, S1720–1

Florida financial condition, including receipts by source, expenditures by function, and fund balances, FY92, annual rpt, S1717–3

Georgia financial condition, including revenues by source, expenditures by function and object, and fund balances, FY92, annual rpt, S1860–1

Hawaii economic conditions, including employment, population, tourism, and construction, quarterly rpt, S2090–2

Hawaii financial condition, including revenues by source, expenditures by function, and fund balances, FY92, annual rpt, S2020–1

Idaho financial condition, including revenues by source and expenditures by object, by agency and/or fund, FY92, annual rpt, S2215–1

Illinois financial condition, including funding for individual capital projects, FY92, annual rpt, S2415–1

Illinois higher education appropriations for capital projects, by type of instn, FY91-93, annual rpt, S2475–1.2

Indiana financial condition, including revenues by source, expenditures by function and object, and fund balances, by agency, FY92, annual rpt, S2570–1

Iowa financial condition, including revenues by source, expenditures by function, and bonded debt, FY92 and trends, annual rpt, S2860–4

Kansas financial condition, including revenues by source, expenditures by function and object, and fund balances, FY92, annual rpt, S2900–1

Kentucky financial condition, including revenues by source, expenditures by function and object, fund balances, and bonded debt, FY92, annual rpt, S3120–1

Louisiana financial condition, including revenues by source, expenditures by function, and fund balances, FY92 and trends, annual rpt, S3285–2

Maine financial condition, including revenues by source, expenditures by function and object, and fund balances, FY92, annual rpt, S3420–1

Maryland financial condition, including revenues by source, expenditures by function, fund balances, and bonded debt, FY92 and trends, annual rpt, S3685–2

Massachusetts financial condition, including revenues by source, and expenditures by function, by fund, FY92 and trends, annual rpt, S3777–1

Michigan financial condition, including revenues by source, expenditures by function, and fund balances, FY92 and trends, annual rpt, S3985–2

Minnesota financial condition, including revenues by source, expenditures by function, fund balances, and bonded debt, FY92 and trends, annual rpt, S4180–1

Mississippi financial condition, including revenues by source, expenditures by function and object, and detail by agency, FY92 and trends, annual rpt, S4346–1

Missouri financial condition, including fund finances, tax collections and distribution, and State treasury activity, FY92 and trends, annual rpt, S4570–1

Missouri financial condition, including revenues by source, expenditures by function, and fund balances, FY92, annual rpt, S4475–1

Montana financial condition, including revenues by source, expenditures by function, and fund balances, FY92, annual rpt, S4653–1

Nebraska correctional instn construction expenditures, FY92, annual rpt, S4850–1

Nebraska financial condition, including revenues by source, expenditures by function and agency, and fund balances, FY92, annual rpt, S4825–1

Nevada financial condition, including fund revenues by source, expenditures by function, and bonded debt, FY92, annual rpt, S5025–1

New Hampshire financial condition, with revenues by source, expenditures by function or object, and fund balances, FY92 and trends, annual rpt, S5175–1

New Jersey financial condition, including revenues by source, expenditures by function, fund balances, and bonded debt, FY92, annual rpt, S5455–1

New Mexico financial condition, including receipts by source, expenditures by agency and function, fund balances, and bonded debt, FY91, annual rpt, S5585–1

New York State financial condition, including revenues by source, expenditures by function, and fund balances, FY93, annual rpt, S5710–1

North Carolina financial condition, including revenues by source, expenditures by function, fund balances, and bonded debt, FY92, annual rpt, S5897–1

North Dakota financial condition, including revenues by source, expenditures by function, fund balances, and bonded debt, FY92, annual rpt, S6162–1

State funding for capital projects

Ohio financial condition, including revenues by source, expenditures by function, and fund balances, FY92, annual rpt, S6255–1

Oregon financial condition, including revenues by source, expenditures by function, and fund statements, FY92, annual rpt, S6603–2

Pennsylvania financial condition, including revenues by source, expenditures by function, and fund balances, FY92 and trends, annual rpt, S6810–4

Pennsylvania statistical abstract, general data, 1992 recurring rpt, U4130–6.2

Rhode Island financial condition, including revenues by source, expenditures by function, and fund balances, FY92 and trends, annual rpt, S6930–1

South Carolina financial condition, including receipts by source, expenditures by function, fund balances, and bonded debt, FY92, annual rpt, S7127–1

South Dakota financial condition, including revenues by source, expenditures by function, fund balances, and bonded debt, FY92, annual rpt, S7330–1

South Dakota public higher education facility construction funding, by instn, 1965-92, annual rpt, S7375–1

Tennessee financial condition, including revenues by source, expenditures by function and object, and fund balances, FY92, annual rpt, S7505–1

Tennessee higher education finances, student aid and expenses, and faculty and salaries, by instn, 1992/93 and trends, annual rpt, S7525–1.2

Tennessee public school finances, by county, city, and school district, 1991/92, annual rpt, S7490–2.4

Texas financial condition, including revenues by source, expenditures by function, and bonded indebtedness, FY92, annual rpt, S7655–3

Texas financial condition, including revenues by source, expenditures by function and dept, and investments, with data for over 400 individual funds, FY92, annual rpt, S7655–2.2

Utah financial condition, including revenues by source, expenditures by function and agency, and fund balances, FY92, annual rpt, S7795–1

Utah public school revenues by source and expenditures by object, by State fund and school district, FY92, annual rpt, S7815–1.2

Vermont financial condition, including revenues by source, expenditures by function, fund balances, and bonded debt, FY92, annual rpt, S8035–1

Virginia financial condition, including revenues by source, expenditures by function, and fund balances, FY92 and trends, annual rpt, S8170–1

Washington State financial condition, including revenues by source, expenditures by function, fund balances, and bonded debt, FY92, annual rpt, S8345–3

Wisconsin financial condition, including revenues by source, expenditures by function and object, and fund balances, FY92, annual rpt, S8675–3

Wisconsin financial condition, including revenues by source, expenditures by function and object, and fund balances, FY93, annual rpt, S8675–2

see also Under State government spending for general State financial and budget data

State funding for commerce

see State funding for economic development

see State government spending

State funding for conservation

see State funding for natural resources and conservation

State funding for construction

see State funding for capital projects

State funding for corrections

Budget and capital expenditures for corrections by State, and cost of care by instn, as of June 1992, annual rpt, A1305–3

Correctional instn admin, inmates, facilities, costs, parole and probation, and staffing, for local, State, and Federal systems, 1992 annual series, R4300–1

Expenditure trends for corrections, with comparisons to incarceration rates, by State, 1993 article, B8500–2.520

Expenditures by State, 1991, biennial rpt, S8780–1.2

Expenditures of State govts by fund source and function, by State, FY90-92, annual rpt, A7118–1

Expenditures of State/local govts for corrections, by State, FY91, semiannual rpt, B8500–1.10

General fund balance data, including trends in appropriations for selected functions, by State, FY91-93, annual rpt, A7470–4.10

Jails and adult detention facilities, inmates, staff, and operating summary, by State and instn, Dec 1992, recurring directory, A1305–1

Statistical profiles of 50 States and DC, general data, 1993 annual almanac, C4712–1

State and local:

Alabama financial condition, including revenues by source, expenditures by function and object, and fund balances, by fund and agency, FY92, annual rpt, S0129–1

Alabama statistical abstract, general data, 1992 recurring rpt, U5680–2.10

Alaska corrections system admin, including inmate and probationer/parolee offenses and demographic characteristics, 1991 annual rpt, S0287–1

Alaska financial condition, including revenues by source, expenditures by function, fund balances, and bond obligations, FY92 and trends, annual rpt, S0275–1

Arizona correctional instn admin, including inmates by criminal background and demographic characteristics, FY92, annual rpt, S0464–2

Arizona financial condition, including revenues by source, expenditures by function, and fund balances, FY91, annual rpt, S0450–2

Arkansas financial condition, including revenues by source, expenditures by function and locality, and fund balances, FY91-92, biennial rpt, S0780–1

Arkansas financial condition, including revenues by source, expenditures by function and object, and fund balances, FY92, annual rpt, S0670–1

Index by Subjects and Names

California correctional instn population, parole and probation, and justice system expenditures, 1987-92, annual rpt, S0910–1.2

California criminal justice system expenditures and employment, by type of agency or function, 1982-91, annual rpt, S0910–2.1

California financial condition, including revenues by source, expenditures by agency and function, fund balances, and bonded debt, FY92 and trends, annual rpt, S0815–1

Colorado financial condition, including receipts by source, and expenditures by function, FY92 and trends, annual rpt, S0980–1

Connecticut financial condition, including revenues by source, expenditures by function, and bonded debt, FY92, annual rpt, S1170–1, S1170–2

DC statistical profile, general data, 1992 annual rpt, S1535–3.8

Florida correctional instns, admin, and inmates by criminal background and demographic characteristics, FY92 annual rpt, S1720–1

Florida financial condition, including receipts by source, expenditures by function, and fund balances, FY92, annual rpt, S1717–1, S1717–3

Georgia corrections dept operations and costs, FY92, annual rpt, S1872–1

Georgia financial condition, including revenues by source, expenditures by function and object, and fund balances, FY92, annual rpt, S1860–1

Illinois corrections dept admin, including inmates and characteristics, finances, and staff, FY91-93 and trends, annual rpt, S2425–1

Illinois financial condition, including revenues by source, and expenditures by object, function, and agency, FY92, annual rpt, S2415–1

Indiana financial condition, including revenues by source, expenditures by function and object, and fund balances, by agency, FY92, annual rpt, S2570–1

Iowa financial condition, including revenues by source, expenditures by function, and bonded debt, FY92 and trends, annual rpt, S2860–4

Kentucky financial condition, including revenues by source, expenditures by function and object, fund balances, and bonded debt, FY92, annual rpt, S3120–1

Louisiana financial condition, including revenues by source, expenditures by function, and fund balances, FY92 and trends, annual rpt, S3285–2

Maine financial condition, including revenues by source, expenditures by function and object, and fund balances, FY92, annual rpt, S3420–1

Michigan correctional instns, admin, and inmates by selected demographic characteristics, 1991 and trends, annual rpt, S3960–1

Michigan financial condition, including revenues by source, expenditures by function, and fund balances, FY92 and trends, annual rpt, S3985–2

Minnesota financial condition, including revenues by source, expenditures by function, fund balances, and bonded debt, FY92 and trends, annual rpt, S4180–1

Index by Subjects and Names — State funding for courts

Mississippi financial condition, including revenues by source, expenditures by function and object, and detail by agency, FY92 and trends, annual rpt, S4346–1

Missouri financial condition, including revenues and expenditures by agency, and tax collections and distribution, FY92 and trends, annual rpt, S4570–1.1

Montana financial condition, including revenues by source, expenditures by function, and fund balances, FY92, annual rpt, S4653–1

Nebraska financial condition, including revenues by source, expenditures by function and agency, and fund balances, FY92, annual rpt, S4825–1

Nebraska prison inmate care costs, by item and instn, FY92 and trends, annual rpt, S4850–1

Nevada financial condition, including fund revenues by source, expenditures by function, and bonded debt, FY92, annual rpt, S5025–1

New Jersey financial condition, including revenues by source, expenditures by function, fund balances, and bonded debt, FY92, annual rpt, S5455–1

New York State financial condition, including revenues by source, expenditures by function, and fund balances, FY93, annual rpt, S5710–1

North Carolina financial condition, including revenues by source, expenditures by function, fund balances, and bonded debt, FY92, annual rpt, S5897–1

North Dakota financial condition, including revenues by source, expenditures by function, fund balances, and bonded debt, FY92, annual rpt, S6162–1

Ohio correctional instn admissions and releases, inmate characteristics, programs, finances, and staffing, FY91 and trends, annual rpt, S6370–1

Ohio financial condition, including revenues by source, expenditures by function, and fund balances, FY92, annual rpt, S6255–1

Oklahoma correctional instn admin, including inmate characteristics, incarceration costs, and data by instn, FY91, annual rpt, S6420–1

Oklahoma financial condition, including revenues by source, expenditures by function, and fund balances, FY91, annual rpt, S6438–1

Pennsylvania financial condition, including revenues by source, expenditures by function, and fund balances, FY92 and trends, annual rpt, S6810–4

Rhode Island financial condition, including revenues by source, expenditures by function, and fund balances, FY92 and trends, annual rpt, S6930–1

South Carolina correctional instns, admin, and inmates by criminal offense and demographic characteristics, FY92 and trends, annual rpt, S7135–1

South Carolina financial condition, including receipts by source, expenditures by function, fund balances, and bonded debt, FY92, annual rpt, S7127–1

South Dakota corrections dept finances and staff, FY92, annual rpt, S7296–1

South Dakota financial condition, including revenues by source, expenditures by function, fund balances, and bonded debt, FY92, annual rpt, S7330–1

Tennessee correctional instn admin, with inmate characteristics, and corrections dept finances and staff, FY92, annual rpt, S7480–1

Tennessee statistical abstract, general data, 1992/93 annual rpt, U8710–2.19

Texas financial condition, including revenues by source, expenditures by function, and bonded indebtedness, FY92, annual rpt, S7655–3

Texas financial condition, including revenues by source, expenditures by function and dept, and investments, with data for over 400 individual funds, FY92, annual rpt, S7655–2.2

Utah financial condition, including revenues by source, expenditures by function and agency, and fund balances, FY92, annual rpt, S7795–1

Vermont financial condition, including revenues by source, expenditures by function, fund balances, and bonded debt, FY92, annual rpt, S8035–1

Wisconsin financial condition, including revenues by source, expenditures by function and object, and fund balances, FY93, annual rpt, S8675–2

Wyoming correctional instn admin, finances, inmate characteristics, and staff, and probation and parole activities, FY92 annual rpt, S8883–1

Wyoming financial condition, including revenues by source, expenditures by function, and fund balances, FY92 and trends, annual rpt, S8875–1

see also Under State government spending for general State financial and budget data

State funding for courts

State and local:

Alabama court caseloads and dispositions, by type of court and case, and location, with judicial dept finances, FY92 and trends, annual rpt, S0118–1

Alaska court cases and dispositions, by type of court and case, and location, with judicial dept finances and personnel, FY92 and trends, annual rpt, S0290–1

Arizona court cases and dispositions, by type of case and court, with judicial personnel and finances, by county and city, FY92, annual rpt, S0525–1

Arkansas financial condition, including revenues by source, expenditures by function and locality, and fund balances, FY91-92, biennial rpt, S0780–1

California correctional instn population, parole and probation, and justice system expenditures, 1987-92, annual rpt, S0910–1.2

California court expenditures, by function, FY92, annual rpt, S0905–1.1

California criminal justice system expenditures and employment, by type of agency or function, 1982-91, annual rpt, S0910–2.1

California financial condition, including revenues by source, expenditures by agency and function, fund balances, and bonded debt, FY92 and trends, annual rpt, S0815–1

Colorado court cases and dispositions, by type of court and case, and location, with judicial dept finances, FY92 and trends, annual rpt, S1035–1

Connecticut financial condition, including revenues by source, expenditures by function, and bonded debt, FY92, annual rpt, S1170–1

Connecticut judicial dept personnel and finances, FY91-92, biennial rpt, S1220–1.1

DC court cases and dispositions, by type of case, and judicial system finances, 1992 and trends, annual rpt, S1515–1

Delaware court caseloads and dispositions, by type of court and case, and by county, with judicial dept finances, FY92, annual rpt, S1360–1

Florida financial condition, including receipts by source, expenditures by function, and fund balances, FY92, annual rpt, S1717–1, S1717–3

Georgia court cases and dispositions, by type of court and case, and location, with judicial dept finances and personnel, FY92, annual rpt, S1903–1

Georgia financial condition, including revenues by source, expenditures by function and object, and fund balances, FY92, annual rpt, S1860–1

Hawaii judicial system appropriations, revenues, and expenditures, FY92, annual rpt, S2115–1.1

Illinois financial condition, including revenues by source, and expenditures by object, function, and agency, FY92, annual rpt, S2415–1

Indiana court cases and dispositions by type of court and case, and location, with judicial system finances and personnel, 1992, annual rpt, S2703–1

Indiana financial condition, including revenues by source, expenditures by function and object, and fund balances, by agency, FY92, annual rpt, S2570–1

Iowa court cases, processing, and dispositions, by type of court and district, with judicial dept appropriations and personnel, 1992 and trends, annual rpt, S2815–1

Iowa financial condition, including revenues by source, expenditures by function, and bonded debt, FY92 and trends, annual rpt, S2860–4

Kentucky financial condition, including revenues by source, expenditures by function and object, fund balances, and bonded debt, FY92, annual rpt, S3120–1

Louisiana judiciary share of State budget, FY93, annual rpt, S3375–1

Maine court cases and dispositions, by type and location, FY92 and trends, annual rpt, S3463–1

Maryland court finances and personnel, by court level and judicial agency, FY92, annual rpt, S3600–1

Massachusetts court cases and dispositions, including probation dept collections, 1992 and trends, annual rpt, S3807–1

Missouri financial condition, including revenues by source, expenditures by function, and fund balances, FY92, annual rpt, S4475–1

Montana financial condition, including revenues by source, expenditures by function, and fund balances, FY92, annual rpt, S4653–1

New Jersey financial condition, including revenues by source, expenditures by function, fund balances, and bonded debt, FY92, annual rpt, S5455–1

State funding for courts

New Mexico court cases and dispositions, by type of court and case, and location, with judicial system finances and personnel, FY92, annual rpt, S5623–1

New Mexico financial condition, including receipts by source, expenditures by agency and function, fund balances, and bonded debt, FY91, annual rpt, S5585–1

North Carolina court cases and dispositions, by type of court and case, and location, with judicial dept finances and personnel, FY91, annual rpt, S5950–1

North Dakota court caseloads and dispositions, by type of case and court, and location, with judicial dept finances, 1991-92, annual rpt, S6210–1

North Dakota financial condition, including revenues by source, expenditures by function, fund balances, and bonded debt, FY92, annual rpt, S6162–1

Oklahoma financial condition, including revenues by source, expenditures by function, and fund balances, FY91, annual rpt, S6438–1

Oklahoma judicial system funding and expenditures, FY92, annual rpt, S6493–1.1

Oregon financial condition, including revenues by source, expenditures by function, and fund statements, FY92, annual rpt, S6603–2

Pennsylvania court admin and finances, 1991 annual rpt, S6900–1.1

Rhode Island judicial budget, FY88-92, annual rpt, S6965–1

South Carolina court cases and dispositions, by type of court and location, with judicial dept finances and employees, 1992 and trends, annual rpt, S7197–1

South Carolina financial condition, including receipts by source, expenditures by function, fund balances, and bonded debt, FY92, annual rpt, S7127–1

South Dakota court cases and dispositions by type of case, and judicial system finances and personnel, by jurisdiction, FY92 and trends, annual rpt, S7395–1

Tennessee statistical abstract, general data, 1992/93 annual rpt, U8710 2.19

Texas financial condition, including revenues by source, expenditures by function and dept, and investments, with data for over 400 individual funds, FY92, annual rpt, S7655–2.2

Texas judicial system appropriations, by purpose, FY88-92, annual rpt, S7703–1

Utah financial condition, including revenues by source, expenditures by function and agency, and fund balances, FY92, annual rpt, S7795–1

Virginia court caseloads, processing, and dispositions, by type of court and case, with judicial dept personnel and finances, by location, 1992 and trends, annual rpt, S8300–1

Washington State court cases and dispositions, by type of court and case, and jurisdiction, with judicial finances and personnel, 1992 and trends, annual rpt, S8339–1

Wisconsin financial condition, including revenues by source, expenditures by function and object, and fund balances, FY93, annual rpt, S8675–2

Wyoming financial condition, including revenues by source, expenditures by function, and fund balances, FY92 and trends, annual rpt, S8875–1

see also Under State government spending for general State financial and budget data

State funding for economic development

Tourism dev offices of State govts, activities, personnel, and budgets, by State, 1992 survey, annual rpt, R9375–2

Travel promotion office budgets by State, FY92, annual rpt, C2140–1.2

State and local:

Alabama financial condition, including revenues by source, expenditures by function and object, and fund balances, by fund and agency, FY92, annual rpt, S0129–1

Alaska financial condition, including revenues by source, expenditures by function, fund balances, and bond obligations, FY92 and trends, annual rpt, S0275–1

Arkansas financial condition, including revenues by source, expenditures by function and locality, and fund balances, FY91-92, biennial rpt, S0780–1

Arkansas financial condition, including revenues by source, expenditures by function and object, and fund balances, FY92, annual rpt, S0670–1

California financial condition, including revenues by source, expenditures by agency and function, fund balances, and bonded debt, FY92 and trends, annual rpt, S0815–1

Colorado financial condition, including receipts by source, and expenditures by function, FY92 and trends, annual rpt, S0980–1

Connecticut financial condition, including revenues by source, expenditures by function, and bonded debt, FY92, annual rpt, S1170–1, S1170–2

DC financial condition, including receipts by source, expenditures by object or function, and fund balances, FY92, annual rpt, S1507–1

DC statistical profile, general data, 1992 annual rpt, S1535–3.3

Georgia financial condition, including revenues by source, expenditures by function and object, and fund balances, FY92, annual rpt, S1860–1

Hawaii financial condition, including revenues by source, expenditures by function, and fund balances, FY92, annual rpt, S2020–1

Hawaii tourism promotion and visitors bur expenditures, 1992 annual rpt, S2090–1.7

Idaho financial condition, including revenues by source and expenditures by object, by agency and/or fund, FY92, annual rpt, S2215–1

Illinois financial condition, including revenues by source, and expenditures by object, function, and agency, FY92, annual rpt, S2415–1

Indiana financial condition, including revenues by source, expenditures by function and object, and fund balances, by agency, FY92, annual rpt, S2570–1

Iowa financial condition, including revenues by source, expenditures by function, and bonded debt, FY92 and trends, annual rpt, S2860–4

Index by Subjects and Names

Iowa State treasury financial operations, including receipts, disbursements, and detailed investment activity, FY92, annual rpt, S2885–1

Kentucky economic impact of Toyota Motor Corp plant installation, including related State costs, employment, and benefits to other States, 1980s-2005, U7138–1.4

Kentucky financial condition, including revenues by source, expenditures by function and object, fund balances, and bonded debt, FY92, annual rpt, S3120–1

Louisiana financial condition, including revenues by source, expenditures by function, and fund balances, FY92 and trends, annual rpt, S3285–2

Maine financial condition, including revenues by source, expenditures by function and object, and fund balances, FY92, annual rpt, S3420–1

Maryland financial condition, including revenues by source, expenditures by function, fund balances, and bonded debt, FY92 and trends, annual rpt, S3685–2

Massachusetts financial condition, including revenues by source, and expenditures by function, by fund, FY92 and trends, annual rpt, S3777–1

Michigan financial condition, including revenues by source, expenditures by function, and fund balances, FY92 and trends, annual rpt, S3985–2

Minnesota financial condition, including revenues by source, expenditures by function, fund balances, and bonded debt, FY92 and trends, annual rpt, S4180–1

Mississippi financial condition, including revenues by source, expenditures by function and object, and detail by agency, FY92 and trends, annual rpt, S4346–1

Missouri financial condition, including revenues by source, expenditures by function, and fund balances, FY92, annual rpt, S4475–1

Montana financial condition, including revenues by source, expenditures by function, and fund balances, FY92, annual rpt, S4653–1

Nebraska financial condition, including revenues by source, expenditures by function and agency, and fund balances, FY92, annual rpt, S4825–1

Nevada financial condition, including fund revenues by source, expenditures by function, and bonded debt, FY92, annual rpt, S5025–1

New Jersey financial condition, including revenues by source, expenditures by function, fund balances, and bonded debt, FY92, annual rpt, S5455–1

New Mexico financial condition, including receipts by source, expenditures by agency and function, fund balances, and bonded debt, FY91, annual rpt, S5585–1

North Carolina financial condition, including revenues by source, expenditures by function, fund balances, and bonded debt, FY92, annual rpt, S5897–1

North Dakota financial condition, including revenues by source, expenditures by function, fund balances, and bonded debt, FY92, annual rpt, S6162–1

Ohio financial condition, including revenues by source, expenditures by function, and fund balances, FY92, annual rpt, S6255–1

Index by Subjects and Names

State funding for education

Oklahoma financial condition, including revenues by source, expenditures by function, and fund balances, FY91, annual rpt, S6438–1

Oregon financial condition, including revenues by source, expenditures by function, and fund statements, FY92, annual rpt, S6603–2

Pennsylvania financial condition, including revenues by source, expenditures by function, and fund balances, FY92 and trends, annual rpt, S6810–4

Pennsylvania statistical abstract, general data, 1992 recurring rpt, U4130–6.2

Rhode Island financial condition, including revenues by source, expenditures by function, and fund balances, FY92 and trends, annual rpt, S6930–1

South Dakota financial condition, including revenues by source, expenditures by function, fund balances, and bonded debt, FY92, annual rpt, S7330–1

Tennessee financial condition, including revenues by source, expenditures by function and object, and fund balances, FY92, annual rpt, S7505–1

Texas financial condition, including revenues by source, expenditures by function, and bonded indebtedness, FY92, annual rpt, S7655–3

Texas financial condition, including revenues by source, expenditures by function and dept, and investments, with data for over 400 individual funds, FY92, annual rpt, S7655–2.2

Utah financial condition, including revenues by source, expenditures by function and agency, and fund balances, FY92, annual rpt, S7795–1

Utah small business dev program, with awards granted, economic impact, and profiles of 10 recipient companies, 1992 article, U8960–2.503

Vermont financial condition, including revenues by source, expenditures by function, fund balances, and bonded debt, FY92, annual rpt, S8035–1

Virginia financial condition, including revenues by source, expenditures by function, and fund balances, FY92 and trends, annual rpt, S8170–1

Washington State financial condition, including revenues by source, expenditures by function, fund balances, and bonded debt, FY92, annual rpt, S8345–3

Wisconsin financial condition, including revenues by source, expenditures by function and object, and fund balances, FY92, annual rpt, S8675–3

Wisconsin financial condition, including revenues by source, expenditures by function and object, and fund balances, FY93, annual rpt, S8675–2

see also Under State government spending for general State financial and budget data

State funding for education

Catholic secondary school operations and finances, including enrollment by race-ethnicity and family income, 1991/92 and trends, biennial rpt, A7375–5

Economic dev condition indicators, including economic performance, business vitality, growth capacity, and tax/fiscal system, by State, 1993 annual rpt, R4225–1.1

Elementary/secondary education expenditures per pupil compared to natl average, for 10 States with highest and lowest spending, FY92, article, B8500–2.509

Expenditures for education and welfare as percents of State govt spending, by State, FY91, article, B8500–2.503

Expenditures for education per pupil and as percent of State/local govt spending, by State, 1993 articles, B8500–2.515

Expenditures of State govts by fund source and function, by State, FY90-92, annual rpt, A7118–1

Expenditures of State/local govts for education, by State, 1993 semiannual rpt, B8500–1.7

Expenditures per capita of State and local govts for education, by State, FY91, biennial rpt, S8780–1.2

General fund appropriation trends for elementary/secondary and higher education, by State, FY93, article, B8500–2.506

General fund balance data, including trends in appropriations for selected functions, by State, FY91-93, annual rpt, A7470–4.10

Govt finances, including revenues by source, expenditures by function, and debt, detailed data for Federal, State, and local govts, 1993 annual rpt, R9050–1

Statistical profiles of 50 States and DC, general data, 1993 annual almanac, C4712–1

Urban public school performance compared to natl goals for year 2000, with data on students, teachers, and finances, for 47 systems, 1990/91 and trends, A4425–4

State and local:

Alabama elementary and secondary school enrollment, staff, pupil transportation, and finances, by district, 1991/92, annual rpt, S0124–1

Alabama financial condition, including revenues by source, expenditures by function and object, and fund balances, by fund and agency, FY92, annual rpt, S0129–1

Alabama State tax collections for education trust fund, FY90-93, annual rpt, U5680–3

Alaska financial condition, including revenues by source, expenditures by function, fund balances, and bond obligations, FY92 and trends, annual rpt, S0275–1

Alaska public schools, enrollment, staff, and finances, by district, FY92, annual rpt, S0295–2

Arizona elementary and secondary school enrollment, staff, and finances, by school district and county, FY92 and trends, annual rpt, S0470–1

Arizona financial condition, including revenues by source, expenditures by function, and fund balances, FY91, annual rpt, S0450–2

Arizona financial condition, including revenues by source, expenditures by function, and fund balances, FY92, annual rpt, S0450–1

Arkansas financial condition, including revenues by source, expenditures by function and locality, and fund balances, FY91-92, biennial rpt, S0780–1

Arkansas financial condition, including revenues by source, expenditures by function and object, and fund balances, FY92, annual rpt, S0670–1

Arkansas public school revenues by source, expenditures by function and object, and indebtedness, 1991/92 and trends, annual rpt, S0660–1.3

California financial condition, including revenues by source, expenditures by agency and function, fund balances, and bonded debt, FY92 and trends, annual rpt, S0815–1

California public school appropriations, FY66-94, annual rpt, S0827–3

Colorado public school revenues by source, and expenditures by category, by school district, 1990, annual rpt, S1000–4.3

Connecticut education dept staff and expenditures, by div, 1991/92, annual rpt, S1185–1

Connecticut financial condition, including revenues by source, expenditures by function, and bonded debt, FY92, annual rpt, S1170–1

Connecticut public school data, including enrollment, staff, programs, finances, and student characteristics, 1991/92, biennial rpt, S1185–3

DC financial condition, including receipts by source, expenditures by object or function, and fund balances, FY92, annual rpt, S1507–1

Delaware public education finances, govt aid by program and school district, 1991/92, annual rpt, S1430–1

Florida financial condition, including receipts by source, expenditures by function, and fund balances, FY92, annual rpt, S1717–1, S1717–3

Georgia financial condition, including revenues by source, expenditures by function and object, and fund balances, FY92, annual rpt, S1860–1

Hawaii financial condition, including revenues by source, expenditures by function, and fund balances, FY92, annual rpt, S2020–1

Idaho economic profile, general data, 1992 recurring rpt, S2218–2.3

Idaho financial condition, including revenues by source and expenditures by object, by agency and/or fund, FY92, annual rpt, S2215–1

Idaho school district revenues by source, and expenditures by function, by district and fund, FY92, annual rpt, S2225–2

Illinois financial condition, including revenues by source, and expenditures by object, function, and agency, FY92, annual rpt, S2415–1

Illinois public school revenues and expenditures by district, with data on busing, State aid claims, and per capita costs, 1990/91, annual rpt, S2440–1.3

Indiana elementary and secondary school enrollment and finances, by district and county, annual rpt series, S2608–2

Indiana financial condition, including revenues by source, expenditures by function and object, and fund balances, by agency, FY92, annual rpt, S2570–1

Iowa financial condition, including revenues by source, expenditures by function, and bonded debt, FY92 and trends, annual rpt, S2860–4

State funding for education

Kansas income tax collections transferred to school districts, FY87-92, annual rpt, S3020–1

Kansas school district revenues by source and expenditures by object, 1990/91, annual rpt, S2945–1

Kentucky financial condition, including revenues by source, expenditures by function and object, fund balances, and bonded debt, FY92, annual rpt, S3120–1

Kentucky public education profiles, with data by region and district, 1991/92 and trends, annual rpt, S3110–1

Kentucky public school finances, staff, and enrollment, by district, 1989/90-1990/91, biennial rpt, S3110–2

Louisiana elementary/secondary school operations, including enrollment, staff, finances, and detail by school district, 1991/92 and trends, annual rpt, S3280–1

Louisiana financial condition, including revenues by source, expenditures by function, and fund balances, FY92 and trends, annual rpt, S3285–2

Maine financial condition, including revenues by source, expenditures by function and object, and fund balances, FY92, annual rpt, S3420–1

Maine public school enrollment, facilities, staff, and finances, with selected data by county and for private schools, 1991 and trends, annual rpt, S3435–1

Maryland elementary and secondary education data, by county, 1991/92 and trends, annual rpt, S3610–2.13

Maryland elementary and secondary education data, by county, 1991/92, annual rpt, S3610–2.9

Maryland elementary and secondary education statistical summary, with data by county, 1991/92-1992/93 and trends, annual rpt, S3610–1

Massachusetts public elementary/secondary education summary data, 1989/90-1991/92 and trends, annual rpt, S3810–3

Massachusetts tax collections by type, and distributions to local areas, FY91 and trends, annual rpt, S3917–1

Michigan financial condition, including revenues by source, expenditures by function, and fund balances, FY92 and trends, annual rpt, S3985–2

Michigan school district financial and enrollment data, with rankings, 1991/92, annual rpt, S3965–3

Minnesota financial condition, including revenues by source, expenditures by function, fund balances, and bonded debt, FY92 and trends, annual rpt, S4180–1

Minnesota public school enrollment, staff, and finances, by district and county, 1991/92 and trends, annual rpt, S4165–1

Mississippi public school enrollment, staff and salaries, and finances, by district, 1991/92 and trends, annual rpt, S4340–1

Missouri financial condition, including fund finances, tax collections and distribution, and State treasury activity, FY92 and trends, annual rpt, S4570–1

Missouri financial condition, including revenues by source, expenditures by function, and fund balances, FY92, annual rpt, S4475–1

Missouri school finances, enrollment, grads, and staff, by county and school district, 1991/92, annual rpt, S4505–1

Montana financial condition, including revenues by source, expenditures by function, and fund balances, FY92, annual rpt, S4653–1

Nebraska financial condition, including revenues by source, expenditures by function and agency, and fund balances, FY92, annual rpt, S4825–1

Nebraska public school finances, including receipts by source and disbursements by function, by county and district, 1988/89, annual rpt, S4865–3

Nevada public school enrollment, test scores, teachers, and finances, by school district, 1990/91 and trends, annual rpt, S5035–2

New Hampshire elementary and secondary school revenues by source and expenditures by function, 1991/92, annual tables, S5200–1.12

New Hampshire school building aid, by school district, 1993/94, annual table, S5200–1.14

New Jersey financial condition, including revenues by source, expenditures by function, fund balances, and bonded debt, FY92, annual rpt, S5455–1

New Mexico elementary/secondary school statistics, including grads, student test results, and finances, by school district, 1989/90-1991/92, annual rpt, S5575–4

New Mexico financial condition, including receipts by source, expenditures by agency and function, fund balances, and bonded debt, FY91, annual rpt, S5585–1

New York State statistical yearbook, general data, 1992 annual rpt, U5100–1.6

North Carolina financial condition, including revenues by source, expenditures by function, fund balances, and bonded debt, FY92, annual rpt, S5897–1

North Carolina public school enrollment, grads, staff, and finances, with data by race, sex, and local district, 1991/92-1992/93 and trends, annual rpt, S5915–1

North Dakota financial condition, including revenues by source, expenditures by function, fund balances, and bonded debt, FY92, annual rpt, S6162–1

North Dakota public school revenues by source, expenditures by function, mill levies, and taxable value, by district, 1992/93 annual rpt, S6180–4

Ohio financial condition, including revenues by source, expenditures by function, and fund balances, FY92, annual rpt, S6255–1

Ohio public school enrollment, finances, special programs, and staff, 1991/92 and trends, annual rpt, S6265–2

Ohio special education expenditures, instructional hours, and enrollment, by service type and school district, 1991/92 and trends, annual rpt, S6265–1

Oklahoma financial condition, including revenues by source, expenditures by function, and fund balances, FY91, annual rpt, S6438–1

Oklahoma public school finances, personnel, enrollment, and facilities, by county and district, 1991/92 and trends, annual rpt, S6423–1

Index by Subjects and Names

Oklahoma public school performance indicators, including students and achievement, finances, and staff, by district, 1990/91-1991/92 and trends, annual rpt, S6423–2

Oklahoma statistical abstract, general data, 1992 annual rpt, U8130–2.5

Oregon financial condition, including revenues by source, expenditures by function, and fund statements, FY92, annual rpt, S6603–2

Oregon public school revenues by source and fund, and expenditures by fund, function, and object, 1991/92, annual rpt, S6590–1.16

Oregon public school revenues by source and fund, and expenditures by fund, function, and object, 1992/93, annual rpt, S6590–1.17

Oregon public school revenues by source, by school district and county, 1992/93, annual rpt, S6590–1.21

Pennsylvania elementary/secondary and higher education enrollment, grads, staff, and finances, by instn type, 1981/82-1996/97, recurring rpt, S6790–5.10

Pennsylvania financial condition, including revenues by source, expenditures by function, and fund balances, FY92 and trends, annual rpt, S6810–4

Rhode Island education expenditures by function and source of funds, by school district, 1991/92, annual rpt, S6970–1.2

Rhode Island financial condition, including revenues by source, expenditures by function, and fund balances, FY92 and trends, annual rpt, S6930–1

South Carolina financial condition, including receipts by source, expenditures by function, fund balances, and bonded debt, FY92, annual rpt, S7127–1

South Carolina school district appropriation trends, FY79-94, annual rpt, S7125–3.3

South Carolina teachers salary schedules, educational revenues by source, and expenditures by function, by school district, 1991/92, annual rpt, S7145–1.5

South Dakota financial condition, including revenues by source, expenditures by function, fund balances, and bonded debt, FY92, annual rpt, S7330–1

South Dakota school enrollment, finances, grads, and staff, by district, 1991/92 and trends, annual rpt, S7315–1

Tennessee financial condition, including revenues by source, expenditures by function and object, and fund balances, FY92, annual rpt, S7505–1

Tennessee public school finances, by county, city, and school district, 1991/92, annual rpt, S7490–2.4

Texas financial condition, including revenues by source, expenditures by function, and bonded indebtedness, FY92, annual rpt, S7655–3

Texas financial condition, including revenues by source, expenditures by function and dept, and investments, with data for over 400 individual funds, FY92, annual rpt, S7655–2

Utah financial condition, including revenues by source, expenditures by function and agency, and fund balances, FY92, annual rpt, S7795–1

Index by Subjects and Names

Utah govt statistical review, fiscal and socioeconomic data, 1993 annual rpt, R9380–1.8

Utah public school revenues by source and expenditures by object, by State fund and school district, FY92, annual rpt, S7815–1.2

Utah tax revenues by source, and distribution to localities and State funds, FY92 and trends, annual rpt, S7905–1

Virginia financial condition, including revenues by source, expenditures by function, and fund balances, FY92 and trends, annual rpt, S8170–1

Virginia public school enrollment, grads, finances, and staff, by county and municipality, 1991/92, annual rpt, S8190–3

Washington State financial condition, including revenues by source, expenditures by function, fund balances, and bonded debt, FY92, annual rpt, S8345–3

West Virginia public school finances, enrollment, staff, and programs, by county, 1992/93 and trends, annual rpt, S8540–4

Wisconsin elementary and secondary school enrollment, staff, costs, and State aid, by school district, 1992/93 and trends, annual rpt, S8795–2

Wisconsin financial condition, including revenues by source, expenditures by function and object, and fund balances, FY92, annual rpt, S8675–3

Wisconsin financial condition, including revenues by source, expenditures by function and object, and fund balances, FY93, annual rpt, S8675–2

Wyoming financial condition, including revenues by source, expenditures by function, and fund balances, FY92 and trends, annual rpt, S8875–1

Wyoming public school revenues by source, expenditures by program and object, and bonded debt, by district, 1991/92, annual rpt, S8890–1.3

see also State funding for higher education

see also State funding for medical education

see also State funding for vocational education

see also Student aid

see also Under State government spending for general State financial and budget data

State funding for employment

Unemployment insurance trends, including data on unemployment, worker characteristics, coverage, benefits, and State govt finances, 1940s-90, R9260–18

State and local:

Arkansas financial condition, including revenues by source, expenditures by function and locality, and fund balances, FY91-92, biennial rpt, S0780–1

California financial condition, including revenues by source, expenditures by agency and function, fund balances, and bonded debt, FY92 and trends, annual rpt, S0815–1

Colorado financial condition, including receipts by source, and expenditures by function, FY92 and trends, annual rpt, S0980–1

Connecticut financial condition, including revenues by source, expenditures by function, and bonded debt, FY92, annual rpt, S1170–1, S1170–2

DC financial condition, including receipts by source, expenditures by object or function, and fund balances, FY92, annual rpt, S1507–1

DC statistical profile, general data, 1992 annual rpt, S1535–3.3

Florida financial condition, including receipts by source, expenditures by function, and fund balances, FY92, annual rpt, S1717–1, S1717–3

Georgia financial condition, including revenues by source, expenditures by function and object, and fund balances, FY92, annual rpt, S1860–1

Hawaii financial condition, including revenues by source, expenditures by function, and fund balances, FY92, annual rpt, S2020–1

Idaho financial condition, including revenues by source and expenditures by object, by agency and/or fund, FY92, annual rpt, S2215–1

Illinois financial condition, including revenues by source, and expenditures by object, function, and agency, FY92, annual rpt, S2415–1

Indiana financial condition, including revenues by source, expenditures by function and object, and fund balances, by agency, FY92, annual rpt, S2570–1

Iowa financial condition, including revenues by source, expenditures by function, and bonded debt, FY92 and trends, annual rpt, S2860–4

Kansas financial condition, including revenues by source, expenditures by function and object, and fund balances, FY92, annual rpt, S2900–1

Maine financial condition, including revenues by source, expenditures by function and object, and fund balances, FY92, annual rpt, S3420–1

Michigan financial condition, including revenues by source, expenditures by function, and fund balances, FY92 and trends, annual rpt, S3985–2

Mississippi financial condition, including revenues by source, expenditures by function and object, and detail by agency, FY92 and trends, annual rpt, S4346–1

Missouri financial condition, including revenues and expenditures by agency, and tax collections and distribution, FY92 and trends, annual rpt, S4570–1.1

Missouri financial condition, including revenues by source, expenditures by function, and fund balances, FY92, annual rpt, S4475–1

Montana financial condition, including revenues by source, expenditures by function, and fund balances, FY92, annual rpt, S4653–1

Nevada financial condition, including fund revenues by source, expenditures by function, and bonded debt, FY92, annual rpt, S5025–1

New Jersey financial condition, including revenues by source, expenditures by function, fund balances, and bonded debt, FY92, annual rpt, S5455–1

New York State financial condition, including revenues by source, expenditures by function, and fund balances, FY93, annual rpt, S5710–1

State funding for energy programs

North Carolina financial condition, including revenues by source, expenditures by function, fund balances, and bonded debt, FY92, annual rpt, S5897–1

North Dakota financial condition, including revenues by source, expenditures by function, fund balances, and bonded debt, FY92, annual rpt, S6162–1

Ohio financial condition, including revenues by source, expenditures by function, and fund balances, FY92, annual rpt, S6255–1

Oregon financial condition, including revenues by source, expenditures by function, and fund statements, FY92, annual rpt, S6603–2

Rhode Island financial condition, including revenues by source, expenditures by function, and fund balances, FY92 and trends, annual rpt, S6930–1

South Carolina financial condition, including receipts by source, expenditures by function, fund balances, and bonded debt, FY92, annual rpt, S7127–1

South Dakota financial condition, including revenues by source, expenditures by function, fund balances, and bonded debt, FY92, annual rpt, S7330–1

Tennessee financial condition, including revenues by source, expenditures by function and object, and fund balances, FY92, annual rpt, S7505–1

Texas financial condition, including revenues by source, expenditures by function, and bonded indebtedness, FY92, annual rpt, S7655–3

Texas financial condition, including revenues by source, expenditures by function and dept, and investments, with data for over 400 individual funds, FY92, annual rpt, S7655–2.2

Wisconsin financial condition, including revenues by source, expenditures by function and object, and fund balances, FY92, annual rpt, S8675–3

Wisconsin financial condition, including revenues by source, expenditures by function and object, and fund balances, FY93, annual rpt, S8675–2

Wyoming financial condition, including revenues by source, expenditures by function, and fund balances, FY92 and trends, annual rpt, S8875–1

see also State and local employees pay

see also State funding for vocational education

see also State retirement systems

see also Under State government spending for general State financial and budget data

State funding for energy programs

State and local:

Alaska electric power residential bill subsidy program, rates paid to participating utilities, 1992, annual rpt, S0280–4

Alaska financial condition, including revenues by source, expenditures by function, fund balances, and bond obligations, FY92 and trends, annual rpt, S0275–1

Arizona financial condition, including revenues by source, expenditures by function, and fund balances, FY91, annual rpt, S0450–2

Arkansas financial condition, including revenues by source, expenditures by function and locality, and fund balances, FY91-92, biennial rpt, S0780–1

State funding for energy programs

California financial condition, including revenues by source, expenditures by agency and function, fund balances, and bonded debt, FY92 and trends, annual rpt, S0815–1

Indiana financial condition, including revenues by source, expenditures by function and object, and fund balances, by agency, FY92, annual rpt, S2570–1

Montana low-income energy assistance cases and payments, by county, monthly rpt, S4755–1

Nebraska financial condition, including revenues by source, expenditures by function and agency, and fund balances, FY92, annual rpt, S4825–1

New Jersey financial condition, including revenues by source, expenditures by function, fund balances, and bonded debt, FY92, annual rpt, S5455–1

New York State financial condition, including revenues by source, expenditures by function, and fund balances, FY93, annual rpt, S5710–1

North Carolina financial condition, including revenues by source, expenditures by function, fund balances, and bonded debt, FY92, annual rpt, S5897–1

North Dakota financial condition, including revenues by source, expenditures by function, fund balances, and bonded debt, FY92, annual rpt, S6162–1

Oregon financial condition, including revenues by source, expenditures by function, and fund statements, FY92, annual rpt, S6603–2

South Carolina financial condition, including receipts by source, expenditures by function, fund balances, and bonded debt, FY92, annual rpt, S7127–1

South Dakota financial condition, including revenues by source, expenditures by function, fund balances, and bonded debt, FY92, annual rpt, S7330–1

South Dakota low-income energy assistance clients and payments, by county, FY92, annual rpt, S7385–1.2

Tennessee financial condition, including revenues by source, expenditures by function and object, and fund balances, FY92, annual rpt, S7505–1

Texas financial condition, including revenues by source, expenditures by function and dept, and investments, with data for over 400 individual funds, FY92, annual rpt, S7655–2.2

see also Under State government spending for general State financial and budget data

State funding for environmental protection

see State funding for natural resources and conservation

State funding for health and hospitals

Funding of govt health care programs by source, Medicare enrollments, and Medicaid recipients, 1960s-91, annual rpt, A5173–2.2

Govt finances, including revenues by source, expenditures by function, and debt, detailed data for Federal, State, and local govts, 1993 annual rpt, R9050–1

Sexually transmitted disease and human immunodeficiency virus (HIV) program expenditures, by State, 1989, A5160–10

Statistical profiles of 50 States and DC, general data, 1993 annual almanac, C4712–1

Substance abuse treatment programs, funding by source, and client characteristics, for alcohol and drug services, by State, FY91 and trends, annual rpt, A7112–1

Teaching hospital house staff stipend/benefit cost funding sources, by ownership, 1992/93, annual rpt, A3273–3

State and local:

Alabama financial condition, including revenues by source, expenditures by function and object, and fund balances, by fund and agency, FY92, annual rpt, S0129–1

Alabama public health dept activities, including services provided, inspection and licensing activity, staff and finances, and vital statistics and health data, 1992 annual rpt, S0175–3

Alaska financial condition, including revenues by source, expenditures by function, fund balances, and bond obligations, FY92 and trends, annual rpt, S0275–1

Arizona financial condition, including revenues by source, expenditures by function, and fund balances, FY91, annual rpt, S0450–2

Arizona financial condition, including revenues by source, expenditures by function, and fund balances, FY92, annual rpt, S0450–1

Arkansas children's medical service State and Federal funding, FY89-91, annual rpt, S0700–2.3

Arkansas financial condition, including revenues by source, expenditures by function and locality, and fund balances, FY91-92, biennial rpt, S0780–1

Arkansas financial condition, including revenues by source, expenditures by function and object, and fund balances, FY92, annual rpt, S0670–1

California cigarette tax Proposition 99 mandating spending for health education and research, actual and projected expenditures by program category, FY90-94, article, A2623–1.511

California financial condition, including revenues by source, expenditures by agency and function, fund balances, and bonded debt, FY92 and trends, annual rpt, S0815–1

Connecticut financial condition, including revenues by source, expenditures by function, and bonded debt, FY92, annual rpt, S1170–1

DC financial condition, including receipts by source, expenditures by object or function, and fund balances, FY92, annual rpt, S1507–1

DC statistical profile, general data, 1992 annual rpt, S1535–3.5

Florida financial condition, including receipts by source, expenditures by function, and fund balances, FY92, annual rpt, S1717–1, S1717–3

Georgia financial condition, including revenues by source, expenditures by function and object, and fund balances, FY92, annual rpt, S1860–1

Hawaii financial condition, including revenues by source, expenditures by function, and fund balances, FY92, annual rpt, S2020–1

Index by Subjects and Names

Idaho financial condition, including revenues by source and expenditures by object, by agency and/or fund, FY92, annual rpt, S2215–1

Illinois financial condition, including revenues by source, and expenditures by object, function, and agency, FY92, annual rpt, S2415–1

Indiana financial condition, including revenues by source, expenditures by function and object, and fund balances, by agency, FY92, annual rpt, S2570–1

Iowa financial condition, including revenues by source, expenditures by function, and bonded debt, FY92 and trends, annual rpt, S2860–4

Louisiana financial condition, including revenues by source, expenditures by function, and fund balances, FY92 and trends, annual rpt, S3285–2

Maryland medical assistance payments and recipients, by program, type of service, location, demographic characteristics, and facility, FY92 and trends, annual rpt, S3635–3

Massachusetts financial condition, including revenues by source, and expenditures by function, by fund, FY92 and trends, annual rpt, S3777–1

Michigan financial condition, including revenues by source, expenditures by function, and fund balances, FY92 and trends, annual rpt, S3985–2

Minnesota financial condition, including revenues by source, expenditures by function, fund balances, and bonded debt, FY92 and trends, annual rpt, S4180–1

Mississippi financial condition, including revenues by source, expenditures by function and object, and detail by agency, FY92 and trends, annual rpt, S4346–1

Missouri financial condition, including revenues and expenditures by agency, and tax collections and distribution, FY92 and trends, annual rpt, S4570–1.1

Missouri financial condition, including revenues by source, expenditures by function, and fund balances, FY92, annual rpt, S4475–1

Montana financial condition, including revenues by source, expenditures by function, and fund balances, FY92, annual rpt, S4653–1

Nebraska financial condition, including revenues by source, expenditures by function and agency, and fund balances, FY92, annual rpt, S4825–1

Nevada financial condition, including fund revenues by source, expenditures by function, and bonded debt, FY92, annual rpt, S5025–1

New Jersey financial condition, including revenues by source, expenditures by function, fund balances, and bonded debt, FY92, annual rpt, S5455–1

New Mexico financial condition, including receipts by source, expenditures by agency and function, fund balances, and bonded debt, FY91, annual rpt, S5585–1

New York State financial condition, including revenues by source, expenditures by function, and fund balances, FY93, annual rpt, S5710–1

New York State statistical yearbook, general data, 1992 annual rpt, U5100–1.11

Index by Subjects and Names

North Carolina financial condition, including revenues by source, expenditures by function, fund balances, and bonded debt, FY92, annual rpt, S5897–1

North Dakota financial condition, including revenues by source, expenditures by function, fund balances, and bonded debt, FY92, annual rpt, S6162–1

Ohio financial condition, including revenues by source, expenditures by function, and fund balances, FY92, annual rpt, S6255–1

Oklahoma financial condition, including revenues by source, expenditures by function, and fund balances, FY91, annual rpt, S6438–1

Oregon financial condition, including revenues by source, expenditures by function, and fund statements, FY92, annual rpt, S6603–2

South Carolina financial condition, including receipts by source, expenditures by function, fund balances, and bonded debt, FY92, annual rpt, S7127–1

South Dakota financial condition, including revenues by source, expenditures by function, fund balances, and bonded debt, FY92, annual rpt, S7330–1

Tennessee financial condition, including revenues by source, expenditures by function and object, and fund balances, FY92, annual rpt, S7505–1

Texas financial condition, including revenues by source, expenditures by function, and bonded indebtedness, FY92, annual rpt, S7655–3

Texas financial condition, including revenues by source, expenditures by function and dept, and investments, with data for over 400 individual funds, FY92, annual rpt, S7655–2.2

Texas indigent health care finances and utilization, with data by county, district, public hospital, and medical school, 1986-91, U8850–8.7

Texas State and local health depts finances, employment, and service area characteristics, FY91 and trends, U8850–8.6

Utah financial condition, including revenues by source, expenditures by function and agency, and fund balances, FY92, annual rpt, S7795–1

Utah govt statistical review, fiscal and socioeconomic data, 1993 annual rpt, R9380–1.9

Washington State public assistance clients and service costs, by client characteristics, program, and county, FY90, annual rpt, S8420–2

Wisconsin financial condition, including revenues by source, expenditures by function and object, and fund balances, FY92, annual rpt, S8675–3

Wisconsin financial condition, including revenues by source, expenditures by function and object, and fund balances, FY93, annual rpt, S8675–2

Wyoming financial condition, including revenues by source, expenditures by function, and fund balances, FY92 and trends, annual rpt, S8875–1

see also Medicaid

see also State funding for medical education

see also Under State government spending for general State financial and budget data

State funding for higher education

Appropriation trends for higher education, by State, FY91-93, article, B8500–2.501

Appropriations for higher education, by State, instn, and function, 1993/94, annual feature, C2175–1.538

Appropriations of tax funds for higher education, by State, instn, and function, FY92-93 and trends, annual rpt, A8970–1

Community and junior college revenues by source and expenditures by function, and selected student characteristics, FY92, annual rpt, A6705–1

Expenditures of State govts by fund source and function, by State, FY90-92, annual rpt, A7118–1

Expenditures of State govts for higher education, by State, 1990/91 and trends, semiannual rpt, B8500–1.7

Expenditures per capita for higher education, by State, FY91, biennial rpt, S8780–1.2

Funding for higher education as percent of State/local spending, by State, FY91 and trends, article, B8500–2.516

Govt finances, including revenues by source, expenditures by function, and debt, detailed data for Federal, State, and local govts, 1993 annual rpt, R9050–1

Higher education instns, faculty, students, degrees, and finances, detailed data by State, 1993 annual rpt, C2175–1.531

Southern States higher education enrollment, degrees, appropriations, tuition/fees, and faculty compensation, by instn type, for 15 States, 1990/91, annual rpt, A8945–31

Southern States higher education financial data, by State, 1970s-92, biennial fact book, A8945–1.6

Southern States public higher education revenue shares from State and local govt and tuition, by State, 1981/82 and 1991/92, A8945–27.12

Western States higher education student exchange program enrollment and support fees, by program and instn, for 15 States, 1992/93, annual rpt, A9385–1

State and local:

Alabama Dept of Education grants/benefits to postsecondary instns, FY92, annual rpt, S0124–1.1

Alabama financial condition, including revenues by source, expenditures by function and object, and fund balances, by fund and agency, FY92, annual rpt, S0129–1

Alaska financial condition, including revenues by source, expenditures by function, fund balances, and bond obligations, FY92 and trends, annual rpt, S0275–1

Arizona financial condition, including revenues by source, expenditures by function, and fund balances, FY91, annual rpt, S0450–2

Arizona financial condition, including revenues by source, expenditures by function, and fund balances, FY92, annual rpt, S0450–1

Arkansas financial condition, including revenues by source, expenditures by function and locality, and fund balances, FY91-92, biennial rpt, S0780–1

State funding for higher education

Arkansas financial condition, including revenues by source, expenditures by function and object, and fund balances, FY92, annual rpt, S0670–1

Arkansas higher education finances, including revenues by source, expenditures by function, and State appropriations, by public instn, FY80s-95, biennial rpt, S0690–4

Arkansas public higher education finances and enrollment, with comparisons to US and selected other States, 1990-92, article, U5930–1.502

California financial condition, including revenues by source, expenditures by agency and function, fund balances, and bonded debt, FY92 and trends, annual rpt, S0815–1

California higher education systems funding by source and expenditures by program category, with enrollment data, FY60s-94, annual rpt, S0827–3

Colorado financial condition, including receipts by source, and expenditures by function, FY92 and trends, annual rpt, S0980–1

Connecticut financial condition, including revenues by source, expenditures by function, and bonded debt, FY92, annual rpt, S1170–1, S1170–2

DC financial condition, including receipts by source, expenditures by object or function, and fund balances, FY92, annual rpt, S1507–1

Delaware postsecondary education finances, enrollment, and degrees conferred, by instn, FY94 annual rpt, S1425–1

Florida financial condition, including receipts by source, expenditures by function, and fund balances, FY92, annual rpt, S1717–1, S1717–3

Florida higher education enrollment, degree programs, staff, and finances, by State-supported instn, with student and staff characteristics, 1991/92 annual rpt, S1725–1

Georgia financial condition, including revenues by source, expenditures by function and object, and fund balances, FY92, annual rpt, S1860–1

Georgia statistical abstract, general data, 1992-93 biennial rpt, U6730–1.2

Hawaii financial condition, including revenues by source, expenditures by function, and fund balances, FY92, annual rpt, S2020–1

Idaho financial condition, including revenues by source and expenditures by object, by agency and/or fund, FY92, annual rpt, S2215–1

Illinois financial condition, including revenues by source, and expenditures by object, function, and agency, FY92, annual rpt, S2415–1

Illinois higher education staff, salaries, student cost and aid, and finances, by instn, 1993 annual rpt, S2475–1.2

Indiana financial condition, including revenues by source, expenditures by function and object, and fund balances, by agency, FY92, annual rpt, S2570–1

Iowa financial condition, including revenues by source, expenditures by function, and bonded debt, FY92 and trends, annual rpt, S2860–4

State funding for higher education

Iowa postsecondary enrollment, degrees, staff, and finances, by instn, 1990/91, annual rpt, S2755–1

Kentucky financial condition, including revenues by source, expenditures by function and object, fund balances, and bonded debt, FY92, annual rpt, S3120–1

Kentucky higher education enrollment, degrees, staff, and finances, by State-supported instn, 1983-92, annual rpt, S3130–3

Louisiana education dept expenditures by function, 1990/91-1991/92, annual rpt, S3280–1.1

Louisiana financial condition, including revenues by source, expenditures by function, and fund balances, FY92 and trends, annual rpt, S3285–2

Maryland financial condition, including revenues by source, expenditures by function, fund balances, and bonded debt, FY92 and trends, annual rpt, S3685–2

Michigan financial condition, including revenues by source, expenditures by function, and fund balances, FY92 and trends, annual rpt, S3985–2

Minnesota financial condition, including revenues by source, expenditures by function, fund balances, and bonded debt, FY92 and trends, annual rpt, S4180–1

Minnesota postsecondary education finances, and enrollment by student characteristics, by type of school system, 1970s-93, biennial rpt, S4195–2.2

Mississippi financial condition, including revenues by source, expenditures by function and object, and detail by agency, FY92 and trends, annual rpt, S4346–1

Mississippi higher education enrollment and degrees, by level and field, and finances, by State-supported instn, 1991/92, annual rpt, S4360–1

Missouri financial condition, including revenues and expenditures by agency, and tax collections and distribution, FY92 and trends, annual rpt, S4570–1.1

Missouri financial condition, including revenues by source, expenditures by function, and fund balances, FY92, annual rpt, S4475–1

Missouri higher education enrollment, degrees, libraries, staff, and finances, by instn, 1992 and trends, annual rpt, S4520–3

Montana financial condition, including revenues by source, expenditures by function, and fund balances, FY92, annual rpt, S4653–1

Nebraska financial condition, including revenues by source, expenditures by function and agency, and fund balances, FY92, annual rpt, S4825–1

Nevada financial condition, including fund revenues by source, expenditures by function, and bonded debt, FY92, annual rpt, S5025–1

New Jersey financial condition, including revenues by source, expenditures by function, fund balances, and bonded debt, FY92, annual rpt, S5455–1

New Mexico financial condition, including receipts by source, expenditures by agency and function, fund balances, and bonded debt, FY91, annual rpt, S5585–1

Index by Subjects and Names

New York State financial condition, including revenues by source, expenditures by function, and fund balances, FY93, annual rpt, S5710–1

North Carolina financial condition, including revenues by source, expenditures by function, fund balances, and bonded debt, FY92, annual rpt, S5897–1

North Dakota financial condition, including revenues by source, expenditures by function, fund balances, and bonded debt, FY92, annual rpt, S6162–1

Ohio financial condition, including revenues by source, expenditures by function, and fund balances, FY92, annual rpt, S6255–1

Oklahoma financial condition, including revenues by source, expenditures by function, and fund balances, FY91, annual rpt, S6438–1

Oregon financial condition, including revenues by source, expenditures by function, and fund statements, FY92, annual rpt, S6603–2

Pennsylvania financial condition, including revenues by source, expenditures by function, and fund balances, FY92 and trends, annual rpt, S6810–4

Rhode Island financial condition, including revenues by source, expenditures by function, and fund balances, FY92 and trends, annual rpt, S6930–1

South Carolina financial condition, including receipts by source, expenditures by function, fund balances, and bonded debt, FY92, annual rpt, S7127–1

South Carolina higher education enrollment, degrees, staff, and finances, by instn, 1992 and trends, annual rpt, S7185–2

South Dakota financial condition, including revenues by source, expenditures by function, fund balances, and bonded debt, FY92, annual rpt, S7330–1

South Dakota public higher education finances, staff, enrollment, degrees, and facilities, by instn, FY93 annual rpt, S7375–1

Tennessee financial condition, including revenues by source, expenditures by function and object, and fund balances, FY92, annual rpt, S7505–1

Tennessee higher education finances, student aid and expenses, and faculty and salaries, by instn, 1992/93 and trends, annual rpt, S7525–1.2

Texas financial condition, including revenues by source, expenditures by function, and bonded indebtedness, FY92, annual rpt, S7655–3

Texas financial condition, including revenues by source, expenditures by function and dept, and investments, with data for over 400 individual funds, FY92, annual rpt, S7655–2.2

Texas higher education appropriations, by instn, FY92-93 and trends, annual rpt, S7657–1.3

Utah financial condition, including revenues by source, expenditures by function and agency, and fund balances, FY92, annual rpt, S7795–1

Utah govt statistical review, fiscal and socioeconomic data, 1993 annual rpt, R9380–1.8

Utah higher education degrees, enrollment, staff, and finances, by public instn, with selected comparisons to instns in other States, 1993/94 annual rpt, S7895–2

Vermont higher education revenues by source, expenditures by function, and tuition/fees, by instn, and student aid trends, 1992 annual rpt, S8035–2.3

Virginia financial condition, including revenues by source, expenditures by function, and fund balances, FY92 and trends, annual rpt, S8170–1

Washington State financial condition, including revenues by source, expenditures by function, fund balances, and bonded debt, FY92, annual rpt, S8345–3

West Virginia higher education revenues by source and expenditures by function, by instn, FY92 and trends, annual rpt, S8533–1.2

Wisconsin financial condition, including revenues by source, expenditures by function and object, and fund balances, FY92, annual rpt, S8675–3

Wisconsin financial condition, including revenues by source, expenditures by function and object, and fund balances, FY93, annual rpt, S8675–2

Wyoming financial condition, including revenues by source, expenditures by function, and fund balances, FY92 and trends, annual rpt, S8875–1

see also State funding for medical education

see also Student aid

see also Under State government spending for general State financial and budget data

State funding for highways and streets

Capital and maintenance outlays, and hwy construction expenditures, by State, 1993 annual rpt, A0865–1.3

Construction contracting plans for hwys and bridges, by State, 1993, annual feature, C5800 2.512

Expenditures for hwys, by State, 1991, semiannual rpt, B8500–1.11

Govt finances, including revenues by source, expenditures by function, and debt, detailed data for Federal, State, and local govts, 1993 annual rpt, R9050–1

Statistical profiles of 50 States and DC, general data, 1993 annual almanac, C4712–1

State and local:

Alabama financial condition, including revenues by source, expenditures by function and object, and fund balances, by fund and agency, FY92, annual rpt, S0129–1

Arizona financial condition, including revenues by source, expenditures by function, and fund balances, FY91, annual rpt, S0450–2

Arizona statistical abstract, general data, 1993 recurring rpt, U5850–2.18

Arkansas financial condition, including revenues by source, expenditures by function and locality, and fund balances, FY91-92, biennial rpt, S0780–1

California financial condition, including revenues by source, expenditures by agency and function, fund balances, and bonded debt, FY92 and trends, annual rpt, S0815–1

State funding for housing

Colorado financial condition, including receipts by source, and expenditures by function, FY92 and trends, annual rpt, S0980–1

Connecticut financial condition, including revenues by source, expenditures by function, and bonded debt, FY92, annual rpt, S1170–1

DC statistical profile, general data, 1992 annual rpt, S1535–3.7

Florida financial condition, including receipts by source, expenditures by function, and fund balances, FY92, annual rpt, S1717–1, S1717–3

Florida statistical abstract, general data, 1992 annual rpt, U6660–1.13

Georgia statistical abstract, general data, 1992-93 biennial rpt, U6730–1.8

Hawaii financial condition, including revenues by source, expenditures by function, and fund balances, FY92, annual rpt, S2020–1

Hawaii tax collections and allocations, by type, for State and counties, FY91-92 and trends, annual rpt, S2120–1

Idaho financial condition, including revenues by source and expenditures by object, by agency and/or fund, FY92, annual rpt, S2215–1

Illinois financial condition, including revenues by source, and expenditures by object, function, and agency, FY92, annual rpt, S2415–1

Indiana financial condition, including revenues by source, expenditures by function and object, and fund balances, by agency, FY92, annual rpt, S2570–1

Louisiana financial condition, including revenues by source, expenditures by function, and fund balances, FY92 and trends, annual rpt, S3285–2

Maine financial condition, including revenues by source, expenditures by function and object, and fund balances, FY92, annual rpt, S3420–1

Massachusetts financial condition, including revenues by source, and expenditures by function, by fund, FY92 and trends, annual rpt, S3777–1

Michigan financial condition, including revenues by source, expenditures by function, and fund balances, FY92 and trends, annual rpt, S3985–2

Minnesota financial condition, including revenues by source, expenditures by function, fund balances, and bonded debt, FY92 and trends, annual rpt, S4180–1

Mississippi financial condition, including revenues by source, expenditures by function and object, and detail by agency, FY92 and trends, annual rpt, S4346–1

Missouri financial condition, including fund finances, tax collections and distribution, and State treasury activity, FY92 and trends, annual rpt, S4570–1

Missouri financial condition, including revenues by source, expenditures by function, and fund balances, FY92, annual rpt, S4475–1

Montana financial condition, including revenues by source, expenditures by function, and fund balances, FY92, annual rpt, S4653–1

Nebraska financial condition, including revenues by source, expenditures by function and agency, and fund balances, FY92, annual rpt, S4825–1

Nevada financial condition, including fund revenues by source, expenditures by function, and bonded debt, FY92, annual rpt, S5025–1

Nevada statistical abstract, general data, 1992 biennial rpt, S5005–1.13

New Hampshire financial condition, with revenues by source, expenditures by function or object, and fund balances, FY92 and trends, annual rpt, S5175–1

New Jersey financial condition, including revenues by source, expenditures by function, fund balances, and bonded debt, FY92, annual rpt, S5455–1

New Mexico financial condition, including receipts by source, expenditures by agency and function, fund balances, and bonded debt, FY91, annual rpt, S5585–1

New York State financial condition, including revenues by source, expenditures by function, and fund balances, FY93, annual rpt, S5710–1

North Carolina financial condition, including revenues by source, expenditures by function, fund balances, and bonded debt, FY92, annual rpt, S5897–1

North Dakota financial condition, including revenues by source, expenditures by function, fund balances, and bonded debt, FY92, annual rpt, S6162–1

Ohio financial condition, including revenues by source, expenditures by function, and fund balances, FY92, annual rpt, S6255–1

Oklahoma financial condition, including revenues by source, expenditures by function, and fund balances, FY91, annual rpt, S6438–1

Oklahoma statistical abstract, general data, 1992 annual rpt, U8130–2.5, U8130–2.16

Oregon financial condition, including revenues by source, expenditures by function, and fund statements, FY92, annual rpt, S6603–2

Pennsylvania financial condition, including revenues by source, expenditures by function, and fund balances, FY92 and trends, annual rpt, S6810–4

Rhode Island financial condition, including revenues by source, expenditures by function, and fund balances, FY92 and trends, annual rpt, S6930–1

South Carolina financial condition, including receipts by source, expenditures by function, fund balances, and bonded debt, FY92, annual rpt, S7127–1

Tennessee financial condition, including revenues by source, expenditures by function and object, and fund balances, FY92, annual rpt, S7505–1

Tennessee statistical abstract, general data, 1992/93 annual rpt, U8710–2.9

Tennessee tax revenues by source and apportionments to counties, cities, and funds, FY91-92 and trends, biennial rpt, S7570–1

Texas financial condition, including revenues by source, expenditures by function, and bonded indebtedness, FY92, annual rpt, S7655–3

Texas financial condition, including revenues by source, expenditures by function and dept, and investments, with data for over 400 individual funds, FY92, annual rpt, S7655–2.2

Utah govt statistical review, fiscal and socioeconomic data, 1993 annual rpt, R9380–1.10

Utah statistical abstract, general data, 1993 triennial rpt, U8960–1.13

Vermont financial condition, including revenues by source, expenditures by function, fund balances, and bonded debt, FY92, annual rpt, S8035–1

Virginia financial condition, including revenues by source, expenditures by function, and fund balances, FY92 and trends, annual rpt, S8170–1

Washington State financial condition, including revenues by source, expenditures by function, fund balances, and bonded debt, FY92, annual rpt, S8345–3

West Virginia statistical handbook, general data, 1992 annual rpt, R9385–1.2

Wisconsin financial condition, including revenues by source, expenditures by function and object, and fund balances, FY93, annual rpt, S8675–2

Wyoming financial condition, including revenues by source, expenditures by function, and fund balances, FY92 and trends, annual rpt, S8875–1

see also Under State government spending for general State financial and budget data

State funding for historical sites and museums *see* State funding for arts and culture

State funding for housing

Property tax relief benefits under "circuit-breaker" and other tax-relief programs, for selected metro areas, 1992, R3834–16

Statistical profiles of 50 States and DC, general data, 1993 annual almanac, C4712–1

State and local:

Alabama financial condition, including revenues by source, expenditures by function and object, and fund balances, by fund and agency, FY92, annual rpt, S0129–1

Alaska financial condition, including revenues by source, expenditures by function, fund balances, and bond obligations, FY92 and trends, annual rpt, S0275–1

Arkansas financial condition, including revenues by source, expenditures by function and locality, and fund balances, FY91-92, biennial rpt, S0780–1

California financial condition, including revenues by source, expenditures by agency and function, fund balances, and bonded debt, FY92 and trends, annual rpt, S0815–1

Connecticut financial condition, including revenues by source, expenditures by function, and bonded debt, FY92, annual rpt, S1170–1, S1170–2

DC financial condition, including receipts by source, expenditures by object or function, and fund balances, FY92, annual rpt, S1507–1

DC statistical profile, general data, 1992 annual rpt, S1535–3.3, S1535–3.4

Hawaii financial condition, including revenues by source, expenditures by function, and fund balances, FY92, annual rpt, S2020–1

State funding for housing

Indiana financial condition, including revenues by source, expenditures by function and object, and fund balances, by agency, FY92, annual rpt, S2570–1

Iowa financial condition, including revenues by source, expenditures by function, and bonded debt, FY92 and trends, annual rpt, S2860–4

Kentucky financial condition, including revenues by source, expenditures by function and object, fund balances, and bonded debt, FY92, annual rpt, S3120–1

Louisiana financial condition, including revenues by source, expenditures by function, and fund balances, FY92 and trends, annual rpt, S3285–2

Michigan financial condition, including revenues by source, expenditures by function, and fund balances, FY92 and trends, annual rpt, S3985–2

Minnesota financial condition, including revenues by source, expenditures by function, fund balances, and bonded debt, FY92 and trends, annual rpt, S4180–1

Mississippi financial condition, including revenues by source, expenditures by function and object, and detail by agency, FY92 and trends, annual rpt, S4346–1

Missouri financial condition, including revenues by source, expenditures by function, and fund balances, FY92, annual rpt, S4475–1

Montana financial condition, including revenues by source, expenditures by function, and fund balances, FY92, annual rpt, S4653–1

Nevada financial condition, including fund revenues by source, expenditures by function, and bonded debt, FY92, annual rpt, S5025–1

New Jersey financial condition, including revenues by source, expenditures by function, fund balances, and bonded debt, FY92, annual rpt, S5455–1

New York State financial condition, including revenues by source, expenditures by function, and fund balances, FY93, annual rpt, S5710–1

North Carolina financial condition, including revenues by source, expenditures by function, fund balances, and bonded debt, FY92, annual rpt, S5897–1

North Dakota financial condition, including revenues by source, expenditures by function, fund balances, and bonded debt, FY92, annual rpt, S6162–1

Oregon financial condition, including revenues by source, expenditures by function, and fund statements, FY92, annual rpt, S6603–2

Pennsylvania financial condition, including revenues by source, expenditures by function, and fund balances, FY92 and trends, annual rpt, S6810–4

Pennsylvania statistical abstract, general data, 1992 recurring rpt, U4130–6.2

Rhode Island financial condition, including revenues by source, expenditures by function, and fund balances, FY92 and trends, annual rpt, S6930–1

South Carolina financial condition, including receipts by source, expenditures by function, fund balances, and bonded debt, FY92, annual rpt, S7127–1

South Dakota financial condition, including revenues by source, expenditures by function, fund balances, and bonded debt, FY92, annual rpt, S7330–1

Tennessee financial condition, including revenues by source, expenditures by function and object, and fund balances, FY92, annual rpt, S7505–1

Texas financial condition, including revenues by source, expenditures by function, and bonded indebtedness, FY92, annual rpt, S7655–3

Texas financial condition, including revenues by source, expenditures by function and dept, and investments, with data for over 400 individual funds, FY92, annual rpt, S7655–2.2

Utah financial condition, including revenues by source, expenditures by function and agency, and fund balances, FY92, annual rpt, S7795–1

Vermont financial condition, including revenues by source, expenditures by function, fund balances, and bonded debt, FY92, annual rpt, S8035–1

Virginia financial condition, including revenues by source, expenditures by function, and fund balances, FY92 and trends, annual rpt, S8170–1

Wisconsin financial condition, including revenues by source, expenditures by function and object, and fund balances, FY92, annual rpt, S8675–3

Wisconsin financial condition, including revenues by source, expenditures by function and object, and fund balances, FY93, annual rpt, S8675–2

see also Public housing

see also Under State government spending for general State financial and budget data

State funding for law enforcement

see State funding for corrections

see State funding for courts

see State funding for public safety

State funding for legislative functions

see State government spending

State funding for libraries

Appropriations, expenditures, salaries, and staff, for State library agencies by State, 1992 annual rpt, A3862–1

Expenditures for public libraries, for 5 States with highest and lowest per capita spending, 1991, article, C1852–1.509

Library and book trade reference info, including public and academic library funding, construction, and operations, by State and instn, 1992, annual compilation, C1650–3

Library construction, costs, and funding sources, by State, city, instn, and library type, FY92 and trends, annual article, C1852–1.501

Statistical profiles of 50 States and DC, general data, 1993 annual almanac, C4712–1

State and local:

Alabama public libraries, finances, holdings, circulation, staff, and population served, by library, FY92, annual rpt, S0180–1

Arizona public library holdings, circulation, finances, and staff, by instn and county, FY92, annual rpt, S0495–1

Arkansas financial condition, including revenues by source, expenditures by function and locality, and fund balances, FY91-92, biennial rpt, S0780–1

Index by Subjects and Names

Arkansas higher education finances, including revenues by source, expenditures by function, and State appropriations, by public instn, FY80s-95, biennial rpt, S0690–4

California financial condition, including revenues by source, expenditures by agency and function, fund balances, and bonded debt, FY92 and trends, annual rpt, S0815–1

California library finances, staff, holdings, and services, by library type and facility, FY92, annual rpt, S0825–2

Colorado public library finances and operations, by instn, 1991, annual rpt, S1000–3.1

Connecticut financial condition, including revenues by source, expenditures by function, and bonded debt, FY92, annual rpt, S1170–1

Florida public libraries, finances, holdings, staff, and services, by system and library, FY92, annual rpt, S1800–2

Idaho public library holdings, staff, services, circulation, and finances, by instn, FY92, annual rpt, S2282–1

Illinois public library holdings, staff, and finances, by instn, FY92, annual rpt, S2535–2

Indiana financial condition, including revenues by source, expenditures by function and object, and fund balances, by agency, FY92, annual rpt, S2570–1

Indiana public and other library holdings, circulation, finances, and staff, by instn, 1992 or FY92, annual rpt, S2655–1

Louisiana public library finances, holdings, circulation, and personnel, by library system, FY92, annual rpt, S3275–1

Maryland public library operating income and expenditures, staff, holdings, and population served, by county, FY92, annual rpt, S3610–5

Missouri public, special, and academic libraries, finances, holdings, circulation, staff, and services, by location, FY92, annual rpt, S4520–2

Montana financial condition, including revenues by source, expenditures by function, and fund balances, FY92, annual rpt, S4653–1

Nebraska public libraries, finances, holdings, circulation, staff, and population served, by instn, FY91, annual rpt, S4910–1

Nevada library and staff directories for public and academic libraries, with data on holdings, operations, and finances, FY92, annual rpt, S5095–1

New Jersey public library finances, holdings, circulation, and staff, by county and library, 1991, annual rpt, S5385–2

New Mexico public library operations and finances, by instn, FY92, annual rpt, S5627–1

New York State public library finances, staff, holdings, and services, by library and county, 1991, annual rpt, S5745–2

North Carolina public libraries, finances, holdings, and personnel, by library system, FY91, annual rpt, S5910–1

North Dakota public library finances, holdings, staff, and operations, by instn, FY91, annual rpt, S6180–5

Ohio public, academic, and other library finances, holdings, and staff, by library and location, 1992 and trends, annual rpt, S6320–1

Index by Subjects and Names

State funding for local areas

Oklahoma financial condition, including revenues by source, expenditures by function, and fund balances, FY91, annual rpt, S6438–1

Oklahoma public and institutional library holdings, circulation, finances, and staff, by facility, FY92, annual rpt, S6470–1

Oregon library finances, staff, holdings, and services, for public, academic, and special libraries by instn, FY92 and trends, annual rpt, S6635–1

Pennsylvania public and institutional library personnel, holdings, circulation, and finances, by county and facility, FY92, annual rpt, S6790–2

Pennsylvania statistical abstract, general data, 1992 recurring rpt, U4130–6.4

South Carolina public and institutional libraries, finances, services, holdings, and staff, by library, FY92, annual rpt, S7210–1

Texas financial condition, including revenues by source, expenditures by function and dept, and investments, with data for over 400 individual funds, FY92, annual rpt, S7655–2.2

Texas public libraries, holdings, circulation, staff, and finances, by library and location, FY91, annual rpt, S7710–1

Vermont libraries, finances, resources, and circulation, by city and library, FY91-92, biennial rpt, S8080–1

Virginia public library operations and finances, by instn, FY92, annual rpt, S8275–1

Washington State public libraries, finances, holdings, circulation, staff, and population served, by instn, 1992, annual rpt, S8375–1

West Virginia public, academic, and special library operations and/or finances, by instn, 1991/92, annual rpt, S8590–1

Wisconsin Blue Book, general data, 1993-94 biennial rpt, S8780–1.2

Wisconsin financial condition, including revenues by source, expenditures by function and object, and fund balances, FY93, annual rpt, S8675–2

Wisconsin libraries, operations, and finances, by library type, instn, and location, 1992, annual rpt, S8795–1

Wyoming public library holdings, staff, circulation, and finances, by county, FY92, annual rpt, S8855–3

see also Under State government spending for general State financial and budget data

State funding for local areas

Capital project financing methods of local govt, by population size, metro status, and census div, 1991 survey, A5800–2.112

City fiscal condition, including budget trends and adjustments, and influencing factors, by region and population size, Mar-Apr 1993 survey, annual rpt, A8012–1.23

Economic dev condition indicators, including economic performance, business vitality, growth capacity, and tax/fiscal system, by State, 1993 annual rpt, R4225–1.1

Expenditures of State/local govts, with detail by selected function, by State, 1993 semiannual rpt, B8500–1.5

Fiscal crisis State aid programs for local govts, and financial reporting requirements, by State, summer 1992, A7470–4.13

General fund revenues, expenditures, and balances, and budget stabilization funds, by State, FY92-94 and trends, semiannual rpt, A7955–1

Govt finances, including revenues by source, expenditures by function, and debt, detailed data for Federal, State, and local govts, 1993 annual rpt, R9050–1

Intergovtl transfers by function, FY54, FY80, and FY90, article, U7860–1.503

Recycling curbside program State grant funding status of municipalities, July 1991 survey, B0230–2

Recycling curbside program State grant practices, July 1991 survey, B0230–1

State and local:

Alabama financial condition, including revenues by source, expenditures by function and object, and fund balances, by fund and agency, FY92, annual rpt, S0129–1

Alaska tax exemption provisions for senior citizens and disabled veterans, and State reimbursements to local areas, FY92 and trends, annual rpt, S0285–1

Arizona tax revenues by source, tax rates, and disbursements to local areas, FY92 and trends, annual rpt, S0515–1

Arkansas financial condition, including revenues by source, expenditures by function and locality, and fund balances, FY91-92, biennial rpt, S0780–1

California financial condition, including revenues by source, expenditures by agency and function, fund balances, and bonded debt, FY92 and trends, annual rpt, S0815–1

California sales/use tax collections and permits, and tax revenue distributions to localities, FY92 and trends, annual rpt, S0835–1.3

Colorado sales tax distributions to counties and cities, FY92, annual rpt, S1075–1.5

Florida State govt disbursements to local areas, by source of funds, FY92, annual rpt, S1717–1

Georgia financial condition, including revenues by source, expenditures by function and object, and fund balances, FY92, annual rpt, S1860–1

Hawaii tax collections and allocations, by type, for State and counties, FY91-92 and trends, annual rpt, S2120–1

Idaho sales tax revenue sharing distribution, by city and county, FY92, annual rpt, S2295–1

Indiana financial condition, including revenues by source, expenditures by function and object, and fund balances, by agency, FY92, annual rpt, S2570–1

Indiana public welfare expenditures, by program and funding source, FY92, annual rpt, S2623–1.8

Kansas financial condition, including revenues by source, expenditures by function and object, and fund balances, FY92, annual rpt, S2900–1

Maryland local govt financial condition, including revenues by source, expenditures by function, and debt obligations, FY92 and trends, annual rpt, S3618–1.1

Maryland State funds transferred to counties, FY92, annual rpt, S3685–2

Massachusetts financial condition, including revenues by source, and expenditures by function, by fund, FY92 and trends, annual rpt, S3777–1

Massachusetts tax collections by type, and distributions to local areas, FY91 and trends, annual rpt, S3917–1

Mississippi tax collections by type, and disbursements, with selected sales and income tax data by locality and industry, FY92 and trends, annual rpt, S4435–1

Missouri financial condition, including revenues and expenditures by agency, and tax collections and distribution, FY92 and trends, annual rpt, S4570–1.1

Nebraska tax revenues by type, tax rates and exemptions, and aid distribution to local areas, with data by county and city, 1991, annual rpt, S4950–1

New Jersey municipal and county data book, general data, 1992 annual rpt, C4712–4

New Mexico tax revenues and disbursements, with data by tax type, county, and city, FY91-92 and trends, annual rpt, S5660–1

New York State financial condition, including revenues by source, expenditures by function, and fund balances, FY93, annual rpt, S5710–1

New York State statistical yearbook, general data, 1992 annual rpt, U5100–1.6, U5100–1.10

North Carolina court system fee and fine collections distributed to local govts, by county, FY91, annual rpt, S5950–1

Ohio financial condition, including revenues by source, expenditures by function, and fund balances, FY92, annual rpt, S6255–1

Ohio tax revenues and collections, by tax type, with distributions and property assessments by county, and corporate taxes by industry, FY92 annual rpt, S6390–1

Oklahoma statistical abstract, general data, 1992 annual rpt, U8130–2.5

Oklahoma tax revenues by source, and distribution to local govts and State funds, FY92 and trends, annual rpt, S6495–1

Oregon financial condition, including revenues by source, expenditures by function, and fund statements, FY92, annual rpt, S6603–2

Pennsylvania statistical abstract, general data, 1992 recurring rpt, U4130–6.2

Rhode Island State assistance to individual cities and towns, by type, FY92, annual rpt, S6930–1

Rhode Island statistical almanac, general data, 1993 annual rpt, C7975–1.1

South Carolina county govt finances, including property value and tax assessments, by county, FY92, annual rpt, S7127–2

South Carolina economic condition, including agriculture, finance, and govt financial data, 1970s-92, annual rpt, S7125–3.1

South Carolina insurance dept county allocation of fire dept premium taxes, 1991, annual rpt, S7195–1

South Dakota tax revenues by source, aid distributed to local areas, and property tax valuations, FY92 annual rpt, S7380–1

State funding for local areas

Tennessee financial condition, including revenues by source, expenditures by function and object, and fund balances, FY92, annual rpt, S7505–1

Tennessee statistical abstract, general data, 1992/93 annual rpt, U8710–2.15

Tennessee tax revenues by source and apportionments to counties, cities, and funds, FY91-92 and trends, biennial rpt, S7570–1

Texas financial condition, including revenues by source, expenditures by function and dept, and investments, with data for over 400 individual funds, FY92, annual rpt, S7655–2

Texas State and local health depts finances, employment, and service area characteristics, FY91 and trends, U8850–8.6

Utah public lands by govt owner, and Federal land payments to State and local govts, with data by county, 1992 article, U8960–2.502

Utah public school revenues by source and expenditures by object, by State fund and school district, FY92, annual rpt, S7815–1.2

Utah tax revenues by source, and distribution to localities and State funds, FY92 and trends, annual rpt, S7905–1

Washington State revenues by source, and distributions by tax and locality, FY92 and trends, annual rpt, S8415–1.1

Washington State treasury operations, including receipts, disbursements, aid to localities, and investments, by fund, FY92, annual rpt, S8455–1

Wisconsin financial condition, including revenues by source, expenditures by function and object, and fund balances, FY92, annual rpt, S8675–3

Wisconsin financial condition, including revenues by source, expenditures by function and object, and fund balances, FY93, annual rpt, S8675–2

Wyoming financial condition, including revenues by source, expenditures by function, and fund balances, FY92 and trends, annual rpt, S8875–1

Wyoming State treasurer financial transactions, including revenues, investments, and disbursements by local area, FY92 and trends, annual rpt, S9010–1

Wyoming tax collections and distribution, and property valuation, with data by property type and location, FY92 and trends, annual rpt, S8990–1

see also Under State government spending for general State financial and budget data

State funding for medical education

Appropriations of tax funds for higher education, by State, instn, and function, FY92-93 and trends, annual rpt, A8970–1

Nursing higher education program finances, faculty and clinical practice, and clinic/center operations, by instn characteristics, 1992/93 biennial rpt, A0615–5

Optometry school revenues by source, and student financial aid, by instn, 1991/92, annual survey, A3370–2

Osteopathy college enrollment, student and faculty characteristics, and finances, 1992/93 and trends, annual rpt, A0620–1

State and local:

Arizona financial condition, including revenues by source, expenditures by function, and fund balances, FY91, annual rpt, S0450–2

Arkansas financial condition, including revenues by source, expenditures by function and locality, and fund balances, FY91-92, biennial rpt, S0780–1

Connecticut financial condition, including revenues by source, expenditures by function, and bonded debt, FY92, annual rpt, S1170–2

Florida higher education enrollment, degree programs, staff, and finances, by State-supported instn, with student and staff characteristics, 1991/92 annual rpt, S1725–1

Illinois higher education staff, salaries, student cost and aid, and finances, by instn, 1993 annual rpt, S2475–1.2

New Jersey financial condition, including revenues by source, expenditures by function, fund balances, and bonded debt, FY92, annual rpt, S5455–1

Oklahoma financial condition, including revenues by source, expenditures by function, and fund balances, FY91, annual rpt, S6438–1

South Dakota public higher education finances, staff, enrollment, degrees, and facilities, by instn, FY93 annual rpt, S7375–1

Tennessee higher education finances, student aid and expenses, and faculty and salaries, by instn, 1992/93 and trends, annual rpt, S7525–1.2

Texas financial condition, including revenues by source, expenditures by function and dept, and investments, with data for over 400 individual funds, FY92, annual rpt, S7655–2.2

Wisconsin financial condition, including revenues by source, expenditures by function and object, and fund balances, FY92, annual rpt, S8675–3

Wisconsin financial condition, including revenues by source, expenditures by function and object, and fund balances, FY93, annual rpt, S8675–2

see also Under State government spending for general State financial and budget data

State funding for natural resources and conservation

Govt finances, including revenues by source, expenditures by function, and debt, detailed data for Federal, State, and local govts, 1993 annual rpt, R9050–1

Recycling curbside program State grant funding status of municipalities, July 1991 survey, B0230–2

Recycling curbside program State grant practices, July 1991 survey, B0230–1

Statistical profiles of 50 States and DC, general data, 1993 annual almanac, C4712–1

State and local:

Alabama financial condition, including revenues by source, expenditures by function and object, and fund balances, by fund and agency, FY92, annual rpt, S0129–1

Alaska financial condition, including revenues by source, expenditures by function, fund balances, and bond obligations, FY92 and trends, annual rpt, S0275–1

Index by Subjects and Names

Arizona financial condition, including revenues by source, expenditures by function, and fund balances, FY91, annual rpt, S0450–2

Arizona financial condition, including revenues by source, expenditures by function, and fund balances, FY92, annual rpt, S0450–1

Arkansas financial condition, including revenues by source, expenditures by function and locality, and fund balances, FY91-92, biennial rpt, S0780–1

Arkansas financial condition, including revenues by source, expenditures by function and object, and fund balances, FY92, annual rpt, S0670–1

California financial condition, including revenues by source, expenditures by agency and function, fund balances, and bonded debt, FY92 and trends, annual rpt, S0815–1

Colorado financial condition, including receipts by source, and expenditures by function, FY92 and trends, annual rpt, S0980–1

Connecticut financial condition, including revenues by source, expenditures by function, and bonded debt, FY92, annual rpt, S1170–1, S1170–2

Florida financial condition, including receipts by source, expenditures by function, and fund balances, FY92, annual rpt, S1717–1, S1717–3

Georgia financial condition, including revenues by source, expenditures by function and object, and fund balances, FY92, annual rpt, S1860–1

Hawaii financial condition, including revenues by source, expenditures by function and object, and fund balances, FY92, annual rpt, S2020–1

Idaho financial condition, including revenues by source and expenditures by object, by agency and/or fund, FY92, annual rpt, S2215–1

Illinois financial condition, including revenues by source, and expenditures by object, function, and agency, FY92, annual rpt, S2415–1

Indiana financial condition, including revenues by source, expenditures by function and object, and fund balances, by agency, FY92, annual rpt, S2570–1

Iowa financial condition, including revenues by source, expenditures by function, and bonded debt, FY92 and trends, annual rpt, S2860–4

Kentucky financial condition, including revenues by source, expenditures by function and object, fund balances, and bonded debt, FY92, annual rpt, S3120–1

Louisiana financial condition, including revenues by source, expenditures by function, and fund balances, FY92 and trends, annual rpt, S3285–2

Maine financial condition, including revenues by source, expenditures by function and object, and fund balances, FY92, annual rpt, S3420–1

Maryland financial condition, including revenues by source, expenditures by function, fund balances, and bonded debt, FY92 and trends, annual rpt, S3685–2

Massachusetts financial condition, including revenues by source, and expenditures by function, by fund, FY92 and trends, annual rpt, S3777–1

Index by Subjects and Names

State funding for parks and recreation

Michigan financial condition, including revenues by source, expenditures by function, and fund balances, FY92 and trends, annual rpt, S3985–2

Minnesota financial condition, including revenues by source, expenditures by function, fund balances, and bonded debt, FY92 and trends, annual rpt, S4180–1

Mississippi financial condition, including revenues by source, expenditures by function and object, and detail by agency, FY92 and trends, annual rpt, S4346–1

Mississippi statistical abstract, general data, 1992 annual rpt, U3255–4.10

Missouri financial condition, including fund finances, tax collections and distribution, and State treasury activity, FY92 and trends, annual rpt, S4570–1

Missouri financial condition, including revenues by source, expenditures by function, and fund balances, FY92, annual rpt, S4475–1

Montana financial condition, including revenues by source, expenditures by function, and fund balances, FY92, annual rpt, S4653–1

Nebraska conservation tax receipts, 1990-91, annual rpt, S4950–1.3

Nevada financial condition, including fund revenues by source, expenditures by function, and bonded debt, FY92, annual rpt, S5025–1

New Jersey financial condition, including revenues by source, expenditures by function, fund balances, and bonded debt, FY92, annual rpt, S5455–1

New Mexico financial condition, including receipts by source, expenditures by agency and function, fund balances, and bonded debt, FY91, annual rpt, S5585–1

New York State financial condition, including revenues by source, expenditures by function, and fund balances, FY93, annual rpt, S5710–1

North Carolina financial condition, including revenues by source, expenditures by function, fund balances, and bonded debt, FY92, annual rpt, S5897–1

North Dakota financial condition, including revenues by source, expenditures by function, fund balances, and bonded debt, FY92, annual rpt, S6162–1

Ohio financial condition, including revenues by source, expenditures by function, and fund balances, FY92, annual rpt, S6255–1

Oklahoma financial condition, including revenues by source, expenditures by function, and fund balances, FY91, annual rpt, S6438–1

Oregon financial condition, including revenues by source, expenditures by function, and fund statements, FY92, annual rpt, S6603–2

Pennsylvania financial condition, including revenues by source, expenditures by function, and fund balances, FY92 and trends, annual rpt, S6810–4

Pennsylvania statistical abstract, general data, 1992 recurring rpt, U4130–6.8

Rhode Island financial condition, including revenues by source, expenditures by function, and fund balances, FY92 and trends, annual rpt, S6930–1

South Carolina financial condition, including receipts by source, expenditures by function, fund balances, and bonded debt, FY92, annual rpt, S7127–1

South Dakota financial condition, including revenues by source, expenditures by function, fund balances, and bonded debt, FY92, annual rpt, S7330–1

Tennessee financial condition, including revenues by source, expenditures by function and object, and fund balances, FY92, annual rpt, S7505–1

Texas financial condition, including revenues by source, expenditures by function, and bonded indebtedness, FY92, annual rpt, S7655–3

Texas financial condition, including revenues by source, expenditures by function and dept, and investments, with data for over 400 individual funds, FY92, annual rpt, S7655–2.2

Utah financial condition, including revenues by source, expenditures by function and agency, and fund balances, FY92, annual rpt, S7795–1

Vermont financial condition, including revenues by source, expenditures by function, fund balances, and bonded debt, FY92, annual rpt, S8035–1

Virginia financial condition, including revenues by source, expenditures by function, and fund balances, FY92 and trends, annual rpt, S8170–1

Washington State financial condition, including revenues by source, expenditures by function, fund balances, and bonded debt, FY92, annual rpt, S8345–3

Wisconsin Blue Book, general data, 1993-94 biennial rpt, S8780–1.2

Wisconsin financial condition, including revenues by source, expenditures by function and object, and fund balances, FY92, annual rpt, S8675–3

Wisconsin financial condition, including revenues by source, expenditures by function and object, and fund balances, FY93, annual rpt, S8675–2

Wyoming financial condition, including revenues by source, expenditures by function, and fund balances, FY92 and trends, annual rpt, S8875–1

see also State funding for energy programs

see also State funding for parks and recreation

see also Under State government spending for general State financial and budget data

State funding for parks and recreation

State and local:

Alabama financial condition, including revenues by source, expenditures by function and object, and fund balances, by fund and agency, FY92, annual rpt, S0129–1

Alaska financial condition, including revenues by source, expenditures by function, fund balances, and bond obligations, FY92 and trends, annual rpt, S0275–1

Arkansas financial condition, including revenues by source, expenditures by function and locality, and fund balances, FY91-92, biennial rpt, S0780–1

Arkansas financial condition, including revenues by source, expenditures by function and object, and fund balances, FY92, annual rpt, S0670–1

California financial condition, including revenues by source, expenditures by agency and function, fund balances, and bonded debt, FY92 and trends, annual rpt, S0815–1

Florida financial condition, including receipts by source, expenditures by function, and fund balances, FY92, annual rpt, S1717–1

Idaho financial condition, including revenues by source and expenditures by object, by agency and/or fund, FY92, annual rpt, S2215–1

Illinois financial condition, including revenues by source, and expenditures by object, function, and agency, FY92, annual rpt, S2415–1

Indiana financial condition, including revenues by source, expenditures by function and object, and fund balances, by agency, FY92, annual rpt, S2570–1

Kentucky financial condition, including revenues by source, expenditures by function and object, fund balances, and bonded debt, FY92, annual rpt, S3120–1

Louisiana financial condition, including revenues by source, expenditures by function, and fund balances, FY92 and trends, annual rpt, S3285–2

Maine financial condition, including revenues by source, expenditures by function and object, and fund balances, FY92, annual rpt, S3420–1

Michigan financial condition, including revenues by source, expenditures by function, and fund balances, FY92 and trends, annual rpt, S3985–2

Mississippi financial condition, including revenues by source, expenditures by function and object, and detail by agency, FY92 and trends, annual rpt, S4346–1

Missouri financial condition, including revenues by source, expenditures by function, and fund balances, FY92, annual rpt, S4475–1

Montana financial condition, including revenues by source, expenditures by function, and fund balances, FY92, annual rpt, S4653–1

Nebraska financial condition, including revenues by source, expenditures by function and agency, and fund balances, FY92, annual rpt, S4825–1

Nevada financial condition, including fund revenues by source, expenditures by function, and bonded debt, FY92, annual rpt, S5025–1

New Hampshire financial condition, with revenues by source, expenditures by function or object, and fund balances, FY92 and trends, annual rpt, S5175–1

New Jersey financial condition, including revenues by source, expenditures by function, fund balances, and bonded debt, FY92, annual rpt, S5455–1

New York State financial condition, including revenues by source, expenditures by function, and fund balances, FY93, annual rpt, S5710–1

North Dakota financial condition, including revenues by source, expenditures by function, fund balances, and bonded debt, FY92, annual rpt, S6162–1

Ohio financial condition, including revenues by source, expenditures by function, and fund balances, FY92, annual rpt, S6255–1

State funding for parks and recreation

Oklahoma financial condition, including revenues by source, expenditures by function, and fund balances, FY91, annual rpt, S6438–1

Rhode Island financial condition, including revenues by source, expenditures by function, and fund balances, FY92 and trends, annual rpt, S6930–1

South Carolina financial condition, including receipts by source, expenditures by function, fund balances, and bonded debt, FY92, annual rpt, S7127–1

South Dakota financial condition, including revenues by source, expenditures by function, fund balances, and bonded debt, FY92, annual rpt, S7330–1

Tennessee financial condition, including revenues by source, expenditures by function and object, and fund balances, FY92, annual rpt, S7505–1

Texas financial condition, including revenues by source, expenditures by function, and bonded indebtedness, FY92, annual rpt, S7655–3

Texas financial condition, including revenues by source, expenditures by function and dept, and investments, with data for over 400 individual funds, FY92, annual rpt, S7655–2.2

Utah financial condition, including revenues by source, expenditures by function and agency, and fund balances, FY92, annual rpt, S7795–1

Wisconsin Blue Book, general data, 1993-94 biennial rpt, S8780–1.2

Wisconsin financial condition, including revenues by source, expenditures by function and object, and fund balances, FY92, annual rpt, S8675–3

see also Under State government spending for general State financial and budget data

State funding for public safety

Expenditures of State/local govts for law enforcement, by State, FY91, semiannual rpt, B8500–1.10

Govt finances, including revenues by source, expenditures by function, and debt, detailed data for Federal, State, and local govts, 1993 annual rpt, R9050–1

Statistical profiles of 50 States and DC, general data, 1993 annual almanac, C4712–1

State and local:

Alabama statistical abstract, general data, 1992 recurring rpt, U5680–2.10

Arizona financial condition, including revenues by source, expenditures by function, and fund balances, FY91, annual rpt, S0450–2

Arizona financial condition, including revenues by source, expenditures by function, and fund balances, FY92, annual rpt, S0450–1

Arizona statistical abstract, general data, 1993 recurring rpt, U5850–2.12

Arkansas financial condition, including revenues by source, expenditures by function and locality, and fund balances, FY91-92, biennial rpt, S0780–1

Arkansas financial condition, including revenues by source, expenditures by function and object, and fund balances, FY92, annual rpt, S0670–1

California financial condition, including revenues by source, expenditures by

agency and function, fund balances, and bonded debt, FY92 and trends, annual rpt, S0815–1

California railroad crossing protection/maintenance and grade separation project funding, FY92 annual rpt, S0930–1

Colorado financial condition, including receipts by source, and expenditures by function, FY92 and trends, annual rpt, S0980–1

Connecticut financial condition, including revenues by source, expenditures by function, and bonded debt, FY92, annual rpt, S1170–1

DC financial condition, including receipts by source, expenditures by object or function, and fund balances, FY92, annual rpt, S1507–1

DC govt criminal justice expenditures, by function, FY87-91, annual rpt, S1535–2

Florida financial condition, including receipts by source, expenditures by function, and fund balances, FY92, annual rpt, S1717–1, S1717–3

Georgia financial condition, including revenues by source, expenditures by function and object, and fund balances, FY92, annual rpt, S1860–1

Hawaii data book, general data, 1992 annual rpt, S2090–1.4

Idaho financial condition, including revenues by source and expenditures by object, by agency and/or fund, FY92, annual rpt, S2215–1

Illinois financial condition, including revenues by source, and expenditures by object, function, and agency, FY92, annual rpt, S2415–1

Indiana financial condition, including revenues by source, expenditures by function and object, and fund balances, by agency, FY92, annual rpt, S2570–1

Iowa financial condition, including revenues by source, expenditures by function, and bonded debt, FY92 and trends, annual rpt, S2860–4

Kentucky financial condition, including revenues by source, expenditures by function and object, fund balanccs, and bonded debt, FY92, annual rpt, S3120–1

Louisiana financial condition, including revenues by source, expenditures by function, and fund balances, FY92 and trends, annual rpt, S3285–2

Maine financial condition, including revenues by source, expenditures by function and object, and fund balances, FY92, annual rpt, S3420–1

Michigan financial condition, including revenues by source, expenditures by function, and fund balances, FY92 and trends, annual rpt, S3985–2

Minnesota financial condition, including revenues by source, expenditures by function, fund balances, and bonded debt, FY92 and trends, annual rpt, S4180–1

Mississippi financial condition, including revenues by source, expenditures by function and object, and detail by agency, FY92 and trends, annual rpt, S4346–1

Missouri financial condition, including revenues and expenditures by agency, and tax collections and distribution, FY92 and trends, annual rpt, S4570–1.1

Index by Subjects and Names

Montana financial condition, including revenues by source, expenditures by function, and fund balances, FY92, annual rpt, S4653–1

Nevada financial condition, including fund revenues by source, expenditures by function, and bonded debt, FY92, annual rpt, S5025–1

New Mexico financial condition, including receipts by source, expenditures by agency and function, fund balances, and bonded debt, FY91, annual rpt, S5585–1

North Carolina financial condition, including revenues by source, expenditures by function, fund balances, and bonded debt, FY92, annual rpt, S5897–1

North Dakota financial condition, including revenues by source, expenditures by function, fund balances, and bonded debt, FY92, annual rpt, S6162–1

Ohio financial condition, including revenues by source, expenditures by function, and fund balances, FY92, annual rpt, S6255–1

Oklahoma financial condition, including revenues by source, expenditures by function, and fund balances, FY91, annual rpt, S6438–1

Oregon financial condition, including revenues by source, expenditures by function, and fund statements, FY92, annual rpt, S6603–2

Rhode Island financial condition, including revenues by source, expenditures by function, and fund balances, FY92 and trends, annual rpt, S6930–1

South Carolina financial condition, including receipts by source, expenditures by function, fund balances, and bonded debt, FY92, annual rpt, S7127–1

South Carolina insurance dept county allocation of fire dept premium taxes, 1991, annual rpt, S7195–1

Tennessee financial condition, including revenues by source, expenditures by function and object, and fund balances, FY92, annual rpt, S7505–1

Tennessee statistical abstract, general data, 1992/93 annual rpt, U8710–2.19

Texas financial condition, including revenues by source, expenditures by function and dept, and investments, with data for over 400 individual funds, FY92, annual rpt, S7655–2.2

Utah financial condition, including revenues by source, expenditures by function and agency, and fund balances, FY92, annual rpt, S7795–1

Wisconsin financial condition, including revenues by source, expenditures by function and object, and fund balances, FY93, annual rpt, S8675–2

see also Under State government spending for general State financial and budget data

State funding for public works

see State funding for capital projects

see State funding for highways and streets

State funding for social welfare

Economic dev condition indicators, including economic performance, business vitality, growth capacity, and tax/fiscal system, by State, 1993 annual rpt, R4225–1.1

Expenditure levels of State/local govts, and selected program costs, by State, 1993 semiannual rpt, B8500–1.8

Index by Subjects and Names

State funding for social welfare

Expenditures for education and welfare as percents of State govt spending, by State, FY91, article, B8500–2.503

Expenditures of State govts by fund source and function, by State, FY90-92, annual rpt, A7118–1

General assistance benefits for single person, with comparison to fair market rent for an efficiency apartment, for 44 metro areas, 1992, R3834–16

Govt finances, including revenues by source, expenditures by function, and debt, detailed data for Federal, State, and local govts, 1993 annual rpt, R9050–1

Medicaid child and total recipients, expenditures, and other program characteristics, and child health summary, by State, FY91, annual rpt, A0565–1

Public assistance program State funding and tax changes, by State, with analysis of impact on the poor, FY92-93, annual rpt, R3834–9

Statistical profiles of 50 States and DC, general data, 1993 annual almanac, C4712–1

State and local:

Alabama financial condition, including revenues by source, expenditures by function and object, and fund balances, by fund and agency, FY92, annual rpt, S0129–1

Alabama public welfare and social service cases, recipients, and payments, by program and county, monthly rpt, S0150–1

Arizona financial condition, including revenues by source, expenditures by function, and fund balances, FY91, annual rpt, S0450–2

Arizona financial condition, including revenues by source, expenditures by function, and fund balances, FY92, annual rpt, S0450–1

Arizona public assistance recipients and payments, by program, county, and district, monthly rpt, S0465–4

Arkansas financial condition, including revenues by source, expenditures by function and locality, and fund balances, FY91-92, biennial rpt, S0780–1

Arkansas financial condition, including revenues by source, expenditures by function and object, and fund balances, FY92, annual rpt, S0670–1

Arkansas human services dept finances and operations, including service recipient characteristics, by program, FY91 and trends, annual rpt, S0700–2

California financial condition, including revenues by source, expenditures by agency and function, fund balances, and bonded debt, FY92 and trends, annual rpt, S0815–1

Colorado welfare and social services expenditures and caseloads, by county and/or program, FY91, annual rpt, S1085–1

Connecticut financial condition, including revenues by source, expenditures by function, and bonded debt, FY92, annual rpt, S1170–1

DC financial condition, including receipts by source, expenditures by object or function, and fund balances, FY92, annual rpt, S1507–1

Delaware public assistance recipients, funds available, and payments, by program, with selected data by county, monthly rpt, S1385–1

Georgia financial condition, including revenues by source, expenditures by function and object, and fund balances, FY92, annual rpt, S1860–1

Georgia State constitutional amendment on trust fund for indigent care, election results by county, Nov 1992, biennial rpt, S1955–1

Hawaii data book, general data, 1992 annual rpt, S2090–1.11

Hawaii financial condition, including revenues by source, expenditures by function, and fund balances, FY92, annual rpt, S2020–1

Idaho public welfare program expenditures and recipients, with data by county, quarterly rpt, S2250–1

Illinois financial condition, including revenues by source, and expenditures by object, function, and agency, FY92, annual rpt, S2415–1

Illinois public assistance program cases, recipients, and payments, by program and county, FY91-92 and trends, annual rpt, S2520–2

Indiana financial condition, including revenues by source, expenditures by function and object, and fund balances, by agency, FY92, annual rpt, S2570–1

Indiana public assistance program participation, expenditures, and services, by county, FY92 and trends, annual rpt, S2623–1

Iowa ADC and SSI program recipients, and expenditures, by county, monthly rpt, S2802–1

Iowa financial condition, including revenues by source, expenditures by function, and bonded debt, FY92 and trends, annual rpt, S2860–4

Kentucky AFDC and SSI recipients and payments, by county, monthly rpt, S3140–2

Kentucky financial condition, including revenues by source, expenditures by function and object, fund balances, and bonded debt, FY92, annual rpt, S3120–1

Kentucky Medicaid recipients and payments, by program, county, and type of medical service, monthly rpt, S3140–5

Maine financial condition, including revenues by source, expenditures by function and object, and fund balances, FY92, annual rpt, S3420–1

Maryland welfare program statistics, and welfare fraud investigations, by county, monthly rpt, S3645–2

Michigan public assistance program cases, recipients, and payments, detailed data by county, monthly rpt, S4010–1

Minnesota financial condition, including revenues by source, expenditures by function, fund balances, and bonded debt, FY92 and trends, annual rpt, S4180–1

Minnesota public welfare program recipients and expenditures, by county, 1992, semiannual rpt, S4202–1

Mississippi financial condition, including revenues by source, expenditures by function and object, and detail by agency, FY92 and trends, annual rpt, S4346–1

Mississippi public welfare and social service cases, recipients, and payments, by program and county, FY92, annual rpt, S4357–1

Mississippi statistical abstract, general data, 1992 annual rpt, U3255–4.12

Missouri financial condition, including revenues and expenditures by agency, and tax collections and distribution, FY92 and trends, annual rpt, S4570–1.1

Missouri financial condition, including revenues by source, expenditures by function, and fund balances, FY92, annual rpt, S4475–1

Missouri public welfare and medical assistance recipients, expenditures, and case processing, by program and county, FY92 and trends, annual rpt, S4575–2

Montana financial condition, including revenues by source, expenditures by function, and fund balances, FY92, annual rpt, S4653–1

Montana welfare and medical assistance program cases and payments, by county and type of service, monthly rpt, S4755–1

Nebraska financial condition, including revenues by source, expenditures by function and agency, and fund balances, FY92, annual rpt, S4825–1

Nebraska public welfare cases, recipients, and payments, by program and county, FY92 and trends, annual rpt, S4957–1

Nevada statistical abstract, general data, 1992 biennial rpt, S5005–1.2, S5005–1.8

New Jersey financial condition, including revenues by source, expenditures by function, fund balances, and bonded debt, FY92, annual rpt, S5455–1

New Jersey public welfare cases, recipients, payments, and case processing, by program and county or city, monthly rpt, S5415–1

New Mexico financial condition, including receipts by source, expenditures by agency and function, fund balances, and bonded debt, FY91, annual rpt, S5585–1

New York State public assistance and social service program statistics, by State area and source of funds, 1991 and trends, annual rpt, S5800–2

New York State statistical yearbook, general data, 1992 annual rpt, U5100–1.11

North Carolina financial condition, including revenues by source, expenditures by function, fund balances, and bonded debt, FY92, annual rpt, S5897–1

North Carolina public welfare programs, cases, recipients, staff, and finances, by county, 1st half FY93, semiannual rpt, S5940–2

North Dakota financial condition, including revenues by source, expenditures by function, fund balances, and bonded debt, FY92, annual rpt, S6162–1

Ohio financial condition, including revenues by source, expenditures by function, and fund balances, FY92, annual rpt, S6255–1

Oklahoma financial condition, including revenues by source, expenditures by function, and fund balances, FY91, annual rpt, S6438–1

Oklahoma public welfare program expenditures, recipients, and services, by program and county, FY92 and trends, annual rpt, S6455–1

State funding for social welfare

Oklahoma statistical abstract, general data, 1992 annual rpt, U8130–2.10

Oregon financial condition, including revenues by source, expenditures by function, and fund statements, FY92, annual rpt, S6603–2

Oregon public welfare caseloads, recipients, and expenditures, by program, city, county, and State region, monthly rpt, S6615–8

Pennsylvania statistical abstract, general data, 1992 recurring rpt, U4130–6.5

Rhode Island financial condition, including revenues by source, expenditures by function, and fund balances, FY92 and trends, annual rpt, S6930–1

South Carolina public welfare recipients, payments, and case processing, by county and program, monthly rpt, S7252–1

South Dakota financial condition, including revenues by source, expenditures by function, fund balances, and bonded debt, FY92, annual rpt, S7330–1

South Dakota welfare expenditures, by program, MSA, and county, FY92, annual rpt, S7385–1

Tennessee financial condition, including revenues by source, expenditures by function and object, and fund balances, FY92, annual rpt, S7505–1

Tennessee statistical abstract, general data, 1992/93 annual rpt, U8710–2.18

Texas financial condition, including revenues by source, expenditures by function, and bonded indebtedness, FY92, annual rpt, S7655–3

Texas financial condition, including revenues by source, expenditures by function and dept, and investments, with data for over 400 individual funds, FY92, annual rpt, S7655–2.2

Texas welfare and social services program expenditures, recipients, and fraud cases, by county and/or program, FY92 and trends, annual rpt, S7695–1

Utah financial condition, including revenues by source, expenditures by function and agency, and fund balances, FY92, annual rpt, S7795–1

Utah govt statistical review, fiscal and socioeconomic data, 1993 annual rpt, R9380–1.9

Utah statistical abstract, general data, 1993 triennial rpt, U8960–1.6

Washington State financial condition, including revenues by source, expenditures by function, fund balances, and bonded debt, FY92, annual rpt, S8345–3

Washington State public assistance clients and service costs, by client characteristics, program, and county, FY90, annual rpt, S8420–2

West Virginia statistical handbook, general data, 1992 annual rpt, R9385–1.2

West Virginia welfare and social service program caseloads and expenditures, by county, monthly rpt, S8560–2

Wisconsin Blue Book, general data, 1993-94 biennial rpt, S8780–1.2

Wisconsin financial condition, including revenues by source, expenditures by function and object, and fund balances, FY92, annual rpt, S8675–3

Wisconsin financial condition, including revenues by source, expenditures by function and object, and fund balances, FY93, annual rpt, S8675–2

Wyoming financial condition, including revenues by source, expenditures by function, and fund balances, FY92 and trends, annual rpt, S8875–1

Wyoming welfare and social service recipients and expenditures, by program and county, FY92, annual rpt, S8908–1

see also State retirement systems

see also Under State government spending for general State financial and budget data

State funding for transportation

Expenditures of State govts by fund source and function, by State, FY90-92, annual rpt, A7118–1

Expenditures of State/local govts for transportation, by State, 1990-91, semiannual rpt, B8500–1.11

Expenditures on facilities/services, by transport mode, 1992 annual rpt, R4815–1

Mass transit industry statistics, including govt funding, vehicle purchasing, and bus production, 1992/93 annual fact book, C1575–3.501

Mass transit system finances and operations, including govt assistance, 1976-92, annual rpt, A2650–1.1

Motorcycle operator education program sites, grads, instructors, and funding info, by State, 1991, annual rpt, A6485–1.2

School bus funding and operations issues, with median State pupil transportation budgets, 1991/92-1993/94, annual article, C1575–1.504

School bus pupil transportation, accident, and expenditure statistics, by State, 1993 annual feature, C1575–1.502

State and local:

Alabama financial condition, including revenues by source, expenditures by function and object, and fund balances, by fund and agency, FY92, annual rpt, S0129–1

Alaska financial condition, including revenues by source, expenditures by function, fund balances, and bond obligations, FY92 and trends, annual rpt, S0275–1

Arizona financial condition, including revenues by source, expenditures by function, and fund balances, FY91, annual rpt, S0450–2

Arizona financial condition, including revenues by source, expenditures by function, and fund balances, FY92, annual rpt, S0450–1

Arkansas financial condition, including revenues by source, expenditures by function and locality, and fund balances, FY91-92, biennial rpt, S0780–1

Arkansas financial condition, including revenues by source, expenditures by function and object, and fund balances, FY92, annual rpt, S0670–1

California financial condition, including revenues by source, expenditures by agency and function, fund balances, and bonded debt, FY92 and trends, annual rpt, S0815–1

California railroad crossing protection/maintenance and grade separation project funding, FY92 annual rpt, S0930–1

Connecticut financial condition, including revenues by source, expenditures by function, and bonded debt, FY92, annual rpt, S1170–1, S1170–2

Florida financial condition, including receipts by source, expenditures by function, and fund balances, FY92, annual rpt, S1717–1, S1717–3

Georgia financial condition, including revenues by source, expenditures by function and object, and fund balances, FY92, annual rpt, S1860–1

Georgia State constitutional amendment on trust fund for transportation, election results by county, Nov 1992, biennial rpt, S1955–1

Hawaii financial condition, including revenues by source, expenditures by function, and fund balances, FY92, annual rpt, S2020–1

Illinois financial condition, including revenues by source, and expenditures by object, function, and agency, FY92, annual rpt, S2415–1

Indiana financial condition, including revenues by source, expenditures by function and object, and fund balances, by agency, FY92, annual rpt, S2570–1

Iowa financial condition, including revenues by source, expenditures by function, and bonded debt, FY92 and trends, annual rpt, S2860–4

Kansas financial condition, including revenues by source, expenditures by function and object, and fund balances, FY92, annual rpt, S2900–1

Kentucky financial condition, including revenues by source, expenditures by function and object, fund balances, and bonded debt, FY92, annual rpt, S3120–1

Louisiana financial condition, including revenues by source, expenditures by function, and fund balances, FY92 and trends, annual rpt, S3285–2

Maine financial condition, including revenues by source, expenditures by function and object, and fund balances, FY92, annual rpt, S3420–1

Maryland financial condition, including revenues by source, expenditures by function, fund balances, and bonded debt, FY92 and trends, annual rpt, S3685–2

Massachusetts financial condition, including revenues by source, and expenditures by function, by fund, FY92 and trends, annual rpt, S3777–1

Michigan financial condition, including revenues by source, expenditures by function, and fund balances, FY92 and trends, annual rpt, S3985–2

Minnesota financial condition, including revenues by source, expenditures by function, fund balances, and bonded debt, FY92 and trends, annual rpt, S4180–1

Mississippi financial condition, including revenues by source, expenditures by function and object, and detail by agency, FY92 and trends, annual rpt, S4346–1

Missouri financial condition, including fund finances, tax collections and distribution, and State treasury activity, FY92 and trends, annual rpt, S4570–1

Missouri financial condition, including revenues by source, expenditures by function, and fund balances, FY92, annual rpt, S4475–1

State government

Montana financial condition, including revenues by source, expenditures by function, and fund balances, FY92, annual rpt, S4653–1

Nebraska financial condition, including revenues by source, expenditures by function and agency, and fund balances, FY92, annual rpt, S4825–1

New Jersey financial condition, including revenues by source, expenditures by function, fund balances, and bonded debt, FY92, annual rpt, S5455–1

New Mexico financial condition, including receipts by source, expenditures by agency and function, fund balances, and bonded debt, FY91, annual rpt, S5585–1

New York State financial condition, including revenues by source, expenditures by function, and fund balances, FY93, annual rpt, S5710–1

North Carolina financial condition, including revenues by source, expenditures by function, fund balances, and bonded debt, FY92, annual rpt, S5897–1

North Dakota financial condition, including revenues by source, expenditures by function, fund balances, and bonded debt, FY92, annual rpt, S6162–1

Ohio financial condition, including revenues by source, expenditures by function, and fund balances, FY92, annual rpt, S6255–1

Oklahoma financial condition, including revenues by source, expenditures by function, and fund balances, FY91, annual rpt, S6438–1

Oregon financial condition, including revenues by source, expenditures by function, and fund statements, FY92, annual rpt, S6603–2

Pennsylvania statistical abstract, general data, 1992 recurring rpt, U4130–6.9

Rhode Island financial condition, including revenues by source, expenditures by function, and fund balances, FY92 and trends, annual rpt, S6930–1

South Carolina financial condition, including receipts by source, expenditures by function, fund balances, and bonded debt, FY92, annual rpt, S7127–1

South Dakota financial condition, including revenues by source, expenditures by function, fund balances, and bonded debt, FY92, annual rpt, S7330–1

Texas financial condition, including revenues by source, expenditures by function and dept, and investments, with data for over 400 individual funds, FY92, annual rpt, S7655–2.2

Utah financial condition, including revenues by source, expenditures by function and agency, and fund balances, FY92, annual rpt, S7795–1

Utah tax revenues by source, and distribution to localities and State funds, FY92 and trends, annual rpt, S7905–1

Vermont financial condition, including revenues by source, expenditures by function, fund balances, and bonded debt, FY92, annual rpt, S8035–1

Virginia financial condition, including revenues by source, expenditures by function, and fund balances, FY92 and trends, annual rpt, S8170–1

Washington State financial condition, including revenues by source, expenditures by function, fund balances, and bonded debt, FY92, annual rpt, S8345–3

Wisconsin financial condition, including revenues by source, expenditures by function and object, and fund balances, FY92, annual rpt, S8675–3

Wisconsin financial condition, including revenues by source, expenditures by function and object, and fund balances, FY93, annual rpt, S8675–2

Wyoming financial condition, including revenues by source, expenditures by function, and fund balances, FY92 and trends, annual rpt, S8875–1

see also State funding for highways and streets

see also Under State government spending for general State financial and budget data

State funding for urban development

see State funding for economic development

see State funding for local areas

State funding for vocational education

Appropriations for higher education, by State, instn, and function, 1993/94, annual feature, C2175–1.S38

Appropriations of tax funds for higher education, by State, instn, and function, FY92-93 and trends, annual rpt, A8970–1

State and local:

Alabama elementary and secondary school enrollment, staff, pupil transportation, and finances, by district, 1991/92, annual rpt, S0124–1

Arkansas financial condition, including revenues by source, expenditures by function and locality, and fund balances, FY91-92, biennial rpt, S0780–1

Arkansas financial condition, including revenues by source, expenditures by function and object, and fund balances, FY92, annual rpt, S0670–1

California financial condition, including revenues by source, expenditures by agency and function, fund balances, and bonded debt, FY92 and trends, annual rpt, S0815–1

Connecticut education dept staff and expenditures, by div, 1991/92, annual rpt, S1185–1

Delaware public education revenues by source, and expenditures by function and program, 1991/92, annual rpt, S1430–1.4

Indiana financial condition, including revenues by source, expenditures by function and object, and fund balances, by agency, FY92, annual rpt, S2570–1

Indiana public school funding for vocational education, by district, 1991/92, annual table, S2608–2.2, S2608–2.11

Kansas school district revenues by source and expenditures by object, 1990/91, annual rpt, S2945–1

Louisiana education dept revenues by source and expenditures by function, 1991/92 and trends, annual rpt, S3280–1.1

Missouri public school finances, staff, students, and programs, detailed data, 1991/92, annual rpt, S4505–1.1

Montana financial condition, including revenues by source, expenditures by function, and fund balances, FY92, annual rpt, S4653–1

Oklahoma financial condition, including revenues by source, expenditures by function, and fund balances, FY91, annual rpt, S6438–1

South Dakota financial condition, including revenues by source, expenditures by function, fund balances, and bonded debt, FY92, annual rpt, S7330–1

Tennessee higher education finances, student aid and expenses, and faculty and salaries, by instn, 1992/93 and trends, annual rpt, S7525–1.2

Tennessee public school finances, by county, city, and school district, 1991/92, annual rpt, S7490–2.4

Texas financial condition, including revenues by source, expenditures by function and dept, and investments, with data for over 400 individual funds, FY92, annual rpt, S7655–2.2

Utah public school revenues by source and expenditures by object, by State fund and school district, FY92, annual rpt, S7815–1.2

Virginia public school enrollment, grads, finances, and staff, by county and municipality, 1991/92, annual rpt, S8190–3

Wisconsin financial condition, including revenues by source, expenditures by function and object, and fund balances, FY93, annual rpt, S8675–2

Wyoming penitentiary vocational education funding, by program, FY92, annual rpt, S8883–1

see also Under State government spending for general State financial and budget data

State government

Air pollutant (sulfur dioxide) emission allowance trading program, State regulatory issues and related data by State and major utility, 1992 rpt, A8195–12

Election results for Federal offices and Governor, by State, county, major city, and party, with voter registration and turnout, 1992 and trends, biennial rpt, C2500–1

Fiscal issues for State govts, including employment, programs, revenues, and expenditures, with data by State, series, U5085–2

Info resources mgmt, including data on budgets, staff, and organizational structure, by State, 1991, biennial rpt, A7121–1

Social and economic devs relevant to State govt policy decisions, with data by State, semimonthly rpt, B8500–2

Social, economic, and govtl indicators, with rankings by State, 1993 semiannual rpt, B8500–1

Water resources planning status and activities, by State, 1991 rpt, A8195–11

State and local:

Delaware public opinion on performance of selected branches of State govt, Feb 1991 survey, R8825–11

see also Federal aid to States

see also Federal-State relations

see also Government assets and liabilities

see also Gubernatorial vetoes

see also Interstate compacts

see also State and local employees

see also State and local employees pay

State government

see also State and local taxes
see also State bonds
see also State budgets
see also State constitutional amendments
see also State constitutional conventions
see also State courts
see also State forests
see also State funding for agriculture
see also State funding for arts and culture
see also State funding for capital projects
see also State funding for corrections
see also State funding for courts
see also State funding for economic development
see also State funding for education
see also State funding for employment
see also State funding for energy programs
see also State funding for health and hospitals
see also State funding for higher education
see also State funding for highways and streets
see also State funding for housing
see also State funding for libraries
see also State funding for local areas
see also State funding for medical education
see also State funding for natural resources and conservation
see also State funding for parks and recreation
see also State funding for public safety
see also State funding for social welfare
see also State funding for transportation
see also State funding for vocational education
see also State government revenues
see also State government spending
see also State legislatures
see also State-local relations
see also State parks
see also State police
see also State retirement systems
see also under By Government Agency in the "Index by Categories"
see also under By State in the "Index by Categories"
see also under names of individual States

State government debt
see Government assets and liabilities
see Public debt

State government revenues
Finances of govt, including revenues by source, expenditures by function, and debt, detailed data for Federal, State, and local govts, 1993 annual rpt, R9050–1
Fiscal issues for State govts, including budget balances, revenues, and expenditures, with data by State, series, A7470–4
General fund revenues, expenditures, and balances, and budget stabilization funds, by State, FY92-94 and trends, semiannual rpt, A7955–1
General revenues from total and own sources, by State, 1993 semiannual rpt, B8500–1.3
Lottery net revenue per capita and as percent of total State revenue, for 17 States, FY85 and FY91, article, B8500–2.S21
Medical malpractice insurance State joint underwriting assn (JUA) financial condition, for 11 States, 1991, annual rpt, A0375–1

Pari-mutuel wagering activity, attendance, purse distribution, and govt revenue, by State and Canadian Province, 1990 and trends, annual rpt, A3363–1
Statistical profiles of 50 States and DC, general data, 1993 annual almanac, C4712–1
Utility and transportation regulatory agency activities, scope of jurisdiction, finances, and employees, by agency, 1991/92 annual rpt, A7015–2

State and local:
Alabama financial condition, including revenues by source, expenditures by function and object, and fund balances, by fund and agency, FY92, annual rpt, S0129–1
Alabama statistical abstract, general data, 1992 recurring rpt, U5680–2.6
Alaska financial condition, including revenues by source, expenditures by function, fund balances, and bond obligations, FY92 and trends, annual rpt, S0275–1
Arizona financial condition, including revenues by source, expenditures by function, and fund balances, FY91, annual rpt, S0450–2
Arizona financial condition, including revenues by source, expenditures by function, and fund balances, FY92, annual rpt, S0450–1
Arizona statistical abstract, general data, 1993 recurring rpt, U5850–2.10
Arkansas financial condition, including revenues by source, expenditures by function and locality, and fund balances, FY91-92, biennial rpt, S0780–1
Arkansas financial condition, including revenues by source, expenditures by function and object, and fund balances, FY92, annual rpt, S0670–1
California financial condition, including revenues by source, expenditures by agency and function, fund balances, and bonded debt, FY92 and trends, annual rpt, S0815–1
California statistical abstract, general data, 1992 annual rpt, S0840–2.13
Colorado financial condition, including receipts by source, and expenditures by function, FY92 and trends, annual rpt, S0980·1
Connecticut financial condition, including revenues by source, expenditures by function, and bonded debt, FY92, annual rpt, S1170–1, S1170–2
DC financial condition, including receipts by source, expenditures by object or function, and fund balances, FY92, annual rpt, S1507–1
DC statistical profile, general data, 1992 annual rpt, S1535–3.2, S1535–3.7
Florida financial condition, including receipts by source, expenditures by function, and fund balances, FY92, annual rpt, S1717–1, S1717–3
Florida statistical abstract, general data, 1992 annual rpt, U6660–1.23
Georgia financial condition, including revenues by source, expenditures by function and object, and fund balances, FY92, annual rpt, S1860–1
Georgia statistical abstract, general data, 1992-93 biennial rpt, U6730–1.11

Hawaii data book, general data, 1992 annual rpt, S2090–1.9, S2090–1.13
Hawaii financial condition, including revenues by source, expenditures by function, and fund balances, FY92, annual rpt, S2020–1
Idaho economic profile, general data, 1992 recurring rpt, S2218–2.4
Idaho financial condition, including revenues by source and expenditures by object, by agency and/or fund, FY92, annual rpt, S2215–1
Illinois financial condition, including revenues by source, and expenditures by object, function, and agency, FY92, annual rpt, S2415–1
Illinois Public Aid Dept Collections Bureau recoveries, with detail by type, FY88-92, annual rpt, S2520–2
Indiana financial condition, including revenues by source, expenditures by function and object, and fund balances, by agency, FY92, annual rpt, S2570–1
Iowa financial condition, including revenues by source, expenditures by function, and bonded debt, FY92 and trends, annual rpt, S2860–4
Iowa State treasury financial operations, including receipts, disbursements, and detailed investment activity, FY92, annual rpt, S2885–1
Kansas financial condition, including revenues by source, expenditures by function and object, and fund balances, FY92, annual rpt, S2900–1
Kansas revenues by source, with comparisons to 5 neighboring States, FY92 annual rpt, S3020–1
Kansas statistical abstract, general data, 1991/92 annual rpt, U7095–2.11
Kentucky financial condition, including revenues by source, expenditures by function and object, fund balances, and bonded debt, FY92, annual rpt, S3120–1
Louisiana financial condition, including revenues by source, expenditures by function, and fund balances, FY92 and trends, annual rpt, S3285–2
Maine financial condition, including revenues by source, expenditures by function and object, and fund balances, FY92, annual rpt, S3420–1
Maryland financial condition, including revenues by source, expenditures by function, fund balances, and bonded debt, FY92 and trends, annual rpt, S3685–2
Maryland statistical abstract, general data, 1993-94 biennial rpt, S3605–1.7
Massachusetts financial condition, including revenues by source, and expenditures by function, by fund, FY92 and trends, annual rpt, S3777–1
Michigan child/spousal support collection program revenues and disbursements, by county, 1992, annual rpt, S3962–1.2
Michigan financial condition, including revenues by source, expenditures by function, and fund balances, FY92 and trends, annual rpt, S3985–2
Minnesota financial condition, including revenues by source, expenditures by function, fund balances, and bonded debt, FY92 and trends, annual rpt, S4180–1
Mississippi financial condition, including revenues by source, expenditures by function and object, and detail by agency, FY92 and trends, annual rpt, S4346–1

Index by Subjects and Names

State government spending

Mississippi State govt revenues, by source, FY92, annual rpt, S4435–1

Mississippi statistical abstract, general data, 1992 annual rpt, U3255–4.11

Missouri financial condition, including fund finances, tax collections and distribution, and State treasury activity, FY92 and trends, annual rpt, S4570–1

Missouri financial condition, including revenues by source, expenditures by function, and fund balances, FY92, annual rpt, S4475–1

Montana financial condition, including revenues by source, expenditures by function, and fund balances, FY92, annual rpt, S4653–1

Montana Revenue Dept collections from tax and nontax sources, FY88-92, biennial rpt, S4750–1.1

Nebraska financial condition, including revenues by source, expenditures by function and agency, and fund balances, FY92, annual rpt, S4825–1

Nevada financial condition, including fund revenues by source, expenditures by function, and bonded debt, FY92, annual rpt, S5025–1

Nevada statistical abstract, general data, 1992 biennial rpt, S5005–1.8

New Hampshire financial condition, with revenues by source, expenditures by function or object, and fund balances, FY92 and trends, annual rpt, S5175–1

New Jersey casino control commission revenues by source, FY91-92, annual rpt, S5360–1

New Jersey financial condition, including revenues by source, expenditures by function, fund balances, and bonded debt, FY92, annual rpt, S5455–1

New Mexico business and economic activity indicators, monthly rpt, U7980 1

New Mexico financial condition, including receipts by source, expenditures by agency and function, fund balances, and bonded debt, FY91, annual rpt, S5585–1

New Mexico public utility commission receipts and disbursements, FY92, annual rpt, S5645–1

New York State financial condition, including revenues by source, expenditures by function, and fund balances, FY93, annual rpt, S5710–1

New York State statistical yearbook, general data, 1992 annual rpt, U5100–1.5, U5100–1.15

North Carolina financial condition, including revenues by source, expenditures by function, fund balances, and bonded debt, FY92, annual rpt, S5897–1

North Dakota financial condition, including revenues by source, expenditures by function, fund balances, and bonded debt, FY92, annual rpt, S6162–1

Ohio financial condition, including revenues by source, expenditures by function, and fund balances, FY92, annual rpt, S6255–1

Ohio State govt revenues by source, FY92, annual rpt, S6390–1.1

Oklahoma financial condition, including revenues by source, expenditures by function, and fund balances, FY91, annual rpt, S6438–1

Oklahoma statistical abstract, general data, 1992 annual rpt, U8130–2.5

Oregon financial condition, including revenues by source, expenditures by function, and fund statements, FY92, annual rpt, S6603–2

Pennsylvania financial condition, including revenues by source, expenditures by function, and fund balances, FY92 and trends, annual rpt, S6810–4

Pennsylvania statistical abstract, general data, 1992 recurring rpt, U4130–6.6

Rhode Island financial condition, including revenues by source, expenditures by function, and fund balances, FY92 and trends, annual rpt, S6930–1

Rhode Island statistical almanac, general data, 1993 annual rpt, C7975–1.1

South Carolina economic condition, including agriculture, finance, and govt financial data, 1970s-92, annual rpt, S7125–3.1

South Carolina financial condition, including receipts by source, expenditures by function, fund balances, and bonded debt, FY92, annual rpt, S7127–1

South Carolina statistical abstract, general data, 1993 annual rpt, S7125–1.2

South Dakota financial condition, including revenues by source, expenditures by function, fund balances, and bonded debt, FY92, annual rpt, S7330–1

Tennessee financial condition, including revenues by source, expenditures by function and object, and fund balances, FY92, annual rpt, S7505–1

Tennessee statistical abstract, general data, 1992/93 annual rpt, U8710–2.15

Texas financial condition, including revenues by source, expenditures by function, and bonded indebtedness, FY92, annual rpt, S7655–3

Texas financial condition, including revenues by source, expenditures by function and dept, and investments, with data for over 400 individual funds, FY92, annual rpt, S7655–2

Texas insurance dept finances, including revenues, expenditures, and fund balances, FY92, annual rpt, S7700–1

Utah financial condition, including revenues by source, expenditures by function and agency, and fund balances, FY92, annual rpt, S7795–1

Utah govt statistical review, fiscal and socioeconomic data, 1993 annual rpt, R9380–1.5

Utah statistical abstract, general data, 1993 triennial rpt, U8960–1.7

Vermont financial condition, including revenues by source, expenditures by function, fund balances, and bonded debt, FY92, annual rpt, S8035–1

Virginia financial condition, including revenues by source, expenditures by function, and fund balances, FY92 and trends, annual rpt, S8170–1

Virginia State constitutional amendment creating a Revenue Stabilization Fund, election results by county and independent city, 1992, annual rpt, S8195–1

Washington State financial condition, including revenues by source, expenditures by function, fund balances, and bonded debt, FY92, annual rpt, S8345–3

Washington State treasury operations, including receipts, disbursements, aid to localities, and investments, by fund, FY92, annual rpt, S8455–1

West Virginia statistical handbook, general data, 1992 annual rpt, R9385–1.2, R9385–1.6

Wisconsin Blue Book, general data, 1993-94 biennial rpt, S8780–1.2

Wisconsin financial condition, including revenues by source, expenditures by function and object, and fund balances, FY92, annual rpt, S8675–3

Wisconsin financial condition, including revenues by source, expenditures by function and object, and fund balances, FY93, annual rpt, S8675–2

Wyoming financial condition, including revenues by source, expenditures by function, and fund balances, FY92 and trends, annual rpt, S8875–1

Wyoming general fund revenues by source, FY83-92, annual rpt, S8855–1

Wyoming State treasurer financial transactions, including revenues, investments, and disbursements by local area, FY92 and trends, annual rpt, S9010–1

see also Estate tax

see also Excise tax

see also Federal aid to States

see also Gift tax

see also Income taxes

see also License taxes and fees

see also Mineral leases

see also Oil and gas leases

see also Property tax

see also Revenue sharing

see also Sales tax

see also Severance taxes

see also State and local taxes

see also State budgets

see also Tolls

see also Unemployment insurance tax

State government spending

Charity gambling receipts, net proceeds, and State regulatory staff and finances, by State, various years FY90-92, article, C2176–1.512

Expenditures of State govts by fund source and function, by State, FY90-92, annual rpt, A7118–1

Expenditures of State/local govts, with detail by selected function, by State, 1993 semiannual rpt, B8500–1.5

Finances of govt, including revenues by source, expenditures by function, and debt, detailed data for Federal, State, and local govts, 1993 annual rpt, R9050–1

Fiscal conditions for New York and selected other States, including tax revenues, expenditures, and taxation of corporate profits, 1992 article, A8825–1.502

Fiscal issues for State govts, including budget balances, revenues, and expenditures, with data by State, series, A7470–4

General fund appropriation trends, with detail for education, prisons, AFDC, and Medicaid, by State, FY93, article, B8500–2.506

General fund expenditure changes proposed by Governors, by State, FY94, article, B8500–2.513

State government spending

General fund revenues, expenditures, and balances, and budget stabilization funds, by State, FY92-94 and trends, semiannual rpt, A7955–1

Medical malpractice insurance State joint underwriting assn (JUA) financial condition, for 11 States, 1991, annual rpt, A0375–1

Statistical profiles of 50 States and DC, general data, 1993 annual almanac, C4712–1

Utility and transportation regulatory agency activities, scope of jurisdiction, finances, and employees, by agency, 1991/92 annual rpt, A7015–2

State and local:

Alabama financial condition, including revenues by source, expenditures by function and object, and fund balances, by fund and agency, FY92, annual rpt, S0129–1

Alaska financial condition, including revenues by source, expenditures by function, fund balances, and bond obligations, FY92 and trends, annual rpt, S0275–1

Arizona financial condition, including revenues by source, expenditures by function, and fund balances, FY91, annual rpt, S0450–2

Arizona financial condition, including revenues by source, expenditures by function, and fund balances, FY92, annual rpt, S0450–1

Arizona State spending levels by function, views of economic analysts, 1991-93, annual survey article, U0282–1.504

Arizona statistical abstract, general data, 1993 recurring rpt, U5850–2.10

Arkansas financial condition, including revenues by source, expenditures by function and locality, and fund balances, FY91-92, biennial rpt, S0780–1

Arkansas financial condition, including revenues by source, expenditures by function and object, and fund balances, FY92, annual rpt, S0670–1

California financial condition, including revenues by source, expenditures by agency and function, fund balances, and bonded debt, FY92 and trends, annual rpt, S0815–1

California general fund appropriations by category, FY68-94, annual rpt, S0827–3

California statistical abstract, general data, 1992 annual rpt, S0840–2.13

California tax board administrative expenses and activities, FY91-92, annual rpt, S0835–1.1

Colorado financial condition, including receipts by source, and expenditures by function, FY92 and trends, annual rpt, S0980–1

Colorado State govt tax admin expenditures, FY92 and trends, annual rpt, S1075–1.1

Connecticut financial condition, including revenues by source, expenditures by function, and bonded debt, FY92, annual rpt, S1170–1, S1170–2

Connecticut State constitutional amendment to limit State govt spending, election results by location, 1992, biennial rpt, S1265–1

DC financial condition, including receipts by source, expenditures by object or function, and fund balances, FY92, annual rpt, S1507–1

DC govt expenditures by agency, FY87-91, annual rpt, S1535–2

DC statistical profile, general data, 1992 annual rpt, S1535–3.2

Florida financial condition, including receipts by source, expenditures by function, and fund balances, FY92, annual rpt, S1717–1, S1717–3

Florida statistical abstract, general data, 1992 annual rpt, U6660–1.23

Georgia financial condition, including revenues by source, expenditures by function and object, and fund balances, FY92, annual rpt, S1860–1

Georgia statistical abstract, general data, 1992-93 biennial rpt, U6730–1.11

Hawaii data book, general data, 1992 annual rpt, S2090–1.9, S2090–1.13

Hawaii financial condition, including revenues by source, expenditures by function, and fund balances, FY92, annual rpt, S2020–1

Idaho economic profile, general data, 1992 recurring rpt, S2218–2.4

Idaho financial condition, including revenues by source and expenditures by object, by agency and/or fund, FY92, annual rpt, S2215–1

Illinois financial condition, including revenues by source, and expenditures by object, function, and agency, FY92, annual rpt, S2415–1

Illinois statistical abstract, general data, 1992 annual rpt, U6910–2

Indiana financial condition, including revenues by source, expenditures by function and object, and fund balances, by agency, FY92, annual rpt, S2570–1

Iowa financial condition, including revenues by source, expenditures by function, and bonded debt, FY92 and trends, annual rpt, S2860–4

Iowa State treasury financial operations, including receipts, disbursements, and detailed investment activity, FY92, annual rpt, S2885–1

Kansas business activity indicators, quarterly rpt, U7095–1

Kansas expenditures by function and object, with comparisons to 5 neighboring States, FY92 annual rpt, S3020–1

Kansas financial condition, including revenues by source, expenditures by function and object, and fund balances, FY92, annual rpt, S2900–1

Kansas statistical abstract, general data, 1991/92 annual rpt, U7095–2.11

Kentucky financial condition, including revenues by source, expenditures by function and object, fund balances, and bonded debt, FY92, annual rpt, S3120–1

Louisiana financial condition, including revenues by source, expenditures by function, and fund balances, FY92 and trends, annual rpt, S3285–2

Maine financial condition, including revenues by source, expenditures by function and object, and fund balances, FY92, annual rpt, S3420–1

Maryland financial condition, including revenues by source, expenditures by function, fund balances, and bonded debt, FY92 and trends, annual rpt, S3685–2

Maryland statistical abstract, general data, 1993-94 biennial rpt, S3605–1.7

Massachusetts financial condition, including revenues by source, and expenditures by function, by fund, FY92 and trends, annual rpt, S3777–1

Michigan child/spousal support collection program revenues and disbursements, by county, 1992, annual rpt, S3962–1.2

Michigan financial condition, including revenues by source, expenditures by function, and fund balances, FY92 and trends, annual rpt, S3985–2

Minnesota financial condition, including revenues by source, expenditures by function, fund balances, and bonded debt, FY92 and trends, annual rpt, S4180–1

Mississippi financial condition, including revenues by source, expenditures by function and object, and detail by agency, FY92 and trends, annual rpt, S4346–1

Missouri financial condition, including fund finances, tax collections and distribution, and State treasury activity, FY92 and trends, annual rpt, S4570–1

Missouri financial condition, including revenues by source, expenditures by function, and fund balances, FY92, annual rpt, S4475–1

Montana financial condition, including revenues by source, expenditures by function, and fund balances, FY92, annual rpt, S4653–1

Nebraska financial condition, including revenues by source, expenditures by function and agency, and fund balances, FY92, annual rpt, S4825–1

Nevada financial condition, including fund revenues by source, expenditures by function, and bonded debt, FY92, annual rpt, S5025–1

Nevada statistical abstract, general data, 1992 biennial rpt, S5005–1.8

New Hampshire financial condition, with revenues by source, expenditures by function or object, and fund balances, FY92 and trends, annual rpt, S5175–1

New Jersey casino control commission expenditures by object, FY91-92, annual rpt, S5360–1

New Jersey financial condition, including revenues by source, expenditures by function, fund balances, and bonded debt, FY92, annual rpt, S5455–1

New Mexico financial condition, including receipts by source, expenditures by agency and function, fund balances, and bonded debt, FY91, annual rpt, S5585–1

New Mexico public utility commission receipts and disbursements, FY92, annual rpt, S5645–1

New Mexico tax dept budget and expenditures, by detailed item, FY91-92 and trends, annual rpt, S5660–1.1

New York State financial condition, including revenues by source, expenditures by function, and fund balances, FY93, annual rpt, S5710–1

New York State statistical yearbook, general data, 1992 annual rpt, U5100–1.5

North Carolina financial condition, including revenues by source, expenditures by function, fund balances, and bonded debt, FY92, annual rpt, S5897–1

North Dakota financial condition, including revenues by source, expenditures by function, fund balances, and bonded debt, FY92, annual rpt, S6162–1

Index by Subjects and Names

State legislatures

Ohio Dept of Taxation expenditures for personal service and maintenance/equipment, FY92, annual rpt, S6390–1.1

Ohio financial condition, including revenues by source, expenditures by function, and fund balances, FY92, annual rpt, S6255–1

Oklahoma financial condition, including revenues by source, expenditures by function, and fund balances, FY91, annual rpt, S6438–1

Oklahoma statistical abstract, general data, 1992 annual rpt, U8130–2.5

Oklahoma tax revenues by source, and distribution to local govts and State funds, FY92 and trends, annual rpt, S6495–1

Oregon financial condition, including revenues by source, expenditures by function, and fund statements, FY92, annual rpt, S6603–2

Pennsylvania financial condition, including revenues by source, expenditures by function, and fund balances, FY92 and trends, annual rpt, S6810–4

Pennsylvania statistical abstract, general data, 1992 recurring rpt, U4130–6.6

Rhode Island financial condition, including revenues by source, expenditures by function, and fund balances, FY92 and trends, annual rpt, S6930–1

Rhode Island statistical almanac, general data, 1993 annual rpt, C7975–1.1

South Carolina economic condition, including agriculture, finance, and govt financial data, 1970s-92, annual rpt, S7125–3.1

South Carolina financial condition, including receipts by source, expenditures by function, fund balances, and bonded debt, FY92, annual rpt, S7127–1

South Carolina statistical abstract, general data, 1993 annual rpt, S7125–1.2

South Carolina tax commission expenses by object, FY92, annual rpt, S7255–1.1

South Dakota financial condition, including revenues by source, expenditures by function, fund balances, and bonded debt, FY92, annual rpt, S7330–1

Tennessee financial condition, including revenues by source, expenditures by function and object, and fund balances, FY92, annual rpt, S7505–1

Tennessee statistical abstract, general data, 1992/93 annual rpt, U8710–2.15, U8710–2.20

Texas financial condition, including revenues by source, expenditures by function, and bonded indebtedness, FY92, annual rpt, S7655–3

Texas financial condition, including revenues by source, expenditures by function and dept, and investments, with data for over 400 individual funds, FY92, annual rpt, S7655–2

Texas insurance dept finances, including revenues, expenditures, and fund balances, FY92, annual rpt, S7700–1

Utah financial condition, including revenues by source, expenditures by function and agency, and fund balances, FY92, annual rpt, S7795–1

Utah govt statistical review, fiscal and socioeconomic data, 1993 annual rpt, R9380–1.5

Utah statistical abstract, general data, 1993 triennial rpt, U8960–1.7

Vermont financial condition, including revenues by source, expenditures by function, fund balances, and bonded debt, FY92, annual rpt, S8035–1

Virginia dept of taxation expenditures by program, FY92, annual rpt, S8305–1.1

Virginia financial condition, including revenues by source, expenditures by function, and fund balances, FY92 and trends, annual rpt, S8170–1

Washington State financial condition, including revenues by source, expenditures by function, fund balances, and bonded debt, FY92, annual rpt, S8345–3

Washington State treasury operations, including receipts, disbursements, aid to localities, and investments, by fund, FY92, annual rpt, S8455–1

West Virginia statistical handbook, general data, 1992 annual rpt, R9385–1.2, R9385–1.6

Wisconsin Blue Book, general data, 1993-94 biennial rpt, S8780–1.2

Wisconsin financial condition, including revenues by source, expenditures by function and object, and fund balances, FY92, annual rpt, S8675–3

Wisconsin financial condition, including revenues by source, expenditures by function and object, and fund balances, FY93, annual rpt, S8675–2

Wyoming financial condition, including revenues by source, expenditures by function, and fund balances, FY92 and trends, annual rpt, S8875–1

Wyoming State treasurer financial transactions, including revenues, Investments, and disbursements by local area, FY92 and trends, annual rpt, S9010–1

see also State budgets

see also State funding for agriculture

see also State funding for arts and culture

see also State funding for capital projects

see also State funding for corrections

see also State funding for courts

see also State funding for economic development

see also State funding for education

see also State funding for employment

see also State funding for energy programs

see also State funding for health and hospitals

see also State funding for higher education

see also State funding for highways and streets

see also State funding for housing

see also State funding for libraries

see also State funding for local areas

see also State funding for medical education

see also State funding for natural resources and conservation

see also State funding for parks and recreation

see also State funding for public safety

see also State funding for social welfare

see also State funding for transportation

see also State funding for vocational education

State initiatives

see Referenda

State legislatures

Black elected officials, by office, govt level, and State or city, Jan 1992 and trends, annual article, R5685–4.502

Fiscal issues for State govts, including budget balances, revenues, and expenditures, with data by State, series, A7470–4

Minority shares of State legislatures, for women, blacks, and Hispanics, by State, 1993 semiannual rpt, B8500–1.1

Recycling curbside programs, State legislator views on operations, funding, and recycled materials, July 1991 survey, B0230–1

State tax increases, with political party of Governors and legislators before vs after subsequent elections, for 17 States, 1991-92, U5085–2.8

Statistical profiles of 50 States and DC, general data, 1993 annual almanac, C4712–1

Turnover rate in State legislatures, by State, 1984-91, article, B8500–2.506

Women in State senates and houses/assemblies, by party and State, 1993 and trends, recurring rpt, U4510–1.63, U4510–1.67

Women State senate and house candidates and officeholders, by party and State, 1992 and trends, recurring rpt, U4510–1.64

State and local:

Alaska election results, and voter registration and turnout, by district and precinct, 1992 general election, biennial rpt, S0337–1

Arizona election results and voter registration, by county and/or district, 1992 general election, biennial rpt, S0520–1

Arizona statistical abstract, general data, 1993 recurring rpt, U5850–2.11

Arkansas election results, by district and/or county, 1992 general election, biennial rpt, S0775–1

California election results, and voter registration and turnout, by district and/or county, 1992 and trends, biennial rpt, S0934–1

California socioeconomic and govtl data for municipalities, counties, and school districts, 1993 annual rpt, C4712–3

Colorado election results and voter registration, by political party, and county and/or district, 1992, biennial rpt, S1090–1

Connecticut election results and voter registration and turnout, by location, 1992 general election, biennial rpt, S1265–1

Delaware election results, by district and/or county, 1992 general election, biennial rpt, S1365–1

Florida election results, by county and/or district, 1992 general election, biennial rpt, S1800–1

Florida statistical abstract, general data, 1992 annual rpt, U6660–1.21

Georgia election results by county, 1992 general election, biennial rpt, S1955–1

Hawaii data book, general data, 1992 annual rpt, S2090–1.8

Hawaii election results, and voter registration by sex, by district and precinct, 1992, biennial series, S2077–1

State legislatures

Idaho election results and voter registration, by county and/or district and precinct, 1992 general election, biennial rpt, S2305–1

Illinois election results, and voter registration trends, by county and/or district, 1992 general election, biennial rpt, S2445–1

Indiana election results, by county and district, with voter registration, 1992 primary and general elections, biennial rpt, S2702–1

Iowa election results, by county and/or district, 1992 general election, biennial rpt, S2865–1

Kansas election results, by county and district, 1992 primary and general elections, biennial rpt, S3030–1

Kentucky election results, by county, district, and circuit, 1992, annual rpt, S3213–1

Maine election results, by district, county, and municipality, 1992 general election, biennial rpt, S3490–1

Massachusetts election results and voter registration, by local area, 1992 and trends, biennial rpt, S3920–1

Michigan election results and voter registration, by county and/or district, 1992 general election, biennial rpt, S4020–1

Minnesota election results and voter registration, by locality, 1992 primary and general elections, biennial rpt, S4255–1

Mississippi statistical abstract, general data, 1992 annual rpt, U3255–4.13

Missouri election results and voter registration, by district and/or county, with directory of govt officials, 1992 general election, biennial rpt, S4580–1

Nebraska election results, and voter registration by party, by county and/or district, 1992 general and primary elections, biennial rpt, S4955–1

Nevada election results, and voter registration and turnout, by county, 1992 general election, biennial rpt, S5125–1

New Hampshire election results, by county and locality, 1992, biennial rpt, S5255–1

New Jersey election results and voter registration, by location, 1992 general election, annual rpt, S5440–1

New Mexico election results, and voter registration by party, by location, 1992 general election, biennial rpt, S5655–1

New York State general election results by county and district, Nov 1992, biennial rpt, S5750–1

North Carolina election results, by county and/or district, 1992 general election, biennial rpt, S5920–1

North Dakota election results and historical trends, including data on ballot measures and detail by location, 1880s-1992, biennial rpt, U8080–1

Ohio election results and voter registration, by local area, 1991-92 and trends, biennial rpt, S6380–1

Oklahoma election results and voter registration, by county and/or district, 1992, biennial rpt, S6425–1

Oklahoma statistical abstract, general data, 1992 annual rpt, U8130–2.6

Oregon election results and voter registration and turnout, by county and/or district, 1992 general election, biennial rpt, S6665–1

South Dakota election results, and voter registration by party, by county, 1992 general election, biennial rpt, S7390–1

Tennessee election results, by district and/or county, 1992 general election, biennial rpt, S7580–1

Tennessee statistical abstract, general data, 1992/93 annual rpt, U8710–2.14

Texas election results and voter registration, by district and/or county, 1992 general election, biennial series, S7750–1

Utah election results and voter registration and turnout, by county and/or district, 1992 general election, biennial rpt, S7875–1

Utah legislature membership, by party affiliation, 1940s-93, triennial rpt, U8960–1.8

Virginia election results by jurisdiction, and voter registration and turnout, 1992 and Jan 1993 elections, annual rpt, S8195–1

Washington State election results and voter registration, by county and/or district, 1992 general election, annual rpt, S8425–1

West Virginia election results and voter registration, by county and party, 1992 and trends, biennial rpt, S8630–1

Wisconsin Blue Book, general data, 1993-94 biennial rpt, S8780–1, S8780–1.3

Wyoming election results by county, district, and precinct, 1992, annual rpt and govtl directory, S9000–1

see also Gubernatorial vetoes

State-local relations

City fiscal condition, including budget trends and adjustments, and influencing factors, by region and population size, Mar-Apr 1993 survey, annual rpt, A8012–1.23

City officials views on State govt attitude toward local govts, 1992 survey, annual rpt, A8012–1.21

State and local:

Maine State constitutional amendment requiring State funding for all municipal govt mandates, election results by local area, 1992, biennial rpt, S3490–1

see also State funding for local areas

State parks

Acreage of State park land, visitors, and revenue as percent of budget, by State, 1991, semiannual rpt, B8500–1.12

Statistical profiles of 50 States and DC, general data, 1993 annual almanac, C4712–1

State and local:

Arizona statistical abstract, general data, 1993 recurring rpt, U5850–2.8

California statistical abstract, general data, 1992 annual rpt, S0840–2.1

Florida statistical abstract, general data, 1992 annual rpt, U6660–1.19

Hawaii data book, general data, 1992 annual rpt, S2090–1.7

Idaho economic profile, general data, 1992 recurring rpt, S2218–2.10

Illinois statistical abstract, general data, 1992 annual rpt, U6910–2

Maine statistical summary, general economic and social data, 1992 recurring rpt, S3434–1

Mississippi statistical abstract, general data, 1992 annual rpt, U3255–4.16

Index by Subjects and Names

Nevada statistical abstract, general data, 1992 biennial rpt, S5005–1.9

New Mexico State and natl park visits, monthly business activity rpt, U7980–1

New York State statistical yearbook, general data, 1992 annual rpt, U5100–1.15

Oklahoma statistical abstract, general data, 1992 annual rpt, U8130–2.21

Pennsylvania statistical abstract, general data, 1992 recurring rpt, U4130–6.8

South Carolina statistical abstract, general data, 1993 annual rpt, S7125–1.14

Tennessee statistical abstract, general data, 1992/93 annual rpt, U8710–2.12

Utah statistical abstract, general data, 1993 triennial rpt, U8960–1.17

West Virginia Natural Resource Dept law enforcement employees, and arrests by offense, offender age, and district, 1991, annual rpt, S8610–1

West Virginia statistical handbook, general data, 1992 annual rpt, R9385–1.7

Wisconsin Blue Book, general data, 1993-94 biennial rpt, S8780–1.2

see also State funding for parks and recreation

State police

State and local:

California criminal justice system expenditures and employment, by function, 1987-92, annual rpt, S0910–1.2

California criminal justice system expenditures and employment, by type of agency or function, 1982-91, annual rpt, S0910–2.1

Colorado crimes and arrests, by offense and location, with offender characteristics, and assaults on police, 1992, annual rpt, S1068–1

Connecticut crimes and arrests, and law enforcement employment by sex, 1992, annual rpt, S1256–1

Delaware State police traffic arrests by violation, accident investigations by troop, and law enforcement activity, 1988-92, annual rpt, S1435–1

Idaho crimes and arrests, law enforcement employees by sex, and assaults on officers, by local agency and county, 1992, annual rpt, S2275–2

Illinois crimes and arrests, by offense, with data by location and offender characteristics, 1991, annual rpt, S2536–1

Kentucky crimes and arrests, law enforcement employment, and assaults on police, 1992, annual rpt, S3150–1

Maryland law enforcement employment by sex, criminal offenses and arrests, and assaults on police, by local agency and county, 1991-92, annual rpt, S3665–1

Michigan crimes and arrests, by offense, with officers killed by dept type, 1992 and trends, annual rpt, S3997–1

Mississippi statistical abstract, general data, 1992 annual rpt, U3255–4.9

New Jersey law enforcement employment, by agency, and assaults on officers, 1992 and trends, annual rpt, S5430–1.4

New York State police info network entries and inquiries, 1983-90, annual rpt, U5100–1.8

Oregon crimes by offense, law enforcement employees by sex, and assaults on police, by local agency, 1992 and trends, annual rpt, S6603–3.2

Index by Subjects and Names

State retirement systems

Pennsylvania crimes and arrests, by offense, with data by location and offender characteristics, 1992 and trends, annual rpt, S6860–1

Virginia crimes and arrests by offense, and law enforcement employment, by location and reporting agency, 1992, annual rpt, S8295–2.2

Washington State crimes and clearances, and law enforcement employment, by reporting agency, 1992, annual rpt, S8440–1

West Virginia crimes and arrests by offense, agency type, and county, with data on law enforcement employment and assaults on officers, 1990-91, annual rpt, S8610–1

State prisons

see Correctional institutions

State retirement systems

- Assets of State pension funds as percent of projected and accumulated benefit obligations, by State, 1993 article, B8500–2.519
- Coverage, assets, and benefits paid, for private and govt pension and retirement programs, 1991 and trends, biennial fact book, A1325–1.3
- Educational and public employee retirement plan characteristics and finances, with detail for selected individual plans, 1990/91 and trends, recurring rpt, A7640–18
- Employee benefit plan asset rankings of top 1,000 funds, with selected fund investment data, 1992, annual feature, C2710–2.504
- Finances of State-administered public employee retirement systems, with detail by State, FY90 and trends, annual rpt, R9050–1.4
- Financial solvency of State govts, based on per capita assets, debt, and pension fund surplus or deficit, by State, 1993 article, B8500–2.521
- Funding shortfalls for underfunded pension funds in 9 States, 1993 article, C5800–7.540
- Health benefit plan funding patterns, coverage and HMO participation by State, and cost mgmt practices, 1993 annual article, C2425–1.506
- Investments of State retirement systems to meet capital gaps, distribution by type of economically targeted investment (ETI), 1993, article, C2710–2.519
- Pension fund ratios of investment earnings and assets to benefit payments, and investment returns, by State, FY91, article, B8500–2.503
- Pension funds with largest surpluses and deficits, for selected top States, 1993 article, C2710–2.519
- Southern States teacher retirement and health insurance plan characteristics and costs as a percent of salaries, for 15 States, 1993 rpt, A8945–34

State and local:

- Alabama financial condition, including revenues by source, expenditures by function and object, and fund balances, by fund and agency, FY92, annual rpt, S0129–1
- Alaska financial condition, including revenues by source, expenditures by function, fund balances, and bond obligations, FY92 and trends, annual rpt, S0275–1

Arizona financial condition, including revenues by source, expenditures by function, and fund balances, FY91, annual rpt, S0450–2

- Arkansas financial condition, including revenues by source, expenditures by function and locality, and fund balances, FY91-92, biennial rpt, S0780–1
- Arkansas financial condition, including revenues by source, expenditures by function and object, and fund balances, FY92, annual rpt, S0670–1
- California financial condition, including revenues by source, expenditures by agency and function, fund balances, and bonded debt, FY92 and trends, annual rpt, S0815–1
- Colorado financial condition, including receipts by source, and expenditures by function, FY92 and trends, annual rpt, S0980–1
- Connecticut financial condition, including revenues by source, expenditures by function, and bonded debt, FY92, annual rpt, S1170–2
- DC financial condition, including receipts by source, expenditures by object or function, and fund balances, FY92, annual rpt, S1507–1
- DC statistical profile, general data, 1992 annual rpt, S1535–3.2
- Florida financial condition, including receipts by source, expenditures by function, and fund balances, FY92, annual rpt, S1717–3
- Florida statistical abstract, general data, 1992 annual rpt, U6660–1.23
- Georgia financial condition, including revenues by source, expenditures by function and object, and fund balances, FY92, annual rpt, S1860–1
- Hawaii data book, general data, 1992 annual rpt, S2090–1.9, S2090–1.11
- Hawaii financial condition, including revenues by source, expenditures by function, and fund balances, FY92, annual rpt, S2020–1
- Idaho financial condition, including revenues by source and expenditures by object, by agency and/or fund, FY92, annual rpt, S2215–1
- Idaho school district revenues by source, and expenditures by function, by district and fund, FY92, annual rpt, S2225–2
- Illinois appropriations to State university retirement system, by instn, FY88-93, annual rpt, S2475–1.2
- Illinois financial condition, including revenues by source, and expenditures by object, function, and agency, FY92, annual rpt, S2415–1
- Indiana financial condition, including revenues by source, expenditures by function and object, and fund balances, by agency, FY92, annual rpt, S2570–1
- Iowa financial condition, including revenues by source, expenditures by function, and bonded debt, FY92 and trends, annual rpt, S2860–4
- Iowa State treasury financial operations, including receipts, disbursements, and detailed investment activity, FY92, annual rpt, S2885–1
- Kansas financial condition, including revenues by source, expenditures by function and object, and fund balances, FY92, annual rpt, S2900–1

Kentucky financial condition, including revenues by source, expenditures by function and object, fund balances, and bonded debt, FY92, annual rpt, S3120–1

- Louisiana financial condition, including revenues by source, expenditures by function, and fund balances, FY92 and trends, annual rpt, S3285–2
- Maine financial condition, including revenues by source, expenditures by function and object, and fund balances, FY92, annual rpt, S3420–1
- Maryland elementary and secondary education data, by county, 1991/92, annual rpt, S3610–2.6, S3610–2.7, S3610–2.9
- Maryland financial condition, including revenues by source, expenditures by function, fund balances, and bonded debt, FY92 and trends, annual rpt, S3685–2
- Massachusetts financial condition, including revenues by source, and expenditures by function, by fund, FY92 and trends, annual rpt, S3777–1
- Michigan financial condition, including revenues by source, expenditures by function, and fund balances, FY92 and trends, annual rpt, S3985–2
- Minnesota financial condition, including revenues by source, expenditures by function, fund balances, and bonded debt, FY92 and trends, annual rpt, S4180–1
- Mississippi financial condition, including revenues by source, expenditures by function and object, and detail by agency, FY92 and trends, annual rpt, S4346–1
- Missouri financial condition, including revenues and expenditures by agency, and tax collections and distribution, FY92 and trends, annual rpt, S4570–1.1
- Missouri financial condition, including revenues by source, expenditures by function, and fund balances, FY92, annual rpt, S4475–1
- Montana financial condition, including revenues by source, expenditures by function, and fund balances, FY92, annual rpt, S4653–1
- Nebraska financial condition, including revenues by source, expenditures by function and agency, and fund balances, FY92, annual rpt, S4825–1
- Nevada financial condition, including fund revenues by source, expenditures by function, and bonded debt, FY92, annual rpt, S5025–1
- New Hampshire financial condition, with revenues by source, expenditures by function or object, and fund balances, FY92 and trends, annual rpt, S5175–1
- New Jersey financial condition, including revenues by source, expenditures by function, fund balances, and bonded debt, FY92, annual rpt, S5455–1
- New York State financial condition, including revenues by source, expenditures by function, and fund balances, FY93, annual rpt, S5710–1
- New York State insurance industry devs, finances, and regulatory activity, 1990/91 and trends, annual rpt, S5770–3
- New York State insurance industry financial and underwriting data, by company and line of coverage, 1991, annual rpt, S5770–2

State retirement systems

New York State statistical yearbook, general data, 1992 annual rpt, U5100–1.5

North Carolina financial condition, including revenues by source, expenditures by function, fund balances, and bonded debt, FY92, annual rpt, S5897–1

North Dakota financial condition, including revenues by source, expenditures by function, fund balances, and bonded debt, FY92, annual rpt, S6162–1

Ohio financial condition, including revenues by source, expenditures by function, and fund balances, FY92, annual rpt, S6255–1

Oklahoma financial condition, including revenues by source, expenditures by function, and fund balances, FY91, annual rpt, S6438–1

Oregon financial condition, including revenues by source, expenditures by function, and fund statements, FY92, annual rpt, S6603–2

Pennsylvania financial condition, including revenues by source, expenditures by function, and fund balances, FY92 and trends, annual rpt, S6810–4

Rhode Island financial condition, including revenues by source, expenditures by function, and fund balances, FY92 and trends, annual rpt, S6930–1

South Carolina financial condition, including receipts by source, expenditures by function, fund balances, and bonded debt, FY92, annual rpt, S7127–1

South Dakota financial condition, including revenues by source, expenditures by function, fund balances, and bonded debt, FY92, annual rpt, S7330–1

Tennessee financial condition, including revenues by source, expenditures by function and object, and fund balances, FY92, annual rpt, S7505–1

Texas financial condition, including revenues by source, expenditures by function, and bonded indebtedness, FY92, annual rpt, S7655–3

Texas financial condition, including revenues by source, expenditures by function and dept, and investments, with data for over 400 individual funds, FY92, annual rpt, S7655–2

Utah financial condition, including revenues by source, expenditures by function and agency, and fund balances, FY92, annual rpt, S7795–1

Utah statistical abstract, general data, 1993 triennial rpt, U8960–1.6

Vermont financial condition, including revenues by source, expenditures by function, fund balances, and bonded debt, FY92, annual rpt, S8035–1

Virginia financial condition, including revenues by source, expenditures by function, and fund balances, FY92 and trends, annual rpt, S8170–1

Washington State financial condition, including revenues by source, expenditures by function, fund balances, and bonded debt, FY92, annual rpt, S8345–3

Wisconsin financial condition, including revenues by source, expenditures by function and object, and fund balances, FY92, annual rpt, S8675–3

Wisconsin financial condition, including revenues by source, expenditures by function and object, and fund balances, FY93, annual rpt, S8675–2

Wyoming financial condition, including revenues by source, expenditures by function, and fund balances, FY92 and trends, annual rpt, S8875–1

Wyoming State deferred compensation program for govt employees, participation and finances, FY92, annual rpt, S9010–1

State supreme courts

see State courts

State taxation

see State and local taxes

State trust funds

see Government trust funds

see Unemployment trust funds

States

see Gross State Product

see terms beginning with State

see under By State in the "Index by Categories"

see under names of individual States

Stationery

see Paper and paper products

Statistical compendia

Alabama county data book, 1992 annual rpt, S0121–2

Alabama municipal data book, 1992 recurring rpt, S0121–5

Alabama statistical abstract, 1992 recurring rpt, U5680–2

Arizona statistical abstract, 1993 recurring rpt, U5850–2

Arkansas socioeconomic trends, by MSA and/or county, 1993 annual rpt, U5935–1

California socioeconomic and govtl data for municipalities, counties, and school districts, 1993 annual rpt, C4712–3

California statistical abstract, 1992 annual rpt, S0840–2

DC statistical profile, 1992 annual rpt, S1535–3

Delaware data book, 1993 annual rpt, S1375–4

Florida county data book, 1992/93 annual rpt, C6360–1

Florida municipal and county profiles, 1991 annual rpt, C4712–6

Florida statistical abstract, 1992 annual rpt, U6660–1

Georgia county guide, 1993 annual rpt, U6750–1

Georgia statistical abstract, 1992-93 biennial rpt, U6730–1

Hawaii data book, 1992 annual rpt, S2090–1

Idaho economic profile, 1992 recurring rpt, S2218–2

Illinois statistical abstract, 1992 annual rpt, U6910–2

Kansas statistical abstract, 1991/92 annual rpt, U7095–2

Kentucky economic statistics, 1993 annual rpt, S3104–1

Latin America statistical abstract, 1992 annual rpt, U6250–1

Maine statistical summary, 1992 recurring rpt, S3434–1

Maryland statistical abstract, 1993-94 biennial rpt, S3605–1

Massachusetts municipal and county profiles, general data, 1992 annual rpt, C4712–2

Index by Subjects and Names

Mississippi statistical abstract, 1992 annual rpt, U3255–4

Nebraska statistical handbook, discontinued biennial rpt, S4855–1

Nevada statistical abstract, 1992 biennial rpt, S5005–1

New Jersey municipal data book, 1992 annual rpt, C4712–4

New York State municipal and county profiles, 1993 annual rpt, C4712–7

New York State statistical yearbook, 1992 annual rpt, U5100–1

Oklahoma statistical abstract, 1992 annual rpt, U8130–2

Pennsylvania statistical abstract, 1992 recurring rpt, U4130–6

Rhode Island statistical almanac, 1993 annual rpt, C7975–1

South Carolina statistical abstract, 1993 annual rpt, S7125–1

State social, economic, and govtl indicators, with rankings, 1993 semiannual rpt, B8500–1

State statistical profiles for 50 States and DC, 1993 annual almanac, C4712–1

Tennessee statistical abstract, 1992/93 annual rpt, U8710–2

Utah govt statistical review, 1993 annual rpt, R9380–1

Utah statistical abstract, 1993 triennial rpt, U8960–1

West Virginia statistical handbook, 1992 annual rpt, R9385–1

Wisconsin Blue Book, 1993-94 biennial rpt, S8780–1

Statistical programs and activities

Corporate earnings forecasting error analysis, 1973-90, article, C3950–1.525

Labor market behavior, natl longitudinal surveys data users handbook and bibl, 1993 recurring rpt, U3780–2

Physician participation in clinical and economic profiling programs, by specialty, sex, and employer type, 1992, article, A2200–5.1

see also Accounting and auditing

see also Bibliographies

see also Business outlook and attitude surveys

see also Census of Population and Housing

see also Classifications

see also Consumer surveys

see also Economic and econometric models

see also Information storage and retrieval systems

see also Media use surveys

see also Methodology

see also Opinion and attitude surveys

see also Statistical compendia

Statistical Research Inc.

Telephone Yellow Pages directory use among consumers, with detail by respondent characteristics, 1992 survey, annual rpt, A9500–2

Statistical Surveys Inc.

Recreational vehicle trailer and motorhome sales change, by region, monthly rpt, C8950–2

Steel industry

see Iron and steel industry

Stein, Aryeh D.

"Behavioral Risk Factors and Preventive Health Measures, Massachusetts, 1986-90", S3850–3

Stephan, Roger

"Profiles of Alaska's Public School Districts, FY92", S0295–2

Stereo systems

see Home video and audio equipment

Sterilization

see Sexual sterilization

Stimulants

see Drug abuse and treatment

see Drugs

Stock exchanges

- Corporate acquisitions and purchase prices, by exchange where traded, 1990-92, annual article, C4683–1.505
- Foreign stock exchange price indexes, by exchange, 1991-92, annual fact book, B6625–1.1
- Foreign stock market performance, for 10 exchanges, 1992, recurring feature, C5800–7.509
- Foreign stock market performance, for 11 exchanges, 1st half 1993, recurring feature, C5800–7.533
- Foreign stock market performance, with data for selected major corporations, biweekly rpt quarterly feature, C3950–1.506, C3950–1.512, C3950–1.521, C3950–1.525
- Latin America stock exchange profiles for 7 countries, with market capitalization, trading volume, and return rates, 1993 articles, C2710–2.507
- Market capitalization, for 6 industrial and 7 emerging countries, 1993 and trends, annual feature, C8900–1.520
- Performance of stock markets in 16 countries, 1992, annual article, C8900–1.507
- Securities industry analyses, with data on underwriting and trading activity, and financial trends, periodic rpt, A8825–1
- Spain, Madrid stock exchange performance by industry sector, and 20 leading stocks with greatest gains or losses, 1992, article, A8955–1.502
- Trading activity on NASDAQ vs other major US and foreign exchanges, 1992 and trends, annual rpt, A7105–1
- Trading volume on NYSE and other leading exchanges, 1982-92, annual fact book, B6625–1.1

see also New York Stock Exchange

see also Securities

see also Stockbrokers

Stock market

see Stock exchanges

Stockbrokers

- Commissions, fees, analysts, offices, and brokers, for 18 brokerage firms, 1993 annual article, C8900–1.528
- Financial performance data for 4 major brokerage firms, 1992 articles, C3950–1.502
- Income and employment for 8 major securities firms, 1992, article, C5800–7.509
- Investment mgmt firms, assets and operating data for approx 900 instns, Jan 1993, annual feature, C2710–2.511
- Natl Assn of Securities Dealers membership, 1980-1st half 1992, recurring article, A8825–1.501
- Natl Assn of Securities Dealers membership, 1980-3rd qtr 1992, recurring article, A8825–1.503
- Natl Assn of Securities Dealers membership, 1987-May 1993, recurring article, A8825–1.505
- Natl Assn of Securities Dealers registered market makers, by State, 1992, annual rpt, A7105–1
- New York Stock Exchange activity, including stock volume and prices, credit distribution, and member firm characteristics, 1992 and trends, annual fact book, B6625–1
- Operating and financial composite ratios for corporations, with establishments and receipts, for approx 200 industries, by asset size, FY90, annual rpt, C7800–1
- Public opinion on honesty/ethical standards of selected occupations, 1992 Gallup Polls and trends, C4040–1.501
- Shopping center financial and operating data, with detail by type of tenant, US and Canada, 1991, triennial rpt, R9285–1

State and local:

- Arizona statistical abstract, general data, 1993 recurring rpt, U5850–2.22
- Connecticut securities broker-dealers and investment agent registrations, 1991 and trends, annual rpt, S1160–1
- DC statistical profile, general data, 1992 annual rpt, S1535–3.4
- Idaho stockbrokers/dealers and agents licensed, FY89-92, annual rpt, S2235–1
- Oregon securities regulatory section activity, including licensed brokers, 1992, annual rpt, S6616–1

Stockholders' equity

see Business assets and liabilities, general

see Business assets and liabilities, specific industry

Stockholm, Sweden

Deaths related to alcohol abuse, by sex and cause, 1987, article, A2623–1.508

Stockpiling

Silver market activity worldwide and in US, including production, consumption by end use, stocks, trade, and prices, by country, 1988-92, annual rpt, B4300–1

see also Strategic Petroleum Reserve

Stocks

see Agricultural stocks

see Business inventories

see Coal stocks

see Energy stocks and inventories

see Options trading

see Petroleum stocks

see Securities

see Stock exchanges

see Stockbrokers

see Stockpiling

Stolen property

see Property damage and loss

see Robbery and theft

see Shoplifting

Stone products and quarries

- Cost indexes for construction, equipment, and labor, by type and location, weekly rpt quarterly feature, C5800–2.534, C5800–2.547
- Financial ratios and performance, for over 350 SIC 4-digit industries, FY88-92, annual rpt, A6400–3
- Operating and financial composite ratios for corporations, with establishments and receipts, for approx 200 industries, by asset size, FY90, annual rpt, C7800–1
- Production trends and outlook for stone product industries, with data by region, 1992 annual article, C0125–6

State and local:

- Hawaii data book, general data, 1992 annual rpt, S2090–1.20
- Mississippi statistical abstract, general data, 1992 annual rpt, U3255–4.10
- New York State statistical yearbook, general data, 1992 annual rpt, U5100–1.2
- Pennsylvania statistical abstract, general data, 1992 recurring rpt, U4130–6.8
- Utah statistical abstract, general data, 1993 triennial rpt, U8960–1.10

see also Abrasive materials

see also Cement and concrete

see also Oil shale

see also Phosphate

see also Potash

Storage

see Cold storage and refrigeration

see Warehouses

Storms

- Deaths in major disasters since 1865, by category, annual rpt, A8375–2.1
- Hurricane Andrew total insured and business establishment damages in Florida and Louisiana, 1992, article, C1200–5.502
- Hurricane deaths and property damage caused by most serious storms since 1900, 1992 annual rpt, U6660–1.8
- Hurricanes and other named storms, predicted vs actual, with meteorological info, 1992, article, C6985–2.503
- Hurricanes and related deaths, 1965-91, and insured property loss for 10 most costly hurricanes, 1969-92, annual rpt, A5650–1.4
- Insurance (property/casualty) losses from Aug 1992 Hurricane Andrew, for 20 underwriters with greatest loss, 1992 article, C1050–1.503
- Tornadoes and related deaths and injuries, by State, 1991, with natl trends from 1965, annual rpt, A5650–1.4

State and local:

- Florida (South) economic impacts of Hurricane Andrew, including insurance payments, unemployment, and tax and lottery sales shortfalls, 1992 article, C5800–7.503
- Hawaii data book, general data, 1992 annual rpt, S2090–1.5
- Oklahoma tornadoes, deaths, and injuries, by county, 1950-91, annual rpt, U8130–2.1
- Rhode Island statistical almanac, general data, 1993 annual rpt, C7975–1

see also Floods

Strategic Defense Initiative

Budget for SDI, by detailed program, FY89-93, annual rpt, A0250–2.2

Strategic materials

State and local:

Colorado property assessed valuation, and summary production data, for strategic minerals by county, 1991-92, annual rpt, S1055–3

see also Stockpiling

see also Strategic Petroleum Reserve

see also Uranium

Strategic Petroleum Reserve

Strategic Petroleum Reserve

Stocks in reserve, 1977-93, periodic basic data book, A2575–14.4

Stocks in SPR, 1983-93, annual feature, C6985–1.513

World oil, gas, and refined product stocks, trade, and consumption, by country and world area, 1991 and trends, annual compilation, C6985–9.2

Strawberries

see Fruit and fruit products

Streams

see Rivers and waterways

Streets

see Highways, streets, and roads

see Traffic engineering

Stress

see Mental health and illness

Strikes and lockouts

see Work stoppages

Stroke

see Cerebrovascular diseases

see Circulatory diseases

Student aid

Appropriations for higher education, by State, instn, and function, 1993/94, annual feature, C2175–1.538

Appropriations of tax funds for higher education, by State, instn, and function, FY92-93 and trends, annual rpt, A8970–1

Athletes on athletic scholarships graduation rates after 6 years, by sex and Natl Collegiate Athletic Assn Div I instn, summer 1991, recurring feature, C2175–1.522

Athletes on athletic scholarships graduation rates after 6 years, by sex, race, and Natl Collegiate Athletic Assn Div I instn, summer 1992, recurring feature, C2175–1.527

Athletes with scholarships, enrollment and graduation rates, by sex, race-ethnicity, and major sport, for Natl Collegiate Athletic Assn Div I instns, 1992/93, annual rpt, A7440–4

Budget of US higher education funding, by agency and program, FY92-94, annual feature, C2175–1.516

Catholic secondary school operations and finances, including enrollment by race-ethnicity and family income, 1991/92 and trends, biennial rpt, A7375–5

Community and junior college revenues by source and expenditures by function, and selected student characteristics, FY92, annual rpt, A6705–1

Dental advanced education program stipends by class level, by instn, 1992/93 annual rpt, A1475–10

Dental school student expenses and financial aid, by instn, US and Canada, 1991/92 or 1992/93, annual rpt, A1475–3.2

Doctoral degree recipient characteristics, including citizenship status, source of support, field of study, and instn, 1990/91 and trends, annual rpt, R6000–7

Ecologist personal and professional characteristics, including research activity and funding, with data by field, Mar 1992 survey, recurring rpt, A4685–1

Federal guaranteed student loan default rates, with detail for proprietary school students, 1988-91, article, C2175–1.528

Federal student loan default rates, by State, and for top 50 lenders and top 10 guarantee agencies, 1991, article, C2175–1.532

Foreign students enrolled in US higher education instns, by instn, State, country of origin, and demographic characteristics, 1991/92 and trends, annual rpt, R5580–1

Higher education appropriations for FY94 compared to spending in FY93, by program, recurring feature, C2175–1.527, C2175–1.536

Higher education financial aid applicant characteristics, American College Testing (ACT) program, discontinued annual trend rpt, R1960–3

Higher education financial aid applicant characteristics, American College Testing (ACT) program, 1993/94, annual rpt, R1960–5

Higher education freshmen attitudes and characteristics, degree and career plans, and financial aid sources, by sex and instn type, fall 1992, annual survey, U6215–1

Higher education freshmen attitudes and characteristics, degree and career plans, and financial aid sources, fall 1992, annual survey summary, C2175–1.505

Higher education instns, faculty, students, degrees, and finances, detailed data by State, 1993 annual rpt, C2175–1.531

Higher education intercollegiate women's sports participation, and scholarship recommendations of Natl Collegiate Athletic Assn gender equity task force, by sport, 1993 rpt, A7440–6

Higher education State-administered student aid awards, by program and State, 1992/93 and trends, annual rpt, A7140–1

Hispanic American students receiving financial aid, by source, with comparison to whites, 1986/87, annual compilation, C6775–3.2

Library education fellowships/traineeships awarded by Dept of Education, and scholarship recipients and donors, 1993 annual compilation, C1650–3

Library/info science school enrollment, staff and student characteristics, finances, and curricula, by school and degree program, 1991/92, annual rpt, A3235–1

Loan delinquency rates for approx 10 types of consumer bank loans, and repossession data, by State, quarterly rpt, A0950–1

Medical school programs, fees, applicants, admissions, and enrollment, with data by age, sex, minority group, and instn, 1992/93 and trends, annual rpt, A3273–10

Medical school revenues by source, student aid, and staff, by instn type, 1989/90 and/or 1990/91, article, A3273–8.503

Natl Merit Scholars college major choices, by sex, 1982-88, recurring rpt, A3960–2.1

Natl Merit Scholars freshman enrollment in top 64 higher education instns, 1992, annual feature, C2175–1.505

Optometry school faculty, enrollment and degrees, policies and programs, and finances, by instn, 1991/92, annual survey, A3370–2

Osteopathy college enrollment, student and faculty characteristics, and finances, 1992/93 and trends, annual rpt, A0620–1

Osteopathy student debt, including types of loans used, for freshmen and seniors, 1991/92, annual survey rpt, A0620–2

Physics and astronomy bachelor degree recipient anticipated sources of support for 1st-year graduate study, 1992 and trends, annual survey, A1960–3

Private elementary and secondary school enrollment, staff, and finances, with detail for minorities, by school type and region, 1980s-1992/93, annual rpt, A6835–3

Psychology doctoral degree recipient employment and demographic characteristics, and finances, 1990/91, biennial survey rpt, A2620–4

Psychology grad depts, faculty characteristics, enrollment, and student aid, US and Canada, 1990/91 and trends, annual rpt, A2620–3

Public health school expenditures for student aid, by fund source and instn (unnamed), FY92, annual rpt, A3372–3

Science and engineering grad students and doctorates with Fed Govt support, by agency, by sex and race-ethnicity, 1980s-90s, recurring rpt, A3960–2.1

Social work higher education programs, faculty and student characteristics, and student aid, with data by instn, 1992 and trends, annual rpt, A4515–1

Southern States higher education student aid data, by State, 1990s and trends, biennial fact book, A8945–1.4

State student aid expenditures, by State, 1991/92-1992/93, annual feature, C2175–1.515

Western States higher education tuition/fees, by resident status, State, and public instn, with State-funded student aid summaries, 1992/93 and trends, annual rpt, A9385–3

Women/girls student aid program support by foundations, with comparisons to total grants, 1990, A9405–1.2

State and local:

California higher education systems funding by source and expenditures by program category, with enrollment data, FY60s-94, annual rpt, S0827–3

Delaware postsecondary education finances, enrollment, and degrees conferred, by instn, FY94 annual rpt, S1425–1

Florida higher education enrollment, degree programs, staff, and finances, by State-supported instn, with student and staff characteristics, 1991/92 annual rpt, S1725–1

Illinois higher education staff, salaries, student cost and aid, and finances, by instn, 1993 annual rpt, S2475–1.2

Illinois statistical abstract, general data, 1992 annual rpt, U6910–2

Indiana financial condition, including revenues by source, expenditures by function and object, and fund balances, by agency, FY92, annual rpt, S2570–1

Iowa postsecondary enrollment, degrees, staff, and finances, by instn, 1990/91, annual rpt, S2755–1

Kentucky higher education enrollment, degrees, staff, and finances, by State-supported instn, 1983-92, annual rpt, S3130–3

Minnesota postsecondary education finances, and enrollment by student characteristics, by type of school system, 1970s-93, biennial rpt, S4195–2.2

Index by Subjects and Names

Students

Mississippi higher education enrollment and degrees, by level and field, and finances, by State-supported instn, 1991/92, annual rpt, S4360–1

Missouri higher education enrollment, degrees, libraries, staff, and finances, by instn, 1992 and trends, annual rpt, S4520–3

New Mexico high school students eligible for and receiving scholarships under State Scholar Program, by school district, 1991/92, annual rpt, S5575–4

North Carolina higher education student costs, admissions, housing, and financial aid, by instn, 1992/93 annual rpt, U8013–1.3

Pennsylvania higher education revenues, expenditures, and endowment funds, by instn type, FY91 and trends, annual rpt, S6790–5.4

Pennsylvania higher education revenues, expenditures, and endowment funds, by instn type, FY92 and trends, annual rpt, S6790–5.16

South Carolina higher education instn expenditures, student loans, and State appropriations for private college tuition aid grants, 1993 annual rpt, S7185–2

South Dakota public higher education finances, staff, enrollment, degrees, and facilities, by instn, FY93 annual rpt, S7375–1

Tennessee higher education finances, student aid and expenses, and faculty and salaries, by instn, 1992/93 and trends, annual rpt, S7525–1.2

Texas higher education student aid awards and recipients, by program and instn type, FY92, annual rpt, S7657–1.3

Utah higher education degrees, enrollment, staff, and finances, by public instn, with selected comparisons to instns in other States, 1993/94 annual rpt, S7895–2

Vermont higher education revenues by source, expenditures by function, and tuition/fees, by instn, and student aid trends, 1992 annual rpt, S8035–2.3

see also Pell Grant Program

see also School lunch and breakfast programs

see also Work-study programs

Student discipline

Black student suspension and corporal punishment rates, with comparisons to whites, 1988, R3840–21

Catholic vs public school ratings for selected aspects of education and environment, public opinion by respondent characteristics, July 1992 survey, A7375–8

School bus fleet director views on weapons-related problems, for urban, suburban, and rural locations, July 1993 survey, annual article, C1575–1.507

State and local:

Louisiana public school suspensions and expulsions, by grade level and parish, 1991/92, annual rpt, S3280–1.1

Massachusetts elementary/secondary student suspension rates, by grade level, 1989/90, annual rpt, S3810–3

Student employment

see Temporary and seasonal employment

see Work-study programs

see Youth employment

Student housing

Higher education freshmen attitudes and characteristics, degree and career plans, and financial aid sources, by sex and instn type, fall 1992, annual survey, U6215–1

State and land-grant university tuition/fees, and room and board charges, by type of professional program and/or instn, fall 1991-92, annual rpt, A7150–4

State and local:

Arkansas population in instns and other group quarters, 1990, census rpt, U5935–7

California population in instns and other group quarters, 1990, census rpt, S0840–9

Florida higher education enrollment, degree programs, staff, and finances, by State-supported instn, with student and staff characteristics, 1991/92 annual rpt, S1725–1

Illinois higher education staff, salaries, student cost and aid, and finances, by instn, 1993 annual rpt, S2475–1.2

New Jersey population in instns and other group quarters, by county, 1990, census rpt, S5425–19

North Carolina higher education student costs, admissions, housing, and financial aid, by instn, 1992/93 annual rpt, U8013–1.3

Pennsylvania higher education tuition/fees, and room and board charges, by instn, 1992/93 and trends, annual rpt, S6790–5.3

Pennsylvania population in instns and other group quarters, 1990, census rpt, U4130–13

South Dakota public higher education finances, staff, enrollment, degrees, and facilities, by instn, FY93 annual rpt, S7375–1

Student loans

see Student aid

Student unrest

Freshmen activities in past year, and willingness to participate in student demonstrations, by sex and instn type, fall 1992, annual survey, U6215–1

see also Riots and disorders

Students

Aircraft pilot (student) certificates issued by FAA, 1964-92, annual rpt, A5120–2.2

Alcohol consumption of college students per week, by region, 1990, survey article, C2175–1.522

American College Test (ACT) scores by student characteristics, with student views on schools and education plans, 1992 and trends, annual rpt, R1960–6

Athletes with scholarships, enrollment and graduation rates, by sex, race-ethnicity, and major sport, for Natl Collegiate Athletic Assn Div 1 instns, 1992/93, annual rpt, A7440–4

Catholic vs public school ratings for selected aspects of education and environment, public opinion by respondent characteristics, July 1992 survey, A7375–8

Dental student admission test scores and pre-dental grade averages, by instn, 1992/93, annual rpt, A1475–4.1

Drug, alcohol, and tobacco use and attitudes among high school seniors and 4th-6th graders, 1993 survey article, B6045–1.504

Elementary/secondary new teacher views on teaching and quality of schools, after 2nd year of teaching, spring 1992 survey, B6045–2

Elementary/secondary prospective teacher characteristics and opinions, survey of persons interested in alternative certification routes, 1992, R6350–7

Elementary/secondary school parental selection program participation and enrollment share, for 7 States with statewide programs, 1992, R3810–7

Elementary/secondary teacher views on education policy issues and selected reform proposals, Jan-Feb 1993 survey, B6045–7

Freshmen attitudes and characteristics, degree and career plans, and financial aid sources, by sex and instn type, fall 1992, annual survey, U6215–1

Freshmen attitudes and characteristics, degree and career plans, and financial aid sources, fall 1992, annual survey summary, C2175–1.505

Hard goods manufacturers opinions on need for Federal action on student competence and worker literacy, 1993 annual survey rpt, A1800–1

High school sophomore participation rates in selected extracurricular activities, by socioeconomic status, 1990, R4800–2.503

High school student abuse of alcohol, cigarettes, and marijuana as affected by junior high prevention program, 1993 article, A2623–1.508

High school students sexual activity and condom use, by sex and race-ethnicity, 1993 article, C4215–1.505

High school vocational-academic program integration, pilot project evaluative data including achievement test results, student and teacher attitudes, and curricula, 1990, A8945–33

Higher education admissions dept activity, including trends in applications received, recruitment, staff, and budgets, 1992-93, annual rpt, A6695–1

Higher education student level of familiarity with 35 corporations, 1993 survey article, C1200–1.503

Higher education student use of and attitudes toward alcohol, drugs, and tobacco products, by sex and region, 1989-91 surveys, annual rpt, U4950–1

Kenya elementary, secondary, and vocational students sexual experience, by selected characteristics, 1989, article, A5160–6.505

Medical education and careers, views of college undergrads and advisors, Feb/Mar 1990 survey, article, A3273–8.506

Medical school applications and acceptances to selective schools by student grade point average (GPA), 1982-89, article, A3273–8.502

Medical school Asian vs white student performance indicators at Jefferson Medical School, including standardized test scores, 1981-92, article, A3273–8.503

Medical school grad plans for practicing in socioeconomically deprived areas, and specialty certification, for minority and nonminority grads, 1982-92, article, A3273–8.507

Students

Medical school policies regarding students with human immunodeficiency virus (HIV), 1990/91, article, A3273–8.503

Medical school student mental health service availability, Oct 1991 survey, article, A3273–8.506

Medical students plans for practicing in socioeconomically deprived areas, for entering vs graduating students, 1987 and 1991, A3273–8.501

Mexico drug use among students, by substance and region, 1976 and 1986, annual rpt, U6250–1.15

Nursing grad student reasons for pursuing degrees, and employment expectations, 1993 survey article, A8010–3.503

Nursing student (male) reasons for career choice and intended specialty, 1993 survey article, A8010–3.503

Opinions of 8th graders on courses in 4 subject areas, by sex and race-ethnicity, 1988, R4800–2.512

Osteopathy student debt and career plans, by student characteristics, 1991/92 and trends, annual survey rpt, A0620–2

Pharmacy degree program applications, enrollment, and degrees conferred, by student characteristics and instn, 1990/91 and trends, annual rpt, A0630–9

Public health school applicant, student, and grad characteristics, by instn, 1991/92 and trends, annual rpt, A3372–3

Public school student distribution and mathematics proficiency ratings by frequency of changing schools in past 2 years, by region, 1992, R4800–2.520

Risk factors at home and school correlated with child abuse and reading ability, and special instructional efforts correlated with drug use, 1992 article, A8680–1.501

School bus loading/unloading accident fatalities, by circumstances, location, and victim age and sex, 1991 and trends, annual rpt, S3040–2

Secondary school student sexual harassment experience at school, for 8-11th graders, by sex, 1993 survey, article, R4800–2.519

Southern States use of reporting systems to track college performance of recent high school grads, for 15 States, 1992, A8945–32

Urban League National Education Initiative population served, and opinions of students and parents, 1991 survey, article, A8510–1.1

Women and minorities in professional fields, detailed education and labor force data, 1980s-91, with historical trends, recurring rpt, A3960–2

Zambia student views on sexual behavior and treatment of persons infected with AIDS virus, by respondent characteristics, 1990 survey, article, A5160–6.503

State and local:

California public school students with limited and fluent English proficiency, by 1st language, grade level, and county, 1992 and trends, annual rpt, S0825–10

Colorado higher education library staff, including student assistants, by instn, 1992, biennial rpt, S1000–3.2

Connecticut public high school grads and postgraduate activities, 1991, biennial rpt, S1185–3

Florida higher education enrollment, degree programs, staff, and finances, by State-supported instn, with student and staff characteristics, 1991/92 annual rpt, S1725–1

Florida 8th-9th grade children of immigrants characteristics, attitudes, and discrimination experience, 1992, survey article, R4800–2.522

Idaho academic library student assistants, by instn, 1992, annual feature, A5370–1

Kentucky economically disadvantaged student shares of enrollment, by region and district, 1991/92 and trends, annual rpt, S3110–1

Missouri American College Test (ACT) scores, by participant characteristics and/or higher education instn, 1993 annual rpt, S4520–3.1

Missouri higher education enrollment, degrees, libraries, staff, and finances, by instn, 1992 and trends, annual rpt, S4520–3

Missouri public school student performance on educational tests, and grad postgraduation activities, 1991/92 and trends, annual rpt, S4505–1.1

New Jersey high school grad postgraduation plans, by county, fall 1991, annual rpt, S5385–1.1

New Mexico elementary/secondary students enrolled in advanced placement classes, by school district, 1991/92 annual rpt, S5575–4

North Carolina high school grads and postgraduation plans, by local district, 1991/92 and trends, annual rpt, S5915–1

North Carolina higher education enrollment, degrees, libraries, staff, and student characteristics, finances, and housing, by instn, 1992/93 and trends, annual rpt, U8013–1

North Dakota students age 6-18, by county, 1981 and 1991, annual planning rpt, S6140–2

Pennsylvania high school grads postgraduation activities, by county, 1991/92, annual rpt, S6790–5.14

South Carolina high school grad postgraduation activities, by school district, 1991, annual rpt, S7145–1.3

Vermont high school seniors and grads postgraduation plans or activities, 1992 annual rpt, S8035–2.2

Virginia public high school grads and postgraduation activity, by county and municipality, 1991/92, annual rpt, S8190–3

see also Black students

see also Educational enrollment

see also Foreign students

see also School dropouts

see also Student aid

see also Student discipline

see also Student housing

see also Student unrest

see also Truancy from school

Submerged lands

see also Offshore oil and gas

Subscription TV

see Television

Subsidies

Canada motion picture and TV subsidy expenditures by 2 natl organizations, by Province, FY92, article, C9380–1.503

Index by Subjects and Names

Low-income housing supply-demand, costs, physical conditions, and public assistance, with data by race-ethnicity, for 44 metro areas, 1980s-91, R3834–16

Nonprofit organization Federal mail subsidies, and 3rd-class mail volume, 1980-93, article, C2176–1.506

Nonprofit organization mail rates for 1993, and rates proposed by Congress for 1994-99, article, C2176–1.521

Nonprofit organization mail rates proposed by House of Representatives panel, 1993-99, article, C2176–1.513

Religious congregation use of discounted postal rates, 1992 survey, recurring rpt, A5435–4

Shipbuilding govt aid programs in 6 OECD countries, and impact on US industry, 1993 recurring rpt, A8900–8

State and local:

DC, Washington Metro Area Transit Authority operating subsidy and cost recovery, FY86-91, annual rpt, S1535–3.7

Wyoming State govt lost earnings due to subsidy investments, FY92 annual rpt, S9010–1

see also Agricultural production quotas and price supports

see also Agricultural subsidies

see also Federal aid programs

see also Federal aid to arts and humanities

see also Federal aid to education

see also Federal aid to higher education

see also Federal aid to highways

see also Federal aid to housing

see also Federal aid to law enforcement

see also Federal aid to libraries

see also Federal aid to local areas

see also Federal aid to medical education

see also Federal aid to medicine

see also Federal aid to rural areas

see also Federal aid to States

see also Federal aid to transportation

see also Federal aid to vocational education

see also Federal funding for energy programs

see also Federal funding for research and development

see also Rent supplements

see also State funding for agriculture

see also State funding for arts and culture

see also State funding for capital projects

see also State funding for corrections

see also State funding for courts

see also State funding for economic development

see also State funding for education

see also State funding for employment

see also State funding for energy programs

see also State funding for health and hospitals

see also State funding for higher education

see also State funding for highways and streets

see also State funding for housing

see also State funding for libraries

see also State funding for local areas

see also State funding for medical education

see also State funding for natural resources and conservation

see also State funding for parks and recreation

see also State funding for public safety

see also State funding for social welfare

see also State funding for transportation
see also State funding for vocational education
see also Tax expenditures
see also Tax incentives and shelters
see also Trade adjustment assistance

Subsidized housing
see Public housing

Substance abuse
see Alcohol abuse and treatment
see Drug abuse and treatment

Suburbs
- Commercial real estate market conditions and outlook, for industrial and office properties, by US metro area and selected foreign city, 1992-93, annual survey, A8916–1
- Lodging industry facilities, sales, and occupancy, with top 42-100 properties in 5 market categories, 1993 annual rpt, C7000–5
- Office building detailed income and expense data, and energy use, US and Canada, by building characteristics, metro area, and US region, 1991 and trends, annual rpt, A5600–2
- Population, and effective buying income, rankings of approx 300 suburbs, 1992, annual rpt, C1200–1.511
- Restaurant sales, population age 25-44, and household income, with detail for suburban areas, 1991, article, C1200–5.501

State and local:
- DC employment, earnings, and hours, by industry, with unemployment insurance data, monthly rpt, S1527–3
- Minnesota public welfare program recipients and expenditures, by county, 1992, semiannual rpt, S4202–1
- *see also* Neighborhoods
- *see also* Urban renewal
- *see also* under By Urban-Rural and Metro-Nonmetro in the "Index by Categories"

Subways
- Mass transit system finances and operations, passengers, and employment, by mode, US and Canada, 1990-91 and trends, annual rpt, A2650–1
- Operations of railroads and rail rapid transit, data and related articles, monthly rpt, C8400–1

State and local:
- DC statistical profile, general data, 1992 annual rpt, S1535–3.7

Sudan
- Energy intl sourcebook, with detail on oil and gas industry operations, supply-demand, and prices, for approx 80 countries, 1970s-91, annual compilation, C6985–10.2

Sudden Infant Death Syndrome
see Infant mortality

Sugar industry and products
- Exports of farm products, by detailed commodity and country of destination, US and California, 1991, annual rpt, B9520–1
- Futures trading on Coffee, Sugar, and Cocoa Exchange, with related data including deliveries by country and/or port, 1992 and trends, annual rpt, B2275–1
- Indonesia agricultural production trends and impacts of govt policies, for 5 major food crops, 1970s-80s, R5620–1.37

Latin America statistical abstract, general data by country, 1992 annual rpt, U6250–1.16, U6250–1.24, U6250–1.25
- Operating and financial composite ratios for corporations, with establishments and receipts, for approx 200 industries, by asset size, FY90, annual rpt, C7800–1
- Production, consumption, stocks, trade, and prices for approx 100 basic commodities, including by country and producing State, commodity yearbook for 1993, C2400–1, C2400–2
- Retail prices for selected consumer items in approx 300 cities, quarterly rpt, A0150–1
- Sales and consumer expenditures, for food store products by type, 1991-92, annual feature, C4655–1.510
- Supermarket sales by detailed product type, 1992 and trends, annual feature, C5225–1.507

State and local:
- California field crops production, acreage, yield, and prices, by commodity and county, 1992 and trends, annual rpt, S0850–1.4
- Colorado agricultural production, marketing, and finances, by commodity and/or county, with farms and acreage, 1992 and trends, annual rpt, S0985–1
- Florida field crop acreage, yield, production, and value, by commodity and/or county, 1992 and trends, annual rpt, S1685–1.4
- Hawaii agricultural production and marketing, by commodity and island, 1987-91, annual rpt, S2030–1
- Hawaii counties population and economic indicators, 1993 annual rpt series, B3500–2
- Hawaii data book, general data, 1992 annual rpt, S2090–1.13, S2090–1.17, S2090–1.19, S2090–1.22
- Hawaii economic conditions, including employment, population, tourism, and construction, quarterly rpt, S2090–2
- Hawaii economic indicators, bimonthly rpt, B3500–1
- Louisiana agricultural production, marketing, and finances, by commodity or parish, 1985-91, annual rpt, U2740–1
- Michigan agricultural production, marketing, and finances, by commodity or county, 1987-91, annual rpt, S3950–1
- Minnesota agricultural production, marketing, and finances, by county or commodity, and farms and acreage, 1992 and trends, annual rpt, S4130–1
- Montana agricultural production, marketing, and finances, by commodity and county, 1991 and trends, annual rpt, S4655–1
- Nebraska agricultural production, marketing, and finances, by commodity and/or county, and farms and acreage, 1991 and trends, annual rpt, S4835–1
- North Dakota agricultural production and marketing, by commodity and county, and farm finances, 1992 and trends, annual rpt, U3600–1
- Ohio agricultural production, marketing, and finances, by commodity and county, with farms and acreage, 1990-91 and trends, annual rpt, S6240–1
- Texas agricultural production, marketing, and finances, by commodity and county, and farms and farmland, 1991 and trends, annual rpt series, S7630–1

Wyoming agricultural production, marketing, and finances, by county and/or commodity, and farms, acreage, and value, 1992 and trends, annual rpt, S8860–1
- Wyoming property assessed valuations and tax levies, by property type, tax purpose, and location, 1992 and trends, annual rpt, S8990–1.2
- *see also* Candy and confectionery products
- *see also* Syrups and sweeteners

Suicide
- Black American health and vital statistics data, with comparisons to whites, 1970s-91, annual compilation, C6775–2.2
- Black youth suicide rates, with comparisons to whites, by sex and age, 1989, R3840–21
- Correctional instn inmate suicides, by sex, by State and Canadian Province, as of June 1992, annual rpt, A1305–3
- Deaths from accidents compared with other causes, by age and sex, 1992 and trends, annual rpt, A8375–2.1
- Latin America statistical abstract, general data by country, 1992 annual rpt, U6250–1.15
- Mexico suicides and attempts, by circumstances and victim characteristics, 1980-84, annual rpt, U6250–1.15
- Nurse suicides by age, and correlation with smoking status, 1976-88, article, A2623–1.504
- Older population age 60/over views on religion importance and resources for suicide prevention, 1993 survey feature, R8780–1.504
- Public opinion on legalization of physician-assisted suicide in selected situations, Dec 1992 Gallup Poll, C4040–1.506
- State social, economic, and govtl indicators, with rankings, 1993 semiannual rpt, B8500–1

State and local:
- Alabama suicide deaths, by race and county, with detail for teenagers, 1992 and trends, annual rpt, S0175–2
- Alaska vital statistics, including births, deaths by cause, marriages, divorces, adoptions, and population, by demographic characteristics and location, 1990, annual rpt, S0315–1
- Arkansas vital statistics, including births, deaths by cause, marriages, and divorces, by age, sex, race, and county, 1991 and trends, annual rpt, S0685–1
- California correctional instn inmate suicides and attempted suicides, 1970-91, annual rpt, S0820–1
- California vital statistics, including population, births, and deaths by cause, by demographic characteristics and county, 1990 and trends, annual rpt, S0865–1
- Colorado vital statistics, including population, births, deaths by cause, abortion, marriage and divorce, and adoption, by demographic characteristics and location, 1990 and trends, annual rpt, S1010–1
- Connecticut vital statistics, including births, deaths by cause, marriages, and divorces, by demographic characteristics and location, 1989, annual rpt, S1200–1
- Delaware vital statistics, including births, deaths by cause, and marriages and

Suicide

dissolutions, by demographic characteristics and location, 1990, annual rpt, S1385–2

- Florida deaths by selected cause, and incidence of selected communicable diseases, by county, 1992 annual rpt, S1746–1.1
- Florida vital statistics, including population, births, deaths by cause, and marriages and dissolutions, by location and demographic characteristics, 1992 and trends, annual rpt, S1745–3
- Georgia county guide, general data, 1993 annual rpt, U6750–1
- Georgia vital statistics, including deaths by cause, demographic characteristics, and location, 1991 and trends, annual rpt, S1895–1.2
- Hawaii health dept activities and services, including vital statistics and disease control, by location, 1990, annual rpt, S2065–1
- Idaho vital statistics, including births, deaths by cause, abortions, marriages, and divorces, by demographic characteristics and county, 1991 and trends, annual rpt, S2250–2
- Iowa suicides, with detail for teenagers, 1991, annual rpt, S2795–1
- Kansas vital statistics, including population, births, deaths by cause, abortions, marriages, and divorces, by demographic characteristics and location, 1991 and trends, annual rpt, S2975–1
- Kentucky vital statistics, including births, deaths by cause, marriages and divorces, and population, by demographic characteristics and county, 1991, annual rpt, S3140–1
- Louisiana vital statistics, including population, births, deaths by cause, reportable diseases, marriages, and divorces, by demographic characteristics and locality, 1989-90 and trends, annual rpt, S3295–1
- Maine vital statistics, including births, deaths by cause, abortions, and marriages and divorces, by demographic characteristics and location, 1991 and trends, annual rpt, S3460 2
- Maryland vital statistics, including population, births, deaths by cause, marriages, and divorces, by demographic characteristics and location, 1989 and trends, annual rpt, S3635–1
- Massachusetts vital statistics, including births, deaths by cause, marriages, divorces, and population, by locality and demographic characteristics, 1990 and trends, annual rpt, S3850–1
- Michigan vital statistics, including births, deaths, marriages, divorces/annulments, and communicable diseases, by location and demographic characteristics, 1990 and trends, annual rpt, S4000–3
- Minnesota vital statistics, including population, births, abortions, deaths, marriages, and divorces, by location and demographic characteristics, 1991 and trends, annual rpt, S4190–2
- Mississippi vital statistics, including births, deaths by cause, marriages, and divorces, by demographic characteristics and location, 1992 and trends, annual rpt, S4350–1
- Missouri vital statistics, including population, births, deaths by cause, and marriages and divorces, by location and demographic characteristics, 1992 and trends, annual rpt, S4518–1
- Montana vital statistics, including births, deaths by cause, abortion, disease, and marriage and divorce, by demographic characteristics and county, 1990-91 and trends, annual rpt, S4690–1
- Nebraska vital statistics, including births, deaths, marriages, divorces, and population, by demographic characteristics and location, 1991 and trends, annual rpt, S4885–1
- Nevada suicides, by method, decedent characteristics, and county, 1989 and trends, annual rpt, S5075–1
- New Hampshire vital statistics, including population, births, deaths by cause, marriages, and divorces, by location and demographic characteristics, 1991 and trends, annual rpt, S5215–1
- New Jersey vital statistics, including births, deaths, population, communicable diseases, and marriages and divorces, by demographic characteristics and location, 1990 and trends, annual rpt, S5405–1
- New Mexico vital statistics, including population, births, deaths, and disease, by location and demographic characteristics, 1991 and trends, annual rpt, S5605–1
- New York State prison inmate suicides in State and local facilities, 1978-91, annual rpt, S5760–3.4
- New York State vital statistics, including population, births, deaths by cause, reportable diseases, and marriages and dissolutions, by demographic characteristics and/or location, 1990 and trends, annual rpt, S5765–1
- North Carolina deaths and rates, by cause and county, 1991 and trends, annual rpt, S5927–1.2
- North Dakota vital statistics, including births, deaths by cause, marriages and divorces, and abortions, by demographic characteristics and/or county, 1991 and trends, annual rpt, S6105–2
- Ohio vital statistics, including births, deaths by cause, marriages, divorces, and population, by demographic characteristics and location, 1991 and trends, annual rpt, S6285–1
- Oregon vital statistics, including births, deaths by cause, communicable diseases, marriages, and divorces, by age, sex, race-ethnicity, and county, 1991 and trends, annual rpt, S6615–5
- Rhode Island vital statistics, including population, births, deaths, marriages, and divorces, by demographic characteristics and locality, 1989 and trends, annual rpt, S6995–1
- South Carolina deaths, by detailed cause, age, sex, and race, 1990, annual rpt, S7175–2
- South Carolina vital statistics, including births, deaths by cause, marriages, and divorces, by age, sex, race, and location, 1990 and trends, annual rpt, S7175–1
- South Dakota vital statistics, including births, deaths, marriage and divorce, and communicable disease, by demographic characteristics and county, 1991 and trends, annual rpt, S7345–1

Index by Subjects and Names

- Tennessee correctional instn incidents, including disturbances, assaults, and deaths, FY91-92, annual rpt, S7480–1
- Tennessee vital statistics, including births, deaths by cause, marriages, divorces, and population, by demographic characteristics and location, 1991 and trends, annual rpt, S7520–2
- Texas vital statistics, including births, deaths by cause, abortions, marriages, and divorces, by location and demographic characteristics, 1991 and trends, annual rpt, S7685–1
- Utah vital statistics, including births, deaths by cause, and population, by county and demographic characteristics, 1990 and trends, annual rpt, S7835–1
- Vermont vital statistics, including population, births, deaths by cause, abortions, marriages, and divorces, by location and demographic characteristics, 1991 and trends, annual rpt, S8054–1
- Virginia vital statistics, including births, deaths by cause, marriages and divorces, and communicable disease, by demographic characteristics and location, 1991 and trends, annual rpt, S8225–1
- Washington State vital statistics, including births, deaths by cause, and population, by demographic characteristics and location, 1991 and trends, annual rpt, S8363–1
- West Virginia vital statistics, including births, deaths by cause, marriages, and divorces, by location and demographic characteristics, 1991 and trends, annual rpt, S8560–1
- Wisconsin vital statistics, including population, births, deaths by cause, and marriages and dissolutions, by county and demographic characteristics, 1991 and trends, annual rpt, S8715–4
- Wyoming vital statistics, including population, births, deaths by cause, marriages, and divorces, by demographic characteristics and county, 1991 and trends, annual rpt, S8920–2

Sulfur

see Nonmetallic minerals and mines

Sulfuric acid

see Chemicals and chemical industry

Summer employment

see Temporary and seasonal employment

Summer homes

see Second homes

Sunglass Association of America

Sales of sunglasses, and prices, by retail outlet type, 1992, article, C5150–3.516

Sunglasses

see Personal care products

Superconductivity

see Energy research and development

Superior courts

see State courts

Supermarkets

see Food stores

Supernatural phenomena

Youth belief in supernatural phenomena, 1978-92 surveys, R8780–1.502

Supervisors and managers

see Executives and managers

Supplemental Security Income

State social, economic, and govtl indicators, with rankings, 1993 semiannual rpt, B8500–1.8

Index by Subjects and Names

State supplement to SSI for elderly living alone, and purchasing power, by State, FY92-93, annual rpt, R3834–9

Statistical profiles of 50 States and DC, general data, 1993 annual almanac, C4712–1

State and local:

- Arizona public assistance recipients and payments, by program, county, and district, monthly rpt, S0465–4
- DC statistical profile, general data, 1992 annual rpt, S1535–3.5
- Delaware public assistance recipients, funds available, and payments, by program, with selected data by county, monthly rpt, S1385–1
- Florida SSI cases and payments, by district and county, FY92, annual rpt, S1717–1
- Georgia county guide, general data, 1993 annual rpt, U6750–1
- Georgia statistical abstract, general data, 1992-93 biennial rpt, U6730–1.13
- Iowa ADC and SSI program recipients, and expenditures, by county, monthly rpt, S2802–1
- Kentucky AFDC and SSI recipients and payments, by county, monthly rpt, S3140–2
- Kentucky Medicaid recipients and payments, by program, county, and type of medical service, monthly rpt, S3140–5
- Michigan public assistance program cases, recipients, and payments, detailed data by county, monthly rpt, S4010–1
- Minnesota public welfare program recipients and expenditures, by county, 1992, semiannual rpt, S4202–1
- Missouri public welfare and medical assistance recipients, expenditures, and case processing, by program and county, FY92 and trends, annual rpt, S4575–2
- Nebraska public welfare cases, recipients, and payments, by program and county, FY92 and trends, annual rpt, S4957–1
- Nevada statistical abstract, general data, 1992 biennial rpt, S5005–1.2
- New Jersey public welfare cases, recipients, payments, and case processing, by program and county or city, monthly rpt, S5415–1
- New York State SSI program statistics, by State area, 1991, annual rpt, S5800–2.3
- Pennsylvania statistical abstract, general data, 1992 recurring rpt, U4130–6.5
- South Carolina public welfare recipients, payments, and case processing, by county and program, monthly rpt, S7252–1
- South Dakota welfare and social services recipients and payments, by program, MSA, and county, FY92, annual rpt, S7385–1
- Tennessee statistical abstract, general data, 1992/93 annual rpt, U8710–2.18
- Utah statistical abstract, general data, 1993 triennial rpt, U8960–1.6
- Wyoming welfare and social service recipients and expenditures, by program and county, FY92, annual rpt, S8908–1

Supplementary wage benefits

see Employee benefits

Supreme Court

- Public confidence in selected societal instns, 1993 Gallup Poll and trends, C4040–1.510, R8780–1.508

Public interest in news items on nomination of Ruth Ginsburg to Supreme Court, July/Aug 1993 survey, C8915–1.504

- Public opinion on credibility of Anita Hill vs Clarence Thomas in Supreme Court confirmation hearings for Thomas, Oct 1991-92 Gallup Polls, C4040–1.504
- Public opinion on preferred political ideology of next Supreme Court justice appointee, Mar 1993 Gallup Poll, C4040–1.509
- Public opinion on Supreme Court nominee Ruth Bader Ginsberg, and court ideology, June 1993 Gallup Poll, C4040–1.512

Surety bonds

- Construction companies performing bonded work, with bonded share of revenues, by type of business, 1993, annual survey rpt, A4155–1
- Insurance (property/casualty) premiums, loss ratios, and market shares, for general liability, medical malpractice, fidelity, and surety, 1991 and trends, annual article, C1050–1.502
- Oil/gas offshore platforms installed and removed in Gulf of Mexico, bonding requirements, and Minerals Management Service liability for abandoned equipment, 1993 article, C6985–2.508
- Premiums written, by type of insurance or line, 1991 and trends, annual rpt, A5650–1.2
- Premiums written, loss ratios, and market shares for property and casualty insurance, by line, leading company, and State, 1992 and trends, annual article, C1050–1.509

State and local:

- Alabama insurance industry financial and underwriting data, by company and line of coverage, 1991, annual rpt, S0160–1
- Alaska insurance industry underwriting and investment data, by company and type of insurance, with regulatory info, 1991 and trends, annual rpt, S0280–3
- Arizona insurance industry financial and underwriting data, by company and type of insurance, with regulatory info, 1992, annual rpt, S0483–1
- Connecticut insurance industry financial and underwriting data, by company and type of insurance, 1991, annual rpt, S1222–1
- Florida insurance industry financial and underwriting data, by company and line of coverage, 1991, annual rpt, S1760–1
- Idaho insurance industry financial and underwriting data, by company and type of insurance, with regulatory data, 1991, annual rpt, S2260–1
- Iowa fidelity/surety insurance premiums and losses, by company, 1992, annual rpt, S2760–1
- Kansas court bond forfeitures, by case type, district, and county, FY92, annual rpt, S3035–1
- Kansas insurance industry financial and underwriting data, by company and type of insurance, with regulatory info, 1992, annual rpt, S2990–1
- Missouri insurance industry financial and underwriting data, by company and type of insurance, with regulatory info, 1992, annual rpt, S4527–1
- Nebraska insurance premiums and losses by detailed line of coverage, by company, 1992, annual rpt, S4890–1

Oklahoma insurance industry financial and underwriting data, by company and type of insurance, with regulatory info, 1992, annual rpt, S6462–1

- Pennsylvania insurance industry financial and underwriting data, by company and line of coverage, 1991, with FY92 regulatory info, annual rpt, S6835–1
- Rhode Island insurance industry financial and underwriting data, by company and line of coverage, 1990, with FY91 regulatory info, annual rpt, S6945–2
- Utah insurance industry financial and underwriting data, by company and line of coverage, with regulatory info, 1991, annual rpt, S7845–1
- West Virginia insurance industry financial and underwriting data, by company and line of coverage, with regulatory info, 1991, annual rpt, S8575–1
- Wisconsin insurance industry financial and underwriting data, by company and line of coverage, with regulatory info, 1992, annual rpt, S8755–1

Surface area

see Land area

see Water area

Surfactants

see Soap and detergent industry

Surgeons and surgery

- Economic aspects of physician medical practice, detailed data by specialty, 1991-92 and trends, annual compilation, A2200–5
- Health care utilization review organization denial incidence for 21 surgical procedures, 1990, A1865–1.506
- Health insurance coverage and finances, and health care costs and facilities, by selected demographic characteristics, 1940s-91, annual rpt, A5173–2
- HMO cesarean section delivery coverage rates, by plan characteristics, 1990, annual rpt, A5150–2.2
- Hospital financial and operating data, including ambulatory surgery and emergency service utilization, semimonthly rpt quarterly feature, A1865–1.506, A1865–1.512
- Hospital outpatient share of surgical procedures, by census div, 1981 and 1991, article, A1865–1.501
- Hospital outpatient surgery revenue shares and outlook, 1992-94, article, A1865–1.509
- Hospital outpatient top 10 nonsurgical and surgical procedures performed, 1991, 1997, and 2002, article, A1865–1.502
- Hospital patient admission rates and length of stay, by diagnosis and procedure, payment source, age, sex, and region, 1991, B4455–4
- Hospital patient admissions, length of stay, operative procedures, and discharges by patient characteristics, 1990 or 1991 and trends, annual fact book, A1275–1.2
- Hospital patient charges and length of stay, by diagnosis and procedure, payment source, age, and region, 1991, B4455–5
- Hospital patient discharges and length of stay, by diagnosis, type of operation, age, and region, 1991, annual rpt series, B4455–1
- Hospital patient discharges and length of stay, by diagnostic related group (DRG), payment source, age, and region, 1991, annual rpt series, B4455–3

Surgeons and surgery

Hysterectomy prevalence by women's demographic characteristics, 1988 surveys, article, A2623–1.503

Medical group patient ambulatory surgery cases, by specialty, 1991, annual rpt, A6365–1

Medical school faculty and compensation, by dept, academic rank, degree, and region, 1992/93, annual rpt, A3273–2

Outpatient surgery procedures performed in hospitals and nonhospital settings, by selected procedure, 1993 article, A1865–1.518

Prostate surgery procedures, costs, and hospital stay, with data by census div and State, 1991 and trends, article, B6045–1.503

Psychiatric hospital operating data, including number of surgical procedures, 1981-91, article, A1865–1.512

Supply, finances, operative procedures, practice specialties, and education, surgeons and all physicians, 1993 annual fact book, A1275–1

Supply of physicians, by detailed specialty and location, 1992 and trends, annual rpt, A2200–3

Tonsillectomy/adenoidectomy procedures, costs, and hospital stay, with data by census div and State, 1991 and trends, article, B6045–1.502

Veterinary surgery teaching methods used at 27 US and Canadian veterinary schools, 1993 article, A3100–2.521

Veterinary surgical procedure frequency and new grad proficiency expectations of veterinarians, Illinois study, 1993 survey article, A3100–2.511

State and local:

California births by cesarean section, with detail by county, 1990 and trends, annual rpt, S0865–1

Colorado births by type of delivery, monthly 1990, annual rpt, S1010–1

Colorado hysterectomy prevalence, by age, 1990, recurring rpt, S1010–3

Delaware births, by type of place and attendant, and method of delivery, 1990, annual rpt, S1385–2

Florida hospital utilization and facilities for selected procedures, and ambulatory surgical centers, by county, 1992 annual rpt, S1746–1.2

Kentucky Medicaid recipients and payments, by program, county, and type of medical service, monthly rpt, S3140–5

Maine births by type of delivery, 1991, annual rpt, S3460–2

Massachusetts cesarean deliveries compared to total births, by age and race-ethnicity of mother and by hospital, 1990, annual rpt, S3850–1

Mississippi births by method of delivery and race, 1992, annual rpt, S4350–1

Missouri births by type of delivery, by race, county, and city, 1992, annual rpt, S4518–1

Montana inpatient and outpatient surgeries, by hospital, 1991, annual rpt, S4690–2

Nebraska births by method of delivery, 1991, annual rpt, S4885–1

New Hampshire births by cesarean section, by county and town, 1991, annual rpt, S5215–1

North Carolina births by cesarean section, by local area, 1991, annual rpt, S5927–1.1

South Carolina cesarean delivery rates, by hospital, 1990-91, annual rpt, S7125–1.10

Tennessee births by method of delivery, including cesarean section, 1991, annual rpt, S7520–2

Texas hospitals, operations, utilization, and finances, by type, ownership, size, and metro-nonmetro status, 1970s-91, U8850–8.3

Vermont births by type and place of delivery, 1991, annual rpt, S8054–1

Washington State births by type of delivery, 1991, annual rpt, S8363–1

Washington State hospital cesarean section delivery rates correlated with hospital and patient characteristics, 1987, article, A2623–1.510

West Virginia births by cesarean section, by county, 1991, annual rpt, S8560–1

Wisconsin cesarean deliveries and total births, 1970s-91, annual rpt, S8715–4

Wyoming births by method of delivery, by county, 1991, annual rpt, S8920–2

see also Medical transplants

Suriname

Energy intl sourcebook, with detail on oil and gas industry operations, supply-demand, and prices, for approx 80 countries, 1970s-91, annual compilation, C6985–10.2

Surplus government property

State and local:

Arkansas financial condition, including revenues by source, expenditures by function and locality, and fund balances, FY91-92, biennial rpt, S0780–1

Nebraska prison industries and Federal Surplus Property programs expenditures, FY92, annual rpt, S4850–1

Texas financial condition, including revenues by source, expenditures by function and dept, and investments, with data for over 400 individual funds, FY92, annual rpt, S7655–2.2

Surveillance

see Electronic surveillance

Survey techniques

see Methodology

Surveys

see Business outlook and attitude surveys

see Consumer surveys

see Cost-of-doing-business surveys

see Market research

see Media use surveys

see Methodology

see Opinion and attitude surveys

see Political attitudes and ideology

see Statistical programs and activities

Sutten, Kerry

"Federal Spending in the Northeast and Midwest: FY92", R8490–35

"Trends in Manufacturing in the Northeast-Midwest", R8490–48

Sweden

Coal industry supply-demand, employment, and trade, by country, 1990-91 and trends, annual rpt, A7400–2.2

Electronics industry trade and/or production trends by product category for 33 countries, with general economic profiles, 1993 annual rpt, A4725–1.4

Index by Subjects and Names

Infant mortality rates, by cause and characteristics of mother, 1983-86, article, A2623–1.503

Machine tool industry operating data by country and product, 1992 and trends, annual rpt, A3179–2.2

Motor vehicle world production, sales, trade, and registrations, by country, world area, manufacturer, and make, 1991 and trends, annual rpt, A0865–2.1

Newsprint shipments from 3 Scandinavian countries, total and to US, monthly rpt, A1630–4

Nuclear power generation and capacity, for 12 operating reactors, 1993 article, B6800–1.506

Nuclear reactors in operation, with capacity, electricity generation, and construction, by unit and country, 1992, annual rpt, B6800–2.2

Steel industry employment at 3 plants, and costs of early retirement and employee assistance programs, 1970s-86, R9260–16

see also Stockholm, Sweden

see also under By Foreign Country or World Area in the "Index by Categories"

Sweeteners

see Honey and beekeeping

see Sugar industry and products

see Syrups and sweeteners

Swimming

High school sports all-time records for boys and girls events, with school and student participation for 1991/92, annual rpt, A7830–2

Participation in 53 sports, by demographic characteristics, State, and census div, 1992, annual rpt series, A8485–3

State and local:

DC statistical profile, general data, 1992 annual rpt, S1535–3.6

Hawaii data book, general data, 1992 annual rpt, S2090–1.7

see also Marine accidents and safety

Swine

see Livestock and livestock industry

Switzerland

Electronics industry trade and/or production trends by product category for 33 countries, with general economic profiles, 1993 annual rpt, A4725–1.4

Machine tool industry operating data by country and product, 1992 and trends, annual rpt, A3179–2.2

Motion picture attendance for top 10 films, 1992, C9380–1.535

Motor vehicle world production, sales, trade, and registrations, by country, world area, manufacturer, and make, 1991 and trends, annual rpt, A0865–2.1

Nuclear reactors in operation, with capacity, electricity generation, and construction, by unit and country, 1992, annual rpt, B6800–2.2

see also under By Foreign Country or World Area in the "Index by Categories"

Sydney, Australia

Smoker and ex-smoker belief in smoking as cause for selected diseases, and reasons for continuing to smoke, western Sydney study, 1993 article, A2623–1.504

Symbols

see National signs and symbols

Index by Subjects and Names

Synthetic fibers and fabrics

Canada manufactured fibers imports and exports, by fiber type and trading partner, 1989-1st 9 months 1992, recurring feature, C3460–1.504

Canada manufactured fibers imports and exports, by fiber type and trading partner, 1989-92, recurring feature, C3460–1.506

Canada manufactured fibers imports and exports, by fiber type and trading partner, 1990-1st half 1993, recurring feature, C3460–1.512

Carpet and rug industry shipments by type, PPI, and US trade by country, 1991 and trends, annual rpt, A3800–1

Cellulosic fiber production and capacity, 1981-92, article, A1250–1.505

Chemical and related industries production, finances, operating ratios, employment, and trade, by country, company, and chemical, 1980s-92, annual feature, A1250–1.530

Clothing (women's and children's) garments imported, by type and fabric, recurring rpt, A5900–1

Consumption and trade by type of fiber and product, 1988-92, annual survey, C3460–1.511

Employment in textile manufactured fiber industry, for US, Europe, and selected Asian countries, 1980-91, annual feature, C3460–1.505

Foreign trade in manufactured textile fibers, detailed data by type and country, 1989-92, annual rpt, C3460–1.504

Nylon fiber production capacity, by country or world area, 1992, article, A1250–1.534

Polyester fiber production capacity worldwide, with shares for Asia vs other areas, 1985 and 1993, article, A1250–1.525

Production and trade of manufactured fibers, and mill fiber consumption, by country, 1989-91, annual feature, C3460–1.503

Production, capacity, and utilization rates, by manufactured fiber type, 1982-92, annual article, C3460–1.503

Production capacity for manufactured textile fibers, by product type and country or world region, 1980-94, annual feature, C3460–1.510

Production, consumption, and trade, detailed monthly and annual data by fiber and fabric type, monthly rpt, C3460–1

Production, consumption, stocks, trade, and prices for approx 100 basic commodities, including by country and producing State, commodity yearbook for 1993, C2400–1, C2400–2

Production of plastics and synthetic fibers, by type, 1992 and trends, annual article, A1250–1.520

Production plants for fiber products, by State and region, 1992 annual directory, C3460–1.501

World manufactured fiber production in 1988-92, and capacity as of Mar 1993 and Dec 1994, by product type and country or world region, annual rpt, C3460–1.508, C3460–1.509

Synthetic fuels

see also Alcohol fuels

see also Biomass energy

Synthetic lubricants

see Chemicals and chemical industry

Synthetic products

see Chemicals and chemical industry

see Plastics and plastics industry

see Rubber and rubber industry

see Synthetic fibers and fabrics

Syphilis

see Sexually transmitted diseases

Syria

Energy intl sourcebook, with detail on oil and gas industry operations, supply-demand, and prices, for approx 80 countries, 1970s-91, annual compilation, C6985–10.2

Syrups and sweeteners

Aspartame sugar substitute sales and market shares for 5 leading brands, year ended July 1993, article, C2710–1.545

Beverage industry data, including high fructose corn syrup and artificial sweetener production, prices, and/or demand, 1992/93 annual rpt, C0125–3.2

Brewers consumption of agricultural products, by commodity, FY64-91, annual rpt, A3455–1.1

Consumption per capita of sweeteners, by type, 1985-92, annual rpt, A4200–1

Maple syrup production and value, US and 11 leading States, 1992-93, annual rpt, S6760–1

Production, consumption, stocks, trade, and prices for approx 100 basic commodities, including by country and producing State, commodity yearbook for 1993, C2400–1, C2400–2

Sales and consumer expenditures, for food store products by type, 1991-92, annual feature, C4655–1.510

Supermarket sales by detailed product type, 1992 and trends, annual feature, C5225–1.507

Women's weight changes correlated with use of artificial sweeteners, by weight class, 1992 article, B6045–1.501

State and local:

Hawaii agricultural production and marketing, by commodity and island, 1987-91, annual rpt, S2030–1

Hawaii data book, general data, 1992 annual rpt, S2090–1.22

New York State maple syrup production, prices, and value, 1983-93, annual rpt, S5700–1

Pennsylvania maple syrup production and value, 1993 and trends, annual rpt, S6760–1

Vermont maple syrup production, price, and value, 1979-89, biennial rpt, S7978–1

see also Honey and beekeeping

Taiwan

Chemical and related industries production, finances, operating ratios, employment, and trade, by country, company, and chemical, 1980s-92, annual feature, A1250–1.530

Economic indexes for US and other industrial countries, and leading and coincident indicators, monthly rpt, U1245–1

Economic indexes for US and selected other countries, composites of leading indicators, monthly rpt, R4105–6

Tariffs and foreign trade controls

Electronics industry trade and/or production trends by product category for 33 countries, with general economic profiles, 1993 annual rpt, A4725–1.4

Energy intl sourcebook, with detail on oil and gas industry operations, supply-demand, and prices, for approx 80 countries, 1970s-91, annual compilation, C6985–10.2

Machine tool industry operating data by country and product, 1992 and trends, annual rpt, A3179–2.2

Motor vehicle world production, sales, trade, and registrations, by country, world area, manufacturer, and make, 1991 and trends, annual rpt, A0865–2.1

Nuclear reactors in operation, with capacity, electricity generation, and construction, by unit and country, 1992, annual rpt, B6800–2.2

Silver supply-demand by country and end use, with prices, futures trading, and market analyses, 1993 and trends, annual rpt, A8902–4

Textile mill consumption of manufactured fibers, cotton, and wool, for selected countries, 1984-91, annual feature, C3460–1.501

Talc

see Nonmetallic minerals and mines

Talcove, Haywood J.

"Soliciting Foreign Business To Meet Economic Development Goals", A5800–2.115

Tank, Andrew

"Information for Strategic Decisions", R4105–78.25

Tanker ships

World oil tanker and gas liquid carrier fleets, by size, 1992 annual rpt, C6985–5.2

World oil tanker fleet ships and characteristics, by country of registry, 1989 and trends, periodic basic data book, A2575–14.5

see also Oil spills

Tanks

see Military vehicles

Tanning industry

see Hides and skins

see Leather industry and products

Tape recordings

see Audiovisual equipment

see Recording industry

Tar

see Asphalt and tar

Tariffs and foreign trade controls

China trade value with US, with detail for Illinois exports, and US tariff rates and collections, for top 20-25 commodities, 1992 article, U6910–1.502

Contraceptive import regulations, imports, and prices in developing countries, by method and country, 1980s-90, R8720–1.1

Distilled spirits trade and duty rates, by product type, 1992 and trends, annual rpt, C4775–1.1

Hard goods industry foreign competition, and manufacturers views on trade issues, by product line, 1993 annual survey rpt, A1800–1

High-technology industry CEO characteristics, and views on mgmt issues including compensation and foreign trade, June 1992 survey, B4490–2.34

Tariffs and foreign trade controls

Import quotas for sugar and cotton imposed by US, by Latin American country, 1992 annual rpt, U6250–1.25

Japan auto exports to US compared to voluntary quotas, by manufacturer, 1993 and/or 1994, recurring article, C2710–3.529

Japan auto exports to US voluntary quotas, by manufacturer, FY81-93, article, R5650–2.531

Latin America statistical abstract, general data by country, 1992 annual rpt, U6250–1.26

Mexico energy tariffs for fuels and equipment, and phaseout schedule under North American Free Trade Agreement, 1993 article, C6985–1.544

Oil import fee and 3 other energy tax options considered by Clinton Admin, cost estimates by State and region, 1993 rpt, R8490–49

Paper industry tariff reductions on US-Canada trade, by product grade, 1988-93, annual rpt, C3975–5.2

Paper manufacturing machinery import tariff rates for selected countries, 1993 annual rpt, C3975–5.1

Shoe industry imports and duty rates under TSUSA, 1992 annual rpt, A4957–1

Uranium import quotas from 6 Commonwealth of Independent States Republics, 1993 article, B6790–1.501

Wine customs duties, by product type, 1992, annual rpt, C4775–2.2

see also Dumping

Tax amnesty

see Tax delinquency and evasion

Tax appeals

see Tax protests and appeals

Tax audits

see Accounting and auditing

Tax courts and cases

see Tax laws and courts

Tax credits

see Tax expenditures

see Tax incentives and shelters

Tax delinquency and evasion

State and local:

Arizona revenue dept tax audit billings and delinquent tax collections, FY92, annual rpt, S0515–1

California business tax noncompliance, most frequent types and kinds of business involved, FY92, annual rpt, S0835–1

Indiana property value and tax levies, collections, credits, and deductions, by county and type, 1991, annual rpt, S2570–1.1

Kentucky delinquent property tax collections, FY82-91, annual rpt, S3120–1

Maryland property valuations, taxes, and tax delinquencies, FY83-92, annual rpt, S3685–2

Massachusetts delinquent tax collections through 11 settlement agreements and 4 collection agencies, FY91, annual rpt, S3917–1

Montana revenue collections by tax type, and taxable establishments, production, and income, FY91-92 and trends, biennial rpt, S4750–1.1

Ohio delinquent property taxes, by county, 1991, annual rpt, S6390–1.5

South Carolina delinquent tax accounts, by county, FY92, annual rpt, S7127–2

South Carolina tax collections from audits and delinquent accounts, FY92, annual rpt, S7255–1.1

Utah delinquent tax collections, with comparison to collection costs, FY84-92, annual rpt, S7905–1

Washington State property tax collections and delinquency, by county, 1991 and trends, annual rpt, S8415–1.2

Tax exempt organizations

Investment mgmt firms in intl investing, tax-exempt assets and operating data for top firms, 1993, annual feature, C2710–2.514

Organizations exempt from Federal income tax, by asset size and organization type, 1993 article, C2425–1.507

Organizations exempt from Federal income tax, by type, 1991-92, annual article, C2176–1.517

Religious congregation views on criteria for tax-exempt status for organizations, 1992 survey, recurring rpt, A5435–4

State and local:

California property tax assessments and exemptions, by type of property, city, county, and company, FY93 and trends, annual rpt, S0835–1.2

Colorado property assessed valuation by detailed property type, and tax levy and revenue by local district, by county, 1991-92, annual rpt, S1055–3

DC tax exempt properties with highest assessed values, July 1992, annual rpt, S1507–1

Indiana property value and tax levies, collections, credits, and deductions, by county and type, 1991, annual rpt, S2570–1.1

Ohio tax exempt property assessments, by type of property and county, 1991 and trends, annual rpt, S6390–1.5

Pennsylvania statistical abstract, general data, 1992 recurring rpt, U4130–6.2

Utah statistical abstract, general data, 1993 triennial rpt, U8960–1.16

see also Nonprofit organizations and foundations

Tax exempt securities

Investment mgmt firms, assets and operating data for approx 900 instns, Jan 1993, annual feature, C2710–2.511

see also Industrial revenue bonds

see also Municipal bonds

Tax expenditures

Value of top 10 tax expenditure provisions, FY92, R8490–47

Tax incentives and shelters

Broadcasting station seller tax deferment certificates granted by FCC for sales to minority buyers, by ethnic group, 1978-1st half 1993, article, C1850–14.537

Charitable deductions claimed on tax returns by income level, and percent of returns with claims, 1991 and trends, article, C2176–1.515

Corporate charitable contributions, by donor characteristics and detailed type of recipient, 1991 and trends, annual rpt, R4105–8

Federal income tax returns, liabilities, deductions, and credits, by State and region, 1988 or 1990, R8490–47

Home office deductions, number and value of claims, 1992, article, C5800–7.512

Investment tax credit correlation with equipment investment levels, 1960-90, A1310–1.16

Real estate investment advisors tax-exempt and total assets by type, top 76 firms, 1993, annual feature, C2710–2.520

Religious congregations tax-exempt status, and views on importance of tax incentives for contributions, 1992 survey, recurring rpt, A5435–4

State and local:

Alaska State and local taxation, including taxes by type, property values, public debt, and tax shelters, by locale, 1992 and trends, annual rpt, S0285–1

Arizona income tax credits by type, and claimants, FY89-92, annual rpt, S0515–1

Arkansas homeowner property tax relief fund transactions, FY91-92, biennial rpt, S0780–1

California individual and corporate income tax returns and property tax assistance, by income class and county, 1990 and trends, annual rpt, S0855–1

California senior citizen/disabled property tax and renters assistance, by income level and county, 1991, annual rpt, S0840–2.13

Colorado personal, corporate, and fiduciary income tax returns filed, liabilities, credits, and refunds, FY92 and trends, annual rpt, S1075–1.3

DC statistical profile, general data, 1992 annual rpt, S1535–3.2, S1535–3.3

Delaware data book, general data, 1993 annual rpt, S1375–4

Hawaii data book, general data, 1992 annual rpt, S2090–1.9

Idaho business inventory sales tax exemption reimbursements, and circuit-breaker property tax relief claimants and benefits, by county, 1992 annual rpt, S2295–1

Indiana property value and tax levies, collections, credits, and deductions, by county and type, 1991, annual rpt, S2570–1.1

Iowa tax credits impact summary, including number of taxpayers and credit values, 1991, annual rpt, S2860–3

Kansas tax refunds for food sales tax and property tax homestead program, FY92 and trends, annual rpt, S3020–1

Maryland individual income tax return filings, and income and tax liability data, by city, county, and income group, 1991, annual rpt, S3685–1

Mississippi regular and elderly/disabled homestead tax exemption applications and reimbursements, by county and school district, 1989-91, annual rpt, S4435–1

Missouri senior citizens tax credit claims and refunds, FY88-92, annual rpt, S4570–1.1

Montana personal and corporate tax credits claimed by type, 1990-91, biennial rpt, S4750–1.1

Nebraska tax revenues by type, tax rates and exemptions, and aid distribution to local areas, with data by county and city, 1991, annual rpt, S4950–1

New Mexico income tax rebates and credits, by type, with detail by income level, FY91-92 annual rpt, S5660–1.2

Index by Subjects and Names

Taxation

Ohio income tax credits claimed, including home heating energy program, FY92 annual rpt, S6390–1.3

South Carolina homestead and merchants inventory exemption reimbursements to local govts, by county, 1991, annual rpt, S7127–2

South Carolina income tax credits and exemptions, FY92, annual rpt, S7255–1.2

South Dakota tax collection allowances, by type, FY92, annual rpt, S7380–1.1

Utah property tax relief claims and amounts, by program, 1991, annual rpt, S7905–1

Vermont tax credits taken in State individual income tax returns, 1991, annual rpt, S8125–1

Washington State senior citizen property tax exemption, applicants and amounts, by county, 1992, annual rpt, S8415–1.3

Wyoming State deferred compensation program for govt employees, participation and finances, FY92, annual rpt, S9010–1

see also Individual retirement arrangements

see also Tax exempt organizations

see also Tax exempt securities

see also Tax expenditures

Tax laws and courts

State and local:

- Arizona court cases and dispositions, by type of case and court, with judicial personnel and finances, by county and city, FY92, annual rpt, S0525–1
- DC court cases and dispositions, by type of case, and judicial system finances, 1992 and trends, annual rpt, S1515–1
- Hawaii court cases and dispositions, by type of court and case, and judicial circuit, FY92 and trends, annual rpt, S2115–1.2
- Hawaii tax dept case activity before State courts, FY92, annual rpt, S2120–1
- Indiana tax court caseload and dispositions, 1992, annual rpt, S2703–1.1
- Iowa court cases, processing, and dispositions, by type of court and district, with judicial dept appropriations and personnel, 1992 and trends, annual rpt, S2815–1
- Texas court cases and dispositions, by type of court and case, and location, FY92, annual rpt, S7703–1

see also Tax protests and appeals

Tax loopholes

see Tax incentives and shelters

Tax protests and appeals

Municipal govt use of property tax increment financing for infrastructure dev, with revenues vs project costs, and complaints, 1993 rpt, A5800–1.1

State and local:

- Arkansas income tax protest fund transactions, FY91-92, biennial rpt, S0780–1
- Colorado property tax abatement/refund petitions and dispositions, by county, 1992 and trends, annual rpt, S1055–3
- Hawaii tax appeals case activity before boards of review, FY92, annual rpt, S2120–1
- Iowa individual income tax abatements, with taxes, penalty, and interest, 1992, annual rpt, S2860–3

Tax reform

Budget of US proposed by Clinton Admin, with data on spending impacts by program, deficit reduction, and tax changes, FY93-98, R3834–17

Charitable contributions plans of affluent business owners as affected by 1993 tax laws, 1993 survey article, C2176–1.519

Economic impact of 4 major tax acts in 5 years following enactment, and outlook for Clinton Admin FY94 proposals, 1993 article, R9050–3.507

Energy tax options considered by Clinton Admin, total and per-household cost estimates by State and region, 1993 rpt, R8490–49

Federal revenue impact of selected tax reforms, 1993-97, annual rpt, C2500–2

Federal tax reform proposed by Clinton Admin effect on disposable income of high-income households, by income level, 1993 article, C2710–3.547

Federal tax revenue changes resulting from FY94 Federal budget, FY94-93, article, R9050–3.508

Increases in taxes proposed by Clinton Admin, impact by State, 1993 annual rpt, R8490–11

Increases in taxes proposed by Clinton Admin, impact by State, 1993 article, R9050–3.503

Manufacturing executives views on most beneficial tax reform measures, 1993 survey article, C1850–4.507

Public opinion on potential tax increases under consideration by Clinton Admin, Jan 1993 survey, C5800–7.514

State shares of upper-level income tax increases proposed by Clinton Admin, compared to population, for 10 States most and least affected, 1993 article, C8900–1.510

State tax changes enacted, with impact on revenues, by tax type and State, FY93 and trends, annual rpt, A7470–4.9

State tax reforms and impact on revenues, by State, FY94, semiannual rpt, A7955–1

State tax revenue changes expected from tax reforms, by State, FY93, article, B8500–2.503

State tax revenue changes expected from tax reforms, with detail for 14 States, FY93, article, B8500–2.502

State and local:

- Arizona revenues and economic analysts outlook for economic impact of 7 proposed tax changes, 1993 article, U0282–1.508
- Arkansas State constitutional amendment on personal property tax, election results by county, Nov 1992, biennial rpt, S0775–1
- Colorado State constitutional amendment on levying of State taxes, election results by county, 1992, biennial rpt, S1090–1
- Florida referendum concerning tax law changes, election results by county, 1992, biennial rpt, S1800–1
- Michigan referenda to limit property and homestead taxes, election results by county, Nov 1992, biennial rpt, S4020–1
- Oklahoma State constitutional amendments concerning tax reform, election results by county, 1992, biennial rpt, S6425–1
- Oregon referendum on property/renters tax relief, election results by county, 1992, biennial rpt, S6665–1
- South Dakota State tax reform measures, election results by county, 1992, biennial rpt, S7390–1

Tax sharing

see Revenue sharing

Taxation

Amusement park operating and financial data, including data for US and foreign parks, miniature golf, waterparks, and games, 1992, annual rpt, A5700–1

College freshmen attitudes on increasing taxes for the wealthy, by sex and instn type, fall 1992, annual survey, U6215–1

Congressional Member views on legislative priorities, Federal deficit, and tax increases, by political party, Dec 1992 survey, article, C8900–1.507

Electric utility financial and operating data, by State and census div, 1991 and trends, annual rpt, A4700–1

Federal expenditures by category, with comparisons to taxes paid, by State and region, FY92 and trends, annual rpt, R8490–35

Federal tax burden, by State and region, FY81 and FY91, annual rpt, R8490–11

Federal tax burden compared to grants received, by State, FY91, semiannual rpt, B8500–1.6

Federal tax burden per capita, by State, FY93 and trends, annual article, R9050–3.505

Federal tax burden under current policy and Clinton Admin proposal, with comparison to Germany, UK, and Japan, by income level, 1993 article, C8900–1.511

Federal tax increases and investment incentives in deficit reduction package signed Aug 1993, with detail for 9 provisions, 1993 article, C5800–2.541

Federal tax receipts as a percent of GNP, forecasts by qtr, monthly rpt, A7000–1

Federal tax revenues, by principal source, FY57-91, annual rpt, A3455–1.6

Federal tax revenues from States compared to Federal spending levels, and State per capita gain or loss from Federal taxes and spending, by State, FY92, article, B8500–2.521

Federal tax revenues from States compared to Federal spending levels, by State, FY91, article, B8500–2.502

GDP relation to tax revenues, US and 22 countries, 1960-91, annual rpt, R9050–1.1

Govt finances, including revenues by source, expenditures by function, and debt, detailed data for Federal, State, and local govts, 1993 annual rpt, R9050–1

Govt finances, taxation, and related issues, series, R9050–15

Govt finances, taxation, and spending policies, periodic rpt, R9050–3

Hard goods manufacturers and representatives views on tax issues and tax liability trends, by product line, 1993 annual survey rpt, A1800–1

Health care expenditures of families, including insurance premiums by source of coverage, and taxes by type, by income group, 1987, R4700–20

Insurance industry employment, payroll, share of GSP, and premium taxes, by State, 1992 annual rpt, A0375–2

Japan govt supplemental budget, and tax revenue forecasts, FY92, article, R5650–2.503

Taxation

Labor time required to earn the equivalent of yearly and daily taxes, with detail by State, 1993 annual feature, R9050–3.504

Latin America statistical abstract, general data by country, 1992 annual rpt, U6250–1.30

Public opinion on tax increases and Clinton Admin plans, Feb 1993 Gallup Poll, C4040–1.508, C4040–1.509

Public opinion on use of tax revenues to send children to public/other school selected by their parents, July 1992 survey, A7375–8

Railroad (Class I) financial and operating data, with detail by company, 1982-91, annual rpt, A3275–8.2

Railroad (Class I) financial condition, operations, and employment, by company and district, 1992, annual rpt, A3275–7

Railroad operating revenues, expenses by type, and financial condition, 1920s-92, annual rpt, A3275–5.1

Travel impact on State economies, with detail by industry sector, 1990 and trends, annual rpt, R9375–7

Trends in tax revenues, for Federal, State, and local govts, FY86-91, article, C8900–1.526

Urban public school systems independent vs dependent tax authority status, and percent using selected tax types, for 47 systems, 1990/91, A4425–4

State and local:

California, Federal revenue collections by type of tax, FY91, annual rpt, S0840–2.13

Hawaii data book, general data, 1992 annual rpt, S2090–1.9

Tennessee statistical abstract, general data, 1992/93 annual rpt, U8710–2.15

Utah govt statistical review, fiscal and socioeconomic data, 1993 annual rpt, R9380–1.3

Utah statistical abstract, general data, 1993 triennial rpt, U8960–1.7

West Virginia Federal taxes collected, by tax type, FY82-91, annual rpt, R9385–1.6

see also Agricultural finance
see also Estate tax
see also Excise tax
see also Fuel tax
see also Gift tax
see also Income taxes
see also License taxes and fees
see also Property tax
see also Revenue sharing
see also Sales tax
see also Severance taxes
see also Social security tax
see also State and local taxes
see also Tariffs and foreign trade controls
see also Tax delinquency and evasion
see also Tax exempt organizations
see also Tax expenditures
see also Tax incentives and shelters
see also Tax laws and courts
see also Tax protests and appeals
see also Tax reform
see also Unemployment insurance tax
see also User fees
see also Windfall profit tax
see also Withholding tax

Taxicabs

Business traveler and trip characteristics, including mode, purpose, and lodging, 1991, annual rpt, R9375–12

Motor vehicle fleet operating and financial data, including fleets by type, registrations by make and model, and top lessors, 1970s-93, annual rpt, C1575–2.507

Sales industry costs, including compensation, training, and travel and related expenses, with data by metro area, 1992 and trends, annual survey, C1200–1.508

State and local:

Arizona traffic accidents, fatalities, and injuries, by vehicle type, circumstances, location, and driver and victim characteristics, 1991 and trends, annual rpt, S0530–1

Connecticut traffic accidents, fatalities, and injuries, by vehicle type, circumstance, location, and driver and victim characteristics, 1992, annual rpt, S1275–1

Florida traffic accidents, fatalities, and injuries, by vehicle type, circumstance, location, and driver and victim characteristics, 1992 and trends, annual rpt, S1750–2

Hawaii data book, general data, 1992 annual rpt, S2090–1.18

Idaho traffic accidents, fatalities, and injuries, by circumstances, location, vehicle type, and driver and victim characteristics, 1992, annual rpt, S2315–1

Kentucky traffic accidents, fatalities, and injuries, by circumstances, location, vehicle type, and driver characteristics, 1992 and trends, annual rpt, S3150–2

Louisiana traffic accidents, fatalities, and injuries, by circumstances, location, and driver characteristics, 1991 and trends, annual rpt, S3345–2

Minnesota traffic accidents, fatalities, and injuries, by type of vehicle and circumstances, and driver and victim characteristics, 1992 and trends, annual rpt, S4230–2

Nevada traffic accidents, fatalities, and injuries, by circumstances, location, and vehicle type, 1992 and trends, annual rpt, S5140–1

New Jersey fatal traffic accidents and fatalities, by vehicle type, location, and circumstances, and driver and victim characteristics, 1992 and trends, annual rpt, S5430–2

North Carolina traffic accidents, fatalities, and injuries, by circumstances, location, vehicle type, and driver and victim characteristics, 1992 and trends, annual rpt, S5990–1

North Dakota traffic accidents, fatalities, and injuries, by circumstances, location, vehicle type, and driver and victim characteristics, 1992 and trends, annual rpt, S6217–1

Ohio traffic accidents, fatalities, and injuries, by circumstances, location, driver and victim characteristics, and vehicle type, 1991 and trends, annual rpt, S6290–1

Rhode Island traffic accidents, fatalities, and injuries, by circumstances, community, and driver and victim characteristics, 1991, annual rpt, S7025–1

Index by Subjects and Names

Tennessee statistical abstract, general data, 1992/93 annual rpt, U8710–2.9

Texas trade, transportation, and public utilities employment, by SIC 2- and 3-digit industry and detailed occupation, 2nd qtr 1991, triennial survey rpt, S7675–1.31

Tea

Production, consumption, stocks, trade, and prices for approx 100 basic commodities, including by country and producing State, commodity yearbook for 1993, C2400–1, C2400–2

Supermarket sales by detailed product type, 1992 and trends, annual feature, C5225–1.507

Vending machine sales by product type, and machines on location, 1992 and trends, annual rpt, C9470–1

Teacher education

Doctoral degree recipient characteristics, including citizenship status, source of support, field of study, and instn, 1990/91 and trends, annual rpt, R6000–7

Elementary/secondary education data, with detail for mathematics including test scores and teacher preparation, by State, 1993 biennial rpt, A4355–1

Elementary/secondary prospective teacher characteristics and opinions, survey of persons interested in alternative certification routes, 1992, R6350–7

Opinions of educators on teacher education and school reform goals, 1992 recurring survey rpt, A3375–1

Psychology grad depts, faculty characteristics, enrollment, and student aid, US and Canada, 1990/91 and trends, annual rpt, A2620–3

Science and math elementary/secondary education, including student and teacher characteristics, and requirements, by State, 1991/92, biennial rpt, A4355–3

Southern States higher education degree conferrals, by sex, race-ethnicity, level, and selected field, by State, 1990s and trends, biennial fact book, A8945–1.3

State-approved teacher education instns, and number affiliated with natl accreditation council, by State, 1993 article, R4800–2.512

Women and minorities in professional fields, detailed education and labor force data, 1991 and trends, recurring rpt, A3960–2.3

State and local:

Arkansas higher education FTE enrollment, and student credit hour production by program area, by academic level and instn, 1991/92 and trends, annual rpt, S0690–2

Colorado public school staff and salaries, by selected characteristics, county, and district, fall 1992 and trends, annual rpt, S1000–2.2

Delaware teacher certificates issued, and employment status of education grads, by subject area, 1991/92, annual rpt, S1430–1.3

Kentucky public school pupil/teacher ratios and teacher certification status, by region and district, 1991/92 and trends, annual rpt, S3110–1

Louisiana public school instructional staff by degree level, 1989/90-1991/92, annual rpt, S3280–1.1

Index by Subjects and Names — Teachers

Maryland elementary and secondary education data, by county, 1992/93, annual rpt, S3610–2.1

Mississippi public school instructional personnel, by position, training level, and age group, 1991/92 and trends, annual rpt, S4340–1.1

Ohio special education teacher training expenditures, 1988/89-1991/92, annual rpt, S6265–1

South Carolina educational employees and training, by school district, 1991/92, annual rpt, S7145–1.4

Tennessee public school teachers and educational level, by sex, county, city, and school district, 1991/92, annual rpt, S7490–2.1

Texas higher education student aid awards and recipients, by program and instn type, FY92, annual rpt, S7657–1.3

Utah statistical abstract, general data, 1993 triennial rpt, U8960–1.3

West Virginia new teachers trained in-State and elsewhere, by subject area and county, 1992/93, annual rpt, S8540–4.2

West Virginia teacher certifications, by field and instn, 1991/92, annual rpt, S8533–1.1

Teachers

Abuse incidence from students reported by teachers, by type of school location, 1991, R4800–2.513

Black American educational statistics, with comparisons to whites, 1970s-92, annual compilation, C6775–2.3

Business school doctoral degrees awarded and faculty positions filled and vacant, by field, 1991/92-1993/94, annual feature, A0065–2.502

Catholic colleges, elementary and high schools, enrollment, and teachers, by diocese and State, 1993 annual compilation, C4950–1

Catholic educational instns, enrollment, and teachers, 1993 annual almanac, C6885–1

Catholic schools, enrollment, and teachers, by region, State, and diocese, 1992/93 and trends, annual rpt, A7375–1

Catholic secondary school operations and finances, including enrollment by race-ethnicity and family income, 1991/92 and trends, biennial rpt, A7375–5

Catholic vs public school ratings for selected aspects of education and environment, public opinion by respondent characteristics, July 1992 survey, A7375–8

Child day care center salaries, health benefits, and turnover, for centers in 5 States or local areas, 1992 survey, annual article, A3865–2

Child day care center staff compensation, health benefits, and turnover, 1992 and trends, A3865–3

Computer Internet intl network use by elementary/secondary school teachers, 1993 survey article, R4800–2.522

Dental school faculty positions, by instn and type of dept, US and Canada, 1992, annual rpt, A1475–3.2

Dental school faculty, support personnel, and staff characteristics, by instn, 1992/93, annual rpt, A1475–4.5

Elementary/secondary new teacher views on teaching and quality of schools, after 2nd year of teaching, spring 1992 survey, B6045–2

Elementary/secondary new teacher views on teaching, and reasons for leaving profession, spring 1992 survey, article, B6045–1.504

Elementary/secondary prospective teacher characteristics and opinions, survey of persons interested in alternative certification routes, 1992, R6350–7

Elementary/secondary public and private school teachers changing schools, with reason for move, 1993 feature, R4800–2.506

Elementary/secondary teacher views on education policy issues and selected reform proposals, Jan-Feb 1993 survey, B6045–7

Elementary/secondary teachers staying at same school, changing schools, and leaving teaching, by school level and highest degree earned, 1988/89, R4800–2.502

Employment, hiring, and labor turnover data for elementary/secondary teachers, for 57 districts, Oct 1990-91, R6350–7

Europe Jewish schools, enrollment, and teachers, in France and UK, 1981/82-1991/92, article, A2050–1.1

Foreign scholars in US higher education instns, by instn, State, and country of origin, 1989/90-1991/92, annual rpt, R5580–1

Foreign scholars teaching/researching at US universities, for top 12-13 instns and countries of origin, 1991/92, article, C2175–1.502

High school vocational-academic program integration, pilot project evaluative data including achievement test results, student and teacher attitudes, and curricula, 1990, A8945–33

Higher Education Chronicle, with data and articles on enrollment, finances, and faculty and salaries, weekly rpt, C2175–1

Higher education faculty and salaries at private instns, by discipline and academic rank, 1992/93, annual rpt, A3900–4

Higher education faculty and salaries at public instns with and without collective bargaining contracts, by discipline and academic rank, 1992/93, annual rpt, A3900–5

Higher education faculty and tenure, by sex, race, and selected discipline, 1980s-91, with historical trends, recurring rpt, A3960–2

Higher education faculty compensation and employment, detailed data by rank, sex, and instn, 1992/93 and trends, annual rpt, A0800–1

Higher education full-time faculty, for 108 instns, US and Canada, 1991/92 annual rpt, A3365–1

Higher education instn policies and practices, including changes in faculty, enrollment, and finances, 1993 annual survey, A1410–1.38

Higher education instns, faculty, students, degrees, and finances, detailed data by State, 1993 annual rpt, C2175–1.531

Higher education, 2-year college enrollment, degrees, faculty and staff, and tuition/fees, by instn and State, 1992 annual directory, A0640–1

Hispanic American educational statistics, with comparisons to whites, 1970s-92, annual compilation, C6775–3.2

Latin America statistical abstract, general data by country, 1992 annual rpt, U6250–1.8

Law school enrollment by minority status, degrees conferred, staff, and library holdings, by instn, 1992/93 and trends, annual rpt, A0970–1

Library/info science school enrollment, staff and student characteristics, finances, and curricula, by school and degree program, 1991/92, annual rpt, A3235–1

Mathematics dept faculty, salaries, enrollment, and degree recipient characteristics, 1991/92 and trends, annual survey, A2085–1

Medical school faculty and compensation, by dept, academic rank, degree, and region, 1992/93, annual rpt, A3273–2

Minority teacher shares in math, biology, chemistry, and other high school subjects, by State, 1989, recurring rpt, A3960–2.2

Nursing college faculty and salaries, by personal and instn characteristics, 1992/93, annual rpt, A0615–1

Nursing higher education program finances, faculty and clinical practice, and clinic/center operations, by instn characteristics, 1992/93 biennial rpt, A0615–5

Nursing schools, programs, enrollment, student and staff characteristics, and grads, 1991 and trends, annual rpt, A8010–1

OECD member countries spending on elementary/secondary and higher education, with data on enrollment and teachers, for 15 countries, 1987, A1600–4

Optometry school faculty, enrollment and degrees, policies and programs, and finances, by instn, 1991/92, annual survey, A3370–2

Osteopathy college enrollment, student and faculty characteristics, and finances, 1992/93 and trends, annual rpt, A0620–1

Political science higher education dept characteristics, including faculty, salaries, enrollment, and finances, 1991/92 annual rpt, A2617–1

Private elementary and secondary school enrollment, staff, and finances, with detail for minorities, by school type and region, 1980s-1992/93, annual rpt, A6835–3

Psychology grad depts, faculty characteristics, enrollment, and student aid, US and Canada, 1990/91 and trends, annual rpt, A2620–3

Public health school faculty characteristics, by instn, fall 1991, recurring rpt, A3372–1

Public opinion on barring homosexuals from teaching school, for US, 9 European countries, and 3 Soviet Union Republics, 1991 survey, C8915–8.1

Public opinion on honesty/ethical standards of selected occupations, 1992 Gallup Polls and trends, C4040–1.501

Public opinion on school problems, quality, and proposed reforms, by respondent characteristics, 1993 annual Gallup Poll, A8680–1.503

Science and math elementary/secondary education, including student and teacher characteristics, and requirements, by State, 1991/92, biennial rpt, A4355–3

Teachers

Social work higher education programs, faculty and student characteristics, and student aid, with data by instn, 1992 and trends, annual rpt, A4515–1

Southern States higher education faculty and administrator characteristics and salaries, by instn type, 1990s and trends, biennial fact book, A8945–1.5

State social, economic, and govtl indicators, with rankings, 1993 semiannual rpt, B8500–1.7

Statistical profiles of 50 States and DC, general data, 1993 annual almanac, C4712–1

Theological school enrollment, staff and compensation, and finances, with data by instn, 1991/92 and trends, annual rpt, A3376–1

Urban public school performance compared to natl goals for year 2000, with data on students, teachers, and finances, for 47 systems, 1990/91 and trends, A4425–4

State and local:

Alabama public school teacher, principal, and other staff positions, by school district, 1991/92, annual rpt, S0124–1.2

Alaska public schools, enrollment, staff, and finances, by district, FY92, annual rpt, S0295–2

Alaska school teachers and admin personnel, FY92 annual rpt, S0275–1

Arizona elementary and secondary school enrollment, staff, and finances, by school district and county, FY92 and trends, annual rpt, S0470–1

Arizona higher education instns, enrollment, and faculty, with comparisons to population, 1990, article, U0280–1.511

Arizona statistical abstract, general data, 1993 recurring rpt, U5850–2.4

Arkansas public school enrollment, grads, staff, and finances, by county and school, 1991/92 and trends, annual rpt, S0660–1

California private school full- and part-time teachers, 1987/88-1992/93, annual rpt, S0825–8

California public school enrollment, grads, and staff, by race-ethnicity, 1992/93 and trends, annual rpt, S0825–9

California public school limited-English-proficiency enrollment, teachers, and programs, by 1st language, grade level, and county, 1992 and trends, annual rpt, S0825–10

California socioeconomic and govtl data for municipalities, counties, and school districts, 1993 annual rpt, C4712–3

Colorado public school staff and salaries, by selected characteristics, county, and district, fall 1992 and trends, annual rpt, S1000–2.2

Connecticut public school data, including enrollment, staff, programs, finances, and student characteristics, 1991/92, biennial rpt, S1185–3

DC statistical profile, general data, 1992 annual rpt, S1535–3.6

Delaware school enrollment, grads, staff, finances, and facilities, by county, school district, and/or instn, 1991/92, annual rpt, S1430–1

Florida higher education enrollment, degree programs, staff, and finances, by State-supported instn, with student and staff characteristics, 1991/92 annual rpt, S1725–1

Index by Subjects and Names

Georgia county guide, general data, 1993 annual rpt, U6750–1

Georgia statistical abstract, general data, 1992-93 biennial rpt, U6730–1.2

Hawaii data book, general data, 1992 annual rpt, S2090–1.3

Idaho public school personnel characteristics and salaries by position, and teachers and enrollment by school district, 1992/93, annual rpt, S2225–3

Illinois elementary and secondary school staff, by sex and county, with data on certification, 1990/91, annual rpt, S2440–1.2

Illinois higher education staff, salaries, student cost and aid, and finances, by instn, 1993 annual rpt, S2475–1.2

Indiana public school teachers and pupil/teacher ratios, by district, 1991/92, annual table, S2608–2.9

Indiana public school teachers and pupil/teacher ratios, by grade level and district, 1990/91, annual table, S2608–2.8

Iowa postsecondary enrollment, degrees, staff, and finances, by instn, 1990/91, annual rpt, S2755–1

Kansas school enrollment, grads, staff, and finances, by county, school district, and/or school, 1990/91, annual rpt, S2945–1

Kentucky higher education enrollment, degrees, staff, and finances, by State-supported instn, 1983-92, annual rpt, S3130–3

Kentucky public school finances, staff, and enrollment, by district, 1989/90-1990/91, biennial rpt, S3110–2

Kentucky public school pupil/teacher ratios and teacher certification status, by region and district, 1991/92 and trends, annual rpt, S3110–1

Louisiana elementary/secondary school operations, including enrollment, staff, finances, and detail by school district, 1991/92 and trends, annual rpt, S3280–1

Maine educational services employment, by detailed occupation, Apr 1991, triennial survey, S3465–1.26

Maine public school enrollment, facilities, staff, and finances, with selected data by county and for private schools, 1991 and trends, annual rpt, S3435–1

Maryland elementary and secondary education data, by county, Oct 1992, annual rpt, S3610–2.12

Maryland elementary and secondary education data, by county, 1992/93, annual rpt, S3610–2.10

Maryland elementary and secondary education statistical summary, with data by county, 1991/92-1992/93 and trends, annual rpt, S3610–1

Maryland statistical abstract, general data, 1993-94 biennial rpt, S3605–1.2

Massachusetts public elementary/secondary education summary data, 1989/90-1991/92 and trends, annual rpt, S3810–3

Michigan school district pupil-teacher ratios, by district, 1991/92, annual rpt, S3965–3

Minnesota public school enrollment, staff, and finances, by district and county, 1991/92 and trends, annual rpt, S4165–1

Mississippi public school enrollment, staff and salaries, and finances, by district, 1991/92 and trends, annual rpt, S4340–1

Missouri higher education faculty, by rank, tenure status, age, and instn, fall 1992 and trends, annual rpt, S4520–3.3

Missouri public school finances, staff, students, and programs, detailed data, 1991/92, annual rpt, S4505–1.1

Nebraska elementary and secondary schools, enrollment by grade, and staff, with data by school district and county, annual series, S4865–2

Nevada public school enrollment, test scores, teachers, and finances, by school district, 1990/91 and trends, annual rpt, S5035–2

Nevada statistical abstract, general data, 1992 biennial rpt, S5005–1.7

New Jersey municipal and county data book, general data, 1992 annual rpt, C4712–4

New Jersey public school teachers, administrators, staff, and salaries, by county, 1991/92, annual rpt, S5385–1.2

North Carolina higher education faculty by rank, sex, and highest degree earned, by instn, fall 1992, annual rpt, U8013–1.2

North Carolina public school enrollment, grads, staff, and finances, with data by race, sex, and local district, 1991/92-1992/93 and trends, annual rpt, S5915–1

North Dakota elementary and secondary school staff characteristics and salaries, by position, region, and enrollment size, 1992/93 annual rpt, S6180–3

North Dakota elementary and secondary schools, enrollment, and staff, by school type and location, 1992/93 annual directory, S6180–2

Oklahoma public school performance indicators, including students and achievement, finances, and staff, by district, 1990/91-1991/92 and trends, annual rpt, S6423–2

Oklahoma school personnel, including teachers by degree level and experience, 1991/92, annual rpt, S6423–1.2

Oregon elementary and secondary public school enrollment by race-ethnicity and teachers, by instn, Oct 1992, annual rpt, S6590–1.1

Oregon elementary and secondary public school personnel by position, by county, Oct 1991, annual rpt, S6590–1.2

Oregon elementary and secondary schools and student/teacher ratios, by school type and size, Oct 1992, annual rpt, S6590–1.7

Pennsylvania elementary/secondary and higher education enrollment, grads, staff, and finances, by instn type, 1981/82-1996/97, recurring rpt, S6790–5.10

Pennsylvania higher education faculty employment, compensation, and tenure status, by sex and type of instn, 1991/92 and trends, annual rpt, S6790–5.5

Pennsylvania higher education faculty employment, compensation, and tenure status, by sex and type of instn, 1992/93 and trends, annual rpt, S6790–5.13

Pennsylvania public school personnel and salary data, by position and district, 1992/93 and trends, annual rpt, S6790–5.12

Index by Subjects and Names

Pennsylvania vocational education enrollment, student characteristics, and faculty, by program and/or school, 1991/92 and trends, annual rpt, S6790–5.7

Rhode Island statistical almanac, general data, 1993 annual rpt, C7975–1.1

South Carolina educational employees and training, by school district, 1991/92, annual rpt, S7145–1.4

South Carolina higher education enrollment, degrees, staff, and finances, by instn, 1992 and trends, annual rpt, S7185–2

South Dakota public higher education finances, staff, enrollment, degrees, and facilities, by instn, FY93 annual rpt, S7375–1

South Dakota school enrollment, finances, grads, and staff, by district, 1991/92 and trends, annual rpt, S7315–1

Tennessee higher education finances, student aid and expenses, and faculty and salaries, by instn, 1992/93 and trends, annual rpt, S7525–1.2

Tennessee public school teachers and highest educational level, by sex, county, city, and school district, 1991/92, annual rpt, S7490–2.1

Texas elementary/secondary education personnel and salaries, by district and county, 1991/92, annual rpt, S7670–1.4

Texas elementary/secondary education personnel, by sex and race-ethnicity, by district and county, 1991/92, annual rpt, S7670–1.3

Texas higher education enrollment and faculty, by race-ethnicity, sex, and instn, 1991/92 and trends, annual rpt, S7657–1.1

Utah govt statistical review, fiscal and socioeconomic data, 1993 annual rpt, R9380–1.8

Utah higher education degrees, enrollment, staff, and finances, by public instn, with selected comparisons to instns in other States, 1993/94 annual rpt, S7895–2

Utah public schools, enrollment, attendance, personnel, and finances, by school district, 1991/92, annual rpt, S7815–1

Virginia public school enrollment, grads, finances, and staff, by county and municipality, 1991/92, annual rpt, S8190–3

West Virginia higher education faculty characteristics and salary, by instn, 1992 and trends, annual rpt, S8533–1.2

West Virginia public and private schools, enrollment, grads, and staff, by county, 1991/92, annual rpt, S8540–3

West Virginia public school finances, enrollment, staff, and programs, by county, 1992/93 and trends, annual rpt, S8540–4

Wisconsin elementary and secondary school enrollment, staff, costs, and State aid, by school district, 1992/93 and trends, annual rpt, S8795–2

Wyoming public school staff and salaries, by position and district, 1991/92, annual rpt, S8890–1.2

see also Educational employees pay

see also Faculty tenure

see also Teacher education

Teaching aids and devices

see Audiovisual education

see Educational materials

Technical assistance

see International assistance

see Military assistance

Technical education

Cuba enrollment at technical schools and universities, 1970/71-1984/85, annual rpt, U6250–1.8

Engineering degrees awarded, by State, instn, and field, with detail for women, minorities, and foreign students, 1991/92, annual rpt, A0685–1

Engineering program enrollment, by instn, field, and State, with detail for women, minorities, and foreign students, fall 1992, annual rpt, A0685–2

Foreign students enrolled in US higher education instns, by instn, State, country of origin, and demographic characteristics, 1991/92 and trends, annual rpt, R5580–1

Higher education, 2-year college enrollment, degrees, faculty and staff, and tuition/fees, by instn and State, 1992 annual directory, A0640–1

Salaries of scientists, engineers, technicians, and other professionals, by employee and employer characteristics, 1990s and trends, biennial rpt, A3960–1

Salary and job offers for college grads, by field of study, type of employer, and degree level, by region, interim rpt series, A3940–1

Salary and job offers for college grads, by field of study, type of employer, and degree level, series, A3940–2

Women and minorities in professional fields, detailed education and labor force data, 1980s-91, with historical trends, recurring rpt, A3960–2

State and local:

Alabama statistical abstract, general data, 1992 recurring rpt, U5680–2.4

Arkansas higher education enrollment by student characteristics and geographic origins, by instn, fall 1991 and trends, annual rpt, S0690–1

Arkansas higher education finances, including revenues by source, expenditures by function, and State appropriations, by public instn, FY80s-95, biennial rpt, S0690–4

Arkansas higher education FTE enrollment, and student credit hour production by program area, by academic level and instn, 1991/92 and trends, annual rpt, S0690–2

Illinois higher education enrollment, degrees, staff, and finances, by public and private instn and student characteristics, 1993 annual rpt, S2475–1

Iowa postsecondary enrollment, degrees, staff, and finances, by instn, 1990/91, annual rpt, S2755–1

Maryland elementary and secondary education statistical summary, with data by county, 1991/92-1992/93 and trends, annual rpt, S3610–1

Minnesota postsecondary education finances, and enrollment by student characteristics, by type of school system, 1970s-93, biennial rpt, S4195–2.2

North Carolina higher education enrollment, degrees, libraries, staff, and student

Technology transfer

characteristics, finances, and housing, by instn, 1992/93 and trends, annual rpt, U8013–1

Pennsylvania higher education degrees conferred, by level, sex, race-ethnicity, instn type, and field of study, 1991/92 and trends, annual rpt, S6790–5.15

Pennsylvania vocational education enrollment, student characteristics, and faculty, by program and/or school, 1991/92 and trends, annual rpt, S6790–5.7

Pennsylvania vocational education 1989/90 grad employment status, by program, 1991 survey, annual rpt, S6790–5.6

South Carolina higher education enrollment, degrees, staff, and finances, by instn, 1992 and trends, annual rpt, S7185–2

South Carolina statistical abstract, general data, 1993 annual rpt, S7125–1.6

Tennessee higher education enrollment, finances, staff, and programs, by instn, 1992/93 and trends, annual rpt, S7525–1

Texas higher education enrollment, faculty, curricula, and finances, by instn, 1991/92 and trends, annual rpt, S7657–1

see also Agricultural education

see also Scientific education

see also Vocational education and training

Technicians

see Clinical laboratory technicians

see Scientists and technicians

Technological innovations

- Electronics industry conditions and outlook, including mgmt issues, global expansion, and most promising new technologies, views of CEOs, 1992/93 survey, annual feature, C1850–2.506
- Hazardous waste site cleanup innovative technologies used by EPA Superfund program, by type of contaminant, Oct 1992, article, C5800–2.537
- Manufacturing use of selected new types of technology, by employment size, 1988, annual rpt, R2800–2

see also Automation

see also Energy research and development

see also Fiber optics

see also Industrial robots

see also Lasers

see also Patents

see also Research

see also Research and development

see also Technology transfer

Technology

see Research

see Research and development

see Science and technology

see Technological innovations

see Technology transfer

Technology transfer

- Coal industry executive concern about mining technology sales/exports to developing countries with large coal reserves, Mar 1993 survey, article, C5226–1.511
- Hard goods manufacturers opinions on establishing centers for technology transfer between companies, by product line, 1993 annual survey rpt, A1800–1
- Japan technology imports and exports, with detail by industry and trading partner, FY91 and trends, annual article, R5650–2.557

Technology transfer

Natl Technology Transfer Center telephone info service users, by State and industry sector, Oct 1992-Aug 1993, C5800–4.533

Technomic Inc.

Restaurant sales and units, for 50 fastest-growing chains, 1991-92, annual article, C1200–5.513

Teenage pregnancy

- Abortion, birth, and pregnancy rates for teenagers, by race, age group, and State, 1988, article, A5160–1.504
- Black American health and vital statistics data, with comparisons to whites, 1970s-91, annual compilation, C6775–2.2
- Black children and youth population, economic, health, and education data, with comparisons to whites, 1993 rpt, R3840–21
- Child and maternal health status indicators, with data by race and State, 1992 annual rpt, R3840–5
- Child health and well-being indicators, with selected household characteristics, by State, 1993 annual rpt, R3832–1
- Childbearing among teenagers by marital status and race, 1990, article, A8510–1.1
- Education continuation programs for teenage parents, program and participant characteristics, Arizona study, 1985-89, article, A5160–1.505
- Education deficiency indicators for mothers age 18-19, by State, 1993 biennial rpt, A4355–1
- Latin America statistical abstract, general data by country, 1992 annual rpt, U6250–1.6
- Low-income families and children, health and welfare indicators, with data by State and city, 1992 annual rpt, R3840–11
- Male youth contraception and paternity attitudes and behavior, correlation with selected characteristics, 1988 survey, article, A5160–1.502
- School-based health clinics effect on student pregnancy rates, St Paul Minn study, 1971/72-1986/87, article, A5160–1.502
- Socioeconomic effects of unplanned childbearing among teenage girls, by race, 1993 article, A5160–1.505
- State economic dev condition indicators, including economic performance, business vitality, growth capacity, and tax/fiscal system, by State, 1993 annual rpt, R4225–1.1
- State social, economic, and govtl indicators, with rankings, 1993 semiannual rpt, B8500–1.9
- Statistical profiles of 50 States and DC, general data, 1993 annual almanac, C4712–1
- Substance abuse correlated with risky sexual behavior among teenage pregnant women, 1988/89 Northwest metro area study, article, A5160–1.501
- Urban public school systems pregnancy prevention, infant care, and parenting programs for teenagers, for 47 systems, 1990/91, A4425–4

State and local:

Alabama vital statistics, including population, births, deaths by cause, marriages, and divorces, by location and demographic characteristics, 1992 and trends, annual rpt, S0175–2

Alaska vital statistics, including births, deaths by cause, marriages, divorces, adoptions, and population, by demographic characteristics and location, 1990, annual rpt, S0315–1

Arkansas vital statistics, including births, deaths by cause, marriages, and divorces, by age, sex, race, and county, 1991 and trends, annual rpt, S0685–1

California vital statistics, including population, births, and deaths by cause, by demographic characteristics and county, 1990 and trends, annual rpt, S0865–1

Colorado births to teenagers, by age group and local area, 1991, annual planning rpt, S1040–3.1

Colorado vital statistics, including population, births, deaths by cause, abortion, marriage and divorce, and adoption, by demographic characteristics and location, 1990 and trends, annual rpt, S1010–1

Connecticut vital statistics, including births, deaths by cause, marriages, and divorces, by demographic characteristics and location, 1989, annual rpt, S1200–1

Delaware vital statistics, including births, deaths by cause, and marriages and dissolutions, by demographic characteristics and location, 1990, annual rpt, S1385–2

Florida vital statistics, including population, births, deaths by cause, and marriages and dissolutions, by location and demographic characteristics, 1992 and trends, annual rpt, S1745–3

Georgia vital statistics, including population, births, abortions, marriages, and divorces, by demographic characteristics and location, 1991 and trends, annual rpt, S1895–1.1

Hawaii health dept activities and services, including vital statistics and disease control, by location, 1990, annual rpt, S2065–1

Idaho vital statistics, including births, deaths by cause, abortions, marriages, and divorces, by demographic characteristics and county, 1991 and trends, annual rpt, S2250–2

Iowa vital statistics, including population, births, deaths by cause, marriages, and divorces, by demographic characteristics and location, 1991 and trends, annual rpt, S2795–1

Kansas vital statistics, including population, births, deaths by cause, abortions, marriages, and divorces, by demographic characteristics and location, 1991 and trends, annual rpt, S2975–1

Kentucky vital statistics, including births, deaths by cause, marriages and divorces, and population, by demographic characteristics and county, 1991, annual rpt, S3140–1

Louisiana vital statistics, including population, births, deaths by cause, reportable diseases, marriages, and divorces, by demographic characteristics and locality, 1989-90 and trends, annual rpt, S3295–1

Maine vital statistics, including births, deaths by cause, abortions, and marriages and divorces, by demographic characteristics and location, 1991 and trends, annual rpt, S3460–2

Index by Subjects and Names

Maryland vital statistics, including population, births, deaths by cause, marriages, and divorces, by demographic characteristics and location, 1989 and trends, annual rpt, S3635–1

Massachusetts vital statistics, including births, deaths by cause, marriages, divorces, and population, by locality and demographic characteristics, 1990 and trends, annual rpt, S3850–1

Michigan labor force planning rpt, including characteristics of Job Training Partnership Act eligible population by State area, 1993 annual rpt, S3980–1.2

Michigan vital statistics, including births, deaths, marriages, divorces/annulments, and communicable diseases, by location and demographic characteristics, 1990 and trends, annual rpt, S4000–3

Minnesota vital statistics, including population, births, abortions, deaths, marriages, and divorces, by location and demographic characteristics, 1991 and trends, annual rpt, S4190–2

Mississippi vital statistics, including births, deaths by cause, marriages, and divorces, by demographic characteristics and location, 1992 and trends, annual rpt, S4350–1

Missouri vital statistics, including population, births, deaths by cause, and marriages and divorces, by location and demographic characteristics, 1992 and trends, annual rpt, S4518–1

Montana vital statistics, including births, deaths by cause, abortion, disease, and marriage and divorce, by demographic characteristics and county, 1990-91 and trends, annual rpt, S4690–1

Nebraska vital statistics, including births, deaths, marriages, divorces, and population, by demographic characteristics and location, 1991 and trends, annual rpt, S4885–1

Nevada vital statistics, including births, abortions, and deaths by cause, by county and demographic characteristics, 1989 and trends, annual rpt, S5075–1

New Hampshire vital statistics, including population, births, deaths by cause, marriages, and divorces, by location and demographic characteristics, 1991 and trends, annual rpt, S5215–1

New Jersey vital statistics, including births, deaths, population, communicable diseases, and marriages and divorces, by demographic characteristics and location, 1990 and trends, annual rpt, S5405–1

New Mexico vital statistics, including population, births, deaths, and disease, by location and demographic characteristics, 1991 and trends, annual rpt, S5605–1

New York State vital statistics, including population, births, deaths by cause, reportable diseases, and marriages and dissolutions, by demographic characteristics and/or location, 1990 and trends, annual rpt, S5765–1

North Carolina public school pregnant students in exceptional programs, 1992/93, annual rpt, S5915–1.1

North Dakota vital statistics, including births, deaths by cause, marriages and divorces, and abortions, by demographic characteristics and/or county, 1991 and trends, annual rpt, S6105–2

Index by Subjects and Names

Ohio vital statistics, including births, deaths by cause, marriages, divorces, and population, by demographic characteristics and location, 1991 and trends, annual rpt, S6285–1

Oregon vital statistics, including teenage pregnancies and abortions by demographic characteristics, 1991 and trends, annual rpt, S6615–5

Pennsylvania labor force planning rpt, including data on populations with employability problems, FY92 annual rpt, S6845–3.3

Rhode Island vital statistics, including population, births, deaths, marriages, and divorces, by demographic characteristics and locality, 1989 and trends, annual rpt, S6995–1

South Carolina teenage pregnancies and outcomes, by county, 1990, annual rpt, S7145–1.1

South Carolina vital statistics, including births, deaths by cause, marriages, and divorces, by age, sex, race, and location, 1990 and trends, annual rpt, S7175–1

South Dakota vital statistics, including births, deaths, marriage and divorce, and communicable disease, by demographic characteristics and county, 1991 and trends, annual rpt, S7345–1

Tennessee pregnancies, births, fetal deaths, and abortions, by race and age of mother, 1991, annual rpt, S7520–2

Tennessee statistical abstract, general data, 1992/93 annual rpt, U8710–2.17

Texas vital statistics, including births, deaths by cause, abortions, marriages, and divorces, by location and demographic characteristics, 1991 and trends, annual rpt, S7685–1

Utah vital statistics, including births, deaths by cause, and population, by county and demographic characteristics, 1990 and trends, annual rpt, S7835–1

Vermont vital statistics, including population, births, deaths by cause, abortions, marriages, and divorces, by location and demographic characteristics, 1991 and trends, annual rpt, S8054–1

Virginia vital statistics, including births, deaths by cause, marriages and divorces, and communicable disease, by demographic characteristics and location, 1991 and trends, annual rpt, S8225–1

Washington State vital statistics, including births, deaths by cause, and population, by demographic characteristics and location, 1991 and trends, annual rpt, S8363–1

West Virginia vital statistics, including births, deaths by cause, marriages, and divorces, by location and demographic characteristics, 1991 and trends, annual rpt, S8560–1

Wisconsin vital statistics, including population, births, deaths by cause, and marriages and dissolutions, by county and demographic characteristics, 1991 and trends, annual rpt, S8715–4

Wyoming vital statistics, including population, births, deaths by cause, marriages, and divorces, by demographic characteristics and county, 1991 and trends, annual rpt, S8920–2

Teenagers

see Youth

Telecommunication

Asynchronous transfer mode (ATM) transmission technology market value for computer applications, by type, 1993-97, article, C4725–3.515

Cable TV system mgmt personnel views on alternate access and personal communications services, including joint ventures with telephone companies, Jan 1993 survey, article, C2965–1.509

China telecommunication industry debt levels, with detail for top 4 cities, 1989, article, A9315–1.503

Cost of telecommunication as percent of total business costs or shipments value, by industry, 1992 article, U8710–1.501

Financial performance and growth rankings for approx 1,000 top corporations, with comparisons by industry group, 1993 annual rpt, C3950–1.505

Food marketers mgmt info system operations, employment, and finances, for wholesalers and retailers by sales size, 1993 and trends, annual survey, A4950–7

Integrated services digital network (ISDN) planned use, by Bell regional holding company, 1993-95, article, C4725–3.509

Integrated services digital network (ISDN) planned use, for Bell regional holding companies and 1 major independent carrier, 1993-94, article, C4725–3.506

Interactive media system profiles, including operating sites and price data, for 12 companies, 1993 feature, C2710–1.520

Market devs in electronics industry, including employment, factory sales, prices, and foreign trade trends, monthly rpt, A4725–2

Multinatl telecommunication operations, including number of countries with selected types of equipment, services, and staff, for 6 major carriers, 1993 article, C1850–5.520

New York Stock Exchange communication devices in use, 1983-92, annual fact book, B6625–1.2

Public relations firms and depts purchasing of selected types of support services, computer software, and telecommunications, 1992 survey, article, A8770–1.501

Public telecommunication network outages, customers affected, and average downtime, by cause, 1990/91, article, C4725–3.505

Retail industry inventory mgmt current and planned use of selected types of telecommunication equipment, by outlet type, 1993 survey, C5150–4.506

Shipment value, employment, and foreign trade, for electronics industry, by sector and product type, 1980s-92, annual rpt, A4725–1.2

State govt info resources mgmt, including data on budgets, staff, and organizational structure, by State, 1991, biennial rpt, A7121–1

State regulatory data for telecommunication services, by State, 1991/92 annual rpt, A7015–3

Teleconferencing equipment and network/services market value worldwide for audio, video, and multimedia sectors, 1992-96, article, C7000–4.510

Telephones and telephone industry

Testing equipment market value, for T-1/T-3 high-capacity telecommunication systems, 1992-97, article, C4725–3.514

Video teleconferencing customer use of public vs private networks, 1993, article, C4725–3.508

Videoconferencing substitution for air/high-speed surface travel, Boston, Mass study, 1993, 2010, and 2030, article, C5800–4.528

Wireless communication equipment worldwide shipments, by application type, 1992 and 1996, article, C1850–2.507

State and local:

California public utility and transportation regulatory data, including revenue requests and rates of return by company, FY92 annual rpt, S0930–1

DC statistical profile, general data, 1992 annual rpt, S1535–3.2

see also Audiovisual equipment

see also Communications satellites

see also Educational broadcasting

see also Electronic mail systems

see also Fiber optics

see also Information storage and retrieval systems

see also Mobile radio

see also Public broadcasting

see also Radio

see also Telegraph

see also Telephones and telephone industry

see also Television

Telecommuting

see Home-based offices and workers

see Personnel management

Telegraph

Utility regulatory agency policies and practices, and industry financial and operating data, by utility type and agency, 1991/92 annual rpt, A7015–3

Western Union offices in US and North Carolina, 1989-90, annual rpt, S5917–2

State and local.

South Dakota property tax and valuations, by property type and locality, FY92 annual rpt, S7380–1.2

Washington State public service and utility companies property value, by company and county, 1992, annual rpt, S8415–1.4

Wyoming property assessed valuations and tax levies, by property type, tax purpose, and location, 1992 and trends, annual rpt, S8990–1.2

Telemarketing

see Direct marketing

Telephones and telephone industry

Answering machines advantages vs disadvantages, public opinion, 1993 survey article, C1200–4.505

Australia new telephone service demand index, and other economic indicators, monthly rpt, U1245–1

Auto buyer plans regarding cellular telephone installation, 1992 article, C1575–2.501

Auto fleet acquisition plans, including cellular telephone installation, 1992 survey, article, C1575–2.503

Bills, average monthly residential, for electric power and other energy, and telephone, in approx 300 cities, quarterly rpt, A0150–1

Cable TV homes passed, subscribers, and finances, for telephone, cable, and direct broadcast satellite company systems, 2000, article, C1850–14.516

Telephones and telephone industry

Index by Subjects and Names

Cable TV multiple system operator subscriber base overlaps with telephone company service areas, for 9 cable and 8 telephone companies, 1993 article, C1850–14.541

Capital expenditure plans and network profiles, by company, 1992 annual article, C4725–3.502

Capital expenditures, residential subscribers, and cable miles by type, for 8 telephone and 4 cable TV companies, 1993 article, C8900–1.513

Cellular car telephone benefits and drawbacks cited by small business executives, 1993 survey article, C4687–1.508

Cellular telephone equipment sales and subscribers, 1985, 1991, and 1996, article, C2000–1.504

China telecommunication data, including telephones, digital lines, debt levels, and cellular network operations, by location, 1980s-95, articles, A9315–1.503

Congressional campaign fund finances, with expenditures by item and contributions by donor type, by candidate, district, and State, 1990 elections, C2500–6

Cordless telephone unit sales distribution by technology type, 1993 and 1996, article, C1850–2.510

Corporate fleet vehicle driver maintenance habits, model preferences, and cellular telephone and credit card use, 1993 survey, article, C1575–2.509

Direct marketing industry devs, including telemarketing activity and consumer response, 1992/93 annual rpt, A4620–1.2

EC telephones per 1,000 population, by country, 1988, R5025–9

Europe cellular telephone market penetration, for 11 countries, 1993 article, C2710–1.509

Financial ratios and performance, for over 350 SIC 4-digit industries, FY88-92, annual rpt, A6400–3

Foreign telephone company stock price and returns after privatization, for 12 firms, 1993 article, C2710–2.516

Higher education admissions dept use of toll-free telephone numbers, 1991-92, annual rpt, A6695–1

Holding company finances, operations, and subsidiaries, by company, Dec 1991, annual rpt, A9360–1

Latin America statistical abstract, general data by country, 1992 annual rpt, U6250–1.4

Life expectancy, shipments, and manufacturers market shares, for appliances by type, 1993 annual article, C2000–1.510

Local exchange carrier finances, equipment, and employment, by company, 1991 and trends, annual rpt, A9360–2

Long-distance carrier advertising expenditures and market shares, for top 3 companies, 1991-92, annual rpt, C2710–1.547

Long-distance telephone market value, and market shares for 4 major companies, 1984 and 1992, article, C8900–1.515

Magazine pay-per-call ("900" numbers) telephone services, with user costs and success ratings, for 11 publications, 1993 feature, C2575–1.504

Medical group financial and operating data, by practice characteristics, 1991, annual rpt, A6365–2

Revenues from toll-free ("800" number) service, for top 3 long-distance carriers and all others, 1992-97, article, C1200–1.504

Revenues in 1992, and stock gains since 1984 breakup of AT&T, for 7 Bell regional holding companies, 1993 article, C5800–7.552

Sales (distributor units) of consumer electronics products by type, 1991-93, annual article, C2000–1.503

Sales (factory) of corded, cordless, and cellular telephones, and telephone answering devices, 1988-92, annual rpt, A4725–4

Sales of telephones, answering devices, and related equipment, and telephone system installed base, 1981-91, annual rpt, A4725–1

Shopping center financial and operating data, with detail by type of tenant, US and Canada, 1991, triennial rpt, R9285–1

Southeastern States local residential telephone rates, for 11 States, 1989, article, U8710–1.501

State govt travel office use of toll-free (800) numbers, including number of lines and inquiries received, by State, 1992 survey, annual rpt, R9375–2

Telephone industry mgmt and technical devs, weekly rpt, C4725–3

Utility regulatory agency policies and practices, and industry financial and operating data, by utility type and agency, 1991/92 annual rpt, A7015–3

Worker reasons cited for not answering business telephone calls, 1993 survey feature, C4687–1.510

World telephone service, including access lines by type, and intl calling patterns, with comparisons to population, by area and country, 1990-91, annual rpt, B0350–1

Yellow Pages directory use among consumers, with detail by respondent characteristics, 1992 survey, annual rpt, A9500–2

Yellow Pages publisher revenues and advertising agency/media buying service billings, for top 10-15 firms, 1992, article, C2710–1.546

State and local:

Alabama households with no telephone, by municipality, 1990, recurring rpt, S0121–5

Alaska public utility financial and operating data, by company and utility type, 1991 and trends, with FY92 regulatory info, annual rpt, S0280–4

Arizona statistical abstract, general data, 1993 recurring rpt, U5850–2.19

Arkansas housing units by presence of telephone, 1990, census rpt, U5935–7

Arkansas public utility financial, operating, and regulatory data, by utility type and company, 1992 annual rpt, S0757–1

California emergency telephone service user surcharge, and universal service tax revenue, FY78-92, annual rpt, S0835–1.6

California housing units by presence of telephone, 1990, census rpt, S0840–9

California public utility and transportation regulatory data, including revenue requests and rates of return by company, FY92 annual rpt, S0930–1

California statistical abstract, general data, 1992 annual rpt, S0840–2.10

Colorado property assessed valuation, by property type and county, and for regulated industries by company, 1991-92, annual rpt, S1055–3

Florida public utility regulatory and operating data, by company and utility type, 1992 and trends, annual rpt, S1790–1

Florida statistical abstract, general data, 1992 annual rpt, U6660–1.14

Georgia statistical abstract, general data, 1992-93 biennial rpt, U6730–1.8

Hawaii data book, general data, 1992 annual rpt, S2090–1.16

Idaho public utilities regulatory data, including finances of service fund used to offset small phone company costs, FY92, annual rpt, S2290–1

Illinois telephone utility financial and operating data, by company, 1992, annual rpt, S2410–2

Kansas statistical abstract, general data, 1991/92 annual rpt, U7095–2.3

Maine housing units lacking telephones, by local area, 1990 census rpt, S3465–9

Maryland statistical abstract, general data, 1993-94 biennial rpt, S3605–1.10

Montana telephone company taxes paid and property values, and 911 emergency system fee collections, FY88-92, biennial rpt, S4750–1

Nebraska public service commission regulatory activities, with financial and operating data for individual railroads and telephone companies, FY91-92 biennial rpt, S4940–1

New Jersey housing units by presence of telephone, by county, 1990, census rpt, S5425–19

New York State public utility financial and operating data, by utility type and company, 1988-92, annual rpt, S5795–1

North Carolina public utility financial, operating, and regulatory data, by utility type and company, 1990 and trends, annual rpt, S5917–2

Oklahoma statistical abstract, general data, 1992 annual rpt, U8130–2.17

Pennsylvania housing units by presence of telephone, 1990, census rpt, U4130–13

Pennsylvania statistical abstract, general data, 1992 recurring rpt, U4130–6.9

Rhode Island housing units lacking telephones, by county and municipality, 1990 census rpt, S6930–9

South Carolina public service commission regulatory activities, with financial and operating data for individual utilities and railroads, FY92 annual rpt, S7235–1

South Carolina statistical abstract, general data, 1993 annual rpt, S7125–1.11

South Dakota percent change in telephone service in approx 20 cities, quarterly rpt, U8595–1

South Dakota property tax and valuations, by property type and locality, FY92 annual rpt, S7380–1.2

Tennessee public utility and transportation commission regulatory activities, with industry financial and operating data, 1991-92 biennial rpt, S7565–1

Index by Subjects and Names

Television

Tennessee statistical abstract, general data, 1992/93 annual rpt, U8710-2.8

Utah economic and business activity review and indicators, monthly rpt, U8960-2

Utah statistical abstract, general data, 1993 triennial rpt, U8960-1.13

Vermont public utility financial and operating data, by company, 1986-91, biennial rpt, S8100-1

Washington State public service and utility companies property value, by company and county, 1992, annual rpt, S8415-1.4

Washington State telecommunication industry financial and operating data, by company, 1988-91, annual rpt, S8450-1.5

Wisconsin business and residential telephone lines net gain, monthly rpt, S8750-1

Wyoming property assessed valuations and tax levies, by property type, tax purpose, and location, 1992 and trends, annual rpt, S8990-1.2

see also Direct marketing

see also Mobile radio

Television

- Advertisement "infomercial" acceptance by TV stations, and trends over past 2 years, Nov 1992 survey, article, C2710-1.509
- Advertisement recall by consumers, top brands or companies, 1st qtr 1993 and trends, article, C2710-1.530
- Advertising cost per 30-second spot for prime-time TV programs, 1993/94 season, article, C2710-1.543
- Advertising costs for 19 TV network special event programs, 1993, article, C2710-1.515
- Advertising expenditures by medium for top 100 advertisers, with comparisons to earnings and sales, and detail by product type and brand, 1991-92, annual rpt, C2710-1.547
- Advertising expenditures for local, spot, and syndicated TV, with detail for top 5 advertisers, 1992, article, C2710-1.516
- Advertising expenditures for local, spot, syndicated, and network TV, with detail for top 10 network advertisers, 3rd qtr 1991-92, article, C2710-1.505
- Advertising expenditures for top 25 network TV advertisers, with detail for 4 networks, 1992, annual article, C2710-1.515
- Advertising expenditures on 4 major TV networks, for top 10 network advertisers, 1st qtr 1993, article, C2710-1.528
- Advertising expenditures on 4 major TV networks, for top 10 network advertisers, 2nd qtr 1992-93, article, C2710-1.541
- Advertising exposure value for top 19 sports event telecasts (primarily auto races), 1992, article, C2710-3.529
- Advertising on TV monitors in selected public places, and on premium cable channels, reactions of marketing professionals and general public, Oct 1992 surveys, article, C2710-1.512
- Advertising purchasing plans and views of media executives, and leading agencies and advertisers, 1993 annual survey feature, C2710-1.528
- Advertising revenue trends from total, local, and natl spot ads, weekly rpt recurring article, C1850-14.509, C1850-14.514, C1850-14.536
- Advertising unpaid "plugs" on TV programs, including by program and product type, and network, Apr 1993, article, C2710-1.535
- Audience familiarity and popularity ratings of top 10 network prime-time programs, Nov 1982 and 1992, article, C2710-1.515
- Audience ratings and shares for 5 late night programs, Sept 1993 and trends, article, C2710-1.549
- Audience ratings and shares for 9 late night programs and/or segments, 1993 article, C2710-1.529
- Audience ratings for network TV and 13 leading programs, impact of out-of-home viewing, Oct-Nov 1992, article, C2710-1.519
- Audience ratings for 4 networks and top 10 programs among households earning $60,000/over, Oct 1992-Jan 1993, C2710-1.517
- Audience share predictions of advertising agency representatives, by TV network and program, 1993/94 season, annual article, C1850-14.530
- Audience shares and ratings for made-for-TV movies, Sept 1991-Aug 1992, annual feature, C9380-1.511
- Audience shares and ratings for top prime-time specials, Sept 1991-Aug 1992, annual feature, C9380-1.511
- Audience shares for 38 new network series, as projected by advertising agency executives, 1993/94, annual article, C2710-1.529
- Baseball broadcasting, including TV and radio originators, and rights payments, by major league team, 1993 annual article, C1850-14.515
- Baseball major league viewership, and provisions of new network contract, public opinion, May 1993 Gallup Poll, C4040-1.511
- Basketball (professional) broadcast coverage, by team, 1993/94, article, C1850-14.540
- Broadcast industries and cable TV devs, including data on finances, advertising, ratings, and licensing, weekly rpt, C1850-14
- Commercials most requested by advertising agencies, top 10 in 1992, article, C2710-1.511
- Consumer expectations of economic conditions and change in income, and intended durable goods purchases by type, Conference Board monthly survey, R4105-4
- Current event and issue coverage by TV and print news media, analysis of selected topics, bimonthly rpt, R3823-1
- EC TVs per 1,000 population, by country, 1988, R5025-9
- Europe TV advertising rates and countries and households reached, for 7 pan-Europe channels, 1993 article, C2710-1.517
- Europe TV viewership, for govt-run and commercial TV in 6 countries, Nov/Dec 1992, article, C2710-1.523
- Europe TVs per 1,000 persons, for EC and European Free Trade Assn countries, 1993, article, C8900-1.504
- Factory sales and shipments, foreign trade, and operating data for the electronics industry, by product category, 1980s-92, annual rpt, A4725-1
- Financial ratios and performance, for over 350 SIC 4-digit industries, FY88-92, annual rpt, A6400-3
- Football (college and professional) broadcast coverage and rights payments, by team, 1993 annual article, C1850-14.534
- Football Super Bowl TV advertising airtime and costs for 6 advertisers, Jan 1993, article, C5800-7.512
- Football Super Bowl XXVII TV advertising units purchased, for 15 major advertisers, Jan 1993, article, C2710-1.509
- Football Super Bowl XXVII TV broadcast time devoted to game vs commercials, Jan 1993, article, C2710-1.512
- Holiday vs typical evening TV audience size, 1992 article, C2710-1.503
- Home shopper characteristics, and subscribers, revenues, and ownership shares for 2 TV home shopping networks, 1993 article, C5800-7.538
- Home shopping network sales and stores, for 2 companies, 1993 annual feature, C5150-3.514
- Home shopping network sales, income, and homes reached, FY92, article, C5150-3.516
- Households with TV, by census div, State, county, Nielsen market area, and time zone, Jan 1994, annual rpt, B6670-2
- Households with TVs, and member population by age and sex, by market area, county, State, and/or census div, 1992/93, annual rpt, B0525-3
- Households with TVs, and population, by race-ethnicity, sex, and age, by market area, 1992/93, annual rpt, B0525-4
- Interactive TV services and costs, consumer opinions, Sept 1993 survey, article, C2710-1.549
- Latin America statistical abstract, general data by country, 1992 annual rpt, U6250-1.4
- Market shares for color TVs, for 5 manufacturers, 1987 92, article, C1850-2.508
- Mass media company revenues for leading firms, with detail by medium, 1991-92, annual feature, C2710-1.540
- Network revenues, profits, and audience ratings, for 4 networks, 1992, article, C5800-7.545
- News (local) TV program audience ratings, with data for top stations, 1992 articles, C1850-14.501, C1850-14.502, C1850-14.503
- Oil industry advertising expenditures for network and spot TV, including cable networks and syndicated programs, by company, 1991-92, annual fact book, C4680-1.507
- Older viewers age 50/over TV audience ratings, for top 10 prime-time programs, 1992 article, C2710-1.503
- Prime-time program ratings and audience, and TV market devs in US and abroad, weekly rpt, C9380-1
- Professional ethics code use, sources, and revisions, for newspaper and TV news journalists, 1993 survey article, A8605-1.504
- Program providers for major network prime-time, 1969-91, article, C2710-1.512
- Public broadcasting station revenues, and data on general system operations and audience, series, R4250-1

Television

Public confidence in selected societal instns, 1993 Gallup Poll and trends, C4040–1.510, R8780–1.508

Public interest in news items on TV violence warnings, and ratings of network news coverage, by respondent characteristics, July/Aug 1993 survey, C8915–1.504

Public opinion on natl issues and public TV coverage, views of leaders and general public, 1992 series, R8825–10

Public opinion on TV violence and overall quality, with detail for entertainment and news shows, by respondent characteristics, Feb 1993 survey, C8915–11.1

Public preference for TV talk shows hosted by Jay Leno vs David Letterman, Dec 1992 Gallup Poll, C4040–1.506

Public TV broadcasting hours, by type of program, producer, and distributor, 1974-90, recurring rpt, R4250–1.15

Sales (distributor units) of consumer electronics products by type, 1991-93, annual article, C2000–1.503

Sales, trade, and industry devs for consumer electronics, by product type, 1970s-92, annual rpt, A4725–4

Sales volume projections for high-definition TV (HDTV) vs digital TV (DTV), biennially 1994-2000, article, C1850–2.506

Spanish-language program audience ratings, for top 10 programs among Hispanic viewers, Oct/Nov 1992, article, C2710–1.510

Spanish-language program audience ratings, for top 20 programs among Hispanic viewers, Oct/Nov 1992, article, C4575–1.504

Spanish-language TV network market penetration, and cable/satellite connections, for 2-3 major networks, 1993 feature, C4575–1.504

Spanish-language TV network revenues, operating loss, and cash flow, for 2 major networks, 1989-92, article, C4575–1.502

Sports program viewing hours of households, for network, syndicated, and cable TV, 1985 and 1992, article, C2710–1.548

Station employment and compensation, by position, and benefits, 1991, biennial rpt, A6635–9

Station group owner companies ranked by market penetration, with stations owned, 1992/93, recurring article, C1850–14.516

Station group owner companies ranked by market penetration, with stations owned, 1993 recurring article, C1850–14.524

Station ownership changes and transaction value, 1954-92, annual article, C1850–14.510

Stations in operation, commercial and noncommercial UHF and VHF, 1988-92, annual rpt, A4725–4

Stations on the air and authorized, by type, weekly rpt, C1850–14

Statistical profiles of 50 States and DC, general data, 1993 annual almanac, C4712–1

Syndicated TV program episodes available, by program, weekly rpt recurring table, C9380–1.511

Viewership by major programming source, 1992, annual rpt, A4620–1.2

Viewership patterns for prime-time TV, and household income, by household cable TV status, 1992/93, C2710–1.520

Violence levels and audience ratings for 6 most violent TV programs, Sept-Dec 1992, article, C5800–7.542

Violence on TV and Govt regulation, opinions of advertising industry magazine readers, Oct 1993 survey, article, C2710–1.551

World audience reach by region, for 5 TV networks with intl markets, 1990-91, annual feature, C2710–1.506

State and local:

Alabama county data book, general data, 1992 annual rpt, S0121–2

Alabama statistical abstract, general data, 1992 recurring rpt, U5680–2.2

Arizona statistical abstract, general data, 1993 recurring rpt, U5850–2.19

DC expenditures of motion picture/TV industry, 1987-91, annual rpt, S1535–3.3

Georgia statistical abstract, general data, 1992-93 biennial rpt, U6730–1.8

Hawaii data book, general data, 1992 annual rpt, S2090–1.16, S2090–1.23

Kansas statistical abstract, general data, 1991/92 annual rpt, U7095–2.13

Maryland statistical abstract, general data, 1993-94 biennial rpt, S3605–1.8

Mississippi statistical abstract, general data, 1992 annual rpt, U3255–4.7

Oklahoma statistical abstract, general data, 1992 annual rpt, U8130–2.17

Tennessee statistical abstract, general data, 1992/93 annual rpt, U8710–2.8

Utah statistical abstract, general data, 1993 triennial rpt, U8960–1.13

see also Broadcast payments and rights

see also Cable television

see also Educational broadcasting

see also Home video and audio equipment

see also Political broadcasting

Television Bureau of Advertising

Political advertising expenditures on local and network TV, biennially 1980-92, article, C1850–14.502

TV advertising expenditures for local and spot ads, for top 5 product categories, 1991-93, article, C1850–14.526

TV station advertising revenue trends for total, local, and natl spot ads, weekly rpt recurring article, C1850–14.509, C1850–14.514, C1850–14.536

Temperature

see Weather

Temporary and seasonal employment

Amusement park seasonal employment by age group and earnings, with detail for miniature golf and waterparks, 1992, annual rpt, A5700–1

College freshmen attitudes and characteristics, degree and career plans, and financial aid sources, by sex and instn type, fall 1992, annual survey, U6215–1

Corporate staffing practices, including use of temporary workers and consultants or freelancers, by occupation type, 1993 survey, annual rpt, B6850–5

State and local:

Alaska employment of youths age 15-21, by occupation, industry, and sex, July-Sept 1992, article, S0320–1.509

Arizona summer youth employment through Job Training Partnership Act, by service delivery area, 1991-92, article, S0465–1.501

DC statistical profile, general data, 1992 annual rpt, S1535–3.3

Oklahoma Job Training Partnership Act funding for youth summer employment programs, by service delivery area, 1993, article, S6430–2.502

Utah summer job openings, by industry div, 1993, annual article, S7820–3.505

see also Migrant workers

see also Youth employment

Tennessee

Agricultural production and marketing, by commodity and county, with farms, acreage, and value, 1992 and trends, annual rpt, S7460–1

Banks and other financial instns financial condition, by instn, 1992 annual rpt, S7507–1

Business activity indicators, quarterly journal, U8710–1

Correctional instn admin, with inmate characteristics, and corrections dept finances and staff, FY92, annual rpt, S7480–1

Court cases and dispositions, by type of court and case, and county, FY92, annual rpt, S7585–1

Economic indicator trends and forecasts, and business executives views on selected issues, 1993 annual articles, U8710–1.502

Economic indicator trends and forecasts, with data by industry div and manufacturing group, 1982-2001, annual rpt, S7560–1

Election results, by district and/or county, 1992 general election, biennial rpt, S7580–1

Elementary and secondary school enrollment, staff, finances, and operations, by county, city, and school district, 1991/92, annual rpt, S7490–2

Employment, hours, and earnings, by industry group and MSA, monthly rpt, S7495–2

Employment, wages, and unemployment insurance contributions, by county and industry, 1991, annual rpt, S7495–1

Govt financial condition, including revenues by source, expenditures by function and object, and fund balances, FY92, annual rpt, S7505–1

Govt regulatory and inspection activity involving securities, fire prevention, insurance, and occupational licenses, FY91, annual rpt, S7466–1

Health behavior risk factor surveillance survey results, by respondent characteristics, 1986-90, annual rpt, S7520–3

Higher education enrollment, finances, staff, and programs, by instn, 1992/93 and trends, annual rpt, S7525–1

Insurance industry financial and underwriting data, by company and type of insurance, with regulatory info, 1991, annual rpt, S7466–1

Markets with daily newspapers, demographic and economic info by geographic area, US and Canada, 1993 annual rpt, C3250–1

Oil/gas industry production, finances, exploration, and reserves, by State, 1992 and trends, annual rpt, A5425–1.1

Personal income per capita, by county and MSA, 1990-91, recurring article, S7495–2.507

Index by Subjects and Names

Tests

Population, by age, sex, race, and county, 1990-2010, recurring rpt, S7560–2

Statistical abstract of Tennessee, detailed social, govtl, and economic data, 1992/93 annual rpt, U8710–2

Statistical profiles of 50 States and DC, general data, 1993 annual almanac, C4712–1

Tax revenues by source and apportionments to counties, cities, and funds, FY91-92 and trends, biennial rpt, S7570–1

Utility and transportation commission regulatory activities, with industry financial and operating data, 1991-92 biennial rpt, S7565–1

Utility and transportation regulatory agency activities, scope of jurisdiction, finances, and employees, by agency, 1991/92 annual rpt, A7015–2

Vital statistics, including births, deaths by cause, marriages, divorces, and population, by demographic characteristics and location, 1991 and trends, annual rpt, S7520–2

see also Knoxville, Tenn.

see also Memphis, Tenn.

see also under By City and By County in the "Index by Categories"

see also under By State in the "Index by Categories"

Tennessee River

Capital investment in waterfront plants/terminals, and river freight traffic, 1930s-90, annual rpt, U8710–2.9

Tennessee Valley Authority

Electric power use and cost, by distributor and consuming sector, and generating plants and capacity, 1992/93 annual rpt, U8710–2.10

Tennis

High school sports all-time records for boys and girls events, with school and student participation for 1991/92, annual rpt, A7830–2

Participation in 53 sports, by demographic characteristics, State, and census div, 1992, annual rpt series, A8485–3

Price of tennis balls in approx 300 cities, quarterly rpt, A0150–1

State and local:

Hawaii data book, general data, 1992 annual rpt, S2090–1.7

Tenure

see Faculty tenure

see Job tenure

Term limitations

see Officials

Terrain

see Topography

Territories of the U.S.

AFDC payments and error rates, by State and territory, FY92 annual rpt, S2623–1.2

Aircraft civil and military joint-use facilities, by State and selected territory, 1991, annual rpt, A0250–2.3

Aviation (general) aircraft active, landing facilities, pilots, and operating data, by FAA region and State, 1993 annual rpt, A5120–2

Bar exam results and admissions, by State and territory, 1992 and trends, annual rpt, A7458–1

Boat registrations, 1990-91, annual rpt, A8055–1

Boating (recreational) industry trends, including sales, foreign trade, and registrations by geographic area, 1980s-92, annual feature, C2425–4

Bowling assn finances and membership, and bowling establishments and lanes, by State and other area, 1991/92 and trends, annual rpt, A1015–1

Catholic population, clergy, and instns, by diocese and State, 1993 annual compilation, C4950–1

Catholic population, clergy, instns, missionaries, and religious order membership, US and worldwide, 1993 annual almanac, C6885–1

Correctional instns, inmates, staff, and cost of care, by instn, US and Canada, with operating summary by State or Province, 1992, annual directory, A1305–3

Ecologist employment characteristics, including location of employer, Mar 1992 survey, recurring rpt, A4685–1

Electric utility income and operating data, by type of company and for individual locally owned utilities, 1993 annual directory, A2625–1.501

Foundations and grants, by State and territory, 1991, annual article, C2176–1.504

General Educational Dev (GED) testing programs and results, by jurisdiction, 1992 and trends, annual rpt, A1410–16

Higher education enrollment in Texas public instns, by territory of origin, fall 1991, annual rpt, S7657–1.1

Higher education R&D funding by source, by State and for US territories, FY91, annual feature, C2175–1.503

Higher education tuition/fees and room charges, by instn, fall 1991-92, annual rpt, A7150–4

Higher education, 2-year college enrollment, degrees, faculty and staff, and tuition/fees, by instn and State, 1992 annual directory, A0640–1

Insurance (property/casualty) finances and operations, with accident and disaster data, 1991 and trends, annual rpt, A5650–1

Library and book trade reference info, including public and academic library funding, construction, and operations, by State and instn, 1992, annual compilation, C1650–3

Life insurance company mortgage and real estate holdings, by State and outlying area, 1991, biennial fact book, A1325–1.4

Mass transit funding from territorial and/or Federal govts, by territory, FY91, annual fact book, C1575–3.501

Medical group practice characteristics, including specialties, form of organization, and location, 1991 and trends, recurring rpt, A2200–7

Medicare and Medicaid recipients and benefits paid, 1991, annual rpt, A5173–2.2

Military commissary sales by location, FY92, annual feature, A2072–2.501

Mutual fund sales, by State and census div, and for Canada and US territories, 1991, annual rpt, A6025–1.2

Newspaper prices per copy for daily editions, by State and territory, 1992, annual article, A8605–1.507

Nursing schools, programs, enrollment, student and staff characteristics, and grads, 1991 and trends, annual rpt, A8010–1

Oil refining capacity of oil companies, by company and plant, 1993 annual fact book, C4680–1.507

Pharmacy degree program enrollment, by student State or territory of residence, by instn, fall 1991, annual rpt, A0630–9

Physicians by detailed specialty and location, 1992 and trends, annual rpt, A2200–3

Political science higher education dept characteristics, including faculty, salaries, enrollment, and finances, 1991/92 annual rpt, A2617–1

Private elementary and secondary school enrollment, staff, and finances, with detail for minorities, by school type and region, 1980s-1992/93, annual rpt, A6835–3

Public broadcasting revenues from State sources, by State and territory, FY91, annual rpt, R4250–1.19

Science and math elementary/secondary education, including student and teacher characteristics, by State and/or territory, 1993 biennial rpt, A4355–3

Telephone service worldwide, including access lines by type, and intl calling patterns, with comparisons to population, by world area and country, 1990-91, annual rpt, B0350–1

Tourism dev offices of State govts, activities, personnel, and budgets, by State, 1992 survey, annual rpt, R9375–2

Veterinarians by location and type of employment, 1990 and 1992, article, A3100–2.522

Veterinarians by professional characteristics and location, and financial and education summaries, 1993 annual directory, A3100–1

Workers compensation law coverage, benefits, and other info, by State, outlying area, and Canadian Province, 1993 annual rpt, A3840–2

State and local:

Missouri higher education enrollment by student characteristics and residence location, by instn, fall 1992 and trends, annual rpt, S4520–3.2

see also American Samoa

see also Guam

see also Panama Canal

see also Puerto Rico

see also Trust Territory of the Pacific Islands

see also U.S. Virgin Islands

Terrorism

Building systems engineer views on influence of terror threats and World Trade Center bombing on own designs and specifications, 1993 article, C1850–12.506

Public opinion on terrorism fears, Mar 1993 Gallup Polls and trends, C4040–1.509

see also Assassination

see also Bombs

Testing equipment

see Instruments and measuring devices

Tests

see Drug and alcohol testing

see Educational tests

see High school equivalency tests

Tests

see Medical examinations and tests
see Occupational testing and certification
see Quality control and testing

Tetanus

see Infective and parasitic diseases

Texas

- Agricultural production, marketing, and finances, by commodity and county, and farms and farmland, 1991 and trends, annual rpt series, S7630–1
- Bank financial performance trends, 1988-92, article, A6400–2.507
- Citrus fruit production and marketing data for major producing States, 1991/92 and trends, annual rpt, S1685–1.1
- Coal (lignite) production, 1980-2005, article, C5226–1.501
- Correctional instn inmates by criminal background and demographic characteristics, FY92, annual rpt, S7660–1
- Court cases and dispositions, by type of court and case, and location, with judicial dept personnel, FY92, annual rpt, S7703–1
- Crimes and arrests, by offense, location, and offender characteristics, with data on law enforcement employment, and assaults on officers, 1992 and trends, annual rpt, S7735–2
- Economic indicators for 10 Western States, including forecasts from selected organizations, monthly rpt, U0282–2
- Election results and voter registration, by district and/or county, 1992 general election, biennial series, S7750–1
- Electric utility financial and operating data, 9 largest investor-owned utilities, 1988-92, annual rpt, S7740–1
- Elementary and secondary education data, by school district and county, annual series, S7670–1
- Employment, by SIC 2- and 3-digit industry and detailed occupation, series, S7675–1
- Employment, hours, and earnings, by MSA and industry group, and unemployment insurance, monthly rpt, S7675–3
- Govt financial condition, including revenues by source, expenditures by function, and bonded indebtedness, FY92, annual rpt, S7655–3
- Govt financial condition, including revenues by source, expenditures by function and dept, and investments, with data for over 400 individual funds, FY92, annual rpt, S7655–2
- Health behavior risk factor surveillance survey results, by respondent characteristics, 1991 and trends, annual rpt, S7685–2
- Health care system policy research, including data on providers and finances, utilization, and insurance, series, U8850–8
- Higher education enrollment, faculty, curricula, and finances, by instn, 1991/92 and trends, annual rpt, S7657–1
- Insurance dept activities, with industry financial and underwriting data by line of coverage, FY92 annual rpt, S7700–1
- Labor force planning rpt, including labor force, employment by industry, income, and population, 1993 annual rpt, S7675–2
- Library holdings, circulation, staff, and finances, by public library and location, FY91, annual rpt, S7710–1
- Markets with daily newspapers, demographic and economic info by geographic area, US and Canada, 1993 annual rpt, C3250–1
- Medical malpractice insurance State joint underwriting assn (JUA) financial condition, for 11 States, 1991, annual rpt, A0375–1
- Mexico-Texas transportation system analysis, including bilateral trade, operations by transport mode, and data by locale, 1993 rpt, U8850–9
- Natural gas utility financial and operating data, by city and company, 1991, with regulatory info, annual rpt, S7745–1
- Oil and gas wells and footage drilled, by type of well, State, and offshore location, quarterly rpt, A2575–6
- Oil/gas industry production, finances, exploration, and reserves, by State, 1992 and trends, annual rpt, A5425–1.1
- Population by age, sex, race-ethnicity, and county, July 1991, annual rpt, S7645–2
- Population by age, sex, race-ethnicity, and county, 1990-2030, recurring rpt, S7645–3
- Population by city, town, and county, 1980 and 1990-91, annual rpt, S7645–1
- Printing (prepress) industry conditions for Dallas/Houston area, 1993 survey article, C1850–10.505
- Statistical profiles of 50 States and DC, general data, 1993 annual almanac, C4712–1
- Utility and transportation regulatory agency activities, scope of jurisdiction, finances, and employees, by agency, 1991/92 annual rpt, A7015–2
- Vital statistics, including births, deaths by cause, abortions, marriages, and divorces, by location and demographic characteristics, 1991 and trends, annual rpt, S7685–1
- Welfare and social services program expenditures, recipients, and fraud cases, by county and/or program, FY92 and trends, annual rpt, S7695–1

see also Dallas, Tex.
see also Fort Worth, Tex.
see also Harris County, Tex.
see also under By City and By County in the "Index by Categories"
see also under By State in the "Index by Categories"

Textbooks

- Book publishing industry financial and operating data, by publisher type and size, and subject category, 1991 and trends, annual rpt, A3274–2
- Dental school undergrad student expenses, by type and instn, 1992/93, annual rpt, A1475–4.3
- Prices for textbooks, by subject area, 1978-92, annual compilation, C1650–3.4

State and local:

- Alabama public school revenues by source and expenditures by object, by district, 1991/92, annual rpt, S0124–1.2
- Arkansas public school revenues by source, expenditures by function and object, and indebtedness, 1991/92 and trends, annual rpt, S0660–1.3
- Indiana public school expenditures by category, by district, FY92, annual tables, S2608–2.1
- Kansas school district revenues by source and expenditures by object, 1990/91, annual rpt, S2945–1
- Maryland elementary and secondary education data, by county, 1991/92 and trends, annual rpt, S3610–2.13
- Maryland elementary and secondary education data, by county, 1991/92, annual rpt, S3610–2.6, S3610–2.7
- Missouri school finances, enrollment, grads, and staff, by county and school district, 1991/92, annual rpt, S4505–1
- Oklahoma school revenues and expenditures, by program, county, and district, FY92, annual rpt, S6423–1.1
- Tennessee public school finances, by county, city, and school district, 1991/92, annual rpt, S7490–2.4
- Virginia public school enrollment, grads, finances, and staff, by county and municipality, 1991/92, annual rpt, S8190–3

Textile industry and fabrics

- Canada manufactured fibers imports and exports, by fiber type, 1989-92, C3460–1.510
- Canada textile fiber consumption and foreign trade, by fiber type, 1981-91, annual feature, C3460–1.507
- Consumption and imports of textile fiber and products by type, 1992 and trends, annual article, C3460–1.507
- Consumption and trade by type of fiber and product, 1988-92, annual survey, C3460–1.511
- Consumption of cotton and other fibers in textile production, by detailed end use, 1990-92, annual rpt, A7485–1
- Corporate performance ratings by executives for leading companies in 32 industries, 1993 annual survey feature, C8900–1.508
- Dye sales by process, and worldwide production, 1993 article, C5800–8.505
- Economic performance indicators and outlook, with industry trends and devs, monthly rpt, C5226–3
- Financial data for approx 170 textile and clothing companies, with industry statistical summary, 1991-92 and trends, annual rpt, C3400–5
- Financial performance and growth rankings for approx 1,000 top corporations, with comparisons by industry group, 1993 annual rpt, C3950–1.505
- Financial performance indicators for 32 textile companies, FY92 and trends, annual rpt, B8130–1
- Financial ratios and performance, for over 350 SIC 4-digit industries, FY88-92, annual rpt, A6400–3
- Latin America statistical abstract, general data by country, 1992 annual rpt, U6250–1.16
- Mexico textile fiber consumption and foreign trade, by fiber type, 1980s-92, C3460–1.510
- Mill financial and operating trends and outlook, 1988-93, annual article, C5226–3.502
- Operating and financial composite ratios for corporations, with establishments and receipts, for approx 200 industries, by asset size, FY90, annual rpt, C7800–1

Index by Subjects and Names

Production, consumption, and trade, detailed monthly and annual data by fiber and fabric type, monthly rpt, C3460–1

Production, consumption, stocks, trade, and prices for approx 100 basic commodities, including by country and producing State, commodity yearbook for 1993, C2400–1, C2400–2

Production, shipments, trade, and consumption, by type of fiber, 1992 and trends, annual article, C3460–1.505

Shopping center financial and operating data, with detail by type of tenant, US and Canada, 1991, triennial rpt, R9285–1

World manufactured fiber production in 1988-92, and capacity as of Mar 1993 and Dec 1994, by product type and country or world region, annual rpt, C3460–1.508, C3460–1.509

State and local:

Florida statistical abstract, general data, 1992 annual rpt, U6660–1.12

see also Carpets and rugs

see also Clothing and clothing industry

see also Cotton

see also Natural fibers

see also Silk

see also Synthetic fibers and fabrics

see also Wool and wool trade

see also under By Industry in the "Index by Categories"

Thailand

Electronics industry trade and/or production trends by product category for 33 countries, with general economic profiles, 1993 annual rpt, A4725–1.4

Energy intl sourcebook, with detail on oil and gas industry operations, supply-demand, and prices, for approx 80 countries, 1970s-91, annual compilation, C6985–10.2

Machine tool industry operating data by country and product, 1992 and trends, annual rpt, A3179–2.2

Motor vehicle world production, sales, trade, and registrations, by country, world area, manufacturer, and make, 1991 and trends, annual rpt, A0865–2.1

Mutual funds investing in Thailand, returns, assets, and other financial data, for 8 funds, 1993 article, C3950–1.527

Offshore oil/gas exploration in Gulf of Thailand, size and operator for 13 tracts licensed in Thai and Cambodian sectors, 1991-92, article, C6985–2.503

Refugee repatriated population coming from 7 Thailand camp sites, for 8 Cambodia reception centers, Mar-Nov 1992, R9372–2.502

Silver supply-demand by country and end use, with prices, futures trading, and market analyses, 1993 and trends, annual rpt, A8902–4

Theater

Broadway plays, musicals, revivals, and flops, 1899/1900-1992/93, annual feature, C9380–1.529

Broadway stage shows with over 1,000 performances, ranking of top shows, May 1993, annual feature, C9380–1.529

Financial ratios and performance, for over 350 SIC 4-digit industries, FY88-92, annual rpt, A6400–3

Nonprofit professional theater finances and operations, 1992 and trends, annual survey, A9065–1

Nonprofit professional theater finances and operations, 1992, article, C2176–1.509

Nonprofit theater income distribution by source, 1992, annual rpt, A0700–1.2

Receipts, attendance, and shows and weeks played, 1992/93 and trends, annual features, C9380–1.529

Ticket sales and industry devs, for theater and film, with detail for Broadway and road shows, and top films, weekly rpt, C9380–1

Theft

see Motor vehicle theft

see Robbery and theft

Therapy

see Occupational therapy

see Physical therapy

see Rehabilitation of the disabled

Thermal power

see Geothermal resources

Third World countries

see Developing countries

Thor, Carl

"Perspectives '93", R2800–2

Thrift institutions

see Savings institutions

Throat disorders

see Nose and throat disorders

Thurgood, Delores H.

"Summary Report, 1991: Doctorate Recipients from U.S. Universities", R6000–7

Tidal waves

see Tsunamis

Tijuana, Mexico

Women maquiladora worker characteristics and incidence of psychological problems, 1990 study, article, A2623–1.503

Timber

see Forests and forestry

see Lumber industry and products

Time

see Daylight Savings Time

Time deposits

see Bank deposits

see Certificates of deposit

Timesharing (resort)

see Resort timesharing

Tin and tin industry

Latin America statistical abstract, general data by country, 1992 annual rpt, U6250–1.23, U6250–1.25

Production, consumption, stocks, trade, and prices for approx 100 basic commodities, including by country and producing State, commodity yearbook for 1993, C2400–1, C2400–2

Supply-demand for selected metals and nonmetallic minerals, with price data, US and worldwide, 1992-93 and trends, annual feature, C5226–2.505

Tires and tire industry

Auto pneumatic tire casings production and stocks, commodity yearbook Jan-Sept 1993 updates, C2400–2

Auto pneumatic tire casings production and stocks, monthly 1982-92, commodity yearbook, C2400–1

Financial ratios and performance, for over 350 SIC 4-digit industries, FY88-92, annual rpt, A6400–3

Hispanic American career professional and business owner views on motor vehicle fleet tire brands used, 1993 survey, article, C4575–1.504

Tobacco industry and products

Japan abandoned and recycled scrap tire volume, with detail by recycled tire use, 1991, article, C2150–3.503

Life of tires by type of road surface, 1993 article, C1575–2.505

Production, trade, inventories, and/or shipments of tires and inner tubes, by vehicle type, monthly rpt suspended coverage, A8810–1

Retail aftermarket sales performance of tire maintenance products, 1993 annual feature, C0125–1.503

Shipments of original equipment and replacement tires by type, 1991-92, annual fact book, C4680–1.507

State and local:

Nebraska receipts from fees on tire sales, 1990-91, annual rpt, S4950–1.3

Titanium

see Metals and metal industries

Tobacco industry and products

Advertising expenditures by medium for top 100 advertisers, with comparisons to earnings and sales, and detail by product type and brand, 1991-92, annual rpt, C2710–1.547

Advertising expenditures in magazines, with detail for top 4 publications, 1981 and 1991, article, C2575–1.503

Canada tobacco exports to US, and cigarette retail vs black market prices, 1992 article, C3950–1.503

Cigarette added tax burden from proposed increase to finance health care reform, by State, with natl average price and taxes, 1993 article, R9050–3.509

Cigarette added tax burden from proposed increase to finance health care reform, with detail for 8 States, 1993 article, C5800–7.549

Cigarette advertisements containing coupons/other promotions, shares for 4 major and all other companies, 1991-92, article, C2710–1.536

Cigarette and other tobacco product taxation, by State, 1950s-92, annual rpt, A9075–2

Cigarette market shares, for premium and discount brands of 6 leading companies, 1991-92, article, C8130–1.510

Cigarette premium and discount brand market shares by manufacturer, with detail for leading premium brands, 1981 and 1992, article, C3950–1.514

Cigarette tow worldwide production, 1988-92, annual rpt, C3460–1.508, C3460–1.509

Corporate performance ratings by executives for leading companies in 32 industries, 1993 annual survey feature, C8900–1.508

Drugstore chains financial performance and marketing operations, with sales by product type, 1993 annual feature, C5150–2.510

Financial performance and growth rankings for approx 1,000 top corporations, with comparisons by industry group, 1993 annual rpt, C3950–1.505

Financial ratios and performance, for over 350 SIC 4-digit industries, FY88-92, annual rpt, A6400–3

Food store tobacco sales as percent of total, by company size and region, 1991-92, annual rpts, A4950–5

Tobacco industry and products

Higher education student use of and attitudes toward alcohol, drugs, and tobacco products, by sex and region, 1989-91 surveys, annual rpt, U4950–1

Latin America statistical abstract, general data by country, 1992 annual rpt, U6250–1.16, U6250–1.24

Military commissary sales, by region, product type, and individual store, FY92, annual feature, A2072–2.501

Military post exchange (Army/Air Force), sales of tobacco products, FY81-92, article, C0500–1.508

Northeast States cigarette excise and State sales taxes per pack, for 8 States, Jan 1993, article, R9050–3.502

Operating and financial composite ratios for corporations, with establishments and receipts, for approx 200 industries, by asset size, FY90, annual rpt, C7800–1

Production, consumption, stocks, trade, and prices for approx 100 basic commodities, including by country and producing State, commodity yearbook for 1993, C2400–1, C2400–2

Retail prices for selected consumer items in approx 300 cities, quarterly rpt, A0150–1

Retail sales by outlet type, and discount chain sales in major depts, by product category, 1992, annual feature, C8130–1.507

Sales and consumer expenditures, for food store products by type, 1991-92, annual feature, C4655–1.510

Sales volume shares by retail outlet type, for approx 300 food, drug, and other product categories, 1993 annual feature, C4655–1.504

Shopping center financial and operating data, with detail by type of tenant, US and Canada, 1991, triennial rpt, R9285–1

Student use of and attitudes toward alcohol, drugs, and tobacco products, 1993 survey article, B6045–1.504

Supermarket sales by detailed product type, 1992 and trends, annual feature, C5225–1.507

Supply-demand summary and other tobacco industry indicators, 1992 annual rpt, A9075–1

Vending machine sales by product type, and machines on location, 1992 and trends, annual rpt, C9470–1

State and local:

Colorado smokeless tobacco product use, by sex and age, 1990, recurring rpt, S1010–3

Florida field crop acreage, yield, production, and value, by commodity and/or county, 1992 and trends, annual rpt, S1685–1.4

Florida statistical abstract, general data, 1992 annual rpt, U6660–1.12

Georgia agricultural production, marketing, and finances, by commodity and/or county, and farms and acreage, 1991 and trends, annual rpt, S1855–1

Hawaii data book, general data, 1992 annual rpt, S2090–1.23

Iowa smokeless tobacco product use, by demographic characteristics, 1991, annual rpt, S2795–2

Kentucky agricultural production, marketing, and finances, by commodity and county; and farms, acreage, and value; 1992 and trends, annual rpt, S3085–1

Massachusetts State initiative on establishment of health protection fund financed by tobacco excise tax, election results by locality, 1992, biennial rpt, S3920–1

Missouri agricultural production, marketing, and finances, by commodity and/or county, and farms and acreage, 1988-92, annual rpt, S4480–1

Montana tobacco product tax collections, FY88-92, biennial rpt, S4750–1.1

North Carolina agricultural production, marketing, and finances, by commodity and county, 1991 and trends, annual rpt, S5885–1

North Dakota smokeless tobacco product use, 1991, annual rpt, S6105–3

Ohio agricultural production, marketing, and finances, by commodity and county, with farms and acreage, 1990-91 and trends, annual rpt, S6240–1

Pennsylvania agricultural production, marketing, and finances, by county and commodity, and farms and acreage, 1992 and trends, annual rpt, S6760–1

South Carolina agricultural production and finances, by commodity and county, 1991-92 and trends, annual rpt, U1075–3

Tennessee agricultural production and marketing, by commodity and county, with farms, acreage, and farm value, 1992 and trends, annual rpt, S7460–1

West Virginia agricultural production, marketing, and finances, by commodity or county, 1991 and trends, annual rpt, S8510–1

Wisconsin agricultural production, marketing, and finances, by commodity and county, and farms, acreage, and sales, 1992 and trends, annual rpt, S8680–1

see also Smoking

see also under By Industry in the "Index by Categories"

Tobacco tax

see Excise tax

Toiletries

see Cosmetics and toiletries

Tolls

Public hwy and toll road revenues, expenditures, and debt, by item, 1954-91, annual rpt, R9050–1.4

State and local:

Indiana financial condition, including revenues by source, expenditures by function and object, and fund balances, by agency, FY92, annual rpt, S2570–1

New York State statistical yearbook, general data, 1992 annual rpt, U5100–1.13

Tomatoes

see Vegetables and vegetable products

Tonga

Oil and gas exploration activity, with seismic lines laid, 1970-88, article, C6985–1.503

Tools

Financial ratios and performance, for over 350 SIC 4-digit industries, FY88-92, annual rpt, A6400–3

Machine tool and other manufacturing technology exports and imports, by country of destination and origin, and by detailed product type, monthly rpt, A3179–3

Machine tool production, shipments, trade, finances, orders, and use, US and worldwide, 1992 and trends, annual rpt, A3179–2

Index by Subjects and Names

Machine tool shipments and new orders for domestic and foreign markets, and backlog, monthly press release, A3179–1

Machine tool world production, trade, and consumption, by country, 1991-92, annual article, C7000–7.503

Metalworking industry devs, with machine tool orders and shipments, monthly rpt, C7000–7

Opinions of consumer hard goods manufacturers and representatives on business issues and outlook, by product line, 1992 annual survey rpt, A1800–1

see also Agricultural machinery and equipment

see also Lawn and garden equipment

Topography

Latin America statistical abstract, general data by country, 1992 annual rpt, U6250–1.1

Statistical profiles of 50 States and DC, general data, 1993 annual almanac, C4712–1

State and local:

Arizona statistical abstract, general data, 1993 recurring rpt, U5850–2.1

California socioeconomic and govtl data for municipalities, counties, and school districts, 1993 annual rpt, C4712–3

Florida municipal and county statistical profiles, general data, 1991 annual rpt, C4712–6

Florida statistical abstract, general data, 1992 annual rpt, U6660–1.8

Hawaii data book, general data, 1992 annual rpt, S2090–1.5

Idaho economic profile, general data, 1992 recurring rpt, S2218–2.7

Maryland statistical abstract, general data, 1993-94 biennial rpt, S3605–1.3

Massachusetts municipal and county profiles, general data, 1992 annual rpt, C4712–2

Oklahoma statistical abstract, general data, 1992 annual rpt, U8130–2.1

Tennessee statistical abstract, general data, 1992/93 annual rpt, U8710–2.12

Wisconsin Blue Book, general data, 1993-94 biennial rpt, S8780–1.2

see also Arid zones

see also Lakes and lakeshores

see also Land area

see also Rivers and waterways

see also Seashores

see also Tropics

see also Water area

Tornadoes

see Storms

Torts

Costs of tort cases, with comparison to economic output, 1991 and 2000, article, C1850–12.504

Costs of tort cases, with detail for medical malpractice and comparisons to 10 other countries, 1991, article, A1865–1.503

Medical malpractice premium reductions under proposed tort reform, 1993-2000, R4865–9

Reform legislation enacted, by State, 1986-92, annual rpt, A5650–1.3

State appellate and trial court caseloads and dispositions, by case type and State, 1991 and trends, annual rpt, R6600–1

Urban small claims and traffic court caseloads, processing, dispositions, judgments, and litigant satisfaction, for 3-12 jurisdictions, 1990, R6600–5

State and local:
Alaska court cases and dispositions, by type of court and case, and location, with judicial dept finances and personnel, FY92 and trends, annual rpt, S0290–1
Arizona court cases and dispositions, by type of case and court, with judicial personnel and finances, by county and city, FY92, annual rpt, S0525–1
Hawaii court cases and dispositions, by type of court and case, and judicial circuit, FY92 and trends, annual rpt, S2115–1.2
Indiana court cases and dispositions by type of court and case, and location, with judicial system finances and personnel, 1992, annual rpt, S2703–1
Iowa court cases, processing, and dispositions, by type of court and district, with judicial dept appropriations and personnel, 1992 and trends, annual rpt, S2815–1
Kansas court cases, including analysis of tort case jury awards and data by county, FY92, annual rpt, S3035–1
Maryland court caseloads and dispositions, by type of court and case, and county, with judicial personnel and finances, FY92 and trends, annual rpt, S3600–1
Massachusetts court cases and dispositions, by type of court and case, and location, FY92 and trends, annual rpt, S3807–1
New Mexico court cases and dispositions, by type of court and case, and location, with judicial system finances and personnel, FY92, annual rpt, S5623–1
Ohio court caseload and case disposition, by type of court and case, and location, 1992, annual rpt, S6385–1
Tennessee court cases and dispositions, by type of court and case, and county, FY92, annual rpt, S7585–1
Texas court cases and dispositions, by type of court and case, and location, FY92, annual rpt, S7703–1
Utah schools tort liability fund finances, by school district, FY92, annual rpt, S7815–1.2
Washington State court cases and dispositions, by type of court and case, and jurisdiction, with judicial finances and personnel, 1992 and trends, annual rpt, S8339–1

Tourism
see Travel and tourism

Towers, Perrin, Forster and Crosby
Health care costs as percent of payroll, for companies in regional vs corporate alliances under Clinton Admin reforms, by company type, 1993 article, C5800–7.550
Nonprofit organization executive salaries, by title and organization type, 1993, annual article, C2176–1.519
Tort case costs, with comparison to economic output, 1991 and 2000, article, C1850–12.504
Tort case costs, with detail for medical malpractice and comparisons to 10 other countries, 1991, article, A1865–1.503

Towne-Oller and Associates Inc.
Allergy medication market shares, for top 5 nonprescription brands, year ended Jan 1993, article, C2710–1.518
Beauty care and cosmetics new product sales performance for top brands in selected categories, biweekly rpt recurring feature, C5150–2.504, C5150–2.505, C5150–2.510, C5150–2.511
Cosmetics sales and market shares in food stores/drugstores, for 11 marketers, year ended June 1993, article, C2710–1.546
Drugstore artificial fingernail product sales trends, for 5 top brands, year ended June 1993, article, C5150–2.519
Drugstore chains top-selling products, and leading manufacturers, 1993 annual article, C5150–2.520
Drugstore health and beauty aid product sales, for 26 fastest-growing product categories, 1992, article, C5150–2.505
Drugstore sales of oral care and other dental-related products, by product type, years ended July 1991-92, articles, C5150–2.502
Drugstore sales shares for blank video vs audio cassette tapes, year ended Feb 1992-93, article, C5150–2.513
Ethnic beauty care product sales distribution by product type, 1991-92, article, C5150–2.506
Ethnic cosmetics and hair care product sales distribution by product category, year ended July 1992-93, article, C5150–2.520
First aid product, antiseptic, and elastic/health support product sales, year ended Apr 1993, article, C5150–2.515
Food store sales of total and private label analgesics and cold remedies, year ended Feb 1993, article, C2710–1.526
Health/beauty aid product supermarket sales growth, by product category, monthly rpt quarterly article, C5225–1.503, C5225–1.505, C5225–1.507, C5225–1.510
Laxative sales and market shares, for top 5 brands and private label, year ended May 1993, article, C2710–1.532
Lice treatment product market shares, including top 5 brands, year ended May 1993, article, C5150–2.517
Oral care product sales trends by product type and manufacturer, year ended June 1993 vs 1992, article, C4655–1.511
Supermarket health/beauty aid product sales shares for private label brands, 1986 and 1991-92, article, C5225–1.502
Supermarket sales of health/beauty care products by detailed type, year ended June 1993, article, C4655–1.511

Toxic substances
see Hazardous substances
see Pesticides
see Poisoning and drug reaction

Toxic waste
see Hazardous waste and disposal

Toyota Motor Corp.
State and local:
Kentucky economic impact of Toyota Motor Corp plant installation, including related State costs, employment, and benefits to other States, 1980s-2005, U7138–1.4

Toys and games
Advertising expenditures by medium for top 100 advertisers, with comparisons to earnings and sales, and detail by product type and brand, 1991-92, annual rpt, C2710–1.547
Amusement equipment in use, and revenue, by type of equipment including video games and pinball machines, 1982 and 1990-92, annual rpt, C9470–1

Amusement park operating and financial data, including data for US and foreign parks, miniature golf, waterparks, and games, 1992, annual rpt, A5700–1
Discount chain consumer natl brand preferences, by product category and chain, and by age group, 1993 survey, annual feature, C5150–3.521
Discount chain top-selling natl brands cited by managers, by product category, chain, and region, 1993 survey, annual feature, C5150–3.520
Discount store sales and productivity data for 20 depts, 1993 annual feature, C5150–3.516
Discount stores, sales, and earnings, for top chains, with detail by specialty, 1993 annual feature, C5150–3.514
Financial performance and growth rankings for approx 1,000 top corporations, with comparisons by industry group, 1993 annual rpt, C3950–1.505
Financial ratios and performance, for over 350 SIC 4-digit industries, FY88-92, annual rpt, A6400–3
Retail prices for selected consumer items in approx 300 cities, quarterly rpt, A0150–1
Retail sales by outlet type, and discount chain sales in major depts, by product category, 1992, annual feature, C8130–1.507
Sales and consumer expenditures, for food store products by type, 1991-92, annual feature, C4655–1.510
Shipments and value, by type of toy and game, 1991-92, annual rpt, A9095–1
Shipments of toys, and orders received, canceled, and/or on hand, monthly rpt, A9095–2
Shopping center financial and operating data, with detail by type of tenant, US and Canada, 1991, triennial rpt, R9285 1
Supermarket sales of nonfood products, by detailed product type, 1992, annual feature, C5225–1.508
see also Electronic games
see also Sporting goods

Trace metals
see also Lead poisoning and pollution

Tractors
see Agricultural machinery and equipment

Trade
see Agricultural exports and imports
see Arms trade
see Balance of payments
see Barter exchange
see Coal exports and imports
see Foreign trade
see Foreign trade promotion
see International assistance
see Interstate commerce
see Marketing
see Military assistance
see Natural gas exports and imports
see Petroleum exports and imports
see Retail trade
see Tariffs and foreign trade controls
see Trade adjustment assistance
see Trade agreements
see Wholesale trade

Trade adjustment assistance
Federal budget trends, including spending by program, State, and region, FY81-94, annual rpt, R8490–11

Trade adjustment assistance

State and local:
Maine trade adjustment participants and costs, overall and in 4 industries, 1987-92, article, S3465–2.501
see also Dumping

Trade agreements
China business review, including trade with US and other countries, and economic activity, bimonthly rpt, A9315–1
General Agreement on Trade and Tariffs (GATT) chronology, with number of countries participating and value of trade covered, 1947-91, R4105–82.2
Hard goods manufacturers views on US-Mexico and North American free trade agreements, by product line, 1993 annual survey rpt, A1800–1
Hispanic American leaders support for North American Free Trade Agreement, 1993 annual survey article, C4575–1.511
North American Free Trade Agreement devs for auto industry, with data on Mexico vehicle production and US total and auto trade with Mexico and Canada, 1980s-91, R8490–43
North American Free Trade Agreement, public interest in news items and opinions on related issues, by respondent characteristics, Sept 1993 survey, C8915–1.505
North American Free Trade Agreement, public support and desired conditions, with detail for 3 States, 1993 survey, annual rpt, A4965–1
Public opinion in US, Canada, and Mexico on North American Free Trade Agreement, Aug-Sept 1992 Gallup Poll and trends, C4040–1.503
Public opinion on North American Free Trade Agreement, Mar 1993 Gallup Poll and trends, C4040–1.510
see also Tariffs and foreign trade controls

Trade balances
see Balance of payments
see Foreign trade

Trade promotion
see Foreign trade promotion

Trade regulation
see Consumer protection
see Copyright
see Interstate commerce
see License taxes and fees
see Licenses and permits
see Patents
see Price regulation
see Tariffs and foreign trade controls
see Trade adjustment assistance
see Trademarks

Trade unions
see Labor unions

Trademarks
Corporate logos, consumer rankings of 5 best and worst, 1993 survey article, C5800–7.547
Corporate logos, consumer rankings of 6 best and worst, spring 1993 survey, article, C2710–1.544
Hard goods manufacturers legal actions concerning patent/trademark infringement by foreign firms, by product line, 1993 annual survey rpt, A1800–1
Retail licensed product sales, by product category and property type, 1992, article, C5150–2.521

Retail licensed product sales, by product category, 1991-92, annual article, C8130–1.507
Retail licensed product sales, by product category, 1992, article, C5150–3.513
Sports league licensed merchandise sales, for 5 professional and collegiate leagues, 1992, article, C0500–1.507
Textile and clothing trademarks, with business info and financial data for approx 170 companies, 1992 annual rpt, C3400–5

Trading cards
see Printing and publishing industry

Traffic accident fatalities
Black American health and vital statistics data, with comparisons to whites, 1970s-91, annual compilation, C6775–2.2
Black children and youth population, economic, health, and education data, with comparisons to whites, 1993 rpt, R3840–21
Deaths and disabling injuries from accidents, by detailed type, victim characteristics, circumstances, and location, 1992 and trends, annual rpt, A8375–2
Deaths and rates, and fatal accidents by urban-rural location, and driver sex and age, 1991 and trends, annual rpt, A5650–1.4
Deaths and rates, by type of accident, State, and foreign country, 1900s-92, annual rpt, A0865–1.3
Deaths from transportation accidents, trends by mode, 1992 annual rpt, R4815–1
Driver fatalities in frontal impact accidents, for autos equipped with airbags vs seat belts only, 1985-91, article, A2623–1.507
Fleet vehicle accidents, injuries and fatalities, and property damage, 4th qtr 1992, recurring feature, C1575–2.505
Fuel tank fire related fatalities before and after Govt standards for fuel system integrity, by location of tank, 1981-86, article, A2623–1.510
Hazardous materials transportation accidents and related fatalities, 1970 and 1980-92, annual rpt, A3850–1
Japan and US health care system data, including expenditures, facilities, insurance coverage, and population health indicators, 1993 article, R5650–2.515
Latin America statistical abstract, general data by country, 1992 annual rpt, U6250–1.15
Mass transit passenger death and injury rates, by transportation mode, 1990, article, C1575–3.502
Motorcycle accident and fatality statistics, with detail by State, 1991 and trends, annual rpt, A6485–1.2
Motorcycle registrations, accidents, and fatalities, by State, 1991, annual rpt, A6490–2
School bus loading/unloading accident fatalities, by circumstances, location, and victim age and sex, 1991 and trends, annual rpt, S3040–2
School bus loading/unloading accident fatalities, by victim age, 1969-92, article, C1575–1.501
School bus pupil transportation, accident, and expenditure statistics, by State, 1993 annual feature, C1575–1.502

State social, economic, and govtl indicators, with rankings, 1993 semiannual rpt, B8500–1.11
Statistical profiles of 50 States and DC, general data, 1993 annual almanac, C4712–1
Traffic safety devs, with accident statistics by State, bimonthly rpt, A8375–1
Truck (pickup) fatal crash rates for all and side-impact/fire crashes, for 3 major manufacturers, 1993 article, C8900–1.516
Trucks in fatal accidents, by driver-related factor, 1990, C2150–4.503

State and local:
Alabama traffic accidents, fatalities, and injuries, by circumstances, vehicle type, and driver and victim characteristics, 1992, annual rpt, S0185–1
Alabama vital statistics, including population, births, deaths by cause, marriages, and divorces, by location and demographic characteristics, 1992 and trends, annual rpt, S0175–2
Alaska traffic accidents, fatalities, and injuries, by vehicle type, circumstance, location, and driver and victim characteristics, 1991 and trends, annual rpt, S0360–1
Alaska vital statistics, including births, deaths by cause, marriages, divorces, adoptions, and population, by demographic characteristics and location, 1990, annual rpt, S0315–1
Arizona traffic accidents, fatalities, and injuries, by vehicle type, circumstances, location, and driver and victim characteristics, 1991 and trends, annual rpt, S0530–1
Arkansas traffic accidents, fatalities, and injuries, by vehicle type, circumstances, location, and driver and victim characteristics, 1991, annual rpt, S0692–1
Arkansas vital statistics, including births, deaths by cause, marriages, and divorces, by age, sex, race, and county, 1991 and trends, annual rpt, S0685–1
California traffic accidents, fatalities, and injuries, by vehicle type, circumstances, location, and driver and victim characteristics, 1991 and trends, annual rpt, S0885–1
California vital statistics, including population, births, and deaths by cause, by demographic characteristics and county, 1990 and trends, annual rpt, S0865–1
Colorado vital statistics, including population, births, deaths by cause, abortion, marriage and divorce, and adoption, by demographic characteristics and location, 1990 and trends, annual rpt, S1010–1
Connecticut traffic accidents, fatalities, and injuries, by vehicle type, circumstance, location, and driver and victim characteristics, 1992, annual rpt, S1275–1
Connecticut vital statistics, including births, deaths by cause, marriages, and divorces, by demographic characteristics and location, 1989, annual rpt, S1200–1
Delaware traffic accidents, fatalities, and injuries, by circumstances, location, and vehicle type, and driver and victim characteristics, 1992 and trends, annual rpt, S1435–1

Index by Subjects and Names

Traffic accident fatalities

Delaware vital statistics, including births, deaths by cause, and marriages and dissolutions, by demographic characteristics and location, 1990, annual rpt, S1385–2

Florida deaths by selected cause, and incidence of selected communicable diseases, by county, 1992 annual rpt, S1746–1.1

Florida traffic accidents, fatalities, and injuries, by vehicle type, circumstance, location, and driver and victim characteristics, 1992 and trends, annual rpt, S1750–2

Florida vital statistics, including population, births, deaths by cause, and marriages and dissolutions, by location and demographic characteristics, 1992 and trends, annual rpt, S1745–3

Georgia statistical abstract, general data, 1992-93 biennial rpt, U6730–1.8

Georgia vital statistics, including deaths by cause, demographic characteristics, and location, 1991 and trends, annual rpt, S1895–1.2

Hawaii data book, general data, 1992 annual rpt, S2090–1.18

Hawaii health dept activities and services, including vital statistics and disease control, by location, 1990, annual rpt, S2065–1

Hawaii traffic accidents, injuries, and fatalities, by circumstances, location, and driver and victim characteristics, 1986 and trends, annual rpt, S2125–1

Idaho traffic accidents, fatalities, and injuries, by circumstances, location, vehicle type, and driver and victim characteristics, 1992, annual rpt, S2315–1

Idaho vital statistics, including births, deaths by cause, abortions, marriages, and divorces, by demographic characteristics and county, 1991 and trends, annual rpt, S2250–2

Illinois traffic accidents, fatalities, and injuries, by circumstances, location, and driver and victim characteristics, 1991 and trends, annual rpt, S2540–1

Indiana traffic accidents, fatalities, and injuries, by circumstances, location, and vehicle type, and driver and victim characteristics, 1992, annual rpt, S2675–1

Iowa vital statistics, including population, births, deaths by cause, marriages, and divorces, by demographic characteristics and location, 1991 and trends, annual rpt, S2795–1

Kansas traffic accidents, fatalities, and injuries, by vehicle type, location, circumstances, and driver and victim characteristics, 1992, annual rpt, S3040–1

Kansas vital statistics, including population, births, deaths by cause, abortions, marriages, and divorces, by demographic characteristics and location, 1991 and trends, annual rpt, S2975–1

Kentucky traffic accidents, fatalities, and injuries, by circumstances, location, vehicle type, and driver characteristics, 1992 and trends, annual rpt, S3150–2

Kentucky vital statistics, including births, deaths by cause, marriages and divorces, and population, by demographic characteristics and county, 1991, annual rpt, S3140–1

Louisiana traffic accidents, fatalities, and injuries, by circumstances, location, and driver characteristics, 1991 and trends, annual rpt, S3345–2

Louisiana vital statistics, including population, births, deaths by cause, reportable diseases, marriages, and divorces, by demographic characteristics and locality, 1989-90 and trends, annual rpt, S3295–1

Maine traffic accidents, fatalities, and injuries, by accident circumstances, vehicle type and make, and driver and victim characteristics, 1992, annual rpt, S3475–2

Maine vital statistics, including births, deaths by cause, abortions, and marriages and divorces, by demographic characteristics and location, 1991 and trends, annual rpt, S3460–2

Maryland traffic accidents, fatalities, and injuries, by circumstances, location, vehicle type, and driver and victim characteristics, 1992, annual rpt, S3665–4

Maryland vital statistics, including population, births, deaths by cause, marriages, and divorces, by demographic characteristics and location, 1989 and trends, annual rpt, S3635–1

Massachusetts vital statistics, including births, deaths by cause, marriages, divorces, and population, by locality and demographic characteristics, 1990 and trends, annual rpt, S3850–1

Michigan traffic accidents, fatalities, and injuries, by vehicle type, circumstance, location, and driver and victim characteristics, 1991 and trends, annual rpt, S3997–2

Michigan vital statistics, including births, deaths, marriages, divorces/annulments, and communicable diseases, by location and demographic characteristics, 1990 and trends, annual rpt, S4000–3

Minnesota traffic accidents, fatalities, and injuries, by type of vehicle and circumstances, and driver and victim characteristics, 1992 and trends, annual rpt, S4230–2

Minnesota vital statistics, including population, births, abortions, deaths, marriages, and divorces, by location and demographic characteristics, 1991 and trends, annual rpt, S4190–2

Mississippi school busing accidents, fatalities, and injuries, 1991/92, annual rpt, S4340–1.2

Mississippi statistical abstract, general data, 1992 annual rpt, U3255–4.9

Mississippi vital statistics, including births, deaths by cause, marriages, and divorces, by demographic characteristics and location, 1992 and trends, annual rpt, S4350–1

Missouri traffic accidents, fatalities, and injuries, by circumstances, location, and driver and victim characteristics, 1992 and trends, annual rpt, S4560–1

Missouri vital statistics, including population, births, deaths by cause, and marriages and divorces, by location and demographic characteristics, 1992 and trends, annual rpt, S4518–1

Montana traffic accidents, fatalities, and injuries, by circumstances, location, and driver and victim characteristics, 1992 and trends, annual rpt, S4705–2

Montana vital statistics, including births, deaths by cause, abortion, disease, and marriage and divorce, by demographic characteristics and county, 1990-91 and trends, annual rpt, S4690–1

Nebraska traffic accidents, fatalities, and injuries, by circumstances, location, vehicle type, and driver and victim characteristics, 1992, annual rpt, S4953–1

Nebraska vital statistics, including births, deaths, marriages, divorces, and population, by demographic characteristics and location, 1991 and trends, annual rpt, S4885–1

Nevada traffic accidents, fatalities, and injuries, by circumstances, location, and vehicle type, 1992 and trends, annual rpt, S5140–1

Nevada vital statistics, including births, abortions, and deaths by cause, by county and demographic characteristics, 1989 and trends, annual rpt, S5075–1

New Hampshire vital statistics, including population, births, deaths by cause, marriages, and divorces, by location and demographic characteristics, 1991 and trends, annual rpt, S5215–1

New Jersey fatal traffic accidents and fatalities, by vehicle type, location, and circumstances, and driver and victim characteristics, 1992 and trends, annual rpt, S5430–2

New Jersey vital statistics, including births, deaths, population, communicable diseases, and marriages and divorces, by demographic characteristics and location, 1990 and trends, annual rpt, S5405–1

New Mexico traffic accidents, fatalities, and injuries, by vehicle type, circumstances, location, and driver and victim characteristics, 1992 and trends, annual rpt, S5665–1

New Mexico vital statistics, including population, births, deaths, and disease, by location and demographic characteristics, 1991 and trends, annual rpt, S5605–1

New York State traffic accidents, fatalities, and injuries, by circumstances, location, vehicle type, and driver and victim characteristics, 1991 and trends, annual rpt, S5790–1

New York State vital statistics, including population, births, deaths by cause, reportable diseases, and marriages and dissolutions, by demographic characteristics and/or location, 1990 and trends, annual rpt, S5765–1

North Carolina deaths and rates, by cause and county, 1991 and trends, annual rpt, S5927–1.2

North Carolina traffic accidents, fatalities, and injuries, by circumstances, location, vehicle type, and driver and victim characteristics, 1992 and trends, annual rpt, S5990–1

North Dakota traffic accidents, fatalities, and injuries, by circumstances, location, vehicle type, and driver and victim characteristics, 1992 and trends, annual rpt, S6217–1

Traffic accident fatalities

North Dakota vital statistics, including births, deaths by cause, marriages and divorces, and abortions, by demographic characteristics and/or county, 1991 and trends, annual rpt, S6105–2

Ohio traffic accidents, fatalities, and injuries, by circumstances, location, driver and victim characteristics, and vehicle type, 1991 and trends, annual rpt, S6290–1

Ohio vital statistics, including births, deaths by cause, marriages, divorces, and population, by demographic characteristics and location, 1991 and trends, annual rpt, S6285–1

Oklahoma traffic accidents, fatalities, and injuries, by circumstances, location, and driver and victim characteristics, 1992 and trends, annual rpt, S6482–1

Oregon vital statistics, including births, deaths by cause, communicable diseases, marriages, and divorces, by age, sex, race-ethnicity, and county, 1991 and trends, annual rpt, S6615–5

Pennsylvania traffic accidents, fatalities, and injuries, by circumstances, location, driver characteristics, and vehicle type, 1991, annual rpt, S6905–3

Rhode Island statistical almanac, general data, 1993 annual rpt, C7975–1.1

Rhode Island traffic accidents, fatalities, and injuries, by circumstances, community, and driver and victim characteristics, 1992, annual rpt, S7025–1

Rhode Island vital statistics, including population, births, deaths, marriages, and divorces, by demographic characteristics and locality, 1989 and trends, annual rpt, S6995–1

South Carolina deaths, by detailed cause, age, sex, and race, 1990, annual rpt, S7175–2

South Carolina traffic accidents, fatalities, and injuries, by circumstances, location, and driver and victim characteristics, 1992 and trends, annual rpt, S7190–2

South Carolina vital statistics, including births, deaths by cause, marriages, and divorces, by age, sex, race, and location, 1990 and trends, annual rpt, S7175–1

South Dakota traffic accidents, fatalities, and injuries, by circumstances, location, vehicle type, and driver and victim characteristics, 1992 and trends, annual rpt, S7300–3

South Dakota vital statistics, including births, deaths, marriage and divorce, and communicable disease, by demographic characteristics and county, 1991 and trends, annual rpt, S7345–1

Tennessee vital statistics, including births, deaths by cause, marriages, divorces, and population, by demographic characteristics and location, 1991 and trends, annual rpt, S7520–2

Texas vital statistics, including births, deaths by cause, abortions, marriages, and divorces, by location and demographic characteristics, 1991 and trends, annual rpt, S7685–1

Utah traffic accidents and fatalities by circumstances, location, driver and victim characteristics, and vehicle type, 1992 and trends, annual rpt, S7890–2

Utah vital statistics, including births, deaths by cause, and population, by county and demographic characteristics, 1990 and trends, annual rpt, S7835–1

Vermont vital statistics, including population, births, deaths by cause, abortions, marriages, and divorces, by location and demographic characteristics, 1991 and trends, annual rpt, S8054–1

Virginia traffic accidents, fatalities, and injuries, by circumstances, location, and driver and victim characteristics, 1991 and trends, annual rpt, S8282–1

Virginia vital statistics, including births, deaths by cause, marriages and divorces, and communicable disease, by demographic characteristics and location, 1991 and trends, annual rpt, S8225–1

Washington State traffic accidents, fatalities, and injuries, by circumstances, vehicle type, and location, with driver and victim characteristics, 1992 and trends, annual rpt, S8428–1

Washington State vital statistics, including births, deaths by cause, and population, by demographic characteristics and location, 1991 and trends, annual rpt, S8363–1

West Virginia traffic accidents, fatalities, and injuries, by circumstance and location, and driver and victim characteristics, 1992, annual rpt, S8645–1

West Virginia vital statistics, including births, deaths by cause, marriages, and divorces, by location and demographic characteristics, 1991 and trends, annual rpt, S8560–1

Wisconsin traffic accidents, fatalities, and injuries, by circumstances, location, vehicle type, and driver and victim characteristics, 1992 and trends, annual rpt, S8815–1

Wisconsin vital statistics, including population, births, deaths by cause, and marriages and dissolutions, by county and demographic characteristics, 1991 and trends, annual rpt, S8715–4

Wyoming traffic accidents, fatalities, and injuries, by circumstances, location, vehicle type, and driver and victim characteristics, 1992 and trends, annual rpt, S9007–1

Wyoming vital statistics, including population, births, deaths by cause, marriages, and divorces, by demographic characteristics and county, 1991 and trends, annual rpt, S8920–2

Traffic accidents and safety

Auto insurance collision coverage experiences for autos and other vehicles, by make and series, for recent model years, 1993 annual rpt series, A5200–1

Crash test results for selected auto or light truck models, weekly rpt recurring feature, C2710–3.511, C2710–3.533

Crash tests trends, including number of vehicles crashed and percent passing, for 16 manufacturers, 1979-93, article, C2710–3.551

Fleet vehicle accidents, and vehicles and mileage, by fleet type and company (unnamed), 1991 and trends, annual rpt, A8375–3

Fleet vehicle accidents, injuries and fatalities, and property damage, 4th qtr 1992, recurring feature, C1575–2.505

Injuries and deaths from accidents, by detailed type, victim characteristics, circumstances, and location, 1992 and trends, annual rpt, A8375–2

Index by Subjects and Names

Injuries and deaths from accidents by type, and selected incidence and economic loss data, 1991 and trends, annual rpt, A5650–1.4

Mass transit passenger death and injury rates, by transportation mode, 1990, article, C1575–3.502

Motorcycle accident and fatality statistics, with detail by State, 1991 and trends, annual rpt, A6485–1.2

Motorcycle registrations, accidents, and fatalities, by State, 1991, annual rpt, A6490–2

Personal injury jury verdict award trends, with data by case type and for awards exceeding $1 million, 1960s-92, annual rpt, C5180–1

Personal injury protection insurance claim frequencies for 1990-92 model autos and other vehicles, by make and model, annual rpt, A5200–3

Regulatory agency activities, including motor carrier safety program staff, costs, inspections, arrests, and fines, by agency, 1991/92 annual rpt, A7015–4

School bus insurance claim frequencies for leading types of accidents, 1993 article, C1575–1.504

School bus pupil transportation, accident, and expenditure statistics, by State, 1993 annual feature, C1575–1.502

Traffic safety devs, with accident statistics by State, bimonthly rpt, A8375–1

Truck (pickup) side-impact crashes and related fuel leaks/fires, for 3 major manufacturers, Michigan study, 1982-91, article, C2710–3.536

Work-related auto accidents, injuries and fatalities, and costs, with detail for fleet vehicles by type, 1991, annual rpt, C1575–2.507

State and local:

Alabama county data book, general data, 1992 annual rpt, S0121–2

Alabama traffic accidents, fatalities, and injuries, by circumstances, vehicle type, and driver and victim characteristics, 1992, annual rpt, S0185–1

Alaska traffic accidents, fatalities, and injuries, by vehicle type, circumstance, location, and driver and victim characteristics, 1991 and trends, annual rpt, S0360–1

Arizona statistical abstract, general data, 1993 recurring rpt, U5850–2.18

Arizona traffic accidents, fatalities, and injuries, by vehicle type, circumstances, location, and driver and victim characteristics, 1991 and trends, annual rpt, S0530–1

Arkansas public school bus accidents, injuries, deaths, and property damage, 1989/90-1991/92, annual rpt, S0660–1.3

Arkansas traffic accidents, fatalities, and injuries, by vehicle type, circumstances, location, and driver and victim characteristics, 1991, annual rpt, S0692–1

California resident views on whether passengers should be allowed to ride in backs of pickup trucks, 1991 annual rpt, S0865–2

California statistical abstract, general data, 1992 annual rpt, S0840–2.10

Traffic engineering

California traffic accidents, fatalities, and injuries, by vehicle type, circumstances, location, and driver and victim characteristics, 1991 and trends, annual rpt, S0885–1

Connecticut traffic accidents, fatalities, and injuries, by vehicle type, circumstance, location, and driver and victim characteristics, 1992, annual rpt, S1275–1

DC statistical profile, general data, 1992 annual rpt, S1535–3.7

Delaware traffic accidents, fatalities, and injuries, by circumstances, location, and vehicle type, and driver and victim characteristics, 1992 and trends, annual rpt, S1435–1

Florida county data book, 1992/93 annual rpt, C6360–1

Florida statistical abstract, general data, 1992 annual rpt, U6660–1.13

Florida traffic accidents, fatalities, and injuries, by vehicle type, circumstance, location, and driver and victim characteristics, 1992 and trends, annual rpt, S1750–2

Georgia county guide, general data, 1993 annual rpt, U6750–1

Hawaii data book, general data, 1992 annual rpt, S2090–1.18

Hawaii traffic accidents, injuries, and fatalities, by circumstances, location, and driver and victim characteristics, 1986 and trends, annual rpt, S2125–1

Idaho traffic accidents, fatalities, and injuries, by circumstances, location, vehicle type, and driver and victim characteristics, 1992, annual rpt, S2315–1

Illinois statistical abstract, general data, 1992 annual rpt, U6910–2

Illinois traffic accidents, fatalities, and injuries, by circumstances, location, and driver and victim characteristics, 1991 and trends, annual rpt, S2540–1

Indiana traffic accidents, fatalities, and injuries, by circumstances, location, and vehicle type, and driver and victim characteristics, 1992, annual rpt, S2675–1

Kansas traffic accidents, fatalities, and injuries, by vehicle type, location, circumstances, and driver and victim characteristics, 1992, annual rpt, S3040–1

Kentucky traffic accidents, fatalities, and injuries, by circumstances, location, vehicle type, and driver characteristics, 1992 and trends, annual rpt, S3150–2

Louisiana traffic accidents, fatalities, and injuries, by circumstances, location, and driver characteristics, 1991 and trends, annual rpt, S3345–2

Maine traffic accidents, fatalities, and injuries, by accident circumstances, vehicle type and make, and driver and victim characteristics, 1992, annual rpt, S3475–2

Maryland traffic accidents, fatalities, and injuries, by circumstances, location, vehicle type, and driver and victim characteristics, 1992, annual rpt, S3665–4

Michigan traffic accidents, fatalities, and injuries, by vehicle type, circumstance, location, and driver and victim characteristics, 1991 and trends, annual rpt, S3997–2

Minnesota traffic accidents, fatalities, and injuries, by type of vehicle and circumstances, and driver and victim characteristics, 1992 and trends, annual rpt, S4230–2

Mississippi school busing accidents, fatalities, and injuries, 1991/92, annual rpt, S4340–1.2

Mississippi statistical abstract, general data, 1992 annual rpt, U3255–4.9

Missouri traffic accidents, fatalities, and injuries, by circumstances, location, and driver and victim characteristics, 1992 and trends, annual rpt, S4560–1

Montana traffic accidents, fatalities, and injuries, by circumstances, location, and driver and victim characteristics, 1992 and trends, annual rpt, S4705–2

Nebraska traffic accidents, fatalities, and injuries, by circumstances, location, vehicle type, and driver and victim characteristics, 1992, annual rpt, S4953–1

Nevada statistical abstract, general data, 1992 biennial rpt, S5005–1.13

Nevada traffic accidents, fatalities, and injuries, by circumstances, location, and vehicle type, 1992 and trends, annual rpt, S5140–1

New Jersey fatal traffic accidents and fatalities, by vehicle type, location, and circumstances, and driver and victim characteristics, 1992 and trends, annual rpt, S5430–2

New Mexico motor carrier safety inspection outcomes, FY91-92 annual rpt, S5660–1

New Mexico traffic accidents, fatalities, and injuries, by vehicle type, circumstances, location, and driver and victim characteristics, 1992 and trends, annual rpt, S5665–1

New York State statistical yearbook, general data, 1992 annual rpt, U5100–1.13

New York State traffic accidents, fatalities, and injuries, by circumstances, location, vehicle type, and driver and victim characteristics, 1991 and trends, annual rpt, S5790–1

North Carolina traffic accidents, fatalities, and injuries, by circumstances, location, vehicle type, and driver and victim characteristics, 1992 and trends, annual rpt, S5990–1

North Dakota traffic accidents, fatalities, and injuries, by circumstances, location, vehicle type, and driver and victim characteristics, 1992 and trends, annual rpt, S6217–1

Ohio traffic accidents, fatalities, and injuries, by circumstances, location, driver and victim characteristics, and vehicle type, 1991 and trends, annual rpt, S6290–1

Oklahoma statistical abstract, general data, 1992 annual rpt, U8130–2.16

Oklahoma traffic accidents, fatalities, and injuries, by circumstances, location, and driver and victim characteristics, 1992 and trends, annual rpt, S6482–1

Pennsylvania traffic accidents, fatalities, and injuries, by circumstances, location, driver characteristics, and vehicle type, 1991, annual rpt, S6905–3

Rhode Island traffic accidents, fatalities, and injuries, by circumstances, community, and driver and victim characteristics, 1992, annual rpt, S7025–1

South Carolina statistical abstract, general data, 1993 annual rpt, S7125–1.15

South Carolina traffic accidents, fatalities, and injuries, by circumstances, location, and driver and victim characteristics, 1992 and trends, annual rpt, S7190–2

South Dakota traffic accidents, fatalities, and injuries, by circumstances, location, vehicle type, and driver and victim characteristics, 1992 and trends, annual rpt, S7300–3

Tennessee public school bus accidents, injuries, and fatalities, by county, city, and school district, 1991/92, annual rpt, S7490–2.3

Tennessee statistical abstract, general data, 1992/93 annual rpt, U8710–2.19

Utah traffic accidents and fatalities by circumstances, location, driver and victim characteristics, and vehicle type, 1992 and trends, annual rpt, S7890–2

Virginia traffic accidents, fatalities, and injuries, by circumstances, location, and driver and victim characteristics, 1991 and trends, annual rpt, S8282–1

Washington State traffic accidents, fatalities, and injuries, by circumstances, vehicle type, and location, with driver and victim characteristics, 1992 and trends, annual rpt, S8428–1

West Virginia traffic accidents, fatalities, and injuries, by circumstance and location, and driver and victim characteristics, 1992, annual rpt, S8645–1

Wisconsin Blue Book, general data, 1993-94 biennial rpt, S8780–1.2

Wisconsin traffic accidents, fatalities, and injuries, by circumstances, location, vehicle type, and driver and victim characteristics, 1992 and trends, annual rpt, S8815–1

Wyoming traffic accidents, fatalities, and injuries, by circumstances, location, vehicle type, and driver and victim characteristics, 1992 and trends, annual rpt, S9007–1

see also Driver education

see also Driving while intoxicated

see also Motor vehicle defects

see also Motor vehicle safety devices

see also Pedestrians

see also State funding for public safety

see also Traffic accident fatalities

see also Traffic engineering

see also Traffic laws and courts

Traffic courts and cases

see Traffic laws and courts

Traffic engineering

Safety issues, including road signs and signals, and improvements for elderly drivers, views of traffic safety magazine readers, Nov/Dec 1992 survey, article, A8375–1.503

State and local:

Alabama accidents, by type of traffic control in place, 1992, annual rpt, S0185–1

Alaska traffic accidents, by type of road defect and traffic control device in place, 1991, annual rpt, S0360–1

Arkansas accidents, by type of road defect and traffic control device in place, 1991, annual rpt, S0692–1

Traffic engineering

California traffic accidents involving traffic control defects, 1991, annual rpt, S0885–1

Connecticut traffic accidents involving inoperational traffic signal, 1992, annual rpt, S1275–1

DC street lights, signalized intersections, and sidewalk and alley mileage, FY91, annual rpt, S1535–3.7

Idaho traffic accidents, by type of traffic control in place, 1992, annual rpt, S2315–1

Maine traffic accidents, by type of traffic control in place, 1992, annual rpt, S3475–2

Minnesota traffic accidents, by type of traffic control in place, 1992, annual rpt, S4230–2

Montana traffic accidents, fatalities, and injuries, by type of road defect and traffic control, 1992, annual rpt, S4705–2

New York State traffic accidents, by type of traffic control, 1991, annual rpt, S5790–1

North Carolina traffic accidents by type of traffic control in use, 1992, annual rpt, S5990–1

Pennsylvania traffic accidents, by type of traffic control in place, 1991, annual rpt, S6905–3

Rhode Island traffic accidents, by type of traffic control in place, 1992, annual rpt, S7025–1

South Carolina traffic accidents, by type of traffic control in place, 1992, annual rpt, S7190–2

Utah traffic accidents by type of traffic control in place, 1992, annual rpt, S7890–2

Virginia traffic accidents and fatalities, by type of traffic control in place, 1991, annual rpt, S8282–1

Wisconsin traffic accidents in construction zones, and by type of traffic control in place, 1992, annual rpt, S8815–1

Wyoming traffic accidents, by type of traffic control in place, 1992, annual rpt, S9007–1

Traffic laws and courts

Motor vehicle noise standards and seat belt use laws, by State, 1993 annual rpt, A0865–1.3

Seat belt use laws, correlation with public use, 1992 survey, annual rpt, C8111–2

State appellate and trial court caseloads and dispositions, by case type and State, 1991 and trends, annual rpt, R6600–1

State legislation status for alcohol-related, safety device use, and speed limit laws, by State, 1993 annual rpt, A8375–2.3

Urban small claims and traffic court caseloads, processing, dispositions, judgments, and litigant satisfaction, for 3-12 jurisdictions, 1990, R6600–5

State and local:

Alabama court caseloads and dispositions, by type of court and case, and location, with judicial dept finances, FY92 and trends, annual rpt, S0118–1

Alaska court cases and dispositions, by type of court and case, and location, with judicial dept finances and personnel, FY92 and trends, annual rpt, S0290–1

Arizona court cases and dispositions, by type of case and court, with judicial personnel and finances, by county and city, FY92, annual rpt, S0525–1

Arkansas court caseloads and dispositions, by type of court and case, and location, FY92 and trends, annual rpt, S0647–1

California court cases and dispositions, by type of case and court, and location, FY92 and trends, annual rpt, S0905–1.2, S0905–2

California criminal justice system detailed data, by offense, county, age, race-ethnicity, and sex, 1991 and trends, annual rpt, S0910–2

Colorado court cases and dispositions, by type of court and detailed case type, FY92 and trends, annual rpt, S1035–1.2

Connecticut court caseloads and dispositions, by type of court and case, and court location, with judicial dept finances, FY91-92, biennial rpt, S1220–1

DC court cases and dispositions, by type of case, and judicial system finances, 1992 and trends, annual rpt, S1515–1

Delaware court caseloads and dispositions, by type of court and case, and by county, with judicial dept finances, FY92, annual rpt, S1360–1

Florida county data book, 1992/93 annual rpt, C6360–1

Georgia county guide, general data, 1993 annual rpt, U6750–1

Georgia court cases and dispositions, by type of court and case, and location, with judicial dept finances and personnel, FY92, annual rpt, S1903–1

Hawaii court cases and dispositions, by type of court and case, and judicial circuit, FY92 and trends, annual rpt, S2115–1.2

Indiana court cases and dispositions by type of court and case, and location, with judicial system finances and personnel, 1992, annual rpt, S2703–1

Kansas court caseloads and disposition, by type of court and case, and location, FY92, annual rpt, S3035–1

Louisiana court caseloads and dispositions, by type of court and case, and jurisdiction, 1992 and trends, annual rpt, S3375–1

Louisiana traffic law violation convictions, 1991, annual rpt, S3345–2

Maine court cases and dispositions, by type and location, FY92 and trends, annual rpt, S3463–1

Maryland court caseloads and dispositions, by type of court and case, and county, with judicial personnel and finances, FY92 and trends, annual rpt, S3600–1

Massachusetts court cases and dispositions, by type of court and case, and location, FY92 and trends, annual rpt, S3807–1

Michigan court caseloads and dispositions, by type of court and case, and court location, 1992 and trends, annual rpt, S3962–1

Nebraska court cases and dispositions, by type of court and case, and location, 1992 and trends, annual rpt, S4965–2

Nevada traffic accidents by posted speed limit, and speed of errant vehicle, 1992, annual rpt, S5140–1

New Mexico court cases and dispositions, by type of court and case, and location, with judicial system finances and personnel, FY92, annual rpt, S5623–1

New York State statistical yearbook, general data, 1992 annual rpt, U5100–1.13

New York State traffic violation citations, and convictions by county, 1991, annual rpt, S5790–1

North Carolina court cases and dispositions, by type of court and case, and location, with judicial dept finances and personnel, FY91, annual rpt, S5950–1

North Carolina traffic accidents involving driving violations, 1992, annual rpt, S5990–1

North Dakota court caseloads and dispositions, by type of case and court, and location, with judicial dept finances, 1991-92, annual rpt, S6210–1

North Dakota traffic accidents involving violations, by urban-rural location and violation type, 1992, annual rpt, S6217–1

Ohio court caseload and case disposition, by type of court and case, and location, 1992, annual rpt, S6385–1

Ohio traffic convictions, by violation, with detail for drinking drivers, 1991 annual rpt, S6290–1

Oklahoma court cases and dispositions, by type of court and case, with judicial system finances, by county or jurisdiction, FY92, annual rpt, S6493–1

Oklahoma Hwy Patrol citations by type of traffic violation, 1988-92, annual rpt, S6482–1

Oregon traffic crimes and arrests, 1992 and trends, annual rpt, S6603–3

Pennsylvania court caseloads and dispositions, by type of court and case, and county, 1991, annual rpt, S6900–1.2

South Carolina court cases and dispositions, by type of court and location, with judicial dept finances and employees, 1992 and trends, annual rpt, S7197–1

South Carolina statistical abstract, general data, 1993 annual rpt, S7125–1.15

South Dakota traffic violation arrests and fines, by type of offense, FY92, annual rpt, S7395–1

Texas court cases and dispositions, by type of court and case, and location, FY92, annual rpt, S7703–1

Vermont court cases and dispositions, by type of court and case, and location, FY92 annual rpt, S8120–1

Virginia court caseloads, processing, and dispositions, by type of court and case, with judicial dept personnel and finances, by location, 1992 and trends, annual rpt, S8300–1

Virginia traffic accidents involving speeding and other driving violations, 1991, annual rpt, S8282–1

Washington State court cases and dispositions, by type of court and case, and jurisdiction, with judicial finances and personnel, 1992 and trends, annual rpt, S8339–1

Washington State traffic accidents, including driver law violations, 1992, annual rpt, S8428–1

West Virginia court caseloads and dispositions, by type of court and case, and judicial circuit, 1992 and trends, annual rpt, S8537–1

West Virginia traffic accidents on hwy segments with 65 mph speed limit, 1992, annual rpt, S8645–1

Wisconsin traffic accidents, including citations issued, 1992 and trends, annual rpt, S8815–1

Index by Subjects and Names

Wyoming traffic accidents, including driver law violations charged, 1992, annual rpt, S9007–1

see also Driving while intoxicated

Traffic violations

see Traffic accidents and safety

see Traffic laws and courts

Training

see Apprenticeship

see Employee development

see Job Training Partnership Act

see Manpower training programs

see Military training

see Vocational education and training

Tranquilizers

see Drug abuse and treatment

see Drugs

Transient housing

Travel trips and traveler characteristics, including mode, purpose, type of lodging, and area of destination and origin, quarterly rpt, R9375–14

State and local:

Arizona, Phoenix area temporary winter resident characteristics, including expenditures, dwelling type, and region of residence, 1992/93, article, U0280–1.508

Hawaii transient accommodation tax and fee collections, FY91-92, annual rpt, S2120–1

see also Emergency shelters

see also Hotels and motels

see also Resort timesharing

Transportation and transportation equipment

Aluminum shipments by end-use market and product type, 1982-92, annual rpt, A0400–2.1

Boat trailers sales and ownership, 1992, annual feature, C2425–4

Business failures and liabilities, by detailed industry, cause, length of operation, and location, 1991-92 and trends, annual rpt, C3150–8

China and US socioeconomic and infrastructure indicators comparison, 1993 rpt, R4105–82.8

Congressional campaign finances, with detailed data for individual Members, and leading contributors by type and industry, 1990 election and trends, biennial rpt, R3828–2.2

Corporate performance ratings by executives for leading companies in 32 industries, 1993 annual survey feature, C8900–1.508

Cost-of-living indexes and retail prices for selected consumer items in approx 300 cities, quarterly rpt, A0150–1

EC transportation infrastructure and use indicators, by country, 1988, R5025–9

Economic impact of travel on States, with detail by industry sector, 1990 and trends, annual rpt, R9375–7

Engineers salaries by industry group, census div, selected metro area, and years since college degree, 1993, annual survey rpt, A0685–5

Engineers salaries by industry group, census div, selected metro area, degree level, and years since college degree, 1993, annual survey rpt, A0685–3

Executive compensation and components, by industry div and major manufacturing group, 1991, annual rpt, R4105–19

Expenditures for natl transportation, personal and total, by expenditure type and mode, 1970s-92, annual rpt, A0865–1.2

Transportation and transportation equipment

Financial ratios and performance, for over 350 SIC 4-digit industries, FY88-92, annual rpt, A6400–3

Food service industry rankings by market segment, for leading organizations, 1992, annual feature, C1850–3.509

Food service industry sales and establishments, with growth outlook, by market segment, 1993 annual feature, C1850–3.503

Fortune magazine ranking of top 50-100 companies in 8 nonindustrial sectors, with financial and employment data, 1992, annual feature, C8900–1.516

Fortune magazine ranking of top 50-100 companies worldwide in 8 nonindustrial sectors, with financial and employment data, 1993 annual feature, C8900–1.522

Latin America statistical abstract, general data by country, 1992 annual rpt, U6250–1.3, U6250–1.13, U6250–1.32

Mexico-Texas transportation system analysis, including bilateral trade, operations by transport mode, and data by locale, 1993 rpt, U8850–9

Oil and refined products transported between PAD districts, by mode, 1983-91, annual compilation, C6985–9.4

Operating and financial composite ratios for corporations, with establishments and receipts, for approx 200 industries, by asset size, FY90, annual rpt, C7800–1

Plastics industry production and sales by resin type, consumption by end-use market, and operating characteristics, 1992 and trends, annual rpt, A8920–1

Regulatory agency policies and practices for motor carriers and railroads, by agency, 1991/92 annual rpt, A7015–4

Service to daily newspaper markets in US and Canada, by mode and company, 1993 annual rpt, C3250–1

Statistical profiles of 50 States and DC, general data, 1993 annual almanac, C4712–1

Trends in transportation operations and finances, by mode, 1991 annual rpt, R4815–1

Vehicle registrations and mileage, licensed drivers, traffic deaths, road mileage, and gasoline and auto prices, 1932 and 1992, C2150–4.501

World transportation infrastructure, and passenger and freight traffic by mode, by country, 1992/93 biennial rpt, R9455–1.5

State and local:

Alabama statistical abstract, general data, 1992 recurring rpt, U5680–2.16

California property tax assessments and exemptions, by type of property, city, county, and company, FY93 and trends, annual rpt, S0835–1.2

California public utility and transportation regulatory data, including revenue requests and rates of return by company, FY92 annual rpt, S0930–1

DC statistical profile, general data, 1992 annual rpt, S1535–3.7

Florida statistical abstract, general data, 1992 annual rpt, U6660–1.12, U6660–1.13

Hawaii data book, general data, 1992 annual rpt, S2090–1.18

Idaho motor carrier regulation activity, FY88-92, annual rpt, S2290–1

Maine employment in trade, utilities, and transportation SIC 2-digit industries, by detailed occupation, 2nd qtr 1991, triennial rpt, S3465–1.25

Nebraska motor transportation regulatory activities, FY91-92, biennial rpt, S4940–1

Nebraska transportation-related statistics, 1982-91, annual rpt, S4825–1

New Mexico economic trends and outlook, by industry div, 1982-92, annual article, U7980–1.503

North Carolina employment in trade, transportation, communications, utilities, govt, and education, by detailed occupation, 2nd qtr 1991, triennial rpt, S5917–5.2

Pennsylvania statistical abstract, general data, 1992 recurring rpt, U4130–6.9

South Dakota social services for elderly, with recipients by race-ethnicity, FY92, annual rpt, S7385–1.1

Tennessee public utility and transportation commission regulatory activities, with industry financial and operating data, 1991-92 biennial rpt, S7565–1

Texas trade, transportation, and public utilities employment, by SIC 2- and 3-digit industry and detailed occupation, 2nd qtr 1991, triennial survey rpt, S7675–1.31

Utah statistical abstract, general data, 1993 triennial rpt, U8960–1.13

Washington State public service and utility companies property value, by company and county, 1992, annual rpt, S8415–1.4

Wyoming property assessed valuations and tax levies, by property type, tax purpose, and location, 1992 and trends, annual rpt, S8990–1.2

see also Air travel

see also Aircraft

see also Airlines

see also Automobiles

see also Aviation accidents and safety

see also Bicycles

see also Boats and boating

see also Bridges and tunnels

see also Buses

see also Canals

see also Commuting

see also Drivers licenses

see also Federal aid to transportation

see also Freight

see also Gasoline

see also Harbors and ports

see also Hazardous substances transport

see also High-speed ground transportation

see also Highways, streets, and roads

see also Inland water transportation

see also Marine accidents and safety

see also Materials handling equipment

see also Military vehicles

see also Motor fuels

see also Motor vehicle fleets

see also Motor vehicle industry

see also Motor vehicle registrations

see also Motor vehicle sales

see also Motorcycles

see also Natural gas pipelines

see also Parking facilities

see also Passenger ships

see also Pipelines

Transportation and transportation equipment

see also Railroad accidents and safety
see also Railroads
see also Recreational vehicles
see also Rivers and waterways
see also Ships and shipping
see also State funding for transportation
see also Subways
see also Tanker ships
see also Taxicabs
see also Traffic accident fatalities
see also Traffic accidents and safety
see also Transportation energy use
see also Travel and tourism
see also Trucks and trucking industry
see also Urban transportation
see also under By Industry in the "Index by Categories"

Transportation Department

see Department of Transportation

Transportation energy use

- Aircraft operating data, including fuel use, by model, 1992, annual rpt, A0325–5
- Airline fuel consumption and costs, by type of service, 1992, annual article, C7000–4.508
- Airline fuel consumption and costs, monthly rpt, C7000–4
- Airline fuel consumption and costs, 1977-91, annual rpt, A0250–2.3
- Alternative motor fuel use and outlook, including data on costs and by fuel type and selected country, 1993 annual rpt, C6985–3.2
- Coal industry supply-demand, employment, and trade, by country, 1990-91 and trends, annual rpt, A7400–2.2
- Consumption of energy, by fuel source and sector, 1984-91, annual rpt, A1775–3.6
- Consumption of petroleum by transport mode, 1992 annual rpt, R4815–1
- Diesel fuel hwy use trends and outlook, 1989-2010, article, C6985–1.549
- Electric utility customers, sales, and revenues, by user sector, bimonthly rpt quarterly table, A4700–4
- Electric utility financial and operating data, by State and census div, 1991 and trends, annual rpt, A4700–1
- Energy consumption by fuel type and sector, 1970s-2010, annual rpt, C6985–5
- Ethanol demand, with detail for transportation uses in California and US, 1992/93-2000/2001, article, C6985–1.533
- Fuel consumption by vehicle type, and corporate fuel economy ratings by manufacturer, 1993 annual rpt, A0865–1.3
- Gasoline consumption and vehicle fuel efficiency trends, including data by vehicle type and State, 1970s-92, annual fact book, C4680–1.507
- Gasoline demand and travel outlook, and supply data, 1992-93, article, C6985–1.534
- Gasoline demand, monthly rpt, R9375–1
- General aviation fuel use, by aircraft type, FY87-2004, annual rpt, A5120–2.3
- Japan energy supply-demand and outlook, by fuel source, 1980s-2000, recurring article, R5650–2.536
- Mass transit rail system energy efficiency ratings, for 14 systems in US and Canada, 1993 article, C1575–3.506

Mass transit system finances and operations, passengers, and employment, by mode, US and Canada, 1990-91 and trends, annual rpt, A2650–1

- Motor vehicle fuel economy for 1994 models, EPA estimates by model and size group, annual feature, C2710–3.550, C2710–3.551
- Motor vehicle fuel economy ratings, with EPA estimates for 1993 models, annual data book, C2710–3.531
- Motorcycle fuel economy data, by engine size, 1992, annual rpt, A6485–1.2
- Natural gas sales by consuming sector, monthly rpt, A1775–2
- Oil and gas industry exploration, production, refining, demand, finance, prices, and reserves, by State and country or world area, 1992 and trends, periodic basic data book, A2575–14.5
- Oil supply-demand, marketing, prices, finances, and employment, detailed data for US and Canada, by product, company, and location, 1993 annual fact book, C4680–1.507
- Railroad (Class I) freight service expenditures by category, and diesel fuel consumption, with detail for 7 companies, 1991, article, C8400–1.508
- Railroad diesel fuel consumption and costs, by company and district, 1992, annual rpt, A3275–7
- Railroad diesel fuel consumption and fuel efficiency, 1982-91, annual rpt, A3275–8.2
- Railroad financial performance, including fuel use and costs, and returns on investment for 11 companies, 1990-93, article, C8400–1.509
- Railroad fuel consumption and cost, and revenue ton-miles generated, 1920s-92, annual rpt, A3275–5
- Sourcebook of oil and gas industry operations and finances, and world supply-demand situation, 1970s-91, annual compilation, C6985–9
- State social, economic, and govtl indicators, with rankings, 1993 semiannual rpt, B8500–1.11
- Statistical profiles of 50 States and DC, general data, 1993 annual almanac, C4712–1
- Supply-demand by energy source and consuming sector, 1947-2010, periodic basic data book, A2575–14.1
- World energy supply-demand, by fuel source and sector, by region and country, 1992/93 biennial rpt, R9455–1.7

State and local:

- Alabama statistical abstract, general data, 1992 recurring rpt, U5680–2.12, U5680–2.16
- Arizona statistical abstract, general data, 1993 recurring rpt, U5850–2.18, U5850–2.20
- California statistical abstract, general data, 1992 annual rpt, S0840–2.10
- Florida statistical abstract, general data, 1992 annual rpt, U6660–1.15
- Georgia statistical abstract, general data, 1992-93 biennial rpt, U6730–1.8
- Hawaii data book, general data, 1992 annual rpt, S2090–1.17, S2090–1.18
- Hawaii fuel consumed and fuel taxes allocated, by type and use, FY91-92, annual rpt, S2120–1

Index by Subjects and Names

- Illinois electric utility sales and operating revenues, energy sold, and customers served, by class of service and company, 1991-92, annual rpt, S2410–1.2
- Kansas statistical abstract, general data, 1991/92 annual rpt, U7095–2.13
- Maryland and US gasoline gallonage sold, 1979-91, biennial rpt, S3605–1.10
- Mississippi consumption of motor fuel and liquefied compressed gas on hwys, and taxes collected, monthly FY92, annual rpt, S4435–1
- Mississippi statistical abstract, general data, 1992 annual rpt, U3255–4.14
- Nebraska motor carrier fuel use and taxes, 1991 and trends, annual rpt, S4950–1.3
- Nevada statistical abstract, general data, 1992 biennial rpt, S5005–1.11
- New York State statistical yearbook, general data, 1992 annual rpt, U5100–1.12, U5100–1.13
- North Carolina public utility financial, operating, and regulatory data, by utility type and company, 1990 and trends, annual rpt, S5917–2
- Ohio gasoline and special fuels consumption, FY88-92, annual rpt, S6390–1.4
- Oklahoma statistical abstract, general data, 1992 annual rpt, U8130–2.16
- Pennsylvania energy supply-demand and prices by fuel type, with electric power info by utility, 1960s-90, recurring rpt, S6810–3
- Pennsylvania statistical abstract, general data, 1992 recurring rpt, U4130–6.9
- South Carolina economic condition, including energy and transportation data, 1970s-92, annual rpt, S7125–3.3
- South Carolina statistical abstract, general data, 1993 annual rpt, S7125–1.8
- Tennessee statistical abstract, general data, 1992/93 annual rpt, U8710–2.9, U8710–2.10
- Utah hwy mileage and expenditures, aviation and motor fuel consumption, and bus travel, various years 1940-92, annual rpt, R9380–1.10
- Utah statistical abstract, general data, 1993 triennial rpt, U8960–1.13
- Virginia motor vehicle registrations, mileage, and fuel consumption, 1982-91, annual rpt, S8282–1
- Washington State electric utility customers, sales, and revenues, by customer class and utility, 1982-91, annual rpt, S8450–1.2
- Wisconsin Blue Book, general data, 1993-94 biennial rpt, S8780–1.2
- Wisconsin oil use, by consuming sector, 1981-90, annual rpt, S8675–3

Transports

see Naval vessels

Trapping

see Hunting and trapping

Travel agencies

- Airline commissions to travel agents, and passenger revenues, by US and foreign carrier, 1st half 1993 and trends, annual article, C7000–4.511
- Business traveler characteristics, including use of travel agencies, 1991, annual rpt, R9375–12
- Establishments and financial data, with agencies by State, 1980s-91, annual rpt, C2140–1.4

Index by Subjects and Names

Travel and tourism

Financial ratios and performance, for over 350 SIC 4-digit industries, FY88-92, annual rpt, A6400–3

Sales (air travel) of top 20 agencies, 1991, recurring rpt, R9375–6

Shopping center financial and operating data, with detail by type of tenant, US and Canada, 1991, triennial rpt, R9285–1

Travel trips and traveler characteristics, including mode, purpose, type of lodging, and area of destination and origin, quarterly rpt, R9375–14

State and local:

Hawaii data book, general data, 1992 annual rpt, S2090–1.23

Travel and tourism

Asia tourist arrivals and daily expenditures in 6 countries, 1993 article, C2710–1.549

Business travel costs trends, by type of expense, 1992-94, article, C1200–1.513

Business traveler and trip characteristics, including mode, purpose, and lodging, 1991, annual rpt, R9375–12

China intl tourist arrivals and tourism earnings, 1988-92, article, A9315–1.506

Congressional campaign fund finances, with expenditures by item and contributions by donor type, by candidate, district, and State, 1990 elections, C2500–6

Consumer complaint and inquiry activity of Better Business Burs, by detailed type of business, 1992, annual rpt, A4350–1

Cruise ships capacity and per diem cost, by ship, 1993 feature, C1200–4.503

Economic impact of travel on States, with detail by industry sector, 1990 and trends, annual rpt, R9375–7

Foreign visitors arriving in US from top 10 foreign countries, 1993, article, C1200–4.505

Incentive programs for consumers, employees, and dealers, with expenditures by industry and incentive type, 1991-92, annual feature, C1200–4.502

Incentive programs for dealers, with purpose, performance measures, and types of awards, 1993 and trends, annual survey article, C1200–4.505

Incentive travel programs for sales promotion, with destinations, and expenditures of top 10 user industries, 1993 survey, annual article, C1200–4.510

Industry devs in travel/tourism, including summary data on travel indicators, monthly rpt, R9375–1

Intercity passenger travel market shares for auto, air, bus, and rail transportation, 1993 article, C1575–3.507

Latin America statistical abstract, general data by country, 1992 annual rpt, U6250–1.14

Library/info science school faculty receiving travel funds, and amounts, by school, 1991/92, annual rpt, A3235–1.1

Motor vehicle use by owner and trip characteristics, and urban and rural travel mileage, with data by mode and State, 1993 annual rpt, A0865–1.3

Motorcycle use and user characteristics, licensed operators, and State requirements, 1992 annual rpt, A6485–1.2

Niagara Falls visitors, hotel rooms and occupancy rates, and unemployment rates, for Ontario and New York sides, 1993 article, C5800–7.544

Rankings for selected travel and tourism indicators, including data for top 20 States, cities, countries, businesses, and other measures, 1992 recurring rpt, R9375–6

Sales industry costs, including compensation, training, and travel and related expenses, with data by metro area, 1992 and trends, annual survey, C1200–1.508

Sourcebook of oil and gas industry, with comparisons to vehicle registrations and use, 1960s-91, annual compilation, C6985–9.5

State economic dev condition indicators, including economic performance, business vitality, growth capacity, and tax/fiscal system, by State, 1993 annual rpt, R4225–1.1

State social, economic, and govtl indicators, with rankings, 1993 semiannual rpt, B8500–1.2, B8500–1.11

State tourism dev offices activities, personnel, and budgets, by State, 1992 survey, annual rpt, R9375–2

Statistical profiles of 50 States and DC, general data, 1993 annual almanac, C4712–1

Travel trips and traveler characteristics, including mode, purpose, type of lodging, and area of destination and origin, quarterly rpt, R9375–14

Vacation plans of consumers in US and abroad within 6 months, and travel mode, monthly rpt bimonthly table, R4105–4

World travel and tourism trends, with traveler and trip characteristics, industry devs, and detail by country and US location, 1992 annual rpt, C2140–1

State and local:

Alabama, Mobile Harbor waterborne freight and passenger traffic, 1951-89, recurring rpt, U5680–2.16

Alaska, Ketchikan cruise ship, airline, and hwy tourism indicators, 1982-91, article, S0320–1.502

Alaska motor vehicle miles traveled, 1982-91, annual rpt, S0360–1

Arizona border crossings from Mexico, by city, 1970-91, recurring rpt, U5850–2.8

Arizona hwy traffic, recreational area visitors, and intl border crossings, by local area, 1984-93, semiannual rpt, U5850–1.1

Arizona statistical abstract, general data, 1993 recurring rpt, U5850–2.18

Arizona vehicle miles traveled, 1977-91, annual rpt, S0530–1

California motor vehicle miles traveled, 1991 and trends, annual rpt, S0885–1

California travel-related expenditures, by type of business, 1991 and trends, annual rpt, S0840–3

Colorado tourism promotion tax collections, by county and industry, FY89-92, annual rpt, S1075–1.5

DC statistical profile, general data, 1992 annual rpt, S1535–3.3

Delaware motor vehicle travel mileage, 1992 and trends, annual rpt, S1435–1

Florida motor vehicle miles traveled, 1972-92, annual rpt, S1750–2

Florida statistical abstract, general data, 1992 annual rpt, U6660–1.13, U6660–1.19

Hawaii counties population and economic indicators, 1993 annual rpt series, B3500–2

Hawaii data book, general data, 1992 annual rpt, S2090–1.7, S2090–1.13, S2090–1.18, S2090–1.23

Hawaii economic conditions, including employment, population, tourism, and construction, quarterly rpt, S2090–2

Hawaii economic indicators, bimonthly rpt, B3500–1

Hawaii tourists, by origin, 1990-92, article, C1200–4.507

Hawaii vehicle miles traveled, by county, 1986, annual rpt, S2125–1

Idaho economic profile, general data, 1992 recurring rpt, S2218–2.10

Idaho motor club financial data, by company, Dec 1991, annual rpt, S2260–1

Idaho motor vehicle travel mileage, 1991-92, annual rpt, S2315–1

Illinois motor vehicle travel mileage, 1982-91, annual rpt, S2540–1

Indiana vehicle miles traveled, 1991-92, annual rpt, S2675–1

Kansas motor vehicle travel mileage, 1992, annual rpt, S3040–1

Louisiana vehicle miles traveled, 1991, annual rpt, S3345–2

Maryland statistical abstract, general data, 1993-94 biennial rpt, S3605–1.5

Michigan vehicle miles traveled, 1948-91, annual rpt, S3997–2

Minnesota vehicle miles traveled, 1983-92, annual rpt, S4230–2

Missouri motor vehicle travel mileage, 1991-92, annual rpt, S4560–1

Nevada hwy traffic flow, 1980-91, annual rpt, U7920–2

Nevada statistical abstract, general data, 1992 biennial rpt, S5005–1.13

Nevada vehicle travel miles, with detail by hwy system and county, 1992 and trends, annual rpt, S5140–1

New Mexico, Albuquerque characteristics, and vacation site selection criteria, views of North Central States residents, spring 1993 survey, article, U7980–1.505

New Mexico economic trends and outlook, by industry div, 1982-92, annual article, U7980–1.503

New Mexico motor vehicle travel mileage, 1983-92, annual rpt, S5665–1

New York State statistical yearbook, general data, 1992 annual rpt, U5100–1.13, U5100–1.15

New York State vehicle miles traveled, 1982-91, annual rpt, S5790–1

North Carolina motor vehicle travel mileage, 1940-92, annual rpt, S5990–1

North Dakota tourism-related employment and earnings, by type of business, 1988 and 1991, annual planning rpt, S6140–2

North Dakota vehicle miles traveled, 1990-92, annual rpt, S6217–1

Ohio vehicle miles traveled, 1980-91, annual rpt, S6290–1

Oklahoma vehicle miles traveled, 1960-92, annual rpt, S6482–1

Oregon economic conditions, including population, construction, income, employment, industry, and foreign trade data, 1991, annual rpt, S6585–3

Pennsylvania statistical abstract, general data, 1992 recurring rpt, U4130–6.2

Travel and tourism

South Carolina motor vehicle miles traveled, 1963-92, annual rpt, S7190–2
South Carolina statistical abstract, general data, 1993 annual rpt, S7125–1.14
South Dakota judicial system personnel and travel mileage for official functions, FY92, annual rpt, S7395–1
South Dakota motor vehicle travel miles, 1961-92, annual rpt, S7300–3
Tennessee travel economic impact, with detail by county, 1985-89, annual rpt, U8710–2.12
Utah economic and business activity review and indicators, monthly rpt, U8960–2
Utah motor vehicle travel mileage, 1934-92, annual rpt, S7890–2
Utah statistical abstract, general data, 1993 triennial rpt, U8960–1.17
Virginia motor vehicle registrations, mileage, and fuel consumption, 1982-91, annual rpt, S8282–1
Washington State vehicle travel mileage, 1992 and trends, annual rpt, S8428–1
West Virginia motor vehicle miles traveled, 1992, annual rpt, S8645–1
Wisconsin Blue Book, general data, 1993-94 biennial rpt, S8780–1.2
Wisconsin vehicle travel miles, 1978-92, annual rpt, S8815–1
Wyoming motor vehicle miles traveled, 1982-92, annual rpt, S9007–1
see also Air travel
see also Passports and visas
see also Transportation energy use
see also Travel agencies
see also Travelers checks

Travelers checks

State and local:
Oklahoma licensed money order agencies, by company, FY92 annual rpt, S6415–1

Treasury Department

see Department of Treasury

Treaties and conventions

Chemical use reduction and phaseout schedule under intl ozone protcction treaty, for 6 ozone-harming substances, 1992 article, A1250–1.506
Japan govt public works contracts let under US-Japan Major Projects Agreement, with bids submitted and won by US firms, 1988-92, article, R5650–2.537
Military forces in Europe, for US, NATO, Soviet Union, and Eastern Europe, prior to and after Conventional Forces in Europe (CFE) treaty, 1991, annual rpt, C2500–2
see also Trade agreements

Trees

see Forests and forestry

Trial courts

see State courts

Trials

Public opinion on Federal prosecution of Los Angeles police officers in Rodney King brutality case, and outcomes, Apr 1993 Gallup Poll, C4040–1.510
Public opinion on news items concerning 2nd Rodney King police brutality trial and Los Angeles riots after 1st trial, by race-ethnicity, Apr/May 1993 survey, C8915–1.503
Public opinion on prosecution of Los Angeles police officers in Rodney King brutality case, and outcomes, Feb 1993 Gallup Poll, C4040–1.508

Rape service agency staff views on influence of 2 highly publicized trials on women's likelihood of reporting rape, 1990-92 surveys, R8375–1

State and local:
Alaska court cases and dispositions, by type of court and case, and location, with judicial dept finances and personnel, FY92 and trends, annual rpt, S0290–1
Arizona court cases and dispositions, by type of case and court, with judicial personnel and finances, by county and city, FY92, annual rpt, S0525–1
California court activity, including caseloads and dispositions, by case type and court, and location, FY92 and trends, annual rpt, S0905–1
California court cases and dispositions, by type of case and court, and location, FY92 and trends, annual rpt, S0905–2
Colorado court cases and dispositions, by type of court and detailed case type, FY92 and trends, annual rpt, S1035–1.2
Connecticut court caseloads and dispositions, by type of court and case, and court location, FY91-92, biennial rpt, S1220–1.2
DC court cases and dispositions, by type of case, and judicial system finances, 1992 and trends, annual rpt, S1515–1
Delaware court caseloads and dispositions, by type of court and case, and by county, with judicial dept finances, FY92, annual rpt, S1360–1
Florida court cases and dispositions, by type of court and case, and location, 1992, annual rpt, S1805–1
Hawaii court cases and dispositions, by type of court and case, and judicial circuit, FY92 and trends, annual rpt, S2115–1.2
Indiana court cases and dispositions by type of court and case, and location, with judicial system finances and personnel, 1992, annual rpt, S2703–1
Iowa court cases, processing, and dispositions, by type of court and district, with judicial dept appropriations and personnel, 1992 and trends, annual rpt, S2815–1
Kansas court caseloads and disposition, by type of court and case, and location, FY92, annual rpt, S3035–1
Louisiana court caseloads and dispositions, by type of court and case, and jurisdiction, 1992 and trends, annual rpt, S3375–1
Maine court cases and dispositions, by type and location, FY92 and trends, annual rpt, S3463–1
Maryland court caseloads and dispositions, by type of court and case, and county, with judicial personnel and finances, FY92 and trends, annual rpt, S3600–1
Massachusetts court cases and dispositions, by type of court and case, and location, FY92 and trends, annual rpt, S3807–1
Michigan court caseloads and dispositions, by type of court and case, and court location, 1992 and trends, annual rpt, S3962–1
New Mexico court cases and dispositions, by type of court and case, and location, with judicial system finances and personnel, FY92, annual rpt, S5623–1

New York State crimes and arrests by offense and demographic characteristics, and court activity and corrections, 1991 and trends, annual rpt, S5760–3
North Carolina court cases and dispositions, by type of court and case, and location, with judicial dept finances and personnel, FY91, annual rpt, S5950–1
Ohio court caseload and case disposition, by type of court and case, and location, 1992, annual rpt, S6385–1
Oklahoma court cases and dispositions, by type of court and case, with judicial system finances, by county or jurisdiction, FY92, annual rpt, S6493–1
Pennsylvania court caseloads and dispositions, by type of court and case, and county, 1991, annual rpt, S6900–1.2
Rhode Island court cases and dispositions, by type of court and case, and county, 1987-91, annual rpt, S6965–1
South Carolina court cases and dispositions, by type of court and location, with judicial dept finances and employees, 1992 and trends, annual rpt, S7197–1
South Dakota court cases and dispositions by type of case, and judicial system finances and personnel, by jurisdiction, FY92 and trends, annual rpt, S7395–1
Tennessee court cases and dispositions, by type of court and case, and county, FY92, annual rpt, S7585–1
Texas court cases and dispositions, by type of court and case, and location, FY92, annual rpt, S7703–1
Vermont court cases and dispositions, by type of court and case, and location, FY92 annual rpt, S8120–1
Virginia court caseloads, processing, and dispositions, by type of court and case, with judicial dept personnel and finances, by location, 1992 and trends, annual rpt, S8300–1
Washington State court cases and dispositions, by type of court and case, and jurisdiction, with judicial finances and personnel, 1992 and trends, annual rpt, S8339–1
West Virginia court caseloads and dispositions, by type of court and case, and judicial circuit, 1992 and trends, annual rpt, S8537–1
see also Domestic relations courts and cases
see also Juries
see also Juvenile courts and cases
see also Probate courts and cases
see also Small claims courts and cases
see also Tax laws and courts
see also Traffic laws and courts

TriBrook Group, Inc.

Hospital planning activity, including construction plans and influence of anticipated health care reform, 1993 survey, article, A1865–1.523

Trichinosis

see Food and waterborne diseases

Trinidad and Tobago

Energy intl sourcebook, with detail on oil and gas industry operations, supply-demand, and prices, for approx 80 countries, 1970s-91, annual compilation, C6985–10.2
Motor vehicle world production, sales, trade, and registrations, by country, world area, manufacturer, and make, 1991 and trends, annual rpt, A0865–2.1

Index by Subjects and Names

Oil refinery capacity for govt-owned company, oil products supply-demand data, and energy use by selected fuel type, 1990 or 1991, article, C6985–1.518

Trophies
see Awards, medals, and prizes

Tropics
Latin America statistical abstract, general data by country, 1992 annual rpt, U6250–1.2

Troy, Kathryn
"Managing Corporate Communications in a Competitive Climate", R4105–78.24

Troy, Leo
"Almanac of Business and Industrial Financial Ratios, 1993 Edition", C7800–1

Truancy from school
State and local:
California criminal justice system detailed data, by offense, county, age, race-ethnicity, and sex, 1991 and trends, annual rpt, S0910–2.2
DC juvenile court case activity, including referrals by offense and age, 1992 and trends, annual rpt, S1515–1
Illinois crimes and arrests, by offense, with data by location and offender characteristics, 1991, annual rpt, S2536–1
New Hampshire arrests, by offense and offender age, sex, and race-ethnicity, 1991, annual rpt, S5250–2.2
North Carolina court cases and dispositions, by type of court and case, and location, with judicial dept finances and personnel, FY91, annual rpt, S5950–1
Utah juvenile offenses by detailed offense type, by month, 1992, annual rpt, S7890–3

Trucks and trucking industry
Accidents involving fleet vehicles, and vehicles and mileage, by fleet type and company (unnamed), 1991 and trends, annual rpt, A8375–3
Beverage distribution operations and costs, including fleet size, maintenance, and purchase plans, 1992 survey, annual rpt, C0125–3.2
Collision coverage insurance claims and payments experience for autos and other vehicles, by make and series, for recent model years, 1993 annual rpt series, A5200–1
Dealership financial data, and sales of trucks by weight class and make, 1993 annual rpt, A7330–1
Equipment distributor financial data, by company type, sales size, and rural vs metro market, FY91 and trends, annual rpt, A8505–4
Fatal accidents involving trucks, by driver-related factor, 1990, C2150–4.503
Financial ratios and performance, for over 350 SIC 4-digit industries, FY88-92, annual rpt, A6400–3
Fuel economy, EPA estimates for 1994 model light trucks, vans, and specialty vehicles, by model, annual feature, C2710–3.551
Leased truck fleet characteristics, including weight class and annual mileage, biennially 1970-92, biennial survey article, C1575–2.503

Light truck accessory purchasing patterns of owners, and owner characteristics, 1993 annual survey feature, C2150–10.506
Light truck market shares in top 10 States and buyer characteristics for 3 leading makes, and general truck market characteristics, 1993 article, C2150–3.510
Light truck owner do-it-yourself maintenance activity by type, 1992 article, C0125–1.501
Logistics trends and devs, including data on costs, finances of major carriers by mode, and foreign trade, 1993 annual compilation, C2150–1.506
Market data book on production, sales, registrations, prices, options, and dealerships, with data by make and country, 1993 annual rpt, C2710–3.531
Mexico-Texas transportation system analysis, including bilateral trade, operations by transport mode, and data by locale, 1993 rpt, U8850–9
New motor vehicle registrations, including imports, by make and model, monthly rpt, C7715–3
Number of cars and trucks in use, newly registered, and scrapped, 1947-92, annual rpt, C7715–2
Operating and financial composite ratios for corporations, with establishments and receipts, for approx 200 industries, by asset size, FY90, annual rpt, C7800–1
Personal injury protection insurance claim frequencies for 1990-92 model autos and other vehicles, by make and model, annual rpt, A5200–3
Production, sales, and market analysis, by manufacturer and make/model, with industry news and devs, weekly rpt, C2710–3
Production, sales, trade, and vehicle use, detailed data on motor vehicle industry by vehicle type, State, and country, 1900s-92, annual rpt, A0865–1
Registrations by State and Canadian Province, fuel consumption, and mileage, 1993 annual fact book, C4680–1.507
Regulatory agency policies and practices for motor carriers and railroads, by agency, 1991/92 annual rpt, A7015–4
Sales in US of Japanese vs US light trucks, vans, and sport/utility vehicles, by vehicle size class and model, 1989-92, article, R5650–2.529
Sales of trucks by type, weight, and make, 1970s-92, annual feature, C2150–4.503
Service to daily newspaper markets in US and Canada, by mode and company, 1993 annual rpt, C3250–1
Theft insurance claims and payments experience for 1990-92 model autos and other vehicles, by make and model, annual rpt, A5200–2
Traffic accident rates, fleets, and vehicles, 1992 and trends, annual rpt, A8375–2.3
Traffic accidents involving defective trucks, by type of defective part, 1984-88, article, C1575–2.511
Traffic fatal crash rates for pickup trucks of 3 major manufacturers, with detail for crashes involving side-impact/fire, 1993 article, C8900–1.516
Travel miles, fuel consumed, and registrations, 3 vehicle types, 1947-91, periodic basic data book, A2575–14.5

Trucks and trucking industry

Trends in transportation operations and finances, by mode, 1991 annual rpt, R4815–1
Used pickup truck (3/4 ton) resale value, replacement cost, and depreciation, 1993 article, C1575–2.505
World production, sales, trade, and registrations of motor vehicles, by country, world area, manufacturer, and make, 1991 and trends, annual rpt, A0865–2

State and local:
Alabama statistical abstract, general data, 1992 recurring rpt, U5680–2.16
Alabama traffic accidents, fatalities, and injuries, by circumstances, vehicle type, and driver and victim characteristics, 1992, annual rpt, S0185–1
Alaska traffic accidents, fatalities, and injuries, by vehicle type, circumstance, location, and driver and victim characteristics, 1991 and trends, annual rpt, S0360–1
Arizona statistical abstract, general data, 1993 recurring rpt, U5850–2.18
Arizona traffic accidents, fatalities, and injuries, by vehicle type, circumstances, location, and driver and victim characteristics, 1991 and trends, annual rpt, S0530–1
Arkansas traffic accidents, fatalities, and injuries, by vehicle type, circumstances, location, and driver and victim characteristics, 1991, annual rpt, S0692–1
California motor carrier investigations, disciplinary actions, and fines assessed, FY92, annual rpt, S0930–1
California resident views on whether passengers should be allowed to ride in backs of pickup trucks, 1991 annual rpt, S0865–2
California traffic accidents, fatalities, and injuries, by vehicle type, circumstances, location, and driver and victim characteristics, 1991 and trends, annual rpt, S0885–1
Colorado truck inspection activities, with detail by port of entry, FY90-92, annual rpt, S1075–1.4
Connecticut traffic accidents, fatalities, and injuries, by vehicle type, circumstance, location, and driver and victim characteristics, 1992, annual rpt, S1275–1
Delaware traffic accidents involving trucks, and truck weight enforcement stops and arrests, 1992 and trends, annual rpt, S1435–1
Florida traffic accidents, fatalities, and injuries, by vehicle type, circumstance, location, and driver and victim characteristics, 1992 and trends, annual rpt, S1750–2
Hawaii data book, general data, 1992 annual rpt, S2090–1.18
Hawaii traffic accidents, injuries, and fatalities, by circumstances, location, and driver and victim characteristics, 1986 and trends, annual rpt, S2125–1
Idaho economic profile, general data, 1992 recurring rpt, S2218–2.8
Idaho traffic accidents, fatalities, and injuries, by circumstances, location, vehicle type, and driver and victim characteristics, 1992, annual rpt, S2315–1

Trucks and trucking industry

Illinois traffic accidents, fatalities, and injuries, by circumstances, location, and driver and victim characteristics, 1991 and trends, annual rpt, S2540–1

Indiana traffic accidents, fatalities, and injuries, by circumstances, location, and vehicle type, and driver and victim characteristics, 1992, annual rpt, S2675–1

Kansas traffic accidents, fatalities, and injuries, by vehicle type, location, circumstances, and driver and victim characteristics, 1992, annual rpt, S3040–1

Kentucky commercial and farm truck registrations, by county, 1991, annual rpt, S3104–1.3

Kentucky traffic accidents, fatalities, and injuries, by circumstances, location, vehicle type, and driver characteristics, 1992 and trends, annual rpt, S3150–2

Louisiana traffic accidents, fatalities, and injuries, by circumstances, location, and driver characteristics, 1991 and trends, annual rpt, S3345–2

Maine traffic accidents, fatalities, and injuries, by accident circumstances, vehicle type and make, and driver and victim characteristics, 1992, annual rpt, S3475–2

Maryland traffic accidents, fatalities, and injuries, by circumstances, location, vehicle type, and driver and victim characteristics, 1992, annual rpt, S3665–4

Michigan traffic accidents, fatalities, and injuries, by vehicle type, circumstance, location, and driver and victim characteristics, 1991 and trends, annual rpt, S3997–2

Minnesota traffic accidents, fatalities, and injuries, by type of vehicle and circumstances, and driver and victim characteristics, 1992 and trends, annual rpt, S4230–2

Mississippi statistical abstract, general data, 1992 annual rpt, U3255–4.6

Missouri traffic accidents, fatalities, and injuries, by circumstances, location, and driver and victim characteristics, 1992 and trends, annual rpt, S4560–1

Montana freight line companies, income, and taxes paid, FY88-92, biennial rpt, S4750–1.1

Montana traffic accidents, fatalities, and injuries, by circumstances, location, and driver and victim characteristics, 1992 and trends, annual rpt, S4705–2

Nebraska traffic accidents, fatalities, and injuries, by circumstances, location, vehicle type, and driver and victim characteristics, 1992, annual rpt, S4953–1

Nevada traffic accidents, fatalities, and injuries, by circumstances, location, and vehicle type, 1992 and trends, annual rpt, S5140–1

New Jersey fatal traffic accidents and fatalities, by vehicle type, location, and circumstances, and driver and victim characteristics, 1992 and trends, annual rpt, S5430–2

New Mexico motor carrier registrations and fees by county, port-of-entry revenue collections, and safety inspection outcomes, FY91-92 annual rpt, S5660–1

New Mexico traffic accidents, fatalities, and injuries, by vehicle type, circumstances, location, and driver and victim characteristics, 1992 and trends, annual rpt, S5665–1

New York State traffic accidents, fatalities, and injuries, by circumstances, location, vehicle type, and driver and victim characteristics, 1991 and trends, annual rpt, S5790–1

North Carolina employment in trade, transportation, communications, utilities, govt, and education, by detailed occupation, 2nd qtr 1991, triennial rpt, S5917–5.2

North Carolina public utility financial, operating, and regulatory data, by utility type and company, 1990 and trends, annual rpt, S5917–2

North Carolina traffic accidents, fatalities, and injuries, by circumstances, location, vehicle type, and driver and victim characteristics, 1992 and trends, annual rpt, S5990–1

North Dakota traffic accidents, fatalities, and injuries, by circumstances, location, vehicle type, and driver and victim characteristics, 1992 and trends, annual rpt, S6217–1

Ohio traffic accidents, fatalities, and injuries, by circumstances, location, driver and victim characteristics, and vehicle type, 1991 and trends, annual rpt, S6290–1

Oregon referendum on banning triple truck-trailer combinations from hwys, election results by county, 1992, biennial rpt, S6665–1

Pennsylvania traffic accidents, fatalities, and injuries, by circumstances, location, driver characteristics, and vehicle type, 1991, annual rpt, S6905–3

Rhode Island traffic accidents, fatalities, and injuries, by circumstances, community, and driver and victim characteristics, 1992, annual rpt, S7025–1

South Carolina motor carrier finances and regulation, including inspections, violations, arrests, and fines, FY92 and trends, annual rpt, S7235–1

South Carolina traffic accidents, fatalities, and injuries, by circumstances, location, and driver and victim characteristics, 1992 and trends, annual rpt, S7190–2

South Dakota traffic accidents, fatalities, and injuries, by circumstances, location, vehicle type, and driver and victim characteristics, 1992 and trends, annual rpt, S7300–3

Tennessee statistical abstract, general data, 1992/93 annual rpt, U8710–2.9

Texas trade, transportation, and public utilities employment, by SIC 2- and 3-digit industry and detailed occupation, 2nd qtr 1991, triennial survey rpt, S7675–1.31

Utah traffic accidents and fatalities by circumstances, location, driver and victim characteristics, and vehicle type, 1992 and trends, annual rpt, S7890–2

Virginia traffic accidents, fatalities, and injuries, by circumstances, location, and driver and victim characteristics, 1991 and trends, annual rpt, S8282–1

Washington State traffic accidents, fatalities, and injuries, by circumstances, vehicle

type, and location, with driver and victim characteristics, 1992 and trends, annual rpt, S8428–1

West Virginia traffic accidents, fatalities, and injuries, by circumstance and location, and driver and victim characteristics, 1992, annual rpt, S8645–1

Wisconsin traffic accidents, fatalities, and injuries, by circumstances, location, vehicle type, and driver and victim characteristics, 1992 and trends, annual rpt, S8815–1

Wyoming traffic accidents, fatalities, and injuries, by circumstances, location, vehicle type, and driver and victim characteristics, 1992 and trends, annual rpt, S9007–1

see also Freight

see also Motor vehicle fleets

see also Motor vehicle industry

see also under By Industry in the "Index by Categories"

Trust funds

Administration of trust funds and estate planning, analyses of trust portfolios, investments, and economic outlook, monthly rpt, C2425–2

Bank (master trust/custodial) assets and operating data for top instns, 1993 annual directory, C2710–2.522

Directory of master and directed trusts, assets managed and services offered, approx 40 instns, 1992 annual feature, C2425–1.502

Directory of trust instns and assets managed, approx 5,000 depts, US and Canada, 1993 annual feature, C2425–2.501

Higher education instn endowment fund and investment pool characteristics and performance, by instn, FY92, annual survey rpt, A6705–2

Institutional fund mgmt and investment trends and devs, biweekly rpt, C2710 2

Insurance, foreign surplus lines companies trust funds on deposit in US, by company, Dec 1991, annual rpt, S7466–1

Mutual fund industry financial data, by type of investor and financial instn intermediary, 1991 and trends, annual rpt, A6025–1.2

Unit investment trust sales volume and value, by trust type, maturity period, and insurance features, monthly rpt, A6025–7

State and local:

Arizona statistical abstract, general data, 1993 recurring rpt, U5850–2.22

California bank trust dept assets and liabilities, Dec 1992, annual rpt, S0810–1

Colorado banks and trust companies, financial condition by instn, 1992, annual rpt, S1070–2

Connecticut banks trust dept accounts and trust funds, by instn, Dec 1991, annual rpt, S1160–1

Delaware court caseloads and dispositions, by type of court and case, and by county, with judicial dept finances, FY92, annual rpt, S1360–1

Kansas court caseloads and disposition, by type of court and case, and location, FY92, annual rpt, S3035–1

Oregon financial instns, financial condition by instn, Dec 1992 and trends, annual rpt, S6616–1

Index by Subjects and Names

Tuberculosis

South Carolina financial instns (State-chartered) financial condition, including data by instn, FY92 annual rpt, S7165–1

Vermont bank trust dept aggregate balance sheet, and State Home Mortgage Guarantee Board trust fund finances, 1991-92, annual rpt, S7995–2

Vermont court cases and dispositions, by type of court and case, and location, FY92 annual rpt, S8120–1

West Virginia bank trust dept accounts and assets, 1990-91, annual rpt, S8530–1

Wisconsin banks trust dept assets, 1992, annual rpt, S8685–1

see also Government trust funds

Trust Territory of the Pacific Islands

Hospital directory, with utilization, expenses, and personnel, by instn, type, and location, 1992, annual rpt, A1865–3

Physicians by detailed specialty and location, 1992 and trends, annual rpt, A2200–3

see also Northern Mariana Islands

Tsunamis

State and local:

Hawaii data book, general data, 1992 annual rpt, S2090–1.5

Tuberculosis

Cases of tuberculosis, for 10 States, 1991, article, A1865–1.510

Hospital patient discharges and length of stay, by diagnosis, type of operation, age, and region, 1991, annual rpt series, B4455–1

Swine slaughtered, tuberculosis-infected carcass incidence, and carcass value and loss, 1976-88, article, A3100–2.519

State and local:

Alabama public health dept activities, including services provided, inspection and licensing activity, staff and finances, and vital statistics and health data, 1992 annual rpt, S0175–3

Alabama vital statistics, including population, births, deaths by cause, marriages, and divorces, by location and demographic characteristics, 1992 and trends, annual rpt, S0175–2

Arizona tuberculosis control program cases and payments, by county and district, monthly rpt, S0465–4

Arkansas vital statistics, including births, deaths by cause, marriages, and divorces, by age, sex, race, and county, 1991 and trends, annual rpt, S0685–1

California vital statistics, including population, births, and deaths by cause, by demographic characteristics and county, 1990 and trends, annual rpt, S0865–1

Colorado vital statistics, including population, births, deaths by cause, abortion, marriage and divorce, and adoption, by demographic characteristics and location, 1990 and trends, annual rpt, S1010–1

Connecticut vital statistics, including births, deaths by cause, marriages, and divorces, by demographic characteristics and location, 1989, annual rpt, S1200–1

Florida deaths by selected cause, and incidence of selected communicable diseases, by county, 1992 annual rpt, S1746–1.1

Florida vital statistics, including population, births, deaths by cause, and marriages and dissolutions, by location and demographic characteristics, 1992 and trends, annual rpt, S1745–3

Hawaii health dept activities and services, including vital statistics and disease control, by location, 1990, annual rpt, S2065–1

Idaho vital statistics, including births, deaths by cause, abortions, marriages, and divorces, by demographic characteristics and county, 1991 and trends, annual rpt, S2250–2

Iowa vital statistics, including population, births, deaths by cause, marriages, and divorces, by demographic characteristics and location, 1991 and trends, annual rpt, S2795–1

Kansas vital statistics, including population, births, deaths by cause, abortions, marriages, and divorces, by demographic characteristics and location, 1991 and trends, annual rpt, S2975–1

Louisiana vital statistics, including population, births, deaths by cause, reportable diseases, marriages, and divorces, by demographic characteristics and locality, 1989-90 and trends, annual rpt, S3295–1

Maine vital statistics, including births, deaths by cause, abortions, and marriages and divorces, by demographic characteristics and location, 1991 and trends, annual rpt, S3460–2

Maryland vital statistics, including population, births, deaths by cause, marriages, and divorces, by demographic characteristics and location, 1989 and trends, annual rpt, S3635–1

Massachusetts vital statistics, including births, deaths by cause, marriages, divorces, and population, by locality and demographic characteristics, 1990 and trends, annual rpt, S3850–1

Michigan vital statistics, including births, deaths, marriages, divorces/annulments, and communicable diseases, by location and demographic characteristics, 1990 and trends, annual rpt, S4000–3

Minnesota vital statistics, including population, births, abortions, deaths, marriages, and divorces, by location and demographic characteristics, 1991 and trends, annual rpt, S4190–2

Mississippi vital statistics, including births, deaths by cause, marriages, and divorces, by demographic characteristics and location, 1992 and trends, annual rpt, S4350–1

Missouri vital statistics, including population, births, deaths by cause, and marriages and divorces, by location and demographic characteristics, 1992 and trends, annual rpt, S4518–1

Montana vital statistics, including births, deaths by cause, abortion, disease, and marriage and divorce, by demographic characteristics and county, 1990-91 and trends, annual rpt, S4690–1

Nebraska vital statistics, including births, deaths, marriages, divorces, and population, by demographic characteristics and location, 1991 and trends, annual rpt, S4885–1

New Hampshire vital statistics, including population, births, deaths by cause, marriages, and divorces, by location and demographic characteristics, 1991 and trends, annual rpt, S5215–1

New Jersey vital statistics, including births, deaths, population, communicable diseases, and marriages and divorces, by demographic characteristics and location, 1990 and trends, annual rpt, S5405–1

New Mexico vital statistics, including population, births, deaths, and disease, by location and demographic characteristics, 1991 and trends, annual rpt, S5605–1

New York State vital statistics, including population, births, deaths by cause, reportable diseases, and marriages and dissolutions, by demographic characteristics and/or location, 1990 and trends, annual rpt, S5765–1

North Dakota vital statistics, including births, deaths by cause, marriages and divorces, and abortions, by demographic characteristics and/or county, 1991 and trends, annual rpt, S6105–2

Ohio vital statistics, including births, deaths by cause, marriages, divorces, and population, by demographic characteristics and location, 1991 and trends, annual rpt, S6285–1

Oregon vital statistics, including births, deaths by cause, communicable diseases, marriages, and divorces, by age, sex, race-ethnicity, and county, 1991 and trends, annual rpt, S6615–5

Rhode Island vital statistics, including population, births, deaths, marriages, and divorces, by demographic characteristics and locality, 1989 and trends, annual rpt, S6995–1

South Carolina deaths, by detailed cause, age, sex, and race, 1990, annual rpt, S7175–2

South Carolina vital statistics, including births, deaths by cause, marriages, and divorces, by age, sex, race, and location, 1990 and trends, annual rpt, S7175–1

South Dakota vital statistics, including births, deaths, marriage and divorce, and communicable disease, by demographic characteristics and county, 1991 and trends, annual rpt, S7345–1

Tennessee vital statistics, including births, deaths by cause, marriages, divorces, and population, by demographic characteristics and location, 1991 and trends, annual rpt, S7520–2

Texas vital statistics, including births, deaths by cause, abortions, marriages, and divorces, by location and demographic characteristics, 1991 and trends, annual rpt, S7685–1

Utah vital statistics, including births and deaths by cause, by demographic characteristics and location, 1990, annual rpt, S7835–1.2

Vermont vital statistics, including population, births, deaths by cause, abortions, marriages, and divorces, by location and demographic characteristics, 1991 and trends, annual rpt, S8054–1

Virginia vital statistics, including births, deaths by cause, marriages and divorces, and communicable disease, by demographic characteristics and location, 1991 and trends, annual rpt, S8225–1

Tuberculosis

Washington State vital statistics, including births, deaths by cause, and population, by demographic characteristics and location, 1991 and trends, annual rpt, S8363–1

West Virginia vital statistics, including births, deaths by cause, marriages, and divorces, by location and demographic characteristics, 1991 and trends, annual rpt, S8560–1

Wisconsin vital statistics, including population, births, deaths by cause, and marriages and dissolutions, by county and demographic characteristics, 1991 and trends, annual rpt, S8715–4

see also under By Disease in the "Index by Categories"

Tucson, Ariz.

Economic condition, including employment and sales, by industry, 1985-93, semiannual rpt, U5850–1.2

see also under By City in the "Index by Categories"

Tuition and fees

- Catholic secondary school operations and finances, including enrollment by race-ethnicity and family income, 1991/92 and trends, biennial rpt, A7375–5
- Community and junior college revenues by source and expenditures by function, and selected student characteristics, FY92, annual rpt, A6705–1
- Dental advanced education programs, enrollment, grads, and finances, by instn and State, 1992/93 annual rpt, A1475–10
- Dental allied education enrollment, grads, and tuition, by instn, 1992/93 annual rpt, A1475–5
- Dental school admission policies, applicants, enrollment, and tuition and fees, by instn, 1992/93, annual rpt, A1475–4.1
- Dental school applications, enrollment, grads, and tuition/fees, by instn, 1992 and trends, annual rpt, A1475–4.2
- Dental school student expenses and financial aid, by instn, US and Canada, 1991/92 or 1992/93, annual rpt, A1475–3.2
- Dental school undergrad student expenses, by type and instn, 1992/93, annual rpt, A1475–4.3
- Higher education instn total costs of tuition, room, board, and fees, for 8 major private instns, 1993/94 and trends, article, C8900–1.514
- Higher education instns, faculty, students, degrees, and finances, detailed data by State, 1993 annual rpt, C2175–1.531
- Higher education spending share covered by tuition/other charges, and change in student charges, by State, FY91, article, B8500–2.516
- Higher education tuition/fees at approx 3,000 individual instns, 1992/93-1993/94, annual feature, C2175–1.535
- Higher education tuition/fees at premier public university, by State, 1992/93 and trends, article, B8500–2.501
- Higher education tuition/fees, errata, C2175–1.503
- Higher education, 2-year college enrollment, degrees, faculty and staff, and tuition/fees, by instn and State, 1992 annual directory, A0640–1
- Law school enrollment by minority status, degrees conferred, staff, and library holdings, by instn, 1992/93 and trends, annual rpt, A0970–1

Library/info science school tuition/fees, by degree program and instn, fall 1992, annual rpt, A3235–1.2

Medical school programs, fees, applicants, admissions, and enrollment, with data by age, sex, minority group, and instn, 1992/93 and trends, annual rpt, A3273–10

Nursing school tuitions, by program type, 1990/91-1991/92, annual rpt, A8010–1

Optometry student expenditures, for residents and nonresidents, by instn, 1991/92, annual survey, A3370–2

Osteopathy college student expenditures, for public and private instns, 1984/85-1991/92, annual rpt, A0620–1

Private elementary and secondary school enrollment, staff, and finances, with detail for minorities, by school type and region, 1980s-1992/93, annual rpt, A6835–3

Southern States higher education enrollment, degrees, appropriations, tuition/fees, and faculty compensation, by instn type, for 15 States, 1990/91, annual rpt, A8945–31

Southern States higher education student aid data, by State, 1990s and trends, biennial fact book, A8945–1.4

Southern States public higher education in- and out-of-State undergrad tuition/fees, by instn type and State, 1991/92, A8945–27.11

Southern States public higher education revenue shares from State and local govt and tuition, by State, 1981/82 and 1991/92, A8945–27.12

State and land-grant university tuition/fees, and room and board charges, by type of professional program and/or instn, fall 1991-92, annual rpt, A7150–4

State social, economic, and govtl indicators, with rankings, 1993 semiannual rpt, B8500–1.7

Theological school enrollment, staff and compensation, and finances, with data by instn, 1991/92 and trends, annual rpt, A3376–1

Western States higher education student exchange program enrollment and support fees, by program and instn, for 15 States, 1992/93, annual rpt, A9385–1

Western States higher education tuition/fees, by resident status, State, and public instn, with State-funded student aid summaries, 1992/93 and trends, annual rpt, A9385–3

State and local:

- Arkansas higher education finances, including revenues by source, expenditures by function, and State appropriations, by public instn, FY80s-95, biennial rpt, S0690–4
- Arkansas public higher education finances and enrollment, with comparisons to US and selected other States, 1990-92, article, U5930–1.502
- California higher education systems funding by source and expenditures by program category, with enrollment data, FY60s-94, annual rpt, S0827–3
- Delaware postsecondary education finances, enrollment, and degrees conferred, by instn, FY94 annual rpt, S1425–1
- Florida higher education enrollment, degree programs, staff, and finances, by

Index by Subjects and Names

State-supported instn, with student and staff characteristics, 1991/92 annual rpt, S1725–1

- Hawaii data book, general data, 1992 annual rpt, S2090–1.3
- Illinois higher education staff, salaries, student cost and aid, and finances, by instn, 1993 annual rpt, S2475–1.2
- Iowa postsecondary enrollment, degrees, staff, and finances, by instn, 1990/91, annual rpt, S2755–1
- Kentucky higher education enrollment, degrees, staff, and finances, by State-supported instn, 1983-92, annual rpt, S3130–3
- Minnesota postsecondary education finances, and enrollment by student characteristics, by type of school system, 1970s-93, biennial rpt, S4195–2.2
- Mississippi higher education enrollment and degrees, by level and field, and finances, by State-supported instn, 1991/92, annual rpt, S4360–1
- Missouri higher education enrollment, degrees, libraries, staff, and finances, by instn, 1992 and trends, annual rpt, S4520–3
- New Hampshire elementary and secondary school revenues by source and expenditures by function, 1991/92, annual tables, S5200–1.12
- North Carolina higher education student costs, admissions, housing, and financial aid, by instn, 1992/93 annual rpt, U8013–1.3
- Oregon public school revenues by source and fund, and expenditures by fund, function, and object, 1991/92, annual rpt, S6590–1.16
- Oregon public school revenues by source and fund, and expenditures by fund, function, and object, 1992/93, annual rpt, S6590–1.17
- Pennsylvania higher education revenues, expenditures, and endowment funds, by instn type, FY91 and trends, annual rpt, S6790–5.4
- Pennsylvania higher education revenues, expenditures, and endowment funds, by instn type, FY92 and trends, annual rpt, S6790–5.16
- Pennsylvania higher education tuition/fees, and room and board charges, by instn, 1992/93 and trends, annual rpt, S6790–5.3
- Rhode Island education expenditures by function and source of funds, by school district, 1991/92, annual rpt, S6970–1.2
- South Carolina higher education enrollment, degrees, staff, and finances, by instn, 1992 and trends, annual rpt, S7185–2
- South Carolina statistical abstract, general data, 1993 annual rpt, S7125–1.6
- South Dakota public higher education finances, staff, enrollment, degrees, and facilities, by instn, FY93 annual rpt, S7375–1
- Tennessee higher education finances, student aid and expenses, and faculty and salaries, by instn, 1992/93 and trends, annual rpt, S7525–1.2
- Tennessee public school finances, by county, city, and school district, 1991/92, annual rpt, S7490–2.4

Index by Subjects and Names

Utah higher education degrees, enrollment, staff, and finances, by public instn, with selected comparisons to instns in other States, 1993/94 annual rpt, S7895–2

Vermont higher education revenues by source, expenditures by function, and tuition/fees, by instn, and student aid trends, 1992 annual rpt, S8035–2.3

West Virginia higher education faculty characteristics and salary, by instn, 1992 and trends, annual rpt, S8533–1.2

West Virginia public school revenues by source, including tuition from patrons, by county, 1993 annual rpt, S8540–4.1

see also Student aid

Tulsa, Okla.

Business activity indicators for Oklahoma, monthly rpt, U8130–1

Employment, hours, and earnings, by industry, monthly rpt, S6430–2

Statistical abstract of Oklahoma, detailed social, economic, and govtl data, 1992 annual rpt, U8130–2

see also under By City in the "Index by Categories"

Tungsten

see Metals and metal industries

Tunisia

Energy intl sourcebook, with detail on oil and gas industry operations, supply-demand, and prices, for approx 80 countries, 1970s-91, annual compilation, C6985–10.2

Tunnels

see Bridges and tunnels

Turkey

Electronics industry trade and/or production trends by product category for 33 countries, with general economic profiles, 1993 annual rpt, A4725–1.4

Energy intl sourcebook, with detail on oil and gas industry operations, supply-demand, and prices, for approx 80 countries, 1970s-91, annual compilation, C6985–10.2

Entertainment industry devs, including motion picture theater screens, films produced, and TV and home video markets, 1993 feature, C9380–1.521

Household appliance production, by type, for 7 manufacturers, 1993 feature, C2000–1.511

Motor vehicle world production, sales, trade, and registrations, by country, world area, manufacturer, and make, 1991 and trends, annual rpt, A0865–2.1

see also under By Foreign Country in the "Index by Categories" or World Area

Turkeys

see Poultry industry and products

Turnersville, N.J.

Discount store ratings and shopping patterns of consumers in 3 market areas, including expenditures, by leading chain, 1992 surveys, article, C5150–3.503

Turnover of labor

see Labor turnover

Turnpikes

State and local:

Maryland tollway traffic by facility, 1982-92, biennial rpt, S3605–1.10

Pennsylvania Turnpike passenger and commercial vehicle use, by interchange, FY89-90, recurring rpt, U4130–6.9

Turpentine

see Gum and wood chemicals

TVA

see Tennessee Valley Authority

Twins

see Plural births

Tyler, Jacob E.

"Military Base Closings Information Packet", R8490–45

Typewriters

see Business machines and equipment

UFOs

see Astronomy

Ukraine

Foreign trade with US, by commodity, 1992 and 1st 5 months 1992-93, article, U2030–1.511

Nuclear reactors in operation, with capacity, electricity generation, and construction, by unit and country, 1992, annual rpt, B6800–2.2

Public opinion in Russia, Ukraine, and Lithuania on political and economic issues and devs, 1991-92 surveys, C8915–10

Public opinion in 9 European countries and 3 Soviet Union Republics on political, economic, and social issues, 1991 survey, C8915–8

Ulcers

see Digestive diseases

Umm al-Qaiwain

see United Arab Emirates

Underdeveloped countries

see Developing countries

Underground economy

Canada cigarette prices on black market compared to legal retail trade, 1992 article, C3950–1.503

Soviet Union public opinion on black marketeers, for Russia, Ukraine, and Lithuania, 1991 survey, C8915–8.2

Underwriters

see Insurance and insurance industry

see Investment banking

Unemployment

see Employment and unemployment, general

see Employment and unemployment, specific industry

see Public welfare programs

see Social security

see Unemployment insurance

see Unemployment insurance tax

see Work incentive programs

Unemployment insurance

Benefit coverage and exhaustions under State and Federal programs, and unemployment rates, with data by State, 1992-93 and trends, R3834–18

Benefits paid and insured unemployment, by State, 1990, biennial rpt, S8780–1.2

Federal budget trends, including spending by program, State, and region, FY81-94, annual rpt, R8490–11

Foreign economic indexes, and leading and coincident indicators for US and other industrial countries, monthly rpt, U1245–1

Govt finances, including revenues by source, expenditures by function, and debt, detailed data for Federal, State, and local govts, 1993 annual rpt, R9050–1

Poor children age 5/under in families receiving unemployment insurance benefits, by family type, 1990-91, annual rpt, U1260–2

State social, economic, and govtl indicators, with rankings, 1993 semiannual rpt, B8500–1.14

Trends in unemployment insurance, including data on unemployment, worker characteristics, coverage, benefits, and State govt finances, 1940s-90, R9260–18

State and local:

Arizona court cases and dispositions, by type of case and court, with judicial personnel and finances, by county and city, FY92, annual rpt, S0525–1

Arizona employment trends by occupational group, including comparisons to unemployment insurance claims by industry div, 1990-92, article, S0465–1.507

Arizona statistical abstract, general data, 1993 recurring rpt, U5850–2.7

California statistical abstract, general data, 1992 annual rpt, S0840–2.5

California unemployment insurance initial claims and weeks claimed, bimonthly rpt, S0840–1

Colorado employment, unemployment, hours, and earnings, with job service activities, monthly rpt, S1040–4

Connecticut unemployment insurance claims, benefits, employer contributions, and fund reserve, monthly rpt, S1235–1

DC employment, earnings, and hours, by industry, with unemployment insurance data, monthly rpt, S1527–3

DC statistical profile, general data, 1992 annual rpt, S1535–3.3

DC unemployment insurance outlay, benefits, and weeks compensated, monthly rpt recurring feature, S1527–3.501

Delaware data book, general data, 1993 annual rpt, S1375–4

Delaware employment, earnings, and hours, by locality and industry, and unemployment insurance activity, monthly rpt, S1405–2

Florida statistical abstract, general data, 1992 annual rpt, U6660–1.7

Georgia statistical abstract, general data, 1992-93 biennial rpt, U6730–1.13

Georgia unemployment insurance claims, benefits, taxes received, and trust fund balance, monthly rpt, S1905–1

Hawaii data book, general data, 1992 annual rpt, S2090–1.11, S2090–1.12

Hawaii economic indicators, bimonthly rpt, B3500–1

Illinois statistical abstract, general data, 1992 annual rpt, U6910–2

Kansas business activity indicators, quarterly rpt, U7095–1

Louisiana insured unemployed by occupation and industry div, by race and MSA, monthly rpt quarterly table, S3320–2

Louisiana job service openings and applicants, and characteristics of Job Training Partnership Act target population and insured unemployed, 1993 annual planning rpt, S3320–1.2

Louisiana unemployment insurance payment review results, 1993, annual table, S3320–2

Maine employment, unemployment, and earnings, by industry group, MSA, and labor area, monthly rpt, S3465–2

Unemployment insurance

Maine unemployment insurance payment review results, 1992, annual article, S3465–2.504

Maryland statistical abstract, general data, 1993-94 biennial rpt, S3605–1.4

Maryland unemployment insurance claims and payments, with detail by State region, monthly rpt, S3605–2

Massachusetts employment, hours, and earnings, by industry and local area, with unemployment insurance claims, monthly rpt, S3808–1

Massachusetts program to help unemployed start a business, impact on need for unemployment insurance benefits, 1993 article, C4687–1.507

Michigan public assistance applications approved and denied, and cases closed, by reason and county, monthly rpt quarterly tables, S4010–1

Michigan unemployment insurance claimants, by State area, June 1992, annual planning rpt, S3980–1.2

Michigan unemployment insurance claims, payments, and exhaustions, monthly rpt, S3980–2

Mississippi statistical abstract, general data, 1992 annual rpt, U3255–4.4

Mississippi unemployment insurance claimant characteristics, 1991/92, annual planning rpt, S4345–1.2

Missouri employment, earnings, and hours, and employment security program activity, by industry and/or county, FY92 and trends, annual rpt, S4530–2.3

Montana layoffs, workers affected, and unemployment insurance claims, by industry div, quarterly rpt, S4710–1

Nebraska unemployment insurance claim trends, quarterly rpt, S4895–2

New Hampshire unemployment insurance claims, monthly rpt, S5205–1

New Jersey economic indicators, including employment, building permits, and retail trade, monthly rpt, S5425–1

New Jersey unemployment insurance repeat claimant characteristics, 1984-88, article, S5425–1.505

New Mexico business and economic activity indicators, monthly rpt, U7980–1

New Mexico unemployment insurance claims and payments, monthly rpt, S5624–2

New Mexico unemployment insurance payment review results, 1992, annual article, S5624–2.507

New York State business activity indicators, quarterly rpt, S5735–2

New York State business and economic indicators, by MSA, county, and industry, 1980s-91, annual rpt, S5735–3

New York State statistical yearbook, general data, 1992 annual rpt, U5100–1.3

North Dakota covered employment and earnings by industry, and unemployment insurance benefits and fund balance, 1991 and trends, annual planning rpt, S6140–2

Ohio unemployment insurance applicants, claims, and payments, monthly rpt, S6270–1

Oklahoma business activity indicators, monthly rpt, U8130–1

Oklahoma employment, hours, and earnings, by industry and MSA, with unemployment insurance and job service activities, monthly rpt, S6430–2

Oklahoma statistical abstract, general data, 1992 annual rpt, U8130–2.10

Oregon ex-service personnel unemployment claims filed, 1st qtr 1989-3rd qtr 1993, article, S6592–1.503

Pennsylvania business activity indicators, monthly rpt, U4110–1

Pennsylvania characteristics of the insured unemployed, 1986-91, annual planning rpt, S6845–3.3

Pennsylvania statistical abstract, general data, 1992 recurring rpt, U4130–6.3

Pennsylvania unemployment insurance claims, benefits, and fund activity, monthly rpt, S6845–1

Rhode Island labor force planning rpt, including population, employment by industry, job openings, and characteristics of insured unemployed, 1993 annual rpt, S6980–3

Rhode Island statistical almanac, general data, 1993 annual rpt, C7975–1.1

South Carolina labor force planning rpt, detailed data on employment, hours, wages, turnover, and characteristics of job service applicants, 1992 annual rpt, S7155–3.2

South Dakota unemployment insurance caseload and recipient characteristics, monthly rpt, S7355–1

Tennessee business activity indicators, quarterly journal, U8710–1

Tennessee statistical abstract, general data, 1992/93 annual rpt, U8710–2.3, U8710–2.18

Tennessee unemployment insurance claims, benefits paid, and trust fund balance, with comparison to Federal benefit programs, monthly rpt, S7495–2

Tennessee unemployment insurance claims, 1989-92, annual rpt, S7560–1

Texas employment, hours, and earnings, by MSA and industry group, and unemployment insurance, monthly rpt, S7675–3

Utah economic and business activity review and indicators, monthly rpt, U8960–2

Utah govt statistical review, fiscal and socioeconomic data, 1993 annual rpt, R9380–1.9

Utah statistical abstract, general data, 1993 triennial rpt, U8960–1.4, U8960–1.6

Utah unemployment insurance coverage, benefits, and payments, 1991-92, article, S7820–3.509

Virginia economic indicators, including new business incorporations and employment data, quarterly rpt, S8205–4

West Virginia statistical handbook, general data, 1992 annual rpt, R9385–1.3

West Virginia unemployment insurance claims and benefits, monthly rpt, S8534–1

Wisconsin unemployment compensation claims and exhaustees, monthly rpt, S8750–1

Wyoming employment by industry group and county, with unemployment insurance and job service activities, monthly rpt, S8895–1

see also State funding for employment
see also Unemployment insurance tax
see also Unemployment trust funds

Unemployment insurance tax

Employee benefit payments and employer cost/payroll ratios, by industry, detailed type of benefit, and firm size, 1991, annual rpt, A3840–1

Higher education instn employee retirement and insurance benefits, prevalence and expenditures, by type of instn and region, 1991, biennial survey, A9025–3

State social, economic, and govtl indicators, with rankings, 1993 semiannual rpt, B8500–1.14

State tax rates and collections, by tax type and State, FY02-92, annual rpt, R9050–1.5

Trends in unemployment insurance, including data on tax rates and collections, 1940s-90, R9260–18

State and local:

Connecticut unemployment insurance claims, benefits, employer contributions, and fund reserve, monthly rpt, S1235–1

Delaware data book, general data, 1993 annual rpt, S1375–4

Georgia unemployment insurance claims, benefits, taxes received, and trust fund balance, monthly rpt, S1905–1

Hawaii tax collections and allocations, by type, for State and counties, FY91-92 and trends, annual rpt, S2120–1

Mississippi statistical abstract, general data, 1992 annual rpt, U3255–4.4

Missouri unemployment insurance contribution data, including tax rates, 1938-91, annual rpt, S4530–2.3

New Hampshire unemployment compensation fund contributions, benefits, interest, and balance, monthly rpt, S5205–1

Ohio unemployment insurance claims, benefits, contributions, and active employer accounts, monthly rpt, S6270–1

Tennessee employment, wages, and unemployment insurance contributions, by county and industry, 1991, annual rpt, S7495–1

Tennessee statistical abstract, general data, 1992/93 annual rpt, U8710–2.3

Utah statistical abstract, general data, 1993 triennial rpt, U8960–1.6

Unemployment trust funds

State unemployment insurance reserve balance, with comparison to total and covered payroll, and insolvency trends, 1940s-91, R9260–18

Status of unemployment insurance trust funds, rankings of 16 weakest States by 3 measures, 1st qtr 1993, R3834–18

State and local:

Arkansas financial condition, including revenues by source, expenditures by function and locality, and fund balances, FY91-92, biennial rpt, S0780–1

California statistical abstract, general data, 1992 annual rpt, S0840–2.5

Colorado financial condition, including receipts by source, and expenditures by function, FY92 and trends, annual rpt, S0980–1

Connecticut unemployment insurance claims, benefits, employer contributions, and fund reserve, monthly rpt, S1235–1

DC statistical profile, general data, 1992 annual rpt, S1535–3.3

Index by Subjects and Names

United Kingdom

Georgia statistical abstract, general data, 1992-93 biennial rpt, U6730–1.13

Georgia unemployment insurance claims, benefits, taxes received, and trust fund balance, monthly rpt, S1905–1

Hawaii tax allocations, by fund, FY91-92, annual rpt, S2120–1

Louisiana financial condition, including revenues by source, expenditures by function, and fund balances, FY92 and trends, annual rpt, S3285–2

Massachusetts financial condition, including revenues by source, and expenditures by function, by fund, FY92 and trends, annual rpt, S3777–1

Minnesota financial condition, including revenues by source, expenditures by function, fund balances, and bonded debt, FY92 and trends, annual rpt, S4180–1

Mississippi financial condition, including revenues by source, expenditures by function and object, and detail by agency, FY92 and trends, annual rpt, S4346–1

Mississippi statistical abstract, general data, 1992 annual rpt, U3255–4.4

Missouri employment, earnings, and hours, and employment security program activity, by industry and/or county, FY92 and trends, annual rpt, S4530–2.3

Montana financial condition, including revenues by source, expenditures by function, and fund balances, FY92, annual rpt, S4653–1

Nebraska financial condition, including revenues by source, expenditures by function and agency, and fund balances, FY92, annual rpt, S4825–1

Nevada financial condition, including fund revenues by source, expenditures by function, and bonded debt, FY92, annual rpt, S5025–1

New Hampshire unemployment compensation fund contributions, benefits, interest, and balance, monthly rpt, S5205–1

New Jersey financial condition, including revenues by source, expenditures by function, fund balances, and bonded debt, FY92, annual rpt, S5455–1

New Mexico unemployment trust fund finances, monthly rpt recurring feature, S5624–2.504, S5624–2.509, S5624–2.510

North Dakota unemployment compensation trust fund income, interest, benefits, and balance, 1971-91, annual planning rpt, S6140–2

Oklahoma unemployment insurance trust fund balance, monthly rpt, S6430–2

Pennsylvania financial condition, including revenues by source, expenditures by function, and fund balances, FY92 and trends, annual rpt, S6810–4

Pennsylvania unemployment insurance claims, benefits, and fund activity, monthly rpt, S6845–1

South Carolina financial condition, including receipts by source, expenditures by function, fund balances, and bonded debt, FY92, annual rpt, S7127–1

South Dakota unemployment trust fund balance, monthly rpt, S7355–1

Tennessee unemployment insurance claims, benefits paid, and trust fund balance, monthly rpt, S7495–2

Tennessee unemployment insurance program assets, 1950s-90, annual rpt, U8710–2.18

Texas financial condition, including revenues by source, expenditures by function, and bonded indebtedness, FY92, annual rpt, S7655–3

Texas financial condition, including revenues by source, expenditures by function and dept, and investments, with data for over 400 individual funds, FY92, annual rpt, S7655–2.2

Utah financial condition, including revenues by source, expenditures by function and agency, and fund balances, FY92, annual rpt, S7795–1

West Virginia unemployment compensation fund balance, monthly rpt, S8534–1

Unfair trade practices

see Dumping

Unfilled orders

see Business orders

Unions

see Labor unions

United Arab Emirates

- Energy intl sourcebook, with detail on oil and gas industry operations, supply-demand, and prices, for approx 80 countries, 1970s-91, annual compilation, C6985–10.2
- Oil industry ownership structure for Abu Dhabi govt-owned company, 1993 article, C6985–1.542
- see *also* Organization of Petroleum Exporting Countries
- see *also* under By Foreign Country or World Area in the "Index by Categories"

United Arab Republic

see Egypt

United Auto Workers

Auto manufacturers union labor costs by component, for domestic vs Japanese-owned companies, 1993 article, C2150–3.509

United Kingdom

- Abortions obtained by Irish women in England, patient characteristics and contraceptive use by marital status, 1988-90, article, A5160–1.501
- Advertising campaign reactions of consumers in US, UK, and France, 1993 survey article, C2710–1.529
- Audio equipment market value, 1982-92, article, C2000–1.510
- Books (academic) published and prices, by subject area, 1985 and 1990-92, annual compilation, C1650–3.4
- Charitable contributions and percent of population making donations, 1987-1990/91, annual rpt, A0700–1.2
- Chemical industry capital spending distribution, by sector, 1992-95, article, A1250–1.520
- Coal industry devs, including consumption trends, mine closures and related employment, and British Coal Corp output, 1992 articles, C5226–2.501
- Coal industry supply-demand, employment, and trade, by country, 1990-91 and trends, annual rpt, A7400–2.2
- Coal production, longwall faces, and employees, by mine and operating status, for Govt-owned company, 1991-92, article, C5226–1.510
- Corporate acquisitions, participants and prices for top 5 transactions, bimonthly rpt quarterly feature, C4683–1

Economic indexes for US and other industrial countries, and leading and coincident indicators, monthly rpt, U1245–1

- Economic indexes for US and selected other countries, composites of leading indicators, monthly rpt, R4105–6
- Economic indicators, including trade with US, import shares for 4 other countries, and population by country and city, 1993 articles, C4687–1.510
- Electronics industry trade and/or production trends by product category for 33 countries, with general economic profiles, 1993 annual rpt, A4725–1.4
- Energy intl sourcebook, with detail on oil and gas industry operations, supply-demand, and prices, for approx 80 countries, 1970s-91, annual compilation, C6985–10.2
- Entertainment industry devs, including motion picture screens, boxoffice receipts, leading films, and TV and VCR use, 1993 feature, C9380–1.513
- Machine tool industry operating data by country and product, 1992 and trends, annual rpt, A3179–2.2
- Military personnel hospital admissions and deaths due to selected diseases, for African troops serving in UK army, 1819-36, article, A2623–1.502
- Motion picture theater screens, for top 4-8 and all other exhibitors in Germany, Spain, France, and UK, 1992, C9380–1.531
- Motor vehicle world production, sales, trade, and registrations, by country, world area, manufacturer, and make, 1991 and trends, annual rpt, A0865–2.1
- Nuclear reactors in operation, with capacity, electricity generation, and construction, by unit and country, 1992, annual rpt, B6800–2.2
- Offshore gas field dev in southern North Sea, with operator, reserves, and production rate, 1993 article, C6985–2.505
- Offshore oil/gas wells drilled, and fields by operating status, 1991-97, article, C6985–1.546
- Oil revenue tax impact on companies operating in North Sea, by company, 1993-96, article, C6985–1.525
- Oil supply-demand and marketing, including UK retail outlets by company, and service station product sales, 1989-90, annual fact book, C4680–1.507
- Public opinion in UK and US on British monarchy, and separation of Prince Charles and Princess Diana, Dec 1992 Gallup Poll, C4040–1.506
- Public opinion in UK and US on most important events in last 60 years, 1993 article, A0610–1.504
- Public opinion in 9 European countries and 3 Soviet Union Republics on political, economic, and social issues, 1991 survey, C8915–8
- Public opinion poll results deviation from natl election outcome, 1992 polls, article, A0610–1.503
- R&D expenditures, with govt spending by recipient type, 1990-91 and trends, article, C1850–6.505

United Kingdom

Silver market activity worldwide and in US, including production, consumption by end use, stocks, trade, and prices, by country, 1988-92, annual rpt, B4300–1
Silver supply-demand by country and end use, with prices, futures trading, and market analyses, 1993 and trends, annual rpt, A8902–4
Swine breeding stock porcine stress syndrome mutation prevalence by breed, in US, Canada, and UK, 1993 article, A3100–2.520
see also under By Foreign Country or World Area in the "Index by Categories"

United Nations

Cambodia peacekeeping personnel serving in UN forces from top 20 countries, Jan 1993, article, R5650–2.540
Latin America voting support for US stance in UN issues, with comparison to other US aid recipients, by country, 1992 annual rpt, U6250–1.9
Public opinion in US on selected foreign policy issues, with detail for 3 States, 1993 survey, annual rpt, A4965–1
Public opinion in US on UN, Mar 1993 Gallup Poll and trends, C4040–1.510
Public opinion in US on UN performance, June 1993 Gallup Poll, C4040–1.512

Universities

see Higher education

University of Tennessee, Center for Business and Economic Research

Tennessee economic indicator trends and forecasts, with data by industry div and manufacturing group, 1982-2001, annual rpt, S7560–1

Unmanned space programs

see Communications satellites
see Space programs

Uranium

Capital spending plans for new mines and plants, by mineral and company, and mine production values, 1993 annual feature, C5226–2.503
Latin America statistical abstract, general data by country, 1992 annual rpt, U6250–1.23
Marketing of uranium, terms of transactions for major selling-buying countries or areas, and price index and earnings data in allied industries, monthly rpt, B6800–1
Sales of uranium under near-term contracts, and near- and long-term transactions, 1992 annual article, B6800–1.502
Supply-demand and price data for energy resources, including by country and producing State, commodity yearbook for 1993, C2400–1
Supply-demand and price data for energy resources, including by country and producing State, commodity yearbook Jan-Sept 1993 updates, C2400–2
Supply-demand for selected metals and nonmetallic minerals, with price data, US and worldwide, 1992-93 and trends, annual feature, C5226–2.505
Supply-demand trends and devs in nuclear power generation and fuel processing worldwide, with related data on individual reactor capacity and completion status, quarterly rpt, B6790–1
World uranium supply-demand and prices, with data by country and company, 1992 and trends, annual rpt, B6800–2

State and local:

Utah statistical abstract, general data, 1993 triennial rpt, U8960–1.10
Wyoming uranium production and assessed valuation, by county, and severance and ad valorem taxes, FY92 annual rpt, S8990–1.2
see also Radioactive waste and disposal

Urban areas

Child poverty rate compared to total US, for aggregate population age 5-17 of 47 major urban areas, 1980 and 1990, A4425–4
Latin America statistical abstract, general data by country, 1992 annual rpt, U6250–1.5, U6250–1.12, U6250–1.13
Middle East population trend and demographic characteristics, by country, 1993 rpt, R8750–2.59
State economic dev condition disparity between urban and rural areas, by State, 1993 annual rpt, R4225–1
State, regional, and census div urban shares of population and land area, 1990, annual data sheet, R8750–9
World population size and characteristics, GNP, and land area, by region and/or country, 1993 annual data sheet, R8750–5
World population size in developing vs developed countries, with detail for urban areas, by country, 1960-2005, R8720–1.1
World population urban share, total and in more vs less developed regions, 1970-2015, R8750–1.503
World population urban share, with detail for developing and developed countries, 1950-2025, article, R8750–1.505

State and local:

New Jersey Index crimes in urban areas, 1992 and trends, annual rpt, S5430–1.3
see also Central business districts
see also Central cities
see also Cities
see also City and town planning
see also Community development
see also Federal aid to local areas
see also Federal-local relations
see also Local government
see also Local government annexation
see also Marketing areas
see also Metropolitan Statistical Areas
see also Neighborhoods
see also Open space land programs
see also Relocation
see also State-local relations
see also Suburbs
see also Urban renewal
see also Urban transportation
see also Zoning and zoning laws
see also under By City and By SMSA in the "Index by Categories"
see also under By Urban-Rural and Metro-Nonmetro in the "Index by Categories"

Urban planning

see City and town planning

Urban renewal

State and local:

DC statistical profile, general data, 1992 annual rpt, S1535–3.3, S1535–3.4
Maryland local govt financial condition, including revenues by source, expenditures by function, and debt obligations, FY92 and trends, annual rpt, S3618–1.1

Index by Subjects and Names

see also Community Development Block Grants
see also Open space land programs
see also Relocation

Urban transportation

Deaths from transportation accidents, and passenger miles, by mode, 1991 and trends, annual rpt, A8375–2.4
Finances and operations of US and Canada urban mass transit systems, including passengers and energy use, by mode, 1990-91 and trends, annual rpt, A2650–1
Mass transit industry trends and devs, articles and special features, bimonthly rpt, C1575–3
Operating and financial composite ratios for corporations, with establishments and receipts, for approx 200 industries, by asset size, FY90, annual rpt, C7800–1
State economic dev condition indicators, including economic performance, business vitality, growth capacity, and tax/fiscal system, by State, 1993 annual rpt, R4225–1.1
State social, economic, and govtl indicators, with rankings, 1993 semiannual rpt, B8500–1.6, B8500–1.11

State and local:

DC statistical profile, general data, 1992 annual rpt, S1535–3.7
New York State statistical yearbook, general data, 1992 annual rpt, U5100–1.13
North Carolina employment in trade, transportation, communications, utilities, govt, and education, by detailed occupation, 2nd qtr 1991, triennial rpt, S5917–5.2
Ohio permissive tax collections for mass transit, by county and transit authority, 1987-91, annual rpt, S6390–1.5
Pennsylvania mass transit fleet characteristics and passengers, including senior citizens, by agency, 1988/89-1989/90, recurring rpt, U4130–6.9
Texas trade, transportation, and public utilities employment, by SIC 2- and 3-digit industry and detailed occupation, 2nd qtr 1991, triennial survey rpt, S7675–1.31
Washington State sales/use tax distributions for public transportation, by transit district, FY90-92, annual rpt, S8415–1.1
Wisconsin Blue Book, general data, 1993-94 biennial rpt, S8780–1.2
see also Buses
see also Commuting
see also Railroads
see also Subways
see also Taxicabs
see also Traffic engineering

Urogenital diseases

Death rates from urinary tract cancer, for men age 45-84, by age group, State, and census div, 1979-89, article, B6045–1.503
Hospital patient admission rates and length of stay, by diagnosis and procedure, payment source, age, sex, and region, 1991, B4455–4
Hospital patient charges and length of stay, by diagnosis and procedure, payment source, age, and region, 1991, B4455–5
Hospital patient discharges and length of stay, by diagnosis, type of operation, age, and region, 1991, annual rpt series, B4455–1

Index by Subjects and Names

Urogenital diseases

Hospital patient discharges and length of stay, by diagnostic related group (DRG), payment source, age, and region, 1991, annual rpt series, B4455–3

Hospital psychiatric patients with selected physical disorders, length of stay by age, sex, and region, 1991, annual rpt series, B4455–2

Prostate surgery procedures, costs, and hospital stay, with data by census div and State, 1991 and trends, article, B6045–1.503

State and local:

Alabama vital statistics, including population, births, deaths by cause, marriages, and divorces, by location and demographic characteristics, 1992 and trends, annual rpt, S0175–2

Alaska vital statistics, including births, deaths by cause, marriages, divorces, adoptions, and population, by demographic characteristics and location, 1990, annual rpt, S0315–1

Arkansas kidney disease patients receiving services, by county, FY90, annual rpt, S0700–2

Arkansas vital statistics, including births, deaths by cause, marriages, and divorces, by age, sex, race, and county, 1991 and trends, annual rpt, S0685–1

California vital statistics, including population, births, and deaths by cause, by demographic characteristics and county, 1990 and trends, annual rpt, S0865–1

Colorado vital statistics, including population, births, deaths by cause, abortion, marriage and divorce, and adoption, by demographic characteristics and location, 1990 and trends, annual rpt, S1010–1

Connecticut vital statistics, including births, deaths by cause, marriages, and divorces, by demographic characteristics and location, 1989, annual rpt, S1200–1

Delaware vital statistics, including births, deaths by cause, and marriages and dissolutions, by demographic characteristics and location, 1990, annual rpt, S1385–2

Florida dialysis centers and stations, by district and county, 1992, annual rpt, S1746–1.2

Florida vital statistics, including population, births, deaths by cause, and marriages and dissolutions, by location and demographic characteristics, 1992 and trends, annual rpt, S1745–3

Georgia vital statistics, including deaths by cause, demographic characteristics, and location, 1991 and trends, annual rpt, S1895–1.2

Hawaii health dept activities and services, including vital statistics and disease control, by location, 1990, annual rpt, S2065–1

Idaho vital statistics, including births, deaths by cause, abortions, marriages, and divorces, by demographic characteristics and county, 1991 and trends, annual rpt, S2250–2

Iowa vital statistics, including population, births, deaths by cause, marriages, and divorces, by demographic characteristics and location, 1991 and trends, annual rpt, S2795–1

Kansas vital statistics, including population, births, deaths by cause, abortions, marriages, and divorces, by demographic characteristics and location, 1991 and trends, annual rpt, S2975–1

Kentucky Medicaid recipients and payments, by program, county, and type of medical service, monthly rpt, S3140–5

Kentucky vital statistics, including births, deaths by cause, marriages and divorces, and population, by demographic characteristics and county, 1991, annual rpt, S3140–1

Louisiana vital statistics, including population, births, deaths by cause, reportable diseases, marriages, and divorces, by demographic characteristics and locality, 1989-90 and trends, annual rpt, S3295–1

Maine vital statistics, including births, deaths by cause, abortions, and marriages and divorces, by demographic characteristics and location, 1991 and trends, annual rpt, S3460–2

Maryland vital statistics, including population, births, deaths by cause, marriages, and divorces, by demographic characteristics and location, 1989 and trends, annual rpt, S3635–1

Massachusetts vital statistics, including births, deaths by cause, marriages, divorces, and population, by locality and demographic characteristics, 1990 and trends, annual rpt, S3850–1

Michigan vital statistics, including births, deaths, marriages, divorces/annulments, and communicable diseases, by location and demographic characteristics, 1990 and trends, annual rpt, S4000–3

Minnesota vital statistics, including population, births, abortions, deaths, marriages, and divorces, by location and demographic characteristics, 1991 and trends, annual rpt, S4190–2

Mississippi vital statistics, including births, deaths by cause, marriages, and divorces, by demographic characteristics and location, 1992 and trends, annual rpt, S4350–1

Missouri vital statistics, including population, births, deaths by cause, and marriages and divorces, by location and demographic characteristics, 1992 and trends, annual rpt, S4518–1

Montana vital statistics, including births, deaths by cause, abortion, disease, and marriage and divorce, by demographic characteristics and county, 1990-91 and trends, annual rpt, S4690–1

Nebraska vital statistics, including births, deaths, marriages, divorces, and population, by demographic characteristics and location, 1991 and trends, annual rpt, S4885–1

Nevada vital statistics, including births, abortions, and deaths by cause, by county and demographic characteristics, 1989 and trends, annual rpt, S5075–1

New Hampshire vital statistics, including population, births, deaths by cause, marriages, and divorces, by location and demographic characteristics, 1991 and trends, annual rpt, S5215–1

New Jersey vital statistics, including births, deaths, population, communicable

diseases, and marriages and divorces, by demographic characteristics and location, 1990 and trends, annual rpt, S5405–1

New Mexico vital statistics, including population, births, deaths, and disease, by location and demographic characteristics, 1991 and trends, annual rpt, S5605–1

New York State vital statistics, including population, births, deaths by cause, reportable diseases, and marriages and dissolutions, by demographic characteristics and/or location, 1990 and trends, annual rpt, S5765–1

North Carolina deaths and rates, by cause and county, 1991 and trends, annual rpt, S5927–1.2

North Dakota vital statistics, including births, deaths by cause, marriages and divorces, and abortions, by demographic characteristics and/or county, 1991 and trends, annual rpt, S6105–2

Ohio vital statistics, including births, deaths by cause, marriages, divorces, and population, by demographic characteristics and location, 1991 and trends, annual rpt, S6285–1

Oregon vital statistics, including births, deaths by cause, communicable diseases, marriages, and divorces, by age, sex, race-ethnicity, and county, 1991 and trends, annual rpt, S6615–5

Rhode Island vital statistics, including population, births, deaths, marriages, and divorces, by demographic characteristics and locality, 1989 and trends, annual rpt, S6995–1

South Carolina deaths, by detailed cause, age, sex, and race, 1990, annual rpt, S7175–2

South Carolina vital statistics, including births, deaths by cause, marriages, and divorces, by age, sex, race, and location, 1990 and trends, annual rpt, S7175–1

South Dakota renal disease services recipients and payments, FY92, annual rpt, S7385–1.1

South Dakota vital statistics, including births, deaths, marriage and divorce, and communicable disease, by demographic characteristics and county, 1991 and trends, annual rpt, S7345–1

Tennessee vital statistics, including births, deaths by cause, marriages, divorces, and population, by demographic characteristics and location, 1991 and trends, annual rpt, S7520–2

Texas vital statistics, including births, deaths by cause, abortions, marriages, and divorces, by location and demographic characteristics, 1991 and trends, annual rpt, S7685–1

Utah vital statistics, including births, deaths by cause, and population, by county and demographic characteristics, 1990 and trends, annual rpt, S7835–1

Vermont vital statistics, including population, births, deaths by cause, abortions, marriages, and divorces, by location and demographic characteristics, 1991 and trends, annual rpt, S8054–1

Virginia vital statistics, including births, deaths by cause, marriages and divorces, and communicable disease, by demographic characteristics and location, 1991 and trends, annual rpt, S8225–1

Urogenital diseases

Washington State vital statistics, including births, deaths by cause, and population, by demographic characteristics and location, 1991 and trends, annual rpt, S8363–1

West Virginia vital statistics, including births, deaths by cause, marriages, and divorces, by location and demographic characteristics, 1991 and trends, annual rpt, S8560–1

Wisconsin vital statistics, including population, births, deaths by cause, and marriages and dissolutions, by county and demographic characteristics, 1991 and trends, annual rpt, S8715–4

Wyoming vital statistics, including population, births, deaths by cause, marriages, and divorces, by demographic characteristics and county, 1991 and trends, annual rpt, S8920–2

see also Sexually transmitted diseases

see also under By Disease in the "Index by Categories"

Uruguay

Statistical abstract of Latin America, detailed social, govtl, and economic data, 1992 annual rpt, U6250–1

see also under By Foreign Country or World Area in the "Index by Categories"

U.S. Budget

see Budget of the U.S.

U.S. Coast Guard

see Coast Guard

U.S. International Development Cooperation Agency

see also Agency for International Development

U.S. Natural Gas Clearinghouse

Southwest US natural gas prices, approx 15 pipelines in 4 States, weekly rpt monthly table, C6985–1

U.S. Postal Service

Budget receipts and outlays of Fed Govt, by source and function, 1920s-93, annual rpt, R9050–1.3

Direct marketing mgmt info, including consumer complaints and handling, and mail volume and rates, 1992/93 annual rpt, A4620–1.5

Newspaper use of selected delivery methods and 3rd-class mail discounts for nonsubscriber/total-market products, fall 1992 survey, article, A8605–1.509

Nonprofit organization Federal mail subsidies, and 3rd-class mail volume, 1980-93, article, C2176–1.506

Nonprofit organization mail rates for 1993, and rates proposed by Congress for 1994-99, article, C2176–1.521

Nonprofit organization mail rates proposed by House of Representatives panel, 1993-99, article, C2176–1.513

Religious congregation use of discounted postal rates, 1992 survey, recurring rpt, A5435–4

State and local:

Arizona statistical abstract, general data, 1993 recurring rpt, U5850–2.19

Florida statistical abstract, general data, 1992 annual rpt, U6660–1.14

Hawaii data book, general data, 1992 annual rpt, S2090–1.16

Mississippi statistical abstract, general data, 1992 annual rpt, U3255–4.7

Oregon food stamps issued through mail, with loss rates, monthly rpt, S6615–8

Tennessee postal revenues, by facility, 1980-90, annual rpt, U8710–2.8

Utah statistical abstract, general data, 1993 triennial rpt, U8960–1.13

see also Postal employees

see also Postal service

U.S. savings bonds

Sales of US savings bonds, New York State and US, quarterly rpt, S5735–2

State and local:

Texas financial condition, including revenues by source, expenditures by function and dept, and investments, with data for over 400 individual funds, FY92, annual rpt, S7655–2.2

Utah statistical abstract, general data, 1993 triennial rpt, U8960–1.15

U.S. statutes

Congressional organization, major legislative and budget actions, and agency and program appropriations, 102nd Congress, 2nd session, 1992, annual rpt, C2500–2

see also Education Consolidation and Improvement Act

see also Elementary and Secondary Education Act

see also under specific subject matter of statutes

U.S. territories

see American Samoa

see Guam

see Panama Canal

see Puerto Rico

see Territories of the U.S.

see Trust Territory of the Pacific Islands

see U.S. Virgin Islands

U.S. Virgin Islands

Accidental deaths, by State and type, 1992, annual rpt, A8375–2.1

Aircraft civil and military joint-use facilities, by State and selected territory, 1991, annual rpt, A0250–2.3

Airports and communities in North America served by regional vs larger airlines, by carrier and location, 1993 annual rpt, A8795–1.2

Black elected officials, by office, govt level, and State, Jan 1993, annual article, R5685–4.505

Black elected officials, by office, govt level, and State or city, Jan 1992 and trends, annual article, R5685–4.502

Foreign students enrolled in US higher education instns, by instn, State, country of origin, and demographic characteristics, 1991/92 and trends, annual rpt, R5580–1

Foundations and finances, FY91, annual rpt, R4900–1

Higher education enrollment, by State and public instn, fall 1992, annual rpt, A7150–5

Hospital directory, with utilization, expenses, and personnel, by instn, type, and location, 1992, annual rpt, A1865–3

Judicial system salaries for judges and court administrators, by State and territory, and for Federal system, July 1993, semiannual rpt, R6600–2

Mathematics proficiency results on Natl Assessment of Educational Progress test, with comparisons to classroom and teacher characteristics, 1993 biennial rpt, A4355–1

Nursing programs (State-approved) for practical/vocational nurses, including

Index by Subjects and Names

admissions, enrollment, and grads, by instn, State, and territory, 1992, annual directory, A8010–5

Nursing programs (State-approved) for registered nurses, including admissions, enrollment, and grads, by instn, State, and territory, 1992, annual directory, A8010–4

Physicians by detailed specialty and location, 1992 and trends, annual rpt, A2200–3

Traffic accident deaths, bimonthly rpt, A8375–1

Transportation regulatory agency policies and practices for motor carriers and railroads, by agency, 1991/92 annual rpt, A7015–4

Trust instns and assets managed, approx 5,000 depts, US and Canada, 1993 annual directory, C2425–2.501

Unemployment insurance trends, including data on unemployment, worker characteristics, coverage, benefits, and State govt finances, 1940s-90, R9260–18

Utility and transportation regulatory agency activities, scope of jurisdiction, finances, and employees, by agency, 1991/92 annual rpt, A7015–2

Utility regulatory agency policies and practices, and industry financial and operating data, by utility type and agency, 1991/92 annual rpt, A7015–3

Water resources planning status and activities, with data water withdrawals and supply shortages, 1991 rpt, A8195–11

State and local:

Oklahoma commuting patterns, including interstate and international travel, and detailed data by county, 1990 and trends, S6416–2

USDA

see Department of Agriculture

User fees

FCC regulatory fees for telecommunication industries under Clinton Admin proposed budget, by company category, FY94, article, C1850–14.533

Telephone directory assistance charges, policies of State and Canadian Province utility regulatory agencies, 1991/92 annual rpt, A7015–3

Transportation taxes and user fees paid to Federal and State govts, 1992 annual rpt, R4815–1

TV station FCC user fees vs cash flow, by market size or per cable subscriber, 1993 article, C1850–14.534

State and local:

Arizona public land grazing fees and components, 1989-93, annual rpt, U5830–1

Idaho telephone user surcharges to offset small phone company costs, FY92, annual rpt, S2290–1

see also Tolls

USMC

see Marine Corps

USSR

see Soviet Union

Utah

Agricultural production, marketing, and finances, by commodity and county, with farms and acreage, 1992 and trends, annual rpt, S7800–1

Index by Subjects and Names

Banks and other financial instns, financial condition by instn, FY93 and trends, annual rpt, S7830–1

Business and economic activity review and indicators for Utah, monthly rpt, U8960–2

Business firms, wages, and employment, by firm size, SIC 2-digit industry, and county, 1st qtr 1992, annual rpt, S7820–1

Corrections inmates, parolees, and probationers, by criminal background and demographic characteristics, with system finances, FY92 and trends, annual rpt, S7810–1

Crimes and arrests, by offense, county, and local agency, with law enforcement employment and assaults on officers, 1992 and trends, annual rpt, S7890–3

Economic and demographic trends, by county and district, 1960-91, annual rpt, S7832–2

Economic indicators for 10 Western States, including forecasts from selected organizations, monthly rpt, U0282–2

Election results and voter registration and turnout, by county and/or district, 1992 general election, biennial rpt, S7875–1

Elementary and secondary school enrollment, attendance, personnel, and finances, by school district, 1991/92, annual rpt, S7815–1

Employment, hours, and earnings, by industry, monthly rpt, S7820–3

Financial condition, including revenues by source, expenditures by function and agency, and fund balances, FY92, annual rpt, S7795–1

Govt statistical review for Utah, with social and economic data, 1993 annual rpt, R9380–1

Health behavior risk factor surveillance survey results, by respondent characteristics, 1991, annual rpt, S7835–3

Higher education degrees, enrollment, staff, and finances, by public instn, with selected comparisons to instns in other States, 1993/94 annual rpt, S7895–2

Homeless shelter population characteristics, individual shelter capacity, and related housing data, 1991-92, annual rpt, S7808–2

Human immunodeficiency virus (HIV) victim sexual partner notification program results, including HIV testing outcome for partners, 1988-90, article, A2623–1.512

Insurance industry financial and underwriting data, by company and line of coverage, with regulatory info, 1991, annual rpt, S7845–1

Labor force characteristics, employment and unemployment, hours, and earnings, with data by industry and locale, 1992 and trends, annual rpt, S7820–10

Libraries, services, staff, and finances, by public library, 1992, annual rpt, S7808–1

Markets with daily newspapers, demographic and economic info by geographic area, US and Canada, 1993 annual rpt, C3250–1

Marriages and divorces, by participant characteristics and location, 1990 and trends, annual rpt, S7835–2

Oil/gas industry production, finances, exploration, and reserves, by State, 1992 and trends, annual rpt, A5425–1.1

Personal income, with detail by source and county, 1992 annual article, S7820–3.501

Population data, 1990 census rpt series, S7832–3

Statistical abstract of Utah, detailed social, govtl, and economic data, 1993 triennial rpt, U8960–1

Statistical profiles of 50 States and DC, general data, 1993 annual almanac, C4712–1

Tax revenues by source, and distribution to localities and State funds, FY92 and trends, annual rpt, S7905–1

Traffic accidents and fatalities by circumstances, location, driver and victim characteristics, and vehicle type, 1992 and trends, annual rpt, S7890–2

Utility and transportation regulatory agency activities, scope of jurisdiction, finances, and employees, by agency, 1991/92 annual rpt, A7015–2

Vital statistics, including births, deaths by cause, and population, by county and demographic characteristics, 1990 and trends, annual rpt, S7835–1

see also Salt Lake City, Utah

see also Salt Lake County, Utah

see also Utah County, Utah

see also Weber County, Utah

see also under By City and By County in the "Index by Categories"

see also under By State in the "Index by Categories"

Utah County, Utah

Homeless shelter capacity and population characteristics for Utah, with detail for selected counties, 1991-92, annual rpt, S7808–2

Utilities

see Public utilities

Utility Data Institute

Electric power generating capacity of nonutility coal- or coke-fired plants entering commercial service in 1992, for 8 plants, 1993 article, C5226–1.512

Uzbekistan

Oil reserves in eastern Uzbekistan, by field, 1993 article, C6985–1.541

Vacant and abandoned property

Oil stripper well abandonments, by State, 1971-92, periodic basic data book, A2575–14.2

Oil stripper well abandonments, 1973-92, annual rpt, A5425–2.1

Oil/gas offshore platforms installed and removed in Gulf of Mexico, bonding requirements, and Minerals Management Service liability for abandoned equipment, 1993 article, C6985–2.508

State and local:

Arizona revenue collections from unclaimed property, FY87-92, annual rpt, S0515–1

Colorado property assessed valuation by detailed property type, and tax levy and revenue by local district, by county, 1991-92, annual rpt, S1055–3

DC vacant lot nuisance citations, maintenance, and liens charged, FY88-91, annual rpt, S1535–3.7

Vacations and holidays

Hawaii data book, general data, 1992 annual rpt, S2090–1.5

Idaho tax statistics, including collections, and data by county and city, FY92 and trends, annual rpt, S2295–1

Illinois Dept of Financial Instns unclaimed property div operations, including interstate finances, FY91 and trends, annual rpt, S2457–2

Indiana financial condition, including revenues by source, expenditures by function and object, and fund balances, by agency, FY92, annual rpt, S2570–1

Montana revenue collections from sale of abandoned property, FY88-92, biennial rpt, S4750–1.1

Tennessee abandoned land fund financial condition, FY92, annual rpt, S7505–1

see also Abandoned buildings

Vacation homes

see Second homes

Vacations and holidays

Books as Christmas gifts, public opinion, 1990-92 surveys, article, C1852–2.503

Business forms manufacturing plant employment and compensation data, by region, 1992 and trends, biennial rpt, A5785–4

Canada photographic and/or home video recording equipment use, by subject or occasion, 1992 survey, recurring rpt, A8695–4

Chambers of commerce vacation and leave policies, 1992, annual rpt, A3840–3

Christmas gift expenditure plans, Dec 1992 Gallup Poll and trends, C4040–1.506

Christmas holiday season sales gain for 12 retail companies, 1992, article, C5800–7.510

Christmas retail sales trends and outlook, 1992-93, article, C5150–3.517

Christmas season advertising budget plans of retailers, by medium, 1991-92, survey article, C1850–14.504

Christmas spending patterns of consumers, views of discount retailers, 1992 survey article, C8130–1.502

Christmas spending plans of consumers, by region, age, and income, Nov 1992 survey, annual rpt, R4105–81.10

Consumer vacation plans for US and foreign travel within 6 months, and travel mode, monthly rpt bimonthly table, R4105–4

Corporate spending levels for customer holiday gifts, 1993 article, C1200–1.512

Employee benefit payments and employer cost/payroll ratios, by industry, detailed type of benefit, and firm size, 1991, annual rpt, A3840–1

Employee vacation weeks in 1st year of service, for US and 5 foreign countries, 1993 feature, C1200–4.503

Food store manager hours per week, and Sundays worked and pay policy, by sales size, year ended Mar 1993, annual survey, A4950–6

Gift product categories consumers plan to buy for 1992 holiday season, 1992 survey article, C5150–3.503

Greeting card sales volume by holiday, 1993, article, C4655–1.511

Hospital (teaching) house staff benefits, by region and ownership, 1992/93, annual rpt, A3273–3

Vacations and holidays

House of Representatives staff characteristics, salaries, and benefits by position, 1992 and trends, recurring rpt, R4140–1

Japan work hours vs time off, 1970s-92, article, C2710–1.536

Jewelry industry price expectations for top-selling items for 1993 Christmas season, 1993 survey, annual article, C2150–7.507

Manufacturing workers annual hours worked and days off, for 7 countries, 1990 or 1991, article, C5800–7.539

Motion picture boxoffice receipts during Thanksgiving-New Year holiday period, 1987-91, article, C9380–1.505

Motion picture boxoffice receipts for top 10 films on Memorial Day weekends, 1980s-92, C9380–1.527

Photographic equipment use, by reason or occasion, 1993 survey, recurring rpt, A8695–2

R&D professionals full use of paid vacation time, 1992, annual article, C1850–6.509

Snack food industry holiday promotional activity and perceived effectiveness, 1991-92, annual rpt, A8905–1

Travel trips and traveler characteristics, including mode, purpose, type of lodging, and area of destination and origin, quarterly rpt, R9375–14

TV audience size on holidays vs typical evenings, 1992 article, C2710–1.503

TV station personnel and compensation, by position, and benefits, 1991, biennial rpt, A6635–9

Worker annual hours of labor and amount of paid vacation, for 12 industrialized countries, 1993 feature, C4215–1.507

State and local:

Arizona proposition requiring legal holiday measure submission for vote, election results by county, 1992, biennial rpt, S0520–1

Arizona traffic accidents, fatalities, and injuries, by vehicle type, circumstances, location, and driver and victim characteristics, 1991 and trends, annual rpt, S0530–1

California traffic accidents, fatalities, and injuries, by vehicle type, circumstances, location, and driver and victim characteristics, 1991 and trends, annual rpt, S0885–1

Delaware traffic accidents, fatalities, and injuries, by circumstances, location, and vehicle type, and driver and victim characteristics, 1992 and trends, annual rpt, S1435–1

Florida traffic accidents, fatalities, and injuries, by vehicle type, circumstance, location, and driver and victim characteristics, 1992 and trends, annual rpt, S1750–2

Georgia and US retail sales during Christmas season, 1982-92, article, U6730–2.501

Hawaii data book, general data, 1992 annual rpt, S2090–1.7

Illinois traffic accidents, fatalities, and injuries, by circumstances, location, and driver and victim characteristics, 1991 and trends, annual rpt, S2540–1

Kansas traffic accidents, fatalities, and injuries, by vehicle type, location,

circumstances, and driver and victim characteristics, 1992, annual rpt, S3040–1

Kentucky traffic accidents, fatalities, and injuries, by circumstances, location, vehicle type, and driver characteristics, 1992 and trends, annual rpt, S3150–2

Louisiana traffic accidents, fatalities, and injuries, by circumstances, location, and driver characteristics, 1991 and trends, annual rpt, S3345–2

Michigan traffic accidents, fatalities, and injuries, by vehicle type, circumstance, location, and driver and victim characteristics, 1991 and trends, annual rpt, S3997–2

Minnesota traffic accidents, fatalities, and injuries, by type of vehicle and circumstances, and driver and victim characteristics, 1992 and trends, annual rpt, S4230–2

Missouri traffic accidents, fatalities, and injuries, by circumstances, location, and driver and victim characteristics, 1992 and trends, annual rpt, S4560–1

Montana traffic accidents, fatalities, and injuries, by circumstances, location, and driver and victim characteristics, 1992 and trends, annual rpt, S4705–2

New Jersey fatal traffic accidents and fatalities, by vehicle type, location, and circumstances, and driver and victim characteristics, 1992 and trends, annual rpt, S5430–2

New Mexico traffic accidents, fatalities, and injuries, by vehicle type, circumstances, location, and driver and victim characteristics, 1992 and trends, annual rpt, S5665–1

New York State traffic accidents, fatalities, and injuries, by circumstances, location, vehicle type, and driver and victim characteristics, 1991 and trends, annual rpt, S5790–1

North Carolina traffic accidents, fatalities, and injuries, by circumstances, location, vehicle type, and driver and victim characteristics, 1992 and trends, annual rpt, S5990–1

North Dakota traffic accidents, fatalities, and injuries, by circumstances, location, vehicle type, and driver and victim characteristics, 1992 and trends, annual rpt, S6217–1

Ohio traffic accidents, fatalities, and injuries, by circumstances, location, driver and victim characteristics, and vehicle type, 1991 and trends, annual rpt, S6290–1

Oklahoma traffic accidents, fatalities, and injuries, by circumstances, location, and driver and victim characteristics, 1992 and trends, annual rpt, S6482–1

South Carolina traffic accidents, fatalities, and injuries, by circumstances, location, and driver and victim characteristics, 1992 and trends, annual rpt, S7190–2

South Dakota employee benefits for full- and part-time workers, 1993 article, S7355–1.502

South Dakota traffic accidents, fatalities, and injuries, by circumstances, location, vehicle type, and driver and victim characteristics, 1992 and trends, annual rpt, S7300–3

Index by Subjects and Names

Virginia traffic accidents, fatalities, and injuries, by circumstances, location, and driver and victim characteristics, 1991 and trends, annual rpt, S8282–1

Wisconsin traffic accidents, fatalities, and injuries, by circumstances, location, vehicle type, and driver and victim characteristics, 1992 and trends, annual rpt, S8815–1

Wyoming traffic accidents, fatalities, and injuries, by circumstances, location, vehicle type, and driver and victim characteristics, 1992 and trends, annual rpt, S9007–1

Vaccination and vaccines

Childhood immunization rates by State, price per dose for 5 vaccines, and polio immunization rates for 74 countries, 1992 annual rpt, R3840–5.1

Developing countries child survival efforts, with selected child and maternal health indicators, 1980s-90, R8720–1.2

Developing countries vaccination rates, for children age 12-23 months, and tetanus toxoid for pregnant women, by country, 1985-92 surveys, U2520–1.51

Hospital (teaching) policies on house staff immunization, 1992/93, annual rpt, A3273–3

Latin America statistical abstract, general data by country, 1992 annual rpt, U6250–1.7

Polio immunization rates among children, by selected country, 1990, annual rpt, R3840–11.1

Rabies control/prevention costs, and cost-benefit analysis for vaccinating wild raccoons, New Jersey study, 1992 article, A3100–2.504

World polio immunization rate, for children age 1, for 50 countries, 1990, semiannual rpt, B8500–1.16

World 1-year-old child population share immunized against selected diseases, by country, 1990, biennial rpt, R9455–1.5

State and local:

Alabama public health dept activities, including services provided, inspection and licensing activity, staff and finances, and vital statistics and health data, 1992 annual rpt, S0175–3

Delaware student immunization rates by vaccine type and county, 1991/92, annual rpt, S1430–1.6

Oregon measles cases, by vaccination status, 1989-91, annual rpt, S6615–5

Vandalism

State and local:

Alabama juvenile and adult arrests, by type of offense, 1992, annual rpt, S0119–1.1

Arizona arrests by offense, offender characteristics, and county, 1992, annual rpt, S0505–2.2

Arkansas crimes and arrests, by offense, victim and offender characteristics, and location, 1992 and trends, annual rpt, S0652–1

California criminal justice system detailed data, by offense, county, age, race-ethnicity, and sex, 1991 and trends, annual rpt, S0910–2.2

Colorado crimes and arrests, by offense and location, with offender characteristics, and assaults on police, 1992, annual rpt, S1068–1

Index by Subjects and Names

Connecticut arrests, by offense, offender characteristics, and local agency, 1992, annual rpt, S1256–1.2

DC criminal justice system summary, including crimes and arrests, criminal procedure, prisoners, and parole, 1991 and trends, annual rpt, S1535–2

Florida crimes and arrests, by offense, with data by victim and offender characteristics, 1992, annual rpt, S1770–1

Hawaii crimes and arrests, by offense, with data by county and victim-offender characteristics, 1992, annual rpt, S2035–1

Idaho vandalism offenses by local agency and county, and value of damaged property, 1992, annual rpt, S2275–2

Illinois crimes and arrests, by offense, with data by location and offender characteristics, 1991, annual rpt, S2536–1

Kansas crimes and arrests, by offense, with data by location, agency, and victim-offender characteristics, 1992 and trends, annual rpt, S2925–1.1

Kansas school vandalism cost, 1990/91, annual rpt, S2945–1

Kentucky arrests by county and offense, and law enforcement employment by agency, 1992, annual rpt, S3150–1.2

Maine arrests of adults and juveniles, by offense, age, and sex, 1991, annual rpt, S3475–1.2

Maryland crimes and arrests, by offense, location, and offender characteristics, with law enforcement employment and assaults on officers, 1992 and trends, annual rpt, S3665–1

Michigan crimes and arrests, by offense, with data by location and offender characteristics, 1992 and trends, annual rpt, S3997–1

Missouri crimes and arrests, by offense and location, with victim and offender characteristics, 1991 and trends, annual rpt, S4560–2

Montana crimes and clearances, by offense and jurisdiction, 1992, annual rpt, S4705–1

New Hampshire arrests, by offense and offender age, sex, and race-ethnicity, 1991, annual rpt, S5250–2.2

North Carolina arrests by detailed offense, offender characteristics, and county, 1991-92, annual rpt, S5955–1.2

North Dakota crimes and arrests, by offense, location, and offender characteristics, and law enforcement employment, 1991 and trends, annual rpt, S6060–1

Oklahoma crimes and arrests, by offense, with victim and offender characteristics, 1990-92, annual rpt, S6465–1.1

Oregon crimes and arrests, by offense, with data by county, local agency, and offender characteristics, 1992 and trends, annual rpt, S6603–3

Pennsylvania crimes and arrests, by offense, with data by location and offender characteristics, 1992 and trends, annual rpt, S6860–1

South Carolina crimes and arrests, by detailed offense, offender characteristics, and location, 1992 and trends, annual rpt, S7205–1.2

Texas arrests, by age, sex, race-ethnicity, and offense, 1992, annual rpt, S7735–2.2

Utah crimes and arrests, by offense, county, and local agency, 1992 and trends, annual rpt, S7890–3

Virginia crimes and arrests by offense, and law enforcement employment, by location and reporting agency, 1992, annual rpt, S8295–2.2

Washington State crimes and arrests, by offense, with data by location and offender characteristics, 1992 and trends, annual rpt, S8440–1

West Virginia crimes and arrests, by offense, location, and offender characteristics, 1990-91, annual rpt, S8610–1

Wisconsin crimes and arrests, by offense, offender characteristics, county, and local agency, 1992 and trends, annual rpt, S8771–1

Wyoming adult and juvenile arrests, by offense, county, and local jurisdiction, 1991, annual rpt, S8867–3.2

Varnishes
see Paints and varnishes

Vasectomy
see Sexual sterilization

VCRs
see Video recordings and equipment

Vegetable oils
see Oils, oilseeds, and fats

Vegetable seeds
see Seeds

Vegetables and vegetable products

Exports of farm products, by detailed commodity and country of destination, US and California, 1991, annual rpt, B9520–1

Farms (vegetable) financial performance and ratios, FY88-92, annual rpt, A6400–3

Latin America statistical abstract, general data by country, 1992 annual rpt, U6250–1.24

Production, consumption, stocks, trade, and prices for approx 100 basic commodities, including by country and producing State, commodity yearbook for 1993, C2400–1, C2400–2

Restaurant patron salad ordering patterns, and trends in vegetable prices and consumption, 1992 article, A8200–1.501

Restaurants (table service) offering locally and organically grown produce, 1992, recurring rpt, A8200–11

Retail prices for selected consumer items in approx 300 cities, quarterly rpt, A0150–1

Sales and consumer expenditures, for food store products by type, 1991-92, annual feature, C4655–1.510

Sales volume shares by retail outlet type, for approx 300 food, drug, and other product categories, 1993 annual feature, C4655–1.504

Supermarket produce dept sales and performance indicators, 1992 and trends, annual article, C4655–1.511

Supermarket sales by detailed product type, 1992 and trends, annual feature, C5225–1.507

State and local:

Alabama agricultural production, marketing, and income, by county and/or commodity, and farms and acreage, 1992 and trends, annual rpt, S0090–1

Vegetables and vegetable products

Alaska agricultural production and marketing, by district and commodity, 1960s-92, annual rpt, U5750–1

Arizona agricultural production, marketing, and finances, by commodity and county, 1988-92, annual rpt, U5830–1

Arkansas agricultural production, marketing, and finances, by commodity and county, with farms and acreage, 1992 and trends, annual rpt, U5920–1

California field crops production, acreage, yield, and prices, by commodity and county, 1992 and trends, annual rpt, S0850–1.4

California vegetable production, marketing, and prices, by commodity and use, 1992 and trends, annual rpt, S0850–1.3

Colorado agricultural production, marketing, and finances, by commodity and/or county, with farms and acreage, 1992 and trends, annual rpt, S0985–1

Florida vegetable, melon, and strawberry production, acreage, yield, shipments, and exports, 1991/92 and trends, annual rpt, S1685–1.2

Georgia agricultural production, marketing, and finances, by commodity and/or county, and farms and acreage, 1991 and trends, annual rpt, S1855–1

Hawaii agricultural production and marketing, by commodity and island, 1987-91, annual rpt, S2030–1

Illinois agricultural production, marketing, and finances, by county or commodity, and farms and farmland, 1991 and trends, annual rpt, S2390–1

Kansas agricultural production, marketing, and finances, by county and/or commodity, and farm acreage and value, 1992 and trends, annual rpt, S2915–1

Louisiana agricultural production, marketing, and finances, by commodity or parish, 1985-91, annual rpt, U2740–1

Michigan agricultural production, marketing, and finances, by commodity or county, 1987-91, annual rpt, S3950–1

Minnesota agricultural production, marketing, and finances, by county or commodity, and farms and acreage, 1992 and trends, annual rpt, S4130–1

Nebraska agricultural production, marketing, and finances, by commodity and/or county, and farms and acreage, 1991 and trends, annual rpt, S4835–1

New Jersey agricultural production, marketing, and finances, by commodity and/or county, and farms and acreage, 1986-91, annual rpt, S5350–1

New Mexico agricultural production, marketing, and finances, by commodity and county, with farms and acreage, 1991 and trends, annual rpt, S5530–1

New York State agricultural production, marketing, and finances, by commodity and/or county, and farms and acreage, 1992 and trends, annual rpt, S5700–1

North Carolina agricultural production, marketing, and finances, by commodity and county, 1991 and trends, annual rpt, S5885–1

North Dakota agricultural production and marketing, by commodity and county, and farm finances, 1992 and trends, annual rpt, U3600–1

Vegetables and vegetable products

Ohio agricultural production, marketing, and finances, by commodity and county, with farms and acreage, 1990-91 and trends, annual rpt, S6240–1

Oklahoma agricultural production, marketing, and finances, by commodity and county, 1992 and trends, annual rpt, S6405–1

Oregon agricultural production, marketing, and finances, by commodity and/or county, with farms and acreage, 1991 and trends, annual rpt, S6575–1

Pennsylvania agricultural production, marketing, and finances, by county and commodity, and farms and acreage, 1992 and trends, annual rpt, S6760–1

South Carolina agricultural production and finances, by commodity and county, 1991-92 and trends, annual rpt, U1075–3

Tennessee agricultural production and marketing, by commodity and county, with farms, acreage, and farm value, 1992 and trends, annual rpt, S7460–1

Texas agricultural production, marketing, and finances, by commodity and county, and farms and farmland, 1991 and trends, annual rpt series, S7630–1

Utah agricultural production, marketing, and finances, by commodity and county, with farms and acreage, 1992 and trends, annual rpt, S7800–1

Washington State agricultural production, marketing, and finances, by commodity and/or county, 1992 and trends, annual rpt, S8328–1

Wisconsin agricultural production, marketing, and finances, by commodity and county, and farms, acreage, and sales, 1992 and trends, annual rpt, S8680–1

Wyoming agricultural production, marketing, and finances, by county and/or commodity, and farms, acreage, and value, 1992 and trends, annual rpt, S8860–1

see also Potatoes

Vegetation

see Plants and vegetation

Vending machines and stands

Convenience stores offering special services, including vending machines, 1992 and trends, annual survey rpt, A6735–1, A6735–2

Financial ratios and performance, for over 350 SIC 4-digit industries, FY88-92, annual rpt, A6400–3

Food service industry sales trends and forecast, by market segment, 1990-93, annual feature, A8200–1.502

Military post exchange (Army/Air Force) and Veterans Canteen Service vending sales, by region and store, FY92, annual rpt, A2072–2.502

Sales by product type, and machines on location, 1992 and trends, annual rpt, C9470–1

Shipments of vending machines, 1983-92, annual feature, C2000–1.505

State and local:

Illinois crimes and arrests, by offense, with data by location and offender characteristics, 1991, annual rpt, S2536–1

Kansas larceny offenses and value of stolen property, by type of theft and location, 1992, annual rpt, S2925–1.1

South Carolina coin-operated device license sales, FY92, annual rpt, S7255–1.2

Venereal diseases

see Sexually transmitted diseases

Venezuela

Coal industry supply-demand, employment, and trade, by country, 1990-91 and trends, annual rpt, A7400–2.2

Energy intl sourcebook, with detail on oil and gas industry operations, supply-demand, and prices, for approx 80 countries, 1970s-91, annual compilation, C6985–10.2

Motor vehicle world production, sales, trade, and registrations, by country, world area, manufacturer, and make, 1991 and trends, annual rpt, A0865–2.1

Oil fields, production, and reserves, in govt-owned production units available for private contract, 1992 article, C6985–1.506

Oil industry operations of govt-owned company, including exploration, marketing, and employment, 1976 and 1988-92, article, C6985–1.542

Presidential decrees by admin, purpose, and ministry, and business and govt leader views on presidential power, 1992 rpt, U6250–1.22

Statistical abstract of Latin America, detailed social, govtl, and economic data, 1992 annual rpt, U6250–1

see also Organization of Petroleum Exporting Countries

see also under By Foreign Country or World Area in the "Index by Categories"

Venture capital

Age of new businesses at time of venture capital financing, 1985/86-1991/92, article, C4687–1.502

Commitments of venture capital, 1986-92, article, C4687–1.510

Economic impact of venture-capital-backed companies, including job creation, capital and R&D investments, and selected growth rates, 1985-91, A8515–2

Electronics and total investments, and portfolio value, for approx 75 venture capital firms, 1993 annual feature, C1850–2.509

Employee benefit funds assets, for funds investing in venture capital, 1992, annual feature, C2710–2.504

Finances and operations of venture capital industry, 1991 and trends, annual rpt, A8515–1

Higher education instn endowment fund and investment pool characteristics and performance, by instn, FY92, annual survey rpt, A6705–2

State economic dev condition indicators, including economic performance, business vitality, growth capacity, and tax/fiscal system, by State, 1993 annual rpt, R4225–1.1

Venture Development Corp.

Electronic uninterruptible power supply sales, 1991-96, article, C1850–2.502

Venture Economics Inc.

Commitments of venture capital, 1986-92, article, C4687–1.510

Vermont

Agricultural production, marketing, and finances, by commodity, with data on govt inspections and funding, 1989-90 biennial rpt, S7978–1

Index by Subjects and Names

Banks and other financial instns, financial condition by instn, 1992 and trends, annual rpt, S7995–2

Court cases and dispositions, by type of court and case, and location, FY92 annual rpt, S8120–1

Elementary and secondary school enrollment, by grade, sex, race-ethnicity, school, and county, 1992/93 and trends, annual rpt, S8020–1

Govt financial condition, including revenues by source, expenditures by function, fund balances, and bonded debt, FY92, annual rpt, S8035–1

Higher education info, including degrees conferred, enrollment, and finances, by instn, 1992 annual rpt, S8035–2

Income tax State returns, taxes, refunds, and credits, by income class and locality, 1991, annual rpt, S8125–1

Insurance industry financial and underwriting data, by company and type of insurance, 1991, annual rpt, S7995–1

Labor force planning rpt, including population, employment by industry, and job service applicant characteristics, 1993 annual rpt, S8025–2

Libraries, finances, resources, and circulation, by city and library, FY91-92, biennial rpt, S8080–1

Markets with daily newspapers, demographic and economic info by geographic area, US and Canada, 1993 annual rpt, C3250–1

Statistical profiles of 50 States and DC, general data, 1993 annual almanac, C4712–1

Utilities financial and operating data, by company, 1986-91, biennial rpt, S8100–1

Utility and transportation regulatory agency activities, scope of jurisdiction, finances, and employees, by agency, 1991/92 annual rpt, A7015–2

Vital statistics, including population, births, deaths by cause, abortions, marriages, and divorces, by location and demographic characteristics, 1991 and trends, annual rpt, S8054–1

see also under By City and By County in the "Index by Categories"

see also under By State in the "Index by Categories"

Veronis, Suhler and Associates

Book expenditure trends and outlook, for consumer and professional/educational books by type, 1987-97, article, C1852–2.520

Media use trends by medium, 1987-91, article, C9380–1.504

Veterans

Homeless population characteristics in 29 cities, 1991/92, annual rpt, A9330–9

State and local:

Alaska civilian veterans by area and sex, with number age 65/over, and distribution by period of service, 1990, article, S0320–1.511

Alaska tax exemption provisions for senior citizens and disabled veterans, and State reimbursements to local areas, FY92 and trends, annual rpt, S0285–1

Arkansas Census of Population and Housing detailed findings, 1990, U5935–7

California Census of Population and Housing detailed findings, 1990, S0840–9

Index by Subjects and Names — Veterinary medicine

California veteran population, by sex and period of service, Mar 1989-91, annual planning rpt, S0830–2

Florida county data book, 1992/93 annual rpt, C6360–1

Florida statistical abstract, general data, 1992 annual rpt, U6660–1.1

Georgia county guide, general data, 1993 annual rpt, U6750–1

Hawaii data book, general data, 1992 annual rpt, S2090–1.10

Hawaii deaths by veteran status and age, 1990, annual rpt, S2065–1.2

Maine Census of Population and Housing summary findings, by local area, 1990, S3465–9

Massachusetts correctional instn inmate socioeconomic characteristics and criminal background, by instn, Jan 1992 and trends, annual rpt, S3805–1

Michigan veterans population and labor force, total and disadvantaged, by State area, 1980, annual planning rpt, S3980–1.2

Mississippi statistical abstract, general data, 1992 annual rpt, U3255–4.13

Mississippi veterans by period served, and labor force status of Vietnam era veterans by age, by race, 1993/94, annual planning rpt, S4345–1.1

New Jersey Census of Population and Housing detailed findings, by county, 1990, S5425–19

Pennsylvania Census of Population and Housing detailed findings, with selected data by county and municipality, 1990, U4130–13

Pennsylvania statistical abstract, general data, 1992 recurring rpt, U4130–6.1

Rhode Island Census of Population and Housing detailed findings, by county and municipality, 1990, S6930–9

Tennessee statistical abstract, general data, 1992/93 annual rpt, U8710–2.1

Utah corrections inmates, parolees, and probationers, by criminal background and demographic characteristics, FY92 and trends, annual rpt, S7810–1

Utah homeless shelter population characteristics, individual shelter capacity, and related housing data, 1991-92, annual rpt, S7808–2

Wisconsin Blue Book, general data, 1993-94 biennial rpt, S8780–1.2

Wisconsin correctional instn admissions by inmate characteristics, including need for special services, 1991, annual rpt, S8692–1.2

Wisconsin correctional instn inmate characteristics, by sex and instn, Dec 1991, semiannual rpt, S8692–1.5

Wisconsin correctional instn inmate characteristics, by sex and instn, June 1991, semiannual rpt, S8692–1.1

see also Retired military personnel

see also Veterans benefits and pensions

see also Veterans education

see also Veterans employment

see also Veterans health facilities and services

see also Veterans housing

Veterans Administration

see Department of Veterans Affairs

Veterans benefits and pensions

Budget receipts and outlays of Fed Govt, by source and function, 1920s-93, annual rpt, R9050–1.3

Payments and recipients for selected Federal entitlement programs, by State and region, early 1990s, R8490–47

Student aid applicant untaxed income sources, American College Testing (ACT) program, 1992, annual rpt, R1960–5

State and local:

Arizona statistical abstract, general data, 1993 recurring rpt, U5850–2.7

California property tax assessments and exemptions, by type of property, city, county, and company, FY93 and trends, annual rpt, S0835–1.2

Georgia county guide, general data, 1993 annual rpt, U6750–1

Illinois statistical abstract, general data, 1992 annual rpt, U6910–2

Indiana property value and tax levies, collections, credits, and deductions, by county and type, 1991, annual rpt, S2570–1.1

North Dakota financial condition, including revenues by source, expenditures by function, fund balances, and bonded debt, FY92, annual rpt, S6162–1

South Carolina revenue shared with county govts, by tax or fund type, FY92, annual rpt, S7127–2

Texas financial condition, including revenues by source, expenditures by function and dept, and investments, with data for over 400 individual funds, FY92, annual rpt, S7655–2.2

Wisconsin Blue Book, general data, 1993-94 biennial rpt, S8780–1.2

Wisconsin financial condition, including revenues by source, expenditures by function and object, and fund balances, FY92, annual rpt, S8675–3

Wyoming property tax exemptions granted veterans, by county, 1992, annual rpt, S8990–1.2

see also Veterans education

see also Veterans health facilities and services

see also Veterans housing

Veterans education

Higher education freshmen attitudes and characteristics, degree and career plans, and financial aid sources, by sex and instn type, fall 1992, annual survey, U6215–1

State and local:

Missouri public school finances, staff, students, and programs, detailed data, 1991/92, annual rpt, S4505–1.1

New York State veterans and nursing scholarships, 1986/87-1990/91, annual rpt, U5100–1.10

North Dakota higher education enrollment, by veteran status and instn, fall 1992, annual rpt, S6110–1

Veterans employment

State and local:

California statistical abstract, general data, 1992 annual rpt, S0840–2.3

Colorado job service applicant characteristics, FY93 annual planning rpt, S1040–3.2

DC employment, earnings, and hours, by industry, with unemployment insurance data, monthly rpt, S1527–3

Louisiana job service openings and applicants, and characteristics of Job Training Partnership Act target population and insured unemployed, 1993 annual planning rpt, S3320–1.2

Michigan labor force planning rpt, including characteristics of Job Training Partnership Act eligible population by State area, 1993 annual rpt, S3980–1.2

Mississippi veterans by period served, and labor force status of Vietnam era veterans by age, by race, 1993/94, annual planning rpt, S4345–1.1

Missouri employment, earnings, and hours, and employment security program activity, by industry and/or county, FY92 and trends, annual rpt, S4530–2.3

New Hampshire job service applicant characteristics, monthly rpt, S5205–1

Pennsylvania labor force and population characteristics, FY92 annual planning rpt, S6845–3.1

South Carolina labor force planning rpt, detailed data on employment, hours, wages, turnover, and characteristics of job service applicants, 1992 annual rpt, S7155–3.2

Vermont labor force by employment status, and job service openings and applicant characteristics, 1993 annual planning rpt, S8025–2.2

Veterans health facilities and services

General Educational Dev (GED) testing programs and results in VA hospitals, 1992, annual rpt, A1410–16

Teaching hospital house staff stipends, benefits, and expenditures, by region and ownership, 1992/93 and trends, annual rpt, A3273–3

State and local:

Colorado public welfare expenditures by program, including veterans nursing homes, FY91, annual rpt, S1085–1

Florida statistical abstract, general data, 1992 annual rpt, U6660–1.20

Oklahoma statistical abstract, general data, 1992 annual rpt, U8130–2.9

Wisconsin Blue Book, general data, 1993-94 biennial rpt, S8780–1.2

see also Veterans benefits and pensions

Veterans hospitals

see Veterans health facilities and services

Veterans housing

Mobile/manufactured home VA loans, monthly rpt, A6325–1

Mortgage delinquency and foreclosure rates, and residential loans serviced, by type, State, and census div and region, quarterly rpt, A6450–1

State and local:

Utah statistical abstract, general data, 1993 triennial rpt, U8960–1.11

Veterans loans

see Veterans benefits and pensions

Veterans pensions

see Veterans benefits and pensions

Veterinary medicine

Aquatic animal course availability in veterinary schools, with faculty and enrollment, by instn, 1991/92, article, A3100–2.S09

Associates in veterinary practice job characteristics and attitudes, 1992 survey, article, C9480–1.505

Veterinary medicine

Caseloads of companion and farm animals, by type of animal and veterinary practice, 1991, survey article, A3100–2.518

Computer and network info services use in home and office, by practice type, 1992 survey, articles, A3100–2.501, A3100–2.502

Employment, starting salaries, benefits, and personal characteristics of veterinary school grads, 1992, annual survey article, A3100–2.504

Enrollment in veterinary school academic and clinical grad programs, quinquennially 1967-92, article, A3100–2.513

Enrollment in veterinary schools by sex, program, instn, and place of residence, US and Canada, 1992/93, annual article, A3100–2.516

Equine veterinarian characteristics and finances, and practice profile, 1992 survey and trends, annual article, C9480–1.503

Expenses as percent of revenues, by category and type of practice, 1990-91, annual survey article, C9480–1.501

Fees charged for selected services, and average client transaction, by region and type of practice, 1993, annual survey, C9480–1.507

Finances and operations of veterinary practices, articles and devs, monthly rpt, C9480–1

Finances of veterinary practices, including income, expenses by item, and financial ratios, by type of practice, 1991, biennial survey article, A3100–2.510

Financial ratios and performance, for over 350 SIC 4-digit industries, FY88-92, annual rpt, A6400–3

Income (money vs real) of veterinarians, by type of employment, biennially 1983-91, biennial article, A3100–2.512

Income of veterinarians, by number of years since graduation and type of practice or employer, 1991, biennial survey article, A3100–2.508

Income of veterinarians by selected personal and practice characteristics, 1992, annual survey article, C9480–1.506

Income of veterinarians, by type of employment, 1991, biennial survey article, A3100–2.506

Loan applications and dispositions, by veterinarian experience, 1992 survey, article, A3100–2.519

Parrots and other psittacines captive breeding info, including breeder use of veterinarians, 1990, annual survey rpt, R9200–14

Public health school faculty characteristics, by instn, fall 1991, recurring rpt, A3372–1

Public/corporate sector veterinarian professional characteristics, 1993 survey, article, A3100–2.520

Salaries of veterinary school grads by type of employment, and educational debt, 1992, annual survey article, A3100–2.503

Surgery teaching methods used at US and Canadian veterinary schools, for 27 instns, 1993 article, A3100–2.521

Surgical procedure frequency and new veterinary grad proficiency expectations of veterinarians, Illinois study, 1993 survey article, A3100–2.511

Veterinarians by location and type of employment, 1990 and 1992, article, A3100–2.522

Veterinarians by professional activity, Dec 1992, annual article, A3100–2.508

Veterinarians by professional characteristics and location, and financial and education summaries, 1993 annual directory, A3100–1

Veterinarians professional news and clinical devs, semimonthly journal, A3100–2

Women and minorities in professional fields, detailed education and labor force data, 1991 and trends, recurring rpt, A3960–2.3

State and local:

Florida county data book, 1992/93 annual rpt, C6360–1

Florida statistical abstract, general data, 1992 annual rpt, U6660–1.9

Veto

see Gubernatorial vetoes

see Presidential vetoes

Vetter, Betty M.

"Professional Women and Minorities: A Total Human Resource Data Compendium, 10th Edition", A3960–2

Victims of crime

see Crime and criminals

see Crime victim compensation

Video cassette recorders

see Video recordings and equipment

Video discs

see Video recordings and equipment

Video games

see Electronic games

Video recordings and equipment

Advertising on rental video tapes, reactions of marketing professionals and general public, Oct 1992 surveys, article, C2710–1.512

Camcorder factory sales value and volume, 1985-92, article, C8130–1.506

Children's prerecorded video cassette unit sales, by retail outlet type, Nov/Dec 1992, article, C8130–1.505

Consumer ownership, purchasing patterns, and use of home video equipment, 1993 survey and trends, recurring rpt, A8695–2

Convenience stores offering special services, including video cassette rentals, 1992 and trends, annual survey rpt, A6735–1, A6735–2

Discount chain consumer natl brand preferences, by product category and chain, and by age group, 1993 survey, annual feature, C5150–3.521

Discount chain top-selling natl brands cited by managers, by product category, chain, and region, 1993 survey, annual feature, C5150–3.520

Factory sales and/or shipments of home video and audio equipment, by product type, 1980s-92, annual rpt, A4725–1.1

Financial ratios and performance, for over 350 SIC 4-digit industries, FY88-92, annual rpt, A6400–3

Higher education admissions dept use of admission videos, 1991-92, annual rpt, A6695–1

Library video cassette holdings, by general topic and instn type, 1993 article, C1852–1.507

Market devs for video cassette sales and rentals, including VCR ownership in US and abroad, weekly rpt, C9380–1

Sales (distributor units) of consumer electronics products by type, 1991-93, annual article, C2000–1.503

Sales distribution and prices of prerecorded video cassettes by retail outlet, genre, and/or region, 1992-93, article, C8130–1.508

Sales of prerecorded video cassettes, 1993-2000, article, C5150–3.514

Sales, trade, and industry devs for consumer electronics, by product type, 1970s-92, annual rpt, A4725–4

Shopping center financial and operating data, with detail by type of tenant, US and Canada, 1991, triennial rpt, R9285–1

Sports and sports/fitness video cassette unit sales, 1988-92, article, C8130–1.503

Supermarket in-store video rental and sales availability, and shopper use, 1993 and trends, annual survey rpt, A4950–3

Supermarket video cassette rental dept operations and outlook, 1993 survey article, C4655–1.508

Supermarket video rentals, 1992 and trends, annual feature, C5225–1.507

State and local:

Hawaii data book, general data, 1992 annual rpt, S2090–1.23

North Carolina public libraries, finances, holdings, and personnel, by library system, FY91, annual rpt, S5910–1

Videotex

see Information storage and retrieval systems

Vietnam

Child and infant mortality rates before, during, and after Vietnam war, with detail by regional area, 1993 article, A2623–1.510

Energy intl sourcebook, with detail on oil and gas industry operations, supply-demand, and prices, for approx 80 countries, 1970s-91, annual compilation, C6985–10.2

Offshore oil/gas exploration activity, with operator, location, and well depth and/or status, 1992-94, article, C6985–2.506

see also Indochinese refugees

Violence

Catholic vs public school ratings for selected aspects of education and environment, public opinion by respondent characteristics, July 1992 survey, A7375–8

Elementary/secondary school violence incidents involving guns, by school level, incident type, and cause, 1993 feature, C4215–1.508

Foundation spending or allocations for violence prevention programs, with year grant making began, 1993 article, C2176–1.519

Public interest in news items on TV network program violence warnings, by respondent characteristics, July/Aug 1993 survey, C8915–1.504

Public opinion on TV violence and overall quality, with detail for entertainment and news shows, by respondent characteristics, Feb 1993 survey, C8915–11.1

Teacher abuse from students, prevalence by type of school location, 1991, R4800–2.513

Teachers feeling unsafe during and after school hours, prevalence by type of school location, 1991, A4425–4

TV program violence levels and audience ratings, for 6 most violent programs, Sept-Dec 1992, article, C5800–7.542

TV violence and Govt regulation, opinions of advertising industry magazine readers, Oct 1993 survey, article, C2710–1.551

State and local:

Maine State court activities, including threat-related matters handled by security officers, 1988-FY92, annual rpt, S3463–1

see also Assassination

see also Assault

see also Assaults on police

see also Child abuse and neglect

see also Crime and criminals

see also Domestic violence

see also Homicide

see also Rape

see also Riots and disorders

see also Terrorism

see also War

Virgin Islands

see U.S. Virgin Islands

Virginia

Business activity indicators, by local area, monthly rpt, U1120–1

Court caseloads, processing, and dispositions, by type of court and case, with judicial dept personnel and finances, by location, 1992 and trends, annual rpt, S8300–1

Crimes and arrests, by offense, location, and offender characteristics, with law enforcement employment, and assaults on officers, 1992, annual rpt, S8295–2

Economic indicators for Virginia, including new business incorporations and employment data, quarterly rpt, S8205–4

Election results by jurisdiction, and voter registration and turnout, 1992 and Jan 1993 elections, annual rpt, S8195–1

Elementary and secondary public school enrollment, grads, finances, and staff, by county and municipality, 1991/92, annual rpt, S8190–3

Elementary/secondary school enrollment and high school grads, with detail by school district, 1980/81-2012/2013, annual rpt, U9080–20

Finance companies financial condition, by instn, Dec 1992, annual rpt, S8180–3

Financial instns (State-chartered), financial condition by instn and instn type, Dec 1992, annual rpt, S8180–2

Govt financial condition, including revenues by source, expenditures by function, and fund balances, FY92 and trends, annual rpt, S8170–1

GSP in current and constant dollars, by industry, with comparisons to Southeast region GSP and US GDP, 1963-89, recurring rpt, U9080–6

Income distribution and income tax returns filed, by locality, 1990, annual rpt, U9080–1

Insurance industry financial and underwriting data, by company and line of coverage, annual rpt discontinued coverage, S8180–1

Labor force, hours, and earnings, with data by industry group and locality, monthly rpt, S8205–6

Library operations and finances, by instn, FY92, annual rpt, S8275–1

Markets with daily newspapers, demographic and economic info by geographic area, US and Canada, 1993 annual rpt, C3250–1

Medical malpractice insurance State joint underwriting assn (JUA) financial condition, for 11 States, 1991, annual rpt, A0375–1

Nursing school administrator and hospital executive views on nursing graduate skills, 1992 survey, article, A1865–1.503

Oil/gas industry production, finances, exploration, and reserves, by State, 1992 and trends, annual rpt, A5425–1.1

Personal income, total and per capita, by local area and major source, 1980-90, annual rpt, U9080–7

Population and net migration, by local area, 1990-91, annual rpt, U9080–9

Population, by location, selected years 1980-2010, recurring rpt, S8205–7

Statistical profiles of 50 States and DC, general data, 1993 annual almanac, C4712–1

Tax revenues by type, county, and independent city, FY92 and trends, annual rpt, S8305–1

Taxable sales, by kind of business and locality, 1991 and trends, annual rpt, U9080–8

Traffic accidents, fatalities, and injuries, by circumstances, location, and driver and victim characteristics, 1991 and trends, annual rpt, S8282–1

Utility and transportation regulatory agency activities, scope of jurisdiction, finances, and employees, by agency, 1991/92 annual rpt, A7015–2/92

Vital statistics, including births, deaths by cause, marriages, and divorces, by demographic characteristics and location, 1991 and trends, annual rpt, S8225–1

Welfare cases, recipients, and expenditures, by program, county, and city, suspended quarterly rpt, S8293–2

Youth population by age, by county and city, with summary by sex and detail for disabled youth, Jan 1993, triennial rpt, S8190–1

see also under By City and By County in the "Index by Categories"

see also under By State in the "Index by Categories"

Virginia Hospital Association

Nursing school administrator and hospital executive views on nursing graduate skills, 1992 survey, article, A1865–1.503

Vision

Contact lens care product market value, with shares by product and retail outlet type, 1987-95, article, C5150–2.513

State and local:

Hawaii health dept family health services and recipients, including school health programs, 1990 annual rpt, S2065–1.5

Indiana welfare cases and payments for eye treatment, by county, FY91-92, annual rpt, S2623–1.8

Montana social services program cases, by county and type of service, monthly rpt quarterly tables, S4755–1

Ohio special education services for visually handicapped children, by school district, 1991/92 and trends, annual rpt, S6265–1

see also Blind

see also Eye diseases and defects

see also Optometry

Vital statistics

Asia and Pacific countries population characteristics, series, R4500–1

Catholic population, marriages, deaths, and baptisms, with detail by country or world area, 1993 annual almanac, C6885–1

Latin America statistical abstract, general data by country, 1992 annual rpt, U6250–1.6

Population, marriages, births, and income data, by locality, 1993 annual jewelry industry almanac, C2150–7.509

Statistical profiles of 50 States and DC, general data, 1993 annual almanac, C4712–1

US vital statistics update, monthly rpt, R8750–1

World population growth factors, with selected vital statistics for countries with highest and lowest values, 1993 article, R8750–1.508

State and local:

Alabama county data book, general data, 1992 annual rpt, S0121–2

Alabama public health dept activities, including services provided, inspection and licensing activity, staff and finances, and vital statistics and health data, 1992 annual rpt, S0175–3

Alabama statistical abstract, general data, 1992 recurring rpt, U5680–2.17

Alabama vital statistics, including population, births, deaths by cause, marriages, and divorces, by location and demographic characteristics, 1992 and trends, annual rpt, S0175–2

Alaska vital statistics, including births, deaths by cause, marriages, divorces, adoptions, and population, by demographic characteristics and location, 1990, annual rpt, S0315–1

Arizona statistical abstract, general data, 1993 recurring rpt, U5850–2.3

Arkansas vital statistics, including births, deaths by cause, marriages, and divorces, by age, sex, race, and county, 1991 and trends, annual rpt, S0685–1

California statistical abstract, general data, 1992 annual rpt, S0840–2.5

California vital statistics, including population, births, and deaths by cause, by demographic characteristics and county, 1990 and trends, annual rpt, S0865–1

Colorado vital statistics, including population, births, deaths by cause, abortion, marriage and divorce, and adoption, by demographic characteristics and location, 1990 and trends, annual rpt, S1010–1

Connecticut vital statistics, including births, deaths by cause, marriages, and divorces, by demographic characteristics and location, 1989, annual rpt, S1200–1

Florida county data book, 1992/93 annual rpt, C6360–1

Florida statistical abstract, general data, 1992 annual rpt, U6660–1.3

Florida vital statistics, including population, births, deaths by cause, and marriages and dissolutions, by location and demographic characteristics, 1992 and trends, annual rpt, S1745–3

Vital statistics

Index by Subjects and Names

Georgia county guide, general data, 1993 annual rpt, U6750–1

Georgia statistical abstract, general data, 1992-93 biennial rpt, U6730–1.1

Georgia vital statistics, including population, births, abortions, deaths by cause, marriages, and divorces, by demographic characteristics and location, 1991 and trends, annual rpt, S1895–1

Hawaii data book, general data, 1992 annual rpt, S2090–1.2

Hawaii health dept activities and services, including vital statistics and disease control, by location, 1990, annual rpt, S2065–1

Idaho economic profile, general data, 1992 recurring rpt, S2218–2.2

Idaho vital tatistics, including births, deaths by cause, abortions, marriages, and divorces, by demographic characteristics and county, 1991 and trends, annual rpt, S2250–2

Illinois statistical abstract, general data, 1992 annual rpt, U6910–2

Iowa vital statistics, including population, births, deaths by cause, marriages, and divorces, by demographic characteristics and location, 1991 and trends, annual rpt, S2795–1

Kansas statistical abstract, general data, 1991/92 annual rpt, U7095–2.2

Kansas vital statistics, including population, births, deaths by cause, abortions, marriages, and divorces, by demographic characteristics and location, 1991 and trends, annual rpt, S2975–1

Kentucky vital statistics, including births, deaths by cause, marriages and divorces, and population, by demographic characteristics and county, 1991, annual rpt, S3140–1

Louisiana vital statistics, including population, births, deaths by cause, reportable diseases, marriages, and divorces, by demographic characteristics and locality, 1989-90 and trends, annual rpt, S3295–1

Maine vital statistics, including births, deaths by cause, abortions, and marriages and divorces, by demographic characteristics and location, 1991 and trends, annual rpt, S3460–2

Maryland statistical abstract, general data, 1993-94 biennial rpt, S3605–1.1

Maryland vital statistics, including population, births, deaths by cause, marriages, and divorces, by demographic characteristics and location, 1989 and trends, annual rpt, S3635–1

Massachusetts vital statistics, including births, deaths by cause, marriages, divorces, and population, by locality and demographic characteristics, 1990 and trends, annual rpt, S3850–1

Michigan vital statistics, including births, deaths, marriages, divorces/annulments, and communicable diseases, by location and demographic characteristics, 1990 and trends, annual rpt, S4000–3

Minnesota vital statistics, including population, births, abortions, deaths, marriages, and divorces, by location and demographic characteristics, 1991 and trends, annual rpt, S4190–2

Mississippi statistical abstract, general data, 1992 annual rpt, U3255–4.2

Mississippi vital statistics, including births, deaths by cause, marriages, and divorces, by demographic characteristics and location, 1992 and trends, annual rpt, S4350–1

Missouri vital statistics, including population, births, deaths by cause, and marriages and divorces, by location and demographic characteristics, 1992 and trends, annual rpt, S4518–1

Montana vital statistics, including births, deaths by cause, abortion, disease, and marriage and divorce, by demographic characteristics and county, 1990-91 and trends, annual rpt, S4690–1

Nebraska vital statistics, including births, deaths, marriages, divorces, and population, by demographic characteristics and location, 1991 and trends, annual rpt, S4885–1

Nevada statistical abstract, general data, 1992 biennial rpt, S5005–1.2

Nevada vital statistics, including births, abortions, and deaths by cause, by county and demographic characteristics, 1989 and trends, annual rpt, S5075–1

New Hampshire vital statistics, including population, births, deaths by cause, marriages, and divorces, by location and demographic characteristics, 1991 and trends, annual rpt, S5215–1

New Jersey vital statistics, including births, deaths, population, communicable diseases, and marriages and divorces, by demographic characteristics and location, 1990 and trends, annual rpt, S5405–1

New Mexico vital statistics, including population, births, deaths, and disease, by location and demographic characteristics, 1991 and trends, annual rpt, S5605–1

New York State statistical yearbook, general data, 1992 annual rpt, U5100–1.1

New York State vital statistics, including population, births, deaths by cause, reportable diseases, and marriages and dissolutions, by demographic characteristics and/or location, 1990 and trends, annual rpt, S5765–1

North Carolina vital statistics, including population, births, deaths by cause, marriages, and divorces, by local area, 1991 and trends, annual rpt, S5927–1

North Dakota vital statistics, including births, deaths by cause, marriages and divorces, and abortions, by demographic characteristics and/or county, 1991 and trends, annual rpt, S6105–2

Ohio vital statistics, including births, deaths by cause, marriages, divorces, and population, by demographic characteristics and location, 1991 and trends, annual rpt, S6285–1

Oklahoma statistical abstract, general data, 1992 annual rpt, U8130–2.2

Oregon vital statistics, including births, deaths by cause, communicable diseases, marriages, and divorces, by age, sex, race-ethnicity, and county, 1991 and trends, annual rpt, S6615–5

Pennsylvania statistical abstract, general data, 1992 recurring rpt, U4130–6.1

Rhode Island vital statistics, including population, births, deaths, marriages, and

divorces, by demographic characteristics and locality, 1989 and trends, annual rpt, S6995–1

South Carolina statistical abstract, general data, 1993 annual rpt, S7125–1.16

South Carolina vital statistics, including births, deaths by cause, marriages, and divorces, by age, sex, race, and location, 1990 and trends, annual rpt, S7175–1

South Dakota vital statistics, including births, deaths, marriage and divorce, and communicable disease, by demographic characteristics and county, 1991 and trends, annual rpt, S7345–1

Tennessee statistical abstract, general data, 1992/93 annual rpt, U8710–2.17

Tennessee vital statistics, including births, deaths by cause, marriages, divorces, and population, by demographic characteristics and location, 1991 and trends, annual rpt, S7520–2

Texas vital statistics, including births, deaths by cause, abortions, marriages, and divorces, by location and demographic characteristics, 1991 and trends, annual rpt, S7685–1

Utah govt statistical review, fiscal and socioeconomic data, 1993 annual rpt, R9380–1.1

Utah statistical abstract, general data, 1993 triennial rpt, U8960–1.2

Utah vital statistics, including births, deaths by cause, and population, by county and demographic characteristics, 1990 and trends, annual rpt, S7835–1

Vermont vital statistics, including population, births, deaths by cause, abortions, marriages, and divorces, by location and demographic characteristics, 1991 and trends, annual rpt, S8054–1

Virginia vital statistics, including births, deaths by cause, marriages and divorces, and communicable disease, by demographic characteristics and location, 1991 and trends, annual rpt, S8225–1

Washington State vital statistics, including births, deaths by cause, and population, by demographic characteristics and location, 1991 and trends, annual rpt, S8363–1

West Virginia statistical handbook, general data, 1992 annual rpt, R9385–1.8

West Virginia vital statistics, including births, deaths by cause, marriages, and divorces, by location and demographic characteristics, 1991 and trends, annual rpt, S8560–1

Wisconsin Blue Book, general data, 1993-94 biennial rpt, S8780–1.2

Wisconsin vital statistics, including population, births, deaths by cause, and marriages and dissolutions, by county and demographic characteristics, 1991 and trends, annual rpt, S8715–4

Wyoming vital statistics, including population, births, deaths by cause, marriages, and divorces, by demographic characteristics and county, 1991 and trends, annual rpt, S8920–2

see also Births

see also Child mortality

see also Deaths

see also Life expectancy

see also Marriage and divorce

see also Traffic accident fatalities

Index by Subjects and Names

Vitamins and nutrients

Animal selenium deficiency and toxicosis cases in livestock/wildlife, by State, 1992 survey, article, A3100–2.510

Calcium supplement lead content, by type of supplement, 1993 article, A2623–1.510

Death rates correlated with vitamin/mineral supplement use and selected other population characteristics, by sex, 1993 article, A2623–1.506

Health condition and preventive health care and safety practices of adults, by respondent characteristics, 1992 and trends, annual survey rpt, C8111–2

Sales and consumer expenditures, for food store products by type, 1991-92, annual feature, C4655–1.510

see also Cholesterol

VLSI Research Inc.

Semiconductor production equipment sales, 1992-94, C1850–6.510

Vocational education and training

Hard goods manufacturers opinions on Federal spending for worker training, by product line, 1993 annual survey rpt, A1800–1

High school vocational-academic program integration, pilot project evaluative data including achievement test results, student and teacher attitudes, and curricula, 1990, A8945–33

Higher education instns, faculty, students, degrees, and finances, detailed data by State, 1993 annual rpt, C2175–1.531

Jail vocational training programs and participants, for 90 local systems, 1992 annual rpt, R4300–1.4

OECD member countries vocational education teachers and/or pupils, 1980s, A1600–4

Southern States higher education enrollment, degrees, appropriations, tuition/fees, and faculty compensation, by instn type, for 15 States, 1990/91, annual rpt, A8945–31

Urban school systems job training programs, and high school grads by postgraduation activity, for 47 systems, 1990/91, A4425–4

State and local:

Alaska public schools, enrollment, staff, and finances, by district, FY92, annual rpt, S0295–2

Connecticut public school data, including enrollment, staff, programs, finances, and student characteristics, 1991/92, biennial rpt, S1185–3

Delaware data book, general data, 1993 annual rpt, S1375–4

Delaware special and vocational education programs funding and enrollment, 1991/92, annual rpt, S1430–1

Georgia statistical abstract, general data, 1992-93 biennial rpt, U6730–1.2

Idaho economic profile, general data, 1992 recurring rpt, S2218–2.3

Indiana AFDC and food stamp recipient training/employment service program participation and expenditures, by type of aid, FY92 annual rpt, S2623–1.5

Louisiana elementary/secondary school operations, including enrollment, staff, finances, and detail by school district, 1991/92 and trends, annual rpt, S3280–1

Maine public school enrollment, facilities, staff, and finances, with selected data by county and for private schools, 1991 and trends, annual rpt, S3435–1

Maryland elementary and secondary education data, by county, 1991/92, annual rpt, S3610–2.7

Maryland elementary and secondary education statistical summary, with data by county, 1991/92-1992/93 and trends, annual rpt, S3610–1

Massachusetts public elementary/secondary education summary data, 1989/90-1991/92 and trends, annual rpt, S3810–3

Massachusetts public elementary/secondary school enrollment by grade, by district, Oct 1992, annual rpt, S3810–4

Massachusetts public elementary/secondary school expenditures per pupil by program, by district, 1991/92, annual rpt, S3810–5

Minnesota postsecondary education finances, and enrollment by student characteristics, by type of school system, 1970s-93, biennial rpt, S4195–2.2

Minnesota public school enrollment, staff, and finances, by district and county, 1991/92 and trends, annual rpt, S4165–1

Mississippi statistical abstract, general data, 1992 annual rpt, U3255–4.3

Mississippi vocational education enrollment and courses offered, by program, 1991/92, annual rpt, S4340–1.2

Missouri higher education student grant and academic scholarship program awards, by instn, FY93 and trends, annual rpt, S4520–3.2

Missouri public school finances, staff, students, and programs, detailed data, 1991/92, annual rpt, S4505–1.1

Nevada public school enrollment, test scores, teachers, and finances, by school district, 1990/91 and trends, annual rpt, S5035–2

New Jersey public schools, enrollment, grads, and student characteristics, by county, 1991/92, annual rpt, S5385–1.1

North Dakota elementary and secondary schools, enrollment, and staff, by school type and location, 1992/93 annual directory, S6180–2

Ohio correctional instn admissions and releases, inmate characteristics, programs, finances, and staffing, FY91 and trends, annual rpt, S6370–1

Ohio public school enrollment, finances, special programs, and staff, 1991/92 and trends, annual rpt, S6265–2

Oklahoma statistical abstract, general data, 1992 annual rpt, U8130–2.8

Pennsylvania elementary/secondary and higher education enrollment, grads, staff, and finances, by instn type, 1981/82-1996/97, recurring rpt, S6790–5.10

Pennsylvania higher education enrollment, by student characteristics and instn, 1992 and trends, annual rpt, S6790–5.9

Pennsylvania higher education State technical school enrollment by student residence location, 1992 and trends, biennial rpt, S6790–5.8

Pennsylvania public and nonpublic school enrollment, by grade, race-ethnicity, sex, and county, 1991/92 and trends, annual rpt, S6790–5.1

Vocational education and training

Pennsylvania public school dropout characteristics, with reasons for leaving school and subsequent activities, 1991/92 and trends, annual rpt, S6790–5.11

Pennsylvania statistical abstract, general data, 1992 recurring rpt, U4130–6.4

Pennsylvania vocational education enrollment, student characteristics, and faculty, by program and/or school, 1991/92 and trends, annual rpt, S6790–5.7

Pennsylvania vocational education 1989/90 grad employment status, by program, 1991 survey, annual rpt, S6790–5.6

Rhode Island educational enrollment, grads, and finances, by district or community, 1991/92 or fall 1992, annual rpt, S6970–1

South Carolina educational enrollment, by school type or level, program, race, and location, 1991/92, annual rpt, S7145–1.3

Tennessee correctional instn vocational education grads, by instn and subject area, FY92, annual rpt, S7480–1

Tennessee higher education enrollment, finances, staff, and programs, by instn, 1992/93 and trends, annual rpt, S7525–1

Tennessee statistical abstract, general data, 1992/93 annual rpt, U8710–2.16

Texas educational employment, by SIC 3-digit industry and detailed occupation, Apr 1991, triennial survey rpt, S7675–1.28

Utah higher education degrees, enrollment, staff, and finances, by public instn, with selected comparisons to instns in other States, 1993/94 annual rpt, S7895–2

Utah public schools, enrollment, attendance, personnel, and finances, by school district, 1991/92, annual rpt, S7815–1

Vermont postsecondary education enrollment, including proprietary schools, by instn, 1992, S8035–2.2

West Virginia vocational education programs, enrollment, funding, and grad employment placements, 1993 annual rpt, S8540–4

Wisconsin Blue Book, general data, 1993-94 biennial rpt, S8780–1.2

Wisconsin correctional instn admissions by inmate characteristics, including need for special services, 1991, annual rpt, S8692–1.2

Wisconsin correctional instn inmate characteristics, by sex and instn, Dec 1991, semiannual rpt, S8692–1.5

Wyoming penitentiary educational programs and participation, FY85-92, annual rpt, S8883–1

see also Agricultural education

see also Apprenticeship

see also Business education

see also Employee development

see also Federal aid to vocational education

see also Industrial arts

see also Job Training Partnership Act

see also Manpower training programs

see also Scientific education

see also Sheltered workshops

see also State funding for vocational education

see also Vocational rehabilitation

Vocational rehabilitation

Index by Subjects and Names

Vocational rehabilitation

State and local:

Alabama vocational rehabilitation caseloads, and Federal and State appropriations, FY87-92, annual rpt, S0124–1.1

Arkansas vocational rehabilitation expenditures, impact on earnings and employment, and client characteristics, FY91 annual rpt, S0700–2.4

DC statistical profile, general data, 1992 annual rpt, S1535–3.5

Maryland vocational rehabilitation case activity, by county and disability, 1992, annual rpt, S3610–1

Missouri public school finances, staff, students, and programs, detailed data, 1991/92, annual rpt, S4505–1.1

Missouri public welfare and medical assistance recipients, expenditures, and case processing, by program and county, FY92 and trends, annual rpt, S4575–2

Montana social services program cases, by county and type of service, with rehabilitation cost per case, monthly rpt quarterly tables, S4755–1

South Carolina statistical abstract, general data, 1993 annual rpt, S7125–1.10

Washington State public assistance clients and service costs, by client characteristics, program, and county, FY90, annual rpt, S8420–2

see also Sheltered workshops

Voice mail

see Electronic mail systems

see Telecommunication

Volcanoes

Latin America statistical abstract, general data by country, 1992 annual rpt, U6250–1.1

State and local:

Hawaii data book, general data, 1992 annual rpt, S2090–1.5

Voluntary military service

Physics and astronomy bachelor degree recipients postgraduation employment, by type of employer, 1991/92 and trends, annual survey, A1960–3

Urban public high school grads by type of postgraduation activity, for 47 systems, 1990/91, A4425–4

State and local:

Arkansas Census of Population and Housing detailed findings, 1990, U5935–7

California Census of Population and Housing detailed findings, 1990, S0840–9

Connecticut public high school grads and postgraduate activities, 1991, biennial rpt, S1185–3

Massachusetts high school grads in class of 1989, postgrad activities, by city and school system, 1992 annual rpt, C4712–2

Missouri postgraduation activities of high school grads, by sex, 1990/91, annual rpt, S4505–1.1

New Hampshire high school grads and postgraduation activities, by school, county, and sex, 1991, annual tables, S5200–1.2

New Hampshire high school grads and postgraduation activities, by school, county, and sex, 1992, annual tables, S5200–1.15

New Jersey Census of Population and Housing detailed findings, by county, 1990, S5425–19

New York State high school grads and postgraduation activities, by municipality and school district, 1991, annual rpt, C4712–7

North Carolina high school grads and postgraduation plans, by local district, 1991/92 and trends, annual rpt, S5915–1

Pennsylvania Census of Population and Housing detailed findings, with selected data by county and municipality, 1990, U4130–13

Pennsylvania high school grads postgraduation activities, by county, 1991/92, annual rpt, S6790–5.14

Pennsylvania public school dropout characteristics, with reasons for leaving school and subsequent activities, 1991/92 and trends, annual rpt, S6790–5.11

Pennsylvania vocational education 1989/90 grad employment status, by program, 1991 survey, annual rpt, S6790–5.6

Rhode Island Census of Population and Housing detailed findings, by county and municipality, 1990, S6930–9

South Dakota public high school grads, by sex and postgraduation status, 1992, annual rpt, S7315–1.1

see also National Guard

Volunteers

Blood bank operating profiles, arranged by State, 1993 biennial directory, A0612–1

Catholic charity social service agency activities, clients, finances, and personnel, 1991 and trends, annual rpt, A3810–1

College freshmen social and academic activities in past year, by sex and instn type, fall 1992, annual survey, U6215–1

Corporate programs encouraging employee volunteering, including methods used to encourage volunteering, obstacles, benefits, and costs, 1992 survey, C2176–1.511, R4105–78.26

Elementary/secondary student required community service desirability, public opinion by respondent characteristics, 1993 annual Gallup Poll, A8680–1.503

Family volunteering benefits and disadvantages, views of volunteer organizations, 1992 survey article, C2176–1.501

Fire dept employment and personnel practices, including eligibility requirements and testing, by population size, metro status, and census div, 1991 survey, recurring rpt, A5800–2.116

Fundraising professionals characteristics, including volunteer activity, 1992 survey, recurring rpt, A8455–1

Higher education admissions dept use of alumni and student volunteers, 1993, annual rpt, A6695–1

Hospital pharmacy volunteers weekly hours, 1991, annual survey, B5165–3

Japan corporate affiliate philanthropic activity in US, for service and manufacturing operations, 1992, survey article, R5650–2.560

Museums and related instns staff and volunteers, by instn type, 1989/90 survey, A0750–1.1

Religious congregation characteristics, including membership, activities, staff, and finances, 1992 survey, recurring rpt, A5435–4

Teenage volunteer activities and characteristics, with comparisons to adults, 1991, survey article, C2176–1.503

Youth age 12-17 charitable contributions, volunteer activity, and views on related issues, by respondent characteristics, 1992 survey, biennial rpt, A5435–5

State and local:

Arizona public library holdings, circulation, finances, and staff, by instn and county, FY92, annual rpt, S0495–1

Colorado higher education library contributed staff services, by instn, 1992, biennial rpt, S1000–3.2

Florida fire depts, and paid and volunteer firefighters, by city and county, 1991 annual rpt, C4712–6

Florida public library personnel, including volunteers, by instn, FY92, annual rpt, S1800–2

Iowa public library finances and operations, by county, size of population served, and library, FY92, annual rpt, S2778–1

Kentucky public library finances and operations, by county, FY92, annual rpt, S3165–1

Maine court child advocacy program volunteers, caseloads, and children served, FY86-92, annual rpt, S3463–1

Maryland public school volunteers, 1992, annual rpt, S3610–1

Montana public library holdings, staff, circulation, and finances, by library, FY92, annual rpt, S4725–1

Oregon library finances, staff, holdings, and services, for public, academic, and special libraries by instn, FY92 and trends, annual rpt, S6635–1

Pennsylvania public and institutional library personnel, holdings, circulation, and finances, by county and facility, FY92, annual rpt, S6790–2

South Carolina public and institutional libraries, finances, services, holdings, and staff, by library, FY92, annual rpt, S7210–1

South Carolina public welfare service volunteers and contributions, by county, monthly rpt, S7252–1

Texas public library volunteer hours served, by library and location, FY91, annual rpt, S7710–1

see also Voluntary military service

Voter registration

Black elected officials, and characteristics of voting age population, with comparisons to whites, 1970s-91, annual compilation, C6775–2.4

Hispanic American elected officials, registered voters, and voting, with comparisons to whites, 1970s-91, annual compilation, C6775–3.3

Latin America statistical abstract, general data by country, 1992 annual rpt, U6250–1.9

Population of voting age, and voter registration and turnout, by State, with registration detail by county, major city, and district, 1992, biennial rpt, C2500–1

Presidential primary election results and voter registration by county and district, by State, 1992 and trends, C2500–7

Registered voters by party and State, 1992, annual rpt, C2500–2

Index by Subjects and Names

Wards, city

Statistical profiles of 50 States and DC, general data, 1993 annual almanac, C4712–1

Trends in voter turnout and registration, by sex, 1960s-92, U4510–1.70

Urban public school systems voter registration programs, for 47 school systems, 1990/91, A4425–4

State and local:

Alaska election results, and voter registration and turnout, by district and precinct, 1992 general election, biennial rpt, S0337–1

Arizona election results and voter registration, by county and/or district, 1992 general election, biennial rpt, S0520–1

Arizona statistical abstract, general data, 1993 recurring rpt, U5850–2.11

California election results, and voter registration and turnout, by district and/or county, 1992 and trends, biennial rpt, S0934–1

California socioeconomic and govtl data for municipalities, counties, and school districts, 1993 annual rpt, C4712–3

Colorado election results and voter registration, by political party, and county and/or district, 1992, biennial rpt, S1090–1

Colorado voter registration at State and county offices, FY92, annual rpt, S1075–1.4

Connecticut election results and voter registration and turnout, by location, 1992 general election, biennial rpt, S1265–1

DC election results and turnout, and voter registration, by ward and precinct, 1992, biennial series, S1525–1

Florida election results and voter registration, by county, 1992, biennial rpt, S1800–1

Florida municipal and county statistical profiles, general data, 1991 annual rpt, C4712–6

Florida statistical abstract, general data, 1992 annual rpt, U6660–1.21

Georgia county guide, general data, 1993 annual rpt, U6750–1

Hawaii election results, and voter registration by sex, by district and precinct, 1992, biennial series, S2077–1

Idaho election results and voter registration, by county and/or district and precinct, 1992 general election, biennial rpt, S2305–1

Illinois election results, and voter registration trends, by county and/or district, 1992 general election, biennial rpt, S2445–1

Indiana election results, by county and district, with voter registration, 1992 primary and general elections, biennial rpt, S2702–1

Kansas election results and voter registration, by party and county, 1992 primary and general elections, biennial rpt, S3030–1

Massachusetts election results and voter registration, by local area, 1992 and trends, biennial rpt, S3920–1

Massachusetts municipal and county profiles, general data, 1992 annual rpt, C4712–2

Michigan election results and voter registration, by county and/or district, 1992 general election, biennial rpt, S4020–1

Minnesota election results and voter registration, by locality, 1992 primary and general elections, biennial rpt, S4255–1

Missouri election results and voter registration, by district and/or county, with directory of govt officials, 1992 general election, biennial rpt, S4580–1

Montana election results and voter registration, by county and/or district, 1992 general election, biennial rpt, S4760–1

Nebraska election results, and voter registration by party, by county and/or district, 1992 general and primary elections, biennial rpt, S4955–1

Nevada election results, and voter registration and turnout, by county, 1992 general election, biennial rpt, S5125–1

New Hampshire election results, by county and locality, 1992, biennial rpt, S5255–1

New Jersey election results and voter registration, by location, 1992 general election, annual rpt, S5440–1

New Mexico election results, and voter registration by party, by location, 1992 general election, biennial rpt, S5655–1

North Carolina election results, with voter registration by party and race-ethnicity, by county, 1992, biennial rpt, S5920–1

Ohio election results and voter registration, by local area, 1991-92 and trends, biennial rpt, S6380–1

Oklahoma voter registration by party, by county, Nov 1992, biennial rpt, S6425–1

Oregon election results and voter registration and turnout, by county and/or district, 1992 general election, biennial rpt, S6665–1

Pennsylvania statistical abstract, general data, 1992 recurring rpt, U4130–6.6

South Carolina revenue shared with county govts, by tax or fund type, FY92, annual rpt, S7127–2

South Carolina voters registered and voting in general election, by county, Nov 1992, annual rpt, S7145–1.1

South Dakota election results, and voter registration by party, by county, 1992 general election, biennial rpt, S7390–1

Texas election results and voter registration, by district and/or county, 1992 general election, biennial series, S7750–1

Utah statistical abstract, general data, 1993 triennial rpt, U8960–1.8

Virginia election results by jurisdiction, and voter registration and turnout, 1992 and Jan 1993 elections, annual rpt, S8195–1

Washington State election results and voter registration, by county and/or district, 1992 general election, annual rpt, S8425–1

West Virginia election results and voter registration, by county and party, 1992 and trends, biennial rpt, S8630–1

Voting

see Elections

see Voter registration

Wage controls

see also Minimum wage

Wages and salaries

see Agricultural wages

see Earnings, general

see Earnings, specific industry

see Educational employees pay

see Federal pay

see Government pay

see Labor costs and cost indexes

see Minimum wage

see Payroll

see State and local employees pay

Wall coverings

Cotton and other fiber consumption in textile production, by detailed end use, 1990-92, annual rpt, A7485–1

Wallace, Jeff

"Demographic State of the State: A Report to the Governor and Legislature on Commuting Patterns for Oklahoma from the 1990 Census", S6416–2

War

Congressional appropriations for Persian Gulf War, FY92, annual rpt, C2500–2

Public opinion in UK and US on reasons for citing World War II as most important event in past 60 years, by age, 1993 article, A0610–1.504

Public opinion on Persian Gulf war, Nov 1990-Jan 1991, with analysis of polling issues, 1993 article, A0610–1.502

Public opinion on Vietnam and selected other wars, Jan 1993 Gallup Poll and trends, C4040–1.507

Vietnam child and infant mortality rates before, during, and after Vietnam war, with detail by regional area, 1993 article, A2623–1.510

State and local:

Colorado income tax return checkoff contributions for the Persian Gulf Desert Storm operations, FY92, annual rpt, S1075–1.3

see also Arms control and disarmament

see also Civil defense

see also Military intervention

see also Military personnel

see also National defense

see also War casualties

War casualties

State and local:

California vital statistics, including population, births, and deaths by cause, by demographic characteristics and county, 1990 and trends, annual rpt, S0865–1

Hawaii residents serving in military, veterans, and war casualties by conflict, 1992 annual rpt, S2090–1.10

Tennessee vital statistics, including births, deaths by cause, marriages, divorces, and population, by demographic characteristics and location, 1991 and trends, annual rpt, S7520–2

Wisconsin Blue Book, general data, 1993-94 biennial rpt, S8780–1.2

War relief

see also Refugees

Wards, city

State and local:

DC crimes and rates by ward, 1991, annual rpt, S1535–2

DC statistical profile, general data, 1992 annual rpt, S1535–3.1

Wards, city

see also Electoral districts and precincts

Warehouses

- Aluminum inventories of London Metal Exchange in US warehouses in 7 cities, monthly rpt, A0400–1
- Construction contract awards by type of project, weekly rpt, C5800–2
- Electrical equipment wholesalers, sales, employment, and facility size, top 250 companies, 1992, annual article, C4725–5.506
- Financial ratios and performance, for over 350 SIC 4-digit industries, FY88-92, annual rpt, A6400–3
- Food marketers financial and operating data, by company size and region, 1991-92, annual rpts, A4950–5
- Home improvement industry sales and operations, for top distributors, cooperatives, and marketing organizations, 1991-92, annual feature, C5150–6.502
- Industry devs, including warehouse use of automation and materials handling equipment, 1993 articles, C2150–1.506
- Operating costs as percent of sales, by expense category, 1988-91, article, C2150–1.504
- Operational characteristics of warehouses, including size, employees, and starting wage, 1992-93, C2150–1.508
- Real estate market conditions and outlook for industrial property, including construction, prices, and sales and leasing activity, by metro area, 1992-93, annual survey, A8916–1
- Real estate market conditions and outlook, including space, rent, transactions, and prices, for major metro areas, 1993 annual rpt, B2800–3
- Rental rates and other property data for warehouse facilities, for major metro areas by region, mid-1993, annual rpt, B2800–6
- Retail industry inventory mgmt, warehousing, and distribution operations, by outlet type, 1993 survey, C5150–4.506
- Supermarket produce dept sales and performance indicators, 1992 and trends, annual article, C4655–1.511

State and local:

- Colorado property assessed valuation by detailed property type, and tax levy and revenue by local district, by county, 1991-92, annual rpt, S1055–3
- Nebraska public service commission regulatory activities, with financial and operating data for individual railroads and telephone companies, FY91-92 biennial rpt, S4940–1
- North Carolina employment in trade, transportation, communications, utilities, govt, and education, by detailed occupation, 2nd qtr 1991, triennial rpt, S5917–5.2
- Texas trade, transportation, and public utilities employment, by SIC 2- and 3-digit industry and detailed occupation, 2nd qtr 1991, triennial survey rpt, S7675–1.31

see also Cold storage and refrigeration

see also Grain storage and facilities

Warranties

see Guarantees and warranties

Warren, Melinda

"Mixed Message: An Analysis of the 1994 Federal Regulatory Budget", U9640–1

Warships

see Naval vessels

Washing machines

see Household appliances and equipment

Washington

see D.C.

see Washington State

Washington State

- Agricultural production, marketing, and finances, by commodity and/or county, 1992 and trends, annual rpt, S8328–1
- Banks and other financial instns, financial condition by type of instn, 1992 and trends, annual rpt, S8325–1
- Correctional instn inmate population, admissions and releases, with demographic characteristics and data by instn, quarterly rpt, S8337–1
- Court cases and dispositions, by type of court and case, and jurisdiction, with judicial finances and personnel, 1992 and trends, annual rpt, S8339–1
- Crimes and arrests, by offense, location, and offender characteristics, with data on law enforcement employment, and assaults on officers, 1992 and trends, annual rpt, S8440–1
- Dairy farms affected by Nov 1990 flood, with cattle deaths and economic loss, 1993 article, A3100–2.512
- Economic indicators for 10 Western States, including forecasts from selected organizations, monthly rpt, U0282–2
- Election results and voter registration, by county and/or district, 1992 general election, annual rpt, S8425–1
- Electric utility financial and operating data, by company, 1982-91, annual rpt, S8450–1.2
- Employment, earnings, and hours, by labor market area and industry group, monthly rpt, S8340–3
- Govt financial condition, including revenues by source, expenditures by function, fund balances, and bonded debt, FY92, annual rpt, S8345–3
- Hospital cesarean section delivery rates correlated with hospital and patient characteristics, 1987, article, A2623–1.510
- Libraries (public) finances, holdings, circulation, staff, and population served, by instn, 1992, annual rpt, S8375–1
- Markets with daily newspapers, demographic and economic info by geographic area, US and Canada, 1993 annual rpt, C3250–1
- Natural gas utilities financial and operating data, by company, 1982-91, annual rpt, S8450–1.3
- Population and demographic characteristics, and housing units, by county and/or city, 1992 and trends, annual rpt, S8345–4
- Public assistance clients and service costs, by client characteristics, program, and county, FY90, annual rpt, S8420–2
- Statistical profiles of 50 States and DC, general data, 1993 annual almanac, C4712–1

Index by Subjects and Names

- Tax revenue by source and county, with property tax rates and assessed valuation, FY92 and trends, annual rpt, S8415–1
- Telecommunication industry financial and operating data, by company, 1988-91, annual rpt, S8450–1.5
- Traffic accidents, fatalities, and injuries, by circumstances, vehicle type, and location, with driver and victim characteristics, 1992 and trends, annual rpt, S8428–1
- Treasury operations, including receipts, disbursements, aid to localities, and investments, by fund, FY92, annual rpt, S8455–1
- Utility and transportation regulatory agency activities, scope of jurisdiction, finances, and employees, by agency, 1991/92 annual rpt, A7015–2
- Vital statistics, including births, deaths, and population, by demographic characteristics and location, 1991 and trends, annual rpt, S8363–1
- Water utilities financial and operating data, by company, 1988-90, annual rpt, S8450–1.1
- Water utilities financial and operating data, by company, 1989-91, annual rpt, S8450–1.4

see also Asotin County, Wash.

see also Seattle, Wash.

see also under By City and By County in the "Index by Categories"

see also under By State in the "Index by Categories"

Washoe County, Nev.

- Business and economic activity indicators for Nevada and local areas, 1980-91, annual rpt, U7920–2
- Casino finances and employment, by location and gaming revenue range, FY92, annual rpt, S5062–1
- Health behavior risk factor surveillance survey results for Nevada, by location and respondent characteristics, 1991, annual rpt, S5075–3

Waste management

- *see* Environmental pollution and control
- *see* Environmental services industry
- *see* Hazardous waste and disposal
- *see* Landfills
- *see* Radioactive waste and disposal
- *see* Recycling of waste materials
- *see* Refuse and refuse disposal
- *see* Sewage and wastewater systems

Wastepaper

- *see* Paper and paper products
- *see* Recycling of waste materials

Wastewater

see Sewage and wastewater systems

Watches and clocks

- Jewelry industry statistics on sales, marketing, trade, and employment, with customer characteristics, 1993 annual almanac, C2150–7.509
- Manufacturing and marketing trends, new product dev, prices, trade, and related indicators, monthly rpt, C2150–7
- Radio clock factory sales, 1983-92, annual rpt, A4725–1.1
- Sales and prices of watches, by retail outlet type, 1992, article, C5150–3.516
- Shipments of household appliances, by detailed product type, 1991-98, annual articles, C2000–1.503

Index by Subjects and Names

Water area

Inland water square mileage, and miles of coastal shoreline, by State, 1993 annual feature, C2425–4

Statistical profiles of 50 States and DC, general data, 1993 annual almanac, C4712–1

State and local:

Arizona statistical abstract, general data, 1993 recurring rpt, U5850–2.1

Arizona water area by county, 1993 annual rpt, U5830–1

California statistical abstract, general data, 1992 annual rpt, S0840–2.1

DC statistical profile, general data, 1992 annual rpt, S1535–3.6

Florida county data book, 1992/93 annual rpt, C6360–1

Florida statistical abstract, general data, 1992 annual rpt, U6660–1.8

Georgia county guide, general data, 1993 annual rpt, U6750–1

Georgia statistical abstract, general data, 1992-93 biennial rpt, U6730–1.1

Hawaii data book, general data, 1992 annual rpt, S2090–1.5

Illinois statistical abstract, general data, 1992 annual rpt, U6910–2

Massachusetts municipal and county profiles, general data, 1992 annual rpt, C4712–2

Mississippi statistical abstract, general data, 1992 annual rpt, U3255–4.16

New Hampshire water area, by county and city, 1993 biennial rpt, S5255–1

New Jersey municipal and county data book, general data, 1992 annual rpt, C4712–4

New York State municipal and county statistical profiles, general data, 1993 annual rpt, C4712–7

Pennsylvania statistical abstract, general data, 1992 recurring rpt, U4130–6.1

South Carolina statistical abstract, general data, 1993 annual rpt, S7125–1.1, S7125–1.4

Tennessee statistical abstract, general data, 1992/93 annual rpt, U8710–2.12

Utah statistical abstract, general data, 1993 triennial rpt, U8960–1.17

Wisconsin Blue Book, general data, 1993-94 biennial rpt, S8780–1.2

see also Water supply and use

Water pollution

City fiscal condition, including perceived impact of spending to meet EPA drinking water standards, Mar-Apr 1993 survey, annual rpt, A8012–1.23

City govt costs to enforce Fed Govt regulations including Clean Water Act and Safe Drinking Water Act, FY93-98, A9330–12

Estuary characteristics and concentrations of nitrogen and phosphorus, by estuary, 1992/93 biennial rpt, R9455–1.7

Lake Erie contaminant levels in herring gull eggs, 1970 and 1980-92, annual rpt, A3850–1

Oil industry environmental performance, with data on toxic chemical releases, oil spills, occupational injury/illness, and corporate spending, 1990 and trends, annual rpt, A2575–27

Pulp and paper industry capital spending plans of US and Canadian companies, by purpose and geographic area, 1992-94, annual survey article, C3975–2.503

State economic dev condition indicators, including economic performance, business vitality, growth capacity, and tax/fiscal system, by State, 1993 annual rpt, R4225–1.1

State social, economic, and govtl indicators, with rankings, 1993 semiannual rpt, B8500–1.15

State and local:

Hawaii data book, general data, 1992 annual rpt, S2090–1.5

Hawaii environmental quality and public health control, inspection, licensing, and enforcement activities, 1990, annual rpt, S2065–1.6

Missouri State water pollution control bonds, FY92, annual rpt, S4570–1.2

Pennsylvania statistical abstract, general data, 1992 recurring rpt, U4130–6.8

Vermont pesticide monitoring activities, including wells tested for herbicides and nitrates, 1989-90, biennial rpt, S7978–1

see also Food and waterborne diseases

see also Marine pollution

see also Oil spills

Water power

Capacity developed and undeveloped, by census div, 1986-90, biennial rpt, U6730–1.8

see also Dams

see also Hydroelectric power

Water resources development

Construction cost indexes for water projects, by expenditure category, weekly rpt quarterly feature, C5800–2.534

Planning status and activities for water resources, with data on water systems by type, withdrawals, and supply shortages, and detail by State, 1991 rpt, A8195–11

State and local:

California statistical abstract, general data, 1992 annual rpt, S0840–2.7

Wyoming State govt water dev revenues, appropriations, and expenditures, with data by project, FY92 annual rpt, S8875–1

see also Aquaculture

see also Canals

see also Flood control

see also Hydroelectric power

see also Inland water transportation

see also Irrigation

see also Marine resources

see also Water power

see also Water supply and use

Water skiing

see Sports and athletics

Water supply and use

Apartment building (conventionally financed) detailed income and expense ratios for US and Canada, by building type, metro area, and US region, 1991 and trends, annual rpt, A5600–1

Apartment building (federally subsidized) detailed income and expense ratios, by building and subsidy type, building age, metro area, and region, 1991 and trends, annual rpt, A5600–5

Chemical consumption for water treatment, by chemical type, 1990 and 2000, article, C5800–8.507

City govt costs to enforce Fed Govt regulations including Clean Water Act and Safe Drinking Water Act, FY93-98, A9330–12

Condominium, cooperative, and planned unit dev detailed expenses, for US and Canada, by building characteristics, metro area, and US region, 1991, annual rpt, A5600–3

Construction contract awards by type of project, weekly rpt, C5800–2

Construction cost indexes for water projects, by expenditure category, weekly rpt quarterly feature, C5800–2.534

Consumption of bottled and tap water per capita, 1981-92, annual article, C0125–2.504

Consumption of water per capita, 1979-91, annual rpt, C0125–3.1

Developing countries population access to safe drinking water and sanitation services, by urban-rural status and country, 1988-90, R8720–1.2

Higher education physical plant operations, costs, employment, salaries, and energy use, by instn and region, 1991/92, recurring rpt, A3183–1

Household water average costs, for US and 13 States, 1990/91, article, B8500–2.505

Latin America statistical abstract, general data by country, 1992 annual rpt, U6250–1.6, U6250–1.7

Office building detailed income and expense data, and energy use, US and Canada, by building characteristics, metro area, and US region, 1991 and trends, annual rpt, A5600–2

Operating and financial composite ratios for corporations, with establishments and receipts, for approx 200 industries, by asset size, FY90, annual rpt, C7800–1

Planning status and activities for water resources, with data on water systems by type, withdrawals, and supply shortages, and detail by State, 1991 rpt, A8195–11

Population per million cubic meters of water, for selected world areas and countries, 1990 and 2025, article, R8750–1.502

Shopping center detailed income and expense data, by building characteristics, metro area, and region, 1991, annual rpt, A5600–6

Tap water characteristics in daily newspaper markets in US and Canada, 1993 annual rpt, C3250–1

Utility regulatory agency policies and practices, and industry financial and operating data, by utility type and agency, 1991/92 annual rpt, A7015–3

World water resources supply-demand conditions and outlook, with population size and growth factors, by region and selected country, 1992 rpt, R8750–2.57

World water supply and use data, including population with access to drinking water, and withdrawal by major use, by country, 1992/93 biennial rpt, R9455–1.5, R9455–1.7

State and local:

Alabama municipal data book, general data, 1992 recurring rpt, S0121–5

Alaska public utility financial and operating data, by company and utility type, 1991 and trends, with FY92 regulatory info, annual rpt, S0280–4

Alaska senior citizen tax deferment for sewer/water system assessments, by municipality, FY92, annual rpt, S0285–1

Water supply and use

Arizona statistical abstract, general data, 1993 recurring rpt, U5850–2.1, U5850–2.16

Arizona water production from oil and gas fields, by field, operator, and well, monthly rpt, S0473–1

Arkansas Census of Population and Housing detailed findings, 1990, U5935–7

Arkansas public utility financial, operating, and regulatory data, by utility type and company, 1992 annual rpt, S0757–1

California Census of Population and Housing detailed findings, 1990, S0840–9

California public utility and transportation regulatory data, including revenue requests and rates of return by company, FY92 annual rpt, S0930–1

California statistical abstract, general data, 1992 annual rpt, S0840–2.7

Colorado property assessed valuation, by property type and county, and for regulated industries by company, 1991-92, annual rpt, S1055–3

Colorado water court case filings and claims, by location, FY92 and trends, annual rpt, S1035–1.2

DC statistical profile, general data, 1992 annual rpt, S1535–3.7

Florida statistical abstract, general data, 1992 annual rpt, U6660–1.8

Florida water and sewer dept regulatory activities, 1992, annual rpt, S1790–1

Georgia county guide, general data, 1993 annual rpt, U6750–1

Georgia statistical abstract, general data, 1992-93 biennial rpt, U6730–1.4

Hawaii data book, general data, 1992 annual rpt, S2090–1.5

Hawaii environmental quality and public health control, inspection, licensing, and enforcement activities, 1990, annual rpt, S2065–1.6

Kansas statistical abstract, general data, 1991/92 annual rpt, U7095–2.3

Louisiana Census of Population and Housing summary findings, by local area, 1990 and trends, U8010–4

Maine Census of Population and Housing summary findings, by local area, 1990, S3465–9

Mississippi statistical abstract, general data, 1992 annual rpt, U3255–4.10

Nevada statistical abstract, general data, 1992 biennial rpt, S5005–1.9

New Jersey Census of Population and Housing detailed findings, by county, 1990, S5425–19

New Jersey municipal and county data book, general data, 1992 annual rpt, C4712–4

New Mexico public utility operating, financial, and regulatory data, by utility type, FY92 annual rpt, S5645–1

New York State public utility financial and operating data, by utility type and company, 1988-92, annual rpt, S5795–1

North Carolina public utility financial, operating, and regulatory data, by utility type and company, 1990 and trends, annual rpt, S5917–2

Pennsylvania Census of Population and Housing detailed findings, with selected data by county and municipality, 1990, U4130–13

Pennsylvania housing data from Census of Population and Housing, by county and municipality, 1990, C1595–14

Pennsylvania statistical abstract, general data, 1992 recurring rpt, U4130–6.1, U4130–6.9

Rhode Island Census of Population and Housing detailed findings, by county and municipality, 1990, S6930–9

South Carolina public service commission regulatory activities, with financial and operating data for individual utilities and railroads, FY92 annual rpt, S7235–1

South Carolina statistical abstract, general data, 1993 annual rpt, S7125–1.4

Tennessee public utility and transportation commission regulatory activities, with industry financial and operating data, 1991-92 biennial rpt, S7565–1

Tennessee statistical abstract, general data, 1992/93 annual rpt, U8710–2.12

Texas trade, transportation, and public utilities employment, by SIC 2- and 3-digit industry and detailed occupation, 2nd qtr 1991, triennial survey rpt, S7675–1.31

Vermont private water systems residential customers and rates, by company, Dec 1991, biennial rpt, S8100–1

Washington State water utilities financial and operating data, by company, 1988-90, annual rpt, S8450–1.1

Washington State water utilities financial and operating data, by company, 1989-91, annual rpt, S8450–1.4

see also Bottled water

see also Dams

see also Food and waterborne diseases

see also Irrigation

see also Reservoirs

see also Water pollution

see also Weather

Waters, Somerset R.

"Travel Industry World Yearbook: The Big Picture, 1992", C2140–1

Waterways

see Canals

see Harbors and ports

see Inland water transportation

see Lakes and lakeshores

see Rivers and waterways

Wayman, Neva

"Arkansas State and County Economic Data", U5935–1

Wealth

Billionaire profiles and sources of wealth, for persons/families worldwide worth 1 billion/more, 1993 annual feature, C3950–1.518

Billionaire profiles and sources of wealth, for 101 wealthiest persons/families worldwide, 1993 annual feature, C8900–1.518

Black American earnings, income, and poverty data, with comparisons to whites, 1980s-91, annual compilation, C6775–2.7

Black American per capita net worth compared to whites, with detail for selected types of assets, 1993 article, C4215–1.507

Black American socioeconomic status, with comparisons to whites and data by region, 1960s-92, annual compilation, A8510–1.1

College freshmen attitudes on increasing taxes for the wealthy, by sex and instn type, fall 1992, annual survey, U6215–1

Index by Subjects and Names

Economic indicator historical trends, 1900s-92, annual rpt, R9050–1.2

Forbes profile of 400 wealthiest individuals, with info on family background, income, and assets, 1993 annual feature, C3950–1.526

Hispanic American households with income over $35,000, by income group and leading State, 1989, article, C4575–1.501

Hispanic American income and poverty data, with comparisons to whites, 1980s-91, annual compilation, C6775–3.5

Hispanic American 50 wealthiest individuals or families, with info on background, assets, and net worth, 1993, annual feature, C4575–1.505

Household assets and debts by type, by household composition, 1989, article, C4215–1.502

Household income and population of 50 wealthiest counties, 1991, annual almanac, C2150–7.509

Household wealth and income data by income level, including assets by type and detail by age group, 1989 and trends, R4700–17

Men age 69-84 net assets, by race, 1990 survey, U3780–9

Minority population characteristics, employment, and voting patterns by detailed race-ethnicity, with comparisons to whites, 1980s-2040, R8750–2.58

Private assets and liabilities trends, by economic sector, decennially 1950-90, U9640–2.14

Student aid applicant characteristics, including assets, American College Testing (ACT) program, 1993/94, annual rpt, R1960–5

State and local:

California total and taxable high-income tax returns, with largest deductions/credits claimed, 1990 and trends, annual rpt, S0855–1

Hawaii data book, general data, 1992 annual rpt, S2090–1.13

Maryland local wealth vs State aid per pupil, by county, 1992/93, annual rpt, S3610–1

Maryland public school appropriations compared to local revenues, wealth, and assessed property value, 1991/92, annual rpt, S3610–2.9

Tennessee statistical abstract, general data, 1992/93 annual rpt, U8710–2.2

see also Business assets and liabilities, general

see also Business assets and liabilities, specific industry

see also Gross Domestic Product

see also Gross National Product

see also Income taxes

see also Investments

see also Money supply

see also National income and product accounts

see also Personal and household income

see also Personal debt

see also Poverty

see also Property

see also Savings

see also under By Income in the "Index by Categories"

Index by Subjects and Names

Weapons systems

see Arms trade
see Military assistance
see Military weapons
see Missiles and rockets

Weather

Climatological data for daily newspaper market areas in US and Canada, 1993 annual rpt, C3250–1

Climatological data for 22 cities, 1992 recurring rpt, S2218–2.7

Damage value caused by 7 weather-related disasters occurring in 1988-93, article, C5800–7.548

Heating degree days, by census div and State, 1990/91-1991/92 and 30-year average, annual rpt, A1775–3.6

Heating or cooling degree days by census div, weekly rpt monthly table, C6985–1

Heating/cooling equipment industry data, with average heating and cooling degree days, by census div, 1991-92, annual rpt, C1800–1

School bus loading/unloading accident fatalities, by circumstances, location, and victim age and sex, 1991 and trends, annual rpt, S3040–2

State and local:

Alabama precipitation and average temperature, by State area, monthly 1992, annual rpt, S0090–1

Alabama traffic accidents, fatalities, and injuries, by circumstances, vehicle type, and driver and victim characteristics, 1992, annual rpt, S0185–1

Alaska climatological data, by weather station, 1993 annual rpt, U5750–1

Alaska traffic accidents, fatalities, and injuries, by vehicle type, circumstance, location, and driver and victim characteristics, 1991 and trends, annual rpt, S0360–1

Arizona monthly precipitation and temperature, and freeze dates, by weather station, 1992 and trends, annual rpt, U5830–1

Arizona statistical abstract, general data, 1993 recurring rpt, U5850–2.1

Arizona traffic accidents, fatalities, and injuries, by vehicle type, circumstances, location, and driver and victim characteristics, 1991 and trends, annual rpt, S0530–1

Arkansas precipitation and average temperatures, by district, monthly 1992, annual rpt, U5920–1

Arkansas traffic accidents, fatalities, and injuries, by vehicle type, circumstances, location, and driver and victim characteristics, 1991, annual rpt, S0692–1

California rainfall by weather station, 1991/92-1992/93, annual rpt, S0850–1.5

California statistical abstract, general data, 1992 annual rpt, S0840–2.1

California traffic accidents, fatalities, and injuries, by vehicle type, circumstances, location, and driver and victim characteristics, 1991 and trends, annual rpt, S0885–1

Colorado precipitation, by district, 1992 and trends, annual rpt, S0985–1

Connecticut traffic accidents, fatalities, and injuries, by vehicle type, circumstance, location, and driver and victim characteristics, 1992, annual rpt, S1275–1

Delaware data book, general data, 1993 annual rpt, S1375–4

Delaware traffic accidents, fatalities, and injuries, by circumstances, location, and vehicle type, and driver and victim characteristics, 1992 and trends, annual rpt, S1435–1

Florida statistical abstract, general data, 1992 annual rpt, U6660–1.8

Georgia precipitation and average temperature, by crop reporting district, monthly 1991, annual rpt, S1855–1

Georgia statistical abstract, general data, 1992-93 biennial rpt, U6730–1.4

Hawaii data book, general data, 1992 annual rpt, S2090–1.5

Hawaii precipitation, by month and station, 1991, annual rpt, S2030–1

Idaho economic profile, general data, 1992 recurring rpt, S2218–2.7

Idaho traffic accidents, fatalities, and injuries, by circumstances, location, vehicle type, and driver and victim characteristics, 1992, annual rpt, S2315–1

Illinois average precipitation and temperature, by crop reporting district, monthly 1991, annual rpt, S2390–1

Indiana traffic accidents, fatalities, and injuries, by circumstances, location, and vehicle type, and driver and victim characteristics, 1992, annual rpt, S2675–1

Kansas precipitation and temperatures, by State district, monthly 1992, annual rpt, S2915–1

Kansas statistical abstract, general data, 1991/92 annual rpt, U7095–2.7

Kentucky temperature and precipitation, by region, weather station, and crop district, monthly 1992, annual rpt, S3085–1

Kentucky traffic accidents, fatalities, and injuries, by circumstances, location, vehicle type, and driver characteristics, 1992 and trends, annual rpt, S3150–2

Louisiana traffic accidents, fatalities, and injuries, by circumstances, location, and driver characteristics, 1991 and trends, annual rpt, S3345–2

Maine statistical summary, general economic and social data, 1992 recurring rpt, S3434–1

Maine traffic accidents, fatalities, and injuries, by accident circumstances, vehicle type and make, and driver and victim characteristics, 1992, annual rpt, S3475–2

Maryland statistical abstract, general data, 1993-94 biennial rpt, S3605–1.3

Maryland traffic accidents, fatalities, and injuries, by circumstances, location, vehicle type, and driver and victim characteristics, 1992, annual rpt, S3665–4

Michigan traffic accidents, fatalities, and injuries, by vehicle type, circumstance, location, and driver and victim characteristics, 1991 and trends, annual rpt, S3997–2

Minnesota precipitation and frost dates, by district and weather station, 1993 annual rpt, S4130–1

Minnesota traffic accidents, fatalities, and injuries, by type of vehicle and circumstances, and driver and victim characteristics, 1992 and trends, annual rpt, S4230–2

Mississippi statistical abstract, general data, 1992 annual rpt, U3255–4.16

Missouri precipitation, snowfall, and average temperatures, by weather station and/or county, monthly 1992, annual rpt, S4480–1

Missouri traffic accidents, fatalities, and injuries, by circumstances, location, and driver and victim characteristics, 1992 and trends, annual rpt, S4560–1

Montana precipitation and growing season, by county and station, 1990-91, annual rpt, S4655–1

Montana traffic accidents, fatalities, and injuries, by circumstances, location, and driver and victim characteristics, 1992 and trends, annual rpt, S4705–2

Nebraska temperatures and precipitation, by State crop reporting district, monthly 1991 and trends, annual rpt, S4835–1

Nebraska traffic accidents, fatalities, and injuries, by circumstances, location, vehicle type, and driver and victim characteristics, 1992, annual rpt, S4953–1

Nevada precipitation and frost-free days, by weather station, 1991-92, annual rpt, S5010–1

Nevada statistical abstract, general data, 1992 biennial rpt, S5005–1.9

Nevada traffic accidents, fatalities, and injuries, by circumstances, location, and vehicle type, 1992 and trends, annual rpt, S5140–1

New Jersey fatal traffic accidents and fatalities, by vehicle type, location, and circumstances, and driver and victim characteristics, 1992 and trends, annual rpt, S5430–2

New Jersey freeze dates and frost-free days, by county and weather station, 1992 annual rpt, S5350–1

New Mexico average freeze dates and precipitation, by county and weather station, 1991, annual rpt, S5530–1

New Mexico traffic accidents, fatalities, and injuries, by vehicle type, circumstances, location, and driver and victim characteristics, 1992 and trends, annual rpt, S5665–1

New York State temperatures, precipitation, and heating degree days, by weather station, monthly 1992, annual rpt, S5700–1

New York State traffic accidents, fatalities, and injuries, by circumstances, location, vehicle type, and driver and victim characteristics, 1991 and trends, annual rpt, S5790–1

North Carolina precipitation and average temperature, by district, monthly 1991, annual rpt, S5885–1

North Carolina traffic accidents, fatalities, and injuries, by circumstances, location, vehicle type, and driver and victim characteristics, 1992 and trends, annual rpt, S5990–1

North Dakota precipitation, temperature, and growing season, by weather station, 1992 and trends, annual rpt, U3600–1

North Dakota traffic accidents, fatalities, and injuries, by circumstances, location, vehicle type, and driver and victim characteristics, 1992 and trends, annual rpt, S6217–1

Weather

Ohio growing season temperature and precipitation, and deviation from normal, by weather station, 1991, annual rpt, S6240–1

Ohio heating degree days and temperature effect on natural gas supply-demand, 1990-92, annual rpt, S6355–1

Ohio traffic accidents, fatalities, and injuries, by circumstances, location, driver and victim characteristics, and vehicle type, 1991 and trends, annual rpt, S6290–1

Oklahoma average precipitation and temperature, by district, monthly 1992, annual rpt, S6405–1

Oklahoma statistical abstract, general data, 1992 annual rpt, U8130–2.1

Oregon precipitation by weather station, monthly 1991, annual rpt, S6575–1

Pennsylvania frost dates, temperature, and precipitation by area and/or weather station, 1992, annual rpt, S6760–1

Pennsylvania heating degree days, by city, 1976/77-1990/91, recurring rpt, S6810–3

Pennsylvania statistical abstract, general data, 1992 recurring rpt, U4130–6.8

Pennsylvania traffic accidents, fatalities, and injuries, by circumstances, location, driver characteristics, and vehicle type, 1991, annual rpt, S6905–3

Rhode Island traffic accidents, fatalities, and injuries, by circumstances, community, and driver and victim characteristics, 1992, annual rpt, S7025–1

South Carolina statistical abstract, general data, 1993 annual rpt, S7125–1.4

South Carolina traffic accidents, fatalities, and injuries, by circumstances, location, and driver and victim characteristics, 1992 and trends, annual rpt, S7190–2

South Dakota precipitation, by weather station, 1991-92, annual rpt, S7280–1

South Dakota traffic accidents, fatalities, and injuries, by circumstances, location, vehicle type, and driver and victim characteristics, 1992 and trends, annual rpt, S7300–3

Tennessee precipitation by month, and freeze dates by county, 1993 annual rpt, S7460–1

Tennessee statistical abstract, general data, 1992/93 annual rpt, U8710–2.12

Texas heating degree days in 25 largest cities, 1990-91, annual rpt, S7745–1

Texas rainfall, by crop reporting district, 1988-91, annual rpt, S7630–1.1

Utah temperature, precipitation, and growing season, by weather station, 1960s-92, annual rpt, S7800–1

Utah traffic accidents and fatalities by circumstances, location, driver and victim characteristics, and vehicle type, 1992 and trends, annual rpt, S7890–2

Virginia traffic accidents, fatalities, and injuries, by circumstances, location, and driver and victim characteristics, 1991 and trends, annual rpt, S8282–1

Washington State precipitation and average temperatures, by weather station, 1992, annual rpt, S8328–1

West Virginia precipitation and average temperatures, by weather station, monthly 1991, annual rpt, S8510–1

West Virginia traffic accidents, fatalities, and injuries, by circumstance and location, and driver and victim characteristics, 1992, annual rpt, S8645–1

Wisconsin Blue Book, general data, 1993-94 biennial rpt, S8780–1.2

Wisconsin precipitation and temperature, by month and weather station, 1992, annual rpt, S8680–1

Wisconsin traffic accidents, fatalities, and injuries, by circumstances, location, vehicle type, and driver and victim characteristics, 1992 and trends, annual rpt, S8815–1

Wyoming monthly temperature and precipitation, and temperature extremes, by weather station, 1991-92, annual rpt, S8860–1

Wyoming traffic accidents, fatalities, and injuries, by circumstances, location, vehicle type, and driver and victim characteristics, 1992 and trends, annual rpt, S9007–1

see also Drought

see also Floods

see also Global climate change

see also Storms

Webb, Patrick

"Famine in Ethiopia: Policy Implications of Coping Failure at National and Household Levels", R5620–1.36

Weber County, Utah

Homeless shelter capacity and population characteristics for Utah, with detail for selected counties, 1991-92, annual rpt, S7808–2

WEFA Group

Foreign trade deficit of US, top 5 countries, 1993, article, C8900–1.510

Wegner, Merrill

"Military Base Closings Information Packet", R8490–45

"Rough Cuts: The Continuing Decline of Defense Dollars for the Northeast-Midwest Region", R8490–44

Weight

see Birthweight

see Body measurements

see Dieting and dietetic products

see Obesity

Weights and measures

State and local:

Vermont weights and measures inspection activity, 1989-90 biennial rpt, S7978–1

Weitzman, Murray S.

"Giving and Volunteering, 1992: Volunteering and Giving Among American Teenagers 12 to 17 Years of Age", A5435–5

Welfare

see Public welfare programs

see Social security

see State funding for social welfare

Welfare mothers

see Aid to Families with Dependent Children

Welgoss, Bill

"Producers Drive Slowly on the Road to Recovery", C0125–5

West Indies

see Caribbean area

West Virginia

Agricultural production, marketing, and finances, by commodity or county, 1991 and trends, annual rpt, S8510–1

Banks and other financial instns, composite financial data, with selected data by instn, 1990-91, annual rpt, S8530–1

Index by Subjects and Names

Court caseloads and dispositions, by type of court and case, and judicial circuit, 1992 and trends, annual rpt, S8537–1

Crimes and arrests, by offense, location, and offender characteristics, with data on law enforcement employment and assaults on officers, 1990-91, annual rpt, S8610–1

Election results and voter registration, by county and party, 1992 and trends, biennial rpt, S8630–1

Elementary and secondary school finances, enrollment, staff, and programs, by county, 1992/93 and trends, annual rpt, S8540–4

Elementary and secondary schools, enrollment, grads, and staff, by county, for public and private schools, 1991/92, annual rpt, S8540–3

Employment, unemployment, hours, and earnings, with job service activities, monthly rpt, S8534–1

Higher education enrollment, degrees, faculty and student characteristics, and finances, by instn, 1992/93 and trends, annual rpt, S8533–1

Insurance industry financial and underwriting data, by company and line of coverage, with regulatory info, 1991, annual rpt, S8575–1

Labor force planning rpt, including population, employment, and job service activities, with data by county and service delivery area, 1993 annual rpt, S8534–2

Library operations and/or finances for public, academic, and special libraries, by instn, 1991/92, annual rpt, S8590–1

Markets with daily newspapers, demographic and economic info by geographic area, US and Canada, 1993 annual rpt, C3250–1

Oil/gas industry production, finances, exploration, and reserves, by State, 1992 and trends, annual rpt, A5425–1.1

Property tax levy rates, by purpose and locale, FY93, annual rpt, S8640–3

Property valuations and tax levies by property class, and levies by purpose, by county, 1992/93 and trends, annual rpt, S8640–2

Statistical handbook of West Virginia, social, govtl, and economic data, 1992 annual rpt, R9385–1

Statistical profiles of 50 States and DC, general data, 1993 annual almanac, C4712–1

Traffic accidents, fatalities, and injuries, by circumstance and location, and driver and victim characteristics, with economic losses, 1992, annual rpt, S8645–1

Utility and transportation regulatory agency activities, scope of jurisdiction, finances, and employees, by agency, 1991/92 annual rpt, A7015–2

Vital statistics, including births, deaths by cause, marriages, and divorces, by location and selected demographic characteristics, 1991 and trends, annual rpt, S8560–1

Welfare and social service program caseloads and expenditures, by county, monthly rpt, S8560–2

see also under By City and By County in the "Index by Categories"

see also under By State in the "Index by Categories"

Index by Subjects and Names

Wheat

Western States

Bookstore employee salaries and benefits, 1992 survey, article, C1852–2.501

College grad job and salary offers, by field of study, type of employer, occupation, and degree level, interim rpt, A3940–1.4, A3940–1.7

Compensation costs for employees, by component, Mar 1992, article, S1040–4.503

Compensation costs for employees, by component, Mar 1993, article, S1040–4.508

Corrections data, including prisoners and capacity, and related data on population and crime, for 13 States, 1980s-90, A4375–13

Corrections incarceration rates, for Utah and other Western States, June 1992, annual rpt, S7810–1

Cost-of-living index, by component, for selected Western cities, monthly rpt quarterly table, S7820–3.503, S7820–3.506, S7820–3.507

Drought-response capability summary for Western region, 1990 survey, A8195–11

Economic data, including employment and construction activity, for 3 West Coast States, various months 1992-93, article, A6400–2.504

Economic indicator trends for 9 Western States, 1980-91, annual rpt, U7920–2

Economic indicator trends in approx 15 Western States, 1990s, annual rpt, B3520–1

Economic indicators for 10 Western States, including forecasts from selected organizations, monthly rpt, U0282–2

Economic profile of Idaho, with comparisons to other Western States, 1992 recurring rpt, S2218–2

Farm workers, hours, and wages, 1992-93, annual rpt, S5010–1

Higher education student exchange program enrollment and support fees, by program and instn, for 15 Western States, 1992/93, annual rpt, A9385–1

Higher education tuition/fees, by resident status, State, and public instn, with State-funded student aid summaries, 1992/93 and trends, annual rpt, A9385–3

Hospital patient discharges and length of stay, by diagnosis, type of operation, and age, 1991, annual rpt, B4455–1.5

Hospital patient discharges and length of stay, by diagnostic related group (DRG), payment source, and age, 1991, annual rpt, B4455–3.5

Hospital psychiatric patient discharges and length of stay, by diagnosis, age, and sex, 1991, annual rpt, B4455–2.5

Income per capita and Federal expenditures, for selected Western States, 1982-91, annual article, U7980–1.503

Labor force data for US and 7 Western States, monthly rpt, S1040–4

Low-income housing supply-demand, costs, physical conditions, and public assistance, for 11 Western metro areas, 1992 rpt, R3834–16.5

Lumber harvest, and distribution of timberland by ownership, for Washington State/Oregon, 1993 article, C3975–2.511

Lumber industry production in Western States and counties, with acreage owned, employment, and sawmill operations, 1980s-92, annual rpt, A9395–1

Lumber production peak level compared to demand outlook and Clinton Admin harvest plan, for Northwest region, 1993 article, C1850–8.509

Natural gas pipeline project construction spending, jobs created, and property tax benefits, for 4 Western States, 1992 article, C6780–2.501

Paper and pulp mills on West Coast shut down, including capacity, 1993 article, C3975–2.509

Pay (average annual), for Mountain-Plains region and 10 component States, 1991, article, U7860–1.505

Pay (average annual) for 10 Western States, 1990-91, annual article, S0465–1.502

Personal income in 15 Western States, 1988-91, U7980–1.501

Plastics processing plant operating costs in 16 Western metro areas, 1993 article, C5800–12.512

Population and land area in urban and rural areas, for 12 Western States, 1990, article, U0280–1.502

Printing industry devs, including sales trends and printer views on business conditions, 1992 feature, C1850–10.503

Statistical abstract of Nevada, with comparisons to other Western States, 1992 biennial rpt, S5005–1

Statistical abstract of Utah, with comparisons to other Western States, 1993 triennial rpt, U8960–1

Travel time to work, population, and land area, for 18 Western urban areas, 1990, article, U0280–1.511

Wage and personal income levels compared to total US, by region and for 10 Western States, 1991 and trends, article, U0280–1.505

see also Southwestern States

see also under By Region in the "Index by Categories"

see also under names of individual States

Wharton Econometric Forecasting Associates *see* WEFA Group

Wheat

Chicago Board of Trade futures and options trading in financial instruments and agricultural commodities, 1992, annual rpt, B2120–1

Exports of farm products, by detailed commodity and country of destination, US and California, 1991, annual rpt, B9520–1

Futures trading volume and prices at Kansas City Board of Trade grain market, with natl production by State, 1992, annual rpt, B1530–1

Latin America statistical abstract, general data by country, 1992 annual rpt, U6250–1.24, U6250–1.25

Production, consumption, price, and trade trends, 1992 annual rpt, A7310–1

Production, consumption, stocks, trade, and prices for approx 100 basic commodities, including by country and producing State, commodity yearbook for 1993, C2400–1, C2400–2

Production, prices, and futures and options trading activity on Minneapolis exchange, 1992 and trends, annual rpt, B6110–1

State and local:

Alabama agricultural production, marketing, and income, by county and/or commodity, and farms and acreage, 1992 and trends, annual rpt, S0090–1

Arizona agricultural production, marketing, and finances, by commodity and county, 1988-92, annual rpt, U5830–1

Arkansas agricultural production, marketing, and finances, by commodity and county, with farms and acreage, 1992 and trends, annual rpt, U5920–1

California field crops production, acreage, yield, and prices, by commodity and county, 1992 and trends, annual rpt, S0850–1.4

Colorado agricultural production, marketing, and finances, by commodity and/or county, with farms and acreage, 1992 and trends, annual rpt, S0985–1

Florida field crop acreage, yield, production, and value, by commodity and/or county, 1992 and trends, annual rpt, S1685–1.4

Georgia agricultural production, marketing, and finances, by commodity and/or county, and farms and acreage, 1991 and trends, annual rpt, S1855–1

Illinois agricultural production, marketing, and finances, by county or commodity, and farms and farmland, 1991 and trends, annual rpt, S2390–1

Kansas agricultural production, marketing, and finances, by county and/or commodity, and farm acreage and value, 1992 and trends, annual rpt, S2915–1

Kentucky agricultural production, marketing, and finances, by commodity and county; and farms, acreage, and value; 1992 and trends, annual rpt, S3085–1

Louisiana agricultural production, marketing, and finances, by commodity or parish, 1985-91, annual rpt, U2740–1

Michigan agricultural production, marketing, and finances, by commodity or county, 1987-91, annual rpt, S3950–1

Minnesota agricultural production, marketing, and finances, by county or commodity, and farms and acreage, 1992 and trends, annual rpt, S4130–1

Missouri agricultural production, marketing, and finances, by commodity and/or county, and farms and acreage, 1988-92, annual rpt, S4480–1

Montana agricultural production, marketing, and finances, by commodity and county, 1991 and trends, annual rpt, S4655–1

Nebraska agricultural production, marketing, and finances, by commodity and/or county, and farms and acreage, 1991 and trends, annual rpt, S4835–1

Nevada agricultural production, marketing, and finances, by county and commodity, and farms and acreage, 1992 and trends, annual rpt, S5010–1

New Jersey agricultural production, marketing, and finances, by commodity and/or county, and farms and acreage, 1986-91, annual rpt, S5350–1

New Mexico agricultural production, marketing, and finances, by commodity and county, with farms and acreage, 1991 and trends, annual rpt, S5530–1

New York State agricultural production, marketing, and finances, by commodity and/or county, and farms and acreage, 1992 and trends, annual rpt, S5700–1

Wheat

North Carolina agricultural production, marketing, and finances, by commodity and county, 1991 and trends, annual rpt, S5885–1

North Dakota agricultural production and marketing, by commodity and county, and farm finances, 1992 and trends, annual rpt, U3600–1

Ohio agricultural production, marketing, and finances, by commodity and county, with farms and acreage, 1990-91 and trends, annual rpt, S6240–1

Oklahoma agricultural production, marketing, and finances, by commodity and county, 1992 and trends, annual rpt, S6405–1

Oregon agricultural production, marketing, and finances, by commodity and/or county, with farms and acreage, 1991 and trends, annual rpt, S6575–1

Pennsylvania agricultural production, marketing, and finances, by county and commodity, and farms and acreage, 1992 and trends, annual rpt, S6760–1

South Carolina agricultural production and finances, by commodity and county, 1991-92 and trends, annual rpt, U1075–3

South Dakota agricultural production, marketing, and finances, by commodity and county, and farms and acreage, 1992 and trends, annual rpt, S7280–1

Tennessee agricultural production and marketing, by commodity and county, with farms, acreage, and farm value, 1992 and trends, annual rpt, S7460–1

Texas agricultural production, marketing, and finances, by commodity and county, and farms and farmland, 1991 and trends, annual rpt series, S7630–1

Utah agricultural production, marketing, and finances, by commodity and county, with farms and acreage, 1992 and trends, annual rpt, S7800–1

Washington State agricultural production, marketing, and finances, by commodity and/or county, 1992 and trends, annual rpt, S8328–1

West Virginia agricultural production, marketing, and finances, by commodity or county, 1991 and trends, annual rpt, S8510–1

Wisconsin agricultural production, marketing, and finances, by commodity and county, and farms, acreage, and sales, 1992 and trends, annual rpt, S8680–1

Wyoming agricultural production, marketing, and finances, by county and/or commodity, and farms, acreage, and value, 1992 and trends, annual rpt, S8860–1

Wheelchairs

see Prosthetics and orthotics

White collar workers

see Executives and managers

see Professional and technical workers

White House

Public visits to White House, 1987-91, annual rpt, S1535–3.3

Wholesale membership clubs

see Consumer cooperatives

Wholesale Price Index

see Producer Price Index

Wholesale trade

Air conditioning/refrigeration wholesaler sales trend and outlook, by region, quarterly 1992-93, annual rpt, C1800–1

Auto aftermarket jobber wholesale buying patterns, including product sources and use of distribution groups, 1993 article, C2150–10.504

Auto aftermarket warehouse distributor membership, for 15 programmed distribution groups, 1993 article, C2150–10.505

Autos (used), wholesale and retail sales of franchised new car dealerships, 1982-92, annual rpt, A7330–1

Beverage distribution operations and costs, including fleet size, maintenance, and purchase plans, 1992 survey, annual rpt, C0125–3.2

Book publishing industry financial and operating data, by publisher type and size, and subject category, 1991 and trends, annual rpt, A3274–2

Business executives expectations for coming qtr, attitudes on key indicators, with trends and data by census div, quarterly rpt, C3150–4

Business failures and liabilities, by detailed industry, cause, length of operation, and location, 1991-92 and trends, annual rpt, C3150–8

Construction machinery distributor sales indexes, and inventory-sales ratio, weekly rpt monthly table, C5800–2

Consumer electronics product sales, trade, and industry devs, by product type, 1970s-92, annual rpt, A4725–4

Drug wholesale company revenues, market shares, and operating ratios, for 7 major firms, 1992-93, article, C3950–1.511

Electrical equipment sales and marketing, special articles and features, monthly rpt, C4725–5

Electrical equipment wholesaler market conditions, by geographic area, 1992 annual article, C4725–5.501

Electrical equipment wholesalers, sales, employment, and facility size, top 250 companies, 1992, annual article, C4725–5.506

Electronics industry factory sales and shipments, foreign trade, and operating data, by product category, 1980s-92, annual rpt, A4725–1

Executive compensation and components, by industry div and major manufacturing group, 1991, annual rpt, R4105–19

Financial ratios and performance, for over 350 SIC 4-digit industries, FY88-92, annual rpt, A6400–3

Food marketers financial and operating data, by company size and region, 1991-92, annual rpts, A4950–5

Food store industry structure, sales, operations, and business outlook, by type of store, 1993 annual rpt, C5225–1.505

Fuel oil dealer operations, with heating and cooling equipment services, by region, 1992 annual survey, C4680–2

Home improvement industry sales and operations, for top distributors, cooperatives, and marketing organizations, 1991-92, annual feature, C5150–6.502

Hospital pharmacy wholesale purchasing, 1991, annual survey, B5165–3

Household appliance factory unit shipments, by product type, 1992 and trends, annual rpt, A3350–4

Index by Subjects and Names

Household appliance industry shipments, by product type, 1991-98, annual articles, C2000–1.503

Household appliance sales by distributors, by product type and State, 1992, annual rpt, A3350–2

Industrial distributors activities including inventory mgmt, materials handling, and traffic, monthly rpt, C2150–1

Jewelry and watch manufacturing and marketing trends, new product dev, prices, trade, and related indicators, monthly rpt, C2150–7

Jewelry industry statistics on sales, marketing, trade, and employment, with customer characteristics, 1993 annual almanac, C2150–7.509

Liquor consumption, trade, and sales volume or shipments, by product type and State, 1991 and trends, annual rpt, A4650–3

Liquor market statistics, including sales, consumption, trade, distillery operations, and govtl info, with data by company, brand, and location, 1992 and trends, annual rpt, C4775–1

Motorcycle wholesale sales, by type and for top 10 States, 1987-91, annual rpt, A6485–1.1

Operating and financial composite ratios for corporations, with establishments and receipts, for approx 200 industries, by asset size, FY90, annual rpt, C7800–1

Paper distribution industry business activity, sales and performance trends, and mgmt devs, monthly rpt, A8140–3

Security equipment dealer purchasing from distributors, by type of equipment and company size, 1992 survey, article, C1850–13.509

Statistical profiles of 50 States and DC, general data, 1993 annual almanac, C4712–1

Steel service center business conditions and outlook, monthly survey, A8990–2

Wine market statistics, including sales, production, trade, and consumer characteristics, with data by company, brand, and geographic area, 1992 and trends, annual rpt, C4775–2

State and local:

Alabama statistical abstract, general data, 1992 recurring rpt, U5680–2.18

Arizona economic condition, including population, employment and earnings, and business activity, by industry and locality, 1985-93, semiannual rpt, U5850–1.1

Arizona statistical abstract, general data, 1993 recurring rpt, U5850–2.21

Arkansas socioeconomic trends, by MSA and/or county, 1993 annual rpt, U5935–1

California milk sales, by sector, type of trade, and container type and size, 1992 and trends, annual rpt, S0850–1.6

California statistical abstract, general data, 1992 annual rpt, S0840–2.11

Florida statistical abstract, general data, 1992 annual rpt, U6660–1.16

Georgia statistical abstract, general data, 1992-93 biennial rpt, U6730–1.7

Hawaii data book, general data, 1992 annual rpt, S2090–1.23

Illinois statistical abstract, general data, 1992 annual rpt, U6910–2

Kansas statistical abstract, general data, 1991/92 annual rpt, U7095–2.8

Kentucky economic statistics, general data, 1993 annual rpt, S3104–1.3

Maine employment in trade, utilities, and transportation SIC 2-digit industries, by detailed occupation, 2nd qtr 1991, triennial rpt, S3465–1.25

Maryland statistical abstract, general data, 1993-94 biennial rpt, S3605–1.5

Mississippi statistical abstract, general data, 1992 annual rpt, U3255–4.5

Mississippi wholesale businesses, sales, and tax collected, by industry group, city, and county, FY92, annual rpt, S4435–1

New Hampshire wholesale and retail trade employment, by SIC 2-digit industry and detailed occupation, 1991, triennial rpt, S5205–2.26

New Mexico and US retail, wholesale, and service industry establishments, sales, payroll, and employment, 1977 and 1987, U7980–1.502

New Mexico economic trends and outlook, by industry div, 1982-92, annual article, U7980–1.503

New York State business activity indicators, quarterly rpt, S5735–2

New York State statistical yearbook, general data, 1992 annual rpt, U5100–1.2

North Carolina employment in trade, transportation, communications, utilities, govt, and education, by detailed occupation, 2nd qtr 1991, triennial rpt, S5917–5.2

Pennsylvania statistical abstract, general data, 1992 recurring rpt, U4130–6.2

South Carolina statistical abstract, general data, 1993 annual rpt, S7125–1.3

Tennessee statistical abstract, general data, 1992/93 annual rpt, U8710–2.7

Texas trade, transportation, and public utilities employment, by SIC 2- and 3-digit industry and detailed occupation, 2nd qtr 1991, triennial survey rpt, S7675–1.31

Utah statistical abstract, general data, 1993 triennial rpt, U8960–1.14

see also Agricultural marketing

see also Auctions

see also Industrial distribution

see also Warehouses

see also under By Industry in the "Index by Categories"

Wicherski, Marlene

"Characteristics of Graduate Departments of Psychology, 1990/91", A2620–3

"1991 Doctorate Employment Survey", A2620–4

"1992/93 Faculty Salaries in Graduate Departments of Psychology", A2620–1

Widows and widowers

Quality of life indicators for widows of older men surveyed in 1966, by race, 1990 survey, U3780–9

see also Old-Age, Survivors, Disability, and Health Insurance

see also under By Marital Status in the "Index by Categories"

Widstrand, Carl

"Population and Water Resources: A Delicate Balance", R8750–2.57

Wild, Cathleen

"Corporate Volunteer Programs: Benefits to Business", R4105–78.26

Wilderness areas

World land area and use, including wilderness areas, by country, 1988, biennial rpt, R9455–1.5

State and local:

Arizona statistical abstract, general data, 1993 recurring rpt, U5850–2.8

Nevada wilderness areas and recommended acreage, 1992 biennial rpt, S5005–1.9

Wildlife and wildlife conservation

World wildlife habitat areas and losses, protection measures, and trade in wildlife products, by country, 1992/93 biennial rpt, R9455–1.6

State and local:

Arizona State initiative defining unlawful methods of taking wildlife, election results by county, 1992, biennial rpt, S0520–1

Arizona statistical abstract, general data, 1993 recurring rpt, U5850–2.8

Colorado income tax return checkoff contributions, for selected causes, FY92 and trends, annual rpt, S1075–1.3

Delaware court caseloads and dispositions, by type of court and case, and by county, with judicial dept finances, FY92, annual rpt, S1360–1

Kansas court caseloads and disposition, by type of court and case, and location, FY92, annual rpt, S3035–1

Montana income tax checkoffs, by purpose, 1987-91, biennial rpt, S4750–1.1

Nevada wild horse and burro inventories, territories, removals, and adoptions, 1990 and trends, biennial rpt, S5005–1.9

Pennsylvania game and sport fish released by species and county, 1992 recurring rpt, U4130–6.8

Virginia income tax return checkoff contributions to wildlife program, 1990, annual rpt, S8305–1.1

Wisconsin Blue Book, general data, 1993-94 biennial rpt, S8780–1.2

see also Birds and bird conservation

see also Endangered species

see also Hunting and trapping

see also Wildlife refuges

see also Zoological parks

Wildlife refuges

State and local:

Hawaii data book, general data, 1992 annual rpt, S2090–1.7

Utah payments from Fed Govt wildlife refuge revenue sharing program, for 3 counties, 1991, article, U8960–2.502

Wilkie, James W.

"Statistical Abstract of Latin America", U6250–1

Williamson, Michelle

"Demographic State of the State: A Report to the Governor and Legislature on Commuting Patterns for Oklahoma from the 1990 Census", S6416–2

Wills and testaments

Charitable contributions, by type of donor and recipient, 1992 and trends, annual rpt, A0700–1

Charitable contributions in wills, bequest or gift characteristics by type of donation, 1993 article, C2176–1.518

Trust fund admin and estate planning, analyses of trust portfolios, investments, and economic outlook, monthly rpt, C2425–2

see also Estate tax

see also Probate courts and cases

Wilmington, Del.

Court caseloads and dispositions, by type of case, FY91-92, annual rpt, S1360–1

Labor force by employment status, monthly rpt, S1405–2

Population by age and sex, 1990-2020, recurring rpt, S1375–3

Vital statistics, including births, deaths by cause, and marriages and dissolutions, by demographic characteristics, 1990, annual rpt, S1385–2

see also under By City in the "Index by Categories"

Wilshire Associates

State pension fund assets as percent of projected and accumulated benefit obligations, by State, 1993 article, B8500–2.519

State pension fund shortfalls, for 9 States with underfunded plans, 1993 article, C5800–7.540

State pension funds with largest surpluses and deficits, for selected top States, 1993 article, C2710–2.519

Wilson, Pamela

"Current Statistics on White Collar Employees", A1570–1

Wilson, Reginald

"Minorities in Higher Education: 11th Annual Status Report", A1410–10

Wind

see Storms

see Wind energy

Wind energy

State and local:

Hawaii data book, general data, 1992 annual rpt, S2090–1.17

Windfall profit tax

Federal receipts under the windfall profit tax, quarterly 1980-85, periodic basic data book, A2575–14.3

Oil and gas industry expenditures for exploration, dev, and production, 1991 and trends, annual survey rpt, A2575–20

Windows

see Glass and glass industry

Wine and winemaking

Consumption and sales of beverages, by type, leading company, and brand, 1992 and trends, annual rpt, C4775–1.4

Consumption of wine compared to distilled spirits and beer, by State, 1991, annual rpt, A4650–3

Exports of farm products, by detailed commodity and country of destination, US and California, 1991, annual rpt, B9520–1

Imports from 5 countries, and consumer purchase outlets, 1993 article, A8955–1.503

Market statistics, including sales, production, trade, and consumer characteristics, with data by company, brand, and geographic area, 1992 and trends, annual rpt, C4775–2

Retail prices for selected consumer items in approx 300 cities, quarterly rpt, A0150–1

Sales and consumer expenditures, for food store products by type, 1991-92, annual feature, C4655–1.510

Sales and market shares for top 24 wine companies, and imports, 1990-92, recurring article, C2710–1.544

Wine and winemaking

Sales, consumption, and marketing devs for beverage industry, monthly rpt, C0125–2

Sales volume shares by retail outlet type, for approx 300 food, drug, and other product categories, 1993 annual feature, C4655–1.504

Shipments and per capita consumption of alcoholic beverages, by type, census div, and State, 1981-91, annual rpt, A3455–1.4

Supermarket sales by detailed product type, 1992 and trends, annual feature, C5225–1.507

State and local:

Arkansas fruit tree and vine inventory, by variety and age, 1992, annual rpt, U5920–1

California wine, beer, and distilled spirits consumption, and excise tax collections, FY35-92, annual rpt, S0835–1.5

Michigan agricultural production, marketing, and finances, by commodity or county, 1987-91, annual rpt, S3950–1

Nebraska beer, alcohol, and wine gallonage and tax revenues, 1991 and trends, annual rpt, S4950–1.3

New York State grape consumption in wine and juice processing, 1983-92, annual rpt, S5700–1

Oregon wine grape acreage and production, and wineries, by variety and county, 1990-91, annual rpt, S6575–1

Washington State wine grape production and prices, by variety, 1988-92, annual rpt, S8328–1

Winter sports

Participation in 53 sports, by demographic characteristics, State, and census div, 1992, annual rpt series, A8485–3

see also Skiing

Winterle, Mary J.

"Work Force Diversity: Corporate Challenges, Corporate Responses", R4105–78.22

Wiretapping

see Electronic surveillance

Wirthlin Group

Health care professional views on managing overuse of high-technology patient procedures, 1993 survey article, A1865–1.522

Health care reform priorities of general public vs health professionals, including importance of ethics and alternative medicine, 1993 survey article, A1865–1.522

Wisconsin

Agricultural production, marketing, and finances, by commodity and county, with farms, acreage, and sales, 1992 and trends, annual rpt, S8680–1

Bank financial condition, by instn and city, with regulatory info, 1992 and trends, annual rpt, S8685–1

Correctional instn inmates, by criminal background and selected characteristics, series, S8692–1

Crime rates compared with incarceration rates, for California, Wisconsin, and Minnesota, 1970s-90, A7575–1.12

Crimes and arrests, by offense, offender characteristics, county, and local agency, with law enforcement employment and assaults on officers, 1992 and trends, annual rpt, S8771–1

Economic indicators, including employment and earnings by industry group, monthly rpt, S8750–1

Elementary and secondary school enrollment, staff, costs, and State aid, by school district, 1992/93 and trends, annual rpt, S8795–2

Govt financial condition, including revenues by source, expenditures by function and object, and fund balances, FY92, annual rpt, S8675–3

Govt financial condition, including revenues by source, expenditures by function and object, and fund balances, FY93, annual rpt, S8675–2

Insurance industry financial and underwriting data, by company and line of coverage, with regulatory info, 1992, annual rpt, S8755–1

Library operations and finances, by library type, instn, and location, 1992, annual rpt, S8795–1

Markets with daily newspapers, demographic and economic info by geographic area, US and Canada, 1993 annual rpt, C3250–1

Medical malpractice insurance State joint underwriting assn (JUA) financial condition, for 11 States, 1991, annual rpt, A0375–1

Population, by age, sex, and county, with components of change, quinquennially 1990-2020, recurring rpt, S8675–4

Savings and loan assns (State-chartered) financial condition, by instn, 1992 and trends, annual rpt, S8807–1

Statistical Blue Book, detailed govtl, social, and economic reference info and data, 1993-94 biennial rpt, S8780–1

Statistical profiles of 50 States and DC, general data, 1993 annual almanac, C4712–1

Traffic accidents, fatalities, and injuries, by circumstances, location, vehicle type, and driver and victim characteristics, 1992 and trends, annual rpt, S8815–1

Utility and transportation regulatory agency activities, scope of jurisdiction, finances, and employees, by agency, 1991/92 annual rpt, A7015–2

Vital statistics, including population, births, deaths by cause, and marriages and dissolutions, by county and demographic characteristics, 1991 and trends, annual rpt, S8715–4

see also Milwaukee, Wis.

see also under By City and By County in the "Index by Categories"

see also under By State in the "Index by Categories"

Withholding tax

State tax revenue from personal, corporate, and sales taxes, by State and region, quarterly rpt, U5085–1

State and local:

Arizona tax revenues by source, tax rates, and disbursements to local areas, FY92 and trends, annual rpt, S0515–1

Arkansas income tax withholding fund finances, FY91-92, biennial rpt, S0780–1

Hawaii tax collections and allocations, by type, for State and counties, FY91-92 and trends, annual rpt, S2120–1

Ohio employer withholding and individual tax returns and collections, FY91-92, annual rpt, S6390–1.3

Index by Subjects and Names

Wolff, Edward N.

"Rich Get Increasingly Richer: Latest Data on Household Wealth During the 1980s", R4700–17

Women

Artificial sweetener use correlated with weight changes, by weight class, 1992 article, B6045–1.501

Black children living in female-headed families, with comparisons to whites, selected years 1959-91, R3840–21

Bowling (women's) assn membership and league activities, by city, State, and country, 1991/92, annual rpt, A9415–1

Breast cancer deaths correlated with occupation, by race, 1979-87, article, A2623–1.511

Business grad school programs for executives, female share of enrollment in 20 instns, 1993 article, C5800–7.552

Business school female faculty salaries by academic rank, 1992/93 annual rpt, A0605–1

Catholic public opinion on ordination of women as priests, 1974-93 surveys, R8780–1.510

Child support/alimony recipient share of female-headed families, 1989, annual rpt, R3832–1

Clothing (women's) discount store sales volume for 4 special sizes, by product type, 1st half 1992-93, article, C5150–3.521

Clothing (women's) with imprinted designs, market shares by retail outlet type and design category, Apr 1992-Mar 1993, article, C5150–3.513

Clothing (women's jeans) market shares for top 8 and all other manufacturers, 1993 article, C5150–3.518

Clothing (women's sleepwear) sales volume, by product type, 1st half 1992-93, article, C5150–3.521

Contraceptive (oral) use correlation with risks of ovarian, endometrial, cervical, and breast cancers, 1993 article, A5160–1.502

Contraceptive implant vs oral method user characteristics, Aug-Dec 1991 Baltimore study, article, A5160–1.506

Contraceptive use and perceived effectiveness by women, by method, marital status, and pregnancy exposure, 1987 and 1992 surveys, article, A5160–1.505

Corporate boards of directors composition, compensation, and practices, by industry sector, 1991 and trends, annual survey rpt, B5000–3

Corporate boards of directors with women and minority members, and board membership by sex and race-ethnicity, 1991/92, B4490–2.36

Cosmetics and fragrances shopping patterns, with views on store attributes, by outlet type, 1993 survey, annual feature, C5150–2.516

Deaths of women from AIDS and related conditions, 1988, article, A2623–1.501

Dental school applications, enrollment, grads, and tuition/fees, by instn, 1992 and trends, annual rpt, A1475–4.2

Dental school female enrollment, by level, 1991/92-1992/93, annual rpt, A1475–3.1

Index by Subjects and Names

Women

Developing countries family planning and child survival efforts, by country and selected demographic characteristics, 1980s-90, R8720–1

Diabetes incidence correlated with smoking status, 1976-88 study, article, A2623–1.504

Doctoral degree recipient characteristics, including citizenship status, source of support, field of study, and instn, 1990/91 and trends, annual rpt, R6000–7

Drugs under dev for selected diseases affecting older adults and women, 1989-93, A1865–1.519

EC public support of feminist goals, correlation with social characteristics, by sex, 1983 survey, article, A0610–1.502

Elected women officials, by level of govt and State, various years 1985-92, annual rpt, S7125–1.9

Elected women officials in public offices, by State, 1993 annual almanac, C4712–1

Engineering degrees awarded, by State, instn, and field, with detail for women, minorities, and foreign students, 1991/92, annual rpt, A0685–1

Engineering program enrollment, by instn, field, and State, with detail for women, minorities, and foreign students, fall 1992, annual rpt, A0685–2

Europe public opinion on quality of life for men vs women, for 9 countries and 3 Soviet Union Republics, 1991 survey, C8915–8.1, C8915–9

Family planning and fertility trends, and contraceptives effectiveness, safety, and availability, by method, series, U2520–1

Family planning devs worldwide, with data on fertility, contraceptive use, and family size preferences, quarterly rpt, A5160–6

Federal judgeship presidential appointments, with detail for women, blacks, and Hispanics, 1963-92, annual rpt, C2500–2

Golf participation of women, including share of total and professional golfers, and course pros/directors by sex, 1993 article, C5800–7.524

Grants made by women's funds, and spending distribution by purpose, 1985-92, article, C2176–1.514

Health care preventive practices, including frequency of Pap smears, mammograms, and breast self-exams, 1992 and trends, annual survey rpt, C8111–2

Health research results, including data on women's use of health services and incidence of selected health problems, 1993 articles, A2623–1.503

Higher education administrator views on representation of women among staff and students, 1993 survey, article, C2175–1.529

Higher education administrator views on women's presence in various positions, and steps taken to improve status of women, 1993 annual survey, A1410–1.38

Higher education enrollment shares for women, by State, fall 1991, annual rpt, C2175–1.531

Higher education freshmen attitudes and characteristics, degree and career plans, and financial aid sources, by sex and instn type, fall 1992, annual survey, U6215–1

Higher education intercollegiate women's sports participation, and scholarship recommendations of Natl Collegiate Athletic Assn gender equity task force, by sport, 1993 rpt, A7440–6

Hispanic American elected female officials, by govt level, 1992 annual directory, A6844–1

Hispanic American women's alcohol consumption compared to acculturation levels and other demographic characteristics, 1982-84, article, A2623–1.508

House of Representatives women members elected in Nov 1992, by marital status, own and children's ages, abortion views, and political party, 1992 article, C5800–7.504

Housing issues for women, with data on household composition, tenure, and characteristics, 1992, A8657–5

Jeweler views on women's jewelry purchasing trends, 1993 survey article, C2150–7.510

Latin America land reform program, percent of beneficiaries who are women, by country, 1992 annual rpt, U6250–1.2

Latin America women's suffrage effect on voter participation, by country, 1992 annual report, U6250–1.9

Law school enrollment, degrees conferred, and staff, with detail for women, by instn, 1992/93 and trends, annual rpt, A0970–1

Medical school total and women students and grads, decennially 1960/61-1990/91 and 1991/92, annual fact book, A1275–1.1

Middle East married women age 15-49 use of contraception, by country, various years 1987-92, R8750–2.59

Military personnel by race-ethnicity, total and women, FY90, article, R8750–1.504

Municipal govt composition, including percent of city council members who are women, by population size, census div, and location and govt type, 1991, A5800–1.1

Nonprofit foundation involvement of women and minorities, series, A9405–1

Obesity and related activity and weight-loss indicators in women age 18-30, by race, 1985-86, article, A2623–1.502

Officials (women) in elective office, news and statistics, series, U4510–4

Officials (women) in Federal, State, and local govt offices, fact sheet series, U4510–1

Opinions of women on income vs cost of living, and general concerns, 1992 feature, C4215–1.502

Osteopathy college enrollment, student and faculty characteristics, and finances, 1992/93 and trends, annual rpt, A0620–1

Personal care product use and shopping patterns, with preferred outlets and brands, 1993 survey and trends, annual feature, C5150–2.515

Political action committees (PACs) funds raised and candidates supported, for 42 women's PACs, 1992, U4510–4.4

Popularity ranking of selected world figures, 1991-92, R8780–1.506

Popularity ratings of selected world figures, 1991-92, annual Gallup Poll, C4040–1.506

Public interest in news items concerning Clinton Admin decision to allow women military personnel to serve in combat roles, Apr/May 1993 survey, C8915–1.503

Sexual behavior and disease risk among women, including data on multiple partners and condom use, by selected characteristics, 1988, article, A5160–1.501

Sexual partners number for women age 15-44, by marital status, 1993 rpt, A5160–10

Sexually transmitted disease prevention using various contraceptive methods, review of research results, 1992 article, A2623–1.501

Shoe sales by retail outlet type, for women's and men's shoes, 1991-92, article, C5150–3.515

Shoes (women's) sales volume by retail outlet type, 1990-92, article, C5150–3.511

Smoking patterns among women age 18-44, by race and age group, 1987 survey, article, A2623–1.511

Southern States elected women officials, State and local, for 8 States, 1985, 1988, and 1992, annual rpt, U3255–4.13

Southern States higher education enrollment, by type of instn, with detail for women and minorities, by State, 1978-92, biennial fact book, A8945–1.2

State legislature female member shares, by State, 1993, semiannual rpt, B8500–1.1

Supermarket promotions use by women, for 6 types of promotions, 1988 and 1992, survey article, C1200–4.507

Theological seminary enrollment in Canada and US, with detail for women and minorities, 1992 and trends, annual rpt, C0105–1

Topless sunbathing by women on public beaches, public opinion on legality, July/Aug 1992 Gallup Poll, C4040–1.502

Travel patterns among women, including private and public transport use by trip purpose, 1990, annual rpt, A0865–1.3

State and local:

California and US women of childbearing age, by age group, 1988-90, annual rpt, S0865–1

Florida women elected officials, State and local, 1985, 1988, and 1992, annual rpt, U6660–1.21

New York State women age 60/over, by county, 1990, annual rpt, U5100–1.1

Pennsylvania female-headed households with children below poverty, by county and municipality, 1989, census rpt, C1595–15

South Carolina female population age 15-44, by race, 1971-90, annual rpt, S7175–1

Utah married women, and marriage and divorce data, 1960s-90, annual rpt, S7835–2

Utah women's use of mammography, breast exams, and Pap smear tests, by respondent characteristics, 1991, annual rpt, S7835–3

see also Families and households
see also Fertility
see also Maternity
see also Maternity benefits
see also Sex discrimination

Women

see also Teenage pregnancy
see also Women-owned businesses
see also Women's employment
see also under By Sex in the "Index by Categories"

Women-owned businesses

Hispanic-owned high-technology company characteristics, including number owned by women, for top 50 firms, 1992, annual article, C4575–1.510

State and local:

Florida statistical abstract, general data, 1992 annual rpt, U6660–1.9

Hawaii data book, general data, 1992 annual rpt, S2090–1.15

Kansas statistical abstract, general data, 1991/92 annual rpt, U7095–2.8

Kentucky economic statistics, general data, 1993 annual rpt, S3104–1.1

Pennsylvania statistical abstract, general data, 1992 recurring rpt, U4130–6.2

Women's employment

Auto dealership service dept operations and profit outlook, including employment of women mechanics, 1993 annual survey, article, C2710–3.537

Black American labor force and employment data, with comparisons to whites, 1970s-91, annual compilation, C6775–2.6

Business grad school women's share of tenured and tenure-track faculty, for 6 schools with highest and lowest shares, 1992 article, C5800–7.506

Catholic charity agency female personnel, 1991 and trends, annual rpt, A3810–1

Chemical and related industries production, finances, operating ratios, employment, and trade, by country, company, and chemical, 1980s-92, annual feature, A1250–1.530

Chemist salaries and employment, by employee and employer characteristics, Mar 1993 and trends, annual article, A1250–1.532

Child health and well-being indicators, with selected household characteristics, by State, 1993 annual rpt, R3832–1

College grad recruiting practices and hiring trends, with data on starting salaries and layoffs, by type of employer, 1992/93 annual survey rpt, U3130–1

Communications industries conditions for women, including opportunities, sexual harassment, and income compared to men, Dec 1992 survey, article, C2710–1.528

Corporate employee transfers, and relocation policies, assistance, and costs, 1992, annual survey, B0600–1

Dental school faculty, support personnel, and staff characteristics, by instn, 1992/93, annual rpt, A1475–4.5

Doctoral degree women recipients employment plans, by race-ethnicity and employer type, 1991, annual rpt, R6000–7

Electronics industry factory sales and shipments, foreign trade, and operating data, by product category, 1980s-92, annual rpt, A4725–1

Elementary/secondary school superintendents personal and professional characteristics and views, 1992 survey rpt, A0775–5

Food (take-out) market characteristics, including employment status of female head of household, May 1992 survey, A8200–21

Food nutrition awareness and health concerns, including shopping and consumption patterns, by respondent characteristics, 1993 survey, annual rpt, A4950–36

Food service industry employee characteristics, and minority-owned establishments and sales, 1993 article, A8200–1.508

Geoscience faculty salaries by rank and for women, with data on minority faculty members, 1991/92 and trends, annual rpt, A1785–4

Govt employment of women, with data by race-ethnicity and State, series, U5090–1

Higher education instns, faculty, students, degrees, and finances, detailed data by State, 1993 annual rpt, C2175–1.531

Higher education president personal and professional characteristics, 1990 and trends, recurring rpt, A1410–12

Labor force and education data for women and minorities in professional fields, 1980s-91, with historical trends, recurring rpt, A3960–2

Labor force participation of women, by marital status, 1900-1990, B6045–1.503

Mexico, Tijuana female maquiladora worker characteristics and incidence of psychological problems, 1990 study, article, A2623–1.503

Mothers of children age 5/under labor force participation rates, by State and major city, 1990, annual rpt, R3840–11

Occupational group distribution of employed women, by race, 1980 and trends, article, A8510–1.1

Physicians (female) by detailed specialty, and location, 1992 and trends, annual rpt, A2200–3.1

Professional women's employment, with detail by race-ethnicity and for 3 occupations, 1990 and trends, article, R8750–1.511

Public broadcasting full-time employment, with detail for women and minorities, by job category, 1977-92, recurring rpt, R4250–1.23

Public opinion on social, political, and economic issues, detailed data, 1972-91 surveys, annual rpt, U6395–1

Science and math elementary/secondary education, including student and teacher characteristics, and requirements, by State, 1991/92, biennial rpt, A4355–3

Shoe industry production, employment, trade, marketing, and related data, by SIC 2- to 5-digit code or product type, 1992 annual rpt, A4957–1.2

Small business views on employment trends for women, minorities, immigrants, and the disabled, and related mgmt issues, 1993 survey article, C4687–1.503

State social, economic, and govtl indicators, with rankings, 1993 semiannual rpt, B8500–1.2

Supermarket shopper practices, attitudes, and expenditures, by respondent characteristics, 1993 and trends, annual survey rpt, A4950–3

Index by Subjects and Names

Surgeons in residence and practice, with female and foreign medical grads by specialty and type of activity, 1993 annual fact book, A1275–1.1

Teachers at preschool, elementary, and secondary levels, percent who are women, for selected OECD member countries, 1980s, A1600–4

Trends in women's employment and earnings, with comparisons to men, and detail by occupation and worker characteristics, 1990s and trends, annual rpt, A1570–2

Unemployment insurance trends, including data on unemployment, worker characteristics, coverage, benefits, and State govt finances, 1940s-90, R9260–18

White-collar work force trends, including employment, earnings, and unionization, with data by occupation, sex, and educational attainment, 1990s and trends, annual rpt, A1570–1

World labor force participation of women, by country, 1990, biennial rpt, R9455–1.5

State and local:

Arkansas Census of Population and Housing detailed findings, 1990, U5935–7

California Census of Population and Housing detailed findings, 1990, S0840–9

California statistical abstract, general data, 1992 annual rpt, S0840–2.3

Colorado job service applicant characteristics, FY93 annual planning rpt, S1040–3.2

Florida statistical abstract, general data, 1992 annual rpt, U6660–1.6

Kentucky labor force planning rpt, including population and labor force characteristics, and employment by industry, 1991 and trends, annual rpt, S3140–3

Louisiana job service openings and applicants, and characteristics of Job Training Partnership Act target population and insured unemployed, 1993 annual planning rpt, S3320–1.2

Maine Census of Population and Housing summary findings, by local area, 1990, S3465–9

Maine female labor force, employment, and unemployment, monthly rpt, S3465–2

Michigan labor force planning rpt, including employment by industry, and characteristics of Job Training Partnership Act eligible population, 1993 annual rpt, S3980–1

Mississippi labor force planning rpt, including population, employment, and characteristics of unemployed and disadvantaged, 1993 annual rpt, S4345–1

Montana employment and unemployment, earnings, and hours, by location and/or industry, quarterly rpt, S4710–1

Montana female employment by industry div and county, 1993-94 annual planning rpt, S4710–3

Nevada female and total employment for 25 occupations with highest and lowest shares of female workers, 1990, article, S5040–1.503

Nevada statistical abstract, general data, 1992 biennial rpt, S5005–1.6

New Jersey Census of Population and Housing detailed findings, by county, 1990, S5425–19

Index by Subjects and Names — Work conditions

New York State employment, earnings, and hours, by county, selected metro area, and industry group, monthly rpt, S5775–1

Pennsylvania Census of Population and Housing detailed findings, with selected data by county and municipality, 1990, U4130–13

Pennsylvania employment distribution by sex and occupational group, and women shares of employment in selected occupations, 1980 and/or 1990, article, S6845–1.502

Pennsylvania labor force planning rpt, including population characteristics, employment and job openings by industry and occupation, and income trends, FY92 annual rpt, S6845–3

Rhode Island Census of Population and Housing detailed findings, by county and municipality, 1990, S6930–9

Rhode Island labor force planning rpt, including population, employment by industry, job openings, and characteristics of insured unemployed, 1993 annual rpt, S6980–3

South Carolina employment, earnings, and hours, by industry group and locality, monthly rpt, S7155–2

South Carolina labor force planning rpt, detailed data on employment, hours, wages, turnover, and characteristics of job service applicants, 1992 annual rpt, S7155–3.2

Utah women's share of employment in selected occupations, 1970, 1980, and 1990, article, S7820–3.508

Vermont labor force by employment status, and job service openings and applicant characteristics, 1993 annual planning rpt, S8025–2.2

West Virginia employment, unemployment, hours, and earnings, with job service activities, monthly rpt, S8534–1

Wyoming women's employment by industry div, 1990-92, article, S8895–1.506

see also Women-owned businesses

see also under By Sex in the "Index by Categories"

Wood

see Lumber industry and products

Wood chemicals

see Gum and wood chemicals

Wood fuel

State and local:

Florida statistical abstract, general data, 1992 annual rpt, U6660–1.15

New York State statistical yearbook, general data, 1992 annual rpt, U5100–1.15

Wool and wool trade

Consumption and trade by type of fiber and product, 1988-92, annual survey, C3460–1.511

Exports of farm products, by detailed commodity and country of destination, US and California, 1991, annual rpt, B9520–1

Fiber Organon, detailed monthly and annual data on industry production, consumption, and trade, by fiber and fabric type, monthly rpt, C3460–1

Latin America statistical abstract, general data by country, 1992 annual rpt, U6250–1.24, U6250–1.25

Production by world region and country, and consumption and trade, 1950s-92, annual article, C3460–1.502

Production, consumption, stocks, trade, and prices for approx 100 basic commodities, including by country and producing State, commodity yearbook for 1993, C2400–1, C2400–2

Textile mill consumption of manufactured fibers, cotton, and wool, by country, 1989-91, annual feature, C3460–1.503

World demand for wool, 1988-92, annual rpt, C3460–1.508, C3460–1.509

State and local:

Alaska agricultural production and marketing, by district and commodity, 1960s-92, annual rpt, U5750–1

Arizona agricultural production, marketing, and finances, by commodity and county, 1988-92, annual rpt, U5830–1

California livestock production and marketing, with comparisons to US, 1983-92, annual rpt, S0850–1.2

Colorado agricultural production, marketing, and finances, by commodity and/or county, with farms and acreage, 1992 and trends, annual rpt, S0985–1

Illinois agricultural production, marketing, and finances, by county or commodity, and farms and farmland, 1991 and trends, annual rpt, S2390–1

Kansas agricultural production, marketing, and finances, by county and/or commodity, and farm acreage and value, 1992 and trends, annual rpt, S2915–1

Kentucky agricultural production, marketing, and finances, by commodity and county; and farms, acreage, and value; 1992 and trends, annual rpt, S3085–1

Louisiana agricultural production, marketing, and finances, by commodity or parish, 1985-91, annual rpt, U2740–1

Michigan agricultural production, marketing, and finances, by commodity or county, 1987-91, annual rpt, S3950–1

Minnesota agricultural production, marketing, and finances, by county or commodity, and farms and acreage, 1992 and trends, annual rpt, S4130–1

Missouri agricultural production, marketing, and finances, by commodity and/or county, and farms and acreage, 1988-92, annual rpt, S4480–1

Montana agricultural production, marketing, and finances, by commodity and county, 1991 and trends, annual rpt, S4655–1

Nebraska agricultural production, marketing, and finances, by commodity and/or county, and farms and acreage, 1991 and trends, annual rpt, S4835–1

Nevada agricultural production, marketing, and finances, by county and commodity, and farms and acreage, 1992 and trends, annual rpt, S5010–1

New Jersey agricultural production, marketing, and finances, by commodity and/or county, and farms and acreage, 1986-91, annual rpt, S5350–1

New Mexico agricultural production, marketing, and finances, by commodity and county, with farms and acreage, 1991 and trends, annual rpt, S5530–1

New York State agricultural production, marketing, and finances, by commodity and/or county, and farms and acreage, 1992 and trends, annual rpt, S5700–1

North Dakota agricultural production and marketing, by commodity and county, and farm finances, 1992 and trends, annual rpt, U3600–1

Ohio agricultural production, marketing, and finances, by commodity and county, with farms and acreage, 1990-91 and trends, annual rpt, S6240–1

Oklahoma agricultural production, marketing, and finances, by commodity and county, 1992 and trends, annual rpt, S6405–1

Oregon agricultural production, marketing, and finances, by commodity and/or county, with farms and acreage, 1991 and trends, annual rpt, S6575–1

Pennsylvania agricultural production, marketing, and finances, by county and commodity, and farms and acreage, 1992 and trends, annual rpt, S6760–1

South Dakota agricultural production, marketing, and finances, by commodity and county, and farms and acreage, 1992 and trends, annual rpt, S7280–1

Tennessee agricultural production and marketing, by commodity and county, with farms, acreage, and farm value, 1992 and trends, annual rpt, S7460–1

Texas agricultural production, marketing, and finances, by commodity and county, and farms and farmland, 1991 and trends, annual rpt series, S7630–1

Utah agricultural production, marketing, and finances, by commodity and county, with farms and acreage, 1992 and trends, annual rpt, S7800–1

Vermont agricultural production, marketing, and finances, by commodity, with data on govt inspections and funding, 1989-90 biennial rpt, S7978–1

Washington State agricultural production, marketing, and finances, by commodity and/or county, 1992 and trends, annual rpt, S8328–1

West Virginia agricultural production, marketing, and finances, by commodity or county, 1991 and trends, annual rpt, S8510–1

Wisconsin agricultural production, marketing, and finances, by commodity and county, and farms, acreage, and sales, 1992 and trends, annual rpt, S8680–1

Wyoming agricultural production, marketing, and finances, by county and/or commodity, and farms, acreage, and value, 1992 and trends, annual rpt, S8860–1

Work conditions

Americans with Disabilities Act employment-related complaints filed with Equal Employment Opportunity Commission, for top 10 States, Mar 1993, article, C1200–5.511

Bartender views on day of the week when most job-related complaints are heard from patrons, 1993 survey feature, C1850–3.509

Cable TV system mgmt salaries by selected characteristics, and views on job satisfaction, Mar/Apr 1993 survey, articles, C1858–1.502

Catalog industry employee job satisfaction, by region, 1992, annual rpt, A4620–1.2

Coal industry personnel earnings and employment history, US and Canada, 1993 survey article, C5226–1.507

Communications industries conditions for women, including opportunities, sexual harassment, and income compared to men, Dec 1992 survey, article, C2710–1.528

Work conditions

Corporate executive job characteristics, series, B4490–2

Corporate personnel mgmt devs, including work force diversity, health care and family-related benefits, counseling services, and competitiveness, 1993 survey, B6850–6

Disabled worker complaint filings with Equal Employment Opportunity Commission under Americans with Disabilities Act, through Feb 1993, article, C5800–7.520

Diversity mgmt program effect on worker opinions concerning quality of work life, 1993 survey article, C1850–2.511

Elementary/secondary school superintendents personal and professional characteristics and views, 1992 survey rpt, A0775–5

Employee satisfaction with and views on importance of selected job aspects, 1973-92 surveys, article, C4687–1.501

Food/beverage manufacturing mgmt views on job responsibilities and satisfaction, and effect of affirmative action, by sex, 1992 survey, annual article, C2150–6.502

Health care professionals dissatisfaction with selected aspects of their jobs, 1992 survey, article, A1865–1.511

Hispanic American professional views on work conditions at own company, with ratings of regions and top 19-20 companies and industries, 1993 survey article, C4575–1.504

Industrial mgmt magazine reader views on job enjoyment and problems, 1992 survey article, C7000–3.501

Loyalty between companies and employees, views of industrial mgmt magazine readers, 1993 survey article, C7000–3.506

Occupational injuries/illnesses and fatalities, lost workdays, and employee views on workplace safety, with data by State, 1992 annual rpt, R8335–1.1

Personnel mgmt professional activities, job satisfaction, employer performance, and obstacles encountered, spring 1993 survey, A8907–2

Psychology doctoral degree recipient employment and demographic characteristics, and finances, 1990/91, biennial survey rpt, A2620–4

Public opinion on job satisfaction and related topics, May 1993 Gallup Poll, C4040–1.511

Public opinion on work-related issues, 1993 survey article, C5800–7.545

Researcher employment situation, including job satisfaction and employer characteristics, 1992 survey, annual article, C1850–6.505

Security equipment industry personnel income, education, work conditions, and activities, 1993 survey, annual article, C1850–13.510

Sexual harassment complaints received by Equal Employment Opportunity Commission, 1987-92, article, C1850–2.507

Veterinary practice nonowner associate job characteristics and attitudes, 1992 survey, article, C9480–1.505

see also Employee performance and appraisal

see also Job tenure

see also Occupational health and safety

Work incentive programs

Earnings and AFDC payment impact of 13 local work-welfare programs, 1993 article, A8510–1.1

State and local:

Arkansas human services dept finances and operations, including Medicaid payments by type of service, FY91 and trends, annual rpt, S0700–2.3

New Mexico self-support program participants and reimbursed expenses, with welfare savings, by county, monthly rpt quarterly feature, S5620–2

New York State AFDC and home relief recipients participating in employment service programs, by program, 1991, annual rpt, S5800–2.1

Work release

see Prison work programs

Work stoppages

Aerospace industry strikes, workers involved, and work-days idle, 1979-91, annual rpt, A0250–2.5

Auto assembly plant shutdowns, with production losses, by plant, weekly rpt, C2710–3

Canada, British Columbia Province paper industry strikes and capacity affected, by company and mill, 1992, annual rpt, C3975–5.2

Latin America statistical abstract, general data by country, 1992 annual rpt, U6250–1.13

Newspaper strikes impact on newsprint consumption, monthly rpt, A1630–4

Newspaper strikes impact on newsprint consumption, 1974-92, annual rpt, A1630–8

State and local:

Colorado labor disputants, monthly rpt, S1040–4

Delaware persons involved in work stoppages, monthly rpt, S1405–2

Hawaii data book, general data, 1992 annual rpt, S2090–1.12, S2090–1.22

Hawaii economic conditions, including employment, population, tourism, and construction, quarterly rpt, S2090–2

Maine statistical summary, general economic and social data, 1992 recurring rpt, S3434–1

Maine workers involved in labor-mgmt disputes, monthly rpt, S3465–2

Michigan public assistance applications approved and denied, and cases closed, by reason and county, monthly rpt quarterly tables, S4010–1

Montana workers involved in labor-mgmt disputes, quarterly rpt, S4710–1

Nevada labor force involved in work stoppages, quarterly rpt, S5040–1

New Hampshire workers involved in labor-mgmt disputes, monthly rpt, S5205–1

New York State statistical yearbook, general data, 1992 annual rpt, U5100–1.3

Oregon labor force and employment statistics, including data by industry, monthly rpt, S6592–1, S6615–2

Pennsylvania workers involved in labor disputes, monthly rpt, S6845–1

Rhode Island workers involved in labor disputes, Jan 1991-June 1993, annual planning rpt, S6980–3

Index by Subjects and Names

Washington State employment, earnings, and hours, by labor market area and industry group, monthly rpt, S8340–3

West Virginia workers involved in labor-mgmt disputes, monthly rpt, S8534–1

Wisconsin workers involved in labor disputes, monthly rpt, S8750–1

Work-study programs

Higher education freshmen attitudes and characteristics, degree and career plans, and financial aid sources, by sex and instn type, fall 1992, annual survey, U6215–1

Library/info science school part-time support staff, including students, by school, 1991/92, annual rpt, A3235–1.1

Southern States higher education student aid data, by State, 1990s and trends, biennial fact book, A8945–1.4

State and local:

Iowa postsecondary enrollment, degrees, staff, and finances, by instn, 1990/91, annual rpt, S2755–1

Minnesota postsecondary education finances, and enrollment by student characteristics, by type of school system, 1970s-93, biennial rpt, S4195–2.2

North Carolina higher education student costs, admissions, housing, and financial aid, by instn, 1992/93 annual rpt, U8013–1.3

Texas higher education student aid awards and recipients, by program and instn type, FY92, annual rpt, S7657–1.3

Utah higher education degrees, enrollment, staff, and finances, by public instn, with selected comparisons to instns in other States, 1993/94 annual rpt, S7895–2

Work training

see Employee development

see Job Training Partnership Act

see Manpower training programs

see Vocational education and training

Worker adjustment assistance

see Trade adjustment assistance

Worker incentives

see Employee bonuses and work incentives

Workers

see Agricultural labor

see Blue collar workers

see Clerical workers

see Employment and unemployment, general

see Employment and unemployment, specific industry

see Job tenure

see Labor supply and demand

see Migrant workers

see Production workers

see Professional and technical workers

see Sales workers

see Service workers

Workers compensation

Analysis of workers compensation laws, including coverage, benefits, and other info, by State, outlying area, and Canadian Province, 1993 annual rpt, A3840–2

Carpentry claim payouts in 5 States with highest and lowest amounts, 1989, article, C4300–1.508

Cases and distribution of compensation paid, by part of body injured, 1991, annual rpt, A8375–4

Cases, deaths, and compensation paid, by accident and injury type, State, and Canadian Province, 1993 annual rpt, A8375–2.2

Index by Subjects and Names

Workers compensation

Claim distribution by cause of injury, 1993 article, C1575–1.505

Construction industry workers compensation claim volume and insurance structure, by type of business, 1993, annual survey rpt, A4155–1

Construction workers compensation insurance rates, by type of work and State, 1993, article, C5800–2.547

Cost of covered medical expenditures by source of funds, and claims and average costs by injury type, 1990 and trends, annual rpt, A5173–2

Employee benefit payments and employer cost/payroll ratios, by industry, detailed type of benefit, and firm size, 1991, annual rpt, A3840–1

Higher education instn employee retirement and insurance benefits, prevalence and expenditures, by type of instn and region, 1991, biennial survey, A9025–3

Insurance (property/casualty) premiums, loss ratios, and market shares, for workers compensation, 1991 and trends, annual article, C1050–1.501

Insurance premiums written for workers compensation, 1982-91, annual rpt, A5650–1.2

Premiums written and operating ratios in property/casualty insurance, by company type and line of coverage, 1988-92, annual article, C1050–1.504

Premiums written, loss ratios, and market shares for property and casualty insurance, by line, leading company, and State, 1992 and trends, annual article, C1050–1.509

Residual market underwriting loss or gain, burden, and market shares, by State, 1991 and trends, annual rpt, A0375–3

Restaurant assn workers compensation self-insurance fund premium pool and enrollment, for 9 States, 1992, article, C1200–5.507

Small corporation mgmt views on workers compensation claims, costs, and State regulation, Aug 1992 survey, C4687–1.501

Workplace safety and health data, including injury and death incidence, govt regulation and spending, and workers compensation, with data by State, 1992 annual rpt, R8335–1

State and local:

Alabama insurance industry financial and underwriting data, by company and line of coverage, 1991, annual rpt, S0160–1

Alaska insurance industry underwriting and investment data, by company and type of insurance, with regulatory info, 1991 and trends, annual rpt, S0280–3

Arizona financial condition, including revenues by source, expenditures by function, and fund balances, FY91, annual rpt, S0450–2

Arizona insurance industry financial and underwriting data, by company and type of insurance, with regulatory info, 1992, annual rpt, S0483–1

Arkansas financial condition, including revenues by source, expenditures by function and locality, and fund balances, FY91-92, biennial rpt, S0780–1

California statistical abstract, general data, 1992 annual rpt, S0840–2.3

Connecticut insurance industry financial and underwriting data, by company and type of insurance, 1991, annual rpt, S1222–1

DC statistical profile, general data, 1992 annual rpt, S1535–3.3

Delaware data book, general data, 1993 annual rpt, S1375–4

Florida insurance industry financial and underwriting data, by company and line of coverage, 1991, annual rpt, S1760–1

Florida State employees medical claims, and costs by type, for HMO vs fee-for-service plans, 1993 article, C5800–2.534

Florida statistical abstract, general data, 1992 annual rpt, U6660–1.7

Georgia financial condition, including revenues by source, expenditures by function and object, and fund balances, FY92, annual rpt, S1860–1

Hawaii data book, general data, 1992 annual rpt, S2090–1.12

Idaho economic profile, general data, 1992 recurring rpt, S2218–2.4

Idaho insurance industry financial and underwriting data, by company and type of insurance, with regulatory data, 1991, annual rpt, S2260–1

Indiana financial condition, including revenues by source, expenditures by function and object, and fund balances, by agency, FY92, annual rpt, S2570–1

Iowa insurance industry financial and underwriting data, by company and type of insurance, 1992, annual rpt, S2760–1

Kansas insurance industry financial and underwriting data, by company and type of insurance, with regulatory info, 1992, annual rpt, S2990–1

Kentucky financial condition, including revenues by source, expenditures by function and object, fund balances, and bonded debt, FY92, annual rpt, S3120–1

Louisiana financial condition, including revenues by source, expenditures by function, and fund balances, FY92 and trends, annual rpt, S3285–2

Maine court cases and dispositions, by type and location, FY92 and trends, annual rpt, S3463–1

Minnesota financial condition, including revenues by source, expenditures by function, fund balances, and bonded debt, FY92 and trends, annual rpt, S4180–1

Mississippi financial condition, including revenues by source, expenditures by function and object, and detail by agency, FY92 and trends, annual rpt, S4346–1

Missouri financial condition, including fund finances, tax collections and distribution, and State treasury activity, FY92 and trends, annual rpt, S4570–1

Missouri insurance industry financial and underwriting data, by company and type of insurance, with regulatory info, 1992, annual rpt, S4527–1

Missouri labor and industrial relations dept activity, with data on work injuries, worker rights, and labor force, FY92 and trends, annual rpt, S4530–2

Nebraska court cases and dispositions, by type of court and case, and location, 1992 and trends, annual rpt, S4965–2

Nebraska insurance premiums and losses by detailed line of coverage, by company, 1992, annual rpt, S4890–1

New Jersey financial condition, including revenues by source, expenditures by function, fund balances, and bonded debt, FY92, annual rpt, S5455–1

New Mexico tax revenues and disbursements, by detailed tax type, and property valuation data, FY91-92 and trends, annual rpt, S5660–1.2

New Mexico workers compensation claims and rates, by industry div, 1992, article, S5624–2.510

New York State insurance industry devs, finances, and regulatory activity, 1990/91 and trends, annual rpt, S5770–3

New York State insurance industry financial and underwriting data, by company and line of coverage, 1991, annual rpt, S5770–2

New York State statistical yearbook, general data, 1992 annual rpt, U5100–1.3

North Dakota trust fund balances, and income vs claims analysis, FY92 and trends, annual rpt, S6162–1

Ohio court caseload and case disposition, by type of court and case, and location, 1992, annual rpt, S6385–1

Ohio financial condition, including revenues by source, expenditures by function, and fund balances, FY92, annual rpt, S6255–1

Oklahoma insurance industry financial and underwriting data, by company and type of insurance, with regulatory info, 1992, annual rpt, S6462–1

Oklahoma statistical abstract, general data, 1992 annual rpt, U8130–2.15

Pennsylvania financial condition, including revenues by source, expenditures by function, and fund balances, FY92 and trends, annual rpt, S6810–4

Pennsylvania insurance industry financial and underwriting data, by company and line of coverage, 1991, with FY92 regulatory info, annual rpt, S6835–1

Rhode Island insurance industry financial and underwriting data, by company and line of coverage, 1990, with FY91 regulatory info, annual rpt, S6945–2

South Carolina financial condition, including receipts by source, expenditures by function, fund balances, and bonded debt, FY92, annual rpt, S7127–1

South Dakota financial condition, including revenues by source, expenditures by function, fund balances, and bonded debt, FY92, annual rpt, S7330–1

Tennessee court cases and dispositions, by type of court and case, and county, FY92, annual rpt, S7585–1

Tennessee statistical abstract, general data, 1992/93 annual rpt, U8710–2.18

Texas court cases and dispositions, by type of court and case, and location, FY92, annual rpt, S7703–1

Texas financial condition, including revenues by source, expenditures by function, and bonded indebtedness, FY92, annual rpt, S7655–3

Texas insurance dept regulatory activities, with industry financial and underwriting data by line of coverage, FY92 annual rpt, S7700–1

Utah financial condition, including revenues by source, expenditures by function and agency, and fund balances, FY92, annual rpt, S7795–1

Workers compensation

Utah insurance industry financial and underwriting data, by company and line of coverage, with regulatory info, 1991, annual rpt, S7845–1

Utah statistical abstract, general data, 1993 triennial rpt, U8960–1.6

Vermont financial condition, including revenues by source, expenditures by function, fund balances, and bonded debt, FY92, annual rpt, S8035–1

Washington State financial condition, including revenues by source, expenditures by function, fund balances, and bonded debt, FY92, annual rpt, S8345–3

West Virginia insurance industry financial and underwriting data, by company and line of coverage, with regulatory info, 1991, annual rpt, S8575–1

West Virginia workers compensation accidents reported by county, and program finances, FY83-92, annual rpt, R9385–1.2

West Virginia workers compensation claim benefits paid, monthly rpt, S8534–1

Wisconsin insurance industry financial and underwriting data, by company and line of coverage, with regulatory info, 1992, annual rpt, S8755–1

Wyoming financial condition, including revenues by source, expenditures by function, and fund balances, FY92 and trends, annual rpt, S8875–1

see also Disability benefits and insurance

see also State funding for employment

see also Unemployment insurance

Working women and mothers

see Women's employment

Worrell, Kay

"Corporate Directors' Compensation, 1993 Edition", R4105–7

Wrecking and demolition

Public housing authority operations and finances, including housing unit demolition, by agency size and region, 1990 rpt, A6800–1

Revenues for top 20 contractors specializing in demolition/wrecking, 1992, annual article, C5800–2.548

State and local:

Arizona statistical abstract, general data, 1993 recurring rpt, U5850–2.15

Connecticut construction activity and value, by type of structure and location, 1992 and trends, annual rpt, S1212–1

Delaware housing construction activity, with data on demolitions and mobile home sales, by locality, 1992 and trends, annual rpt, S1387–1

Hawaii data book, general data, 1992 annual rpt, S2090–1.21

New Jersey residential construction activity and costs, by location, 1991 and trends, annual rpt, S5425–3

Wright, Killen and Co.

Oil refinery, ethylene, and gas processing Gulf Coast plants profitability analyses, weekly rpt monthly tables, C6985–1

Writers and writing

Ecologist personal and professional characteristics, including publishing activity by type of publication, Mar 1992 survey, recurring rpt, A4685–1

Magazine use of gender-specific vocabulary, and ratio of male to female readers, for 8 consumer publications, 1993 feature, C2575–1.507

Medical research journal article multiple author incidence, for 2 radiation oncology publications, with data by author country and instn, 1983-87, article, A3273–8.502

Medical school medicine dept chairmen article publishing activity, 1979-90, article, A3273–8.510

Salaries of scientists, engineers, technicians, and other professionals, by employee and employer characteristics, 1990s and trends, biennial rpt, A3960–1

see also Books and bookselling

see also Language use and ability

Writing ability

see Educational tests

see Language use and ability

Writing instruments

see Office supplies

Wyoming

Agricultural production, marketing, and income, by county and/or commodity, and farms and acreage, 1992 and trends, annual rpt, S8860–1

Correctional instn admin, finances, inmate characteristics, and staff, and probation and parole activities, FY92, annual rpt, S8883–1

Crimes and arrests, by offense, location, and offender characteristics, with data on law enforcement employment and assaults on officers, 1991 and trends, annual rpt, S8867–3

Election results by county, district, and precinct, 1992, annual rpt and govtl directory, S9000–1

Elementary and secondary school enrollment, staff, and finances, by county and district, 1991/92, annual rpt series, S8890–1

Employment by industry group and county, with unemployment insurance and job service activities, monthly rpt, S8895–1

Financial transactions of State treasurer, including revenues, investments, and disbursements by local area, FY92 and trends, annual rpt, S9010–1

Govt financial condition, including revenues by source, expenditures by function, and fund balances, FY92 and trends, annual rpt, S8875–1

Library holdings, staff, circulation, and finances, by county, FY92, annual rpt, S8855–3

Markets with daily newspapers, demographic and economic info by geographic area, US and Canada, 1993 annual rpt, C3250–1

Oil/gas industry production, finances, exploration, and reserves, by State, 1992 and trends, annual rpt, A5425–1.1

Sales and use tax revenue by industry div and/or retail sector, by county, FY81-92, annual rpt, S8855–1

Statistical profiles of 50 States and DC, general data, 1993 annual almanac, C4712–1

Tax collections and distribution, and property valuation, with data by property type and location, FY92 and trends, annual rpt, S8990–1

Traffic accidents, fatalities, and injuries, by circumstances, location, vehicle type, and driver and victim characteristics, 1992 and trends, annual rpt, S9007–1

Index by Subjects and Names

Uranium reserves and resources in Green Mountain/Sheep Mountain region, by deposit, 1993 article, B6790–1.503

Utility and transportation regulatory agency activities, scope of jurisdiction, finances, and employees, by agency, 1991/92 annual rpt, A7015–2

Vital statistics, including births, deaths by cause, marriages, and divorces, by demographic characteristics and county, 1991 and trends, annual rpt, S8920–2

Welfare and social services recipients and expenditures, by program and county, FY92, annual rpt, S8908–1

see also Laramie County, Wyo.

see also Natrona County, Wyo.

see also under By City and By County in the "Index by Categories"

see also under By State in the "Index by Categories"

X-rays

Hospital patient admission rates and length of stay, by diagnosis and procedure, payment source, age, sex, and region, 1991, B4455–4

Hospital patient charges and length of stay, by diagnosis and procedure, payment source, age, and region, 1991, B4455–5

Shipment value, employment, and foreign trade, for electronics industry, by sector and product type, 1980s-92, annual rpt, A4725–1.2

State and local:

Kentucky Medicaid recipients and payments, by program, county, and type of medical service, monthly rpt, S3140–5

Xenos, Peter

"Trends in Female and Male Age at Marriage and Celibacy in Asia", R4500–1.64

Xylene

see Chemicals and chemical industry

Yankee Group Inc.

Computer network hub market value, with market shares for 6 leading and all other manufacturers, 1993 article, C1850–2.504

Yankelovich Clancy Shulman

Environmental claims by marketers influence on consumer purchasing decisions, 1992 survey feature, C1200–4.501

Hispanic American views on characteristics of public TV vs 4 other networks, 1992 survey, R4250–1.24

Yankelovich Partners

Children's consumer attitudes and savings practices, Dec 1992-Jan 1993 survey, article, C2710–1.531

Consumer views on clothing shopping experience, and activities cited as status symbols, 1989 and/or 1992, survey article, C8130–1.506

Restaurant patron rights, views of consumers, operators, and critics, 1992-93 surveys, article, C1850–3.511

Yarn

see Textile industry and fabrics

Index by Subjects and Names

Youth employment

Yellow Pages
see Advertising
see Directories

Yellowstone National Park
Vital statistics for residents of Yellowstone Natl Park, including births, deaths, and marriages, 1991 and trends, annual rpt, S8920–2
Vital statistics for residents of Yellowstone Natl Park, including population and pregnancy outcomes, 1980 and 1990-91, annual rpt, S4690–1

Yemen
Energy intl sourcebook, with detail on oil and gas industry operations, supply-demand, and prices, for approx 80 countries, 1970s-91, annual compilation, C6985–10.2

Yogurt
see Dairy industry and products

Young, Arthur, and Co.
see Ernst and Young Co.

Youth
Abortion attitudes of teenage boys, by respondent characteristics, 1988 survey, article, A5160–1.505
Black children and youth population, economic, health, and education data, with comparisons to whites, 1993 rpt, R3840–21
Charitable and volunteer activity of youth age 12-17, and views on related issues, by respondent characteristics, 1992 survey, biennial rpt, A5435–5
Condom use and attitudes among sexually active young men, by race-ethnicity, 1988 and 1991 surveys, article, A5160–1.504
Developing countries female population age 15-19, with data on marriage, maternity, and contraception use rates, various years 1977-90, R8720–1.1
Drivers and driving fatalities total and nighttime share for youths age 15-20, and juvenile blood alcohol limits in 17 States with low limits, 1993 article, A8375–1.506
Expenditures by teenagers, distribution by product category, 1993 survey, article, C5150–3.518
Firearm experience and attitudes of youth age 10-19, Apr-May 1993 survey, article, R4800–2.522
Health condition and health service use and sources for youth age 10-15, with data by insurance status, 1988, article, A2623–1.509
Homeless population characteristics in 29 cities, 1991/92, annual rpt, A9330–9
Income and expenditures of teenagers, and girls cosmetics use and views on drugstore marketing, 1993 articles, C5150–2.508
Latin America youth sexual experience, by sex, for selected cities and countries, 1985-91 surveys, U2520–1.51
Minority population characteristics, with employment and/or school enrollment status of youths age 16-24 by race-ethnicity, 1991, R8750–2.58
Natl longitudinal surveys data users handbook and bibl, 1993 recurring rpt, U3780–2
Opinions of youth on environmental and population issues, 1992 survey, R8780–1.503

Radio audience size, leading stations and formats, and advertising rates and revenues, by market area, recurring rpt, C3165–1
Religious beliefs of teenagers, and approval of interracial and interfaith marriages, by respondent characteristics, 1993 survey feature, R8780–1.507
Religious practices of teenagers, and views on selected social issues, by religion, 1991-93 surveys, R8780–1.510
Religious questions of interest to teenagers, and church donation practices, with detail by religion, 1993 surveys, R8780–1.509
Restaurant patronage patterns of population age 18-24, 1991, article, A8200–1.504
Sexual activity and number of partners among urban women age 15-19, by race, 1971-88, article, A5160–1.501
Smoking among teenagers vs price of cigarettes, for US and Canada, 1982 and 1992, article, C5800–7.519
Social issues of concern to teenagers, and spending trends, 1993 article, C2710–1.541
Supernatural phenomena, teenagers beliefs, 1978-92 surveys, R8780–1.502
Urban poverty rate compared to total US, for aggregate population age 5-17 of 47 major urban areas, 1980 and 1990, A4425–4
Volunteer activities and characteristics of teenagers vs adults, 1991, survey article, C2176–1.503
World population size and characteristics, GNP, and land area, by region and/or country, 1993 annual data sheet, R8750–5

State and local:
Georgia total and teenage suicides, by county, 1982-91, annual rpt, U6750–1
Illinois traffic accidents, fatalities, and injuries, involvement of youthful drivers, 1991 and trends, annual rpt, S2540–1
Kentucky teenage drivers involved in traffic accidents, 1989-92, annual rpt, S3150–2
Louisiana traffic accidents involving drivers age 15-20 years, with data on alcohol use, 1991, annual rpt, S3345–2
Michigan traffic accident injuries and fatalities involving alcohol, for victims age 18-20, 1989-91, annual rpt, S3997–2
Montana youth population by sex and age, 1990 and 1992, annual rpt, S4705–1
Nebraska population age 20/under, by age, sex, and county, June 1992, annual rpt, S4865–2.6
New Jersey traffic accident fatalities involving alcohol, for drivers age 17-20, 1992, annual rpt, S5430–2
New Mexico traffic accidents involving teenagers and young adults, 1992 and trends, annual rpt, S5665–1
Ohio traffic accidents involving youthful drivers, with data on alcohol use, 1991, annual rpt, S6290–1
Oregon adolescent suicide attempts and deaths, by county, method, and victim characteristics, 1991 and trends, annual rpt, S6615–5
South Carolina participation in teen companion program for youths with parents in State employment program, monthly rpt, S7252–1

Utah marriages involving persons under age 20, and subsequent divorce rates, 1990 and trends, annual rpt, S7835–2
Utah total and school-age population, 1995-2020, annual rpt, R9380–1.1
Washington State public assistance clients and service costs, by client characteristics, program, and county, FY90, annual rpt, S8420–2
Washington State youthful drivers involved in traffic accidents, 1992 and trends, annual rpt, S8428–1
Wyoming individualized youth service cases and expenditures, by county, FY92, annual rpt, S8908–1
Wyoming traffic accidents, fatalities, and injuries, involvement of youthful drivers, 1992, annual rpt, S9007–1

see also Child mortality
see also Children
see also Elementary and secondary education
see also Foster home care
see also Higher education
see also Juvenile courts and cases
see also Juvenile delinquency
see also Juvenile detention and correctional institutions
see also Missing persons and runaways
see also School dropouts
see also Student discipline
see also Students
see also Teenage pregnancy
see also Temporary and seasonal employment
see also Youth employment
see also under By Age in the "Index by Categories"

Youth employment
Black American socioeconomic status, including health, education, politics, crime, and employment, with comparisons to whites, 1993 annual compilation, C6775–2
Black American socioeconomic status, with comparisons to whites and data by region, 1960s-92, annual compilation, A8510–1.1
Black children and youth population, economic, health, and education data, with comparisons to whites, 1993 rpt, R3840–21
Charitable contributions and volunteer activity of youth age 12-17, by employment status, 1992 survey, biennial rpt, A5435–5
College freshmen attitudes and characteristics, degree and career plans, and financial aid sources, by sex and instn type, fall 1992, annual survey, U6215–1
Hispanic American employment status of high school and college students, with comparison to whites, 1991, annual compilation, C6775–3.2
Issues of child/youth employment, with data on number of child workers, occupational deaths and injuries, and Federal and State regulation, 1992 rpt, R8335–2
Job Corps youth training program funding, enrollment capacity, and participants by selected characteristics, 1981-94, article, R4800–2.515
Labor force age 16-24, by age group, Apr and July 1993, article, S0465–1.508
Metro area poor neighborhood unemployment rates for youths age 16-19, with comparison to US and detail by race-ethnicity, 1990, A4425–4

Youth employment

Statistical profiles of 50 States and DC, general data, 1993 annual almanac, C4712–1

Unemployment rates among youths by State, and by age and educational attainment, 1992 annual rpt, R3840–11.2

Unemployment rates for youths age 20, with detail for high school grads and dropouts, by sex and race, 1963-67 and 1983-87, article, C4687–1.511

State and local:

Alaska employment of youths age 15-21, by occupation, industry, and sex, July-Sept 1992, article, S0320–1.509

Arizona summer youth employment through Job Training Partnership Act, by service delivery area, 1991-92, article, S0465–1.501

Arizona youth not in school/not graduated by labor force status, by county, 1990, recurring rpt, U5850–2.4

Arkansas Census of Population and Housing detailed findings, 1990, U5935–7

California Census of Population and Housing detailed findings, 1990, S0840–9

California employment statistics, by demographic characteristics, industry, MSA, and county, monthly rpt, S0830–1

California statistical abstract, general data, 1992 annual rpt, S0840–2.3

Colorado labor force planning rpt, including population, employment by industry, and job service applicants, FY94 annual rpt, S1040–3

Connecticut public high school grads and postgraduate activities, 1991, biennial rpt, S1185–3

DC public school grad employment status 6 months after graduation, 1988-91, annual rpt, S1605–2

DC statistical profile, general data, 1992 annual rpt, S1535–3.3

Georgia statistical abstract, general data, 1992-93 biennial rpt, U6730–1.3

Hawaii data book, general data, 1992 annual rpt, S2090–1.12

Louisiana job service openings and applicants, and characteristics of Job Training Partnership Act target population and insured unemployed, 1993 annual planning rpt, S3320–1.2

Maine Census of Population and Housing summary findings, by local area, 1990, S3465–9

Maryland statistical abstract, general data, 1993-94 biennial rpt, S3605–1.4

Massachusetts high school grads in class of 1989, postgrad activities, by city and school system, 1992 annual rpt, C4712–2

Michigan labor force planning rpt, including employment by industry, and characteristics of Job Training Partnership Act eligible population, 1993 annual rpt, S3980–1

Michigan youth summer labor force and employment data, 1992-93 and trends, article, S3980–2.501

Missouri postgraduation activities of high school grads, by sex, 1990/91, annual rpt, S4505–1.1

New Hampshire high school grads and postgraduation activities, by school, county, and sex, 1991, annual tables, S5200–1.2

New Hampshire high school grads and postgraduation activities, by school, county, and sex, 1992, annual tables, S5200–1.15

New Jersey Census of Population and Housing detailed findings, by county, 1990, S5425–19

New Jersey high school grad postgraduation plans, by county, fall 1991, annual rpt, S5385–1.1

New Jersey unemployment rates for youths and Hispanics, and by race and sex, 1991-92, annual article, S5425–1.503

New Mexico labor force planning rpt, including population characteristics, and employment by industry and occupation, 1993 annual rpt, S5624–1

New York State high school grads and postgraduation activities, by municipality and school district, 1991, annual rpt, C4712–7

North Carolina high school grads and postgraduation plans, by local district, 1991/92 and trends, annual rpt, S5915–1

Oklahoma Job Training Partnership Act funding for youth summer employment programs, by service delivery area, 1993, article, S6430–2.502

Pennsylvania Census of Population and Housing detailed findings, with selected data by county and municipality, 1990, U4130–13

Pennsylvania high school grads postgraduation activities, by county, 1991/92, annual rpt, S6790–5.14

Pennsylvania labor force planning rpt, including population characteristics, employment and job openings by industry and occupation, and income trends, FY92 annual rpt, S6845–3

Pennsylvania youth unemployment rate, with detail for vocational education grads and comparison to US, 1990, annual rpt, S6790–5.6

Rhode Island Census of Population and Housing detailed findings, by county and municipality, 1990, S6930–9

South Carolina labor force planning rpt, detailed data on employment, hours, wages, turnover, and characteristics of job service applicants, 1992 annual rpt, S7155–3.2

South Dakota public high school grads, by sex and postgraduation status, 1992, annual rpt, S7315–1.1

Tennessee labor force age 16-19, by employment status and county, 1992, article, S7495–2.504

Vermont labor force by employment status, and job service openings and applicant characteristics, 1993 annual planning rpt, S8025–2.2

see also Apprenticeship

see also Child labor

see also Temporary and seasonal employment

Youth services schools

see Juvenile detention and correctional institutions

Yugoslavia

Energy intl sourcebook, with detail on oil and gas industry operations, supply-demand, and prices, for approx 80 countries, 1970s-91, annual compilation, C6985–10.2

Motor vehicle world production, sales, trade, and registrations, by country, world area, manufacturer, and make, 1991 and trends, annual rpt, A0865–2.1

Refugee/displaced population within former Yugoslavia, by region of origin and present location, Jan 1993, R9372–2.504

see also Bosnia and Herzegovina

see also Serbia

Zaire

Contraceptive community-based distribution program costs and effectiveness, 1980s, article, A5160–6.505

Energy intl sourcebook, with detail on oil and gas industry operations, supply-demand, and prices, for approx 80 countries, 1970s-91, annual compilation, C6985–10.2

Zambia

Fertilizer use by small farms in Eastern Province Zambia, 1980s, R5620–1.38

Student views on sexual behavior and treatment of persons infected with AIDS virus, by respondent characteristics, 1990 survey, article, A5160–6.503

Zapata, Hector O.

"Agricultural Statistics and Prices for Louisiana, 1985-91", U2740–1

Zimbabwe

Motor vehicle world production, sales, trade, and registrations, by country, world area, manufacturer, and make, 1991 and trends, annual rpt, A0865–2.1

Zimmerman & Associates

Hospital accounts receivable average days outstanding, 1989-92, article, A1865–1.509

Zinc and zinc industry

Capital spending plans for new mines and plants, by mineral and company, and mine production values, 1993 annual feature, C5226–2.503

Latin America statistical abstract, general data by country, 1992 annual rpt, U6250–1.23, U6250–1.25

Production, consumption, stocks, trade, and prices for approx 100 basic commodities, including by country and producing State, commodity yearbook for 1993, C2400–1, C2400–2

Supply-demand for selected metals and nonmetallic minerals, with price data, US and worldwide, 1992-93 and trends, annual feature, C5226–2.505

State and local:

Pennsylvania statistical abstract, general data, 1992 recurring rpt, U4130–6.8

Zip codes

Consumer buying power survey of population, income, and sales by product line, with detail for top 100 zip code areas, 1992, annual rpt, C1200–1.514

State and local:

Florida statistical abstract, general data, 1992 annual rpt, U6660–1.14

see also Neighborhoods

Zoning and zoning laws

Local govt land use planning commissions composition and activities, and commissioner characteristics, 1987 and trends, recurring rpt, A2615–2

State and local:
DC property use vs zoning status, and zoning commission activities, 1992 annual rpt, S1535–3.1
see also Building permits

Zoological parks

Operations and finances for museums and related instns, by type, budget size, governing authority, and region, 1989/90 survey, A0750–1

State and local:
Hawaii data book, general data, 1992 annual rpt, S2090–1.7

Zoology

see also Animals
see also Birds and bird conservation
see also Wildlife and wildlife conservation

Index
by Categories

Index by Categories

Geographic Breakdowns

By Census Division	741
By City	743
By County	753
By Foreign Country or World Area	770
By Region	778
By SMSA or MSA	784
By State	787
By Urban-Rural and Metro-Nonmetro	797

Economic Breakdowns

By Commodity	801
By Government Agency	805
By Income	807
By Individual Company or Institution	810
By Industry	834
By Occupation	842

Demographic Breakdowns

By Age	846
By Disease	856
By Educational Attainment	858
By Marital Status	862
By Race	864
By Sex	874

The Index by Categories contains references to all publications, tables, and groups of tables that contain breakdowns of statistical data by any or several of the above 20 standard categories.

CATEGORY DETAIL

The amount of detail provided in the various category index breakdowns may vary considerably:

Breakdowns "By sex" or "By urban-rural" are, by definition, complete. Breakdowns "By county" encompass county-level data and also data shown by various additional types of sub-State areas (e.g. labor market areas, health care districts, State judicial districts); the type of area is generally specified in the notation of content listed under the category terms. Breakdowns "By State" are generally complete unless specific limitations are noted, and usually include D.C.

Breakdowns "By race" frequently show white and nonwhite or white, black, and other. When additional race-ethnicity breakdowns are included, they are indexed specifically in the Index of Subjects and Names (i.e. Asian Americans, Indians, Hispanic Americans) as well as under the category "By race." Summary data on ethnic groups and minorities may be found under the heading "Minority groups" in the Index by Subjects and Names.

The greatest variation in the detail of category breakdowns occurs in such categories as "By city," "By foreign country," "By industry," "By commodity," and "By occupation." For these categories, we try, whenever possible, to indicate the degree of detail in the notations of content and in the abstract of the publication.

USE OF SUBJECT HEADINGS

Within each of the categories, references have been grouped according to the subject matter of the publication or the statistical content being indexed. The following 21 subheadings have been used for this purpose.

Agriculture and Food — Covers all agricultural data, including commercial fishing; fertilizer industry; agricultural credit; agricultural land; farm population and labor; food except retail prices; restaurants and food service industry; and beer, wine, and liquor data.

See also Natural Resources, Environment, and Pollution, for forestry data, additional conservation data Prices and Cost of Living, for retail food prices Public Welfare and Social Security, for food stamp data

Banking, Finance, and Insurance — Covers all data on financial institutions including banking and insurance; consumer credit; bankruptcy; securities markets; futures trading; and money supply, interest rates, and other financial indicators.

See also Agriculture and Food, for agricultural credit Government and Defense, for government debt and securities Health and Vital Statistics, for health insurance data Housing and Construction, for mortgage data Industry and Commerce, for general economic indicators Transportation and Travel, for auto insurance data

Communications — Covers all data on industries in this sector, including finances, output, employment, occupational safety, and rates and regulation; advertising industry; Postal Service; and use of print and broadcast media.

Education — Covers all data on education in general, including schools, faculty, students, graduates, finances, and libraries.

See also Health and Vital Statistics, for medical and dental schools and health manpower training Labor and Employment, for employment training programs Science and Technology, for education exclusively in science and engineering Veterans Affairs, for GI Bill and other veterans' education

Energy Resources and Demand — Covers supply, consumption, and conservation of all types of energy. Includes exploration, extraction, R&D, transportation, distribution, and waste disposal of all energy forms; data on energy industries; and energy use and costs.

See also Government and Defense, for fuel tax data Health and Vital Statistics, for accidents and occupational health in energy industries, including mines

Geography and Climate — Covers all data on weather, climate, oceanography, storms and other natural disasters; and land area and topography.

See also Natural Resources, Environment, and Pollution, for data on water supply

Government and Defense — Covers all data on government in general, including activities, finances, programs, and personnel; all data on defense activities and foreign affairs; taxes in general, including individual income taxes; coinage; elections and voting; and municipal and industrial revenue bonds.

See also Health and Vital Statistics, for military medicine
Industry and Commerce, for corporate income tax data

Health and Vital Statistics — Covers all data on health condition, disease, and disability; occupational health and safety; medical care, costs, and insurance; medical facilities; health personnel and their education; fertility; life expectancy; family planning; marriage and divorce; and vital statistics.

See also Industry and Commerce, for drugstore operations and finances
Public Welfare and Social Security, for data on Medicare, Medicaid, and social security disability recipients
Transportation and Travel, for all transportation accidents
Veterans Affairs, for data on veterans' health and VA medical facilities

Housing and Construction — Covers all data on housing condition, finance, and occupancy; all data on the construction industry; all mortgages; urban renewal and community development; government aid for housing or communities; and real estate business.

See also Natural Resources, Environment and Pollution, for construction of dams, sewer plants, etc.
Transportation and Travel, for construction of highways and bridges

Income — Covers all data on personal and family income; earnings (in general, and in industries not covered by other subject headings); and related data on wealth and poverty status.

See also Agriculture and Food, for farm income data
Industry and Commerce, for business income
Public Welfare and Social Security, for income maintenance data

Industry and Commerce — Covers all data on industry in general, including production, finances, payrolls, and profits; productivity; trade and marketing; foreign trade, tariffs, and balance of payments; foreign investments; corporate income taxes; and economic indicators in general.

See also Agriculture and Food, for food industry operations
Communications, and Transportation and Travel, for manufacturing in those industries
Science and Technology, for data on high-technology industries

Labor and Employment — Covers all data on the labor force and employment (in general, and in industries not covered by other subject headings), including characteristics, hours, working conditions, employee benefits, and pensions; unemployment; labor unions; and employment training programs.

See also Health and Vital Statistics, for data on occupational health and safety
Income, for earnings data
Industry and Commerce, for general industry data

Law Enforcement — Covers all data on crime and the characteristics of criminals; all data on the criminal justice system, including police, lawyers, courts, prisons, and sentences; and legal education.

Natural Resources, Environment, and Pollution — Covers all data on natural resource supply and conservation, including forests, public lands, and wildlife; land use; water supply, dams, and flood control; environmental quality; all types of pollutants; wastes in general, including sewage disposal; oil spills; radioactivity in the environment; and water utilities.

See also Agriculture and Food, for conservation specifically related to agriculture
†Energy Resources and Demand, for additional data on energy reserves, disposal of wastes from energy production, and nuclear power
Health and Vital Statistics, for occupational hazards and for the health effects of pollutants

Population — Covers all data on population size; characteristics of the population in general; demographic groups such as youth, women, or blacks; migration; religion; adoptions; and general public opinion.

See also Health and Vital Statistics, for data on births, deaths, family planning, and fertility

Prices and Cost of Living — Covers prices in general, both wholesale and retail; price indexes; consumer costs and expenditures; and inflation.

See also Education, for tuition costs
Energy Resources and Demand, for consumer prices and utility bills
Health and Vital Statistics, for medical costs

Public Welfare and Social Security — Covers all data related to social security program, including Medicare and disability insurance; welfare, public assistance, and medical assistance (Medicaid); food stamps and school lunch programs; social services; and charitable organizations and philanthropic activities.

See also Health and Vital Statistics, for data on workers compensation and disabled persons
Labor and Employment, for unemployment insurance

Recreation and Leisure — Covers all data on recreation activities and recreation industries. Includes sport fishing, hunting, boating, parks, museums, the performing arts, and the gaming industry.

See also Education, for libraries
Transportation and Travel, for data on travel and lodging

Science and Technology — Covers scientific activities, private and government funding, employment, and education; space programs; inventions and patents; and high-technology.

See also Agriculture and Food, for agricultural sciences
Energy Resources and Demand, for R&D in energy fields
Geography and Climate, for data on weather

Transportation and Travel — Covers all data on specific transportation industries and modes of travel, including finances, operations, employment, and regulation; transportation accidents and safety; motor vehicle insurance and use; tourism and tourist characteristics; passports; hotel and motel data; and freight and shipments data when emphasis is on mode.

See also Energy Resources and Demand, for pipeline data
Industry and Commerce, for general industry output and shipments

Veterans Affairs — Covers everything that relates exclusively to veterans, including education, health, VA hospitals, housing and VA home loans, employment and employment programs, pensions, and disability payments.

Index by Categories

GEOGRAPHIC BREAKDOWNS

BY CENSUS DIVISION

Agriculture and Food

Alcoholic beverage shipments and per capita consumption, by type, census div, and State, 1980s-91, annual rpt, A3455–1.4

Brewing industry finances and operations, including consumption, trade, and taxes, with data by State and census div, 1991 and trends, annual rpt, A3455–1

Convenience stores with gasoline marketing operations, by chain company, census div, and State, 1992, annual article, C4680–1.502

Convenience stores with gasoline marketing operations, by chain company, census div, and State, 1993, annual article, C4680–1.510

Eating/drinking establishment revenues, by census div, 1992 feature, C1850–10.503

Food service industry sales, market shares, establishments, and business activity indicators, by location, 1992, annual feature, C1200–5.515

Food service industry wage rates for hourly employees, by position, census div, State, and selected metro area, 1992, recurring rpt, A8200–14

Food service sales outlook, by industry segment and census div, 1992-93 and trends, annual feature, C5150–5.504

Food/beverage manufacturers mgmt salaries, by selected employee characteristics, 1992 survey, annual article, C2150–6.502

Restaurant (chicken specialty) establishments by census div, 1992 annual article, C1200–5.509

Restaurant (hamburger) establishments by census div, and sales and units for top 10 chains, 1993 annual article, C1200–5.504

Restaurant (Italian food) establishments by census div, 1992, annual article, C1200–5.508

Restaurant (Mexican food) establishments by census div, and sales and/or units for top 4-5 chains, 1993 annual article, C1200–5.514

Restaurant (pizza) establishments by census div, and sales and units for top 10 chains, 1992, annual article, C1200–5.506

Restaurant (sandwich) establishments by census div, 1992, annual article, C1200–5.503

Restaurant (seafood) establishments by census div, 1992, article, C1200–5.516

Restaurant industry expansion outlook and operating data, by census div and MSA, 1993 annual articles, C1850–3.506

Restaurant sales forecast, by census div and State, 1992-93, annual feature, A8200–1.502

Supermarket sales, effective buying income, and population, by State and census div, 1991, annual rpt, C3400–6

Banking, Finance, and Insurance

Bank deposits and savings capital, by census div, 1992 feature, C1850–10.501

Life insurance in force by State and census div, 1991, biennial fact book, A1325–1.1

Mutual fund sales, by State and census div, and for Canada and US territories, 1991, annual rpt, A6025–1.2

Communications

Direct marketing industry devs, including advertising patterns, finances, target market characteristics, and consumer attitudes, 1992/93 annual rpt, A4620–1

TV and total households, and member population by age and sex, by market area, county, State, and/or census div, 1992/93, annual rpt, B0525–3

TV households by census div, State, county, Nielsen market area, and time zone, Jan 1994, annual rpt, B6670–2

Education

Doctoral degree recipients postdoctoral employment by census div, by sex, 1990/91, annual rpt, R6000–7

Higher education faculty salaries by academic rank and instn type, by census div, 1992/93, annual rpt, A0800–1

Librarians (special) salaries by age, sex, and census div, 1992, article, C1852–1.503

Librarians (special) salaries, by location, work setting, and personal characteristics, US and Canada, 1992 and trends, biennial survey rpt, A8965–1

Librarians at universities and research instns by minority group, and salaries by position and experience, by census div, 1992 annual survey, A3365–2

Library (public) materials budget average percent change, by census div, FY93, annual article, C1852–1.502

Energy Resources and Demand

Coal deliveries and prices for individual electric power plants, by utility, State, and census div, monthly rpt, A7400–9

Cogeneration project capacity, operating status, and natural gas demand, by census div, Sept 1990, annual rpt, C6985–3.2

Electric power (steam) plants, capacity, generation, and fuel use and costs, by fuel type, utility, and location, 1991, annual rpt, A7400–7

Electric power generating equipment scheduled shipments to industrial customers, by State and census div, as of Jan 1992, annual rpt, A4700–2.2

Electric power production by type of fuel, and utility coal consumption and stocks, by census div, monthly rpt, A7400–8

Electric utility financial and operating data, by State and census div, 1991 and trends, annual rpt, A4700–1

Electric utility fuel costs and consumption, by type and census div, 1990-91, articles, A4700–4.501

Electric utility plants and generating capacity, by State and census div, Dec 1991, annual rpt, C5800–28.507

Energy (BTU) tax proposed by Clinton Admin, including impact by census div, 1993 article, C6985–1.524

Natural gas heat equipment shipments, and customers and gas heat shares by census div, 1993 annual fact book, C4680–1.507

Natural gas industry composite income statement, with sales and prices by consuming sector and census div, quarterly rpt, A1775–1

Natural gas industry detailed operating and financial data, by State and census div, 1960s-91, annual rpt, A1775–3

Natural gas prices by consuming sector and census div, 1982-91, annual rpt, S7745–1

Natural gas storage capacity and additions, by census div, 1986-2000, article, C6985–1.552

Water power capacity developed and undeveloped, by census div, 1986-90, biennial rpt, U6730–1.8

Geography and Climate

Heating degree days, by census div and State, 1990/91-1991/92 and 30-year average, annual rpt, A1775–3.6

Heating or cooling degree days by census div, weekly rpt monthly table, C6985–1

Heating/cooling equipment industry data, with average heating and cooling degree days, by census div, 1991-92, annual rpt, C1800–1

Land area, by region, census div, and State, 1991 annual data sheet, R8750–9

Government and Defense

County manager salaries, by sex, county size, census div, and metro status, July 1992, annual rpt, A5800–1.3

Defense receipts per capita, with comparison to natl average for procurement, personnel, and research components, by census div, 1983, R4700–19

DOD prime contract awards, by type of contractor and census div, FY89-91, annual rpt, A0250–2.4, A0250–2.5

Fire dept employment and personnel practices, including eligibility requirements and testing, by population size, metro status, and census div, 1991 survey, recurring rpt, A5800–2.116

Local govt capital improvement financing methods, by population size, metro status, and census div, 1991 survey, A5800–2.112

Municipal and county govt structure, public services, finances, and intergovtl relations, 1993 annual rpt, A5800–1

Municipal council committee use and policies, by population size, metro status, and census div, 1991 survey, A5800–2.114

Municipal govt annexation activity, and population and land area affected, by city, State, and census div, 1980-91, A5800–1.2

Health and Vital Statistics

Cancer (urinary tract) death rates for men age 45-84, by age, State, and census div, 1979-89, article, B6045–1.503

BY CENSUS DIVISION

Hospital outpatient share of surgical procedures, by census div, 1981 and 1991, article, A1865–1.501

Hospital pharmacy operating data, by instn type and size, and census div, 1991, annual survey, B5165–3

Hospital shares offering geriatric services, by census div, 1991, article, A1865–1.505

Hospital staff shortage trends, by census div, 1991 survey, article, A1865–1.504

Hospitals by census div, 1991, annual rpt series, B4455–1

Infant mortality rates by race, State, and census div, 1987-89, annual rpt, S6285–1

Infant mortality rates from sudden infant death syndrome, by race, census div, and State, 1980 and 1988, article, B6045–1.502

Medical group practice characteristics, including specialties, form of organization, and location, 1991 and trends, recurring rpt, A2200–7

Physician practice economic aspects, detailed data by specialty, 1991-92 and trends, annual compilation, A2200–5

Physicians by detailed specialty and location, 1992, annual rpt, A2200–3.2

Prostate surgery procedures, costs, and hospital stay, with data by census div and State, 1991 and trends, article, B6045–1.503

Rabies cases in animals, distribution by census div, 1st 11 months 1992, article, A3100–2.506

Tonsillectomy/adenoidectomy procedures, costs, and hospital stay, with data by census div and State, 1991 and trends, article, B6045–1.502

Veterinarians by location and type of employment, 1990 and 1992, article, A3100–2.522

Vital statistics summary by census div and State, including births by race and deaths by major cause, 1989-90, annual rpt, S3295–1

State and local:

Oregon marriage dissolutions, by duration of marriage, and census div and State where ceremony performed, 1991, annual rpt, S6615–5

Housing and Construction

Commercial real estate inventory, vacancy, and construction, for industrial and office properties, by census div, 1992, annual survey, A8916–1

Mobile/manufactured home production, shipments, and financing, with data by State and census div, monthly rpt, A6325–1

Mortgage delinquency and foreclosure rates, and residential loans serviced, by type, State, and census div and region, quarterly rpt, A6450–1

Income

Association executives compensation, by position, assn type, and census div, with personnel practices and benefit provisions, 1992, biennial rpt, A2900–3

Consumer buying power survey of population, income, and sales by kind of business, by census div, State, MSA, county, and city, 1992, annual rpt, C1200–1.511

Consumer buying power survey of population, income, and sales by product line, by State, metro area, county, and census div, 1993 annual rpt, C1200–1.514

Household income with and without cost-of-living adjustment, by census div and population size, 1991, annual article, U0280–1.501

Professional worker salaries, by employee and employer characteristics, with detail for scientists and engineers, 1990s and trends, biennial rpt, A3960–1

Industry and Commerce

Business executives expectations for coming qtr, attitudes on key indicators, with trends and data by census div, quarterly rpt, C3150–4

Business failures and liabilities, by detailed industry, cause, length of operation, and location, 1991-92 and trends, annual rpt, C3150–8

Business failures and liabilities, by industry, census div, State, and major city, monthly rpt, C3150–2

Consumer buying power survey of population, income, and sales by kind of business, by census div, State, MSA, county, and city, 1992, annual rpt, C1200–1.511

Consumer buying power survey of population, income, and sales by product line, by State, metro area, county, and census div, 1993 annual rpt, C1200–1.514

Consumer expectations of economic conditions, by census div, Conference Board monthly survey, R4105–4

Discount chain sales and merchandising, including data by dept, leading chain, and location, 1992 and trends, annual feature, C8130–1.507

Discount stores and membership wholesale clubs, by State and census div, 1992, annual feature, C5150–3.516

Drugstore (independent pharmacy) financial and operating data, by store characteristics, 1991 and trends, annual survey, B5165–1

Economic characteristics and dev goals of local areas that solicit foreign investment, by population size, metro status, and census div, 1993 survey rpt, A5800–2.115

Electrical equipment distributor sales forecasts, by census div and State, 1992-93, annual article, C4725–5.502

Electrical equipment wholesaler market conditions, by geographic area, 1992 annual article, C4725–5.501

Hardware retail store composite finances and operations, by census div, 1991, annual rpt, A8275–1.1

Incorporations (new), by State and census div, monthly rpt, C3150–3

Interior design top 200 firms, fees, and business volume, by census div, 1993 annual article, C1850–7.501

Newsprint consumption by State and census div, 1989-90, annual rpt, A8610–1

Newsprint shipments by census div of destination, for US, Canada, and North America, monthly rpt, A1630–4

Paper and paperboard industry financial and operating data, by product, census div, and State, 1970s-95, annual rpt, A1630–6.2

Paper and pulp production capacity, by census div, 1980s-94, annual rpt, C3975–5.1

Paper, paperboard, and wood pulp industry capacity and material consumption, by grade and census div, 1970s-95, annual rpt, A1630–7

Index by Categories

Paper, paperboard, wood pulp, and recovered paper production and mills, and pulpwood production, by State and census div, 1991, article, A1630–5.502

Paperboard packaging industry corrugated and folding carton box plants and equipment, by census div and for Canada, 1990-92, annual article, C0125–4.501

Photographic equipment and supplies, consumer ownership, purchasing patterns, and use, 1993 survey and trends, recurring rpt, A8695–2

Pulp and paper industry capital spending plans of US and Canadian companies, by purpose and geographic area, 1992-94, annual survey article, C3975–2.503

Shoe industry sales indicators, by census div, 1987 and 1991, annual rpt, A4957–1.1

Labor and Employment

Corporate employee relocations, including census divs most often moved to and declined, 1992, annual rpt, B0600–1

Labor union success rates in NLRB elections, by industry group and census div, and for public utility plants by employment size, 1985-90, article, C6985–6.506

Planning profession employment and salaries, by type of employer, demographic and professional characteristics, and location, 1991 and trends, biennial rpt, A2615–1

Law Enforcement

Law school grad employment and salaries, by type of employer, location, and grad characteristics, 1992 and trends, annual rpt, A6505–1

Legal services industry receipts, by census div, 1992 feature, C1850–10.502

Local govt police liability lawsuits, claim and settlement amounts, and legal costs, by population size, census div, and/or case type, 1990/91 survey, A5800–2.113

Natural Resources, Environment and Pollution

Chemical hazard emergency response planning by local govts, including public notification methods, by locality, 1993 rpt, A5800–4.34

Population

Churches and membership, by denomination, census div, State, and county, 1990, R4985–1

Consumer buying power survey of population, income, and sales by kind of business, by census div, State, MSA, county, and city, 1992, annual rpt, C1200–1.511

Consumer buying power survey of population, income, and sales by product line, by State, metro area, county, and census div, 1993 annual rpt, C1200–1.514

Immigrant households, income, and home ownership rates by origin and length of US residence, and 15 cities with most new immigrants, 1993 article, C4300–1.512

Jewish population by world area, country, and US census div, State, and city, 1990-92, annual compilation, A2050–1

Latin America ancestry reported by US population, by region and census div, 1980, annual rpt, U6250–1.14

Older population characteristics, for persons age 65/over and 85/over, by census div and State, 1990 and trends, article, B6045–1.502

Population by age group, by census div and State, Apr 1990, article, B6045–1.501

Index by Categories

BY CITY

Population size and selected characteristics, by region, census div, and State, 1991 and trends, annual data sheet, R8750–9

Religious congregation characteristics, including membership, activities, staff, and finances, 1992 survey, recurring rpt, A5435–4

State and local:

Alaska migration patterns by US region and census div, 1980-90, annual rpt, S0320–4

Prices and Cost of Living

Cost-of-living indexes, and adjustment impact on household income, by census div and population size, 1991, annual article, U0280–1.501

Public Welfare and Social Security

Charitable contributions of corporations, by location of hq, 1991, annual rpt, R4105–8

Foundation assets, income, and grants by type of recipient, with data for top organizations and by location, 1991 and trends, annual rpt, R4900–1

Foundations, assets, and contributions, by organization type and census div, with top 100 organizations, FY91, annual article, C2176–1.507

Foundations, assets, gifts received, expenditures, and grants, by State and census div, 1991 and trends, annual article, C2176–1.516

Fundraising professionals characteristics, earnings, and benefits, 1992 survey, recurring rpt, A8455–1

Recreation and Leisure

Participation in 53 sports, by demographic characteristics, State, and census div, 1992, annual rpt series, A8485–3

Sporting goods purchaser characteristics, by product category, 1992, annual survey rpt, A8485–4

Sporting goods purchases, by product and outlet type, census div, and purchaser characteristics, with average prices, 1992 and trends, annual survey, A8485–2

Science and Technology

Chemist and chemical engineer salaries, employment status, and demographic and professional characteristics, 1993, annual rpt, A1250–4

Chemistry and chemical engineering grad starting salaries, employment status, demographic characteristics, and advanced study plans, 1991/92, annual rpt, A1250–2

Ecologist employment characteristics, including location of employer, Mar 1992 survey, recurring rpt, A4685–1

Engineers salaries by industry group, census div, selected metro area, and years since college degree, 1993, annual survey rpt, A0685–5

Engineers salaries by industry group, census div, selected metro area, degree level, and years since college degree, 1993, annual survey rpt, A0685–3

Physical science R&D spending, and grad students, distribution by census div, 1991, annual feature, A1250–1.537

Physics and astronomy enrollment and degrees awarded, by type of instn and census div, 1991/92-1992/93 and trends, annual rpt, A1960–2.1

Psychology grad dept faculty salaries, by academic rank, years in rank, census div, and sex, 1992/93 and trends, annual rpt, A2620–1

Transportation and Travel

Aerospace industry employment distribution by census div, 1991, annual rpt, A0250–2.5

Business traveler and trip characteristics, including mode, purpose, and lodging, 1991, annual rpt, R9375–12

Hotel room occupancy rates, by census div, 1990-1st half 1992, article, A6450–2.501

State travel office total and advertising budgets, by census div, FY93, annual rpt, R9375–2

Travel trips and traveler characteristics, including mode, purpose, type of lodging, and area of destination and origin, quarterly rpt, R9375–14

Traveler and trip characteristics, 1990, annual rpt, C2140–1.2

State and local:

Hawaii visitors, by residence and demographic characteristics, 1991 and trends, annual rpt, S2090–1.7

BY CITY

Agriculture and Food

Citrus fruit receipts at selected cities, by source and transport mode, 1991/92, annual rpt, S1685–1.1

Coffee, Sugar, and Cocoa Exchange trading activity, with related data including deliveries and stocks by country and/or port, 1992 and trends, annual rpt, B2275–1

Farms, and livestock and crop values, by State, MSA, county, city, and Canadian Province, 1993 annual rpt, C3250–1

Food service industry wage rates for hourly employees, by position, census div, State, and selected metro area, 1992, recurring rpt, A8200–14

Food store industry sales and operations, for 52 market areas, 1992, annual rpt, C5225–1.505

Restaurants with independent owners ranked among top 100 in sales, for top 5 cities, 1992, annual article, C1850–3.505

Supermarket prices for selected grocery items in 4-7 chains in 7 metro areas, Apr 1993, article, C4655–1.507

Tobacco leaf and product exports by customs district, 1991, annual rpt, A9075–1

State and local:

California commercial fish landings, by species and port, 1991, annual rpt, S0840–2.7

Florida vegetable, melon, and strawberry shipments to 25 US and Canadian cities, 1991/92, annual rpt, S1685–1.2

Banking, Finance, and Insurance

Banks and savings instn establishments and deposits in daily newspaper markets in US and Canada, 1993 annual rpt, C3250–1

Shareholders of NYSE member firms, for 45 metro areas, 1990, annual fact book, B6625–1.1

Trust instns and assets managed, approx 5,000 depts, US and Canada, 1993 annual directory, C2425–2.501

State and local:

Alabama financial instns (State-chartered), financial condition, with deposits and assets by instn, FY92 annual rpt, S0110–1

Connecticut financial instns and branch offices, by instn and city, 1991, annual rpt, S1160–1

Georgia banks and other financial instns, financial condition by instn type, and assets by instn and city, Dec 1992, annual rpt, S1865–1

Illinois bank and trust companies (State-chartered) financial condition and status changes, by instn and city, FY92, annual rpt, S2395–1

Indiana financial instns (State-chartered) financial condition, including assets by instn arranged by city, 1991 and trends, annual rpt, S2625–1

Iowa bank and trust companies (State-chartered), financial condition by instn arranged by city, FY92 annual rpt, S2760–2

Kentucky financial instns condition, including assets by instn and city, with regulatory info, 1992 and trends, annual rpt, S3121–1

Louisiana financial instns (State-chartered), financial condition by instn arranged by city, with regulatory info, Dec 1992, annual rpt, S3265–1

Michigan banks and other financial instns, financial condition by instn, with regulatory info, 1992 and trends, annual rpt, S3957–1

Minnesota financial instns (State-regulated), financial condition by instn, 1991-92, annual rpt, S4140–3

Mississippi banks and other financial instns, by city, Dec 1992, annual rpt, S4325–1

Mississippi statistical abstract, general data, 1992 annual rpt, U3255–4

Oregon bank deposits, by instn grouped by county and city, Dec 1992, annual rpt, S6616–1

South Carolina financial instns (State-chartered) financial condition, including data by instn, FY92 annual rpt, S7165–1

Tennessee banks and other financial instns financial condition, by instn and city, 1992 annual rpt, S7507–1

Tennessee statistical abstract, general data, 1992/93 annual rpt, U8710–2

Virginia consumer finance companies net loans receivable, by instn arranged by city, Dec 1992, annual rpt, S8180–3

Virginia financial instns (State-chartered), financial condition by instn and instn type, Dec 1992, annual rpt, S8180–2

West Virginia banks and other financial instns, composite financial condition, with selected data by instn, 1990-91, annual rpt, S8530–1

Wisconsin banks financial condition, by instn and city, with regulatory info, 1992 and trends, annual rpt, S8685–1

Communications

Advertising agency billings for leading firms in top 20 US and top 10 foreign market areas, 1991-92, annual rpt, C2710–1.522

Broadcast tower current and proposed Federal land lease rates, for radio or TV stations in 6 cities, 1993 article, C1850–14.534

Business card use trends, for 15 cities, 1987-92, article, C4687–1.505

Cable TV industry devs, including leading multiple system operators and systems, finances, advertising, and data by network and service, biweekly rpt, C1858–1, C2965–1

BY CITY

Canada daily newspaper circulation, by publication and city, 6-month periods ended Sept 1992 and Mar 1993, semiannual rpt, A3385–3.2

China telecommunication data, including telephones, digital lines, debt levels, and cellular network operations, by location, 1980s-95, articles, A9315–1.503

Hispanic American marketing devs, including advertising expenditures by medium and effectiveness in leading market areas, 1992 annual features, C4575–1.502

Motion pictures with highest boxoffice receipts, and screens showing, for selected foreign cities, weekly rpt, C9380–1

Newspaper (daily) circulation, by US publication and city, 6-month periods ended Sept 1992 and Mar 1993, semiannual rpt, A3385–3.1

Newspaper (weekly) circulation, by US and Canadian publication and city, 6-month periods ended Sept 1992 and Mar 1993, semiannual rpt, A3385–3.3

Newspaper circulation in daily paper markets in US and Canada, by company, 1993 annual rpt, C3250–1

Newspaper single-copy sales as a percent of total circulation, for 5 Southeastern cities, selected years 1975-91, article, A8605–1.509

Radio audience ratings and program format, for top stations in leading metro markets, weekly rpt recurring article, C1850–14.506, C1850–14.507, C1850–14.508, C1850–14.521, C1850–14.531, C1850–14.542

Radio audience ratings for 6 news/talk format stations in 4 major cities, spring 1993, article, C1850–14.539

Radio audience size, leading stations and formats, and advertising rates and revenues, by market area, recurring rpt, C3165–1

Telephone exchange access lines worldwide, with comparison to population, by country and selected city, 1990-91, annual rpt, B0350–1

TV and cable TV households in top 20 market areas, Nielsen vs Arbitron estimates, biweekly rpt recurring feature, C1858 1.504, C2965–1.507, C2965–1.510

TV and total households, and member population by age and sex, by market area, county, State, and/or census div, 1992/93, annual rpt, B0525–3

TV audience ratings and shares for President Clinton's budget presentation, in 12 cities, Aug 1993, article, C9380–1.536

TV audience ratings for sign-on to sign-off period and late news programs, for 6-7 stations in top 3 metro markets, May 1993, article, C1850–14.523

TV audience ratings for sign-on to sign-off period and late news programs, for 6-7 stations in top 5 metro markets, Feb 1993, article, C1850–14.515

TV households and population by race-ethnicity, sex, and age, by market area, 1992/93, annual rpt, B0525–4

TV households and ranking among top 100 market areas, for 46 areas changing rank, 1992/93-1993/94, C1850–14.538

TV households by census div, State, county, Nielsen market area, and time zone, Jan 1994, annual rpt, B6670–2

TV station audience ratings and shares in 5-8 pm timeslot, for 5-7 stations in top 10 market areas, Feb 1993 sweeps period, recurring feature, C9380–1.516

TV station audience ratings and shares in 5-8 pm timeslot, for 5-7 stations in top 10 market areas, May 1993 sweeps period, recurring feature, C9380–1.527

TV station audience ratings and shares in 5-8 pm timeslot, for 5-7 stations in top 10 market areas, Nov 1992 sweeps period, recurring feature, C9380–1.505

TV station audience ratings in 5-8 pm and late news timeslots, for 5-7 stations in top 10 market areas, May 1993 sweeps period, recurring feature, C9380–1.531

TV station revenues, for top 20 cities, 1993, C1850–14.518

State and local:

Alabama statistical abstract, general data, 1992 recurring rpt, U5680–2

Alaska public utility rates, by utility type and community, June 1992, annual rpt, S0280–4

Arizona statistical abstract, general data, 1993 recurring rpt, U5850–2

California telephone bills, by city, Jan 1992, annual rpt, S0840–2.10

Florida statistical abstract, general data, 1992 annual rpt, U6660–1

Georgia statistical abstract, general data, 1992-93 biennial rpt, U6730–1

Kansas daily newspaper circulation by city and newspaper, 1985-91, annual rpt, U7095–2.13

Maryland statistical abstract, general data, 1993-94 biennial rpt, S3605–1

Mississippi statistical abstract, general data, 1992 annual rpt, U3255–4

New York State public broadcast stations, operation, and State aid, FY90-91, annual rpt, U5100–1.10

Oklahoma statistical abstract, general data, 1992 annual rpt, U8130–2

Rhode Island *Providence Journal-Bulletin* circulation, by city and county, FY92, annual rpt, C7975–1.1

Tennessee statistical abstract, general data, 1992/93 annual rpt, U8710–2

Utah statistical abstract, general data, 1993 triennial rpt, U8960–1

Education

Catholic colleges, elementary and high schools, enrollment, and teachers, by diocese and State, 1993 annual compilation, C4950–1

Catholic educational instns and enrollment, by State and diocese, 1993 annual almanac, C6885–1

Catholic schools, enrollment, and teachers, by region, State, and diocese, 1992/93 and trends, annual rpt, A7375–1

Library building referenda election results, by instn and location, FY92 and trends, annual article, C1852–1.508

Library construction, costs, and funding sources, by State, city, instn, and library type, FY92 and trends, annual article, C1852–1.501

Library construction, costs, and funding sources, by State, city, instn, and library type, FY92 and trends, annual compilation, C1650–3.4

School district enrollment, for top 100 districts, fall 1990, R4800–2.518

Index by Categories

Teacher employment, hiring, and labor turnover data, for 57 districts, Oct 1990-91, R6350–7

Urban public school performance compared to natl goals for year 2000, with data on students, teachers, and finances, for 47 systems, 1990/91 and trends, A4425–4

State and local:

Alabama elementary and secondary school enrollment, staff, pupil transportation, and finances, by district, 1991/92, annual rpt, S0124–1

Alabama municipal data book, general data, 1992 recurring rpt, S0121–5

Alabama statistical abstract, general data, 1992 recurring rpt, U5680–2

Alaska high school grads as percent of population over age 25, total and Native American, by borough and census area, 1980 and 1990, article, S0320–1.504

Alaska population, housing, income, and education data, by demographic characteristics and/or locality, 1990/91 and trends, annual rpt, S0320–4

California socioeconomic and govtl data for municipalities, counties, and school districts, 1993 annual rpt, C4712–3

Colorado public school enrollment, finances, and student and staff characteristics, by locality, 1991 annual rpt series, S1000–4

Colorado public school enrollment, finances, and student and staff characteristics, by locality, 1992 annual rpt series, S1000–2

Connecticut public library staff, holdings, circulation, and finances, by library and town, FY91, annual rpt, S1242–1

Delaware data book, general data, 1993 annual rpt, S1375–4

Delaware school enrollment, grads, staff, finances, and facilities, by county, school district, and/or instn, 1991/92, annual rpt, S1430–1

Florida municipal and county statistical profiles, general data, 1991 annual rpt, C4712–6

Georgia public school data, by county and city, 1993 annual rpt, U6750–1

Idaho public and nonpublic school enrollment by grade, by school district and/or county, Sept 1992, annual rpt, S2225–1

Illinois elementary and secondary school enrollment, staff, and finances, by county and district, 1990/91 and trends, annual rpt, S2440–1

Illinois public library holdings, staff, and finances, by instn, FY92, annual rpt, S2535–2

Indiana elementary and secondary school enrollment and finances, by district and county, annual rpt series, S2608–2

Indiana public and other library holdings, circulation, finances, and staff, by instn, 1992 or FY92, annual rpt, S2655–1

Iowa public library finances and operations, by county, size of population served, and library, FY92, annual rpt, S2778–1

Kansas school enrollment, grads, staff, and finances, by county, school district, and/or school, 1990/91, annual rpt, S2945–1

Kansas statistical abstract, general data, 1991/92 annual rpt, U7095–2

Maryland General Educational Dev (GED) test results, by test center, FY92, annual rpt, S3610–1

Index by Categories

BY CITY

Massachusetts municipal and county profiles, general data, 1992 annual rpt, C4712–2

Massachusetts public elementary/secondary school enrollment by grade, by district, Oct 1992, annual rpt, S3810–4

Massachusetts public elementary/secondary school expenditures per pupil by program, by district, 1991/92, annual rpt, S3810–5

Massachusetts public library finances, holdings, and circulation, by municipality, FY92, annual rpt, S3870–1

Michigan school district financial and enrollment data, with rankings, 1991/92, annual rpt, S3965–3

Minnesota public school enrollment, staff, and finances, by district and county, 1991/92 and trends, annual rpt, S4165–1

Mississippi public school enrollment, staff and salaries, and finances, by district, 1991/92, annual rpt, S4340–1.3

Mississippi statistical abstract, general data, 1992 annual rpt, U3255–4

Missouri public school finances, enrollment, and staff, by county and school district, 1991/92, annual rpt, S4505–1.2

Missouri public, special, and academic libraries, finances, holdings, circulation, staff, and services, by location, FY92, annual rpt, S4520–2

Montana public library holdings, staff, circulation, and finances, by library, FY92, annual rpt, S4725–1

Nebraska public libraries, finances, holdings, circulation, staff, and population served, by instn, FY91, annual rpt, S4910–1

New Hampshire elementary and secondary education statistics, with selected data by school district, annual rpt series, S5200–1

New Hampshire public library finances and operations, by library and/or location, 1991, annual rpt, S5227–1

New Jersey municipal and county data book, general data, 1992 annual rpt, C4712–4

New Mexico public library operations and finances, by instn, FY92, annual rpt, S5627–1

New York State municipal and county statistical profiles, general data, 1993 annual rpt, C4712–7

New York State statistical yearbook, general data, 1992 annual rpt, U5100–1

North Carolina public libraries, finances, holdings, and personnel, by library system, FY91, annual rpt, S5910–1

North Carolina public school enrollment, grads, staff, and finances, with data by race, sex, and local district, 1991/92-1992/93 and trends, annual rpt, S5915–1

Ohio public, academic, and other library finances, holdings, and staff, by library and location, 1992 and trends, annual rpt, S6320–1

Oregon library finances, staff, holdings, and services, for public, academic, and special libraries by instn, FY92 and trends, annual rpt, S6635–1

Pennsylvania public school personnel and salary data, by position and district, 1992/93 and trends, annual rpt, S6790–5.12

Pennsylvania statistical abstract, general data, 1992 recurring rpt, U4130–6

Rhode Island educational enrollment, grads, and finances, by district or community, 1991/92 or fall 1992, annual rpt, S6970–1

Rhode Island statistical almanac, general data, 1993 annual rpt, C7975–1

South Dakota school enrollment, finances, grads, and staff, by district, 1991/92 and trends, annual rpt, S7315–1

Tennessee public school enrollment, staff, finances, and operations, by county, city, and school district, 1991/92, annual rpt, S7490–2

Tennessee statistical abstract, general data, 1992/93 annual rpt, U8710–2

Texas elementary and secondary education data, by school district and county, annual series, S7670–1

Texas public libraries, holdings, circulation, staff, and finances, by library and location, FY91, annual rpt, S7710–1

Utah employment by detailed occupation, and educational attainment by age group, by sex and race-ethnicity, with detail for 7 urban areas, 1990 census rpt, S7832–3.4

Vermont libraries, finances, resources, and circulation, by city and library, FY91-92, biennial rpt, S8080–1

Virginia public library operations and finances, by instn, FY92, annual rpt, S8275–1

Virginia public school enrollment and high school grads, with detail by school district, 1980/81-2012/2013, annual rpt, U9080–20

Virginia public school enrollment, grads, finances, and staff, by county and municipality, 1991/92, annual rpt, S8190–3

Washington State public libraries, finances, holdings, circulation, staff, and population served, by instn, 1992, annual rpt, S8375–1

West Virginia public, academic, and special library operations and/or finances, by instn, 1991/92, annual rpt, S8590–1

Wisconsin elementary and secondary school enrollment, staff, costs, and State aid, by school district, 1992/93 and trends, annual rpt, S8795–2

Wisconsin libraries, operations, and finances, by library type, instn, and location, 1992, annual rpt, S8795–1

Energy Resources and Demand

Canada natural gas production outlook to 2010, domestic use and foreign trade, and exports to US via 8 delivery points, 1993 article, C6985–1.529

Coal trade by customs district, 1988-91, annual rpt, A7400–2.1

Electric utility income and operating data, by type of company and for individual locally owned utilities, 1993 annual directory, A2625–1.501

Gasoline (unleaded) and diesel fuel prices, by selected city, July-Dec 1992, annual rpt, C1575–2.507

Gasoline (unleaded) and diesel fuel prices, by selected city, monthly rpt, C1575–2

Gasoline prices, by city and PAD district, weekly rpt, C6985–1

Gasoline prices in approx 50 cities, selected years 1920-92, periodic basic data book, A2575–14.3

Natural gas and competing fuel prices, selected cities, 1991/92 annual rpt, A7015–3

Oil and refined products imports, by importing company, port, and country of origin, monthly rpt, A2575–12

Utility (electric and gas) billings for residential, commercial, and/or industrial service in selected cities, 1991, recurring rpt, S2218–2.6

State and local:

Alaska public utility rates, by utility type and community, June 1992, annual rpt, S0280–4

California diesel fuel wholesale prices before and after EPA low-sulfur requirements, for 6 cities, Aug and Oct 1993, article, C6985–1.551

California gas and electric bills, by city, Jan 1992, annual rpt, S0840–2.10

Florida statistical abstract, general data, 1992 annual rpt, U6660–1

Georgia statistical abstract, general data, 1992-93 biennial rpt, U6730–1

Pennsylvania coal exports by customs district, 1982-90, recurring rpt, S6810–3

Tennessee statistical abstract, general data, 1992/93 annual rpt, U8710–2

Texas natural gas utility financial and operating data, by city and company, 1991, with regulatory info, annual rpt, S7745–1

Geography and Climate

Climatological data for 22 cities, 1992 recurring rpt, S2218–2.7

Latin America statistical abstract, general data by country, 1992 annual rpt, U6250–1.1

State and local:

Arizona statistical abstract, general data, 1993 recurring rpt, U5850–2

California socioeconomic and govtl data for municipalities, counties, and school districts, 1993 annual rpt, C4712–3

Florida municipal and county statistical profiles, general data, 1991 annual rpt, C4712–6

Florida statistical abstract, general data, 1992 annual rpt, U6660 1

Georgia statistical abstract, general data, 1992-93 biennial rpt, U6730–1

Hawaii data book, general data, 1992 annual rpt, S2090–1

Idaho economic profile, general data, 1992 recurring rpt, S2218–2

Maine land area and population density, by local area, 1990 census rpt, S3465–7

Maryland climatological data, by weather station, 1960-90, biennial rpt, S3605–1.3

Maryland land area, by county and taxing jurisdiction, 1993 annual rpt, S3618–1.2

Massachusetts municipal and county profiles, general data, 1992 annual rpt, C4712–2

Nevada climatological data, by weather station, 1992 biennial rpt, S5005–1.9

New Hampshire land and water area, by county and city, 1993 biennial rpt, S5255–1

New Jersey municipal and county data book, general data, 1992 annual rpt, C4712–4

New York State municipal and county statistical profiles, general data, 1993 annual rpt, C4712–7

Oklahoma statistical abstract, general data, 1992 annual rpt, U8130–2

Pennsylvania heating degree days, by city, 1976/77-1990/91, recurring rpt, S6810–3

Pennsylvania statistical abstract, general data, 1992 recurring rpt, U4130–6

South Carolina statistical abstract, general data, 1993 annual rpt, S7125–1

BY CITY

Index by Categories

Tennessee statistical abstract, general data, 1992/93 annual rpt, U8710–2

Texas heating degree days in 25 largest cities, 1990-91, annual rpt, S7745–1

Virginia land area, by county and independent city, 1991, annual rpt, S8305–1.3

Government and Defense

Black elected officials, by office, govt level, and State or city, Jan 1992 and trends, annual article, R5685–4.502

City govt costs to enforce Fed Govt regulations including environmental laws, for 314 cities, FY93, with summary projections to FY98, A9330–12

Commercial building property taxes as percent of gross rent, for 26 metro areas, 1993 article, A6450–2.506

Congressional campaign contributions from individual donors and political action committees, for top 20 metro areas, 1990 election, biennial rpt, R3828–2.1

Economic indicators affecting local real estate markets, including DOD spending and manufacturing employment share, by locale, 1992, article, A6450–2.509

Election results for Federal offices and Governor, and voter registration, for 6 major metro areas, and by city in selected States, 1992, biennial rpt, C2500–1

Govt revenues by source and expenditures by function, 52 largest cities, FY90, annual rpt, R9050–1.6

Hispanic Americans on elected councils in 20 cities with largest Hispanic populations, 1980, annual rpt, U6250–1.5

Hispanic-owned business availability vs use for city govt contracts by type, and status of contract award disparity studies, for 5-10 cities, 1993 article, C4575–1.510

Local govt activities and structure, finances, and employment, series, A5800–4

Lodging tax rates, for 5 cities with highest rates, 1993 feature, C1200–1.513

Municipal and county govt structure, public services, finances, and intergovtl relations, 1993 annual rpt, A5800–1

Municipal govt annexation activity, and population and land area affected, by city, State, and census div, 1980-91, A5800–1.2

Tax burdens and rates, for largest city in each State, 1993 annual rpt, R9380–1.7

Tax rates on office space in 12 cities, 1993, R9050–15.7

Western States region State/local taxes and tax rates, for 10 major cities, FY92 annual rpt, S7905–1

State and local:

Alabama municipal data book, general data, 1992 recurring rpt, S0121–5

Alaska election results, and voter registration and turnout, by district and precinct, 1992 general election, biennial rpt, S0337–1

Alaska State and local taxation, including taxes by type, property values, public debt, and tax shelters, by locale, 1992 and trends, annual rpt, S0285–1

Arizona statistical abstract, general data, 1993 recurring rpt, U5850–2

Arizona tax revenues by source, tax rates, and disbursements to local areas, FY92 and trends, annual rpt, S0515–1

Arkansas financial condition, including revenues by source, expenditures by function and locality, and fund balances, FY91-92, biennial rpt, S0780–1

California election and referenda detailed results, by jurisdiction, 1992, biennial rpt, S0934–1.2

California socioeconomic and govtl data for municipalities, counties, and school districts, 1993 annual rpt, C4712–3

California tax collections (excluding income tax), by locality, company, and type of tax, FY92 and trends, annual rpt, S0835–1

Colorado property assessed valuation by detailed property type, and tax levy and revenue by local district, by county, 1991-92, annual rpt, S1055–3

Colorado retail sales and sales tax revenue, by county, city, and kind of business, FY92 and trends, annual rpt, S1075–1.5

Connecticut election results and voter registration and turnout, by location, 1992 general election, biennial rpt, S1265–1

Delaware data book, general data, 1993 annual rpt, S1375–4

Florida municipal and county statistical profiles, general data, 1991 annual rpt, C4712–6

Florida State govt disbursements to local areas, by source of funds, FY92, annual rpt, S1717–1

Florida statistical abstract, general data, 1992 annual rpt, U6660–1

Georgia statistical abstract, general data, 1992-93 biennial rpt, U6730–1

Idaho tax statistics, including collections, and data by county and city, FY92 and trends, annual rpt, S2295–1

Illinois property valuation and tax rates, by county and district, 1990/91, annual rpt, S2440–1.3

Iowa retail sales and use tax filings data, and establishments reporting, by county and city, and by kind of business, quarterly rpt, S2860–1

Kansas local sales tax collections, by county and city, FY91-92, annual rpt, S3020–1

Kansas statistical abstract, general data, 1991/92 annual rpt, U7095–2

Maine election results, by district, county, and municipality, 1992 general election, biennial rpt, S3490–1

Maine statistical summary, general economic and social data, 1992 recurring rpt, S3434–1

Maryland individual income tax return filings, and income and tax liability data, by city, county, and income group, 1991, annual rpt, S3685–1

Maryland local govt financial condition, including revenues by source, expenditures by function, and debt obligations, FY92 and trends, annual rpt, S3618–1

Massachusetts election results and voter registration, by local area, 1992 and trends, biennial rpt, S3920–1

Massachusetts municipal and county profiles, general data, 1992 annual rpt, C4712–2

Minnesota election results and voter registration, by locality, 1992 primary and general elections, biennial rpt, S4255–1

Mississippi statistical abstract, general data, 1992 annual rpt, U3255–4

Mississippi tax collections by type, and disbursements, with selected sales and income tax data by locality and industry, FY92 and trends, annual rpt, S4435–1

Missouri financial condition, including revenues and expenditures by agency, and tax collections and distribution, FY92 and trends, annual rpt, S4570–1.1

Montana taxable property values by city and town, 1991-92, biennial rpt, S4750–1.2

Nebraska tax revenues by type, tax rates and exemptions, and aid distribution to local areas, with data by county and city, 1991, annual rpt, S4950–1

New Hampshire election results, by county and locality, 1992, biennial rpt, S5255–1

New Jersey election results and voter registration, by location, 1992 general election, annual rpt, S5440–1

New Jersey municipal and county data book, general data, 1992 annual rpt, C4712–4

New Mexico tax revenues and disbursements, with data by tax type, county, and city, FY91-92 and trends, annual rpt, S5660–1

New York State municipal and county statistical profiles, general data, 1993 annual rpt, C4712–7

New York State statistical yearbook, general data, 1992 annual rpt, U5100–1

Ohio election results, and voter registration, by county and subdivision, 1991-92 and trends, biennial rpt, S6380–1

Oklahoma statistical abstract, general data, 1992 annual rpt, U8130–2

Pennsylvania statistical abstract, general data, 1992 recurring rpt, U4130–6

Rhode Island State assistance to individual cities and towns, by type, FY92, annual rpt, S6930–1

Rhode Island statistical almanac, general data, 1993 annual rpt, C7975–1

South Carolina local option sales/use tax collections, by county and city, FY92, annual rpt, S7255–1.3

South Dakota tax revenues by source, aid distributed to local areas, and property tax valuations, FY92 annual rpt, S7380–1

Tennessee statistical abstract, general data, 1992/93 annual rpt, U8710–2

Tennessee tax revenues by source and apportionments to counties, cities, and funds, FY91-92 and trends, biennial rpt, S7570–1

Utah govt statistical review, fiscal and socioeconomic data, 1993 annual rpt, R9380–1

Utah tax revenues by source, and distribution to localities and State funds, FY92 and trends, annual rpt, S7905–1

Vermont individual State income tax returns, by income class and locality, 1991, annual rpt, S8125–1.1

Virginia DOD expenditures by category, by county and city, FY89-91, article, S8205–4.502

Virginia DOD military and civilian employment by service branch, by region, locale, and installation, 1991 and trends, article, S8205–4.501

Virginia election results by jurisdiction, and voter registration and turnout, 1992 and Jan 1993 elections, annual rpt, S8195–1

Virginia tax revenues by type, county, and independent city, FY92 and trends, annual rpt, S8305–1

Washington State local govt annexations, by county and city, Apr 1990-92, annual rpt, S8345–4

Washington State treasury operations, including receipts, disbursements, aid to localities, and investments, by fund, FY92, annual rpt, S8455–1

Index by Categories

BY CITY

West Virginia fire protection classification ratings, by town and fire district, 1991, annual rpt, S8575–1

West Virginia property tax levy rates, by purpose and locale, FY93, annual rpt, S8640–3

Wisconsin Blue Book, general data, 1993-94 biennial rpt, S8780–1.3

Wisconsin property values and taxes, by school district, 1992/93, annual rpt, S8795–2

Wyoming election results by county, district, and precinct, 1992, annual rpt and govtl directory, S9000–1

Wyoming State treasurer financial transactions, including revenues, investments, and disbursements by local area, FY92 and trends, annual rpt, S9010–1

Wyoming tax collections and distribution, and property valuation, with data by property type and location, FY92 and trends, annual rpt, S8990–1

Health and Vital Statistics

- AIDS cases, for top 10 metro areas, 1993 article, C4215–1.505
- Eye bank activity in US and abroad, including donations by type, source, and donor characteristics, and data by individual bank, 1992 and trends, annual rpt, A4743–1
- Health insurance employee benefit costs, 10 metro areas with highest and lowest rates compared to natl average, 1992 article, C4687–1.501
- Health insurance group plan cost indicators, for 400 cities, 1989, B6095–1, B6095–2
- Health insurance managed care and nonmanaged care top 10 market areas, with population, 1992, article, A1865–1.510
- Hospital (teaching) house staff stipends in 37 metro areas, 1992/93, annual rpt, A3273–3
- Hospital directory, with utilization, expenses, and personnel, by instn, type, and location, 1992, annual rpt, A1865–3
- Hospital emergency dept visits for non-urgent, urgent, and emergent care, in 4 metro areas, Nov 1991, article, A1865–1.514
- Human immunodeficiency virus (HIV) infection rates among clients at sexually transmitted disease, drug treatment, and counseling/testing facilities in 14 cities, 1988-90, article, A2623–1.506
- Measles cases in preschool children, health care providers used and welfare status, in 5 metro areas, 1989-90, article, A2623–1.508
- Nurse average earnings in 7 major cities, by position, 1992 rpt, U8850–8.2
- Surgery costs for selected procedures, in 7 metro areas, 1992, annual rpt, A5173–2.3

State and local:

- Alabama vital statistics, including population, births, deaths by cause, marriages, and divorces, by location and demographic characteristics, 1992 and trends, annual rpt, S0175–2
- Colorado vital statistics, including population, births, deaths by cause, abortion, marriage and divorce, and adoption, by demographic characteristics and location, 1990 and trends, annual rpt, S1010–1
- Connecticut vital statistics, including births, deaths by cause, marriages, and divorces, by demographic characteristics and location, 1989, annual rpt, S1200–1
- Florida vital statistics, including population, births, deaths by cause, and marriages and dissolutions, by location and demographic characteristics, 1992 and trends, annual rpt, S1745–3
- Georgia vital statistics, including population, births, abortions, deaths by cause, marriages, and divorces, by demographic characteristics and location, 1991 and trends, annual rpt, S1895–1
- Iowa vital statistics, including population, births, deaths by cause, marriages, and divorces, by demographic characteristics and location, 1991 and trends, annual rpt, S2795–1
- Kansas vital statistics, including population, births, deaths by cause, abortions, marriages, and divorces, by demographic characteristics and location, 1991 and trends, annual rpt, S2975–1
- Louisiana vital statistics, including population, births, deaths by cause, reportable diseases, marriages, and divorces, by demographic characteristics and locality, 1989-90 and trends, annual rpt, S3295–1
- Massachusetts vital statistics, including births, deaths by cause, marriages, divorces, and population, by locality and demographic characteristics, 1990 and trends, annual rpt, S3850–1
- Michigan vital statistics, including births and deaths by selected city, 1990, annual rpt, S4000–3
- Minnesota vital statistics, including population, births, abortions, deaths, marriages, and divorces, by location and demographic characteristics, 1991 and trends, annual rpt, S4190–2
- Mississippi statistical abstract, general data, 1992 annual rpt, U3255–4
- Mississippi vital statistics, including births, deaths by cause, marriages, and divorces, by demographic characteristics and location, 1992 and trends, annual rpt, S4350–1
- Missouri vital statistics, including population, births, deaths by cause, and marriages and divorces, by location and demographic characteristics, 1992 and trends, annual rpt, S4518–1
- Nebraska vital statistics, including births, deaths, marriages, divorces, and population, by demographic characteristics and location, 1991 and trends, annual rpt, S4885–1
- New Hampshire vital statistics, including population, births, deaths by cause, marriages, and divorces, by location and demographic characteristics, 1991 and trends, annual rpt, S5215–1
- New Mexico vital statistics, including population, births, deaths, and disease, by location and demographic characteristics, 1991 and trends, annual rpt, S5605–1
- New York State vital statistics, including population, births, deaths by cause, reportable diseases, and marriages and dissolutions, by demographic characteristics and/or location, 1990 and trends, annual rpt, S5765–1
- North Carolina vital statistics, including population, births, deaths, marriages, and divorces, by local area, 1991 and trends, annual rpt, S5927–1.1
- Ohio vital statistics, including births, deaths by cause, marriages, divorces, and population, by demographic characteristics and location, 1991 and trends, annual rpt, S6285–1
- Oklahoma statistical abstract, general data, 1992 annual rpt, U8130–2
- Oregon births and deaths by city, and deaths by detailed cause in 3 major cities, 1991, annual rpt, S6615–5
- Pennsylvania statistical abstract, general data, 1992 recurring rpt, U4130–6
- Rhode Island vital statistics, including population, births, deaths, marriages, and divorces, by demographic characteristics and locality, 1989 and trends, annual rpt, S6995–1
- South Carolina vital statistics, including births, deaths by cause, marriages, and divorces, by age, sex, race, and location, 1990 and trends, annual rpt, S7175–1
- Tennessee statistical abstract, general data, 1992/93 annual rpt, U8710–2
- Tennessee vital statistics, including births, deaths by cause, marriages, divorces, and population, by demographic characteristics and location, 1991 and trends, annual rpt, S7520–2
- Texas physicians insured against professional liability, with data on premiums and claims, and detail by specialty and/or age, sex, and city, 1978-91, U8850–8.8
- Texas State and local health depts finances, employment, and service area characteristics, FY91 and trends, U8850–8.6
- Texas vital statistics, including births, deaths by cause, abortions, marriages, and divorces, by location and demographic characteristics, 1991 and trends, annual rpt, S7685–1
- Utah vital statistics, including births and deaths by cause, by demographic characteristics and location, 1990, annual rpt, S7835–1.2
- Vermont vital statistics, including population, births, deaths by cause, abortions, marriages, and divorces, by location and demographic characteristics, 1991 and trends, annual rpt, S8054–1
- Virginia vital statistics, including births, deaths by cause, marriages and divorces, and communicable disease, by demographic characteristics and location, 1991 and trends, annual rpt, S8225–1
- Washington State vital statistics, including births, deaths by cause, and population, by demographic characteristics and location, 1991 and trends, annual rpt, S8363–1
- West Virginia vital statistics, including births, deaths by cause, marriages, and divorces, by location and demographic characteristics, 1991 and trends, annual rpt, S8560–1
- Wisconsin live births, and total, fetal, and infant deaths, by county and selected city, 1991, annual rpt, S8715–4

Housing and Construction

Apartment building (conventionally financed) detailed income and expense ratios for US and Canada, by building type, metro area, and US region, 1991 and trends, annual rpt, A5600–1

BY CITY

Index by Categories

Apartment building (federally subsidized) detailed income and expense ratios, by building and subsidy type, building age, metro area, and region, 1991 and trends, annual rpt, A5600–5

China real estate prices per square foot of property offered in Hong Kong, for 9 Chinese cities, 1st qtr 1993, article, A9315–1.506

Commercial real estate market conditions and outlook, for industrial and office properties, by US metro area and selected foreign city, 1992-93, annual survey, A8916–1

Commercial real estate market conditions and outlook, for industrial and office properties in major metro areas, 1993 annual rpt, B2800–3

Condominium, cooperative, and planned unit dev detailed expenses, for US and Canada, by building characteristics, metro area, and US region, 1991, annual rpt, A5600–3

Construction (nonresidential) cost indexes for 21 metro areas, with cost increase by region, monthly rpt quarterly feature, C5800–15

Construction cost indexes for 20 cities in Europe, North America, and Pacific region, 4th qtr 1989-3rd qtr 1992, article, C5800–2.502

Construction cost indexes in 20 major cities, 1967-92, annual article, C5800–2.521

Construction industry materials prices by selected item, and cost indexes for construction, wages, and materials, approx 20 cities, weekly rpt, C5800–2

Construction industry wage and other cost trends, selected cities, weekly rpt quarterly feature, C5800–2.547

Home buyer (1st-time and repeat) profile, and transaction characteristics, including prices and financing, by region and for 18 metro areas, 1990-92, annual survey rpt, B2150–1

Home ownership rates in 10 metro areas with highest and lowest rates, 1992, C4300–1.510

Home prices for typical high-income homes in 29 metro areas, 1992, article, B8500–2.518

Homebuilder closings, for top 5 companies in 50 market areas, 1992, annual feature, C4300–1.507

Housing permit and remodeling activity, for 9 metro areas, semimonthly rpt, C1850–8

Housing permit, approval, and other regulatory compliance fees in 8 cities, 1992, article, C4300–1.510

Housing price forecast and trends, and mortgage foreclosure rate projections, for 43 metro areas or regions in rank order, 1993 article, A6450–2.509

Housing starts for 50 leading metro areas, 1990-93, annual article, C4300–1.503

Industrial and high-technology facilities availability, rental rates, and sale prices, for major metro areas by region, mid-1993, annual rpt, B2800–6

Lot (vacant) supply and absorption rate, for 15 metro areas, 1993 article, C4300–1.511

Low-income housing assistance availability indicators for 28 cities, 1991/92, annual rpt, A9330–9

Low-income housing supply-demand, costs, physical conditions, and public assistance, with data by race-ethnicity, for 44 metro areas, 1980s-91, R3834–16

Office space construction, for 14 metro areas, 1993 article, C8900–1.520

Real estate market outlook for top 13 metro areas, as rated by institutional investors, 1993, article, C4300–1.505

State and local:

Alabama municipal data book, general data, 1992 recurring rpt, S0121–5

Alabama statistical abstract, general data, 1992 recurring rpt, U5680–2

Arizona building permits issued and value, by type, size, and location, monthly rpt quarterly table, U0280–1.503, U0280–1.506, U0280–1.509

Arizona statistical abstract, general data, 1993 recurring rpt, U5850–2

California construction activity, and building vacancy rates, by selected metro area, 1992 and trends, annual rpt, S0840–3.1

California socioeconomic and govtl data for municipalities, counties, and school districts, 1993 annual rpt, C4712–3

Connecticut construction activity and value, by type of structure and location, 1992 and trends, annual rpt, S1212–1

Delaware housing construction activity, with data on demolitions and mobile home sales, by locality, 1992 and trends, annual rpt, S1387–1

Florida building permits, value by county, city, and type of construction, monthly rpt, U6660–5

Florida county data book, 1992/93 annual rpt, C6360–1

Florida municipal and county statistical profiles, general data, 1991 annual rpt, C4712–6

Florida statistical abstract, general data, 1992 annual rpt, U6660–1

Hawaii, Honolulu apartment rents compared to other major US cities, 1993, annual rpt, S2090–1.21

Idaho construction activity and value, by city and county, monthly rpt, B3900–1

Kansas statistical abstract, general data, 1991/92 annual rpt, U7095–2

Maine Census of Population and Housing summary findings, by local area, 1990, S3465–7, S3465–8, S3465–9

Massachusetts municipal and county profiles, general data, 1992 annual rpt, C4712–2

New Jersey municipal and county data book, general data, 1992 annual rpt, C4712–4

New Jersey residential construction activity and costs, by location, 1991 and trends, annual rpt, S5425–3

New Mexico business and economic activity indicators, monthly rpt, U7980–1

New York State business activity indicators, quarterly rpt, S5735–2

New York State municipal and county statistical profiles, general data, 1993 annual rpt, C4712–7

New York State statistical yearbook, general data, 1992 annual rpt, U5100–1

Oklahoma statistical abstract, general data, 1992 annual rpt, U8130–2

Pennsylvania housing data from Census of Population and Housing, by county and municipality, 1990, C1595–14

Rhode Island Census of Population and Housing detailed findings, by county and municipality, 1990, S6930–9

Rhode Island statistical almanac, general data, 1993 annual rpt, C7975–1

Tennessee statistical abstract, general data, 1992/93 annual rpt, U8710–2

Utah statistical abstract, general data, 1993 triennial rpt, U8960–1

Washington State population and demographic characteristics, and housing units, by county and/or city, 1992 and trends, annual rpt, S8345–4

Income

Association executives compensation, by metro area, 1992, biennial rpt, A2900–3

Black child poverty rates, with comparisons to whites, for major cities, 1989, R3840–21

Computer/info systems salaries for 24 positions, with detail for 6 major cities, 1993 survey, annual article, C1850–5.518

Consumer buying power survey of population, income, and sales by kind of business, by census div, State, MSA, county, and city, 1992, annual rpt, C1200–1.511

Consumer buying power survey of population, income, and sales by product line, by State, metro area, county, and census div, 1993 annual rpt, C1200–1.514

Earnings of workers, principal industries in daily newspaper markets in US and Canada, 1993 annual rpt, C3250–1

Logistics manager salaries, top 10 metro areas, Nov 1992 survey, annual article, C1850–11

Markets with daily newspapers, demographic and economic info by geographic area, US and Canada, 1993 annual rpt, C3250–1

Pay (average annual) in 22 cities, 1986 and 1991, article, S0465–1.502

Poverty rate in 29 cities, 1990, annual rpt, A9330–9

Poverty rates among children in 200 cities, with detail by race-ethnicity, 1989 and trends, R3840–20.2

Professional worker salaries, by employee and employer characteristics, with detail for scientists and engineers, 1990s and trends, biennial rpt, A3960–1

State and local:

Alabama municipal data book, general data, 1992 recurring rpt, S0121–5

Alaska population, housing, income, and education data, by demographic characteristics and/or locality, 1990/91 and trends, annual rpt, S0320–4

California socioeconomic and govtl data for municipalities, counties, and school districts, 1993 annual rpt, C4712–3

Florida statistical abstract, general data, 1992 annual rpt, U6660–1

Hawaii data book, general data, 1992 annual rpt, S2090–1

Kentucky economic statistics, general data, 1993 annual rpt, S3104–1.4

Massachusetts municipal and county profiles, general data, 1992 annual rpt, C4712–2

New Jersey municipal and county data book, general data, 1992 annual rpt, C4712–4

New York State municipal and county statistical profiles, general data, 1993 annual rpt, C4712–7

Pennsylvania Census of Population and Housing detailed findings, with selected data by county and municipality, 1990, U4130–13

Pennsylvania income data from Census of Population and Housing, by county and municipality, 1989, C1595–15

Index by Categories BY CITY

Rhode Island Census of Population and Housing detailed findings, by county and municipality, 1990, S6930–9

South Carolina statistical abstract, general data, 1993 annual rpt, S7125–1

Tennessee statistical abstract, general data, 1992/93 annual rpt, U8710–2

Utah govt statistical review, fiscal and socioeconomic data, 1993 annual rpt, R9380–1

Utah labor force characteristics, employment and unemployment, hours, and earnings, with data by industry and locale, 1992 and trends, annual rpt, S7820–10

Utah personal income and household data, by location and race-ethnicity, 1990 census rpt, S7832–3.3

Vermont individual State income tax returns, by income class and locality, 1991, annual rpt, S8125–1.1

Virginia income distribution and income tax returns filed, by locality, 1990, annual rpt, U9080–1

Virginia total and per capita personal income, by local area and major source, 1980-90, annual rpt, U9080–7

Industry and Commerce

Aluminum inventories of London Metal Exchange in US warehouses in 7 cities, monthly rpt, A0400–1

Black Americans preference for US products, with detail for 5 cities, 1993 survey feature, C4215–1.510

Black-owned enterprises ranked among top 100, with aggregate revenue and employment, for 7 cities with black mayors, 1992, article, C4215–1.509

Business executives ratings of ports, highways, and intl air service, with daily number of intl flights, for top 6-8 cities, 1993 article, C2150–1.504

Business failures and liabilities, by detailed industry, cause, length of operation, and location, 1991-92 and trends, annual rpt, C3150–8

Business failures and liabilities, by industry, census div, State, and major city, monthly rpt, C3150–2

China consumer goods sales by city, 1990, article, A9315–1.501

Cigarette exports by customs district, 1991, annual rpt, A9075–1

Cities rated as best for business by Fortune magazine, socioeconomic profiles of top 60 metro areas, 1992 annual article, C8900–1.501

Consumer buying power survey of population, income, and sales by kind of business, by census div, State, MSA, county, and city, 1992, annual rpt, C1200–1.511

Consumer buying power survey of population, income, and sales by product line, by State, metro area, county, and census div, 1993 annual rpt, C1200–1.514

Electrical equipment wholesaler market conditions, by geographic area, 1992 annual article, C4725–5.501

Foreign trade volume and value handled by top 20 ports, 1992, recurring article, C2150–1.506

Forest products foreign trade at 30 leading ports, 1991-92, annual article, C3975–2.512

Fortune 500 largest industrial corporation hqs in top 13 cities, 1992 and trends, annual feature, C8900–1.513

Fortune 500 largest service corporation hqs in top 6 cities, 1992, annual feature, C8900–1.516

Iron and steel imports, by US customs district and port, 1992, annual rpt, A2000–2.2

Iron ore shipments in US and Canada, with detail by Great Lakes port, monthly rpt, A2010–2

Machine tools in use, by type and city, 1989, annual rpt, A3179–2.1

Mexico retail sales, population, persons per household, and average earnings, for 5 major cities, 1993 articles, C5150–6.508

Office building detailed income and expense data, and energy use, US and Canada, by building characteristics, metro area, and US region, 1991 and trends, annual rpt, A5600–2

Retail stores and shopping centers in daily newspaper markets in US and Canada, by company, 1993 annual rpt, C3250–1

Shopping center detailed income and expense data, by building characteristics, metro area, and region, 1991, annual rpt, A5600–6

Trade activity at 15-16 leading US ports, with detail for Baltimore, 1989-91, biennial rpt, S3605–1.10

Western States plastics processing plant operating costs, by item, in 16 metro areas, 1993 article, C5800–12.512

State and local:

Alabama, Mobile Customs District foreign trade, by port and leading commodity and country, 1992 recurring rpt, U5680–2.7

Alabama statistical abstract, general data, 1992 recurring rpt, U5680–2

Arizona statistical abstract, general data, 1993 recurring rpt, U5850–2

California commercial and industrial vacancy rates in 10 State areas or cities, bimonthly rpt, S0840–1

California imports and exports, by customs district, 1983-91, annual rpt, S0840–2.11

Colorado retail sales and sales tax revenue, by county, city, and kind of business, FY92 and trends, annual rpt, S1075–1.5

Florida shopping center rents and vacancy rates in 8 metro areas, 1993 article, C5150–4.508

Georgia statistical abstract, general data, 1992-93 biennial rpt, U6730–1

Hawaii data book, general data, 1992 annual rpt, S2090–1

Indiana business conditions analysis for selected local areas, quarterly rpt semiannual feature, U2160–1.502, U2160–1.504

Iowa retail sales and use tax filings data, and establishments reporting, by county and city, and by kind of business, FY91, annual supplement, S2860–1.501

Iowa retail sales and use tax filings data, and establishments reporting, by county and city, and by kind of business, FY92, annual supplement, S2860–1.502

Mississippi statistical abstract, general data, 1992 annual rpt, U3255–4

Mississippi tax collections by type, and disbursements, with selected sales and income tax data by locality and industry, FY92 and trends, annual rpt, S4435–1

Nebraska business and economic activity indicators, monthly rpt, U7860–1

Nebraska sales tax revenues and taxable sales, by county, city, and detailed industry, 1990-91, annual rpt, S4950–1.2

New Mexico retail receipts, by city, monthly business activity rpt, U7980–1

Oklahoma business activity indicators, monthly rpt, U8130–1

Oklahoma statistical abstract, general data, 1992 annual rpt, U8130–2

Rhode Island statistical almanac, general data, 1993 annual rpt, C7975–1

South Carolina business gross receipts, by county and city, 1991, annual rpt, S7255–1.3

South Dakota business activity review, including selected data by city and industry, quarterly rpt, U8595–1

South Dakota gross sales/use tax purchases and taxable retail sales, by county and selected city, bimonthly rpt, U8595–2

Tennessee statistical abstract, general data, 1992/93 annual rpt, U8710–2

Utah business establishments, employment, and wages, by community, 1992, annual rpt, S7820–10

Utah taxable retail sales by city, FY92, annual rpt, R9380–1.6

Virginia taxable sales, by kind of business and locality, 1991 and trends, annual rpt, U9080–8

Labor and Employment

Economic indicators affecting local real estate markets, including DOD spending and manufacturing employment share, by locale, 1992, article, A6450–2.509

Employment and worker earnings, for principal industries in daily newspaper markets in US and Canada, 1993 annual rpt, C3250–1

Employment trends and outlook, for 10 metro areas with greatest projected growth, 1982-2002, article, C8900–1.519

Jobs lost or gained, for 5 cities with greatest losses and gains since June 1990, C8900–1.524

Latin America statistical abstract, general data by country, 1992 annual rpt, U6250–1.12

Unemployment rate in DC and approx 25 central cities, monthly rpt, S1527–3

Unemployment rate in 29 cities, Aug 1991-92, annual rpt, A9330–9

State and local:

Alabama municipal data book, general data, 1992 recurring rpt, S0121–5

California employment in 17 metro areas, Aug 1992-93, article, S0840–1.505

Delaware data book, general data, 1993 annual rpt, S1375–4

Kansas statistical abstract, general data, 1991/92 annual rpt, U7095–2

Maine Census of Population and Housing summary findings, by local area, 1990, S3465–9

Maine statistical summary, general economic and social data, 1992 recurring rpt, S3434–1

Massachusetts employment, hours, and earnings, by industry and local area, with unemployment insurance claims, monthly rpt, S3808–1

Massachusetts municipal and county profiles, general data, 1992 annual rpt, C4712–2

New Jersey municipal and county data book, general data, 1992 annual rpt, C4712–4

BY CITY

Index by Categories

New York State municipal and county statistical profiles, general data, 1993 annual rpt, C4712–7

North Dakota full- and part-time employment shares by sex, for 8 metro areas, 1993 annual planning rpt, S6140–2

Pennsylvania Census of Population and Housing detailed findings, with selected data by county and municipality, 1990, U4130–13

Pennsylvania employment and commuting data from Census of Population and Housing, by county and municipality, 1990, C1595–16

Pennsylvania statistical abstract, general data, 1992 recurring rpt, U4130–6

Rhode Island Census of Population and Housing detailed findings, by county and municipality, 1990, S6930–9

Rhode Island labor force planning rpt, including population, employment by industry, job openings, and characteristics of insured unemployed, 1993 annual rpt, S6980–3

Rhode Island statistical almanac, general data, 1993 annual rpt, C7975–1

South Carolina labor force and unemployment in selected cities, monthly rpt, S7155–2

Utah employment by detailed occupation, and educational attainment by age group, by sex and race-ethnicity, with detail for 7 urban areas, 1990 census rpt, S7832–3.4

Utah labor force characteristics, employment and unemployment, hours, and earnings, with data by industry and locale, 1992 and trends, annual rpt, S7820–10

Virginia cities in Washington MSA, unemployment rates, monthly rpt, S1527–3

Virginia labor force, hours, and earnings, with data by industry group and locality, monthly rpt, S8205–6

Wisconsin employment, hours, and earnings, by selected area, monthly rpt, S8750–1

Wyoming labor force by employment status, for 3 cities, monthly 1992, S8895–1.506

Law Enforcement

Crimes in cities with population over 400,000, 1991, annual rpt, S1535–2

Divorce caseloads and processing times by case characteristics, with domestic court judicial staff, for 16 urban jurisdictions, 1989 and/or 1990, R6600–6

Law school grad employment and salaries, by type of employer, location, and grad characteristics, 1992 and trends, annual rpt, A6505–1

Municipal police personnel salaries, by position and city, 1992, recurring rpt, A5800–4.32

Urban small claims and traffic court caseloads, processing, dispositions, judgments, and litigant satisfaction, for 3-12 jurisdictions, 1990, R6600–5

State and local:

Alabama crimes and arrests, by offense and location, with law enforcement employment, 1992 and trends, annual rpt, S0119–1

Alabama municipal data book, general data, 1992 recurring rpt, S0121–5

Alabama statistical abstract, general data, 1992 recurring rpt, U5680–2

Alaska court cases and dispositions, by type of court and case, and location, with judicial dept finances and personnel, FY92 and trends, annual rpt, S0290–1

Arizona court cases and dispositions, by type of case and court, with judicial personnel and finances, by county and city, FY92, annual rpt, S0525–1

Arizona statistical abstract, general data, 1993 recurring rpt, U5850–2

California court cases and dispositions, by type of case and court, and location, FY92 and trends, annual rpt, S0905–2

California socioeconomic and govtl data for municipalities, counties, and school districts, 1993 annual rpt, C4712–3

Connecticut crimes and arrests, by offense, with data by local agency, and victim-offender characteristics, 1992, annual rpt, S1256–1

Delaware alderman's court caseloads and dispositions, by city, FY92, annual rpt, S1360–1

Florida "habitual offender" sentencing laws effect on prison population, with data by circuit court and offender characteristics, 1993 rpt, A7575–5

Florida municipal and county statistical profiles, general data, 1991 annual rpt, C4712–6

Florida statistical abstract, general data, 1992 annual rpt, U6660–1

Georgia statistical abstract, general data, 1992-93 biennial rpt, U6730–1

Idaho crimes and arrests, by offense, with data by location and offender characteristics, 1992 and trends, annual rpt, S2275–2

Illinois crimes and arrests, by offense, with data by location and offender characteristics, 1991, annual rpt, S2536–1

Illinois statistical abstract, general data, 1992 annual rpt, U6910–2

Indiana court cases and dispositions by type of court and case, and location, with judicial system finances and personnel, 1992, annual rpt, S2703–1

Kansas crimes and arrests, by offense, with data by location, agency, and victim-offender characteristics, 1992 and trends, annual rpt, S2925–1

Kansas statistical abstract, general data, 1991/92 annual rpt, U7095–2

Kentucky crimes and arrests, by offense, with data by location and offender characteristics, 1992, annual rpt, S3150–1

Louisiana court caseloads and dispositions, by type of court and case, and jurisdiction, 1992 and trends, annual rpt, S3375–1

Maine court cases and dispositions, by type and location, FY92 and trends, annual rpt, S3463–1

Maine crimes reported, by offense, county, and local agency, 1991, annual rpt, S3475–1.2

Maryland crimes and arrests, law enforcement employment by sex, and assaults on police, by municipality, 1991-92, annual rpt, S3665–1

Massachusetts correctional instn inmate socioeconomic characteristics and criminal background, by instn, Jan 1992 and trends, annual rpt, S3805–1

Massachusetts court cases and dispositions, by type of court and case, and location, FY92 and trends, annual rpt, S3807–1

Massachusetts municipal and county profiles, general data, 1992 annual rpt, C4712–2

Michigan court caseloads and dispositions, by type of court and case, and court location, 1992 and trends, annual rpt, S3962–1

Mississippi statistical abstract, general data, 1992 annual rpt, U3255–4

Missouri crimes and arrests, by offense and location, with victim and offender characteristics, 1991 and trends, annual rpt, S4560–2

New Hampshire Index crimes reported, by agency and county, 1991, annual rpt, S5250–2.2

New Jersey crimes, population and land area, and law enforcement personnel by sex, by county and municipality, 1992 and trends, annual rpt, S5430–1.3

New Jersey municipal and county data book, general data, 1992 annual rpt, C4712–4

New York State criminal justice activities, by offense, location, local agency, and demographic characteristics, 1991 and trends, annual rpt, S5760–3

New York State municipal and county statistical profiles, general data, 1993 annual rpt, C4712–7

North Dakota court caseloads and dispositions, by type of case and court, and location, with judicial dept finances, 1991-92, annual rpt, S6210–1

North Dakota crimes and arrests, by offense, location, and offender characteristics, and law enforcement employment, 1991 and trends, annual rpt, S6060–1

Ohio court caseload and case disposition, by type of court and case, and location, 1992, annual rpt, S6385–1

Pennsylvania crimes and arrests, by offense, with data by location and offender characteristics, 1992 and trends, annual rpt, S6860–1

South Carolina court cases and dispositions, by type of court and location, with judicial dept finances and employees, 1992 and trends, annual rpt, S7197–1

Tennessee statistical abstract, general data, 1992/93 annual rpt, U8710–2

Texas court cases and dispositions, by type of court and case, and location, FY92, annual rpt, S7703–1

Virginia court caseloads, processing, and dispositions, by type of court and case, with judicial dept personnel and finances, by location, 1992 and trends, annual rpt, S8300–1

Virginia crimes and arrests by offense, and law enforcement employment, by location and reporting agency, 1992, annual rpt, S8295–2.2

Washington State court cases and dispositions, by type of court and case, and jurisdiction, with judicial finances and personnel, 1992 and trends, annual rpt, S8339–1

Washington State crimes and arrests, by offense, with data by location and offender characteristics, 1992 and trends, annual rpt, S8440–1

West Virginia crimes and rates, by major offense and city, 1991, annual rpt, S8610–1.1

Wyoming crimes and arrests, by offense, with data by location and victim and offender characteristics, 1991 and trends, annual rpt, S8867–3

Index by Categories

BY CITY

Natural Resources, Environment and Pollution

Air pollution attributable to road transportation, by substance, for 14 cities worldwide, 1992/93 biennial rpt, R9455–1.4

Child well-being indicators based on social, economic, and environmental factors, for 239 MSAs, with detail by component county and city, 1980s-90s, R9700–2

City govt costs to enforce Fed Govt regulations including environmental laws, for 314 cities, FY93, with summary projections to FY98, A9330–12

Environmental regulation costs under Federal mandates, summary projections for 6 cities, 1993 rpt, U9640–3

Plastics recycling program collection costs in 18 communities, 1992 rpt, A4375–14

Recycled newspaper exports by port of embarkation, 1981-92, annual rpt, A1630–8

Southeastern cities failing to meet natl ozone standards, with number of days exceeding standards, 1988-90, annual rpt, U8710–2.12

Wastepaper prices by grade, for 4 market areas, 1980-92, annual rpt, C3975–5.4

State and local:

Alaska public utility rates, by utility type and community, June 1992, annual rpt, S0280–4

California statistical abstract, general data, 1992 annual rpt, S0840–2

Florida statistical abstract, general data, 1992 annual rpt, U6660–1

New Jersey municipal and county data book, general data, 1992 annual rpt, C4712–4

Population

Black American population and share, in 10 cities with largest black population, and largest black share, 1990, article, A8510–1.1

Capital and largest city population, by State, 1993 annual almanac, C4712–1

Catholic population, clergy, and instns, by diocese and State, 1992, annual almanac, C6885–1

Catholic population, clergy, and instns, by diocese and State, 1993 annual compilation, C4950–1

Child and maternal health and welfare indicators, by selected city, 1992 annual rpt, R3840–11

Child well-being indicators based on social, economic, and environmental factors, for 239 MSAs, with detail by component county and city, 1980s-90s, R9700–2

Commonwealth of Independent States region population by sex, urban vs rural status, Republic, and selected city, 1986, R4105–82.4

Consumer buying power survey of population, income, and sales by kind of business, by census div, State, MSA, county, and city, 1992, annual rpt, C1200–1.511

Consumer buying power survey of population, income, and sales by product line, by State, metro area, county, and census div, 1993 annual rpt, C1200–1.514

Developing countries urban population, and share living in informal settlements, for 13 cities, 1993 rpt, A5800–1.1

Europe Jewish population, with social and demographic characteristics, for 10-12 countries, 1930s-91, article, A2050–1.1

Hispanic American population in top 20 cities, 1980, annual rpt, U6250–1.5

Hispanic American vs total population, for 35 cities with Hispanic mayors as of 1993, article, C4575–1.511

Jewish population by world area, country, and US census div, State, and city, 1990-92, annual compilation, A2050–1

Latin America statistical abstract, general data by country, 1992 annual rpt, U6250–1.5, U6250–1.17

Markets with daily newspapers, demographic and economic info by geographic area, US and Canada, 1993 annual rpt, C3250–1

Metro area low-income housing supply-demand, with data on population, income, and poverty and unemployment rates, for 44 metro areas, 1980s-91, R3834–16

Mexico economic indicators, including population by major city, 1993 articles, C4687–1.512

Middle East population trend and demographic characteristics, by country, 1993 rpt, R8750–2.59

Minority population characteristics, employment, and voting patterns by detailed race-ethnicity, with comparisons to whites, 1980s-2040, R8750–2.58

Population and black shares in large cities with black mayors, Jan 1992, annual article, R5685–4.502

Population growth rates for 5 fastest- and slowest-growing metro areas, 1990-2010, C4300–1.508

World rankings of 10 largest cities by population size, 1990 and 1992, article, R8750–1.505

World telephone exchange access lines, with comparison to population, by country and selected city, 1990-91, annual rpt, B0350–1

State and local.

Alabama municipal data book, general data, 1992 recurring rpt, S0121–5

Alabama statistical abstract, general data, 1992 recurring rpt, U5680–2

Alabama vital statistics, including population, births, deaths by cause, marriages, and divorces, by location and demographic characteristics, 1992 and trends, annual rpt, S0175–2

Alaska, Denali Borough population characteristics and income, with detail by local area, 1990-91, article, S0320–1.509

Alaska, Northwest Arctic Borough population characteristics and income, with detail by local area, 1990, article, S0320–1.512

Alaska population, by city, 1992, annual rpt, S0285–1

Alaska population, housing, income, and education data, by demographic characteristics and/or locality, 1990/91 and trends, annual rpt, S0320–4

California socioeconomic and govtl data for municipalities, counties, and school districts, 1993 annual rpt, C4712–3

California statistical abstract, general data, 1992 annual rpt, S0840–2

Connecticut population, by county, town, and health district, 1989, annual rpt, S1200–1

Florida county data book, 1992/93 annual rpt, C6360–1

Florida municipal and county statistical profiles, general data, 1991 annual rpt, C4712–6

Florida population, by city, county, and MSA, Apr 1992 and trends, annual rpt, U6660–4

Florida statistical abstract, general data, 1992 annual rpt, U6660–1

Georgia population trends and characteristics, by city and county, 1993 annual rpt, U6750–1

Georgia statistical abstract, general data, 1992-93 biennial rpt, U6730–1

Hawaii data book, general data, 1992 annual rpt, S2090–1

Idaho economic profile, general data, 1992 recurring rpt, S2218–2

Idaho population by city, 1980 and 1990, annual rpt, S2250–2

Iowa vital statistics, including population, births, deaths by cause, marriages, and divorces, by demographic characteristics and location, 1991 and trends, annual rpt, S2795–1

Kansas statistical abstract, general data, 1991/92 annual rpt, U7095–2

Kansas vital statistics, including population, births, deaths by cause, abortions, marriages, and divorces, by demographic characteristics and location, 1991 and trends, annual rpt, S2975–1

Kentucky economic statistics, general data, 1993 annual rpt, S3104–1.4

Maine Census of Population and Housing summary findings, by local area, 1990, S3465–7, S3465–8, S3465–9

Maine statistical summary, general economic and social data, 1992 recurring rpt, S3434–1

Maryland population, by county and taxing jurisdiction, 1993 annual rpt, S3618–1.2

Maryland statistical abstract, general data, 1993-94 biennial rpt, S3605–1

Massachusetts municipal and county profiles, general data, 1992 annual rpt, C4712 2

Massachusetts vital statistics, including births, deaths by cause, marriages, divorces, and population, by locality and demographic characteristics, 1990 and trends, annual rpt, S3850–1

Mississippi population, by race and city, 1990, annual rpt, S4350–1

Missouri population by city, 1980 and 1990, biennial rpt, S4580–1

Missouri vital statistics, including population, births, deaths by cause, and marriages and divorces, by location and demographic characteristics, 1992 and trends, annual rpt, S4518–1

Montana population, by city, county, and library service area, 1990, annual rpt, S4725–1

Nevada statistical abstract, general data, 1992 biennial rpt, S5005–1

New Hampshire population, by county and city, 1970, 1980, and 1990, biennial rpt, S5255–1

New Hampshire population by town, 1991, annual rpt, S5215–1

New Jersey cities without public libraries, population in 1990, annual rpt, S5385–2.1

New Jersey crimes, population and land area, and law enforcement personnel by sex, by county and municipality, 1992 and trends, annual rpt, S5430–1.3

New Jersey municipal and county data book, general data, 1992 annual rpt, C4712–4

BY CITY

New Mexico population, by city, 1980 and 1990, annual rpt, S5605–1.4

New Mexico population, by county and city, 1980 and 1990, annual planning rpt, S5624–1

New York State municipal and county statistical profiles, general data, 1993 annual rpt, C4712–7

New York State population, for 9 major cities, decennially 1930-90, annual rpt, S5710–1

New York State statistical yearbook, general data, 1992 annual rpt, U5100–1

New York State vital statistics, including population, births, deaths by cause, reportable diseases, and marriages and dissolutions, by demographic characteristics and/or location, 1990 and trends, annual rpt, S5765–1

Ohio vital statistics, including births, deaths by cause, marriages, divorces, and population, by demographic characteristics and location, 1991 and trends, annual rpt, S6285–1

Oklahoma population projections, by age, sex, and locality, with data on fertility and migration, 1990-2020, recurring rpt, S6416–1

Oklahoma statistical abstract, general data, 1992 annual rpt, U8130–2

Oregon population, by city, 1991, annual rpt, S6615–5

Pennsylvania Census of Population and Housing detailed findings, with selected data by county and municipality, 1990, U4130–13

Pennsylvania statistical abstract, general data, 1992 recurring rpt, U4130–6

Rhode Island Census of Population and Housing detailed findings, by county and municipality, 1990, S6930–9

Rhode Island labor force planning rpt, including population, employment by industry, job openings, and characteristics of insured unemployed, 1993 annual rpt, S6980–3

Rhode Island statistical almanac, general data, 1993 annual rpt, C7975–1

Rhode Island vital statistics, including population, births, deaths, marriages, and divorces, by demographic characteristics and locality, 1989 and trends, annual rpt, S6995–1

South Carolina population, by age, race-ethnicity, sex, and locality, 1990 and trends, annual planning rpt, S7155–3.1

South Carolina statistical abstract, general data, 1993 annual rpt, S7125–1

Tennessee population by race, county, and city, 1991 and trends, annual rpt, S7520–2

Tennessee statistical abstract, general data, 1992/93 annual rpt, U8710–2

Texas population by city, town, and county, 1980 and 1990-91, annual rpt, S7645–1

Utah employment by detailed occupation, and educational attainment by age group, by sex and race-ethnicity, with detail for 7 urban areas, 1990 census rpt, S7832–3.4

Utah govt statistical review, fiscal and socioeconomic data, 1993 annual rpt, R9380–1

Utah statistical abstract, general data, 1993 triennial rpt, U8960–1

Vermont population, by age, sex, and locality, 1991 and trends, annual planning rpt, S8025–2.1

Vermont population, by town, 1990, biennial rpt, S8080–1

Vermont vital statistics, including population, births, deaths by cause, abortions, marriages, and divorces, by location and demographic characteristics, 1991 and trends, annual rpt, S8054–1

Virginia population and net migration, by local area, 1990-91, annual rpt, U9080–9

Virginia population by race and location, 1991 and trends, annual rpt, S8225–1

Virginia population trends and projections by location, 1980-2000, recurring rpt, S8205–7

Virginia youth population by age, by county and city, with detail for disabled youth, Jan 1993, triennial rpt, S8190–1

Washington State population and demographic characteristics, and housing units, by county and/or city, 1992 and trends, annual rpt, S8345–4

Washington State vital statistics, including births, deaths by cause, and population, by demographic characteristics and location, 1991 and trends, annual rpt, S8363–1

West Virginia population, by MSA and component county and city, 1980 and 1990, annual planning rpt, S8534–2

West Virginia population by selected city, 1990, annual rpt, S8560–1

Wisconsin Blue Book, general data, 1993-94 biennial rpt, S8780–1.2

Prices and Cost of Living

Cost-of-living indexes and retail prices for selected consumer items in approx 300 cities, quarterly rpt, A0150–1

Cost-of-living indexes for housing and other items, for 51 metro areas, 4th qtr 1992, article, U0280–1.510

CPI for selected urban areas, 1991-92, annual rpt, U8130–2.22

Urban CPI, selected cities, 1991, annual rpt, U8710–2.2

Western cities cost-of-living index, by component, selected cities, monthly rpt quarterly table, S7820–3.503, S7820–3.506, S7820–3.507

State and local:

Alaska cost-of-living indicators for selected items and local areas, with comparisons to other US cities, 1992 annual article, S0320–1.501

Arizona cost of living and income, by city, 1991, annual article, U0280–1.501

Hawaii, Honolulu executive cost-of-living index compared to major cities worldwide, Mar 1992, annual rpt, S2090–1.14

Nebraska cost-of-living indicators by component, for 6 cities, with comparisons to other US cities, quarterly rpt, S4895–2

Oregon cost-of-living index, for 4 cities and Portland metro area, 4th qtr 1991, annual rpt, S6585–3

Tennessee cost-of-living indexes by component, for 11 metro areas, 4th qtr 1992, article, S7495–2.503

Public Welfare and Social Security

Emergency food and shelter supply-demand and assisted housing availability in 28-29 cities, with data on homeless population characteristics, 1991/92, annual rpt, A9330–9

Homeless shelter costs and utilization, for 8 cities, 1992 annual rpt, S7808–2

Index by Categories

United Way large organizations in 39 cities, funds raised in 1991-92 and 1992 goals, recurring article, C2176–1.503

United Way local organization funds drive results, and/or trend in allocations to charities, by city, 1991-92, article, C2176–1.515

United Way local organization funds drive results, errata, C2176–1.516

United Way local organizations in 16 cities, funds raised in 1991-92 and 1992 goals, recurring article, C2176–1.502

State and local:

Alaska AFDC caseloads and expenditures by region and municipality, and client self-sufficiency project survey data, 1993 article, S0320–1.503

Maryland public welfare caseloads by local dept of social services, monthly rpt, S3645–2

Nebraska social services recipients and payments, by local office, FY92, annual rpt, S4957–1.2

New Jersey public welfare cases, recipients, payments, and case processing, by program and county or city, monthly rpt, S5415–1

Oregon public welfare caseloads, recipients, and expenditures, by program, city, county, and State region, monthly rpt, S6615–8

Wisconsin State appropriations for food service for elderly, by school district, FY92, annual rpt, S8795–2

Recreation and Leisure

Arts fundraising through united arts funds (UAFs), with fund operations, income by source, and allocations, by UAF, 1992 and trends, annual rpt, A1315–2

Arts fundraising through united arts funds (UAFs), with top 10 UAFs in funds raised by source, 1992, annual article, C2176–1.513

Baseball American League player and team performance, and public attendance, 1992 and trends, annual rpt, A2068–1

Baseball Natl League player and team performance, and public attendance, 1992 and trends, annual rpt, A8015–1

Bowling (women's) assn membership and league activities, by city, State, and country, 1991/92, annual rpt, A9415–1

Bowling assn finances and membership, and bowling establishments and lanes, by State and other area, 1991/92 and trends, annual rpt, A1015–1

Olympic summer games profits or losses, by host city, 1976-96, with funds raised to date for Atlanta Ga 1996 games, article, C8900–1.514

Science and Technology

R&D facility construction costs, with cost indexes for 23 cities, 1993 article, C1850–6.504

Transportation and Travel

Air passenger (non-US resident) arrivals from overseas, by port of entry, 1988 and 1992, C7000–4.510

Airport freight traffic at top 20 airports, 1992, annual article, C2150–1.506

Airport passenger traffic and aircraft movements, for top 30 airports worldwide, 1991, C7000–4.501

Airport passenger traffic at top 32 airports worldwide, 1992, C7000–4.508

Airport passenger traffic at top 50 airports worldwide, 1990, annual rpt, C2140–1.5

Index by Categories

BY COUNTY

Airport regional and other daily flight departures for 10 airports with most regional flights, 1993 article, C5800–4.517

Airport runway incursions at 15 major airports, year ended June 1992-93, article, C5800–4.526

Airports and communities in North America served by regional vs larger airlines, by carrier and location, 1993 annual rpt, A8795–1.2

Auto ownership in US and Canadian cities, 1993 annual rpt, C3250–1

Commuting times for 14 metro areas with longest average times, 1992 feature, C4300–1.502

Hotel property value trends, for 5 metro areas with greatest gains and losses, 1991 vs 1990, C1200–5.502

Lodging industry occupancy rates, by major city, 1990-91, annual rpt, C2140–1.4

Mass transit use by commuters, and high occupancy vehicle roadway mileage, by selected metro area, 1992 annual rpt, A2650–1.1

Mexico-Texas transportation system analysis, including bilateral trade, operations by transport mode, and data by locale, 1993 rpt, U8850–9

Motor vehicle assemblies by city and State, 1992, annual rpt, A0865–1.1

Rail transit system Federal funding for new rail starts, for 26 cities, 1993, article, C8400–1.501

Sales industry costs for travel and related expenses, including incentive travel by destination, 1992 annual survey, C1200–1.508

Southeastern States waterborne shipments and receipts, for 6 cities, 1988 and trends, biennial rpt, U6730–1.8

Traffic accident deaths for 433 cities in US and Canada, 1991-92, annual rpt, A8375–2.3

Transportation service to daily newspaper markets in US and Canada, by mode and company, 1993 annual rpt, C3250–1

Travel and tourism rankings for selected indicators, including data for top 20 States, cities, countries, businesses, and other measures, 1992 recurring rpt, R9375–6

Western States travel times to work, population, and land area, for 18 urban areas, 1990, article, U0280–1.511

State and local:

Alabama statistical abstract, general data, 1992 recurring rpt, U5680–2

Alaska traffic accidents, fatalities, and injuries, by vehicle type, circumstance, location, and driver and victim characteristics, 1991 and trends, annual rpt, S0360–1

Arizona border crossings from Mexico, by city, 1970-91, recurring rpt, U5850–2.8

Arizona intl border crossings, between Mexico and 6 cities, 1985-93, semiannual rpt, U5850–1.1

Arizona statistical abstract, general data, 1993 recurring rpt, U5850–2

Arizona traffic accidents, fatalities, and injuries, by vehicle type, circumstances, location, and driver and victim characteristics, 1991 and trends, annual rpt, S0530–1

Arkansas traffic accidents, fatalities, and injuries, by vehicle type, circumstances, location, and driver and victim characteristics, 1991, annual rpt, S0692–1

California traffic accidents, fatalities, and injuries, by vehicle type, circumstances, location, and driver and victim characteristics, 1991 and trends, annual rpt, S0885–1

Colorado truck inspection activities by port of entry, FY92, annual rpt, S1075–1.4

Connecticut traffic accidents, fatalities, and injuries, by vehicle type, circumstance, location, and driver and victim characteristics, 1992, annual rpt, S1275–1

Florida statistical abstract, general data, 1992 annual rpt, U6660–1

Hawaii airport and harbor traffic, by facility, 1992 annual rpt, S2090–1.18

Illinois air passenger enplanements, by airport, 1986-90, annual rpt, U6910–2

Illinois traffic accidents, fatalities, and injuries, by circumstances, location, and driver and victim characteristics, 1991 and trends, annual rpt, S2540–1

Kansas traffic accidents, fatalities, and injuries, by vehicle type, location, circumstances, and driver and victim characteristics, 1992, annual rpt, S3040–1

Louisiana traffic accidents, fatalities, and injuries, by circumstances, location, and driver characteristics, 1991 and trends, annual rpt, S3345–2

Michigan traffic accidents, fatalities, and injuries, by vehicle type, circumstance, location, and driver and victim characteristics, 1991 and trends, annual rpt, S3997–2

Minnesota traffic accidents, fatalities, and injuries, by type of vehicle and circumstances, and driver and victim characteristics, 1992 and trends, annual rpt, S4230–2

Mississippi statistical abstract, general data, 1992 annual rpt, U3255–4

Missouri traffic accidents, fatalities, and injuries, by circumstances, location, and driver and victim characteristics, 1992 and trends, annual rpt, S4560–1

New Jersey fatal traffic accidents and fatalities, by vehicle type, location, and circumstances, and driver and victim characteristics, 1992 and trends, annual rpt, S5430–2

New Mexico motor carrier inspection activity and revenue collections by port of entry, and vehicle registration activity by local office, FY90-92, annual rpt, S5660–1.2

New Mexico traffic accidents, fatalities, and injuries, by vehicle type, circumstances, location, and driver and victim characteristics, 1992 and trends, annual rpt, S5665–1

New York State statistical yearbook, general data, 1992 annual rpt, U5100–1

North Carolina traffic accidents, fatalities, and injuries, by circumstances, location, vehicle type, and driver and victim characteristics, 1992 and trends, annual rpt, S5990–1

North Dakota traffic accidents, fatalities, and injuries, by circumstances, location, vehicle type, and driver and victim characteristics, 1992 and trends, annual rpt, S6217–1

Ohio traffic accidents, fatalities, and injuries, by circumstances, location, driver and victim characteristics, and vehicle type, 1991 and trends, annual rpt, S6290–1

Oklahoma statistical abstract, general data, 1992 annual rpt, U8130–2

Rhode Island statistical almanac, general data, 1993 annual rpt, C7975–1

Rhode Island traffic accidents, fatalities, and injuries, by circumstances, community, and driver and victim characteristics, 1992, annual rpt, S7025–1

South Dakota traffic accidents, fatalities, and injuries, by circumstances, location, vehicle type, and driver and victim characteristics, 1992 and trends, annual rpt, S7300–3

Tennessee statistical abstract, general data, 1992/93 annual rpt, U8710–2

Utah traffic accidents and fatalities by circumstances, location, driver and victim characteristics, and vehicle type, 1992 and trends, annual rpt, S7890–2

Virginia traffic accidents, fatalities, and injuries, by circumstances, location, and driver and victim characteristics, 1991 and trends, annual rpt, S8282–1

Washington State traffic accidents, fatalities, and injuries, by circumstances, vehicle type, and location, with driver and victim characteristics, 1992 and trends, annual rpt, S8428–1

West Virginia traffic accidents, fatalities, and injuries, by circumstance and location, and driver and victim characteristics, 1992, annual rpt, S8645–1

Wisconsin traffic accidents, fatalities, and injuries, by circumstances, location, vehicle type, and driver and victim characteristics, 1992 and trends, annual rpt, S8815–1

Wyoming traffic accidents, fatalities, and injuries, by circumstances, location, vehicle type, and driver and victim characteristics, 1992 and trends, annual rpt, S9007–1

BY COUNTY

Agriculture and Food

Farms, and livestock and crop values, by State, MSA, county, city, and Canadian Province, 1993 annual rpt, C3250–1

State and local:

Alabama agricultural production, marketing, and income, by county and/or commodity, and farms and acreage, 1992 and trends, annual rpt, S0090–1

Alabama county data book, general data, 1992 annual rpt, S0121–2

Alabama statistical abstract, general data, 1992 recurring rpt, U5680–2

Arizona agricultural production, marketing, and finances, by commodity and county, 1988-92, annual rpt, U5830–1

Arizona statistical abstract, general data, 1993 recurring rpt, U5850–2

Arkansas agricultural production, marketing, and finances, by commodity and county, with farms and acreage, 1992 and trends, annual rpt, U5920–1

Arkansas socioeconomic trends, by MSA and/or county, 1993 annual rpt, U5935–1

California agricultural statistics, including production, acreage, finances, and marketing, by commodity, annual rpt series, S0850–1

California statistical abstract, general data, 1992 annual rpt, S0840–2

Colorado agricultural production, marketing, and finances, by commodity and/or county, with farms and acreage, 1992 and trends, annual rpt, S0985–1

BY COUNTY

Index by Categories

Florida agricultural statistics, including production, finances, and shipment data for citrus, dairy, and other sectors, by commodity and/or county, 1993 annual rpt series, S1685–1

Florida county data book, 1992/93 annual rpt, C6360–1

Florida statistical abstract, general data, 1992 annual rpt, U6660–1

Georgia agricultural production, marketing, and finances, by commodity and/or county, and farms and acreage, 1991 and trends, annual rpt, S1855–1

Georgia county guide, general data, 1993 annual rpt, U6750–1

Georgia statistical abstract, general data, 1992-93 biennial rpt, U6730–1

Hawaii agricultural production and marketing, by commodity and island, 1987-91, annual rpt, S2030–1

Hawaii data book, general data, 1992 annual rpt, S2090–1

Illinois agricultural production, marketing, and finances, by county or commodity, and farms and farmland, 1991 and trends, annual rpt, S2390–1

Illinois statistical abstract, general data, 1992 annual rpt, U6910–2

Kansas agricultural production, marketing, and finances, by county and/or commodity, and farm acreage and value, 1992 and trends, annual rpt, S2915–1

Kansas statistical abstract, general data, 1991/92 annual rpt, U7095–2

Kentucky agricultural production, marketing, and finances, by commodity and county; and farms, acreage, and value; 1992 and trends, annual rpt, S3085–1

Louisiana agricultural production, marketing, and finances, by commodity or parish, 1985-91, annual rpt, U2740–1

Michigan agricultural production, marketing, and finances, by commodity or county, 1987-91, annual rpt, S3950–1

Minnesota agricultural production, marketing, and finances, by county or commodity, and farms and acreage, 1992 and trends, annual rpt, S4130 1

Mississippi statistical abstract, general data, 1992 annual rpt, U3255–4

Missouri agricultural production, marketing, and finances, by commodity and/or county, and farms and acreage, 1988-92, annual rpt, S4480–1

Montana agricultural production, marketing, and finances, by commodity and county, 1991 and trends, annual rpt, S4655–1

Montana farmland acreage and value, by county, 1991-92, biennial rpt, S4750–1.2

Nebraska agricultural production, marketing, and finances, by commodity and/or county, and farms and acreage, 1991 and trends, annual rpt, S4835–1

Nebraska farmer/rancher/fisherman income tax returns, and income, by county, 1990, annual rpt, S4950–1.1

Nevada agricultural production, marketing, and finances, by county and commodity, and farms and acreage, 1992 and trends, annual rpt, S5010–1

Nevada statistical abstract, general data, 1992 biennial rpt, S5005–1

New Jersey agricultural production, marketing, and finances, by commodity and/or county, and farms and acreage, 1986-91, annual rpt, S5350–1

New Mexico agricultural production, marketing, and finances, by commodity and county, with farms and acreage, 1991 and trends, annual rpt, S5530–1

New York State agricultural production, marketing, and finances, by commodity and/or county, and farms and acreage, 1992 and trends, annual rpt, S5700–1

New York State statistical yearbook, general data, 1992 annual rpt, U5100–1

North Carolina agricultural production, marketing, by commodity and county, 1991 and trends, annual rpt, S5885–1

North Dakota agricultural production and marketing, by commodity and county, and farm finances, 1992 and trends, annual rpt, U3600–1

North Dakota farmland, acres in conservation reserve program, and sales and average prices, by county, 1993 annual planning rpt, S6140–2

Ohio agricultural production, marketing, and finances, by commodity and county, with farms and acreage, 1990-91 and trends, annual rpt, S6240–1

Oklahoma agricultural production, marketing, and finances, by commodity and county, 1992 and trends, annual rpt, S6405–1

Oklahoma statistical abstract, general data, 1992 annual rpt, U8130–2

Oregon agricultural production, marketing, and finances, by commodity and/or county, with farms and acreage, 1991 and trends, annual rpt, S6575–1

Pennsylvania agricultural production, marketing, and finances, by county and commodity, and farms and acreage, 1992 and trends, annual rpt, S6760–1

Pennsylvania statistical abstract, general data, 1992 recurring rpt, U4130–6

South Carolina agricultural production and finances, by commodity and county, 1991-92 and trends, annual rpt, U1075–3

South Carolina economic activity indicators, including employment by industry div, by county, 1993 annual rpt, S7145–1.2

South Carolina statistical abstract, general data, 1993 annual rpt, S7125–1

South Dakota agricultural production, marketing, and finances, by commodity and county, and farms and acreage, 1992 and trends, annual rpt, S7280–1

Tennessee agricultural production and marketing, by commodity and county, with farms, acreage, and farm value, 1992 and trends, annual rpt, S7460–1

Tennessee statistical abstract, general data, 1992/93 annual rpt, U8710–2

Texas agricultural production, marketing, and finances, by commodity and county, and farms and farmland, 1991 and trends, annual rpt series, S7630–1

Utah agricultural production, marketing, and finances, by commodity and county, with farms and acreage, 1992 and trends, annual rpt, S7800–1

Utah statistical abstract, general data, 1993 triennial rpt, U8960–1

Vermont dairy industry plants and operations, by county, 1988-89, biennial rpt, S7978–1

Washington State agricultural production, marketing, and finances, by commodity and/or county, 1992 and trends, annual rpt, S8328–1

West Virginia agricultural production, marketing, and finances, by commodity or county, 1991 and trends, annual rpt, S8510–1

Wisconsin agricultural production, marketing, and finances, by commodity and county, and farms, acreage, and sales, 1992 and trends, annual rpt, S8680–1

Wisconsin Blue Book, general data, 1993-94 biennial rpt, S8780–1.2

Wyoming agricultural production, marketing, and finances, by county and/or commodity, and farms, acreage, and value, 1992 and trends, annual rpt, S8860–1

Banking, Finance, and Insurance

State and local:

Alabama county data book, general data, 1992 annual rpt, S0121–2

Alabama statistical abstract, general data, 1992 recurring rpt, U5680–2

Arizona statistical abstract, general data, 1993 recurring rpt, U5850–2

Arkansas socioeconomic trends, by MSA and/or county, 1993 annual rpt, U5935–1

Florida statistical abstract, general data, 1992 annual rpt, U6660–1

Georgia county guide, general data, 1993 annual rpt, U6750–1

Georgia statistical abstract, general data, 1992-93 biennial rpt, U6730–1

Hawaii data book, general data, 1992 annual rpt, S2090–1

Illinois banks (State-chartered) financial condition, by county, FY92, annual rpt, S2395–1

Illinois real estate title insurance premiums written, by county, 1990, annual rpt, S2457–2

Illinois statistical abstract, general data, 1992 annual rpt, U6910–2

Kansas statistical abstract, general data, 1991/92 annual rpt, U7095–2

Kentucky economic statistics, general data, 1993 annual rpt, S3104–1.3

Maine financial instn assets, deposits, and loans, by type of instn and county, 1982-92, annual rpt, S3473–1

Maryland statistical abstract, general data, 1993-94 biennial rpt, S3605–1

Mississippi banks and branch offices, by county and city, Dec 1992, annual rpt, S4325–1

Mississippi statistical abstract, general data, 1992 annual rpt, U3255–4

New Jersey banks and other financial instns, assets and liabilities by instn, 1992 and trends, annual rpt, S5355–1

New York State statistical yearbook, general data, 1992 annual rpt, U5100–1

Oklahoma banks and bank holding companies by asset size, and asset concentration by location and among top instns, 1984-90, article, U8130–1.502

Oklahoma statistical abstract, general data, 1992 annual rpt, U8130–2

Oregon bank deposits, by instn grouped by county and city, Dec 1992, annual rpt, S6616–1

Pennsylvania statistical abstract, general data, 1992 recurring rpt, U4130–6

South Carolina statistical abstract, general data, 1993 annual rpt, S7125–1

Tennessee statistical abstract, general data, 1992/93 annual rpt, U8710–2

Index by Categories

BY COUNTY

Wisconsin Blue Book, general data, 1993-94 biennial rpt, S8780–1.2

Communications

- TV and total households, and member population by age and sex, by market area, county, State, and/or census div, 1992/93, annual rpt, B0525–3
- TV households by census div, State, county, Nielsen market area, and time zone, Jan 1994, annual rpt, B6670–2

State and local:

- Alabama county data book, general data, 1992 annual rpt, S0121–2
- Arizona statistical abstract, general data, 1993 recurring rpt, U5850–2
- Florida statistical abstract, general data, 1992 annual rpt, U6660–1
- Hawaii data book, general data, 1992 annual rpt, S2090–1
- Rhode Island *Providence Journal-Bulletin* circulation, by city and county, FY92, annual rpt, C7975–1.1
- Tennessee statistical abstract, general data, 1992/93 annual rpt, U8710–2

Education

- School bus fleet rankings, top 74 districts and 26 contractors, 1992 survey, annual article, C1575–1.501
- Teacher employment, hiring, and labor turnover data, for 57 districts, Oct 1990-91, R6350–7

State and local:

- Alabama county data book, general data, 1992 annual rpt, S0121–2
- Alabama elementary and secondary school enrollment, staff, pupil transportation, and finances, by district, 1991/92, annual rpt, S0124–1
- Alabama public libraries, finances, holdings, circulation, staff, and population served, by library, FY92, annual rpt, S0180–1
- Alabama statistical abstract, general data, 1992 recurring rpt, U5680–2
- Alaska high school grads as percent of population over age 25, total and Native American, by borough and census area, 1980 and 1990, article, S0320–1.504
- Alaska population, housing, income, and education data, by demographic characteristics and/or locality, 1990/91 and trends, annual rpt, S0320–4
- Alaska public schools, enrollment, staff, and finances, by district, FY92, annual rpt, S0295–2
- Arizona elementary and secondary school enrollment, staff, and finances, by school district and county, FY92 and trends, annual rpt, S0470–1
- Arizona public library holdings, circulation, finances, and staff, by instn and county, FY92, annual rpt, S0495–1
- Arizona statistical abstract, general data, 1993 recurring rpt, U5850–2
- Arkansas higher education enrollment by student characteristics and geographic origins, by instn, fall 1991 and trends, annual rpt, S0690–1
- Arkansas public school enrollment, grads, staff, and finances, by county and school, 1991/92 and trends, annual rpt, S0660–1
- Arkansas socioeconomic trends, by MSA and/or county, 1993 annual rpt, U5935–1
- California private schools, enrollment by grade, grads, and staff, with data by county, 1992/93 and trends, annual rpt, S0825–8

California public school enrollment, grads, and teachers, by race-ethnicity and county, 1992/93 and trends, annual rpt, S0825–9

- California public school limited-English-proficiency enrollment, teachers, and programs, by 1st language, grade level, and county, 1992 and trends, annual rpt, S0825–10
- California public schools, enrollment by grade, and grads, by county, 1992/93 and trends, annual rpt, S0825–7
- California socioeconomic and govtl data for municipalities, counties, and school districts, 1993 annual rpt, C4712–3
- Colorado public school enrollment and dropouts, by local area, 1991/92, annual planning rpt, S1040–3.1
- Colorado public school enrollment, finances, and student and staff characteristics, by locality, 1991 annual rpt series, S1000–4
- Colorado public school enrollment, finances, and student and staff characteristics, by locality, 1992 annual rpt series, S1000–2
- Delaware data book, general data, 1993 annual rpt, S1375–4
- Delaware school enrollment, grads, staff, finances, and facilities, by county, school district, and/or instn, 1991/92, annual rpt, S1430–1
- Florida county data book, 1992/93 annual rpt, C6360–1
- Florida higher education enrollment, by State and Florida county of residence, fall 1991, annual rpt, S1725–1
- Florida municipal and county statistical profiles, general data, 1991 annual rpt, C4712–6
- Florida statistical abstract, general data, 1992 annual rpt, U6660–1
- Georgia county guide, general data, 1993 annual rpt, U6750–1
- Georgia statistical abstract, general data, 1992-93 biennial rpt, U6730–1
- Hawaii data book, general data, 1992 annual rpt, S2090–1
- Idaho economic profile, general data, 1992 recurring rpt, S2218–2
- Idaho public and nonpublic school enrollment by grade, by school district and/or county, Sept 1992, annual rpt, S2225–1
- Idaho public library holdings, staff, services, circulation, and finances, by instn, FY92, annual rpt, S2282–1
- Idaho public school personnel characteristics and salaries by position, and teachers and enrollment by school district, 1992/93, annual rpt, S2225–3
- Idaho school district revenues by source, and expenditures by function, by district and fund, FY92, annual rpt, S2225–2
- Illinois elementary and secondary school enrollment, staff, and finances, by county and district, 1990/91 and trends, annual rpt, S2440–1
- Illinois public library holdings, staff, and finances, by instn, FY92, annual rpt, S2535–2
- Illinois statistical abstract, general data, 1992 annual rpt, U6910–2
- Indiana elementary and secondary school enrollment and finances, by district and county, annual rpt series, S2608–2
- Indiana public and other library holdings, circulation, finances, and staff, by instn, 1992 or FY92, annual rpt, S2655–1

Iowa public library finances and operations, by county, size of population served, and library, FY92, annual rpt, S2778–1

- Kansas school enrollment, grads, staff, and finances, by county, school district, and/or school, 1990/91, annual rpt, S2945–1
- Kansas statistical abstract, general data, 1991/92 annual rpt, U7095–2
- Kentucky public education profiles, with data by region and district, 1991/92 and trends, annual rpt, S3110–1
- Kentucky public library finances and operations, by county, FY92, annual rpt, S3165–1
- Kentucky public school finances, staff, and enrollment, by district, 1989/90-1990/91, biennial rpt, S3110–2
- Kentucky school revenue bonds issued, by district, FY92, annual rpt, S3120–1
- Louisiana elementary/secondary school operations, including enrollment, staff, finances, and detail by school district, 1991/92 and trends, annual rpt, S3280–1
- Louisiana public library finances, holdings, circulation, and personnel, by parish library system, FY92, annual rpt, S3275–1
- Maine public school enrollment, facilities, staff, and finances, with selected data by county and for private schools, 1991 and trends, annual rpt, S3435–1
- Maryland elementary and secondary education data, by county, annual rpt series, S3610–2
- Maryland elementary and secondary education statistical summary, with data by county, 1991/92-1992/93 and trends, annual rpt, S3610–1
- Maryland public library operating income and expenditures, staff, holdings, and population served, by county, FY92, annual rpt, S3610–5
- Maryland statistical abstract, general data, 1993-94 biennial rpt, S3605–1
- Massachusetts municipal and county profiles, general data, 1992 annual rpt, C4712–2
- Massachusetts public elementary/secondary school enrollment by grade, by district, Oct 1992, annual rpt, S3810–4
- Massachusetts public elementary/secondary school expenditures per pupil by program, by district, 1991/92, annual rpt, S3810–5
- Minnesota public school enrollment, staff, and finances, by district and county, 1991/92 and trends, annual rpt, S4165–1
- Mississippi property tax assessments and levies by type, by county and school district, 1991/92, annual rpt, S4340–1.3
- Mississippi statistical abstract, general data, 1992 annual rpt, U3255–4
- Missouri higher education enrollment by student characteristics and residence location, by instn, fall 1992 and trends, annual rpt, S4520–3.2
- Missouri public school finances, enrollment, and staff, by county and school district, 1991/92, annual rpt, S4505–1.2
- Missouri public, special, and academic libraries, finances, holdings, circulation, staff, and services, by location, FY92, annual rpt, S4520–2
- Montana public school enrollment by grade, and grads, by school, county, race-ethnicity, and sex, 1992 and trends, annual rpt, S4740–1

BY COUNTY

Index by Categories

Nebraska elementary and secondary schools, enrollment by grade, and staff, with data by school district and county, annual series, S4865–2

Nebraska elementary/secondary private school enrollment shares, for 21 counties, 1990, article, U7860–1.502

Nebraska public school finances, including receipts by source and disbursements by function, by county and district, 1988/89, annual rpt, S4865–3

Nevada public school enrollment, test scores, teachers, and finances, by school district, 1990/91 and trends, annual rpt, S5035–2

Nevada statistical abstract, general data, 1992 biennial rpt, S5005–1

New Hampshire high school grads and postgraduation activities, by school, county, and sex, 1991, annual tables, S5200–1.2

New Hampshire high school grads and postgraduation activities, by school, county, and sex, 1992, annual tables, S5200–1.15

New Hampshire public library finances and operations, by library and/or location, 1991, annual rpt, S5227–1

New Jersey municipal and county data book, general data, 1992 annual rpt, C4712–4

New Jersey public library finances, holdings, circulation, and staff, by county and library, 1991, annual rpt, S5385–2

New Jersey public schools, enrollment, and student and staff characteristics, and nonpublic schools and enrollment, by county, 1991/92, annual rpt, S5385–1

New Mexico elementary/secondary school statistics, including grads, student test results, and finances, by school district, 1989/90-1991/92, annual rpt, S5575–4

New Mexico high school enrollment and dropouts, by county, 1991/92, annual planning rpt, S5624–1

New Mexico public library operations and finances, by instn, FY92, annual rpt, S5627–1

New York State municipal and county statistical profiles, general data, 1993 annual rpt, C4712–7

New York State public library finances, staff, holdings, and services, by library and county, 1991, annual rpt, S5745–2

New York State statistical yearbook, general data, 1992 annual rpt, U5100–1

North Carolina higher education enrollment, by student characteristics, and State and county of residence, fall 1992 and trends, annual rpt, U8013–1.1

North Carolina public libraries, finances, holdings, and personnel, by library system, FY91, annual rpt, S5910–1

North Carolina public school enrollment, grads, staff, and finances, with data by race, sex, and local district, 1991/92-1992/93 and trends, annual rpt, S5915–1

North Dakota elementary and secondary schools, enrollment, and staff, by school type and location, 1992/93 annual directory, S6180–2

North Dakota higher education enrollment, by level, instn, county, and selected student characteristics, fall 1992 and trends, annual rpt, S6110–1

North Dakota public school revenues by source, expenditures by function, mill levies, and taxable value, by district, 1992/93 annual rpt, S6180–4

Ohio public, academic, and other library finances, holdings, and staff, by library and location, 1992 and trends, annual rpt, S6320–1

Ohio special education expenditures, instructional hours, and enrollment, by service type and school district, 1991/92 and trends, annual rpt, S6265–1

Oklahoma public school finances, personnel, enrollment, and facilities, by county and district, 1991/92 and trends, annual rpt, S6423–1

Oklahoma public school performance indicators, including students and achievement, finances, and staff, by district, 1990/91-1991/92 and trends, annual rpt, S6423–2

Oklahoma statistical abstract, general data, 1992 annual rpt, U8130–2

Oregon elementary and secondary education enrollment and finances, including data by school district and county, annual rpt series, S6590–1

Oregon population share with bachelor's degree/higher, by county, 1990, article, S6615–2.502

Pennsylvania public and institutional library personnel, holdings, circulation, and finances, by county and facility, FY92, annual rpt, S6790–2

Pennsylvania public and nonpublic high school grads, sex, race-ethnicity, and county, 1991/92 and trends, annual rpt, S6790–5.14

Pennsylvania public and nonpublic school enrollment, by grade, race-ethnicity, sex, and county, 1991/92 and trends, annual rpt, S6790–5.1

Pennsylvania public and nonpublic school enrollment, by grade, race-ethnicity, sex, and county, 1992/93 and trends, annual rpt, S6790–5.17

Pennsylvania public school personnel and salary data, by position and district, 1992/93 and trends, annual rpt, S6790–5.12

Pennsylvania statistical abstract, general data, 1992 recurring rpt, U4130–6

Rhode Island educational enrollment, grads, and finances, by district or community, 1991/92 or fall 1992, annual rpt, S6970–1

South Carolina educational characteristics and socioeconomic indicators, by school district and county, 1991/92, annual rpt, S7145–1

South Carolina higher education freshman enrollment by State and South Carolina county of residence, fall 1992, annual rpt, S7185–2

South Carolina public and private schools, enrollment, and grads, by county, 1990/91 and trends, annual planning rpt, S7155–3.3

South Carolina public library per capita bookstocks, circulation, and local support, by county, FY92, annual rpt, S7210–1

South Carolina statistical abstract, general data, 1993 annual rpt, S7125–1

South Dakota public higher education instn enrollment, by student county of residence, by instn, fall 1992, annual rpt, S7375–1

South Dakota school enrollment, finances, grads, and staff, by district, 1991/92 and trends, annual rpt, S7315–1

Tennessee higher education enrollment, by county of residence, fall 1984-92, annual rpt, S7525–1.1

Tennessee public school enrollment, staff, finances, and operations, by county, city, and school district, 1991/92, annual rpt, S7490–2

Tennessee statistical abstract, general data, 1992/93 annual rpt, U8710–2

Tennessee value of food donated by USDA distributed to schools, by county, 1992/93, annual rpt, S7460–1

Texas elementary and secondary education data, by school district and county, annual series, S7670–1

Texas higher education enrollment in public instns, by county of origin, fall 1991, annual rpt, S7657–1.1

Texas public libraries, holdings, circulation, staff, and finances, by library and location, FY91, annual rpt, S7710–1

Utah govt statistical review, fiscal and socioeconomic data, 1993 annual rpt, R9380–1

Utah higher education enrollment, by county and instn, fall 1992, annual rpt, S7895–2

Utah public libraries, services, staff, and finances, by library, 1992, annual rpt, S7808–1

Utah public school enrollment, personnel, programs, and finances, by school district, 1991/92 annual rpt, S7815–1.2

Utah statistical abstract, general data, 1993 triennial rpt, U8960–1

Vermont elementary and secondary school enrollment by grade, sex, race-ethnicity, school, and county, 1992/93 and trends, annual rpt, S8020–1

Virginia public library operations and finances, by instn, FY92, annual rpt, S8275–1

Virginia public school enrollment and high school grads, with detail by school district, 1980/81-2012/2013, annual rpt, U9080–20

Virginia public school enrollment, grads, finances, and staff, by county and municipality, 1991/92, annual rpt, S8190–3

Washington State public libraries, finances, holdings, circulation, staff, and population served, by instn, 1992, annual rpt, S8375–1

West Virginia public, academic, and special library operations and/or finances, by instn, 1991/92, annual rpt, S8590–1

West Virginia public and private schools, enrollment, grads, and staff, by county, 1991/92, annual rpt, S8540–3

West Virginia public school finances, enrollment, staff, and programs, by county, 1992/93 and trends, annual rpt, S8540–4

Wisconsin Blue Book, general data, 1993-94 biennial rpt, S8780–1.2

Wisconsin libraries, operations, and finances, by library type, instn, and location, 1992, annual rpt, S8795–1

Wyoming public library holdings, staff, circulation, and finances, by county, FY92, annual rpt, S8855–3

Wyoming public school enrollment, staff, and finances, by county and district, 1991/92, annual rpt series, S8890–1

Index by Categories

BY COUNTY

Energy Resources and Demand

State and local:

Alabama county data book, general data, 1992 annual rpt, S0121–2

Alabama statistical abstract, general data, 1992 recurring rpt, U5680–2

California statistical abstract, general data, 1992 annual rpt, S0840–2

Florida statistical abstract, general data, 1992 annual rpt, U6660–1

Hawaii data book, general data, 1992 annual rpt, S2090–1

Kansas oil and gas production, by county, 1991, annual rpt, S3020–1

Kansas statistical abstract, general data, 1991/92 annual rpt, U7095–2

Mississippi statistical abstract, general data, 1992 annual rpt, U3255–4

Missouri coal mine production, by county, FY92, annual rpt, S4530–2.1

Montana low-income energy assistance cases and payments, by county, monthly rpt, S4755–1

Montana oil and gas production and taxes paid, by county, 1990-91, biennial rpt, S4750–1.1

New York State home energy assistance program statistics, by State area, FY91, annual rpt, S5800–2.3

New York State statistical yearbook, general data, 1992 annual rpt, U5100–1

Ohio home heating energy credit program assistance, by county, winter 1991/92, annual rpt, S6390–1.3

Oklahoma statistical abstract, general data, 1992 annual rpt, U8130–2

South Carolina statistical abstract, general data, 1993 annual rpt, S7125–1

South Dakota low-income energy assistance clients and payments, by MSA and county, FY92, annual rpt, S7385–1.2

Tennessee statistical abstract, general data, 1992/93 annual rpt, U8710–2

West Virginia underground and surface coal production, by county, 1982-91, annual rpt, R9385–1.7

Geography and Climate

State and local:

Alabama county data book, general data, 1992 annual rpt, S0121–2

Alabama statistical abstract, general data, 1992 recurring rpt, U5680–2

Arizona statistical abstract, general data, 1993 recurring rpt, U5850–2

Arkansas land area by county, 1987, annual rpt, U5920–1

California socioeconomic and govtl data for municipalities, counties, and school districts, 1993 annual rpt, C4712–3

California statistical abstract, general data, 1992 annual rpt, S0840–2

Florida land and water area, by county, 1992/93 annual rpt, C6360–1

Florida municipal and county statistical profiles, general data, 1991 annual rpt, C4712–6

Florida statistical abstract, general data, 1992 annual rpt, U6660–1

Georgia land and water area, by county, 1990, annual rpt, U6750–1

Georgia precipitation and average temperature, by crop reporting district, monthly 1991, annual rpt, S1855–1

Georgia statistical abstract, general data, 1992-93 biennial rpt, U6730–1

Hawaii data book, general data, 1992 annual rpt, S2090–1

Idaho economic profile, general data, 1992 recurring rpt, S2218–2

Illinois average precipitation and temperature, by crop reporting district, monthly 1991, annual rpt, S2390–1

Illinois statistical abstract, general data, 1992 annual rpt, U6910–2

Kansas statistical abstract, general data, 1991/92 annual rpt, U7095–2

Kentucky economic statistics, general data, 1993 annual rpt, S3104–1

Kentucky land and water area, by county, 1983, annual rpt, S3085–1

Maine land area and population density, by local area, 1990 census rpt, S3465–7

Maryland land area, by county and taxing jurisdiction, 1993 annual rpt, S3618–1.2

Maryland statistical abstract, general data, 1993-94 biennial rpt, S3605–1

Mississippi statistical abstract, general data, 1992 annual rpt, U3255–4

Montana precipitation and growing season, by county and station, 1990-91, annual rpt, S4655–1

Nebraska temperatures and precipitation, by State crop reporting district, monthly 1991 and trends, annual rpt, S4835–1

Nevada statistical abstract, general data, 1992 biennial rpt, S5005–1

New Hampshire land and water area, by county and city, 1993 biennial rpt, S5255–1

New Jersey freeze dates and frost-free days, by county and weather station, 1992 annual rpt, S5350–1

New Jersey municipal and county data book, general data, 1992 annual rpt, C4712–4

New Mexico average freeze dates and precipitation, by county and weather station, 1991, annual rpt, S5530 1

New York State municipal and county statistical profiles, general data, 1993 annual rpt, C4712–7

New York State statistical yearbook, general data, 1992 annual rpt, U5100–1

North Carolina precipitation and average temperature, by district, monthly 1991, annual rpt, S5885–1

Oklahoma average precipitation and temperature, by district, monthly 1992, annual rpt, S6405–1

Oklahoma statistical abstract, general data, 1992 annual rpt, U8130–2

Pennsylvania statistical abstract, general data, 1992 recurring rpt, U4130–6

South Carolina land area, by county, 1993 annual rpt, S7145–1.5

South Carolina statistical abstract, general data, 1993 annual rpt, S7125–1

Tennessee statistical abstract, general data, 1992/93 annual rpt, U8710–2

Utah land area by county, 1990, annual article, U8960–2.504

Utah population and land area, by county, 1990, annual rpt, S7835–1.1

Utah statistical abstract, general data, 1993 triennial rpt, U8960–1

Virginia land area, by county and independent city, 1991, annual rpt, S8305–1.3

Wisconsin Blue Book, general data, 1993-94 biennial rpt, S8780–1.2

Government and Defense

DOD prime contracts awarded, for top 20 counties, 1984, R4700–19

Economic indicators affecting local real estate markets, including DOD spending and manufacturing employment share, by locale, 1992, article, A6450–2.509

Election results for Federal offices and Governor, by State, county, major city, and party, with voter registration and turnout, 1992 and trends, biennial rpt, C2500–1

Hispanic American population shares in 17 congressional districts that elected Hispanic Representatives in Nov 1992, article, C4575–1.502

Local govt activities and structure, finances, and employment, series, A5800–4

Municipal and county govt structure, public services, finances, and intergovtl relations, 1993 annual rpt, A5800–1

Presidential primary election results and voter registration by county and district, by State, 1992 and trends, C2500–7

State and local:

Alabama county data book, general data, 1992 annual rpt, S0121–2

Alabama election results, by district and/or county, 1992 general election, biennial rpt, S0205–1

Alabama statistical abstract, general data, 1992 recurring rpt, U5680–2

Alaska election results, and voter registration and turnout, by district and precinct, 1992 general election, biennial rpt, S0337–1

Alaska military personnel, housing arrangements, and defense expenditures, by census area and borough, 1993 article, S0320–1.511

Arizona election results and voter registration, by county and/or district, 1992 general election, biennial rpt, S0520–1

Arizona property tax levy accounts receivable, by county, 1991 and trends, annual rpt, S0450–1

Arizona statistical abstract, general data, 1993 recurring rpt, U5850–2

Arizona tax revenues by source, tax rates, and disbursements to local areas, FY92 and trends, annual rpt, S0515–1

Arkansas election results, by district and/or county, 1992 general election, biennial rpt, S0775–1

Arkansas financial condition, including revenues by source, expenditures by function and locality, and fund balances, FY91-92, biennial rpt, S0780–1

California economic condition, including population, employment and earnings, income, business activity, and taxation, 1960s-92, annual rpt, S0840–3.2

California election results, and voter registration and turnout, by district and/or county, 1992 and trends, biennial rpt, S0934–1

California individual taxable income reported by source, deductions and credits by type, and tax returns, by income class and county, 1990, annual rpt, S0855–1.1

California socioeconomic and govtl data for municipalities, counties, and school districts, 1993 annual rpt, C4712–3

California statistical abstract, general data, 1992 annual rpt, S0840–2

BY COUNTY

Index by Categories

California tax collections (excluding income tax), by locality, company, and type of tax, FY92 and trends, annual rpt, S0835–1

Colorado election results and voter registration, by political party, and county and/or district, 1992, biennial rpt, S1090–1

Colorado property assessed valuation by detailed property type, and tax levy and revenue by local district, by county, 1991-92, annual rpt, S1055–3

Colorado tax revenues by type, with selected data by county and city, FY92 and trends, annual rpt, S1075–1

Connecticut election results and voter registration and turnout, by location, 1992 general election, biennial rpt, S1265–1

Delaware data book, general data, 1993 annual rpt, S1375–4

Delaware election results, by district and/or county, 1992 general election, biennial rpt, S1365–1

Florida county data book, 1992/93 annual rpt, C6360–1

Florida election results, by county and/or district, 1992 general election, biennial rpt, S1800–1

Florida municipal and county statistical profiles, general data, 1991 annual rpt, C4712–6

Florida State govt disbursements to local areas, by source of funds, FY92, annual rpt, S1717–1

Florida statistical abstract, general data, 1992 annual rpt, U6660–1

Georgia county guide, general data, 1993 annual rpt, U6750–1

Georgia election results by county, 1992 general election, biennial rpt, S1955–1

Georgia statistical abstract, general data, 1992-93 biennial rpt, U6730–1

Georgia tax revenues, by type and county, FY92 annual rpt, S1950–1.2

Hawaii data book, general data, 1992 annual rpt, S2090–1

Hawaii election results, and voter registration by sex, by district and precinct, 1992, biennial series, S2077–1

Hawaii tax collections and allocations, by type, for State and counties, FY91-92 and trends, annual rpt, S2120–1

Idaho election results and voter registration, by county and/or district and precinct, 1992 general election, biennial rpt, S2305–1

Idaho tax statistics, including collections, and data by county and city, FY92 and trends, annual rpt, S2295–1

Illinois election results, and voter registration trends, by county and/or district, 1992 general election, biennial rpt, S2445–1

Illinois property valuation and tax rates, by county and district, 1990/91, annual rpt, S2440–1.3

Indiana election results, by county and district, with voter registration, 1992 primary and general elections, biennial rpt, S2702–1

Indiana property value and tax levies, collections, credits, and deductions, by county and type, 1991, annual rpt, S2570–1.1

Iowa election results, by county and/or district, 1992 general election, biennial rpt, S2865–1

Iowa individual income tax return filings, income, taxes paid, and credits, by income bracket, and filings by county, 1991, annual rpt, S2860–3

Iowa retail sales and use tax filings data, and establishments reporting, by county and city, and by kind of business, quarterly rpt, S2860–1

Kansas county economic dev planning, including data on population and incorporated cities, by county, 1993 article, U7095–1.502

Kansas election results, by county and district, 1992 primary and general elections, biennial rpt, S3030–1

Kansas statistical abstract, general data, 1991/92 annual rpt, U7095–2

Kansas tax collections by tax type, and property values, with data by county, FY92 and trends, annual rpt, S3020–1

Kentucky election results, by county, district, and circuit, 1992, annual rpt, S3213–1

Louisiana presidential election results, by parish and precinct, 1992 general election, quadrennial rpt, S3370–3

Maine election results, by district, county, and municipality, 1992 general election, biennial rpt, S3490–1

Maryland election results, by county and district, 1992 general election, biennial rpt, S3615–1

Maryland individual income tax return filings, and income and tax liability data, by city, county, and income group, 1991, annual rpt, S3685–1

Maryland local govt financial condition, including revenues by source, expenditures by function, and debt obligations, FY92 and trends, annual rpt, S3618–1

Maryland State property taxes receivable, tax rates, and fund transferrals, by county, FY92 and trends, annual rpt, S3685–2

Maryland statistical abstract, general data, 1993-94 biennial rpt, S3605–1

Massachusetts election results and voter registration, by local area, 1992 and trends, biennial rpt, S3920–1

Michigan election results and voter registration, by county and/or district, 1992 general election, biennial rpt, S4020–1

Minnesota election results and voter registration, by locality, 1992 primary and general elections, biennial rpt, S4255–1

Mississippi statistical abstract, general data, 1992 annual rpt, U3255–4

Mississippi tax collections by type, and disbursements, with selected sales and income tax data by locality and industry, FY92 and trends, annual rpt, S4435–1

Missouri election results and voter registration, by district and/or county, with directory of govt officials, 1992 general election, biennial rpt, S4580–1

Missouri financial condition, including revenues and expenditures by agency, and tax collections and distribution, FY92 and trends, annual rpt, S4570–1.1

Montana election results and voter registration, by county and/or district, 1992 general election, biennial rpt, S4760–1

Montana tax collections by tax type, and property value by county, FY91-92 and trends, biennial rpt, S4750–1

Nebraska election results, and voter registration by party, by county and/or district, 1992 general and primary elections, biennial rpt, S4955–1

Nebraska State and local govt employment, by county, 1991, article, U7860–1.502

Nebraska tax revenues by type, tax rates and exemptions, and aid distribution to local areas, with data by county and city, 1991, annual rpt, S4950–1

Nevada election results, and voter registration and turnout, by county, 1992 general election, biennial rpt, S5125–1

Nevada statistical abstract, general data, 1992 biennial rpt, S5005–1

New Hampshire election results, by county and locality, 1992, biennial rpt, S5255–1

New Hampshire Federal employment, by occupation and county, 1992, triennial rpt, S5205–2.25

New Jersey election results and voter registration, by location, 1992 general election, annual rpt, S5440–1

New Jersey municipal and county data book, general data, 1992 annual rpt, C4712–4

New Mexico election results, and voter registration by party, by location, 1992 general election, biennial rpt, S5655–1

New Mexico tax revenues and disbursements, with data by tax type, county, and city, FY91-92 and trends, annual rpt, S5660–1

New York State general election results by county and district, Nov 1992, biennial rpt, S5750–1

New York State municipal and county statistical profiles, general data, 1993 annual rpt, C4712–7

New York State statistical yearbook, general data, 1992 annual rpt, U5100–1

North Carolina election results, by county and/or district, 1992 general election, biennial rpt, S5920–1

North Carolina supplemental tax receipts for education, by school district, 1991/92, annual rpt, S5915–1.1

North Dakota election results and historical trends, including data on ballot measures and detail by location, 1880s-1992, biennial rpt, U8080–1

North Dakota election results, by location, 1992 general election, biennial rpt, S6205–1

Ohio election results and voter registration, by local area, 1991-92 and trends, biennial rpt, S6380–1

Ohio tax revenues and collections, by tax type, with distributions and property assessments by county, and corporate taxes by industry, FY92 annual rpt, S6390–1

Oklahoma election results and voter registration, by county and/or district, 1992, biennial rpt, S6425–1

Oklahoma statistical abstract, general data, 1992 annual rpt, U8130–2

Oregon election results and voter registration and turnout, by county and/or district, 1992 general election, biennial rpt, S6665–1

Pennsylvania statistical abstract, general data, 1992 recurring rpt, U4130–6

Pennsylvania tax collections by tax type, with data by county and industry, FY92 and trends, annual rpt, S6885–1

South Carolina county govt finances, including property value and tax assessments, by county, FY92, annual rpt, S7127–2

Index by Categories

BY COUNTY

South Carolina income tax returns, distribution by taxable income, by county, 1991, annual rpt, S7145-1.2

South Carolina insurance dept county allocation of fire dept premium taxes, 1991, annual rpt, S7195-1

South Carolina statistical abstract, general data, 1993 annual rpt, S7125-1

South Carolina tax returns and collections, property assessments, and taxable sales, with data by county and industry group, FY92, annual rpt, S7255-1

South Carolina tax revenues shared with county govts, by county and type of tax, FY91, annual rpt, S7125-3.1

South Carolina voters registered and voting in general election, by county, Nov 1992, annual rpt, S7145-1.1

South Dakota election results, and voter registration by party, by county, 1992 general election, biennial rpt, S7390-1

South Dakota tax revenues by source, aid distributed to local areas, and property tax valuations, FY92 annual rpt, S7380-1

Tennessee election results, by district and/or county, 1992 general election, biennial rpt, S7580-1

Tennessee statistical abstract, general data, 1992/93 annual rpt, U8710-2

Tennessee tax revenues by source and apportionments to counties, cities, and funds, FY91-92 and trends, biennial rpt, S7570-1

Texas election results and voter registration, by district and/or county, 1992 general election, biennial series, S7750-1

Utah election results and voter registration and turnout, by county and/or district, 1992 general election, biennial rpt, S7875-1

Utah govt statistical review, fiscal and socioeconomic data, 1993 annual rpt, R9380-1

Utah public lands by govt owner, and Federal land payments to State and local govts, with data by county, 1992 article, U8960-2.502

Utah statistical abstract, general data, 1993 triennial rpt, U8960-1

Utah tax revenues by source, and distribution to localities and State funds, FY92 and trends, annual rpt, S7905-1

Vermont individual State income tax returns, and property and sales tax refunds, by income class and locality, 1991, annual rpt, S8125-1

Virginia DOD expenditures by category, by county and city, FY89-91, article, S8205-4.502

Virginia election results by jurisdiction, and voter registration and turnout, 1992 and Jan 1993 elections, annual rpt, S8195-1

Virginia tax revenues by type, county, and independent city, FY92 and trends, annual rpt, S8305-1

Washington State election results and voter registration, by county and/or district, 1992 general election, annual rpt, S8425-1

Washington State local govt annexations, by county and city, Apr 1990-92, annual rpt, S8345-4

Washington State tax revenue by source and county, with property tax rates and assessed valuation, FY92 and trends, annual rpt, S8415-1

Washington State treasury operations, including receipts, disbursements, aid to localities, and investments, by fund, FY92, annual rpt, S8455-1

West Virginia election results and voter registration, by county and party, 1992 and trends, biennial rpt, S8630-1

West Virginia property tax levy rates, by purpose and locale, FY93, annual rpt, S8640-3

West Virginia property valuations and tax levies by property class, and levies by purpose, by county, 1992/93 and trends, annual rpt, S8640-2

West Virginia statistical handbook, general data, 1992 annual rpt, R9385-1

Wisconsin Blue Book, general data, 1993-94 biennial rpt, S8780-1.2, S8780-1.3

Wisconsin property tax relief and shared revenue payments, by county, FY93, annual rpt, S8675-2.1

Wyoming election results by county, district, and precinct, 1992, annual rpt and govtl directory, S9000-1

Wyoming sales and use tax revenue by industry div and/or retail sector, by county, FY81-92, annual rpt, S8855-1

Wyoming State treasurer financial transactions, including revenues, investments, and disbursements by local area, FY92 and trends, annual rpt, S9010-1

Wyoming tax collections and distribution, and property valuation, with data by property type and location, FY92 and trends, annual rpt, S8990-1

Health and Vital Statistics

Health care atlas, including births and deaths, communicable disease, manpower, and facilities and utilization, by county, 1992 annual rpt, S1746-1

Physicians by detailed specialty and location, 1992, annual rpt, A2200-3.2

State and local:

Alabama county data book, general data, 1992 annual rpt, S0121-2

Alabama statistical abstract, general data, 1992 recurring rpt, U5680-2

Alabama vital statistics, including population, births, deaths by cause, marriages, and divorces, by location and demographic characteristics, 1992 and trends, annual rpt, S0175-2

Alaska vital statistics, including births, deaths by cause, marriages, divorces, adoptions, and population, by demographic characteristics and location, 1990, annual rpt, S0315-1

Arizona Indian population, education, housing, health, and employment characteristics, with detail by reservation, 1970s-91, recurring rpt, U5850-2.9

Arizona statistical abstract, general data, 1993 recurring rpt, U5850-2

Arkansas vital statistics, including births, deaths by cause, marriages, and divorces, by age, sex, race, and county, 1991 and trends, annual rpt, S0685-1

California statistical abstract, general data, 1992 annual rpt, S0840-2

California vital statistics, including population, births, and deaths by cause, by demographic characteristics and county, 1990 and trends, annual rpt, S0865-1

Colorado vital statistics, including population, births, deaths by cause, abortion, marriage and divorce, and adoption, by demographic characteristics and location, 1990 and trends, annual rpt, S1010-1

Connecticut vital statistics, including births, deaths by cause, marriages, and divorces, by demographic characteristics and location, 1989, annual rpt, S1200-1

Delaware vital statistics, including births, deaths by cause, and marriages and dissolutions, by demographic characteristics and location, 1990, annual rpt, S1385-2

Florida county data book, 1992/93 annual rpt, C6360-1

Florida statistical abstract, general data, 1992 annual rpt, U6660-1

Florida vital statistics, including population, births, deaths by cause, and marriages and dissolutions, by location and demographic characteristics, 1992 and trends, annual rpt, S1745-3

Georgia county guide, general data, 1993 annual rpt, U6750-1

Georgia health behavior risk factor surveillance survey results, by health district, 1991, annual rpt, S1895-2

Georgia statistical abstract, general data, 1992-93 biennial rpt, U6730-1

Georgia vital statistics, including population, births, abortions, deaths by cause, marriages, and divorces, by demographic characteristics and location, 1991 and trends, annual rpt, S1895-1

Hawaii data book, general data, 1992 annual rpt, S2090-1

Hawaii health dept activities and services, including vital statistics and disease control, by location, 1990, annual rpt, S2065-1

Idaho vital statistics, including births, deaths by cause, abortions, marriages, and divorces, by demographic characteristics and county, 1991 and trends, annual rpt, S2250-2

Illinois mental health facility patient population and characteristics, by facility, location, and treatment category, FY93, annual rpt, S2505-1

Illinois statistical abstract, general data, 1992 annual rpt, U6910-2

Iowa vital statistics, including population, births, deaths by cause, marriages, and divorces, by demographic characteristics and location, 1991 and trends, annual rpt, S2795-1

Kansas statistical abstract, general data, 1991/92 annual rpt, U7095-2

Kansas vital statistics, including population, births, deaths by cause, abortions, marriages, and divorces, by demographic characteristics and location, 1991 and trends, annual rpt, S2975-1

Kentucky health behavior risk factor surveillance survey results, by State area and respondent characteristics, 1988-90, annual rpt, S3140-6

Kentucky vital statistics, including births, deaths by cause, marriages and divorces, and population, by demographic characteristics and county, 1991, annual rpt, S3140-1

Louisiana vital statistics, including population, births, deaths by cause, reportable diseases, marriages, and divorces, by demographic characteristics and locality, 1989-90 and trends, annual rpt, S3295-1

BY COUNTY

Index by Categories

Maine vital statistics, including births, deaths by cause, abortions, and marriages and divorces, by demographic characteristics and location, 1991 and trends, annual rpt, S3460–2

Maryland statistical abstract, general data, 1993-94 biennial rpt, S3605–1

Maryland vital statistics, including population, births, deaths by cause, marriages, and divorces, by demographic characteristics and location, 1989 and trends, annual rpt, S3635–1

Massachusetts vital statistics, including births, deaths by cause, marriages, divorces, and population, by locality and demographic characteristics, 1990 and trends, annual rpt, S3850–1

Michigan drug/alcohol abusers admitted to treatment programs, by State area, FY91, annual planning rpt, S3980–1.2

Michigan vital statistics, including births, deaths, marriages, divorces/annulments, and communicable diseases, by location and demographic characteristics, 1990 and trends, annual rpt, S4000–3

Minnesota vital statistics, including population, births, abortions, deaths, marriages, and divorces, by location and demographic characteristics, 1991 and trends, annual rpt, S4190–2

Mississippi statistical abstract, general data, 1992 annual rpt, U3255–4

Mississippi vital statistics, including births, deaths by cause, marriages, and divorces, by demographic characteristics and location, 1992 and trends, annual rpt, S4350–1

Missouri occupational disability and death incidents, by county, 1991, annual rpt, S4530–2.2

Missouri vital statistics, including population, births, deaths by cause, and marriages and divorces, by location and demographic characteristics, 1992 and trends, annual rpt, S4518–1

Montana vital statistics, including births, deaths by cause, abortion, disease, and marriage and divorce, by demographic characteristics and county, 1990-91 and trends, annual rpt, S4690–1

Nebraska vital statistics, including births, deaths, marriages, divorces, and population, by demographic characteristics and location, 1991 and trends, annual rpt, S4885–1

Nevada statistical abstract, general data, 1992 biennial rpt, S5005–1

Nevada vital statistics, including births, abortions, and deaths by cause, by county and demographic characteristics, 1989 and trends, annual rpt, S5075–1

New Hampshire vital statistics, including population, births, deaths by cause, marriages, and divorces, by location and demographic characteristics, 1991 and trends, annual rpt, S5215–1

New Jersey vital statistics, including births, deaths, population, communicable diseases, and marriages and divorces, by demographic characteristics and location, 1990 and trends, annual rpt, S5405–1

New Mexico vital statistics, including population, births, deaths, and disease, by location and demographic characteristics, 1991 and trends, annual rpt, S5605–1

New York State statistical yearbook, general data, 1992 annual rpt, U5100–1

New York State vital statistics, including population, births, deaths by cause, reportable diseases, and marriages and dissolutions, by demographic characteristics and/or location, 1990 and trends, annual rpt, S5765–1

North Carolina vital statistics, including population, births, deaths by cause, marriages, and divorces, by local area, 1991 and trends, annual rpt, S5927–1

North Dakota physicians and nurses, by county, 1992, annual planning rpt, S6140–2

North Dakota vital statistics, including births, deaths by cause, marriages and divorces, and abortions, by demographic characteristics and/or county, 1991 and trends, annual rpt, S6105–2

Ohio vital statistics, including births, deaths by cause, marriages, divorces, and population, by demographic characteristics and location, 1991 and trends, annual rpt, S6285–1

Oklahoma statistical abstract, general data, 1992 annual rpt, U8130–2

Oregon vital statistics, including births, deaths by cause, communicable diseases, marriages, and divorces, by age, sex, race-ethnicity, and county, 1991 and trends, annual rpt, S6615–5

Pennsylvania statistical abstract, general data, 1992 recurring rpt, U4130–6

Rhode Island vital statistics, including population, births, deaths, marriages, and divorces, by demographic characteristics and locality, 1989 and trends, annual rpt, S6995–1

South Carolina statistical abstract, general data, 1993 annual rpt, S7125–1

South Carolina teenage pregnancies and outcomes, by county, 1990, annual rpt, S7145–1.1

South Carolina vital statistics, including births, deaths by cause, marriages, and divorces, by age, sex, race, and location, 1990 and trends, annual rpt, S7175–1

South Dakota vital statistics, including births, deaths, marriage and divorce, and communicable disease, by demographic characteristics and county, 1991 and trends, annual rpt, S7345–1

Tennessee statistical abstract, general data, 1992/93 annual rpt, U8710–2

Tennessee vital statistics, including births, deaths by cause, marriages, divorces, and population, by demographic characteristics and location, 1991 and trends, annual rpt, S7520–2

Texas indigent health care finances and utilization, with data by county, district, public hospital, and medical school, 1986-91, U8850–8.7

Texas nursing employment, demand outlook, earnings, and education, by selected characteristics, various years 1971-91, U8850–8.2

Texas State and local health depts finances, employment, and service area characteristics, FY91 and trends, U8850–8.6

Texas vital statistics, including births, deaths by cause, abortions, marriages, and divorces, by location and demographic characteristics, 1991 and trends, annual rpt, S7685–1

Utah marriages and divorces, by participant characteristics and location, 1990 and trends, annual rpt, S7835–2

Utah statistical abstract, general data, 1993 triennial rpt, U8960–1

Utah vital statistics, including births, deaths by cause, and population, by county and demographic characteristics, 1990 and trends, annual rpt, S7835–1

Vermont vital statistics, including population, births, deaths by cause, abortions, marriages, and divorces, by location and demographic characteristics, 1991 and trends, annual rpt, S8054–1

Virginia vital statistics, including births, deaths by cause, marriages and divorces, and communicable disease, by demographic characteristics and location, 1991 and trends, annual rpt, S8225–1

Washington State noninstitutional population with disabilities, by severity and county, 1990, annual rpt, S8345–4

Washington State vital statistics, including births, deaths by cause, and population, by demographic characteristics and location, 1991 and trends, annual rpt, S8363–1

West Virginia vital statistics, including births, deaths by cause, marriages, and divorces, by location and demographic characteristics, 1991 and trends, annual rpt, S8560–1

West Virginia workers compensation accidents reported by county, and program finances, FY83-92, annual rpt, R9385–1.2

Wisconsin Blue Book, general data, 1993-94 biennial rpt, S8780–1.2

Wisconsin vital statistics, including population, births, deaths by cause, and marriages and dissolutions, by county and demographic characteristics, 1991 and trends, annual rpt, S8715–4

Wyoming vital statistics, including population, births, deaths by cause, marriages, and divorces, by demographic characteristics and county, 1991 and trends, annual rpt, S8920–2

Housing and Construction

State and local:

Alabama county data book, general data, 1992 annual rpt, S0121–2

Alabama statistical abstract, general data, 1992 recurring rpt, U5680–2

Alaska population, housing, income, and education data, by demographic characteristics and/or locality, 1990/91 and trends, annual rpt, S0320–4

Arizona building permits issued and value, by type, size, and location, monthly rpt quarterly table, U0280–1.503, U0280–1.506, U0280–1.509

Arizona statistical abstract, general data, 1993 recurring rpt, U5850–2

Arkansas property assessments, by county, decennially 1970-90 and 1992, annual rpt, U5935–1

California housing median prices by State region, 1992, annual rpt, S0840–3.1

California socioeconomic and govtl data for municipalities, counties, and school districts, 1993 annual rpt, C4712–3

California statistical abstract, general data, 1992 annual rpt, S0840–2

Connecticut construction activity and value, by type of structure and location, 1992 and trends, annual rpt, S1212–1

Index by Categories

BY COUNTY

Delaware housing construction activity, with data on demolitions and mobile home sales, by locality, 1992 and trends, annual rpt, S1387–1

Florida building permits, value by county, city, and type of construction, monthly rpt, U6660–5

Florida county data book, 1992/93 annual rpt, C6360–1

Florida municipal and county statistical profiles, general data, 1991 annual rpt, C4712–6

Florida statistical abstract, general data, 1992 annual rpt, U6660–1

Georgia, Atlanta area housing permits issued and forecast, by county, quarterly rpt, U1880–2

Georgia county guide, general data, 1993 annual rpt, U6750–1

Georgia statistical abstract, general data, 1992-93 biennial rpt, U6730–1

Hawaii construction authorized, including single- and multi-family housing, by county, quarterly rpt, S2090–2

Hawaii data book, general data, 1992 annual rpt, S2090–1

Idaho construction activity and value, by city and county, monthly rpt, B3900–1

Illinois statistical abstract, general data, 1992 annual rpt, U6910–2

Kansas statistical abstract, general data, 1991/92 annual rpt, U7095–2

Louisiana Census of Population and Housing summary findings, by local area, 1990 and trends, U8010–4

Maine Census of Population and Housing summary findings, by local area, 1990, S3465–7, S3465–8, S3465–9

Maryland statistical abstract, general data, 1993-94 biennial rpt, S3605–1

New Jersey Census of Population and Housing detailed findings, by county, 1990, S5425–19

New Jersey municipal and county data book, general data, 1992 annual rpt, C4712–4

New Jersey residential construction activity and costs, by location, 1991 and trends, annual rpt, S5425–3

New York State municipal and county statistical profiles, general data, 1993 annual rpt, C4712–7

New York State statistical yearbook, general data, 1992 annual rpt, U5100–1

Oklahoma statistical abstract, general data, 1992 annual rpt, U8130–2

Pennsylvania building permits authorized, by MSA and selected county, monthly rpt quarterly table, U4110–1.501, U4110–1.503, U4110–1.505, U4110–1.507

Pennsylvania building permits issued and value, by construction type, county, and MSA, 1992, annual article, U4110–1.506

Pennsylvania housing data from Census of Population and Housing, by county and municipality, 1990, C1595–14

Pennsylvania statistical abstract, general data, 1992 recurring rpt, U4130–6

Rhode Island Census of Population and Housing detailed findings, by county and municipality, 1990, S6930–9

South Carolina statistical abstract, general data, 1993 annual rpt, S7125–1

Tennessee statistical abstract, general data, 1992/93 annual rpt, U8710–2

Utah statistical abstract, general data, 1993 triennial rpt, U8960–1

Washington State population and demographic characteristics, and housing units, by county and/or city, 1992 and trends, annual rpt, S8345–4

Income

Black child poverty rates for 50 counties with highest rates, with comparisons to whites, 1989, R3840–21

Consumer buying power survey of population, income, and sales by kind of business, by census div, State, MSA, county, and city, 1992, annual rpt, C1200–1.511

Consumer buying power survey of population, income, and sales by product line, by State, metro area, county, and census div, 1993 annual rpt, C1200–1.514

Markets with daily newspapers, demographic and economic info by geographic area, US and Canada, 1993 annual rpt, C3250–1

Poverty rates among children in 89 counties, 1989, R3840–20.2

State and local:

Alabama county data book, general data, 1992 annual rpt, S0121–2

Alabama statistical abstract, general data, 1992 recurring rpt, U5680–2

Alaska per capita and family median income, by school district, FY92 annual report, S0295–2

Alaska population, housing, income, and education data, by demographic characteristics and/or locality, 1990/91 and trends, annual rpt, S0320–4

Alaska resident vs nonresident workers and earnings, by local area, 1991, article, S0320–1.508

Arizona statistical abstract, general data, 1993 recurring rpt, U5850–2

Arkansas population, per capita income, and economic vitality index, by county and/or metro area, 1980s-90, article, U5930–1.501

Arkansas socioeconomic trends, by MSA and/or county, 1993 annual rpt, U5935–1

California economic condition, including population, employment and earnings, income, business activity, and taxation, 1960s-92, annual rpt, S0840–3.2

California socioeconomic and govtl data for municipalities, counties, and school districts, 1993 annual rpt, C4712–3

California statistical abstract, general data, 1992 annual rpt, S0840–2

Colorado per capita income, by county, 1989-91, annual article, S1040–4.507

Colorado personal income per capita, and population in poverty, by county or local area, FY94 annual planning rpt, S1040–3

Florida county data book, 1992/93 annual rpt, C6360–1

Florida statistical abstract, general data, 1992 annual rpt, U6660–1

Georgia county guide, general data, 1993 annual rpt, U6750–1

Georgia personal income and employment, by MSA, county, and metro-nonmetro status, 1990-91, article, U6730–2.505

Georgia personal income, by MSA, county, and metro-nonmetro status, errata, U6730–2.501

Georgia statistical abstract, general data, 1992-93 biennial rpt, U6730–1

Georgia taxable personal income, by county, 1990, annual rpt, S1950–1.2

Hawaii data book, general data, 1992 annual rpt, S2090–1

Idaho economic profile, general data, 1992 recurring rpt, S2218–2

Illinois statistical abstract, general data, 1992 annual rpt, U6910–2

Kansas economic outlook, with income data for selected State areas, 1993 annual articles, U7095–1.501

Kansas statistical abstract, general data, 1991/92 annual rpt, U7095–2

Kentucky economic statistics, general data, 1993 annual rpt, S3104–1

Kentucky labor force planning rpt, including population and labor force characteristics, and employment by industry, 1991 and trends, annual rpt, S3140–3

Louisiana total and per capita personal income, by parish, 1989-91, annual planning rpt, S3320–1.1

Maryland individual income tax return filings, and income and tax liability data, by city, county, and income group, 1991, annual rpt, S3685–1

Maryland statistical abstract, general data, 1993-94 biennial rpt, S3605–1

Massachusetts municipal and county profiles, general data, 1992 annual rpt, C4712–2

Michigan personal income per capita, by county, 1980 and 1990, annual planning rpt, S3980–1.2

Mississippi income by source, county, and MSA, and wages by industry group, 1993 annual planning rpt, S4345–1.4

Mississippi statistical abstract, general data, 1992 annual rpt, U3255–4

Mississippi taxpayers, taxable income, and gross tax, by county, FY92, annual rpt, S4435–1

Missouri prevailing wage determinations, by county, FY92, annual rpt, S4530–2.1

Montana personal income by county, 1989-91, annual planning rpt, S4710–3

Nebraska personal income and tax liability, by county, 1990, annual rpt, S4950–1

Nebraska transfer payments, by component and State area, with comparisons to total personal income, 1990-91 and trends, article, U7860–1.504

Nebraska transfer payments per capita, with share of personal income, by county, 1990, article, U7860–1.505

Nevada personal and family income by county, and average wages in selected counties, 1992 annual rpt, S5040–4

Nevada statistical abstract, general data, 1992 biennial rpt, S5005–1

New Hampshire employment and wages covered by unemployment insurance, by industry div and county, 1992 and trends, article, S5205–1.501

New Hampshire per capita income, by county, 1987-90, recurring rpt, S5205–7

New Jersey Census of Population and Housing detailed findings, by county, 1990, S5425–19

New Jersey covered wages, by county, 1990-91, annual article, S5425–1.501

New Jersey covered wages, by county, 1991-92, annual article, S5425–1.507

New Jersey municipal and county data book, general data, 1992 annual rpt, C4712–4

BY COUNTY

Index by Categories

New Jersey personal income, by county, 1991 and trends, recurring feature, S5425–1.506

New Mexico per capita income, and families in poverty, by county, 1993 annual rpt, S5605–1

New Mexico personal and family income, and poverty rates, by county, 1989-90, annual planning rpt, S5624–1

New Mexico personal income by county and MSA, 1990-91, S5624–2.508

New Mexico population in poverty, by race-ethnicity and county, 1990, S5620–2.501

New Mexico poverty rates by county, 1990, S5624–2.505

New York State average earnings, by industry, county, and labor market area, 1987-91, annual feature, S5775–1.501

New York State municipal and county statistical profiles, general data, 1993 annual rpt, C4712–7

New York State public assistance recipients earned income, by State area, 1991, annual rpt, S5800–2.1

New York State statistical yearbook, general data, 1992 annual rpt, U5100–1

North Carolina personal income by county, 1990, annual rpt, S5915–1.1

North Dakota population living in poverty, by sex, county, and State region, 1993 annual planning rpt, S6140–2

Ohio individual income tax returns filed, income, and tax liability, by income class and county, 1990, annual rpt, S6390–1.3

Oklahoma per capita income and poverty rates, by county, 1990, S6455–1.1

Oklahoma statistical abstract, general data, 1992 annual rpt, U8130–2

Oregon covered employment, payroll, and average earnings, by county and industry, 1991, article, S6615–2.502

Oregon median family income, by county, 1989, article, S6615–2.502

Oregon population in poverty, by county, monthly rpt, S6615–8

Oregon poverty rate by State region, 1990 and 1992, article, S6592–1.502

Pennsylvania Census of Population and Housing detailed findings, with selected data by county and municipality, 1990, U4130–13

Pennsylvania income data from Census of Population and Housing, by county and municipality, 1989, C1595–15

Pennsylvania individual income tax returns and taxable income, by county, 1990, annual rpt, S6885–1

Pennsylvania personal income and wages, by county, FY92 annual planning rpt, S6845–3.2

Pennsylvania personal income, by type, industry div, MSA, and county, 1993 annual article, U4110–1.506

Pennsylvania statistical abstract, general data, 1992 recurring rpt, U4130–6

Rhode Island Census of Population and Housing detailed findings, by county and municipality, 1990, S6930–9

South Carolina economic activity indicators, including employment by industry div, by county, 1993 annual rpt, S7145–1.2

South Carolina income and poverty, by county, 1992 annual planning rpt, S7155–3.3

South Carolina per capita income by county, Dec 1991, annual rpt, S7125–3.2

South Carolina statistical abstract, general data, 1993 annual rpt, S7125–1

South Dakota total and per capita personal income, by county, 1989-91, annual article, U8595–1.503

Tennessee employment, wages, and unemployment insurance contributions, by county and industry, 1991, annual rpt, S7495–1

Tennessee per capita income, by county and MSA, 1990-91, recurring article, S7495–2.507

Tennessee statistical abstract, general data, 1992/93 annual rpt, U8710–2

Texas per capita income, by county and MSA, 1985 and 1990, annual planning rpt, S7675–2

Utah business firms, wages, and employment, by firm size, SIC 2-digit industry, and county, 1st qtr 1992, annual rpt, S7820–1

Utah govt statistical review, fiscal and socioeconomic data, 1993 annual rpt, R9380–1

Utah individual income tax returns and adjusted gross income, by county, 1991, annual rpt, S7905–1

Utah labor force characteristics, employment and unemployment, hours, and earnings, with data by industry and locale, 1992 and trends, annual rpt, S7820–10

Utah payroll wages, by county and planning district, 1991-92, S7820–3.506

Utah personal income and household data, by location and race-ethnicity, 1990 census rpt, S7832–3.3

Utah personal income, by source, industry, and county, 1993 annual article, U8960–2.506

Utah personal income, with detail by source and county, 1992 annual article, S7820–3.501

Utah statistical abstract, general data, 1993 triennial rpt, U8960–1

Vermont individual State income tax returns, and property and sales tax refunds, by income class and locality, 1991, annual rpt, S8125–1

Vermont per capita income by county, 1986-91, annual planning rpt, S8025–2.1

Virginia income distribution and income tax returns filed, by locality, 1990, annual rpt, U9080–1

Virginia total and per capita personal income, by local area and major source, 1980-90, annual rpt, U9080–7

Washington State household and and per capita income, by county, 1989-90, annual rpt, S8345–4

West Virginia economically disadvantaged population by age group, and personal income, by county, 1993 annual planning rpt, S8534–2

West Virginia per capita income, by county, 1989, annual rpt, S8560–1

West Virginia statistical handbook, general data, 1992 annual rpt, R9385–1

Wisconsin Blue Book, general data, 1993-94 biennial rpt, S8780–1.2

Wyoming employment, payroll, and wages, by county, monthly rpt quarterly feature, S8895–1.502, S8895–1.504, S8895–1.506, S8895–1.508

Wyoming Native American population, unemployment, and poverty rates, by county and/or reservation, 1990, article, S8895–1.501

Industry and Commerce

Consumer buying power survey of population, income, and sales by kind of business, by census div, State, MSA, county, and city, 1992, annual rpt, C1200–1.511

Consumer buying power survey of population, income, and sales by product line, by State, metro area, county, and census div, 1993 annual rpt, C1200–1.514

Lumber industry production in Western States and counties, with acreage owned, employment, and sawmill operations, 1980s-92, annual rpt, A9395–1

Receipts in manufacturing and nonmanufacturing, for top 15 counties, 1992, article, C1200–1.509

Retail sales by kind of business, rankings by MSA, city, and county, 1993 annual rpt, C3250–1

State and local:

Alabama county data book, general data, 1992 annual rpt, S0121–2

Alabama retail sales, by kind of business, MSA, and county, monthly business activity rpt, U5680–1

Alabama statistical abstract, general data, 1992 recurring rpt, U5680–2

Arizona population, employment, and industry activity, for 13 nonmetro counties, 1985-93, semiannual rpt, U5850–1.2

Arizona statistical abstract, general data, 1993 recurring rpt, U5850–2

Arkansas socioeconomic trends, by MSA and/or county, 1993 annual rpt, U5935–1

California statistical abstract, general data, 1992 annual rpt, S0840–2

California taxable sales, by kind of business and county, FY92, annual rpt, S0835–1.3

Colorado retail sales and sales tax revenue, by county, city, and kind of business, FY92 and trends, annual rpt, S1075–1.5

Florida county data book, 1992/93 annual rpt, C6360–1

Florida statistical abstract, general data, 1992 annual rpt, U6660–1

Georgia county guide, general data, 1993 annual rpt, U6750–1

Georgia statistical abstract, general data, 1992-93 biennial rpt, U6730–1

Georgia taxable retail sales, by county, 1991, annual rpt, S1950–1.2

Georgia taxable sales, by kind of business and location, 1991-92, annual article, U6730–2.503

Hawaii data book, general data, 1992 annual rpt, S2090–1

Hawaii economic indicators, bimonthly rpt, B3500–1

Idaho taxable sales and sales taxes paid, by county, FY92, annual rpt, S2295–1

Illinois economic and business activity indicators, including data by industry and county, bimonthly rpt, S2405–2

Illinois statistical abstract, general data, 1992 annual rpt, U6910–2

Iowa retail sales and use tax filings data, and establishments reporting, by county and city, and by kind of business, FY91, annual supplement, S2860–1.501

Iowa retail sales and use tax filings data, and establishments reporting, by county and city, and by kind of business, FY92, annual supplement, S2860–1.502

Index by Categories

BY COUNTY

Kansas retail sales and tax activity trends, by urban-rural area and county, 1980-91, article, U7095–1.502

Kansas statistical abstract, general data, 1991/92 annual rpt, U7095–2

Kansas taxable retail sales, by area and kind of business, quarterly rpt, U7095–1

Kentucky economic statistics, general data, 1993 annual rpt, S3104–1.3

Maryland statistical abstract, general data, 1993-94 biennial rpt, S3605–1

Mississippi statistical abstract, general data, 1992 annual rpt, U3255–4

Mississippi tax collections by type, and disbursements, with selected sales and income tax data by locality and industry, FY92 and trends, annual rpt, S4435–1

Montana mine production and taxes paid, by county, 1990-91, biennial rpt, S4750–1.1

Montana new businesses, by labor force area and county, 1991-92, annual planning rpt, S4710–3

Montana new businesses enrolling in unemployment insurance program, by labor market area, quarterly rpt, S4710–1

Nebraska sales tax revenues and taxable sales, by county, city, and detailed industry, 1990-91, annual rpt, S4950–1.2

Nevada business and economic activity indicators, with comparisons to other Western States, 1980-91, annual rpt, U7920–2

Nevada statistical abstract, general data, 1992 biennial rpt, S5005–1

New York State business and economic indicators, by MSA, county, and industry, 1980s-91, annual rpt, S5735–3

New York State statistical yearbook, general data, 1992 annual rpt, U5100–1

Oklahoma statistical abstract, general data, 1992 annual rpt, U8130–2

Pennsylvania statistical abstract, general data, 1992 recurring rpt, U4130–6

Rhode Island statistical almanac, general data, 1993 annual rpt, C7975–1

South Carolina business establishments, and taxable sales, by county and city, 1991, annual rpt, S7255–1.3

South Carolina economic activity indicators, including employment by industry div, by county, 1993 annual rpt, S7145–1.2

South Carolina statistical abstract, general data, 1993 annual rpt, S7125–1

South Dakota gross sales/use tax purchases and taxable retail sales, by county and selected city, bimonthly rpt, U8595–2

South Dakota taxable sales by locality, quarterly rpt, U8595–1

Tennessee statistical abstract, general data, 1992/93 annual rpt, U8710–2

Utah business activity indicators, by county, 1988-91, annual feature, U8960–2.501

Utah business activity indicators, by county, 1989-92, annual feature, U8960–2.507

Utah business establishments, startups, and closings, by industry div and location, 1992, annual rpt, S7820–10

Utah economic and business activity review and indicators, monthly rpt, U8960–2

Utah economic and demographic trends, by county and district, 1960-91, annual rpt, S7832–2

Utah statistical abstract, general data, 1993 triennial rpt, U8960–1

Utah taxable retail sales by county, FY92, annual rpt, R9380–1.6

Utah taxable retail sales by county, 1986-91, annual rpt, S7905–1

Virginia business activity indicators, by local area, monthly rpt, U1120–1

Virginia taxable sales, by kind of business and locality, 1991 and trends, annual rpt, U9080–8

Washington State new business establishments, by county and industry, FY88-92, annual rpt, S8415–1.1

West Virginia statistical handbook, general data, 1992 annual rpt, R9385–1

Labor and Employment

State and local:

Alabama business activity indicators, monthly rpt, U5680–1

Alabama county data book, general data, 1992 annual rpt, S0121–2

Alabama statistical abstract, general data, 1992 recurring rpt, U5680–2

Alaska employment and unemployment, hours, and earnings, by area and/or industry, monthly rpt, S0320–1

Alaska unemployment rate, by school district, FY92 annual report, S0295–2

Arizona employment and unemployment, by county and industry, with production worker hours and earnings, monthly rpt, S0465–1

Arizona occupational profiles, with employment and job outlook, by industry div, occupation, and county, series, S0465–2

Arizona population, employment, and industry activity, for 13 nonmetro counties, 1985-93, semiannual rpt, U5850–1.2

Arizona statistical abstract, general data, 1993 recurring rpt, U5850–2

Arizona unemployment rates as reported by Census Bur vs BLS and State Dept of Economic Security, by county, 1980 and 1990, article, U0280–1.511

Arkansas business and economic activity indicators, quarterly rpt, U5930–1

Arkansas labor force, employment, and unemployment, by MSA, county, and labor area, 1980-92, annual rpt, S0662–2

Arkansas socioeconomic trends, by MSA and/or county, 1993 annual rpt, U5935–1

Arkansas vocational rehabilitation expenditures, impact on earnings and employment, and client characteristics, FY91 annual rpt, S0700–2.4

California employment statistics, by demographic characteristics, industry, MSA, and county, monthly rpt, S0830–1

California statistical abstract, general data, 1992 annual rpt, S0840–2

Colorado employment and unemployment, by location, monthly rpt, S1040–4

Colorado labor force planning rpt, including population, employment by industry, and job service applicants, FY94 annual rpt, S1040–3

DC MSA unemployment rates, by city and county, monthly rpt, S1527–3

Delaware employment, earnings, and hours, by locality and industry, and unemployment insurance activity, monthly rpt, S1405–2

Delaware employment projections, by county, 1990-2020, recurring rpt, S1375–3

Florida county data book, 1992/93 annual rpt, C6360–1

Florida employment and unemployment, by industry div and location, monthly rpt, S1765–3

Florida statistical abstract, general data, 1992 annual rpt, U6660–1

Georgia county guide, general data, 1993 annual rpt, U6750–1

Georgia labor force by employment status, by county, monthly rpt, S1905–1

Georgia personal income and employment, by MSA, county, and metro-nonmetro status, 1990-91, article, U6730–2.505

Georgia statistical abstract, general data, 1992-93 biennial rpt, U6730–1

Hawaii data book, general data, 1992 annual rpt, S2090–1

Hawaii labor force by employment status, industry, and county, quarterly rpt, S2090–2

Idaho economic profile, general data, 1992 recurring rpt, S2218–2

Idaho employment by industry, by county and labor market area, monthly 1991, annual rpt, S2230–2

Illinois economic and business activity indicators, including data by industry and county, bimonthly rpt, S2405–2

Illinois statistical abstract, general data, 1992 annual rpt, U6910–2

Iowa labor force supply-demand data, including population, earnings, and employment by industry and occupation, 1993 annual rpt, S2784–3

Kansas business activity indicators, quarterly rpt, U7095–1

Kansas statistical abstract, general data, 1991/92 annual rpt, U7095–2

Kentucky economic statistics, general data, 1993 annual rpt, S3104–1

Kentucky labor force planning rpt, including population and labor force characteristics, and employment by industry, 1991 and trends, annual rpt, S3140–3

Louisiana labor force, employment, and unemployment, by parish and MSA, monthly rpt, S3320–2

Louisiana labor force planning rpt, including population and labor force characteristics, unemployment claimants, and data by parish and MSA, 1993 annual rpt, S3320–1

Maine Census of Population and Housing summary findings, by local area, 1990, S3465–9

Maine employment, unemployment, and earnings, by industry group, MSA, and labor area, monthly rpt, S3465–2

Maryland labor force, employment, earnings, and hours, with data by industry and location, monthly rpt, S3605–2

Maryland statistical abstract, general data, 1993-94 biennial rpt, S3605–1

Massachusetts employment, hours, and earnings, by industry and local area, with unemployment insurance claims, monthly rpt, S3808–1

Massachusetts municipal and county profiles, general data, 1992 annual rpt, C4712–2

Michigan employment, hours, and earnings, with detail by industry and local area, monthly rpt, S3980–2

Michigan labor force planning rpt, including selected data by county and service delivery area, 1993 annual rpt, S3980–1

BY COUNTY

Index by Categories

Minnesota employment, hours, and earnings, by industry group and locality, monthly rpt, S4205–1

Mississippi statistical abstract, general data, 1992 annual rpt, U3255–4

Missouri employment, earnings, and hours, and employment security program activity, by industry and/or county, FY92 and trends, annual rpt, S4530–2.3

Missouri labor force by employment status, by MSA, labor market area, and county, monthly rpt, S4530–3

Montana employment and unemployment, earnings, and hours, by location and/or industry, quarterly rpt, S4710–1

Montana labor force planning rpt, including population, income, and employment and job openings by industry and occupation, with selected data by county, 1993-94 annual rpt, S4710–3

Nebraska employment and unemployment, by industry group and locality, quarterly rpt, S4895–2

Nevada employment, hours, and earnings, by industry, and unemployment by county, quarterly rpt, S5040–1

Nevada statistical abstract, general data, 1992 biennial rpt, S5005–1

New Hampshire employment, hours, and earnings, by industry and area, monthly rpt, S5205–1

New Hampshire labor force and population by race, sex, and age, and employment by industry div, statewide and by county, 1992 recurring rpt, S5205–7

New Jersey Census of Population and Housing detailed findings, by county, 1990, S5425–19

New Jersey municipal and county data book, general data, 1992 annual rpt, C4712–4

New Mexico employment, hours, and earnings, by labor market area and industry, monthly rpt, S5624–2

New Mexico labor force planning rpt, including population characteristics, and employment by industry and occupation, 1993 annual rpt, S5624–1

New York State employment, earnings, and hours, by county, selected metro area, and industry group, monthly rpt, S5775–1

New York State insured employed, by county, quarterly rpt, S5735–2

New York State municipal and county statistical profiles, general data, 1993 annual rpt, C4712–7

New York State statistical yearbook, general data, 1992 annual rpt, U5100–1

North Carolina labor force and employment by industry, by county, MSA, labor area, and planning region, 1991 and trends, annual rpt, S5917–4

North Dakota employment, hours, and earnings, by industry div and/or location, monthly rpt, S6140–4

North Dakota labor force planning rpt, including population, employment, and earnings, with data by industry and county, 1993 annual rpt, S6140–2

Oklahoma labor force by employment status, and unemployment insurance data, by service delivery area and/or county, monthly rpt, S6430–2

Oklahoma statistical abstract, general data, 1992 annual rpt, U8130–2

Oklahoma unemployment rates, and AFDC employment program placements, by county, FY92 annual rpt, S6455–1

Oregon covered employment, payroll, and average earnings, by county and industry, 1991, article, S6615–2.502

Oregon labor force by employment status, by MSA and county, monthly rpt recurring feature, S6592–1.501, S6615–2.502, S6615–2.503

Oregon labor force by employment status, difference between census and Current Population Survey estimates, by county and MSA, 1990, article, S6615–2.501

Pennsylvania Census of Population and Housing detailed findings, with selected data by county and municipality, 1990, U4130–13

Pennsylvania employment and commuting data from Census of Population and Housing, by county and municipality, 1990, C1595–16

Pennsylvania employment and unemployment rate, by county, monthly rpt quarterly table, U4110–1.501, U4110–1.503, U4110–1.505, U4110–1.507

Pennsylvania labor force and employment data, by county and labor market area, monthly rpt, S6845–1

Pennsylvania labor force planning rpt, including population characteristics, employment and job openings by industry and occupation, and income trends, FY92 annual rpt, S6845–3

Pennsylvania statistical abstract, general data, 1992 recurring rpt, U4130–6

Rhode Island Census of Population and Housing detailed findings, by county and municipality, 1990, S6930–9

Rhode Island statistical almanac, general data, 1993 annual rpt, C7975–1

South Carolina economic activity indicators, including employment by industry div, by county, 1993 annual rpt, S7145–1.2

South Carolina labor force, employment, and unemployment, by county, monthly rpt, S7155–2

South Carolina labor force planning rpt, detailed data on employment, hours, wages, turnover, and characteristics of job service applicants, 1992 annual rpt, S7155–3.2

South Carolina statistical abstract, general data, 1993 annual rpt, S7125–1

South Carolina unemployment rates by county, Oct 1988-Oct 1991, annual rpt, S7125–3.2

South Dakota labor force, employment, and unemployment, and unemployment insurance weeks claimed, by county, monthly rpt, S7355–1

Tennessee employment, wages, and unemployment insurance contributions, by county and industry, 1991, annual rpt, S7495–1

Tennessee labor force age 16-19, by employment status and county, 1992, article, S7495–2.504

Tennessee statistical abstract, general data, 1992/93 annual rpt, U8710–2

Tennessee unemployment rate by county, monthly rpt, S7495–2

Utah business firms, wages, and employment, by firm size, SIC 2-digit industry, and county, 1st qtr 1992, annual rpt, S7820–1

Utah employment and unemployment, by planning district and county, monthly rpt, S7820–3

Utah govt statistical review, fiscal and socioeconomic data, 1993 annual rpt, R9380–1

Utah labor force characteristics, employment and unemployment, hours, and earnings, with data by industry and locale, 1992 and trends, annual rpt, S7820–10

Utah statistical abstract, general data, 1993 triennial rpt, U8960–1

Vermont labor force, and women's employment shares, by county, 1992, annual planning rpt, S8025–2.2

Virginia labor force, hours, and earnings, with data by industry group and locality, monthly rpt, S8205–6

Washington State employment, earnings, and hours, by labor market area and industry group, monthly rpt, S8340–3

West Virginia labor force, by employment status, county, and labor market area, monthly rpt, S8534–1

West Virginia labor force planning rpt, including population, employment, and job service activities, with data by county and service delivery area, 1993 annual rpt, S8534–2

West Virginia statistical handbook, general data, 1992 annual rpt, R9385–1

Wisconsin employment, hours, and earnings, by selected area, monthly rpt, S8750–1

Wyoming employment by industry group and county, with unemployment insurance and job service activities, monthly rpt, S8895–1

Wyoming work force employed in and out of county of residence, and out of State, by county, 1990, article, S8895–1.503

Law Enforcement

Jail facilities, population, costs, and staff and salaries, for 90 local systems, 1992 annual rpt, R1300 1.4

State and local:

Alabama county data book, general data, 1992 annual rpt, S0121–2

Alabama court caseloads and dispositions, by type of court and case, and location, with judicial dept finances, FY92 and trends, annual rpt, S0118–1

Alabama crimes and arrests, by offense and location, with law enforcement employment, 1992 and trends, annual rpt, S0119–1

Alabama statistical abstract, general data, 1992 recurring rpt, U5680–2

Alaska court cases and dispositions, by type of court and case, and location, with judicial dept finances and personnel, FY92 and trends, annual rpt, S0290–1

Alaska prison inmates and probationers/parolees, by place of residence upon admission, 1991, annual rpt, S0287–1

Arizona court cases and dispositions, by type of case and court, with judicial personnel and finances, by county and city, FY92, annual rpt, S0525–1

Arizona crimes and arrests, by offense, county, and offender characteristics, 1992, annual rpt, S0505–2

Arizona prison inmates by county of commitment, June 1992, annual rpt, S0464–2

Index by Categories

BY COUNTY

Arizona statistical abstract, general data, 1993 recurring rpt, U5850–2

Arkansas child abuse/neglect cases, with detail for sexual abuse, by county, FY91, annual rpt, S0700–2.2

Arkansas court caseloads and dispositions, by type of court and case, and location, FY92 and trends, annual rpt, S0647–1

Arkansas crimes and arrests, by offense, victim and offender characteristics, and location, 1992 and trends, annual rpt, S0652–1

Arkansas juvenile detention center commitments, by county, 1991, annual rpt, S0700–2.2

California correctional instn inmates, by offense, demographic characteristics, and instn, Dec 1992, semiannual rpt, S0820–2

California correctional instn inmates, with criminal background and demographic characteristics, 1991 and trends, annual rpt, S0820–1

California court cases and dispositions, by type of case and court, and location, FY92 and trends, annual rpt, S0905–1.2, S0905–2

California criminal justice system detailed data, by offense, county, age, race-ethnicity, and sex, 1991 and trends, annual rpt, S0910–2.2

California socioeconomic and govtl data for municipalities, counties, and school districts, 1993 annual rpt, C4712–3

Colorado court cases and dispositions, by type of court and detailed case type, FY92 and trends, annual rpt, S1035–1.2

Colorado crimes and arrests, by offense and location, with offender characteristics, and assaults on police, 1992, annual rpt, S1068–1

Connecticut court caseloads and dispositions, by type of court and case, and court location, FY91-92, biennial rpt, S1220–1.2

Connecticut Index crime rates, by county and offense, 1992, annual rpt, S1256–1.1

Delaware court caseloads and dispositions, by type of court and case, and by county, with judicial dept finances, FY92, annual rpt, S1360–1

Delaware crimes and arrests, by offense, county, and victim-offender characteristics, 1991 and trends, annual rpt, S1375–5

Florida correctional instns, admin, and inmates by criminal background and demographic characteristics, FY92 annual rpt, S1720–1

Florida county data book, 1992/93 annual rpt, C6360–1

Florida court cases and dispositions, by type of court and case, and location, 1992, annual rpt, S1805–1

Florida municipal and county statistical profiles, general data, 1991 annual rpt, C4712–6

Florida statistical abstract, general data, 1992 annual rpt, U6660–1

Georgia county guide, general data, 1993 annual rpt, U6750–1

Georgia court cases and dispositions, by type of court and case, and location, with judicial dept finances and personnel, FY92, annual rpt, S1903–1

Georgia crimes and arrests, by offense, with data by location and offender characteristics, 1992 and trends, annual rpt, S1901–1

Georgia statistical abstract, general data, 1992-93 biennial rpt, U6730–1

Hawaii crimes and arrests, by offense, with data by county and victim-offender characteristics, 1992, annual rpt, S2035–1

Hawaii data book, general data, 1992 annual rpt, S2090–1

Idaho crimes and arrests, by offense, with data by location and offender characteristics, 1992 and trends, annual rpt, S2275–2

Illinois crimes and arrests, by offense, with data by location and offender characteristics, 1991, annual rpt, S2536–1

Illinois statistical abstract, general data, 1992 annual rpt, U6910–2

Indiana child abuse and neglect cases by county and victim and perpetrator characteristics, FY92 annual rpt, S2623–1.7

Indiana court cases and dispositions by type of court and case, and location, with judicial system finances and personnel, 1992, annual rpt, S2703–1

Iowa court cases and dispositions by district, and scheduled violations handled by court clerks, by county, 1992 and trends, annual rpt, S2815–1

Kansas court caseloads and disposition, by type of court and case, and location, FY92, annual rpt, S3035–1

Kansas court-ordered correctional instn admissions, and parolees, by county, FY92, annual rpt, S2940–1

Kansas crimes and arrests, by offense, with data by location, agency, and victim-offender characteristics, 1992 and trends, annual rpt, S2925–1

Kansas statistical abstract, general data, 1991/92 annual rpt, U7095–2

Kentucky crimes and arrests, by offense, with data by location and offender characteristics, 1992, annual rpt, S3150–1

Kentucky prison releases, by age group and State area, 1991, annual planning rpt, S3140–3

Louisiana court caseloads and dispositions, by type of court and case, and jurisdiction, 1992 and trends, annual rpt, S3375–1

Maine court cases and dispositions, by type and location, FY92 and trends, annual rpt, S3463–1

Maine crimes and arrests, by offense, with data by county, reporting agency, and offender age and sex, 1991, annual rpt, S3475–1

Maryland court caseloads and dispositions, by type of court and case, and county, with judicial personnel and finances, FY92 and trends, annual rpt, S3600–1

Maryland crimes and arrests, law enforcement employment by sex, and assaults on police, by local agency and county, 1991-92, annual rpt, S3665–1

Maryland statistical abstract, general data, 1993-94 biennial rpt, S3605–1

Massachusetts correctional instn inmate socioeconomic characteristics and criminal background, by instn, Jan 1992 and trends, annual rpt, S3805–1

Massachusetts court cases and dispositions, by type of court and case, and location, FY92 and trends, annual rpt, S3807–1

Michigan court caseloads and dispositions, by type of court and case, and court location, 1992 and trends, annual rpt, S3962–1

Michigan crimes and arrests, by offense, with data by location and offender characteristics, 1992 and trends, annual rpt, S3997–1

Michigan prison admissions by sentencing county, and criminal court dispositions by district and circuit, 1991, annual rpt, S3960–1

Mississippi statistical abstract, general data, 1992 annual rpt, U3255–4

Missouri correctional instn admissions by county of sentencing, FY93, annual rpt, S4501–1

Missouri crimes and arrests, by offense and location, with victim and offender characteristics, 1991 and trends, annual rpt, S4560–2

Montana crimes and clearances, by offense and jurisdiction, 1992, annual rpt, S4705–1

Nebraska court cases and dispositions, by type of court and case, and location, 1992 and trends, annual rpt, S4965–2

New Hampshire Index crimes reported, by county, 1990-91, annual rpt, S5250–2.2

New Jersey correctional instn population by county of commitment, Dec 1991, annual rpt, S5370–1

New Jersey crimes and arrests, by offense, with data by location and offender characteristics, 1992 and trends, annual rpt, S5430–1

New Jersey municipal and county data book, general data, 1992 annual rpt, C4712–4

New Mexico court cases and dispositions, by type of court and case, and location, with judicial system finances and personnel, FY92, annual rpt, S5623–1

New York State correctional instn inmates released, by criminal background, sentence, and demographic characteristics, 1991 and trends, recurring rpt series, S5725–1

New York State court cases and dispositions, by type of court and case, and jurisdiction, 1991, annual rpt, S5730–1

New York State criminal justice activities, by offense, location, and local agency, with law enforcement employment, 1991 and trends, annual rpt, S5760–3

New York State local jail/penitentiary inmates by offense, sentence, and demographic characteristics, by county or facility, 1991, annual rpt, S5724–2

New York State municipal and county statistical profiles, general data, 1993 annual rpt, C4712–7

New York State statistical yearbook, general data, 1992 annual rpt, U5100–1

North Carolina correctional instn admissions, separations, and population, by county of conviction, FY93, semiannual rpt, S5900–1

North Carolina court cases and dispositions, by type of court and case, and location, with judicial dept finances and personnel, FY91, annual rpt, S5950–1

North Carolina crimes and arrests, by offense, with data by location and offender characteristics, 1992 and trends, annual rpt, S5955–1

North Dakota court caseloads and dispositions, by type of case and court, and location, with judicial dept finances, 1991-92, annual rpt, S6210–1

BY COUNTY

Index by Categories

North Dakota crimes and arrests, by offense, location, and offender characteristics, and law enforcement employment, 1991 and trends, annual rpt, S6060–1

Ohio correctional instn admissions and releases, inmate characteristics, programs, finances, and staffing, FY91 and trends, annual rpt, S6370–1

Ohio court caseload and case disposition, by type of court and case, and location, 1992, annual rpt, S6385–1

Oklahoma correctional instn admin, with data by district and county, FY91, annual rpt, S6420–1

Oklahoma court cases and dispositions, by type of court and case, with judicial system finances, by county or jurisdiction, FY92, annual rpt, S6493–1

Oklahoma Crime Index offenses, by county and reporting agency, 1990-92, annual rpt, S6465–1.2

Oklahoma statistical abstract, general data, 1992 annual rpt, U8130–2

Oregon crimes and arrests, by offense, with data by county, local agency, and offender characteristics, 1992 and trends, annual rpt, S6603–3

Pennsylvania court caseloads and dispositions, by type of court and case, and county, with judicial system finances, 1991, annual rpt, S6900–1

Pennsylvania crimes and arrests, by offense, with data by location and offender characteristics, 1992 and trends, annual rpt, S6860–1

Pennsylvania State correctional instn admin, and inmates by type of offense and demographic characteristics, 1990 and trends, annual rpt, S6782–1

Pennsylvania statistical abstract, general data, 1992 recurring rpt, U4130–6

Rhode Island court cases and dispositions, by type of court and case, and county, 1987-91, annual rpt, S6965–1

South Carolina correctional instns, admin, and inmates by criminal offense and demographic characteristics, FY92 and trends, annual rpt, S7135–1

South Carolina court cases and dispositions, by type of court and location, with judicial dept finances and employees, 1992 and trends, annual rpt, S7197–1

South Carolina crime rates, by county, 1991, annual rpt, S7145–1.1

South Carolina crimes and arrests, by detailed offense, offender characteristics, and location, 1992 and trends, annual rpt, S7205–1.2

South Carolina statistical abstract, general data, 1993 annual rpt, S7125–1

South Dakota court cases and dispositions by type of case, and judicial system finances and personnel, by jurisdiction, FY92 and trends, annual rpt, S7395–1

Tennessee correctional instn admissions, by county of conviction, FY92, annual rpt, S7480–1

Tennessee court cases and dispositions, by type of court and case, and county, FY92, annual rpt, S7585–1

Tennessee statistical abstract, general data, 1992/93 annual rpt, U8710–2

Texas court cases and dispositions, by type of court and case, and location, FY92, annual rpt, S7703–1

Texas criminal offenses, by local agency, 1992, annual rpt, S7735–2.2

Utah crimes and arrests, by offense, county, and local agency, 1992 and trends, annual rpt, S7890–3

Vermont court cases and dispositions, by type of court and case, and location, FY92 annual rpt, S8120–1

Virginia court caseloads, processing, and dispositions, by type of court and case, with judicial dept personnel and finances, by location, 1992 and trends, annual rpt, S8300–1

Virginia crimes and arrests by offense, and law enforcement employment, by location and reporting agency, 1992, annual rpt, S8295–2.2

Washington State correctional instn admissions by county of conviction, quarterly rpt, S8337–1

Washington State court cases and dispositions, by type of court and case, and jurisdiction, with judicial finances and personnel, 1992 and trends, annual rpt, S8339–1

Washington State crimes and arrests, by offense, with data by location and offender characteristics, 1992 and trends, annual rpt, S8440–1

West Virginia court caseloads and dispositions, by type of court and case, and judicial circuit, 1992 and trends, annual rpt, S8537–1

West Virginia crimes and arrests, by offense, location, and offender characteristics, 1990-91, annual rpt, S8610–1

Wisconsin correctional instn inmates, by criminal background and selected characteristics, series, S8692–1

Wisconsin crimes and arrests, by offense, offender characteristics, county, and local agency, 1992 and trends, annual rpt, S8771–1

Wisconsin prison inmate releases, by county of commitment and intended residence, by sex, 1991, annual rpt, S8692–1.3

Wyoming correctional instn inmates, probationers, and parolees, by county, FY92, annual rpt, S8883–1

Wyoming crimes and arrests, by offense, with data by location and victim and offender characteristics, 1991 and trends, annual rpt, S8867–3

Natural Resources, Environment and Pollution

Child well-being indicators based on social, economic, and environmental factors, for 239 MSAs, with detail by component county and city, 1980s-90s, R9700–2

State and local:

Alabama county data book, general data, 1992 annual rpt, S0121–2

Alabama statistical abstract, general data, 1992 recurring rpt, U5680–2

Arizona statistical abstract, general data, 1993 recurring rpt, U5850–2

California statistical abstract, general data, 1992 annual rpt, S0840–2

Florida county data book, 1992/93 annual rpt, C6360–1

Florida statistical abstract, general data, 1992 annual rpt, U6660–1

Georgia county guide, general data, 1993 annual rpt, U6750–1

Georgia statistical abstract, general data, 1992-93 biennial rpt, U6730–1

Hawaii data book, general data, 1992 annual rpt, S2090–1

Maryland statistical abstract, general data, 1993-94 biennial rpt, S3605–1

Montana property values, by detailed property class and type, with land acreage by use, by county, 1991-92 and trends, biennial rpt, S4750–1.2

Nevada statistical abstract, general data, 1992 biennial rpt, S5005–1

New Jersey municipal and county data book, general data, 1992 annual rpt, C4712–4

New York State hazardous waste disposal law violations, by local area, 1991, annual rpt, S5760–3.3

New York State statistical yearbook, general data, 1992 annual rpt, U5100–1

North Carolina water/sewer systems and customers, by county, Dec 1990, annual rpt, S5917–2

Pennsylvania statistical abstract, general data, 1992 recurring rpt, U4130–6

South Carolina statistical abstract, general data, 1993 annual rpt, S7125–1

Tennessee statistical abstract, general data, 1992/93 annual rpt, U8710–2

Tennessee timberland by ownership and county, 1989, annual rpt, S7460–1

Utah public lands by govt owner, and Federal land payments to State and local govts, with data by county, 1992 article, U8960–2.S02

Washington State forest land and value, by county, 1992, annual rpt, S8415–1.3

Population

Child well-being indicators based on social, economic, and environmental factors, for 239 MSAs, with detail by component county and city, 1980s-90s, R9700–2

Churches and membership, by denomination, census div, State, and county, 1990, R4985–1

Consumer buying power survey of population, income, and sales by kind of business, by census div, State, MSA, county, and city, 1992, annual rpt, C1200–1.511

Consumer buying power survey of population, income, and sales by product line, by State, metro area, county, and census div, 1993 annual rpt, C1200–1.514

Market area population and characteristics, households, income, and retail outlets, for 21 leading areas, 1993 feature, C2710–1.538

Markets with daily newspapers, demographic and economic info by geographic area, US and Canada, 1993 annual rpt, C3250–1

Older population age 65/over, for 10 counties with largest increase, 1990, C4300–1.508

State and local:

Alabama county data book, general data, 1992 annual rpt, S0121–2

Alabama population trends by race, with detail for 20 counties comprising Black Belt region, 1880-1990, U0340–1.6

Alabama statistical abstract, general data, 1992 recurring rpt, U5680–2

Alabama vital statistics, including population, births, deaths by cause, marriages, and divorces, by location and demographic characteristics, 1992 and trends, annual rpt, S0175–2

Index by Categories

BY COUNTY

Alaska population, housing, income, and education data, by demographic characteristics and/or locality, 1990/91 and trends, annual rpt, S0320–4

Alaska vital statistics, including births, deaths by cause, marriages, divorces, adoptions, and population, by demographic characteristics and location, 1990, annual rpt, S0315–1

Arizona population, employment, and industry activity, for 13 nonmetro counties, 1985-93, semiannual rpt, U5850–1.2

Arizona population projections by county, 1993-2002 and quinquennially 2005-2040, semiannual rpt, U5850–1.1

Arizona statistical abstract, general data, 1993 recurring rpt, U5850–2

Arizona temporary winter residents and expenditures, and mobile home and trailer park spaces and occupancy, by local area, winter 1992/93, annual article, U0280–1.508

Arkansas population, per capita income, and economic vitality index, by county and/or metro area, 1980s-90, article, U5930–1.501

Arkansas socioeconomic trends, by MSA and/or county, 1993 annual rpt, U5935–1

California economic condition, including population, employment and earnings, income, business activity, and taxation, 1960s-92, annual rpt, S0840–3.2

California population by age, sex, race-ethnicity, and county, decennially 1990-2040, recurring rpt, S0840–4

California population by county, July 1990, annual rpt, S0855–1.1

California population by county, 1990-92, annual planning rpt, S0830–2

California population by county, 1991 and trends, annual rpt, S0885–1

California socioeconomic and govtl data for municipalities, counties, and school districts, 1993 annual rpt, C4712–3

California statistical abstract, general data, 1992 annual rpt, S0840–2

California vital statistics, including population, births, and deaths by cause, by demographic characteristics and county, 1990 and trends, annual rpt, S0865–1

Colorado population by county, 1980, 1990, and July 1991, annual rpt, S1075–1

Colorado vital statistics, including population, births, deaths by cause, abortion, marriage and divorce, and adoption, by demographic characteristics and location, 1990 and trends, annual rpt, S1010–1

Connecticut population, by county, town, and health district, 1989, annual rpt, S1200–1

Delaware population, by age, sex, race, and locality, 1990-2020, recurring rpt, S1375–3

Delaware population, by county, 1970-2010, annual rpt, S1385–2

Florida county data book, 1992/93 annual rpt, C6360–1

Florida municipal and county statistical profiles, general data, 1991 annual rpt, C4712–6

Florida population and household composition, series, U6660–3

Florida population, by city, county, and MSA, Apr 1992 and trends, annual rpt, U6660–4

Florida population, by race-ethnicity, age, and county, 1992 annual rpt, S1746–1.1

Florida statistical abstract, general data, 1992 annual rpt, U6660–1

Florida vital statistics, including population, births, deaths by cause, and marriages and dissolutions, by location and demographic characteristics, 1992 and trends, annual rpt, S1745–3

Georgia county guide, general data, 1993 annual rpt, U6750–1

Georgia population by county, 1992, annual rpt, S1901–1

Georgia statistical abstract, general data, 1992-93 biennial rpt, U6730–1

Georgia vital statistics, including population, births, abortions, deaths by cause, marriages, and divorces, by demographic characteristics and location, 1991 and trends, annual rpt, S1895–1

Hawaii civilian and military population, by county and island, 1980 and 1989-90, annual rpt, S2065–1.2

Hawaii data book, general data, 1992 annual rpt, S2090–1

Idaho economic profile, general data, 1992 recurring rpt, S2218–2

Idaho population by county, 1980 and 1990, annual rpt, S2250–2

Illinois statistical abstract, general data, 1992 annual rpt, U6910–2

Indiana welfare dept juvenile wards, and population, by county, 1990 or June 1992, annual rpt, S2623–1.7

Iowa labor force supply-demand data, including population, earnings, and employment by industry and occupation, 1993 annual rpt, S2784–3

Iowa vital statistics, including population, births, deaths by cause, marriages, and divorces, by demographic characteristics and location, 1991 and trends, annual rpt, S2795–1

Kansas population, by selected county, 1989-90, annual articles, U7095–1.501

Kansas statistical abstract, general data, 1991/92 annual rpt, U7095–2

Kansas vital statistics, including population, births, deaths by cause, abortions, marriages, and divorces, by demographic characteristics and location, 1991 and trends, annual rpt, S2975–1

Kentucky economic statistics, general data, 1993 annual rpt, S3104–1

Kentucky labor force planning rpt, including population and labor force characteristics, and employment by industry, 1991 and trends, annual rpt, S3140–3

Kentucky vital statistics, including births, deaths by cause, marriages and divorces, and population, by demographic characteristics and county, 1991, annual rpt, S3140–1

Louisiana Census of Population and Housing summary findings, by local area, 1990 and trends, U8010–4

Louisiana labor force planning rpt, including population and labor force characteristics, unemployment claimants, and data by parish and MSA, 1993 annual rpt, S3320–1

Louisiana population by parish, 1980, 1990, and 1992, annual rpt, S3280–1.1

Louisiana vital statistics, including population, births, deaths by cause, reportable diseases,

marriages, and divorces, by demographic characteristics and locality, 1989-90 and trends, annual rpt, S3295–1

Maine Census of Population and Housing summary findings, by local area, 1990, S3465–7, S3465–8, S3465–9

Maine population, by age, sex, and county, 1991, annual rpt, S3460–2

Maine statistical summary, general economic and social data, 1992 recurring rpt, S3434–1

Maryland homeless children, by region and county, 1991/92, annual rpt, S3610–1

Maryland population, by county and taxing jurisdiction, 1993 annual rpt, S3618–1.2

Maryland statistical abstract, general data, 1993-94 biennial rpt, S3605–1

Maryland vital statistics, including population, births, deaths by cause, marriages, and divorces, by demographic characteristics and location, 1989 and trends, annual rpt, S3635–1

Massachusetts municipal and county profiles, general data, 1992 annual rpt, C4712–2

Massachusetts vital statistics, including births, deaths by cause, marriages, divorces, and population, by locality and demographic characteristics, 1990 and trends, annual rpt, S3850–1

Michigan labor force planning rpt, including selected data by county and service delivery area, 1993 annual rpt, S3980–1

Michigan population, by age, sex, race, and county, 1990 and trends, annual rpt, S4000–3

Minnesota population, by age, sex, and county, 1991, annual rpt, S4190–2

Mississippi population, by race and county, 1990, annual rpt, S4350–1

Mississippi population trends, and households, by county and MSA, 1993 annual planning rpt, S4345–1.4

Mississippi statistical abstract, general data, 1992 annual rpt, U3255–4

Missouri vital statistics, including population, births, deaths by cause, and marriages and divorces, by location and demographic characteristics, 1992 and trends, annual rpt, S4518–1

Montana labor force planning rpt, including population, income, and employment and job openings by industry and occupation, with selected data by county, 1993-94 annual rpt, S4710–3

Montana population, by city, county, and library service area, 1990, annual rpt, S4725–1

Montana population, with detail by county, 1990-91 and trends, annual rpt, S4690–1

Nebraska population age 20/under, by age, sex, and county, June 1992, annual rpt, S4865–2.6

Nebraska population and migration rates, with detail by age group and county, 1980-90, article, U7860–1.508

Nebraska vital statistics, including births, deaths, marriages, divorces, and population, by demographic characteristics and location, 1991 and trends, annual rpt, S4885–1

Nevada business and economic activity indicators, with comparisons to other Western States, 1980-91, annual rpt, U7920–2

BY COUNTY

Index by Categories

Nevada population, by county, 1980-89, annual rpt, S5075–1

Nevada population by county, 1992-93 and 1997, annual rpt, S5040–4

Nevada statistical abstract, general data, 1992 biennial rpt, S5005–1

New Hampshire labor force and population by race, sex, and age, and employment by industry div, statewide and by county, 1992 recurring rpt, S5205–7

New Hampshire population, by county and city, 1970, 1980, and 1990, biennial rpt, S5255–1

New Hampshire population by county, 1991 and trends, annual rpt, S5215–1

New Jersey Census of Population and Housing detailed findings, by county, 1990, S5425–19

New Jersey crimes, population and land area, and law enforcement personnel by sex, by county and municipality, 1992 and trends, annual rpt, S5430–1.3

New Jersey municipal and county data book, general data, 1992 annual rpt, C4712–4

New Jersey population, by race and Hispanic ethnicity, sex, age, and county, 1990, annual rpt, S5405–1

New Mexico population by age, sex, county, and State region, 1980 and 1990, U7980–6

New Mexico population, by race-ethnicity, county, and city, 1993 annual planning rpt, S5624–1

New Mexico population size and components of change, by county, 1990-91, article, U7980–1.503

New Mexico vital statistics, including population, births, deaths, and disease, by location and demographic characteristics, 1991 and trends, annual rpt, S5605–1

New York State municipal and county statistical profiles, general data, 1993 annual rpt, C4712–7

New York State statistical yearbook, general data, 1992 annual rpt, U5100–1

New York State vital statistics, including population, births, deaths by cause, reportable diseases, and marriages and dissolutions, by demographic characteristics and/or location, 1990 and trends, annual rpt, S5765–1

North Carolina vital statistics, including population, births, deaths, marriages, and divorces, by local area, 1991 and trends, annual rpt, S5927–1.1

North Dakota children by age and/or sex, by county, Aug 1991, annual education directory, S6180–2

North Dakota labor force planning rpt, including population, employment, and earnings, with data by industry and county, 1993 annual rpt, S6140–2

North Dakota population, by county, 1991, annual rpt, S6105–2

Ohio population by age, sex, and county, with summary components of change, quinquennially 1990-2015, recurring rpt, S6260–3

Ohio vital statistics, including births, deaths by cause, marriages, divorces, and population, by demographic characteristics and location, 1991 and trends, annual rpt, S6285–1

Oklahoma population by county, 1990-92, annual rpt, S6465–1.2

Oklahoma population projections, by age, sex, and locality, with data on fertility and migration, 1990-2020, recurring rpt, S6416–1

Oklahoma statistical abstract, general data, 1992 annual rpt, U8130–2

Oregon population, by age, sex, and county, 1991 and trends, annual rpt, S6615–5

Oregon population by county and place of residence in 1990 vs 1985, article, S6592–1.501

Oregon population by county, July 1991-92, article, S6615–2.502

Pennsylvania Census of Population and Housing detailed findings, with selected data by county and municipality, 1990, U4130–13

Pennsylvania labor force and population characteristics, FY92 annual planning rpt, S6845–3.1

Pennsylvania statistical abstract, general data, 1992 recurring rpt, U4130–6

Rhode Island Census of Population and Housing detailed findings, by county and municipality, 1990, S6930–9

Rhode Island labor force planning rpt, including population, employment by industry, job openings, and characteristics of insured unemployed, 1993 annual rpt, S6980–3

Rhode Island vital statistics, including population, births, deaths, marriages, and divorces, by demographic characteristics and locality, 1989 and trends, annual rpt, S6995–1

South Carolina population, by county and demographic characteristics, 1992 annual planning rpt, S7155–3

South Carolina population, by race, age, and county, 1990 and trends, annual rpt, S7175–1

South Carolina population characteristics, by county, 1993 annual rpt, S7145–1.1

South Carolina statistical abstract, general data, 1993 annual rpt, S7125 1

Tennessee population, by age, sex, race, and county, 1990-2010, recurring rpt, S7560–2

Tennessee population by race, county, and city, 1991 and trends, annual rpt, S7520–2

Tennessee statistical abstract, general data, 1992/93 annual rpt, U8710–2

Texas population, by age, sex, race-ethnicity, and county, July 1991, annual rpt, S7645–2

Texas population by city, town, and county, 1980 and 1990-91, annual rpt, S7645–1

Texas population, by county and race-ethnicity, 1990-2030, recurring rpt, S7645–3

Utah govt statistical review, fiscal and socioeconomic data, 1993 annual rpt, R9380–1

Utah population by urban-rural status and/or county, 1990 and 1992, annual rpt, S7800–1

Utah population estimates and components, including data by county, 1992 and trends, annual article, U8960–2.504

Utah statistical abstract, general data, 1993 triennial rpt, U8960–1

Utah vital statistics, including population by county, 1990 and trends, annual rpt, S7835–1.1

Vermont population, by age, sex, and locality, 1991 and trends, annual planning rpt, S8025–2.1

Vermont vital statistics, including population, births, deaths by cause, abortions, marriages, and divorces, by location and demographic characteristics, 1991 and trends, annual rpt, S8054–1

Virginia population and net migration, by local area, 1990-91, annual rpt, U9080–9

Virginia population by race and location, 1991 and trends, annual rpt, S8225–1

Virginia population trends and projections by location, 1980-2000, recurring rpt, S8205–7

Virginia youth population by age, by county and city, with detail for disabled youth, Jan 1993, triennial rpt, S8190–1

Washington State population and demographic characteristics, and housing units, by county and/or city, 1992 and trends, annual rpt, S8345–4

Washington State vital statistics, including births, deaths by cause, and population, by demographic characteristics and location, 1991 and trends, annual rpt, S8363–1

West Virginia labor force planning rpt, including population, employment, and job service activities, with data by county and service delivery area, 1993 annual rpt, S8534–2

West Virginia population, by county and demographic characteristics, 1990 and trends, annual rpt, S8560–1

West Virginia statistical handbook, general data, 1992 annual rpt, R9385–1

Wisconsin Blue Book, general data, 1993-94 biennial rpt, S8780–1.1, S8780–1.2

Wisconsin population, by age, sex, and county, with components of change, quinquennially 1990-2020, recurring rpt, S8675–4

Wisconsin population by county, Jan 1992, annual rpt, S8675–2.1

Wisconsin vital statistics, including population, births, deaths by cause, and marriages and dissolutions, by county and demographic characteristics, 1991 and trends, annual rpt, S8715–4

Wyoming Native American population, unemployment, and poverty rates, by county and/or reservation, 1990, article, S8895–1.501

Wyoming vital statistics, including population, births, deaths by cause, marriages, and divorces, by demographic characteristics and county, 1991 and trends, annual rpt, S8920–2

Prices and Cost of Living

State and local:

Florida price level index, by major item and county, 1991, annual rpt, U6660–1.24

Maryland household expenditures for retail goods by purchase outlet type, by county, 1990, biennial rpt, S3605–1.6

Public Welfare and Social Security

State and local:

Alabama county data book, general data, 1992 annual rpt, S0121–2

Alabama public welfare and social service cases, recipients, and payments, by program and county, monthly rpt, S0150–1

Alaska AFDC caseloads and expenditures by region and municipality, and client self-sufficiency project survey data, 1993 article, S0320–1.503

Index by Categories BY COUNTY

Arizona public assistance recipients and payments, by program, county, and district, monthly rpt, S0465–4

Arizona school food service program meals served, expenditures, and value of donated commodities, by school district and county, 1991/92, annual rpt, S0470–1

Arizona statistical abstract, general data, 1993 recurring rpt, U5850–2

Arkansas human services dept finances and operations, including service recipient characteristics, by program, FY91 and trends, annual rpt, S0700–2

California public welfare cases, recipients, and expenditures, by program and county, monthly rpt, S0935–2

Colorado welfare and social services expenditures and caseloads, by county and/or program, FY91, annual rpt, S1085–1

Delaware public assistance recipients, funds available, and payments, by program, with selected data by county, monthly rpt, S1385–1

Florida AFDC and SSI cases and payments, by district and county, FY92, annual rpt, S1717–1

Florida county data book, 1992/93 annual rpt, C6360–1

Florida statistical abstract, general data, 1992 annual rpt, U6660–1

Georgia county guide, general data, 1993 annual rpt, U6750–1

Georgia statistical abstract, general data, 1992-93 biennial rpt, U6730–1

Hawaii data book, general data, 1992 annual rpt, S2090–1

Idaho public welfare program expenditures and recipients, with data by county, quarterly rpt, S2250–1

Illinois public assistance program cases, recipients, and payments, by program and county, FY91-92 and trends, annual rpt, S2520–2

Illinois statistical abstract, general data, 1992 annual rpt, U6910–2

Indiana public assistance program participation, expenditures, and services, by county, FY92 and trends, annual rpt, S2623–1

Iowa ADC and SSI program recipients, and expenditures, by county, monthly rpt, S2802–1

Kansas statistical abstract, general data, 1991/92 annual rpt, U7095–2

Kentucky AFDC and SSI recipients and payments, by county, monthly rpt, S3140–2

Kentucky Medicaid recipients and payments, by program, county, and type of medical service, monthly rpt, S3140–5

Louisiana labor market info, including population receiving AFDC and food stamps, by area, 1992, annual planning rpt, S3320–1.2

Maryland medical assistance payments and recipients, by program, type of service, location, demographic characteristics, and facility, FY92 and trends, annual rpt, S3635–3

Maryland statistical abstract, general data, 1993-94 biennial rpt, S3605–1

Maryland welfare program statistics, and welfare fraud investigations, by county, monthly rpt, S3645–2

Michigan public assistance program cases, recipients, and payments, detailed data by county, monthly rpt, S4010–1

Minnesota public welfare program recipients and expenditures, by county, 1992, semiannual rpt, S4202–1

Mississippi public welfare and social service cases, recipients, and payments, by program and county, FY92, annual rpt, S4357–1

Mississippi statistical abstract, general data, 1992 annual rpt, U3255–4

Missouri public welfare and medical assistance recipients and payments, by program and county, FY92, annual rpt, S4575–2

Montana welfare and medical assistance program cases and payments, by county and type of service, monthly rpt, S4755–1

Nebraska public welfare cases, recipients, and payments, by program and county, FY92, annual rpt, S4957–1.2

New Jersey public welfare cases, recipients, payments, and case processing, by program and county or city, monthly rpt, S5415–1

New Mexico food stamp recipients, by county, Jan 1993, annual planning rpt, S5624–1

New Mexico public assistance cases, expenditures, and case processing, by program and county, monthly rpt, S5620–2

New York State public assistance and social service program statistics, by State area and source of funds, 1991 and trends, annual rpt, S5800–2

New York State statistical yearbook, general data, 1992 annual rpt, U5100–1

North Carolina public welfare programs, cases, recipients, staff, and finances, by county, 1st half FY93, semiannual rpt, S5940–2

Oklahoma public welfare program expenditures, recipients, and services, by program and county, FY92 and trends, annual rpt, S6455–1

Oklahoma statistical abstract, general data, 1992 annual rpt, U8130–2

Oregon public welfare caseloads, recipients, and/or expenditures, by program and county, monthly rpt, S6615–8

Pennsylvania statistical abstract, general data, 1992 recurring rpt, U4130–6

South Carolina public welfare recipients, payments, and case processing, by county and program, monthly rpt, S7252–1

South Carolina statistical abstract, general data, 1993 annual rpt, S7125–1

South Carolina students eligible for free or reduced-price lunches, by school district, Oct 1991, annual rpt, S7145–1.3

South Dakota welfare and social services recipients, by program, MSA, and county, FY92, annual rpt, S7385–1.2

Tennessee statistical abstract, general data, 1992/93 annual rpt, U8710–2

Texas welfare and social services program expenditures, recipients, and fraud cases, by county and/or program, FY92 and trends, annual rpt, S7695–1

Utah govt statistical review, fiscal and socioeconomic data, 1993 annual rpt, R9380–1

Utah statistical abstract, general data, 1993 triennial rpt, U8960–1

Washington State public assistance clients and service costs, by client characteristics, program, and county, FY90, annual rpt, S8420–2

West Virginia welfare and social service program caseloads and expenditures, by county, monthly rpt, S8560–2

Wisconsin Blue Book, general data, 1993-94 biennial rpt, S8780–1.2

Wyoming welfare and social service recipients and expenditures, by program and county, FY92, annual rpt, S8908–1

Recreation and Leisure

Arts fundraising through united arts funds (UAFs), with fund operations, income by source, and allocations, by UAF, 1992 and trends, annual rpt, A1315–2

State and local:

Alabama county data book, general data, 1992 annual rpt, S0121–2

Florida statistical abstract, general data, 1992 annual rpt, U6660–1

Hawaii data book, general data, 1992 annual rpt, S2090–1

Maryland statistical abstract, general data, 1993-94 biennial rpt, S3605–1

Mississippi statistical abstract, general data, 1992 annual rpt, U3255–4

Nevada statistical abstract, general data, 1992 biennial rpt, S5005–1

New Jersey casino service industry establishments and revenues, by county, FY92, annual rpt, S5360–1

New York State motorboat and snowmobile registrations, by county, 1991, annual rpt, S5790–1

New York State statistical yearbook, general data, 1992 annual rpt, U5100–1

Pennsylvania statistical abstract, general data, 1992 recurring rpt, U4130–6

South Carolina statistical abstract, general data, 1993 annual rpt, S7125–1

Washington State commercial boats and assessed values, by county, 1992, annual rpt, S8415–1.3

Transportation and Travel

State and local:

Alabama county data book, general data, 1992 annual rpt, S0121–2

Arizona statistical abstract, general data, 1993 recurring rpt, U5850–2

Arizona traffic accidents, fatalities, and injuries, by vehicle type, circumstances, location, and driver and victim characteristics, 1991 and trends, annual rpt, S0530–1

Arkansas traffic accidents, fatalities, and injuries, by vehicle type, circumstances, location, and driver and victim characteristics, 1991, annual rpt, S0692–1

California statistical abstract, general data, 1992 annual rpt, S0840–2

California traffic accidents, fatalities, and injuries, by vehicle type, circumstances, location, and driver and victim characteristics, 1991 and trends, annual rpt, S0885–1

Colorado motor vehicle fees, taxes, and registrations, by license plate type and/or county, 1991, annual rpt, S1075–1.4

Delaware traffic accidents, fatalities, and injuries, by circumstances, location, and vehicle type, and driver and victim characteristics, 1992 and trends, annual rpt, S1435–1

BY COUNTY

Florida county data book, 1992/93 annual rpt, C6360–1

Florida statistical abstract, general data, 1992 annual rpt, U6660–1

Florida traffic accidents, fatalities, and injuries, by vehicle type, circumstance, location, and driver and victim characteristics, 1992 and trends, annual rpt, S1750–2

Georgia auto registrations, by county, 1991, annual rpt, S1950–1.2

Georgia county guide, general data, 1993 annual rpt, U6750–1

Georgia statistical abstract, general data, 1992-93 biennial rpt, U6730–1

Hawaii data book, general data, 1992 annual rpt, S2090–1

Hawaii traffic accidents, motor vehicle registrations, and drivers registered and involved in accidents, by county, 1986 and trends, annual rpt, S2125–1

Hawaii visitors and hotel occupancy and room rates, by county, quarterly rpt, S2090–2

Hawaii visitors and hotel occupancy rates, by county or island, bimonthly rpt, B3500–1

Idaho traffic accidents, fatalities, and injuries, by circumstances, location, vehicle type, and driver and victim characteristics, 1992, annual rpt, S2315–1

Illinois statistical abstract, general data, 1992 annual rpt, U6910–2

Illinois traffic accidents, fatalities, and injuries, by circumstances, location, and driver and victim characteristics, 1991 and trends, annual rpt, S2540–1

Kansas motor vehicle registrations, by vehicle type and county, 1991, annual rpt, S3020–1

Kansas statistical abstract, general data, 1991/92 annual rpt, U7095–2

Kansas traffic accidents, fatalities, and injuries, by vehicle type, location, circumstances, and driver and victim characteristics, 1992, annual rpt, S3040–1

Kentucky economic statistics, general data, 1993 annual rpt, S3104–1.3

Kentucky traffic accidents, fatalities, and injuries, by circumstances, location, vehicle type, and driver characteristics, 1992 and trends, annual rpt, S3150–2

Louisiana traffic accidents, fatalities, and injuries, by circumstances, location, and driver characteristics, 1991 and trends, annual rpt, S3345–2

Maryland statistical abstract, general data, 1993-94 biennial rpt, S3605–1

Maryland traffic accidents, fatalities, and injuries, by circumstances, location, vehicle type, and driver and victim characteristics, 1992, annual rpt, S3665–4

Michigan traffic accidents, fatalities, and injuries, and vehicle registrations and revenues, by county, 1991 and trends, annual rpt, S3997–2

Minnesota traffic accidents, fatalities, and injuries, by type of vehicle and circumstances, and driver and victim characteristics, 1992 and trends, annual rpt, S4230–2

Mississippi motor vehicle registrations, by county, FY92, annual rpt, S4435–1

Mississippi statistical abstract, general data, 1992 annual rpt, U3255–4

Missouri traffic accidents, fatalities, and injuries, by circumstances, location, and driver and victim characteristics, 1992 and trends, annual rpt, S4560–1

Montana traffic accidents, fatalities, and injuries, by circumstances, location, and driver and victim characteristics, 1992 and trends, annual rpt, S4705–2

Nebraska traffic accidents, fatalities, and injuries, by circumstances, location, vehicle type, and driver and victim characteristics, 1992, annual rpt, S4953–1

Nevada statistical abstract, general data, 1992 biennial rpt, S5005–1

Nevada traffic accidents, fatalities, and injuries, by circumstances, location, and vehicle type, 1992 and trends, annual rpt, S5140–1

New Jersey fatal traffic accidents and fatalities, by vehicle type, location, and circumstances, and driver and victim characteristics, 1992 and trends, annual rpt, S5430–2

New Mexico licensed drivers and motor vehicle registrations, by county, FY91-92 annual rpt, S5660–1.2

New Mexico traffic accidents, fatalities, and injuries, by vehicle type, circumstances, location, and driver and victim characteristics, 1992 and trends, annual rpt, S5665–1

New York State statistical yearbook, general data, 1992 annual rpt, U5100–1

New York State traffic accidents, fatalities, and injuries, by circumstances, location, vehicle type, and driver and victim characteristics, 1991 and trends, annual rpt, S5790–1

North Carolina traffic accidents, fatalities, and injuries, by circumstances, location, vehicle type, and driver and victim characteristics, 1992 and trends, annual rpt, S5990–1

North Dakota traffic accidents, fatalities, and injuries, by circumstances, location, vehicle type, and driver and victim characteristics, 1992 and trends, annual rpt, S6217–1

Ohio traffic accidents, fatalities, and injuries, by circumstances, location, driver and victim characteristics, and vehicle type, 1991 and trends, annual rpt, S6290–1

Oklahoma commuting patterns, including interstate and international travel, and detailed data by county, 1990 and trends, S6416–2

Oklahoma statistical abstract, general data, 1992 annual rpt, U8130–2

Oklahoma traffic accidents, fatalities, and injuries, by circumstances, location, and driver and victim characteristics, 1992 and trends, annual rpt, S6482–1

Pennsylvania statistical abstract, general data, 1992 recurring rpt, U4130–6

Pennsylvania traffic accidents, fatalities, and injuries, by circumstances, location, driver characteristics, and vehicle type, 1991, annual rpt, S6905–3

Rhode Island statistical almanac, general data, 1993 annual rpt, C7975–1

South Carolina statistical abstract, general data, 1993 annual rpt, S7125–1

South Carolina traffic accidents, fatalities, injuries, and economic loss, and vehicle registrations, by county, 1992 and trends, annual rpt, S7190–2

Index by Categories

South Dakota traffic accidents, fatalities, and injuries, by circumstances, location, vehicle type, and driver and victim characteristics, 1992 and trends, annual rpt, S7300–3

South Dakota workers and intercounty commuters, for counties with highest rates of commuting, 1990, S7355–1.501

Tennessee commuting patterns by county, for primary counties of 5 MSAs, 1990, S7495–2.505

Tennessee statistical abstract, general data, 1992/93 annual rpt, U8710–2

Utah traffic accidents and fatalities by circumstances, location, driver and victim characteristics, and vehicle type, 1992 and trends, annual rpt, S7890–2

Virginia traffic accidents, fatalities, and injuries, by circumstances, location, and driver and victim characteristics, 1991 and trends, annual rpt, S8282–1

Washington State traffic accidents, fatalities, and injuries, by circumstances, vehicle type, and location, with driver and victim characteristics, 1992 and trends, annual rpt, S8428–1

West Virginia statistical handbook, general data, 1992 annual rpt, R9385–1

West Virginia traffic accidents, fatalities, injuries, and economic loss, by county, 1992, annual rpt, S8645–1

Wisconsin Blue Book, general data, 1993-94 biennial rpt, S8780–1.2

Wisconsin traffic accidents, fatalities, and injuries, by circumstances, location, vehicle type, and driver and victim characteristics, 1992 and trends, annual rpt, S8815–1

Wyoming traffic accidents, fatalities, and injuries, by circumstances, location, vehicle type, and driver and victim characteristics, 1992 and trends, annual rpt, S9007–1

Veterans Affairs

State and local:

Alaska civilian veterans by area and sex, with number age 65/over, and distribution by period of service, 1990, article, S0320 1.511

Florida county data book, 1992/93 annual rpt, C6360–1

Georgia county guide, general data, 1993 annual rpt, U6750–1

Illinois statistical abstract, general data, 1992 annual rpt, U6910–2

Michigan veterans population and labor force, total and disadvantaged, by State area, 1980, annual planning rpt, S3980–1.2

Mississippi expenditures of Veterans Admin, by object and county, 1991, annual rpt, U3255–4.13

Pennsylvania statistical abstract, general data, 1992 recurring rpt, U4130–6

Pennsylvania veteran labor force data, by county, 1990, annual planning rpt, S6845–3.1

Tennessee statistical abstract, general data, 1992/93 annual rpt, U8710–2

BY FOREIGN COUNTRY OR WORLD AREA

Agriculture and Food

Baked goods (cookies and crackers) market shares, sales growth, and consumption, for top 5-6 countries, 1993 feature, C2710–1.509

Bottled water market shares, sales growth, and consumption, for top 6 countries, 1993 feature, C2710–1.513

Index by Categories

BY FOREIGN COUNTRY OR WORLD AREA

Brewing industry financial and operating data, including consumption, trade, and taxes, 1991 and trends, annual rpt, A3455–1

Cereal market shares for selected manufacturers, by world region, 1989-92, C2710–1.527

Chocolate market shares, sales growth, and consumption, for top 6-8 countries, 1992 feature, C2710–1.504

Citrus fruit production in selected countries, and US exports by country of destination, 1991/92 and trends, annual rpt, S1685–1.1

Coffee, Sugar, and Cocoa Exchange trading activity, with related data including deliveries and stocks by country and/or port, 1992 and trends, annual rpt, B2275–1

Corn and refined products supply and demand trends, US and by foreign country, 1993 annual rpt, A4200–1

Corn trade worldwide, with detail for US and selected other countries or areas, 1985/86-1992/93, annual rpt, S8680–1

Cotton and wool production by world region and country, and consumption and trade, 1950s-92, annual article, C3460–1.502

Distilled spirits trade, consumption, and prices, by product type and country, 1992 and trends, annual rpt, C4775–1

Exports of farm products, by detailed commodity and country of destination, US and California, 1991, annual rpt, B9520–1

Farm equipment foreign trade, by equipment type and country, 1986-91, annual feature, C3450–1.501

Fertilizer (phosphate) production distribution by type, and demand by world area, 1993 article, C5800–8.511

Fig industry production, acreage, and prices in California, with US consumption and imports by country, 1950s-92, annual rpt, A3750–1

Ice cream/frozen dessert production, and exports from US, by country, 1992 annual rpt, A5825–1

Latin America statistical abstract, general data by country, 1992 annual rpt, U6250–1.2, U6250–1.7, U6250–1.12, U6250–1.13, U6250–1.16, U6250–1.24, U6250–1.25, U6250–1.26

Liquor exports and imports, by product type and country, 1991, annual rpt, A4650–3

Macadamia nut imports, by country of origin, 1991, annual rpt, S2030–1

Meat and related products and poultry trade, production, and consumption, by country, 1990 and trends, annual rpt, A2100–1.2

Popcorn market shares, with consumption data for microwave popcorn, for top 5-7 countries, 1993 feature, C2710–1.517

Production, consumption, stocks, trade, and prices for approx 100 basic commodities, including by country and producing State, commodity yearbook for 1993, C2400–1, C2400–2

Soft drink foreign capital investments, for Coca Cola and Pepsi Cola in 9 emerging foreign markets, 1993 article, C5800–7.543

Soybean production and foreign trade data, by country, 1980s-93, annual rpt, B8480–1

Wheat exports by destination, production in 28 countries, and supply-demand summary for leading countries, 1992 annual rpt, A7310–1

Wine imports from 5 countries, 1990-91, article, A8955–1.503

Wine market statistics, including sales, production, trade, and consumer characteristics, with data by company, brand, and geographic area, 1992 and trends, annual rpt, C4775–2

World agriculture and food supply data, by country, 1992/93 biennial rpt, R9455–1.6

World Culinary Olympics awards won by US and other top natl teams, 1992, article, C5150–5.501

State and local:

Arizona farmland holdings of foreign owners, by selected country and county, Dec 1992, annual rpt, U5830–1

California agricultural exports distribution by destination country, 1991, annual rpt, S0840–3.1

Hawaii farmland holdings of foreign owners, with detail by selected country, 1991, annual rpt, S2030–1

Illinois farmland holdings of foreign owners, by county, country, and land use, 1990, annual rpt, U6910–2

Nevada farmland holdings of foreign owners, by county and country, Dec 1992, annual rpt, S5010–1

Oklahoma and US farmland holdings of foreign owners, by country, Dec 1992, annual rpt, S6405–1

Wisconsin dairy cattle exports by country of destination, 1989-92, annual rpt, S8680–1

Banking, Finance, and Insurance

American depositary receipt (ADR) capital raised, distribution by issuer country, 1st half 1993, article, C2710–2.519

Bank financial and/or operating ratios, for 6 EC countries and US, 1991, article, A8955–1.502

Business Week economic indicators, including exchange rates for selected currencies, weekly rpt, C5800–7

Dollar exchange rates for approx 30 countries, monthly rpt, A7400–3

Foreign securities listed on NYSE, by world region, 1992, annual fact book, B6625–1.1

Insurance premiums for life and non-life business, top 10 countries, 1990, annual rpt, A5650–1.1

Investment of US tax-exempt assets in intl and global equities, top 5 countries of investment, 1993, annual feature, C2710 2.511

Japan yen exchange rates with US dollar and 8 other currencies, 1992 and trends, annual article, R5650–2.511

Latin America statistical abstract, general data by country, 1992 annual rpt, U6250–1.27, U6250–1.28, U6250–1.29, U6250–1.30, U6250–1.33

Latin America stock exchange profiles for 7 countries, with market capitalization, trading volume, and return rates, 1993 articles, C2710–2.507

Life insurance in force in foreign countries, and ratio to natl income, by country, 1992 biennial fact book, A1325–1.7

Mutual fund investment company assets, for US and 16 foreign countries, 1986-91, annual rpt, A6025–1.1

NASDAQ over-the-counter securities issues, and terminal installations, by country, 1993 annual rpt, A7105–1

Securities market participation by foreign and US investors, by world area and country, quarterly rpt, A8825–2

Securities of foreign countries sold in US, volume and value of private placements under SEC Rule 144A, by country, 1990-1st half 1993, article, A8825–1.506

Stock market performance, for 10 foreign exchanges, 1992, recurring feature, C5800–7.509

Stock market performance, for 11 foreign exchanges, 1st half 1993, recurring feature, C5800–7.533

Stock market performance in selected developed and emerging markets, biweekly rpt quarterly feature, C3950–1.506, C3950–1.512, C3950–1.521, C3950–1.525

Stock market performance in 16 countries, 1992, annual article, C8900–1.507

World financial market devs including economic and monetary trends and forecasts for 15 industrial countries, bimonthly rpt, B6200–2

State and local:

California foreign bank offices, with financial condition, by instn and hq country, Dec 1992, annual rpt, S0810–1

Florida foreign bank offices and assets, by hq country, Dec 1990-91, annual rpt, U6660–1.17

Iowa State govt investment data, including number of foreign companies deemed unacceptable due to business in South Africa, by country, FY92 annual rpt, S2885–1

Communications

Advertising (TV/cinema) awards won by leading agencies and/or countries, 1993 annual article, C2710–1.532, C2710–1.533

Advertising agency income, billings by medium, employees, and offices, for leading US and/or foreign agencies, 1992 and trends, annual rpt, C2710–1.522

Advertising importance to public in 20 countries, 1993 survey article, C2710–1.549

Advertising spending trends, for 11 countries, 1992-93, article, C2710–1.532

Advertising worldwide media and marketing, with data for leading periodicals, and expenditures by top advertiser and country, 1992 annual feature, C2710–1.506

Book exports to Canada, Japan, UK, and 7 world regions, by subject category, 1991 and trends, annual rpt, A3274–2

Book production, costs, and trade, by country, 1993 annual compilation, C1650–3.4

Catalog industry executive views in US on best foreign markets, 1991 survey, annual rpt, A4620–1.5

Developing countries women's views on family planning messages, and TV and radio ownership rates, by country, 1985-92 surveys, U2520–1.51

EC video cassette rental and sales revenues, by country, 1991, articles, C9380–1.503

Europe advertising costs for 4 media, by country, with comparisons to US, 1992, article, C2710–1.532

BY FOREIGN COUNTRY OR WORLD AREA

Index by Categories

Europe advertising expenditure outlook by medium, for 12 countries, 1993 vs 1992, article, C2710–1.513

Europe cellular telephone market penetration, for 11 countries, 1993 article, C2710–1.509

Europe consumer socioeconomic characteristics and attitudes regarding direct mail, with data by country, 1992/93 annual rpt, A4620–1.5

Europe motion picture subsidy activity of European Film Distribution Office (EFDO), for 12 countries, 1988-92, article, C9380–1.540

Europe TV programming shares purchased from foreign sources, total and from major suppliers, for 16 countries, 1993 article, C1850–14.508

Europe TV viewership, for govt-run and commercial TV in 6 countries, Nov/Dec 1992, article, C2710–1.523

Latin America home video market indicators, for 8 countries, 1993 feature, C9380–1.519

Latin America statistical abstract, general data by country, 1992 annual rpt, U6250–1.4

Motion picture foreign productions, boxoffice receipts, rental income, and top films in selected countries, weekly rpt, C9380–1

Motion picture rental income for US releases in top 15 foreign countries, 1990-92, annual feature, C9380–1.530

Newspaper (daily) sales per 1,000 inhabitants, and advertising revenue, by country, 1988 and 1991-92, article, A8605–1.508

Periodical subscription prices, by subject area, and by country or world region of origin, 1993 and trends, annual article, C1852–1.506

Postal service rates for 1st-class mail, for US and 13 foreign countries, Dec 1991, annual rpt, A4620–1.5

Telephone service worldwide, including access lines by type, and intl calling patterns, with comparisons to population, by world area and country, 1990-91, annual rpt, B0350–1

TV and home video market indicators for 17 countries, 1993 feature, C9380–1.520

TV penetration and related market indicators in 14 countries, 1993 features, C9380–1.543

Education

Africa public universities, enrollment, and expenditures per student, for 12-34 countries, 1993 article, C2175–1.524

Developing countries family planning efforts, with data on socioeconomic and health conditions compared to developed countries, by country, 1980s-90, R8720–1.1

Doctoral degree foreign recipients in US, by country of origin, 1990/91, annual rpt, R6000–7

Govt spending on preschool-12th grade education in US and 5 other industrialized countries, 1980s, R8335–2

Higher education enrollment of foreign students, by instn, discipline, State, and country of origin, 1991/92, annual feature, C2175–1.501

Higher education foreign scholars engaged in research/teaching, for top 12-13 US instns and countries of origin, 1991/92, article, C2175–1.502

Higher education foreign students, by country of study and origin, 1991/92 and trends, annual rpt, R5580–1

Higher education foreign students in US instns, and science/engineering degree share of population age 22, by country, 1992 recurring rpt, A3960–2.1

Higher education instn language study abroad programs, including countries or world areas of study, 1993 annual survey, A1410–1.38

Higher education, 2-year college enrollment, degrees, faculty and staff, and tuition, for instns in selected countries, 1992 annual directory, A0640–1

Latin America statistical abstract, general data by country, 1992 annual rpt, U6250–1.8

Library automated systems installations by world region, 1993 annual articles, C1852–1.505, C1852–1.506

Library/info science school foreign students, by country of origin, fall 1992, annual rpt, A3235–1.2

Literacy rates and educational attainment, by sex and country, 1992/93 biennial rpt, R9455–1.5

Mathematics doctoral degree recipients by world region of citizenship, 1991/92, annual rpt, A2085–1.1

OECD member countries spending on elementary/secondary and higher education, with data on enrollment and teachers, for 15 countries, 1987, A1600–4

Student achievement test scores in math and science, by selected country, 1991, recurring rpt, A3960–2.1

State and local:

Florida foreign students enrolled in State-supported universities, by instn and country, fall 1991, annual rpt, S1725–1

Kentucky higher education foreign student enrollment by country of origin, fall 1992, annual rpt, S3130–3

Energy Resources and Demand

Africa (West) natural gas reserves, for 7 countries, 1993 article, C6985–2.504

Coal foreign trade activity, by country of origin and destination, monthly rpt, A7400–3

Coal industry executive views on country or region posing greatest competitive threat, Mar 1993 survey, article, C5226–1.511

Coal industry supply-demand, employment, and trade, by country, with summary data on world energy resources, 1992 annual rpt, A7400–2

Coalbed degasification emissions recovered, used, and vented, for 7 major coal producing countries, 1992 article, C6985–1.507

Commonwealth of Independent States natural gas exports, and price trends, by destination country, 1993 article, C6985–1.514, C6985–1.515

Electric power plant capacity on order outside North America, for developed and developing countries by region, 1993-2000, article, C6985–6.509

Electric power production and capacity, top 15 countries, 1990, annual rpt, A4700–1

Energy exploration, rotary drilling rigs in operation, by world area and country, monthly rpt, B4675–1

Energy intl sourcebook, with detail on oil and gas industry operations, supply-demand, and prices, for approx 80 countries, 1970s-91, annual compilation, C6985–10

Energy prices for distillate oil and natural gas, for US and 5-6 other countries, 1993 article, C6985–1.524

Gasoline prices and tax component, for US and 6 foreign countries, 1992 annual rpt, C2140–1.3

Latin America statistical abstract, general data by country, 1992 annual rpt, U6250–1.23, U6250–1.25

Middle East offshore oil and gas reserves and production, for 12 countries, 1992, article, C6985–2.505

Natural gas processing plants, capacity, and production, by company, State, and country, 1993 annual rpt, C6985–1.537

Natural gas production and drilling activity, trade, and consumption, by country or world area, 1989-91, annual rpt, A1775–3.2

Natural gas reserves and supply distances to Germany, by selected country or area, Jan 1993, article, C6780–1.504

Nuclear generating capacity added, by reactor and country, 1992, annual article, B6790–1.502

Nuclear power plant (non-US) capacity factors and cumulative generation, by plant, 1993 annual feature, B6790–1.503

Nuclear power plants and utilization, for 7 countries, 1987-92, recurring article, R5650–2.536

Offshore oil and gas wells, reserves, and production, by country, 1990-93, annual article, C6985–2.508

Offshore oil/gas fields developed in past 15 years with reserves of 5-20 million barrels, by world area, 1993 article, C6985–2.509

Offshore oil/gas production system projects under construction or planned, by company and country, 1992 annual feature, C6985–2.501

Offshore oil/gas subsea reserves, wells completed, and expected production, by field in 5 world regions, for projects due onstream in 1993/94, article, C6985–2.507

Oil (crude) prices, production, and US imports, by country, 1992-93, annual article, C6985–1.539

Oil and gas drilling and production technology devs, including drilling rigs in operation by world area, monthly rpt, C4420–1

Oil and gas fields by size, by country or world area, Dec 1989, article, C6985–1.516

Oil and gas industry exploration, production, refining, demand, finance, prices, and reserves, by State and country or world area, 1993 and trends, periodic basic data book, A2575–14

Oil and gas industry intl exploration, drilling, production, refining, stock, price, and financial data, weekly rpt, C6985–1

Oil and gas industry trends, with data by company, State, and country, 1993 annual compilation, C6985–4

Oil and gas intl supply-demand, exploration, refining, reserves, and industry finances, basic data by country and company, 1993 annual rpt, C6985–3

Index by Categories

BY FOREIGN COUNTRY OR WORLD AREA

Oil and gas pipeline mileage under construction or planned in 1993, for 5 world areas, Canada, and US, annual article, C6985–1.515

Oil and gas production by country, 1986-91, annual rpt, A7400–2.1

Oil and gas sourcebook, with industry operations and finances, and world supply-demand situation, 1970s-91, annual compilation, C6985–9

Oil and gas supply-demand and industry operations, with trends by country and producing State, 1970s-2010, annual rpt, C6985–5

Oil and refined products imports, by importing company, port, and country of origin, monthly rpt, A2575–12

Oil exports from Ecuador and Venezuela, by country of destination, 1992 annual rpt, U6250–1.25

Oil imports of US, by country and world area, 1983-93, annual feature, C6985–1.513

Oil imports of US, by country, 1960-91, recurring rpt, S6810–3

Oil refineries, petrochemical processing facilities, and pipelines, construction and costs, by country and company, weekly rpt semiannual list, C6985–1.524, C6985–1.551

Oil refinery capacity worldwide, by process, with data by country, company, and US State, 1992 annual feature, C6985–1.508

Oil reserves, production, refining capacity, and refined product prices, by world area and country, 1992 and trends, annual fact book, C4680–1.507

Oil reserves worldwide, by region, 1979-92, annual rpt, A5425–1.2

Oil world reserves and production, by country, company, and field, 1992 annual feature, C6985–1.509

Oil/gas deep well drilling, success ratios, and costs, by world area, 1990-92, annual article, C4420–1.503

Oil/gas drilling coiled tubing units in use, by tubing size and world region, 3rd-4th qtr 1992, article, C4420–1.502

Oil/gas drilling coiled tubing units in use, by world region and country, Oct 1992, article, C4420–1.501

Oil/gas reserve additions and replacement costs, for selected countries and world areas, 1988-92, article, C6985–1.530

Oil/gas seismic exploration land and marine crews, by world area, weekly rpt quarterly feature, C6985–1.515, C6985–1.521

Oil/natural gas liquids production, and crude oil trade, by world area, 1991 and 1997, article, C6985–1.515

Pipeline construction projects planned in foreign countries, including costs, by company, 1994, annual feature, C6780–2.504

Russia oil exports to 8 former Soviet Republics, and oil and gas prices, 1993 article, U2030–1.511

Seismic crews operating, by country or world area, 1987-92, annual rpt, C6985–3.5

Seismic exploration land crews and vessels, by world area or country, quarterly press release, A8912–2

Southeast Asia offshore oil/gas fields and platforms planned, by country, 1993-97, article, C6985–2.501

Uranium marketing, terms of transactions for major selling-buying countries or areas, and price index and earnings data in allied industries, monthly rpt, B6800–1

Uranium oxide deliveries to US utilities, distribution by country of origin, 1991-92, article, B6790–1.503

Uranium supply-demand and prices worldwide, and nuclear power industry devs, with data by country and company, 1992 and trends, annual rpt, B6800–2

World energy supply-demand, by fuel source and sector, by region and country, 1992/93 biennial rpt, R9455–1.3, R9455–1.7

State and local:

Pennsylvania coal exports, by country of destination, 1982-90, recurring rpt, S6810–3

Geography and Climate

Coastline and maritime zone length, by country, 1992/93 biennial rpt, R9455–1.7

Land area, by country, 1993 annual data sheet, R8750–5

Latin America statistical abstract, general data by country, 1992 annual rpt, U6250–1.1

World land area and use, by country, 1992/93 biennial rpt, R9455–1.5

Government and Defense

Cambodia peacekeeping personnel serving in UN forces from top 20 countries, Jan 1993, article, R5650–2.540

Developing countries govt spending for health, education, and defense, with total budget and detail for family planning by program, by country, 1980s-90, R8720–1.1

Europe public opinion on political, economic, and social issues, for 9 countries and 3 Soviet Union Republics, 1991 survey, C8915–8

Europe public opinion on political, economic, and social issues of interest to foreign investors, for 9 countries and 3 Soviet Union Republics, 1991 survey, C8915–9

Federal employee foreign travel allowance rates per diem, by country or city, June 1992, annual rpt, C2140–1.5

Federal tax burden under current policy and Clinton Admin proposal, with comparison to Germany, UK, and Japan, by income level, 1993 article, C8900–1.511

Gasoline tax rates and consumption, hwy miles, and persons per car, for US and 7 foreign countries, 1993 article, R9050–3.507

Gasoline taxes and rates, with detail by State and comparisons to 7 foreign countries, 1993 rpt, R9050–15.6

GDP reductions budgeted in US and 5 European countries, 1st half 1993, article, C5800–7.505

Gold coins issued by 60 countries, with country rankings by total gold use, 1992 and trends, annual rpt, A5145–1

Govt bond market ratings for 31 countries, 1993 article, C2710–2.520

Grants and credits issued by US Govt to foreign countries, by country and world region, 1946-90, annual rpt, R9050–1.3

Indebtedness of foreign countries to US, by country and world region, FY54-92, annual rpt, R9050–1.3

Infrastructure dev share of OECD countries foreign assistance, for 11 donor countries, 1991, article, C5800–2.527

Latin America statistical abstract, general data by country, 1992 annual rpt, U6250–1.9, U6250–1.11, U6250–1.12, U6250–1.30

Military post exchange sales, retail and other, by service branch, location, and store, FY92 and trends, annual rpt, A2072–2.502

Military US commissary sales by location, FY92, annual feature, A2072–2.501

Military weapon purchases from US, for top 5 foreign countries, since Aug 1990, 1993 article, C8900–1.509

Municipal govt officials directory, by city, for US, Canada, and 15 other countries, 1993 annual rpt, A5800–1

OECD Dev Assistance Committee contributions, by member and recipient country, 1987-91, annual article, R5650–2.507

OECD Dev Assistance Committee contributions, by member country, 1988-92, annual article, R5650–2.550

R&D spending and share of GNP, with govt funding by purpose, for US and 3 other industrial countries, 1989, article, R5650–2.521

Silver coins issued by 83 countries, with country rankings by total silver use, 1992 and trends, annual rpt, A8902–2

Tax (value-added) rates and revenues for 6 industrial countries, 1993 article, C8900–1.515

Tax revenues as percent of GNP, for US and 22 other countries, 1960-91, annual rpt, R9050–1.1

World govt spending and debt indicators, by country, 1992/93 biennial rpt, R9455–1.5

World official dev assistance received or granted, total and as percent of GNP, by country, 1989 and trends, biennial rpt, R9455–1.5

Health and Vital Statistics

Accidental deaths and death rates, with detail for occupational accidents, by country, 1993 annual rpt, A8375–2

Africa women's premarital sexual experience and childbearing, for 7 Sub-Saharan countries, 1986-89, article, A5160–6.503

AIDS cases and deaths in Western Hemisphere countries, 1986-89, annual rpt, U6250–1.6

Asia and Pacific countries population characteristics, series, R4500–1

Child gender preferences in developing countries, with data on family composition and child health, by country, 1980s, article, A5160–6.501

Child health and well-being indicators, for 6 countries, 1993 annual rpt, R3832–1

Contraceptive use among married women worldwide, by world region and country, 1993 annual data sheet, R8750–5

Contraceptive use and methods among postpartum women in 25 developing countries, 1980s, article, A5160–6.501

Death rates, by sex and age, for 14 foreign countries, 1990 and trends, article, B6045–1.503

Developing countries contraceptive failure rates, by user urban-rural residence and education, for 15 countries, 1986-89 surveys, article, A5160–6.504

Developing countries family planning and child survival efforts, by country and selected demographic characteristics, 1980s-90, R8720–1

BY FOREIGN COUNTRY OR WORLD AREA

Index by Categories

Developing countries sexual sterilization prevalence and interest among women, by country, 1993 article, A5160–6.503

Eye bank activity, including tissue shared with banks in other world areas, 1992, annual rpt, A4743–1

Family planning and fertility trends, and contraceptives effectiveness, safety, and availability, by method, series, U2520–1

Family planning service costs in 13 developing countries, by contraceptive method and service type, 1980s, article, A5160–6.502

Fertility rates and preferences, and contraceptive use, among women in 18 developing countries, 1980s, article, A5160–6.501

Health care expenditures as percent of GDP and per capita, for 15 OECD countries, 1970, 1980, and 1990, annual fact book, A1275–1.4

Health data, including AIDS cases by world region, and hospitalization length for selected diseases in 5 countries, 1992 annual rpt, A5173–2.4

Hearing aid exports to Canada, Japan, and 5 world regions, quarterly rpt, A5185–1

Hospital recruiting of foreign nurses, with source countries, by region, 1993 and trends, annual survey rpt, A6500–1

Infant and child mortality and low-weight birth rates, and child polio immunization rates, by selected country, 1992 annual rpt, R3840–5.1, R3840–11.1

Infant mortality rates for 39 countries, 1982, annual rpt, S6285–1

Latin America fertility and contraceptive use rates, for 11 countries, 1992, article, R8750–1.504

Latin America statistical abstract, general data by country, 1992 annual rpt, U6250–1.6, U6250–1.7

Medical research journal article multiple author incidence, for 2 radiation oncology publications, with data by author country and instn, 1983-87, article, A3273–8.502

Optometry school foreign students by country of residence, by instn, 1991/92, annual survey, A3370–2

Pharmacy degree program foreign student enrollment, by country of origin, fall 1991, annual rpt, A0630–9

Veterinary school enrollment by student State or country of residence, by instn, 1992/93, annual article, A3100–2.516

World population and health indicators, with detail by region and country, 1992/93 biennial rpt, R9455–1.2, R9455–1.5

World vital statistics, for top 50 countries in births, deaths, infant mortality, and life expectancy, 1992, semiannual rpt, B8500–1.16

State and local:

Hawaii leprosy patients registered, by place of birth, 1983-90, annual rpt, S2065–1.4

Housing and Construction

Architectural and engineering design firm countries of operation, for leading firms, 1992, annual article, C5800–2.522

Building materials prices, for 10 materials in 20 countries, 1993 article, C5800–2.521

Construction contractors working abroad, and contract values, by location of contracts, 1991-92, annual rpt, C5800–2.529

Construction cost indicators for selected countries, with data by project and material type, 1992 article, C5800–2.502

Construction design firms foreign billings, specialties, and work locations, for top 200 intl firms, 1992, annual article, C5800–2.538

Construction intl companies foreign and total contract values, with data by country or world region, for top 225 firms, 1992, annual feature, C5800–2.542

Eastern Europe housing starts, with detail for 4 countries, 1992-2000, article, C4300–1.504

Europe construction industry domestic and foreign mergers/acquisitions, for 23 Eastern and Western European countries, 1992 article, C5800–2.507

Latin America statistical abstract, general data by country, 1992 annual rpt, U6250–1.7, U6250–1.13

Income

Africa income per capita, by country, 1987, annual rpt, C2140–1.3

Billionaires by country, 1993 annual feature, C3950–1.518

Earnings of manufacturing production workers, US and 6 foreign countries, 1982-91, annual rpt, A3179–2.3

Latin America statistical abstract, general data by country, 1992 annual rpt, U6250–1.12, U6250–1.13, U6250–1.18

Shoe industry production workers compensation, US vs 7 other countries, 1981-91, annual rpt, A4957–1.2

Industry and Commerce

Accounts receivable average days outstanding, for US and 12 foreign countries, 1993 article, C4687–1.505

Air conditioning/refrigeration equipment trade, by country or world area, 1991-92, annual rpt, C1800–1

Aluminum production by world area, 1991, article, C5800–8.506

Aluminum production, consumption, and trade, by country and/or world area, 1982-92, annual rpt, A0400–2.2

Asia foreign investment inflow, with detail for US and Japanese investment, for 8-9 countries, FY85-92, article, R5650–2.555

Asia household appliance import trends of US, for 7 product types from 8 source countries, 1991 vs 1987, C2000–1.502

Asia textile manufactured fiber production and capacity, for 4 countries, monthly rpt semiannual survey, C3460–1.502

Canada economic indicators, including US trade, import shares for 8 other countries, and population by Province, 1993 articles, C4687–1.508

Canada manufactured fibers imports and exports, by fiber type and trading partner, 1989-1st 9 months 1992, recurring feature, C3460–1.504

Canada manufactured fibers imports and exports, by fiber type and trading partner, 1989-92, recurring feature, C3460–1.506

Canada manufactured fibers imports and exports, by fiber type and trading partner, 1990-1st half 1993, recurring feature, C3460–1.512

Carpet and rug industry shipments by type, PPI, and US trade by country, 1991 and trends, annual rpt, A3800–1

Chemical and related industries production, finances, operating ratios, employment, and trade, by country, company, and chemical, 1980s-92, annual feature, A1250–1.530

Chemical exports and imports, by trading partner and product category, 1992, article, A1250–1.521

Chemical exports by world region, 1980, 1986, and 1991, article, A1250–1.534

Chemical industry foreign trade and other operating data, for US and selected foreign countries, 1970s-92, annual rpt, A3850–1

Chemical industry shipment value, for US, Japan, and 7 European countries, 1991, article, C5800–8.505

Chemical industry worldwide production and trade, selected data by country and world area, 1988-92, annual feature, A1250–1.507

Competitiveness indicators for US vs other major industrial countries, including investments, productivity, exports, and per capita GDP, 1993 annual rpt, A4475–1

Computers (personal) per 1,000 population, for US, Canada, Europe, Japan, and other areas, 1993 article, C8900–1.519

Copper exports and imports, by country of origin or destination, 1987-91, annual rpt, S0497–1

Copper mine production and brass mill product supply in selected countries, 1972-92, annual rpt, A4175–1

Corporate acquisitions of US companies, for top 5 acquiring countries, bimonthly rpt quarterly feature, C4683–1

Corporate acquisitions of US firms abroad and foreign firms in US, 6 countries with most transactions, 1992, annual compilation, C4683–1.504

Corporate alternative minimum tax impacts on capital investment costs, including data by industry and type of equipment, and comparisons to 7 other countries, 1991 rpt, A1310–4

Corporate financial data for 500 largest foreign companies, by country, 1993 annual feature, C3950–1.519

Corporate intl acquisitions and value, with detail by selected country and for 19 major deals involving German firms, 1991-92 and trends, article, A5135–2.1

Corporate market value of top 1,000 firms worldwide, with related financial data, by company and country, 1993 annual feature, C5800–7.536

Corporate mergers, acquisitions, and divestitures, with buyers and sellers by location, 1992 and trends, annual rpt, B6020–1

Corporate public image advertising abroad, including specific areas targeted, 1992, triennial survey rpt, A3357–1

Coupons redeemed per household, in US, Canada, and 5 European countries, 1992, article, C2710–1.549

Current account and trade balances, for 13 OECD countries, 1991 or 1992, article, U6910–1.501

Czechoslovakia chemical and aggregate leading industries investments of US and 5 European countries, 1992, article, A1250–1.520

Diamond (cut but unset) exports and imports, for top 8 trading partners and all others, 1st half 1993, article, C2150–7.512

Index by Categories

BY FOREIGN COUNTRY OR WORLD AREA

Diamond (polished) exports and imports, for top 10 trading partners and all others, 1991, article, C2150–7.501

Diamond production value, by country, 1992, article, C5226–2.510

Eastern Europe foreign investments from 7 leading countries, 12 months ended Sept 1992, article, C5800–7.511

Eastern/Central Europe foreign trade with OECD and EC, with data by country and commodity, 1980s-90, R5025–10

EC cargo traffic and GNP shares for member countries or groups, 1993 article, C2150–6.504

EC chemical trade with Eastern Europe, with detail by trading partner for Germany, 1993 article, A1250–1.540

EC corporate acquisitions by Japanese firms, with detail for 5 countries, 1988-1st half 1992, article, C4683–1.501

EC economic indicators relating to proposed economic unification, by country, 1992 rpt, R5025–9

Economic growth rate, and direct investment abroad, for 5 countries, 1993 article, C8900–1.520

Economic indexes for US and selected other countries, composites of leading indicators, monthly rpt, R4105–6

Economic indicator forecasts for 6 countries, 1990s, annual rpt, B3520–1

Economic indicators for selected countries and world regions, 1992 and trends, annual rpt, A3179–2.3

Economic leading and coincident index trends for US and other industrial countries, monthly rpt, U1245–1

Economic performance and democracy measures for 16-20 countries, 1982-92, article, C5800–7.531

Economic trends and outlook, by country and region, 1993 annual feature, C8900–1.520

Electronic connector device market growth, by selected world area, 1986-96, article, C1850–2.501

Electronics industry market data, including foreign trade by country and product type, 1992 and trends, annual rpt, A4725–1

Electronics industry market devs, including foreign trade by major trading partner, monthly rpt, A4725–2

Electronics industry share of firms with market presence and production facilities in 8 foreign countries or world areas, 1993 and 1998, annual feature, C1850–2.506

Electronics market value, and percent change in GDP, for 12 countries, 1991-94, article, C1850–2.506

Electronics trade, by product category, detailed type, and country, monthly rpt, A4725–3

Europe chemical production outlook, for 7 countries, 1992-93, annual article, A1250–1.511

Europe computer advertising expenditures, for top 15 manufacturers, with detail by country, 1992, article, C2710–1.527

Europe corporate acquisitions activity by country and industry, and price and participants for top transactions, 1992 and trends, annual article, C4683–1.504

Europe electronic components market value, with detail for 8 countries, 1991, article, C1850–2.501

Europe electronics market value, for 8 countries, with comparisons to US and Japan, 1992 and 1994, article, C1850–2.502

Europe fine chemicals producers and total capacity, with detail for 7 countries, 1992, article, A1250–1.519

Europe govt-owned companies likely to be privatized, govt ownership share and value for 25 firms in 6 countries, 1993 article, C5800–7.537

Europe household appliance production, sales, and market shares, by country, product type, and manufacturer, 1991-92, annual feature, C2000–1.508

Europe public opinion on political, economic, and social issues, for 9 countries and 3 Soviet Union Republics, 1991 survey, C8915–8

Europe public opinion on political, economic, and social issues of interest to foreign investors, for 9 countries and 3 Soviet Union Republics, 1991 survey, C8915–9

Europe socioeconomic summaries, for EC and European Free Trade Assn countries, 1992-93, article, C8900–1.504

Exports of the US distribution by country or world region of destination, 1992, article, C4575–1.510

Exports of the US shares for top 5 destination countries, 1993 articles, C4687–1.512

Foreign trade deficit of US, for top 5 countries, 1993, article, C8900–1.510

Foreign trade in services and merchandise, by trading partner, 1986-92, article, A3892–1.503

Fortune magazine ranking of top 50-100 companies worldwide in 8 nonindustrial sectors, with financial and employment data, 1993 annual feature, C8900–1.522

Fortune 500 largest industrial corporations worldwide, with financial and employment data, 1992, annual feature, C8900–1.520

Franchise operations abroad, by country and type of business, 1991, annual rpt, A5820–1

GDP for top 20 countries, 1990, recurring rpt, R9375–6

GDP trends by country or region, 1992-94, article, C8900–1.527

Germany (West) and US foreign investment activity, by country, 1980-91, annual rpt, A5135–2.2

GNP per capita, by world region and country, 1991, annual data sheet, R8750–5

GNP total and per capita, for 50 countries, 1989, semiannual rpt, B8500–1.16

Gold consumption for jewelry, for top 10 countries, 1988-92, article, C2150–7.510

Gold consumption shares for coinage, for top 10 and all other countries, 1991, article, C2150–7.501

Gold mine production for 65 countries, 1992-96, annual rpt, A5145–2

Gold producers and exploration spending of US-owned companies, for operations in US, Canada, Australia, Latin America, and elsewhere, 1989-92, articles, C5226–2.506

Hard goods US manufacturers views on foreign competitors and potential export markets, by product line, 1993 annual survey rpt, A1800–1

Home improvement industry sales, stores, and other operating data, for leading foreign chains by country, 1991-92, annual feature, C5150–6.503

Import value from top 10 countries, 1985-91, article, U6910–1.502

Indium refinery production and capacity, and reserves, by country or world area, 1991, article, C5226–2.505

Industrial gas market value, by country or world region, 1991, article, C5800–8.502

Industrial plant and equipment investment trends, for US and 6 foreign countries, 1972-91, C7000–7.502

Investment and savings rates, and industrial equipment current value vs costs, for US and selected other countries, 1993 rpt, A1310–2.2

Iran imports by country of origin, 1977 and 1990, R4105–82.7

Iron and steel industry world production, and trade of US products, by country, 1992 and trends, annual rpt, A2000–2

Iron ore production, by country, 1982-91, article, C5226–2.502

Iron ore trade and production, by country, 1983-92, annual rpt, A2010–3.2

Japan and US foreign trade and investments, with detail by country, 1988-92, annual feature, R5650–2.552

Japan export shares for selected regions of destination, and export share of GNP compared to 5 other countries, 1992 article, R5650–2.504

Japan foreign aid contributions, by type and recipient region and country, 1987-91, annual article, R5650–2.507

Japan foreign dev aid, including distribution by recipient region, 1988-97, article, C5800–2.545

Japan foreign direct investments, with data by industry and investing country/world area, 1950s-93, annual article, R5650–2.544

Japan foreign investment rate of return on sales by world region, and overseas share of production, with detail by industry, FY84-91, article, R5650–2.559

Japan foreign investment trends, by country and industry, FY88-Mar 1993, annual article, R5650–2.533

Japan household appliance exports and imports, with detail by trading partner, by appliance type, 1985-91, article, C2000–1.504

Jewelry industry statistics on sales, marketing, trade, and employment, with customer characteristics, 1993 annual almanac, C2150–7.509

Korea (South) petrochemical and thermoplastics production and foreign trade, with detail by trading partner, 1992 and trends, article, C5800–8.510

Latin America economic indicators affecting business climate, with data on motor vehicle and oil industries and detail by country, 1992 rpt, R4105–82.6

Latin America statistical abstract, general data by country, 1992 annual rpt, U6250–1.4, U6250–1.16, U6250–1.23, U6250–1.24, U6250–1.25, U6250–1.26, U6250–1.29, U6250–1.32

Lumber exports from US to Pacific Rim, by country and product type, monthly rpt, A1630–2

BY FOREIGN COUNTRY OR WORLD AREA

Index by Categories

Lumber industry exports by destination, and imports from Canada and all other countries, 1984-92, annual rpt, A9395–1

Machine tool and other manufacturing technology exports and imports, by country of destination and origin, and by detailed product type, monthly rpt, A3179–3

Machine tool production, shipments, trade, finances, orders, and use, US and worldwide, 1992 and trends, annual rpt, A3179–2

Machine tool world production, trade, and consumption, by country, 1991-92, annual article, C7000–7.503

Magnesium imports of US and Japan from China and Commonwealth of Independent States, with worldwide demand by application or world region, 1992-93, article, A1250–1.544

Manganese ore imports for use in iron and steel industry, by country of origin, 1988-92, annual rpt, A2000–2.3

Manufacturing industry comparisons for US and 7-11 other countries, including output, compensation costs, and productivity, 1993 rpt, R8490–48

Manufacturing productivity and unit labor costs, and capital-GNP ratio, US and selected other countries, 1950s-90, annual rpt, R9050–1.2

Metal production, consumption, and reserves, for selected metals by country, 1990 and trends, biennial rpt, R9455–1.7

Mexico textile manufactured fiber imports and exports, by country of origin and destination, 1990-1st half 1993, C3460–1.512

Mineral exploration activities, expenses, and staff, for foreign and domestic operations of US and Canadian companies, 1991, article, C5226–2.508

Minerals supply-demand for selected commodities, US and worldwide, 1990s, annual feature, C5226–2.505

Mining govt royalty and corporate income tax rates, for 12 countries, 1993 article, C5226–2.506

Mining industry capital investment, by world area, 1993 annual feature, C5226–2.503

Newsprint capacity trends, and announced changes by company, by country, monthly rpt, A1630–4

Newsprint foreign trade, worldwide production, and capacity data by company, by country, 1970s-94, annual rpt, A1630–8

Newsprint production, consumption, trade, prices, and mill capacity, with data by world area, 1991-92 and trends, annual rpt, A8610–1

Nylon fiber production capacity, by country or world area, 1992, article, A1250–1.534

Paper, paperboard, and wood pulp industry capacity, by grade and country or world area, 1991 and 1995, annual rpt, A1630–7

Paperboard (kraft linerboard) exports, for 10 major supplying countries, and by world region, 1991 and/or 1992, article, A1630–5.504

Pesticide market value, by world region or country, 1990-91, article, A1250–1.501

Phosphate reserves and deposits, by country and selected US State, 1990, annual rpt, U6660–1.10

Phosphate rock production worldwide, by country, 1987-91, article, C5226–2.504

Plastics (polypropylene) foreign trade balance, by world area, 1991 and 1995, article, C6985–1.533

Plastics production capacity for specified resins, by major company and world region, monthly rpt recurring table, C5800–12.502

Potash exports by US and Canadian producers, by type and country of destination, monthly rpt quarterly tables, A8720–2

Potash imports, by State and country of origin, quarterly rpt, A8720–4

Potash production, inventories, and sales and exports by State, Canadian Province, and country of destination, monthly rpt, A8720–1

Private label product market shares in selected product categories, by selected country, 1988-93, C2710–1.536

Production, consumption, stocks, trade, and prices for approx 100 basic commodities, including by country and producing State, commodity yearbook for 1993, C2400–1, C2400–2

Productivity and related indicators, trend analysis for US and other industrial countries, 1980s-92, annual rpt, R2800–2

Profits (foreign) of US companies, distribution by country or world region, 1991, article, C5800–7.546

Pulp and paper industry operations and finances, US and Canada, with detail by company and product grade, and world production and trade summary, 1993 annual rpt, C3975–5

Rubber (synthetic) consumption by type, for 4 world regions, 1992 and 1997, article, C5800–8.504

Rubber demand, for synthetic and natural rubber, by world area, 1992-93 and 1997, article, A1250–1.524

Services sales to foreign persons by foreign affiliates of US companies, by country and industry, 1986-90, article, A3892–1.501

Shoe industry production and operating data, including trade by country, retail sales, and consumer expenditures, quarterly rpt, A4957–2

Shoe industry production, employment, trade, marketing, and related data, by SIC 2- to 5-digit code or product type, 1992 annual rpt, A4957–1.2

Silver market activity worldwide and in US, including production, consumption by end use, stocks, trade, and prices, by country, 1988-92, annual rpt, B4300–1

Silver mine production for 60 countries, 1992-96, annual rpt, A8902–1

Silver supply-demand by country and end use, with prices, futures trading, and market analyses, 1993 and trends, annual rpt, A8902–4

Soviet Union foreign trade with approx 20 countries, monthly rpt recurring feature, U2030–1.502

Soviet Union foreign trade with 5 Eastern European countries, monthly rpt recurring feature, U2030–1.503

Spain foreign trade and investment devs, by country and industry, 1991 and trends, articles, A8955–1.502

Spain, Madrid exports, by destination country or area, 1991, article (in Spanish), A8955–1.501

Steel consumption worldwide, with detail by selected country or world area, 1990-93, 1995, and 2000, annual article, C7000–8.502

Steel industry restructuring devs, with data on production, employment, and worker assistance, and selected detail by company, for 8-12 countries, 1970s-90, R9260–16

Steel production by country and world area, monthly rpt, A7400–3

Sulfur (oil-based) recovery plant capacity and production, by company and country, Jan 1993, annual feature, C6985–1.537

Sulfur production and reserves, by country, 1991-92, article, C5226–2.508

Textile manufactured fiber exports, by country of destination, 1991-1st half 1993, annual feature, C3460–1.512

Textile manufactured fiber production and capacity, by product type and country or world region, 1993 annual rpt, C3460–1.508, C3460–1.509

Textile manufactured fiber production capacity, by product type and country or world region, 1980-94, annual feature, C3460–1.510

Textile manufactured fibers imports, by country of origin, monthly rpt, C3460–1

Textile manufactured fibers production and trade, and mill consumption, by country, 1989-91, annual feature, C3460–1.503

Textile manufactured fibers trade, detailed data by type and country, 1989-92, annual rpt, C3460–1.504

UK economic indicators, including US trade, import shares for 4 other countries, and population by country and city, 1993 articles, C4687–1.510

Watch imports by country of origin, 1991-92, article, C2150–7.511

Watch production, purchasing, and export prices, by country and/or type, 1992 and trends, article, C2150–7.510

Wood chemicals (naval stores) production, consumption, and trade, US and foreign, 1992 and trends, annual rpt, C6585–1

World economic trends, for 7 industrial countries, 1984-92, article, U2160–1.502

World financial market devs including economic and monetary trends and forecasts for 15 industrial countries, bimonthly rpt, B6200–2

World foreign trade patterns, and US multinatl corporation views on intellectual property protection, by country or world area, 1991 rpt, R4105–82.2

World GNP, and GDP by sector, by country, 1989 and trends, biennial rpt, R9455–1.5

State and local:

Alabama export values for 6 countries of destination, 1990, annual rpt, U5680–3

Alabama, Port of Mobile foreign trade, by leading commodity and country, 1992 recurring rpt, U5680–2.7

Georgia affiliates of foreign companies, with facilities, employment and investment, by hq country, 1991 and trends, biennial rpt, U6730–1.6

Georgia exports, by industry group and country of destination, and exporting business establishments, 1993 article, U6730–2.502

Index by Categories

BY FOREIGN COUNTRY OR WORLD AREA

Hawaii foreign trade and direct investment, by country, 1992 annual rpt, S2090–1.24

Idaho exports value by major country or region of destination, 1987-91, recurring rpt, S2218–2.9

Illinois export values for top 10 countries of destination, 1989-92, S2405–2.503

Iowa exports to top 10 countries of destination, 1991, annual rpt, S2784–3

Maine foreign trade value by country of destination, 1992 recurring rpt, S3434–1

Maryland, Port of Baltimore imports and exports, by country, 1991, biennial rpt, S3605–1.10

New Jersey foreign-owned business establishments and employment, by leading owner country and industry div, 1987, article, S5425–1.501

North Dakota exports, by country of destination, 1991, annual rpt, S6140–2

Oregon exports value, for top 5 destinations and commodity types, 1991, annual rpt, S6585–3

Pennsylvania, ports of Philadelphia foreign trade, by commodity and country, 1990 and trends, recurring rpt, U4130–6.2

South Carolina foreign investments by investing country, 1991 and trends, annual rpt, S7125–1.3

South Dakota exports to top 20 countries of destination, with detail for Canada and Mexico by commodity, 1991, article, U8595–1.502

Washington State intl trade, by major trading partner, 1982-91, annual rpt, S8345–3

Labor and Employment

Chemical process industry employment in 23 countries, 1991-92, article, C5800–8.509

Corporate employee intl relocations, including continents most often moved to and from, 1992, annual rpt, B0600–1

Employment and investments abroad of US multinatl firms, and foreign compensation and unemployment data, for 10 countries, 1970s-93, article, C8900–1.504

Labor cost per hour in US, Germany, France, UK, and Japan, 1988 and 1992, article, C5800–7.517

Latin America statistical abstract, general data by country, 1992 annual rpt, U6250–1.12, U6250–1.13

Manufacturing workers annual hours worked and days off, for 7 countries, 1990 or 1991, article, C5800–7.539

Persian Gulf region foreign workers and labor force share, for 6 countries, 1975 and 1990, R8750–2.59

Production worker compensation costs for 25 countries and 3 country groups, 1992, article, S0465–1.508

Southeastern States employment at foreign-owned firms, by hq country, 1990, annual rpt, U8710–2.20

Unemployment rates for US, Japan, EC, and 5 European countries, 1993, article, C8900–1.526

Vacation weeks given to 1st-year employees in US and 5 foreign countries, 1993 feature, C1200–4.503

Worker annual hours of labor and amount of paid vacation, for 12 industrialized countries, 1993 feature, C4215–1.507

World labor force, including women's share, by country, 1970s-2000, biennial rpt, R9455–1.5

Law Enforcement

Latin America statistical abstract, general data by country, 1992 annual rpt, U6250–1.15

Lawyers compared to population, for US and 5 other countries, 1993 article, C2425–2.503

Tort case costs as percent of GDP, for US and 10 other countries, 1991, article, A1865–1.503

Natural Resources, Environment and Pollution

Developing countries population access to safe drinking water and sanitation services, by urban-rural status and country, 1988-90, R8720–1.2

Environmental services revenues by world region and selected country, 1991 and 1996, article, A1250–1.530

Europe municipal solid waste volume, with detail for plastics, by country, 1990, annual encyclopedia, C5800–12.503

Forest and other wooded land, protected forest, and forest products production value, by world region, 1993 article, C3975–2.506

Japan exports of water and nonvehicle air filtering/purifying equipment, with detail by major importing country, 1988-92, article, R5650–2.532

Latin America statistical abstract, general data by country, 1992 annual rpt, U6250–1.2, U6250–1.6

Tropical forest acreage lost in 50 countries, and selected deforestation rates, 1981-85, annual rpt, U6250–1.24

Wastepaper exports, by country of destination and grade, 1991, annual rpt, C3975–5.4

Water supply outlook, population per million cubic meters in selected world areas and countries, 1990 and 2025, article, R8750–1.502

World resource issues and environmental devs, by region and country, 1992/93 biennial rpt, R9455–1

World water resources supply-demand conditions and outlook, with population size and growth factors, by region and selected country, 1992 rpt, R8750–2.57

Population

Asia and Pacific countries population characteristics, series, R4500–1

Catholic population, clergy, and instns, and US missionaries by sex and order, by country or world region, 1993 annual almanac, C6885–1

Developing countries family planning efforts, with data on socioeconomic and health conditions compared to developed countries, by country, 1980s-90, R8720–1.1

EC population and GDP trends for 4 countries and all others, and foreign population shares by country, 1992 rpt, R5025–9

Europe consumer socioeconomic characteristics and attitudes regarding direct mail, with data by country, 1992/93 annual rpt, A4620–1.5

Europe public opinion on political, economic, and social issues, for 9 countries and 3 Soviet Union Republics, 1991 survey, C8915–8

Foreign-born population, by world region of origin, decennially 1960-90, article, R8750–1.511

Hispanic American population, by country of ethnic origin, 1990, article, C4575–1.511

Immigrant households, income, and home ownership rates by origin and length of US residence, and 15 cities with most new immigrants, 1993 article, C4300–1.512

Immigrants admitted to US, Florida, and 6 MSAs, by country of birth, 1990, annual rpt, U6660–1.1

Jewish population by world area, country, and US census div, State, and city, 1990-92, annual compilation, A2050–1

Latin America statistical abstract, general data by country, 1992 annual rpt, U6250–1.1, U6250–1.5, U6250–1.10, U6250–1.14, U6250–1.17

Legal immigrants not covered by Immigration Reform and Control Act, from top 15 and all other countries of origin, FY91, article, R8750–1.501

Middle East population trend and demographic characteristics, by country, 1993 rpt, R8750–2.59

Population age 65/over as percent of population age 15-64, for 7 countries, 1985, 1995, and 2005, article, R5650–2.546

Population and growth rates for 130 countries, with rankings, 1960s-87, annual rpt, U6250–1.5

Population profiles of selected countries and world areas, monthly rpt, R8750–1

Population shares foreign born, for US and 5 European countries, 1985 and 1990, article, C5800–7.535

Population size and characteristics, GNP, and land area, by world region and/or country, 1993 annual data sheet, R8750–5

Population size and projections, for top 50 countries, 1993 semiannual rpt, B8500–1.16

Public opinion in US on country that represents greatest danger, Jan 1993 survey, C8915–1.501

Refugee arrival activity worldwide, and US admission and asylum data, by country, 1992 annual feature, R9372–2.503

Refugee arrivals, asylum, and quotas, by world area or country of origin, monthly rpt, R9372–2

Refugee assistance budgets, for State Dept programs by world area, FY93-94, annual article, R9372–2.506

Refugee asylum application processing staff, and claims filed, for US and 8 foreign countries, 1993 article, R9372–2.507

Refugees, resettlement, and intl aid devs, by country, 1992, annual rpt, R9372–1

Religious preferences in 19 countries, 1991-92 surveys, R8780–1.503

World population and health indicators, with detail by region and country, 1992/93 biennial rpt, R9455–1.2, R9455–1.5

World telephone service, with comparison to population and households, by area and country, 1990-91, annual rpt, B0350–1

State and local:

California legal immigrants, distribution by country of origin, 1986-90, article, R9372–2.509

DC refugee resettlement cases, by world area of origin, 1987-91, annual rpt, S1535–3.5

Hawaii resident ancestry and birthplace, and immigrants, by country, 1980s-91, annual rpt, S2090–1.1

BY FOREIGN COUNTRY OR WORLD AREA

Maryland foreign-born population, by country of birth, 1990, biennial rpt, S3605–1.1

Tennessee and US naturalized citizens, by country of birth, 1980-89, annual rpt, U8710–2.1

Prices and Cost of Living

Consumer price trends, for Canada, Japan, and 4 European countries, 1976-92, article, A6450–2.503

Latin America statistical abstract, general data by country, 1992 annual rpt, U6250–1.18, U6250–1.31

Public Welfare and Social Security

Latin America statistical abstract, general data by country, 1992 annual rpt, U6250–1.7

Worldwide charitable contributions of US corporations, by recipient type and country or world area, 1990 and trends, R4105–78.23

Worldwide charitable contributions of US corporations, by recipient type and country or world area, 1993 article, C2176–1.507

State and local:

Utah homeless shelter population without US citizenship, by world region of origin, July 1992, annual rpt, S7808–2

Recreation and Leisure

Bicycle import shares and value, by country of origin, 1992 and trends, annual rpt, A3470–1

Bowling (women's) assn membership and league activities, by city, State, and country, 1991/92, annual rpt, A9415–1

Bowling assn finances and membership, and bowling establishments and lanes, by State and other area, 1991/92 and trends, annual rpt, A1015–1

Science and Technology

Chemical R&D activity, employment, and funding, by selected country, 1993 annual feature, A1250–1.537

Ecologist employment characteristics, including world region of employer, Mar 1992 survey, recurring rpt, A4685–1

European Space Agency Columbus space station dev contribution shares by country, 1992 article, C5800–4.503

High-technology US company foreign acquisitions, distribution among top 4 and all other hq countries, Oct 1988-Apr 1992, C1850–2.503, C1850–6.501

Japan technology imports and exports, with detail by industry and trading partner, FY91 and trends, annual article, R5650–2.557

Latin America statistical abstract, general data by country, 1992 annual rpt, U6250–1.8

Mathematics and science test scores worldwide for students age 13, for 14 countries, 1990, annual rpt, R3840–11.1

Patents from US issued to foreign residents, for top 50 countries, 1992, semiannual rpt, B8500–1.16

Patents issued by US to persons/firms in 15 leading and all other foreign countries, FY91-92, article, A1250–1.515

Patents issued in US, for top 10 countries, 1991-92, C1850–6.507

R&D expenditure summary for US and 9 foreign countries, 1992, annual feature, C5800–7.534

R&D spending trends for US, Germany, Japan, and France, 1985-91, article, C1850–6.511

Spacecraft launchings by country, 1991 and trends, annual rpt, A0250–2.2

World space flight devs and records, with launches and orbiting equipment by country, and detail for US programs, 1992 and trends, annual rpt, B9170–1

Transportation and Travel

Aerospace industry foreign trade, by major trading partner, 1987-91, annual rpt, A0250–2.4

Aircraft (general aviation) and hours flown, by world region, 1981-91, annual rpt, A5120–2.1

Aircraft (jet) world inventory, orders, and deliveries, by type of aircraft and individual owner/operator, 1992 and trends, annual rpt, B1582–1

Airline capacity shares for US vs natl flag carriers, for 6 countries, 1993 article, C7000–4.507

Airline market activity, including traffic, financial performance, employment, and fleet composition, by carrier and world area, 1992, annual feature, C7000–4.508

Airline passenger jet requirements projected to 2011, by world region, with traffic and fleet trends and outlook, 1993 annual rpt, B3075–1

Airline passenger traffic, by world region, 1991-95, article, C5800–4.524

Asia tourist arrivals and daily expenditures in 6 countries, 1993 article, C2710–1.549

Auto and light truck trade, with detail by trading partner, weekly rpt quarterly table, C2710–3.513, C2710–3.524, C2710–3.539

Auto import dealer franchises by country of origin and make, 1992-93, annual article, C2710–3.519

Auto parts total trade balance, with import and export value by major trading partner, 1985-92, article, R5650–2.523

Bicycle import shares and value, by country of origin, 1992 and trends, annual rpt, A3470–1

Europe auto market, including buyer preferences and market shares for selected manufacturers, by country, Aug/Sept 1992 survey, article, C2710–1.523

Europe auto sales, by country and/or manufacturer, weekly rpt monthly tables, C2710–3

Helicopters in civil aviation, production, trade, utilization, accidents, and landing facilities, 1993 annual rpt, A5190–1

Incentive travel programs for sales promotion, with destinations, and expenditures of top 10 user industries, 1993 survey, annual article, C1200–4.510

Latin America motor vehicle production and sales, and Mexico auto exports, by country or world region, 1992, article, C2710–3.553

Latin America statistical abstract, general data by country, 1992 annual rpt, U6250–1.3, U6250–1.14, U6250–1.15

Logistics cost as percent of GDP, for US, Japan, and 3 world regions, 1993 annual article, C2150–1.506

Motor vehicle industry detailed production, sales, trade, and vehicle use and ownership data, by vehicle type, State, and country, 1900s-92, annual rpt, A0865–1

Motor vehicle production and sales, by country and manufacturer, 1992 and trends, annual data book, C2710–3.531

Index by Categories

Motor vehicle production shares by country or world region, 1993 article, C8900–1.526

Motor vehicle world production, sales, trade, and registrations, by country, world area, manufacturer, and make, 1991 and trends, annual rpt, A0865–2

Shipbuilding govt aid programs in 6 OECD countries, and impact on US industry, 1993 recurring rpt, A8900–8

State govt travel offices foreign promotional budget allocations, by selected country, by State, 1992 survey, annual rpt, R9375–2

Traffic accident fatalities and rates, and vehicle registrations, by country, 1986-91, annual rpt, A8375–2.3

Traffic accident fatalities and seat belt use laws, by country, 1993 annual rpt, A0865–1.3

Travel and tourism rankings for selected indicators, including data for top 20 States, cities, countries, businesses, and other measures, 1992 recurring rpt, R9375–6

Travel and tourism trends in US and worldwide, with traveler and trip characteristics, and data by local area, 1992 annual rpt, C2140–1

Visitor arrivals in US from top 10 foreign countries, 1993, article, C1200–4.505

World transportation infrastructure, and passenger and freight traffic by mode, by country, 1992/93 biennial rpt, R9455–1.5

State and local:

Hawaii visitors, by residence and demographic characteristics, 1991 and trends, annual rpt, S2090–1.7

Oklahoma commuting patterns, including interstate and international travel, and detailed data by county, 1990 and trends, S6416–2

South Carolina foreign visitors, length of stay, and expenditures, by selected country, 1987-91, annual rpt, S7125–1.14

BY REGION

Agriculture and Food

Alcohol use patterns among high school seniors, by region, 1993 survey article, B6045–1.504

Alcoholic beverage drinker characteristics, 1992, annual rpt, C4775–2.2

Distilled spirits consumption, and consumer characteristics and buying habits, 1992 and trends, annual rpt, C4775–1.3

Farm price support Federal payments, by State and region, FY82, FY88, and FY92, R8490–47

Fish processing and wholesaling plants and employment, by region and selected State, 1990, annual rpt, U6660–1.10

Food (single-serving packaged) use by consumers, by region, 1993 survey article, C1850–1.509

Food away from home expenditures, by household characteristics and for 26 MSAs, 1991, recurring rpt, A8200–13

Food marketers financial and operating data, by company size and region, 1991-92, annual rpts, A4950–5

Food marketing mgmt personnel compensation, by position, by company sales size and region, year ended Mar 1993, annual survey, A4950–6

Index by Categories

BY REGION

Food nutrition awareness and health concerns, including shopping and consumption patterns, by respondent characteristics, 1993 survey, annual rpt, A4950–36

Food store industry structure, sales, operations, and business outlook, by type of store, 1993 annual rpt, C5225–1.505

Food store sales by region, 1990-91, annual rpt, C3400–6

Food take-out consumer characteristics, consumption patterns, and attitudes, May 1992 survey, A8200–21

Ice cream and frozen dessert production, by region, 1992 and trends, annual rpt, A5825–1.1

Meat and poultry demand, prices, and processor operations and finances, with data on meat production, 1991 and trends, annual rpt, A2100–1.1

Restaurant (table service) operations and menu offerings, and related consumer views and practices by demographic characteristics, 1992, recurring rpt, A8200–11

Restaurant patronage patterns, expenditures, and food preferences, 1992 survey, recurring feature, C1850–3.501

Restaurant smoking policy importance to consumers, and views on smoking acceptability in restaurants and other public places, by selected characteristics, Jan 1993 survey, A8200–8.15

Snack food sales, consumption, and prices, by snack type and region, with data on industry operations and outlook, 1992 and trends, annual rpt, A8905–1

Soft drink consumption indexes by region, 1992, annual article, C0125–2.504

Supermarket (independent) sales and operating ratios, by store type, sales size, and region, 1991, annual survey, A4950–4

Supermarket attributes considered by shoppers in evaluating service quality, by respondent characteristics, fall 1992 survey, A4950–37.2

Supermarket bakery and deli consumer shopping frequency, by region, 1993 annual survey article, C5225–1.508

Supermarket bakery depts and consumer shopping frequency, by region, 1991 and/or 1992, annual article, C5225–1.504

Supermarket shopper practices, attitudes, and expenditures, by respondent characteristics, 1993 and trends, annual survey rpt, A4950–3

Supermarkets opened, remodeled, and closed, including store features, dev costs, and rent, by region and sales size, 1992 and trends, annual rpt, A4950–2

Turkey hatchery operations by region, 1992, annual rpt, S1685–1.3

Wheat inspected for export, by variety and port, June 1991-May 1992, annual rpt, A7310–1

State and local:

Oregon floriculture product shipments, by destination, 1991, annual rpt, S6575–1

Wisconsin cattle shipments, by region of destination, 1989-92, annual rpt, S8680–1

Banking, Finance, and Insurance

Accounting grad supply-demand, including detail by sex, race-ethnicity, and region, 1991/92 and trends, annual rpt, A1885–1

Bank failures and outlays by FDIC, by State and region, 1990-92, R8490–47

Bank market value rankings and related finances, for leading instns by region, 1993 annual feature, C5800–7.521

Bank profitability indicators for approx 50 instns, with regional rankings, weekly rpt quarterly article, C5800–7.503, C5800–7.519, C5800–7.528, C5800–7.541

Home equity lending activity and practices of financial instns, by region, asset size, and instn type, 1992, annual rpt, A4160–3

Mortgage insurance premiums written, by region, 1988-91, annual rpt, A6455–1

Public opinion on business use of personal info, and consumer examination of own credit rpt by selected characteristics, 1992 survey, annual rpt, B3280–2

Real estate investment advisor assets managed, distribution by region, 1992-93, annual feature, C2710–2.520

Venture capital resources under mgmt, by region, 1990-91, annual rpt, A8515–1

Communications

Advertising agency salaries, by position and region, 1992-93, article, C2710–1.505

Cable TV system mgmt salaries by selected characteristics, and views on job satisfaction, Mar/Apr 1993 survey, articles, C1858–1.502

Direct marketing industry devs, including advertising patterns, finances, target market characteristics, and consumer attitudes, 1992/93 annual rpt, A4620–1

Magazine circulation director and manager compensation, by region, sex, age, and publication characteristics, 1992 survey, annual article, C2575–1.502

Magazine compensation of ad sales personnel, by region, sex, age, and publication characteristics, 1993 survey, annual article, C2575–1.516

Magazine compensation of editorial personnel, by region, sex, age, and publication characteristics, 1993 survey, annual article, C2575–1.512

Magazine production director and manager compensation, by region, sex, age, and publication characteristics, 1993 survey, annual article, C2575–1.510

News events followed most closely by public, and opinion on media coverage and selected current issues, by respondent characteristics, recurring rpt, C8915–1

Public opinion on the media and related issues, by respondent characteristics, series, C8915–11

Radio ownership, audience characteristics, and advertising revenues and effectiveness, with selected comparisons to other media, 1993 annual rpt, A8789–1

Telephone Yellow Pages directory use among consumers, with detail by respondent characteristics, 1992 survey, annual rpt, A9500–2

TV households by census div, State, county, Nielsen market area, and time zone, Jan 1994, annual rpt, B6670–2

Video cassette (prerecorded) sales distribution by region, 1992, article, C8130–1.508

Education

Catholic schools, enrollment, and teachers, by region, State, and diocese, 1992/93 and trends, annual rpt, A7375–1

Catholic secondary school operations and finances, by region, 1991/92 and trends, biennial rpt, A7375–5

Catholic vs public school performance, and support for parental school selection funded by govt, public opinion by respondent characteristics, July 1992 survey, A7375–8

Foreign students enrolled in US higher education instns, by instn, State, country of origin, and demographic characteristics, 1991/92 and trends, annual rpt, R5580–1

High school grads by race-ethnicity and region, 1985/86-1994/95, annual rpt, A1410–10

Higher education administrative salaries in doctorate-granting public universities, approx 80 positions by region, 1992/93, annual survey rpt, U5960–1

Higher education enrollment trends for 1st-time freshmen, by region, fall 1992, annual rpt, A7150–5

Higher education instn employee retirement and insurance benefits, prevalence and expenditures, by type of instn and region, 1991, biennial survey, A9025–3

Higher education instns with budget and enrollment increases, and faculty reductions, by region, 1993 annual survey, A1410–1.38

Higher education physical plant operations, costs, employment, salaries, and energy use, by instn and region, 1991/92, recurring rpt, A3183–1

Higher education student weekly alcohol consumption, by region, 1990, survey article, C2175–1.522

Librarian salaries for 6 positions, for public and academic libraries by region, 1993, annual rpt, A2070–3

Library school grad placements and salaries, by region, sex, instn, and library type, with detail for minorities, 1992 and trends, annual article, C1852–1.512

Library school grads, placements, and salaries, by region and sex, 1991 and trends, annual compilation, C1650–3.3

Library/info science school enrollment, staff and student characteristics, finances, and curricula, by school and degree program, 1991/92, annual rpt, A3235–1

Political science higher education dept characteristics, including faculty, salaries, enrollment, and finances, 1991/92 annual rpt, A2617–1

Private elementary and secondary school enrollment, staff, and finances, with detail for minorities, by school type and region, 1980s-1992/93, annual rpt, A6835–3

Public school student distribution and mathematics proficiency ratings by frequency of changing schools in past 2 years, by region, 1992, R4800–2.520

Social work higher education programs and faculty, with data by region, 1992 and trends, annual rpt, A4515–1.1

Energy Resources and Demand

Coal deliveries and prices at electric power plants, by Bur of Mines producing district, monthly rpt, A7400–9

Coal exports and imports, by customs district, monthly rpt, A7400–3

Coal industry executive views on industry public image, by region, Mar 1993 survey, article, C5226–1.507

BY REGION

Index by Categories

Coal industry personnel earnings and employment history, US and Canada, 1993 survey article, C5226–1.507

Electric light/power construction cost indexes, by region, 1971-92, annual rpt, A4700–1

Electric power (steam) plants, capacity, generation, and fuel use and costs, by fuel type, utility, and location, 1991, annual rpt, A7400–7

Electric power generating equipment orders and shipments, and capacity addition trends, with data by location and facility, 1991 annual rpt, A4700–2

Electric power output trends, by region, year ended Jan 1993, C6985–6.505

Electric power peak summer demand percent change, by region, 1993 vs 1992, article, C6985–6.512

Electric power plants planned and under construction in 1993, by type, utility, and region, and forecast capacity for 1993-2001, annual feature, C5800–28.503

Electric power production, by region, monthly rpt, C5800–28

Electric power summer demand and resources, by region, June-Sept 1993, annual article, C5800–28.508

Electric power supply-demand, and utility capacities and fuel requirements, detailed data by US and Canadian region, 1992-2002, annual rpt, A8630–2

Electric power transmission facility additions/upgrades planned, by facility and region, winter 1992/93, C5800–28.504

Electric utilities financial performance and growth of approx 80 firms arranged by region, 1993 annual rpt, C3950–1.505

Electric utility capacity additions and plans, by region, 1991-2001, annual feature, C5800–28.507

Electric utility capital spending, by function and region, and capacity addition plans, 1992-97, annual article, C6985–6.503

Electric utility construction and capacity outlook, including data by region and fuel source, 1992-2001, annual feature, C5800–28.501

Electric utility financial and operating ratios, by region, 1990, annual article, A2625–1.501

Electric utility State/local taxes/contributions as percent of revenues, for public and private utilities by region, 1990, article, A2625–1.501

Fuel oil dealer operations, with heating and cooling equipment services, by region, 1992 annual survey, C4680–2

Fuel oil dealer sales, customers, and equipment lines, by region, 1992, annual fact book, C4680–1.507

Fuel used for residential heating, cooking, and clothes drying, by region, 1970s-91, annual rpt, A1775–3.7

Gasoline prices by census region, 1978-92, periodic basic data book, A2575–14.3

Gasoline prices by grade and region, monthly rpt, C4680–1

Hydroelectric developed and undeveloped generating capacity, by region, 1993 article, C6985–6.507

Natural gas potential reserve estimates in 7 regions, Dec 1992 and trends, biennial rpt, R8765–1

Natural gas prices by region, monthly rpt, A1775–2

Natural gas resources by region, 1993, article, C6985–1.527

Oil (crude) production by PAD district, 1st half 1992-93, annual article, C6985–1.539

Oil and gas drilling workover rigs active, by region, Apr 1987-Dec 1991, annual compilation, C6985–9.1

Oil and gas industry intl exploration, drilling, production, refining, stock, price, and financial data, weekly rpt, C6985–1

Oil and gas industry trends, with data by company, State, and country, 1993 annual compilation, C6985–4

Oil and gas supply-demand, trade, and industry exploration and operations, by product and PAD district, 1993 annual feature, C6985–1.513

Oil and refined products production, stocks, and imports, by PAD district and product, weekly rpt, A2575–1

Oil products demand, by PAD district, monthly 1983-91, annual compilation, C6985–9.2

Oil products transported between PAD districts, by mode, 1983-91, annual compilation, C6985–9.4

Oil refinery crude runs, by district, 1982-91, annual rpt, C6985–5.2

Oil refinery runs, refineries operating and shutdown, and imports, by PAD district, 1993 and trends, periodic basic data book, A2575–14.4

Oil refining capacity that could be lost due to clean air legislation, by PAD district, 1992 article, C6985–1.509

Oil supply-demand, marketing, prices, finances, and employment, detailed data for US and Canada, by product, company, and location, 1993 annual fact book, C4680–1.507

Refinery cost index for residual fuel oil, by PAD district, quarterly 1989-92, article, C6985–1.536

State and local:

Ohio electric utility coal supply, by source region, Jan 1990-June 1992, annual rpt, S6355–1

Geography and Climate

Land area, by region, census div, and State, 1991 annual data sheet, R8750–9

Government and Defense

Army/Air Force post exchange and commissary sales, by dept and US and foreign region, FY91, annual rpt, A2072–1

City fiscal condition, including budget trends and adjustments, and influencing factors, by region and population size, Mar-Apr 1993 survey, annual rpt, A8012–1.23

Congressional voting patterns and support for President, by region, 1992 and trends, annual rpt, C2500–2

DOD contract and payroll spending, military and civilian personnel, installations, and cutbacks, by State and region, various years FY81-93, R8490–44

Energy (BTU) tax proposed by Clinton Admin average household cost, by region 1993 feature, C4300–1.506

Energy (BTU) tax proposed by Clinton Admin, expected effects on number and capacity of oil refineries by region, 1993 article, C6985–1.528

Energy tax options considered by Clinton Admin, total and per-household cost estimates by State and region, 1993 rpt, R8490–49

Federal budget trends, including spending by program, State, and region, FY81-94, annual rpt, R8490–11

Federal entitlement program payments and recipients by program, and income tax return data, by State and region, early 1990s, R8490–47

Federal expenditures by category, by State and region, FY92 and trends, annual rpt, R8490–35

Military base closure/realignment and impact on personnel, with data on spending and installations, by State, region, and base, 1988-93, R8490–45

Military commissary sales by region, monthly rpt, C0500–1

Military commissary sales, by region, product type, and individual store, FY92, annual feature, A2072–2.501

Military post exchange sales, retail and other, by service branch, location, and store, FY92 and trends, annual rpt, A2072–2.502

Municipal and county govt structure, public services, finances, and intergovtl relations, 1993 annual rpt, A5800–1

Presidential election results, by State and region, 1992, annual rpt, C2500–2

Public opinion on Clinton Admin policies and actions, by respondent characteristics, series, C8915–7

Public opinion on issues concerning politics and the press, by respondent characteristics, series, C8915–4

State govt finances and related indicators, by region, 1993 semiannual rpt, A7955–1

State govt spending trends by fund source and function, regional summaries, FY90-92, annual rpt, A7118–1

State tax revenue from personal, corporate, and sales taxes, by State and region, quarterly rpt, U5085–1

Health and Vital Statistics

AIDS deaths in hospitals vs at home, by region and decedent characteristics, 1988 and trends, article, A2623–1.512

AIDS incidence in the workplace by region and industry, and employer testing and other policies, 1993 and trends, A2075–20.14

Blood bank collection and transfusion data, and shipments by region, 1993 annual rpt, A0612–2

Depression incidence among blacks and whites by selected demographic characteristics, 1984 survey, article, A2623–1.504

Disabled persons use of home care services, with costs, payment sources, and types of care, by selected characteristics, 1992, R4865–15

Dogs blastomycosis respiratory disease incidence, by region and dog characteristics, 1980-90, article, A3100–2.503

Ear tube implantation prevalence in children, by demographic characteristics and reasons for implant, 1988, article, A2623–1.509

Health care specialist and health-related company CEO income, public perceptions vs actual amounts, by respondent characteristics, 1991-93, R4865–13

Index by Categories

BY REGION

Health condition and preventive health care and safety practices of adults, by respondent characteristics, 1992 and trends, annual survey rpt, C8111–2

Health insurance coverage and finances, and health care costs and facilities, by selected demographic characteristics, 1940s-91, annual rpt, A5173–2

Health insurance enrollment distribution by type of plan, by region, 1992, article, A1865–1.511

Higher education student use of and attitudes toward alcohol, drugs, and tobacco products, by sex and region, 1989-91 surveys, annual rpt, U4950–1

HMO benefits, enrollment and utilization, staffing, finances, and relations with employers, by plan characteristics, 1990-91, annual rpt, A5150–2

HMO enrollment share of population, by region, July 1992, article, A1865–1.513

Hospital (teaching) house staff stipends, benefits, and expenditures, by region and ownership, 1992/93, annual rpt, A3273–3

Hospital CEO demographic and professional characteristics, perquisites, and views on mgmt issues, Oct 1992 survey, recurring rpt, B4490–2.35

Hospital employee health care benefits, including coverage for mental health/substance abuse and AIDS, and data by region, 1992 survey, article, A1865–1.505

Hospital industry financial and operating indicators, with detail for Medicare, by instn characteristics and location, 1988-92, annual rpt, B1880–1

Hospital patient admission rates and length of stay, by diagnosis and procedure, payment source, age, sex, and region, 1991, B4455–4

Hospital patient admissions, length of stay, operative procedures, and discharges by patient characteristics, 1990 or 1991 and trends, annual fact book, A1275–1.2

Hospital patient charges and length of stay, by diagnosis and procedure, payment source, age, and region, 1991, B4455–5

Hospital patient discharges and length of stay, by diagnosis, type of operation, age, and region, 1991, annual rpt series, B4455–1

Hospital patient discharges and length of stay, by diagnostic related group (DRG), payment source, age, and region, 1991, annual rpt series, B4455–3

Hospital psychiatric patient discharges and length of stay, by diagnosis, age, sex, and region, 1991, annual rpt series, B4455–2

Hospital recruiting of nurses and allied health personnel, with budget, vacancies, turnover, and compensation, 1993 and trends, annual survey rpt, A6500–1

Hospital revenue shares from outpatient services and managed care plans, by region, 1992-94, article, A1865–1.505

Human immunodeficiency virus (HIV) testing and posttest counseling rates, by demographic characteristics, 1989, article, A2623–1.501

Medicaid Federal grants, recipients, and benefits by type of service, with selected public health funding factors, by State and region, various years 1974-94, R8490–46

Medical care CPI trends, by region and for 27 MSAs, 1988-92, annual article, B6045–1.502

Medical group financial and operating data, by practice characteristics, 1991, annual rpt, A6365–2

Medical group mgmt compensation, by demographic and practice characteristics, 1992, annual rpt, A6365–3

Medical group physician and allied personnel compensation and productivity, by specialty, and demographic and practice characteristics, 1991, annual rpt, A6365–1

Medical school faculty and compensation, by dept, academic rank, degree, and region, 1992/93, annual rpt, A3273–2

Medical school faculty physician and allied personnel compensation and productivity, by academic rank, sex, and specialty, 1991, annual rpt, A6365–5

Nurse practitioner average salaries, by region, 1990, U8850–8.2

Nursing college deans and salaries, by personal and instn characteristics, 1992/93, annual rpt, A0615–2

Nursing college faculty and salaries, by personal and instn characteristics, 1992/93, annual rpt, A0615–1

Nursing home resident mental health care use, by resident and home characteristics, and provider type, 1985/86 survey, article, A2623–1.505

Nursing school enrollment and grads, by degree level, sex, race-ethnicity, and instn type and location, 1992/93 and trends, annual rpt, A0615–4

Nursing schools, programs, enrollment, student and staff characteristics, and grads, 1991 and trends, annual rpt, A8010–1

Physician compensation in group practices and HMOs, by specialty and region, 1992 survey and trends, annual rpt, B7450–2

Physician practice characteristics, including use of electronic billing, and participation in statistical profiling programs, by region, 1992, articles, A2200–5.1

Physician professional liability insurance premiums, and claim incidence and amounts, by region, 1982-89, U8850–8.8

Physician visit volume forecast for outpatients with indemnity insurance coverage, by region, 1993 article, A1865–1.524

Physicians by detailed specialty and location, 1992, annual rpt, A2200–3.2

Smoking acceptability in restaurants and other public places, and importance of restaurant smoking policy, views of consumers by selected characteristics, Jan 1993 survey, A8200–8.15

Veterinarian fees, and average client transaction, by region and type of practice, 1993, annual survey, C9480–1.507

Veterinarian income by selected personal and practice characteristics, 1992, annual survey article, C9480–1.506

Women's use of mammography and Pap smear tests, by demographic characteristics, 1987 survey, article, A2623–1.503

Housing and Construction

Apartment building (conventionally financed) detailed income and expense ratios for US and Canada, by building type, metro area, and US region, 1991 and trends, annual rpt, A5600–i

Apartment building (federally subsidized) detailed income and expense ratios, by building and subsidy type, building age, metro area, and region, 1991 and trends, annual rpt, A5600–5

Apartment complex mgmt income and expenses, and vacancy and turnover rates, by region and metro area, 1992, annual survey rpt, A6497–1

Condominium, cooperative, and planned unit dev detailed expenses, for US and Canada, by building characteristics, metro area, and US region, 1991, annual rpt, A5600–3

Construction (industrial) contract awards, by region, weekly rpt monthly table, C5800–2

Construction (nonresidential) cost indexes for 21 metro areas, with cost increase by region, monthly rpt quarterly feature, C5800–15

Construction company finances, by region, 1992, article, C5800–2.513

Construction contract awards by region, weekly rpt recurring feature, C5800–2.505, C5800–2.521, C5800–2.530, C5800–2.543

Construction contract value, by construction type and region, including floor area and number of residential units, 1992-93, annual rpt, C5800–15.501, C5800–15.504, C5800–15.507, C5800–26, C5800–29

Construction contract value, by project type, State, and region, 1991-93, annual feature, C5800–2.512

Construction industry finances and operations, by type of business and region, 1992-93, annual survey rpt, A4155–1

Construction nonunion wages and benefit levels, by craft and region, 1992, article, C5800–2.534

Heating/cooling system characteristics of new housing units, by region, 1990-91, annual rpt, C1800–1

Home buyer (1st-time and repeat) profile, and transaction characteristics, including prices and financing, by region and for 18 metro areas, 1990-92, annual survey rpt, B2150–1

Home improvement industry retail sales, by region, 1991-92, annual feature, C5150–6.503

Homebuilder average salaries and bonuses by position, by company sales size and region, 1992, C4300–1.509

Homebuilder financial and operating data, including detail by location, for top 400 builders, 1993 annual feature, C1850–8.507

Homebuilder hours spent driving each day, by region, 1993 feature, C4300–1.512

Homebuilder operations and finances, by region and sales size group, 1992 survey, article, C4300–1.501

Homebuilder outlook for land availability and costs, with detail by region, 1993 survey, article, C1850–8.510

Homebuilder sources for acquisition, dev, and construction loans, by region and company size, 1992 survey, article, C4300–1.501

Housing assistance Federal grants by State and region, for HOPE and HOME programs, FY92, R8490–42

Housing market conditions in US regions and selected MSAs, including construction, rental vacancies, and prices, by type of housing, quarterly rpt, B5190–1

BY REGION

Index by Categories

Housing permits and starts, by region, monthly rpt, A6450–2

Housing prices, by region, 1970-92, annual rpt, S7125–3.1

Housing sales and average prices, by region, 1987-91, annual rpt, S7125–1.11

Housing sales shares for new vs existing homes, by region, 1992, C4300–1.507

Housing sales shares to 1st-time buyers, by region, 1992, C4300–1.510

Housing sales, with price and affordability data, by region, State, and metro area, monthly rpt, A7000–2

Housing starts and mobile home placements, by region, 1984-92, annual rpt, A9395–1

Housing starts and sales by region and/or leading metro area, 1990-93, annual article, C4300–1.503

Housing starts, sales, and prices, by region, monthly rpt, A7000–1

Industrial and high-technology facilities availability, rental rates, and sale prices, for major metro areas by region, mid-1993, annual rpt, B2800–6

Low-income housing supply-demand, costs, and physical conditions, with data by race-ethnicity, for 44 metro areas, by region, 1980s-91, R3834–16

Mobile/manufactured home production, shipments, and financing, with data by State and census div, monthly rpt, A6325–1

Mortgage delinquency and foreclosure rates, and residential loans serviced, by type, State, and census div and region, quarterly rpt, A6450–1

Public housing authority operations and finances, including unit vacancy rates and demolition by region, by agency size, 1990 rpt, A6800–1

Public opinion on trend in home value, by region, 3rd qtr 1993 and trends, article, U7475–2.504, U7475–2.505

Real estate property managers characteristics and compensation, including types of property managed, 1989 surveys, recurring rpt, A5600–4

Real estate residential brokerage firm finances and operations, with data by region and company size, 1990/91 and trends, article, A7000–1.502

Income

Black American earnings, income, and poverty data, with comparisons to whites, 1980s-91, annual compilation, C6775–2.7

Black American socioeconomic status, with comparisons to whites and data by region, 1960s-92, annual compilation, A8510–1.1

College grad job and salary offers, by field of study, type of employer and occupation, and degree level, by region, interim rpt series, A3940–1

Federal Medicaid funding factors, including per capita personal income, taxable resources, and poverty population, by State and region, 1980s-91, R8490–46

Hispanic American income and poverty data, with comparisons to whites, 1980s-91, annual compilation, C6775–3.5

Industrial distribution personnel compensation, by position and selected other characteristics, 1992 survey, annual article, C1850–4.501

Manufacturing industry trends including employment, earnings, establishments, and GSP, by State and region, 1970s-92, R8490–48

Nonprofit organization executive compensation, by position, organization characteristics, and region, 1993, annual article, C2176–1.519

Paper and pulp industry average wages and wage increases, by region, 1993 annual rpt, C3975–5.1

Plastics processing industry salaries for managers, supervisors, salespersons, and engineers, by region, 1992, biennial rpt, A8920–3

Poverty shares by race-ethnicity, by region, 1991, R3834–15

Professional worker salaries and employment, by employee and employer characteristics, with detail for scientists and engineers, 1990s and trends, biennial rpt, A3960–1

Public relations compensation, by employee and company characteristics, 1993 survey, annual article, A8770–1.503

Retail industry distribution center wages, by region, 1993 survey, C5150–4.506

Wage and personal income levels compared to total US, by region, 1991 and trends, article, U0280–1.505

Industry and Commerce

Air conditioning/refrigeration wholesaler sales trend and outlook, by region, quarterly 1992-93, annual rpt, C1800–1

Business formations, failures, and bankruptcies, by region, FY92 vs FY91, article, C4687–1.511

Business forms manufacturing plant employment and compensation data, by region, 1992 and trends, biennial rpt, A5785–4

CEOs region of birth, for small companies with rapid growth, 1993 survey article, C5800–7.551

Concrete (ready-mixed) industry production and operating trends and outlook, by region, 1992 survey, annual article, C0125–5

Container (fiber box) shipments by end-use industry and region, and other industry operating data, 1940s-92, annual rpt, A4875–1

Corporate mergers, acquisitions, and divestitures, with buyers and sellers by location, 1992 and trends, annual rpt, B6020–1

Discount chain top-selling natl brands cited by managers, by product category, chain, and region, 1993 survey, annual feature, C5150–3.520

Discount store health/beauty aid dept size, and stores with prescription depts, by region, 1986-91, annual article, C5150–3.502

Drugstore chain and brand preferences of consumers, with data by product type and region, 1992 annual survey feature, C5150–2.503

Drugstore sales and merchandising trends, by product type and market area, 1992 annual feature, C5150–2.503

Exports to Mexico and Canada, value and share of total trade by region and State, 1991, R8490–43

Freight carrier revenues, net income, and operating ratios, for top 7-15 less-than-truckload carriers by region, 1991-92, annual article, C2150–1.506

Gross regional product and outlook, by region, 1991-93, semiannual article, C8900–1.507

Gross regional product and outlook, by region, 1992-94, semiannual article, C8900–1.520

Hispanic American professional views on work conditions at own company, with ratings of regions and top 19-20 companies and industries, 1993 survey article, C4575–1.504

Hispanic-owned business outlook for selected performance indicators, with data by region, monthly rpt quarterly feature, C4575–1.510

Home-based businesses and home workers linked to offices by telecommunication, distribution by region, 1993 article, C4725–3.S04

Home furnishings retailer financial and operating data, by firm characteristics and region, 1992 and trends, annual rpt, A7975–1

Industrial product sales trends, by region, monthly rpt recurring feature, C1850–4

Iron and steel imports, by US customs district and port, 1992, annual rpt, A2000–2.2

Iron ore production, shipments, trade, and plant inventories and consumption, US and Canada, 1992 and trends, annual rpt, A2010–3

Jewelry business openings and failures, and general economic indicators, by region, monthly rpt, C2150–7

Jewelry industry sales and profit outlook, by region, 1993 survey, annual article, C2150–7.507

Jewelry industry statistics on sales, marketing, trade, and employment, with customer characteristics, 1993 annual almanac, C2150–7.509

Lumber industry supply-demand, sales, trade, and employment, monthly rpt, A1630–1

Manufacturing industry trends including employment, earnings, establishments, and GSP, by State and region, 1970s-92, R8490–48

Metal heat treatment industry billings, for Michigan, Canada, and 7 regions, monthly press release, A6376–1

Newsprint shipments, and consumption by newspapers, by region and State, 1979-92, annual rpt, A1630–8

Office building detailed income and expense data, and energy use, US and Canada, by building characteristics, metro area, and US region, 1991 and trends, annual rpt, A5600–2

Office product dealer financial and operating data, by sales volume and region, 1991 and trends, annual rpt, A8110–1

Paper and paperboard industry financial and operating data, by product, region, and State, 1992 and trends, annual rpt, A1630–6

Paper and pulp mills by State, and production and use trends, by region, 1993 annual rpt, C3975–5.1, C3975–5.3, C3975–5.4

Paper, paperboard, and wood pulp industry capacity, distribution by region, 1980-95, annual rpt, A1630–7

Paperboard corrugated/solid fiber product shipments, by region, monthly rpt, C0125–4

Plastics processing industry employment, compensation practices, and union representation, by region, 1992, annual survey rpt, A8920–2

Index by Categories

BY REGION

Plastics processing industry financial and operating ratios, by processing activity, sales size, and region, 1992, annual rpt, A8920–4

Printing (small press) industry sales trends, by region, 1989-91, article, C1850–10.503

Pulp and paper industry salaries, by region, 1992 survey, annual article, C3975–2.503

Pulp and paper mill machine maintenance operations and personnel, by region and grade, 1992 survey, recurring article, C3975–2.504

Pulpwood receipts, consumption, residues, and inventories, by region, monthly rpt, A1630–5

Rental equipment industry financial data, by revenue size group and region, and for Canada, 1991 and trends, annual rpt, A2665–1

Salary budget increases and structure, by industry and region, and for Canada, 1993-94 and trends, annual survey rpt, A1295–1

Security equipment industry devs, including share of companies with increased revenues, by region, Oct-Nov 1992 survey, annual feature, C1850–13.503

Shoe industry production by region and State, 1984-91, annual rpt, A4957–1.2

Shopping center detailed income and expense data, by building characteristics, metro area, and region, 1991, annual rpt, A5600–6

Shopping center financial and operating data, with detail by type of tenant, US and Canada, 1991, triennial rpt, R9285–1

State govt finances and related indicators, by region, 1993, semiannual rpt, A7955–1

Stone products (sand/gravel and crushed stone) production trends and outlook, with data by region, 1992 annual article, C0125–6

Sulfur recovery from oil refineries and natural gas plants vs mine production, and sales by PAD district, 1982-91, article, C6985–1.514

Textile fiber product manufacturers, with plants by State and region, 1992 annual directory, C3460–1.501

Labor and Employment

Black American labor force and employment data, with comparisons to whites, 1970s-91, annual compilation, C6775–2.6

College grad employment opportunities by region, views of employers, 1992/93, annual survey rpt, U3130–1

College grad job and salary offers, by field of study, type of employer and occupation, and degree level, by region, interim rpt series, A3940–1

College grad recruiting activity of employers, by region, 1992 annual rpt, A3940–3

Employee benefit payments as percent of payroll, by industry and region, 1991, annual rpt, A3840–1

Employment and unemployment, by race, sex, and region, 1991, annual article, A8510–1.1

Employment trends, total and manufacturing, by region, quarterly rpt, B5190–1

Executive job vacancy index, by industry, job function, and region, quarterly rpt, B5000–5

Hiring costs and new hires, by industry, State, region, and employer characteristics, 1992 and trends, annual survey rpt, A4740–2

Hiring plans of employers in coming qtr, by industry div and region, quarterly rpt, B5275–1

Hiring trends by region, 1991-92, annual survey rpt, B6850–3

Hispanic American labor force and employment data, with comparisons to whites, 1980s-91, annual compilation, C6775–3.4

Labor cost indexes for private industry, by region, Mar 1993 and trends, article, S1040–4.508

Labor cost indexes for private industry, by region, Sept 1991-92, June 1992, and trends, article, S1040–4.503

Manufacturing industry trends including employment, earnings, establishments, and GSP, by State and region, 1970s-92, R8490–48

Women's employment and earnings, with comparisons to men, and detail by occupation and worker characteristics, 1990s and trends, annual rpt, A1570–2

Law Enforcement

Crime victims per 1,000 population, by demographic characteristics, 1991, article, R8750–1.505

Motor vehicle thefts, by region and type of vehicle, 1991, annual rpt, A0865–1.2

Police collective bargaining experience of city govts, including negotiator, methods, 3rd-party interference, and union tactics, by region, 1992, A5800–1.1

Police officers killed, by region and circumstances, 1992, annual rpt, S0119–1.2

Natural Resources, Environment and Pollution

Food marketers solid waste disposal practices, by type of material, by region, 1991, annual rpt, A4960–5.2

Forestland owned by commercial forest industry, and timber harvest, by region, 1987, annual rpt, A1630–6.3

Waste fuel boiler/industrial furnace applications to EPA for continued use, by region, May 1992, article, C5800–8.505

Population

Black American population and demographic characteristics, with comparisons to whites, 1970s-2080, annual compilation, C6775–2.1

Gallup Poll public attitude surveys, results and sample characteristics, monthly rpt, C4040–1

Hispanic American household ownership of selected luxury items, by region, 1991, article, C4575–1.501

Hispanic American population and demographic characteristics, with comparisons to whites, 1993 annual compilation, C6775–3.1

Households by housing tenure status, region, and age of household head, quarterly rpt, B5190–1

Latin America ancestry reported by US population, by region and census div, 1980, annual rpt, U6250–1.14

Older population growth rate compared to population age 64/under, by region and metro status, decennially 1960-90, article, R8750–1.506

Population by State and region, 1980 and 1992, annual rpt, R8490–11

Population size and selected characteristics, by region, census div, and State, 1991 and trends, annual data sheet, R8750–9

Religion and related social issues, public opinions and attitudes, monthly survey, R8780–1

State and local:

Alaska migration patterns by US region and census div, 1980-90, annual rpt, S0320–4

Arizona, Phoenix area temporary winter resident characteristics, including expenditures, dwelling type, and region of residence, 1992/93, article, U0280–1.508

South Carolina population by birthplace, 1990, annual rpt, S7125–1.13

Prices and Cost of Living

Christmas spending plans of consumers, by region, age, and income, Nov 1992 survey, annual rpt, R4105–81.10

Consumer attitudes on economic conditions and personal financial situation, monthly survey, U7475–2

Public Welfare and Social Security

Catholic charity social service agency services and population served, by region and State, 1991, annual rpt, A3810–1

Corporate charitable contributions to arts programs, distribution by industry div and region, 1988 and 1991, recurring rpt, A3690–1

Transfer payments by State and region, 1990-91, biennial rpt, S3605–1.6

United Way local organization fundraising trends, by State and region, 1991-92, article, C2176–1.515

Youth age 12-17 charitable contributions and volunteer activity, by respondent characteristics, 1992 survey, biennial rpt, A5435–5.1

State and local:

Utah homeless shelter population, by region of origin, July 1992, annual rpt, S7808–2

Recreation and Leisure

Art museum salaries for 37 positions, by region, population size served, and budget size, FY93, annual rpt, A3290–1

Boating (recreational) industry trends, including sales, foreign trade, and registrations by geographic area, 1980s-92, annual feature, C2425–4

Bowling assn finances and membership, and bowling establishments and lanes, by State and other area, 1991/92 and trends, annual rpt, A1015–1

Museums and related instns operations and finances, by type, budget size, governing authority, and region, 1989/90 survey, A0750–1

Recreational vehicle trailer and motorhome sales change, by region, monthly rpt, C8950–2

Science and Technology

Engineer compensation, by work and employee characteristics, and region and metro area, 1992, annual rpt, A8460–1

Mathematics proficiency on Natl Assessment of Educational Progress test, by State and region, 1992, biennial rpt, A4355–3.1

Physics and astronomy bachelor degree recipients postgraduation plans and demographic characteristics, 1991/92 and trends, annual survey, A1960–3

Physics grads employment status, by region, 1990/91, annual rpt, A1960–1

BY REGION

Index by Categories

Transportation and Travel

Airline travel frequency, destination, and purpose, by traveler characteristics, 1992 survey and trends, annual rpt, A0325–6

Auto dealer satisfaction with manufacturer natl advertising campaigns, by region, 1993 survey article, C2710–1.518, C2710–3.521

Auto do-it-yourself (DIY) maintenance activity, by type and consumer characteristics, 1993 and trends, annual survey, C0125–1.506

Auto fleet operating costs by region, 1992, annual rpt, C1575–2.507

Auto purchaser characteristics, 1993, annual rpt, A0865–1.2

Auto sales and leases, distribution by region, 1993 feature, C1575–2.505

Autos (used) average auction prices, by make, model, year, and region, monthly rpt, C1575–2

Aviation (general) aircraft active, landing facilities, pilots, and operating data, by FAA region and State, 1993 annual rpt, A5120–2

Freight carrier quality ratings by shippers, by company and region, 1993 annual survey article, C2150–1.507

Hotel real estate sales transactions, with prices, financing methods, and industry performance data, by region, 1991 and trends, article, A6450–2.501

Hwy and bridge construction contracting plans, by region and State, 1993, annual feature, C5800–2.512

Lodging industry occupancy and room rates, by region, 1990-91, annual rpt, C2140–1.4

Motor vehicle fleet manager earnings, and personal and professional characteristics, 1993 article, C1575–2.506

Motor vehicle fleet operating costs by type and region, 1991-92, article, C1575–2.508

Motorcycles in use, and distribution of retail sales and market value, by region, 1991, annual rpt, A6485 1.1

Railroad (Class I) financial condition, operations, and employment, by company and district, 1992, annual rpt, A3275–7

Railroad (Class I) traffic, employment, finances, and equipment, by district and State, 1920s-92, annual rpt, A3275–5

Travel trips and traveler characteristics, including mode, purpose, type of lodging, and area of destination and origin, quarterly rpt, R9375–14

BY SMSA OR MSA

Agriculture and Food

Farms, and livestock and crop values, by State, MSA, county, city, and Canadian Province, 1993 annual rpt, C3250–1

Food away from home expenditures, by household characteristics and for top 10 MSAs, 1991, article, A8200–1.507

Food away from home expenditures, by household characteristics and for 26 MSAs, 1991, recurring rpt, A8200–13

Food service industry sales, market shares, establishments, and business activity indicators, by location, 1992, annual feature, C1200–5.515

Food store market shares and outlets, by company and store type, for approx 350 metro areas in US and Canada, with industry operating data, 1993 annual rpt, C3400–6

Liquor sales volume, by product type and leading metro area, 1992, annual rpt, C4775–1.1

Restaurant industry expansion outlook and operating data, by census div and MSA, 1993 annual articles, C1850–3.506

Wine market statistics, including sales and consumption by metro area, 1992 and trends, annual rpt, C4775–2.1

State and local:

Illinois statistical abstract, general data, 1992 annual rpt, U6910–2

Banking, Finance, and Insurance

State and local:

Arizona statistical abstract, general data, 1993 recurring rpt, U5850–2

Arkansas socioeconomic trends, by MSA and/or county, 1993 annual rpt, U5935–1

Georgia statistical abstract, general data, 1992-93 biennial rpt, U6730–1

Illinois statistical abstract, general data, 1992 annual rpt, U6910–2

Kentucky economic statistics, general data, 1993 annual rpt, S3104–1.4

New York State statistical yearbook, general data, 1992 annual rpt, U5100–1

Oklahoma banks and bank holding companies by asset size, and asset concentration by location and among top instns, 1984-90, article, U8130–1.502

South Carolina statistical abstract, general data, 1993 annual rpt, S7125–1

Tennessee statistical abstract, general data, 1992/93 annual rpt, U8710–2

Education

Librarians (special) salaries, by location, work setting, and personal characteristics, US and Canada, 1992 and trends, biennial survey rpt, A8965–1

Energy Resources and Demand

Gasoline prices, by selected MSA, 1990-92, annual fact book, C4680–1.507

Gasoline prices in approx 30 MSAs, 1978-92, periodic basic data book, A2575–14.3

State and local:

Nevada statistical abstract, general data, 1992 biennial rpt, S5005–1

Pennsylvania industrial electric power sales, by MSA, monthly rpt quarterly tables, U4110–1.501, U4110–1.503, U4110–1.505, U4110–1.507

South Dakota low-income energy assistance clients and payments, by MSA and county, FY92, annual rpt, S7385–1.2

Geography and Climate

State and local:

South Carolina statistical abstract, general data, 1993 annual rpt, S7125–1

Health and Vital Statistics

Medical care CPI trends, by region and for 27 MSAs, 1988-92, annual article, B6045–1.502

Physicians by detailed specialty and location, 1992, annual rpt, A2200–3.2

State and local:

Georgia statistical abstract, general data, 1992-93 biennial rpt, U6730–1

Georgia vital statistics, including population, births, abortions, deaths by cause, marriages, and divorces, by demographic characteristics and location, 1991 and trends, annual rpt, S1895–1

Illinois statistical abstract, general data, 1992 annual rpt, U6910–2

Housing and Construction

Apartment complex mgmt income and expenses, and vacancy and turnover rates, by region and metro area, 1992, annual survey rpt, A6497–1

Housing market conditions in US regions and selected MSAs, including construction, rental vacancies, and prices, by type of housing, quarterly rpt, B5190–1

Housing sales, with price and affordability data, by region, State, and metro area, monthly rpt, A7000–2

State and local:

Arizona statistical abstract, general data, 1993 recurring rpt, U5850–2

California residential and nonresidential building permit value, by MSA, 1992, annual rpt, S0840–3.1

Georgia construction permit values and employment, by MSA, errata, U6730–2.501

Georgia statistical abstract, general data, 1992-93 biennial rpt, U6730–1

Illinois statistical abstract, general data, 1992 annual rpt, U6910–2

Louisiana Census of Population and Housing summary findings, by local area, 1990 and trends, U8010–4

New York State business activity indicators, quarterly rpt, S5735–2

New York State statistical yearbook, general data, 1992 annual rpt, U5100–1

Oklahoma real estate loan rejection rates for whites and minorities by income level, statewide and by MSA, 1991, article, U8130–1.504

Oklahoma statistical abstract, general data, 1992 annual rpt, U8130–2

Pennsylvania building permits authorized, by MSA and selected county, monthly rpt quarterly table, U4110–1.501, U4110–1.503, U4110–1.505, U4110–1.507

Pennsylvania building permits issued and value, by construction type, county, and MSA, 1992, annual article, U4110–1.506

Pennsylvania economic indicators, by MSA, monthly rpt quarterly tables, U4110–1.501, U4110–1.503, U4110–1.505, U4110 1.507

South Carolina statistical abstract, general data, 1993 annual rpt, S7125–1

Tennessee statistical abstract, general data, 1992/93 annual rpt, U8710–2

Income

Consumer buying power survey of population, income, and sales by kind of business, by census div, State, MSA, county, and city, 1992, annual rpt, C1200–1.511

Consumer buying power survey of population, income, and sales by product line, by State, metro area, county, and census div, 1993 annual rpt, C1200–1.514

Consumer socioeconomic profiles, for top 50 MSAs ranked by supermarket sales, 1991, annual rpt, C3400–6

Earnings index for 27 MSAs and 4 occupational groups, 1990, biennial rpt, S3605–1.6

Markets with daily newspapers, demographic and economic info by geographic area, US and Canada, 1993 annual rpt, C3250–1

Metro area household income trends for central cities vs suburbs, and employment data, for 78 largest MSAs, 1993 rpt, A8012–1.22

State and local:

Index by Categories

BY SMSA OR MSA

Alabama statistical abstract, general data, 1992 recurring rpt, U5680–2

Arizona statistical abstract, general data, 1993 recurring rpt, U5850–2

Arkansas population, income, and employment trends, by MSA, 1973-2040, article, U5930–1.503

Arkansas population, per capita income, and economic vitality index, by county and/or metro area, 1980s-90, article, U5930–1.501

Arkansas socioeconomic trends, by MSA and/or county, 1993 annual rpt, U5935–1

California employment statistics, by demographic characteristics, industry, MSA, and county, monthly rpt, S0830–1

Connecticut employment, hours, and earnings, by labor market area and industry, and selected economic indicators, monthly rpt, S1235–1

Florida statistical abstract, general data, 1992 annual rpt, U6660–1

Georgia personal income and employment, by MSA, county, and metro-nonmetro status, 1990-91, article, U6730–2.505

Georgia statistical abstract, general data, 1992-93 biennial rpt, U6730–1

Illinois statistical abstract, general data, 1992 annual rpt, U6910–2

Indiana per capita personal income, by MSA and for metro vs nonmetro areas, 1991, U2160–1.504

Kansas statistical abstract, general data, 1991/92 annual rpt, U7095–2

Kentucky economic statistics, general data, 1993 annual rpt, S3104–1.4

Louisiana employment, hours, and earnings, by industry and MSA, monthly rpt, S3320–2

Massachusetts employment, hours, and earnings, by industry and local area, with unemployment insurance claims, monthly rpt, S3808–1

Mississippi income by source, county, and MSA, and wages by industry group, 1993 annual planning rpt, S4345–1.4

Mississippi statistical abstract, general data, 1992 annual rpt, U3255–4

Missouri employment, earnings, and hours, by industry and MSA, monthly rpt, S4530–3

Nebraska manufacturing and service worker hours and earnings, by selected industry group and locality, quarterly rpt, S4895–2

Nebraska transfer payments, by component and State area, with comparisons to total personal income, 1990-91 and trends, article, U7860–1.504

New Hampshire employment, hours, and earnings, by industry and area, monthly rpt, S5205–1

New Mexico personal income by county and MSA, 1990-91, S5624–2.508

New York State employment, earnings, and hours, by county, selected metro area, and industry group, monthly rpt, S5775–1

Ohio employment, hours, and earnings, by industry and MSA, with job service and unemployment insurance activities, monthly rpt, S6270–1

Oklahoma statistical abstract, general data, 1992 annual rpt, U8130–2

Pennsylvania personal income, by type, industry div, MSA, and county, 1993 annual article, U4110–1.506

Pennsylvania statistical abstract, general data, 1992 recurring rpt, U4130–6

Pennsylvania wage and earnings data, by MSA, 1983-90, annual planning rpt, S6845–3.2

South Carolina statistical abstract, general data, 1993 annual rpt, S7125–1

South Carolina total and per capita income, by MSA, 1988-90, annual planning rpt, S7155–3.3

Tennessee employment, hours, and earnings, by industry group and MSA, monthly rpt, S7495–2

Tennessee per capita income, by county and MSA, 1990-91, recurring article, S7495–2.507

Tennessee statistical abstract, general data, 1992/93 annual rpt, U8710–2

Texas employment, hours, and earnings, by MSA and industry group, and unemployment insurance, monthly rpt, S7675–3

Texas per capita income, by county and MSA, 1985 and 1990, annual planning rpt, S7675–2

Utah personal income and household data, by location and race-ethnicity, 1990 census rpt, S7832–3.3

Utah statistical abstract, general data, 1993 triennial rpt, U8960–1

Virginia income distribution and income tax returns filed, by locality, 1990, annual rpt, U9080–1

Virginia total and per capita personal income, by local area and major source, 1980-90, annual rpt, U9080–7

Industry and Commerce

Consumer buying power survey of population, income, and sales by kind of business, by census div, State, MSA, county, and city, 1992, annual rpt, C1200–1.511

Consumer buying power survey of population, income, and sales by product line, by State, metro area, county, and census div, 1993 annual rpt, C1200–1.514

Retail outlets for selected leading chains in 21 media market areas, 1992, C2710–1.538

Retail sales by kind of business, rankings by MSA, city, and county, 1993 annual rpt, C3250–1

Sales industry costs, including compensation, training, and travel and related expenses, with data by metro area, 1992 and trends, annual survey, C1200–1.508

State and local:

Alabama retail sales, by kind of business, MSA, and county, monthly business activity rpt, U5680–1

Alabama statistical abstract, general data, 1992 recurring rpt, U5680–2

Arizona statistical abstract, general data, 1993 recurring rpt, U5850–2

Arkansas socioeconomic trends, by MSA and/or county, 1993 annual rpt, U5935–1

Florida statistical abstract, general data, 1992 annual rpt, U6660–1

Georgia statistical abstract, general data, 1992-93 biennial rpt, U6730–1

Georgia taxable sales, by kind of business and location, 1991-92, annual article, U6730–2.503

Illinois retail sales trends, by location type and MSA, 3rd qtr 1991-92, article, U6910–1.502

Illinois statistical abstract, general data, 1992 annual rpt, U6910–2

Kansas taxable retail sales, by area and kind of business, quarterly rpt, U7095–1

Nevada statistical abstract, general data, 1992 biennial rpt, S5005–1

New York State business activity indicators, quarterly rpt, S5735–2

New York State business and economic indicators, by MSA, county, and industry, 1980s-91, annual rpt, S5735–3

New York State statistical yearbook, general data, 1992 annual rpt, U5100–1

Oklahoma business activity indicators, monthly rpt, U8130–1

Oklahoma statistical abstract, general data, 1992 annual rpt, U8130–2

Pennsylvania statistical abstract, general data, 1992 recurring rpt, U4130–6

Tennessee statistical abstract, general data, 1992/93 annual rpt, U8710–2

Virginia business activity indicators, by local area, monthly rpt, U1120–1

Virginia taxable sales, by kind of business and locality, 1991 and trends, annual rpt, U9080–8

Labor and Employment

Employment to population ratios, and unemployment rates, by race and leading MSA, 1991, annual article, A8510–1.1

Employment trends, total and manufacturing, approx 50 MSAs, quarterly rpt, B5190–1

Metro area household income trends for central cities vs suburbs, and employment data, for 78 largest MSAs, 1993 rpt, A8012–1.22

Unemployment rate in DC and approx 40 other MSAs, monthly rpt, S1527–3

State and local:

Alabama business activity indicators, monthly rpt, U5680–1

Alabama statistical abstract, general data, 1992 recurring rpt, U5680–2

Arizona statistical abstract, general data, 1993 recurring rpt, U5850–2

Arkansas business and economic activity indicators, quarterly rpt, U5930–1

Arkansas labor force, employment, and unemployment, by MSA, county, and labor area, 1980-92, annual rpt, S0662–2

Arkansas socioeconomic trends, by MSA and/or county, 1993 annual rpt, U5935–1

California economic condition, including population, employment and earnings, income, business activity, and taxation, 1993 annual rpt, S0840–3

California employment statistics, by demographic characteristics, industry, MSA, and county, monthly rpt, S0830–1

California statistical abstract, general data, 1992 annual rpt, S0840–2

Colorado employment and unemployment, by location, monthly rpt, S1040–4

Colorado labor force by employment status, by local area, 1991-92, annual planning rpt, S1040–3.1

Connecticut employment, hours, and earnings, by labor market area and industry, and selected economic indicators, monthly rpt, S1235–1

Florida employment and unemployment, by industry div and location, monthly rpt, S1765–3

Florida statistical abstract, general data, 1992 annual rpt, U6660–1

BY SMSA OR MSA

Index by Categories

Georgia employment, earnings, and hours, by major industry group and MSA, monthly rpt, S1905–1

Georgia personal income and employment, by MSA, county, and metro-nonmetro status, 1990-91, article, U6730–2.505

Georgia statistical abstract, general data, 1992-93 biennial rpt, U6730–1

Illinois statistical abstract, general data, 1992 annual rpt, U6910–2

Iowa labor force supply-demand data, including population, earnings, and employment by industry and occupation, 1993 annual rpt, S2784–3

Kansas business activity indicators, quarterly rpt, U7095–1

Kansas statistical abstract, general data, 1991/92 annual rpt, U7095–2

Kentucky economic statistics, general data, 1993 annual rpt, S3104–1.4

Louisiana employment, hours, and earnings, by industry and MSA, monthly rpt, S3320–2

Louisiana labor force planning rpt, including population and labor force characteristics, unemployment claimants, and data by parish and MSA, 1993 annual rpt, S3320–1

Massachusetts employment, hours, and earnings, by industry and local area, with unemployment insurance claims, monthly rpt, S3808–1

Michigan employment, hours, and earnings, with detail by industry and local area, monthly rpt, S3980–2

Minnesota employment by industry div and MSA, 1992, article, S4205–3.501

Minnesota employment, hours, and earnings, by industry group and locality, monthly rpt, S4205–1

Mississippi statistical abstract, general data, 1992 annual rpt, U3255–4

Missouri employment, earnings, and hours, by industry and MSA, monthly rpt, S4530–3

Missouri labor force and unemployment rates, by MSA and county, FY92, annual rpt, S4530–2.3

Nebraska employment and unemployment, by industry group and locality, quarterly rpt, S4895–2

Nevada statistical abstract, general data, 1992 biennial rpt, S5005–1

New Hampshire employment, hours, and earnings, by industry and area, monthly rpt, S5205–1

New Jersey employment, by labor market area, Mar 1992, annual article, S5425–1.503

New York State business activity indicators, quarterly rpt, S5735–2

New York State employment, earnings, and hours, by county, selected metro area, and industry group, monthly rpt, S5775–1

New York State statistical yearbook, general data, 1992 annual rpt, U5100–1

North Carolina labor force and employment by industry, by county, MSA, labor area, and planning region, 1991 and trends, annual rpt, S5917–4

North Dakota employment, hours, and earnings, by industry div and/or location, monthly rpt, S6140–4

Ohio employment, hours, and earnings, by industry and MSA, with job service and unemployment insurance activities, monthly rpt, S6270–1

Oklahoma statistical abstract, general data, 1992 annual rpt, U8130–2

Oregon labor force by employment status, by MSA and county, monthly rpt recurring feature, S6592–1.501, S6615–2.502, S6615–2.503

Oregon labor force by employment status, difference between census and Current Population Survey estimates, by county and MSA, 1990, article, S6615–2.501

Pennsylvania economic indicators, by MSA, monthly rpt quarterly tables, U4110–1.501, U4110–1.503, U4110–1.505, U4110–1.507

Pennsylvania labor force and employment data, by county and labor market area, monthly rpt, S6845–1

Pennsylvania labor force planning rpt, including population characteristics, employment and job openings by industry and occupation, and income trends, FY92 annual rpt, S6845–3

Pennsylvania statistical abstract, general data, 1992 recurring rpt, U4130–6

South Carolina employment, earnings, and hours, by industry group and locality, monthly rpt, S7155–2

South Carolina labor force planning rpt, detailed data on employment, hours, wages, turnover, and characteristics of job service applicants, 1992 annual rpt, S7155–3.2

South Carolina statistical abstract, general data, 1993 annual rpt, S7125–1

Tennessee employment, hours, and earnings, by industry group and MSA, monthly rpt, S7495–2

Tennessee statistical abstract, general data, 1992/93 annual rpt, U8710–2

Texas employment, hours, and earnings, by MSA and industry group, and unemployment insurance, monthly rpt, S7675–3

Utah employment and unemployment, by MSA, monthly rpt, S7820–3

Virginia labor force, hours, and earnings, with data by industry group and locality, monthly rpt, S8205–6

Washington State employment, earnings, and hours, by labor market area and industry group, monthly rpt, S8340–3

West Virginia employment by industry and MSA, FY92, annual planning rpt, S8534–2

West Virginia employment, unemployment, hours, and earnings, with job service activities, monthly rpt, S8534–1

Wisconsin employment, hours, and earnings, by selected area, monthly rpt, S8750–1

Law Enforcement

State and local:

Alabama crimes and arrests, by offense and location, with law enforcement employment, 1992 and trends, annual rpt, S0119–1

Alabama statistical abstract, general data, 1992 recurring rpt, U5680–2

Georgia crimes and arrests, by offense, with data by location and offender characteristics, 1992 and trends, annual rpt, S1901–1

Georgia statistical abstract, general data, 1992-93 biennial rpt, U6730–1

Massachusetts correctional instn inmate socioeconomic characteristics and criminal background, by instn, Jan 1992 and trends, annual rpt, S3805–1

Pennsylvania crimes and arrests, by offense, with data by location and offender characteristics, 1992 and trends, annual rpt, S6860–1

Pennsylvania statistical abstract, general data, 1992 recurring rpt, U4130–6

Tennessee statistical abstract, general data, 1992/93 annual rpt, U8710–2

Texas correctional instn inmates by criminal background and demographic characteristics, FY92, annual rpt, S7660–1

Natural Resources, Environment and Pollution

Child well-being indicators based on social, economic, and environmental factors, for 239 MSAs, with detail by component county and city, 1980s-90s, R9700–2

Population

Black American population and demographic characteristics, with comparisons to whites, 1970s-2080, annual compilation, C6775–2.1

Child well-being indicators based on social, economic, and environmental factors, for 239 MSAs, with detail by component county and city, 1980s-90s, R9700–2

Consumer buying power survey of population, income, and sales by kind of business, by census div, State, MSA, county, and city, 1992, annual rpt, C1200–1.511

Consumer buying power survey of population, income, and sales by product line, by State, metro area, county, and census div, 1993 annual rpt, C1200–1.514

Consumer socioeconomic profiles, for top 50 MSAs ranked by supermarket sales, 1991, annual rpt, C3400–6

Drinking age population, by major metro area, 1991-92, annual rpt, C4775–1.3, C4775–2.2

Hispanic American population and demographic characteristics, with comparisons to whites, 1993 annual compilation, C6775–3.1

Immigrants admitted to US, Florida, and 6 MSAs, by country of birth, 1990, annual rpt, U6660–1.1

Market area population and characteristics, households, income, and retail outlets, for 21 leading areas, 1993 feature, C2710–1.538

Markets with daily newspapers, demographic and economic info by geographic area, US and Canada, 1993 annual rpt, C3250–1

State and local:

Alabama statistical abstract, general data, 1992 recurring rpt, U5680–2

Arkansas population, income, and employment trends, by MSA, 1973-2040, article, U5930–1.503

Arkansas population, per capita income, and economic vitality index, by county and/or metro area, 1980s-90, article, U5930–1.501

Arkansas socioeconomic trends, by MSA and/or county, 1993 annual rpt, U5935–1

Florida population, by city, county, and MSA, Apr 1992 and trends, annual rpt, U6660–4

Florida statistical abstract, general data, 1992 annual rpt, U6660–1

Georgia population by MSA, 1992, annual rpt, S1901–1

Georgia statistical abstract, general data, 1992-93 biennial rpt, U6730–1

Index by Categories

Georgia vital statistics, including population, births, abortions, deaths by cause, marriages, and divorces, by demographic characteristics and location, 1991 and trends, annual rpt, S1895–1

Illinois statistical abstract, general data, 1992 annual rpt, U6910–2

Kansas statistical abstract, general data, 1991/92 annual rpt, U7095–2

Kentucky economic statistics, general data, 1993 annual rpt, S3104–1.4

Louisiana Census of Population and Housing summary findings, by local area, 1990 and trends, U8010–4

Louisiana population, by race, sex, and location, 1992, annual planning rpt, S3320–1.1

Mississippi population trends, and households, by county and MSA, 1993 annual planning rpt, S4345–1.4

Mississippi statistical abstract, general data, 1992 annual rpt, U3255–4

New York State statistical yearbook, general data, 1992 annual rpt, U5100–1

Oklahoma population projections, by age, sex, and locality, with data on fertility and migration, 1990-2020, recurring rpt, S6416–1

Oklahoma statistical abstract, general data, 1992 annual rpt, U8130–2

Pennsylvania labor force and population characteristics, FY92 annual planning rpt, S6845–3.1

Pennsylvania statistical abstract, general data, 1992 recurring rpt, U4130–6

South Carolina population, by age, race-ethnicity, sex, and locality, 1990 and trends, annual planning rpt, S7155–3.1

South Carolina statistical abstract, general data, 1993 annual rpt, S7125–1

Tennessee statistical abstract, general data, 1992/93 annual rpt, U8710–2

Virginia population and net migration, by local area, 1990-91, annual rpt, U9080–9

Virginia population trends and projections by location, 1980-2000, recurring rpt, S8205–7

West Virginia population, by MSA and component county and city, 1980 and 1990, annual planning rpt, S8534–2

Prices and Cost of Living

Cost-of-living indexes by item, by MSA, quarterly rpt, A0150–1

State and local:

California CPI for State and 3 metro areas, with change by component, 1993 annual rpt, S0840–3

California statistical abstract, general data, 1992 annual rpt, S0840–2

Public Welfare and Social Security

State and local:

Illinois statistical abstract, general data, 1992 annual rpt, U6910–2

South Dakota welfare and social services recipients, by program, MSA, and county, FY92, annual rpt, S7385–1.2

Science and Technology

Engineer compensation, by work and employee characteristics, and region and metro area, 1992, annual rpt, A8460–1

Veterans Affairs

State and local:

Illinois statistical abstract, general data, 1992 annual rpt, U6910–2

BY STATE

Agriculture and Food

Agricultural crop and livestock production, rankings by State, 1992, annual rpt, S3085–1

Alcoholic beverage purchase restrictions and tax rates, by State, 1993 annual rpt, C4775–1.2

Alcoholic beverage shipments and per capita consumption, by type, census div, and State, 1980s-91, annual rpt, A3455–1.4

Appalachia farm real estate value, by State, 1985-91, annual rpt, S8510–1

Brewing industry finances and operations, including consumption, trade, and taxes, with data by State and census div, 1991 and trends, annual rpt, A3455–1

Catfish and trout operations and sales, by selected State, 1990-92, annual rpt, S5885–1

Convenience stores, by State, 1980-92, annual survey rpt, A6735–2

Convenience stores with gasoline marketing operations, by chain company, census div, and State, 1992, annual article, C4680–1.502

Convenience stores with gasoline marketing operations, by chain company, census div, and State, 1993, annual article, C4680–1.510

Corn refiner purchases of goods/services, and corn farmer acreage, yield, production, and income from refiners, by State, 1993 annual rpt, A4200–1

Cotton production and acreage in 4 States, and ginning rates in 14 States, 1992, C5226–3.505

Farm cash receipts, for top 20 agricultural States, 1992, annual rpt, S0850–1.5

Farm income per capita, by State, 1991, article, B8500–2.503

Farm marketing and govt payment cash receipts, by State, 1991, annual rpt, S5885–1

Farm price support Federal payments, by State and region, FY82, FY88, and FY92, R8490–47

Farm property value, and land rents, by State, 1993 and trends, annual rpt, S6760–1

Farm real estate values, by State, 1984-93, annual rpt, S5700–1

Farm real estate values, by State, 1986-93, annual rpt, S5010–1

Farms, acreage, assets, debt, equity, and income, by State, 1993-94 biennial rpt, S8780–1.2

Farms, and livestock and crop values, by State, MSA, county, city, and Canadian Province, 1993 annual rpt, C3250–1

Fish processing and wholesaling plants and employment, by region and selected State, 1990, annual rpt, U6660–1.10

Flour milling companies and capacity, in US by State, Canada, Mexico, and Central American and Caribbean area countries, 1993 annual directory and buyers guide, C8450–3

Food service industry sales, market shares, establishments, and business activity indicators, by location, 1992, annual feature, C1200–5.515

Food service industry wage rates for hourly employees, by position, census div, State, and selected metro area, 1992, recurring rpt, A8200–14

BY STATE

Food store industry sales and operations, by State, 1992, annual rpt, C5225–1.505

Grain crop acreage, production, and yield, by commodity and State, 1992 and trends, annual rpt, B2120–1

Grain elevators and capacity in US and Canada, by type and State or Province, with ranking of top storage companies, 1993 annual directory and buyers guide, C8450–2

Grain production and yield in States served by Minneapolis exchange, with area elevator receipts and shipments by mode, 1992 and trends, annual rpt, B6110–1.1

Grain production, by crop and State, 1990-92, annual rpt, B1530–1

Honey production, stocks, and value, and bee colonies, US and 16 leading States, 1992, annual rpt, S6760–1

Ice cream and frozen dessert production, by State, 1992, annual rpt, A5825–1.1

Liquor consumption, trade, and sales volume or shipments, by product type and State, 1991 and trends, annual rpt, A4650–3

Liquor market statistics, including sales, consumption, trade, distillery operations, and govtl info, with data by company, brand, and location, 1992 and trends, annual rpt, C4775–1

Livestock, dairy, and poultry inventories, marketings, and finances, and shipments in and out of Florida, by State, 1992 and trends, annual rpt, S1685–1.3

Livestock inventory by State and species, Jan 1993, annual rpt, S0850–1.2

Livestock operations and inventories, cash receipts, and slaughtering plants, by animal species and State, 1992 annual rpt, A2100–1.1

Milk cows on farms, production, and income, by State, 1992, annual rpt, S0850–1.6

North Central States agricultural export value, for 7 States by commodity, 1988-91, annual rpt, S4835–1

Production, consumption, stocks, trade, and prices for approx 100 basic commodities, including by country and producing State, commodity yearbook for 1993, C2400–1, C2400–2

Restaurant assn workers compensation self-insurance fund premium pool and enrollment, for 9 States, 1992, article, C1200–5.507

Restaurant sales forecast, by census div and State, 1992-93, annual feature, A8200–1.502

Soft drink manufacturing plants, by State, 1981-91, annual rpt, C0125–3.1

Soybean acreage, yield, and production, by State, 1970-92, annual rpt, B8480–1

State social, economic, and govtl indicators, with rankings, 1993 semiannual rpt, B8500–1.2, B8500–1.12

Statistical profiles of 50 States and DC, general data, 1993 annual almanac, C4712–1

Supermarket sales, effective buying income, and population, by State and census div, 1991, annual rpt, C3400–6

Tobacco cash receipts in 16 States, 1991, annual rpt, A9075–1

Wheat production and prices in selected States, 1980s-92, annual rpt, A7310–1

Wine market statistics, including sales, production, trade, and consumer

BY STATE

Index by Categories

characteristics, with data by company, brand, and geographic area, 1992 and trends, annual rpt, C4775–2

State and local:

Colorado livestock inshipments from selected States, 1985-92, annual rpt, S0985–1

Kansas livestock inshipments, by State of origin, 1987-91, annual rpt, U7095–2.15

Kansas livestock inshipments, by State of origin, 1987-92, annual rpt, S2915–1

Missouri feeder pig shipment distribution by State of destination, 1992, annual rpt, S4480–1

New Mexico cattle shipments by State of origin and destination, 1991, annual rpt, S5530–1

Texas cattle and sheep inshipments and outshipments, by State, 1991, annual rpt, S7630–1.2

Wisconsin livestock outshipments, by State of destination, 1992 and trends, annual rpt, S8680–1

Banking, Finance, and Insurance

Bank failures and outlays by FDIC, by State and region, 1990-92, R8490–47

Insurance (property/casualty) companies, premiums written, loss ratios, and market shares of leading firms, by State, 1992, annual article, C1050–1.509

Insurance (property/casualty) finances and operations, with related accident, disaster, and crime incidence data, 1991 and trends, annual rpt, A5650–1

Insurance (property/casualty) premiums, market shares, and leading underwriters, for general liability, medical malpractice, fidelity, and surety, by State, 1991, annual article, C1050–1.502

Insurance (property/casualty) premiums, market shares, and leading underwriters, for workers compensation, by State, 1991, annual article, C1050–1.501

Insurance industry employment, payroll, share of GSP, and premium taxes, by State, 1992 annual rpt, A0375–2

Life insurance industry fact book on operations and finances, 1991 and trends, biennial rpt, A1325–1

Loan delinquency rates for approx 10 types of consumer bank loans, and repossession data, by State, quarterly rpt, A0950–1

Medical malpractice insurance State joint underwriting assn (JUA) financial condition, for 11 States, 1991, annual rpt, A0375–1

Mutual fund sales, by State, 1991, annual rpt, A6025–1

NASDAQ over-the-counter securities issuers, and registered brokers, by State, 1992, annual rpt, A7105–1

Savings instn economic issues and devs, with quarterly data on financial condition by instn type and State, monthly rpt, A8813–1

Statistical profiles of 50 States and DC, general data, 1993 annual almanac, C4712–1

Trust instns and assets managed, approx 5,000 depts, US and Canada, 1993 annual directory, C2425–2.501

Unit investment trust sales volume and value, by State, monthly rpt annual feature, A6025–7

Venture capital under mgmt and newly disbursed, by State, 1991, annual rpt, A8515–1

State and local:

Illinois Dept of Financial Instns unclaimed property div operations, including interstate finances with 24 reciprocal States, FY91, annual rpt, S2457–2

Communications

Cable TV equipped public and private elementary and secondary schools, by State, 1993 article, C2965–1.510

Direct marketing establishments and receipts, for direct mail and catalog/mail order houses, 1987, annual rpt, A4620–1.2

Magazine (farm) circulation, by State and publication, 6-month periods ended Dec 1992 and June 1993, semiannual rpt, A3385–3.4

Newspaper circulation and market penetration, for 22 States, 1992, article, A8605–1.507

Newspaper prices per copy for daily editions, by State, 1992, annual article, A8605–1.507

Public broadcasting revenues from State sources, by State and territory, FY91, annual rpt, R4250–1.19

Statistical profiles of 50 States and DC, general data, 1993 annual almanac, C4712–1

Telephone independent companies and access lines, by State, Dec 1991, annual rpt, A9360–2

Telephone local residential service rates for 11 Southeastern States, 1989, article, U8710–1.501

TV and total households, and member population by age and sex, by market area, county, State, and/or census div, 1992/93, annual rpt, B0525–3

TV households by census div, State, county, Nielsen market area, and time zone, Jan 1994, annual rpt, B6670–2

Utility regulatory agency policies and practices, and industry financial and operating data, by utility type and agency, 1991/92 annual rpt, A7015–3

Education

Black American educational statistics, with comparisons to whites, 1970s-92, annual compilation, C6775–2.3

Catholic colleges, elementary and high schools, enrollment, and teachers, by diocese and State, 1993 annual compilation, C4950–1

Catholic educational instns and enrollment, by State and diocese, 1993 annual almanac, C6885–1

Catholic schools, enrollment, and teachers, by region, State, and diocese, 1992/93 and trends, annual rpt, A7375–1

Doctoral degree recipients by sex and field of study, by State of doctoral instn, 1990/91, annual rpt, R6000–7

Educational attainment, and education finances, by State, 1993-94 biennial rpt, S8780–1.2

Educational expenditures vs personal income, by State, FY91, annual rpt, R9380–1.8

Elementary/secondary education data, with detail for mathematics including test scores and teacher preparation, by State, 1993 biennial rpt, A4355–1

Elementary/secondary education expenditures per pupil and as percent of State/local govt spending, by State, 1993 articles, B8500–2.515

Elementary/secondary education expenditures per pupil compared to natl average, for 10 States with highest and lowest spending, FY92, article, B8500–2.509

Elementary/secondary prospective teacher characteristics, including States where they want to teach, 1992 survey, R6350–7

Elementary/secondary school parental selection, parent and general public views, and local program characteristics and results, 1992 rpt, R3810–7

Elementary/secondary school revenues, expenditures, and teacher salaries, by State, 1940s-91, annual rpt, R9050–1.6

Elementary/secondary student computer use at school, by State, 1989, article, B8500–2.506

Elementary/secondary students with math teachers emphasizing algebra and geometry, by State, 1990, article, R4800–2.522

General Educational Dev (GED) testing programs and results, by jurisdiction, 1992 and trends, annual rpt, A1410–16

High school dropout rates among youth age 16-19, for 5 States with lowest and highest rates, 1990, annual rpt, S2784–3

High school grads, by State, 1991/92-2008/09, article, C2175–1.537

Higher education appropriation trends, by State, FY91-93, article, B8500–2.501

Higher education appropriations and tuition, by State, and Vermont enrollment by State of residence, 1992 annual rpt, S8035–2

Higher education appropriations, by State, instn, and function, 1993/94, annual feature, C2175–1.538

Higher education appropriations from tax funds, by State, instn, and function, FY92-93 and trends, annual rpt, A8970 1

Higher education average tuition and charges, by institutional category and State, 1990/91, annual rpt, S6790–5.3

Higher education data for selected States, with detail for Minnesota, 1993 biennial rpt, S4195–2.2

Higher education enrollment, by State and public instn, fall 1992, annual rpt, A7150–5

Higher education enrollment of foreign students, by instn, discipline, State, and country of origin, 1991/92, annual feature, C2175–1.501

Higher education enrollment of foreign students, by instn, State, country of origin, and demographic characteristics, 1991/92 and trends, annual rpt, R5580–1

Higher education enrollment of minority and foreign students, with comparison to whites, by sex, State, and instn type, fall 1991, recurring feature, C2175–1.506

Higher education faculty average salaries by rank, at approx 2,000 instns arranged by State, 1992/93, annual feature, C2175–1.516

Higher education faculty compensation and employment, detailed data by rank, sex, and instn, 1992/93 and trends, annual rpt, A0800–1

Higher education financial issues, with data on college attendance rates and instn administrative costs, for 11-18 States, 1988 or 1990, article, B8500–2.510

Index by Categories

BY STATE

Higher education funding as percent of State/local spending, and share of spending covered by tuition/other charges, by State, FY91 and trends, article, B8500–2.516

Higher education funding trends by State, 1993 annual rpt, S0827–3

Higher education instn Fed Govt R&D obligations per capita, by State, FY90, article, B8500–2.501

Higher education instns, faculty, students, degrees, and finances, detailed data by State, 1993 annual rpt, C2175–1.531

Higher education involvement of minorities, including enrollment and degrees awarded, by race-ethnicity, sex, and State, 1970s-91, annual rpt, A1410–10

Higher education on-campus crime incidence and arrests by selected offense, by instn and State, 1991/92, C2175–1.506

Higher education public instn finances and enrollment for 7 Southwestern States, with comparisons to US and selected other States, 1990-92, article, U5930–1.502

Higher education R&D funding by source, by State and for US territories, FY91, annual feature, C2175–1.503

Higher education State-administered student aid awards, by program and State, 1992/93 and trends, annual rpt, A7140–1

Higher education student charges, by State and land-grant instn, and type of professional program, fall 1991-92, annual rpt, A7150–4

Higher education student Federal loan default rates, by State, and for top 50 lenders and top 10 guarantee agencies, 1991, article, C2175–1.532

Higher education tuition/fees at approx 3,000 individual instns, by State, 1992/93-1993/94, annual feature, C2175 1.535

Higher education tuition/fees at premier public university, by State, 1992/93 and trends, article, B8500–2.501

Higher education, 2-year college enrollment, degrees, faculty and staff, and tuition/fees, by instn and State, 1992 annual directory, A0640–1

Hispanic American educational statistics, with comparisons to whites, 1970s-92, annual compilation, C6775–3.2

Library and book trade reference info, including public and academic library funding, construction, and operations, by State and instn, 1992, annual compilation, C1650–3

Library building referenda election results, by instn and location, FY92 and trends, annual article, C1852–1.508

Library construction, costs, and funding sources, by State, city, instn, and library type, FY92 and trends, annual article, C1852–1.501

Library expenditures and circulation, for 5 States with highest and lowest levels, 1991, article, C1852–1.509

Library financial and operational rankings, by State, FY91, annual rpt, S2778–1

Library school grad placements and salaries, by region, sex, instn, and library type, with detail for minorities, 1992 and trends, annual article, C1852–1.512

Library State agency appropriations, expenditures, salaries, and staff, by State, 1992 annual rpt, A3862–1

Middle Atlantic States higher education faculty salaries at public and private instns, for 7 States, 1991/92, annual rpt, S6790–5.13

Minority enrollment share for higher education, and high school grads by race-ethnicity, by State, 1990s and trends, recurring rpt, A3960–2.1

Minority student and teacher shares in public schools, with detail for math and science teachers, by State, 1989, recurring rpt, A3960–2.2

North Central States higher education tuition/fees, for public instns in 8 States, FY89-92, annual rpt, S7375–1

Northeastern States higher education enrollment trend, for 12 States, 1990 vs 1980, annual rpt, S6790–5.9

School bus funding and operations issues, including capital spending for 3-5 States with greatest increase or decrease, 1991/92-1992/93, annual article, C1575–1.504

School bus pupil transportation, accident, and expenditure statistics, by State, 1993 annual feature, C1575–1.502

School district funding data, high school graduation and dropout rates, and Head Start program enrollment, by State, 1990 or FY90, annual rpt, R3840–11

Southeastern States school expenditures and staff salaries, for 12 States and US, 1990/91-1991/92, annual rpt, S4340–1.1

Southeastern States teacher average salaries, for 12 States, FY88-94, annual rpt, S7125–3.3

Southern States higher education enrollment, degrees, appropriations, tuition/fees, and faculty compensation, by instn type, for 15 States, 1990/91, annual rpt, A8945–31

Southern States higher education enrollment, degrees, faculty, and finances, for 15 States, 1990s and trends, biennial fact book, A8945–1

Southern States higher education-related data for 15 States, fact book update series, A8945–27

Southern States teacher retirement and health insurance plan characteristics and costs as a percent of salaries, for 15 States, 1993 rpt, A8945–34

Southern States use of reporting systems to track college performance of recent high school grads, for 15 States, 1992, A8945–32

State social, economic, and govtl indicators, with rankings, 1993 semiannual rpt, B8500–1.7

Statistical profiles of 50 States and DC, general data, 1993 annual almanac, C4712–1

Student aid expenditures, by State, 1991/92-1992/93, annual feature, C2175–1.515

Teacher education instns with State approval, and number affiliated with natl accreditation council, by State, 1993 article, R4800–2.512

Teacher salaries, by State, 1991/92, annual rpt, S6790–5.12

Textbook and educational material sales compared to school enrollment and expenditures, by State, 1990-91, annual rpt, A3274–2

Western States higher education student exchange program enrollment and support fees, by program and instn, for 15 States, 1992/93, annual rpt, A9385–1

Western States higher education tuition/fees, by resident status, State, and public instn, with State-funded student aid summaries, 1992/93 and trends, annual rpt, A9385–3

State and local:

Arkansas higher education enrollment by student characteristics and geographic origins, by instn, fall 1991 and trends, annual rpt, S0690–1

Delaware educational personnel by State awarding bachelors degree, 1991/92, annual rpt, S1430–1.3

Florida higher education enrollment, by State and Florida county of residence, fall 1991, annual rpt, S1725–1

Illinois college freshman enrollment, by State of residence, fall 1992, annual rpt, S2475–1.1

Kentucky higher education enrollment, for top 10 States of student origin, fall 1992, annual rpt, S3130–3

Missouri higher education enrollment, including by student residence and transfer student origin, fall 1992, annual rpt, S4520–3

North Carolina higher education enrollment, by student characteristics, and State and county of residence, fall 1992 and trends, annual rpt, U8013–1.1

North Dakota postsecondary enrollment by instn and State of residence, fall 1992, annual rpt, S6110–1

Pennsylvania higher education students by State of residence and academic level, and undergrad migration patterns by State, 1993 biennial rpt, S6790–5.8

South Carolina higher education freshman enrollment by State and South Carolina county of residence, fall 1992, annual rpt, S7185–2

Tennessee higher education enrollment, by State of residence, fall 1992, annual rpt, S7525–1.1

Texas higher education enrollment in public instns, by State of origin, fall 1991, annual rpt, S7657–1.1

Energy Resources and Demand

Coal deliveries and prices for individual electric power plants, by utility, State, and census div, monthly rpt, A7400–9

Coal leases issued by Fed Govt, including acreage, sales, and royalties, for 10 States, FY91, article, C5226–1.510

Coal longwall mining operations, by company and State, 1993, annual article, C5226–1.504

Coal preparation plants and capacity in US, Canada, and Mexico, by company, 1993 biennial feature, C5226–1.511

Electric bills, average monthly residential, for 10 States, 1980-91, annual rpt, S5917–2

Electric power (steam) plants, capacity, generation, and fuel use and costs, by fuel type, utility, and location, 1991, annual rpt, A7400–7

Electric power generated and fuel use by type, for individual steam plants by utility and State, monthly rpt, A7400–8

Electric power generating equipment scheduled shipments to industrial customers, by State and census div, as of Jan 1992, annual rpt, A4700–2.2

SRI 1993 789

BY STATE

Electric utility demand-side mgmt program impact on electricity demand in 8 States, by 2000, article, C4725–5.502

Electric utility financial and operating data, by State and census div, 1991 and trends, annual rpt, A4700–1

Electric utility income and operating data, by type of company and for individual locally owned utilities, 1993 annual directory, A2625–1.501

Electric utility plants and generating capacity, by State and census div, Dec 1991, annual rpt, C5800–28.507

Energy consumption by State, 1965-89, recurring rpt, U5680–2.12

Gasoline service stations, by State, 1993 and trends, annual article, C4680–1.505

Industrial electric power and natural gas costs, by State, 1991 or 1992, article, C5800–12.512

Natural gas industry detailed operating and financial data, by State and census div, 1960s-91, annual rpt, A1775–3

Natural gas processing plants, capacity, and production, by company, State, and country, 1993 annual rpt, C6985–1.537

Oil and gas deep well drilling, success ratios, and costs, by State and for offshore, 1991-92, annual article, C4420–1.502

Oil and gas drilling and production technology devs, including drilling rigs in operation by State, monthly rpt, C4420–1

Oil and gas drilling costs, and wells and footage drilled, by State, offshore location, and type of well, 1991, annual rpt, A2575–9

Oil and gas industry exploration, production, refining, demand, finance, prices, and reserves, by State and country or world area, 1993 and trends, periodic basic data book, A2575–14

Oil and gas industry intl exploration, drilling, production, refining, stock, price, and financial data, weekly rpt, C6985–1

Oil and gas industry trends, with data by company, State, and country, 1993 annual compilation, C6985–4

Oil and gas intl supply-demand, exploration, refining, reserves, and industry finances, basic data by country and company, 1993 annual rpt, C6985–3

Oil and gas pipeline construction costs, mileage, and operating and financial data, by location and/or company, 1991 and trends, annual feature, C6985–1.504

Oil and gas sourcebook, with industry operations and finances, and world supply-demand situation, 1970s-91, annual compilation, C6985–9

Oil and gas supply-demand and industry operations, with trends by country and producing State, 1970s-2001, annual rpt, C6985–5

Oil and gas supply-demand, trade, and industry exploration and operations, by product and State, 1993 annual feature, C6985–1.513

Oil and gas wells and footage drilled, by type of well, State, and offshore location, quarterly rpt, A2575–6

Oil and lease condensate production by State, Texas district, and selected month, weekly rpt, A2575–1

Oil industry employment by segment, by State, 1991, periodic basic data book, A2575–14.7

Oil refinery capacity worldwide, by process, with data by country, company, and US State, 1992 annual feature, C6985–1.508

Oil supply-demand, marketing, prices, finances, and employment, detailed data for US and Canada, by product, company, and location, 1993 annual fact book, C4680–1.507

Oil/gas industry production, finances, exploration, and reserves, by State, 1992 and trends, annual rpt, A5425–1

Oil/gas wells drilled and planned, and oil production, by State, 1992-93, annual article, C6985–1.539

Southeastern States electric power generation capacity additions as percent of installed base, for 11 States, 1992-2000 article, C5800–28.506

State social, economic, and govtl indicators, with rankings, 1993 semiannual rpt, B8500–1.12

Statistical profiles of 50 States and DC, general data, 1993 annual almanac, C4712–1

Sulfur dioxide emission allowance trading program, State regulatory issues and related data by State and major utility, 1992 rpt, A8195–12

Utility regulatory agency policies and practices, and industry financial and operating data, by utility type and agency, 1991/92 annual rpt, A7015–3

Western States natural gas pipeline project construction spending, jobs created, and property tax benefits, for 4 States, 1992 article, C6780–2.501

State and local:

Pennsylvania coal shipments, by end use and State of destination, 1985 and 1990, recurring rpt, S6810–3

Geography and Climate

Heating degree days, by census div and State, 1990/91-1991/92 and 30-year average, annual rpt, A1775–3.6

Land area, by region, census div, and State, 1991 annual data sheet, R8750–9

Land area by State, including Federal and State lands, 1991, annual rpt, A6485–1.2

Statistical profiles of 50 States and DC, general data, 1993 annual almanac, C4712–1

Tornadoes and related deaths and injuries, by State, 1991, annual rpt, A5650–1.4

Water mileage, inland and coastal, by State and territory, 1993 annual feature, C2425–4

Western States population and land area in urban and rural areas, for 12 States, 1990, article, U0280–1.502

Government and Defense

Alcoholic beverage purchase restrictions and tax rates, by State, 1993 annual rpt, C4775–1.2

Black Americans elected to House of Representatives, vote shares by district and State, Nov 1992, article, R5685–4.501

Black elected officials, by office, govt level, and State, Jan 1993, annual article, R5685–4.505

Black elected officials, by office, govt level, and State or city, Jan 1992 and trends, annual article, R5685–4.502

Bonds issued, retired, and outstanding, by level of govt and State, FY90, annual rpt, R9050–1.4

Index by Categories

Brewers and other distillers tax payments to Federal and State govts, FY91 and trends, annual rpt, A3455–1.6

Budget receipts and outlays of Fed Govt, by source and function, 1920s-93, annual rpt, R9050–1.3

Child labor regulatory activity evaluation, and number of inspectors and specialists, by State, 1992 rpt, R8335–2

Cigarette added tax burden from proposed increase to finance health care reform, by State, with natl average price and taxes, 1993 article, R9050–3.509

Cigarette added tax burden from proposed increase to finance health care reform, with detail for 8 States, 1993 article, C5800–7.549

Congressional campaign finances and results, with data by candidate, State, and for leading contributors by type, 1990 election and trends, biennial rpt, R3828–3

Congressional campaign fund finances, with expenditures by item and contributions by donor type, by candidate, district, and State, 1990 elections, C2500–6

Congressional term limitation initiative voting results in 14 States, 1992, article, A1865–1.507

Congressional voting for 7 bills, for House Members from districts with at least 15% black population, by State, 1993 article, R5685–4.503

Congressional voting patterns and support for President, by State, 1992, annual rpt, C2500–2

Defense contracts value per capita vs US average by State, and value of R&D awards to businesses and educational instns for top 6-10 States, 1950s-84, R4700–19

Defense expenditures and personnel, by State, 1992, article, S0320–1.511

Defense industries job losses from budget cuts, with loss outlook for 1997, for 10 States, 1993 article, C8900–1.508

Defense-related product as percent of total product, for top 10 States, 1992, article, C5800–7.531

Defense share of output, for top 15 States, 1991, article, S8205–4.503

DOD contract and payroll spending, military and civilian personnel, installations, and cutbacks, by State and region, various years FY81-93, R8490–44

Economic dev condition indicators, including economic performance, business vitality, growth capacity, and tax/fiscal system, by State, 1993 annual rpt, R4225–1

Elected black and female officials, by level of govt and State, 1993 annual rpt, S7125–1.9

Election results for Federal offices and Governor, by State, county, major city, and party, with voter registration and turnout, 1992 and trends, biennial rpt, C2500–1

Election results for presidential, congressional, and gubernatorial races, and congressional term limitation referenda, by State, 1992, annual rpt, C2500–2

Employment (Federal civilian), ranking by State, Dec 1990, biennial rpt, S3605–1.4

Employment in govt, by level and State, Oct 1991, annual rpt, R9380–1.3

Employment in govt, by level and State, 1991 and trends, annual rpt, R9050–1

Index by Categories

BY STATE

Energy (BTU) tax proposed by Clinton Admin, burden per household and by economic sector, by State, 1993 article, R9050–3.505

Energy (BTU) tax proposed by Clinton Admin, resulting job losses by State, 1994-98, article, R9050–3.506

Energy tax options considered by Clinton Admin, total and per-household cost estimates by State and region, 1993 rpt, R8490–49

Expenditures of State govts by fund source and function, by State, FY90-92, annual rpt, A7118–1

Federal budget trends, including spending by program, State, and region, FY81-94, annual rpt, R8490–11

Federal entitlement program payments and recipients by program, and income tax return data, by State and region, early 1990s, R8490–47

Federal expenditures by category, by State and region, FY92 and trends, annual rpt, R8490–35

Federal payments in lieu of taxes on public lands, by State, 1991, article, U8960–2.502

Federal tax burden and spending, by State, FY93 annual rpt, R9050–15.5

Federal tax burden per capita, by State, FY93 and trends, annual article, R9050–3.505

Federal taxes and spending per capita, by State, 1992, article, R9050–3.506

Fiscal conditions for New York and selected other States, including tax revenues, expenditures, and taxation of corporate profits, 1992 article, A8825–1.502

Fiscal issues for State govts, including budget balances, revenues, and expenditures, with data by State, series, A7470–4

Fiscal issues for State govts, including employment, programs, revenues, and expenditures, with data by State, series, U5085–2

Fuel tax rates and revenues, by State, 1992 and trends, annual rpt, C4680–1.507

Gasoline taxes and rates, by State, 1993 article, R9050–3.507

Gasoline taxes and rates, with detail by State and comparisons to 7 foreign countries, 1993 rpt, R9050–15.6

General fund revenues, expenditures, and balances, and budget stabilization funds, by State, FY92-94 and trends, semiannual rpt, A7955–1

Governor salaries in 10 States with highest and lowest pay, 1992 article, C5800–7.506

Govt finances, including revenues by source, expenditures by function, and debt, detailed data for Federal, State, and local govts, 1993 annual rpt, R9050–1

Hispanic American elected officials by office and State, with related population characteristics, 1992 annual directory, A6844–1

Hispanic American voter candidate preferences in 1992 presidential election, in 5 States, Oct 1992 survey, article, C4575–1.501

Hispanic Americans in elected offices in 15 States with largest Hispanic populations, 1980, annual rpt, U6250–1.5

Lottery advertising budget and agency, by State, FY92, article, C2710–1.526

Military base closure/realignment and impact on personnel, with data on spending and installations, by State, region, and base, 1988-93, R8490–45

Military commissary sales by location, FY92, annual feature, A2072–2.501

Municipal govt annexation activity, and population and land area affected, by city, State, and census div, 1980-91, A5800–1.2

Northeast States cigarette excise and State sales taxes per pack, for 8 States, Jan 1993, article, R9050–3.502

Oil industry severance/production taxes paid, by State, 1970-90, annual compilation, C6985–9.3

Pari-mutuel wagering activity, attendance, purse distribution, and govt revenue, by State and Canadian Province, 1990 and trends, annual rpt, A3363–1

Payments of State/local taxes, FY91, and rates by type of tax, Jan 1993, by State, annual rpt, R9380–1.7

Pension fund shortfalls for underfunded plans in 9 States, 1993 article, C5800–7.540

Pension funds with largest surpluses and deficits, for selected top States, 1993 article, C2710–2.519

Presidential primary election results and voter registration by county and district, by State, 1992 and trends, C2500–7

Property tax State/local collections, by State, FY80 and FY91, recurring article, R9050–3.508

Property tax State/local collections, with comparison to income, by State, FY80 and FY91, R9050–15.7

Southern States population, personal income, and State/local revenues and expenditures, by State, 1950s-2010, biennial fact book, A8945–1.1

State and local govt employee wages compared to private sector, with detail by sex and State, 1989 and trends, R4/00–21

State economic and social devs relevant to policy decisions, with data by State, semimonthly rpt, B8500–2

State funding changes for public assistance programs, and tax changes, by State, with analysis of impact on the poor, FY92-93, annual rpt, R3834–9

State govt employment and finances, by State, 1993-94 biennial rpt, S8780–1.2

State govt info resources mgmt, including data on budgets, staff, and organizational structure, by State, 1991, biennial rpt, A7121–1

State shares of upper-level income tax increases proposed by Clinton Admin, compared to population, for 10 States most and least affected, 1993 article, C8900–1.510

State social, economic, and govtl indicators, with rankings, 1993 semiannual rpt, B8500–1

State tax revenue from personal, corporate, and sales taxes, by State and region, quarterly rpt, U5085–1

State/local revenues from selected sources, State rankings, FY90, annual rpt, U8130–2.5

Statistical profiles of 50 States and DC, general data, 1993 annual almanac, C4712–1

Tax collections and rates, with comparison to personal income, by State, FY81-93, R9050–14

Tax increases proposed by Clinton Admin, impact by State, 1993 article, R9050–3.503

Tax levels as measured by date average taxpayer earns enough to pay yearly taxes, by State, 1993, annual feature, R9050–3.504

Tax revenues of States per capita, by State, 1991, annual rpt, S4950–1

Tax revenues per capita and compared to personal income, by State, FY91 and trends, article, R9050–3.501

Taxes compared to income, and labor time required to earn the equivalent of yearly and daily taxes, by State, 1993 and trends, annual rpt, R9050–15.4

Tobacco products taxation, by State, 1950s-92, annual rpt, A9075–2

Transportation regulatory agency policies and practices for motor carriers and railroads, by agency, 1991/92 annual rpt, A7015–4

Transportation-related revenues of individual States, by type, 1991-92, annual rpt, A0865–1.3

Utility and transportation regulatory agency activities, scope of jurisdiction, finances, and employees, by agency, 1991/92 annual rpt, A7015–2

Utility regulatory agency policies and practices, and industry financial and operating data, by utility type and agency, 1991/92 annual rpt, A7015–3

Western States expenditures of Fed Govt, for 9 States, 1984-91, annual article, U7980–1.503

Women officials in Federal, State, and local govt offices, fact sheet series, U4510–1

Women's employment in govt, with data by race-ethnicity and State, series, U5090–1

Health and Vital Statistics

Abortion legality support as affected by survey question formulation, with detail for 6 States, Sept/Oct 1989 survey, article, A5160–1.504

Accidental deaths and disabling injuries, by detailed type, victim characteristics, circumstances, and location, 1992 and trends, annual rpt, A8375–2

AIDS cases, for top 10 States/territories, 1993 article, C4215–1.505

AIDS incidence rates among white and Hispanic population, by State, 1991, article, A2623–1.506

AIDS prison inmate cases, deaths, and testing, by State and for Federal system, 1991-92, annual rpt, R4300–1.1

AIDS quarantine use and complaint handling by States in cases of infected individuals whose behavior increases transmission risk, by State, 1981-90, article, A2623–1.512

Animal selenium deficiency and toxicosis cases in livestock/wildlife, by State, 1992 survey, article, A3100–2.510

Birds (pet) tested for Newcastle disease in 5 States, with results and disease flowchart, 1991, article, A3100–2.503

Blood bank operating profiles, arranged by State, 1993 biennial directory, A0612–1

Cancer (urinary tract) death rates for men age 45-84, by age, State, and census div, 1979-89, article, B6045–1.503

Cancer incidence and mortality, including data by State, sex, and body site, 1993 and trends, annual rpt, A1175–1

BY STATE

Index by Categories

Child and maternal health status indicators, with data by race and State, 1992 annual rpt, R3840–5

Child health and well-being indicators, with selected household characteristics, by State, 1993 annual rpt, R3832–1

Death rates for 4 leading causes, by State, 1989, annual fact book, A1275–1.5

Dental advanced education programs, enrollment, grads, and finances, by instn and State, 1992/93 annual rpt, A1475–10

Dental allied education enrollment, grads, and tuition, by instn, 1992/93 annual rpt, A1475–5

Dental school distribution of 1st-year and predoctoral students by State of residence, by instn, 1992/93, annual rpt, A1475–3.1

Disabled persons expenditures for home care services, by State, 1992, R4865–15

Drowning deaths, for top 10 States, 1990, B6045–1.504

Drug prescription writing authority for nurse practitioners and physician assistants, by State, 1991/92, U8850–8.4

Health behavior risk factor surveillance survey results, by State, 1990, recurring rpt, S1010–3

Health behavior risk factor surveillance survey results, by State, 1991, annual rpt, S1895–2, S6105–3

Health benefit plans for State employees, coverage and HMO participation by State, 1993 annual article, C2425–1.506

Health care employment in top 10 States, June 1993, article, A1865–1.522

Health care spending and insurance coverage under current law vs plans of presidential candidates Bush and Clinton, by State, 1993-2005, R4865–9

Health insurance benefits mandated by law in each State, and State program provisions in 2 States, 1991, U8850–8.1

Health insurance coverage lack, and population with high out-of-pocket expenses, by State and selected characteristics, 1993, R4865–14

Health insurance data, including HMOs, govt programs, facilities and utilization, and related health info, by State, 1992 annual rpt, A5173–2

Health insurance employer premiums for typical employee coverage as a percent of natl average, by State, Mar 1992, article, B8500–2.505

Health insurance low-cost "barebones" plan characteristics and persons covered, for 29 States waiving mandated benefits, 1992/93, R4865–16

Health insurance, non-elderly adults lacking coverage by State, with Medicaid coverage rates for 16 States, 1991 and trends, article, B8500–2.508

Hearing aid unit sales, by type and State, and trade summary, quarterly rpt, A5185–1

HMO enrollment as percent of population, for top 5 States, 1992, A1865–1.515

HMOs and enrollment, and preferred provider organizations (PPOs), by State, 1993 annual fact book, A1275–1.3

Hospital (public) revenues per capita, by State, 1991, article, B8500–2.518

Hospital costs per day and per stay, by State, 1990, annual rpt, A5650–1.4

Hospital directory, with utilization, expenses, and personnel, by instn, type, and location, 1992, annual rpt, A1865–3

Hospital emergency dept visits per 1,000 population, by State, 1990, article, B8500–2.501

Hospital industry financial and operating indicators, with detail for Medicare, by instn characteristics and location, 1988-92, annual rpt, B1880–1

Hysterectomy prevalence in 16 States, 1988 surveys, article, A2623–1.503

Infant mortality rates by race, State, and census div, 1987-89, annual rpt, S6285–1

Infant mortality rates from sudden infant death syndrome, by race, census div, and State, 1980 and 1988, article, B6045–1.502

Infant, neonatal, and adult mortality rates, and percent of births to single mothers, by selected characteristics, 1970s-89, annual rpt, S1385–2

Marriages and divorces, by State, 1991 and trends, biennial rpt, S8780–1.2

Medicaid Federal grants, recipients, and benefits by type of service, with selected public health funding factors, by State and region, various years 1974-94, R8490–46

Medicaid matching funds raised by States from sources other than general fund as a percent of Federal Medicaid grants, by State, FY93, article, B8500–2.509

Medical group practice characteristics, including specialties, form of organization, and location, 1991 and trends, recurring rpt, A2200–7

Nursing home insurance adequacy as means of making care affordable to elderly, with detail by age and/or State, 1992 and 2005, R4865–12

Nursing programs (State-approved) for practical/vocational nurses, including admissions, enrollment, and grads, by instn, State, and territory, 1992, annual directory, A8010–5

Nursing programs (State-approved) for registered nurses, including admissions, enrollment, and grads, by instn, State, and territory, 1992, annual directory, A8010–4

Nursing schools, programs, enrollment, student and staff characteristics, and grads, 1991 and trends, annual rpt, A8010–1

Optometry school students by State of residence, by instn, 1991/92, annual survey, A3370–2

Osteopathic physicians by State and other location, July 1993, annual rpt, A0620–1

Pharmacy degree program enrollment and degrees conferred, by State, fall 1991, annual rpt, A0630–9

Physicians by detailed specialty and location, 1992 and trends, annual rpt, A2200–3

Prostate surgery procedures, costs, and hospital stay, with data by census div and State, 1991 and trends, article, B6045–1.503

Rabies cases in wild and domestic animals and humans, by State, 1992 annual article, A3100–2.504

Sexually transmitted disease and human immunodeficiency virus (HIV) program expenditures, by State, 1989, A5160–10

Southern States children age 17/under lacking health insurance and eligible for Medicaid, with detail by age and family income, for 6-17 States, 1991, R9000–1

State social, economic, and govtl indicators, with rankings, 1993 semiannual rpt, B8500–1.1, B8500–1.9

Statistical profiles of 50 States and DC, general data, 1993 annual almanac, C4712–1

Substance abuse treatment programs, funding by source, and client characteristics, for alcohol and drug services, by State, FY91 and trends, annual rpt, A7112–1

Surgeons in practice per 100,000 population, by State, 1990, annual fact book, A1275–1.1

Teenage abortions, births, and pregnancies, by State, 1988, article, A5160–1.504

Tonsillectomy/adenoidectomy procedures, costs, and hospital stay, with data by census div and State, 1991 and trends, article, B6045–1.502

Tuberculosis cases, for 10 States, 1991, article, A1865–1.510

Veterinarians by location and type of employment, 1990 and 1992, article, A3100–2.522

Veterinarians by professional characteristics and location, and financial and education summaries, 1993 annual directory, A3100–1

Veterinary school enrollment by student State or country of residence, by instn, 1992/93, annual article, A3100–2.516

Vital statistics summary by State, including births by race and deaths by major cause, 1989-90, annual rpt, S3295–1

Women's unintended pregnancy risk and eligibility for subsidized family planning services, by State, 1990, article, A5160–1.502

Workers compensation insurance residual market underwriting loss or gain, burden, and market shares, by State, 1991 and trends, annual rpt, A0375–3

Workers compensation law coverage, benefits, and other info, by State, outlying area, and Canadian Province, 1993 annual rpt, A3840–2

Workers compensation residential carpentry claim payouts in 5 States with highest and lowest amounts, 1989, article, C4300–1.508

Workplace safety and health data, including injury and death incidence, govt regulation and spending, and workers compensation, with data by State, 1992 annual rpt, R8335–1

State and local:

Alabama marriages, by State of residence of bride and groom, 1992, annual rpt, S0175–2

Arkansas marriages, by State of residence of bride and groom, 1991, annual rpt, S0685–1

Colorado vital statistics, including abortions by State of residence, 1990, annual rpt, S1010–1

Maine abortions by patient State of residence, 1991, annual rpt, S3460–2

Michigan vital events involving residents and nonresidents, by place of origin or occurrence, 1990, annual rpt, S4000–3

Minnesota abortions and marriages involving nonresidents, by State of origin, 1991, annual rpt, S4190–2

Oregon marriage dissolutions, by duration of marriage, and census div and State where ceremony performed, 1991, annual rpt, S6615–5

South Dakota births and induced abortions, by State of occurrence and/or residence, 1991, annual rpt, S7345–1

Utah marriages and divorces by State of residence or occurrence, 1990 and trends, annual rpt, S7835–2

Vermont vital statistics, including births, deaths, marriages, and abortions, by State of residence or occurrence, 1991, annual rpt, S8054–1

Virginia births, deaths, and marriages involving residents of Virginia and other States, by State, 1991, annual rpt, S8225–1

West Virginia resident births and deaths by State of occurrence, 1991 and trends, annual rpt, S8560–1

Housing and Construction

Construction (residential) cost increases, for top 11 States, 1992 vs 1991, C4300–1.511

Construction contract value, by project type, State, and region, 1991-93, annual feature, C5800–2.512

Construction workers compensation insurance rates, by type of work and State, 1993, article, C5800–2.547

Eastern States housing units by primary heating fuel, for 14 New England and Middle Atlantic States, 1990, article, C4680–1.501

Homebuilder financial and operating data, including detail by location, for top 400 builders, 1993 annual feature, C1850–8.507

Housing assistance Federal grants by State and region, for HOPE and HOME programs, FY92, R8490–42

Housing sales, with price and affordability data, by region, State, and metro area, monthly rpt, A7000–2

Mobile homes, and share of total homes, by State, 1990, article, C5150–6.501

Mobile/manufactured home production, shipments, and financing, with data by State and census div, monthly rpt, A6325–1

Mortgage delinquency and foreclosure rates, and residential loans serviced, by type, State, and census div and region, quarterly rpt, A6450–1

Real estate broker ratings of market conditions and outlook in 20 States, 1992 survey article, C4300–1.501

Rental costs compared to household and minimum wage income, by State or major city, 1992 annual rpt, R3840–11

Residential building permits issued per 1,000 population, and permit trends, by State, 1992-93, article, B8500–2.523

Sales of existing homes, by State, quarterly rpt, B5190–1

State social, economic, and govtl indicators, with rankings, 1993 semiannual rpt, B8500–1.2

Statistical profiles of 50 States and DC, general data, 1993 annual almanac, C4712–1

Western States housing permits, for approx 15 States, 1990s, annual rpt, B3520–1

Income

Black child poverty rates, with comparisons to whites, by State, 1989, R3840–21

Consumer buying power survey of population, income, and sales by kind of business, by census div, State, MSA, county, and city, 1992, annual rpt, C1200–1.511

Consumer buying power survey of population, income, and sales by product line, by State, metro area, county, and census div, 1993 annual rpt, C1200–1.514

Earned income, by industry and State, 1991, biennial rpt, S8780–1.2

Federal Medicaid funding factors, including per capita personal income, taxable resources, and poverty population, by State and region, 1980s-91, R8490–46

Household income trends, with number and distribution of households by income level and State, 1980 and 1990, article, U8960–2.505

Income (personal), by State, 1991 vs 1982, semiannual rpt, U5850–1

Income (personal) by State, 1992 annual rpt, S7155–3.3

Income (personal) in 20 States with highest and lowest averages, 1991, annual rpt, C2140–1.2

Income (personal) per capita, and child poverty rates, by State, 1993 biennial rpt, A4355–1

Income (personal), total and per capita, by State, 1970s-91, annual rpt, R9050–1.2

Income and poverty indicators, by State, 1980s-90, recurring rpt, U5680–2.9

Income comparisons among upper, middle, and lower income groups, by State, 1979-89, R3834–13, R3834–14

Income comparisons between top and bottom quintiles, by State, late 1980s, article, B8500–2.506

Income per capita by State, 1990, annual rpt, S6845–3.2

Income per capita, for selected Eastern and top 10 States, 1992, recurring feature, S5425–1.506

Logistics personnel salary indexes in 21 States, 1993 annual article, C2150–1.508

Manufacturing industry trends including employment, earnings, establishments, and GSP, by State and region, 1970s-92, R8490–48

Markets with daily newspapers, demographic and economic info by geographic area, US and Canada, 1993 annual rpt, C3250–1

Midwest personal income in 7 States, quarterly rpt, U8595–1

Mountain-Plains region average annual pay, with detail for 10 States, 1991, article, U7860–1.505

New England per capita income by State, with comparison to other regions, 1988-92, annual rpt, S6980–3

Planning profession employment and salaries, by type of employer, demographic and professional characteristics, and location, 1991 and trends, biennial rpt, A2615–1

Poverty among children by race-ethnicity, by State, 1989 and trends, R3840–20.1

Poverty shares by race-ethnicity, by State, 1990, R3834–15

Professional worker salaries, by employee and employer characteristics, with detail for scientists and engineers, 1990s and trends, biennial rpt, A3960–1

Southeastern States poverty levels and median income, for 7 States, 1990, annual rpt, U5680–3

Southern States population, personal income, and State/local revenues and expenditures, by State, 1950s-2010, biennial fact book, A8945–1.1

Southwestern States annual average pay, by industry div, for 8 States, 1990-91, article, S5624–2.501

State social, economic, and govtl indicators, with rankings, 1993 semiannual rpt, B8500–1.2, B8500–1.14

Statistical profiles of 50 States and DC, general data, 1993 annual almanac, C4712–1

Western States average annual pay, for 10 States, 1990-91, annual article, S0465–1.502

Western States per capita income in selected States, 1982 and 1986-91, annual article, U7980–1.503

Western States personal income, for approx 15 States, 1990s, annual rpt, B3520–1

Western States total and per capita personal income, by State, 1988-91, U7980–1.501

Industry and Commerce

Auto assembly plant installation economic impact, for Toyota Motor Corp Kentucky plant, for US and 6 States, 1991-92 and 1996, U7138–1.4

Black-owned business firms, sales/receipts, employment, and payroll, by industry div and State, 1982 and/or 1987, annual compilation, C6775–2.8

Black-owned businesses share of sales/receipts, for 10 leading States, 1987, article, A8510–1.1

Black-owned businesses, top 100 by State, 1992, annual feature, C4215–1.507

Blast furnaces in operation, Canada and US by State, monthly 1992, annual rpt, A2010–3.3

Business cost indexes, for 6 least and 6 most expensive States, 1993 article, C8900–1.509

Business failures and liabilities, by detailed industry, cause, length of operation, and location, 1991-92 and trends, annual rpt, C3150–8

Business failures and liabilities, by industry, census div, State, and major city, monthly rpt, C3150–2

Chemical industry companies, production, employment, earnings, and exports, for top 30 producing States, 1993 annual rpt, A3850–1

Consumer buying power survey of population, income, and sales by kind of business, by census div, State, MSA, county, and city, 1992, annual rpt, C1200–1.511

Consumer buying power survey of population, income, and sales by product line, by State, metro area, county, and census div, 1993 annual rpt, C1200–1.514

Copper mine production in selected States, 1972-92, annual rpt, A4175–1

Corporate mergers, acquisitions, and divestitures, with buyers and sellers by location, 1992 and trends, annual rpt, B6020–1

Discount chain sales and merchandising, including data by dept, leading chain, and location, 1992 and trends, annual feature, C8130–1.507

Discount stores and membership wholesale clubs, by State and census div, 1992, annual feature, C5150–3.516

Economic dev condition indicators, including economic performance, business vitality, growth capacity, and tax/fiscal system, by State, 1993 annual rpt, R4225–1

BY STATE

Index by Categories

Economic performance indexes by State, semimonthly rpt quarterly article, B8500–2.504, B8500–2.510, B8500–2.516, B8500–2.522

Electrical equipment distributor sales forecasts, by census div and State, 1992-93, annual article, C4725–5.502

Electrical equipment wholesaler market conditions, by geographic area, 1992 annual article, C4725–5.501

Exports to Mexico and Canada, value and share of total trade by region and State, 1991, R8490–43

Fastener sales for 10 leading States, selected years 1980-91, C1850–4.502

Fortune 500 largest industrial corporations and financial performance, by hq State, 1992 and trends, annual feature, C8900–1.513

Fortune 500 largest service corporations and financial performance, by hq State, 1992, annual feature, C8900–1.516

Hispanic-owned leading businesses and revenues, for top 10 States, 1992, annual feature, C4575–1.507

Household appliance sales by distributors, by product type and State, 1992, annual rpt, A3350–2

Incorporations (new), by State and census div, monthly rpt, C3150–3

Jewelry industry statistics on sales, marketing, trade, and employment, with customer characteristics, 1993 annual almanac, C2150–7.509

Lumber industry production in Western States and counties, with acreage owned, employment, and sawmill operations, 1980s-92, annual rpt, A9395–1

Machine tool industry employment, by State, 1991, annual rpt, A3179–2.1

Manufacturing exports value per capita, by State, 1992, article, B8500–2.512

Manufacturing industry trends including employment, earnings, establishments, and GSP, by State and region, 1970s-92, R8490–48

Manufacturing value added and wages per hour, for 9 States with highest and lowest values, 1991, article, B8500–2.516

Manufacturing value added, by State, 1985 and 1990, biennial rpt, S8780–1.2

Metal (primary) manufacturing plants, by type and State, 1993, annual article, C7000–8.504

Mexico exports for 4 US States, including shares by transport mode, 1991, U8850–9

Mexico exports of selected US States, 1987-90, annual rpt, U6250–1.26

Mineral (nonfuel) production value in 6 leading States, 1989, triennial rpt, S0465–2.33

Newsprint consumption by State and census div, 1989-90, annual rpt, A8610–1

Newsprint recycled product consumption goals in 24 States, 1993 annual rpt, C3975–5.3

Newsprint shipments, and consumption by newspapers, by region and State, 1979-92, annual rpt, A1630–8

North Central States business establishments, and wages by industry div, for 9 States, 1993 annual rpt, S6140–2

Northeast region newspaper publisher recycled newsprint purchasing goals vs supply, for 6-8 States, 1992-2000, A4375–15

Paper and paperboard industry financial and operating data, by product, census div, and State, 1970s-95, annual rpt, A1630–6.2

Paper and pulp mills by State, and production in top States, 1993 annual rpt, C3975–5.1, C3975–5.4

Paper, paperboard, wood pulp, and recovered paper production and mills, and pulpwood production, by State and census div, 1991, article, A1630–5.502

Phosphate reserves of 7 producing States, 1990, annual rpt, U6660–1.10

Phosphate rock reserves, and phosphoric acid production capacity, for 7 States, 1993 annual feature, C5226–2.505

Potash imports, by State and country of origin, quarterly rpt, A8720–4

Potash production and sales in Canada and US, by Province and State, 1991-92, monthly rpt annual tables, A8720–2

Potash production, inventories, and sales and exports by State, Canadian Province, and country of destination, monthly rpt, A8720–1

Production, consumption, stocks, trade, and prices for approx 100 basic commodities, including by country and producing State, commodity yearbook for 1993, C2400–1, C2400–2

Retail sales for 9 kinds of business by market area in US and Canada, with rankings by MSA, city, and county, 1993 annual rpt, C3250–1

Shoe industry production, employment and earnings, and plant closings, by selected State, 1991 and trends, annual rpt, A4957–1.2

Small privately held companies, 500 fastest growing by State, 1993 annual feature, C4687–1.512

Southeastern States agricultural receipts, and GSP and employment trends, for Tennessee and neighboring States, 1979-90, annual rpt, S7560–1

Southeastern States economic indicators, including population and income, for 12 States, 1970s-92, annual rpt, S7125–3.3

Southeastern States GSP, for 7 States, 1977 and 1989, annual rpt, U5680–3

State economic and social devs relevant to policy decisions, with data by State, semimonthly rpt, B8500–2

State social, economic, and govtl indicators, with rankings, 1993 semiannual rpt, B8500–1.2

Statistical profiles of 50 States and DC, general data, 1993 annual almanac, C4712–1

Steel production, by State, 1988-92, annual rpt, A2000–2.3

Textile fiber product manufacturers, with plants by State and region, 1992 annual directory, C3460–1.501

Textile finishing machinery in place, by selected State, June 1983 and 1988, annual rpt, A3800–1

Western States economic indicator trends, for 9 States, 1980-91, annual rpt, U7920–2

Western States economic indicators, including forecasts from selected organizations, for 10 States, monthly rpt, U0282–2

Labor and Employment

Americans with Disabilities Act employment-related complaints filed with Equal Employment Opportunity Commission, for top 10 States, Mar 1993, article, C1200–5.511

Electronics industry production and operating data, including employment for top 5 States by selected product type, 1991, annual rpt, A4725–1

Employment trends by State, May 1992-93, article, B8500–2.519

Employment trends for 19 States with greatest growth and 10 with greatest decline, Nov 1992 vs 1991, article, B8500–2.507

Hiring costs and new hires, by industry, State, region, and employer characteristics, 1992 and trends, annual survey rpt, A4740–2

Jobs added for 12 States with fastest employment growth rates, Feb 1992-Feb 1993, article, S4205–3.501

Labor force by educational attainment, sex, and age group, by State, 1990, article, U8960–2.509

Manufacturing employment change, by State, Nov 1992 vs 1991, article, B8500–2.509

Manufacturing employment share, and growth compared to total employment, by State, Feb 1993, article, B8500–2.513

Manufacturing employment trends and shares of work force, by State, Sept 1992, article, B8500–2.504

Manufacturing employment trends by State, July 1993 vs July 1992, article, B8500–2.523

Manufacturing exports share of private sector employment, by State, 1989, article, B8500–2.508

Manufacturing industry trends including employment, earnings, establishments, and GSP, by State and region, 1970s-92, R8490–48

Manufacturing job trends, for 20 States with greatest proportion of manufacturing employment, May 1991-May 1993, C8900–1.523

Military base proposed closures effect on total employment, by State, 1993, article, B8500–2.513

Nonfarm employment, by State, quarterly rpt, U5085–1

Nonprofit organizations employment, with comparison to population, by State, 1990, article, C2176–1.505

Planning profession employment and salaries, by type of employer, demographic and professional characteristics, and location, 1991 and trends, biennial rpt, A2615–1

Southwestern States employment trends, by industry div, for 6 States, Mar and July 1992-93, S5624–2.510

Southwestern States employment trends, by industry div, for 6 States, Mar 1992-93, S5624–2.507

Southwestern States employment trends, for 6 States, June 1991-93, S5624–2.509

State social, economic, and govtl indicators, with rankings, 1993 semiannual rpt, B8500–1.2, B8500–1.14

Statistical profiles of 50 States and DC, general data, 1993 annual almanac, C4712–1

Unemployment insurance coverage under State and Federal programs, unemployment rates, and benefit exhaustions, with data by State, 1992-93 and trends, R3834–18

Unemployment insurance covered unemployment rates by State, and 10 States with highest and/or lowest covered employment and average wages, various years 1948-90, R9260–18

Index by Categories

BY STATE

Unemployment rates by State, 1991, annual rpt, S7155–3.2

Unemployment rates by State, 1991-92, annual article, S5425–1.503

Unemployment rates for Florida and 10 other populous States, monthly rpt, S1765–3

Unemployment rates in 10 largest States, Sept 1993, with change from Mar 1991, article, C5800–7.552

Western States employment and unemployment, 7 States, monthly rpt, S1040–4

Western States employment, for approx 15 States, 1990s, annual rpt, B3520–1

Law Enforcement

Bar exam results and admissions, by State and territory, 1992 and trends, annual rpt, A7458–1

Child abuse/neglect cases reported by type, and fatalities, by State, 1992 and trends, annual rpt, A7456–1

Correctional inmates and expenditures, by State, 1993-94 biennial rpt, S8780–1.2

Correctional instn admin, inmates, facilities, costs, parole and probation, and staffing, for local, State, and Federal systems, 1992 annual series, R4300–1

Correctional instns, inmates, staff, and cost of care, by instn, US and Canada, with operating summary by State or Province, 1992, annual directory, A1305–3

Corrections funding trends, incarceration rates, and prisoners sentenced to 1 year/more, by State, 1993 article, B8500–2.520

Court caseloads and dispositions, for State appellate and trial courts by case type and State, 1991 and trends, annual rpt, R6600–1

Crime Index offense rate rankings, by State, 1991, annual rpt, S6060–1

Crime Index offenses and rates, by State, 1991, annual rpt, S5955–1.2

Crime Index rates for total, violent, and property crime, by State, 1991, annual rpt, S2035–1

Crime rates for property, robbery, burglary, and vehicle theft offenses, by State, 1993 article, C1050–1.511

Criminal justice system expenditures and employment, by State, 1988, recurring rpt, U5680–2.10

Drunk driving laws and deterrents, by State, 1993 annual rpt, A5650–1

Higher education on-campus crime incidence and arrests by selected offense, by instn and State, 1991/92, C2175–1.506

Jails and adult detention facilities, inmates, staff, and operating summary, by State and instn, Dec 1992, recurring directory, A1305–1

Judicial system salaries for judges and court administrators, by State and territory, and for Federal system, July 1993, semiannual rpt, R6600–2

Juvenile State instn custody prevalence rates by sex, age, and race-ethnicity, for 16 States, 1991, A7575–1.13

Law school enrollment by minority status, degrees conferred, staff, and library holdings, by instn, 1992/93 and trends, annual rpt, A0970–1

Law school grad employment and salaries, by type of employer, location, and grad characteristics, 1992 and trends, annual rpt, A6505–1

Motor vehicle thefts, by State, 1990-91, annual rpt, A0865–1.2

Personal injury jury verdict awards exceeding $1 million, by State, 1987-92, annual rpt, C5180–1

Prison work program inmate participation rates, for top 4-6 States, FY92 annual rpt, S7810–1

Prisoners on death row by sex and race-ethnicity, and executions, by State, 1992 and trends, annual rpt, A1305–3

Property crime incidence, by offense and State, 1991, annual rpt, A5650–1.4

Seat belt use laws by State, including effective date and provisions, 1993 annual rpt, A5650–1

Small claims vs total civil filings in general and limited jurisdiction courts, with small claims limits, by State, 1990, R6600–5

State social, economic, and govtl indicators, with rankings, 1993 semiannual rpt, B8500–1.10

Statistical profiles of 50 States and DC, general data, 1993 annual almanac, C4712–1

Tort reform legislation enacted, by State, 1986-92, annual rpt, A5650–1.3

Western States corrections data, including prisoners and capacity, and related data on population and crime, for 13 States, 1980s-90, A4375–13

State and local:

Kansas parole and probation interstate compact cases, by sending and receiving State, June 1992, annual rpt, S2940–1

Wyoming penitentiary inmate admissions, by State of residence, FY92, annual rpt, S8883–1

Natural Resources, Environment and Pollution

Auto battery recycling legislation provisions, by State, June 1992, article, C0125 1.502

Northeastern States plastic recycling program collection methods, and manufacturers of plastic products, for 10 States, 1992 rpt, A4375–14

Planning status and activities for water resources, with data on water systems by type, withdrawals, and supply shortages, and detail by State, 1991 rpt, A8195–11

State social, economic, and govtl indicators, with rankings, 1993 semiannual rpt, B8500–1.12, B8500–1.15

Statistical profiles of 50 States and DC, general data, 1993 annual almanac, C4712–1

Tree farms and acreage, US and 16 States, 1991-92, annual rpt, U6660–1.10

Utility regulatory agency policies and practices, and industry financial and operating data, by utility type and agency, 1991/92 annual rpt, A7015–3

Water residential average costs, for US and 13 States, 1990/91, article, B8500–2.505

Population

Black American population and demographic characteristics, with comparisons to whites, 1970s-2080, annual compilation, C6775–2.1

Catholic population, clergy, and instns, by diocese and State, 1992, annual almanac, C6885–1

Catholic population, clergy, and instns, by diocese and State, 1993 annual compilation, C4950–1

Child and maternal health and welfare indicators, by State, FY90 or 1990, annual rpt, R3840–11.2

Child health and well-being indicators, with selected household characteristics, by State, 1993 annual rpt, R3832–1

Children under age 15 share of population, for 10 States with highest and lowest shares, 1940 and 1990, B6045–1.501

Churches and membership, by denomination, census div, State, and county, 1990, R4985–1

Consumer buying power survey of population, income, and sales by kind of business, by census div, State, MSA, county, and city, 1992, annual rpt, C1200–1.511

Consumer buying power survey of population, income, and sales by product line, by State, metro area, county, and census div, 1993 annual rpt, C1200–1.514

Drinking age population, by State, 1991-92, annual rpt, C4775–1.3, C4775–2.2

Foreign-born shares of population age 17/under, for top 10 States and DC, 1990, article, R8750–1.509

Hispanic American households with income over $35,000, by income group and leading State, 1989, article, C4575–1.501

Hispanic American population and demographic characteristics, with comparisons to whites, 1993 annual compilation, C6775–3.1

Hispanic American population in top 15 States, 1980, annual rpt, U6250–1.5

Immigrants by intended State of residence, and Hispanic origin population by State, 1992 annual rpt, U6250–1.14

Jewish population by world area, country, and US census div, State, and city, 1990-92, annual compilation, A2050–1

Markets with daily newspapers, demographic and economic info by geographic area, US and Canada, 1993 annual rpt, C3250–1

Older population characteristics, for persons age 65/over and 85/over, by census div and State, 1990 and trends, article, B6045–1.502

Population and households, by State, selected years 1960-91, annual rpt, R9050–1.2

Population by age group, by census div and State, Apr 1990, article, B6045–1.501

Population by State and region, 1980 and 1992, annual rpt, R8490–11

Population characteristics and higher education data, by State, 1993 annual rpt, C2175–1.531

Population in areas "dry" for beer, by State, 1982-91, annual rpt, A3455–1.6

Population size and annual change, by State, 1992, article, B8500–2.508

Population size and selected characteristics, by region, census div, and State, 1991 and trends, annual data sheet, R8750–9

Puerto Rican immigrants with college education, percent living in 4 leading US States, 1982-88, article, C4575–1.506

Refugee arrivals, by State, 1992 annual feature, R9372–2.503

Social indicators and quality of life, Southern and selected other States, 1992 annual rpt, U6660–1.25

Southern States population, personal income, and State/local revenues and expenditures, by State, 1950s-2010, biennial fact book, A8945–1.1

BY STATE

Index by Categories

Spanish-language speakers and English-speaking ability, for 11 States, 1990, article, C4575–1.508

State migration patterns, with native population share by State, and residence changes in past 5 years including between selected States, 1990, article, B8500–2.512

State social, economic, and govtl indicators, with rankings, 1993 semiannual rpt, B8500–1.1

Statistical profiles of 50 States and DC, general data, 1993 annual almanac, C4712–1

Western States population and land area in urban and rural areas, for 12 States, 1990, article, U0280–1.502

Western States population, for approx 15 States, 1991-94, annual rpt, B3520–1

State and local:

Alaska in- and out-migration, by selected State, 1980-90, annual rpt, S0320–4

Maryland in- and out-migration, by State, 1989/90, biennial rpt, S3605–1.1

Prices and Cost of Living

Foreign student living expenses, by State, 1992/93, annual rpt, R5580–1

Household average expenditures for retail goods, rankings by State, 1990, biennial rpt, S3605–1.6

Newspaper prices per copy for daily editions, by State, 1992, annual article, A8605–1.507

Public Welfare and Social Security

AFDC cost-of-living increase changes, by selected State, FY94, semiannual rpt, A7955–1

AFDC legal standards and maximum payments, by State, Jan 1992, annual rpt, S2623–1.2

AFDC recipients, by State, Sept 1991, annual rpt, R9380–1.9

Benefits (maximum) paid for AFDC, general assistance, and SSI, by State, with population shares receiving AFDC and food stamps in selected States, 1993 article, B8500–2.515

Catholic charity social service agency services and population served, by region and State, 1991, annual rpt, A3810–1

Charity gambling gross receipts and net proceeds to charity, by State, 1992, article, C2176–1.520

Charity gambling receipts, net proceeds, and State regulatory staff and finances, by State, various years FY90-92, article, C2176–1.512

Disability benefit programs of Social Security Admin, initial claims processing times and number pending, by State, FY88-93, R4865–11

Foundation assets, income, and grants by type of recipient, with data for top organizations and by location, 1991 and trends, annual rpt, R4900–1

Foundations and grants, by State and territory, 1991, annual article, C2176–1.504

Foundations, assets, gifts received, expenditures, and grants, by State and census div, 1991 and trends, annual article, C2176–1.516

Medicaid actual vs budgeted change in spending, by State, FY92, article, B8500–2.507

Medicaid child and total recipients, expenditures, and other program characteristics, and child health summary, by State, FY91, annual rpt, A0565–1

Medicaid expenditures compared to general spending, by State, FY88 and FY91, annual rpt, S7560–1

Medicaid Federal grants as a percent of total costs, by State, FY93, B8500–2.514

Medicaid home health care payments per recipient, for 16 highest and 17 lowest States, FY91, article, B8500–2.511

Medicaid pregnancy services expansion efforts, including eligibility, outreach activities, and obstetrician reimbursement, by State, 1993 article, A5160–1.506

Medicaid recipients as percent of population in poverty, by State, FY90, article, B8500–2.501

Medicare and Medicaid recipients and benefits paid, by State, 1991, annual rpt, A5173–2.2

Medicare participation rates among physicians, and Federal and State Medicaid payments, by State, 1993 annual fact book, A1275–1.5

Payments and contributions for selected social insurance programs, by State, 1940s-92, annual rpt, R9050–1.1

Public assistance Medicaid recipients by eligibility basis, and AFDC benefits, for 10-14 States, 1992 rpt, U8850–8.5

Public assistance program State funding and tax changes, by State, with analysis of impact on the poor, FY92-93, annual rpt, R3834–9

Refugee assistance Federal outlays under State Legalization Impact Assistance Grants program, with shares for 7 States, 1992, article, A1865–1.523

Social Security beneficiaries and payments, by State, 1989, annual rpt, U8130–2.10

Social Security retirement income per capita, and payment trends, by State, FY92, article, B8500–2.516

State social, economic, and govtl indicators, with rankings, 1993 semiannual rpt, B8500–1.8, B8500–1.9

Statistical profiles of 50 States and DC, general data, 1993 annual almanac, C4712–1

Transfer payments by State and region, 1990-91, biennial rpt, S3605–1.6

United Way local organization fundraising trends, by State and region, 1991-92, article, C2176–1.515

Welfare expenditures, by State, FY91, biennial rpt, S8780–1.2

Welfare program payments and/or error rates, for AFDC and Medicaid, by State, FY92 annual rpt, S2623–1

Recreation and Leisure

Boat ownership, registrations, and sales, by boat type and/or State, including data for related equipment, 1992 annual rpt, A8055–1

Boating (recreational) industry trends, including sales, foreign trade, and registrations by geographic area, 1980s-92, annual feature, C2425–4

Bowling (women's) assn membership and league activities, by city, State, and country, 1991/92, annual rpt, A9415–1

Bowling assn finances and membership, and bowling establishments and lanes, by State and other area, 1991/92 and trends, annual rpt, A1015–1

Fishing and hunting license revenues and holders, top 20 States, FY89, recurring rpt, R9375–6

Pari-mutuel wagering activity, attendance, purse distribution, and govt revenue, by State and Canadian Province, 1990 and trends, annual rpt, A3363–1

Parks and forests (national) visitors, for top 20 States, 1992 recurring rpt, R9375–6

Participation in 53 sports, by demographic characteristics, State, and census div, 1992, annual rpt series, A8485–3

State social, economic, and govtl indicators, with rankings, 1993 semiannual rpt, B8500–1.12

Science and Technology

Astronomy enrollment and degrees awarded, by level, State, and instn, 1991/92-1992/93, annual rpt, A1960–2.3

Engineering degrees awarded, by State, instn, and field, with detail for women, minorities, and foreign students, 1991/92, annual rpt, A0685–1

Engineering program enrollment, by instn, field, and State, with detail for women, minorities, and foreign students, fall 1992, annual rpt, A0685–2

Hispanic-owned high-technology company hq locations, for top 50 firms, 1993 annual article, C4575–1.510

Physics enrollment and degrees awarded, by level, State, and instn, 1991/92-1992/93, annual rpt, A1960–2.2

Science and math elementary/secondary education, including student and teacher characteristics, and requirements, by State, 1991/92, biennial rpt, A4355–3

Science courses in high school, percent of students taking biology, chemistry, and physics, by State, 1991/92, article, A1250–1.534

State social, economic, and govtl indicators, with rankings, 1993 semiannual rpt, B8500–1.13

Technology transfer info requests received by Federal toll-free telephone service, by State, Oct 1992-Aug 1993, C5800–4.533

Transportation and Travel

Aircraft facilities by type including heliports, by State, 1991, annual rpt, A0250–2.3

Airports and communities in North America served by regional vs larger airlines, by carrier and location, 1993 annual rpt, A8795–1.2

Auto insurance passenger and commercial premiums, market shares, and loss ratios, with rankings of States and 20 leading firms, 1992, annual article, C1050–1.511

Auto insurance premiums written, and autos insured through shared market plans, by State, 1993 annual rpt, A5650–1

Aviation (general) aircraft active, landing facilities, pilots, and operating data, by FAA region and State, 1993 annual rpt, A5120–2

Drivers licensed, by sex, State, and Canadian Province, 1993 annual fact book, C4680–1.507

Federal transit funding received per dollar contributed to Mass Transit Account, by State, 1991, C1575–3.507

Helipads/helistops by State, 1993 annual rpt, A5190–1

Hwy and bridge construction contracting plans, by State, 1993, annual feature, C5800–2.512

Index by Categories

Hwy construction cost and bid price trends, by State, weekly rpt quarterly feature, C5800–2.508, C5800–2.521, C5800–2.534, C5800–2.547

Interstate migration patterns indicated by household goods shipments, by State, 1992, annual press release, B0210–1, B9300–1

Mass transit funding from State and/or Federal govts, by State and territory, FY91, annual fact book, C1575–3.501

Mass transit service providers by State, 1992 annual rpt, A2650–1.1

Motor vehicle dealership financial and operating data, including sales and employment by State, 1970s-93, annual rpt, A7330–1

Motor vehicle fleets and vehicles, and State auto insurance, registration, and tax requirements, by State, 1993 annual rpt, C1575–2.507

Motor vehicle industry detailed production, sales, trade, and vehicle use and ownership data, by vehicle type, State, and country, 1900s-92, annual rpt, A0865–1

Motor vehicle odometer tampering prevalence by State, 1st half 1991, article, C1575–2.504

Motor vehicle production, and registrations by manufacturer, by State, 1993 annual data book, C2710–3.531

Motor vehicle production by State, 1993 model year, annual article, C2710–3.551

Motor vehicle registrations by vehicle type, by State and Canadian Province, 1993 annual fact book, C4680–1.507

Motorcycle market devs, including production, sales, imports, dealer operations, and owner characteristics, 1991 and trends, annual rpt, A6485–1

Motorcycle operator licensing procedures, operators, and vehicle registrations, by State, 1993 annual rpt, A6490–1

Motorcycle registrations, accidents, and fatalities, by State, 1991, annual rpt, A6490–2

North Central States airport operations and air traffic control activities, for 8 States, 1989, annual rpt, U6910–2

Railroad employment and track mileage, by State, 1992, annual rpt, A3275–5

Railroad operating data, including top commodities handled, employment and wages, and retirement system, by State, 1991, annual rpt, A3275–10

Railroads, employment, and track mileage, by State, 1991 and trends, annual rpt, A3275–8

Regulatory agency policies and practices for motor carriers and railroads, by agency, 1991/92 annual rpt, A7015–4

Road/bridge special project Federal funding, for 25 States, FY92, annual rpt, C2500–2

School bus loading/unloading accident fatalities, by circumstances, location, and victim age and sex, 1991 and trends, annual rpt, S3040–2

State social, economic, and govtl indicators, with rankings, 1993 semiannual rpt, B8500–1.11

Statistical profiles of 50 States and DC, general data, 1993 annual almanac, C4712–1

Tourism dev offices of State govts, activities, personnel, and budgets, by State, 1992 survey, annual rpt, R9375–2

BY URBAN-RURAL AND METRO-NONMETRO

Traffic accident deaths, school bus accidents, and legislation status of selected laws, by State, 1992 and trends, annual rpt, A8375–2.3

Traffic accident fatalities and rates, by State, 1990-91, annual rpt, A0865–1.3

Traffic safety devs, with accident statistics by State, bimonthly rpt, A8375–1

Travel and tourism rankings for selected indicators, including data for top 20 States, cities, countries, businesses, and other measures, 1992 recurring rpt, R9375–6

Travel and tourism trends in US and worldwide, with traveler and trip characteristics, and data by local area, 1992 annual rpt, C2140–1

Travel impact on State economies, with detail by industry sector, 1990 and trends, annual rpt, R9375–7

Truck (light) market shares for top 10 States, 1993 article, C2150–3.510

State and local:

Arizona traffic accidents, by residence of driver, 1991, annual rpt, S0530–1

Florida registrations of out-of-State vehicles, by State of previous registration, 1987-91, annual rpt, U6660–1.13

Florida tourist arrivals, by mode and State of origin, 1991, annual rpt, U6660–1.19

Montana traffic accidents, by place of vehicle registration, 1992, annual rpt, S4705–2

Nevada traffic accidents, by neighboring State of driver residence, 1992, annual rpt, S5140–1

Oklahoma commuting patterns, including interstate and international travel, and detailed data by county, 1990 and trends, S6416–2

South Carolina traffic accidents, by home State of driver, 1992, annual rpt, S7190–2

Wyoming traffic accidents, by driver licensing State, 1992, annual rpt, S9007–1

BY URBAN-RURAL AND METRO-NONMETRO

Agriculture and Food

Convenience store investment for new urban vs rural outlets, 1992 and trends, annual survey rpt, A6735–1, A6735–2

Convenience store investment per new outlet, by object, urban vs rural, 1988-92, annual fact book, C4680–1.507

Distilled spirits consumption, and consumer characteristics and buying habits, 1992 and trends, annual rpt, C4775–1.3

Food service industry sales, market shares, establishments, and business activity indicators, by location, 1992, annual feature, C1200–5.515

Restaurant (table service) operations and menu offerings, and related consumer views and practices by demographic characteristics, 1992, recurring rpt, A8200–11

Restaurant industry financial and operating data, by establishment characteristics and location, 1992, annual rpt, A8200–3

Restaurant smoking policy importance to consumers, and views on smoking acceptability in restaurants and other public places, by selected characteristics, Jan 1993 survey, A8200–8.15

Wine and other alcoholic beverage consumption, and consumer characteristics and buying habits, 1993 annual rpt, C4775–2.2

State and local:

Illinois statistical abstract, general data, 1992 annual rpt, U6910–2

Banking, Finance, and Insurance

Bank noncurrent loans/leases, and losses, by type of loan, asset size, and metro status, 1992, semiannual rpt, A6400–4

Public opinion on business use of personal info, and consumer examination of own credit rpt by selected characteristics, 1992 survey, annual rpt, B3280–2

State and local:

Illinois statistical abstract, general data, 1992 annual rpt, U6910–2

Oklahoma banks and bank holding companies by asset size, and asset concentration by location and among top instns, 1984-90, article, U8130–1.502

Education

Catholic schools, by urban-rural location, 1981/82 and 1992/93, annual rpt, A7375–1

Elementary/secondary new teacher views on teaching and quality of schools, after 2nd year of teaching, spring 1992 survey, B6045–2

Elementary/secondary prospective teacher characteristics and opinions, survey of persons interested in alternative certification routes, 1992, R6350–7

Elementary/secondary teacher views on education policy issues and selected reform proposals, with data by school location type, Jan-Feb 1993 survey, B6045–7

Latin America statistical abstract, general data by country, 1992 annual rpt, U6250–1.8

School bus fleet director salaries, and experience of weapons-related problems, by location type, July 1993 survey, annual article, C1575–1.507

School bus transportation share of district budgets, by district location type, 1993 annual feature, C1575–1.502

Teacher abuse from students, prevalence by type of school location, 1991, R4800–2.513

Urban public school performance compared to natl goals for year 2000, with selected comparisons to other location types and total US, 1990/91 and trends, A4425–4

State and local:

Colorado public school enrollment, finances, and student and staff characteristics, by locality, 1992 annual rpt series, S1000–2

Iowa library urban and rural population served, by county, FY92, annual rpt, S2778–1

Massachusetts elementary/secondary school districts and enrollment, by type of community, Oct 1991, annual rpt, S3810–3

Tennessee statistical abstract, general data, 1992/93 annual rpt, U8710–2

Geography and Climate

Western States population and land area in urban and rural areas, for 12 States, 1990, article, U0280–1.502

State and local:

Georgia statistical abstract, general data, 1992-93 biennial rpt, U6730–1

Hawaii data book, general data, 1992 annual rpt, S2090–1

BY URBAN-RURAL AND METRO-NONMETRO

Index by Categories

Government and Defense

City fiscal condition, including budget trends and adjustments, and influencing factors, by region and population size, Mar-Apr 1993 survey, annual rpt, A8012–1.23

County manager salaries, by sex, county size, census div, and metro status, July 1992, annual rpt, A5800–1.3

House of Representatives district offices, by district type, 1992 recurring rpt, R4140–1

Municipal and county govt structure, public services, finances, and intergovtl relations, 1993 annual rpt, A5800–1

State and local:

Idaho property tax urban and rural rates, by county, 1992, annual rpt, S2295–1

Iowa retail sales/use tax by population size group, FY91, annual supplement, S2860–1.501

Iowa retail sales/use tax by population size group, FY92, annual supplement, S2860–1.502

Kansas economic dev planning in urban and rural counties, 1993 article, U7095–1.502

Health and Vital Statistics

AIDS cases in metro and nonmetro areas, 1992 annual rpt, A5173–2.4

China women's fertility patterns correlated with socioeconomic characteristics, in 6 Provinces, 1987, article, A5160–6.502

Contraceptive (oral) use errors among women in Botswana, Egypt, Zimbabwe, and Indonesia, by demographic characteristics, 1987-89 surveys, article, A5160–6.504

Depression incidence among blacks and whites by selected demographic characteristics, 1984 survey, article, A2623–1.504

Developing countries contraceptive failure rates, by user urban-rural residence and education, for 15 countries, 1986-89 surveys, article, A5160–6.504

Developing countries family planning and child survival efforts, by country and selected demographic characteristics, 1980s-90, R8720–1

Developing countries fertility, family planning, sexual behavior, and child health indicators, with selected detail by demographic characteristics, 1984-92 surveys, U2520–1.51

Disabled persons use of home care services, with costs, payment sources, and types of care, by selected characteristics, 1992, R4865–15

Elderly population receiving selected medical procedures and diagnostic tests, by race and urban-rural residence, 1986, article, A2623–1.509

Health care specialist and health-related company CEO income, public perceptions vs actual amounts, by respondent characteristics, 1991-93, R4865–13

Health insurance coverage and finances, and health care costs and facilities, by selected demographic characteristics, 1940s-91, annual rpt, A5173–2

Home health care agency use by Medicare patients, by type of service and urban-rural residence, 1987, article, A2623–1.505

Hospital admissions, bed-size group and urban-rural location, 1981 and 1991, article, A1865–1.514

Hospital emergency dept use, by location and patient insurance coverage status, 1990 and trends, A1865–1.508

Hospital industry financial and operating indicators, with detail for Medicare, by instn characteristics and location, 1988-92, annual rpt, B1880–1

Hospital worker shortage trends reported by urban and rural facilities, 1991 survey, article, A1865–1.501

Hospitals by urban-rural location, 1991, B4455–4, B4455–5

Hospitals by urban-rural location, 1991, annual rpt, B4455–1

Hospitals by urban-rural location, 1991, annual rpt series, B4455–3

Hospitals with and without psychiatric units, by urban-rural location, 1991, annual rpt series, B4455–2

Human immunodeficiency virus (HIV) testing and posttest counseling rates, by demographic characteristics, 1989, article, A2623–1.501

Latin America statistical abstract, general data by country, 1992 annual rpt, U6250–1.6, U6250–1.12

Nursing higher education program clinics/centers operated by urban-rural location, FY92, biennial rpt, A0615–5

Nursing home resident mental health care use, by resident and home characteristics, and provider type, 1985/86 survey, article, A2623–1.505

Older population health condition indicators and insurance coverage, by urban-rural status, 1993 article, A1865–1.522

Osteopathy students career plans, including population size of hometown and intended location of practice, 1991/92, annual survey rpt, A0620–2

Physician practice economic aspects, detailed data by specialty, 1991-92 and trends, annual compilation, A2200–5

Physician rural vs nonrural area background and practice plans, with data by sex, 1993 article, A3273–8.505

Physicians by detailed specialty, location, age, sex, and board certification status, 1992 and trends, annual rpt, A2200–3.1

Physicians in total and nonmetro areas, by professional activity, 1970, 1980, and 1990, annual fact book, A1275–1.1

Smoking acceptability in restaurants and other public places, and importance of restaurant smoking policy, views of consumers by selected characteristics, Jan 1993 survey, A8200–8.15

Women's sexual behavior and disease risk, including data on multiple partners and condom use, by selected characteristics, 1988, article, A5160–1.501

Women's use of mammography and Pap smear tests, by demographic characteristics, 1987 survey, article, A2623–1.503

World population and health indicators, with detail by region and country, 1992/93 biennial rpt, R9455–1.5

State and local:

Alabama births by urban-rural residence, race, and age of mother, 1992, annual rpt, S0175–2

Colorado vital statistics, including population, births, deaths by cause, abortion, marriage and divorce, and adoption, by demographic characteristics and location, 1990 and trends, annual rpt, S1010–1

Georgia vital statistics, including population, births, abortions, deaths by cause,

marriages, and divorces, by demographic characteristics and location, 1991 and trends, annual rpt, S1895–1

New Mexico vital statistics, including population, births, deaths, and disease, by location and demographic characteristics, 1991 and trends, annual rpt, S5605–1

Texas births and deaths in rural areas and selected cities, by county, 1991, annual rpt, S7685–1

Texas hospitals, operations, utilization, and finances, by type, ownership, size, and metro-nonmetro status, 1970s-91, U8850–8.3

Texas nursing employment, demand outlook, earnings, and education, by selected characteristics, various years 1971-91, U8850–8.2

Utah vital statistics, including births by characteristics of mother and child, by location, 1990 and trends, annual rpt, S7835–1.1

Washington State hospital cesarean section delivery rates correlated with hospital and patient characteristics, 1987, article, A2623–1.510

Housing and Construction

State and local:

Arizona statistical abstract, general data, 1993 recurring rpt, U5850–2

Arkansas Census of Population and Housing detailed findings, 1990, U5935–7

California Census of Population and Housing detailed findings, 1990, S0840–9

Georgia statistical abstract, general data, 1992-93 biennial rpt, U6730–1

Illinois statistical abstract, general data, 1992 annual rpt, U6910–2

New Jersey Census of Population and Housing detailed findings, by county, 1990, S5425–19

New York State statistical yearbook, general data, 1992 annual rpt, U5100–1

Pennsylvania Census of Population and Housing detailed findings, with selected data by county and municipality, 1990, U4130–13

Pennsylvania housing data from Census of Population and Housing, by county and municipality, 1990, C1595–14

Income

Black American earnings, income, and poverty data, with comparisons to whites, 1980s-91, annual compilation, C6775–2.7

Black American socioeconomic status, with comparisons to whites and data by region, 1960s-92, annual compilation, A8510–1.1

Consumer buying power survey of population, income, and sales by product line, by State, metro area, county, and census div, 1993 annual rpt, C1200–1.514

Hispanic American income and poverty data, with comparisons to whites, 1980s-91, annual compilation, C6775–3.5

Latin America statistical abstract, general data by country, 1992 annual rpt, U6250–1.12

Poor children age 5/under, with demographic and family characteristics, 1991 and trends, annual rpt, U1260–2

Poverty shares by race-ethnicity, for rural vs urban areas, 1991, R3834–15

State and local:

Florida statistical abstract, general data, 1992 annual rpt, U6660–1

Index by Categories

BY URBAN-RURAL AND METRO-NONMETRO

Georgia personal income and employment, by MSA, county, and metro-nonmetro status, 1990-91, article, U6730–2.505

Georgia statistical abstract, general data, 1992-93 biennial rpt, U6730–1

Illinois statistical abstract, general data, 1992 annual rpt, U6910–2

Indiana per capita personal income, by MSA and for metro vs nonmetro areas, 1991, U2160–1.504

Mississippi statistical abstract, general data, 1992 annual rpt, U3255–4

Nebraska transfer payments, by component and State area, with comparisons to total personal income, 1990-91 and trends, article, U7860–1.504

Pennsylvania metro-nonmetro lower-living-standard income level, by family size, FY92 annual planning rpt, S6845–3.3

Virginia income distribution and income tax returns filed, by locality, 1990, annual rpt, U9080–1

Virginia total and per capita personal income, by local area and major source, 1980-90, annual rpt, U9080–7

West Virginia per capita personal income, by metro-nonmetro status, 1989-90, annual planning rpt, S8534–2

Industry and Commerce

Business incubator facilities in urban, suburban, and rural locations, 1991, annual rpt, A7360–1

Canada photographic and video equipment and supplies ownership, purchasing patterns, and use, by household characteristics, 1992 survey, recurring rpt, A8695–4

Consumer buying power survey of population, income, and sales by product line, by State, metro area, county, and census div, 1993 annual rpt, C1200–1.514

Drugstore (independent pharmacy) financial and operating data, by store characteristics, 1991 and trends, annual survey, B5165–1

Hardware finances and operations, for hardware stores, home centers, and lumber/building material outlets, by trade area size, 1991, annual rpt series, A8275–1

Midwest business and economic conditions in metro and nonurban areas, by sector and State, bankers opinions, spring 1993 survey, semiannual rpt, B6785–1

Photographic equipment and supplies, consumer ownership, purchasing patterns, and use, 1993 survey and trends, recurring rpt, A8695–2

State and local:

Georgia exporting business establishments, by hq metro-nonmetro location, 1993 article, U6730–2.502

Georgia taxable sales, by kind of business and location, 1991-92, annual article, U6730–2.503

Illinois retail sales, by business and location type, 1991-92, article, U6910–1.501

Illinois retail sales trends, by location type and MSA, 3rd qtr 1991-92, article, U6910–1.502

Illinois statistical abstract, general data, 1992 annual rpt, U6910–2

Kansas retail sales and tax activity trends, by urban-rural area and county, 1980-91, article, U7095–1.502

Virginia taxable sales, by kind of business and locality, 1991 and trends, annual rpt, U9080–8

Labor and Employment

Planning profession employment and salaries, by type of employer, demographic and professional characteristics, and location, 1991 and trends, biennial rpt, A2615–1

State and local:

Arizona employment and unemployment, by county and industry, with production worker hours and earnings, monthly rpt, S0465–1

Georgia personal income and employment, by MSA, county, and metro-nonmetro status, 1990-91, article, U6730–2.505

Illinois statistical abstract, general data, 1992 annual rpt, U6910–2

Kansas service industries employment growth compared to population growth, for metro and nonmetro areas, 1980-90, article, U7095–1.502

Mississippi statistical abstract, general data, 1992 annual rpt, U3255–4

Wisconsin employment forecast for selected metro vs total nonmetro areas, monthly rpt quarterly table, S8750–1.504

Law Enforcement

Crime victims per 1,000 population, by demographic characteristics, 1991, article, R8750–1.505

State and local:

Alabama statistical abstract, general data, 1992 recurring rpt, U5680–2

Hawaii crimes and arrests, by offense, with data by county and victim-offender characteristics, 1992, annual rpt, S2035–1

Illinois crimes and arrests, by offense, with data by location and offender characteristics, 1991, annual rpt, S2536–1

Maine crimes reported, by offense and urban-rural status, 1991, annual rpt, S3475–1.2

Michigan crimes and arrests, by offense, with data by location and offender characteristics, 1992 and trends, annual rpt, S3997–1

Missouri crimes and arrests, by offense and location, with victim and offender characteristics, 1991 and trends, annual rpt, S4560–2

New Jersey crimes, population and land area, and law enforcement personnel by sex, by county and municipality, 1992 and trends, annual rpt, S5430–1.3

New York State correctional instn inmates released, by criminal background, sentence, and demographic characteristics, 1991 and trends, recurring rpt series, S5725–1

North Carolina crimes by offense, and law enforcement employment, by local agency, 1991-92, annual rpt, S5955–1.1

North Dakota crimes and arrests, by offense, location, and offender characteristics, and law enforcement employment, 1991 and trends, annual rpt, S6060–1

Pennsylvania crimes and arrests, by offense, with data by location and offender characteristics, 1992 and trends, annual rpt, S6860–1

Virginia court caseloads, processing, and dispositions, by type of court and case, with judicial dept personnel and finances, by location, 1992 and trends, annual rpt, S8300–1

West Virginia crimes and arrests by offense, and assaults on police officers, for rural and municipal agencies, 1990-91, annual rpt, S8610–1

Wisconsin crimes and arrests, by offense, offender characteristics, county, and local agency, 1992 and trends, annual rpt, S8771–1

Natural Resources, Environment and Pollution

Developing countries population access to safe drinking water and sanitation services, by urban-rural status and country, 1988-90, R8720–1.2

Latin America statistical abstract, general data by country, 1992 annual rpt, U6250–1.6, U6250–1.7

Water and sanitation facilities access of world population, by urban-rural status and country, 1992/93 biennial rpt, R9455–1.5

Population

Black American population and demographic characteristics, with comparisons to whites, 1970s-2080, annual compilation, C6775–2.1

Black children and youth population, economic, health, and education data, with comparisons to whites, 1993 rpt, R3840–21

Churches and/or membership, by metro size class and in nonmetro areas, by denomination, 1990, R4985–1

Commonwealth of Independent States region population by sex, urban vs rural status, Republic, and selected city, 1986, R4105–82.4

Consumer buying power survey of population, income, and sales by product line, by State, metro area, county, and census div, 1993 annual rpt, C1200–1.514

Gallup Poll public attitude surveys, results and sample characteristics, monthly rpt, C4040–1

Hispanic American population and demographic characteristics, with comparisons to whites, 1993 annual compilation, C6775–3.1

Older population growth rate compared to population age 64/under, by region and metro status, decennially 1960-90, article, R8750–1.506

Population distribution and selected characteristics by location type, with detail by race, 1991, article, A8510–1.1

Religious congregation characteristics, including membership, activities, staff, and finances, 1992 survey, recurring rpt, A5435–4

Statistical profiles of 50 States and DC, general data, 1993 annual almanac, C4712–1

Western States population and land area in urban and rural areas, for 12 States, 1990, article, U0280–1.502

Women's housing issues, with data on household composition, tenure, and characteristics, 1992, A8657–5

World population and health indicators, with detail by region and country, 1992/93 biennial rpt, R9455–1.5

State and local:

Alabama county data book, general data, 1992 annual rpt, S0121–2

Alabama statistical abstract, general data, 1992 recurring rpt, U5680–2

BY URBAN-RURAL AND METRO-NONMETRO

Index by Categories

Alaska population, housing, income, and education data, by demographic characteristics and/or locality, 1990/91 and trends, annual rpt, S0320–4

Arizona population trends and projections, and net migration, for 2 urban and total nonurban areas, 1960s-2010, annual article, U0280–1.504

Arizona statistical abstract, general data, 1993 recurring rpt, U5850–2

Arkansas Census of Population and Housing detailed findings, 1990, U5935–7

California Census of Population and Housing detailed findings, 1990, S0840–9

Colorado vital statistics, including population, births, deaths by cause, abortion, marriage and divorce, and adoption, by demographic characteristics and location, 1990 and trends, annual rpt, S1010–1

Florida statistical abstract, general data, 1992 annual rpt, U6660–1

Georgia county guide, general data, 1993 annual rpt, U6750–1

Georgia statistical abstract, general data, 1992-93 biennial rpt, U6730–1

Georgia vital statistics, including population, births, abortions, deaths by cause, marriages, and divorces, by demographic characteristics and location, 1991 and trends, annual rpt, S1895–1

Hawaii data book, general data, 1992 annual rpt, S2090–1

Illinois statistical abstract, general data, 1992 annual rpt, U6910–2

Iowa urban and farm and nonfarm rural population, 1990, annual rpt, S2784–3

Kansas statistical abstract, general data, 1991/92 annual rpt, U7095–2

Kentucky economic statistics, general data, 1993 annual rpt, S3104–1

Louisiana Census of Population and Housing summary findings, by local area, 1990 and trends, U8010–4

Missouri urban vs rural population, decennially 1900-90, annual rpt, S4475–1

Nevada statistical abstract, general data, 1992 biennial rpt, S5005–1

New Jersey Census of Population and Housing detailed findings, by county, 1990, S5425–19

Oklahoma population projections, by age, sex, and locality, with data on fertility and migration, 1990-2020, recurring rpt, S6416–1

Pennsylvania Census of Population and Housing detailed findings, with selected data by county and municipality, 1990, U4130–13

Pennsylvania statistical abstract, general data, 1992 recurring rpt, U4130–6

Rhode Island Census of Population and Housing detailed findings, by county and municipality, 1990, S6930–9

South Carolina population characteristics, by county, 1993 annual rpt, S7145–1.1

South Carolina statistical abstract, general data, 1993 annual rpt, S7125–1

Tennessee population projections by age, sex, and county metro status, 1990-2010, article, U8710–1.501

Tennessee statistical abstract, general data, 1992/93 annual rpt, U8710–2

Utah govt statistical review, fiscal and socioeconomic data, 1993 annual rpt, R9380–1

Utah population by urban-rural status and/or county, 1990 and 1992, annual rpt, S7800–1

Utah statistical abstract, general data, 1993 triennial rpt, U8960–1

Utah vital statistics, including population in urban and rural counties, 1990, annual rpt, S7835–1.1

Virginia population and net migration, by local area, 1990-91, annual rpt, U9080–9

Wisconsin Blue Book, general data, 1993-94 biennial rpt, S8780–1.2

Public Welfare and Social Security

State and local:

Florida statistical abstract, general data, 1992 annual rpt, U6660–1

Illinois statistical abstract, general data, 1992 annual rpt, U6910–2

Minnesota public welfare program recipients and expenditures, for urban and rural counties, 1992, semiannual rpt, S4202–1

Recreation and Leisure

Boating-related activities participation, by market area size, 1991, annual feature, C2425–4

Participation in 53 sports, by demographic characteristics, State, and census div, 1992, annual rpt series, A8485–3

Sporting goods purchaser characteristics, by product category, 1992, annual survey rpt, A8485–4

Science and Technology

Ecologist employment characteristics, including location of employer, Mar 1992 survey, recurring rpt, A4685–1

Transportation and Travel

Motorcycle use and user characteristics, licensed operators, and State requirements, 1992 annual rpt, A6485–1.2

Road mileage and vehicle miles of travel, by urban-rural status, by State, 1993 annual rpt, A0865–1.3

School bus loading/unloading accident fatalities, by circumstances, location, and victim age and sex, 1991 and trends, annual rpt, S3040–2

Statistical profiles of 50 States and DC, general data, 1993 annual almanac, C4712–1

Traffic accidents and fatalities, by urban-rural location, 1991, annual rpt, A5650–1.4

Traffic accidents, fatalities, and injuries, by vehicle type, circumstances, location, and driver and victim characteristics, 1992 and trends, annual rpt, A8375–2.3

Truck equipment distributor financial data, by company type, sales size, and rural vs metro market, FY91 and trends, annual rpt, A8505–4

Vehicle miles traveled on urban streets and rural roads, and fuel consumed, by vehicle type, 1991, annual fact book, C4680–1.507

State and local:

Alaska traffic accidents, fatalities, and injuries, by vehicle type, circumstance, location, and driver and victim characteristics, 1991 and trends, annual rpt, S0360–1

Arizona statistical abstract, general data, 1993 recurring rpt, U5850–2

Arizona traffic accidents, fatalities, and injuries, by vehicle type, circumstances, location, and driver and victim characteristics, 1991 and trends, annual rpt, S0530–1

Arkansas traffic accidents, fatalities, and injuries, by vehicle type, circumstances, location, and driver and victim characteristics, 1991, annual rpt, S0692–1

California statistical abstract, general data, 1992 annual rpt, S0840–2

California traffic accidents, fatalities, and injuries, by vehicle type, circumstances, location, and driver and victim characteristics, 1991 and trends, annual rpt, S0885–1

Florida statistical abstract, general data, 1992 annual rpt, U6660–1

Hawaii data book, general data, 1992 annual rpt, S2090–1

Idaho traffic accidents, fatalities, and injuries, by circumstances, location, vehicle type, and driver and victim characteristics, 1992, annual rpt, S2315–1

Illinois traffic accidents, fatalities, and injuries, by circumstances, location, and driver and victim characteristics, 1991 and trends, annual rpt, S2540–1

Indiana traffic accidents, fatalities, and injuries, by circumstances, location, and vehicle type, and driver and victim characteristics, 1992, annual rpt, S2675–1

Kansas traffic accidents, fatalities, and injuries, by vehicle type, location, circumstances, and driver and victim characteristics, 1992, annual rpt, S3040–1

Kentucky traffic accidents, fatalities, and injuries, by circumstances, location, vehicle type, and driver characteristics, 1992 and trends, annual rpt, S3150–2

Louisiana traffic accidents, fatalities, and injuries, by circumstances, location, and driver characteristics, 1991 and trends, annual rpt, S3345–2

Maine traffic accidents, fatalities, and injuries, by accident circumstances, vehicle type and make, and driver and victim characteristics, 1992, annual rpt, S3475–2

Michigan traffic accidents, fatalities, and injuries, by vehicle type, circumstance, location, and driver and victim characteristics, 1991 and trends, annual rpt, S3997–2

Minnesota traffic accidents, fatalities, and injuries, by type of vehicle and circumstances, and driver and victim characteristics, 1992 and trends, annual rpt, S4230–2

Missouri traffic accidents, fatalities, and injuries, by circumstances, location, and driver and victim characteristics, 1992 and trends, annual rpt, S4560–1

Montana traffic accidents, fatalities, and injuries, by circumstances, location, and driver and victim characteristics, 1992 and trends, annual rpt, S4705–2

Nebraska traffic accidents, fatalities, and injuries, by circumstances, location, vehicle type, and driver and victim characteristics, 1992, annual rpt, S4953–1

Nevada statistical abstract, general data, 1992 biennial rpt, S5005–1

Nevada traffic accidents, fatalities, and injuries, by circumstances, location, and vehicle type, 1992 and trends, annual rpt, S5140–1

New Mexico traffic accidents, fatalities, and injuries, by vehicle type, circumstances, location, and driver and victim characteristics, 1992 and trends, annual rpt, S5665–1

Index by Categories

BY COMMODITY

New York State traffic accidents, fatalities, and injuries, by circumstances, location, vehicle type, and driver and victim characteristics, 1991 and trends, annual rpt, S5790–1

North Carolina traffic accidents, fatalities, and injuries, by circumstances, location, vehicle type, and driver and victim characteristics, 1992 and trends, annual rpt, S5990–1

North Dakota traffic accidents, fatalities, and injuries, by circumstances, location, vehicle type, and driver and victim characteristics, 1992 and trends, annual rpt, S6217–1

Ohio traffic accidents, fatalities, and injuries, by circumstances, location, driver and victim characteristics, and vehicle type, 1991 and trends, annual rpt, S6290–1

Oklahoma traffic accidents, fatalities, and injuries, by circumstances, location, and driver and victim characteristics, 1992 and trends, annual rpt, S6482–1

South Carolina traffic accidents, fatalities, and injuries, by circumstances, location, and driver and victim characteristics, 1992 and trends, annual rpt, S7190–2

South Dakota traffic accidents, fatalities, and injuries, by circumstances, location, vehicle type, and driver and victim characteristics, 1992 and trends, annual rpt, S7300–3

Tennessee statistical abstract, general data, 1992/93 annual rpt, U8710–2

Utah statistical abstract, general data, 1993 triennial rpt, U8960–1

Utah traffic accidents and fatalities by circumstances, location, driver and victim characteristics, and vehicle type, 1992 and trends, annual rpt, S7890–2

Washington State traffic accidents, fatalities, and injuries, by circumstances, vehicle type, and location, with driver and victim characteristics, 1992 and trends, annual rpt, S8428–1

West Virginia traffic accidents, fatalities, and injuries, by circumstance and location, and driver and victim characteristics, 1992, annual rpt, S8645–1

Wisconsin Blue Book, general data, 1993-94 biennial rpt, S8780–1.2

Wisconsin traffic accidents, fatalities, and injuries, by circumstances, location, vehicle type, and driver and victim characteristics, 1992 and trends, annual rpt, S8815–1

Wyoming traffic accidents, fatalities, and injuries, by circumstances, location, vehicle type, and driver and victim characteristics, 1992 and trends, annual rpt, S9007–1

Veterans Affairs

State and local:

Illinois statistical abstract, general data, 1992 annual rpt, U6910–2

ECONOMIC BREAKDOWNS

BY COMMODITY

Agriculture and Food

Aquaculture production and value, with data on FDA-approved drugs available, for selected types of animals, 1991, article, A3100–2.514

Beverage consumption, and market shares, by beverage type, 1981-92, annual article, C0125–2.504

Beverage industry sales, production, consumption, and trade, by company, brand, and product type, 1991 and trends, annual rpt, C0125–3.1

Black American farm characteristics, with comparisons to all farms, 1987, annual compilation, C6775–2.8

Brewers grain and other agricultural products consumption, by commodity, FY64-91, annual rpt, A3455–1.1

Chicago Board of Trade futures and options trading in financial instruments and agricultural commodities, 1992, annual rpt, B2120–1

Commodity Credit Corp losses and price support costs, by commodity, FY91 and trends, annual rpt, R9050–1.3

Convenience store sales, gross margin, and inventory turnover, by product category, 1992 and trends, annual survey rpt, A6735–1, A6735–2

Ethiopia famine analysis, including crop production, food consumption, and cereal price trends in affected areas, 1992 rpt, R5620–1.36

Exports of farm products, by detailed commodity and country of destination, US and California, 1991, annual rpt, B9520–1

Farm prices paid for selected production commodities, 1986-91, annual rpt, S5350–1

Farm prices paid for selected production commodities, 1989-92, annual rpt, S8680–1

Farm value per acre, for tobacco vs 7 other crops, 1991, annual rpt, A9075–1

Field crop pesticide and fertilizer use for 4 major crops, 1992, article, A1250–1.542

Food industry new product introductions, with data by product category, 1992, annual article, C2150–6.505

Food nutrition awareness and health concerns, including shopping and consumption patterns, by respondent characteristics, 1993 survey, annual rpt, A4950–36

Food service product consumption trends, for 7 menu items, 1983 and 1992, article, C1850–3.503

Food store industry structure, sales, operations, and business outlook, by type of store, 1993 annual rpt, C5225–1.505

Food store product sales, consumer expenditures, and price changes, by product type, 1991-92, annual feature, C4655–1.510

Grain futures and options trading activity on Minneapolis exchange, with production, price, and disposition data for area served, 1992 and trends, annual rpt, B6110–1

Hispanic American farm characteristics, with comparisons to all farms, 1987, annual compilation, C6775–3.6

Latin America statistical abstract, general data by country, 1992 annual rpt, U6250–1.16, U6250–1.24, U6250–1.25, U6250–1.26

Mexico food consumption, distribution by commodity group, 1993 article, C2150–6.509

Production, consumption, stocks, trade, and prices for approx 100 basic commodities,

including by country and producing State, commodity yearbook for 1993, C2400–1, C2400–2

Restaurant menu practices, including items offered, and info on nutrition, ingredients, and preparation, 1987 and 1992, A8200–22

Restaurant patronage patterns, expenditures, and food preferences, 1992 survey, recurring feature, C1850–3.501

Restaurant/food service menu item popularity, 1993 survey, recurring article, C1850–3.514

Shopping center food service tenants financial and operating data, by type of food served, 1991, triennial rpt, R9285–1

Supermarket health/beauty aid private label sales shares, for top 10 product categories, 1993 article, C8130–1.504

Supermarket prices for selected grocery items in 4-7 chains in 7 metro areas, Apr 1993, article, C4655–1.507

Supermarket sales by detailed product type, 1992 and trends, annual feature, C5225–1.507

Supermarket sales of nonfood products, by detailed product type, 1992, annual feature, C5225–1.508

Vending machine sales by product type, and machines on location, 1992 and trends, annual rpt, C9470–1

State and local:

Alabama agricultural production, marketing, and income, by county and/or commodity, and farms and acreage, 1992 and trends, annual rpt, S0090–1

Alabama statistical abstract, general data, 1992 recurring rpt, U5680–2

Alaska agricultural production and marketing, by district and commodity, 1960s-92, annual rpt, U5750–1

Arizona agricultural production, marketing, and finances, by commodity and county, 1988-92, annual rpt, U5830–1

Arizona statistical abstract, general data, 1993 recurring rpt, U5850–2

Arkansas agricultural production, marketing, and finances, by commodity and county, with farms and acreage, 1992 and trends, annual rpt, U5920–1

California agricultural statistics, including production, acreage, finances, and marketing, by commodity, annual rpt series, S0850–1

California statistical abstract, general data, 1992 annual rpt, S0840–2

Colorado agricultural production, marketing, and finances, by commodity and/or county, with farms and acreage, 1992 and trends, annual rpt, S0985–1

Florida agricultural statistics, including production, finances, and shipment data for citrus, dairy, and other sectors, by commodity and/or county, 1993 annual rpt series, S1685–1

Florida statistical abstract, general data, 1992 annual rpt, U6660–1

Georgia agricultural production, marketing, and finances, by commodity and/or county, and farms and acreage, 1991 and trends, annual rpt, S1855–1

Georgia county guide, general data, 1993 annual rpt, U6750–1

Georgia statistical abstract, general data, 1992-93 biennial rpt, U6730–1

BY COMMODITY

Index by Categories

Hawaii agricultural production and marketing, by commodity and island, 1987-91, annual rpt, S2030–1

Hawaii data book, general data, 1992 annual rpt, S2090–1

Idaho economic profile, general data, 1992 recurring rpt, S2218–2

Illinois agricultural production, marketing, and finances, by county or commodity, and farms and farmland, 1991 and trends, annual rpt, S2390–1

Illinois statistical abstract, general data, 1992 annual rpt, U6910–2

Kansas agricultural production, marketing, and finances, by county and/or commodity, and farm acreage and value, 1992 and trends, annual rpt, S2915–1

Kansas farm prices received, by selected commodity, quarterly rpt, U7095–1

Kansas statistical abstract, general data, 1991/92 annual rpt, U7095–2

Kentucky agricultural production, marketing, and finances, by commodity and county; and farms, acreage, and value; 1992 and trends, annual rpt, S3085–1

Kentucky economic statistics, general data, 1993 annual rpt, S3104–1.1

Louisiana agricultural production, marketing, and finances, by commodity or parish, 1985-91, annual rpt, U2740–1

Maryland statistical abstract, general data, 1993-94 biennial rpt, S3605–1

Michigan agricultural production, marketing, and finances, by commodity or county, 1987-91, annual rpt, S3950–1

Minnesota agricultural production, marketing, and finances, by county or commodity, and farms and acreage, 1992 and trends, annual rpt, S4130–1

Mississippi statistical abstract, general data, 1992 annual rpt, U3255–4

Missouri agricultural production, marketing, and finances, by commodity and/or county, and farms and acreage, 1988-92, annual rpt, S4480–1

Montana agricultural production, marketing, and finances, by commodity and county, 1991 and trends, annual rpt, S4655–1

Nebraska agricultural production, marketing, and finances, by commodity and/or county, and farms and acreage, 1991 and trends, annual rpt, S4835–1

Nevada agricultural production, marketing, and finances, by county and commodity, and farms and acreage, 1992 and trends, annual rpt, S5010–1

Nevada statistical abstract, general data, 1992 biennial rpt, S5005–1

New Jersey agricultural production, marketing, and finances, by commodity and/or county, and farms and acreage, 1986-91, annual rpt, S5350–1

New Mexico agricultural production, marketing, and finances, by commodity and county, with farms and acreage, 1991 and trends, annual rpt, S5530–1

New York State agricultural production, marketing, and finances, by commodity and/or county, and farms and acreage, 1992 and trends, annual rpt, S5700–1

New York State statistical yearbook, general data, 1992 annual rpt, U5100–1

North Carolina agricultural production, marketing, and finances, by commodity and county, 1991 and trends, annual rpt, S5885–1

North Dakota agricultural production and marketing, by commodity and county, and farm finances, 1992 and trends, annual rpt, U3600–1

Ohio agricultural production, marketing, and finances, by commodity and county, with farms and acreage, 1990-91 and trends, annual rpt, S6240–1

Oklahoma agricultural production, marketing, and finances, by commodity and county, 1992 and trends, annual rpt, S6405–1

Oklahoma statistical abstract, general data, 1992 annual rpt, U8130–2

Oregon agricultural production, marketing, and finances, by commodity and/or county, with farms and acreage, 1991 and trends, annual rpt, S6575–1

Oregon economic conditions, including population, construction, income, employment, industry, and foreign trade data, 1991, annual rpt, S6585–3

Pennsylvania agricultural production, marketing, and finances, by county and commodity, and farms and acreage, 1992 and trends, annual rpt, S6760–1

Pennsylvania statistical abstract, general data, 1992 recurring rpt, U4130–6

South Carolina agricultural production and cash receipts for selected crops, 1970s-91, annual rpt, S7125–3.1

South Carolina agricultural production and finances, by commodity and county, 1991-92 and trends, annual rpt, U1075–3

South Carolina statistical abstract, general data, 1993 annual rpt, S7125–1

South Dakota agricultural production and prices received by farmers, by commodity, quarterly rpt, U8595–1

South Dakota agricultural production, marketing, and finances, by commodity and county, and farms and acreage, 1992 and trends, annual rpt, S7280–1

South Dakota field crop acreage, by crop, 1991-92 and intended 1993, recurring table, U8595–1.S03

Tennessee agricultural production and marketing, by commodity and county, with farms, acreage, and farm value, 1992 and trends, annual rpt, S7460–1

Tennessee statistical abstract, general data, 1992/93 annual rpt, U8710–2

Texas agricultural production, marketing, and finances, by commodity and county, and farms and farmland, 1991 and trends, annual rpt series, S7630–1

Utah agricultural production, marketing, and finances, by commodity and county, with farms and acreage, 1992 and trends, annual rpt, S7800–1

Utah statistical abstract, general data, 1993 triennial rpt, U8960–1

Vermont agricultural production, marketing, and finances, by commodity, with data on govt inspections and funding, 1989-90 biennial rpt, S7978–1

Washington State agricultural production, marketing, and finances, by commodity and/or county, 1992 and trends, annual rpt, S8328–1

West Virginia agricultural production, marketing, and finances, by commodity or county, 1991 and trends, annual rpt, S8510–1

Wisconsin agricultural production, marketing, and finances, by commodity and county, and farms, acreage, and sales, 1992 and trends, annual rpt, S8680–1

Wisconsin Blue Book, general data, 1993-94 biennial rpt, S8780–1.2

Wyoming agricultural production, marketing, and finances, by county and/or commodity, and farms, acreage, and value, 1992 and trends, annual rpt, S8860–1

Banking, Finance, and Insurance

Chicago Board of Trade futures and options trading in financial instruments and agricultural commodities, 1992, annual rpt, B2120–1

Futures and options contract open interest (outstanding commitments), on foreign exchanges, by commodity and exchange, monthly rpt, A5040–6

Futures and options trading activity by exchange, and selected indicators for investors, 1992 and trends, commodity yearbook, C2400–1

Futures and options trading volume by commodity and exchange, 1988-92, annual rpt, A5040–1

Futures and options trading volume on foreign exchanges, by commodity and exchange, monthly rpt, A5040–5

Futures contract open interest (outstanding commitments), by commodity and exchange, monthly rpt, A5040–4

Futures trading volume and prices at Kansas City Board of Trade grain market, with natl production by State, 1992, annual rpt, B1530–1

Futures trading volume by commodity and exchange, monthly rpt, A5040–2

Options trading volume by commodity, securities index, and exchange, monthly rpt, A5040–3

Communications

Advertising expenditures, by medium and product category, 1991-92, annual rpt, C2710–1.S47

Direct marketing industry devs, including advertising patterns, finances, target market characteristics, and consumer attitudes, 1992/93 annual rpt, A4620–1

Energy Resources and Demand

Oil refinery construction, operating, and materials costs, Nelson-Farrar Cost Indexes, weekly rpt monthly and quarterly tables, C6985–1

Government and Defense

Military commissary frozen food sales, for top 10 commodities, FY92 and trends, article, C0500–1.S03

Military commissary sales, by region, product type, and individual store, FY92, annual feature, A2072–2.S01

Military commissary sales of top 10 beverage types, with coffee sales trend by region, 1991/92, article, C0500–1.S04

Military post exchange and commissary sales, by product category, for military resale agencies, FY91 and trends, annual rpt, A2072–1

Military post exchange sales, by product dept and US and overseas region, FY92, annual rpt, A2072–2.S02

State and local:

Maryland sales and service tax rates, by commodity and county, FY92, annual rpt, S3618–1.2

Wyoming mineral production and taxable valuation, by county, and severance and ad valorem taxes, FY92 annual rpt, S8990–1.2

Index by Categories

BY COMMODITY

Housing and Construction

Construction materials PPI, by commodity, 1987-90, annual rpt, U6660–1.11

Industry and Commerce

- Appliance industry shipments, by product type, 1991-98, annual articles, C2000–1.503
- Appliance life expectancy, shipments, and manufacturers market share, by product type, 1993 annual article, C2000–1.510
- Business gift-giving practices, including types of gifts and top 10 industry users, 1993 survey, annual article, C1200–4.508
- Canada economic indicators, including US trade, import shares for 8 other countries, and population by Province, 1993 articles, C4687–1.508
- Chemical and related industries production, finances, operating ratios, employment, and trade, by country, company, and chemical, 1980s-92, annual feature, A1250–1.530
- Chemical industry finances and operations, with data by industry segment and product, 1970s-92, annual rpt, A3850–1
- Chemical industry worldwide production and trade, selected data by country and world area, 1988-92, annual feature, A1250–1.507
- Chemical production, top 50 chemicals, 1992 and trends, annual article, A1250–1.520
- China business review, including trade with US and other countries, and economic activity, bimonthly rpt, A9315–1
- China industrial and agricultural production, and foreign trade and investment, with detail for leading commodities, 1980s-92, annual feature, A9315–1.504
- China trade value with US, with detail for Illinois exports, and US tariff rates and collections, for top 20-25 commodities, 1992 article, U6910–1.502
- Commonwealth of Independent States, Russia and Ukraine foreign trade with US, by commodity, 1992 and 1st 5 months 1992-93, article, U2030–1.511
- Consumer goods containing plastic, imports and exports by product type, monthly rpt quarterly table, C5800–12.501, C5800–12.505, C5800–12.508, C5800–12.511
- Convenience store sales, profit, and inventory turnover rates, by product type, 1991-92, annual fact book, C4680–1.507
- Czechoslovakia chemical production by product, and sales, exports, and employment of leading firms, by Republic, 1990-92, article, A1250–1.509
- Discount chain consumer natl brand preferences, by product category and chain, and by age group, 1993 survey, annual feature, C5150–3.521
- Discount chain sales and merchandising, including data by dept, leading chain, and location, 1992 and trends, annual feature, C8130–1.507
- Discount chain top-selling natl brands cited by managers, by product category, chain, and region, 1993 survey, annual feature, C5150–3.520
- Discount wholesale membership club top food and nonfood products purchased for families and business, 1992 article, C8130–1.501
- Drugstore chain and brand preferences of consumers, with data by product type and region, 1992 annual survey feature, C5150–2.503
- Drugstore chain pharmacy dept performance, with sales by product type, 1992, annual feature, C5150–2.511
- Drugstore chains financial performance and marketing operations, with sales by product type, 1993 annual feature, C5150–2.510
- Drugstore sales and merchandising trends, by product type and market area, 1992 annual feature, C5150–2.503
- Eastern/Central Europe foreign trade with OECD and EC, with data by country and commodity, 1980s-90, R5025–10
- Electronics industry factory sales and shipments, foreign trade, and operating data, by product category, 1980s-92, annual rpt, A4725–1
- Electronics industry market devs, including employment, factory sales, prices, and foreign trade trends, monthly rpt, A4725–2
- Electronics industry market trends and outlook, including product sales and shipments, employment, and leading manufacturers, monthly rpt, C1850–2
- Electronics trade, by product category, detailed type, and country, monthly rpt, A4725–3
- Forecasts of natl income and product account components and related indicators, quarterly rpt, U1880–1
- Foreign trade through California ports, by product category, 1991, annual rpt, S0840–3.1
- Foreign trade value with Japan and EC, for 5 types of commodities, 1993 article, C8900–1.516
- Germany (West) bilateral trade with US, by commodity, 1980, 1985, and 1990, annual rpt, A5135–2.2
- Health and beauty aid product sales shares by outlet type, by product category, 1991 and trends, annual article, C5225–1.501
- Health/beauty aid sales trends by product category and outlet type, 1992, article, A2072–2.501
- Household appliance factory unit shipments, by product type, 1992 and trends, annual rpt, A3350–4
- Household appliance industry manufacturing and market trends, by product type, various years 1920-94, biennial rpt, A3350–3
- Household appliance sales by distributors, by product type and State, 1992, annual rpt, A3350–2
- Household appliance shipments, by product type, with articles and special features on industry trends and devs, monthly rpt, C2000–1
- Household equipment shipments by product type, 1983-92, annual feature, C2000–1.505
- Import penetration for selected manufactured products, 1981 and 1991, R8490–48
- Japan and US foreign trade and investments, with detail by commodity, 1988-92, annual feature, R5650–2.552
- Japan electronics industry output change, by type of product, 1992, article, C8900–1.511
- Japan export share of production, for selected product categories, 1987-91, article, R5650–2.504
- Japan imports from US, for top 10 product categories, 1st 8 months 1992, article, C8900–1.502
- Japan-Indonesia foreign trade, by commodity, 1988-92, article, R5650–2.534
- Jewelry and watch manufacturing and marketing trends, new product dev, prices, trade, and related indicators, monthly rpt, C2150–7
- Latin America statistical abstract, general data by country, 1992 annual rpt, U6250–1.16, U6250–1.23, U6250–1.25, U6250–1.26
- Machine tool and other manufacturing technology exports and imports, by country of destination and origin, and by detailed product type, monthly rpt, A3179–3
- Men's grocery product purchasing, with comparisons to women, by detailed product type, 1992 article, C5225–1.501
- Metals and ferroalloys, current price quotations, by commodity, monthly rpt, C5226–2
- Mexico economic indicators, including US trade value for 10 commodities, 1993 articles, C4687–1.512
- Minerals supply-demand for selected commodities, with price data, US and worldwide, 1992-93 and trends, annual feature, C5226–2.505
- Mining industry capital spending plans for new mines and plants, by mineral and company, 1993 annual feature, C5226–2.503
- Minority consumer purchasing by product type, and ownership of selected electronics, for blacks, Hispanics, and Asians, 1992/93 survey, article, C2710–1.513
- Paper/paperboard packaging use, by type and end-use market, 1993 annual rpt, C3975–5.4
- Plastics and resin sales by material and major market, foreign trade, and capacity by company, 1991-92, annual feature, C5800–12.504
- Plastics resin production, sales/captive use, and trade, by resin type and/or use, monthly rpt, A8920–5
- Private label product sales, for 19 product categories, 1993 article, C5150–3.505
- Private label product sales in food, mass merchandise, and drugstores, with detail for top 14 product categories, year ended May 1993, article, C5150–3.519
- Production, consumption, stocks, trade, and prices for approx 100 basic commodities, including by country and producing State, commodity yearbook for 1993, C2400–1, C2400–2
- Retail outlet type sales volume shares, for approx 300 food, drug, and other product categories, 1993 annual feature, C4655–1.504
- Russia and aggregate other former Soviet Republics foreign trade with US, with detail for selected commodities, 1st 9 months 1992, U2030–1.505
- Russia foreign trade, by selected commodity, 1st 5 months 1993, article, U2030–1.509
- Russia foreign trade with US, with detail for selected commodities, 1st half 1992, U2030–1.503
- Russia foreign trade with US, with detail for selected commodities, 1st 4 months 1992-93, U2030–1.510
- Russia military-industrial complex share of production for 16 products, 1992 feature, U2030–1.503

BY COMMODITY

Shopping center financial and operating data, with detail by type of tenant, US and Canada, 1991, triennial rpt, R9285–1

Soviet Union and Russia foreign trade, by selected commodity, 1990-92, U2030–1.508

Soviet Union industrial production by commodity, monthly rpt recurring feature, U2030–1.507

Soviet Union production of selected commodities, with comparisons to US, 1985 or 1986, R4105–82.4

Spain, Catalonia region exports and imports, by product category, 1991, article, A8955–1.501

Spain, Madrid export and import value, by product type, 1990-91, article, A8955–1.502

UK economic indicators, including US trade, import shares for 4 other countries, and population by country and city, 1993 articles, C4687–1.510

Vending machine sales by product type, and machines on location, 1992 and trends, annual rpt, C9470–1

State and local:

- Alabama export values for top 5 commodities, 1990, annual rpt, U5680–3
- Alabama statistical abstract, general data, 1992 recurring rpt, U5680–2
- Arizona mineral production and value, by mineral type, 1991 and trends, annual rpt, S0497–1
- Arizona statistical abstract, general data, 1993 recurring rpt, U5850–2
- Arkansas nonfuel mineral production, by commodity, 1991-92, annual article, U5930–1.503
- California statistical abstract, general data, 1992 annual rpt, S0840–2
- Georgia statistical abstract, general data, 1992-93 biennial rpt, U6730–1
- Hawaii data book, general data, 1992 annual rpt, S2090–1
- Idaho economic profile, general data, 1992 recurring rpt, S2218–2
- Kansas mineral production and value, by mineral, 1989-91, annual rpt, U7095–2.16
- Kentucky economic statistics, general data, 1993 annual rpt, S3104–1.1
- Maryland statistical abstract, general data, 1993-94 biennial rpt, S3605–1
- Mississippi statistical abstract, general data, 1992 annual rpt, U3255–4
- Missouri mineral production, by commodity and company, FY92 and trends, annual rpt, S4530–2.1
- Nevada statistical abstract, general data, 1992 biennial rpt, S5005–1
- New Mexico mineral production, by type, 1982 and 1986-92, annual article, U7980–1.503
- New York State statistical yearbook, general data, 1992 annual rpt, U5100–1
- Oregon exports value, for top 5 destinations and commodity types, 1991, annual rpt, S6585–3
- Pennsylvania statistical abstract, general data, 1992 recurring rpt, U4130–6
- South Carolina statistical abstract, general data, 1993 annual rpt, S7125–1
- South Dakota exports to top 20 countries of destination, with detail for Canada and Mexico by commodity, 1991, article, U8595–1.502

Tennessee statistical abstract, general data, 1992/93 annual rpt, U8710–2

Utah statistical abstract, general data, 1993 triennial rpt, U8960–1

Law Enforcement

State and local:

Alabama, value of property stolen and recovered, by type of property, 1992, annual rpt, S0119–1.1

Arizona, value of property stolen and recovered, and damaged by arson, by property type, 1992, annual rpt, S0505–2.1

Arkansas, value of property stolen, recovered, and damaged by arson, by type, 1992 and trends, annual rpt, S0652–1

California, value of property stolen, recovered, and damaged by arson, by property type, 1987-92, annual rpt, S0910–1.1

Colorado, value of property stolen and recovered, and property damage, by property type, 1992, annual rpt, S1068–1

Connecticut, value of property stolen and recovered, by type, 1992, annual rpt, S1256–1.1

Delaware, value of property stolen and recovered, by type, 1989-91, annual rpt, S1375–5

Florida, value of property stolen and recovered, by property type, 1992, annual rpt, S1770–1

Hawaii, value of property stolen and recovered, by property type and county, 1992, annual rpt, S2035–1

Kansas, value of property stolen and recovered, by type of item, location, and offense, 1992, annual rpt, S2925–1.1

Kentucky, value of property stolen and recovered, by property type, 1992, annual rpt, S3150–1.1

Maine, value of property stolen and recovered, by county and type of property, 1990-91, annual rpt, S3475–1.1

Michigan, value of property stolen and recovered, by property type, 1992 and trends, annual rpt, S3997–1

New Hampshire, value of property stolen, recovered, and destroyed by arson, by property type, 1991, annual rpt, S5250–2.1

New Jersey, value of property stolen, recovered, and damaged, by county and/or property type, 1992, annual rpt, S5430–1

New York State, value of property stolen and recovered, by type, 1991, annual rpt, S5760–3.1

North Carolina, value of property stolen and recovered, by property type, 1992, annual rpt, S5955–1.1

North Dakota, value of property stolen and recovered, by property type, 1991, annual rpt, S6060–1

Oklahoma, value of property stolen and recovered, and arson damage, by property type, 1990-92, annual rpt, S6465–1

Pennsylvania, value of items stolen and recovered, by property type, 1992, annual rpt, S6860–1

Texas property stolen and destroyed by arson, by property type, 1992, annual rpt, S7735–2.1

Utah, value of property stolen and recovered, by type, 1992, annual rpt, S7890–3

Index by Categories

Virginia, value of property stolen, recovered, and damaged, by offense and property type, 1991-92, annual rpt, S8295–2.1

Washington State, value of property stolen and recovered, by property type, 1992, annual rpt, S8440–1

Wisconsin, value of property stolen and recovered, by property type, 1992, annual rpt, S8771–1

Wyoming, value of property stolen and recovered, by type, 1991, annual rpt, S8867–3.1

Natural Resources, Environment and Pollution

Recycling curbside program operations, funding, and recycled materials, municipal official views and summary program characteristics, July 1991 survey, B0230–2

Prices and Cost of Living

Business Week economic indicators, including prices for selected commodities, weekly rpt, C5800–7

Commodity price trends, with detail for selected commodities or groups, biweekly rpt quarterly feature, C3950–1.505, C3950–1.513, C3950–1.519, C3950–1.524

Consumer expenditures by item and age group, 1991 and trends, annual rpt, A0865–1.2

Food CPI, by item, 1992, annual rpt, C5225–1.505

Germany (East vs West) prices of selected food and nonfood items, 1988, R4105–82.3

Japan CPI by item, 1988-92, annual compilation, R5650–2.552

Latin America statistical abstract, general data by country, 1992 annual rpt, U6250–1.31

Personal consumption expenditures, by product or service, 1920s-91, annual rpt, R9050–1.2

Price index trends, by commodity, 1913-91, recurring rpt, U5680–2.14

Pulp, paper, and allied products PPI, by detailed item, 1985-92, annual rpt, A1630–6.4

Urban consumers CPI monthly trends, by item, quarterly rpt, U8595–1

Wealthy lifestyles, comparative prices of selected goods and services, 1976 and 1993, annual article, C3950–1.526

World commodity prices and price indexes, by selected commodity, 1975-89, biennial rpt, R9455–1.5

State and local:

- Alaska cost-of-living indicators for selected items and local areas, with comparisons to other US cities, 1992 annual article, S0320–1.501
- Arizona, Phoenix CPI by item, monthly rpt quarterly table, U0280–1.501, U0280–1.504, U0280–1.507, U0280–1.510
- Arizona, Phoenix CPI by item, 1992 and trends, annual article, U0280–1.505
- California CPI in 2 major metro areas, by item, 1992, annual rpt, S0840–3.1
- California statistical abstract, general data, 1992 annual rpt, S0840–2
- Colorado, Denver area CPI, by component, 1st half 1992, semiannual feature, S1040–4.501

Index by Categories

BY GOVERNMENT AGENCY

Colorado, Denver area CPI, by component, 2nd half 1992, semiannual feature, S1040–4.504

DC CPI by item, monthly rpt bimonthly feature, S1527–3.501, S1527–3.502, S1527–3.503, S1527–3.504, S1527–3.505

Florida statistical abstract, general data, 1992 annual rpt, U6660–1

Hawaii data book, general data, 1992 annual rpt, S2090–1

Hawaii, Honolulu CPI by major item, quarterly rpt, S2090–2

Kansas City daily cash grain prices, by commodity, 1992, annual rpt, B1530–1

Nebraska cost-of-living indicators by component, for 6 cities, with comparisons to other US cities, quarterly rpt, S4895–2

New York State statistical yearbook, general data, 1992 annual rpt, U5100–1

Pennsylvania, Philadelphia and Pittsburgh CPI, by major item, monthly rpt quarterly table, U4110–1.501, U4110–1.503, U4110–1.505, U4110–1.507

Public Welfare and Social Security

State and local:

Arkansas food assistance distributions to school and instn programs, by commodity, FY91, annual rpt, S0700–2.3

Nebraska food distributed to low-income families, amount and value of 25 commodities, FY92, annual rpt, S4957–1.1

New York State food distribution program staples distributed, by county, FY90, annual rpt, U5100–1.11

Recreation and Leisure

Musical instrument and accessory shipment volume and/or retail value, and foreign trade, by product type, 1992 and trends, annual rpt, A6848–1

Sporting goods purchases, by product and outlet type, census div, and purchaser characteristics, with average prices, 1992 and trends, annual survey, A8485–2

Toy and game shipments and value, by type, 1991-92, annual rpt, A9095–1

Transportation and Travel

Auto maintenance activity and product purchasing, for imported vehicle owners, 1991 and 1993 surveys, annual article, C2150–10.508

Auto maintenance market, including consumer product purchase patterns and do-it-yourself activity, 1993 annual survey feature, C2150–10.504

Auto parts/supplies and repair aftermarket sales performance, by product group, 1993 annual feature, C0125–1.503

Mexico-Texas transportation system analysis, including bilateral trade, operations by transport mode, and data by locale, 1993 rpt, U8850–9

Motor vehicle industry materials consumption by type, and factory installations by component, 1993 annual rpt, A0865–1

Railroad (Class I) financial condition, operations, and employment, by company and district, 1992, annual rpt, A3275–7

Railroad freight car loadings by commodity, and ton-miles, weekly press release, A3275–2

Railroad freight car loadings by commodity, piggyback carloadings, and revenue ton-miles, monthly rpt, C8400–1

Railroad freight loads and revenues, by commodity, 1991-92, annual rpt, A3275–5.2

Railroad freight tons originated, and revenue shares, by commodity, 1982-91, annual rpt, A3275–8.2

Railroad operating data, including top commodities handled, employment and wages, and retirement system, by State, 1991, annual rpt, A3275–10

Transportation cost ratios for approx 150 commodities, 2 alternative measures, 1992 article, U5930–1.501

State and local:

Alabama statistical abstract, general data, 1992 recurring rpt, U5680–2

Hawaii data book, general data, 1992 annual rpt, S2090–1

Nebraska railroad revenue freight traffic, by commodity, 1990-91, biennial rpt, S4940–1

North Carolina railroad revenue freight tonnage, by commodity, Dec 1990, annual rpt, S5917–2

Oklahoma statistical abstract, general data, 1992 annual rpt, U8130–2

Tennessee statistical abstract, general data, 1992/93 annual rpt, U8710–2

Wisconsin Blue Book, general data, 1993-94 biennial rpt, S8780–1.2

BY GOVERNMENT AGENCY

Communications

Regulatory agency policies and practices, and industry financial and operating data, by utility type and agency, 1991/92 annual rpt, A7015–3

Education

Budget of US higher education funding, by agency and program, FY92-94, annual feature, C2175–1.516

Educational exchange program Federal funding, by agency, 1992, article, C2175–1.528

Southern States higher education Federal funding, by agency and State, 1989/90, biennial fact book, A8945–1.6

State and local:

California State agency library staff, expenditures, holdings, and activities, by library, FY92, annual rpt, S0825–2

Florida higher education contract and grant awards for State instns, by sponsoring Federal agency, 1991/92, annual rpt, S1725–1

Maryland higher education funding, by instn and Federal agency, FY90, biennial rpt, S3605–1.2

Energy Resources and Demand

Federal Govt energy consumption, by agency and source, FY78-92, periodic basic data book, A2575–14.1

Regulatory agency policies and practices, and industry financial and operating data, by utility type and agency, 1991/92 annual rpt, A7015–3

Government and Defense

Budget receipts and outlays of Fed Govt, by source and function, 1920s-93, annual rpt, R9050–1.3

Congressional organization, major legislative and budget actions, and agency and program appropriations, 102nd Congress, 2nd session, 1992, annual rpt, C2500–2

Federal regulatory agency costs and staff, for approx 50 agencies, FY70s-94, annual rpt, U9640–1

Japan Office of Trade and Investment Ombudsman cases, by world area of origin and jurisdictional ministry, 1982-July 1993, article, R5650–2.553

Transportation regulatory agency policies and practices for motor carriers and railroads, by agency, 1991/92 annual rpt, A7015–4

Utility and transportation regulatory agency activities, scope of jurisdiction, finances, and employees, by agency, 1991/92 annual rpt, A7015–2

Utility regulatory agency policies and practices, and industry financial and operating data, by utility type and agency, 1991/92 annual rpt, A7015–3

State and local:

Alabama Federal aid by agency and program, FY85-90, recurring rpt, U5680–2.6

Alabama financial condition, including revenues by source, expenditures by function and object, and fund balances, by fund and agency, FY92, annual rpt, S0129–1

Alaska financial condition, including revenues by source, expenditures by function, fund balances, and bond obligations, FY92 and trends, annual rpt, S0275–1

Arizona financial condition, including revenues by source, expenditures by function, and fund balances, FY92, annual rpt, S0450–1

California financial condition, including revenues by source, expenditures by agency and function, fund balances, and bonded debt, FY92 and trends, annual rpt, S0815–1

California statistical abstract, general data, 1992 annual rpt, S0840–2

Colorado financial condition, including receipts by source, and expenditures by function, FY92 and trends, annual rpt, S0980–1

Connecticut financial condition, including revenues by source, expenditures by function, and bonded debt, FY92, annual rpt, S1170–1, S1170–2

DC govt expenditures, by agency, FY87-91, annual rpt, S1535–2

Florida financial condition, including receipts by source, expenditures by function, and fund balances, FY92, annual rpt, S1717–1, S1717–3

Florida statistical abstract, general data, 1992 annual rpt, U6660–1

Georgia financial condition, including revenues by source, expenditures by function and object, and fund balances, FY92, annual rpt, S1860–1

Georgia statistical abstract, general data, 1992-93 biennial rpt, U6730–1

Hawaii data book, general data, 1992 annual rpt, S2090–1

Hawaii financial condition, including revenues by source, expenditures by function, and fund balances, FY92, annual rpt, S2020–1

Idaho financial condition, including revenues by source and expenditures by object, by agency and/or fund, FY92, annual rpt, S2215–1

Illinois financial condition, including revenues by source, and expenditures by object, function, and agency, FY92, annual rpt, S2415–1

BY GOVERNMENT AGENCY

Indiana financial condition, including revenues by source, expenditures by function and object, and fund balances, by agency, FY92, annual rpt, S2570–1

Iowa financial condition, including revenues by source, expenditures by function, and bonded debt, FY92 and trends, annual rpt, S2860–4

Iowa State treasury financial operations, including receipts, disbursements, and detailed investment activity, FY92, annual rpt, S2885–1

Kentucky financial condition, including revenues by source, expenditures by function and object, fund balances, and bonded debt, FY92, annual rpt, S3120–1

Louisiana financial condition, including revenues by source, expenditures by function, and fund balances, FY92 and trends, annual rpt, S3285–2

Maine financial condition, including revenues by source, expenditures by function and object, and fund balances, FY92, annual rpt, S3420–1

Maryland, Fed Govt expenditures, by function, agency, and county, FY91, biennial rpt, S3605–1.13

Maryland financial condition, including revenues by source, expenditures by function, fund balances, and bonded debt, FY92 and trends, annual rpt, S3685–2

Massachusetts financial condition, including revenues by source, and expenditures by function, by fund, FY92 and trends, annual rpt, S3777–1

Michigan financial condition, including revenues by source, expenditures by function, and fund balances, FY92 and trends, annual rpt, S3985–2

Minnesota financial condition, including revenues by source, expenditures by function, fund balances, and bonded debt, FY92 and trends, annual rpt, S4180–1

Mississippi financial condition, including revenues by source, expenditures by function and object, and detail by agency, FY92 and trends, annual rpt, S4346–1

Mississippi statistical abstract, general data, 1992 annual rpt, U3255–4

Missouri financial condition, including fund finances, tax collections and distribution, and State treasury activity, FY92 and trends, annual rpt, S4570–1

Montana financial condition, including revenues by source, expenditures by function, and fund balances, FY92, annual rpt, S4653–1

Nebraska financial condition, including revenues by source, expenditures by function and agency, and fund balances, FY92, annual rpt, S4825–1

Nevada financial condition, including fund revenues by source, expenditures by function, and bonded debt, FY92, annual rpt, S5025–1

Nevada statistical abstract, general data, 1992 biennial rpt, S5005–1

New Jersey financial condition, including revenues by source, expenditures by function, fund balances, and bonded debt, FY92, annual rpt, S5455–1

New Mexico financial condition, including receipts by source, expenditures by agency and function, fund balances, and bonded debt, FY91, annual rpt, S5585–1

New York State financial condition, including revenues by source, expenditures by function, and fund balances, FY93, annual rpt, S5710–1

New York State statistical yearbook, general data, 1992 annual rpt, U5100–1

North Carolina financial condition, including revenues by source, expenditures by function, fund balances, and bonded debt, FY92, annual rpt, S5897–1

North Dakota financial condition, including revenues by source, expenditures by function, fund balances, and bonded debt, FY92, annual rpt, S6162–1

Ohio financial condition, including revenues by source, expenditures by function, and fund balances, FY92, annual rpt, S6255–1

Oklahoma financial audit narrative summary, with data on Federal expenditures by agency and program, FY91, annual rpt, S6410–1

Oklahoma financial condition, including revenues by source, expenditures by function, and fund balances, FY91, annual rpt, S6438–1

Oklahoma statistical abstract, general data, 1992 annual rpt, U8130–2

Oklahoma tax revenues by source, and distribution to local govts and State funds, FY92 and trends, annual rpt, S6495–1

Oregon financial condition, including revenues by source, expenditures by function, and fund statements, FY92, annual rpt, S6603–2

Pennsylvania financial condition, including revenues by source, expenditures by function, and fund balances, FY92 and trends, annual rpt, S6810–4

Pennsylvania statistical abstract, general data, 1992 recurring rpt, U4130–6.6

Rhode Island financial condition, including revenues by source, expenditures by function, and fund balances, FY92 and trends, annual rpt, S6930–1

Rhode Island statistical almanac, general data, 1993 annual rpt, C7975–1

South Carolina financial condition, including receipts by source, expenditures by function, fund balances, and bonded debt, FY92, annual rpt, S7127–1

South Dakota financial condition, including revenues by source, expenditures by function, fund balances, and bonded debt, FY92, annual rpt, S7330–1

Tennessee financial condition, including revenues by source, expenditures by function and object, and fund balances, FY92, annual rpt, S7505–1

Texas financial condition, including revenues by source, expenditures by function, and bonded indebtedness, FY92, annual rpt, S7655–3

Texas govt revenues, expenditures, and cash balances, by fund and dept, FY92, annual rpt, S7655–2

Utah financial condition, including revenues by source, expenditures by function and agency, and fund balances, FY92, annual rpt, S7795–1

Vermont financial condition, including revenues by source, expenditures by function, fund balances, and bonded debt, FY92, annual rpt, S8035–1

Washington State financial condition, including revenues by source, expenditures by function, fund balances, and bonded debt, FY92, annual rpt, S8345–3

Index by Categories

Washington State treasury operations, including receipts, disbursements, aid to localities, and investments, by fund, FY92, annual rpt, S8455–1

West Virginia statistical handbook, general data, 1992 annual rpt, R9385–1

Wisconsin Blue Book, general data, 1993-94 biennial rpt, S8780–1.2

Wisconsin financial condition, including revenues by source, expenditures by function and object, and fund balances, FY92, annual rpt, S8675–3

Wisconsin financial condition, including revenues by source, expenditures by function and object, and fund balances, FY93, annual rpt, S8675–2

Wyoming financial condition, including revenues by source, expenditures by function, and fund balances, FY92 and trends, annual rpt, S8875–1

Wyoming State employees by agency, July 1991-92, annual rpt, S8875–1

Health and Vital Statistics

State and local:

Texas State and local health depts finances, employment, and service area characteristics, FY91 and trends, U8850–8.6

Housing and Construction

Construction-related Federal program funding proposed by Clinton Admin, by agency, FY93-94, article, C5800–2.524

Construction value and activities of top 25 Federal or State govt agencies, FY92, annual article, C1850–9.501

Public housing authority operations, including households served, staff, and waiting list, for 22 local agencies, 1993 rpt, A6800–2

Industry and Commerce

Hard goods manufacturers and representatives views on govt regulation, including agencies responsible for problems, by product line, 1993 annual survey rpt, A1800–1

Law Enforcement

State and local:

Alabama crimes and arrests, by offense and location, with law enforcement employment, 1992 and trends, annual rpt, S0119–1

Arizona law enforcement employment by sex, by local agency, Oct 1992, annual rpt, S0505–2.2

Arkansas crimes and arrests, and law enforcement personnel, by agency, 1992, annual rpt, S0652–1

Colorado crimes and arrests, by offense and law enforcement agency, 1992, annual rpt, S1068–1

Connecticut crimes and arrests, by offense, with data by local agency, and victim-offender characteristics, 1992, annual rpt, S1256–1

Delaware crimes reported and cleared, by reporting agency, 1988-91, annual rpt, S1375–5

Idaho crimes and arrests, law enforcement employment, and assaults on officers, by local agency, 1992 and trends, annual rpt, S2275–2

Illinois crimes and arrests, by offense, with data by location and offender characteristics, 1991, annual rpt, S2536–1

Kansas crimes and arrests, by offense, with data by location, agency, and victim-offender characteristics, 1992 and trends, annual rpt, S2925–1

Index by Categories

BY INCOME

Kentucky crimes and arrests, by offense, with data by location and offender characteristics, 1992, annual rpt, S3150–1

Maine administrative court cases and disposition, by agency, 1983-FY92, annual rpt, S3463–1

Maine crimes reported, by offense, county, and local agency, 1991, annual rpt, S3475–1.2

Maryland crimes and arrests, law enforcement employment by sex, and assaults on police, by local agency and county, 1991-92, annual rpt, S3665–1

Michigan crimes and arrests, by offense, with data by location and offender characteristics, 1992 and trends, annual rpt, S3997–1

Missouri crimes and arrests, by offense and location, with victim and offender characteristics, 1991 and trends, annual rpt, S4560–2

Montana crimes and clearances, by offense and jurisdiction, 1992, annual rpt, S4705–1

New Hampshire Index crimes reported, by agency and county, 1991, annual rpt, S5250–2.2

New Jersey law enforcement employment, by agency, and assaults on officers, 1992 and trends, annual rpt, S5430–1.4

New York State criminal justice activities, by offense, location, and local agency, with law enforcement employment, 1991 and trends, annual rpt, S5760–3

New York State statistical yearbook, general data, 1992 annual rpt, U5100–1

North Carolina crimes by offense, and law enforcement employment, by local agency, 1991-92, annual rpt, S5955–1.1

North Dakota crimes and arrests, by offense, location, and offender characteristics, and law enforcement employment, 1991 and trends, annual rpt, S6060–1

Oklahoma Crime Index offenses, by county and reporting agency, 1990-92, annual rpt, S6465–1.2

Oregon crimes by offense, law enforcement employees by sex, and assaults on police, by local agency, 1992 and trends, annual rpt, S6603–3.2

Pennsylvania crimes and arrests, by offense, location, and offender characteristics, with law enforcement employment, 1992 and trends, annual rpt, S6860–1

South Carolina crimes and arrests, by detailed offense, offender characteristics, and location, 1992 and trends, annual rpt, S7205–1.2

Texas criminal offenses, by local agency, 1992, annual rpt, S7735–2.2

Utah crimes and arrests, by offense, county, and local agency, 1992 and trends, annual rpt, S7890–3

Virginia crimes and arrests by offense, and law enforcement employment, by location and reporting agency, 1992, annual rpt, S8295–2.2

Washington State crimes and arrests, by offense, with data by location and offender characteristics, 1992 and trends, annual rpt, S8440–1

West Virginia crimes and arrests, by offense and local agency, 1990-91, annual rpt, S8610–1.2

Wisconsin crimes and arrests, by offense, offender characteristics, county, and local agency, 1992 and trends, annual rpt, S8771–1

Wyoming crimes and arrests, by offense, with data by location and victim and offender characteristics, 1991 and trends, annual rpt, S8867–3

Natural Resources, Environment and Pollution

Environmental research spending of Fed Govt, by agency, FY92, article, A1250–1.508

Regulatory agency policies and practices, and industry financial and operating data, by utility type and agency, 1991/92 annual rpt, A7015–3

Southeastern States federally owned land, by agency, for 12 States, Sept 1989, annual rpt, U8710–2.12

State and local:

California statistical abstract, general data, 1992 annual rpt, S0840–2

Nevada statistical abstract, general data, 1992 biennial rpt, S5005–1

Utah public lands by govt owner, and Federal land payments to State and local govts, with data by county, 1992 article, U8960–2.502

Science and Technology

Ecologist research grant sources, and funding activity of selected Govt agencies, 1992 recurring rpt, A4685–1

Federal expenditures for research, by selected agency, 1981, 1987, and 1993, article, A1250–1.514

Federal outlays for science/technology-related programs, changes proposed by Clinton Admin, by agency, 1994-98, article, A1250–1.517

Japan govt R&D expenditures, by agency, FY92, article, C1850–6.504

Japan R&D expenditures, by funding and performing sector, govt agency, and industry, FY70s-93, annual article, R5650–2.557

R&D budget authority for FY92-93, and Clinton Admin proposal for FY94, by agency and function, 1993 article, A1250–1.521

R&D funding in Budget of US for 7 agencies in FY93, with Clinton Admin request and congressional appropriation for FY94, annual article, A1250–1.534, A1250–1.544

R&D laboratory budgets and facilities of 6 Federal agencies, 1993 article, C5800–7.531

R&D obligations of Fed Govt, by field and agency, FY86-93, annual feature, A1250–1.537

R&D program funding in higher education instns, by State and selected agency, FY90, annual rpt, C2175–1.531

Science and engineering grad students and doctorates with Fed Govt support, by agency, by sex and race-ethnicity, 1980s-90s, recurring rpt, A3960–2.1

Transportation and Travel

Federal outlays for transportation R&D and planning, by agency, 1992 annual rpt, R4815–1

Regulatory agency policies and practices for motor carriers and railroads, by agency, 1991/92 annual rpt, A7015–4

State and local:

Arkansas traffic accidents, by county and investigating agency, 1991, annual rpt, S0692–1

Delaware traffic accidents, by reporting agency, 1991-92, annual rpt, S1435–1

Nevada traffic accidents, by investigating agency, 1992, annual rpt, S5140–1

Pennsylvania mass transit fleet characteristics and passengers, including senior citizens, by agency, 1988/89-1989/90, recurring rpt, U4130–6.9

South Carolina traffic accidents, fatalities, and injuries, by investigating agency, 1992, annual rpt, S7190–2

Utah hwy user revenue distributions, by agency, FY87-92, annual rpt, R9380–1.10

BY INCOME

Agriculture and Food

Distilled spirits consumption, and consumer characteristics and buying habits, 1992 and trends, annual rpt, C4775–1.3

Food away from home expenditures, by household characteristics and for top 10 MSAs, 1991, article, A8200–1.507

Food away from home expenditures, by household characteristics and for 26 MSAs, 1991, recurring rpt, A8200–13

Food catering market, including consumer attendance at catered events by sex and income, 1992 survey, article, A8200–1.503

Food nutrition awareness and health concerns, including shopping, preparation, and consumption patterns, by respondent characteristics, 1992 survey, annual rpt, A4950–36

Food service industry employee characteristics, and minority-owned establishments and sales, 1993 article, A8200–1.508

Food shopper characteristics, for households shopping wholesale membership clubs vs supermarkets, 1992 survey, article, C2710–1.511

Food take-out consumer characteristics, consumption patterns, and attitudes, May 1992 survey, A8200–21

Restaurant (table service) operations and menu offerings, and related consumer views and practices by demographic characteristics, 1992, recurring rpt, A8200–11

Restaurant smoking policy importance to consumers, and views on smoking acceptability in restaurants and other public places, by selected characteristics, Jan 1993 survey, A8200–8.15

Snack food consumption patterns, by snack type and consumer characteristics, 1989/90 and trends, recurring rpt, A8905–2

Supermarket bakery and deli shoppers, by income, 1993 annual survey article, C5225–1.508

Supermarket shopper practices, attitudes, and expenditures, by respondent characteristics, 1993 and trends, annual survey rpt, A4950–3

Supermarket shopper views on quality of customer service and importance of selected factors, by respondent characteristics, 1991-92 surveys, A4950–37

BY INCOME

Wine and other alcoholic beverage consumption, and consumer characteristics and buying habits, 1993 annual rpt, C4775–2.2

Banking, Finance, and Insurance

Bank CEO demographic and professional characteristics, attitudes, and compensation, Apr 1992 survey, annual rpt, B4490–2.33

Life insurance purchases and ownership, by consumer and household characteristics, 1991 and trends, biennial fact book, A1325–1.1

Population lacking insurance coverage, by family income level, 1991, article, C8900–1.516

Public opinion on business use of personal info, and consumer examination of own credit rpt by selected characteristics, 1992 survey, annual rpt, B3280–2

Shareholders of NYSE member firms, by demographic characteristics and metro area, 1970s-90, annual fact book, B6625–1.1

Communications

Direct marketing industry devs, including advertising patterns, finances, target market characteristics, and consumer attitudes, 1992/93 annual rpt, A4620–1

Magazine promotion dept activities, and executive characteristics and salary, Nov 1992 survey, article, C2575–1.506

Newspaper reader socioeconomic characteristics, 1993 annual rpt, A8605–4

Public opinion on the media and related issues, by respondent characteristics, series, C8915–11

Telephone Yellow Pages directory use among consumers, with detail by respondent characteristics, 1992 survey, annual rpt, A9500–2

Education

American College Test (ACT) scores by student characteristics, with student views on schools and education plans, 1992 and trends, annual rpt, R1960–6

Catholic secondary school operations and finances, including enrollment by race-ethnicity and family income, 1991/92 and trends, biennial rpt, A7375–5

Catholic vs public school performance, and support for parental school selection funded by govt, public opinion by respondent characteristics, July 1992 survey, A7375–8

Higher education financial aid applicant characteristics, American College Testing (ACT) program, 1993/94, annual rpt, R1960–5

Higher education freshmen parental income, occupations, and education, by student sex and instn type, fall 1992, annual survey, U6215–1

Librarians at universities and research instns, salaries by sex, type of position, and instn, FY92 and trends, annual survey, A3365–2

Political science higher education dept faculty by salary level, 1991/92, annual rpt, A2617–1

Scholastic Aptitude Test (SAT) participants and/or scores, by education of parents, income, and race-ethnicity, 1992, C4215–1.501

State and local:

Minnesota postsecondary student scholarship/grant awards, by income level and educational system, FY91-92, biennial rpt, S4195–2.2

Missouri American College Test (ACT) scores, by participant characteristics and/or higher education instn, 1993 annual rpt, S4520–3.1

New Jersey, Montclair parents use of selected info sources in choosing elementary/secondary school under parental selection program, by income level, 1989/90, R3810–7

Pennsylvania public school personnel and salary data, by position and district, 1992/93 and trends, annual rpt, S6790–5.12

Energy Resources and Demand

Motor fuel expenditure share of posttax income, by income class, 1993 article, C6985–1.516

Government and Defense

Black elected officials, and characteristics of voting age population, with comparisons to whites, 1970s-91, annual compilation, C6775–2.4

Energy (BTU) tax proposed by Clinton Admin as a percent of household income, by income level, 1993 article, R9050–3.502

Federal income tax changes proposed in Clinton Admin budget, with impacts by income level, 1993 rpt, R3834–17

Federal income tax revenue by income bracket, 1916-90, annual rpt, R9050–1.3

Federal tax burden under current policy and Clinton Admin proposal, with comparison to Germany, UK, and Japan, by income level, 1993 article, C8900–1.511

Gasoline tax payments as a percent of family income, by income level, 1993 article, R9050–3.502

Gasoline tax payments as a percent of family income, by income level, 1993 rpt, R9050–15.6

Hispanic American elected officials, registered voters, and voting, with comparisons to whites, 1970s-91, annual compilation, C6775–3.3

Hispanic American vs non-Hispanic voter turnout, by demographic characteristics, Nov 1992 election, article, C4575–1.511

Public opinion on Clinton Admin policies and actions, by respondent characteristics, series, C8915–7

Public opinion on issues concerning politics and the press, by respondent characteristics, series, C8915–4

Sales tax as percent of annual and lifetime household income, by income category, 1989, article, C8900–1.513

State/local tax burden by family income, by State, 1991, semiannual rpt, B8500–1.4

State and local:

California individual and corporate income tax returns and property tax assistance, by income class and county, 1990 and trends, annual rpt, S0855–1

California senior citizen/disabled property tax and renters assistance, by income level and county, 1991, annual rpt, S0840–2.13

California statistical abstract, general data, 1992 annual rpt, S0840–2

DC statistical profile, general data, 1992 annual rpt, S1535–3

Delaware data book, general data, 1993 annual rpt, S1375–4

Georgia personal income tax returns, taxable income, and taxes paid, by income bracket and county, 1990, annual rpt, S1950–1.2

Index by Categories

Georgia statistical abstract, general data, 1992-93 biennial rpt, U6730–1

Hawaii data book, general data, 1992 annual rpt, S2090–1

Iowa individual income tax return filings, income, taxes paid, and credits, by income bracket, and filings by county, 1991, annual rpt, S2860–3

Maryland individual income tax return filings, and income and tax liability data, by city, county, and income group, 1991, annual rpt, S3685–1

Nebraska personal and corporate income tax returns filed, tax credits and liability, and income, by county and/or income group, 1990, annual rpt, S4950–1.1

New Mexico personal income returns, tax liability, rebates, and credits, by income class, 1990-91, annual rpt, S5660–1.2

New York State statistical yearbook, general data, 1992 annual rpt, U5100–1

Ohio individual income tax returns filed, income, and tax liability, by income class and county, 1990, annual rpt, S6390–1.3

Pennsylvania individual income tax returns, and taxable income by source, by income class, 1990, annual rpt, S6885–1

Pennsylvania statistical abstract, general data, 1992 recurring rpt, U4130–6

South Carolina income tax returns, distribution by taxable income, by county, 1991, annual rpt, S7145–1.2

South Carolina income tax returns, exemptions, and liability, by income class, 1991, annual rpt, S7255–1.2

South Carolina statistical abstract, general data, 1993 annual rpt, S7125–1

Utah govt statistical review, fiscal and socioeconomic data, 1993 annual rpt, R9380–1

Utah individual income tax returns and adjusted gross income, by income class, 1991, annual rpt, S7905–1

Utah statistical abstract, general data, 1993 triennial rpt, U8960–1

Vermont individual State income tax returns, and property and sales tax refunds, by income class and locality, 1991, annual rpt, S8125–1

Virginia personal and corporate income tax returns filed, taxable income, and tax, 1990 or FY92 and trends, annual rpt, S8305–1.1

West Virginia statistical handbook, general data, 1992 annual rpt, R9385–1

Health and Vital Statistics

Child and maternal health indicators and insurance coverage, by race-ethnicity and other demographic characteristics, 1992 annual rpt, R3840–5.1

Child health insurance coverage rates for employment-related insurance, by income and race-ethnicity, 1977, 1987, and 2000, annual rpt, R3840–11.1

Dental problems/treatment-related time lost from work or school, by demographic characteristics, 1989, article, A2623–1.502

Disabled persons use of home care services, with costs, payment sources, and types of care, by selected characteristics, 1992, R4865–15

Drugs (prescription) use, expenditures, and financing methods among population age 65/older and 64/under, by patient characteristics, 1987, R4865–8

Index by Categories

BY INCOME

Health care expenditures of families, including insurance premiums by source of coverage, and taxes by type, by income group, 1987, R4700–20

Health care specialist and health-related company CEO income, public perceptions vs actual amounts, by respondent characteristics, 1991-93, R4865–13

Health condition and preventive health care and safety practices of adults, by respondent characteristics, 1992 and trends, annual survey rpt, C8111–2

Health insurance coverage lack, and population with high out-of-pocket expenses, by State and selected characteristics, 1993, R4865–14

Health insurance coverage lack by sex, race, employment status, and household income level, 1993 feature, C4215–1.506

Health insurance employer-paid benefits coverage, and tax revenues that would be generated if benefits were taxed, by income group, 1991, article, C3950–1.505

Hysterectomy prevalence by women's demographic characteristics, 1988 surveys, article, A2623–1.503

Incidence of illness and injury, and hospitalization and mortality data, by selected demographic characteristics, 1992 annual rpt, A5173–2.4

Nursing center (community) staff and client characteristics, and services, 1990 survey, article, A8010–3.506

Nursing higher education program clinic patient characteristics, FY92, biennial rpt, A0615–5

Osteopathy student debt and career plans, by student characteristics, 1991/92 and trends, annual survey rpt, A0620–2

Sexual behavior among heterosexuals, including data on demographic characteristics, number of partners, and condom use, 1990/91 survey, article, A5160–1.506

Smoking acceptability in restaurants and other public places, and importance of restaurant smoking policy, views of consumers by selected characteristics, Jan 1993 survey, A8200–8.15

Southern States children age 17/under lacking health insurance and eligible for Medicaid, with detail by age and family income, for 6-17 States, 1991, R9000–1

Veterinarian income by selected personal and practice characteristics, 1992, annual survey article, C9480–1.506

Veterinarians by type of employment, by income group, 1991, biennial survey article, A3100–2.506

Women's use of mammography and Pap smear tests, by demographic characteristics, 1987 survey, article, A2623–1.503

State and local:

Alabama health behavior risk factor surveillance survey results, by respondent characteristics, 1988-89, recurring rpt, S0175–6

Colorado resident awareness of AIDS virus, by income, 1990, recurring rpt, S1010–3

Connecticut health insurance coverage rate, by respondent characteristics and behavior risk factors, 1991 survey, S1200–3

Georgia health behavior risk factor surveillance survey results, by respondent characteristics, 1991 and trends, annual rpt, S1895–2

Hawaii health dept activities and services, including vital statistics and disease control, by location, 1990, annual rpt, S2065–1

Kentucky health behavior risk factor surveillance survey results, by State area and respondent characteristics, 1988-90, annual rpt, S3140–6

Massachusetts health behavior risk factor surveillance survey results, by respondent characteristics, 1986-90, recurring rpt, S3850–3

Michigan health behavior risk factor surveillance survey results, by respondent characteristics, 1991, annual rpt, S4000–4

Nevada health behavior risk factor surveillance survey results, by location and respondent characteristics, 1991, annual rpt, S5075–3

New York State health behavior risk factor surveillance survey results, by respondent characteristics, 1990, recurring rpt, S5765–3

North Dakota health behavior risk factor surveillance survey results, by respondent characteristics, 1991 and trends, annual rpt, S6105–3

Pennsylvania health behavior risk factor surveillance survey results, by respondent characteristics, 1991, annual rpt, S6820–4

South Carolina statistical abstract, general data, 1993 annual rpt, S7125–1

Texas health behavior risk factor surveillance survey results, by respondent characteristics, 1991 and trends, annual rpt, S7685–2

Utah health behavior risk factor surveillance survey results, by respondent characteristics, 1991, annual rpt, S7835–3

Washington State hypertension incidence by selected socioeconomic characteristics, 1990, annual rpt, S8363–1

Housing and Construction

Home buyer (1st-time and repeat) profile, and transaction characteristics, including prices and financing, by region and for 18 metro areas, 1990-92, annual survey rpt, B2150–1

Mortgage approval rates, by neighborhood characteristics and applicant race-ethnicity and income level, 1990, article, A8510–1.1

Public housing authority operations and finances, including resident characteristics, by agency size, 1989, A6800–1

Real estate property managers characteristics and compensation, including types of property managed, 1989 surveys, recurring rpt, A5600–4

State and local:

Arizona, Phoenix housing affordable prices and monthly payments, by income level, 1993 annual feature, U0280–1.505

Arizona statistical abstract, general data, 1993 recurring rpt, U5850–2

Oklahoma real estate loan rejection rates for whites and minorities by income level, statewide and by MSA, 1991, article, U8130–1.504

Income

Household wealth and income data by income level, including assets by type and detail by age group, 1989 and trends, R4700–17

Household wealth by asset type, income level, and race, 1984, article, A8510–1.1

Income comparisons among upper, middle, and lower income groups, by State, 1979-89, R3834–13, R3834–14

Minimum wage workers distribution by family income level, 1993 article, C8900–1.512

State and local:

California individual and corporate income tax returns and property tax assistance, by income class and county, 1990 and trends, annual rpt, S0855–1

California statistical abstract, general data, 1992 annual rpt, S0840–2

Georgia personal income tax returns, taxable income, and taxes paid, by income bracket and county, 1990, annual rpt, S1950–1.2

Georgia statistical abstract, general data, 1992-93 biennial rpt, U6730–1

Hawaii data book, general data, 1992 annual rpt, S2090–1

Iowa individual income tax return filings, income, taxes paid, and credits, by income bracket, and filings by county, 1991, annual rpt, S2860–3

Maryland individual income tax return filings, and income and tax liability data, by city, county, and income group, 1991, annual rpt, S3685–1

Montana income from selected sources, by income level, as reported on State tax returns, 1990-91, biennial rpt, S4750–1.1

Nebraska personal and corporate income tax returns filed, tax credits and liability, and income, by county and/or income group, 1990, annual rpt, S4950–1.1

New Mexico personal income returns, tax liability, rebates, and credits, by income class, 1990-91, annual rpt, S5660–1.2

Ohio individual income tax returns filed, income, and tax liability, by income class and county, 1990, annual rpt, S6390–1.3

Pennsylvania individual income tax returns, and taxable income by source, by income class, 1990, annual rpt, S6885–1

Pennsylvania statistical abstract, general data, 1992 recurring rpt, U4130–6

South Carolina income tax returns, exemptions, and liability, by income class, 1991, annual rpt, S7255–1.2

South Carolina statistical abstract, general data, 1993 annual rpt, S7125–1

Utah govt statistical review, fiscal and socioeconomic data, 1993 annual rpt, R9380–1

Utah individual income tax returns and adjusted gross income, by income class, 1991, annual rpt, S7905–1

Utah statistical abstract, general data, 1993 triennial rpt, U8960–1

Vermont individual State income tax returns, and property and sales tax refunds, by income class and locality, 1991, annual rpt, S8125–1

Virginia personal and corporate income tax returns filed, taxable income, and tax, 1990 or FY92 and trends, annual rpt, S8305–1.1

Industry and Commerce

Canada photographic and video equipment and supplies ownership, purchasing patterns, and use, by household characteristics, 1992 survey, recurring rpt, A8695–4

BY INCOME

Consumer expectations of economic conditions, by household income, Conference Board monthly survey, R4105–4

Discount store expenditures of consumers, by selected characteristics, 1993 article, C5150–3.509

Discount store shopper characteristics, use of natl vs regional discounters, and types of clothing purchased, 1990 and 1992, article, C8130–1.506

Photographic equipment and supplies, consumer ownership, purchasing patterns, and use, 1993 survey and trends, recurring rpt, A8695–2

Retail outlet consumer preference indexes, by selected demographic characteristics, 1993 annual feature, C4655–1.504

Security equipment industry personnel income, education, work conditions, and activities, 1993 survey, annual article, C1850–13.510

Labor and Employment

Pension benefits and coverage as affected by job tenure and mobility, with data by plan type and worker characteristics, 1993 rpt, R9260–17

State and local:

Missouri vocational rehabilitants by earnings level at referral and completion, FY92, annual rpt, S4505–1.1

New Jersey unemployment insurance repeat claimant characteristics, 1984-88, article, S5425–1.505

Law Enforcement

Black American crime, arrest, and incarceration data, with comparisons to whites, 1970s-91, annual compilation, C6775–2.5

Crime victims per 1,000 population, by demographic characteristics, 1991, article, R8750–1.505

Incarcerated mothers and their children, with data on characteristics, child caregivers, visitation, and support program use, 1991/92, A7575–4

Population

Black American earnings, income, and poverty data, with comparisons to whites, 1980s-91, annual compilation, C6775–2.7

Black American socioeconomic status, with comparisons to whites and data by region, 1960s-92, annual compilation, A8510 1.1

Consumer buying power survey of population, income, and sales by kind of business, by census div, State, MSA, county, and city, 1992, annual rpt, C1200–1.511

Ethiopia famine impacts and responses by household income group, 1980s, R5620–1.36

Families and unrelated individuals, by income level, 1987-91, annual rpt, A4957–1.1

Families by income, 1991, annual rpt, R9050–1.2

Gallup Poll public attitude surveys, results and sample characteristics, monthly rpt, C4040–1

Hispanic American households with income over $35,000, by income group and leading State, 1989, article, C4575–1.501

Hispanic American income and poverty data, with comparisons to whites, 1980s-91, annual compilation, C6775–3.5

Household income trends, with number and distribution of households by income level and State, 1980 and 1990, article, U8960–2.505

Market area population and characteristics, households, income, and retail outlets, for 21 leading areas, 1993 feature, C2710–1.538

Men age 69-84 quality of life indicators, including health, finances, family, and employment, by race, 1990 survey, U3780–9

Religion and related social issues, public opinions and attitudes, monthly survey, R8780–1

Russia population distribution by monthly income, Aug 1992, U2030–1.504

State and local:

Arizona Indian population, education, housing, health, and employment characteristics, with detail by reservation, 1970s-91, recurring rpt, U5850–2.9

Arizona, Phoenix area temporary winter resident characteristics, including expenditures, dwelling type, and region of residence, 1992/93, article, U0280–1.508

Arizona statistical abstract, general data, 1993 recurring rpt, U5850–2

Arkansas Census of Population and Housing detailed findings, 1990, U5935–7

California Census of Population and Housing detailed findings, 1990, S0840–9

Florida county data book, 1992/93 annual rpt, C6360–1

Florida statistical abstract, general data, 1992 annual rpt, U6660–1

Georgia county guide, general data, 1993 annual rpt, U6750–1

Hawaii data book, general data, 1992 annual rpt, S2090–1

Indiana population and family characteristics, 1990, article, U2160–1.501

Kansas households by income class, by selected county, 1989, annual articles, U7095–1.501

Kentucky labor force planning rpt, including population and labor force characteristics, and employment by industry, 1991 and trends, annual rpt, S3140–3

Louisiana Census of Population and Housing summary findings, by local area, 1990 and trends, U8010–4

Maine Census of Population and Housing summary findings, by local area, 1990, S3465–9

Maryland statistical abstract, general data, 1993-94 biennial rpt, S3605–1

Nebraska northeastern counties families and households, poverty rates, and income by source, by population size, 1989, article, U7860–1.509

New Jersey Census of Population and Housing detailed findings, by county, 1990, S5425–19

Pennsylvania Census of Population and Housing detailed findings, with selected data by county and municipality, 1990, U4130–13

Pennsylvania statistical abstract, general data, 1992 recurring rpt, U4130–6

Rhode Island Census of Population and Housing detailed findings, by county and municipality, 1990, S6930–9

South Carolina statistical abstract, general data, 1993 annual rpt, S7125–1

Utah personal income and household data, by location and race-ethnicity, 1990 census rpt, S7832–3.3

Index by Categories

Utah statistical abstract, general data, 1993 triennial rpt, U8960–1

Prices and Cost of Living

Christmas spending plans of consumers, by region, age, and income, Nov 1992 survey, annual rpt, R4105–81.10

Consumer attitudes on economic conditions and personal financial situation, monthly survey, U7475–2

Cost-of-living indexes by income group, 1991, annual article, U0280–1.501

Public Welfare and Social Security

Arts/humanities organization charitable contribution donor characteristics, 1993 survey article, C2176–1.507

Charitable and total average deductions claimed on tax returns, by income level, 1991, article, C2176–1.515

Charitable contributions, and share of households making donations, by income level, 1989, article, C2176–1.505

Recreation and Leisure

Boating-related activities participation, by household income, 1991, annual feature, C2425–4

Participation in 53 sports, by demographic characteristics, State, and census div, 1992, annual rpt series, A8485–3

Sporting goods purchaser characteristics, by product category, 1992, annual survey rpt, A8485–4

Sporting goods purchases, by product and outlet type, census div, and purchaser characteristics, with average prices, 1992 and trends, annual survey, A8485–2

Science and Technology

Ecologist personal and professional characteristics, including research activity and funding, with data by field, Mar 1992 survey, recurring rpt, A4685–1

Psychology grad dept faculty salaries, by academic rank, years in rank, census div, and sex, 1992/93 and trends, annual rpt, A2620–1

Transportation and Travel

Airline travel frequency, destination, and purpose, by traveler characteristics, 1992 survey and trends, annual rpt, A0325–6

Auto dealership service dept operations and profit outlook, and manager compensation, 1993 annual survey, article, C2710 3.537

Business traveler and trip characteristics, including mode, purpose, and lodging, 1991, annual rpt, R9375–12

Motorcycle use and user characteristics, licensed operators, and State requirements, 1992 annual rpt, A6485–1.2

Travel trips and traveler characteristics, including mode, purpose, type of lodging, and area of destination and origin, quarterly rpt, R9375–14

Traveler and trip characteristics, 1990, annual rpt, C2140–1.2

State and local:

Hawaii data book, general data, 1992 annual rpt, S2090–1

BY INDIVIDUAL COMPANY OR INSTITUTION

Agriculture and Food

Beer industry production, capacity, and sales volume, including top brands and brewers, 1982-92, annual feature, C0125–2.503

Beer shipments, for top 10 domestic brands, 1992, annual article, C2710–1.507

Index by Categories

BY INDIVIDUAL COMPANY OR INSTITUTION

Beverage consumption and sales, by type, leading company, and brand, 1992 and trends, annual rpt, C4775–1.4, C4775–2.3

Beverage market shares, for top 10 soft drink, bottled water, and beer brands, 1992, article, C5150–2.515

Beverage product market shares and sales, by company and/or brand, 1991 and trends, annual rpt, C0125–3.1

Candy (gummy) sales, total and for top 10 manufacturers, 1992-93, article, C2710–1.548

Candy sales and market shares, for top 10 brands, 1991-92, article, C2710–1.518

Candy sales in mass merchandise and drugstores, with 5 top-selling novelty brands, 1992, article, C5150–3.519

Cereal coupon advertisement shares for top 5 companies, 1991/92, article, C2710–1.511

Cereal market shares for selected manufacturers, by world region, 1989-92, C2710–1.527

Coffee market shares by company, for regular and instant brands, 1990-92, annual article, C2710–1.531

Convenience store outlets, gasoline sales, and average store size, by company, 1993 annual fact book, C4680–1.507

Convenience stores operated or planned, and gasoline sales, by chain company, 1993 annual article, C4680–1.509

Convenience stores with gasoline marketing operations, by chain company, census div, and State, 1992, annual article, C4680–1.502

Convenience stores with gasoline marketing operations, by chain company, census div, and State, 1993, annual article, C4680–1.510

Flour milling companies and capacity, in US by State, Canada, Mexico, and Central American and Caribbean area countries, 1993 annual directory and buyers guide, C8450–3

Food marketing industry "share groups," membership and facilitating organization for 15 groups, 1993 article, C4655–1.508

Food plant construction/expansion project info, cost, and employees, by company, 1992, annual feature, C2150–6.506

Food service (institutional) financial and operating data, for leading firms by market segment, 1993 recurring feature, C1850–3.511

Food service CEO compensation, with comparisons to company performance, for top 75 executives, FY92, article, C1200–5.513

Food service industry financial and operating data, for top 100 chains and companies, FY91-93, annual feature, C5150–5.509

Food service industry sales and establishments, for top 400 chains and other organizations, 1992, annual feature, C1850–3.509

Food service initial public stock offerings and prices, for 12 companies, 1992, C5150–5.503

Food store market shares and outlets, by company and store type, for approx 350 metro areas in US and Canada, with industry operating data, 1993 annual rpt, C3400–6

Food store sales and market shares, for private label products and top 4 brands in 6 product categories, 1992, article, C2710–1.521

Fruit juice purchasing by consumers, for leading brands, 1993 survey article, C5150–3.510

Grain elevators and capacities in Minneapolis-St Paul and Duluth-Superior switching districts, 1992, annual rpt, B6110–1.1

Grain elevators and capacity in US and Canada, by type and State or Province, with ranking of top storage companies, 1993 annual directory and buyers guide, C8450–2

Liquor market statistics, including sales, consumption, trade, distillery operations, and govtl info, with data by company, brand, and location, 1992 and trends, annual rpt, C4775–1

Liquor sales for top 36 brands, 1991-92, annual article, C2710–1.513

Meat company sales and slaughterhouse capacity, for top 20 firms, 1992 annual rpt, A2100–1.1

Restaurant (fast-food) chain sales, for top 6 companies, 1990, annual rpt, C2140–1.4

Restaurant (hamburger) establishments by census div, and sales and units for top 10 chains, 1993 annual article, C1200–5.504

Restaurant (Mexican food) establishments by census div, and sales and/or units for top 4-5 chains, 1993 annual article, C1200–5.514

Restaurant (Mexican food) sales, for top 5 chains, 1991, article, C1200–5.507

Restaurant (pizza) establishments by census div, and sales and units for top 10 chains, 1992, annual article, C1200–5.506

Restaurant (steak house/saloon) establishments, for 6 leading chains, 1992 article, C5150–5.502

Restaurant company stock price change, for 10 firms with greatest declines and gains, 1993 article, C5150–5.505, C5150–5.508, C5150–5.513

Restaurant company stock prices, for 10 firms with greatest declines and gains, Nov 1991-92, C5150–5.503

Restaurant franchises and sales, and franchisee fees and investment required, by leading company, 1993 annual feature, C1200–5.512

Restaurant minority franchisees, and minority-managed units, for 12 major chains, Sept 1993, article, C5150–5.511

Restaurant quality ratings among consumers, for most popular chains, 1993 annual feature, C1850–3.504

Restaurant sales and operations of 20 organizations with outstanding marketing concepts, 1993 article, C1850–3.508

Restaurant sales and units, for 50 fastest-growing chains, 1991-92, annual article, C1200–5.513

Restaurant State assn staff, payroll, locations represented, and political action committee spending, for organizations in 14 States, 1993 article, C1200–5.510

Restaurants with independent owners, sales, seating capacity, average check size, and patrons served, top 100 instns, 1992, annual article, C1850–3.505

Soft drink consumption and market shares, by company and brand, and by flavor, 1985-92, annual article, C0125–2.504

Soft drink coupons issued by top 5 companies, 1991-92, article, C2710–1.532

Supermarket chain stores, total and with pharmacies, top 46 chain companies, 1993 annual feature, C5150–2.511

Supermarket prices for selected grocery items in 4-7 chains in 7 metro areas, Apr 1993, article, C4655–1.507

Supermarket product sales and market shares, for top brands in selected product categories, weekly rpt monthly table, C2710–1

Tractor performance test results, by manufacturer and model, 1983-92, annual rpt, C3450–1.502

Water (bottled) sales, by company and brand, 1991-92, annual article, C0125–2.504

Wine market statistics, including sales, production, trade, and consumer characteristics, with data by company, brand, and geographic area, 1992 and trends, annual rpt, C4775–2

Wine sales and market shares for top 24 wine companies, and imports, 1990-92, recurring article, C2710–1.544

State and local:

Kansas grain facilities and capacity serving Kansas City Board of Trade, by company, 1992, annual rpt, B1530–1

Banking, Finance, and Insurance

Bank (master trust/custodial) assets and operating data for top instns, 1993 annual directory, C2710–2.522

Bank acquisitions of savings instns that have converted to stock ownership, participants, assets, and price data for 10 recent transactions, 1993 article, C3950–1.517

Bank assets, equity, performance, and market value, top 50 instns worldwide, 1993 annual feature, C5800–7.535

Bank assets, for top 12 instns worldwide, 1992, article, C5800–7.529

Bank assets, market capitalization, and financial ratios, for 6 largest instns, June 1993, article, C3950–1.527

Bank assets, share of nonperforming loans, and stock performance, for 10 major instns, 1993 article, C3950–1.526

Bank financial performance, including assets, loans, deposits, and operating ratios, top 100 instns, 1992, annual feature, C5800–7.526

Bank loans for corporate mergers/acquisitions, top 10 lending instns, 1992, article, C4683–1.504

Black-owned enterprises financial and operating data, for top 100 firms and auto dealerships and for top 15-25 financial instns, 1992 and trends, annual feature, C4215–1.507

Business Week investment indicators, including best and worst performing stocks and mutual funds, weekly rpt, C5800–7

Canada Govt-insured mortgage-backed securities issuance value, by issuer, 1987-93, article, A6450–2.508

Commodity futures investment performance and assets, for 10 largest managed funds, 1992 article, C5800–7.504

Corporate dividend yield trends for 10 companies with large increases, 1992 vs 1991, article, C4215–1.506

BY INDIVIDUAL COMPANY OR INSTITUTION

Index by Categories

Corporate dividend yields and payout ratios, for selected industries and companies, biweekly rpt quarterly feature, C3950-1.504, C3950-1.510, C3950-1.517, C3950-1.523

Corporate stock investment performance and earnings outlook, approx 900 companies, 1992 annual feature, C5800-7.509

Credit card market value and shares, for 5 major cards, 1992, article, C2710-1.516

Eximbank commercial aircraft loan and guarantee authorizations for individual customers, FY87-91, annual rpt, A0250-2.4

Finance company assets, commercial paper issuances, and bank guarantees, for selected leading companies, 1989-91, R4700-22

Financial advisors in corporate mergers/acquisitions, top instns ranked by activity, 1992, annual compilation, C4683-1.503

Financial instns performance, for 10 small/midsize instns with high returns on equity, 1992 article, C3950-1.502

Financial performance and growth rankings for approx 1,000 top corporations, with comparisons by industry group, 1993 annual rpt, C3950-1.505

Forbes investment indicators, including best and worst performing stocks, biweekly rpt, C3950-1

Foreign stock exchange price indexes, by exchange, 1991-92, annual fact book, B6625-1.1

Futures and options contract open interest (outstanding commitments), on foreign exchanges, by commodity and exchange, monthly rpt, A5040-6

Futures and options trading activity by exchange, and selected indicators for investors, 1992 and trends, commodity yearbook, C2400-1

Futures and options trading volume by commodity and exchange, 1988-92, annual rpt, A5040-1

Futures and options trading volume on foreign exchanges, by commodity and exchange, monthly rpt, A5040-5

Futures contract open interest (outstanding commitments), by commodity and exchange, monthly rpt, A5040-4

Futures trading volume by commodity and exchange, monthly rpt, A5040-2

Higher education student Federal loan default rates, by State, and for top 50 lenders and top 10 guarantee agencies, 1991, article, C2175-1.532

Insurance (accident/health) premiums and underwriting ratios, for top 300 firms, 1991, annual article, C1050-2.502

Insurance (life/health) assets of top 100 firms, with A M Best Co financial ratings, 1993 annual article, C1050-2.511

Insurance (life/health) capital/surplus, for top 100 companies, 1987-91, annual article, C1050-2.504

Insurance (life/health) capital/surplus, for top 100 companies, 1988-92, annual article, C1050-2.512

Insurance (life/health) company assets, for top 100 firms, 1987-91, article, C1050-2.506

Insurance (life/health) company assets, net operating gain, and return on equity, for 100 largest firms, 1992, article, C1050-2.510

Insurance (life/health) company formations, retirements, mergers, and name changes, by company, 1992 and trends, annual article, C1050-2.506

Insurance (life/health) income and expense data, for top 100 companies, 1992, annual article, C1050-2.511

Insurance (life/health) industry asset allocation and investment yields, for top 125 US and Canadian companies, 1992 and trends, annual article, C1050-2.512

Insurance (life/health) industry separate account assets, for top 15 firms, 1991, recurring article, C1050-2.505

Insurance (property/casualty) asset composition and investment yield, for top 100 firms, 1991 and trends, annual article, C1050-1.502

Insurance (property/casualty) company assets, for top 100 firms, 1987-91, article, C1050-1.505

Insurance (property/casualty) company formations, retirements, mergers, and name changes, by company, 1992 and trends, annual article, C1050-1.506

Insurance (property/casualty) company net premiums written, for top 100 firms, 1987-91, article, C1050-1.506

Insurance (property/casualty) income and expense data, for top 100 companies, 1992, article, C1050-1.511

Insurance (property/casualty) losses from Aug 1992 Hurricane Andrew, for 20 underwriters with greatest loss, 1992 article, C1050-1.503

Insurance (property/casualty) premium-expense ratios for top 100 companies, 1991, article, C1050-1.504

Insurance (property/casualty) premiums, loss ratios, and market shares, for top 20 general liability, medical malpractice, fidelity, and surety underwriters, 1991 and trends, annual article, C1050-1.502

Insurance (property/casualty) premiums, loss ratios, and market shares, for top 20 workers compensation underwriters, 1991 and trends, annual article, C1050-1.501

Insurance (property/casualty) premiums of top 100 firms, with A M Best Co financial ratings, 1993 annual article, C1050-1.510

Insurance (property/casualty) premiums written by top 250 companies and groups, 1992, annual article, C1050-1.508

Insurance (property/casualty) premiums written, loss ratios, and market shares, by line, leading company, and State, 1992 and trends, annual article, C1050-1.509

Insurance company acquisitions by foreign firms, participants and price for major purchases of property/casualty and life/health insurers, 1988-92, article, C1050-1.503, C1050-2.503

Insurance flexible-premium retirement annuity policy 5-year performance, by company, 1988-92, annual article, C1050-2.507

Insurance, foreign surplus lines companies trust funds on deposit in US, by company, Dec 1991, annual rpt, S7466-1

Insurance policy comparisons, for life and health insurance by type of policy and company, monthly rpt recurring feature, C1050-2.502, C1050-2.504, C1050-2.506, C1050-2.507, C1050-2.508, C1050-2.512

Investment banks with black owners, value of securities issues managed, for top 13 instns, Dec 1992, article, C4215-1.507

Investment mgmt companies new business, rankings of top 10 firms in selected categories, 1992, annual feature, C2710-2.506

Investment mgmt consultants, with data on clients and staff, 1992 annual feature, C2710-2.501

Investment mgmt firm assets managed in index funds, top firms, Dec 1992, semiannual article, C2710-2.505

Investment mgmt firm assets managed in index funds, top firms, Mar 1993, semiannual article, C2710-2.516

Investment mgmt firms, assets and operating data for approx 900 instns, Jan 1993, annual feature, C2710-2.511

Investment mgmt firms in intl investing, tax-exempt assets and operating data for top firms, 1993, annual feature, C2710-2.514

Investment performance of foreign stocks, for 100 traded on US exchanges, and 500 largest foreign companies, 1993 annual feature, C3950-1.519

Investment performance of leading funds with institutional investors, by fund and type, biweekly rpt quarterly feature, C2710-2.502, C2710-2.506, C2710-2.507, C2710-2.512, C2710-2.513, C2710-2.518, C2710-2.519

Investment return for portfolios recommended by 42 advisory newsletters, 1993 article, C3950-1.522

Japan bank market capitalization trends for 14 major instns, Apr 1992-June 1993, article, C2710-2.515

Japan bank profits and nonperforming loans, for 21 leading instns, FY92, article, R5650-2.533

Korea (South) stock fund market capitalization, price, asset value, and premium/discount trends, for 16 funds, 1993 article, C3950-1.508

Latin America loan exposure of 27 US banks, 1986, annual rpt, U6250-1.28

Life insurance (credit) policies in force and issued, for top 100 companies, 1991, annual article, C1050-2.504

Life insurance (universal) policy 5-year performance, by company, 1988-92, annual article, C1050-2.511

Life insurance (universal, whole, and term) sales results, for 115 companies, 1992, annual article, C1050-2.511

Life insurance annuity premium income and fund deposits of top 200 insurers, 1991, annual article, C1050-2.501

Life insurance average policy issued and in force, for 150 companies, 1981 and 1987-91, annual article, C1050-2.502

Life insurance average policyholder premiums and dividends, 10-year dividend scale comparisons, by insurer, 1993 annual article, C1050-2.510

Life insurance average policyholder premiums and dividends, 20-year dividend scale comparisons, by insurer, 1993 annual article, C1050-2.509

Life insurance policy comparisons, for single-premium deferred annuity policies, by company, 1992 annual article, C1050-2.501

Index by Categories

BY INDIVIDUAL COMPANY OR INSTITUTION

Life insurance policy comparisons, for universal life contracts, monthly rpt quarterly feature, C1050-2.502, C1050-2.505, C1050-2.508, C1050-2.511

Life insurance policy lapse ratios, for 150 companies, 1987-91, annual article, C1050-2.502

Life insurance policy 5-year performance, for single-premium deferred annuity policies, by company, 1987-91, annual article, C1050-2.501

Life insurance premium-expense ratios for top 100 companies, 1991, article, C1050-2.503

Life insurance premium income of top 500 US/Canadian life/health insurers, 1992 and trends, annual article, C1050-2.509

Life insurance sales and insurance in force, for top 25-135 issuers of ordinary, group, and industrial life policies, 1992, annual article, C1050-2.510

Life insurance sales, policies in force, and assets, for top 100 US/Canadian life/health insurers, 1992, annual article, C1050-2.509

Life insurance variable annuity and variable life premiums/deposits, for top life/health insurers, 1992, annual article, C1050-2.512

Life insurance variable annuity fund premium income and deposits, for top life/health insurers, 1991, annual article, C1050-2.503

Mortgage lender ranking trends based on originations and servicing volume, for top instns, 1970s-92, article, A6450-2.509

Mutual fund assets and investment performance, for 273 top performing funds, 1993 recurring article, C8900-1.528

Mutual fund assets and investment performance, for 276 top performing funds, 1992 recurring article, C8900-1.511

Mutual fund assets and investment performance, 105 closed-end equity and 120 closed-end fixed-income funds, 1993 annual feature, C5800-7.517

Mutual fund assets and investment performance, 555 fixed-income funds, 1993 annual feature, C5800-7.516

Mutual fund assets and investment performance, 760 equity funds, 1993 annual feature, C5800-7.515

Mutual fund assets and investment return, for 5 funds and their namesake "clones," 1993 article, C3950-1.521

Mutual fund assets and returns, for 10 major foreign-based funds, 1992 article, C3950-1.502

Mutual fund investment performance, by fund, June 1993 and trends, annual compilation, C3950-1.522

Mutual fund investment performance, for approx 1,000 established stock/balanced, taxable bond, and municipal bond funds, 1993 annual article, C3950-1.508

Mutual fund investment performance, for best and/or worst equity, and taxable and tax-free bond funds, 1992, annual feature, C5800-7.509

Mutual fund investment performance of best- and worst-performing funds, biweekly rpt semiannual feature, C3950-1.501, C3950-1.514

Mutual fund investment performance, with detail for best- and worst-performing funds in selected categories, weekly rpt recurring article, C5800-7.523, C5800-7.533, C5800-7.549

Mutual fund investment returns and assets, for 50 funds selected on basis of long-term performance, 1993 annual article, C4215-1.505

Mutual fund mgmt company assets and market shares, for top 25 firms, Sept 1992, article, C5800-7.511

Mutual fund mgmt company stock performance data, for 8 firms, 1993 article, C3950-1.523

Mutual funds (money market) financial performance and rankings of over 850 funds, with background info for investors, 1992 and trends, annual directory, C4682-2

Mutual funds financial performance and rankings of over 2,400 funds, with background info for investors, 1992 and trends, annual directory, C4682-1

Mutual funds pretax and after-tax return trends and tax liability for 50 largest funds, and ranking of 30 funds with highest and lowest liability, 1993 article, C5800-7.547

Mutual funds used most by defined contribution retirement plans, rankings of top equity and income funds by assets, May 1993, semiannual article, C2710-2.517

Mutual funds used most by defined contribution retirement plans, rankings of top equity and income funds by assets, 1993 semiannual article, C2710-2.505

Mutual funds used most by defined contribution retirement plans, rankings of top equity and income funds by investment performance trends, biweekly rpt quarterly feature, C2710-2.505, C2710-2.509, C2710-2.517

Mutual private equity funds value of closings and funds raised, for 13 funds, 1993 article, C2710-2.511

Options trading volume by commodity, securities index, and exchange, monthly rpt, A5040-3

Real estate investment advisors tax-exempt and total assets by type, top 76 firms, 1993, annual feature, C2710-2.520

Real estate investment mgmt companies, pension fund and other managed assets, and investment info, by company, 1992 annual directory, C2425-1.501

Real estate investment mgmt companies, pension fund and other managed assets, and investment info, by company, 1993 annual directory, C2425-1.507

Securities initial public offerings and value, and funds raised, for top 10 underwriters, 1992, article, C4687-1.507

Securities initial public offerings, performance of best and worst issues, and leading underwriters, 1993 annual article, C3950-1.517

Securities initial public offerings, performance of leading issues and underwriters, biweekly rpt quarterly feature, C3950-1.507, C3950-1.520, C3950-1.527

Securities investment return and dividends per share, for 5-50 best and worst performing stocks on 3 exchanges, 1992, annual article, C8900-1.507

Securities listed on NYSE, rankings of leading stocks by trading volume and market value, 1992, annual fact book, B6625-1.1

Securities traded over-the-counter on NASDAQ market, trading volume and price performance, for over 4,500 issues, 1992 and trends, annual rpt, A7105-1

Silver futures trading volume and open interest, by exchange, 1970-93, annual rpt, A8902-4

Small business investment company fund performance, assets, and number of companies in portfolio, for 6 funds, 1992 article, C3950-1.504

Small company earnings per share outlook of security analysts, for 18-80 companies, 1992-93, article, C3950-1.504

Spain insurance premiums for 10 leading underwriting groups, 1992, annual article, C1050-1.510

Spain, Madrid stock exchange performance by industry sector, and 20 leading stocks with greatest gains or losses, 1992, article, A8955-1.502

Spain mutual fund assets and corporate affiliation, for top 5 managers, 1993 article, A8955-1.503

Stock investment returns for 6 "blue chip" stocks vs S&P 500, 1982-92, article, C8900-1.503

Stock price, and earnings outlook through 1994, for 30 Dow Jones Industrials, article, C3950-1.527

Stockbroker commissions, fees, analysts, offices, and brokers, for 18 firms, 1993 annual article, C8900-1.528

Thailand investing mutual fund returns, assets, and other financial data, for 8 funds, 1993 article, C3950-1.527

Treasury bond (30-year) interest rate forecasts of 16 economists, year-end 1993-94, article, C8900-1.526

Trust instns and assets managed, approx 5,000 depts, US and Canada, 1993 annual directory, C2425-2.501

Trusts, master and directed, assets managed and services offered, approx 40 instns, 1992 annual directory, C2425-1.502

Venture capital firm portfolio value, and electronics and total investments, for approx 100 firms, 1993 annual feature, C1850-2.509

State and local:

Alabama credit union assets, for top 100 instns, 1990, recurring rpt, U5680-2.6

Alabama financial instns (State-chartered) financial condition, with deposits and assets by instn, FY92 annual rpt, S0110-1

Alabama insurance industry financial and underwriting data, by company and line of coverage, 1991, annual rpt, S0160-1

Alaska bank assets and liabilities of individual commercial and savings instns, quarterly rpt, S0280-2

Alaska insurance industry underwriting and investment data, by company and type of insurance, with regulatory info, 1991 and trends, annual rpt, S0280-3

Arizona bank balance sheets and branches, individual State and natl instns, quarterly rpt, S0460-2

Arizona credit union balance sheets, members, and branches, by instn, quarterly rpt, S0460-4

BY INDIVIDUAL COMPANY OR INSTITUTION

Index by Categories

Arizona insurance industry financial and underwriting data, by company and type of insurance, with regulatory info, 1992, annual rpt, S0483–1

Arizona savings and loan assn balance sheets and branches, individual State and natl instns, quarterly rpt, S0460–1

Arkansas banks and other financial instns, financial condition by instn, June 1992, annual rpt, S0632–1

Arkansas State govt investment holdings and funds on deposit with banks and savings and loan assns, by instn, FY92, biennial rpt, S0780–1

California banks and trust companies, financial condition by instn, with regulatory info, Dec 1992, annual rpt, S0810–1

California insurance industry financial and underwriting data, by company and type of insurance, with regulatory info, 1991, annual rpt, S0900–1

Colorado banks and trust companies, financial condition by instn, 1992, annual rpt, S1070–2

Colorado savings and loan assn financial condition, by instn, 1992, annual rpt, S1070–3

Connecticut banks and other financial instns, financial condition by instn, 1991 and trends, annual rpt, S1160–1

Connecticut insurance industry financial and underwriting data, by company and type of insurance, 1991, annual rpt, S1222–1

Delaware bank loans to students, by lending instn, FY88-92, annual rpt, S1425–1

Delaware financial instns, assets and branches, by instn, 1992, annual rpt, S1375–4

Florida insurance industry financial and underwriting data, by company and line of coverage, 1991, annual rpt, S1760–1

Georgia banks and other financial instns, financial condition by instn type, and assets by instn and city, Dec 1992, annual rpt, S1865–1

Idaho banks and other financial instns, financial condition, with data by instn and loan activity analysis, FY92 or 1991, annual rpt, S2235–1

Idaho insurance industry financial and underwriting data, by company and type of insurance, with regulatory data, 1991, annual rpt, S2260–1

Illinois bank and trust companies (State-chartered) financial condition and status changes, by instn, FY92, annual rpt, S2395–1

Indiana financial instns (State-chartered) financial condition, including assets by instn arranged by city, 1991 and trends, annual rpt, S2625–1

Iowa bank and trust companies (State-chartered), financial condition by instn arranged by city, FY92 annual rpt, S2760–2

Iowa insurance industry financial and underwriting data, by company and type of insurance, 1992, annual rpt, S2760–1

Kansas insurance industry financial and underwriting data, by company and type of insurance, with regulatory info, 1992, annual rpt, S2990–1

Kentucky financial instns condition, including assets by instn and city, with regulatory info, 1992 and trends, annual rpt, S3121–1

Louisiana financial instns (State-chartered), financial condition by instn arranged by city, with regulatory info, Dec 1992, annual rpt, S3265–1

Maine banks and other financial instns, financial condition by instn, June 1992, annual rpt, S3473–2

Maryland bank branches, assets, liabilities, and deposits, 9 largest instns, Dec 1991, biennial rpt, S3605–1.8

Maryland banks and credit unions (State-chartered) financial condition by instn, with regulatory data, FY92 annual rpt, S3655–2

Maryland insurance industry financial and underwriting data, by company and type of insurance, with regulatory info, 1991, annual rpt, S3655–1

Michigan banks and other financial instns, financial condition by instn, with regulatory info, 1992 and trends, annual rpt, S3957–1

Michigan insurance industry financial and underwriting data, by company and type of insurance, with regulatory info, 1991, annual rpt, S3983–1

Minnesota financial instns (State-regulated), financial condition by instn, 1991-92, annual rpt, S4140–3

Minnesota insurance industry financial and underwriting data, by company and line of coverage, 1991, annual rpt, S4140–4

Mississippi bank and credit union assets, by instn, Dec 1992, annual rpt, S4325–1

Mississippi bank assets, by instn and city, Dec 1991, annual rpt, U3255–4.8

Missouri banks and trust companies (State-chartered) financial condition, by instn, FY91-92 and trends, biennial rpt, S4502–1

Missouri insurance industry financial and underwriting data, by company and type of insurance, with regulatory info, 1992, annual rpt, S4527–1

Missouri State treasury investments, summary balance sheets, bonded debt, and deposits in individual banks, FY92, annual rpt, S4570–1.2

Nebraska insurance industry financial and underwriting data, by company and line of coverage, with regulatory info, 1992, annual rpt, S4890–1

New Hampshire insurance industry financial data by company, 1991, with FY92 regulatory info, annual rpt, S5220–1

New Jersey banks and other financial instns, assets and liabilities by instn, 1992 and trends, annual rpt, S5355–1

New Jersey insurance industry financial and underwriting data, by company and type of insurance, 1990, annual rpt, S5420–1

New Mexico financial instns, financial and operating data by instn, with regulatory activities, 1992, annual rpt, S5652–1

New York State insurance company assets or premiums, for top 10 life, property/casualty, and auto insurers, 1990, annual rpt, U5100–1.7

New York State insurance industry financial and underwriting data, by company and line of coverage, 1991, annual rpt, S5770–2

New York State insurance industry overview, with data on rate changes by company, and finances of companies in liquidation, 1991, annual rpt, S5770–3

Oklahoma financial instns, and insurance company finances, 1992 annual rpt, U8130–2.20

Oklahoma insurance industry financial and underwriting data, by company and type of insurance, with regulatory info, 1992, annual rpt, S6462–1

Oklahoma licensed money order agencies, by company, FY92 annual rpt, S6415–1

Oregon financial instns, financial condition by instn, Dec 1992 and trends, annual rpt, S6616–1

Pennsylvania insurance industry financial and underwriting data, by company and line of coverage, 1991, with FY92 regulatory info, annual rpt, S6835–1

Rhode Island banks and other financial instns (State-chartered), assets and liabilities, by instn, 1991, annual rpt, S6945–1

Rhode Island insurance industry financial and underwriting data, by company and line of coverage, 1990, with FY91 regulatory info, annual rpt, S6945–2

South Carolina financial instns (State-chartered) financial condition, including data by instn, FY92 annual rpt, S7165–1

South Carolina insurance industry financial and underwriting data, by company, 1991, with FY92 regulatory info, annual rpt, S7195 1

South Dakota insurance industry financial and underwriting data, by company and type of insurance, with regulatory info, 1991-92, annual rpt, S7300–2

Tennessee bank assets and financial ratios, by instn, Dec 1989, annual rpt, U8710–2.13

Tennessee banks and other financial instns financial condition, by instn and city, 1992 annual rpt, S7507–1

Tennessee insurance industry financial and underwriting data, by company and type of insurance, with regulatory info, 1991, annual rpt, S7466–1

Texas insurance companies in liquidation, financial data by company, FY92, annual rpt, S7700–1

Utah banks and other financial instns, financial condition by instn, FY93 and trends, annual rpt, S7830–1

Utah financial instn lending to students, by instn, FY92, annual rpt, S7895–2

Utah insurance industry financial and underwriting data, by company and line of coverage, with regulatory info, 1991, annual rpt, S7845–1

Vermont banks and other financial instns, financial condition by instn, 1992 and trends, annual rpt, S7995–2

Vermont insurance industry financial and underwriting data, by company and type of insurance, 1991, annual rpt, S7995–1

Virginia consumer finance companies financial condition, by instn, Dec 1992, annual rpt, S8180–3

Virginia financial instns (State-chartered), financial condition by instn and instn type, Dec 1992, annual rpt, S8180–2

Washington State banks finances by instn, 1992, annual rpt, S8325–1

West Virginia banks and other financial instns, composite financial condition, with selected data by instn, 1990-91, annual rpt, S8530–1

Index by Categories

BY INDIVIDUAL COMPANY OR INSTITUTION

West Virginia insurance industry financial and underwriting data, by company and line of coverage, with regulatory info, 1991, annual rpt, S8575–1

Wisconsin banks financial condition, by instn and city, with regulatory info, 1992 and trends, annual rpt, S8685–1

Wisconsin insurance industry financial and underwriting data, by company and line of coverage, with regulatory info, 1992, annual rpt, S8755–1

Wisconsin savings and loan assns and savings banks (State-chartered) financial condition, by instn, 1992 and trends, annual rpt, S8807–1

Wyoming State govt cash deposits in financial instns, by instn, FY92, annual rpt, S9010–1

Communications

Advertising agencies with multinatl clients, including countries in which they advertise, 1993 annual article, C2710–1.545

Advertising agency employment, for top 16 firms, Oct 1991-92, annual feature, C2710–1.505

Advertising agency income and billings, for top 10-20 multinatl firms in Latin America, Europe, and Asia/Pacific, 1992, annual article, C2710–1.527

Advertising agency income, billings by medium, employees, and offices, for leading US and/or foreign agencies, 1992 and trends, annual rpt, C2710–1.522

Advertising cost per 30-second spot for prime-time TV programs, 1993/94 season, article, C2710–1.543

Advertising expenditures by medium for top 100 advertisers, with comparisons to earnings and sales, and detail by product type and brand, 1991-92, annual rpt, C2710–1.547

Advertising expenditures for top 10 advertisers, 1st qtr 1992-93, article, C2710–3.544

Advertising expenditures for top 200 brands, by selected medium, weekly rpt quarterly feature, C2710–1.502, C2710–1.512, C2710–1.525, C2710–1.540

Advertising expenditures for top 25 network TV advertisers, with detail for 4 networks, 1992, annual article, C2710–1.515

Advertising expenditures of corporations and assns, by medium, 1988-92, and top 10 advertisers for 1992, annual article, A8770–1.504

Advertising worldwide media and marketing, with data for leading periodicals, and expenditures by top advertiser and country, 1992 annual feature, C2710–1.506

Book industry bestsellers and weeks on bestseller list, 1992, annual feature, C1852–2.505

Book industry bestsellers, hardcover and paperback, and copies in print, 1992, annual articles, C1852–2.509

Book publishing income and profit margin, for 16 companies, 1991-92, article, C1852–2.519

Book publishing sales, for top 11 general trade publishers, 1991-92, article, C1852–2.524

Book superstore sales and outlets for top 6 chains, Jan 1993, article, C1852–2.514

Books reviewed by specific publications, 1991-92, annual compilation, C1650–3.4

Bookstore chain sales, for leading companies, weekly rpt quarterly feature, C1852–2.519, C1852–2.524

Bookstores and sales of 11 largest trade bookstore chains, 1991-92, article, C1852–2.516

Broadcast (TV and radio) coverage and rights payments to college and professional football teams, 1993 annual article, C1850–14.534

Broadcast (TV and radio) coverage of professional basketball teams, 1993/94, article, C1850–14.540

Broadcast industries and cable TV devs, including data on finances, advertising, ratings, and licensing, weekly rpt, C1850–14

Broadcasting advertising industry assn chief executive salaries, for 4 assns, 1993 features, C1850–14.511

Broadcasting and related electronic communications companies revenues and earnings, top 100 companies, 1992, annual article, C1850–14.526

Broadcasting of major league baseball, with TV and radio originators, and rights payments, by team, 1993 annual article, C1850–14.515

Broadcasting revenues and profits, by source, for 3 major networks, 1992, annual article, C1850–14.522

Broadcasting stations ownership changes and transaction values, 1992, annual article, C1850–14.510

Cable TV advertising expenditures for top 5 advertisers in 7 product categories, biweekly rpt quarterly feature, C1858–1.502, C1858–1.508, C2965–1.505, C2965–1.511

Cable TV advertising interconnect subscribers, for top 50 interconnects, June 1993, recurring feature, C1858–1.505

Cable TV advertising interconnect subscribers, for top 50 interconnects, Sept 1993, recurring feature, C1858–1.508

Cable TV industry devs, including leading multiple system operators and systems, finances, advertising, and data by network and service, biweekly rpt, C1858–1, C2965–1

Cable TV multiple system operator subscriber base overlaps with telephone company service areas, for 9 cable and 8 telephone companies, 1993 article, C1850–14.541

Cable TV publicly owned systems, with subscribers and channels, 1993 annual directory, A2625–1.501

Cable TV ratings and households reached, by network, weekly rpt quarterly feature, C1850–14.506, C1850–14.517, C1850–14.530, C1850–14.540

Cable TV subscriber household shares, for top 10 and all other companies, 1993 article, C8900–1.518

Cable TV subscribers for 13 major companies owned by newspaper companies, Dec 1992, article, A8605–1.510

Cable TV subscribers of top 8 cable companies not affiliated with telephone companies, 1993 article, C4725–3.517

Cable TV wireless system subscribers, for top 8 companies, 1993 article, C1850–14.532

Canada daily newspaper circulation, by publication and city, 6-month periods ended Sept 1992 and Mar 1993, semiannual rpt, A3385–3.2

Cellular telephone subscribers, potential customers, and market penetration, for 10 companies, 1992, article, C4725–3.512

China cellular telephone network subscribers and capacity, by location and supplier, 1991, articles, A9315–1.503

Communications industries trade assn chief executive salaries, for 12 assns, 1993 feature, C1850–14.506

Communications regulatory agency activities, including rate reviews by company, 1991/92 annual rpt, A7015–3

Communications satellites in orbit and proposed, including owners and number of transponders, 1993 annual feature, C1850–14.512

Corporate magazines, including readership, for 10 publications, 1993 article, C1200–1.509

Direct marketing billings in US and worldwide, for top direct response agencies, 1991-92, annual articles, C2710–1.535

Direct marketing industry devs, including advertising patterns, finances, target market characteristics, and consumer attitudes, 1992/93 annual rpt, A4620–1

Entertainment industry devs and ticket sales, with detail for Broadway and road shows, and top films, weekly rpt, C9380–1

Entertainment industry mergers and acquisitions, including participants and value, 3rd qtr 1992, article, C9380–1.502

Entertainment industry securities issues, for 5 companies, 3rd qtr 1992, article, C9380–1.502

Europe public relations firms with US ties, including data on worldwide offices and activities, by company, 1993 article, A8770–1.505

Europe TV advertising rates and countries and households reached, for 7 pan-Europe channels, 1993 article, C2710–1.517

Football Super Bowl XXVII TV advertising units purchased, for 15 major advertisers, Jan 1993, article, C2710–1.509

Foreign advertising accounts budgets, and prospective and current ad agencies, for selected companies/brands, weekly rpt recurring feature, C2710–1.504, C2710–1.509, C2710–1.513, C2710–1.517, C2710–1.523, C2710–1.527, C2710–1.532, C2710–1.536, C2710–1.545, C2710–1.549

France public relations firms with US ties, including data on fees and staff, by company, 1993 article, A8770–1.503

Hispanic American marketing devs, including leading advertisers and media, and market characteristics, 1992 annual features, C4575–1.502

Interactive media system profiles, including operating sites and price data, for 12 companies, 1993 feature, C2710–1.520

Japan motion picture rental income, by distributor, 1991 and 1st 9 months 1992, article, C9380–1.502

Magazine (boating) advertising page trends, for 6 publications, 1990-Aug 1993, article, C2575–1.516

Magazine (parenting) advertising pages and revenues, for 4 publications, 1989-92, article, C2575–1.508

Magazine advertising pages and revenues, by publication, weekly rpt monthly tables, C2710–1

BY INDIVIDUAL COMPANY OR INSTITUTION

Index by Categories

Magazine advertising revenues and pages, for top 50 publications, 1991-92, annual feature, C2575–1.518

Magazine advertising revenues, for top 5 group publishers, 1st qtr 1993, article, C2710–1.526

Magazine charitable contributions, with beneficiary, sponsor, and amount, for 11 publications, 1992, C2575–1.508

Magazine circulation and advertising rates, for US and Canadian publications, 1988-92, annual rpt, A3385–1

Magazine circulation and paper sources, for 39 publications using recycled paper, 1993 annual rpt, C3975–5.3

Magazine circulation, by US and Canadian publication, 6-month periods ended Dec 1992 and June 1993, semiannual rpt, A3385–3.4

Magazine circulation, for top 200 consumer publications and top 10 nonpaid circulation magazines, 1st half 1993, semiannual article, C2710–1.541

Magazine circulation, for top 200 consumer publications and top 12 nonpaid circulation magazines, 2nd half 1992, semiannual article, C2710–1.514

Magazine circulation, for top 50-100 publications, 1991-92, annual feature, C2575–1.518

Magazine pay-per-call ("900" numbers) telephone services, with user costs and success ratings, for 11 publications, 1993 feature, C2575–1.504

Magazine prices and sales, for 20 magazines with highest and lowest subscription and single-copy prices, 1993 article, C2575–1.509

Magazine revenues, advertising pages, and circulation, for top 300 publications, 1992, annual article, C2710–1.531

Magazine revenues, circulation, advertising, and rates, for top 500 consumer and business publications, 1992, annual article, C2575–1.515

Magazine total and foreign circulation, and prices, for 10 publications with significant foreign readership, 1993 article, C2575–1.511

Magazine use of desktop publishing/electronic systems for pre-press operations, including hardware and software brands used, May 1993 survey, article, C2575–1.514

Magazine use of gender-specific vocabulary, and ratio of male to female readers, for 8 consumer publications, 1993 feature, C2575–1.507

Magazines (country lifestyle) subscribers, price, and reader age and income, for 7 publications, 1993 article, C2575–1.507

Magazines targeted to gay/lesbian audience, with circulation and advertising rates, for 7 publications, 1993 feature, C2710–1.509

Market research industry devs, including revenues and operations of leading firms, 1991-92, annual feature, C2710–1.550

Mass media company revenues for leading firms, with detail by medium, 1991-92, annual feature, C2710–1.540

Motion picture Academy Award best picture nominee films attended and preferred by public, Feb 1993 survey, C8915–1.502

Motion picture Academy Award nominations, by film and distributor, 1993, annual feature, C9380–1.514

Motion picture boxoffice receipts for films winning Academy Awards for best picture, with share received after award, 1984-91, C9380–1.520

Motion picture boxoffice receipts in US for foreign films winning Academy Awards, 1972-91, C9380–1.508

Motion picture foreign productions, boxoffice receipts, rental income, and top films in selected countries, weekly rpt, C9380–1

Motion picture production starts, by company, weekly rpt recurring feature, C9380–1

Motion picture rental income for all-time top films, 1993 annual feature, C9380–1.514, C9380–1.525

Motion picture rental income for films winning Academy Awards for best actor or actress but not for best picture, 1960-90, C9380–1.510

Motion picture rental income for films winning Academy Awards for best picture, 1937-91, C9380–1.509

Motion picture rental income, rankings of top all-time films, 1993 annual feature, C9380–1.509

Motion picture rental income, rankings of top films, 1992, annual feature, C9380–1.509

Motion picture theater screens, for top 4-8 and all other exhibitors in Germany, Spain, France, and UK, 1992, C9380–1.531

News media coverage of current events and issues, with data for selected networks or publications, bimonthly rpt, R3823–1

Newspaper (daily) circulation, by US publication and city, 6-month periods ended Sept 1992 and Mar 1993, semiannual rpt, A3385–3.1

Newspaper (weekly) circulation, by US and Canadian publication and city, 6-month periods ended Sept 1992 and Mar 1993, semiannual rpt, A3385–3.3

Newspaper advertising expenditures, with top advertisers, and top advertising agencies in billings, 1992, C2710–1.524

Newspaper circulation and newsprint consumption of 15 largest daily newspapers and companies, 1991, annual rpt, C3975–5.3

Newspaper circulation for daily and Sunday editions of top 100 papers, 6-month period ended Mar 1993, semiannual article, C2710–1.526

Newspaper circulation for daily and Sunday editions of top 100 papers, 6-month period ended Sept 1992, semiannual article, C2710–1.502

Newspaper circulation for leading publishers and world publications, with newsprint consumption data, 1992 annual rpt, A8610–1

Newspaper circulation in daily paper markets in US and Canada, by company, 1993 annual rpt, C3250–1

Newspaper family ownership or control, circulation, and dailies published, for top 25 newspaper groups, 1992 article, A8605–1.501

Newspaper journalists minority shares, for 50 leading publications, 1992-93, article, A8605–1.507

Newspapers and circulation for top 45 publishers, and advertising linage and revenues for 9 publishers, 1993 annual rpt, A1630–8

Newspapers and circulation of top 20 owners, and circulation of top 20 publications, Sept 1992, annual rpt, A8605–4

Public broadcasting station major gifts, with comparison to total donation value, for 7 stations, 1991-93, article, C2176–1.522

Public opinion on credibility of selected news media organizations, reporters, and public figures, 1985, 1989, and 1993 surveys, C8915–1.502

Publisher advertising revenues, for top 10 companies, 1st half 1993, C2710–1.538

Publisher advertising revenues, for top 10 companies, 1st 9 months 1992-93, C2710–1.551

Publisher advertising revenues, for top 10 companies, 1992, C2710–1.513

Publishing employment and productivity indicators, for 10 companies, 1992-93, article, C1852–2.521

Radio (public) audience and market population shares for blacks and Hispanics, for 6-13 stations, 1991, R4250–1.18

Radio advertising expenditures for top 50 advertisers, 1992, annual rpt, A8789–1

Radio audience ratings and program format, for top stations in leading metro markets, weekly rpt recurring article, C1850–14.506, C1850–14.507, C1850–14.508, C1850–14.521, C1850–14.531, C1850–14.542

Radio audience size, leading stations and formats, and advertising rates and revenues, by market area, recurring rpt, C3165–1

Radio networks audience age 12/over and 25-54, for top 15 networks, fall 1992 and trends, semiannual article, C1850–14.514

Radio networks audience age 12/over, for top 15 networks, spring 1993 and trends, semiannual article, C1850–14.538

Radio station group owners ranked by total Arbitron rating, with stations owned and ratings, for top 25 companies, summer 1992, article, C1850–14.502

Recording industry sales of Spanish-language music, for 6 leading and all other companies, 1992, article, C4575–1.508

Sales promotion income, for top sales promotion and promotional services agencies, 1991-92, annual feature, C2710–1.527

Telecommunication company capital expenditures, residential subscribers, and cable miles by type, for 8 telephone and 4 cable TV companies, 1993 article, C8900–1.513

Telecommunication multinatl operations, including number of countries with selected types of equipment, services, and staff, for 6 major carriers, 1993 article, C1850–5.520

Telephone company integrated services digital network (ISDN) planned use, by Bell regional holding company, 1993-95, article, C4725–3.509

Telephone company integrated services digital network (ISDN) planned use, for Bell regional holding companies and 1 major independent carrier, 1993-94, article, C4725–3.506

Telephone company revenues, access lines, and vulnerability to local services competition, by major company, 1992 and trends, article, C4725–3.511

Index by Categories

BY INDIVIDUAL COMPANY OR INSTITUTION

Telephone company stock prices and returns after privatization, for 12 foreign firms, 1993 article, C2710–2.516

Telephone holding company finances, operations, and subsidiaries, by company, Dec 1991, annual rpt, A9360–1

Telephone industry capital expenditure plans and network profiles, by company, 1992 annual article, C4725–3.502

Telephone local exchange carrier finances, equipment, and employment, by company, 1991 and trends, annual rpt, A9360–2

Telephone long-distance carrier revenues from toll-free ("800" number) service, for top 3 companies and all others, 1992-97, article, C1200–1.504

Telephone long-distance market value, with market shares for 4 major carriers, 1984 and 1992, article, C8900–1.515

Telephone Yellow Pages publisher revenues and advertising agency/media buying service billings, for top 10-15 firms, 1992, article, C2710–1.546

TV (color) market shares, for 5 manufacturers, 1987-92, article, C1850–2.508

TV advertisement recall by consumers, top brands or companies, 1st qtr 1993 and trends, article, C2710–1.530

TV advertising billings or expenditures, for top 10 agencies and top 15 advertisers, 1991-92, annual feature, C2710–1.528

TV advertising expenditures for top 10 broadcast TV network advertisers, 1st qtr 1992-93, C1850–14.527

TV advertising expenditures for top 10 network advertisers, 3rd qtr 1991-92, article, C2710–1.505

TV advertising expenditures for top 5 advertisers on local, spot, and syndicated TV, 1992, article, C2710–1.516

TV advertising expenditures on 4 major networks, for top 10 network advertisers, 1st qtr 1993, article, C2710–1.528

TV advertising expenditures on 4 major networks, for top 10 network advertisers, 2nd qtr 1992-93, article, C2710–1.541

TV advertising exposure value for top 19 sports event telecasts (primarily auto races), 1992, article, C2710–3.529

TV audience familiarity and popularity ratings of top 10 network prime-time programs, Nov 1982 and 1992, article, C2710–1.515

TV audience ratings and shares for 5 late night programs, Sept 1993 and trends, article, C2710–1.549

TV audience ratings and shares for 9 late night programs and/or segments, 1993 article, C2710–1.529

TV audience ratings for 4 networks and top 10 programs among households earning $60,000/over, Oct 1992-Jan 1993, C2710–1.517

TV audience share predictions of advertising agency representatives, by network and program, 1993/94 season, annual article, C1850–14.530

TV audience shares and ratings for made-for-TV movies, Sept 1991-Aug 1992, annual feature, C9380–1.511

TV audience shares for 38 new network series, as projected by advertising agency executives, 1993/94, annual article, C2710–1.529

TV out-of-home viewing impact on ratings for all network TV and 13 leading programs, Oct-Nov 1992, article, C2710–1.519

TV prime-time program ratings and audience, by program, weekly rpt, C9380–1

TV prime-time programs and hours sold by top producers, 1992/93 season, annual article, C1850–14.523

TV prime-time special audience ratings and share, for top shows broadcast Sept 1991-Aug 1992, annual feature, C9380–1.511

TV program advertising costs, for 19 network special event programs, 1993, article, C2710–1.515

TV Spanish-language program audience ratings, for top 10 programs among Hispanic viewers, Oct/Nov 1992, article, C2710–1.510

TV Spanish-language program audience ratings, for top 20 programs among Hispanic viewers, Oct/Nov 1992, article, C4575–1.504

TV station audience ratings and shares in 5-8 pm timeslot, for 5-7 stations in top 10 market areas, Feb 1993 sweeps period, recurring feature, C9380–1.516

TV station audience ratings and shares in 5-8 pm timeslot, for 5-7 stations in top 10 market areas, May 1993 sweeps period, recurring feature, C9380–1.527

TV station audience ratings and shares in 5-8 pm timeslot, for 5-7 stations in top 10 market areas, Nov 1992 sweeps period, recurring feature, C9380–1.505

TV station audience ratings in 5-8 pm and late news timeslots, for 5-7 stations in top 10 market areas, May 1993 sweeps period, recurring feature, C9380–1.531

TV station group owner companies ranked by market penetration, with stations owned, 1992/93, recurring article, C1850–14.516

TV station group owner companies ranked by market penetration, with stations owned, 1993 recurring article, C1850–14.524

TV syndicated program audience ratings, for 13 new programs, Sept 1993, recurring feature, C1850–14.540

TV syndicated program audience ratings, for 17 new programs, May 1992-93, recurring article, C1850–14.524

TV syndicated program audience ratings, for 19 new programs, Feb 1992-93, recurring article, C1850–14.514

Veterinary journal error rates of reference citations made in articles, for 6 major journals, 1990, article, A3100–2.507

State and local:

Alabama newspaper circulation by paper, and radio and TV stations, 1992 recurring rpt, U5680–2.2

Alaska public utility financial and operating data, by company and utility type, 1991 and trends, with FY92 regulatory info, annual rpt, S0280–4

Arizona newspapers circulation, by city and publication, 1991, recurring rpt, U5850–2.19

Arkansas public utility financial, operating, and regulatory data, by utility type and company, 1992 annual rpt, S0757–1

California public utility and transportation regulatory data, including revenue requests and rates of return by company, FY92 annual rpt, S0930–1

Florida newspapers circulation by publication, and telephone company exchanges and access lines, 1992 annual rpt, U6660–1.14

Florida public utility regulatory and operating data, by company and utility type, 1992 and trends, annual rpt, S1790–1

Hawaii newspaper circulation of 11 publications, 1988/89-1991/92, annual rpt, S2090–1.16

Idaho public utility regulatory data, and commission finances, FY92, annual rpt, S2290–1

Illinois telephone utility financial and operating data, by company, 1992, annual rpt, S2410–2

Kansas daily newspaper circulation by city and newspaper, 1985-91, annual rpt, U7095–2.13

Maryland newspaper circulation by paper, 1991, biennial rpt, S3605–1.8

Mississippi newspapers and radio and TV stations, 1992 annual rpt, U3255–4.7

Montana public utility and transportation property assessments, by county and company, 1991-92, biennial rpt, S4750–1.2

Nebraska public service commission regulatory activities, with financial and operating data for individual railroads and telephone companies, FY91-92 biennial rpt, S4940–1

New York State public broadcast stations, operation, and State aid, FY90-91, annual rpt, U5100–1.10

New York State public utility financial and operating data, by utility type and company, 1988-92, annual rpt, S5795–1

North Carolina public utility financial, operating, and regulatory data, by utility type and company, 1990 and trends, annual rpt, S5917–2

Oklahoma communications services, by company, 1992 annual rpt, U8130–2.17

South Carolina public service commission regulatory activities, with financial and operating data for individual utilities and railroads, FY92 annual rpt, S7235–1

Tennessee newspaper circulation by paper, and radio and TV stations by city, 1992/93 annual rpt, U8710–2.8

Utah newspaper circulation by publication, and telephone company access lines, 1993 triennial rpt, U8960–1.13

Vermont public utility financial and operating data, by company, 1986-91, biennial rpt, S8100–1

Washington State public service and utility companies property value, by company and county, 1992, annual rpt, S8415–1.4

Washington State telecommunication industry financial and operating data, by company, 1988-91, annual rpt, S8450–1.5

Education

Business grad school characteristics, for 20 instns ranked 21-40 in a 1992 ratings survey, article, C5800–7.531

Business grad school programs for executives, with data on revenues, enrollment, tuition, and participant characteristics, by instn, 1993 feature, C5800–7.552

Business school enrollment by degree level, for top 10 instns, fall 1992, annual feature, A0605–2.501

Business school entrepreneurship courses offered at 20 schools, 1993 article, C5800–7.551

BY INDIVIDUAL COMPANY OR INSTITUTION

Index by Categories

Catholic universities/colleges enrollment by instn, 1993 annual almanac, C6885–1

College football bowl games, payments to participating teams, 1992/93, annual feature, C2175–1.503

Corporate education contribution levels, and programs supported, for 119 companies, 1992 survey, annual article, C8900–1.502

Doctoral degree recipient characteristics, including citizenship status, source of support, field of study, and instn, 1990/91 and trends, annual rpt, R6000–7

Education journal editorial practices and characteristics, for 54 publications, 1993 recurring survey article, A8680–1.502

Educational and public employee retirement plan characteristics and finances, with detail for selected individual plans, 1990/91, recurring rpt, A7640–18.2

Elementary/secondary education foundation grants and value, for top 10 recipients, 1990/91, article, R4800–2.522

Elementary/secondary private school endowments, for top 9 instns, 1993 article, R4800–2.521

Elementary/secondary school superintendents membership in selected professional assns, 1992 survey rpt, A0775–5

Europe-US academic collaboration project Education Dept grants awarded to 23 US instns, 1993 article, C2175–1.538

Federal higher education funding earmarked for projects at specific instns, FY93, article, C2175–1.525

Financial support of educational instns from contributions, with top instns, by instn and donor type, 1991/92 and trends, article, C2176–1.514

Higher education academic term length, by semester, for 20 public and private instns, 1968/69 and 1993/94, article, C2175–1.536

Higher education appropriations, by State, instn, and function, 1993/94, annual feature, C2175–1.538

Higher education appropriations for selected public instns, FY90-93, annual rpt, S0827–3

Higher education appropriations from tax funds, by State, instn, and function, FY92-93 and trends, annual rpt, A8970 1

Higher education endowment funds of 419 instns, market values, June 1991-92, annual feature, C2175–1.508

Higher education enrollment, by State and public instn, fall 1992, annual rpt, A7150–5

Higher education enrollment, full-time faculty, and doctoral fields and grads, for 108 instns, US and Canada, 1991/92 annual rpt, A3365–1

Higher education enrollment of foreign students, by instn, discipline, State, and country of origin, 1991/92, annual feature, C2175–1.501

Higher education enrollment of minority and foreign students at approx 3,100 instns, fall 1991, recurring feature, C2175–1.510

Higher education faculty average salaries by rank, at approx 2,000 instns arranged by State, 1992/93, annual feature, C2175–1.516

Higher education faculty compensation and employment, detailed data by rank, sex, and instn, 1992/93 and trends, annual rpt, A0800–1

Higher education Fed Govt obligations for R&D, top US and Southern instns, 1989/90, biennial fact book, A8945–1.6

Higher education Fed Govt obligations, for top 100 instns, FY91, annual feature, C2175–1.528

Higher education foreign scholars engaged in research/teaching, for top 12-13 instns and countries of origin, 1991/92, article, C2175–1.502

Higher education foreign students and nonstudent scholars, by State and instn, 1991/92, annual rpt, R5580–1

Higher education funding and Federal aid for R&D, for top 100 instns, FY91, annual feature, C2175–1.502

Higher education instn endowment fund and investment pool characteristics and performance, by instn, FY92, annual survey rpt, A6705–2

Higher education instns ranked by number of patents received, for top 22 instns, 1992, article, C2175–1.512

Higher education on-campus crime incidence and arrests by selected offense, by instn and State, 1991/92, C2175–1.506

Higher education physical plant operations, costs, employment, salaries, and energy use, by instn and region, 1991/92, recurring rpt, A3183–1

Higher education private instn salaries and benefits of chief executives and top 5 earners, and total expenditures, by instn, FY91 or FY92, article, C2175–1.519

Higher education student athlete vs total graduation rates after 6 years, by sex, race, and Natl Collegiate Athletic Assn Div I instn, summer 1991, recurring feature, C2175–1.522, C2175–1.527

Higher education tuition/fees at approx 3,000 individual instns, 1992/93-1993/94, annual feature, C2175–1.535

Higher education voluntary support, by type of instn and donor, with top recipient instns and use, 1991/92 and trends, annual feature, C2175–1.525

Higher education, 2-year college enrollment, degrees, faculty and staff, and tuition/fees, by instn and State, 1992 annual directory, A0640–1

Journalism/mass communication enrollment and grads by level, by instn, sex, race-ethnicity, and field, 1990/91 and trends, annual article, A3225–1

Librarians at universities and research instns, salaries by sex, type of position, and instn, FY92 and trends, annual survey, A3365–2

Library (research) holdings, expenditures by type, and staff, for 120 academic and nonacademic instns, US and Canada, FY92, annual rpt, A3365–1

Library (research) holdings, staff, and expenditures, for instns in US and Canada, 1991/92, annual feature, C2175–1.511

Library and book trade reference info, including public and academic library funding, construction, and operations, by State and instn, 1992, annual compilation, C1650–3

Library automated system installations worldwide and in US, and vendor revenues, by vendor, 1992 and trends, annual articles, C1852–1.505, C1852–1.506

Library building referenda election results, by instn and location, FY92 and trends, annual article, C1852–1.508

Library construction, costs, and funding sources, by State, city, instn, and library type, FY92 and trends, annual article, C1852–1.501

Library school grad placements and salaries, by region, sex, instn, and library type, with detail for minorities, 1992 and trends, annual article, C1852–1.512

Library/info science school enrollment, staff and student characteristics, finances, and curricula, by school and degree program, 1991/92, annual rpt, A3235–1

Natl Merit Scholars freshman enrollment in top 64 higher education instns, 1992, annual feature, C2175–1.505

School bus fleet contractor fleets, pupils transported, and districts under contract, for top 50 contractors, 1993, article, C1575–1.505

School bus fleet rankings, top 74 districts and 26 contractors, 1992 survey, annual article, C1575–1.501

Social work higher education programs, faculty and student characteristics, and student aid, by instn, 1992, annual rpt, A4515–1.2

Southern States higher education instn library collections, staff, and expenditures, for 26 instns, 1990/91 and trends, biennial fact book, A8945–1.6

State and land-grant university tuition/fees, and room and board charges, by type of professional program and/or instn, fall 1991-92, annual rpt, A7150–4

Theological school enrollment, staff and compensation, and finances, with data by instn, 1991/92 and trends, annual rpt, A3376–1

Western States higher education faculty salaries at 14 universities, by academic rank, 1991/92, biennial rpt, S5005–1.7

Western States higher education student exchange program enrollment and support fees, by program and instn, for 15 States, 1992/93, annual rpt, A9385–1

Western States higher education tuition/fees, by resident status, State, and public instn, with State-funded student aid summaries, 1992/93 and trends, annual rpt, A9385–3

State and local:

Alabama higher education enrollment and degrees conferred, by instn, 1990 and trends, recurring rpt, U5680–2.4

Alabama public libraries, finances, holdings, circulation, staff, and population served, by library, FY92, annual rpt, S0180–1

Alabama university campus crimes and law enforcement employment, by instn, 1988-90, recurring rpt, U5680–2.10

Alaska higher education enrollment, by instn, 1982-92, annual rpt, S0275–1

Arizona higher education enrollment, by instn, 1970s-92, recurring rpt, U5850–2.4

Arizona higher education enrollment, by public instn, 1982-91, annual rpt, S0450–2

Arizona public library holdings, circulation, finances, and staff, by instn and county, FY92, annual rpt, S0495–1

Arkansas higher education degrees conferred, by level, discipline, student race and sex, and instn, 1990/91 and trends, annual rpt, S0690–3

Arkansas higher education enrollment by student characteristics and geographic origins, by instn, fall 1991 and trends, annual rpt, S0690–1

Index by Categories

BY INDIVIDUAL COMPANY OR INSTITUTION

Arkansas higher education finances, including revenues by source, expenditures by function, and State appropriations, by public instn, FY80s-95, biennial rpt, S0690–4

Arkansas higher education FTE enrollment, and student credit hour production by program area, by academic level and instn, 1991/92 and trends, annual rpt, S0690–2

Arkansas public school teachers, and enrollment by grade, by county, district, and school, Oct 1992, annual rpt, S0660–1

California library finances, staff, holdings, and services, by library type and facility, FY92, annual rpt, S0825–2

California postsecondary education enrollment and degrees, by sex, race-ethnicity, and instn, 1990/91, annual series, S0827–2

Colorado library finances and operations, including staff, holdings, and population served, by instn and library type, series, S1000–3

Connecticut public library staff, holdings, circulation, and finances, by library and town, FY91, annual rpt, S1242–1

DC higher education enrollment, by level and instn, 1988/89-1991/92, annual rpt, S1535–3.6

DC public school enrollment, by school, 1991/92, annual rpt, S1535–3.1

DC public school finances, enrollment, grads, and test scores, with data by school, 1987/88-1991/92, annual rpt, S1605–2

Delaware postsecondary education finances, enrollment, and degrees conferred, by instn, FY94 annual rpt, S1425–1

Delaware school enrollment, grads, staff, finances, and facilities, by county, school district, and/or instn, 1991/92, annual rpt, S1430–1

Florida higher education enrollment, by instn, 1990 and trends, annual rpt, U6660–1.4

Florida higher education enrollment, by instn, 1992/93 annual rpt, C6360–1

Florida higher education enrollment, degree programs, staff, and finances, by State-supported instn, with student and staff characteristics, 1991/92 annual rpt, S1725–1

Florida public libraries, finances, holdings, staff, and services, by system and library, FY92, annual rpt, S1800–2

Florida public library operations, and community college finances, 1992 annual rpt, U6660–1.20

Georgia higher education degrees conferred, enrollment, and finances, by instn, 1990/91-1991/92 and trends, biennial rpt, U6730–1.2

Georgia higher education enrollment by sex, by instn, 1991, annual rpt, U6750–1

Georgia State-supported higher education instn assets and liabilities, by instn, FY92, annual rpt, S1860–1

Hawaii college and university enrollment, degrees conferred, and library operations, by instn, 1992 annual rpt, S2090–1.3

Idaho academic library staff, expenditures, and holdings, by instn, 1992, annual feature, A5370–1

Idaho higher education enrollment by level, and degree and vocational programs offered, by instn, 1992 recurring rpt, S2218–2.3

Idaho public library holdings, staff, services, circulation, and finances, by instn, FY92, annual rpt, S2282–1

Illinois criminal offenses for campus, railroad, and other special police forces, 1991, annual rpt, S2536–1

Illinois elementary and secondary enrollment at 7 State funded instns, by funding agency, 1990/91, annual rpt, S2440–1.1

Illinois higher education enrollment, degrees, staff, and finances, by public and private instn and student characteristics, 1993 annual rpt, S2475–1

Illinois higher education instn security personnel, and crimes by offense, by instn, 1991, annual rpt, U6910–2

Illinois public library holdings, staff, and finances, by instn, FY92, annual rpt, S2535–2

Illinois statistical abstract, general data, 1992 annual rpt, U6910–2

Indiana enrollment in private schools, by grade and instn, 1992/93, annual table, S2608–2.7

Indiana high school enrollment by grade and sex, by county and school, 1992/93, annual table, S2608–2.5

Indiana higher education enrollment, for top 20 instns, fall 1990, annual rpt, S2570–1.1

Indiana public and other library holdings, circulation, finances, and staff, by instn, 1992 or FY92, annual rpt, S2655–1

Iowa postsecondary enrollment, degrees, staff, and finances, by instn, 1990/91, annual rpt, S2755–1

Iowa public library finances and operations, by county, size of population served, and library, FY92, annual rpt, S2778–1

Kansas private school enrollment, attendance, and teachers, by instn, 1990/91, annual rpt, S2945–1

Kansas public and private college enrollment, by instn, 1991/92, annual rpt, U7095–2.5

Kentucky higher education enrollment, degrees, staff, and finances, by State-supported instn, 1983-92, annual rpt, S3130–3

Louisiana public library finances, holdings, circulation, and personnel, by library system, FY92, annual rpt, S3275–1

Maine higher education enrollment and programs, by instn, 1992 recurring rpt, S3434–1

Maine 1-room schools, with enrollment, fall 1991, annual rpt, S3435–1

Maryland higher education enrollment, degrees, faculty, and finances, by instn, 1993-94 biennial rpt, S3605–1.2

Maryland public school enrollment and staff, by county and instn, 1992/93, annual rpt, S3610–2.8

Minnesota postsecondary education interstate tuition reciprocity, by selected instn, 1993 biennial rpt, S4195–2.2

Minnesota public library holdings, staff, services, circulation, and finances, by library, 1991, annual rpt, S4165–2

Mississippi higher education enrollment and degrees, by level and field, and finances, by State-supported instn, 1991/92, annual rpt, S4360–1

Mississippi higher education enrollment and degrees conferred, by instn, 1992 annual rpt, U3255–4.3

Mississippi public library holdings and operations, by library and city, FY91, annual rpt, U3255–4.3

Missouri higher education enrollment, degrees, libraries, staff, and finances, by instn, 1992 and trends, annual rpt, S4520–3

Missouri public, special, and academic libraries, finances, holdings, circulation, staff, and services, by location, FY92, annual rpt, S4520–2

Montana higher education enrollment, by instn, 1983-92, annual rpt, S4653–1

Montana public library holdings, staff, circulation, and finances, by library, FY92, annual rpt, S4725–1

Montana public school enrollment by grade, and grads, by school, county, race-ethnicity, and sex, 1992 and trends, annual rpt, S4740–1

Nebraska elementary and secondary schools, enrollment by grade, and staff, with data by school district and county, annual series, S4865–2

Nebraska public libraries, finances, holdings, circulation, staff, and population served, by instn, FY91, annual rpt, S4910–1

Nevada higher education enrollment, degrees, faculty, and selected finances, by instn, 1967/68-1991/92, biennial rpt, S5005–1.7

Nevada library and staff directories for public and academic libraries, with data on holdings, operations, and finances, FY92, annual rpt, S5095–1

New Hampshire high school grads and postgraduation activities, by school, county, and sex, 1991, annual tables, S5200–1.2

New Hampshire high school grads and postgraduation activities, by school, county, and sex, 1992, annual tables, S5200–1.15

New Hampshire public library finances and operations, by library and/or location, 1991, annual rpt, S5227–1

New Hampshire public secondary school enrollment, by instn, Oct 1992, annual table, S5200–1.7

New Jersey crimes by offense, and law enforcement employees, by higher education instn, 1992, annual rpt, S5430–1

New Jersey public library finances, holdings, circulation, and staff, by county and library, 1991, annual rpt, S5385–2

New Mexico public library operations and finances, by instn, FY92, annual rpt, S5627–1

New York State public library finances, staff, holdings, and services, by library and county, 1991, annual rpt, S5745–2

New York State university system enrollment, degrees, and employment, by campus, 1992 annual rpt, U5100–1.10

North Carolina higher education enrollment, degrees, libraries, staff, and student characteristics, finances, and housing, by instn, 1992/93 and trends, annual rpt, U8013–1

North Carolina public libraries, finances, holdings, and personnel, by library system, FY91, annual rpt, S5910–1

North Dakota elementary and secondary school staff, by position and college attended, 1992/93 annual rpt, S6180–3

North Dakota elementary and secondary schools, enrollment, and staff, by school type and location, 1992/93 annual directory, S6180–2

BY INDIVIDUAL COMPANY OR INSTITUTION

Index by Categories

North Dakota higher education enrollment, by level, instn, county, and selected student characteristics, fall 1992 and trends, annual rpt, S6110–1

North Dakota public library finances, holdings, staff, and operations, by instn, FY91, annual rpt, S6180–5

Ohio public, academic, and other library finances, holdings, and staff, by library and location, 1992 and trends, annual rpt, S6320–1

Oklahoma higher education enrollment and State funding, by instn, 1992 annual rpt, U8130–2.8

Oklahoma library holdings and operations, by instn, FY91, annual rpt, U8130–2.21

Oklahoma public and institutional library holdings, circulation, finances, and staff, by facility, FY92, annual rpt, S6470–1

Oregon elementary and secondary public school enrollment by race-ethnicity and teachers, by instn, Oct 1992, annual rpt, S6590–1.1

Oregon library finances, staff, holdings, and services, for public, academic, and special libraries by instn, FY92 and trends, annual rpt, S6635–1

Oregon private and parochial schools, enrollment, and grads, with detail by school, county, and religious affiliation, 1992/93, annual rpt, S6590–1.19

Oregon public high school completers, by instn, county, sex, and race-ethnicity, 1992, annual rpt, S6590–1.10

Oregon public middle school enrollment, by instn, Oct 1992, annual rpt, S6590–1.11

Oregon public secondary school enrollment, by instn, Oct 1992, annual rpt, S6590–1.13

Pennsylvania higher education enrollment, by student characteristics and instn, 1992 and trends, annual rpt, S6790–5.9

Pennsylvania higher education funding by purpose, and library holdings, operations, and staff, by instn, 1992 recurring rpt, U4130–6.4

Pennsylvania higher education tuition/fees, and room and board charges, by instn, 1992/93 and trends, annual rpt, S6790–5.3

Pennsylvania public and institutional library personnel, holdings, circulation, and finances, by county and facility, FY92, annual rpt, S6790–2

Pennsylvania vocational education enrollment, student characteristics, and faculty, by program and/or school, 1991/92 and trends, annual rpt, S6790–5.7

Rhode Island grads of public, nonpublic, and State-operated high schools, by sex and instn, June 1992, annual rpt, S6970–1.1

Rhode Island higher education enrollment, finances, and facilities, by instn, 1993 annual rpt, C7975–1

Rhode Island higher education financial data, by instn, FY92, annual rpt, S6930–1

South Carolina enrollment in public higher education, by instn, fall 1990-91, annual planning rpt, S7155–3.3

South Carolina higher education enrollment and tuition, by instn, fall 1991 and trends, annual rpt, S7125–1.6

South Carolina higher education enrollment, degrees, staff, and finances, by instn, 1992 and trends, annual rpt, S7185–2

South Carolina public and institutional libraries, finances, services, holdings, and staff, by library, FY92, annual rpt, S7210–1

South Dakota public higher education finances, staff, enrollment, degrees, and facilities, by instn, FY93 annual rpt, S7375–1

Tennessee higher education degrees conferred and enrollment, and public library expenditures, staff, and services, by instn, 1992/93 annual rpt, U8710–2.16

Tennessee higher education enrollment, finances, staff, and programs, by instn, 1992/93 and trends, annual rpt, S7525–1

Texas elementary and secondary education enrollment by race-ethnicity, by school, district, and county, 1991/92, annual rpt, S7670–1.1

Texas higher education enrollment, faculty, curricula, and finances, by instn, 1991/92 and trends, annual rpt, S7657–1

Texas public libraries, holdings, circulation, staff, and finances, by library and location, FY91, annual rpt, S7710–1

Utah college president salaries by instn, 1992, annual rpt, R9380–1.5

Utah higher education and private elementary and secondary revenues and/or enrollment, by instn, 1993 triennial rpt, U8960–1.3

Utah higher education degrees, enrollment, staff, and finances, by public instn, with selected comparisons to instns in other States, 1993/94 annual rpt, S7895–2

Utah higher education instns revenues, expenditures, and enrollments, by instn, 1993 annual rpt, R9380–1.8

Utah private school enrollment, by race-ethnicity, sex, and instn, Oct 1991, annual rpt, S7815–1.2

Utah public libraries, services, staff, and finances, by library, 1992, annual rpt, S7808–1

Vermont elementary and secondary school enrollment by grade, sex, race-ethnicity, school, and county, 1992/93 and trends, annual rpt, S8020–1

Vermont higher education info, including degrees conferred, enrollment, and finances, by instn, 1992 annual rpt, S8035–2

Vermont libraries, finances, resources, and circulation, by city and library, FY91-92, biennial rpt, S8080–1

Virginia public library operations and finances, by instn, FY92, annual rpt, S8275–1

Washington State public libraries, finances, holdings, circulation, staff, and population served, by instn, 1992, annual rpt, S8375–1

West Virginia education professional certificates issued to grads of selected higher education instns, 1991/92, annual rpt, S8540–3

West Virginia higher education enrollment, degrees, faculty and student characteristics, and finances, by instn, 1992/93 and trends, annual rpt, S8533–1

West Virginia higher education finances, enrollment, and degrees conferred, by instn, FY82-91, annual rpt, R9385–1.4

West Virginia public, academic, and special library operations and/or finances, by instn, 1991/92, annual rpt, S8590–1

Wisconsin libraries, operations, and finances, by library type, instn, and location, 1992, annual rpt, S8795–1

Wisconsin postsecondary education enrollment, by instn, 1992/93 and trends, biennial rpt, S8780–1.2

Wyoming public school enrollment, by sex, race-ethnicity, school, and district, 1991/92 and trends, annual rpt, S8890–1.2

Energy Resources and Demand

Air pollutant (sulfur dioxide) emission allowance sales at EPA auction, with cumulative allowances and amount and number of bids by company, Mar 1993, article, C6985–6.507

Alternative fuel (biodiesel) derived from vegetable oils or animal fats, manufacturing capacity of 14 plants worldwide, 1993 article, C5800–8.504

China nuclear power generating capacity by unit, uranium resources by Province, and uranium processing capacity by plant, 1993 article, B6800–1.509

China oil exploration joint venture contracts, with location, land area, and participating companies, 1993 article, C6985–1.550

Coal deliveries and prices for individual electric power plants, by utility, State, and census div, monthly rpt, A7400–9

Coal imports for electric utilities, by country of origin and utility, 1980s-91, annual rpt, A7400–2.1

Coal industry executive views on companies and regional assns providing most leadership, and top companies in 4 aspects of operations, Mar 1993 survey, article, C5226–1.509

Coal longwall mining operations, by company and location, 1993, annual article, C5226–1.504

Coal preparation plants and capacity in US, Canada, and Mexico, by company, 1993 biennial feature, C5226–1.511

Distribution utilities pipeline facilities, distribution, and revenue data, by selected major company, 1991, annual rpt, A1775–3.3

Ecuador oil production by domestic and foreign company, oil consumption, and outlays of govt-owned holding company, 1990s-2010, article, C6985–1.518

Electric power (steam) plants, capacity, generation, and fuel use and costs, by fuel type, utility, and location, 1991, annual rpt, A7400–7

Electric power generated and fuel use by type, for individual steam plants by utility and State, monthly rpt, A7400–8

Electric power generating capacity additions, by facility, 1991-92, annual rpt, A4700–2.1

Electric power plants planned and under construction in 1993, by type, utility, and region, and forecast capacity for 1993-2001, annual feature, C5800–28.503

Electric power residential costs for 12 utilities with highest and lowest rates, summer 1992, annual article, C6985–6.508

Electric power residential costs for 12 utilities with highest and lowest rates, winter 1991/92, annual article, C6985–6.502

Electric power transmission facility additions/upgrades planned, by facility and region, winter 1992/93, C5800–28.504

Index by Categories

BY INDIVIDUAL COMPANY OR INSTITUTION

Electric utility customers by type, and direct load-control budgets for 1993, for 17 companies, 1993 article, C5800–28.508

Electric utility financial and investment performance indicators, for top 50 companies, 1991, article, C5800–28.501

Electric utility financial and operating performance rankings, top 100 utilities, 1992, annual article, C6985–6.508

Electric utility fuel consumption for 7 natural-gas-fired combined-cycle power plants, 1993 article, C5800–28.509

Electric utility generating unit additions and retirements, by utility, 1993-2002, annual rpt, A8630–2

Electric utility income and operating data, by type of company and for individual locally owned utilities, 1993 annual directory, A2625–1.501

Electric utility operating data, including generating capacity and efficiency, peak demand, and fuel consumption, top 100 utilities, 1992, annual article, C6985–6.512

Electric utility power delivery equipment voltage level upgrades completed or planned, and system characteristics, for 20 substations, 1993 article, C6985–6.512

Electric utility revenues, sales, and distribution operating/maintenance expenses, for top 20 companies, 1990-91, article, C6985–6.501

Electric utility spot coal purchases, for approx 20 utilities, monthly rpt, C5226–1

Electric utility sulfur dioxide emission allowance bids and purchases at EPA auction, by company, 1993 article, C5800–28.508

Ethanol capacity operating and planned/under construction, by company and plant, 1992 article, A1250–1.501

Europe oil refinery desulfurization requirements, for 18 companies, 1997 and 2002, article, C6985–1.547

Finland nuclear generation and capacity of operating reactors, and capacity of nonnuclear plants to be commissioned by 2000, 1993 article, B6800–1.507

France oil refinery capacity by process, and capital outlays for unleaded gasoline projects, for selected companies, 1993 article, C6985–1.547

Fuel economy averages for motor vehicles, by manufacturer, 1970s-93, annual rpt, A0865–1.3

Fuel economy, EPA estimates for 1994 model vehicles, by model and size group, annual feature, C2710–3.550, C2710–3.551

Gasoline unattended-site retail outlets, franchises/marketers, and average transactions, for 6 retail chains, 1993 article, C4680–1.511

Gulf of Mexico Federal oil/gas leases relinquished by top 5 companies, 1st half 1993, article, C6985–2.509

Gulf of Mexico oil/gas wells drilled by operator, 1st qtr 1993, article, C6985–2.508

Gulf of Mexico total and undrilled Federal oil/gas leases relinquished, by company, 1992, article, C6985–2.505

Indonesia coal production, by company, 1984-90, annual rpt, A7400–2.2

Italy oil refinery capacity and throughput, by company and plant, 1990-91 or 1992, article, C6985–1.523

Liquefied natural gas trade by country and outlook, and trading contracts in effect with participants, 1993 article, C6985–1.535

Midwest electric utilities prices paid for Powder River Basin coal, for 15 plants, 1991, article, A4700–4.501

Motor vehicle fuel economy ratings, with EPA estimates for 1993 models, annual data book, C2710–3.531

Myanmar oil and gas production and potential yield, and leased acreage by company and basin, 1992 article, C6985–1.506

Natural gas distribution utility and pipeline company financial and operating data, top 500 companies, 1992, annual article, C6780–1.505

Natural gas processing plants, capacity, and production, by company, State, and country, 1993 annual rpt, C6985–1.537

Natural gas spot prices for 7 pipelines, monthly 1986-91, annual compilation, C6985–9.3

Natural gas throughput of top 10 interstate pipelines, 1991 and trends, article, C6780–1.502

Natural gas utility pipeline mileage and distribution services, pipeline breakage risk, and number of customers, for 21 utilities, 1991, article, C6780–1.503

Natural gas well completions in tight gas sands formations, for top 25 operators, cumulative through 1992, article, C6985–1.501

Norway offshore reserves of oil, gas, and natural gas liquids, for 5 new fields, with operator and location, 1993 article, C6985 2.509

Nuclear power generation and fuel processing trends and devs worldwide, with related data on individual reactor capacity and completion status, quarterly rpt, B6790–1

Nuclear power plant (non-US) capacity factors and cumulative generation, by plant, 1993 annual feature, B6790–1.503

Nuclear power plant capacity factors and cumulative generation, by plant, 1993 annual feature, B6790–1.502

Nuclear reactors in operation, with capacity, electricity generation, and construction, by unit and country, 1992, annual rpt, B6800–2.2

Offshore oil/gas production system projects under construction or planned, by company and country, 1992 annual feature, C6985–2.501

Offshore oil/gas support vessel fleet characteristics, by company, 1993 annual article, C6985–2.505

Oil and gas independent company finances and operations, for approx 50 companies, 1991-92, semiannual article, C6985–1.504

Oil and gas industry financial and operating data, rankings for top 300 US and top 100 non-US companies, 1991-92, annual feature, C6985–1.547

Oil and gas industry operations and finances of 20-30 major companies, 1991 and trends, periodic basic data book, A2575–14

Oil and gas industry trends, with data by company, State, and country, 1993 annual compilation, C6985–4

Oil and gas intl supply-demand, exploration, refining, reserves, and industry finances, basic data by country and company, 1993 annual rpt, C6985–3

Oil and gas lease sales in Gulf of Mexico, with top bidders, weekly rpt recurring article, C6985–1.522, C6985–1.547

Oil and gas pipeline construction costs, mileage, and operating and financial data, by location and/or company, 1991 and trends, annual feature, C6985–1.504

Oil and gas research grant awards of American Chemical Society Petroleum Research Fund, by recipient, 1993 recurring feature, A1250–1.514, A1250–1.525, A1250–1.538

Oil and refined products imports, by importing company, port, and country of origin, monthly rpt, A2575–12

Oil change fast service outlet independent and franchise establishments, for top 7 chains, 1992, article, C4680–1.503

Oil company earnings, for approx 20 companies, monthly rpt quarterly article, C4680–1.501, C4680–1.504, C4680–1.506, C4680–1.510

Oil company R&D expenditures, for 17 firms, 1981-92, article, C6985–1.536

Oil exploration/production expenditures of US and foreign companies in US, Canada, and elsewhere, 1992-93, annual article, C6985–1.515

Oil industry income and operating data, for approx 20 major companies, 1991-92, annual article, C6985–1.533

Oil industry income, net profits, and selected operating data, approx 25 companies, weekly rpt quarterly article, C6985–1.520, C6985–1 534, C6985–1.545

Oil industry income, net profits, and selected operating data, approx 50 companies, 1st 9 months 1991-92, article, C6985–1.511

Oil industry operations of govt-owned companies in 4 Middle Eastern or Latin American countries, 1993 articles, C6985–1.542

Oil refineries for sale, with current owner and crude capacity, 1993 article, C6985–1.539

Oil refineries, petrochemical processing facilities, and pipelines, construction and costs, by country and company, weekly rpt semiannual list, C6985–1.524, C6985–1.551

Oil refineries shutdown as of Jan 1993, with distillation capacity, by company and PAD district, periodic basic data book, A2575–14.4

Oil refineries shutdown, including crude capacity, by company, 1992-93, article, C4680–1.508

Oil refiners net income, for top 22 companies, 1st 9 months 1991-92, article, C6985–1.507

Oil refinery capacity, for 10 plants up for sale, Aug 1993, article, C4680–1.510

Oil refinery capacity worldwide, by process, with data by country, company, and US State, 1992 annual feature, C6985–1.508

Oil refinery desulfurization projects and capacity, by company, 1993 article, C6985–1.549

BY INDIVIDUAL COMPANY OR INSTITUTION

Index by Categories

Oil supply-demand, marketing, prices, finances, and employment, detailed data for US and Canada, by product, company, and location, 1993 annual fact book, C4680–1.507

Oil world reserves and production, by country, company, and field, 1992 annual feature, C6985–1.509

Oil/gas deepwater drilling activity, with data by company, 1993, annual feature, C6985–2.510

Oil/gas industry occupational injury, illness, and employment data, by function, for 136 companies, 1991, annual rpt, A2575–4

Oil/gas well blowouts and associated financial loss, by operator and location, 1960-91, article, C6985–1.532

Peru oil production for govt-owned and 4 private companies, 1992-94, article, C6985–1.525

Pipeline construction projects planned in foreign countries, including costs, by company, 1994, annual feature, C6780–2.504

Pipeline construction projects planned in US, Canada, and other countries, including costs, by pipeline type and company, 1993 annual feature, C6780–2.502

Pipeline/gas utility automated control and acquisition system market shares, for 8 leading and all other manufacturers, 1991, article, C6985–1.501

Spain oil refinery distillation capacity and crude runs to stills, by company and refinery, 1991, article, C6985–1.522

Spain oil refining capacity and utilization, and employment, for 3 refineries, 1993 article, A8955–1.503

Sulfur dioxide emission allowance trading program, State regulatory issues and related data by State and major utility, 1992 rpt, A8195–12

Sweden nuclear power generation and capacity, for 12 operating reactors, 1993 article, B6800–1.506

UK coal mine closures and related employment, for 31 mines, Oct 1992-Mar 1993, article, C5226–2.501

UK offshore gas field dev in southern North Sea, with operator, reserves, and production rate, 1993 article, C6985–2.505

UK oil revenue tax impact on oil companies operating in North Sea, by company, 1993-96, article, C6985–1.525

Uranium anti-dumping petition against former Soviet Union, with participating companies and ownership, and export quotas for 6 Republics, 1992 article, B6800–1.501

Uranium conversion and enrichment suppliers, and fuel fabrication facilities, with plant capacities, 1992 annual rpt, B6800–2.1

Uranium production, reserves, and ownership interests, for 4 largest intl producers, by country and mine, 1990s-2003 article, B6800–1.508

Uranium reserves, capacity, and operating status of in situ leach mining projects, 1993 article, B6790–1.501

Utility regulatory agency activities, including rate reviews by company, 1991/92 annual rpt, A7015–3

Vietnam offshore oil/gas exploration activity, with operator, location, and well depth and/or status, 1992-94, article, C6985–2.506

State and local:

Alaska public utility financial and operating data, by company and utility type, 1991 and trends, with FY92 regulatory info, annual rpt, S0280–4

Arizona oil and gas production, by field, operator, and well, monthly rpt, S0473–1

Arkansas oil and gas production by field, and disposition, monthly rpt, S0737–1

Arkansas public utility financial, operating, and regulatory data, by utility type and company, 1992 annual rpt, S0757–1

California diesel fuel refining capacity, with projected impact of new State law, for 9 major refiners and aggregate independents, 1993-94, article, C6985–1.544

California diesel fuel supply under compliance with and variance from low-aromatics regulations, with detail for selected refiners, 1993-94, article, C4680–1.511

California fuel distributors sales volume and taxes assessed, by fuel type and company, FY92 and trends, annual rpt, S0835–1.4

California hydroelectric plants and capacity, 1992 annual rpt, S0840–2.7

California public utility and transportation regulatory data, including revenue requests and rates of return by company, FY92 annual rpt, S0930–1

Florida electric and gas utility operations by company, and nuclear power plant capacities, 1992 annual rpt, U6660–1.15

Florida oil and gas production by field, 1988-90, annual rpt, U6660–1.15

Florida public utility regulatory and operating data, by company and utility type, 1992 and trends, annual rpt, S1790–1

Idaho public utility regulatory data, and commission finances, FY92, annual rpt, S2290–1

Illinois electric and gas utility sales and operating revenues, and customers served, by class of service and company, 1991-92, annual rpt series, S2410–1

Maryland electric utility residential operating data, by company, 1991, biennial rpt, S3605–1.10

Montana public utility and transportation property assessments, by county and company, 1991-92, biennial rpt, S4750–1.2

Nevada oil and geothermal energy production, by site, 1990 and trends, biennial rpt, S5005–1.11

Nevada residential electricity consumption, revenues, and bills, by utility, 1990 and trends, biennial rpt, S5005–1.11

New Mexico public utility rate adjustment cases and dispositions, by company, FY92 annual rpt, S5645–1

New York State electric and gas utility financial and operating data, by company and consuming sector, 1990, annual rpt, U5100–1.12

New York State electric utility demand-side mgmt expenditures, and resulting demand reductions, for 7 companies, 1993-94, article, C6985–6.505

New York State public utility financial and operating data, by utility type and company, 1988-92, annual rpt, S5795–1

North Carolina public utility financial, operating, and regulatory data, by utility type and company, 1990 and trends, annual rpt, S5917–2

Ohio natural gas and electricity supply-demand by utility and consuming sector, 1992-93 and trends, annual rpt, S6355–1

Pennsylvania energy supply-demand and prices by fuel type, with electric power info by utility, 1960s-90, recurring rpt, S6810–3

South Carolina electric utility financial and operating data, by company and/or supplier, 1993 annual rpt, S7125–1.8

South Carolina public service commission regulatory activities, with financial and operating data for individual utilities and railroads, FY92 annual rpt, S7235–1

Tennessee electric power distributors energy use, sales, and rates, for individual cooperatives using TVA power, 1990, annual rpt, U8710–2.10

Texas electric utility financial and operating data, 9 largest investor-owned utilities, 1988-92, annual rpt, S7740–1

Texas natural gas utility financial and operating data, by city and company, 1991, with regulatory info, annual rpt, S7745–1

Vermont public utility financial and operating data, by company, 1986-91, biennial rpt, S8100–1

Washington State electric utility financial and operating data, by company, 1982-91, annual rpt, S8450–1.2

Washington State natural gas utility financial and operating data, by company, 1982-91, annual rpt, S8450–1.3

Washington State public service and utility companies property value, by company and county, 1992, annual rpt, S8415–1.4

Geography and Climate

State and local:

Alaska climatological data, by weather station, 1993 annual rpt, U5750–1

Arizona climatological data, by weather station, 1989, recurring rpt, U5850–2.1

Arizona Indian population, education, housing, health, and employment characteristics, with detail by reservation, 1970s-91, recurring rpt, U5850–2.9

Arizona monthly precipitation and temperature, and freeze dates, by weather station, 1992 and trends, annual rpt, U5830–1

California climatological data, by weather station, 1992 annual rpt, S0840–2.1

California rainfall by weather station, 1991/92-1992/93, annual rpt, S0850–1.5

Florida climatological data, by weather station, 1992 annual rpt, U6660–1.8

Hawaii climatological data, by weather station, 1992 annual rpt, S2090–1.5

Hawaii precipitation, by month and station, 1991, annual rpt, S2030–1

Kentucky precipitation, by weather station and crop district, Apr-Sept 1992, annual rpt, S3085–1

Maryland climatological data, by weather station, 1960-90, biennial rpt, S3605–1.3

Minnesota precipitation and frost dates, by district and weather station, 1993 annual rpt, S4130–1

Missouri precipitation, snowfall, and average temperatures, by weather station and/or county, monthly 1992, annual rpt, S4480–1

Nevada climatological data, by weather station, 1992 biennial rpt, S5005–1.9

Index by Categories

BY INDIVIDUAL COMPANY OR INSTITUTION

Nevada precipitation and frost-free days, by weather station, 1991-92, annual rpt, S5010–1

New Jersey freeze dates and frost-free days, by county and weather station, 1992 annual rpt, S5350–1

New Mexico average freeze dates and precipitation, by county and weather station, 1991, annual rpt, S5530–1

New York State temperatures, precipitation, and heating degree days, by weather station, monthly 1992, annual rpt, S5700–1

North Dakota precipitation, temperature, and growing season, by weather station, 1992 and trends, annual rpt, U3600–1

Ohio growing season temperature and precipitation, and deviation from normal, by weather station, 1991, annual rpt, S6240–1

Oregon precipitation by weather station, monthly 1991, annual rpt, S6575–1

Pennsylvania frost dates, temperature, and precipitation by area and/or weather station, 1992, annual rpt, S6760–1

South Dakota precipitation, by weather station, 1991-92, annual rpt, S7280–1

Tennessee climatological data, by weather station, 1992/93 annual rpt, U8710–2.12

Utah temperature, precipitation, and growing season, by weather station, 1960s-92, annual rpt, S7800–1

Washington State precipitation and average temperatures, by weather station, 1992, annual rpt, S8328–1

West Virginia precipitation and average temperatures, by weather station, monthly 1991, annual rpt, S8510–1

Wisconsin Indian reservation population and acreage, by reservation and tribe, 1990 or 1992, biennial rpt, S8780–1.2

Wisconsin precipitation and temperature, by month and weather station, 1992, annual rpt, S8680–1

Wyoming monthly temperature and precipitation, and temperature extremes, by weather station, 1991-92, annual rpt, S8860–1

Government and Defense

Aerospace and defense industries financial performance, with data for approx 200 major US and foreign companies, FY92 and trends, annual feature, C5800–4.519

Aerospace contractors, NASA and DOD, top 30 companies, FY87-91, annual rpt, A0250–2.5

Aluminum manufacturer financial effects of energy (BTU) tax proposed by Clinton Admin, with production and capacity data, for 5 companies, 1993-96, article, C5226–2.506

Coast Guard post exchange system sales, by individual exchange, FY91, annual rpt, A2072–1

Congressional campaign finances, with detailed data for individual Members, and leading contributors by type and industry, 1990 election and trends, biennial rpt, R3828–2

Defense Commissary Agency payments to 406 suppliers receiving $1 million/more, FY92, article, C0500–1.506

Defense contractor military sales, and share of total sales, for top 10 contractors, 1991, article, C8900–1.509

Defense contractor stock performance outlook, for 8 firms, 1993 article, C5800–7.546

Defense industries conversion to nonmilitary production, with data on defense contracts and spending, top contractors, and employment by occupation, 1980s and trends, R4700–19

Gold coins issued, face value, gold content, and physical characteristics, by mint, for 60 issuing countries, 1992, annual rpt, A5145–1

Japan defense budget allocations by equipment type, procurement, and value of contracts for top 10 contractors, various periods FY82-95, article, R5650–2.518

Japan defense contract value for top 10 contractors, FY91-92, article, R5650–2.533

Military base closures/realignments proposed, with personnel affected, for 18 Northeastern and Midwestern States, by service branch and base, 1993, R8490–45

Military commissary construction contract value and completion dates, by military base, 1993 article, C0500–1.503

Military commissary prices compared to retail grocery stores, for 6 bases, Sept 1992, article, C0500–1.505

Military commissary sales, by region, product type, and individual store, FY92, annual feature, A2072–2.501

Military personnel and retirees affected by proposed post exchange/commissary closures at 17 bases, 1993 article, C0500–1.508

Military post exchange (Army/Air Force), sales of approx 700 top supplier companies, for year ended Jan 1993, annual feature, C0500–1.505

Military post exchange (Navy) sales of approx 200 supplier companies, and sales by Navy store and dept, FY92 and trends, annual feature, C0500–1.507

Military post exchange sales increases for top 5 exchanges, by service branch, Dec 1992 vs 1991, C0500–1.505

Military post exchange sales, retail and other, by service branch, location, and store, FY92 and trends, annual rpt, A2072–2.502

Military retirees affected by post exchange/commissary closures at 7 bases, 1994, C0500–1.505

Military retirees affected by post exchange/commissary closures at 9 bases, 1993, C0500–1.504

Political consulting companies ranked by payments from congressional campaigns, for top 15 firms by area of expertise, 1990 elections, C2500–6

Silver coins issued, face value, silver content, and physical characteristics, by mint, for 83 countries, 1992, annual rpt, A8902–2

Women's political action committees (PACs) funds raised and candidates supported, for 42 PACs, 1992, U4510–4.4

State and local:

Alaska defense contract values for top 5 contractors, 1992, article, S0320–1.511

Arizona receipts and expenditures of State-supported instns, by instn, FY92, annual rpt, S0450–1

Arkansas State-controlled instn finances, FY91-92, biennial rpt, S0780–1

California financial condition of State-supported instns, FY92 and trends, annual rpt, S0815–1

California military base closures, with impact on employment, 1993 annual rpt, S0840–3.1

California tax collections (excluding income tax), by locality, company, and type of tax, FY92 and trends, annual rpt, S0835–1

Colorado regulated industries assessed property valuation, by company, 1991-92, annual rpt, S1055–3

Connecticut appropriations and expenditures, by State-supported instn and function, FY92, annual rpt, S1170–1

DC govt workers unionized, by union, 1991, annual rpt, S1535–3.2

Hawaii DOD military and civilian personnel, by installation, Sept 1991, annual rpt, S2090–1.10

Idaho State govt disbursements for State-supported instns, FY92, annual rpt, S2215–1

Illinois financial condition of State-supported instns, FY92, annual rpt, S2415–1

Iowa State treasury financial operations, including funds in individual banking instns, and detailed investments, FY92, annual rpt, S2885–1

Kansas financial data for individual capital projects and State-supported instns, FY92, annual rpt, S2900–1

Massachusetts delinquent tax collections through 11 settlement agreements and 4 collection agencies, FY91, annual rpt, S3917–1

Mississippi public utilities tax assessments, by company, 1985-91, annual rpt, S4435–1

Missouri nonappropriated finances for State-controlled instns, FY92, annual rpt, S4570–1.1

Nevada assessed property values for top 10 owners, FY92, annual rpt, S5025–1

Nevada property assessed valuation of top 10 property owners, FY92, biennial rpt, S5005–1.8

New Mexico revenues and expenditures, investments, and bonded debt, for State-controlled instns, FY91, annual rpt, S5585–1

New York/New Jersey Port Authority operating revenues and net income, for 10 properties, 1992, article, C3950–1.511

Texas revenues, expenditures, and cash balances of individual State-supported instns, FY92, annual rpt, S7655–2.2

Utah finances for State-controlled instns, FY92, annual rpt, S7795–1

Virginia DOD military and civilian employment by service branch, by region, locale, and installation, 1991 and trends, article, S8205–4.501

Washington State bonded debt, by State-controlled instn, FY92, annual rpt, S8345–3

Health and Vital Statistics

Allergy medication market shares, for top 5 nonprescription brands, year ended Jan 1993, article, C2710–1.518

Ambulance company revenues, net income, and stock performance, for 4 firms, 1993 article, C3950–1.523

Blood bank operating profiles, arranged by State, 1993 biennial directory, A0612–1

BY INDIVIDUAL COMPANY OR INSTITUTION

Index by Categories

Cancer research grants provided by American Cancer Society, by recipient instn, FY92, annual rpt, A1175–1

Catholic facilities for elderly and handicapped persons, by type and State, 1993 annual almanac, C6885–1

Dental advanced education programs, enrollment, grads, and finances, by instn and State, 1992/93 annual rpt, A1475–10

Dental allied education enrollment, grads, and tuition, by instn, 1992/93 annual rpt, A1475–5

Dental school enrollment and grads, program characteristics, and faculty, by US and Canadian instn, 1992/93, annual rpt, A1475–3

Dental school programs, enrollment, and finances by instn, annual rpt series, A1475–4

Drug new products approved by FDA, including review time needed and prior foreign approval, by drug, 1992, article, C5150–2.507

Drug sales, for 9 chiral drugs containing molecules that can exist in mirror image forms, 1990, article, C5800–8.512

Drug wholesale company revenues, market shares, and operating ratios, for 7 major firms, 1992-93, article, C3950–1.511

Drugs (prescription) top 100 brands in sales, 1992, annual feature, C5150–2.511

Drugs (prescription) top 200 brands and top 100 generic products, 1992 annual pharmacy reference guide, C5150–2.503

Drugs (prescription) use, expenditures, prices, and profit trends, with data by patient characteristics and for top 20 brands, 1992 rpt, R4865–8

Eye bank activity in US and abroad, including donations by type, source, and donor characteristics, and data by individual bank, 1992 and trends, annual rpt, A4743 1

Health-related company CEO income, for 10 leading health insurance and 3 major drug companies, 1991-92, R4865–13

HMO enrollment, with detail for pure vs open-ended plans, for top 10 HMOs, July 1992, article, A1865–1.513

Hospital directory, with utilization, expenses, and personnel, by instn, type, and location, 1992, annual rpt, A1865–3

Laxative sales and market shares, for top 5 brands and private label, year ended May 1993, article, C2710–1.532

Lice treatment product market shares, including top 5 brands, year ended May 1993, article, C5150–2.517

Magnetic resonance imaging (MRI) machine manufacturer sales and stock performance, for 6 companies, 1992 article, C3950–1.504

Medical research journal article multiple author incidence, for 2 radiation oncology publications, with data by author country and instn, 1983-87, article, A3273–8.502

Medical school combined baccalaureate-MD program characteristics and class size at 28 schools, 1991/92, article, A3273–8.501

Medical school tuition and fees, applicants and entrants, and enrollment, by individual US and Canadian instn, 1992/93, annual rpt, A3273–10

Nursing programs (State-approved) for practical/vocational nurses, including admissions, enrollment, and grads, by instn, State, and territory, 1992, annual directory, A8010–5

Nursing programs (State-approved) for registered nurses, including admissions, enrollment, and grads, by instn, State, and territory, 1992, annual directory, A8010–4

Occupational health and safety govt regulatory activities, including inspections, fines, and data by State and company, 1992 annual rpt, R8335–1.2

Occupational safety record of top company in approx 400 SIC 4-digit industries, 1992 annual rpt, A8375–4

Oil/gas industry occupational injury, illness, and employment data, by function, for 136 companies, 1991, annual rpt, A2575–4

Optometry school faculty, enrollment and degrees, policies and programs, and finances, by instn, 1991/92, annual survey, A3370–2

Osteopathy college applications and enrollment, and student characteristics, by instn, 1992/93 and trends, annual rpt, A0620–1

Pharmaceutical industry financial performance, for 10 major companies, 1993 article, C8900–1.514

Pharmacy degree program applications, enrollment, and degrees conferred, by student characteristics and instn, 1990/91 and trends, annual rpt, A0630–9

Physician group credit ratings, and employment, for 9 groups rated by Standard & Poors Corp, 1993 article, A1865–1.516

Physicians by instn of graduation and period degree received, 1992, annual rpt, A2200–3.1

Pregnancy home test kit market shares, for top 5 and all other brands, 1992, articles, C5150–2.511

Public health school applicant, student, and grad characteristics, by instn, 1991/92 and trends, annual rpt, A3372–3

Public health school faculty characteristics, by instn, fall 1991, recurring rpt, A3372–1

Veterinary school aquatic animal course availability, faculty, and enrollment, by instn, 1991/92, article, A3100–2.509

Veterinary school enrollment by sex, program, instn, and place of residence, US and Canada, 1992/93, annual article, A3100–2.516

Veterinary surgery teaching methods used at 27 US and Canadian veterinary schools, 1993 article, A3100–2.521

Voluntary health agency revenues, and expenditures by function, for 39 major organizations, FY90, annual rpt, A7973–1

Workplace accidents resulting in most fatalities since 1987, by employer, 1992 annual rpt, R8335–1.1

State and local:

Alabama births in hospitals, by sex and race, by instn and county, 1992, annual rpt, S0175–2

Alabama hospital facilities, patient data, staff, and expenses, by instn, 1991, recurring rpt, U5680–2.8

Arkansas mental health program clients served, by facility, FY91, annual rpt, S0700–2.4

California State mental hospital admissions, population, deaths, and discharges, by instn, FY92, annual rpt, S0840–2.5

DC hospital and nursing home beds and use by facility, and ambulance trips by hospital of destination, 1992 annual rpt, S1535–3.1, S1535–3.5, S1535–3.8

Delaware live births, by place of birth, 1990, annual rpt, S1385–2

Florida health care atlas, including health facilities and equipment, and allied health program enrollment by instn, 1992 annual rpt, S1746–1.2

Hawaii health care facility bed capacity, by type of care and instn, 1990, annual rpt, S2065–1.7

Hawaii membership and dues in 4 HMOs, 1988-91, annual rpt, S2090–1.15

Illinois mental health facility patient population and characteristics, by facility, location, and treatment category, FY93, annual rpt, S2505–1

Louisiana vital statistics, including population, births, deaths by cause, reportable diseases, marriages, and divorces, by demographic characteristics and locality, 1989-90 and trends, annual rpt, S3295–1

Maine births by medical facility, 1991, annual rpt, S3460–2

Massachusetts births, by method of delivery, characteristics of mother, and payment sources, by hospital, 1990, annual rpt, S3850–1

Montana health care facility capacity, utilization, and finances, by instn, 1991, annual rpt, S4690–2

Nevada hospital ownership, finances, and utilization, by facility, FY90, annual rpt, S5005–1.2

Nevada total and low-weight births, and birthweight-related deaths, by individual hospital, 1985-89, annual rpt, S5075–1

New Hampshire births, by county and for residents of 3 neighboring States, by hospital, 1991, annual rpt, S5215–1

New Mexico births, by health facility and type of attendant, by county, 1991, annual rpt, S5605–1.4

New York State psychiatric center admissions, residents, and persons served, by facility, FY90, annual rpt, U5100–1.11

North Carolina public defender and assigned counsel caseloads and costs, including State mental hospital hearings, FY91, annual rpt, S5950–1

Oklahoma beds and/or admissions in hospitals and other health care facilities, by instn, 1992 annual rpt, U8130–2.9

Pennsylvania hospital finances and utilization, by facility, 1989, recurring rpt, U4130–6.5

Rhode Island health facilities and capacity, by instn, 1993 annual rpt, C7975–1

South Carolina health facility statistics, for mental health and other hospitals, 1993 annual rpt, S7125–1.10

Texas indigent health care finances and utilization, with data by county, district, public hospital, and medical school, 1986-91, U8850–8.7

Utah hospital beds and utilization, by instn, FY90, triennial rpt, U8960–1.2

Utah vital statistics, including births by instn and location, 1990, annual rpt, S7835–1.2

Vermont births and deaths by location, including individual instns, 1991, annual rpt, S8054–1

Wisconsin mental instn inmates and capacity, by instn, FY60-92, biennial rpt, S8780–1.2

Index by Categories

BY INDIVIDUAL COMPANY OR INSTITUTION

Housing and Construction

Apartment units owned by top 10 companies, 1993, C4300–1.508

Architectural and engineering design firm billings, for top 500 firms, 1992, annual article, C5800–2.522

Building design/construction company revenues and operations, for top 300 firms, 1991, annual feature, C1850–9.502

Building owner value of properties owned and additions, and construction in progress, top 700 owner firms, 1991, annual article, C5800–2.504

Construction contract values, total and foreign, with rankings of top 400 contractors, 1992, annual rpt, C5800–2.529

Construction equipment positive and negative attributes cited by contractors, for 6 manufacturers, 1993 survey article, C5800–2.519

Construction mgmt firm total and foreign contract values for top 100 firms, and employee compensation by position, 1992 and trends, annual article, C5800–2.533

Construction specialty firm revenues, and contract values, by specialty, for top 600 contractors, 1992, annual article, C5800–2.548

Homebuilder financial and operating data, including detail by location, for top 400 builders, 1993 annual feature, C1850–8.507

Housing construction, revenues, and closings of top 100 homebuilding companies, 1992, annual feature, C4300–1.507

Housing starts forecasts by 10 industry analysts, 1993, annual article, C4300–1.503

Intl construction design firms foreign billings, specialties, and work locations, for top 200 firms, 1992, annual article, C5800–2.538

Intl construction firms foreign and total contract values, for top 225 firms, 1992, annual feature, C5800–2.542

Japan real estate investment in Hawaii and California since 1985, with buyer, purchase price, and current value for 9 properties, 1993 article, C3950–1.517

Mortgage purchasing from loan originators, with volume purchased by 78 leading instns, 1991-92, article, A6450–2.502

State and local:

Alaska property assessment contract revaluation costs, by contractor and municipality, 1992, annual rpt, S0285–1

Arizona Indian population, education, housing, health, and employment characteristics, with detail by reservation, 1970s-91, recurring rpt, U5850–2.9

DC commercial, residential, and tax exempt properties with highest assessed values, July 1992, annual rpt, S1507–1

Hawaii seating capacity for selected stadiums, theaters, and churches, and heights of tallest structures, 1992 annual rpt, S2090–1.21

Illinois financial condition, including funding for individual capital projects, FY92, annual rpt, S2415–1.2

New York City major commercial property sales and lease transactions, including participants and square footage involved, 1992, annual rpt, B2800–5

Income

Billionaire profiles and sources of wealth, for persons/families worldwide worth 1 billion/more, 1993 annual feature, C3950–1.518

Billionaire profiles and sources of wealth, for 101 wealthiest persons/families worldwide, 1993 annual feature, C8900–1.518

CEO compensation measures, for top 10 executives among 100 leading natl advertisers, 1992 article, C2710–1.505

Corporate CEO compensation compared to company performance, for 200 executives, 1992, annual article, C8900–1.517

Corporate CEO compensation in 800 firms, with sales and profit data, 1993 annual article, C3950–1.515

Corporate executive compensation for top executives at approx 400 companies, by industry group, 1992 and trends, annual survey, C5800–7.525

Corporate executive compensation, with company revenues, for 20 highly paid executives in US, Germany, and Japan, 1993 article, C3950–1.516

Forbes profile of 400 wealthiest individuals, with info on family background, income, and assets, 1993 annual feature, C3950–1.526

Hispanic American 50 wealthiest individuals or families, with info on background, assets, and net worth, 1993, annual feature, C4575–1.505

Japan corporate CEOs compensation, for 50 largest companies, 1991, article, C5800–7.525

Sales and marketing executive compensation, for top 100 executives, with company sales and profit data, 1992 annual article, C1200–1.501

State and local:

Hawaii wealthiest individuals, with age and net worth, 1992, annual rpt, S2090–1.13

Industry and Commerce

Air conditioning manufacturer market shares, for top 8 and all other companies, 1992, annual rpt, C1800–1

Aluminum production capacity for top 20 producers, 1982-92, annual rpt, A0400–2.1

Appliance manufacturers market shares, by product type, 1992, annual article, C2000–1.510

Australia chemical production capacity for 7 major producers of petrochemicals and polymers, 1993 article, A1250–1.531

Beauty care and cosmetics new product sales performance for top brands in selected categories, biweekly rpt recurring feature, C5150–2.504, C5150–2.505, C5150–2.510, C5150–2.511

Black-owned enterprises financial and operating data, for top 100 firms and auto dealerships and for top 15-25 financial instns, 1992 and trends, annual feature, C4215–1.507

Black-owned franchises, with type of business and startup costs, top 50 companies, 1993 annual article, C4215–1.510

Business Week economic, business, and investment devs, with related statistical indicators, weekly rpt, C5800–7

Canada home improvement sales and outlets, for 4-5 leading retail chains and buying groups, 1992, articles, C5150–6.508

Carbon dioxide pipelines in Texas/New Mexico Permian Basin region, with ownership, mileage, and throughput capacity, 1993 article, C6985–1.542

Chemical (ethylene oxide) plants worldwide involved in explosions, and new ethoxylation capacity by company, 1992 article, C5800–8.502

Chemical and allied industries earnings, sales, and profit margins, by company, weekly rpt quarterly article, A1250–1.502, A1250–1.514, A1250–1.525, A1250–1.536

Chemical and related industries production, finances, operating ratios, employment, and trade, by country, company, and chemical, 1980s-92, annual feature, A1250–1.530

Chemical company sales and profits, for top 50 producers worldwide, 1992, annual article, A1250–1.533

Chemical industry capital spending, US and worldwide, for 19 US and 6 European companies, 1988-93, annual article, A1250–1.508

Chemical industry Intl Organization for Standardization (ISO 9000) registrations of US and non-US facilities, for 27 companies, 1992/93, article, A1250–1.516

Chemical industry methyl tertiary butyl ether (MTBE) capacity, and polyethylene capacity additions, by company and plant, 1993 articles, A1250–1.541

Chemical industry sales and operating summary for top 100 companies, 1992, annual article, A1250–1.523

Chemical industry sales and operating summary for top 50 companies, FY68, article, A1250–1.523

Chemical industry stock performance, for 30 companies, 1992, article, A1250–1.510

China business review, including trade with US and other countries, and economic activity, bimonthly rpt, A9315–1

China private sector industrial project dev costs, for 10 projects being considered by Intl Finance Corp, 1993 article, A9315–1.504

Cigarette advertisements containing coupons/other promotions, shares for 4 major and all other companies, 1991-92, article, C2710–1.536

Cigarette market shares, for premium and discount brands of 6 leading companies, 1991-92, article, C8130–1.510

Cigarette premium and discount brand market shares by manufacturer, with detail for leading premium brands, 1981 and 1992, article, C3950–1.514

Clothing (women's jeans) market shares for top 8 and all other manufacturers, 1993 article, C5150–3.518

Clothing and shoe industries financial performance indicators for 72 companies, FY92 and trends, annual rpt, B8130–2

Clothing discount and off-price store sales and outlets, for top 10 chains, 1993 article, C5150–3.513

Computer (mini/micro) use and networking, including software in use, 1992 survey and trends, annual article, C1850–5.502

Computer (personal) company revenues for top 50 firms worldwide, and top 50 marketing in North America, 1991, annual article, C1850–5.503

BY INDIVIDUAL COMPANY OR INSTITUTION

Index by Categories

Computer-aided design, manufacturing, and engineering (CAD/CAM/CAE) revenues, with market shares for 10 companies, 1992, article, C7000-7.501

Computer-aided design, manufacturing, and engineering (CAD/CAM/CAE) revenues worldwide, with market shares for 10 companies, 1993, article, C5800-4.513

Computer company advertising expenditures, for top 5 advertisers in selected media, 1st half 1992, C2710-1.502

Computer company revenues and earnings, for top 10 companies making network software, 1993 article, C8900-1.521

Computer educational networks for children, subscribers and prices for 5 networks, 1993 article, C8900-1.524

Computer industry advertising expenditures, for top 10 manufacturers and magazines, 1st half 1992-93, article, C2710-1.542

Computer manufacturer advertising expenditures and pages in magazines, for top 12 firms, 1st 8 months 1992-93, article, C2710-1.548

Computer software company revenues and employment, for top 100 firms worldwide, 1992, annual article, C1850-5.520

Computer software with sales/marketing applications, installations sold and product characteristics, by vendor, 1992 annual directory, C1200-1.502

Computer system purchasing and expansion plans of businesses, including data by manufacturer, 1993 survey and trends, annual article, C1850-5.513

Computer systems integration consultant revenues and market shares, for top 5 companies, 1993, article, C8900-1.526

Computer/info systems companies revenues and other financial data, for top 100 firms worldwide and in North America, 1992 and trends, annual rpt, C1850-5.514

Computer/info systems marketing and manufacturing news and analytical articles, semimonthly rpt, C1850-5

Consumer photographic and video equipment ownership and use, including film and 1-use camera brands preferred, 1993 survey, recurring rpt, A8695-2

Convenience store finances and number of stores, for 5 chains with bankruptcy filings, 1991-92, article, C4680-1.505

Copper production in US for 1987-91, and smelter capacity in North America in 1991, by company, annual rpt, S0497-1

Corporate acquisition impact on stock prices, and leading financial advisors in selected industries, 1993 annual compilation, C4683-1.502

Corporate CEO characteristics, compensation, and company finances, for officers of top 1,000 firms, 1993 annual feature, C5800-7.549

Corporate event sponsorship expenditures, for top 13 companies, 1992, article, C1200-1.512

Corporate financial losses, for 10 firms with all-time largest annual loss, 1993 article, C5800-7.517

Corporate initiatives for communicating benefits info to employees, profiles of 19 firms, 1993 rpt, R4105-78.28

Corporate market value of top 100 firms in developing countries, by company, 1993 annual feature, C5800-7.536

Corporate market value of top 1,000 firms worldwide, with related financial data, by company and country, 1993 annual feature, C5800-7.536

Corporate market value rankings of top 1,000 firms, with sales, profits, assets, and related data, by company and industry, 1993 annual feature, C5800-7.521

Corporate merger/acquisition leading cancellations, with participants and prices, 1992, annual article, C4683-1.504

Corporate mergers, acquisitions, and divestitures, with prices, payment methods, and characteristics of participants, 1992 and trends, annual rpt, B6020-1

Corporate mergers, acquisitions, divestitures, joint ventures, and other agreements involving US and/or foreign companies, bimonthly rpt, C4683-1

Corporate mergers and acquisitions, top transactions and acquiring companies, 1992, annual compilation, C4683-1.504

Corporate performance ratings by executives for leading companies in 32 industries, 1993 annual survey feature, C8900-1.508

Corporate productivity, employment, sales, and operating income, for 46 companies with outstanding productivity improvement, 1992 and trends, C5800-7.532

Corporate sales, earnings, and stock performance, for 100 fastest-growing companies, 1993 annual article, C8900-1.521

Corporate sales, profits, return on equity, price/earnings ratio, and earnings per share, approx 900 corporations, with industry rankings, weekly rpt quarterly article, C5800-7.503, C5800-7.519, C5800-7.528, C5800-7.541

Corporate tender offer prices for 10 largest bids, 1992, annual article, C4683-1.504

Corporations with rapid growth, financial data for 250 firms, 1993 feature, C5800-7.551

Cosmetics sales and market shares in food stores/drugstores, for 11 marketers, year ended June 1993, article, C2710-1.546

Cosmetics use indexes among women by age group, for selected brands, 1993 articles, C5150-2.514

Czechoslovakia chemical production by product, and sales, exports, and employment of leading firms, by Republic, 1990-92, article, A1250-1.509

Diapers (disposable) couponed advertisement shares for top 3 and all other manufacturers, 1991/92, article, C2710-1.517

Discount chain consumer natl brand preferences, by product category and chain, and by age group, 1993 survey, annual feature, C5150-3.521

Discount chain sales and merchandising, including data by dept, leading chain, and location, 1992 and trends, annual feature, C8130-1.507

Discount chain stores, total and with pharmacies, for 10 chains, 1993 annual feature, C5150-2.511

Discount chain top-selling natl brands cited by managers, by product category, chain, and region, 1993 survey, annual feature, C5150-3.520

Discount regional chain sales and stores, for 8 leading chains, 1993 article, C5150-3.517

Discount retail company executive compensation, for 75 highest-paid executives, 1992, annual feature, C5150-3.518

Discount store ratings and shopping patterns of consumers in 3 market areas, including expenditures, by leading chain, 1992 surveys, article, C5150-3.503

Discount store sales and earnings, for approx 40 major companies, monthly rpt recurring feature, C8130-1

Discount store sales trends for selected leading chains, biweekly rpt monthly feature, C5150-3

Discount stores, sales, and earnings, for top chains, with detail by specialty, 1993 annual feature, C5150-3.514

Discount wholesale membership club sales and stores, for 9 major chains, 1992, annual article, C8130-1.501

Drugstore advertising shares for top 10 stationery/home office product types and brands, Aug 1992, article, C5150-2.501

Drugstore artificial fingernail product sales trends, for 5 top brands, year ended June 1993, article, C5150-2.519

Drugstore chain and brand preferences of consumers, with data by product type and region, 1992 annual survey feature, C5150-2.503

Drugstore chain pharmacy outlets for top 24 companies, 1993, annual feature, C5150-2.511

Drugstore chain stores use of scanning equipment, by chain, 1993 feature, C5150-2.512

Drugstore chains financial performance and marketing operations, by US and Canadian company, 1993 annual feature, C5150-2.511

Drugstore chains top-selling over-the-counter products, year ended June 1993, article, C5150-2.521

Drugstore chains top-selling products, and leading manufacturers, 1993 annual article, C5150-2.520

Eastern Europe public opinion on selected Western companies, for 6 countries and 3 Soviet Union Republics, 1991 survey, C8915-8.2

Economic indicator forecasts for GDP, inflation, unemployment, and Treasury bond rates, by approx 10 forecasting organizations, monthly rpt, R4105-80

Economic indicator forecasts for 30 countries by approx 50 forecasting organizations, including GDP, inflation, unemployment, and interest rates, 1992-94, R4105-6.502

Electric utility asset diversification, with selected comparisons to financial performance, for 35 companies, 1990 and 1992, article, A4700-4.505

Electrical equipment wholesalers, sales, employment, and facility size, top 250 companies, 1992, annual article, C4725-5.506

Electronics company financial data and business info for approx 500 companies, 1991-92 and trends, annual rpt, C3400-4

Electronics company financial performance, for top 100 multinatl firms, 1992 annual feature, C1850-2.502

Electronics company financial performance, ranking of top 200 firms, 1992 and trends, annual feature, C1850-2.509

Index by Categories

BY INDIVIDUAL COMPANY OR INSTITUTION

Electronics company revenues, funding, and employment, for 25 companies started in the recent past, 1993 recurring article, C1850–2.505

Electronics contract manufacturing sales of top 6 contractors, with selected detail by major customer, 1993 annual feature, C1850–2.510

Electronics industry market trends and outlook, including product sales and shipments, employment, and leading manufacturers, monthly rpt, C1850–2

Ethylene plants under dev and capacity, by process and company, 1993 article, C5800–8.508

Europe and worldwide computer chip sales for top 12 companies ranked by sales in Europe, 1991, article, C5800–7.508

Europe chemical company earnings trends, for 12 companies, 1st-2nd half 1992, article, A1250–1.517

Europe companies acquired by US companies, and transaction value, for top 10 transactions, 1984–92, C1575–2.506

Europe computer advertising expenditures, for top 15 manufacturers, with detail by country, 1992, article, C2710–1.527

Europe corporate acquisitions involving companies from different and same countries, price and participants for top transactions, 1992, annual article, C4683–1.504

Europe electronics industry financial performance, for top 50 companies, FY91 or FY92, annual article, C1850–2.501

Europe govt-owned companies likely to be privatized, govt ownership share and value for 25 firms in 6 countries, 1993 article, C5800–7.537

Europe household appliance production, sales, and market shares, by country, product type, and manufacturer, 1991-92, annual feature, C2000–1.508

Europe plastic bottle recycler capacity, for 9 companies, 1993 annual encyclopedia, C5800–12.503

Europe retail clothing chain stores and sales, for 5 major chains, 1993 article, C2710–1.517

Export sales ranking of top 50 companies, 1992, annual feature, C8900–1.517

Facial skin care product sales, for top 5 brands, 1992, article, C5150–2.510

Financial performance and growth rankings for approx 1,000 top corporations, with comparisons by industry group, 1993 annual rpt, C3950–1.505

Forbes 500 top companies in sales, profits, assets, market value, and productivity, with stock and employment data, 1992, annual rpt, C3950–1.513

Forecasts for GDP, prices, prime interest rate, and unemployment, 50 economists, 1992-93, annual feature, C5800–7.509

Foreign investments in US, foreign companies, and US multinatls, financial data for top 100-500 in each category, 1992, annual feature, C3950–1.519

Forest products foreign trade at 30 leading ports, 1991-92, annual article, C3975–2.512

Fortune magazine ranking of top 50-100 companies in 8 nonindustrial sectors, with financial and employment data, 1992, annual feature, C8900–1.516

Fortune magazine ranking of top 50-100 companies worldwide in 8 nonindustrial sectors, with financial and employment data, 1993 annual feature, C8900–1.522

Fortune 500 largest industrial corporations, sales, financial, and stock performance data by company, 1992, annual feature, C8900–1.513

Fortune 500 largest industrial corporations worldwide, with financial and employment data, 1992, annual feature, C8900–1.520

Gases used in electronics industry, market value worldwide and shares for top 5 and all other suppliers, 1992, article, C1850–2.504

GDP forecasts by 20 economists, 2nd qtr 1993-2nd qtr 1994, annual article, C5800–7.533

Germany vs US market value and employment of leading firms in 5 industries, and value of 19 major intl acquisitions/mergers involving German firms, 1993 articles, A5135–2.1

Hair care product sales trends, for top 10 brands in drugstores, with comparisons to mass merchandise and food/drug stores, year ended June 1993, articles, C5150–2.519

Higher education student level of familiarity with 35 corporations, 1993 survey article, C1200–1.503

Hispanic American professional views on work conditions at own company, with ratings of regions and top 19-20 companies and industries, 1993 survey article, C4575–1.504

Hispanic-owned business sales and employment, for top 500 companies, 1992, annual feature, C4575–1.507

Hispanic-owned business sales and employment, for 100 fastest-growing companies, 1988-92, annual feature, C4575–1.509

Home improvement industry sales and operations, for top distributors, cooperatives, and marketing organizations, 1991-92, annual feature, C5150–6.502

Home improvement industry sales and operations, for top retailers, 1992 and trends, annual feature, C5150–6.503

Home improvement industry sales and related data, by product category and for top 10 chains, 1992, article, C4725–5.507

Home improvement industry sales, stores, and other operating data, for leading foreign chains by country, 1991-92, annual feature, C5150–6.503

Home improvement store finances and operations, for 6 major chains, 1991, annual rpt, A8275–1

Home improvement store sales and stores, for 5 leading chains, 1993 article, C1850–4.505

Home improvement stores and sales, for 10 major chains in US and Europe, 1993 article, C5150–6.507

Household use indexes for medicated skin care and children's pain reliever products, by brand, for white vs black households, 1993 article, C5150–2.520

Industrial design awards won by leading design firms and manufacturers, 1993 and trends, annual article, C5800–7.531

Industrial distributor sales, branches, employment, and operating profiles, for top 50 companies, 1992, annual article, C1850–4.506

Industrial distributor sales, employment, and inventory turns, for top 25 companies with sales of $5 million/less, 1991, annual article, C1850–4.503

Information technology company sales and employment, for 25 innovative firms, 1993 article, C8900–1.525

Interior design industry financial and employment data, top 100 firms, 1993 annual article, C1850–7.501

Interior design industry financial and employment data, 2nd 100 largest firms, 1993 annual article, C1850–7.502

Iron ore shipments grade analyses, by grade name and mining company, US and Canada, 1992, annual rpt, A2010–3.3

Israel company stock performance, sales, and market value, for 14 firms traded on US exchanges, 1993 article, C3950–1.523

Japan export share of production, for selected steel, motor vehicle, and electronics companies, FY84 and FY91, article, R5650–2.504

Japan GNP growth forecasts of 6 organizations, FY93-94, article, R5650–2.558

Japan GNP or GDP growth and current account balance, forecasts of 6 organizations, 1993 article, R5650–2.538

Japan machine tool manufacturer sales, and income or loss, for 6 leading companies, FY93, article, C7000–7.504

Japan personal computer market shares for 5 major and all other manufacturers, 1992, article, C8900–1.519

Japan steel sheet dumping margins in US, for 4 leading and all other companies, 1993 article, R5650–2.512, R5650–2.539

Jewelry trade assns financial performance data, for 5 organizations, 1991 or FY92, article, C2150–7.505

Latin America company sales and employment, for 20 leading firms, 1992 annual rpt, U6250–1.29

Leveraged buyout transactions and value, with leading participants and industries, 1992 annual feature, C4683–1.501

Lotion (hand/body) market shares, for top 9 brands and private label, 1993 article, C2710–1.530

Market research firm performance ratings among electronics/computer industry clients, for 14 companies, 1993 survey, article, C1850–2.511

Market value of top 20 companies worldwide, 1972, 1982, and 1992, article, C8900–1.514

Marketing executive views on technology use and future importance, including companies cited as top users, July/Aug 1992 survey, article, C2710–1.510

Methanol supply-demand outlook in North America, Europe, and worldwide, with capacity by company, 1993 article, C6985–1.522

Mexico lobbyists in US income from Mexican Govt, for 8 major Hispanic firms or individuals, 1991-93, article, C4575–1.510

Minerals supply-demand for selected commodities, US and worldwide, with data by company, 1992 and trends, annual feature, C5226–2.505

Mining companies shares of Western world nonfuel mine production, for top 50 companies worldwide, 1991, article, C5226–2.511

BY INDIVIDUAL COMPANY OR INSTITUTION

Index by Categories

Mining industry capital spending plans for new mines and plants, by mineral and company, 1993 annual feature, C5226–2.503

Mining industry return on equity, with impact of 3 proposed mineral royalty rates for Federal lands, for selected companies, 1991, article, C5226–2.506

Multinatl companies sales and intl share, for 50 smaller firms, 1992, article, C5800–7.544

Newsprint capacity announced changes, by company and country, monthly rpt, A1630–4

Newsprint capacity announced changes, by company and country, 1980s-94, annual rpt, A1630–8

Newsprint production, consumption, trade, prices, and mill capacity, with data by world area, 1991-92 and trends, annual rpt, A8610–1

Newsprint recycling capacity, demand, and wastepaper consumption, for Northeast US and Eastern Canada, with data by mill, various years 1988-2000, A4375–15

Oral care product sales in food stores, for 12 manufacturers, year ended June 1993, article, C4655–1.511

Packaging expenditures of top 7 manufacturers, 1992, article, C1850–1.508

Paper (coated) recycled products, with percent of content from waste, by manufacturer, 1993 annual feature, C2575–1.518

Paper and paperboard industry outlook as forecast by 6 industry analysts, 1993, annual article, C3975–2.503

Paper industry sales and earnings of individual companies in US and Canada, monthly rpt quarterly feature, C3975–2.502, C3975–2.503, C3975–2.505, C3975–2.506, C3975 2.508, C3975–2.511, C3975–2.512

Paper, paperboard, and wood pulp industry announced mill capacity expansions, by company, 1992 annual rpt, A1630–7

Petrochemical foreign ownership shares for major companies investing in US plants, for 2 product types, 1992, article, C6985–1.522

Pipeline projects with polypropylene coatings, by operating company, 1992 article, C6985–1.507

Plastics (degradable) production capacity and costs, for 13 companies, 1993 annual encyclopedia, C5800–12.503

Plastics (polyethylene) market shares for 3 major producers, by product type, Jan 1993, article, C5800–12.511

Plastics (polyethylene terephthalate) reclamation capacity, for 3 integrated fiber manufacturers, 1993 article, C5800–12.513

Plastics and resin sales by material and major market, foreign trade, and capacity by company, 1991-92, annual feature, C5800–12.504

Plastics production capacity for specified resins, by major company and/or world region, monthly rpt recurring table, C5800–12.502, C5800–12.504, C5800–12.506, C5800–12.507, C5800–12.509, C5800–12.510, C5800–12.512, C5800–12.513

Plastics specialty materials manufacturer income, R&D expenditures, and stock performance, for 10 companies, 1992, article, C3950–1.511

Printing (quick) sales, employment, and establishments, for top companies, 1992 article, C1850–10.503

Printing company sales, employment, and equipment, for top 101 North American firms, 1993 annual feature, C1850–10.512

Privately held corporation revenues and employment, for 400 largest firms, 1992 annual article, C3950–1.503

Pulp and paper industry expansion plans, for US and Canadian mills, 1993 annual survey article, C3975–2.503

Pulp and paper industry operations and finances, US and Canada, with detail by company and product grade, and world production and trade summary, 1993 annual rpt, C3975–5

Pulp and paper industry production, capacity, consumption, trade, and sales/earnings data, including profiles for selected companies and sectors, monthly rpt, C3975–2

Pulp and paper mill Intl Organization for Standardization (ISO 9000) certification data, for 40 mills, 1993 survey, annual article, C3975–2.508

Retail chain construction activity, capital expenditures, and number of new stores, for leading firms, 1991-92, annual feature, C5150–4.503

Retail chain financial data and business info for approx 240 US and Canadian companies, 1991-92 and trends, annual rpt, C3400–2

Retail chain performance indexes and ratios, for top 38 chains, 1986-91, annual article, C5150–4.502

Retail chain revenues, profits, and stores, top 100 chains, with selected data by outlet type, 1991-92, annual articles, C5150–4.508

Retail chain sales, for selected leading companies, monthly rpt, C5150–4

Retail credit operations, including selected cards offered, by outlet type, 1992 annual survey, C5150–4.504

Retail general merchandise chain sales, earnings, and stores, for top companies worldwide, with detail for selected areas, 1991-92, annual feature, C5150–3.516

Retail outlets for selected leading chains in 21 media market areas, 1992, C2710–1.538

Retail store financial performance indicators, for 98 public firms, FY92 and trends, annual rpt, B8130–4

Retail stores and shopping centers in daily newspaper markets in US and Canada, by company, 1993 annual rpt, C3250–1

Retailer views on top 6 manufacturers for forming retail-supplier partnerships, 1993 survey article, C1200–4.509

Russia bleached pulp and chlorine production, by pulp/paper mill, 1990, article, C3975–2.504

Sales executive ratings of corporate sales forces, by industry sector and sales function, 1993 annual survey article, C1200–1.512

Sales growth for 10 companies outperforming 5-year average of S&P Industrial Index firms, 1992 article, C5800–7.502

Security equipment industry revenues, accounts, and operating data, for 100 leading companies, 1992, annual feature, C1850–13.507

Shopping center expansion plans of top 10 developers, with square footage added, and new centers, 1991-92, annual article, C5150–4.506

Small companies with high 5-year returns on equity, financial performance and chief executive characteristics, for top 200 firms, 1992 annual article, C3950–1.501

Small companies with sales under $150 million, financial data for top 100 growth firms, 1993 annual article, C5800–7.529

Small companies with sales under $25 million, financial and operating data for top 100 public firms, 1992 and trends, annual feature, C4687–1.507

Small privately held companies sales, employment, and other data, for 500 fastest growing firms, 1988 and 1992, annual feature, C4687–1.512

South Africa uranium production facilities by company, with other activities, operating status, and 1992 production, article, B6800–1.505

Spain chemical process industry sales and employment of top 15 companies, and production capacity and utilization of major chemicals, 1991, article, C5800–8.511

Steel (galvanized) hot-dip production lines capacity, for 6 new lines added by 5 companies, 1993 article, C7000–8.503

Steel industry operating trends and devs, including profiles of 4 major companies, 1960-90, U9640–2.15

Steel mill employment, capacity, shipments, and other operating info, for individual mini and market mills, 1992 annual feature, C7000–8.501

Sulfur (oil-based) recovery plant capacity and production, by company and country, Jan 1993, annual feature, C6985–1.537

Tall oil fractionating capacity of US and foreign companies, 1992, annual rpt, C6585–1

Tampon product market value, with shares for top 4 and all other manufacturers, 1992, article, C2710–1.513

Textile and clothing companies financial data, for approx 170 firms, with industry statistical summary, 1991-92 and trends, annual rpt, C3400–5

Textile fiber product manufacturers, with plants by State and region, 1992 annual directory, C3460–1.501

Textile industry financial performance indicators for 32 companies, FY92 and trends, annual rpt, B8130–1

Textile industry sales and earnings, selected companies, monthly rpt recurring table, C5226–3.501

Toothbrush market shares, for top 9 brands and private label, year ended Apr 1993, article, C2710–1.530

Toothpaste promotional advertisements for 4 companies, 1st half 1992-93, article, C2710–1.540

Turkey household appliance production, by type, for 7 manufacturers, 1993 feature, C2000–1.511

Uranium conversion capacity and 1993 commitments, for 5 suppliers worldwide, article, B6800–1.504

Index by Categories

BY INDIVIDUAL COMPANY OR INSTITUTION

Western States economic indicators, including forecasts from selected organizations, for 10 States, monthly rpt, U0282–2

Women's use and shopping patterns for personal care products, with preferred outlets and brands, 1993 survey and trends, annual feature, C5150–2.515

State and local:

Arizona copper industry operations, including production, capacity, and reserves, by company and mine, with US and intl comparisons, 1991 and trends, annual rpt, S0497–1

Arizona economic indicators, including forecasts from 16 forecasting organizations, monthly rpt, U0282–1

Florida, Miami convention revenue loss due to black boycott, for 5 organizations and aggregate 20 others, 1993 article, C4215–1.509

Georgia-based Fortune 500 firms, 1991, biennial rpt, U6730–1.6

Hawaii corporations, sales, employment, and revenues, for selected firms, 1992 annual rpt, S2090–1.15

Hawaii shopping center characteristics, by center, 1992 annual rpt, S2090–1.23

Kentucky employment and number of plants, for top 58 manufacturers, 1992, annual rpt, S3120–1

Maine industrial parks and site features, 1992 recurring rpt, S3434–1

Minnesota-based Fortune 500 corporation sales, assets, and net income, by company, 1991, annual rpt, S4180–1

Mississippi employment and number of plants, top 25 companies, FY92 annual rpt, S4346–1

Mississippi new and expanded industry employment and investment, by company, 1991, annual rpt, U3255–4.5

Missouri mineral production, by commodity and company, FY92 and trends, annual rpt, S4530–2.1

South Carolina largest manufacturing employers, and Fortune 500 companies, 1993 annual rpt, S7125–1.3

South Carolina new firm investments, and plant closings and employment affected, by company, 1991, annual planning rpt, S7155–3.2

Utah small business dev program, with awards granted, economic impact, and profiles of 10 recipient companies, 1992 article, U8960–2.503

Utah timber production volume and value from natl forests, 1960-92, triennial rpt, U8960–1.9

Washington State corporate assessed property value, for top 10 firms, FY92, annual rpt, S8345–3

Labor and Employment

Canada, British Columbia Province paper industry strikes and capacity affected, by company and mill, 1992, annual rpt, C3975–5.2

Corporate employee training policies and spending as a percent of payroll, for 8 companies with outstanding programs, 1993 article, C8900–1.511

Employee benefit plan asset rankings of top 1,000 funds, with selected fund investment data, 1992, annual feature, C2710–2.504

Labor union membership, for 10 largest unions, 1981 and 1991, article, C8900–1.508

Layoffs by major companies, public awareness, Jan 1993 survey, C8915–1.501

Pension fund assets, for top 300 funds worldwide, 1992, annual feature, C2710–2.515

Pension fund guaranteed benefit liability shares unfunded, for 50 funds with largest underfunding, 1991, article, C2710–2.502

Pension fund portfolio characteristics and investment performance, 4th qtr 1992, semiannual feature, C3950–1.509

Plastics processing employee representation by 7 labor unions, by region, 1992, annual survey rpt, A8920–2

Puerto Rico employment of 10 largest US companies manufacturing under IRS Code Section 936, 1993 article, C5800–7.532

Steel industry restructuring devs, with data on production, employment, and worker assistance, and selected detail by company, for 8-12 countries, 1970s-90, R9260–16

State and local:

Alabama employment for top 20 private employers, 1991, annual rpt, S0129–1

Alaska employment for top 100 companies, with distribution by industry div, 1992, annual article, S0320–1.510

Alaska, Juneau employment for top 10 firms, 1992, article, S0320–1.512

Alaska, Ketchikan employment for top 10 firms, 1991, article, S0320–1.502

Alaska, Northwest Arctic Borough employment for top 8 firms, 1992, article, S0320–1.512

Arizona employment for top 10 employers, FY91, annual rpt, S0450–2

DC top 10 business and nonprofit employers, 1992, annual rpt, S1535–3.3

Florida 50 largest employers and location of corporate hq, 1992 annual rpt, U6660–1.6

Georgia employment for top 50 employers, 1991, biennial rpt, U6730–1.3

Idaho employment for 94 largest employers, 1992 recurring rpt, S2218–2.5

Illinois employment for top 30 companies, Jan 1993, S2405–2.502

Iowa top 10-50 employers, 1982 and 1992, annual rpt, S2784–3

Louisiana top 25 private employers, 1st qtr 1992, annual rpt, S3285–2

Missouri top 15 employers, 1991, annual rpt, S4475–1

New Jersey employment, for 50 largest employers, 1991, annual rpt, S5455–1

New York State largest private employers, 1990, annual rpt, U5100–1.3

North Carolina employment for top 25 employers, June 1992, annual rpt, S5897–1

Oklahoma major employers by size, 1990, annual rpt, U8130–2.3

Oregon employment for top 39 private employers, FY92 annual rpt, S6603–2

Oregon employment for top 50 employers, Sept 1992, article, S6592–1.501

Pennsylvania 50 largest employers, Mar 1991, annual planning rpt, S6845–3.2

South Carolina employees of 25 largest manufacturing firms, Dec 1991, annual rpt, S7127–1

Tennessee employment for top 50 companies, FY92 annual rpt, S7505–1

Utah employees of 47 largest employers, Dec 1991, annual rpt, S7795–1

Utah employment at 46 largest employers, Dec 1992, S7820–3.509

Utah employment for 54 largest employers, Dec 1992, annual rpt, S7820–10

Wyoming Native American unemployment rates, by reservation, 1990, article, S8895–1.501

Law Enforcement

Bankruptcy attorneys in 6 legal firms, 1987 and 1992, article, C5800–7.512

Correctional instns, inmates, staff, and cost of care, by instn, US and Canada, with operating summary by State or Province, 1992, annual directory, A1305–3

Higher education on-campus crime incidence and arrests by selected offense, by instn and State, 1991/92, C2175–1.506

Jail facilities, population, costs, and staff and salaries, for 90 local systems, 1992 annual rpt, R4300–1.4

Jails and adult detention facilities, inmates, staff, and operating summary, by State and instn, Dec 1992, recurring directory, A1305–1

Law school enrollment by minority status, degrees conferred, staff, and library holdings, by instn, 1992/93 and trends, annual rpt, A0970–1

State and local:

Alabama university campus crimes and law enforcement employment, by instn, 1988-90, recurring rpt, U5680–2.10

Alaska correctional instn inmates, by facility, 1991-92, annual rpt, S0275–1

Alaska corrections system admin, including costs at specific prisons and community centers, FY91, annual rpt, S0287–1

Arizona prison construction activity, including new beds and costs, FY92 annual rpt, S0464–2

California correctional instn inmates, by offense, demographic characteristics, and instn, Dec 1992, semiannual rpt, S0820–2

California correctional instn inmates, with criminal background and demographic characteristics, 1991 and trends, annual rpt, S0820–1

DC prison and detention facility population, by facility, 1987-91, annual rpt, S1535–3.8

Florida correctional instns, admin, and inmates by criminal background and demographic characteristics, FY92 annual rpt, S1720–1

Georgia prison inmates and operations, by instn, FY92, annual rpt, S1872–1

Illinois correctional instn capacity, by facility, FY74-93, annual rpt, S2425–1

Iowa correctional instn admissions, releases, and inmate characteristics, by instn, monthly rpt, S2770–1

Kansas correctional instn inmate population, by instn, FY91-92, annual rpt, U7095–2.12

Kansas correctional instn inmates, by offense, demographic characteristics, and instn, FY92 and trends, annual rpt, S2940–1

Kansas crimes reported by agency, including correctional instns and parks, 1992, annual rpt, S2925–1.1

Maryland assaults against spouses, by military installation, 1992, annual rpt, S3665–1

Maryland correctional instn education programs enrollment and completions, by instn, 1991/92, annual rpt, S3610–1

BY INDIVIDUAL COMPANY OR INSTITUTION

Index by Categories

Maryland correctional instns population and per capita costs, by instn, FY92, biennial rpt, S3605–1.9

Massachusetts correctional instn inmate socioeconomic characteristics and criminal background, by instn, Jan 1992 and trends, annual rpt, S3805–1

Michigan correctional instns, admin, and inmates by selected demographic characteristics, 1991 and trends, annual rpt, S3960–1

Missouri correctional instn population, by instn, FY93, annual rpt, S4501–1

Nebraska correctional instn admin, with inmates by criminal background and demographic characteristics, by instn, FY92 and trends, annual rpt, S4850–1

Nevada prisoners and prison operating capacity, by instn, 1985-91, biennial rpt, S5005–1.4

New Jersey correctional instn inmates, by offense, sentence length, demographic characteristics, and instn, Dec 1991 annual rpt, S5370–1

New York State correctional inmate population by instn, and community dispute resolution program cases and dispositions by facility, 1992 annual rpt, U5100 1.8

New York State correctional instn inmate population and capacity, by local facility, 1991, annual rpt, S5760–3.4

New York State local jail/penitentiary inmates by offense, sentence, and demographic characteristics, by county or facility, 1991, annual rpt, S5724–2

North Carolina correctional instn admissions, separations, and population, with inmate characteristics, FY93, semiannual rpt, S5900–1

North Dakota local correctional instn adult and juvenile inmate characteristics, by instn, 1991 and trends, annual rpt, S6060–3

Oklahoma correctional instn admin, including inmate characteristics, incarceration costs, and data by instn, FY91, annual rpt, S6420–1

Oklahoma State treatment centers and programs for juveniles, resident population movement by instn, FY92, annual rpt, S6455–1.2

Pennsylvania State correctional instn admin, and inmates by type of offense and demographic characteristics, 1990 and trends, annual rpt, S6782–1

South Carolina correctional instns, admin, and inmates by criminal offense and demographic characteristics, FY92 and trends, annual rpt, S7135–1

South Carolina juvenile correctional inmates vs instn capacity, by instn, FY91-92, annual rpt, S7125–1.5

Tennessee correctional instn inmates, capacity, and per capita expenditures, by instn, FY90, annual rpt, U8710–2.19

Tennessee correctional instn population, capacity, costs, and vocational training grads, by instn, FY92, annual rpt, S7480–1

Texas correctional instn inmates, by sex and instn, Aug 1992, annual rpt, S7660–1

Washington State correctional instn inmates by demographic characteristics, and prison capacity, by instn, quarterly rpt, S8337–1

Wisconsin correctional instn inmates and capacity, by instn, FY60-92, biennial rpt, S8780–1.2

Wisconsin correctional instn inmates, by criminal background and selected characteristics, series, S8692–1

Wyoming correctional instn admin, finances, inmate characteristics, and staff, and probation and parole activities, FY92 annual rpt, S8883–1

Natural Resources, Environment and Pollution

Air pollutants released in 1987 and 1991, for 4 companies with highest emissions in 1987, article, C5800–7.530

Biogas organic waste recycling project characteristics, including production capacity, for 12 major projects worldwide, 1993 article, C5800–8.507

Chemical company waste reduction activities, for 8 firms, 1992 article, A1250–1.503

Chemical industry toxic chemical releases by 10 firms and environmental spending by 20 firms, 1993 article, A1250–1.533

Developing countries debt acquisition in exchange for conservation program funding, summary of programs in 11 countries including participating organizations, Nov 1991, biennial rpt, R9455–1.6

Environmental engineering professional views on career and top employers, May 1993, annual survey article, C5800–2.546

Environmental records and summary financial data for 10 leading and 20 other manufacturers rated by Fortune magazine, 1993 article, C8900–1.520

Industrial emission-control equipment market shares for top 10 and all other manufacturers, 1991, article, A4700–4.501

Natl forests in US and 8 Southern States, timber stand improvement needs and acreage needing reforestation, by forest, FY91, annual rpt, U3255–4.10

Timberland holdings of major paper companies, 1993 annual rpt, C3975–5.1

Utility regulatory agency activities, including rate reviews by company, 1991/92 annual rpt, A7015–3

World heritage site mgmt problems, by world region and site, 1992/93 biennial rpt, R9455–1.6

State and local:

Alaska public utility financial and operating data, by company and utility type, 1991 and trends, with FY92 regulatory info, annual rpt, S0280–4

Arizona reservoir storage capacity, by reservoir, 1984-91, recurring rpt, U5850–2.1

Arizona water production from oil and gas fields, by field, operator, and well, monthly rpt, S0473–1

Arizona wilderness designated acreage, by area, 1990, recurring rpt, U5850–2.8

Arkansas public utility financial, operating, and regulatory data, by utility type and company, 1992 annual rpt, S0757–1

California dams and reservoirs, and water supply and use, 1992 annual rpt, S0840–2.7

California, Los Angeles area oil refinery emissions allocations, by company, 1994, 2000, and 2003, article, C6985–1.552

California public utility and transportation regulatory data, including revenue requests and rates of return by company, FY92 annual rpt, S0930–1

Florida natl forest acreage, by county and forest, 1991, annual rpt, U6660–1.10

Florida residential water rates and population served, by utility, 1988/89, annual rpt, U6660–1.8

Hawaii air quality testing by station, and water pollution penalties by facility, 1990 annual rpt, S2065–1.6

Hawaii fish counts by species at selected sites, FY92, annual rpt, S2090–1.20

Hawaii land acreage owned by 6 largest landowners, 1989-91, annual rpt, S2090–1.6

Nevada wilderness areas and recommended acreage, and water supply by reservoir, 1992 biennial rpt, S5005–1.9

New York State public utility financial and operating data, by utility type and company, 1988-92, annual rpt, S5795–1

North Carolina water and sewer utility finances, customers, and systems, by company, 1990, annual rpt, S5917–2

South Carolina public service commission regulatory activities, with financial and operating data for individual utilities and railroads, FY92 annual rpt, S7235–1

Vermont private water systems residential customers and rates, by company, Dec 1991, biennial rpt, S8100–1

Washington State water utilities financial and operating data, by company, 1988-90, annual rpt, S8450–1.1

Washington State water utilities financial and operating data, by company, 1989-91, annual rpt, S8450–1.4

Wyoming State govt water dev appropriations and expenditures, by project, FY92 annual rpt, S8875–1

Population

Cambodia repatriated refugee population coming from 7 Thailand camp sites, for 8 reception centers, Mar-Nov 1992, R9372–2.502

Church membership and contributions, by Protestant denomination, US and Canada, 1991 or 1992, annual article, C2176–1.518

Churches and membership, by denomination, census div, State, and county, 1990, R4985–1

Churches, membership, clergy, and contributions, by denomination, US and Canada, 1991-92, annual rpt, C0105–1

Refugees resettled in US under voluntary agency sponsorship, with detail for 12 top agencies, FY92, R9372–2.505

State and local:

Arizona Indian population, education, housing, health, and employment characteristics, with detail by reservation, 1970s-91, recurring rpt, U5850–2.9

Idaho population on 5 Indian reservations, by race-ethnicity, 1990, recurring rpt, S2218–2.2

Utah Indian reservation population characteristics, by reservation, 1990, census rpt, S7832–3.3

Public Welfare and Social Security

Charitable contributions, including donors and recipients of gifts, and foundation assets and grants, 1993 annual rpt, A0700–1

Index by Categories

BY INDIVIDUAL COMPANY OR INSTITUTION

Charitable contributions of largest corporate donors (unnamed), and relation to income, 1991, annual rpt, R4105–8

Employee contributions to non-United Way funds through on-the-job campaigns, with data for selected individual funds, 1989-92, article, C2176–1.502

Foundation assets, income, and grants by type of recipient, with data for top organizations and by location, 1991 and trends, annual rpt, R4900–1

Foundation board trustees by sex and race-ethnicity, for 25 leading private, community, and corporate foundations, 1989 and trends, A9405–1.1

Foundation board trustees by sex and race-ethnicity, for 25 leading private, community, and corporate foundations, 1991 and trends, A9405–1.2

Foundation grants of $5.7 million/over, with recipient, donor, and purpose, 1991, annual article, C2176–1.504

Foundations (community-based) asset value, grants paid, and gifts received, for top 50 organizations, 1992, annual article, C2176–1.518

Foundations, assets, and contributions, by organization type and census div, with top 100 organizations, FY91, annual article, C2176–1.507

Japan corporate affiliate charitable foundations in US, with assets and contributions, by company, various years 1989-93, article, R5650–2.560

Nonprofit foundation grants awarded and assets, top 50 foundations, 1991, annual feature, C2175–1.520

Nonprofit organization executive compensation, with comparison to organization income, by leading organization, FY91 or FY92, article, C2176–1.509

Nonprofit organizations private support, income, and services and fundraising costs, for top 400 organizations, FY91 or FY92, annual article, C2176–1.501

Philanthropy trends and devs, including data on nonprofit organization activities and finances, and corporate and individual giving, biweekly rpt, C2176–1

Somalia aid efforts, including expenditures and personnel, for selected charitable organizations, 1993 article, C2176–1.504

Voluntary health agency revenues, and expenditures by function, for 39 major organizations, FY90, annual rpt, A7973–1

State and local:

DC homeless shelter capacity and use, by facility, FY91, annual rpt, S1535–3.5

Maryland medical assistance payments and recipients, by program, type of service, location, demographic characteristics, and facility, FY92 and trends, annual rpt, S3635–3

Utah homeless shelter facilities and utilization, 1991-92, annual rpt, S7808–2

Recreation and Leisure

Amusement park attendance, for top 20 parks, 1991, annual rpt, C2140–1.2

Arts fundraising through united arts funds (UAFs), with fund operations, income by source, and allocations, by UAF, 1992 and trends, annual rpt, A1315–2

Arts fundraising through united arts funds (UAFs), with top 10 UAFs in funds raised by source, 1992, annual article, C2176–1.513

Baseball American League player and team performance, and public attendance, 1992 and trends, annual rpt, A2068–1

Baseball broadcasting, including TV and radio originators, and rights payments, by major league team, 1993 annual article, C1850–14.515

Baseball Natl League player and team performance, and public attendance, 1992 and trends, annual rpt, A8015–1

Basketball (professional) broadcast coverage, by team, 1993/94, article, C1850–14.540

Football (college) bowl game payments to participating teams, 1992/93, annual feature, C2175–1.503

Football (college and professional) broadcast coverage and rights payments, by team, 1993 annual article, C1850–14.534

Natl Park Service areas acreage, visits, and overnight stays for top 20 areas, 1990 or 1991, recurring rpt, R9375–6

Recreational vehicle towables and motorhome manufacturer market shares, for top 10 companies, 1992, annual article, C8950–2.502

Resort hotel profiles, including room rates and facilities, 1992 annual survey, C1200–1.508

Sports pay-per-view packages on cable TV, including number of games and prices, for 11 professional teams, 1993 article, C1850–14.522

Theater, Broadway stage shows with over 1,000 performances, ranking of top shows, May 1993, annual feature, C9380–1.529

Theater receipts and attendance for individual shows on Broadway, weekly rpt, C9380–1

Theme park attendance, top 20 parks, 1989, recurring rpt, R9375–6

Video game manufacturer sales and stock performance, for 6 companies, 1993 article, C3950–1.521

State and local:

Arizona State and natl park visitors, by area, 1980-91, recurring rpt, U5850–2.8

Arizona visitors to parks and other recreational areas, by site, 1985-93, semiannual rpt, U5850–1.1

California park and recreation area acreage, 1992 annual rpt, S0840–2.1

DC museum, memorial, and White House visits, 1987-91, annual rpt, S1535–3.3

Florida park and memorial attendance, 1992 annual rpt, U6660–1.19

Hawaii museums and other cultural attractions attendance, and performing arts productions by organization, 1992 annual rpt, S2090–1.7

Idaho State park and Alpine skiing area facilities, by site, 1992 recurring rpt, S2218–2.10

Illinois park and recreation area acreage and attendance, and fish hatchery and game farm acreage, by site, 1992 annual rpt, U6910–2

Maine ski areas, parks, and other recreational facilities, 1992 recurring rpt, S3434–1

Mississippi park and recreation areas, 1992 annual rpt, U3255–4.16

Nebraska pari-mutuel wagering and taxes paid, by organization, 1991, annual rpt, S4950–1.3

Nevada State park acreage and visitors, by park, 1985-90, biennial rpt, S5005–1.9

New Jersey casino revenues and operations for 12 facilities, with State regulatory activities, 1992 and trends, annual rpt, S5360–1

New York State attendance at recreational and camping sites, 1992 annual rpt, U5100–1.15

Oklahoma horse racing days, attendance, and wager, by track, 1990, annual rpt, U8130–2.21

Oklahoma State park attendance, by site, FY89-92, annual rpt, U8130–2.21

Pennsylvania historic sites and State and natl park attendance, by site or park, 1986-90, recurring rpt, U4130–6.8

South Carolina State park facilities and attendance, by park and use, 1993 annual rpt, S7125–1.14

Tennessee natl and State park and recreation area acreage and visitors, by site, 1992/93 annual rpt, U8710–2.12

Utah natl and State park area acreage, and visits, by site, 1993 triennial rpt, U8960–1.17

West Virginia State park and forest attendance by site, FY83-92, annual rpt, R9385–1.7

Wisconsin State recreational facilities and historic sites, and visitors, by site, 1991 and trends, biennial rpt, S8780–1.2

Science and Technology

Astronomy enrollment and degrees awarded, by level, State, and instn, 1991/92-1992/93, annual rpt, A1960–2.3

Biotechnology company income and earnings, for approx 30 firms, 1991-92, recurring article, A1250–1.518

Biotechnology company income and earnings, for approx 30 firms, 3rd qtr and 1st nine months 1992, recurring article, A1250–1.504

Chemical industry R&D spending, for 27 companies, 1987-93, annual article, A1250–1.511

Chemicals R&D spending in Federal, industrial, and academic sectors, with data by company and instn, 1980s-93, annual feature, A1250–1.537

Chemistry and chemical engineering degrees awarded, by level, sex, and instn, 1991/92 and trends, annual articles, A1250–1.535

Chemists employment terminations by 6 companies, Oct 1990-Dec 1991, recurring article, A1250–1.507

Chemists employment terminations by 7 companies, 1990-92, recurring article, A1250–1.536

Ecologist characteristics, including membership in various professional organizations, and school awarding higher education degree, Mar 1992 survey, recurring rpt, A4685–1

Engineering degrees awarded, by State, instn, and field, with detail for women, minorities, and foreign students, 1991/92, annual rpt, A0685–1

Engineering program enrollment, by instn, field, and State, with detail for women, minorities, and foreign students, fall 1992, annual rpt, A0685–2

Engineering schools granting degrees to women, minorities, and foreign students, leading instns, 1991, recurring rpt, A3960–2.3

BY INDIVIDUAL COMPANY OR INSTITUTION

High-technology company market value, for top 10 firms, July 1993, article, C8900–1.521

High-technology small companies with rapid growth, employment and sales data for 25 firms, 1993 article, C5800–7.551

Hispanic-owned high-technology company sales and employment, for top 50 firms, 1992, annual article, C4575–1.510

Japan patent applications of top 10 companies, 1987-91, C1850–6.506

Paper industry R&D spending, by company, 1989-91, annual rpt, C3975–5.1

Patent activity for approx 200 US and foreign firms in 13 industries, 1992 and trends, article, C5800–7.540

Photonics-related patents issued to top 10 manufacturers, 1992, article, C1850–6.508

Physics enrollment and degrees awarded, by level, State, and instn, 1991/92-1992/93, annual rpt, A1960–2.2

R&D expenditures, and sales and profits, for approx 900 firms, 1992, annual feature, C5800–7.534

Spacecraft launches by individual vehicle, with launch success and orbital status, 1992 and trends, annual rpt, B9170–1

State and local:

Pennsylvania advanced technology center funding under govt partnership program, FY92, recurring rpt, U4130–6.2

Pennsylvania R&D and science/engineering financing from Fed Govt, by higher education instn, 1989, recurring rpt, U4130–6.4

Utah high-technology industry trends, with R&D spending, and employment of major firms, 1986-92, recurring article, U8960–2.508

Transportation and Travel

Aerospace and defense industries financial performance, with data for approx 200 major US and foreign companies, FY92 and trends, annual feature, C5800–4 519

Aerospace industry, civil and military production, R&D, trade, employment, and finances, with Federal funding data, 1991 and trends, annual rpt, A0250–2

Aerospace/defense industry capital investments as percent of sales, for 4 major companies, 1989 and 1991, article, C5800–4.516

Aircraft (business/personal) shipments by model, for approx 20 manufacturers, weekly rpt quarterly table, C5800–30.503, C5800–30.505, C5800–30.509

Aircraft (jet) order cancellations and deferrals by airline, and aircraft in storage by model, 1992 article, C7000–4.502

Aircraft (jet) orders from 5-6 manufacturers worldwide, by model, monthly rpt quarterly feature, C7000–4.502, C7000–4.505

Aircraft (jet) world inventory, leasing activity, orders, and deliveries, by type of aircraft and individual owner/operator, 1992 and trends, annual rpt, B1582–1

Aircraft (regional) fleets, by carrier and manufacturer, and top models in use, 1992, annual rpt, A8795–1

Aircraft (turbine-powered) in service and on order, by manufacturer and model, for over 900 airlines worldwide, Dec 1992, annual rpt, B3370–1

Aircraft shipments and net billings, by general aviation manufacturer and/or model, quarterly rpt, A5120–1

Airline (regional) traffic, aircraft, subsidy payments, and services, by carrier and location, 1992 and trends, annual rpt, A8795–1

Airline commissions to travel agents, and passenger revenues, by US and foreign carrier, 1st half 1993 and trends, annual article, C7000–4.511

Airline expenditures on inflight meals, for 9 major carriers and all others, 1992, article, C1200–5.516

Airline finances and operations of scheduled carriers, summary statistics, 1992 and trends, annual rpt, A0325–5

Airline financial performance, by carrier, monthly rpt quarterly table, C7000–4.501, C7000–4.504, C7000–4.508, C7000–4.509

Airline fleet average age, for 10 major carriers, 1993 article, C8900–1.507

Airline fleet units owned, leased, and on order, by model, July 1993, and planned changes for 2nd half 1993, article, C5800–4.530

Airline food service expenditures, by carrier, 1st 9 months 1992 and trends, annual article, C7000–4.507

Airline Hawaii-US mainland route market shares, for top 9 and all other carriers, 1990, article, B3500–1.502

Airline industry devs including passenger and cargo traffic activity and fuel costs, with worldwide passenger traffic, by carrier, monthly rpt, C7000–4

Airline intl and domestic passenger-kilometers flown by top 15 carriers worldwide, 1992, article, C5800–4.524

Airline jet fleet leased vs owned, and operating lease expenses, by major carrier, 1993 annual article, C7000–4.508

Airline market activity, including traffic, financial performance, employment, and fleet composition, by US and foreign carrier, 1991-92, annual feature, C7000–4.508

Airline passengers boarded, and voluntary and involuntary denied boardings, by carrier, monthly rpt quarterly table, C7000–4.502, C7000–4.506

Airline pilots, and compensation per flight crew member, for 9 carriers, 1992, article, C5800–4.528

Airline revenues or earnings or losses, for 10 largest carriers, 1992, article, C8900–1.517

Airline revenues, profits, and passenger traffic, for top 50 carriers worldwide, 1991, article, C8900–1.501

Airline traffic and finances worldwide, by carrier, 1993 annual feature, C7000–4.511

Airline traffic and financial forecasts, and fleet acquisition and disposal plans, by US and foreign carrier, 1993 annual article, C7000–4.503

Airport freight traffic at top 20 airports, 1992, annual article, C2150–1.506

Airport passenger and freight traffic at top 20 airports, 1992, annual rpt, A0325–5

Airport regional and other daily flight departures for 10 airports with most regional flights, 1993 article, C5800–4.517

Index by Categories

Airport runway incursions at 15 major airports, year ended June 1992-93, article, C5800–4.526

Auto advertising expenditures outside US by top 10 manufacturers, and billings for auto accounts changing agencies, 1993 article, C2710–1.509

Auto aftermarket chain sales, income, and stores, for 8 companies, 1989-91, C2150–10.501

Auto aftermarket company financial and operating data, including sales, income, stores, and inventory turns, for 8-12 public firms, 1993 article, C2150–10.508

Auto aftermarket retail sales, and number of stores and service bays, for top 100 chains, 1993 annual article, C2150–10.507

Auto aftermarket warehouse distributor membership, for 15 programmed distribution groups, 1993 article, C2150–10.505

Auto and other vehicle characteristics, for 1993 models, annual rpt, A5200–5

Auto and truck customer sales satisfaction index, by leading model, 1992-93, annual article, C2710–3.535

Auto and truck models and/or makes with fewest problems for buyers, with summaries for US, Asian, and European manufacturers, 1993 and trends, article, C2710–3.532

Auto and truck sales and market share summary, with data by vehicle type, manufacturer, and leading make and model, 1st qtr 1992-93, C2150–3.507

Auto customer satisfaction index after 3 years of ownership, for top 14 nameplates, 1993, article, C2710–3.517

Auto customer satisfaction index, by leading model, 1992-93, annual article, C2710–3.538

Auto dealer fleet vehicle sales, for top 30 dealers, 1992 article, C1575–2.501

Auto dealer franchise desirability rating for top 33 makes, winter 1992 93, survey article, C2710–3.525

Auto dealer satisfaction with manufacturers, index for top 15 makes, 1991-92, survey article, C2710–3.512

Auto dealer views on dealer assn and manufacturer advertising programs, including natl campaign spending levels by medium, with data by vehicle make, 1993 survey article, C2710–1.518, C2710–3.521

Auto dealership sales per outlet, by make, 1988-92, annual article, C2710–3.520

Auto dealerships, including domestic and import outlets, and franchises by make, 1993 and trends, annual article, C2710–3.519

Auto dependability index after 5 years of ownership, for top 12 nameplates, 1992-93, article, C2710–3.524

Auto fleet acquisition plans, including data by manufacturer, 1992 survey, article, C1575–2.503

Auto fleet dealer award recipients, and top dealer sales by make, 1992, annual feature, C1575–2.508

Auto fleet registrations by model, by size class, 1992-93 models, annual feature, C1575–2.510

Auto fleet use of fuel credit cards, with detail for 6 oil company cards, 1993 survey article, C1575–2.505

Index by Categories

BY INDIVIDUAL COMPANY OR INSTITUTION

Auto industry financial performance of top 3 US auto manufacturers, weekly rpt quarterly table, C2710–3.501, C2710–3.516, C2710–3.527, C2710–3.538, C2710–3.541

Auto industry performance indicators for 3 major manufacturers, 1970s-92, annual article, C2150–3.506

Auto industry revenues and stock performance, for 3 major vehicle manufacturers and approx 50 suppliers, weekly rpt quarterly feature, C2710–3.518, C2710–3.532, C2710–3.545

Auto insurance claims cost and frequency, and low-speed crash repair costs, selected makes and series, 1993 annual rpt, A5650–1.4

Auto insurance collision coverage experiences for autos and other vehicles, by make and series, for recent model years, 1993 annual rpt series, A5200–1

Auto insurance passenger and commercial premiums, market shares, and loss ratios, with rankings of States and 20 leading firms, 1992, annual article, C1050–1.511

Auto insurance personal injury protection claim frequencies, 1990-92 model autos and other vehicles, annual rpt, A5200–3

Auto insurance theft coverage experiences, for 1990-92 model autos and other vehicles, by make and model, annual rpt, A5200–2

Auto maintenance activity of imported vehicle owners, including nameplates owned, 1993 survey, annual article, C2150–10.508

Auto manufacturer advertising agency changes, including billings involved, for 11 firms, 1991-92, article, C2710–1.501

Auto market data book on production, sales, registrations, prices, options, dealerships, and industry finances, with data by make and country, 1993 annual rpt, C2710–3.531

Auto news and devs, with production and sales data and market analysis, US and foreign, by manufacturer and make/model, weekly rpt, C2710–3

Auto original equipment supplier North American sales of top 50 firms, with worldwide sales and components made, 1991-92, annual data book, C2710–3.531

Auto problems for buyers, for 7 European manufacturers, 1993 article, C2710–3.533

Auto purchasing and plans, including makes most likely to be purchased, by age group, 1993 survey article, C2710 1.539

Auto registrations, with detail for vehicle fleets by type, by manufacturer and make, weekly rpt quarterly feature, C2710–3.507, C2710–3.521, C2710–3.536, C2710–3.546

Auto rental company fleet size, and auto manufacturers shares of ownership and vehicles, for 8 rental companies, 1993 article, C2710–3.521

Autos (used) average auction prices, by make, model, year, and region, monthly rpt, C1575–2

Autos and light trucks/vans in top 100 corporate fleets, 1993, annual feature, C1575–2.504

Autos and light trucks/vans in 2nd 100 largest corporate fleets, 1993, annual feature, C1575–2.506

Black-owned enterprises financial and operating data, for top 100 firms and auto dealerships and for top 15-25 financial instns, 1992 and trends, annual feature, C4215–1.507

Bus (urban) fleets of 100 largest transit systems in US or Canada, 1993, annual article, C1575–3.507

Bus company fleets, for top 50 private operators in US and Canada, 1993 annual feature, C1575–3.503

Buses/vans owned or leased by major transit systems, top 41 and all other manufacturers, 1992 annual rpt, A2650–1.2

Business aircraft and helicopter accidents, with circumstances, fatalities, and model involved, weekly rpt quarterly feature, C5800–30

Canada auto dealer satisfaction with manufacturers, ratings for 21 makes, 1992 survey, article, C2710–3.518

Corporate auto fleet driver model preferences and use of selected auto service chains, oil and gasoline brands, and credit card types, 1993 survey, article, C1575–2.509

Cruise ships capacity and per diem cost, by ship, 1993 feature, C1200–4.503

Europe airline revenues and govt ownership share, for 8 major carriers, 1992 article, C8900–1.501

Europe airline revenues and market shares, for 8 major carriers, 1991, article, C5800–4.512

Europe auto market, including buyer preferences and market shares for selected manufacturers, by country, Aug/Sept 1992 survey, article, C2710–1.523

Europe auto sales, by country and/or manufacturer, weekly rpt monthly tables, C2710–3

Europe sport-utility vehicle unit sales, for 8 manufacturers and all others, 1992, article, C2150–3.506

Freight carrier quality ratings by shippers, by mode and company, 1993 annual survey article, C2150–1.507

Helicopters in civil aviation, production, trade, utilization, accidents, and landing facilities, 1993 annual rpt, A5190–1

Hispanic American career professional and business owner views on motor vehicle fleet composition by make, and tire brands used, 1993 survey, article, C4575–1.504

Hispanic-owned business motor vehicle fleet composition, and makes driven by chief executives, 1992 annual survey feature, C4575–1.501

Japan auto exports to US compared to voluntary quotas, by manufacturer, 1993 and/or 1994, recurring article, C2710–3.529

Japan auto exports to US voluntary quotas, by manufacturer, FY81-93, article, R5650–2.531

Japan auto manufacturer US auto parts purchases, and auto production in US and Canada compared to US firms, with selected detail by company and plant, 1993 article, R5650–2.523

Japan auto sales in US, with comparison to domestic manufacturers, 1985-92, annual article, R5650–2.511

Japan motor vehicle trade with US, and auto registrations by domestic and import make, 1987-92, article, R5650–2.543

Lodging industry facilities, sales, and occupancy, with top 42-100 properties in 5 market categories, 1993 annual rpt, C7000–5

Logistics trends and devs, including data on costs, finances of major carriers by mode, and foreign trade, 1993 annual compilation, C2150–1.506

Mass transit rail cars by type, for top 10 systems, 1992/93 annual fact book, C1575–3.501

Mass transit rail system energy efficiency ratings, for 14 systems in US and Canada, 1993 article, C1575–3.506

Mass transit rail system revenue passenger miles per vehicle hour, for 14 systems in US and Canada, 1993 article, C1575–3.505

Mass transit system operators in major cities ranked by passenger trips, by mode, FY91, annual rpt, A2650–1.1

Mexico auto and truck production for domestic and export markets, for top 5 and all other manufacturers, 1990-91, R4105–82.6

Mexico auto production and planned foreign investments, by manufacturer, 1992 rpt, R8490–43

Mexico foreign-owned motor vehicle plants and employment by company, and hq countries of auto parts industry foreign participants, 1993 article, C2150–3.505

Mexico motor vehicle sales, and domestic and export production, for 5 manufacturers, weekly rpt monthly tables, C2710–3

Mexico original auto equipment supplier plants and locations, with major products and customers, by company, 1993 article, C2710–3.550

Motor vehicle assembly plant production, by State and Canadian Province, manufacturer, model, and plant, 1993 model year, annual article, C2710–3.551

Motor vehicle assembly plant shutdown schedules for model changeovers/vacations, by US and Canadian plant, 1993 annual feature, C2710–3.537

Motor vehicle component manufacturers total and component sales, for top 13 companies worldwide, 1993 article, C2150–3.509

Motor vehicle crash test results for selected auto or light truck models, weekly rpt recurring feature, C2710–3.511, C2710–3.533

Motor vehicle fleet accidents, and vehicles and mileage, by fleet type and company (unnamed), 1991 and trends, annual rpt, A8375–3

Motor vehicle fleet lessors ranked by number of cars and truck managed, for top 15 companies, 1983 and 1993, C1575–2.510

Motor vehicle fleet operating and financial data, including fleets by type, registrations by make and model, and top lessors, 1970s-93, annual rpt, C1575–2.507

Motor vehicle fleet size, with makes and/or models used, for 7 major corporate fleets, 1993-94, article, C2710–3.553

Motor vehicle fuel economy for 1994 models, EPA estimates by model and size group, annual feature, C2710–3.550, C2710–3.551

Motor vehicle industry car and truck sales, by make and for top 10 vehicles, 1992-93 model years, annual article, C2710–3.551

BY INDIVIDUAL COMPANY OR INSTITUTION

Index by Categories

Motor vehicle industry labor productivity in North America, for 27 truck and 29 auto plants, 1992, article, C2150–3.503

Motor vehicle new model dev costs and production requirements, for 3 major manufacturers, 1993 article, C8900–1.518

Motor vehicle new registrations, including imports, by make and model, monthly rpt, C7715–3

Motor vehicle plant capacity, production, employment, and productivity, for 12 plants in 6 countries, 1993 article, C2150–3.504

Motor vehicle plant die change operations, efficiency scores for teams at 9 plants, 1992 annual article, C2150–3.501

Motor vehicle production and sales by manufacturer and/or make, and world leading producers, 1993 annual rpt, A0865–1.1

Motor vehicle production, revenues, and profits, for top 30 manufacturers worldwide, 1992, article, C8900–1.526

Motor vehicle rental fleet registrations of vehicles sold under buy-back programs of 11 manufacturers, 1990-93, C1575–2.503

Motor vehicle retail prices, for autos, light trucks, and vans, by make, model, and body style, 1993 model year, C2710–3.504

Motor vehicle sales, for selected auto and truck manufacturers, 1993 annual rpt, A7330–1

Motor vehicle sales, forecasts by 10 auto industry analysts, 1993, annual article, C2710–3.510

Motor vehicle sales, forecasts by 9 auto industry analysts, 1993-94, annual article, C2710–3.538

Motor vehicle world production, sales, trade, and registrations, by country, world area, manufacturer, and make, 1990-91 and trends, annual rpt, A0865–2

Motorcycle manufacturer market share, top 6 makes, 1987-91, annual rpt, A6485–1.1

Public utility truck/van fleets, for top 40 companies, 1992, annual feature, C1575–2.502

Railroad (Class I) financial condition, operations, and employment, by company and district, 1992, annual rpt, A3275–7

Railroad (Class I) freight service expenditures by category, and diesel fuel consumption, with detail for 7 companies, 1991, article, C8400–1.508

Railroad (Class I) traffic, employment, finances, and equipment, for 13 companies, 1992, annual rpt, A3275–5.4

Railroad financial and operating trends, including data by company, 1982-91, annual rpt, A3275–8

Railroad financial performance and expenses, by Class I railroad and district, quarterly rpt, A3275–1

Railroad financial performance, including fuel use and costs, and returns on investment for 11 companies, 1990-93, article, C8400–1.509

Railroad passenger cars delivered, undelivered backlog, and new orders outlook, by purchaser, 1993 annual feature, C8400–1.503

Resort hotel profiles, including room rates and facilities, 1992 annual survey, C1200–1.508

Shipbuilding (naval vessel) activity in private shipyards, including contracts, deliveries, and ongoing construction, 1993 recurring rpt, A8900–6

Shipbuilding govt aid in 6 OECD countries, with detail for specific contracts and shipyards, 1993 recurring rpt, A8900–8

Sports car 2-seat model sales, for 15 models, 1992, article, C2150–3.505

Tourism receipts and travel-related industry finances, US and foreign, with detail by company, 1992 annual rpt, C2140–1

Transportation regulatory agency activities, including rate reviews by company, 1991, annual rpt, A7015–4

Transportation service to daily newspaper markets in US and Canada, by mode and company, 1993 annual rpt, C3250–1

Travel and tourism rankings for selected indicators, including data for top 20 States, cities, countries, businesses, and other measures, 1992 recurring rpt, R9375–6

Truck (heavy-/medium-duty) manufacturers ranked by desirability of franchises, dealer views, May and Nov 1992, article, C2710–3.525

Truck fleet financial and operating data for top 200 freight carriers, 1992 and trends, annual feature, C2150–4.504

Truck sales by vehicle make and diesel engine manufacturer, 1991-92, annual feature, C2150–4.503

Trucks (light), sport/utility, and van fleet registrations, by model, 1st half 1992-93 model years, annual feature, C1575–2.510

State and local:

Alabama waterborne freight by river and at Mobile Harbor, and State licensed airports, 1992 recurring rpt, U5680–2.16

Arizona aircraft traffic, by airport, FY91, recurring rpt, U5850–2.18

California public utility and transportation regulatory data, including revenue requests and rates of return by company, FY92 annual rpt, S0930–1

California traffic accidents resulting in deaths and injuries, by vehicle make, 1983, 1987, and 1991, annual rpt, S0885–1

Florida airport and port traffic, and railroad track mileage by company, 1992 annual rpt, U6660–1.13

Hawaii airport and harbor traffic by facility, and top motor vehicle makes registered, 1992 annual rpt, S2090–1.18

Idaho railroad track mileage, by carrier, 1992 recurring rpt, S2218–2.8

Illinois air passenger enplanements, by airport, 1986-90, annual rpt, U6910–2

Illinois criminal offenses for campus, railroad, and other special police forces, 1991, annual rpt, S2536–1

Maine traffic accidents, fatalities, and injuries, by vehicle make, 1992, annual rpt, S3475–2

Maryland tollway traffic by facility, 1982-92, biennial rpt, S3605–1.10

Mississippi rail transport operations, by carrier, 1992 annual rpt, U3255–4.6

Montana public utility and transportation property assessments, by county and company, 1991-92, biennial rpt, S4750–1.2

Nebraska public service commission regulatory activities, with financial and operating data for individual railroads and telephone companies, FY91-92 biennial rpt, S4940–1

Nevada air passenger traffic at 2 major airports, 1980-91, biennial rpt, S5005–1.13

New Mexico traffic accidents, fatalities, and injuries, by Indian pueblo or reservation, 1992, annual rpt, S5665–1

New York State waterborne and air traffic, by port, canal, and airport; and urban transportation operations by transit authority; 1992 annual rpt, U5100–1.13

North Carolina public utility financial, operating, and regulatory data, by utility type and company, 1990 and trends, annual rpt, S5917–2

Oklahoma railroad track mileage, by railroad, 1991, annual rpt, U8130–2.16

South Carolina public service commission regulatory activities, with financial and operating data for individual utilities and railroads, FY92 annual rpt, S7235–1

South Carolina waterborne trade by port, and railroad and bus operations by company, 1993 annual rpt, S7125–1.15

Tennessee airports and river terminals, 1992/93 annual rpt, U8710–2.9

Texas railroad and airport operating data, 1992, U8850–9

Washington State public service and utility companies property value, by company and county, 1992, annual rpt, S8415–1.4

Wisconsin waterborne freight traffic by commodity, by port, 1990, biennial rpt, S8780–1.2

Wyoming traffic accidents involving motorcycles, by accident severity and vehicle make, 1992, annual rpt, S9007–1

Veterans Affairs

State and local:

Florida VA health facilities utilization, by instn, FY90, annual rpt, U6660–1.20

BY INDUSTRY

Banking, Finance, and Insurance

Business Week investment indicators, including major stock indexes, and best and worst performing industries, weekly rpt, C5800–7

Corporate dividend yields and payout ratios, for selected industries and companies, biweekly rpt quarterly feature, C3950–1.504, C3950–1.510, C3950–1.517, C3950–1.523

Corporate stock investment performance and earnings outlook, approx 900 companies by industry, 1992 annual feature, C5800–7.509

Financial performance and growth rankings for approx 1,000 top corporations, with comparisons by industry group, 1993 annual rpt, C3950–1.505

Forbes investment indicators, including best and worst performing industries, biweekly rpt, C3950–1

Investment performance of selected stock indexes, biweekly rpt quarterly feature, C2710–2.502, C2710–2.507, C2710–2.514

Mutual fund common stock portfolio holdings by industry, 1990-91, annual rpt, A6025–1.1

SBA loan distribution by industry div, FY92, C4687–1.509

Securities initial public offerings, for 5 most active industries, biweekly rpt quarterly feature, C3950–1.507, C3950–1.520, C3950–1.527

Index by Categories

BY INDUSTRY

Securities listed on NYSE and market value, by industry group, 1992, annual fact book, B6625–1.1

Securities traded over-the-counter on NASDAQ market, trading volume and price performance, for over 4,500 issues, 1992 and trends, annual rpt, A7105–1

Small business loan risk ratings by bankers, for 10 most and least risky industries, 1993 article, C4687–1.503

Spain, Madrid stock exchange performance by industry sector, and 20 leading stocks with greatest gains or losses, 1992, article, A8955–1.502

Venture capital disbursements, and new and follow-on investments, by industry group, selected years 1986-91, annual rpt, A8515–1

Venture capital funding for electronics and selected other industries, 1991-92, article, C1850–2.509

State and local:

Oklahoma statistical abstract, general data, 1992 annual rpt, U8130–2

Wisconsin consumer credit licensing and regulatory activity, including complaints handled by line of business, 1992 and trends, annual rpt, S8685–1

Communications

Advertising (outdoor) expenditures, for top 10 industry or product categories, 1992, recurring article, C2710–1.517

Advertising expenditures as percents of sales and profits, by SIC 4-digit industry, 1993, annual article, C2710–1.537

Cable TV advertising expenditures, for top 20 industry categories, 1992, article, C1850–14.515

Direct marketing industry devs, including advertising patterns, finances, target market characteristics, and consumer attitudes, 1992/93 annual rpt, A4620–1

Radio advertising expenditures by advertiser kind of business, 1992 and trends, annual rpt, A8789–1

Telecommunication costs as percent of total business costs or shipments value, by industry, by industry, 1992 article, U8710–1.501

State and local:

Hawaii data book, general data, 1992 annual rpt, S2090–1

Education

Librarians (special) salaries, by location, work setting, and personal characteristics, US and Canada, 1992 and trends, biennial survey rpt, A8965–1

Political science faculty taking nonacademic jobs, by type of employer, 1991/92, annual rpt, A2617–1

Energy Resources and Demand

Electric power cost as percent of product shipment value, by SIC 2-digit industry, 1985-90, annual rpt, A4700–1

Manufacturing energy consumption per dollar of value added, by industry group, 1993 article, C7000–3.507

Natural gas sales and revenues, by user industry group, 1970s-91, annual rpt, A1775–3.4

Government and Defense

Congressional campaign finances, with detailed data for individual Members, and leading contributors by type and industry, 1990 election and trends, biennial rpt, R3828–2

Defense industries conversion to nonmilitary production, with data on defense contracts and spending, top contractors, and employment by occupation, 1980s and trends, R4700–19

World privatization of govt businesses, by method of transfer, industry sector, and natl economy type, 1980-87, R4105–82.5

State and local:

Colorado retail sales and sales tax revenue, by county, city, and kind of business, FY92 and trends, annual rpt, S1075–1.5

Connecticut sales/use tax revenues, by industry category, FY92, annual rpt, S1170–2

Florida statistical abstract, general data, 1992 annual rpt, U6660–1

Georgia sales and use tax receipts, by type of business, FY92 annual rpt, S1950–1.2

Iowa retail sales and use tax filings data, and establishments reporting, by county and city, and by kind of business, quarterly rpt, S2860–1

Kansas sales tax collections and alcoholic beverage licensees, by kind of business, FY91-92, annual rpt, S3020–1

Kansas statistical abstract, general data, 1991/92 annual rpt, U7095–2

Maryland statistical abstract, general data, 1993-94 biennial rpt, S3605–1

Minnesota defense contract awards, with detail by industry and impact on employment, FY85-92, article, S4205–3.501

Mississippi tax collections by type, and disbursements, with selected sales and income tax data by locality and industry, FY92 and trends, annual rpt, S4435–1

Nebraska sales tax revenues and taxable sales, by county, city, and detailed industry, 1990-91, annual rpt, S4950–1.2

New Mexico business tax returns and taxable receipts, by industry div and county, FY90-92, annual rpt, S5660–1.2

New York State statistical yearbook, general data, 1992 annual rpt, U5100–1

Ohio business property assessment data, by property class and industry, 1991 and trends, annual rpt, S6390–1.5

Ohio corporate franchise tax returns filed, income, and tax liability, by industry div, 1991, annual rpt, S6390–1.2

Pennsylvania sales and use tax collections, by industry div and county, FY91-92, annual rpt, S6885–1

South Carolina sales tax collections by industrial category, FY75-92, annual rpt, S7125–3.1

South Carolina tax returns and collections, property assessments, and taxable sales, with data by county and industry group, FY92, annual rpt, S7255–1

Virginia defense purchases compared to total output, by industry div and selected group, 1991, with outlook for 1997, article, S8205–4.503

Wyoming sales and use tax revenue by industry div and/or retail sector, by county, FY81-92, annual rpt, S8855–1

Health and Vital Statistics

Accidental deaths by industry div, 1991, annual article, A8375–1.501

AIDS incidence in the workplace by region and industry, and employer testing and other policies, 1993 and trends, A2075–20.14

Health insurance costs for employers for indirectly subsidizing uninsured and Medicare/Medicaid patients, by industry div, 1993 article, C5800–7.520

Health insurance enrollment distribution, for employer-provided plans by type, by region and industry, 1992, article, A1865–1.511

Health insurance provision by employers, and health plan costs per employee, by industry div, 1991 and trends, annual rpt, A5173–2

Occupational accidents and deaths, by industry group or div, 1991, annual rpt, A1775–3.9

Occupational injuries, illnesses, and deaths, by industry group, with workdays lost, 1991-92 and trends, annual rpt, A8375–2.2

Occupational injuries/illnesses and deaths, and workdays lost, by detailed industry, 1991 and trends, annual rpt, A8375–4

Occupational injury and illness incidence and lost workdays, by industry div, 1989-90, annual rpt, A5173–2.4

Physician visit volume forecast for outpatients enrolled in HMOs, by employer industry, 1993 article, A1865–1.524

South Africa industrial accident rates, for 5 industries, 1993 article, C5226–2.505

Youth work-related injuries, by age and selected industry, 1990, R8335–2

State and local:

Alabama occupational deaths, by industry div and age group, 1992, annual rpt, S0175–2

California statistical abstract, general data, 1992 annual rpt, S0840–2

Florida work-related injuries, by accident type and industry div, 1990, annual rpt, U6660–1.7

Idaho occupational deaths, by industry div and victim age, 1990-91, annual rpt, S2250–2

Idaho workers compensation insurance rates per $100 of payroll, by selected industry, with comparisons to neighboring States, 1992, recurring rpt, S2218–2.4

Iowa accidental deaths, by type and industry, 1991, annual rpt, S2795–1

Iowa occupational injury/illness rate, by industry div, 1990-91, annual rpt, S2784–3

Kansas deaths by selected cause, by decedents industry of employment, 1991, annual rpt, S2975–1

Minnesota occupational deaths by age group, by industry div, 1990-91, annual rpt, S4190–2

Missouri occupational disability and death incidents, and compensation costs, by industry, 1991, annual rpt, S4530–2.2

Missouri work-related deaths, by industry div, age, and sex, 1992, annual rpt, S4518–1

Nebraska births by mother's tobacco and alcohol use during pregnancy, by occupation and industry div, 1991, annual rpt, S4885–1

Nebraska occupational deaths, by industry div and victim age, 1991, annual rpt, S4885–1

Oklahoma statistical abstract, general data, 1992 annual rpt, U8130–2

Oregon accidental deaths by industry div, 1991, annual rpt, S6615–5

South Carolina statistical abstract, general data, 1993 annual rpt, S7125–1

BY INDUSTRY

Wyoming occupational deaths, by sex, age, and industry div, 1991, annual rpt, S8920–2

Housing and Construction

Building owner value of construction in progress, for top 10 firms in 8 industry groups, 1991, annual article, C5800–2.504

State and local:

Arizona statistical abstract, general data, 1993 recurring rpt, U5850–2

Income

- College grad job and salary offers, by field of study, type of employer and occupation, and degree level, by region, interim rpt series, A3940–1
- College grad job and salary offers, by field of study, type of employer and occupation, and degree level, series, A3940–2
- College grad recruiting practices and hiring trends, with data on starting salaries and layoffs, by type of employer, 1992/93 annual survey rpt, U3130–1
- Computer/info systems salaries for 24 positions, by industry sector and location, 1993 survey, annual article, C1850–5.518
- Corporate boards of directors compensation practices and amounts, by industry group, 1991-92, annual rpt, R4105–7
- Corporate executive compensation for top executives at approx 400 companies, by industry group, 1992 and trends, annual survey, C5800–7.525
- Earnings of workers, principal industries in daily newspaper markets in US and Canada, by company, 1993 annual rpt, C3250–1
- Executive compensation and components, by industry div and major manufacturing group, 1991, annual rpt, R4105–19
- Forecasts of natl income and product account components and related indicators, quarterly rpt, U1880–1
- Japan wage negotiation results, by industry, spring 1993, article, R5650–2.522
- Japan wages for regular and manufacturing employees, by industry, 1988-92, annual compilation, R5650–2.552
- Latin America statistical abstract, general data by country, 1992 annual rpt, U6250–1.13
- Logistics manager salaries, by position, industry, and selected characteristics, Nov 1992 survey, annual article, C1850–11
- Mexico industrial worker hourly earnings in 7 industries, with comparisons to US, 1990, article, C5800–7.524
- Professional worker salaries, by employee and employer characteristics, with detail for scientists and engineers, 1990s and trends, biennial rpt, A3960–1
- Salary ranges for selected positions, by industry or profession, 1993 article, C4215–1.503
- Trade assn executives compensation, by industry div, 1992, biennial rpt, A2900–3

State and local:

- Alabama statistical abstract, general data, 1992 recurring rpt, U5680–2
- Alaska employment and unemployment, hours, and earnings, by area and/or industry, monthly rpt, S0320–1
- Arizona economic condition, including population, employment and earnings, and business activity, by industry and locality, 1985-93, semiannual rpt, U5850–1.1
- Arizona employment and unemployment, by county and industry, with production worker hours and earnings, monthly rpt, S0465–1
- Arizona statistical abstract, general data, 1993 recurring rpt, U5850–2
- California economic condition, including population, employment and earnings, income, business activity, and taxation, 1960s-92, annual rpt, S0840–3.2
- California employment statistics, by demographic characteristics, industry, MSA, and county, monthly rpt, S0830–1
- California personal income from business/professional sources, by industry div, 1990, annual rpt, S0855–1.1
- California statistical abstract, general data, 1992 annual rpt, S0840–2
- Colorado average annual pay by industry div, 1992, S1040–4.508
- Connecticut employment, hours, and earnings, by labor market area and industry, and selected economic indicators, monthly rpt, S1235–1
- DC annual average pay, by industry div, 1990-91, annual article, S1527–3.501
- DC employment, earnings, and hours, by industry, with unemployment insurance data, monthly rpt, S1527–3
- DC statistical profile, general data, 1992 annual rpt, S1535–3
- Delaware employment, earnings, and hours, by locality and industry, and unemployment insurance activity, monthly rpt, S1405–2
- Florida statistical abstract, general data, 1992 annual rpt, U6660–1
- Georgia and Atlanta MSA forecast employment by industry group and income by source, quarterly rpt, U1880–2
- Georgia employment, earnings, and hours, by major industry group and MSA, monthly rpt, S1905–1
- Georgia statistical abstract, general data, 1992-93 biennial rpt, U6730–1
- Hawaii data book, general data, 1992 annual rpt, S2090–1
- Hawaii economic indicators, bimonthly rpt, B3500–1
- Idaho economic profile, general data, 1992 recurring rpt, S2218–2
- Illinois business activity indicators, quarterly rpt, U6910–1
- Illinois statistical abstract, general data, 1992 annual rpt, U6910–2
- Kansas business activity indicators, quarterly rpt, U7095–1
- Kansas statistical abstract, general data, 1991/92 annual rpt, U7095–2
- Kentucky economic statistics, general data, 1993 annual rpt, S3104–1
- Kentucky pay and earnings by industry div, and individual industry shares of wages, 1980s-91, annual planning rpt, S3140–3
- Louisiana employment, hours, and earnings, by industry and MSA, monthly rpt, S3320–2
- Louisiana production workers average hours and earnings, by industry, monthly 1992, annual planning rpt, S3320–1.1
- Maine employment, unemployment, and earnings, by industry group, MSA, and labor area, monthly rpt, S3465–2
- Maine statistical summary, general economic and social data, 1992 recurring rpt, S3434–1
- Maryland labor force, employment, earnings, and hours, with data by industry and location, monthly rpt, S3605–2
- Maryland statistical abstract, general data, 1993-94 biennial rpt, S3605–1
- Massachusetts employment, hours, and earnings, by industry and local area, with unemployment insurance claims, monthly rpt, S3808–1
- Michigan employment, hours, and earnings, with detail by industry and local area, monthly rpt, S3980–2
- Michigan labor force planning rpt, including population characteristics, and earnings in selected industries, 1993 annual rpt, S3980–1.1
- Minnesota employment, hours, and earnings, by industry group and locality, monthly rpt, S4205–1
- Mississippi income by source, county, and MSA, and wages by industry group, 1993 annual planning rpt, S4345–1.4
- Mississippi statistical abstract, general data, 1992 annual rpt, U3255–4
- Missouri employment, earnings, and hours, and employment security program activity, by industry and/or county, FY92 and trends, annual rpt, S4530–2.3
- Missouri employment, earnings, and hours, by industry and MSA, monthly rpt, S4530–3
- Montana average hours and earnings, by industry, 1991-92, annual planning rpt, S4710–3
- Montana employment and unemployment, earnings, and hours, by location and/or industry, quarterly rpt, S4710–1
- Nebraska manufacturing and service worker hours and earnings, by selected industry group and locality, quarterly rpt, S4895–2
- Nevada business and economic activity indicators, with comparisons to other Western States, 1980-91, annual rpt, U7920–2
- Nevada employment, hours, and earnings, by industry, and unemployment by county, quarterly rpt, S5040–1
- Nevada statistical abstract, general data, 1992 biennial rpt, S5005–1
- New Hampshire employment, hours, and earnings, by industry and area, monthly rpt, S5205–1
- New Jersey economic indicators, including employment, building permits, and retail trade, monthly rpt, S5425–1
- New Mexico business and economic activity indicators, monthly rpt, U7980–1
- New Mexico employment, hours, and earnings, by labor market area and industry, monthly rpt, S5624–2
- New York State employment, earnings, and hours, by county, selected metro area, and industry group, monthly rpt, S5775–1
- New York State statistical yearbook, general data, 1992 annual rpt, U5100–1
- North Carolina employment, hours, and earnings, by industry group, with job placements, monthly rpt, S5917–3
- North Dakota labor force planning rpt, including population, employment, and earnings, with data by industry and county, 1993 annual rpt, S6140–2
- Ohio employment, hours, and earnings, by industry and MSA, with job service and unemployment insurance activities, monthly rpt, S6270–1

Index by Categories

BY INDUSTRY

Ohio personal income by industry div, 1982-91, annual rpt, S6255–1

Oklahoma employment, hours, and earnings, by industry and MSA, with unemployment insurance and job service activities, monthly rpt, S6430–2

Oregon labor force and employment statistics, including data by industry, monthly rpt, S6592–1, S6615–2

Pennsylvania earnings, by industry group, 1991, annual planning rpt, S6845–3.2

Pennsylvania employment, hours, and earnings, by industry, monthly rpt, S6845–1

Pennsylvania personal income, by type, industry div, MSA, and county, 1993 annual article, U4110–1.506

Pennsylvania statistical abstract, general data, 1992 recurring rpt, U4130–6

Rhode Island employment, hours, and earnings, by industry, monthly rpt, S6980–1

Rhode Island statistical almanac, general data, 1993 annual rpt, C7975–1

South Carolina economic condition, including employment, manufacturing, and income, 1970s-92, annual rpt, S7125–3.2

South Carolina employment, earnings, and hours, by industry group and locality, monthly rpt, S7155–2

South Carolina labor force planning rpt, including population, employment, income, and job service activities, 1992 annual rpt, S7155–3

South Carolina statistical abstract, general data, 1993 annual rpt, S7125–1

South Dakota employment, earnings, and hours for selected industries and areas, with characteristics of unemployed and job service activities, monthly rpt, S7355–1

South Dakota personal income, by industry source, 1990-92, annual article, U8595–1.503

Tennessee economic indicator trends and forecasts, with data by industry div and manufacturing group, 1982-2001, annual rpt, S7560–1

Tennessee employment, hours, and earnings, by industry group and MSA, monthly rpt, S7495–2

Tennessee employment, wages, and unemployment insurance contributions, by county and industry, 1991, annual rpt, S7495–1

Tennessee statistical abstract, general data, 1992/93 annual rpt, U8710–2

Texas employment, hours, and earnings, by MSA and industry group, and unemployment insurance, monthly rpt, S7675–3

Utah business firms, wages, and employment, by firm size, SIC 2-digit industry, and county, 1st qtr 1992, annual rpt, S7820–1

Utah employment, hours, and earnings, by industry, monthly rpt, S7820–3

Utah govt statistical review, fiscal and socioeconomic data, 1993 annual rpt, R9380–1

Utah labor force characteristics, employment and unemployment, hours, and earnings, with data by industry and locale, 1992 and trends, annual rpt, S7820–10

Utah personal income, by source, industry, and county, 1993 annual article, U8960–2.506

Utah statistical abstract, general data, 1993 triennial rpt, U8960–1

Vermont earnings by selected industry group, 1991-92, annual planning rpt, S8025–2.1

Virginia earnings trends by industry div, 1991 vs 1990, annual rpt, U9080–7

Virginia labor force, hours, and earnings, with data by industry group and locality, monthly rpt, S8205–6

Washington State employment, earnings, and hours, by labor market area and industry group, monthly rpt, S8340–3

West Virginia employment, unemployment, hours, and earnings, with job service activities, monthly rpt, S8534–1

West Virginia production worker hours and earnings, by industry group, 1990-91, annual planning rpt, S8534–2

West Virginia statistical handbook, general data, 1992 annual rpt, R9385–1

Wisconsin Blue Book, general data, 1993-94 biennial rpt, S8780–1.2

Wisconsin economic indicators, including employment and earnings by industry group, monthly rpt, S8750–1

Wyoming employment, payroll, and wages, by industry div, 1991, S8895–1.505

Wyoming employment, payroll, and wages, by industry div, 1991-92, S8895–1.509

Wyoming employment, payroll, and wages, by industry div, 3rd qtr 1991-4th qtr 1992, S8895–1.508

Wyoming payroll and wages by industry div, and personal income, with comparisons to US, 1987-92, article, S8895–1.507

Industry and Commerce

Aluminum shipments by end-use market and product type, 1982-92, annual rpt, A0400–2.1

Automation spending for sales, marketing, and customer service applications, by industry, 1993 article, C1200–1.505

Black-owned business firms, sales/receipts, employment, and payroll, by industry div and State, 1982 and/or 1987, annual compilation, C6775–2.8

Black-owned franchises, distribution of top 50 companies, and franchise ownership and financing patterns, by industry group, 1993 annual article, C4215–1.510

Black-owned leading business sales, by industry, 1992, annual feature, C4215–1.507

Black-owned vs total businesses and receipts, by industry div, 1987, annual article, A8510–1.1

Business failures and liabilities, by detailed industry, cause, length of operation, and location, 1991-92 and trends, annual rpt, C3150–8

Business failures and liabilities, by industry, census div, State, and major city, monthly rpt, C3150–2

Business failures and liabilities, by industry group, quarterly rpt, C3150–6

Business gift-giving practices, including types of gifts and top 10 industry users, 1993 survey, annual article, C1200–4.508

Business incubator facilities finances and operations, including services offered and tenant characteristics, 1991, annual rpt, A7360–1

Business Week industrial production indicators, for selected industries, weekly rpt, C5800–7

Canada manufacturing employees, wages, value added, and shipments, top 10 industry groups, 1987, annual rpt, C3975–5.2

Capital assets required to earn a dollar of annual revenue, by industry div and major manufacturing group, 1991, article, A4700–4.503

Chambers of commerce dues and membership accounts, by type of business, 1992, annual rpt, A3840–3

China business review, including trade with US and other countries, and economic activity, bimonthly rpt, A9315–1

Consumer buying power survey of population, income, and sales by kind of business, by census div, State, MSA, county, and city, 1992, annual rpt, C1200–1.511

Consumer complaint and inquiry activity of Better Business Burs, by detailed type of business, 1992, annual rpt, A4350–1

Container (fiber box) shipments by end-use industry and region, and other industry operating data, 1940s-92, annual rpt, A4875–1

Corporate acquisitions of US firms abroad and foreign firms in US, by industry, 1992, annual compilation, C4683–1.504

Corporate alternative minimum tax impacts on capital investment costs, including data by industry and type of equipment, and comparisons to 7 other countries, 1991 rpt, A1310–4

Corporate boards of directors composition, compensation, and practices, by industry sector, 1991 and trends, annual survey rpt, B5000–3

Corporate market value rankings of top 1,000 firms, with sales, profits, assets, and related data, by company and industry, 1993 annual feature, C5800–7.521

Corporate merger/acquisition activity, with leading financial advisors, by selected industry, 1993 annual compilation, C4683–1.502

Corporate mergers, acquisitions, and divestitures, with prices, payment methods, and characteristics of participants, 1992 and trends, annual rpt, B6020–1

Corporate mergers, acquisitions, and other agreements involving US companies, by SIC code, bimonthly rpt quarterly feature, C4683–1

Corporate performance ratings by executives for leading companies in 32 industries, 1993 annual survey feature, C8900–1.508

Corporate profits, dividend payments, depreciation charges, and capital investment, by industry, 1920s-91, annual rpt, R9050–1.2

Corporate sales, profits, return on equity, price/earnings ratio, and earnings per share, approx 900 corporations, with industry rankings, weekly rpt quarterly article, C5800–7.503, C5800–7.519, C5800–7.528, C5800–7.541

Corporate use of employee stock option plans, by industry div, Nov/Dec 1992 survey, R4105–78.31

Corporate use of employees working from outside locations using computers/modems ("telecommuting"), by industry div, 1993 survey rpt, B6850–7

Corporate use of selected variable pay and recognition programs, with objectives and success, by industry div, Oct 1992 survey and trends, R4105–78.27

BY INDUSTRY

Index by Categories

Corporate work force reduction prevalence by industry sector, assistance provided displaced workers, and reduction effects, 1992 survey, article, C4215–1.504

Customer satisfaction with service over the telephone, by selected industry, 1993 article, C4687–1.508

Earnings per share change, for 24 industries, 1992-94, article, C8900–1.519

Europe computer/info systems spending plans, by industry and application, 1993 vs 1992, survey article, C1850–2.504

Europe corporate acquisitions activity by country and industry, and price and participants for top transactions, 1992 and trends, annual article, C4683–1.504

Europe public opinion on political, economic, and social issues, for 9 countries and 3 Soviet Union Republics, 1991 survey, C8915–8.2

Europe public opinion on political, economic, and social issues of interest to foreign investors, for 9 countries and 3 Soviet Union Republics, 1991 survey, C8915–9

Financial performance and growth rankings for approx 1,000 top corporations, with comparisons by industry group, 1993 annual rpt, C3950–1.505

Financial ratios and performance, for over 350 SIC 4-digit industries, FY88-92, annual rpt, A6400–3

Forbes 500 top companies in sales, profits, assets, market value, and productivity, with stock and employment data, 1992, annual rpt, C3950–1.513

Fortune magazine ranking of top 50-100 companies worldwide in 8 nonindustrial sectors, with financial and employment data, 1993 annual feature, C8900–1.522

Fortune 500 largest industrial corporations, sales, financial, and stock performance data by company, 1992, annual feature, C8900–1.513

Fortune 500 largest industrial corporations worldwide, with financial and employment data, 1992, annual feature, C8900–1.520

Franchise operations and finances, by type of business, 1991/92 and trends, annual rpt, A5820–1

Germany (West) foreign investment activity, by country and industry, 1984-91, annual rpt, A5135–2.2

Hard goods manufacturers and representatives opinions on business issues, by product line, 1993 annual survey rpt, A1800–1

Hispanic American professional views on work conditions at own company, with ratings of regions and top 19-20 companies and industries, 1993 survey article, C4575–1.504

Hispanic-owned businesses and revenues, by industry div for aggregate top 500 firms, and sales of top 10 companies in 8 industries, 1992, annual feature, C4575–1.507

Hispanic-owned businesses and sales, 100 fastest-growing companies by industry, 1988-92, annual feature, C4575–1.509

Incentive programs for consumers, employees, and dealers, with expenditures by industry and incentive type, 1991-92, annual feature, C1200–4.502

Incentive programs for consumers, with methods used and expenditures for top 10 industries, 1993 annual survey article, C1200–4.506

Incentive programs for salespeople, with expenditures of top 10 user industries, 1993 survey, annual article, C1200–4.511

Indonesia GDP, by industry, 1970s-88, R5620–1.37

Iron and steel industry shipments, by product type and consuming industry, 1992 and trends, annual rpt, A2000–2.2

Japan business shares of value added, and extent of govt regulation, by industry div, Mar 1989, article, R5650–2.501

Japan economic profile, including govt finances, industrial production, foreign trade and investments, and comparisons to US, 1988-92, annual feature, R5650–2.552

Japan foreign direct investments, with data by industry and investing country/world area, 1950s-93, annual article, R5650–2.544

Japan foreign investment in US, by selected industry, 1985-91, article, R5650–2.509

Japan foreign investment rate of return on sales by world region, and overseas share of production, with detail by industry, FY84-91, article, R5650–2.559

Japan foreign investment trends, by country and industry, FY88-Mar 1993, annual article, R5650–2.533

Latin America statistical abstract, general data by country, 1992 annual rpt, U6250–1.16, U6250–1.26, U6250–1.29, U6250–1.32

Leveraged buyout transactions and value, with leading participants and industries, 1992 annual feature, C4683–1.501

Machine tools in use, by type, age, and industry, 1989, annual rpt, A3179–2.1

Manufacturing foreign investment projects started by 5 most active US industries, 1991, article, C1850–2.502

Manufacturing production and operating data, including equipment purchases, by selected industry, 1993 and trends, annual rpt, A3179–2.3

Manufacturing shipment values for 25 largest SIC 4-digit industries, 1993, annual rpt, A8920–1.1

Manufacturing shipments forecast, for selected industries, 1993 article, C7000–3.504

Metalworking industry capital spending plans, by equipment type and industry group, 1989-93, annual survey, C4080–1

Mexico GDP components, including shares by industry div, and services trade with US by industry group, 1980-92, article, A3892–1.504

Mexico investment of US vs other countries, by industry sector, 1929-87, U6250–1.21

North American Free Trade Agreement outlook for 12 major industries, with employment and Mexico trade value, by industry, 1991, article, C8900–1.513

Operating and financial composite ratios for corporations, with establishments and receipts, for approx 200 industries, by asset size, FY90, annual rpt, C7800–1

Paper/paperboard packaging use, by type and end-use market, 1993 annual rpt, C3975–5.4

Paperboard folding carton shipment trends, by market sector, 1991-92, article, C0125–4.502

Plastics and resin sales by material and major market, foreign trade, and capacity by company, 1991-92, annual feature, C5800–12.504

Plastics industry production and sales by resin type, consumption by end-use market, and operating characteristics, 1992 and trends, annual rpt, A8920–1

Plastics product manufacturers in 9 SIC 4-digit industries, with detail for Northeast region and States, 1987, A4375–14

Productivity and related indicators, trend analysis for US and other industrial countries, 1980s-92, annual rpt, R2800–2

Quality assurance programs of North American companies, by industry sector, 1992 annual survey rpt, B6850–2

Retail sales by kind of business, 1991-92, article, U6730–2.503

Retail sales for 9 kinds of business by market area in US and Canada, with rankings by MSA, city, and county, 1993 annual rpt, C3250–1

Salary budget increases and structure, by industry and region, and for Canada, 1993-94 and trends, annual survey rpt, A1295–1

Sales executive ratings of corporate sales forces, by industry sector and sales function, 1993 annual survey article, C1200–1.512

Sales industry costs, including advertising expenditures as percent of sales, by industry, 1992 annual survey, C1200–1.508

Sales per employee of large vs small companies, for 6 industries in which smaller companies outperform larger ones, 1993 article, C5800–7.551

Services export value for top 24 and all other industry groups, 1991, article, A3892–1.501

Services sales to foreign persons by foreign affiliates of US companies, by country and industry, 1986-90, article, A3892–1.501

Shipment value for selected manufacturing industry groups, 1986-87, annual rpt, C3975–5.1

Shipment values and employment for top 25 manufacturing and nonmanufacturing industries, 1992, article, C1200–1.509

Shopping center financial and operating data, with detail by type of tenant, US and Canada, 1991, triennial rpt, R9285–1

Silver supply-demand by country and end use, with prices, futures trading, and market analyses, 1993 and trends, annual rpt, A8902–4

Small business incubator facilities tenants by industry sector, 1993 article, C4687–1.503

Small businesses with sales under $25 million, top 100 firms by industry sector, 1993 annual feature, C4687–1.507

Small privately held companies, distribution of 500 fastest growing by industry, 1993 annual feature, C4687–1.512

Soviet Union GDP distribution by industry sector, 1985, R4105–82.4

Spain foreign trade and investment devs, by country and industry, 1991 and trends, articles, A8955–1.502

Spain industrial production distribution by industry group, for Catalonia and Aragon regions, 1992 articles, A8955–1.501

Spain market conditions for 15 industries judged to be good prospects for US investment, 1992 feature, A8955–1.501

Statistical profiles of 50 States and DC, general data, 1993 annual almanac, C4712–1

Index by Categories

BY INDUSTRY

World export distribution by industry div, 1989, R4105–82.2

State and local:

- Alabama retail sales, by kind of business, MSA, and county, monthly business activity rpt, U5680–1
- Alabama statistical abstract, general data, 1992 recurring rpt, U5680–2
- Arizona economic condition, including population, employment and earnings, and business activity, by industry and locality, 1985-93, semiannual rpt, U5850–1
- Arizona retail sales, by kind of business, 1992, annual article, U0280–1.507
- Arizona taxable sales, and property assessments, by industry classification and county, FY92 and trends, annual rpt, S0515–1
- Arizona temporary winter resident impact on employment and consumer expenditures, by industry div, winter 1992/93, annual article, U0280–1.508
- California corporate income reported and tax returns, by industry, 1989-90, annual rpt, S0855–1.2
- California economic condition, including population, employment and earnings, income, business activity, and taxation, 1993 annual rpt, S0840–3
- California statistical abstract, general data, 1992 annual rpt, S0840–2
- California taxable sales, by kind of business and county, FY92, annual rpt, S0835–1.3
- Colorado retail sales and sales tax revenue, by county, city, and kind of business, FY92 and trends, annual rpt, S1075–1.5
- DC statistical profile, general data, 1992 annual rpt, S1535–3
- Florida county data book, 1992/93 annual rpt, C6360–1
- Florida statistical abstract, general data, 1992 annual rpt, U6660–1
- Georgia county guide, general data, 1993 annual rpt, U6750–1
- Georgia exports, by industry group and country of destination, and exporting business establishments, 1993 article, U6730–2.502
- Georgia statistical abstract, general data, 1992-93 biennial rpt, U6730–1
- Georgia taxable sales, by kind of business and location, 1991-92, annual article, U6730–2.503
- Hawaii data book, general data, 1992 annual rpt, S2090–1
- Hawaii economic indicators, bimonthly rpt, B3500–1
- Idaho economic profile, general data, 1992 recurring rpt, S2218–2
- Idaho input-output analysis multipliers by major industry group, 1993 article, S2245–2.501
- Illinois business activity indicators, quarterly rpt, U6910–1
- Illinois export values for top 10 industries, 1989-92, S2405–2.503
- Illinois exports to China, value for top 10 industries, 1989-91, article, U6910–1.502
- Illinois statistical abstract, general data, 1992 annual rpt, U6910–2
- Indiana business conditions analysis for selected local areas, quarterly rpt semiannual feature, U2160–1.502, U2160–1.504

Iowa retail sales and use tax filings data, and establishments reporting, by county and city, and by kind of business, FY91, annual supplement, S2860–1.501

- Iowa retail sales and use tax filings data, and establishments reporting, by county and city, and by kind of business, FY92, annual supplement, S2860–1.502
- Kansas service industries employment and economic growth, with comparisons to other industries, 1980s-90, article, U7095–1.502
- Kansas statistical abstract, general data, 1991/92 annual rpt, U7095–2
- Kansas taxable retail sales, by area and kind of business, quarterly rpt, U7095–1
- Kentucky economic statistics, general data, 1993 annual rpt, S3104–1
- Maine statistical summary, general economic and social data, 1992 recurring rpt, S3434–1
- Maryland statistical abstract, general data, 1993-94 biennial rpt, S3605–1
- Mississippi statistical abstract, general data, 1992 annual rpt, U3255–4
- Mississippi tax collections by type, and disbursements, with selected sales and income tax data by locality and industry, FY92 and trends, annual rpt, S4435–1
- Missouri retail sales by kind of business, 1982-91, annual rpt, S4475–1
- Montana corporate income tax returns filed, and tax liability, by industry div, FY91-92, biennial rpt, S4750–1.1
- Montana new businesses, by industry div, 1990-92, annual planning rpt, S4710–3
- Montana sales for agriculture compared to 4 other major industries, 1989-91, annual rpt, S4655–1
- Nebraska sales tax revenues and taxable sales, by county, city, and detailed industry, 1990-91, annual rpt, S4950–1.2
- Nevada business establishments by industry div, by MSA and selected county, 2nd qtr 1992, annual rpt, S5040–4
- Nevada statistical abstract, general data, 1992 biennial rpt, S5005–1
- New Jersey foreign-owned business establishments, employment, payroll, and shipments/sales, by industry div, 1987, article, S5425–1.501
- New Mexico business and economic activity indicators, monthly rpt, U7980–1
- New York State business activity indicators, quarterly rpt, S5735–2
- New York State business and economic indicators, by MSA, county, and industry, 1980s-91, annual rpt, S5735–3
- New York State statistical yearbook, general data, 1992 annual rpt, U5100–1
- Ohio corporate franchise tax returns filed, income, and tax liability, by industry div, 1991, annual rpt, S6390–1.2
- Oklahoma business activity indicators, monthly rpt, U8130–1
- Oklahoma statistical abstract, general data, 1992 annual rpt, U8130–2
- Pennsylvania retail sales, by kind of business, monthly rpt, U4110–1
- Pennsylvania statistical abstract, general data, 1992 recurring rpt, U4130–6
- Rhode Island statistical almanac, general data, 1993 annual rpt, C7975–1
- South Carolina economic condition, including employment, manufacturing, and income, 1970s-92, annual rpt, S7125–3.2

South Carolina statistical abstract, general data, 1993 annual rpt, S7125–1

- South Dakota taxable retail sales for top 10 counties, by industry div, bimonthly rpt, U8595–2
- South Dakota taxable sales, by SIC 2-digit industry, FY92, annual rpt, S7380–1.1
- Tennessee economic indicator trends and forecasts, with data by industry div and manufacturing group, 1982-2001, annual rpt, S7560–1
- Tennessee statistical abstract, general data, 1992/93 annual rpt, U8710–2
- Texas GSP by industry div, 1983-92, annual rpt, S7655–3
- Utah business establishments, and business startups and closings, by industry, 1992 and trends, annual rpt, S7820–10
- Utah govt statistical review, fiscal and socioeconomic data, 1993 annual rpt, R9380–1
- Utah statistical abstract, general data, 1993 triennial rpt, U8960–1
- Virginia GSP in current and constant dollars, by industry, with comparisons to Southeast region GSP and US GDP, 1963-89, recurring rpt, U9080–6
- Virginia ports export value, total and for 16 industries, 1989 and 1991, U1120–1.501
- Virginia retail sales by kind of business, by local area, monthly rpt, U1120–1
- Virginia taxable retail sales by kind of business, FY92, annual rpt, S8305–1.2
- Virginia taxable sales, by kind of business and locality, 1991 and trends, annual rpt, U9080–8
- Washington State new business establishments, by county and industry, FY88-92, annual rpt, S8415–1.1
- West Virginia statistical handbook, general data, 1992 annual rpt, R9385–1
- Wisconsin Blue Book, general data, 1993-94 biennial rpt, S8780–1.2
- Wyoming payroll and wages by industry div, and personal income, with comparisons to US, 1987-92, article, S8895–1.507

Labor and Employment

- Black American labor force and employment data, with comparisons to whites, 1970s-91, annual compilation, C6775–2.6
- Black American share of work force, by industry div, 1991, article, A8510–1.1
- Black employment shares for 10 fastest-growing industries, 1993 feature, C4215–1.503
- College grad hiring plans by industry, with data on campus visits, starting salaries, and minority hires, 1991/92-1992/93, annual rpt, A3940–3
- College grad job and salary offers, by field of study, type of employer and occupation, and degree level, by region, interim rpt series, A3940–1
- College grad job and salary offers, by field of study, type of employer and occupation, and degree level, series, A3940–2
- College grad recruiting practices and hiring trends, with data on starting salaries and layoffs, by type of employer, 1992/93 annual survey rpt, U3130–1
- Corporate work force reduction incidence, by industry, Aug-Sept 1992 survey, annual rpt, A2075–20.9
- Displaced workers by sex, race-ethnicity, industry div, and occupation, with characteristics of new employment, 1987-92, article, S0465–1.506

BY INDUSTRY

Index by Categories

Employee benefit payments and employer cost/payroll ratios, by industry, detailed type of benefit, and firm size, 1991, annual rpt, A3840–1

Employee layoffs by industry div, 1991-92, annual survey rpt, B6850–3

Employee workplace skill needs and training programs in place, by industry sector, 1993 survey, annual rpt, B6850–4

Employer use of basic skills remedial training programs, by major industry group, Jan-Mar 1993 survey, annual rpt, A2075–20.13

Employment and worker earnings, for principal industries in daily newspaper markets in US and Canada, 1993 annual rpt, C3250–1

Employment by industry div and major industry group, 1975, 1990, and 2005, article, A3892–1.503

Employment distribution by industry div, by State, 1991, semiannual rpt, B8500–1.2

Employment growth projections accuracy analysis for BLS, by occupation and industry div, 1993 article, S4205–3.501

Employment in business and industry, hiring plans for college grads, by field, salary, and degree, 1993 annual survey rpt, U3730–1

Executive job vacancy index, by industry, job function, and region, quarterly rpt, B5000–5

Flexible work schedules offered by employers, and workers with flexible schedules by occupation and industry div, 1993 article, S0465–1.504

Forecasts of natl income and product account components and related indicators, quarterly rpt, U1880–1

Fortune 500 largest industrial corporations employment, by company and industry, 1992, annual feature, C8900–1.513

Hiring costs and new hires, by industry, State, region, and employer characteristics, 1992 and trends, annual survey rpt, A4740–2

Hiring plans of employers in coming qtr, by industry div and region, quarterly rpt, B5275–1

Hispanic American labor force and employment data, with comparisons to whites, 1980s-91, annual compilation, C6775–3.4

Indonesia employment by industry sector, 1971 and 1980, R5620–1.37

Japan employment index and labor productivity, by industry, 1988-92, annual compilation, R5650–2.552

Job creation outlook for midsize companies, distribution by industry div, 1993 article, C8900–1.517

Labor union membership compared to total workers, by sex, race and Hispanic ethnicity, occupation, and industry div, 1991-92, article, S0465–1.505

Labor union success rates in NLRB elections, by industry group and census div, and for public utility plants by employment size, 1985-90, article, C6985–6.506

Latin America statistical abstract, general data by country, 1992 annual rpt, U6250–1.12

Layoffs announced by corportions, with distribution by industry, 1st half 1993, article, C8900–1.521

Layoffs announced by top 10 industries, 1st 7 months 1993, article, C8900–1.524

Pension benefits and coverage as affected by job tenure and mobility, with data by plan type and worker characteristics, 1993 rpt, R9260–17

Small corporations offering employee equity incentives and 401(k) plans, by selected industry, 1992-93, survey article, C4687–1.502

Southeastern States mass layoffs, by industry div, 1991, article, S7495–2.501

Statistical profiles of 50 States and DC, general data, 1993 annual almanac, C4712–1

Unemployment insurance trends, including data on unemployment, worker characteristics, coverage, benefits, and State govt finances, 1940s-90, R9260–18

West Coast employment by industry div, and construction activity, for 3 States, various months 1992-93, article, A6400–2.504

State and local:

Alabama business activity indicators, monthly rpt, U5680–1

Alabama county data book, general data, 1992 annual rpt, S0121–2

Alabama economic trends and outlook, 1980s-93, annual rpt, U5680–3

Alabama statistical abstract, general data, 1992 recurring rpt, U5680–2

Alaska employment and unemployment, hours, and earnings, by area and/or industry, monthly rpt, S0320–1

Alaska employment for top 100 companies, with distribution by industry div, 1992, annual article, S0320–1.510

Arizona economic condition, including population, employment and earnings, and business activity, by industry and locality, 1985-93, semiannual rpt, U5850–1

Arizona economic trends and forecast, monthly rpt quarterly article, U0280–1.503, U0280–1.506, U0280–1.509

Arizona employment and earnings for selected leading industries, 1982-91, article, U0280–1.502

Arizona employment and unemployment, by county and industry, with production worker hours and earnings, monthly rpt, S0465–1

Arizona employment distribution by industry div and occupational group, 1990, article, U0280–1.502

Arizona employment trends and outlook, by industry div, 1989-94, annual article, U0282–1.510

Arizona occupational profiles, with employment and job outlook, by industry div, occupation, and county, series, S0465–2

Arizona statistical abstract, general data, 1993 recurring rpt, U5850–2

Arkansas Census of Population and Housing detailed findings, 1990, U5935–7

Arkansas employment distribution and growth rates, by industry div and county, 1982-92, article, U5930–1.504

California Census of Population and Housing detailed findings, 1990, S0840–9

California economic condition, including population, employment and earnings, income, business activity, and taxation, 1993 annual rpt, S0840–3

California economic indicators, bimonthly rpt, S0840–1

California employment statistics, by demographic characteristics, industry, MSA, and county, monthly rpt, S0830–1

California labor force planning rpt, including population characteristics, and employment by industry, 1992 annual rpt, S0830–2

California statistical abstract, general data, 1992 annual rpt, S0840–2

Colorado employment, unemployment, hours, and earnings, with job service activities, monthly rpt, S1040–4

Colorado labor force planning rpt, including population, employment by industry, and job service applicants, FY94 annual rpt, S1040–3

Connecticut employment, hours, and earnings, by labor market area and industry, and selected economic indicators, monthly rpt, S1235–1

DC employment, earnings, and hours, by industry, with unemployment insurance data, monthly rpt, S1527–3

DC statistical profile, general data, 1992 annual rpt, S1535–3

Delaware data book, general data, 1993 annual rpt, S1375–4

Delaware employment, earnings, and hours, by locality and industry, and unemployment insurance activity, monthly rpt, S1405–2

Florida county data book, 1992/93 annual rpt, C6360–1

Florida employment and unemployment, by industry div and location, monthly rpt, S1765–3

Florida statistical abstract, general data, 1992 annual rpt, U6660–1

Georgia and Atlanta MSA forecast employment by industry group and income by source, quarterly rpt, U1880–2

Georgia, Atlanta summer 1996 Olympic games projected impact on State employment in 39 industries, 1992 article, U6730–2.501

Georgia employment, earnings, and hours, by major industry group and MSA, monthly rpt, S1905–1

Georgia statistical abstract, general data, 1992-93 biennial rpt, U6730–1

Hawaii data book, general data, 1992 annual rpt, S2090–1

Hawaii economic indicators, bimonthly rpt, B3500–1

Hawaii labor force by employment status, industry, and county, quarterly rpt, S2090–2

Idaho and US economic trends and forecasts, quarterly rpt, S2245–2

Idaho economic profile, general data, 1992 recurring rpt, S2218–2

Idaho employment by industry, by county and labor market area, monthly 1991, annual rpt, S2230–2

Illinois business activity indicators, quarterly rpt, U6910–1

Illinois economic and business activity indicators, including data by industry and county, bimonthly rpt, S2405–2

Illinois statistical abstract, general data, 1992 annual rpt, U6910–2

Indiana employment by industry div, 1990, annual rpt, S2570–1.1

Index by Categories

BY INDUSTRY

Indiana employment trends, with comparison to US, by industry div, 1993 article, U2160–1.504

Iowa labor force supply-demand data, including population, earnings, and employment by industry and occupation, 1993 annual rpt, S2784–3

Kansas business activity indicators, quarterly rpt, U7095–1

Kansas statistical abstract, general data, 1991/92 annual rpt, U7095–2

Kentucky economic statistics, general data, 1993 annual rpt, S3104–1

Kentucky labor force planning rpt, including population and labor force characteristics, and employment by industry, 1991 and trends, annual rpt, S3140–3

Louisiana employment, hours, and earnings, by industry and MSA, monthly rpt, S3320–2

Louisiana labor force planning rpt, including population and labor force characteristics, unemployment claimants, and data by parish and MSA, 1993 annual rpt, S3320–1

Maine employment, by SIC 2-digit industry and detailed occupation, triennial series, S3465–1

Maine employment, unemployment, and earnings, by industry group, MSA, and labor area, monthly rpt, S3465–2

Maine statistical summary, general economic and social data, 1992 recurring rpt, S3434–1

Maryland labor force, employment, earnings, and hours, with data by industry and location, monthly rpt, S3605–2

Maryland statistical abstract, general data, 1993-94 biennial rpt, S3605–1

Massachusetts employment, hours, and earnings, by industry and local area, with unemployment insurance claims, monthly rpt, S3808–1

Michigan employment by industry, 1993 annual planning rpt, S3980–1.1

Michigan employment, hours, and earnings, with detail by industry and local area, monthly rpt, S3980–2

Minnesota employment, hours, and earnings, by industry group and locality, monthly rpt, S4205–1

Minnesota employment trends and outlook by industry, 1993 articles, S4205–3.501

Mississippi statistical abstract, general data, 1992 annual rpt, U3255–4

Mississippi unemployment insurance claimants, and employment and job growth, by industry, 1993 annual planning rpt, S4345–1.2

Missouri employment, earnings, and hours, and employment security program activity, by industry and/or county, FY92 and trends, annual rpt, S4530–2.3

Missouri employment, earnings, and hours, by industry and MSA, monthly rpt, S4530–3

Montana employment and unemployment, earnings, and hours, by location and/or industry, quarterly rpt, S4710–1

Montana labor force planning rpt, including population, income, and employment and job openings by industry and occupation, with selected data by county, 1993-94 annual rpt, S4710–3

Nebraska business and economic activity indicators, monthly rpt, U7860–1

Nebraska employment and unemployment, by industry group and locality, quarterly rpt, S4895–2

Nevada business and economic activity indicators, with comparisons to other Western States, 1980-91, annual rpt, U7920–2

Nevada employment, hours, and earnings, by industry, and unemployment by county, quarterly rpt, S5040–1

Nevada labor force conditions and outlook, with data by industry, MSA, and county, 1992 annual rpt, S5040–4

Nevada statistical abstract, general data, 1992 biennial rpt, S5005–1

New Hampshire employment, by SIC 2- and 3-digit industry and detailed occupation, series, S5205–2

New Hampshire employment, hours, and earnings, by industry and area, monthly rpt, S5205–1

New Hampshire labor force and population by race, sex, and age, and employment by industry div, statewide and by county, 1992 recurring rpt, S5205–7

New Jersey Census of Population and Housing detailed findings, by county, 1990, S5425–19

New Jersey economic indicators, including employment, building permits, and retail trade, monthly rpt, S5425–1

New Mexico business and economic activity indicators, monthly rpt, U7980–1

New Mexico employment, hours, and earnings, by labor market area and industry, monthly rpt, S5624–2

New Mexico labor force planning rpt, including population characteristics, and employment by industry and occupation, 1993 annual rpt, S5624–1

New Mexico workers compensation claims and rates, by industry div, 1992, article, S5624–2.510

New York State business activity indicators, quarterly rpt, S5735–2

New York State business and economic indicators, by MSA, county, and industry, 1980s-91, annual rpt, S5735–3

New York State employment, earnings, and hours, by county, selected metro area, and industry group, monthly rpt, S5775–1

New York State statistical yearbook, general data, 1992 annual rpt, U5100–1

North Carolina employment, hours, and earnings, by industry group, with job placements, monthly rpt, S5917–3

North Carolina employment in SIC 2-digit industries, by detailed occupation, triennial rpt series, S5917–5

North Carolina labor force and employment by industry, by county, MSA, labor area, and planning region, 1991 and trends, annual rpt, S5917–4

North Dakota employment, hours, and earnings, by industry div and/or location, monthly rpt, S6140–4

North Dakota labor force planning rpt, including population, employment, and earnings, with data by industry and county, 1993 annual rpt, S6140–2

Ohio employment, hours, and earnings, by industry and MSA, with job service and unemployment insurance activities, monthly rpt, S6270–1

Oklahoma business activity indicators, monthly rpt quarterly data, U8130–1

Oklahoma employment and unemployment insurance data, by industry, monthly rpt, S6430–2

Oklahoma statistical abstract, general data, 1992 annual rpt, U8130–2

Oregon economic conditions, including population, construction, income, employment, industry, and foreign trade data, 1991, annual rpt, S6585–3

Oregon labor force and employment statistics, including data by industry, monthly rpt, S6592–1, S6615–2

Pennsylvania business activity indicators, monthly rpt, U4110–1

Pennsylvania Census of Population and Housing detailed findings, with selected data by county and municipality, 1990, U4130–13

Pennsylvania economic trends and outlook for gross regional product, personal income, and employment, 1980s-93, annual article, U4110–1.504

Pennsylvania employment and commuting data from Census of Population and Housing, by county and municipality, 1990, C1595–16

Pennsylvania employment, hours, and earnings, by industry, monthly rpt, S6845–1

Pennsylvania labor force planning rpt, including population characteristics, employment and job openings by industry and occupation, and income trends, FY92 annual rpt, S6845–3

Pennsylvania statistical abstract, general data, 1992 recurring rpt, U4130–6

Rhode Island Census of Population and Housing detailed findings, by county and municipality, 1990, S6930–9

Rhode Island employment, hours, and earnings, by industry, monthly rpt, S6980–1

Rhode Island labor force planning rpt, including population, employment by industry, job openings, and characteristics of insured unemployed, 1993 annual rpt, S6980–3

Rhode Island statistical almanac, general data, 1993 annual rpt, C7975–1

South Carolina economic activity indicators, including employment by industry div, by county, 1993 annual rpt, S7145–1.2

South Carolina economic condition, including employment, manufacturing, and income, 1970s-92, annual rpt, S7125–3.2

South Carolina employment, earnings, and hours, by industry group and locality, monthly rpt, S7155–2

South Carolina labor force planning rpt, including population, employment, income, and job service activities, 1992 annual rpt, S7155–3

South Carolina statistical abstract, general data, 1993 annual rpt, S7125–1

South Dakota business activity review, including selected data by city and industry, quarterly rpt, U8595–1

South Dakota employment, earnings, and hours for selected industries and areas, with characteristics of unemployed and job service activities, monthly rpt, S7355–1

Tennessee economic indicator trends and forecasts, with data by industry div and manufacturing group, 1982-2001, annual rpt, S7560–1

BY INDUSTRY

Tennessee employment, hours, and earnings, by industry group and MSA, monthly rpt, S7495–2

Tennessee employment, wages, and unemployment insurance contributions, by county and industry, 1991, annual rpt, S7495–1

Tennessee statistical abstract, general data, 1992/93 annual rpt, U8710–2

Texas employment, by SIC 2- and 3-digit industry and detailed occupation, series, S7675–1

Texas employment, hours, and earnings, by MSA and industry group, and unemployment insurance, monthly rpt, S7675–3

Texas labor force planning rpt, including labor force, employment by industry, income, and population, 1993 annual rpt, S7675–2

Utah business firms, wages, and employment, by firm size, SIC 2-digit industry, and county, 1st qtr 1992, annual rpt, S7820–1

Utah employment and wages for workers born in Utah vs other States, by industry div, 3rd qtr 1992, article, S7820–3.507

Utah employment, by industry div, county, and district, 1960-91, annual rpt, S7832–2

Utah employment, hours, and earnings, by industry, monthly rpt, S7820–3

Utah govt statistical review, fiscal and socioeconomic data, 1993 annual rpt, R9380–1

Utah labor force characteristics, employment and unemployment, hours, and earnings, with data by industry and locale, 1992 and trends, annual rpt, S7820–10

Utah nonagricultural employment by industry div and level of govt, monthly business activity rpt, U8960–2

Utah statistical abstract, general data, 1993 triennial rpt, U8960–1

Utah summer job openings, by industry div, 1993, annual article, S7820–3.505

Vermont labor force by employment status, and job service openings and applicant characteristics, 1993 annual planning rpt, S8025–2.2

Virginia employment and GSP, by industry div, 1989, recurring rpt, U9080–6

Virginia employment by industry div, 1991-92, U1120–1.503

Virginia labor force, hours, and earnings, with data by industry group and locality, monthly rpt, S8205–6

Washington State employment, earnings, and hours, by labor market area and industry group, monthly rpt, S8340–3

West Virginia employment, unemployment, hours, and earnings, with job service activities, monthly rpt, S8534–1

West Virginia labor force planning rpt, including population, employment, and job service activities, with data by county and service delivery area, 1993 annual rpt, S8534–2

West Virginia statistical handbook, general data, 1992 annual rpt, R9385–1

Wisconsin Blue Book, general data, 1993-94 biennial rpt, S8780–1.2

Wisconsin economic indicators, including employment and earnings by industry group, monthly rpt, S8750–1

Wyoming employment by industry group and county, with unemployment insurance and job service activities, monthly rpt, S8895–1

Natural Resources, Environment and Pollution

Chemical (toxic) environmental releases, for 10 leading industries, 1990, annual rpt, A2575–27

State and local:

Georgia water use and toxic chemical releases, by industry div, 1990 and trends, biennial rpt, U6730–1.4

Pennsylvania statistical abstract, general data, 1992 recurring rpt, U4130–6

Tennessee pollution abatement operating costs, by industry, 1989 and trends, annual rpt, U8710–2.4

Prices and Cost of Living

Japan WPI by industry and end-use category, 1988-92, annual compilation, R5650–2.552

State and local:

Maryland household expenditures for retail goods by purchase outlet type, by county, 1990, biennial rpt, S3605–1.6

Public Welfare and Social Security

Corporate charitable contributions, by donor characteristics and detailed type of recipient, 1991 and trends, annual rpt, R4105–8

Corporate charitable contributions to arts programs, distribution by industry div and region, 1988 and 1991, recurring rpt, A3690–1

Science and Technology

Chemist and chemical engineer salaries, employment status, and demographic and professional characteristics, 1993, annual rpt, A1250–4

Chemistry and chemical engineering grad starting salaries, employment status, demographic characteristics, and advanced study plans, 1991/92, annual rpt, A1250–2

Engineer compensation, by work and employee characteristics, and region and metro area, 1992, annual rpt, A8460–1

Engineers salaries by industry group, census div, selected metro area, and years since college degree, 1993, annual survey rpt, A0685–5

Engineers salaries by industry group, census div, selected metro area, degree level, and years since college degree, 1993, annual survey rpt, A0685–3

France R&D expenditures for 9 leading industry groups, 1993 article, C1850–6.509

High-technology employment growth rates for top 10 industries, 1993 article, C1850–6.510

Industrial R&D expenditures, by industry group, 1992-93, annual survey rpt, A5510–1

Japan R&D expenditures, by funding and performing sector, govt agency, and industry, FY70s-93, annual article, R5650–2.557

Japan technology imports and exports, with detail by industry and trading partner, FY91 and trends, annual article, R5650–2.557

Patent activity for approx 200 US and foreign firms in 13 industries, 1992 and trends, article, C5800–7.540

R&D budget trends for 9 industries, 1992-93, annual article, C1850–6.503

Index by Categories

R&D expenditures, and sales and profits, for approx 900 corporations, by industry, 1992, annual feature, C5800–7.534

R&D spending, by selected manufacturing industry group, 1991, annual rpt, C3975–5.1

Scientist/engineer employment, and chemists and salaries, by industry, 1993 annual feature, A1250–1.537

State and local:

Utah employment in high-technology industries, 1986-92, recurring article, U8960–2.508

Transportation and Travel

Business traveler and trip characteristics, including mode, purpose, and lodging, 1991, annual rpt, R9375–12

Incentive travel programs for sales promotion, with destinations, and expenditures of top 10 user industries, 1993 survey, annual article, C1200–4.510

Motor vehicle, dealership, and related industries operating data, with data by State and industry segment, 1990s and trends, annual rpt, A0865–1.3

Motor vehicle fleet accidents, and vehicles and mileage, by fleet type and company (unnamed), 1991 and trends, annual rpt, A8375–3

Travel impact on State economies, with detail by industry sector, 1990 and trends, annual rpt, R9375–7

State and local:

Alabama statistical abstract, general data, 1992 recurring rpt, U5680–2

Hawaii jobs and income generated by visitor expenditures, by industry sector, 1991, annual rpt, S2090–1.7

Tennessee statistical abstract, general data, 1992/93 annual rpt, U8710–2

BY OCCUPATION

Agriculture and Food

Distilled spirits consumption, and consumer characteristics and buying habits, 1992 and trends, annual rpt, C4775–1.3

Food away from home expenditures, by household characteristics and for 26 MSAs, 1991, recurring rpt, A8200–13

Food marketing mgmt personnel compensation, by position, by company sales size and region, year ended Mar 1993, annual survey, A4950–6

Food service black and Hispanic shares of employment, with detail for 8 occupations, 1992, article, C5150–5.511

Food service industry employee characteristics, and minority-owned establishments and sales, 1993 article, A8200–1.508

Food service wages and employment, for 18 positions, 1992 survey, biennial article, A8200–1.503

Food/beverage manufacturers mgmt salaries, by selected employee characteristics, 1992 survey, annual article, C2150–6.502

Wine and other alcoholic beverage consumption, and consumer characteristics and buying habits, 1993 annual rpt, C4775–2.2

Banking, Finance, and Insurance

Life insurance purchases and ownership, by consumer and household characteristics, 1991 and trends, biennial fact book, A1325–1.1

Index by Categories

BY OCCUPATION

Shareholders of NYSE member firms, by demographic characteristics and metro area, 1970s-90, annual fact book, B6625–1.1

Communications

Direct marketing industry devs, including advertising patterns, finances, target market characteristics, and consumer attitudes, 1992/93 annual rpt, A4620–1

Newspaper reader socioeconomic characteristics, 1993 annual rpt, A8605–4

State and local:

Maine employment in trade, utilities, and transportation SIC 2-digit industries, by detailed occupation, 2nd qtr 1991, triennial rpt, S3465–1.25

Education

Elementary/secondary prospective teacher characteristics and opinions, survey of persons interested in alternative certification routes, 1992, R6350–7

Higher education administrative salaries, by position and instn type, 1992/93, annual feature, C2175–1.507

Higher education administrative salaries, for 167 positions, by instn type and budget size, 1992/93, annual rpt, A3900–1

Higher education administrative salaries in doctorate-granting public universities, approx 80 positions by region, 1992/93, annual survey rpt, U5960–1

Higher education freshmen career choices, by race-ethnicity and sex, 1992 recurring rpt, A3960–2.1

Higher education freshmen parental income, occupations, and education, by student sex and instn type, fall 1992, annual survey, U6215–1

Higher education physical plant operations, costs, employment, salaries, and energy use, by instn and region, 1991/92, recurring rpt, A3183–1

State and local:

Alabama public school staff positions, by district, 1991/92, annual rpt, S0124–1.2

Arkansas public school staff and salaries, by sex and position, 1990/91-1991/92, annual rpt, S0660–1.2

Colorado public school staff and salaries, by selected characteristics, county, and district, fall 1992 and trends, annual rpt, S1000–2.2

Georgia statistical abstract, general data, 1992-93 biennial rpt, U6730–1

Idaho public school personnel characteristics and salaries by position, and teachers and enrollment by school district, 1992/93, annual rpt, S2225–3

Kansas public school certified personnel, by position, 1990/91, annual rpt, S2945–1

Maine educational services employment, by detailed occupation, Apr 1991, triennial survey, S3465–1.26

Massachusetts elementary/secondary school expenditures per pupil for occupational programs by type, by district, 1991/92, annual rpt, S3810–5

Mississippi public school noninstructional staff, by occupation, 1991/92, annual rpt, S4340–1.1

Nebraska elementary and secondary school personnel, by sex and assignment, 1992/93, annual rpt, S4865–2.7

New Hampshire govt and education employment by detailed occupation, 1991 or 1992, triennial rpt, S5205–2.25

North Carolina public school personnel by sex, race, and source of funds, by occupation and local district, 1992/93, annual rpt, S5915–1

North Dakota elementary and secondary school staff characteristics and salaries, by position, region, and enrollment size, 1992/93 annual rpt, S6180–3

Pennsylvania public school personnel and salary data, by position and district, 1992/93 and trends, annual rpt, S6790–5.12

Pennsylvania statistical abstract, general data, 1992 recurring rpt, U4130–6

Tennessee public school staff, by position, county, city, and school district, 1991/92 annual rpt, S7490–2.1

Texas educational employment, by SIC 3-digit industry and detailed occupation, Apr 1991, triennial survey rpt, S7675–1.28

Utah public school personnel and salaries, by detailed position and district, 1991/92, annual rpt, S7815–1.2

West Virginia public school personnel and salaries, by position, 1991/92, annual rpt, S8540–3

Wyoming public school staff and salaries, by position and district, 1991/92, annual rpt, S8890–1.2

Energy Resources and Demand

Coal industry personnel earnings and employment history, US and Canada, 1993 survey article, C5226–1.507

State and local:

Maine employment in trade, utilities, and transportation SIC 2-digit industries, by detailed occupation, 2nd qtr 1991, triennial rpt, S3465–1.25

Government and Defense

Black elected officials, and characteristics of voting age population, with comparisons to whites, 1970s-91, annual compilation, C6775–2.4

County govt officials salaries, by position, region, and county size, July 1992 and trends, annual rpt, A5800–1.3

Defense industries conversion to nonmilitary production, with data on defense contracts and spending, top contractors, and employment by occupation, 1980s and trends, R4700–19

Federal Govt salaries for typical positions, 1993 annual rpt, R9380–1.4

Hispanic American elected officials, registered voters, and voting, with comparisons to whites, 1970s-91, annual compilation, C6775–3.3

Local govt land use planning commissions composition and activities, and commissioner characteristics, 1987 and trends, recurring rpt, A2615–2

Municipal govt officials salaries, by position, region, form of govt, and city size, July 1992 and trends, annual rpt, A5800–1.3

State and local govt employee wages compared to private sector, with data on employee characteristics, 1989, R4700–21

State and local:

Maine govt employment, by level and detailed occupation, May 1991 or Mar 1992, triennial survey, S3465–1.27

New Hampshire govt and education employment by detailed occupation, 1991 or 1992, triennial rpt, S5205–2.25

Texas State and local govt employment, by detailed occupation, May 1991, triennial survey rpt, S7675–1.30

Health and Vital Statistics

Dental problems/treatment-related time lost from work or school, by demographic characteristics, 1989, article, A2623–1.502

Health care employment for 16 fastest-growing occupations, 1990 and 2005, article, A1865–1.514

Musculoskeletal disability incidences in men and women correlated with occupations, 1992 article, A2623–1.501

Older men deaths by cause, by smoking and drinking habits, race, and occupation, 1966-90, U3780–9

Smoking status of men and women by occupation, and smoker characteristics, 1985 and/or 1990, article, B6045–1.501

Women's deaths from breast cancer correlated with occupation, by race, 1979-87, article, A2623–1.511

State and local:

Alabama statistical abstract, general data, 1992 recurring rpt, U5680–2

Florida county data book, 1992/93 annual rpt, C6360–1

Florida health care atlas, including manpower by occupation and health care facilities by type, by district and county, 1992 annual rpt, S1746–1.2

Kansas deaths by selected cause, by occupation of decedent, 1991, annual rpt, S2975–1

Maine deaths, by sex, age, and occupational group, 1991, annual rpt, S3460–2

Nebraska births by mother's tobacco and alcohol use during pregnancy, by occupation and industry div, 1991, annual rpt, S4885–1

Nevada suicides, by decedent occupation and age, 1989, annual rpt, S5075–1

South Carolina statistical abstract, general data, 1993 annual rpt, S7125–1

Wisconsin deaths by occupation, by age, sex, and cause, 1991, annual rpt, S8715–4

Housing and Construction

Construction industry wage rates, by craft and selected city, 1993, article, C5800–2.547

Construction nonunion wages and benefit levels, by craft and region, 1992, article, C5800–2.534

Income

Black American earnings, income, and poverty data, with comparisons to whites, 1980s-91, annual compilation, C6775–2 7

College grad job and salary offers, by field of study, type of employer and occupation, and degree level, by region, interim rpt series, A3940–1

College grad job and salary offers, by field of study, type of employer and occupation, and degree level, series, A3940–2

Computer-related occupation salary ranges, for 22 occupations, 1992, article, C4215–1.503

Computer/info systems salaries for 24 positions, by industry sector and location, 1993 survey, annual article, C1850–5.518

Earnings by sex and detailed occupation, 1983 and 1991, annual rpt, S6845–3.2

Earnings index for 27 MSAs and 4 occupational groups, 1990, biennial rpt, S3605–1.6

BY OCCUPATION

Index by Categories

Hispanic American income and poverty data, with comparisons to whites, 1980s-91, annual compilation, C6775–3.5

Jewelry store employee compensation, by position, 1992 annual survey article, C2150–7.501

Jewelry store employee earnings, by position, with detail by sex for managers and sales workers, 1990-91, annual almanac, C2150–7.509

Plastics processing industry employment, compensation practices, and union representation, by region, 1992, annual survey rpt, A8920–2

Plastics processing industry salaries for managers, supervisors, salespersons, and engineers, by region, 1992, biennial rpt, A8920–3

Professional worker salaries, by employee and employer characteristics, with detail for scientists and engineers, 1990s and trends, biennial rpt, A3960–1

Salary ranges for selected positions, by industry or profession, 1993 article, C4215–1.503

White-collar work force trends, including employment, earnings, and unionization, with data by occupation, sex, and educational attainment, 1990s and trends, annual rpt, A1570 1

Women's employment and earnings, with comparisons to men, and detail by occupation and worker characteristics, 1990s and trends, annual rpt, A1570–2

State and local:

- Alaska job openings and hourly wages for positions advertised with State employment service, by occupation, July 1991-92, article, S0320–1.505
- Delaware data book, general data, 1993 annual rpt, S1375–4
- Hawaii data book, general data, 1992 annual rpt, S2090–1
- Idaho economic profile, general data, 1992 recurring rpt, S2218–2
- Montana wage rates for employers certified to hire alien workers, for selected occupations, quarterly rpt, S4710–1
- New Mexico wages for selected occupations, Sept 1992, annual planning rpt, S5624–1
- South Carolina labor force planning rpt, detailed data on employment, hours, wages, turnover, and characteristics of job service applicants, 1992 annual rpt, S7155–3.2
- Utah entry-level wages for 20 unskilled or semiskilled occupations, 1993 annual article, S7820–3.505
- Utah monthly salaries by occupation, July 1992, annual article, S7820–3.503

Industry and Commerce

Corporate boards of directors composition, compensation, and practices, by industry sector, 1991 and trends, annual survey rpt, B5000–3

Small corporation outside directors, by occupation, 1993 article, C4687–1.508

State and local:

Maryland building materials/garden supplies industry employment and wages, by industry and occupational group, June 1991, article, S3605–2.501

Labor and Employment

Black American employment shares, and employment growth, by occupation, 1990-2005, article, A8510–1.1

Black American labor force and employment data, with comparisons to whites, 1970s-91, annual compilation, C6775–2.6

Black employment share and salaries, for 16 occupations with significant employment growth projected for 2005, 1993 feature, C4215–1.503

College grad job and salary offers, by field of study, type of employer and occupation, and degree level, by region, interim rpt series, A3940–1

College grad job and salary offers, by field of study, type of employer and occupation, and degree level, series, A3940–2

Corporate human resources executive views on outlook for recruiting personnel in selected occupational groups, Sept/Oct 1991 survey, R4105–78.21

Corporate staffing practices, including use of temporary workers and consultants or freelancers, by occupation type, 1993 survey, annual rpt, B6850–5

Displaced workers by sex, race-ethnicity, industry div, and occupation, with characteristics of new employment, 1987-92, article, S0465–1.506

Employee satisfaction with work compared to 5 years ago, by occupational group, 1992 survey article, C4687–1.501

Employment by race and sex, by occupational group, 1991, annual article, A8510–1.1

Employment distribution by major occupational group, by State, 1991, semiannual rpt, B8500–1.2

Employment growth projections accuracy analysis for BLS, by occupation and industry div, 1993 article, S4205–3.501

Employment in 1990 and growth through 2005, by detailed occupation, article, C8900–1.519

Flexible work schedules offered by employers, and workers with flexible schedules by occupation and industry div, 1993 article, S0465–1.504

Hispanic American labor force and employment data, with comparisons to whites, 1980s-91, annual compilation, C6775–3.4

Hispanic American vs nonminority employment, by occupational group and sex, 1992, article, C4575–1.511

Labor union membership compared to total workers, by sex, race and Hispanic ethnicity, occupation, and industry div, 1991-92, article, S0465–1.505

Latin America immigrants to US and naturalized citizens, by country and occupation, 1992 annual rpt, U6250–1.14

Latin America statistical abstract, general data by country, 1992 annual rpt, U6250–1.12

Minority population characteristics, employment, and voting patterns by detailed race-ethnicity, with comparisons to whites, 1980s-2040, R8750–2.58

Pension benefits and coverage as affected by job tenure and mobility, with data by plan type and worker characteristics, 1993 rpt, R9260–17

Statistical profiles of 50 States and DC, general data, 1993 annual almanac, C4712–1

White-collar work force trends, including employment, earnings, and unionization,

with data by occupation, sex, and educational attainment, 1990s and trends, annual rpt, A1570–1

Women and minorities in professional fields, detailed education and labor force data, 1980s-91, with historical trends, recurring rpt, A3960–2

Women's employment and earnings, with comparisons to men, and detail by occupation and worker characteristics, 1990s and trends, annual rpt, A1570–2

State and local:

- Alaska employment of youths age 15-21, by occupation, industry, and sex, July-Sept 1992, article, S0320–1.509
- Alaska job openings and hourly wages for positions advertised with State employment service, by occupation, July 1991-92, article, S0320–1.505
- Arizona employment distribution by industry div and occupational group, 1990, article, U0280–1.502
- Arizona employment trends by occupational group, including comparisons to unemployment insurance claims by industry div, 1990-92, article, S0465–1.507
- Arizona occupational profiles, with employment and job outlook, by industry div, occupation, and county, series, S0465–2
- Arkansas Census of Population and Housing detailed findings, 1990, U5935–7
- California Census of Population and Housing detailed findings, 1990, S0840–9
- California registered apprentices, by trade, race-ethnicity, and sex, 1991 and trends, annual rpt, S0840–2.3
- California statistical abstract, general data, 1992 annual rpt, S0840–2
- Colorado employment growth by occupation, 1992-97, article, S1040–4.506
- Colorado labor force planning rpt, including population, employment by industry, and job service applicants, FY94 annual rpt, S1040–3
- DC statistical profile, general data, 1992 annual rpt, S1535–3
- Florida county data book, 1992/93 annual rpt, C6360–1
- Florida statistical abstract, general data, 1992 annual rpt, U6660–1
- Georgia county guide, general data, 1993 annual rpt, U6750–1
- Georgia employment and job openings, by detailed occupation, 1990-2005, article, U6730–2.504
- Georgia statistical abstract, general data, 1992-93 biennial rpt, U6730–1
- Hawaii data book, general data, 1992 annual rpt, S2090–1
- Idaho economic profile, general data, 1992 recurring rpt, S2218–2
- Indiana, Indianapolis employment trends by occupational group, with comparisons to 5 other metro areas, 1980-90, article, U2160–1.504
- Iowa labor force supply-demand data, including population, earnings, and employment by industry and occupation, 1993 annual rpt, S2784–3
- Kansas employment by occupational group and type of worker, by selected county, 1990 and trends, annual articles, U7095–1.501

Index by Categories

BY OCCUPATION

Kentucky job openings and employment in fastest-growing occupations, 1987-2000, annual planning rpt, S3140–3

Louisiana Census of Population and Housing summary findings, by local area, 1990 and trends, U8010–4

Louisiana insured unemployed by occupation and industry div, by race and MSA, monthly rpt quarterly table, S3320–2

Louisiana labor force planning rpt, including population and labor force characteristics, unemployment claimants, and data by parish and MSA, 1993 annual rpt, S3320–1

Maine employment, by SIC 2-digit industry and detailed occupation, triennial series, S3465–1

Massachusetts municipal and county profiles, general data, 1992 annual rpt, C4712–2

Michigan employment projections by occupation, 1988-2000, annual planning rpt, S3980–1.2

Mississippi labor force planning rpt, including population, employment, and characteristics of unemployed and disadvantaged, 1993 annual rpt, S4345–1

Montana labor force planning rpt, including population, income, and employment and job openings by industry and occupation, with selected data by county, 1993-94 annual rpt, S4710–3

Nebraska labor force distribution by occupational group, by sex, 1940, article, U7860–1.507

Nevada employment and job opening outlook for 6 rapidly growing occupations, through 1996, article, S5040–1.502

Nevada female and total employment for 25 occupations with highest and lowest shares of female workers, 1990, article, S5040–1.503

New Hampshire employment, by SIC 2- and 3-digit industry and detailed occupation, series, S5205–2

New Hampshire job service activities, including applicant characteristics and job openings, monthly rpt, S5205–1

New Jersey Census of Population and Housing detailed findings, by county, 1990, S5425–19

New Jersey employment in 4 nonmanufacturing industry divs, by occupation, 1987 and 1990, article, S5425–1.506

New Jersey municipal and county data book, general data, 1992 annual rpt, C4/12–4

New Mexico labor force planning rpt, including population characteristics, and employment by industry and occupation, 1993 annual rpt, S5624–1

New York State municipal and county statistical profiles, general data, 1993 annual rpt, C4712–7

New York State statistical yearbook, general data, 1992 annual rpt, U5100–1

North Carolina employment, hours, and earnings, by industry group, with job placements, monthly rpt, S5917–3

North Carolina employment in SIC 2-digit industries, by detailed occupation, triennial rpt series, S5917–5

North Dakota employment by selected occupation, 1980 and 1988, article, S6140–4.501

North Dakota employment outlook for approx 30 occupations with most growth, decline, and openings, 1988-2000, article, S6140–4.502

Oklahoma employment distribution by industry div and occupation, 1980 and 1989-90, article, U8130–1.501

Pennsylvania Census of Population and Housing detailed findings, with selected data by county and municipality, 1990, U4130–13

Pennsylvania employment and commuting data from Census of Population and Housing, by county and municipality, 1990, C1595–16

Pennsylvania employment distribution by sex and occupational group, and women shares of employment in selected occupations, 1980 and/or 1990, article, S6845–1.502

Pennsylvania high school grads postgraduation work activity, by occupational group and county, 1991/92, annual rpt, S6790–5.14

Pennsylvania labor force planning rpt, including population characteristics, employment and job openings by industry and occupation, and income trends, FY92 annual rpt, S6845–3

Pennsylvania statistical abstract, general data, 1992 recurring rpt, U4130–6

Rhode Island Census of Population and Housing detailed findings, by county and municipality, 1990, S6930–9

Rhode Island labor force planning rpt, including population, employment by industry, job openings, and characteristics of insured unemployed, 1993 annual rpt, S6980–3

Rhode Island statistical almanac, general data, 1993 annual rpt, C7975–1

South Carolina employment, with annual job openings due to job creation and worker separations, by occupation, 1990-2000, S7155–2.501

South Carolina labor force planning rpt, including population, employment, income, and job service activities, 1992 annual rpt, S7155–3

South Carolina statistical abstract, general data, 1993 annual rpt, S7125–1

South Dakota unemployed, by occupational group, monthly rpt, S7355–1

Tennessee labor force by employment status, and employment by sex and race, by occupational group and industry div, 1992, articles, S7495–2.506

Tennessee State boards certification activity, by occupation, FY91, annual rpt, S7466–1

Tennessee statistical abstract, general data, 1992/93 annual rpt, U8710–2

Texas employment, by SIC 2- and 3-digit industry and detailed occupation, series, S7675–1

Utah employment by detailed occupation, and educational attainment by age group, by sex and race-ethnicity, with detail for 7 urban areas, 1990 census rpt, S7832–3.4

Utah labor force characteristics, employment and unemployment, hours, and earnings, with data by industry and locale, 1992 and trends, annual rpt, S7820–10

Utah statistical abstract, general data, 1993 triennial rpt, U8960–1

Utah women's share of employment in selected occupations, 1970, 1980, and 1990, article, S7820–3.508

Vermont labor force by employment status, and job service openings and applicant characteristics, 1993 annual planning rpt, S8025–2.2

West Virginia employment, unemployment, hours, and earnings, with job service activities, monthly rpt, S8534–1

West Virginia labor force planning rpt, including population, employment, and job service activities, with data by county and service delivery area, 1993 annual rpt, S8534–2

Law Enforcement

State and local:

California judicial system employment by position, sex, and race-ethnicity, with minority utilization rates and parity targets, Jan 1993, annual rpt, S0905–1.1

Florida "habitual offender" sentencing laws effect on prison population, with data by circuit court and offender characteristics, 1993 rpt, A7575–5

Massachusetts correctional instn inmate socioeconomic characteristics and criminal background, by instn, Jan 1992 and trends, annual rpt, S3805–1

Pennsylvania corrections dept staff and job openings, by position and instn, 1990, annual rpt, S6782–1

Population

Social prestige ratings among general public, for 77 occupations, 1989, survey article, C7000–3.509

State and local:

Hawaii data book, general data, 1992 annual rpt, S2090–1

Recreation and Leisure

Arts fundraising through united arts funds (UAFs), with contributions from professionals by selected occupation, by UAF, 1992, annual rpt, A1315–2

Sporting goods purchaser characteristics, by product category, 1992, annual survey rpt, A8485–4

Transportation and Travel

Auto do-it-yourself (DIY) maintenance activity, by type and consumer characteristics, 1993 and trends, annual survey, C0125–1.506

Business traveler and trip characteristics, including mode, purpose, and lodging, 1991, annual rpt, R9375–12

Motorcycle use and user characteristics, licensed operators, and State requirements, 1992 annual rpt, A6485–1.2

Railroad employment and earnings, by occupational group, company, and district, 1992, annual rpt, A3275–7

Railroad employment and wages, by occupational group, 1991 and trends, annual rpt, A3275–8.2

Railroad employment, payroll, and hours, with data by occupational class and company, 1920s-92, annual rpt, A3275–5.4

Transportation employment in specialized occupations, trends by mode, 1992 annual rpt, R4815–1

Travel trips and traveler characteristics, including mode, purpose, type of lodging, and area of destination and origin, quarterly rpt, R9375–14

State and local:

Hawaii data book, general data, 1992 annual rpt, S2090–1

BY OCCUPATION

Maine employment in trade, utilities, and transportation SIC 2-digit industries, by detailed occupation, 2nd qtr 1991, triennial rpt, S3465–1.25

Texas railroad employment, by detailed occupation, May 1991, triennial survey rpt, S7675–1.29

Virginia traffic accidents, by driver occupation, 1991, annual rpt, S8282–1

Washington State traffic accidents, including safety restraint use by driver occupation, 1992, annual rpt, S8428–1

DEMOGRAPHIC BREAKDOWNS

BY AGE

Agriculture and Food

Black American farm and farm operator characteristics, with comparisons to all farms, 1987, annual compilation, C6775–2.8

Distilled spirits consumption, and consumer characteristics and buying habits, 1992 and trends, annual rpt, C4775–1.3

Food away from home expenditures, by household characteristics and for top 10 MSAs, 1991, article, A8200–1.507

Food away from home expenditures, by household characteristics and for 26 MSAs, 1991, recurring rpt, A8200–13

Food away from home expenditures of consumers compared to population size, by age group, 1993 article, C1200–5.516

Food expenditure trends for food at home, by age group, 1990s, article, C5225–1.506

Food nutrition awareness and health concerns, including shopping and consumption patterns, by respondent characteristics, 1993 survey, annual rpt, A4950–36

Food service industry employee characteristics, and minority-owned establishments and sales, 1993 article, A8200–1.508

Food take-out consumer characteristics, consumption patterns, and attitudes, May 1992 survey, A8200–21

Hispanic American farm and farm operator characteristics, with comparisons to all farms, 1987, annual compilation, C6775–3.6

Juice drink paper box container preferences, by consumer age group, 1992 survey, C1850–1.501

Restaurant (quick-service) operations, including most popular menu items, and patron age, use of promotions, and views on smoking, 1992, article, A8200–1.509

Restaurant (table service) operations and menu offerings, and related consumer views and practices by demographic characteristics, 1992, recurring rpt, A8200–11

Restaurant customer traffic shares by age, and expenditures for food away from home by age of household head, 1990 or 1991, article, A8200–1.504

Restaurant customer traffic shares by age, with detail for upscale establishments, 1992, article, A8200–1.511

Restaurant dessert operations and consumer ordering patterns, 1992 survey rpt, A8200–20

Restaurant smoking policy importance to consumers, and views on smoking acceptability in restaurants and other public places, by selected characteristics, Jan 1993 survey, A8200–8.15

Snack food consumption patterns, by snack type and consumer characteristics, 1989/90 and trends, recurring rpt, A8905–2

Supermarket bakery and deli shoppers, by age group, 1993 annual survey article, C5225–1.508

Supermarket bakery dept shopping frequency, by shopper age, 1991-92, annual article, C5225–1.504

Supermarket shopper practices, attitudes, and expenditures, by respondent characteristics, 1993 and trends, annual survey rpt, A4950–3

Supermarket shopper views on quality of customer service and importance of selected factors, by respondent characteristics, 1991-92 surveys, A4950–37

Wine and other alcoholic beverage consumption, and consumer characteristics and buying habits, 1993 annual rpt, C4775–2.2

State and local:

Oklahoma farm operators by age group, 1978, 1982, and 1987, annual rpt, S6405–1

Wisconsin dairy farmers by age group, Dec 1992, annual rpt, S8680–1

Banking, Finance, and Insurance

Bank CEO demographic and professional characteristics, attitudes, and compensation, Apr 1992 survey, annual rpt, B4490–2.33

Home equity loan distribution by borrower age, by financial instn type, asset size, and region, 1992, annual rpt, A4160–3

Life insurance benefit payments, by payment method and characteristics of beneficiaries and insured, 1940s-91, biennial fact book, A1325–1.2

Life insurance purchases and ownership, by consumer and household characteristics, 1991 and trends, biennial fact book, A1325–1.1

Shareholders of NYSE member firms, by demographic characteristics and metro area, 1970s-90, annual fact book, B6625–1.1

Communications

Advertiser views on most desirable age group target of advertising, 1993 annual survey feature, C2710–1.528

Direct marketing industry devs, including advertising patterns, finances, target market characteristics, and consumer attitudes, 1992/93 annual rpt, A4620–1

Magazine circulation director and manager compensation, by region, sex, age, and publication characteristics, 1992 survey, annual article, C2575–1.502

Magazine compensation of ad sales personnel, by region, sex, age, and publication characteristics, 1993 survey, annual article, C2575–1.516

Magazine compensation of editorial personnel, by region, sex, age, and publication characteristics, 1993 survey, annual article, C2575–1.512

Magazine production director and manager compensation, by region, sex, age, and publication characteristics, 1993 survey, annual article, C2575–1.510

Magazine promotion dept activities, and executive characteristics and salary, Nov 1992 survey, article, C2575–1.506

News events followed most closely by public, and opinion on media coverage and selected current issues, by respondent characteristics, recurring rpt, C8915–1

Newspaper reader socioeconomic characteristics, 1993 annual rpt, A8605–4

Public opinion on the media and related issues, by respondent characteristics, series, C8915–11

Radio audience age distribution compared to general population, 1986 and 1992, article, C1850–14.525

Radio audience size, leading stations and formats, and advertising rates and revenues, by market area, recurring rpt, C3165–1

Radio ownership, audience characteristics, and advertising revenues and effectiveness, with selected comparisons to other media, 1993 annual rpt, A8789–1

Telephone Yellow Pages directory use among consumers, with detail by respondent characteristics, 1992 survey, annual rpt, A9500–2

TV households and population by age and sex, by market area, 1992/93, annual rpt, B0525–3

TV households and population by race-ethnicity, sex, and age, by market area, 1992/93, annual rpt, B0525–4

TV interactive hardware price and service fees acceptable to consumers, by age, Sept 1993 survey, article, C2710–1.549

TV syndicated program audience shares and ratings, by daypart and audience characteristics, Nov 1991-92, article, C9380–1.511

Education

Black American educational statistics, with comparisons to whites, 1970s-92, annual compilation, C6775–2.3

Catholic vs public school performance, and support for parental school selection funded by govt, public opinion by respondent characteristics, July 1992 survey, A7375–8

Community and junior college revenues by source and expenditures by function, and selected student characteristics, FY92, annual rpt, A6705–1

Elementary/secondary prospective teacher characteristics and opinions, survey of persons interested in alternative certification routes, 1992, R6350–7

Elementary/secondary school superintendents personal and professional characteristics and views, 1992 survey rpt, A0775–5

General Educational Dev (GED) testing data, by age and jurisdiction, 1992, annual rpt, A1410–16

Higher education freshmen attitudes and characteristics, degree and career plans, and financial aid sources, by sex and instn type, fall 1992, annual survey, U6215–1

Higher education president personal and professional characteristics, 1990 and trends, recurring rpt, A1410–12

Index by Categories

BY AGE

Higher education president personal and professional characteristics, 1990, article, C2175–1.533

Hispanic American educational statistics, with comparisons to whites, 1970s-92, annual compilation, C6775–3.2

Latin America statistical abstract, general data by country, 1992 annual rpt, U6250–1.8

Librarians (special) salaries by age, sex, and census div, 1992, article, C1852–1.503

Librarians (special) salaries, by location, work setting, and personal characteristics, US and Canada, 1992 and trends, biennial survey rpt, A8965–1

Library/info science school enrollment, staff and student characteristics, finances, and curricula, by school and degree program, 1991/92, annual rpt, A3235–1

Public opinion on school problems, quality, and proposed reforms, by respondent characteristics, 1993 annual Gallup Poll, A8680–1.503

Social work higher education programs, faculty and student characteristics, and student aid, with data by instn, 1992 and trends, annual rpt, A4515–1

Southern States higher education enrollment and rates, by age group and State, 1987 and 1989, biennial fact book, A8945–1.2

Women and minorities in professional fields, detailed education and labor force data, 1980s-91, with historical trends, recurring rpt, A3960–2

State and local:

Arkansas higher education enrollment by student characteristics and geographic origins, by instn, fall 1991 and trends, annual rpt, S0690–1

Colorado public school staff and salaries, by selected characteristics, county, and district, fall 1992 and trends, annual rpt, S1000–2.2

Florida higher education enrollment, degree programs, staff, and finances, by State-supported instn, with student and staff characteristics, 1991/92 annual rpt, S1725–1

Georgia statistical abstract, general data, 1992-93 biennial rpt, U6730–1

Hawaii data book, general data, 1992 annual rpt, S2090–1

Idaho public school personnel characteristics and salaries by position, and teachers and enrollment by school district, 1992/93, annual rpt, S2225–3

Illinois higher education enrollment and degrees, by level, instn, field of instruction, and student characteristics, 1992 and trends, annual rpt, S2475–1.1

Illinois special education enrollment, by age and type of handicap, 1990/91, annual rpt, S2440–1.1

Kentucky higher education enrollment and degrees conferred, by age group, 1983-92, annual rpt, S3130–3

Maine high school equivalency diploma recipients, by age, 1971/72-1991/92, annual rpt, S3435–1

Minnesota postsecondary education finances, and enrollment by student characteristics, by type of school system, 1970s-93, biennial rpt, S4195–2.2

Mississippi public school instructional personnel, by position, training level, and age group, 1991/92 and trends, annual rpt, S4340–1.1

Missouri higher education enrollment and faculty, by age and instn, fall 1992, annual rpt, S4520–3

Nevada statistical abstract, general data, 1992 biennial rpt, S5005–1

New Jersey public school teachers, administrators, staff, and salaries, by county, 1991/92, annual rpt, S5385–1.2

North Carolina higher education enrollment, by student characteristics, and State and county of residence, fall 1992 and trends, annual rpt, U8013–1.1

North Dakota elementary and secondary school staff characteristics and salaries, by position, region, and enrollment size, 1992/93 annual rpt, S6180–3

North Dakota higher education enrollment, by level, instn, county, and selected student characteristics, fall 1992 and trends, annual rpt, S6110–1

Ohio special education enrollment, by age and type of handicap, Dec 1991, annual rpt, S6265–2

Pennsylvania public school dropout characteristics, with reasons for leaving school and subsequent activities, 1991/92 and trends, annual rpt, S6790–5.11

Pennsylvania public school personnel and salary data, by position and district, 1992/93 and trends, annual rpt, S6790–5.12

Pennsylvania vocational education teachers, by age group and program, 1991/92, annual rpt, S6790–5.7

South Dakota public higher education enrollment and faculty, by age group and instn, fall 1992, annual rpt, S7375–1

South Dakota teacher salaries, by age group, 1991/92, annual rpt, S7315–1.2

Tennessee higher education enrollment, including by age, sex, race, and instn, fall 1992 and trends, annual rpt, S7525–1.1

Tennessee public school bus drivers, by age group, 1991/92, annual rpt, S7490–2.3

Utah adult education enrollment, by age, sex, and school district, 1991/92, annual rpt, S7815–1.2

Utah employment by detailed occupation, and educational attainment by age group, by sex and race-ethnicity, with detail for 7 urban areas, 1990 census rpt, S7832–3.4

Utah higher education enrollment by age, sex, and instn, 1991/92 and trends, annual rpt, S7895–2

Vermont higher education enrollment by instn, and student aid recipients, by sex and age, 1992 annual rpt, S8035–2

Virginia public school students and promotion, by grade and age, 1991/92, annual rpt, S8190–3

West Virginia higher education enrollment, degrees, faculty and student characteristics, and finances, by instn, 1992/93 and trends, annual rpt, S8533–1

Government and Defense

Black elected officials, and characteristics of voting age population, with comparisons to whites, 1970s-91, annual compilation, C6775–2.4

Hispanic American elected officials, registered voters, and voting, with comparisons to whites, 1970s-91, annual compilation, C6775–3.3

Hispanic American vs non-Hispanic voter turnout, by demographic characteristics, Nov 1992 election, article, C4575–1.511

House of Representatives staff characteristics, salaries, and benefits by position, 1992 and trends, recurring rpt, R4140–1

House of Representatives women members elected in Nov 1992, by own and children's ages, article, C5800–7.504

Local govt land use planning commissions composition and activities, and commissioner characteristics, 1987 and trends, recurring rpt, A2615–2

Public opinion on Clinton Admin policies and actions, by respondent characteristics, series, C8915–7

Public opinion on issues concerning politics and the press, by respondent characteristics, series, C8915–4

State and local govt employee wages compared to private sector, with data on employee characteristics, 1989, R4700–21

State and local:

Florida statistical abstract, general data, 1992 annual rpt, U6660–1

Hawaii data book, general data, 1992 annual rpt, S2090–1

Oklahoma statistical abstract, general data, 1992 annual rpt, U8130–2

South Carolina statistical abstract, general data, 1993 annual rpt, S7125–1

Health and Vital Statistics

Accidental deaths and disabling injuries, by detailed type, victim characteristics, circumstances, and location, 1992 and trends, annual rpt, A8375–2

Bangladesh women's fertility rates, expected additional births, and unwanted births, by age, 1989, article, A5160–6.502

Black American health and vital statistics data, with comparisons to whites, 1970s-91, annual compilation, C6775–2.2

Cancer (urinary tract) death rates for men age 45-84, by age, State, and census div, 1979-89, article, B6045–1.503

Child and maternal health indicators and insurance coverage, by race-ethnicity and other demographic characteristics, 1992 annual rpt, R3840–5.1

Cocaine user characteristics, including criminal behavior and health condition, with comparison to nonusers, 1991 and trends, article, A2623–1.510

Contraceptive (oral) use errors among women in Botswana, Egypt, Zimbabwe, and Indonesia, by demographic characteristics, 1987-89 surveys, article, A5160–6.504

Death rates by age and sex, for US and 14 other countries, 1991 and trends, article, B6045–1.503

Death shares for 4 leading causes, by age group, 1989, B6045–1.501

Dental problems/treatment-related time lost from work or school, by demographic characteristics, 1989, article, A2623–1.502

Depression incidence among blacks and whites by selected demographic characteristics, 1984 survey, article, A2623–1.504

Developing countries contraceptive use rates for married women, by selected characteristics, by country, various years, 1974-91, R8720–1.1

Developing countries fertility, family planning, sexual behavior, and child health indicators, with selected detail by demographic characteristics, 1984-92 surveys, U2520–1.51

BY AGE

Index by Categories

Disability rates and probable duration, by age group, 1993 article, A3100–2.505

Europe prenatal care levels by demographic characteristics, for 3 countries, with comparisons to US, 1993 article, A2623–1.503

Eye bank activity in US and abroad, including donations by type, source, and donor characteristics, and data by individual bank, 1992 and trends, annual rpt, A4743–1

Fire death rates, by age group, 1982-91, annual rpt, A5650–1.4

Health care specialist and health-related company CEO income, public perceptions vs actual amounts, by respondent characteristics, 1991-93, R4865–13

Health condition and preventive health care and safety practices of adults, by respondent characteristics, 1992 and trends, annual survey rpt, C8111–2

Health insurance coverage and finances, and health care costs and facilities, by selected demographic characteristics, 1940s-91, annual rpt, A5173–2

Health insurance coverage lack, and population with high out-of-pocket expenses, by State and selected characteristics, 1993, R4865–14

Hip fracture incidence rates in US and Hong Kong, by age and sex, 1988/89, article, A2623–1.507

HMO enrollment and utilization patterns, by plan characteristics and member sex and age, 1990-91, annual rpt, A5150–2.2

Hospital CEO demographic and professional characteristics, perquisites, and views on mgmt issues, Oct 1992 survey, recurring rpt, B4490–2.35

Hospital patient admission rates and length of stay, by diagnosis and procedure, payment source, age, sex, and region, 1991, B4455–4

Hospital patient admissions, length of stay, operative procedures, and discharges by patient characteristics, 1990 or 1991 and trends, annual fact book, A1275–1.2

Hospital patient charges and length of stay, by diagnosis and procedure, payment source, age, and region, 1991, B4455–5

Hospital patient discharges and length of stay, by diagnosis, type of operation, age, and region, 1991, annual rpt series, B4455–1

Hospital patient discharges and length of stay, by diagnostic related group (DRG), payment source, age, and region, 1991, annual rpt series, B4455–3

Hospital psychiatric patient discharges and length of stay, by diagnosis, age, sex, and region, 1991, annual rpt series, B4455–2

Human immunodeficiency virus (HIV) testing and posttest counseling rates, by demographic characteristics, 1989, article, A2623–1.501

Hysterectomy prevalence by women's demographic characteristics, 1988 surveys, article, A2623–1.503

Latin America statistical abstract, general data by country, 1992 annual rpt, U6250–1.6

Life expectancy and mortality rates, by age, race, and sex, 1900-92, annual article, B6045–1.504

Life expectancy, by age, sex, and race, 1991 and trends, biennial fact book, A1325–1.6

Medical school programs, fees, applicants, admissions, and enrollment, with data by age, sex, minority group, and instn, 1992/93 and trends, annual rpt, A3273–10

Men's sexual behavior, including condom use, and AIDS knowledge and risks, by selected characteristics, 1991 survey, articles, A5160–1.503

Mexico suicides and attempts, by circumstances and victim characteristics, 1980-84, annual rpt, U6250–1.15

Nurse suicides by age, and correlation with smoking status, 1976-88, article, A2623–1.504

Nursing center (community) staff and client characteristics, and services, 1990 survey, article, A8010–3.506

Nursing higher education program faculty and clinic patient characteristics, 1992/93 biennial rpt, A0615–5

Nursing home insurance adequacy as means of making care affordable to elderly, with detail by age and/or State, 1992 and 2005, R4865–12

Nursing home resident mental health care use, by resident and home characteristics, and provider type, 1985/86 survey, article, A2623–1.505

Older men deaths, by age at death, race, and occupation, 1966-90, U3780–9

Osteopathy student debt and career plans, by student characteristics, 1991/92 and trends, annual survey rpt, A0620–2

Philippines birth outcomes by maternal characteristics, 1983/84 Cebu metro area study, article, A5160–6.505

Physician practice characteristics, detailed data by specialty, type of practice and location, and age, 1992 and trends, annual rpt, A2200–5

Physicians by detailed specialty, location, age, sex, and board certification status, 1992 and trends, annual rpt, A2200–3.1

Sexual activity with multiple partners and strangers, by population characteristics, 1988-90 surveys, article, A5160–1.503

Sexual behavior among adults, including extramarital sex, condom use, and impact of AIDS, by demographic characteristics, 1990 survey, article, A2623–1.512

Sexual behavior among heterosexuals, including data on demographic characteristics, number of partners, and condom use, 1990/91 survey, article, A5160–1.506

Smoking acceptability in restaurants and other public places, and importance of restaurant smoking policy, views of consumers by selected characteristics, Jan 1993 survey, A8200–8.15

Smoking status of men and women by occupation, and smoker characteristics, 1985 and/or 1990, article, B6045–1.501

Southern States children age 17/under lacking health insurance and eligible for Medicaid, with detail by age and family income, for 6-17 States, 1991, R9000–1

Substance abuse treatment programs, funding by source, and client characteristics, for alcohol and drug services, by State, FY91 and trends, annual rpt, A7112–1

Sweden infant mortality rates, by cause and characteristics of mother, 1983-86, article, A2623–1.503

Women's sexual behavior and disease risk, including data on multiple partners and condom use, by selected characteristics, 1988, article, A5160–1.501

Women's smoking patterns, among persons age 18-44 by race and age group, 1987 survey, article, A2623–1.511

Women's use of mammography and Pap smear tests, by demographic characteristics, 1987 survey, article, A2623–1.503

Workers injured compared to labor force, by age, 1992 annual rpt, R8335–1.1

Youth work-related injuries, by age and selected industry, 1990, R8335–2

Zambia student views on sexual behavior and treatment of persons infected with AIDS virus, by respondent characteristics, 1990 survey, article, A5160–6.503

State and local:

Alabama health behavior risk factor surveillance survey results, by respondent characteristics, 1988-89, recurring rpt, S0175–6

Alabama vital statistics, including population, births, deaths by cause, marriages, and divorces, by location and demographic characteristics, 1992 and trends, annual rpt, S0175–2

Alaska vital statistics, including births, deaths by cause, marriages, divorces, adoptions, and population, by demographic characteristics and location, 1990, annual rpt, S0315–1

Arkansas drug and alcohol treatment and prevention program expenditures, success rates, and client characteristics, FY91 annual rpt, S0700–2.1

Arkansas mental health program clients served, by age, race, county, and facility, FY91, annual rpt, S0700 2.4

Arkansas vital statistics, including births, deaths by cause, marriages, and divorces, by age, sex, race, and county, 1991 and trends, annual rpt, S0685–1

California health behavior risk factor surveillance survey results, by respondent characteristics, 1991 and trends, annual rpt, S0865–2

California statistical abstract, general data, 1992 annual rpt, S0840–2

California vital statistics, including population, births, and deaths by cause, by demographic characteristics and county, 1990 and trends, annual rpt, S0865–1

Colorado health behavior risk factor surveillance survey results, by respondent characteristics, 1990, recurring rpt, S1010–3

Colorado vital statistics, including population, births, deaths by cause, abortion, marriage and divorce, and adoption, by demographic characteristics and location, 1990 and trends, annual rpt, S1010–1

Connecticut health insurance coverage rate, by respondent characteristics and behavior risk factors, 1991 survey, S1200–3

Connecticut vital statistics, including births, deaths by cause, marriages, and divorces, by demographic characteristics and location, 1989, annual rpt, S1200–1

DC statistical profile, general data, 1992 annual rpt, S1535–3

Index by Categories

BY AGE

Delaware vital statistics, including births, deaths by cause, and marriages and dissolutions, by demographic characteristics and location, 1990, annual rpt, S1385–2

Florida births by race and characteristics of mother, with detail for low-weight births, by county, 1990, annual rpt, S1746–1.1

Florida statistical abstract, general data, 1992 annual rpt, U6660–1

Florida vital statistics, including population, births, deaths by cause, and marriages and dissolutions, by location and demographic characteristics, 1992 and trends, annual rpt, S1745–3

Georgia health behavior risk factor surveillance survey results, by respondent characteristics, 1991 and trends, annual rpt, S1895–2

Georgia statistical abstract, general data, 1992-93 biennial rpt, U6730–1

Georgia vital statistics, including population, births, abortions, deaths by cause, marriages, and divorces, by demographic characteristics and location, 1991 and trends, annual rpt, S1895–1

Hawaii data book, general data, 1992 annual rpt, S2090–1

Hawaii health dept activities and services, including vital statistics and disease control, by location, 1990, annual rpt, S2065–1

Idaho economic profile, general data, 1992 recurring rpt, S2218–2.2

Idaho vital statistics, including births, deaths by cause, abortions, marriages, and divorces, by demographic characteristics and county, 1991 and trends, annual rpt, S2250–2

Illinois mental health facility patient population and characteristics, by facility, location, and treatment category, FY93, annual rpt, S2505–1

Iowa health behavior risk factor surveillance survey results, by respondent characteristics, 1991, annual rpt, S2795–2

Iowa vital statistics, including population, births, deaths by cause, marriages, and divorces, by demographic characteristics and location, 1991 and trends, annual rpt, S2795–1

Kansas statistical abstract, general data, 1991/92 annual rpt, U7095–2

Kansas vital statistics, including population, births, deaths by cause, abortions, marriages, and divorces, by demographic characteristics and location, 1991 and trends, annual rpt, S2975–1

Kentucky health behavior risk factor surveillance survey results, by State area and respondent characteristics, 1988-90, annual rpt, S3140–6

Kentucky vital statistics, including births, deaths by cause, marriages and divorces, and population, by demographic characteristics and county, 1991, annual rpt, S3140–1

Louisiana vital statistics, including population, births, deaths by cause, reportable diseases, marriages, and divorces, by demographic characteristics and locality, 1989-90 and trends, annual rpt, S3295–1

Maine vital statistics, including births, deaths by cause, abortions, and marriages and divorces, by demographic characteristics and location, 1991 and trends, annual rpt, S3460–2

Maryland vital statistics, including population, births, deaths by cause, marriages, and divorces, by demographic characteristics and location, 1989 and trends, annual rpt, S3635–1

Massachusetts health behavior risk factor surveillance survey results, by respondent characteristics, 1986-90, recurring rpt, S3850–3

Massachusetts vital statistics, including births, deaths by cause, marriages, divorces, and population, by locality and demographic characteristics, 1990 and trends, annual rpt, S3850–1

Michigan health behavior risk factor surveillance survey results, by respondent characteristics, 1991, annual rpt, S4000–4

Michigan vital statistics, including births, deaths, marriages, divorces/annulments, and communicable diseases, by location and demographic characteristics, 1990 and trends, annual rpt, S4000–3

Minnesota vital statistics, including population, births, abortions, deaths, marriages, and divorces, by location and demographic characteristics, 1991 and trends, annual rpt, S4190–2

Mississippi statistical abstract, general data, 1992 annual rpt, U3255–4

Mississippi vital statistics, including births, deaths by cause, marriages, and divorces, by demographic characteristics and location, 1992 and trends, annual rpt, S4350–1

Missouri vital statistics, including population, births, deaths by cause, and marriages and divorces, by location and demographic characteristics, 1992 and trends, annual rpt, S4518–1

Montana long-term and personal care facilities patients, by age, sex, and instn, 1991, annual rpt, S4690–2

Montana vital statistics, including births, deaths by cause, abortion, disease, and marriage and divorce, by demographic characteristics and county, 1990-91 and trends, annual rpt, S4690–1

Nebraska vital statistics, including births, deaths, marriages, divorces, and population, by demographic characteristics and location, 1991 and trends, annual rpt, S4885–1

Nevada health behavior risk factor surveillance survey results, by location and respondent characteristics, 1991, annual rpt, S5075–3

Nevada statistical abstract, general data, 1992 biennial rpt, S5005–1

Nevada vital statistics, including births, abortions, and deaths by cause, by county and demographic characteristics, 1989 and trends, annual rpt, S5075–1

New Hampshire vital statistics, including population, births, deaths by cause, marriages, and divorces, by location and demographic characteristics, 1991 and trends, annual rpt, S5215–1

New Jersey vital statistics, including births, deaths, population, communicable diseases, and marriages and divorces, by demographic characteristics and location, 1990 and trends, annual rpt, S5405–1

New Mexico vital statistics, including population, births, deaths, and disease, by location and demographic characteristics, 1991 and trends, annual rpt, S5605–1

New York State health behavior risk factor surveillance survey results, by respondent characteristics, 1990, recurring rpt, S5765–3

New York State statistical yearbook, general data, 1992 annual rpt, U5100–1

New York State vital statistics, including population, births, deaths by cause, reportable diseases, and marriages and dissolutions, by demographic characteristics and/or location, 1990 and trends, annual rpt, S5765–1

North Carolina vital statistics, including population, births, deaths, marriages, and divorces, by local area, 1991 and trends, annual rpt, S5927–1.1

North Dakota health behavior risk factor surveillance survey results, by respondent characteristics, 1991 and trends, annual rpt, S6105–3

North Dakota vital statistics, including births, deaths by cause, marriages and divorces, and abortions, by demographic characteristics and/or county, 1991 and trends, annual rpt, S6105–2

Ohio vital statistics, including births, deaths by cause, marriages, divorces, and population, by demographic characteristics and location, 1991 and trends, annual rpt, S6285–1

Oregon vital statistics, including births, deaths by cause, communicable diseases, marriages, and divorces, by age, sex, race-ethnicity, and county, 1991 and trends, annual rpt, S6615–5

Pennsylvania health behavior risk factor surveillance survey results, by respondent characteristics, 1991, annual rpt, S6820–4

Rhode Island vital statistics, including population, births, deaths, marriages, and divorces, by demographic characteristics and locality, 1989 and trends, annual rpt, S6995–1

South Carolina deaths, by detailed cause, age, sex, and race, 1990, annual rpt, S7175–2

South Carolina statistical abstract, general data, 1993 annual rpt, S7125–1

South Carolina vital statistics, including births, deaths by cause, marriages, and divorces, by age, sex, race, and location, 1990 and trends, annual rpt, S7175–1

South Dakota vital statistics, including births, deaths, marriage and divorce, and communicable disease, by demographic characteristics and county, 1991 and trends, annual rpt, S7345–1

Tennessee health behavior risk factor surveillance survey results, by respondent characteristics, 1986-90, annual rpt, S7520–3

Tennessee vital statistics, including births, deaths by cause, marriages, divorces, and population, by demographic characteristics and location, 1991 and trends, annual rpt, S7520–2

Texas fertility and survival rates, by age and race-ethnicity, 1990, recurring rpt, S7645–3

Texas health behavior risk factor surveillance survey results, by respondent characteristics, 1991 and trends, annual rpt, S7685–2

Texas nursing employment, demand outlook, earnings, and education, by selected characteristics, various years 1971-91, U8850–8.2

BY AGE

Texas physicians insured against professional liability, with data on premiums and claims, and detail by specialty and/or age, sex, and city, 1978-91, U8850–8.8

Texas vital statistics, including births, deaths by cause, abortions, marriages, and divorces, by location and demographic characteristics, 1991 and trends, annual rpt, S7685–1

Utah health behavior risk factor surveillance survey results, by respondent characteristics, 1991, annual rpt, S7835–3

Utah marriages and divorces, by participant characteristics and location, 1990 and trends, annual rpt, S7835–2

Utah vital statistics, including births, deaths by cause, and population, by county and demographic characteristics, 1990 and trends, annual rpt, S7835–1

Vermont vital statistics, including population, births, deaths by cause, abortions, marriages, and divorces, by location and demographic characteristics, 1991 and trends, annual rpt, S8054–1

Virginia vital statistics, including births, deaths by cause, marriages and divorces, and communicable disease, by demographic characteristics and location, 1991 and trends, annual rpt, S8225–1

Washington State vital statistics, including births, deaths by cause, and population, by demographic characteristics and location, 1991 and trends, annual rpt, S8363–1

West Virginia vital statistics, including births, deaths by cause, marriages and divorces, by location and demographic characteristics, 1991 and trends, annual rpt, S8560–1

Wisconsin vital statistics, including population, births, deaths by cause, and marriages and dissolutions, by county and demographic characteristics, 1991 and trends, annual rpt, S8715–4

Wyoming vital statistics, including population, births, deaths by cause, marriages, and divorces, by demographic characteristics and county, 1991 and trends, annual rpt, S8920–2

Housing and Construction

Home rental rates by householder age, 1982-92, article, A7000–1.503

Public housing authority income and expenses, resident and property characteristics, and unit vacancy and turnover rates, various years FY77-1992, A6800–2

Real estate property managers characteristics and compensation, including types of property managed, 1989 surveys, recurring rpt, A5600–4

State and local:

Arkansas Census of Population and Housing detailed findings, 1990, U5935–7

California Census of Population and Housing detailed findings, 1990, S0840–9

New Jersey Census of Population and Housing detailed findings, by county, 1990, S5425–19

Pennsylvania Census of Population and Housing detailed findings, with selected data by county and municipality, 1990, U4130–13

Income

Black American earnings, income, and poverty data, with comparisons to whites, 1980s-91, annual compilation, C6775–2.7

Black American socioeconomic status, with comparisons to whites and data by region, 1960s-92, annual compilation, A8510–1.1

Hispanic American income and poverty data, with comparisons to whites, 1980s-91, annual compilation, C6775–3.5

Household wealth and income data by income level, including assets by type and detail by age group, 1989 and trends, R4700–17

Industrial distribution personnel compensation, by position and selected other characteristics, 1992 survey, annual article, C1850–4.501

Logistics manager salaries, by position, industry, and selected characteristics, Nov 1992 survey, annual article, C1850–11

Poverty rates by age group, 1979 and 1991, annual rpt, U1260–2

Professional worker salaries, by employee and employer characteristics, with detail for scientists and engineers, 1990s and trends, biennial rpt, A3960–1

Women's employment and earnings, with comparisons to men, and detail by occupation and worker characteristics, 1990s and trends, annual rpt, A1570–2

State and local:

Arizona statistical abstract, general data, 1993 recurring rpt, U5850–2

Arkansas Census of Population and Housing detailed findings, 1990, U5935–7

California Census of Population and Housing detailed findings, 1990, S0840–9

Colorado low-income population, by age and local area, 1990, annual planning rpt, S1040–3.1

Kentucky labor force planning rpt, including population and labor force characteristics, and employment by industry, 1991 and trends, annual rpt, S3140–3

Louisiana Census of Population and Housing summary findings, by local area, 1990 and trends, U8010–4

Mississippi characteristics of economically disadvantaged and Job Training Partnership Act eligible population, 1993/94, annual planning rpt, S4345–1.3

New Jersey Census of Population and Housing detailed findings, by county, 1990, S5425–19

Pennsylvania Census of Population and Housing detailed findings, with selected data by county and municipality, 1990, U4130–13

South Carolina statistical abstract, general data, 1993 annual rpt, S7125–1

West Virginia economically disadvantaged population, by county and age group, 1991, annual planning rpt, S8534–2

Industry and Commerce

Canada photographic and video equipment and supplies ownership, purchasing patterns, and use, by household characteristics, 1992 survey, recurring rpt, A8695–4

CEO characteristics and compensation, for small companies with rapid growth, 1993 survey article, C5800–7.551

Consumer expectations of economic conditions, by age of household head, Conference Board monthly survey, R4105–4

Index by Categories

Cosmetics use indexes among women by age group, for selected brands, 1993 articles, C5150–2.514

Discount chain consumer natl brand preferences, by product category and chain, and by age group, 1993 survey, annual feature, C5150–3.521

Photographic equipment and supplies, consumer ownership, purchasing patterns, and use, 1993 survey and trends, recurring rpt, A8695–2

Private label product characteristics and purchasing factors as seen by consumers, by selected characteristics, 1991 survey, article, C0125–1.504

Retail outlet consumer preference indexes, by selected demographic characteristics, 1993 annual feature, C4655–1.504

Sales worker incidence of reaching plateaus in productivity by age group, and mgmt views on reasons and solutions, 1993 survey article, C1200–1.509

Shoe sales by age of wearer, 1987 and 1991, annual rpt, A4957–1.1

Women's use and shopping patterns for personal care products, by age group, 1993 survey and trends, annual feature, C5150–2.515

Labor and Employment

Black American labor force and employment data, with comparisons to whites, 1970s-91, annual compilation, C6775–2.6

Hispanic American labor force and employment data, with comparisons to whites, 1980s-91, annual compilation, C6775–3.4

Japan population share age 55/over who are employed, by age group and sex, 1987-92, article, R5650–2.549

Labor force by sex and age, 1980s-2005, annual rpt, R9050–1.2

Labor force participation, by sex and age group, 1975, 1990, and 2005, annual rpt, A1570–1

Pension benefits and coverage as affected by job tenure and mobility, with data by plan type and worker characteristics, 1993 rpt, R9260–17

Planning profession employment and salaries, by type of employer, demographic and professional characteristics, and location, 1991 and trends, biennial rpt, A2615–1

Unemployment insurance trends, including data on unemployment, worker characteristics, coverage, benefits, and State govt finances, 1940s-90, R9260–18

Women's employment and earnings, with comparisons to men, and detail by occupation and worker characteristics, 1990s and trends, annual rpt, A1570–2

Youth employment estimates among ages 12-17, 1990, R8335–2

State and local:

Arkansas vocational rehabilitation expenditures, impact on earnings and employment, and client characteristics, FY91 annual rpt, S0700–2.4

California labor force planning rpt, including population characteristics, and employment by industry, 1992 annual rpt, S0830–2

DC statistical profile, general data, 1992 annual rpt, S1535–3

Delaware data book, general data, 1993 annual rpt, S1375–4

Index by Categories

BY AGE

Hawaii data book, general data, 1992 annual rpt, S2090–1

Louisiana job service openings and applicants, and characteristics of Job Training Partnership Act target population and insured unemployed, 1993 annual planning rpt, S3320–1.2

Michigan labor force planning rpt, including employment by industry, and characteristics of Job Training Partnership Act eligible population, 1993 annual rpt, S3980–1

Mississippi labor force planning rpt, including population, employment, and characteristics of unemployed and disadvantaged, 1993 annual rpt, S4345–1

New Hampshire labor force and population by race, sex, and age, and employment by industry div, statewide and by county, 1992 recurring rpt, S5205–7

New Jersey insured unemployed characteristics, monthly rpt, S5425–1

New Mexico labor force planning rpt, including population characteristics, and employment by industry and occupation, 1993 annual rpt, S5624–1

Pennsylvania labor force planning rpt, including population characteristics, employment and job openings by industry and occupation, and income trends, FY92 annual rpt, S6845–3

South Carolina labor force planning rpt, detailed data on employment, hours, wages, turnover, and characteristics of job service applicants, 1992 annual rpt, S7155–3.2

Utah labor force and percent without high school diploma, by sex, age group, and/or race-ethnicity, 1990, article, U8960–2.509

Utah statistical abstract, general data, 1993 triennial rpt, U8960–1

Vermont labor force by employment status, and job service openings and applicant characteristics, 1993 annual planning rpt, S8025–2.2

West Virginia labor force planning rpt, including population, employment, and job service activities, with data by county and service delivery area, 1993 annual rpt, S8534–2

Law Enforcement

Arrests by age for selected offenses, 1991, annual rpt, A5650–1.4

Black American crime, arrest, and incarceration data, with comparisons to whites, 1970s-91, annual compilation, C6775–2.5

Correctional instns, inmates, staff, and cost of care, by instn, US and Canada, with operating summary by State or Province, 1992, annual directory, A1305–3

Crime victims per 1,000 population, by demographic characteristics, 1991, article, R8750–1.505

Household crime victimization rates for burglary, larceny, and motor vehicle theft, by age of victim, 1987-90, article, C1850–13.506

Juvenile State instn custody prevalence rates by sex, age, and race-ethnicity, for 16 States, 1991, A7575–1.13

Law school grad employment and salaries, by type of employer, location, and grad characteristics, 1992 and trends, annual rpt, A6505–1

Rape incidence by victim age group, 1990-92 surveys, R8375–1

State and local:

Alabama arrests by offender age and offense, 1992, annual rpt, S0119–1.1

Alaska corrections system admin, including inmate and probationer/parolee offenses and demographic characteristics, 1991 annual rpt, S0287–1

Arizona arrests and murder victims, by age, sex, and race-ethnicity, 1992, annual rpt, S0505–2

Arizona correctional instn admin, including inmates by criminal background and demographic characteristics, FY92, annual rpt, S0464–2

Arizona juvenile court referrals and adjudication activity, by age and sex, FY92, annual rpt, S0525–1

Arizona statistical abstract, general data, 1993 recurring rpt, U5850–2

Arkansas child abuse and neglect victims, by age, sex, and race, FY91, annual rpt, S0700–2.2

Arkansas crimes and arrests, by offense, victim and offender characteristics, and location, 1992 and trends, annual rpt, S0652–1

Arkansas juvenile detention center and community program admissions, by age and sex, 1989-91, annual rpt, S0700–2.2

California correctional instn inmates, by offense, demographic characteristics, and instn, Dec 1992, semiannual rpt, S0820–2

California correctional instn inmates, with criminal background and demographic characteristics, 1991 and trends, annual rpt, S0820–1

California crimes and arrests, clearances, and arrest dispositions, with data by offense and offender characteristics, 1987-92, annual rpt, S0910–1.1

California criminal justice system detailed data, by offense, county, age, race-ethnicity, and sex, 1991 and trends, annual rpt, S0910–2.2

Colorado homicide offenders and victims, by age, sex, and race-ethnicity, 1991-92, annual rpt, S1068–1

Connecticut crimes and arrests, by offense, with data by local agency, and victim-offender characteristics, 1992, annual rpt, S1256–1

DC arrests, homicide offenders and victims, and juvenile drug test results, by age, 1991 and trends, annual rpt, S1535–2

DC juvenile court case activity, including referrals by offense and age, 1992 and trends, annual rpt, S1515–1

DC statistical profile, general data, 1992 annual rpt, S1535–3

Florida correctional instns, admin, and inmates by criminal background and demographic characteristics, FY92 annual rpt, S1720–1

Georgia correctional instns, admin, and inmate characteristics, FY92, annual rpt, S1872–1

Georgia county guide, general data, 1993 annual rpt, U6750–1

Georgia crimes and arrests, by offense, with data by location and offender characteristics, 1992 and trends, annual rpt, S1901–1

Georgia statistical abstract, general data, 1992-93 biennial rpt, U6730–1

Hawaii crimes and arrests, by offense, with data by county and victim-offender characteristics, 1992, annual rpt, S2035–1

Idaho crimes and arrests, by offense, with data by location and offender characteristics, 1992 and trends, annual rpt, S2275–2

Illinois corrections dept admin, including inmates and characteristics, finances, and staff, FY91-93 and trends, annual rpt, S2425–1

Indiana child abuse and neglect cases by county and victim and perpetrator characteristics, FY92 annual rpt, S2623–1.7

Iowa correctional instn admissions, releases, and inmate characteristics, by instn, monthly rpt, S2770–1

Kansas correctional instn inmates, by offense, demographic characteristics, and instn, FY92 and trends, annual rpt, S2940–1

Kansas crimes and arrests, by offense, with data by location, agency, and victim-offender characteristics, 1992 and trends, annual rpt, S2925–1.1

Kansas statistical abstract, general data, 1991/92 annual rpt, U7095–2

Kentucky crimes and arrests, by offense, with data by location and offender characteristics, 1992, annual rpt, S3150–1

Kentucky prison releases, by age group and State area, 1991, annual planning rpt, S3140–3

Maine crimes and arrests, by offense, with data by county, reporting agency, and offender age and sex, 1991, annual rpt, S3475–1

Maryland crimes and arrests, by offense, location, and offender characteristics, with law enforcement employment and assaults on officers, 1992 and trends, annual rpt, S3665–1

Maryland statistical abstract, general data, 1993-94 biennial rpt, S3605–1

Massachusetts correctional instn inmate socioeconomic characteristics and criminal background, by instn, Jan 1992 and trends, annual rpt, S3805–1

Michigan correctional instns, admin, and inmates by selected demographic characteristics, 1991 and trends, annual rpt, S3960–1

Michigan crimes and arrests, with murder victims by race, sex, and age, 1992, annual rpt, S3997–1

Mississippi statistical abstract, general data, 1992 annual rpt, U3255–4

Missouri correctional instn admissions, releases, and inmate characteristics, FY93, annual rpt, S4501–1

Nebraska correctional instn admin, with inmates by criminal background and demographic characteristics, by instn, FY92 and trends, annual rpt, S4850–1

New Hampshire crimes and arrests, by offense, jurisdiction, and offender characteristics, 1991 and trends, annual rpt, S5250–2

New Jersey correctional instn inmates, by offense, sentence length, demographic characteristics, and instn, Dec 1991 annual rpt, S5370–1

BY AGE

Index by Categories

New Jersey crimes and arrests, by offense, with data by location and offender characteristics, 1992 and trends, annual rpt, S5430–1

New York State arrests, homicide victims and offenders, and prisoners, by demographic characteristics, 1991, annual rpt, S5760–3

New York State attorney registrations, by year of birth, 1991, annual rpt, S5730–1

New York State children and youth involved in family court cases, by age, sex, and county, 1991, annual rpt, S5730–1

New York State correctional instn inmates released, by criminal background, sentence, and demographic characteristics, 1991 and trends, recurring rpt series, S5725–1

New York State local jail/penitentiary inmates by offense, sentence, and demographic characteristics, by county or facility, 1991, annual rpt, S5724–2

New York State statistical yearbook, general data, 1992 annual rpt, U5100–1

North Carolina correctional instn admissions, separations, and population, with inmate characteristics, FY93, semiannual rpt, S5900–1

North Carolina crimes and arrests, by offense, with data by location and offender characteristics, 1992 and trends, annual rpt, S5955–1

North Dakota crimes and arrests, by offense, location, and offender characteristics, and law enforcement employment, 1991 and trends, annual rpt, S6060–1

North Dakota local correctional instn adult and juvenile inmate characteristics, by instn, 1991 and trends, annual rpt, S6060–3

Ohio correctional instn admissions and releases, inmate characteristics, programs, finances, and staffing, FY91 and trends, annual rpt, S6370–1

Oklahoma crimes and arrests, by offense, with data by local agency and victim and offender characteristics, 1990-92, annual rpt, S6465–1

Oregon crimes and arrests, by offense, with detail on bias crimes and data by victim and offender characteristics, 1992 and trends, annual rpt, S6603–3.1

Pennsylvania crimes and arrests, by offense, with data by location and offender characteristics, 1992 and trends, annual rpt, S6860–1

Pennsylvania State correctional instn admin, and inmates by type of offense and demographic characteristics, 1990 and trends, annual rpt, S6782–1

South Carolina correctional instns, admin, and inmates by criminal offense and demographic characteristics, FY92 and trends, annual rpt, S7135–1

South Carolina crimes and arrests, by offense, with data by location and victim-offender characteristics, and assaults on officers, 1992 and trends, annual rpt, S7205–1

South Carolina statistical abstract, general data, 1993 annual rpt, S7125–1

Tennessee correctional instn admin, with inmate characteristics, and corrections dept finances and staff, FY92, annual rpt, S7480–1

Texas appellate and trial judge demographic characteristics, Sept 1992, annual rpt, S7703–1

Texas arrests, by age, sex, race-ethnicity, and offense, 1992, annual rpt, S7735–2.2

Texas correctional instn inmates by criminal background and demographic characteristics, FY92, annual rpt, S7660–1

Utah corrections inmates, parolees, and probationers, by criminal background and demographic characteristics, FY92 and trends, annual rpt, S7810–1

Utah murder victims and offenders, by age group, 1992, annual rpt, S7890–3

Virginia crimes and arrests, by offense, with data by location and offender characteristics, 1992, annual rpt, S8295–2

Washington State correctional instn inmate population, admissions, and releases, by demographic characteristics, quarterly rpt, S8337–1

Washington State crimes and arrests, by offense, with data by location and offender characteristics, 1992 and trends, annual rpt, S8440–1

West Virginia arrests and murder victims, by age, 1990-91, annual rpt, S8610–1.1

Wisconsin correctional instn inmates, by criminal background and selected characteristics, series, S8692–1

Wisconsin crimes and arrests, by offense, offender characteristics, county, and local agency, 1992 and trends, annual rpt, S8771–1

Wyoming correctional instn admin, finances, inmate characteristics, and staff, and probation and parole activities, FY92 annual rpt, S8883–1

Wyoming crimes and arrests, by offense, with data by location and victim and offender characteristics, 1991 and trends, annual rpt, S8867–3

Population

Births and fertility, by selected newborn and maternal characteristics, 1990, article, R8750–1.510

Black American population and demographic characteristics, with comparisons to whites, 1970s-2080, annual compilation, C6775–2.1

Black American socioeconomic status, with comparisons to whites and data by region, 1960s-92, annual compilation, A8510–1.1

Black children and youth population, economic, health, and education data, with comparisons to whites, 1993 rpt, R3840–21

Children's living arrangements, by parents characteristics and child age and race-ethnicity, 1992, article, B6045–1.504

Children's living arrangements, by parents characteristics and child race-ethnicity, 1991, article, B6045–1.503

Consumer buying power survey of population, income, and sales by kind of business, by census div, State, MSA, county, and city, 1992, annual rpt, C1200–1.511

Consumer buying power survey of population, income, and sales by product line, by State, metro area, county, and census div, 1993 annual rpt, C1200–1.514

Consumer socioeconomic profiles, for top 50 MSAs ranked by supermarket sales, 1991, annual rpt, C3400–6

Europe Jewish population, with social and demographic characteristics, for 10-12 countries, 1930s-91, article, A2050–1.1

Gallup Poll public attitude surveys, results and sample characteristics, monthly rpt, C4040–1

Hispanic American socioeconomic status, including education, politics, income, and employment, with comparisons to whites, 1993 annual compilation, C6775–3

Households by housing tenure status, region, and age of household head, quarterly rpt, B5190–1

Male population by age, quinquennially 1995-2025, annual rpt, A3880–1

Market area population and characteristics, households, income, and retail outlets, for 21 leading areas, 1993 feature, C2710–1.538

Minority population characteristics, employment, and voting patterns by detailed race-ethnicity, with comparisons to whites, 1980s-2040, R8750–2.58

Minority population share, by age group, 1992 and 2025, article, R8750–1.506

Population age structure, decennially 1970-2040, article, U0280–1.507

Population age 3-34, by age group, 1960-88, recurring rpt, A3960–2.1

Population by age group, by census div and State, Apr 1990, article, B6045–1.501

Population by age group, by State, Canadian Province, and local area, 1993 annual rpt, C3250–1

Population by age, 1960s-2050, annual rpt, R9050–1.2

Population trends and projections, by age and sex, 1980s-2080, annual rpt, A4957–1.1

Public opinion in UK and US on reasons for citing World War II as most important event in past 60 years, by age, 1993 article, A0610–1.504

Public opinion on expected change in privacy protection of consumer info by year 2000, by age and education level, 1992 survey and trends, annual rpt, B3280–2

Refugee arrivals, by sex and age, FY83-92, R9372–2.507

Religion and related social issues, public opinions and attitudes, monthly survey, R8780–1

Russia public opinion on political and economic issues and devs, by selected characteristics, 1991-92 surveys, C8915–10

Solitary living population, by age and sex, 1990, 1995, and 2000, article, C4655–1.506

Southern States population, personal income, and State/local revenues and expenditures, by State, 1950s-2010, biennial fact book, A8945–1.1

Statistical profiles of 50 States and DC, general data, 1993 annual almanac, C4712–1

Women's housing issues, with data on household composition, tenure, and characteristics, 1992, A8657–5

World female population age 15-49, with marriage/cohabitation rate in developing countries, by age group and country, 1990, R8720–1.1

World population and health indicators, with detail by region and country, 1992/93 biennial rpt, R9455–1.5

World population distribution by age group, for top 50 countries, 1992, semiannual rpt, B8500–1.16

State and local:

Index by Categories

BY AGE

Alabama population by age group, 1990, 2000, and 2015, article, U5680–1.503

Alabama statistical abstract, general data, 1992 recurring rpt, U5680–2

Alabama vital statistics, including population, births, deaths by cause, marriages, and divorces, by location and demographic characteristics, 1992 and trends, annual rpt, S0175–2

Alaska population, housing, income, and education data, by demographic characteristics and/or locality, 1990/91 and trends, annual rpt, S0320–4

Alaska vital statistics, including births, deaths by cause, marriages, divorces, adoptions, and population, by demographic characteristics and location, 1990, annual rpt, S0315–1

Arizona Indian population, education, housing, health, and employment characteristics, with detail by reservation, 1970s-91, recurring rpt, U5850–2.9

Arizona, Phoenix area temporary winter resident characteristics, including expenditures, dwelling type, and region of residence, 1992/93, article, U0280–1.508

Arizona statistical abstract, general data, 1993 recurring rpt, U5850–2

Arkansas adoptions by child age, race, and sex, FY91, annual rpt, S0700–2.2

Arkansas Census of Population and Housing detailed findings, 1990, U5935–7

California and US women of childbearing age, by age group, 1988-90, annual rpt, S0865–1

California Census of Population and Housing detailed findings, 1990, S0840–9

California labor force planning rpt, including population characteristics, and employment by industry, 1992 annual rpt, S0830–2

California population by age, sex, race-ethnicity, and county, decennially 1990-2040, recurring rpt, S0840–4

California socioeconomic and govtl data for municipalities, counties, and school districts, 1993 annual rpt, C4712–3

California statistical abstract, general data, 1992 annual rpt, S0840–2

Colorado vital statistics, including population, births, deaths by cause, abortion, marriage and divorce, and adoption, by demographic characteristics and location, 1990 and trends, annual rpt, S1010–1

Connecticut population, by age and sex, 1989, annual rpt, S1200–1

DC statistical profile, general data, 1992 annual rpt, S1535–3

Delaware population, by age, sex, race, and locality, 1990-2020, recurring rpt, S1375–3

Delaware vital statistics, including births, deaths by cause, and marriages and dissolutions, by demographic characteristics and location, 1990, annual rpt, S1385–2

Florida county data book, 1992/93 annual rpt, C6360–1

Florida municipal and county statistical profiles, general data, 1991 annual rpt, C4712–6

Florida population by age, sex, and race, by county, 1990, 1992, and quinquennially 1995-2010, annual rpt, U6660–3.46

Florida population by age, sex, and race, by county, 1990-91 and quinquennially 1995-2010, annual rpt, U6660–3.43

Florida population, by race-ethnicity, age, and county, 1992 annual rpt, S1746–1.1

Florida population distribution by age group, by county, Apr 1991 and trends, annual rpt, U6660–4

Florida statistical abstract, general data, 1992 annual rpt, U6660–1

Florida vital statistics, including population, births, deaths by cause, and marriages and dissolutions, by location and demographic characteristics, 1992 and trends, annual rpt, S1745–3

Georgia county guide, general data, 1993 annual rpt, U6750–1

Georgia statistical abstract, general data, 1992-93 biennial rpt, U6730–1

Georgia vital statistics, including population by demographic characteristics and location, 1991, annual rpt, S1895–1.3

Hawaii data book, general data, 1992 annual rpt, S2090–1

Hawaii homeless population, by age, 1992, annual rpt, S2090–1.21

Idaho economic profile, general data, 1992 recurring rpt, S2218–2.2

Idaho population by age and sex, 1990, annual rpt, S2250–2

Illinois statistical abstract, general data, 1992 annual rpt, U6910–2

Indiana population by age group, 1981-91, annual rpt, S2570–1.1

Kansas statistical abstract, general data, 1991/92 annual rpt, U7095–2

Kansas vital statistics, including population, births, deaths by cause, abortions, marriages, and divorces, by demographic characteristics and location, 1991 and trends, annual rpt, S2975–1

Kentucky economic statistics, general data, 1993 annual rpt, S3104–1

Kentucky labor force planning rpt, including population and labor force characteristics, and employment by industry, 1991 and trends, annual rpt, S3140–3

Kentucky vital statistics, including births, deaths by cause, marriages and divorces, and population, by demographic characteristics and county, 1991, annual rpt, S3140–1

Louisiana Census of Population and Housing summary findings, by local area, 1990 and trends, U8010–4

Maine Census of Population and Housing summary findings, by local area, 1990, S3465–7, S3465–8

Maine population, by age, sex, and county, 1991, annual rpt, S3460–2

Maryland statistical abstract, general data, 1993-94 biennial rpt, S3605–1

Maryland vital statistics, including population, births, deaths by cause, marriages, and divorces, by demographic characteristics and location, 1989 and trends, annual rpt, S3635–1

Massachusetts municipal and county profiles, general data, 1992 annual rpt, C4712–2

Massachusetts vital statistics, including births, deaths by cause, marriages, divorces, and population, by locality and demographic characteristics, 1990 and trends, annual rpt, S3850–1

Michigan labor force planning rpt, including employment by industry, and characteristics of Job Training Partnership Act eligible population, 1993 annual rpt, S3980–1

Michigan population, by age, sex, race, and county, 1990, annual rpt, S4000–3

Minnesota population, by age, sex, and county, 1991, annual rpt, S4190–2

Mississippi population, by age, race, sex, and educational attainment, 1993/94, annual planning rpt, S4345–1.1

Mississippi population, by age, sex, and race, 1990, annual rpt, S4350–1

Mississippi statistical abstract, general data, 1992 annual rpt, U3255–4

Nebraska population age 20/under, by age, sex, and county, June 1992, annual rpt, S4865–2.6

Nebraska population and migration rates, with detail by age group and county, 1980-90, article, U7860–1.508

Nevada statistical abstract, general data, 1992 biennial rpt, S5005–1

New Hampshire labor force and population by race, sex, and age, and employment by industry div, statewide and by county, 1992 recurring rpt, S5205–7

New Jersey Census of Population and Housing detailed findings, by county, 1990, S5425–19

New Jersey municipal and county data book, general data, 1992 annual rpt, C4712–4

New Jersey population, by race-ethnicity, sex, age, and county, 1990, annual rpt, S5405–1

New Mexico population by age, sex, county, and State region, 1980 and 1990, U7980–6

New Mexico population, by age, 1990-2020, annual planning rpt, S5624–1

New Mexico vital statistics, including population, births, deaths, and disease, by location and demographic characteristics, 1991 and trends, annual rpt, S5605–1

New York State adoptions, by sex, age, and race-ethnicity, 1991, annual rpt, S5800–2.3

New York State municipal and county statistical profiles, general data, 1993 annual rpt, C4712–7

New York State statistical yearbook, general data, 1992 annual rpt, U5100–1

New York State vital statistics, including population, births, deaths by cause, reportable diseases, and marriages and dissolutions, by demographic characteristics and/or location, 1990 and trends, annual rpt, S5765–1

North Dakota children by age and/or sex, by county, Aug 1991, annual education directory, S6180–2

Ohio population by age, sex, and county, with summary components of change, quinquennially 1990-2015, recurring rpt, S6260–3

Ohio vital statistics, including births, deaths by cause, marriages, divorces, and population, by demographic characteristics and location, 1991 and trends, annual rpt, S6285–1

Oklahoma population projections, by age, sex, and locality, with data on fertility and migration, 1990-2020, recurring rpt, S6416–1

Oklahoma statistical abstract, general data, 1992 annual rpt, U8130–2

Oregon population, by age and sex, 1950s-91, annual rpt, S6615–5

BY AGE

Index by Categories

Pennsylvania Census of Population and Housing detailed findings, with selected data by county and municipality, 1990, U4130–13

Pennsylvania statistical abstract, general data, 1992 recurring rpt, U4130–6

Rhode Island labor force planning rpt, including population, employment by industry, job openings, and characteristics of insured unemployed, 1993 annual rpt, S6980–3

Rhode Island statistical almanac, general data, 1993 annual rpt, C7975–1

Rhode Island vital statistics, including population, births, deaths, marriages, and divorces, by demographic characteristics and locality, 1989 and trends, annual rpt, S6995–1

South Carolina labor force planning rpt, including population, employment, income, and job service activities, 1992 annual rpt, S7155–3

South Carolina population, by race, age, and county, 1990 and trends, annual rpt, S7175–1

South Carolina population characteristics, by county, 1993 annual rpt, S7145–1.1

South Carolina statistical abstract, general data, 1993 annual rpt, S7125–1

Tennessee population, by age, sex, race, and county, 1990-2010, recurring rpt, S7560–2

Tennessee population projections by age, sex, and county metro status, 1990-2010, article, U8710–1.501

Tennessee statistical abstract, general data, 1992/93 annual rpt, U8710–2

Texas disabled persons above and below poverty level, by age group, FY92, annual rpt, S7695–1

Texas labor force planning rpt, including labor force, employment by industry, income, and population, 1993 annual rpt, S7675–2

Texas population, by age, sex, and race-ethnicity, 1990, recurring rpt, S7645–3

Texas population, by age, sex, race-ethnicity, and county, July 1991, annual rpt, S7645–2

Utah govt statistical review, fiscal and socioeconomic data, 1993 annual rpt, R9380–1

Utah statistical abstract, general data, 1993 triennial rpt, U8960–1

Vermont population, by age, sex, and locality, 1991 and trends, annual planning rpt, S8025–2.1

Vermont vital statistics, including population, births, deaths by cause, abortions, marriages, and divorces, by location and demographic characteristics, 1991 and trends, annual rpt, S8054–1

Virginia youth population by age, by county and city, with detail for disabled youth, Jan 1993, triennial rpt, S8190–1

Washington State population and demographic characteristics, and housing units, by county and/or city, 1992 and trends, annual rpt, S8345–4

Washington State vital statistics, including births, deaths by cause, and population, by demographic characteristics and location, 1991 and trends, annual rpt, S8363–1

West Virginia labor force planning rpt, including population, employment, and job service activities, with data by county and service delivery area, 1993 annual rpt, S8534–2

West Virginia population, by county and demographic characteristics, 1990 and trends, annual rpt, S8560–1

Wisconsin population, by age, sex, and county, with components of change, quinquennially 1990-2020, recurring rpt, S8675–4

Wisconsin vital statistics, including population, births, deaths by cause, and marriages and dissolutions, by county and demographic characteristics, 1991 and trends, annual rpt, S8715–4

Prices and Cost of Living

Christmas spending plans of consumers, by region, age, and income, Nov 1992 survey, annual rpt, R4105–81.10

Consumer attitudes on economic conditions and personal financial situation, monthly survey, U7475–2

Consumer expenditures by item and age group, 1991 and trends, annual rpt, A0865–1.2

Public Welfare and Social Security

Arts/humanities organization charitable contribution donor characteristics, 1993 survey article, C2176–1.507

Fundraising professionals characteristics, earnings, and benefits, 1992 survey, recurring rpt, A8455–1

Youth age 12-17 charitable contributions, volunteer activity, and views on related issues, by respondent characteristics, 1992 survey, biennial rpt, A5435–5

State and local:

Arkansas human services dept finances and operations, including Medicaid payments by type of service, FY91 and trends, annual rpt, S0700–2.3

California AFDC recipients by selected characteristics, June 1988-90, annual planning rpt, S0830–2

Florida statistical abstract, general data, 1992 annual rpt, U6660–1

Georgia statistical abstract, general data, 1992-93 biennial rpt, U6730–1

Hawaii data book, general data, 1992 annual rpt, S2090–1

Maryland medical assistance payments and recipients, by program, type of service, location, demographic characteristics, and facility, FY92 and trends, annual rpt, S3635–3

Michigan ADC children served, by age and county, monthly rpt semiannual tables, S4010–1.503, S4010–1.505

Michigan children in day care, by age group and county, monthly rpt quarterly tables, S4010–1

Michigan welfare registrants by age, June 1992, annual planning rpt, S3980–1.2

New York State public assistance recipients and adoptions, by sex and age, 1991, annual rpt, S5800–2

New York State statistical yearbook, general data, 1992 annual rpt, U5100–1

Oklahoma public welfare program recipients and payments, and recipient characteristics, by county and type of service, FY92, annual rpt, S6455–1.2

Pennsylvania statistical abstract, general data, 1992 recurring rpt, U4130–6

Texas Medicaid expenditures by category, and recipient characteristics and medical services received, 1975 and 1980-91, U8850–8.5

Utah homeless shelter population characteristics, individual shelter capacity, and related housing data, 1991-92, annual rpt, S7808–2

Washington State public assistance clients and service costs, by client characteristics, program, and county, FY90, annual rpt, S8420–2

West Virginia welfare and social service programs, including number of children in foster care, by age, monthly rpt, S8560–2

Recreation and Leisure

Amusement park seasonal employment by age group, with detail for miniature golf and waterparks, 1992, annual rpt, A5700–1

Participation in 53 sports, by demographic characteristics, State, and census div, 1992, annual rpt series, A8485–3

Sporting goods purchaser characteristics, by product category, 1992, annual survey rpt, A8485–4

Sporting goods purchases, by product and outlet type, census div, and purchaser characteristics, with average prices, 1992 and trends, annual survey, A8485–2

Science and Technology

Chemist and chemical engineer salaries, employment status, and demographic and professional characteristics, 1993, annual rpt, A1250–4

Chemist salaries and employment, by employee and employer characteristics, Mar 1993 and trends, annual article, A1250–1.532

Chemistry and chemical engineering grad starting salaries, employment status, demographic characteristics, and advanced study plans, 1991/92, annual rpt, A1250–2

Ecologist personal and professional characteristics, including research activity and funding, with data by field, Mar 1992 survey, recurring rpt, A4685–1

High-technology industry CEO characteristics, and views on mgmt issues including compensation and foreign trade, June 1992 survey, B4490–2.34

Physics and astronomy bachelor degree recipients postgraduation plans and demographic characteristics, 1991/92 and trends, annual survey, A1960–3

Physics and astronomy grads employment status, by sex, age, subfield, citizenship, degree, and employer type, with salary info, 1990/91, annual rpt, A1960–1

Psychology doctoral degree recipient employment and demographic characteristics, and finances, 1990/91, biennial survey rpt, A2620–4

Transportation and Travel

Aircraft pilots by age and type of certificate, 1992, annual rpt, A5120–2.2

Airline travel frequency, destination, and purpose, by traveler characteristics, 1992 survey and trends, annual rpt, A0325–6

Auto customer preference for US vs Japanese cars, by age, 1993 survey article, C2150–3.508

Auto do-it-yourself (DIY) maintenance activity, by type and consumer characteristics, 1993 and trends, annual survey, C0125–1.506

Index by Categories

BY AGE

Auto maintenance activity by consumer age, for imported vehicle owners, 1991 and 1993 surveys, annual article, C2150–10.508

Auto purchasing and plans, including makes most likely to be purchased, by age group, 1993 survey article, C2710–1.539

Business traveler and trip characteristics, including mode, purpose, and lodging, 1991, annual rpt, R9375–12

Motor vehicle drivers, accident involvement, and fatally injured drunk drivers, by age, 1991 and trends, annual rpt, A5650–1.4

Motor vehicle fleet manager earnings, and personal and professional characteristics, 1993 article, C1575–2.506

Motor vehicle ownership and use patterns by owner characteristics, and licensed drivers, 1990s and trends, annual rpt, A0865–1

Motorcycle use and user characteristics, licensed operators, and State requirements, 1992 annual rpt, A6485–1.2

Public transportation riders distribution by age group, 1993 article, C1575–3.505

School bus loading/unloading accident fatalities, by circumstances, location, and victim age and sex, 1991 and trends, annual rpt, S3040–2

School bus loading/unloading accident fatalities, by victim age, 1969-91, annual feature, C1575–1.502

School bus loading/unloading accident fatalities, by victim age, 1969-92, article, C1575–1.501

Traffic accidents, fatalities, and injuries, by vehicle type, circumstances, location, and driver and victim characteristics, 1992 and trends, annual rpt, A8375–2.3

Travel trips and traveler characteristics, including mode, purpose, type of lodging, and area of destination and origin, quarterly rpt, R9375–14

Traveler and trip characteristics, 1990, annual rpt, C2140–1.2

Trucks (light) accessory purchasing, and owner characteristics, 1993 annual survey feature, C2150–10.506

State and local:

Alabama traffic accidents, fatalities, and injuries, by circumstances, vehicle type, and driver and victim characteristics, 1992, annual rpt, S0185–1

Alaska traffic accidents, fatalities, and injuries, by vehicle type, circumstance, location, and driver and victim characteristics, 1991 and trends, annual rpt, S0360–1

Arizona traffic accidents, fatalities, and injuries, by vehicle type, circumstances, location, and driver and victim characteristics, 1991 and trends, annual rpt, S0530–1

Arkansas traffic accidents, fatalities, and injuries, by vehicle type, circumstances, location, and driver and victim characteristics, 1991, annual rpt, S0692–1

California statistical abstract, general data, 1992 annual rpt, S0840–2

California traffic accidents, fatalities, and injuries, by vehicle type, circumstances, location, and driver and victim characteristics, 1991 and trends, annual rpt, S0885–1

Connecticut traffic accidents, fatalities, and injuries, by vehicle type, circumstance, location, and driver and victim characteristics, 1992, annual rpt, S1275–1

Delaware traffic accidents, fatalities, and injuries, by circumstances, location, and vehicle type, and driver and victim characteristics, 1992 and trends, annual rpt, S1435–1

Florida statistical abstract, general data, 1992 annual rpt, U6660–1

Florida traffic accidents, fatalities, and injuries, by vehicle type, circumstance, location, and driver and victim characteristics, 1992 and trends, annual rpt, S1750–2

Hawaii data book, general data, 1992 annual rpt, S2090–1

Hawaii motor vehicle drivers registered, and persons involved in accidents, by sex and/or age, 1986, annual rpt, S2125–1

Idaho traffic accidents, fatalities, and injuries, by circumstances, location, vehicle type, and driver and victim characteristics, 1992, annual rpt, S2315–1

Illinois traffic accidents, fatalities, and injuries, by circumstances, location, and driver and victim characteristics, 1991 and trends, annual rpt, S2540–1

Indiana traffic accidents, fatalities, and injuries, by circumstances, location, and vehicle type, and driver and victim characteristics, 1992, annual rpt, S2675–1

Kansas licensed drivers, by age group, 1991, annual rpt, S3020–1

Kansas traffic accidents, fatalities, and injuries, by vehicle type, location, circumstances, and driver and victim characteristics, 1992, annual rpt, S3040–1

Kentucky traffic accidents, fatalities, and injuries, by circumstances, location, vehicle type, and driver characteristics, 1992 and trends, annual rpt, S3150–2

Louisiana traffic accidents, fatalities, and injuries, by circumstances, location, and driver characteristics, 1991 and trends, annual rpt, S3345–2

Maine traffic accidents, fatalities, and injuries, by accident circumstances, vehicle type and make, and driver and victim characteristics, 1992, annual rpt, S3475–2

Maryland traffic accidents, fatalities, and injuries, by circumstances, location, vehicle type, and driver and victim characteristics, 1992, annual rpt, S3665–4

Michigan traffic accidents, fatalities, and injuries, by vehicle type, circumstance, location, and driver and victim characteristics, 1991 and trends, annual rpt, S3997–2

Minnesota traffic accidents, fatalities, and injuries, by type of vehicle and circumstances, and driver and victim characteristics, 1992 and trends, annual rpt, S4230–2

Missouri traffic accidents, fatalities, and injuries, by circumstances, location, and driver and victim characteristics, 1992 and trends, annual rpt, S4560–1

Montana traffic accidents, fatalities, and injuries, by circumstances, location, and driver and victim characteristics, 1992 and trends, annual rpt, S4705–2

Nebraska traffic accidents, fatalities, and injuries, by circumstances, location, vehicle type, and driver and victim characteristics, 1992, annual rpt, S4953–1

Nevada drivers and pedestrians involved in traffic accidents, by age, 1992, annual rpt, S5140–1

Nevada statistical abstract, general data, 1992 biennial rpt, S5005–1

New Jersey fatal traffic accidents and fatalities, by vehicle type, location, and circumstances, and driver and victim characteristics, 1992 and trends, annual rpt, S5430–2

New Mexico licensed drivers, by sex, age, and county, July 1990-92, annual rpt, S5660–1.2

New Mexico traffic accidents, fatalities, and injuries, by vehicle type, circumstances, location, and driver and victim characteristics, 1992 and trends, annual rpt, S5665–1

New York State statistical yearbook, general data, 1992 annual rpt, U5100–1

New York State traffic accidents, fatalities, and injuries, by circumstances, location, vehicle type, and driver and victim characteristics, 1991 and trends, annual rpt, S5790–1

North Carolina traffic accidents, fatalities, and injuries, by circumstances, location, vehicle type, and driver and victim characteristics, 1992 and trends, annual rpt, S5990–1

North Dakota traffic accidents, fatalities, and injuries, by circumstances, location, vehicle type, and driver and victim characteristics, 1992 and trends, annual rpt, S6217–1

Ohio traffic accidents, fatalities, and injuries, by circumstances, location, driver and victim characteristics, and vehicle type, 1991 and trends, annual rpt, S6290–1

Oklahoma statistical abstract, general data, 1992 annual rpt, U8130–2

Oklahoma traffic accidents, fatalities, and injuries, by circumstances, location, and driver and victim characteristics, 1992 and trends, annual rpt, S6482–1

Pennsylvania traffic accidents, fatalities, and injuries, by circumstances, location, driver characteristics, and vehicle type, 1991, annual rpt, S6905–3

Rhode Island traffic accidents, fatalities, and injuries, by circumstances, community, and driver and victim characteristics, 1992, annual rpt, S7025–1

South Carolina statistical abstract, general data, 1993 annual rpt, S7125–1

South Carolina traffic accidents, fatalities, and injuries, by circumstances, location, and driver and victim characteristics, 1992 and trends, annual rpt, S7190–2

South Dakota traffic accidents, fatalities, and injuries, by circumstances, location, vehicle type, and driver and victim characteristics, 1992 and trends, annual rpt, S7300–3

Tennessee statistical abstract, general data, 1992/93 annual rpt, U8710–2

Utah traffic accidents and fatalities by circumstances, location, driver and victim characteristics, and vehicle type, 1992 and trends, annual rpt, S7890–2

Virginia traffic accidents, fatalities, and injuries, by circumstances, location, and driver and victim characteristics, 1991 and trends, annual rpt, S8282–1

Washington State traffic accidents, fatalities, and injuries, by circumstances, vehicle type, and location, with driver and victim characteristics, 1992 and trends, annual rpt, S8428–1

BY AGE

West Virginia statistical handbook, general data, 1992 annual rpt, R9385–1
West Virginia traffic accidents, fatalities, and injuries, by circumstance and location, and driver and victim characteristics, 1992, annual rpt, S8645–1
Wisconsin Blue Book, general data, 1993-94 biennial rpt, S8780–1.2
Wisconsin traffic accidents, fatalities, and injuries, by circumstances, location, vehicle type, and driver and victim characteristics, 1992 and trends, annual rpt, S8815–1
Wyoming traffic accidents, fatalities, and injuries, by circumstances, location, vehicle type, and driver and victim characteristics, 1992 and trends, annual rpt, S9007–1

Veterans Affairs

State and local:

Florida VA health facilities utilization, by patient characteristics and instn, FY90, annual rpt, U6660–1.20
Pennsylvania statistical abstract, general data, 1992 recurring rpt, U4130–6

BY DISEASE

Agriculture and Food

Calf deaths and related costs, by disease, 1987/88 Colorado study, article, A3100–2.518

Education

Higher education enrollment of disabled students, by sex and type of disability, 1983-91, recurring rpt, A3960–2.1
Higher education freshmen with physical disabilities, by type, fall 1992, annual survey, U6215–1

State and local:

Arizona special education expenditures by program type, by county and school district, 1991/92, annual rpt, S0470–1
Delaware special education enrollment by type of handicap, school, and district, Sept 1991, annual rpt, S1430–1.2
Illinois special education enrollment, by age and type of handicap, 1990/91, annual rpt, S2440–1.1
Louisiana special education enrollment, by type of handicap and district, 1991/92, annual rpt, S3280–1.2
Maryland special education enrollment by county and disability, 1991/92, annual rpt, S3610–1
Missouri special education students served, by type of handicap, FY92, annual rpt, S4505–1.1
Nevada statistical abstract, general data, 1992 biennial rpt, S5005–1.7
North Carolina special education enrollment, by type of handicap and local district, 1992/93, annual rpt, S5915–1.1
Ohio special education enrollment, by age and type of handicap, Dec 1991, annual rpt, S6265–2
South Dakota special education students, by handicapping condition, 1991/92, annual rpt, S7315–1.1
Tennessee special education enrollment, by county, city, district, and type of handicap, 1991/92, annual rpt, S7490–2.3
Utah special education enrollment, by type of handicap and school district, 1991/92, annual rpt, S7815–1.2
Wyoming special education students, by disability and district, 1992, annual rpt, S8890–1.2

Index by Categories

Health and Vital Statistics

Accidental deaths and disabling injuries, by detailed type, victim characteristics, circumstances, and location, 1992 and trends, annual rpt, A8375–2
Africa military personnel hospital admissions and deaths due to selected diseases, for African troops serving in UK army, 1819-36, article, A2623–1.502
AIDS victims reported causes of death, including mention of AIDS on death certificates by patient characteristics, 1987-89, article, A2623–1.512
Black American health and vital statistics data, with comparisons to whites, 1970s-91, annual compilation, C6775–2.2
Child welfare indicators, including incidence of 4 preventable childhood diseases, and youth death rates by leading cause, 1992 annual rpt, R3840–11.1
Death rates for leading causes, and leading diagnoses in Medicare hospitalizations, 1993 annual fact book, A1275–1.5
Death rates for selected leading causes, by State, 1990, semiannual rpt, B8500–1.9
Deaths by leading cause, 1991 and trends, biennial fact book, A1325–1.6
Deaths by selected cause, for industrialized vs developing countries, 1992/93 biennial rpt, R9455–1.2
Drugs under dev for selected diseases affecting older adults and women, 1989-93, A1865–1.519
Eye bank activity, including donors by cause of death, and patients needing corneal transplants by diagnosis, 1992, annual rpt, A4743–1
Health voluntary agency finances, for approx 35 organizations associated with specific diseases, FY90, annual rpt, A7973–1
Hospital patient admission rates and length of stay, by diagnosis and procedure, payment source, age, sex, and region, 1991, B4455–4
Hospital patient admissions, length of stay, operative procedures, and discharges by patient characteristics, 1990 or 1991 and trends, annual fact book, A1275–1.2
Hospital patient charges and length of stay, by diagnosis and procedure, payment source, age, and region, 1991, B4455–5
Hospital patient discharges and length of stay, by diagnosis, type of operation, age, and region, 1991, annual rpt series, B4455–1
Hospital patient discharges and length of stay, by diagnostic related group (DRG), payment source, age, and region, 1991, annual rpt series, B4455–3
Hospital psychiatric patient discharges and length of stay, by diagnosis, age, sex, and region, 1991, annual rpt series, B4455–2
Incidence of illness and injury, and hospitalization and mortality data, by selected demographic characteristics, 1992 annual rpt, A5173–2.4
Infant deaths from 9 leading causes, 1993 feature, C4215–1.511
Infant mortality rates by leading cause of death, by race, 1989, annual rpt, R3840–5.1
Latin America statistical abstract, general data by country, 1992 annual rpt, U6250–1.6

Occupational injuries/illnesses and fatalities, lost workdays, and employee views on workplace safety, with data by State, 1992 annual rpt, R8335–1.1
Older men deaths by cause, by smoking and drinking habits, race, and occupation, 1966-90, U3780–9
Older population incidence of selected medical conditions, by urban-rural status, 1993 article, A1865–1.522
Research expenditures by NIH, and incidence, for cystic fibrosis, multiple sclerosis, muscular dystrophy, and scleroderma, 1993 article, C5800–7.546
Sexually transmitted disease incidence, risk, and govt funding data, by disease, 1993 rpt, A5160–10
Sweden infant mortality rates, by cause and characteristics of mother, 1983-86, article, A2623–1.503

State and local:

Alabama public health dept activities, including services provided, inspection and licensing activity, staff and finances, and vital statistics and health data, 1992 annual rpt, S0175–3
Alabama statistical abstract, general data, 1992 recurring rpt, U5680–2.8, U5680–2.17
Alabama vital statistics, including population, births, deaths by cause, marriages, and divorces, by location and demographic characteristics, 1992 and trends, annual rpt, S0175–2
Alaska vital statistics, including births, deaths by cause, marriages, divorces, adoptions, and population, by demographic characteristics and location, 1990, annual rpt, S0315–1
Arizona statistical abstract, general data, 1993 recurring rpt, U5850–2.3
Arkansas vital statistics, including births, deaths by cause, marriages, and divorces, by age, sex, race, and county, 1991 and trends, annual rpt, S0685–1
California death rates and estimated alcohol-related mortality, by cause and demographic characteristics, 1980-89, article, A2623–1.508
California statistical abstract, general data, 1992 annual rpt, S0840–2.5
California vital statistics, including population, births, and deaths by cause, by demographic characteristics and county, 1990 and trends, annual rpt, S0865–1
Colorado vital statistics, including population, births, deaths by cause, abortion, marriage and divorce, and adoption, by demographic characteristics and location, 1990 and trends, annual rpt, S1010–1
Connecticut vital statistics, including births, deaths by cause, marriages, and divorces, by demographic characteristics and location, 1989, annual rpt, S1200–1
DC statistical profile, general data, 1992 annual rpt, S1535–3.5
Delaware vital statistics, including births, deaths by cause, and marriages and dissolutions, by demographic characteristics and location, 1990, annual rpt, S1385–2
Florida county data book, 1992/93 annual rpt, C6360–1
Florida deaths by cause, communicable disease incidence, and hospital utilization, 1992 annual rpt, S1746–1

Index by Categories

BY DISEASE

Florida statistical abstract, general data, 1992 annual rpt, U6660–1.3

Florida vital statistics, including population, births, deaths by cause, and marriages and dissolutions, by location and demographic characteristics, 1992 and trends, annual rpt, S1745–3

Georgia county guide, general data, 1993 annual rpt, U6750–1

Georgia statistical abstract, general data, 1992-93 biennial rpt, U6730–1.1

Georgia vital statistics, including deaths by cause, demographic characteristics, and location, 1991 and trends, annual rpt, S1895–1.2

Hawaii data book, general data, 1992 annual rpt, S2090–1.2

Hawaii health dept activities and services, including vital statistics and disease control, by location, 1990, annual rpt, S2065–1

Idaho vital statistics, including births, deaths by cause, abortions, marriages, and divorces, by demographic characteristics and county, 1991 and trends, annual rpt, S2250–2

Illinois mental health facility patient population and characteristics, by facility, location, and treatment category, FY93, annual rpt, S2505–1

Illinois statistical abstract, general data, 1992 annual rpt, U6910–2

Iowa vital statistics, including population, births, deaths by cause, marriages, and divorces, by demographic characteristics and location, 1991 and trends, annual rpt, S2795–1

Kansas vital statistics, including population, births, deaths by cause, abortions, marriages, and divorces, by demographic characteristics and location, 1991 and trends, annual rpt, S2975–1

Kentucky vital statistics, including births, deaths by cause, marriages and divorces, and population, by demographic characteristics and county, 1991, annual rpt, S3140–1

Louisiana vital statistics, including population, births, deaths by cause, reportable diseases, marriages, and divorces, by demographic characteristics and locality, 1989-90 and trends, annual rpt, S3295–1

Maine vital statistics, including births, deaths by cause, abortions, and marriages and divorces, by demographic characteristics and location, 1991 and trends, annual rpt, S3460–2

Maryland statistical abstract, general data, 1993-94 biennial rpt, S3605–1.1

Maryland vital statistics, including population, births, deaths by cause, marriages, and divorces, by demographic characteristics and location, 1989 and trends, annual rpt, S3635–1

Massachusetts vital statistics, including births, deaths by cause, marriages, divorces, and population, by locality and demographic characteristics, 1990 and trends, annual rpt, S3850–1

Michigan vital statistics, including births, deaths, marriages, divorces/annulments, and communicable diseases, by location and demographic characteristics, 1990 and trends, annual rpt, S4000–3

Minnesota vital statistics, including population, births, abortions, deaths, marriages, and divorces, by location and demographic characteristics, 1991 and trends, annual rpt, S4190–2

Mississippi statistical abstract, general data, 1992 annual rpt, U3255–4.2

Mississippi vital statistics, including births, deaths by cause, marriages, and divorces, by demographic characteristics and location, 1992 and trends, annual rpt, S4350–1

Missouri vital statistics, including population, births, deaths by cause, and marriages and divorces, by location and demographic characteristics, 1992 and trends, annual rpt, S4518–1

Montana vital statistics, including births, deaths by cause, abortion, disease, and marriage and divorce, by demographic characteristics and county, 1990-91 and trends, annual rpt, S4690–1

Nebraska vital statistics, including births, deaths, marriages, divorces, and population, by demographic characteristics and location, 1991 and trends, annual rpt, S4885–1

Nevada statistical abstract, general data, 1992 biennial rpt, S5005–1.2

Nevada vital statistics, including births, abortions, and deaths by cause, by county and demographic characteristics, 1989 and trends, annual rpt, S5075–1

New Hampshire vital statistics, including population, births, deaths by cause, marriages, and divorces, by location and demographic characteristics, 1991 and trends, annual rpt, S5215–1

New Jersey vital statistics, including births, deaths, population, communicable diseases, and marriages and divorces, by demographic characteristics and location, 1990 and trends, annual rpt, S5405–1

New Mexico vital statistics, including population, births, deaths, and disease, by location and demographic characteristics, 1991 and trends, annual rpt, S5605–1

New York State statistical yearbook, general data, 1992 annual rpt, U5100–1

New York State vital statistics, including population, births, deaths by cause, reportable diseases, and marriages and dissolutions, by demographic characteristics and/or location, 1990 and trends, annual rpt, S5765–1

North Carolina deaths and rates, by cause and county, 1991 and trends, annual rpt, S5927–1.2

North Dakota vital statistics, including births, deaths by cause, marriages and divorces, and abortions, by demographic characteristics and/or county, 1991 and trends, annual rpt, S6105–2

Ohio vital statistics, including births, deaths by cause, marriages, divorces, and population, by demographic characteristics and location, 1991 and trends, annual rpt, S6285–1

Oklahoma statistical abstract, general data, 1992 annual rpt, U8130–2.9

Oregon vital statistics, including births, deaths by cause, communicable diseases, marriages, and divorces, by age, sex, race-ethnicity, and county, 1991 and trends, annual rpt, S6615–5

Pennsylvania statistical abstract, general data, 1992 recurring rpt, U4130–6.1

Rhode Island vital statistics, including population, births, deaths, marriages, and divorces, by demographic characteristics and locality, 1989 and trends, annual rpt, S6995–1

South Carolina deaths, by detailed cause, age, sex, and race, 1990, annual rpt, S7175–2

South Carolina statistical abstract, general data, 1993 annual rpt, S7125–1.10, S7125–1.16

South Carolina vital statistics, including births, deaths by cause, marriages, and divorces, by age, sex, race, and location, 1990 and trends, annual rpt, S7175–1

South Dakota vital statistics, including births, deaths, marriage and divorce, and communicable disease, by demographic characteristics and county, 1991 and trends, annual rpt, S7345–1

Tennessee statistical abstract, general data, 1992/93 annual rpt, U8710–2.17

Tennessee vital statistics, including births, deaths by cause, marriages, divorces, and population, by demographic characteristics and location, 1991 and trends, annual rpt, S7520–2

Texas vital statistics, including births, deaths by cause, abortions, marriages, and divorces, by location and demographic characteristics, 1991 and trends, annual rpt, S7685–1

Utah statistical abstract, general data, 1993 triennial rpt, U8960–1.2

Utah vital statistics, including births, deaths by cause, and population, by county and demographic characteristics, 1990 and trends, annual rpt, S7835–1

Vermont vital statistics, including population, births, deaths by cause, abortions, marriages, and divorces, by location and demographic characteristics, 1991 and trends, annual rpt, S8054–1

Virginia vital statistics, including births, deaths by cause, marriages and divorces, and communicable disease, by demographic characteristics and location, 1991 and trends, annual rpt, S8225–1

Washington State vital statistics, including births, deaths by cause, and population, by demographic characteristics and location, 1991 and trends, annual rpt, S8363–1

West Virginia vital statistics, including births, deaths by cause, marriages, and divorces, by location and demographic characteristics, 1991 and trends, annual rpt, S8560–1

Wisconsin vital statistics, including population, births, deaths by cause, and marriages and dissolutions, by county and demographic characteristics, 1991 and trends, annual rpt, S8715–4

Wyoming vital statistics, including population, births, deaths by cause, marriages, and divorces, by demographic characteristics and county, 1991 and trends, annual rpt, S8920–2

Labor and Employment

State and local:

Arkansas vocational rehabilitation expenditures, impact on earnings and employment, and client characteristics, FY91 annual rpt, S0700–2.4

BY DISEASE

Maryland vocational rehabilitation case activity, by county and disability, 1992, annual rpt, S3610–1

Law Enforcement

Law school grad employment and salaries, for grads with selected disabilities, 1992, annual rpt, A6505–1

Public Welfare and Social Security

State and local:

Montana rehabilitation and visual services program caseload by type of disability, by county, monthly rpt quarterly table, S4755–1

Transportation and Travel

State and local:

New York State traffic fatalities and injuries, by injury type, 1991, annual rpt, S5790–1

BY EDUCATIONAL ATTAINMENT

Agriculture and Food

- Distilled spirits consumption, and consumer characteristics and buying habits, 1992 and trends, annual rpt, C4775–1.3
- Food nutrition awareness and health concerns, including shopping and consumption patterns, by respondent characteristics, 1993 survey, annual rpt, A4950–36
- Food service industry employee characteristics, and minority-owned establishments and sales, 1993 article, A8200–1.508
- Food take-out consumer characteristics, consumption patterns, and attitudes, May 1992 survey, A8200–21
- Food/beverage manufacturers mgmt salaries, by selected employee characteristics, 1992 survey, annual article, C2150–6.502
- Restaurant smoking policy importance to consumers, and views on smoking acceptability in restaurants and other public places, by selected characteristics, Jan 1993 survey, A8200–8.15
- Wine and other alcoholic beverage consumption, and consumer characteristics and buying habits, 1993 annual rpt, C4775–2.2

Banking, Finance, and Insurance

- Bank CEO demographic and professional characteristics, attitudes, and compensation, Apr 1992 survey, annual rpt, B4490–2.33
- Life insurance purchases and ownership, by consumer and household characteristics, 1991 and trends, biennial fact book, A1325–1.1
- Shareholders of NYSE member firms, by demographic characteristics and metro area, 1970s-90, annual fact book, B6625–1.1

State and local:

South Dakota accounting firm recruiters views on tax curriculum for accounting undergraduates, and degree levels of students hired, fall 1992 survey, article, U8595–1.504

Communications

- Direct marketing industry devs, including advertising patterns, finances, target market characteristics, and consumer attitudes, 1992/93 annual rpt, A4620–1
- News events followed most closely by public, and opinion on media coverage and selected current issues, by respondent characteristics, recurring rpt, C8915–1

Public opinion on the media and related issues, by respondent characteristics, series, C8915–11

- Telephone Yellow Pages directory use among consumers, with detail by respondent characteristics, 1992 survey, annual rpt, A9500–2
- **Education**
- Black American educational statistics, with comparisons to whites, 1970s-92, annual compilation, C6775–2.3
- Catholic vs public school performance, and support for parental school selection funded by govt, public opinion by respondent characteristics, July 1992 survey, A7375–8
- Elementary/secondary school superintendents personal and professional characteristics and views, 1992 survey rpt, A0775–5
- Elementary/secondary teachers staying at same school, changing schools, and leaving teaching, by school level and highest degree earned, 1988/89, R4800–2.502
- Foreign students enrolled in US higher education instns, by instn, State, country of origin, and demographic characteristics, 1991/92 and trends, annual rpt, R5580–1
- General Educational Dev (GED) examinees by highest grade completed, by jurisdiction, 1992, annual rpt, A1410–16
- Higher education degrees awarded, by level, sex, race-ethnicity, and field, 1990s and trends, recurring rpt, A3960–2.1
- Higher education degrees conferred, by level, sex, discipline, and race-ethnicity, 1990/91, recurring feature, C2175–1.523
- Higher education faculty characteristics, including highest degree earned and parent educational attainment, 1990, recurring rpt, A3960–2.2
- Higher education freshmen parental income, occupations, and education, by student sex and instn type, fall 1992, annual survey, U6215–1
- Higher education instns, faculty, students, degrees, and finances, detailed data by State, 1993 annual rpt, C2175–1.531
- Higher education president personal and professional characteristics, 1990 and trends, recurring rpt, A1410–12
- Higher education president personal and professional characteristics, 1990, article, C2175–1.533
- Hispanic American educational statistics, with comparisons to whites, 1970s-92, annual compilation, C6775–3.2
- Japan higher education foreign students, with detail for US students by funding source, by academic level, 1993 article, R5650–2.527
- Librarians (special) salaries, by location, work setting, and personal characteristics, US and Canada, 1992 and trends, biennial survey rpt, A8965–1
- Mathematics proficiency results on Natl Assessment of Educational Progress tests, by parental education, 1990, article, U8710–1.503
- Parent expectations of their 8th grade children's ultimate educational attainment, 1988, article, R4800–2.509
- Scholastic Aptitude Test (SAT) participants and/or scores, by education of parents, income, and race-ethnicity, 1992, C4215–1.501

State and local:

Index by Categories

- Arizona librarians by educational attainment, by library and county, FY92, annual rpt, S0495–1
- Arkansas higher education degrees conferred, by level, discipline, student race and sex, and instn, 1990/91 and trends, annual rpt, S0690–3
- Colorado public school staff and salaries, by selected characteristics, county, and district, fall 1992 and trends, annual rpt, S1000–2.2
- DC public school teacher salaries by degree level, 1987/88-1991/92, annual rpt, S1605–2
- DC statistical profile, general data, 1992 annual rpt, S1535–3
- Delaware educational personnel by degree level, 1991/92, annual rpt, S1430–1.3
- Florida statistical abstract, general data, 1992 annual rpt, U6660–1
- Idaho public school personnel characteristics and salaries by position, and teachers and enrollment by school district, 1992/93, annual rpt, S2225–3
- Illinois higher education enrollment and degrees, by level, instn, field of instruction, and student characteristics, 1992 and trends, annual rpt, S2475 1.1
- Iowa postsecondary enrollment, degrees, staff, and finances, by instn, 1990/91, annual rpt, S2755–1
- Iowa public library professional staff, by highest degree attained, FY92, annual rpt, S2778–1
- Kentucky higher education enrollment, degrees, staff, and finances, by State-supported instn, 1983-92, annual rpt, S3130–3
- Louisiana public school instructional staff by degree level, 1989/90-1991/92, annual rpt, S3280–1.1
- Maryland elementary and secondary education data, by county, 1992/93, annual rpt, S3610–2.1
- Maryland statistical abstract, general data, 1993-94 biennial rpt, S3605–1
- Massachusetts public library employees by educational attainment, FY92 annual rpt, S3870–1
- Mississippi higher education enrollment and degrees, by level and field, and finances, by State-supported instn, 1991/92, annual rpt, S4360–1
- Missouri higher education degrees conferred, by level, sex, race-ethnicity, instn, and field of study, FY92 and trends, annual rpt, S4520–3.3
- Missouri public school administrators and teachers, by degree level, 1991/92, annual rpt, S4505–1.1
- New Hampshire public school teacher salary schedules, by professional degree level and school district, 1992/93, annual table, S5200–1.3
- New Jersey public school teachers, administrators, staff, and salaries, by county, 1991/92, annual rpt, S5385–1.2
- North Carolina higher education degrees conferred by level, and faculty by highest degree earned, by instn, 1991/92, annual rpt, U8013–1.2
- North Carolina public school staff characteristics, including highest degree held, 1992/93, annual rpt, S5915–1.1

Index by Categories

BY EDUCATIONAL ATTAINMENT

North Dakota elementary and secondary school staff characteristics and salaries, by position, region, and enrollment size, 1992/93 annual rpt, S6180–3

Ohio public school staff by degree status, 1981/82 and 1991/92, annual rpt, S6265–2

Oklahoma teachers by degree level and experience, 1991/92, annual rpt, S6423–1.2

Pennsylvania elementary/secondary and higher education enrollment, grads, staff, and finances, by instn type, 1981/82-1996/97, recurring rpt, S6790–5.10

Pennsylvania higher education degrees conferred, by level, sex, race-ethnicity, instn type, and field of study, 1990/91 and trends, annual rpt, S6790–5.2

Pennsylvania higher education degrees conferred, by level, sex, race-ethnicity, instn type, and field of study, 1991/92 and trends, annual rpt, S6790–5.15

Pennsylvania public school personnel and salary data, by position and district, 1992/93 and trends, annual rpt, S6790–5.12

Pennsylvania statistical abstract, general data, 1992 recurring rpt, U4130–6

Pennsylvania vocational education teachers by educational attainment and program, 1991/92, annual rpt, S6790–5.7

South Carolina educational employees and training, by school district, 1991/92, annual rpt, S7145–1.4

South Dakota public higher education degrees awarded, and faculty by degree level, by instn, FY93 annual rpt, S7375–1

South Dakota teacher salaries, by education, 1991/92, annual rpt, S7315–1.2

Tennessee higher education degrees conferred, by instn, recipient race-ethnicity and sex, and level, 1991/92, annual rpt, S7525–1.2

Tennessee public school teachers and educational level, by sex, county, city, and school district, 1991/92, annual rpt, S7490–2.1

Tennessee statistical abstract, general data, 1992/93 annual rpt, U8710–2

Utah statistical abstract, general data, 1993 triennial rpt, U8960–1

Vermont higher education degrees conferred, by level, field, sex, and instn, 1991/92 and trends, annual rpt, S8035–2.1

West Virginia higher education enrollment, degrees, faculty and student characteristics, and finances, by instn, 1992/93 and trends, annual rpt, S8533–1

West Virginia teachers and salaries, by degree level, 1992/93 and trends, annual rpt, S8540–4.2

West Virginia teachers by degree level, by county, 1991/92, annual rpt, S8540–3

Wisconsin, Milwaukee educational attainment of parents with children in public schools, and in private schools under school selection program, by sex, 1989/90-1990/91, R3810–7

Government and Defense

Black elected officials, and characteristics of voting age population, with comparisons to whites, 1970s-91, annual compilation, C6775–2.4

Hispanic American elected officials, registered voters, and voting, with comparisons to whites, 1970s-91, annual compilation, C6775–3.3

Hispanic American vs non-Hispanic voter turnout, by demographic characteristics, Nov 1992 election, article, C4575–1.511

House of Representatives staff characteristics, salaries, and benefits by position, 1992 and trends, recurring rpt, R4140–1

Municipal govt composition, including mayors by education level and race-ethnicity, 1991, A5800–1.1

Public opinion on issues concerning politics and the press, by respondent characteristics, series, C8915–4

State and local:

Wisconsin State legislators demographic characteristics, 1983-93, biennial rpt, S8780–1.1

Health and Vital Statistics

Alcohol abuse risk correlated with education, by age group, 1980-85 studies, article, A2623–1.508

China women's fertility patterns correlated with socioeconomic characteristics, in 6 Provinces, 1987, article, A5160–6.502

Contraceptive (oral) use errors among women in Botswana, Egypt, Zimbabwe, and Indonesia, by demographic characteristics, 1987-89 surveys, article, A5160–6.504

Dental school enrollment, by level of prior education and instn, 1992/93, annual rpt, A1475–3.1

Dental school 1st-year enrollment by level of predoctoral education, 1969/70-1992/93, annual rpt, A1475–4.2

Developing countries contraceptive failure rates, by user urban-rural residence and education, for 15 countries, 1986-89 surveys, article, A5160–6.504

Developing countries contraceptive use and tetanus vaccination rates for women, by selected characteristics, by country, various years, 1974-91, R8720–1

Developing countries fertility, family planning, sexual behavior, and child health indicators, with selected detail by demographic characteristics, 1984-92 surveys, U2520–1.51

Health care specialist and health-related company CEO income, public perceptions vs actual amounts, by respondent characteristics, 1991-93, R4865–13

Health condition and preventive health care and safety practices of adults, by respondent characteristics, 1992 and trends, annual survey rpt, C8111–2

Hospital personnel recruiter educational background, by region, 1993 and trends, annual survey rpt, A6500–1

Hysterectomy prevalence by women's demographic characteristics, 1988 surveys, article, A2623–1.503

Medical group mgmt compensation, by demographic and practice characteristics, 1992, annual rpt, A6365–3

Men's sexual behavior, including condom use, and AIDS knowledge and risks, by selected characteristics, 1991 survey, articles, A5160–1.503

Nursing center (community) staff and client characteristics, and services, 1990 survey, article, A8010–3.506

Nursing college deans and salaries, by personal and instn characteristics, 1992/93, annual rpt, A0615–2

Nursing school enrollment and grads, by degree level, sex, race-ethnicity, and instn type and location, 1992/93 and trends, annual rpt, A0615–4

Nursing schools, programs, enrollment, student and staff characteristics, and grads, 1991 and trends, annual rpt, A8010–1

Optometry school faculty, enrollment and degrees, policies and programs, and finances, by instn, 1991/92, annual survey, A3370–2

Osteopathy college enrollment, student and faculty characteristics, and finances, 1992/93 and trends, annual rpt, A0620–1

Pharmacy degree program applications, enrollment, and degrees conferred, by student characteristics and instn, 1990/91 and trends, annual rpt, A0630–9

Public health school applicant, student, and grad characteristics, by instn, 1991/92 and trends, annual rpt, A3372–3

Public health school faculty characteristics, by instn, fall 1991, recurring rpt, A3372–1

Sexual behavior among adults, including extramarital sex, condom use, and impact of AIDS, by demographic characteristics, 1990 survey, article, A2623–1.512

Sexual behavior among heterosexuals, including data on demographic characteristics, number of partners, and condom use, 1990/91 survey, article, A5160–1.506

Smoking acceptability in restaurants and other public places, and importance of restaurant smoking policy, views of consumers by selected characteristics, Jan 1993 survey, A8200–8.15

Smoking status of men and women by occupation, and smoker characteristics, 1985 and/or 1990, article, B6045–1.501

Sweden infant mortality rates, by cause and characteristics of mother, 1983-86, article, A2623–1.503

Women's use of mammography and Pap smear tests, by demographic characteristics, 1987 survey, article, A2623–1.503

Zambia student views on sexual behavior and treatment of persons infected with AIDS virus, by respondent characteristics, 1990 survey, article, A5160–6.503

State and local:

Alabama health behavior risk factor surveillance survey results, by respondent characteristics, 1988-89, recurring rpt, S0175–6

Alabama vital statistics, including population, births, deaths by cause, marriages, and divorces, by location and demographic characteristics, 1992 and trends, annual rpt, S0175–2

Alaska births, by mother's race and education, 1990, annual rpt, S0315–1

Colorado births, by characteristics of mother, 1990, annual rpt, S1010–1

Connecticut births by race-ethnicity and education of mother, 1989, annual rpt, S1200–1

Connecticut health insurance coverage rate, by respondent characteristics and behavior risk factors, 1991 survey, S1200–3

Delaware vital statistics, including births, deaths by cause, and marriages and dissolutions, by demographic characteristics and location, 1990, annual rpt, S1385–2

BY EDUCATIONAL ATTAINMENT

Georgia health behavior risk factor surveillance survey results, by respondent characteristics, 1991 and trends, annual rpt, S1895–2

Hawaii health dept activities and services, including vital statistics and disease control, by location, 1990, annual rpt, S2065–1

Idaho live births, by education of mother, onset of prenatal care, and county, 1991, annual rpt, S2250–2

Kansas marriages and dissolutions, by education of husband and wife, 1991, annual rpt, S2975–1

Kentucky births by characteristics of mother and child, by county, 1991, annual rpt, S3140–1

Kentucky health behavior risk factor surveillance survey results, by State area and respondent characteristics, 1988-90, annual rpt, S3140–6

Maine vital statistics, including births, deaths by cause, abortions, and marriages and divorces, by demographic characteristics and location, 1991 and trends, annual rpt, S3460–2

Massachusetts health behavior risk factor surveillance survey results, by respondent characteristics, 1986-90, recurring rpt, S3850–3

Michigan health behavior risk factor surveillance survey results, by respondent characteristics, 1991, annual rpt, S4000–4

Minnesota vital statistics, including population, births, abortions, deaths, marriages, and divorces, by location and demographic characteristics, 1991 and trends, annual rpt, S4190–2

Mississippi vital statistics, including births, deaths by cause, marriages, and divorces, by demographic characteristics and location, 1992 and trends, annual rpt, S4350–1

Missouri abortions by education of patient, 1992, annual rpt, S4518–1

Montana births by mothers education and number of children, 1990-91, annual rpt, S4690–1

Nebraska vital statistics, including births, deaths, marriages, divorces, and population, by demographic characteristics and location, 1991 and trends, annual rpt, S4885–1

Nevada health behavior risk factor surveillance survey results, by location and respondent characteristics, 1991, annual rpt, S5075–3

New Hampshire marriages by education of bride and groom, 1991, annual rpt, S5215–1

New Jersey births by educational attainment of mother and onset of prenatal care, 1990, annual rpt, S5405–1

New Mexico vital statistics, including population, births, deaths, and disease, by location and demographic characteristics, 1991 and trends, annual rpt, S5605–1

New York State health behavior risk factor surveillance survey results, by respondent characteristics, 1990, recurring rpt, S5765–3

North Dakota abortions, by demographic characteristics of patient, 1991, annual rpt, S6105–2

North Dakota health behavior risk factor surveillance survey results, by respondent characteristics, 1991 and trends, annual rpt, S6105–3

Ohio births by education, age, and race of mother, 1991, annual rpt, S6285–1

Oregon vital statistics, including births, deaths by cause, communicable diseases, marriages, and divorces, by age, sex, race-ethnicity, and county, 1991 and trends, annual rpt, S6615–5

Pennsylvania health behavior risk factor surveillance survey results, by respondent characteristics, 1991, annual rpt, S6820–4

Rhode Island marriages, by education of husband and wife, 1989, annual rpt, S6995–1

South Carolina births by educational attainment of mother, by county and race, 1990, annual rpt, S7175–1

South Carolina statistical abstract, general data, 1993 annual rpt, S7125–1

Tennessee health behavior risk factor surveillance survey results, by respondent characteristics, 1986-90, annual rpt, S7520–3

Texas health behavior risk factor surveillance survey results, by respondent characteristics, 1991 and trends, annual rpt, S7685–2

Texas nursing employment, demand outlook, earnings, and education, by selected characteristics, various years 1971-91, U8850–8.2

Utah health behavior risk factor surveillance survey results, by respondent characteristics, 1991, annual rpt, S7835–3

Utah marriages and divorces, by participant characteristics and location, 1990 and trends, annual rpt, S7835–2

Utah vital statistics, including births by characteristics of child and parents, by location, 1990, annual rpt, S7835–1.2

Vermont vital statistics, including population, births, deaths by cause, abortions, marriages, and divorces, by location and demographic characteristics, 1991 and trends, annual rpt, S8054–1

Virginia vital statistics, including births, deaths by cause, marriages and divorces, and communicable disease, by demographic characteristics and location, 1991 and trends, annual rpt, S8225–1

Washington State hypertension incidence by selected socioeconomic characteristics, 1990, annual rpt, S8363–1

West Virginia births by education of mother and level of prenatal care, 1991, annual rpt, S8560–1

Wisconsin births by education and race-ethnicity of mother, 1991, annual rpt, S8715–4

Wyoming births by onset of prenatal care, age and education of mother, and county, 1991, annual rpt, S8920–2

Housing and Construction

Real estate property managers characteristics and compensation, including types of property managed, 1989 surveys, recurring rpt, A5600–4

Income

Black American earnings, income, and poverty data, with comparisons to whites, 1980s-91, annual compilation, C6775–2.7

Index by Categories

College grad job and salary offers, by field of study, type of employer and occupation, and degree level, by region, interim rpt series, A3940–1

College grad job and salary offers, by field of study, type of employer and occupation, and degree level, series, A3940–2

Hispanic American income and poverty data, with comparisons to whites, 1980s-91, annual compilation, C6775–3.5

Income of full-time adult workers, by sex and education, 1979-89, annual rpt, S7125–1.6

Logistics manager salaries, by position, industry, and selected characteristics, Nov 1992 survey, annual article, C1850–11

Planning profession employment and salaries, by type of employer, demographic and professional characteristics, and location, 1991 and trends, biennial rpt, A2615–1

Poor children age 5/under, with demographic and family characteristics, 1990 and trends, annual rpt, U1260–2

Professional worker salaries, by employee and employer characteristics, with detail for scientists and engineers, 1990s and trends, biennial rpt, A3960–1

Salaries of new college grads, by degree level and field, 1991/92-1992/93, annual rpt, A3940–3

White-collar work force trends, including employment, earnings, and unionization, with data by occupation, sex, and educational attainment, 1990s and trends, annual rpt, A1570–1

Women's employment and earnings, with comparisons to men, and detail by occupation and worker characteristics, 1990s and trends, annual rpt, A1570–2

Industry and Commerce

Canada photographic and video equipment and supplies ownership, purchasing patterns, and use, by household characteristics, 1992 survey, recurring rpt, A8695–4

CEO characteristics and compensation, for small companies with rapid growth, 1993 survey article, C5800–7.551

Private label product characteristics and purchasing factors as seen by consumers, by selected characteristics, 1991 survey, article, C0125–1.504

Retail outlet consumer preference indexes, by selected demographic characteristics, 1993 annual feature, C4655–1.504

Security equipment industry personnel income, education, work conditions, and activities, 1993 survey, annual article, C1850–13.510

Labor and Employment

Black American labor force and employment data, with comparisons to whites, 1970s-91, annual compilation, C6775–2.6

College grad job and salary offers, by field of study, type of employer and occupation, and degree level, by region, interim rpt series, A3940–1

College grad job and salary offers, by field of study, type of employer and occupation, and degree level, series, A3940–2

Employee views on most important job aspects, by education, 1992 survey article, C4687–1.501

Employment in business and industry, hiring plans for college grads, by field, salary, and degree, 1993 annual survey rpt, U3730–1

Index by Categories

BY EDUCATIONAL ATTAINMENT

Labor force by educational attainment, sex, and age group, by State, 1990, article, U8960–2.509

Men age 18-29 employment in manufacturing, by education, 1973 and 1986, annual rpt, R8335–1.1

Minority population characteristics, employment, and voting patterns by detailed race-ethnicity, with comparisons to whites, 1980s-2040, R8750–2.58

White-collar work force trends, including employment, earnings, and unionization, with data by occupation, sex, and educational attainment, 1990s and trends, annual rpt, A1570–1

Women and minorities in professional fields, detailed education and labor force data, 1980s-91, with historical trends, recurring rpt, A3960–2

State and local:

Arkansas vocational rehabilitation expenditures, impact on earnings and employment, and client characteristics, FY91 annual rpt, S0700–2.4

Colorado job service applicant characteristics, FY93 annual planning rpt, S1040–3.2

DC statistical profile, general data, 1992 annual rpt, S1535–3

Mississippi characteristics of economically disadvantaged and Job Training Partnership Act eligible population, 1993/94, annual planning rpt, S4345–1.3

New Jersey unemployment insurance repeat claimant characteristics, 1984-88, article, S5425–1.505

Vermont labor force by employment status, and job service openings and applicant characteristics, 1993 annual planning rpt, S8025–2.2

Law Enforcement

Incarcerated mothers and their children, with data on characteristics, child caregivers, visitation, and support program use, 1991/92, A7575–4

State and local:

Arizona correctional instn admin, including inmates by criminal background and demographic characteristics, FY92, annual rpt, S0464–2

Florida correctional instns, admin, and inmates by criminal background and demographic characteristics, FY92 annual rpt, S1720–1

Florida "habitual offender" sentencing laws effect on prison population, with data by circuit court and offender characteristics, 1993 rpt, A7575–5

Georgia correctional instns, admin, and inmate characteristics, FY92, annual rpt, S1872–1

Iowa correctional instn admissions, releases, and inmate characteristics, by instn, monthly rpt, S2770–1

Kansas correctional instn inmates, by offense, demographic characteristics, and instn, FY92 and trends, annual rpt, S2940–1

Kansas law enforcement employees by demographic characteristics and local agency, with assaults on police by circumstance, 1992, annual rpt, S2925–1.2

Kansas statistical abstract, general data, 1991/92 annual rpt, U7095–2

Massachusetts correctional instn inmate socioeconomic characteristics and criminal background, by instn, Jan 1992 and trends, annual rpt, S3805–1

Missouri correctional instn admissions, releases, and inmate characteristics, FY93, annual rpt, S4501–1

New York State correctional instn inmate population and characteristics, and probation and parole, 1991 and trends, annual rpt, S5760–3.4

New York State local jail/penitentiary inmates by offense, sentence, and demographic characteristics, by county or facility, 1991, annual rpt, S5724–2

New York State statistical yearbook, general data, 1992 annual rpt, U5100–1

North Carolina correctional instn admissions, separations, and population, with inmate characteristics, FY93, semiannual rpt, S5900–1

South Dakota correctional instn admin, including inmates by criminal background and demographic characteristics, FY92 and trends, annual rpt, S7296–1

Texas appellate and trial judge demographic characteristics, Sept 1992, annual rpt, S7703–1

Texas correctional instn inmates by criminal background and demographic characteristics, FY92, annual rpt, S7660–1

Utah corrections inmates, parolees, and probationers, by criminal background and demographic characteristics, FY92 and trends, annual rpt, S7810–1

Wisconsin correctional instn inmates, by criminal background and selected characteristics, series, S8692–1

Wyoming correctional instn admin, finances, inmate characteristics, and staff, and probation and parole activities, FY92 annual rpt, S8883–1

Population

Black American socioeconomic status, including health, education, politics, crime, and employment, with comparisons to whites, 1993 annual compilation, C6775–2

Black children and youth population, economic, health, and education data, with comparisons to whites, 1993 rpt, R3840–21

Children's living arrangements, by parents characteristics and child age and race-ethnicity, 1992, article, B6045–1.504

Children's living arrangements, by parents characteristics and child race-ethnicity, 1991, article, B6045–1.503

Gallup Poll public attitude surveys, results and sample characteristics, monthly rpt, C4040–1

Hispanic American socioeconomic status, including education, politics, income, and employment, with comparisons to whites, 1993 annual compilation, C6775–3

Latin America statistical abstract, general data by country, 1992 annual rpt, U6250–1.8

Men age 69-84 quality of life indicators, including health, finances, family, and employment, by race, 1990 survey, U3780–9

Minority population characteristics, employment, and voting patterns by detailed race-ethnicity, with comparisons to whites, 1980s-2040, R8750–2.58

Older population age 65/over educational attainment, by race-ethnicity, 1970, 1980, and 1990, B6045–1.504

Population by age, race, sex, and educational attainment, 1991 and trends, articles, A8510–1.1

Public opinion on expected change in privacy protection of consumer info by year 2000, by age and education level, 1992 survey and trends, annual rpt, B3280–2

Religion and related social issues, public opinions and attitudes, monthly survey, R8780–1

Russia public opinion on political and economic issues and devs, by selected characteristics, 1991-92 surveys, C8915–10

Statistical profiles of 50 States and DC, general data, 1993 annual almanac, C4712–1

State and local:

Alabama statistical abstract, general data, 1992 recurring rpt, U5680–2

Arizona Indian population, education, housing, health, and employment characteristics, with detail by reservation, 1970s-91, recurring rpt, U5850–2.9

Arizona, Phoenix area temporary winter resident characteristics, including expenditures, dwelling type, and region of residence, 1992/93, article, U0280–1.508

Arizona population age 25/over, distribution by education, 1990, article, U0280–1.502

Arizona statistical abstract, general data, 1993 recurring rpt, U5850–2

Arkansas Census of Population and Housing detailed findings, 1990, U5935–7

California Census of Population and Housing detailed findings, 1990, S0840–9

DC statistical profile, general data, 1992 annual rpt, S1535–3

Florida county data book, 1992/93 annual rpt, C6360–1

Florida statistical abstract, general data, 1992 annual rpt, U6660–1

Georgia county guide, general data, 1993 annual rpt, U6750–1

Hawaii data book, general data, 1992 annual rpt, S2090–1

Kansas population by educational level, by selected county, 1990, annual articles, U7095–1.501

Kansas statistical abstract, general data, 1991/92 annual rpt, U7095–2

Kentucky economic statistics, general data, 1993 annual rpt, S3104–1.3

Kentucky labor force planning rpt, including population and labor force characteristics, and employment by industry, 1991 and trends, annual rpt, S3140–3

Louisiana Census of Population and Housing summary findings, by local area, 1990 and trends, U8010–4

Maryland statistical abstract, general data, 1993-94 biennial rpt, S3605–1

Massachusetts municipal and county profiles, general data, 1992 annual rpt, C4712–2

Mississippi population, by age, race, sex, and educational attainment, 1993/94, annual planning rpt, S4345–1.1

New Jersey Census of Population and Housing detailed findings, by county, 1990, S5425–19

New Jersey municipal and county data book, general data, 1992 annual rpt, C4712–4

New Mexico population age 25/over by educational attainment, 1990, annual planning rpt, S5624–1

BY EDUCATIONAL ATTAINMENT

New York State municipal and county statistical profiles, general data, 1993 annual rpt, C4712–7

New York State statistical yearbook, general data, 1992 annual rpt, U5100–1

Oregon population educational attainment, health and life insurance coverage, rent, and poverty, 1990 and 1992, article, S6592–1.502

Pennsylvania Census of Population and Housing detailed findings, with selected data by county and municipality, 1990, U4130–13

Rhode Island Census of Population and Housing detailed findings, by county and municipality, 1990, S6930–9

South Carolina statistical abstract, general data, 1993 annual rpt, S7125–1

Utah employment by detailed occupation, and educational attainment by age group, by sex and race-ethnicity, with detail for 7 urban areas, 1990 census rpt, S7832–3.4

Utah statistical abstract, general data, 1993 triennial rpt, U8960–1

Washington State population and demographic characteristics, and housing units, by county and/or city, 1992 and trends, annual rpt, S8345–4

Public Welfare and Social Security

Catholic charity social service agency staff by level of education, 1991, annual rpt, A3810–1

Fundraising professionals characteristics, earnings, and benefits, 1992 survey, recurring rpt, A8455–1

Recreation and Leisure

Participation in 53 sports, by demographic characteristics, State, and census div, 1992, annual rpt series, A8485–3

Sporting goods purchaser characteristics, by product category, 1992, annual survey rpt, A8485–4

Sporting goods purchases, by product and outlet type, census div, and purchaser characteristics, with average prices, 1992 and trends, annual survey, A8485–2

Science and Technology

Chemist and chemical engineer salaries, employment status, and demographic and professional characteristics, 1993, annual rpt, A1250–4

Chemist employment and salaries, by degree level and industry, 1993, annual feature, A1250–1.537

Chemist salaries and employment, by employee and employer characteristics, Mar 1993 and trends, annual article, A1250–1.532

Chemistry and chemical engineering degrees awarded, by level, sex, and instn, 1991/92 and trends, annual articles, A1250–1.535

Chemistry and chemical engineering grad starting salaries, employment status, demographic characteristics, and advanced study plans, 1991/92, annual rpt, A1250–2

Engineer compensation, by work and employee characteristics, and region and metro area, 1992, annual rpt, A8460–1

Engineering degrees awarded, by State, instn, and field, with detail for women, minorities, and foreign students, 1991/92, annual rpt, A0685–1

Engineers salaries by industry group, census div, selected metro area, degree level, and years since college degree, 1993, annual survey rpt, A0685–3

High-technology industry CEO characteristics, and views on mgmt issues including compensation and foreign trade, June 1992 survey, B4490–2.34

Physics and astronomy enrollment and degrees, annual survey of US college depts, series, A1960–2

Physics and astronomy grads employment status, by sex, age, subfield, citizenship, degree, and employer type, with salary info, 1990/91, annual rpt, A1960–1

R&D professional salaries and employment characteristics, 1993 and trends, annual article, C1850–6.509

Transportation and Travel

Airline travel frequency, destination, and purpose, by traveler characteristics, 1992 survey and trends, annual rpt, A0325–6

Auto purchaser characteristics, 1993, annual rpt, A0865–1.2

Business traveler and trip characteristics, including mode, purpose, and lodging, 1991, annual rpt, R9375–12

Motor vehicle fleet manager earnings, and personal and professional characteristics, 1993 article, C1575–2.506

Motorcycle use and user characteristics, licensed operators, and State requirements, 1992 annual rpt, A6485–1.2

Travel trips and traveler characteristics, including mode, purpose, type of lodging, and area of destination and origin, quarterly rpt, R9375–14

BY MARITAL STATUS

Agriculture and Food

Food consumption patterns, including types of ethnic foods prepared/eaten at home by marital status, 1993 survey, annual rpt, A4950–36

Food service industry employee characteristics, and minority-owned establishments and sales, 1993 article, A8200–1.508

Supermarket shopper practices, attitudes, and expenditures, by respondent characteristics, 1993 and trends, annual survey rpt, A4950–3

Communications

Direct marketing industry devs, including advertising patterns, finances, target market characteristics, and consumer attitudes, 1992/93 annual rpt, A4620–1

Education

Doctoral degree recipient characteristics, including citizenship status, source of support, field of study, and instn, 1990/91 and trends, annual rpt, R6000–7

Elementary/secondary prospective teacher characteristics and opinions, survey of persons interested in alternative certification routes, 1992, R6350–7

Elementary/secondary school superintendents personal and professional characteristics and views, 1992 survey rpt, A0775–5

Foreign students enrolled in US higher education instns, by instn, State, country of origin, and demographic characteristics, 1991/92 and trends, annual rpt, R5580–1

Higher education faculty characteristics, including marital status, 1990, recurring rpt, A3960–2.2

Higher education financial aid applicant characteristics, American College Testing (ACT) program, 1993/94, annual rpt, R1960–5

Higher education freshmen parental marital status, by student sex and instn type, fall 1992, annual survey, U6215–1

Higher education president personal and professional characteristics, 1990 and trends, recurring rpt, A1410–12

Higher education president personal and professional characteristics, 1990, article, C2175–1.533

State and local:

North Dakota higher education enrollment, by level, instn, county, and selected student characteristics, fall 1992 and trends, annual rpt, S6110–1

Government and Defense

Federal income tax liability and effective rates, by taxable bracket, 1965-90, annual rpt, R9050–1.3

House of Representatives staff characteristics, salaries, and benefits by position, 1992 and trends, recurring rpt, R4140–1

House of Representatives women members elected in Nov 1992, by marital status, article, C5800–7.504

State and local:

California individual taxable income reported by source, deductions and credits by type, and tax returns, by income class and county, 1990, annual rpt, S0855–1.1

Iowa individual income tax returns filed, by filing status and county, 1991, annual rpt, S2860–3

Vermont individual State income tax returns by marital status, by income class and locality, 1991, annual rpt, S8125–1.1

Wisconsin State legislators demographic characteristics, 1983-93, biennial rpt, S8780–1.1

Health and Vital Statistics

Depression incidence among blacks and whites by selected demographic characteristics, 1984 survey, article, A2623–1.504

Disabled persons use of home care services, with costs, payment sources, and types of care, by selected characteristics, 1992, R4865–15

Disabled workers return to work rates, by marital status, 1992 annual rpt, A5173–2.4

Drugs (prescription) use, expenditures, and financing methods among population age 65/older and 64/under, by patient characteristics, 1987, R4865–8

Europe prenatal care levels by demographic characteristics, for 3 countries, with comparisons to US, 1993 article, A2623–1.503

Hispanic Americans sexual behavior, including number of partners, by sex and marital status, 1991 survey, article, A5160–1.505

Irish women obtaining abortions in England, characteristics and contraceptive use by marital status, 1988-90, article, A5160–1.501

Men's sexual behavior, including condom use, and AIDS knowledge and risks, by selected characteristics, 1991 survey, articles, A5160–1.503

Mexico suicides and attempts, by circumstances and victim characteristics, 1980-84, annual rpt, U6250–1.15

Nursing home resident mental health care use, by resident and home characteristics, and provider type, 1985/86 survey, article, A2623–1.505

Index by Categories

BY MARITAL STATUS

Osteopathy student debt and career plans, by student characteristics, 1991/92 and trends, annual survey rpt, A0620–2

Sexual activity with multiple partners and strangers, by population characteristics, 1988-90 surveys, article, A5160–1.503

Sexual behavior among adults, including extramarital sex, condom use, and impact of AIDS, by demographic characteristics, 1990 survey, article, A2623–1.512

Sexual behavior among heterosexuals, including data on demographic characteristics, number of partners, and condom use, 1990/91 survey, article, A5160–1.506

Teenage childbearing by marital status and race, 1990, article, A8510–1.1

Veterinary school grad employment, starting salaries, benefits, and personal characteristics, by sex, 1992, annual survey article, A3100–2.504

Women's contraceptive use and views on effectiveness, by method, marital status, and pregnancy exposure, 1987 and 1992 surveys, article, A5160–1.505

Women's number of sexual partners, by marital status, 1993 rpt, A5160–10

Women's sexual behavior and disease risk, including data on multiple partners and condom use, by selected characteristics, 1988, article, A5160–1.501

Women's use of mammography and Pap smear tests, by demographic characteristics, 1987 survey, article, A2623–1.503

Zambia student views on sexual behavior and treatment of persons infected with AIDS virus, by respondent characteristics, 1990 survey, article, A5160–6.503

State and local:

Alabama health behavior risk factor surveillance survey results, by respondent characteristics, 1988-89, recurring rpt, S0175–6

Alabama vital statistics, including population, births, deaths by cause, marriages, and divorces, by location and demographic characteristics, 1992 and trends, annual rpt, S0175–2

Alaska vital statistics, including births, deaths by cause, marriages, divorces, adoptions, and population, by demographic characteristics and location, 1990, annual rpt, S0315–1

Arkansas births, abortions, and fetal deaths, by marital status of mother, 1991, annual rpt, S0685–1

California vital statistics, including population, births, and deaths by cause, by demographic characteristics and county, 1990 and trends, annual rpt, S0865–1

Colorado vital statistics, including population, births, deaths by cause, abortion, marriage and divorce, and adoption, by demographic characteristics and location, 1990 and trends, annual rpt, S1010–1

Connecticut health insurance coverage rate, by respondent characteristics and behavior risk factors, 1991 survey, S1200–3

Connecticut vital statistics, including births, deaths by cause, marriages, and divorces, by demographic characteristics and location, 1989, annual rpt, S1200–1

DC statistical profile, general data, 1992 annual rpt, S1535–3

Delaware births, and infant and neonatal deaths, by race, marital status, and age of mother, 1986-89, annual rpt, S1385–2

Delaware marriages, by previous marital status, 1990, annual rpt, S1385–2

Florida births by race and characteristics of mother, with detail for low-weight births, by county, 1990, annual rpt, S1746–1.1

Hawaii health dept activities and services, including vital statistics and disease control, by location, 1990, annual rpt, S2065–1

Idaho vital statistics, including births, deaths by cause, abortions, marriages, and divorces, by demographic characteristics and county, 1991 and trends, annual rpt, S2250–2

Iowa vital statistics, including population, births, deaths by cause, marriages, and divorces, by demographic characteristics and location, 1991 and trends, annual rpt, S2795–1

Kansas vital statistics, including population, births, deaths by cause, abortions, marriages, and divorces, by demographic characteristics and location, 1991 and trends, annual rpt, S2975–1

Kentucky births by characteristics of mother and child, by county, 1991, annual rpt, S3140–1

Kentucky health behavior risk factor surveillance survey results, by State area and respondent characteristics, 1988-90, annual rpt, S3140–6

Louisiana vital statistics, including population, births, deaths by cause, reportable diseases, marriages and divorces, by demographic characteristics and locality, 1989-90 and trends, annual rpt, S3295–1

Maine vital statistics, including births, deaths by cause, abortions, and marriages and divorces, by demographic characteristics and location, 1991 and trends, annual rpt, S3460–2

Maryland marriages by previous marital status of bride and groom, 1989, annual rpt, S3635–1

Massachusetts health behavior risk factor surveillance survey results, by respondent characteristics, 1986-90, recurring rpt, S3850–3

Massachusetts vital statistics, including births, deaths by cause, marriages, divorces, and population, by locality and demographic characteristics, 1990 and trends, annual rpt, S3850 1

Michigan deaths, by age, race, sex, and marital status, 1990, annual rpt, S4000–3

Minnesota births and abortions, by women's marital status, 1991, annual rpt, S4190–2

Mississippi vital statistics, including births, deaths by cause, marriages, and divorces, by demographic characteristics and location, 1992 and trends, annual rpt, S4350–1

Missouri vital statistics, including population, births, deaths by cause, and marriages and divorces, by location and demographic characteristics, 1992 and trends, annual rpt, S4518–1

Montana vital statistics, including births, deaths by cause, abortion, disease, and marriage and divorce, by demographic characteristics and county, 1990-91 and trends, annual rpt, S4690–1

Nebraska vital statistics, including births, deaths, marriages, divorces, and population, by demographic characteristics and location, 1991 and trends, annual rpt, S4885–1

Nevada vital statistics, including births, abortions, and deaths by cause, by county and demographic characteristics, 1989 and trends, annual rpt, S5075–1

New Hampshire births to teenage mothers, by marital status and county, 1987-91, annual rpt, S5215–1

New Jersey vital statistics, including births, deaths, population, communicable diseases, and marriages and divorces, by demographic characteristics and location, 1990 and trends, annual rpt, S5405–1

New Mexico abortions by patient characteristics, 1991 and trends, annual rpt, S5605–1.1

New York State health behavior risk factor surveillance survey results, by respondent characteristics, 1990, recurring rpt, S5765–3

North Dakota abortions, by demographic characteristics of patient, 1991, annual rpt, S6105–2

North Dakota health behavior risk factor surveillance survey results, by respondent characteristics, 1991 and trends, annual rpt, S6105–3

Oregon vital statistics, including births, deaths by cause, communicable diseases, marriages, and divorces, by age, sex, race-ethnicity, and county, 1991 and trends, annual rpt, S6615–5

Rhode Island vital statistics, including population, births, deaths, marriages, and divorces, by demographic characteristics and locality, 1989 and trends, annual rpt, S6995–1

South Carolina statistical abstract, general data, 1993 annual rpt, S7125–1

South Carolina vital statistics, including births, deaths by cause, marriages, and divorces, by age, sex, race, and location, 1990 and trends, annual rpt, S7175–1

Tennessee marriages, by previous marital status, 1991, annual rpt, S7520–2

Tennessee statistical abstract, general data, 1992/93 annual rpt, U8710–2

Utah health behavior risk factor surveillance survey results, by respondent characteristics, 1991, annual rpt, S7835–3

Utah marriages and divorces, by participant characteristics and location, 1990 and trends, annual rpt, S7835–2

Utah vital statistics, including births by characteristics of mother and child, by location, 1990, annual rpt, S7835–1.2

Vermont vital statistics, including population, births, deaths by cause, abortions, marriages, and divorces, by location and demographic characteristics, 1991 and trends, annual rpt, S8054–1

Virginia marriages, by previous marital status of couple and race of groom, 1991, annual rpt, S8225–1

Washington State vital statistics, including deaths by cause and decedent characteristics, 1991, annual rpt, S8363–1

West Virginia vital statistics, including deaths by cause, marriages, and divorces, by location and demographic characteristics, 1991 and trends, annual rpt, S8560–1

BY MARITAL STATUS

Wisconsin births by marital status and race-ethnicity of mother, 1991, annual rpt, S8715–4

Wyoming vital statistics, including population, births, deaths by cause, marriages, and divorces, by demographic characteristics and county, 1991 and trends, annual rpt, S8920–2

Housing and Construction

Home buyer (1st-time and repeat) profile, and transaction characteristics, including prices and financing, by region and for 18 metro areas, 1990-92, annual survey rpt, B2150–1

Income

Black American earnings, income, and poverty data, with comparisons to whites, 1980s-91, annual compilation, C6775–2.7

Hispanic American income and poverty data, with comparisons to whites, 1980s-91, annual compilation, C6775–3.5

Industry and Commerce

- Canada photographic and video equipment and supplies ownership, purchasing patterns, and use, by household characteristics, 1992 survey, recurring rpt, A8695–4
- Diamond jewelry purchases, prices paid, and purchaser characteristics, 1993 annual almanac, C2150–7.509

Labor and Employment

Black American labor force and employment data, with comparisons to whites, 1970s-91, annual compilation, C6775–2.6

Women's labor force participation, by marital status, 1900-1990, B6045–1.503

State and local:

- Arkansas vocational rehabilitation expenditures, impact on earnings and employment, and client characteristics, FY91 annual rpt, S0700–2.4
- California labor force planning rpt, including population characteristics, and employment by industry, 1992 annual rpt, S0830–2
- Florida statistical abstract, general data, 1992 annual rpt, U6660–1
- Georgia statistical abstract, general data, 1992 93 bicnnial rpt, U6730–1
- Utah labor force characteristics, employment and unemployment, hours, and earnings, with data by industry and locale, 1992 and trends, annual rpt, S7820–10
- Utah statistical abstract, general data, 1993 triennial rpt, U8960–1

Law Enforcement

Incarcerated mothers and their children, with data on characteristics, child caregivers, visitation, and support program use, 1991/92, A7575–4

State and local:

- Alaska corrections system admin, including inmate and probationer/parolee offenses and demographic characteristics, 1991 annual rpt, S0287–1
- Arizona correctional instn admin, including inmates by criminal background and demographic characteristics, FY92, annual rpt, S0464–2
- Arizona statistical abstract, general data, 1993 recurring rpt, U5850–2
- California correctional instn inmates, with criminal background and demographic characteristics, 1991 and trends, annual rpt, S0820–1

Florida "habitual offender" sentencing laws effect on prison population, with data by circuit court and offender characteristics, 1993 rpt, A7575–5

- Georgia correctional instns, admin, and inmate characteristics, FY92, annual rpt, S1872–1
- Indiana child abuse and neglect cases by county and victim and perpetrator characteristics, FY92 annual rpt, S2623–1.7
- Iowa correctional instn admissions, releases, and inmate characteristics, by instn, monthly rpt, S2770–1
- Massachusetts correctional instn inmate socioeconomic characteristics and criminal background, by instn, Jan 1992 and trends, annual rpt, S3805–1
- Missouri correctional instn admissions, releases, and inmate characteristics, FY93, annual rpt, S4501–1
- North Carolina correctional instn admissions, separations, and population, with inmate characteristics, FY93, semiannual rpt, S5900–1
- Pennsylvania State correctional instn admin, and inmates by type of offense and demographic characteristics, 1990 and trends, annual rpt, S6782–1
- Utah corrections inmates, parolees, and probationers, by criminal background and demographic characteristics, FY92 and trends, annual rpt, S7810–1
- Wisconsin correctional instn admissions by inmate characteristics, including need for special services, 1991, annual rpt, S8692–1.2
- Wyoming correctional instn admin, finances, inmate characteristics, and staff, and probation and parole activities, FY92 annual rpt, S8883–1

Population

- Black American population and demographic characteristics, with comparisons to whites, 1970s-2080, annual compilation, C6775–2.1
- Hispanic American population and demographic characteristics, with comparisons to whites, 1993 annual compilation, C6775–3.1
- Men age 69-84 quality of life indicators, including health, finances, family, and employment, by race, 1990 survey, U3780–9
- Population distribution by marital status, by sex and race, 1991, article, A8510–1.1
- Statistical profiles of 50 States and DC, general data, 1993 annual almanac, C4712–1
- Women's housing issues, with data on household composition, tenure, and characteristics, 1992, A8657–5

State and local:

- Alabama statistical abstract, general data, 1992 recurring rpt, U5680–2
- Arizona statistical abstract, general data, 1993 recurring rpt, U5850–2
- Arkansas Census of Population and Housing detailed findings, 1990, U5935–7
- California Census of Population and Housing detailed findings, 1990, S0840–9
- Florida county data book, 1992/93 annual rpt, C6360–1
- Florida statistical abstract, general data, 1992 annual rpt, U6660–1

Index by Categories

- Hawaii data book, general data, 1992 annual rpt, S2090–1
- Illinois statistical abstract, general data, 1992 annual rpt, U6910–2
- New Jersey Census of Population and Housing detailed findings, by county, 1990, S5425–19
- Pennsylvania Census of Population and Housing detailed findings, with selected data by county and municipality, 1990, U4130–13
- South Carolina statistical abstract, general data, 1993 annual rpt, S7125–1

Public Welfare and Social Security

State and local:

California statistical abstract, general data, 1992 annual rpt, S0840–2

Science and Technology

Ecologist personal and professional characteristics, including research activity and funding, with data by field, Mar 1992 survey, recurring rpt, A4685–1

Transportation and Travel

- Business traveler and trip characteristics, including mode, purpose, and lodging, 1991, annual rpt, R9375–12
- Motorcycle use and user characteristics, licensed operators, and State requirements, 1992 annual rpt, A6485–1.2
- Travel trips and traveler characteristics, including mode, purpose, type of lodging, and area of destination and origin, quarterly rpt, R9375–14
- Traveler and trip characteristics, 1990, annual rpt, C2140–1.2

BY RACE

Agriculture and Food

- Alcohol use patterns among high school seniors, by race, 1993 survey article, B6045–1.504
- Distilled spirits consumption, and consumer characteristics and buying habits, 1992 and trends, annual rpt, C4775–1.3
- Food nutrition awareness and health concerns, including shopping and consumption patterns, by respondent characteristics, 1993 survey, annual rpt, A4950–36
- Food service industry employee characteristics, and minority-owned establishments and sales, 1993 article, A8200–1.508
- Food service patronage patterns, by race-ethnicity, June 1992-May 1993, article, A8200–1.510
- Restaurant smoking policy importance to consumers, and views on smoking acceptability in restaurants and other public places, by selected characteristics, Jan 1993 survey, A8200–8.15
- Restaurant/lodging industries executives/managers, by sex and race-ethnicity, 1992, article, C5150–5.511
- Wine and other alcoholic beverage consumption, and consumer characteristics and buying habits, 1993 annual rpt, C4775–2.2

State and local:

Florida statistical abstract, general data, 1992 annual rpt, U6660–1

Index by Categories

BY RACE

Banking, Finance, and Insurance

Accounting grad supply-demand, including detail by sex, race-ethnicity, and region, 1991/92 and trends, annual rpt, A1885–1

Small business owners financing sources and experience of discrimination in lending, by race-ethnicity, 1993 survey feature, C4215–1.512

Communications

News events followed most closely by public, and opinion on media coverage and selected current issues, by respondent characteristics, recurring rpt, C8915–1

Public opinion on the media and related issues, by respondent characteristics, series, C8915–11

TV home shoppers vs average shoppers, TV viewing time and race-ethnicity, 1993 feature, C1850–14.514

TV households and population by race-ethnicity, sex, and age, by market area, 1992/93, annual rpt, B0525–4

TV news coverage of Los Angeles riots following Rodney King police brutality case verdict, with source characteristics, and detail by network, Apr-May 1992, article, R3823–1.506

TV news coverage of Rodney King police brutality case, with reporter and source characteristics, and detail by network, Mar 1991-Apr 1992, article, R3823–1.505

TV news stories by sex and race-ethnicity of reporter or anchor, with detail by network, 1992, annual article, R3823–1.503

Education

American College Test (ACT) scores, by sex and race-ethnicity, 1993, annual article, C2175–1.534

American College Test (ACT) scores by student characteristics, with student views on schools and education plans, 1992 and trends, annual rpt, R1960–6

Black American educational statistics, with comparisons to whites, 1970s-92, annual compilation, C6775–2.3

Black colleges enrollment distribution by student race-ethnicity, 1993 article, C4215–1.509

Catholic school enrollment by ethnic group, 1982/83 and 1991/92-1992/93, annual rpt, A7375–1

Catholic secondary school operations and finances, including enrollment by race-ethnicity and family income, 1991/92 and trends, biennial rpt, A7375 5

Catholic vs public school performance, and support for parental school selection funded by govt, views of Catholics by race-ethnicity, July 1992 survey, A7375–8

Community and junior college revenues by source and expenditures by function, and selected student characteristics, FY92, annual rpt, A6705–1

Doctoral degree recipient characteristics, including citizenship status, source of support, field of study, and instn, 1990/91 and trends, annual rpt, R6000–7

Doctoral degrees conferred and recipient characteristics, by field, 1992, annual feature, C2175–1.535

Elementary/secondary new teacher views on teaching and quality of schools, after 2nd year of teaching, spring 1992 survey, B6045–2

Elementary/secondary prospective teacher characteristics and opinions, survey of persons interested in alternative certification routes, 1992, R6350–7

Elementary/secondary school superintendents personal and professional characteristics and views, 1992 survey rpt, A0775–5

Elementary/secondary teacher views on education policy issues and selected reform proposals, with data by race-ethnicity, Jan-Feb 1993 survey, B6045–7

Higher education bachelors and masters degrees conferred, by sex and race-ethnicity, 1990, C4215–1.503

Higher education degrees conferred, by level, sex, discipline, and race-ethnicity, 1990/91, recurring feature, C2175–1.523

Higher education employment, by position type and race-ethnicity, 1991/92, C2175–1.507

Higher education enrollment by race-ethnicity, by State, fall 1991, annual rpt, C2175–1.531

Higher education enrollment of minority and foreign students at approx 3,100 instns, fall 1991, recurring feature, C2175–1.510

Higher education enrollment of minority and foreign students, with comparison to whites, by sex, State, and instn type, fall 1991, recurring feature, C2175–1.506

Higher education freshmen attitudes and characteristics, degree and career plans, and financial aid sources, by sex and instn type, fall 1992, annual survey, U6215–1

Higher education involvement of minorities, including enrollment and degrees awarded, by race-ethnicity, sex, and State, 1970s-91, annual rpt, A1410–10

Higher education minority student enrollment trends, 1993 annual survey, A1410–1.38

Higher education president personal and professional characteristics, 1990 and trends, recurring rpt, A1410–12

Higher education president personal and professional characteristics, 1990, article, C2175–1.533

Higher education student athlete enrollment and graduation rates, by sex, race-ethnicity, and major sport, for Natl Collegiate Athletic Assn Div I instns, 1992/93, annual rpt, A7440–4

Higher education student athlete vs total graduation rates after 6 years, by sex, race, and Natl Collegiate Athletic Assn Div I instn, summer 1991, recurring feature, C2175–1.522, C2175–1.527

Higher education undergrad and grad enrollment by race-ethnicity, fall 1990, article, C4215–1.508

Higher education, 2-year college enrollment by minority status, by instn and State, Oct 1990-91, annual directory, A0640–1

Journalism/mass communication enrollment and grads by level, by instn, sex, race-ethnicity, and field, 1990/91 and trends, annual article, A3225–1

Librarians (special) salaries, by location, work setting, and personal characteristics, US and Canada, 1992 and trends, biennial survey rpt, A8965–1

Librarians at universities and research instns, by minority group and census div, FY92, annual survey, A3365–2

Library/info science school enrollment, staff and student characteristics, finances, and curricula, by school and degree program, 1991/92, annual rpt, A3235–1

Mathematics dept faculty and doctoral degree recipient characteristics, including salaries, 1991/92 and trends, annual survey, A2085–1.1

Natl Assessment of Educational Progress test reading scores of students at 3 ages, by race-ethnicity, 1971-90, article, R4800–2.504

Political science higher education dept faculty and salaries, by sex and race-ethnicity, 1991/92, annual rpt, A2617–1

Private elementary and secondary school enrollment, staff, and finances, with detail for minorities, by school type and region, 1980s-1992/93, annual rpt, A6835–3

Public opinion on school problems, quality, and proposed reforms, by respondent characteristics, 1993 annual Gallup Poll, A8680–1.503

Public school improvement outlook and funding adequacy, views of parents by race and Hispanic ethnicity, Feb 1993 survey, article, R4800–2.517

Scholastic Aptitude Test (SAT) participants and/or scores, by education of parents, income, and race-ethnicity, 1992, C4215–1.501

Social work higher education programs, faculty and student characteristics, and student aid, with data by instn, 1992 and trends, annual rpt, A4515–1

Southern States higher education faculty and administrator characteristics and salaries, by instn type, 1990s and trends, biennial fact book, A8945–1.5

Statistical profiles of 50 States and DC, general data, 1993 annual almanac, C4712–1

Student attitudes on courses in 4 subject areas, for 8th graders by sex and race-ethnicity, 1988, R4800–2.512

Theological school enrollment by degree level, by sex and race-ethnicity, fall 1992 and trends, annual rpt, A3376–1

Urban public school performance compared to natl goals for year 2000, with data by race-ethnicity and sex, 1990/91, A4425–4

Western States higher education grad student exchange program enrollment, by race-ethnicity, for 13 States, fall 1992, annual rpt, A9385–1

Women and minorities in professional fields, detailed education and labor force data, 1980s-91, with historical trends, recurring rpt, A3960–2

State and local:

Alabama public school enrollment, dropouts, and grads, by race and school system, 1991/92, annual rpt, S0124–1.1

Alabama statistical abstract, general data, 1992 recurring rpt, U5680–2

Alaska public schools, enrollment, staff, and finances, by district, FY92, annual rpt, S0295–2

Arizona elementary and secondary school enrollment, by grade and race-ethnicity, 1991/92, annual rpt, S0470–1

Arizona statistical abstract, general data, 1993 recurring rpt, U5850–2

Arkansas higher education degrees conferred, by level, discipline, student race and sex, and instn, 1990/91 and trends, annual rpt, S0690–3

Arkansas higher education enrollment by student characteristics and geographic origins, by instn, fall 1991 and trends, annual rpt, S0690–1

BY RACE

Index by Categories

Arkansas public school enrollment and grads, by race-ethnicity and sex, 1991/92, annual rpt, S0660–1.1

California postsecondary education enrollment and degrees, by sex, race-ethnicity, and instn, 1990/91, annual series, S0827–2

California public school enrollment, grads, and staff, by race-ethnicity, 1992/93 and trends, annual rpt, S0825–9

Colorado public school enrollment, finances, and student and staff characteristics, by locality, 1992 annual rpt series, S1000–2

Connecticut public school data, including enrollment, staff, programs, finances, and student characteristics, 1991/92, biennial rpt, S1185–3

DC public school enrollment, by race-ethnicity, 1987/88-1991/92, annual rpt, S1605–2

DC statistical profile, general data, 1992 annual rpt, S1535–3

Delaware postsecondary instn enrollment and degrees conferred, by race-ethnicity, FY94 annual rpt, S1425–1

Delaware public and nonpublic school student and staff characteristics, 1991/92, annual rpt, S1430–1

Florida county data book, 1992/93 annual rpt, C6360–1

Florida higher education enrollment, degree programs, staff, and finances, by State-supported instn, with student and staff characteristics, 1991/92 annual rpt, S1725–1

Florida statistical abstract, general data, 1992 annual rpt, U6660–1

Georgia county guide, general data, 1993 annual rpt, U6750–1

Idaho public school personnel characteristics and salaries by position, and teachers and enrollment by school district, 1992/93, annual rpt, S2225–3

Illinois higher education enrollment and degrees, by level, instn, field of instruction, and student characteristics, 1992 and trends, annual rpt, S2475–1.1

Illinois public school enrollment and dropouts, by race-ethnicity, 1990/91, annual rpt, S2440–1.1

Illinois statistical abstract, general data, 1992 annual rpt, U6910–2

Iowa postsecondary enrollment, degrees, staff, and finances, by instn, 1990/91, annual rpt, S2755–1

Kentucky higher education enrollment and degrees conferred, by race, 1983-92, annual rpt, S3130–3

Louisiana elementary/secondary school operations, including enrollment, staff, finances, and detail by school district, 1991/92 and trends, annual rpt, S3280–1

Maryland elementary and secondary education data, by county, 1991/92, annual rpt, S3610–2.3

Maryland elementary and secondary education data, by county, 1992 and trends, annual rpt, S3610–2.4

Maryland elementary and secondary education data, by county, 1992/93, annual rpt, S3610–2.8

Maryland public school enrollment and achievement test scores by race-ethnicity, and teachers by race, with detail by county, 1992, annual rpt, S3610–1

Maryland public school professional staff, by function, sex, race, and county, Oct 1992, annual rpt, S3610–2.12

Massachusetts elementary/secondary school enrollment, by sex and race-ethnicity, Oct 1980 and 1991, annual rpt, S3810–3

Minnesota enrollment distribution by race-ethnicity, and minority student shares by district and county, 1991/92 and trends, annual rpt, S4165–1

Minnesota postsecondary education finances, and enrollment by student characteristics, by type of school system, 1970s-93, biennial rpt, S4195–2.2

Mississippi high school grads, by sex and race-ethnicity, 1991/92, annual rpt, S4340–1.1

Missouri higher education enrollment and degrees granted, by sex, race-ethnicity, and instn, 1992 and trends, annual rpt, S4520–3

Montana public school enrollment by grade, and grads, by school, county, race-ethnicity, and sex, 1992 and trends, annual rpt, S4740–1

Nebraska elementary and secondary school enrollment, by race-ethnicity, school district, and county, 1992/93, annual rpt, S4865–2.5

Nevada public school enrollment and teachers, by race-ethnicity and school district, 1990/91, annual rpt, S5035–2

Nevada statistical abstract, general data, 1992 biennial rpt, S5005–1

New Jersey public schools, enrollment, and student and staff characteristics, and nonpublic schools and enrollment, by county, 1991/92, annual rpt, S5385–1

New Mexico elementary/secondary school enrollment by race-ethnicity, 1991/92, annual rpt, S5575–4

New Mexico high school enrollment and dropouts, by race-ethnicity, 1991/92, annual planning rpt, S5624–1

New York State statistical yearbook, general data, 1992 annual rpt, U5100–1

North Carolina higher education enrollment, degrees, libraries, staff, and student characteristics, finances, and housing, by instn, 1992/93 and trends, annual rpt, U8013–1

North Carolina public school enrollment, grads, staff, and finances, with data by race, sex, and local district, 1991/92-1992/93 and trends, annual rpt, S5915–1

North Dakota elementary and secondary school enrollment, by race-ethnicity, Sept 1992, annual directory, S6180–2

North Dakota elementary and secondary school staff characteristics and salaries, by position, region, and enrollment size, 1992/93 annual rpt, S6180–3

North Dakota higher education enrollment, by level, instn, county, and selected student characteristics, fall 1992 and trends, annual rpt, S6110–1

Oklahoma public school enrollment shares by race-ethnicity, 1989 and 1992, annual rpt, S6423–2

Oregon elementary and secondary public school enrollment by race-ethnicity and teachers, by instn, Oct 1992, annual rpt, S6590–1.1

Oregon public high school completers, by instn, county, sex, and race-ethnicity, 1992, annual rpt, S6590–1.10

Oregon public school enrollment, by county, grade, and race-ethnicity, Oct 1992, annual rpt, S6590–1.9

Pennsylvania educational statistics by level and/or type of education, series, S6790–5

Rhode Island public school enrollment by type of instn, grade, sex, race-ethnicity, and district, 1991/92 or fall 1992, annual rpt, S6970–1.1

South Carolina educational enrollment, by school type or level, program, race, and location, 1991/92, annual rpt, S7145–1.3

South Carolina higher education degrees awarded, by sex and race, FY91, annual planning rpt, S7155–3.3

South Carolina higher education enrollment, degrees, staff, and finances, by instn, 1992 and trends, annual rpt, S7185–2

South Carolina statistical abstract, general data, 1993 annual rpt, S7125–1

South Dakota elementary/secondary school enrollment, grads, and dropouts, by race-ethnicity, 1991/92, annual rpt, S7315–1.1

South Dakota public higher education enrollment and faculty, by race-ethnicity and instn, FY93 annual rpt, S7375–1

Tennessee higher education and vocational enrollment and grads, by race-ethnicity, 1991/92, annual rpt, S7525–1

Texas elementary and secondary education enrollment by race-ethnicity, by school, district, and county, 1991/92, annual rpt, S7670–1.1

Texas elementary/secondary education personnel, by sex and race-ethnicity, by district and county, 1991/92, annual rpt, S7670–1.3

Texas higher education enrollment and faculty, by race-ethnicity, sex, and instn, 1991/92 and trends, annual rpt, S7657–1.1

Utah employment by detailed occupation, and educational attainment by age group, by sex and race-ethnicity, with detail for 7 urban areas, 1990 census rpt, S7832–3.4

Utah public school enrollment, dropouts, and grads, by race-ethnicity, 1991/92, annual rpt, S7815–1.2

Vermont elementary and secondary school enrollment by grade, sex, race-ethnicity, school, and county, 1992/93 and trends, annual rpt, S8020–1

Virginia public school dropouts by race-ethnicity and sex, by county and municipality, 1991/92, annual rpt, S8190–3

West Virginia higher education enrollment, degrees, faculty and student characteristics, and finances, by instn, 1992/93 and trends, annual rpt, S8533–1

Wisconsin elementary and secondary school enrollment, staff, costs, and State aid, by school district, 1992/93 and trends, annual rpt, S8795–2

Wyoming public school enrollment, by sex, race-ethnicity, school, and district, 1991/92 and trends, annual rpt, S8890–1.2

Government and Defense

Black elected officials, and characteristics of voting age population, with comparisons to whites, 1970s-91, annual compilation, C6775–2.4

Index by Categories

BY RACE

Black voter participation, with detail for persons age 18-24 and comparisons to whites, biennially 1972-90, R3840–21

Congress minority membership after Nov 1990 and 1992 elections, by race-ethnicity, article, C4215–1.504

House of Representatives staff characteristics, salaries, and benefits by position, 1992 and trends, recurring rpt, R4140–1

Local govt land use planning commissions composition and activities, and commissioner characteristics, 1987 and trends, recurring rpt, A2615–2

Local officials in municipal and county govt, demographic profiles and job functions, 1993 annual rpt, A5800–1

Military personnel by race-ethnicity, total and women, FY90, article, R8750–1.504

Minority population characteristics, employment, and voting patterns by detailed race-ethnicity, with comparisons to whites, 1980s-2040, R8750–2.58

Public opinion on Clinton Admin policies and actions, by respondent characteristics, series, C8915–7

Public opinion on issues concerning politics and the press, by respondent characteristics, series, C8915–4

Voter turnout and registration trends, by race-ethnicity and/or sex, 1960s-92, U4510–1.70

Women candidates in State-level elections, outcome summaries including campaign funds raised, voting by sex, and winner's race-ethnicity, 1992, U4510–4.4

Women's employment in govt, with data by race-ethnicity and State, series, U5090–1

State and local:

DC statistical profile, general data, 1992 annual rpt, S1535–3

Florida county data book, 1992/93 annual rpt, C6360–1

Florida statistical abstract, general data, 1992 annual rpt, U6660–1

Georgia county guide, general data, 1993 annual rpt, U6750–1

Hawaii data book, general data, 1992 annual rpt, S2090–1

North Carolina election results, with voter registration by party and race-ethnicity, by county, 1992, biennial rpt, S5920–1

Oklahoma statistical abstract, general data, 1992 annual rpt, U8130–2

South Carolina statistical abstract, general data, 1993 annual rpt, S7125–1

Tennessee statistical abstract, general data, 1992/93 annual rpt, U8710–2

Wisconsin Blue Book, general data, 1993-94 biennial rpt, S8780–1.2

Health and Vital Statistics

Abortion attitudes of teenage boys, by respondent characteristics, 1988 survey, article, A5160–1.505

AIDS cases, by sex and race-ethnicity, through June 1992, article, C4215–1.503

AIDS deaths in hospitals vs at home, by region and decedent characteristics, 1988 and trends, article, A2623–1.512

AIDS stigmatizing attitudes and beliefs prevalence among general public, with detail by race and sex, 1990/91 surveys, article, A2623–1.506

AIDS survival rates correlated with victim race, summary of research results, 1993 article, A2623–1.512

Asthma incidence among children, by race-ethnicity, with detail by Hispanic ethnic origin, 1993 article, A2623–1.506

Births by race, 1960-90, recurring rpt, A3960–2.1

Black American health and vital statistics data, with comparisons to whites, 1970s-91, annual compilation, C6775–2.2

Black American socioeconomic status, with data on life expectancy, death rates, and teenage pregnancy, and comparisons to whites, 1993 article, A8510–1.1

Cancer survival rates by body site, by race, 1960-88, annual rpt, A1175–1

Child and maternal health status indicators, with data by race and State, 1992 annual rpt, R3840–5

Child health and well-being indicators, by race-ethnicity, 1993 annual rpt, R3832–1

Child health indicators, including infant mortality, birthweight, and prenatal care, by race and State, 1989, annual rpt, A0565–1

Children age 9-10 cardiovascular disease risk factor incidence, for girls by race, 1992 article, A2623–1.502

Children's orthopedic internal fixation device implantation prevalence, and results, with detail by demographic characteristics, 1988, article, A2623–1.509

Cholesterol level correlated with alcohol consumption frequency, by race and sex, 1976-80, article, A2623–1.508

Cocaine user characteristics, including criminal behavior and health condition, with comparison to nonusers, 1991 and trends, article, A2623–1.510

Condom use and attitudes among sexually active young men, by race-ethnicity, 1988 and 1991 surveys, article, A5160–1.504

Death rates by age, sex, and race, 1991 and trends, article, B6045–1.503

Dental problems/treatment-related time lost from work or school, by demographic characteristics, 1989, article, A2623–1.502

Dental school enrollment and grads, by sex and race-ethnicity, 1992/93 annual rpt, A1475–3.1

Dental school faculty, support personnel, and staff characteristics, by instn, 1992/93, annual rpt, A1475–4.5

Dental school student attrition, by reason and student characteristics, 1991/92 and trends, annual rpt, A1475–4.4

Depression incidence among blacks and whites by selected demographic characteristics, 1984 survey, article, A2623–1.504

Drug use at work among workers age 19-27, by sex and race-ethnicity, 1984, annual rpt, R8335–1.1

Drugs (prescription) use, expenditures, and financing methods among population age 65/older and 64/under, by patient characteristics, 1987, R4865–8

Ear tube implantation prevalence in children, by demographic characteristics and reasons for implant, 1988, article, A2623–1.509

Elderly population receiving selected medical procedures and diagnostic tests, by race and urban-rural residence, 1986, article, A2623–1.509

Eye bank activity in US and abroad, including donations by type, source, and donor characteristics, and data by individual bank, 1992 and trends, annual rpt, A4743–1

Health care specialist and health-related company CEO income, public perceptions vs actual amounts, by respondent characteristics, 1991-93, R4865–13

Health condition and preventive health care and safety practices of adults, by respondent characteristics, 1992 and trends, annual survey rpt, C8111–2

Health indicators, including hypertension and lung cancer rates, and cancer and heart disease/stroke deaths, by sex and race-ethnicity, 1993 feature, C4215–1.511

Health insurance coverage and finances, and health care costs and facilities, by selected demographic characteristics, 1940s-91, annual rpt, A5173–2

Health insurance coverage lack, and population with high out-of-pocket expenses, by State and selected characteristics, 1993, R4865–14

Health insurance coverage lack by race, 1989-91, article, C4215–1.507

Health insurance coverage lack by sex, race, employment status, and household income level, 1993 feature, C4215–1.506

Human immunodeficiency virus (HIV) testing and posttest counseling rates, by demographic characteristics, 1989, article, A2623–1.501

Hysterectomy prevalence by women's demographic characteristics, 1988 surveys, article, A2623–1.503

Infant mortality rates from sudden infant death syndrome, by race, census div, and State, 1980 and 1988, article, B6045–1.502

Life expectancy and mortality rates, by age, race, and sex, 1900-92, annual article, B6045–1.504

Life expectancy at birth, by race, decennially 1960-90, annual fact book, A1275–1.5

Life expectancy, by age, sex, and race, 1991 and trends, biennial fact book, A1325–1.6

Low-income families and children, health and welfare indicators, with data by State and city, 1992 annual rpt, R3840–11

Measles cases in preschool children, health care providers used and welfare status, by race-ethnicity, 1989-90, article, A2623–1.508

Medical school programs, fees, applicants, admissions, and enrollment, with data by age, sex, minority group, and instn, 1992/93 and trends, annual rpt, A3273–10

Men's sexual behavior, including condom use, and AIDS knowledge and risks, by selected characteristics, 1991 survey, articles, A5160–1.503

Nursing center (community) staff and client characteristics, and services, 1990 survey, article, A8010–3.506

Nursing college deans, by race-ethnicity, 1992/93, annual rpt, A0615–2

Nursing college faculty, by race-ethnicity, 1992/93, annual rpt, A0615–1

Nursing higher education program faculty and clinic patient characteristics, 1992/93 biennial rpt, A0615–5

Nursing home resident mental health care use, by resident and home characteristics, and provider type, 1985/86 survey, article, A2623–1.505

Nursing school enrollment and grads, by degree level, sex, race-ethnicity, and instn type and location, 1992/93 and trends, annual rpt, A0615–4

BY RACE

Index by Categories

Nursing schools, programs, enrollment, student and staff characteristics, and grads, 1991 and trends, annual rpt, A8010–1

Optometry school faculty, enrollment and degrees, policies and programs, and finances, by instn, 1991/92, annual survey, A3370–2

Organs donated by type, by race of donor, 1990, article, C4215–1.501

Osteopathy college enrollment, student and faculty characteristics, and finances, 1992/93 and trends, annual rpt, A0620–1

Osteopathy student debt and career plans, by student characteristics, 1991/92 and trends, annual survey rpt, A0620–2

Pharmacy degree program applications, enrollment, and degrees conferred, by student characteristics and instn, 1990/91 and trends, annual rpt, A0630–9

Public health school applicant, student, and grad characteristics, by instn, 1991/92 and trends, annual rpt, A3372–3

Public health school faculty characteristics, by instn, fall 1991, recurring rpt, A3372–1

Sexual activity and condom use among high school students by sex, and adolescent/adult AIDS cases, by race-ethnicity, 1993 article, C4215–1.505

Sexual activity with multiple partners and strangers, by population characteristics, 1988-90 surveys, article, A5160–1.503

Sexual behavior among adults, including extramarital sex, condom use, and impact of AIDS, by demographic characteristics, 1990 survey, article, A2623–1.512

Sexual behavior among heterosexuals, including data on demographic characteristics, number of partners, and condom use, 1990/91 survey, article, A5160–1.506

Smoking acceptability in restaurants and other public places, and importance of restaurant smoking policy, views of consumers by selected characteristics, Jan 1993 survey, A8200–8.15

Smoking status of men and women by occupation, and smoker characteristics, 1985 and/or 1990, article, B6045–1.501

Substance abuse treatment programs, funding by source, and client characteristics, for alcohol and drug services, by State, FY91 and trends, annual rpt, A7112–1

Teenage abortion, birth, and pregnancy rates, by race, 1988, article, A5160–1.504

Women's calorie intake during pregnancy and lactation, by race and poverty status, 1985-86 study, article, A2623–1.510

Women's deaths from breast cancer correlated with occupation, by race, 1979-87, article, A2623–1.511

Women's obesity and related activity and weight-loss indicators, by race, 1985-86, article, A2623–1.502

Women's sexual behavior and disease risk, including data on multiple partners and condom use, by selected characteristics, 1988, article, A5160–1.501

Women's smoking patterns, among persons age 18-44 by race and age group, 1987 survey, article, A2623–1.511

Women's use of mammography and Pap smear tests, by demographic characteristics, 1987 survey, article, A2623–1.503

Women's weight gain during pregnancy and retained weight after birth, by race, 1988, article, A2623–1.510

Youth age 10-15 health condition and health service use and sources, with data by insurance status, by race-ethnicity, 1988, article, A2623–1.509

State and local:

Alabama health behavior risk factor surveillance survey results, by respondent characteristics, 1988-89, recurring rpt, S0175–6

Alabama statistical abstract, general data, 1992 recurring rpt, U5680–2

Alabama vital statistics, including population, births, deaths by cause, marriages, and divorces, by location and demographic characteristics, 1992 and trends, annual rpt, S0175–2

Alaska vital statistics, including births, deaths by cause, marriages, divorces, adoptions, and population, by demographic characteristics and location, 1990, annual rpt, S0315–1

Arizona statistical abstract, general data, 1993 recurring rpt, U5850–2

Arkansas drug and alcohol treatment and prevention program expenditures, success rates, and client characteristics, FY91 annual rpt, S0700–2.1

Arkansas mental health program clients served, by age, race, county, and facility, FY91, annual rpt, S0700–2.4

Arkansas vital statistics, including births, deaths by cause, marriages, and divorces, by age, sex, race, and county, 1991 and trends, annual rpt, S0685–1

California death rates and estimated alcohol-related mortality, by cause and demographic characteristics, 1980-89, article, A2623–1.508

California health behavior risk factor surveillance survey results, by respondent characteristics, 1991 and trends, annual rpt, S0865–2

California vital statistics, including population, births, and deaths by cause, by demographic characteristics and county, 1990 and trends, annual rpt, S0865–1

Colorado health behavior risk factor surveillance survey results, by respondent characteristics, 1990, recurring rpt, S1010–3

Colorado vital statistics, including population, births, deaths by cause, abortion, marriage and divorce, and adoption, by demographic characteristics and location, 1990 and trends, annual rpt, S1010–1

Connecticut health insurance coverage rate, by respondent characteristics and behavior risk factors, 1991 survey, S1200–3

Connecticut vital statistics, including births, deaths by cause, marriages, and divorces, by demographic characteristics and location, 1989, annual rpt, S1200–1

DC statistical profile, general data, 1992 annual rpt, S1535–3

Delaware vital statistics, including births, deaths by cause, and marriages and dissolutions, by demographic characteristics and location, 1990, annual rpt, S1385–2

Florida births by race and characteristics of mother, with detail for low-weight births, by county, 1990, annual rpt, S1746–1.1

Florida county data book, 1992/93 annual rpt, C6360–1

Florida statistical abstract, general data, 1992 annual rpt, U6660–1

Florida vital statistics, including population, births, deaths by cause, and marriages and dissolutions, by location and demographic characteristics, 1992 and trends, annual rpt, S1745–3

Georgia county guide, general data, 1993 annual rpt, U6750–1

Georgia statistical abstract, general data, 1992-93 biennial rpt, U6730–1

Georgia vital statistics, including population, births, abortions, deaths by cause, marriages, and divorces, by demographic characteristics and location, 1991 and trends, annual rpt, S1895–1

Hawaii health dept activities and services, including vital statistics and disease control, by location, 1990, annual rpt, S2065–1

Idaho vital statistics, including births, deaths by cause, abortions, marriages, and divorces, by demographic characteristics and county, 1991 and trends, annual rpt, S2250–2

Illinois mental health facility patient population and characteristics, by facility, location, and treatment category, FY93, annual rpt, S2505–1

Illinois statistical abstract, general data, 1992 annual rpt, U6910–2

Iowa vital statistics, including population, births, deaths by cause, marriages, and divorces, by demographic characteristics and location, 1991 and trends, annual rpt, S2795–1

Kansas vital statistics, including population, births, deaths by cause, abortions, marriages, and divorces, by demographic characteristics and location, 1991 and trends, annual rpt, S2975–1

Kentucky health behavior risk factor surveillance survey results, by State area and respondent characteristics, 1988-90, annual rpt, S3140–6

Kentucky vital statistics, including births, deaths by cause, marriages and divorces, and population, by demographic characteristics and county, 1991, annual rpt, S3140–1

Louisiana vital statistics, including population, births, deaths by cause, reportable diseases, marriages, and divorces, by demographic characteristics and locality, 1989-90 and trends, annual rpt, S3295–1

Maine births by race-ethnicity of mother, and abortions by patient characteristics, 1991, annual rpt, S3460–2

Maryland statistical abstract, general data, 1993-94 biennial rpt, S3605–1

Maryland vital statistics, including population, births, deaths by cause, marriages, and divorces, by demographic characteristics and location, 1989 and trends, annual rpt, S3635–1

Massachusetts health behavior risk factor surveillance survey results, by respondent characteristics, 1986-90, recurring rpt, S3850–3

Massachusetts vital statistics, including births, deaths by cause, marriages, divorces, and population, by locality and demographic characteristics, 1990 and trends, annual rpt, S3850–1

Michigan health behavior risk factor surveillance survey results, by respondent characteristics, 1991, annual rpt, S4000–4

Index by Categories

BY RACE

Michigan vital statistics, including births, deaths, marriages, divorces/annulments, and communicable diseases, by location and demographic characteristics, 1990 and trends, annual rpt, S4000–3

Minnesota vital statistics, including population, births, abortions, deaths, marriages, and divorces, by location and demographic characteristics, 1991 and trends, annual rpt, S4190–2

Mississippi statistical abstract, general data, 1992 annual rpt, U3255–4

Mississippi vital statistics, including births, deaths by cause, marriages, and divorces, by demographic characteristics and location, 1992 and trends, annual rpt, S4350–1

Missouri vital statistics, including population, births, deaths by cause, and marriages and divorces, by location and demographic characteristics, 1992 and trends, annual rpt, S4518–1

Montana vital statistics, including births, deaths by cause, abortion, disease, and marriage and divorce, by demographic characteristics and county, 1990-91 and trends, annual rpt, S4690–1

Nebraska vital statistics, including births, deaths, marriages, divorces, and population, by demographic characteristics and location, 1991 and trends, annual rpt, S4885–1

Nevada vital statistics, including births, abortions, and deaths by cause, by county and demographic characteristics, 1989 and trends, annual rpt, S5075–1

New Jersey vital statistics, including births, deaths, population, communicable diseases, and marriages and divorces, by demographic characteristics and location, 1990 and trends, annual rpt, S5405–1

New Mexico vital statistics, including population, births, deaths, and disease, by location and demographic characteristics, 1991 and trends, annual rpt, S5605–1

New York State health behavior risk factor surveillance survey results, by respondent characteristics, 1990, recurring rpt, S5765–3

New York State statistical yearbook, general data, 1992 annual rpt, U5100–1

New York State vital statistics, including population, births, deaths by cause, reportable diseases, and marriages and dissolutions, by demographic characteristics and/or location, 1990 and trends, annual rpt, S5765–1

North Carolina vital statistics, including population, births, deaths, marriages, and divorces, by local area, 1991 and trends, annual rpt, S5927–1.1

North Dakota health behavior risk factor surveillance survey results, by respondent characteristics, 1991 and trends, annual rpt, S6105–3

North Dakota vital statistics, including births, deaths by cause, marriages and divorces, and abortions, by demographic characteristics and/or county, 1991 and trends, annual rpt, S6105–2

Ohio vital statistics, including births, deaths by cause, marriages, divorces, and population, by demographic characteristics and location, 1991 and trends, annual rpt, S6285–1

Oklahoma statistical abstract, general data, 1992 annual rpt, U8130–2

Oregon vital statistics, including births, deaths by cause, communicable diseases, marriages, and divorces, by age, sex, race-ethnicity, and county, 1991 and trends, annual rpt, S6615–5

Rhode Island vital statistics, including population, births, deaths, marriages, and divorces, by demographic characteristics and locality, 1989 and trends, annual rpt, S6995–1

South Carolina deaths, by detailed cause, age, sex, and race, 1990, annual rpt, S7175–2

South Carolina statistical abstract, general data, 1993 annual rpt, S7125–1

South Carolina vital statistics, including births, deaths by cause, marriages, and divorces, by age, sex, race, and location, 1990 and trends, annual rpt, S7175–1

South Dakota vital statistics, including births, deaths, marriage and divorce, and communicable disease, by demographic characteristics and county, 1991 and trends, annual rpt, S7345–1

Tennessee health behavior risk factor surveillance survey results, by respondent characteristics, 1986-90, annual rpt, S7520–3

Tennessee statistical abstract, general data, 1992/93 annual rpt, U8710–2

Tennessee vital statistics, including births, deaths by cause, marriages, divorces, and population, by demographic characteristics and location, 1991 and trends, annual rpt, S7520–2

Texas fertility and survival rates, by age and race-ethnicity, 1990, recurring rpt, S7645–3

Texas health behavior risk factor surveillance survey results, by respondent characteristics, 1991 and trends, annual rpt, S7685–2

Texas local health dept service area population by race-ethnicity, for 22 local areas, 1990, U8850–8.6

Texas nursing employment, demand outlook, earnings, and education, by selected characteristics, various years 1971-91, U8850–8.2

Texas vital statistics, including births, deaths by cause, abortions, marriages, and divorces, by location and demographic characteristics, 1991 and trends, annual rpt, S7685–1

Utah marriages and divorces, by participant characteristics and location, 1990 and trends, annual rpt, S7835–2

Utah vital statistics, including births, deaths by cause, and population, by county and demographic characteristics, 1990 and trends, annual rpt, S7835–1

Vermont vital statistics, including population, births, deaths by cause, abortions, marriages, and divorces, by location and demographic characteristics, 1991 and trends, annual rpt, S8054–1

Virginia vital statistics, including births, deaths by cause, marriages and divorces, and communicable disease, by demographic characteristics and location, 1991 and trends, annual rpt, S8225–1

Washington State vital statistics, including births, deaths by cause, and population, by demographic characteristics and location, 1991 and trends, annual rpt, S8363–1

West Virginia vital statistics, including births, deaths by cause, marriages, and divorces, by location and demographic characteristics, 1991 and trends, annual rpt, S8560–1

Wisconsin vital statistics, including population, births, deaths by cause, and marriages and dissolutions, by county and demographic characteristics, 1991 and trends, annual rpt, S8715–4

Wyoming vital statistics, including population, births, deaths by cause, marriages, and divorces, by demographic characteristics and county, 1991 and trends, annual rpt, S8920–2

Housing and Construction

Low-income housing supply-demand, costs, physical conditions, and public assistance, with data by race-ethnicity, for 44 metro areas, 1980s-91, R3834–16

Mortgage approval rates, by neighborhood characteristics and applicant race-ethnicity and income level, 1990, article, A8510–1.1

Public housing authority operations and finances, including resident characteristics, by agency size, 1989, A6800–1

State and local:

Alabama statistical abstract, general data, 1992 recurring rpt, U5680–2

Arizona statistical abstract, general data, 1993 recurring rpt, U5850–2

Arkansas Census of Population and Housing detailed findings, 1990, U5935–7

California Census of Population and Housing detailed findings, 1990, S0840–9

Florida statistical abstract, general data, 1992 annual rpt, U6660–1

Georgia statistical abstract, general data, 1992-93 biennial rpt, U6730–1

Maine Census of Population and Housing summary findings, by local area, 1990, S3465–7

New Jersey Census of Population and Housing detailed findings, by county, 1990, S5425–19

New York State statistical yearbook, general data, 1992 annual rpt, U5100–1

Oklahoma real estate loan rejection rates for whites and minorities by income level, statewide and by MSA, 1991, article, U8130–1.504

Pennsylvania Census of Population and Housing detailed findings, with selected data by county and municipality, 1990, U4130–13

Rhode Island statistical almanac, general data, 1993 annual rpt, C7975–1

South Carolina statistical abstract, general data, 1993 annual rpt, S7125–1

Income

Black American earnings, income, and poverty data, with comparisons to whites, 1980s-91, annual compilation, C6775–2.7

Black American socioeconomic status, with comparisons to whites and data by region, 1960s-92, annual compilation, A8510–1.1

Child poverty by State and for 200 cities and 89 counties, with State and city detail by race-ethnicity, 1989 and trends, R3840–20

Earnings by sex and race-ethnicity, 1992 feature, C4215–1.502

Earnings of black and Hispanic workers by sex compared to white men, selected years 1963-91, annual rpt, A1570–2

BY RACE

Index by Categories

Household income and/or wealth for whites vs nonwhites, by age, income group, and family type, 1989 and trends, R4700–17

Money income by race, 1990-93, article, C4215–1.502

Planning profession employment and salaries, by type of employer, demographic and professional characteristics, and location, 1991 and trends, biennial rpt, A2615–1

Poor children age 5/under, with demographic and family characteristics, 1991 and trends, annual rpt, U1260–2

Poverty indicators for white population, with comparisons to blacks and Hispanics and data by State, 1990-91, R3834–15

Professional worker salaries, by employee and employer characteristics, with detail for scientists and engineers, 1990s and trends, biennial rpt, A3960–1

Wealth and value of selected types of assets per capita, by race, 1993 article, C4215–1.507

State and local:

Arizona household income and poverty rates, by race-ethnicity, 1989, article, U0280–1.502

Arizona statistical abstract, general data, 1993 recurring rpt, U5850–2

Arkansas Census of Population and Housing detailed findings, 1990, U5935–7

California Census of Population and Housing detailed findings, 1990, S0840–9

Florida county data book, 1992/93 annual rpt, C6360–1

Georgia county guide, general data, 1993 annual rpt, U6750–1

Iowa population share in poverty, by race-ethnicity, 1990, annual rpt, S2784–3

Kentucky labor force planning rpt, including population and labor force characteristics, and employment by industry, 1991 and trends, annual rpt, S3140–3

Louisiana Census of Population and Housing summary findings, by local area, 1990 and trends, U8010–4

Mississippi characteristics of economically disadvantaged and Job Training Partnership Act eligible population, 1993/94, annual planning rpt, S4345–1.3

New Jersey Census of Population and Housing detailed findings, by county, 1990, S5425–19

New Mexico population in poverty, by race-ethnicity and county, 1990, S5620–2.501

New Mexico population in poverty, by race-ethnicity, 1989, annual rpt, S5624–1

New Mexico residents in poverty, by race-ethnicity, 1979 and 1989, annual rpt, S5605–1.1

Pennsylvania Census of Population and Housing detailed findings, with selected data by county and municipality, 1990, U4130–13

South Carolina statistical abstract, general data, 1993 annual rpt, S7125–1

Utah personal income and household data, by location and race-ethnicity, 1990 census rpt, S7832–3.3

Washington State population and demographic characteristics, and housing units, by county and/or city, 1992 and trends, annual rpt, S8345–4

Industry and Commerce

Business formation rate by race-ethnicity, 1993 article, C4687–1.510

Consumer shopping practices, including methods used to cut back on expenditures and learn about products, for blacks vs non-blacks, 1993 survey feature, C4215–1.510

Corporate boards of directors with women and minority members, and board membership by sex and race-ethnicity, 1991/92, B4490–2.36

Cosmetics sales to general population and black consumers, distribution by outlet type, 1991, article, C5150–2.502

Drugstore marketing to ethnic minorities, with related consumer indicators for blacks or by race, 1993 articles, C5150–2.518

Household use indexes for medicated skin care and children's pain reliever products, by brand, for white vs black households, 1993 article, C5150–2.520

Minority-owned business establishments and gross receipts compared to total US, by race-ethnicity, 1987, article, C4215–1.507

Private label product characteristics and purchasing factors as seen by consumers, by selected characteristics, 1991 survey, article, C0125–1.504

Retail outlet consumer preference indexes, by selected demographic characteristics, 1993 annual feature, C4655–1.504

Retail outlet selection factors cited by consumers, by race, 1993 survey article, C4215–1.509

State and local:

Hawaii data book, general data, 1992 annual rpt, S2090–1

Labor and Employment

Black American labor force and employment data, with comparisons to whites, 1970s-91, annual compilation, C6775–2.6

Displaced workers by sex, race-ethnicity, industry div, and occupation, with characteristics of new employment, 1987-92, article, S0465–1.506

Job Corps youth training program funding, enrollment capacity, and participants by selected characteristics, 1981-94, article, R4800–2.515

Labor force by employment status, by race, 1991-93, article, C4215–1.502

Labor force data, by race and sex, 1993 annual compilation, A8510–1.1

Labor force size, entrants, and leavers, by sex and race-ethnicity, 1990-2005, article, R8750–1.507

Labor union membership compared to total workers, by sex, race and Hispanic ethnicity, occupation, and industry div, 1991-92, article, S0465–1.505

Men age 18-29 employment in manufacturing, and mean earnings, by race-ethnicity, 1970s-86, annual rpt, R8335–1.1

Minority employment levels among businesses in minority communities, by owner race, 1993 article, C4215–1.510

Minority population characteristics, employment, and voting patterns by detailed race-ethnicity, with comparisons to whites, 1980s-2040, R8750–2.58

Pension benefits and coverage as affected by job tenure and mobility, with data by plan type and worker characteristics, 1993 rpt, R9260–17

Planning profession employment and salaries, by type of employer, demographic and professional characteristics, and location, 1991 and trends, biennial rpt, A2615–1

Sales workers by sex and race-ethnicity, 1990, article, C1200–1.512

Statistical profiles of 50 States and DC, general data, 1993 annual almanac, C4712–1

Women and minorities in professional fields, detailed education and labor force data, 1980s-91, with historical trends, recurring rpt, A3960–2

Women professionals employment, with detail by race-ethnicity and for 3 occupations, 1990 and trends, article, R8750–1.511

Women's labor force participation, by race-ethnicity, 1973-92, annual rpt, A1570–2

Work force by occupational group, by race, Mar 1993, annual rpt, A1570–1

Youth age 20 unemployment rates, with detail for high school grads and dropouts, by sex and race, 1963-67 and 1983-87, article, C4687–1.511

Youth employment shares by race and Hispanic ethnicity, among ages 15-17, 1991, R8335–2

State and local:

Arkansas Census of Population and Housing detailed findings, 1990, U5935–7

Arkansas vocational rehabilitation expenditures, impact on earnings and employment, and client characteristics, FY91 annual rpt, S0700–2.4

California Census of Population and Housing detailed findings, 1990, S0840–9

California employment statistics, by demographic characteristics, industry, MSA, and county, monthly rpt, S0830–1

California labor force planning rpt, including population characteristics, and employment by industry, 1992 annual rpt, S0830–2

California registered apprentices, by trade, race-ethnicity, and sex, 1991 and trends, annual rpt, S0840–2.3

Colorado job service applicant characteristics, FY93 annual planning rpt, S1040–3.2

DC statistical profile, general data, 1992 annual rpt, S1535–3

Florida statistical abstract, general data, 1992 annual rpt, U6660–1

Georgia county guide, general data, 1993 annual rpt, U6750–1

Georgia statistical abstract, general data, 1992-93 biennial rpt, U6730–1

Hawaii data book, general data, 1992 annual rpt, S2090–1

Indiana, Indianapolis employment trends for executives and machinists by sex and race, with comparisons to 5 other metro areas, 1980-90, article, U2160–1.504

Kentucky labor force planning rpt, including population and labor force characteristics, and employment by industry, 1991 and trends, annual rpt, S3140–3

Louisiana Census of Population and Housing summary findings, by local area, 1990 and trends, U8010–4

Louisiana insured unemployed by occupation and industry div, by race and MSA, monthly rpt quarterly table, S3320–2

Louisiana labor force planning rpt, including population and labor force characteristics, unemployment claimants, and data by parish and MSA, 1993 annual rpt, S3320–1

Index by Categories BY RACE

Maryland statistical abstract, general data, 1993-94 biennial rpt, S3605–1

Maryland vocational rehabilitation center client characteristics, 1992, annual rpt, S3610–1

Michigan labor force planning rpt, including employment by industry, and characteristics of Job Training Partnership Act eligible population, 1993 annual rpt, S3980–1

Mississippi labor force planning rpt, including population, employment, and characteristics of unemployed and disadvantaged, 1993 annual rpt, S4345–1

Mississippi statistical abstract, general data, 1992 annual rpt, U3255–4

Montana employment and unemployment, by race-ethnicity and county, 1990, annual planning rpt, S4710–3

New Hampshire job service applicant characteristics, monthly rpt, S5205–1

New Hampshire labor force and population by race, sex, and age, and employment by industry div, statewide and by county, 1992 recurring rpt, S5205–7

New Jersey Census of Population and Housing detailed findings, by county, 1990, S5425–19

New Jersey insured unemployed characteristics, monthly rpt, S5425–1

New Jersey unemployment rates by race and sex, 1991-92, annual article, S5425–1.503

New Mexico labor force planning rpt, including population characteristics, and employment by industry and occupation, 1993 annual rpt, S5624–1

New York State statistical yearbook, general data, 1992 annual rpt, U5100–1

Oklahoma statistical abstract, general data, 1992 annual rpt, U8130–2

Pennsylvania Census of Population and Housing detailed findings, with selected data by county and municipallty, 1990, U4130–13

Pennsylvania employment and commuting data from Census of Population and Housing, by county and municipality, 1990, C1595–16

Pennsylvania labor force and population characteristics, FY92 annual planning rpt, S6845–3.1

Pennsylvania statistical abstract, general data, 1992 recurring rpt, U4130–6

South Carolina labor force planning rpt, detailed data on employment, hours, wages, turnover, and characteristics of job service applicants, 1992 annual rpt, S7155–3.2

South Carolina statistical abstract, general data, 1993 annual rpt, S7125–1

South Dakota employment, earnings, and hours for selected industries and areas, with characteristics of unemployed and job service activities, monthly rpt, S7355–1

Tennessee labor force by employment status, and employment by sex and race, by occupational group and industry div, 1992, articles, S7495–2.506

Tennessee statistical abstract, general data, 1992/93 annual rpt, U8710–2

Utah employment by detailed occupation, and educational attainment by age group, by sex and race-ethnicity, with detail for 7 urban areas, 1990 census rpt, S7832–3.4

Utah labor force and percent without high school diploma, by sex, age group, and/or race-ethnicity, 1990, article, U8960–2.509

Vermont labor force by employment status, and job service openings and applicant characteristics, 1993 annual planning rpt, S8025–2.2

West Virginia labor force planning rpt, including population, employment, and job service activities, with data by county and service delivery area, 1993 annual rpt, S8534–2

Wyoming employment and unemployment by sex and race-ethnicity, by county, 1990, S8895–1.505

Law Enforcement

Black American crime, arrest, and incarceration data, with comparisons to whites, 1970s-91, annual compilation, C6775–2.5

Correctional instn inmates and staff, and probationers, by sex and race, by State and for Federal system, and for major jails, Jan 1992, annual series, R4300–1

Correctional instns, inmates, staff, and cost of care, by instn, US and Canada, with operating summary by State or Province, 1992, annual directory, A1305–3

Crime victims per 1,000 population, by demographic characteristics, 1991, article, R8750–1.505

Incarcerated mothers and their children, with data on characteristics, child caregivers, visitation, and support program use, 1991/92, A7575–4

Juvenile State instn custody prevalence rates by sex, age, and race-ethnicity, for 16 States, 1991, A7575–1.13

Law school enrollment by minority status, degrees conferred, staff, and library holdings, by instn, 1992/93 and trends, annual rpt, A0970–1

Law school grad employment and salaries, by type of employer, location, and grad characteristics, 1992 and trends, annual rpt, A6505–1

Prisoners on death row, by State, sex, and race-ethnicity, 1992 and trends, annual rpt, A1305–3

State and local:

Alabama crimes and arrests, by victim and offender characteristics, 1992, annual rpt, S0119–1.1

Alaska corrections system admin, including inmate and probationer/parolee offenses and demographic characteristics, 1991 annual rpt, S0287–1

Alaska State court system employees, by race-ethnicity, FY92, annual rpt, S0290–1

Arizona arrests and murder victims, by age, sex, and race-ethnicity, 1992, annual rpt, S0505–2

Arizona correctional instn admin, including inmates by criminal background and demographic characteristics, FY92, annual rpt, S0464–2

Arizona statistical abstract, general data, 1993 recurring rpt, U5850–2

Arkansas child abuse and neglect victims, by age, sex, and race, FY91, annual rpt, S0700–2.2

Arkansas crimes and arrests, by offense, victim and offender characteristics, and location, 1992 and trends, annual rpt, S0652–1

California correctional instn inmates, by offense, demographic characteristics, and instn, Dec 1992, semiannual rpt, S0820–2

California correctional instn inmates, with criminal background and demographic characteristics, 1991 and trends, annual rpt, S0820–1

California crimes and arrests, clearances, and arrest dispositions, with data by offense and offender characteristics, 1987-92, annual rpt, S0910–1.1

California criminal justice system detailed data, by offense, county, age, race-ethnicity, and sex, 1991 and trends, annual rpt, S0910–2.2

California judicial system employment by position, sex, and race-ethnicity, with minority utilization rates and parity targets, Jan 1993, annual rpt, S0905–1.1

Colorado homicide offenders and victims, by age, sex, and race-ethnicity, 1991-92, annual rpt, S1068–1

Connecticut crimes and arrests, by offense, with data by local agency, and victim-offender characteristics, 1992, annual rpt, S1256–1

DC court committee members by race-ethnicity and sex, by committee, 1992, annual rpt, S1515–1

Delaware crimes and arrests, by offense, county, and victim-offender characteristics, 1991 and trends, annual rpt, S1375–5

Delaware public opinion on criminal sentencing, prison alternatives, and related issues, Feb 1991 survey, R8825–11

Florida correctional instns, admin, and inmates by criminal background and demographic characteristics, FY92 annual rpt, S1720–1

Florida county data book, 1992/93 annual rpt, C6360–1

Florida "habitual offender" sentencing laws effect on prison population, with data by circuit court and offender characteristics, 1993 rpt, A7575–5

Florida statistical abstract, general data, 1992 annual rpt, U6660–1

Georgia correctional instns, admin, and inmate characteristics, FY92, annual rpt, S1872–1

Georgia county guide, general data, 1993 annual rpt, U6750–1

Georgia crimes and arrests, by offense, with data by location and offender characteristics, 1992 and trends, annual rpt, S1901–1

Georgia statistical abstract, general data, 1992-93 biennial rpt, U6730–1

Hawaii crimes and arrests, by offense, with data by county and victim-offender characteristics, 1992, annual rpt, S2035–1

Idaho crimes and arrests, by offense, with data by location and offender characteristics, 1992 and trends, annual rpt, S2275–2

Illinois corrections dept admin, including inmates and characteristics, finances, and staff, FY91-93 and trends, annual rpt, S2425–1

Illinois crimes and arrests, by offender characteristics, 1990-91, annual rpt, S2536–1

Indiana child abuse and neglect cases by county and victim and perpetrator characteristics, FY92 annual rpt, S2623–1.7

Iowa correctional instn admissions, releases, and inmate characteristics, by instn, monthly rpt, S2770–1

BY RACE

Kansas correctional instn inmates, by offense, demographic characteristics, and instn, FY92 and trends, annual rpt, S2940–1

Kansas crimes and arrests, with victim, offender, and law enforcement employee characteristics, 1992, annual rpt, S2925–1

Kansas statistical abstract, general data, 1991/92 annual rpt, U7095–2

Kentucky crimes and arrests, by offense, with data by location and offender characteristics, 1992, annual rpt, S3150–1

Maryland crimes and arrests, by offense, location, and offender characteristics, with law enforcement employment and assaults on officers, 1992 and trends, annual rpt, S3665–1

Massachusetts correctional instn inmate socioeconomic characteristics and criminal background, by instn, Jan 1992 and trends, annual rpt, S3805–1

Michigan correctional instns, admin, and inmates by selected demographic characteristics, 1991 and trends, annual rpt, S3960–1

Michigan crimes and arrests, with murder victims by race, sex, and age, 1992, annual rpt, S3997–1

Mississippi statistical abstract, general data, 1992 annual rpt, U3255–4

Missouri correctional instn admissions, releases, and inmate characteristics, FY93, annual rpt, S4501–1

Missouri crimes and arrests, by offense and location, with victim and offender characteristics, 1991 and trends, annual rpt, S4560–2

Nebraska correctional instn admin, with inmates by criminal background and demographic characteristics, by instn, FY92 and trends, annual rpt, S4850–1

New Hampshire arrests, by offense and offender age, sex, and race-ethnicity, 1991, annual rpt, S5250–2.2

New Jersey correctional instn inmates, by offense, sentence length, demographic characteristics, and instn, Dec 1991 annual rpt, S5370–1

New Jersey crimes and arrests, by offense, with data by location and offender characteristics, 1992 and trends, annual rpt, S5430–1

New York State arrests, homicide victims and offenders, and prisoners, by demographic characteristics, 1991, annual rpt, S5760–3

New York State correctional instn inmates released, by criminal background, sentence, and demographic characteristics, 1991 and trends, recurring rpt series, S5725–1

New York State local jail/penitentiary inmates by offense, sentence, and demographic characteristics, by county or facility, 1991, annual rpt, S5724–2

New York State statistical yearbook, general data, 1992 annual rpt, U5100–1

North Carolina correctional instn admissions, separations, and population, with inmate characteristics, FY93, semiannual rpt, S5900–1

North Carolina crimes and arrests, by offense, with data by location and offender characteristics, 1992 and trends, annual rpt, S5955–1

North Dakota crimes and arrests, by offense, location, and offender characteristics, and law enforcement employment, 1991 and trends, annual rpt, S6060–1

North Dakota local correctional instn adult and juvenile inmate characteristics, by instn, 1991 and trends, annual rpt, S6060–3

Ohio correctional instn admissions and releases, inmate characteristics, programs, finances, and staffing, FY91 and trends, annual rpt, S6370–1

Oklahoma correctional instn admin, including inmate characteristics, incarceration costs, and data by instn, FY91, annual rpt, S6420–1

Oklahoma crimes and arrests, by offense, with data by local agency and victim and offender characteristics, 1990-92, annual rpt, S6465–1

Oregon crimes and arrests, by offense, with detail on bias crimes and data by victim and offender characteristics, 1992 and trends, annual rpt, S6603–3.1

Pennsylvania crimes and arrests, by offense, with data by location and offender characteristics, 1992 and trends, annual rpt, S6860–1

Pennsylvania State correctional instn admin, and inmates by type of offense and demographic characteristics, 1990 and trends, annual rpt, S6782–1

Pennsylvania statistical abstract, general data, 1992 recurring rpt, U4130–6

South Carolina correctional instns, admin, and inmates by criminal offense and demographic characteristics, FY92 and trends, annual rpt, S7135–1

South Carolina crimes and arrests, by offense, with data by location and victim-offender characteristics, and assaults on officers, 1992 and trends, annual rpt, S7205–1

South Carolina statistical abstract, general data, 1993 annual rpt, S7125–1

South Dakota correctional instn admin, including inmates by criminal background and demographic characteristics, FY92 and trends, annual rpt, S7296 1

Tennessee correctional instn admin, with inmate characteristics, and corrections dept finances and staff, FY92, annual rpt, S7480–1

Tennessee statistical abstract, general data, 1992/93 annual rpt, U8710–2

Texas correctional instn inmates by criminal background and demographic characteristics, FY92, annual rpt, S7660–1

Texas criminal offenders and victims by race-ethnicity and selected offense, 1992, annual rpt, S7735–2

Utah corrections inmates, parolees, and probationers, by criminal background and demographic characteristics, FY92 and trends, annual rpt, S7810–1

Utah murder victims and offenders, by race-ethnicity, 1992, annual rpt, S7890–3

Virginia crimes and arrests, by offense, with data by location and offender characteristics, 1992, annual rpt, S8295–2

Washington State correctional instn inmate population, admissions, and releases, by demographic characteristics, quarterly rpt, S8337–1

Washington State crimes and arrests, by offense, with data by location and offender characteristics, 1992 and trends, annual rpt, S8440–1

West Virginia arrests and murder victims, by race-ethnicity, 1990-91, annual rpt, S8610–1.1

Wisconsin correctional instn inmates, by criminal background and selected characteristics, series, S8692–1

Wisconsin crimes and arrests, by offense, offender characteristics, county, and local agency, 1992 and trends, annual rpt, S8771–1

Wyoming correctional instn admin, finances, inmate characteristics, and staff, and probation and parole activities, FY92 annual rpt, S8883–1

Wyoming homicide victim and offender characteristics, and arrests by offense and age, 1991, annual rpt, S8867–3.1

Population

Births and fertility, by selected newborn and maternal characteristics, 1990, article, R8750–1.510

Black American socioeconomic status, including health, education, politics, crime, and employment, with comparisons to whites, 1993 annual compilation, C6775–2

Black American socioeconomic status, with comparisons to whites, 1993 annual compilation, A8510–1

Black children and youth population, economic, health, and education data, with comparisons to whites, 1993 rpt, R3840–21

Census of Population and Housing undercounts, by race and sex, 1990 Census and trends, annual rpt, C2500–2

Child health and well-being indicators, by race-ethnicity, 1993 annual rpt, R3832–1

Children's living arrangements, by parents characteristics and child age and race-ethnicity, 1992, article, B6045–1.504

Children's living arrangements, by parents characteristics and child race-ethnicity, 1991, article, B6045–1.503

Children's living arrangements, by race-ethnicity, decennially 1960-90, B6045–1.502

Consumer buying power survey of population, income, and sales by product line, by State, metro area, county, and census div, 1993 annual rpt, C1200–1.514

Gallup Poll public attitude surveys, results and sample characteristics, monthly rpt, C4040–1

Homeless population characteristics in 29 cities, 1991/92, annual rpt, A9330–9

Immigrant share of population growth by race-ethnicity, 1992-2010, article, C5800–7.533

Japan public image in US, with data on US attitudes toward the Japanese by race, 1993 survey article, R5650–2.520

Low-income families and children, health and welfare indicators, with data by State and city, 1992 annual rpt, R3840–11

Market area population and characteristics, households, income, and retail outlets, for 21 leading areas, 1993 feature, C2710–1.538

Married couples by race and Hispanic ethnicity of husband and wife, 1991, annual compilation, C6775–3.1

Men age 69-84 quality of life indicators, including health, finances, family, and employment, by race, 1990 survey, U3780–9

Minority population characteristics, employment, and voting patterns by detailed race-ethnicity, with comparisons to whites, 1980s-2040, R8750–2.58

Index by Categories

BY RACE

Older population age 65/over educational attainment, by race-ethnicity, 1970, 1980, and 1990, B6045–1.504

Population by race and detailed ethnic group, 1992 recurring rpt, A3960–2.1

Population by race-ethnicity, 1985, 1991, and 2000, article, C2150–6.504

Religion and related social issues, public opinions and attitudes, monthly survey, R8780–1

Religious congregation characteristics, including membership, activities, staff, and finances, 1992 survey, recurring rpt, A5435–4

Southern States population, personal income, and State/local revenues and expenditures, by State, 1950s-2010, biennial fact book, A8945–1.1

Statistical profiles of 50 States and DC, general data, 1993 annual almanac, C4712–1

Teenage girls unplanned childbearing effects on socioeconomic condition, by race, 1993 article, A5160–1.505

Women's housing issues, with data on household composition, tenure, and characteristics, 1992, A8657–5

State and local:

Alabama county data book, general data, 1992 annual rpt, S0121–2

Alabama population trends by race, with detail for 20 counties comprising Black Belt region, 1880-1990, U0340–1.6

Alabama statistical abstract, general data, 1992 recurring rpt, U5680–2

Alabama vital statistics, including population, births, deaths by cause, marriages, and divorces, by location and demographic characteristics, 1992 and trends, annual rpt, S0175–2

Alaska population, housing, income, and education data, by demographic characteristics and/or locality, 1990/91 and trends, annual rpt, S0320–4

Alaska vital statistics, including births, deaths by cause, marriages, divorces, adoptions, and population, by demographic characteristics and location, 1990, annual rpt, S0315–1

Arizona statistical abstract, general data, 1993 recurring rpt, U5850–2

Arkansas adoptions by child age, race, and sex, FY91, annual rpt, S0700–2.2

Arkansas Census of Population and Housing detailed findings, 1990, U5935–7

Arkansas population, by race, 1920-91, annual rpt, S0685–1

California Census of Population and Housing detailed findings, 1990, S0840–9

California labor force planning rpt, including population characteristics, and employment by industry, 1992 annual rpt, S0830–2

California population by age, sex, race-ethnicity, and county, decennially 1990-2040, recurring rpt, S0840–4

California socioeconomic and govtl data for municipalities, counties, and school districts, 1993 annual rpt, C4712–3

California statistical abstract, general data, 1992 annual rpt, S0840–2

Colorado vital statistics, including population, births, deaths by cause, abortion, marriage and divorce, and adoption, by demographic characteristics and location, 1990 and trends, annual rpt, S1010–1

DC statistical profile, general data, 1992 annual rpt, S1535–3

Delaware population, by age, sex, race, and locality, 1990-2020, recurring rpt, S1375–3

Delaware vital statistics, including births, deaths by cause, and marriages and dissolutions, by demographic characteristics and location, 1990, annual rpt, S1385–2

Florida county data book, 1992/93 annual rpt, C6360–1

Florida municipal and county statistical profiles, general data, 1991 annual rpt, C4712–6

Florida population by age, sex, and race, by county, 1990, 1992, and quinquennially 1995-2010, annual rpt, U6660–3.46

Florida population by age, sex, and race, by county, 1990-91 and quinquennially 1995-2010, annual rpt, U6660–3.43

Florida population, by race-ethnicity, age, and county, 1992 annual rpt, S1746–1.1

Florida statistical abstract, general data, 1992 annual rpt, U6660–1

Florida vital statistics, including population, births, deaths by cause, and marriages and dissolutions, by location and demographic characteristics, 1992 and trends, annual rpt, S1745–3

Georgia county guide, general data, 1993 annual rpt, U6750–1

Georgia statistical abstract, general data, 1992-93 biennial rpt, U6730–1

Georgia vital statistics, including population, births, abortions, deaths by cause, marriages, and divorces, by demographic characteristics and location, 1991 and trends, annual rpt, S1895–1

Hawaii data book, general data, 1992 annual rpt, S2090–1

Idaho economic profile, general data, 1992 recurring rpt, S2218–2.2

Idaho population by race-ethnicity, 1990, annual rpt, S2250–2

Illinois statistical abstract, general data, 1992 annual rpt, U6910–2

Kansas statistical abstract, general data, 1991/92 annual rpt, U7095–2

Kentucky economic statistics, general data, 1993 annual rpt, S3104–1

Kentucky labor force planning rpt, including population and labor force characteristics, and employment by industry, 1991 and trends, annual rpt, S3140–3

Kentucky vital statistics, including births, deaths by cause, marriages and divorces, and population, by demographic characteristics and county, 1991, annual rpt, S3140–1

Louisiana Census of Population and Housing summary findings, by local area, 1990 and trends, U8010–4

Louisiana population, by race, sex, and location, 1992, annual planning rpt, S3320–1.1

Maine Census of Population and Housing summary findings, by local area, 1990, S3465–7, S3465–8

Maryland statistical abstract, general data, 1993-94 biennial rpt, S3605–1

Maryland vital statistics, including population, births, deaths by cause, marriages, and divorces, by demographic characteristics and location, 1989 and trends, annual rpt, S3635–1

Massachusetts municipal and county profiles, general data, 1992 annual rpt, C4712–2

Massachusetts vital statistics, including births, deaths by cause, marriages, divorces, and population, by locality and demographic characteristics, 1990 and trends, annual rpt, S3850–1

Michigan labor force planning rpt, including employment by industry, and characteristics of Job Training Partnership Act eligible population, 1993 annual rpt, S3980–1

Michigan population, by age, sex, race, and county, 1990, annual rpt, S4000–3

Mississippi population, by age, race, sex, and educational attainment, 1993/94, annual planning rpt, S4345–1.1

Mississippi population, by age, sex, race, and location, 1990, annual rpt, S4350–1

Mississippi statistical abstract, general data, 1992 annual rpt, U3255–4

Nevada statistical abstract, general data, 1992 biennial rpt, S5005–1

New Hampshire labor force and population by race, sex, and age, and employment by industry div, statewide and by county, 1992 recurring rpt, S5205–7

New Jersey Census of Population and Housing detailed findings, by county, 1990, S5425–19

New Jersey municipal and county data book, general data, 1992 annual rpt, C4712–4

New Jersey population, by race-ethnicity, sex, age, and county, 1990, annual rpt, S5405–1

New Mexico population, by race-ethnicity and county, 1990 and trends, annual planning rpt, S5624–1

New Mexico vital statistics, including population, births, deaths, and disease, by location and demographic characteristics, 1991 and trends, annual rpt, S5605–1

New York State adoptions, by sex, age, and race-ethnicity, 1991 and trends, annual rpt, S5800–2.3

New York State municipal and county statistical profiles, general data, 1993 annual rpt, C4712–7

New York State statistical yearbook, general data, 1992 annual rpt, U5100–1

New York State vital statistics, including population, births, deaths by cause, reportable diseases, and marriages and dissolutions, by demographic characteristics and/or location, 1990 and trends, annual rpt, S5765–1

North Carolina vital statistics, including population, births, deaths, marriages, and divorces, by local area, 1991 and trends, annual rpt, S5927–1.1

Ohio vital statistics, including births, deaths by cause, marriages, divorces, and population, by demographic characteristics and location, 1991 and trends, annual rpt, S6285–1

Oklahoma statistical abstract, general data, 1992 annual rpt, U8130–2

Pennsylvania Census of Population and Housing detailed findings, with selected data by county and municipality, 1990, U4130–13

Pennsylvania statistical abstract, general data, 1992 recurring rpt, U4130–6

Rhode Island labor force planning rpt, including population, employment by

BY RACE

industry, job openings, and characteristics of insured unemployed, 1993 annual rpt, S6980–3

Rhode Island statistical almanac, general data, 1993 annual rpt, C7975–1

Rhode Island vital statistics, including population, births, deaths, marriages, and divorces, by demographic characteristics and locality, 1989 and trends, annual rpt, S6995–1

South Carolina labor force planning rpt, including population, employment, income, and job service activities, 1992 annual rpt, S7155–3

South Carolina population characteristics, by county, 1993 annual rpt, S7145–1.1

South Carolina population, total and women age 15-44, by race, 1990 and trends, annual rpt, S7175–1

South Carolina statistical abstract, general data, 1993 annual rpt, S7125–1

Tennessee population, by age, sex, race, and county, 1990-2010, recurring rpt, S7560–2

Tennessee population by race, 1972-91, annual rpt, S7520–2

Tennessee statistical abstract, general data, 1992/93 annual rpt, U8710–2

Texas labor force planning rpt, including labor force, employment by industry, income, and population, 1993 annual rpt, S7675–2

Texas population, by age, sex, race-ethnicity, and county, July 1991, annual rpt, S7645–2

Texas population, by county and race-ethnicity, 1990-2030, recurring rpt, S7645–3

Utah employment by detailed occupation, and educational attainment by age group, by sex and race-ethnicity, with detail for 7 urban areas, 1990 census rpt, S7832–3.4

Utah govt statistical review, fiscal and socioeconomic data, 1993 annual rpt, R9380–1

Utah population distribution and selected characteristics, by race-ethnicity, 1990, S7820–3.504

Utah statistical abstract, general data, 1993 triennial rpt, U8960–1

Virginia population by race and location, 1991 and trends, annual rpt, S8225–1

Washington State population and demographic characteristics, and housing units, by county and/or city, 1992 and trends, annual rpt, S8345–4

West Virginia labor force planning rpt, including population, employment, and job service activities, with data by county and service delivery area, 1993 annual rpt, S8534–2

West Virginia population, by race-ethnicity, 1990, annual rpt, S8560–1

Wisconsin Blue Book, general data, 1993-94 biennial rpt, S8780–1.2

Wisconsin vital statistics, including population, births, deaths by cause, and marriages and dissolutions, by county and demographic characteristics, 1991 and trends, annual rpt, S8715–4

Public Welfare and Social Security

Arts/humanities organization charitable contribution donor characteristics, 1993 survey article, C2176–1.507

Foundation board trustees by sex and race-ethnicity, for 25 leading private, community, and corporate foundations, 1989 and trends, A9405–1.1

Foundation board trustees by sex and race-ethnicity, for 25 leading private, community, and corporate foundations, 1991 and trends, A9405–1.2

Foundation employment distribution by sex, race, and minority status, by position type, 1993, article, C2176–1.520

Foundation finances, and personnel and governing board characteristics, by organization characteristics, 1991/92, article, C2176–1.506

Nonprofit foundation boards, officers, and staff, by sex and race, 1992, annual rpt, A0700–1.1

Public assistance and social insurance program participation among whites, blacks, and Hispanics, 1991, R3834–15

Volunteer activities and characteristics of teenagers vs adults, 1991, survey article, C2176–1.503

Youth age 12-17 charitable contributions, volunteer activity, and views on related issues, by respondent characteristics, 1992 survey, biennial rpt, A5435–5

State and local:

Arkansas human services dept finances and operations, including service recipient characteristics, by program, FY91 and trends, annual rpt, S0700–2

California AFDC recipients by selected characteristics, June 1988-90, annual planning rpt, S0830–2

California statistical abstract, general data, 1992 annual rpt, S0840–2

Georgia statistical abstract, general data, 1992-93 biennial rpt, U6730–1

Hawaii data book, general data, 1992 annual rpt, S2090–1

Indiana public assistance program participation, expenditures, and services, by county, FY92 and trends, annual rpt, S2623–1

Maryland medical assistance payments and recipients, by program, type of service, location, demographic characteristics, and facility, FY92 and trends, annual rpt, S3635–3

Michigan public assistance recipients, by race-ethnicity and county, monthly rpt quarterly tables, S4010–1

Michigan welfare registrants by race-ethnicity, June 1992, annual planning rpt, S3980–1.2

New Mexico public welfare recipient characteristics, by program, monthly rpt quarterly table, S5620–2

New York State adoptions, by sex, age, and race-ethnicity, 1991 and trends, annual rpt, S5800–2.3

New York State statistical yearbook, general data, 1992 annual rpt, U5100–1

Oklahoma public welfare program recipients and payments, and recipient characteristics, by county and type of service, FY92, annual rpt, S6455–1.2

Pennsylvania statistical abstract, general data, 1992 recurring rpt, U4130–6

South Dakota social services for elderly, with recipients by race-ethnicity, FY92, annual rpt, S7385–1.1

Texas Medicaid expenditures by category, and recipient characteristics and medical services received, 1975 and 1980-91, U8850–8.5

Utah homeless shelter population characteristics, individual shelter capacity, and related housing data, 1991-92, annual rpt, S7808–2

Washington State public assistance clients and service costs, by client characteristics, program, and county, FY90, annual rpt, S8420–2

Science and Technology

Chemist and chemical engineer salaries, employment status, and demographic and professional characteristics, 1993, annual rpt, A1250–4

Chemistry and chemical engineering grad starting salaries, employment status, demographic characteristics, and advanced study plans, 1991/92, annual rpt, A1250–2

Ecologist personal and professional characteristics, including research activity and funding, with data by field, Mar 1992 survey, recurring rpt, A4685–1

Engineering degrees awarded, by State, instn, and field, with detail for women, minorities, and foreign students, 1991/92, annual rpt, A0685–1

Engineering program enrollment, by instn, field, and State, with detail for women, minorities, and foreign students, fall 1992, annual rpt, A0685–2

Geoscience enrollment and degrees awarded, by sex, race-ethnicity, and discipline, 1991/92, annual rpt, A1785–3

Physics and astronomy bachelor degree recipients postgraduation plans and demographic characteristics, 1991/92 and trends, annual survey, A1960–3

Physics degrees awarded, by level, sex, and minority group, 1991/92, annual rpt, A1960–2.1

Psychology doctoral degree recipient employment and demographic characteristics, and finances, 1990/91, biennial survey rpt, A2620–4

Psychology grad depts, faculty characteristics, enrollment, and student aid, US and Canada, 1990/91 and trends, annual rpt, A2620–3

Science and math elementary/secondary education, including student and teacher characteristics, by State, 1991/92, biennial rpt, A4355–3.1

Transportation and Travel

Airline travel frequency, destination, and purpose, by traveler characteristics, 1992 survey and trends, annual rpt, A0325–6

Veterans Affairs

State and local:

Mississippi veterans by period served, and labor force status of Vietnam era veterans by age, by race, 1993/94, annual planning rpt, S4345–1.1

BY SEX

Agriculture and Food

Alcohol use patterns among high school seniors, by sex, 1993 survey article, B6045–1.504

Black American farm and farm operator characteristics, with comparisons to all farms, 1987, annual compilation, C6775–2.8

Children's consumption of 6 food product types, by sex, 1990 survey, article, C2710–1.512

Index by Categories

BY SEX

Convenience store employee characteristics, 1992, annual survey rpt, A6735–1

Distilled spirits consumption, and consumer characteristics and buying habits, 1992 and trends, annual rpt, C4775–1.3

Food catering market, including consumer attendance at catered events by sex and income, 1992 survey, article, A8200–1.503

Food nutrition awareness and health concerns, including consumption patterns, by respondent characteristics, 1993 survey, annual rpt, A4950–36

Food service industry employee characteristics, and minority-owned establishments and sales, 1993 article, A8200–1.508

Food store managers by sex, 1991, annual rpt, A4950–5.2

Food take-out consumer characteristics, consumption patterns, and attitudes, May 1992 survey, A8200–21

Food/beverage manufacturing mgmt salaries, responsibility, job satisfaction, and views on effect of affirmative action, by sex, 1992 survey, annual article, C2150–6.502

Hispanic American farm and farm operator characteristics, with comparisons to all farms, 1987, annual compilation, C6775–3.6

Older population restaurant menu item preferences, by sex, 1992, article, A8200–1.510

Restaurant (table service) operations and menu offerings, and related consumer views and practices by demographic characteristics, 1992, recurring rpt, A8200–11

Restaurant dessert operations and consumer ordering patterns, 1992 survey rpt, A8200–20

Restaurant patron salad ordering patterns, by sex, 1991, article, A8200–1.501

Restaurant smoking policy importance to consumers, and views on smoking acceptability in restaurants and other public places, by selected characteristics, Jan 1993 survey, A8200–8.15

Restaurant/food service mgmt compensation, characteristics, and views, including data by position, 1992 survey, annual article, C1850–3.502

Restaurant/lodging industries executives/managers, by sex and race-ethnicity, 1992, article, C5150–5.511

Snack food consumption patterns, by snack type and consumer characteristics, 1989/90 and trends, recurring rpt, A8905–2

Supermarket shopper practices, attitudes, and expenditures, by respondent characteristics, 1993 and trends, annual survey rpt, A4950–3

Supermarket shopper views on quality of customer service and importance of selected factors, by respondent characteristics, 1991-92 surveys, A4950–37

Wine and other alcoholic beverage consumption, and consumer characteristics and buying habits, 1993 annual rpt, C4775–2.2

State and local:

Florida statistical abstract, general data, 1992 annual rpt, U6660–1

Banking, Finance, and Insurance

Accounting grad supply-demand, including detail by sex, race-ethnicity, and region, 1991/92 and trends, annual rpt, A1885–1

Life insurance benefit payments, by payment method and characteristics of beneficiaries and insured, 1940s-91, biennial fact book, A1325–1.2

Life insurance purchases and ownership, by consumer and household characteristics, 1991 and trends, biennial fact book, A1325–1.1

Shareholders of NYSE member firms, by demographic characteristics and metro area, 1970s-90, annual fact book, B6625–1.1

Communications

Advertising content and practices cited as offensive by women vs men, 1993 survey article, C1200–4.507

Advertising costs for selected media, with detail by audience sex, 1993 article, A8605–1.505

Cable TV system mgmt salaries by selected characteristics, and views on job satisfaction, Mar/Apr 1993 survey, articles, C1858–1.502

Children reading selected written material, and listening to radio, by sex, 1990 survey, article, C2710–1.512

Communications industries employee income by sex and experience, Dec 1992 survey, article, C2710–1.528

Direct marketing industry devs, including advertising patterns, finances, target market characteristics, and consumer attitudes, 1992/93 annual rpt, A4620–1

Magazine circulation director and manager compensation, by region, sex, age, and publication characteristics, 1992 survey, annual article, C2575–1.502

Magazine compensation of ad sales personnel, by region, sex, age, and publication characteristics, 1993 survey, annual article, C2575–1.516

Magazine compensation of editorial personnel, by region, sex, age, and publication characteristics, 1993 survey, annual article, C2575–1.512

Magazine production director and manager compensation, by region, sex, age, and publication characteristics, 1993 survey, annual article, C2575–1.510

Magazine promotion dept activities, and executive characteristics and salary, Nov 1992 survey, article, C2575 1.506

Magazine use of gender-specific vocabulary, and ratio of male to female readers, for 8 consumer publications, 1993 feature, C2575–1.507

News events followed most closely by public, and opinion on media coverage and selected current issues, by respondent characteristics, recurring rpt, C8915–1

Newspaper employment, and weekday edition readership, by sex, 1992 and trends, annual rpt, A8605–4

Newspaper front page references, bylines, and photo subjects involving men vs women, 1993, article, A8605–1.507

Newspaper readership by sex, 1992-93, article, A8605–1.511

Public opinion on the media and related issues, by respondent characteristics, series, C8915–11

Radio audience size, leading stations and formats, and advertising rates and revenues, by market area, recurring rpt, C3165–1

Radio ownership, audience characteristics, and advertising revenues and effectiveness, with selected comparisons to other media, 1993 annual rpt, A8789–1

Telephone Yellow Pages directory use among consumers, with detail by respondent characteristics, 1992 survey, annual rpt, A9500–2

TV (public) members vs general public with college degrees, by sex, 1992 survey rpt, R4250–1.22

TV audience ratings by sex, for 3 major networks, 1992/93, article, C9380–1.523

TV audience shares of 10 syndicated action/adventure programs, for viewers age 18-49 by sex, May 1993, article, C1850–14.535

TV households and population by age and sex, by market area, 1992/93, annual rpt, B0525–3

TV households and population by race-ethnicity, sex, and age, by market area, 1992/93, annual rpt, B0525–4

TV news stories by sex and race-ethnicity of reporter or anchor, with detail by network, 1992, annual article, R3823–1.503

TV syndicated program audience shares and ratings, by daypart and audience characteristics, Nov 1991-92, article, C9380–1.511

Education

American College Test (ACT) scores, by sex and race-ethnicity, 1993, annual article, C2175–1.534

American College Test (ACT) scores by student characteristics, with student views on schools and education plans, 1992 and trends, annual rpt, R1960–6

Black American educational statistics, with comparisons to whites, 1970s-92, annual compilation, C6775–2.3

Business and total higher education degrees awarded, by level and sex, 1962/63-1990/91, article, A0605–2.502

Catholic secondary school salaries for religious teachers by sex, 1987/88-1991/92, biennial rpt, A7375–5

Catholic vs public school performance, and support for parental school selection funded by govt, public opinion by respondent characteristics, July 1992 survey, A7375–8

Community and junior college revenues by source and expenditures by function, and selected student characteristics, FY92, annual rpt, A6705–1

Developing countries family planning efforts, with data on socioeconomic and health conditions compared to developed countries, by country, 1980s-90, R8720–1.1

Doctoral degree recipient characteristics, including citizenship status, source of support, field of study, and instn, 1990/91 and trends, annual rpt, R6000–7

Doctoral degrees conferred and recipient characteristics, by field, 1992, annual feature, C2175–1.535

Elementary/secondary prospective teacher characteristics and opinions, survey of persons interested in alternative certification routes, 1992, R6350–7

BY SEX

Index by Categories

Elementary/secondary school superintendents personal and professional characteristics and views, 1992 survey rpt, A0775–5

Foreign students enrolled in US higher education instns, by instn, State, country of origin, and demographic characteristics, 1991/92 and trends, annual rpt, R5580–1

High school sports all-time records for boys and girls events, with school and student participation for 1991/92, annual rpt, A7830–2

Higher education administrative salaries, for 167 positions, by sex and instn type, 1992/93, annual rpt, A3900–1

Higher education bachelors and masters degrees conferred, by sex and race-ethnicity, 1990, C4215–1.503

Higher education degree fields of men and women earning all, bachelors, and advanced degrees, 1990, article, U7860–1.505

Higher education degrees conferred, by level, sex, discipline, and race-ethnicity, 1990/91, recurring feature, C2175–1.523

Higher education enrollment and degrees by sex, and high school grads, 1992-2003, annual feature, C2175–1.504

Higher education enrollment and grads, and faculty and librarian salaries, by sex, 1993 annual rpt, A1570–2

Higher education enrollment of foreign students, by sex, 1991/92, annual feature, C2175–1.501

Higher education enrollment of minority and foreign students, with comparison to whites, by sex, State, and instn type, fall 1991, recurring feature, C2175–1.506

Higher education faculty average salaries, by rank and sex, 1992/3, annual feature, C2175–1.516

Higher education faculty compensation and employment, detailed data by rank, sex, and instn, 1992/93 and trends, annual rpt, A0800–1

Higher education freshmen attitudes and characteristics, degree and career plans, and financial aid sources, by sex and instn type, fall 1992, annual survey, U6215–1

Higher education involvement of minorities, including enrollment and degrees awarded, by race-ethnicity, sex, and State, 1970s-91, annual rpt, A1410–10

Higher education president personal and professional characteristics, 1990 and trends, recurring rpt, A1410–12

Higher education president personal and professional characteristics, 1990, article, C2175–1.533

Higher education student athlete enrollment and graduation rates, by sex, race-ethnicity, and major sport, for Natl Collegiate Athletic Assn Div I instns, 1992/93, annual rpt, A7440–4

Higher education student athlete vs total graduation rates after 6 years, by sex, race, and Natl Collegiate Athletic Assn Div I instn, summer 1991, recurring feature, C2175–1.522, C2175–1.527

Higher education tenured faculty, by sex and State, 1990/91, annual rpt, C2175–1.531

Hispanic American educational statistics, with comparisons to whites, 1970s-92, annual compilation, C6775–3.2

Journalism/mass communication enrollment and grads by level, by instn, sex, race-ethnicity, and field, 1990/91 and trends, annual article, A3225–1

Latin America statistical abstract, general data by country, 1992 annual rpt, U6250–1.8

Librarians (special) salaries by age, sex, and census div, 1992, article, C1852–1.503

Librarians (special) salaries, by location, work setting, and personal characteristics, US and Canada, 1992 and trends, biennial survey rpt, A8965–1

Librarians at universities and research instns, salaries by sex, type of position, and instn, FY92 and trends, annual survey, A3365–2

Library school grad placements and salaries, by region, sex, instn, and library type, with detail for minorities, 1992 and trends, annual article, C1852–1.512

Library school grads, placements, and salaries, by region and sex, 1991 and trends, annual compilation, C1650–3.3

Library/info science school enrollment, staff and student characteristics, finances, and curricula, by school and degree program, 1991/92, annual rpt, A3235–1

Literacy rates and educational attainment, by sex and country, 1992/93 biennial rpt, R9455–1.5

Mathematics dept faculty, salaries, enrollment, and degree recipient characteristics, 1991/92 and trends, annual survey, A2085–1

Middle East literacy rates by sex and country, various years 1983-90, R8750–2.59

Political science higher education dept faculty and salaries, by sex and race-ethnicity, 1991/92, annual rpt, A2617–1

Private elementary and secondary school staff, and administrative salaries, by position and sex, 1991/92-1992/93, annual rpt, A6835–3

Secondary school student sexual harassment experience at school, for 8-11th graders, by sex, 1993 survey, article, R4800 2.519

Social work higher education programs, faculty and student characteristics, and student aid, with data by instn, 1992 and trends, annual rpt, A4515–1

Southern States higher education enrollment, degrees, faculty, and finances, for 15 States, 1990s and trends, biennial fact book, A8945–1

Statistical profiles of 50 States and DC, general data, 1993 annual almanac, C4712–1

Student attitudes on courses in 4 subject areas, for 8th graders by sex and race-ethnicity, 1988, R4800–2.512

Theological school enrollment by degree level, by sex and race-ethnicity, fall 1992 and trends, annual rpt, A3376–1

Urban public school performance compared to natl goals for year 2000, with data by race-ethnicity and sex, 1990/91 and trends, A4425–4

Western States higher education grad student exchange program enrollment, by sex, for 13 States, fall 1992, annual rpt, A9385–1

Women and minorities in professional fields, detailed education and labor force data, 1980s-91, with historical trends, recurring rpt, A3960–2

State and local:

Alabama public school enrollment, dropouts, and grads, by sex and school system, 1991/92, annual rpt, S0124–1.1

Alaska public schools, enrollment, staff, and finances, by district, FY92, annual rpt, S0295–2

Arizona statistical abstract, general data, 1993 recurring rpt, U5850–2

Arkansas higher education degrees conferred, by level, discipline, student race and sex, and instn, 1990/91 and trends, annual rpt, S0690–3

Arkansas higher education enrollment by student characteristics and geographic origins, by instn, fall 1991 and trends, annual rpt, S0690–1

Arkansas public school enrollment, grads, and staff, and private school grads, by sex, 1991/92, annual rpt, S0660–1

California postsecondary education enrollment and degrees, by sex, race-ethnicity, and instn, 1990/91, annual series, S0827–2

California public school enrollment by grade, and staff by position, by sex and race-ethnicity, 1992/93, annual rpt, S0825–9

Colorado public school enrollment, finances, and student and staff characteristics, by locality, 1992 annual rpt series, S1000–2

Connecticut public school data, including enrollment, staff, programs, finances, and student characteristics, 1991/92, biennial rpt, S1185–3

DC statistical profile, general data, 1992 annual rpt, S1535–3

Delaware postsecondary instn enrollment and degrees conferred, by sex, FY94 annual rpt, S1425–1

Delaware public school student and staff characteristics, 1991/92, annual rpt, S1430–1

Florida county data book, 1992/93 annual rpt, C6360–1

Florida higher education enrollment, degree programs, staff, and finances, by State-supported instn, with student and staff characteristics, 1991/92 annual rpt, S1725–1

Florida statistical abstract, general data, 1992 annual rpt, U6660–1

Georgia county guide, general data, 1993 annual rpt, U6750–1

Georgia statistical abstract, general data, 1992-93 biennial rpt, U6730–1

Hawaii data book, general data, 1992 annual rpt, S2090–1

Idaho public school personnel characteristics and salaries by position, and teachers and enrollment by school district, 1992/93, annual rpt, S2225–3

Illinois higher education enrollment, degrees, staff, and finances, by public and private instn and student characteristics, 1993 annual rpt, S2475–1

Illinois public and/or private school staff, and high school grads and dropouts, by sex, 1990/91 annual rpt, S2440–1

Illinois statistical abstract, general data, 1992 annual rpt, U6910–2

Indiana high school enrollment by grade and sex, by county and school, 1992/93, annual table, S2608–2.5

Iowa postsecondary enrollment, degrees, staff, and finances, by instn, 1990/91, annual rpt, S2755–1

Kansas public and private school grads and dropouts, by sex, 1990/91, annual rpt, S2945–1

Index by Categories

BY SEX

Kentucky higher education enrollment and degrees conferred, by sex, 1983-92, annual rpt, S3130–3

Kentucky public school finances, staff, and enrollment, by district, 1989/90-1990/91, biennial rpt, S3110–2

Louisiana elementary/secondary school operations, including enrollment, staff, finances, and detail by school district, 1991/92 and trends, annual rpt, S3280–1

Maine elementary and secondary school students retained, dropouts, and expulsions, by sex and grade, 1990/91, annual rpt, S3435–1

Maryland elementary and secondary education data, by county, Oct 1992, annual rpt, S3610–2.12

Maryland elementary and secondary education data, by county, 1991/92, annual rpt, S3610–2.3

Maryland elementary and secondary education data, by county, 1992 and trends, annual rpt, S3610–2.4

Maryland teachers by sex and race, and student achievement test scores by sex, 1992, annual rpt, S3610–1

Massachusetts elementary/secondary school enrollment, by sex and race-ethnicity, Oct 1980 and 1991, annual rpt, S3810–3

Minnesota postsecondary education finances, and enrollment by student characteristics, by type of school system, 1970s-93, biennial rpt, S4195–2.2

Mississippi high school grads, by sex, 1966/67-1991/92, annual rpt, S4340–1.1

Mississippi higher education enrollment by sex, by State-supported off-campus center, 1991/92, annual rpt, S4360–1

Mississippi statistical abstract, general data, 1992 annual rpt, U3255–4

Missouri higher education enrollment and degrees granted, by sex, race-ethnicity, and instn, 1992 and trends, annual rpt, S4520–3

Missouri public school enrollment, grads, dropouts, and personnel and salaries, by sex, 1991/92 and trends, annual rpt, S4505–1.1

Montana public school enrollment by grade, and grads, by school, county, race-ethnicity, and sex, 1992 and trends, annual rpt, S4740–1

Nebraska elementary and secondary school enrollment and personnel, by sex, annual series, S4865–2

New Hampshire high school grads and postgraduation activities, by school, county, and sex, 1991, annual tables, S5200–1.2

New Hampshire high school grads and postgraduation activities, by school, county, and sex, 1992, annual tables, S5200–1.15

New Jersey public schools, enrollment, and student and staff characteristics, and nonpublic schools and enrollment, by county, 1991/92, annual rpt, S5385–1

New Mexico high school enrollment and dropouts, by sex, 1991/92, annual planning rpt, S5624–1

North Carolina higher education enrollment, degrees, libraries, staff, and student characteristics, finances, and housing, by instn, 1992/93 and trends, annual rpt, U8013–1

North Carolina public school enrollment, grads, staff, and finances, with data by race, sex, and local district, 1991/92-1992/93 and trends, annual rpt, S5915–1

North Dakota elementary and secondary school enrollment, and high school grads, by sex, 1992/93 annual directory, S6180–2

North Dakota elementary and secondary school staff characteristics and salaries, by position, region, and enrollment size, 1992/93 annual rpt, S6180–3

North Dakota higher education enrollment, by level, instn, county, and selected student characteristics, fall 1992 and trends, annual rpt, S6110–1

Oklahoma high school grads, by county and sex, 1991/92, annual rpt, S6423–1.2

Oklahoma statistical abstract, general data, 1992 annual rpt, U8130–2

Oregon public high school completers, by instn, county, sex, and race-ethnicity, 1992, annual rpt, S6590–1.10

Pennsylvania educational statistics by level and/or type of education, series, S6790–5

Pennsylvania statistical abstract, general data, 1992 recurring rpt, U4130–6

Rhode Island public school enrollment by type of instn, grade, sex, race-ethnicity, and district, 1991/92 or fall 1992, annual rpt, S6970–1.1

South Carolina higher education degrees awarded, by sex and race, FY91, annual planning rpt, S7155–3.3

South Carolina higher education enrollment, degrees, staff, and finances, by instn, 1992 and trends, annual rpt, S7185–2

South Carolina statistical abstract, general data, 1993 annual rpt, S7125–1

South Dakota elementary/secondary school enrollment, grads, and staff, by sex, 1991/92, annual rpt, S7315–1

South Dakota public higher education enrollment and faculty, by sex and instn, fall 1992, annual rpt, S7375–1

Tennessee higher education and vocational enrollment and grads, by sex and race-ethnicity, 1991/92, annual rpt, S7525–1

Tennessee public school staff by sex, county, city, and school district, 1991/92, annual rpt, S7490–2

Tennessee statistical abstract, general data, 1992/93 annual rpt, U8710–2

Texas elementary/secondary education personnel, by sex and race-ethnicity, by district and county, 1991/92, annual rpt, S7670–1.3

Texas higher education enrollment and faculty, by race-ethnicity, sex, and instn, 1991/92 and trends, annual rpt, S7657–1.1

Utah employment by detailed occupation, and educational attainment by age group, by sex and race-ethnicity, with detail for 7 urban areas, 1990 census rpt, S7832–3.4

Utah higher education enrollment and degrees awarded, by sex and instn, 1991/92 and trends, annual rpt, S7895–2

Utah public school enrollment, dropouts, and grads, by sex, race-ethnicity, and district, 1991/92, annual rpt, S7815–1.2

Utah statistical abstract, general data, 1993 triennial rpt, U8960–1

Vermont elementary and secondary school enrollment by grade, sex, race-ethnicity, school, and county, 1992/93 and trends, annual rpt, S8020–1

Vermont higher education enrollment, degrees, and student aid, by sex, 1992 annual rpt, S8035–2

Virginia public school dropouts by race-ethnicity and sex, by county and municipality, 1991/92, annual rpt, S8190–3

West Virginia higher education enrollment, degrees, faculty and student characteristics, and finances, by instn, 1992/93 and trends, annual rpt, S8533–1

West Virginia public and private school enrollment and grads, by sex, 1991/92, annual rpt, S8540–3

Wisconsin Blue Book, general data, 1993-94 biennial rpt, S8780–1.2

Wisconsin, Milwaukee educational attainment of parents with children in public schools, and in private schools under school selection program, by sex, 1989/90-1990/91, R3810–7

Wyoming public school staff by position, enrollment, and high school grads, by sex and district, 1991/92, annual rpt series, S8890–1

Government and Defense

Black elected officials, and characteristics of voting age population, with comparisons to whites, 1970s-91, annual compilation, C6775–2.4

Black elected officials, by sex, 1970-92, annual article, R5685–4.502

County manager salaries, by sex, county size, census div, and metro status, July 1992, annual rpt, A5800–1.3

Elections involving women candidates or outcomes affected by gender gaps, voting by sex, 1992, U4510–4.4

Federal employment of scientists and engineers, by field and sex, 1989, article, A1250–1.523

Hispanic American elected official characteristics, 1992, annual directory, A6844–1

Hispanic American elected officials, registered voters, and voting, with comparisons to whites, 1970s-91, annual compilation, C6775–3.3

Hispanic American vs non-Hispanic voter turnout, by demographic characteristics, Nov 1992 election, article, C4575–1.511

House of Representatives staff characteristics, salaries, and benefits by position, 1992 and trends, recurring rpt, R4140–1

Local govt land use planning commissions composition and activities, and commissioner characteristics, 1987 and trends, recurring rpt, A2615–2

Local officials in municipal and county govt, demographic profiles and job functions, 1993 annual rpt, A5800–1

Political comparisons by sex, including voting patterns, party affiliation, presidential performance ratings, and opinions on issues, 1950s-92, U4510–1.65

Public opinion on Clinton Admin policies and actions, by respondent characteristics, series, C8915–7

Public opinion on issues concerning politics and the press, by respondent characteristics, series, C8915–4

State and local govt employee wages compared to private sector, with detail by sex and State, 1989 and trends, R4700–21

BY SEX

State/local govt employees in low-paying vs other jobs, by sex, 1990, U5090–1.3

Voter turnout and registration trends, by race-ethnicity and/or sex, 1960s-92, U4510–1.70

State and local:

Colorado registered voters, by sex and county, 1992, biennial rpt, S1090–1

DC statistical profile, general data, 1992 annual rpt, S1535–3

Hawaii data book, general data, 1992 annual rpt, S2090–1

Hawaii election results, and voter registration by sex, by district and precinct, 1992, biennial series, S2077–1

New York State statistical yearbook, general data, 1992 annual rpt, U5100–1

Oklahoma statistical abstract, general data, 1992 annual rpt, U8130–2

Pennsylvania statistical abstract, general data, 1992 recurring rpt, U4130–6

South Carolina statistical abstract, general data, 1993 annual rpt, S7125–1

Tennessee statistical abstract, general data, 1992/93 annual rpt, U8710–2

Wisconsin Blue Book, general data, 1993-94 biennial rpt, S8780–1.1, S8780–1.2

Health and Vital Statistics

- Accidental deaths and disabling injuries, by detailed type, victim characteristics, circumstances, and location, 1992 and trends, annual rpt, A8375–2
- AIDS cases among whites and Hispanics, by sex and transmission category, 1988-91, article, A2623–1.506
- AIDS cases, by sex and race-ethnicity, through June 1992, article, C4215–1.503
- AIDS deaths in hospitals vs at home, by region and decedent characteristics, 1988 and trends, article, A2623–1.512
- AIDS stigmatizing attitudes and beliefs prevalence among general public, with detail by race and sex, 1990/91 surveys, article, A2623–1.506
- Asia population age at 1st marriage, by sex and country, 1890s-1980s, R4500–1.64
- Births by sex, 1933-90, recurring rpt, A3960–2.1
- Black American health and vital statistics data, with comparisons to whites, 1970s-91, annual compilation, C6775–2.2
- Cancer incidence and mortality, including data by State, sex, and body site, 1993 and trends, annual rpt, A1175–1
- Child gender preferences in developing countries, with data on family composition and child health by sex, by country, 1980s, article, A5160–6.501
- Children's orthopedic internal fixation device implantation prevalence, and results, with detail by demographic characteristics, 1988, article, A2623–1.509
- Cholesterol level correlated with alcohol consumption frequency, by race and sex, 1976-80, article, A2623–1.508
- Cocaine user characteristics, including criminal behavior and health condition, with comparison to nonusers, 1991 and trends, article, A2623–1.510
- Death rates by age and sex, for US and 14 other countries, 1991 and trends, article, B6045–1.503
- Death rates for selected causes among exercising population, by sex, 1992 article, B6045–1.501

Dental problems/treatment-related time lost from work or school, by demographic characteristics, 1989, article, A2623–1.502

Dental school applicants and 1st-year enrollment, by sex and instn, 1992/93, annual rpt, A1475–4.1

Dental school enrollment and grads, by sex and race-ethnicity, 1992/93 annual rpt, A1475–3.1

Dental school faculty, support personnel, and staff characteristics, by instn, 1992/93, annual rpt, A1475–4.5

Dental school student attrition, by reason and student characteristics, 1991/92 and trends, annual rpt, A1475–4.4

Depression incidence among blacks and whites by selected demographic characteristics, 1984 survey, article, A2623–1.504

Depression incidence by period of birth and sex, 1993 article, A2623–1.507

Developing countries family planning efforts, with data on socioeconomic and health conditions compared to developed countries, by country, 1980s-90, R8720–1.1

Developing countries fertility, family planning, sexual behavior, and child health indicators, with selected detail by demographic characteristics, 1984-92 surveys, U2520–1.51

Disabled persons use of home care services, with costs, payment sources, and types of care, by selected characteristics, 1992, R4865–15

Drug use at work among workers age 19-27, by sex and race-ethnicity, 1984, annual rpt, R8335–1.1

Drugs (prescription) use, expenditures, and financing methods among population age 65/older and 64/under, by patient characteristics, 1987, R4865–8

Ear tube implantation prevalence in children, by demographic characteristics and reasons for implant, 1988, article, A2623–1.509

Germany (East vs West) life expectancy by sex, 1988, R4105–82.3

Health condition and preventive health care and safety practices of adults, by respondent characteristics, 1992 and trends, annual survey rpt, C8111–2

Health indicators, including hypertension and lung cancer rates, and cancer and heart disease/stroke deaths, by sex and race-ethnicity, 1993 feature, C4215–1.511

Health insurance coverage and finances, and health care costs and facilities, by selected demographic characteristics, 1940s-91, annual rpt, A5173–2

Health insurance coverage lack, and population with high out-of-pocket expenses, by State and selected characteristics, 1993, R4865–14

Health insurance coverage lack by sex, race, employment status, and household income level, 1993 feature, C4215–1.506

Higher education student use of and attitudes toward alcohol, drugs, and tobacco products, by sex and region, 1989-91 surveys, annual rpt, U4950–1

Hip fracture incidence rates in US and Hong Kong, by age and sex, 1988/89, article, A2623–1.507

Hispanic American AIDS cases and deaths, by sex, with comparisons to whites, 1984-91, annual compilation, C6775–3.6

Index by Categories

Hispanic Americans sexual activity with multiple partners, with comparison to whites, by sex, 1991 survey, article, A5160–1.505

HMO enrollment and utilization patterns, by plan characteristics and member sex and age, 1990-91, annual rpt, A5150–2.2

Home health care patient characteristics, 1993 article, A1865–1.516

Hospital patient admission rates and length of stay, by diagnosis and procedure, payment source, age, sex, and region, 1991, B4455–4

Hospital patient admissions, length of stay, operative procedures, and discharges by patient characteristics, 1990 or 1991 and trends, annual fact book, A1275–1.2

Hospital psychiatric patient discharges and length of stay, by diagnosis, age, sex, and region, 1991, annual rpt series, B4455–2

Human immunodeficiency virus (HIV) testing and posttest counseling rates, by demographic characteristics, 1989, article, A2623–1.501

Infant mortality rates, by sex and race, 1989, article, A8510–1.1

Japan and US health indicators, including population longevity, by sex, 1990, article, R5650–2.515

Kenya elementary, secondary, and vocational students sexual experience, by selected characteristics, 1989, article, A5160–6.505

Latin America statistical abstract, general data by country, 1992 annual rpt, U6250–1.6

Life expectancy and mortality rates, by age, race, and sex, 1900-92, annual article, B6045–1.504

Life expectancy at birth by sex, by world region and/or country, 1993 annual data sheet, R8750–5

Life expectancy at birth, by sex, decennially 1960-90, annual fact book, A1275–1.5

Life expectancy, by age, sex, and race, 1991 and trends, biennial fact book, A1325–1.6

Medical group mgmt compensation, by demographic and practice characteristics, 1992, annual rpt, A6365–3

Medical group physician and allied personnel compensation and productivity, by specialty, and demographic and practice characteristics, 1991, annual rpt, A6365–1

Medical school faculty physician and allied personnel compensation and productivity, by academic rank, sex, and specialty, 1991, annual rpt, A6365–5

Medical school programs, fees, applicants, admissions, and enrollment, with data by age, sex, minority group, and instn, 1992/93 and trends, annual rpt, A3273–10

Mexico suicides and attempts, by circumstances and victim characteristics, 1980-84, annual rpt, U6250–1.15

Musculoskeletal disability incidences in men and women correlated with occupations, 1992 article, A2623–1.501

New England elderly population smoking status correlated with dental problems, by sex, 1993 article, A2623–1.511

Nursing college deans, by sex, 1992/93, annual rpt, A0615–2

Nursing college faculty and salaries, by personal and instn characteristics, 1992/93, annual rpt, A0615–1

Index by Categories

BY SEX

Nursing higher education program faculty and clinic patient characteristics, 1992/93 biennial rpt, A0615–5

Nursing home resident mental health care use, by resident and home characteristics, and provider type, 1985/86 survey, article, A2623–1.505

Nursing school enrollment and grads, by degree level, sex, race-ethnicity, and instn type and location, 1992/93 and trends, annual rpt, A0615–4

Nursing schools, programs, enrollment, student and staff characteristics, and grads, 1991 and trends, annual rpt, A8010–1

Nutrition labeling law changes potential impact on public health condition, by sex, 1993 article, A2623–1.507

Optometry school faculty, enrollment and degrees, policies and programs, and finances, by instn, 1991/92, annual survey, A3370–2

Osteopathy college enrollment, student and faculty characteristics, and finances, 1992/93 and trends, annual rpt, A0620–1

Osteopathy student debt and career plans, by student characteristics, 1991/92 and trends, annual survey rpt, A0620–2

Pharmacy degree program applications, enrollment, and degrees conferred, by student characteristics and instn, 1990/91 and trends, annual rpt, A0630–9

Physician internal medicine specialty residency training and general practice selection, by sex, 1993 article, A3273–8.505

Physician participation in clinical and economic profiling programs, by specialty, sex, and employer type, 1992, article, A2200–5.1

Physician rural vs nonrural area background and practice plans, with data by sex, 1993 article, A3273–8.505

Physicians by detailed specialty, location, age, sex, and board certification status, 1992 and trends, annual rpt, A2200–3.1

Public health school applicant, student, and grad characteristics, by instn, 1991/92 and trends, annual rpt, A3372–3

Public health school faculty characteristics, by instn, fall 1991, recurring rpt, A3372–1

Sexual activity and condom use among high school students by sex, and adolescent/adult AIDS cases, by race-ethnicity, 1993 article, C4215–1.505

Sexual activity with multiple partners and strangers, by population characteristics, 1988-90 surveys, article, A5160–1.503

Sexual activity with multiple partners, incidence by sex and age, 1988/89, article, A5160–1.501

Sexual behavior among adults, including extramarital sex, condom use, and impact of AIDS, by demographic characteristics, 1990 survey, article, A2623–1.512

Sexual behavior among heterosexuals, including data on demographic characteristics, number of partners, and condom use, 1990/91 survey, article, A5160–1.506

Sexually transmitted disease infection risk to men vs women from unprotected intercourse, by disease, 1993 rpt, A5160–10

Smoking acceptability in restaurants and other public places, and importance of

restaurant smoking policy, views of consumers by selected characteristics, Jan 1993 survey, A8200–8.15

Smoking habits of workers as affected by workplace smoking restrictions, by sex, 1989-90 Washington State study, article, A2623–1.509

Smoking status of men and women by occupation, and smoker characteristics, 1985 and/or 1990, article, B6045–1.501

Statistical profiles of 50 States and DC, general data, 1993 annual almanac, C4712–1

Substance abuse treatment programs, funding by source, and client characteristics, for alcohol and drug services, by State, FY91 and trends, annual rpt, A7112–1

Sweden, Stockholm deaths related to alcohol abuse, by sex and cause, 1987, article, A2623–1.508

Veterinarian (equine) characteristics and finances, and practice profile, 1992 survey and trends, annual article, C9480–1.503

Veterinarian income by selected personal and practice characteristics, 1992, annual survey article, C9480–1.506

Veterinarians by professional characteristics and location, and financial and education summaries, 1993 annual directory, A3100–1

Veterinary school enrollment by sex, program, instn, and place of residence, US and Canada, 1992/93, annual article, A3100–2.516

Veterinary school grad employment, starting salaries, benefits, and personal characteristics, by sex, 1992, annual survey article, A3100–2.504

Vitamin/mineral supplement use correlated with death rates, by sex and selected other characteristics, 1993 article, A2623–1.506

World life expectancy, by sex, for top 50 countries, 1992, semiannual rpt, B8500–1.16

Zambia student views on sexual behavior and treatment of persons infected with AIDS virus, by respondent characteristics, 1990 survey, article, A5160–6.503

State and local:

Alabama health behavior risk factor surveillance survey results, by respondent characteristics, 1988-89, recurring rpt, S0175–6

Alabama statistical abstract, general data, 1992 recurring rpt, U5680–2

Alabama vital statistics, including population, births, deaths by cause, marriages, and divorces, by location and demographic characteristics, 1992 and trends, annual rpt, S0175–2

Alaska vital statistics, including births, deaths by cause, marriages, divorces, adoptions, and population, by demographic characteristics and location, 1990, annual rpt, S0315–1

Arizona Indian population, education, housing, health, and employment characteristics, with detail by reservation, 1970s-91, recurring rpt, U5850–2.9

Arizona statistical abstract, general data, 1993 recurring rpt, U5850–2

Arkansas drug and alcohol treatment and prevention program expenditures, success rates, and client characteristics, FY91 annual rpt, S0700–2.1

Arkansas vital statistics, including births, deaths by cause, marriages, and divorces, by age, sex, race, and county, 1991 and trends, annual rpt, S0685–1

California death rates and estimated alcohol-related mortality, by cause and demographic characteristics, 1980-89, article, A2623–1.508

California health behavior risk factor surveillance survey results, by respondent characteristics, 1991 and trends, annual rpt, S0865–2

California statistical abstract, general data, 1992 annual rpt, S0840–2

California vital statistics, including population, births, and deaths by cause, by demographic characteristics and county, 1990 and trends, annual rpt, S0865–1

Colorado health behavior risk factor surveillance survey results, by respondent characteristics, 1990, recurring rpt, S1010–3

Colorado vital statistics, including population, births, deaths by cause, abortion, marriage and divorce, and adoption, by demographic characteristics and location, 1990 and trends, annual rpt, S1010–1

Connecticut health behavior risk factor surveillance survey results, including data on obesity incidence by sex, 1989-91, annual rpt, S1200–2

Connecticut vital statistics, including births, deaths by cause, marriages, and divorces, by demographic characteristics and location, 1989, annual rpt, S1200–1

DC statistical profile, general data, 1992 annual rpt, S1535–3

Delaware vital statistics, including births, deaths by cause, and marriages and dissolutions, by demographic characteristics and location, 1990, annual rpt, S1385–2

Florida community college health care program enrollment and completers, by sex and program, 1991, annual rpt, S1746–1.2

Florida statistical abstract, general data, 1992 annual rpt, U6660–1

Florida vital statistics, including population, births, deaths by cause, and marriages and dissolutions, by location and demographic characteristics, 1992 and trends, annual rpt, S1745–3

Georgia health behavior risk factor surveillance survey results, by respondent characteristics, 1991 and trends, annual rpt, S1895–2

Hawaii data book, general data, 1992 annual rpt, S2090–1

Hawaii health dept activities and services, including vital statistics and disease control, by location, 1990, annual rpt, S2065–1

Idaho vital statistics, including births, deaths by cause, abortions, marriages, and divorces, by demographic characteristics and county, 1991 and trends, annual rpt, S2250–2

Illinois mental health facility patient population and characteristics, by facility, location, and treatment category, FY93, annual rpt, S2505–1

Iowa health behavior risk factor surveillance survey results, by respondent characteristics, 1991, annual rpt, S2795–2

Iowa vital statistics, including population, births, deaths by cause, marriages, and

BY SEX

Index by Categories

divorces, by demographic characteristics and location, 1991 and trends, annual rpt, S2795–1

- Kansas vital statistics, including population, births, deaths by cause, abortions, marriages, and divorces, by demographic characteristics and location, 1991 and trends, annual rpt, S2975–1
- Kentucky health behavior risk factor surveillance survey results, by State area and respondent characteristics, 1988-90, annual rpt, S3140–6
- Kentucky vital statistics, including births, deaths by cause, marriages and divorces, and population, by demographic characteristics and county, 1991, annual rpt, S3140–1
- Louisiana vital statistics, including population, births, deaths by cause, reportable diseases, marriages, and divorces, by demographic characteristics and locality, 1989-90 and trends, annual rpt, S3295–1
- Maine vital statistics, including births, deaths by cause, abortions, and marriages and divorces, by demographic characteristics and location, 1991 and trends, annual rpt, S3460–2
- Maryland statistical abstract, general data, 1993-94 biennial rpt, S3605–1
- Maryland vital statistics, including population, births, deaths by cause, marriages, and divorces, by demographic characteristics and location, 1989 and trends, annual rpt, S3635–1
- Massachusetts health behavior risk factor surveillance survey results, by respondent characteristics, 1986-90, recurring rpt, S3850–3
- Massachusetts vital statistics, including births, deaths by cause, marriages, divorces, and population, by locality and demographic characteristics, 1990 and trends, annual rpt, S3850–1
- Michigan health behavior risk factor surveillance survey results, by respondent characteristics, 1991, annual rpt, S4000–4
- Michigan vital statistics, including births, deaths, marriages, divorces/annulments, and communicable diseases, by location and demographic characteristics, 1990 and trends, annual rpt, S4000–3
- Minnesota vital statistics, including population, births, abortions, deaths, marriages, and divorces, by location and demographic characteristics, 1991 and trends, annual rpt, S4190–2
- Mississippi statistical abstract, general data, 1992 annual rpt, U3255–4
- Mississippi vital statistics, including births, deaths by cause, marriages, and divorces, by demographic characteristics and location, 1992 and trends, annual rpt, S4350–1
- Missouri vital statistics, including population, births, deaths by cause, and marriages and divorces, by location and demographic characteristics, 1992 and trends, annual rpt, S4518–1
- Montana long-term and personal care facilities patients, by age, sex, and instn, 1991, annual rpt, S4690–2
- Montana vital statistics, including births, deaths by cause, abortion, disease, and marriage and divorce, by demographic characteristics and county, 1990-91 and trends, annual rpt, S4690–1

Nebraska vital statistics, including births, deaths, marriages, divorces, and population, by demographic characteristics and location, 1991 and trends, annual rpt, S4885–1

- Nevada health behavior risk factor surveillance survey results, by location and respondent characteristics, 1991, annual rpt, S5075–3
- Nevada vital statistics, including births, abortions, and deaths by cause, by county and demographic characteristics, 1989 and trends, annual rpt, S5075–1
- New Hampshire vital statistics, including population, births, deaths by cause, marriages, and divorces, by location and demographic characteristics, 1991 and trends, annual rpt, S5215–1
- New Jersey vital statistics, including births, deaths, population, communicable diseases, and marriages and divorces, by demographic characteristics and location, 1990 and trends, annual rpt, S5405–1
- New Mexico vital statistics, including population, births, deaths, and disease, by location and demographic characteristics, 1991 and trends, annual rpt, S5605–1
- New York State health behavior risk factor surveillance survey results, by respondent characteristics, 1990, recurring rpt, S5765–3
- New York State statistical yearbook, general data, 1992 annual rpt, U5100–1
- New York State vital statistics, including population, births, deaths by cause, reportable diseases, and marriages and dissolutions, by demographic characteristics and/or location, 1990 and trends, annual rpt, S5765–1
- North Carolina vital statistics, including population, births, deaths, marriages, and divorces, by local area, 1991 and trends, annual rpt, S5927–1.1
- North Dakota health behavior risk factor surveillance survey results, by respondent characteristics, 1991 and trends, annual rpt, S6105–3
- North Dakota vital statistics, including births, deaths by cause, marriages and divorces, and abortions, by demographic characteristics and/or county, 1991 and trends, annual rpt, S6105–2
- Ohio vital statistics, including births, deaths by cause, marriages, divorces, and population, by demographic characteristics and location, 1991 and trends, annual rpt, S6285–1
- Oregon vital statistics, including births, deaths by cause, communicable diseases, marriages, and divorces, by age, sex, race-ethnicity, and county, 1991 and trends, annual rpt, S6615–5
- Pennsylvania health behavior risk factor surveillance survey results, by respondent characteristics, 1991, annual rpt, S6820–4
- Rhode Island vital statistics, including population, births, deaths, marriages, and divorces, by demographic characteristics and locality, 1989 and trends, annual rpt, S6995–1
- South Carolina deaths, by detailed cause, age, sex, and race, 1990, annual rpt, S7175–2
- South Carolina statistical abstract, general data, 1993 annual rpt, S7125–1

South Carolina vital statistics, including births, deaths by cause, marriages, and divorces, by age, sex, race, and location, 1990 and trends, annual rpt, S7175–1

- South Dakota vital statistics, including births, deaths, marriage and divorce, and communicable disease, by demographic characteristics and county, 1991 and trends, annual rpt, S7345–1
- Tennessee health behavior risk factor surveillance survey results, by respondent characteristics, 1986-90, annual rpt, S7520–3
- Tennessee vital statistics, including births, deaths by cause, marriages, divorces, and population, by demographic characteristics and location, 1991 and trends, annual rpt, S7520–2
- Texas health behavior risk factor surveillance survey results, by respondent characteristics, 1991 and trends, annual rpt, S7685–2
- Texas nursing employment, demand outlook, earnings, and education, by selected characteristics, various years 1971-91, U8850–8.2
- Texas physicians insured against professional liability, with data on premiums and claims, and detail by specialty and/or age, sex, and city, 1978-91, U8850–8.8
- Texas survival rates, by age, sex, and race-ethnicity, 1989/90, recurring rpt, S7645–3
- Texas vital statistics, including births, deaths by cause, abortions, marriages, and divorces, by location and demographic characteristics, 1991 and trends, annual rpt, S7685–1
- Utah marriages and divorces, by participant characteristics and location, 1990 and trends, annual rpt, S7835–2
- Utah vital statistics, including births, deaths by cause, and population, by county and demographic characteristics, 1990 and trends, annual rpt, S7835–1
- Vermont vital statistics, including population, births, deaths by cause, abortions, marriages, and divorces, by location and demographic characteristics, 1991 and trends, annual rpt, S8054–1
- Virginia vital statistics, including births, deaths by cause, marriages and divorces, and communicable disease, by demographic characteristics and location, 1991 and trends, annual rpt, S8225–1
- Washington State vital statistics, including births, deaths by cause, and population, by demographic characteristics and location, 1991 and trends, annual rpt, S8363–1
- West Virginia vital statistics, including births, deaths by cause, marriages, and divorces, by location and demographic characteristics, 1991 and trends, annual rpt, S8560–1
- Wisconsin vital statistics, including population, births, deaths by cause, and marriages and dissolutions, by county and demographic characteristics, 1991 and trends, annual rpt, S8715–4
- Wyoming vital statistics, including population, births, deaths by cause, marriages, and divorces, by demographic characteristics and county, 1991 and trends, annual rpt, S8920–2

Index by Categories

BY SEX

Income

Black American earnings, income, and poverty data, with comparisons to whites, 1980s-91, annual compilation, C6775–2.7

Black American socioeconomic status, with comparisons to whites and data by region, 1960s-92, annual compilation, A8510–1.1

College grad job and salary offers, by field of study, job function, and sex, series, A3940–2

Earnings by sex and detailed occupation, 1983 and 1991, annual rpt, S6845–3.2

Earnings by sex and race-ethnicity, 1992 feature, C4215–1.502

Earnings of college vs high school grads, by sex, 1979 and 1989, R4105–80.501

Higher education grad earnings superiority over high school grads, share attributable to computer skills, by sex, 1991, article, C8900–1.515

Hispanic American income and poverty data, with comparisons to whites, 1980s-91, annual compilation, C6775–3.5

Hospital fundraising personnel salaries, by position, sex, experience, and hospital size, 1993 and trends, annual article, C2176–1.517

Income of full-time adult workers, by sex and education, 1979-89, annual rpt, S7125–1.6

Jewelry store employee earnings, by position, with detail by sex for managers and sales workers, 1990-91, annual almanac, C2150–7.509

Jewelry store salary ranges for managers and sales workers by sex, 1992 annual survey article, C2150–7.501

Planning profession employment and salaries, by type of employer, demographic and professional characteristics, and location, 1991 and trends, biennial rpt, A2615–1

Professional worker salaries, by employee and employer characteristics, with detail for scientists and engineers, 1990s and trends, biennial rpt, A3960–1

Public relations compensation, by employee and company characteristics, 1993 survey, annual article, A8770–1.503

White-collar work force trends, including employment, earnings, and unionization, with data by occupation, sex, and educational attainment, 1990s and trends, annual rpt, A1570–1

Women's employment and earnings, with comparisons to men, and detail by occupation and worker characteristics, 1990s and trends, annual rpt, A1570–2

State and local:

Arizona statistical abstract, general data, 1993 recurring rpt, U5850–2

Arkansas Census of Population and Housing detailed findings, 1990, U5935–7

California Census of Population and Housing detailed findings, 1990, S0840–9

Hawaii data book, general data, 1992 annual rpt, S2090–1

Mississippi characteristics of economically disadvantaged and Job Training Partnership Act eligible population, 1993/94, annual planning rpt, S4345–1.3

New Jersey Census of Population and Housing detailed findings, by county, 1990, S5425–19

North Dakota population living in poverty, by sex, county, and State region, 1993 annual planning rpt, S6140–2

Pennsylvania Census of Population and Housing detailed findings, with selected data by county and municipality, 1990, U4130–13

Pennsylvania vocational education 1989/90 grad wages, by sex, 1991 survey, annual rpt, S6790–5.6

Industry and Commerce

Canada photographic and video equipment and supplies ownership, purchasing patterns, and use, by household characteristics, 1992 survey, recurring rpt, A8695–4

CEO characteristics and compensation, for small companies with rapid growth, 1993 survey article, C5800–7.551

Corporate boards of directors with women and minority members, and board membership by sex and race-ethnicity, 1991/92, B4490–2.36

Diamond jewelry purchases, prices paid, and purchaser characteristics, 1993 annual almanac, C2150–7.509

Discount store expenditures of consumers, by selected characteristics, 1993 article, C5150–3.509

Discount store shopper characteristics, use of natl vs regional discounters, and types of clothing purchased, 1990 and 1992, article, C8130–1.506

Grocery product purchasing by men, with comparisons to women, by detailed product type, 1992 article, C5225–1.501

Photographic equipment and supplies, consumer ownership, purchasing patterns, and use, 1993 survey and trends, recurring rpt, A8695–2

Private label product characteristics and purchasing factors as seen by consumers, by selected characteristics, 1991 survey, article, C0125–1.504

Labor and Employment

Black American labor force and employment data, with comparisons to whites, 1970s-91, annual compilation, C6775–2.6

College grad hiring plans by industry, with data on campus visits, starting salaries, and minority hires, 1991/92-1992/93, annual rpt, A3940–3

College grad job and salary offers, by field of study, job function, and sex, series, A3940–2

Displaced workers by sex, race-ethnicity, industry div, and occupation, with characteristics of new employment, 1987-92, article, S0465–1.506

Germany (East vs West) employment as a percent of total population, by sex, 1988, R4105–82.3

Hispanic American labor force and employment data, with comparisons to whites, 1980s-91, annual compilation, C6775–3.4

Hispanic American vs nonminority employment, by occupational group and sex, 1992, article, C4575–1.511

Japan population share age 55/over who are employed, by age group and sex, 1987-92, article, R5650–2.549

Job Corps youth training program funding, enrollment capacity, and participants by selected characteristics, 1981-94, article, R4800–2.515

Labor force by sex and age, 1980s-2005, annual rpt, R9050–1.2

Labor force data, by race and sex, 1993 annual compilation, A8510–1.1

Labor force size, entrants, and leavers, by sex and race-ethnicity, 1990-2005, article, R8750–1.507

Labor union membership compared to total workers, by sex, race and Hispanic ethnicity, occupation, and industry div, 1991-92, article, S0465–1.505

Latin America statistical abstract, general data by country, 1992 annual rpt, U6250–1.12

Pension benefits and coverage as affected by job tenure and mobility, with data by plan type and worker characteristics, 1993 rpt, R9260–17

Planning profession employment and salaries, by type of employer, demographic and professional characteristics, and location, 1991 and trends, biennial rpt, A2615–1

Retirement age and duration trends, by sex, various periods 1950-2005, article, R8750–1.505

Sales workers by sex and race-ethnicity, 1990, article, C1200–1.512

Shoe industry employment by sex, 1984-1st half 1992, annual rpt, A4957–1.2

Statistical profiles of 50 States and DC, general data, 1993 annual almanac, C4712–1

Unemployment insurance trends, including data on unemployment, worker characteristics, coverage, benefits, and State govt finances, 1940s-90, R9260–18

White-collar work force trends, including employment, earnings, and unionization, with data by occupation, sex, and educational attainment, 1990s and trends, annual rpt, A1570–1

Women and minorities in professional fields, detailed education and labor force data, 1980s-91, with historical trends, recurring rpt, A3960–2

Women's employment and earnings, with comparisons to men, and detail by occupation and worker characteristics, 1990s and trends, annual rpt, A1570–2

Youth age 20 unemployment rates, with detail for high school grads and dropouts, by sex and race, 1963-67 and 1983-87, article, C4687–1.511

State and local:

Alaska employment of youths age 15-21, by occupation, industry, and sex, July-Sept 1992, article, S0320–1.509

Arkansas Census of Population and Housing detailed findings, 1990, U5935–7

Arkansas vocational rehabilitation expenditures, impact on earnings and employment, and client characteristics, FY91 annual rpt, S0700–2.4

California Census of Population and Housing detailed findings, 1990, S0840–9

California employment statistics, by demographic characteristics, industry, MSA, and county, monthly rpt, S0830–1

California labor force planning rpt, including population characteristics, and employment by industry, 1992 annual rpt, S0830–2

California registered apprentices by trade, and union membership by industry, by sex, 1991 and trends, annual rpt, S0840–2.3

Colorado labor force planning rpt, including population, employment by industry, and job service applicants, FY94 annual rpt, S1040–3

SRI 1993 881

BY SEX

Index by Categories

DC statistical profile, general data, 1992 annual rpt, S1535–3

Delaware data book, general data, 1993 annual rpt, S1375–4

Florida statistical abstract, general data, 1992 annual rpt, U6660–1

Georgia county guide, general data, 1993 annual rpt, U6750–1

Georgia statistical abstract, general data, 1992-93 biennial rpt, U6730–1

Hawaii data book, general data, 1992 annual rpt, S2090–1

Indiana, Indianapolis employment trends for executives and machinists by sex and race, with comparisons to 5 other metro areas, 1980-90, article, U2160–1.504

Kentucky labor force planning rpt, including population and labor force characteristics, and employment by industry, 1991 and trends, annual rpt, S3140–3

Louisiana Census of Population and Housing summary findings, by local area, 1990 and trends, U8010–4

Louisiana labor force planning rpt, including population and labor force characteristics, unemployment claimants, and data by parish and MSA, 1993 annual rpt, S3320–1

Maine Census of Population and Housing summary findings, by local area, 1990, S3465–9

Maryland statistical abstract, general data, 1993-94 biennial rpt, S3605–1

Maryland vocational rehabilitation center client characteristics, 1992, annual rpt, S3610–1

Michigan labor force planning rpt, including employment by industry, and characteristics of Job Training Partnership Act eligible population, 1993 annual rpt, S3980–1

Mississippi labor force planning rpt, including population, employment, and characteristics of unemployed and disadvantaged, 1993 annual rpt, S4345–1

Mississippi statistical abstract, general data, 1992 annual rpt, U3255–4

Missouri job corps program enrollment, by sex, 1989-91, annual rpt, S4530–2.3

Montana employment by sex, by industry div and county, 1993-94 annual planning rpt, S4710–3

Nebraska labor force distribution by occupational group, by sex, 1940, article, U7860–1.507

Nevada female and total employment for 25 occupations with highest and lowest shares of female workers, 1990, article, S5040–1.503

Nevada statistical abstract, general data, 1992 biennial rpt, S5005–1

New Hampshire job service applicant characteristics, monthly rpt, S5205–1

New Hampshire labor force and population by race, sex, and age, and employment by industry div, statewide and by county, 1992 recurring rpt, S5205–7

New Jersey Census of Population and Housing detailed findings, by county, 1990, S5425–19

New Jersey insured unemployed characteristics, monthly rpt, S5425–1

New Jersey unemployment rates by race and sex, 1991-92, annual article, S5425–1.503

New Mexico labor force planning rpt, including population characteristics, and employment by industry and occupation, 1993 annual rpt, S5624–1

New York State statistical yearbook, general data, 1992 annual rpt, U5100–1

North Dakota full- and part-time employment shares by sex, for 8 metro areas, 1993 annual planning rpt, S6140–2

Oklahoma statistical abstract, general data, 1992 annual rpt, U8130–2

Oregon labor force participation, by sex, 1940-90, article, S6615–2.501

Pennsylvania Census of Population and Housing detailed findings, with selected data by county and municipality, 1990, U4130–13

Pennsylvania employment and commuting data from Census of Population and Housing, by county and municipality, 1990, C1595–16

Pennsylvania employment distribution by sex and occupational group, and women shares of employment in selected occupations, 1980 and/or 1990, article, S6845–1.502

Pennsylvania labor force planning rpt, including population characteristics, employment and job openings by industry and occupation, and income trends, FY92 annual rpt, S6845–3

Pennsylvania statistical abstract, general data, 1992 recurring rpt, U4130–6

Rhode Island Census of Population and Housing detailed findings, by county and municipality, 1990, S6930–9

Rhode Island labor force planning rpt, including population, employment by industry, job openings, and characteristics of insured unemployed, 1993 annual rpt, S6980–3

Rhode Island statistical almanac, general data, 1993 annual rpt, C7975–1

South Carolina labor force planning rpt, detailed data on employment, hours, wages, turnover, and characteristics of job service applicants, 1992 annual rpt, S7155–3.2

South Carolina statistical abstract, general data, 1993 annual rpt, S7125–1

South Dakota employment, earnings, and hours for selected industries and areas, with characteristics of unemployed and job service activities, monthly rpt, S7355–1

Tennessee labor force by employment status, and employment by sex and race, by occupational group and industry div, 1992, articles, S7495–2.506

Tennessee statistical abstract, general data, 1992/93 annual rpt, U8710–2

Utah employment by detailed occupation, and educational attainment by age group, by sex and race-ethnicity, with detail for 7 urban areas, 1990 census rpt, S7832–3.4

Utah labor force and percent without high school diploma, by sex, age group, and/or race-ethnicity, 1990, article, U8960–2.509

Utah labor force characteristics, employment and unemployment, hours, and earnings, with data by industry and locale, 1992 and trends, annual rpt, S7820–10

Utah statistical abstract, general data, 1993 triennial rpt, U8960–1

Vermont labor force by employment status, and job service openings and applicant characteristics, 1993 annual planning rpt, S8025–2.2

Washington State population and demographic characteristics, and housing units, by county and/or city, 1992 and trends, annual rpt, S8345–4

West Virginia labor force planning rpt, including population, employment, and job service activities, with data by county and service delivery area, 1993 annual rpt, S8534–2

Wyoming employment and unemployment by sex and race-ethnicity, by county, 1990, S8895–1.505

Law Enforcement

Black American crime, arrest, and incarceration data, with comparisons to whites, 1970s-91, annual compilation, C6775–2.5

Correctional instn inmates and staff, and probationers, by sex and race, by State and for Federal system, and for major jails, Jan 1992, annual series, R4300–1

Correctional instns, inmates, staff, and cost of care, by instn, US and Canada, with operating summary by State or Province, 1992, annual directory, A1305–3

Crime victims per 1,000 population, by demographic characteristics, 1991, article, R8750–1.505

Jails and adult detention facilities, inmates, staff, and operating summary, by State and instn, Dec 1992, recurring directory, A1305–1

Juvenile State instn custody prevalence rates by sex, age, and race-ethnicity, for 16 States, 1991, A7575–1.13

Law school enrollment and staff, total and female, by instn, 1992/93 and trends, annual rpt, A0970–1

Law school grad employment and salaries, by type of employer, location, and grad characteristics, 1992 and trends, annual rpt, A6505–1

Mexico criminal suspects and sentenced delinquents, by sex, 1976-84, annual rpt, U6250–1.15

Personal injury jury verdict awards in wrongful death cases, by sex, 1992 and trends, annual rpt, C5180–1

Prisoners on death row, by State, sex, and race-ethnicity, 1992 and trends, annual rpt, A1305–3

State and local:

Alabama crimes and arrests, by offense and offender characteristics, and law enforcement employment by sex, 1992 and trends, annual rpt, S0119–1

Alaska corrections system admin, including inmate and probationer/parolee offenses and demographic characteristics, 1991 annual rpt, S0287–1

Alaska State court system employees, by sex, FY92, annual rpt, S0290–1

Arizona arrests, murder victims, and law enforcement employment, by sex, 1992, annual rpt, S0505–2

Arizona correctional instn admin, including inmates by criminal background and demographic characteristics, FY92, annual rpt, S0464–2

Arizona juvenile court referrals and adjudication activity, by age and sex, FY92, annual rpt, S0525–1

Arizona statistical abstract, general data, 1993 recurring rpt, U5850–2

Index by Categories

BY SEX

Arkansas child abuse and neglect victims, by age, sex, and race, FY91, annual rpt, S0700–2.2

Arkansas crimes and arrests, by victim and offender characteristics, with law enforcement employment data, 1992 and trends, annual rpt, S0652–1

Arkansas juvenile detention center and community program admissions, by age and sex, 1989-91, annual rpt, S0700–2.2

California correctional instn inmates, by offense, demographic characteristics, and instn, Dec 1992, semiannual rpt, S0820–2

California correctional instn inmates, with criminal background and demographic characteristics, 1991 and trends, annual rpt, S0820–1

California crimes and arrests, clearances, and arrest dispositions, with data by offense and offender characteristics, 1987-92, annual rpt, S0910–1.1

California criminal justice system detailed data, by offense, county, age, race-ethnicity, and sex, 1991 and trends, annual rpt, S0910–2

California felons newly received and paroled, by sex, 1988-90, annual planning rpt, S0830–2

California judicial system employment by position, sex, and race-ethnicity, with minority utilization rates and parity targets, Jan 1993, annual rpt, S0905–1.1

California statistical abstract, general data, 1992 annual rpt, S0840–2

Colorado crimes and arrests, by offense and location, with offender characteristics, and assaults on police, 1992, annual rpt, S1068–1

Connecticut crimes and arrests, by offense and offender characteristics, and law enforcement employment by sex, 1992, annual rpt, S1256–1

DC arrests, and juvenile drug test results, by sex, 1991, annual rpt, S1535–2

DC court committee members by race-ethnicity and sex, and juvenile case referrals by defendant sex, 1992 and trends, annual rpt, S1515–1

DC statistical profile, general data, 1992 annual rpt, S1535–3

Delaware crimes and arrests, by offense, county, and victim-offender characteristics, 1991 and trends, annual rpt, S1375–5

Florida correctional instns, admin, and inmates by criminal background and demographic characteristics, FY92 annual rpt, S1720–1

Florida county data book, 1992/93 annual rpt, C6360–1

Florida crimes and arrests, by offense, with data by victim and offender characteristics, 1992, annual rpt, S1770–1

Florida "habitual offender" sentencing laws effect on prison population, with data by circuit court and offender characteristics, 1993 rpt, A7575–5

Florida statistical abstract, general data, 1992 annual rpt, U6660–1

Georgia correctional instns, admin, and inmate characteristics, FY92, annual rpt, S1872–1

Georgia county guide, general data, 1993 annual rpt, U6750–1

Georgia crimes and arrests, by offense, with data by location and offender characteristics, 1992 and trends, annual rpt, S1901–1

Georgia statistical abstract, general data, 1992-93 biennial rpt, U6730–1

Hawaii crimes and arrests, by offense, with data by county and victim-offender characteristics, 1992, annual rpt, S2035–1

Hawaii data book, general data, 1992 annual rpt, S2090–1

Idaho crimes and arrests, by offender characteristics, and law enforcement employment by sex, 1992, annual rpt, S2275–2

Illinois corrections dept admin, including inmates and characteristics, finances, and staff, FY91-93 and trends, annual rpt, S2425–1

Illinois crimes and arrests, by offender characteristics, 1990-91, annual rpt, S2536–1

Indiana child abuse and neglect cases by county and victim and perpetrator characteristics, FY92 annual rpt, S2623–1.7

Iowa correctional instn admissions, releases, and inmate characteristics, by instn, monthly rpt, S2770–1

Kansas correctional instn inmates, by offense, demographic characteristics, and instn, FY92 and trends, annual rpt, S2940–1

Kansas crimes and arrests, with victim, offender, and law enforcement employee characteristics, 1992, annual rpt, S2925–1

Kansas statistical abstract, general data, 1991/92 annual rpt, U7095–2

Kentucky crimes and arrests, by offense and offender characteristics, and law enforcement employment by sex, 1992, annual rpt, S3150–1

Maine crimes and arrests, and law enforcement employment, by sex, 1991, annual rpt, S3475–1

Maryland arrests by offense, and law enforcement personnel by local agency and county, by sex, 1992, annual rpt, S3665–1

Maryland statistical abstract, general data, 1993-94 biennial rpt, S3605–1

Massachusetts correctional instn inmate socioeconomic characteristics and criminal background, by instn, Jan 1992 and trends, annual rpt, S3805–1

Massachusetts court jury dept activities, with data on juror selection and service by sex, by county, 1992, annual rpt, S3807–1

Michigan correctional instns, admin, and inmates by selected demographic characteristics, 1991 and trends, annual rpt, S3960–1

Michigan crimes and arrests, with murder victims by race, sex, and age, 1992, annual rpt, S3997–1

Mississippi statistical abstract, general data, 1992 annual rpt, U3255–4

Missouri correctional instn admissions, releases, and inmate characteristics, FY93, annual rpt, S4501–1

Missouri crimes and arrests, by offense and location, with victim and offender characteristics, 1991 and trends, annual rpt, S4560–2

Nebraska correctional instn admin, with inmates by criminal background and demographic characteristics, by instn, FY92 and trends, annual rpt, S4850–1

New Hampshire crimes and arrests, by offense, jurisdiction, and offender characteristics, 1991 and trends, annual rpt, S5250–2

New Jersey crimes and arrests by victim-offender characteristics, and law enforcement employment by sex, 1992 and trends, annual rpt, S5430–1

New York State arrests, homicide victims and offenders, law enforcement employees, and prisoners, by demographic characteristics, 1991, annual rpt, S5760–3

New York State children and youth involved in family court cases, by sex and county, 1991, annual rpt, S5730–1

New York State correctional instn inmates released, by criminal background, sentence, and demographic characteristics, 1991 and trends, recurring rpt series, S5725–1

New York State local jail/penitentiary inmates by offense, sentence, and demographic characteristics, by county or facility, 1991, annual rpt, S5724–2

New York State statistical yearbook, general data, 1992 annual rpt, U5100–1

North Carolina correctional instn admissions, separations, and population, with inmate characteristics, FY93, semiannual rpt, S5900–1

North Carolina crimes and arrests by offender characteristics, and law enforcement employment by sex, 1991-92, annual rpt, S5955–1

North Dakota crimes and arrests, by offender characteristics, and law enforcement employment by sex, 1991, annual rpt, S6060–1

North Dakota local correctional instn adult and juvenile inmate characteristics, by instn, 1991 and trends, annual rpt, S6060–3

Ohio correctional instn admissions and releases, inmate characteristics, programs, finances, and staffing, FY91 and trends, annual rpt, S6370–1

Oklahoma correctional instn admin, including inmate characteristics, incarceration costs, and data by instn, FY91, annual rpt, S6420–1

Oklahoma crimes and arrests, including offenders, homicide victims, and law enforcement employment, by sex, 1992 annual rpt, S6465–1

Oregon crimes and arrests, by offense and offender characteristics, and law enforcement employment by sex, 1992, annual rpt, S6603–3

Pennsylvania law enforcement employees by local agency, arrests by criminal offense, and victims and offenders, by sex, 1992, annual rpt, S6860–1

Pennsylvania State correctional instn admin, and inmates by type of offense and demographic characteristics, 1990 and trends, annual rpt, S6782–1

Pennsylvania statistical abstract, general data, 1992 recurring rpt, U4130–6

South Carolina correctional instns, admin, and inmates by criminal offense and demographic characteristics, FY92 and trends, annual rpt, S7135–1

South Carolina crimes and arrests, by offense, with data by location and victim-offender characteristics, and assaults on officers, 1992 and trends, annual rpt, S7205–1

South Carolina statistical abstract, general data, 1993 annual rpt, S7125–1

South Dakota correctional instn admin, including inmates by criminal background and demographic characteristics, FY92 and trends, annual rpt, S7296–1

BY SEX

Index by Categories

Tennessee correctional instn admin, with inmate characteristics, and corrections dept finances and staff, FY92, annual rpt, S7480–1

Tennessee statistical abstract, general data, 1992/93 annual rpt, U8710–2

Texas correctional instn inmates by criminal background and demographic characteristics, FY92, annual rpt, S7660–1

Texas crimes and arrests, by offense, with data by location and offender characteristics, 1992 and trends, annual rpt, S7735–2

Utah corrections inmates, parolees, and probationers, by criminal background and demographic characteristics, FY92 and trends, annual rpt, S7810–1

Utah murder victims and offenders, by sex, 1992, annual rpt, S7890–3

Virginia crimes and arrests by offender characteristics, and law enforcement employment by sex, 1992, annual rpt, S8295–2

Washington State correctional instn inmate population, admissions, and releases, by demographic characteristics, quarterly rpt, S8337–1

Washington State crimes and arrests, by victim and offender characteristics, and law enforcement employment by sex, 1992 and trends, annual rpt, S8440–1

West Virginia crimes and arrests, by offense and offender characteristics, and law enforcement employment by sex, 1990-91, annual rpt, S8610–1

Wisconsin correctional instn inmates, by criminal background and selected characteristics, series, S8692–1

Wisconsin crimes and arrests, by offense, offender characteristics, county, and local agency, 1992 and trends, annual rpt, S8771–1

Wyoming correctional instn admin, finances, inmate characteristics, and staff, and probation and parole activities, FY92 annual rpt, S8883–1

Wyoming crimes and arrests, by offender characteristics, and law enforcement employment by sex, 1991, annual rpt, S8867–3

Population

Black American socioeconomic status, including health, education, politics, crime, and employment, with comparisons to whites, 1993 annual compilation, C6775–2

Bolivia population by sex, 1990-2000, annual rpt, U6250–1.5

Catholic missionaries from US, by sex and world region, 1993 annual almanac, C6885–1

Census of Population and Housing undercounts, by race and sex, 1990 Census and trends, annual rpt, C2500–2

Commonwealth of Independent States region population by sex, urban vs rural status, Republic, and selected city, 1986, R4105–82.4

EC public support of feminist goals, correlation with social characteristics, by sex, 1983 survey, article, A0610–1.502

Gallup Poll public attitude surveys, results and sample characteristics, monthly rpt, C4040–1

Germany (West) and US comparative socioeconomic statistics, 1970s-91, annual rpt, A5135–2.2

Hispanic American socioeconomic status, including education, politics, income, and employment, with comparisons to whites, 1993 annual compilation, C6775–3

Homeless population characteristics in 29 cities, 1991/92, annual rpt, A9330–9

Household composition and living arrangement data for women vs men, 1992, A8657–5

Market area population and characteristics, households, income, and retail outlets, for 21 leading areas, 1993 feature, C2710–1.538

Older population shares by sex, for 5 States with greatest increases and declines in population age 65/over and 85/over, 1980-90, article, B6045–1.502

Population by age, race, sex, and educational attainment, 1991 and trends, articles, A8510–1.1

Population by race-ethnicity, sex, and educational status, 1992 recurring rpt, A3960–2.1

Population trends and projections, by age and sex, 1980s-2080, annual rpt, A4957–1.1

Refugee arrivals, by sex and age, FY83-92, R9372–2.507

Religion and related social issues, public opinions and attitudes, monthly survey, R8780–1

Russia public opinion on political and economic issues and devs, by selected characteristics, 1991-92 surveys, C8915–10

Solitary living population, by age and sex, 1990, 1995, and 2000, article, C4655–1.506

Statistical profiles of 50 States and DC, general data, 1993 annual almanac, C4712–1

State and local:

Alabama vital statistics, including population, births, deaths by cause, marriages, and divorces, by location and demographic characteristics, 1992 and trends, annual rpt, S0175–2

Alaska population, housing, income, and education data, by demographic characteristics and/or locality, 1990/91 and trends, annual rpt, S0320–4

Alaska vital statistics, including births, deaths by cause, marriages, divorces, adoptions, and population, by demographic characteristics and location, 1990, annual rpt, S0315–1

Arizona Indian population, education, housing, health, and employment characteristics, with detail by reservation, 1970s-91, recurring rpt, U5850–2.9

Arizona, Phoenix area temporary winter resident characteristics, including expenditures, dwelling type, and region of residence, 1992/93, article, U0280–1.508

Arizona statistical abstract, general data, 1993 recurring rpt, U5850–2

Arkansas adoptions by child age, race, and sex, FY91, annual rpt, S0700–2.2

Arkansas Census of Population and Housing detailed findings, 1990, U5935–7

California Census of Population and Housing detailed findings, 1990, S0840–9

California labor force planning rpt, including population characteristics, and employment by industry, 1992 annual rpt, S0830–2

California population by age, sex, race-ethnicity, and county, decennially 1990-2040, recurring rpt, S0840–4

California socioeconomic and govtl data for municipalities, counties, and school districts, 1993 annual rpt, C4712–3

Colorado labor force planning rpt, including population, employment by industry, and job service applicants, FY94 annual rpt, S1040–3

Colorado vital statistics, including population, births, deaths by cause, abortion, marriage and divorce, and adoption, by demographic characteristics and location, 1990 and trends, annual rpt, S1010–1

Connecticut population, by age and sex, 1989, annual rpt, S1200–1

DC statistical profile, general data, 1992 annual rpt, S1535–3

Delaware population, by age, sex, race, and locality, 1990-2020, recurring rpt, S1375–3

Delaware vital statistics, including births, deaths by cause, and marriages and dissolutions, by demographic characteristics and location, 1990, annual rpt, S1385–2

Florida municipal and county statistical profiles, general data, 1991 annual rpt, C4712–6

Florida population by age, sex, and race, by county, 1990, 1992, and quinquennially 1995-2010, annual rpt, U6660–3.46

Florida population by age, sex, and race, by county, 1990-91 and quinquennially 1995-2010, annual rpt, U6660–3.43

Florida statistical abstract, general data, 1992 annual rpt, U6660–1

Florida vital statistics, including population, births, deaths by cause, and marriages and dissolutions, by location and demographic characteristics, 1992 and trends, annual rpt, S1745–3

Georgia county guide, general data, 1993 annual rpt, U6750–1

Georgia statistical abstract, general data, 1992-93 biennial rpt, U6730–1

Georgia vital statistics, including population by demographic characteristics and location, 1991, annual rpt, S1895–1.3

Hawaii data book, general data, 1992 annual rpt, S2090–1

Idaho economic profile, general data, 1992 recurring rpt, S2218–2.2

Idaho population by age and sex, 1990, annual rpt, S2250–2

Illinois statistical abstract, general data, 1992 annual rpt, U6910–2

Kansas statistical abstract, general data, 1991/92 annual rpt, U7095–2

Kansas vital statistics, including population, births, deaths by cause, abortions, marriages, and divorces, by demographic characteristics and location, 1991 and trends, annual rpt, S2975–1

Kentucky economic statistics, general data, 1993 annual rpt, S3104–1

Kentucky labor force planning rpt, including population and labor force characteristics, and employment by industry, 1991 and trends, annual rpt, S3140–3

Kentucky vital statistics, including births, deaths by cause, marriages and divorces, and population, by demographic characteristics and county, 1991, annual rpt, S3140–1

Index by Categories

BY SEX

Louisiana Census of Population and Housing summary findings, by local area, 1990 and trends, U8010–4

Louisiana population, by race, sex, and location, 1992, annual planning rpt, S3320–1.1

Maine Census of Population and Housing summary findings, by local area, 1990, S3465–7, S3465–8

Maine population, by age, sex, and county, 1991, annual rpt, S3460–2

Maryland statistical abstract, general data, 1993-94 biennial rpt, S3605–1

Maryland vital statistics, including population, births, deaths by cause, marriages, and divorces, by demographic characteristics and location, 1989 and trends, annual rpt, S3635–1

Massachusetts municipal and county profiles, general data, 1992 annual rpt, C4712–2

Massachusetts vital statistics, including births, deaths by cause, marriages, divorces, and population, by locality and demographic characteristics, 1990 and trends, annual rpt, S3850–1

Michigan labor force planning rpt, including employment by industry, and characteristics of Job Training Partnership Act eligible population, 1993 annual rpt, S3980–1

Michigan population, by age, sex, race, and county, 1990, annual rpt, S4000–3

Minnesota population, by age, sex, and county, 1991, annual rpt, S4190–2

Mississippi population, by age, race, sex, and educational attainment, 1993/94, annual planning rpt, S4345–1.1

Mississippi population, by age, sex, and race, 1990, annual rpt, S4350–1

Montana youth population by sex and age, 1990 and 1992, annual rpt, S4705–1

Nebraska population age 20/under, by age, sex, and county, June 1992, annual rpt, S4865–2.6

Nevada statistical abstract, general data, 1992 biennial rpt, S5005–1

New Hampshire labor force and population by race, sex, and age, and employment by industry div, statewide and by county, 1992 recurring rpt, S5205–7

New Jersey Census of Population and Housing detailed findings, by county, 1990, S5425–19

New Jersey municipal and county data book, general data, 1992 annual rpt, C4712–4

New Jersey population, by race and Hispanic ethnicity, sex, age, and county, 1990, annual rpt, S5405–1

New Mexico population, by age and sex, 1990, annual planning rpt, S5624–1

New Mexico population, by age, sex, and race-ethnicity, 1990, annual rpt, S5605–1.1

New Mexico population by age, sex, county, and State region, 1980 and 1990, U7980–6

New York State adoptions, by sex, age, and race-ethnicity, 1991, annual rpt, S5800–2.3

New York State municipal and county statistical profiles, general data, 1993 annual rpt, C4712–7

New York State statistical yearbook, general data, 1992 annual rpt, U5100–1

New York State vital statistics, including population, births, deaths by cause, reportable diseases, and marriages and dissolutions, by demographic characteristics and/or location, 1990 and trends, annual rpt, S5765–1

North Carolina vital statistics, including population, births, deaths, marriages, and divorces, by local area, 1991 and trends, annual rpt, S5927–1.1

North Dakota children by age and/or sex, by county, Aug 1991, annual education directory, S6180–2

Ohio population by age, sex, and county, with summary components of change, quinquennially 1990-2015, recurring rpt, S6260–3

Ohio vital statistics, including births, deaths by cause, marriages, divorces, and population, by demographic characteristics and location, 1991 and trends, annual rpt, S6285–1

Oklahoma population projections, by age, sex, and locality, with data on fertility and migration, 1990-2020, recurring rpt, S6416–1

Oklahoma statistical abstract, general data, 1992 annual rpt, U8130–2

Oregon population, by age and sex, 1950s-91, annual rpt, S6615–5

Pennsylvania Census of Population and Housing detailed findings, with selected data by county and municipality, 1990, U4130–13

Pennsylvania statistical abstract, general data, 1992 recurring rpt, U4130–6

Rhode Island statistical almanac, general data, 1993 annual rpt, C7975–1

Rhode Island vital statistics, including population, births, deaths, marriages, and divorces, by demographic characteristics and locality, 1989 and trends, annual rpt, S6995 1

South Carolina labor force planning rpt, including population, employment, income, and job service activities, 1992 annual rpt, S7155–3

South Carolina statistical abstract, general data, 1993 annual rpt, S7125–1

Tennessee population, by age, sex, race, and county, 1990-2010, recurring rpt, S7560–2

Tennessee population projections by age, sex, and county metro status, 1990-2010, article, U8710–1.501

Tennessee statistical abstract, general data, 1992/93 annual rpt, U8710–2

Texas labor force planning rpt, including labor force, employment by industry, income, and population, 1993 annual rpt, S7675–2

Texas population, by age, sex, and race-ethnicity, 1990, recurring rpt, S7645–3

Texas population, by age, sex, race-ethnicity, and county, July 1991, annual rpt, S7645–2

Utah statistical abstract, general data, 1993 triennial rpt, U8960–1

Vermont population, by age, sex, and locality, 1991 and trends, annual planning rpt, S8025–2.1

Vermont vital statistics, including population, births, deaths by cause, abortions, marriages, and divorces, by location and demographic characteristics, 1991 and trends, annual rpt, S8054–1

Virginia population age 19/under, by age and sex, Jan 1993, triennial rpt, S8190–1

Washington State population and demographic characteristics, and housing units, by county and/or city, 1992 and trends, annual rpt, S8345–4

Washington State vital statistics, including births, deaths by cause, and population, by demographic characteristics and location, 1991 and trends, annual rpt, S8363–1

West Virginia labor force planning rpt, including population, employment, and job service activities, with data by county and service delivery area, 1993 annual rpt, S8534–2

West Virginia population, by sex, 1990, annual rpt, S8560–1

Wisconsin Blue Book, general data, 1993-94 biennial rpt, S8780–1.2

Wisconsin population, by age, sex, and county, with components of change, quinquennially 1990-2020, recurring rpt, S8675–4

Wisconsin vital statistics, including population, births, deaths by cause, and marriages and dissolutions, by county and demographic characteristics, 1991 and trends, annual rpt, S8715–4

Public Welfare and Social Security

Foundation board trustees by sex and race-ethnicity, for 25 leading private, community, and corporate foundations, 1989 and trends, A9405–1.1

Foundation board trustees by sex and race-ethnicity, for 25 leading private, community, and corporate foundations, 1991 and trends, A9405–1.2

Foundation employment distribution by sex, race, and minority status, by position type, 1993, article, C2176–1.520

Foundation finances, and personnel and governing board characteristics, by organization characteristics, 1991/92, article, C2176–1.506

Fundraising professionals characteristics, earnings, and benefits, 1992 survey, recurring rpt, A8455–1

Nonprofit foundation boards, officers, and staff, by sex and race, 1992, annual rpt, A0700–1.1

Social Security recipient mean age at start of benefits, 1950-2005, article, R8750–1.505

Volunteer activities and characteristics of teenagers vs adults, 1991, survey article, C2176–1.503

Youth age 12-17 charitable contributions, volunteer activity, and views on related issues, by respondent characteristics, 1992 survey, biennial rpt, A5435–5

State and local:

Arkansas human services dept finances and operations, including Medicaid payments by type of service, FY91 and trends, annual rpt, S0700–2.3

California AFDC recipients by selected characteristics, June 1988-90, annual planning rpt, S0830–2

California statistical abstract, general data, 1992 annual rpt, S0840–2

Georgia statistical abstract, general data, 1992-93 biennial rpt, U6730–1

Hawaii data book, general data, 1992 annual rpt, S2090–1

Maryland medical assistance payments and recipients, by program, type of service,

BY SEX

Index by Categories

location, demographic characteristics, and facility, FY92 and trends, annual rpt, S3635–3

Michigan welfare registrants by sex, June 1992, annual planning rpt, S3980–1.2

New Mexico public welfare recipient characteristics, by program, monthly rpt quarterly table, S5620–2

New York State public assistance recipients and adoptions, by sex and age, 1991, annual rpt, S5800–2

New York State statistical yearbook, general data, 1992 annual rpt, U5100–1

Oklahoma public welfare program recipients and payments, and recipient characteristics, by county and type of service, FY92, annual rpt, S6455–1.2

South Carolina teen companion program for children of welfare parents, participation by sex, monthly rpt, S7252–1

Texas Medicaid expenditures by category, and recipient characteristics and medical services received, 1975 and 1980-91, U8850–8.5

Utah homeless shelter population characteristics, individual shelter capacity, and related housing data, 1991-92, annual rpt, S7808–2

Recreation and Leisure

Golf course pros/directors by sex, 1993 article, C5800–7.524

Participation in 53 sports, by demographic characteristics, State, and census div, 1992, annual rpt series, A8485–3

Sporting goods purchaser characteristics, by product category, 1992, annual survey rpt, A8485–4

Sporting goods purchases, by product and outlet type, census div, and purchaser characteristics, with average prices, 1992 and trends, annual survey, A8485–2

Science and Technology

Chemist and chemical engineer salaries, employment status, and demographic and professional characteristics, 1993, annual rpt, A1250 4

Chemist salaries and employment, by employee and employer characteristics, Mar 1993 and trends, annual article, A1250–1.532

Chemistry and chemical engineering degrees awarded, by level, sex, and instn, 1991/92 and trends, annual articles, A1250–1.535

Chemistry and chemical engineering grad starting salaries, employment status, demographic characteristics, and advanced study plans, 1991/92, annual rpt, A1250–2

Ecologist personal and professional characteristics, including research activity and funding, with data by field, Mar 1992 survey, recurring rpt, A4685–1

Engineer compensation, by work and employee characteristics, and region and metro area, 1992, annual rpt, A8460–1

Engineering degrees awarded, by State, instn, and field, with detail for women, minorities, and foreign students, 1991/92, annual rpt, A0685–1

Engineering program enrollment, by instn, field, and State, with detail for women, minorities, and foreign students, fall 1992, annual rpt, A0685–2

Geoscience enrollment and degrees awarded, by sex, race-ethnicity, and discipline, 1991/92, annual rpt, A1785–3

Latin America statistical abstract, general data by country, 1992 annual rpt, U6250–1.8

Physics and astronomy bachelor degree recipients postgraduation plans and demographic characteristics, 1991/92 and trends, annual survey, A1960–3

Physics and astronomy grads employment status, by sex, age, subfield, citizenship, degree, and employer type, with salary info, 1990/91, annual rpt, A1960–1

Physics degrees awarded, by level, sex, and minority group, 1991/92, annual rpt, A1960–2.1

Psychology doctoral degree recipient employment and demographic characteristics, and finances, 1990/91, biennial survey rpt, A2620–4

Psychology grad dept faculty salaries, by academic rank, years in rank, census div, and sex, 1992/93 and trends, annual rpt, A2620–1

Psychology grad depts, faculty characteristics, enrollment, and student aid, US and Canada, 1990/91 and trends, annual rpt, A2620–3

Science and math elementary/secondary education, including student and teacher characteristics, and requirements, by State, 1991/92, biennial rpt, A4355–3

Transportation and Travel

Airline travel frequency, destination, and purpose, by traveler characteristics, 1992 survey and trends, annual rpt, A0325–6

Auto do-it-yourself (DIY) maintenance activity, by type and consumer characteristics, 1993 and trends, annual survey, C0125–1.506

Business traveler and trip characteristics, including mode, purpose, and lodging, 1991, annual rpt, R9375–12

Drivers licensed, by sex, State, and Canadian Province, 1993 annual fact book, C4680–1.507

Motor vehicle drivers, accident involvement, and fatally injured drunk drivers, by sex, 1991 and trends, annual rpt, A5650–1.4

Motor vehicle drivers in fatal accidents, by blood alcohol content, by sex, 1982-90, article, A8375–1.505

Motor vehicle fleet manager earnings, and personal and professional characteristics, 1993 article, C1575–2.506

Motor vehicle ownership and use patterns by owner characteristics, and licensed drivers, 1990s and trends, annual rpt, A0865–1

Motorcycle use and user characteristics, licensed operators, and State requirements, 1992 annual rpt, A6485–1.2

School bus loading/unloading accident fatalities, by circumstances, location, and victim age and sex, 1991 and trends, annual rpt, S3040–2

Travel trips and traveler characteristics, including mode, purpose, type of lodging, and area of destination and origin, quarterly rpt, R9375–14

Traveler and trip characteristics, 1990, annual rpt, C2140–1.2

Trucks (light) accessory purchasing, and owner characteristics, 1993 annual survey feature, C2150–10.506

State and local:

Alabama traffic accidents, fatalities, and injuries, by circumstances, vehicle type, and driver and victim characteristics, 1992, annual rpt, S0185–1

Alaska traffic accidents, fatalities, and injuries, by vehicle type, circumstance, location, and driver and victim characteristics, 1991 and trends, annual rpt, S0360–1

Arizona traffic accidents, fatalities, and injuries, by vehicle type, circumstances, location, and driver and victim characteristics, 1991 and trends, annual rpt, S0530–1

Arkansas traffic accidents, fatalities, and injuries, by vehicle type, circumstances, location, and driver and victim characteristics, 1991, annual rpt, S0692–1

California statistical abstract, general data, 1992 annual rpt, S0840–2

California traffic accidents, fatalities, and injuries, by vehicle type, circumstances, location, and driver and victim characteristics, 1991 and trends, annual rpt, S0885–1

Connecticut traffic accidents, fatalities, and injuries, by vehicle type, circumstance, location, and driver and victim characteristics, 1992, annual rpt, S1275–1

Delaware traffic accidents, fatalities, and injuries, by circumstances, location, and vehicle type, and driver and victim characteristics, 1992 and trends, annual rpt, S1435–1

Florida statistical abstract, general data, 1992 annual rpt, U6660–1

Florida traffic accidents, fatalities, and injuries, by vehicle type, circumstance, location, and driver and victim characteristics, 1992 and trends, annual rpt, S1750–2

Georgia statistical abstract, general data, 1992-93 biennial rpt, U6730–1

Hawaii data book, general data, 1992 annual rpt, S2090–1

Hawaii motor vehicle drivers registered, and persons involved in accidents, by sex and/or age, 1986, annual rpt, S2125–1

Idaho traffic accidents, fatalities, and injuries, by circumstances, location, vehicle type, and driver and victim characteristics, 1992, annual rpt, S2315–1

Illinois traffic accidents, fatalities, and injuries, by circumstances, location, and driver and victim characteristics, 1991 and trends, annual rpt, S2540–1

Indiana traffic accidents, fatalities, and injuries, by circumstances, location, and vehicle type, and driver and victim characteristics, 1992, annual rpt, S2675–1

Kansas traffic accidents, fatalities, and injuries, by vehicle type, location, circumstances, and driver and victim characteristics, 1992, annual rpt, S3040–1

Kentucky traffic accidents, fatalities, and injuries, by circumstances, location, vehicle type, and driver characteristics, 1992 and trends, annual rpt, S3150–2

Louisiana traffic accidents, fatalities, and injuries, by circumstances, location, and driver characteristics, 1991 and trends, annual rpt, S3345–2

Maine traffic accidents, fatalities, and injuries, by accident circumstances, vehicle type and make, and driver and victim characteristics, 1992, annual rpt, S3475–2

Maryland traffic accidents, fatalities, and injuries, by circumstances, location, vehicle type, and driver and victim characteristics, 1992, annual rpt, S3665–4

Index by Categories BY SEX

Michigan traffic accidents, fatalities, and injuries, by vehicle type, circumstance, location, and driver and victim characteristics, 1991 and trends, annual rpt, S3997–2

Minnesota traffic accidents, fatalities, and injuries, by type of vehicle and circumstances, and driver and victim characteristics, 1992 and trends, annual rpt, S4230–2

Missouri pedestrian fatalities and injuries, by sex and age group, 1992, annual rpt, S4560–1

Montana traffic accidents, fatalities, and injuries, by circumstances, location, and driver and victim characteristics, 1992 and trends, annual rpt, S4705–2

Nebraska traffic accidents, fatalities, and injuries, by circumstances, location, vehicle type, and driver and victim characteristics, 1992, annual rpt, S4953–1

Nevada statistical abstract, general data, 1992 biennial rpt, S5005–1

Nevada traffic accidents, by driver age and sex, 1992, annual rpt, S5140–1

New Jersey fatal traffic accidents and fatalities, by vehicle type, location, and circumstances, and driver and victim characteristics, 1992 and trends, annual rpt, S5430–2

New Mexico licensed drivers, by sex, age, and county, July 1990-92, annual rpt, S5660–1.2

New Mexico traffic accidents, fatalities, and injuries, by vehicle type, circumstances, location, and driver and victim characteristics, 1992 and trends, annual rpt, S5665–1

New York State statistical yearbook, general data, 1992 annual rpt, U5100–1

New York State traffic accidents, fatalities, and injuries, by circumstances, location, vehicle type, and driver and victim characteristics, 1991 and trends, annual rpt, S5790–1

North Carolina traffic accidents, fatalities, and injuries, by circumstances, location, vehicle type, and driver and victim characteristics, 1992 and trends, annual rpt, S5990–1

North Dakota traffic accidents, fatalities, and injuries, by circumstances, location, vehicle type, and driver and victim characteristics, 1992 and trends, annual rpt, S6217–1

Ohio traffic accidents, fatalities, and injuries, by circumstances, location, driver and victim characteristics, and vehicle type, 1991 and trends, annual rpt, S6290–1

Oklahoma traffic accidents, fatalities, and injuries, by circumstances, location, and driver and victim characteristics, 1992 and trends, annual rpt, S6482–1

Pennsylvania traffic accidents, fatalities, and injuries, by circumstances, location, driver characteristics, and vehicle type, 1991, annual rpt, S6905–3

Rhode Island traffic accidents, fatalities, and injuries, by circumstances, community, and driver and victim characteristics, 1992, annual rpt, S7025–1

South Carolina statistical abstract, general data, 1993 annual rpt, S7125–1

South Carolina traffic accidents, fatalities, and injuries, by circumstances, location, and driver and victim characteristics, 1992 and trends, annual rpt, S7190–2

South Dakota traffic accidents, fatalities, and injuries, by circumstances, location, vehicle type, and driver and victim characteristics, 1992 and trends, annual rpt, S7300–3

Utah traffic accidents and fatalities by circumstances, location, driver and victim characteristics, and vehicle type, 1992 and trends, annual rpt, S7890–2

Virginia traffic accidents, fatalities, and injuries, by circumstances, location, and driver and victim characteristics, 1991 and trends, annual rpt, S8282–1

Washington State traffic accidents, fatalities, and injuries, by circumstances, vehicle type, and location, with driver and victim characteristics, 1992 and trends, annual rpt, S8428–1

West Virginia traffic accidents, fatalities, and injuries, by circumstance and location, and driver and victim characteristics, 1992, annual rpt, S8645–1

Wisconsin traffic accidents, fatalities, and injuries, by circumstances, location, vehicle type, and driver and victim characteristics, 1992 and trends, annual rpt, S8815–1

Wyoming traffic accidents, fatalities, and injuries, by circumstances, location, vehicle type, and driver and victim characteristics, 1992 and trends, annual rpt, S9007–1

Veterans Affairs

State and local:

Alaska civilian veterans by area and sex, with number age 65/over, and distribution by period of service, 1990, article, S0320–1.511

California veteran population, by sex and period of service, Mar 1989-91, annual planning rpt, S0830–2

Georgia county guide, general data, 1993 annual rpt, U6750–1

Wisconsin Blue Book, general data, 1993-94 biennial rpt, S8780–1.2

Index by Issuing Sources

Index by Issuing Sources

Names of issuing sources generally appear in natural word order, with publication titles listed below. Periodicity and SRI microfiche status also are shown for each title. Where issuing source names have been inverted for purposes of alphabetization by surname (e.g., Best, A. M., Co.), a cross-reference from natural word order is provided.

University research centers are listed first by university, and secondly by specific center or department issuing the report. In general, titles of State reports are listed under State issuing sources at the department or agency level, with cross-references provided, as necessary, from names of responsible State subagencies.

A. C. Nielsen Co.
see Nielsen Media Research

A. M. Best Co.
see Best, A. M., Co.

AAFRC Trust for Philanthropy
see American Association of Fund-Raising Counsel Trust for Philanthropy, A0700–1

Abingdon Press
Yearbook of American and Canadian Churches, 1993, [Annual, SRI/MF/excerpts] C0105–1

ACCRA
Cost of Living Index, [Quarterly, SRI/MF/complete, delayed] A0150–1

Administrative Management Society
AMS Management Salaries Report, [Annual, discontinued] A0175–2
AMS Office Benefits Survey Report for the U.S. and Canada, [Annual, discontinued] A0175–5
AMS Office, Professional, and Data Processing Salaries Report, [Annual, discontinued] A0175–1
AMS Office Turnover Survey Report for the U.S. and Canada, [Biennial, discontinued] A0175–4

Advanstar Communications
Aftermarket Business, [Monthly, SRI/MF/not filmed] C0125–1
Beverage Industry, [Monthly, SRI/MF/not filmed] C0125–2
Beverage Industry, Annual Manual 92/93, [Annual, SRI/MF/not filmed] C0125–3
Paperboard Packaging, [Monthly, SRI/MF/not filmed] C0125–4
Pit and Quarry: Review/Outlook, [Monthly (selected issue), SRI/MF/not filmed] C0125–6
Ready Mix: Review/Outlook, [Bimonthly (selected issue), SRI/MF/not filmed] C0125–5

Aerospace Industries Association of America
Aerospace Facts and Figures, 1992-93, [Annual, SRI/MF/complete] A0250–2

AFL-CIO
see American Federation of Labor and Congress of Industrial Organizations

Air-Conditioning and Refrigeration Institute
News Release from the Air-Conditioning and Refrigeration Institute, [Monthly, SRI/MF/complete, shipped quarterly] A0300–1

Air Transport Association of America
Air Transport, 1993, [Annual, SRI/MF/complete] A0325–5
Air Travel Survey, 1992, [Annual, SRI/MF/not filmed] A0325–6
Preliminary Scheduled Cargo Traffic Statistics, U.S. Scheduled Airline Industry, [Monthly, SRI/MF/complete, shipped quarterly] A0325–2
Preliminary Scheduled Passenger Traffic Statistics: U.S. Scheduled Airline Industry, [Monthly, SRI/MF/complete, shipped quarterly] A0325–1

Alabama Administrative Office of Courts
Alabama Judicial System Annual Report, FY92, [Annual, SRI/MF/complete] S0118–1

Alabama Agricultural Statistics Service
see Alabama Department of Agriculture and Industries, S0090–1

Alabama Board of Education
see Alabama Department of Education, S0124–1

Alabama Criminal Justice Information Center
1992 Crime in Alabama, [Annual, SRI/MF/complete] S0119–1

Alabama Department of Agriculture and Industries
Alabama Agricultural Statistics, 1991 Revised, 1992 Preliminary, [Annual, SRI/MF/complete] S0090–1

Alabama Department of Banking
Annual Report of Superintendent of Banks of the State of Alabama, for the Fiscal Year Ending Sept. 30, 1992, [Annual, SRI/MF/complete] S0110–1

Alabama Department of Economic and Community Affairs
Alabama County Data Book, 1992-93, [Annual, SRI/MF/complete] S0121–2
Alabama Municipal Data Book, 1993, [Recurring (irreg.), SRI/MF/complete] S0121–5

Alabama Department of Education
State of Alabama Department of Education Annual Report, 1992: Statistical and Financial Data for 1991/92, [Annual, SRI/MF/complete] S0124–1

Alabama Department of Finance
State of Alabama Comprehensive Annual Financial Report for the Fiscal Year Ended Sept. 30, 1992, [Annual, SRI/MF/complete, current & previous year reports] S0129–1

Alabama Department of Human Resources
Statistics, Alabama Department of Human Resources, [Monthly, SRI/MF/complete, shipped quarterly] S0150–1

Alabama Department of Insurance
1992 Alabama Insurance Report: Business of 1991, Company Directory, [Annual, SRI/MF/complete] S0160–1

Alabama Department of Public Health
Alabama Department of Public Health Summary Report of the State Health Officer, 1992, [Annual, SRI/MF/complete] S0175–3
Lifestyles of Health: Behavioral Risk Factor Surveillance Report, Alabama, 1989, [Recurring (irreg.), SRI/MF/complete] S0175–6
1992 Alabama Vital Events, [Annual, SRI/MF/complete, current & previous year reports] S0175–2

Alabama Department of Public Safety
1992 Alabama Accident Summary, Statewide Accidents, [Annual, SRI/MF/complete] S0185–1

Alabama Public Library Service
Alabama Public Library Service: Library Directory and 1992 Statistical Report, [Annual, SRI/MF/complete] S0180–1

Alabama Secretary of State
State of Alabama Certified Vote Totals, Nov. 3, 1992, General Election, [Biennial, SRI/MF/complete] S0205–1

Alan Guttmacher Institute
see Guttmacher, Alan, Institute

Alaska Agricultural Statistics Service
see University of Alaska: Agricultural and Forestry Experiment Station, U5750–1

Alaska Court System
Alaska Court System 1992 Annual Report, [Annual, SRI/MF/complete] S0290–1

Alaska Department of Administration
State of Alaska Comprehensive Annual Financial Report for the Fiscal Year July 1, 1991-June 30, 1992, [Annual, SRI/MF/complete] S0275–1

Alaska Department of Commerce and Economic Development
Alaska Public Utilities Commission Annual Report to the Legislature, FY92, [Annual, SRI/MF/complete] S0280–4
Comparative Statement of Assets, Liabilities, and Capital Accounts of Alaska Banks, [Quarterly, SRI/MF/complete] S0280–2
State of Alaska Division of Insurance 54th Annual Report, 1991 Calendar Year, Fiscal Year 1992, [Annual, SRI/MF/complete] S0280–3

Alaska Department of Community and Regional Affairs
Alaska Taxable, 1992, [Annual, SRI/MF/complete] S0285–1

Alaska Department of Corrections
Alaska Corrections in Review, 1991 Report, [Annual, SRI/MF/complete] S0287–1

Alaska Department of Education
Education in Alaska: Report to the People, [Annual, discontinued] S0295–1
Profiles of Alaska's Public School Districts, FY92, [Annual, SRI/MF/complete, current & previous year reports] S0295–2

Alaska Department of Health and Social Services
Alaska Bureau of Vital Statistics 1990 Annual Report, [Annual, SRI/MF/complete] S0315–1

Alaska Department of Labor

Index by Issuing Sources

Alaska Department of Labor
Alaska Economic Trends, [Monthly, SRI/MF/complete, shipped quarterly] S0320–1
Alaska Population Overview: 1991 Estimates, [Annual, SRI/MF/complete] S0320–4

Alaska Department of Transportation and Public Facilities
1991 Alaska Traffic Accidents, [Annual, SRI/MF/complete] S0360–1

Alaska Office of the Lieutenant Governor
State of Alaska Official Returns, Nov. 3, 1992 General Election, [Biennial, SRI/MF/complete] S0337–1

ALCOA
see Aluminum Company of America

Alliance of American Insurers
Insurance Industry: A Key Player in the U.S. Economy, [Annual, SRI/MF/complete] A0375–2
1991 Financial Condition of Medical Malpractice JUAs, [Annual, SRI/MF/complete] A0375–1
1991 Residual Markets Workers Compensation, [Annual, SRI/MF/complete] A0375–3

Allied Van Lines
Allied Van Lines Magnet States Report, [Annual, SRI/MF/complete] B0210–1

Aluminum Association
Aluminum Situation, [Monthly, SRI/MF/complete, shipped quarterly] A0400–1
Aluminum Statistical Review for 1992, [Annual, SRI/MF/complete] A0400–2

Aluminum Company of America
1991 Solid Waste Management Study: Legislators, [Monograph, SRI/MF/complete] B0230–1
1991 Solid Waste Management Study: Municipal Decision Makers, [Monograph, SRI/MF/complete] B0230–2

American Academy of Pediatrics
Medicaid State Reports, FY91, [Annual, SRI/MF/complete] A0565–1

American Assembly of Collegiate Schools of Business
Newsline, [Quarterly, SRI/MF/excerpts] A0605–2
1992-93 Salary Survey, [Annual, SRI/MF/complete] A0605–1

American Association for Public Opinion Research
Public Opinion Quarterly, [Quarterly, SRI/MF/excerpts] A0610–1

American Association of Blood Banks
American Association of Blood Banks 1992 Annual Report, [Annual, SRI/MF/complete] A0612–2
1993 Directory of Community Blood Centers, [Biennial, SRI/MF/complete] A0612–1

American Association of Colleges of Nursing
1992-93 Special Report on Institutional Resources and Budgets in Baccalaureate and Graduate Programs in Nursing, [Biennial, SRI/MF/complete] A0615–5
1992/93 Enrollment and Graduations in Baccalaureate and Graduate Programs in Nursing, [Annual, SRI/MF/complete] A0615–4
1992/93 Faculty Salaries in Baccalaureate and Graduate Programs in Nursing, [Annual, SRI/MF/complete] A0615–1

1992/93 Salaries of Deans in Baccalaureate and Graduate Programs in Nursing, [Annual, SRI/MF/complete] A0615–2

American Association of Colleges of Osteopathic Medicine
Debts and Career Plans of Osteopathic Medical Students in 1992, [Annual, SRI/MF/complete] A0620–2
1993 Annual Statistical Report, [Annual, SRI/MF/complete] A0620–1

American Association of Colleges of Pharmacy
Profile of Pharmacy Students, [Annual, SRI/MF/complete] A0630–9

American Association of Community Colleges
Community, Technical, and Junior Colleges Statistical Yearbook, 1992 Edition, [Annual, SRI/MF/not filmed] A0640–1

American Association of Dental Schools
Annual Report on Dental Education, 1992/93, [Annual, SRI/MF/complete] A1475–3

American Association of Engineering Societies
Engineering and Technology Degrees, 1992, [Annual, SRI/MF/complete, delayed] A0685–1
Engineering and Technology Enrollments, Fall 1992, [Annual, SRI/MF/complete, delayed] A0685–2
Engineers' Salaries: Special Industry Report, 1993, [Annual, SRI/MF/complete, delayed] A0685–3
Professional Income of Engineers, 1993, [Annual, SRI/MF/complete, delayed] A0685–5

American Association of Fund-Raising Counsel Trust for Philanthropy
Giving USA 1993 Edition: The Annual Report on Philanthropy for the Year 1992, [Annual, SRI/MF/complete, delayed] A0700–1

American Association of Museums
Data Report from the 1989 National Museum Survey, [Monograph, SRI/MF/complete] A0750–1

American Association of School Administrators
1992 Study of the American School Superintendency, [Monograph, SRI/MF/complete] A0775–5

American Association of State Colleges and Universities
Estimates of Fall 1992 Enrollment at Public, Four-Year Institutions, [Annual, SRI/MF/complete] A7150–5
Student Charges at Public Institutions: Annual Survey, 1991/92, [Annual, SRI/MF/complete] A7150–4

American Association of University Professors
Academe: The Annual Report on the Economic Status of the Profession, 1992/93, [Bimonthly (selected issue), SRI/MF/complete, delayed] A0800–1

American Association of Yellow Pages Publishers
see Yellow Pages Publishers Association

American Automobile Manufacturers Association
AAMA Motor Vehicle Facts and Figures '93, [Annual, SRI/MF/not filmed] A0865–1
World Motor Vehicle Data, 1993 Edition, [Annual, SRI/MF/complete, delayed] A0865–2

American Bankers Association
Consumer Credit Delinquency Bulletin, [Quarterly, SRI/MF/not filmed] A0950–1

American Bar Association
Review of Legal Education in the U.S., Fall 1992, [Annual, SRI/MF/complete] A0970–1

American Bowling Congress
ABC 1991-92 Annual Report, [Annual, SRI/MF/complete] A1015–1

American Cancer Society
Cancer Facts and Figures, 1993, [Annual, SRI/MF/complete] A1175–1

American Chamber of Commerce Researchers Association
see ACCRA

American Chemical Society
Chemical and Engineering News, [Weekly, SRI/MF/excerpts, shipped quarterly] A1250–1
Salaries 1993: Analysis of the American Chemical Society's 1993 Survey of Salaries and Employment, [Annual, SRI/MF/complete] A1250–4
Starting Salaries of Chemists and Chemical Engineers, 1992: Analysis of the American Chemical Society's Survey of Graduates in Chemistry and Chemical Engineering, [Annual, SRI/MF/complete] A1250–2

American College of Surgeons
Socio-Economic Factbook for Surgery, 1993, [Annual, SRI/MF/not filmed] A1275–1

American College Testing Program
High School Profile Report, Normative Data: HS Graduating Class of 1992 National Report, [Annual, SRI/MF/complete] R1960–6
Profile of Financial Aid Applicants: Historical Trend Data, [Annual, discontinued] R1960 3
Profile of Financial Aid Applicants, 1993/94, [Annual, SRI/MF/complete] R1960–5

American Compensation Association
1993-94 Report on the Salary Budget Survey, [Annual, SRI/MF/complete] A1295–1

American Correctional Association
Directory: Juvenile and Adult Correctional Departments, Institutions, Agencies, and Paroling Authorities, 1993, [Annual, SRI/MF/complete, delayed] A1305–3
1993-95 National Jail and Adult Detention Directory, [Recurring (irreg.), SRI/MF/complete, delayed] A1305–1

American Council for Capital Formation
Congressional Testimony Reports, [Series, SRI/MF/complete] A1310–2
Economic Effects of the Corporate Alternative Minimum Tax, [Monograph, SRI/MF/complete] A1310–4
Impact of President Clinton's Tax Proposals on Capital Formation, [Monograph, SRI/MF/complete] A1310–2.2
Investment Tax Credit and Economic Growth, [Monograph, SRI/MF/complete] A1310–1.16
Special Reports (ACCF), [Series, SRI/MF/complete] A1310–1

American Council for Nationalities Service
Refugee Reports, [Monthly, SRI/MF/complete, delayed] R9372–2

Index by Issuing Sources

American Petroleum Institute

World Refugee Survey, 1993, [Annual, SRI/MF/complete, delayed] R9372–1

American Council for the Arts
United Arts Fundraising 1992, [Annual, SRI/MF/complete] A1315–2

American Council of Life Insurance
1992 Life Insurance Fact Book, [Biennial, SRI/MF/complete] A1325–1

American Council on Education
American College President: A 1993 Edition, [Recurring (irreg.), SRI/MF/complete] A1410–12
American Freshman: National Norms for Fall 1992, [Annual, SRI/MF/complete] U6215–1
Campus Trends, 1993, [Annual, SRI/MF/complete] A1410–1.38
Higher Education Panel Reports, [Series, SRI/MF/complete] A1410–1
Minorities in Higher Education: 11th Annual Status Report, [Annual, SRI/MF/not filmed] A1410–10
1992 GED Statistical Report, [Annual, SRI/MF/complete] A1410–16

American Dental Association
Annual Report on Advanced Dental Education, 1992/93, [Annual, SRI/MF/complete, current & previous year reports] A1475–10
Annual Report on Allied Dental Education, 1992/93, [Annual, SRI/MF/complete, current & previous year reports] A1475–5
Annual Report on Dental Education, 1992/93, [Annual, SRI/MF/complete] A1475–3
Dental School Admissions, 1992/93, [Annual, SRI/MF/complete] A1475–4.1
Dental School Faculty and Support Staff, 1992/93, [Annual, SRI/MF/complete] A1475–4.5
Dental School Trend Analysis, 1992/93, [Annual, SRI/MF/complete] A1475–4.2
Dental School Tuition, 1992/93, [Annual, SRI/MF/complete] A1475–4.3
Dental Student Attrition, 1992/93, [Annual, SRI/MF/complete] A1475–4.4
Supplements to Dental Education, 1992/93 Annual Report, [Series, SRI/MF/complete] A1475–4

American Federation of Labor and Congress of Industrial Organizations
Current Statistics on White Collar Employees, [Annual, SRI/MF/not filmed] A1570–1
Salaried and Professional Women: Relevant Statistics, [Annual, SRI/MF/not filmed] A1570–2

American Federation of Teachers
International Comparison of Public Spending on Education, [Monograph, SRI/MF/complete] A1600–4

American Footwear Industries Association
see Footwear Industries of America

American Forest and Paper Association
Bilateral Trade: Canada, A Fact Sheet on U.S.-Canadian Wood Products Trade, [Monthly, SRI/MF/complete, shipped quarterly] A1630–3
Exports: Pacific Rim, A Fact Sheet on U.S. Wood Product Exports to the Pacific Rim, [Monthly, SRI/MF/complete, shipped quarterly] A1630–2
Newsprint Division Annual Statistical Summary '92, [Annual, SRI/MF/complete, current & previous year reports] A1630–8

Newsprint Division Monthly Statistical Report, [Monthly, SRI/MF/complete, shipped quarterly] A1630–4
Paper, Paperboard, and Wood Pulp Monthly Statistical Summary, [Monthly, SRI/MF/complete, shipped quarterly] A1630–5
Paper, Paperboard, Pulp Capacity and Fiber Consumption, 1991-95, [Annual, SRI/MF/complete] A1630–7
Statistical Roundup, [Monthly, with quarterly supplements, SRI/MF/complete, shipped quarterly] A1630–1
Statistics of Paper, Paperboard, and Wood Pulp, 1993, [Annual, SRI/MF/complete] A1630–6

American Gas Association
Gas Facts, 1991 Data: A Statistical Record of the Gas Utility Industry, [Annual, SRI/MF/complete] A1775–3
Gas Stats: Monthly Gas Utility Statistical Report, [Monthly, SRI/MF/complete, shipped quarterly] A1775–2
Gas Stats: Quarterly Report of Gas Industry Operations, [Quarterly, SRI/MF/complete] A1775–1

American Geological Institute
AGI Faculty Salary Report, 1992, [Annual, SRI/MF/complete] A1785–4
American Geological Institute Survey of Students in the Geosciences, 1991-92, [Annual, SRI/MF/complete] A1785–3

American Hardware Manufacturers Association
1993 Government Relations Survey, [Annual, SRI/MF/complete] A1800–1

American Hospital Association
American Hospital Association Guide to the Health Care Field, 1993 Edition, [Annual, SRI/MF/not filmed] A1865–3
Hospitals & Health Networks, [Semimonthly, SRI/MF/not filmed] A1865–1

American Institute of Certified Public Accountants
Supply of Accounting Graduates and the Demand for Public Accounting Recruits, 1993, [Annual, SRI/MF/not filmed] A1885–1

American Institute of Physics
Data on Astronomy Enrollments and Degrees, [Annual, SRI/MF/complete] A1960–2.3
Data on Physics Enrollments and Degrees: A Supplement, [Annual, SRI/MF/complete] A1960–2.2
Employment Survey, 1991, [Annual, SRI/MF/complete] A1960–1
Enrollments and Degrees, [Annual, SRI/MF/complete] A1960–2.1
Physics and Astronomy Enrollments and Degrees, [Annual series, SRI/MF/complete] A1960–2
1991/92 Survey of Physics and Astronomy Bachelor's Degree Recipients, [Annual, SRI/MF/complete] A1960–3

American Iron and Steel Institute
Annual Statistical Report, American Iron and Steel Institute, 1992, [Annual, SRI/MF/complete] A2000–2

American Iron Ore Association
Iron Ore Report U.S. and Canada, [Monthly, SRI/MF/not filmed] A2010–1
Iron Ore, 1992, [Annual, SRI/MF/not filmed] A2010–3

Shipments of U.S. and Canadian Iron Ore Destined to U.S. and Canada, [Monthly, SRI/MF/not filmed] A2010–2

American Jewish Committee
American Jewish Year Book, 1993, [Annual, SRI/MF/excerpts] A2050–1

American League of Professional Baseball Clubs
1993 American League Red Book, [Annual, SRI/MF/complete] A2068–1

American Library Association
ALA Survey of Librarian Salaries, 1993, [Annual, SRI/MF/complete] A2070–3

American Logistics Association
ALA 1992-93 Worldwide Directory and Fact Book, [Annual, SRI/MF/complete] A2072–1
Interservice, [Quarterly, SRI/MF/excerpts] A2072–2

American Management Association
AMA Research Reports, [Series, SRI/MF/complete] A2075–20
1992 AMA Survey on Downsizing and Assistance to Displaced Workers, [Annual, SRI/MF/complete] A2075–20.9
1992 AMA Survey on Marketing in a Recessionary Economy, [Monograph, SRI/MF/complete] A2075–20.10
1993 AMA Survey on Basic Skills Testing and Training, [Annual, SRI/MF/complete] A2075–20.13
1993 AMA Survey on HIV and AIDS Related Policies, [Monograph, SRI/MF/complete] A2075–20.14
1993 AMA Survey on Managing Cultural Diversity, [Monograph, SRI/MF/complete] A2075–20.11
1993 AMA Survey on Workplace Drug Testing and Drug Abuse Policies, [Annual, SRI/MF/complete] A2075–20.12

American Mathematical Society
1992 Annual AMS-MAA Survey, [Annual, SRI/MF/complete] A2085–1

American Meat Institute
Meat Industry Financial Operating Survey, [Annual, discontinued] A2100–2
1992 Meat and Poultry Facts, [Annual, SRI/MF/complete] A2100–1

American Medical Association
Medical Groups in the U.S., A Survey of Practice Characteristics, 1993 Edition, [Recurring (irreg.), SRI/MF/complete] A2200–7
Physician Characteristics and Distribution in the U.S., 1993 Edition, [Annual, SRI/MF/complete] A2200–3
Socioeconomic Characteristics of Medical Practice, 1993, [Annual, SRI/MF/complete] A2200–5

American Newspaper Publishers Association
see Newspaper Association of America

American Paper Institute
see American Forest and Paper Association

American Petroleum Institute
Basic Petroleum Data Book: Petroleum Industry Statistics, [3 times per year, SRI/MF/complete] A2575–14
Energy Prices and Externalities, [Monograph, SRI/MF/complete] A2575–28
Estimated Costs and Benefits of Retrofitting Aboveground Petroleum Industry Storage Tanks with Release Prevention Barriers, [Monograph, SRI/MF/complete] A2575–26

American Petroleum Institute

Imported Crude Oil and Petroleum Products, [Monthly, SRI/MF/complete] A2575–12

Monthly Completion Report for U.S. Oil, Gas and Dry Wells, [Monthly, SRI/MF/complete, shipped quarterly] A2575–3

Monthly Statistical Report, Estimated U.S. Petroleum Balance, [Monthly, SRI/MF/complete, shipped quarterly] A2575–2

Petroleum Industry Environmental Performance, 1992, [Annual, SRI/MF/complete] A2575–27

Quarterly Completion Report, [Quarterly, SRI/MF/complete] A2575–6

Summary of Occupational Injuries, Illnesses and Fatalities in the Petroleum Industry, [Annual, SRI/MF/complete] A2575–4

U.S. Crude Oil Distillation Refining Capacity Survey, [Annual, discontinued] A2575–7

U.S. Petroleum Supply: History, Prospects, and Policy Implications, [Monograph, SRI/MF/complete] A2575–25

Weekly Statistical Bulletin, [Weekly, SRI/MF/complete, shipped quarterly] A2575–1

1991 Joint Association Survey on Drilling Costs, [Annual, SRI/MF/complete] A2575–9

1991 Survey on Oil and Gas Expenditures: Exploration, Development, Production, [Annual, SRI/MF/complete] A2575–20

American Planning Association

Personnel Practices in Planning Offices, [Monograph, SRI/MF/complete] A2615–3

Planners' Salaries and Employment Trends, 1991, [Biennial, SRI/MF/complete] A2615–1

Planning Commission: Its Composition and Function, 1987, [Recurring (irreg.), SRI/MF/complete] A2615–2

American Political Science Association

APSA Survey of Political Science Departments, 1991-92, [Annual, SRI/MF/complete] A2617–1

American Productivity and Quality Center

Perspectives '93, [Annual, SRI/MF/complete] R2800–2

American Psychological Association

Characteristics of Graduate Departments of Psychology, 1990/91, [Annual, SRI/MF/complete] A2620–3

1991 Doctorate Employment Survey, [Biennial, SRI/MF/complete] A2620–4

1992/93 Faculty Salaries in Graduate Departments of Psychology, [Annual, SRI/MF/complete] A2620–1

American Public Health Association

American Journal of Public Health, [Monthly, SRI/MF/excerpts] A2623–1

American Public Power Association

Public Power, [Bimonthly, SRI/MF/excerpts, delayed] A2625–1

American Public Transit Association

Transit Fact Book, 1992 Edition, [Annual, SRI/MF/complete] A2650–1

American Rental Association

Cost of Doing Business Survey, 1991, [Annual, SRI/MF/complete] A2665–1

American Shoe Center

see Footwear Industries of America

American Society for Quality Control

ASQC/Gallup Survey on Quality Leadership Roles of Corporate Executives and Directors, [Monograph, SRI/MF/complete] A2800–3

American Society of Association Executives

Association Executive Compensation Study, 8th Edition, [Biennial, SRI/MF/complete] A2900–3

American Telephone and Telegraph Co.

see AT&T Communications, B0350–1

American Trucking Associations

Monthly Truck Tonnage Report, [Monthly, SRI/MF/complete, shipped quarterly] A3075–1

American Veterinary Medical Association

Journal of the American Veterinary Medical Association, [Semimonthly, SRI/MF/excerpts, shipped quarterly] A3100–2

1993 AVMA Directory, [Annual, SRI/MF/excerpts] A3100–1

AMT—The Association for Manufacturing Technology

Industry Estimates: Machine Tool Orders and Shipments, [Monthly, SRI/MF/complete, shipped quarterly] A3179–1

U.S. Foreign Trade in Manufacturing Technology, [Monthly, SRI/MF/complete, shipped quarterly] A3179–3

1993-94 Economic Handbook of the Machine Tool Industry, [Annual, SRI/MF/complete] A3179–2

API

see American Petroleum Institute

APPA—The Association of Higher Education Facilities Officers

1991/92 Comparative Costs and Staffing Report for College and University Facilities, [Recurring (irreg.), SRI/MF/complete] A3183–1

Appalachian State University

1992/93 National Faculty Salary Survey by Discipline and Rank in Private Colleges and Universities, [Annual, SRI/MF/complete, delayed] A3900–4

1992/93 National Faculty Salary Survey by Discipline and Rank in Public Colleges and Universities, [Annual, SRI/MF/complete, delayed] A3900–5

Arbitron Co.

Television Ethnic Population Book, 1992-93, [Annual, SRI/MF/complete] B0525–4

Television Universe Estimates Summary, 1992-93, [Annual, SRI/MF/complete] B0525–3

Argus Agronomics

Implement and Tractor, [7 issues per year, SRI/MF/excerpts, shipped quarterly] C0495–1

Arizona Agricultural Statistics Service

see University of Arizona: Arizona Agricultural Statistics Service, U5830–1

Arizona Banking Department

Condensed Statement of Reports for State and Federal Savings and Loan Associations, Arizona, [Quarterly, SRI/MF/complete] S0460–1

Condensed Statement of Reports of State and National Banks of Arizona, [Quarterly, SRI/MF/complete] S0460–2

Condensed Statement of Reports, State Credit Unions, Arizona, [Quarterly, SRI/MF/complete] S0460–4

Arizona Department of Administration

State of Arizona Annual Financial Report, 1991-92, [Annual, SRI/MF/complete] S0450–1

State of Arizona Comprehensive Annual Financial Report for the Fiscal Year Ended June 30, 1991, [Annual, SRI/MF/complete] S0450–2

Arizona Department of Corrections

FY92 Annual Report, Arizona Department of Corrections, [Annual, SRI/MF/complete] S0464–2

Arizona Department of Economic Security

Arizona Economic Trends, [Monthly, SRI/MF/complete, shipped quarterly] S0465–1

Arizona Occupational Profiles, [Series, SRI/MF/complete] S0465–2

Statistical Bulletin, Arizona Department of Economic Security, Family Assistance Administration, [Monthly, with annual supplement, SRI/MF/complete, shipped quarterly] S0465–4

Arizona Department of Education

Annual Report of the Superintendent of Public Instruction, Statistical and Financial Data for FY91-92, Arizona, [Annual, SRI/MF/complete] S0470–1

Arizona Department of Insurance

80th Annual Report of the Department of Insurance, State of Arizona, for the Year Ending Dec. 31, 1992, [Annual, SRI/MF/complete] S0483–1

Arizona Department of Library, Archives and Public Records

Arizona Public Library Statistics, 1991-92, [Annual, SRI/MF/complete] S0495–1

Arizona Department of Mines and Mineral Resources

Primary Copper Industry of Arizona in 1991, [Annual, SRI/MF/complete] S0497–1

Arizona Department of Public Safety

Arizona Uniform Crime Report, 1992, [Annual, SRI/MF/complete] S0505–2

Arizona Department of Revenue

Arizona Department of Revenue 1992 Annual Report, [Annual, SRI/MF/complete] S0515–1

Arizona Department of Transportation

Arizona Traffic Accident Summary, 1991, [Annual, SRI/MF/complete] S0530–1

Arizona Geological Survey

Oil, Gas, and Helium Production Report, Arizona, [Monthly, SRI/MF/complete, shipped quarterly] S0473–1

Arizona Office of the Secretary of State

State of Arizona Official Canvass, General Election, Nov. 3, 1992, [Biennial, SRI/MF/complete] S0520–1

Arizona Oil and Gas Conservation Commission

see Arizona Geological Survey, S0473–1

Arizona State University: Bureau of Business and Economic Research

see Arizona State University: Center for Business Research, U0280–1

Arizona State University: Center for Business Research

Arizona Business, [Monthly, SRI/MF/complete, shipped quarterly] U0280–1

Index by Issuing Sources

Arizona State University: Economic Outlook Center

Arizona Blue Chip Economic Forecast, [Monthly, SRI/MF/complete, shipped quarterly.] U0282–1

Western Blue Chip Economic Forecast, [Monthly, SRI/MF/complete, shipped quarterly] U0282–2

Arizona Supreme Court

Arizona Courts, [Annual, SRI/MF/complete] S0525–1

Arkansas Administrative Office of the Courts

Annual Report of the Arkansas Judiciary, FY91-92: Statistical Supplement of All Arkansas Courts, [Annual, SRI/MF/complete] S0647–1

Arkansas Agricultural Statistics Service

see University of Arkansas: Agricultural Experiment Station, U5920–1

Arkansas Bank Department

78th Annual Report of the Bank Commissioner of Arkansas, 1992, [Annual, SRI/MF/complete] S0632–1

Arkansas Crime Information Center

Crime in Arkansas, 1992, [Annual, SRI/MF/complete] S0652–1

Arkansas Department of Education

Statistical Summary for the Public Schools of Arkansas, 1990-92, [Annual, SRI/MF/complete] S0660–1

Arkansas Department of Finance and Administration

Arkansas Comprehensive Annual Financial Report for Fiscal Year Ended June 30, 1992, [Annual, SRI/MF/complete] S0670–1

Arkansas Department of Health

Arkansas Vital Statistics, 1991, [Annual, SRI/MF/complete] S0685–1

Arkansas Department of Higher Education

Annual Full-Time Equivalent Enrollment and Student Semester Credit Hour Production in Arkansas State Institutions of Higher Education, 1991/92, [Annual, SRI/MF/complete] S0690–2

Annual Summary Report of Degrees Granted by Arkansas Institutions of Higher Education, 1990/91, [Annual, SRI/MF/complete] S0690–3

Fact Book on Arkansas Public Higher Education, [Biennial, SRI/MF/complete, current & previous biennial reports] S0690–4

On-Campus Enrollment and Geographic Origins in Arkansas Higher Education, Fall 1991, [Annual, SRI/MF/complete] S0690–1

Arkansas Department of Human Services

Arkansas Department of Human Services 1991 Statistical Report, [Annual, SRI/MF/complete, current & previous year reports] S0700–2

Arkansas Employment Security Department

Arkansas Labor Force Statistics: Annual Averages, 1980-92, [Annual, SRI/MF/complete] S0662–2

Arkansas Highway and Transportation Department

Arkansas Traffic Accident Data, 1991, [Annual, SRI/MF/complete] S0692–1

Arkansas Judicial Department

see Arkansas Administrative Office of the Courts

Arkansas Office of the Secretary of State

Arkansas 1992 General Election, [Biennial, SRI/MF/complete] S0775–1

Arkansas Office of the Treasurer

Biennial Report of the Treasurer of State of the State of Arkansas for the Biennial Period Beginning July 1, 1990 and Ending June 30, 1992, [Biennial, SRI/MF/complete] S0780–1

Arkansas Oil and Gas Commission

Arkansas Oil and Gas Statistical Bulletin, [Monthly, SRI/MF/complete, shipped quarterly] S0737–1

Arkansas Public Service Commission

Arkansas Public Service Commission 1992 Annual Report, [Annual, SRI/MF/complete] S0757–1

Army Times Publishing Co.

Military Market, [Monthly, SRI/MF/excerpts, shipped quarterly] C0500–1

Arthur Andersen

Franchising in the Economy, 1989-92, [Annual, SRI/MF/complete] A5820–1

Association for Education in Journalism and Mass Communication

Journalism Educator, [Quarterly (selected issue), SRI/MF/excerpts] A3225–1

Association for Library and Information Science Education

Library and Information Science Education Statistical Report, 1993, [Annual, SRI/MF/complete, delayed] A3235–1

Association of American Medical Colleges

Academic Medicine, [Monthly, SRI/MF/excerpts, shipped quarterly] A3273–8

Council of Teaching Hospitals Survey of Housestaff Stipends, Benefits, and Funding, 1992, [Annual, SRI/MF/complete] A3273–3

Medical School Admission Requirements, 1994/95 U.S. and Canada, [Annual, SRI/MF/complete] A3273–10

Report on Medical School Faculty Salaries, 1992/93, [Annual, SRI/MF/complete] A3273–2

Association of American Publishers

1991 Industry Statistics, [Annual, SRI/MF/complete, delayed] A3274–2

Association of American Railroads

Analysis of Class I Railroads, 1992, [Annual, SRI/MF/complete] A3275–7

Railroad Facts, 1993 Edition, [Annual, SRI/MF/complete, current & previous year reports] A3275–5

Railroad Revenues, Expenses, and Income: Class I Railroads in the U.S., [Quarterly, SRI/MF/complete] A3275–1

Railroad Ten-Year Trends, 1982-91, [Annual, SRI/MF/complete] A3275–8

Railroads and States, [Annual, SRI/MF/complete] A3275–10

Trends: Carloadings of Major Railroads, [Weekly, SRI/MF/complete, shipped quarterly] A3275–2

Trends: U.S. Rail Freight Car and Locomotive Acquisition, [Quarterly, SRI/MF/complete] A3275–3

Association of Art Museum Directors

Association of Art Museum Directors 1993 Salary Survey, [Annual, SRI/MF/complete] A3290–1

Audit Bureau of Circulations

Association of Home Appliance Manufacturers

Appliance Sales by Distributors, States, 1992, [Annual, SRI/MF/complete current & previous year reports] A3350–2

Factory Shipments of Appliances: Historical Data, [Annual, SRI/MF/complete] A3350–4

Major Home Appliance Industry Fact Book, [Biennial, SRI/MF/not filmed] A3350–3

Major Home Appliance Industry Shipments, [Monthly, SRI/MF/complete, shipped quarterly] A3350–1

Association of National Advertisers

Corporate Advertising Practices, 1992, [Triennial, SRI/MF/complete] A3357–1

Association of Racing Commissioners International

Pari-Mutuel Racing, 1990, [Annual, SRI/MF/complete] A3363–1

Association of Research Libraries

ARL Annual Salary Survey, 1992, [Annual, SRI/MF/complete] A3365–2

ARL Statistics, 1991-92, [Annual, SRI/MF/complete] A3365–1

Association of Schools and Colleges of Optometry

Annual Survey of Optometric Educational Institutions: Survey Results July 1991-June 1992, [Annual, SRI/MF/complete] A3370–2

Association of Schools of Public Health

U.S. Schools of Public Health Data Report on Applicants, New Enrollments, and Students, Fall 1992, and Graduates and Expenditures, 1991/92, with Trends Analysis for 1974/75 Through Fall 1992, [Annual, SRI/MF/complete, current & previous year reports] A3372–3

U.S. Schools of Public Health: Data Report on Faculty, 1991-92, [Recurring (irreg.), SRI/MF/complete] A3372–1

Association of Teacher Educators

2nd ATE Survey of Critical Issues in Teacher Education, [Recurring (irreg.), SRI/MF/complete] A3375–1

Association of Theological Schools in the U.S. and Canada

Fact Book on Theological Education for the Academic Year 1992/93, [Annual, SRI/MF/complete] A3376–1

AT&T Communications

World's Telephones: A Statistical Compilation as of Jan. 1991-92, [Annual, SRI/MF/not filmed] B0350–1

Atlas Van Lines

Atlas Van Lines 26th Annual Survey of Corporate Relocation Policies, [Annual, SRI/MF/complete] B0600–1

Auburn University: Center for Demographic and Cultural Research

CDCR Population Reports, [Series, SRI/MF/complete] U0340–1

Population Changes in Alabama's Black Belt: 1880-1990, [Monograph, SRI/MF/complete] U0340–1.6

Audit Bureau of Circulations

ABC Magazine Trend Report, 1988-92, [Annual, SRI/MF/complete] A3385–1

FAS-FAX: Canadian Daily Newspapers, Circulation Averages, [Semiannual, SRI/MF/complete] A3385–3.2

FAS-FAX Reports, [Series, SRI/MF/complete] A3385–3

Audit Bureau of Circulations

FAS-FAX: U.S. and Canadian Periodicals, Circulation Averages, [Semiannual, SRI/MF/complete] A3385–3.4

FAS-FAX: U.S. and Canadian Weekly Newspapers, Circulation Averages, [Semiannual, SRI/MF/complete] A3385–3.3

FAS-FAX: U.S. Daily Newspapers, Circulation Averages, [Semiannual, SRI/MF/complete] A3385–3.1

Battelle Memorial Institute

Probable Levels of R&D Expenditures in 1993: Forecast and Analysis, [Annual, SRI/MF/complete] R3300–1

Beer Institute

Brewing Industry in the U.S.: Brewers Almanac, 1992, [Annual, SRI/MF/not filmed] A3455–1

Best, A. M., Co.

Best's Review: Life/Health Insurance Edition, [Monthly, SRI/MF/not filmed] C1050–2

Best's Review: Property/Casualty Insurance Edition, [Monthly, SRI/MF/not filmed] C1050–1

Better Homes and Gardens

How Consumers Evaluate Service in Their Supermarket, 1991, [Monograph, SRI/MF/complete] A4950–37.1

How To Win and Influence Shoppers, 1992, [Monograph, SRI/MF/complete] A4950–37.2

Service Advantage, [SRI/MF/complete] A4950–37

Bicycle Manufacturers Association of America

1992 Bicycle Market in Review, [Annual, SRI/MF/complete] A3470–1

Bill Communications

Incentive/ Managing and Marketing Through Motivation, [Monthly, SRI/MF/excerpts, shipped quarterly] C1200–4

Restaurant Business, [18 issues per year, SRI/MF/excerpts, shipped quarterly] C1200–5

Sales and Marketing Management, [Monthly, and special annual issues, SRI/MF/excerpts, shipped quarterly] C1200–1

Board of Trade of Kansas City, Missouri

1992 Annual Statistical Report, The Board of Trade of Kansas City, Missouri, Inc., [Annual, SRI/MF/complete] B1530–1

Bobit Publishing Co.

Automotive Fleet, [Monthly, SRI/MF/excerpts, shipped quarterly] C1575–2

Metro Magazine, [Bimonthly, and annual Fact Book issue, SRI/MF/excerpts] C1575–3

School Bus Fleet, [Bimonthly, SRI/MF/excerpts] C1575–1

Boeing Commercial Airplane Group

World Jet Airplane Inventory, Year-End 1992, [Annual, SRI/MF/complete] B1582–1

BonData

Pennsylvania Employment and Transportation Table, 1990 Census by County and Municipality, [Monograph, SRI/MF/complete] C1595–16

Pennsylvania General Income/Poverty Table, 1990 Census by County and Municipality, [Monograph, SRI/MF/complete] C1595–15

Pennsylvania Housing Table, 1990 Census by County and Municipality, [Monograph, SRI/MF/complete] C1595–14

Bowker Magazine Group

see Cahners Publishing: Bowker Magazine Group, C1852–1, C1852–2

Bowker, R. R., Co.

Bowker Annual: Library and Book Trade Almanac, 38th Edition, 1993, [Annual, SRI/MF/not filmed] C1650–3

Official Catholic Directory, 1993 General Summary, [Annual, SRI/MF/excerpts] C4950–1

Broadcast Cable Financial Management Association

1991 Television Employee Compensation and Fringe Benefits Report, [Biennial, SRI/MF/complete] A6635–9

Business Committee for the Arts

BCA Report: 1992 National Survey of Business Support to the Arts, [Recurring (irreg.), SRI/MF/complete] A3690–1

Business News Publishing Co.

Air Conditioning, Heating, and Refrigeration News: 1993 Statistical Panorama, [Weekly (selected issue), SRI/MF/excerpts] C1800–1

Cahners Publishing: Bowker Magazine Group

Library Journal, [Semimonthly, SRI/MF/excerpts, shipped quarterly] C1852–1

Publishers Weekly, [Weekly, SRI/MF/excerpts, shipped quarterly] C1852–2

Cahners Publishing Co.

Broadcasting & Cable, [Weekly, SRI/MF/excerpts, shipped quarterly] C1850–14

Building Design and Construction, [Monthly (selected issues), SRI/MF/excerpts] C1850–9

Datamation, [Semimonthly, SRI/MF/excerpts, shipped quarterly] C1850–5

Electronic Business Buyer, [Monthly, SRI/MF/excerpts, shipped quarterly] C1850–2

Graphic Arts Monthly, [Monthly, SRI/MF/excerpts, shipped quarterly] C1850–10

Industrial Distribution, [Monthly, SRI/MF/excerpts, shipped quarterly] C1850–4

Interior Design, [Monthly (selected issues), SRI/MF/excerpts] C1850–7

Packaging, [Monthly, SRI/MF/excerpts, shipped quarterly] C1850–1

Professional Builder, [Monthly, SRI/MF/excerpts, shipped quarterly] C1850–8

R&D, [Monthly, SRI/MF/excerpts, shipped quarterly] C1850–6

Restaurants and Institutions, [Biweekly, SRI/MF/excerpts, shipped quarterly] C1850–3

Security, [Monthly, SRI/MF/excerpts, shipped quarterly] C1850–12

Security Distributing and Marketing, [Monthly, SRI/MF/excerpts, shipped quarterly] C1850–13

Traffic Management: Annual Salary Survey, [Monthly (selected issue), SRI/MF/excerpts] C1850–11

Variety, [Weekly, SRI/MF/not filmed] C9380–1

Index by Issuing Sources

California Agricultural Statistics Service

see California Department of Food and Agriculture, S0850–1

California Banking Department

California State Banking Department 83rd Annual Report, 1992, [Annual, SRI/MF/complete] S0810–1

California Board of Equalization

California State Board of Equalization Annual Report, Fiscal Year Ending June 30, 1992, [Annual, SRI/MF/complete] S0835–1

California Department of Corrections

California Prisoners and Parolees, 1991, [Annual, SRI/MF/complete] S0820–1

Characteristics of Population in California State Prisons by Institution, Dec. 31, 1992, [Semiannual, SRI/MF/complete] S0820–2

California Department of Education

California Library Statistics, 1993, [Annual, SRI/MF/complete, current & previous year reports] S0825–2

Enrollment and Staff in California Private Schools, 1992/93, [Annual, SRI/MF/complete] S0825–8

Enrollment in California Public Schools, 1992/93, [Annual, SRI/MF/complete] S0825–7

Language Census Report for California Public Schools, 1992, [Annual, SRI/MF/complete] S0825–10

Racial or Ethnic Distribution of Staff and Students in California Public Schools, 1992-93, [Annual, SRI/MF/complete] S0825–9

California Department of Finance

California Economic Indicators, [Bimonthly, SRI/MF/complete] S0840–1

California Statistical Abstract, 1992, [Annual, SRI/MF/complete] S0840–2

Economic Report of the Governor, 1993, California, [Annual, SRI/MF/complete] S0840–3

Projected Total Population of California Counties, [Recurring (irreg.), SRI/MF/complete] S0840–4

1990 Census of Population and Housing, Summary Tape File 3, California, [Monograph, SRI/MF/complete] S0840–9

California Department of Food and Agriculture

California Agricultural Statistics, [Annual series, SRI/MF/complete] S0850–1

California Agriculture: Statistical Review 1992, [Annual, SRI/MF/complete] S0850–1.5

California Dairy Industry Statistics, 1992, [Annual, SRI/MF/complete] S0850–1.6

California Field Crops Statistics, 1983-92; County Data, 1991-92, [Annual, SRI/MF/complete] S0850–1.4

California Fruit and Nut Statistics, 1983-92, [Annual, SRI/MF/complete] S0850–1.1

California Livestock Statistics, 1992, [Annual, SRI/MF/complete] S0850–1.2

California Vegetable Crops: Acreage, Production and Value, 1983-92, [Annual, SRI/MF/complete] S0850–1.3

California Department of Health Services

California Behavioral Risk Factor Survey, 1991 Update, [Annual, SRI/MF/complete] S0865–2

Index by Issuing Sources

Vital Statistics of California, 1990, [Annual, SRI/MF/complete] S0865–1

California Department of Highway Patrol 1991 Annual Report of Fatal and Injury Motor Vehicle Traffic Accidents, California, [Annual, SRI/MF/complete] S0885–1

California Department of Insurance 124th Annual Report of the Insurance Commissioner of the State of California, for the Year Ending Dec. 31, 1991, [Annual, SRI/MF/complete] S0900–1

California Department of Justice California Criminal Justice Profile, 1991, Statewide, [Annual, SRI/MF/complete] S0910–2 Crime and Delinquency in California, 1992, [Annual, SRI/MF/complete, current & previous year reports] S0910–1

California Department of Social Services Public Welfare in California, [Monthly, SRI/MF/complete, shipped quarterly] S0935–2

California Employment Development Department Annual Planning Information, California, 1991, [Annual, SRI/MF/complete] S0830–2 California Labor Market Bulletin, [Monthly, SRI/MF/complete, shipped quarterly] S0830–1

California Fig Advisory Board 1992 Statistical Review of the California Fig Industry, [Annual, SRI/MF/complete] A3750–1

California Fig Institute 1992 Statistical Review of the California Fig Industry, [Annual, SRI/MF/complete] A3750–1

California Franchise Tax Board California Franchise Tax Board 1991 Annual Report, [Annual, SRI/MF/complete, current & previous year reports] S0855–1

California Judicial Council Annual Data Reference: 1991-92 Caseload Data by Individual Courts, Judicial Council of California, [Annual, SRI/MF/complete] S0905–2 1993 Annual Report, Judicial Council of California, [Annual, SRI/MF/complete] S0905–1

California Office of the Controller Annual Report of the State of California, Budgetary Basis, Fiscal Year Ended June 30, 1992, [Annual, SRI/MF/complete] S0815–1

California Office of the Secretary of State Certified Statement of Vote, Nov. 3, 1992, General Election, California, [Biennial, SRI/MF/complete] S0934–1

California Postsecondary Education Commission Data Abstracts Series, [Series, SRI/MF/complete] S0827–2 Degree Type Data Abstract, June 1990-July 1991, California, [Annual, SRI/MF/complete] S0827–2.2 Fiscal Profiles, 1993, [Annual, SRI/MF/complete, current & previous year reports] S0827–3 Postsecondary Student Enrollments by Student Level, Fall 1991, California, [Annual, SRI/MF/complete] S0827–2.1

California Public Utilities Commission Annual Report, 1991-92, California Public Utilities Commission, [Annual, SRI/MF/complete] S0930–1

California State Library see California Department of Education, S0825–2

Capital Cities Media CableVision, [Biweekly, SRI/MF/not filmed] C1858–1

Carnegie Foundation for the Advancement of Teaching School Choice, [Monograph, SRI/MF/complete] R3810–7

Carpet and Rug Institute Carpet and Rug Industry Review, 1992, [Annual, SRI/MF/complete] A3800–1

Catholic Charities USA 1991 Annual Survey, Catholic Charities USA, [Annual, SRI/MF/complete] A3810–1

Center for Healthcare Industry Performance Studies 1993 Almanac of Hospital Financial and Operating Indicators, [Annual, SRI/MF/complete, current & previous year reports] B1880–1

Center for Human Resource Research see Ohio State University—Center for Human Resource Research

Center for International Business Cycle Research International Economic Indicators, [Monthly, SRI/MF/complete, delayed] U1245–1 Recession-Recovery Watch, [Quarterly, SRI/MF/complete] U1245–2 Service Sector Indicators, [Monthly, SRI/MF/complete, shipped quarterly] U1245–3

Center for Media and Public Affairs Media Monitor, [Bimonthly, SRI/MF/complete] R3823–1

Center for Research in Ambulatory Health Care Administration Cost Survey: 1992 Report Based on 1991 Data, [Annual, SRI/MF/complete] A6365–2 Membership Compensation Survey: 1992 Report Based on 1992 Data, [Annual, SRI/MF/complete] A6365–3 Physician Compensation and Production Survey: 1992 Report Based on 1991 Data, [Annual, SRI/MF/complete] A6365–1

Center for Responsive Politics Cash Constituents of Congress, [Monograph, SRI/MF/complete] R3828–3 Open Secrets: Encyclopedia of Congressional Money and Politics, [Biennial, SRI/MF/complete] R3828–2

Center for the Study of Social Policy Kids Count Data Book: State Profiles of Child Well-Being, [Annual, SRI/MF/complete] R3832–1

Center for the Study of the States States and the Poor: How Budget Decisions Affected Low Income People in 1992, [Annual, SRI/MF/complete] R3834–9

Center on Budget and Policy Priorities Changes in Income Disparities in Selected States Over the 1980s, [Monograph, SRI/MF/complete] R3834–14 End of the Line? What the End of Emergency Unemployment Benefits Means, [Monograph, SRI/MF/complete] R3834–18

Child Care Employee Project

New Direction: The Clinton Budget and Economic Plan, [Monograph, SRI/MF/complete] R3834–17 Place to Call Home: The Low Income Housing Crisis in 44 Major Metropolitan Areas, [Series, SRI/MF/complete] R3834–16 States and the Poor: How Budget Decisions Affected Low Income People in 1992, [Annual, SRI/MF/complete] R3834–9 Where Have All the Dollars Gone? A State-by-State Analysis of Income Disparities Over the 1980s, [Monograph, SRI/MF/complete] R3834–13 White Poverty in America, [Monograph, SRI/MF/complete] R3834–15

Chamber of Commerce of the U.S. Economic Outlook: Chamber of Commerce of the U.S., [Quarterly, SRI/MF/complete] A3840–6 Employee Benefits, 1992 Edition, [Annual, SRI/MF/complete] A3840–1 1993 Analysis of Workers' Compensation Laws, [Annual, SRI/MF/complete] A3840–2 1993 Survey of Local Chambers of Commerce, [Annual, SRI/MF/not filmed] A3840–3

Chase, Dana, Publications Appliance, [Monthly, SRI/MF/not filmed] C2000–1

Chemical Banking Corporation Economic Report, [Bimonthly, SRI/MF/complete] B2000–2 Financial Digest, [Biweekly, SRI/MF/complete, shipped quarterly] B2000–1

Chemical Manufacturers Association U.S. Chemical Industry Statistical Handbook, 1993, [Annual, SRI/MF/complete] A3850–1

Chicago Board of Trade Wheat Grower: Wheat Facts 1992, [Annual, SRI/MF/complete] A7310–1 1992 Statistical Annual Supplement, [Annual, SRI/MF/not filmed] B2120–1

Chicago Sun-Times Pocket Guide to the Chicago Market, [Annual, suspended] C2130–1

Chicago Title and Trust Family of Title Insurers Who's Buying Houses in America: The Chicago Title and Trust Family of Title Insurers' 17th Annual Survey of Recent Home Buyers, [Annual, SRI/MF/complete] B2150–1

Chief Officers of State Library Agencies 1992 State Library Agencies Financial Survey, [Annual, SRI/MF/complete, current & previous year reports] A3862–1

Child and Waters Travel Industry World Yearbook: The Big Picture, 1992, [Annual, SRI/MF/not filmed] C2140–1

Child Care Employee Project Child Care Employee News: 1992 Salary Survey Summary, [Quarterly (selected issue), SRI/MF/complete] A3865–2 National Child Care Staffing Study Revisited: Four Years in the Life of Center-Based Child Care, [Monograph, SRI/MF/complete] A3865–3

Children's Defense Fund

Children's Defense Fund
Child Poverty Data from the 1990 Census, [SRI/MF/complete, delayed] R3840–20
Health of America's Children, 1992, [Annual, SRI/MF/complete, delayed] R3840–5
Progress and Peril: Black Children in America, [Monograph, SRI/MF/complete, delayed] R3840–21
State of America's Children, 1992, [Annual, SRI/MF/complete, delayed] R3840–11

Chilton Co.
Chilton's Automotive Industries, [Monthly, SRI/MF/excerpts, shipped quarterly] C2150–3
Chilton's Automotive Marketing, [Monthly, SRI/MF/excerpts, shipped quarterly] C2150–10
Chilton's Commercial Carrier Journal, [Monthly, SRI/MF/excerpts, shipped quarterly] C2150–4
Chilton's Food Engineering, [Monthly, SRI/MF/excerpts, shipped quarterly] C2150–6
Distribution: The Transportation & Business Logistics Magazine, [Monthly, SRI/MF/excerpts, shipped quarterly] C2150–1
Jewelers' Circular-Keystone, [Monthly, SRI/MF/not filmed] C2150–7

Chilton Publications
CableVision, [Biweekly, SRI/MF/not filmed] C1858–1

China Business Forum
China Business Review, [Bimonthly, SRI/MF/not filmed] A9315–1

Chronicle of Higher Education, Inc.
Chronicle of Higher Education, [Weekly, SRI/MF/excerpts, shipped quarterly] C2175–1

Chronicle of Philanthropy
Chronicle of Philanthropy, [Biweekly, SRI/MF/excerpts] C2176–1

Clemson University: South Carolina Agricultural Experiment Station
South Carolina Crop, Livestock and Poultry Statistics, 1991-93, [Annual, SRI/MF/complete] U1075–3

Clothing Manufacturers Association of the U.S.A.
Special Statistical Report on Profit, Production, and Sales Trends in the Men's and Boys' Tailored Clothing Industry, [Annual, SRI/MF/not filmed] A3880–1

Coal Exporters Association of the U.S.
International Coal, 1992 Edition, [Annual, SRI/MF/not filmed] A7400–2

Coalition of Service Industries
Service Economy, [Quarterly, SRI/MF/complete] A3892–1

Coffee, Sugar and Cocoa Exchange
Coffee, Sugar and Cocoa Exchange 1992 Statistical Annual, [Annual, SRI/MF/complete] B2275–1

College and University Personnel Association
1992/93 Administrative Compensation Survey, [Annual, SRI/MF/complete, delayed] A3900–1
1992/93 National Faculty Salary Survey by Discipline and Rank in Private Colleges and Universities, [Annual, SRI/MF/complete, delayed] A3900–4
1992/93 National Faculty Salary Survey by Discipline and Rank in Public Colleges and Universities, [Annual, SRI/MF/complete, delayed] A3900–5

College of William and Mary: Bureau of Business Research
Virginia Business Report, [Monthly, SRI/MF/complete, shipped quarterly] U1120–1

College Placement Council
CPC Salary Survey: A Study of 1992-93 Beginning Offers, [Annual series, SRI/MF/complete, delayed] A3940–2
CPC Salary Survey: Regional Interim Reports, [Annual series, SRI/MF/complete, delayed] A3940–1
Recruiting '93, [Annual, SRI/MF/complete, delayed] A3940–3

College Retirement Equities Fund
see Teachers Insurance and Annuity Association, A9025–3

Colorado Agricultural Statistics Service
see Colorado Department of Agriculture, S0985–1

Colorado Department of Administration
Colorado Comprehensive Annual Financial Report for the Year Ended June 30, 1992, [Annual, SRI/MF/complete] S0980–1

Colorado Department of Agriculture
Colorado Agricultural Statistics, 1992 Preliminary, 1991 Revised, [Annual, SRI/MF/complete] S0985–1

Colorado Department of Education
Certificated Personnel and Related Information, Fall 1992, [Annual, SRI/MF/complete] S1000–2.2
Pupil Membership and Related Information, Fall 1992, [Annual, SRI/MF/complete] S1000–2.1
Revenues and Expenditures, 1991, [Annual, SRI/MF/complete] S1000–4.3
Statistical Series: Colorado Department of Education, [Annual series, SRI/MF/complete] S1000–2, [Annual series, SRI/MF/complete] S1000–4
Statistics and Input-Output Measures for Colorado Academic Libraries, 1992, [Biennial, SRI/MF/complete] S1000–3.2
Statistics and Input-Output Measures for Colorado Public Libraries, 1991, [Annual, SRI/MF/complete] S1000–3.1
Statistics for Colorado Libraries, [Series, SRI/MF/complete] S1000–3

Colorado Department of Health
Colorado Behavioral Risk Factor Surveillance System, 1990, [Recurring (irreg.), SRI/MF/complete] S1010–3
Colorado Vital Statistics, 1990, [Annual, SRI/MF/complete] S1010–1

Colorado Department of Labor and Employment
Annual Planning Information Report, Program Year 1993 (July 1993-June 1994), Colorado, [Annual, SRI/MF/complete] S1040–3
Colorado Labor Force Review, [Monthly, SRI/MF/complete, shipped quarterly] S1040–4

Colorado Department of Local Affairs
State of Colorado, 1992: 22nd Annual Report, Division of Property Taxation, [Annual, SRI/MF/complete] S1055–3

Colorado Department of Public Safety
Crime in Colorado: Annual Report, 1992, [Annual, SRI/MF/complete] S1068–1

Colorado Department of Regulatory Agencies
Financial Report on Colorado State Chartered Savings and Loan Associations and Credit Unions, 1992, [Annual, SRI/MF/complete] S1070–3

Index by Issuing Sources

83rd Annual Report of the State Bank Commissioner of the State of Colorado, 1992, [Annual, SRI/MF/complete] S1070–2

Colorado Department of Revenue
Annual Report 1992, Colorado Department of Revenue, [Annual, SRI/MF/complete] S1075–1

Colorado Department of Social Services
Colorado Department of Social Services Expenditures During FY91, [Annual, SRI/MF/complete] S1085–1

Colorado Department of State
State of Colorado Abstract of Votes Cast, 1992, [Biennial, SRI/MF/complete] S1090–1

Colorado Judicial Department
Colorado Judicial Department Annual Report, 1992, [Annual, SRI/MF/complete] S1035–1

Columbia University: Center for International Business Cycle Research
International Economic Indicators, [Monthly, SRI/MF/complete, delayed] U1245–1
Recession-Recovery Watch, [Quarterly, SRI/MF/complete] U1245–2
Service Sector Indicators, [Monthly, SRI/MF/complete, shipped quarterly] U1245–3

Columbia University: National Center for Children in Poverty
Five Million Children: 1993 Update, [Annual, SRI/MF/complete, current & previous year reports] U1260–2

Commission on Professionals in Science and Technology
Professional Women and Minorities: A Total Human Resource Data Compendium, 10th Edition, [Recurring (irreg.), SRI/MF/complete, delayed] A3960–2
Salaries of Scientists, Engineers, and Technicians: A Summary of Salary Surveys, 16th Edition, [Biennial, SRI/MF/complete] A3960–1

Commodity Research Bureau
Knight-Ridder CRB Commodity Year Book Statistical Supplement, [3 per year, SRI/MF/complete] C2400–2
Knight-Ridder CRB Commodity Year Book, 1993, [Annual, SRI/MF/complete] C2400–1

Communication Channels
Boating Industry: The Boating Business, 1992, [Monthly (selected issue), SRI/MF/excerpts] C2425–4
Pension World, [Monthly, SRI/MF/excerpts, shipped quarterly] C2425–1
Trusts and Estates, [Monthly, SRI/MF/excerpts, shipped quarterly] C2425–2

Conference Board
Availability of a Quality Work Force, [Monograph, SRI/MF/complete] R4105–78.21
Benefit Communications: Enhancing the Employer's Investment, [Monograph, SRI/MF/complete] R4105–78.28
Bright Christmas 1992, [Annual, SRI/MF/complete] R4105–81.10
China at the Crossroads, [Monograph, SRI/MF/complete] R4105–82.8
Conference Board Reports, [Series, SRI/MF/complete] R4105–78

Index by Issuing Sources

Consumer Confidence Survey, [Monthly, SRI/MF/complete, shipped quarterly] R4105–4

Corporate Boards and Corporate Governance, [Monograph, SRI/MF/complete] R4105–78.29

Corporate Contributions, 1991, [Annual, SRI/MF/complete] R4105–8

Corporate Directors' Compensation, 1993 Edition, [Annual, SRI/MF/complete] R4105–7

Corporate Support of Dropout Prevention and Work Readiness, [Monograph, SRI/MF/complete] R4105–78.30

Corporate Volunteer Programs: Benefits to Business, [Monograph, SRI/MF/complete] R4105–78.26

Does Quality Work? A Review of Relevant Studies, [Monograph, SRI/MF/complete] R4105–78.32

Economic Times, [Monthly, SRI/MF/complete, shipped quarterly] R4105–80

Foreign Business Activity in the Former U.S.S.R., [Monograph, SRI/MF/complete] R4105–82.4

German Reunification, [Monograph, SRI/MF/complete] R4105–82.3

Global Business White Papers, [Series, SRI/MF/complete] R4105–82

Global Contributions of U.S. Corporations, [Monograph, SRI/MF/complete] R4105–78.23

Gulf War, [Monograph, SRI/MF/complete] R4105–82.1

Information for Strategic Decisions, [Monograph, SRI/MF/complete] R4105–78.25

International Economic Scoreboard, [Monthly, SRI/MF/complete, shipped quarterly] R4105–6

Islamic Fundamentalism, [Monograph, SRI/MF/complete] R4105–82.7

Latin America: A Region in Transition, [Monograph, SRI/MF/complete] R4105–82.6

Managing Corporate Communications in a Competitive Climate, [Monograph, SRI/MF/complete] R4105–78.24

Privatization, [Monograph, SRI/MF/complete] R4105–82.5

Recession and the Consumer, [Monograph, SRI/MF/complete] R4105–81.9

Special Consumer Survey Reports, [Series, SRI/MF/complete] R4105–81

Stock Options: Motivating Through Ownership, [Monograph, SRI/MF/complete] R4105–78.31

Top Executive Compensation, 1992 Edition, [Annual, SRI/MF/complete] R4105–19

Uruguay Round of GATT, [Monograph, SRI/MF/complete] R4105–82.2

Variable Pay: Nontraditional Programs for Motivation and Reward, [Monograph, SRI/MF/complete] R4105–78.27

Work Force Diversity: Corporate Challenges, Corporate Responses, [Monograph, SRI/MF/complete] R4105–78.22

Conference of State Court Administrators

State Court Caseload Statistics: Annual Report 1991, [Annual, SRI/MF/complete] R6600–1

Congressional Management Foundation

1992 U.S. House of Representatives Employment Practices: A Study of Staff Salary, Tenure, Demographics and Benefits, [Recurring (irreg.), SRI/MF/complete] R4140–1

Congressional Quarterly, Inc.

America Votes 20: A Handbook of Contemporary American Election Statistics, [Biennial, SRI/MF/not filmed] C2500–1

Cash Constituents of Congress, [Monograph, SRI/MF/complete] R3828–3

Congressional Quarterly Almanac: 102nd Congress, 2nd Session, 1992, [Annual, SRI/MF/not filmed] C2500–2

Handbook of Campaign Spending: Money in the 1990 Congressional Races, [Monograph, SRI/MF/not filmed] C2500–6

Open Secrets: Encyclopedia of Congressional Money and Politics, [Biennial, SRI/MF/complete] R3828–2

Presidential Primaries and Caucuses, 1992: A Handbook of Election Statistics, [Monograph, SRI/MF/not filmed] C2500–7

Conlon, Thomas R., and Associates

Study of Executive Compensation Plan Design, 1992, [Biennial, SRI/MF/complete] B2535–1

Connecticut Department of Banking

Annual Report of the Banking Commissioner of the State of Connecticut, for the Year Ended Dec. 31, 1991, [Annual, SRI/MF/complete] S1160–1

Connecticut Department of Education

Profile of Our Schools: The Condition of Education in Connecticut, 1991/92, [Biennial, SRI/MF/complete] S1185–3

Statement of Activities, 1991/92, Connecticut Department of Education, [Annual, SRI/MF/complete] S1185–1

Town and School District Profiles, [Annual, discontinued] S1185–2

Connecticut Department of Health Services

Behavioral Risk Factor Surveillance System, Connecticut, 1989-91, [Annual, SRI/MF/complete] S1200–2

Health Insurance Coverage in Connecticut, [Monograph, SRI/MF/complete] S1200–3

State of Connecticut 142nd Registration Report of Births, Marriages, Divorces, and Deaths for the Year Ending Dec. 31, 1989, [Annual, SRI/MF/complete] S1200–1

Connecticut Department of Housing

Connecticut Housing Production and Permit Authorized Construction: 1992, [Annual, SRI/MF/complete] S1212–1

Connecticut Department of Public Safety

Crime in Connecticut, 1992, [Annual, SRI/MF/complete] S1256–1

Connecticut Department of Transportation

Connecticut Motor Vehicle Traffic Accident Data, 1992, [Annual, SRI/MF/complete] S1275–1

Connecticut Insurance Department

State of Connecticut 126th Annual Report of the Insurance Commissioner, [Annual, SRI/MF/complete] S1222–1

Corporation for Public Broadcasting

Connecticut Judicial Branch

Biennial Report of the Connecticut Judicial Branch, July 1, 1990-June 30, 1992, [Biennial, SRI/MF/complete] S1220–1

Connecticut Labor Department

Labor Situation, [Monthly, SRI/MF/complete, shipped quarterly] S1235–1

Connecticut Office of the Comptroller

Report of the State Comptroller to the Governor for the Fiscal Year Ended June 30, 1992, Connecticut, [Annual, SRI/MF/complete] S1170–1

State of Connecticut Comprehensive Annual Financial Report for the Fiscal Year Ended June 30, 1992, [Annual, SRI/MF/complete] S1170–2

Connecticut Office of the Secretary of the State

Statement of Vote, General Election, Nov. 3, 1992, Connecticut, [Biennial, SRI/MF/complete] S1265–1

Connecticut State Library

Connecticut Public Library Statistical Summary and Salary Survey, FY91, [Annual, SRI/MF/complete] S1242–1

Construction Financial Management Association

1993 Construction Industry Annual Financial Survey, [Annual, SRI/MF/complete, current & previous year reports] A4155–1

Consultative Group on International Economic and Monetary Affairs

see Group of Thirty

Consumer Bankers Association

1993 Automobile Finance Study: An Analysis of the December, 1992 Survey, [Annual, SRI/MF/complete] A4160–2

1993 Home Lending Survey for Year End 1992, [Annual, SRI/MF/complete] A4160–3

1993 Small Business Banking Study: An Analysis of the September Survey, [Annual, SRI/MF/complete] A4160–5

Copper Development Association

Annual Data, 1993: Copper, Brass, Bronze; Copper Supply and Consumption, 1972-92, [Annual, SRI/MF/complete] A4175–1

Corn Refiners Association

Corn Annual, 1993, [Annual, SRI/MF/complete] A4200–1

Cornell University: New York State College of Agriculture and Life Sciences

Agricultural Finance Review, [Annual, SRI/MF/complete] U1380–4

Corporation for Enterprise Development

1993 Development Report Card for the States, [Annual, SRI/MF/complete, delayed] R4225–1

Corporation for Public Broadcasting

African-American Public Television Viewing, [Monograph, SRI/MF/complete] R4250–1.17

Asian-Americans and Public Television, [Monograph, SRI/MF/complete] R4250–1.16

Average Revenue Profiles for Public Broadcasting Stations, FY91, [Annual, SRI/MF/complete] R4250–1.20

Covering the Nation's Most Important Issues: What Public Broadcasting Can Do To Increase Public Understanding, [Monograph, SRI/MF/complete] R8825–10.1

Corporation for Public Broadcasting

Do Members Use Public Television Differently? An Exploratory Study, [Monograph, SRI/MF/complete] R4250-1.22

Highlights from the Public Television Programming Survey, 1990, [Recurring (irreg.), SRI/MF/complete] R4250-1.15

Hispanic Public Television Viewing, [Monograph, SRI/MF/complete] R4250-1.24

Public Broadcasting Stations' Income from State Governments and State Colleges and Universities Ranked State-by-State, FY91, [Annual, SRI/MF/complete] R4250-1.19

Public Broadcasting's Coverage of Issues and Programming Themes, [Series, SRI/MF/complete] R8825-10

Public Radio Listening by Hispanics and African-Americans, [Monograph, SRI/MF/complete] R4250-1.18

Research Notes, [Series, SRI/MF/complete] R4250-1

Second Look at Public Television: Leaders and the American Public Assess Its Coverage of Issues and Programming Themes, [Monograph, SRI/MF/complete] R8825-10.2

Summary Highlights: Full-Time Employees of Public Broadcasting, 1977-92, [Recurring (irreg.), SRI/MF/complete] R4250 1.23

Viewer and Listener Membership Income for Public Television and Radio Grantees, FY91, [Annual, SRI/MF/complete] R4250-1.21

Council of Better Business Bureaus Annual Inquiry and Complaint Summary, 1992, [Annual, SRI/MF/complete] A4350-1

Council of Chief State School Officers Analysis of State Education Indicators: State Profiles and NAEP Results Related to State Policies and Practices, 1993, [Biennial, SRI/MF/complete] A4355-1 State Indicators of Science and Mathematics Education, 1993, [Biennial, SRI/MF/complete] A4355-3

Council of Graduate Departments of Psychology Characteristics of Graduate Departments of Psychology, 1990/91, [Annual, SRI/MF/complete] A2620-3

Council of State Governments Changing West: Corrections, [Monograph, SRI/MF/complete] A4375-13 North American Newsprint Industry: Transitions to Recycling, [Monograph, SRI/MF/complete] A4375-15 Study of Markets for Post Consumer Plastics for Northeast Recycling Council, [Monograph, SRI/MF/complete] A4375-14 1992 State Library Agencies Financial Survey, [Annual, SRI/MF/complete, current & previous year reports] A3862-1

Council of the Great City Schools National Urban Education Goals: Baseline Indicators, 1990-91, [Monograph, SRI/MF/complete] A4425-4

Council on Competitiveness Competitiveness Index, 1993, [Annual, SRI/MF/complete] A4475-1

Index by Issuing Sources

Council on Social Work Education Statistics on Social Work Education in the U.S.: 1992, [Annual, SRI/MF/complete] A4515-1

Cowles Business Media Folio: The Magazine for Magazine Management, [Semimonthly, SRI/MF/excerpts, shipped quarterly] C2575-1

Crain Communications Advertising Age, [Weekly, SRI/MF/excerpts] C2710-1 Automotive News, [Weekly, SRI/MF/excerpts] C2710-3 Pensions & Investments, [Biweekly, SRI/MF/excerpts, shipped quarterly] C2710-2

Criminal Justice Institute Corrections Yearbook, 1992, [Annual, SRI/MF/complete] R4300-1 Corrections Yearbook, 1992: Adult Corrections, [Annual, SRI/MF/complete] R4300-1.1 Corrections Yearbook, 1992: Jail Systems, [Annual, SRI/MF/complete] R4300-1.4 Corrections Yearbook, 1992: Juvenile Corrections, [Annual, SRI/MF/complete] R4300-1.2 Corrections Yearbook, 1992: Probation and Parole, [Annual, SRI/MF/complete] R4300-1.3

Cushman & Wakefield Across the Nation: Industrial, Mid-Year 1993, [Annual, SRI/MF/complete] B2800-6 Across the Nation: Office, [Quarterly, SRI/MF/complete] B2800-4 Business America Real Estate Monitor, [Annual, discontinued] B2800-1 Focus on Marketrends, 1993, [Annual, SRI/MF/complete] B2800-3 1993 Focus on Manhattantrends, [Annual, SRI/MF/complete] B2800-5

Daily Racing Form, Inc. Survey on Sports Attendance, [Annual, suspended] C2825-1

Dana Chase Publications *see* Chase, Dana, Publications

Delaware Administrative Office of the Courts 1992 Annual Report of the Delaware Judiciary, [Annual, SRI/MF/complete] S1360-1

Delaware Board of Education Report of Educational Statistics, 1991/92, Delaware, [Annual, SRI/MF/complete] S1430-1

Delaware Commissioner of Elections Official Results, 1992 General Election, Delaware, [Biennial, SRI/MF/complete] S1365-1

Delaware Department of Health and Social Services Delaware Vital Statistics Annual Report, 1990, [Annual, SRI/MF/complete] S1385-2 Public Assistance Statistical Report, Delaware, [Monthly, final issue, SRI/MF/complete, shipped quarterly] S1385-1

Delaware Department of Labor Delaware Digest Labor Market Monthly, [Monthly, SRI/MF/complete, shipped quarterly] S1405-2

Delaware Department of Public Instruction Report of Educational Statistics, 1991/92, Delaware, [Annual, SRI/MF/complete] S1430-1

Delaware Department of Public Safety 1992 Annual Traffic Statistical Report, Delaware, [Annual, SRI/MF/complete] S1435-1

Delaware Development Office *see* Delaware Executive Office of the Governor, S1375-3, S1375-4

Delaware Executive Office of the Governor Crime in Delaware, 1991: An Analysis of Uniform Crime Data, [Annual, SRI/MF/complete] S1375-5 Delaware Data Book, [Annual, SRI/MF/complete] S1375-4 Delaware Population Consortium Population Projections, Version 1992.0, [Recurring (irreg.), SRI/MF/complete] S1375-3

Delaware Higher Education Commission Data Book: Financing Postsecondary Education in Delaware for FY94, [Annual, SRI/MF/complete] S1425-1

Delaware State Housing Authority Housing Production in Delaware, 1992, [Annual, SRI/MF/complete] S1387-1

Delaware Statistical Analysis Center *see* Delaware Executive Office of the Governor, S1375-5

Deloitte & Touche Restaurant Industry Operations Report 1993, [Annual, SRI/MF/complete] A8200-3

Direct Marketing Association 1992-93 Statistical Fact Book: Current Information About Direct Marketing, [Annual, SRI/MF/complete] A4620-1

Distilled Spirits Council of the U.S. 1991 Statistical Information for the U.S. Liquor Industry, [Annual, SRI/MF/complete] A4650-3

District of Columbia Board of Elections and Ethics District of Columbia Elections, 1992, [Biennial series, SRI/MF/complete, current and previous biennial reports] S1525-1

District of Columbia Courts District of Columbia Courts Annual Report, 1992, [Annual, SRI/MF/complete] S1515-1

District of Columbia Department of Employment Services Metropolitan Washington, D.C., Area Labor Summary, [Monthly, SRI/MF/complete, shipped quarterly] S1527-3

District of Columbia Executive Office of the Mayor Indices: A Statistical Index to District of Columbia Services, [Annual, SRI/MF/complete] S1535-3 1991 Crime and Justice Report for the District of Columbia, [Annual, SRI/MF/complete] S1535-2

District of Columbia Office of the Controller District of Columbia Comprehensive Annual Financial Report, Year Ended Sept. 30, 1992, [Annual, SRI/MF/complete] S1507-1

District of Columbia Public Schools Five Year Statistical Glance at D.C. Public Schools: School Years 1987/88-1991/92, [Annual, SRI/MF/complete] S1605-2

Index by Issuing Sources

Diversified Publishing Group
CableVision, [Biweekly, SRI/MF/not filmed] C2965–1

Donoghue Organization
see IBC/Donoghue, Inc.

Douglas Aircraft Co.
Outlook for Commercial Aircraft, 1992-2011, [Annual, SRI/MF/complete] B3075–1

Duke University: Center on East-West Trade, Investment, and Communications
Journal of Soviet Nationalities, [Quarterly, discontinued] U1520–1

Dun and Bradstreet
Business Expectations, [Quarterly, SRI/MF/complete] C3150–4
Monthly Business Failures, [Monthly, SRI/MF/complete, shipped quarterly] C3150–2
New Business Incorporations, [Monthly, SRI/MF/complete, shipped quarterly] C3150–3
Quarterly Business Failures, [Quarterly, SRI/MF/complete] C3150–6
1991-92 Business Failure Record, Dun and Bradstreet, [Annual, SRI/MF/complete] C3150–8

Duncan's American Radio, Inc.
American Radio, [5 per year, SRI/MF/complete] C3165–1

Earl G. Graves Publishing Co.
see Graves, Earl G., Publishing Co.

East-West Center: Program on Population
Papers of the Program on Population, [Series, SRI/MF/complete] R4500–1
Trends in Female and Male Age at Marriage and Celibacy in Asia, [Monograph, SRI/MF/complete] R4500–1.64

Ecological Society of America
Profiles of Ecologists: Results of a Survey of the Membership of the Ecological Society of America, [Recurring (irreg.), SRI/MF/complete] A4685–1

Economic Policy Institute
Converting the Cold War Economy: Investing in Industries, Workers, and Communities, [Monograph, SRI/MF/complete] R4700–19
Effects of Diminished Economic Opportunities on Social Stress: Heart Attacks, Stroke, and Crime, [Monograph, SRI/MF/complete] R4700–18
Impact of Health Care Financing on Family Budgets, [Monograph, SRI/MF/complete] R4700–20
Parallel Banking System, [Monograph, SRI/MF/complete] R4700–22
Rich Get Increasingly Richer: Latest Data on Household Wealth During the 1980s, [Monograph, SRI/MF/complete] R4700–17
Still Neglecting Public Investment: The FY94 Budget Outlook, [Monograph, SRI/MF/complete] R4700–23
Truth About Public Employees: Underpaid or Overpaid?, [Monograph, SRI/MF/complete] R4700–21

Edison Electric Institute
Electric Perspectives, [Bimonthly, SRI/MF/excerpts] A4700–4
Statistical Yearbook of the Electric Utility Industry, 1991, [Annual, SRI/MF/complete, delayed] A4700–1

1991 Electric Power Equipment Report, [Annual, SRI/MF/complete, delayed] A4700–2

Editor & Publisher Co.
Editor & Publisher Market Guide, 1993, [Annual, SRI/MF/complete, delayed] C3250–1

Editorial Projects in Education
Education Week, [Weekly, SRI/MF/excerpts, shipped quarterly] R4800–2

Elections Research Center
America Votes 20: A Handbook of Contemporary American Election Statistics, [Biennial, SRI/MF/not filmed] C2500–1

Electronic Industries Association
Electronic Market Data Book, 1993 Edition, [Annual, SRI/MF/complete] A4725–1
Electronic Market Trends, [Monthly, SRI/MF/complete] A4725–2
Electronics Foreign Trade, [Monthly, SRI/MF/complete] A4725–3
U.S. Consumer Electronics Industry in Review, 1993, [Annual, SRI/MF/not filmed] A4725–4

Eli Lilly and Co.
see Lilly, Eli, and Co.

Employment Management Association
National Cost Per Hire Data, 1992, [Annual, SRI/MF/complete] A4740–2

Engineering Manpower Commission
see American Association of Engineering Societies

Engineering, Workforce Commission
see American Association of Engineering Societies

Eno Transportation Foundation
Transportation in America, 10th Edition, [Annual, SRI/MF/not filmed] R4815–1

Equifax Inc.
Harris-Equifax Consumer Privacy Survey, 1992, [Annual, SRI/MF/complete] B3280–2

Ernst and Young
Monthly Statistical Report, Resins, [Monthly, with annual summary, SRI/MF/complete, shipped quarterly] A8920–5

Exxon Corp.
Turbine-Engined Fleets of the World's Airlines, 1993 Survey, [Annual, SRI/MF/complete] B3370–1

Eye Bank Association of America
Eye Banking Statistics, [Annual, SRI/MF/complete] A4743–1

Fairchild Fashion & Merchandising Group
Fairchild's Electronics Industry Financial Directory, 1992/93, [Annual, SRI/MF/complete, delayed] C3400–4
Fairchild's Retail Stores Financial Directory, 1992/93, [Annual, SRI/MF/complete, delayed] C3400–2
Fairchild's Textile and Apparel Financial Directory, 1992/93, [Annual, SRI/MF/complete, delayed] C3400–5
SN '93 Distribution Study of Grocery Store Sales, [Annual, SRI/MF/complete, delayed] C3400–6

Families USA Foundation
Comparative Analysis of the Presidential Candidates' Health Plans, [Monograph, SRI/MF/complete] R4865–9
Going to Mexico: Priced Out of American Health Care, [Monograph, SRI/MF/complete] R4865–10

Florida Department of Corrections

Half of Us: Families Priced Out of Health Protection, [Monograph, SRI/MF/complete] R4865–14
Heavy Burden of Home Care, [Monograph, SRI/MF/complete] R4865–15
Making Them Wait for Social Security Disability Benefits, [Monograph, SRI/MF/complete] R4865–11
No Sale: The Failure of Barebones Insurance, [Monograph, SRI/MF/complete] R4865–16
Nursing Home Insurance: Who Can Afford It?, [Monograph, SRI/MF/complete] R4865–12
Prescription Costs: America's Other Drug Crisis, [Monograph, SRI/MF/complete] R4865–8
They Make That Much?, [Monograph, SRI/MF/complete] R4865–13

Farm Press Publications
Implement and Tractor, [7 issues per year, SRI/MF/excerpts, shipped quarterly] C3450–1

Fiber Economics Bureau
Fiber Organon, [Monthly, SRI/MF/complete, shipped quarterly] C3460–1

Fibre Box Association
Fibre Box Industry Annual Report, 1992, [Annual, SRI/MF/complete] A4875–1

First Hawaiian Bank
County Profiles, [Series, SRI/MF/complete] B3500–2
Economic Indicators, Hawaii, [Bimonthly, SRI/MF/complete] B3500–1
Honolulu County in 1993, [Annual, SRI/MF/complete] B3500–2.2
Kauai County in 1992 and 1993, [Annual, SRI/MF/complete] B3500–2.1
Maui County in 1993, [Annual, SRI/MF/complete] B3500–2.3

First Interstate Bancorp
Forecast 1993-94, [Annual, with interim update, SRI/MF/complete] B3520–1

First Security Bank of Idaho
Idaho Construction Report, [Monthly, SRI/MF/complete, shipped quarterly] B3900–1

Florida Agency for Health Care Administration
1992 Florida Health Care Atlas, [Annual, SRI/MF/complete] S1746–1

Florida Agricultural Statistics Service
see Florida Department of Agriculture and Consumer Services, S1685–1

Florida Department of Agriculture and Consumer Services
Florida Agricultural Statistics, [Annual series, SRI/MF/complete] S1685–1
Florida Agricultural Statistics, Citrus Summary, 1991-92, [Annual, SRI/MF/complete] S1685–1.1
Florida Agricultural Statistics, Field Crops Summary, 1992, [Annual, SRI/MF/complete] S1685–1.4
Florida Agricultural Statistics, Livestock, Dairy, and Poultry Summary, 1992, [Annual, SRI/MF/complete] S1685–1.3
Florida Agricultural Statistics, Vegetable Summary, 1991-92, [Annual, SRI/MF/complete] S1685–1.2

Florida Department of Corrections
Florida Department of Corrections 1991/92 Annual Report, [Annual, SRI/MF/complete] S1720–1

Florida Department of Education

Index by Issuing Sources

Florida Department of Education
Fact Book, 1991/92, State University System of Florida, [Annual, SRI/MF/complete] S1725–1

Florida Department of Health and Rehabilitative Services
Annual Statistical Report, Florida Department of Health and Rehabilitative Services, [Annual, discontinued] S1745–4
Florida Vital Statistics, 1992, [Annual, SRI/MF/complete, current & previous year reports] S1745–3

Florida Department of Highway Safety and Motor Vehicles
Florida Traffic Crash Data, 1992, [Annual, SRI/MF/complete] S1750–2

Florida Department of Insurance
Report of the Department of Insurance, State of Florida, 1992, [Annual, SRI/MF/complete] S1760–1

Florida Department of Labor and Employment Security
Florida Labor Market Trends, [Monthly, SRI/MF/complete, shipped quarterly] S1765–3

Florida Department of Law Enforcement
Crime in Florida, 1992 Annual Report, [Annual, SRI/MF/complete] S1770–1

Florida Department of State
Nov. 3, 1992 General Election Results, Florida, [Biennial, SRI/MF/complete] S1800–1
1993 Florida Library Directory with Statistics, [Annual, SRI/MF/complete] S1800–2

Florida Office of the Comptroller
Florida Comprehensive Annual Financial Report, Fiscal Year Ended June 30, 1992, [Annual, SRI/MF/complete] S1717–3
State of Florida Annual Report of the Comptroller, FY92, [Annual, SRI/MF/complete] S1717–1

Florida Public Service Commission
Florida Public Service Commission, 1992 Annual Report, [Annual, SRI/MF/complete] S1790–1

Florida Supreme Court
Florida County Court Summary Report, 1992, [Annual, SRI/MF/complete] S1805–1

Food Marketing Institute
Food Marketing Industry Speaks, 1992-93, [Annual, SRI/MF/complete, delayed] A4950–5
Information Systems Study, 1993, [Annual, SRI/MF/complete, current & previous year reports, current report delayed] A4950–7
Operating Results of Independent Supermarkets, 1991, [Annual, SRI/MF/complete, delayed] A4950–4
Service Advantage, [SRI/MF/complete] A4950–37
Shopping for Health, 1993: A Report on Diet, Nutrition and Ethnic Foods, [Annual, SRI/MF/complete, current & previous reports, current report delayed] A4950–36
Trends: Consumer Attitudes and the Supermarket, 1993, [Annual, SRI/MF/complete, delayed] A4950–3
1991-92 Annual Financial Review: The Annual Report of the Supermarket Companies, [Annual, SRI/MF/complete, delayed] A4950–1

1992-93 Management Compensation Study for Wholesalers and Large Retailers, [Annual, SRI/MF/complete, delayed] A4950–6
1993 Facts About Store Development, [Annual, SRI/MF/complete, delayed] A4950–2

Footwear Industries of America
Footwear Manual, [Annual, SRI/MF/complete, delayed] A4957–1
Statistical Reporter: Quarterly Report, [Quarterly, SRI/MF/complete] A4957–2

Forbes, Inc.
Forbes, [Biweekly, SRI/MF/excerpts, shipped quarterly] C3950–1

Foreign Policy Association
National Opinion Ballot Report, [Annual, SRI/MF/complete] A4965–1

Foundation Center
Foundation Giving: Yearbook of Facts and Figures on Private, Corporate and Community Foundations, [Annual, SRI/MF/complete] R4900–1

Foundation for International Business Cycle Research
International Economic Indicators, [Monthly, SRI/MF/complete, delayed] U1245–1

Freeman, Miller, Publications
Pulp and Paper, [Monthly, SRI/MF/excerpts, shipped quarterly] C3975–2
Pulp and Paper: 1993 North American Factbook, [Annual, SRI/MF/complete, delayed] C3975–5
Wood Technology, [Bimonthly, SRI/MF/excerpts] C3975–1

Futures Industry Association
International Open Interest Report, [Monthly, SRI/MF/complete, shipped quarterly] A5040–6
International Report: International Volume, [Monthly, SRI/MF/complete, shipped quarterly] A5040–5
Monthly Options Report: Volume of Options Contracts Traded, [Monthly, SRI/MF/complete, shipped quarterly] A5040–3
Monthly Volume Report: Volume of Futures Contracts Traded, [Monthly, SRI/MF/complete, shipped quarterly] A5040–2
Open Interest Report: Open Interest of Last Trading Day, [Monthly, SRI/MF/complete, shipped quarterly] A5040–4
Volume of Futures and Options Trading on U.S. Futures Exchanges, 1968-92, [Annual, SRI/MF/complete] A5040–1

Gallup Poll
Gallup Poll Monthly, [Monthly, SRI/MF/not filmed] C4040–1

Gardner Publications
Production: 1993 Capital Spending Survey, [Annual, SRI/MF/complete] C4080–1

Gas Appliance Manufacturers Association
Statistical Highlights, [Monthly, with annual supplements, SRI/MF/complete, shipped quarterly] A5100–1

General Aviation Manufacturers Association
General Aviation Airplane Shipment Report, [Quarterly, SRI/MF/complete] A5120–1
General Aviation Statistical Databook, 1993 Edition, [Annual, SRI/MF/complete] A5120–2

Georgia Agricultural Statistics Service
see Georgia Department of Agriculture, S1855–1

Georgia Bureau of Investigation
1992 Summary Report, Georgia Uniform Crime Reporting Program, [Annual, SRI/MF/complete] S1901–1

Georgia Crime Information Center
see Georgia Bureau of Investigation, S1901–1

Georgia Department of Agriculture
Georgia Agricultural Facts, 1992 Edition, [Annual, SRI/MF/complete] S1855–1

Georgia Department of Audits
Report of the State Auditor of Georgia, Year Ended June 30, 1992, [Annual, SRI/MF/complete] S1860–1

Georgia Department of Banking and Finance
Department of Banking and Finance, State of Georgia: 73rd Annual Report, Year Ending Dec. 31, 1992, [Annual, SRI/MF/complete] S1865–1

Georgia Department of Corrections
Georgia Department of Corrections 1992 Annual Report, [Annual, SRI/MF/complete] S1872–1

Georgia Department of Human Resources
Georgia Vital Statistics Report, 1991, [Annual, SRI/MF/complete] S1895–1
Lifestyle Behaviors of Adult Residents of the State of Georgia: Behavioral Risk Factor Survey, 1991, [Annual, SRI/MF/complete] S1895–2

Georgia Department of Labor
Georgia Labor Market Trends, [Monthly, SRI/MF/complete, shipped quarterly] S1905–1

Georgia Department of Revenue
Georgia Department of Revenue 1992 Statistical Report, [Annual, SRI/MF/complete] S1950 1

Georgia Judicial Council
19th Annual Report on the Work of the Georgia Courts, FY92, [Annual, SRI/MF/complete] S1903–1

Georgia Office of the Secretary of State
State of Georgia General Election Nov. 3, 1992, [Biennial, SRI/MF/complete] S1955–1

Georgia State University: Economic Forecasting Center
Forecast of Georgia and Atlanta, [Quarterly, SRI/MF/complete] U1880–2
Forecast of the Nation, [Quarterly, SRI/MF/complete] U1880–1
Monthly Projections, [Monthly, SRI/MF/complete, shipped quarterly] U1880–3

German American Chamber of Commerce
U.S.-German Economic Yearbook, 1992, [Annual, SRI/MF/complete] A5135–2

Glenmary Research Center
Churches and Church Membership in the U.S., 1990, [Monograph, SRI/MF/not filmed] R4985–1

Gold Institute
Modern Gold Coinage, 1992, [Annual, SRI/MF/complete, delayed] A5145–1
World Mine Production of Gold, 1992-96, [Annual, SRI/MF/complete] A5145–2

Goldhirsh Group
INC., [Monthly, SRI/MF/excerpts, shipped quarterly] C4687–1

Index by Issuing Sources

Graves, Earl G., Publishing Co.
Black Enterprise, [Monthly, SRI/MF/not filmed] C4215–1

Group Health Association of America
HMO Industry Profile 1992 Edition, [Annual, SRI/MF/complete] A5150–2

Group of Thirty
EMU and the Regions, [Monograph, SRI/MF/complete] R5025–9
Threat of Managed Trade to Transforming Economies, [Monograph, SRI/MF/complete] R5025–10
Why Now? Change and Turmoil in U.S. Banking, [Monograph, SRI/MF/complete] R5025–8

Guttmacher, Alan, Institute
Family Planning Perspectives, [Bimonthly, SRI/MF/complete] A5160–1
International Family Planning Perspectives, [Quarterly, SRI/MF/complete] A5160–6
Testing Positive: Sexually Transmitted Disease and the Public Health Response, [Monograph, SRI/MF/complete] A5160–10

Handy and Harman
Silver Market, 1992, 77th Annual Review, [Annual, SRI/MF/complete] B4300–1

Hanley-Wood
Builder, [Monthly, SRI/MF/not filmed] C4300–1

Hart Publications
Petroleum Engineer International, [Monthly, SRI/MF/not filmed] C4420–1

Harvard University: Russian Research Center
RRC Economic Newsletter, [Monthly, SRI/MF/complete, shipped quarterly] U2030–1

Hawaii Agricultural Statistics Service
see Hawaii Department of Agriculture, S2030–1

Hawaii Department of Accounting and General Services
State of Hawaii Comprehensive Annual Financial Report for the Fiscal Year Ended June 30, 1992, [Annual, SRI/MF/complete] S2020–1

Hawaii Department of Agriculture
Statistics of Hawaiian Agriculture, 1991, [Annual, SRI/MF/complete] S2030–1

Hawaii Department of Business, Economic Development and Tourism
Quarterly Statistical and Economic Report, State of Hawaii, [Quarterly, SRI/MF/complete] S2090–2
State of Hawaii Data Book, 1992: A Statistical Abstract, [Annual, SRI/MF/complete] S2090–1

Hawaii Department of Health
Annual Report Statistical Supplement, 1990, State of Hawaii Department of Health, [Annual, SRI/MF/complete] S2065–1

Hawaii Department of Planning and Economic Development
see Hawaii Department of Business, Economic Development and Tourism

Hawaii Department of Taxation
Department of Taxation Annual Report, 1991-92, Hawaii, [Annual, SRI/MF/complete] S2120–1

Hawaii Department of the Attorney General
Crime in Hawaii, 1992: A Review of Uniform Crime Reports, [Annual, SRI/MF/complete] S2035–1

Hawaii Department of Transportation
Major Traffic Accidents, State of Hawaii, 1986, [Annual, SRI/MF/complete] S2125–1

Hawaii Office of the Lieutenant Governor
General Election and Special Election for the Office of Hawaiian Affairs, Nov. 3, 1992, Hawaii, [Biennial, SRI/MF/complete] S2077–1.2
Primary and Special Election, Sept. 19, 1992, Hawaii, [Biennial, SRI/MF/complete] S2077–1.1
Result of Votes Cast, 1992, State of Hawaii, [Biennial series, SRI/MF/complete] S2077–1

Hawaii Supreme Court
Judiciary, State of Hawaii: Annual Report, July 1, 1991-June 30, 1992, [Annual, SRI/MF/complete] S2115–1

HCIA, Inc.
Geriatric Length of Stay by Diagnosis and Operation, U.S., 1992-93, [Annual, SRI/MF/complete, delayed] B4455–1.6
Length of Stay, by Diagnosis and Operation, 1992-93, [Annual series, SRI/MF/complete, delayed] B4455–1
Length of Stay by DRG and Payment Source, 1992-93, [Annual series, SRI/MF/complete, delayed] B4455–3
Pediatric Length of Stay by Diagnosis and Operation, U.S., 1992-93, [Annual, SRI/MF/complete, delayed] B4455–1.7
Psychiatric Length of Stay by Diagnosis, 1992-93, [Annual series, SRI/MF/complete, delayed] B4455–2
1993 Hospital Admission Rates, [Monograph, SRI/MF/complete, delayed] B4455–4
1993 Hospital Inpatient Charges, [Monograph, SRI/MF/complete, delayed] B4455–5

Health Insurance Association of America
Source Book of Health Insurance Data, 1992, [Annual, SRI/MF/complete] A5173–2

Health Insurance Institute
see Health Insurance Association of America

Healthcare Knowledge Resources
see HCIA, Inc.

Hearing Industries Association
HIA Statistical Report, [Quarterly, SRI/MF/complete] A5185–1

Heidrick and Struggles
Bank CEO Leadership Challenge: Anticipating and Directing Change. A Survey of the Top 300 Banks' Chief Executives, [Annual, SRI/MF/complete] B4490–2.33
Forging the Vision: Survey of U.S. Technology Chief Executives, [Monograph, SRI/MF/complete] B4490–2.34
Health Care Chief Executive, [Recurring (irreg.), SRI/MF/complete] B4490–2.35
New Diversity: Women and Minorities on Corporate Boards, [Monograph, SRI/MF/complete] B4490–2.36
Profile Series, [Series, SRI/MF/complete] B4490–2

Helicopter Association International
1993 Helicopter Annual, [Annual, SRI/MF/complete] A5190–1

Highway Loss Data Institute
Insurance Collision Report, [Series, SRI/MF/complete] A5200–1
Insurance Injury Report: 1990-92 Passenger Cars, Large Vans, Pickups, and Utility Vehicles, [Annual, SRI/MF/complete] A5200–3
Insurance Losses by Vehicle Density, 1990-92 Models, [Monograph, SRI/MF/complete] A5200–4.31
Insurance Special Reports, [Series, SRI/MF/complete] A5200–4
Insurance Theft Report: 1990-92 Passenger Cars, Vans, Pickups, and Utility Vehicles, [Annual, SRI/MF/complete] A5200–2
Trends in Injury and Collision: Losses by Car Size, 1979-89 Model Passenger Cars, [Monograph, SRI/MF/complete] A5200–4.30
Vehicle Descriptions, 1993 Models, [Annual, SRI/MF/complete] A5200–5

Hispanic Business, Inc.
Hispanic Business, [Monthly, SRI/MF/excerpts, shipped quarterly] C4575–1

Home Center Institute
Bottom Line Report: Detailed Cost-of-Doing Business Data for Home Centers, 1992, [Annual, SRI/MF/complete] A8275–1.2
Financial Operating Reports, [Annual series, SRI/MF/complete] A8275–1
Management Report: Detailed Cost-of-Doing Business Data for Hardware Stores, 1992, [Annual, SRI/MF/complete] A8275–1.1
Profit Report: Detailed Cost-of-Doing Business Data for Retail Lumber Outlets, 1992, [Annual, SRI/MF/complete] A8275–1.3

Howfrey Communications
Supermarket Business, [Monthly, SRI/MF/excerpts, shipped quarterly] C4655–1

Hughes Christensen
International Rotary Drilling Rig Report, [Monthly, SRI/MF/complete, shipped quarterly] B4675–1

Hunter Publishing
Fuel Oil News: The Oil Heating Industry: 1992, [Monthly (selected issue), SRI/MF/excerpts] C4680–2
NPN—National Petroleum News, [Monthly, SRI/MF/excerpts, shipped quarterly] C4680–1

IBC/Donoghue, Inc.
IBC/Donoghue Money Fund Directory, 1993 Edition, [Annual, SRI/MF/complete] C4682–2
IBC/Donoghue Mutual Funds Almanac, 24th Edition, 1993, [Annual, SRI/MF/complete] C4682–1

Idaho Department of Commerce
Idaho Facts, [Recurring (irreg.), SRI/MF/complete] S2218–2

Idaho Department of Education
Annual Statistical Report, 1992/93: Public School Certified and Non-Certified Personnel, Idaho, [Annual, SRI/MF/complete] S2225–3
Financial Summaries, Idaho School Districts, FY92, [Annual, SRI/MF/complete] S2225–2
Idaho Department of Education Public and Nonpublic School Membership, 1992/93 School Year (as Reported Sept. 25, 1992), [Annual, SRI/MF/complete] S2225–1

Idaho Department of Employment

Idaho Department of Employment
Basic Economic Data for Idaho, 1991, [Annual, SRI/MF/complete] S2230–2

Idaho Department of Finance
State of Idaho Department of Finance 74th Annual Report, [Annual, SRI/MF/complete] S2235–1

Idaho Department of Health and Welfare
Quarterly Welfare Statistical Bulletin, Idaho, [Quarterly, SRI/MF/complete] S2250–1
1991 Annual Summary of Vital Statistics, Idaho, [Annual, SRI/MF/complete] S2250–2

Idaho Department of Insurance
91st Annual Report: State of Idaho, Department of Insurance, for the Year Ended December 31, 1991, [Annual, SRI/MF/complete] S2260–1

Idaho Department of Law Enforcement
Crime in Idaho, 1992, [Annual, SRI/MF/complete] S2275–2

Idaho Department of Revenue and Taxation
Idaho State Tax Commission 1992 Annual Report, [Annual, SRI/MF/complete] S2295–1

Idaho Department of Transportation
State of Idaho Motor Vehicle Traffic Accidents, Statewide Report, Jan. 1, 1992-Dec. 31, 1992, [Annual, SRI/MF/complete] S2315–1

Idaho Division of Financial Management
see Idaho Office of the Governor, S2245–2

Idaho Library Association
Idaho Librarian: Statistics for Idaho Academic Libraries, [Quarterly (selected issue), SRI/MF/excerpts] A5370–1

Idaho Office of the Auditor
State of Idaho Annual Report of the State Auditor, Fiscal Year Ended June 30, 1992, [Annual, SRI/MF/complete] S2215–1

Idaho Office of the Governor
Idaho Economic Forecast, [Quarterly, SRI/MF/complete] S2245–2

Idaho Office of the Secretary of State
Abstract of Votes Cast at the General Election, Nov. 3, 1992, State of Idaho, [Biennial, SRI/MF/complete] S2305–1

Idaho Public Utilities Commission
1992 Idaho Public Utilities Commission Annual Report, [Annual, SRI/MF/complete] S2290–1

Idaho State Library
Idaho Public Library Statistics, FY92, [Annual, SRI/MF/complete, current & previous year reports] S2282–1

IDD, Inc.
Mergers and Acquisitions, [Bimonthly, SRI/MF/excerpts] C4683–1

Illinois Agricultural Statistics Service
see Illinois Department of Agriculture, S2390–1

Illinois Board of Education
1991 Annual Statistical Report of the Illinois State Board of Education, [Annual, SRI/MF/complete] S2440–1

Illinois Board of Elections
State of Illinois Official Vote Cast at the General Election, Nov. 3, 1992, [Biennial, SRI/MF/complete] S2445–1

Illinois Board of Higher Education
Data Book on Illinois Higher Education, [Annual, SRI/MF/complete] S2475–1

Illinois Commerce Commission
Illinois Electric Utilities: A Comparative Study of Electric Sales Statistics for Calendar Years 1992 and 1991, [Annual, SRI/MF/complete] S2410–1.2
Illinois Gas Utilities: A Comparative Study of Gas Sales Statistics for Calendar Years 1992 and 1991, [Annual, SRI/MF/complete] S2410–1.1
Illinois Utilities Statistics, [Annual series, SRI/MF/complete] S2410–1
Operating Statistics of Telephone Companies in Illinois for Calendar Year 1992, [Annual, SRI/MF/complete] S2410–2

Illinois Commissioner of Banks and Trust Companies
Commissioner of Banks and Trust Companies, State of Illinois July 1, 1991-June 30, 1992 Report, [Annual, SRI/MF/complete, current & previous year reports] S2395–1

Illinois Department of Agriculture
Illinois Agricultural Statistics, 1992, [Annual, SRI/MF/complete] S2390–1

Illinois Department of Commerce and Community Affairs
Illinois Economic Summary, [Quarterly, SRI/MF/complete] S2405–2

Illinois Department of Corrections
Human Services Plan, FY91-93, Volume III, Illinois, [Annual, SRI/MF/complete] S2425–1
Jail and Detention Statistics and Information, Illinois, [Annual, suspended] S2425–2

Illinois Department of Financial Institutions
Illinois Department of Financial Institutions FY91 Annual Report, [Annual, SRI/MF/complete] S2457–2

Illinois Department of Law Enforcement
see Illinois Department of State Police, S2536–1

Illinois Department of Mental Health and Developmental Disabilities
Illinois Mental Health Statistics, FY93, [Annual, SRI/MF/complete] S2505–1

Illinois Department of Public Aid
Illinois Department of Public Aid Annual Report, FY91 and FY92, [Annual, SRI/MF/complete] S2520–2

Illinois Department of State Police
Crime in Illinois, 1991, [Annual, SRI/MF/complete] S2536–1

Illinois Department of Transportation
1991 Illinois Crash Facts and Statistics, [Annual, SRI/MF/complete] S2540–1

Illinois Office of the Comptroller
Illinois Annual Reports, 1992, [Annual series, SRI/MF/complete] S2415–1

Illinois Office of the Secretary of State
Illinois Public Library Statistics: A Guide for Librarians and Trustees, 1991-92, [Annual, SRI/MF/complete] S2535–2

Illinois Public Utilities Division
see Illinois Commerce Commission, S2410–1, S2410–2

Illinois State Library
see Illinois Office of the Secretary of State, S2535–2

Inc. Publishing Co.
INC., [Monthly, SRI/MF/excerpts, shipped quarterly] C4687–1

Independent Petroleum Association of America
Petroleum Independent: The Oil and Natural Gas Producing Industry in Your State, 1993-94, [Monthly (selected issue), SRI/MF/complete] A5425–1
U.S. Petroleum Statistics, 1992 Data Updated, [Annual, SRI/MF/complete] A5425–2
1991 Joint Association Survey on Drilling Costs, [Annual, SRI/MF/complete] A2575–9

Independent Sector
From Belief to Commitment: The Community Service Activities and Finances of Religious Congregations in the U.S., 1993 Edition, [Recurring (irreg.), SRI/MF/complete] A5435–4
Giving and Volunteering, 1992: Volunteering and Giving Among American Teenagers 12 to 17 Years of Age, [Biennial, SRI/MF/complete] A5435–5

Indiana Department of Education
General Fund Summary of Expenditures by Program and Per Pupil Costs, July 1, 1991-June 30, 1992, Indiana, [Annual, SRI/MF/complete, current & 2 previous reports] S2608–2.1
Indiana Department of Education Reports, [Series, SRI/MF/complete] S2608–2
Number of Pupils Enrolled in Nonpublic Schools, 1992/93, Indiana, [Annual, SRI/MF/complete, current & 5 previous reports] S2608–2.7
Number of Pupils Enrolled in Public Schools, 1992/93, Indiana, [Annual, SRI/MF/complete] S2608–2.6
Revenue from State Sources for July 1, 1991-June 30, 1992, Indiana, [Annual, SRI/MF/complete] S2608–2.2
School Corporation Wealth Ratio, 1991/92; Assessments and Tax Rates Payable for 1992, Indiana, [Annual, SRI/MF/complete] S2608–2.3
Summary of Expenditures by Object and Percent of Total Expenditures for July 1, 1990-June 30, 1991, Indiana, [Annual, SRI/MF/complete] S2608–2.4
Summary of Expenditures by Object and Percent of Total Expenditures for July 1, 1991-June 30, 1992, Indiana, [Annual, SRI/MF/complete] S2608–2.10
Summary of Indebtedness—Principal Outstanding, as of June 30, 1992, Indiana, [Annual, SRI/MF/complete] S2608–2.12
Summary of Receipts, 1991/92, Indiana, [Annual, SRI/MF/complete] S2608–2.11
1990/91 Pupil/Teacher Ratio Report, Indiana, [Annual, SRI/MF/complete, current & 3 previous reports] S2608–2.8
1991/92 Public Pupil/Teacher Ratio, Indiana, [Annual, SRI/MF/complete] S2608–2.9
1992/93 Public High School Enrollment Report, Indiana, [Annual, SRI/MF/complete] S2608–2.5

Indiana Department of Financial Institutions
Department of Financial Institutions Annual Report, Year Ended Dec. 31, 1991, State of Indiana, [Annual, SRI/MF/complete] S2625–1

Index by Issuing Sources

Indiana Department of Public Welfare
see Indiana Family and Social Services Administration, S2623–1

Indiana Family and Social Services Administration
Indiana Division of Family and Children FY92 Annual Report, [Annual, SRI/MF/complete] S2623–1

Indiana Office of the Auditor
Indiana Comprehensive Annual Financial Report for the Fiscal Year Ended June 30, 1992, [Annual, SRI/MF/complete] S2570–1

Indiana Office of the Secretary of State
1992 Election Report, State of Indiana, [Biennial, SRI/MF/complete] S2702–1

Indiana State Library
Statistics of Indiana Libraries, 1992, [Annual, SRI/MF/complete] S2655–1

Indiana State Police Department
Summary of Motor Vehicle Traffic Accidents in Indiana, 1992, [Annual, SRI/MF/complete] S2675–1

Indiana Supreme Court
1992 Indiana Judicial Report, [Annual, SRI/MF/complete] S2703–1

Indiana University: Indiana Business Research Center
Indiana Business Review, [Quarterly, SRI/MF/complete] U2160–1

Industrial Research Institute
Industrial Research Institute's Annual R&D Trends Survey, [Annual, SRI/MF/complete] A5510–1

Information Publications
Almanac of the 50 States: Basic Data Profiles with Comparative Tables, [Annual, SRI/MF/complete] C4712–1
Black Americans: A Statistical Sourcebook, 1993 Edition, [Annual, SRI/MF/complete] C6775–2
California Cities, Towns, and Counties, 1993, [Annual, SRI/MF/complete] C4712–3
Florida Municipal Profiles, 1991-92, [Annual, SRI/MF/complete.] C4712–6
Hispanic Americans: A Statistical Sourcebook, 1993 Edition, [Annual, SRI/MF/complete] C6775–3
Massachusetts Municipal Profiles, 1992-93, [Annual, SRI/MF/complete, current & previous year reports] C4712–2
New Jersey Municipal Data Book, 1992-93 Edition, [Annual, SRI/MF/complete] C4712–4
New York State Municipal Profiles, 1993, [Annual, SRI/MF/complete] C4712–7

Institute for Enterprise Advancement
see National Federation of Independent Business, A7815–1

Institute for Social Research
see University of Michigan—Institute for Social Research

Institute of International Education
Open Doors 1991/92: Report on International Educational Exchange, [Annual, SRI/MF/not filmed] R5580–1

Institute of Real Estate Management
Certified Property Manager Profile and Compensation Study, 1989 Revised Edition, [Recurring (irreg.), SRI/MF/complete, delayed] A5600–4
Expense Analysis, 1992: Condominiums, Co-ops, and PUDs, [Annual, SRI/MF/complete, delayed] A5600–3

Income/Expense Analysis, 1992: Conventional Apartments, [Annual, SRI/MF/complete, delayed] A5600–1
Income/Expense Analysis, 1992: Federally-Assisted Apartments, [Annual, SRI/MF/complete, delayed] A5600–5
Income/Expense Analysis, 1992: Office Buildings, [Annual, SRI/MF/complete, delayed] A5600–2
Income/Expense Analysis, 1992: Shopping Centers, [Annual, SRI/MF/complete, delayed] A5600–6

Insurance Information Institute
Fact Book: 1993 Property/Casualty Insurance Facts, [Annual, SRI/MF/complete] A5650–1

International Association of Amusement Parks and Attractions
IAAPA 1992 Amusement Industry Abstract, [Annual, SRI/MF/complete] A5700–1

International Business Communications
IBC/Donoghue Money Fund Directory, 1993 Edition, [Annual, SRI/MF/complete] C4682–2
IBC/Donoghue Mutual Funds Almanac, 24th Edition, 1993, [Annual, SRI/MF/complete] C4682–1

International Business Forms Industries
Perspective 92, [Annual, SRI/MF/complete] A5785–2
1991-92 Ratio Study, [Annual, SRI/MF/complete] A5785–3
1992 Production Employees Cost Survey, [Biennial, SRI/MF/complete] A5785–4

International City/County Management Association
Baseline Data Reports, [Series, SRI/MF/not filmed] A5800–2
Capital Improvement Financing, 1991, [Monograph, SRI/MF/not filmed] A5800–2.112
Financial Aspects of Police Liability, [Monograph, SRI/MF/not filmed] A5800–2.113
Fire Personnel Practices, [Recurring (irreg.), SRI/MF/not filmed] A5800–2.116
Local Emergency Response Plans, [Monograph, SRI/MF/not filmed] A5800–4.34
Local Government Infrastructure Financing, [Monograph, SRI/MF/not filmed] A5800–4.33
Municipal Year Book, 1993, [Annual, SRI/MF/not filmed] A5800–1
Police Salaries, 1992, [Recurring (irreg.), SRI/MF/not filmed] A5800–4.32
Soliciting Foreign Business To Meet Economic Development Goals, [Monograph, SRI/MF/not filmed] A5800–2.115
Special Data Issues, [Series, SRI/MF/not filmed] A5800–4
Use of Council Committees in Local Governments, [Monograph, SRI/MF/not filmed] A5800–2.114

International Food Policy Research Institute
Economic Incentives and Comparative Advantage in Indonesian Food Crop Production, [Monograph, SRI/MF/complete] R5620–1.37
Famine in Ethiopia: Policy Implications of Coping Failure at National and Household Levels, [Monograph, SRI/MF/complete] R5620–1.36

Iowa Department of Human Services

Fertilizer Use on Smallholder Farms in Eastern Province, Zambia, [Monograph, SRI/MF/complete] R5620–1.38
Research Reports, [Series, SRI/MF/complete] R5620–1

International Franchise Association
Franchising in the Economy, 1989-92, [Annual, SRI/MF/complete] A5820–1

International Ice Cream Association
Latest Scoop Worldwide: Facts and Figures on Ice Cream and Related Products, [Annual, SRI/MF/complete] A5825–1

International Ladies Garment Workers Union
Conditions in the Women's Garment Industry, [1-3 issues per year, SRI/MF/complete] A5900–1

International Mass Retail Association
Ernst & Young/IMRA Survey of Retail Loss Prevention Trends, [Annual] A5940–2
Operating Results of Mass Retail Stores and the Mass Retailers' Merchandising Report, [Annual, discontinued] A5940–6

International Trade Association of Commercial Heat Treaters
Analysis of National Billings: Commercial Heat Treaters, [Monthly, SRI/MF/complete, shipped quarterly] A6376–1

Intertec Publishing Corp.
Electrical Wholesaling, [Monthly, SRI/MF/excerpts, shipped quarterly] C4725–5
Grounds Maintenance: 1992 Salary Survey, [Monthly (selected issue), SRI/MF/not filmed] C4725–6
Telephony, [Weekly, SRI/MF/excerpts, shipped quarterly] C4725–3

Investment Company Institute
Mutual Fund Fact Book: Industry Trends and Statistics for 1991, [Annual, SRI/MF/complete] A6025–1
Trends in Mutual Fund Activity, [Monthly, SRI/MF/complete, shipped quarterly] A6025–5
Unit Investment Trust Statistics, [Monthly, SRI/MF/complete] A6025–7

Iowa College Student Aid Commission
Information Digest of Postsecondary Education in Iowa, 1990/91, [Annual, SRI/MF/complete] S2755–1

Iowa Department of Commerce
Annual Report of the Superintendent of Banking of the State of Iowa, for the Year Ending June 30, 1992, [Annual, SRI/MF/complete] S2760–2
1993 Report of the Insurance Division of Iowa, [Annual, SRI/MF/complete, current & previous year reports] S2760–1

Iowa Department of Corrections
Monthly Statistical Movement Summary for Iowa Department of Corrections, [Monthly, SRI/MF/complete, shipped quarterly] S2770–1

Iowa Department of Cultural Affairs
Iowa Public Library Statistics, 1991-92, [Annual, SRI/MF/complete] S2778–1

Iowa Department of Employment Services
Condition of Employment, 1993, Iowa, [Annual, SRI/MF/complete] S2784–3

Iowa Department of Human Services
Monthly Public Assistance Statistical Report, Iowa, [Monthly, SRI/MF/complete, shipped quarterly] S2802–1

Iowa Department of Public Health

Iowa Department of Public Health
Iowa Health Risk Behaviors, 1991 Final Report, [Annual, SRI/MF/complete] S2795–2
Vital Statistics, Iowa 1991, [Annual, SRI/MF/complete] S2795–1

Iowa Department of Revenue and Finance
Comprehensive Annual Financial Report for the Fiscal Year Ended June 30, 1992, Iowa, [Annual, SRI/MF/complete, current & previous year reports] S2860–4
Iowa Retail Sales and Use Tax Report, [Quarterly, with annual supplement, SRI/MF/complete] S2860–1
1991 Iowa Individual Income Tax Annual Statistical Report: 1991 Returns Filed in 1992, [Annual, SRI/MF/complete] S2860–3

Iowa Division of Banking
see Iowa Department of Commerce, S2760–2

Iowa Division of Insurance
see Iowa Department of Commerce, S2760–1

Iowa Judicial Department
1992 Annual Statistical Report: Report to the Supreme Court of Iowa by the State Court Administrator, [Annual, SRI/MF/complete] S2815–1

Iowa Office of the Secretary of State
General Election, Nov. 3, 1992: Official Canvass Summary, Iowa, [Biennial, SRI/MF/complete] S2865–1

Iowa State University: North Central Regional Center for Rural Development
Cooperative Extension Services' Role in Business Incubator Educational Programs, [Monograph, SRI/MF/complete] U2410–3

Iowa Treasurer
Annual Report, 1992, Treasurer of the State of Iowa, [Annual, SRI/MF/complete] S2885–1

Japan Economic Institute
JEI Report, [Weekly, in 2 parts, SRI/MF/excerpts, shipped quarterly] R5650–2

Jewish Publication Society
American Jewish Year Book, 1993, [Annual, SRI/MF/excerpts] A2050–1

Jobson Publishing Corp.
Jobson's Liquor Handbook, 1993, [Annual, SRI/MF/not filmed] C4775–1
Jobson's Wine Handbook, 1993, [Annual, SRI/MF/not filmed] C4775–2

Johns Hopkins University: Population Information Program
Population Reports, [Series, SRI/MF/complete] U2520–1
Reproductive Revolution: New Survey Findings, [Monograph, SRI/MF/complete] U2520–1.51

Joint Center for Political and Economic Studies
Focus, [Monthly, SRI/MF/complete] R5685–4

Journal Publications
Seafood Business, [Bimonthly (selected issues), SRI/MF/excerpts] C4825–3

Kansas Agricultural Statistics
see Kansas Board of Agriculture, S2915–1

Kansas Board of Agriculture
Kansas Farm Facts, 1993, [Annual, SRI/MF/complete] S2915–1

Kansas Bureau of Investigation
see Kansas Office of the Attorney General, S2925–1

Kansas City Board of Trade
see Board of Trade of Kansas City, Missouri

Kansas Department of Administration
Kansas Annual Financial Report for Period July 1, 1991-June 30, 1992, [Annual, SRI/MF/complete] S2900–1

Kansas Department of Corrections
Statistical Profile of the FY92 Offender Population, Kansas Department of Corrections, [Annual, SRI/MF/complete] S2940–1

Kansas Department of Health and Environment
Annual Summary of Vital Statistics, Kansas, 1991, [Annual, SRI/MF/complete] S2975–1

Kansas Department of Insurance
123rd Annual Report of the Kansas Insurance Department, for Year Ending Dec. 31, 1992, [Annual, SRI/MF/complete] S2990–1

Kansas Department of Revenue
Annual Report, Fiscal Year Ending June 30, 1992, State of Kansas Department of Revenue, [Annual, SRI/MF/complete] S3020–1

Kansas Department of Transportation
Kansas Traffic Accident Facts, 1992, [Annual, SRI/MF/complete, current & previous year reports] S3040–1
School Bus Loading and Unloading Survey, Calendar Year 1991, School Year 1991/92, [Annual, SRI/MF/complete, current & previous year reports] S3040–2

Kansas Office of the Attorney General
Crime in Kansas, 1992, [Annual, SRI/MF/complete] S2925–1

Kansas Office of the Secretary of State
Election Statistics, State of Kansas, 1992 Presidential Preference Primary, Primary and General Elections, [Biennial, SRI/MF/complete] S3030–1

Kansas State Board of Education
Annual Statistical Report, Summary 1990/91, Kansas State Board of Education, [Annual, SRI/MF/complete] S2945–1

Kansas Supreme Court
Annual Report of the Courts of Kansas, FY92, [Annual, SRI/MF/complete] S3035–1

KEDI, Inc.
see Kent Economic and Development Institute, Inc.

Kenedy, P. J., and Sons
Official Catholic Directory, 1993 General Summary, [Annual, SRI/MF/excerpts] C4950–1

Kent Economic and Development Institute, Inc.
KEDI Economic Survey, [Monthly, SRI/MF/complete, delayed] B4950–1

Kentucky Agricultural Statistics Service
see Kentucky Department of Agriculture, S3085–1

Kentucky Cabinet for Economic Development
1993 Kentucky Deskbook of Economic Statistics, [Annual, SRI/MF/complete] S3104–1

Index by Issuing Sources

Kentucky Cabinet for Human Resources
Health Behavior Trends, 1988-90: Kentucky Lifestyles, [Annual, SRI/MF/complete] S3140–6
Kentucky Annual Labor Market Planning Information, Program Year 1993, [Annual, SRI/MF/complete] S3140–3
Medicaid Services in Kentucky, [Monthly, with annual supplement, SRI/MF/complete] S3140–5
Public Assistance in Kentucky, [Monthly, with annual supplements, SRI/MF/complete, shipped quarterly] S3140–2
1991 Vital Statistics Report, Kentucky, [Annual, SRI/MF/complete] S3140–1

Kentucky Council on Higher Education
1983-92 Kentucky Institutions of Higher Education Information Digest, [Annual, SRI/MF/complete] S3130–3

Kentucky Department for Administration
see Kentucky Finance and Administration Cabinet, S3120–1

Kentucky Department for Libraries and Archives
Statistical Report of Kentucky Public Libraries, Fiscal Year 1991-92, [Annual, SRI/MF/complete] S3165–1

Kentucky Department of Agriculture
Kentucky Agricultural Statistics, 1992-93, [Annual, SRI/MF/complete] S3085–1

Kentucky Department of Education
Biennial Report, 1989-91, Kentucky Department of Education, [Biennial, SRI/MF/complete] S3110–2
Profiles of Kentucky Public Schools, FY92, [Annual, SRI/MF/complete] S3110–1

Kentucky Department of Financial Institutions
Kentucky Department of Financial Institutions Annual Report, Dec. 31, 1992, [Annual, SRI/MF/complete] S3121–1

Kentucky Department of Justice
Crime in Kentucky, 1992, [Annual, SRI/MF/complete] S3150–1
Kentucky Traffic Accident Facts, 1992 Report, [Annual, SRI/MF/complete] S3150–2

Kentucky Finance and Administration Cabinet
Commonwealth of Kentucky Comprehensive Annual Financial Report, for the Year Ended June 30, 1992, [Annual, SRI/MF/complete] S3120–1

Kentucky Office of the Secretary of State
Official Primary and General Election Returns for 1992, Kentucky, [Annual, SRI/MF/complete, current & previous year reports] S3213–1

Kentucky State Police
see Kentucky Department of Justice, S3150–1, S3150–2

Knight-Ridder Financial Publishing
Knight-Ridder CRB Commodity Year Book Statistical Supplement, [3 per year, SRI/MF/complete] C2400–2
Knight-Ridder CRB Commodity Year Book, 1993, [Annual, SRI/MF/complete] C2400–1

Korn/Ferry International
Board of Directors 19th Annual Study, 1992, [Annual, SRI/MF/complete] B5000–3
National Index of Executive Vacancies, [Quarterly, SRI/MF/complete] B5000–5

Index by Issuing Sources

Kriegte Enterprises
Naval Stores Review, 1992 International Yearbook, [Annual, SRI/MF/not filmed] C6585–1

Kurt Salmon Associates
see Salmon, Kurt, Associates

Lebhar-Friedman
Chain Store Age Executive, [Monthly, SRI/MF/excerpts, shipped quarterly] C5150–4
Discount Store News, [Biweekly, SRI/MF/excerpts] C5150–3
Drug Store News, [Biweekly, SRI/MF/excerpts] C5150–2
National Home Center News, [Biweekly, SRI/MF/excerpts] C5150–6
Nation's Restaurant News, [Weekly, SRI/MF/excerpts, shipped quarterly] C5150–5

Life Insurance Marketing and Research Association
Monthly Survey of Life Insurance Sales in Canada, [Monthly, SRI/MF/complete, shipped quarterly] A6225–2
Monthly Survey of Life Insurance Sales in the U.S., [Monthly, SRI/MF/complete, shipped quarterly] A6225–1

Lilly, Eli, and Co.
Lilly Digest, 1992, [Annual, SRI/MF/complete] B5165–1
Lilly Hospital Pharmacy Survey, 1992, [Annual, SRI/MF/complete] B5165–3

Lomas Mortgage USA
U.S. Housing Markets, [Quarterly, SRI/MF/not filmed] B5190–1

Louisiana Agricultural Statistics Service
see Louisiana State University: Department of Agricultural Economics and Agribusiness, U2740–1

Louisiana Department of Commerce
Reports of the State Banks, Savings Banks, Savings and Loan Associations, Credit Unions, Consumer Credit, and Sale of Checks in the State of Louisiana, 1992, [Annual, SRI/MF/complete] S3265–1

Louisiana Department of Culture, Recreation, and Tourism
Public Libraries in Louisiana, Statistical Report, 1992, [Annual, SRI/MF/complete] S3275–1

Louisiana Department of Education
Louisiana Department of Education 143rd Annual Financial and Statistical Report, 1991/92, [Annual, SRI/MF/complete] S3280–1

Louisiana Department of Health and Hospitals
1989-90 Vital Statistics of Louisiana, [Annual, SRI/MF/complete, current & previous year reports] S3295–1

Louisiana Department of Labor
Louisiana Annual Planning Report, [Annual, SRI/MF/complete] S3320–1
Louisiana Labor Market Information, [Monthly, SRI/MF/complete, shipped quarterly] S3320–2

Louisiana Department of Public Safety and Corrections
1991 Louisiana Traffic Records Data Report, [Annual, SRI/MF/complete] S3345–2

Louisiana Division of Administration
see Louisiana Office of the Governor, S3285–2

Louisiana Office of the Governor
State of Louisiana Comprehensive Annual Financial Report, for the Year Ended June 30, 1992, [Annual, SRI/MF/complete] S3285–2

Louisiana Office of the Secretary of State
State of Louisiana General Election Returns, Nov. 3, 1992, [Quadrennial, SRI/MF/complete] S3370–3

Louisiana State University: Center for Energy Studies
Louisiana Energy Indicators, [Quarterly, suspended] U2730–1

Louisiana State University: Department of Agricultural Economics and Agribusiness
Agricultural Statistics and Prices for Louisiana, 1985-91, [Annual, SRI/MF/complete] U2740–1

Louisiana Supreme Court
1992 Annual Report of the Judicial Council, Supreme Court of Louisiana, [Annual, SRI/MF/complete] S3375–1

LRP Publications
Current Award Trends in Personal Injury, 1993 Edition, [Annual, SRI/MF/complete, delayed] C5180–1

Maclean Hunter Media, Inc.
Progressive Grocer, [Monthly, SRI/MF/not filmed] C5225–1

Maclean Hunter Publishing Co.
Coal, [Monthly, SRI/MF/not filmed] C5226–1
E&MJ, [Monthly, SRI/MF/not filmed] C5226–2
Textile World, [Monthly, SRI/MF/not filmed] C5226–3

Maine Administrative Office of the Courts
see Maine Judicial Branch, S3463–1

Maine Department of Administrative and Financial Services
State of Maine Financial Report for Period July 1, 1991-June 30, 1992, [Annual, SRI/MF/complete] S3420–1

Maine Department of Business Occupational and Professional Regulation
see Maine Department of Professional and Financial Regulation

Maine Department of Economic and Community Development
Maine: A Statistical Summary, [Recurring (irreg.), SRI/MF/complete] S3434–1

Maine Department of Education
1991 Maine Educational Facts, [Annual, SRI/MF/complete] S3435–1

Maine Department of Human Services
Maine Vital Statistics, 1991, [Annual, SRI/MF/complete] S3460–2

Maine Department of Labor
Maine Labor Market Digest, [Monthly, SRI/MF/complete, shipped quarterly] S3465–2
Maine Occupational Staffing, [Series, SRI/MF/complete] S3465–1
Maine Occupational Staffing for Educational Services Industry, Apr. 1991, [Triennial, SRI/MF/complete] S3465–1.26
Maine Occupational Staffing for Federal Government (Mar. 1992), State Government (May 1991), Local Government (May 1991), [Triennial, SRI/MF/complete] S3465–1.27
Maine Occupational Staffing for Wholesale Trade, Retail Trade, Transportation, Communications, Electric, Gas, and Sanitary Services, Second Quarter 1991, [Triennial, SRI/MF/complete] S3465–1.25

Maryland Department of Education

1990 Census: Summary Population and Housing Characteristics, Maine, [Monograph, SRI/MF/complete] S3465–7
1990 Census: Summary Social, Economic, and Housing Characteristics, Maine, [Monograph, SRI/MF/complete] S3465–9
1990 Census, Volume I Profiles, Maine: Selected Population and Housing Characteristics from Summary Tape File 1, [Series, SRI/MF/complete] S3465–8

Maine Department of Professional and Financial Regulation
Economic Area Survey, Dec. 31, 1992, Maine, [Annual, SRI/MF/complete] S3473–1
Status of Maine's Financial Institutions, [Annual, SRI/MF/complete, current & previous year reports] S3473–2

Maine Department of Public Safety
Crime in Maine, 1991, [Annual, SRI/MF/complete] S3475–1
Maine Department of Public Safety 1992 Statewide Accident Data, [Annual, SRI/MF/complete] S3475–2

Maine Department of the Secretary of State
State of Maine General Election Tabulation, Nov. 3, 1992, [Biennial series, SRI/MF/complete] S3490–1

Maine Judicial Branch
Annual Report, FY92, State of Maine Judicial Branch, [Annual, SRI/MF/complete] S3463–1

Manpower, Inc.
Manpower, Inc. Employment Outlook Survey, [Quarterly, SRI/MF/complete] B5275–1

Manufactured Housing Institute
Manufacturing Report, [Monthly, SRI/MF/complete, shipped quarterly] A6325–1

Maryland Administrative Board of Election Laws
State of Maryland Nov. 3, 1992 General Election Returns, [Biennial, SRI/MF/complete] S3615–1

Maryland Administrative Office of the Courts
Annual Report of the Maryland Judiciary, 1991-92, [Annual, SRI/MF/complete] S3600–1

Maryland Comptroller of the Treasury
State of Maryland Comprehensive Annual Financial Report for the Year Ended June 30, 1992, [Annual, SRI/MF/complete] S3685–2
Summary Report 1991, Maryland Income Tax Division, [Annual, SRI/MF/complete] S3685–1

Maryland Department of Economic and Employment Development
Maryland Monthly Labor Review, [Monthly, SRI/MF/complete, shipped quarterly] S3605–2
1993-94 Maryland Statistical Abstract, [Biennial, SRI/MF/complete] S3605–1

Maryland Department of Education
Analysis of Professional Salaries: Maryland Public Schools, Oct. 1991, [Annual, SRI/MF/complete] S3610–2.2
Analysis of Professional Salaries: Maryland Public Schools, Oct. 1992, [Annual, SRI/MF/complete] S3610–2.11
Fact Book, 1992/93: A Statistical Handbook, [Annual, SRI/MF/complete] S3610–1

Maryland Department of Education

Grade Organization: Enrollment by Race/Ethnicity and Professional Staff at School Level, Sept. 30, 1992, Maryland, [Annual, SRI/MF/complete] S3610–2.8

Maryland Public Library Statistics, FY92, [Annual, SRI/MF/complete] S3610–5

Maryland Public School Enrollment by Sex and Race/Ethnicity, Sept. 30, 1992, [Annual, SRI/MF/complete] S3610–2.4

Maryland Public Schools, [Series, SRI/MF/complete] S3610–2

Number of Maryland Public Schools by Organization and Enrollment, Sept. 30, 1992, [Annual, SRI/MF/complete] S3610–2.5

Professional Salary Schedules, Maryland Public Schools, 1992/93, [Annual, SRI/MF/complete] S3610–2.1

Professional Staff by Assignment, Race/Ethnicity and Gender, Maryland Public Schools, Oct. 1992, [Annual, SRI/MF/complete, current & previous year reports] S3610–2.12

Selected Financial Data, Maryland Public Schools, 1991/92: Part 1, Revenue, Wealth, and Effort, [Annual, SRI/MF/complete] S3610–2.9

Selected Financial Data, Maryland Public Schools, 1991/92: Part 2, Expenditures, [Annual, SRI/MF/complete] S3610–2.7

Selected Financial Data, Maryland Public Schools, 1991/92: Part 3, Analysis of Costs, [Annual, SRI/MF/complete] S3610–2.6

Selected Financial Data, Maryland Public Schools, 1991/92: Part 4, Ten Year Summary, [Annual, SRI/MF/complete] S3610–2.13

Staff Employed at School and Central Office Levels, Maryland Public Schools, 1992/93, [Annual, SRI/MF/complete] S3610–2.10

Summary of Attendance, Maryland Public Schools, 1991/92, [Annual, SRI/MF/complete] S3610–2.3

Maryland Department of Employment and Training

see Maryland Department of Economic and Employment Development

Maryland Department of Fiscal Services

Local Government Finances in Maryland for the Fiscal Year Ended June 30, 1992, [Annual, SRI/MF/complete] S3618–1

Maryland Department of Health and Mental Hygiene

Annual Vital Statistics Report, Maryland, 1989, [Annual, SRI/MF/complete, current & previous year reports] S3635–1

Maryland Medical Care Programs: The Year in Review, FY92, [Annual, SRI/MF/complete] S3635–3

Maryland Department of Human Resources

Income Maintenance Administration Monthly Statistical Report, Maryland, [Monthly, with annual supplement, SRI/MF/complete, shipped quarterly] S3645–2

Maryland Department of Licensing and Regulation

121st Annual Report of the Insurance Commissioner of the State of Maryland, [Annual, SRI/MF/complete] S3655–1

82nd Annual Report of the Bank Commissioner of the State of Maryland, June 30, 1992, [Annual, SRI/MF/complete] S3655–2

Maryland Department of Public Safety and Correctional Services

Maryland Automated Accident Reporting System: National Safety Council Report, Statewide, 1992, [Annual, SRI/MF/complete] S3665–4

1992 State of Maryland Uniform Crime Reports, [Annual, SRI/MF/complete] S3665–1

Massachusetts Board of Library Commissioners

Massachusetts Public Library Data, 1992, [Annual, SRI/MF/complete] S3870–1

Massachusetts Department of Correction

Statistical Description of Residents of Massachusetts Correctional Institutions on Jan. 1, 1992, [Annual, SRI/MF/complete] S3805–1

Massachusetts Department of Education

Individual School Report, Oct. 1, 1992, Massachusetts, [Annual, SRI/MF/complete] S3810–4

Information About Public Education in Massachusetts, [Annual, SRI/MF/complete] S3810–3

1991-92 Per Pupil Expenditures by Program, Massachusetts, [Annual, SRI/MF/complete, current & previous year reports] S3810–5

Massachusetts Department of Employment and Training

see Massachusetts Executive Office of Economic Affairs, S3808–1

Massachusetts Department of Public Health

Annual Report, Vital Statistics of Massachusetts, 1990, [Annual, SRI/MF/complete] S3850–1

Behavioral Risk Factors and Preventive Health Measures, Massachusetts, 1986-90, [Recurring (irreg.), SRI/MF/complete] S3850–3

Massachusetts Department of Revenue

Annual Report, FY91, Massachusetts Department of Revenue, [Annual, SRI/MF/complete] S3917–1

Massachusetts Executive Office for Administration and Finance

Commonwealth of Massachusetts Comprehensive Annual Financial Report for the Fiscal Year Ended June 30, 1992, [Annual, SRI/MF/completc] S3777–1

Massachusetts Executive Office of Economic Affairs

Massachusetts Employment Review, [Monthly, SRI/MF/complete, shipped quarterly] S3808–1

Occupational Profiles: Massachusetts, [Triennial, discontinued] S3808–2

Massachusetts Office of the Chief Administrative Justice of the Trial Court

Massachusetts Trial Court Interim Annual Report, 1992, [Annual, SRI/MF/complete] S3807–1

Massachusetts Office of the Secretary of State

Massachusetts Election Statistics, 1992, [Biennial, SRI/MF/complete] S3920–1

Mathematical Association of America

1992 Annual AMS-MAA Survey, [Annual, SRI/MF/complete] A2085–1

McDonnell Douglas Corp.

Outlook for Commercial Aircraft, 1992-2011, [Annual, SRI/MF/complete] B3075–1

Index by Issuing Sources

McGraw-Hill

Architectural Record, [Monthly, SRI/MF/not filmed] C5800–15

Aviation Week and Space Technology, [Weekly, SRI/MF/not filmed] C5800–4

Business Week, [Weekly, SRI/MF/not filmed] C5800–7

Chemical Engineering, [Monthly, SRI/MF/not filmed] C5800–8

Dodge/Sweet's Construction Outlook '93, [Annual, SRI/MF/complete] C5800–26

Electrical World, [Monthly, SRI/MF/not filmed] C5800–28

ENR, [Weekly, SRI/MF/not filmed] C5800–2

Modern Plastics, [Monthly, SRI/MF/not filmed] C5800–12

Weekly of Business Aviation, [Weekly, SRI/MF/excerpts, shipped quarterly] C5800–30

1993 Dodge/Sweet's Construction Outlook, Updates, [2 per year, SRI/MF/complete] C5800–29

Medical Group Management Association

Academic Practice Faculty Compensation and Production Survey: 1992 Report Based on 1991 Data, [Annual, SRI/MF/complete] A6365–5

Cost Survey: 1992 Report Based on 1991 Data, [Annual, SRI/MF/complete] A6365–2

Membership Compensation Survey: 1992 Report Based on 1992 Data, [Annual, SRI/MF/complete] A6365–3

Physician Compensation and Production Survey: 1992 Report Based on 1991 Data, [Annual, SRI/MF/complete] A6365–1

Merrill Lynch Business Brokerage and Valuation

Mergerstat Review, 1992, [Annual, SRI/MF/complete, delayed] B6020–1

Metal Treating Institute

Analysis of National Billings: Commercial Heat Treaters, [Monthly, SRI/MF/complete, shipped quarterly] A6376–1

Metropolitan Life Insurance Co.

Metropolitan Life Survey of the American Teacher, 1992, the Second Year. New Teachers' Expectations and Ideals: A Survey of New Teachers Who Completed Their Second Year of Teaching in Public Schools in 1992, [Annual, SRI/MF/complete] B6045–2

Metropolitan Life Survey of the American Teacher, 1993: Teachers Respond to President Clinton's Education Proposals, [Annual, SRI/MF/complete] B6045–7

Statistical Bulletin, Metropolitan Life Insurance Co., [Quarterly, SRI/MF/complete, delayed] B6045–1

Michigan Agricultural Statistics Service

see Michigan Department of Agriculture, S3950–1

Michigan Board of Education

Michigan K-12 School Districts Ranked by Selected Financial Data, 1991/92, [Annual, SRI/MF/complete] S3965–3

Michigan Court Administrative Office

Michigan State Courts Annual Report, 1992, [Annual, SRI/MF/complete, current & previous year reports] S3962–1

Index by Issuing Sources

Michigan Department of Agriculture
Michigan Agricultural Statistics, 1992, [Annual, SRI/MF/complete] S3950–1

Michigan Department of Commerce
Michigan Financial Institutions Bureau 1992 Annual Report, [Annual, SRI/MF/complete] S3957–1

Michigan Department of Corrections
Michigan Department of Corrections 1991 Statistical Report, [Annual, SRI/MF/complete] S3960–1

Michigan Department of Education
see Michigan Board of Education, S3965–3

Michigan Department of Labor
Annual Planning Information Report, Program Year 1993, Michigan, [Annual, SRI/MF/complete] S3980–1
Michigan's Labor Market News, [Monthly, SRI/MF/complete, shipped quarterly] S3980–2

Michigan Department of Licensing and Regulation
Michigan Insurance Bureau Annual Statistical Report for the Year Ending Dec. 31, 1991, [Annual, SRI/MF/complete] S3983–1

Michigan Department of Management and Budget
Comprehensive Annual Financial Report of the State of Michigan, Fiscal Year Ended Sept. 30, 1992, [Annual, SRI/MF/complete] S3985–2

Michigan Department of Public Health
Health Risk Behaviors, 1991, Michigan, [Annual, SRI/MF/complete] S4000–4
Michigan Health Statistics, 1990, [Annual, SRI/MF/complete] S4000–3

Michigan Department of Social Services
Assistance Payments Statistics, Michigan, [Monthly, SRI/MF/complete] S4010–1

Michigan Department of State Police
Michigan Traffic Crash Facts, 1991, [Annual, SRI/MF/complete] S3997–2
1992 Uniform Crime Report for the State of Michigan, [Annual, SRI/MF/complete] S3997–1

Michigan Employment Security Commission
see Michigan Department of Labor, S3980–1, S3980–2

Michigan Secretary of State
State of Michigan General Election, Nov. 3, 1992, [Biennial, SRI/MF/complete] S4020–1

Michigan State University: Career Development and Placement Services
Recruiting Trends, 1992-93: A Study of Businesses, Industries, and Governmental Agencies Employing New College Graduates, [Annual, SRI/MF/complete] U3130–1

Mid-Continent Oil and Gas Association
1991 Joint Association Survey on Drilling Costs, [Annual, SRI/MF/complete] A2575–9

Miller Freeman Publications
see Freeman, Miller, Publications

Milliman & Robertson, Inc.
Group Comprehensive Major Medical Net Claim Cost Relationships by Area, [Monograph, SRI/MF/not filmed] B6095–1
Group Health Insurance Costs Most in Los Angeles: 73 Percent Higher Than National Average, [Monograph, SRI/MF/not filmed] B6095–2

Missouri Department of Consumer Affairs, Regulation and Licensing

Minneapolis Grain Exchange
110th Statistical Annual, Year Ending Dec. 31, 1992, Minneapolis Grain Exchange, [Annual, SRI/MF/complete] B6110–1

Minnesota Agricultural Statistics Service
see Minnesota Department of Agriculture, S4130–1

Minnesota Department of Agriculture
Minnesota Agriculture Statistics, 1993, [Annual, SRI/MF/complete] S4130–1

Minnesota Department of Commerce
Minnesota Department of Commerce Annual Insurance Supplement, 1991, [Annual, SRI/MF/complete] S4140–4
State of Minnesota, Division of Financial Examinations, 1992 Annual Report, [Annual, SRI/MF/complete, current & previous year reports] S4140–3

Minnesota Department of Education
Minnesota Libraries: Minnesota Public Library Statistics, 1991, [Quarterly (selected issue), SRI/MF/complete] S4165–2
School District Profiles, 1991/92, Minnesota, [Annual, SRI/MF/complete] S4165–1

Minnesota Department of Finance
State of Minnesota Comprehensive Annual Financial Report, for the Year Ended June 30, 1992, [Annual, SRI/MF/complete] S4180–1

Minnesota Department of Health
Minnesota Health Statistics, 1991, [Annual, SRI/MF/complete, current & previous year reports] S4190–2

Minnesota Department of Human Services
Summary of Minnesota Public Assistance Trends, CY92, [Semiannual, SRI/MF/complete, current & 2 previous semiannual reports] S4202–1

Minnesota Department of Jobs and Training
Minnesota Labor Market Review, [Monthly, SRI/MF/complete, shipped quarterly] S4205–1
Minnesota Labor Market Trends, [Quarterly, SRI/MF/complete] S4205–3

Minnesota Department of Public Safety
Minnesota Motor Vehicle Crash Facts, 1992, [Annual, SRI/MF/complete] S4230–2

Minnesota Department of Public Service
Minnesota Department of Public Service Biennial Report, [Biennial, discontinued] S4235–1

Minnesota Department of Revenue
Minnesota State Individual income Tax, [Annual, discontinued] S4250–1

Minnesota Higher Education Coordinating Board
Report to the Governor and 1993 Legislature, Minnesota Higher Education Coordinating Board, [Biennial, SRI/MF/complete] S4195–2

Minnesota Office of the Secretary of State
Minnesota Election Results, 1992: Presidential Primary Election, State Primary Election, and State General Election, [Biennial, SRI/MF/complete] S4255–1

Mississippi Auditor of Public Accounts
see Mississippi Department of Finance and Administration, S4346–1

Mississippi Board of Trustees of State Institutions of Higher Learning
Statistical Report of Information Regarding the Enrollment, Student Credit Hours, Degrees Conferred, and Finances of the State-Supported Universities in Mississippi for the Summer of 1991 and the Regular 1991/92 Session, [Annual, SRI/MF/complete] S4360–1

Mississippi Department of Banking and Consumer Finance
Annual Report of the Department of Banking and Consumer Finance, State of Mississippi, Jan. 1, 1992-Dec. 31, 1992, [Annual, SRI/MF/complete] S4325–1

Mississippi Department of Education
Annual Report of the State Superintendent of Public Education to the Legislature of Mississippi, 1993: Statistical Reports 1991/92, [Annual, SRI/MF/complete] S4340–1

Mississippi Department of Finance and Administration
Mississippi Comprehensive Annual Financial Report, 1992, [Annual, SRI/MF/complete] S4346–1

Mississippi Department of Health
Vital Statistics, Mississippi, 1992, [Annual, SRI/MF/complete, current & previous year reports] S4350–1

Mississippi Department of Human Services
Annual Report, FY92, Mississippi Department of Human Services, [Annual, SRI/MF/complete] S4357–1

Mississippi Employment Security Commission
Annual Planning Information, State of Mississippi, PY93, [Annual, SRI/MF/complete] S4345–1

Mississippi State University: College of Business and Industry
Mississippi Statistical Abstract, 1992, [Annual, SRI/MF/complete] U3255–4

Mississippi Tax Commission
Mississippi State Tax Commission Annual Report, FYE June 30, 1992, [Annual, SRI/MF/complete] S4435–1

Missouri Agricultural Statistics Service
see Missouri Department of Agriculture, S4480–1

Missouri Coordinating Board for Higher Education
Annual Report Missouri Coordinating Board for Higher Education, [Annual, discontinued coverage] S4520–1
Directory of Missouri Libraries: Public, Special, College and University, Statistics for FY92, [Annual, SRI/MF/complete] S4520–2
Statistical Summary of Missouri Higher Education, 1992/93, with State Profile of ACT-Tested Students Graduating from High School, Spring 1992, [Annual, SRI/MF/complete, current & previous year reports] S4520–3

Missouri Department of Agriculture
Missouri Farm Facts, 1993, [Annual, SRI/MF/complete, current & previous year reports] S4480–1

Missouri Department of Consumer Affairs, Regulation and Licensing
see Missouri Department of Economic Development

Missouri Department of Corrections

Missouri Department of Corrections
Missouri Department of Corrections Institutional Admission and Release Report for FY93, [Annual, SRI/MF/complete] S4501–1

Missouri Department of Economic Development
23rd Biennial Report of the Division of Finance of the Department of Economic Development, State of Missouri, [Biennial, SRI/MF/complete] S4502–1

Missouri Department of Elementary and Secondary Education
143rd Report of the Public Schools of Missouri for the School Year Ending June 30, 1992, [Annual, SRI/MF/complete] S4505–1

Missouri Department of Health
Missouri Vital Statistics, 1992, [Annual, SRI/MF/complete, current & previous year reports] S4518–1

Missouri Department of Insurance
Annual Report and Statistical Data, Compiled for the Year Ending Dec. 31, 1992, Missouri, [Annual, SRI/MF/complete] S4527–1

Missouri Department of Labor and Industrial Relations
Annual Report, 1992, Missouri Department of Labor and Industrial Relations, [Annual, SRI/MF/complete] S4530–2
Missouri Area Labor Trends, [Monthly, SRI/MF/complete, shipped quarterly] S4530–3

Missouri Department of Public Safety
Missouri Traffic Crashes, 1993 Edition, [Annual, SRI/MF/complete] S4560–1
1991 Missouri Crime and Arrest Digest, [Annual, SRI/MF/complete] S4560–2

Missouri Department of Revenue
Component Unit Financial Report of the Missouri Department of Revenue, Fiscal Year Ended June 30, 1992, [Annual, SRI/MF/complete] S4570–1

Missouri Department of Social Services
FY92 Annual Report Statistical Information, Missouri Division of Family Services, [Annual, SRI/MF/complete] S4575–2

Missouri Insurance Division
see Missouri Department of Insurance

Missouri Office of Administration
State of Missouri Comprehensive Annual Financial Report, Fiscal Year Ended June 30, 1992, [Annual, SRI/MF/complete] S4475–1

Missouri Office of the Secretary of State
Missouri Roster, 1993-94: A Directory of State, District, and County Officials, [Biennial, SRI/MF/complete] S4580–1

Missouri Office of the State Treasurer
see Missouri Department of Revenue, S4570–1

Missouri State Board of Education
143rd Report of the Public Schools of Missouri for the School Year Ending June 30, 1992, [Annual, SRI/MF/complete] S4505–1

Missouri State Library
see Missouri Coordinating Board for Higher Education, S4520–2

MLR Enterprises
see IDD, Inc.

Montana Agricultural Statistics Service
see Montana Department of Agriculture, S4655–1

Montana Board of Crime Control
see Montana Department of Justice, S4705–1

Montana Department of Administration
Montana Comprehensive Annual Financial Report for the Fiscal Year Ended June 30, 1992, [Annual, SRI/MF/complete] S4653–1

Montana Department of Agriculture
Montana Agricultural Statistics, 1992, [Annual, SRI/MF/complete] S4655–1

Montana Department of Health and Environmental Sciences
Montana Health Data Book and Medical Facilities Inventory, 1992, [Annual, SRI/MF/complete] S4690–2
Montana Vital Statistics, 1990-91, [Annual, SRI/MF/complete] S4690–1

Montana Department of Justice
Crime in Montana, 1992 Annual Report, [Annual, SRI/MF/complete] S4705–1
Montana Annual Traffic Statistical Report, 1992, [Annual, SRI/MF/complete] S4705–2

Montana Department of Labor and Industry
Montana Annual Planning Information, 1993-94, [Annual, SRI/MF/complete] S4710–3
Montana Employment and Labor Force Trends, [Quarterly, SRI/MF/complete] S4710–1

Montana Department of Revenue
Biennial Report of the Montana Department of Revenue for the Period July 1, 1990 to June 30, 1992, [Biennial, SRI/MF/complete] S4750–1

Montana Department of Social and Rehabilitation Services
Statistical Report, Montana, [Monthly, with fiscal year summary, SRI/MF/complete, shipped quarterly] S4755–1

Montana Highway Patrol
see Montana Department of Justice, S4705–2

Montana Library Commission
Montana Public Library Statistics for July 1991-June 1992, [Annual, SRI/MF/complete] S4725–1

Montana Office of Public Instruction
Montana Public School Enrollment Data, School Year 1992/93, [Annual, SRI/MF/complete] S4740–1

Montana Office of the Secretary of State
Official 1992 General Election Canvass, Montana, [Biennial, SRI/MF/complete] S4760–1

Montana State Library
see Montana Library Commission, S4725–1

Morgan Guaranty Trust Co. of New York
World Financial Markets, [Bimonthly, SRI/MF/complete] B6200–2

Morris, Robert, Associates
Journal of Commercial Lending, [Monthly, SRI/MF/not filmed] A6400–2
Research Report: Insured Commercial Bank Noncurrent Loan and Loss Statistics for 1992, [Semiannual, SRI/MF/not filmed] A6400–4
RMA Annual Statement Studies, 1992, [Annual, SRI/MF/not filmed] A6400–3

Mortgage Bankers Association of America
Financial Statements and Operating Ratios for the Mortgage Banking Industry, 1989, [Annual, SRI/MF/complete] A6450–3
Mortgage Banking, [Monthly, SRI/MF/excerpts, shipped quarterly] A6450–2
National Delinquency Survey, [Quarterly, SRI/MF/complete] A6450–1

Mortgage Insurance Companies of America
1992-93 Factbook and Membership Directory, Mortgage Insurance Companies of America, [Annual, SRI/MF/not filmed] A6455–1

Motor Vehicle Manufacturers Association of the U.S.
see American Automobile Manufacturers Association

Motorcycle Industry Council
1992 Motorcycle Statistical Annual, [Annual, SRI/MF/complete] A6485–1

Motorcycle Safety Foundation
Cycle Safety Info: Motorcycle Accident Statistics, 1991, [Annual, SRI/MF/complete] A6490–2
Cycle Safety Info: State Motorcycle Operator Licensing, 1993, [Annual, SRI/MF/complete] A6490–1

NALEO Educational Fund
1992 National Roster of Hispanic Elected Officials, [Annual, SRI/MF/not filmed] A6844–1

National Academy of Sciences—National Research Council
Summary Report, 1991: Doctorate Recipients from U.S. Universities, [Annual, SRI/MF/complete] R6000–7

National Apartment Association
1993 Survey of Income and Expenses in Rental Apartment Communities, [Annual, SRI/MF/complete] A6497–1

National Association for Health Care Recruitment
National Association for Health Care Recruitment Recruitment Survey, [Annual, SRI/MF/complete] A6500–1

National Association for Law Placement
Class of 1992 Employment Report and Salary Survey, [Annual, SRI/MF/complete] A6505–1

National Association of Broadcasters
1991 Television Employee Compensation and Fringe Benefits Report, [Biennial, SRI/MF/complete] A6635–9

National Association of Business Economists
NABE Industry Survey, [Quarterly, SRI/MF/complete, delayed] A6650–4
NABE Outlook, [Quarterly, SRI/MF/complete, delayed] A6650–5
NABE Policy Survey, [Semiannual, SRI/MF/complete, delayed] A6650–6

National Association of College Admission Counselors
Admission Trends Survey, [Annual, SRI/MF/complete, current & previous year reports] A6695–1

National Association of College and University Business Officers
Comparative Financial Statistics for Public Two-Year Colleges: FY92 National Sample, [Annual, SRI/MF/complete] A6705–1
1992 NACUBO Endowment Study, [Annual, SRI/MF/complete] A6705–2

Index by Issuing Sources

National Cotton Council of America

National Association of Convenience Stores
1993 Convenience Store Industry Fact Book, [Annual, SRI/MF/complete] A6735–2
1993 State of the Industry: Convenience Store Industry Totals, Trends, and Averages, [Annual, SRI/MF/complete] A6735–1

National Association of Fleet Administrators
NAFA Fleet Executive: The Magazine for Vehicle Management, [Monthly, SRI/MF/excerpts, shipped quarterly] A6755–1

National Association of Home Builders
Builder, [Monthly, SRI/MF/not filmed] C4300–1

National Association of Housing and Redevelopment Officials
Local Housing Authorities in the 1990s, [Monograph, SRI/MF/complete] A6800–2
Many Faces of Public Housing, [Monograph, SRI/MF/complete] A6800–1

National Association of Independent Schools
NAIS Statistics: Financial Aid, Financial Operations, Enrollment, Staffing, [Annual, discontinued] A6835–2
NAIS Statistics: Tuitions, Teacher and Administrator Salaries, [Annual, discontinued] A6835–1
NAIS Statistics, 1992, [Annual, SRI/MF/not filmed] A6835–3

National Association of Latino Elected and Appointed Officials Educational Fund
1992 National Roster of Hispanic Elected Officials, [Annual, SRI/MF/not filmed] A6844–1

National Association of Music Merchants
Music USA 1993: Statistical Review of the U.S. Music Products Industry, [Annual, SRI/MF/not filmed] A6848–1

National Association of Nurse Recruiters
National Association for Health Care Recruitment Recruitment Survey, [Annual, SRI/MF/complete] A6500–1

National Association of Purchasing Management
Report on Business, [Monthly, SRI/MF/complete, shipped quarterly] A6910–1

National Association of Realtors
Home Sales, [Monthly, final issues, SRI/MF/complete, shipped quarterly] A7000–2
Real Estate Outlook, [Monthly, SRI/MF/complete, shipped quarterly] A7000–1

National Association of Regulatory Utility Commissioners
Annual Report on Utility and Carrier Regulation, [Annual, discontinued] A7015–1
Profiles of Regulatory Agencies of the U.S. and Canada, Yearbook 1991-92, [Annual, SRI/MF/complete, delayed] A7015–2
Transportation Regulatory Policy in the U.S. and Canada, Annual Compilation 1991-92, [Annual, SRI/MF/complete, delayed] A7015–4
Utility Regulatory Policy in the U.S. and Canada, Compilation 1991-92, [Annual, SRI/MF/complete, delayed] A7015–3

National Association of Secondary School Principals
Salaries Paid Principals and Assistant Principals, 1992/93 School Year, [Annual, SRI/MF/complete] A7085–2

National Association of Securities Dealers
1993 NASDAQ Fact Book and Company Directory, [Annual, SRI/MF/complete] A7105–1

National Association of State Alcohol and Drug Abuse Directors
State Resources and Services Related to Alcohol and Other Drug Abuse Problems, FY91, [Annual, SRI/MF/complete] A7112–1

National Association of State Budget Officers
Fiscal Survey of States, [Semiannual, SRI/MF/complete, current & previous semiannual reports] A7955–1
State Expenditure Report, 1992, [Annual, SRI/MF/complete] A7118–1

National Association of State Information Resource Executives
State Information Resource Management Organizational Structures: 1992 NASIRE Biennial Report, [Biennial, SRI/MF/complete] A7121–1

National Association of State Information Systems
see National Association of State Information Resource Executives

National Association of State Racing Commissioners
see Association of Racing Commissioners International

National Association of State Scholarship and Grant Programs
NASSGP 24th Annual Survey Report, 1992/93 Academic Year, [Annual, SRI/MF/complete] A7140–1

National Association of State Universities and Land-Grant Colleges
Estimates of Fall 1992 Enrollment at Public, Four-Year Institutions, [Annual, SRI/MF/complete] A7150–5
Student Charges at Public Institutions: Annual Survey, 1991/92, [Annual, SRI/MF/complete] A7150–4

National Association of Wheat Growers
Wheat Grower: Wheat Facts 1992, [Annual, SRI/MF/complete] A7310–1

National Automobile Dealers Association
NADA Data 1993: Economic Impact of America's New Car and Truck Dealers, [Annual, SRI/MF/complete] A7350–1

National Business Incubation Association
State of the Business Incubation Industry, 1991, [Annual, SRI/MF/complete] A7360–1

National Catholic Educational Association
Dollars and Sense: Catholic High Schools and Their Finances, 1992, [Biennial, SRI/MF/complete] A7375–5
People's Poll on Schools and School Choice: A New Gallup Survey, [Monograph, SRI/MF/complete] A7375–8
U.S. Catholic Elementary and Secondary Schools, 1992/93: Annual Statistical Report on Schools, Enrollment and Staffing, [Annual, SRI/MF/complete] A7375–1

National Center for Education Information
Who Wants To Teach?, [Monograph, SRI/MF/complete] R6350–7

National Center for State Courts
Divorce Courts: Case Management, Case Characteristics, and the Pace of Litigation in 16 Urban Jurisdictions, [Monograph, SRI/MF/not filmed] R6600–6
Small Claims and Traffic Courts: Case Management Procedures, Case Characteristics, and Outcomes in 12 Urban Jurisdictions, [Monograph, SRI/MF/not filmed] R6600–5
State Court Caseload Statistics: Annual Report 1991, [Annual, SRI/MF/complete] R6600–1
Survey of Judicial Salaries, [Semiannual, SRI/MF/not filmed] R6600–2

National Coal Association
International Coal Review, [Monthly, with annual edition, SRI/MF/not filmed] A7400–3
International Coal, 1992 Edition, [Annual, SRI/MF/not filmed] A7400–2
Power Plant Deliveries, [Monthly, SRI/MF/not filmed] A7400–9
Steam Electric Market Analysis, [Monthly, SRI/MF/not filmed] A7400–8
Steam Electric Plant Factors, 1992, [Annual, SRI/MF/not filmed] A7400–7

National Coalition of United Arts Funds
United Arts Fundraising 1992, [Annual, SRI/MF/complete] A1315–2

National Collegiate Athletic Association
Final Report of the NCAA Gender-Equity Task Force, [Monograph, SRI/MF/complete] A7440–6
1993 NCAA Division I Graduation-Rates Summary, [Annual, SRI/MF/complete] A7440–4

National Committee for Prevention of Child Abuse
Current Trends in Child Abuse Reporting and Fatalities: The Results of the 1992 Annual Fifty State Survey, [Annual, SRI/MF/complete] A7456–1

National Conference of Bar Examiners
1992 Bar Examination Statistics, [Annual, SRI/MF/complete] A7458–1

National Conference of State Legislatures
Legislative Finance Papers, [Series, SRI/MF/complete] A7470–4
State Budget Actions, 1992, [Annual, SRI/MF/complete] A7470–4.10
State Fiscal Outlook for 1993, [Annual, SRI/MF/complete] A7470–4.11
State Fiscal Update: Feb. 1993, [Monograph, SRI/MF/complete] A7470–4.12
State Fiscal Update: Mar. 1993., [Monograph, SRI/MF/complete] A7470–4.14
State Programs to Assist Distressed Local Governments, [Monograph, SRI/MF/complete] A7470–4.13
State Tax Actions, 1992, [Annual, SRI/MF/complete] A7470–4.9

National Coordinating Committee on Medical Malpractice JUAs
1991 Financial Condition of Medical Malpractice JUAs, [Annual, SRI/MF/complete] A0375–1

National Cotton Council of America
Cotton Counts Its Customers: The Quantity of Cotton Consumed in Final Uses in the U.S., Revised 1990-91 and Preliminary 1992, [Annual, SRI/MF/not filmed] A7485–1

National Council for U.S.-China Trade

National Council for U.S.-China Trade *see* U.S.-China Business Council

National Council of Churches Yearbook of American and Canadian Churches, 1993, [Annual, SRI/MF/excerpts] C0105–1

National Council on Crime and Delinquency Does Imprisonment Reduce Crime? A Critique of 'Voodoo' Criminology, [Monograph, SRI/MF/complete] A7575–3

Does Involvement in Religion Help Prisoners Adjust to Prison?, [Monograph, SRI/MF/complete] A7575–1.11

Juveniles Taken into Custody Research Program: Estimating the Prevalence of Juvenile Custody by Race and Gender, [Monograph, SRI/MF/complete] A7575–1.13

NCCD Focus, [Series, SRI/MF/complete] A7575–1

'Prisons Pay' Studies: Research or Ideology, [Monograph, SRI/MF/complete] A7575–1.12

Reforming Florida's Unjust, Costly and Ineffective Sentencing Laws, [Monograph, SRI/MF/complete] A7575–5

Why Punish the Children? A Reappraisal of the Children of Incarcerated Mothers in America, [Monograph, SRI/MF/complete] A7575–4

National Data Consultants Florida County Perspectives, 1992-93 Edition, [Annual, SRI/MF/complete, delayed] C6360–1

National Education Association Retirement and Retiree Health Benefits Provisions Survey, 1990-91, [Recurring (irreg.), SRI/MF/complete, current & previous reports] A7640–18

National Electric Reliability Council *see* North American Electric Reliability Council

National Federation of Independent Business NFIB Quarterly Economic Report for Small Business, [Quarterly, SRI/MF/complete, delayed] A7815–1

National Federation of State High School Associations National High School Sports Record Book, 1993 Edition, [Annual, SRI/MF/complete] A7830–2

National Forest Products Association *see* American Forest and Paper Association

National Governors' Association Fiscal Survey of States, [Semiannual, SRI/MF/complete, current & previous semiannual reports] A7955–1

National Health Council Report on Voluntary Health Agency Revenue and Expenses, FY90, [Annual, SRI/MF/complete] A7973–1

National Home Furnishings Association NHFA Annual Operating Experiences Report, [Annual, SRI/MF/complete, current & previous year reports] A7975–1

National League for Nursing Nursing and Health Care, [Monthly, SRI/MF/excerpts, shipped quarterly] A8010–3

Nursing Data Review, 1993, [Annual, SRI/MF/complete] A8010–1

State-Approved Schools of Nursing: L.P.N./L.V.N., 1993, [Annual, SRI/MF/complete, delayed] A8010–5

State-Approved Schools of Nursing: R.N., 1993, [Annual, SRI/MF/complete] A8010–4

National League of Cities 'All in It Together': Cities, Suburbs and Local Economic Regions, [Monograph, SRI/MF/complete] A8012–1.22

City Fiscal Conditions in 1993, [Annual, SRI/MF/complete] A8012–1.23

Research Reports on America's Cities, [Series, SRI/MF/complete] A8012–1

State of America's Cities: The Ninth Annual Opinion Survey of Municipal Elected Officials, [Annual, SRI/MF/complete] A8012–1.21

National League of Professional Baseball Clubs National League Green Book, 1993, [Annual, SRI/MF/excerpts] A8015–1

National Machine Tool Builders' Association *see* AMT—The Association for Manufacturing Technology

National Marine Manufacturers Association Boating 1992, [Annual, SRI/MF/complete] A8055–1

National Mass Retailing Institute *see* International Mass Retail Association

National Office Products Association NOPA Dealer Operating Results, 1992, [Annual, SRI/MF/not filmed] A8110–1

National Opinion Research Center *see* University of Chicago: National Opinion Research Center

National Paper Trade Association NPTA Management News, [Monthly, SRI/MF/excerpts, shipped quarterly] A8140–3

National Regulatory Research Institute Integrated Resource Planning for Water Utilities, [Monograph, SRI/MF/complete] A8195–11

Public Utility Commission Implementation of the Clean Air Act's Allowance Trading Program, [Monograph, SRI/MF/complete] A8195–12

National Research Council *see* National Academy of Sciences—National Research Council

National Restaurant Association Consumer Attitude and Behavior Studies, [Series, SRI/MF/complete] A8200–8

Off-Premises Market, [Monograph, SRI/MF/complete] A8200–21

Restaurant Industry Operations Report 1993, [Annual, SRI/MF/complete] A8200–3

Restaurant Spending: Consumer Expenditures on Food Away from Home, 1991, [Recurring (irreg.), SRI/MF/complete] A8200–13

Restaurants USA, [Monthly, SRI/MF/complete, shipped quarterly] A8200–1

Smoking in Restaurants: A Consumer Attitude Survey, [Monograph, SRI/MF/complete] A8200–8.15

Spotlight on Desserts, [Monograph, SRI/MF/complete] A8200–20

Survey of Wage Rates for Hourly Employees, 1992, [Recurring (irreg.), SRI/MF/complete] A8200–14

Tableservice Restaurant Trends, 1993, [Recurring (irreg.), SRI/MF/complete] A8200–11

1992 Menu Analysis, [Monograph, SRI/MF/complete] A8200–22

National Retail Hardware Association Bottom Line Report: Detailed Cost-of-Doing Business Data for Home Centers, 1992, [Annual, SRI/MF/complete] A8275–1.2

Financial Operating Reports, [Annual series, SRI/MF/complete] A8275–1

Management Report: Detailed Cost-of-Doing Business Data for Hardware Stores, 1992, [Annual, SRI/MF/complete] A8275–1.1

Profit Report: Detailed Cost-of-Doing Business Data for Retail Lumber Outlets, 1992, [Annual, SRI/MF/complete] A8275–1.3

National Safe Workplace Institute Basic Information on Workplace Safety and Health in the U.S., 1992 Edition, [Annual, SRI/MF/complete] R8335–1

Sacrificing America's Youth: The Problem of Child Labor and the Response of Government, [Monograph, SRI/MF/complete] R8335–2

National Safety Council Accident Facts, 1993 Edition, [Annual, SRI/MF/complete, delayed] A8375–2

Fleet Accident Rates, 1992, [Annual, SRI/MF/complete, delayed] A8375–3

Traffic Safety, [Bimonthly, SRI/MF/complete, delayed] A8375–1

Work Injury and Illness Rates, 1992, [Annual, SRI/MF/complete, delayed] A8375–4

National Society of Fund Raising Executives NSFRE Profile: 1992 Membership Survey, [Recurring (irreg.), SRI/MF/complete] A8455–1

National Society of Professional Engineers Professional Engineer Income and Salary Survey, 1993, [Annual, SRI/MF/complete] A8460–1

National Sporting Goods Association Lifestyle Characteristics of 1992 Sporting Goods Consumers, [Annual, SRI/MF/complete, delayed] A8485–4

Sporting Goods Market in 1993, [Annual, SRI/MF/complete] A8485–2

Sports Participation in 1992, [Series, SRI/MF/complete, delayed] A8485–3

National Truck Equipment Association 1992 Distributor Profit Survey Report, [Annual, SRI/MF/complete] A8505–4

National Urban League State of Black America, 1993, [Annual, SRI/MF/complete, delayed] A8510–1

National Venture Capital Association National Venture Capital Association 1991 Annual Report, [Annual, SRI/MF/complete] A8515–1

Third Annual Economic Impact of Venture Capital Study, [Annual, SRI/MF/complete] A8515–2

National Victim Center Rape in America, [Monograph, SRI/MF/not filmed] R8375–1

Naval Stores Review Naval Stores Review, 1992 International Yearbook, [Annual, SRI/MF/not filmed] C6585–1

Nebraska Agricultural Statistics Service *see* Nebraska Department of Agriculture, S4835–1

Index by Issuing Sources

Nebraska Department of Administrative Services

State of Nebraska Comprehensive Annual Financial Report, Year Ended June 30, 1992, [Annual, SRI/MF/complete] S4825–1

Nebraska Department of Agriculture 1991/92 Nebraska Agricultural Statistics, [Annual, SRI/MF/complete] S4835–1

Nebraska Department of Correctional Services Nebraska Department of Correctional Services, 18th Annual Report, FY91/92, [Annual, SRI/MF/complete] S4850–1

Nebraska Department of Economic Development Nebraska Statistical Handbook, [Biennial, discontinued] S4855–1

Nebraska Department of Education Financial Report of Public School District, All Classes, School Year 1988/89, Nebraska, [Annual, SRI/MF/complete] S4865–3

Nebraska Elementary and Secondary Education, [Series, SRI/MF/complete] S4865–2

Nebraska Department of Health Nebraska Department of Health 1991 Vital Statistics Report, [Annual, SRI/MF/complete] S4885–1

Nebraska Department of Insurance Summary of Insurance Business in Nebraska for the Year 1992, [Annual, SRI/MF/complete, current & previous year reports] S4890–1

Nebraska Department of Labor Nebraska Labor Market Information Quarterly, [Quarterly, with annual summary, SRI/MF/complete] S4895–2

Nebraska Department of Revenue 1991 Annual Report, Nebraska Department of Revenue, [Annual, SRI/MF/complete, current & previous year reports] S4950–1

Nebraska Department of Roads State of Nebraska 1992 Traffic Accident Facts Annual Report, [Annual, SRI/MF/complete] S4953–1

Nebraska Department of Social Services Nebraska Department of Social Services Annual Report, 1992, [Annual, SRI/MF/complete] S4957–1

Nebraska Library Commission Nebraska Public Library Profile: 1990-91 Statistical Data, [Annual, SRI/MF/complete] S4910–1

Nebraska Office of the Secretary of State Official Report of the Board of State Canvassers of the State of Nebraska: Primary Election, May 12, 1992; General Election, Nov. 3, 1992, [Biennial, SRI/MF/complete] S4955–1

Nebraska Public Service Commission Nebraska Public Service Commission Biennial Report, July 1, 1990-June 30, 1992, [Biennial, SRI/MF/complete] S4940–1

Nebraska Supreme Court Nebraska Supreme Court 1992 Annual Report, [Annual, SRI/MF/complete, current & previous year reports] S4965–2

Nevada Agricultural Statistics Service see Nevada Department of Agriculture, S5010–1

Nevada Department of Administration Nevada Statistical Abstract, 1992 Edition, [Biennial, SRI/MF/complete] S5005–1

Nevada Department of Agriculture Nevada Agricultural Statistics, 1993, [Annual, SRI/MF/complete] S5010–1

Nevada Department of Education Nevada Education in 1991/92: A Status Report, [Annual, SRI/MF/complete] S5035–2

Nevada Department of Human Resources Behavioral Risk Factor Surveillance, Nevada, 1992, [Annual, SRI/MF/complete] S5075–3

Nevada Vital Statistics Report, 1989, [Annual, SRI/MF/complete] S5075–1

Nevada Department of Transportation Nevada Traffic Accidents, 1992, [Annual, SRI/MF/complete] S5140–1

Nevada Employment Security Department Economic Update, Nevada, [Quarterly, SRI/MF/complete] S5040–1

Nevada Area Labor Review, 1992-93: 1992 Economic Activity and 1993 Outlook, [Annual, SRI/MF/complete] S5040–4

Nevada Gaming Control Board Nevada Gaming Abstract, 1992, [Annual, SRI/MF/complete] S5062–1

Nevada Office of the Controller State of Nevada Comprehensive Annual Financial Report for the Fiscal Year Ended June 30, 1992, [Annual, SRI/MF/complete] S5025–1

Nevada Office of the Secretary of State 1992 General Election Returns, Nevada, [Biennial, SRI/MF/complete] S5125–1

Nevada State Library and Archives Library Directory and Statistics, 1993, [Annual, SRI/MF/complete] S5095–1

New Hampshire Department of Administrative Services State of New Hampshire Comprehensive Annual Financial Report for the Fiscal Year Ended June 30, 1992, [Annual, SRI/MF/complete] S5175–1

New Hampshire Department of Education Cost per Pupil by District, 1991/92, New Hampshire, [Annual, SRI/MF/complete] S5200–1.5

Educational Statistics for New Hampshire, [Annual series, SRI/MF/complete] S5200–1

Enrollments in Grades 9-12 in New Hampshire Approved Public Secondary Schools and Approved Public Academies, Oct. 1, 1992, [Annual, SRI/MF/complete] S5200–1.7

Estimated Building Aid for 1993/94, New Hampshire, [Annual, SRI/MF/complete] S5200–1.14

Estimated Expenditures of School Districts, 1992/93, New Hampshire, [Annual, SRI/MF/complete] S5200–1.6

Fact Sheet: Approved Elementary, Middle, Junior High, and Senior High Schools (by District for School Year 1991/92), New Hampshire, [Annual, SRI/MF/complete] S5200–1.13

Fall Enrollments by School Administrative Unit, 1992/93, New Hampshire, [Annual, SRI/MF/complete] S5200–1.8

Fall Enrollments in New Hampshire Public Schools and Approved Public Academies, Oct. 1, 1992, [Annual, SRI/MF/complete] S5200–1.10

New Hampshire Department of State

New Hampshire Public High School Graduates: Graduating Class of 1991, [Annual, SRI/MF/complete] S5200–1.2

New Hampshire Public High School Graduates: Graduating Class of 1992, [Annual, SRI/MF/complete] S5200–1.15

State Average Cost per Pupil and Total Expenditures, 1991/92, New Hampshire, [Annual, SRI/MF/complete] S5200–1.4

State Totals—Fall Enrollments, 1991/92, New Hampshire, [Annual, SRI/MF/complete] S5200–1.1

State Totals—Fall Enrollments, 1992/93, New Hampshire, [Annual, SRI/MF/complete] S5200–1.9

Teacher Salary Schedules, 1992/93: New Hampshire School Districts, [Annual, SRI/MF/complete] S5200–1.3

Total Net Revenue and Expenditures of School Districts, 1991/92, New Hampshire, [Annual, SRI/MF/complete] S5200–1.12

Valuations, Property Tax Assessments, and School Tax Rates of School Districts, 1992/93, New Hampshire, [Annual, SRI/MF/complete] S5200–1.17

1991/92 Average Daily Membership Based upon Attendance and Residence, New Hampshire, [Annual, SRI/MF/complete] S5200–1.11

1992 Equalized Valuation per Pupil, 1991/92, of New Hampshire School Districts, [Annual, SRI/MF/complete] S5200–1.16

New Hampshire Department of Employment Security

Annual Planning Information, New Hampshire, [Annual, discontinued] S5205–3

Economic and Labor Market Projections for New Hampshire and Its Counties: FY92 and FY93, [Recurring (irreg.), SRI/MF/complete] S5205–7

Economic Conditions in New Hampshire, [Monthly, SRI/MF/complete, shipped quarterly] S5205–1

New Hampshire Labor Market Areas Planning Guide, [Annual, discontinued] S5205–6

New Hampshire Occupational Employment Statistics, [Series, SRI/MF/complete] S5205–2

New Hampshire Staffing Patterns in Government and Educational Services, 1991, [Triennial, SRI/MF/complete] S5205–2.25

New Hampshire Staffing Patterns in Wholesale and Retail Trade, 1991, [Triennial, SRI/MF/complete] S5205–2.26

New Hampshire Department of Health and Human Services

Vital Statistics Report for the State of New Hampshire, 1991, [Annual, SRI/MF/complete] S5215–1

New Hampshire Department of Safety Crime in New Hampshire, 1991, [Annual, SRI/MF/complete] S5250–2

New Hampshire Department of State State of New Hampshire Manual for the General Court, 1993, [Biennial, SRI/MF/complete] S5255–1

New Hampshire Insurance Department

New Hampshire Insurance Department
141st Annual Report of the New Hampshire Insurance Department for the Fiscal Year July 1, 1991-June 30, 1992, [Annual, SRI/MF/complete] S5220–1

New Hampshire State Library
New Hampshire Library Statistics, 1991, [Annual, SRI/MF/complete] S5227–1

New Jersey Agricultural Statistics Service
see New Jersey Department of Agriculture, S5350–1

New Jersey Casino Control Commission
1992 Annual Report of the New Jersey Casino Control Commission, [Annual, SRI/MF/complete] S5360–1

New Jersey Department of Agriculture
New Jersey Agriculture, 1992, [Annual, SRI/MF/complete] S5350–1

New Jersey Department of Banking
State of New Jersey, Commissioner of Banking, Annual Report, 1992, [Annual, SRI/MF/complete] S5355–1

New Jersey Department of Corrections
Annual Report: Offenders in New Jersey Correctional Institutions on Dec. 31, 1991, by Selected Characteristics, [Annual, SRI/MF/complete] S5370–1

New Jersey Department of Education
New Jersey Public Library Statistics, 1991, [Annual, SRI/MF/complete] S5385–2
Vital Educational Statistics, 1991/92, New Jersey, [Annual, SRI/MF/complete] S5385–1

New Jersey Department of Health
New Jersey Health Statistics, 1990, [Annual, SRI/MF/complete] S5405–1

New Jersey Department of Human Services
Economic Assistance Statistics, New Jersey, [Monthly, SRI/MF/complete, shipped quarterly] S5415–1

New Jersey Department of Insurance
New Jersey Department of Insurance 1990 Annual Report, [Annual, SRI/MF/complete, current & previous year reports] S5420–1

New Jersey Department of Labor
New Jersey Building Permits, 1991 Annual Summary, [Annual, SRI/MF/complete] S5425–3
New Jersey Economic Indicators, [Monthly, SRI/MF/complete, shipped quarterly] S5425–1
Profiling New Jersey II, [Monograph, SRI/MF/complete] S5425–19

New Jersey Department of Law and Public Safety
Fatal Motor Vehicle Accident Comparative Data Report, 1992, New Jersey State Police, [Annual, SRI/MF/complete] S5430–2
Uniform Crime Reports, State of New Jersey, 1992, [Annual, SRI/MF/complete] S5430–1

New Jersey Department of State
State of New Jersey General Election Results by Municipality, [Annual, discontinued] S5440–2
State of New Jersey Results of the General Election Held Nov. 3, 1992, by County and Municipality, [Annual, SRI/MF/complete] S5440–1

New Jersey Department of the Treasury
New Jersey Comprehensive Annual Financial Report, June 30, 1992, [Annual, SRI/MF/complete] S5455–1

New Jersey State Data Center
see New Jersey Department of Labor, S5425–19

New Jersey State Police Division
see New Jersey Department of Law and Public Safety, S5430–1, S5430–2

New Mexico Agricultural Statistics Service
see New Mexico Department of Agriculture, S5530–1

New Mexico Department of Agriculture
New Mexico Agricultural Statistics, 1991, [Annual, SRI/MF/complete] S5530–1

New Mexico Department of Education
New Mexico Accountability Report, 1991/92, [Annual, SRI/MF/complete] S5575–4
New Mexico School District and Student Achievement Profiles, [Annual, discontinued] S5575–2

New Mexico Department of Finance and Administration
Annual Financial Report, for 79th Fiscal Year Ending June 30, 1991, New Mexico, [Annual, SRI/MF/complete] S5585–1

New Mexico Department of Health
Selected Health Statistics, New Mexico, 1991, [Annual, SRI/MF/complete, current & previous year reports] S5605–1

New Mexico Department of Human Services
New Mexico Income Support Division Monthly Statistical Report, [Monthly, SRI/MF/complete] S5620–2

New Mexico Department of Labor
New Mexico Labor Market Annual Planning Indicators, [Annual, SRI/MF/complete] S5624–1
New Mexico Labor Market Review, [Monthly, SRI/MF/complete, shipped quarterly] S5624–2

New Mexico Department of Taxation and Revenue
New Mexico Taxation and Revenue Department Combined Annual Reports, 79th and 80th Fiscal Years (1990-91 and 1991-92), [Annual, SRI/MF/complete] S5660–1

New Mexico Employment Security Department
see New Mexico Department of Labor

New Mexico Highway and Transportation Department
New Mexico Traffic Crash Data, 1992, [Annual, SRI/MF/complete] S5665–1

New Mexico Judicial Branch
New Mexico State Courts 1992 Annual Report, [Annual, SRI/MF/complete] S5623–1

New Mexico Office of the Secretary of State
State of New Mexico Official Returns: 1992 General Election, [Biennial, SRI/MF/complete] S5655–1

New Mexico Public Service Commission
New Mexico Public Service Commission 48th Annual Report, July 1, 1991-June 30, 1992, [Annual, SRI/MF/complete] S5645–1

New Mexico Regulation and Licensing Department
78th Annual Report, New Mexico Financial Institutions Division, 1992, [Annual, SRI/MF/complete] S5652–1

New Mexico State Library
New Mexico Public Library Statistics, FY92, [Annual, SRI/MF/complete, current & previous year reports] S5627–1

New York Agricultural Statistics Service
see New York State Department of Agriculture and Markets, S5700–1

New York State Board of Elections
New York State General Election Vote, Nov. 3, 1992, [Biennial, SRI/MF/complete] S5750–1

New York State Commission of Correction
Statewide Compilation of Data from 1991 Sheriffs' Annual Reports, New York State, [Annual, SRI/MF/complete] S5724–2

New York State Department of Agriculture and Markets
New York Agricultural Statistics, 1992-93, [Annual, SRI/MF/complete] S5700–1

New York State Department of Audit and Control
State of New York Comprehensive Annual Financial Report, for Fiscal Year Ended Mar. 31, 1993, [Annual, SRI/MF/complete] S5710–1

New York State Department of Commerce
see New York State Department of Economic Development

New York State Department of Correctional Services
Characteristics of Inmates Committed and Discharged, New York State, [Series, SRI/MF/complete] S5725–1
Characteristics of Inmates Discharged, 1991, [Recurring (irreg.), SRI/MF/complete] S5725–1.1

New York State Department of Economic Development
New York State Business Fact Book, 1992, [Annual, SRI/MF/complete] S5735–3
New York State Business Statistics, [Quarterly, with annual summary, SRI/MF/complete] S5735–2

New York State Department of Health
New York State Behavioral Risk Factor Surveillance System, 1990 Reports, [Recurring (irreg.), SRI/MF/complete] S5765–3
Vital Statistics of New York State, 1990, [Annual, SRI/MF/complete] S5765–1

New York State Department of Labor
Employment Review, New York State, [Monthly, SRI/MF/complete] S5775–1

New York State Department of Motor Vehicles
1991 Motor Vehicle Statistics, Accidents, License and Registration Statistical Data, New York State, [Annual, SRI/MF/complete, current & previous year reports] S5790–1

New York State Department of Public Service
Financial Statistics of the Major Privately Owned Utilities in New York State, 1992, [Annual, SRI/MF/complete, current & previous year reports] S5795–1

New York State Department of Social Services
Statistical Supplement to the 1991 Annual Report of the New York State Department of Social Services, [Annual, SRI/MF/complete, current & previous year reports] S5800–2

New York State Education Department
1991 Public and Association Libraries Statistics, New York State, [Annual, SRI/MF/complete] S5745–2

Index by Issuing Sources

Northeast-Midwest Institute

New York State Executive Department
1991 Crime and Justice Annual Report, New York, [Annual, SRI/MF/complete] S5760–3

New York State Insurance Department
Loss and Expense Ratios: Insurance Expense Exhibits, New York State, [Annual, discontinued] S5770–1
Statistical Tables from Annual Statements, New York State Insurance Department, [Annual, SRI/MF/complete, current & previous year reports] S5770–2
133rd Annual Report of the Superintendent of Insurance, New York State, [Annual, SRI/MF/complete] S5770–3

New York State Office of Court Administration
14th Annual Report of the Chief Administrator of the Courts, State of New York, 1992, [Annual, SRI/MF/complete] S5730–1

New York State Office of the State Comptroller
State of New York Comprehensive Annual Financial Report, for Fiscal Year Ended Mar. 31, 1993, [Annual, SRI/MF/complete] S5710–1

New York State Public Service Commission
see New York State Department of Public Service, S5795–1

New York Stock Exchange
Fact Book for the Year 1992, [Annual, SRI/MF/complete] B6625–1

Newspaper Association of America
Facts About Newspapers '93, [Annual, SRI/MF/complete] A8605–4
Presstime, [Monthly, SRI/MF/excerpts, shipped quarterly] A8605–1

Newsprint Information Committee
Newspaper and Newsprint Facts at a Glance, 1992-93, [Annual, SRI/MF/complete] A8610–1

Nielsen Media Research
U.S. Television Household Estimates, [Annual, SRI/MF/complete, current & previous year reports] B6670–2

NMTBA—The Association for Manufacturing Technology
see AMT—The Association for Manufacturing Technology

NORC
see University of Chicago: National Opinion Research Center

North American Electric Reliability Council
Electricity Supply and Demand, 1993-2002, [Annual, SRI/MF/complete] A8630–2

North Carolina Agricultural Statistics Division
see North Carolina Department of Agriculture, S5885–1

North Carolina Board of Elections
State Board of Elections Registration Statistics as of Oct. 5, 1992, and Abstract of Votes Cast in the General Election Held on Nov. 3, 1992, North Carolina, [Biennial, SRI/MF/complete] S5920–1

North Carolina Department of Agriculture
North Carolina Agricultural Statistics, 1992, [Annual, SRI/MF/complete] S5885–1

North Carolina Department of Correction
North Carolina Department of Correction Statistical Abstract, [Semiannual, SRI/MF/complete, current & previous semiannual reports] S5900–1

North Carolina Department of Cultural Resources
Statistics and Directory of North Carolina Public Libraries, 1990-91, [Annual, SRI/MF/complete] S5910–1

North Carolina Department of Economic and Community Development
Civilian Labor Force Estimates for North Carolina, 1981-91, [Annual, SRI/MF/complete] S5917–4
North Carolina Utilities Commission: 1992 Report, [Annual, SRI/MF/complete] S5917–2
Occupational Employment in Selected Nonmanufacturing Industries and Government in North Carolina, 1991, [Triennial, SRI/MF/complete] S5917–5.2
Occupational Employment Reports, North Carolina, [Series, SRI/MF/complete] S5917–5
State Labor Summary, North Carolina, [Monthly, SRI/MF/complete, shipped quarterly] S5917–3

North Carolina Department of Environment, Health, and Natural Resources
North Carolina Vital Statistics, 1991, [Annual, SRI/MF/complete] S5927–1

North Carolina Department of Human Resources
Statistical Journal, July 1, 1992-Dec. 31, 1992, North Carolina, [Semiannual, SRI/MF/complete, current & previous semiannual reports] S5940–2

North Carolina Department of Justice
State of North Carolina Uniform Crime Report, 1992, [Annual, SRI/MF/complete] S5955–1

North Carolina Department of Public Instruction
Statistical Profile, 1993 North Carolina Public Schools, [Annual, SRI/MF/complete] S5915–1

North Carolina Department of Transportation
North Carolina Traffic Accident Facts, 1992, [Annual, SRI/MF/complete] S5990–1

North Carolina Employment Security Commission
see North Carolina Department of Economic and Community Development, S5917–3, S5917–4, S5917–5

North Carolina Judicial Department
North Carolina Courts, 1990-91: Annual Report of the Administrative Office of the Courts, [Annual, SRI/MF/complete] S5950–1

North Carolina Office of the State Controller
Comprehensive Annual Financial Report for the Year Ended June 30, 1992, North Carolina, [Annual, SRI/MF/complete] S5897–1

North Dakota Agricultural Statistics Service
see North Dakota State University: Agricultural Experiment Station, U3600–1

North Dakota Board of Higher Education
Fall 1992 Enrollment, North Dakota Institutions of Higher Education, [Annual, SRI/MF/complete] S6110–1

North Dakota Department of Health and Consolidated Laboratories
North Dakota 1991 Vital Statistics Report, [Annual, SRI/MF/complete] S6105–2
Report on the 1991 Behavioral Health Risks of North Dakotans, [Annual, SRI/MF/complete] S6105–3

North Dakota Department of Public Instruction
Administrative and Instructional Personnel in North Dakota, 1992/93, [Annual, SRI/MF/complete] S6180–3
North Dakota Educational Directory, 1992/93, [Annual, SRI/MF/complete] S6180–2
North Dakota Library Statistics, FY91, [Annual, SRI/MF/complete] S6180–5
School Finance Facts, North Dakota, [Annual, SRI/MF/complete] S6180–4

North Dakota Department of Transportation
1992 North Dakota Vehicular Crash Facts, [Annual, SRI/MF/complete] S6217–1

North Dakota Highway Department
see North Dakota Department of Transportation

North Dakota Job Service
Annual Planning Report, 1993, North Dakota, [Annual, SRI/MF/complete] S6140–2
North Dakota Labor Market Advisor, [Monthly, SRI/MF/complete, shipped quarterly] S6140–4

North Dakota Office of Management and Budget
State of North Dakota Comprehensive Annual Financial Report for the Fiscal Year Ended June 30, 1992, [Annual, SRI/MF/complete] S6162–1

North Dakota Office of the Attorney General
Crime in North Dakota: 1991, [Annual, SRI/MF/complete] S6060–1
North Dakota Correctional Facilities Report, [Annual, discontinued] S6060–2
Supervision and Incarceration: 1991, North Dakota, [Annual, SRI/MF/complete] S6060–3

North Dakota Office of the Secretary of State
North Dakota Official Abstract of Votes Cast at the General Election Held Nov. 3, 1992, [Biennial, SRI/MF/complete] S6205–1

North Dakota State Library
North Dakota Library Statistics, FY91, [Annual, SRI/MF/complete] S6180–5

North Dakota State University: Agricultural Experiment Station
North Dakota Agricultural Statistics, 1993, [Annual, SRI/MF/complete] U3600–1

North Dakota Supreme Court
North Dakota Courts Annual Report, 1992, [Annual, SRI/MF/complete] S6210–1

Northeast-Midwest Congressional Coalition
Budget and the Region, Fiscal 1994, [Annual, SRI/MF/complete] R8490–11
Military Base Closings Information Packet, [Monograph, SRI/MF/complete, current & previous reports] R8490–45

Northeast-Midwest Institute
Budget and the Region, Fiscal 1994, [Annual, SRI/MF/complete] R8490–11
Federal Spending in the Northeast and Midwest: FY92, [Annual, SRI/MF/complete] R8490–35
Hope and Home: Program Descriptions and Possible Changes, [Monograph, SRI/MF/complete] R8490–42
Military Base Closings Information Packet, [Monograph, SRI/MF/complete, current & previous reports] R8490–45
North American Free Trade Agreement's Auto Text in Strategic Context, [Monograph, SRI/MF/complete] R8490–43

Northeast-Midwest Institute

Regional Dimensions of the Crisis in Health Care Financing, [Monograph, SRI/MF/complete] R8490-46

Rough Cuts: The Continuing Decline of Defense Dollars for the Northeast-Midwest Region, [Monograph, SRI/MF/complete] R8490-44

State-by-State Impacts of Energy Tax Alternatives, [Monograph, SRI/MF/complete] R8490-49

Trends in Manufacturing in the Northeast-Midwest, [Monograph, SRI/MF/complete] R8490-48

Where Have All the Dollars Gone? Regional Patterns in Entitlement Spending, [Monograph, SRI/MF/complete] R8490-47

Northeast-Midwest Senate Coalition Budget and the Region, Fiscal 1994, [Annual, SRI/MF/complete] R8490-11

Northeast Recycling Council North American Newsprint Industry: Transitions to Recycling, [Monograph, SRI/MF/complete] A4375-15 Study of Markets for Post Consumer Plastics for Northeast Recycling Council, [Monograph, SRI/MF/complete] A4375-14

Northwestern University: Placement Center Northwestern Lindquist-Endicott Report, 1993: A National Survey of 258 Well-Known Business and Industrial Organizations, [Annual, SRI/MF/not filmed] U3730-1

Norwest Corp. Economic Indicators: Spring 1993 Regional Economic Survey, [Bimonthly (selected issues), SRI/MF/complete, Spring 1993 & Fall 1992 reports] B6785-1

Nuclear Assurance Corp. Focus: Quarterly Report on the Nuclear Fuel Cycle, [Quarterly, SRI/MF/not filmed] B6790-1

NUEXCO NUEXCO Review, [Monthly, SRI/MF/complete, shipped quarterly] B6800-1 NUEXCO Review, 1992, [Annual, SRI/MF/complete] B6800-2

Numbers & Concepts Black Americans: A Statistical Sourcebook, 1993 Edition, [Annual, SRI/MF/complete] C6775-2 Hispanic Americans: A Statistical Sourcebook, 1993 Edition, [Annual, SRI/MF/complete] C6775-3

Ohio Agricultural Statistics Service see Ohio Department of Agriculture, S6240-1

Ohio Bureau of Employment Services Ohio Labor Market Review, [Monthly, with annual summary, SRI/MF/complete, shipped quarterly] S6270-1

Ohio Data Users Center see Ohio Department of Development, S6260-3

Ohio Department of Agriculture Ohio Department of Agriculture Annual Report for 1991, [Annual, SRI/MF/complete] S6240-1

Ohio Department of Development Population Projections, Ohio and Counties by Age and Sex: 1990 to 2015, [Recurring (irreg.), SRI/MF/complete] S6260-3

Ohio Department of Education Annual Financial and Statistical Report, School Year 1991/92, Division of Special Education, Ohio, [Annual, SRI/MF/complete] S6265-1 Annual Report, 1991-92, State Board of Education, Ohio, [Annual, SRI/MF/complete] S6265-2

Ohio Department of Health 1991 Report of Vital Statistics, Ohio, [Annual, SRI/MF/complete] S6285-1

Ohio Department of Highway Safety Ohio Department of Highway Safety 1991 Crash Facts, [Annual, SRI/MF/complete] S6290-1

Ohio Department of Rehabilitation and Correction Ohio Department of Rehabilitation and Correction FY91 Annual Report, [Annual, SRI/MF/complete] S6370-1

Ohio Department of Taxation Annual Report of the State of Ohio Department of Taxation for the Fiscal Year Ending June 30, 1992, [Annual, SRI/MF/complete] S6390-1

Ohio Office of Budget and Management Ohio Comprehensive Annual Financial Report for the Fiscal Year Ended June 30, 1992, [Annual, SRI/MF/complete] S6255-1

Ohio Office of the Secretary of State Ohio Election Statistics for 1991-92, [Biennial, SRI/MF/complete] S6380-1

Ohio Public Utilities Commission Ohio Short Term Forecast of Utility Fuels, 1992-93, [Annual, SRI/MF/complete] S6355-1

Ohio State Board of Education see Ohio Department of Education, S6265-2

Ohio State Library Statistics of Ohio Libraries, 1993, [Annual, SRI/MF/complete] S6320-1

Ohio State University—Center for Human Resource Research NLS Handbook, 1993: The National Longitudinal Surveys, [Recurring (irreg.), SRI/MF/complete, current & previous year reports] U3780-2 NLS Older Male Sample Revisited: A Unique Data Base for Gerontological Research, [Monograph, SRI/MF/complete] U3780-9

Ohio Supreme Court Ohio Courts Summary, 1992, [Annual, SRI/MF/complete] S6385-1

Oildom Publishing Co. Pipeline & Utilities Construction, [Monthly, SRI/MF/excerpts, shipped quarterly] C6780-2 Pipeline and Gas Journal, [Monthly, SRI/MF/excerpts, shipped quarterly] C6780-1

Oklahoma Agricultural Statistics Service see Oklahoma Department of Agriculture, S6405-1

Oklahoma Banking Department Report of the Bank Commissioner of the State of Oklahoma, 1992, [Annual, SRI/MF/complete] S6415-1

Oklahoma Bureau of Investigation State of Oklahoma Uniform Crime Report, Annual Report, Jan.-Dec. 1992, [Annual, SRI/MF/complete] S6465-1

Oklahoma Department of Agriculture Oklahoma Agricultural Statistics, 1992, [Annual, SRI/MF/complete] S6405-1

Oklahoma Department of Commerce Demographic State of the State: A Report to the Governor and Legislature on Commuting Patterns for Oklahoma from the 1990 Census, [Annual, SRI/MF/complete] S6416-2 Population Projections for Oklahoma, 1990-2020, [Recurring (irreg.), SRI/MF/complete] S6416-1 Statistical Abstract of Oklahoma, 1992, [Annual, SRI/MF/complete] U8130-2

Oklahoma Department of Corrections Oklahoma Department of Corrections FY91 Annual Report, [Annual, SRI/MF/complete] S6420-1

Oklahoma Department of Education Results 1992: Oklahoma Educational Indicators Program, [Annual, SRI/MF/complete] S6423-2 1991/92 Annual Report: Oklahoma State Department of Education, [Annual, SRI/MF/complete] S6423-1

Oklahoma Department of Human Services Oklahoma Department of Human Services FY92 Annual Report, [Annual, SRI/MF/complete] S6455-1

Oklahoma Department of Libraries Roster and Statistics of Oklahoma Public and Institutional Libraries, July 1, 1991-June 30, 1992, [Annual, SRI/MF/complete] S6470-1

Oklahoma Department of Public Safety 1992 Oklahoma Traffic Accident Facts, [Annual, SRI/MF/complete] S6482-1

Oklahoma Election Board State of Oklahoma Election Results and Statistics, 1992, [Biennial, SRI/MF/complete] S6425-1

Oklahoma Employment Security Commission Oklahoma Labor Market, [Monthly, SRI/MF/complete, shipped quarterly] S6430-2

Oklahoma Insurance Department 86th Annual Report and Directory, 1993, Oklahoma, [Annual, SRI/MF/complete, current & previous year reports] S6462-1

Oklahoma Office of State Finance Oklahoma Comprehensive Annual Financial Report for the Fiscal Year Ended June 30, 1991, [Annual, SRI/MF/complete] S6438-1

Oklahoma Office of the State Auditor and Inspector State of Oklahoma Single Audit for the Year Ended June 30, 1991, [Annual, SRI/MF/complete] S6410-1

Oklahoma State Data Center see Oklahoma Department of Commerce, S6416-1, S6416-2

Oklahoma Supreme Court State of Oklahoma: The Judiciary Annual Report, FY92, [Annual, SRI/MF/complete] S6493-1

Oklahoma Tax Commission Annual Report of the Oklahoma Tax Commission, Fiscal Year Ended June 30, 1992, [Annual, SRI/MF/complete] S6495-1

Older Women's League Room for Improvement: The Lack of Affordable, Adaptable and Accessible Housing for Midlife and Older Women, [Monograph, SRI/MF/complete] A8657-5

Index by Issuing Sources

Olsten Corporation

HR Strategies, [Annual, SRI/MF/complete] B6850–5

Managing Today's Automated Workplace, [Monograph, SRI/MF/complete] B6850–7

Managing Today's Human Resource Priorities, [Annual, SRI/MF/complete] B6850–3

Quality Programs and Practices, [Annual, SRI/MF/complete] B6850–2

Skills for Success, [Annual, SRI/MF/complete] B6850–4

Workplace Social Issues, [Recurring (irreg.), SRI/MF/complete, current & previous reports] B6850–6

Olsten Forum on Human Resource Issues and Trends

HR Strategies, [Annual, SRI/MF/complete] B6850–5

Managing Today's Automated Workplace, [Monograph, SRI/MF/complete] B6850–7

Managing Today's Human Resource Priorities, [Annual, SRI/MF/complete] B6850–3

Quality Programs and Practices, [Annual, SRI/MF/complete] B6850–2

Skills for Success, [Annual, SRI/MF/complete] B6850–4

Workplace Social Issues, [Recurring (irreg.), SRI/MF/complete, current & previous reports] B6850–6

Oregon Agricultural Statistics Service

see Oregon Department of Agriculture, S6575–1

Oregon Department of Agriculture

1991-92 Oregon Agriculture and Fisheries Statistics, [Annual, SRI/MF/complete] S6575–1

Oregon Department of Education

Actual and Projected Public School Average Daily Membership and Enrollment, Oregon, [Annual, SRI/MF/complete] S6590–1.12

Audited 1991/92 Per Student Current Expenditures, Oregon, [Annual, SRI/MF/complete] S6590–1.18

Budgeted 1992/93 Per Student Current Expenditures, Oregon, [Annual, SRI/MF/complete] S6590–1.3

Cumulative Enrollment Summary and Average Daily Membership Attending, Year Ending June 30, 1992, Oregon, [Annual, SRI/MF/complete] S6590–1.4

Full-Time Equivalency of Public School District Personnel, by County as of Oct. 1, 1992, Oregon, [Annual, SRI/MF/complete] S6590–1.2

Grades Offered by Oregon Regular Schools, 1992/93, [Annual, SRI/MF/complete] S6590–1.6

Number of Public Schools, 1992/93, Oregon, [Annual, SRI/MF/complete] S6590–1.5

Oregon Educational Statistics, [Annual series, SRI/MF/complete] S6590–1

Oregon Public Middle Schools, 1992/93, with Oct. 1, 1992 Membership by Grade, [Annual, SRI/MF/complete] S6590–1.11

Oregon Public School Racial-Ethnic Summary, by County and by Grade, Oct. 1, 1992, [Annual, SRI/MF/complete] S6590–1.9

Oregon Public Secondary Schools, 1992/93, with Oct. 1, 1992 Membership by Grade, [Annual, SRI/MF/complete] S6590–1.13

Oregon School District Financial Elections, 1992, [Annual, SRI/MF/complete] S6590–1.15

Oregon School Districts, July 1, 1992, [Annual, SRI/MF/complete] S6590–1.14

Oregon School Districts Levying Authority, 1992/93, [Annual, SRI/MF/complete] S6590–1.20

Public and Private High School Graduates, Actual and Projected, Oregon, [Annual, SRI/MF/complete] S6590–1.8

School Districts Budget Summary, 1992/93, Oregon, [Annual, SRI/MF/complete] S6590–1.17

Student-Teacher Ratios in Oregon Regular Schools as of Oct. 1, 1992, [Annual, SRI/MF/complete] S6590–1.7

Summary of 1992/93 Oregon Private and Parochial Schools, [Annual, SRI/MF/complete] S6590–1.19

Summary of 1992/93 School District and ESD Budget Resources and Taxes Levied, Oregon, [Annual, SRI/MF/complete] S6590–1.21

1991/92 School Districts Audit Summary, Oregon, [Annual, SRI/MF/complete] S6590–1.16

1992 High School Completers, Oregon Public Schools, [Annual, SRI/MF/complete] S6590–1.10

1992/93 Summary of Organization, Students, and Staff in Oregon Public Schools, [Annual, SRI/MF/complete] S6590–1.1

Oregon Department of Human Resources

Adult and Family Services Division Public Assistance Programs, Branch and District Data, Oregon, [Monthly, SRI/MF/complete, shipped quarterly] S6615–8

Oregon Industrial Outlook, [Biennial, discontinued] S6615–9

Oregon Labor Trends, [Monthly, SRI/MF/complete, shipped quarterly] S6615–2

Oregon Vital Statistics Annual Report, 1991, [Annual, SRI/MF/complete] S6615–5

Oregon Department of Insurance and Finance

Annual Report, 1992, Oregon Department of Insurance and Finance, Division of Finance and Corporate Securities, [Annual, SRI/MF/complete] S6616–1

Oregon Economic Development Department

Economic Profile of Oregon, Update 1992, [Annual, SRI/MF/complete] S6585–3

Oregon Employment Department

Oregon Labor Trends, [Monthly, SRI/MF/complete, shipped quarterly] S6592–1

Oregon Executive Department

Oregon Comprehensive Annual Financial Report for the Year Ended June 30, 1992, [Annual, SRI/MF/complete] S6603–2

Report of Criminal Offenses and Arrests, 1992, Oregon, [Annual, SRI/MF/complete, current & previous year reports] S6603–3

Oregon Office of the Secretary of State

Official Abstract of Votes, General Election, Nov. 3, 1992, State of Oregon, [Biennial, SRI/MF/complete] S6665–1

Oregon State Library

Directory and Statistics of Oregon Libraries, 1992, [Annual, SRI/MF/complete] S6635–1

Our Sunday Visitor, Inc.

1993 Catholic Almanac, [Annual, SRI/MF/excerpts, current & previous year reports] C6885–1

Oxford University Press

World Resources, 1992-93, [Biennial, SRI/MF/complete] R9455–1

P. J. Kenedy and Sons

see Kenedy, P. J., and Sons

Pennsylvania Agricultural Statistics Service

see Pennsylvania Department of Agriculture, S6760–1

Pennsylvania Department of Agriculture

1992-93 Statistical Summary and Pennsylvania Department of Agriculture Annual Report, [Annual, SRI/MF/complete] S6760–1

Pennsylvania Department of Corrections

1990 Annual Statistical Report, State Correctional System, Pennsylvania, [Annual, SRI/MF/complete] S6782–1

Pennsylvania Department of Education

Colleges and Universities: Basic Student Charges, 1992/93, Pennsylvania, [Annual, SRI/MF/complete] S6790–5.3

Colleges and Universities: Degrees and Awards Conferred, 1990/91, Pennsylvania, [Annual, SRI/MF/complete] S6790–5.2

Colleges and Universities: Degrees and Awards Conferred, 1991/92, Pennsylvania, [Annual, SRI/MF/complete] S6790–5.15

Colleges and Universities: Faculty and Staff, 1991/92, Pennsylvania, [Annual, SRI/MF/complete] S6790–5.5

Colleges and Universities: Faculty and Staff, 1992/93, Pennsylvania, [Annual, SRI/MF/complete] S6790–5.13

Colleges and Universities: Fall Enrollments, 1992, Pennsylvania, [Annual, SRI/MF/complete] S6790–5.9

Colleges and Universities: Finance, 1990/91, Pennsylvania, [Annual, SRI/MF/complete] S6790–5.4

Colleges and Universities: Finance, 1991/92, Pennsylvania, [Annual, SRI/MF/complete] S6790–5.16

Colleges and Universities: Residence of Students, Fall 1992, Pennsylvania, [Biennial, SRI/MF/complete] S6790–5.8

Education Statistics: Projections to 1996/97, Pennsylvania, [Recurring (irreg.), SRI/MF/complete] S6790–5.10

Public, Private and Nonpublic Schools: Enrollments, 1991/92, Pennsylvania, [Annual, SRI/MF/complete] S6790–5.1

Public, Private and Nonpublic Schools: Enrollments, 1992/93, Pennsylvania, [Annual, SRI/MF/complete] S6790–5.17

Public, Private and Nonpublic Schools: High School Graduates, 1991/92, Pennsylvania, [Annual, SRI/MF/complete] S6790–5.14

Public Schools: Personnel, 1992/93, Pennsylvania, [Annual, SRI/MF/complete] S6790–5.12

Public Secondary School Dropouts in Pennsylvania, 1991/92, [Annual, SRI/MF/complete] S6790–5.11

Statistical Reports, [Series, SRI/MF/complete] S6790–5

Pennsylvania Department of Education

Vocational-Technical Education: Education and Employment Status of 1989/90 Completers, [Annual, SRI/MF/complete] S6790-5.6

Vocational-Technical Education: Secondary Program Statistics, 1991/92, Pennsylvania, [Annual, SRI/MF/complete] S6790-5.7

1991-92 Pennsylvania Library Statistics, [Annual, SRI/MF/complete, current & previous year reports] S6790-2

Pennsylvania Department of Health Health Risks of Pennsylvania Adults, 1991, [Annual, SRI/MF/complete] S6820-4

Pennsylvania Department of Labor and Industry

Annual Planning Information Report for Pennsylvania, FY92, [Annual, SRI/MF/complete] S6845-3

Pennsylvania's Labor Force: A Monthly Statistical Analysis, [Monthly, SRI/MF/complete, shipped quarterly] S6845-1

Pennsylvania Department of Revenue FY91-92 Statistical Supplement to the Pennsylvania Tax Compendium, [Annual, SRI/MF/complete, current & previous year reports] S6885-1

Pennsylvania Department of Transportation Pennsylvania Department of Transportation 1991 Statistical Summary Report, [Annual, SRI/MF/complete] S6905-3

Pennsylvania Insurance Department Annual Statistical Report of the Insurance Department of the Commonwealth of Pennsylvania for the Period July 1, 1991-June 30, 1992, [Annual, SRI/MF/complete] S6835-1

Pennsylvania Office of the Governor Comprehensive Annual Financial Report for the Fiscal Year Ended June 30, 1992, Pennsylvania, [Annual, SRI/MF/complete] S6810-4 Pennsylvania Energy Profile, 1960-90, [Recurring (irreg.), SRI/MF/complete] S6810-3

Pennsylvania State Data Center see Pennsylvania State University: Pennsylvania State Data Center, U4130-6, U4130-13

Pennsylvania State Library see Pennsylvania Department of Education, S6790-2

Pennsylvania State Police Uniform Crime Report: Commonwealth of Pennsylvania, Annual Report, 1992, [Annual, SRI/MF/complete] S6860-1

Pennsylvania State University: Pennsylvania State Data Center

1990 General Income Characteristics: Pennsylvania, [Monograph, SRI/MF/complete] U4130-13

1992 Pennsylvania Statistical Abstract, [Recurring (irreg.), SRI/MF/complete] U4130-6

Pennsylvania State University: Smeal College of Business Administration Pennsylvania Business Survey, [Monthly, SRI/MF/complete, shipped quarterly] U4110-1

Pennsylvania Supreme Court Report of the Administrative Office, Pennsylvania Supreme Court, [Annual, SRI/MF/complete] S6900-1

PennWell Publishing Co.

Electric Light and Power, [Monthly, SRI/MF/excerpts, shipped quarterly] C6985-6

Energy Statistics Sourcebook, 7th Edition, [Annual, SRI/MF/complete, delayed] C6985-9

International Energy Statistics Sourcebook, 2nd Edition, [Annual, SRI/MF/complete, delayed] C6985-10

International Petroleum Encyclopedia, 1993, [Annual, SRI/MF/excerpts, delayed] C6985-3

Offshore, [Monthly, SRI/MF/not filmed] C6985-2

Oil and Gas Journal, [Weekly, SRI/MF/not filmed] C6985-1

Oil and Gas Journal Data Book, 1993 Edition, [Annual, SRI/MF/complete, delayed] C6985-4

Oil Industry Outlook, 9th Edition, 1993-97, [Annual, SRI/MF/complete, delayed] C6985-5

Penton Publishing

Air Transport World, [Monthly, SRI/MF/not filmed] C7000-4

American Machinist, [Monthly, SRI/MF/not filmed] C7000-7

Foundry Management and Technology, [Monthly, SRI/MF/not filmed] C7000-2

Industry Week, [Semimonthly, SRI/MF/not filmed] C7000-3

Lodging Hospitality: Lodging's 400 Top Performers, [Monthly (selected issue), SRI/MF/excerpts] C7000-5

Lodging Hospitality: 1993 Almanac, [Monthly (selected issue), SRI/MF/excerpts] C7000-6

33: Metal Producing, [Monthly, SRI/MF/not filmed] C7000-8

Petroleum Independent Publishers, Inc. Petroleum Independent: The Oil and Natural Gas Producing Industry in Your State, 1993-94, [Monthly (selected issue), SRI/MF/complete] A5425-1

Phi Delta Kappa Phi Delta Kappan, [10 issues per year, SRI/MF/excerpts, shipped quarterly] A8680-1

Photo Marketing Association International 1992 Canadian Consumer Photographic Survey, [Recurring (irreg.), SRI/MF/not filmed] A8695-4

1993 Consumer Photographic Survey, [Recurring (Irreg.), SRI/MF/not filmed] A8695-2

Physician Executive Management Center Practitioner Compensation in Group Practice and HMOs: A 1992 Report, [Annual, SRI/MF/complete] B7450-2

Polk, R. L., and Co. Passenger Car and Truck Scrappage and Growth in the U.S., [Annual, SRI/MF/complete] C7715-2

Pocket Summary of Registrations: New Cars, New Trucks, [Monthly, SRI/MF/complete, shipped quarterly] C7715-3

Population Council Family Planning and Child Survival Programs as Assessed in 1991, [Monograph, SRI/MF/complete] R8720-1

Population Reference Bureau

America's Minorities - The Demographics of Diversity, [Monograph, SRI/MF/complete] R8750-2.58

Middle East Population Puzzle, [Monograph, SRI/MF/complete] R8750-2.59

Population and Water Resources: A Delicate Balance, [Monograph, SRI/MF/complete] R8750-2.57

Population Bulletin, [Series, SRI/MF/complete] R8750-2

Population Today, [Monthly, SRI/MF/complete, shipped quarterly] R8750-1

U.S. Population Data Sheet, [Annual, SRI/MF/complete] R8750-9

1993 World Population Data Sheet, [Annual, SRI/MF/complete] R8750-5

Potash and Phosphate Institute Potash Summary Report, [Monthly, SRI/MF/complete, shipped quarterly] A8720-1

Statistical Report: Potash Imports, [Quarterly, with annual summaries, SRI/MF/complete] A8720-4

Statistical Report: Potash Production, Inventory, Disappearance, and Sales, [Monthly, final issues, SRI/MF/complete, shipped quarterly] A8720-2

Statistical Report: Press Release, Potash Sales, [Quarterly, SRI/MF/complete] A8720-5

Potential Gas Committee Potential Supply of Natural Gas in the U.S. (Dec. 31, 1992), [Biennial, SRI/MF/complete] R8765-1

Premiere Publishing Fuel Oil News: The Oil Heating Industry: 1992, [Monthly (selected issue), SRI/MF/excerpts] C4680-2

Prentice-Hall, Inc. Almanac of Business and Industrial Financial Ratios, 1993 Edition, [Annual, SRI/MF/not filmed] C7800-1

Prevention Magazine Shopping for Health, 1993: A Report on Diet, Nutrition and Ethnic Foods, [Annual, SRI/MF/complete, current & previous reports, current report delayed] A4950-36

Princeton Religion Research Center Emerging Trends, [Monthly, SRI/MF/complete, shipped quarterly] R8780-1

Progressive Grocer, Inc. see Maclean Hunter Media, Inc.

Providence Journal Co. 1993 Journal-Bulletin Rhode Island Almanac, 107th Annual Edition, [Annual, SRI/MF/excerpts] C7975-1

Public Agenda Foundation Public Broadcasting's Coverage of Issues and Programming Themes, [Series, SRI/MF/complete] R8825-10

Punishing Criminals: The People of Delaware Consider the Options, [Monograph, SRI/MF/complete] R8825-11

Public Relations Society of America Public Relations Journal, [Monthly, SRI/MF/excerpts, shipped quarterly] A8770-1

Index by Issuing Sources

Sosland Publishing Co.

Public Utility Commission of Texas
1992 Texas Electric Utility Company Profiles, [Annual, SRI/MF/complete] S7740–1

R. L. Polk and Co.
see Polk, R. L., and Co.

R. R. Bowker Co.
see Bowker, R. R., Co.

Radio Advertising Bureau
Radio Marketing Guide and Fact Book for Advertisers, 1993-94, [Annual, SRI/MF/complete] A8789–1

Reed Publishing USA
Variety, [Weekly, SRI/MF/not filmed] C9380–1

Regional Airline Association
RAA Annual Report '93, 20th Anniversary Issue, [Annual, SRI/MF/complete] A8795–1

Rhode Island Administrative Office of State Courts
State of Rhode Island Report on the Judiciary, 1991, [Annual, SRI/MF/complete] S6965–1

Rhode Island Department of Administration
Census 90: Selected Social Characteristics for Rhode Island Counties, Cities, and Towns, [Monograph, SRI/MF/complete] S6930–9
Comprehensive Annual Financial Report of the State of Rhode Island and Providence Plantations for the Fiscal Year Ended June 30, 1992, [Annual, SRI/MF/complete] S6930–1

Rhode Island Department of Business Regulation
129th Annual Report of the Insurance Division Made to the General Assembly, 1991, Rhode Island, [Annual, SRI/MF/complete] S6945–2
85th Annual Report of the Division of Banking to the General Assembly, 1992, Rhode Island, [Annual, SRI/MF/complete] S6945–1

Rhode Island Department of Elementary and Secondary Education
1991/92 Statistical Tables, Rhode Island Department of Elementary and Secondary Education, [Annual, SRI/MF/complete] S6970–1

Rhode Island Department of Employment and Training
Labor Market Information for Rhode Island Planners, 1993, [Annual, SRI/MF/complete, current & previous year reports] S6980–3
Rhode Island Employment Bulletin, [Monthly, SRI/MF/complete, shipped quarterly] S6980–1

Rhode Island Department of Health
Vital Statistics Annual Report, 1989, Rhode Island, [Annual, SRI/MF/complete] S6995–1

Rhode Island Department of Transportation
1992 Motor Vehicle Accident Statistics, Rhode Island, [Annual, SRI/MF/complete, current & previous year reports] S7025–1

Rhode Island Office of the State Court Administrator
see Rhode Island Administrative Office of State Courts, S6965–1

Robert Morris Associates
see Morris, Robert, Associates

Rodale Press
Prevention Index 1993: A Report Card on the Nation's Health, [Annual, SRI/MF/complete] C8111–2

Rubber Manufacturers Association
Monthly Tire Report, [Monthly, suspended coverage] A8810–1

Rutgers University: Center for the American Woman and Politics
CAWP News and Notes, [Series, SRI/MF/complete] U4510–4
Fact Sheets, [Series, SRI/MF/complete] U4510–1
Gender Gap, [Monograph, SRI/MF/complete] U4510–1.65
Sex Differences in Voter Turnout, [Monograph, SRI/MF/complete] U4510–1.70
Statewide Elective Executive Women, 1993, [Recurring (irreg.), SRI/MF/complete] U4510–1.62, U4510–1.73
Women in Elective Office, 1993, [Recurring (irreg.), SRI/MF/complete] U4510–1.72
Women in State Legislatures, 1993, [Recurring (irreg.), SRI/MF/complete] U4510–1.63, U4510–1.67
Women in the U.S. Congress, 1993, [Annual, SRI/MF/complete] U4510–1.61, [Annual, SRI/MF/complete] U4510–1.69
Women in the U.S. House of Representatives, 1993, [Recurring (irreg.), SRI/MF/complete] U4510–1.60, U4510–1.68
Women in the U.S. Senate, 1922-93, [Recurring (irreg.), SRI/MF/complete] U4510–1.59, U4510–1.71
Women Moving into State Legislatures, 1974-93, [Recurring (irreg.), SRI/MF/complete] U4510–1.64
Women of Color in Elective Office, 1993, [Annual, SRI/MF/complete] U4510–1.66

Salmon, Kurt, Associates
KSA Perspective: Apparel and Footwear Profiles for 1992, [Annual, SRI/MF/complete] B8130–2
KSA Perspective: Retail Profile for 1992, [Annual, SRI/MF/complete] B8130–4
KSA Perspective: Textile Profile for 1992, [Annual, SRI/MF/complete] B8130–1

Savings and Community Bankers of America
Economic Outlook, [Monthly with quarterly supplements, SRI/MF/complete, shipped quarterly] A8813–1

Schwartz Publications
Discount Merchandiser, [Monthly, SRI/MF/not filmed] C8130–1

Scientific Manpower Commission
see Commission on Professionals in Science and Technology

Securities Industry Association
Foreign Activity: An Analysis of Foreign Participation in the U.S. Securities Markets, [Quarterly, with updates, SRI/MF/complete, shipped quarterly.] A8825–2
Securities Industry Trends: An Analysis of Emerging Trends in the Securities Industry, [6-8 issues per year, SRI/MF/complete, shipped quarterly] A8825–1

Shipbuilders Council of America
International Shipbuilding Aid, [Recurring (irreg.), SRI/MF/complete] A8900–8
Naval Shipbuilding, [Recurring (irreg.), SRI/MF/complete, current & previous reports] A8900–6

Silver Institute
Modern Silver Coinage, 1992, [Annual, SRI/MF/complete, delayed] A8902–2
Silver Institute Letter: Worldwide Information on Silver, [Bimonthly, SRI/MF/complete] A8902–3
World Mine Production of Silver in 1992 with Projections for 1993-96, [Annual, SRI/MF/complete] A8902–1
World Silver Survey, 1993, [Annual, SRI/MF/complete, delayed] A8902–4

Simmons-Boardman Publishing Corp.
Railway Age, [Monthly, SRI/MF/excerpts, shipped quarterly] C8400–1

Small Motor Manufacturers Association
Market Survey Motor Production Reports, [Quarterly, SRI/MF/complete] A8904–1

Snack Food Association
1992 Snack Food Association Consumer Snacking Behavior Report, [Recurring (irreg.), SRI/MF/complete] A8905–2
1993 Snack Food Association State-of-the-Industry Report, [Annual, SRI/MF/complete, current & previous year reports] A8905–1

Society for Human Resource Management
SHRM Work and Family Survey Report, 1992, [Monograph, SRI/MF/complete] A8907–1
1993 SHRM Survey: Human Resource Practices and Job Satisfaction, [Monograph, SRI/MF/complete] A8907–2

Society of Exploration Geophysicists
International Seismic Crew Count, [Quarterly, SRI/MF/complete] A8912–2
Monthly Seismic Crew Count, [Monthly, SRI/MF/complete, shipped quarterly] A8912–1

Society of Industrial and Office Realtors
Comparative Statistics of Industrial and Office Real Estate Markets, 1993 Guide, [Annual, SRI/MF/complete] A8916–1

Society of the Plastics Industry
Facts and Figures of the U.S. Plastics Industry, 1993 Edition, [Annual, SRI/MF/complete] A8920–1
Financial and Operating Ratios Survey, 1992 Plastics Processing Companies, [Annual, SRI/MF/complete] A8920–4
Monthly Statistical Report, Resins, [Monthly, with annual summary, SRI/MF/complete, shipped quarterly] A8920–5
Salary and Sales Policy, 1992, Plastics Processing Companies, [Biennial, SRI/MF/complete] A8920–3
1992 Labor Survey, Plastics Processing Companies, [Annual, SRI/MF/complete] A8920–2

Sosland Publishing Co.
Milling and Baking News: 1993 Grain Guide, North American Grain Yearbook, [Annual, SRI/MF/excerpts] C8450–2
Milling and Baking News: 1993 Milling Directory & Buyer's Guide, [Annual, SRI/MF/excerpts] C8450–3

South Carolina Agricultural Statistics Service

South Carolina Agricultural Statistics Service *see* Clemson University: South Carolina Agricultural Experiment Station, U1075–3

South Carolina Board of Financial Institutions South Carolina State Board of Financial Institutions Annual Report, 1991-92, [Annual, SRI/MF/complete] S7165–1

South Carolina Budget and Control Board South Carolina Statistical Abstract, 1993, [Annual, SRI/MF/complete] S7125–1 1993 Economic Report, The State of South Carolina, [Annual, SRI/MF/complete] S7125–3

South Carolina Commission on Higher Education South Carolina Higher Education Statistical Abstract, 15th Edition, [Annual, SRI/MF/complete] S7185–2

South Carolina Department of Corrections South Carolina Department of Corrections Annual Report, 1991-92, [Annual, SRI/MF/complete] S7135–1

South Carolina Department of Education Rankings of the Counties and School Districts of South Carolina, 1991/92, [Annual, SRI/MF/complete] S7145–1

South Carolina Department of Health and Environmental Control Detailed Mortality Statistics, South Carolina, 1990, [Annual, SRI/MF/complete] S7175–2 South Carolina Vital and Morbidity Statistics, 1990, [Annual, SRI/MF/complete] S7175–1

South Carolina Department of Highways and Public Transportation 1992 South Carolina Traffic Accident Fact Book, [Annual, SRI/MF/complete] S7190–2

South Carolina Department of Insurance South Carolina Department of Insurance Annual Report, 1991-92, [Annual, SRI/MF/complete] S7195–1

South Carolina Department of Social Services Statistical Report, South Carolina Department of Social Services, [Monthly, SRI/MF/complete, shipped quarterly] S7252–1

South Carolina Employment Security Commission South Carolina Labor Market Review, 1992, [Annual, SRI/MF/complete] S7155–3 South Carolina's Employment Trends, [Monthly, SRI/MF/complete, shipped quarterly] S7155–2

South Carolina Judicial Department South Carolina Judicial Department Annual Report, 1992, [Annual, SRI/MF/complete] S7197–1

South Carolina Law Enforcement Division Crime in South Carolina, 1992, [Annual, SRI/MF/complete] S7205–1

South Carolina Office of Comptroller General South Carolina Office of the Comptroller General, Annual Report, 1991-92, [Annual, SRI/MF/complete] S7127–2 State of South Carolina Comprehensive Annual Financial Report for the Fiscal Year Ended June 30, 1992, [Annual, SRI/MF/complete] S7127–1

South Carolina Public Service Commission Public Service Commission of South Carolina Annual Report, 1991-92, [Annual, SRI/MF/complete, current & previous year reports] S7235–1

South Carolina State Library South Carolina State Library Annual Report, 1991-92, [Annual, SRI/MF/complete] S7210–1

South Carolina Tax Commission South Carolina Tax Commission Annual Report, 1991-92, [Annual, SRI/MF/complete] S7255–1

South Dakota Agricultural Statistics Service *see* South Dakota Department of Agriculture, S7280–1

South Dakota Board of Regents FY93 Fact Book, South Dakota Board of Regents, [Annual, SRI/MF/complete] S7375–1

South Dakota Department of Agriculture South Dakota Agricultural Statistics, 1992-93, [Annual, SRI/MF/complete] S7280–1

South Dakota Department of Commerce and Regulation Guide to the Division of Insurance and Comparative Statement, [Annual, SRI/MF/complete] S7300–2 1992 South Dakota Motor Vehicle Traffic Accident Summary, [Annual, SRI/MF/complete] S7300–3

South Dakota Department of Corrections South Dakota Department of Corrections Annual Report, July 1, 1991-June 30, 1992, [Annual, SRI/MF/complete] S7296–1

South Dakota Department of Education and Cultural Affairs South Dakota Educational Statistics Digest, 1991/92, [Annual, SRI/MF/complete] S7315–1

South Dakota Department of Health South Dakota Vital Statistics and Health Status: 1991, [Annual, SRI/MF/complete] S7345–1

South Dakota Department of Labor South Dakota Labor Bulletin, [Monthly, SRI/MF/complete, shipped quarterly] S7355–1

South Dakota Department of Revenue South Dakota Department of Revenue Annual Report, FY92, [Annual, SRI/MF/complete] S7380–1

South Dakota Department of Social Services South Dakota Department of Social Services Annual Statistical Report, FY92, [Annual, SRI/MF/complete] S7385–1

South Dakota Insurance Division *see* South Dakota Department of Commerce and Regulation, S7300–2

South Dakota Office of Executive Management Comprehensive Annual Financial Report for the Year Ended June 30, 1992, South Dakota, [Annual, SRI/MF/complete] S7330–1

South Dakota Office of Highway Safety *see* South Dakota Department of Commerce and Regulation, S7300–3

South Dakota Office of the Secretary of State Official Election Returns and Registration Figures for South Dakota, General Election, Nov. 3, 1992, [Biennial, SRI/MF/complete] S7390–1

Index by Issuing Sources

South Dakota Supreme Court South Dakota Courts: The State of the Judiciary and 1992 Annual Report of the South Dakota Unified Judicial System, [Annual, SRI/MF/complete] S7395–1

Southern Illinois University: Core Institute, Student Health Program Alcohol and Drugs on American College Campuses, [Annual, SRI/MF/complete] U4950–1

Southern Institute on Children and Families Uninsured Children in the South, [Monograph, SRI/MF/complete] R9000–1

Southern Regional Education Board Case of the Shrinking State Share, [Monograph, SRI/MF/complete] A8945–27.12 Cost of Teacher Benefits in the SREB States, [Monograph, SRI/MF/complete] A8945–34 Majority of Students Attend Large Public Colleges, [Monograph, SRI/MF/complete] A8945–27.10 Making High Schools Work Through Integration of Academic and Vocational Education, [Monograph, SRI/MF/complete] A8945–33 Readiness for College: College-to-School Reporting in the SREB States, [Monograph, SRI/MF/complete] A8945–32 SREB Fact Book Bulletins, [Series, SRI/MF/complete] A8945–27 SREB Fact Book on Higher Education, 1992, [Biennial, SRI/MF/complete] A8945–1 SREB-State Data Exchange, 1990-91, [Annual, SRI/MF/complete] A8945–31 Tuition, Required Fees, and Total Cost of Attendance, [Monograph, SRI/MF/complete] A8945–27.11

Soyatech Inc. '93 Soya Bluebook, [Annual, SRI/MF/complete] B8480–1

Spain-USA Chamber of Commerce Business Link, [Quarterly, SRI/MF/complete] A8955–1

Special Libraries Association SLA Biennial Salary Survey, 1993, [Biennial, with annual updates, SRI/MF/complete] A8965–1

State Higher Education Executive Officers State Higher Education Appropriations, 1992/93, [Annual, SRI/MF/complete] A8970–1

State Justice Institute Divorce Courts: Case Management, Case Characteristics, and the Pace of Litigation in 16 Urban Jurisdictions, [Monograph, SRI/MF/not filmed] R6600–6 Small Claims and Traffic Courts: Case Management Procedures, Case Characteristics, and Outcomes in 12 Urban Jurisdictions, [Monograph, SRI/MF/not filmed] R6600–5 State Court Caseload Statistics: Annual Report 1991, [Annual, SRI/MF/complete] R6600–1

State Policy Research, Inc. State Policy Reports, [Semimonthly, SRI/MF/complete, delayed] B8500–2 States in Profile: The State Policy Reference Book, 1993, [Semiannual, SRI/MF/complete, delayed, current & previous semiannual reports] B8500–1

Index by Issuing Sources

State University of New York: Center for the Study of the States

Anatomy and Magnitude of State Tax Increases in 1992, [Annual, SRI/MF/complete] U5085–2.9

Credit Rating Changes: An Indicator of State Fiscal Stress, [Monograph, SRI/MF/complete] U5085–2.6

Impact of the Clinton Economic Plan on the States, [Monograph, SRI/MF/complete] U5085–2.10

Local Taxes Outpace State Taxes, [Monograph, SRI/MF/complete] U5085–2.11

State and Local Employment in the 1980s: How Did It Grow?, [Monograph, SRI/MF/complete] U5085–2.7

State Fiscal Briefs, [Series, SRI/MF/complete] U5085–2

State Revenue Report, [Quarterly, SRI/MF/complete] U5085–1

Trends in Federal Aid to States Since 1989: Not What Many People Assume, [Monograph, SRI/MF/complete] U5085–2.12

What Do the 1992 Election Results Say About State Fiscal Policy?, [Monograph, SRI/MF/complete] U5085–2.8

State University of New York: Center for Women in Government

Women in Public Service, [Series, SRI/MF/complete] U5090–1

Women Still 'Stuck' in Low-Level Jobs, [Monograph, SRI/MF/complete] U5090–1.3

State University of New York: Nelson A. Rockefeller Institute of Government

1992 New York State Statistical Yearbook, [Annual, SRI/MF/complete] U5100–1

Steel Service Center Institute

Business Conditions, [Monthly, in 2 parts, SRI/MF/not filmed] A8990–2

Tax Foundation

Corporate Tax Burden, [Recurring (irreg.), SRI/MF/complete] R9050–15.2

Facts and Figures on Government Finance: 1993 Edition, [Annual, SRI/MF/complete, delayed] R9050–1

President's Fiscal Year 1994 Budget, [Recurring (irreg.), SRI/MF/complete] R9050–15.3

Price of Mobility: Gasoline Taxes in America, [Monograph, SRI/MF/complete] R9050–15.6

Property Taxes on the Rise Again Across Nation, [Monograph, SRI/MF/complete] R9050–15.7

Special Report: Survey of State Tax Rates and Collections, [Monograph, SRI/MF/complete] R9050–14

Special Report: Value of Typical American Family's 1992 Income Eroded by Taxes and Inflation, [Annual, SRI/MF/complete, current & previous year reports] R9050–13

Special Reports (Tax Foundation), [Series, SRI/MF/complete] R9050–15

Tax Features, [Monthly, SRI/MF/complete, shipped quarterly] R9050–3

Tax Freedom Day 1993, [Annual, SRI/MF/complete] R9050–15.4

Washington's Largest Monument: The National Debt, [Monograph, SRI/MF/complete] R9050–15.1

1993 Federal Tax Burden by State, [Annual, SRI/MF/complete] R9050–15.5

Tayloe Murphy Institute

see University of Virginia—Center for Public Service

Teachers Insurance and Annuity Association

College and University Employee Retirement and Insurance Benefits Cost Survey, [Biennial, SRI/MF/complete] A9025–3

Tennessee Agricultural Statistics Service

see Tennessee Department of Agriculture, S7460–1

Tennessee Department of Agriculture

Tennessee Agriculture, 1993, [Annual, SRI/MF/complete] S7460–1

Tennessee Department of Commerce and Insurance

Annual Report of the Department of Commerce and Insurance, Business of 1991, Tennessee, [Annual, SRI/MF/complete] S7466–1

Tennessee Department of Correction

Tennessee Department of Correction FY91-92 Annual Report, [Annual, SRI/MF/complete] S7480–1

Tennessee Department of Education

Annual Statistical Report of the Department of Education for the Scholastic Year Ending June 30, 1992, State of Tennessee, [Annual, SRI/MF/complete] S7490–2

Tennessee Department of Employment Security

Covered Employment and Wages by Industry, Statewide and by County in Tennessee, 1991, [Annual, SRI/MF/complete] S7495–1

Labor Market Report, Tennessee, [Monthly, SRI/MF/complete, shipped quarterly] S7495–2

Tennessee Department of Finance and Administration

Tennessee Comprehensive Annual Financial Report for the Year Ended June 30, 1992, [Annual, SRI/MF/complete] S7505–1

Tennessee Department of Financial Institutions

Tennessee Department of Financial Institutions 19th Annual Report, 1992, [Annual, SRI/MF/complete] S7507–1

Tennessee Department of Health

Annual Bulletin of Vital Statistics for the Year 1991, Tennessee, [Annual, SRI/MF/complete] S7520–2

1990 Annual Report of Tennessee Behavioral Risk Factors, [Annual, SRI/MF/complete] S7520–3

Tennessee Department of Revenue

Biennial Report, FY90-91, FY91-92, Tennessee Department of Revenue, [Biennial, SRI/MF/complete] S7570–1

Tennessee Higher Education Commission

Statistical Abstract of Tennessee Higher Education, 1992/93, [Annual, SRI/MF/complete] S7525–1

Tennessee Office of the Secretary of State

Certification of Election Returns for the General Election Held Nov. 3, 1992, Tennessee, [Biennial, SRI/MF/complete] S7580–1

Tennessee Public Service Commission

Tennessee Public Service Commission 1991-92 Annual Report, [Biennial, SRI/MF/complete] S7565–1

Texas Education Agency

Tennessee State Planning Office

Economic Report to the Governor of the State of Tennessee on the State's Economic Outlook, [Annual, SRI/MF/complete] S7560–1

Population Estimates for the State of Tennessee, [Recurring (irreg.), SRI/MF/complete] S7560–2

Tennessee Supreme Court

Tennessee Judicial Council Annual Report, 1991-92, [Annual, SRI/MF/complete] S7585–1

Texas Agricultural Statistics Service

see Texas Department of Agriculture, S7630–1

Texas Comptroller of Public Accounts

Texas Comprehensive Annual Financial Report, for the Year Ending Aug. 31, 1992, [Annual, SRI/MF/complete] S7655–3

Texas 1992 Annual Cash Report for the Year Ended Aug. 31, 1992, [Annual, SRI/MF/complete] S7655–2

Texas Department of Agriculture

1991 Texas Agricultural Cash Receipts and Price Statistics, [Annual, SRI/MF/complete] S7630–1.3

1991 Texas Agricultural Statistics, [Annual, SRI/MF/complete] S7630–1

1991 Texas Crop Statistics, [Annual, SRI/MF/complete] S7630–1.1

1991 Texas Livestock Statistics, [Annual, SRI/MF/complete] S7630–1.2

Texas Department of Commerce

Estimates of the Total Population of Counties in Texas by Age, Sex, and Race/Ethnicity for July 1, 1991, [Annual, SRI/MF/complete] S7645–2

Estimates of the Total Populations of Counties and Places in Texas, July 1, 1991, [Annual, SRI/MF/complete] S7645–1

Projections of the Population of Texas and Counties in Texas by Age, Sex, and Race/Ethnicity for 1990-2030, [Recurring (irreg.), SRI/MF/complete] S7645–3

Texas Department of Corrections

see Texas Department of Criminal Justice

Texas Department of Criminal Justice

1992 Fiscal Year Statistical Report, Texas Department of Criminal Justice, [Annual, SRI/MF/complete] S7660–1

Texas Department of Health

Texas Vital Statistics, 1991, [Annual, SRI/MF/complete] S7685–1

1991 Texas Behavioral Risk Factor Surveillance: Final Overview, [Annual, SRI/MF/complete] S7685–2

Texas Department of Human Services

1992 Annual Report, Texas Department of Human Services, [Annual, SRI/MF/complete] S7695–1

Texas Department of Insurance

1992 Annual Report, Texas Department of Insurance, [Annual, SRI/MF/complete] S7700–1

Texas Department of Public Safety

Crime in Texas, 1992, [Annual, SRI/MF/complete] S7735–2

Texas Education Agency

Table I. Fall 1991/92 Personnel Roster: FTE Counts by Personnel Types and Subtypes, by Sex and Ethnicity, State Totals, Texas, [Annual, SRI/MF/complete] S7670–1.3

Texas Education Agency

Table II. Fall 1991/92 Personnel Roster: FTE Counts and Base Salaries by Personnel Type, State Totals, Texas, [Annual, SRI/MF/complete] S7670–1.4

Texas Education Statistics, [Annual series, SRI/MF/complete] S7670–1

Texas Public School Membership by Ethnic Group: Campus Report, Count and Percent, Fall 1991/92 PEIMS Data, [Annual, SRI/MF/complete] S7670–1.1

Total Enrollment by Grade, 1991/92 PEIMS Data, Texas, [Annual, SRI/MF/complete] S7670–1.2

Texas Employment Commission

Industry Staffing Patterns for Education, Apr. 1991, [Triennial, SRI/MF/complete] S7675–1.28

Industry Staffing Patterns for Railroads, May 1991, [Triennial, SRI/MF/complete] S7675–1.29

Industry Staffing Patterns for Selected Trade and Regulated Industries, 2nd Quarter 1991, [Triennial, SRI/MF/complete] S7675–1.31

Industry Staffing Patterns for State and Local Government, May 1991, [Triennial, SRI/MF/complete] S7675–1.30

Texas Labor Market Review, [Monthly, SRI/MF/complete, shipped quarterly] S7675–3

Texas Occupational Employment Statistics, [Series, SRI/MF/complete] S7675–1

Texas Planning Information, PY93, [Annual, SRI/MF/complete] S7675–2

Texas Higher Education Coordinating Board

Statistical Report, FY92, Texas Higher Education Coordinating Board, [Annual, SRI/MF/complete] S7657–1

Texas Judicial Council

Texas Judicial System Annual Report, FY92, [Annual, SRI/MF/complete] S7703–1

Texas Office of the Secretary of State

Official General Election Returns, Nov. 3, 1992, Texas, [Biennial series, SRI/MF/complete] S7750–1

Texas Railroad Commission

Gas Utilities Annual Report, Fiscal Year 1992, Railroad Commission of Texas, [Annual, SRI/MF/complete] S7745–1

Texas State Data Center

see Texas Department of Commerce, S7645 1, S7645–2, S7645–3

Texas State Library

Texas Public Library Statistics for 1991, [Annual, SRI/MF/complete] S7710–1

Texas Transportation/Gas Utilities Division

see Texas Railroad Commission, S7745–1

Theatre Communications Group

Theatre Facts 92, [Annual, SRI/MF/complete, delayed] A9065–1

Thomas R. Conlon and Associates

see Conlon, Thomas R., and Associates

Time, Inc.

Fortune, [Biweekly, SRI/MF/excerpts, shipped quarterly] C8900–1

Times Journal Co.

Military Market, [Monthly, SRI/MF/excerpts, shipped quarterly] C0500–1

Times Mirror Center for the People & the Press

Campaign '92: Voters Say 'THUMBS UP' to Campaign, Process and Coverage. Survey XIII, [Monograph, SRI/MF/complete] C8915–4.24

Index by Issuing Sources

Clinton's Press Judged as Less Fair Than Bush's and Reagan's, [Monograph, SRI/MF/complete] C8915–7.4

Less Support for Clintonomics Over the Back Fence, [Monograph, SRI/MF/complete] C8915–7.1

Outlook for Business in the New Europe, [Monograph, SRI/MF/complete] C8915–9

People, the Press and Politics, [Series, SRI/MF/complete] C8915–4

Policy Surveys, [Series, SRI/MF/complete] C8915–7

Public Opinion in Gridlock Over Clinton Economic Package, [Monograph, SRI/MF/complete] C8915–7.3

Public, Their Doctors, and Health Care Reform, [Monograph, SRI/MF/complete] C8915–7.2

Pulse of Europe: A Survey of Political and Social Values and Attitudes, [Monograph, SRI/MF/complete] C8915–8

Russians Rethink Democracy: The Pulse of Europe II, [Monograph, SRI/MF/complete] C8915–10

The Press and Campaign '92: A Self Assessment, [Monograph, SRI/MF/complete] C8915–4.25

Times Mirror Media Monitor, [Series, SRI/MF/complete] C8915–11

Times Mirror News Interest Index, [Recurring (irreg.), SRI/MF/complete] C8915–1

TV Violence: More Objectionable in Entertainment Than in Newscasts, [Monograph, SRI/MF/complete] C8915–11.1

TL Enterprises

RV Business, [Monthly, SRI/MF/excerpts, shipped quarterly] C8950–2

Tobacco Institute

Tax Burden on Tobacco: Historical Compilation, 1992, [Annual, SRI/MF/complete] A9075–2

Tobacco Industry Profile, 1992, [Annual, SRI/MF/complete] A9075–1

Toy Manufacturers of America

Monthly Market Trend Reports, [Monthly, SRI/MF/complete, shipped quarterly] A9095–2

National Statistics Program: Shipments, 1992 vs. 1991, [Annual, SRI/MF/complete] A9095–1

Trade Records Analysis of Flora and Fauna in Commerce

see TRAFFIC (U.S.A.)

TRAFFIC (U.S.A.)

1991 Psittacine Captive Breeding Survey: A Survey of Private Aviculture in the U.S., [Annual, SRI/MF/complete, current & previous year reports] R9200–14

TRW, Inc.

Space Log, 1992, [Annual, SRI/MF/complete] B9170–1

ULI—The Urban Land Institute

see Urban Land Institute

United Nations Development Programme

World Resources, 1992-93, [Biennial, SRI/MF/complete] R9455–1

United Nations Environment Programme

World Resources, 1992-93, [Biennial, SRI/MF/complete] R9455–1

United Van Lines

United Van Lines Migration Study, [Annual, SRI/MF/complete] B9300–1

University of Alabama: Center for Business and Economic Research

Alabama Business and Economic Indicators, [Monthly, SRI/MF/complete, shipped quarterly] U5680–1

Alabama Economic Outlook, 1993, [Annual, SRI/MF/complete] U5680–3

Economic Abstract of Alabama, [Recurring (irreg.), SRI/MF/complete] U5680–2

University of Alaska: Agricultural and Forestry Experiment Station

Alaska Agricultural Statistics, 1993, [Annual, SRI/MF/complete] U5750–1

University of Arizona: Arizona Agricultural Statistics Service

1992 Arizona Agricultural Statistics, [Annual, SRI/MF/complete] U5830–1

University of Arizona: Economic and Business Research Program

Arizona Economic Indicators, [Semiannual, SRI/MF/complete, Fall 1992 & Spring 1993 reports] U5850–1

Arizona Statistical Abstract: 1993 Data Handbook, [Recurring (irreg.), SRI/MF/not filmed] U5850–2

University of Arkansas: Agricultural Experiment Station

Arkansas Agricultural Statistics, 1992, [Annual, SRI/MF/complete] U5920–1

University of Arkansas: Arkansas Institute for Economic Advancement

Arkansas State and County Economic Data, [Annual, SRI/MF/complete] U5935–1

1990 Census of Population and Housing STF3A Profile, Arkansas, [Monograph, SRI/MF/complete] U5935–7

University of Arkansas: Bureau of Business and Economic Research

Arkansas Business and Economic Review, [Quarterly, SRI/MF/complete] U5930–1

University of Arkansas: Office of Institutional Research

26th Annual Rank-Order Distribution of Administrative Salaries Paid, 1992/93, [Annual, SRI/MF/complete] U5960–1

University of California at Los Angeles: Graduate School of Education

American Freshman: National Norms for Fall 1992, [Annual, SRI/MF/complete] U6215 1

University of California at Los Angeles: Latin American Center

Statistical Abstract of Latin America, [Annual, SRI/MF/not filmed] U6250–1

University of Chicago: National Opinion Research Center

General Social Surveys, 1972-91: Cumulative Codebook Supplement, [Annual, SRI/MF/complete] U6395–1

University of Chicago Press

Public Opinion Quarterly, [Quarterly, SRI/MF/excerpts] A0610–1

University of Colorado: Business Research Division

Tourism's Top Twenty: Fast Facts on Travel and Tourism, 1992 Edition, [Recurring (irreg.), SRI/MF/complete, current & previous reports] R9375–6

University of Florida: Bureau of Economic and Business Research

Building Permit Activity in Florida, [Monthly, with annual summary, SRI/MF/complete, shipped quarterly] U6660–5

Index by Issuing Sources

Florida Estimates of Population, Apr. 1, 1992, [Annual, SRI/MF/complete] U6660–4

Number of Households and Average Household Size in Florida: Apr. 1, 1992, [Annual, SRI/MF/complete] U6660–3.45

Population Projections by Age, Sex, and Race for Florida and Its Counties, 1991-2010, [Annual, SRI/MF/complete] U6660–3.43

Population Projections by Age, Sex, and Race for Florida and Its Counties, 1992-2010, [Annual, SRI/MF/complete] U6660–3.46

Population Studies Bulletin, [Series, SRI/MF/complete] U6660–3

Projections of Florida Population by County, 1992-2020, [Annual, SRI/MF/complete] U6660–3.44

1992 Florida Statistical Abstract, [Annual, SRI/MF/complete] U6660–1

University of Georgia: Cooperative Extension Service

Georgia County Guide, 12th Edition, 1993, [Annual, SRI/MF/complete] U6750–1

University of Georgia: Terry College of Business

Georgia Business and Economic Conditions, [Bimonthly, SRI/MF/complete] U6730–2

Georgia Statistical Abstract, 1992-93, [Biennial, SRI/MF/complete] U6730–1

University of Illinois: Bureau of Economic and Business Research

Illinois Business Review, [Quarterly, SRI/MF/complete] U6910–1

1992 Illinois Statistical Abstract, [Annual, SRI/MF/complete] U6910–2

University of Kansas: Institute for Public Policy and Business Research

Kansas Business Review, [Quarterly, SRI/MF/complete] U7095–1

Kansas Statistical Abstract, 1991-92, [Annual, SRI/MF/complete] U7095–2

University of Kentucky: Center for Business and Economic Research

Economic Significance of Toyota Motor Manufacturing, U.S.A., Inc., in Kentucky, [Monograph, SRI/MF/complete] U7138–1.4

Review and Perspective, [Series, SRI/MF/complete] U7138–1

University of Michigan—Institute for Social Research

Surveys of Consumers, Monthly Report, [Monthly, SRI/MF/complete] U7475–2

University of Nebraska: Bureau of Business Research

Business in Nebraska, [Monthly, SRI/MF/complete, shipped quarterly] U7860–1

University of Nevada: Bureau of Business and Economic Research

Nevada Business and Economic Indicators, [Annual, SRI/MF/complete] U7920–2

Nevada Review of Business and Economics, [Semiannual, discontinued] U7920–1

University of New Mexico: Bureau of Business and Economic Research

Census in New Mexico: Changes in the Age and Sex Composition of Counties Between 1980 and 1990, [Monograph, SRI/MF/complete] U7980–6

New Mexico Business, Current Economic Report, [Monthly, SRI/MF/complete, shipped quarterly] U7980–1

U.S. Travel Data Center

University of New Orleans: Division of Business and Economic Research

Louisiana FactBook, [Monograph, SRI/MF/not filmed] U8010–4

University of North Carolina

Statistical Abstract of Higher Education in North Carolina, 1992/93, [Annual, SRI/MF/complete] U8013–1

University of North Dakota: Bureau of Governmental Affairs

North Dakota Votes, [Biennial, SRI/MF/complete] U8080–1

University of Oklahoma: Center for Economic and Management Research

Oklahoma Business Bulletin, [Monthly, SRI/MF/complete, shipped quarterly] U8130–1

Statistical Abstract of Oklahoma, 1992, [Annual, SRI/MF/complete] U8130–2

University of South Dakota: Business Research Bureau

South Dakota Business Review, [Quarterly, SRI/MF/complete] U8595–1

South Dakota Data Supplement, [Bimonthly, SRI/MF/complete] U8595–2

University of Tennessee: Center for Business and Economic Research

Survey of Business, [Quarterly, SRI/MF/complete] U8710–1

Tennessee Statistical Abstract, 1992/93, [Annual, SRI/MF/complete] U8710–2

University of Texas: Lyndon B. Johnson School of Public Affairs

Mid-Level Practitioners: Their Role in Providing Quality Health Care, [Monograph, SRI/MF/complete] U8850–8.4

Nurses in Texas: Nurse Aides to Advanced Nurse Practitioners, 1971-91, [Monograph, SRI/MF/complete] U8850–8.2

Overview of the Indigent Health Care System in Texas, [Monograph, SRI/MF/complete] U8850–8.7

Policy Research Project on Health Care Cost and Access: Working Papers, [Series, SRI/MF/complete] U8850–8

Professional Liability Insurance in Texas, [Monograph, SRI/MF/complete] U8850–8.8

Public Health System in Texas, [Monograph, SRI/MF/complete] U8850–8.6

State Initiatives to Establish Basic Health Insurance Plans, [Monograph, SRI/MF/complete] U8850–8.1

Texas Medicaid Program, [Monograph, SRI/MF/complete] U8850–8.5

Texas-Mexico Multimodal Transportation, [Monograph, SRI/MF/complete] U8850–9

Texas Provider Utilization and Financial Data, [Monograph, SRI/MF/complete] U8850–8.3

University of Utah: Bureau of Economic and Business Research

Statistical Abstract of Utah, 1993, [Triennial, SRI/MF/complete] U8960–1

Utah Economic and Business Review, [Monthly, SRI/MF/complete, shipped quarterly] U8960–2

University of Virginia—Center for Public Service

Projections of Educational Statistics to 2012, [Annual, SRI/MF/complete, current & previous year reports] U9080–20

Taxable Sales in Virginia, 1991, [Annual, The SRI/MF/complete] U9080–8

Virginia Gross State Product, 1963-89, [Recurring (irreg.), SRI/MF/complete] U9080–6

Virginia Personal Income, 1980-90, [Annual, SRI/MF/complete] U9080–7

1990 Virginia AGI: Distribution of Virginia Adjusted Gross Income by Income Class and Locality, [Annual, SRI/MF/complete] U9080–1

1991 Estimates of the Population of Virginia Counties and Cities, [Annual, SRI/MF/complete] U9080–9

Upjohn Institute for Employment Research

Banking the Furnace: Restructuring of the Steel Industry in Eight Countries, [Monograph, SRI/MF/complete] R9260–16

Pension Policy for a Mobile Labor Force, [Monograph, SRI/MF/complete] R9260–17

Unemployment Insurance in the U.S.: The First Half Century, [Monograph, SRI/MF/complete] R9260–18

Urban Land Institute

Dollars and Cents of Shopping Centers, 1993: A Study of Receipts and Expenses in Shopping Center Operations, [Triennial, SRI/MF/not filmed] R9285–1

US-China Business Council

China Business Review, [Bimonthly, SRI/MF/not filmed] A9315–1

U.S. Committee for Refugees

Refugee Reports, [Monthly, SRI/MF/complete, delayed] R9372–2

World Refugee Survey, 1993, [Annual, SRI/MF/complete, delayed] R9372–1

U.S. Conference of Mayors

Impact of Unfunded Federal Mandates on U.S. Cities: A 314 City Survey, [Monograph, SRI/MF/complete] A9330–12

Status Report on Hunger and Homelessness in America's Cities: 1992, [Annual, SRI/MF/complete] A9330–9

U.S. Data on Demand, Inc.

States in Profile: The State Policy Reference Book, 1993, [Semiannual, SRI/MF/complete, delayed, current & previous semiannual reports] B8500–1

U.S. Independent Telephone Association *see* U.S. Telephone Association

U.S. Telephone Association

Holding Company Report, [Annual, SRI/MF/complete] A9360–1

Statistics of the Local Exchange Carriers, 1992, [Annual, SRI/MF/complete, delayed] A9360–2

U.S. Travel Data Center

Impact of Travel on State Economies, 1990, [Annual, SRI/MF/complete] R9375–7

Survey of State Travel Offices, 1992-93, [Annual, SRI/MF/complete] R9375–2

Tourism's Top Twenty: Fast Facts on Travel and Tourism, 1992 Edition, [Recurring (irreg.), SRI/MF/complete, current & previous reports] R9375–6

Travel Market Report, [Quarterly, SRI/MF/complete] R9375–14

Travel Printout, [Monthly, SRI/MF/complete, shipped quarterly] R9375–1

1991 Survey of Business Travelers, [Annual, SRI/MF/complete] R9375–12

Utah Agricultural Statistics Service

see Utah Department of Agriculture, S7800–1

Utah Board of Regents/Office of the Commissioner of Higher Education

Utah System of Higher Education Data Book, 1993/94, [Annual, SRI/MF/complete] S7895–2

Utah Department of Administrative Services

State of Utah Comprehensive Annual Financial Report for the Fiscal Year Ended June 30, 1992, [Annual, SRI/MF/complete] S7795–1

Utah Department of Agriculture

1993 Utah Agricultural Statistics, [Annual, SRI/MF/complete] S7800–1

Utah Department of Community and Economic Development

Utah Public Library Service, 1992: An Annual Report, [Annual, SRI/MF/complete] S7808–1

Utah's 1992 Homeless Count, [Annual, SRI/MF/complete] S7808–2

Utah Department of Corrections

Utah Department of Corrections 1992 Annual Report, [Annual, SRI/MF/complete] S7810–1

Utah Department of Employment Security

Annual Report of Labor Market Information, 1992, Utah, [Annual, SRI/MF/complete] S7820–10

Utah Employers, Employment and Wages by Size, 1992, [Annual, SRI/MF/complete] S7820–1

Utah Labor Market Report, [Monthly, SRI/MF/complete, shipped quarterly] S7820–3

Utah Department of Financial Institutions

13th Annual and 47th Report of the Commissioner of Financial Institutions, State of Utah, for the Period July 1, 1992-June 30, 1993, [Annual, SRI/MF/complete] S7830 1

Utah Department of Health

Behavioral Risk Factor Surveillance System Summary Report, Utah, 1991, [Annual, SRI/MF/complete] S7835–3

Utah's Marriage and Divorce: 1990, [Annual, SRI/MF/complete] S7835–2

Utah's Vital Statistics Annual Report, 1990, [Annual, SRI/MF/complete] S7835–1

Utah Department of Public Safety

Crime in Utah, 1992, [Annual, SRI/MF/complete] S7890–3

Utah Traffic Accident Summary, 1992, [Annual, SRI/MF/complete] S7890–2

Utah Foundation

Statistical Review of Government in Utah, 36th Annual Edition, 1993, [Annual, SRI/MF/complete] R9380–1

Utah Insurance Department

Utah Insurance Department: Business of 1991, [Annual, SRI/MF/complete] S7845–1

Utah Office of Education

Annual Report of the Utah State Superintendent of Public Instruction, 1991-92, [Annual, SRI/MF/complete] S7815–1

Utah Office of the Governor

Equal Employment Opportunity Data for Utah, [Monograph, SRI/MF/complete] S7832–3.4

Income of Utah, [Monograph, SRI/MF/complete] S7832–3.3

1990 Census Briefs, [Series, SRI/MF/complete] S7832–3

1992 Utah Economic and Demographic Profiles, [Annual, SRI/MF/complete] S7832–2

Utah Office of the Lieutenant Governor/Secretary of State

State of Utah General Election Report, Nov. 3, 1992, [Biennial, SRI/MF/complete] S7875–1

Utah Tax Commission

Annual Report of the Utah State Tax Commission, July 1, 1991-June 30, 1992, [Annual, SRI/MF/complete] S7905–1

Variety, Inc.

Variety, [Weekly, SRI/MF/not filmed] C9380–1

Vending Times, Inc.

Vending Times: Census of the Industry Issue, 1993, [Monthly (selected issue), SRI/MF/not filmed] C9470–1

Vermont Department of Agriculture

Agriculture of Vermont, 45th Biennial Report of the Vermont Department of Agriculture, 1989-90, [Biennial, SRI/MF/complete] S7978–1

Vermont Department of Banking, Insurance and Securities

Annual Report of the Bank Commissioner of the State of Vermont, for the Year Ended Dec. 31, 1992, [Annual, SRI/MF/complete] S7995–2

Annual Report of the Insurance Commissioner of the State of Vermont for the Year Ended June 30, 1992, [Annual, SRI/MF/complete] S7995–1

Vermont Department of Education

Elementary-Secondary Public School Enrollment, 1992/93 School Year, Vermont, [Annual, SRI/MF/complete] S8020–1

Vermont Department of Employment and Training

Vermont Annual Planning Information, 1993, [Annual, SRI/MF/complete, current & previous year reports] S8025–2

Vermont Department of Finance and Management

State of Vermont Comprehensive Annual Financial Report, For the Year Ended June 30, 1992, [Annual, SRI/MF/complete] S8035–1

Vermont Postsecondary Education Information Sourcebook, 1992, [Annual, SRI/MF/complete] S8035–2

Vermont Department of Health

1991 Annual Report of Vital Statistics in Vermont, [Annual, SRI/MF/complete] S8054–1

Vermont Department of Libraries

Vermont Department of Libraries 12th Biennial Report, Statistics of Local Libraries, July 1, 1990-June 30, 1992; Vermont Library Directory, 1993, [Biennial, SRI/MF/complete] S8080–1

Vermont Department of Taxes

1991 Vermont Tax Statistics, [Annual, SRI/MF/complete] S8125–1

Vermont Public Service Department

State of Vermont Department of Public Service Biennial Reports, July 1, 1986-June 30, 1992, [Biennial, SRI/MF/complete] S8100–1

Vermont Supreme Court

Judicial Statistics, State of Vermont, for the Year Ending June 30, 1992, [Annual, SRI/MF/complete] S8120–1

Veterinary Medicine Publishing Co.

Veterinary Economics, [Monthly, SRI/MF/excerpts, shipped quarterly] C9480–1

Virginia Board of Elections

Commonwealth of Virginia Official Election Results, 1992, [Annual, SRI/MF/complete] S8195–1

Virginia Center for Health Statistics

see Virginia Department of Health, S8225–1

Virginia Corporation Commission

Consumer Finance Licensees Operating in Virginia at the Close of Business Dec. 31, 1992: Supplement to the 1992 Annual Report of the Bureau of Financial Institutions, [Annual, SRI/MF/complete] S8180–3

Insurance Company Statistical Report, [Annual, discontinued coverage] S8180–1

1992 Annual Report of the Bureau of Financial Institutions, State Corporation Commission, Commonwealth of Virginia, [Annual, SRI/MF/complete] S8180–2

Virginia Department of Education

Superintendent's Summary: School Census Returns, 1992, Virginia, [Triennial, SRI/MF/complete] S8190–1

1991/92 Superintendent's Annual Report for Virginia, [Annual, SRI/MF/complete] S8190–3

Virginia Department of Health

Virginia 1991 Vital Statistics Annual Report, [Annual, SRI/MF/complete] S8225–1

Virginia Department of Motor Vehicles

1991 Virginia Traffic Crash Facts, [Annual, SRI/MF/complete] S8282–1

Virginia Department of Social Services

Public Welfare Statistics, Virginia, [Quarterly, suspended] S8293–2

Virginia Department of State Police

Crime in Virginia, 1992, [Annual, SRI/MF/complete] S8295–2

Virginia Department of Taxation

Virginia Department of Taxation Annual Report, FY92, [Annual, SRI/MF/complete] S8305–1

Virginia Employment Commission

Virginia Economic Indicators, [Quarterly, SRI/MF/complete] S8205–4

Virginia Labor Market Review, [Monthly, SRI/MF/complete, shipped quarterly] S8205–6

Virginia Population Projections, 2010, [Recurring (irreg.), SRI/MF/complete] S8205–7

Virginia Office of the Comptroller

Report of the Comptroller to the Governor of Virginia: A Comprehensive Annual Financial Report for the Fiscal Year Ended June 30, 1992, [Annual, SRI/MF/complete] S8170–1

Virginia State Library and Archives

Virginia Public Library Statistics, 1991-92, [Annual, SRI/MF/complete] S8275–1

Virginia Supreme Court

Virginia State of the Judiciary Report, 1992, [Annual, SRI/MF/complete] S8300–1

Index by Issuing Sources

Washington Office of Administrator for the Courts

Report of the Courts of Washington, 1992, [Annual, SRI/MF/complete] S8339–1

Washington State Agricultural Statistics Service

see Washington State Department of Agriculture, S8328–1

Washington State Criminal Justice Training Commission

Crime in Washington State, Annual Report, 1992, [Annual, SRI/MF/complete] S8440–1

Washington State Department of Agriculture

Washington Agricultural Statistics, 1992-93, [Annual, SRI/MF/complete] S8328–1

Washington State Department of Corrections

Client Characteristics and Population Movement Report, Washington State, [Quarterly, SRI/MF/complete] S8337–1

Washington State Department of General Administration

1992 Annual Report from the Supervisor of Banking, Washington State, [Annual, SRI/MF/complete] S8325–1

Washington State Department of Health

Washington State Vital Statistics, 1991, [Annual, SRI/MF/complete] S8363–1

Washington State Department of Revenue

Tax Statistics, 1992, Washington State, [Annual, SRI/MF/complete] S8415–1

Washington State Department of Social and Health Services

DSHS County Data Report, FY90, Washington State, [Annual, SRI/MF/complete] S8420–2

Washington State Employment Security Department

Washington Labor Market, [Monthly, SRI/MF/complete, shipped quarterly] S8340–3

Washington State Library

Washington Public Library Statistics, 1992, [Annual, SRI/MF/complete] S8375–1

Washington State Office of Financial Management

Washington State Comprehensive Annual Financial Report for the Fiscal Year Ended June 30, 1992, [Annual, SRI/MF/complete] S8345–3

1992 Population Trends for Washington State, [Annual, SRI/MF/complete] S8345–4

Washington State Office of the Secretary of State

Official Returns of the State General Election, Nov. 3, 1992, State of Washington, [Annual, SRI/MF/complete] S8425–1

Washington State Office of the Treasurer

Washington State Treasurer, 1992 Annual Report, [Annual, SRI/MF/complete] S8455–1

Washington State Traffic Safety Commission

1992 Traffic Collisions in Washington State: Data Summary and Highway Safety Problem Analysis, [Annual, SRI/MF/complete] S8428–1

Washington State Uniform Crime Reporting

Crime in Washington State, Annual Report, 1992, [Annual, SRI/MF/complete] S8440–1

Washington State Utilities and Transportation Commission

Annual Statistics of Electric Companies, 1982-91, Washington State, [Annual, SRI/MF/complete] S8450–1.2

Annual Statistics of Gas Companies, 1982-91, Washington State, [Annual, SRI/MF/complete] S8450–1.3

Annual Statistics of Telecommunications Companies, 1991, Washington State, [Annual, SRI/MF/complete] S8450–1.5

Annual Statistics of Water Companies, 1988-90, [Annual, SRI/MF/complete] S8450–1.1

Annual Statistics of Water Companies, 1989-91, [Annual, SRI/MF/complete] S8450–1.4

Statistics of Utility Companies, Washington State, [Annual series, SRI/MF/complete] S8450–1

Washington University: Center for the Study of American Business

Changes and Challenges: The Transformation of the U.S. Steel Industry, [Monograph, SRI/MF/complete] U9640–2.15

Changing Structures and Strategies: Survey of American Manufacturing Executives, [Monograph, SRI/MF/complete] U9640–4

Mixed Message: An Analysis of the 1994 Federal Regulatory Budget, [Annual, SRI/MF/complete] U9640–1

Policy Study Series, [Series, SRI/MF/complete] U9640–2

Unfunded Federal Mandates: Environmentalism's Achilles Heel?, [Monograph, SRI/MF/complete] U9640–3

1980s: A Decade of Debt?, [Monograph, SRI/MF/complete] U9640–2.14

West Virginia Department of Agriculture

West Virginia Agricultural Statistics, 1992, [Annual, SRI/MF/complete] S8510–1

West Virginia Department of Banking

90th Annual Report of Financial Institutions, Year Ending Dec. 31, 1991, West Virginia, [Annual, SRI/MF/complete] S8530–1

West Virginia Department of Commerce, Labor and Environmental Resources

Annual Planning Information, West Virginia, Program Year 1993, [Annual, SRI/MF/complete] S8534–3

West Virginia Economic Summary, [Monthly, with annual supplement, SRI/MF/complete, shipped quarterly] S8534–1

West Virginia Department of Education

Annual Report: 1991/92 Educational Statistical Summary, West Virginia, [Annual, SRI/MF/complete] S8540–3

Public Education Source Book, 1993, West Virginia, [Annual, SRI/MF/complete] S8540–4

West Virginia Department of Health and Human Resources

Statistics, West Virginia Department of Health and Human Resources, [Monthly, SRI/MF/complete, shipped quarterly] S8560–2

45th Annual Report: Vital Health Statistics of West Virginia, 1991, [Annual, SRI/MF/complete] S8560–1

Wisconsin Department of Administration

West Virginia Department of Human Services

see West Virginia Department of Health and Human Resources

West Virginia Department of Insurance

83rd Annual Report of the Insurance Commissioner of the State of West Virginia, Year Ending Dec. 31, 1991, [Annual, SRI/MF/complete] S8575–1

West Virginia Department of Public Safety

Crime in West Virginia, 1991, [Annual, SRI/MF/complete] S8610–1

West Virginia Department of Tax and Revenue

Classified Assessed Valuation Taxes Levied, 1992 Tax Year, Fiscal Year Ending June 30, 1993, West Virginia, [Annual, SRI/MF/complete] S8640–2

Rates of Levy: State, County, School, and Municipal, 1992 Tax Year, Fiscal Year Ending June 30, 1993, West Virginia, [Annual, SRI/MF/complete] S8640–3

West Virginia Department of Transportation

1992 West Virginia Crash Data, [Annual, SRI/MF/complete] S8645–1

West Virginia Division of Employment Security

see West Virginia Department of Commerce, Labor and Environmental Resources

West Virginia Library Commission

West Virginia Library Commission 1992 Statistical Report, [Annual, SRI/MF/complete] S8590–1

West Virginia Office of the Secretary of State

State of West Virginia 1992 Election Returns, [Biennial, SRI/MF/complete] S8630–1

West Virginia Research League

West Virginia Research League 1992 Statistical Handbook, [Annual, SRI/MF/complete] R9385–1

West Virginia State College and University Systems

Statistical Profile of Higher Education in West Virginia, 1992/93, [Annual, SRI/MF/complete] S8533–1

West Virginia Supreme Court of Appeals

West Virginia State Court System Caseload Report for Calendar Year 1992, [Annual, SRI/MF/complete] S8537–1

Western Interstate Commission for Higher Education

Tuition, Fees and Financial Aid in Public Higher Education in the West, 1992/93, [Annual, SRI/MF/complete] A9385–3

WICHE Student Exchange Programs, Statistical Report, Academic Year 1992/93, [Annual, SRI/MF/complete] A9385–1

Western Wood Products Association

1992 Statistical Yearbook of the Western Lumber Industry, [Annual, SRI/MF/not filmed] A9395–1

Wisconsin Agricultural Statistics Service

see Wisconsin Department of Agriculture, Trade and Consumer Protection, S8680–1

Wisconsin Department of Administration

Annual Fiscal Report (Budgetary Basis), State of Wisconsin, 1993, [Annual, SRI/MF/complete, current & previous year reports] S8675–2

Wisconsin Comprehensive Annual Financial Report for the Fiscal Year Ended June 30, 1992, [Annual, SRI/MF/complete, current & previous year reports] S8675–3

Wisconsin Department of Administration

Wisconsin Population Projections, 1990-2020, [Recurring (irreg.), SRI/MF/complete] S8675–4

Wisconsin Department of Agriculture, Trade and Consumer Protection
Wisconsin Agricultural Statistics, 1993, [Annual, SRI/MF/complete] S8680–1

Wisconsin Department of Corrections
Calendar Year Summary Report of Population Movement, 1991, Wisconsin, [Annual, SRI/MF/complete] S8692–1.4
Fiscal Year Summary of Population Movement, 1992, [Annual, SRI/MF/complete] S8692–1.6
Offenders Admitted to Adult Correctional Institutions, 1991, Wisconsin, [Annual, SRI/MF/complete] S8692–1.2
Offenders Released from Adult Correctional Institutions, 1991, [Annual, SRI/MF/complete] S8692–1.3
Residents in Wisconsin Adult Correctional Facilities on Dec. 31, 1991, [Semiannual, SRI/MF/complete] S8692–1.5
Residents in Wisconsin Adult Correctional Facilities on June 30, 1991, [Semiannual, SRI/MF/complete] S8692–1.1
Statistical Bulletins, Wisconsin Department of Corrections, [Annual series, SRI/MF/complete] S8692–1

Wisconsin Department of Health and Social Services
Vital Statistics, 1991, Wisconsin, [Annual, SRI/MF/complete, current & previous year reports] S8715–4

Wisconsin Department of Industry, Labor and Human Relations
Wisconsin Economic Indicators, [Monthly, SRI/MF/complete, shipped quarterly] S8750–1

Wisconsin Department of Public Instruction
Basic Facts About Wisconsin's Elementary and Secondary Schools, 1992/93, [Annual, SRI/MF/complete] S8795–2
Wisconsin Library Service Record, 1992, [Annual, SRI/MF/complete] S8795–1

Wisconsin Department of Transportation
1992 Wisconsin Traffic Crash Facts, [Annual, SRI/MF/complete, current & previous year reports] S8815–1

Wisconsin Legislative Reference Bureau
State of Wisconsin 1993-94 Blue Book, [Biennial, SRI/MF/complete] S8780–1

Wisconsin Office of Commissioner of Banking
Wisconsin 1992 Annual Report, Office of Commissioner of Banking, [Annual, SRI/MF/complete] S8685–1

Wisconsin Office of Commissioner of Savings and Loan
96th Annual Report on the Condition of Wisconsin Savings and Loan Associations and Savings Banks, [Annual, SRI/MF/complete] S8807–1

Wisconsin Office of Justice Assistance
Wisconsin Crime and Arrests, 1992, [Annual, SRI/MF/complete] S8771–1

Wisconsin Office of the Commissioner of Insurance
Wisconsin Insurance Report, Business of 1992, [Annual, SRI/MF/complete, current & previous year reports] S8755–1

Women and Foundations/Corporate Philanthropy
Challenge of Diversifying Philanthropic Leadership, [Monograph, SRI/MF/complete] A9405–1.1

Far From Done Reports, [Series, SRI/MF/complete] A9405–1
Getting It Done: From Commitment to Action on Funding for Women and Girls, [Monograph, SRI/MF/complete] A9405–1.2

Women's International Bowling Congress
Women's International Bowling Congress 1991-92 Annual Report, [Annual, SRI/MF/complete] A9415–1

World Resources Institute
World Resources, 1992-93, [Biennial, SRI/MF/complete] R9455–1

World Wildlife Fund
1991 Psittacine Captive Breeding Survey: A Survey of Private Aviculture in the U.S., [Annual, SRI/MF/complete, current & previous year reports] R9200–14

World Wildlife Fund-U.S.
see TRAFFIC (U.S.A.)

Worldtariff
California Agricultural Exports Annual Bulletin and Statistical Appendix, 1991, [Annual, SRI/MF/complete, delayed] B9520–1

Wyoming Agricultural Statistics Service
see Wyoming Department of Agriculture, S8860–1

Wyoming Board of Charities and Reform
see Wyoming Department of Corrections, S8883–1

Wyoming Department of Administration and Information
Wyoming Public Library Statistics, FY92, [Annual, SRI/MF/complete] S8855–3
Wyoming Sales and Use Tax Revenue Report, 1992, [Annual, SRI/MF/complete] S8855–1

Wyoming Department of Agriculture
Wyoming Agricultural Statistics, 1993, [Annual, SRI/MF/complete] S8860–1

Wyoming Department of Corrections
State of Wyoming 1992 Annual Report of the Department of Corrections, [Annual, SRI/MF/complete] S8883–1

Wyoming Department of Education
Statistical Report Series, Wyoming, [Annual Series, SRI/MF/complete] S8890–1
1991/92 Wyoming Public Schools Fund Accounting and Reporting, [Annual, SRI/MF/complete] S8890–1.3
1992 School District Property Valuations, Mill Levies, and Bonded Debt, Wyoming, [Annual, SRI/MF/complete] S8890–1.1
1992 School Districts Fall Report of Staff, Teachers/Pupils/Schools, and Enrollments, Wyoming, [Annual, SRI/MF/complete] S8890–1.2

Wyoming Department of Employment
Wyoming Labor Force Trends, [Monthly, SRI/MF/complete, shipped quarterly] S8895–1

Wyoming Department of Family Services
Management Information and Statistical Report, FY92, Wyoming, [Annual, SRI/MF/complete] S8908–1

Wyoming Department of Health
Wyoming Vital Statistics, 1991, [Annual, SRI/MF/complete] S8920–2

Wyoming Department of Revenue
Wyoming Department of Revenue 1992 Annual Report, [Annual, SRI/MF/complete] S8990–1

Index by Issuing Sources

Wyoming Employment Security Commission
see Wyoming Department of Employment

Wyoming Office of the Attorney General
Crime in Wyoming, Jan.-Dec. 1991, [Annual, SRI/MF/complete] S8867–3

Wyoming Office of the Auditor
State of Wyoming Comprehensive Annual Financial Report for Fiscal Year Ended June 30, 1992, [Annual, SRI/MF/complete] S8875–1

Wyoming Office of the Secretary of State
1993 Wyoming Official Directory and 1992 Election Returns, [Annual, SRI/MF/complete] S9000–1

Wyoming Office of the Treasurer
Annual Report of the Treasurer of the State of Wyoming, for the Period July 1, 1991-June 30, 1992, [Annual, SRI/MF/complete] S9010–1

Wyoming Transportation Department
Wyoming's Comprehensive Report on Traffic Accidents, 1992, [Annual, SRI/MF/complete] S9007–1

Yellow Pages Publishers Association
Yellow Pages Industry Usage Study, 1992, [Annual, SRI/MF/complete] A9500–2

Zero Population Growth
Children's Stress Index, [Monograph, SRI/MF/complete] R9700–2

Index by Titles

Index by Titles

Titles are listed alphabetically in natural word order, as they appear in the Abstracts Section. Titles beginning with numbers (e.g., "1990 Census...") appear at the end of the index. Where appropriate, alternate word orders of titles have also been provided.

In addition to publication titles, individual report titles within a publication series are indexed. Titles of articles from periodicals are not included unless so well known as to be a useful searching tool.

AAMA Motor Vehicle Facts and Figures '93, A0865–1

ABC Magazine Trend Report, 1988-92, A3385–1

ABC 1991-92 Annual Report, A1015–1

Abstract of Votes Cast at the General Election, Nov. 3, 1992, State of Idaho, S2305–1

Academe: The Annual Report on the Economic Status of the Profession, 1992/93, A0800–1

Academic Medicine, A3273–8

Academic Practice Faculty Compensation and Production Survey: 1992 Report Based on 1991 Data, A6365–5

Accident Facts, 1993 Edition, A8375–2

Across the Nation: Industrial, Mid-Year 1993, B2800–6

Across the Nation: Office, B2800–4

Actual and Projected Public School Average Daily Membership and Enrollment, Oregon, S6590 1.12

Administrative and Instructional Personnel in North Dakota, 1992/93, S6180–3

Administrative Compensation Survey, A3900–1

Admission Trends Survey, A6695–1

Adult and Family Services Division Public Assistance Programs, Branch and District Data, Oregon, S6615–8

Advertising Age, C2710–1

Aerospace Facts and Figures, 1992-93, A0250–2

African-American Public Television Viewing, R4250–1.17

Aftermarket Business, C0125–1

AGI Faculty Salary Report, 1992, A1785–4

Agricultural Finance Review, U1380–4

Agricultural Statistics and Prices for Louisiana, 1985-91, U2740–1

Agriculture of Vermont, 45th Biennial Report of the Vermont Department of Agriculture, 1989-90, S7978–1

Air Conditioning, Heating, and Refrigeration News: 1993 Statistical Panorama, C1800–1

Air Transport World, C7000–4

Air Transport, 1993, A0325–5

Air Travel Survey, 1992, A0325–6

ALA Survey of Librarian Salaries, 1993, A2070–3

ALA 1992-93 Worldwide Directory and Fact Book, A2072–1

Alabama Accident Summary, Statewide Accidents, S0185–1

Alabama Agricultural Statistics, 1991 Revised, 1992 Preliminary, S0090–1

Alabama Business and Economic Indicators, U5680–1

Alabama County Data Book, 1992-93, S0121–2

Alabama Department of Public Health Summary Report of the State Health Officer, 1992, S0175–3

Alabama Economic Outlook, 1993, U5680–3

Alabama Insurance Report, S0160–1

Alabama Judicial System Annual Report, FY92, S0118–1

Alabama Municipal Data Book, 1993, S0121–5

Alabama Public Library Service: Library Directory and 1992 Statistical Report, S0180–1

Alabama Vital Events, S0175–2

Alaska Agricultural Statistics, 1993, U5750–1

Alaska Bureau of Vital Statistics 1990 Annual Report, S0315–1

Alaska Corrections in Review, 1991 Report, S0287–1

Alaska Court System 1992 Annual Report, S0290–1

Alaska Economic Trends, S0320–1

Alaska Population Overview: 1991 Estimates, S0320–4

Alaska Public Utilities Commission Annual Report to the Legislature, FY92, S0280–4

Alaska Taxable, 1992, S0285–1

Alaska Traffic Accidents, S0360–1

Alcohol and Drugs on American College Campuses, U4950–1

'All in It Together': Cities, Suburbs and Local Economic Regions, A8012–1.22

Allied Van Lines Magnet States Report, B0210–1

Almanac of Business and Industrial Financial Ratios, 1993 Edition, C7800–1

Almanac of Hospital Financial and Operating Indicators, B1880–1

Almanac of the 50 States: Basic Data Profiles with Comparative Tables, C4712–1

Aluminum Situation, A0400–1

Aluminum Statistical Review for 1992, A0400–2

AMA Research Reports, A2075–20

AMA Survey of Downsizing and Assistance to Displaced Workers, A2075–20.9

AMA Survey on Basic Skills Testing and Training, A2075–20.13

AMA Survey on HIV and AIDS Related Policies, 1993, A2075–20.14

AMA Survey on Managing Cultural Diversity, 1993, A2075–20.11

AMA Survey on Marketing in a Recessionary Economy, 1992, A2075–20.10

AMA Survey on Workplace Drug Testing and Drug Abuse Policies, A2075–20.12

America Votes 20: A Handbook of Contemporary American Election Statistics, C2500–1

American Association of Blood Banks 1992 Annual Report, A0612–2

American College President: A 1993 Edition, A1410–12

American Family Losing Ground to Taxes and Inflation, R9050–13

American Freshman: National Norms for Fall 1992, U6215–1

American Geological Institute Survey of Students in the Geosciences, 1991-92, A1785–3

American Hospital Association Guide to the Health Care Field, 1993 Edition, A1865–3

American Jewish Year Book, 1993, A2050–1

American Journal of Public Health, A2623–1

American League Red Book, A2068–1

American Logistics Association Worldwide Directory and Fact Book, A2072–1

American Machinist, C7000–7

American Mathematical Society Annual Survey, A2085–1

American Radio, C3165–1

America's Minorities - The Demographics of Diversity, R8750–2.58

AMS Management Salaries Report, A0175–2

AMS Office Benefits Survey Report for the U.S. and Canada, A0175–5

AMS Office, Professional, and Data Processing Salaries Report, A0175–1

AMS Office Turnover Survey Report for the U.S. and Canada, A0175–4

AMT Industry Estimates: Machine Tool Orders and Shipments, A3179–1

Analysis of Class I Railroads, 1992, A3275–7

Analysis of National Billings: Commercial Heat Treaters, A6376–1

Analysis of Professional Salaries: Maryland Public Schools, Oct. 1991, S3610–2.2

Analysis of Professional Salaries: Maryland Public Schools, Oct. 1992, S3610–2.11

Analysis of State Education Indicators: State Profiles and NAEP Results Related to State Policies and Practices, 1993, A4355–1

Analysis of Workers' Compensation Laws, A3840–2

Anatomy and Magnitude of State Tax Increases in 1992, U5085–2.9

Annual AMS-MAA Survey, A2085–1

Annual Bulletin of Vital Statistics for the Year 1991, Tennessee, S7520–2

Annual Consumer Expenditures Study, C4655–1.510

Annual Data Reference: 1991-92 Caseload Data by Individual Courts, Judicial Council of California, S0905–2

Annual Data, 1993: Copper, Brass, Bronze; Copper Supply and Consumption, 1972-92, A4175–1

Annual Financial and Statistical Report, School Year 1991/92, Division of Special Education, Ohio, S6265–1

Annual Financial Report, for 79th Fiscal Year Ending June 30, 1991, New Mexico, S5585–1

Annual Financial Review: The Annual Report of the Supermarket Companies, A4950–1

Annual Fiscal Report

Index by Titles

Annual Fiscal Report (Budgetary Basis), State of Wisconsin, 1992, S8675–2

Annual Fiscal Report (Budgetary Basis), State of Wisconsin, 1993, S8675–2

Annual Full-Time Equivalent Enrollment and Student Semester Credit Hour Production in Arkansas State Institutions of Higher Education, 1991/92, S0690–2

Annual Inquiry and Complaint Summary, 1992, A4350–1

Annual National Survey of Recent Home Buyers, B2150–1

Annual Planning Information, California, 1991, S0830–2

Annual Planning Information, New Hampshire, S5205–3

Annual Planning Information Report for Pennsylvania, FY92, S6845–3

Annual Planning Information Report, Program Year 1993 (July 1993-June 1994), Colorado, S1040–3

Annual Planning Information Report, Program Year 1993, Michigan, S3980–1

Annual Planning Information, State of Mississippi, PY93, S4345–1

Annual Planning Information, West Virginia, Program Year 1993, S8534–2

Annual Planning Report, 1993, North Dakota, S6140–2

Annual Rank-Order Distribution of Administrative Salaries Paid, U5960–1

Annual Report and Directory, Oklahoma, S6462–1

Annual Report and Statistical Data, Compiled for the Year Ending Dec. 31, 1992, Missouri, S4527–1

Annual Report, Fiscal Year Ending June 30, 1992, State of Kansas Department of Revenue, S3020–1

Annual Report from the Supervisor of Banking, Washington State, S8325–1

Annual Report, FY91, Massachusetts Department of Revenue, S3917–1

Annual Report, FY92, Mississippi Department of Human Services, S4357–1

Annual Report, FY92, State of Maine Judicial Branch, S3463–1

Annual Report, Judicial Council of California, S0905–1

Annual Report Missouri Coordinating Board for Higher Education, S4520–1

Annual Report, Nebraska Department of Revenue, S4950–1

Annual Report of Fatal and Injury Motor Vehicle Traffic Accidents, California, S0885–1

Annual Report of Financial Institutions, Year Ending Dec. 31, 1991, West Virginia, S8530–1

Annual Report of Labor Market Information, 1992, Utah, S7820–10

Annual Report of Superintendent of Banks of the State of Alabama, for the Fiscal Year Ending Sept. 30, 1992, S0110–1

Annual Report of Tennessee Behavioral Risk Factors, S7520–3

Annual Report of the Arkansas Judiciary, FY91-92: Statistical Supplement of All Arkansas Courts, S0647–1

Annual Report of the Bank Commissioner of Arkansas, S0632–1

Annual Report of the Bank Commissioner of the State of Maryland, S3655–2

Annual Report of the Bank Commissioner of the State of Vermont, for the Year Ended Dec. 31, 1992, S7995–2

Annual Report of the Banking Commissioner of the State of Connecticut, for the Year Ended Dec. 31, 1991, S1160–1

Annual Report of the Bureau of Financial Institutions, State Corporation Commission, Commonwealth of Virginia, S8180–2

Annual Report of the Chief Administrator of the Courts, State of New York, S5730–1

Annual Report of the Commissioner of Financial Institutions, State of Utah, S7830–1

Annual Report of the Courts of Kansas, FY92, S3035–1

Annual Report of the Delaware Judiciary, S1360–1

Annual Report of the Department of Banking and Consumer Finance, State of Mississippi, Jan. 1, 1992-Dec. 31, 1992, S4325–1

Annual Report of the Department of Commerce and Insurance, Business of 1991, Tennessee, S7466–1

Annual Report of the Department of Insurance, State of Arizona, S0483–1

Annual Report of the Division of Banking to the General Assembly, Rhode Island, S6945–1

Annual Report of the Insurance Commissioner of the State of California, S0900–1

Annual Report of the Insurance Commissioner of the State of Maryland, S3655–1

Annual Report of the Insurance Commissioner of the State of Vermont for the Year Ended June 30, 1992, S7995–1

Annual Report of the Insurance Commissioner of the State of West Virginia, S8575–1

Annual Report of the Insurance Commissioner, State of Utah, S7845–1

Annual Report of the Judicial Council, Supreme Court of Louisiana, S3375–1

Annual Report of the Kansas Insurance Department, S2990–1

Annual Report of the Maryland Judiciary, 1991-92, S3600–1

Annual Report of the New Hampshire Insurance Department, S5220–1

Annual Report of the New Mexico Financial Institutions Division, S5652–1

Annual Report of the North Dakota Judicial System, S6210–1

Annual Report of the Oklahoma Tax Commission, Fiscal Year Ended June 30, 1992, S6495–1

Annual Report of the Regional Airline Association, A8795–1

Annual Report of the South Dakota Unified Judicial System, S7395–1

Annual Report of the State Bank Commissioner of the State of Colorado, S1070–2

Annual Report of the State of California, Budgetary Basis, Fiscal Year Ended June 30, 1992, S0815–1

Annual Report of the State of Ohio Department of Taxation for the Fiscal Year Ending June 30, 1992, S6390–1

Annual Report of the State Superintendent of Public Education to the Legislature of Mississippi, 1993: Statistical Reports 1991/92, S4340–1

Annual Report of the Superintendent of Banking of the State of Iowa, for the Year Ending June 30, 1992, S2760–2

Annual Report of the Superintendent of Insurance to the New York Legislature, S5770–3

Annual Report of the Superintendent of Public Instruction, Statistical and Financial Data for FY91-92, Arizona, S0470–1

Annual Report of the Treasurer of the State of Wyoming, for the Period July 1, 1991-June 30, 1992, S9010–1

Annual Report of the Treasurer, State of Washington, S8455–1

Annual Report of the Utah State Superintendent of Public Instruction, 1991-92, S7815–1

Annual Report of the Utah State Tax Commission, July 1, 1991-June 30, 1992, S7905–1

Annual Report of Vital Statistics in Vermont, S8054–1

Annual Report: Offenders in New Jersey Correctional Institutions on Dec. 31, 1991, by Selected Characteristics, S5370–1

Annual Report: Oklahoma State Department of Education, S6423–1

Annual Report on Advanced Dental Education, 1991/92, A1475–10

Annual Report on Advanced Dental Education, 1992/93, A1475–10

Annual Report on Allied Dental Education, 1991/92, A1475–5

Annual Report on Allied Dental Education, 1992/93, A1475–5

Annual Report on Dental Education, 1992/93, A1475–3

Annual Report on the Condition of Wisconsin Savings and Loan Associations and Savings Banks, S8807–1

Annual Report on the Work of the Georgia Courts, S1903–1

Annual Report on Utility and Carrier Regulation, A7015–1

Annual Report: State of Idaho, Department of Insurance, S2260–1

Annual Report Statistical Information, Missouri Division of Family Services, S4575–2

Annual Report Statistical Supplement, 1990, State of Hawaii Department of Health, S2065–1

Annual Report, Texas Department of Human Services, S7695–1

Annual Report, Texas Department of Insurance, S7700–1

Annual Report, Vital Statistics of Massachusetts, 1990, S3850–1

Annual Report, 1991-92, California Public Utilities Commission, S0930–1

Annual Report, 1991-92, State Board of Education, Ohio, S6265–2

Annual Report: 1991/92 Educational Statistical Summary, West Virginia, S8540–3

Annual Report 1992, Colorado Department of Revenue, S1075–1

Annual Report, 1992, Missouri Department of Labor and Industrial Relations, S4530–2

Annual Report, 1992, Oregon Department of Insurance and Finance, Division of Finance and Corporate Securities, S6616–1

Annual Report, 1992, Treasurer of the State of Iowa, S2885–1

Annual Statement Studies, RMA, A6400–3

Annual Statistical Report, American Association of Colleges of Osteopathic Medicine, A0620–1

Annual Statistical Report, American Iron and Steel Institute, 1992, A2000–2

Index by Titles

Biennial Report of the

Annual Statistical Report, Florida Department of Health and Rehabilitative Services, S1745–4

Annual Statistical Report of the Department of Education for the Scholastic Year Ending June 30, 1992, State of Tennessee, S7490–2

Annual Statistical Report of the Illinois State Board of Education, S2440–1

Annual Statistical Report of the Insurance Department of the Commonwealth of Pennsylvania for the Period July 1, 1991-June 30, 1992, S6835–1

Annual Statistical Report of the Michigan Insurance Bureau, S3983–1

Annual Statistical Report: Report to the Supreme Court of Iowa by the State Court Administrator, S2815–1

Annual Statistical Report, State Correctional System, Pennsylvania, S6782–1

Annual Statistical Report, Summary 1990/91, Kansas State Board of Education, S2945–1

Annual Statistical Report, The Board of Trade of Kansas City, Missouri, Inc., B1530–1

Annual Statistical Report, 1992/93: Public School Certified and Non-Certified Personnel, Idaho, S2225–3

Annual Statistics of Electric Companies, 1982-91, Washington State, S8450–1.2

Annual Statistics of Gas Companies, 1982-91, Washington State, S8450–1.3

Annual Statistics of Telecommunications Companies, 1991, Washington State, S8450–1.5

Annual Statistics of Water Companies, 1988-90, S8450–1.1

Annual Statistics of Water Companies, 1989-91, S8450–1.4

Annual Summary of Vital Statistics, Idaho, S2250–2

Annual Summary of Vital Statistics, Kansas, 1991, S2975–1

Annual Summary Report of Degrees Granted by Arkansas Institutions of Higher Education, 1990/91, S0690–3

Annual Supplement to 1993 Analysis of Workers Compensation Laws, A3840–2

Annual Survey, Catholic Charities USA, A3810–1

Annual Survey of Optometric Educational Institutions: Survey Results July 1991-June 1992, A3370–2

Annual Traffic Statistical Report, Delaware, S1435–1

Annual Vital Statistics Report, Maryland, 1988, S3635–1

Annual Vital Statistics Report, Maryland, 1989, S3635–1

Annual Vital Statistics Series: Volume I, S7175–1

Annual Vital Statistics Series, Volume II, S7175–2

Appliance, C2000–1

Appliance Sales by Distributors, States, 1991, A3350–2

Appliance Sales by Distributors, States, 1992, A3350–2

Appropriations of State Tax Funds for Operating Expenses of Higher Education, A8970–1

APSA Survey of Political Science Departments, 1991-92, A2617–1

Architectural Record, C5800–15

Arizona Agricultural Statistics, U5830–1

Arizona Blue Chip Economic Forecast, U0282–1

Arizona Business, U0280–1

Arizona Courts, S0525–1

Arizona Department of Corrections Annual Report, S0464–2

Arizona Department of Revenue 1992 Annual Report, S0515–1

Arizona Economic Indicators, U5850–1

Arizona Economic Trends, S0465–1

Arizona Labor Market Newsletter, S0465–1

Arizona Occupational Profiles, S0465–2

Arizona Occupational Profiles: Construction, S0465–2.34

Arizona Occupational Profiles: Finance, Insurance and Real Estate, S0465–2.36

Arizona Occupational Profiles: Mining, S0465–2.33

Arizona Occupational Profiles: Services, S0465–2.35

Arizona Public Library Statistics, 1991-92, S0495–1

Arizona Statistical Abstract: 1993 Data Handbook, U5850–2

Arizona Traffic Accident Summary, 1991, S0530–1

Arizona Uniform Crime Report, 1992, S0505–2

Arkansas Agricultural Statistics, 1992, U5920–1

Arkansas Business and Economic Review, U5930–1

Arkansas Comprehensive Annual Financial Report for Fiscal Year Ended June 30, 1992, S0670–1

Arkansas Department of Human Services 1990 Statistical Report, S0700–2

Arkansas Department of Human Services 1991 Statistical Report, S0700–2

Arkansas Labor Force Statistics: Annual Averages, 1980-92, S0662–2

Arkansas Oil and Gas Statistical Bulletin, S0737–1

Arkansas Public Service Commission 1992 Annual Report, S0757–1

Arkansas State and County Economic Data, U5935–1

Arkansas Traffic Accident Data, 1991, S0692–1

Arkansas Vital Statistics, 1991, S0685–1

Arkansas 1992 General Election, S0775–1

ARL Annual Salary Survey, 1992, A3365–2

ARL Statistics, 1991-92, A3365–1

Asian-Americans and Public Television, R4250–1.16

ASQC/Gallup Survey on Quality Leadership Roles of Corporate Executives and Directors, A2800–3

Assistance Payments Statistics, Michigan, S4010–1

Association Executive Compensation Study, 8th Edition, A2900–3

Association of American Publishers Industry Statistics, A3274–2

Association of Art Museum Directors 1993 Salary Survey, A3290–1

ATE Survey of Critical Issues in Teacher Education, A3375–1

Atlas Van Lines 26th Annual Survey of Corporate Relocation Policies, B0600–1

Audited 1991/92 Per Student Current Expenditures, Oregon, S6590–1.18

Automobile Finance Study, A4160–2

Automotive Fleet, C1575–2

Automotive Industries, C2150–3

Automotive News, C2710–3

Availability of a Quality Work Force, R4105–78.21

Average Daily Membership Based upon Attendance and Residence, New Hampshire, S5200–1.11

Average Revenue Profiles for Public Broadcasting Stations, FY91, R4250–1.20

Aviation Week and Space Technology, C5800–4

AVMA Directory, A3100–1

Bank CEO Leadership Challenge: Anticipating and Directing Change. A Survey of the Top 300 Banks' Chief Executives, B4490–2.33

Banking the Furnace: Restructuring of the Steel Industry in Eight Countries, R9260–16

Bar Examination Statistics, A7458–1

Baseline Data Reports, A5800–2

Baseline Data Reports. Capital Improvement Financing, 1991, A5800–2.112

Baseline Data Reports. Financial Aspects of Police Liability, A5800–2.113

Baseline Data Reports. Fire Personnel Practices, A5800–2.116

Baseline Data Reports. Soliciting Foreign Business To Meet Economic Development Goals, A5800–2.115

Baseline Data Reports. Use of Council Committees in Local Governments, A5800–2.114

Basic Economic Data for Idaho, 1991, S2230–2

Basic Facts About Wisconsin's Elementary and Secondary Schools, 1992/93, S8795–2

Basic Information on Workplace Safety and Health in the U.S., 1992 Edition, R8335–1

Basic Petroleum Data Book: Petroleum Industry Statistics, A2575–14

BCA Report: 1992 National Survey of Business Support to the Arts, A3690–1

Behavioral Risk Factor Surveillance, Nevada, 1992, S5075–3

Behavioral Risk Factor Surveillance System, Connecticut, 1989-91, S1200–2

Behavioral Risk Factor Surveillance System Summary Report, Utah, 1991, S7835–3

Behavioral Risk Factors and Preventive Health Measures, Massachusetts, 1986-90, S3850–3

Benefit Communications: Enhancing the Employer's Investment, R4105–78.28

Best's Review. Life/Health Insurance Edition, C1050–2

Best's Review: Property/Casualty Insurance Edition, C1050–1

Beverage Industry, C0125–2

Beverage Industry, Annual Manual 92/93, C0125–3

Bicycle Market in Review, A3470–1

Biennial Report, FY90-91, FY91-92, Tennessee Department of Revenue, S7570–1

Biennial Report of the Connecticut Judicial Branch, July 1, 1990-June 30, 1992, S1220–1

Biennial Report of the Division of Finance of the Department of Economic Development, Missouri, S4502–1

Biennial Report of the Montana Department of Revenue for the Period July 1, 1990 to June 30, 1992, S4750–1

Biennial Report of the

Index by Titles

Biennial Report of the Treasurer of State of the State of Arkansas for the Biennial Period Beginning July 1, 1990 and Ending June 30, 1992, S0780–1

Biennial Report, 1989-91, Kentucky Department of Education, S3110–2

Bilateral Trade: Canada, A Fact Sheet on U.S.-Canadian Wood Products Trade, A1630–3, A7870–5

Black Americans: A Statistical Sourcebook, 1993 Edition, C6775–2

Black Enterprise, C4215–1

Board of Directors 19th Annual Study, 1992, B5000–3

Boating Industry: The Boating Business, 1992, C2425–4

Boating 1992, A8055–1

Bottom Line Report: Detailed Cost-of-Doing Business Data for Home Centers, 1992, A8275–1.2

Bowker Annual: Library and Book Trade Almanac, 38th Edition, 1993, C1650–3

Bowling Is Something Special, A1015–1

Brewers Almanac, A3455–1

Brewing Industry in the U.S.: Brewers Almanac, 1992, A3455–1

Bright Christmas 1992, R4105–81.10

Broadcasting & Cable, C1850–14

Budget and the Region, Fiscal 1994, R8490–11

Budgeted 1992/93 Per Student Current Expenditures, Oregon, S6590–1.3

Builder, C4300–1

Building Design and Construction, C1850–9

Building Permit Activity in Florida, U6660–5

Business America Real Estate Monitor, B2800–1

Business Aviation, C5800–30

Business Conditions, A8990–2

Business Expectations, C3150–4

Business Failure Record, Dun and Bradstreet, C3150–8

Business in Nebraska, U7860–1

Business Link, A8955–1

Business Statistics, New York State, S5735–2

Business Week, C5800–7

CableVision, C1858-1, C2965–1

Calendar Year Summary Report of Population Movement, 1991, Wisconsin, S8692–1.4

California Agricultural Exports Annual Bulletin and Statistical Appendix, 1991, B9520–1

California Agricultural Statistics, S0850–1

California Agriculture: Statistical Review 1992, S0850–1.5

California Behavioral Risk Factor Survey, 1991 Update, S0865–2

California Cities, Towns, and Counties, 1993, C4712–3

California Criminal Justice Profile, 1991, Statewide, S0910–2

California Dairy Industry Statistics, 1992, S0850–1.6

California Economic Indicators, S0840–1

California Field Crops Statistics, 1983-92; County Data, 1991-92, S0850–1.4

California Franchise Tax Board 1990 Annual Report, S0855–1

California Franchise Tax Board 1991 Annual Report, S0855–1

California Fruit and Nut Statistics, 1983-92, S0850–1.1

California Labor Market Bulletin, S0830–1

California Library Statistics, 1992, S0825–2

California Library Statistics, 1993, S0825–2

California Livestock Statistics, 1992, S0850–1.2

California Prisoners and Parolees, 1991, S0820–1

California State Banking Department 83rd Annual Report, 1992, S0810–1

California State Board of Equalization Annual Report, Fiscal Year Ending June 30, 1992, S0835–1

California Statistical Abstract, 1992, S0840–2

California Vegetable Crops: Acreage, Production and Value, 1983-92, S0850–1.3

Campaign '92: Voters Say 'THUMBS UP' to Campaign, Process and Coverage. Survey XIII, C8915–4.24

Campus Trends, 1993, A1410–1.38

Canadian Consumer Photographic Survey, A8695–4

Cancer Facts and Figures, 1993, A1175–1

Capital Improvement Financing, 1991, A5800–2.112

Cargo Flown in Scheduled Domestic and International Service: U.S. Airline Industry, A0325–2

Carpet and Rug Industry Review, 1992, A3800–1

Case of the Shrinking State Share, A8945–27.12

Cash Constituents of Congress, R3828–3

Catholic Almanac, C6885–1

CAWP News and Notes, U4510–4

CDCR Population Reports, U0340–1

Census Briefs, Utah, S7832–3

Census in New Mexico: Changes in the Age and Sex Composition of Counties Between 1980 and 1990, U7980–6

Census in New Mexico, Volume II, U7980–6

Census of Population and Housing STF3A Profile, Arkansas, 1990, U5935–7

Census of Population and Housing, Summary Tape File 3, California, 1990, S0840–9

Census 90: Selected Social Characteristics for Rhode Island Counties, Cities, and Towns, S6930–9

Certificated Personnel and Related Information, Fall 1992, S1000–2.2

Certification of Election Returns for the General Election Held Nov. 3, 1992, Tennessee, S/580–1

Certified Property Manager Profile and Compensation Study, 1989 Revised Edition, A5600–4

Certified Statement of Vote, Nov. 3, 1992, General Election, California, S0934–1

Chain Store Age Executive, C5150–4

Challenge of Diversifying Philanthropic Leadership, A9405–1.1

Changes and Challenges: The Transformation of the U.S. Steel Industry, U9640–2.15

Changes in Income Disparities in Selected States Over the 1980s, R3834–14

Changing Structures and Strategies: Survey of American Manufacturing Executives, U9640–4

Changing West: Corrections, A4375–13

Characteristics of Graduate Departments of Psychology, 1990/91, A2620–3

Characteristics of Inmates Committed and Discharged, New York State, S5725–1

Characteristics of Inmates Discharged, 1991, S5725–1.1

Characteristics of Population in California State Prisons by Institution, Dec. 31, 1992, S0820–2

Chemical and Engineering News, A1250–1

Chemical Engineering, C5800–8

Chicago Board of Trade Statistical Annual Supplement, B2120–1

Child Care Employee News: 1992 Salary Survey Summary, A3865–2

Child Poverty Data from the 1990 Census, R3840–20

Children's Stress Index, R9700–2

Chilton's Automotive Industries, C2150–3

Chilton's Automotive Marketing, C2150–10

Chilton's Commercial Carrier Journal, C2150–4

Chilton's Food Engineering, C2150–6

Chilton's Jewelers' Circular-Keystone, C2150–7

China at the Crossroads, R4105–82.8

China Business Review, A9315–1

Chronicle of Higher Education, C2175–1

Chronicle of Philanthropy, C2176–1

Churches and Church Membership in the U.S., 1990, R4985–1

City Fiscal Conditions in 1993, A8012–1.23

Civilian Labor Force Estimates for North Carolina, 1981-91, S5917–4

Class of 1992 Employment Report and Salary Survey, A6505–1

Classified Assessed Valuation Taxes Levied, 1992 Tax Year, Fiscal Year Ending June 30, 1993, West Virginia, S8640 2

Client Characteristics and Population Movement Report, Washington State, S8337–1

Clinton's Press Judged as Less Fair Than Bush's and Reagan's, C8915–7.4

Coal, C5226–1

Coffee, Sugar and Cocoa Exchange 1992 Statistical Annual, B2275–1

College and University Employee Retirement and Insurance Benefits Cost Survey, A9025–3

Colleges and Universities: Basic Student Charges, 1992/93, Pennsylvania, S6790–5.3

Colleges and Universities: Degrees and Awards Conferred, 1990/91, Pennsylvania, S6790–5.2

Colleges and Universities: Degrees and Awards Conferred, 1991/92, Pennsylvania, S6790–5.15

Colleges and Universities: Faculty and Staff, 1991/92, Pennsylvania, S6790–5.5

Colleges and Universities: Faculty and Staff, 1992/93, Pennsylvania, S6790–5.13

Colleges and Universities: Fall Enrollments, 1992, Pennsylvania, S6790–5.9

Colleges and Universities: Finance, 1990/91, Pennsylvania, S6790–5.4

Colleges and Universities: Finance, 1991/92, Pennsylvania, S6790–5.16

Colleges and Universities: Residence of Students, Fall 1992, Pennsylvania, S6790–5.8

Colorado Agricultural Statistics, 1992 Preliminary, 1991 Revised, S0985–1

Colorado Behavioral Risk Factor Surveillance System, 1990, S1010–3

Colorado Comprehensive Annual Financial Report for the Year Ended June 30, 1992, S0980–1

Colorado Department of Revenue Annual Report, S1075–1

Index by Titles

Colorado Department of Social Services Expenditures During FY91, S1085–1

Colorado Educational Statistical Series, S1000–2, S1000–4

Colorado Educational Statistical Series: Certificated Personnel and Related Information, S1000–2.2

Colorado Educational Statistical Series: Pupil Membership and Related Information, S1000–2.1

Colorado Educational Statistical Series: Revenues and Expenditures, S1000–4.3

Colorado Judicial Department Annual Report, 1992, S1035–1

Colorado Labor Force Review, S1040–4

Colorado Vital Statistics, 1990, S1010–1

Commercial Carrier Journal, C2150–4

Commissioner of Banks and Trust Companies, State of Illinois, July 1, 1990-June 30, 1991 Report, S2395–1

Commissioner of Banks and Trust Companies, State of Illinois July 1, 1991-June 30, 1992 Report, S2395–1

Commodity Year Book, C2400–1

Commodity Year Book Statistical Supplement, C2400–2

Commonwealth of Kentucky Comprehensive Annual Financial Report, for the Year Ended June 30, 1992, S3120–1

Commonwealth of Massachusetts Comprehensive Annual Financial Report for the Fiscal Year Ended June 30, 1992, S3777–1

Commonwealth of Virginia Official Election Results, 1992, S8195–1

Community, Technical, and Junior Colleges Statistical Yearbook, 1992 Edition, A0640–1

Comparative Analysis of the Presidential Candidates' Health Plans, R4865–9

Comparative Costs and Staffing Report for College and University Facilities, A3183–1

Comparative Financial Statistics for Public Two Year Colleges: FY92 National Sample, A6705–1

Comparative Statement of Assets, Liabilities, and Capital Accounts of Alaska Banks, S0280–2

Comparative Statement of Insurance Business in South Dakota, S7300–2

Comparative Statistics of Industrial and Office Real Estate Markets, 1993 Guide, A8916–1

Competitiveness Index, 1993, A4475–1

Component Unit Financial Report of the Missouri Department of Revenue, Fiscal Year Ended June 30, 1992, S4570–1

Comprehensive Annual Financial Report for the Fiscal Year Ended June 30, 1991, Iowa, S2860–4

Comprehensive Annual Financial Report for the Fiscal Year Ended June 30, 1992, Iowa, S2860–4

Comprehensive Annual Financial Report for the Fiscal Year Ended June 30, 1992, Pennsylvania, S6810–4

Comprehensive Annual Financial Report for the Year Ended June 30, 1992, North Carolina, S5897–1

Comprehensive Annual Financial Report for the Year Ended June 30, 1992, South Dakota, S7330–1

Comprehensive Annual Financial Report of the State of Michigan, Fiscal Year Ended Sept. 30, 1992, S3985–2

Comprehensive Annual Financial Report of the State of Rhode Island and Providence Plantations for the Fiscal Year Ended June 30, 1992, S6930–1

Condensed Statement of Reports for State and Federal Savings and Loan Associations, Arizona, S0460–1

Condensed Statement of Reports of State and National Banks of Arizona, S0460–2

Condensed Statement of Reports, State Credit Unions, Arizona, S0460–4

Condition of Employment, 1993, Iowa, S2784–3

Conditions in the Women's Garment Industry, A5900–1

Conference Board Reports, R4105–78

Congressional Quarterly Almanac: 102nd Congress, 1st Session, 1991, C2500–2

Congressional Quarterly Almanac: 102nd Congress, 2nd Session, 1992, C2500–2

Congressional Testimony Reports, A1310–2

Connecticut Annual Report of the State Comptroller, S1170–1

Connecticut Behavioral Health Risks, S1200–2

Connecticut Housing Production and Permit Authorized Construction: 1992, S1212–1

Connecticut Labor Situation, S1235–1

Connecticut Motor Vehicle Traffic Accident Data, 1992, S1275–1

Connecticut Public Library Statistical Summary and Salary Survey, FY91, S1242–1

Construction Industry Annual Financial Survey, A4155–1

Consumer Attitude and Behavior Studies, A8200–8

Consumer Confidence Survey, R4105–4

Consumer Credit Delinquency Bulletin, A0950–1

Consumer Finance Licensees Operating in Virginia at the Close of Business Dec. 31, 1992: Supplement to the 1992 Annual Report of the Bureau of Financial Institutions, S8180–3

Consumer Photographic Survey, A8695–2

Convenience Store Industry Fact Book, A6735–2

Converting the Cold War Economy: Investing in Industries, Workers, and Communities, R4700–19

Cooperative Extension Services' Role in Business Incubator Educational Programs, U2410–3

Corn Annual, 1993, A4200–1

Corporate Advertising Practices, 1992, A3357–1

Corporate Boards and Corporate Governance, R4105–78.29

Corporate Contributions, 1991, R4105–8

Corporate Directors' Compensation, 1993 Edition, R4105–7

Corporate Support of Dropout Prevention and Work Readiness, R4105–78.30

Corporate Tax Burden, R9050–15.2

Corporate Volunteer Programs: Benefits to Business, R4105–78.26

Corrections Yearbook, 1992, R4300–1

Corrections Yearbook, 1992: Adult Corrections, R4300–1.1

Corrections Yearbook, 1992: Jail Systems, R4300–1.4

Corrections Yearbook, 1992: Juvenile Corrections, R4300–1.2

Crime in Washington State,

Corrections Yearbook, 1992: Probation and Parole, R4300–1.3

Cost of Doing Business Survey, 1991, A2665–1

Cost of Living Index, A0150–1, A1225–1

Cost of Teacher Benefits in the SREB States, A8945–34

Cost Per Hire Survey Report, A4740–2

Cost per Pupil by District, 1991/92, New Hampshire, S5200–1.5

Cost Survey: 1992 Report Based on 1991 Data, A6365–2

Cotton Counts Its Customers: The Quantity of Cotton Consumed in Final Uses in the U.S., Revised 1990-91 and Preliminary 1992, A7485–1

Council of Teaching Hospitals Survey of Housestaff Stipends, Benefits, and Funding, 1992, A3273–3

County Profiles, B3500–2

Covered Employment and Wages by Industry, Statewide and by County in Tennessee, 1991, S7495–1

Covering the Nation's Most Important Issues: What Public Broadcasting Can Do To Increase Public Understanding, R8825–10.1

CPC Salary Survey: A Study of 1992-93 Beginning Offers, A3940–2

CPC Salary Survey: Regional Interim Reports, A3940–1

Credit Rating Changes: An Indicator of State Fiscal Stress, U5085–2.6

Crime and Delinquency in California, 1991, S0910–1

Crime and Delinquency in California, 1992, S0910–1

Crime and Justice Annual Report, New York, S5760–3

Crime and Justice Report for the District of Columbia, S1535–2

Crime in Alabama, S0119–1

Crime in Arizona, S0505–2

Crime in Arkansas, 1992, S0652–1

Crime in Colorado: Annual Report, 1992, S1068–1

Crime in Connecticut, 1992, S1256–1

Crime in Delaware, 1991: An Analysis of Uniform Crime Data, S1375–5

Crime in Florida, 1992 Annual Report, S1770–1

Crime in Hawaii, 1992: A Review of Uniform Crime Reports, S2035–1

Crime in Idaho, 1992, S2275–2

Crime in Illinois, 1991, S2536–1

Crime in Kansas, 1992, S2925–1

Crime in Kentucky, 1992, S3150–1

Crime in Maine, 1991, S3475–1

Crime in Maryland, S3665–1

Crime in Michigan, Uniform Crime Report, S3997–1

Crime in Montana, 1992 Annual Report, S4705–1

Crime in New Hampshire, 1991, S5250–2

Crime in New Jersey, S5430–1

Crime in North Carolina, S5955–1

Crime in North Dakota: 1991, S6060–1

Crime in Oklahoma, S6465–1

Crime in Pennsylvania: Uniform Crime Report, S6860–1

Crime in South Carolina, 1992, S7205–1

Crime in Texas, 1992, S7735–2

Crime in Utah, 1992, S7890–3

Crime in Virginia, 1992, S8295–2

Crime in Washington State, Annual Report, 1992, S8440–1

Crime in West Virginia, 1991

Index by Titles

Crime in West Virginia, 1991, S8610–1
Crime in Wyoming, Jan.-Dec. 1991, S8867–3
Crossing to Mexico: Priced Out of American Health Care, R4865–10
Cumulative Enrollment Summary and Average Daily Membership Attending, Year Ending June 30, 1992, Oregon, S6590–1.4
CUPA National Faculty Salary Survey by Discipline and Rank, in Private Colleges and Universities, A3900–4
CUPA National Faculty Salary Survey by Discipline and Rank, in Public Colleges and Universities, A3900–5
Current Award Trends in Personal Injury, 1993 Edition, C5180–1
Current Company Practices in the Use of Corporate Advertising, A3357–1
Current Economic Indicators: New Business Incorporations, C3150–3
Current Statistics on White Collar Employees, A1570–1
Current Trends in Child Abuse Reporting and Fatalities: The Results of the 1992 Annual Fifty State Survey, A7456–1
Cycle Safety Info: Motorcycle Accident Statistics, 1991, A6490–2
Cycle Safety Info: State Motorcycle Operator Licensing, 1993, A6490–1

Data Abstracts Series, S0827–2
Data Abstracts Series: Degree Type Data Abstract, June 1990-July 1991, California, S0827–2.2
Data Abstracts Series: Postsecondary Student Enrollments by Student Level, Fall 1991, California, S0827–2.1
Data Book: Financing Postsecondary Education in Delaware for FY94, S1425–1
Data Book on Illinois Higher Education, S2475–1
Data on Astronomy Enrollments and Degrees, A1960 2.3
Data on Physics Enrollments and Degrees: A Supplement, A1960–2.2
Data Report from the 1989 National Museum Survey, A0750–1
Datamation, C1850–5
Debts and Career Plans of Osteopathic Medical Students in 1992, A0620–2
Degree Type Data Abstract, June 1990-July 1991, California, S0827–2.2
Delaware Data Book, S1375–4
Delaware Digest Labor Market Monthly, S1405–2
Delaware Population Consortium Population Projections, Version 1992.0, S1375–3
Delaware Vital Statistics Annual Report, 1990, S1385–2
Demographic State of the State: A Report to the Governor and Legislature on Commuting Patterns for Oklahoma from the 1990 Census, S6416–2
Dental School Admissions, 1992/93, A1475–4.1
Dental School Faculty and Support Staff, 1992/93, A1475–4.5
Dental School Trend Analysis, 1992/93, A1475–4.2
Dental School Tuition, 1992/93, A1475–4.3
Dental Student Attrition, 1992/93, A1475–4.4
Department of Banking and Finance, State of Georgia: 73rd Annual Report, Year Ending Dec. 31, 1992, S1865–1

Department of Financial Institutions Annual Report, Year Ended Dec. 31, 1991, State of Indiana, S2625–1
Department of Taxation Annual Report, 1991-92, Hawaii, S2120–1
Detailed Mortality Statistics, South Carolina, 1990, S7175–2
Development Report Card for the States, R4225–1
Directory and Statistics of Oregon Libraries, 1992, S6635–1
Directory: Juvenile and Adult Correctional Departments, Institutions, Agencies, and Paroling Authorities, 1993, A1305–3
Directory of Community Blood Centers, A0612–1
Directory of Missouri Libraries: Public, Special, College and University, Statistics for FY92, S4520–2
Discount Merchandiser, C8130–1
Discount Store News, C5150–3
Distribution Study of Grocery Store Sales, C3400–6
Distribution: The Transportation & Business Logistics Magazine, C2150–1
Distributor Profit Survey Report, A8505–4
District of Columbia Comprehensive Annual Financial Report, Year Ended Sept. 30, 1992, S1507–1
District of Columbia Courts Annual Report, 1992, S1515–1
District of Columbia Elections, 1990, S1525–1
District of Columbia Elections, 1992, S1525–1
Divorce Courts: Case Management, Case Characteristics, and the Pace of Litigation in 16 Urban Jurisdictions, R6600–6
Do Members Use Public Television Differently? An Exploratory Study, R4250–1.22
Doctorate Employment Survey, A2620–4
Dodge/Sweet's Construction Outlook, Updates, C5800–29
Dodge/Sweet's Construction Outlook '93, C5800–26
Does Imprisonment Reduce Crime? A Critique of 'Voodoo' Criminology, A7575–3
Does Involvement in Religion Help Prisoners Adjust to Prison?, A7575–1.11
Does Quality Work? A Review of Relevant Studies, R4105–78.32
Dollars and Cents of Shopping Centers, 1993: A Study of Receipts and Expenses in Shopping Center Operations, R9285–1
Dollars and Sense: Catholic High Schools and Their Finances, 1992, A7375–5
Donoghue's Money Fund Directory, C4682–2
Donoghue's Mutual Funds Almanac, C4682–1
Drug Store News, C5150–2
DSHS County Data Report, FY90, Washington State, S8420–2
Dun and Bradstreet Business Expectations Survey, C3150–4
Dun and Bradstreet Business Failure Record, C3150–8

E&MJ, C5226–2
Economic Abstract of Alabama, U5680–2
Economic and Labor Market Projections for New Hampshire and Its Counties: FY92 and FY93, S5205–7

Economic Area Survey, Dec. 31, 1992, Maine, S3473–1
Economic Assistance Statistics, New Jersey, S5415–1
Economic Conditions in New Hampshire, S5205–1
Economic Effects of the Corporate Alternative Minimum Tax, A1310–4
Economic Handbook of the Machine Tool Industry, A3179–2
Economic Incentives and Comparative Advantage in Indonesian Food Crop Production, R5620–1.37
Economic Indicators: County Profiles, B3500–2
Economic Indicators: Fall 1992 Regional Economic Survey, B6785–1
Economic Indicators, Hawaii, B3500–1
Economic Indicators: Spring 1993 Regional Economic Survey, B6785–1
Economic Newsletter, Russian Research Center, U2030–1
Economic Outlook, A8813–1
Economic Outlook: Chamber of Commerce of the U.S., A3840–6
Economic Profile of Oregon, Update 1992, S6585–3
Economic Report, B2000–2
Economic Report of the Governor, 1993, California, S0840–3
Economic Report, The State of South Carolina, S7125–3
Economic Report to the Governor of the State of Tennessee on the State's Economic Outlook, S7560–1
Economic Significance of Toyota Motor Manufacturing, U.S.A., Inc., in Kentucky, U7138–1.4
Economic Times, R4105–80
Economic Update, Nevada, S5040–1
Editor & Publisher Market Guide, 1993, C3250–1
Education in Alaska: Report to the People, S0295–1
Education Statistics: Projections to 1996/97, Pennsylvania, S6790–5.10
Education Week, R4800–2
Educational Statistics for New Hampshire, S5200–1
Effects of Diminished Economic Opportunities on Social Stress: Heart Attacks, Stroke, and Crime, R4700–18
EL&P: Electric Light and Power, C6985–6
Election in North Dakota, U8080–1
Election Report, State of Indiana, S2702–1
Election Statistics, State of Kansas, 1992 Presidential Preference Primary, Primary and General Elections, S3030–1
Electric Light and Power, C6985–6
Electric Perspectives, A4700–4
Electric Power Equipment Report, A4700–2
Electrical Wholesaling, C4725–5
Electrical World, C5800–28
Electricity Supply and Demand, 1993-2002, A8630–2
Electronic Business, C1850–2
Electronic Business Buyer, C1850–2
Electronic Market Data Book, 1993 Edition, A4725–1
Electronic Market Trends, A4725–2
Electronics Foreign Trade, A4725–3
Elementary-Secondary Public School Enrollment, 1992/93 School Year, Vermont, S8020–1

Index by Titles

EMA Report of National Cost Per Hire Data, A4740–2
Emerging Trends, R8780–1
Employee Benefits, 1992 Edition, A3840–1
Employment Outlook Survey, Manpower, Inc., B5275–1
Employment Review, New York State, S5775–1
Employment Survey, 1991, A1960–1
EMU and the Regions, R5025–9
End of the Line? What the End of Emergency Unemployment Benefits Means, R3834–18
Energy Prices and Externalities, A2575–28
Energy Statistics Sourcebook, 7th Edition, C6985–9
Engineering and Mining Journal, C5226–2
Engineering and Technology Degrees, 1992, A0685–1
Engineering and Technology Enrollments, Fall 1992, A0685–2
Engineering News-Record, C5800–2
Engineers' Salaries: Special Industry Report, 1993, A0685–3
ENR, C5800–2
Enrollment and Graduations in Baccalaureate and Graduate Programs in Nursing, A0615–4
Enrollment and Staff in California Private Schools, 1992/93, S0825–8
Enrollment in California Public Schools, 1992/93, S0825–7
Enrollments and Degrees, A1960–2.1
Enrollments at Public, Four-Year Colleges and Universities: Annual Survey, A7150–5
Enrollments in Grades 9-12 in New Hampshire Approved Public Secondary Schools and Approved Public Academies, Oct. 1, 1992, S5200–1.7
Equal Employment Opportunity Data for Utah, S7832–3.4
Equalized Valuation per Pupil of New Hampshire School Districts, S5200–1.16
Ernst & Young/IMRA Survey of Retail Loss Prevention Trends, A5940 2
Estimated Building Aid for 1993/94, New Hampshire, S5200–1.14
Estimated Costs and Benefits of Retrofitting Aboveground Petroleum Industry Storage Tanks with Release Prevention Barriers, A2575–26
Estimated Distributor Sales by State, A3350–2
Estimated Expenditures of School Districts, 1992/93, New Hampshire, S5200–1.6
Estimates of Fall 1992 Enrollment at Public, Four-Year Institutions, A7150–5
Estimates of the Population of Virginia Counties and Cities, U9080–9
Estimates of the Total Population of Counties in Texas by Age, Sex, and Race/Ethnicity for July 1, 1991, S7645–2
Estimates of the Total Populations of Counties and Places in Texas, July 1, 1991, S7645–1
Expense Analysis, 1992: Condominiums, Co-ops, and PUDs, A5600–3
Exports: Pacific Rim, A Fact Sheet on U.S. Wood Product Exports to the Pacific Rim, A1630–2, A7870–4
Eye Banking Statistics, A4743–1

Fact Book for the Year 1992, B6625–1
Fact Book on Arkansas Public Higher Education, S0690–4

Florida Public Service

Fact Book on Arkansas Public Higher Education Finance, S0690–4
Fact Book on Theological Education for the Academic Year 1992/93, A3376–1
Fact Book, South Dakota Board of Regents, S7375–1
Fact Book, 1991/92, State University System of Florida, S1725–1
Fact Book, 1992/93: A Statistical Handbook, S3610–1
Fact Book: 1993 Property/Casualty Insurance Facts, A5650–1
Fact Sheet: Approved Elementary, Middle, Junior High, and Senior High Schools (by District for School Year 1991/92), New Hampshire, S5200–1.13
Fact Sheets, U4510–1
Factbook and Membership Directory, Mortgage Insurance Companies of America, A6455–1
Factory Shipments of Appliances: Historical Data, A3350–4
Facts About Newspapers '93, A8605–4
Facts About Store Development, A4950–2
Facts and Figures of the U.S. Plastics Industry, 1993 Edition, A8920–1
Facts and Figures on Government Finance: 1993 Edition, R9050–1
Faculty Salaries in Baccalaureate and Graduate Programs in Nursing, A0615–1
Faculty Salaries in Graduate Departments of Psychology, A2620–1
Fairchild's Electronics Industry Financial Directory, 1992/93, C3400–4
Fairchild's Retail Stores Financial Directory, 1992/93, C3400–2
Fairchild's Textile and Apparel Financial Directory, 1992/93, C3400–5
Fall Enrollments by School Administrative Unit, 1992/93, New Hampshire, S5200–1.8
Fall Enrollments in New Hampshire Public Schools and Approved Public Academies, Oct. 1, 1992, S5200–1.10
Fall 1992 Enrollment, North Dakota Institutions of Higher Education, S6110–1
Family Assistance Administration Statistical Bulletin, S0465–4
Family Planning and Child Survival Programs as Assessed in 1991, R8720–1
Family Planning Perspectives, A5160–1
Famine in Ethiopia: Policy Implications of Coping Failure at National and Household Levels, R5620–1.36
Far From Done Reports, A9405–1
FAS-FAX: Canadian Daily Newspapers, Circulation Averages, A3385–3.2
FAS-FAX Reports, A3385–3
FAS-FAX: U.S. and Canadian Periodicals, Circulation Averages, A3385–3.4
FAS-FAX: U.S. and Canadian Weekly Newspapers, Circulation Averages, A3385–3.3
FAS-FAX: U.S. Daily Newspapers, Circulation Averages, A3385–3.1
Fatal Motor Vehicle Accident Comparative Data Report, 1992, New Jersey State Police, S5430–2
Federal Spending in the Northeast and Midwest: FY92, R8490–35
Federal Tax Burden by State, R9050–15.5
Fertilizer Use on Smallholder Farms in Eastern Province, Zambia, R5620–1.38
Fiber Organon, C3460–1
Fibre Box Industry Annual Report, 1992, A4875–1

Final Report of the NCAA Gender-Equity Task Force, A7440–6
Financial and Operating Ratios Survey, 1992 Plastics Processing Companies, A8920–4
Financial Aspects of Police Liability, A5800–2.113
Financial Condition of Medical Malpractice JUAs, A0375–1
Financial Digest, B2000–1
Financial Operating Reports, A8275–1
Financial Report, Maine, S3420–1
Financial Report of Public School District, All Classes, School Year 1988/89, Nebraska, S4865–3
Financial Report on Colorado State Chartered Savings and Loan Associations and Credit Unions, 1992, S1070–3
Financial Statements and Operating Ratios for the Mortgage Banking Industry, 1989, A6450–3
Financial Statistics of the Major Privately Owned Utilities in New York State, 1991, S5795–1
Financial Statistics of the Major Privately Owned Utilities in New York State, 1992, S5795–1
Financial Summaries, Idaho School Districts, FY92, S2225–2
Fire Personnel Practices, A5800–2.116
Fiscal Profiles, 1992, S0827–3
Fiscal Profiles, 1993, S0827–3
Fiscal Survey of States, A7955–1
Fiscal Year Statistical Report, Texas Department of Criminal Justice, S7660–1
Fiscal Year Summary of Population Movement, 1992, S8692–1.6
Five Million Children: 1992 Update, U1260–2
Five Million Children: 1993 Update, U1260–2
Five Year Statistical Glance at D.C. Public Schools: School Years 1987/88-1991/92, S1605–2
Fleet Accident Rates, 1992, A8375–3
Fleet Executive, A6755–1
Florida Agricultural Statistics, S1685–1
Florida Agricultural Statistics, Citrus Summary, 1991-92, S1685–1.1
Florida Agricultural Statistics, Field Crops Summary, 1992, S1685–1.4
Florida Agricultural Statistics, Livestock, Dairy, and Poultry Summary, 1992, S1685–1.3
Florida Agricultural Statistics, Vegetable Summary, 1991-92, S1685–1.2
Florida Comprehensive Annual Financial Report, Fiscal Year Ended June 30, 1992, S1717–3
Florida County Court Summary Report, 1992, S1805–1
Florida County Perspectives, 1992-93 Edition, C6360–1
Florida Department of Corrections 1991/92 Annual Report, S1720–1
Florida Department of Insurance Annual Report, S1760–1
Florida Estimates of Population, Apr. 1, 1992, U6660–4
Florida Health Care Atlas, S1746–1
Florida Labor Market Trends, S1765–3
Florida Library Directory with Statistics, S1800–2
Florida Municipal Profiles, 1991-92, C4712–6
Florida Public Service Commission, 1992 Annual Report, S1790–1

Florida Statistical Abstract

Index by Titles

Florida Statistical Abstract, U6660–1
Florida Traffic Crash Data, 1992, S1750–2
Florida Vital Statistics, 1991, S1745–3
Florida Vital Statistics, 1992, S1745–3
Focus, R5685–4
Focus on Manhattantrends, B2800–5
Focus on Marketrends, 1993, B2800–3
Focus: Quarterly Report on the Nuclear Fuel Cycle, B6790–1
Folio: The Magazine for Magazine Management, C2575–1
Food Marketing Industry Speaks, 1992-93, A4950–5
Footwear Manual, A4957–1
Forbes, C3950–1
Forecast of Georgia and Atlanta, U1880–2
Forecast of the Nation, U1880–1
Forecast 1993-94, B3520–1
Foreign Activity: An Analysis of Foreign Participation in the U.S. Securities Markets, A8825–2
Foreign Business Activity in the Former U.S.S.R., R4105–82.4
Forest Industries, C3975–1
Forging the Vision: Survey of U.S. Technology Chief Executives, B4490–2.34
Fortune, C8900–1
Fortune Directory of the Largest U.S. Industrial corporations, C8900–1.513
Foundation Giving: Yearbook of Facts and Figures on Private, Corporate and Community Foundations, R4900–1
Foundry Management and Technology, C7000–2
Franchising in the Economy, 1989-92, A5820–1
From Belief to Commitment: The Community Service Activities and Finances of Religious Congregations in the U.S., 1993 Edition, A5435–4
Fuel Oil News: The Oil Heating Industry: 1992, C4680–2
Full-Time Equivalency of Public School District Personnel, by County as of Oct. 1, 1992, Oregon, S6590–1.2
FY90-91 Statistical Supplement to the Pennsylvania Tax Compendium, S6885–1
FY91-92 Statistical Supplement to the Pennsylvania Tax Compendium, S6885–1
FY92 Annual Report, Arizona Department of Corrections, S0464–2
FY92 Annual Report Statistical Information, Missouri Division of Family Services, S4575–2
FY93 Fact Book, South Dakota Board of Regents, S7375–1

Gallup Poll Monthly, C4040–1
GAMA Statistical Highlights, A5100–1
Gas Facts, 1991 Data: A Statistical Record of the Gas Utility Industry, A1775–3
Gas Stats: Monthly Gas Utility Statistical Report, A1775–2
Gas Stats: Quarterly Report of Gas Industry Operations, A1775–1
Gas Utilities Annual Report, Fiscal Year 1992, Railroad Commission of Texas, S7745–1
GED Statistical Report, A1410–16
Gender Gap, U4510–1.65
General Aviation Aircraft Shipment Report, A5120–1
General Aviation Airplane Shipment Report, A5120–1

General Aviation Statistical Databook, 1993 Edition, A5120–2
General Election and Special Election for the Office of Hawaiian Affairs, Nov. 3, 1992, Hawaii, S2077–1.2
General Election, Nov. 3, 1992: Official Canvass Summary, Iowa, S2865–1
General Election Results, Florida, S1800–1
General Election Returns, Nevada, S5125–1
General Fund Summary of Expenditures by Program and Per Pupil Costs, July 1, 1989-June 30, 1990, Indiana, S2608–2.1
General Fund Summary of Expenditures by Program and Per Pupil Costs, July 1, 1990-June 30, 1991, Indiana, S2608–2.1
General Fund Summary of Expenditures by Program and Per Pupil Costs, July 1, 1991-June 30, 1992, Indiana, S2608–2.1
General Income Characteristics: Pennsylvania, 1990, U4130–13
General Social Surveys, 1972-91: Cumulative Codebook Supplement, U6395–1
Georgia Agricultural Facts, 1992 Edition, S1855–1
Georgia Business and Economic Conditions, U6730–2
Georgia County Guide, 12th Edition, 1993, U6750–1
Georgia Department of Corrections 1992 Annual Report, S1872–1
Georgia Department of Revenue 1992 Statistical Report, S1950–1
Georgia Labor Market Trends, S1905–1
Georgia State University Forecast: Georgia and Atlanta, U1880–2
Georgia State University Forecast: The Nation, U1880–1
Georgia Statistical Abstract, 1992-93, U6730–1
Georgia Uniform Crime Reporting Program, Summary Report, S1901–1
Georgia Vital Statistics Report, 1991, S1895–1
Geriatric Length of Stay by Diagnosis and Operation, U.S., 1992-93, B4455–1.6
German Reunification, R4105–82.3
Getting It Done: From Commitment to Action on Funding for Women and Girls, A9405–1.2
Giving and Volunteering, 1992: Volunteering and Giving Among American Teenagers 12 to 17 Years of Age, A5435 5
Giving USA 1993 Edition: The Annual Report on Philanthropy for the Year 1992, A0700–1
Global Business White Papers, R4105–82
Global Business White Papers: China at the Crossroads, R4105–82.8
Global Business White Papers: Foreign Business Activity in the Former U.S.S.R., R4105–82.4
Global Business White Papers: German Reunification, R4105–82.3
Global Business White Papers: Gulf War, R4105–82.1
Global Business White Papers: Islamic Fundamentalism, R4105–82.7
Global Business White Papers: Latin America—A Region in Transition, R4105–82.6
Global Business White Papers: Privatization, R4105–82.5
Global Business White Papers: Uruguay Round of GATT, R4105–82.2

Global Contributions of U.S. Corporations, R4105–78.23
Going to Mexico: Priced Out of American Health Care, R4865–10
Government Relations Survey, A1800–1
Grade Organization: Enrollment by Race/Ethnicity and Professional Staff at School Level, Sept. 30, 1992, Maryland, S3610–2.8
Grades Offered by Oregon Regular Schools, 1992/93, S6590–1.6
Graduation-Rates Summary, Division I, A7440–4
Grain Guide: North American Grain Yearbook, C8450–2
Graphic Arts Monthly, C1850–10
Grounds Maintenance: 1992 Salary Survey, C4725–6
Group Comprehensive Major Medical Net Claim Cost Relationships by Area, B6095–1
Group Health Insurance Costs Most in Los Angeles: 73 Percent Higher Than National Average, B6095–2
GSU Economic Forecasting Center: Monthly Projections, U1880–3
Guide to the Division of Insurance and Comparative Statement, S7300–2
Gulf War, R4105–82.1

Half of Us: Families Priced Out of Health Protection, R4865–14
Handbook of Campaign Spending: Money in the 1990 Congressional Races, C2500–6
Harris-Equifax Consumer Privacy Survey, 1992, B3280–2
Health Behavior Trends, 1988-90: Kentucky Lifestyles, S3140–6
Health Care Chief Executive, B4490–2.35
Health Insurance Coverage in Connecticut, S1200–3
Health of America's Children, 1992, R3840–5
Health Risk Behaviors, 1991, Michigan, S4000–4
Health Risks of Pennsylvania Adults, 1991, S6820–4
Heavy Burden of Home Care, R4865–15
Helicopter Annual, A5190–1
HIA Statistical Report, A5185–1
High School Completers, Oregon Public Schools, S6590–1.10
High School Profile Report, Normative Data: HS Graduating Class of 1992 National Report, R1960–6
Higher Education Panel Reports, A1410–1
Highlights from the Public Television Programming Survey, 1990, R4250–1.15
Hispanic Americans: A Statistical Sourcebook, 1993 Edition, C6775–3
Hispanic Business, C4575–1
Hispanic Public Television Viewing, R4250–1.24
HMO Industry Profile 1992 Edition, A5150–2
Holding Company Report, A9360–1
Home Appliance Newsline, A3350–1
Home Buyers Survey, B2150–1
Home Equity Loan Study, A4160–3
Home Lending Survey, A4160–3
Home Sales, A7000–2
Honolulu County in 1993, B3500–2.2
Hope and Home: Program Descriptions and Possible Changes, R8490–42

Index by Titles

Hospital Admission Rates, B4455–4
Hospital Finance Almanac, B1880–1
Hospital Inpatient Charges, B4455–5
Hospitals & Health Networks, A1865–1
Housing Production in Delaware, 1992, S1387–1
How Consumers Evaluate Service in Their Supermarket, 1991, A4950–37.1
How To Win and Influence Shoppers, 1992, A4950–37.2
HR Strategies, B6850–5
Human Services Plan, FY91-93, Volume III, Illinois, S2425–1

IAAPA 1992 Amusement Industry Abstract, A5700–1
IBC/Donoghue Money Fund Directory, 1993 Edition, C4682–2
IBC/Donoghue Mutual Funds Almanac, 24th Edition, 1993, C4682–1
Idaho Construction Report, B3900–1
Idaho Department of Education Public and Nonpublic School Membership, 1992/93 School Year (as Reported Sept. 25, 1992), S2225–1
Idaho Economic Forecast, S2245–2
Idaho Facts, S2218–2
Idaho Librarian: Statistics for Idaho Academic Libraries, A5370–1
Idaho Public Library Statistics, FY91, S2282–1
Idaho Public Library Statistics, FY92, S2282–1
Idaho Public Utilities Commission Annual Report, S2290–1
Idaho State Tax Commission 1992 Annual Report, S2295–1
Idaho Vital Statistics, S2250–2
Illinois Agricultural Statistics, 1992, S2390–1
Illinois Annual Reports, 1992, S2415–1
Illinois Business Review, U6910–1
Illinois Crash Facts and Statistics, S2540–1
Illinois Department of Financial Institutions FY91 Annual Report, S2457–2
Illinois Department of Public Aid Annual Report, FY91 and FY92, S2520–2
Illinois Economic Summary, S2405–2
Illinois Electric Utilities: A Comparative Study of Electric Sales Statistics for Calendar Years 1992 and 1991, S2410–1.2
Illinois Gas Utilities: A Comparative Study of Gas Sales Statistics for Calendar Years 1992 and 1991, S2410–1.1
Illinois Mental Health Statistics, FY93, S2505–1
Illinois Public Library Statistics: A Guide for Librarians and Trustees, 1991-92, S2535–2
Illinois Statistical Abstract, U6910–2
Illinois Utilities Statistics, S2410–1
Illustrated Analysis of North Carolina Traffic Accident Statistics, S5990–1
Impact of Health Care Financing on Family Budgets, R4700–20
Impact of President Clinton's Tax Proposals on Capital Formation, A1310–2.2
Impact of the Clinton Economic Plan on the States, U5085–2.10
Impact of Travel on State Economies, 1990, R9375–7
Impact of Unfunded Federal Mandates on U.S. Cities: A 314 City Survey, A9330–12
Implement and Tractor, C0495–1, C3450–1
Imported Crude Oil and Petroleum Products, A2575–12

INC., C4687–1
Incentive/ Managing and Marketing Through Motivation, C1200–4
Income Maintenance Administration Monthly Statistical Report, Maryland, S3645–2
Income of Utah, S7832–3.3
Income/Expense Analysis, 1992: Conventional Apartments, A5600–1
Income/Expense Analysis, 1992: Federally-Assisted Apartments, A5600–5
Income/Expense Analysis, 1992: Office Buildings, A5600–2
Income/Expense Analysis, 1992: Shopping Centers, A5600–6
Indiana Business Review, U2160–1
Indiana Comprehensive Annual Financial Report for the Fiscal Year Ended June 30, 1992, S2570–1
Indiana Department of Education Reports, S2608–2
Indiana Department of Financial Institutions Annual Report, S2625–1
Indiana Department of Public Welfare Annual Report, S2623–1
Indiana Division of Family and Children FY92 Annual Report, S2623–1
Indiana Judicial Report, S2703–1
Indices: A Statistical Index to District of Columbia Services, S1535–3
Individual School Report, Oct. 1, 1992, Massachusetts, S3810–4
Industrial Distribution, C1850–4
Industrial Research Institute's Annual R&D Trends Survey, A5510–1
Industry Estimates: Machine Tool Orders and Shipments, A3179–1
Industry Staffing Patterns for Education, Apr. 1991, S7675–1.28
Industry Staffing Patterns for Railroads, May 1991, S7675–1.29
Industry Staffing Patterns for Selected Trade and Regulated Industries, 2nd Quarter 1991, S7675–1.31
Industry Staffing Patterns for State and Local Government, May 1991, S7675–1.30
Industry Statistics, A3274–2
Industry Week, C7000–3
Information About Public Education in Massachusetts, S3810–3
Information Digest, Kentucky Institutions of Higher Education, S3130–3
Information Digest of Postsecondary Education in Iowa, 1990/91, S2755–1
Information for Strategic Decisions, R4105–78.25
Information Systems Study, 1992, A4950–7
Information Systems Study, 1993, A4950–7
Insurance Collision Report, A5200–1
Insurance Collision Report: Initial Results for 1993 Vehicles, A5200–1.2
Insurance Collision Report: 1990-92 Passenger Cars, Vans, Pickups, and Utility Vehicles, A5200–1.1
Insurance Commissioner's Annual Report, State of West Virginia, S8575–1
Insurance Company Statistical Report, S8180–1
Insurance Division Annual Report Made to the General Assembly, Rhode Island, S6945–2
Insurance Industry: A Key Player in the U.S. Economy, A0375–2
Insurance Injury Report: 1990-92 Passenger Cars, Large Vans, Pickups, and Utility Vehicles, A5200–3

Insurance Losses by Vehicle Density, 1990-92 Models, A5200–4.31
Insurance Special Reports, A5200–4
Insurance Theft Report: 1990-92 Passenger Cars, Vans, Pickups, and Utility Vehicles, A5200–2
Integrated Resource Planning for Water Utilities, A8195–11
Interior Design, C1850–7
International Coal Review, A7400–3
International Coal, 1992 Edition, A7400–2
International Comparison of Public Spending on Education, A1600–4
International Economic Indicators, U1245–1
International Economic Scoreboard, R4105–6
International Energy Statistics Sourcebook, 2nd Edition, C6985–10
International Family Planning Perspectives, A5160–6
International Index of Executive Vacancies, B5000–5
International Open Interest Report, A5040–6
International Petroleum Encyclopedia, 1993, C6985–3
International Report: International Volume, A5040–5
International Rotary Drilling Rig Report, B4675–1
International Seismic Crew Count, A8912–2
International Shipbuilding Aid, A8900–8
Interservice, A2072–2
Investment Tax Credit and Economic Growth:, A1310–1.16
Iowa Health Risk Behaviors, 1991 Final Report, S2795–2
Iowa Individual Income Tax Annual Statistical Report, S2860–3
Iowa Public Library Statistics, 1991-92, S2778–1
Iowa Retail Sales and Use Tax Report, S2860–1
Iron Ore Report U.S. and Canada, A2010–1
Iron Ore, 1992, A2010–3
Islamic Fundamentalism, R4105–82.7

Jail and Detention Statistics and Information, Illinois, S2425–2
JCK: Jewelers' Circular-Keystone, C2150–7
JEI Report, R5650–2
Jewelers' Circular-Keystone, C2150–7
Jobson's Liquor Handbook, 1993, C4775–1
Jobson's Wine Handbook, 1993, C4775–2
Joint Association Survey on Drilling Costs, A2575–9
Journal-Bulletin Rhode Island Almanac, C7975–1
Journal of Commercial Lending, A6400–2
Journal of Soviet Nationalities, U1520–1
Journal of the American Veterinary Medical Association, A3100–2
Journalism Educator, A3225–1
Judicial Statistics, State of Vermont, for the Year Ending June 30, 1992, S8120–1
Judiciary, State of Hawaii: Annual Report, July 1, 1991-June 30, 1992, S2115–1
Juveniles Taken into Custody Research Program: Estimating the Prevalence of Juvenile Custody by Race and Gender, A7575–1.13

Kansas Annual Financial Report for Period July 1, 1991-June 30, 1992, S2900–1

Kansas Business Review

Index by Titles

Kansas Business Review, U7095–1
Kansas Farm Facts, 1993, S2915–1
Kansas Statistical Abstract, 1991-92, U7095–2
Kansas Traffic Accident Facts, 1991, S3040–1
Kansas Traffic Accident Facts, 1992, S3040–1
Kauai County in 1992 and 1993, B3500–2.1
KEDI Economic Survey, B4950–1
Kentucky Agricultural Statistics, 1992-93, S3085–1
Kentucky Annual Labor Market Planning Information, Program Year 1993, S3140–3
Kentucky Department of Financial Institutions Annual Report, Dec. 31, 1992, S3121–1
Kentucky Deskbook of Economic Statistics, S3104–1
Kentucky Traffic Accident Facts, 1992 Report, S3150–2
Kentucky Vital Statistics Report, S3140–1
Kids Count Data Book: State Profiles of Child Well-Being, R3832–1
Knight-Ridder CRB Commodity Year Book Statistical Supplement, C2400–2
Knight-Ridder CRB Commodity Year Book, 1993, C2400–1
KSA Perspective: Apparel and Footwear Profiles for 1992, B8130–2
KSA Perspective: Retail Profile for 1992, B8130–4
KSA Perspective: Textile Profile for 1992, B8130–1

Labor Market Information for Rhode Island Planners, 1992, S6980–3
Labor Market Information for Rhode Island Planners, 1993, S6980–3
Labor Market Information Newsletter, S6430–2
Labor Market Report, Tennessee, S7495–2
Labor Market Review, Virginia, S8205–6
Labor Situation, S1235–1
Labor Survey, Plastics Processing Companies, A8920–2
Language Census Report for California Public Schools, 1992, S0825–10
Latest Scoop Worldwide: Facts and Figures on Ice Cream and Related Products, A5825–1
Latin America: A Region in Transition, R4105–82.6
Leading National Advertisers, C2710–1.547
Legislative Finance Papers, A7470–4
Length of Stay by Diagnosis and Operation, North Central Region, B4455–1.3
Length of Stay by Diagnosis and Operation, Northeastern Region, B4455–1.2
Length of Stay by Diagnosis and Operation, Southern Region, B4455–1.4
Length of Stay by Diagnosis and Operation, U.S., B4455–1.1
Length of Stay by Diagnosis and Operation, U.S. Geriatric, B4455–1.6
Length of Stay by Diagnosis and Operation, U.S., Pediatric, B4455–1.7
Length of Stay by Diagnosis and Operation, Western Region, B4455–1.5
Length of Stay, by Diagnosis and Operation, 1992-93, B4455–1
Length of Stay by DRG and Payment Source, North Central Region, B4455–3.3
Length of Stay by DRG and Payment Source, Northeastern Region, B4455–3.2

Length of Stay by DRG and Payment Source, Southern Region, B4455–3.4
Length of Stay by DRG and Payment Source, U.S., B4455–3.1
Length of Stay by DRG and Payment Source, Western Region, B4455–3.5
Length of Stay by DRG and Payment Source, 1992-93, B4455–3
Less Support for Clintonomics Over the Back Fence, C8915–7.1
Library and Information Science Education Statistical Report, 1993, A3235–1
Library Directory and Statistics, 1993, S5095–1
Library Journal, C1852–1
Life Insurance Fact Book, A1325–1
Lifestyle Behaviors of Adult Residents of the State of Georgia: Behavioral Risk Factor Survey, 1991, S1895–2
Lifestyle Characteristics of 1992 Sporting Goods Consumers, A8485–4
Lifestyles of Health: Behavioral Risk Factor Surveillance Report, Alabama, 1989, S0175–6
Lilly Digest, 1992, B5165–1
Lilly Hospital Pharmacy Survey, 1992, B5165–3
Local Emergency Response Plans, A5800–4.34
Local Government Finances in Maryland for the Fiscal Year Ended June 30, 1992, S3618–1
Local Government Infrastructure Financing, A5800–4.33
Local Housing Authorities in the 1990s, A6800–2
Local Taxes Outpace State Taxes, U5085–2.11
Lodging Hospitality: Lodging's 400 Top Performers, C7000–5
Lodging Hospitality: 1993 Almanac, C7000–6
Loss and Expense Ratios: Insurance Expense Exhibits, New York State, S5770–1
Louisiana Annual Planning Report, S3320–1
Louisiana Department of Education 143rd Annual Financial and Statistical Report, 1991/92, S3280–1
Louisiana Energy Indicators, U2730–1
Louisiana FactBook, U8010–4
Louisiana Labor Market Information, S3320–2
Louisiana Traffic Records Data Report, S3345–2

Machine Tool Orders and Shipments: Industry Estimates, A3179–1
Magazine Trend Report, A3385–1
Maine: A Statistical Summary, S3434–1
Maine Department of Public Safety 1992 Statewide Accident Data, S3475–2
Maine Educational Facts, S3435–1
Maine Labor Market Digest, S3465–2
Maine Occupational Staffing, S3465–1
Maine Occupational Staffing for Educational Services Industry, Apr. 1991, S3465–1.26
Maine Occupational Staffing for Federal Government (Mar. 1992), State Government (May 1991), Local Government (May 1991), S3465–1.27
Maine Occupational Staffing for Wholesale Trade, Retail Trade, Transportation, Communications, Electric, Gas, and Sanitary Services, Second Quarter 1991, S3465–1.25

Maine Vital Statistics, 1991, S3460–2
Major Home Appliance Industry Fact Book, A3350–3
Major Home Appliance Industry Shipments, A3350–1
Major Traffic Accidents, State of Hawaii, 1986, S2125–1
Majority of Students Attend Large Public Colleges, A8945–27.10
Making High Schools Work Through Integration of Academic and Vocational Education, A8945–33
Making Them Wait for Social Security Disability Benefits, R4865–11
Management Compensation Study for Wholesalers and Large Retailers, A4950–6
Management Information and Statistical Report, FY92, Wyoming, S8908–1
Management Report: Detailed Cost-of-Doing Business Data for Hardware Stores, 1992, A8275–1.1
Managing Corporate Communications in a Competitive Climate, R4105–78.24
Managing Today's Automated Workplace, B6850–7
Managing Today's Human Resource Priorities, B6850–3
Manpower, Inc. Employment Outlook Survey, B5275–1
Manufactured Housing Institute Manufacturing Report, A6325–1
Manufacturing Report, A6325–1
Many Faces of Public Housing, A6800–1
Market Survey Motor Production Reports, A8904–1
Maryland Automated Accident Reporting System: National Safety Council Report, Statewide, 1992, S3665–4
Maryland Income Tax Division, Summary Report, S3685–1
Maryland Medical Care Programs: The Year in Review, FY92, S3635–3
Maryland Monthly Labor Review, S3605–2
Maryland Public Library Statistics, FY92, S3610–5
Maryland Public School Enrollment by Sex and Race/Ethnicity, Sept. 30, 1992, S3610–2.4
Maryland Public Schools, S3610–2
Maryland Statistical Abstract, S3605–1
Massachusetts Election Statistics, 1992, S3920–1
Massachusetts Employment Review, S3808–1
Massachusetts Municipal Profiles, 1991-92, C4712–2
Massachusetts Municipal Profiles, 1992-93, C4712–2
Massachusetts Public Library Data, 1992, S3870–1
Massachusetts Trial Court Interim Annual Report, 1992, S3807–1
Maui County in 1993, B3500–2.3
Meat and Poultry Facts, A2100–1
Meat Industry Financial Operating Survey, A2100–2
Meatfacts, A2100–1
Media Monitor, R3823–1
Medicaid Services in Kentucky, S3140–5
Medicaid State Reports, FY91, A0565–1
Medical Groups in the U.S., A Survey of Practice Characteristics, 1993 Edition, A2200–7
Medical School Admission Requirements, 1994/95 U.S. and Canada, A3273–10

Index by Titles

Meeting the Challenge: Condition of Education in Connecticut, Elementary and Secondary, S1185–3
Membership Compensation Survey: 1992 Report Based on 1992 Data, A6365–3
Menu Analysis, 1992, A8200–22
Mergers and Acquisitions, C4683–1
Mergerstat Review, 1992, B6020–1
Metal Producing, C7000–8
Metro Magazine, C1575–3
Metropolitan Life Insurance Co. Statistical Bulletin, B6045–1
Metropolitan Life Survey of the American Teacher, 1992, the Second Year. New Teachers' Expectations and Ideals: A Survey of New Teachers Who Completed Their Second Year of Teaching in Public Schools in 1992, B6045–2
Metropolitan Life Survey of the American Teacher, 1993: Teachers Respond to President Clinton's Education Proposals, B6045–7
Metropolitan Washington, D.C., Area Labor Summary, S1527–3
Michigan Agricultural Statistics, 1992, S3950–1
Michigan Department of Corrections 1991 Statistical Report, S3960–1
Michigan Financial Institutions Bureau 1992 Annual Report, S3957–1
Michigan Health Statistics, 1990, S4000–3
Michigan Insurance Bureau Annual Statistical Report for the Year Ending Dec. 31, 1991, S3983–1
Michigan K-12 School Districts Ranked by Selected Financial Data, 1991/92, S3965–3
Michigan State Courts Annual Report, 1991, S3962–1
Michigan State Courts Annual Report, 1992, S3962–1
Michigan Traffic Crash Facts, 1991, S3997–2
Michigan's Labor Market News, S3980–2
Mid-Level Practitioners: Their Role in Providing Quality Health Care, U8850–8.4
Middle East Population Puzzle, R8750–2.59
Military Base Closings Information Packet, R8490–45
Military Market, C0500–1
Milling and Baking News: 1993 Grain Guide, North American Grain Yearbook, C8450–2
Milling and Baking News: 1993 Milling Directory & Buyer's Guide, C8450–3
Milling Directory & Buyer's Guide, C8450–3
Minneapolis Grain Exchange Statistical Annual, B6110–1
Minnesota Agriculture Statistics, 1993, S4130–1
Minnesota Department of Commerce Annual Insurance Supplement, 1991, S4140–4
Minnesota Department of Public Service Biennial Report, S4235–1
Minnesota Election Results, 1992: Presidential Primary Election, State Primary Election, and State General Election, S4255–1
Minnesota Health Statistics, 1990, S4190–2
Minnesota Health Statistics, 1991, S4190–2
Minnesota Labor Market Review, S4205–1
Minnesota Labor Market Trends, S4205–3
Minnesota Libraries: Minnesota Public Library Statistics, 1991, S4165–2
Minnesota Motor Vehicle Crash Facts, 1992, S4230–2
Minnesota State Individual income Tax, S4250–1

Minorities in Higher Education: 11th Annual Status Report, A1410–10
Mississippi Comprehensive Annual Financial Report, 1992, S4346–1
Mississippi State Tax Commission Annual Report, FYE June 30, 1992, S4435–1
Mississippi Statistical Abstract, 1992, U3255–4
Missouri Area Labor Trends, S4530–3
Missouri Crime and Arrest Digest, S4560–2
Missouri Department of Corrections Institutional Admission and Release Report for FY93, S4501–1
Missouri Department of Labor and Industrial Relations Annual Report, S4530–2
Missouri Farm Facts, 1992, S4480–1
Missouri Farm Facts, 1993, S4480–1
Missouri Roster, 1993-94: A Directory of State, District, and County Officials, S4580–1
Missouri Traffic Crashes, 1993 Edition, S4560–1
Missouri Vital Statistics, 1992, S4518–1
Mixed Message: An Analysis of the 1994 Federal Regulatory Budget, U9640–1
Modern Gold Coinage, 1992, A5145–1
Modern Plastics, C5800–12
Modern Silver Coinage, 1992, A8902–2
Money Fund Directory, C4682–2
Montana Agricultural Statistics, 1992, S4655–1
Montana Annual Planning Information, 1993-94, S4710–3
Montana Annual Traffic Statistical Report, 1992, S4705–2
Montana Comprehensive Annual Financial Report for the Fiscal Year Ended June 30, 1992, S4653–1
Montana Employment and Labor Force Trends, S4710–1
Montana Health Data Book and Medical Facilities Inventory, 1992, S4690–2
Montana Public Library Statistics for July 1991-June 1992, S4725–1
Montana Public School Enrollment Data, School Year 1992/93, S4740–1
Montana Vital Statistics, 1990-91, S4690–1
Monthly Business Failures, C3150–2
Monthly Completion Report for U.S. Oil, Gas and Dry Wells, A2575–3
Monthly Completion Report: Report on Well Completions in the U.S., A2575–3
Monthly Market Trend Reports, A9095–2
Monthly Options Report: Volume of Options Contracts Traded, A5040–3
Monthly Projections, U1880–3
Monthly Public Assistance Statistical Report, Iowa, S2802–1
Monthly Seismic Crew Count, A8912–1
Monthly Statistical Movement Summary for Iowa Department of Corrections, S2770–1
Monthly Statistical Report, Estimated U.S. Petroleum Balance, A2575–2
Monthly Statistical Report, Resins, A8920–5
Monthly Survey of Life Insurance Sales in Canada, A6225–2
Monthly Survey of Life Insurance Sales in the U.S., A6225–1
Monthly Tire Report, A8810–1
Monthly Truck Tonnage Report, A3075–1
Monthly Volume Report: Volume of Futures Contracts Traded, A5040–2
Mortgage Banking, A6450–2
Motor Vehicle Accident Statistics, Rhode Island, S7025–1

NCAA Division I

Motor Vehicle Facts and Figures, A0865–1
Motor Vehicle Statistics, Accidents, License and Registration Statistical Data, New York State, S5790–1
Motorcycle Statistical Annual, A6485–1
Municipal Year Book, 1993, A5800–1
Music USA 1993: Statistical Review of the U.S. Music Products Industry, A6848–1
Mutual Fund Fact Book: Industry Trends and Statistics for 1991, A6025–1
Mutual Funds Almanac, C4682–1

NABE Industry Survey, A6650–4
NABE Outlook, A6650–5
NABE Policy Survey, A6650–6
NACUBO Endowment Study, A6705–2
NADA Data 1993: Economic Impact of America's New Car and Truck Dealers, A7330–1
NAFA Fleet Executive: The Magazine for Vehicle Management, A6755–1
NAHCR Recruitment Survey, A6500–1
NAIS Statistics: Financial Aid, Financial Operations, Enrollment, Staffing, A6835–2
NAIS Statistics: Tuitions, Teacher and Administrator Salaries, A6835–1
NAIS Statistics, 1992, A6835–3
NAPM Insights: Report on Business, A6910–1
NASDAQ Fact Book and Company Directory, A7105–1
NASSGP 24th Annual Survey Report, 1992/93 Academic Year, A7140–1
National Association for Health Care Recruitment Survey, A6500–1
National Association of State Scholarship and Grant Programs, Annual Survey Report, A7140–1
National Child Care Staffing Study Revisited: Four Years in the Life of Center-Based Child Care, A3865–3
National Cost Per Hire Data, 1992, A4740–2
National Delinquency Survey, A6450–1
National Faculty Salary Survey by Discipline and Rank, in Private Colleges and Universities, A3900–4
National Faculty Salary Survey by Discipline and Rank, in Public Colleges and Universities, A3900–5
National High School Sports Record Book, 1993 Edition, A7830–2
National Home Center News, C5150–6
National Index of Executive Vacancies, B5000–5
National Jail and Adult Detention Directory, A1305–1
National League Green Book, 1993, A8015–1
National Opinion Ballot Report, A4965–1
National Petroleum News, C4680–1
National Roster of Hispanic Elected Officials, A6844–1
National Statistics Program: Shipments, 1992 vs. 1991, A9095–1
National Urban Education Goals: Baseline Indicators, 1990-91, A4425–4
National Venture Capital Association 1991 Annual Report, A8515–1
Nation's Restaurant News, C5150–5
Naval Shipbuilding, A8900–6
Naval Stores Review, 1992 International Yearbook, C6585–1
NCAA Division I Graduation-Rates Summary, A7440–4

NCCD Focus

Index by Titles

NCCD Focus, A7575–1

Nebraska Agricultural Statistics, S4835–1

Nebraska Department of Correctional Services, 18th Annual Report, FY91/92, S4850–1

Nebraska Department of Health 1991 Vital Statistics Report, S4885–1

Nebraska Department of Social Services Annual Report, 1992, S4957–1

Nebraska Elementary and Secondary Education, S4865–2

Nebraska Elementary and Secondary Education: Membership by Race and Sex, 1992-93, S4865–2.5

Nebraska Elementary and Secondary Education: Membership Data, 1992-93, S4865–2.2

Nebraska Elementary and Secondary Education: Membership History, 1992-93, S4865–2.3

Nebraska Elementary and Secondary Education: Ranking by Membership, 1992-93, S4865–2.4

Nebraska Elementary and Secondary Education: School District Census, 1992-93, S4865–2.6

Nebraska Elementary and Secondary Education: School District Data, 1992-93, S4865–2.1

Nebraska Elementary and Secondary Education: Staffing Data, 1992-93, S4865–2.7

Nebraska Labor Market Information Quarterly, S4895–2

Nebraska Public Library Profile: 1990-91 Statistical Data, S4910–1

Nebraska Public Service Commission Biennial Report, July 1, 1990-June 30, 1992, S4940–1

Nebraska Statistical Handbook, S4855–1

Nebraska Supreme Court 1991 Annual Report, S4965–2

Nebraska Supreme Court 1992 Annual Report, S4965–2

Nevada Agricultural Statistics, 1993, S5010–1

Nevada Area Labor Review, 1992-93: 1992 Economic Activity and 1993 Outlook, S5040–4

Nevada Business and Economic Indicators, U7920–2

Nevada Economic Update, S5040–1

Nevada Education in 1991/92: A Status Report, S5035–2

Nevada Gaming Abstract, 1992, S5062–1

Nevada Library Directory and Statistics, S5095–1

Nevada Review of Business and Economics, U7920–1

Nevada Statistical Abstract, 1992 Edition, S5005–1

Nevada Traffic Accidents, 1992, S5140–1

Nevada Vital Statistics Report, 1989, S5075–1

New Business Incorporations, C3150–3

New Direction: The Clinton Budget and Economic Plan, R3834–17

New Directions: Texas Department of Human Services Annual Report, S7695–1

New Diversity: Women and Minorities on Corporate Boards, B4490–2.36

New Hampshire Labor Market Areas Planning Guide, S5205–6

New Hampshire Library Statistics, 1991, S5227–1

New Hampshire Occupational Employment Statistics, S5205–2

New Hampshire Public High School Graduates: Graduating Class of 1991, S5200–1.2

New Hampshire Public High School Graduates: Graduating Class of 1992, S5200–1.15

New Hampshire Staffing Patterns in Government and Educational Services, 1991, S5205–2.25

New Hampshire Staffing Patterns in Wholesale and Retail Trade, 1991, S5205–2.26

New Jersey Agriculture, 1992, S5350–1

New Jersey Building Permits, 1991 Annual Summary, S5425–3

New Jersey Casino Control Commission Annual Report, S5360–1

New Jersey Comprehensive Annual Financial Report, June 30, 1992, S5455–1

New Jersey Department of Insurance 1989 Annual Statistical Report, S5420–1

New Jersey Department of Insurance 1990 Annual Report, S5420–1

New Jersey Economic Indicators, S5425–1

New Jersey Health Statistics, 1990, S5405–1

New Jersey Municipal Data Book, 1992-93 Edition, C4712–4

New Jersey Public Library Statistics, 1991, S5385–2

New Mexico Accountability Report, 1991/92, S5575–4

New Mexico Agricultural Statistics, 1991, S5530–1

New Mexico Business, Current Economic Report, U7980–1

New Mexico Financial Institutions Division Annual Report, S5652–1

New Mexico Income Support Division Monthly Statistical Report, S5620–2

New Mexico Labor Market Annual Planning Indicators, S5624–1

New Mexico Labor Market Review, S5624–2

New Mexico Public Library Statistics, FY91, S5627–1

New Mexico Public Library Statistics, FY92, S5627–1

New Mexico Public Service Commission 48th Annual Report, July 1, 1991-June 30, 1992, S5645–1

New Mexico School District and Student Achievement Profiles, S5575 2

New Mexico State Courts 1992 Annual Report, S5623–1

New Mexico Taxation and Revenue Department Combined Annual Reports, 79th and 80th Fiscal Years (1990-91 and 1991-92), S5660–1

New Mexico Traffic Crash Data, 1992, S5665–1

New York Agricultural Statistics, 1992-93, S5700–1

New York State Behavioral Risk Factor Surveillance System, 1990 Reports, S5765–3

New York State Business Fact Book, 1992, S5735–3

New York State Business Statistics, S5735–2

New York State General Election Vote, Nov. 3, 1992, S5750–1

New York State Municipal Profiles, 1993, C4712–7

New York State Statistical Yearbook, U5100–1

News Release from the Air-Conditioning and Refrigeration Institute, A0300–1

Newsline, A0605–2

Newspaper and Newsprint Facts at a Glance, 1992-93, A8610–1

Newsprint Division Annual Statistical Summary '91, A1630–8

Newsprint Division Annual Statistical Summary '92, A1630–8

Newsprint Division Monthly Statistical Report, A1630–4, A2500–3

NFIB Quarterly Economic Report for Small Business, A7815–1

NHFA Annual Operating Experiences Report, A7975–1

Nielsen Annual Review of Retail Drugstore Trends, C5150–2.503

NLS Handbook, 1992: The National Longitudinal Surveys, U3780–2

NLS Handbook, 1993: The National Longitudinal Surveys, U3780–2

NLS Older Male Sample Revisited: A Unique Data Base for Gerontological Research, U3780–9

No Sale: The Failure of Barebones Insurance, R4865–16

NOPA Dealer Operating Results, 1992, A8110–1

North American Free Trade Agreement's Auto Text in Strategic Context, R8490–43

North American Newsprint Industry: Transitions to Recycling, A4375–15

North Carolina Agricultural Statistics, 1992, S5885–1

North Carolina Courts, 1990-91: Annual Report of the Administrative Office of the Courts, S5950–1

North Carolina Department of Correction Statistical Abstract, S5900–1

North Carolina Traffic Accident Facts, 1992, S5990–1

North Carolina Utilities Commission: 1992 Report, S5917–2

North Carolina Vital Statistics. Vol. 1: Births, Deaths, Population, Marriages, Divorces, S5927–1.1

North Carolina Vital Statistics. Vol. 2: Leading Causes of Mortality, S5927–1.2

North Carolina Vital Statistics, 1991, S5927–1

North Dakota Agricultural Statistics, 1993, U3600–1

North Dakota Correctional Facilities Report, S6060–2

North Dakota Courts Annual Report, 1992, S6210–1

North Dakota Educational Directory, 1992/93, S6180–2

North Dakota Labor Market Advisor, S6140–4

North Dakota Library Statistics, FY91, S6180–5

North Dakota Official Abstract of Votes Cast at the General Election Held Nov. 3, 1992, S6205–1

North Dakota Vehicular Crash Facts, S6217–1

North Dakota Votes, U8080–1

North Dakota 1991 Vital Statistics Report, S6105–2

Northwestern Lindquist-Endicott Report, 1993: A National Survey of 258 Well-Known Business and Industrial Organizations, U3730–1

Index by Titles

Nov. 3, 1992 General Election Results, Florida, S1800–1
NPN—National Petroleum News, C4680–1
NPTA Management News, A8140–3
NSFRE Profile: 1992 Membership Survey, A8455–1
NUEXCO Monthly Report, B6800–1
NUEXCO Review, B6800–1
NUEXCO Review, 1992, B6800 2
Number of Households and Average Household Size in Florida: Apr. 1, 1992, U6660–3.45
Number of Maryland Public Schools by Organization and Enrollment, Sept. 30, 1992, S3610–2.5
Number of Public Schools, 1992/93, Oregon, S6590–1.5
Number of Pupils Enrolled in Nonpublic Schools, Fall 1987, Indiana, S2608–2.7
Number of Pupils Enrolled in Nonpublic Schools, Fall 1988, Indiana, S2608–2.7
Number of Pupils Enrolled in Nonpublic Schools, 1989/90, Indiana, S2608–2.7
Number of Pupils Enrolled in Nonpublic Schools, 1990/91, Indiana, S2608–2.7
Number of Pupils Enrolled in Nonpublic Schools, 1991/92, Indiana, S2608–2.7
Number of Pupils Enrolled in Nonpublic Schools, 1992/93, Indiana, S2608–2.7
Number of Pupils Enrolled in Public Schools, 1992/93, Indiana, S2608–2.6
Nurses in Texas: Nurse Aides to Advanced Nurse Practitioners, 1971-91, U8850–8.2
Nursing and Health Care, A8010–3
Nursing Data Review, 1993, A8010–1
Nursing Home Insurance: Who Can Afford It?, R4865–12

Occupational Employment in Selected Nonmanufacturing Industries and Government in North Carolina, 1991, S5917–5.?
Occupational Employment Reports, North Carolina, S5917–5
Occupational Profiles: Massachusetts, S3808–2
Off-Premises Market, A8200–21
Offenders Admitted to Adult Correctional Institutions, 1991, Wisconsin, S8692–1.2
Offenders Released from Adult Correctional Institutions, 1991, S8692–1.3
Official Abstract of Votes, General Election, Nov. 3, 1992, State of Oregon, S6665–1
Official Catholic Directory, 1993 General Summary, C4950–1
Official Election Returns and Registration Figures for South Dakota, General Election, Nov. 3, 1992, S7390–1
Official General Election Returns, Nov. 3, 1992, Texas, S7750–1
Official Primary and General Election Returns for 1991, Kentucky, S3213–1
Official Primary and General Election Returns for 1992, Kentucky, S3213–1
Official Report of the Board of State Canvassers of the State of Nebraska: Primary Election, May 12, 1992; General Election, Nov. 3, 1992, S4955–1
Official Results, 1992 General Election, Delaware, S1365–1
Official Returns of the State General Election, Nov. 3, 1992, State of Washington, S8425–1

Official 1992 General Election Canvass, Montana, S4760–1
Offshore, C6985–2
Offshore, Incorporating The Oilman, C6985–2
Ohio Comprehensive Annual Financial Report for the Fiscal Year Ended June 30, 1992, S6255–1
Ohio Courts Summary, 1992, S6385–1
Ohio Department of Agriculture Annual Report for 1991, S6240–1
Ohio Department of Highway Safety 1991 Crash Facts, S6290–1
Ohio Department of Rehabilitation and Correction FY91 Annual Report, S6370–1
Ohio Election Statistics for 1991-92, S6380–1
Ohio Labor Market Information: Labor Market Review, S6270–1
Ohio Labor Market Review, S6270–1
Ohio Short Term Forecast of Utility Fuels, 1992-93, S6355–1
Oil and Gas Journal, C6985–1
Oil and Gas Journal Data Book, 1993 Edition, C6985–4
Oil and Natural Gas Producing Industry in Your State, A5425–1
Oil, Gas, and Helium Production Report, Arizona, S0473–1
Oil Industry Outlook, 9th Edition, 1993-97, C6985–5
Oklahoma Agricultural Statistics, 1992, S6405–1
Oklahoma Business Bulletin, U8130–1
Oklahoma Comprehensive Annual Financial Report for the Fiscal Year Ended June 30, 1991, S6438–1
Oklahoma Department of Corrections FY91 Annual Report, S6420–1
Oklahoma Department of Human Services FY92 Annual Report, S6455–1
Oklahoma Labor Market, S6430–2
Oklahoma Traffic Accident Facts, S6482–1
On-Campus Enrollment and Geographic Origins in Arkansas Higher Education, Fall 1991, S0690–1
Open Doors 1991/92: Report on International Educational Exchange, R5580–1
Open Interest Report: Open Interest of Last Trading Day, A5040–4
Open Secrets: Encyclopedia of Congressional Money and Politics, R3828–2
Operating Results of Independent Supermarkets, 1991, A4950–4
Operating Results of Mass Retail Stores and the Mass Retailers' Merchandising Report, A5940–6
Operating Statistics of Telephone Companies in Illinois for Calendar Year 1992, S2410–2
Oregon Agriculture and Fisheries Statistics, S6575–1
Oregon Comprehensive Annual Financial Report for the Year Ended June 30, 1992, S6603–2
Oregon Educational Statistics, S6590–1
Oregon Industrial Outlook, S6615–9
Oregon Labor Trends, S6592–1, S6615–2
Oregon Public Middle Schools, 1992/93, with Oct. 1, 1992 Membership by Grade, S6590–1.11
Oregon Public School Racial-Ethnic Summary, by County and by Grade, Oct. 1, 1992, S6590–1.9
Oregon Public Secondary Schools, 1992/93, with Oct. 1, 1992 Membership by Grade, S6590–1.13

Petroleum Industry

Oregon School District Financial Elections, 1992, S6590–1.15
Oregon School District Tax Bases, S6590–1.20
Oregon School Districts, July 1, 1992, S6590–1.14
Oregon School Districts Levying Authority, 1992/93, S6590–1.20
Oregon Vital Statistics Annual Report, 1991, S6615–5
Outlook for Business in the New Europe, C8915–9
Outlook for Commercial Aircraft, 1992-2011, B3075–1
Overview of the Indigent Health Care System in Texas, U8850–8.7

Packaging, C1850–1
Paper, Paperboard, and Wood Pulp Monthly Statistical Summary, A1630–5, A2500–2
Paper, Paperboard, Pulp Capacity and Fiber Consumption, 1991-95, A1630–7
Paperboard Packaging, C0125–4
Papers of the Program on Population, R4500–1
Parallel Banking System, R4700–22
Pari-Mutuel Racing, 1990, A3363–1
Passenger Car and Truck Scrappage and Growth in the U.S., C7715–2
Passenger Traffic Statistics, U.S. Scheduled Airline Industry, A0325–1
Pediatric Length of Stay by Diagnosis and Operation, U.S., 1992-93, B4455–1.7
Pennsylvania Business Survey, U4110–1
Pennsylvania Department of Transportation 1991 Statistical Summary Report, S6905–3
Pennsylvania Employment and Transportation Table, 1990 Census by County and Municipality, C1595–16
Pennsylvania Energy Profile, 1960-90, S6810–3
Pennsylvania General Income/Poverty Table, 1990 Census by County and Municipality, C1595–15
Pennsylvania Housing Table, 1990 Census by County and Municipality, C1595–14
Pennsylvania Library Statistics, S6790–2
Pennsylvania Statistical Abstract, U4130–6
Pennsylvania's Labor Force: A Monthly Statistical Analysis, S6845–1
Pension Policy for a Mobile Labor Force, R9260–17
Pension World, C2425–1
Pensions & Investments, C2710–2
People, the Press and Politics, C8915–4
People's Poll on Schools and School Choice: A New Gallup Survey, A7375–8
Per Pupil Expenditures by Program, Massachusetts, S3810–5
Personnel Practices in Planning Offices, A2615–3
Personnel Roster: Salary Reports, Texas, S7670–1.4
Personnel Roster: Sex and Ethnicity Reports, Texas, S7670–1.3
Perspective 92, A5785–2
Perspectives '93, R2800–2
Petroleum Engineer International, C4420–1
Petroleum Independent: The Oil and Natural Gas Producing Industry in Your State, 1993-94, A5425–1
Petroleum Industry Environmental Performance, 1992, A2575–27

Phi Delta Kappan

Index by Titles

Phi Delta Kappan, A8680–1
Physician Characteristics and Distribution in the U.S., 1993 Edition, A2200–3
Physician Compensation and Production Survey: 1992 Report Based on 1991 Data, A6365–1
Physics and Astronomy Enrollments and Degrees, A1960–2
Pipeline & Utilities Construction, C6780–2
Pipeline and Gas Journal, C6780–1
Pit and Quarry: Review/Outlook, C0125–6
Place to Call Home: The Low Income Housing Crisis in 44 Major Metropolitan Areas, R3834–16
Planners' Salaries and Employment Trends, 1991, A2615–1
Planning Commission: Its Composition and Function, 1987, A2615–2
Plastics Processing Companies, Annual Labor Survey, A8920–2
Plastics Processing Companies: Financial and Operating Ratios, A8920–4
Pocket Guide to the Chicago Market, C2130–1
Pocket Summary of Registrations: New Cars, New Trucks, C7715–3
Police Salaries, 1992, A5800–4.32
Policy Research Project on Health Care Cost and Access: Working Papers, U8850–8
Policy Study Series, U9640–2
Policy Surveys, C8915–7
Population and Water Resources: A Delicate Balance, R8750–2.57
Population Bulletin, R8750–2
Population Changes in Alabama's Black Belt: 1880-1990, U0340–1.6
Population Estimates for the State of Tennessee, S7560–2
Population Projections by Age, Sex, and Race for Florida and Its Counties, 1991-2010, U6660–3.43
Population Projections by Age, Sex, and Race for Florida and Its Counties, 1992-2010, U6660–3.46
Population Projections for Oklahoma, 1990-2020, S6416–1
Population Projections, Ohio and Counties by Age and Sex: 1990 to 2015, S6260–3
Population Reports, U2520–1
Population Reports, CDCR, U0340–1
Population Reports. Reproductive Revolution: New Survey Findings, U2520–1.51
Population Studies Bulletin, U6660–3
Population Today, R8750–1
Population Trends for Washington State, S8345–4
Postsecondary Student Enrollments by Student Level, Fall 1991, California, S0827–2.1
Potash Imports: Statistical Report, A8720–4
Potash Production, Inventory, Disappearance, and Sales: Statistical Report, A8720–2
Potash Sales: Statistical Report, Press Release, A8720–5
Potash Summary Report, A8720–1
Potential Supply of Natural Gas in the U.S. (Dec. 31, 1992), R8765–1
Power Plant Deliveries, A7400–9
Practitioner Compensation in Group Practice and HMOs: A 1992 Report, B7450–2
Preliminary Scheduled Cargo Traffic Statistics, U.S. Scheduled Airline Industry, A0325–2
Preliminary Scheduled Passenger Traffic Statistics: U.S. Scheduled Airline Industry, A0325–1

Prescription Costs: America's Other Drug Crisis, R4865–8
Presidential Primaries and Caucuses, 1992: A Handbook of Election Statistics, C2500–7
President's Fiscal Year 1994 Budget, R9050–15.3
Presstime, A8605–1
Prevention Index 1993: A Report Card on the Nation's Health, C8111–2
Price of Mobility: Gasoline Taxes in America, R9050–15.6
Primary and Special Election, Sept. 19, 1992, Hawaii, S2077–1.1
Primary Copper Industry of Arizona in 1991, S0497–1
'Prisons Pay' Studies: Research or Ideology, A7575–1.12
Privatization, R4105–82.5
Probable Levels of R&D Expenditures in 1993: Forecast and Analysis, R3300–1
Production Employees Cost Survey, A5785–4
Production: 1993 Capital Spending Survey, C4080–1
Productivity Perspectives, R2800–2
Professional Builder, C1850–8
Professional Engineer Income and Salary Survey, 1993, A8460–1
Professional Income of Engineers, 1993, A0685–5
Professional Liability Insurance in Texas, U8850–8.8
Professional Salary Schedules, Maryland Public Schools, 1992/93, S3610–2.1
Professional Staff by Assignment, Race/Ethnicity and Gender, Maryland Public Schools, Oct. 1991, S3610–2.12
Professional Staff by Assignment, Race/Ethnicity and Gender, Maryland Public Schools, Oct. 1992, S3610–2.12
Professional Women and Minorities: A Total Human Resource Data Compendium, 10th Edition, A3960–2
Profile of Financial Aid Applicants: Historical Trend Data, R1960–3
Profile of Financial Aid Applicants, 1993/94, R1960–5
Profile of Our Schools: The Condition of Education in Connecticut, 1991/92, S1185–3
Profile of Pharmacy Students, A0630–9
Profile Series, B4490–2
Profiles of Alaska's Public School Districts, FY91, S0295–2
Profiles of Alaska's Public School Districts, FY92, S0295–2
Profiles of Ecologists: Results of a Survey of the Membership of the Ecological Society of America, A4685–1
Profiles of Kentucky Public Schools, FY92, S3110–1
Profiles of Regulatory Agencies of the U.S. and Canada, Yearbook 1991-92, A7015–2
Profiling New Jersey II, S5425–19
Profit Report: Detailed Cost-of-Doing Business Data for Retail Lumber Outlets, 1992, A8275–1.3
Progress and Peril: Black Children in America, R3840–21
Progressive Grocer, C5225–1
Projected Total Population of California Counties, S0840–4
Projections of Educational Statistics to 2011, U9080–20
Projections of Educational Statistics to 2012, U9080–20

Projections of Florida Population by County, 1992-2020, U6660–3.44
Projections of the Population of Texas and Counties in Texas by Age, Sex, and Race/Ethnicity for 1990-2030, S7645–3
Property Taxes on the Rise Again Across Nation, R9050–15.7
PRRC Emerging Trends, R8780–1
Psittacine Captive Breeding Survey: A Survey of Private Aviculture in the U.S., R9200–14
Psychiatric Length of Stay by Diagnosis: North Central Region, B4455–2.3
Psychiatric Length of Stay by Diagnosis: Northeastern Region, B4455–2.2
Psychiatric Length of Stay by Diagnosis: Southern Region, B4455–2.4
Psychiatric Length of Stay by Diagnosis, U.S., B4455–2.1
Psychiatric Length of Stay by Diagnosis: Western Region, B4455–2.5
Psychiatric Length of Stay by Diagnosis, 1992-93, B4455–2
Public and Association Libraries Statistics, New York State, S5745–2
Public and Nonpublic School Enrollment, Idaho Department of Education, S2225–1
Public and Private High School Graduates, Actual and Projected, Oregon, S6590–1.8
Public Assistance in Kentucky, S3140–2
Public Assistance Statistical Report, Delaware, S1385–1
Public Broadcasting Stations' Income from State Governments and State Colleges and Universities Ranked State-by-State, FY91, R4250–1.19
Public Broadcasting's Coverage of Issues and Programming Themes, R8825–10
Public Education Source Book, 1993, West Virginia, S8540–4
Public Health System in Texas, U8850–8.6
Public High School Enrollment Report, Indiana, S2608–2.5
Public Libraries in Louisiana, Statistical Report, 1992, S3275–1
Public Opinion in Gridlock Over Clinton Economic Package, C8915–7.3
Public Opinion Quarterly, A0610–1
Public Power, A2625–1
Public, Private and Nonpublic Schools: Enrollments, 1991/92, Pennsylvania, S6790–5.1
Public, Private and Nonpublic Schools: Enrollments, 1992/93, Pennsylvania, S6790–5.17
Public, Private and Nonpublic Schools: High School Graduates, 1991/92, Pennsylvania, S6790–5.14
Public Pupil/Teacher Ratio, Indiana, S2608–2.9
Public Radio Listening by Hispanics and African-Americans, R4250–1.18
Public Relations Journal, A8770–1
Public Schools: Personnel, 1992/93, Pennsylvania, S6790–5.12
Public Secondary School Dropouts in Pennsylvania, 1991/92, S6790–5.11
Public Service Commission of South Carolina Annual Report, 1990-91, S7235–1
Public Service Commission of South Carolina Annual Report, 1991-92, S7235–1
Public, Their Doctors, and Health Care Reform, C8915–7.2
Public Utility Commission Implementation of the Clean Air Act's Allowance Trading Program, A8195–12

Index by Titles

Public Welfare in California, S0935–2
Public Welfare Statistics, Virginia, S8293–2
Publishers Weekly, C1852–2
Pulp and Paper, C3975–2
Pulp and Paper: 1993 North American Factbook, C3975–5
Pulse of Europe: A Survey of Political and Social Values and Attitudes, C8915–8
Punishing Criminals: The People of Delaware Consider the Options, R8825–11
Pupil Membership and Related Information, Fall 1992, S1000–2.1
Pupil/Teacher Ratio Report, Indiana, S2608–2.8

Quality Programs and Practices, B6850–2
Quarterly Business Expectations, C3150–4
Quarterly Business Failures, C3150–6
Quarterly Completion Report, A2575–6
Quarterly Statistical and Economic Report, State of Hawaii, S2090–2
Quarterly Welfare Statistical Bulletin, Idaho, S2250–1

R&D, C1850–6
RAA Annual Report '93, 20th Anniversary Issue, A8795–1
Racial or Ethnic Distribution of Staff and Students in California Public Schools, 1992-93, S0825–9
Radio Facts for Advertisers, A8789–1
Radio Marketing Guide and Fact Book for Advertisers, 1993-94, A8789–1
Railroad Facts, 1992 Edition, A3275–5
Railroad Facts, 1993 Edition, A3275–5
Railroad Revenues, Expenses, and Income: Class I Railroads in the U.S., A3275–1
Railroad Ten-Year Trends, 1982-91, A3275–8
Railroads and States, A3275–10
Railway Age, C8400–1
Rankings of the Counties and School Districts of South Carolina, 1991/92, S7145–1
Rape in America, R8375–1
Rates of Levy: State, County, School, and Municipal, 1992 Tax Year, Fiscal Year Ending June 30, 1993, West Virginia, S8640–3
Ratio Study, A5785–3
RB: Restaurant Business, C1200–5
Readiness for College: College-to-School Reporting in the SREB States, A8945–32
Ready Mix: Review/Outlook, C0125–5
Real Estate Outlook, A7000–1
Recession and the Consumer, R4105–81.9
Recession-Recovery Watch, U1245–2
Recruiting Trends, 1992-93: A Study of Businesses, Industries, and Governmental Agencies Employing New College Graduates, U3130–1
Recruiting '93, A3940–3
Reforming Florida's Unjust, Costly and Ineffective Sentencing Laws, A7575–5
Refugee Reports, R9372–2
Regional Dimensions of the Crisis in Health Care Financing, R8490–46
Report of Criminal Offenses and Arrests, 1991, Oregon, S6603–3
Report of Criminal Offenses and Arrests, 1992, Oregon, S6603–3
Report of Educational Statistics, 1991/92, Delaware, S1430–1

Report of the Administrative Office, Pennsylvania Supreme Court, S6900–1
Report of the Bank Commissioner of the State of Oklahoma, 1992, S6415–1
Report of the Comptroller to the Governor of Virginia: A Comprehensive Annual Financial Report for the Fiscal Year Ended June 30, 1992, S8170–1
Report of the Courts of Washington, 1992, S8339–1
Report of the Department of Insurance, State of Florida, 1992, S1760–1
Report of the Insurance Division of Iowa, S2760–1
Report of the Public Schools of Missouri, S4505–1
Report of the State Auditor of Georgia, Year Ended June 30, 1992, S1860–1
Report of the State Comptroller to the Governor for the Fiscal Year Ended June 30, 1992, Connecticut, S1170–1
Report of Vital Statistics, Ohio, S6285–1
Report on Business, A6910–1
Report on Medical School Faculty Salaries, 1992/93, A3273–2
Report on the Health Behaviors of Iowans, 1991, S2795–2
Report on the Salary Budget Survey, A1295–1
Report on the 1991 Behavioral Health Risks of North Dakotans, S6105–3
Report on Voluntary Health Agency Revenue and Expenses, FY90, A7973–1
Report to the Governor and 1993 Legislature, Minnesota Higher Education Coordinating Board, S4195–2
Reports of the State Banks, Savings Banks, Savings and Loan Associations, Credit Unions, Consumer Credit, and Sale of Checks in the State of Louisiana, 1992, S3265–1
Reproductive Revolution: New Survey Findings, U2520–1.51
Research and Development, C1850–6
Research League Statistical Handbook, R9385–1
Research Notes, R4250–1
Research Report: Insured Commercial Bank Noncurrent Loan and Loss Statistics for 1992, A6400–4
Research Reports, R5620–1
Research Reports on America's Cities, A8012–1
Residents in Wisconsin Adult Correctional Facilities on Dec. 31, 1991, S8692–1.5
Residents in Wisconsin Adult Correctional Facilities on June 30, 1991, S8692–1.1
Residual Markets Workers Compensation, A0375–3
Restaurant Business, C1200–5
Restaurant Industry Operations Report 1993, A8200–3
Restaurant Spending: Consumer Expenditures on Food Away from Home, 1991, A8200–13
Restaurants and Institutions, C1850–3
Restaurants USA, A8200–1
Result of Votes Cast, 1992, State of Hawaii, S2077–1
Results 1992: Oklahoma Educational Indicators Program, S6423–2
Retirement and Retiree Health Benefits Provisions Survey, 1990-91, A7640–18
Retirement Provisions Survey, A7640–18

School Districts Audit

Revenue from State Sources for July 1, 1991-June 30, 1992, Indiana, S2608–2.2
Revenues and Expenditures, 1991, S1000–4.3
Review and Perspective, U7138–1
Review of Legal Education in the U.S., Fall 1992, A0970–1
Rhode Island Accident Location Reporting System 1991 Summary Tables, S7025–1
Rhode Island Almanac, C7975–1
Rhode Island Comprehensive Annual Financial Report, S6930–1
Rhode Island Department of Elementary and Secondary Education, Statistical Tables, S6970–1
Rhode Island Employment Bulletin, S6980–1
Rich Get Increasingly Richer: Latest Data on Household Wealth During the 1980s, R4700–17
RMA Annual Statement Studies, 1992, A6400–3
Room for Improvement: The Lack of Affordable, Adaptable and Accessible Housing for Midlife and Older Women, A8657–5
Roster and Statistics of Oklahoma Public and Institutional Libraries, July 1, 1991-June 30, 1992, S6470–1
Rough Cuts: The Continuing Decline of Defense Dollars for the Northeast-Midwest Region, R8490–44
RRC Economic Newsletter, U2030–1
Rubber Manufacturers Association's Monthly Tire and Inner Tube Report, A8810–1
Russians Rethink Democracy: The Pulse of Europe II, C8915–10
RV Business, C8950–2

Sacrificing America's Youth: The Problem of Child Labor and the Response of Government, R8335–2
Salaried and Professional Women: Relevant Statistics, A1570–2
Salaries of Deans in Baccalaureate and Graduate Programs in Nursing, A0615–2
Salaries of Scientists, Engineers, and Technicians: A Summary of Salary Surveys, 16th Edition, A3960–1
Salaries Paid Principals and Assistant Principals, 1992/93 School Year, A7085–2
Salaries 1993: Analysis of the American Chemical Society's 1993 Survey of Salaries and Employment, A1250–4
Salary and Sales Policy, 1992, Plastics Processing Companies, A8920–3
Salary Survey, A0605–1
Sales and Marketing Management, C1200–1
School Bus Fleet, C1575–1
School Bus Loading and Unloading Survey, Calendar Year 1990, School Year 1990/91, S3040–2
School Bus Loading and Unloading Survey, Calendar Year 1991, School Year 1991/92, S3040–2
School Choice, R3810–7
School Corporation Wealth Ratio, 1991/92; Assessments and Tax Rates Payable for 1992, Indiana, S2608–2.3
School District Profiles, 1991/92, Minnesota, S4165–1
School District Property Valuations, Mill Levies, and Bonded Debt, Wyoming, S8890–1.1
School Districts Audit Summary, Oregon, S6590–1.16

School Districts Budget

School Districts Budget Summary, 1992/93, Oregon, S6590–1.17

School Districts Fall Report of Staff, Teachers/Pupils/Schools, and Enrollments, Wyoming, S8890–1.2

School Finance Facts, North Dakota, S6180–4

Seafood Business, C4825–3

Second Look at Public Television: Leaders and the American Public Assess Its Coverage of Issues and Programming Themes, R8825–10.2

Securities Industry Trends: An Analysis of Emerging Trends in the Securities Industry, A8825–1

Security, C1850–12

Security Distributing and Marketing, C1850–13

Selected Financial Data, Maryland Public Schools, 1991/92: Part 1, Revenue, Wealth, and Effort, S3610–2.9

Selected Financial Data, Maryland Public Schools, 1991/92: Part 2, Expenditures, S3610–2.7

Selected Financial Data, Maryland Public Schools, 1991/92: Part 3, Analysis of Costs, S3610–2.6

Selected Financial Data, Maryland Public Schools, 1991/92: Part 4, Ten Year Summary, S3610–2.13

Selected Health Statistics, New Mexico, 1990, S5605–1

Selected Health Statistics, New Mexico, 1991, S5605–1

Selected Population and Housing Characteristics from Summary Tape File 1, 1990 Census. Volume I Profiles, Maine, S3465–8

Service Advantage, A4950–37

Service Economy, A3892–1

Service Sector Indicators, U1245–3

Sex Differences in Voter Turnout, U4510–1.70

Shipments of U.S. and Canadian Iron Ore Destined to U.S. and Canada, A2010–2

Shopping for Health: A Report on Food and Nutrition, A4950–36

Shopping for Health, 1993: A Report on Diet, Nutrition and Ethnic Foods, A4950–36

SHRM Survey, 1993: Human Resource Practices and Job Satisfaction, A8907–2

SHRM Work and Family Survey Report, 1992, A8907–1

Silver Institute Letter: Worldwide Information on Silver, A8902–3

Silver Market, 1992, 77th Annual Review, B4300–1

Skills for Success, B6850–4

SLA Biennial Salary Survey, 1993, A8965–1

Small Business Banking Study: An Analysis of the September Survey, A4160–5

Small Claims and Traffic Courts: Case Management Procedures, Case Characteristics, and Outcomes in 12 Urban Jurisdictions, R6600–5

Smoking in Restaurants: A Consumer Attitude Survey, A8200–8.15

SN '93 Distribution Study of Grocery Store Sales, C3400–6

Snack Food Association Consumer Snacking Behavior Report, A8905–2

Snack Food Association State-of-the-Industry Report, A8905–1

Socio-Economic Factbook for Surgery, 1993, A1275–1

Index by Titles

Socioeconomic Characteristics of Medical Practice, 1993, A2200–5

Soliciting Foreign Business To Meet Economic Development Goals, A5800–2.115

Solid Waste Management Study, 1991: Legislators, B0230–1

Solid Waste Management Study, 1991: Municipal Decision Makers, B0230–2

Source Book of Health Insurance Data, 1992, A5173–2

South Carolina Agricultural Statistics, U1075–3

South Carolina Crop, Livestock and Poultry Statistics, 1991-93, U1075–3

South Carolina Department of Corrections Annual Report, 1991-92, S7135–1

South Carolina Department of Insurance Annual Report, 1991-92, S7195–1

South Carolina Economic Report, S7125–3

South Carolina Higher Education Statistical Abstract, 15th Edition, S7185–2

South Carolina Judicial Department Annual Report, 1992, S7197–1

South Carolina Labor Market Review, 1992, S7155–3

South Carolina Office of the Comptroller General, Annual Report, 1991-92, S7127–2

South Carolina State Board of Financial Institutions Annual Report, 1991-92, S7165–1

South Carolina State Library Annual Report, 1991-92, S7210–1

South Carolina Statistical Abstract, 1993, S7125–1

South Carolina Tax Commission Annual Report, 1991-92, S7255–1

South Carolina Traffic Accident Fact Book, S7190–2

South Carolina Vital and Morbidity Statistics, 1990, S7175–1

South Carolina's Employment Trends, S7155–2

South Dakota Agricultural Statistics, 1992-93, S7280–1

South Dakota Business Review, U8595–1

South Dakota Courts: The State of the Judiciary and 1992 Annual Report of the South Dakota Unified Judicial System, S7395–1

South Dakota Data Supplement, U8595–2

South Dakota Department of Corrections Annual Report, July 1, 1991-June 30, 1992, S7296–1

South Dakota Department of Revenue Annual Report, FY92, S7380–1

South Dakota Department of Social Services Annual Statistical Report, FY92, S7385–1

South Dakota Educational Statistics Digest, 1991/92, S7315–1

South Dakota Labor Bulletin, S7355–1

South Dakota Motor Vehicle Traffic Accident Summary, S7300–3

South Dakota Vital Statistics and Health Status: 1991, S7345–1

Soya Bluebook, B8480–1

Space Log, 1992, B9170–1

Special Consumer Survey Reports, R4105–81

Special Data Issues, A5800–4

Special Data Issues: Local Emergency Response Plans, A5800–4.34

Special Data Issues: Local Government Infrastructure Financing, A5800–4.33

Special Data Issues: Police Salaries, A5800–4.32

Special Report on Institutional Resources and Budgets in Baccalaureate and Graduate Programs in Nursing, A0615–5

Special Report: Survey of State Tax Rates and Collections, R9050–14

Special Report: Value of Typical American Family's 1992 Income Eroded by Taxes and Inflation, R9050–13

Special Reports (ACCF), A1310–1

Special Reports (Tax Foundation), R9050–15

Special Statistical Report on Profit, Production, and Sales Trends in the Men's and Boys' Tailored Clothing Industry, A3880–1

Sporting Goods Market in 1993, A8485–2

Sports Participation in 1992, A8485–3

Spotlight on Desserts, A8200–20

SREB Fact Book Bulletins, A8945–27

SREB Fact Book on Higher Education, 1992, A8945–1

SREB-State Data Exchange, 1990-91, A8945–31

Staff Employed at School and Central Office Levels, Maryland Public Schools, 1992/93, S3610–2.10

Starting Salaries of Chemists and Chemical Engineers, 1992: Analysis of the American Chemical Society's Survey of Graduates in Chemistry and Chemical Engineering, A1250–2

State and Local Employment in the 1980s: How Did It Grow?, U5085–2.7

State-Approved Schools of Nursing: L.P.N./L.V.N., 1993, A8010–5

State-Approved Schools of Nursing: R.N., 1993, A8010–4

State Average Cost per Pupil and Total Expenditures, 1991/92, New Hampshire, S5200–1.4

State Board of Elections Registration Statistics as of Oct. 5, 1992, and Abstract of Votes Cast in the General Election Held on Nov. 3, 1992, North Carolina, S5920–1

State Budget Actions, 1992, A7470–4.10

State-by-State Impacts of Energy Tax Alternatives, R8490–49

State Court Caseload Statistics: Annual Report 1991, R6600–1

State Education Indicators, A4355–1

State Expenditure Report, 1992, A7470–4.10

State Fiscal Briefs, U5085–2

State Fiscal Outlook for 1993, A7470–4.11

State Fiscal Update: Feb. 1993, A7470–4.12

State Fiscal Update: Mar. 1993., A7470–4.14

State Higher Education Appropriations, 1992/93, A8970–1

State Indicators of Science and Mathematics Education, 1993, A4355–3

State Information Resource Management Organizational Structures: 1992 NASIRE Biennial Report, A7121–1

State Initiatives to Establish Basic Health Insurance Plans, U8850–8.1

State Labor Summary, North Carolina, S5917–3

State Library Agencies Financial Survey, A3862–1

State of Alabama Certified Vote Totals, Nov. 3, 1992, General Election, S0205–1

State of Alabama Comprehensive Annual Financial Report for the Fiscal Year Ended Sept. 30, 1991, S0129–1

State of Alabama Comprehensive Annual Financial Report for the Fiscal Year Ended Sept. 30, 1992, S0129–1

Index by Titles

Statistical Report of

State of Alabama Department of Education Annual Report, 1992: Statistical and Financial Data for 1991/92, S0124–1

State of Alaska Comprehensive Annual Financial Report for the Fiscal Year July 1, 1991-June 30, 1992, S0275–1

State of Alaska Division of Insurance 54th Annual Report, 1991 Calendar Year, Fiscal Year 1992, S0280–3

State of Alaska Official Returns, Nov. 3, 1992 General Election, S0337–1

State of America's Children, 1992, R3840–11

State of America's Cities: The Ninth Annual Opinion Survey of Municipal Elected Officials, A8012–1.21

State of Arizona Annual Financial Report, 1991-92, S0450–1

State of Arizona Comprehensive Annual Financial Report for the Fiscal Year Ended June 30, 1991, S0450–2

State of Arizona Official Canvass, General Election, Nov. 3, 1992, S0520–1

State of Black America, 1993, A8510–1

State of Colorado Abstract of Votes Cast, 1992, S1090–1

State of Colorado, 1992: 22nd Annual Report, Division of Property Taxation, S1055–3

State of Connecticut Comprehensive Annual Financial Report for the Fiscal Year Ended June 30, 1992, S1170–2

State of Connecticut 126th Annual Report of the Insurance Commissioner, S1222–1

State of Connecticut 142nd Registration Report of Births, Marriages, Divorces, and Deaths for the Year Ending Dec. 31, 1989, S1200–1

State of Florida Annual Report of the Comptroller, FY92, S1717–1

State of Georgia General Election Nov. 3, 1992, S1955–1

State of Hawaii Comprehensive Annual Financial Report for the Fiscal Year Ended June 30, 1992, S2020–1

State of Hawaii Data Book, 1992: A Statistical Abstract, S2090–1

State of Idaho Annual Report of the State Auditor, Fiscal Year Ended June 30, 1992, S2215–1

State of Idaho Department of Finance 74th Annual Report, S2235–1

State of Idaho Motor Vehicle Traffic Accidents, Statewide Report, Jan. 1, 1992-Dec. 31, 1992, S2315–1

State of Illinois Official Vote Cast at the General Election, Nov. 3, 1992, S2445–1

State of Louisiana Comprehensive Annual Financial Report, for the Year Ended June 30, 1992, S3285–2

State of Louisiana General Election Returns, Nov. 3, 1992, S3370–3

State of Maine Financial Report for Period July 1, 1991-June 30, 1992, S3420–1

State of Maine General Election Tabulation, Nov. 3, 1992, S3490–1

State of Maryland Comprehensive Annual Financial Report for the Year Ended June 30, 1992, S3685–2

State of Maryland Nov. 3, 1992 General Election Returns, S3615–1

State of Maryland Uniform Crime Reports, S3665–1

State of Michigan General Election, Nov. 3, 1992, S4020–1

State of Minnesota Comprehensive Annual Financial Report, for the Year Ended June 30, 1992, S4180–1

State of Minnesota, Division of Financial Examinations, 1991 Annual Report, S4140–3

State of Minnesota, Division of Financial Examinations, 1992 Annual Report, S4140–3

State of Missouri Comprehensive Annual Financial Report, Fiscal Year Ended June 30, 1992, S4475–1

State of Nebraska Comprehensive Annual Financial Report, Year Ended June 30, 1992, S4825–1

State of Nebraska 1992 Traffic Accident Facts Annual Report, S4953–1

State of Nevada Comprehensive Annual Financial Report for the Fiscal Year Ended June 30, 1992, S5025–1

State of New Hampshire Comprehensive Annual Financial Report for the Fiscal Year Ended June 30, 1992, S5175–1

State of New Hampshire Manual for the General Court, 1993, S5255–1

State of New Jersey, Commissioner of Banking, Annual Report, 1992, S5355–1

State of New Jersey General Election Results by Municipality, S5440–2

State of New Jersey Results of the General Election Held Nov. 3, 1992, by County and Municipality, S5440–1

State of New Mexico Official Returns: 1992 General Election, S5655–1

State of New York Comprehensive Annual Financial Report, for Fiscal Year Ended Mar. 31, 1993, S5710–1

State of North Carolina Uniform Crime Report, 1992, S5955–1

State of North Dakota Comprehensive Annual Financial Report for the Fiscal Year Ended June 30, 1992, S6162–1

State of Oklahoma Election Results and Statistics, 1992, S6425–1

State of Oklahoma Single Audit for the Year Ended June 30, 1991, S6410–1

State of Oklahoma: The Judiciary Annual Report, FY92, S6493–1

State of Oklahoma Uniform Crime Report, Annual Report, Jan.-Dec. 1992, S6465–1

State of Rhode Island Report on the Judiciary, 1991, S6965–1

State of South Carolina Comprehensive Annual Financial Report for the Fiscal Year Ended June 30, 1992, S7127–1

State of the Business Incubation Industry, 1991, A7360–1

State of the Industry: Convenience Store Industry Totals, Trends, and Averages, A6735–1

State of Utah Comprehensive Annual Financial Report for the Fiscal Year Ended June 30, 1992, S7795–1

State of Utah General Election Report, Nov. 3, 1992, S7875–1

State of Vermont Comprehensive Annual Financial Report, For the Year Ended June 30, 1992, S8035–1

State of Vermont Department of Public Service Biennial Reports, July 1, 1986-June 30, 1992, S8100–1

State of West Virginia 1992 Election Returns, S8630–1

State of Wisconsin 1993-94 Blue Book, S8780–1

State of Wyoming Comprehensive Annual Financial Report for Fiscal Year Ended June 30, 1992, S8875–1

State of Wyoming 1992 Annual Report of the Department of Corrections, S8883–1

State Policy Reports, B8500–2

State Programs to Assist Distressed Local Governments, A7470–4.13

State Resources and Services Related to Alcohol and Other Drug Abuse Problems, FY91, A7112–1

State Revenue Report, U5085–1

State Tax Actions, 1992, A7470–4.9

State Totals—Fall Enrollments, 1991/92, New Hampshire, S5200–1.1

State Totals—Fall Enrollments, 1992/93, New Hampshire, S5200–1.9

Statement of Activities, 1991/92, Connecticut Department of Education, S1185–1

Statement of Vote, General Election, Nov. 3, 1992, Connecticut, S1265–1

States and the Poor: How Budget Decisions Affected Low Income People in 1992, R3834–9

States in Profile: The State Policy Reference Book, 1992, B8500–1

States in Profile: The State Policy Reference Book, 1993, B8500–1

Statewide Compilation of Data from 1991 Sheriffs' Annual Reports, New York State, S5724–2

Statewide Elective Executive Women, 1993, U4510–1.62, U4510–1.73

Statistical Abstract of Higher Education in North Carolina, 1992/93, U8013–1

Statistical Abstract of Latin America, U6250–1

Statistical Abstract of Oklahoma, 1992, U8130–2

Statistical Abstract of Tennessee Higher Education, 1992/93, S7525–1

Statistical Abstract of Utah, 1993, U8960–1

Statistical Annual, Minneapolis Grain Exchange, B6110–1

Statistical Bulletin, Arizona Department of Economic Security, Family Assistance Administration, S0465–4

Statistical Bulletin, Metropolitan Life Insurance Co., B6045–1

Statistical Bulletins, Wisconsin Department of Corrections, S8692–1

Statistical Description of Residents of Massachusetts Correctional Institutions on Jan. 1, 1992, S3805–1

Statistical Fact Book: Current Information About Direct Marketing, A4620–1

Statistical Glance at D.C. Public Schools, S1605–2

Statistical Highlights, A5100–1

Statistical Information for the U.S. Liquor Industry, A4650–3

Statistical Journal, July 1, 1992-Dec. 31, 1992, North Carolina, S5940–2

Statistical Profile of Higher Education in West Virginia, 1992/93, S8533–1

Statistical Profile of the FY92 Offender Population, Kansas Department of Corrections, S2940–1

Statistical Profile, 1993 North Carolina Public Schools, S5915–1

Statistical Report, FY92, Texas Higher Education Coordinating Board, S7657–1

Statistical Report, Montana, S4755–1

Statistical Report of Information Regarding the Enrollment, Student Credit Hours, Degrees Conferred, and Finances of the State-Supported Universities in Mississippi for the Summer of 1991 and the Regular 1991/92 Session, S4360–1

Statistical Report of

Index by Titles

Statistical Report of Kentucky Public Libraries, Fiscal Year 1991-92, S3165–1
Statistical Report: Potash Imports, A8720–4
Statistical Report: Potash Production, Inventory, Disappearance, and Sales, A8720–2
Statistical Report: Potash Sales, A8720–1
Statistical Report: Press Release, Potash Sales, A8720–5
Statistical Report Series, Wyoming, S8890–1
Statistical Report Series, Wyoming: Public Schools Fund Accounting and Reporting, S8890–1.3
Statistical Report Series, Wyoming: School District Property Valuations, Mill Levies, and Bonded Debt, S8890–1.1
Statistical Report Series, Wyoming: School Districts Fall Report of Staff, Teachers/Pupils/Schools, and Enrollments, S8890–1.2
Statistical Report, South Carolina Department of Social Services, S7252–1
Statistical Reporter: Quarterly Report, A4957–2
Statistical Reports, S6790–5
Statistical Review of Government in Utah, 36th Annual Edition, 1993, R9380–1
Statistical Review of the California Fig Industry, A3750–1
Statistical Roundup, A1630–1, A7870–3
Statistical Series: Colorado Department of Education, S1000–2, S1000–4
Statistical Summary and Pennsylvania Department of Agriculture Annual Report, S6760–1
Statistical Summary for the Public Schools of Arkansas, 1990-92, S0660–1
Statistical Summary of Missouri Higher Education, 1991/92, with FY91 Missouri Student Achievement Study Supplement, S4520–3
Statistical Summary of Missouri Higher Education, 1992/93, with State Profile of ACT-Tested Students Graduating from High School, Spring 1992, S4520–3
Statistical Supplement to the Pennsylvania Tax Compendium, S6885–1
Statistical Supplement to the 1990 Annual Report of the New York Department of Social Services, S5800–2
Statistical Supplement to the 1991 Annual Report of the New York State Department of Social Services, S5800–2
Statistical Tables from Annual Statements, New York State Insurance Department, S5770–2
Statistical Yearbook of the Electric Utility Industry, 1991, A4700–1
Statistical Yearbook of the Western Lumber Industry, A9395–1
Statistics, Alabama Department of Human Resources, S0150–1
Statistics and Directory of North Carolina Public Libraries, 1990-91, S5910–1
Statistics and Input-Output Measures for Colorado Academic Libraries, 1992, S1000–3.2
Statistics and Input-Output Measures for Colorado Public Libraries, 1991, S1000–3.1
Statistics for Colorado Libraries, S1000–3
Statistics of Hawaiian Agriculture, 1991, S2030–1
Statistics of Indiana Libraries, 1992, S2655–1
Statistics of Ohio Libraries, 1993, S6320–1

Statistics of Paper, Paperboard, and Wood Pulp, 1993, A1630–6
Statistics of the Local Exchange Carriers, 1992, A9360–2
Statistics of Utility Companies, Washington State, S8450–1
Statistics on Social Work Education in the U.S.: 1992, A4515–1
Statistics, West Virginia Department of Health and Human Resources, S8560–2
Status of Maine's Financial Institutions, S3473–2
Status Report on Hunger and Homelessness in America's Cities: 1992, A9330–9
Steam Electric Market Analysis, A7400–8
Steam Electric Plant Factors, 1992, A7400–7
Still Neglecting Public Investment: The FY94 Budget Outlook, R4700–23
Stock Options: Motivating Through Ownership, R4105–78.31
Student Charges at Public Institutions: Annual Survey, 1991/92, A7150–4
Student-Teacher Ratios in Oregon Regular Schools as of Oct. 1, 1992, S6590–1.7
Study of Executive Compensation Plan Design, 1992, B2535–1
Study of Markets for Post Consumer Plastics for Northeast Recycling Council, A4375–14
Study of the American School Superintendency, 1992, A0775–5
Summary Highlights: Full-Time Employees of Public Broadcasting, 1977-92, R4250–1.23
Summary of Attendance, Maryland Public Schools, 1991/92, S3610–2.3
Summary of Expenditures by Object and Percent of Total Expenditures for July 1, 1990-June 30, 1991, Indiana, S2608–2.4
Summary of Expenditures by Object and Percent of Total Expenditures for July 1, 1991-June 30, 1992, Indiana, S2608–2.10
Summary of Indebtedness—Principal Outstanding, as of June 30, 1992, Indiana, S2608–2.12
Summary of Insurance Business in Nebraska for the Year 1991, S4890–1
Summary of Insurance Business in Nebraska for the Year 1992, S4890–1
Summary of Minnesota Public Assistance Trends, CY91, S4202–1
Summary of Minnesota Public Assistance Trends, CY92, S4202–1
Summary of Minnesota Public Assistance Trends, FY92, S4202–1
Summary of Motor Vehicle Traffic Accidents in Indiana, 1992, S2675–1
Summary of Occupational Injuries, Illnesses and Fatalities in the Petroleum Industry, A2575–4
Summary of Organization, Students, and Staff in Oregon Public Schools, S6590–1.1
Summary of Population Movement, Wisconsin Department of Corrections, S8692–1.4
Summary of Receipts, 1991/92, Indiana, S2608–2.11
Summary of 1992/93 Oregon Private and Parochial Schools, S6590–1.19
Summary of 1992/93 School District and ESD Budget Resources and Taxes Levied, Oregon, S6590–1.21
Summary Population and Housing Characteristics, Maine, 1990 Census, S3465–7
Summary Report, Georgia Uniform Crime Reporting Program, S1901–1

Summary Report, 1991: Doctorate Recipients from U.S. Universities, R6000–7
Summary Report 1991, Maryland Income Tax Division, S3685–1
Summary Social, Economic, and Housing Characteristics, Maine, 1990 Census, S3465–9
Superintendent's Annual Report for Virginia, S8190–3
Superintendent's Summary: School Census Returns, 1992, Virginia, S8190–1
Supermarket Business, C4655–1
Supervision and Incarceration: 1991, North Dakota, S6060–3
Supplement to the Annual Report of the Bureau of Financial Institutions: Consumer Finance Licensees Operating in Virginia, S8180–3
Supplements to Dental Education, 1992/93 Annual Report, A1475–4
Supplements to Dental Education, 1992/93 Annual Report: Dental School Admissions, A1475–4.1
Supplements to Dental Education, 1992/93 Annual Report: Dental School Faculty and Support Staff, A1475–4.5
Supplements to Dental Education, 1992/93 Annual Report: Dental School Trend Analysis, A1475–4.2
Supplements to Dental Education, 1992/93 Annual Report: Dental School Tuition, A1475–4.3
Supplements to Dental Education, 1992/93 Annual Report: Dental Student Attrition, A1475–4.4
Supply of Accounting Graduates and the Demand for Public Accounting Recruits, 1993, A1885–1
Survey of Business, U8710–1
Survey of Business Travelers, R9375–12
Survey of Buying Power, C1200–1.511
Survey of Buying Power: Part II, C1200–1.514
Survey of Departments: American Political Science Association, A2617–1
Survey of Income and Expenses in Rental Apartment Communities, A6497–1
Survey of Judicial Salaries, R6600–2
Survey of Local Chambers of Commerce, A3840–3
Survey of Media Markets, C1200–1.514
Survey of Physics and Astronomy Bachelor's Degree Recipients, A1960–3
Survey of State Travel Offices, 1992-93, R9375–2
Survey of Wage Rates for Hourly Employees, 1992, A8200–14
Survey on Oil and Gas Expenditures: Exploration, Development, Production, A2575–20
Survey on Sports Attendance, C2825–1
Surveys of Consumers, Monthly Report, U7475–2

Table I. Fall 1991/92 Personnel Roster: FTE Counts by Personnel Types and Subtypes, by Sex and Ethnicity, State Totals, Texas, S7670–1.3
Table II. Fall 1991/92 Personnel Roster: FTE Counts and Base Salaries by Personnel Type, State Totals, Texas, S7670–1.4
Tableservice Restaurant Trends, 1993, A8200–11

Index by Titles

Tax Burden on Tobacco: Historical Compilation, 1992, A9075–2

Tax Features, R9050–3

Tax Freedom Day 1993, R9050–15.4

Tax Statistics, 1992, Washington State, S8415–1

Taxable Sales in Virginia, 1991, U9080–8

Teacher Salary Schedules, 1992/93: New Hampshire School Districts, S5200–1.3

Telephony, C4725–3

Television Employee Compensation and Fringe Benefits Report, A6635–9

Television Ethnic Population Book, 1992-93, B0525–4

Television Universe Estimates Summary, 1992-93, B0525–3

Tennessee Agriculture, 1993, S7460–1

Tennessee Comprehensive Annual Financial Report for the Year Ended June 30, 1992, S7505–1

Tennessee Department of Correction FY91-92 Annual Report, S7480–1

Tennessee Department of Financial Institutions 19th Annual Report, 1992, S7507–1

Tennessee Judicial Council Annual Report, 1991-92, S7585–1

Tennessee Labor Market Report, S7495–2

Tennessee Public Service Commission 1991-92 Annual Report, S7565–1

Tennessee Statistical Abstract, 1992/93, U8710–2

Tennessee Vital Statistics, S7520–2

Testing Positive: Sexually Transmitted Disease and the Public Health Response, A5160–10

Texas Agricultural Cash Receipts and Price Statistics, S7630–1.3

Texas Agricultural Statistics, S7630–1

Texas Behavioral Risk Factor Surveillance: Final Overview, S7685–2

Texas Comprehensive Annual Financial Report, for the Year Ending Aug. 31, 1992, S7655–3

Texas Crime Report, S7735–2

Texas Crop Statistics, S7630–1.1

Texas Education Statistics, S7670–1

Texas Electric Utility Company Profiles, S7740–1

Texas Judicial System Annual Report, FY92, S7703–1

Texas Labor Market Review, S7675–3

Texas Livestock Statistics, S7630–1.2

Texas Medicaid Program, U8850–8.5

Texas-Mexico Multimodal Transportation, U8850–9

Texas Occupational Employment Statistics, S7675–1

Texas Occupational Employment Statistics: Industry Staffing Patterns for Education, S7675–1.28

Texas Occupational Employment Statistics: Industry Staffing Patterns for Railroads, S7675–1.29

Texas Occupational Employment Statistics: Industry Staffing Patterns for Selected Trade and Regulated Industries, S7675–1.31

Texas Occupational Employment Statistics: Industry Staffing Patterns for State and Local Government, S7675–1.30

Texas Planning Information, PY93, S7675–2

Texas Provider Utilization and Financial Data, U8850–8.3

Texas Public Library Statistics for 1991, S7710–1

Texas Public School Membership by Ethnic Group: Campus Report, Count and Percent, Fall 1991/92 PEIMS Data, S7670–1.1

Texas Vital Statistics, 1991, S7685–1

Texas 1992 Annual Cash Report for the Year Ended Aug. 31, 1992, S7655–2

Textile World, C5226–3

The Press and Campaign '92: A Self Assessment, C8915–4.25

Theatre Facts 92, A9065–1

They Make That Much?, R4865–13

Third Annual Economic Impact of Venture Capital Study, A8515–2

Thirty-Three: Metal Producing, C7000–8

Threat of Managed Trade to Transforming Economies, R5025–10

Times Mirror Media Monitor, C8915–11

Times Mirror News Interest Index, C8915–1

Tobacco Industry Profile, 1992, A9075–1

Top Executive Compensation, 1992 Edition, R4105–19

Total Enrollment by Grade, 1991/92 PEIMS Data, Texas, S7670–1.2

Total Net Revenue and Expenditures of School Districts, 1991/92, New Hampshire, S5200–1.12

Tourism's Top Twenty: Fast Facts on Travel and Tourism, 1988 Edition, R9375–6

Tourism's Top Twenty: Fast Facts on Travel and Tourism, 1992 Edition, R9375–6

Town and School District Profiles, S1185–2

Traffic Collisions in Washington State: Data Summary and Highway Safety Problem Analysis, S8428–1

Traffic Management: Annual Salary Survey, C1850–11

Traffic Safety, A8375–1

Transit Fact Book, 1992 Edition, A2650–1

Transportation in America, 10th Edition, R4815–1

Transportation Regulatory Policy in the U.S. and Canada, Annual Compilation 1991-92, A7015–4

Travel Industry World Yearbook: The Big Picture, 1992, C2140–1

Travel Market Report, R9375–14

Travel Printout, R9375–1

Trends: Carloadings of Major Railroads, A3275–2

Trends: Consumer Attitudes and the Supermarket, 1993, A4950–3

Trends in Federal Aid to States Since 1989: Not What Many People Assume, U5085–2.12

Trends in Female and Male Age at Marriage and Celibacy in Asia, R4500–1.64

Trends in Injury and Collision: Losses by Car Size, 1979-89 Model Passenger Cars, A5200–4.30

Trends in Manufacturing in the Northeast-Midwest, R8490–48

Trends in Mutual Fund Activity, A6025–5

Trends: U.S. Rail Freight Car and Locomotive Acquisition, A3275–3

Trusts and Estates, C2425–2

Truth About Public Employees: Underpaid or Overpaid?, R4700–21

Tuition, Fees and Financial Aid in Public Higher Education in the West, 1992/93, A9385–3

Tuition, Required Fees, and Total Cost of Attendance, A8945–27.11

Turbine-Engined Fleets of the World's Airlines, 1993 Survey, B3370–1

Utah Employers, Employment

TV Violence: More Objectionable in Entertainment Than in Newscasts, C8915–11.1

Unemployment Insurance in the U.S.: The First Half Century, R9260–18

Unfunded Federal Mandates: Environmentalism's Achilles Heel?, U9640–3

Uniform Crime Report: Commonwealth of Pennsylvania, Annual Report, 1992, S6860–1

Uniform Crime Report for the State of Michigan, S3997–1

Uniform Crime Reports, State of New Jersey, 1992, S5430–1

Uninsured Children in the South, R9000–1

Unit Investment Trust Statistics, A6025–7

United Arts Fundraising 1992, A1315–2

United Van Lines Migration Study, B9300–1

Uruguay Round of GATT, R4105–82.2

U.S. Catholic Elementary and Secondary Schools, 1992/93: Annual Statistical Report on Schools, Enrollment and Staffing, A7375–1

U.S. Chamber of Commerce Economic Outlook, A3840–6

U.S. Chemical Industry Statistical Handbook, 1993, A3850–1

U.S. Consumer Electronics Industry in Review, 1993, A4725–4

U.S. Crude Oil Distillation Refining Capacity Survey, A2575–7

U.S. Foreign Trade in Machine Tools, A3179–3

U.S. Foreign Trade in Manufacturing Technology, A3179–3

U.S.-German Economic Yearbook, 1992, A5135–2

U.S. House of Representatives Employment Practices: A Study of Staff Salary, Tenure, Demographics and Benefits, R4140–1

U.S. Housing Markets, B5190–1

U.S. Petroleum Statistics, 1992 Data Updated, A5425–2

U.S. Petroleum Supply: History, Prospects, and Policy Implications, A2575–25

U.S. Population Data Sheet, R8750–9

U.S. Schools of Public Health Data Report on Applicants, New Enrollments, and Students, Fall 1991, and Graduates and Expenditures, 1991/92, with Trends Analysis for 1974/75 Through Fall 1991, A3372–3

U.S. Schools of Public Health Data Report on Applicants, New Enrollments, and Students, Fall 1992, and Graduates and Expenditures, 1991/92, with Trends Analysis for 1974/75 Through Fall 1992, A3372–3

U.S. Schools of Public Health: Data Report on Faculty, 1991-92, A3372–1

U.S. Television Household Estimates, B6670–2

Use of Council Committees in Local Governments, A5800–2.114

Utah Agricultural Statistics, S7800–1

Utah Department of Corrections 1992 Annual Report, S7810–1

Utah Economic and Business Review, U8960–2

Utah Economic and Demographic Profiles, S7832–2

Utah Employers, Employment and Wages by Size, 1992, S7820–1

Utah Insurance Department:

Utah Insurance Department: Business of 1991, S7845–1
Utah Labor Market Report, S7820–3
Utah Public Library Service, 1992: An Annual Report, S7808–1
Utah System of Higher Education Data Book, 1993/94, S7895–2
Utah Traffic Accident Summary, 1992, S7890–2
Utah's Marriage and Divorce: 1990, S7835–2
Utah's Vital Statistics Annual Report, 1990, S7835–1
Utah's 1992 Homeless Count, S7808–2
Utility Regulatory Policy in the U.S. and Canada, Compilation 1991-92, A7015–3

Valuations, Property Tax Assessments, and School Tax Rates of School Districts, 1992/93, New Hampshire, S5200–1.17
Variable Pay: Nontraditional Programs for Motivation and Reward, R4105–78.27
Variety, C9380–1
Vehicle Descriptions, 1993 Models, A5200–5
Vending Times: Census of the Industry Issue, 1993, C9470–1
Vermont Annual Planning Information, 1992, S8025–2
Vermont Annual Planning Information, 1993, S8025–2
Vermont Department of Libraries 12th Biennial Report, Statistics of Local Libraries, July 1, 1990-June 30, 1992; Vermont Library Directory, 1993, S8080–1
Vermont Postsecondary Education Information Sourcebook, 1992, S8035–2
Vermont Tax Statistics, S8125–1
Veterinary Economics, C9480–1
Viewer and Listener Membership Income for Public Television and Radio Grantees, FY91, R4250–1.21
Virginia AGI: Distribution of Virginia Adjusted Gross Income by Income Class and Locality, U9080–1
Virginia Business Report, U1120–1
Virginia Department of Taxation Annual Report, FY92, S8305–1
Virginia Economic Indicators, S8205–4
Virginia Gross State Product, 1963-89, U9080–6
Virginia Labor Market Review, S8205–6
Virginia Personal Income, 1980-90, U9080–7
Virginia Population Projections, 2010, S8205–7
Virginia Public Library Statistics, 1991-92, S8275–1
Virginia School Census, S8190–1
Virginia State of the Judiciary Report, 1992, S8300–1
Virginia Traffic Facts, S8282–1
Virginia 1991 Vital Statistics Annual Report, S8225–1
Vital Educational Statistics, 1991/92, New Jersey, S5385–1
Vital Health Statistics of West Virginia, S8560–1
Vital Statistics Annual Report, 1989, Rhode Island, S6995–1
Vital Statistics, Iowa 1991, S2795–1
Vital Statistics, Mississippi, 1991, S4350–1
Vital Statistics, Mississippi, 1992, S4350–1
Vital Statistics of California, 1990, S0865–1
Vital Statistics of Louisiana, S3295–1
Vital Statistics of New York State, 1990, S5765–1

Vital Statistics Report for the State of New Hampshire, 1991, S5215–1
Vital Statistics Report, Kentucky, S3140–1
Vital Statistics Report, Nebraska, S4885–1
Vital Statistics, 1990, Wisconsin, S8715–4
Vital Statistics, 1991, Wisconsin, S8715–4
Vocational-Technical Education: Education and Employment Status of 1989/90 Completers, S6790–5.6
Vocational-Technical Education: Secondary Program Statistics, 1991/92, Pennsylvania, S6790–5.7
Volume of Futures and Options Trading on U.S. Futures Exchanges, 1968-92, A5040–1

Washington Agricultural Statistics, 1992-93, S8328–1
Washington Labor Market, S8340–3
Washington Public Library Statistics, 1992, S8375–1
Washington State Comprehensive Annual Financial Report for the Fiscal Year Ended June 30, 1992, S8345–3
Washington State Treasurer, 1992 Annual Report, S8455–1
Washington State Vital Statistics, 1991, S8363–1
Washington's Largest Monument: The National Debt, R9050–15.1
Weekly of Business Aviation, C5800–30
Weekly Statistical Bulletin, A2575–1
West Virginia Agricultural Statistics, 1992, S8510–1
West Virginia and Service Delivery Areas Annual Planning Information, S8534–2
West Virginia Crash Data, S8645–1
West Virginia Economic Summary, S8534–1
West Virginia Educational Statistical Summary, S8540–3
West Virginia Library Commission 1992 Statistical Report, S8590–1
West Virginia Research League 1992 Statistical Handbook, R9385–1
West Virginia State Court System Caseload Report for Calendar Year 1992, S8537–1
Western Blue Chip Economic Forecast, U0282–2
What Do the 1992 Election Results Say About State Fiscal Policy?, U5085–2.8
Wheat Grower: Wheat Facts 1992, A7310–1
Where Have All the Dollars Gone? A State-by-State Analysis of Income Disparities Over the 1980s, R3834–13
Where Have All the Dollars Gone? Regional Patterns in Entitlement Spending, R8490–47
White Poverty in America, R3834–15
Who Wants To Teach?, R6350–7
Who's Buying Houses in America: The Chicago Title and Trust Family of Title Insurers' 17th Annual Survey of Recent Home Buyers, B2150–1
Why Now? Change and Turmoil in U.S. Banking, R5025–8
Why Punish the Children? A Reappraisal of the Children of Incarcerated Mothers in America, A7575–4
WICHE Student Exchange Programs, Statistical Report, Academic Year 1992/93, A9385–1
Wisconsin Agricultural Statistics, 1993, S8680–1
Wisconsin Comprehensive Annual financial Report for the Fiscal Year Ended June 30, 1991, S8675–3

Index by Titles

Wisconsin Comprehensive Annual Financial Report for the Fiscal Year Ended June 30, 1992, S8675–3
Wisconsin Crime and Arrests, 1992, S8771–1
Wisconsin Economic Indicators, S8750–1
Wisconsin Insurance Report, Business of 1991, S8755–1
Wisconsin Insurance Report, Business of 1992, S8755–1
Wisconsin Library Service Record, 1992, S8795–1
Wisconsin Population Projections, 1990-2020, S8675–4
Wisconsin Traffic Accident Facts, S8815–1
Wisconsin Traffic Crash Facts, S8815–1
Wisconsin Vital Statistics, S8715–4
Wisconsin 1992 Annual Report, Office of Commissioner of Banking, S8685–1
Women in Elective Office, 1993, U4510–1.72
Women in Public Service, U5090–1
Women in State Legislatures, 1993, U4510–1.63, U4510–1.67
Women in the U.S. Congress, 1993, U4510–1.61, U4510–1.69
Women in the U.S. House of Representatives, 1993, U4510–1.60, U4510–1.68
Women in the U.S. Senate, 1922-93, U4510–1.59, U4510–1.71
Women Moving into State Legislatures, 1974-93, U4510–1 64
Women of Color in Elective Office, 1993, U4510–1.66
Women Still 'Stuck' in Low-Level Jobs, U5090–1.3
Women's International Bowling Congress 1991-92 Annual Report, A9415–1
Wood Technology, C3975–1
Work Force Diversity: Corporate Challenges, Corporate Responses, R4105–78.22
Work Injury and Illness Rates, 1992, A8375–4
Workplace Social Issues, B6850–6
Workplace Social Issues of the 1990s, B6850–6
World Financial Markets, B6200–2
World Jet Airplane Inventory, Year-End 1992, B1582–1
World Mine Production of Gold, 1992-96, A5145–2
World Mine Production of Silver in 1992 with Projections for 1993-96, A8902–1
World Motor Vehicle Data, 1993 Edition, A0865–2
World Population Data Sheet, R8750–5
World Refugee Survey, 1993, R9372–1
World Resources, 1992-93, R9455–1
World Silver Survey, 1993, A8902–4
World's Telephones: A Statistical Compilation as of Jan. 1991-92, B0350–1
Wyoming Agricultural Statistics, 1993, S8860–1
Wyoming Department of Revenue 1992 Annual Report, S8990–1
Wyoming Labor Force Trends, S8895–1
Wyoming Official Directory and Election Returns, S9000–1
Wyoming Public Library Statistics, FY92, S8855–3
Wyoming Public Schools Fund Accounting and Reporting, S8890–1.3
Wyoming Sales and Use Tax Revenue Report, 1992, S8855–1
Wyoming Vital Statistics, 1991, S8920–2
Wyoming's Comprehensive Report on Traffic Accidents, 1992, S9007–1

Index by Titles

Yearbook of American and Canadian Churches, 1993, C0105–1
Yellow Pages Industry Usage Study, 1992, A9500–2

100 Leading National Advertisers, C2710–1.547
110th Statistical Annual, Year Ending Dec. 31, 1992, Minneapolis Grain Exchange, B6110–1
121st Annual Report of the Insurance Commissioner of the State of Maryland, S3655–1
123rd Annual Report of the Kansas Insurance Department, for Year Ending Dec. 31, 1992, S2990–1
124th Annual Report of the Insurance Commissioner of the State of California, for the Year Ending Dec. 31, 1991, S0900–1
129th Annual Report of the Insurance Division Made to the General Assembly, 1991, Rhode Island, S6945–2
13th Annual and 47th Report of the Commissioner of Financial Institutions, State of Utah, for the Period July 1, 1992-June 30, 1993, S7830–1
133rd Annual Report of the Superintendent of Insurance, New York State, S5770–3
14th Annual Report of the Chief Administrator of the Courts, State of New York, 1992, S5730–1
141st Annual Report of the New Hampshire Insurance Department for the Fiscal Year July 1, 1991-June 30, 1992, S5220–1
143rd Report of the Public Schools of Missouri for the School Year Ending June 30, 1992, S4505–1
19th Annual Report on the Work of the Georgia Courts, FY92, S1903–1
1980s: A Decade of Debt?, U9640–2.14
1983-92 Kentucky Institutions of Higher Education Information Digest, S3130–3
1987-88 Vital Statistics of Louisiana, S3295–1
1987/88 Pupil/Teacher Ratio Report, Indiana, S2608–2.8
1988/89 Pupil/Teacher Ratio Report, Indiana, S2608–2.8
1989-90 Vital Statistics of Louisiana, S3295–1
1989/90 Pupil/Teacher Ratio Report, Indiana, S2608–2.8
1990 Annual Report, Nebraska Department of Revenue, S4950–1
1990 Annual Report of Tennessee Behavioral Risk Factors, S7520–3
1990 Annual Statistical Report, State Correctional System, Pennsylvania, S6782–1
1990 Census Briefs, S7832–3
1990 Census of Population and Housing STF3A Profile, Arkansas, U5935–7
1990 Census of Population and Housing, Summary Tape File 3, California, S0840–9
1990 Census: Summary Population and Housing Characteristics, Maine, S3465–7
1990 Census: Summary Social, Economic, and Housing Characteristics, Maine, S3465–9
1990 Census, Volume 1 Profiles, Maine: Selected Population and Housing Characteristics from Summary Tape File 1, S3465–8
1990 General Income Characteristics: Pennsylvania, U4130–13
1990 Motor Vehicle Statistics, Accidents, License and Registration Statistical Data, New York State, S5790–1

1990 Psittacine Captive Breeding Survey: A Survey of Private Aviculture in the U.S., R9200–14
1990 Virginia AGI: Distribution of Virginia Adjusted Gross Income by Income Class and Locality, U9080–1
1990-91 Pennsylvania Library Statistics, S6790–2
1990-91 Per Pupil Expenditures by Program, Massachusetts, S3810–5
1990/91 Pupil/Teacher Ratio Report, Indiana, S2608–2.8
1991 Alaska Traffic Accidents, S0360–1
1991 Annual Report, Nebraska Department of Revenue, S4950–1
1991 Annual Report of Fatal and Injury Motor Vehicle Traffic Accidents, California, S0885–1
1991 Annual Report of Vital Statistics in Vermont, S8054–1
1991 Annual Statistical Report of the Illinois State Board of Education, S2440–1
1991 Annual Summary of Vital Statistics, Idaho, S2250–2
1991 Annual Survey, Catholic Charities USA, A3810–1
1991 Crime and Justice Annual Report, New York, S5760–3
1991 Crime and Justice Report for the District of Columbia, S1535–2
1991 Doctorate Employment Survey, A2620–4
1991 Electric Power Equipment Report, A4700–2
1991 Estimates of the Population of Virginia Counties and Cities, U9080–9
1991 Financial Condition of Medical Malpractice JUAs, A0375–1
1991 Illinois Crash Facts and Statistics, S2540–1
1991 Industry Statistics, A3274–2
1991 Iowa Individual Income Tax Annual Statistical Report: 1991 Returns Filed in 1992, S2860–3
1991 Joint Association Survey on Drilling Costs, A2575–9
1991 Louisiana Traffic Records Data Report, S3345–2
1991 Maine Educational Facts, S3435–1
1991 Missouri Crime and Arrest Digest, S4560–2
1991 Motor Vehicle Statistics, Accidents, License and Registration Statistical Data, New York State, S5790–1
1991 Psittacine Captive Breeding Survey: A Survey of Private Aviculture in the U.S., R9200–14
1991 Public and Association Libraries Statistics, New York State, S5745–2
1991 Report of Vital Statistics, Ohio, S6285–1
1991 Residual Markets Workers Compensation, A0375–3
1991 Solid Waste Management Study: Legislators, B0230–1
1991 Solid Waste Management Study: Municipal Decision Makers, B0230–2
1991 State Library Agencies Financial Survey, A3862–1
1991 Statistical Information for the U.S. Liquor Industry, A4650–3
1991 Survey of Business Travelers, R9375–12
1991 Survey on Oil and Gas Expenditures: Exploration, Development, Production, A2575–20

1992 Annual Report of the New

1991 Television Employee Compensation and Fringe Benefits Report, A6635–9
1991 Texas Agricultural Cash Receipts and Price Statistics, S7630–1.3
1991 Texas Agricultural Statistics, S7630–1
1991 Texas Behavioral Risk Factor Surveillance: Final Overview, S7685–2
1991 Texas Crop Statistics, S7630–1.1
1991 Texas Livestock Statistics, S7630–1.2
1991 Vermont Tax Statistics, S8125–1
1991 Virginia Traffic Crash Facts, S8282–1
1991 Vital Statistics Report, Kentucky, S3140–1
1991 Wisconsin Traffic Crash Facts, S8815–1
1991-92 Annual Financial Review: The Annual Report of the Supermarket Companies, A4950–1
1991-92 Business Failure Record, Dun and Bradstreet, C3150–8
1991-92 Oregon Agriculture and Fisheries Statistics, S6575–1
1991-92 Pennsylvania Library Statistics, S6790–2
1991-92 Per Pupil Expenditures by Program, Massachusetts, S3810–5
1991-92 Ratio Study, A5785–3
1991/92 Annual Report: Oklahoma State Department of Education, S6423–1
1991/92 Average Daily Membership Based upon Attendance and Residence, New Hampshire, S5200–1.11
1991/92 Comparative Costs and Staffing Report for College and University Facilities, A3183–1
1991/92 Nebraska Agricultural Statistics, S4835–1
1991/92 Public Pupil/Teacher Ratio, Indiana, S2608–2.9
1991/92 School Districts Audit Summary, Oregon, S6590–1.16
1991/92 Statistical Tables, Rhode Island Department of Elementary and Secondary Education, S6970–1
1991/92 Superintendent's Annual Report for Virginia, S8190–3
1991/92 Survey of Physics and Astronomy Bachelor's Degree Recipients, A1960–3
1991/92 Wyoming Public Schools Fund Accounting and Reporting, S8890–1.3
1992 Alabama Accident Summary, Statewide Accidents, S0185–1
1992 Alabama Insurance Report: Business of 1991, Company Directory, S0160–1
1992 Alabama Vital Events, S0175–2
1992 Almanac of Hospital Financial and Operating Indicators, B1880–1
1992 AMA Survey on Downsizing and Assistance to Displaced Workers, A2075–20.9
1992 AMA Survey on Marketing in a Recessionary Economy, A2075–20.10
1992 Annual AMS-MAA Survey, A2085–1
1992 Annual Report from the Supervisor of Banking, Washington State, S8325–1
1992 Annual Report of the Bureau of Financial Institutions, State Corporation Commission, Commonwealth of Virginia, S8180–2
1992 Annual Report of the Delaware Judiciary, S1360–1
1992 Annual Report of the Judicial Council, Supreme Court of Louisiana, S3375–1
1992 Annual Report of the New Jersey Casino Control Commission, S5360–1

1992 Annual Report, Texas

Index by Titles

1992 Annual Report, Texas Department of Human Services, S7695–1
1992 Annual Report, Texas Department of Insurance, S7700–1
1992 Annual Statistical Report: Report to the Supreme Court of Iowa by the State Court Administrator, S2815–1
1992 Annual Statistical Report, The Board of Trade of Kansas City, Missouri, Inc., B1530–1
1992 Annual Traffic Statistical Report, Delaware, S1435–1
1992 Arizona Agricultural Statistics, U5830–1
1992 Bar Examination Statistics, A7458–1
1992 Bicycle Market in Review, A3470–1
1992 Canadian Consumer Photographic Survey, A8695–4
1992 Catholic Almanac, C6885–1
1992 Construction Industry Annual Financial Survey, A4155–1
1992 Crime in Alabama, S0119–1
1992 Distributor Profit Survey Report, A8505–4
1992 Election Report, State of Indiana, S2702–1
1992 Equalized Valuation per Pupil, 1991/92, of New Hampshire School Districts, S5200–1.16
1992 Fiscal Year Statistical Report, Texas Department of Criminal Justice, S7660–1
1992 Florida Health Care Atlas, S1746–1
1992 Florida Statistical Abstract, U6660–1
1992 GED Statistical Report, A1410–16
1992 General Election Returns, Nevada, S5125–1
1992 High School Completers, Oregon Public Schools, S6590–1.10
1992 Idaho Public Utilities Commission Annual Report, S2290–1
1992 Illinois Statistical Abstract, U6910–2
1992 Indiana Judicial Report, S2703–1
1992 Labor Survey, Plastics Processing Companies, A8920–2
1992 Life Insurance Fact Book, A1325–1
1992 Meat and Poultry Facts, A2100–1
1992 Menu Analysis, A8200–22
1992 Motor Vehicle Accident Statistics, Rhode Island, S7025–1
1992 Motorcycle Statistical Annual, A6485–1
1992 NACUBO Endowment Study, A6705–2
1992 National Roster of Hispanic Elected Officials, A6844–1
1992 New York State Statistical Yearbook, U5100–1
1992 North Dakota Vehicular Crash Facts, S6217–1
1992 Oklahoma Traffic Accident Facts, S6482–1
1992 Pennsylvania Statistical Abstract, U4130–6
1992 Population Trends for Washington State, S8345–4
1992 Production Employees Cost Survey, A5785–4
1992 Report of the Insurance Division of Iowa, S2760–1
1992 School District Property Valuations, Mill Levies, and Bonded Debt, Wyoming, S8890–1.1
1992 School Districts Fall Report of Staff, Teachers/Pupils/Schools, and Enrollments, Wyoming, S8890–1.2
1992 Snack Food Association Consumer Snacking Behavior Report, A8905–2

1992 Snack Food Association State-of-the-Industry Report, A8905–1
1992 South Carolina Traffic Accident Fact Book, S7190–2
1992 South Dakota Motor Vehicle Traffic Accident Summary, S7300–3
1992 State Library Agencies Financial Survey, A3862–1
1992 State of Maryland Uniform Crime Reports, S3665–1
1992 Statistical Annual Supplement, B2120–1
1992 Statistical Review of the California Fig Industry, A3750–1
1992 Statistical Yearbook of the Western Lumber Industry, A9395–1
1992 Study of the American School Superintendency, A0775–5
1992 Summary Report, Georgia Uniform Crime Reporting Program, S1901–1
1992 Texas Electric Utility Company Profiles, S7740–1
1992 Traffic Collisions in Washington State: Data Summary and Highway Safety Problem Analysis, S8428–1
1992 Uniform Crime Report for the State of Michigan, S3997–1
1992 U.S. House of Representatives Employment Practices: A Study of Staff Salary, Tenure, Demographics and Benefits, R4140–1
1992 Utah Economic and Demographic Profiles, S7832–2
1992 West Virginia Crash Data, S8645–1
1992 Wisconsin Traffic Crash Facts, S8815–1
1992-93 Factbook and Membership Directory, Mortgage Insurance Companies of America, A6455–1
1992-93 Management Compensation Study for Wholesalers and Large Retailers, A4950–6
1992-93 Salary Survey, A0605–1
1992-93 Special Report on Institutional Resources and Budgets in Baccalaureate and Graduate Programs in Nursing, A0615 5
1992-93 Statistical Fact Book: Current Information About Direct Marketing, A4620–1
1992-93 Statistical Summary and Pennsylvania Department of Agriculture Annual Report, S6760–1
1992/93 Administrative Compensation Survey, A3900–1
1992/93 Enrollment and Graduations in Baccalaureate and Graduate Programs in Nursing, A0615–4
1992/93 Faculty Salaries in Baccalaureate and Graduate Programs in Nursing, A0615–1
1992/93 Faculty Salaries in Graduate Departments of Psychology, A2620–1
1992/93 National Faculty Salary Survey by Discipline and Rank in Private Colleges and Universities, A3900–4
1992/93 National Faculty Salary Survey by Discipline and Rank in Public Colleges and Universities, A3900–5
1992/93 Public High School Enrollment Report, Indiana, S2608–2.5
1992/93 Salaries of Deans in Baccalaureate and Graduate Programs in Nursing, A0615–2
1992/93 Summary of Organization, Students, and Staff in Oregon Public Schools, S6590–1.1
1993 Almanac of Hospital Financial and Operating Indicators, B1880–1

1993 AMA Survey on Basic Skills Testing and Training, A2075–20.13
1993 AMA Survey on HIV and AIDS Related Policies, A2075–20.14
1993 AMA Survey on Managing Cultural Diversity, A2075–20.11
1993 AMA Survey on Workplace Drug Testing and Drug Abuse Policies, A2075–20.12
1993 American League Red Book, A2068–1
1993 Analysis of Workers' Compensation Laws, A3840–2
1993 Annual Report, Judicial Council of California, S0905–1
1993 Annual Statistical Report, A0620–1
1993 Automobile Finance Study: An Analysis of the December, 1992 Survey, A4160–2
1993 AVMA Directory, A3100–1
1993 Catholic Almanac, C6885–1
1993 Construction Industry Annual Financial Survey, A4155–1
1993 Consumer Photographic Survey, A8695–2
1993 Convenience Store Industry Fact Book, A6735–2
1993 Development Report Card for the States, R4225–1
1993 Directory of Community Blood Centers, A0612–1
1993 Dodge/Sweet's Construction Outlook, Updates, C5800–29
1993 Economic Report, The State of South Carolina, S7125–3
1993 Facts About Store Development, A4950–2
1993 Federal Tax Burden by State, R9050–15.5
1993 Florida Library Directory with Statistics, S1800–2
1993 Focus on Manhattantrends, B2800–5
1993 Government Relations Survey, A1800–1
1993 Helicopter Annual, A5190–1
1993 Home Lending Survey for Year End 1992, A4160–3
1993 Hospital Admission Rates, B4455–4
1993 Hospital Inpatient Charges, B4455–5
1993 Journal-Bulletin Rhode Island Almanac, 107th Annual Edition, C7975–1
1993 Kentucky Deskbook of Economic Statistics, S3104–1
1993 NASDAQ Fact Book and Company Directory, A7105–1
1993 NCAA Division I Graduation-Rates Summary, A7440–4
1993 Report of the Insurance Division of Iowa, S2760–1
1993 SHRM Survey: Human Resource Practices and Job Satisfaction, A8907–2
1993 Small Business Banking Study: An Analysis of the September Survey, A4160–5
1993 Snack Food Association State-of-the-Industry Report, A8905–1
1993 State of the Industry: Convenience Store Industry Totals, Trends, and Averages, A6735–1
1993 Survey of Income and Expenses in Rental Apartment Communities, A6497–1
1993 Survey of Local Chambers of Commerce, A3840–3
1993 Utah Agricultural Statistics, S7800–1
1993 World Population Data Sheet, R8750–5
1993 Wyoming Official Directory and 1992 Election Returns, S9000–1

Index by Titles

1993-94 Economic Handbook of the Machine Tool Industry, A3179–2
1993-94 Maryland Statistical Abstract, S3605–1
1993-94 Report on the Salary Budget Survey, A1295–1
1993-95 National Jail and Adult Detention Directory, A1305–1

2nd ATE Survey of Critical Issues in Teacher Education, A3375–1
23rd Biennial Report of the Division of Finance of the Department of Economic Development, State of Missouri, S4502–1
26th Annual Rank-Order Distribution of Administrative Salaries Paid, 1992/93, U5960–1

33: Metal Producing, C7000–8

45th Annual Report: Vital Health Statistics of West Virginia, 1991, S8560–1
46th Annual Consumer Expenditures Study, C4655–1.510

78th Annual Report, New Mexico Financial Institutions Division, 1992, S5652–1
78th Annual Report of the Bank Commissioner of Arkansas, 1992, S0632–1

80th Annual Report of the Department of Insurance, State of Arizona, for the Year Ending Dec. 31, 1992, S0483–1
82nd Annual Report of the Bank Commissioner of the State of Maryland, June 30, 1992, S3655–2
83rd Annual Report of the Insurance Commissioner of the State of West Virginia, Year Ending Dec. 31, 1991, S8575–1
83rd Annual Report of the State Bank Commissioner of the State of Colorado, 1992, S1070–2
85th Annual Report and Directory, 1992, Oklahoma, S6462–1
85th Annual Report of the Division of Banking to the General Assembly, 1992, Rhode Island, S6945–1
86th Annual Report and Directory, 1993, Oklahoma, S6462–1

90th Annual Report of Financial Institutions, Year Ending Dec. 31, 1991, West Virginia, S8530–1
91st Annual Report: State of Idaho, Department of Insurance, for the Year Ended December 31, 1991, S2260–1
'93 Soya Bluebook, B8480–1
96th Annual Report on the Condition of Wisconsin Savings and Loan Associations and Savings Banks, S8807–1

Guide to Selected Standard Classifications

Guide to Selected Standard Classifications

(This guide outlines the major standard classification systems used by various Federal agencies to arrange and present social and economic statistical data.)

Census Regions and Divisions	949
Outlying Areas of the U.S.	949
Federal Reserve Districts	949
Metropolitan Statistical Areas	950
Consolidated Metropolitan Statistical Areas	951
Cities with Population over 100,000	952
Consumer Price Index Cities	952
Standard Industrial Classification	953
Standard Occupational Classification	961
Standard International Trade Classification, Revision 3	964
Uniform Crime Reporting Classification of Offenses	968

Census Divisions and Outlying Areas of the U.S.

CENSUS REGIONS SHOWING DIVISIONS INCLUDED IN EACH:

NORTHEAST
New England
Middle Atlantic

MIDWEST
East North Central
West North Central

SOUTH
South Atlantic
East South Central
West South Central

WEST
Mountain
Pacific

CENSUS DIVISIONS SHOWING STATES INCLUDED IN EACH:

NEW ENGLAND
Maine
New Hampshire
Vermont
Massachusetts
Rhode Island
Connecticut

MIDDLE ATLANTIC
New York
New Jersey
Pennsylvania

EAST NORTH CENTRAL
Ohio
Indiana
Illinois
Michigan
Wisconsin

WEST NORTH CENTRAL
Minnesota
Iowa
Missouri
North Dakota
South Dakota
Nebraska
Kansas

SOUTH ATLANTIC
Delaware
Maryland
District of Columbia
Virginia
West Virginia
North Carolina
South Carolina
Georgia
Florida

EAST SOUTH CENTRAL
Kentucky
Tennessee
Alabama
Mississippi

WEST SOUTH CENTRAL
Arkansas
Louisiana
Oklahoma
Texas

MOUNTAIN
Montana
Idaho
Wyoming
Colorado
New Mexico
Arizona
Utah
Nevada

PACIFIC
Washington
Oregon
California
Alaska
Hawaii

OUTLYING AREAS OF THE UNITED STATES:

American Samoa
Guam
Northern Mariana Islands
Puerto Rico
Republic of Palau
Virgin Islands

Federal Reserve Districts

District 1 (Boston)
Maine, Massachusetts, New Hampshire, Rhode Island, Vermont; most of Connecticut

District 2 (New York)
New York; Puerto Rico, portions of New Jersey; Fairfield Co., Connecticut

District 3 (Philadelphia)
Delaware; portions of New Jersey and Pennsylvania

District 4 (Cleveland)
Ohio; portions of Kentucky, Pennsylvania, West Virginia

District 5 (Richmond)
District of Columbia, Maryland, North & South Carolina, Virginia; portions of West Virginia

District 6 (Atlanta)
Alabama, Florida, Georgia; portions of Louisiana, Mississippi, eastern Tennessee

District 7 (Chicago)
Iowa; portions of Michigan, Illinois, Indiana, Wisconsin

District 8 (St. Louis)
Arkansas; portions of Kentucky, Illinois, Indiana, Mississippi, Missouri, western Tennessee

District 9 (Minneapolis)
Minnesota, Montana, North & South Dakota; portions of Michigan and Wisconsin

District 10 (Kansas City)
Colorado, Kansas, Nebraska, Oklahoma, Wyoming; portions of Missouri, New Mexico

District 11 (Dallas)
Texas; portions of Louisiana, New Mexico

District 12 (San Francisco)
Alaska, Arizona, California, Guam, Hawaii, Idaho, Nevada, Oregon, Utah, Washington

Metropolitan Statistical Areas

Metropolitan Statistical Areas (MSAs) were developed to enable all Federal statistical agencies to use the same boundaries in publishing urban data.

MSA listings are updated annually to reflect changes in inclusion standards or demographic data. The following list, which is current as of Dec. 1992, includes both MSAs and Primary MSAs (PMSAs). Consolidated Metropolitan Statistical Areas (CMSAs), which consist of adjacent PMSAs are listed separately below.

In July 1983 this MSA system replaced a system based on the Standard Metropolitan Statistical Area (SMSA). SMSA titles in use through June 1983 are listed in the SRI 1980–85 Cumulative Index.

Area Code	Area Title
0040	Abilene, TX
0060	Aguadilla, PR
0080	Akron, OH
0120	Albany, GA
0160	Albany-Schenectady-Troy, NY
0200	Albuquerque, NM
0220	Alexandria, LA
0240	Allentown-Bethlehem-Easton, PA
0280	Altoona, PA
0320	Amarillo, TX
0360	Anaheim-Santa Ana, CA (See Orange County, CA)
0380	Anchorage, AK
0400	Anderson, IN (See Indianapolis, IN)
0405	Anderson, SC (See Greenville-Spartanburg-Anderson, SC)
0440	Ann Arbor, MI
0450	Anniston, AL
0460	Appleton-Oshkosh-Neenah, WI
0470	Arecibo, PR
0480	Ashville, NC
0500	Athens, GA
0520	Atlanta, GA
0560	Atlantic-Cape May, NJ
0600	Augusta-Aiken, GA-SC
0620	Aurora-Elgin, IL (See Chicago, IL)
0640	Austin-San Marcos, TX
0680	Bakersfield, CA
0720	Baltimore, MD
0730	Bangor, ME
0740	Barnstable-Yarmouth, MA (new)
0760	Baton Rouge, LA
0780	Battle Creek, MI (See Kalamazoo-Battle Creek, MI)
0840	Beaumont-Port Arthur, TX
0845	Beaver County, PA (See Pittsburgh, PA)
0860	Bellingham, WA
0870	Benton Harbor, MI
0875	Bergen-Passaic, NJ (See New York-Newark, NY-NJ-PA)
0880	Billings, MT
0920	Biloxi-Gulfport-Pascagoula, MS
0960	Binghamton, NY
1000	Birmingham, AL
1010	Bismarck, ND
1020	Bloomington, IN
1040	Bloomington-Normal, IL
1080	Boise City, ID
1120	Boston, MA-NH-ME-CT
1125	Boulder-Longmont, CO
1140	Bradenton, FL (See Sarasota-Bradenton, FL)
1145	Brazoria, TX
1150	Bremerton, WA
1160	Bridgeport, CT
1170	Bristol, CT (See Hartford, CT)
1200	Brockton, MA
1240	Brownsville-Harlingen-San Benito, TX
1260	Bryan-College Station, TX
1280	Buffalo-Niagara Falls, NY
1300	Burlington, NC (See Greensboro-Winston Salem-High Point, NC)
1305	Burlington, VT
1310	Caguas, PR
1320	Canton-Massillon, OH
1350	Casper, WY
1360	Cedar Rapids, IA
1400	Champaign-Urbana, IL
1440	Charleston-North Charleston, SC
1480	Charleston, WV
1520	Charlotte-Gastonia-Rock Hill, NC-SC
1540	Charlottesville, VA
1560	Chattanooga, TN-GA
1580	Cheyenne, WY
1600	Chicago, IL
1620	Chico-Paradise, CA
1640	Cincinnati, OH-KY-IN
1660	Clarksville-Hopkinsville, TN-KY
1680	Cleveland-Lorain-Elyria, OH
1720	Colorado Springs, CO
1740	Columbia, MO
1760	Columbia, SC
1800	Columbus, GA-AL
1840	Columbus, OH
1880	Corpus Christi, TX
1900	Cumberland, MD-WV
1920	Dallas, TX
1930	Danbury, CT
1950	Danville, VA
1960	Davenport-Moline-Rock Island, IA-IL
2000	Dayton-Springfield, OH
2020	Daytona Beach, FL
2030	Decatur, AL
2040	Decatur, IL
2080	Denver, CO
2120	Des Moines, IA
2160	Detroit, MI
2180	Dothan, AL
2190	Dover, DE (new)
2200	Dubuque, IA
2240	Duluth-Superior, MN-WI
2281	Dutchess County, NY
2290	Eau Claire, WI
2320	El Paso, TX
2330	Elkhart-Goshen, IN
2335	Elmira, NY
2340	Enid, OK
2360	Erie, PA
2400	Eugene-Springfield, OR
2440	Evansville-Henderson, IN-KY
2480	Fall River, MA-RI (See Providence-Fall River-Warwick, RI-MA)
2520	Fargo-Moorhead, ND-MN
2560	Fayetteville, NY
2580	Fayetteville-Springdale-Rogers, AR
2600	Fitchburg, Leominster, MA (See Boston, MA-NH-ME-CT)
2640	Flint, MI
2650	Florence, AL
2655	Florence, SC
2670	Fort Collins-Loveland, CO
2680	Fort Lauderdale, FL
2700	Fort Myers-Cape Coral, FL
2710	Fort Pierce-Port St. Lucie, FL
2720	Fort Smith, AR-OK
2750	Fort Walton Beach, FL
2760	Fort Wayne, IN
2800	Forth Worth-Arlington, TX
2840	Fresno, CA
2880	Gadsden, AL
2900	Gainesville, FL
2920	Galveston-Texas City, TX
2960	Gary, IN
2975	Glens Falls, NY
2980	Goldsboro, NC (new)
2985	Grand Forks, ND-MN
3000	Grand Rapids-Muskegon-Holland, MI
3040	Great Falls, MT
3060	Greeley, CO
3080	Green Bay, WI
3120	Greensboro-Winston-Salem-High Point, NC
3150	Greenville, NC (new)
3160	Greenville-Spartanburg-Anderson, SC
3180	Hagerstown, MD
3200	Hamilton-Middletown, OH
3240	Harrisburg-Lebanon-Carlisle, PA
3280	Hartford, CT
3290	Hickory-Morgantown, NC
3320	Honolulu, HI
3350	Houma, LA
3360	Houston, TX
3400	Huntington-Ashland, WV-KY-OH
3440	Huntsville, AL
3480	Indianapolis, IN
3500	Iowa City, IA
3520	Jackson, MI
3560	Jackson, MS
3580	Jackson, TN
3600	Jacksonville, FL
3605	Jacksonville, NC
3610	Jamestown, NY
3620	Janesville-Beloit, WI
3640	Jersey City, NJ (See New York-Newark, NY-NJ-PA)
3660	Johnson City-Kingsport-Bristol, TN-VA
3680	Johntown, PA
3690	Joliet, IL (See Chicago, IL)
3710	Joplin, MO
3720	Kalamazoo-Battle Creek, MI
3740	Kankakee, IL
3760	Kansas City, MO-KS
3800	Kenosha, WI
3810	Killeen-Temple, TX
3840	Knoxville, TN
3850	Kokomo, IN
3870	La Crosse, WI-MN
3880	Lafayette, LA
3920	Lafayette, IN
3960	Lake Charles, LA
3965	Lake County, IL (See Chicago, IL)
3980	Lakeland-Winter Haven, FL
4000	Lancaster, PA
4040	Lansing-East Lansing, MI
4080	Laredo, TX
4100	Las Cruces, NM
4120	Las Vegas, NV-AZ
4150	Lawrence, KS
4160	Lawrence-Haverhill, MA-NH (See Boston, MA-NH-ME-CT)
4200	Lawton, OK
4240	Lewiston-Auburn, ME
4280	Lexington, KY
4320	Lima, OH
4360	Lincoln, NE
4400	Little Rock-North Little Rock, AR
4420	Longview-Marshall, TX
4440	Lorain-Elyria, OH (See Cleveland-Lorain-Elyria, OH)
4480	Los Angeles-Long Beach, CA
4520	Louisville, KY-IN
4560	Lowell, MA-NH (See Boston, MA-NH-ME-CT)
4600	Lubbock, TX
4640	Lynchburg, VA
4680	Macon, GA
4720	Madison, WI
4760	Manchester, NH (See Boston, MA-NH-ME-CT)

Guide to Selected Standard Classifications — Metropolitan Statistical Areas

Code	Area	Code	Area	Code	Area	Code	Area
4800	Mansfield, OH	5720	Norfolk-Virginia Beach-Newport News, VA-NC	6720	Reno, NV	8080	Steubenville-Weirton, OH-WV
4840	Mayaguez, PR	5760	Norwalk, CT (See Stamford-Norwalk, CT)	6740	Richland-Kennewick-Pasco, WA	8120	Stockton-Lodi, CA
4880	McAllen-Edinburg, Mission, TX	5775	Oakland, CA	6760	Richmond-Petersburg, VA	8140	Sumter, SC
4890	Medford-Ashland, OR	5790	Ocala, FL	6780	Riverside-San Bernardino, CA	8160	Syracuse, NY
4900	Melbourne-Titusville-Palm Bay, FL	5800	Odessa-Midland, TX	6800	Roanoke, VA	8200	Tacoma, WA
4920	Memphis, TN-AR-MS	5880	Oklahoma City, OK	6820	Rochester, MN	8240	Tallahassee, FL
4940	Merced, CA	5910	Olympia, WA	6840	Rochester, NY	8280	Tampa-St. Petersburg-Clearwater, FL
5000	Miami, FL	5920	Omaha, NE-IA	6880	Rockford, IL	8320	Terre Haute, IN
5015	Middlesex-Somerset-Hunterdon, NJ (See New York-Newark, NY-NJ-PA)	5945	Orange County, CA	6895	Rocky Mount, NC	8360	Texarkana, TX-Texarkana, AR
5020	Middletown, CT	5950	Orange County, NY	6920	Sacramento, CA	8400	Toledo, OH
	(See Hartford, CT)	5960	Orlando, FL	6960	Saginaw-Bay City-Midland, MI	8440	Topeka, KS
5040	Midland, TX	5990	Owensboro, KY	6980	St. Cloud, MN	8480	Trenton, NJ
	(See Odessa-Midland, TX)	6000	Oxnard-Ventura, CA (See Ventura, CA)	7000	St. Joseph, MO	8520	Tucson, AZ
5080	Milwaukee, Waukesha, WI	6015	Panama City, FL	7040	St. Louis, MO-IL	8560	Tulsa, OK
5120	Minneapolis, St. Paul, MN-WI	6020	Parkersburg-Marietta, WV-OH	7080	Salem, OR	8600	Tuscaloosa, AL
5160	Mobile, AL	6025	Pascagoula, MS (See Biloxi-Gulfport-Pascagoula, MS)	7090	Salem-Gloucester, MA (See Boston, MA-NH-ME-CT)	8640	Tyler, TX
5170	Modesto, CA			7120	Salinas, CA	8680	Utica-Rome, NY
5190	Monmouth-Ocean, NJ (See New York-Newark, NY-NJ-PA)	6060	Pawtucket-Woonsocket-Attleboro, RI-MA (See Providence-Fall River-Warwick, RI-MA)	7160	Salt Lake City-Ogden, UT	8720	Vallejo-Fairfield-Napa, CA
5200	Monroe, LA			7200	San Angelo, TX	8725	Vancouver, WA (See Portland-Vancouver, OR-WA)
5240	Montgomery, AL	6080	Pensacola, FL	7240	San Antonio, TX	8735	Ventura, CA
5280	Muncie, IN	6120	Peoria-Pekin, IL	7320	San Diego, CA	8750	Victoria, TX
5320	Muskegon, MI (See Grand Rapids-Muskegon-Holland, MI)	6160	Philadelphia, PA-NJ	7360	San Francisco, CA	8760	Vineland-Millville-Bridgeton, NJ
5330	Myrtle Beach, SC (new)	6200	Phoenix-Mesa, AZ	7400	San Jose, CA	8780	Visalia-Tulare-Porterville, CA
5345	Naples, FL	6240	Pine Bluff, AR	7440	San Juan-Bayamon, PR	8800	Waco, TX
5350	Nashua, NH	6280	Pittsburgh, PA	7460	San Luis Obispo-Atascadero-Paso Robles, CA (new)	8840	Washington, DC-MD-VA-WV
5360	Nashville, TN	6320	Pittsfield, MA	7480	Santa Barbara-Santa Maria-Lompoc, CA	8880	Waterbury, CT
5380	Nassau-Suffolk, NY (See New York-Newark, NY-NJ-PA)	6360	Ponce, PR	7485	Santa Cruz-Watsonville, CA	8920	Waterloo-Cedar Falls, IA
5400	New Bedford, MA (See Boston, MA-NH-ME-CT)	6400	Portland, ME	7490	Santa Fe, NM	8940	Wausau, WI
		6440	Portland-Vancouver, OR-WA	7500	Santa Rosa, CA	8960	West Palm Beach-Boca Raton, FL
5440	New Britain, CT (See Hartford, CT)	6450	Portsmouth-Dover-Rochester, NH-ME (See Boston, MA-NH-ME-CT)	7510	Sarasota-Bradenton, FL	9000	Wheeling, WV-OH
5480	New Haven-Meriden, CT	6460	Poughkeepsie, NY (See Dutchess County, NY)	7520	Savannah, GA	9040	Wichita, KS
5520	New London-Norwich, CT-RI	6480	Providence-Fall River-Warwick, RI-MA	7560	Scranton-Wilkes-Barre-Hazleton, PA	9080	Wichita Falls, TX
5560	New Orleans, LA	6520	Provo-Orem, UT	7600	Seattle-Bellevue-Everett, WA	9140	Williamsport, PA
5600	New York-Newark, NY-NJ-PA	6560	Pueblo, CO	7610	Sharon, PA	9160	Wilmington-Newark, DE-MD
5640	Newark, NJ (See New York-Newark, NY-NJ-PA)	6580	Punta Gorda, FL (new)	7620	Sheboygan, WI	9200	Wilmington, NC
		6600	Racine, WI	7640	Sherman-Denison, TX	9240	Worcester, MA (See Boston, MA-NH-ME-CT)
5700	Niagara Falls, NY (See Buffalo-Niagara Falls, NY)	6640	Raleigh-Durham-Chapel Hill, NC	7680	Shreveport-Bossier City, LA	9260	Yakima, WA
		6660	Rapid City, SD	7720	Sious City, IA-NE	9270	Yolo, CA
		6680	Reading, PA	7760	Sioux Falls, SD	9280	York, PA
		6690	Redding, CA	7800	South Bend, IN	9320	Youngstown-Warren, OH
				7840	Spokane, WA	9340	Yuba City, CA
				7880	Springfield, IL	9360	Yuma, AZ
				7920	Springfield, MO		
				8000	Springfield, MA		
				8040	Stamford-Norwalk, CT		
				8050	State College, PA		

Consolidated Metropolitan Statistical Areas

Area Code	Area Title	Area Code	Area Title	Area Code	Area Title
07	Boston-Brockton-Nashua, MA-NH-ME-CT	31	Dallas-Fort Worth, TX	77	Philadelphia-Wilmington-Atlantic City, PA-NJ-DE-MD
14	Chicago-Gary-Kenosha, IL-IN-WI	34	Denver-Boulder-Greeley, CO	79	Portland-Salem, OR-WA
21	Cincinnati-Hamilton, OH-KY-IN	35	Detroit-Ann Arbor-Flint, MI	82	Sacramento-Yolo, CA
28	Cleveland-Akron, OH	42	Houston-Galveston-Brazoria, TX	84	San Francisco-Oakland-San Jose, CA
		49	Los Angeles-Riverside-Orange County, CA	87	San Juan-Caguas-Arecibo, PR
		56	Miami-Fort Lauderdale, FL	91	Seattle-Tacoma-Bremerton, WA
		63	Milwaukee-Racine, WI	97	Washington-Baltimore, DC-MD-VA-WV
		70	New York-Northern New Jersey-Long Island, NY-NJ-CT-PA		

Cities With Population Over 100,000

1992 Rank and Population

Rank	City	Population
1	New York, NY	7,311,966
2	Los Angeles, CA	3,489,779
3	Chicago, IL	2,768,483
4	Houston, TX	1,690,180
5	Philadelphia, PA	1,552,572
6	San Diego, CA	1,148,851
7	Dallas, TX	1,022,497
8	Phoenix, AZ	1,012,230
9	Detroit, MI	1,012,110
10	San Antonio, TX	966,437
11	San Jose, CA	801,331
12	Indianapolis, IN	746,538
13	San Francisco, CA	728,921
14	Baltimore, MD	726,096
15	Jacksonville, FL	661,177
16	Columbus, OH	642,987
17	Milwaukee, WI	617,043
18	Memphis, TN	610,275
19	Washington, DC	585,221
20	Boston, MA	551,675
21	El Paso, TX	543,813
22	Seattle, WA	519,598
23	Cleveland, OH	502,539
24	Nashville-Davidson, TN	495,012
25	Austin, TX	492,329
26	New Orleans, LA	489,595
27	Denver, CO	483,852
28	Fort Worth, TX	454,430
29	Oklahoma City, OK	453,995
30	Portland, OR	445,458
31	Long Beach, CA	438,771
32	Kansas City, MO	431,553
33	Virginia Beach, VA	417,061
34	Charlotte, NC	416,294
35	Tucson, AZ	415,079
36	Albuquerque, NM	398,492
37	Atlanta, GA	394,848
38	St. Louis, MO	383,733
39	Sacramento, CA	382,816
40	Fresno, CA	376,130
41	Tulsa, OK	375,307
42	Oakland, CA	373,219
43	Honolulu, HI	371,320
44	Miami, FL	367,016
45	Pittsburgh, PA	366,852
46	Cincinnati, OH	364,278
47	Minneapolis, MN	362,696
48	Omaha, NE	339,671
49	Toledo, OH	329,325
50	Buffalo, NY	323,284
51	Wichita, KS	311,746
52	Mesa, AZ	296,645
53	Colorado Springs, CO	295,815
54	Las Vegas, NV	295,516
55	Santa Ana, CA	288,024
56	Tampa, FL	284,737
57	Arlington, TX	275,907
58	Anaheim, CA	274,162
59	Louisville, KY	271,038
60	St. Paul, MN	268,266
61	Newark, NJ	267,849
62	Corpus Christi, TX	266,412
63	Birmingham, AL	264,984
64	Norfolk, VA	253,768
65	Anchorage, AK	245,866
66	Aurora, CO	239,626
67	Riverside, CA	238,601
68	St. Petersburg, FL	235,306
69	Rochester, NY	234,163
70	Lexington-Fayette, KY	232,562
71	Jersey City, NJ	228,575
72	Baton Rouge, LA	224,704
73	Akron, OH	223,621
74	Raleigh, NC	220,524
75	Stockton, CA	219,621
76	Richmond, VA	202,263
77	Mobile, AL	201,896
78	Lincoln, NE	197,488
79	Shreveport, LA	196,645
80	Jackson, MS	196,231
81	Madison, WI	195,161
82	Des Moines, IA	194,540
83	Montgomery, AL	192,125
84	Hialeah, FL	191,702
85	Grand Rapids, MI	191,230
86	Garland, TX	191,186
87	Greensboro, NC	189,924
88	Bakersfield, CA	187,985
89	Lubbock, TX	187,941
90	Spokane, WA	187,429
91	Yonkers, NY	186,063
92	Columbus, GA	185,744
93	Huntington Beach, CA	185,055
94	Tacoma, WA	183,890
95	Dayton, OH	183,189
96	Fremont, CA	179,300
97	Glendale, CA	177,671
98	Newport News, VA	177,286
99	Little Rock, AR	176,870
100	Orlando, FL	174,215
101	Fort Wayne, IN	173,717
102	San Bernardino, CA	172,451
103	Modesto, CA	172,292
104	Arlington, VA	171,582
105	Knoxville, TX	167,287
106	Chesapeake, VA	166,005
107	Salt Lake City, UT	165,835
108	Worcester, MA	163,414
109	Huntsville, AL	163,319
110	Syracuse, NY	162,835
111	Irving, TX	161,261
112	Amarillo, TX	161,065
113	Glendale, TX	156,165
114	Providence, RI	155,418
115	Springfield, MA	153,466
116	Chattanooga, TN	152,888
117	Fort Lauderdale, FL	148,524
118	Kansas City, KS	146,507
119	Garden Grove, CA	145,874
120	Springfield, MO	145,438
121	Oxnard, CA	144,805
122	Winston-Salem, NC	144,791
123	Chula Vista, CA	144,752
124	Warren, MI	142,494
125	Tempe, AZ	142,139
126	Plano, TX	142,106
127	Rockford, IL	141,679
128	Durham, NC	140,926
129	Pomona, CA	140,364
130	Reno, NV	139,884
131	Oceanside, CA	139,718
132	Paterson, NJ	139,358
133	Flint, MI	139,311
134	Ontario, CA	138,981
135	Savannah, GA	138,908
136	Hampton, VA	137,048
137	Scottsdale, AZ	137,022
138	Bridgeport, CT	137,020
139	Laredo, TX	136,508
140	Torrance, CA	135,642
141	Boise City, ID	135,506
142	Pasadena, CA	132,605
143	Moreno Valley, CA	132,105
144	Hartford, CT	131,995
145	Tallahassee, FL	130,357
146	Evansville, IN	127,566
147	Lansing, MI	126,722
148	Lakewood, CO	125,957
149	Pasadena, TX	125,418
150	New Haven, CT	123,966
151	Hollywood, FL	121,732
152	Topeka, KS	120,257
153	Irvine, CA	119,389
154	Overland Park, KS	119,260
155	Santa Clarita, CA	118,676
156	Sunnyvale, CA	118,438
157	Sterling Heights, MI	118,314
158	Gary, IN	116,702
159	Santa Rosa, CA	116,554
160	Eugene, OR	115,963
161	Beaumont, TX	115,494
162	Fullerton, CA	115,476
163	Hayward, CA	115,189
164	Salinas, CA	114,762
165	Peoria, IL	113,983
166	Vallejo, CA	113,703
167	Orange, CA	113,591
168	Escondido, CA	113,161
169	Alexandria, VA	113,134
170	Independence, MO	112,713
171	Concord, CA	112,688
172	Salem, OR	112,050
173	Cedar Rapids, IA	111,659
174	Inglewood, CA	111,496
175	Rancho Cucamonga, CA	111,161
176	Ann Arbor, MI	109,766
177	Erie, PA	109,267
178	Mesquite, TX	108,324
179	Abilene, TX	108,095
180	Elizabeth, NJ	107,915
181	Stamford, CT	107,590
182	Thousand Oaks, CA	107,522
183	Macon, GA	107,257
184	El Monte, CA	106,935
185	Waterbury, CT	106,904
186	Springfield, IL	106,429
187	Allentown, PA	106,429
188	Lancaster, CA	106,139
189	South Bend, IN	105,942
190	Aurora, IL	105,929
191	Brownsville, TX	105,757
192	Sioux Falls, SD	105,634
193	Grand Prairie, TX	104,482
194	Portsmouth, VA	104,361
195	Waco, TX	103,997
196	Simi Valley, CA	103,813
197	Livonia, MI	101,375
198	Berkeley, CA	101,122
199	Green Bay, WI	100,459
200	Chandler, AZ	100,173

Consumer Price Index Cities

Consumer Price Index data are collected for the following Metropolitan Statistical Areas:

Anchorage, AK
Atlanta, GA
Baltimore, MD
Boston-Lawrence-Salem, MA-NH
Buffalo-Niagara Falls, NY
Chicago-Gary-Lake County, IL-IN-WI
Cincinnati-Hamilton, OH-KY-IN
Cleveland-Akron-Lorain, OH
Dallas-Fort Worth, TX
Denver-Boulder, CO
Detroit-Ann Arbor, MI
Honolulu, HI
Houston-Galveston-Brazoria, TX
Kansas City, MO-KS
Los Angeles-Anaheim-Riverside, CA
Miami-Fort Lauderdale, FL
Milwaukee, WI
Minneapolis-St. Paul, MN-WI
New Orleans, LA
N.Y. Northern N.J.-Long Island, NY-NJ-CT
Phil.-Wilmington-Trenton, PA-NJ-DE-MD
Pittsburgh-Beaver Valley, PA
Portland-Vancouver, OR-WA
St. Louis-East St. Louis, MO-IL
San Diego, CA
San Francisco-Oakland-San Jose, CA
Seattle-Tacoma, WA
Tampa-St. Petersburg-Clearwater, FL
Washington, DC-MD-VA

Standard Industrial Classification

The Standard Industrial Classification (SIC) was developed to classify industrial establishments by the type of activity in which they are engaged, for the purpose of promoting uniformity and comparability of statistical data collected by Federal and State agencies, trade associations, and others. The classification system is at 4 levels: industry divisions, major groups, and individual industries—represented by 1- to 4-digit codes. The following list is taken from the 1987 *Standard Industrial Classification Manual,* which revises the 1972 edition and 1977 supplement. For the 1972/77 version of the classification, please see SRI 1980-1985 Cumulative Index. Abbreviation: nec = not elsewhere classified.

Group and Industry Code

AGRICULTURE, FORESTRY, AND FISHING

01 AGRICULTURAL PRODUCTION—CROPS

- **011 Cash Grains**
  - 0111 Wheat
  - 0112 Rice
  - 0115 Corn
  - 0116 Soybeans
  - 0119 Cash grains, nec
- **013 Field Crops, Except Cash Grains**
  - 0131 Cotton
  - 0132 Tobacco
  - 0133 Sugarcane and sugar beets
  - 0134 Irish potatoes
  - 0139 Field crops, except cash grains, nec
- **016 Vegetables and Melons**
  - 0161 Vegetables and melons
- **017 Fruits and Tree Nuts**
  - 0171 Berry crops
  - 0172 Grapes
  - 0173 Tree nuts
  - 0174 Citrus fruits
  - 0175 Deciduous tree fruits
  - 0179 Fruits and tree nuts, nec
- **018 Horticultural Specialties**
  - 0181 Ornamental nursery products
  - 0182 Food crops grown under cover
- **019 General Farms, Primarily Crop**
  - 0191 General farms, primarily crop

02 AGRICULTURAL PRODUCTION—LIVESTOCK

- **021 Livestock, Except Dairy and Poultry**
  - 0211 Beef cattle feedlots
  - 0212 Beef cattle, except feedlots
  - 0213 Hogs
  - 0214 Sheep and goats
  - 0219 General livestock, nec
- **024 Dairy Farms**
  - 0241 Dairy farms
- **025 Poultry and Eggs**
  - 0251 Broiler, fryer, and roaster chickens
  - 0252 Chicken eggs
  - 0253 Turkeys and turkey eggs
  - 0254 Poultry hatcheries
  - 0259 Poultry and eggs, nec
- **027 Animal Specialties**
  - 0271 Fur-bearing animals and rabbits
  - 0272 Horses and other equines
  - 0273 Animal aquaculture
  - 0279 Animal specialties, nec
- **029 General Farms, Primarily Animal**
  - 0291 General farms, primarily animal

07 AGRICULTURAL SERVICES

- **071 Soil Preparation Services**
  - 0711 Soil preparation services
- **072 Crop Services**
  - 0721 Crop planting and protecting
  - 0722 Crop harvesting
  - 0723 Crop preparation services for market
  - 0724 Cotton ginning
- **074 Veterinary Services**
  - 0741 Veterinary services for livestock
  - 0742 Veterinary services, specialties
- **075 Animal Services, Except Veterinary**
  - 0751 Livestock services, exc. veterinary
  - 0752 Animal specialty services
- **076 Farm Labor and Management Services**
  - 0761 Farm labor contractors
  - 0762 Farm management services
- **078 Landscape and Horticultural Services**
  - 0781 Landscape counseling and planning
  - 0782 Lawn and garden services
  - 0783 Ornamental shrub and tree services

08 FORESTRY

- **081 Timber Tracts**
  - 0811 Timber tracts
- **083 Forest Products**
  - 0831 Forest products
- **085 Forestry Services**
  - 0851 Forestry services

09 FISHING, HUNTING, AND TRAPPING

- **091 Commercial Fishing**
  - 0912 Finfish
  - 0913 Shellfish
  - 0919 Miscellaneous marine products
- **092 Fish Hatcheries and Preserves**
  - 0921 Fish hatcheries and preserves
- **097 Hunting, Trapping, Game Propagation**
  - 0971 Hunting, trapping, game propagation

MINING

10 METAL MINING

- **101 Iron Ores**
  - 1011 Iron ores
- **102 Copper Ores**
  - 1021 Copper ores
- **103 Lead and Zinc Ores**
  - 1031 Lead and zinc ores
- **104 Gold and Silver Ores**
  - 1041 Gold ores
  - 1044 Silver ores
- **106 Ferroalloy Ores, Except Vanadium**
  - 1061 Ferroalloy ores, except vanadium
- **108 Metal Mining Services**
  - 1081 Metal mining services
- **109 Miscellaneous Metal Ores**
  - 1094 Uranium-radium-vanadium ores
  - 1099 Metal ores, nec

12 COAL MINING

- **122 Bituminous Coal and Lignite Mining**
  - 1221 Bituminous coal and lignite—surface
  - 1222 Bituminous coal—underground
- **123 Anthracite Mining**
  - 1231 Anthracite mining
- **124 Coal Mining Services**
  - 1241 Coal mining services

13 OIL AND GAS EXTRACTION

- **131 Crude Petroleum and Natural Gas**
  - 1311 Crude petroleum and natural gas
- **132 Natural Gas Liquids**
  - 1321 Natural gas liquids
- **138 Oil and Gas Field Services**
  - 1381 Drilling oil and gas wells
  - 1382 Oil and gas exploration services
  - 1389 Oil and gas field services, nec

14 NONMETALLIC MINERALS, EXCEPT FUELS

- **141 Dimension Stone**
  - 1411 Dimension stone
- **142 Crushed and Broken Stone**
  - 1422 Crushed and broken limestone
  - 1423 Crushed and broken granite
  - 1429 Crushed and broken stone, nec
- **144 Sand and Gravel**
  - 1442 Construction sand and gravel
  - 1446 Industrial sand
- **145 Clay, Ceramic, & Refractory Minerals**
  - 1455 Kaolin and ball clay
  - 1459 Clay and related minerals, nec
- **147 Chemical and Fertilizer Minerals**
  - 1474 Potash, soda, and borate minerals
  - 1475 Phosphate rock
  - 1479 Chemical and fertilizer mining, nec
- **148 Nonmetallic Minerals Services**
  - 1481 Nonmetallic minerals services
- **149 Miscellaneous Nonmetallic Minerals**
  - 1499 Miscellaneous nonmetallic minerals

CONSTRUCTION

15 GENERAL BUILDING CONTRACTORS

- **152 Residential Building Construction**
  - 1521 Single-family housing construction
  - 1522 Residential construction, nec
- **153 Operative Builders**
  - 1531 Operative builders
- **154 Nonresidential Building Construction**
  - 1541 Industrial buildings and warehouses
  - 1542 Nonresidential construction, nec

16 HEAVY CONSTRUCTION, EX. BUILDING

- **161 Highway and Street Construction**
  - 1611 Highway and street construction

Guide to Selected Standard Classifications

Standard Industrial Classification

162 Heavy Construction, Except Highway
1622 Bridge, tunnel, & elevated highway
1623 Water, sewer, and utility lines
1629 Heavy construction, nec

17 SPECIAL TRADE CONTRACTORS

171 Plumbing, Heating, Air-Conditioning
1711 Plumbing, heating, air-conditioning

172 Painting and Paper Hanging
1721 Painting and paper hanging

173 Electrical Work
1731 Electrical work

174 Masonry, Stonework, and Plastering
1741 Masonry and other stonework
1742 Plastering, drywall, and insulation
1743 Terrazzo, tile, marble, mosaic work

175 Carpentry and Floor Work
1751 Carpentry work
1752 Floor laying and floor work, nec

176 Roofing, Siding, and Sheet Metal Work
1761 Roofing, siding, and sheet metal work

177 Concrete Work
1771 Concrete work

178 Water Well Drilling
1781 Water well drilling

179 Misc. Special Trade Contractors
1791 Structural steel erection
1793 Glass and glazing work
1794 Excavation work
1795 Wrecking and demolition work
1796 Installing building equipment, nec
1799 Special trade contractors, nec

MANUFACTURING

20 FOOD AND KINDRED PRODUCTS

201 Meat Products
2011 Meat packing plants
2013 Sausages and other prepared meats
2015 Poultry slaughtering and processing

202 Dairy Products
2021 Creamery butter
2022 Cheese, natural and processed
2023 Dry, condensed, evaporated products
2024 Ice cream and frozen desserts
2026 Fluid milk

203 Preserved Fruits and Vegetables
2032 Canned specialties
2033 Canned fruits and vegetables
2034 Dehydrated fruits, vegetables, soups
2035 Pickles, sauces, and salad dressings
2037 Frozen fruits and vegetables
2038 Frozen specialties, nec

204 Grain Mill Products
2041 Flour and other grain mill products
2043 Cereal breakfast foods
2044 Rice milling
2045 Prepared flour mixes and doughs
2046 Wet corn milling
2047 Dog and cat food
2048 Prepared feeds, nec

205 Bakery Products
2051 Bread, cake, and related products
2052 Cookies and crackers
2053 Frozen bakery products, except bread

206 Sugar and Confectionery Products
2061 Raw cane sugar
2062 Cane sugar refining
2063 Beet sugar
2064 Candy & other confectionery products

2066 Chocolate and cocoa products
2067 Chewing gum
2068 Salted and roasted nuts and seeds

207 Fats and Oils
2074 Cottonseed oil mills
2075 Soybean oil mills
2076 Vegetable oil mills, nec
2077 Animal and marine fats and oils
2079 Edible fats and oils, nec

208 Beverages
2082 Malt beverages
2083 Malt
2084 Wines, brandy, and brandy spirits
2085 Distilled and blended liquors
2086 Bottled and canned soft drinks
2087 Flavoring extracts and syrups, nec

209 Misc. Food and Kindred Products
2091 Canned and cured fish and seafoods
2092 Fresh or frozen prepared fish
2095 Roasted coffee
2096 Potato chips and similar snacks
2097 Manufactured ice
2098 Macaroni and spaghetti
2099 Food preparations, nec

21 TOBACCO PRODUCTS

211 Cigarettes
2111 Cigarettes

212 Cigars
2121 Cigars

213 Chewing and Smoking Tobacco
2131 Chewing and smoking tobacco

214 Tobacco Stemming and Redrying
2141 Tobacco stemming and redrying

22 TEXTILE MILL PRODUCTS

221 Broadwoven Fabric Mills, Cotton
2211 Broadwoven fabric mills, cotton

222 Broadwoven Fabric Mills, Manmade
2221 Broadwoven fabric mills, manmade

223 Broadwoven Fabric Mills, Wool
2231 Broadwoven fabric mills, wool

224 Narrow Fabric Mills
2241 Narrow fabric mills

225 Knitting Mills
2251 Women's hosiery, except socks
2252 Hosiery, nec
2253 Knit outerwear mills
2254 Knit underwear mills
2257 Weft knit fabric mills
2258 Lace & warp knit fabric mills
2259 Knitting mills, nec

226 Textile Finishing, Except Wool
2261 Finishing plants, cotton
2262 Finishing plants, manmade
2269 Finishing plants, nec

227 Carpets and Rugs
2273 Carpets and rugs

228 Yarn and Thread Mills
2281 Yarn spinning mills
2282 Throwing and winding mills
2284 Thread mills

229 Miscellaneous Textile Goods
2295 Coated fabrics, not rubberized
2296 Tire cord and fabrics
2297 Nonwoven fabrics
2298 Cordage and twine
2299 Textile goods, nec

23 APPAREL AND OTHER TEXTILE PRODUCTS

231 Men's and Boys' Suits and Coats
2311 Men's and boys' suits and coats

232 Men's and Boys' Furnishings
2321 Men's and boys' shirts
2322 Men's & boys' underwear & nightwear
2323 Men's and boys' neckwear
2325 Men's and boys' trousers and slacks
2326 Men's and boys' work clothing
2329 Men's and boys' clothing, nec

233 Women's and Misses' Outerwear
2331 Women's & misses' blouses & shirts
2335 Women's, juniors', & misses' dresses
2337 Women's and misses' suits and coats
2339 Women's and misses' outerwear, nec

234 Women's and Children's Undergarments
2341 Women's and children's underwear
2342 Bras, girdles, and allied garments

235 Hats, Caps, and Millinery
2353 Hats, caps, and millinery

236 Girls' and Children's Outerwear
2361 Girls' & children's dresses, blouses
2369 Girls' and children's outerwear, nec

237 Fur Goods
2371 Fur goods

238 Miscellaneous Apparel and Accessories
2381 Fabric dress and work gloves
2384 Robes and dressing gowns
2385 Waterproof outerwear
2386 Leather and sheep-lined clothing
2387 Apparel belts
2389 Apparel and accessories, nec

239 Misc. Fabricated Textile Products
2391 Curtains and draperies
2392 Housefurnishings, nec
2393 Textile bags
2394 Canvas and related products
2395 Pleating and stitching
2396 Automotive and apparel trimmings
2397 Schiffli machine embroideries
2399 Fabricated textile products, nec

24 LUMBER AND WOOD PRODUCTS

241 Logging
2411 Logging

242 Sawmills and Planing Mills
2421 Sawmills and planing mills, general
2426 Hardwood dimension & flooring mills
2429 Special product sawmills, nec

243 Millwork, Plywood & Structural Members
2431 Millwork
2434 Wood kitchen cabinets
2435 Hardwood veneer and plywood
2436 Softwood veneer and plywood
2439 Structural wood members, nec

244 Wood Containers
2441 Nailed wood boxes and shook
2448 Wood pallets and skids
2449 Wood containers, nec

245 Wood Buildings and Mobile Homes
2451 Mobile homes
2452 Prefabricated wood buildings

249 Miscellaneous Wood Products
2491 Wood preserving
2493 Reconstituted wood products
2499 Wood products, nec

Standard Industrial Classification

Guide to Selected Standard Classifications

25 FURNITURE AND FIXTURES

251 Household Furniture
- 2511 Wood household furniture
- 2512 Upholstered household furniture
- 2514 Metal household furniture
- 2515 Mattresses and bedsprings
- 2517 Wood TV and radio cabinets
- 2519 Household furniture, nec

252 Office Furniture
- 2521 Wood office furniture
- 2522 Office furniture, except wood

253 Public Building & Related Furniture
- 2531 Public building & related furniture

254 Partitions and Fixtures
- 2541 Wood partitions and fixtures
- 2542 Partitions and fixtures, except wood

259 Miscellaneous Furniture and Fixtures
- 2591 Drapery hardware & blinds & shades
- 2599 Furniture and fixtures, nec

26 PAPER AND ALLIED PRODUCTS

261 Pulp Mills
- 2611 Pulp mills

262 Paper Mills
- 2621 Paper mills

263 Paperboard Mills
- 2631 Paperboard mills

265 Paperboard Containers and Boxes
- 2652 Setup paperboard boxes
- 2653 Corrugated and solid fiber boxes
- 2655 Fiber cans, drums & similar products
- 2656 Sanitary food containers
- 2657 Folding paperboard boxes

267 Misc. Converted Paper Products
- 2671 Paper coated & laminated, packaging
- 2672 Paper coated and laminated, nec
- 2673 Bags: plastics, laminated, & coated
- 2674 Bags: uncoated paper & multiwall
- 2675 Die-cut paper and board
- 2676 Sanitary paper products
- 2677 Envelopes
- 2678 Stationery products
- 2679 Converted paper products, nec

27 PRINTING AND PUBLISHING

271 Newspapers
- 2711 Newspapers

272 Periodicals
- 2721 Periodicals

273 Books
- 2731 Book publishing
- 2732 Book printing

274 Miscellaneous Publishing
- 2741 Miscellaneous publishing

275 Commercial Printing
- 2752 Commercial printing, lithographic
- 2754 Commercial printing, gravure
- 2759 Commercial printing, nec

276 Manifold Business Forms
- 2761 Manifold business forms

277 Greeting Cards
- 2771 Greeting cards

278 Blankbooks and Bookbinding
- 2782 Blankbooks and looseleaf binders
- 2789 Bookbinding and related work

279 Printing Trade Services
- 2791 Typesetting
- 2796 Platemaking services

28 CHEMICALS AND ALLIED PRODUCTS

281 Industrial Inorganic Chemicals
- 2812 Alkalies and chlorine
- 2813 Industrial gases
- 2816 Inorganic pigments
- 2819 Industrial inorganic chemicals, nec

282 Plastics Materials and Synthetics
- 2821 Plastics materials and resins
- 2822 Synthetic rubber
- 2823 Cellulosic manmade fibers
- 2824 Organic fibers, noncellulosic

283 Drugs
- 2833 Medicinals and botanicals
- 2834 Pharmaceutical preparations
- 2835 Diagnostic substances
- 2836 Biological products exc. diagnostic

284 Soap, Cleaners, and Toilet Goods
- 2841 Soap and other detergents
- 2842 Polishes and sanitation goods
- 2843 Surface active agents
- 2844 Toilet preparations

285 Paints and Allied Products
- 2851 Paints and allied products

286 Industrial Organic Chemicals
- 2861 Gum and wood chemicals
- 2865 Cyclic crudes and intermediates
- 2869 Industrial organic chemicals, nec

287 Agricultural Chemicals
- 2873 Nitrogenous fertilizers
- 2874 Phosphatic fertilizers
- 2875 Fertilizers, mixing only
- 2879 Agricultural chemicals, nec

289 Miscellaneous Chemical Products
- 2891 Adhesives and sealants
- 2892 Explosives
- 2893 Printing ink
- 2895 Carbon black
- 2899 Chemical preparations, nec

29 PETROLEUM AND COAL PRODUCTS

291 Petroleum Refining
- 2911 Petroleum refining

295 Asphalt Paving and Roofing Materials
- 2951 Asphalt paving mixtures and blocks
- 2952 Asphalt felts and coatings

299 Misc. Petroleum and Coal Products
- 2992 Lubricating oils and greases
- 2999 Petroleum and coal products, nec

30 RUBBER AND MISC. PLASTICS PRODUCTS

301 Tires and Inner Tubes
- 3011 Tires and inner tubes

302 Rubber and Plastics Footwear
- 3021 Rubber and plastics footwear

305 Hose & Belting & Gaskets & Packing
- 3052 Rubber & plastics hose & belting
- 3053 Gaskets, packing and sealing devices

306 Fabricated Rubber Products, NEC
- 3061 Mechanical rubber goods
- 3069 Fabricated rubber products, nec

308 Miscellaneous Plastics Products, NEC
- 3081 Unsupported plastics film & sheet
- 3082 Unsupported plastics profile shapes
- 3083 Laminated plastics plate & sheet
- 3084 Plastics pipe
- 3085 Plastics bottles
- 3086 Plastics foam products
- 3087 Custom compound purchased resins
- 3088 Plastics plumbing fixtures
- 3089 Plastics products, nec

31 LEATHER AND LEATHER PRODUCTS

311 Leather Tanning and Finishing
- 3111 Leather tanning and finishing

313 Footwear Cut Stock
- 3131 Footwear cut stock

314 Footwear, Except Rubber
- 3142 House slippers
- 3143 Men's footwear, except athletic
- 3144 Women's footwear, except athletic
- 3149 Footwear, except rubber, nec

315 Leather Gloves and Mittens
- 3151 Leather gloves and mittens

316 Luggage
- 3161 Luggage

317 Handbags and Personal Leather Goods
- 3171 Women's handbags and purses
- 3172 Personal leather goods, nec

319 Leather Goods, NEC
- 3199 Leather goods, nec

32 STONE, CLAY, AND GLASS PRODUCTS

321 Flat Glass
- 3211 Flat glass

322 Glass and Glassware, Pressed or Blown
- 3221 Glass containers
- 3229 Pressed and blown glass, nec

323 Products of Purchased Glass
- 3231 Products of purchased glass

324 Cement, Hydraulic
- 3241 Cement, hydraulic

325 Structural Clay Products
- 3251 Brick and structural clay tile
- 3253 Ceramic wall and floor tile
- 3255 Clay refractories
- 3259 Structural clay products, nec

326 Pottery and Related Products
- 3261 Vitreous plumbing fixtures
- 3262 Vitreous china table & kitchenware
- 3263 Semivitreous table & kitchenware
- 3264 Porcelain electrical supplies
- 3269 Pottery products, nec

327 Concrete, Gypsum, and Plaster Products
- 3271 Concrete block and brick
- 3272 Concrete products, nec
- 3273 Ready-mixed concrete
- 3274 Lime
- 3275 Gypsum products

328 Cut Stone and Stone Products
- 3281 Cut stone and stone products

329 Misc. Nonmetallic Mineral Products
- 3291 Abrasive products
- 3292 Asbestos products
- 3295 Minerals, ground or treated
- 3296 Mineral wool
- 3297 Nonclay refractories
- 3299 Nonmetallic mineral products, nec

33 PRIMARY METAL INDUSTRIES

331 Blast Furnace and Basic Steel Products
- 3312 Blast furnaces and steel mills
- 3313 Electrometallurgical products
- 3315 Steel wire and related products
- 3316 Cold finishing of steel shapes
- 3317 Steel pipe and tubes

332 Iron and Steel Foundries
- 3321 Gray and ductile iron foundries
- 3322 Malleable iron foundries
- 3324 Steel investment foundries
- 3325 Steel foundries, nec

Guide to Selected Standard Classifications

Standard Industrial Classification

333 Primary Nonferrous Metals
- 3331 Primary copper
- 3334 Primary aluminum
- 3339 Primary nonferrous metals, nec

334 Secondary Nonferrous Metals
- 3341 Secondary nonferrous metals

335 Nonferrous Rolling and Drawing
- 3351 Copper rolling and drawing
- 3353 Aluminum sheet, plate, and foil
- 3354 Aluminum extruded products
- 3355 Aluminum rolling and drawing, nec
- 3356 Nonferrous rolling and drawing, nec
- 3357 Nonferrous wiredrawing & insulating

336 Nonferrous Foundries (Castings)
- 3363 Aluminum die-castings
- 3364 Nonferrous die-casting exc. aluminum
- 3365 Aluminum foundries
- 3366 Copper foundries
- 3369 Nonferrous foundries, nec

339 Miscellaneous Primary Metal Products
- 3398 Metal heat treating
- 3399 Primary metal products, nec

34 FABRICATED METAL PRODUCTS

341 Metal Cans and Shipping Containers
- 3411 Metal cans
- 3412 Metal barrels, drums, and pails

342 Cutlery, Handtools, and Hardware
- 3421 Cutlery
- 3423 Hand and edge tools, nec
- 3425 Saw blades and handsaws
- 3429 Hardware, nec

343 Plumbing and Heating, Except Electric
- 3431 Metal sanitary ware
- 3432 Plumbing fixture fittings and trim
- 3433 Heating equipment, except electric

344 Fabricated Structural Metal Products
- 3441 Fabricated structural metal
- 3442 Metal doors, sash, and trim
- 3443 Fabricated plate work (boiler shops)
- 3444 Sheet metal work
- 3446 Architectural metal work
- 3448 Prefabricated metal buildings
- 3449 Miscellaneous metal work

345 Screw Machine Products, Bolts, Etc.
- 3451 Screw machine products
- 3452 Bolts, nuts, rivets, and washers

346 Metal Forgings and Stampings
- 3462 Iron and steel forgings
- 3463 Nonferrous forgings
- 3465 Automotive stampings
- 3466 Crowns and closures
- 3469 Metal stampings, nec

347 Metal Services, NEC
- 3471 Plating and polishing
- 3479 Metal coating and allied services

348 Ordnance and Accessories, NEC
- 3482 Small arms ammunition
- 3483 Ammunition, exc. for small arms, nec
- 3484 Small arms
- 3489 Ordnance and accessories, nec

349 Misc. Fabricated Metal Products
- 3491 Industrial valves
- 3492 Fluid power valves & hose fittings
- 3493 Steel springs, except wire
- 3494 Valves and pipe fittings, nec
- 3495 Wire springs
- 3496 Misc. fabricated wire products
- 3497 Metal foil and leaf
- 3498 Fabricated pipe and fittings
- 3499 Fabricated metal products, nec

35 INDUSTRIAL MACHINERY AND EQUIPMENT

351 Engines and Turbines
- 3511 Turbines and turbine generator sets
- 3519 Internal combustion engines, nec

352 Farm and Garden Machinery
- 3523 Farm machinery and equipment
- 3524 Lawn and garden equipment

353 Construction and Related Machinery
- 3531 Construction machinery
- 3532 Mining machinery
- 3533 Oil and gas field machinery
- 3534 Elevators and moving stairways
- 3535 Conveyors and conveying equipment
- 3536 Hoists, cranes, and monorails
- 3537 Industrial trucks and tractors

354 Metalworking Machinery
- 3541 Machine tools, metal cutting types
- 3542 Machine tools, metal forming types
- 3543 Industrial patterns
- 3544 Special dies, tools, jigs & fixtures
- 3545 Machine tool accessories
- 3546 Power-driven handtools
- 3547 Rolling mill machinery
- 3548 Welding apparatus
- 3549 Metalworking machinery, nec

355 Special Industry Machinery
- 3552 Textile machinery
- 3553 Woodworking machinery
- 3554 Paper industries machinery
- 3555 Printing trades machinery
- 3556 Food products machinery
- 3559 Special industry machinery, nec

356 General Industrial Machinery
- 3561 Pumps and pumping equipment
- 3562 Ball and roller bearings
- 3563 Air and gas compressors
- 3564 Blowers and fans
- 3565 Packaging machinery
- 3566 Speed changers, drives, and gears
- 3567 Industrial furnaces and ovens
- 3568 Power transmission equipment, nec
- 3569 General industrial machinery, nec

357 Computer and Office Equipment
- 3571 Electronic computers
- 3572 Computer storage devices
- 3575 Computer terminals
- 3577 Computer peripheral equipment, nec
- 3578 Calculating and accounting equipment
- 3579 Office machines, nec

358 Refrigeration and Service Machinery
- 3581 Automatic vending machines
- 3582 Commercial laundry equipment
- 3585 Refrigeration and heating equipment
- 3586 Measuring and dispensing pumps
- 3589 Service industry machinery, nec

359 Industrial Machinery, NEC
- 3592 Carburetors, pistons, rings, valves
- 3593 Fluid power cylinders & actuators
- 3594 Fluid power pumps and motors
- 3596 Scales and balances, exc. laboratory
- 3599 Industrial machinery, nec

36 ELECTRONIC & OTHER ELECTRIC EQUIPMENT

361 Electric Distribution Equipment
- 3612 Transformers, except electronic
- 3613 Switchgear and switchboard apparatus

362 Electrical Industrial Apparatus
- 3621 Motors and generators

- 3624 Carbon and graphite products
- 3625 Relays and industrial controls
- 3629 Electrical industrial apparatus, nec

363 Household Appliances
- 3631 Household cooking equipment
- 3632 Household refrigerators and freezers
- 3633 Household laundry equipment
- 3634 Electric housewares and fans
- 3635 Household vacuum cleaners
- 3639 Household appliances, nec

364 Electric Lighting and Wiring Equipment
- 3641 Electric lamps
- 3643 Current-carrying wiring devices
- 3644 Noncurrent-carrying wiring devices
- 3645 Residential lighting fixtures
- 3646 Commercial lighting fixtures
- 3647 Vehicular lighting equipment
- 3648 Lighting equipment, nec

365 Household Audio and Video Equipment
- 3651 Household audio and video equipment
- 3652 Prerecorded records and tapes

366 Communications Equipment
- 3661 Telephone and telegraph apparatus
- 3663 Radio & TV communications equipment
- 3669 Communications equipment, nec

367 Electronic Components and Accessories
- 3671 Electron tubes
- 3672 Printed circuit boards
- 3674 Semiconductors and related devices
- 3675 Electronic capacitors
- 3676 Electronic resistors
- 3677 Electronic coils and transformers
- 3678 Electronic connectors
- 3679 Electronic components, nec

369 Misc. Electrical Equipment & Supplies
- 3691 Storage batteries
- 3692 Primary batteries, dry and wet
- 3694 Engine electrical equipment
- 3695 Magnetic and optical recording media
- 3699 Electrical equipment & supplies, nec

37 TRANSPORTATION EQUIPMENT

371 Motor Vehicles and Equipment
- 3711 Motor vehicles and car bodies
- 3713 Truck and bus bodies
- 3714 Motor vehicle parts and accessories
- 3715 Truck trailers
- 3716 Motor homes

372 Aircraft and Parts
- 3721 Aircraft
- 3724 Aircraft engines and engine parts
- 3728 Aircraft parts and equipment, nec

373 Ship and Boat Building and Repairing
- 3731 Ship building and repairing
- 3732 Boat building and repairing

374 Railroad Equipment
- 3743 Railroad equipment

375 Motorcycles, Bicycles, and Parts
- 3751 Motorcycles, bicycles, and parts

376 Guided Missiles, Space Vehicles, Parts
- 3761 Guided missiles and space vehicles
- 3764 Space propulsion units and parts
- 3769 Space vehicle equipment, nec

379 Miscellaneous Transportation Equipment
- 3792 Travel trailers and campers
- 3795 Tanks and tank components
- 3799 Transportation equipment, nec

Standard Industrial Classification

Guide to Selected Standard Classifications

38 INSTRUMENTS AND RELATED PRODUCTS

381 Search and Navigation Equipment
3812 Search and navigation equipment

382 Measuring and Controlling Devices
3821 Laboratory apparatus and furniture
3822 Environmental controls
3823 Process control instruments
3824 Fluid meters and counting devices
3825 Instruments to measure electricity
3826 Analytical instruments
3827 Optical instruments and lenses
3829 Measuring & controlling devices, nec

384 Medical Instruments and Supplies
3841 Surgical and medical instruments
3842 Surgical appliances and supplies
3843 Dental equipment and supplies
3844 X-ray apparatus and tubes
3845 Electromedical equipment

385 Ophthalmic Goods
3851 Ophthalmic goods

386 Photographic Equipment and Supplies
3861 Photographic equipment and supplies

387 Watches, Clocks, Watchcases & Parts
3873 Watches, clocks, watchcases & parts

39 MISCELLANEOUS MANUFACTURING INDUSTRIES

391 Jewelry, Silverware, and Plated Ware
3911 Jewelry, precious metal
3914 Silverware and plated ware
3915 Jewelers' materials & lapidary work

393 Musical Instruments
3931 Musical instruments

394 Toys and Sporting Goods
3942 Dolls and stuffed toys
3944 Games, toys, and children's vehicles
3949 Sporting and athletic goods, nec

395 Pens, Pencils, Office, & Art Supplies
3951 Pens and mechanical pencils
3952 Lead pencils and art goods
3953 Marking devices
3955 Carbon paper and inked ribbons

396 Costume Jewelry and Notions
3961 Costume jewelry
3965 Fasteners, buttons, needles, & pins

399 Miscellaneous Manufactures
3991 Brooms and brushes
3993 Signs and advertising specialities
3995 Burial caskets
3996 Hard surface floor coverings, nec
3999 Manufacturing industries, nec

TRANSPORTATION AND PUBLIC UTILITIES

40 RAILROAD TRANSPORTATION

401 Railroads
4011 Railroads, line-haul operating
4013 Switching and terminal services

41 LOCAL AND INTERURBAN PASSENGER TRANSIT

411 Local and Suburban Transportation
4111 Local and suburban transit
4119 Local passenger transportation, nec

412 Taxicabs
4121 Taxicabs

413 Intercity and Rural Bus Transportation
4131 Intercity & rural bus transportation

414 Bus Charter Service
4141 Local bus charter service
4142 Bus charter service, except local

415 School Buses
4151 School buses

417 Bus Terminal and Service Facilities
4173 Bus terminal and service facilities

42 TRUCKING AND WAREHOUSING

421 Trucking & Courier Services, Ex. Air
4212 Local trucking, without storage
4213 Trucking, except local
4214 Local trucking with storage
4215 Courier services, except by air

422 Public Warehousing and Storage
4221 Farm product warehousing and storage
4222 Refrigerated warehousing and storage
4225 General warehousing and storage
4226 Special warehousing and storage, nec

423 Trucking Terminal Facilities
4231 Trucking terminal facilities

43 U.S. POSTAL SERVICE

431 U.S. Postal Service
4311 U.S. Postal Service

44 WATER TRANSPORTATION

441 Deep Sea Foreign Trans. of Freight
4412 Deep sea foreign trans. of freight

442 Deep Sea Domestic Trans. of Freight
4424 Deep sea domestic trans. of freight

443 Freight Trans. on the Great Lakes
4432 Freight trans. on the Great Lakes

444 Water Transportation of Freight, NEC
4449 Water transportation of freight, nec

448 Water Transportation of Passengers
4481 Deep sea passenger trans., ex. ferry
4482 Ferries
4489 Water passenger transportation, nec

449 Water Transportation Services
4491 Marine cargo handling
4492 Towing and tugboat service
4493 Marinas
4499 Water transportation services, nec

45 TRANSPORTATION BY AIR

451 Air Transportation, Scheduled
4512 Air transportation, scheduled
4513 Air courier services

452 Air Transportation, Nonscheduled
4522 Air transportation, nonscheduled

458 Airports, Flying Fields, & Services
4581 Airports, flying fields, & services

46 PIPELINES, EXCEPT NATURAL GAS

461 Pipelines, Except Natural Gas
4612 Crude petroleum pipelines
4613 Refined petroleum pipelines
4619 Pipelines, nec

47 TRANSPORTATION SERVICES

472 Passenger Transportation Arrangement
4724 Travel agencies
4725 Tour operators
4729 Passenger transport arrangement, nec

473 Freight Transportation Arrangement
4731 Freight transportation arrangement

474 Rental of Railroad Cars
4741 Rental of railroad cars

478 Miscellaneous Transportation Services
4783 Packing and crating
4785 Inspection & fixed facilities
4789 Transportation services, nec

48 COMMUNICATIONS

481 Telephone Communications
4812 Radiotelephone communications
4813 Telephone communications, exc. radio

482 Telegraph & Other Communications
4822 Telegraph & other communications

483 Radio and Television Broadcasting
4832 Radio broadcasting stations
4833 Television broadcasting stations

484 Cable and Other Pay TV Services
4841 Cable and other pay TV services

489 Communications Services, NEC
4899 Communications services, nec

49 ELECTRIC, GAS, AND SANITARY SERVICES

491 Electric Services
4911 Electric services

492 Gas Production and Distribution
4922 Natural gas transmission
4923 Gas transmission and distribution
4924 Natural gas distribution
4925 Gas production and/or distribution

493 Combination Utility Services
4931 Electric and other services combined
4932 Gas and other services combined
4939 Combination utilities, nec

494 Water Supply
4941 Water supply

495 Sanitary Services
4952 Sewerage systems
4953 Refuse systems
4959 Sanitary services, nec

496 Steam and Air-Conditioning Supply
4961 Steam and air-conditioning supply

497 Irrigation Systems
4971 Irrigation systems

WHOLESALE TRADE

50 WHOLESALE TRADE—DURABLE GOODS

501 Motor Vehicles, Parts, and Supplies
5012 Automobiles and other motor vehicles
5013 Motor vehicle supplies and new parts
5014 Tires and tubes
5015 Motor vehicle parts, used

502 Furniture and Homefurnishings
5021 Furniture
5023 Homefurnishings

503 Lumber and Construction Materials
5031 Lumber, plywood, and millwork
5032 Brick, stone, & related materials
5033 Roofing, siding, & insulation
5039 Construction materials, nec

504 Professional & Commercial Equipment
5043 Photographic equipment and supplies
5044 Office equipment
5045 Computers, peripherals & software

Guide to Selected Standard Classifications

Standard Industrial Classification

5046 Commercial equipment, nec
5047 Medical and hospital equipment
5048 Ophthalmic goods
5049 Professional equipment, nec

505 Metals and Minerals, Except Petroleum
5051 Metals service centers and offices
5052 Coal and other minerals and ores

506 Electrical Goods
5063 Electrical apparatus and equipment
5064 Electrical appliances, TV & radios
5065 Electronic parts and equipment

507 Hardware, Plumbing & Heating Equipment
5072 Hardware
5074 Plumbing & hydronic heating supplies
5075 Warm air heating & air-conditioning
5078 Refrigeration equipment and supplies

508 Machinery, Equipment, and Supplies
5082 Construction and mining machinery
5083 Farm and garden machinery
5084 Industrial machinery and equipment
5085 Industrial supplies
5087 Service establishment equipment
5088 Transportation equipment & supplies

509 Miscellaneous Durable Goods
5091 Sporting & recreational goods
5092 Toys and hobby goods and supplies
5093 Scrap and waste materials
5094 Jewelry & precious stones
5099 Durable goods, nec

51 WHOLESALE TRADE— NONDURABLE GOODS

511 Paper and Paper Products
5111 Printing and writing paper
5112 Stationery and office supplies
5113 Industrial & personal service paper

512 Drugs, Proprietaries, and Sundries
5122 Drugs, proprietaries, and sundries

513 Apparel, Piece Goods, and Notions
5131 Piece goods & notions
5136 Men's and boys' clothing
5137 Women's and children's clothing
5139 Footwear

514 Groceries and Related Products
5141 Groceries, general line
5142 Packaged frozen foods
5143 Dairy products, exc. dried or canned
5144 Poultry and poultry products
5145 Confectionery
5146 Fish and seafoods
5147 Meats and meat products
5148 Fresh fruits and vegetables
5149 Groceries and related products, nec

515 Farm-Product Raw Materials
5153 Grain and field beans
5154 Livestock
5159 Farm-product raw materials, nec

516 Chemicals and Allied Products
5162 Plastics materials & basic shapes
5169 Chemicals & allied products, nec

517 Petroleum and Petroleum Products
5171 Petroleum bulk stations & terminals
5172 Petroleum products, nec

518 Beer, Wine, and Distilled Beverages
5181 Beer and ale
5182 Wine and distilled beverages

519 Misc. Nondurable Goods
5191 Farm supplies

5192 Books, periodicals, & newspapers
5193 Flowers & florists' supplies
5194 Tobacco and tobacco products
5198 Paints, varnishes, and supplies
5199 Nondurable goods, nec

RETAIL TRADE

52 BUILDING MATERIALS & GARDEN SUPPLIES

521 Lumber and Other Building Materials
5211 Lumber and other building materials

523 Paint, Glass, and Wallpaper Stores
5231 Paint, glass, and wallpaper stores

525 Hardware Stores
5251 Hardware stores

526 Retail Nurseries and Garden Stores
5261 Retail nurseries and garden stores

527 Mobile Home Dealers
5271 Mobile home dealers

53 GENERAL MERCHANDISE STORES

531 Department Stores
5311 Department stores

533 Variety Stores
5331 Variety stores

539 Misc. General Merchandise Stores
5399 Misc. general merchandise stores

54 FOOD STORES

541 Grocery Stores
5411 Grocery stores

542 Meat and Fish Markets
5421 Meat and fish markets

543 Fruit and Vegetable Markets
5431 Fruit and vegetable markets

544 Candy, Nut, and Confectionery Stores
5441 Candy, nut, and confectionery stores

545 Dairy Products Stores
5451 Dairy products stores

546 Retail Bakeries
5461 Retail bakeries

549 Miscellaneous Food Stores
5499 Miscellaneous food stores

55 AUTOMOTIVE DEALERS & SERVICE STATIONS

551 New and Used Car Dealers
5511 New and used car dealers

552 Used Car Dealers
5521 Used car dealers

553 Auto and Home Supply Stores
5531 Auto and home supply stores

554 Gasoline Service Stations
5541 Gasoline service stations

555 Boat Dealers
5551 Boat dealers

556 Recreational Vehicle Dealers
5561 Recreational vehicle dealers

557 Motorcycle Dealers
5571 Motorcycle dealers

559 Automotive Dealers, NEC
5599 Automotive dealers, nec

56 APPAREL AND ACCESSORY STORES

561 Men's & Boys' Clothing Stores
5611 Men's & boys' clothing stores

562 Women's Clothing Stores
5621 Women's clothing stores

563 Women's Accessory & Specialty Stores
5632 Women's accessory & specialty stores

564 Children's and Infants' Wear Stores
5641 Children's and infants' wear stores

565 Family Clothing Stores
5651 Family clothing stores

566 Shoe Stores
5661 Shoe stores

569 Misc. Apparel & Accessory Stores
5699 Misc. apparel & accessory stores

57 FURNITURE AND HOMEFURNISHINGS STORES

571 Furniture and Homefurnishings Stores
5712 Furniture stores
5713 Floor covering stores
5714 Drapery and upholstery stores
5719 Misc. homefurnishings stores

572 Household Appliance Stores
5722 Household appliance stores

573 Radio, Television, & Computer Stores
5731 Radio, TV, & electronic stores
5734 Computer and software stores
5735 Record & prerecorded tape stores
5736 Musical instrument stores

58 EATING AND DRINKING PLACES

581 Eating and Drinking Places
5812 Eating places
5813 Drinking places

59 MISCELLANEOUS RETAIL

591 Drug Stores and Proprietary Stores
5912 Drug stores and proprietary stores

592 Liquor Stores
5921 Liquor stores

593 Used Merchandise Stores
5932 Used merchandise stores

594 Miscellaneous Shopping Goods Stores
5941 Sporting goods and bicycle shops
5942 Book stores
5943 Stationery stores
5944 Jewelry stores
5945 Hobby, toy, and game shops
5946 Camera & photographic supply stores
5947 Gift, novelty, and souvenir shops
5948 Luggage and leather goods stores
5949 Sewing, needlework, and piece goods

596 Nonstore Retailers
5961 Catalog and mail-order houses
5962 Merchandising machine operators
5963 Direct selling establishments

598 Fuel Dealers
5983 Fuel oil dealers
5984 Liquefied petroleum gas dealers
5989 Fuel dealers, nec

599 Retail Stores, NEC
5992 Florists
5993 Tobacco stores and stands
5994 News dealers and newsstands
5995 Optical goods stores
5999 Miscellaneous retail stores, nec

FINANCE, INSURANCE, AND REAL ESTATE

60 DEPOSITORY INSTITUTIONS

601 Central Reserve Depositories
6011 Federal reserve banks
6019 Central reserve depository, nec

Standard Industrial Classification

Guide to Selected Standard Classifications

- **602 Commercial Banks**
  - 6021 National commercial banks
  - 6022 State commercial banks
  - 6029 Commercial banks, nec
- **603 Savings Institutions**
  - 6035 Federal savings institutions
  - 6036 Savings institutions, except federal
- **606 Credit Unions**
  - 6061 Federal credit unions
  - 6062 State credit unions
- **608 Foreign Bank & Branches & Agencies**
  - 6081 Foreign bank & branches & agencies
  - 6082 Foreign trade & international banks
- **609 Functions Closely Related to Banking**
  - 6091 Nondeposit trust facilities
  - 6099 Functions related to deposit banking
- **61 NONDEPOSITORY INSTITUTIONS**
- **611 Federal & Fed.-Sponsored Credit**
  - 6111 Federal & fed.-sponsored credit
- **614 Personal Credit Institutions**
  - 6141 Personal credit institutions
- **615 Business Credit Institutions**
  - 6153 Short-term business credit
  - 6159 Misc. business credit institutions
- **616 Mortgage Bankers and Brokers**
  - 6162 Mortgage bankers and correspondents
  - 6163 Loan brokers
- **62 SECURITY AND COMMODITY BROKERS**
- **621 Security Brokers and Dealers**
  - 6211 Security brokers and dealers
- **622 Commodity Contracts Brokers, Dealers**
  - 6221 Commodity contracts brokers, dealers
- **623 Security and Commodity Exchanges**
  - 6231 Security and commodity exchanges
- **628 Security and Commodity Services**
  - 6282 Investment advice
  - 6289 Security & commodity services, nec
- **63 INSURANCE CARRIERS**
- **631 Life Insurance**
  - 6311 Life insurance
- **632 Medical Service and Health Insurance**
  - 6321 Accident and health insurance
  - 6324 Hospital and medical service plans
- **633 Fire, Marine, and Casualty Insurance**
  - 6331 Fire, marine, and casualty insurance
- **635 Surety Insurance**
  - 6351 Surety insurance
- **636 Title Insurance**
  - 6361 Title insurance
- **637 Pension, Health, and Welfare Funds**
  - 6371 Pension, health, and welfare funds
- **639 Insurance Carriers, NEC**
  - 6399 Insurance carriers, nec
- **64 INSURANCE AGENTS, BROKERS, & SERVICE**
- **641 Insurance Agents, Brokers, & Service**
  - 6411 Insurance agents, brokers, & service
- **65 REAL ESTATE**
- **651 Real Estate Operators and Lessors**
  - 6512 Nonresidential building operators
  - 6513 Apartment building operators
  - 6514 Dwelling operators, exc. apartments
  - 6515 Mobile home site operators
  - 6517 Railroad property lessors
  - 6519 Real property lessors, nec
- **653 Real Estate Agents and Managers**
  - 6531 Real estate agents and managers
- **654 Title Abstract Offices**
  - 6541 Title abstract offices
- **655 Subdividers and Developers**
  - 6552 Subdividers and developers, nec
  - 6553 Cemetery subdividers and developers
- **67 HOLDING AND OTHER INVESTMENT OFFICES**
- **671 Holding Offices**
  - 6712 Bank holding companies
  - 6719 Holding companies, nec
- **672 Investment Offices**
  - 6722 Management investment, open-end
  - 6726 Investment offices, nec
- **673 Trusts**
  - 6732 Educational, religious, etc. trusts
  - 6733 Trusts, nec
- **679 Miscellaneous Investing**
  - 6792 Oil royalty traders
  - 6794 Patent owners and lessors
  - 6798 Real estate investment trusts
  - 6799 Investors, nec

SERVICES

- **70 HOTELS AND OTHER LODGING PLACES**
- **701 Hotels and Motels**
  - 7011 Hotels and motels
- **702 Rooming and Boarding Houses**
  - 7021 Rooming and boarding houses
- **703 Camps and Recreational Vehicle Parks**
  - 7032 Sporting and recreational camps
  - 7033 Trailer parks and campsites
- **704 Membership-Basis Organization Hotels**
  - 7041 Membership-basis organization hotels
- **72 PERSONAL SERVICES**
- **721 Laundry, Cleaning, & Garment Services**
  - 7211 Power Laundries, family & commercial
  - 7212 Garment pressing & cleaners' agents
  - 7213 Linen supply
  - 7215 Coin-operated laundries and cleaning
  - 7216 Drycleaning plants, except rug
  - 7217 Carpet and upholstery cleaning
  - 7218 Industrial launderers
  - 7219 Laundry and garment services, nec
- **722 Photographic Studios, Portrait**
  - 7221 Photographic studios, portrait
- **723 Beauty Shops**
  - 7231 Beauty shops
- **724 Barber Shops**
  - 7241 Barber shops
- **725 Shoe Repair and Shoeshine Parlors**
  - 7251 Shoe repair and shoeshine parlors
- **726 Funeral Service and Crematories**
  - 7261 Funeral service and crematories
- **729 Miscellaneous Personal Services**
  - 7291 Tax return preparation services
  - 7299 Miscellaneous personal services, nec
- **73 BUSINESS SERVICES**
- **731 Advertising**
  - 7311 Advertising agencies
  - 7312 Outdoor advertising services
  - 7313 Radio, TV, publisher representatives
  - 7319 Advertising, nec
- **732 Credit Reporting and Collection**
  - 7322 Adjustment & collection services
  - 7323 Credit reporting services
- **733 Mailing, Reproduction, Stenographic**
  - 7331 Direct mail advertising services
  - 7334 Photocopying & duplicating services
  - 7335 Commercial photography
  - 7336 Commercial art and graphic design
  - 7338 Secretarial & court reporting
- **734 Services to Buildings**
  - 7342 Disinfecting & pest control services
  - 7349 Building maintenance services, nec
- **735 Misc. Equipment Rental & Leasing**
  - 7352 Medical equipment rental
  - 7353 Heavy construction equipment rental
  - 7359 Equipment rental & leasing, nec
- **736 Personnel Supply Services**
  - 7361 Employment agencies
  - 7363 Help supply services
- **737 Computer and Data Processing Services**
  - 7371 Computer programming services
  - 7372 Prepackaged software
  - 7373 Computer integrated systems design
  - 7374 Data processing and preparation
  - 7375 Information retrieval services
  - 7376 Computer facilities management
  - 7377 Computer rental & leasing
  - 7378 Computer maintenance & repair
  - 7379 Computer related services, nec
- **738 Miscellaneous Business Services**
  - 7381 Detective & armored car services
  - 7382 Security systems services
  - 7383 News syndicates
  - 7384 Photofinishing laboratories
  - 7389 Business services, nec
- **75 AUTO REPAIR, SERVICES, AND PARKING**
- **751 Automotive Rentals, No Drivers**
  - 7513 Truck rental and leasing, no drivers
  - 7514 Passenger car rental
  - 7515 Passenger car leasing
  - 7519 Utility trailer rental
- **752 Automobile Parking**
  - 7521 Automobile parking
- **753 Automotive Repair Shops**
  - 7532 Top & body repair & paint shops
  - 7533 Auto exhaust system repair shops
  - 7534 Tire retreading and repair shops
  - 7536 Automotive glass replacement shops
  - 7537 Automotive transmission repair shops
  - 7538 General automotive repair shops
  - 7539 Automotive repair shops, nec
- **754 Automotive Services, Except Repair**
  - 7542 Carwashes
  - 7549 Automotive services, nec
- **76 MISCELLANEOUS REPAIR SERVICES**
- **762 Electrical Repair Shops**
  - 7622 Radio and television repair
  - 7623 Refrigeration service and repair
  - 7629 Electrical repair shops, nec
- **763 Watch, Clock, and Jewelry Repair**
  - 7631 Watch, clock, and jewelry repair
- **764 Reupholstery and Furniture Repair**
  - 7641 Reupholstery and furniture repair

Guide to Selected Standard Classifications

Standard Industrial Classification

- **769 Miscellaneous Repair Shops**
  - 7692 Welding repair
  - 7694 Armature rewinding shops
  - 7699 Repair services, nec
- **78 MOTION PICTURES**
- **781 Motion Picture Production & Services**
  - 7812 Motion picture & video production
  - 7819 Services allied to motion pictures
- **782 Motion Picture Distribution & Services**
  - 7822 Motion picture and tape distribution
  - 7829 Motion picture distribution services
- **783 Motion Picture Theaters**
  - 7832 Motion picture theaters, ex drive-in
  - 7833 Drive-in motion picture theaters
- **784 Video Tape Rental**
  - 7841 Video tape rental
- **79 AMUSEMENT & RECREATION SERVICES**
- **791 Dance Studios, Schools, and Halls**
  - 7911 Dance studios, schools, and halls
- **792 Producers, Orchestras, Entertainers**
  - 7922 Theatrical producers and services
  - 7929 Entertainers & entertainment groups
- **793 Bowling Centers**
  - 7933 Bowling centers
- **794 Commercial Sports**
  - 7941 Sports clubs, managers, & promoters
  - 7948 Racing, including track operation
- **799 Misc. Amusement, Recreation Services**
  - 7991 Physical fitness facilities
  - 7992 Public golf courses
  - 7993 Coin-operated amusement devices
  - 7996 Amusement parks
  - 7997 Membership sports & recreation clubs
  - 7999 Amusement and recreation, nec
- **80 HEALTH SERVICES**
- **801 Offices & Clinics of Medical Doctors**
  - 8011 Offices & clinics of medical doctors
- **802 Offices and Clinics of Dentists**
  - 8021 Offices and clinics of dentists
- **803 Offices of Osteopathic Physicians**
  - 8031 Offices of osteopathic physicians
- **804 Offices of Other Health Practitioners**
  - 8041 Offices and clinics of chiropractors
  - 8042 Offices and clinics of optometrists
  - 8043 Offices and clinics of podiatrists
  - 8049 Offices of health practitioners, nec
- **805 Nursing and Personal Care Facilities**
  - 8051 Skilled nursing care facilities
  - 8052 Intermediate care facilities
  - 8059 Nursing and personal care, nec
- **806 Hospitals**
  - 8062 General medical & surgical hospitals
  - 8063 Psychiatric hospitals
  - 8069 Specialty hospitals exc. psychiatric
- **807 Medical and Dental Laboratories**
  - 8071 Medical laboratories
  - 8072 Dental laboratories
- **808 Home Health Care Services**
  - 8082 Home health care services
- **809 Health and Allied Services, NEC**
  - 8092 Kidney dialysis centers
  - 8093 Specialty outpatient clinics, nec
  - 8099 Health and allied services, nec
- **81 LEGAL SERVICES**
- **811 Legal Services**
  - 8111 Legal services
- **82 EDUCATIONAL SERVICES**
- **821 Elementary and Secondary Schools**
  - 8211 Elementary and secondary schools
- **822 Colleges and Universities**
  - 8221 Colleges and universities
  - 8222 Junior colleges
- **823 Libraries**
  - 8231 Libraries
- **824 Vocational Schools**
  - 8243 Data processing schools
  - 8244 Business and secretarial schools
  - 8249 Vocational schools, nec
- **829 Schools & Educational Services, NEC**
  - 8299 Schools & educational services, nec
- **83 SOCIAL SERVICES**
- **832 Individual and Family Services**
  - 8322 Individual and family services
- **833 Job Training and Related Services**
  - 8331 Job training and related services
- **835 Child Day Care Services**
  - 8351 Child day care services
- **836 Residential Care**
  - 8361 Residential care
- **839 Social Services, NEC**
  - 8399 Social services, nec
- **84 MUSEUMS, BOTANICAL, ZOOLOGICAL GARDENS**
- **841 Museums and Art Galleries**
  - 8412 Museums and art galleries
- **842 Botanical and Zoological Gardens**
  - 8422 Botanical and zoological gardens
- **86 MEMBERSHIP ORGANIZATIONS**
- **861 Business Associations**
  - 8611 Business associations
- **862 Professional Organizations**
  - 8621 Professional organizations
- **863 Labor Organizations**
  - 8631 Labor organizations
- **864 Civic and Social Associations**
  - 8641 Civic and social associations
- **865 Political Organizations**
  - 8651 Political organizations
- **866 Religious Organizations**
  - 8661 Religious organizations
- **869 Membership Organizations, NEC**
  - 8699 Membership organizations, nec
- **87 ENGINEERING & MANAGEMENT SERVICES**
- **871 Engineering & Architectural Services**
  - 8711 Engineering services
  - 8712 Architectural services
  - 8713 Surveying services
- **872 Accounting, Auditing, & Bookkeeping**
  - 8721 Accounting, auditing, & bookkeeping
- **873 Research and Testing Services**
  - 8731 Commercial physical research
  - 8732 Commercial nonphysical research
  - 8733 Noncommercial research organizations
  - 8734 Testing laboratories
- **874 Management and Public Relations**
  - 8741 Management services
  - 8742 Management consulting services
  - 8743 Public relations services
  - 8744 Facilities support services
  - 8748 Business consulting, nec
- **88 PRIVATE HOUSEHOLDS**
- **881 Private Households**
  - 8811 Private households
- **89 SERVICES, NEC**
- **899 Services, NEC**
  - 8999 Services, nec

PUBLIC ADMINISTRATION

- **91 EXECUTIVE, LEGISLATIVE, AND GENERAL**
- **911 Executive Offices**
  - 9111 Executive offices
- **912 Legislative Bodies**
  - 9121 Legislative bodies
- **913 Executive and Legislative Combined**
  - 9131 Executive and legislative combined
- **919 General Government, NEC**
  - 9199 General government, nec
- **92 JUSTICE, PUBLIC ORDER, AND SAFETY**
- **921 Courts**
  - 9211 Courts
- **922 Public Order and Safety**
  - 9221 Police protection
  - 9222 Legal counsel and prosecution
  - 9223 Correctional institutions
  - 9224 Fire protection
  - 9229 Public order and safety, nec
- **93 FINANCE, TAXATION, & MONETARY POLICY**
- **931 Finance, Taxation, & Monetary Policy**
  - 9311 Finance, taxation, & monetary policy
- **94 ADMINISTRATION OF HUMAN RESOURCES**
- **941 Admin. of Educational Programs**
  - 9411 Admin. of educational programs
- **943 Admin. of Public Health Programs**
  - 9431 Admin. of public health programs
- **944 Admin. of Social & Manpower Programs**
  - 9441 Admin. of social & manpower programs
- **945 Administration of Veterans' Affairs**
  - 9451 Administration of veterans' affairs
- **95 ENVIRONMENTAL QUALITY AND HOUSING**
- **951 Environmental Quality**
  - 9511 Air, water, & solid waste management
  - 9512 Land, mineral, wildlife conservation
- **953 Housing and Urban Development**
  - 9531 Housing programs
  - 9532 Urban and community development
- **96 ADMINISTRATION OF ECONOMIC PROGRAMS**
- **961 Admin. of General Economic Programs**
  - 9611 Admin. of general economic programs
- **962 Regulation, Admin. of Transportation**
  - 9621 Regulation, admin. of transportation
- **963 Regulation, Admin. of Utilities**
  - 9631 Regulation, admin. of utilities
- **964 Regulation of Agricultural Marketing**
  - 9641 Regulation of agricultural marketing
- **965 Regulation Misc. Commercial Sectors**
  - 9651 Regulation misc. commercial sectors
- **966 Space Research and Technology**
  - 9661 Space research and technology
- **97 NATIONAL SECURITY AND INTL. AFFAIRS**
- **971 National Security**
  - 9711 National security
- **972 International Affairs**
  - 9721 International affairs

NONCLASSIFIABLE ESTABLISHMENTS

- **99 NONCLASSIFIABLE ESTABLISHMENTS**
- **999 Nonclassifiable Establishments**
  - 9999 Nonclassifiable establishments

Standard Occupational Classification

The Standard Occupational Classification was developed to provide a standardized system of job descriptions and classification codes for all occupations performed for pay or profit, for use in the presentation and analysis of statistical data about occupations. The classification system is at 4 levels, with division titles, 2- and 3-digit occupation group codes, and 4-digit unit group codes.

The classification is presented in the revised 1980 *Standard Occupational Classification Manual,* from which the following list is taken.

Occupation Group Code

EXECUTIVE, ADMINISTRATIVE AND MANAGERIAL OCCUPATIONS

- **11 Officials and Administrators, Public Administration**
  - 111 Legislators
  - 112 Chief Executives and General Administrators
  - 113 Officials and Administrators, Government Agencies

- **12-13 Officials and Administrators, Other**
  - 121 General Managers and Other Top Executives
  - 122 Financial Managers
  - 123 Personnel and Labor Relations Managers
  - 124 Purchasing Managers
  - 125 Managers; Marketing, Advertising, and Public Relations
  - 126 Managers; Engineering, Mathematics, and Natural Sciences
  - 127 Managers; Social Sciences and Related Fields
  - 128 Administrators; Education and Related Fields
  - 131 Managers; Medicine and Health
  - 132 Production Managers, Industrial
  - 133 Construction Managers
  - 134 Public Utilities Managers
  - 135 Managers; Service Organizations
  - 136 Managers; Mining, Quarrying, Well Drilling, and Similar Operations
  - 137 Managers; Administrative Services
  - 139 Officials and Administrators; Other, Not Elsewhere Classified

- **14 Management Related Occupations**
  - 141 Accountants, Auditors, and Other Financial Specialists
  - 142 Management Analysts
  - 143 Personnel, Training, and Labor Relations Specialists
  - 144 Purchasing Agents and Buyers
  - 145 Business and Promotion Agents
  - 147 Inspectors and Compliance Officers
  - 149 Management Related Occupations, Not Elsewhere Classified

ENGINEERS, SURVEYORS AND ARCHITECTS

- **16 Engineers, Surveyors and Architects**
  - 161 Architects
  - 162-3 Engineers
  - 164 Surveyors and Mapping Scientists

NATURAL SCIENTISTS AND MATHEMATICIANS

- **17 Computer, Mathematical, and Operations Research Occupations**
  - 171 Computer Scientists
  - 172 Operations and Systems Researchers and Analysts
  - 173 Mathematical Scientists

- **18 Natural Scientists**
  - 184 Physical Scientists
  - 185 Life Scientists

SOCIAL SCIENTISTS, SOCIAL WORKERS, RELIGIOUS WORKERS, AND LAWYERS

- **19 Social Scientists and Urban Planners**
  - 191 Social Scientists
  - 192 Urban and Regional Planners

- **20 Social, Recreation, and Religious Workers**
  - 203 Social and Recreation Workers
  - 204 Religious Workers

- **21 Lawyers and Judges**
  - 211 Lawyers
  - 212 Judges

TEACHERS, LIBRARIANS, AND COUNSELORS

- **22 Teachers; College, University and Other Postsecondary Institution**

- **23 Teachers, Except Postsecondary Institution**
  - 231 Prekindergarten and Kindergarten Teachers
  - 232 Elementary School Teachers
  - 233 Secondary School Teachers
  - 235 Teachers; Special Education
  - 236 Instructional Coordinators
  - 239 Adult Education and Other Teachers, Not Elsewhere Classified

- **24 Vocational and Educational Counselors**

- **25 Librarians, Archivists, and Curators**
  - 251 Librarians
  - 252 Archivists and Curators

HEALTH DIAGNOSING AND TREATING PRACTITIONERS

- **26 Physicians and Dentists**
  - 261 Physicians
  - 262 Dentists

- **27 Veterinarians**

- **28 Other Health Diagnosing and Treating Practitioners**
  - 281 Optometrists
  - 283 Podiatrists
  - 289 Health Diagnosing and Treating Practitioners, Not Elsewhere Classified

REGISTERED NURSES, PHARMACISTS, DIETITIANS, THERAPISTS, AND PHYSICIAN'S ASSISTANTS

- **29 Registered Nurses**

- **30 Pharmacists, Dietitians, Therapists, and Physician's Assistants**
  - 301 Pharmacists
  - 302 Dietitians
  - 303 Therapists
  - 304 Physician's Assistants

WRITERS, ARTISTS, ENTERTAINERS, AND ATHLETES

- **32 Writers, Artists, Performers, and Related Workers**
  - 321 Authors
  - 322 Designers
  - 323 Musicians and Composers
  - 324 Actors and Directors
  - 325 Painters, Sculptors, Craft-Artists and Artist-Printmakers
  - 326 Photographers
  - 327 Dancers
  - 328 Performers, Not Elsewhere Classified
  - 329 Writers, Artists, and Related Workers; Not Elsewhere Classified

- **33 Editors, Reporters, Public Relations Specialists, and Announcers**
  - 331 Editors and Reporters
  - 332 Public Relations Specialists and Publicity Writers
  - 333 Radio, Television and Other Announcers

- **34 Athletes and Related Workers**

Guide to Selected Standard Classifications

Standard Occupational Classification

HEALTH TECHNOLOGISTS AND TECHNICIANS

36 Health Technologists and Technicians
- 362 Clinical Laboratory Technologists and Technicians
- 363 Dental Hygienists
- 364 Health Record Technologists and Technicians
- 365 Radiologic Technologists and Technicians
- 366 Licensed Practical Nurses
- 369 Health Technologists and Technicians, Not Elsewhere Classified

TECHNOLOGISTS AND TECHNICIANS, EXCEPT HEALTH

37 Engineering and Related Technologists and Technicians
- 371 Engineering Technologists and Technicians
- 372 Drafting Occupations
- 373 Surveying and Mapping Technicians

38 Science Technologists and Technicians
- 382 Biological Technologists and Technicians, Except Health
- 383 Chemical and Nuclear Technologists and Technicians
- 384 Mathematical Technicians
- 389 Science Technologists and Technicians, Not Elsewhere Classified

39 Technicians; Except Health, Engineering, and Science
- 392 Air Traffic Controllers
- 393 Radio and Related Operators
- 396 Legal Technicians
- 397 Programmers
- 398 Technical Writers
- 399 Technicians, Not Elsewhere Classified

MARKETING AND SALES OCCUPATIONS

40 Supervisors; Marketing and Sales Occupations
- 401 Supervisors; Sales Occupations, Insurance, Real Estate, and Business Services
- 402 Supervisors; Sales Occupations, Commodities Except Retail
- 403 Supervisors; Sales Occupations, Retail

41 Insurance, Securities, Real Estate, and Business Service Sales Occupations
- 412 Insurance, Real Estate, and Securities Sales Occupations
- 415 Business Service Sales Occupations

42 Sales Occupations, Commodities Except Retail
- 421 Sales Engineers
- 423 Technical Sales Workers and Service Advisors
- 424 Sales Representatives

43 Sales Occupations, Retail
- 434-5 Salespersons, Commodities
- 436 Sales Occupations; Other

44 Sales Related Occupations
- 444 Appraisers and Related Occupations
- 445 Demonstrators, Promoters, and Models
- 446 Shoppers
- 447 Auctioneers
- 449 Sales Occupations; Other, Not Elsewhere Classified

ADMINISTRATIVE SUPPORT OCCUPATIONS, INCLUDING CLERICAL

45 Supervisors; Administrative Support Occupations, Including Clerical

46-47 Administrative Support Occupations, Including Clerical
- 461 Computer and Peripheral Equipment Operators
- 462 Secretaries, Stenographers and Typists
- 463 General Office Occupations
- 464 Information Clerks
- 466 Correspondence Clerks and Order Clerks
- 469 Record Clerks
- 471 Financial Record Processing Occupations
- 472 Duplicating, Mail and Other Office Machine Operators
- 473 Communications Equipment Operators
- 474 Mail and Message Distributing Occupations
- 475 Material Recording, Scheduling, and Distributing Clerks
- 478 Adjusters, Investigators, and Collectors
- 479 Miscellaneous Administrative Support Occupations, Including Clerical

SERVICE OCCUPATIONS

50 Private Household Occupations
- 502 Day Workers
- 503 Launderers and Ironers
- 504 Cooks, Private Household
- 505 Housekeepers and Butlers
- 506 Child Care Workers, Private Household
- 507 Private Household Cleaners and Servants
- 509 Private Household Occupations, Not Elsewhere Classified

51 Protective Service Occupations
- 511 Supervisors; Service Occupations, Protective
- 512 Firefighting and Fire Prevention Occupations
- 513 Police and Detectives
- 514 Guards

52 Service Occupations, Except Private Household and Protective
- 521 Food and Beverage Preparation and Service Occupations
- 523 Health Service Occupations
- 524 Cleaning and Building Service Occupations, Except Private Household
- 525-6 Personal Service Occupations

AGRICULTURAL, FORESTRY AND FISHING OCCUPATIONS

55 Farm Operators and Managers
- 551 Farmers (Working Proprietors)
- 552 Farm Managers

56 Other Agricultural and Related Occupations
- 561 Farm Occupations, Except Managerial
- 562 Related Agricultural Occupations

57 Forestry and Logging Occupations
- 571 Supervisors; Forestry and Logging Workers
- 572 Forestry Workers, Except Logging
- 573 Timber Cutting and Related Occupations
- 579 Logging Occupations, Not Elsewhere Classified

58 Fishers, Hunters, and Trappers
- 583 Fishers
- 584 Hunters and Trappers

MECHANICS AND REPAIRERS

60 Supervisors; Mechanics and Repairers

61 Mechanics and Repairers
- 611 Vehicle and Mobile Equipment Mechanics and Repairers
- 613 Industrial Machinery Repairers
- 614 Machinery Maintenance Occupations
- 615 Electrical and Electronic Equipment Repairers
- 616 Heating, Air-Conditioning, and Refrigeration Mechanics
- 617 Miscellaneous Mechanics and Repairers

CONSTRUCTION AND EXTRACTIVE OCCUPATIONS

63 Supervisors; Construction and Extractive Occupations
- 631 Supervisors; Construction
- 632 Supervisors; Extractive Occupations

64 Construction Trades
- 641 Brickmasons, Stonemasons, and Hard Tile Setters
- 642 Carpenters and Related Workers
- 643 Electricians and Power Transmission Installers
- 644 Painters, Paperhangers, and Plasterers
- 645 Plumbers, Pipefitters and Steamfitters
- 646-7 Other Construction Trades

65 Extractive Occupations
- 652 Drillers, Oil Well
- 653 Explosive Workers
- 654 Mining Machine Operators
- 656 Extractive Occupations, Not Elsewhere Classified

PRECISION PRODUCTION OCCUPATIONS

67 Supervisors; Precision Production Occupations

68 Precision Production Occupations
- 681-2 Precision Metal Workers
- 683 Precision Woodworkers
- 684 Precision Printing Occupations
- 685 Precision Textile, Apparel and Furnishings Workers
- 686 Precision Workers; Assorted Materials
- 687 Precision Food Production Occupations
- 688 Precision Inspectors, Testers, and Related Workers

69 Plant and System Operators
- 691 Water and Sewage Treatment Plant Operators
- 692 Gas Plant Operators
- 693 Power Plant Operators
- 694 Chemical Plant Operators
- 695 Petroleum Plant Operators
- 696 Miscellaneous Plant or System Operators

PRODUCTION WORKING OCCUPATIONS

71 Supervisors; Production Occupations

73-74 Machine Setup Operators
- 731-2 Metalworking and Plastic Working Machine Setup Operators
- 733 Metal Fabricating Machine Setup Operators
- 734 Metal and Plastic Processing Machine Setup Operators
- 743 Woodworking Machine Setup Operators
- 744 Printing Machine Setup Operators
- 745 Textile Machine Setup Operators
- 746-7 Assorted Materials: Machine Setup Operators

75-76 Machine Operators and Tenders
- 751-2 Metalworking and Plastic Working Machine Operators and Tenders
- 753 Metal Fabricating Machine Operators and Tenders
- 754 Metal and Plastic Processing Machine Operators and Tenders
- 763 Woodworking Machine Operators and Tenders
- 764 Printing Machine Operators and Tenders
- 765 Textile, Apparel and Furnishings Machine Operators and Tenders
- 766-7 Machine Operators and Tenders; Assorted Materials

77 Fabricators, Assemblers, and Hand Working Occupations
- 771 Welders and Solderers
- 772 Assemblers
- 774 Fabricators, Not Elsewhere Classified
- 775 Hand Working Occupations

78 Production Inspectors, Testers, Samplers, and Weighers
- 782 Production Inspectors, Checkers and Examiners
- 783 Production Testers
- 784 Production Samplers and Weighers
- 785 Graders and Sorters, Except Agricultural
- 787 Production Expediters

TRANSPORTATION AND MATERIAL MOVING OCCUPATIONS

81 Supervisors; Transportation and Material Moving Occupations
- 811 Supervisors; Motorized Equipment Operators
- 812 Supervisors; Material Moving Equipment Operators

82 Transportation Occupations
- 821 Motor Vehicle Operators
- 823 Rail Transportation Occupations
- 824 Water Transportation Occupations
- 825 Airplane Pilots and Navigators
- 828 Transportation Inspectors

83 Material Moving Occupations, Except Transportation
- 831 Material Moving Equipment Operators

HANDLERS, EQUIPMENT CLEANERS, HELPERS AND LABORERS

85 Supervisors; Handlers, Equipment Cleaners, Helpers, and Laborers

86 Helpers
- 861 Helpers; Machine Operators and Tenders
- 862 Helpers; Fabricators and Inspectors
- 863 Helpers; Mechanics and Repairers
- 864 Helpers; Construction Trades
- 865 Helpers; Extractive Occupations

87 Handlers, Equipment Cleaners and Laborers
- 871 Construction Laborers
- 872 Freight, Stock, and Material Movers; Hand
- 873 Garage and Service Station Related Occupations
- 874 Parking Lot Attendants
- 875 Vehicle Washers and Equipment Cleaners
- 876 Miscellaneous Manual Occupations

MILITARY OCCUPATIONS

91 Military Occupations

MISCELLANEOUS OCCUPATIONS

99 Miscellaneous Occupations

Standard International Trade Classification, Revision 3

The Standard International Trade Classification (SITC) is a statistical classification of commodities in world trade, developed by the United Nations to facilitate international comparison of commodity trade data. The classification is at 5 levels: sections, divisions, groups, subgroups, and items—represented by 1- to 5-digit codes.

SITC Revision 3 was published in 1986. An earlier classification scheme, Revision 2, was published in 1975.

The 1- to 3-digit codes of Revision 3 are listed below.

Section, Division, and Group Codes

0 FOOD AND LIVE ANIMALS

- **00 Live Animals Other Than Animals of Division 03**
  - 001 Live animals other than animals of division 03
- **01 Meat and Meat Preparations**
  - 011 Meat of bovine animals, fresh, chilled or frozen
  - 012 Other meat and edible meat offal, fresh, chilled or frozen (except meat and meat offal unfit or unsuitable for human consumption)
  - 016 Meat and edible meat offal, salted, in brine, dried or smoked; edible flours and meals of meat or meat offal
  - 017 Meat and edible meat offal, prepared or preserved, n.e.s.
- **02 Dairy Products and Birds' Eggs**
  - 022 Milk and cream and milk products other than butter or cheese
  - 023 Butter and other fats and oils derived from milk
  - 024 Cheese and curd
  - 025 Eggs, birds', and egg yolks, fresh, dried or otherwise preserved, sweetened or not; egg albumin
- **03 Fish (Not Marine Mammals), Crustaceans, Molluscs and Aquatic Invertebrates, and Preparations Thereof**
  - 034 Fish, fresh (live or dead), chilled or frozen
  - 035 Fish, dried, salted or in brine; smoked fish (whether or not cooked before or during the smoking process)
  - 036 Crustaceans, molluscs and aquatic invertebrates, whether in shell or not, fresh (live or dead), chilled, frozen, dried, salted or in brine; crustaceans, in shell, cooked by steaming or boiling in water
  - 037 Fish, crustaceans, molluscs and other aquatic invertebrates, prepared or preserved, n.e.s.
- **04 Cereals and Cereal Preparations**
  - 041 Wheat (including spelt) and meslin, unmilled
  - 042 Rice
  - 043 Barley, unmilled
  - 044 Maize (not including sweet corn) unmilled
  - 045 Cereals, unmilled (other than wheat, rice, barley, and maize)
  - 046 Meal and flour of wheat and flour of meslin
  - 047 Other cereal meals and flours
  - 048 Cereal preparations and preparations of flour or starch of fruits or vegetables
- **05 Vegetables and Fruit**
  - 054 Vegetables, fresh, chilled, frozen or simply preserved (including dried leguminous vegetables); roots, tubers and other edible vegetable products, n.e.s., fresh or dried
  - 056 Vegetables, roots and tubers, prepared or preserved, n.e.s.
  - 057 Fruit and nuts (not including oil nuts), fresh or dried
  - 058 Fruit, preserved, and fruit preparations (excluding fruit juices)
  - 059 Fruit juices (including grape must) and vegetable juices, unfermented and not containing added spirit, whether or not containing added sugar or other sweetening matter
- **06 Sugars, Sugar Preparations and Honey**
  - 061 Sugars, molasses and honey
  - 062 Sugar confectionery
- **07 Coffee, Tea, Cocoa, Spices, and Manufactures Thereof**
  - 071 Coffee and coffee substitutes
  - 072 Cocoa
  - 073 Chocolate and other food preparations containing cocoa, n.e.s.
  - 074 Tea and mate
  - 075 Spices
- **08 Feeding Stuff for Animals (Not Including Unmilled Cereals)**
  - 081 Feeding stuff for animals (not including unmilled cereals)
- **09 Miscellaneous Edible Products and Preparations**
  - 091 Margarine and shortening
  - 098 Edible products and preparations, n.e.s.

1 BEVERAGES AND TOBACCO

- **11 Beverages**
  - 111 Non-alcoholic beverages, n.e.s.
  - 112 Alcoholic beverages
- **12 Tobacco and Tobacco Manufactures**
  - 121 Tobacco, unmanufactured; tobacco refuse
  - 122 Tobacco, manufactured (whether or not containing tobacco substitutes)

2 CRUDE MATERIALS, INEDIBLE, EXCEPT FUELS

- **21 Hides, Skins and Furskins, Raw**
  - 211 Hides and skins (except furskins), raw
  - 212 Furskins, raw (including heads, tails, paws and other pieces or cuttings, suitable for furriers' use), other than hides and skins of group 211
- **22 Oil Seeds and Oleaginous Fruits**
  - 222 Oil seeds and oleaginous fruits of a kind used for the extraction of "soft" fixed vegetable oils (excluding flours and meals)
  - 223 Oil seeds and oleaginous fruits, whole or broken, of a kind used for the extraction of other fixed vegetable oils (including flours and meals of oil seeds or oleaginous fruit, n.e.s.)
- **23 Crude Rubber (Including Synthetic and Reclaimed)**
  - 231 Natural rubber, balata, gutta percha, guayule, chicle and similar natural gums, in primary forms (including latex) or in plates, sheets or strip
  - 232 Synthetic rubber; reclaimed rubber; waste, parings and scrap of unhardened rubber
- **24 Cork and Wood**
  - 244 Cork, natural, raw and waste (including natural cork in blocks or sheets)
  - 245 Fuel wood (excluding wood waste) and wood charcoal
  - 246 Wood in chips or particles and wood waste
  - 247 Wood in the rough or roughly squared
  - 248 Wood, simply worked, and railway sleepers of wood
- **25 Pulp and Waste Paper**
  - 251 Pulp and waste paper
- **26 Textile Fibres (Other Than Wool Tops and Other Combed Wool) and Their Wastes (Not Manufactured Into Yarn or Fabric)**
  - 261 Silk
  - 263 Cotton
  - 264 Jute and other textile bast fibres, n.e.s., raw or processed but not spun; tow and waste of these fibres (including yarn waste and garnetted stock)
  - 265 Vegetable textile fibres (other than cotton and jute), raw or processed but not spun; waste of these fibres
  - 266 Synthetic fibres suitable for spinning
  - 267 Other man-made fibres suitable for spinning and waste of man-made fibres
  - 268 Wool and other animal hair (including wool tops)
  - 269 Worn clothing and other worn textile articles; rags

- **27 Crude Fertilizers, Other Than Those of Division 56, and Crude Minerals (Excluding Coal, Petroleum and Precious Stones)**
  - 272 Fertilizers, crude, other than those of division 56
  - 273 Stone, sand and gravel
  - 274 Sulphur and unroasted iron pyrites
  - 277 Natural abrasives, n.e.s. (including industrial diamonds)
  - 278 Other crude minerals
- **28 Metalliferous Ores and Metal Scrap**
  - 281 Iron ore and concentrates
  - 282 Ferrous waste and scrap; remelting ingots of iron or steel
  - 283 Copper ores and concentrates; copper mattes, cement copper
  - 284 Nickel ores and concentrates; nickel mattes, nickel oxide, sinters and other intermediate products of nickel metallurgy
  - 285 Aluminium ores and concentrates (including alumina)
  - 286 Ores and concentrates of uranium or thorium
  - 287 Ores and concentrates of base metals, n.e.s.
  - 288 Non-ferrous base metal waste and scrap, n.e.s.
  - 289 Ores and concentrates of precious metals; waste, scrap and sweepings of precious metals (other than of gold)
- **29 Crude Animal and Vegetable Materials, n.e.s.**
  - 291 Crude animal materials, n.e.s.
  - 292 Crude vegetable materials, n.e.s.

3 MINERAL FUELS, LUBRICANTS AND RELATED MATERIALS

- **32 Coal, Coke and Briquettes**
  - 321 Coal, whether or not pulverized, but not agglomerated
  - 322 Briquettes, lignite and peat
  - 325 Coke and semi-coke (including char) of coal, of lignite or of peat, whether or not agglomerated; retort carbon
- **33 Petroleum, Petroleum Products and Related Materials**
  - 333 Petroleum oils and oils obtained from bituminous minerals, crude
  - 334 Petroleum oils and oils obtained from bituminous minerals (other than crude); preparations, n.e.s., containing by weight 70% or more of petroleum oils or of oils obtained from bituminous minerals, these oils being the basic constituents of the preparations
  - 335 Residual petroleum products, n.e.s. and related materials
- **34 Gas, Natural and Manufactured**
  - 342 Liquefied propane and butane
  - 343 Natural gas, whether or not liquefied
  - 344 Petroleum gases and other gaseous hydrocarbons, n.e.s.
  - 345 Coal gas, water gas, producer gas and similar gases, other than petroleum gases and other gaseous hydrocarbons

- **35 Electric Current**
  - 351 Electric current

4 ANIMAL AND VEGETABLE OILS, FATS AND WAXES

- **41 Animal Oils and Fats**
  - 411 Animal oils and fats
- **42 Fixed Vegetable Fats and Oils, Crude, Refined or Fractionated**
  - 421 Fixed vegetable fats and oils, "soft", crude, refined or fractionated
  - 422 Fixed vegetable fats and oils, crude, refined or fractionated, other than "soft"
- **43 Animal or Vegetable Fats and Oils, Processed; Waxes of Animal or Vegetable Origin; Inedible Mixtures or Preparations of Animal or Vegetable Fats or Oils, n.e.s.**
  - 431 Animal or vegetable fats and oils, processed, waxes, and inedible mixtures or preparations of animal or vegetable fats or oils, n.e.s.

5 CHEMICALS AND RELATED PRODUCTS, N.E.S.

- **51 Organic Chemicals**
  - 511 Hydrocarbons, n.e.s., and their halogenated, sulphonated, nitrated or nitrosated derivatives
  - 512 Alcohols, phenols, phenol-alcohols, and their halogenated, sulphonated, nitrated or nitrosated derivatives
  - 513 Carboxylic acids and their anhydrides, halides, peroxides and peroxyacids; their halogenated, sulphonated, nitrated or nitrosated derivatives
  - 514 Nitrogen-function compounds
  - 515 Organo-inorganic compounds, heterocyclic compounds, nucleic acids and their salts
  - 516 Other organic chemicals
- **52 Inorganic Chemicals**
  - 522 Inorganic chemical elements, oxides and halogen salts
  - 523 Metallic salts and peroxysalts, of inorganic acids
  - 524 Other inorganic chemicals; organic and inorganic compounds of precious metals
  - 525 Radio-active and associated materials
- **53 Dyeing, Tanning and Colouring Materials**
  - 531 Synthetic organic colouring matter and colour lakes, and preparations based thereon
  - 532 Dyeing and tanning extracts, and synthetic tanning materials
  - 533 Pigments, paints, varnishes and related materials
- **54 Medicinal and Pharmaceutical Products**
  - 541 Medicinal and pharmaceutical products, other than medicaments of group 542
  - 542 Medicaments (including veterinary medicaments)

- **55 Essential Oils and Resinoids and Perfume Materials; Toilet, Polishing and Cleansing Preparations**
  - 551 Essential oils, perfume and flavour materials
  - 553 Perfumery, cosmetics or toilet preparations (excluding soaps)
  - 554 Soap, cleansing and polishing preparations
- **56 Fertilizers (Other Than Those of Group 272)**
  - 562 Fertilizers (other than those of group 272)
- **57 Plastics in Primary Forms**
  - 571 Polymers of ethylene, in primary forms
  - 572 Polymers of styrene, in primary forms
  - 573 Polymers of vinyl chloride or of other halogenated olefins, in primary forms
  - 574 Polyacetals, other polyethers and epoxide resins, in primary forms; polycarbonates, alkyd resins and other polyesters, in primary forms
  - 575 Other plastics, in primary forms
  - 579 Waste, parings and scrap, of plastics
- **58 Plastics in Non-primary Forms**
  - 581 Tubes, pipes and hoses of plastics
  - 582 Plates, sheets, film, foil and strip, of plastics
  - 583 Monofilament of which any cross-sectional dimension exceeds 1 mm, rods, sticks and profile shapes, whether or not surface-worked but not otherwise worked, of plastics
- **59 Chemical Materials and Products, n.e.s.**
  - 591 Insecticides, rodenticides, fungicides, herbicides, anti-sprouting products and plant-growth regulators, disinfectants and similar products, put up in forms or packings for retail sale or as preparations or articles (e.g., sulphur-treated bands, wicks and candles, and fly-papers)
  - 592 Starches, inulin and wheat gluten; albuminoidal substances; glues
  - 593 Explosives and pyrotechnic products
  - 597 Prepared additives for mineral oils and the like; prepared liquids for hydraulic transmission; anti-freezing preparations and prepared de-icing fluids; lubricating preparations
  - 598 Miscellaneous chemical products, n.e.s.

6 MANUFACTURED GOODS CLASSIFIED CHIEFLY BY MATERIAL

- **61 Leather, Leather Manufactures, n.e.s., and Dressed Furskins**
  - 611 Leather
  - 612 Manufactures of leather or of composition leather, n.e.s.; saddlery and harness
  - 613 Furskins, tanned or dressed (including heads, tails, paws and

other pieces or cuttings), unassembled, or assembled (without the addition of other materials), other than those of heading 848.3

62 Rubber Manufactures, n.e.s.

- 621 Materials of rubber (e.g., pastes, plates, sheets, rods, thread, tubes, of rubber)
- 625 Rubber tyres, interchangeable tyre treads, tyre flaps and inner tubes for wheels of all kinds
- 629 Articles of rubber, n.e.s.

63 Cork and Wood Manufactures (Excluding Furniture)

- 633 Cork manufactures
- 634 Veneers, plywood, particle board, and other wood, worked, n.e.s.
- 635 Wood manufactures, n.e.s.

64 Paper, Paperboard, and Articles of Paper Pulp, of Paper or of Paperboard

- 641 Paper and paperboard
- 642 Paper and paperboard, cut to size or shape, and articles of paper or paperboard

65 Textile Yarn, Fabrics, Made-Up Articles, n.e.s., and Related Products

- 651 Textile yarn
- 652 Cotton fabrics, woven (not including narrow or special fabrics)
- 653 Fabrics, woven, of man-made textile materials (not including narrow or special fabrics)
- 654 Other textile fabrics, woven
- 655 Knitted or crocheted fabrics (including tubular knit fabrics, n.e.s., pile fabrics and open-work fabrics), n.e.s.
- 656 Tulles, lace, embroidery, ribbons, trimmings and other small wares
- 657 Special yarns, special textile fabrics and related products
- 658 Made-up articles, wholly or chiefly of textile materials, n.e.s.
- 659 Floor coverings, etc.

66 Non-Metallic Mineral Manufactures, n.e.s.

- 661 Lime, cement, and fabricated construction materials (except glass and clay materials)
- 662 Clay construction materials and refractory construction materials
- 663 Mineral manufactures, n.e.s.
- 664 Glass
- 665 Glassware
- 666 Pottery
- 667 Pearls, precious and semi-precious stones, unworked or worked

67 Iron and Steel

- 671 Pig iron, spiegeleisen, sponge iron, iron or steel granules and powders and ferro-alloys
- 672 Ingots and other primary forms, of iron or steel; semi-finished products of iron or steel
- 673 Flat-rolled products, of iron or non-alloy steel, not clad, plated or coated
- 674 Flat-rolled products of iron or non-alloy steel, clad, plated or coated
- 675 Flat-rolled products of alloy steel
- 676 Iron and steel bars, rods, angles, shapes and sections (including sheet piling)
- 677 Rails and railway track construction material, of iron or steel

- 678 Wire of iron or steel
- 679 Tubes, pipes and hollow profiles, and tube or pipe fittings, of iron or steel

68 Non-Ferrous Metals

- 681 Silver, platinum and other metals of the platinum group
- 682 Copper
- 683 Nickel
- 684 Aluminium
- 685 Lead
- 686 Zinc
- 687 Tin
- 689 Miscellaneous non-ferrous base metals employed in metallurgy, and cermets

69 Manufactures of Metals, n.e.s.

- 691 Structures and parts of structures, n.e.s., of iron, steel or aluminium
- 692 Metal containers for storage or transport
- 693 Wire products (excluding insulated electrical wiring) and fencing grills
- 694 Nails, screws, nuts, bolts, rivets and the like, of iron, steel, copper or aluminium
- 695 Tools for use in the hand or in machines
- 696 Cutlery
- 697 Household equipment of base metal, n.e.s.
- 699 Manufactures of base metal, n.e.s.

7 MACHINERY AND TRANSPORT EQUIPMENT

71 Power Generating Machinery and Equipment

- 711 Steam or other vapour generating boilers, super-heated water boilers, and auxiliary plant for use therewith; and parts thereof
- 712 Steam turbines and other vapour turbines, and parts thereof, n.e.s.
- 713 Internal combustion piston engines, and parts thereof, n.e.s.
- 714 Engines and motors, non-electric (other than those of groups 712, 713 and 718); parts, n.e.s. of these engines and motors
- 716 Rotating electric plant and parts thereof, n.e.s.
- 718 Other power generating machinery and parts thereof, n.e.s.

72 Machinery Specialized for Particular Industries

- 721 Agricultural machinery (excluding tractors) and parts thereof
- 722 Tractors (other than those of headings 744.14 and 744.15)
- 723 Civil engineering and contractors' plant and equipment
- 724 Textile and leather machinery, and parts thereof, n.e.s.
- 725 Paper mill and pulp mill machinery, paper cutting machines and other machinery for the manufacture of paper articles; parts thereof
- 726 Printing and bookbinding machinery, and parts thereof
- 727 Food-processing machines (excluding domestic)
- 728 Other machinery and equipment specialized for particular industries, and parts thereof, n.e.s.

73 Metalworking Machinery

- 731 Machine-tools working by removing metal or other material
- 733 Machine-tools for working metal, sintered metal carbides or cermets, without removing material
- 735 Parts, n.e.s., and accessories suitable for use solely or principally with the machines falling within headings 731 and 733 (including work or tool holders, self-opening dieheads, dividing heads and other special attachments for machine-tools); tool holders for any type of tool for working in the hand
- 737 Metalworking machinery (other than machine-tools), and parts thereof, n.e.s.

74 General Industrial Machinery and Equipment, n.e.s., and Machine Parts, n.e.s.

- 741 Heating and cooling equipment and parts thereof, n.e.s.
- 742 Pumps for liquids, whether or not fitted with a measuring device; liquid elevators; parts for such pumps and liquid elevators
- 743 Pumps (other than pumps for liquids), air or other gas compressors and fans; ventilating or recycling hoods incorporating a fan, whether or not fitted with filters; centrifuges; filtering or purifying apparatus; and parts thereof
- 744 Mechanical handling equipment, and parts thereof, n.e.s.
- 745 Other non-electrical machinery, tools and mechanical apparatus, and parts thereof, n.e.s.
- 746 Ball or roller bearings
- 747 Taps, cocks, valves and similar appliances, for pipes, boiler shells, tanks, vats and the like (including pressure reducing valves and thermostatically controlled valves)
- 748 Transmission shafts (including cam shafts and crank shafts) and cranks; bearing housings and plain shaft bearings; gears and gearing; ball screws; gear boxes and other speed changers (including torque converters); flywheels and pulleys (including pulley blocks); clutches and shaft couplings (including universal joints); and parts thereof
- 749 Non-electric parts and accessories of machinery, n.e.s.

75 Office Machines and Automatic Data Processing Machines

- 751 Office machines
- 752 Automatic data processing machines and units thereof; magnetic or optical readers, machines for transcribing data onto data media in coded form and machines for processing such data, n.e.s.
- 759 Parts and accessories (other than covers, carrying cases and the like) suitable for use solely or principally with machines falling within groups 751 and 752

76 Telecommunications and Sound Recording and Reproducing Apparatus and Equipment

761 Television receivers (including

video monitors and video projectors), whether or not combined, in the same housing, with radio-broadcast receivers or sound or video recording or reproducing apparatus

- 762 Radio-broadcast receivers, whether or not combined, in the same housing, with sound recording or reproducing apparatus or a clock
- 763 Sound recorders or reproducers; television image and sound recorders or reproducers; prepared unrecorded media
- 764 Telecommunications equipment, n.e.s.; and parts, n.e.s., and accessories of apparatus falling within division 76

77 Electrical Machinery, Apparatus and Appliances, n.e.s., and Electrical Parts Thereof (Including Non-Electrical Counterparts, n.e.s. of Electrical Household Type Equipment)

- 771 Electric power machinery (other than rotating electric plant of heading 716), and parts thereof
- 772 Electrical apparatus for switching or protecting electrical circuits or for making connections to or in electrical circuits (e.g., switches, relays, fuses, lightning arresters, voltage limiters, surge suppressors, plugs and sockets, lampholders and junction boxes); electrical resistors (including rheostats and potentiometers), other than heating resistors; printed circuits; boards, panels (including numerical control panels), consoles, desks, cabinets and other bases, equipped with two or more apparatus for switching, protecting or for making connections to or in electrical circuits, for electric control or the distribution of electricity (excluding switching apparatus of heading 764.1)
- 773 Equipment for distributing electricity, n.e.s.
- 774 Electro-diagnostic apparatus for medical, surgical, dental or veterinary sciences and radiological apparatus
- 775 Household type, electrical and non-electrical equipment, n.e.s.
- 776 Thermionic, cold cathode or photo-cathode valves and tubes (e.g., vacuum or vapour or gas filled valves and tubes, mercury arc rectifying valves and tubes, cathode-ray tubes, television camera tubes); diodes, transistors and similar semi-conductor devices; photosensitive semi-conductor devices; light emitting diodes; mounted piezo-electric crystals; electronic integrated circuits and microassemblies; and parts thereof
- 778 Electrical machinery and apparatus, n.e.s.

78 Road Vehicles (Including Air-Cushion Vehicles)

781 Motor cars and other motor vehicles principally designed for the transport of persons (other than public-transport type

vehicles), including station wagons and racing cars

- 782 Motor vehicles for the transport of goods and special purpose motor vehicles
- 783 Road motor vehicles, n.e.s.
- 784 Parts and accessories of the motor vehicles of groups 722, 781, 782 and 783
- 785 Motorcycles (including mopeds) and cycles, motorized and non-motorized; invalid carriages
- 786 Trailers and semi-trailers; other vehicles, not mechanically propelled; specially designed and equipped transport containers

79 Other Transport Equipment

- 791 Railway vehicles (including hovertrains) and associated equipment
- 792 Aircraft and associated equipment; spacecraft (including satellites) and spacecraft launch vehicles; and parts thereof
- 793 Ships, boats (including hovercraft) and floating structures

8 MISCELLANEOUS MANUFACTURED ARTICLES

81 Prefabricated Buildings; Sanitary, Plumbing, Heating and Lighting Fixtures and Fittings, n.e.s.

- 811 Prefabricated buildings
- 812 Sanitary, plumbing and heating fixtures and fittings, n.e.s.
- 813 Lighting fixtures and fittings, n.e.s.

82 Furniture and Parts Thereof; Bedding, Mattresses, Mattress Supports, Cushions and Similar Stuffed Furnishings

821 Furniture and parts thereof; bedding, mattresses, mattress supports, cushions and similar stuffed furnishings

83 Travel Goods, Handbags and Similar Containers

831 Trunks, suit-cases, vanity-cases, executive-cases, brief-cases, school satchels, binocular cases, camera cases, musical instrument cases, spectacle cases, gun cases, holsters and similar containers; travelling bags, toilet bags, rucksacks, handbags, shopping-bags, wallets, purses, map-cases, cigarette-cases, tobacco-pouches, tool bags, sports bags, bottle-cases, jewellery boxes, powder-boxes, cutlery cases and similar containers, of leather or of composition leather, of plastic sheeting, of textile materials, of vulcanized fibre or of paperboard, or wholly or mainly covered with such materials; travel sets for personal toilet, sewing or shoe or clothes cleaning

84 Articles of Apparel and Clothing Accessories

841 Men's or boys' coats, jackets, suits, blazers, trousers, shorts, shirts, underwear, knitwear and similar articles of textile fabrics, not knitted or crocheted (other than those of heading 845.2 or 845.6)

- 842 Women's and girls' coats, capes, jackets, suits, blazers, trousers, shorts, shirts, underwear and similar articles of textile fabrics, not knitted or crocheted (other than those of heading 845.2 or 845.6)
- 843 Men's or boys' coats, capes, jackets, suits, blazers, trousers, shorts, shirts, underwear, nightwear and similar articles of textile fabrics, knitted or crocheted (other than those of heading 845.2 or 845.6)
- 844 Women's or girls' coats, capes, jackets, suits, blazers, trousers, shorts, shirts, underwear, nightwear and similar articles of textile fabrics, knitted or crocheted (other than those of heading 845.2 or 845.6)
- 845 Articles of apparel, of textile fabrics, whether or not knitted or crocheted, n.e.s.
- 846 Clothing accessories, of textile fabrics, whether or not knitted or crocheted (other than those for babies)
- 848 Articles of apparel and clothing accessories of other than textile fabrics; headgear of all materials

85 Footwear

851 Footwear

87 Professional, Scientific and Controlling Instruments and Apparatus, n.e.s.

- 871 Optical instruments and apparatus, n.e.s.
- 872 Instruments and appliances, n.e.s., for medical, surgical, dental or veterinary purposes
- 873 Meters and counters, n.e.s.
- 874 Measuring, checking, analysing and controlling instruments and apparatus, n.e.s.

88 Photographic Apparatus, Equipment and Supplies and Optical Goods, n.e.s.; Watches and Clocks

- 881 Photographic apparatus and equipment, n.e.s.
- 882 Photographic and cinematographic supplies
- 883 Cinematograph film, exposed and developed, whether or not incorporating sound track or consisting only of sound track
- 884 Optical goods, n.e.s.
- 885 Watches and clocks

89 Miscellaneous Manufactured Articles, n.e.s.

- 891 Arms and ammunition
- 892 Printed matter
- 893 Articles, n.e.s. of plastics
- 894 Baby carriages, toys, games and sporting goods
- 895 Office and stationery supplies, n.e.s.
- 896 Works of art, collectors' pieces and antiques
- 897 Jewellery, goldsmiths' and silversmiths' wares, and other articles of precious or semi-precious materials, n.e.s.

898 Musical instruments and parts and accessories thereof; records, tapes and other sound or similar recordings (excluding goods of groups 763, 882 and 883)

899 Miscellaneous manufactured articles, n.e.s.

9 COMMODITIES AND TRANSACTIONS NOT CLASSIFIED ELSEWHERE IN THE SITC

91 Postal Packages Not Classified According to Kind

911 Postal packages not classified according to kind

93 Special Transactions and Commodities Not Classified According to Kind

931 Special transactions and commodities not classified according to kind

96 Coin (Other Than Gold Coin), Not Being Legal Tender

961 Coin (other than gold coin), not being legal tender

97 Gold, Non-Monetary (Excluding Gold Ores and Concentrates)

971 Gold, non-monetary (excluding gold ores and concentrates)

Uniform Crime Reporting Classification of Offenses

Uniform Crime Reporting (UCR) receives crime information through voluntary reports submitted by local law enforcement agencies across the country. In 1966, the FBI began coordinating UCR data collection through designated State level agencies which report Statewide information to the FBI. UCR divides offenses into two major classifications which are designated Part I and Part II offenses, as listed below. Seven of these Part I offenses (excluding arson), because of their seriousness, frequency of occurrence, and likelihood of being reported to police, serve as a crime index and are used to calculate crime rates.

PART I (INDEX) OFFENSES

Violent Crimes
Criminal Homicide
Forcible rape
Robbery
Aggravated Assaults

Property Crimes
Burglary
Larceny/theft
Motor Vehicle Theft
Arson

PART II (NON-INDEX) OFFENSES

Other Assaults
Forgery and Counterfeiting
Fraud
Embezzlement
Stolen Property Offenses
Vandalism
Weapons Offenses
Prostitution and Commercialized Vice
Sex Offenses
Drug Laws
Gambling
Offenses Against the Family and Children
Driving Under the Influence
Liquor Law
Drunkenness
Disorderly Conduct
Vagrancy
All Other Offenses
Suspicion
Curfew and Loitering Laws
Runaways